THE SIXTH Virgin Film Guide

CineBooks

First published in Great Britain in 1997 by
Virgin Books
an imprint of Virgin Publishing Ltd
332 Ladbroke Grove
London W10 5AH

Copyright © CineBooks, a division of
News America Publishing Incorporated 1997

A catalogue record for this book is available from the British Library.

Book design and production by Peter Hajduk and Noel Harrington

ISBN 0 7535 0113 9

Printed and Bound in Finland by WSOY

CONTENTS

PREFACE TO THE SIXTH EDITION

Welcome to the sixth edition of the *Virgin Film Guide*. As with previous volumes, we have brought the *VFG* up to date with full coverage of the films that we consider the most noteworthy from the past 12 months, from foreign treasures like Tran Ahn Hung's *Cyclo* to such Hollywood blockbusters like *Men in Black*. We've also gone back into our vast database to reappraise a few of the films we've had a chance to revisit, while deleting a few of the titles that we felt no longer warranted inclusion. This year also marks the return of our directors index, featuring complete filmographies for notable directors whose films are included in this edition.

The reviews included in this book were selected and condensed from the nearly 40,000 entries in CineBooks's landmark 25-volume reference work, *The Motion Picture Guide*, which covers just about every sound film released in the US. This selection consists not only of the works that we consider the outstanding achievements of world cinema, but also those films that represent key examples of a genre or have some special social, cultural, or historical significance.

Why another film guide? Several reasons. First, every film in this book counts. Other guides may cover more movies, but the *VFG* gives you more information on the films that *matter*. By narrowing our focus, we've been able to include fuller credits than in any other book of this kind—from producer and director through to costume designer and stunt coordinator, as well as up to ten acting credits and characters' names per title. Similarly, our synopses and reviews are longer and more in-depth. Finally, while other guides tend to offer the idiosyncratic opinions of one individual, the *VFG* draws on CineBooks's entire team of film experts. Each is skilled in a different kind of film—from classic Hollywood musicals like *An American in Paris* to low-budget cult favorites like *The Honeymoon Killers*.

Thanks are due to everyone who help shaped this volume, in particular: founding editor James Monaco, who first launched this project; Elaine Collins, our agent at Woods Collins Associates, for her consummately professional handling of business and legal matters; and Noel Harrington, for his artful manipulation of typesetting software. We'd also like to thank all of you who have taken the time to write with your responses. We value your input and hope you'll keep the comments and suggestions flowing to: CineBooks, c/o TV Guide Entertainment Network, 620 Avenue of the Americas, 6th Floor, New York, NY, 10011, USA. You may also visit our site on the World Wide Web at:

`http://www.tvguide.com/movies`

Editors: Ken Fox, Ed Grant, Jo Imeson, Andrew Joseph, Maitland McDonagh
Administration: Michelle Diliberto

New York City
July 1997

HOW TO USE THIS BOOK

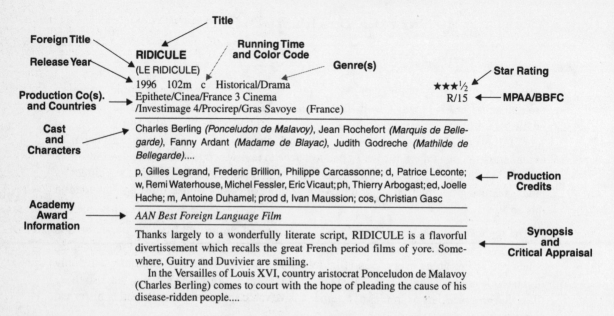

Title

Foreign Title

Release Year

Production Co(s).
and Countries

Cast
and
Characters

Academy
Award
Information

Running Time
and Color Code

Genre(s)

Star Rating

MPAA/BBFC

Production
Credits

Synopsis
and
Critical Appraisal

RIDICULE
(LE RIDICULE)
1996 102m c Historical/Drama
Epithete/Cinea/France 3 Cinema
/Investimage 4/Procirep/Gras Savoye   (France)

★★★½
R/15

Charles Berling *(Ponceludon de Malavoy)*, Jean Rochefort *(Marquis de Belle-garde)*, Fanny Ardant *(Madame de Blayac)*, Judith Godreche *(Mathilde de Bellegarde)*....

p, Gilles Legrand, Frederic Brillion, Philippe Carcassonne; d, Patrice Leconte; w, Remi Waterhouse, Michel Fessler, Eric Vicaut; ph, Thierry Arbogast; ed, Joelle Hache; m, Antoine Duhamel; prod d, Ivan Maussion; cos, Christian Gasc

AAN Best Foreign Language Film

Thanks largely to a wonderfully literate script, RIDICULE is a flavorful divertissement which recalls the great French period films of yore. Some-where, Guitry and Duvivier are smiling.
   In the Versailles of Louis XVI, country aristocrat Ponceludon de Malavoy (Charles Berling) comes to court with the hope of pleading the cause of his disease-ridden people....

Films are listed alphabetically according to the title by which they were first released in the US. If you need to search for a film by a foreign or alternate title, please consult the Alternate Title Index. Films are rated according to the following scale: 5 stars = masterpiece; 4 stars = excellent; 3 stars = good; 2 stars = fair; 1 star = without merit. Half stars are also awarded. Key creative and technical personnel are abbreviated as follows: p (producer); d (director); w (writer); ph (cinematographer); ed (editor); m (music composer); prod d (production designer); art d (art director); fx (special effects); chor (choreographer); cos (costume designer); anim (animator).

The Motion Picture Association of America (MPAA) currently grades films according to the following codes: **G** (GENERAL AUDIENCES—All ages admitted); **PG** (PARENTAL GUIDANCE SUG-GESTED—Some material may not be suitable for children); **PG-13** (PARENTS STRONGLY CAUTIONED—Some material may be inappropriate for children under 13); **R** (RE-STRICTED—Under 17 requires accompanying parent of adult guardian); and **NC-17** (NO CHIL-DREN UNDER 17 ADMITTED). This book also contains ratings issued while earlier systems were in effect, as follows: **GP** (May be considered the equivalent of PG); **M** (Mature Audiences, Parental Guidance Suggested); and **X** (No One Under 17 Admitted).

Since 1982, the following system of classification has been applied in the UK: **U** (Universal—suitable for all); **PG** (Parental Guidance—some scenes may be unsuitable for young children); **12** (passed for those aged 12 and over); **15** (passed for those aged 15 and over); and **18** (passed for those aged 18 and over).   When UK certificates were first introduced in 1913, the categories were simply **U** (Universal) and **A** (Adult; no unaccompanied child admitted). **H** (for Horrific) was introduced as an advisory category in 1932, to be replaced in 1951 by **X** (no admission to those under 16). In 1970, a new system was introduced: **U** (as before); **A** (Advisory; unaccompanied children of 5 and over admitted, but a film in this category could contain material that parents might prefer children under 14 not to see); **AA** (no admission to those under 14); and **X** (no admission to those under 18).

The editors wish to thank the British Board of Film Classification for its assistance.

A

A NOUS LA LIBERTE

1931 104m bw Comedy/Political ★★★★★
SDFS (France) /U

Henri Marchand (*Emile*), Raymond Cordy (*Louis*), Rolla France (*Jeanne*), Paul Olivier (*Paul Imaque*), Jacques Shelly (*Paul*), Andre Michaud (*Foreman*), Germaine Aussey (*Maud*), Alex D'Arcy (*Gigolo*), William Burke (*Old Convict*), Vincent Hyspa (*Old Orator*)

d, Rene Clair; w, Rene Clair; ph, Georges Perinal; ed, Rene Clair, Rene Le Henaff; m, Georges Auric

AAN Best Art Direction: Lazare Meerson

This classic satire on the dehumanization of industrial workers is one of Rene Clair's greatest achievements, preceding Chaplin's indictment of the industrial revolution, MODERN TIMES, by five years. Clair's fast-paced and wickedly funny entertainment centers on the friendship between two prison inmates—Louis (Raymond Cordy), who escapes and becomes a phonograph company tycoon, and Emile (Henri Marchand), who, after he too escapes, is hired at his friend's factory. Filming without a script and giving his actors freedom to improvise, Clair structured his film like an operetta. Georges Auric wrote the music, to which the movements of the assembly lines of actors are choreographed. Clair's message is an angry one—"a bitter pill," as he described it, which "would be more easily swallowed when coated with diverting music." The film earned an Academy Award nomination for Best Interior Decoration.

ABBOTT AND COSTELLO MEET FRANKENSTEIN

1948 83m bw Comedy ★★★★
Universal (U.S.) /U

Bud Abbott (*Chick Young*), Lou Costello (*Wilbur Grey*), Lon Chaney Jr. (*Lawrence Talbot/The Wolf Man*), Bela Lugosi (*Dracula*), Glenn Strange (*The Monster*), Lenore Aubert (*Sandra Mornay*), Jane Randolph (*Joan Raymond*), Frank Ferguson (*McDougal*), Charles Bradstreet (*Dr. Stevens*), Howard Negley (*Harris*)

p, Robert Arthur; d, Charles Barton; w, Robert Lees, Frederic I. Rinaldo, John Grant (based on the novel *Frankenstein* by Mary Shelley); ph, Charles Van Enger; ed, Frank Gross; m, Frank Skinner; fx, David S. Horsley

Hilarious spoof of the classic Universal horror films of the 1930s and early 40s, with Abbott and Costello playing railway porters who unwittingly deliver the "undead" bodies of Frankenstein's monster (Glenn Strange) and Dracula (Bela Lugosi) to a wax museum, where the bodies are revived. Thus awakened, Dracula becomes intent on replacing the catatonic Monster's brain with dim-witted Costello's, because it would make the beast easier to control. Lawrence Talbot (Lon Chaney, Jr.) attempts to help the boys, but he's got problems of his own: he turns into a wolfman whenever there's a full moon. Horror buffs will note that Chaney, Jr., who had played the Monster in THE GHOST OF FRANKENSTEIN, fills in for Strange in the shot where the Monster tosses actress Lenore Aubert out a window. Strange had broken his foot in an accident, and rather than lose three days of shooting, Chaney volunteered to don the makeup once again. After this film's considerable success at the box office, Abbott and Costello made seven more pictures in which they "met" Hollywood monsters, but none were as lively and entertaining as this one.

ABE LINCOLN IN ILLINOIS

1940 110m bw Biography ★★★
RKO (U.S.) /U

Raymond Massey (*Abraham Lincoln*), Gene Lockhart (*Stephen Douglas*), Ruth Gordon (*Mary Todd Lincoln*), Mary Howard (*Ann Rutledge*), Dorothy Tree (*Elizabeth Edwards*), Harvey Stephens (*Ninian Edwards*), Minor Watson (*Joshua Speed*), Alan Baxter (*Billy Herndon*), Howard da Silva (*Jack Armstrong*), Maurice Murphy (*John McNeil*)

p, Max Gordon; d, John Cromwell; w, Grover Jones, Robert E. Sherwood (based on his play); ph, James Wong Howe; ed, George Hively; m, Roy Webb

AAN Best Actor: Raymond Massey; *AAN Best Cinematography:* James Wong Howe

In adapting Robert E. Sherwood's popular play about the early years of Abraham Lincoln, the filmmakers wisely chose Raymond Massey, who played the title role on stage, to reprise his portrayal in the film. Massey heads an impressive cast in a picture spanning thirty years of Lincoln's life, following his career from his beginnings as a woodsman and shopkeeper to his entry into law and politics and culminating with his election as the 16th president of the United States. The film includes some memorable scenes of Lincoln's debates with his longtime political rival, Stephen Douglas (Gene Lockhart), and offers a vivid account of 19th-century life in the Midwest, with particular attention paid to the political processes of the day. Massey's excellent performance earned an Oscar nomination (he lost to James Stewart in THE PHILADELPHIA STORY) and the film was also nominated for Best Cinematography.

ABOMINABLE DR. PHIBES, THE

1971 93m c Horror ★★★
AIP (U.S./U.K.) PG/15

Vincent Price (*Dr. Anton Phibes*), Joseph Cotten (*Dr. Vesalius*), Hugh Griffith (*Rabbi*), Terry-Thomas (*Dr. Longstreet*), Virginia North (*Vulnavia*), Aubrey Woods (*Goldsmith*), Susan Travers (*Nurse Allan*), Alex Scott (*Dr. Hargreaves*), Peter Gilmore (*Dr. Kitaj*), Edward Burnham (*Dr. Dunwoody*)

p, Louis M. Heyward, Ronald S. Dunas; d, Robert Fuest; w, James Whiton, William Goldstein; ph, Norman Warwick; ed, Tristam Cones; m, Basil Kirchin; art d, Bernard Reeves; cos, Elsa Fennell

A delightfully goofy horror film set in England circa 1929, THE ABOMINABLE DR. PHIBES stars Vincent Price as Dr. Anton Phibes, a horribly disfigured madman who enacts an insidious revenge on the team of physicians who failed to save the life of his dear, departed wife (Caroline Munro, seen mostly in photos). His face and voice destroyed in an auto accident, Phibes reconstructs his mutilated visage over the bones that remained, and recovers his lost voice by plugging a cord extended from his neck into a Victrola! The gruesome ends he devises for the doctors are patterned after the plagues brought down on Ramses in ancient Egypt (killer locusts, blood-sucking bats, rabid rats, etc.). Kept at a snappy pace by "Avengers" director Robert Fuest and given a bizarre art deco look by art director Bernard Reeves and set designer Brian Eatwell, this movie is a kitschy homage to the sillier horror pictures of the 1930s and well worth a look. An equally entertaining sequel, DR. PHIBES RISES AGAIN, was released in 1972.

ABSENCE OF MALICE

1981 116m c Drama ★★½
Columbia (U.S.) PG

Paul Newman (*Gallagher*), Sally Field (*Megan*), Bob Balaban (*Rosen*), Melinda Dillon (*Teresa*), Luther Adler (*Malderone*), Barry Primus (*Waddell*), Josef Sommer (*McAdam*), John Harkins (*Davidek*), Don Hood (*Quinn*), Wilford Brimley (*Wells*)

p, Sydney Pollack; d, Sydney Pollack; w, Kurt Luedtke; ph, Owen Roizman; ed, Sheldon Kahn; m, Dave Grusin; prod d, Terence Marsh; cos, Bernie Pollack

AAN Best Actor: Paul Newman; *AAN Best Supporting Actress:* Melinda Dillon; *AAN Best Original Screenplay:* Kurt Luedtke

ABSENT-MINDED PROFESSOR, THE

Gallagher (Paul Newman), the son of a dead mobster, runs a legitimate business in Miami, with his uncle (Luther Adler) his only connection to organized crime. A federal investigator (Bob Balaban) thinks Gallagher knows the details of a labor leader's disappearance, and leaks information to Megan (Sally Field), a reporter who writes a story implicating Gallagher. The story's publication brings tragic results, and Gallagher plots to get revenge. Sydney Pollack's film is a solid, absorbing drama that, in profiling the damage that can result from investigative reporting, presents a counterpoint to ALL THE PRESIDENT'S MEN. Newman, Dillon, and Luedtke received Oscar nominations.

ABSENT-MINDED PROFESSOR, THE

1961 97m bw Comedy/Fantasy ★★★
Walt Disney Productions (U.S.) G/U

Fred MacMurray *(Prof. Ned Brainard)*, Nancy Olson *(Betsy Carlisle)*, Keenan Wynn *(Alonzo Hawk)*, Tommy Kirk *(Bill Hawk)*, Leon Ames *(Rufus Daggett)*, Elliott Reid *(Shelby Ashton)*, Edward Andrews *(Defense Secretary)*, Wally Brown *(Coach Elkins)*, Forrest Lewis *(Officer Kelly)*, James Westerfield *(Officer Hanson)*

p, Walt Disney; d, Robert Stevenson; w, Bill Walsh (based on the story by Samuel W. Taylor); ph, Edward Colman; ed, Cotton Warburton; m, George Bruns; art d, Carroll Clark; fx, Peter Ellenshaw, Eustace Lycett, Robert A. Mattey

AAN Best Cinematography: Edward Colman; *AAN Best Art Direction:* Carroll Clark (Art Direction), Emile Kuri (Set Decoration), Hal Gausman (Set Decoration); *AAN Best Visual Effects:* Robert A Mattey (Special Effects-Visual), Eustace Lycett (Special Effects-Visual)

A wacky comedy in which college professor Ned Brainard (Fred MacMurray) invents flying rubber, which he dubs "flubber." The substance has gravity-defying properties and, when applied to the soles of shoes, allows the wearer to leap to incredible heights. A variety of suitably screwy situations ensue, as the evil Alonzo Hawk (Keenan Wynn) plots to steal the formula for his own personal gain. This is a zanily inventive piece of work, with delightful special effects, which set the style for a long series of live-action Disney films. It earned Oscar nominations for Best Cinematography, Best Art Direction, and Best Special Effects. A 1964 sequel, THE SON OF FLUBBER, was less successful.

ABSOLUTE BEGINNERS

1986 107m c Musical ★★★
Palace/Virgin/Goldcrest (U.K.) PG-13/15

Eddie O'Connell *(Colin)*, Patsy Kensit *(Crepe Suzette)*, David Bowie *(Vendice Partners)*, James Fox *(Henley of Mayfair)*, Ray Davies *(Arthur)*, Mandy Rice-Davies *(Mum)*, Eve Ferret *(Big Jill)*, Tony Hippolyte *(Mr. Cool)*, Graham Fletcher-Cook *(Wizard)*, Joe McKenna *(Fabulous Hoplite)*

p, Stephen Woolley, Chris Brown; d, Julien Temple; w, Christopher Wicking, Richard Burridge, Don MacPherson (based on the novel by Colin MacInnes); ph, Oliver Stapleton; ed, Michael Bradsell, Gerry Hambling, Richard Bedford, Russell Lloyd; m, Gil Evans; prod d, John Beard; art d, Stuart Rose, Ken Wheatley; chor, David Toguri; cos, Sue Blane, David Perry

A visually inventive and energetic pop musical adapted from Colin MacInnes' 1958 cult novel of the same name. ABSOLUTE BEGINNERS is a tale of two swinging English teens, Colin (Eddie O'Connell) and Crepe Suzette (Patsy Kensit), set against the backdrop of emerging youth culture and racial tension in late 1950s London. As Suzette becomes a success in the fashion business and looks set to leave her street roots behind, Colin is torn between his youthful idealism and his desire to do whatever is necessary to lure her back. Though the characterization and plot waver on the transparent, ABSOLUTE BEGINNERS has no shortage of color, movement, and infectious music—it's a perfect example of a music video sensibility applied to a feature-length film. Highlights include songs by jazzman Slim Gaillard ("Selling Out") and The Style Council ("Have You Ever Had It Blue?") and a bravura, one-take opening sequence a la TOUCH OF EVIL.

ABYSS, THE

1989 140m c Science Fiction ★★½
Fox (U.S.) PG-13/12

Ed Harris *(Bud Brigman)*, Mary Elizabeth Mastrantonio *(Lindsey Brigman)*, Michael Biehn *(Lt. Coffey)*, George Robert Klek *(Wilhite)*, John Bedford Lloyd *("Jammer" Willis)*, Christopher Murphy *(Seal Schoenick)*, Adam Nelson *(Ensign Monk)*, J.C. Quinn *("Sonny" Dawson)*, Kimberly Scott *(Lisa "One Night" Standing)*, Capt. Kidd Brewer Jr. *(Lew Finler)*

p, Gale Anne Hurd; d, James Cameron; w, James Cameron; ph, Mikael Salomon, Dennis Skotak; ed, Joel Goodman; m, Alan Silvestri; prod d, Leslie Dilley; art d, Peter Childs; cos, Deborah Everton

AAN Best Cinematography: Mikael Salomon; *AAN Best Art Direction:* Leslie Dilley, Anne Kuljian; *AAN Best Sound:* Don Bassman, Kevin F. Cleary, Richard Overton, Lee Orloff; *AA Best Visual Effects:* John Bruno, Dennis Muren, Hoyt Yeatman, Dennis Skotak

Picture the opening scene of JAWS, except that, in THE ABYSS, it's not a great white shark but an underwater UFO that propels the movie into action. Spotted on sonar by a US nuclear submarine, the "thing" is eerily tracked below deck, where it creates a disaster because of the crew's ensuing panic. The sub sinks onto the ledge of an abyss, and a team of oil riggers, led by foreman Bud Brigman (Ed Harris), is pressed into a rescue mission. The civilian crew is joined by engineer Lindsey Brigman (Mary Elizabeth Mastrantonio), who happens to be Bud's soon-to-be ex-wife, and a group of navy underwater experts headed by Lt. Coffey (Michael Biehn), whose top-secret priority is the 150 nuclear warheads located on the sub. The rescue takes on a new character when the extra-terrestrial force makes its presence known. Despite the fact that most of the action occurs below sea level, THE ABYSS simply recycles elements of the stellar blockbusters it tries so hard to emulate (CLOSE ENCOUNTERS, E.T., and director James Cameron's own ALIENS among them). Unfortunately, it lacks the emotional impact and suspense of its predecessors and is spoiled by a disappointingly inane ending. What ultimately saves the film are its extraordinary sets and phenomenal Oscar-winning visual effects.

ACCIDENT

1967 105m c Drama ★★★★
Royal Avenue Chelsea (U.K.) /PG

Dirk Bogarde *(Stephen)*, Stanley Baker *(Charley)*, Jacqueline Sassard *(Anna)*, Michael York *(William)*, Vivien Merchant *(Rosalind)*, Delphine Seyrig *(Francesca)*, Alexander Knox *(Provost)*, Ann Firbank *(Laura)*, Brian Phelan *(Police Sergeant)*, Terence Rigby *(Plain Clothed Policeman)*

p, Joseph Losey, Norman Priggen; d, Joseph Losey; w, Harold Pinter (based on the novel by Nicholas Mosley); ph, Gerry Fisher; ed, Reginald Beck; m, John Dankworth; art d, Carmen Dillon; cos, Beatrice Dawson, De Luca of Rome

Dirk Bogarde gives a brilliant performance in this psychologically dense and compelling study, scripted by Harold Pinter, of an Oxford don and his infatuation with a beautiful student.

While typing late one night in his country home, Stephen (Dirk Bogarde), an Oxford philosophy professor, hears a crash and runs outside to find two of his pupils trapped inside a smashed car. William (Michael York) is dead, and Anna (Jacqueline Sassard) is in shock, but uninjured. Stephen remembers when he and the aristocratic William first met the Austrian Anna at school; in particular, he recalls a leisurely Sunday lunch spent at his own house. Charley (Stanley Baker), a brash colleague of Stephen's, had been having an affair with Anna, and it had eventually fallen to Stephen to deny the gravity of the situation to Charley's wife.

ACCIDENT is arguably director Joseph Losey's best film, equaling the superb THE SERVANT. There is something about Pinter's obliquely penetrating dialogue that brings out the best in Losey, raising the director's customary cerebral pessimism to new levels of insight. As Stephen, Bogarde brilliantly captures the mentality of his character—a civilized man who has sublimated his sexuality and now finds his fantasies taking over during a mid-life crisis. The rest of the cast is equally excellent, but Stanley Baker stands out as the amoral, but quite likable, Charley.

Losey cleverly scrambles the time scheme of the plot, a la Alain Resnais, most notably in the complex structure of the long Sunday lunch sequence. Like the repressed characters, the visual style of the film is deceptively simple, with the beautiful colors of the serene British countryside used to mask the languorous sensuality and emotional devastation that lies beneath the surface.

ACCIDENTAL TOURIST, THE

1988 121m c Comedy   ★★★★
Warner Bros. (U.S.)   PG

William Hurt *(Macon Leary)*, Kathleen Turner *(Sarah Leary)*, Geena Davis *(Muriel Pritchett)*, Amy Wright *(Rose)*, Bill Pullman *(Julian)*, Robert Gorman *(Alexander Pritchett)*, David Ogden Stiers *(Porter Leary)*, Ed Begley Jr. *(Charles Leary)*, Bradley Mott *(Mr. Loomis)*, Seth Granger *(Ethan)*

p, Lawrence Kasdan, Charles Okun, Michael Grillo; d, Lawrence Kasdan; w, Frank Galati, Lawrence Kasdan (based on the novel by Anne Tyler); ph, John Bailey; ed, Carol Littleton; m, John Williams; prod d, Bo Welch; cos, Ruth Myers

AAN Best Picture; AA Best Supporting Actress: Geena Davis; *AAN Best Adapted Screenplay:* Frank Galati, Lawrence Kasdan; *AAN Best Score:* John Williams

Writer-director Kasdan's fine adaptation of Tyler's novel hinges on Hurt's understated performance as a writer of travel guides for businessmen who hate to travel. Shortly after his wife, Turner (who starred opposite Hurt in Kasdan's BODY HEAT), leaves him, he breaks a leg and moves in with his oddball middle-aged sister and brothers (Wright, Begley, and Stiers). Because his dead son's Welsh corgi has become a disciplinary problem, Hurt calls upon the dog-training services of Davis, a vibrant divorcee. They begin an awkward relationship that is further complicated when Turner wants to patch things up. Kasdan has remained true to the spirit of Tyler's award-winning novel, preserving much of her wonderful dialogue and humor. Hurt's performance is remarkably assured, and Davis beautifully captures her character's insouciance. Less than perfect is Turner, whose capable performance presents a figure somewhat hollow at the center. Although some may find the film slow-moving, its rich characterizations alone makes it well worth watching. Davis won the Best Supporting Actress Oscar. The film was nominated for Best Picture, Best Adapted Screenplay, and Best Original Score.

ACCOMPANIST, THE
(L'ACCOMPAGNATRICE)

1992 110m c Historical/Drama   ★★★½
Film Par Film/Les Films de la Boissiere/Orly Films/Sedif/France 3   PG
Cinema/Paravision International (France)

Richard Bohringer *(Charles Brice)*, Elena Safonova *(Irene Brice)*, Romane Bohringer *(Sophie Vasseur)*, Samuel Labarthe *(Jacques Fabert)*, Julien Rassam *(Benoit Weizman)*, Nelly Borgeaud *(Helene Vasseur - Sophie's Mother)*, Bernard Verley *(Jacques Cenlat)*, Niels Dubost *(Young Civil Servant on the Train)*, Sacha Briquet *(Dignitary)*, Claude Rich *(Minister)*

p, Jean-Louis Livi; d, Claude Miller; w, Claude Miller, Luc Beraud (from the novel by Nina Berberova); ph, Yves Angelo; ed, Albert Jurgenson; prod d, Jean-Pierre Kohut; art d, Michael Howells; cos, Jacqueline Bouchard

Cesar Award-winning actress Romane Bohringer joins her father Richard Bohringer (THE COOK, THE THIEF, HIS WIFE AND HER LOVER) and Elena Safonova (DARK EYES) in this powerful story of betrayal in wartime France; while primarily a story of collaboration, it is also an allegorical tale that could take place at any time, in any culture.

Gifted young pianist Sophie (Bohringer) and her mother endure grinding deprivation in German-occupied Paris. She auditions for classical vocalist Irene (Safonova), who is impressed with her talent and inner toughness, and hires the girl as her accompanist. Captivated by Irene's glamorous life, Sophie rejects her mother and acts as go-between for the singer and her lover, Resistance leader Fabert (Samuel Labarthe). After Irene's husband Charles (Richard Bohringer) insults a Nazi officer, the trio escapes to London. Fabert follows and he

and Irene resume their romance, no longer using Sophie's services; Sophie feels betrayed and becomes a jealous voyeur, with terrible consequences.

Director Claude Miller (THE LITTLE THIEF, GARDE A VUE) skillfully tells a story of seduction, pride, and betrayal, with the help of an outstanding cast. Miller has said he based Charles—as Bohringer seems to have based his performance—on the cuckolded Jewish aristocrat played by Marcel Dalio in Renoir's RULES OF THE GAME. The younger Bohringer is frighteningly good as Sophie; she readily buys into the comfortable life Irene offers, but is never fulfilled, becoming instead more drawn and brittle. One of 1993's most absorbing and poignant dramas.

ACCUSED, THE

1988 110m c Drama   ★★½
Paramount (U.S.)   R/18

Kelly McGillis *(Kathryn Murphy)*, Jodie Foster *(Sarah Tobias)*, Bernie Coulson *(Kenneth Joyce)*, Ann Hearn *(Sally Frazer)*, Steve Antin *(Bob Joiner)*, Tom O'Brien *(Larry)*, Allan Lysell *(Al Massi)*, Leo Rossi *(Cliff Albrecht)*, Carmen Argenziano *(Paul Rudolph)*, Terry David Mulligan *(Det. Duncan)*

p, Stanley R. Jaffe, Sherry Lansing; d, Jonathan Kaplan; w, Tom Topor; ph, Ralf D. Bode; ed, Jerry Greenberg, O. Nicholas Brown; m, Brad Fiedel; prod d, Richard Kent Wilcox

AA Best Actress: Jodie Foster

Only a riveting performance by Jodie Foster lifts THE ACCUSED above the level of a television movie. The story, which bears some resemblance to a much-publicized 1983 incident in Massachusetts, centers on the case of Foster, a tough, sexy young woman who is gang-raped in a neighborhood bar before a crowd of cheering onlookers. District attorney McGillis takes the case. She agrees to a plea bargain in which the rapists admit to reckless endangerment, because she fears her client's sordid past will destroy her credibility in court. After Foster castigates McGillis for selling her out, McGillis devises a new strategy—to put the crowd of onlookers on trial for "criminal solicitation."

Director Jonathan Kaplan and screenwriter Tom Topor purposely paint Foster as a slut in order to strengthen their argument—for no matter how provocatively she was dressed or how erotically she danced, no one can believe that Foster wanted to be gang-raped. Although the filmmakers are well-intentioned, THE ACCUSED is a predictable picture that lacks emotional insight; it works only because of the onscreen bond between Foster, who won a much-deserved Oscar for her performance, and McGillis. Foster charges forward into the frame with explosive energy, carrying the film and proving she has far too much talent to let mediocre material bring her down.

ACE IN THE HOLE

1951 111m bw Drama   ★★★★
Paramount (U.S.)

Kirk Douglas *(Charles Tatum)*, Jan Sterling *(Lorraine)*, Robert Arthur *(Herbie Cook)*, Porter Hall *(Jacob Q. Boot)*, Frank Cady *(Mr. Federber)*, Richard Benedict *(Leo Minosa)*, Ray Teal *(Sheriff)*, Lewis Martin *(McCardle)*, John Berks *(Papa Minosa)*, Frances Dominguez *(Mama Minosa)*

p, Billy Wilder; d, Billy Wilder; w, Billy Wilder, Lesser Samuels, Walter Newman; ph, Charles Lang; ed, Arthur Schmidt; m, Hugo Friedhofer; art d, Hal Pereira, Earl Hedrick

AAN Best Original Screenplay: Lesser Samuels, Walter Newman

A bitter pill, brilliantly done by Billy Wilder. Boozy but ruthlessly ambitious newspaperman, Douglas, down on his luck and desperate to improve his lot as a result of a mining accident, builds a media circus. Gut-busting performance by a growling Douglas, matched easily by snarling Sterling, who gets best line: "I don't pray. Kneeling bags my nylons." An uneasy classic.

ACE VENTURA: PET DETECTIVE

1994 85m C Comedy   ★★★
Ace Productions/Morgan Creek (U.S.)   PG-13/12

Jim Carrey *(Ace Ventura)*, Courteney Cox *(Melissa)*, Sean Young *(Lieutenant Lois Einhorn)*, Tone Loc *(Emilio)*, Dan Marino *(Himself)*, Noble Willingham *(Riddle)*, Troy Evans *(Podacter)*, Raynor Scheine *(Woodstock)*, Udo Kier *(Camp)*, Frank Adonis *(Vinnie)*

p, James G. Robinson; d, Tom Shadyac; w, Jack Bernstein, Tom Shadyac, Jim Carrey (from a story by Jack Bernstein); ph, Julio Macat; ed, Don Zimmerman; m, Ira Newborn; prod d, William A. Elliott; art d, Alan E. Muraoka; fx, Michael N. Arbogast, Matte World Digital; cos, Bobbie Read

ACE VENTURA: PET DETECTIVE marks the ascendance of a new star in film farce, as Jim Carrey elevates this stupid, suprisingly shoddy picture into the comedy stratosphere, mainly thanks to his Gumby-like ability to contort his face and body in the most amazing ways.

Ace Ventura (Jim Carrey) is an alarmingly eccentric private eye who specializes in cases involving animals. He cares far more for wildlife than he does for social niceties, and women and varmints love him right back. Ventura's the perfect man for the job when the aquatic mascot of the Miami Dolphins is kidnapped, but the plot thickens when star quarterback Dan Marino vanishes as well. Only Ace can get back the mammals, win the girl (team employee Melissa, played by Courteney Cox), and evade the strangely obstructive cop Lt. Einhorn (Sean Young).

One of the funniest films to emerge from Hollywood in the 90s, ACE VENTURA claimed huge audiences, despite dismissive reviews. Critics noted that every gag is carried much too far, as if daring the viewer not to laugh, but failed to account for the devoted following Carrey had cultivated with his sometimes grotesque clowning on TV's "In Living Color." Interestingly, Ace is not the typical movie goofball, smart aleck, or idiot savant; he's a genuine weirdo who happens to be stunningly competent at his job. The same can be said for the film's justly popular leading man.

ACROSS 110TH STREET

1972 102m c Crime   ★★★½
UA (U.S.)   R/18

Anthony Quinn *(Capt. Frank Mattelli)*, Yaphet Kotto *(Det. Lt. Pope)*, Anthony Franciosa *(Nick D'Salvio)*, Paul Benjamin *(Jim Harris)*, Ed Bernard *(Joe Logart)*, Richard Ward *(Doc Johnson)*, Norma Donaldson *(Gloria Roberts)*, Antonio Fargas *(Henry Jackson)*, Gilbert Lewis *(Shevvy)*, Marlene Warfield *(Mrs. Jackson)*

p, Ralph Serpe, Fouad Said; d, Barry Shear; w, Luther Davis (based on the novel by Wally Ferris); ph, Jack Priestley; ed, Byron Brandt; m, J.J. Johnson; art d, Perry Watkins

Fast-paced, brutal actioner has three black hoods stealing a fortune from a Mafia-controlled Harlem numbers bank. They are tracked down by crooked cop Quinn, who walks a thin line between his duties as a policeman and his obligations to the Mafia. It's a race to see who gets the thieves first, the Mafia hoods or Quinn and his black partner, Kotto. Smartly edited with terrific location work in New York City. The dependable Kotto is a standout.

ADAM'S RIB

1949 101m bw Comedy   ★★★½
MGM (U.S.)   /A

Spencer Tracy *(Adam Bonner)*, Katharine Hepburn *(Amanda Bonner)*, Judy Holliday *(Doris Attinger)*, Tom Ewell *(Warren Attinger)*, David Wayne *(Kip Lurie)*, Jean Hagen *(Beryl Caighn)*, Hope Emerson *(Olympia La Pere)*, Eve March *(Grace)*, Clarence Kolb *(Judge Reiser)*, Emerson Treacy *(Jules Frikke)*

p, Lawrence Weingarten; d, George Cukor; w, Ruth Gordon, Garson Kanin; ph, George Folsey; ed, George Boemler; m, Miklos Rozsa; art d, Cedric Gibbons, William Ferrari; fx, A. Arnold Gillespie; cos, Walter Plunkett

AAN Best Original Screenplay: Ruth Gordon, Garson Kanin

Delightful, sophisticated comedy sparked by the famous chemistry between Katharine Hepburn and Spencer Tracy. When Tracy, an unyielding DA, prosecutes the client of his lawyer-wife, Hepburn, in an attempted murder case, it unleashes a battle of the sexes that almost wrecks their happy marriage. The defendant is Holliday (in an outstanding debut which led to her getting the "dumb blonde" lead in BORN YESTERDAY), who attempted to shoot a woman who was trysting with Holliday's slippery husband (Ewell, very funny here). Hepburn, an advocate of women's rights, is determined to prove that the prosecution's case is a reflection of sexist double standards, and that Holliday's husband would never be tried for the same actions. This rankles the conservative Tracy, and matters are further complicated when foppish David Wayne begins to move in on Hepburn. Throughout the trial, Tracy and Hepburn's marriage seems headed for the rocks, their courtroom resentments surfacing at home. Eventually, Hepburn wins an acquittal for Holliday through a case based on sexual equality, but admits, as does a petulant Tracy, that there are basic differences between men and women. "*Vive le difference!*" Tracy exclaims, and the marriage and the battle between the sexes go on. A thoroughly witty, sharply directed, fun film from Cukor, with a sprightly, Oscar-nominated script from Gordon and Kanin, ADAM'S RIB succeeds brilliantly through a combination of top talents, especially those of Hepburn and Tracy.

ADDAMS FAMILY VALUES

1993 94m c Comedy/Horror   ★★★
Paramount (U.S.)   PG-13/PG

Anjelica Huston *(Morticia Addams)*, Raul Julia *(Gomez Addams)*, Christopher Lloyd *(Uncle Fester Addams)*, Joan Cusack *(Debbie Jellinsky)*, Christina Ricci *(Wednesday Addams)*, Carol Kane *(Granny Addams)*, Jimmy Workman *(Pugsley Addams)*, Kaitlyn Hooper *(Pubert Addams)*, Kristin Hooper *(Pubert Addams)*, Carel Struycken *(Lurch the Butler)*

p, Scott Rudin; d, Barry Sonnenfeld; w, Paul Rudnick (from the characters created by Charles Addams); ph, Donald Peterman; ed, Arthur Schmidt, Jim Miller; m, Marc Shaiman; prod d, Ken Adam; fx, Alan Munro; chor, Peter Anastos; cos, Theoni V. Aldredge

AAN Best Art Direction: Ken Adam, Marvin March

Like the first ADDAMS FAMILY, this continuation of the macabre clan's misadventures is really just a string of sight gags and one-liners. The good news is that the one-liners are much funnier than the first time, mainly thanks to the increased input of screenwriter Paul Rudnick.

The other major change *chez* Addams is that young Wednesday (Christina Ricci) has entered that "difficult" stage of growing up—boys are starting to pique her interest almost as much as ritual sacrifice. To complicate matters further, the family is upended by the arrival of a new baby of indeterminate gender ("Is it a boy? Is it a girl?"—"It's an Addams!" goes the post-birth exchange, though the infant does sport a Gomez-style mustache). Wednesday and Pugsley (Jimmy Workman) react with unconcealed venom toward their new, rival sibling, showing a keenness to play, not with him, but with his head. Meanwhile, a bogus nanny (Joan Cusack) is scheming to get her hands on Uncle Fester's (Christopher Lloyd) fortune. Her plan involves sending the older children off to an exclusive summer camp, where there are plenty of opportunities to poke fun at the rich, self-obsessed children of rich, self-obsessed parents.

When forced by the camp leader to take part in a cheesy Thanksgiving pageant he has "conceived," Wednesday complains that his work is lacking in both character definition and dramatic structure. The same could be said of ADDAMS FAMILY VALUES but, frankly, we don't give a damn.

ADDAMS FAMILY, THE

1991 99m c Comedy/Horror   ★★½
Orion (U.S.)   PG-13/PG

Anjelica Huston *(Morticia Addams)*, Raul Julia *(Gomez Addams)*, Christopher Lloyd *(Uncle Fester Addams/Gordon Craven)*, Dan Hedaya *(Tully Alford)*, Elizabeth Wilson *(Abigail Craven)*, Judith

Malina *(Granny)*, Carel Struycken *(Lurch)*, Dana Ivey *(Margaret Alford)*, Paul Benedict *(Judge Womack)*, Christina Ricci *(Wednesday Addams)*

p, Scott Rudin; d, Barry Sonnenfeld; w, Caroline Thompson, Larry Wilson (from the characters created by Charles Addams); ph, Owen Roizman; ed, Dede Allen, Jim Miller; m, Marc Shaiman; prod d, Richard MacDonald; art d, Marjorie Stone McShirley; fx, Alan Munro, Chuck Comiskey, Chuck Gaspar; chor, Peter Anastos; cos, Ruth Myers

AAN Best Costume Design: Ruth Myers

This meticulously composed homage owes far more to Charles Addams's original *New Yorker* cartoons than to the short-lived 60s TV series. Unfortunately, the filmmakers were so intent on creating the right look and attitude that they neglected to think about the plot; the result is a series of one-note jokes that no amount of visual style can redeem.

The Addamses are a ghoulish clan delighting in the macabre—the devilish opposite of a rosy, wholesome American family. The debonair Gomez Addams (Raul Julia) and his morbidly elegant wife Morticia (Anjelica Huston) preside over an eccentric household that includes Wednesday (Christina Ricci) and Pugsley (Jimmy Workman), their precociously diabolical offspring; Lurch (Carel Struycken), their aptly named manservant; and Thing (Christopher Hart), a disembodied hand that serves as the family pet. Into this grim but happy bunch come Abigail Craven (Elizabeth Wilson) and her son Gordon (Christopher Lloyd), a con artist duo who, in conspiracy with Tully Alford (Dan Hedaya), the Addams's crooked lawyer, plan to make off with the Addams fortune. The plan revolves around the uncanny resemblance between Gordon and Gomez's long-lost brother, Fester (also played by Lloyd).

Cinematographer-turned-director Barry Sonnenfeld and screenwriters Larry Wilson and Caroline Thompson haven't solved the problem of how to construct a film around a one-joke concept, though the production design is a triumph of post-modern Gothic and there are some effective one-liners (Morticia to a depressed Gomez: "Don't torture yourself, Gomez. That's *my* job.").

ADVENTURES OF BARON MUNCHAUSEN, THE

1989   126m   c   Science Fiction/Fantasy   ★★★
Prominent/Laura/Allied Film Makers   (U.K./West Germany)   PG

John Neville *(Baron Munchausen)*, Eric Idle *(Desmond/Berthold)*, Sarah Polley *(Sally Salt)*, Oliver Reed *(Vulcan)*, Charles McKeown *(Rupert/Adolphus)*, Winston Dennis *(Bill Albrecht)*, Jack Purvis *(Jeremy/Gustavus)*, Valentina Cortese *(Queen Ariadne/Violet)*, Jonathan Pryce *(Horatio Jackson)*, Bill Paterson *(Henry Salt)*

p, Thomas Schuhly, Ray Cooper; d, Terry Gilliam; w, Charles McKeown, Terry Gilliam (based on the stories by Rudolph Erich Raspe); ph, Giuseppe Rotunno; ed, Peter Hollywood; m, Michael Kamen; prod d, Dante Ferretti; art d, Massimo Razzi, Maria Teresa Barbasso; chor, Pino Penesse, Giorgio Rossi; cos, Gabriella Pescucci

AAN Best Art Direction: Dante Ferretti (Art Direction), Francesca Lo Schiavo (Set Decoration); *AAN Best Costume Design:* Gabriella Pescucci; *AAN Best Visual Effects:* Richard Conway, Kent Houston; *AAN Best Makeup:* Maggie Weston, Fabrizio Sforza

Director Terry Gilliam's THE ADVENTURES OF BARON MUNCHAUSEN adapts the tall tales and fables associated with the real-life Karl Friedrich Hieronymous von Munchhausen (1720-97), a German soldier and nobleman. The film begins in a walled city whose denizens suffer under a siege by the army of the Ottoman Empire, and under the government of their evil leader Horatio Jackson (Jonathan Pryce). Within the town, a theater troupe is staging a rendition of the Munchausen saga when an aged man in the audience (John Neville) announces that he's the *real* Baron, and that only he can save them from the siege. He then departs in a makeshift balloon to round up his former cohorts, the superhumanly gifted aides who will help him in his struggle. The narrative is highly episodic and only intermittently engaging, but Gilliam's wildly inventive *mise en scene*, ably assisted by production designer Dante Ferretti, is extraordinary.

ADVENTURES OF BUCKAROO BANZAI: ACROSS THE 8TH DIMENSION, THE

1984   103m   c   Comedy/Science Fiction   ★★½
Sherwood   (U.S.)   PG/15

Peter Weller *(Buckaroo Banzai)*, John Lithgow *(Dr. Emilio Lizardo/Lord John Whorfin)*, Ellen Barkin *(Penny Priddy)*, Jeff Goldblum *(New Jersey)*, Christopher Lloyd *(John Bigboote)*, Lewis Smith *(Perfect Tommy)*, Rosalind Cash *(John Emdall)*, Robert Ito *(Prof. Hikita)*, Pepe Serna *(Reno Nevada)*, Ronald Lacey *(President Widmark)*

p, Neil Canton, W.D. Richter; d, W.D. Richter; w, Earl Mac Rauch; ph, Fred Koenekamp; ed, Richard Marks, George Bowers; m, Michael Boddicker; prod d, J. Michael Riva; art d, Richard Carter, Stephen Dane; fx, Michael Fink; cos, Aggie Guerard Rodgers

Clearly designed as a cult film, this messy trifle is not without its charms. These include the affably weird Goldblum, Lithgow's deliriously overstated mad scientist, and a band of alien invaders who are not emissaries of a vastly superior race, but beer-swilling mediocrities in Hawaiian shirts. Nevertheless, this strange film tries to do too much in too short a time. The title character (Weller) is a nuclear physicist, brain surgeon, and rock-'n'-roll singer who saves the world from the Red Lectroids, aliens from a distant galaxy. As the film opens, Weller is trying to drive his superpowered car through a mountain in an attempt to test the "oscillation overthruster" he has invented. The device is highly coveted by the aliens, who need it in order to return to their own world. Dr. Emilio Lizardo (Lithgow), who conducted the same research decades earlier, escapes from a mental institution and sets up shop again, making plans for world domination in league with the Red Lectroids. Few films appear so obviously to have dropped footage on the cutting-room floor. Punch lines appear without set-ups and set-ups without punch lines. Characters come and go with such bewildering speed that it is virtually impossible to keep track of the story, which jumps around enough to induce motion sickness. BUCKAROO BANZAI has nevertheless earned a loyal cult following among those who are willing to invest time in the roller-coaster ride.

ADVENTURES OF DON JUAN

1949   110m   c   Adventure/Romance   ★★½
Warner Bros.   (U.S.)   /PG

Errol Flynn *(Don Juan)*, Viveca Lindfors *(Queen Margaret)*, Robert Douglas *(Duke de Lorca)*, Alan Hale *(Leporello)*, Romney Brent *(King Phillip III)*, Ann Rutherford *(Donna Elena)*, Robert Warwick *(Count De Polan)*, Jerry Austin *(Don Sebastian)*, Douglas Kennedy *(Don Rodrigo)*, Jean Shepherd *(Donna Carlotta)*

p, Jerry Wald; d, Vincent Sherman; w, George Oppenheimer, Harry Kurnitz (based on the story by Harry Dalmas); ph, Elwood Bredell; ed, Alan Crosland Jr.; m, Max Steiner

AAN Best Art Direction: Edward Carrere, Lyle Reifsnider; *AA Best Costume Design:* Leah Rhodes, Travilla, Marjorie Best

The last of the big-budget swashbucklers for an increasingly dissipated star and an increasingly disappointed studio, DON JUAN offers Flynn as the notorious lover and swordsman of the title: amorous, capricious and somewhat world-weary. The film features the predictable expert duels in resplendent settings, when Flynn is not enjoying the flighty advances of a bevy of luscious contract beauties. Viveca Lindfors is an arresting choice for the Queen of Spain, but her considerable talents are not challenged by routine Hollywood treatment. The film did respectable box office business, but it is evident to the viewer that Flynn is growing a little long in the tooth for leading man roles. Nevertheless, DON JUAN is enjoyable formula fluff and a fitting swan song to Flynn's years as a bankable star.

ADVENTURES OF ICHABOD AND MR. TOAD, THE

1949   68m   c   Animated   ★★★★
Walt Disney Productions   (U.S.)   /A

VOICES OF: Bing Crosby *(Narrator)*, Basil Rathbone, Eric Blore, Pat O'Malley, John Floyardt, Colin Campbell, Campbell Grant, Claud Allister, The Rhythmaires

ADVENTURES OF MARK TWAIN, THE

p, Walt Disney; d, Jack Kinney, Clyde Geronimi, James Algar; w, Erdman Penner, Winston Hibler, Joe Rinaldi, Ted Sears, Homer Brightman, Harry Reeves (based on the story "The Legend of Sleepy Hollow" by Washington Irving and the book *The Wind in the Willows* by Kenneth Grahame)

Split into two sequences, this feature-length cartoon is one of Disney's finest efforts, with attention paid to every animated detail. The first sequence deals with the madcap, aristocratic Mr. Toad of Kenneth Grahame's British classic *The Wind in the Willows*, a haughty amphibian who thinks himself too good for such fellows as Mr. Pig and stuffy Mr. Rat. Toad, who is obsessed with planes and autos, lands through his own recklessness in trouble, debt, and jail, and his friends must rally to get him out and defeat the band of thieving weasels that framed him. The second sequence, concerning the emaciated Ichabod Crane of Washington Irving's "The Legend of Sleepy Hollow", is delightfully narrated by Bing Crosby, who also croons some eerie tunes with the Rhythmaires. Ichabod, the new schoolmaster in a small New England village, has a memorable Halloween night when he is chased by the legendary Headless Horseman. For pure imaginative animation, this pell-mell race through forests and glens is still unequaled. ADVENTURE is superb family entertainment, though very young children may find the climactic sequence of the "Sleepy Hollow" portion too frightening. The two segments have been released separately on videocassette.

ADVENTURES OF MARK TWAIN, THE

1944   130m   bw   Biography   ★★★
Warner Bros.   (U.S.)   /U

Fredric March *(Samuel Clemens)*, Alexis Smith *(Olivia Langdon)*, Donald Crisp *(J. B. Pond)*, Alan Hale *(Steve Gillis)*, C. Aubrey Smith *(Oxford Chancellor)*, John Carradine *(Bret Harte)*, William Henry *(Charles Langdon)*, Robert Barrat *(Horace E. Bixby)*, Walter Hampden *(Jervis Langdon)*, Joyce Reynolds *(Clara Clemens)*

p, Jesse L. Lasky; d, Irving Rapper; w, Alan LeMay, Harry Chandlee (based on an adaptation by Alan LeMay and Harold M. Sherman of biographical material owned by the Mark Twain Co.); ph, Sol Polito, Laurence Butler, Eddie Linden, Don Siegel, James Leicester; ed, Ralph Dawson; m, Max Steiner; art d, John Hughes

AAN Best Score: Max Steiner; *AAN Best Art Direction:* John J Hughes (Art Direction), Fred MacLean (Interior Decoration); *AAN Best Visual Effects:* Paul Detlefsen (Special Effects-Photographic), John Crous (Special Effects-Photographic), Nathan Levinson (Special Effects-Sound)

Cliched but engaging film biography, with a solid performance by Fredric March as the young adventurer who left Hannibal, Missouri, to learn the Mississippi River's tricky ways as a navigator. In one scene, the young navigator is attempting to steer a riverboat through fogbound waters when he hears a deckhand, after throwing out a weight to determine the water's depth, shout: "Mark the twain [twine—the rope tied about the weight] 15 [feet]." Thus the *nom de plume* of one of America's finest writers and humorists. Sharp dialogue sparks the predictable story line as Twain moves from the Mississippi to the West as a newspaper editor, then on to Gold Rush California, where he writes the short story "The Celebrated Jumping Frog of Calaveras County," the success of which launches his literary career. The episodic film chronicles Twain's meetings with the greats of his day (U.S. Grant, Bret Harte, Oliver Wendell Holmes, Ralph Waldo Emerson, etc.), as well as his courtship of and marriage to Olivia Langdon (Alexis Smith), as it follows Twain from young manhood to old age. March imbues his character with quiet nobility, projecting the forceful, courageous soul of the immortal Twain. What's missing is the vinegary, difficult side of Twain that made him as unforgettable a man as he was a writer.

ADVENTURES OF MILO AND OTIS, THE
(KONEKO MONOGATARI)

1989   76m   c   Children's   ★★★
Fuji Television   (Japan)   G/U

Dudley Moore *(Narrator)*

p, Masaru Kakutani, Satoru Ogata; d, Masanori Hata; w, Mark Saltzman (based on a story by Masanori Hata); ph, Hideo Fujii, Shinji Tomita; ed, Chizuko Osada; m, Michael Boddicker

Of all the buddy movies ever made, MILO AND OTIS features one of the most unlikely pairs of friends—a cat and dog that befriend each other on a farm and eventually wander out into the not-so-friendly world. Not a single human being appears onscreen in this delightful live-action entry from Japan. It all starts when the kitten, Milo, decides to take a trip down the river in a box, with his faithful canine chum, Otis, following behind. But soon Otis loses track of his friend, who gets into many adventures. Based on a charming screenplay by Mark Saltzman, this clever children's film contains beautiful nature photography and moments of humor along with many impressive animal stunts. Surely it was no small feat to get bears and dogs, chickens and cats, pigs and cows to work together harmoniously. Shot from the animals' point of view and narrated by Dudley Moore, MILO AND OTIS contains some important messages about the responsibilites of friendship. Slow in spots, but a treat nevertheless.

ADVENTURES OF PRISCILLA, QUEEN OF THE DESERT, THE

1994   102m   c   Musical/Drama/Comedy   ★★★
Latent Image/Specific Films   (Australia)   R/15

Terence Stamp *(Bernadette)*, Hugo Weaving *(Tick/Mitzi)*, Guy Pearce *(Adam/Felicia)*, Bill Hunter *(Bob)*, Sarah Chadwick *(Marion)*, Mark Holmes *(Benji)*, Julia Cortez *(Cynthia)*, Ken Radley *(Frank)*, Alan Dargin *(Aboriginal Man)*, Rebel Russell *(Logowoman)*

p, Al Clark, Michael Hamlyn; d, Stephan Elliott; w, Stephan Elliott; ph, Brian Breheny; ed, Sue Blainey; m, Guy Gross; prod d, Owen Patterson; art d, Colin Gibson; chor, Mark White; cos, Lizzy Gardiner, Tim Chappel

AA Best Costume Design: Lizzy Gardiner, Tim Chappel

This offbeat Australian road movie about a busload of female impersonators became a surprise hit in the US, heralding a wave of cinematic interest in cross-dressing that would embrace everything from WIGSTOCK, a documentary about New York's much-loved open air drag festival, to the star-studded mainstream production, TO WONG FOO, THANKS FOR EVERYTHING, JULIE NEWMAR.

Drag performer Tick/Mitzi (Hugo Weaving) invites recently bereaved transsexual Bernadette (Terence Stamp) to join him and Adam/Felicia (Guy Pearce) on a journey to the outback town of Alice Springs, where they've been invited to put on a show at a casino run by an ex-partner of Tick's. The Priscilla of the title is the dilapidated bus Adam buys for the trip.

PRISCILLA is less concerned with "normalizing" gay lifestyles than earlier cross-dressing comedies such as LA CAGE AUX FOLLES and VICTOR/VICTORIA. The script is spiked with cheeky, occasionally hilarious encounters, like the trio's stroll through a lazy Outback town in flamboyant space-age drag, or Bernadette's deliciously unprintable riposte to a hostile woman in a bar. But the film tends toward pat, sitcom-style resolutions to its potentially interesting conflicts, and cannot sustain the manic, farcical pace of its best moments.

Things truly come alive during the drag performances and rehearsals, boosted by an irrepressible disco soundtrack. The Oscar-winning costumes by Lizzy Gardiner and Tim Chappel are wildly inspired, and the filmmakers indulge themselves—and us—with extended shots of the outrageously attired performers set against the spectacularly barren landscape. The true heart of the movie, though, is Terence Stamp. He may be a little stiff in the show routines but, offstage, he's a revelation, giving a performance of near-perfect restraint and dignity.

ADVENTURES OF ROBIN HOOD, THE

1938   102m   c   Adventure   ★★★★★
Warner Bros.   (U.S.)   /U

Errol Flynn *(Sir Robin of Locksley/Robin Hood)*, Olivia de Havilland *(Maid Marian)*, Basil Rathbone *(Sir Guy of Gisbourne)*, Claude Rains *(Prince John)*, Patric Knowles *(Will Scarlett)*, Eugene Pallette *(Friar Tuck)*, Alan Hale *(Little John)*, Melville Cooper *(High Sheriff of Nottingham)*, Ian Hunter *(King Richard the Lion-Hearted)*, Una O'Connor *(Bess)* p, Henry Blanke; d, Michael Curtiz, William Keighley; w, Norman Reilly Raine, Seton I. Miller (based on the novel *Ivanhoe* by Sir Walter Scott and the opera *Robin Hood* by De Koven-Smith); ph, Sol Polito, Tony Gaudio; ed, Ralph Dawson; m, Erich Wolfgang Korngold; art d, Carl Jules Weyl; cos, Milo Anderson

AAN Best Picture; *AA Best Editing:* Ralph Dawson; *AA Best Score:* Erich Wolfgang Korngold; *AA Best Art Direction:* Carl J. Weyl

When King Richard the Lion-Hearted (Ian Hunter) is captured by Austrians and held for ransom, evil Prince John (Claude Rains) declares himself ruler of England and makes no attempt to secure Richard's safe return. Though John has all the nobles and their armies on his side, it doesn't sway a lone knight, Robin Hood (Errol Flynn), who swears his allegiance to Richard and sets out to raise the ransom money by stealing from the caravans of the rich that cross through Sherwood Forest. Robin is aided by his lady love, Maid Marian (Olivia de Havilland), and his band of merry men, including Little John (Alan Hale) and Friar Tuck (Eugene Pallette), as he battles the false monarch and the villainous Sheriff of Nottingham (Melville Cooper) in his effort to return the throne to its rightful owner. This is one of the truly great adventure films of all time, and features a terrific performance by the perfectly cast Flynn. Handsome, dashing, and athletic, Flynn is everything that Robin Hood should be, with a wicked sense of humor to boot. His adversaries are all memorable villains, particularly Basil Rathbone as the conniving Sir Guy of Gisbourne. Rathbone spent many hours with a fencing instructor to prepare for his climactic duel with Flynn, one of the most exciting battles ever put on film. Only a spirited and extravagant production could do justice to the Robin Hood legend; this film is more than equal to the task. Korngold's score won a well-deserved Oscar, as did the editing and art direction.

ADVENTURES OF ROBINSON CRUSOE, THE

1952   90m   c   Adventure   ★★★½
UA   (Mexico)   /U

Dan O'Herlihy *(Robinson Crusoe)*, Jaime Fernandez *(Friday)*, Felipe de Alba *(Capt. Oberzo)*, Chel Lopez *(Bos'n)*, Jose Chavez, Emilio Garibay *(Leaders of the Mutiny)*

p, Oscar Dancigers, Henry Ehrlich; d, Luis Bunuel; w, Hugo Butler, Luis Bunuel (based on the novel *The Life and Strange Surprising Adventures of Robinson Crusoe* by Daniel Defoe); ph, Alex Phillips; ed, Carlos Savage, Alberto Valenzuela; m, Anthony Collins

AAN Best Actor: Dan O'Herlihy

A fairly faithful adaptation of Daniel Defoe's classic *The Life and Strange Surprising Adventures of Robinson Crusoe*, directed by Bunuel in Mexico. Shipwrecked in a storm, sailor Robinson Crusoe (Dan O'Herlihy) finds himself washed up on the shore of a desert island. All other hands have been killed in the storm, but Crusoe is able to salvage a cat, a dog, and some weapons and provisions from the wreckage. He takes up residence in a cave and begins living as his prehistoric ancestors must have done, all the while striving to overcome his oppressive loneliness. After going 18 years without seeing another human being, he is shocked when a small band of natives visits the island one day. They are about to kill and eat one of their party when Crusoe intervenes, saves the intended victim, and chases off the others. The two develop a strong relationship as they spend another ten years on the island, after which Crusoe is finally returned to civilization by the crew of a ship that anchors offshore.

Bunuel's adaptation is particularly effective in evoking the loneliness of the stranded survivor and in depicting the changes that gradually occur within him as his memories of civilization begin to fade. O'Herlihy earned an Academy Award nomination for his performance, but lost to Marlon Brando for ON THE WATERFRONT.

ADVENTURES OF SHERLOCK HOLMES, THE

1939   85m   bw   Mystery   ★★★★
Fox   (U.S.)   /PG

Basil Rathbone *(Sherlock Holmes)*, Nigel Bruce *(Dr. Watson)*, Ida Lupino *(Ann Brandon)*, Alan Marshal *(Jerrold Hunter)*, Terry Kilburn *(Billy)*, George Zucco *(Prof. Moriarty)*, Henry Stephenson *(Sir Ronald Ramsgate)*, E.E. Clive *(Inspector Bristol)*, Arthur Hohl *(Bassick)*, May Beatty *(Mrs. Jameson)*

p, Gene Markey; d, Alfred Werker; w, Edwin Blum, William A. Drake (based on the play by William Gillette and the works of Arthur Conan Doyle); ph, Leon Shamroy; ed, Robert Bischoff

A taut script and sharp, witty dialogue make this, the second of the Basil Rathbone/Nigel Bruce Sherlock Holmes vehicles, one of the finest crime adventures ever made. Arch-villain Professor Moriarty (Zucco, in the first of many appearances as Holmes's chief nemesis) plots a grand theft by sidetracking Holmes (Rathbone) with two foul murders, one involving Ann Brandon (Lupino). As Holmes investigates the murders, Moriarty begins work on his real goal, stealing the crown jewels from the Tower of London.

ADVENTURES was released a mere six months after THE HOUND OF THE BASKERVILLES and is generally considered superior to its predecessor, thanks to Alfred Werker's direction. Although both films were box office hits, Fox executives thought of the Holmes films as expensive "B" pictures and declined to continue the series at the outbreak of WWII, assuming the public would be uninterested in the 19th century British sleuth. In 1942 Universal reunited Rathbone and Bruce, updated the scenarios to reflect contemporary themes (i.e., Nazi spies), scaled down the production costs and turned out 11 successful, if inferior, installments.

ADVENTURES OF TOM SAWYER, THE

1938   93m   c   Adventure   ★★★½
Selznick   (U.S.)   /U

Tommy Kelly *(Tom Sawyer)*, Jackie Moran *(Huckleberry Finn)*, Ann Gillis *(Becky Thatcher)*, May Robson *(Aunt Polly)*, Walter Brennan *(Muff Potter)*, Victor Jory *(Injun Joe)*, David Holt *(Sid Sawyer)*, Victor Kilian *(Sheriff)*, Nana Bryant *(Mrs. Thatcher)*, Olin Howlin *(Schoolmaster)*

p, David O. Selznick, William H. Wright; d, Norman Taurog; w, John V.A. Weaver (based on the novel by Mark Twain); ph, James Wong Howe, Wilfrid M. Cline; ed, Margaret Clancy

AAN Best Art Direction: Lyle Wheeler (Art Direction)

Mark Twain's beloved Tom Sawyer comes to life in this excellent Selznick production, with Tommy Kelly portraying the brave, mischievous boy. He is caught between the manners of his very proper home, ruled by tough but loving Aunt Polly (May Robson), and the wild, roaming, trouble-seeking nature of his friend Huckleberry Finn, ably portrayed by Jackie Moran. The great Sawyer adventures are faithfully re-created—the conning of the two boys into whitewashing his aunt's fence, a wild ride down the Mississippi on a raft, the witnessing of Injun Joe's crimes and his pursuit of Tom and the terrified Becky Sharp (Ann Gillis) into the giant cave. The incorrigible boys even witness their own funeral ceremony before informing the grieving townsfolk that they are still among the living. A lively production featuring a quick pace, a chilling climax, and a surprising amount of wit.

ADVENTURESS, THE

1946   111m   bw   Spy   ★★★★
Individual   (U.K.)   /U

Deborah Kerr *(Bridie Quilty)*, Trevor Howard *(Lt. David Bayne)*, Raymond Huntley *(Miller)*, Michael Howard *(Hawkins)*, Norman Shelley *(Man in Straw Hat)*, Liam Redmond *(Timothy)*, Brefni O'Rorke *(Michael O'Callaghan)*, James Harcourt *(Grandfather)*, W.G. O'Gorman *(Danny Quilty)*, George Woodbridge *(Steve)*

p, Sidney Gilliat; d, Frank Launder; w, Sidney Gilliat, Frank Launder, Wolfgang Wilhelm; ph, Wilkie Cooper; ed, Thelma Myers; m, William Alwyn

An expertly crafted suspense film that is too often overlooked. Deborah Kerr, making her fifth feature at age 24, appears as an Irish spitfire who has been weaned on her grandfather's tales of British cruelty to the Irish; she leaves her small village of Ballygarry, spouting anti-British venom to a stranger, Huntley, on board a train to Dublin, where the IRA rejects her. But Huntley, a Nazi agent, uses her as a pawn, telling her that he represents another branch of the movement and involving her in the rescue of "one of the lads" imprisoned in a British jail—in reality, another Nazi spy. Howard, as a British intelligence agent, tracks her down and falls in love with her, staying a step behind through one perilous adventure after another, both to protect her and to uncover the Nazi spy ring. This is a highly suspenseful, atmospheric film in the Hitchcock tradition with a sophisticated script by Launder and Gilliat, who authored THE LADY VANISHES. The acting, particularly by Kerr (who won the 1947 New York Film Critics Award for this role and her appearance in BLACK NARCISSUS), Howard, and Huntley, is outstanding.

ADVISE AND CONSENT

1962 140m bw Political   ★★★½
Columbia (U.S.)   /X

Henry Fonda *(Robert Leffingwell)*, Charles Laughton *(Sen. Seabright "Seb" Cooley)*, Don Murray *(Sen. Brigham Anderson)*, Walter Pidgeon *(Sen. Bob Munson)*, Peter Lawford *(Sen. Lafe Smith)*, George Grizzard *(Sen. Fred Van Ackerman)*, Gene Tierney *(Dolly Harrison)*, Franchot Tone *(The President)*, Lew Ayres *(The Vice-President)*, Burgess Meredith *(Herbert Gelman)*

p, Otto Preminger; d, Otto Preminger; w, Wendell Mayes (based on the novel by Allen Drury); ph, Sam Leavitt; ed, Louis Loeffler; m, Jerry Fielding; prod d, Lyle Wheeler; cos, Hope Bryce

Incisive, sometimes brutal, study of American high politics, based on Allen Drury's best-selling novel, featuring outstanding performances from the leads and a great collection of character actors.

Fonda has been appointed Secretary of State, and the film revolves around his appointment's confirmation by the US Senate. Pidgeon and his cohorts are trying to push the appointment through, past such ancient pelicans as Laughton, in a marvelous portrayal of a crusty old Dixiecrat. Murray, a freshman senator whose vote in support of the nomination is vital, will not commit to his party leader, Pidgeon. This leads Grizzard, a ruthless, power-hungry colleague, to attempt to blackmail Murray into siding with his voting block. He digs up Murray's former homosexual activities and threatens to expose him unless he votes "the right way," with unexpectedly tragic results.

In an all-star cast, Laughton shines in his last role, but the subdued work by Tone and Ayres shows how underplaying can sometimes work best before the camera. Though the film sensationalizes politics, Preminger's touch is more precise and cautious than usual; this is a more realistic if less human portrait of the Senate than Capra's MR. SMITH GOES TO WASHINGTON. Both films proved to be unpopular with their role models, who refused to comment on them.

AFRICAN QUEEN, THE

1951 105m c Adventure/Romance/War   ★★★★★
Horizon/Romulus (U.S./U.K.)   /U

Humphrey Bogart *(Charlie Allnut)*, Katharine Hepburn *(Rose Sayer)*, Robert Morley *(Rev. Samuel Sayer)*, Peter Bull *(Captain)*, Theodore Bikel *(1st Officer)*, Walter Gotell *(2nd Officer)*, Gerald Onn *(Petty Officer)*, Peter Swanwick, Richard Marner *(Officers at Shona)*

p, Sam Spiegel; d, John Huston; w, James Agee, John Huston (based on the novel by C.S. Forester); ph, Jack Cardiff; ed, Ralph Kemplen; m, Allan Gray

AA Best Actor: Humphrey Bogart; *AAN Best Actress:* Katharine Hepburn; *AAN Best Director:* John Huston; *AAN Best Screenplay:* James Agee, John Huston

John Huston's THE AFRICAN QUEEN is a film that has everything—adventure, humor, spectacular photography and superb performances.

In his only Oscar-winning performance, Bogart stars as Charlie Allnut, a reprobate who uses his little battered steamer, *The African Queen*, to run supplies to small villages in East Africa at the onset of WWI. At one stop he meets Rose (Katharine Hepburn), the devoted spinster sister of Rev. Samuel Sayer (Robert Morley). When Charlie returns to the village later, he finds that German troops have invaded and Sayer is dead, and he offers to take the distraught Rose back to civilization. Thus begins a perilous and unforgettable journey as Charlie and Rose decide to do their part in the war effort against the Germans.

THE AFRICAN QUEEN's marvelous screenplay was written as a straight drama by James Agee, but director John Huston and his stars give it a lyrical tongue-in-cheek treatment that fills the screen with hilarious humanity. Magnificently filmed on location in Africa by Jack Cardiff, THE AFRICAN QUEEN is Hollywood filmmaking of the highest order.

AFTER DARK, MY SWEET

1990 114m c Crime   ★★★½
Avenue (U.S.)   R/18

Jason Patric *(Collie)*, Rachel Ward *(Fay)*, Bruce Dern *(Uncle Bud)*, George Dickerson *(Doc Goldman)*, James Cotton *(Charlie)*, Corey Carrier *(Jack)*, Rocky Giordani *(Bert)*, Jeanie Moore *(Nanny)*, Tom Wagner *(Counterman)*, Burke Byrnes *(Cop)*

p, Ric Kidney, Robert Redlin; d, James Foley; w, James Foley, Robert Redlin (based on the novel by Jim Thompson); ph, Mark Plummer; ed, Howard Smith; m, Maurice Jarre; art d, Kenneth A. Hardy; fx, Ken Diaz

A latter-day film noir involving the intertwined destinies of three boozy lowlifes. Collie (Jason Patric) is a near-psychopathic ex-boxer who left the ring after killing a competitor. He becomes involved with Fay (Rachel Ward), a seductive, alcoholic widow, and Uncle Bud (Bruce Dern), a sleazy former lawman, and is drawn into their scheme to get rich quick by kidnapping the young scion of a wealthy local family.

AFTER DARK, MY SWEET is based on a 1955 novel by prolific tough-guy novelist Jim Thompson, who worked on the screenplays of THE KILLING and PATHS OF GLORY for Stanley Kubrick, and whose *The Grifters* and *The Kill-Off* were also turned into 1990 releases. Director James Foley (RECKLESS, AT CLOSE RANGE) and cinematographer Mark Plummer deftly conjure the sense of stifling containment that drives these characters to drink or sin, but Robert Redlin's screenplay fails to fully animate their personalities. Patric gives a tremendous, smoldering performance, but Ward fails to convey the mysterious radiance of a convincing femme fatale. Dern rounds out the unappetizing triangle with an unpleasant performance, proving himself a worthy contender in the Dennis Hopper/Harry Dean Stanton creepstakes.

AFTER HOURS

1985 96m c Comedy   ★★★★
Double Play/Geffen (U.S.)   R/15

Griffin Dunne *(Paul Hackett)*, Rosanna Arquette *(Marcy)*, Verna Bloom *(June)*, Tommy Chong *(Pepe)*, Linda Fiorentino *(Kiki)*, Teri Garr *(Julie)*, John Heard *(Tom, the Bartender)*, Richard "Cheech" Marin *(Neil)*, Catherine O'Hara *(Gail)*, Dick Miller *(Waiter)*

p, Amy Robinson, Griffin Dunne, Robert F. Colesberry; d, Martin Scorsese; w, Joseph Minion; ph, Michael Ballhaus; ed, Thelma Schoonmaker; m, Howard Shore; prod d, Jeffrey Townsend; art d, Stephen J. Lineweaver; cos, Rita Ryack

A wickedly funny black comedy that follows the increasingly bizarre series of events that befall hapless word-processer Griffin Dunne after he ventures out of his apartment on the Upper East Side of Manhattan and goes downtown in search of carnal pleasures. On a wild cab ride to SoHo, Dunne loses the only folding money he has on him. When he goes to the loft of the sexy but quirky Rosanna Arquette, he discovers only Linda Fiorentino, working on a papier-mache sculpture. Eventually Arquette shows up, but she's such a hyperactive mass of contradictions that Dunne leaves. However, when he plunks down the 90 cents he has to his name at the subway station, the attendant tells him the fare has gone up to $1.50 this very midnight. He's trapped in SoHo, and things only get worse as the night wears on.

Scorsese is in total command of his visual style in AFTER HOURS, a tightly constructed film that races from scene to scene. The story sprang from the mind of screenwriter Joseph Minion, a Columbia University film student who had written the script for a class. Dunne turns in a superb performance, and we share his mounting frustration, fear, shame, and guilt. Scorsese ordered Dunne to abstain from sex and sleep during filming to increase his anxiety level, and filmed this small gem on location for the small budget of $3.5 million.

AFTER THE FOX

1966   102m   c   Comedy   ★★★
UA   (U.S./U.K./Italy)   /U

Peter Sellers *(Aldo Vanucci)*, Victor Mature *(Tony Powell)*, Britt Ekland *(Gina Romantica)*, Martin Balsam *(Harry)*, Akim Tamiroff *(Okra)*, Paolo Stoppa *(Polio)*, Tino Buazzelli *(Siepi)*, Mac Ronay *(Carlo)*, Lydia Brazzi *(Mama Vanucci)*, Lando Buzzanca *(Police Chief)*

p, John Bryan; d, Vittorio De Sica; w, Neil Simon, Cesare Zavattini; ph, Leonida Barboni; ed, Russell Lloyd; m, Burt Bacharach; art d, Mario Garbuglia; cos, Piero Tosi

A visual delight thanks to director De Sica, this Sellers vehicle is loaded with belly laughs thanks to an uneven but solid script by Simon. As the flamboyantly inept Fox, a *master* thief, Sellers breaks jail in order to arrange the passage to Rome of $3 million in gold bullion stolen in Cairo. After his escape, Sellers pops up almost frame by frame in a host of disguises—a prison doctor, a tourist cameraman, an Italian cop, and a zany New Wave film director, spoofing the avant-garde in a merciless portrayal. Part of that parody has Victor Mature (making a movie within the movie) as an aging star trussed up with corsets and insisting he wear the threadbare trench coat and battered hat from his 1940s films.

Mature is brilliant at mocking his former film noir persona, and interplays memorably with Sellers. In another spoof the Italian actors zestily parody stereotypes of themselves and their country: their casual ways, indifference to authority, and sexual passion. Particularly outstanding are the desert scenes, where De Sica himself is attempting to direct a movie during a violent sandstorm and has his equipment stolen by Sellers and Tamiroff.

AFTER THE REHEARSAL

1984   72m   c   Drama   ★★
Cinematograph/Persona   (Sweden)   R/U

Erland Josephson *(Henrik Vogler)*, Ingrid Thulin *(Rakel)*, Lena Olin *(Anna Egerman)*, Nadja Palmstjerna-Weiss *(Anna at age 12)*, Bertil Guve *(Henrik at age 12)*

p, Jorn Donner; d, Ingmar Bergman; w, Ingmar Bergman; ph, Sven Nykvist; ed, Sylvia Ingemarsson; art d, Anna Asp; cos, Inger Pehrsson

Filmed for Swedish television, AFTER THE REHEARSAL was advertised as Bergman's farewell to cinema (a claim also made upon the release of FANNY AND ALEXANDER in 1983). Partly autobiographical, it concerns an aging theater director, Josephson, who looks back on the pain and suffering he has caused those around him, especially the actresses he has loved and left. After the rehearsal of his fifth production of August Strindberg's *Dream Play*, the director rests on a couch onstage. There he is visited by Olin, a young actress who has returned to the theater in search of a bracelet she supposedly left behind. There is a mutual attraction between actress and director as they discuss their lives and the theater—Josephson revealing that he once had an affair with her mother. Then they imagine what their lives would be like if they were to have an affair.

Although AFTER THE REHEARSAL is blessed with three superb performances (especially Thulin, as a has-been actress who attacks the director for having abandoned her), it is trapped in its staginess, leaving one to wonder why Bergman decided to bring it to the screen (Bob Fosse's revelation on a similar theme was certainly more colorful). Olin, Josephson, and cinematographer Nykvist would meet again a few years later in Philip Kaufman's THE UNBEARABLE LIGHTNESS OF BEING.

AGE OF INNOCENCE, THE

1993   133m   c   Drama/Historical/Romance   ★★★★
Columbia/Cappa/De Fina Productions   (U.S.)   PG/U

Daniel Day-Lewis *(Newland Archer)*, Michelle Pfeiffer *(Countess Ellen Olenska)*, Winona Ryder *(May Welland)*, Alexis Smith *(Louisa Van Der Luyden)*, Geraldine Chaplin *(Mrs. Welland)*, Mary Beth Hurt *(Regina Beaufort)*, Alec McCowen *(Sillerton Jackson)*, Richard E. Grant *(Larry Lefferts)*, Miriam Margolyes *(Mrs. Mingott)*, Robert Sean Leonard *(Ted Archer)*

p, Barbara De Fina; d, Martin Scorsese; w, Jay Cocks, Martin Scorsese (from the novel by Edith Wharton); ph, Michael Ballhaus; ed, Thelma Schoonmaker; m, Elmer Bernstein; prod d, Dante Ferretti; art d, Speed Hopkins, Jean-Michel Hugon; fx, John Ottesen, Illusion Arts Inc.; cos, Gabriella Pescucci, Tirelli Costumi Roma, Barbara Matera Ltd.

AAN Best Adapted Screenplay: Jay Cocks, Martin Scorsese; *AAN Best Supporting Actress:* Winona Ryder; *AAN Best Art Direction:* Dante Ferretti, Robert J. Franco; *AA Best Costume Design:* Gabriella Pescucci; *AAN Best Original Score:* Elmer Bernstein

Rendered with sumptuous, almost painful accuracy, THE AGE OF INNOCENCE, adapted from the novel by Edith Wharton, seems at first glance an unlikely venture for relentlessly contemporary New Yorker Martin Scorsese. But its loving exploration of the arcane workings of a closed society, that of wealthy, well-bred New Yorkers of the 1870s, has more in common than one might expect with Scorsese's earlier work, from MEAN STREETS through GOODFELLAS. Perhaps the film's most remarkable aspect is how alien its underlying assumptions are to a society saturated with "Just Do It!" messages. Beneath the delineation of manners and mannerisms, the examination of lushly appointed decor and clothing, the evocation of a time and a place lost to the forward rush of history, THE AGE OF INNOCENCE rests on a moral struggle all but impossible to imagine in a modern-day setting.

Newland Archer (Daniel Day-Lewis), a respectable but vaguely discontented young lawyer, is engaged to marry the vapid and eminently proper May Welland (Winona Ryder). Their well-ordered lives are disrupted by the return of May's cousin, Ellen Olenska (Michelle Pfeiffer), a countess by virtue of her marriage to a Polish aristocrat. Intelligent, sophisticated, and just a bit too continental after her years abroad, Ellen is at first shunned by New York society, then tolerated after the Archers and the Wellands band together to draw her back into the fold. The film charts the painfully hesitant progress of Ellen and Newland's forbidden romance, no less passionate for being doomed.

THE AGE OF INNOCENCE is a feast for the eyes, and Scorsese brings to stuffy New York society the same keen regard for the rules of social games that characterize his earlier films.

AGNES OF GOD

1985   98m   c   Mystery   ★★★
Columbia   (U.S.)   PG-13/15

Jane Fonda *(Dr. Martha Livingston)*, Anne Bancroft *(Sister Miriam Ruth)*, Meg Tilly *(Sister Agnes)*, Anne Pitoniak *(Dr. Livingston's Mother)*, Winston Rekert *(Detective Langevin)*, Gratien Gelinas *(Father Martineau)*, Guy Hoffman *(Justice Joseph Leveau)*, Gabriel Arcand *(Monsignor)*, Francoise Faucher *(Eve LeClaire)*, Jacques Tourangeau *(Eugene Lyon)*

p, Patrick Palmer, Norman Jewison; d, Norman Jewison; w, John Pielmeier (based on his play); ph, Sven Nykvist; ed, Antony Gibbs; m, Georges Delerue; prod d, Ken Adam; art d, Carol Spier; cos, Renee April

AAN Best Actress: Anne Bancroft; *AAN Best Supporting Actress:* Meg Tilly; *AAN Best Score:* Georges Delerue

Set in a Quebec convent, this well-made mystery raises theological and philosophical questions as it unfolds its tale of the murder of a baby born to a young nun who has no recollection of the infant's conception or delivery. Jane Fonda, a chain-smoking court-appointed psychiatrist, is given the task of determining whether Meg Tilly, a beatific young nun, is sane, sainted, mad, or a murderer. But Anne Bancroft, the convent's mother superior, questions whether the answer to the mystery lies in psychology, setting up a faith-versus-reason confrontation that is the real focus of the film. John Pielmeier's award-winning 1982 play is adapted for the screen here by director Norman Jewison, and though the plot has some annoying holes, the dialogue and the performances are excellent. Both Tilly and Bancroft received Oscar nominations for their work, along with Georges Delerue for his original music score.

AGUIRRE, THE WRATH OF GOD
(AGUIRRE, DER ZORN GOTTES)

1972 90m c Historical ★★★★★
(West Germany) /PG

Klaus Kinski *(Don Lope de Aguirre)*, Ruy Guerra *(Don Pedro de Ursua)*, Del Negro *(Brother Gaspar de Carvajal)*, Helena Rojo *(Inez)*, Cecilia Rivera *(Flores)*, Peter Berling *(Don Fernando de Guzman)*, Alejandro Repulles *(Gonzalez Pizarro)*, Daniel Ades *(Perucho)*, Armando Polanha *(Armando)*, Edward Roland *(Okello)*

p, Werner Herzog; d, Werner Herzog; w, Werner Herzog; ph, Thomas Mauch; ed, Beate Mainka-Jellinghaus; m, Popol Vuh; fx, Juvenal Herrera, Miguel Vasquez

A stunning, terrifying exploration of human obsession descending into madness. Herzog's most powerful fiction film chronicles the Peruvian expedition led by Gonzalez Pizarro (half-brother of the brutal conqueror of the Incas) in search of the legendary city of gold, El Dorado. The film opens in 1560 when Pizarro (Repulles), his men exhausted from their excruciating journey through the dense jungles, decides to send a small party ahead to determine if exploration should continue. Though Don Pedro de Ursua (Guerra) is put in charge, he is challenged by the maniacally ambitious Aguirre (Kinski), who insists against increasingly overwhelming odds that the journey continue, with devastating consequences. The film is based on a journal written by Gaspar de Carvajal, who was one of an army of Spaniards who accompanied the real Gonzalez Pizarro.

Kinski's intensity makes him a remarkable Aguirre; indeed, it is difficult to recall a more intensely driven character in film. His madness is portrayed against an almost hallucinatory environment enhanced by Thomas Mauch's brilliant cinematography and Popol Vuh's spare score. Herzog's cast and crew suffered incredible hardships filming in unexplored regions of South America but as a result the director captured a hostile, mysterious jungle world in such a way as to trivialize complaints that traditional story elements and character development are missing. Just as Aguirre is able to overwhelm the people around him, so the watcher can count on a staggering cinematic experience that assaults the senses.

AH, WILDERNESS!

1935 101m bw Comedy ★★★★
MGM (U.S.) /A

Wallace Beery *(Sid Davis)*, Lionel Barrymore *(Nat Miller)*, Aline MacMahon *(Lily Davis)*, Eric Linden *(Richard Miller)*, Cecilia Parker *(Muriel McComber)*, Spring Byington *(Essie Miller)*, Mickey Rooney *(Tommy Miller)*, Charley Grapewin *(Mr. McComber)*, Frank Albertson *(Arthur Miller)*, Eddie Nugent *(Wint Selby)*

p, Hunt Stromberg; d, Clarence Brown; w, Albert Hackett, Frances Goodrich (based on the play by Eugene O'Neill); ph, Clyde De Vinna; ed, Frank E. Hull; m, Herbert Stothart; art d, Cedric Gibbons, William A. Horning

Eugene O'Neill's only comedy, written in five weeks, is a dream of the sweet, unaffected boyhood he never had, culminating in one long summer during which adolescence struggles into manhood. Eric Linden plays Richard Miller, a young man of sincerity and some charming stupidity. His mother busies herself with household problems, his mischievous brother and unruly sister vex him, his father nervously avoids instructing him in the ways of the world, and his often-inebriated uncle teaches him about life. It's a marvelous slice of Americana, filled with funny and tender scenes as young Richard strives to understand himself and those around him. Mickey Rooney, here playing the younger brother, played the lead role thirteen years later in the musical remake, SUMMER HOLIDAY.

AIR FORCE

1943 124m bw War ★★★½
Warner Bros. (U.S.) /PG

John Ridgely *(Capt. Mike Quincannon)*, Gig Young *(Lt. Bill Williams)*, Arthur Kennedy *(Lt. Tommy McMartin)*, Charles Drake *(Lt. Munchauser)*, Harry Carey *(Sgt. Robby White)*, George Tobias *(Cpl. Weinberg)*, Ward Wood *(Cpl. Peterson)*, Ray Montgomery *(Pvt. Chester)*, John Garfield *(Sgt. Joe Winocki)*, James Brown *(Lt. Tex Rader)*

p, Hal B. Wallis; d, Howard Hawks; w, Dudley Nichols; ph, James Wong Howe, Elmer Dyer; ed, George Amy; m, Franz Waxman; art d, John Hughes; fx, Roy Davidson, Rex Wimpy, H.F. Koenekamp

AAN Best Original Screenplay: Dudley Nichols; *AAN Best Cinematography:* James Wong Howe, Elmer Dyer, Charles Marshall; *AA Best Editing:* George Amy; *AAN Best Visual Effects:* Hans Koenekamp, Rex Wimpy, Nathan Levinson

One of the finest American propaganda films produced during WWII, AIR FORCE fits perfectly into the canon of its director, Howard Hawks. A filmmaker who excels at portraying group action, Hawks tells the story of the "Mary Ann," a B-17 bomber, and its crew. While there is much here the viewer may find offensive (notably the predictable anti-"Jap" rhetoric), Hawks's mesmerizing direction and the assured and emotional performances of the cast, especially Garfield and Carey, draw the viewer in. Though by now beginning to date, Nichols's screenplay is powerful, with dialogue that is both meaningful and believable. The film earned Academy Award nominations for its script and cinematography and won Oscars for editing and special effects. A real fortress, later lost in the Pacific, was used for much of the filming, with interiors photographed inside a $40,000 model. Hawks was a veteran of the Air Corps of WWI, and his own experience and reverence for the service shows in every scene.

AIRPLANE!

1980 88m c Comedy ★★½
Paramount (U.S.) PG

Robert Hays *(Ted Striker)*, Julie Hagerty *(Elaine)*, Kareem Abdul-Jabbar *(Murdock)*, Lloyd Bridges *(McCroskey)*, Peter Graves *(Capt. Oveur)*, Leslie Nielsen *(Dr. Rumack)*, Lorna Patterson *(Randy)*, Robert Stack *(Kramer)*, Stephen Stucker *(Johnny)*, Barbara Billingsley *(Jive Lady)*

p, Jon Davison; d, Jim Abrahams, David Zucker, Jerry Zucker; w, Jim Abrahams, David Zucker, Jerry Zucker; ph, Joseph Biroc; ed, Patrick Kennedy; m, Elmer Bernstein; fx, Bruce Logan; chor, Tom Mahoney; cos, Rosanna Norton

Loaded with slapstick silliness and schoolboy wordplay, featuring tongue-in-cheek performances by familiar television personalities, and mostly just plain goofy, this inventive comedy from the Zucker-Abrahams-Zucker writing-directing team (THE KENTUCKY FRIED MOVIE, THE NAKED GUN) lampoons crisis-in-the-air films like THE CROWDED SKY and ZERO HOUR.

Ted Striker (Robert Hayes), a failed fighter pilot, is forced to take the controls of a commercial jet liner after the captain (Peter Graves) and co-pilot (basketball legend Kareem Abdul-Jabbar) become ill. Encouraged by his stewardess girlfriend (Julie Haggerty) and zany Dr. Rumack (Leslie Nielsen), and receiving ground support from the even zanier Kramer (Robert Stack), Striker does his best to follow the incomprehensible instructions he is given. Meanwhile, passengers become daffy, berserk, sex-crazed, and generally impossible. The onslaught of one-liners and sight gags in AIRPLANE! is so relentless that even the most dour viewer is ultimately won over—or exhausted.

AIRPORT

1970 137m c Disaster ★★
Universal (U.S.) G/PG

Burt Lancaster *(Mel Bakersfeld)*, Dean Martin *(Vernon Demerest)*, Jean Seberg *(Tanya Livingston)*, Jacqueline Bisset *(Gwen Meighen)*, George Kennedy *(Joe Patroni)*, Helen Hayes *(Ada Quonsett)*, Van Heflin *(D.O. Guerrero)*, Maureen Stapleton *(Inez Guerrero)*, Barry Nelson *(Lt. Anson Harris)*, Dana Wynter *(Mrs. Cindy Bakersfeld)* p, Ross Hunter; d, George Seaton, Henry Hathaway; w, George Seaton (based on the novel by Arthur Hailey); ph, Ernest Laszlo; ed, Stuart Gilmore; m, Alfred Newman; art d, Preston Ames, Alexander Golitzen; cos, Edith Head

AAN Best Picture; AA Best Supporting Actress: Helen Hayes; *AAN Best Supporting Actress:* Maureen Stapleton; *AAN Best Adapted Screenplay:* George Seaton; *AAN Best Cinematography:* Ernest Laszlo; *AAN Best Editing:* Stuart Gilmore; *AAN Best Score:* Alfred Newman; *AAN Best Art Direction:* Alexander Golitzen, E. Preston Ames, Jack D. Moore, Mickey S. Michaels; *AAN Best Costume Design:* Edith Head; *AAN Best Sound:* Ronald Pierce, David Moriarty

An empty reshaping of GRAND HOTEL, held together by disaster in the sky.

Heflin smuggles a bomb on board, then blows himself out of an airborne jet, which limps along for more than two hours looking for a place to land while a score of passengers' lives are capsulized. Frantic ground people sweat over microphones and runway equipment, desperately trying to move a stalled plane on the only runway available (during a blizzard!) while ground crew chief Kennedy blathers heroically.

The film cost more than $10 million, and Universal chiefs held their breath. They need not have worried; the production soared beyond a $45 million gross and spawned three, progressively inferior, sequels. Nominated for ten Academy Awards including Best Picture. Both Stapleton and Hayes were nominated for Best Supporting Actress, and Hayes won, proving sentiment and cloying cuteness can conquer any mediocre script. AIRPORT will be remembered as the trailblazer of the disaster epic, one of the most trivial genres in the history of motion pictures.

AKIRA

1988   124m   c   Animated/Action   ★★½
Akira Committee   (Japan)

VOICES OF: Mitsuo Iwara, Nozomu Sasaki, Mami Koyama, Taro Ishida

p, Ryohei Susuki, Shunzo Kato; d, Katsuhiro Otomo; w, Katsuhiro Otomo, Izo Hashimoto (from the graphic novel by Otomo); ph, Katsuji Misawa; m, Shoji Yamashiro; art d, Toshiharu Mizutani; anim, Takashi Nakamura

With this animated epic—adapted from the famous manga series by Katsuhiro Otomo—"Japanimation" jumped from cult to mainstream. Just as comic books have graduated from children's entertainment to sophisticated graphic novels, AKIRA, likewise, sets out to use the animated format in a bold, adult way.

The time is 2019, 31 years after WWIII, during which Tokyo was destroyed by an atomic bomb. The rebuilt Neo Tokyo is an urban hell whose denizens live like rats at the foot of towering skycrapers. The heroes of the movie are a group of teenage biker punks who terrorize the city with their violent gang wars. There is also a group of revolutionaries who are trying to overthrow the oppressive government. The government, meanwhile, is performing strange experiments with a mysterious invention called "Akira." It is part bomb, part god, and potentially destructive: when part of it is injected into a human being, that person is endowed with apocalyptic strength.

The animation shows off the kind of hyperactive filmmaking that would cost millions to produce in a live-action format. The opening sequence finds the biker gang burning down the freeways of Neo Tokyo at maximum speed, presenting the characters and the cityscape from every possible angle. The powerful movement of the movie is exhilarating, but it's all action with little characterization or plot. There is a moral here about mankind's lust for power, but it never clearly emerges from the spectacle of destruction and violence. Ultimately, AKIRA is really all about the animation.

ALADDIN

1992   90m   c   Animated/Comedy/Musical   ★★★★
Walt Disney Productions   (U.S.)   G/U

VOICES OF: Scott Weinger *(Aladdin)*, Robin Williams *(Genie)*, Linda Larkin *(Jasmine)*, Jonathan Freeman *(Jafar)*, Frank Welker *(Abu/Narrator)*, Gilbert Gottfried *(Iago)*, Douglas Seale *(Sultan)*, Lea Salonga *(Singing Jasmine)*, Charlie Adler, Jack Angel

p, John Musker, Ron Clements; d, John Musker, Ron Clements; w, Ron Clements, John Musker, Ted Elliot, Terry Rossio; ed, H. Lee Peterson; m, Alan Menken; art d, Bill Perkins; anim, Ed Gombert, Rasoul Azadani, Kathy Altieri, Vera Lanpher, Don Paul, Steve Goldberg

AA Best Score: Alan Menken; *AA Best Song:* Alan Menken (Music), Tim Rice (Lyrics); *AAN Best Song:* Alan Menken (Music), Howard Ashman (Lyrics); *AAN Best Sound:* Terry Porter, Mel Metcalfe, David J. Hudson, Doc Kane; *AAN Best Sound Effects Editing:* Mark Mangini

A surprisingly hip outing for the Walt Disney company, which catapulted the classic fable into the 1990s, largely thanks to the input of Robin Williams as the voice of the mercurial, motor-mouthed Genie. ALADDIN is a fairy tale with an edge—a popular children's story that will have even the most media-savvy parents straining to keep up with Williams's machine-gun delivery of quips, allusions and imitations.

Animation, it turns out, is an ideal medium for Williams's talents. As he launches into his trademark free-associative riffs, impersonating everyone from Arnold Schwarzenegger to William Buckley to a bevy of harem women, the corresponding images spring to life with breathtaking speed and ingenuity; it would take several viewings to capture all the nuances of these comic cartoon jags.

This is not to say that the Genie-free segments of ALADDIN serve only as down time. The story moves at a brisk pace and is punctuated by some virtuoso sequences, in particular a dizzying magic carpet ride through the cave where the lamp is found. Though the lead characters are, as usual, bland, they're compensated for by a cheeky, entertaining supporting cast. Special mention should go to the mute but expressive magic carpet, and to Iago, hench-parrot of the principal villain, Jafar. Iago's cackling voice was provided by anarchic New York comedian Gilbert Gottfried, and Jafar's evil face was partially modeled, according to the animators, on that of former First Lady Nancy Reagan.

ALAMO, THE

1960   192m   c   War   ★★★
Batjac   (U.S.)   /PG

John Wayne *(Col. David Crockett)*, Richard Widmark *(Col. James Bowie)*, Laurence Harvey *(Col. William Travis)*, Frankie Avalon *(Smitty)*, Patrick Wayne *(Capt. James Butler Bonham)*, Linda Cristal *(Flaca)*, Joan O'Brien *(Mrs. Dickinson)*, Chill Wills *(Beekeeper)*, Joseph Calleia *(Juan Sequin)*, Ken Curtis *(Capt. Almeron Dickinson)*

p, John Wayne; d, John Wayne; w, James Edward Grant; ph, William Clothier; ed, Stuart Gilmore; m, Dimitri Tiomkin; art d, Alfred Ybarra; fx, Lee Zavitz

AAN Best Picture; AAN Best Supporting Actor: Chill Wills; *AAN Best Cinematography:* William H. Clothier; *AAN Best Editing:* Stuart Gilmore; *AAN Best Score:* Dimitri Tiomkin; *AAN Best Song:* Dimitri Tiomkin, Paul Francis Webster; *AA Best Sound:* Gordon E. Sawyer, Fred Hynes

Sprawling, ponderous history lesson that re-creates the defense of the Alamo in 1836 Texas, when 187 Americans and Texicans held off Santa Anna's army of 7,000 men for 13 days. The major focus is on Colonels William Travis (Laurence Harvey), Davy Crockett (John Wayne), and Jim Bowie (Richard Widmark). Wayne, whose Batjac Productions spent some $15 million mounting THE ALAMO (shot in 91 days, with $1.5 million spent re-creating the fort), produced, starred, and directed, with uncredited second-unit assistance from good friend John Ford. The result is an old-fashioned patriotic movie and a rousing epic that performed poorly at the box office, perhaps because it chronicled one of America's most famous military losses. All the pontificating about the joys of freedom becomes irritating, but James Edward Grant's dialogue occasionally crackles with enough humorous wit to hold an audience untill the gripping finale. Originally released at 192 minutes, it was later edited down to 140 minutes, with much of the Ford-directed footage reportedly cut out. The videocassette runs 161 minutes, but fails to recapture the sumptuous Todd-AO wide-screen photography.

ALEXANDER NEVSKY

1938 107m bw Historical/War   ★★★★
Mosfilm (U.S.S.R.)   /PG

Nikolai Cherkassov *(Prince Alexander Yaroslavich Nevsky)*, Nikolai Okhlopkov *(Vassily Buslai)*, A.L. Abrikossov *(Gavrilo Olexich)*, D.N. Orlov *(Ignat. Master Armourer)*, V. Novikov *(Pavsha, Governor of Pskov)*, N.N. Arski *(Domash, Nobleman of Novgorod)*, V.O. Massalitinova *(Amefa Timofeyevna, Mother of Buslai)*, V.S. Ivasbeva *(Olga, a Novgorod Girl)*, A.S. Danilova *(Vassilissa)*, V.L. Ersbov *(Master of the Teutonic Order)*

d, Sergei Eisenstein, D.I. Vassillev; w, Sergei Eisenstein, Peter Pavlenko; ph, Edward Tisse; m, Sergei Prokofiev

Sergei Eisenstein's classic tale of 13th-century Russia is as magnificent today as it must have been in 1938. A formidable achievement of Soviet cinema, this epic concerns the trying period when Russia was invaded by Teutonic knights on one front and Tartars on the other. As a result, the motherland is plundered, and the morale of the people crumbles. Finally, the moody, volatile Prince Nevsky (Nikolai Cherkassov) is summoned to lead his people in their struggle against the oppressors. A valiant and intelligent nobleman, Nevsky forms his army (an undertaking that consumes half the film), then wins a decisive battle at frozen Lake Peipus in 1242.

Eisenstein had the Russian army at his disposal, and the battle scenes, populated with thousands of men, are overwhelming. Wearing terrifying helmets fashioned after gargoyles, ogres, and fierce animals, the Teutonic knights engage the Russian army of peasants and nobles, hacking with sword, spear, and axe until the armor-burdened invaders fall victim to the lake's cracking ice. Eisenstein's attention to detail is meticulous down to the last horse blanket and homemade shoe, and the mounting of his monument to Russia's ancient hero is superb. His career on the verge of collapse, Eisenstein was rewarded for his work (an undeniably propagandist piece with the heroic Nevsky as Stalin and the savage Teutons as the Nazis) by being named head of Mosfilm Studios. The film represents a stylistic departure for Eisenstein, whose was beginning to abandon dialectical montage (e.g., THE BATTLESHIP POTEMKIN) for more conventional narrative methods. Prokofiev's vigorous score has become a concert piece in its own right.

ALEXANDER'S RAGTIME BAND

1938 105m bw Musical   ★★★½
Fox (U.S.)   /U

Tyrone Power *(Roger Grant)*, Alice Faye *(Stella Kirby)*, Don Ameche *(Charlie Dwyer)*, Ethel Merman *(Jerry Allen)*, Jack Haley *(Davey Lane)*, Jean Hersholt *(Prof. Heinrich)*, Helen Westley *(Aunt Sophie)*, John Carradine *(Taxi Driver)*, Paul Hurst *(Bill)*, Wally Vernon *(Himself)*

p, Harry Joe Brown; d, Henry King; w, Kathryn Scola, Lamar Trotti, Michael Sherman; ph, Peverell Marley; ed, Barbara McLean; art d, Bernard Herzbrun, Boris Leven; chor, Seymour Felix; cos, Gwen Wakeling

AAN Best Picture; AAN Best Original Story: Irving Berlin; AAN Best Editing: Barbara McLean; AA Best Score: Alfred Newman; AAN Best Song: Irving Berlin; AAN Best Art Direction: Bernard Herzbrun, Boris Leven

28 of Irving Berlin's greatest songs make this energetic, handsomely mounted production a must-see for musical fans. Spanning the years 1915 through 1938, the film follows the fortunes of Roger Grant (Tyrone Power), a Nob Hill San Franciscan who gives up his classical musical training in favor of playing ragtime. Grant starts his own "Alexander's Ragtime Band" (named for the song) and hires Stella Kirby (Alice Faye) as his singer. He falls in love with Kirby, but has a romantic rival in the shape of Charlie Dwyer (Don Ameche). Berlin was particularly pleased with Faye, of whom he said "I'd rather have Alice Faye introduce my songs than any other singer I know." With her limpid, bovine eyes and her throbbing contralto, Faye is the film's outstanding feature (best moment: her first outing with the band), but fans of the musical will also be interested in seeing young Ethel Merman strut her vintage stuff.

ALFIE

1966 114m c Drama   ★★★½
Lewis Gilbert/Sheldrake (U.K.)   /15

Michael Caine *(Alfie)*, Shelley Winters *(Ruby)*, Millicent Martin *(Siddie)*, Julia Foster *(Gilda)*, Jane Asher *(Annie)*, Shirley Ann Field *(Carla)*, Vivien Merchant *(Lily)*, Eleanor Bron *(The Doctor)*, Denholm Elliott *(Abortionist)*, Alfie Bass *(Harry)*

p, Lewis Gilbert; d, Lewis Gilbert; w, Bill Naughton (based on his play); ph, Otto Heller; ed, Thelma Connell; m, Sonny Rollins

AAN Best Picture; AAN Best Actor: Michael Caine; AAN Best Supporting Actress: Vivien Merchant; AAN Best Adapted Screenplay: Bill Naughton; AAN Best Song: Burt Bacharach (Music), Hal David (Lyrics)

ALFIE is a surprisingly successful exercise in dramatic irony: the title character, a charming mediocrity who fancies himself a ladykiller, delivers a running commentary on his tawdry sexual conquests and penny-ante criminal ambitions, cheerfully oblivious to an audience that knows more about him than he will ever know himself. Screenwriter Bill Naughton had already employed this rather stagy strategy in a play and novel of the same title; that Alfie's extended asides work so well on screen is due to the disarming appearance of naivete with which Michael Caine is able to address the camera.

Alfie uses women shamelessly and without malice; when they demand commitment or emotional engagement from him, he's perplexed. Among a series of lovers, the most shabbily treated are Gilda (Julia Foster), his pregnant common-law wife, and Lily (Vivien Merchant), a married woman who looks for passion but finds pregnancy and abortion, both arranged by Alfie. In its time, the film was praised for its sexual frankness and persuasive rendering of Swinging London; both seem quaint by contemporary standards. Caine's Cockney Don Juan, however, is *sui generis*.

ALGIERS

1938 95m bw Crime   ★★★★
UA (U.S.)   /A

Charles Boyer *(Pepe Le Moko)*, Sigrid Gurie *(Ines)*, Hedy Lamarr *(Gaby)*, Joseph Calleia *(Slimane)*, Gene Lockhart *(Regis)*, Johnny Downs *(Pierrot)*, Alan Hale *(Grandpere)*, Nina Koshetz *(Tania)*, Joan Woodbury *(Aicha)*, Claudia Dell *(Marie)*

p, Walter Wanger; d, John Cromwell; w, John Howard Lawson, James M. Cain (based on the novel *Pepe Le Moko* by Roger D'Ashelbe); ph, James Wong Howe; ed, Otho Lovering, William Reynolds; m, Vincent Scotto, Muhammed Ygner Buchen; art d, Alexander Toluboff; cos, Omar Kiam, Irene

AAN Best Actor: Charles Boyer; AAN Best Supporting Actor: Gene Lockhart; AAN Best Cinematography: James Wong Howe; AAN Best Art Direction: Alexander Toluboff (Art Direction)

Down along the shadowy, labyrinthine alleyways of the Casbah, a notorious bastion in French Algiers that harbors criminals, the viewer is introduced to a remarkable thief and lover, Pepe Le Moko (the charismatic Boyer, a reigning screen sex symbol in 1938). Wanted for stealing jewels, Boyer has fled pursuing Parisian police and taken refuge in the Casbah. Calleia is the crafty French detective who plays a waiting game, watching for the moment the wanted man will step from the Casbah into the arms of his officers. Boyer grows restless, longing for the grand life of Paris, resenting the mooning woman who is devoted to him (Gurie). Lamarr, a dazzling Parisian tourist slumming among criminals, walks into his life and, even though she is engaged, invents excuses to slip back into the Casbah to meet Boyer. The film follows Boyer's and Lamarr's involvement to its fatalistic conclusion, and their love scenes are definitive examples of smoldering continental passion.

Lamarr's role made her an international star, though she subsequently failed to live up to the promise of her debut. Strong supporting performances are contributed by Calleia and Lockhart, the latter's portrayal of an informer garnering him an Oscar nomination for Best Supporting Actor. Director Cromwell reshot this movie almost scene-for-scene from the earlier French version, PEPE LE MOKO, directed by Julien Duvivier and starring Jean Gabin. The film was remade in

1948 as CASBAH with Tony Martin and Yvonne De Carlo. Oddly enough, the expression *Come wiz me to the Casbah* was never uttered onscreen in ALGIERS.

ALI BABA AND THE FORTY THIEVES

1944 87m c Adventure	★★½
Universal (U.S.)	/U

Maria Montez *(Amara)*, Jon Hall *(Ali Baba)*, Turhan Bey *(Jamiel)*, Andy Devine *(Abdullah)*, Kurt Katch *(Hulagu Khan)*, Frank Puglia *(Cassim)*, Fortunio Bonanova *(Baba)*, Moroni Olsen *(Caliph)*, Ramsay Ames *(Nalu)*, Chris-Pin Martin *(Fat Thief)*

p, Paul Malvern; d, Arthur Lubin; w, Edmund Hartmann; ph, George Robinson, W. Howard Greene; ed, Russell Schoengarth; m, Edward Ward; art d, John B. Goodman, Richard H. Riedel; fx, John P. Fulton

This lavish Arabian Nights fantasy follows the exploits of the Caliph of Baghdad's son, who runs off into the desert after his father is killed by raiding Mongols. There he encounters the legendary 40 thieves and watches in amazement as their command, "Open Sesame," magically parts a solid rock wall, revealing a cavernous hiding place filled with treasures. He is adopted by the thieves, dubbed "Ali Baba," and grows up to be their leader. As an adult, Ali sets out to avenge his father's death and to free his land from the reigning Mongols. While the film is set in the ancient Middle East, there is much in the script that is reminiscent of THE ADVENTURES OF ROBIN HOOD, and some elements which draw on the western genre. Lots of fast-paced action, though the dialogue sometimes gets cumbersome, especially in the mouth of Andy Devine. But what self-respecting cult fan can resist the sultry blandishments and snakelike perambulations of Universal's B queen, Maria Montez?

ALICE
(NECO Z ALENKY)

1988 85m c Fantasy	★★★½
Film Four/Condor/SRG/Hessisches Rudfunk	/U
(Switzerland/U.K./West Germany)	

Kristyna Kohoutova *(Alice)*, Camilla Power *(Voice of Alice)*

p, Peter-Christian Fueter; d, Jan Svankmajer; w, Jan Svankmajer (based on *Alice's Adventures in Wonderland* by Lewis Carroll); ph, Svatopluk Maly; ed, Marie Zemanova; anim, Bedrich Glaser

This is a dark, surrealist interpretation of Lewis Carroll's *Alice's Adventures in Wonderland* by the brilliant Czech animator Jan Svankmajer. The director combines live action and puppet animation to create a disturbing vision of Alice's world, filled with images of death and violence. Although all the action takes place within a dream, Svankmajer, in true surrealist spirit, keeps the line between dream and reality ambiguous. Alice is the only live creature in the film, and it is she who supplies the voices of her (often grotesque) animated companions. In one scene typical of Svankmajer's command of dream logic, the girl becomes her own doll. ALICE is macabre, haunting, and very true to the spirit of Carroll's book, exploring the marvels and fears of a child's imagination.

ALICE ADAMS

1935 99m bw Comedy/Drama	★★★★
RKO (U.S.)	/U

Katharine Hepburn *(Alice Adams)*, Fred MacMurray *(Arthur Russell)*, Fred Stone *(Mr. Adams)*, Evelyn Venable *(Mildred Palmer)*, Frank Albertson *(Walter Adams)*, Ann Shoemaker *(Mrs. Adams)*, Charley Grapewin *(Mr. Lamb)*, Grady Sutton *(Frank Dowling)*, Hedda Hopper *(Mrs. Palmer)*, Jonathan Hale *(Mr. Palmer)*

p, Pandro S. Berman; d, George Stevens; w, Dorothy Yost, Mortimer Offner (based on the novel by Booth Tarkington); ph, Robert de Grasse; ed, Jane Loring; m, Max Steiner; art d, Van Nest Polglase; cos, Walter Plunkett

The pathetic, social-climbing heroine of Booth Tarkington's novel was never better played than by Hepburn, who brought a fierce determination, clutching coyness, and tragic optimism to the part. She plays Alice Adams, who lives only a block or two from the wrong side of the tracks, but who pretends that she and her family enjoy the status of her wealthy

peer group—a pretense that grows into a dangerous conviction. Her family of hopeless clods drags her down to grim reality at every turn, yet she tries to escape through rich acquaintances who are really nothing more than chic snobs. They merely tolerate her as a source of amusement, frivolously inviting her to an exclusive party where she meets the man of her dreams: rich, handsome, gracious MacMurray, who plays his part with unexpected sensitivity. He is attracted to her and is conned into believing that her folks are well-to-do. Hepburn inflates their importance and then risks all by inviting her hero to dinner at her home. George Stevens's dinner-party scene is a classically choreographed symphony of tragicomedy that remains with the viewer long after the tacked-on happy ending. Fred Stone, Ann Shoemaker and, young Frank Albertson, as Alice's grasping family, stand out in a capable ensemble cast, but supporting honors are stolen by Hattie McDaniel, in a slovenly turn as a hostess's worst nightmare. The painful yearning behind Alice's character speaks to audiences in a universal way, and the film proved an important stepping stone for 30-year-old director George Stevens, with his first major film, and Hepburn, who won a second Academy Award nomination for the part, after MORNING GLORY in 1933.

ALICE DOESN'T LIVE HERE ANYMORE

1975 112m c Drama	★★★
Warner Bros. (U.S.)	PG/15

Ellen Burstyn *(Alice Hyatt)*, Kris Kristofferson *(David)*, Alfred Lutter *(Tommy Hyatt)*, Billy "Green" Bush *(Donald Hyatt)*, Diane Ladd *(Flo)*, Lelia Goldoni *(Neighbor Bea)*, Harvey Keitel *(Ben Everhart)*, Lane Bradbury *(Ben's Wife)*, Vic Tayback *(Mel)*, Jodie Foster *(Audrey)*

p, David Susskind, Audrey Maas; d, Martin Scorsese; w, Robert Getchell; ph, Kent Wakeford; ed, Marcia Lucas; m, Richard LaSalle; prod d, Toby Rafelson

AA Best Actress: Ellen Burstyn; *AAN Best Supporting Actress:* Diane Ladd; *AAN Best Original Screenplay:* Robert Getchell

After achieving some success with the brilliant, independently made MEAN STREETS, Martin Scorsese was given a chance to direct a mainstream Hollywood film. The result is this effective but uneven work, which chronicles a woman's search for self.

Burstyn stars as an unhappy housewife living in New Mexico with her cruel husband (Bush) and their precocious, somewhat spoiled son (Lutter). When Bush dies, Burstyn and son pack up their belongings and head for Monterey, California, where she hopes to begin the singing career she has always dreamed about. Along the way she has a brief fling with the frightening Keitel, but must take flight when his violent temper erupts. When her car breaks down, she takes a job at an Arizona diner run by crusty Tayback and becomes best pals with salty Diane Ladd. Kristofferson is a rancher who frequents the restaurant, and he and Burstyn soon begin an awkward courtship. Burstyn won a well-deserved Oscar for her performance, and she is matched in expertise by Ladd and Tayback, but the acting cannot conceal the storyline's shortcomings. The film was the inspiration for the television series "Alice" starring Linda Lavin, with Tayback reprising his role as the owner of Mel's Diner. Also receiving Oscar nominations were Ladd for Supporting Actress and Getchell for his screenplay.

ALICE IN THE CITIES
(ALICE IN DEN STADTEN)

1974 110m bw Drama	★★★
Bauer (West Germany)	/U

Rudiger Vogler *(Phillip)*, Yella Rottlander *(Alice)*, Elisabeth Kreuzer *(Lisa)*, Edda Kochi *(Edda)*, Didi Petrikat *(The Girl)*, Ernest Bohm *(The Agent)*, Sam Presti *(The Car Salesman)*, Lois Moran *(Girl at Ticket Counter)*, Hans Hirschmuller, Sybille Baier

p, Peter Genee; d, Wim Wenders; w, Wim Wenders, Veith der Furstenberg; ph, Robby Muller, Martin Schafer; ed, Peter Przygodda, Barbara von Weitershausen

An ancestor of director Wenders's 1984 film PARIS, TEXAS, this low-budget West German picture follows Vogler, a German journalist traveling across the US East Coast in search of a story. He considers Polaroid snapshots a better way to capture America's landscapes, buildings, and signs than writing about them. While trying to return to

Germany, Vogler meets Kreuzer and her nine-year-old daughter, Rottlander, who are also trying to arrange a flight home. Kreuzer mysteriously disappears, leaving Rottlander in Vogler's care, setting up the premise of this hypnotic odyssey, the beginning of a loosely connected Wenders road-movie trilogy (it was followed in 1975 by WRONG MOVE and, one year later, KINGS OF THE ROAD—all three starring Vogler). Like Vogler, Wenders is a documentarian who fills his frame with images of American culture (a hot dog stand, a used car lot, Shea Stadium) and strains of American music ("Under the Boardwalk," Canned Heat, Chuck Berry) to tell his story.

ALICE IN WONDERLAND

1951   74m   c   Fantasy   ★★★½
Walt Disney Productions   (U.S.)   /U

Kathryn Beaumont *(Alice)*, Ed Wynn *(Mad Hatter)*, Richard Haydn *(Caterpillar)*, Sterling Holloway *(Cheshire Cat)*, Jerry Colonna *(March Hare)*, Verna Felton *(Queen of Hearts)*, Pat O'Malley *(Walrus/Carpenter/Dee/Dum)*, Bill Thompson *(White Rabbit/Dodo)*, Heather Angel *(Alice's Sister)*, Joseph Kearns *(Doorknob)*

p, Walt Disney; d, Clyde Geronimi, Hamilton Luske, Wilfred Jackson; w, Winston Hibler, Bill Peet, Joe Rinaldi, William Cottrell, Joe Grant, Del Connell, Ted Sears, Erdman Penner, Milt Banta, Dick Kelsey, Dick Huemer, Tom Oreb, John Walbridge (based on the stories of Lewis Carroll); m, Oliver Wallace; anim, Milt Kahl, Ward Kimball, Franklin Thomas, Eric Larson, John Lounsbery, Oliver M. Johnston, Wolfgang Reitherman, Marc Davis, Les Clark, Norman Ferguson, Josh Meador, Dan MacManus, George Rowley, Blaine Gibson

AAN Best Score: Oliver Wallace

Disney's beautifully animated but slightly chilly rendering of Alice's tale, aimed at a children's market for which Disney eschewed intellectual interpretations of Carroll's story, instead playing it straight as a storybook dream/nightmare. All of Alice's adventures are in place, including her tea party with the Mad Hatter and friends, her meeting with the bewildering Cheshire Cat, and her strange game of croquet with the temperamental Queen of Hearts. The film is dazzling in its use of color and odd shapes and is enhanced by the distinctive voices of Ed Wynn as the Mad Hatter, Sterling Holloway as the Cheshire Cat, Jerry Colonna as the March Hare, and Verna Felton as the Queen of Hearts.

ALICE'S RESTAURANT

1969   111m   c   Drama   ★★★
UA   (U.S.)   R/15

Arlo Guthrie *(Arlo)*, Pat Quinn *(Alice)*, James Broderick *(Ray)*, Michael McClanathan *(Shelly)*, Geoff Outlaw *(Roger)*, Tina Chen *(Marichan)*, Kathleen Dabney *(Karin)*, William Obanhein *(Officer Obie)*, Seth Allan *(Evangelist)*, Monroe Arnold *(Bluegrass)*

p, Hillard Elkins, Joe Manduke; d, Arthur Penn; w, Venable Herndon, Arthur Penn (based on the song "The Alice's Restaurant Massacre" by Arlo Guthrie); ph, Michael Nebbia; ed, Dede Allen; m, Arlo Guthrie

AAN Best Director: Arthur Penn

Arlo Guthrie, son of folk-singing immortal Woody Guthrie, achieved some celebrity in the 1960s with his 18-minute song "The Alice's Restaurant Massacre," in which he tells the tale of his arrest and trial for littering, which led to his being rejected for the draft during the Vietnam War. Director Arthur Penn used a lengthy and bitterly amusing re-creation of the events depicted in the song as the centerpiece for this exploration of the 60s counterculture. Ray Brock (James Broderick) is an aging hippie who buys a church in Stockbridge, Massachusetts, and with his wife, Alice (Pat Quinn), shares the good life with a variety of societal drop-outs. Guthrie drops in long enough to run afoul of the local cop, Obie (William Obanheim, playing himself) and pays a visit to a New York hospital to visit his father who is dying of Hodgkin's disease. To his credit, Penn refused to romanticize his subjects, and the film stands as a fairly accurate chronicle of the times. The real Alice Brock has a small role as one of the hippies.

ALIEN

1979   124m   c   Horror/Science Fiction   ★★★★
Brandywine/Shusett   (U.S.)   R/18

Tom Skerritt *(Dallas)*, Sigourney Weaver *(Ripley)*, Veronica Cartwright *(Lambert)*, Harry Dean Stanton *(Brett)*, John Hurt *(Kane)*, Ian Holm *(Ash)*, Yaphet Kotto *(Parker)*

p, Gordon Carroll, David Giler, Walter Hill; d, Ridley Scott; w, Dan O'Bannon (based on a story by O'Bannon and Ronald Shusett); ph, Derek Vanlint; ed, Terry Rawlings, Peter Weatherley; m, Jerry Goldsmith; prod d, Michael Seymour; fx, Carlo Rambaldi, Bernard Lodge; cos, John Mollo, H.R. Giger, Roger Dicken

AAN Best Art Direction: Michael Seymour, Les Dilley, Roger Christian, Ian Whittaker; *AA Best Visual Effects:* H.R. Giger, Carlo Rambaldi, Brian Johnson, Nick Allder, Denys Ayling

A seminal work of late '70s science fiction, ALIEN remains notable for its influence as well as its excellence.

The crew of the industrial spaceship *Nostromo* lands on the surface of a mysterious planet and discovers a crashed spacecraft. Inside, a strange egg disgorges a multilegged lifeform that latches onto the face of crewman Kane (John Hurt), who, unconscious, is brought back to the *Nostromo*. There, the creature resists all attempts to dislodge it. Soon, however, it disappears, only to turn up dead later as Kane revives, apparently none the worse for wear. The *Nostromo* takes off, and while the crew is having dinner, a snakelike creature erupts from Kane's stomach and vanishes into the bowels of the ship. After jettisoning Kane's body, the crew sets out in search of the alien. Other crew members are soon killed, and warrant officer Ripley (Sigourney Weaver) spearheads the battle against the seemingly indestructible creature.

ALIEN has been described as "a haunted house movie in space," and therein lies its appeal. There's nothing terribly complex or original about the movie, but it is distinguished by its clever and innovative use of B-movie staples in a hi-tech setting. Coming into his own as a director on his second feature, Ridley Scott wrings every possible ounce of suspense and atmosphere out of the proceedings. Swiss artist-designer H.R. Giger supplied the distinctive "bio-mechanical" concepts for the film, which help make the alien one of cinema's scariest creations: a nightmare synthesis of humanoid form, insect-like appendages, and mechanized structure that is all the more effective for not being seen too clearly for most of the film.

The non-star cast acquits itself well, bringing an appealing quality to their characters. One of them, Weaver's Ripley, would develop into one of the genre's most memorable heroines through the subsequent sequels. Perhaps because of its closed-in setting, the movie was an easy target for imitation. Several dozen low-budget copies have appeared since its initial release.

ALIENS

1986   137m   c   Science Fiction   ★★★
Brandywine   (U.S.)   R/18

Sigourney Weaver *(Ripley)*, Carrie Henn *(Newt)*, Michael Biehn *(Cpl. Hicks)*, Paul Reiser *(Burke)*, Lance Henriksen *(Bishop)*, Bill Paxton *(Pvt. Hudson)*, William Hope *(Lt. Gorman)*, Jenette Goldstein *(Pvt. Vasquez)*, Al Matthews *(Sgt. Apone)*, Mark Rolston *(Pvt. Drake)*

p, Gale Anne Hurd; d, James Cameron; w, James Cameron (based on a story by Cameron, David Giler, and Walter Hill and on characters created by Dan O'Bannon and Ronald Shusett); ph, Adrian Biddle; ed, Ray Lovejoy; m, James Horner; prod d, Peter Lamont; art d, Bert Davey, Fred Hole, Michael Lamont, Ken Court; fx, Stan Winston, L.A. Effects Group, John Richardson, Norman Baillie; cos, Emma Porteous

AAN Best Actress: Sigourney Weaver; *AAN Best Editing:* Ray Lovejoy; *AAN Best Score:* James Horner; *AAN Best Art Direction:* Peter Lamont, Crispian Sallis; *AAN Best Sound:* Graham V. Hartstone, Nicolas LeMessurier, Michael A. Carter, Roy Charman; *AA Best Visual Effects:* Robert Skotak, Stan Winston, John Richardson, Suzanne Benson; *AA Best Sound Effects Editing:* Don Sharpe

The long-awaited sequel to the successful ALIEN is a nonstop, high-tech, souped-up war movie, with gung ho marines blasting special-effects creatures, and a genuinely convincing, exciting action heroine. Ripley (Sigourney Weaver) is found in deep space by a salvage ship and brought back to a space station, where Burke (Paul Reiser), a representative of The Company, tells her that she has been unconscious for 57 years. To her horror, Ripley also learns that the planet on which she and her crew found the creature in ALIEN has been colonized. It isn't long, however, until Burke tells her that they've lost contact with the colony and asks her to accompany a platoon of colonial marines to the planet as an adviser. Weaver is superb—tough, smart, and the best fighter, male or female, in the movie. The rest of the small cast also performs well, and director James Cameron handles the action superbly. The cutting is quick, the suspense unrelenting, and the monsters thoroughly frightening.

ALIEN3

1992	135m	c	Science Fiction/Action/Horror	★★½
Fox/Brandywine Productions		(U.S.)		R/18

Sigourney Weaver *(Ripley)*, Charles S. Dutton *(Dillon)*, Charles Dance *(Clemens)*, Paul McGann *(Golic)*, Brian Glover *(Andrews)*, Ralph Brown *(Aaron)*, Danny Webb *(Morse)*, Christopher John Fields *(Rains)*, Holt McCallany *(Junior)*, Lance Henriksen *(Bishop)*

p, Gordon Carroll, Walter Hill, David Giler; d, David Fincher; w, David Giler, Walter Hill, Larry Ferguson (from a story by Vincent Ward, based on characters created by Dan O'Bannon and Ronald Shusett); ph, Alex Thomson; ed, Terry Rawlings; m, Elliot Goldenthal; prod d, Norman Reynolds; art d, James Morahan, Fred Hole; fx, George Gibbs, Richard Edlund, Tom Woodruff Jr., Alec Gillis; cos, Bob Ringwood, David Perry

AAN Best Visual Effects: Richard Edlund, Alec Gillis, Tom Woodruff, Jr., George Gibbs

Cruising through space on the way back from her last battle with the ALIENS, Ripley (Sigourney Weaver) crash-lands on what is possibly the least desirable piece of real-estate in the Galaxy—a run-down, low-tech penal colony inhabited by a bunch of serial killers who have developed their own brand of fundamentalist religion. Ripley—her head shaved as a precaution against lice—holds her own among this unsavory bunch, even getting friendly with the colony's doctor (Charles Dance), a charming Englishman with a mysterious past. Before long, though, it's Ripley's past that comes back to haunt her, as it becomes increasingly clear that her old, double-jawed, acid-blooded friends are back.

ALIEN3 is a would-be blockbuster that is marred by an overlong, clumsily choreographed final chase scene, as the prisoners lure the alien through a seemingly endless series of tunnels in an attempt to trap it. Nevertheless, the absence of high-tech gadgetry, and the almost medieval atmosphere of the colony, put an intriguing, Gothic spin on what could easily have been a tired re-run. Director David Fincher, a 28-year-old music video whiz-kid, has done an impressive job with the visuals, which are artfully composed without drawing undue attention to themselves. Through it all, the incomparable Ms. Weaver does her patented feminist action-hero thing, projecting intelligence, resilience and grim humor.

ALL ABOUT EVE

1950	138m	bw	Drama	★★★★★
Fox	(U.S.)			/U

Bette Davis *(Margo Channing)*, Anne Baxter *(Eve Harrington)*, George Sanders *(Addison De Witt)*, Celeste Holm *(Karen Richards)*, Gary Merrill *(Bill Simpson)*, Hugh Marlowe *(Lloyd Richards)*, Thelma Ritter *(Birdie Coonan)*, Marilyn Monroe *(Miss Casswell)*, Gregory Ratoff *(Max Fabian)*, Barbara Bates *(Phoebe)*

p, Darryl F. Zanuck; d, Joseph L. Mankiewicz; w, Joseph L. Mankiewicz (based on the story "The Wisdom of Eve" by Mary Orr); ph, Milton Krasner; ed, Barbara McLean; m, Alfred Newman; art d, Lyle Wheeler, George W. Davis; fx, Fred Sersen; cos, Edith Head

AA Best Picture; AAN Best Actress: Anne Baxter; *AAN Best Actress:* Bette Davis; *AA Best Supporting Actor:* George Sanders; *AAN Best Supporting Actress:* Celeste Holm; *AAN Best Supporting Actress:* Thelma Ritter; *AA Best Director:* Joseph L. Mankiewicz; *AA Best Screenplay:* Joseph L. Mankiewicz; *AAN Best Cinematography:* Milton Krasner; *AAN Best Editing:* Barbara McLean; *AAN Best Score:* Alfred Newman; *AAN Best Art Direction:* Lyle Wheeler, George W. Davis, Thomas Little, Walter M. Scott; *AA Best Costume Design:* Edith Head, Charles LeMaire; *AA Best Sound:* 20th Century-Fox Sound Department

ALL ABOUT EVE is the consummate backstage story, a film that holds a magnifying glass up to theatrical environs and exposes all the egos, tempers, conspiracies and backstage back-biting that make up the world of make-believe on Broadway. The screenplay, written by Joseph L. Mankiewicz, who also directed, may be the most biting example of hard-boiled wit ever to come out of Hollywood, and it is stylishly performed at a breakneck pace by a uniformly expert cast.

The story, based on Mary Orr's "The Wisdom of Eve," concerns an aging star who befriends a seemingly innocent fan, who wants to take over and inhabit the star's life. Bette Davis won the part of vain, temperamental Margo Channing by default when Claudette Colbert broke her back, and single-handedly revived her career after having been dumped by Warner Bros. Though Mankiewicz and Davis always claimed the character was based on Austrian actress Elisabeth Bergner, Davis enacted her role as a mirror twin of then-fabled Broadway rival Tallulah Bankhead, thus fanning the flames of an already existing feud. EVE was the peak of Anne Baxter's star years and she almost matches Davis in her silky, dangerous portrayal of Eve. These two are supported by a who's who of matchless portraits, including Gary Merrill (whom Davis would fall in love with during filming and later marry), George Sanders (as a poisonous critic), the biting Thelma Ritter, Celeste Holm, and a young Marilyn Monroe as a cynical, dreamy starlet.

EVE won six Oscars: Best Picture, Director, Screenplay, Supporting Actor (Sanders), Costume Design (Edith Head), and Sound Recording. It also was nominated for Cinematography, Art Direction, Score, Editing, and Supporting Actress (Holm and Ritter). Bette Davis was doomed to lose for Best Actress, canceled out by Baxter's shared nomination, and by rival old pro Gloria Swanson for SUNSET BOULEVARD (all lost to rookie Judy Holliday for BORN YESTERDAY). The musical *Applause*, a Broadway success with Lauren Bacall, and later Anne Baxter, was based on EVE.

ALL MY SONS

1948	93m	bw	Drama	★★★½
Universal	(U.S.)			/A

Edward G. Robinson *(Joe Keller)*, Burt Lancaster *(Chris Keller)*, Mady Christians *(Kate Keller)*, Louisa Horton *(Ann Deever)*, Howard Duff *(George Deever)*, Frank Conroy *(Herbert Deever)*, Lloyd Gough *(Jim Bayliss)*, Arlene Francis *(Sue Bayliss)*, Henry Morgan *(Frank Lubey)*, Elisabeth Fraser *(Lydia Lubey)*

p, Chester Erskine; d, Irving Reis; w, Chester Erskine (based on the play by Arthur Miller); ph, Russell Metty; ed, Ralph Dawson; m, Leith Stevens; art d, Bernard Herzbrun, Hilyard Brown; fx, David S. Horsley; cos, Grace Houston

Arthur Miller's powerful drama tells the story of a family being ripped apart by the discovery of the father's corrupt business ethics during WWII (purposefully shipping defective military parts that resulted in the death of 21 men). The windy treatment is beginning to show its age, but is somewhat compensated for by acting of a high order. Robinson provides one of his best performances, showing the human frailty of his character in all its naked fury and shame, a role matched only by Lancaster's tense, taut presence as an embittered war veteran.

ALL OF ME

1984	93m	c	Comedy	★★½
Kings Road	(U.S.)			PG/15

Steve Martin *(Roger Cobb)*, Lily Tomlin *(Edwina Cutwater)*, Victoria Tennant *(Terry Hoskins)*, Madolyn Smith *(Peggy Schuyler)*, Richard Libertini *(Prahka Lasa)*, Dana Elcar *(Burton Schuyler)*, Jason Bernard *(Tyrone Wattell)*, Selma Diamond *(Margo)*, Eric Christmas *(Fred Hoskins)*, Gailard Sartain *(Fulton Norris)*

ALL QUIET ON THE WESTERN FRONT

p, Stephen Friedman; d, Carl Reiner; w, Phil Alden Robinson, Henry Olek (based on the novel *Me Too* by Ed Davis); ph, Richard H. Kline; ed, Bud Molin; m, Patrick Williams; prod d, Edward Carfagno; fx, Bruce Steinheimer; cos, Ray Summers

Roger Cobb (Steve Martin) is a guitar-playing attorney semi-engaged to the daughter of his boss at a large law firm, whose most important client is the very rich, very ill Edwina Cutwater (Lily Tomlin). Through her personal guru, Cutwater is planning a mind/body switch with a beautiful young woman (Victoria Tennant) and needs some help reworking her will. When Cobb is assigned to the case, the transfer goes awry, and the lawyer winds up battling with Cutwater for control of *his* body. Martin does some of his best acting in this film and steals the movie from Tomlin, whose character is, at best, a one-note creation. If you're a Martin fan, you'll love ALL OF ME; if you aren't, there's still enough fun in spots to make it worth your time.

ALL QUIET ON THE WESTERN FRONT

1930 140m bw War   ★★★★★
Universal (U.S.)   /PG

Louis Wolheim *(Katczinsky)*, Lew Ayres *(Paul Baumer)*, John Wray *(Himmelstoss)*, Slim Summerville *(Tjaden)*, Russell Gleason *(Muller)*, William Bakewell *(Albert)*, Scott Kolk *(Leer)*, Walter Rogers *(Behm)*, Ben Alexander *(Kemmerick)*, Owen Davis Jr. *(Peter)*

p, Carl Laemmle Jr.; d, Lewis Milestone; w, Del Andrews, Maxwell Anderson, Lewis Milestone (uncredited), George Abbott (based on the novel by Erich Maria Remarque); ph, Karl Freund, Arthur Edeson; ed, Edgar Adams, Milton Carruth; m, David Broekman; art d, Charles D. Hall, William R. Schmidt; fx, Frank H. Booth

AA Best Picture; *AA Best Director:* Lewis Milestone; *AAN Best Screenplay:* George Abbott, Maxwell Anderson, Del Andrews; *AAN Best Cinematography:* Arthur Edeson

A remarkably faithful adaptation of Erich Maria Remarque's classic pacifist novel, ALL QUIET ON THE WESTERN FRONT is perhaps the greatest antiwar film ever made, holding considerable power even now due to Lewis Milestone's inventive direction.

Set during WWI and told from the German point of view, the story centers on Paul Baumer (Lew Ayres). A sensitive youth, Baumer is recruited by a war-mongering professor (Arnold Lucy) advocating "glory for the Fatherland." Paul and his friends enlist and are trained by Himmelstoss (John Wray), a kindly postmaster turned brutal corporal, then sent to the front lines to taste battle, blood, and death. Paul comes under the protective wing of an old veteran, Katczinsky (Louis Wolheim), who teaches him how to survive the horrors of war.

The film is emotionally draining, and so realistic that it will be forever etched in the mind of any viewer. Milestone's direction is frequently inspired, most notably during the battle scenes. In one such scene, the camera serves as a kind of machine gun, shooting down the oncoming troops as it glides along the trenches. Universal spared no expense during production, converting more than 20 acres of a large California ranch into battlefields occupied by more than 2,000 ex-servicemen extras. After its initial release, some foreign countries refused to run the film. Poland banned it for being pro-German, while the Nazis labeled it anti-German. Joseph Goebbels, later propaganda minister, publicly denounced the film.

ALL QUIET ON THE WESTERN FRONT received an Academy Award as Best Picture and Milestone was honored as Best Director. Originally released with a running time of 140 minutes, the film has suffered many cuts over the years with some prints running as short as 90 minutes. The most recent videotape release restores the film to 130 minutes of running time. An interesting, but now-forgotten, sequel titled THE ROAD BACK, directed by James Whale (THE BRIDE OF FRANKENSTEIN), was made in 1937. The original was remade as a television movie in 1979, with Richard Thomas unsuccessfully trying to match the timeless power of Ayres's performance.

ALL THAT HEAVEN ALLOWS

1955 89m c Drama   ★★★★
Universal (U.S.)   /U

Jane Wyman *(Cary Scott)*, Rock Hudson *(Ron Kirby)*, Agnes Moorehead *(Sara Warren)*, Conrad Nagel *(Harvey)*, Virginia Grey *(Alida Anderson)*, Gloria Talbott *(Kay Scott)*, William Reynolds *(Ned Scott)*, Jacqueline de Wit *(Mona Plash)*, Charles Drake *(Mick Anderson)*, Leigh Snowden *(Jo-Ann)*

p, Ross Hunter; d, Douglas Sirk; w, Peg Fenwick (based on a story by Edna Lee and Harry Lee); ph, Russell Metty; ed, Frank Gross, Fred Baratta; m, Frank Skinner, Joseph Gershenson; art d, Alexander Golitzen, Eric Orbom; cos, Bill Thomas

ALL THAT HEAVEN ALLOWS is a classic Douglas Sirk melodrama with Jane Wyman and Rock Hudson, that was the inspiration for Rainer Werner Fassbinder's ALI, FEAR EATS THE SOUL (1973).

After the death of her husband, New Englander Cary Scott (Jane Wyman) settles into the role of being a lonely, middle-aged widow, and her friend Sara (Agnes Moorehead) tries to get her back into the social scene. Harvey (Conrad Nagel), an elderly family friend, proposes to her, but she turns him down. Cary becomes friendly with her young gardener Ron Kirby (Rock Hudson), and despite their age difference, they fall in love and Ron asks her to marry him. Cary's grown children, Ned (William Reynolds) and Kay (Gloria Talbott), come home for a visit, and they're shocked to learn that she's planning to marry Ron, since he's much younger and from a different social class, and that she intends to move out of the family home. Cary takes Ron to a party to introduce him to her friends, but they're subjected to insults and mockery.

In the 1950s, Douglas Sirk was Universal's house director, turning out a succession of slick, commercially successful soap operas with producer Ross Hunter. On the surface, like most of Sirk's Universal tearjerkers, ALL THAT HEAVEN ALLOWS is a combination of "kitsch, craziness," and trashiness," to use the director's own words, yet, as always, he transforms the wish-fulfillment fantasy cliches into a poignant love story and incisive social critique through his masterful handling of actors and his transcendent mise-en-scene. Sirk draws a superb performance from Wyman, using composition and expressionistic colors to trap her in private, middle-classic prison, framed behind picturesque snow-covered windows, her sad image reflected in objects such as mirrors, furniture, and a television set, creating a pathetic imitation of life. Russell Metty's cinematography brilliantly serves Sirk's style of long takes, reframing the characters through subtle camera movements, and splitting the frame into sections while bathing the foreground and background of a shot with different colors to suggest the emotional state of the characters. A particularly stunning example is when Kay comes home in hysterics after her friends were teasing her about her mother getting married, and the multi-hued glass of a circular window throws a rainbow-pattern across her face as she's crying. With its touching story and stylized treatment, ALL THAT HEAVEN ALLOWS is one of Sirk's finest films.

ALL THAT JAZZ

1979 123m c Musical   ★★★
Columbia (U.S.)   R/15

Roy Scheider *(Joe Gideon)*, Jessica Lange *(Angelique)*, Ann Reinking *(Kate Jagger)*, Leland Palmer *(Audrey Paris)*, Cliff Gorman *(David Newman)*, Ben Vereen *(O'Connor Flood)*, Erzebet Foldi *(Michelle)*, Michael Tolan *(Dr. Ballinger)*, Max Wright *(Joshua Benn)*, William La Messena *(Jonesy Hecht)*

p, Robert Alan Aurthur; d, Bob Fosse; w, Robert Alan Aurthur, Bob Fosse; ph, Giuseppe Rotunno; ed, Alan Heim; m, Ralph Burns; chor, Bob Fosse; cos, Albert Wolsky

AAN Best Picture; *AAN Best Actor:* Roy Scheider; *AAN Best Director:* Bob Fosse; *AAN Best Original Screenplay:* Robert Alan Aurthur, Bob Fosse; *AAN Best Cinematography:* Giuseppe Rotunno; *AA Best Editing:* Alan Heim; *AA Best Score:* Ralph Burns; *AA Best Art Direction:* Philip Rosenberg, Tony Walton, Edward Stewart, Gary Brink; *AA Best Costume Design:* Albert Wolsky

With the possible exception of 2001: A SPACE ODYSSEY (1968), this Fellini-influenced tragicomic musical was probably the most outre work to date when it was nominated for a Best Picture Oscar.

Joe Gideon (Roy Scheider) is a famous New York choreographer who plays as hard as he works. He pops pills, drinks, smokes, and maniacally drives his dancers and himself in preparation for a new musical, while simultaneously editing a movie he directed and trying to keep his daughter, ex-wife, longtime lover, Broadway investors—and his own rampant libido—satisfied. The chores exhaust him; as a result he has a heart attack and cardiac surgery, and begins to hallucinate wild musical numbers archly metaphoric of his own life.

The dancing is frenzied, the dialogue piercing, the photography superb, and the acting first-rate, with non-showman Scheider an illustrious example of casting against type. Parallels between Fosse's own life and that of his onscreen alter ego are clear: Fosse was editing his film LENNY while rehearsing a show, then he suffered a heart attack, recovered, and after more stage success, made this movie. He cast his former lover Ann Reinking as Joe Gideon's fading flame, and basically dissected the life of a flip, doomed, dysfunctional antihero who alternately evokes sympathy, then repulses with his sexual addiction and constant need for ego-gratification. ALL THAT JAZZ is great-looking but not easy to watch; Fosse's indulgent vision at times approaches sour self-loathing, and nothing like the explicit open-heart surgery had been seen on mainstream American screens, let alone the morbid song-and-dance routines in an operating theater.

ALL THE KING'S MEN

1949 109m bw Political   ★★★★★
Columbia (U.S.)   /A

Broderick Crawford (Willie Stark), Joanne Dru (Anne Stanton), John Ireland (Jack Burden), John Derek (Tom Stark), Mercedes McCambridge (Sadie Burke), Shepperd Strudwick (Adam Stanton), Ralph Dumke (Tiny Duffy), Anne Seymour (Lucy Stark), Katherine Warren (Mrs. Burden), Raymond Greenleaf (Judge Stanton)

p, Robert Rossen; d, Robert Rossen; w, Robert Rossen (based on the novel by Robert Penn Warren); ph, Burnett Guffey; ed, Al Clark; m, Louis Gruenberg

AA Best Picture; AA Best Actor: Broderick Crawford; *AAN Best Supporting Actor:* John Ireland; *AA Best Supporting Actress:* Mercedes McCambridge; *AAN Best Director:* Robert Rossen; *AAN Best Screenplay:* Robert Rossen; *AAN Best Editing:* Robert Parrish, Al Clark

Academy Award-winning rise and fall of a rotten politician, based on the Pulitzer Prize-winning novel by Robert Penn Warren. This scathing, grimly realistic film, long a pet project for producer-director-writer Robert Rossen, served as a breakthrough for Broderick Crawford, who had previously been confined to B films. As Willie Stark, Crawford let loose a fierce and awesome acting *tour de force* he never again equaled (and won an Academy Award for his work). The character of Willie Stark himself was most certainly inspired by Louisiana's Huey Pierce Long, the controversial "Kingfish" who ruled the state as governor (and later senator) with an iron hand and an enduring populist appeal, soaking the wealthy and enhancing his personal power unscrupulously. Long's demagoguery, so accurately profiled in this film, ended with his assassination in 1935 by Dr. Carl Austin Weiss, a 29-year-old Baton Rouge physician whose sister may or may not have been raped by Long.

Rossen's film chronicles this life of raw power with compelling scenes, and Crawford's performance is well-supported by the rest of the cast—especially McCambridge, in her film debut, as a conniving political aide. Rossen shot the film in Stockton, California, a working-class town, and enlisted the aid of hundreds of citizens as extras and bit players, adding an edge of authenticity to the production of this hallmark political film.

ALL THE PRESIDENT'S MEN

1976 138m c Political   ★★★★
Warner Bros. (U.S.)   PG/15

Dustin Hoffman (Carl Bernstein), Robert Redford (Bob Woodward), Jack Warden (Harry Rosenfeld), Martin Balsam (Howard Simons), Hal Holbrook (Deep Throat), Jason Robards Jr. (Ben Bradlee), Jane Alexander (Bookkeeper), Meredith Baxter Birney (Debbie Sloan), Ned Beatty (Dardis), Stephen Collins (Hugh Sloan, Jr.)

p, Walter Coblenz; d, Alan J. Pakula; w, William Goldman (based on the book by Carl Bernstein and Bob Woodward); ph, Gordon Willis; ed, Robert Wolfe; m, David Shire; prod d, George Jenkins

AAN Best Picture; AA Best Supporting Actor: Jason Robards; *AAN Best Supporting Actress:* Jane Alexander; *AAN Best Director:* Alan J. Pakula; *AA Best Adapted Screenplay:* William Goldman; *AAN Best Editing:* Robert L. Wolfe; *AA Best Art Direction:* George Jenkins, George Gaines; *AA Best Sound:* Arthur Piantadosi, Les Fresholtz, Dick Alexander, Jim Webb

Landmark movie which combines elements of the political thriller, buddy picture-star vehicle, detective story, 1930s newspaper reporter programmer, and biopic. The two stars play the real-life *Washington Post* reporters who kicked off the Watergate investigation, with Hoffman as the Jewish, street-smart Carl Bernstein and Redford as the WASPy Bob Woodward. Robards, beginning his spate of crusty-ole-codger supporting roles, won an Oscar, as did screenwriter William Goldman. The film features a host of fine character portrayals and a compelling climax that compensates for its length.

ALL THE RIGHT MOVES

1983 91m c Sports   ★½
Fox (U.S.)   R/15

Tom Cruise (Stef), Craig T. Nelson (Nickerson), Lea Thompson (Lisa), Charles Cioffi (Pop), Paul Carafotes (Salvucci), Christopher Penn (Brian), Sandy Faison (Suzie), Paige Price (Tracy), James A. Baffico (Bosko), Donald A. Yanessa (Coach)

p, Stephen Deutsch; d, Michael Chapman; w, Michael Kane; ph, Jan De Bont; ed, David Garfield; m, David Campbell; art d, Mary Ann Biddle; cos, Deborah Hopper, Joseph Roveto

High-school football star Tom Cruise yearns to escape his stifling mill town existence via a sports scholarship but runs afoul of tough coach Craig T. Nelson. This cliche-riddled picture was the directorial debut of veteran cinematographer Michael Chapman, who took no risks in his first time out. Filmed in Johnstown, Pennsylvania, where area coach Don Yanessa acted as technical advisor, also appearing as an opposing coach.

ALL THIS AND HEAVEN TOO

1940 140m bw Romance   ★★★★
Warner Bros. (U.S.)   /U

Bette Davis (Henriette Deluzy Desportes), Charles Boyer (Duke De Praslin), Jeffrey Lynn (Reverend Henry Field), Barbara O'Neil (Duchesse De Praslin), Virginia Weidler (Louise), Walter Hampden (Pasquier), Harry Davenport (Pierre), Fritz Leiber (Abbe Gallard), Helen Westley (Mme. Le Maire), Sibyl Harris (Mlle. Maillard)

p, David Lewis; d, Anatole Litvak; w, Casey Robinson (based on the novel by Rachel Lyman Field); ph, Ernest Haller; ed, Warren Low; m, Max Steiner; art d, Carl Jules Weyl; cos, Orry-Kelly

AAN Best Picture; AAN Best Supporting Actress: Barbara O'Neil; *AAN Best Cinematography:* Ernest Haller

A classic of unrequited love, based on the best-selling Rachel Field novel set in 19th-century France. Governess Davis falls in love with nobleman Boyer who has engaged her to care for his children. Litvak's smooth, understated treatment produces restrained, ageless performances from both stars. Oscar nominee Barbara O'Neil (best remembered as Scarlett O'Hara's mother in GWTW) almost steals the picture in a serpentine portrayal of Boyer's possessive, neurotic wife. This moody, elaborate production, greatly enhanced by its Steiner score, is a deft example of the "women's picture."

ALPHAVILLE

1965 98m bw Science Fiction ★★★★½
Athos (France/Italy) /A

Eddie Constantine (*Lemmy Caution*), Anna Karina (*Natasha Von Braun*), Akim Tamiroff (*Henri Dickson*), Laszlo Szabo (*Doctor*), Howard Vernon (*Prof. Von Braun*), Michel Delahaye (*Von Braun's Assistant*), Jean-Andre Fieschi (*Prof. Heckel*), Jean-Louis Comolli (*Prof. Jeckell*)

p, Andre Michelin; d, Jean-Luc Godard; w, Jean-Luc Godard; ph, Raoul Coutard; ed, Agnes Guillemot; m, Paul Misraki

Jean-Luc Godard's ALPHAVILLE is a poetic, funny, and visually inspired blend of sci-fi, detective-film satire, and political allegory.

Secret agent Lemmy Caution (Eddie Constantine) enters Alphaville in search of his predecessor Henri Dickson (Akim Tamiroff) and Professor Von Braun (Howard Vernon), the inventor of a death ray. Pretending to be a reporter, Lemmy discovers that Alphaville is a cold and loveless automated society that's run by a computer invented by Von Braun called Alpha 60. He meets Von Braun's daughter Natasha (Anna Karina) and finds Dickson at a hotel where dissidents are kept until they commit suicide. After seeing Dickson die, Natasha takes Lemmy to see her father. Von Braun's guards capture Lemmy and he's interrogated by Alpha 60, then given a tour of the computer's control center. There he learns that Von Braun intends to declare war on the Outlands.

ALPHAVILLE is a brilliant satire of an alienated society that has been robbed of its poetry and emotion by science and technology. The film's central conceit—and joke—is that this dystopian futuristic society is actually contemporary France, and the pod-like, conformist mindset of its people already exists. All of the interiors were filmed in dehumanizing glass and concrete office buildings and hotels, filled with sterile corridors and fluorescent computer rooms. All of the exteriors take place in a nocturnal Paris illuminated only by car lights and flashing neon. The casting of Eddie Constantine was inspired, as he had established the character of the hard-boiled dick Lemmy Caution in a series of French movies based on Peter Cheyney's novels. With his trench-coat, fedora, cigarette, and craggy face, Constantine recalls a poor-man's Humphrey Bogart, nonchalantly shooting everything in sight. Raoul Coutard's superbly mobile camerawork and Paul Misraki's excellent score all contribute to a movie that proves that you need neither a huge budget or computer effects to make a classic sci-fi movie, but only imagination.

AMADEUS

1984 158m c Biography/Musical ★★★★★
Orion (U.S.) PG

F. Murray Abraham (*Antonio Salieri*), Tom Hulce (*Wolfgang Amadeus Mozart*), Elizabeth Berridge (*Constanze Mozart*), Simon Callow (*Emanuel Schikaneder*), Roy Dotrice (*Leopold Mozart*), Christine Ebersole (*Katerina Cavalieri*), Jeffrey Jones (*Emperor Joseph II*), Charles Kay (*Count Orsini-Rosenberg*), Kenny Baker (*Parody Commendatore*), Lisbeth Bartlett (*Papagena*)

p, Saul Zaentz; d, Milos Forman; w, Peter Shaffer (based on his play); ph, Miroslav Ondricek; ed, Nena Danevic, Michael Chandler; m, Wolfgang Amadeus Mozart, Antonio Salieri, Giovanni Battista Pergolesi; prod d, Patrizia von Brandenstein; art d, Karel Cerny, Francesco Chianese, Josef Svoboda; fx, Dick Smith; chor, Twyla Tharp; cos, Theodor Pistek

AA Best Picture; *AA Best Actor*: F. Murray Abraham; *AAN Best Actor*: Tom Hulce; *AA Best Director*: Milos Forman; *AA Best Adapted Screenplay*: Peter Shaffer; *AAN Best Cinematography*: Miroslav Ondricek; *AAN Best Editing*: Nena Danevic, Michael Chandler; *AA Best Art Direction*: Patrizia Von Brandenstein, Karel Cerny; *AA Best Costume Design*: Theodor Pistek; *AA Best Sound*: Mark Berger, Tom Scott, Todd Boekelheide, Chris Newman; *AA Best Makeup*: Paul LeBlanc, Dick Smith

Milos Forman's brilliant, Oscar-winning adaptation of Peter Shaffer's hit play, AMADEUS is a fictionalized retelling of the final days of Antonio Salieri.

Salieri (F. Murray Abraham, who won the Best Actor Oscar for his portrayal), a famous composer in Mozart's day but now incarcerated in an insane asylum, begins his final confession to a young cleric. He tells the story of his relationship with Mozart (Tom Hulce), in a 30-year flashback to when he first met the 26-year-old prodigy. Furious that this boor can produce such beautiful music, Salieri determines to keep Mozart's talent from continued recognition.

The discerning but less talented Salieri has great influence in Vienna, being court composer to Joseph II of Austria (Jeffrey Jones), who realizes he knows little about music and therefore allows Salieri to decide what he should hear and whom he should be patron to. After Mozart manages to get the Emperor's ear, his career is launched, and we see him writing and conducting several of his best pieces. Then his friends, health, and resources waste away. He works most feverishly on his "Requiem," commissioned by a masked stranger who is actually Salieri. The effort proves the final stroke against the greater composer's weakened constitution, and he is buried in a pauper's grave.

Milos Forman's direction is flawless, Neville Marriner's musical direction is superb, and the film is a feast for the eyes and ears. Although Forman concentrates on Mozart's more popular works, the prodigious output of Mozart's short life is clearly conveyed. AMADEUS is a must for any music lover, any film lover, or anyone who reveres excellence.

AMARCORD

1974 127m c Comedy ★★★★
F.C./PECF/New World (Italy/France) R/18

Magali Noel (*Gradisca*), Bruno Zanin (*Titta*), Pupella Maggio (*Titta's Mother*), Armando Brancia (*Titta's Father*), Giuseppe Ianigro (*Titta's Grandfather*), Nando Orfei (*Pataca*), Ciccio Ingrassia (*Uncle Teo*), Luigi Rossi (*Lawyer*), Gennaro Ombra (*Bisein*), Josiane Tanzilli (*Volpina*)

p, Franco Cristaldi; d, Federico Fellini; w, Federico Fellini, Tonino Guerra; ph, Giuseppe Rotunno; ed, Ruggero Mastroianni; m, Nino Rota; art d, Danilo Donati

AAN Best Director: Federico Fellini; *AAN Best Original Screenplay*: Federico Fellini, Tonino Guerra; *AA Best Foreign Language Film*:

A pictorial weaving of the bizarre fragments of Fellini's imagination and memory, AMARCORD is set in a seaside village (very similar to Fellini's boyhood town of Rimini) in the 1930s. Through the eyes of the impressionable young Zanin, Fellini takes a penetrating look at family life, religion, love, sex, education, and politics. Among the characters are Zanin's constantly battling mother and father, and a priest who listens to confession only to spark his own deviant imagination. Although Italy is under the control of the Fascists, the regime's oppressiveness remains obscure to the naive villagers, who worship an immense, daunting banner of Il Duce's face. There is hardly a character in AMARCORD left unscathed by Fellini's biting wit, yet the director manages to present them lovingly. Unique personality traits, revelations of personal weakness (and thus humanness), are valued for the color and variety they add to the world. AMARCORD won the Academy Award for Best Foreign Film in 1974.

AMATEUR

1994 105m c Drama/Thriller/Crime ★★★
Union Generale du Cinematographique/True Fiction R/15
Pictures/Zenith Productions/American Playhouse/Theatrical
Films/Channel Four Films/La Sept Cinema (U.S./U.K./France)

Isabelle Huppert (*Isabelle*), Martin Donovan (*Thomas*), Elina Lowensohn (*Sofia*), Damian Young (*Edward*), Chuck Montgomery (*Jan*), David Simonds (*Kurt*), Pamela Stewart (*Officer Melville*), Erica Gimpel (*Irate Woman*), Jan Leslie Harding (*Waitress*), Terry Alexander (*Frank the Cook*)

p, Ted Hope, Hal Hartley; d, Hal Hartley; w, Hal Hartley; ph, Michael Spiller; ed, Steve Hamilton; m, Jeff Taylor; prod d, Steve Rosenzweig; art d, Ginger Tougas; fx, Drew Jiritano; cos, Alexander Welker

AMATEUR wears its themes on its sleeve, and questions of identity are always on the character's minds; everyone wants to change, to be redeemed, but nobody seems to know how.

Handsome, sharply dressed Thomas (Martin Donovan) wakes up in New York's trendy SoHo, unable to remember who he is or how he came to be lying face down on the cobblestone pavement. He stumbles into the fragile arms of Isabelle (Isabelle Huppert), an enigmatic beauty who tends to his head wound and assists him in his search for the secret of his identity. But the more Thomas learns about the man he used to be, the more he wants to emulate Isabelle, a former nun who's remaking herself as a literary pornographer.

A brittle comedy of manners for an ill-mannered age, AMATEUR sounds more engaging than it actually is. This elegantly photographed film features blackmail, attempted murder, amnesia, a stylish European porno star (Elina Lowensohn), and a hair-raising episode of torture—but it's more tedious than piquant. Though fans of Hartley's distinctive blend of coolly arch dialogue and preposterous happenstance won't be disappointed, AMATEUR is exasperatingly clever and ultimately superficial. Surprisingly, the film's last scene abandons the hip detachment that is director Hal Hartley's trademark and lends the film a genuinely poignant punch.

AMERICAN FRIEND, THE

1977   127m   c   Mystery/Thriller   ★★★★
Road Movies   (West Germany)   /15

Dennis Hopper *(Ripley)*, Bruno Ganz *(Jonathan Zimmermann)*, Lisa Kreuzer *(Marianne Zimmermann)*, Gerard Blain *(Raoul Minot)*, Nicholas Ray *(Derwatt)*, Samuel Fuller *(The American)*, Peter Lilienthal *(Marcangelo)*, Daniel Schmid *(Ingraham)*, Jean Eustache *(Friendly Man)*, Rudolf Schundler *(Gantner)*

d, Wim Wenders; w, Wim Wenders (based on the novel *Ripley's Game* by Patricia Highsmith); ph, Robby Muller; ed, Peter Przygodda; m, Jurgen Knieper; art d, Sickerts

Dennis Hopper and Bruno Ganz are superb in Wim Wenders's THE AMERICAN FRIEND, a gripping Hitchockian thriller based on a novel by Patricia Highsmith.

Jonathan Zimmermann (Bruno Ganz), a Hamburg picture-framer and painting-restorer who's suffering from an incurable blood disease, meets Tom Ripley (Dennis Hopper), an American who sells forged paintings in Germany and knows about Jonathan's illness. Because of a perceived slight when the two were introduced, Ripley spreads a rumor that Jonathan's death is imminent, and suggests his name to a criminal associate named Minot (Gerard Blain) who's looking for a non-professional hitman to dispose of his rivals. Jonathan refuses, but changes his mind as his anxiety over his condition increases; he carries out Minot's assignment, shooting a man in the Paris subway. Back in Germany, Minot pays him only half of the proposed fee, telling him he will give him the rest after he performs another killing.

THE AMERICAN FRIEND is a moody and riveting thriller-cum-existential character study that pays homage to the American cinema, not only by its casting of Wenders's two directorial cult-heroes, Nicholas Ray and Samuel Fuller, but also through direct stylistic and thematic references to the work of Alfred Hitchcock, who had made one of his best films, STRANGERS ON A TRAIN (1951) from a Highsmith novel. Wenders handles the thriller aspects of the plot expertly, making it possibly his most accessible film. He also treats the story as an ironic commentary on the influence of American culture on Germany and the uneasy relationship between the two countries, as well as a personal meditation on the acts of looking and seeing. Hopper gives one of the best performances of his career as the devilish Ripley, driving around spouting philosophy into a tape-recorder. Ganz is equally superb as the tortured Jonathan, and both actors brilliantly play off the other's differing acting style. Wenders has categorized THE AMERICAN FRIEND as simply an "entertainment film," but it's a richly textured and deeply rewarding one.

AMERICAN GRAFFITI

1973   110m   c   Comedy   ★★★★½
Universal   (U.S.)   PG

Richard Dreyfus *(Curt)*, Ron Howard *(Steve)*, Paul LeMat *(John)*, Charles Martin Smith *(Terry)*, Cindy Williams *(Laurie)*, Candy Clark *(Debbie)*, Mackenzie Phillips *(Carol)*, Wolfman Jack *(Himself)*, Harrison Ford *(Falfa)*, Bo Hopkins *(Joe)*

p, Francis Ford Coppola, Gary Kurtz; d, George Lucas; w, George Lucas, Gloria Katz, Willard Huyck; ph, Ron Everslage, Jan D'Alquen; ed, Verna Fields, Marcia Lucas; art d, Dennis Clark; cos, Aggie Guerard Rodgers

AAN Best Picture; AAN Best Supporting Actress: Candy Clark; *AAN Best Director:* George Lucas; *AAN Best Adapted Screenplay:* George Lucas, Gloria Katz, Willard Huyck; *AAN Best Editing:* Verna Fields, Marcia Lucas

A hallmark film of the 1970s. In a series of touching and telling vignettes, AMERICAN GRAFFITI follows a memorable crew of small-town teenagers through one momentous night in 1962. Director Lucas' modest, near-verite approach contrasts strikingly with his glitzy following film, STAR WARS.

Steve (Ron Howard), a clean-cut youth, is to leave for college the next day; Curt (Richard Dreyfuss), the class intellectual, is also slated for college but has doubts about his future; Laurie (Cindy Williams), Curt's sister and Steve's girlfriend, is upset by the latter's impending departure; Terry (Charles Martin Smith) is a hopeless nerd who desperately yearns to be "cool"; John (Paul LeMat), who's very cool indeed, drives "the fastest car in the valley" and is constantly being forced to prove that boast. After the school dance, everyone goes cruising. John picks up loquacious 13-year-old Carol (Mackenzie Phillips), thinking she's much older until she climbs aboard his 1932 Ford Deuce Coupe. Steve and Laurie, driving about in his 1958 Impala, clash over their ambitions; he's full of hope for the future, while she's afraid her life is over at 17. Curt goes off in search of the elusive Girl in the White T-Bird, while Terry has an adventure with a reputedly "experienced" older girl (Candy Clark).

Based on George Lucas' own teenage hot-rodding days in Modesto, California, the appeal of AMERICAN GRAFFITI is in its fragmentary scenes; the nervous camera jumps from character to character to present a powerful collage of American youth on the brink of maturity and the complex experiences of the coming decade. The enormous financial and critical success of GRAFFITI—it grossed over $100 million domestically—allowed Lucas the freedom to finance one of the most beloved and highest-grossing films of all time—STAR WARS—and spawned numerous imitations, even inspiring the long-running TV sitcom "Happy Days." The film boosted the careers of a host of young performers including Dreyfuss, Howard, Williams, LeMat, Smith, Clark, Phillips, Harrison Ford, Kathleen Quinlan, and Suzanne Somers.

AMERICAN IN PARIS, AN

1951   113m   c   Musical   ★★★★★
MGM   (U.S.)   /U

Gene Kelly *(Jerry Mulligan)*, Leslie Caron *(Lise Bouvier)*, Oscar Levant *(Adam Cook)*, Georges Guetary *(Henri Baurel)*, Nina Foch *(Milo Roberts)*, Eugene Borden *(George Mattieu)*, Martha Bamattre *(Mathilde Mattieu)*, Mary Jones *(Old Lady Dancer)*, Ann Codee *(Therese)*, George Davis *(Francois)*

p, Arthur Freed; d, Vincente Minnelli; w, Alan Jay Lerner; ph, Alfred Gilks, John Alton; ed, Adrienne Fazan; art d, Cedric Gibbons, Preston Ames; fx, Warren Newcombe; chor, Gene Kelly; cos, Walter Plunkett, Irene Sharaff

AA Best Picture; AAN Best Director: Vincente Minnelli; *AA Best Screenplay:* Alan Jay Lerner; *AA Best Cinematography:* Alfred Gilks, John Alton; *AAN Best Editing:* Adrienne Fazan; *AA Best Score:* Johnny Green, Saul Chaplin; *AA Best Art Direction:* Cedric Gibbons, Preston Ames, Edwin B. Willis, Keogh Gleason; *AA Best Costume Design:* Orry-Kelly, Walter Plunkett, Irene Sharaff

A classic film featuring the timeless music of George and Ira Gershwin, AN AMERICAN IN PARIS has a freshness and charm rare in the musical genre, and it was the film that forever identified MGM as *the* studio for musicals.

Jerry Mulligan (Gene Kelly) is an ex-GI and struggling artist in postwar Paris. His friend Adam Cook (Oscar Levant) is a piano player in a nearby cafe, a sarcastic and morose individual who offers nothing but discouragement to Jerry. However, another friend, Henri Baurel (Georges Guetary), a successful revue singer, is more encouraging. Henri informs his pal that he's going to marry a wonderful girl, an 18-year-old dancer whom he rescued from the Nazis during the war.

Jerry, meanwhile, is discovered by Milo Roberts (Nina Foch), a wealthy patroness who purchases his paintings and encourages her friends to do the same. Innocently enjoying his newfound success, Jerry visits a nightclub and meets Lise (newcomer Leslie Caron, discovered by Kelly in the Ballets des Champs Elysees), falling for her immediately. She fends off his advances but laters agrees to a date, then informs him that she's engaged to Henri. Though they are in love, Jerry and Lise do the noble thing and decide not to meet again.

The plot was showing signs of age far earlier than 1951, but everything else about AN AMERICAN IN PARIS more than compensates: the songs are all Gershwin Brothers standards; Kelly's choreography is breathtaking; the original screenplay by playwright Alan Jay Lerner is alternately witty and touching; and Minnelli's direction feels buoyantly assured. The 17-minute Dufy-inspired ballet (art directors Cedric Gibbons and Preston Ames, along with costume designer Irene Sharaff, also contributed brilliantly to this sequence) is the showstopper here but an underrated standout is "I'll Build a Stairway to Paradise," performed with marvelous elan by Guetary. Although the setting is Paris, very little of the film was actually shot on location; the spectacular scenes were mostly sets built on the lot. AN AMERICAN IN PARIS received a total of seven Academy Awards, plus a special Oscar to Kelly.

AMERICAN MADNESS

1932 75m bw Drama   ★★★
Columbia (U.S.)   /U

Walter Huston (*Dickson*), Pat O'Brien (*Matt*), Kay Johnson (*Mrs. Dickson*), Constance Cummings (*Helen*), Gavin Gordon (*Cluett*), Robert Ellis (*Dude Finlay*), Jeanne Sorel (*Cluett's Secretary*), Walter Walker (*Schultz*), Berton Churchill (*O'Brien*), Arthur Hoyt (*Ives*)

d, Frank Capra; w, Robert Riskin; ph, Joseph Walker; ed, Maurice Wright

Rare Capra work, and one of the few films to properly utilize the genius of the astonishing Walter Huston. Central theme of stressed-out bank president Huston as idealistic individual against the cruelty of the faceless crowd, struck a blow against Hooverism and for FDR's New Deal.

Like the single-set interiors of GRAND HOTEL, Capra filmed AMERICAN MADNESS totally within an enormous bank set, all the action taking place inside board rooms and vaults and behind tellers' cages, moving his camera with fluid truck and dolly shots, boom shots, and quick cuts that keep up the already established frenetic pace. To further create this sense of urgency, Capra cut out all dissolves (a device used to indicate the passing of time). He overlapped speeches and then had his actors hurry through their actions and dialogue.

AMERICAN MADNESS captured authentically the hysteria of the Great Depression; nor does the gratuitous romantic subplot mar its otherwise noble intentions.

AMERICAN WEREWOLF IN LONDON, AN

1981 97m c Comedy/Science Fiction/Horror   ★★★
Universal (U.S.)   R/18

David Naughton (*David Kessler*), Jenny Agutter (*Alex Price*), Griffin Dunne (*Jack Goodman*), John Woodvine (*Dr. Hirsch*), Brian Glover (*Chess Player*), David Schofield (*Dart Player*), Lila Kaye (*Barmaid*), Paul Kember (*Sgt. McManus*), Don McKillop (*Inspector Villiers*), Frank Oz (*Mr. Collins*)

p, George Folsey Jr.; d, John Landis; w, John Landis; ph, Robert Paynter; ed, Malcolm Campbell; m, Elmer Bernstein; art d, Leslie Dilley; fx, Rick Baker; cos, Deborah Nadoolman

AA Best Makeup: Rick Baker

Sit tight: the most literal of the horror excursions into werewolf territory plays it straight for bloody terror. Young man gets bitten by a werewolf on the British moors and chilling special effects ensue, with a hair-raising climax in Piccadilly Circus. Rick Baker deservedly won the first Academy Award for makeup; direction and script by Landis have sharp fangs for laughs and reverence for the genre's history.

AMITYVILLE HORROR, THE

1979 126m c Horror   ★½
INT/American (U.S.)   R/15

James Brolin (*George Lutz*), Margot Kidder (*Kathleen Lutz*), Rod Steiger (*Fr. Delaney*), Don Stroud (*Fr. Bolen*), Natasha Ryan (*Amy*), K.C. Martel (*Greg*), Meeno Peluce (*Matt*), Michael Sacks (*Jeff*), Helen Shaver (*Carolyn*), Val Avery (*Sgt. Gionfriddo*)

p, Ronald Saland, Elliot Geisinger; d, Stuart Rosenberg; w, Sandor Stern (based on the book by Jay Anson); ph, Fred Koenekamp; ed, Robert Brown; m, Lalo Schifrin; art d, Kim Swados; fx, Dell Rheaume

AAN Best Score: Lalo Schifrin

Based on Jay Anson's slimy best-seller, THE AMITYVILLE HORROR reaped a fortune for its studio, American International, just before it went out of business. The film chronicles the trials and tribulations of the hapless Lutz family (headed by Brolin and Kidder) as they discover that the new house they've purchased for a steal in Amityville, NY, is plagued by evil demons that manifest themselves in a variety of disgusting ways (flies, black gook, Rod Steiger overacting as a priest). Schifrin's score received an Oscar nomination. A TV prequel and three dreadful sequels (one in 3-D) followed.

ANASTASIA

1956 105m c Drama   ★★★★
Fox (U.S.)   /U

Ingrid Bergman (*Anastasia*), Yul Brynner (*Bounine*), Helen Hayes (*Empress*), Akim Tamiroff (*Chernov*), Martita Hunt (*Baroness von Livenbaum*), Felix Aylmer (*Russian Chamberlain*), Sacha Pitoeff (*Petrovin*), Ivan Desny (*Prince Paul*), Natalie Schafer (*Lissenskaia*), Gregoire Gromoff (*Stepan*)

p, Buddy Adler; d, Anatole Litvak; w, Arthur Laurents (based on Guy Bolton's adaptation of Marcelle Maurette's play); ph, Jack Hildyard; ed, Bert Bates; m, Alfred Newman; art d, Andre Andrejew, Bill Andrews; cos, Rene Hubert

AA Best Actress: Ingrid Bergman; AAN Best Score: Alfred Newman

The peak of Ingrid bergman's triumphant career. Cheap impostor or grand duchess of Russia and daughter of the last czar? There was no doubt in the mind of any viewer after watching Bergman's sublime performance that Anastasia was the lost and unhappy Romanoff princess. This was Bergman's comeback to American screens after the Rosellini scandal and she played her part with such intense feeling that it won over audiences worldwide and earned her an Academy Award. Climax is Bergman's confrontation with Empress Hayes, the latter's best screen work. The Laurents screenplay is faithful to the Marcelle Maurette play. A grand entry in Hollywood history.

ANATOMY OF A MURDER

1959 160m bw Drama   ★★★★½
Columbia (U.S.)   /15

James Stewart (*Paul Biegler*), Lee Remick (*Laura Manion*), Ben Gazzara (*Lt. Frederick Manion*), Arthur O'Connell (*Parnell McCarthy*), Eve Arden (*Maida*), Kathryn Grant (*Mary Pilant*), Joseph N. Welch (*Judge Weaver*), Brooks West (*Mitch Lodwick*), George C. Scott (*Claude Dancer*), Murray Hamilton (*Alphonse Paquette*)

p, Otto Preminger; d, Otto Preminger; w, Wendell Mayes; ph, Sam Leavitt; ed, Louis Loeffler; m, Duke Ellington

AAN Best Picture; AAN Best Actor: James Stewart; AAN Best Supporting Actor: Arthur O'Connell; AAN Best Supporting Actor: George C Scott; AAN Best Adapted Screenplay: Wendell Mayes; AAN Best Cinematography: Sam Leavitt; AAN Best Editing: Louis R Loeffler

Courtroom histrionics given sizzle and sex by Otto Preminger and Duke Ellington's jazz. Stewart shocked 1950s audiences with his gritty, quirky performance as a confirmed bachelor defense attorney speaking directly about contraceptives, pink panties and rape. Old pros Arden and O'Connell flawlessly support the star performance in a talky tennis game. Gazzarra as a brutal army stud and Remick as his duplicitous, sluttish wife received well-deserved career boosts for their efforts.

The casting of Remick was Preminger's major concern after Lana Turner left the project (actress reportedly slapped director who slapped her back) and Jayne Mansfield backed off from the script. Joseph Welch, who plays the judge, was the famed Army-McCarthy hearings lawyer who would go on to become a real life judge. Even today, when these issues seem tame, the long drama crackles along. The film was nominated for Best Picture and Best Actor (the year BEN-HUR swept the competition) as well as Best Supporting Actor (both O'Connell and George C. Scott), Best Screenplay, Best Cinematography, and Best Film Editing.

ANCHORS AWEIGH

1945 143m c Musical ★★½
MGM (U.S.) /U

Frank Sinatra *(Clarence Doolittle)*, Gene Kelly *(Joseph Brady)*, Kathryn Grayson *(Susan Abbott)*, Jose Iturbi *(Himself)*, Dean Stockwell *(Donald Martin)*, Carlos Ramirez *(Carlos)*, Henry O'Neill *(Adm. Hammond)*, Leon Ames *(Commander)*, Rags Ragland *(Police Sergeant)*, Edgar Kennedy *(Police Captain)*

p, Joe Pasternak; d, George Sidney; w, Isobel Lennart (based on a story by Natalie Marcin); ph, Robert Planck, Charles P. Boyle; ed, Adrienne Fazan; m, George Stoll; art d, Cedric Gibbons, Randall Duell; chor, Gene Kelly; cos, Irene, Kay Dean

AAN Best Picture; AAN Best Actor: Gene Kelly; *AAN Best Cinematography:* Robert Planck, Charles Boyle; *AA Best Score:* Georgie Stoll; *AAN Best Song:* Jule Styne (Music), Sammy Cahn (Lyrics)

This amiable musical of gobs on shore leave in Hollywood lacks the snap of ON THE TOWN but holds up when young Sinatra croons "I Fall in Love Too Easily" and when Kelly gets the chance to dance with animated mouse Jerry of "Tom & Jerry" fame. The technique of live action mixed with cartoons has been done often since then, most notably in 1988's WHO FRAMED ROGER RABBIT, but it has never been done to better advantage than in this film. Pamela Britton's comic relief Brooklyn girl feels more authentic than the sticky sentiments of Pekinese Grayson. A pleasant, mindless diversion.

AND GOD CREATED WOMAN
(ET DIEU CREA LA FEMME)

1956 92m c Drama/Erotic ★★
Iena/UCIL/Cocinor (France) /18

Brigitte Bardot *(Juliette)*, Curt Jurgens *(Eric)*, Jean-Louis Trintignant *(Michel)*, Christian Marquand *(Antoine)*, Georges Poujouly *(Christian)*, Jean Tissier *(M. Vigier-Lefranc)*, Jeanne Marken *(Mme. Morin)*, Marie Glory *(Mme. Tardieu)*, Isabelle Corey *(Lucienne)*, Jean Lefebvre *(Rene)*

p, Raoul J. Levy; d, Roger Vadim; w, Roger Vadim, Raoul Levy; ph, Armand Thirard; ed, Victoria Mercanton; m, Paul Misraki; art d, Jean Andre

. . . but Roger Vadim created Brigitte Bardot. This is the film that made Bardot a household name and liberated French cinema by putting it in the hands of the young and the beautiful. And it managed to do all these things without being very good. The story is a simple one: sexy orphan Juliette (Bardot) marries Michel (Jean-Louis Trintignant), is pursued by the wealthy Eric (Curt Jurgens), and sleeps with Antoine (Christian Marquand), Michel's brother. Nonetheless, Michel fights for Juliette and manages to lure her back. Slight on story, AND GOD CREATED WOMAN is strong on energy, all of it coming from Bardot's brilliant screen presence. Her pouty lips, accentuated breasts, skimpy clothing, and wildly erotic mambo routine late in the film helped whip audiences into a frenzy. They couldn't get enough of her in France, nor could they in America. While her effect on the American film scene was dubious (more and more soft-porn titillation was imported), her effect on the French film industry can be seen in the rise of the *Nouvelle Vague* directors, who were given greater opportunities in light of Vadim's commercial success. Vadim would continue along this same path with diminishing impact on the film world and then try to create "Woman" again in an unsuccessful 1988 remake (in title only) starring Rebecca DeMornay. Bardot went on to enjoy continued success without him, making one wonder if, perhaps, Bardot created Vadim.

AND NOW FOR SOMETHING COMPLETELY DIFFERENT

1971 88m c Comedy ★★★
Columbia (U.K.) PG

Graham Chapman, John Cleese, Eric Idle, Terry Jones, Michael Palin, Terry Gilliam, Carol Cleveland, Connie Booth

p, Patricia Casey; d, Ian MacNaughton; w, Graham Chapman, John Cleese, Terry Gilliam, Eric Idle, Terry Jones, Michael Palin; ph, David Muir; ed, Thom Noble; art d, Colin Grimes; anim, Terry Gilliam

Some of the best of the BBC TV's "Monty Python's Flying Circus" sketches reshot for feature film release. Although the cast is brilliant and the material generally funny, the film fails to take advantage of the big-screen format. The gang from Python did much better with the follow-up film, MONTY PYTHON AND THE HOLY GRAIL.

AND THE SHIP SAILS ON
(E LA NAVE VA)

1983 132m c Comedy ★★★
RAI-TV (Italy/France) /PG

Freddie Jones *(Orlando)*, Barbara Jefford *(Ildebranda Cuffari)*, Victor Poletti *(Fuciletto)*, Peter Cellier *(Sir Reginald)*, Elisa Marinardi *(Teresa Valegnani)*, Norma West *(Sir Reginald's Wife)*, Paolo Paolini *(Orchestra Conductor)*, Sarah Jane Varley *(Dorothy)*, Fiorenzo Serra *(Grand Duke of Harzock)*, Pina Bausch *(Princess Lheremia)*

p, Franco Cristaldi; d, Federico Fellini; w, Federico Fellini, Tonino Guerra; ph, Giuseppe Rotunno; ed, Ruggero Mastroianni; m, Gianfranco Plenizio; art d, Dante Ferretti

A minor, eccentric offering from Fellini, involving an odd assortment of passengers who set sail in 1914 for the small island of Cleo. The purpose of their voyage ("the voyage of life?" one character queries) is to scatter the ashes of their friend, a famous opera diva. While the first-class cabins contain businessmen, opera colleagues, comedians, royalty, and various patrons of the arts, the steerage contains a slew of Serbo-Croatian freedom fighters on the run after assassinating Archduke Ferdinand—the catalysts of WWI. If that isn't enough variety, there is also a rhinoceros on board. Tensions rise when an Austro-Hungarian battleship arrives and demands that the revolutionaries be turned over to their custody.

With a line of logic that is as scattered as the diva's ashes, AND THE SHIP SAILS ON is a frustrating film which never quite comes together, and which has little basis in either psychological or physical reality (it was photographed entirely on Cinecitta sets, which Fellini shows us). The picture is worth watching, if only for the scenes with the rhino and the lengthy opening sequence, which begins as a scratchy, sepia-toned silent film that gradually but gloriously develops into a colorful sound picture.

AND THEN THERE WERE NONE

1945 97m bw Mystery ★★★★
Fox (U.S.)

Barry Fitzgerald *(Judge Quincannon)*, Walter Huston *(Dr. Armstrong)*, Louis Hayward *(Philip Lombard)*, Roland Young *(Blore)*, June Duprez *(Vera Claythorne)*, C. Aubrey Smith *(Gen. Mandrake)*, Judith Anderson *(Emily Brent)*, Mischa Auer *(Prince Starloff)*, Richard Haydn *(Rogers)*, Queenie Leonard *(Mrs. Rogers)*

p, Harry M. Popkin; d, Rene Clair; w, Dudley Nichols (based on the story "Ten Little Niggers" by Agatha Christie); ph, Lucien Andriot; ed, Harvey Manger; art d, Ernst Fegte

This classic Agatha Christie whodunit takes place on a desolate island off the English coast where ten strangers—all with criminal pasts—meet. All have been invited to spend an evening in a sprawling, eerie mansion as guests of maniacal Judge Quincannon (Fitzgerald). Among the colorful characters are the sinister Dr. Armstrong (Huston), the dictatorial General Mandrake (Smith), phony Prince Starloff (Auer), and lovers Philip (Hayward) and Vera (Duprez). It gradually dawns on the terrified guests that they have been marooned on the island for only one purpose—to be murdered one by one in retribution for their transgressions, as per the nursery rhyme "Ten Little Indians."

French director Clair took his time with this production, using his cameras to play cat-and-mouse with each victim and adopting the perfect pace for the story as originally conceived by Christie and tightly adapted by Nichols. The ending of this adaptation differs from Christie's original; the 1965 remake, TEN LITTLE INDIANS, restored the original finale, while the 1974 version, again titled TEN LITTLE INDIANS, used the Clair/Nichols ending.

ANDERSON TAPES, THE

1971 98m c Crime ★★½
Columbia (U.S.) GP/15

Sean Connery (Anderson), Dyan Cannon (Ingrid), Martin Balsam (Haskins), Ralph Meeker (Delaney), Alan King (Angelo), Christopher Walken (The Kid), Val Avery (Parelli), Dick Williams (Spencer), Garrett Morris (Everson), Stan Gottlieb (Pop)

p, Robert M. Weitman; d, Sidney Lumet; w, Frank Pierson (based on the novel by Lawrence Sanders); ph, Arthur J. Ornitz; ed, Joanne Burke; m, Quincy Jones; art d, Philip Rosenberg

A solid, precise, well-made Lumet film, with tough ex-convict Connery, an habitual criminal, looking for a big score immediately upon leaving prison. He goes to the syndicate to seek funds to back a massive robbery, intending to ransack a posh East Side New York apartment building. Rounding up a gang of top-flight thieves, Connery proceeds to plan and carry out his caper, unaware that he is being taped at every turn by various government agencies to discover his links with organized crime. He and his men break into each apartment that is unoccupied—he has determined in advance what tenants are present—and carries out the systematic looting of each place. There are so many lawmen listening in that it seems the whole world is bugged. A good example of the now-neglected caper genre.

ANDY WARHOL'S DRACULA
(DRACULA CERCA SANGUE DI VERGINE E. . . MORI DI SETE)

1974 90m c Horror ★★★
CC Champion & 1/Carlo Ponti-Jean Yanne-Jean-Pierre R/
Rassam (France/Italy)

Joe Dallesandro (Mario), Udo Kier (Dracula), Arno Juerging (Anton), Maxime McKendry (Lady Difiore), Vittorio De Sica (Lord Difiore), Dominique Darel (Rubinia), Stefania Cassini (Saphiria), Roman Polanski (Man in Inn), Gil Cagne (Townsman), Milena Vukotic (Esmeralda)

p, Carlo Ponti, Andrew Braunsberg, Jean-Pierre Rassam, Jean Yanne; d, Paul Morrissey, Antonio Margheriti; w, Paul Morrissey; ph, Luigi Kuveiller; ed, Jed Johnson, Franca Silvi; m, Carlo Gizzi; prod d, Enrico Job; art d, Gianni Giovagnoni; fx, Carlo Rambaldi, Roberto Arcangeli

Shot immediately after ANDY WARHOL'S FRANKENSTEIN with much of the same cast and crew, DRACULA is definitely the better of the two. More like a drug addict than a monster, Dracula (Kier) needs "wirgin" blood to survive, and virgins in his native Romania are in short supply. With his assistant, Juerging, and his sister (in a coffin), Dracula travels to Roman Catholic Italy, where virgins should be more prevalent, and winds up at the crumbling estate of a destitute marquis and his four unmarried daughters. Eager to marry one of his daughters off to the rich Romanian count, the marquis gives Dracula a warm welcome. Unbeknownst to the vampire, however, the two middle daughters have already lost their virginity to a hunky socialist handyman (Dallesandro).

Not so outright disgusting as Warhol's FRANKENSTEIN, DRACULA is stylishly directed, atmospheric, funny, and intense enough to please gorehounds—especially at the climax. Kier makes a wonderful Dracula with his thick accent and goofy mannerisms, but De Sica (director of such neorealist classics as SHOESHINE and THE BICYCLE THIEF) nearly steals the show as the eccentric marquis. Once again Morrissey's distinctive stamp is on the script, but many European sources credit Margheriti as the director. Look for Roman Polanski in a cameo as a goofy villager. Originally rated X by the MPAA, the rating was later changed to an R.

ANGEL AT MY TABLE, AN

1990 156m c Biography/Drama ★★★★
Hibiscus Films/Sharmill Films (New Zealand) R/15

Kerry Fox (Janet Frame), Karen Fergusson (Janet Frame—as a Teenager), Alexia Keogh (Janet Frame—as a Child), Iris Churn (Mum), K.J. Wilson (Dad), Melina Bernecker (Myrtle Frame), Glynis Angell (Isabel Frame), Samantha Townsley (Isabel Frame—as a Teenager), Katherine Murray-Cowper (Isabel Frame—as a Child), Sarah Smuts-Kennedy (June Frame)

p, Bridget Ikin; d, Jane Campion; w, Laura Jones (from the autobiographies To the Is-Land, An Angel at My Table and The Envoy from Mirror City by Janet Frame); ph, Stuart Dryburgh; ed, Veronica Haussler; m, Don McGlashan; prod d, Grant Major; art d, Jackie Gilmore; cos, Glenys Jackson

Lushly photographed and beautifully acted, AN ANGEL AT MY TABLE was the second feature directed by New Zealander Jane Campion, who would win a world-wide reputation with her following film, THE PIANO.

Adapted from the autobiography of novelist and poet Janet Frame (Kerry Fox), the film tells the story of a stubborn, plain, introverted redhead whose thirst for knowledge and determination to be a writer set her apart in her isolated rural community. She's shy as a child; in college, she finds herself increasingly alienated from her fellow students. She feels awkward and ugly, and when her lively, self-confident sister (Glynis Angell) arrives, Janet only looks worse by comparison. She retreats into a life of fantasy and isolation, and eventually has a nervous breakdown. Committed to an institution, Janet is diagnosed—incorrectly, it later turns out—as an incurable schizophrenic. Leaving the hospital, Janet meets Frank Sargeson (Martyn Sanderson), an eccentric writer, who encourages her to broaden her perspectives by traveling. Slowly Janet emerges from her shell, and by the time she returns to New Zealand, some peace (if not exactly happiness) has become possible for her.

Jane Campion has established a reputation for making slightly off-center films in which regular folks get glimpses of the darkness that lurks beneath the surfaces of their lives. An admirer of Frame's novels since she was a teenager, Campion builds her film around a heroine who defies Hollywood conventions; she's not beautiful or sexy or sophisticated, and her adventures are mostly intellectual. Originally shot on 16mm and 1-inch videotape as a 3-part miniseries for Australian TV, then re-edited for 35mm theatrical release, the film doesn't look like a TV movie, except perhaps in the intimacy of its subject.

ANGELS IN THE OUTFIELD

1951 99m c Comedy/Sports ★★★½
MGM (U.S.)

Paul Douglas (Guffy McGovern), Janet Leigh (Jennifer Paige), Keenan Wynn (Fred Bayles), Donna Corcoran (Bridget White), Lewis Stone (Arnold P. Hapgood), Spring Byington (Sr. Edwitha), Bruce Bennett (Saul Hellman), Marvin Kaplan (Timothy Durney), Ellen Corby (Sr. Veronica), Jeff Richards (Dave Rothberg)

p, Clarence Brown; d, Clarence Brown; w, Dorothy Kingsley, George Wells (based on a story by Richard Conlin); ph, Paul C. Vogel; ed, Robert J. Kern; m, Daniele Amfitheatrof

This delightful baseball comedy stars Paul Douglas as Guffy McGovern, the irascible manager of the Pittsburgh Pirates, who are firmly entrenched in the basement of the National League until the prayers of a little girl (Donna Corcoran) prompt the angel Gabriel to intervene. When Guffy sees the divine light and turns over a new leaf, more angels—baseball greats of the past—lend a helping glove, and the Pirates start winning ball games, shooting to the top of the standings. Reporter Jennifer Paige (Janet Leigh) suspects the Pirates are receiving help from above and begins an investigation into the matter. Great performances by all make this a little gem of a film. Dwight Eisenhower, interviewed during his presidency, named this his favorite movie. Note the fleeting presence of Hall of Famers Ty Cobb and Joe DiMaggio.

ANGELS OVER BROADWAY
1940 78m bw Drama   ★★★★
Columbia (U.S.)   /A

Douglas Fairbanks Jr. *(Bill O'Brien)*, Rita Hayworth *(Nina Barona)*, Thomas Mitchell *(Gene Gibbons)*, John Qualen *(Charles Engle)*, George Watts *(Hopper)*, Ralph Theodore *(Dutch Enright)*, Eddie Foster *(Louie Artino)*, Jack Roper *(Eddie Burns)*, Constance Worth *(Sylvia Marbe)*, Richard Bond *(Sylvia's Escort)*

p, Ben Hecht; d, Ben Hecht, Lee Garmes; w, Ben Hecht; ph, Lee Garmes; ed, Gene Havlick; m, George Antheil; art d, Lionel Banks; cos, Ray Howell

AAN Best Original Screenplay: Ben Hecht

One of the more underappreciated films to come out of Hollywood, this marvelous Ben Hecht production annoyed the critics of the day for not pandering to its audience. Four leads and a host of supporting players make a single Broadway night come to life with zip and wit. Mitchell, as a silver-tongued, alcoholic playwright, saves Qualen, who is about to commit suicide after embezzling several thousand dollars. "Dismiss your hearse," Mitchell urges him. "Live, little man, and suffer!" The zany playwright proposes a surefire scheme to dupe some big-time card sharps in a battle royal, using Qualen's stolen loot to build a fortune. Enter slick Fairbanks, who shills for a top-drawer poker game, and his devoted but equally sharp girlfriend Hayworth. Fairbanks spots Qualen as an easy mark and intends to suck him into the game and take him for everything. Nothing, of course, goes according to anyone's plans as Hecht's clever script twists and turns its way to a startling and delightful conclusion.

The performances, particularly by Mitchell and Fairbanks, are captivating, and the dialogue sparkles with Hecht's poetic irony: "This town's a giant dice game—come on seven!" Because the film featured Rita Hayworth, who had been hand-picked for stardom by Columbia's boss Harry Cohn, Hecht was given a relatively free reign on this production, and went unhampered by interfering studio bureaucrats to create an unpredictable Broadway saga. Hecht earned an Academy Award nomination for his original screenplay, but lost to Preston Sturges for THE GREAT MCGINTY.

ANGELS WITH DIRTY FACES
1938 97m bw Crime   ★★★★
Warner Bros. (U.S.)   /PG

James Cagney *(Rocky Sullivan)*, Pat O'Brien *(Jerry Connelly)*, Humphrey Bogart *(James Frazier)*, Ann Sheridan *(Laury Ferguson)*, George Bancroft *(Mac Keefer)*, Billy Halop *(Soapy)*, Bobby Jordan *(Swing)*, Leo Gorcey *(Bim)*, Bernard Punsley *(Hunky)*, Gabriel Dell *(Pasty)*

p, Samuel Bischoff; d, Michael Curtiz; w, John Wexley, Warren Duff (based on a story by Rowland Brown); ph, Sol Polito; ed, Owen Marks; m, Max Steiner; art d, Robert Haas

AAN Best Actor: James Cagney; *AAN Best Director:* Michael Curtiz; *AAN Best Original Screenplay:* Rowland Brown

One of the most stirring, colorful and memorable gangster films of its day, and a perfect summary of Cagney's tough but soft-hearted screen image. As youths, Rocky Sullivan and his pal Jerry Connelly are caught in the act of breaking into a railroad car. Jerry escapes, but Rocky is caught and sent to reform school. The film then jumps ahead several years, with Rocky (now played by Cagney) a hardened criminal, and Jerry (Pat O'Brien) a priest in the neighborhood where the boys grew up. Rocky, recently released from jail, returns to the neighborhood, where a battle begins between the criminal and the priest for the hearts and minds of some tough kids in the neighborhood. Rocky also tries to get his double-crossing ex-partner (Humphrey Bogart) to come up with the $100,000 he owes him.

With Cagney, O'Brien, and Bogart plus the young actors known as the Dead End Kids, the film offers a host of terrific characters, crisp dialogue, and a generous portion of humor. (Particularly funny is the scene in which Rocky gives the young toughs a lesson in how to play basketball.) Films about boyhood friends who go down different paths in life were popular in the 1930s, but the tale was never more effectively told than in this fast-paced drama.

ANIMAL CRACKERS
1930 97m bw Comedy   ★★★½
Paramount (U.S.)   /U

Groucho Marx *(Capt. Jeffrey Spaulding)*, Harpo Marx *(The Professor)*, Chico Marx *(Signor Emanuel Ravelli)*, Zeppo Marx *(Horatio Jamison)*, Lillian Roth *(Arabella Rittenhouse)*, Margaret Dumont *(Mrs. Rittenhouse)*, Louis Sorin *(Roscoe W. Chandler)*, Hal Thompson *(John Parker)*, Margaret Irving *(Mrs. Whitehead)*, Kathryn Reece *(Grace Carpenter)*

d, Victor Heerman; w, Morrie Ryskind (based on the musical play by Morrie Ryskind and George S. Kaufman); ph, George Foley

The second Marx Brothers film is a riotous version of their stage hit.

Mrs. Rittenhouse (Margaret Dumont), a wealthy Long Island matron, throws a lavish party at her mansion, at which the noted African explorer Captain Spaulding (Groucho Marx) is the guest of honor. Mrs. Whitehead, a society rival of Mrs. Rittenhouse's, decides to sabotage the party by substituting a copy of a noted painting that will be unveiled that evening. Meanwhile, Mrs. Rittenhouse's daughter Arabella (Lillian Roth) plans to switch the painting with a copy done by her artist boyfriend John (Hal Thompson), in order to impress art impresario Roscoe W. Chandler (Louis Sorin), whom musicans Ravelli and The Professor (Chico and Harpo Marx) recognize as actually being a former fish peddler named Abie.

ANIMAL CRACKERS is exceedingly stagy and theatrical, even by 1930's standards, but is nevertheless very funny and highly enjoyable. Some of its classic bits include the "Hooray for Captain Spaulding" production number, featuring the melody that Groucho would later adopt as the theme song for his radio and television hit "You Bet Your Life"; the hilarious parody of Eugene O'Neill's *Strange Interlude*, with Spaulding stepping forward and vocalizing his internal thoughts in the middle of a scene; and the usual quota of bad puns. ANIMAL CRACKERS was also the hardest Marx Brothers film to see for many years, having been withheld from circulation from 1958 to 1974 due to a copyright dispute. When it was re-released to theaters in 1974, a whole new generation of Marx Brothers fans were born, and happily, Groucho was still alive to bask in the triumph.

ANIMAL FARM
1955 75m c Animated   ★★
DCA (U.K.)   /U

Maurice Denham *(Voices of the Animals)*, Gordon Heath *(Narrator)*

p, John Halas, Joy Batchelor; d, John Halas, Joy Batchelor; w, John Halas, Joy Batchelor, Lothar Wolff, Borden Mace, Philip Stapp (based on the novel by George Orwell); ph, S.J. Griffiths; m, Matyas Seiber

A cartoon adaptation of George Orwell's classic dystopia, notable as the first feature-length animated British production. The story concerns a barnyard rebellion led by a pig, Napoleon, who perverts the revolutionary cause and takes on all the evil characteristics of the overthrown regime. The animation is satisfactory, and the film has several powerful moments, but the allegorical nature of Orwell's satirical fable is better served in print.

ANNA AND THE KING OF SIAM
1946 128m bw Drama   ★★★★
Fox (U.S.)   /A

Irene Dunne *(Anna)*, Rex Harrison *(the King)*, Linda Darnell *(Tuptin)*, Lee J. Cobb *(Kralahome)*, Gale Sondergaard *(Lady Thiang)*, Mikhail Rasumny *(Alak)*, Dennis Hoey *(Sir Edward)*, Tito Renaldo *(Prince as a Man)*, Richard Lyon *(Louis Owens)*, William Edmunds *(Monshee)*

p, Louis D. Lighton; d, John Cromwell; w, Talbot Jennings, Sally Benson (based on the book by Margaret Landon); ph, Arthur Miller; m, Bernard Wheeler, William Darling; fx, Fred Sersen

AAN Best Supporting Actress: Gale Sondergaard; *AAN Best Screenplay:* Sally Benson, Talbot Jennings; *AA Best Cinematography:* Arthur Miller; *AAN Best Score:* Bernard Herrmann; *AA Best Art Direction:* Lyle Wheeler, William Darling, Thomas Little, Frank E. Hughes

An entertaining, touching tale of an English tutor who travels to Siam in 1862 with her young son. She is hired to educate the harem and 67 children of the rather savage king, who covets Western culture but insists upon maintaining Siam's customs and some particularly barbaric traditions. The story is drawn from the real life of 33-year-old Mrs. Anna Leonowens, brilliantly played by Dunne, who is at first repelled by and later attracted to Harrison, the king (in his first American film), and his different Eastern ways. She also meets and befriends the king's first wife (Sondergaard), long relegated to the back rooms of the imperial palace, and a lovely young addition to the harem (Darnell) who falls tragically in love with another. The supporting cast is uniformly excellent, including Cobb in the role of the king's chief minister. Director Cromwell keeps the well lighted and photographed story brisk and less sentimental than the musical remake, THE KING AND I. Dunne is the perfect British governess, and the theoretically miscast Harrison is simply majestic as the king who gropes toward both sensitivity and Western ideas, battling his authoritarian instincts all the way. It's a wonder that this production, richly costumed and boasting lavish sets, was not done in color.

ANNA CHRISTIE

1930 86m bw Drama   ★★★
MGM (U.S.)   /A

Greta Garbo (Anna Christie), Charles Bickford (Matt Burke), George F. Marion Sr. (Chris Christopherson), Marie Dressler (Marthy Owen), James T. Mack (Johnny the Harp), Lee Phelps (Larry)

d, Clarence Brown; w, Frances Marion (based on the play by Eugene O'Neill); ph, William Daniels; ed, Hugh Wynn; art d, Cedric Gibbons; cos, Adrian

AAN Best Actress: Greta Garbo; *AAN Best Director:* Clarence Brown; *AAN Best Cinematography:* William H Daniels

The public fascination with the mysterious Garbo heightened ANNA CHRISTIE's popularity. Although critics and public alike were justifiably captivated by her husky, accented voice and famous delivery of her opening lines: "Gimme a viskey, ginger ale on the side . . . and don't be stingy, baby!" parts of her performance are exaggerated, reminiscent more of off-key silent-screen posturing than the equally intense but refined technique she would soon master. The sometimes mugging Dressler, on the other hand, in the star-making role of the aging wharf rat who commiserates with Garbo throughout the film, steals every scene she appears in and manages to convey both touching pathos and a rich humanity. Much of the film's creakiness is due to the cumbersome sound equipment that prevented director Clarence Brown from using his noise-making cameras freely. Nominated for an Academy Award for Best Actress for this film and ROMANCE, Garbo remade the film in German with Jacques Feyder (director of THE KISS, Garbo's last silent) and, reportedly, she liked Feyder's version better than Brown's, of which she said, "Isn't it terrible? Who ever saw Swedes act like that?"

ANNA KARENINA

1935 85m bw Drama   ★★★★
MGM (U.S.)   /U

Greta Garbo (Anna Karenina), Fredric March (Vronsky), Freddie Bartholomew (Sergei), Maureen O'Sullivan (Kitty), May Robson (Countess Vronsky), Basil Rathbone (Karenin), Reginald Owen (Stiva), Reginald Denny (Yashvin), Phoebe Foster (Dolly), Gyles Isham (Levin)

p, David O. Selznick; d, Clarence Brown; w, Clemence Dane, Salka Viertel, S.N. Behrman (based on the novel by Leo Tolstoy); ph, William Daniels; ed, Robert J. Kern; m, Herbert Stothart; chor, Marguerite Wallmann, Chester Hale

A remake of the John Gilbert-Greta Garbo silent movie LOVE, this often splendid, moody Garbo vehicle under Clarence Brown's direction tells the tragic Tolstoy tale with great sensitivity. As the immortal Anna of 19th-century St. Petersburg, Garbo plays the pampered wife of Karenin (Rathbone, in fine form), a rich but icy government official. After pleading with her straying married brother (Owen) not to jeopardize his marriage, she ironically meets and falls in love the dashing Captain Vronsky (March). When she asks her husband for a divorce,

she is told that if she makes such an unheard-of move, she will be deprived of her son (Bartholomew). Remorseful but consumed by love, Anna runs off with Vronsky, who resigns his commission. Though happy at first, he soon longs for his carefree army days, and she is pained by her thwarted attempts to spend time with her son. The star-crossed lovers finally argue and separate and when Anna, rushing to the train station upon learning that Vronsky is leaving, sees him saying goodbye to another woman, she throws herself in front of the departing train.

Director Brown, in one of the best of his seven films with Garbo, and ace cinematographer William Daniels, Garbo's favorite, bathe their beloved actress in soft light that caresses her classic features. Adorned in luxurious but subdued gowns appropriate to both her own passionate but understated style and Anna's profound sadness, Garbo is unforgettable as a woman who only briefly experiences carefree happiness, whose desires are crushed by a rigid and unfeeling society. Especially memorable is the finale, as light flashes from the oncoming train alternately reveal and hide Anna's conflicting emotions. Meticulously and sumptuously mounted by producer David O. Selznick, the film carefully pares down Tolstoy's sprawling classic to center almost entirely upon its heroine, but the end result is highly satisfying nonetheless.

ANNA KARENINA

1947 139m bw Drama   ★★★½
Korda/London Films (U.K.)   /PG

Vivien Leigh (Anna Karenina), Ralph Richardson (Alexei Karenin), Kieron Moore (Count Vronsky), Sally Ann Howes (Kitty Scherbatsky), Niall MacGinnis (Levin), Martita Hunt (Princess Betty Tversky), Marie Lohr (Princess Scherbatsky), Michael Gough (Nicholai), Hugh Dempster (Stefan Oblonsky), Mary Kerridge (Dolly Oblonsky)

p, Alexander Korda; d, Julien Duvivier; w, Jean Anouilh, Guy Morgan, Julien Duvivier (based on the novel by Leo Tolstoy); ph, Henri Alekan; ed, Russell Lloyd; m, Constant Lambert; prod d, Andre Andrejew; fx, W. Percy Day; cos, Cecil Beaton

This remake of the Garbo classic has different values and approaches that enhance Vivien Leigh's magnetic performance as the ill-starred Anna, who leaves her stuffy bureaucrat husband, Karenin (Richardson), for an adventurous army officer, Vronsky (Moore), only to be discarded and sent to suicide in front of an onrushing train when husband, child, and lover are lost to her. Unlike the 1935 version, which also downplayed the novel's subplots far more, the psychological elements of this tragedy are underscored and registered with powerful impact through Leigh, whose raw emotions distort and finally destroy a once orderly, though predictably dull, life. Leigh is positively riveting, and Richardson as the priggish, pompous government official is properly vengeful and vexing. Only the very handsome Moore, in the admittedly colorless role as the self-centered lover, is a letdown, delivering a sometimes bland performance. Korda's production, though perhaps overlong, is truly spectacular, with a great supporting cast, countless extras, and authentic 19th-century sets that are mouth-openers. Duvivier's direction is moody and fast-paced, highlighted by sometimes frightening effects, with angles and cuts that reflect the image of a woman slipping deeper and deeper into her own destruction.

ANNE OF THE THOUSAND DAYS

1969 145m c Historical   ★★★★
Universal (U.K.)   M/PG

Richard Burton (King Henry VIII), Genevieve Bujold (Anne Boleyn), Irene Papas (Queen Katherine), Anthony Quayle (Wolsey), John Colicos (Cromwell), Michael Hordern (Thomas Boleyn), Katherine Blake (Elizabeth), Peter Jeffrey (Norfolk), Joseph O'Conor (Fisher), William Squire (Thomas More)

p, Hal B. Wallis; d, Charles Jarrott; w, Bridget Boland, John Hale (adapted by Richard Sokolove, based on the play by Maxwell Anderson); ph, Arthur Ibbetson; ed, Richard Marden; m, Georges Delerue; prod d, Maurice Carter; art d, Lionel Couch; chor, Mary Skeaping; cos, Margaret Furse

AAN Best Picture; *AAN Best Actor:* Richard Burton; *AAN Best Actress:* Genevieve Bujold; *AAN Best Supporting Actor:* Anthony Quayle; *AAN Best Adapted Screenplay:* John Hale, Bridget Boland, Richard Sokolove; *AAN Best Cinematography:* Arthur Ibbetson; *AAN Best Score:* Georges Delerue; *AAN Best Art Direction:* Maurice Carter, Lionel Couch, Patrick McLoughlin; *AA Best Costume Design:* Margaret Furse; *AAN Best Sound:* John Alfred

A superbly acted costume drama, ANNE OF THE THOUSAND DAYS recounts the story of Henry VIII (Richard Burton), who, in 1526, discards his wife, Katherine of Aragon (Irene Papas), in favor of the younger, prettier Anne Boleyn (Genevieve Bujold), who soon proves to be as crafty and ruthless as her sovereign. Resisting Henry's incessant advances, insisting that any child born to them must be decreed legitimate, Anne plays her cat-and-mouse game for six years, while Cardinal Wolsey (Quayle) collapses into ineffectual senility when he fails to have Anne's marriage to another annulled. Only the Iago-like Cromwell (John Colicos) solves the king's dilemma by precipitating a break with the Vatican, naming Henry head of the Church of England, and dispensing with any religious controls over his or Anne's marital status. Although the union produces a daughter, Henry later seizes upon the birth of a stillborn son as an excuse to abandon his queen and and woo the attractive Jane Seymour (Lesley Paterson). After that Anne's days are numbered—one thousand, to be exact.

Based on the 1948 Maxwell Anderson play (a star vehicle for Rex Harrison on Broadway), ANNE OF THE THOUSAND DAYS has a touch of soap opera which helps explain its then-substantial gross of $7 million. But it also boasts lavish sets and handsome photography, an arresting performance by Burton—the epitome of the royal fox and oaf—and well-judged work from Bujold, Papas, and Quayle, all of which make for a rousing, bawdy, and often enlightening historical film. A successful entry in a series of such features made during the 60s, including BECKET (also produced by Wallis), A MAN FOR ALL SEASONS, and THE LION IN WINTER, the film received an Academy Award nomination for Best Picture but lost to John Schlesinger's gritty, contemporary MIDNIGHT COWBOY.

ANNIE GET YOUR GUN

1950 107m c Musical/Western ★★★½
MGM (U.S.) /U

Betty Hutton *(Annie Oakley)*, Howard Keel *(Frank Butler)*, Louis Calhern *(Buffalo Bill)*, J. Carrol Naish *(Chief Sitting Bull)*, Edward Arnold *(Pawnee Bill)*, Keenan Wynn *(Charlie Davenport)*, Benay Venuta *(Dolly Tate)*, Clinton Sundberg *(Foster Wilson)*, James Harrison *(Mac)*, Brad Mora *(Little Jake)*

p, Arthur Freed; d, George Sidney; w, Sidney Sheldon (based on the musical play, book by Herbert Fields and Dorothy Fields); ph, Charles Rosher; ed, James E. Newcom; m, Irving Berlin; art d, Cedric Gibbons, Paul Groesse; fx, A. Arnold Gillespie, Warren Newcombe; chor, Robert Alton

AAN Best Cinematography: Charles Rosher; *AAN Best Editing:* James E. Newcom; *AA Best Score:* Adolph Deutsch, Roger Edens; *AAN Best Art Direction:* Cedric Gibbons, Paul Groesse, Edwin B. Willis, Richard A. Pefferle

Sprightly songfest that, surprisingly, captivated audiences wanting musicals with dancing. There is little dancing throughout, but the tunes became instant standards and the large sets, armies of extras, and Wild West motif offset the missing choreography. In a glove-fitting role, Hutton blasts her way on and off screen as the sharpshooting Annie Oakley Mozie (1860-1926), a homely girl from the Ozarks who becomes queen of Buffalo Bill's renowned Wild West Show, pitting her talents against marksman Frank Butler (Keel). She loves Keel, but her ability to best him keeps driving him away. Finally Sitting Bull (Naish) gives her worthwhile advice before she faces off against Keel one more time. "You miss, you win," the Indian chief tells her, and he's right.

Keel is excellent as the smug star of the show; Naish is likewise top-notch as a shrewd Sitting Bull; Calhern superb as a noble but slippery Buffalo Bill; Arnold solid as his show biz rival; and Wynn his usual truculent self. Standout numbers include "Doin' What Comes Natur'lly" sung by Hutton and siblings, "My Defenses Are Down"

boomed by Keel, "I'm an Indian Too" with Hutton and a horde of leaping, lunging Indians, and the fantastic finale with hundreds of cowboys and Indians, "There's No Business Like Show Business."

MGM execs struggled to find the perfect Annie Oakley, first considering Judy Canova, Betty Garrett, and Doris Day before opting for Judy Garland, who was reportedly fired because of incessant tantrums. Hutton was finally brought in to save the day, which she did with typically unbridled enthusiasm, giving one of her most suitable performances, even though she proved to be no Ethel Merman, who originated the role in the smash Broadway production, when it came to singing the finale. Although the choice of director was similarly muddled by MGM moguls, passing from Busby Berkeley to Charles Walters and finally to George Sidney, the extremely lavish result went on to win the Oscar for Best Score in a Musical, as well as nominations for cinematography, art direction and editing.

ANNIE HALL

1977 93m c Comedy ★★★★
UA (U.S.) PG/15

Woody Allen *(Alvy Singer)*, Diane Keaton *(Annie Hall)*, Tony Roberts *(Rob)*, Carol Kane *(Allison)*, Paul Simon *(Tony Lacey)*, Colleen Dewhurst *(Mom Hall)*, Janet Margolin *(Robin)*, Shelley Duvall *(Pam)*, Christopher Walken *(Duane Hall)*, Donald Symington *(Dad Hall)*

p, Charles H. Joffe; d, Woody Allen; w, Woody Allen, Marshall Brickman; ph, Gordon Willis; ed, Ralph Rosenblum, Wendy Greene Bricmont; art d, Mel Bourne; cos, Ruth Morley, George Newman, Marilyn Putnam, Ralph Lauren, Nancy McArdle

AA Best Picture; *AAN Best Actor:* Woody Allen; *AA Best Actress:* Diane Keaton; *AA Best Director:* Woody Allen; *AA Best Original Screenplay:* Woody Allen, Marshall Brickman

Seminal, hilarious look at contemporary relationships, with Woody Allen playing Alvy Singer, a neurotic, insecure comedy writer (Allen began his own career as a gag writer for the "Tonight Show") who falls madly in love with Annie Hall (Diane Keaton), an aspiring singer. They fumble about in the early stages of their relationship like two teenagers groping toward sex and self-identity, mouthing cliches twisted in the Allen style to the wry, the incisive, and the sublimely ridiculous. They move in together, but he soon becomes so insecure about their affair that he pounces on her every move, interpreting these acts as rejection and disaffection. Eventually their own mutual uncertainty splits them apart and they are left to their careers and to trying again with other partners.

The simplicity of the seemingly impromptu story, set largely in Allen's beloved New York City, is part of ANNIE HALL's undeniable charm, along with Allen's flashbacks to childhood (with side-splitting Jonathan Munk as a young Woody) and constant asides to the camera, a device that sometimes can't help to carry the laughs. Allen moves freely through the flashbacks as a grown man, commenting on various scenes in a technique borrowed from Bergman's WILD STRAWBERRIES. The quip quotient is high (observing that Keaton habitually smokes a joint before they make love, Allen cracks, "Why don't you take sodium pentothal? Then you could sleep through the whole thing!") and Roberts is highly effective as the crass, materialistic sidekick.

ANOTHER WOMAN

1988 84m c Drama ★★★½
Jack Rollins-Charles H. Joffe (U.S.) PG

Gena Rowlands *(Marion Post)*, Mia Farrow *(Hope)*, Ian Holm *(Ken Post)*, Blythe Danner *(Lydia)*, Gene Hackman *(Larry)*, Betty Buckley *(Kathy)*, Martha Plimpton *(Laura Post)*, John Houseman *(Marion's Dad)*, Sandy Dennis *(Claire)*, David Ogden Stiers *(Young Marion's Dad)*

p, Robert Greenhut; d, Woody Allen; w, Woody Allen; ph, Sven Nykvist; ed, Susan E. Morse; prod d, Santo Loquasto; cos, Jeffrey Kurland

ANOTHER WOMAN stars Gena Rowlands as an aging professor who realizes she has led an unemotional life and must look into the past in order to prepare herself for the future. She is married to a physician (Holm), has a close relationship with her stepdaughter (Plimpton), avoids her brother (Yulin), and fears the loss of her ailing father

(Houseman). When she overhears a pregnant psychiatric patient's therapy session, Marion becomes obsessed with knowing all about the woman (Farrow), who reminds her of her younger self.

Full of the hand-wringing and self-consciously intellectual exchanges that characterize Allen's Bergmanesque outings, ANOTHER WOMAN benefits from a superb ensemble cast. An especially endearing final performance comes from the frail and obviously ailing Houseman, who was to die very shortly after the film's release. Nykvist's photography is impeccable, as is Loquasto's spare production design.

ANTHONY ADVERSE

1936   139m   bw   Historical/Romance   ★★
Warner Bros.   (U.S.)   /A

Fredric March *(Anthony Adverse)*, Olivia de Havilland *(Angela Guessippi)*, Edmund Gwenn *(John Bonnyfeather)*, Claude Rains *(Don Luis)*, Anita Louise *(Maria)*, Louis Hayward *(Denis Moore)*, Gale Sondergaard *(Faith Paleologus)*, Steffi Duna *(Neleta)*, Henry O'Neill, Billy Mauch *(Anthony as a Child)*

p, Henry Blanke; d, Mervyn LeRoy; w, Sheridan Gibney (based on the novel by Hervey Allen); ph, Tony Gaudio; ed, Ralph Dawson; m, Erich Wolfgang Korngold; art d, Anton Grot; cos, Milo Anderson

AAN Best Picture; AA Best Supporting Actress: Gale Sondergaard; *AA Best Cinematography:* Gaetano Gaudio; *AA Best Editing:* Ralph Dawson; *AA Best Score:* Leo Forbstein Warner Bros Studio Music Department, Erich Wolfgang Korngold; *AAN Best Art Direction:* Anton Grot

This lavish but overlong film remains true to the 1200-page best-seller on which it is based, though judging by the result one wonders to what extent this is admirable. Popular and acclaimed in its day, and technically highly skilled, ANTHONY ADVERSE substitutes historical pageantry for drama and melodramatic flourish for characterization whenever it gets the chance.

March plays the title role, an illegitimate child whose father (Hayward) is killed in a duel and who is raised in a convent by a gentle priest (O'Neill). Adopted by a kindly Scottish trader (Gwenn), the growing boy soon finds romance with a girl (de Havilland) who aspires to sing grand opera. Although they marry, the couple are separated when a crucial note is blown away by a gust of wind. Anthony goes crazy with despair and jungle fever for several years while managing his stepfather's questionable African interests, and when he returns to Europe he finds his stepfather dead, his wife a diva linked romantically to Napoleon (Rollo Lloyd), and his inheritance jeoparadized by the wicked Don Luis (Rains), who killed his real father back when. The wrap-up includes chicanery, a duel, and a surprise from de Havilland.

This massive but choppy historical soaper, aiming to both jerk tears and swash buckles, now seems inferior to other similar but more modest films. March has his moments, but seems more concerned with appearing young and stalwart than with giving the role the tongue-in-cheek dash it so desperately needs. De Havilland is mere decoration, and it is up to several of the supporting players, particularly Rains and Sondergaard (as a scheming, ambitious housekeeper), to serve as energetic foils to the film's rampant displays of virtue. Grot's sets and Gaudio's cinematography add definite sweep, and Korngold's score is both majestic and melancholic, befitting the romantic tragedy of star-crossed lovers this film would dearly like to be.

ANTONIA'S LINE
(ANTONIA)

1995   104m   c   Drama/Fantasy   ★★
Antonia's Line International/Bergen Film/Prime Time/Bard   /15
Entertainment/NPS Televisie   (Netherlands/Belgium/U.K.)

Willeke van Ammelrooy *(Antonia)*, Els Dottermans *(Danielle)*, Dora van der Groen *(Allegonde)*, Veerle van Overloop *(Therese)*, Jan Decleir *(Bas)*, Mil Seghers *(Crooked Finger)*, Marina de Graaf *(DeeDee)*, Elsie de Brauw *(Lara)*, Thyrza Ravesteijn *(Sarah)*, Jakob Beks *(Daan)*

p, Hans de Weers; d, Marleen Gorris; w, Marleen Gorris; ph, Willy Stassen; ed, Michiel Reichwein, Wim Louwrier; m, Ilona Sekacz; art d, Harry Ammerlaan; fx, Steven van Couwelaar, Olivier de Laveleye; cos, Jany Temime

AA Best Foreign Language Film

ANTONIA'S LINE is a multigenerational chronicle that won the 1996 Academy Award for Best Foreign Language Film.

Elderly Antonia (Willeke van Ammelrooy) decides one morning that this will be the day of her death, and surveys her life. After WW II, she returns to her rural hometown with her young daughter Danielle (Els Dottermans) to take over the family farm. As time goes by, Antonia's farm shelters assorted misfits and outcasts, including two refugees from a neighboring farm run by the ignorant bully Daan (Jakob Beks) and his sons. Antonia has a better relationship with another neighbor, Farmer Bas (Jan Decleir), though she rejects his proposal of marriage. Danielle goes to art school, then returns to the farm to paint. She decides that she wants a child, though not a husband, and gives birth to a daughter, Therese (Veerle van Overloop). Therese is educated at home by the misanthropic genius Crooked Finger (Mil Seghers), and subsequently goes to college. Following some unhappy relationships, she returns to the farm and has a child. On the day of Antonia's death, Therese's daughter, Sarah (Thyrza Ravesteijn), has a vision of a banquet shared by all the past and present residents of the farm.

A succession of events does not a plot make, as ANTONIA'S LINE proves. The film plays like the heavily edited highlights of an eight-hour miniseries, with any gaps filled in by portentous and occasionally inane narration. Characters drift in and out of the film with nothing more substantial than a funny name and a peculiar personality trait. Writer-director Marlene Gorris is less strident here than in her controversial A QUESTION OF SILENCE (1982), although her feminist philosophy at times seems simplistic.

ANTONIO DAS MORTES
(O DRAGAO DA MALADE CONTRA O SANTO GUERREIRO)

1969   100m   c   Action   ★★★½
Grove   (Brazil)   /X

Mauricio do Valle *(Antonio das Mortes)*, Odete Lara *(Laura)*, Othon Bastos *(Teacher)*, Hugo Carvana *(Police Chief)*, Jofre Soares *(Colonel)*, Rosa Maria Penna *(Saint)*

p, Claude-Antoine Mapa; d, Glauber Rocha; w, Glauber Rocha; ph, Alfonso Beato; m, Marlos Nobre

Powerful political film, with mercenary do Valle tracking down insurgents, killing all the members of one band and dispatching the leader in hand-to-hand combat in a wild bullet-ridden finale, only to discover his real sympathies are with the rebels. Clearly indebted to the directors of France's New Wave, Rocha would make greater films; nevertheless, ANTONIO DAS MORTES survives as a landmark in Brazil's emergent *Cinema Novo* by one of its finest filmmakers. Brazil's lush vegetation, mountains, and plains are beautifully photographed in this polemic, which lionizes the likes of revolutionary Che Guevara while indicting the cruel and impersonal landlords of a South American dictatorship.

APACHE

1954   91m   c   Western   ★★★
Hecht/Lancaster   (U.S.)   /U

Burt Lancaster *(Massai)*, Jean Peters *(Nalinle)*, John McIntire *(Al Sieber)*, Charles Bronson *(Hondo)*, John Dehner *(Weddle)*, Paul Guilfoyle *(Santos)*, Ian MacDonald *(Glagg)*, Walter Sande *(Lt. Col. Beck)*, Morris Ankrum *(Dawson)*, Monte Blue *(Geronimo)*

p, Harold Hecht; d, Robert Aldrich; w, James R. Webb (based on the novel *Bronco Apache* by Paul I. Wellman); ph, Ernest Laszlo; ed, Alan Crosland Jr.; m, David Raksin; art d, Nicolai Remisoff

A brutal western in which the acrobatic Lancaster, as one of Geronimo's chiefs, refuses to surrender, conducting a one-man war against the cavalry with knife, arrow, and gun. Swarms of troopers attempt to kill him, led by white scout McIntire, who is sympathetic to the plight of the Native Americans. Lancaster, who co-produced, is in his typically over-earnest mode here, all flashing, gnashing teeth and sweaty armpits. The perspective is notable for its links to several 1950s Westerns beginning with BROKEN ARROW (1950), which revived the social concern for the American Indian which late silent film had explored. Peters is a sensuous and attractive if somewhat glamourized mate for Lancaster, daughter of an Indian (Guilfoyle) who sells out the renegade. Silent screen matinee idol Blue also appears, but is not entirely convincing as Geronimo. UA compelled Lancaster to change the ending of this film; he wanted his hero to be shot to death by troopers after he had made peace and settled down to farm the land. Instead, he is exonerated, despite slaying a dozen men, because he has conducted a legitimate war and is therefore entitled to the provisions of peace settlements accorded warring nations. The end result is suitably lively but compromised cinema.

APARAJITO

1956 113m bw Drama   ★★★★
Epic (India)   /U

Pinaki Sen Gupta *(Apu as a boy)*, Smaran Ghosal *(Apu as an adolescent)*, Karuna Banerji *(Mother)*, Kanu Banerji *(Father)*, Ramani Sen Gupta *(Old Uncle)*, Charu Ghosh *(Nanda Babu)*, Subodh Ganguly *(Headmaster)*, Kali Charan Ray *(Press Proprietor)*, Santi Gupta *(Landlord's Wife)*, K.S. Pandey *(Pandey)*

p, Satyajit Ray; d, Satyajit Ray; w, Satyajit Ray (based on the novel *Pather Panchali* by Bibhutibhusan Bandapadhaya); ph, Subrata Mitra; ed, Dulal Dutta; m, Ravi Shankar; art d, Bansi Chandragupta

The young Apu (Gupta) and his newly widowed mother (Banerji) struggle for existence in a small Indian town. Resisting a life in the priesthood, the boy persuades his mother to send him to school. Having done well in his studies over the years, as a young adult (now played by Ghosal) Apu wins a scholarship to the university in Calcutta. Engulfed in city life and the demands of his schoolwork, Apu gradually forgets about his mother. APARAJITO is the second chapter in THE APU TRILOGY (preceded by PATHER PANCHALI and followed by THE WORLD OF APU), among the finest and certainly the most famous group of films to come out of India, in which director Satyajit Ray, a painter and commercial artist, devoted his time, money, and passion to a personal project that many considered impossible, the cinematic adaptation of the popular Bengali novel *Pather Panchali*. Although very slow-moving and not as involving as the first and third episodes of Apu's fortunes, APARAJITO similarly shows the influence of Italian neorealism and remains a thoughtful, colorful, and poetic story of life in India. The beautiful black-and-white photography is accented by Shankar's traditional sitar score. Winner of the Golden Lion at the 1957 Venice Film Festival.

APARTMENT, THE

1960 125m bw Comedy/Drama   ★★★★★
UA (U.S.)   /PG

Jack Lemmon *(C.C. Baxter)*, Shirley MacLaine *(Fran Kubelik)*, Fred MacMurray *(J.D. Sheldrake)*, Ray Walston *(Mr. Dobisch)*, David Lewis *(Mr. Kirkeby)*, Jack Kruschen *(Dr. Dreyfuss)*, Joan Shawlee *(Sylvia)*, Edie Adams *(Miss Olsen)*, Hope Holiday *(Margie MacDougall)*, Johnny Seven *(Karl Matuschka)*

p, Billy Wilder; d, Billy Wilder; w, Billy Wilder, I.A.L. Diamond; ph, Joseph La Shelle; ed, Daniel Mandell; m, Adolph Deutsch; art d, Alexander Trauner

AA Best Picture; AAN Best Actor: Jack Lemmon; *AAN Best Actress:* Shirley MacLaine; *AAN Best Supporting Actor:* Jack Kruschen; *AA Best Director:* Billy Wilder; *AA Best Original Story and Screenplay:* Billy Wilder, I.A.L. Diamond; *AAN Best Cinematography:* Joseph LaShelle; *AA Best Editing:* Daniel Mandell; *AA Best Art Direction:* Alexander Trauner, Edward G. Boyle; *AAN Best Sound:* Gordon E. Sawyer

Classic Billy Wilder comedy-drama about a put-upon insurance clerk (Lemmon) who rises through the ranks by loaning out his apartment as a trysting-place for his philandering superiors. When one of them (Fred MacMurray) callously casts off his elevator girl-mistress (Shirley MacLaine), causing her to attempt suicide, the clerk lovingly nurses her back to health.

A barbed and occasionally brutal comedy with few illusions about personal or corporate ethics, THE APARTMENT captured one of the singular images of early '60s America; the immense office (designed by Alexander Trauner) in which the human workers, seated behind endless, perfectly aligned rows of identical desks, appear completely subordinate to the dehumanizing mechanisms of conformity and efficiency.

Wilder had promised Lemmon "a plum" in exchange for committing to a drag role in SOME LIKE IT HOT, and this was undeniably it. The actor gives one of the finest performances of his career and is perfectly paired with MacLaine, whose "small business" as the forlorn, neurotic elevator operator is a joy to behold. MacMurray made a great heel, but his fan mail was so opposed to these kinds of portrayals that he comfortably stayed in the Disney camp. Fans of Wilder's character repertory will recognize mainstay Joan Shawlee as the office amazon, hilariously dancing on top of a desk at the Christmas party. Wilder shot the film right up to its finish without knowing the ending, handing his stars wet mimeographed script pages about 20 minutes before the final scenes. Quick readers, Lemmon and MacLaine then nailed it in one take. This film was later adapted into the smash Broadway musical *Promises, Promises*.

APOCALYPSE NOW

1979 139m c War   ★★★★
UA (U.S.)   R/18

Marlon Brando *(Col. Kurtz)*, Robert Duvall *(Lt. Col. Kilgore)*, Martin Sheen *(Capt. Willard)*, Frederic Forrest *(Chef)*, Albert Hall *(Chief)*, Sam Bottoms *(Lance)*, Laurence Fishburne *(Clean)*, Dennis Hopper *(Photojournalist)*, Harrison Ford *(Colonel)*, Scott Glenn *(Civilian)*

p, Francis Ford Coppola; d, Francis Ford Coppola; w, Michael Herr, John Milius, Francis Ford Coppola; ph, Vittorio Storaro; ed, Richard Marks; m, Carmine Coppola, Francis Ford Coppola; prod d, Dean Tavoularis; art d, Angelo Graham; cos, Charles James

AAN Best Picture; AAN Best Supporting Actor: Robert Duvall; *AAN Best Director:* Francis Coppola; *AAN Best Adapted Screenplay:* John Milius, Francis Coppola; *AA Best Cinematography:* Vittorio Storaro; *AAN Best Editing:* Richard Marks, Walter Murch, Gerald B. Greenberg, Lisa Fruchtman; *AAN Best Art Direction:* Dean Tavoularis, Angelo Graham, George R. Nelson; *AA Best Sound:* Walter Murch, Mark Berger, Richard Beggs, Nat Boxer

Francis Ford Coppola's notorious and controversial contribution to the Vietnam movie subgenre remains, despite its flaws, one of the most complex and unforgettable war movies ever made. With a plot structure inspired by Joseph Conrad's *Heart of Darkness*, APOCALYPSE NOW follows Willard (Martin Sheen), a cold and amoral Army captain, as he journeys upriver into Cambodia to assassinate Col. Kurtz (Marlon Brando), a renegade Green Beret who has broken from the American military and set himself up as a god among a tribe of Montagnard warriors, using them to wage his own private war. What follows is a hallucinatory look at the madness of the American involvement in Vietnam.

More than five years in the making, APOCALYPSE NOW became a cause celebre even before it opened. As documented by numerous press accounts and the book *Notes*, a collection of journal entries written by Coppola's wife, Eleanor, the filming in the Philippines was hellish, disaster-plagued, and decadent, beginning with a $12 million budget and going over $31 million before the 238-day shooting schedule ended, with Coppola's own money making up the difference. Eleanor Coppola later used her journals, together with documentary footage shot during the production, as the basis of 1991's HEARTS OF DARKNESS, a fascinating account of the making of the film.

APOLLO 13

1995 140m c Drama/Historical   ★★★½
Imagine Entertainment (U.S.)   PG

Tom Hanks *(Jim Lovell)*, Bill Paxton *(Fred W. Haise)*, Kevin Bacon *(John L. Swigart)*, Gary Sinise *(Ken Mattingly)*, Ed Harris *(Gene Kranz)*, Kathleen Quinlan *(Marilyn Lovell)*, Mary Kate Schellhardt *(Barbara Lovell)*, Emily Ann Lloyd *(Susan Lovell)*, Miko Hughes *(Jeffrey Lovell)*, Max Elliott Slade *(Jay Lovell)* p, Brian Grazer; d, Ron Howard; w, William Broyles Jr., Al Reinert, John Sayles (uncredited); ph, Dean Cundey; ed, Daniel Hanley, Michael Hill; m, James Horner; prod d, Michael Corenblith; art d, David Bomba, Bruce Allan Miller; fx, Matt Sweeney, Robert Legato, Digital Domain; cos, Rita Ryack

AAN Best Picture; AAN Best Supporting Actor: Ed Harris; *AAN Best Supporting Actress:* Kathleen Quinlan; *AAN Best Adapted Screenplay:* William Broyles Jr., Al Reinert; *AAN Best Art Direction:* Eugenio Zanetti; *AA Best Editing:* Mike Hill, Dan Hanley; *AAN Best Dramatic Score:* James Horner; *AA Best Sound:* Rick Dior, Steve Pederson, Scott Millan, David MacMillan; *AAN Best Visual Effects:* Robert Legato, Michael Kanfer, Leslie Ekker, Matt Sweeney

A boy's space adventure with an all-star cast, this blockbuster hit trades heavily on nostalgia for the glory years of the American space program. Paradoxically, it tells the story of 1970's ill-fated Apollo 13 mission, a failure by most standards. It was to be the third moon landing, but the ship malfunctioned in deep space, briefly recapturing the attention of a jaded public. For the better part of a tense week, it seemed that the crew of three — James A. Lovell, Jr. (Tom Hanks), Fred Haise, Jr. (Bill Paxton), and last-minute replacement John L. Swigert, Jr. (Kevin Bacon) — might not be coming back.

Viewers who have seen the eerily prescient MAROONED (1969) may get a sense of *deja vu*. But APOLLO 13 has all the advantages: top-notch special effects, including sequences filmed in a real zero-gravity simulator; attention to every detail, from the epic outer space vistas to the minutiae of life on board the crippled space vehicle; a cast that goes from really good to even better, including Gary Sinise as the unfortunate Ken Mattingly — who was bumped from the Apollo 13 crew at the 11th hour — and Ed Harris as flight director Gene Kranz, who headed up the massive effort to bring the boys home. Still, there's something oddly flat about the film. There's no hint of political or social context (unlike the flawed but fascinating THE RIGHT STUFF); it's all Life Magazine cover shots, and director Ron Howard never digs beyond the surface. Like the real Apollo 13, it gets to the stars, but misses the moon.

APPLAUSE
1929   80m   bw   Drama   ★★★★★
Paramount   (U.S.)

Helen Morgan *(Kitty Darling)*, Joan Peers *(April Darling)*, Fuller Mellish Jr. *(Hitch Nelson)*, Jack Cameron *(Joe King)*, Henry Wadsworth *(Tony)*, Dorothy Cumming *(Mother Superior)*

p, Monta Bell; d, Rouben Mamoulian; w, Garrett Fort (based on the novel by Beth Brown); ph, George Folsey; ed, John Bassler

Morgan, the rage of Broadway musicals and nightclubs during the 1920s, is a fading burlesque singing star—she is shown to age on the stage as her born-in-a-trunk daughter grows up in a convent. The pathetic Morgan is being two-timed by a slippery boy friend. Moreover, she attempts to save her grown-up child from the clutches of fakes and ne'er-do-wells. Poignant though dated, this early talkie is rich in old burlesque backstage atmosphere and has many innovative techniques introduced by Mamoulian in his directorial debut. Then there is Morgan's singing, which is captivating and distinctive. She made her screen debut in this picture and would die of cirrhosis of the liver in 1941 at age 41.

APPRENTICESHIP OF DUDDY KRAVITZ, THE
1974   121m   c   Comedy/Drama   ★★★★
International Cinemedia Centre   (Canada)   PG/15

Richard Dreyfuss *(Duddy)*, Micheline Lanctot *(Yvette)*, Jack Warden *(Max)*, Randy Quaid *(Virgil)*, Joseph Wiseman *(Uncle Benjy)*, Denholm Elliott *(Friar)*, Henry Ramer *(Dingleman)*, Joe Silver *(Farber)*, Zvee Scooler *(Grandfather)*, Robert Goodier *(Calder)*

p, John Kemeny; d, Ted Kotcheff; w, Mordecai Richler (based on his novel); ph, Brian West; ed, Thom Noble; m, Stanley Meyers; prod d, Anne Pritchard

AAN Best Adapted Screenplay: Mordecai Richler (Screenplay), Lionel Chetwynd (Adaptation)

Dreyfuss, a zealous Jewish boy determined to become rich in the world, loses all personal contact with women, friends, and family in his desperate business transactions. A strong, often very funny film that points out the potential emotional loss in the pressure to succeed put on the young by families. Not anti-Semitic, the film means to point out the corruption of youth and power of greed in all young people, not the Jews alone, although the film did receive many negative reactions from Jewish groups, as did the book it is based on. Dreyfuss, who later went on to become one of the better-known faces of the 1970s, turns in an early great performance, making Duddy simultaneously loathsome, funny, and vulnerable. British actor Elliott masterfully portrays the washed-up British director Dreyfuss hires to make Bar Mitzvah movies for his relatives. In the most hilarious scene in the film, Dreyfuss's relatives are stunned to see that "artsy" filmmaker Elliott has juxtaposed Bar Mitzvah scenes with footage detailing African tribal dances celebrating the circumcision rights of the young warriors. Although there are quite a few holes in the script and Dreyfuss is undeniably grating, THE APPRENTICESHIP OF DUDDY KRAVITZ is a sad, funny, memorable film.

AROUND THE WORLD IN 80 DAYS
1956   175m   c   Adventure   ★★★★
Michael Todd   (U.S.)   /U

David Niven *(Phileas Fogg)*, Cantinflas *(Passepartout)*, Shirley MacLaine *(Princess Aouda)*, Robert Newton *(Inspector Fix)*, Charles Boyer *(Monsieur Casse)*, Joe E. Brown *(Station Master)*, Martine Carol *(Tourist)*, John Carradine *(Col. Proctor Stamp)*, Charles Coburn *(Clerk)*, Ronald Colman *(Railway Official)*

p, Michael Todd; d, Michael Anderson; w, S.J. Perelman, John Farrow, James Poe (based on the novel by Jules Verne); ph, Lionel Lindon; ed, Gene Ruggiero, Paul Weatherwax; m, Victor Young; art d, James Sullivan, Ken Adam; fx, Lee Zavitz; chor, Paul Godkin; cos, Miles White

AA Best Picture; AAN Best Director: Michael Anderson; *AA Best Adapted Screenplay:* James Poe, John Farrow, S.J. Perelman; *AA Best Cinematography:* Lionel Lindon; *AA Best Editing:* Gene Ruggiero, Paul Weatherwax; *AA Best Score:* Victor Young; *AAN Best Art Direction:* James W. Sullivan, Ken Adams, Ross J. Dowd; *AAN Best Costume Design:* Miles White

David Niven is the punctual Phileas Fogg of the famous Jules Verne novel, who makes a bet with his fellow club members in London that he can encircle the globe within 80 days—this in 1872, when travel proceeded at a snail's pace. Fogg is accompanied by his bumbling valet (the great Mexican mimic Cantinflas) and along the way picks up a wandering princess (Shirley MacLaine), while being pursued by a London detective (Robert Newton) who believes the globetrotter has somehow robbed the Bank of England. Around these leads an army of 46 famous personalities of the day appear in bit parts. (This was the film that began the trend of stars appearing in cameo roles.) The star-spotting is fun, but so is the adventure, as Fogg journeys by train, ship, hot-air balloon, and elephant across Europe, India, Japan, the Pacific, the US, and the Atlantic in a race to win his bet. The film was shot in more than 100 natural settings and on 140 special sets. Everything about this big, beautiful movie smacks of authenticity, excitement, and massive showmanship. Winner of five Oscars: Best Picture, Best Screenplay, Best Cinematography, Best Score and Best Film Editing.

ARROWSMITH
1931   108m   bw   Drama   ★★½
Goldwyn   (U.S.)   /A

Ronald Colman *(Dr. Martin Arrowsmith)*, Helen Hayes *(Leora)*, A.E. Anson *(Prof. Gottlieb)*, Richard Bennett *(Sondelius)*, Claude King *(Dr. Tubbs)*, Beulah Bondi *(Mrs. Tozer)*, Myrna Loy *(Joyce Lanyon)*, Russell Hopton *(Terry Wickett)*, DeWitt Jennings *(Mr. Tozer)*, John Qualen *(Henry Novak)*

p, Samuel Goldwyn; d, John Ford; w, Sidney Howard (based on the novel by Sinclair Lewis); ph, Ray June; ed, Hugh Bennett; m, Alfred Newman

AAN Best Picture; AAN Best Adapted Screenplay: Sidney Howard; *AAN Best Cinematography:* Ray June; *AAN Best Art Direction:* Richard Day (Art Direction)

Idealistic doctor Ronald Colman is obsessed with finding a cure for bubonic plague and wrestling with his moral conscience in this uneven Sidney Howard adaptation of Sinclair Lewis's novel. Hayes gets the big death scene, Loy gets the sexy seduction bits, John Ford gets the blame. Immensely popular with audiences and listed as one of the year's best films by *The New York Times*, ARROWSMITH was nominated as Best Picture but thankfully lost out to GRAND HOTEL.

ARSENIC AND OLD LACE

1944 118m bw Comedy	★★★½
Warner Bros. (U.S.)	/PG

Cary Grant *(Mortimer Brewster)*, Raymond Massey *(Jonathan Brewster)*, Priscilla Lane *(Elaine Harper)*, Josephine Hull *(Abby Brewster)*, Jean Adair *(Martha Brewster)*, Jack Carson *(O'Hara)*, Edward Everett Horton *(Mr. Witherspoon)*, Peter Lorre *(Dr. Einstein)*, James Gleason *(Lt. Rooney)*, John Alexander *("Teddy Roosevelt" Brewster)*

p, Frank Capra; d, Frank Capra; w, Julius J. Epstein, Philip G. Epstein (based on the play by Joseph Kesselring); ph, Sol Polito; ed, Daniel Mandell; m, Max Steiner; art d, Max Parker; fx, Byron Haskin, Robert Burks

Riotously funny film adaptation of the smash Broadway comedy (which ran for almost four years), coddled and coaxed into hilarious existence by master director Capra. The lovable Brewster sisters are spinster pillars of Brooklyn society, except for their secret penchant for poisoning old male callers with their homemade elderberry wine, to end the men's loneliness! Grant plays their frantic nephew who discovers their serial murders. The punch line that ended the play was cut by censors; the line in occurs after Grant learns he is free of hereditary insanity, and yells elatedly to his fiance: "Elaine! Did you hear? Do you understand? I'm a bastard!" Additional comedic lunacy results from macabre team of Lorre and Massey (the latter in a part made famous on Broadway by Boris Karloff) and Alexander as an eccentric uncle who believes he's Teddy Roosevelt.

ARSENIC was Capra's pet from beginning to end. He saw the play in New York and rushed backstage to buy the property, only to be told that Warner Brothers (his studio was Columbia) had optioned the film rights. He immediately went to the WB studio and had Jack Warner's own people prepare a modest budget, $400,000, for a hectic four-week shooting schedule ($100,000 for the star salary Grant demanded). Capra used only one interior set, that of the spooky old house belonging to the aunts, and an exterior set of the house next to an ancient cemetery. The lighting was low-keyed, from dusk to night, in keeping with the eerie atmosphere. Capra came in on schedule as usual and produced a romping, ripsnorting comedy classic.

ARTHUR

1981 117m c Comedy	★★★
Orion (U.S.)	PG/15

Dudley Moore *(Arthur Bach)*, Liza Minnelli *(Linda Marolla)*, John Gielgud *(Hobson)*, Geraldine Fitzgerald *(Martha Bach)*, Jill Eikenberry *(Susan Johnson)*, Stephen Elliott *(Burt Johnson)*, Ted Ross *(Bitterman)*, Barney Martin *(Ralph Marolla)*, Thomas Barbour *(Stanford Bach)*, Anne DeSalvo *(Gloria)*

p, Robert Greenhut; d, Steve Gordon; w, Steve Gordon; ph, Fred Schuler; ed, Susan E. Morse; m, Burt Bacharach; prod d, Stephen Hendrickson; cos, Jane Greenwood

AAN Best Actor: Dudley Moore; *AA Best Supporting Actor:* John Gielgud; *AAN Best Original Screenplay:* Steve Gordon; *AA Best Song:* Burt Bacharach, Carole Bayer Sager, Christopher Cross, Peter Allen

Dudley Moore plays Arthur Bach, a dissolute playboy who would rather be drunk than face the reality of his great wealth and engagement to WASP witch Susan Johnson (Jill Eikenberry). Arthur, who is looked after by his kindly valet, Hobson (John Gielgud), soon falls for working girl Linda Marolla (Liza Minnelli), whom he prefers to his socialite fiancee. Susan, however, refuses to be shunned, and Arthur's father and grandmother threaten to cut off his inheritance if he continues to see working-class Linda. Moore is predictable as the spoiled scion of wealth, Minnelli is terrific as his candid sweetheart, but Gielgud's loyal yet sarcastic servant steals the film (he was rewarded with a supporting actor Oscar). The highly polished production is well paced and imaginatively directed, although the happy union of prince and pauper is harder to swallow in 1981 than it would have been in 1931, when cinematic escapism brought relief to depression-era audiences. A flat sequel, ARTHUR 2 ON THE ROCKS, was released in 1988.

ASHES AND DIAMONDS
(POPIOL I DIAMENT)

1958 105m bw Drama/War	★★★
(Poland)	/X

Zbigniew Cybulski *(Maciek)*, Ewa Krzyzewski *(Krystyna)*, Adam Pawlikowski *(Andrzej)*, Waclaw Zastrzezynski *(Szczuka)*, Bogumil Kobiela *(Drewnowski)*, Jan Ciecierski *(Porter)*, Stanislaw Milski *(Pienionzek)*, Artur Mlodnicki *(Kotowicz)*, Halina Kwiatkoska *(Mrs. Staniewicz)*, Ignacy Machowski *(Waga)*

d, Andrzej Wajda; w, Andrzej Wajda, Jerzy Andrzejewski (based on the novel by Jerzy Andrzejewski); ph, Jerzy Wojcik; ed, Halina Nawrocka; m, Aroclaw Radio Quintet; art d, Roman Mann; cos, Katarzyna Chodorowicz

After making A GENERATION (1954) and KANAL (1957), Andrzej Wajda completed his loose trilogy of WWII Polish Resistance films with the prize-winning ASHES AND DIAMONDS. Set at the beginning of the transitional period between occupation and socialization, when Communists and old-line partisans were unofficially at war, the movie tells the story of a young Polish veteran who is torn between the habit of violence and his better instincts.

ASHES AND DIAMONDS is not a movie that travels well. To Poles, it provided a rich and provocative portrait of their nation at a crucial and divisive turning point in its history, the transition from war, occupation, resistance, and victory to a new socialistic order. Those moviegoers distanced by time and space may find the film a somewhat elusive and esoteric work. The movie's least parochial element is the lead character, Maciek (Zbigniew Cybulski), a moody and capricious lad who more closely resembles young people of the mid-1950s, when the film was made, than the mid-'40s character he is meant to embody. In a single sequence, Maciek provides his girlfriend and the film s audience with a virtual catalogue of '50s youth attitudes: "Oh, God, how beautiful life could be!" (youthful yearning); "I don't know what is sad and what isn't" (youthful confusion); "I'd like to change certain things" (youthful idealism); "to lead a different life" (youthful frustration); "it's difficult to speak about it" (youthful inarticulateness).

Cybulski was dubbed "the Polish James Dean." He did indeed resemble Dean and spoke some of the same body language, but his performance as Maciek was little more extroverted than any of his American counterpart's screen portrayals. Cybulski was reputed to be, like Maciek, a hard drinker, womanizer, and gadfly, and like Dean, he died young.

Richly composed and photographed, with atmosphere aplenty, ASHES AND DIAMONDS suffers somewhat from an excess of loose plot ends and of underdeveloped characters, perhaps a consequence of having been based on a prestigious novel. Similar in some ways to the contemporaneous films of Carol Reed, it does not match them in lucidity, intrigue, or power.

ASPHALT JUNGLE, THE

1950 112m bw Crime	★★★★½
MGM (U.S.)	/A

Sterling Hayden *(Dix Handley)*, Louis Calhern *(Alonzo D. Emmerich)*, Jean Hagen *(Doll Conovan)*, James Whitmore *(Gus Ninissi)*, Sam Jaffe *(Doc Erwin Riedenschneider)*, John McIntire *(Police Commissioner Hardy)*, Marc Lawrence *(Cobby)*, Barry Kelley *(Lt. Ditrich)*, Anthony Caruso *(Louis Ciavelli)*, Teresa Celli *(Maria Ciavelli)*

p, Arthur Hornblow Jr.; d, John Huston; w, Ben Maddow, John Huston (based on the novel by W.R. Burnett); ph, Harold Rosson; ed, George Boemler; m, Miklos Rozsa; art d, Cedric Gibbons, Randall Duell

AAN Best Supporting Actor: Sam Jaffe; *AAN Best Director:* John Huston; *AAN Best Original Screenplay:* Ben Maddow, John Huston; *AAN Best Cinematography:* Harold Rosson

Adapted by director John Huston and co-screenwriter Ben Maddow from the novel by W.R. Burnett, this classic, often copied but never equaled, focuses on the robbery of a swank jewelry firm, meticulously planned by master criminal "Doc" Erwin Riedenschneider (Sam Jaffe) while imprisoned. Alonzo D. Emmerich (Louis Calhern) is a sleazy lawyer who'll fence the stolen jewels, giving "Doc" and his cohorts $1 million for their labors. The assembled gang includes Dix Handley (Sterling Hayden), a somewhat dumb but standup fellow who has dreams of buying back his father's Kentucky horse ranch; Gus Ninissi (James Whitmore), a tough-as-nails, cat-loving hunchback who runs a diner; and Louis Ciavelli (Anthony Caruso), a professional thief who's enlisted to blow the safe under Riedenschneider's supervision. After carefully drilling the gang members, "Doc" leads the men on the robbery attempt. The safe is blown and the gems secured, but his "perfect" crime immediately unravels.

Huston directed this superb production with tremendous assurance, developing his characters incisively but not at the expense of the rapidly developing plot. Indeed, THE ASPHALT JUNGLE boasts a rogues' gallery of definitive portrayals, led by creepy mastermind Jaffe, whose voyeuristic pursuit of Lolitas finally frames him. Calhern figures nicely as the crooked lawyer who keeps Monroe, in an outstanding cameo that foretold her future stardom. Jean Hagen's moll is a rare lead female performance, poignant and subtly shaded, that is totally devoid of studio-era vanity. Rosson's moody photography and Rozsa's moving score further enhance this *film noir* masterpiece.

ASSAULT, THE

1986 155m c Drama/War ★★★★
Cannon (Netherlands) PG

Derek De Lint *(Anton Steenwijk)*, Marc van Uchelen *(Anton as a Boy)*, Monique Van de Ven *(Truus Coster/Saskia de Graaff)*, John Kraaykamp *(Cor Takes)*, Huub van der Lubbe *(Fake Ploeg/His Father)*, Elly Weller *(Mrs. Beumer)*, Ina van der Molen *(Karin Korteweg)*, Frans Vorstman *(Father Steenwijk)*, Edda Barends *(Mother Steenwijk)*, Caspar De Boer *(Peter Steenwijk)*

p, Fons Rademakers; d, Fons Rademakers; w, Gerard Soeteman (based on the novel by Harry Mulisch); ph, Theo Van de Sande; ed, Kees Linthorst; m, Jurriaan Andriessen; art d, Dorus van der Linden; fx, Harry Wiesenhaan; cos, Anne-Marie van Beverwijk

AA Best Foreign Language Film

A powerful motion picture that poses more questions than it answers, THE ASSAULT will haunt anyone who understands the tragic psychological effects of emotional repression. Spanning a 40-year period, it begins in Holland as the war is waning and the Germans realize they will be beaten. One night while dining by candlelight during curfew, a Dutch family sees a local collaborator killed by a sniper. Fearing that they will be blamed, the family watches in horror as their neighbors drag the body in front of their home. Soon Germans are everywhere, the family is arrested and shot, their house is burned, and the son, Anton (Marc van Uchelen), is taken away to prison. Years later, he becomes a physician, marries, and has his own family, but the memory of that bleak night continues to haunt him.

Winner of the 1986 Academy Award for Best Foreign Film, THE ASSAULT is a powerful indictment of the Nazi horror, although it seldom editorializes. Much more than the war picture it begins as, this documentary-like Dutch film explores lives that have been torn apart by German occupation.

ASSAULT ON PRECINCT 13

1976 91m c Action ★★★½
Turtle (U.S.) R/18

Austin Stoker *(Bishop)*, Darwin Joston *(Wilson)*, Laurie Zimmer *(Leigh)*, Martin West *(Lawson)*, Tony Burton *(Wells)*, Charles Cyphers *(Starker)*, Nancy Loomis *(Julie)*, Peter Bruni *(Ice Cream Man)*, John J. Fox *(Warden)*, Kim Richards *(Kathy)*

p, J.S. Kaplan; d, John Carpenter; w, John Carpenter; ph, Douglas Knapp; ed, John T. Chance; m, John Carpenter; art d, Tommy Wallace; cos, Louise Kyes

Not really a horror film but one that often comes up during discussions of George Romero's NIGHT OF THE LIVING DEAD, this early John Carpenter effort still holds up as one of the director's best works.

A low-budget and taut update of the classic Howard Hawks western RIO BRAVO, set in modern-day Los Angeles, the story concerns a lengthy siege by a multiracial street gang on a soon-to-be-closed police station. The gang has murdered a young girl, whose father runs to the station for help. This man is in a state of shock and cannot speak to the lone cop, Bishop (Austin Stoker), or to the two secretaries (Zimmer and Loomis) waiting for the moving vans to take what's left of the station's file cabinets. Unexpectedly, two death-row prisoners arrive and are put in holding cells until authorities can find a place for them (the state prison is overcrowded). As night falls, the gang attacks in full force, riddling the station with bullets shot from guns with silencers. The gang cuts the electricity and phone lines, rendering the station helpless in the center of the neighborhood. The inmates demand to be let loose so that they can defend themselves and prove themselves honorable men.

The shadowy photography, great editing, snappy dialogue, and a moody synthesizer score by Carpenter himself make ASSAULT ON PRECINCT 13 one of the most successful homages to Hawks, and a triumph in its own right. The parallels with Romero's film are obvious (the street gang is reminiscent of Romero's zombies), and Carpenter, who often borrows character names and situations from films and filmmakers he admires, seems to have intended it that way.

AT CLOSE RANGE

1986 111m c Crime ★★★½
Hemdale (U.S.) R/15

Sean Penn *(Brad Whitewood, Jr.)*, Christopher Walken *(Brad Whitewood, Sr.)*, Mary Stuart Masterson *(Terry)*, Christopher Penn *(Tommy Whitewood)*, Millie Perkins *(Julie Whitewood)*, Eileen Ryan *(Grandmother)*, Alan Autry *(Ernie)*, Candy Clark *(Mary Sue)*, R.D. Call *(Dickie Whitewood)*, Tracey Walter *(Patch)*

p, Elliott Lewitt, Don Guest; d, James Foley; w, Nicholas Kazan (based on a story by Lewitt and Kazan); ph, Juan Ruiz-Anchia; ed, Howard Smith; m, Patrick Leonard; prod d, Peter Jamison; fx, Burt Dalton, Adams Calvert; cos, Hilary Rosenfeld

A chilling and realistic crime film, AT CLOSE RANGE features strong performances by Christopher Walken and Sean Penn. The film follows fresh-out-of-high-school Brad Whitewood, Jr. (Penn), as he struggles against the boredom of his rural existence. Living in a run-down house with his half-brother, Tommy (Christopher Penn, Sean's brother), his grandmother (Eileen Ryan, the Penn boys' mother), and his mother (Millie Perkins), Brad coasts along until two events change his life forever: he falls in love with Terry (Mary Stuart Masterson), and his wayward father (Walken) wanders back on the scene.

Relentlessly grim, AT CLOSE RANGE offers a frightening glimpse at the dark side of American life and poses disturbing questions about family ties. Unfortunately, although director James Foley handles the performances with skill, he also indulges in too many flashy directorial pyrotechnics, muting the emotional impact. Writer Nicholas Kazan (son of director Elia) based his script on the Johnston family murders in Pennsylvania in 1978.

ATLANTIC CITY

1981 104m c Crime/Romance ★★★½
Paramount (U.S./Canada) R/15

Burt Lancaster *(Lou)*, Susan Sarandon *(Sally)*, Kate Reid *(Grace)*, Michel Piccoli *(Joseph)*, Hollis McLaren *(Chrissie)*, Robert Joy *(Dave)*, Al Waxman *(Alfie)*, Robert Goulet *(Singer)*, Moses Znaimer *(Felix)*, Angus MacInnes *(Vinnie)*

p, Denis Heroux; d, Louis Malle; w, John Guare; ph, Richard Ciupka; ed, Suzanne Baron; m, Michel Legrand; prod d, Anne Pritchard; cos, Francois Barbeau

AAN Best Picture; AAN Best Actor: Burt Lancaster; *AAN Best Actress:* Susan Sarandon; *AAN Best Director:* Louis Malle; *AAN Best Original Screenplay:* John Guare (Screenplay)

Richly sad portraits of wasted American lives, filtered through a European sensibility. Burt Lancaster, in a masterful performance, plays Lou, an aging small-time criminal who hangs around Atlantic City doing odd jobs and taking care of the broken-down moll (Kate Reid) of the deceased gangster for whom Lou was a gofer. Living in an invented past, Lou identifies with yesteryear's notorious gangsters and gets involved with sexy would-be croupier, Sally (Susan Sarandon), and her drug-dealing estranged husband (Robert Joy).

Aided by a superb script from playwright John Guare, director Louis Malle (PRETTY BABY, AU REVOIR LES ENFANTS) pulls off a minor coup here, celebrating his wounded characters even as he mercilessly reveals their dreams for the hopeless illusions they really are. He is exceptionally well served by his cast and his location—a gone-to-seed resort town supported, like the principal characters, by memories of glories past.

ATTACK!

1956   107m   bw   War   ★★★
UA   (U.S.)   /A

Jack Palance *(Lt. Costa)*, Eddie Albert *(Capt. Cooney)*, Lee Marvin *(Col. Bartlett)*, Robert Strauss *(Pvt. Bernstein)*, Richard Jaeckel *(Pvt. Snowden)*, Buddy Ebsen *(Sgt. Tolliver)*, William Smithers *(Lt. Woodruff)*, Jon Shepodd *(Cpl. Jackson)*, James Goodwin *(Pvt. Ricks)*, Steven Geray *(Short German)*

p, Robert Aldrich; d, Robert Aldrich; w, James Poe (based on the play "The Fragile Fox" by Norman Brooks); ph, Joseph Biroc; ed, Michael Luciano; m, Frank DeVol

No sensibilities are spared in this brutal portrait of infantry warfare, featuring a powerful performance by Palance. In 1944 Belgium, Albert is a coward who has achieved the rank of captain only because of his father's political power. Because Marvin's political ambitions can be served by Albert's family, he overlooks Albert's imcompetence. But Palance and his platoon (Ebsen, Jaeckel, Strauss) feel victimized, particularly Palance who becomes an almost supernatural force of vengeance. A cynical and grim account of war, ATTACK! features excellent performances from the entire cast and is one of director Aldrich's best films.

ATTACK OF THE KILLER TOMATOES

1978   87m   c   Comedy/Horror   ★
NAI   (U.S.)   PG

David Miller *(Mason Dixon)*, George Wilson *(Jim Richardson)*, Sharon Taylor *(Lois Fairchild)*, Jack Riley *(Agriculture Official)*, Rock Peace *(Wilbur Finletter)*, Eric Christmas *(Senator Polk)*, Al Sklar *(Ted Swan)*, Ernie Meyers *(President)*, Jerry Anderson *(Major Milis)*, Ron Shapiro *(Newspaper Editor)*

p, J. Stephen Peace, John De Bello; d, John De Bello; w, Costa Dillon, J. Stephen Peace, John De Bello; ph, John K. Culley; m, Gordon Goodwin, Paul Sundfur

In a cynical bid for cult success, ATTACK OF THE KILLER TOMATOES employs calculatedly bad acting, ridiculous special effects, and inane dialog. Though it succeeded to some degree in achieving its goal, it's a thoroughly dull, unfunny effort. The film tries too hard at being ridiculous, and though the idea of savage vegetables rolling around the city splattering innocent bystanders sounds funny, actually sitting through nearly 90 minutes of it is enough to make anyone long for ATTACK OF THE 50 FOOT WOMAN. There are some funny song parodies, but that's about it.

AU HASARD, BALTHAZAR

1966   95m   c   Drama   ★★★★★
New Line   (France)

Anne Wiazemsky *(Marie)*, Francois Lafarge *(Gerard)*, Philippe Asselin *(Marie's Father)*, Nathalie Joyaut *(Marie's Mother)*, Walter Green *(Jacques)*, Jean-Claude Guilbert *(Arnold)*, Pierre Klossowski *(Merchant)*, Francois Sullerot *(Baker)*, M.C. Fremont *(Baker's Wife)*, Jean Remignard *(Notary)*

p, Mag Bodard; d, Robert Bresson; w, Robert Bresson; ph, Ghislain Cloquet; ed, Raymond Lamy; m, Jean Wiener; art d, Pierre Charbonnier

This poignant film is a powerful portrait of humanity seen through the life of a donkey. The animal is first the loving plaything of small children in rural France, then a working beast of burden named by a sullen child. As the girl grows up, the donkey's fortunes worsen with the young woman's when she is gang-raped and dies. Her sadistic lover, a leader of a motorcycle gang, tortures the donkey by setting its tail on fire. The donkey's life intersects with the lives of many of its other owners, as well. A brutal farmer owns the animal and beats it, but is finished off in grim irony. Then the donkey has a respite in becoming a momentary circus star, but then again returns to tilling the soil. It ends its days with a simple-minded but loving old man who considers the animal a saint. This great film, made with uncompromising honesty and devastating reality, is, according to Jean-Luc Godard, "the world in an hour and a half." Music includes Franz Schubert's "Piano Sonata No. 20."

AU REVOIR, LES ENFANTS

1987   104m   c   Drama/War   ★★★★½
Nouvelle Editions de Films/MK2/Stella   (France)   PG

Gaspard Manesse *(Julien Quentin)*, Raphael Fejto *(Jean Bonnet)*, Francine Racette *(Mme. Quentin)*, Stanislas Carre de Malberg *(Francois Quentin)*, Philippe Morier-Genoud *(Father Jean)*, Francois Berleand *(Father Michel)*, Francois Negret *(Joseph)*, Peter Fitz *(Muller)*, Pascal Rivet *(Boulanger)*, Benoit Henriet *(Ciron)*

p, Louis Malle; d, Louis Malle; w, Louis Malle; ph, Renato Berta; ed, Emmanuelle Castro; m, Franz Schubert, Camille Saint-Saens; cos, Corinne Jorry

AAN Best Foreign Language Film ; *AAN Best Original Screenplay:* Louis Malle

A delicately rendered and exceptionally moving reminiscence of a boyhood friendship cut short by war. Louis Malle's semi-autobiographical film is set in January, 1944, during the German Occupation of France. Julien (Gaspard Manesse) is a privileged, precocious 12-year old with a doting mother and a superior attitude. Sent away to a provincial Catholic boarding school, he easily outclasses his loutish schoolmates until the arrival of Bonnet (Raphael Fejto), who is cultivated, literate, and oddly circumspect about revealing his background. At first, Julien hopes to expose and humiliate his rival, but their common interests lead to an uneasy alliance and finally friendship. Then Bonnet's secret is revealed: he is a Jew being hidden from the Gestapo by schoolmaster Fr. Jean (Philippe Morier-Genoud).

One of director-producer-writer Malle's most personal projects, AU REVOIR LES ENFANTS can be seen as the completion of a trilogy that began with MURMUR OF THE HEART (1971), a sunny comedy of evolving postwar manners, and continued with a darkly-hued portrait of a teenaged collaborator, LACOMBE LUCIEN (1974). All three films are about maturation during a decade of political upheaval, and each is concerned with choices thrust upon children—choices inevitably compromised by social and familial pressures beyond a child's control. Like the earlier films, AU REVOIR rejects any notion of youthful innocence, making it a bracingly welcome exception to the post-E.T. slew of films romanticizing childhood. Malle is adept at eliciting mature performances from children, and Manesse and Fejto are excellent even by adult standards.

AUNTIE MAME

1958   143m   c   Comedy   ★★★★
Warner Bros.   (U.S.)   /A

Rosalind Russell *(Mame Dennis)*, Forrest Tucker *(Beauregard Burnside)*, Coral Browne *(Vera Charles)*, Fred Clark *(Mr. Babcock)*, Roger Smith *(Patrick Dennis)*, Patric Knowles *(Lindsay Woolsey)*, Peggy Cass *(Agnes Gooch)*, Jan Handzlik *(Patrick Dennis as a Child)*, Joanna Barnes *(Gloria Upson)*, Pippa Scott *(Pegeen Ryan)*

d, Morton Da Costa; w, Betty Comden, Adolph Green (based on the novel *Mame* by Patrick Dennis and the play by Jerome Lawrence, Robert E. Lee); ph, Harry Stradling; ed, William Ziegler; m, Bronislau Kaper; art d, Malcolm Bert; cos, Orry-Kelly

AAN Best Picture; AAN Best Actress: Rosalind Russell; *AAN Best Supporting Actress:* Peggy Cass; *AAN Best Cinematography:* Harry Stradling Sr; *AAN Best Editing:* William Ziegler; *AAN Best Art Direction:* Malcolm Bert (Art Direction), George James Hopkins (Set Decoration)

A showcase for the spectacular talents of Russell, who made the play a Broadway hit. Eccentric, colorful Mame Dennis adopts an orphan boy, exposing him to all manner of extravagant and bizarre characters in the 1920s and 1930s. The film is a trifle overlong and episodic, but Russell is supported in high style by a talented cast. Look for many amusing 1950s art direction and costume touches that are unusual. For once Hollywood agreed that Broadway's casting couldn't be improved; Russell's way with words, her rhythms, speed, and timing are irreplacably, impeccably right.

AUTUMN LEAVES

1956   107m   bw   Drama   ★★★
Columbia   (U.S.)   /X

Joan Crawford *(Milly)*, Cliff Robertson *(Burt Hanson)*, Vera Miles *(Virginia)*, Lorne Greene *(Mr. Hanson)*, Ruth Donnelly *(Liz)*, Shepperd Strudwick *(Dr. Couzzens)*, Selmer Jackson *(Mr. Wetherby)*, Maxine Cooper *(Nurse Evans)*, Marjorie Bennett *(Waitress)*, Frank Gerstle *(Mr. Ramsey)*

p, William Goetz; d, Robert Aldrich; w, Jean Rouveral, Hugo Butler, Lewis Meltzer, Robert Blees; ph, Charles Lang; ed, Michael Luciano; m, H.J. Salter

Butch-bobbed, bug-eyed career gal spinster Crawford meets shy Cliff Robertson and grabs for love, gets a schizo. Released a year after the nihilist film noir classic KISS ME DEADLY, the film recaptured the twisted qualities of the human mind. Labeled a "woman's picture," AUTUMN LEAVES is an intense melodrama about loneliness, despair, and mental illness. Taking a pleasant romantic tale and plunging it into a whirlwind of schizophrenic violence has the same effect as seeing a hammer shatter a shiny piece of glass. Almost like a nightmare going on in Crawford's mind, the film's visual style gets more and more distorted and the lighting very harsh as Robertson's schizophrenia builds. Joan's performance is on the money and the Crawford cult will enjoy her "reading" Lorne Greene and Vera Miles as she chases them down the street ("And you, ya slut!"). The lady later said Robert Aldrich "likes evil things, twisted things." The title song, penned by Joseph Kosma, Jacques Prevert, and Johnny Mercer, was a big hit for Nat King Cole.

AUTUMN SONATA

1978   97m   c   Drama   ★★½
ITC   (Sweden)   PG/15

Ingrid Bergman *(Charlotte)*, Liv Ullmann *(Eva)*, Lena Nyman *(Helena)*, Halvar Bjork *(Viktor)*, Georg Lokkeberg *(Leonardo)*, Knut Wigert *(Professor)*, Eva von Hanno *(Nurse)*, Erland Josephson *(Josef)*, Linn Ullmann *(Eva as a Child)*, Arne Bang-Hansen *(Uncle Otto)*

p, Lew Grade, Martin Starger; d, Ingmar Bergman; w, Ingmar Bergman; ph, Sven Nykvist; ed, Sylvia Ingemarsson; prod d, Anna Asp; cos, Inger Pehrsson

AAN Best Actress: Ingrid Bergman; *AAN Best Original Screenplay:* Ingmar Bergman (Story)

The meeting of the Bergmans is reason alone to see AUTUMN SONATA, the director's exploration of mother-daughter conflict, but whatever cohesion the film projects is a result of Ingrid Bergman, as magnetic as ever in her final film performance. Photographed beautifully by Sven Nykvist, this painful film compels audiences finally to turn away. There is too much talk, talk, talk about feelings and not enough demonstration of them, but like cream, Ingrid keeps rising to the top of the chatter.

AVALON

1990   126m   c   Drama   ★★★
Baltimore Pictures   (U.S.)   PG/U

Armin Mueller-Stahl *(Sam Krichinsky)*, Joan Plowright *(Eva Krichinsky)*, Aidan Quinn *(Jules Kaye)*, Elizabeth Perkins *(Ann Kaye)*, Kevin Pollak *(Izzy Kirk)*, Israel Rubinek *(Nathan Krichinsky)*, Leo Fuchs *(Hymie Krichinsky)*, Eve Gordon *(Dottie Kirk)*, Lou Jacobi *(Gabriel Krichinsky)*, Elijah Wood *(Michael Kaye)*

p, Mark Johnson, Barry Levinson; d, Barry Levinson; w, Barry Levinson; ph, Allen Daviau; ed, Stu Linder; m, Randy Newman; prod d, Norman Reynolds; art d, Fred Hole, Edward Richardson; fx, Allen L. Hall, Thomas R. Burman, Bari Dreiband-Burman; cos, Gloria Gresham

AAN Best Original Screenplay: Barry Levinson; *AAN Best Cinematography:* Allen Daviau; *AAN Best Score:* Randy Newman; *AAN Best Costume Design:* Gloria Gresham

Completing writer-director Barry Levinson's "Baltimore trilogy," which began with the acclaimed DINER and continued with TIN MEN, the autobiographical AVALON is a lyrical, melancholy account of an immigrant family's rise and gradual disintegration.

Immigrating to Baltimore in 1914, Sam Krichinsky (Armin Mueller-Stahl) is reunited with his brothers—Gabriel (Lou Jacobi), Hymie (Leo Fuchs) and Nathan (Israel Rubinek)—and drawn into the "family circle," whose members pool their resources to bring relatives over from the old country. Wallpaper hangers during the week, the brothers are musicians during the weekends, and it is during one of their gigs that Sam meets Eva (Joan Plowright), his future wife. Their son, Jules (Aidan Quinn) does not follow in his father's footsteps as a manual laborer. Instead he becomes a door-to-door salesman, sometimes taking along his young son, Michael (Elijah Wood). During one of these outings, Michael watches in terror as his father is stabbed by a mugger. While recuperating, Jules is given a television set by his family. The only "program" at that time is a nonstop test pattern; nevertheless, Jules glimpses a future in the new invention.

AVALON is concerned with the perils of sacrificing humanity for material success, a sort of 90s cinematic hangover from the "go for it" excesses of the 80s. Allen Daviau's photography is exceptional; Quinn, Mueller-Stahl, and Plowright give commendable performances. Ultimately, though, Levinson's very personal project never acquires a personality of its own.

AWFUL TRUTH, THE

1937   90m   bw   Comedy   ★★★★★
Columbia   (U.S.)   /A

Irene Dunne *(Lucy Warriner)*, Cary Grant *(Jerry Warriner)*, Ralph Bellamy *(Daniel Leeson)*, Alex D'Arcy *(Armand Duvalle)*, Cecil Cunningham *(Aunt Patsy)*, Molly Lamont *(Barbara Vance)*, Esther Dale *(Mrs. Leeson)*, Joyce Compton *(Dixie Belle Lee/Toots Binswanger)*, Robert Allen *(Frank Randall)*, Robert Warwick *(Mr. Vance)*

p, Leo McCarey; d, Leo McCarey; w, Vina Delmar (based on the play by Arthur Richman); ph, Joseph Walker; ed, Al Clark; art d, Stephen Goosson, Lionel Banks; cos, Robert Kalloch

AAN Best Picture; AAN Best Actress: Irene Dunne; *AAN Best Supporting Actor:* Ralph Bellamy; *AA Best Director:* Leo McCarey; *AAN Best Screenplay:* Vina Delmar; *AAN Best Editing:* Al Clark

A superbly lighthearted production, and the epitome of 1930s screwball comedies. Grant tells wife Dunne that he is going on a short Florida vacation, but then spends his time playing poker with the boys, establishing an alibi by burning himself under a sunlamp. When he returns home he finds his wife absent; then she appears with D'Arcy, a dashing voice teacher. Both Grant and Dunne assume that the other has been unfaithful and, after a rousing round of accusations, they decide to accept a 90-day interlocutory divorce. Their main courtroom battle focuses on their pet dog, Mr. Smith (Asta of the "Thin Man" series). As the legal wrangling moves into full swing, Dunne not only continues to see D'Arcy, but befriends Texas oil baron Bellamy. Meanwhile, Grant looks up an old flame, Compton, a sexy nightclub singer. Dunne and Grant go their separate ways, but are still drawn to each other. When Grant begins to fall for socialite Lamont, Dunne invades a party at her mansion, pretending to be drunk and carrying on wildly until Grant escorts her home. She convinces him to drive her to their mountain retreat, where they play a cat-and-mouse game, finally acknowledging that they still love each other.

This classic comedy began life as a 1922 stage hit and had been filmed twice previously—in 1925 as a silent with Agnes Ayres and Warner Baxter, and again in 1929 with Henry Daniell and Ina Claire. Director Leo McCarey maintained the basic premise of the play but improved it greatly, adding sophisticated dialogue and encouraging his actors to improvise around anything they thought funny. THE AWFUL TRUTH was in the can in six weeks, and was such a success that Grant and Dunne were teamed again in another splendid comedy, MY FAVORITE WIFE, and in a touching tearjerker, PENNY SERENADE. The film was nominated for an Academy Award for Best Picture and disappointingly remade in 1953 as LET'S DO IT AGAIN with Jane Wyman and Ray Milland.

B

BABE

1995 94m c Fantasy/Children's/Comedy   ★★★½
Kennedy Miller Productions (Australia)   G/U

Christine Cavanaugh *(Voice of Babe)*, James Cromwell *(Arthur Hoggett)*, Miriam Margolyes *(Voice of Fly)*, Hugo Weaving *(Voice of Rex)*, Danny Mann *(Voice of Ferdinand)*, Miriam Flynn *(Voice of Maa)*, Evelyn Krape *(Voice of Old Ewe)*, Russie Taylor *(Voice of Cat)*, Michael Edward-Stevens *(Voice of Horse)*, Charles Bartlett *(Voice of Cow)*

p, George Miller, Doug Mitchell, Bill Miller; d, Chris Noonan; w, George Miller, Chris Noonan (based on the novel *The Sheep-Pig* by Dick King-Smith); ph, Andrew Lesnie; ed, Marcus D'Arcy, Jay Friedkin; m, Nigel Westlake; prod d, Roger Ford; art d, Colin Gibson; fx, Dave Roberts, Charles Gibson, John Stephenson, Jim Henson's Creature Shop, Rhythm & Hues; cos, Roger Ford; anim, Rhythm & Hues

AAN Best Picture; AAN Best Supporting Actor: James Cromwell; AAN Best Director: Chris Noonan; AAN Best Adapted Screenplay: George Miller, Chris Noonan; AAN Best Art Direction: Roger Ford (Art Direction), Kerrie Brown (set decoration); AAN Best Editing: Marcus D'Arcy; AA Best Visual Effects: Scott E. Anderson, Charles Gibson, Neal Scanlan, John Cox

The kind of movie that slyly seduces even the most unregenerate cynic, BABE is a clever family picture that brings surprising freshness to the timeworn premise of talking barnyard animals.

The title character (voice of Christine Cavanaugh) is a piglet raised for slaughter in a terrifying assembly-line breeding pen. Trucked to a county fair, Babe is won and taken home by taciturn but kind-hearted Farmer Hoggett (James Cromwell). Lonely and ignorant of the barnyard's social hierarchy, the piglet unconditionally befriends all beasts, from the sheepdog bitch Fly (voice of Miriam Margolyes), who becomes Babe's surrogate mother, to the aged ewe Maa (voice of Miriam Flynn). Gradually, Babe is accepted by his fellow animals, but the humans still plan to butcher him for Christmas dinner. In an attempt to make himself useful and save his bacon, Babe learns to herd the farm's unruly gang of sheep. Ultimately, his survival will depend on his performance as the sole "sheep-pig" in a prestigious sheepdog contest.

"A humorous look at the limitations and lunacy of a preordained society," was Universal's drily accurate press-kit summation of BABE, which treads a careful path between G-rated fun and didacticism. True, there's a heavy animal-rights undertone in early scenes of Babe's harsh babe-hood, and a soapy subplot about Rex, a dysfunctional dog with a dark secret, is almost too much. But a sense of whimsy prevails, the tone set by an irresistible chorus of Muppet mice who shrilly announce the story's successive chapters. The voice-over cast, refreshingly devoid of big-name Hollywood stars, is perfect, and the animatronics, done by the Jim Henson Creature Factory (plus an Aussie outfit specializing in robot sheep!), blends neatly with about 500 separate live animal performers.

BABES IN ARMS

1939 93m bw Musical   ★★★
MGM (U.S.)   /U

Mickey Rooney *(Mickey Moran)*, Judy Garland *(Patsy Barton)*, Charles Winninger *(Joe Moran)*, Guy Kibbee *(Judge Black)*, June Preisser *(Rosalie Essex)*, Grace Hayes *(Florrie Moran)*, Betty Jaynes *(Molly Moran)*, Douglas McPhail *(Don Brice)*, Rand Brooks *(Jeff Steele)*, Leni Lynn *(Dody Martini)*

p, Arthur Freed; d, Busby Berkeley; w, Jack McGowan, Kay Van Riper (based on the musical play by Richard Rodgers and Lorenz Hart); ph, Ray June; ed, Frank Sullivan; art d, Cedric Gibbons, Merrill Pye; cos, Dolly Tree

AAN Best Actor: Mickey Rooney; AAN Best Score: Roger Edens, George Stoll

Based on the Rodgers and Hart play of the same name, BABES IN ARMS was the first Rooney/Garland vehicle helmed by Busby Berkeley, and its success set the tone for STRIKE UP THE BAND and BABES ON BROADWAY, their subsequent collaborations. (Garland later teamed with Berkeley and hoofer Gene Kelly for 1942's FOR ME AND MY GAL.)

Joe and Florrie Moran (Charles Winninger and Grace Hayes) are old vaudevillians who begin a touring show featuring many of their senior pals. Their children, Mickey (Rooney) and Molly (Betty Jaynes), want to tag along, but the old folks refuse so, at Patsy Barton's (Garland) urging, Mickey writes a show that he'll star in as well as direct. The determined youngsters must also prove that, contrary to the demands of Martha Steele (Margaret Hamilton), they don't belong in a state-administered trade school.

Only "Where or When" remains from the original score, trampled by the unsubtle Berkeley (whom Garland would grow to loathe). This was the first of the Mickey/Judy "let's put on a show" extravaganzas but it's saved by Rooney's brash nerve and especially by the triple-threat charm of Garland, an performer unequaled in the annals of show business. The storyline here has been reduced to vaudeville corn, but watch Garland's ability to transcend cliche, transforming formulaic dross into critical and box-office gold.

BABES IN TOYLAND

1934 77m bw Fantasy/Musical   ★★★
MGM (U.S.)   /U

Stan Laurel *(Stanley Dum)*, Oliver Hardy *(Oliver Dee)*, Charlotte Henry *(Bo-Peep)*, Felix Knight *(Tom-Tom)*, Henry Brandon *(Barnaby)*, Florence Roberts *(Widow Peep)*, Ferdinand Munier *(Santa Claus)*, William Burress *(Toymaker)*, Virginia Karns *(Mother Goose)*, Johnny Downs *(Little Boy Blue)*

p, Hal Roach; d, Gus Meins, Charles Rogers; w, Nick Grinde, Frank Butler (based on the musical comedy by Victor Herbert); ph, Art Lloyd, Francis Corby; ed, William Terhune, Bert Jordan

Victor Herbert operetta presented as vehicle for comedic genius of Laurel and Hardy. As Stanley Dum and Oliver Dee, L&H become the unsung heroes of Toyland when they avert the marriage of Bo Peep and the evil Barnaby, save the widow's abode (a multilevel shoe), rescue Tom-Tom from his exile to Bogeyland (the highlight), and ultimately rid Toyland of the evil Barnaby forever. A beautiful example of family entertainment, with the "March of the Toys" number offering five minutes of raucous action that ends the film on a high note. BABES was remade, with increasingly diminished returns, by Disney in 1961 with Tommy Sands and Annette Funicello and in 1986 with Keanu Reeves and Drew Barrymore.

BABES ON BROADWAY

1941 121m bw Musical   ★★★½
MGM (U.S.)   /U

Mickey Rooney (*Tommy Williams*), Judy Garland (*Penny Morris*), Fay Bainter (*Miss Jones*), Virginia Weidler (*Barbara Jo*), Ray McDonald (*Ray Lambert*), Richard Quine (*Morton Hammond*), Donald Meek (*Mr. Stone*), Alexander Woollcott (*Himself*), Luis Alberni (*Nick*), James Gleason (*Thornton Reed*)

p, Arthur Freed; d, Busby Berkeley; w, Fred Finklehoffe, Elaine Ryan (based on a story by Burton Lane); ph, Lester White; ed, Frederick Y. Smith; cos, Robert Kalloch

AAN Best Song: Burton Lane (Music), Ralph Freed (Lyrics)

This sequel to BABES IN ARMS is slightly superior, serving up Rooney and Garland in everything from soup to nuts. BROADWAY presents Rooney at his enthusiastic peak, especially when he impersonates Carmen Miranda, but he's still eclipsed by Garland when she sings "F.D.R. Jones". Minstrel finale, and tributes to past theatrical performers are dynamite moments. Trivia fans should watch for Joe Yule, Rooney's father, as Mason, and for the debut of Margaret O'Brien. Burton Lane and Ralph Freed's "How About You?" earned an Oscar nomination.

BABETTE'S FEAST
(BABETTE'S GASTEBUD)

1987 102m c Drama   ★★★½
Panorama/Nordisk/Danish Film Institute (Denmark)   G/U

Ghita Norby (*Narrator*), Stephane Audran (*Babette Hersant*), Jean-Philippe Lafont (*Achille Papin*), Gudmar Wivesson (*Lorenz Lowenhielm as a Young Man*), Jarl Kulle (*Lorenz Lowenhielm as an Old Man*), Bibi Andersson (*Swedish Court Lady-in-Waiting*), Hanne Stensgaard (*Young Philippa*), Bodil Kjer (*Old Philippa*), Vibeke Hastrup (*Young Martina*), Birgitte Federspiel (*Old Martina*)

p, Just Betzer, Bo Christensen; d, Gabriel Axel; w, Gabriel Axel (based on the short story by Isak Dinesen [Karen Blixen]); ph, Henning Kristiansen; ed, Finn Henriksen; m, Per Norgard, Wolfgang Amadeus Mozart; fx, Henning Bahs; cos, Annelise Hauberg, Pia Myrdal, Karl Lagerfeld

AA Best Foreign Language Film

Winner of the Oscar for Best Foreign-Language Film of 1987, this quiet Danish film seemed an unlikely candidate for international success; instead of sex, violence, or nudity, it offers sermons and hymns, a dozen or so elderly Danes, and a feast to end all feasts. An expository flashback opens the film, delving into the frustrated love lives of Hastrup and Stensgaard, the daughters of a prophetic minister in a small town on Denmark's rugged Jutland peninsula. The story then shifts to 1871, as the title character (Audran), whose husband and son were killed by the Paris Communards, arrives from France and enters the employ of the sisters, who are carrying on their now-dead father's ministry. After 14 years of service with the sisters, Babette wins 10,000 francs in the French lottery and uses it to prepare a sumptuous banquet in honor of the minister's 100th birthday. At first, the stoic townspeople are reluctant to participate fully in this "pagan" feast; but ultimately they joyously indulge in Babette's masterwork, and it is revealed that she was once the chef de cuisine at the famous Cafe Anglais in Paris.

A gentle film that metaphorically examines the artist's relationship to her art, BABETTE'S FEAST is the sort of story that one cannot help but find uplifting. The performances—by such art-house favorites as Audran, Federspiel (ORDET), Lafont (BIZET'S CARMEN), and Bergman veterans Kulle and Andersson—are uniformly wonderful. The story on which the film is based was the product of a bet between its author, Karen Blixen (aka Isak Dinesen, whom Meryl Streep portrayed in OUT OF AFRICA), and a friend who suggested that the best way to crack the American market was to write about food.

BABY DOLL

1956 114m bw Drama   ★★★★
Warner Bros. (U.S.)   /X

Karl Malden (*Archie*), Carroll Baker (*Baby Doll*), Eli Wallach (*Silva Vacarro*), Mildred Dunnock (*Aunt Rose Comfort*), Lonny Chapman (*Rock*), Eades Hogue (*Town Marshal*), Noah Williamson (*Deputy*)

p, Elia Kazan; d, Elia Kazan; w, Tennessee Williams (based on his play); ph, Boris Kaufman; ed, Gene Milford; m, Kenyon Hopkins; cos, Anna Hill Johnstone

AAN Best Actress: Carroll Baker; *AAN Best Supporting Actress:* Mildred Dunnock; *AAN Best Adapted Screenplay:* Tennessee Williams; *AAN Best Cinematography:* Boris Kaufman

An explosive, provocative black comedy from Tennessee Williams and Elia Kazan. Williams reworked his one-act play, *27 Wagonloads of Cotton*, into a highly controversial screenplay that *Time* magazine called "possibly the dirtiest American picture ever legally exhibited."

Although BABY DOLL feels tame today, the cinematography and appropriately sleazy setting still have a sizzling effect, especially in a notorious porch-swing tryst between stars Carroll Baker and Eli Wallach. All the performances are masterful, amusing and archtypal in the Williams manner: Karl Malden's yokel, Baker's hothouse virgin, Mildred Dunnock's vague octogenarian (especially hilarious) and Wallach's wily Sicilian all score strongly, though the latter lacks the physical size and power to be a believably threatening stud. Arguably, Kazan has no peer at directing Williams: you can almost feel the moss growing, so authentic is this treatment.

This was Baker's first major role, following her film debut in 1953's EASY TO LOVE, and despite all the moral outrage, she deservedly received an Oscar nomination (she lost to Ingrid Bergman for ANASTASIA), as did the script, Dunnock, and Kaufman's starkly handsome black-and-white photography. At the other end of the spectrum, the Catholic Legion of Decency broadly condemned the film, stating that it "dwells upon carnal suggestiveness." Half the town of Benoit, Mississippi, where the film was shot on location, turned out as extras for this sexual potboiler, presumably from erotic curiosity.

BACHELOR AND THE BOBBY-SOXER, THE

1947 95m bw Comedy   ★★★
RKO (U.S.)   /U

Cary Grant (*Dick*), Myrna Loy (*Margaret*), Shirley Temple (*Susan*), Rudy Vallee (*Tommy*), Ray Collins (*Beemish*), Harry Davenport (*Thaddeus*), Johnny Sands (*Jerry*), Don Beddoe (*Tony*), Lillian Randolph (*Bessie*), Veda Ann Borg (*Agnes Prescott*)

p, Dore Schary; d, Irving Reis; w, Sidney Sheldon; ph, Robert de Grasse, Nicholas Musuraca; ed, Frederic Knudtson; m, Leigh Harline; art d, Albert S. D'Agostino, Carroll Clark; fx, Russell A. Cully; cos, Edward Stevenson

AA Best Original Screenplay: Sidney Sheldon

Judge Loy, impatient with cocky playboy Grant after he has appeared before her because of a nightclub fracas, orders him to indulge Temple's schoolgirl crush until it plays itself out. Silly premise allows sophisticated Grant to explode into side-splitting antics, aping the teenaged set. If you adore Grant, you'll enjoy this farce, but Loy's breezy charm is wasted and Temple has reached that age where her preciousness can be irritating to behold. This was Dore Schary's last personal production before taking over the reins of RKO.

BACHELOR MOTHER

1939 80m bw Comedy   ★★★★½
RKO (U.S.)   /U

Ginger Rogers (*Polly Parrish*), David Niven (*David Merlin*), Charles Coburn (*J. B. Merlin*), Frank Albertson (*Freddie Miller*), E.E. Clive (*Butler*), Elbert Coplen Jr. (*Johnnie*), Ferike Boros (*Mrs. Weiss*), Ernest Truex (*Investigator*), Leonard Penn (*Jerome Weiss*), Paul Stanton (*Hargraves*) p, B.G. DeSylva, Pandro S. Berman; d, Garson Kanin; w, Norman Krasna (based on a story by Felix Jackson); ph, Robert de Grasse; ed, Henry Berman, Robert Wise; m, Roy Webb; art d, Van Nest Polglase, Carroll Clark; fx, Vernon L. Walker; cos, Irene

AAN Best Original Screenplay: Felix Jackson

Although Rogers had starred in four hit films sans Fred Astaire during the mid-1930s, it was really with BACHELOR MOTHER, her first solo effort after the team's separation and RKO's biggest hit of 1939, that she really confirmed that she didn't need to sing or dance to appeal to mass audiences. Notable as an example of the slight relaxation during the late 1930s of Hollywood's self-enforced Production Code, the slightly risqué story features Rogers as a single saleswoman for a large Macy's-like department store who finds a baby on her doorstep, whereupon everyone assumes that she's its mother.

Many of the witty lines apparently went right over the heads of the censors. Niven, delightful in his first major romantic comedy lead, portrays the playboy son of store owner Coburn, falling for Rogers even though he too assumes that she is the child's mother. Director Kanin, here enjoying one of his earliest successes, shapes the material as though he had had decades of experience. The supporting cast is uniformly excellent, especially Albertson and the hilariously befuddled, scene-stealing Coburn ("I don't care who's the father. . . I'm the grandfather!"). Originally made in Hungary in 1935, the film easily outpaces its wet-blanket remake with Debbie Reynolds and Eddie Fisher, BUNDLE OF JOY (1956).

BACK STREET

1941 89m bw Drama ★★★★
Universal (U.S.) /A

Charles Boyer *(Walter Saxel)*, Margaret Sullavan *(Ray Smith)*, Richard Carlson *(Curt Stanton)*, Frank McHugh *(Ed Porter)*, Tim Holt *(Richard Saxel)*, Frank Jenks *(Harry Niles)*, Esther Dale *(Mrs. Smith)*, Samuel S. Hinds *(Felix Darren)*, Peggy Stewart *(Freda Smith)*, Nell O'Day *(Elizabeth Saxel)*

p, Frank Shaw; d, Robert Stevenson; w, Bruce Manning, Felix Jackson (based on the novel by Fannie Hurst); ph, William Daniels; ed, Ted J. Kent; art d, Seward Webb

AAN Best Score: Frank Skinner

This restrained, luminous version of Fannie Hurst's oft-filmed saga is easily the best. BACK STREET's success is largely due to the tragic nobility Boyer and Sullavan invest this story of a woman who remains devoted to a married man. In real life, both actors' fates had the same elements of sad inevitability: Boyer and Sullavan died from barbiturate overdoses which were self-inflicted; Boyer in a depression after his wife passed away and Sullavan as a result of her frustration with increasing deafness. Her complicated nature and tempestuous life was chronicled by her daughter in the book *Haywire*. Sullavan's first three husbands were Henry Fonda, William Wyler, and Leland Hayward.

BACK TO SCHOOL

1986 96m c Comedy ★★★
Paper Clip (U.S.) PG-13/15

Rodney Dangerfield *(Thornton Melon)*, Sally Kellerman *(Diane)*, Burt Young *(Lou)*, Keith Gordon *(Jason Melon)*, Robert Downey Jr. *(Derek)*, Paxton Whitehead *(Philip Barbay)*, Terry Farrell *(Valerie)*, M. Emmet Walsh *(Coach Turnbull)*, Adrienne Barbeau *(Vanessa)*, William Zabka *(Chas)*

p, Chuck Russell; d, Alan Metter; w, Steven Kampmann, Will Aldis, Peter Torokvei, Harold Ramis (based on a story by Dangerfield, Greg Fields, Dennis Snee); ph, Thomas Ackerman; ed, David Rawlins; m, Danny Elfman; prod d, David L. Snyder; fx, Michael Lantieri; cos, Durinda Wood

Broad, crude comedy hit has Rodney Dangerfield as Thornton Melon, the immensely wealthy owner of a chain of "Big Men's" clothing stores. His son Jason (Keith Gordon), a student at Grand Lakes University, has lied and told his father that he is a "big man on campus" and a champion diver. In truth, the boy is a nerdy towel attendant for the diving team and has only one friend, Derek (Robert Downey, Jr.), a self-styled revolutionary. Thornton decides to enroll in the school so

that he will be closer to his son and can help him through his current problems, but finds the task more difficult than he anticipated—money helps, however. The plot is suitably slight, allowing plenty of room for the barrage of jokes that roll off Dangerfield's tongue. The result is unsophisticated, unilluminating, unambitious, and hilarious.

BACK TO THE FUTURE

1985 116m c Science Fiction/Comedy ★★★
Amblin/Universal (U.S.) PG

Michael J. Fox *(Marty McFly)*, Christopher Lloyd *(Dr. Emmett Brown)*, Lea Thompson *(Lorraine Baines)*, Crispin Glover *(George McFly)*, Thomas F. Wilson *(Biff Tannen)*, Claudia Wells *(Jennifer Parker)*, Marc McClure *(Dave McFly)*, Wendie Jo Sperber *(Linda McFly)*, George DiCenzo *(Sam Baines)*, James Tolkan *(Mr. Strickland)*

p, Bob Gale, Neil Canton; d, Robert Zemeckis; w, Robert Zemeckis, Bob Gale; ph, Dean Cundey; ed, Arthur Schmidt, Harry Keramidas; m, Alan Silvestri; prod d, Lawrence G. Paull; art d, Todd Hallowell; fx, Kevin Pike; chor, Brad Jeffries; cos, Deborah L. Scott

AAN Best Original Screenplay: Robert Zemeckis, Bob Gale; *AAN Best Song:* Chris Hayes, Johnny Colla, Huey Lewis; *AAN Best Sound:* Bill Varney, Tennyson Sebastian II, Robert Thirlwell, William B. Kaplan; *AA Best Sound Effects Editing:* Charles L. Campbell, Robert Rutledge

Marty McFly (Michael J. Fox) is a decent teenager who plays an electric guitar, sails about on a skateboard, and courts pretty Claudia Wells. But all is not well in Fox's little world. His father (Crispin Glover) is a milquetoast, his mother (Lea Thompson) is an alcoholic, and his brother and sister (Marc McClure and Wendie Jo Sperber) are decidedly weird. Marty's friend, the positively manic Christopher Lloyd, has been working on a device for time travel. Marty activates the device and finds that he has traveled back to 1955, where he encounters his own parents as teenagers. If that isn't troublesome enough, he also discovers that he doesn't have enough special plutonium fuel to return to the future. All this makes for a snappy, happy, and wonderfully nostalgic outing, with ample time-traveling twists and turns. The laughs are plentiful and the acting by Fox, Thompson, and Glover is superb. Robert Zemeckis's direction, like the technical contributions, is first-rate, and after an ambling start takes off into frenetic, non-stop fun.

BACK TO THE FUTURE PART III

1990 118m c Comedy/Science Fiction/Western ★★★
Steven Spielberg (U.S.) PG

Michael J. Fox *(Marty McFly/Seamus McFly)*, Christopher Lloyd *(Dr. Emmett Brown)*, Mary Steenburgen *(Clara Clayton)*, Thomas F. Wilson *(Buford "Mad Dog" Tannen/Biff Tannen)*, Lea Thompson *(Maggie McFly/Lorraine McFly)*, Elisabeth Shue *(Jennifer)*, Matt Clark *(Bartender)*, Richard Dysart *(Barbed Wire Salesman)*, Pat Buttram, Harry Carey Jr.

p, Bob Gale, Neil Canton; d, Robert Zemeckis; w, Bob Gale (based on a story and characters created by Robert Zemeckis and Bob Gale); ph, Dean Cundey; ed, Arthur Schmidt, Harry Keramidas; m, Alan Silvestri; prod d, Rick Carter; art d, Marjorie Stone McShirley, Jim Teegarden; fx, Ken Ralston, Scott Farrar, Michael Lantieri; chor, Brad Jeffries; cos, Joanna Johnston; anim, Wes Takahashi

Part III finds the FUTURE series back on track. This time, Fox and terrific special effects breathe life into the abandoned western genre with exciting, inventive results. The film also boasts the welcome presence of Mary Steenburgen, playing as sweet and spirited a heroine as has ever crossed a screen.

BACKBEAT

1994 100m c Musical/Drama/Biography ★★★
Polygram/Scala Productions (United Kingdom) R/15

Sheryl Lee *(Astrid Kircherr)*, Stephen Dorff *(Stuart Sutcliffe)*, Ian Hart *(John Lennon)*, Gary Bakewell *(Paul McCartney)*, Chris O'Neill *(George Harrison)*, Scot Williams *(Pete Best)*, Kai Wiesinger *(Klaus Voormann)*, Jennifer Ehle *(Cynthia Powell)*, Wolf Kahler *(Bert Kaempfert)*, James Doherty *(Tony Sheridan)* p, Finola Dwyer, Stephen Woolley; d, Iain Softley; w, Stephen Ward, Iain Softley, Michael Thomas; ph, Ian Wilson; ed, Martin Walsh; prod d, Joseph Bennett, Petra Borghoff; art d, Michael Carlin, Joseph Plagge; cos, Sheena Napier

Set amid the neon tawdriness of Hamburg and the working-class grime of Liverpool, BACKBEAT is about two friends, their band, and the woman who comes between them. The story is a cliche, but the band is the Beatles, and the friends are John Lennon and Stuart Sutcliffe—the real "fifth Beatle" who left the group before they became famous and then died of a brain hemorrhage in 1962.

We first meet Lennon (Ian Hart) and his longtime friend and bandmate Sutcliffe (Stephen Dorff) in a tough Liverpool nightclub, then follow them to Hamburg, where—with Paul (Gary Bakewell), George (Chris O'Neill), and drummer Pete Best (Scot Williams)—they play sleazy clubs and live the low life. Stu falls for Astrid Kirchherr (Sheryl Lee), a German art student and world-class bohemian, and the stage is set for a clash between love and friendship, high continental bohemianism and raucous pop culture.

Those expecting an "early days of the Beatles" saga may be disappointed by BACKBEAT, but those willing to entertain the story of Stu Sutcliffe and his famous friends should enjoy it—though it evokes a time and place better than it establishes characters. Noted producer Don Was (of Was Not Was) assembled a group of indie/grunge music stars, including Thurston Moore, Mike Mills, and Dave Pirner (of Sonic Youth, R.E.M., and Soul Asylum, respectively) as the off-camera band (doing contemporary rock and roll covers, not Beatles songs), and first-time director Iain Softley makes the film more visually distinctive than most music bios.

BACKDRAFT

1991 135m c Action/Thriller/Drama   ★★★
Imagine Films Entertainment/Trilogy Entertainment   R/15
Group/Raffaella Productions   (U.S.)

Kurt Russell (Stephen McCaffrey), William Baldwin (Brian McCaffrey), Robert De Niro (Donald Rimgale), Donald Sutherland (Ronald Bartel), Jennifer Jason Leigh (Jennifer Vaitkus), Scott Glenn (John Adcox), Rebecca De Mornay (Helen McCaffrey), Jason Gedrick (Tim Krizminski), J.T. Walsh (Martin Swayzak), Tony Mockus Sr. (Chief John Fitzgerald)

p, Richard B. Lewis, John Watson, Pen Densham; d, Ron Howard; w, Gregory Widen; ph, Mikael Salomon; ed, Daniel Hanley, Michael Hill; m, Hans Zimmer; prod d, Albert Brenner; art d, Carol Winstead Wood; fx, Allen Hall; chor, Monica Devereux; cos, Jodie Tillen

AAN Best Sound: Gary Summers, Randy Thom, Gary Rydstrom, Glenn Williams; *AAN Best Visual Effects:* Mikael Salomon, Allen Hall, Clay Pinney, Scott Farrar; *AAN Best Sound Effects Editing:* Gary Rydstrom, Richard Hymns

Directed by Ron Howard from a screenplay by former fireman Gregory Widen, BACKDRAFT offers an insider's look at a profession seldom featured in movies. Unfortunately, the film drags when the fire is offscreen, only springing to life when it's the main attraction.

The McCaffrey brothers, Stephen (Kurt Russell) and Brian (William Baldwin), are driven by an intense rivalry that started when they were children. When Brian decides to follow Stephen—who in turn followed their late father—into the fire department, tempers flare. Their antagonistic relationship forces Brian's transfer to another assignment: he's made assistant to Donald Rimgale (Robert De Niro), a fire department investigator who specializes in cases of arson. Rimgale is working on a series of fires involving a "backdraft," in which a smoldering fire, exposed to oxygen, suddenly explodes in a literal fireball. Brian meets Rimgale's nemesis, Ronald Bartel (Donald Sutherland), a compulsive fire starter who dreams of seeing the entire world in flames. The investigation points to a corrupt city alderman (J.T. Walsh), but after consulting with Bartel, Brian begins to suspect his brother.

Despite the novelty of the setting, the family drama that forms BACKDRAFT's core is predictable. What makes BACKDRAFT enthralling is the fire itself. Much—in fact, too much—is made dialoguewise of the fire being a living thing, a kind of beast that slinks in the shadows and preys on the careless, the unsuspecting and the overconfident. But BACKDRAFT's fire more than lives up to expectations. It's

spectacular, yes, but that's not all. Not only do the firefighting scenes evoke a feeling of gritty authenticity, but the fire itself really does seem to be alive. A scene in which a door warps ever-so-slightly, almost imperceptibly outward because a smoldering fire lurks behind it, waiting for the blast of oxygen that will bring it to roaring life, would work just as well in a finely crafted horror movie; the sentience, the subtle and cruel intelligence of the fire seems beyond dispute.

BAD AND THE BEAUTIFUL, THE

1952 116m bw Drama   ★★★★★
MGM (U.S.)   /A

Lana Turner (Georgia Lorrison), Kirk Douglas (Jonathan Shields), Walter Pidgeon (Harry Pebbel), Dick Powell (James Lee Bartlow), Barry Sullivan (Fred Amiel), Gloria Grahame (Rosemary Bartlow), Gilbert Roland (Victor "Gaucho" Ribera), Leo G. Carroll (Henry Whitfield), Vanessa Brown (Kay Amiel), Paul Stewart (Syd Murphy)

p, John Houseman; d, Vincente Minnelli; w, Charles Schnee (based on a story by George Bradshaw); ph, Robert Surtees; ed, Conrad A. Nervig; m, David Raksin; art d, Cedric Gibbons, Edward Carfagno; fx, A. Arnold Gillespie, Warren Newcombe; cos, Helen Rose

AAN Best Actor: Kirk Douglas; *AA Best Supporting Actress:* Gloria Grahame; *AA Best Screenplay:* Charles Schnee; *AA Best Cinematography:* Robert Surtees; *AA Best Art Direction:* Cedric Gibbons, Edward C. Carfagno, Edwin B. Willis, Keogh Gleason; *AA Best Costume Design:* Helen Rose

The rise, fall and resurgence of a loutish Hollywood producer, as told through the eyes of three people he made then alienated. This quintessential movie on movies is an engrossing, seductive Minnelli epic, graced with superb performances.

The three separate stories, revolving around Douglas, a ruthless producer whose cunning ways allow him to climb to the top of the Hollywood heap, are told by star Turner, director Sullivan and writer Powell. Some film buffs believe that Douglas's role model was Val Lewton, the extravagant, driven producer of the 1940s, since Lewton made CAT PEOPLE and Douglas produces "The Cat Men" in the film. However, the character is more likely based on mogul David O. Selznick, particularly his beginnings as a B-film producer, his grooming of future wife Jennifer Jones and his making of a colossal Civil War film which, of course, was GONE WITH THE WIND.

Pidgeon's part is most certainly based upon the cost-conscious B-production chief at MGM, Harry Rapf, for whom Selznick first went to work. Schnee's sharp script, which acutely profiles every type of Hollywood character, from the grubbing agent to the mighty mogul, enables one easily to identify Turner's character with that of Diana Barrymore, the tragedy-struck daughter of the Great Profile, John Barrymore. The Powell role, an excellently understated profile, is best associated with writer F. Scott Fitzgerald, whose romance with Hollywood turned sour and who was married to southern belle Zelda Sayre Fitzgerald.

Cost-conscious MGM used many sets from its previous productions for this film, showing them in their naked construction, such as the sweeping staircase used earlier in Turner's MERRY WIDOW. More "inside" ploys were used in the production; Turner's own makeup man and hairdresser, Del Armstrong and Helen Young, appear in the film in their real-life roles, as does Alyce My, Turner's regular stand-in. Raksin's stirring, moody score is superb. The sets by Edwin B. Willis and Keogh Gleason, especially in the roomy, dust-laden mansions, the movie lots, the sets, and the studio offices, totally reflect the Hollywood that is no more but which is forever preserved in this always-fascinating classic.

BAD BEHAVIOR

1993 100m c Comedy/Drama   ★★★★
Parallax Pictures/Film Four International   (U.K.)   R/15

Stephen Rea (Gerry McAllister), Sinead Cusack (Ellie McAllister), Philip Jackson (Howard Spink), Clare Higgins (Jessica Kennedy), Phil Daniels (The Nunn Brothers), Mary Jo Randle (Winifred Turner), Saira Todd (Sophie Bevan), Amanda Boxer (Linda Marks), Luke Blair (Joe McAllister), Joe Coles (Michael McAllister) p, Sarah Curtis; d, Les Blair; ph, Witold Stok; ed, Martin Walsh; m, John Altman; prod d, Jim Grant; art d, Rebecca M. Harvey; cos, Janty Yates

Lovably shapeless, BAD BEHAVIOR is a shaggy dog story of a film, a low key comedy of domestic relations that finds rueful humor in the frustrating, shabby, but emotionally complex lives of a middle-class Irish family marooned in London.

Ellie (Sinead Cusack) and Gerry (Stephen Rea) McAllister are entering middle age with an air of resigned hopefulness not entirely justified by their circumstances. He's a city planner, she works in a bookstore and oversees their chaotic extended household, which includes a raft of neurotic friends. When con artist Howard Spink (Philip Jackson) convinces Ellie that the house needs fixing, and dispatches physically identical but ethically opposed twin brothers (Phil Daniels) to do the work, the disruption threatens the delicate balance of the McAllisters' marriage.

BAD BEHAVIOR, whose rhythms are slow and unpredictable, dictated by the shifting behavior of its richly imagined and realized characters, violates every rule of Hollywood screenwriting. But it's engagingly laid back and crammed with sharp, unforced observations about the scores of tiny sacrifices that compose the foundation of daily life and, in particular, long-term relationships. Cusack and Rea construct a flawless portrait of a married couple who are neither idealized nor the butt of shallow jokes; their relationship is simultaneously secure and bristling with unresolved conflicts. They know one another well enough to recognize exactly which subjects ought to be left alone, but are made reckless by familiarity (and liquor) and are forever poking at the sore spots. If BAD BEHAVIOR's lack of dramatic focus is sometimes trying, it offers finely nuanced performances and many modest but affecting dramatic moments by way of compensation.

BAD BLOOD
(MAUVAIS SANG)

1987 128m c Crime/Romance   ★★★
Plain Chant/Soprofilms/FR3/CNC/Sofima (France)   /18

Denis Lavant (Alex), Juliette Binoche (Anna), Michel Piccoli (Marc), Hans Meyer (Hans), Julie Delpy (Lise), Carroll Brooks (The American Woman), Hugo Pratt (Boris), Serge Reggiani (Charlie), Mireille Perrier (The Young Mother), Jerome Zucca (Thomas)

p, Philippe Diaz; d, Leos Carax; w, Leos Carax; ph, Jean-Yves Escoffier; ed, Nelly Quettier; m, Benjamin Britten, Serge Prokofiev, Charles Chaplin; art d, Michel Vandestien, Thomas Peckre, Jack Dubus; fx, Guy Trielli; chor, Christine Burgos; cos, Robert Nardone, Dominique Gregogna, Martine Metert

Artsy, occasionally inspired piece by French *wunderkind* Leos Carax, who clearly wants us to know how much he owes to Cocteau and Godard. The pulp-novel plot, which takes a backseat to Carax's moody, romantic visuals, concerns a fictional AIDS-like plague called STBO which one contracts by "making love without love." The majority of those infected are adolescents whose lovemaking had previously been without consequence. The only known serum is locked away at the top of a skyscraper, with a lot of different people trying to get their hands on it. Though the storyline moves in unconvincing fits and starts, Carax gets good performances from his hip young stars—including Denis Lavant, Juliette Binoche and Julie Delpy—and pulls off some bravura set pieces. Worth a look.

BAD COMPANY

1972 93m c Western   ★★★★
Paramount (U.S.)   /15

Jeff Bridges (Jake Rumsey), Barry Brown (Drew Dixon), Jim Davis (Marshal), David Huddleston (Big Joe), John Savage (Loney), Jerry Houser (Arthur Simms), Damon Cofer (Jim Bob Logan), Joshua Hill Lewis (Boog Bookin), Charles Tyner (Farmer), Geoffrey Lewis

p, Stanley R. Jaffe; d, Robert Benton; w, David Newman, Robert Benton; ph, Gordon Willis; ed, Ralph Rosenblum; m, Harvey Schmidt; art d, Robert Gundlach

A highly engaging sleeper. Draft dodging is evidently an old American custom, according to this screenplay by Benton and Newman, the duo who scripted BONNIE AND CLYDE. Marking Benton's directorial debut, BAD COMPANY is a comedy-drama about the Civil War equivalent of the Viet Nam protesters. Instead of going north to Canada, these young men wend their ways west. Bridges, Brown, Houser, Cofer, Savage, and Lewis are a bunch of young Easterners who drift out beyond the Mississippi and encounter several adventures. A segmented movie, BAD COMPANY manages to sustain interest through deft direction and an intelligent screenplay. The movie shows the down side of the Old West: deprivation, the cold, the murders, and very little of the dime-novel glamour that young men read about in their gaslit Manhattan rooms. It's a mixture of comedy and drama—and when it's funny, it's terrific.

BAD DAY AT BLACK ROCK

1955 81m c Drama   ★★★★
MGM (U.S.)   /A

Spencer Tracy (John J. MacReedy), Robert Ryan (Reno Smith), Anne Francis (Liz Wirth), Dean Jagger (Tim Horn), Walter Brennan (Doc Velie), John Ericson (Pete Wirth), Lee Marvin (Hector David), Ernest Borgnine (Coley Trimble), Russell Collins (Mr. Hastings), Walter Sande (Sam)

p, Dore Schary; d, John Sturges; w, Don McGuire, Millard Kaufman (based on a story by Howard Breslin); ph, William Mellor; ed, Newell P. Kimlin; m, Andre Previn; art d, Cedric Gibbons, Malcolm Brown

AAN Best Actor: Spencer Tracy; *AAN Best Director:* John Sturges; *AAN Best Original Screenplay:* Millard Kaufman

In this powerful, lightning-paced film, Tracy plays a one-armed stranger who uncovers a dangerous skeleton in a western hick town's closet, with harrowing results. Tracy is at his subdued, thoughtful best, while Ryan perfectly conveys the ignorance behind racial prejudice and Borgnine and Marvin are memorable heavies. Sturges's direction is superbly timed, and Kaufman's script was so memorable that many of its lines quickly passed into public use.

BAD INFLUENCE

1990 99m c Mystery/Thriller   ★★★
Epic (U.S.)   R/18

Rob Lowe (Alex), James Spader (Michael Boll), Lisa Zane (Claire), Christian Clemenson (Pismo Boll), Kathleen Wilhoite (Leslie), Tony Maggio (Patterson), Marcia Cross (Ruth Fielding)

p, Steve Tisch; d, Curtis Hanson; w, David Koepp; ph, Robert Elswit; ed, Bonnie Koehler; m, Trevor Jones; prod d, Ron Foreman; art d, William S. Combs

Slick thriller that capitalized on Lowe's bad boy publicity. Spader befriends Lowe after the latter comes to his aid in a barroom, and soon finds the creep controlling his life; to describe any of the twists would ruin the surprises in the story. Hanson keeps the film moving along at a quick pace and makes the most of the shifting point of view and weird morality of David Koepp's screenplay.

A curious mixture of styles, BAD INFLUENCE is a Hitchcockian homage (particularly its second half) that's also reminiscent of recent films including AT CLOSE RANGE and the Koepp-scripted APARTMENT ZERO. Spader is most effective here, and Lowe has finally found his niche as a junior league Richard Gere. The tension between the two is well handled and yet never quite explained, which adds to the mysterious "feel" of the movie and gives the characters a sexually ambiguous edge.

BAD LIEUTENANT

1992 96m c Crime/Thriller   ★★★½
Lt. Productions/Edward R. Pressman   NC-17/18
Film Corporation (U.S.)

Harvey Keitel (The Lieutenant), Victor Argo (Bet Cop), Paul Calderon (Cop One), Leonard Thomas (Cop Two), Robin Burrows (Ariane), Frankie Thorn (Nun), Zoe Tamarlaine Lund (Zoe), Victoria Bastel (Bowtay), Paul Hipp (Jesus), Brian McElroy (Lt.'s Son)

p, Edward R. Pressman, Mary Kane; d, Abel Ferrara; w, Zoe Tamarlaine Lund, Abel Ferrara; ph, Ken Kelsch; ed, Anthony Redman; m, Joe Delia; prod d, Charles Lagola; cos, David Sawaryn

The Lieutenant (Harvey Keitel) is a New York City cop who's juggling two lives. At home, he's a family man who just wants the best for his wife and extended flock of relatives. On the job, he's a rogue agent heading for disaster. He drinks too much and has a coke problem; he abuses suspects and extorts sexual favors from prostitutes and drug addicts, including his strung-out mistress (Zoe Tamarlaine Lund, who co-wrote the screenplay and starred in Ferrara's early cult hit, MS. 45); and he's a compulsive gambler deep in hock to the Mafia.

All that changes when a young nun (Frankie Thorn) is brutally raped during a robbery at a convent in Spanish Harlem. The Lieutenant quickly launches his own investigation, figuring that he can use the reward money to pay off his debts. More importantly, his search takes on the aspect of a spiritual quest for redemption, even as he simultaneously indulges in a suicidal gambling spree that increases his indebtedness to an exasperated mob bookie.

The director of such stylish thrillers as CHINA GIRL and KING OF NEW YORK, Abel Ferrara has made his reputation by balancing lurid narratives and lush, seductive visuals. BAD LIEUTENANT is actually an aesthetic throwback to Ferrara's earliest work, 1979's DRILLER KILLER; it is harsh, gritty and utterly uncompromising. The photography has the bleak, documentary look of THE FRENCH CONNECTION, heavy on the hand-held camera; the editing is rough and jarring. One can empathize with the characters, but it's hard to imagine liking any of them.

Harvey Keitel gives an astonishing performance here, playing a tortured soul who simultaneously revels in self-loathing and yearns for absolution. Excellent supporting performances, including Lund's turn as a philosophizing junkie, round out the picture. Though hardly a film for all sensibilities, BAD LIEUTENANT has the courage of its own convictions, and follows them to the bitter end.

BAD NEWS BEARS, THE

1976 102m c Comedy ★★★
Paramount (U.S.) PG

Walter Matthau (Coach Buttermaker), Tatum O'Neal (Manda Whurlizer), Vic Morrow (Roy Turner), Joyce Van Patten (Cleveland), Ben Piazza (Councilman Whitewood), Jackie Earle Haley (Kelly Leak), Alfred Lutter (Ogilvie), Brandon Cruz (Joey Turner), Shari Summers (Mrs. Turner), Joe Brooks (Umpire)

p, Stanley R. Jaffe; d, Michael Ritchie; w, Bill Lancaster; ph, John A. Alonzo; ed, Richard A. Harris; m, Jerry Fielding; prod d, Polly Platt

As amusing for adults as it is for children, this charming, funny film takes a gentle poke at Little League baseball and the American obsession with winning. Morris Buttermaker (Walter Matthau, in a strong comic turn), a one-time minor leaguer, becomes the manager of the Bears, a team of multiracial Little League rejects in southern California. With Morris's help this hapless, foul-mouthed bunch, led by its star female hurler, Manda Whurlizer (Tatum O'Neal), begins improving and winning ball games. Director Michael Ritchie (DOWNHILL RACER, SMILE), working from a script by Burt Lancaster's son, Bill, provides a nice twist on the expected outcome. Although the film could have been preachy, Ritchie handles the story and theme with deftness. So popular was the film that it produced two sequels—THE BAD NEWS BEARS IN BREAKING TRAINING (1977) and THE BAD NEWS BEARS GO TO JAPAN (1978)—and at least one imitation, HERE COME THE TIGERS (1978), plus a TV series.

BAD SLEEP WELL, THE
(WARUI YATSU HODO YOKU NEMURU)
1960 135m bw Drama ★★★
Tanaka-Kurosawa (Japan) /A

Toshiro Mifune (Koichi Nishi), Takeshi Kato (Itakura), Masayuki Mori (Iwabuchi), Takashi Shimura (Moriyama), Akira Nishimura (Shirai), Kamatari Fujiwara (Wada), Gen Shimizu (Miura), Kyoko Kagawa (Keiko), Tatsuya Mihashi (Tatsuo), Kyu Sazanka (Kaneko)

p, Tomoyuki Tanaka, Akira Kurosawa; d, Akira Kurosawa; w, Akira Kurosawa, Shinobu Hashimoto, Hideo Oguni, Ryuzu Kikushima, Eijiro Hisaita; ph, Yuruzu Aizawa; ed, Akira Kurosawa; m, Masaru Sato

Samurai capitalism. One of Akira Kurosawa's most obviously political films, THE BAD SLEEP WELL is a prophetic indictment of Japan's cutthroat, feudalistic approach to business. Nishi (Toshiro Mifune) is a fast-rising young executive about to further his acquisition of power through marriage to Keiko (Kyoko Kagawa), the daughter of the firm's president, Iwabuchi (Masayuki Mori). Nishi, however, is something of a modern-day samurai—a heroic figure who has adopted a new identity in order to avenge the death of his father, a corporate vice president whose death can be traced to Iwabuchi. Nishi's method of revenge is to become part of the family and destroy Iwabuchi from within. But Nishi eventually discovers that there is no room for the noble hero in the ruthless world of high-powered executives and politicians. One of Kurosawa's finest achievements, THE BAD SLEEP WELL becomes even more interesting when viewed as a predecessor to HIGH AND LOW (1963), an equally jaundiced look at Japanese mores.

BADLANDS

1973 94m c Crime/Drama ★★★★★
Pressman Williams/Jill Jakes (U.S.) PG/18

Martin Sheen (Kit), Sissy Spacek (Holly), Warren Oates (Father), Ramon Bieri (Cato), Alan Vint (Deputy), Gary Littlejohn (Sheriff), John Carter (Rich Man), Bryan Montgomery (Boy), Gail Threlkeld (Girl), Charles Fitzpatrick (Clerk)

p, Terrence Malick; d, Terrence Malick; w, Terrence Malick; ph, Brian Probyn, Tak Fujimoto, Stevan Larner; ed, Robert Estrin; m, George Tipton, James Taylor; art d, Jack Fisk; cos, Dona Baldwin

Stark, brutal story obviously based on the Charles Starkweather-Carol Fugate murder spree through Nebraska and surrounding states in 1958, with Sheen playing the killer lashing out against a society that ignores his existence and Spacek as his misguided teenage consort. Sheen is forceful and properly weird as the mass murderer, killing Oates, Spacek's disapproving father, when he forbids his daughter to date him. He then goes on the run, Spacek in tow, randomly killing innocents who cross his path. (Starkweather and Fugate, although she later denied killing anyone, were responsible for the deaths of ten people.) The locale in the movie is changed to South Dakota but almost all the characteristics of the real culprits are intact, the strutting Sheen pretending to be James Dean in REBEL WITHOUT A CAUSE, while Spacek doesn't quite understand what he's all about, but goes along anyway.

Director Malick neither romanticizes nor condemns his subjects, maintaining a low-key approach to the story that results in a fascinating character study. Perhaps Starkweather himself provided the best insight into the character when he stated: "The more I looked at people the more I hated them, because I knowed there wasn't any place for me with the kind of people I knowed." The film did scant box office business, but it remains one of the most impressive directorial debuts ever. While Malick would continue to show promise in the equally impressive DAYS OF HEAVEN, by the end of the 1980s these two films would represent his entire oeuvre.

BAGDAD CAFE

1987 91m c Comedy ★★★½
Pelemele/BR-HR/Project (West Germany) PG

Marianne Sagebrecht (Jasmin Munchgstettner), CCH Pounder (Brenda), Jack Palance (Rudi Cox), Christine Kaufmann (Debbie), Monica Calhoun (Phyllis), Darron Flagg (Sal Junior), George Aquilar (Cahuenga), G. Smokey Campbell (Sal), Hans Stadlbauer (Munchgstettner), Apesanahkwat (Sheriff Arnie)

p, Percy Adlon, Eleonore Adlon; d, Percy Adlon; w, Percy Adlon, Eleonore Adlon, Christopher Doherty (based on a story by Percy Adlon); ph, Bernd Heinl; ed, Norbert Herzner; m, Bob Telson, Johann Sebastian Bach; cos, Elizabeth Warner, Regina Batz

AAN Best Song: Bob Telson (Music & Lyrics)

An adorable oddity. Director Percy Adlon's first English-language film is set in a run-down motel in the middle of the Mojave Desert and, like his earlier art-house hit SUGARBABY, stars the uniquely talented Marianne Sagebrecht (Sagebrecht). Jasmin Munchgstettner (Sagebrecht), a German *hausfrau*, is abandoned in the desert after an argument with her husband. After wandering for some time under the scorching sun, Jasmin checks into a dusty motel run by Brenda (C.C.H. Pounder), a tough-talking, no-nonsense woman who treats her new boarder like some sort of space alien. With time, however, the pair become the best of friends, turning the decrepit diner into the most exciting place west of Las Vegas, and Jasmin becomes one of the most popular entertainers for miles around—especially catching the fancy of Rudi Cox (Jack Palance), a cosmic romantic who desperately wants to paint her portrait. BAGDAD CAFE is a visually exhilarating and consciously modern film, more concerned with projecting an atmosphere or spirit than with telling a story. It's hard not to fall in love with this comic fable about the magic that develops at the meeting of two cultures.

BAKER'S WIFE, THE
(LA FEMME DU BOULANGER)

1938   130m   bw   Comedy   ★★★★
Marcel Pagnol   (France)   /A

Raimu *(Aimable, The Baker)*, Ginette Leclerc *(Aurelie, The Baker's Wife)*, Charles Moulin *(Dominique, The Shepherd)*, Robert Vattier *(The Priest)*, Robert Bassac *(The School Teacher)*, Fernand Charpin *(The Marquis)*, Maximilienne

p, Robert Hakim, Raymond Hakim; d, Marcel Pagnol; w, Marcel Pagnol (based on Jean Giono's novel *Jean Le Bleu*); ph, R. Lendruz, N. Daries; ed, Suzanne de Troeye; m, Vincent Scotto

Raimu, the star of Marcel Pagnol's Marseilles trilogy, here teams again with Pagnol as the baker Aimable, a new addition to a French village that has lacked a quality baker for some time. The tasting of Aimable's first loaves of bread is an event eagerly awaited by all the locals, giving the villagers a chance to take time away from their daily complaints and neighborly disagreements. Aimable takes great pride in his bread—a pride equalled only by his affection for his coquettish wife Aurelie (Ginette Leclerc). The villagers agree that if their new baker's bread is as lovely as his wife, all will be content. Unfortunately for Aimable, however, the handsome shepherd Dominique (Charles Moulin) prefers Aurelie to a brioche, and she prefers his affection to slaving over a hot stove. When they run off together, Aimable is no longer able to continue his baking. Rather than risk losing another baker, the villagers band together in an effort to bring Aurelie back home. A touching comedy that borders on the tragic, THE BAKER'S WIFE is brilliantly acted and directed, and proved one of the most popular French films of all time in the US.

BALL OF FIRE

1941   111m   bw   Comedy   ★★★★★
Goldwyn   (U.S.)   /U

Gary Cooper *(Prof. Bertram Potts)*, Barbara Stanwyck *(Sugarpuss O'Shea)*, Oscar Homolka *(Prof. Gurkakoff)*, Henry Travers *(Prof. Jerome)*, S.Z. Sakall *(Prof. Magenbruch)*, Tully Marshall *(Prof. Robinson)*, Leonid Kinskey *(Prof. Quintana)*, Richard Haydn *(Prof. Oddly)*, Aubrey Mather *(Prof. Peagram)*, Allen Jenkins *(Garbage Man)*

p, Samuel Goldwyn; d, Howard Hawks; w, Charles Brackett, Billy Wilder (based on the story "From A to Z" by Thomas Monroe, Billy Wilder); ph, Gregg Toland; ed, Daniel Mandell; m, Alfred Newman; art d, Perry Ferguson

AAN Best Actress: Barbara Stanwyck; *AAN Best Original Screenplay:* Thomas Monroe, Billy Wilder; *AAN Best Score:* Alfred Newman; *AAN Best Sound:* Thomas Moulton (Sound)

Skewed variation on "Snow White and the Seven Dwarfs," courtesy of Howard Hawks and a zany Wilder-Brackett screenplay. Cooper is a stodgy linguist researching slang for a new encyclopedia. In order to get closer to it, he recruits Stanwyck, as a stripper who knows exactly what color the cat's pajamas should be and why it's 23, not 24 or 22 Skiddoo. Cooper lives in a huge house with seven other longhairs and Stanwyck goes on the lam and moves in. There's a veritable corps de comedy in the character actors here; one look at the cast list will

convince anyone that scene-stealing would have been rampant without the firm Hawks hand. Terrific, crackling dialogue, especially in the slangy, machine-gun mouth of La Stanwyck. Remade as A SONG IS BORN, again by Hawks.

BALLAD OF A SOLDIER

1959   89m   bw   Drama/War   ★★★★★
Mosfilm   (U.S.S.R.)   /U

Vladimir Ivashov *(Alyosha)*, Zhanna Prokhorenko *(Shura)*, Antonina Maximova *(Alyosha's Mother)*, Nikolai Kruchkov *(General)*, Yevgeniy Urbanskiy *(Invalid)*

d, Grigori Chukhrai; w, Valentin Yezhov, Grigori Chukhrai; m, Michael Siv

AAN Best Original Screenplay: Valentin Yoshov, Grigori Chukhrai

A young soldier (Ivashov) fighting on the front during WWII heroically disables two German tanks and is rewarded with a six-day leave. As he makes the long journey home to see his mother (Maximova) he meets a variety of people, both friendly and antagonistic, who need his help. Though he finally makes it to his mother's door, he never gets to spend his leave quite as he intended before having to return to almost certain death at the front.

This startlingly realistic and lovingly detailed picture transcends its dramatic premise to embody on several levels the tale of all the Soviet people. An episodic and visually haunting film with modest but never overdone touches of comedy, romance, and sentimentality, BALLAD OF A SOLDIER is a fine example of the Soviet realist tradition—a style of filmmaking paralleled by the more cinematically innovative techniques of such Soviet directors as Sergei Paradzhanov (SHADOWS OF FORGOTTEN ANCESTORS) and Andrei Tarkovsky (MY NAME IS IVAN). Although the film is nationalistic, this and several of Chukrai's other films (e.g. THE FORTY-FIRST) nevertheless contain a palpable critique of Stalinism and its "cult of the hero," suggesting that humanity is more important than heroism.

BALLAD OF CABLE HOGUE, THE

1970   121m   c   Western   ★★★½
Warner Bros.   (U.S.)   R/PG

Jason Robards Jr. *(Cable Hogue)*, Stella Stevens *(Hildy)*, David Warner *(Joshua)*, Strother Martin *(Bowen)*, Slim Pickens *(Ben)*, L.Q. Jones *(Taggart)*, Peter Whitney *(Cushing)*, R.G. Armstrong *(Quittner)*, Gene Evans *(Clete)*, William Mims *(Jensen)*

p, Phil Feldman, Sam Peckinpah, William Faralla; d, Sam Peckinpah; w, John Crawford, Edmund Penney; ph, Lucien Ballard; ed, Frank Santillo, Lou Lombardo; m, Jerry Goldsmith; art d, Leroy Coleman; cos, Robert Fletcher

Peckinpah demonstrated a sense of humor in THE BALLAD OF CABLE HOGUE that had not been seen since his early TV days when he ran one of the best and most overlooked cowboy shows ever, "The Westerner," starring Brian Keith. CABLE HOGUE is at its best when chronicling how the Old West passed and mercantilism spread across the Great Plains.

Robards is a prospector abandoned in the desert and left to die by Martin and Jones. (They worked together again that same year in THE BROTHERHOOD OF SATAN.) Instead of dying, he finds water in a previously arid spot, opens a rest stop for thirsty travelers, and prospers. Stevens is a whore determined to sleep her way to riches, and after a brief fling with Robards, she decides to move on to greener sheets, fleeing to San Francisco. (This is Stevens's best role and underlines the terrible waste of her career—she's terrific.) Warner pops in and out as a preacher who can't decide whether he should save souls or live a life of dedicated hedonism. Hedonism wins. If you're expecting blood and guts and slow-motion death forget it. Peckinpah decided to make a different movie here, and different it is. Not a hit at the box office, it remains one of his finest efforts, funny, touching and never mawkishly sentimental.

BALLAD OF GREGORIO CORTEZ, THE

1983 104m c Western   ★★★
Embassy (U.S.)   PG/15

Edward James Olmos (Cortez), Tom Bower (Boone Choate), Bruce McGill (Bill Blakely), James Gammon (Sheriff Fly), Alan Vint (Sheriff Trimmell), Timothy Scott (Sheriff Morris), Pepe Serna (Romaldo Cortez), Brion James (Capt. Rogers), Barry Corbin (Abernethy), Rosana DeSoto (Carolot Munoz)

p, Michael Hausman, Moctesuma Esparza; d, Robert M. Young; w, Robert M. Young, Victor Villasenor (based on the novel With His Pistol in His Hands by Americo Paredes); ph, Reynaldo Villalobos, Robert M. Young; ed, Richard Soto; m, W. Michael Lewis, Edward James Olmos; art d, Stuart Wurtzel

Originally developed at Robert Redford's esteemed Sundance Institute, THE BALLAD OF GREGORIO CORTEZ recounts one of the most famous manhunts in Texas history. Gregorio Cortez (Olmos), a San Antonio cowhand, was arrested in 1901 in a case of mistaken identity. Because no one could properly translate into Spanish for him, Cortez fought back and accidentally slew a sheriff in what today might be deemed self-defense. Director Robert M. Young takes us on an 11-day manhunt as Cortez hightails it for Mexico, pursued by the legendary Texas Rangers and a small army of others, none of whom can catch the mercurial fugitive. The press made him a hero, but he turned himself in (after escaping several traps) when he learned that his family had been arrested and were being held as prisoners. Young uses flashbacks to present varying accounts of what happened. The original courthouse and jail where Cortez was held and tried lend authenticity to the setting, and the film provides a compelling historical representation of what life must have been like in the Southwest at the turn of the century, especially for Hispanic citizens and workers.

BALLAD OF NARAYAMA
(NARAYAMA-BUSHI-KO)

1958 98m c Drama   ★★★
Shochiku (Japan)

Kinuyo Tanaka (Orin), Teiji Takahashi (Tatsuhei), Yuko Mochizuki (Tama-Yan), Danko Ichikawa (Kesakichi), Keiko Ogasawara (Mutsu-Yan), Seiji Miyaguchi (Mata-Yan), Yunosuke Ito (Mata-Yan's son), Ken Mitsuda (Teru-Yan)

p, Ryuzo Otani; d, Keisuke Kinoshita; w, Keisuke Kinoshita (based on the novel by Shichiro Fukazawa); ph, Hiroyuki Kusuda; ed, Yoshi Sugihara; m, R. Kineya, M. Nozawa; art d, Kisaku Ito

One of the more notable of the "sensitive" Japanese releases popular on the international art house circuit in the early 1960s. Kinoshita's carefully stylized film depicts the centuries-old tradition of herding the aged and infirm onto the barren wastes of Mount Narayama where the elements soon put them out of their misery and send them to the gods. One woman in her seventies accepts her fate but stoically lingers, surviving on sheer will power. Another victim rebels at being sent to his death on the mountain by his brutal son, who kills the old man and is in turn himself killed.

The production, technically excellent and photographically stunning, distances the audience from the savagery of the drama via its careful, theatrical use of studio sets and lighting and a Kabuki narrator. Unlike the 1983 remake by Shohei Imamura, which emphasizes both the violence of the town's customs and the links between humans and nature via a relentlessly harsh realism, Kinoshita almost pushes the film into the realm of fantasy. Criticized by some as too conservative, this version, while less powerfully dramatic than Imamura's, nevertheless finds its own, different level of resonance.

BALLAD OF NARAYAMA, THE

1983 130m c Drama   ★★★★½
Toei (Japan)   /18

Ken Ogata (Tatsuhei), Sumiko Sakamoto (Orin, His Mother), Takejo Aki (Tamayan, His Wife), Tonpei Hidari (Risuke, His Brother), Shoichi Ozawa (Katsuzo), Seiji Kurasaki (Kesakichi, Older Son), Kaoru Shimamori (Tomekichi, Younger Son), Ryutaro Tatsumi (Matayan), Junko Takada (Matsu), Nijiko Kiyokawa (Old Widow Okane)

p, Goro Kusakabe, Jiro Tomoda; d, Shohei Imamura; w, Shohei Imamura (based on the stories "Narayama Bushi-ko" and "Tohoku No Zunmatachi" by Scichiro Fakazawa); ph, Masao Tochizawa; ed, Hajime Okayasu; m, Shinichiro Ikebe; art d, Nobutaka Yoshino

A remarkable picture based on the award-winning stories by Fakazawa and previously filmed in 1958 under the same title. The story takes place in a 19th century Japanese village plagued by famine. In order to ration food, the village has ritualized the killing of redundant members of the community: newborn males are murdered, while the elderly are carried by their children to the top of Mount Narayama and left to die. Orin (Sakamoto) is a 69-year-old woman thus scheduled for extinction; her son (Ogata) is reluctant to carry out the ritual, but the mother, bound to tradition, is adamant. After finding wives for her children, she begins the arduous journey up the mountain, strapped to her son's back.

In deliberate contrast to the dreamy original, this remake is joltingly realistic. Director Imamura (THE PORNOGRAPHERS), who began as an assistant to Yasujiro Ozu, has a well-known flair for urban low-life; here, he turns to rural brutishness with equally striking results. The film revels in the indecorous (dead babies and a ritual gang-bang are highlights), but everything is rendered with a visual beauty that is probably intentionally incongruous. Winner of the Golden Palm at the 1983 Cannes festival.

BAMBI

1942 70m c Animated/Children's   ★★★★★
Walt Disney Productions (U.S.)   /U

VOICES OF: Bobby Stewart (Bambi), Peter Behn (Thumper), Stan Alexander (Flower), Cammie King (Faline), Donnie Dunagan, Hardie Albright, John Sutherland, Tim Davis, Sam Edwards, Sterling Holloway

p, Walt Disney; d, David Hand; w, Perce Pearce, Larry Morey (based on the story by Felix Salten); m, Frank Churchill, Edward Plumb; anim, Milt Kahl, Eric Larson, Franklin Thomas, Oliver M. Johnston Jr.

AAN Best Score: Frank Churchill, Edward Plumb; AAN Best Song: Frank Churchill (Music), Larry Morey (Lyrics); AAN Best Sound: Sam Slyfield (Sound)

Said to be Walt Disney's own personal favorite of all his films, BAMBI is a brilliantly animated, heart-tugging parable about the cycles of life as reflected in the story of the growth of a young deer.

A fawn named Bambi learns to walk and talk with the help of his friends, a bunny named Thumper and a skunk named Flower. Bambi's mother teaches him about the joys of nature but warns him to stay away from the deadly creature named "Man." One spring day during a visit to a meadow, Bambi's mother is killed by a hunter. Years pass, and Bambi experiences the first pangs of romantic love when he becomes interested in a female deer named Faline. After winning a fight with another male for her affection, he further proves his heroism during a raging forest fire that nearly claims the lives of his friends and Faline.

Originally planned to follow Disney's first animated feature, SNOW WHITE AND THE SEVEN DWARFS (1937), BAMBI wound up taking five years to make. In contrast to the clean lines and bright colors of most Disney cartoons, the drawings in BAMBI have a soft, lush, and almost hazy quality to them, in keeping with the gentleness of the characters. The bittersweet fable is actually geared toward older kids and even adults, dealing with such traumatic subjects as the loss of childhood innocence and the death of a parent; the heartwrenching scene where Bambi's mother is killed has inspired countless nightmares among those who saw it at a very early age. This honest, non-sugarcoated approach to the hard truths of life, however, is what gives BAMBI its lasting emotional power, and makes it stand apart, not only from Disney's cartoons, but from virtually all others as well.

BANANAS

1971 82m c Comedy/War   ★★★
UA (U.S.)   /15

Woody Allen (Fielding Mellish), Louise Lasser (Nancy), Carlos Montalban (Gen. Vargas), Natividad Abascal (Yolanda), Jacobo Morales (Esposito), Miguel Suarez (Luis), David Ortiz (Sanchez), Rene Enriquez (Diaz), Jack Axelrod (Arroyo), Howard Cosell (Himself) p, Charles H. Joffe, Jack Grossberg; d, Woody Allen; w, Woody Allen, Mickey Rose; ph, Andrew Costikyan; ed, Ron Kalish; m, Marvin Hamlisch; prod d, Ed Wittstein; cos, Gene Coffin.

Woody Allen is Fielding Mellish, a neurotic New Yorker who's enamored of a political activist, Nancy (Louise Lasser), Allen's wife at the time), who'll have nothing to do with him because she's totally immersed in the revolution taking place in the banana republic of San Marcos. Wearing Castro-like fatigues and a false red beard, Allen accidentally winds up as president of San Marcos. He returns to the US, is unmasked as a fraud, tried for subversion, and winds up marrying Nancy. Although some of the humor falls flat in this early Allen comedy, his satire of revolutions and revolutionaries is perpetually topical; subsequent events in Central America have only enhanced the film's appeal.

BAND OF OUTSIDERS

1964 95m bw Crime   ★★★
Anouchka/Orsay (France)

Anna Karina (Odile), Claude Brasseur (Arthur), Sami Frey (Franz), Louisa Colpeyn (Mme. Victoria), Daniele Girard (English Teacher), Ernest Menzer (Arthur's Uncle), Chantal Darget (Arthur's Aunt), Michele Seghers (Pupil), Claude Makovski (Pupil), Georges Staquet (Legionnaire)

d, Jean-Luc Godard; w, Jean-Luc Godard (based on the novel Fool's Gold by Dolores Hitchens); ph, Raoul Coutard; ed, Agnes Guillemot, Francoise Collin; m, Michel Legrand

Several years after the success of his debut feature, BREATHLESS, Godard returned to the crime genre and his fascination with American pop culture. Outsiders less by choice than by societal pressures, Odile (Karina), Arthur (Brasseur), and Franz (Frey) meet in an English language class and become fast friends. Odile tells Franz that she lives in a house where a large cache of loot is hidden, and soon he and Arthur, under the influence of the countless Hollywood films and pulp novels they've consumed, decide to burglarize the house. Odile, attracted to both men, completes the criminal triangle.

As anyone who has seen a Godard film might guess, there is very little concern for plot—the attraction of BAND OF OUTSIDERS lies not so much in its actual story as in Godard's telling of it. His voice-over narration is confrontational; his characters talk to the screen; there exists a strange, somewhat uneasy relationship between comedy and violence; and the frame is filled with various allusions to film, literature, and Godard himself. This was his seventh film in only five years and, as in Truffaut's SHOOT THE PIANO PLAYER, it attempts to find a new truth by retelling a familiar story in a new way. Particularly memorable is the trio's nine-second tour of the Louvre.

If this film is less engaged with social and political realities than most of Godard's other work from this period and seems like nothing more than a playful attempt to re-create an old Hollywood genre, one must remember that even a lesser Godard is likely to be much more stimulating than another director's better films. At the height of his impish self-awareness, the filmmaker credits himself here as Jean-Luc Cinema Godard.

BAND WAGON, THE

1953 111m c Musical   ★★★★½
MGM (U.S.)   /U

Fred Astaire (Tony Hunter), Cyd Charisse (Gaby Gerard), Oscar Levant (Lester Marton), Nanette Fabray (Lily Marton), Jack Buchanan (Jeffrey Cordova), James Mitchell (Paul Byrd), Robert Gist (Hal Benton), Thurston Hall (Col. Tripp), Ava Gardner (The Movie Star), LeRoy Daniels (Shoeshine Boy)

p, Arthur Freed; d, Vincente Minnelli; w, Betty Comden, Adolph Green; ph, Harry Jackson; ed, Albert Akst; chor, Michael Kidd, Oliver Smith

AAN Best Original Screenplay: Betty Comden, Adolph Green; AAN Best Score: Adolph Deutsch; AAN Best Costume Design: Mary Ann Nyberg

Seamlessly directed by Vincente Minnelli, THE BAND WAGON is one of the finest musicals ever made. Playing its hackneyed story with tongue firmly in cheek, it simultaneously reflects upon the musical genre, satirizes its conventions and delivers marvelous entertainment. Hollywood dancer Tony Hunter (Astaire) having fallen from favor with the moviegoing public, attempts a comeback on Broadway in a musical written by Lester and Lily Marton (Levant and Fabray, essentially playing the screenwriting team of Comden and Green). The play's arty director, Jeffrey Cordova (Buchanan), makes some misguided staging decisions, while Tony's lead, ballerina Gaby Gerard (Charisse), is less than enamored of him, setting up the problems the players must resolve.

Along the way, we are treated to a tart look at life behind the scenes and a host of highly engaging performances. Astaire has rarely been more appealing—or moving—in a thinly disguised autobiographical role. Fabray and Levant provide the sugar and vinegar in generous doses, Charisse's acting is quite satisfactory and her subdued, earthy sensuality makes her a surprisingly apt dance partner for Astaire, and Buchanan all but steals the film as the hilariously Faust-obsessed, maddeningly brilliant impresario. A low-key highlight is his delightful softshoe with Astaire to "I Guess I'll Have to Change My Plans", but the musical pleasures are many and varied, including "A Shine on Your Shoes," Astaire's romp in a 42nd Street penny arcade; "Dancing in the Dark," Astaire and Charisse's dreamy pas de deux; the legendary "Triplets," featuring a swaddled Buchanan, Astaire, and Fabray; the striking and sexy "Girl Hunt Ballet", a spoof of film noir and hard-boiled detectives; and of course the witty showbiz anthem, "That's Entertainment."

BANDIT QUEEN

1995 129m c Drama/Biography/Political   ★★★½
Film Four International/Kaleidoscope (India/U.K.)   /18

Seema Biswas (Phoolan Devi), Nirmal Pandey (Vikram Mallah), Manjoj Bajpai (Man Singh), Rajesh Vivek (Mustaquim), Raghuvir Yadav (Madho), Govind Namdeo (Sriram), Saurabh Shukla (Kailash), Aditya Srivastava (Puttilal), Agesh Markam (Mad Woman), Anirudh Agarwal (Babu Gujjar)

p, Sundeep Singh Bedi; d, Shekhar Kapur; w, Mala Sen; ph, Ashok Mehta; ed, Renu Saluja; m, Nusrat Fateh Ali Khan; prod d, Eve Mavrakis; art d, Ashok Bhagat; cos, Dolly Ahluwalia

BANDIT QUEEN, a masterful Indian epic based on the life of a latterday woman warrior, makes few concessions to art-house taste, and viewers whose notions of India have been shaped by decorous Merchant/Ivory productions may shrink from its confrontational style.

Unlike the handful of South Asian movies that have drawn international attention over the past decade — e.g., SPICES (1985) and SALAAM BOMBAY! (1988), both directed by filmmakers then associated with the high-minded "parallel cinema" — BANDIT QUEEN has the narrative sweep and visual energy of the best Indian commercial pictures, reflecting the Bollywood background of its formidably talented director, Shekhar Kapur.

This harrowing, wilfully controversial film tells the story of Phoolan Devi (Seema Biswas), the near-legendary leader of a band of dacoits — brigands — who conducted daring raids on landowners in north central India during the late 1970s and early '80s, often distributing the proceeds among lower-caste tenant farmers. Married at the age of 11 and abandoned by her husband after she resisted his sexual demands, Devi became a social outcast, defenseless against the depredations of rural India's exceptionally brutal patriarchy. In a particularly gruesome episode, Devi was gang-raped by most of the upper-caste men in the village of Behmai, Uttar Pradesh; she later took revenge by organizing a massacre that left 20 villagers dead. By the time of her arrest in 1983, Devi was a folk hero, due in no small part to her apparently instinctual feminism: her gang's practice of disrupting the wedding ceremonies of child brides captured the imaginations of both peasant women and urban leftists.

Despite the opening title — "This is a true story" — Kapur's film is less a literal biography than an explication of the popular mythology surrounding Phoolan Devi. As electrically portrayed by Biswas, she's a furious embodiment of shakti — feminine power — and a figure of affronted womanhood that inevitably recalls the abundant rape-revenge subgenre of Indian commercial melodrama (it's no accident that examples of the colossal hoardings used to promote Bollywood movies are prominently visible during the Behmai massacre sequence). Production values are first-rate throughout, notably the mournful score by Nusrat Fateh Ali Khan and cinematographer Ashok Mehta's dazzling use of the unearthly ravine country of Chambral Valley.

BANG THE DRUM SLOWLY

1973 96m c Sports ★★★½
Paramount (U.S.) /AA

Robert De Niro (Bruce Pearson), Michael Moriarty (Henry Wiggen), Vincent Gardenia (Dutch Schnell), Phil Foster (Joe Jaros), Ann Wedgeworth (Katie), Pat McVey (Pearson's Father), Heather Mac-Rae (Holly Wiggen), Selma Diamond (Tootsie), Barbara Babcock, Maurice Rosenfield (Team Owners)

p, Maurice Rosenfield, Lois Rosenfield; d, John Hancock; w, Mark Harris (based on his novel); ph, Richard Shore; ed, Richard Marks; m, Stephen Lawrence; prod d, Robert Gundlach

AAN Best Supporting Actor: Vincent Gardenia

A well-done if depressing film, BANG THE DRUM SLOWLY is a sort of baseball version of "Brian's Song," the TV movie that told the story of the extraordinary friendship between the Chicago Bears' Gale Sayers and Brian Piccolo, who died of cancer. In this film, De Niro is the dying athlete, a journeyman big-league catcher who has contracted Hodgkin's disease. Moriarty, the team's star pitcher, becomes dedicated to his batterymate when he learns of De Niro's fatal illness and prevents him from being sent to the minors. When their teammates find out, they too belatedly make De Niro feel like one of the boys, and, surprisingly, his playing even improves. Alas, it's all a little too late.

One of De Niro's earliest roles—the quintessential bumpkin who wears a smiley-face T-shirt under his sports jacket—it's poles apart from the enigmatic loners that later became his specialty. To prepare for the part, De Niro not only practiced with the Cincinnati Reds, but also traveled to Georgia to perfect his accent. His hard work resulted in a wholly believable performance. Moriarty is also very effective as Henry Wiggen, the central character in a number of baseball novels by Harris, who adapted one of them for this film. Previously done on TV with Paul Newman and Albert Salmi, this version, under Hancock's fine direction, became one of the best baseball movies ever. Vincent Gardenia received an Academy Award nomination for his supporting work as the team's manager, and Foster is wonderful as a coach.

BANK DICK, THE

1940 69m bw Comedy ★★★★½
Universal (U.S.) /U

W.C. Fields (Egbert Souse), Cora Witherspoon (Agatha Souse), Una Merkel (Myrtle Souse), Evelyn Del Rio (Elsie Mae Adele Brunch Souse), Jessie Ralph (Mrs. Hermisillo Brunch), Franklin Pangborn (J. Pinkerton Snoopington), Shemp Howard (Joe Guelpe), Dick Purcell (Mackley Q. Greene), Grady Sutton (Og Oggilby), Russell Hicks (J. Frothingham Waterbury)

d, Edward F. Cline; w, W.C. Fields; ph, Milton Krasner; ed, Arthur Hilton; art d, Jack Otterson

Along with IT'S A GIFT, one of the definitive W.C. Fields films. THE BANK DICK is, as with all the best of Fields, appropriately thin on plot and heavy with hilarious set-pieces which allow "The Great Man" his full comic scope. The cynical, eccentric, bottle-hitting comedian plays an unemployed, henpecked (as usual) family man none-too-eagerly seeking work who accidentally captures a bank robber and is rewarded with a job as guard inside the bank. When not busy bothering customers (as when he apprehends a patron's son brandishing a toy gun), he runs between his deliciously horrid family and The Black Pussy Cat Cafe, where the proprietor (a Three Stooges-less Howard) spends most of his time pouring the guard, his only customer, a series of stiff ones.

The movie is filled with a marvelous series of Fields-patented comic bits, including an especially zany car chase, reminiscent of the best Mack Sennett, where "hostage" Fields once again inadvertantly saves the day. Fields, who wrote the script under the typically improbable pseudonym of Mahatma Kane Jeeves, plays a character named Souse, which he pronounces, in the French manner, as "Sou-say"; the rest of the cast, as might be expected, merely follows the word's English pronunciation. With wonderful supporting work from Witherspoon, Ralph, Pangborn, Sutton, Jack Norton, Pierre Watkin, and many others.

BARBAROSA

1982 90m c Western ★★★½
Universal (U.S.) PG

Willie Nelson (Barbarosa), Gary Busey (Karl), Isela Vega (Josephina), Gilbert Roland (Don Braulio), Danny De La Paz (Eduardo), Alma Martinez (Juanita), George Voskovec (Herman), Sharon Compton (Hilda), Howland Chamberlin (Emil), Harry Caesar (Sims)

p, Paul N. Lazarus III, William D. Wittliff; d, Fred Schepisi; w, William D. Wittliff; ph, Ian Baker; ed, Don Zimmerman, David Ramirez; m, Bruce Smeaton

Country singer Willie Nelson plays the amiable title outlaw who befriends Gary Busey. The two roam the Texas border region, both on the run from family feuds. A beautifully filmed, nicely philosophic and rather old-fashioned western with an elegiac tone, well directed by Australian director Fred Schepisi (BREAKER MORANT), BARBAROSA features uniformly strong acting, with Busey and Nelson making a good team.

BARCELONA

1994 101m c Comedy/Romance/Political ★★★
Film Barcelona/Castle Rock/Westerly Films (U.S.) PG-13/12

Taylor Nichols (Ted Boynton), Christopher Eigeman (Fred Mason), Tushka Bergen (Montserrat), Mira Sorvino (Marta Ferrer), Pep Munne (Ramon), Nuria Badia (Aurora), Hellena Schmied (Greta), Francis Creighton (Frank), Thomas Gibson (Dickie Taylor), Jack Gilpin (The Consul)

p, Whit Stillman; d, Whit Stillman; w, Whit Stillman; ph, John Thomas; ed, Chris Tellefsen; m, Mark Suozzo; prod d, Jose Maria Botines; cos, Edi Giguere

Among stale Hollywood romances like I.Q., SPEECHLESS, and LOVE AFFAIR, Whit Stillman's BARCELONA is the real McCoy, a gossamer blend of *chagrin d'amour*, musical beds, and translation errors in the language of love.

In Spain during the last years of the Cold War, Ted (Taylor Nichols), an American salesman, reluctantly plays host to his cousin, naval officer Fred (Chris Eigeman). Bumming money or embroidering stories about Ted's sexual proclivities, Fred is a tactless but oddly charming loose cannon, and the two become social successes among the young women who work as hostesses for the Spanish Trade Fair. While Ted pursues Montserrat (Tushka Bergen), Fred sleeps with Marta (Mira Sorvino), a pretty but heedless party girl; meanwhile, a rising turmoil of anti-American sentiment threatens their idyll.

Writer-director Stillman (METROPOLITAN) showcases scenic Barcelona as a moonlit love-field where courtship is as likely to be interrupted by a USO bombing as by a lover's betrayal. Political innocents abroad, the cousins also lack the Spaniards' nonchalance in affairs of the heart; despite Fred's obnoxiousness and Ted's uptight theorizing, their genuine guilelessness never fails to shine through. BARCELONA represents a cinematic advance over the tighter but visually drab METROPOLITAN, but Stillman sacrifices pacing here: he has a lot to say and doesn't always have the editorial flair to nail down his sentiments as neatly as he might.

BAREFOOT IN THE PARK

1967 104m c Comedy ★★★½
Paramount (U.S.) /PG

Robert Redford (Paul Bratter), Jane Fonda (Corie Bratter), Charles Boyer (Victor Velasco), Mildred Natwick (Mrs. Ethel Banks), Herb Edelman (Telephone Man), James F. Stone (Delivery Man), Ted Hartley (Frank), Mabel Albertson (Aunt Harriet), Fritz Feld (Restaurant Proprietor)

p, Hal B. Wallis; d, Gene Saks; w, Neil Simon (based on his play); ph, Joseph La Shelle; ed, William Lyon; m, Neal Hefti; cos, Edith Head

AAN Best Supporting Actress: Mildred Natwick

Laughs galore in early first screenplay by Simon, based on his Broadway success. Saks makes a fine impression in his first directorial stint, which features Redford and Fonda living in a small fifth-floor apartment in Greenwich Village. She thinks their place is lovely, but he, ever the conservative attorney, hates it. Boyer plays the slightly zany, womanizing upstairs neighbor who must go through their apartment to reach his. Ever a romantic, Fonda adores the old reprobate and fixes him up with her stodgy mother (Natwick). A series of comic and romantic complications ensues, some of which center around Redford's inability to let himself go—like the night he refused Fonda's entreaties to go barefoot in Central Park on a night when it was 17 degrees out and raining to boot. Love of course finds a way, and Redford finds a way to romp in a manner befitting the film's title. Redford and the Oscar-nominated Natwick, fresh from their Broadway triumph in the play, perform with the ease familiarity brings, and Fonda and Boyer also display the appropriate lightness of touch.

BARFLY

1987 100m c Comedy/Romance ★★★★
Francis Ford Coppola/Golan-Globus (U.S.) R/18

Mickey Rourke (Henry Chinaski), Faye Dunaway (Wanda Wilcox), Alice Krige (Tully Sorenson), Jack Nance (Detective), J.C. Quinn (Jim), Frank Stallone (Eddie), Gloria LeRoy (Grandma Moses), Sandy Martin (Janice), Roberta Bassin (Lilly), Joe Unger (Ben)

p, Barbet Schroeder, Fred Roos, Tom Luddy; d, Barbet Schroeder; w, Charles Bukowski; ph, Robby Muller; ed, Eva Gardos; prod d, Bob Ziembicki; cos, Milena Canonero

Not a film for everyone, but the unrelieved squalor of BARFLY offers its own peculiar fascinations. Director Barbet Schroeder (REVERSAL OF FORTUNE) positions the grungy world of cult writer Charles Bukowski under a cinematic microscope, affording titillating glimpses of lowlife.

Rourke plays Henry Chinaski, a slovenly, hard-drinking, fistfighting scribe who's taken with Wanda Wilcox (Dunaway), a haggard but attractive drunk he meets in a bar. Chinaski's work is admired by wealthy, pretty, self-assured publisher Tully Sorenson (Krige), and that provides the film with a romantic triangle as Wanda and Tully battle for Henry's attentions. Rourke, who turns in the finest performance of his career to date, takes a character who could be seen as pathetic and despicable and makes him, if not a likable hero, at least an understandable one. Dunaway gives an exceptional performance, and Krige is perfect in her role.

The making of BARFLY was nearly as extreme as anything in the film. Producer-director Schroeder had originally commissioned Bukowski to write a screenplay for $20,000, then struggled for years to get the project filmed. Finally, he entered the office of Cannon president Menahem Golan and threatened to cut off a finger unless Cannon made the film. After initially refusing, Golan realized Schroeder's obsession with BARFLY and eventually gave the project the go-ahead. The kind of film people are likely to disagree about strongly.

BARKLEYS OF BROADWAY, THE

1949 109m c Musical ★★★½
MGM (U.S.) /U

Fred Astaire (Josh Barkley), Ginger Rogers (Dinah Barkley), Oscar Levant (Ezra Miller), Billie Burke (Mrs. Belney), Gale Robbins (Shirlene May), Jacques Francois (Jacques Barredout), George Zucco (The Judge), Clinton Sundberg (Bert Felsher), Inez Cooper (Pamela Driscoll), Carol Brewster (Gloria Amboy)

p, Arthur Freed; d, Charles Walters; w, Betty Comden, Adolph Green; ph, Harry Stradling; ed, Albert Akst; m, Lennie Hayton; art d, Cedric Gibbons, Edward Carfagno; chor, Hermes Pan, Robert Alton; cos, Irene; anim, Irving G. Reis

AAN Best Cinematography: Harry Stradling

A very enjoyable if somewhat disappointing reunion for the unbeatable team of Astaire and Rogers. Handsomely produced, THE BARKLEYS OF BROADWAY retells with some but not quite enough wit a thinly disguised version of what was perceived as the duo's actual working relationship. Astaire and Rogers play Josh and Dinah Barkley, an affectionate and highly successful, if sometimes contentious, married

musical comedy team. Trouble comes when Dinah's dramatic ambitions and Josh's jealousy over the attention paid to his wife by a handsome French playwright (Francois) encourage the pair to split both professionally and personally. Although each enjoys considerable solo success, they finally realize they belong together doing musical comedy.

The team's first pairing in ten years, which came about after Astaire's costar in the previous year's highly successful EASTER PARADE, Judy Garland, suffered one of her many breakdowns, it would also prove to be their last together. THE BARKLEYS OF BROADWAY shows neither the screen duo nor screenwriters Comden and Green at their best, despite the sharp support from Levant, Burke, and others. The film's chief weakness is the score by Harry Warren and Ira Gershwin, though Fred and Ginger also reprise George and Ira Gershwin's decade-old classic, "They Can't Take That Away from Me." Oddly enough, the legendary pair most closely approximates their earlier magic during the warm comic and romantic interludes, though their delightful and spirited tap duet to "Bouncin' the Blues" does bring some of their patented incandescence onto the dance floor.

BARRETTS OF WIMPOLE STREET, THE

1934 110m bw Romance/Biography ★★★½
MGM (U.S.) /U

Fredric March (Robert Browning), Norma Shearer (Elizabeth Barrett), Charles Laughton (Edward Moulton Barrett), Maureen O'Sullivan (Henrietta Barrett), Katherine Alexander (Arabel Barrett), Una O'Connor (Wilson), Ian Wolfe (Harry Bevan), Marion Clayton (Bella Hedley), Ralph Forbes (Capt. Surtees Cook), Vernon Downing (Octavius Barrett)

p, Irving Thalberg; d, Sidney Franklin; w, Ernest Vajda, Claudine West, Donald Ogden Stewart (based on the play by Rudolph Besier); ph, William Daniels; ed, Margaret Booth; art d, Cedric Gibbons; cos, Adrian

AAN Best Picture; AAN Best Actress: Norma Shearer

One of the better-known and more typical of MGM's adaptations of famous stage plays, THE BARRETTS OF WIMPOLE STREET is slightly strangled by its own sense of prestige, but proves worthy drama nonetheless. This historical romance tells how the near-invalid Elizabeth Barrett (Shearer) finds happiness and renewed vitality through the love of fellow poet Robert Browning (March), despite the efforts of her dictatorial and overly protective father (played exquisitely by Laughton). Confined to her room with little but her dog and her love of poetry for comfort, Elizabeth cannot even reach out to her brothers and sisters, also under the thumb of their father's tyranny. The battle between father and lover, seemingly simplistic, takes on increasing depth as the drama unfolds.

Though much of the acting is somewhat theatrical, it is also effective on its own terms in this rarefied atmosphere. The climactic moment as Elizabeth struggles out of her father's grasp, realizing that his smothering love for her isn't simply of a paternal nature, is extremely well handled by both Shearer and Laughton. Although the latter's villainy dominates the film, the supporting performances are generally good, particularly those of O'Sullivan as Elizabeth's hapless younger sister and O'Connor as a loyal servant. Not as good as contemporary reviews suggest, but nostalgically charming.

BARRETTS OF WIMPOLE STREET, THE

1956 105m c Romance/Biography ★★★★
MGM (U.K.) /U

Jennifer Jones (Elizabeth), John Gielgud (Barrett), Bill Travers (Robert Browning), Virginia McKenna (Henrietta), Susan Stephen (Bella), Vernon Gray (Capt. Surtees Cook), Jean Anderson (Wilson), Maxine Audley (Arabel), Leslie Phillips (Harry Bevan), Laurence Naismith (Dr. Chambers)

p, Sam Zimbalist; d, Sidney Franklin; w, John Dighton (based on the play by Rudolph Besier); ph, Freddie Young; ed, Frank Clark; m, Bronislau Kaper; art d, Alfred Junge; cos, Elizabeth Haffenden

Sidney Franklin directed both versions of this well-known biopic, originally filmed in 1934. Jones plays poet and near-invalid Elizabeth Barrett, whose father's (Gielgud) almost incestuous adoration for her all but confines her to his London house. She is understandably lonely and depressed; her only companions are her books, her servants, her dog, and her horde of brothers (all wonderfully played by bright young men of the period), Enter Robert Browning (Travers), a fellow poet rich in love and warmth, who sweeps Elizabeth off the couch and into bloom like a morning glory at dawn. Gielgud, in a magnificent performance imbued with understated menace, attempts to smash the relationship before it attains fruition, and the struggle for the young woman's happiness is on. A subtle, lovingly rendered if sometimes leisurely film with fine acting all around and a technical skill which surpasses its worthy 1934 predecessor, THE BARRETTS OF WIMPOLE STREET is very effective drama.

BARRY LYNDON

1975 184m c Historical   ★★★★
Hawk/Peregrine (U.K.)   PG

Ryan O'Neal *(Barry Lyndon)*, Marisa Berenson *(Lady Lyndon)*, Patrick Magee *(The Chevalier)*, Hardy Kruger *(Capt. Potzdorf)*, Steven Berkoff *(Lord Ludd)*, Gay Hamilton *(Nora)*, Leonard Rossiter *(Capt. Quin)*, Godfrey Quigley *(Capt. Grogan)*, Arthur O'Sullivan *(Highwayman)*, Diana Koerner *(German Girl)*

p, Stanley Kubrick; d, Stanley Kubrick; w, Stanley Kubrick (based on the novel by William Makepeace Thackeray); ph, John Alcott; ed, Tony Lawson; m, Leonard Rosenman; prod d, Ken Adam; art d, Roy Walker

AAN Best Picture; AAN Best Director: Stanley Kubrick; *AAN Best Adapted Screenplay:* Stanley Kubrick; *AA Best Cinematography:* John Alcott; *AA Best Score:* Leonard Rosenman; *AA Best Art Direction:* Roy Walker, Ken Adam, Vernon Dixon; *AA Best Costume Design:* Ulla-Britt Soderlund, Milena Canonero

Grave, painterly, and bitterly satirical, BARRY LYNDON baffled viewers who expected picaresque breeziness along the lines of TOM JONES. Kubrick's translation of the Thackeray novel downplays its frivolity and foregrounds its acerbic social critique. With an actor only slightly more expressive than Ryan O'Neal in the lead, this sombre costume epic might have reached the level of tragedy; as it is, the film is langorous to a fault, but so visually delightful and keenly observed that its excesses demand forgiveness.

The title character (Ryan O'Neal) is a rustic Irish boy who falls in love with a local lass (Gay Hamilton). When he threatens to disrupt her financially desirable match with an English officer (Leonard Rossiter), her family tricks him into leaving town. Barry's subsequent adventures encompass triumph and disaster: among other things, he is impressed into (and deserts from) two warring armies, becomes assistant to an itinerant society card sharp, and woos a widowed aristocrat (Marisa Berenson). His decision to marry her—dictated solely by his desire to acquire social standing—is a tragic misstep; thenceforward, Barry's life describes an inexorable downward trajectory.

BARRY LYNDON received mixed notices, but even its detractors had to concede that it was one of the most visually beautiful movies ever shot: Kubrick lavished on his film a kind of attention to period detail that remained unmatched until the release of Scorsese's THE AGE OF INNOCENCE nearly 20 years later. In an effort to recreate the look of 18th-century canvasses, the director resolved to shoot the film wholly without artificial lighting; with cinematographer John Alcott, he pioneered the indoor use of ultra-high-speed color film—some scenes are lit only by candles! Music, as always with Kubrick, is integral to the project; Irish folk tunes by The Chieftains and Schubert's E-minor Trio (which has since become something of a movie cliche) are particularly well used.

BARTON FINK

1991 116m c Comedy/Drama   ★★★½
Circle Films/Barton Circle Productions (U.S.)   R/15

John Turturro *(Barton Fink)*, John Goodman *(Charlie Meadows)*, Judy Davis *(Audrey Taylor)*, Michael Lerner *(Jack Lipnick)*, John Mahoney *(W.P. Mayhew)*, Tony Shalhoub *(Ben Geisler)*, Jon Polito *(Lou Breeze)*, Steve Buscemi *(Chet)*, David Warrilow *(Garland Stanford)*, Richard Portnow *(Detective Mastrionotti)*

p, Ethan Coen; d, Joel Coen; w, Ethan Coen, Joel Coen; ph, Roger Deakins; ed, Roderick Jaynes; m, Carter Burwell; prod d, Dennis Gassner; art d, Leslie McDonald, Bob Goldstein; fx, Robert Spurlock, Laurel Schneider; cos, Richard Hornung

AAN Best Supporting Actor: Michael Lerner; *AAN Best Art Direction:* Dennis Gassner (Art Direction), Nancy Haigh (Set Decoration); *AAN Best Costume Design:* Richard Hornung

The grand-prize winner at the 1991 Cannes festival, BARTON FINK is the fourth installment in the Coen Brothers' series of highly stylized homages to classical Hollywood. But like their earlier films, BARTON FINK is a *tour de force* of cinematic technique that encases a quirky narrative of little depth.

Barton Fink (John Turturro) is an earnest young New York playwright who hits it big with a Depression-era proletarian drama before being reluctantly seduced by a lucrative offer to go to Hollywood and write for the movies. Despite assurances that he will be given free reign by studio boss Jack Lipnick (Michael Lerner), Barton is asked to write a wrestling picture for Wallace Beery. Pent up in a surreal hotel room, Barton suffers acute and hallucinatory writer's block.

Unlike the Coen's previous works (the film noir BLOOD SIMPLE, the screwball comedy RAISING ARIZONA and the gangster film MILLER'S CROSSING), BARTON FINK is not a revisionist take on a classical genre but a bizarre, comic portrayal of the Hollywood studio system of the 1930s and 40s. The principal characters are clearly drawn from actual people in that system: Fink is a thinly veiled version of Clifford Odets, the leftist playwright who departed the socially committed Group Theatre in New York to write screenplays in Hollywood during WWII. And the dipsomaniac writer W.P. Mayhew (John Mahoney) is, of course, William Faulkner.

But the scene-stealer is Jack Lipnick, the larger-than-life movie mogul who is a composite of MGM's Louis B. Mayer and other studio heads. Michael Lerner's portrayal of Lipnick overwhelms even the fine acting of the leading players, not the least of which is Goodman's transformation from a lonely salesman into a psychotic killer. As Barton, John Turturro (DO THE RIGHT THING, MILLER'S CROSSING) can only deadpan his way amid these caricatures while careening from one baffling encounter to the next.

The film's period decor, mood lighting and artful camerawork are beautiful, at times thrilling, to look at. The surrealistic writer's block scenes, in which Barton silently watches wallpaper peel and its paste ooze, are particularly memorable—imagine ERASERHEAD in color. Ultimately, however, the look, sound and feel of this macabre comedy fail to support any coherent theme. The bombastic Philistines of Hollywood, the idealistic artists of the theater and the "common man" are all rather cruelly skewered in the film's finely polished characterizations. Much is denigrated, but little affirmed.

BASIC INSTINCT

1992 122m c Erotic/Thriller   ★★½
Carolco/Le Studio Canal Plus/Basic Inst Inc (U.S.)   R/18

Michael Douglas *(Detective Nick Curran)*, Sharon Stone *(Catherine Tramell)*, George Dzundza *(Gus)*, Jeanne Tripplehorn *(Dr. Beth Gardner)*, Denis Arndt *(Lieutenant Walker)*, Leilani Sarelle *(Roxy)*, Bruce A. Young *(Andrews)*, Chelcie Ross *(Captain Talcott)*, Dorothy Malone *(Hazel Dobkins)*, Wayne Knight *(John Correli)*

p, Alan Marshall; d, Paul Verhoeven; w, Joe Eszterhas; ph, Jan De Bont; ed, Frank J. Urioste; m, Jerry Goldsmith; prod d, Terence Marsh; cos, Ellen Mirojnick

AAN Best Editing: Frank J. Urioste; *AAN Best Score:* Jerry Goldsmith

Directed by Paul Verhoeven (SPETTERS, ROBOCOP), BASIC INSTINCT is a psychological thriller with a liberal helping of soft porn thrown in for good measure.

At first glance, Catherine Tramell (Sharon Stone) seems like a dream date. A successful novelist with a classy psychology degree, Tramell is beautiful, rich, brilliant, and oversexed. There's only one problem. Anyone who has ever been close to Tramell has died in mysterious circumstances—circumstances which have been either recreated or predicted in her novels. Is she an evil genius who tests her brilliance by destroying those around her? Or is she being set up by a diabolical rival? This is what San Francisco cop Nick Curran (Michael

Douglas) must determine after he is called in to investigate the murder of Tramell's boyfriend, a former rock star stabbed to death with an ice pick while engaging in that favorite pastime of rock stars, kinky sex.

Screenwriter Joe Eszterhas's story does generate a degree of suspense, particularly in the scenes where Tramell turns the tables on Curran; she is now writing a book based on *his* life, and rakes up some unpleasant details from the past concerning his "accidental" killing of two innocent tourists. But the screenplay also displays a flaw you would hope not to find in a $3 million script: it makes no logical sense.

The worst things about BASIC INSTINCT, though, are the explicit "love" scenes. They're supposed to contribute to a heady equation in which sex, violence and psychology are fused; instead, they're gratuitous, exploitative, and entirely unerotic.

BASKET CASE

1982   90m   c   Horror   ★★★★
Analysis   (U.S.)   /18

Kevin Van Hentenryck *(Duane Bradley)*, Terri Susan Smith *(Sharon)*, Beverly Bonner *(Casey)*, Lloyd Pace *(Dr. Harold Needleman)*, Diana Browne *(Dr. Judith Kutter)*, Robert Vogel *(Hotel Manager)*, Bill Freeman *(Dr. Julius Lifflander)*, Joe Clarke *(Brian "Mickey" O'Donovan)*, Dorothy Strongin *(Josephine)*, Ruth Neuman *(Aunt)*

p, Edgar Ievins; d, Frank Henenlotter; w, Frank Henenlotter; ph, Bruce Torbet; ed, Frank Henenlotter; m, Gus Russo; fx, Kevin Haney, John Caglione

This ultra-low-budget production was shot over the course of six months on location in the streets, apartments, and flophouses of New York City. It became a hit on the midnight-show circuit and is arguably one of the best horror films of the 1980s. Directed by Frank Henenlotter with as much style as is possible on a miniscule budget, the film centers on Duane (Van Hentenryck), a young man from Glens Falls, New York, who checks into a fleabag hotel on 42nd Street carrying a wicker basket. Inside the basket is his small, horribly misshapen Siamese twin, Belial. Communicating with Duane telepathically, Belial is determined to wreak vengeance on the physicians that separated him from his twin. Meanwhile, however, Duane has met a nice girl (Smith) and begun to make a life of his own, one that doesn't include Belial.

Disturbing, grotesque, and very funny at times, BASKET CASE is a unique work in which imagination triumphs over the limitations of budget. Blown up to 35mm from the 16mm original, the film's grainy, cheap look only enhances the seediness of Henenlotter's milieu, while, in Belial, Henenlotter has come up with one of the most memorable and sympathetic screen monsters since KING KONG. A rather cheap-looking puppet created by Kevin Haney and John Caglione, Belial has a certain shabby charm that has endeared him to horror fans throughout the world. In a film that contains many unforgettable images, perhaps the most startling—and most moving—is a flashback to Belial's childhood, in which the monster's kindly aunt lets the mutant child sit on her lap while reading aloud to him.

BATMAN

1989   126m   C   Science Fiction/Fantasy/Crime   ★★★
Warner Bros.   (U.S.)   PG-13/U

Michael Keaton *(Batman/Bruce Wayne)*, Jack Nicholson *(Joker/Jack Napier)*, Kim Basinger *(Vicki Vale)*, Robert Wuhl *(Alexander Knox)*, Pat Hingle *(Commissioner Gordon)*, Billy Dee Williams *(District Attorney Harvey Dent)*, Michael Gough *(Alfred)*, Jack Palance *(Carl Grissom)*, Jerry Hall *(Alicia)*, Lee Wallace *(Mayor)*

p, Jon Peters, Peter Guber, Chris Kenny; d, Tim Burton; w, Sam Hamm, Warren Skaaren (based on a story by Sam Hamm and characters created by Bob Kane); ph, Roger Pratt; ed, Ray Lovejoy; m, Danny Elfman; prod d, Anton Furst; art d, Leslie Tomkins, Terry Ackland-Snow, Nigel Phelps; cos, Bob Ringwood, Linda Henrikson

AA Best Art Direction: Anton Furst (Art Direction), Peter Young (Set Decoration)

Gotham City, a crime-ridden, debris-strewn, sunless, architecturally incoherent metropolis, is desperately in need of a savior, for the city is in the corrupting grip of crime boss Carl Grissom (Palance). Ace photographer Vicki Vale (Basinger) has been intrigued by the sightings of a mysterious, giant vigilante bat. She meets enigmatic millionaire

Bruce Wayne (Keaton), not suspecting that he's Batman. Wayne is quite taken with the lovely Vicki but is distracted by the wicked ways of Grissom's top henchman, Jack Napier (Nicholson), alias the Joker.

Perhaps it was inevitable, considering all the hype preceding and surrounding its release, that BATMAN would fall a bit flat once it finally reached the screen. Despite its interesting, grim tone and undeniably striking visuals from director Burton and production designer Furst, the film fails to synthesize its strengths into a compelling whole. Its obvious intention to parallel the Joker and Batman as two psychotics, one promoting good and the other evil, doesn't come through with as much impact as it should. The Joker seems maniacal, all right, but hardly as sinister as the silent Batman. In terms of acting, too, Nicholson's campy, full-blown rendering of the Joker (his best moment occurs as he pulls a ridiculously long pistol out of his pants) overshadows the miscast Keaton, whose attempt to be moody and macho gives him all the appeal of plywood.

BATMAN is dark, stylish, and full of "postmodern" touches—but wants to be more so. Given all its potential, it's a shame BATMAN wasn't more. It was, however, easily the biggest box-office hit of 1989, and one of the highest grossing films in history, a testament more to its massive marketing campaign than to its quality.

BATMAN & ROBIN

1997   130m   c   Action/Fantasy   ★★
Warner Bros.   (U.S.)   PG-13/PG

George Clooney *(Batman/Bruce Wayne)*, Chris O'Donnell *(Robin/Dick Grayson)*, Alicia Silverstone *(Batgirl/Barbara Wilson)*, Arnold Schwarzenegger *(Mr. Freeze/Dr. Victor Fries)*, Uma Thurman *(Poison Ivy/Pamela Isley)*, Elle Macpherson *(Julie Madison)*, Vendela K. Thommessen *(Nora Fries)*, Vivica A. Fox *(Ms. B. Haven)*, John Glover *(Dr. Jason Woodrue)*, Michael Gough *(Alfred Pennyworth)*

p, Peter MacGregor-Scott; d, Joel Schumacher; w, Akiva Goldsman (based on the DC Comics characters created by Bob Kane); ph, Stephen Goldblatt; ed, Dennis Virkler; m, Elliot Goldenthal; prod d, Barbara Ling; art d, Richard Holland, Geoff Hubbard; fx, John Dykstra, Andrew Adamson, Matt Sweeney, Pacific Data Images, Warner Digital, Rhythm & Hues Studios; cos, Ingird Ferrin, Robert Turturice

The fourth installment in the Batman franchise, and a victory of set decoration over such incidentals as character and plot.

Beleaguered Gotham City faces a nasty pair of costumed super-psychos: Mr. Freeze (Arnold Schwarzenegger) is stealing diamonds and frosting everyone who gets in his way, while eco-terrorist Poison Ivy (Uma Thurman) is out to wipe all warm-blooded parasites off the face of the earth so her beloved plants can reclaim the top of the food chain. Good thing Batman (George Clooney) doesn't have to go it alone. Not only does he have Robin (Chris O'Donnell) at his side, but he gains a Batgirl when Barbara Wilson (Alicia Silverstone), the niece of Bruce Wayne's loyal butler, Alfred (Michael Gough), comes to stay.

The money is on the screen in the form of empty spectacle, dressed up with ham-fisted homages to METROPOLIS, CASABLANCA, BLOND VENUS, THE BLACK CAT, THE WIZARD OF OZ, A CLOCKWORK ORANGE, Mexican wrestling movies, and much, much more. The whole cumbersome enterprise appears to be fueled by the "wouldn't it be cool?" factor: wouldn't it be cool to tart-up Thurman in green latex and really high heels, then make her talk like Mae West? Wouldn't it be cool to have CLUELESS cutie Silverstone play English school girl (accent optional) by day and cycle slut by night, shimmying into a bullet-braed Batgirl suit for a cat fight with Uma? Wouldn't it be cool to coat Schwarzenegger in silver paint and dress him up like a plastic action figure, marry him to a supermodel (Vendela), *and* have him live in an ice cream store shaped like a snowman? The result is a moving jumble sale of pop-culture allusions and expensive tchotchkes—a gee-whiz kid's movie imagined by perverse adults. How else to reconcile the juvenile puns and the rubber-clad crotch shots?

BATMAN FOREVER

1995   121m   c   Adventure/Action   ★★½
Warner Bros.   (U.S.)   PG-13/PG

Val Kilmer *(Batman/Bruce Wayne)*, Tommy Lee Jones *(Harvey Two-Face/Harvey Dent)*, Jim Carrey *(The Riddler/Edward Nygma)*, Nicole Kidman *(Dr. Chase Meridian)*, Chris O'Donnell *(Robin/Dick Grayson)*, Michael Gough *(Alfred Pennyworth)*, Pat Hingle *(Police Commissioner James Gordon)*, Debi Mazar *(Spice)*, Drew Barrymore *(Sugar)*, Ed Begley Jr. *(Fred Stickley)*

p, Tim Burton, Peter MacGregor-Scott; d, Joel Schumacher; w, Lee Batchler, Janet Scott Batchler, Akiva Goldsman (from a story by Lee Batchler and Janet Scott Batchler based on characters created by Bob Kane); ph, Stephen Goldblatt; ed, Dennis Virkler; m, Elliot Goldenthal; prod d, Barbara Ling; art d, Christopher Burian-Mohr, Joseph P. Lucky; fx, Tommy L. Fisher, John Dykstra, Illusion Arts; cos, Bob Ringwood, Ingrid Ferrin

AAN Best Cinematography: Stephen Goldblatt; *AAN Best Sound:* Donald O. Mitchell, Frank A. Montano, Michael Herbick, Petur Hliddal; *AAN Best Sound Effects:* John Leveque, Bruce Stambler

The third entry in the wildly popular BATMAN cycle boasts a new Batman, new costumes, a revamped Batmobile, and several new characters—including a Robin for the 90s, two super-villains, and yet another blonde love interest. Holy overkill!

It's not easy being the Batman (Val Kilmer). Old enemies, like the visually and psychologically bifurcated Two-Face (Tommy Lee Jones), desire revenge. Beautiful criminal psychologist Dr. Chase Meridian (Nicole Kidman) has designs on his mind and his body. A brilliant but crazed employee of Wayne Enterprises, Edward Nygma (Jim Carrey), is transformed into the Riddler, a fiendishly clever villain who joins forces with Two-Face in a scheme to brainwash the denizens of Gotham City. The emotionally conflicted hero meets the challenge with the help of his faithful butler Alfred (Michael Gough) and his new ward, Dick Grayson (Chris O'Donnell), a vengeance-driven circus acrobat who joins the fight in the heroic persona of Robin.

Warner Bros. brass deemed Tim Burton's BATMAN RETURNS too dark for kiddies, so they hired Joel Schumacher (THE CLIENT) to reimagine the series in ways more friendly to marketing tie-ins. He obliged by serving up "Batman Lite," a product made irresistible by its campy, colorful packaging, but less filling—and less satisfying—than previous incarnations. While Schumacher brings a distinctive sensibility to the project (reminiscent of the 1960s TV show), he lacks an organizing intelligence capable of accommodating so much new material. BATMAN FOREVER is a noisy riot of color with cramped, chaotic and confusing action sequences. Carrey's stylized clowning is perfect for the Riddler, but most of the other talent is wasted or underutilized. At best, it's mildly diverting, brainless fun that feels like a long trailer for a better film.

BATMAN RETURNS

1992   126m   c   Adventure/Crime/Fantasy   ★★½
Warner Bros./Polygram   (U.S.)   PG-13/12

Michael Keaton *(Batman/Bruce Wayne)*, Danny DeVito *(The Penguin/Oswald Cobblepot)*, Michelle Pfeiffer *(Catwoman/Selina Kyle)*, Christopher Walken *(Max Shreck)*, Michael Gough *(Alfred—The Butler)*, Michael Murphy *(The Mayor of Gotham)*, Cristi Conaway *(The Ice Princess)*, Andrew Bryniarski *(Chip Shreck)*, Pat Hingle *(Police Commissioner Gordon)*, Paul Reubens *(Penguin's Father)*

p, Denise DiNovi, Tim Burton; d, Tim Burton; w, Daniel Waters, Sam Hamm (from story by Waters and Hamm based on the characters by Bob Kane); ph, Stefan Czapsky; ed, Chris Lebenzon; m, Danny Elfman; prod d, Bo Welch; art d, Rick Heinrichs; fx, Michael Fink, Dennis Skotak, John Bruno, Craig Barr; cos, Bob Rigwood, Mary Vogt

AAN Best Visual Effects: Michael Fink, Craig Barron, John Bruno, Dennis Skotak; *AAN Best Makeup:* Ve Neill, Ronnie Specter, Stan Winston

Roll up! Roll up! The Bat-circus has come to town. See a whole range of new Bat-gadgets! See Michelle Pfeiffer in a skin-tight leather costume! See Danny DeVito in a lot of makeup! See some *very* expensive sets! Don't look, though, for anything resembling imagination, suspense, or humor.

From the script level, all the way through the direction, acting, and editing, BATMAN RETURNS is as much of a mess as the beleaguered Gotham City in which it is set. The paint-by-numbers story attempts a clumsy balance between fantasy and reality which ends up lost between both worlds. The production design succeeds in creating a comic-book ambience, but director Tim Burton and his screenwriters bring a heavy-handed, plodding realism to bear on what should be pop-mythic material. Neither is the perfunctory plot redeemed by the lavish action sequences; the fights and chases are incoherent and over-the-top, with the result being confusion rather than suspense.

BATTLE OF ALGIERS, THE
(MAARAKAT ALGER)

1965   120m   bw   War   ★★★★
Magna   (Italy/Algeria)   /X

Yacef Saadi *(Kader)*, Jean Martin *(Colonel)*, Brahim Haggiag *(Ali La Pointe)*, Tommaso Neri *(Captain)*, Samia Kerbash *(One of the Girls)*, Fawzia el Kader *(Halima)*, Michele Kerbash *(Fathia)*, Mohamed Ben Kassen *(Petit Omar)*

p, Antonio Musu, Yacef Saadi; d, Gillo Pontecorvo; w, Gillo Pontecorvo, Franco Solinas; ph, Marcello Gatti; ed, Mario Serandrei, Mario Morra; m, Gillo Pontecorvo, Ennio Morricone

AAN Best Foreign Language Film

A powerful battle cry for Marxist revolutionaries, THE BATTLE OF ALGIERS details the struggle for Algerian independence from France. The film opens in 1957, as a tortured Arab prisoner informs against Ali la Pointe (Haggiag), the last surviving member of the FLN (Algerian Liberation Front). As French soldiers surround Ali's apartment, Colonel Mathieu (Martin) issues a final warning to Ali and his family: surrender or be blown to pieces. With the sides clearly laid out—revolutionary vs. colonial authority—the film shifts to 1954, as the Algerian conflict first develops.

Photographed in grainy black and white to suggest the style of documentaries and TV news reports, THE BATTLE OF ALGIERS most closely resembles the neorealism of Roberto Rossellini and the revolutionary editing techniques of Sergei Eisenstein. Like Eisenstein, director Pontecorvo took his camera to the actual locations of the revolution, re-created certain events, and cast local nonprofessionals. Only Martin is a professional actor, while Saadi, the film's coproducer, plays an FLN leader—a character based on his real-life role as the organizer of the resistance and the military commander of the FLN.

The content of the film has been attacked as being too inflammatory; it was reportedly used as a terrorist primer in the late 1960s. Yet it's entirely frank about its politics, something that can't be said of most Hollywood films. What makes the movie's power creditable is Pontecorvo's ability to present combatants on both sides as multidimensional, nonheroic human beings, even though it's obvious where the director's own sentiments lie. The film received the Golden Lion at Venice in 1966.

BATTLE OF BRITAIN

1969   133m   c   War   ★★★½
Spitfire   (U.K.)   G/PG

Harry Andrews *(Senior Civil Servant)*, Michael Caine *(Squadron Leader Canfield)*, Trevor Howard *(Air Vice Marshal Keith Park)*, Curt Jurgens *(Baron von Richter)*, Ian McShane *(Sgt. Pilot Andy)*, Kenneth More *(Group Capt. Baker)*, Laurence Olivier *(Air Chief Marshal Sir Hugh Dowding)*, Nigel Patrick *(Group Capt. Hope)*, Christopher Plummer *(Squadron Leader Harvey)*, Michael Redgrave *(Air Vice Marshal Evill)*

p, Harry Saltzman, S. Benjamin Fisz; d, Guy Hamilton; w, James Kennaway, Wilfred Greatorex; ph, Freddie Young, Bob Huke; ed, Bert Bates; m, William Walton, Ron Goodwin; prod d, Sydney Streeter; art d, Maurice Carter, Bert Davey, Jack Maxsted, William Hutchinson, Gil Parrondo; fx, Cliff Richardson, Glen Robinson

This stirring if slightly overlong saga of England's WWII defense of its homeland features a staggering, star-studded cast, who abet the film's docudrama style with excellent portrayals down the line, despite the restrictions of their roles. Caine, Plummer, and More have the meatier parts, with Susannah York providing the obligatory love interest as Plummer's WAAF wife who hates the war and craves affection. Olivier is in fine form as Sir Hugh Dowding, whose crafty tactics with his limited fighter command induced the Luftwaffe to make fatal errors that led to its destruction, and Robert Shaw is superb as an exhausted but relentlessly tough fighter commander who orders his men again and again into the air.

While the film is a fitting paean to the noble RAF in its "Finest Hour," nodding recognition is also given to the Czech and Polish flyers who fought alongside their British comrades. Except for Jurgens, however, the German actors are mere caricatures of the Nazi high command, with Rolf Stiefel especially ludicrous as a berserk Hitler. The aerial photography of the German bombing and the dogfights between the British and German fighters are spectacular and fascinating; it was the high production value of these segments which cost the producers the bulk of their $12 million investment. Adolf Galland, one of the sharpest German aces to vex the British during WWII, was employed as a technical advisor on the film.

BEACH BLANKET BINGO

1965   100m   c   Musical/Comedy   ★★½
AIP   (U.S.)

Frankie Avalon (Frankie), Annette Funicello (Dee Dee), Deborah Walley (Bonnie Graham), Harvey Lembeck (Eric Von Zipper), John Ashley (Steve Gordon), Jody McCrea (Bonehead), Donna Loren (Donna), Marta Kristen (Lorelei), Linda Evans (Sugar Kane), Timothy Carey (South Dakota Slim)

p, James H. Nicholson, Samuel Z. Arkoff; d, William Asher; w, William Asher, Leo Townsend; ph, Floyd Crosby; ed, Fred R. Feitshans Jr., Eve Newman; m, Les Baxter; art d, Howard Campbell

Probably the best known of the spate of "beach party" films of the 1960s, BEACH BLANKET BINGO provides 100 minutes of silly, mildly amusing entertainment if you're in the right mood. There's trouble in teen paradise when Frankie (Avalon) and Dee Dee (Funicello) clash over his infatuation with singer Sugar Kane (Evans). Meanwhile, a mermaid falls in love with nitwit surfer Bonehead (McCrea), and the nefarious Eric Von Zipper (Lembeck) and his Rat Pack kidnap Sugar. Don Rickles, Buster Keaton, Paul Lynde and others are also on hand, sandwiching their shtick between the musical numbers from Frankie, Annette, and their scantily clad pals.

BEACHES

1988   123m   c   Drama   ★★
Touchstone/Silver Screen Partners IV/Bruckheimer   PG-13/15
South-All Girl   (U.S.)

Bette Midler (C.C. Bloom), Barbara Hershey (Hillary Whitney Essex), John Heard (John Pierce), Spalding Gray (Dr. Richard Milstein), Lainie Kazan (Leona Bloom), James Read (Michael Essex), Grace Johnston (Victoria Essex), Mayim Bialik (C.C., Age 11), Marcie Leeds (Hillary, Age 11)

p, Bonnie Bruckheimer-Martell, Bette Midler, Margaret Jennings South; d, Garry Marshall; w, Mary Agnes Donoghue (based on the novel by Iris Rainer Dart); ph, Dante Spinotti; ed, Richard Halsey; m, Georges Delerue; prod d, Albert Brenner; cos, Robert de Mora

AAN Best Art Direction: Albert Brenner (Art Direction), Garrett Lewis (Set Decoration)

This interminable melodrama purports to be a warm, humorous, and moving look at the relationship of two women over the course of 30 years. In reality BEACHES is a trite, maudlin, and terribly superficial effort of the sub-made-for-TV quality, an insult to anyone who has ever befriended another human being. The film depicts the unlikely friendship of a brassy, Jewish, Bronx-bred singer (Midler) and an icy, WASP-ish, San Francisco-bred socialite (Hershey) from their meeting in Atlantic City until the day the latter is buried, a victim of the kind of disease that seems only to afflict characters in movies like this.

An ego trip for star-executive producer Midler, the film tells its story mostly in flashback and entirely from her character's point of view, while the successful songstress drives a rented car from LA to San Francisco to be with the dying Hershey. Director Marshall fails to bring anything remotely resembling inspiration or spontaneity to screenwriter Donoghue's terribly mundane disease-of-the-week script, leaving the viewer wondering why these two women would even speak to each other, let alone commit themselves to an apparently deeply emotional relationship. The problems they face are wholly synthetic, dealt with in a flash, and forgotten until the next minicrisis comes along. There is no sense of real joy, pain, or struggle here—merely a TV version that is only tangentially related to actual human experience.

BEAR, THE

1989   93m   c   Adventure   ★★★½
Price/Renn   (France)   PG

Jack Wallace (Bill), Tcheky Karyo (Tom), Andre Lacombe (The Dog Handler), Bart the Bear (Kaar), Douce the Bear (Youk)

p, Claude Berri; d, Jean-Jacques Annaud; w, Gerard Brach (based on the novel The Grizzly King by James Oliver Curwood); ph, Philippe Rousselot; ed, Noelle Boisson; m, Philippe Sarde; prod d, Toni Ludi; art d, Heidi Ludi, Antony Greengrow, George Dietz; cos, Corinne Jorry, Francoise Disle; anim, Bretislav Pojar

AAN Best Editing: Noelle Boisson

This deceptively simple wilderness tale began production in 1982 with a four-line synopsis—"A big solitary bear. An orphan bear cub. Two hunters in the forest. The animals' point of view"—and went on to take in more than $100 million before its US release. The plot, practically nonexistent at first, unfolds in British Columbia in 1885, detailing the idyllic daily routine of a bear cub. After the cub's mother is killed in a rockslide, however, the youngster must attempt to bond with a 2000-pound Kodiak male being pursued by a pair of hunters—Bill (Wallace), a calm, calculating veteran, and his young, overeager friend Tom (Karyo).

A far cry from the sweet nature adventures that Disney popularized, THE BEAR is a sublime, graceful tale of human nature told, somewhat paradoxically, through the eyes of an animal. Director Annaud tells his story almost exclusively through visuals, using a bare minimum of dialogue and an elegantly constructed soundtrack composed from the "language" of the bears. Though the film borrows from the sophisticated techniques of such masters of silent film as D.W. Griffith and Robert Flaherty, it gives the feel of having been captured effortlessly by the cameras.

BEAT THE DEVIL

1953   100m   bw   Comedy/Drama   ★★★★
Romulus/Santana   (U.S.)   /U

Humphrey Bogart (Billy Dannreuther), Gina Lollobrigida (Maria Dannreuther), Jennifer Jones (Gwendolyn Chelm), Robert Morley (Peterson), Peter Lorre (O'Hara), Edward Underdown (Harry Chelm), Ivor Barnard (Major Ross), Marco Tulli (Ravello), Marion Perroni (Purser), Alex Pochet (Hotel Manager)

d, John Huston; w, John Huston, Truman Capote (based on the novel by James Helvick); ph, Oswald Morris; ed, Ralph Kemplen; m, Franco Mannino; art d, Wilfred Shingleton

A screwball, wacky comedy that is played as straight as any film noir and is even funnier as a result. Five desperate and disparate men (Bogart, Lorre, Morley, Barnard, and Tulli) are out to garner control over East African land which they believe contains a rich uranium ore lode. Their scuzzy steamer is in port in Italy. Bogart is married to Gina (an odd choice for the role but she proves to be more than adept at the straightfaced comedy). The other four are their "business associates," Bogart and Gina meet another couple, Jones and Underdown. She's in a blonde wig and off-the-wall; he's a prig-and-a-half at first glance but in reality, he's a phony peer. Jones rattles on about her hubby's uranium holdings, all lies. The "associates" think they are being gulled by Bogart when it appears that Bogie is after Jones and Gina is hot for Underdown.

The boat leaves for Africa, then blows up. Seven survivors make it to shore and are taken in by a hostile group of Arabs. Their lives are saved when Bogart manages to charm the evil Arab police chief by promising the man an opportunity to meet his idol, Rita Hayworth. Underdown is supposed to have drowned and this causes Jones, a pathological liar, to tell the truth. The four villains are taken in by the Italian police, then Jones gets a telegram from her still-alive husband and is delighted to learn that Underdown made it to Africa and acquired the uranium-rich land the others yearned for.

If all the aforementioned sounds like a hodge-podge, you're right. But it is such wonderful nonsense—there isn't a moment when the picture doesn't take a left turn when you expect it to turn right. Director Huston, working from a quirky, literate script by Capote, manages to parody a number of his earlier films, including THE MALTESE FALCON, THE TREASURE OF THE SIERRA MADRE, and KEY LARGO. Bogart, who, of course, was in all those films, seems to be having a marvelous time skewering them and gives a memorable performance. The film's humor is not readily apparent, and the movie was quickly rejected by the public upon its release. But today it has achieved something of a cult following and is a sheer delight.

BEAU GESTE

1939 114m bw Adventure/War   ★★★½
Paramount (U.S.)   /A

Gary Cooper (Michael "Beau" Geste), Ray Milland (John Geste), Robert Preston (Digby Geste), Brian Donlevy (Sgt. Markoff), Susan Hayward (Isobel Rivers), J. Carrol Naish (Rasinoff), Albert Dekker (Schwartz), Broderick Crawford (Hank Miller), Charles Barton (Buddy McMonigal), James Stephenson (Maj. Henri de Beaujolais)

p, William A. Wellman; d, William A. Wellman; w, Robert Carson (based on the novel by Percival Christopher Wren); ph, Theodor Sparkuhl, Archie Stout; ed, Thomas Scott; m, Alfred Newman; art d, Hans Dreier, Robert Odell

AAN Best Supporting Actor: Brian Donlevy; *AAN Best Art Direction:* Hans Dreier (Art Direction), Robert Odell (Art Direction)

Gary Cooper enacts the title role with quiet magnificence in this superb adventure tale loaded with drama, action, and mystery. The film opens with a relief column of Legionnaires crossing the desert dunes to Fort Zinderneuf. The fort seems strangely silent and a bugler is sent to investigate. He finds all inside the fort dead, and notices a sergeant on the parapet in whose hand is a note confessing to the theft of a fabulous gem called "the Blue Water." When the column enters the fort, the body of the sergeant is gone. Next the troops hear shots outside the fort and pursue what they think are tribal invaders. The fort suddenly erupts into flames, setting off the arsenal which destroys Zinderneuf.

In a flashback to 15 years earlier, we see three boys, the Geste brothers, at a great English mansion. The boys are cared for by kindly Thatcher, an impoverished blueblood who is so desperate to give the orphaned brothers and another child, Gillis, a good home that she secretly sells the treasured family jewel, the Blue Water, to raise the necessary funds. O'Connor secretly witnesses the transaction and watches Thatcher replace the gem with a fake. Years later, with O'Connor grown into Cooper, his brothers grown into Milland and Preston, and Gillis bloomed into Hayward, the lord of the manor, Huntley, appears seeking the great sapphire. To prevent Thatcher from having to admit her secret transaction, Cooper steals the phony gem, leaves a note for his brothers admitting the theft, and joins the Foreign Legion.

Cooper's great performance is given solid support by Ray Milland and Robert Preston, but Susan Hayward appears only briefly as the love interest and her performance is unmemorable. Brian Donlevy almost steals every scene he's in with a snarling performance that will scare the blazes out of any viewer, and J. Carrol Naish's hyena-like Rasinoff is unforgettable. Great support also comes from veteran heavies Albert Dekker, Harry Woods, and Harold Huber, enacting the mutinous Legionnaires. Broderick Crawford and Charles Barton provide the comic relief as the Gestes' sidekicks.

When director William Wellman was brought in to remake the silent 1926 version of P.C. Wren's captivating story, he was instructed to follow the original almost to the letter, which he did, even using the same location, the spreading desert dunes of Yuma, Arizona, where a new Fort Zinderneuf was completely rebuilt. Paramount executives thought it would be impressive to run the first reel of the silent version before showing the 1939 remake to reviewers, to show what sound could do to improve a classic. It was a scheme that almost blew up in their faces; some reviewers still preferred the silent version, but most felt that the remake was superior.

BEAUTY AND THE BEAST
(LA BELLE ET LA BETE)

1946 90m bw Science Fiction/Fantasy   ★★★★★
Discina (France)   /PG

Jean Marais (Avenant/The Beast/The Prince), Josette Day (Beauty), Marcel Andre (The Merchant), Mila Parely (Adelaide), Nane Germon (Felice), Michel Auclair (Ludovic)

p, Andre Paulve; d, Jean Cocteau; w, Jean Cocteau (based on the fairy tale by Mme. Leprince de Beaumont); ph, Henri Alekan; ed, Claude Iberia; m, Georges Auric; art d, Christian Berard

A masterpiece. The great Jean Cocteau has written that in order for a myth to live it must continually be told and retold, and this is just what Cocteau does in BEAUTY AND THE BEAST—bringing Mme. Marie Leprince de Beaumont's 1757 fairy tale to the screen. Beauty (Josette Day) and the Beast (Jean Marais) are given a new life in the cinema thanks to Cocteau's poetry, Henri Alekan's cinematography, Georges Auric's music, and Christian Berard's art direction. The legend is familiar: a merchant's beautiful daughter saves her father's life by agreeing to visit the diabolical Beast, a fearsome creature with magical powers. Beauty faints with horror upon their first meeting, but gradually grows to love the Beast, finding the soul that exists beneath his gruesome exterior.

While the narrative is basic and familiar, the film's visuals are not. A magical white horse blazes across the screen; the Beast's hands smoke after a kill; the hanging white laundry of Beauty's family billows in the breeze; the Beast's fantastical candelabras are human arms that extend from the walls and emerge from the dinner table. It is a credit to Cocteau's genius (and to that of his collaborators) that he has taken the unreal world of a fairy tale and made it as real as the world around us.

BEAUTY AND THE BEAST

1991 84m c Animated/Musical/Romance   ★★★★½
Walt Disney Productions/Silver Screen Partners IV (U.S.) G/U

VOICES OF: Paige O'Hara (Belle), Robby Benson (Beast), Rex Everhart (Maurice), Richard White (Gaston), Jesse Corti (Le Fou), Angela Lansbury (Mrs. Potts), Jerry Orbach (Lumiere), David Ogden Stiers (Cogsworth/Narrator), Bradley Michael Pierce (Chip), Hal Smith (Philippe)

p, Don Hahn; d, Kirk Wise, Gary Trousdale; w, Linda Woolverton (from the story by Kelly Asbury, Brenda Chapman, Tom Ellery, Kevin Harkey, Robert Lence, Burny Mattinson, Brian Pimental, Joe Ranft, Christopher Sanders and Bruce Woodside); ed, John Carnochan; m, Alan Menken; art d, Brian McEntee; anim, Roger Allers, Ed Ghertner, Lisa Keene, Vera Lanpher, Randy Fullmer, Jim Hillin

AA Best Score: Alan Menken; *AA Best Song:* Alan Menken (Music), Howard Ashman (Lyrics); *AAN Best Picture; AAN Best Sound:* Terry Porter, Mel Metcalfe, David J. Hudson, Doc Kane

BEAUTY AND THE BEAST is a nostalgic feast, drawing shamelessly on the best traditions of screen animation and American musical theater and film. Thoroughly derivative but thoroughly charming.

Belle (Paige O'Hara) is a beautiful young woman in a small French town who dreams of escape, fending off advances from the handsome, but arrogant and chauvinistic Gaston (Richard White). Belle's father is lost in a dark wood and seeks refuge in an enchanted castle, lorded over by the Beast (Robby Benson), a spoiled young prince transformed by an enchantress into a hideous monster. The spell has transformed his castle into a dank, gloomy lair and his servants into household bric-a-brac. Enraged that Maurice has violated the castle grounds, the Beast locks him in a dungeon. When her father's horse returns home without him, Belle sets off in pursuit and finds her way to the castle, where the Beast agrees to let her father leave if she will remain in his stead—forever.

The familiar narrative is strengthened by the independent, self-assured character of Belle. Unlike Disney heroines from Snow White through Ariel, Belle is smart, knows what she wants, and doesn't spend her time pining away for the love of a handsome prince. Howard Ashman and Alan Menken propel the plot and character development along with their tuneful, witty and textured songs. As they enrich the palette of the narrative, they also invite comparison with some of the past glories of the American musical theater—from the opening numbers of *Fiddler on the Roof* and *She Loves Me* (the teeming "Belle" opener), the love soliloquies from *South Pacific* (the touching "Something There" soliloquies of Belle and the Beast), the "Shall We Dance?" waltz from *The King and I* (the soaring "Beauty and the Beast" waltz), to crowd-pleasing production numbers from Jerry Herman's *Hello Dolly* and *Mame* (the boisterous "Be Our Guest").

All this, though, would mean nothing if the animation were not of a standard to compare with the rest of the elements. It is. Using computer wizardry to simulate live-action film techniques like dollies, tracks and pans, the animation succeeds in creating an uncannily realistic world. The filmmakers have used considerable depth of field, permitting action to occur on many levels of the frame, from background to foreground, and to move, not only horizontally, but also back and forth from the camera eye. The camera sweeps above forests and down into castle chambers, and races around characters in 360 degree tracks. This is catnip for the kids, and should keep even the most jaded adults awake for the film's blessedly crisp 84 minutes.

BECKET

1964   148m   c   Historical   ★★★★
Paramount   (U.K.)   /PG

Richard Burton *(Thomas Becket)*, Peter O'Toole *(King Henry II)*, Donald Wolfit *(Bishop Folliot)*, John Gielgud *(King Louis VII)*, Martita Hunt *(Queen Matilda)*, Pamela Brown *(Queen Eleanor)*, Sian Phillips *(Gwendolyn)*, Paolo Stoppa *(Pope Alexander III)*, Gino Cervi *(Cardinal Zambelli)*, David Weston *(Brother John)*

p, Hal B. Wallis; d, Peter Glenville; w, Edward Anhalt (based on the play by Jean Anouilh); ph, Geoffrey Unsworth; ed, Anne V. Coates; m, Laurence Rosenthal; prod d, John Bryan; art d, Maurice Carter; cos, Margaret Furse

AAN Best Picture; AAN Best Actor: Richard Burton; *AAN Best Actor:* Peter O'Toole; *AAN Best Supporting Actor:* John Gielgud; *AAN Best Director:* Peter Glenville; *AA Best Adapted Screenplay:* Edward Anhalt; *AAN Best Cinematography:* Geoffrey Unsworth; *AAN Best Editing:* Anne Coates; *AAN Best Score:* Laurence Rosenthal; *AAN Best Art Direction:* John Bryan, Maurice Carter, Patrick McLoughlin, Robert Cartwright; *AAN Best Costume Design:* Margaret Furse; *AAN Best Sound:* John Cox

This notable improvement over the stage-bound Anouilh play recounts the story of two great friends turned unintentional foes, Becket (Richard Burton) and Henry II (Peter O'Toole). Becket is Henry's chancellor until consecrated Archbishop of Canterbury, almost in jest, by Henry. Becket takes the job seriously and defends the church from royal onslaught. The two men drift further apart as Becket goes deeper into his ecclesiastical role, and the king realizes that his former friend must be killed after the two men meet for an attempted reconciliation in a wonderful scene on horseback at a British beach.

Ostensibly a story regarding the separation of church and state, Anouilh and Anhalt followed history closely and added their own undercurrent of homoerotic tension between the men, although this is so subtle that it was lost on many viewers. All technical credits are excellent and so are the performances. Many wonderful touches abound, including the scene wherein forks are introduced to the court. Wallis, whose career spanned six decades (everything from LITTLE CAESAR, CASABLANCA, and GUNFIGHT AT THE O.K. CORRAL to various Elvis Presley films) established himself in the pantheon of producers with this film.

BECKY SHARP

1935   83m   c   Drama   ★★½
Pioneer   (U.S.)   /A

Miriam Hopkins *(Becky Sharp)*, Frances Dee *(Amelia Sedley)*, Cedric Hardwicke *(Marquis of Steyne)*, Billie Burke *(Lady Bareacres)*, Alison Skipworth *(Miss Crawley)*, Nigel Bruce *(Joseph Sedley)*, Alan Mowbray *(Rawdon Crawley)*, Colin Tapley *(William Dobbin)*, G.P. Huntley Jr. *(George Osborne)*, William Stack *(Pitt Crawley)*

p, Kenneth MacGowan; d, Rouben Mamoulian; w, Francis Edwards Faragoh (based on a play by Langdon Mitchell and *Vanity Fair* by William Makepeace Thackeray); ph, Ray Rennahan; ed, Archie Marshek; m, Roy Webb; prod d, Robert Jones; chor, Russell Lewis

Landmark technicolor, but otherwise very flat indeed. Third version of *Vanity Fair* was a troubled production with original director Lowell Sherman dying, Mamoulian starting over. Hopkins always excelled at predatory roles, but unless flawlessly scripted and sat on by a director, her characterizations invariably went over the top. Watch if you want to see her play to the second balcony, otherwise be on the lookout for rare 1932 version with Myrna Loy. BECKY SHARP wasn't fine enough to make everyone race to film in color; it would take four more years with three mammoth MGM successes—GONE WITH THE WIND and THE WIZARD OF OZ among them—before it started to *really* take off.

BED AND BOARD

1970   95m   c   Drama   ★★½
Carrosse/Valoria   (France/Italy)   /A

Jean-Pierre Leaud *(Antoine)*, Claude Jade *(Christine)*, Hiroko Berghauer *(Kyoko)*, Barbara Laage *(Executive Secretary)*, Daniel Ceccaldi *(M. Darbon)*, Claire Duhamel *(Mme. Darbon)*, Pierre Fabre *(The Sneerer)*, Claude Vega *(Strangler)*, Billy Kearns *(American Customer)*, Daniel Boulanger *(Tenor)*

p, Francois Truffaut; d, Francois Truffaut; w, Francois Truffaut, Claude de Givray, Bernard Revon; ph, Nestor Almendros; art d, Jean Mandaroux

Part of the continuing saga of that fun-loving Frenchman, Antoine Doinel, played hungrily by Leaud. He falls in love with and marries Jade, fathers a child, then experiments with adultery by having an uninteresting affair with Berghauer before the close-out. Director Truffaut's dwelling upon scenes thought to be tender is really a matter of self-indulgence. There simply isn't enough story, and most of the characters remain inert.

BED SITTING ROOM, THE

1969   80m   c   Comedy   ★★★
UA   (U.K.)   /AA

Rita Tushingham *(Penelope)*, Ralph Richardson *(Lord Fortnum)*, Peter Cook *(Inspector)*, Dudley Moore *(Sergeant)*, Spike Milligan *(Mate)*, Michael Hordern *(Blues Martin)*, Roy Kinnear *(Plastic Mac Man)*, Richard Warwick *(Allan)*, Arthur Lowe *(Father)*, Mona Washbourne *(Mother)*

p, Richard Lester; d, Richard Lester; w, John Antrobus, Charles Wood (based on a play by Antrobus and Spike Milligan); ph, David Watkin; ed, John Victor Smith; m, Ken Horne

A field day for funny collection of Brits. Weird picture originated in a well-known weird place, the mind of "Goon Show" alumnus Spike Milligan. An offbeat look at London after the bombs have been dropped, this episodic film follows several Blitz survivors (many of them played by British TV stars) as they make their way through the ruins of their great city. Lowe turns into a parrot, Washbourne becomes a chest of drawers, Tushingham announces that she's 17 months pregnant, and Richardson metamorphoses into a bed sitting room! Although the basic situation may not be the funniest set-up imaginable, the players manage to keep the laughs flying thick and fast. Former Goons Cook and Moore are side-splittingly funny as government bureaucrats; Marty Feldman makes his debut.

BEDAZZLED

1967 104m c Comedy ★★★½
Fox (U.K.) /PG

Peter Cook *(George Spiggot)*, Dudley Moore *(Stanley Moon)*, Eleanor Bron *(Margaret)*, Raquel Welch *(Lillian Lust)*, Alba *(Vanity)*, Robert Russell *(Anger)*, Barry Humphries *(Envy)*, Parnell McGarry *(Gluttony)*, Daniele Noel *(Avarice)*, Howard Goorney *(Sloth)*

p, Stanley Donen; d, Stanley Donen; w, Peter Cook (based on a story by Cook, Dudley Moore); ph, Austin Dempster; ed, Richard Marden; m, Dudley Moore

Chic Faust update by Cook and Moore, latter as Faust, Cook as Satan. Raquel is humorless as usual, upstaged to high hell by sexy Eleanor Bron. Quite good indeed from Stanley Donen. And dig the Julie Andrews bit.

BEDKNOBS AND BROOMSTICKS

1971 117m c Fantasy ★★★
Walt Disney Productions (U.S.) G/U

Angela Lansbury *(Eglantine Price)*, David Tomlinson *(Emelius Browne)*, Roddy McDowall *(Mr. Jelk)*, Sam Jaffe *(Bookman)*, John Ericson *(Col. Heller)*, Bruce Forsyth *(Swinburne)*, Reginald Owen *(Gen. Teagler)*, Tessie O'Shea *(Mrs. Hobday)*, Arthur Gould-Porter *(Capt. Greer)*, Ben Wrigley *(Street Sweeper)*

p, Bill Walsh; d, Robert Stevenson; w, Bill Walsh, Don DaGradi (based on the book by Mary Norton); ph, Frank Phillips; ed, Cotton Warburton; art d, Peter Ellenshaw, John B. Mansbridge; fx, Danny Lee, Eustace Lycett, Alan Maley; cos, Bill Thomas; anim, Ward Kimball

AAN Best Score: Richard M. Sherman, Robert B. Sherman, Irwin Kostal; *AAN Best Song:* Richard M. Sherman, Robert B. Sherman; *AAN Best Art Direction:* John B. Mansbridge, Peter Ellenshaw, Emile Kuri, Hal Gausman; *AAN Best Costume Design:* Bill Thomas; *AA Best Visual Effects:* Alan Maley, Eustace Lycett, Danny Lee

Similar in many ways to MARY POPPINS, BEDKNOBS AND BROOMSTICKS is filled with unique special effects and delightful music. Angela Lansbury stars as Eglantine Price, the owner of a seaside house in England who has three children foisted on her during WWII. At first, the children aren't thrilled about being relocated. Then they learn that Eglantine is studying witchcraft by mail and has much mischief planned for the Nazis if they ever land in England. With a bedstead as their magic carpet, Eglantine takes the kids on a wonderful ride into several fantastic worlds. Animation is neatly mixed with live action, and Lansbury, engaging as ever, heads a capable cast.

BEDTIME FOR BONZO

1951 83m bw Comedy ★★½
Universal (U.S.) /U

Ronald Reagan *(Prof. Peter Boyd)*, Diana Lynn *(Jane)*, Walter Slezak *(Prof. Hans Neumann)*, Lucille Barkley *(Valerie Tillinghast)*, Jesse White *(Babcock)*, Herbert Heyes *(Dean Tillinghast)*, Herb Vigran *(Lt. Daggett)*, Harry Tyler *(Knicksy)*, Edward Clark *(Fosdick)*, Edward Gargan *(Policeman)*

p, Michel Kraike; d, Frederick de Cordova; w, Val Burton, Lou Breslow (based on a story by Raphael Blau, Ted Berkman); ph, Carl Guthrie; ed, Ted J. Kent; m, Frank Skinner

Cult comeuppance. For once Reagan is in synch with his costar, but Bonzo the chimp proved the more able farceur. Animal fans will be saddened to know Bonzo and four stand-ins died tragically in a trailer fire. (Had it been Reagan, young American filmmakers might be better funded today.) The first assignment for Freddie de Cordova, longtime producer of the "Tonight Show." We all gotta start somewhere. A sequel followed—BONZO GOES TO COLLEGE—sans Reagan, who apparently couldn't handle the academic overload.

BEETLEJUICE

1988 92m c Comedy/Horror ★★★½
Geffen (U.S.) PG/15

Alec Baldwin *(Adam Maitland)*, Geena Davis *(Barbara Maitland)*, Michael Keaton *(Betelgeuse)*, Catherine O'Hara *(Delia Deetz)*, Glenn Shadix *(Otho)*, Winona Ryder *(Lydia Deetz)*, Jeffrey Jones *(Charles Deetz)*, Sylvia Sidney *(Juno)*, Patrice Martinez *(Receptionist)*, Robert Goulet *(Maxie Dean)*

p, Richard Hashimoto, Larry Wilson, Michael Bender; d, Tim Burton; w, Michael McDowell, Warren Skaaren (based on a story by McDowell, Larry Wilson); ph, Thomas Ackerman; ed, Jane Kurson; m, Danny Elfman; prod d, Bo Welch; fx, Chuck Gaspar, Robert Short; chor, Chrissy Bocchino; cos, Aggie Guerard Rodgers

AA Best Makeup: Ve Neill, Steve LaPorte, Robert Short

A surreal, demented delight. The long-awaited second film from wunderkind director Tim Burton is a wildly inventive, unique horror comedy that plays like a twisted, surrealistic, cartoon remake of TOPPER (1937). Keaton is in rare form leading the haunt, rivaled by virtuoso Sidney as overloaded other side caseworker. Film won a much deserved Oscar for Best Achievement in Makeup.

BEFORE SUNRISE

1995 101m c Romance/Comedy/Drama ★★★½
Detour Film/Filmhaus/Castle Rock Entertainment (U.S.) R/15

Ethan Hawke *(Jesse)*, Julie Delpy *(Celine)*, Andrea Eckert *(Wife on Train)*, Hanno Poschl *(Husband on Train)*, Karl Bruckschwaiger *(Guy on Bridge)*, Tex Rubinowitz *(Guy on Bridge)*, Erni Mangold *(Palm Reader)*, Dominik Castell *(Street Poet)*, Haymon Maria Buttinger *(Bartender)*, Harold Waiglein *(Guitarist in Club)*

p, Anne Walker-McBay; d, Richard Linklater; w, Richard Linklater, Kim Krizan; ph, Lee Daniel; ed, Sandra Adair; prod d, Florian Reichmann; cos, Florentina Welley

Director Richard Linklater's third feature is a wry, winning portrait of a brief encounter between two young people who meet on a train, spend the night in Vienna and then part, defying Hollywood conventions of character and story development to charming effect.

The film has little plot in the mainstream sense of that term. Jesse (Ethan Hawke), a young American man, meets Celine (Julie Delpy), a French college student, on a train heading to Austria. The two begin to talk, and do little else for the next 101 minutes. Richard Linklater surprised many viewers by making an unapologetically romantic movie after the less conventionally sentimental SLACKER and DAZED AND CONFUSED. But BEFORE SUNRISE is a logical extension of Linklater's interests, particularly intertextual cultural references and rambling philosophical prattle. It feels like an American Eric Rohmer movie (imagine both the best and the worst that implies), defined by intimate yet heated conversations about life, art, love, religion, sex, and politics.

BEFORE SUNRISE leans heavily on the appeal of its leads, who are in virtually every shot and helped develop the dialogue during the improvisational rehearsal period. Ethan Hawke rises to the occasion, delivering a relaxed, engaging performance as Jesse. Julie Delpy of KILLING ZOE and THREE COLORS: WHITE is a revelation as Celine. The film's only real flaw is its failure to address the viewer's nagging feeling that in real life, the sweetly grave Celine would quickly tire of the rather callow Jessie. Still, it's encouraging to see a major Hollywood studio release a film that allows these characters to take center stage and keep it.

BEFORE THE RAIN
(PO DEZJU)

1994 115m c Drama/War/Political ★★★★
Vardar Film/Aim Productions/Noe Productions /15
(Macedonia/U.K./France)

Katrin Cartlidge *(Anne)*, Rade Serbedzija *(Aleksandar)*, Gregoire Colin *(Kiril)*, Labina Mitevska *(Zamira)*, Jay Villiers *(Nick)*, Silvija Stojanovska *(Hana)*, Phyllida Law *(Anne's Mother)*, Josif Josifovski *(Father Marko)*, Boris Delcevski *(Petre)*, Dejan Velkov *(Mate)*

p, Judy Counihan, Cedomir Kolar, Sam Taylor, Cat Villiers; d, Milcho Manchevski; w, Milcho Manchevski; ph, Manuel Teran; ed, Nicolas Gaster; m, Anastasia; prod d, Sharon Lamofsky, David Munns; fx, Valentin Lozey, John Fontana, Vasil Dikov; cos, Caroline Harris, Sue Yelland

Billed as the first feature made in the newly declared republic of Macedonia, formerly a region of Yugoslavia, Milcho Manchevski's film is a glossy, mystical, ultimately pessimistic take on the worldwide ripples caused by the Balkan genocide.

In Manchevski's elliptical three-part narrative, a young monk (Gregoire Colin) shelters a Muslim girl (Labina Mitevska); a trendy Londoner (Katrin Cartlidge, NAKED) struggles with some unanticipated personal consequences of war; a Macedonian photographer (Rade Serbedzija) returns to the village of his childhood and finds it changed beyond recognition. BEFORE THE RAIN won the Golden Lion (Best Picture) award at the 1994 Venice Film Festival and was nominated for that year's best foreign-language film Oscar. Released theatrically in the US in 1995, it enjoyed wide critical acclaim and was sometimes compared to another Oscar nominee, PULP FICTION, which employed a similarly unconventional structure. Though the two films are completely divergent in theme and subject matter, both tell their stories out of chronological order. The circular structure of BEFORE THE RAIN adds to its impact. Near the end of the third segment, the viewer realizes that the three seemingly separate stories are interconnected, and that events are racing toward an inevitable, tragic conclusion.

Technically superior in every department, BEFORE THE RAIN features achingly beautiful Macedonian landscapes, lovingly exploited by cinematographer Manuel Teran. The visually stunning, vibrantly colorful Macedonian segments stand in stark contrast to the harsh, gray London settings. This disparity reiterates one of the film's messages: war in one region affects another, no matter how far removed geographically or culturally.

BEFORE THE REVOLUTION
(PRIMA DELLA REVOLUTIONA)

1964	115m	bw	Drama	★½
Cineriz	(Italy)			/X

Adriana Asti (Gina), Francesco Barilli (Boy), Allen Midgette (Agostino), Morando Morandini (Teacher)

d, Bernardo Bertolucci; w, Bernardo Bertolucci; ph, Aldo Scavarda; ed, Roberto Perpignani; m, Gino Paoli

When the poor friend of an upper-class boy commits suicide, the wealthy lad, Barilli, begins to question his own life and outlook. Considerable appeal in evidence, but only during talking jags.

BEGGAR'S OPERA, THE

1952	94m	c	Musical	★★★
Imperadio	(U.K.)			/U

Laurence Olivier (Capt. MacHeath), Stanley Holloway (Lockit), George Devine (Peachum), Mary Clare (Mrs. Peachum), Athene Seyler (Mrs. Trapes), Dorothy Tutin (Polly Peachum), Daphne Anderson (Lucy Lockit), Hugh Griffith (The Beggar), Margot Grahame (The Actress), Denis Cannan (The Footman)

p, Laurence Olivier, Herbert Wilcox; d, Peter Brook; w, Denis Cannan, Christopher Fry (based on the comic opera by John Gay); ph, Guy Green; ed, Reginald Beck; m, Arthur Bliss

Eclectic, thoughtful, but not an unmitigated smash. The esteemed Brook made his film directing debut with THE BEGGAR'S OPERA, an attempt at re-creating John Gay's original play on film. (It was also done as The Threepenny Opera with a score by Bertolt Brecht and Kurt Weill.) The music in this version is by Sir Arthur Bliss, with lyrics by Christopher Fry (The Lady's Not For Burning) as well as some additional dialogue for the Cannan screenplay. Olivier stars as MacHeath, with Holloway as Lockit, Griffith as the Beggar, and the wonderful Seyler (who gave one of the funniest performances in any comedy in MAKE MINE MINK and for years specialized in classical stage work) as Mrs. Trapes. Olivier provides a play-within-a-play as a prisoner in Newgate who creates an opera based on his own life.

It's all very complex and may have been better done in MAN OF LA MANCHA. This is an ambitious project that never quite comes off. Olivier and Holloway did their own singing, but the others were dubbed. Olivier is no Howard Keel and lacks the inherent sexiness to play MacHeath; he did well to stay out of musicals, unless doing character singing like THE ENTERTAINER. Bold attempt failed at the box office, but, for film enthusiasts, it remains an interesting curiosity.

BEING THERE

1979	130m	c	Comedy	★★★★
Lorimar	(U.S.)			PG/15

Peter Sellers (Chance), Shirley MacLaine (Eve Rand), Melvyn Douglas (Benjamin Rand), Jack Warden (President Bobby), Richard Dysart (Dr. Robert Allenby), Richard Basehart (Vladmir Skrapinov), Ruth Attaway (Louise), David Clennon (Thomas Franklin), Fran Brill (Sally Hayes), Denise DuBarry (Johanna Franklin)

p, Andrew Braunsberg; d, Hal Ashby; w, Jerzy Kosinski (based on his novel); ph, Caleb Deschanel; ed, Don Zimmerman; m, Johnny Mandel; art d, James Schoppe

AAN Best Actor: Peter Sellers; AA Best Supporting Actor: Melvyn Douglas

Deft fable of innocence's wisdom. Jerzy Kosinski's modern fable gets a terrific translation to the screen due to his tight screenplay, capable direction by Ashby, and a marvelous performance by Sellers, one unlike any other in his career. Simpleton becomes wealthy and famous, but flimsy idea goes on too long. MacLaine is funny as the sex-starved wife who at first is amusedly captivated by Sellers then falls in love with him. Deschanel's stunning cinematography also deserves praise, as does Mandel's very appropriate score. Sellers was nominated for a Best Actor Oscar but lost to Dustin Hoffman for KRAMER VS. KRAMER, while Douglas won his second Academy Award for Best Supporting Actor (his first came for HUD in 1963). Filmed in Washington, DC; Los Angeles; and at the Biltmore, the Vanderbilts' North Carolina mansion.

BELLE DE JOUR

1967	100m	c	Drama	★★★★½
Paris	(France)			/18

Catherine Deneuve (Severine Serizy), Jean Sorel (Pierre Serizy), Michel Piccoli (Henri Husson), Genevieve Page (Mme. Anais), Pierre Clementi (Marcel), Francisco Rabal (Hippolyte), Francoise Fabian (Charlotte), Maria Latour (Mathilde), Georges Marchal (The Duke), Macha Meril (Renee Fevret)

p, Robert Hakim, Raymond Hakim; d, Luis Bunuel; w, Luis Bunuel, Jean-Claude Carriere (based on the novel by Joseph Kessel); ph, Sacha Vierny; ed, Walter Spohr; art d, Robert Clavel

A delightful puzzle, and Deneuve's finest hour-and-a-half. She plays a happily married middle-class woman who genuinely loves, but is unable to feel passionate toward, her husband, a successful surgeon. She eventually finds fulfilment of a kind by pursing a career as a high-class, afternoons-only (hence "Belle de Jour") prostitute.

As the film opens, a handsome young 19th-century couple (Jean Sorel, Catherine Deneuve) whisper sweet nothings to each other during a carriage ride through a beautiful country estate. Suddenly and inexplicably angered, the man orders his partner out of the carriage, and has the two drivers drag her to a nearby tree, to which she is tied and subjected to a brutal whipping. The man then casually tells the drivers to rape her. Cut to the young woman lounging in bed in a modern-day Paris bedroom, where she has fantasized the entire sequence. Or has she?

Nothing else in BELLE DE JOUR quite lives up to the exquisite jolt of that first shift from fantasy to reality, or vice versa. Throughout, Bunuel juggles scenes that may be "real" with others that seem like dreams or wish-fulfilments. But, by the end, the technique seems more like a means of toying with the audience than a genuine correlative for the protagonist's conflicted state of mind. The result is almost, but not quite, a great movie—as opaque as its central character, it teases and intrigues, but falls short of delivering emotional satisfaction. Essential viewing, though, if only for Deneuve's signature performance. Pierre Clementi also shines in the role of a brutal young hood who develops an obsession with "Belle." Having been withdrawn from circulation by its producers at the end of the 1970s, BELLE DE JOUR was re-released theatrically (and billed as "presented by Martin Scorsese") in 1995 by Miramax Zoe, a new division of the independent juggernaut devoted to "rescuing" lost French classics.

BELLE EPOQUE

1992   108m   c   Comedy/Historical/Romance   ★★★
Fernando Trueba PC/Lola Films/Anematorgrafo/French   R/15
Productions   (Spain/France/Portugal)

Fernando-Fernan Gomez (Manolo), Jorge Sanz (Fernando), Maribel Verdu (Rocio), Ariadna Gil (Violetta), Miriam Diaz-Aroca (Clara), Penelope Cruz (Luz), Mary Carmen Ramirez (Amalia—Manolo's Wife), Michel Galabru (Danglard—Amalia's Manager), Gabino Diego (Juanito—Rocio's Suitor), Chus Lampreave (Dona Asun—Juanito's Mother)

p, Andres Vincente Gomez; d, Fernando Trueba; w, Rafael Azcona (from a story by Azcona, Jose Louis Garcia Sanchez and Fernando Trueba); ph, Jose Luis Alcaine; ed, Carmen Frias; m, Antoine Duhamel; art d, Juan Botella

AA Best Foreign Language Film

A deftly orchestrated romantic comedy that treats a turbulent historical period lightheartedly, yet without completely avoiding political realities; the film's infectious good spirits spring from an engaging story, well-developed characters, and adroit casting.

"Somewhere in Spain, in 1931." Fernando (Jorge Sanz), a young ex-seminarian defecting from the Army after the King's abdication, befriends Manolo (Fernando Fernan-Gomez), a free-thinking, self-proclaimed "heathen, rebel, and libertine" who invites Fernando to his home. Manolo later takes Fernando to the train station so he can flee to Madrid, but a look at the older man's four daughters compels Fernando to "miss" his train and lodge in Manolo's house. All the daughters—proper young widow Clara (Miriam Diaz-Aroca), frivolous, strong-willed Rocio (Maribel Verdu), aggressive, self-assertive Violeta (Ariadna Gil), and sweet, romantic Luz (Penelope Cruz)—subtly but surely pursue and seduce him, and shy Fernando is confused as to which of the ladies he loves.

Though the plot sounds like a salacious "farmer's daughters" joke, the four sisters are richly enough written to evade stereotypes. BELLE EPOQUE's one miscalculation comes at the denouement, when a tragedy shatters the otherwise merry atmosphere. Clearly meant to bring home the tensions and uncertainty of the time, and as a premonition of the civil war to come, it is an abrupt, unexpected turn, discordant in an otherwise lyrical, lightweight entertainment.

BELLES OF ST. TRINIAN'S, THE

1954   91m   bw   Comedy   ★★★
London Films   (U.K.)   /U

Alastair Sim (Millicent Fritton/ Clarence Fritton), Joyce Grenfell (Sgt. Ruby Gates), George Cole (Flash Harry), Vivienne Martin (Arabella), Eric Pohlmann (Sultan of Makyad), Lorna Henderson (Princess Fatima), Hermione Baddeley (Miss Drownder), Betty Ann Davies (Miss Waters), Renee Houston (Miss Brimmer), Beryl Reid (Miss Dawn)

p, Frank Launder, Sidney Gilliat; d, Frank Launder; w, Frank Launder, Sidney Gilliat, Val Valentine; ph, Stanley Pavey; ed, Thelma Connell; m, Malcolm Arnold

Monstrously fun. This is a very funny comedy based on Ronald Searles's cartoons of a horrid girls' school known as St. Trinian's. The plot has to do with the horsenapping of a famous steed that is foiled by some of the school's pupils. Among the girls' antics is using the school's science lab to make gin, which is then sold by the crooked Flash Harry (George Cole). Alastair Sim is brilliant in two roles, playing the headmistress as well as her ne'er-do-well brother. Joyce Grenfell is also quite amusing as a police spy. This one was a winner, spawning less successful sequels BLUE MURDER AT ST. TRINIAN'S, THE PURE HELL OF ST. TRINIAN'S, and THE GREAT ST. TRINIAN'S TRAIN ROBBERY.

BELLS ARE RINGING

1960   126m   c   Musical/Comedy   ★★★½
MGM   (U.S.)   /U

Judy Holliday (Ella Peterson), Dean Martin (Jeffrey Moss), Fred Clark (Larry Hastings), Eddie Foy Jr. (J. Otto Prantz), Jean Stapleton (Sue), Ruth Storey (Gwynne), Dort Clark (Inspector Barnes), Frank Gorshin (Blake Barton), Ralph Roberts (Francis), Valerie Allen (Olga)

p, Arthur Freed; d, Vincente Minnelli; w, Betty Comden, Adolph Green (based on the musical play by Betty Comden, Adolph Green and Jule Styne); ph, Milton Krasner; ed, Adrienne Fazan; m, Jule Styne, Betty Comden, Adolph Green; art d, George W. Davis, Preston Ames; chor, Charles O'Curran; cos, Walter Plunkett

AAN Best Score: Andre Previn

The last performance of a much-loved star. Judy Holliday reprises her Broadway success in this adaptation of the hit Comden-Green-Jules Styne musical, playing Ella Peterson, who works at a telephone answering service and gets passionately involved in her clients' lives. Hapless playwright Jeffrey Moss (a miscast Dean Martin) is her love interest. In supporting roles, Jean Stapleton scores in one of her earliest appearances, as do Frank Gorshin in the role of a beatnik who wants to be a serious actor and Eddie Foy, Jr., as a bookie; jazz fans will recognize saxophone great Gerry Mulligan, married to Holliday at the time, as Ella's blind date. Vincente Minnelli's film might have benefited from less emphasis on dialogue and more on the musical numbers ("Just in Time" and "The Party's Over" among them), but Holliday is adorable and effortlessly "real" in one of the best roles of her sadly abbreviated career.

BELLS OF ST. MARY'S, THE

1945   126m   bw   Drama   ★★★★
Rainbow   (U.S.)   /U

Bing Crosby (Father Chuck O'Malley), Ingrid Bergman (Sister Benedict), Henry Travers (Mr. Bogardus), Ruth Donnelly (Sister Michael), Joan Carroll (Patsy), Martha Sleeper (Patsy's Mother), William Gargan (Joe Gallagher), Rhys Williams (Dr. McKay), Dick Tyler (Eddie), Una O'Connor (Mrs. Breen)

p, Leo McCarey; d, Leo McCarey; w, Dudley Nichols (based on a story by Leo McCarey); ph, George Barnes; ed, Harry Marker; m, Robert Emmett Dolan; art d, William Flannery; cos, Edith Head

AAN Best Picture; AAN Best Actor: Bing Crosby; *AAN Best Actress:* Ingrid Bergman; *AAN Best Director:* Leo McCarey; *AAN Best Editing:* Harry Marker; *AAN Best Score:* Robert Emmett Dolan; *AAN Best Song:* James Van Heusen (Music), Johnny Burke (Lyrics); *AA Best Sound:* Stephen Dunn

Touchingly sentimental, but strong in all the right places. The sequel to GOING MY WAY is nearly as good as its predecessor. Bing Crosby is trouble-shooting priest Father Chuck O'Malley, who's sent to the financially ailing St. Mary's. There he runs smack into charming, clever Sister Benedict (Ingrid Bergman), a mother superior who rules her students with a gentle but decisive hand. She is too rigid for Father O'Malley and he's too permissive for her, setting up a confrontation of styles that's a joy to behold. It's a gentle, uplifting story, and features some fine songs by Crosby, including "Adeste Fidelis," "In the Land of Beginning Again," and the sprightly "Aren't You Glad You're You." The two leads are seamless all the way home.

BELLY OF AN ARCHITECT, THE

1987   108m   c   Drama   ★★★
Callender   (U.K./Italy)   /15

Brian Dennehy (Stourley Kracklite), Chloe Webb (Louisa Kracklite), Lambert Wilson (Caspasian Speckler), Vanni Corbellini (Frederico), Sergio Fantoni (Io Speckler), Stefania Casini (Flavia Speckler), Alfredo Varelli (Julio Ficcone), Geoffrey Copleston (Caspetti), Francesco Carnelutti (Pastarri), Marino Mase (Trettorio)

p, Colin Callender, Walter Donohue; d, Peter Greenaway; w, Peter Greenaway; ph, Sacha Vierny; ed, John Wilson; m, Wim Mertens, Glenn Branca; art d, Luciana Vedovelli; cos, Maurizio Millenotti

A film to either love or loathe. Exquisitely composed film about obsession reaffirms director Peter Greenaway's reputation as a meticulous visual artist. Stourley Kracklite (Brian Dennehy), a corpulent Chicago architect of some renown, travels to Rome with his considerably younger wife Louisa (Chloe Webb) to oversee an exhibition commemorating the work of Etienne Louis Boullee, a little-known but visionary 18th-century French architect. A handsome young Italian architect, Caspasian Speckler (Lambert Wilson), is in charge of the project's finances, and he covets both Kracklite's control of the exhibition and his wife. Kracklite's world begins to crumble as he becomes obsessed with the chronic abdominal pains from which he suffers, making him oblivious to Speckler's machinations. Dennehy's extraordinary performance buoys the film, and Wilson is entirely convincing as the rival architect, but Webb is badly miscast. The main attractions here are Greenaway's densely textured compositions, each one a triumph of symmetry and design.

BEN-HUR

1959   212m   c   Historical/Religious   ★★★★½
MGM   (U.S.)   /PG

Charlton Heston (Judah Ben Hur), Jack Hawkins (Quintus Arrius), Stephen Boyd (Messala), Haya Harareet (Esther), Hugh Griffith (Sheik Ilderim), Martha Scott (Miriam), Sam Jaffe (Simonides), Cathy O'Donnell (Tirzah), Finlay Currie (Balthasar), Frank Thring (Pontius Pilate)

p, Sam Zimbalist; d, William Wyler; w, Karl Tunberg (based on the novel by Lew Wallace); ph, Robert Surtees; ed, Ralph E. Winters, John Dunning; m, Miklos Rozsa; art d, William A. Horning, Edward Carfagno; fx, A. Arnold Gillespie, Robert MacDonald; cos, Elizabeth Haffenden

AA Best Picture; AA Best Actor: Charlton Heston; AA Best Supporting Actor: Hugh Griffith; AA Best Director: William Wyler; AAN Best Adapted Screenplay: Karl Tunberg; AA Best Cinematography: Robert L. Surtees; AA Best Editing: Ralph E. Winters, John D. Dunning; AA Best Score: Miklos Rozsa; AA Best Art Direction: William A. Horning, Edward C. Carfagno, Hugh Hunt; AA Best Costume Design: Elizabeth Haffenden; AA Best Sound: Franklin E. Milton; AA Best Visual Effects: A. Arnold Gillespie, Robert MacDonald, Milo Lory

Predictable but magnificent and satisfying. In remaking the silent 1927 classic, which starred Ramon Novarro and Francis X. Bushman, quality-conscious director Wyler shines the old chestnut up. Highlights include the galley ship and climatic chariot race with Heston—in a tour de force performance—besieged by the sexy but evil Boyd. (This sequence was actually helmed by action expert Andrew Marton.) Even with the western overtones, the actors make stunning rivals. Majesty is in almost every frame of this film thanks to Wyler, who tells the story in human, understated terms.

Everything about BEN HUR was enormous; more than 300 sets were employed, covering more than 340 acres. The arena housing the chariot race consumed 18 acres, the largest single set in film history. The five-story stands were packed with 8,000 extras, and 40,000 tons of sand were taken from beaches to make the track. Scores of Yugoslavian horses were imported for the spectacular 20-minute race, which took three months to shoot. More than 1000 workers labored for a year to build the colossal arena. Rome's Cinecitta Studios were gutted of more than a million props, and sculptors made more than 200 giant statues. Also unique were the wide-screen cameras employed, 65 millimeters wide, to achieve sharp, deep focus. MGM lavished about $12,500,000 on this stupendous production, which brought them near bankruptcy, but the returns were staggering: a gross of $40 million.

BENJI

1974   85m   c   Children's   ★★★
Mulberry Square   (U.S.)   G/U

Higgins the Dog (Benji), Patsy Garrett (Mary), Allen Fiuzat (Paul), Cynthia Smith (Cindy), Peter Breck (Dr. Chapman), Frances Bavier (Lady with Cat), Terry Carter (Officer Tuttle), Edgar Buchanan (Bill), Tom Lester (Riley), Christopher Connelly (Henry)

p, Joe Camp; d, Joe Camp; w, Joe Camp; ph, Don Reddy; ed, Leon Smith; m, Euel Box; prod d, Harland Wright

AAN Best Song: Euel Box (Music), Betty Box (Lyrics)

A lovable mutt thwarts kidnappers. A-h-h-h-h-h. Much of the film is shot from a dog's-eye view, and this technique works perfectly. The human actors are okay but not as cool as the canine star, a veteran of TV's "Petticoat Junction" series. The title song was nominated for an Oscar! Sequel: FOR THE LOVE OF BENJI.

BENNY & JOON

1993   98m   c   Comedy/Drama   ★★½
MGM   (U.S.)   PG/12

Johnny Depp (Sam), Mary Stuart Masterson (Joon), Aidan Quinn (Benny), Julianne Moore (Ruthie), Oliver Platt (Eric), CCH Pounder (Dr. Garvey), Dan Hedaya (Thomas), Joe Grifasi (Mike), William H. Macy (Randy Burch), Liane Alexandra Curtis (Claudia)

p, Susan Arnold, Donna Roth; d, Jeremiah Chechik; w, Barry Berman (from a story by Berman and Leslie McNeil); ph, John Schwartzman; ed, Carol Littleton; m, Rachel Portman; prod d, Neil Spisak; art d, Pat Tagliaferro; fx, J.D. Streett IV; cos, Aggie Guerard Rodgers

A gentle comedy about two misfits—a schizophrenic girl and a boy whom earlier generations would have called an odd duck—who find love, BENNY & JOON means well but overdoses on whimsy.

Benny Pearl (Aidan Quinn) is a smart, handsome mechanic who has dedicated his life to caring for his sister Joon (Mary Stuart Masterson), a creative free spirit with a dangerous penchant for setting fires. Sam (Johnny Depp) is a lovable misfit who does a fine Buster Keaton imitation but is functionally illiterate and a trial to his family. Sam and Joon complement one another, allowing Benny to date and enjoy a taste of freedom, but when he realizes they've fallen in love, the stage is set for a family crisis.

BENNY & JOON is one in a long line of films in which mental illness is conceived as making people more creative, honest, perceptive, and loving—in a word, better—than sane people. The script appears several times on the verge of testing dangerous waters—there's a hint of incestuous closeness in the siblings' relationship—but always retreats in favor of focusing on how cute Sam and Joon are as they bring a fresh perspective to such mundane activities as cooking: she whips up peanut butter and cereal milkshakes, he mashes potatoes with a tennis racket, and together they make grilled cheese with an iron.

If the performances were as cute and sweet as the characters, the film would need a warning label. But Depp's Sam is delicately touching, a maladjusted waif with both soul and grit, and Masterson resists the temptation to soften Joon.

BERLIN ALEXANDERPLATZ

1979   896m   c   Drama   ★★★★
Bavaria Atelier/RAI/Westdeutscher Rundfunk   (West Germany)

Gunter Lamprecht (Franz Biberkopf), Gottfried John (Reinhold), Barbara Sukowa (Mieze), Hanna Schygulla (Eva), Franz Buchrieser (Meck), Claus Holm (Wirt), Hark Bohm (Luders), Brigitte Mira (Mrs. Bast), Roger Fritz (Herbert), Werner Asam (Fritz)

p, Peter Marthesheimer; d, Rainer Werner Fassbinder; w, Rainer Werner Fassbinder (based on the novel by Alfred Doblin); ph, Xaver Schwarzenberger; ed, Juliane Lorenz, Rainer Werner Fassbinder; m, Peer Raben; art d, Helmut Gassner, Werner Achmann, Jurgen Henze; fx, Theo Nischwitz; cos, Barbara Baum

An astonishing, momumental work. Over the short span of 17 years—from 1965, when he directed his first 10-minute film, up to his death on June 10, 1982—Rainer Werner Fassbinder directed some 90 hours of film and television. BERLIN ALEXANDERPLATZ, an adaptation of Alfred Doblin's massive novel made for German television, runs approximately 15 hours, and makes up one-seventh of Fassbinder's total output. Comprised of 13 episodes and an epilogue, the film stars Gunter Lamprecht as the pimp Franz Biberkopf, released from prison after serving time for murdering a prostitute. Now that he has a certain freedom, he takes to the streets of Berlin in the late 1920s in search of his identity.

Simply recounting the plot does no justice to Fassbinder or the film. What Doblin tried to do in his novel (written from 1927 to 1929) was to put into print the atmosphere of Berlin life. Acknowledging his debt to Doblin, Fassbinder has said, "I had quite simply, without realizing it, made Doblin's fantasy into my life." In that sense, BERLIN ALEX-ANDERPLATZ is not the story of Berlin, but the story of Fassbinder—and in these 15 hours the two are inseparable.

BEST MAN, THE

1964 102m bw Drama ★★★½
UA (U.S.) /A

Henry Fonda *(William Russell)*, Cliff Robertson *(Joe Cantwell)*, Edie Adams *(Mabel Cantwell)*, Margaret Leighton *(Alice Russell)*, Shelley Berman *(Sheldon Bascomb)*, Lee Tracy *(Art Hockstader)*, Ann Sothern *(Mrs. Gamadge)*, Gene Raymond *(Dan Cantwell)*, Kevin McCarthy *(Dick Jensen)*, Mahalia Jackson *(Herself)*

p, Stuart Millar, Lawrence Turman; d, Franklin J. Schaffner; w, Gore Vidal (based on his play); ph, Haskell Wexler; ed, Robert Swink; m, Mort Lindsey; cos, Dorothy Jeakins

AAN Best Supporting Actor: Lee Tracy

Vidal's savage political hornet's nest. Idealist Fonda and hypocrite Robertson do battle for their party's Presidental nomination. Fonda's wife Leighton had held off getting a divorce so as not to hurt her husband's political chances. Lee Tracy is the dying President who hasn't put his support behind either man on the eve of the convention. Robertson has a dossier on Fonda's emotional instability and uses it to get what he wants. Then we learn that Robertson had a rendezvous with another man some years earlier. Will Fonda retaliate? You can see Stevenson in Fonda, McCarthy or Nixon in Robertson, and a bit of Truman in outstanding, Oscar-nominated Tracy, who died before making another film. Gore Vidal's dialogue is razor-sharp as is Haskell Wexler's photography.

BEST YEARS OF OUR LIVES, THE

1946 172m bw Drama/War ★★★★★
Goldwyn (U.S.) /U

Myrna Loy *(Milly Stephenson)*, Fredric March *(Al Stephenson)*, Dana Andrews *(Fred Derry)*, Teresa Wright *(Peggy Stephenson)*, Virginia Mayo *(Marie Derry)*, Cathy O'Donnell *(Wilma Cameron)*, Hoagy Carmichael *(Butch Engle)*, Harold Russell *(Homer Parrish)*, Gladys George *(Hortense Derry)*, Roman Bohnen *(Pat Derry)*

p, Samuel Goldwyn; d, William Wyler; w, Robert E. Sherwood (based on the blank-verse novella *Glory for Me* by MacKinlay Kantor); ph, Gregg Toland; ed, Daniel Mandell; m, Hugo Friedhofer; art d, George Jenkins, Perry Ferguson; cos, Irene Sharaff

AA Best Picture; AA Best Actor: Fredric March; AA Best Supporting Actor: Harold Russell; AA Best Director: William Wyler; AA Best Screenplay: Robert E. Sherwood; AA Best Editing: Daniel Mandell; AA Best Score: Hugo Friedhofer; AAN Best Sound: Gordon Sawyer

The best coming home movie ever made. "I don't care if it doesn't make a nickel," Sam Goldwyn reportedly said of THE BEST YEARS, "I just want every man, woman, and child in America to see it." The colorful producer got the idea for the film after reading a *Life* article about WWII veterans and their difficulties in adjusting to civilian life. With a brilliant script by Robert E. Sherwood, effective direction by William Wyler, masterful photography by Gregg Toland and excellent performances by the entire cast, this film about returning American servicemen is justifiably considered a classic.

Three servicemen—Al Stephenson (Fredric March), Fred Derry (Dana Andrews), and Homer Parrish (Harold Russell)—are shown returning to their hometown, plagued by memories of war and doubts about their future in a country they have difficulty remembering. After sharing space on board the bomber that flies them home, the three take a cab to their separate addresses. The sailor Homer comes home to his girl with a pair of hooks where his hands once were (Russell, the only nonprofessional in the cast, lost his hands in a training accident while in the service); middle-aged Al returns to his loving wife (Myrna Loy), children, and old job as a banker; Fred finds a spouse who has more or less abandoned him, and no prospects for a job.

Although everyone in Hollywood thought Goldwyn would lose his shirt on THE BEST YEARS OF OUR LIVES, it was a massive hit. Russell won a special Oscar for bringing hope to servicemen.

BETRAYAL

1982 95m c Drama ★★★½
Fox (U.K.) R/15

Jeremy Irons *(Jerry)*, Patricia Hodge *(Emma)*, Ben Kingsley *(Robert)*

p, Sam Spiegel; d, David Jones; w, Harold Pinter (based on his play); ph, Mike Fash; ed, John Bloom; m, Dominic Muldowney; prod d, Eileen Diss; cos, Jane Robinson, Jean Muir

AAN Best Adapted Screenplay: Harold Pinter (Screenplay)

Harold Pinter's screenplay for BETRAYAL begins at the end of its story and flashes back to the beginning, permitting the audience full awareness of the outcome as the events unfold, and thus giving those events a weight and structure that linear chronology would not endow on them. Robert (Ben Kingsley) is a book publisher whose wife, Emma (Patricia Hodge), is having an affair with Jerry (Jeremy Irons), a literary agent. The film begins after the affair is over and ends as Jerry and Emma meet. The immensely talented Kingsley is the fulcrum which moves the story backward (or forward, as the case may be). Uttering only a few words, his Robert knows exactly what is going on and conveys a subtle sense of menace. Director David Jones fashions a brisk film, despite having to deal with Pinter's lengthy silences. Hodge, who should have been the center of attraction, comes across as a mite cool—it's hard to see how she inspires passion in these two very different men. Once you've grasped the reverse chronology, the events peel away in layers that produce unexpected insights along the way.

BETSY'S WEDDING

1990 97m c Comedy ★★½
Silver Screen Partners IV/Touchstone (U.S.) R/15

Alan Alda *(Eddie Hopper)*, Joey Bishop *(Eddie's Father)*, Madeline Kahn *(Lola Hopper)*, Anthony LaPaglia *(Stevie Dee)*, Catherine O'Hara *(Gloria Henner)*, Joe Pesci *(Oscar Henner)*, Molly Ringwald *(Betsy Hopper)*, Ally Sheedy *(Connie Hopper)*, Burt Young *(Georgie)*, Julie Bovasso *(Grandma)*

p, Martin Bregman, Louis A. Stroller; d, Alan Alda; w, Alan Alda; ph, Kelvin Pike; ed, Michael Polakow; m, Bruce Broughton; prod d, John Jay Moore; art d, Andrew Moore; fx, Greg Hull; cos, Mary Malin

Nothing new under the sun, except for Anthony LaPaglia, as a Mafia prince courting tough policewoman Ally Sheedy. Otherwise, class conflicts and a wacky wedding, courtesy Alan Alda, whose persona is beginning to grate. Nice to see Madeline Kahn.

BETTY BLUE
(37.2 LE MATIN)

1986 120m c Drama/Erotic ★★★
Constellation/Cargo (France) R/18

Beatrice Dalle *(Betty)*, Jean-Hugues Anglade *(Zorg)*, Consuelo de Haviland *(Lisa)*, Gerard Darmon *(Eddy)*, Clementine Celarie *(Annie)*, Jacques Mathou *(Bob)*, Claude Confortes *(Owner)*, Philippe Laudenbach *(Gyneco Publisher)*, Vincent Lindon *(Policeman Richard)*, Raoul Billeray *(Old Policeman)*

p, Claudie Ossard, Jean-Jacques Beineix; d, Jean-Jacques Beineix; w, Jean-Jacques Beineix (based on the novel *37.2 Le Matin* by Philippe Djian); ph, Jean-Francois Robin; ed, Monique Prim; m, Gabriel Yared; art d, Carlos Conti; fx, Jean-Francois Cousson, Georges Demetreau; cos, Elisabeth Tavernier

AAN Best Foreign Language Film

Jean-Jacques Beineix's attempt to combine the energetic high-gloss finish of his debut feature, DIVA, with the raw poetic intensity of MOON IN THE GUTTER, ends up as an inconsistent and unsatisfying tale of *amour fou* and literary ambition. Dalle embarks on a personal crusade to get her lover's (Anglade) novel published, but has a pretty hard time dealing with rejection notices. Eventually she starts hearing voices, and is finally driven to poke out her own eye. Anglade, best known in the US as the "roller" in SUBWAY, is perfectly cast here, although the best thing about the film is the pouty, 21-year-old Dalle. While not a box-office smash in the US, BETTY BLUE did garner an

Oscar nomination as Best Foreign Language Film. In 1991 Beineix released his original director's cut, at an expanded running time of 182 minutes, in France.

BETWEEN THE LINES

1977 101m c Drama ★★★
Midwest (U.S.) R/15

John Heard (Harry), Lindsay Crouse (Abbie), Jeff Goldblum (Max), Jill Eikenberry (Lynn), Bruno Kirby (David), Gwen Welles (Laura), Stephen Collins (Michael), Lewis J. Stadlen (Stanley), Michael J. Pollard (Hawker), Lane Smith (Roy Walsh)

p, Raphael D. Silver; d, Joan Micklin Silver; w, Fred Barron (based on a story by Barron, David M. Helpern); ph, Kenneth Van Sickle; ed, John Carter; m, Michael Kamen; cos, Patrizia von Brandenstein

Tight little sleeper again demonstrates that Silver is a director with excellent taste and the ability to wring every last penny out of a budget and put it onscreen. The story takes place at an alternative newspaper like the "Village Voice" or "The LA Weekly." Knockout performances all. BETWEEN THE LINES was made for a mere $800,000, and the husband-wife Silver team managed to bring in a first-rate picture.

BEVERLY HILLS COP

1984 105m c Comedy/Crime ★★★
Paramount (U.S.) R/15

Eddie Murphy (Axel Foley), Judge Reinhold (Detective Billy Rosewood), John Ashton (Sgt. Taggart), Lisa Eilbacher (Jenny Summers), Ronny Cox (Lt. Bogomil), Steven Berkoff (Victor Maitland), James Russo (Mikey Tandino), Jonathan Banks (Zack), Stephen Elliott (Chief Hubbard), Gil Hill (Inspector Todd)

p, Don Simpson, Jerry Bruckheimer; d, Martin Brest; w, Daniel Petrie Jr. (based on a story by Daniel Petrie Jr. and Danilo Bach); ph, Bruce Surtees; ed, Billy Weber, Arthur Coburn; m, Harold Faltermeyer; prod d, Angelo Graham; art d, James J. Murakami; fx, Ken Pepiot; cos, Tom Bronson

AAN Best Original Screenplay: Daniel Petrie Jr (Screenplay), Danilo Bach (Story)

A sassy cop; brash, crude and very funny. Murphy's third film was phenomenally successful at the box office, aided substantially by a hit-filled soundtrack. BEVERLY HILLS COP is an entertaining, if empty-headed, cop film in which street-smart Detroit detective Murphy sets out to avenge the murder of a friend. Basically a star vehicle designed to show off the talents of Murphy—it succeeds admirably. The comedy is deftly balanced with the stunningly staged action scenes. Surprisingly, most of the laughs are given to Reinhold and Ashton. Acting honors go to Bronson Pinchot in a brief but career-making turn.

BEYOND THE VALLEY OF THE DOLLS

1970 109m c Erotic/Drama ★★★
Fox (U.S.) NC-17/

Dolly Read (Kelly MacNamara), Cynthia Myers (Casey Anderson), Marcia McBroom (Petronella Danforth), John LaZar (Z-Man), Michael Blodgett (Lance Rocke), David Gurian (Harris Allworth), Edy Williams (Ashley St. Ives), Erica Gavin (Roxanne), Charles Napier (Baxter Wolfe), The Strawberry Alarm Clock

p, Russ Meyer; d, Russ Meyer; w, Roger Ebert; ph, Fred J. Koenekamp; ed, Dann Cahn, Dick Wormel; m, Stu Phillips

Russ Meyer's BEYOND THE VALLEY OF THE DOLLS is an outrageously entertaining cult classic, and probably one of the most bizarre movies ever produced by a major Hollywood studio.

Eager to break into the big time, an all-girl rock band composed of Kelly (Dolly Read), Casey (Cynthia Myers) and Pet (Marcia McBroom) heads for Los Angeles, accompanied by their manager Harris (David Gurian), who's also Kelly's lover. Kelly's aunt introduces the girls to record producer Ronnie "Z-Man" Barzell (John LaZar), who turns the group into stars. As they become successful, Kelly abandons Harris for playboy Lance Rocke (Michael Blodgett), Harris is seduced by a porn star, and Pet falls in love with a law student. Casey, who gets hooked on pills and alcohol, is attracted to Kelly's aunt's lesbian

employee. Things reach a head when Lance and the band members attend a party at Barzell's house; "Z-Man" freaks out and attacks his guests one by one in the guise of a superheroine named "Superwoman."

After losing a fortune on epic flops like DOCTOR DOOLITTLE (1967), Twentieth Century-Fox enlisted Russ Meyer—who had earned millions with low-budget skinflicks—to make a film for them. The result was a film that outraged the industry but turned a huge profit on a $1.2 million budget, despite Fox's trepidation in promoting it. Technically, Meyer's films were always topnotch, and in this, his first widescreen movie, he and cinematographer Fred Koenekamp create some stylish comic-book compositions, splashed with Day-Glo colors.

In addition to a cast of former-Playboy models and other non-actors delivering film critic Ebert's mind-boggling dialogue ("You will drink the black sperm of my vengeance"), there are wild orgies, drug parties, Nazi butlers, and a gruesome Manson-like massacre that reaches a manic pitch of surreal hysteria. BEYOND is often repellent and demented— which is to say it's typical Meyer—but it's also a funny, psychedelic time-capsule.

BHAJI ON THE BEACH

1994 100m c Comedy/Drama ★★★
Channel Four/Umbi Films (United Kingdom) /15

Kim Vithana (Ginder), Jimmi Harkishin (Ranjit), Sarita Khajuria (Hashida), Mo Sesay (Oliver), Lalita Ahmed (Asha), Surendra Kochar (Bina), Shaheen Khan (Simi), Zohra Segal (Pushpa), Nisha Nayar (Ladhu), Renu Kochar (Madhu)

p, Nadine Marsh-Edwards; d, Gurinder Chadha; w, Meera Syal (based on a story by Meera Syal and Gurinder Chadha); ph, John Kenway; ed, Oral Norrie Ottley; m, John Altman, Craig Preuss; prod d, Derek Brown; art d, Helen Raynor; cos, Annie Symons

First-time feature director Gurinder Chadha has called Ken Loach her most important influence, and BHAJI ON THE BEACH, a charming comic drama about women of Punjabi heritage living in urban England, is comparable to the best of Loach's realist comedies.

In a middle-class, mostly Indian neighborhood of Birmingham, housewife Ginder (Kim Vithana) has fled her abusive husband Ranjit (Jimmi Harkishin); she's persuaded by social worker Simi (Shaheen Khan) to join a group of Asian women on a day-trip to the nearby resort town of Blackpool. Along for the ride are Hashida (Sarita Khajuria), a pre-med student who has just discovered she's pregnant; Asha (Lalita Ahmed), a middle-aged newsagent; elderly gossips Pushpa (Zohra Segal) and Bina (Surendra Kochar); and a pair of giggly, assimilated teenagers, Ladhu (Nisha Nayar) and Madhu (Renu Kochar). Ranjit, however, discovers their destination and is soon in hot pursuit.

With remarkable assurance, BHAJI ON THE BEACH sketches a large number of characters who are both universally recognizable and plausible as the product of a particular subculture. Chadha sees herself as primarily a British (as opposed to Indian or female) filmmaker, and BHAJI, like her 1989 short subject I'M BRITISH BUT. . . , is deeply concerned with expanding popular notions of what it means to be British. The film is punctuated with delightful parodies of the Bombay commercial pictures that serve as a cultural umbilicus to Indians across the globe. Asha's consultation with a fearsome statue of Rama quotes the classic costume picture BAIJU BAWRA (1952); scenes of a sluttish Hashida insulting her elders refer to PURAB AUR PASCHIM/EAST AND WEST (1970), a melodrama decrying the insidious influence of Western culture on Indian youth.

BICYCLE THIEF, THE
(LADRI DI BICICLETTE)

1948 90m bw Drama ★★★★★
Mayer/Burstyn (Italy) /U

Lamberto Maggiorani (Antonio), Lianella Carell (Maria), Enzo Staiola (Bruno), Elena Altieri (The Lady), Vittorio Antonucci (The Thief), Gino Saltamerenda (Bajocco), Fausto Guerzoni (Amateur Actor)

p, Vittorio De Sica; d, Vittorio De Sica; w, Cesare Zavattini (based on the novel by Luigi Bartolini); ph, Carlo Montuori; ed, Eraldo Da Roma; m, Alesandro Cicognini; art d, Antonio Traverso

AAN Best Original Screenplay: Cesare Zavattini

A landmark film—honest, beautiful, and deceptively simple. Reviewers praised THE BICYCLE THIEF unanimously upon its first release, which marked one of the finest achievements of Italian neorealism.

Maggiorani is a poor, working-class Italian whose happiness at finding a job gives way to despair when his bicycle—on which his employment depends—is stolen. His search for the bike takes on an epic quality, with Staiola turning in an impossibly heart-wrenching performance as Maggiorani's young son. THE BICYCLE THIEF is a brilliant testament to director Vittorio De Sica's greatness and to the power of neorealism. All roles were played by nonactors, the dialogue is as spare as it can be in a talking picture, and the coarse black-and-white photography makes viewers feel as if they were watching a documentary, though without sacrificing drama.

Cesare Zavattini received an Oscar nomination for his screenplay, and the film received a Special Academy Award as the "most outstanding" foreign film of the year. The film was deftly and affectionately sent up by Mauricio Nichetti in his 1989 feature, THE ICICLE THIEF.

BIG

1988 104m c Comedy ★★★½
Fox (U.S.) PG

Tom Hanks *(Josh Baskin)*, Elizabeth Perkins *(Susan Lawrence)*, Robert Loggia *("Mac" MacMillan)*, John Heard *(Paul Davenport)*, Jared Rushton *(Billy Kopeche)*, David Moscow *(Young Josh)*, Jon Lovitz *(Scotty Brennen)*, Mercedes Ruehl *(Mrs. Baskin)*, Josh Clark *(Mr. Baskin)*, Kimberlee M. Davis *(Cynthia Benson)*

p, James L. Brooks, Robert Greenhut; d, Penny Marshall; w, Gary Ross, Anne Spielberg; ph, Barry Sonnenfeld; ed, Barry Malkin; m, Howard Shore; prod d, Santo Loquasto; chor, Patricia Birch; cos, Judianna Makovsky

AAN Best Actor: Tom Hanks; *AAN Best Original Screenplay:* Gary Ross, Anne Spielberg

The best of the spate of body-switching films in the late 80s. BIG features a brilliant, unforced performance by Tom Hanks as a New Jersey Little Leaguer, who after wishing he were older, suddenly finds himself walking around in a 35-year-old body. Hiding in Manhattan until his friend Rushton can track down the carny fortune-telling machine that granted the wish, Hanks gets a job with a toy manufacturing firm and rises quickly up the corporate ladder thanks to his unique kid's insight. BIG is a winning, charming film, primarily because Hanks makes it work. He is extraordinarily convincing as an adolescent who suddenly finds himself dealing with a new, adult body, responsibilities, and a romantic relationship, while simultaneously trying to survive vicious corporate infighting.

BIG CHILL, THE

1983 103m c Comedy/Drama ★★½
Columbia (U.S.) R/15

Glenn Close *(Sarah)*, Tom Berenger *(Sam)*, William Hurt *(Nick)*, Jeff Goldblum *(Michael)*, Mary Kay Place *(Meg)*, Kevin Kline *(Harold)*, Meg Tilly *(Chloe)*, Don Galloway *(Richard)*, JoBeth Williams *(Karen)*, James Gillis *(Minister)*

p, Michael Shamberg; d, Lawrence Kasdan; w, Lawrence Kasdan, Barbara Benedek; ph, John Bailey; ed, Carol Littleton; prod d, Ida Random

AAN Best Picture; AAN Best Supporting Actress: Glenn Close; *AAN Best Original Screenplay:* Lawrence Kasdan (Screenplay), Barbara Benedek (Screenplay)

THE BIG CHILL is a glib, seriocomic look at a 1980s reunion of a group of old college friends who were radicals during the 1960s, and how their lives have changed since that time. Strong acting and a string of classic rock and soul tunes make up for a superficial script.

A group of former college friends are reunited for a funeral after learning of the suicide of another friend who had been staying at the house of running shoe mogul Harold (Kevin Kline) and his physician wife Sarah (Glenn Close). After the funeral, the group gathers at Harold and Sarah's house for the weekend. As the friends get reacquainted while eating, drinking, flirting, getting stoned and dancing, corporate attorney Meg (Mary Kay Place) announces that she wants to have a baby and begins asking the men in the house if they will do the honors. Sarah encourages Harold to sleep with Meg, and he does so. In the meantime, suburban housewife Karen (JoBeth Williams) pursues TV star Sam (Tom Berenger), whom she's had a crush on since college, and magazine writer Michael (Jeff Goldblum) tries to exploit the whole weekend into an article about the "lost hope" of the '60s generation.

THE BIG CHILL is the ultimate 1980s baby-boomer movie, presenting the definitive portrayal of the emerging yuppie archetype and all its traits: from running shoes, jogging, camcorders, and Motown, to baby-fever, self-analytical narcissism, and guilt-ridden upwardly mobile lifestyles. It is consistently entertaining and wonderfully acted, yet is finally undone by its refusal to deal honestly with the serious issues it raises; director/co-writer Lawrence Kasdan chooses instead to end virtually every scene with a cheap punchline. In the final analysis, the film doesn't amount to much, except to provide a good opportunity for the fine ensemble cast to show off their talents. One interesting cast note is that the character of Alex, who is never seen alive, but whose corpse is shown under the opening credits as it's being dressed for the funeral, was played by a then unknown Kevin Costner.

BIG CLOCK, THE

1948 95m bw Crime ★★★½
Paramount (U.S.)

Ray Milland *(George Stroud)*, Charles Laughton *(Earl Janoth)*, Maureen O'Sullivan *(Georgette Stroud)*, George Macready *(Steven Hagen)*, Rita Johnson *(Pauline York)*, Elsa Lanchester *(Louise Patterson)*, Harold Vermilyea *(Don Klausmeyer)*, Dan Tobin *(Ray Cordette)*, Henry Morgan *(Bill Womack)*, Richard Webb *(Nat Sperling)*

p, Richard Maibaum; d, John Farrow; w, Jonathan Latimer (based on the novel by Kenneth Fearing); ph, John Seitz; ed, Gene Ruggiero; m, Victor Young; art d, Hans Dreier, Roland Anderson, Albert Nozaki; fx, Gordon Jennings; cos, Edith Head

Steady *film noir* production fraught with suspense, twisting its unique plot and characters to a clever and frightening conclusion. Milland is the shrewd editor of *Crimeways* Magazine which is published by Laughton, a megalomaniacal media tycoon who kills his mistress. Milland tries to solve murder, but all clues point back at him! Almost stolen by the eccentric as usual Elsa Lanchester. In 1987, the film was remade with a military setting in NO WAY OUT, starring Kevin Costner and Gene Hackman.

BIG DEAL ON MADONNA STREET
(I SOLTI IGNOTI)

1958 91m bw Comedy/Crime ★★★½
Lux (Italy)

Vittorio Gassman *(Peppe)*, Renato Salvatori *(Mario)*, Rossana Rory *(Norma)*, Carla Gravina *(Nicoletta)*, Claudia Cardinale *(Carmelina)*, Carlo Pisacane *(Capannelle)*, Tiberio Murgia *(Ferribotte)*, Memmo Carotenuto *(Cosimo)*, Marcello Mastroianni *(Tiberio)*, Toto *(Dante)*

p, Franco Cristaldi; d, Mario Monicelli; w, Suso Cecchi D'Amico, Agenore Incrocci, Furio Scarpelli, Mario Monicelli

AAN Best Foreign Language Film

A classic Italian spoof. Vittorio Gassman stars as Peppe, a bungling petty thief who leads a group of incompetent burglars in a plan to loot a jewelry store on Madonna Street. One of the finest examples of Italian comedy to reach American shores (it was nominated for a Best Foriegn Film Oscar in 1958), BIG DEAL ON MADONNA STREET satirizes all those procedural caper films that Hollywood turned out and the foreign homages that followed (such as RIFIFI and BOB LE FLAMBEUR). The entire burglarizing procedure, as directed by Mario Monicelli, is hilarious, thanks to the fine acting and the steady stream of sight gags that recall the classic comedies of silent days. CRACKERS, an unfunny remake from Louis Malle, appeared in 1984, and BIG DEAL ON MADONNA STREET—20 YEARS LATER surfaced in 1985. The film was also unsuccessfully adapted for a broadway musical.

BIG EASY, THE

1987 108m c Crime/Thriller   ★★★
Kings Road (U.S.)   R/15

Dennis Quaid *(Remy McSwain)*, Ellen Barkin *(Anne Osborne)*, Ned Beatty *(Jack Kellom)*, Ebbe Roe Smith *(Detective Dodge)*, John Goodman *(Detective DeSoto)*, Lisa Jane Persky *(Detective McCabe)*, Charles Ludlam *(Lamar)*, Thomas O'Brien *(Bobby)*, James Garrison *(Judge Noland)*, Carol Sutton *(Judge Raskov)*

p, Stephen Friedman; d, Jim McBride; w, Daniel Petrie Jr., Jack Baran; ph, Affonso Beato; ed, Mia Goldman; m, Brad Fiedel; prod d, Jeannine Claudia Oppewall; fx, Bill Purcell; cos, Tracy Tynan

Colorful Cajun *noir*, spicy, romantic, efficient. Hot Noo Ahluns police detective (Dennis Quaid) clashes with assistant district attorney (Ellen Barkin) over cop corruption. The best scenes are the romantic ones; McBride effectively captures the Big Easy, a city that is almost a character in itself, but the ending is contrived. That's the late and beloved New York Ridiculous Theatre impressario Charles Ludlam, out of his corset, as Lamar.

BIG HEAT, THE

1953 89m bw Crime   ★★★★
Columbia (U.S.)   /15

Glenn Ford *(Dave Bannion)*, Gloria Grahame *(Debby Marsh)*, Jocelyn Brando *(Katie Bannion)*, Alexander Scourby *(Mike Lagana)*, Lee Marvin *(Vince Stone)*, Jeanette Nolan *(Bertha Duncan)*, Peter Whitney *(Tierney)*, Willis Bouchey *(Lt. Wilkes)*, Robert Burton *(Gus Burke)*, Adam Williams *(Larry Gordon)*

p, Robert Arthur; d, Fritz Lang; w, Sydney Boehm (based on the serial in the *Saturday Evening Post* by William P. McGivern); ph, Charles Lang; ed, Charles Nelson; m, Daniele Amfitheatrof; art d, Robert Peterson; cos, Jean Louis

A scalding face-full of harsh reality, courtesy Fritz Lang. Starkly photographed and without a continuous score, the absence of which underlines the hard-hitting dialogue and the sound of smacking fists and thudding bullets, this film is as brutal as Lang's M as frightening. Ford, an ex-cop out to avenge the mob murder of his wife, gets upstaged by two performances of incredible power: Grahame and Marvin. Grahame plays a moll who squeals and pays; her performance defines the film noir anti-heroine, and in a world of comedic 1950s sex, she was the real thing, either coming along too late or too soon. Marvin moved his career up a definite notch as the sadistic killer.

This film, along with a spate of others, was spawned by the 1950 US Senate crime investigations conducted via TV, which pinpointed widespread corruption by organized crime throughout America. Fritz Lang's THE BIG HEAT, meaning the heat brought down by the police, is one of the best expose films dealing with the national crime cartel, including HOODLUM EMPIRE, Robert Wise's startling CAPTIVE CITY, and Phil Karlson's hard-hitting KANSAS CITY CONFIDENTIAL. Lang's ferocious gangster film is directed with immaculate care, showing not so much violence on film as the reaction to violence, while examining the victims. A terse script by Boehm and sharp photography by Charles Lang in keeping with the theme contribute to this startling film noir.

BIG KNIFE, THE

1955 111m bw Drama   ★★★½
UA (U.S.)   /A

Jack Palance *(Charles Castle)*, Ida Lupino *(Marion Castle)*, Shelley Winters *(Dixie Evans)*, Wendell Corey *(Smiley Coy)*, Jean Hagen *(Connie Bliss)*, Rod Steiger *(Stanley Hoff)*, Ilka Chase *(Patty Benedict)*, Everett Sloane *(Nat Danziger)*, Wesley Addy *(Hank Teagle)*, Paul Langton *(Buddy Bliss)*

p, Robert Aldrich; d, Robert Aldrich; w, James Poe (based on the play by Clifford Odets); ph, Ernest Laszlo; ed, Michael Luciano; m, Frank DeVol; art d, William Glasgow

Hollywood sterotypes based on Odets but compelling and viciously done with a *tour de force* for Palance, as a tinseltown hunk with a dark, dishonest secret, supported by an amazing cast. Director Aldrich's

unflinching use of a candid, almost documentary style results in a devastating mirror image of Hollywood at its most ruthless. Grim, lacking compassion and uncompromising, irrespective of the name-dropping of real personalities (Kazan, Wilder, Wyler, etc.) to authenticate the atmosphere. The script blares the philosophy that it is not only windy at the top but also lethal.

BIG PARADE, THE
(DA YUE BING)

1987 102m c Drama   ★★★
Guangxi (China)   /15

Huang Xueqi, Sun Chun, Lu Lei, Wu Ruofu

d, Chen Kaige; w, Gao Lili; ph, Zhang Yimou; ed, Zhou Xinxia; m, Qu Xiaosong, Zhao Quiping; prod d, He Qun

Chinese director Chen Kaige's long-awaited second feature, following the critically acclaimed YELLOW EARTH, was a somewhat uneven effort, hampered by a cliched narrative that fails to live up to the brilliance of the imagery.

Set in modern-day China, the film follows a single airborne unit as it undergoes a grueling training session in preparation for the prestigious parade in Beijing celebrating the 35th anniversary of the revolution. Led by a tough drill sergeant who is a veteran of a China-Vietnam conflict, the undisciplined young men are slowly whipped into shape until they becomes a flawless unit capable of marching in perfect order.

In THE BIG PARADE director Kaige strives for something more than what some critics have called the "Chinese FULL METAL JACKET." The film illustrates the conflict between the group and the individual in today's China. This somewhat subversive theme may have been the reason Chinese officials prevented the film's release for two years (it was filmed in 1985). Unfortunately, to Western eyes used to countless war films, the exploration of this theme may be a bit too banal. Although the characters and situations are standard basic training fare, Kaige filled his film with frequently breathtaking visuals.

From the opening helicopter shot which shows miles and miles of troops training on the tarmac to the final slow-motion shots of various units, Kaige continually comes up with beautiful and fascinating images of men in motion. Most remarkable, however, is the sequence where the men are not in motion—the arduous drill where the soldiers must stand still in the blazing sun. The wide-screen shimmers with the brutal heat, and the sweat pours from beneath the soldiers' helmets, presenting a brilliant, unforgettable image of individual human endurance and mass stupidity.

BIG RED ONE, THE

1980 113m c War   ★★★★
Lorimar (U.S.)   PG/15

Lee Marvin *(Sergeant)*, Mark Hamill *(Griff)*, Robert Carradine *(Zab)*, Bobby Di Cicco *(Vinci)*, Kelly Ward *(Johnson)*, Siegfried Rauch *(Schroeder)*, Stephane Audran *(Walloon)*, Serge Marquand *(Ransonnet)*, Charles Macaulay *(General/Captain)*, Alain Doutey *(Broban)*

p, Gene Corman; d, Samuel Fuller; w, Samuel Fuller; ph, Adam Greenberg; ed, David Bretherton, Morton Tubor; m, Dana Koproff; art d, Peter Jamison; fx, Kit West, Peter Dawson, Jeff Clifford

Samuel Fuller's episodic THE BIG RED ONE is a powerful, humorous, and touching autobiographical film that's the last of the great WWII movies.

In 1942, a Sergeant (Lee Marvin) leads a group of raw recruits in the First Infantry Division (nicknamed "the Big Red One"), including a quartet dubbed "The Four Horsemen"—Griff (Mark Hamill), a sharpshooter; Zab (Robert Carradine), an aspiring novelist; Vinci (Bobby Di Cicco), an Italian-American; and Johnson (Kelly Ward), a farmboy. In 1943 Sicily, with the help of a boy whose mother has been killed, they manage to destroy a huge German gun that's concealed at the top of a mountain. On D-Day in 1944, they take part in the Normandy invasion, but get trapped on Omaha Beach. Griff proves himself by eluding enemy gunfire and blowing up a fence, enabling them to escape. The squad then goes to Belgium and recaptures an insane asylum that's being used by the Nazis as their headquarters. In 1945, they experience the worst horror of their wartime careers when they're sent to liberate a concentration camp in Czechoslovakia.

Based in his own WWII experiences, THE BIG RED ONE was a dream project for Samuel Fuller, who had tried to get the film made for decades. Despite the film's limited budget, which necessitated that most of the location shooting be done in Israel, and the continuity lapses due to post-production tinkering, Fuller manages to create one of the most poignant war films ever made. Fuller demonstrates his philosophy that "the only glory in war is surviving," by focusing on the Four Horsemen and through a series of searing scenes filled with unforgettable images (a Nazi hiding behind a giant crucifix in the middle of a battlefield; the terrified eyes of concentration camp prisoners). Real-life ex-Marine Lee Marvin is perfect as the taciturn yet compassionate Sarge, and Robert Carradine is amusing as Zab, the cigar-chomping, pulp-novelist Fuller-surrogate, while the character of Griff is solemnly played by Mark Hamill. Vehemently antimilitaristic, the film celebrates camaraderie and brotherhood and eloquently demonstrates the ultimate futility of war.

BIG SLEEP, THE

1946 118m bw Mystery/Crime   ★★★★★
Warner Bros. (U.S.)   /PG

Humphrey Bogart (Philip Marlowe), Lauren Bacall (Vivian), John Ridgely (Eddie Mars), Louis Jean Heydt (Joe Brody), Elisha Cook Jr. (Jones), Regis Toomey (Bernie Ohls), Sonia Darrin (Agnes), Bob Steele (Canino), Martha Vickers (Carmen), Tom Rafferty (Carol Lundgren)

p, Howard Hawks; d, Howard Hawks; w, William Faulkner, Jules Furthman, Leigh Brackett (based on the novel by Raymond Chandler); ph, Sid Hickox; ed, Christian Nyby; m, Max Steiner; art d, Carl Jules Weyl; fx, Roy Davidson; cos, Leah Rhodes

The most convoluted of the great noir films, based on the first yarn written by Raymond Chandler. THE BIG SLEEP comes magically alive through Hawks's careful direction and Bogart's persona, which is twin to his character of Philip Marlowe.

Summoned to the lavish mansion of General Sternwood (Charles Waldron), Marlowe is hired to investigate blackmailer Geiger (Theodore Von Eltz), a Hollywood smut book dealer who has compromising photos of the general's daughter Carmen (Vickers). The general's real aim, however, is to have Bogart locate his missing confidante Shawn Regan. Marlowe follows his clues to Geiger's home, finding the smut peddler dead and Carmen drugged. Before police arrive, Marlowe secrets Carmen back home and strikes up a romance with the general's other daughter, Vivian (Bacall). With Vivian at the gumshoe's side, Marlowe sinks deeper and deeper into a labyrinthine plot of gambling, blackmail, and murder.

One of the greatest detective films to come out of Hollywood, THE BIG SLEEP is perhaps most notorious for its famous unsolved murder—that of the Sternwood chauffeur. The unwieldy plot, scripted by William Faulkner, kept Hawks busy trying to figure out the puzzle. When Hawks called Chandler to ask the killer's identity, the writer reportedly stated: "How should I know? You figure it out," and hung up. It was on the set of THE BIG SLEEP that the Bogart and Bacall love-team image was cemented, although their first sizzling union on screen was in TO HAVE AND HAVE NOT. Their dazzling star personas, combined with the poetry of both Chandler's and Faulkner's words and Howard Hawks's direction, give THE BIG SLEEP some of the most sexually electric dialogue ever to hit the screen.

BIG TRAIL, THE

1930 125m c/bw Western   ★★★
Fox (U.S.)   /U

John Wayne (Breck Coleman), Marguerite Churchill (Ruth Cameron), El Brendel (Gussie), Tully Marshall (Zeke), Tyrone Power Sr. (Red Flack), David Rollins (Dave Cameron), Frederick Burton (Pa Bascom), Charles Stevens (Lopez), Russ Powell (Windy Bill), Helen Parrish (Honey Girl)

d, Raoul Walsh; w, Jack Peabody, Marie Boyle, Florence Postal, Fred Sersen (based on a story by Hal Evarts and Raoul Walsh); ph, Lucien Andriot, Arthur Edeson; ed, Jack Dennis; m, Arthur Kay; art d, Harold Miles, Fred Sersen

Creaking, but sentimentally grand. Wayne was working as a property man, a kid just out of college, when director John Ford noticed him. When colleague Raoul Walsh was searching for the male lead for his latest project, Ford recommended Wayne, telling Walsh, who appeared in Griffith's THE BIRTH OF A NATION in 1915, and who would go on to become one of the best action directors (OBJECTIVE BURMA, THEY DIED WITH THEIR BOOTS ON) that he "liked the looks of this new kid with a funny walk, like he owned the world."

The film deals with the first covered wagon train to cross the rugged Oregon Trail. There is the traditional Indian attack with pioneers beating off the redskins from their circle of wagons, a spectacular buffalo hunt, and a devastating scene where the entire cast was almost drowned when fording a river during a fierce rainstorm (Walsh always kept the cameras rolling). There is little plot other than the great trek west through the wilderness of Nebraska and Wyoming where the film was shot, with Wayne vying for Churchill's attentions with Tully Marshall and others.

Walsh's direction is superb as he captures the thrilling outdoor action in this epic which cost Fox $2 million to produce, a fortune in those days. Further, the film was one of the first to be made in Grandeur, a 55mm wide-screen color process so impressive that the premiere audience jumped to its feet and cheered at the conclusion. Most viewers, however, only saw the film on the standard 35mm black-and-white screen, and this took away from the film's impact.

Wayne seems uneasy, and it can't have helped that Fox producers insisted that Lumsden Hare, the studio voice coach, teach Wayne to sound like an Englishman in buckskin so that each preciously recorded word could be understood. Wayne next drifted into the oblivion of "poverty row" studios that would have him making sagebrush grinders for nine years until Ford once again came to the rescue by giving him the lead in his classic STAGECOACH.

BILL & TED'S EXCELLENT ADVENTURE

1989 90m c Science Fiction/Comedy   ★★½
Nelson/Interscope/Nelson-Murphey (U.S.)   PG

Keanu Reeves (Ted "Theodore" Logan), Alex Winter (Bill S. Preston), George Carlin (Rufus), Terry Camilleri (Napoleon), Dan Shor (Billy the Kid), Tony Steedman (Socrates), Rod Loomis (Sigmund Freud), Al Leong (Genghis Khan), Jane Wiedlin (Joan of Arc), Robert V. Barron (Abraham Lincoln)

p, Scott Kroopf, Michael S. Murphey, Joel Soisson; d, Stephen Herek; w, Chris Matheson, Ed Solomon; ph, Tim Suhrstedt; ed, Larry Bock, Patrick Rand; m, David Newman; prod d, Roy Forge Smith; art d, Gordon White; chor, Brad Jeffries; cos, Jill Ohanneson

Radical! Pair of rock 'n' roll airheads can't graduate unless they pass history exam. Along comes Carlin from the future to enable dudes to experience history for themselves. Dudes take off without film. Still, BILL & TED has an intangibly charming goofiness about it that is somehow endearing: Here is a movie about teenagers that contains no excessive profanity, no drug references, and no explicit sexual activity.

BILL OF DIVORCEMENT, A

1932 70m bw Drama   ★★★★
Selznick (U.S.)   /A

John Barrymore (Hillary Fairfield), Billie Burke (Margaret Fairfield), Katharine Hepburn (Sydney Fairfield), David Manners (Kit Humphrey), Henry Stephenson (Doctor Alliot), Paul Cavanagh (Gray Meredith), Elizabeth Patterson (Aunt Hester), Gayle Evers (Bassett), Julie Haydon (Party Guest)

p, David O. Selznick; d, George Cukor; w, Howard Estabrook, Harry Wagstaff Gribble (based on the play by Clemence Dane); ph, Sid Hickox; ed, Arthur Roberts; m, Max Steiner; art d, Carroll Clark; cos, Josette De Lima

This was the second, definitive version of three filmings of the Clemence Dane play. (The first was a British silent of 1922, and RKO made a second worthy sound version with Adolphe Menjou and Maureen

O'Hara in 1940.) John Barrymore was at the top of his profession with this performance, and a radiant Katharine Hepburn made her screen debut. Barrymore plays a man who has been living in a mental hospital for many years and who escapes on the day his wife (Burke) is divorcing him. His daughter's (Hepburn) rediscovery of her father, her reaction to the taint of hereditary mental illness in the family, and the wife's desire to remarry make for a compact and compelling drama.

Barrymore is simply superb, director George Cukor eliciting a lost, sensitive and caring man from beneath the occasional bravado. Hepburn, who was to work with Cukor nine more times in films and TV, was only 24 at the time. Her appearance was electric and sent critics reaching for new superlatives.

BILLY BATHGATE

1991	106m	c	Crime/Drama/Romance	★★★
Touchstone	(U.S.)			R/15

Dustin Hoffman (Dutch Schultz), Nicole Kidman (Drew Preston), Loren Dean (Billy Bathgate), Bruce Willis (Bo Weinberg), Steven Hill (Otto Berman), Steve Buscemi (Irving), Billy Jaye (Mickey), John Costelloe (Lulu), Tim Jerome (Dixie Davis), Stanley Tucci (Lucky Luciano)

p, Arlene Donovan, Robert F Colesberry; d, Robert Benton; w, Tom Stoppard (from the novel by E.L. Doctorow); ph, Nestor Almendros; ed, Alan Heim, Robert Reitano, David Ray; m, Mark Isham; prod d, Patrizia Von Brandenstein; art d, Tim Galvin, Dennis Bradford, John Willett; fx, Joe Unsinn, Michael Landati; chor, Patricia Birch; cos, Joseph G. Aulisi

Despite an impressive array of talent, the ingredients never catch fire in this oddly lifeless adaptation of E.L. Doctorow's acclaimed novel.

Billy Bathgate (Loren Dean), an enterprising street kid from the Depression-era Bronx slums, bluffs and charms his way into the upper echelons of Dutch Schultz's (Hoffman) gang by helping expose the duplicity of Schultz's trusted lieutenant, Bo Weinberg (Bruce Willis). Dumped from a tugboat wearing cement overshoes, Weinberg leaves behind a rich girlfriend, Drew Preston (Nicole Kidman), who takes up with Schultz. It becomes Billy's main job to take care of Drew, as Schultz, already in decline, is preoccupied with fighting federal tax-evasion charges in the courts and rising mafioso Lucky Luciano (Stanley Tucci) on the streets.

Doctorow's multileveled plotting becomes BILLY BATHGATE's greatest liability: Stoppard's script and Benton's direction are so preoccupied with keeping the lines of action clear that they fail to establish a consistent mood or a strong point of view—the novel's real strengths. The casting also works against any lasting impact. The highly-touted Dean emerges here as just another generic brat-packer, wholly out of his expressive range. Kidman is too cool a beauty to evoke the hungry sexuality of the novel's Drew, for whom men were literally willing to die. Hoffman is, as usual, technically flawless, but on a gut level he fails even to erase memories of James Remar's searing portrayal of Schulz in THE COTTON CLUB. Only Steven Hill's performance, as Schultz's level-headed accountant, suggests the rough lyricism of Doctorow's elegy to the bad men who built America.

BILLY LIAR

1963	98m	bw	Drama	★★★★
Vic Films Ltd.	(U.K.)			/PG

Tom Courtenay (Billy Fisher), Julie Christie (Liz), Wilfred Pickles (Geoffrey Fisher), Mona Washbourne (Alice Fisher), Ethel Griffies (Florence), Finlay Currie (Duxbury), Rodney Bewes (Arthur Crabtree), Helen Fraser (Barbara), George Innes (Eric Stamp), Leonard Rossiter (Shadrack)

p, Joseph Janni; d, John Schlesinger; w, Keith Waterhouse, Willis Hall (based on their play); ph, Denys Coop; ed, Roger Cherrill; m, Richard Rodney Bennett; art d, Ray Simon

One of the seminal British working-class films of the 1960s, BILLY LIAR is a first-rate comedy-fantasy that features Tom Courtenay in a role which Albert Finney had played in the stage version by Waterhouse and Hall.

No one will argue the plot's derivation—James Thurber's classic short story "The Secret Life of Walter Mitty," with Courtenay as Billy Fisher, a dreamer who works for a funeral director, but who retreats into a fantasy world. Billy is also a pathological liar who, as Oscar Wilde once said, doesn't lie for gain, just for the sheer joy of lying. Billy is involved with three young women, two of whom share an engagement ring. Christie, in one of her earliest roles, is terrific as an adventurous young woman willing to overlook anything the charming Billy tosses at her.

All the secondary roles are sharply etched and wonderfully acted under the sure hand of John Schlesinger in his third feature. Although his two earlier films, TERMINUS and A KIND OF LOVING, were superb, it was really with this film that Schlesinger garnered widespread attention. A later stage musical and TV series were based on the same story.

BILOXI BLUES

1988	107m	c	Comedy/War	★★★½
Rastar	(U.S.)			PG-13/15

Matthew Broderick (Eugene Morris Jerome), Christopher Walken (Sgt. Merwin J. Toomey), Matt Mulhern (Joseph Wykowski), Corey Parker (Arnold Epstein), Markus Flanagan (Roy Selridge), Casey Siemaszko (Donald Carney), Michael Dolan (James J. Hennessey), Penelope Ann Miller (Daisy Hannigan), Park Overall (Rowena), Alan Pottinger (Peek)

p, Ray Stark; d, Mike Nichols; w, Neil Simon (based on his play); ph, Bill Butler; ed, Sam O'Steen; m, Georges Delerue; prod d, Paul Sylbert; cos, Ann Roth

BILOXI BLUES works better than the script alone would suggest, thanks to the skillful direction of Nichols and excellent performances from Broderick and Walken.

An adaptation of Simon's autobiographical play, the film follows New Yorker Broderick through his Army basic training in Biloxi, Mississippi, in the last days of WWII. The Biloxi heat gets him down, as does his strange drill sergeant, Walken, whose sadism works in quiet, mysterious ways, sowing dissent among his troops. Weeks of bad food, long marches, and humiliation are somewhat relieved when Broderick falls in love with Miller while on weekend leave. When his buddies find Broderick's notes and read his hurtful remarks about them—including his musings about whether Parker is homosexual—the aspiring writer discovers just how powerful words can be.

Successfully opening up Simon's popular play, Nichols avoids presenting the jokes in the sitcom formula typical of Simon, as set-ups to big punchlines. Broderick brings appealing nuances to the role he created onstage, and Walken makes his sergeant a quietly chilling, ambiguous character. An intelligent, tightly constructed film which manages to satirize both the military and the process of growing up.

BIRD

1988	161m	c	Biography	★★★★
Malpaso	(U.S.)			R/15

Forest Whitaker (Charlie "Yardbird" Parker), Diane Venora (Chan Richardson Parker), Michael Zelniker (Red Rodney), Samuel E. Wright (Dizzy Gillespie), Keith David (Buster Franklin), Michael McGuire (Brewster), James Handy (Esteves), Damon Whitaker (Young Bird), Morgan Nagler (Kim), Arlen Dean Snyder (Dr. Heath)

p, Clint Eastwood; d, Clint Eastwood; w, Joel Oliansky; ph, Jack N. Green; ed, Joel Cox; m, Lennie Niehaus; fx, Joe Day

AA Best Sound: Les Fresholtz, Dick Alexander, Vern Poore, Burton Willie D

A tribute to the life and genius of saxophonist Charlie Parker, BIRD is a collage of passages from Parker's remarkable life, from his childhood in Kansas City, through his tumultuous interracial relationship with Chan Richardson, to his tragic death at the age of 34.

Derived mostly from Chan Parker's unpublished memoir, *Life in E-Flat*, the story is told through an intricate structure that jumps backward and forward in an ambitious attempt to create a narrative and visual equivalent to Parker's complicated music. In a remarkable directorial effort, Eastwood shows a great flair for atmosphere and composition and presents a nuanced, complex, humane portrait of

Parker's talents, obstacles, virtues and failings. Whitaker gives a towering performance as the tortured musical genius, and Venora is equally impressive as the independent, compassionate Chan.

Wisely opting to use Parker's actual solos on the soundtrack instead of having a modern musician re-create them, Eastwood and musical director Lennie Niehaus took several previously unreleased recordings of Parker and digitally stripped away his accompanists (mostly because of poor recording techniques that featured Bird at the expense of the others), replacing them with modern musicians.

BIRD WITH THE CRYSTAL PLUMAGE, THE
(L'UCELLO DALLE PLUME DI CRISTALLO)

1969   98m   c   Horror   ★★★★
Glazier   (Italy/West Germany)   PG/18

Tony Musante *(Sam Dalmas)*, Suzy Kendall *(Julia)*, Eva Renzi *(Monica)*, Enrico Maria Salerno *(Morosini)*, Mario Adorf *(Berto)*, Renato Romano *(Dover)*, Umberto Raho *(Ranieri)*

p, Salvatore Argento; d, Dario Argento; w, Dario Argento; ph, Vittorio Storaro; m, Ennio Morricone

A heart-stopping horror melodrama with excellent acting from all involved. Director Argento, here essaying his first film, uses humor, much like Hitchcock, to complement the suspense, but you never feel the master is being ripped off.

Walking home one night, Musante, a Yank scribe in Rome, sees Renzi being murdered in an art gallery. He can't make out the killer's face, but the police decide to garnish his passport, as this is but one of several murders of lone women. Musante cooperates with the police but also conducts his own investigation, which takes him into the underbelly of the Eternal City.

Memorable characters abound and Storaro's sensational camera work and Morricone's score highlight their seedy milieu aptly. Several terrifying sequences come one after another, but none are gratuitous and the film never wallows in its violence. With a different title and better marketing, this compelling film, which had considerable influence on what would become known as the "slasher" genre in the 1980s, would have been a smash.

BIRDCAGE, THE

1996   118m   c   Comedy   ★★
Icarus Productions/United Artists   (U.S.)   R/15

Robin Williams *(Armand Goldman)*, Gene Hackman *(Senator Keeley)*, Nathan Lane *(Albert)*, Dianne Wiest *(Louise Keeley)*, Dan Futterman *(Val Goldman)*, Calista Flockhart *(Barbara Keeley)*, Hank Azaria *(Agador)*, Christine Baranski *(Katharine)*, Tom McGowan *(Harry Radman)*, Grant Heslov *(Photographer)*

p, Mike Nichols; d, Mike Nichols; w, Elaine May (based on the screenplay *La Cage Aux Folles* by Jean Poiret, Francis Veber, Edouard Molinaro, and Marcello Danon, adapted from the stage play by Jean Poiret); ph, Emmanuel Lubezki; ed, Arthur Schmidt; prod d, Bo Welch; art d, Tom Duffield; fx, Stan Parks, Syd Dutton, Bill Taylor, Illusion Arts, Inc.; chor, Vincent Paterson; cos, Ann Roth

AAN Best Art Direction: Bo Welch, Cheryl Carasik

In this flaccid remake of LA CAGE AUX FOLLES, Robin Williams and Nathan Lane play Armand and Albert, a middle-aged couple whose life together might be a model of bourgeois domesticity if they weren't both men. Armand owns a flashy Florida drag club called the Birdcage, and Albert is the unconvincing star attraction—it's not really clear who's clamoring to see this tubby, wholesome clown in a frock, but never mind. They're thrown into a tizz when their son (Dan Futterman)—he's actually Armand's kid by his ex-wife (Christine Baranski), but Albert might as well be his mother—announces his engagement to the daughter of a right-wing senator (Gene Hackman) who champions "family values." The Ozzie and Harriet of the drag set agree to play it straight for a night with the prospective in-laws, and tediously predictable complications ensue.

Unsurprisingly, the film rests on grotesque stereotypes of gay men (though it tries to have it both ways by flogging a simplistic plea for tolerance). What might be a surprise, given the talents involved, is how relentlessly unfunny it is. But this is drag comedy aimed squarely at middle America, where cuddly, sexless queens who sing show tunes,

wear silly clothes, and cook delightful meals are good for an indulgent laugh. The biggest chuckles come courtesy of the couple's swishy Latin houseboy (Hank Azaria), who not only talks funny and executes a classic pratfall with the best of them, but also looks adorable in a Carmen Miranda-inspired halter top.

BIRDMAN OF ALCATRAZ

1962   147m   bw   Prison/Biography   ★★★½
UA   (U.S.)   /A

Burt Lancaster *(Robert Stroud)*, Karl Malden *(Harvey Shoemaker)*, Thelma Ritter *(Elizabeth Stroud)*, Betty Field *(Stella Johnson)*, Neville Brand *(Bull Ransom)*, Edmond O'Brien *(Tom Gaddis)*, Hugh Marlowe *(Roy Comstock)*, Telly Savalas *(Feto Gomez)*, Crahan Denton *(Kramer)*, James Westerfield *(Jess Younger)*

p, Stuart Miller, Guy Trosper; d, John Frankenheimer; w, Guy Trosper (based on the book by Thomas E. Gaddis); ph, Burnett Guffey; ed, Edward Mann; m, Elmer Bernstein

AAN Best Actor: Burt Lancaster; *AAN Best Supporting Actor:* Telly Savalas; *AAN Best Supporting Actress:* Thelma Ritter; *AAN Best Cinematography:* Burnett Guffey

In a story based on fact, Lancaster plays surly, withdrawn inmate Robert Stroud, sentenced to life in prison, who cures a sick bird which flies into his cell one day, and later becomes an internationally recognized ornithologist. Fighting against an overly protective mother (Ritter) and a truculent warden (Malden), Stroud is nonetheless able to continue his research even when sent to Alcatraz, the notorious "Rock" in San Francisco Bay, home to only the most incorrigible prisoners. Finally, though, after an abortive romance (Field) and a prison riot which he helps quell, Stroud is able to tell his remarkable story to writer Tom Gaddis (O'Brien, playing the author of the film's source biography), who brings it to the world.

THE BIRDMAN OF ALCATRAZ has great production values, moving if sometimes plodding, overly deliberate scripting, and efficient direction from black-and-white specialist Frankenheimer which strives mightily to overcome the essentially static nature of the storyline. Lancaster's star turn in the title role, typically bravura yet more restrained than usual, plays a vital role in holding this lengthy movie together while staving off sentimentality in the process. Nominated for Best Actor, Lancaster lost to Gregory Peck for his role in TO KILL A MOCKINGBIRD. Malden is typically Malden, but Savalas, as one of Stroud's fellow inmates, and the reliable Ritter make the most of their roles and received supporting Oscar nominations, as did Guffey's skillful cinematography.

BIRDS, THE

1963   120m   c   Horror   ★★★★
Universal   (U.S.)   /15

Rod Taylor *(Mitch Brenner)*, Tippi Hedren *(Melanie Daniels)*, Jessica Tandy *(Lydia Brenner)*, Suzanne Pleshette *(Annie Hayworth)*, Veronica Cartwright *(Cathy Brenner)*, Ethel Griffies *(Mrs. Bundy)*, Charles McGraw *(Sebastian Sholes)*, Ruth McDevitt *(Mrs. MacGruder)*, Joe Mantell *(Salesman)*, Doodles Weaver *(Fisherman)*

p, Alfred Hitchcock; d, Alfred Hitchcock; w, Evan Hunter (based on the story by Daphne du Maurier); ph, Robert Burks; ed, George Tomasini; m, Bernard Herrmann; prod d, Norman Deming; fx, Ub Iwerks; cos, Edith Head

AAN Best Visual Effects: Ub Iwerks

Hitchcock's follow-up to PSYCHO (1960) was yet another groundbreaking addition to the horror genre and further revealed the master director's darker obsessions.

Loosely based on a Daphne du Maurier short story, the action is set in Bodega Bay and follows bored, spoiled socialite Melanie Daniels (Hedren) as she romantically pursues dashing lawyer Mitch Brenner (Taylor). Tension soon develops among Melanie, schoolteacher Annie Hayworth, Mitch's former flame (Pleshette), and Mitch's domineering mother (Tandy). The emotional interplay is interrupted (and reflected) by the sudden and unexplained attack of thousands of birds on the area.

Hailed as one of Hitchcock's masterpieces by some and despised by others, THE BIRDS is certainly among the director's more complex and fascinating works. Volumes have been written about the film, with each writer picking it apart scene by scene in order to prove his or her particular critical theory—mostly of the psychoanalytic variety. Be that as it may, even those who grow impatient with the slow build-up or occasional dramatic lapses cannot deny the terrifying power of many of the film's haunting images: the bird point-of-view shot of Bodega Bay, the birds slowly gathering on the playground monkey bars, the attack on the children's birthday party, Melanie trapped in the attic, and the final ambiguous shot of the defeated humans leaving Bodega Bay while the thousands of triumphant birds gathered on the ground watch them go.

BIRDY

1984　120m　c　Drama/War　★★★★½
Malton　(U.S.)　R/15

Matthew Modine *(Birdy)*, Nicolas Cage *(Al Columbato)*, John Harkins *(Dr. Weiss)*, Sandy Baron *(Mr. Columbato)*, Karen Young *(Hannah Rourke)*, Bruno Kirby *(Renaldi)*, Nancy Fish *(Mrs. Prevost)*, George Buck *(Birdy's Father)*, Delores Sage *(Birdy's Mother)*, Robert L. Ryan *(Joe Sagessa)*

p, Alan Marshall; d, Alan Parker; w, Sandy Kroopf, Jack Behr (based on the novel by William Wharton); ph, Michael Seresin; ed, Gerry Hambling; m, Peter Gabriel; prod d, Geoffrey Kirkland; art d, Armin Ganz, Stewart Campbell; cos, Kristi Zea

BIRDY is one of those rare movies that successfully brings a psychological novel to the screen without sacrificing its saliency or complexity.

Although the book by William Wharton is set in the days after WWII, the film has been updated to the post-Vietnam era to tell the story of the deep friendship between Birdy (Modine) and Al Columbato (Cage), a pair of young men whose lives have been scarred by the war experience. Birdy has had an obsessive affinity for birds since childhood (scenes of which are shown in flashback), but in the period after his wartime service he believes he has actually been transformed into a bird. As a result he is confined to a military mental hospital. His best friend, Al (who was physically wounded in Vietnam), is determined to bring Birdy back to the real world.

One of the most bizarre accounts of postwar trauma, BIRDY succeeds because of an excellent, nuanced screenplay, supple direction by Parker, and the outstanding performances of both Cage and Modine. Modine's sensitive portrayal of the young man who transcends species boundaries is spellbinding; Cage is at once affable, concerned, and frustrated. Full of moments which will linger in the memory (such as the flashbacks showing Birdy's attempts to fly or the film's final scene), the film is at once stark, compassionate and hilarious. A fresh and welcome alternative to such "realistic" postwar films as COMING HOME, WHO'LL STOP THE RAIN, and ROLLING THUNDER. Winner of the 1985 Special Grand Jury Prize at Cannes.

BISHOP'S WIFE, THE

1947　105m　bw　Comedy/Drama/Fantasy　★★★
RKO　(U.S.)　/U

Cary Grant *(Dudley)*, David Niven *(Henry Brougham)*, Loretta Young *(Julia Brougham)*, Monty Woolley *(Prof. Wutheridge)*, James Gleason *(Sylvester)*, Gladys Cooper *(Mrs. Hamilton)*, Elsa Lanchester *(Matilda)*, Sara Haden *(Mildred Cassaway)*, Karolyn Grimes *(Debby Brougham)*, Tito Vuolo *(Maggenti)*

p, Samuel Goldwyn; d, Henry Koster; w, Robert E. Sherwood, Leonardo Bercovici (based on a novel by Robert Nathan); ph, Gregg Toland; ed, Monica Collingwood; m, Hugo Friedhofer; art d, Charles Henderson; cos, Irene Sharaff

AAN Best Picture; AAN Best Director: Henry Koster; *AAN Best Editing:* Monica Collingwood; *AAN Best Score:* Hugo Friedhofer; *AA Best Sound:* Goldwyn Sound Department

A warm, sentimental comedy-fantasy, a follow-up to the similar but superior IT'S A WONDERFUL LIFE.

Niven plays an Episcopalian bishop praying for money to build a new church. His marriage is apparently over and his faith is quivering when Grant, an angel who uses his powers so sparingly that he might

have been from the Welcome Wagon, arrives on the scene. Young, as Niven's wife, never learns Cary is from Up There as he unobtrusively helps her and Niven achieve some peace on earth and goodwill toward each other.

Under Koster's typically smooth direction, everyone seems to be having a good time, enjoying the script without mocking its blandness. The picture runs on a bit long and it does pale by comparison to the book, but it was a welcome smile in 1947 and has the same effect today. Popular and acclaimed in its day, the film was rather surprisingly nominated for Best Picture of the year.

BITTER RICE

1949　107m　bw　Drama　★★★
DEG　(Italy)　/A

Silvana Mangano *(Silvana)*, Doris Dowling *(Francesca)*, Vittorio Gassman *(Walter)*, Raf Vallone *(Marco)*, Checco Rissone *(Aristide)*, Nico Pepe *(Beppe)*, Andriana Sivieri *(Celeste)*, Lia Croelli *(Amelia)*, Maria Grazia Francia *(Gabriella)*, Ann Maestri *(Irene)*

p, Dino De Laurentiis; d, Giuseppe De Santis; w, Giuseppe De Santis, Carlo Lizzani, Gianni Puccini (based on a story by Giuseppe De Santis, Carlo Lizzani); ph, Otello Martelli; m, Goffredo Petrassi

AAN Best Original Screenplay: Giuseppe De Santis, Carlo Lizzani

One of the earliest examples of how the Italian neorealist cinema of the 1940s succumbed to the dictates of Hollywood star glamor, BITTER RICE is nevertheless a good, moody film which captures the bare survival atmosphere of Italy after WWII, when the country lay in ruins and everyone scraped for a living.

In this case it's the buxom, somewhat glamorized Mangano, who parades about in a bursting sweater, short-shorts and artfully torn nylons as she works with hundreds of other women in the rice fields of the Po Valley. (Notably, Mangano's presence in this film, shaped by future husband De Laurentiis, prefigures the arrival of the so-called Italian "sexpot" actresses of the 1950s, whose ranks included Gina Lollbrigida and Sophia Loren).

The story, less involved with the effects of the war and poverty than earlier neorealist efforts, concerns the young woman and her involvement with two men, one down-to-earth, respectable but weak (Vallone), the other brutal, criminal yet magnetic (Gassman). The acting is fine and De Santis's direction shows great compositional skill with both camera and figure movement. Hardly a compelling critique of worker exploitation, BITTER RICE is still potent in its sensual, naturalistic depiction of love on straw bunks and sex offered along the highway.

BIZET'S CARMEN

1984　152m　c　Opera　★★★
Marcel Dassault/Opera/Gaumont　(France/Italy)　PG

Julia Migenes-Johnson *(Carmen)*, Placido Domingo *(Don Jose)*, Ruggero Raimondi *(Escamillo)*, Faith Esham *(Micaela)*, Jean-Philippe Lafont *(Dancairo)*, Gerard Garino *(Remendado)*, Susan Daniel *(Mercedes)*, Lilian Watson *(Frasquita)*, Jean Paul Bogart *(Zuniga)*, Francois Le Roux *(Morales)*

p, Patrice Ledoux; d, Francesco Rosi; w, Francesco Rosi, Tonino Guerra (based on the story by Prosper Merimee and the opera "Carmen" by Georges Bizet); ph, Pasqualino De Santis; ed, Ruggero Mastroianni, Colette Semprun; m, Georges Bizet; prod d, Enrico Job; chor, Antonio Gades; cos, Enrico Job

For those who like like their Bizet straight, this is probably the best of the opera's many adaptations to date. In this relatively straightforward rendering of the classic tale, the sensuous Migenes-Johnson plays Carmen, a cigarette factory worker who ruins the life of a Spanish officer (Domingo).

The film's chief plus is Rosi's direction, at once low-key in its documentary realism and fiery in its passion and detail. By taking their actors and cameras into the Andalusian landscape of Spain, Rosi and cinematographer De Santis have succeeded in giving a different and entirely valid feel to the well-worn saga. The choreographer, Antonio Gades, performed similar duties on the Carlos Saura version, and Lorin Maazel's handling of the music is a standout. A serious drawback is Migenes-Johnson's voice; she seems to have been cast more for her looks than her vocal talents.

BLACK AND WHITE IN COLOR
(LA VICTOIRE EN CHANTANT)
1976 100m c Drama/War   ★★★
Allied Artists (France)   PG/A

Jean Carmet *(Sgt. Bosselet)*, Jacques Dufilho *(Paul Rechampot)*,
Catherine Rouvel *(Marinette)*, Jacques Spiesser *(Hubert Fresnoy)*,
Dora Doll *(Maryvonne)*, Maurice Barrier *(Caprice)*, Claude Legros
(Jacques Rechampot), Jacques Monnet *(Pere Simon)*, Peter Berling
(Pere Jean De La Croix), Marius Beugre Boignan *(Barthelemy)*

p, Arthur Cohn, Jacques Perrin, Giorgio Silagni; d, Jean-Jacques
Annaud; w, Jean-Jacques Annaud, Georges Conchon; ph, Claude
Agostini; ed, Francoise Bonnot; m, Pierre Bachelet; art d, Max Douy

AA Best Foreign Language Film

The winner of the 1976 Oscar for Best Foreign Film, this first feature
from Annaud (THE NAME OF THE ROSE) is set in a French colonial
outpost in 1915.

When Spiesser, a conscientious young geologist, writes home to
Paris to lament the "dangers" of Africa (chief among which is boredom), he begs for newspapers and books from home. Some time later
the papers arrive, bringing the news—six months late—that France is
at war with Germany. This poses a bit of a problem at the outpost for a
number of reasons: the colonists are friendly with a group of neighboring Germans; their commander, Carmet, has never been in battle; and
they have no trained army. Rising to the challenge, Carmet conscripts
all the healthy male natives who live near the outpost and teaches them
to speak French, operate bayonets, wear shoes, and sing "La Marseillaise." Ultimately, the natives are even honored with French names.

A biting satire on war, colonialism, and French patriotism which
sometimes does not escape the character types it aims to parody,
BLACK AND WHITE IN COLOR juxtaposes scenes of gaiety and
humor with the brutalities of racism and war. The result is something
of a combination of Philippe de Broca's cult antiwar satire, KING OF
HEARTS, and Jamie Uys's THE GODS MUST BE CRAZY. Deserving of special mention is the playful score by Bachelet.

BLACK CAT, THE
1934 70m bw Horror   ★★★★½
Universal (U.S.)   /15

Boris Karloff *(Hjalmar Poelzig)*, Bela Lugosi *(Dr. Vitus Verdegast)*,
David Manners *(Peter Allison)*, Julie Bishop *(Joan Allison)*, Lucille
Lund *(Karen)*, Egon Brecher *(Majordomo)*, Henry Armetta *(Ser-
geant)*, Albert Conti *(Lieutenant)*, Anna Duncan *(Maid)*, Herman Bing
(Car Steward)

p, Carl Laemmle Jr.; d, Edgar G. Ulmer; w, Edgar G. Ulmer, Peter
Ruric (based on the story by Edgar Allan Poe); ph, John Mescall; ed,
Ray Curtiss; art d, Charles D. Hall

The first and best teaming of horror stars Karloff and Lugosi was this
bizarre, haunting, and hypnotic film by director Ulmer.

Not an adaptation of Poe but rather a strikingly effective evocation
of the twisted world of his literature, the story concerns a young couple,
Peter (Manners) and Joan (Wells), who meet mysterious scientist Dr.
Vitus Verdegast (Lugosi) while on their honeymoon in Budapest. The
trio wind up at the home of Verdegast's old "friend" Hjalmar Poelzig
(Karloff), an architect living atop a mountain in a modernistic, Art Deco
mansion.

As it turns out, Poelzig is the leader of a satanic cult who, as a
commander during WWI, caused the capture of Verdegast and the
deaths of thousands of their countrymen in a bloody battle. While
Verdegast rotted in prison, the architect stole his wife, who later died
(he keeps her corpse in a glass case), then married Verdegast's daughter.
Verdegast has now come for revenge, and Peter and Joan find themselves caught in a deadly game of cat and mouse.

A remarkable study of evil containing some unusually brutal scenes
in its frenzied climax, THE BLACK CAT is still one of the most
affecting horrors the genre has ever produced. With supreme directorial
skill, Ulmer infuses the film with an overwhelming sense of unease,
eroticism, and dread that remains powerful to this day. The literate
script, magnificent set design, superbly fluid camerawork, and stunning
performances by Karloff (whose character was inspired by occult

hedonist Aleister Crowley) and Lugosi lend the film a timeless quality.
Ulmer would go on to direct such low-budget classics as DETOUR
(1945), but this is his masterpiece.

BLACK CAULDRON, THE
1985 82m c Animated   ★★★½
Walt Disney Productions/Silver Screen Partners II (U.S.)   PG/U

VOICES OF: Grant Bardsley *(Taran)*, Susan Sheridan *(Eilonwy)*,
Freddie Jones *(Dallben)*, Nigel Hawthorne *(Fflewddur)*, Arthur Malet
(King Eidilleg), John Byner *(Gurgi/Doli)*, Lindsay Rich, Brandon Call,
Gregory Levinson *(Fairfolk)*, Eda Reiss Merin *(Orddu)*

p, Joe Hale; d, Ted Berman, Richard Rich; w, David Jonas, Vance
Gerry, Ted Berman, Richard Rich, Joe Hale, Al Wilson, Roy Morita,
Peter Young, Art Stevens, Rosemary Anne Sisson, Roy Edward
Disney (based on the five novels of the series *The Chronicles of
Prydain* by Lloyd Alexander); ed, Jim Melton, Jim Koford, Armetta
Jackson; m, Elmer Bernstein; anim, Walt Stanchfield

A glorious return to the days at Disney when animation was full and
detail was everything, THE BLACK CAULDRON is betrayed by a
routine storyline which fails to grip the imagination in the same way
that such classics as PINOCCHIO or DUMBO do, but it's a remarkable
achievement nonetheless.

A familiar sword-and-sorcery yarn, the story tells of Taran, an
aspiring warrior, and his battle supreme with the villainous Horned
King, who wants to gain possession of the Black Cauldron, a source of
supernatural power. Taran knows that if the Horned King gets the
Cauldron, civilization will cease. Taran is joined in his struggle by
Eilonwy, a princess; a psychic pig named Hen Wen; Gurgi, a sycophan-
tic creature; and a bevy of minifairies.

Only the second animated feature to be shot in 70mm (the first such
widescreen extravaganza being 1959's SLEEPING BEAUTY), THE
BLACK CAULDRON used more than 2.5 million drawings to bring
its tale vividly to life. Every leaf has been patiently drawn, the depth of
field is remarkable, the angles are chosen with care, and the result is a
state-of-the-art cartoon that should be seen by anyone who loves the
craft. Despite its drawbacks as entertainment, it remains one of the best
technical cartoon features ever produced by Disney.

BLACK NARCISSUS
1946 100m c Drama   ★★★★½
Archer (U.K.)   /15

Deborah Kerr *(Sister Clodagh)*, Sabu *(Dilip Rai)*, David Farrar *(Mr.
Dean)*, Flora Robson *(Sister Philippa)*, Jean Simmons *(Kanchi)*,
Esmond Knight *(Gen. Toda Rai)*, Kathleen Byron *(Sister Ruth)*, Jenny
Laird *(Sister Honey)*, Judith Furse *(Sister Briony)*, May Hallatt *(Angu
Ayah)*

p, Michael Powell, Emeric Pressburger; d, Michael Powell, Emeric
Pressburger; w, Michael Powell, Emeric Pressburger (based on the
novel by Rumer Godden); ph, Jack Cardiff; ed, Reginald Mills; m,
Brian Easdale

AA Best Cinematography: Jack Cardiff; *AA Best Art Direction:* Alfred
Junge (Art Direction)

A stunner from one of the great collaborative teams in the history of
cinema and an anomaly in British film of the 1940s. Powell and
Pressburger continued their string of daring, idiosyncratic films (LIFE
AND DEATH OF COLONEL BLIMP, A MATTER OF LIFE AND
DEATH, THE RED SHOES) with this full-blown melodrama concerning a group of Anglican nuns who attempt to establish a school and
hospital at an ancient ruler's castle-cum-bordello high in the Himalayas.

Kerr is highly effective as the young, ambitious Sister Clodagh,
given her first taste of authority but bedeviled by the climate, the
natives, the cynical but sexy British government agent Mr. Dean
(Farrar) and her own and her colleagues' emotional weaknesses. In-
dian-born juvenile actor Sabu, in his last major role, plays a rich,
bejeweled young general (who wears Black Narcissus perfume) bewitched by a seductive native girl (Simmons, in an odd but highly
effective bit of casting). The turbulent chain of events reaches its climax

when Sister Ruth (Byron, superb in a performance which should have insured her career) becomes unhinged over her desires for Mr. Dean and her jealousy of Sister Clodagh.

An odd, unsettling film which suggests the dangers of both emotional restraint and unchecked passion, BLACK NARCISSUS is also one of the most visually beautiful films ever made in color. The acting of the leads excels, and they are splendidly abetted by Robson, Furst, and Laird as the other nuns and by Knight and Hallatt as, respectively, a paternal ruler and a hilariously cynical housekeeper.

Full of hysteria (especially at the cathartic climax, where Byron's makeup antedates that of THE EXORCIST) and continuing Powell and Pressburger's implicit critique of British stiff-upper-lip attitudes, BLACK NARCISSUS was ahead of its time, prefiguring the later melodramas of everyone from Sirk to Fassbinder to Ken Russell. The scenes where Sister Clodagh recalls her happy, romantic days before entering the convent were at first cut by censors. The film deservedly won the Oscars for color cinematography and art direction.

BLACK ORPHEUS
(ORFEU NEGRO)

1959 100m c Drama ★★★½
Lopert (France/Italy/Brazil) /A

Breno Mello (Orfeo), Marpessa Dawn (Eurydice), Lourdes de Oliveira (Mira), Lea Garcia (Serafina), Adhemar da Silva (Death), Alexandro Constantino (Hermes), Waldetar de Souza (Chico), Jorge dos Santos (Benedito), Aurino Cassanio (Zeca)

p, Sacha Gordine; d, Marcel Camus; w, Jacques Viot, Marcel Camus (based on the play "Orfeu da Conceicao" by Vinicius de Moraes); ph, Jean Bourgoin; ed, Andree Feix; m, Antonio Carlos Jobim, Luiz Bonfa

AA Best Foreign Language Film

The Orpheus myth is transplanted onto the soil of Rio de Janeiro during Carnival—the one time of the year that calls for unrestrained celebration, music, dance, and costumes.

Orfeo (Mello) is a streetcar conductor and guitarist engaged to Mira (de Oliveira), an exotic and vivacious woman who lives as if every day were Carnival. However, anyone familiar with the legend of Orpheus (as the man in Rio's marriage office is) knows that he is destined to love Eurydice (Dawn—oddly enough, a dancer born in Pittsburgh), personified here as a newcomer to Rio who arrives in town to visit her cousin Serafina (Garcia). Eurydice has fled her hometown because she was being followed by a mysterious stranger, one who has followed her to Rio and has disguised himself as Death for Carnival. In order to save Eurydice, Orfeo must travel into the Underworld and bring her back to the world of the living.

From the opening shot, in which two Brazilian musicians literally burst through the frame, one can sense the explosiveness of BLACK ORPHEUS. Like Carnival, the film frame dances, the soundtrack sings, and the costumes swirl in an explosion of color and light. Besides its exhilarating style, however, the well-acted film works as an effective translation of the classic Greek myth into a Brazilian romance.

More successful as a travelogue of Brazilian scenery than an exploration of the country's folk culture, BLACK ORPHEUS was the second film from Camus, a Frenchman who traveled to Brazil to make this picture and would never again repeat its success. BLACK ORPHEUS received instant international acclaim and was honored with the Golden Palm at Cannes and the Academy Award for Best Foreign Film.

BLACK RAIN
(KUROI AME)

1989 123m bw Drama ★★★½
Imamura/Hayashibara/Tohokushinsha (Japan) /PG

Yoshiko Tanaka (Yasuko), Kazuo Kitamura (Shigematsu), Etsuko Ichihara (Shigako), Shoichi Ozawa (Shokichi), Norihei Miki (Kotaro), Keisuke Ishida (Yuichi)

p, Hisa Iino; d, Shohei Imamura; w, Shohei Imamura, Toshiro Ishido (based on a novel by Masuji Ibuse); ph, Takashi Kawamata; ed, Hajime Okayasu; m, Toru Takemitsu; art d, Hisao Inagaki

A potent if flawed study of the dropping of the atomic bomb on Hiroshima and its aftereffects, focusing on the dark destiny of one family caught in the holocaust.

The film opens with the bombing, showing the blinding flash of light, the shock wave that disintegrates people and buildings, and the black rain falling on young Yasuko (Tanaka), her aunt Shigako (Ichihara) and her uncle Shigematsu (Kitamura), which exposes them all to radiation poisoning. Five years pass, and the family's main problem is now the difficulty of finding a husband for Yasuko, whose contamination leaves her a pariah in the community. The locals have become used to funeral processions and to the taking of various home remedies; the desperate Shigako even turns to a noisy charlatan of a faith healer. Yasuko gradually becomes involved with Yuichi (Ishida), whose nerves have been shattered by the war, but the couple's time together is fatefully limited.

Imamura films his story in stark, elegant black and white, creating both haunting imagery (e.g. the escaping townspeople looking back at the mushroom cloud forming behind them) and a distance from the story's drama. Similar distancing is evoked by the soap opera treatment of the story and the bewildered resignation of the protagonists, never once expressing either real rage or sorrow at their plight. What is less clear is the critical perspective Imamura (or the audience) can take via such distancing. The problems of traditional Japanese formality are highlighted, as are the prejudices held by the Japanese against the bomb's victims (hibakusha in Japanese) and the horrors of warfare which bring about such conditions, but no single critique is fully fleshed out.

The film is full of touching moments, but at times the emotional resonance is characteristic of second-rate Hollywood, as when Yuichi's phobia of the sounds of moving vehicles vanishes during an ambulance ride at the film's end. In short, the film is powerfully grim but does not capture the horror of the bomb's blast, it is full of cool observation yet cannot resist idealizing the central family unit.

BLACK ROBE

1991 100m c Adventure/Drama/Historical ★★★½
Alliance Entertainment/Samson Productions/Cinegramme V R/15
(Canada/Australia)

Lothaire Bluteau (Father Laforgue), Aden Young (Daniel), Sandrine Holt (Annuka), August Schellenberg (Chomina), Tantoo Cardinal (Chomina's Wife), Billy Two Rivers (Ougebmat), Lawrence Bayne (Neehatin), Harrison Liu (Awondoie), Wesley Cote (Oujita), Frank Wilson (Father Jerome)

p, Robert Lantos, Stephane Reichel, Sue Milliken; d, Bruce Beresford; w, Brian Moore (from novel Black Robe by Brian Moore); ph, Peter James; ed, Tim Wellburn; m, Georges Delerue; prod d, Herbert Pinter; art d, Gavin Mitchell; fx, Louis Craig, Francois Dagenais, Darren Perks; cos, Renee April, John Hay

Despite an occasionally plodding screenplay, this white-man-in-the-wilderness drama goes DANCES WITH WOLVES one better by showing more genuine respect for its subject. Directed by Bruce Beresford, BLACK ROBE was adapted by Brian Moore from his own novel, which, in turn, was based on letters and journals written by Jesuit missionaries, whom the Indians dubbed "black robes," in the New World during the 17th century.

The story revolves around Father Laforgue (JESUS OF MONTREAL's Lothaire Bluteau) who is sent by Champlain (Jean Brousseau), the founder and governor of Quebec, 1,500 miles north to a frontier Jesuit mission to assist in the conversion of the Huron tribe to Catholicism in 1634. Pledging to guide and protect Laforgue, Algonquin leader Chomina (August Schellenberg) brings his wife, young son and beautiful teenage daughter Annuka (Sandrine Holt), as well as a small party of braves and their families. Driven as much by his passion for Annuka as his aspirations to the priesthood, young French settler Daniel (Aden Young) also volunteers to accompany Laforgue on what turns into a grueling journey.

Returning to the theme of his first international hit, BREAKER MORANT, as well as the more recent MISTER JOHNSON, Beresford's emphasis in BLACK ROBE is on European presumption in forcing native peoples to adopt Western culture. Nevertheless, BLACK ROBE tries to distinguish itself by pretending to a basic, at times brutal, "honesty" in its depiction of native culture. The Indians in BLACK ROBE aren't the starry-eyed noble savages that strain credibility in DANCES WITH WOLVES. Far from it: there are scenes of Indian brutishness that rival anything in overtly racist Hollywood films. These are balanced by a sympathetic portrayal of Laforgue's Indian companions, who appear as relatively complex human beings. Their spiritual beliefs ultimately impress Laforgue, though it happens too late to be of much help to anyone.

BLACK STALLION, THE

1979 118m c Adventure ★★★★
UA (U.S.) G/U

Kelly Reno (*Alec Ramsey*), Mickey Rooney (*Henry Dailey*), Teri Garr (*Alec's Mother*), Clarence Muse (*Snoe*), Hoyt Axton (*Alec's Father*), Michael Higgins (*Neville*), Ed McNamara (*Jake*), Doghmi Larbi (*The Arab*), John Burton, John Buchanan (*Jockeys*)

p, Tom Sternberg, Fred Roos; d, Carroll Ballard; w, Melissa Mathison, Jeanne Rosenberg, William D. Wittliff (based on the novel by Walter Farley); ph, Caleb Deschanel; ed, Robert Dalva; m, Carmine Coppola

AAN Best Supporting Actor: Mickey Rooney; *AAN Best Editing:* Robert Dalva

This touching and beautifully photographed, if slightly overlong, tale of a boy and his horse follows the escapades of young Alec Ramsey (Reno), who is traveling across the ocean with his father.

The ship sinks, and Alec is saved by Black, a handsome Arabian stallion the boy had befriended earlier in the journey. After being shipwrecked on a deserted island, Alec and Black are rescued and returned to their small-town home. Eventually, Black is cared for by former horse trainer Henry Dailey (Rooney), who later takes Kelly under his wing to be trained as a jockey. Naturally, it all leads up to the big race—a stunningly photographed sequence brimming with tension.

A simple film, sentimental but not mawkish, as enjoyable for adults as it is for children, THE BLACK STALLION is one of the finest movies about children and horses since Elizabeth Taylor was seen in NATIONAL VELVET. It's also a pleasure to see Rooney back in the saddle again, so to speak, and his lively character turn won him a much-deserved Oscar nomination for Best Supporting Actor. A sequel, THE BLACK STALLION RETURNS (1983), is more a Saharan adventure than a sports picture.

BLACK SUNDAY
(LA MASCHERA DEL DEMONIO)

1960 83m bw Horror ★★★★½
AIP (Italy) /AA

Barbara Steele (*Witch Princess Katia*), John Richardson (*Dr. Gorobee*), Ivo Garrani (*Prince*), Andrea Cecchi (*Dr. Choma*), Arturo Dominici (*Javutich*), Enrico Olivieri (*Constantin*), Antonio Pierfederici (*the Pope*), Clara Bindi (*Innkeeper*), Germana Dominici (*His Daughter*), Mario Passante (*Nikita*)

p, Massimo De Rita; d, Mario Bava; w, Ennio De Concini, Mario Serandrei (based on a story by Nikolai Gogol); ph, Mario Bava, Ubaldo Terzano; ed, Mario Serandrei; m, Les Baxter; art d, Giorgio Giovannini

In 1630, a beautiful witch princess, Asa (Barbara Steele), who is a vampire, and her lover, Juvato (Arturo Dominici), are put to death by her vengeful brother. He has iron masks with spikes on the inside placed on both of their faces and then sledgehammered home. Two hundred years later, blood is accidentally spilled on Asa's face and she rises from the dead along with Juvato to wreak revenge on the descendants of those who executed her—including her look-alike, Katia (also played by Steele).

Beautifully photographed in black and white by Bava himself, BLACK SUNDAY is hypnotic and compelling. From the brutal opening to the resurrection of the vampires and the horrors that follow, Bava's camera effortlessly glides through the fogbound sets, presenting one incredible image after another. Bava exhibits a comparable command of sound and music—or the lack thereof—with some sequences played out in virtual silence. Steele is magnificent in her dual role as

vengeful devil and vestal virgin. As the resurrected Asa, her beautiful face is both seductive and horrifying, bearing the terrible holes punched by the iron mask. The role catapulted her to horror-movie stardom.

Unfortunately, when released in the US by American International Pictures, BLACK SUNDAY was badly dubbed and a bombastic Les Baxter score was imposed over the original by Roberto Nicolosi. Another, less bastardized version is available from California-based Sinister Cinema.

BLACK SUNDAY

1977 143m c Action ★★★★
Paramount (U.S.) R/15

Robert Shaw (*Kabakov*), Bruce Dern (*Lander*), Marthe Keller (*Dahlia*), Fritz Weaver (*Corley*), Steven Keats (*Moshevsky*), Bekim Fehmiu (*Fasil*), Michael V. Gazzo (*Muzi*), William Daniels (*Pugh*), Walter Gotell (*Col. Riaf*), Victor Campos (*Nageeb*)

p, Robert Evans; d, John Frankenheimer; w, Ernest Lehman, Ivan Moffat, Kenneth Ross; ph, John A. Alonzo; ed, Tom Rolf; m, John Williams

One of the best of the disaster films of the 1970s, the genuinely disturbing BLACK SUNDAY is likely to cause nightmares long after you've seen it. Keller and Fehmiu portray "Black September" agents (in a takeoff on the killers who terrorized the 1972 Olympics) who plan to hijack the Goodyear Blimp and send it into the teeming Super Bowl crowd firing thousands of steel darts. Dern, in typical and fine form as a deranged Vietnam veteran, is hired to pilot the killer blimp. Shaw, as an Israeli major, and Weaver, playing a heroic FBI agent, smoothly represent law and order. The scene where the blimp comes over the top of Miami's Orange Bowl is guaranteed to have you squirming in your seat. Far superior to the similar TWO MINUTE WARNING (1976), BLACK SUNDAY benefits from its technical skill, drawn-out suspense and developed characterizations, though the film could have been even more effectively tight with a shorter running time.

BLACK SWAN, THE

1942 85m c Adventure ★★★★½
Fox (U.S.) /A

Tyrone Power (*James Waring*), Maureen O'Hara (*Margaret Denby*), Laird Cregar (*Capt. Henry Morgan*), Thomas Mitchell (*Tommy Blue*), George Sanders (*Capt. Billy Leech*), Anthony Quinn (*Wogan*), George Zucco (*Lord Denby*), Edward Ashley (*Roger Ingram*), Fortunio Bonanova (*Don Miguel*), Stuart Robertson (*Capt. Graham*)

p, Robert Bassler; d, Henry King; w, Ben Hecht, Seton I. Miller (based on the novel by Rafael Sabatini); ph, Leon Shamroy; ed, Barbara McLean; m, Alfred Newman; art d, Richard Day, James Basevi; cos, Earl Luick

AA Best Cinematography: Leon Shamroy; *AAN Best Score:* Alfred Newman; *AAN Best Visual Effects:* Fred Sersen, Roger Heman, George Leverett

Along with THE MARK OF ZORRO, the peak of Tyrone Power's career as a swashbuckler.

A sweeping pirate epic with Power as an aide to notorious buccaneer Henry Morgan (Cregar), the film opens with Morgan pardoned from the gallows and sent to Jamaica as its new governor. Trying to prevent his former associates from continuing their villainous activities, Morgan encounters resistance from two renegades (Sanders and Quinn). Power, meanwhile, falls for the daughter (O'Hara) of the former governor, but she spurns his brazen advances. Although kidnapping her and taking her along on his warship doesn't initially help matters, things change when Sanders and Quinn overpower his ship, forcing Power to fight for the woman he loves.

The story and dialogue smack of the Errol Flynn adventure CAPTAIN BLOOD, but the film employs its cliches with such overwhelming vigor and good humor that they seem like old friends. Even though his physique isn't quite up to the more beefcake aspects of the hardsell by the producers, Power is full of marvelous dash and derring-do. Cregar, all hearty bravado, is equally wonderful, his enormous body bedecked in wigs and finery, and the practically unrecognizable Sanders, sporting a thick red wig and beard, is quite effective as a less civilized type of villain than those he usually played. The ravishing, flame-haired, underrated O'Hara, too, is in her element as the feisty heroine and the result of all this happy casting is lavish Hollywoodiana at its sporting best.

BLACKBOARD JUNGLE

1955 100m bw Drama ★★★½
MGM (U.S.) /X

Glenn Ford *(Richard Dadier)*, Anne Francis *(Anne Dadier)*, Louis Calhern *(Jim Murdock)*, Margaret Hayes *(Lois Judby Hammond)*, John Hoyt *(Mr. Warneke)*, Richard Kiley *(Joshua Y. Edwards)*, Emile Meyer *(Mr. Halloran)*, Warner Anderson *(Dr. Bradley)*, Basil Ruysdael *(Prof. A.R. Kraal)*, Sidney Poitier *(Gregory W. Miller)*

p, Pandro S. Berman; d, Richard Brooks; w, Richard Brooks (based on the novel by Evan Hunter); ph, Russell Harlan; ed, Ferris Webster; m, Charles Wolcott; art d, Cedric Gibbons, Randall Duell

AAN Best Original Screenplay: Richard Brooks; *AAN Best Cinematography:* Russell Harlan; *AAN Best Editing:* Ferris Webster; *AAN Best Art Direction:* Cedric Gibbons (Art Direction), Randall Duell (Art Direction), Edwin B Willis (Set Decoration), Henry Grace (Set Decoration)

This searing if somewhat overrated condemnation of juvenile delinquency brought attention to some of the problems afflicting urban high schools and is notable as a reflection of certain 1950s social mores. Rendered in effectively grainy black and white and using violence with considerable impact, the dutifully sincere screenplay by director Brooks unfortunately substitutes a more upbeat ending for Evan Hunter's original.

Ford, in a typically edgy but likable, effective performance, is a newly returned veteran who takes his first teaching job in an inner-city school. He soons runs afoul of some of his tougher students, who are only hanging around until they are old enough to get jobs. Several story lines run through the film: Ford's wife (Francis, failing to transcend an ill-conceived part), tries to convince him to find another job; another teacher (Kiley) thinks he can reason with the kids but soon finds out how wrong he is; an aging teacher (Calhern) just wants to survive until he can retire; and a pretty young teacher (Hayes) is frightened by her new assignment.

Vic Morrow is excellent as the leader of a gang of thugs, as is Poitier in a star-making performance, though at age 31 he unfortunately doesn't convince as a high school student. Future director Paul Mazursky and Jamie Farr (then Jameel Farah) play other students. BLACKBOARD JUNGLE also brought rock'n'roll to movie audiences with a bang courtesy of Bill Haley and the Comets, who sing "Rock Around the Clock."

BLACKMAIL

1929 75m bw Mystery ★★★★
Elstree/Wardour/British Intl. (U.K.) /15

Anny Ondra *(Alice White)*, John Longden *(Frank Webber)*, Donald Calthrop *(Tracy)*, Cyril Ritchard *(The Artist)*, Sara Allgood *(Mrs. White)*, Charles Paton *(Mr. White)*, Harvey Braban *(Inspector)*, Phyllis Monkman *(Gossip)*, Hannah Jones *(Landlady)*, Percy Parsons *(Crook)*

p, John Maxwell; d, Alfred Hitchcock; w, Alfred Hitchcock, Benn W. Levy, Charles Bennett (based on the play by Charles Bennett); ph, Jack Cox; ed, Emile De Ruelle; m, John Hubert Bath, Henry Stafford, John Reynders

The first all-talkie for both Great Britain and Alfred Hitchcock, this adaptation of a 1928 play stars Ondra as Alice White, a young British woman who is to be married to Scotland Yard detective Frank Webber (Longden). Alice, however, is drawn to a handsome artist (Ritchard), whom she ends up stabbing when he tries to force her to model nude. Of course, she soon falls prey to the crime of the title and of course her boyfriend heads up the murder investigation.

Although BLACKMAIL was completed and released as a silent film, Hitchcock was ordered by the studio to add some dialogue sequences for a "talkie" release in some specially equipped theaters. The main problem was Ondra's heavy Polish accent. Rather than reshoot all of her scenes, though, actress Joan Barry was brought in to dub the star's voice. This procedure was crude in those historic early

sound days: Barry had to be positioned off camera next to Ondra and speak the lines as the leading lady mouthed them, and to some extent the effort shows in Ondra's somewhat strained performance. The film, though, was a great success, artistically and technically. Even though the film contains scenes obviously shot silent to which one telling sound was later added, the exploration of the medium's new capabilities is downright palpable. Moodily filmed in an effectively Germanic style, with a neat supporting turn by Calthrop and fine set pieces such as the chase through the British Museum, BLACKMAIL still plays well, and is a suitable precursor to the master director's later work. In one of his earliest cameos, Hitchcock appears as a subway rider annoyed by a pesky boy while trying to read a book.

BLACULA

1972 92m c Horror ★★★
AIP (U.S.) PG/X

William Marshall *(Blacula)*, Vonetta McGee *(Tina)*, Denise Nicholas *(Michelle)*, Thalmus Rasulala *(Gordon Thomas)*, Gordon Pinsent *(Lt. Peters)*, Charles McCauley *(Dracula)*, Emily Yancy *(Nancy)*, Lance Taylor Sr. *(Swenson)*, Ted Harris *(Bobby)*, Rick Metzler *(Billy)*

p, Joseph T. Naar; d, William Crain; w, Joan Torres, Raymond Koenig; ph, John Stevens; ed, Allan Jacobs; m, Gene Page; art d, Walter Scott Herndon

An off-the-wall hellraiser. Hilarious blaxploitation pic has Dracula biting black prince, who, two hundred years later, is taking a bite out of Hollywood. To die for. So much that a sequel followed in 1973 with an even more engaging title—SCREAM, BLACULA, SCREAM.

BLADE RUNNER

1982 114m c Science Fiction ★★★★
The Ladd Company/Sir Run Run Shaw (U.S.) R/15

Harrison Ford *(Rick Deckard)*, Rutger Hauer *(Roy Batty)*, Sean Young *(Rachael)*, Edward James Olmos *(Gaff)*, M. Emmet Walsh *(Bryant)*, Daryl Hannah *(Pris)*, William Sanderson *(J.F. Sebastian)*, Brion James *(Leon)*, Joseph Turkel *(Tyrell)*, Joanna Cassidy *(Zhora)*

p, Michael Deeley; d, Ridley Scott; w, Hampton Fancher, David Peoples (based on the novel "Do Androids Dream of Electric Sheep" by Philip K. Dick); ph, Jordan Cronenweth; ed, Terry Rawlings; m, Vangelis; art d, David L. Snyder; fx, Douglas Trumbull, Richard Yuricich, David Dryer; cos, Charles Knode, Michael Kaplan

AAN Best Art Direction: Lawrence G. Paull (Art Direction), David L. Snyder (Art Direction), Linda DeScenna (Set Decoration); *AAN Best Visual Effects:* Douglas Trumbull, Richard Yuricich, David Dryer

One of the most visually influential science fiction films ever made, BLADE RUNNER has a history as labyrinthine as any of its futuristic film noir sets. A fascinatingly contemplative detective story about a world-weary android-killer and his renegade prey, it has attracted a sizeable cult audience and retains a unique place in cinema.

Los Angeles, year 2019. Cynical ex-cop Deckard (Harrison Ford) is a retired assassin of rogue androids (called "replicants"). His former boss, Bryant (M. Emmet Walsh), presses him into service: he is to kill a group of physically superior replicants that are on the loose after escaping from an "off-world" colony. Deckard visits the Tyrell Corporation, where he encounters mogul Eldon Tyrell (Joseph Turkel) and his assistant, Rachael (Sean Young). Tyrell informs Deckard that Rachael is a new breed of replicant—implanted with memories, she believes herself to be human. Bent on speaking to Tyrell in order to find out what their "termination dates" are, two of the replicants—Roy Batty (Rutger Hauer) and Pris (Daryl Hannah)—insinuate themselves into the home of geneticist J.F. Sebastian (William Sanderson), who created the replicant design for Tyrell. In the meantime, two more of the replicants have been disposed of and Deckard has become romantically obsessed with Rachael.

A critical and commercial flop in its initial, 116-minute domestic release, BLADE RUNNER has been shown in numerous versions in the years since. Most notable are the original theatrical cut, an "unrated version" (featuring additional violent footage) prepared for home-video release, and director Ridley Scott's official "director's cut," which offered some key variations on the original theatrical version of the film. Whatever the version, and for all its stylistic achievements and excesses, this "future noir" contains performances as stunning as its look: Ford's pained, taciturn Deckard; Hauer's doomed, dangerous, tragic Batty; Sanderson's naive yet knowing Sebastian; and Young's icily cool yet terrified Rachael. The moody musical score evokes classic noir without sinking into caricature, and the pre-computer-animation special effects seem more lifelike than their sometimes sterile-looking counterparts in films made a decade later.

BLADE RUNNER stands as a tough, idiosyncratic, and highly original vision of the future that asks meaningful questions about the nature of being human. Despite its imperfections and occasionally muddy plot points, BLADE RUNNER successfully combines and transcends the sci-fi and detective genres to forge a serious drama, that stands head and shoulders above the cartoonlike approach of many of its popular genre brethren.

BLAZING SADDLES

1974 93m c Comedy/Western   ★★½
Warner Bros. (U.S.)   R/15

Cleavon Little (Bart), Gene Wilder (Jim), Slim Pickens (Taggart), David Huddleston (Olson Johnson), Liam Dunn (Reverend Johnson), Alex Karras (Mongo), John Hillerman (Howard Johnson), George Furth (Van Johnson), Mel Brooks (Governor Lepetomane/Indian Chief), Harvey Korman (Hedley Lamarr)

p, Michael Hertzberg; d, Mel Brooks; w, Mel Brooks, Norman Steinberg, Andrew Bergman, Richard Pryor, Alan Uger (based on a story by Andrew Bergman); ph, Joseph Biroc; ed, John C. Howard, Danford B. Greene; m, John Morris; prod d, Peter Wooley; chor, Alan Johnson; cos, Vittorio Nino Novarese

AAN Best Supporting Actress: Madeline Kahn; AAN Best Editing: John C Howard, Danford Greene; AAN Best Song: John Morris (Music), Mel Brooks (Lyrics)

A lewd spoof of westerns and racial prejudice; enough laughs to cover the fact that it is, essentially, a stupid movie. Little is terrific as a black sheriff who has been hired so that the citizens of the town will panic and sell their land out cheap to speculators who plan to run a railroad through town. When the village turns on Little, he must call on the jail's only con, Wilder, who was at one time the fastest gun in the West. Last fifteen minutes of the movie are an obvious cop-out and the humor is often toilet level, but in addition to Little, Kahn scores big (in a takeoff of Marlene Dietrich's saloon belles), as do Karras and Korman. What really lessens SADDLES is that its intentions aren't clear. Its humor provoked no thinking; insensitive moviegoers assumed the racial putdowns and cowboy crudeness were deliberate. The public loved the film—it stands as the highest grossing western in history—$45 million plus! But they loved it for all the wrong reasons.

BLITHE SPIRIT

1945 96m c Fantasy   ★★★★
Cineguild (U.K.)   /U

Rex Harrison (Charles Condomine), Constance Cummings (Ruth Condomine), Kay Hammond (Elvira), Margaret Rutherford (Madame Arcati), Hugh Wakefield (Dr. Bradman), Joyce Carey (Mrs. Bradman), Jacqueline Clark (Edith)

p, Noel Coward; d, David Lean; w, Noel Coward, David Lean, Anthony Havelock-Allan (based on the play by Noel Coward); ph, Ronald Neame; ed, Jack Harris; m, Richard Addinsell; art d, C.P. Norman

AA Best Visual Effects: Thomas Howard (Special Effects-Visual)

A quicksilver cocktail. Novelist conjures up late first wife who can't resist causing trouble in his second marriage. Dry, but hilarious, Noel Coward romp, delivered seamlessly by David Lean. And stolen by Rutherford, the most inept, adorable medium ever. But the cinematography leaves something to be desired and only the Coward wit keeps this from not being a TOPPER rehash.

BLOB, THE

1958 85m c Science Fiction   ★½
Paramount (U.S.)   /18

Steve McQueen (Steve), Aneta Corseaut (Judy), Earl Rowe (Police Lieutenant), Olin Howlin (Old Man), Stephen Chase, John Benson, Vincent Barbi, Tom Ogen, Julie Cousins, Ralph Roseman

p, Jack H. Harris; d, Irvin S. Yeaworth Jr.; w, Theodore Simonson, Kate Phillips (based on an idea by Irvine H. Millgate); ph, Thomas E. Spalding; ed, Alfred Hillman; m, Jean Yeaworth

Jack H. Harris, the cheapie producer who went on to make the forgettable MOTHER GOOSE A GO-GO, struck it rich with this silly picture that gave McQueen his first starring role after a few supporting jobs in SOMEBODY UP THERE LIKES ME and NEVER LOVE A STRANGER. It's a teenage horror tale as McQueen and Corseaut tell their tiny Pennsylvania town that they've seen this purple goop that's eating people up. Naturally, no one believes them.

A sequel was made called BEWARE THE BLOB, also known as SON OF BLOB. The title was what brought the people in to see this otherwise undistinguished movie. McQueen plays his role with believability, as he did almost everything in his brief career. The oddest thing about the movie is the title song by Hal David and a 29-year-old composer named Burt Bacharach. It's not a bad tune.

BLONDE VENUS

1932 92m bw Drama   ★★★★
Paramount (U.S.)   /PG

Marlene Dietrich (Helen Faraday), Herbert Marshall (Edward Faraday), Cary Grant (Nick Townsend), Dickie Moore (Johnny Faraday), Francis Sayles (Charlie Blaine), Robert Emmett O'Connor (Dan O'Connor), Gene Morgan (Ben Smith), Rita La Roy (Taxi Belle Hooper), Sidney Toler (Detective Wilson), Morgan Wallace (Dr. Pierce)

d, Josef von Sternberg; w, Jules Furthman, S.K. Lauren (based on a story by von Sternberg); ph, Bert Glennon; m, Oscar Poteker; art d, Wiard Ihnen; cos, Travis Banton

Dietrich suffers, for once; Von Sternberg's paen to the pain of love in all its variations is so lovingly rendered that the shoestring story looks almost seamless. No one ever looked lovelier after sinking to the gutter than Dietrich—even her tatters are photographed to maximum effect. Dickie Moore was perhaps the most beautiful little boy ever in movies and the two male stars are there to bask in all that is Dietrich. She also appears in her hallmark top hat, white tie and tails singing "You Little So and So" but the sequence that lives on and on is the gorilla surprise and "Hot Voodoo," a highpoint of expressionistic eroticism, replete with blonde afro. Lensed two years before the code; hopefully your copy won't have the skinny-dipping opening deleted.

BLOOD AND SAND

1941 123m c Drama   ★★★★
Fox (U.S.)   /PG

Tyrone Power (Juan Gallardo), Linda Darnell (Carmen Espinosa), Rita Hayworth (Dona Sol des Muire), Anthony Quinn (Manolo de Palma), Alla Nazimova (Senora Augustias), J. Carrol Naish (Garabato), John Carradine (Nacional), Laird Cregar (Natalio Curro), Lynn Bari (Encarnacion), Vincente Gomez (Guitarist)

p, Robert T. Kane; d, Rouben Mamoulian; w, Jo Swerling (based on the novel Sangre y Arena by Vicente Blasco Ibanez); ph, Ernest Palmer, Ray Rennahan; ed, Robert Bischoff; m, Alfred Newman; art d, Richard Day, Joseph C. Wright; chor, Hermes Pan, Budd Boetticher; cos, Travis Banton

AA Best Cinematography: Ernest Palmer, Ray Rennahan; AAN Best Art Direction: Richard Day, Joseph C. Wright, Thomas Little

Lavish, tragic mural that owes its pizazz to Mamoulian's use of color and composition; BLOOD AND SAND is like watching the great Spanish Masters do animation. Remake of the great Valentino triumph seems a little flat, mainly because Power lacks the magnetism and danger of his predecessor.

Students of sex symbolism should have fun comparing Darnell and Hayworth, although both ladies are still a light year away from possessing the full extent of their erotic powers. Hayworth, who won Donna Sol over Maria Montez and because Carole Landis refused to dye her hair red, became a contender for pin-up queen as a result of the film. As usual, she lacks the fatality of the greatest seductresses and looks unhappy, but all flaws go out the window when the lady starts to flamenco. The best performances are delivered by the compelling Nazimova and young Anthony Quinn. Ernest Palmer and Ray Rennahan won Oscars for the lush cinematography.

BLOOD SIMPLE

1984 97m c Crime/Thriller ★★★★
River Road (U.S.) /18

John Getz (Ray), Frances McDormand (Abby), Dan Hedaya (Julian Marty), M. Emmet Walsh (Private Detective Visser), Samm-Art Williams (Maurice), Deborah Neumann (Debra), Raquel Gavia (Landlady), Van Brooks (Man from Lubbock), Senor Marco (Mr. Garcia), William Creamer (Old Cracker)

p, Ethan Coen; d, Joel Coen; w, Ethan Coen, Joel Coen; ph, Barry Sonnenfeld; ed, Roderick Jaynes, Don Wiegmann, Peggy Connolly; m, Carter Burwell; prod d, Jane Musky; fx, Loren Bivens; cos, Sara Medina-Pape

Stylish shoestring noir; an admirable filmmaking debut for the brothers Coen—Ethan (producer) and Joel (director).

Walsh is a sleazy private eye hired by Texas strip bar owner Hedaya to kill his wife McDormand and her lover Getz. Instead, Walsh fakes the double hit by doctoring photographs and then fills Hedaya with lead. When Getz discovers Hedaya in a pool of blood, he goes "simple"—foolishly cleaning up after the murder on the assumption that McDormand committed it. His actions distorted by his blinding passion, Getz then takes the body to an empty field to bury it, only to find that he, by a brutal twist of fate, is being buried.

Drawing from the crime novels of James M. Cain, BLOOD SIMPLE'S characters have none of the Cain complexities one might hope for, existing simply as chess pieces to further flashy stylistics. The Coens' concern isn't emotional intensity but bravura camera moves and chic lighting of cinematographer Sonnenfeld.

McDormand is wonderfully naturalistic as the not-too-bright girl with a homey sensuality, and Hedaya somehow manages to be vile yet sympathetic. Hailed by some as the best American independent film, BLOOD SIMPLE was completed on an astonishingly small budget of less than $1.5 million and looks as if it cost ten times as much.

BLOOD WEDDING

1981 72m c Dance ★★★
Libra (Spain) /U

Antonio Gades (Leonardo), Christina Hoyos (Bride), Juan Antonio Jimenez (Groom), Pilar Cardenas (Mother), Carmen Villena (Wife), El Guito, Elvira Andres, Marisa Nella, Lario Diaz, Azucena Flores

p, Emiliano Piedra; d, Carlos Saura; w, Antonio Artero (based on the play by Federico Garcia Lorca, adapted by Alfredo Manas); ph, Teo Escamilla; ed, Pablo del Amo

For dance lovers only. Much-touted meeting of filmmaker Carlos Saura, choreographer Antonio Gades, and playwright Federico Garcia Lorca has been often overly received. BLOOD WEDDING opens backstage as the dancers pour in, open their makeup cases, fix their hair, and apply their greasepaint. Some time later, Gades and his troupe move out into their rehearsal space and begin practicing their flamenco version of Garcia Lorca's play. The film runs an economical 72 minutes.

BLOW OUT

1981 108m c Mystery ★★★★
Filmways (U.S.) R/18

John Travolta (Jack), Nancy Allen (Sally), John Lithgow (Burke), Dennis Franz (Karp), Peter Boyden (Sam), Curt May (Frank), Ernest McClure (Jim), Dave Roberts (Anchorman), Maurice Copeland (Jack), Claire Carter (Anchorwoman)

p, George Litto; d, Brian De Palma; w, Brian De Palma; ph, Vilmos Zsigmond; ed, Paul Hirsch; m, Pino Donaggio; prod d, Paul Sylbert; cos, Vicki Sanchez

An homage to BLOW-UP that far outstrips the original in emotional immediacy, political sophistication, and visual style. Jack Terry (John Travolta) is a sound-effects recorder who specializes in sounds for trashy porn-slasher films. While out recording one night, he hears a tire blow out and sees a car swerve off a bridge and into the water. He jumps in and saves Sally (Nancy Allen), a prostitute who was with a now-drowned politician. The media and the dead man's associates are all convinced it was an accident, but Jack hears something on his tape recording—a gunshot that precedes the blow out. Using Sally as bait, Jack begins a cat-and-mouse game to find the killer.

Like most of De Palma's films, BLOW OUT is replete with cinematic quotes and inside jokes; this time, however, there's real substance behind the flashy attitudinizing. De Palma, in a grim mood of post-Watergate disillusionment, is here concerned with the role of violence in American history: shades of Chappaquiddick and the Kennedy assassinations are everywhere; a psychotic CIA agent (chillingly played by John Lithgow) stands in for American idealism gone murderously wrong; the bloody climax is played out amidst a surreally rendered Bicentennial celebration. Travolta gives a sensitive performance, as does the director's then-wife Nancy Allen. The film's emphasis on the role of sound technology in movie-making is unusual and instructive.

BLOWUP

1966 111m c Drama/Mystery ★★★½
Bridge Films (U.K./Italy) /18

David Hemmings (Thomas), Vanessa Redgrave (Jane), Sarah Miles (Patricia), Jane Birkin (Teenager #1), Gillian Hills (Teenager #2), Peter Bowles (Ron), Harry Hutchinson (Shopkeeper), John Castle (Patricia's Artist Husband), Susan Broderick (Antique Shop Owner), Mary Khal (Fashion Editor)

p, Carlo Ponti; d, Michelangelo Antonioni; w, Michelangelo Antonioni, Tonino Guerra, Edward Bond (based on the short story, "Final del Juego," by Julio Cortazar); ph, Carlo di Palma; ed, Frank Clarke; m, Herbie Hancock, The Yardbirds; cos, Jocelyn Richards

AAN Best Director: Michelangelo Antonioni; AAN Best Original Screenplay: Michelangelo Antonioni (Screenplay), Tonino Guerra (Screenplay), Edward Bond (Screenplay)

Pop-culture icon that has become a cult classic. Antonioni's adaptation of Cortazar's short story is an engrossing study of imagery and one's perception of the image. Set against the backdrop of 1960s London, BLOWUP follows fashionable young photographer Hemmings as he passively snaps his way through a world of drugs, models and parties. While wandering through a quiet park, he begins taking photos of two lovers embracing. One of them, Redgrave, chases after him and demands that he return the negatives. Later, after developing the photos, Hemmings thinks he sees something in the background—a man with a gun aimed at the back of Redgrave's partner. Returning that evening to the park, Hemmings finds the man's corpse. But the following morning, when he revisits the scene, the corpse has vanished . . .

In its time one of the most financially successful art films ever made, BLOW-UP marked Antonioni's leap into the commercial arena, after an early career largely confined to film festivals. From the perspective of the 90s, though, it's hard to see what all the fuss was about. The "swinging 60s" stuff looks as dated as the Herbie Hancock score sounds, Hemmings is a difficult actor to care about, and the neo-surrealist touches are downright irritating. There are moments of humor, though it's hard to gauge how many of them are intentional. Jane Birkin makes her screen debut, as one of the two giggling teenagers who "wrestle" with Hemmings.

BLUE
(TROIS COULEURS: BLEU)

1993 97m c Drama   ★★★

Marin Karmitz Productions/Tor Film Studios/CAB   R/15
Productions   (France/Poland/Switzerland)

Juliette Binoche *(Julie)*, Benoit Regent *(Olivier)*, Florence Pernel *(Sandrine)*, Charlotte Very *(Lucille)*, Emmanuelle Riva *(The Mother)*, Helene Vincent *(Journalist)*, Philippe Volter *(Estate Agent)*, Hugues Quester *(Patrice)*, Florence Vignon *(Copyist)*, Yann Tregouet *(Antoine)*

p, Marin Karmitz; d, Krzysztof Kieslowski; w, Krzysztof Kieslowski, Krzysztof Piesiewicz; ph, Slawomir Idziak; ed, Jacques Witta; m, Zbigniew Preisner; prod d, Claude Lenoir; cos, Virginie Viard

In this first section of his THREE COLORS trilogy, director Krzysztof Kieslowski's noted visual style is amply on display: images are transformed from the familiar into the unearthly, with a sense of dislocation permeating the whole.

When Julie (Juliette Binoche) survives a car crash that claims the lives of her classical composer husband Patrice (Hugues Quester) and young child, she attempts suicide. After her convalescence, she instructs her lawyers to dispose of the family estate and all her belongings, and disappears, moving into an apartment in an unfamiliar new neighborhood. Julie hears that a composer friend and former lover, Olivier (Benoit Regent), has been asked to complete a piece that her husband had been working on for an important series of concerts. With Olivier's help, she confronts the facts of her husband's past and reckons with the mysteries surrounding his music.

While BLUE might at first be seen as a kind of elegy to genius, as Julie seems to have dedicated her life to upholding the myth of her husband's brilliance, it gradually turns into an examination of things that aren't what they seem to be. Juliette Binoche is almost always on screen and Kieslowski and his camera seem enchanted by her, perpetually finding new ways to photograph her coolly beautiful face. The music, by Zbignew Preisner, is heard mostly in short snippets, but swells to a full-length finale at the end, revealing itself as rather kitschy and bland.

BLUE

1994 76m c Documentary/Biography/Experimental   ★★★½
Baselisk Communications/Uplink/Channel Four   (U.K.)

VOICES OF: Derek Jarman, John Quentin, Nigel Terry, Tilda Swinton

p, James Mackay, Takashi Asai; d, Derek Jarman; w, Derek Jarman; m, Simon Fisher Turner

BLUE is British militant gay filmmaker Derek Jarman's final film, and the only one to bring his anger to bear explicitly on the disease that finally claimed him. Constructed in layers of sound and orchestral bridges over an unvarying blue matte screen, the film is a meditation on many things—life, love, politics, metabolism. "All that concerns life and death is transacting within me," the voiceover claims.

The unapologetically poetic narration combines observations and epiphanies, at times seemingly lifted straight from journal entries, with an ongoing description of the body's failings against the onslaught of AIDS. The latter provides the film with its narrative engine, as the sense of sight, the filmmaker's most precious, slowly departs, summoning up a lifetime of remembered images as it passes. Formally, BLUE accomplishes several things that no other feature in memory does. The unvarying blue, and the hypnagogic imagery it encourages, has the curious effect of highlighting the dimensions of the screen itself, locating the film in the room with the viewer, rather than drawing the spectator into the frame. Second, with its preponderance of classically-trained voices and the liberal use of atmospheric sound, the piece works largely as radio broadcasts once did, marshalling the inherent drama in the physics of the medium—"His Master's Voice" captured point-blank with maximized acoustics, something that location sound precludes in the interest of "realism."

BLUE ANGEL, THE
(DER BLAUE ENGEL)

1930 99m bw Drama   ★★★★★

UFA   (Germany)

Emil Jannings *(Prof. Immanuel Rath)*, Marlene Dietrich *(Lola Frohlich)*, Kurt Gerron *(Kiepert, a Magician)*, Rosa Valetti *(Guste, his Wife)*, Hans Albers *(Mazeppa)*, Eduard von Winterstein *(Principal of the School)*, Reinhold Bernt *(The Clown)*, Hans Roth *(Beadle)*, Rolf Muller *(Angst, a Student)*, Robert Klein-Lork *(Goldstaub, a Student)*

p, Erich Pommer; d, Josef von Sternberg; w, Robert Liebmann, Karl Vollmoeller, Carl Zuckmayer (based on the novel *Professor Unrat* by Heinrich Mann); ph, Gunther Rittau, Hans Schneeberger; ed, S.K. Winston; m, Friedrick Hollander

The one and only; an unqualified masterpiece and milestone. Grim, ritualistic rise and fall of a respectable man at the hands of a heartless tramp is still one of the most horrifying studies of human degradation ever made. THE BLUE ANGEL's international success can be attributed to any number of elements: The immortal Jannings, UFA's greatest actor and a victim of the transition from silents to sound, is astounding in an essentially silent performance; Dietrich is wholly captivating in her first role with Sternberg—a creative union from which arose the Dietrich persona that would become internationally recognizable. It is, however, the genius of Sternberg to which THE BLUE ANGEL owes its greatness. His use of lighting, composition and of silence as sound, his overall creation of a world that can seduce and destroy even its most upstanding citizen, attest to this filmmaker's greatness and to the stature of THE BLUE ANGEL. Filmed simultaneously in German and English, the film is available in two, slightly differing, videotape versions—in German with English subtitles, and in English, the former preferable to the latter.

BLUE COLLAR

1978 110m c Drama   ★★★

T.A.T.   (U.S.)   R/18

Richard Pryor *(Zeke Brown)*, Harvey Keitel *(Jerry Bartkowski)*, Yaphet Kotto *(Smokey)*, Ed Begley Jr. *(Bobby Joe)*, Harry Bellaver *(Eddie Johnson)*, George Memmoli *(Jenkins)*, Lucy Saroyan *(Arlene Bartowski)*, Lane Smith *(Clarence Hill)*, Cliff De Young *(John Burrows)*, Borah Silver *(Miller)*

p, Don Guest; d, Paul Schrader; w, Paul Schrader, Leonard Schrader (based on materials by Sidney A. Glass); ph, Bobby Byrne; ed, Tom Rolf; m, Jack Nitzsche, Ry Cooder; cos, Ron Dawson, Alice Rush

Unionism, corruption, and betrayal in a Detroit auto plant. The directorial debut of Paul Schrader, who wrote TAXI DRIVER for Martin Scorsese, is one of surprisingly few films concerned with the pressures and politics of the workplace, where, after all, most adults spend nearly half their waking hours. Co-workers Pryor and Keitel have learned the hard way that union jobs no longer guarantee middle-class comfort; their friend, cynical ex-con Kotto, suggests that they rob a safe in the office of their union local. The break-in yields little cash, but they find an incriminating ledger with which they hope to blackmail the union leadership. The union, unresponsive and complacent when it comes to worker complaints, reacts with deadly efficiency when its power is threatened.

A key film for an era of diminishing expectations, BLUE COLLAR depicts big business and big labor as collaborators, expertly manipulating class resentment and racial tension so as to keep the work force divided. The precipitous decline of American unionism since the film's release may blunt the film's impact, however: many viewers will now have cause to reflect that a corrupt union is better than no union at all. The three leads—particularly Pryor, in an essentially non-comedic role—are remarkable.

BLUE DAHLIA, THE

1946 96m bw Mystery ★★★½
Paramount (U.S.) /A

Alan Ladd *(Johnny Morrison)*, Veronica Lake *(Joyce Harwood)*, William Bendix *(Buzz Wanchek)*, Howard da Silva *(Eddie Harwood)*, Doris Dowling *(Helen Morrison)*, Tom Powers *(Capt. Hendrickson)*, Hugh Beaumont *(George Copeland)*, Howard Freeman *(Corelli)*, Don Costello *(Leo)*, Will Wright *("Dad" Newell)*

p, John Houseman; d, George Marshall; w, Raymond Chandler (based on his story); ph, Lionel Lindon; ed, Arthur Schmidt; m, Victor Young; art d, Hans Dreier, Walter Tyler; cos, Edith Head

AAN Best Original Screenplay: Raymond Chandler

Tidy *film noir* , although we prefer Ladd and Lake in THIS GUN FOR HIRE. This is the only film script Raymond Chandler did directly for the screen, and the script reflects his hard-boiled, grim wit. Ladd returns from the service, finds wife has become a tramp. When she's murdered, he has to clear himself. Taut film still plays like house afire.

BLUE SKIES

1946 104m c Musical ★★★
Paramount (U.S.) /U

Bing Crosby *(Johnny Adams)*, Fred Astaire *(Jed Potter)*, Joan Caulfield *(Mary O'Hara)*, Billy De Wolfe *(Tony)*, Olga San Juan *(Nita Nova)*, Mikhail Rasumny *(Francois)*, Frank Faylen *(Mack)*, Victoria Horne *(Martha Nurse)*, Karolyn Grimes *(Mary Elizabeth)*

p, Sol C. Siegel; d, Stuart Heisler; w, Arthur Sheekman (based on an idea by Irving Berlin, adapted by Allan Scott); ph, Charles Lang, William Snyder; ed, LeRoy Stone; fx, Gordon Jennings, Paul K. Lerpae, Farclot Edouart; chor, Hermes Pan

AAN Best Score: Robert Emmett Dolan; *AAN Best Song:* Irving Berlin (Music & Lyrics)

Forty-two song cues and 30 full numbers held together by a plot of tissue paper. But with these two, who cares? Score by Berlin features Astaire's classic "Puttin' On the Ritz", and both guys dueting on "A Couple of Song and Dance Men". Easy all the way.

BLUE SKY

1994 101m c Drama ★★★
Prairie Films/Heathrow Productions/Orion (U.S.) PG-13/

Jessica Lange *(Carly Marshall)*, Tommy Lee Jones *(Captain Hank Marshall)*, Powers Boothe *(Vince Johnson)*, Carrie Snodgress *(Vera Johnson)*, Amy Locane *(Alex Marshall)*, Chris O'Donnell *(Glenn Johnson)*, Mitchell Ryan *(Ray Stevens)*, Dale Dye *(Colonel Mike Anwalt)*, Tim Scott *(Ned Owens)*, Annie Ross *(Lydia)*

p, Robert H. Solo; d, Tony Richardson; w, Rama Laurie Stagner, Jerry Leichtling, Arlene Sarner (from a story by Rama Laurie Stagner); ph, Steve Yaconelli; ed, Robert K. Lambert; m, Jack Nitzche; prod d, Timian Alsaker; art d, Gary John Constable; cos, Jane Robinson

AA Best Actress: Jessica Lange

The late Tony Richardson's BLUE SKY was the last of Orion's pre-bankruptcy films to see the light of day, and seems a more fitting swan song for Arthur Krim's widely respected company than, say, CLIFFORD. But despite the director's pedigree (TOM JONES, THE LONELINESS OF THE LONG-DISTANCE RUNNER), this picture feels somehow enervated, perhaps reflecting Richardson's struggles with AIDS during its 1991 filming.

At the dawn of the 1960s, Major Hank Marshall (Tommy Lee Jones), a US Army nuclear engineer, favors underground nuclear testing, despite the preference of army brass for open-air detonations. His wife Carly (Jessica Lange), a Barbie-doll bourgeoise, is slowly being suffocated by domestic torpor and encroaching age.

Jones is excellent here, as always, but the selling point is clearly Lange's seductive, damaged, mercurial Carly. She is both an American version of BETTY BLUE, allowed the full dramatic range of hysteria, and a more corrosive update of Auntie Mame or Jean Brodie—a charismatic kook whose eccentricities, in the end, aren't so charming once it becomes clear that she's seriously ill. And despite the implausible quality of some of the melodrama—it's a comparatively muted

throwback to the glossy melos of the 1950s—BLUE SKY is a welcome alternative view of domesticity in a field increasingly devoted to half-baked "family values."

BLUE STEEL

1990 102m c Thriller ★★★
Lightning/Precision/Mack-Taylor (U.S.) R/18

Jamie Lee Curtis *(Megan Turner)*, Ron Silver *(Eugene Hunt)*, Clancy Brown *(Nick Mann)*, Elizabeth Pena *(Tracy Perez)*, Louise Fletcher *(Shirley Turner)*, Philip Bosco *(Frank Turner)*, Kevin Dunn *(Assistant Chief Stanley Hoyt)*, Richard Jenkins *(Attorney Mel Dawson)*, Markus Flannagan *(Husband)*, Mary Mara *(Wife)*

p, Edward R. Pressman, Oliver Stone, Michael Rauch; d, Kathryn Bigelow; w, Kathryn Bigelow, Eric Red; ph, Amir Mokri; ed, Lee Percy; m, Brad Fiedel; prod d, Toby Corbett; fx, Steve Kirshoff; cos, Richard Shissler

Suspenseful and relentlessly stylish, BLUE STEEL is a slick, crypto-feminist thriller from Kathryn Bigelow (NEAR DARK, POINT BREAK), a gifted action director with a feel for the eroticism of violence.

During her first night on the job, rookie cop Megan Turner (Jamie Lee Curtis) breaks up a supermarket robbery and kills the gunman, whose pistol ends up in the hands of customer Eugene Hunt (Ron Silver). Hunt, a deranged Wall Street broker, takes the gun home and inscribes Megan's name on the bullets; obsessed with Megan, he begins a killing spree. Meanwhile, Megan has problems of her own: her mother (Louise Fletcher) is being abused by her father (Philip Bosco); she hasn't had a date in months. Enter Hunt, who sweeps the unsuspecting Megan off her feet with fancy dinners and thrilling helicopter rides. But Hunt has more than romance on his mind: he's grooming Megan for a role in his murderous fantasies.

BLUE STEEL's greatest pleasure is its smashing cinematography, courtesy of Amir Mokri (who has given several Wayne Wang films a distinctive look), but also owing much to Bigelow's distinctive pop aesthetics. The dependable Curtis adds depth to what might have been a stock character; Silver is convincingly vicious and seductive. Lest we fail to take the film seriously, the screenplay (written by Bigelow with longtime collaborator Eric Red) drops some unobtrusive hints about violence as a tool of patriarchy.

BLUE VELVET

1986 120m c Mystery ★★★
DEG (U.S.) R/18

Kyle MacLachlan *(Jeffrey Beaumont)*, Isabella Rossellini *(Dorothy Vallens)*, Dennis Hopper *(Frank Booth)*, Laura Dern *(Sandy Williams)*, Hope Lange *(Mrs. Williams)*, Dean Stockwell *(Ben)*, George Dickerson *(Detective Williams)*, Priscilla Pointer *(Mrs. Beaumont)*, Frances Bay *(Aunt Barbara)*, Jack Harvey *(Mr. Beaumont)*

p, Fred Caruso; d, David Lynch; w, David Lynch; ph, Frederick Elmes; ed, Duwayne Dunham; m, Angelo Badalamenti; prod d, Patricia Norris; fx, Greg Hull, George Hill; cos, Gloria Laughride

AAN Best Director: David Lynch

Weirdness, big time. The seamy side of small town Americana from—who else?—David Lynch. When archetypal college student Jeffrey Beaumont (MacLachlan) finds a severed human ear in a deserted field, he enlists the help of innocent high-schooler Sandy (Dern) in finding the body to which it once belonged. The key to the mystery is nightclub chanteuse Dorothy Vallens (Rossellini), whose husband and child are being held hostage by the demoniacal Frank Booth (Hopper), who sexually torments the singer in exchange for the safety of her loved ones. Eventually Jeffrey probes so deeply into this dark and troubling mystery that he comes face to face with Booth, the very embodiment of evil. As if to demonstrate the film's premise that people would prefer to avoid the dark side of life—the sadism, perversions, fetishism, drug addiction, and violence—many critics complained that BLUE VELVET was "dangerous" in its exploration of these traits, contending that these taboos were better left in the closet. Director David Lynch addresses that belief here—Hopper, the voice of evil, demands that people not look at him, while MacLachlan, the voice of good, not only looks but fights back. All of this revolves around the film's mystery elements, which are on a par with the innocent whodunit mentality of a Hardy Boys-Nancy Drew episode, although the rest of the film is deeply disquieting and sexually aggressive, not to be seen by those easily repulsed. There are certain similarities between this film and Alfred Hitchcock's 1943 classic SHADOW OF A DOUBT, in which Joseph Cotten's "Uncle Charlie" is a demented murderer whose diseased presence threatens a quiet California town. Surprisingly, for a picture so steeped in controversy as it was, BLUE VELVET *did* earn Lynch a Best Director Oscar nomination. In addition to the Bobby Vinton title tune, the film prominently features the Roy Orbison tune "In Dreams," and a lush score by Angelo Badalamenti. Depending on your point of view, either dark-sidedly brilliant or garbage heaped on top of whipped cream.

BLUES BROTHERS, THE

1980   133m   c   Comedy   ★★½
Universal   (U.S.)   R/15

John Belushi *(Joliet Jake)*, Dan Aykroyd *(Elwood)*, James Brown *(Rev. Cleophus James)*, Cab Calloway *(Curtis)*, Ray Charles *(Ray)*, Carrie Fisher *(Mystery Woman)*, Aretha Franklin *(Soul Food Cafe Owner)*, Henry Gibson *(Nazi Leader)*, John Candy *(Burton Mercer)*, Murphy Dunne *(Murph)*

p, Robert K. Weiss; d, John Landis; w, John Landis, Dan Aykroyd; ph, Stephen Katz; ed, George Folsey Jr.; m, Ira Newborn; cos, Deborah Nadoolman

THE BLUES BROTHERS is a monument to waste, noise and misplaced cool, but it does have its engagingly nutty moments. The premise for this $30 million flick is that blue-eyed soul brothers Jake and Elwood (John Belushi and Dan Aykroyd) need to raise $5,000 for their old orphanage. With no other motivation, they systematically destroy the city of Chicago. One of the most self-indulgent films of the 1980s, THE BLUES BROTHERS shows the dangers of giving untold sums of money to brash young directors. The highlights are few, but telling—all of the black performers score in their brief roles, especially Franklin and Calloway. Unfortunately, these performers's legitimate "soul" underlines the Blues Brothers's assumed soul. Henry Gibson is funny as a George Rockwell-type Nazi, and Frank Oz of Muppet fame makes a rare on-screen appearance as a corrections officer. This film has one pace—breakneck—and doesn't allow the audience to breathe, rest, or care about anyone or anything. It's worth noting that its big budget exceeded the amount Chaplin, Keaton, Laurel and Hardy, Charlie Chase, Harry Langdon, and Ben Turpin used to make *all* their films.

BLUME IN LOVE

1973   115m   c   Comedy   ★★★
Warner Bros.   (U.S.)   R/15

George Segal *(Blume)*, Susan Anspach *(Nina Blume)*, Kris Kristofferson *(Elmo)*, Marsha Mason *(Arlene)*, Shelley Winters *(Mrs. Cramer)*, Donald Muhich *(Analyst)*, Paul Mazursky *(Blume's Partner)*

p, Paul Mazursky; d, Paul Mazursky; w, Paul Mazursky; ph, Bruce Surtees; ed, Donn Cambern; prod d, Pato Guzman

Sympathetic but self-indulgent masculine version of Mazursky's AN UNMARRIED WOMAN, a few years later. Segal is splendid as the lovesick lawyer who lusts after his ex, Anspach, who has taken up with Kristofferson. Mason is formidable as a woman waiting for divorced men. Mazursky, working without Larry Tucker for the first time, lets the picture get away from him a few times and does not edit with as tight an eye as for his previous films. His jaundiced look at love in California allows him to have some fun satirizing early 1970s types like Gottlieb (the bass player in the Limelighters group) as a guru and Denison as a Yoga leader. Winters is hysterical in a small role as a wife trying to decide whether or not to divorce her lecherous husband. Mazursky gave himself a role as Segal's partner which may explan moments when film feels unfocused.

BOB & CAROL & TED & ALICE

1969   104m   c   Comedy   ★★★
Columbia   (U.S.)   R/15

Natalie Wood *(Carol)*, Robert Culp *(Bob)*, Elliott Gould *(Ted)*, Dyan Cannon *(Alice)*, Horst Ebersberg *(Horst)*, Lee Bergere *(Emelio)*, Donald Muhich *(Psychiatrist)*, Noble Lee Holderread Jr. *(Sean)*, K.T. Stevens *(Phyllis)*, Celeste Yarnall *(Susan)*

p, Larry Tucker; d, Paul Mazursky; w, Paul Mazursky, Larry Tucker; ph, Charles Lang; m, Quincy Jones; chor, Miriam Nelson; cos, Moss Mabry

AAN Best Supporting Actor: Elliott Gould; *AAN Best Supporting Actress:* Dyan Cannon; *AAN Best Adapted Screenplay:* Paul Mazursky, Larry Tucker; *AAN Best Cinematography:* Charles B Lang

Screwing around, '60s style, and beginning to look very dated and self-indulgent. Helped not at all by bad ending. Gould and especially Cannon come off with top honors; they were nominated for Academy Awards, as was the story and cinematography.

BOB LE FLAMBEUR

1955   98m   bw   Crime   ★★★★
Studios Jenner/OGC/La Cyme/Play Art   (France)

Isabelle Corey *(Anne)*, Daniel Cauchy *(Paolo)*, Roger Duchesne *(Bob Montagne)*, Guy Decomble *(Inspector Ledru)*, Andre Garret *(Roger)*, Gerard Buhr *(Marc)*, Claude Cerval *(Jean)*, Colette Fleury *(Suzanne—Jean's Wife)*, Simone Paris *(Yvonne)*, Howard Vernon *(McKimmie)*

p, Jean-Pierre Melville; d, Jean-Pierre Melville; w, Jean-Pierre Melville, Auguste le Breton; ph, Henri Decae; ed, Monique Bonnot; m, Eddie Barclay, Jo Boyer; art d, Claude Bouxin, Jean-Pierre Melville

The lightest movie of Jean-Pierre Melville's career, BOB LE FLAMBEUR is the story of an aging gambler and his attempt to end a lifelong streak of bad luck by pulling off the ultimate heist. Considered an important precursor of the French New Wave, this low-budget film was described by its creator as "not a pure *policier,* but a comedy of manners" and also as "a love-letter to Paris."

Bob the Gambler (Roger Duchesne), a 50-year-old ex-thief who is down on his luck, is seated in a cafe with Paulo (Daniel Cauchy), an admiring young protege, when in walks Anne (Isabelle Corey), a sexy teenager, accompanied by Marc (Gerard Buhr), a pimp. Bob scares Marc off and then treats Anne to dinner, lectures her, and stakes her to a hotel bed while Paulo flirts with her. Days later, Bob puts Anne up in his apartment, no strings attached; he soon finds that Paulo and she have become romantically involved. Bob and his friend, Roger (Andre Garret), visit the Deauville Casino, where Roger bumps into Jean (Claude Cerval), an old pal and now a croupier. Jean tells Roger that the casino safe contains hundreds of millions of francs. Roger relays the information to Bob, who decides to hold the place up.

Melville wrote the initial draft of BOB LE FLAMBEUR before he had seen THE ASPHALT JUNGLE (1950). Realizing that he couldn't match the grim power of the John Huston caper classic, he turned his own scenario into something of a comedy. In the title role of Bob, he cast Duchesne, who had been a major French star before WWII but had since drifted into shadier areas of employment. The director discovered 15-year-old Corey on a Paris street and cast her as Anne. Alarmingly closer to "fille" than a femme fatale, the seductively insouciant Anne became, in Corey's hands, one of the screen's great erotic figures of the 1950s.

At once a charming entertainment, a resonant character study, an ironic morality tale, and a bittersweet celebration of Montmartre, BOB LE FLAMBEUR reinforces Melville's reputation as one of history's premier filmmakers in the same way that Shakespeare's comedies enhance his reputation as a major tragedian. In foregrounding the wit and drollery that lurk beneath the surface of such weighty masterpieces as LES ENFANTS TERRIBLES (1949) and LE SAMOURAI (1967), BOB LE FLAMBEUR rounds out Melville's resume and secures him a berth in the cinema's pantheon.

BOB ROBERTS

1992 105m c Comedy/Political ★★½
The Bob Roberts Co./Working Title/Polygram (U.S./U.K.) R/15

Tim Robbins *(Bob Roberts)*, Giancarlo Esposito *(Bugs Raplin)*, Ray Wise *(Chet MacGregor)*, Alan Rickman *(Lukas Hart, III)*, Gore Vidal *(Senator Brickley Paiste)*, James Spader *(News Anchor Chuck Marin)*, Helen Hunt *(Reporter Rose Pondell)*, Peter Gallagher *(News Anchor Dan Riley)*, Susan Sarandon *(News Anchor Tawna Titan)*, Fred Ward *(News Anchor Chip Daley)*

p, Forrest Murray; d, Tim Robbins; w, Tim Robbins; ph, Jean Lepine; ed, Lisa Churgin; m, David Robbins; prod d, Richard Hoover; art d, Gary Kosko; cos, Bridget Kelly

BOB ROBERTS is a smart, funny pseudo-documentary about a conservative folk-singer who campaigns to become U.S. Senator for Pennsylvania, cloaking his extreme right-wing views in the radical rhetoric of the 1960s.

Directed and written by its star, Tim Robbins, the film began life as a sketch for "Saturday Night Live" in 1985. Much of it feels like an extended "SNL" gag (one of the funniest sequences has the would-be Senator appearing on a thinly disguised version of the show called "Cutting Edge Live"), but Robbins has also clearly learned a lot from his work with Robert Altman on THE PLAYER.

Like Altman's best films, BOB ROBERTS builds a freewheeling, multi-layered portrait of its characters' world where what happens in the background of a scene is often as entertaining—and revealing—as what we're "supposed" to be looking at. And like THE PLAYER, Robbins's new film is peppered with cameos by celebrities including Susan Sarandon, Peter Gallagher and Fred Ward. Gore Vidal plays Roberts's opponent, an articulate, old-style Democrat whose campaign is tainted by allegations of an extra-marital affair.

Onto this hybrid of NASHVILLE and SPINAL TAP Robbins has layered a sub-plot worthy of J.F.K., featuring an investigative reporter played by Giancarlo Esposito. He claims to have evidence linking Robbins's right-hand man Lukas Hart, III (Alan Rickman), to S&L-financed drug-running, but pays dearly for his discovery.

Although the conspiracy theory helps keep BOB ROBERTS moving, the real joy of the film is in the incidental details: songs such as "Wall Street Rap," the video for which features pin-striped financiers celebrating the joys of wealth; the recurrent Bob Dylan pastiches, including a Roberts album titled "Bob on Bob"; and hilariously on-the-mark cameos from the likes of James Spader as a vacuous local newscaster, and Bob Balaban, as the spineless producer of "Cutting Edge Live."

BOCCACCIO '70

1962 150m c Fantasy/Comedy ★★½
TCF (France/Italy) /X

THE RAFFLE: Sophia Loren *(Zoe)*, Luigi Gillianni *(Gaetano)*, Alfio Vita *(Cuspet)*, THE JOB: Romy Schneider *(Pupe)*, Tomas Milian *(The Count)*, Romolo Valli, Paolo Stoppa, THE TEMPTATION OF DR. ANTONIO: Anita Ekberg *(Anita)*, Peppino de Filippo *(Dr. Antonio)*, Dante Maggio

p, Carlo Ponti, Antonio Cervi; d, Federico Fellini, Vittorio De Sica, Luchino Visconti; w, Federico Fellini, Ennio Flaiano, Tullio Pinelli, Suso Cecchi D'Amico, Luchino Visconti, Cesare Zavattini; ph, Giuseppe Rotunno, Otello Marelli; m, Nino Rota, Nino Rota, Armando Trovajoli

Three unconnected episodes dealing with modern stories the producers would have you think Boccaccio might have written if alive; from the lack of content and characterization, Boccaccio would have used a pseudonym for these turgid tales. The film is only an excuse to parade the Amazonian attributes of Ekberg and Loren, with Schneider thrown in for dramatic license. In one story, Ekberg is a billboard image that comes to life in a dream conjured by a middle-aged lecher. In "The Raffle," Loren plays a woman who operates a shooting gallery and is the sex prize of a Saturday night raffle. To accommodate a country bumpkin who begs to win the raffle, she fixes the drawing but does not deliver the goods; to show she is a noble slattern, however, Loren spreads the word that she has dallied with the clod so he will become

a hero to his crowd. Schneider's segment is almost lost between these two stories; she plays a secretary in love with the boss and sacrificing her personal life for the ungrateful wretch. Contrived and spotty.

BODY AND SOUL

1947 104m bw Sports ★★★★½
Enterprise (U.S.) /A

John Garfield *(Charlie Davis)*, Lilli Palmer *(Peg Born)*, Hazel Brooks *(Alice)*, Anne Revere *(Anna Davis)*, William Conrad *(Quinn)*, Joseph Pevney *(Shorty Polaski)*, Canada Lee *(Ben)*, Lloyd Goff *(Roberts)*, Art Smith *(David Davis)*, James Burke *(Arnold)*

p, Bob Roberts; d, Robert Rossen; w, Abraham Polonsky; ph, James Wong Howe; ed, Robert Parrish; m, Hugo Friedhofer; art d, Nathan Juran; cos, Marion Herwood Keyes

AAN Best Actor: John Garfield; AAN Best Original Screenplay: Abraham Polonsky; AA Best Editing: Francis Lyon, Robert Parrish

The fight film to which all others are compared. John Garfield portrays Charlie Davis, a Jewish prizefighter whose parents want him to hang up the gloves and get an education. When his father is killed in a bomb explosion, however, the proud Charlie prevents his mother (Anne Revere) from accepting government relief, turns pro, and by hook and crook, rises quickly to the top, winning the championship from Ben (onetime welterweight Canada Lee), who is left with a life-threatening blood clot in his brain. As the champ, Charlie slides into a dissipated lifestyle and throws over his artist girlfriend, Peg Born (Lilli Palmer), for a floozy (Hazel Brooks), falling deeper into the clutches of the gangster who owns him (Lloyd Goff) in the process. Garfield's riveting, Oscar-nominated performance lifts BODY AND SOUL to the masterpiece level, as do Robert Rossen's superb direction, the marvelous photography of James Wong Howe and the Oscar-winning editing. The fight sequences, in particular, brought a kind of realism to the genre that had never before existed (Howe wore skates and rolled around the ring shooting the fight scenes with a hand-held camera). A knockout on all levels.

BODY HEAT

1981 113m c Crime/Erotic ★★★½
Ladd (U.S.) R/18

William Hurt *(Ned Racine)*, Kathleen Turner *(Matty Walker)*, Richard Crenna *(Edmund Walker)*, Ted Danson *(Peter Lowenstein)*, J.A. Preston *(Oscar Grace)*, Mickey Rourke *(Teddy Lewis)*, Kim Zimmer *(Mary Ann)*, Jane Hallaren *(Stella)*, Lanna Saunders *(Roz Kraft)*, Michael Ryan *(Miles Hardin)*

p, Fred T. Gallo; d, Lawrence Kasdan; w, Lawrence Kasdan; ph, Richard H. Kline; ed, Carol Littleton; m, John Barry; cos, Renie Conley

An excellent crime drama in the style of Raymond Chandler, James M. Cain, and Dashiell Hammett. Director-writer Lawrence Kasdan borrows liberally in style from 1940s *film noir* and incorporates a plot reminiscent of DOUBLE INDEMNITY, but he adds a steamy sexuality more in keeping with contemporary films. Set in Florida, the movie follows the ill-fated course of Ned Racine (William Hurt), a rather dim-witted attorney who gets deeply involved with sultry Matty Walker (Kathleen Turner), a woman who wants her husband dead. Hurt gives a superior performance—we can actually see him thinking, rather painfully—while Turner makes a fine *femme fatale* after the model of Lauren Bacall. Ted Danson is also excellent as a slightly nerdy lawyer-friend of Ned's; Mickey Rourke, in one of his early screen appearances, shows the promise of things to come; and the other supporting roles are likewise well handled.

BODYGUARD, THE

1992 114m c Romance/Thriller ★★
TIG Productions/Kasdan Pictures (U.S.) R/15

Kevin Costner *(Frank Farmer)*, Whitney Houston *(Rachel Marron)*, Gary Kemp *(Sy Spector)*, Bill Cobbs *(Devaney)*, Ralph Waite *(Herb Farmer)*, Tomas Arana *(Portman)*, Michele Lamar Richards *(Nicki)*, Mike Starr *(Tony)*, Christopher Birt *(Henry)*, DeVaughn Nixon *(Fletcher)*

p, Lawrence Kasdan, Jim Wilson, Kevin Costner; d, Mick Jackson; w, Lawrence Kasdan (from his story); ph, Andrew Dunn; ed, Richard A. Harris, Donn Cambern; m, Alan Silvestri; prod d, Jeffrey Beecroft; art d, William Ladd Skinner; cos, Susan Nininger

AAN Best Song: David Foster (Music), Linda Thompson (Lyrics); *AAN Best Song:* Jud Friedman (Music), Allan Rich (Lyrics)

Based on a screenplay by Lawrence Kasdan, THE BODYGUARD is a dreary, turgid melodrama featuring the much ballyhooed debut of pop diva Whitney Houston.

Frank Farmer (Kevin Costner) is an ex-secret serviceman who, racked with guilt because he was off duty the day President Reagan was shot, is now a bodyguard for hire. His latest client is Rachel Marron (Whitney Houston), a pop singer and Academy Award nominee who has recently begun receiving death threats. After a budding romance between the two is quashed by Farmer as a matter of professional protocol, it turns out the threats have been emanating from Rachel's jealous sister Nicki (Michele Lamar Richards), who has hired an assassin to kill Rachel. After accidentally doing away with Nicki, the killer makes a second attempt at the climactic Academy Awards ceremony, during which Rachel takes a very long, slow walk to the podium. . . .

THE BODYGUARD should have remained in Kasdan's drawer. It echoes the worst aspects of previous flops like THE FAN and THE OSCAR without any attempt at reworking the lame plots and weak characters of those films. Instead, director Mick Jackson glosses over the shoddiness with a cheap-jack MTV burnish that ultimately serves to highlight the shortcomings of the narrative. As an actress, Whitney Houston is competent but bland; someone must have liked her forgettable songs, however, since the soundtrack album was a best seller.

BONNIE AND CLYDE

1967   111m   c   Crime   ★★★★½
Warner Bros.   (U.S.)   /18

Warren Beatty (*Clyde Barrow*), Faye Dunaway (*Bonnie Parker*), Michael J. Pollard (*C.W. Moss*), Gene Hackman (*Buck Barrow*), Estelle Parsons (*Blanche*), Denver Pyle (*Frank Hamer*), Dub Taylor (*Ivan Moss*), Evans Evans (*Velma Davis*), Gene Wilder (*Eugene Grizzard*), James Stiver (*Grocery Store Owner*)

p, Warren Beatty; d, Arthur Penn; w, David Newman, Robert Benton; ph, Burnett Guffey; ed, Dede Allen; m, Charles Strouse; art d, Dean Tavoularis; fx, Danny Lee; cos, Theadora Van Runkle

AAN Best Picture; AAN Best Actor: Warren Beatty; *AAN Best Actress:* Faye Dunaway; *AAN Best Supporting Actor:* Gene Hackman; *AAN Best Supporting Actor:* Michael J. Pollard; *AA Best Supporting Actress:* Estelle Parsons; *AAN Best Director:* Arthur Penn; *AAN Best Original Story and Screenplay:* David Newman, Robert Benton; *AA Best Cinematography:* Burnett Guffey; *AAN Best Costume Design:* Theadora Van Runkle

Landmark gangster film that made a huge commercial and cultural splash. The seminal script by David Newman and Robert Benton struck a nerve with the 1967 youth culture as it reimagined the two rural Depression-era outlaws as largely sympathetic nonconformists. The film set new standards for screen violence but it alternated its scenes of mayhem with lyrical interludes and jaunty slapstick sequences accompanied by spirited banjo music. While unusual for a Hollywood feature, such jarring shifts in tone were typical of the genre-bending works of French New Wave directors Francois Truffaut and Jean-Luc Godard, both of whom were slated to direct the feature at various points in its genesis.

Producer/star Beatty cajoled Warner Brothers into financing the production and selected Arthur Penn to direct. Penn initially aimed at realism, constructing scenes based on Walker Evans photographs and NRA posters, but a competing nostalgic impulse won out. The Oscar-winning cinematography of Burnett Guffey served up the Dust Bowl on a sumptuous Technicolor platter, and historical accuracy was jettisoned in favor of glossy romanticization. In the process, the story took on the quality of a folk ballad.

As portrayed by Beatty and Dunaway, Clyde Barrow and Bonnie Parker were just plain folks who liked to pose for photographs and rob banks. As one ad campaign proclaimed, "They are young, they are in love, they kill people." The rest of the Barrow gang is portrayed by a powerhouse group of supporting players: Gene Hackman, Estelle Parsons (who won the Oscar for Best Supporting Actress), and Michael J. Pollard. Gene Wilder also makes his screen debut as a nervous mortician.

BONNIE AND CLYDE grossed $23 million and became Warner's second best box-office attraction up to that time, after MY FAIR LADY. Despite its controversial nature, the film was nominated for nine Oscars (it only won two).

BOOM TOWN

1940   117m   bw   Drama   ★★½
MGM   (U.S.)   /A

Clark Gable (*Big John McMasters*), Spencer Tracy (*Square John Sand*), Claudette Colbert (*Betsy Bartlett*), Hedy Lamarr (*Karen Vanmeer*), Frank Morgan (*Luther Aldrich*), Lionel Atwill (*Harry Compton*), Chill Wills (*Harmony Jones*), Marion Martin (*Whitey*), Minna Gombell (*Spanish Eva*), Joe Yule (*Ed Murphy*)

p, Sam Zimbalist; d, Jack Conway; w, John Lee Mahin (based on a story by James Edward Grant); ph, Harold Rosson; ed, Blanche Sewell; m, Franz Waxman; art d, Cedric Gibbons, Eddie Imazu; cos, Adrian, Gile Steele

AAN Best Cinematography: Harold Rosson; *AAN Best Visual Effects:* A. Arnold Gillespie (Special Effects-Photographic), Douglas Shearer (Special Effects-Sound)

More of a "pop" than a "boom". Lavish MGM production in which the studio paired its greatest male stars, Gable and Tracy, for the last time. The story concerns two oilmen whose financial ups and downs are interwoven with their romantic entanglements. Against a backdrop of gushing oil wells and East Coast wheeling and dealing, Gable steals his friend's true love (Colbert) and then cheats on her with another (Lamarr). Tracy, noble and stoic to the end, works behind the scenes to protect his former love.

A slick, fast-moving film, BOOM TOWN displays a queer obsession with earning and losing money by the million. The star power, with little of value to hang onto, does its professional best to boost the lumpy storyline. The biggest hit of 1940, this mediocre film earned Oscar nominations for Best Cinematography and Best Special Effects.

BOOMERANG

1947   88m   bw   Mystery   ★★★★
Fox   (U.S.)   /A

Dana Andrews (*Henry L. Harvey*), Jane Wyatt (*Mrs. Harvey*), Lee J. Cobb (*Chief Robinson*), Cara Williams (*Irene Nelson*), Arthur Kennedy (*John Waldron*), Sam Levene (*Woods*), Taylor Holmes (*Wade*), Robert Keith (*McCreery*), Ed Begley (*Harris*), Philip Coolidge (*Crossman*)

p, Louis de Rochemont; d, Elia Kazan; w, Richard Murphy (based on the *Reader's Digest* article "The Perfect Case" by Anthony Abbott); ph, Norbert Brodine; ed, Harmon Jones; m, David Buttolph

AAN Best Original Screenplay: Richard Murphy

A chilling *film noir* about the murder of a priest, the subsequent arrest and trial of a jobless drifter, and the efforts of a young state's attorney to uncover the truth. Closely based on the actual 1924 murder (still unsolved) of Fr. Hubert Dahme in Bridgeport, Connecticut, the film was directed by the young Elia Kazan in a highly effective, semi-documentary style. Kazan shot most of the film on location, using high-contrast cinematography and an extremely mobile camera to create a palpable sense of urgency. Producer Louis de Rochemont had earlier been responsible for the "March of Time" newsreel series, as well as the naturalistic features THE HOUSE ON 92ND STREET and 13 RUE MADELEINE.

BORN ON THE FOURTH OF JULY

1989   140m   c   Drama/War   ★★★
Fourth of July   (U.S.)   R/18

Tom Cruise *(Ron Kovic)*, Bryan Larkin *(Young Ron)*, Raymond J. Barry *(Mr. Kovic)*, Caroline Kava *(Mrs. Kovic)*, Josh Evans *(Tommy Kovic)*, Seth Allen *(Young Tommy)*, Jamie Talisman *(Jimmy Kovic)*, Sean Stone *(Young Jimmy)*, Anne Bobby *(Susanne Kovic)*, Jenna von Oy *(Young Susanne)*

p, A. Kitman Ho, Oliver Stone; d, Oliver Stone; w, Oliver Stone, Ron Kovic (based on his autobiography); ph, Robert Richardson; ed, David Brenner; m, John Williams; prod d, Bruno Rubeo; art d, Victor Kempster, Richard L. Johnson; cos, Judy Ruskin

AAN Best Picture; *AAN Best Actor*: Tom Cruise; *AA Best Director*: Oliver Stone; *AAN Best Adapted Screenplay*: Oliver Stone, Ron Kovic; *AAN Best Cinematography*: Robert Richardson; *AA Best Editing*: David Brenner, Joe Hutshing; *AAN Best Score*: John Williams; *AAN Best Sound*: Michael Minkler, Gregory H. Watkins, Wylie Stateman, Tod A. Maitland

Oliver Stone (PLATOON) returns to the Vietnam War era but here the focus is primarily on the homefront and the aftershocks of war. Ambitious matinee idol Tom Cruise stars in a showy change-of-pace characterization as Ron Kovic in the autobiographical story of a gung ho young man who went proudly off to Vietnam, came back home in a wheelchair, and, after a traumatic interval, became a high profile antiwar activist.

The film begins with a depiction of Kovic's youth in Massapequa, New York, where he is raised to be a deeply patriotic, God-fearing, macho all-American athelete. As such, he eagerly enlists in the Marines and ships off to Vietnam, convinced of the justness of the American cause. He becomes increasingly confused and disoriented after he accidentally kills one of his own men in a firefight. He later receives a bullet wound that leaves him paralyzed from the waist down. Back in the home of his family which no longer understands him, he degenerates into a drunken, self-pitying dropout. After a dissolute sequence in Mexico, he somehow gets a grip on himself, confronts his changed feelings about his life and his country, and becomes an antiwar activist, thereby regaining his self-respect.

Stone's film is undeniably emotionally powerful but problematic because it lingers on the pathos of Kovic's condition while skirting the less visually dramatic aspects of the character. Kovic clearly undergoes a political conversion but it is never dealt with directly—he changes during a fadeout. The effect is as unintentionally jarring as if a reel of the film were missing. The critique of masculinity is far more thoughtful and compelling than the vague ruminations about war. Nonetheless Cruise's impassioned performance as Kovic is an impressive accomplishment.

BORN YESTERDAY

1951   103m   bw   Comedy   ★★★★
Columbia   (U.S.)   /U

Judy Holliday *(Billie Dawn)*, Broderick Crawford *(Harry Brock)*, William Holden *(Paul Verrall)*, Howard St. John *(Jim Devery)*, Frank Otto *(Eddie)*, Larry Oliver *(Norval Hedges)*, Barbara Brown *(Mrs. Hedges)*, Grandon Rhodes *(Sanborn)*, Claire Carleton *(Helen)*, Smoki Whitfield *(Bootblack)*

p, S. Sylvan Simon; d, George Cukor; w, Albert Mannheimer (based on the play by Garson Kanin); ph, Joseph Walker; ed, Charles Nelson; m, Frederick Hollander; cos, Jean Louis

AAN Best Picture; *AA Best Actress*: Judy Holliday; *AAN Best Director*: George Cukor; *AAN Best Screenplay*: Albert Mannheimer; *AAN Best Costume Design*: Jean Louis

The highlight of this lively Garson Kanin Broadway comedy is the most delightful "dumb blonde" to ever grace the screen, Holliday, in a role she originated on stage and nearly did not get to re-create on screen. As the malaprop-tossing mistress of scrap metal tycoon Crawford, she is unknowingly put in nominal charge of his shady empire so that he can cover his tracks. Though no paragon of high culture himself, Crawford is embarrassed by his paramour's lack of social refinement. He hires her a tutor, Holden, who actually plans to write a series of articles exposing Crawford's slippery operations. The PYGMALION-like process of changing the tasteless yet street-savvy Holliday into a cultured lady is loaded with laughs and inoffensive sexual innuendoes. The situation gets more complicated as Holliday and Holden fall in love.

Crawford is frightening yet funny as the tycoon and Holden is effective in his appealing if low-key role. But Holliday is the film's most enduring treasure. Indeed, she was so effective as a dumb blonde that she was typecast in most of her subsequent films. Holliday's priceless characterization earned her an Oscar for Best Actress (one of BORN YESTERDAY's five nominations including: Best Picture, Best Direction, Best Screenplay, and Best Costume Design), a considerable achievement in light of her stellar competition that year: Gloria Swanson in SUNSET BOULEVARD and Bette Davis in ALL ABOUT EVE. A sheer delight, even if one only remembers the classic gin rummy scene.

BOUDU SAVED FROM DROWNING

1932   84m   bw   Comedy   ★★★½
Pathe   (France)   /15

Michel Simon *(Boudu)*, Charles Granval *(Monsieur Lestingois)*, Marcelle Hainia *(Madama Lestingois)*, Severine Lerczynska *(Anne-Marie)*, Jean Daste *(Student)*, Max Dalban *(Godin)*, Jean Gehret *(Vigour)*, Jacques Becker *(Poet on a Bench)*, Jane Pierson *(Rose, the Neighbor's Maid)*, George Darnoux *(Marriage Guest)*

p, Michel Simon, Jean Gehret; d, Jean Renoir; w, Jean Renoir (based on a play by Rene Fauchois); ph, Jean-Paul Alphen; ed, Marguerite Renoir; m, Leo Daniderff, Johann Strauss; art d, Hugues Laurent, Jean Castanier

This social comedy is another masterpiece from Renoir. Made in 1932 but lost, then finally released in 1967 in the US, this film is a timeless satire on middle-class values centering on Boudu (Michel Simon), an archetypal tramp about to commit suicide in grief, apparently, over the loss of his dog. He leaps into the Seine from the Pont des Arts, but is saved by bourgeois bookseller Lestingois (Charles Granval), who takes Boudu home and tries to start him on the road to a productive, responsible life. Boudu, however, is a protohippie—a long-haired, bearded believer in freedom and anarchy. During his stay in Lastingois' very proper household, he turns the place into a shambles, seduces Lestingois' wife (Marcelle Hainia), and, after he strikes it rich in the lottery, marries the family's gold-digging maid (Severine Lerczynska). He is then faced with the choice of living as a socially responsible adult in a tuxedo or reasserting his own independence. Told in Renoir's characteristically liberating realist humanist manner and exquisitely photographed, the story is immeasurably aided by Simon's extraordinary portrayal of Boudu. As Renoir has written: "Everything that an actor can be in a film, Michel Simon is in BOUDU. Everything!" Crudely remade in 1986 as DOWN AND OUT IN BEVERLY HILLS, starring Nick Nolte.

BOUND

1996   107m   c   Crime/Thriller   ★★★½
Dino De Laurentiis Communications/Spelling Films   (U.S.)   R/18

Jennifer Tilly *(Violet)*, Gina Gershon *(Corky)*, Joe Pantoliano *(Caesar)*, John P. Ryan *(Mickey Malnato)*, Christopher Meloni *(Johnnie Marconi)*, Richard Sarafian *(Gino Marzzone)*, Barry Kivel *(Shelly)*, Mary Mara *(Bartender)*, Peter Spellos *(Lou)*, Susie Bright *(Jesse)*

p, Andrew Lazar, Stuart Boros; d, Larry Wachowski, Andy Wachowski; w, Larry Wachowski, Andy Wachowski; ph, Bill Pope; ed, Zach Staenberg; m, Don Davis; prod d, Eve Cauley; art d, Robert Goldstein, Andrea Dopaso; fx, Lou Carlucci; cos, Lizzy Gardiner

With its fast-paced dialogue, slick characterizations, and brash cinematography, BOUND is a clever, exceptionally stylish twist on the edge-of-the-seat thriller.

Soon after she starts renovating her Chicago high-rise apartment, ex-con Corky (Gina Gershon) meets neighbor Violet (Jennifer Tilly), who lives with mobster Caesar (Joe Pantoliano). Sick of Caesar and attracted to her new friend, Violet becomes romantically involved with Corky. Violet and Corky scheme to steal $2 million that Caesar is supposed to present to a Mafia boss. Their carefully thought-out plan starts to go awry when Caesar decides not to run for his life but to stay and prove a rival mobster guilty of stealing the cash.

It is to the credit of first-time writers-directors Andy and Larry Wachowski that BOUND remains suspenseful without stretching the plot's plausibility beyond the breaking point. The lesbian twist on the "young lovers dupe the rich boyfriend-husband" plot heightens the suspense,but it's not just a gimmick: the relationship is sexy, tender, and believable. But in this truly American film, the women are eventually brought into crisis situations due to emotional frailty and lack of physical strength. Is using traditional "feminine" traits as a plot device sexist? Probably, but the dynamic set up here between Violet and Corky is genuine and exciting, and the audience is set up to root for them.

Gershon is a wonder as Corky. While publicity was given to the fact that a "lesbian expert" was consulted for the script, Gershon's method of preparing for her role by studying how classic male actors played their love scenes is what makes her performance unique and powerful. Pantoliano's Caesar is also a terrific creation. He's smarter than he looks, tougher than people expect, and likable enough to keep the conflict honest.

BOUND FOR GLORY

1976   147m   c   Biography   ★★★★
UA   (U.S.)   PG

David Carradine (*Woody Guthrie*), Ronny Cox (*Ozark Bule*), Melinda Dillon (*Mary Guthrie*), Gail Strickland (*Pauline*), John Lehne (*Locke*), Ji-Tu Cumbuka (*Slim Snedeger*), Randy Quaid (*Luther Johnson*), Elizabeth Macey (*Liz Johnson*), Allan Miller (*Agent*)

p, Robert F. Blumofe, Harold Leventhal; d, Hal Ashby; w, Robert Getchell (based on the autobiography of Woody Guthrie); ph, Haskell Wexler; ed, Robert C. Jones, Pembroke J. Herring

AAN Best Picture; *AAN Best Adapted Screenplay:* Robert Getchell; *AA Best Cinematography:* Haskell Wexler; *AAN Best Editing:* Robert Jones, Pembroke J. Herring; *AA Best Score:* Leonard Rosenman; *AAN Best Costume Design:* William Theiss

A moving, brilliantly photographed picture that portrays the legendary eccentric folksinger Woody Guthrie in a trip across Depression-era America. Carradine is memorable as the penniless Okie who rides a train to California but is stopped at the border because the state is having difficulty providing for those that have arrived already. Carradine sneaks across the border and meets Quaid, and the two team up to look for work. Cox is an Ozark folk singer who periodically visits the labor camps to lighten the load of these poor men's lives. At one of the meetings, Carradine joins in the singing and Cox is so impressed that he gets him a job on the radio. Success is almost immediate, but Guthrie's social conscience compels him to use the radio as a political organ for recounting the travails of the farm workers he knows so intimately. He is told to cut out the politicking or leave. He chooses to be fired. Later he gets offered a chance to play the big time at Hollywood's Coconut Grove provided that he'll commercialize his work. No surprises here. He hits the road, hoping to bring the message of his music to people he meets along the way.

This is a superior biopic. Viewers get to see Guthrie warts and all. That easily half the audience is too young to know who he was should not matter. This is the story of an artist with deeply held political principles, a remarkable quality in any age. At 147 minutes, this film could lose a quarter of an hour or more with no loss to the drama.

Haskell Wexler proves again that he is a master of evocative cinematography as he uses the camera to its best advantage in every frame of this Hal Ashby directed film. Robert Getchell adapted Guthrie's autobiography for the screenplay but Ashby and his editor made extensive contributions.

BOY FRIEND, THE

1971   108m   c   Musical   ★★★½
MGM   (U.K.)   G/U

Twiggy (*Polly Browne*), Christopher Gable (*Tony Brockhurst*), Moyra Fraser (*Madame Dubonnet*), Max Adrian (*Max*), Bryan Pringle (*Percy*), Catherine Wilmer (*Lady Brockhurst*), Murray Melvin (*Alphonse*), Georgina Hale (*Fay*), Sally Bryant (*Nancy*), Vladek Sheybal (*De Thrill*)

p, Ken Russell; d, Ken Russell; w, Ken Russell (based on a play by Sandy Wilson); ph, David Watkin; ed, Michael Bradsell; art d, Simon Holland; chor, Christopher Gable, Terry Gilbert, Gillian Gregory; cos, Shirley Russell

AAN Best Score: Peter Maxwell Davies (Adaptation), Peter Greenwell (Adaptation)

Ken Russell's dizzy, affectionate homage to 1930s musicals and Busby Berkeley is for many his best film. Twiggy is the assistant stage manager who gets her big chance when star Glenda Jackson hurts her ankle. "Come back a star," the director tells her, and that's just what she does. (The same line was spoken by Warner Baxter to Ruby Keeler in 42ND STREET.) Russell's bombastic direction has never looked so right. Musical numbers (the film's song score received an Oscar nomination) are uniformly well done, and include "I Could Be Happy", "The Boy Friend", "Won't You Charleston With Me?", "Fancy Forgetting", "Sur La Plage", "A Room In Bloomsbury", "Safety In Numbers", "It's Never Too Late To Fall In Love", "Poor Little Pierette", "Riviera", "The You Don't Want To Play With Me Blues" (Sandy Wilson), "All I Do Is Dream Of You", "You Are My Lucky Star" (Nacio Herb Brown, Arthur Freed) and "Any Old Iron" (Charles Collins, E.A. Shepherd, Fred Terry).

THE BOY FRIEND is a sincere celebration of the musical from a camp point of view. And let it be said Russell discovered Tommy Tune many years before Broadway did.

BOYS FROM BRAZIL, THE

1978   123m   c   Thriller/War   ★★★½
Fox   (U.S./U.K.)   R/18

Gregory Peck (*Josef Mengele*), Laurence Olivier (*Ezra Lieberman*), James Mason (*Eduard Seibert*), Lilli Palmer (*Esther Lieberman*), Uta Hagen (*Frieda Maloney*), Rosemary Harris (*Mrs. Doring*), John Dehner (*Henry Wheelock*), John Rubinstein (*David Bennett*), Anne Meara (*Mrs. Curry*), Steve Guttenberg (*Barry Kohler*)

p, Martin Richards, Stanley O'Toole; d, Franklin J. Schaffner; w, Heywood Gould (based on the novel by Ira Levin); ph, Henri Decae; ed, Robert Swink; m, Jerry Goldsmith; cos, Anthony Mendleson

AAN Best Actor: Laurence Olivier; *AAN Best Editing:* Robert E Swink; *AAN Best Score:* Jerry Goldsmith

This fast-moving picture features a battle of wits between the "Angel of Death," Nazi war criminal Josef Mengele (Gregory Peck), and fictional Nazi hunter Ezra Lieberman (Laurence Olivier, his character seemingly based on real-life Nazi hunter Simon Wiesenthal), in a farfetched plot having to do with the cloning of Hitler. Mengele's plan is to harvest hundreds of young men (all of whom have been raised in environments nearly identical to the one that Hitler grew up in) in an attempt to replicate the Fuhrer's upbringing as well as his genetic structure. The picture barrels along for about 115 minutes, but then falls apart in a wildly ludicrous finale. The cast is great—including Peck, Olivier, James Mason, Denholm Elliott, and even Steve Guttenberg (in one of his first roles). The film is compelling, albeit pretty silly in its elaborate "what if?" plot mechanications.

BOYS OF ST. VINCENT, THE

1993   210m   c   Drama   ★★★★½
Les Productions Tele-Action/National Film
Board of Canada   (Canada)

Henry Czerny (*Peter Lavin*), Johnny Morina (*Kevin Reevey—age 10*), Sebastian Spence (*Kevin Reevey—age 25*), Brian Dodd (*Steven Lunny—age 10*), David Hewlett (*Steven Lunny—age 25*), Jonathan

Lewis *(Eddie Linnane)*, Jeremy Keefe *(Mike Sproule)*, Philip Dinn *(Mike Finn)*, Brian Dooley *(Detective Noseworthy)*, Greg Thomey *(Brother Glackin)*

p, Sam Grana; d, John N. Smith; w, Des Walsh, John N. Smith, Sam Grana; ph, Pierre Letarte; ed, Werner Nold, Andre Corriveau; m, Neil Smolar; prod d, Real Ouellette

This two-part made-for-TV Canadian movie proved one of the most emotionally devastating films released in the US in 1994. THE BOYS OF ST. VINCENT was inspired by a notorious case involving the alleged sexual abuse of dozens of children by Christian Brothers in a Catholic-administered orphanage.

Part One is set in 1975 Newfoundland at St. Vincent, a nightmarish institution where the authoritarian Brother Peter Lavin (Henry Czerny) extorts sexual favors from young boys. Part Two opens 15 years later in Montreal, Quebec, with the arrest of Lavin, now married and the father of two pre-teen sons. THE BOYS OF ST. VINCENT does not flinch from depicting the physical and emotional horrors endured by the boys but, despite the sensational subject-matter, its approach is restrained and non-exploitative. The film is neither an anti-Catholic nor homophobic diatribe but, rather, a dark and impressively complex critique of the abuse of power. Henry Czerny gives a terrifying but exquisitely modulated performance, roaming the corridors under his command with a crucifix jammed in his belt like a six-gun. Watching this martinet try to "mother" a small child is genuinely unnerving. Perhaps one of the greatest achievements of BOYS, though, is the emergence of Lavin as more understandably human in the second half. The verdict on Lavin is not disclosed, but it hardly matters; when the survivors on both sides are left so damaged, the idea of legal justice being served is small consolation.

BOYS TOWN

1938 96m bw Drama ★★★
MGM (U.S.) /A

Spencer Tracy *(Father Edward Flanagan)*, Mickey Rooney *(Whitey Marsh)*, Henry Hull *(Dave Morris)*, Leslie Fenton *(Dan Farrow)*, Addison Richards *(The Judge)*, Edward Norris *(Joe Marsh)*, Gene Reynolds *(Tony Ponessa)*, Minor Watson *(The Bishop)*, Jonathan Hale *(John Hargraves)*, Bobs Watson *(Pee Wee)*

p, John W. Considine Jr.; d, Norman Taurog; w, John Meehan, Dore Schary; w, based on a story by Dore Schary, Eleanore Griffin; ph, Sidney Wagner; ed, Elmo Veron; m, Edward Ward; art d, Cedric Gibbons, Urie McCleary; fx, Slavko Vorkapich

AAN Best Picture; AA Best Actor: Spencer Tracy; *AAN Best Director:* Norman Taurog; *AA Best Original Story:* Eleanore Griffin, Dore Schary; *AAN Best Screenplay:* John Meehan, Dore Schary

One of the more overrated films of its era. Not surprisingly one of MGM tyrant Louis B. Mayer's favorite films, this sentimental wallow dramatizes the real-life story of Father Edward Flanagan, founder of the famous Boys Town for errant youths. What sounds like ideal "truth is stranger than fiction" material, with inspiration to boot, comes across as stilted, overly sanctimonious moralizing. Father Flanagan's efforts against incredible obstacles vanish with a magic flourish of the scriptwriter's pen, and the generally reliable Tracy, one of the most talented and engaging actors of his day, compounds these errors with a performance dripping with piety. Tracy always claimed that his Oscar for Best Actor here belonged to Flanagan (he even sent the priest his statuette); the Academy should have bypassed the actor entirely and simply donated the crockery to Flanagan for his humanitarian activities. The soft-focus closeups of the film's star weren't needed to soften Tracy's likably craggy features; they were there to canonize the film's hero with a phony cinematic halo. Director Taurog, a competent but unimaginative contract man, was chosen for this epic because of his past success with child actors. Credit the electrifying 18-year-old Mickey Rooney with lending some edge to a picture that is soft, soft, soft. Also highly effective is the genuinely sweet child actor Bobs Watson, able to turn on the tears without batting an eyelid. Too respectful of its subject matter, BOYS TOWN is well-crafted and smoothly paced, probably most entertaining for those who can down maple syrup without benefit of pancakes. Nominated for Best Picture and Best Director, the film won an Oscar for Best Original Story.

BOYZ N THE HOOD

1991 107m c Drama ★★★★
Both Inc./Columbia (U.S.) R/15

Laurence Fishburne *(Furious Styles)*, Ice Cube *(Doughboy Baker)*, Cuba Gooding Jr. *(Tre Styles)*, Nia Long *(Brandi)*, Morris Chestnut *(Ricky Baker)*, Tyra Ferrell *(Mrs. Baker)*, Angela Bassett *(Reva Styles)*, Meta King *(Brandi's Mom)*, Whitman Mayo *(The Old Man)*, Hudhail Al-Amir *(SAT Man)*

p, Steve Nicolaides; d, John Singleton; w, John Singleton; ph, Charles Mills; ed, Bruce Cannon; m, Stanley Clarke; art d, Bruce Bellamy

AAN Best Director: John Singleton; *AAN Best Original Screenplay:* John Singleton

John Singleton's debut feature is a low-key morality drama about the strained bonds of family and friendship in the midst of social disorder.

The film begins in South Central Los Angeles, circa 1984, where ten-year-old Tre Styles (Desi Arnez Hines II) is confronted with the violence of everyday life in the streets of his ghettoized, African-American neighborhood. After being entrusted by his divorced mother Reva (Angela Bassett) to her ex-husband Furious (Larry Fishburne), Tre receives moral guidance from his loving but disciplinarian father. Growing up he befriends the brothers who live across the street, bad-assed Doughboy and shy Ricky, who dreams of playing professional football. After Doughboy spends seven years in prison for juvenile crimes, the three are reunited during their last year of high school.

Tre (Cuba Gooding, Jr.) and Ricky (Morris Chestnut) are the inseparable good kids, while Doughboy (Ice Cube) leads the crew of bitter and combative boys in the 'hood. USC recruiters offer Ricky an athletic scholarship, while Tre and his girlfriend Brandi (Nia Long) discuss the possibility of getting married—after completing their college educations. But chaotic forces overwhelm even these best and brightest in their efforts to escape the terrors of their neighborhood.

"Increase the peace." The words which appear at the conclusion of BOYZ N THE HOOD ring out as a simple, intelligent, and urgent plea, befitting Singleton's powerful, unpretentious dramatization of life in a modern L.A. ghetto. Like fellow black filmmaker Spike Lee, Singleton fills his work with references to the particulars of black life: from little Tre's precocious lecture on Afrocentric history, to Furious's lessons about racial genocide and culturally biased IQ tests, to Brandi and Tre's destinations at historically black colleges Spelman and Morehouse. The ensemble cast makes good on Singleton's true-to-life script, with particularly strong work performances by rap star-turned-actor Ice Cube as Doughboy and the understated Larry Fishburne as Furious Styles. Positive figures—Furious, Tre, Brandi—are rendered perhaps too virtuous, and Singleton becomes a bit preachy in the closing scenes, but an overt "message" movie may be the only appropriate response to the ongoing social crisis addressed by BOYZ N THE HOOD.

BRAINSTORM

1965 105m bw Thriller ★★★
Warner Bros. (U.S.) /15

Jeffrey Hunter *(Jim Grayam)*, Anne Francis *(Lorrie Benson)*, Dana Andrews *(Cort Benson)*, Viveca Lindfors *(Dr. E. Larstadt)*, Stacy Harris *(Josh Reynolds)*, Kathie Browne *(Angie DeWitt)*, Phillip Pine *(Dr. Ames)*, Michael Pate *(Dr. Mills)*, Robert McQueeney *(Sgt. Dawes)*, Strother Martin *(Mr. Clyde)*

p, William Conrad; d, William Conrad; w, Mann Rubin (based on a story by Larry Marcus); ph, Sam Leavitt; ed, William Ziegler; m, George Duning

Creepy yet contrived suspense film stars Hunter as a young scientist who saves distraught Francis from committing suicide. The pair fall in love, but Francis' rotten husband Andrews (who drove her to the brink of suicide in the first place) digs up the file on Hunter's earlier mental instability. He exacts his revenge by framing the scientist for obscene phone calls and other misdeeds so as to create the impression that he's cracking up again. Hunter and Francis retaliate with a plot to murder Andrews. Hunter expects to get a light sentence with an insanity defense since everyone is convinced he's crazy anyway. Hunter figures that he will be placed in a cushy mental institution, recover after a decent interval, and walk off scot-free into the waiting arms of Francis. Of course things don't work out as they plan. . . .

Fine cast directed by actor Conrad, TV's "Cannon," in a clever and taut visual style. Good, spare musical score by George Duning.

BRAM STOKER'S DRACULA

1992 130m c Horror/Romance/Fantasy ★★★½
Columbia/American Zoetrope/Osiris Films (U.S.) R/18

Gary Oldman (Count Vlad Dracul/Dracula), Winona Ryder (Mina Murray/Elisabeta), Anthony Hopkins (Professor Abraham Van Helsing), Keanu Reeves (Jonathan Harker), Richard E. Grant (Dr. Jack Seward), Cary Elwes (Lord Arthur Holmwood), Bill Campbell (Quincey P. Morris), Sadie Frost (Lucy Westenra), Tom Waits (R.M. Renfield), Monica Bellucci (Dracula's Bride)

p, Francis Ford Coppola, Fred Fuchs, Charles Mulvehill; d, Francis Ford Coppola; w, James V. Hart (from the novel Dracula by Bram Stoker); ph, Michael Ballhaus; ed, Nicholas C. Smith, Glen Scantlebury, Anne Goursaud; m, Wojciech Kilar; prod d, Thomas Sanders; art d, Andrew Precht; cos, Eiko Ishioka

AAN Best Art Direction: Thomas Sanders, Garrett Lewis; AA Best Costume Design: Eiko Ishioka; AA Best Makeup: Greg Cannom, Michele Burke, Matthew W. Mungle; AA Best Sound Effects Editing: Tom C. McCarthy, David E. Stone

Francis Ford Coppola's lavish new version of Bram Stoker's classic novel is a visual cornucopia, overstuffed with images of both beauty and grotesque horror.

Coppola has assembled a virtual Who's Who of young screen heartthrobs, all of whom—from Winona Ryder to Gary Oldman to Keanu Reeves to Cary Elwes—do their stuff against a range of brilliantly realized settings. Count Dracula's Transylvanian lair has a deliberately tongue-in-cheek, mythological aura, and Victorian England is brought to life through meticulous, and humorous, production design.

DRACULA also boasts some impressive special effects, and Coppola clearly enjoys recreating the cutting-edge technology of the late 19th century, from a primitive blood-transfusion apparatus to the earliest moving pictures.

The problem is that the visual pyrotechnics and period detail tend to blunt the dramatic impact of a narrative that's pretty bloodless to begin with. James V. Hart's screenplay sticks fairly close to Stoker's novel but loses steam after about 20 minutes, when continual cutting between different storylines creates more confusion than tension.

It's also hard to gauge the tone of this adaptation. Hart sets up an archly romantic relationship between the Count (Oldman) and a beautiful young woman (Ryder) who's a dead ringer for the love he lost centuries earlier. The couple's "love conquers all" scenes can't be taken seriously, but it's not entirely clear how ironic DRACULA is intended to be.

Not, that is, until the late arrival of Anthony Hopkins as Professor Van Helsing. Hopkins clearly recognizes this big, overblown, theme park ride for what it is, and wisely decides to inject some campy humor into the proceedings. The resulting combination is fun—but not as much fun as BUFFY THE VAMPIRE SLAYER.

BRASSED OFF

1996 107m c Drama ★★★
Prominent Features/Channel Four (U.K.) R/15

Pete Postlethwaite (Danny), Tara Fitzgerald (Gloria), Ewan McGregor (Andy), Stephen Tompkinson (Phil), Jim Carter (Harry), Philip Jackson (Jim), Peter Martin (Ernie), Sue Johnston (Vera), Mary Healey (Ida), Lill Roughley (Rita)

p, Steve Abbott; d, Mark Herman; w, Mark Herman; ph, Andy Collins; ed, Mike Ellis; m, Trevor Jones; prod d, Don Taylor; cos, Amy Roberts

As shameless and manipulative a tearjerker as any Hollywood fable of the no-hoper who wins the impossible win, this Yorkshire-set tale of political perfidy and the triumph of the common man spreads a thin layer of mining-town grit over the feel-good formula and pretends to be tough. But don't be fooled—this really is a HOW GREEN WAS MY VALLEY for the '90s.

Retired miner Danny (Pete Postlethwaite), who hides his portentous cough from everyone, even his nearest and dearest, lives to lead the Grimley Colliery Band, whose members are drawn from the ranks of the local pit workers. He's got his eyes on a national brass-band competition at the Royal Albert Hall, but the amateur musicians have more pressing worries, providing the film with its many subplots. The Grimley mine is slated to close, which will leave them all jobless and with little hope of finding work in their one-industry town. Will the miners stick together and vote to keep the pit open, or will management divide and conquer? Does Danny's sad-sack son Phil (Stephen Tompkinson), who supplements his income by dressing as a kiddie party clown, stand a chance of luring back his estranged wife? Will hard-luck lad Andy (Ewan McGregor) and lovely local-lass-made-bad Gloria (Tara Fitzgerald)—who plays a sweet flugelhorn solo but secretly works for management—pair off? These aren't really questions: Anyone who goes to the pictures with some regularity can figure out the answers. But solid performances all around keep the plot-plates spinning, and anyone in the mood for a good cry will find many appropriate moments at which to pull out the hankies.

BRAVEHEART

1995 177m c Historical/Drama/Adventure ★★★
Icon Productions/The Ladd Co./Marquis R/15
Film/Paramount (U.S.)

Mel Gibson (William Wallace), Sophie Marceau (Princess Isabelle), Patrick McGoohan (Longshanks—King Edward I), Catherine McCormack (Murron), Brendan Gleeson (Hamish), James Cosmo (Campbell), David O'Hara (Stephen), Angus McFadyen (Robert the Bruce), Ian Bannen (The Leper), Peter Hanly (Prince Edward)

p, Mel Gibson, Alan Ladd Jr., Bruce Davey; d, Mel Gibson; w, Randall Wallace; ph, John Toll; ed, Steven Rosenblum; m, James Horner; prod d, Thomas Sanders; art d, Dan Dorrance; fx, Nick Allder; cos, Charles Knode

AA Best Picture; AA Best Director: Mel Gibson; AAN Best Original Screenplay: Randall Wallace; AA Best Cinematography: John Toll; AAN Best Costume Design: Charles Knode; AAN Best Editing: Steven Rosenblum; AA Best Makeup: Peter Frampton, Paul Pattison, Lois Burwell; AAN Best Dramatic Score: James Horner; AAN Best Sound: Andy Nelson, Scott Millan, Anna Behlmer, Brian Simmons; AA Best Sound Effects: Lon Bender, Per Hallberg

A massive, sweaty, sloppy and extremely heavy-handed epic, BRAVEHEART won Mel Gibson a Best Directing Oscar and delivers enough visceral excitement to make it an ideal rainy afternoon matinee.

As a boy, Scottish hero-to-be Sir William Wallace (Mel Gibson) witnesses the vicious treachery of King Edward I (Patrick McGoohan) when he slaughters a group of unarmed landowners. Educated abroad, Wallace returns as an adult to the tiny hamlet of Ellerslie to raise crops and children. After defending his wife from English rapists, he's forced to flee and begins enlisting locals in a bloody revolt. Wallace leads his army against the superior English forces at Stirling, beating them through cunning and bravery, and is declared "Guardian of Scotland." He takes his army into England, capturing the city of York. Sparks fly when he encounters comely Princess Isabelle (Sophie Marceau), but her husband, Prince Edward (Peter Hanly), in a performance that amounts to a homophobic caricature, schemes to destroy Wallace, who is soon betrayed by Robert the Bruce and Scottish aristocrats.

Although BRAVEHEART's scale is impressive, Gibson's attempt to create an old fashioned epic a la EL CID or SPARTACUS is not entirely successful. The pace is uneven and Gibson's abuse of slow motion reduces many dramatic scenes to tedium, though John Toll's gorgeous cinematography and Thomas Sanders's detailed, thoroughly authentic production design help overcome the film's sluggishness. And the fight sequences are truly outstanding: bloody, amazingly brutal, and efficiently edited, they create a compelling sense of the way it must have felt to be in the thick of brutal battle.

BRAZIL

1985   131m   c   Fantasy/Science Fiction   ★★★½
Terry Gilliam   (U.K.)   R/15

Jonathan Pryce *(Sam Lowry)*, Robert De Niro *(Tuttle)*, Katherine Helmond *(Ida Lowry)*, Ian Holm *(Kurtzmann)*, Bob Hoskins *(Spoor)*, Michael Palin *(Jack Lint)*, Ian Richardson *(Warrenn)*, Peter Vaughan *(Helpmann)*, Kim Greist *(Jill Layton)*, Jim Broadbent *(Dr. Jaffe)*

p, Arnon Milchan; d, Terry Gilliam; w, Terry Gilliam, Tom Stoppard, Charles McKeown; ph, Roger Pratt; ed, Julian Doyle; m, Michael Kamen; prod d, Norman Garwood; art d, John Beard, Keith Pain; fx, George Gibbs, Richard Conway; cos, James Acheson

AAN Best Original Screenplay: Terry Gilliam (Screenplay), Tom Stoppard (Screenplay), Charles McKeown (Screenplay); *AAN Best Art Direction:* Norman Garwood (Art Direction), Maggie Gray (Set Decoration)

Black humor dons its darkest robes in BRAZIL. Blindingly obtuse, excessively morose, the film is nevertheless dazzling in its inventive and massive sets and spectacular in its techniques. The theme is latter-day Orwell, well beyond 1984. The place could be anywhere in the future, where citizens of the regime live subterranean existences. One of these punctilious moles is Sam Lowry (Jonathan Pryce), a mundane statistician working in the Ministry of Information. He and millions of others work and live in a world crowded with a huge snakelike ductwork that heats, cools, and generally keeps the community going, when it works. A disaster, of sorts, is set off when a bug in the computer system causes everything to go haywire by altering the arrest record for a terrorist named Tuttle (Robert De Niro) to read Buttle. Lowry investigates the mistaken identity and discovers the girl of his fantasies, Jill Layton (Kim Greist). But in doing so he brings the scrutiny of superiors upon himself. The art direction (which earned the film an Academy Award nomination, as did the screenplay) and the special effects are nothing less than stunning. The storyline is a bit confusing—fragmented through interjected scenes and dizzying cross-cutting—so that some viewers may not grasp the sense of it all until it's almost over, and perhaps that's the point. Perhaps not. The plot's weaknesses become painfully apparent about halfway through the film. Still, BRAZIL is a powerful work that is both bleakly funny and breathtakingly assured. Following TIME BANDITS with this film, Gilliam firmly established himself as a director possessing true vision and remarkable style; few fantasy-film directors can compare with him. Haunting, lyrical and trendsetting, BRAZIL—a black comedy that remains ahead of its time—is one of the most audacious fantasies ever made.

BREAKDOWN

1997   c   Thriller   ★★★
Dino De Laurentiis/Spelling Films   (U.S.)   R/

Kurt Russell *(Jeff Taylor)*, J.T. Walsh *(Red Barr)*, Kathleen Quinlan *(Amy Taylor)*, M.C. Gainey *(Earl)*, Jack Noseworthy *(Billy)*, Ritch Brinkley *(Al)*, Rex Linn *(Sheriff Boyd)*, Moira Harris *(Arleen)*, Kim Robillard *(Deputy Len Carver)*, Thomas Kopache *(Calhoun)*

p, Dino De Laurentiis, Martha De Laurentiis; d, Jonathan Mostow; w, Jonathan Mostow, Sam Montogomery (based on a story by Jonathan Mostow); ph, Doug Milsome; ed, Derek Brechin, Kevin Stitt; m, Basil Poledouris; prod d, Victoria Paul; cos, Terry Dresbach

A tough little nail-biter that proves that classic suspense techniques are alive and well. There's nothing too ambitious or deeply significant going on: just a frantic guy, a missing wife, and a whole lot of ominous, empty road.

Massachusetts couple Jeff and Amy Taylor (Kurt Russell and Kathleen Quinlan) are driving cross-country in their shiny new car, heading for a fresh start in San Diego. Somewhere south of the boondocks and in the middle of nowhere, the car breaks down. Friendly trucker Red Barr (J.T. Walsh) offers them a lift to Belle's Diner, just a short piece down the road. Amy goes, Jeff stays with the car. And then she's gone. The police can't help and the locals are taciturn: they don't take much to strangers—or are they hiding something? Jeff's second-worst fears are realized when he learns that Amy has been kidnapped by Red and

his gang of smirking, backwoods highwaymen, and if he doesn't come up with more cash than he can possibly get his hands on, they're going to kill her.

This lean, tautly directed thriller preys on urban paranoia about the American heartland, the suspicion that far from being full of friendly folks and good, old-fashioned family values, it's a deceptively pretty cesspool teeming with perverted, inbred predators just waiting to show some soft-bellied big city folks that their fancy ways don't mean doodly-squat. There are echoes of Stephen Spielberg's DUEL and Roman Polanski's FRANTIC, as well as ROADGAMES, DELIVERANCE, THE HITCHER, and THE HILLS HAVE EYES. But director-cowriter Mostow isn't interested in homages: he's just looking to crank up the suspense bit by miserable bit, and does a very skillful job of it.

BREAKER MORANT

1980   107m   c   Drama/War   ★★★
South Australian Film   (Australia)   /A

Edward Woodward *(Lt. Harry Morant)*, Jack Thompson *(Maj. J.F. Thomas)*, John Waters *(Capt. Alfred Taylor)*, Bryan Brown *(Lt. Peter Handcock)*, Rod Mullinar *(Maj. Charles Bolton)*, Lewis Fitz-Gerald *(Lt. George Witton)*, Charles Tingwell *(Lt. Col. Denny)*, Vincent Ball *(Lt. Ian (Johnny) Hamilton)*, Frank Wilson *(Dr. Johnson)*, Terence Donovan *(Capt. Simon Hunt)*

p, Matt Carroll; d, Bruce Beresford; w, Bruce Beresford, Jonathan Hardy, David Stevens (based on a play by Kenneth Ross); ph, Don McAlpine; ed, William Anderson; m, Phil Cunneen; cos, Anna Senior

AAN Best Adapted Screenplay: Jonathan Hardy (Screenplay), David Stevens (Screenplay), Bruce Beresford (Screenplay)

A good court-martial drama in the old-fashioned style. Set during the Boer War—fought in South Africa between the descendants of Dutch colonists (the Boers) and the British during the years 1899-1902—BREAKER MORANT chronicles an obscure incident in 1901 when three Australian soldiers stationed in South Africa to assist the British were court martialed for executing enemy prisoners. Fighting what was, in essence, a guerrilla war, Lt. Harry "Breaker" Morant (Edward Woodward) ordered the executions acting under the orders of the British command. One of these prisoners turns out to have been a German citizen fighting alongside the Boers. Eager to maintain a good relationship with Germany, the British decide to make scapegoats of the Australians. Capably directed by Australian Bruce Beresford and well acted, BREAKER MORANT is a fascinating and satisfying experience. Unfolding his film in flashback during testimony at the trial, Beresford skillfully translates Kenneth Ross' play to the screen with an eye for historical accuracy.

BREAKFAST AT TIFFANY'S

1961   115m   c   Drama   ★★★★½
Paramount   (U.S.)   /PG

Audrey Hepburn *(Holly Golightly)*, George Peppard *(Paul Varjak)*, Patricia Neal *(2-E)*, Buddy Ebsen *(Doc Golightly)*, Martin Balsam *(O.J. Berman)*, Mickey Rooney *(Mr. Yunioshi)*, Jose-Luis de Vilallonga *(Jose da Silva Perriera)*, John McGiver *(Tiffany's Clerk)*, Dorothy Whitney *(Mag Wildwood)*, Stanley Adams *(Rusty Trawler)*

p, Martin Jurow, Richard Shepherd; d, Blake Edwards; w, George Axelrod (based on the novella by Truman Capote); ph, Franz Planer; ed, Howard Smith; m, Henry Mancini; cos, Edith Head

AAN Best Actress: Audrey Hepburn; *AAN Best Adapted Screenplay:* George Axelrod; *AA Best Score:* Henry Mancini; *AA Best Song:* Henry Mancini, Johnny Mercer; *AAN Best Art Direction:* Hal Pereira, Roland Anderson, Sam Comer, Ray Moyer

Capote's novella comes to glorious if slightly sentimentalized onscreen life with Hepburn gamboling through the film as the fey, ever-charming Holly Golightly. Peppard, never again quite so appealing, is Paul, the upstairs neighbor both intrigued and puzzled by Holly's erratic behavior: throwing all-night bashes for dozens of friends one moment, a lonely neurotic the next. Also mysterious are her visits to an imprisoned ganglord (Alan Reed) and to nightclub powder rooms, from which she emerges with $50 in cash each time. Paul, too, has a puzzling relationship with a wealthy woman (Neal) which prevents his growing love for

Holly from flowering. Finally, though, answers come in the form of Doc (Ebsen), a visitor from rural Texas who reveals some of the truth behind Holly's surface sophistication.

The film is well cast, with the exception of Rooney as a Japanese neighbor—a racist grotesque—driven to frenzy by Holly's noisy soirees. Balsam, as Holly's agent, offers a significant insight into his client's personality midway through the film when he notes: "She's a phony, all right, but a *real* phony." Amusingly helmed by director Edwards, romantic to the *n*th degree, and likely to disappoint only those devoted to Capote's novel, BREAKFAST AT TIFFANY'S is one of the great New York films, swathing the city in a layers of dewy love and glossy chic. The song, "Moon River," memorably crooned by Hepburn, won an Oscar and went on to become a popular favorite.

BREAKFAST CLUB, THE
1985   97m   c   Drama   ★★★
A&M   (U.S.)   R/15

Emilio Estevez (*Andrew Clark*), Paul Gleason (*Richard Vernon*), Anthony Michael Hall (*Brian Johnson*), John Kapelos (*Carl*), Judd Nelson (*John Bender*), Molly Ringwald (*Claire Standish*), Ally Sheedy (*Allison Reynolds*), Perry Crawford (*Allison's Father*), Mary Christian (*Brian's Sister*), Ron Dean (*Andy's Father*)

p, Ned Tanen, John Hughes; d, John Hughes; w, John Hughes; ph, Thomas Del Ruth; ed, Dede Allen; m, Keith Forsey, Gary Chang; prod d, John W. Corso; fx, Bill Schirmer; chor, Dorain Grusman; cos, Marilyn Vance, Christian Zamiata

Of the plethora of teen-based films released in 1985, THE BREAKFAST CLUB stands as one of the best, but it's still not exactly a shining example of the genre. Set in suburban Chicago, the film features five high school students from different social backgrounds who must spend a Saturday sitting in the school library as punishment for various infractions. Estevez, a star wrestler, is the jock; Ringwald portrays a rich, spoiled "princess"; Hall is a nerdy "brain;" Sheedy plays an introverted loner; and Nelson is a rebellious punk. Nelson fixes the library doors so they will remain closed, giving the students a little privacy. Confronting their values head on, with an articulate and sarcastic verbal assault, Nelson works on the others until they slowly begin talking with one another. THE BREAKFAST CLUB, paradoxically, is one of the few teen-oriented films that truly addresses the troubles of its characters, yet it falters in dealing with the issues raised. Director-writer Hughes, though he gives the material a sense of fun and achieves several moments of genuine warmth, too often resorts to obvious cliches, stereotypes, and easy answers, and throws in the near-obligatory rock video as well. His cast, on the other hand, is a fine ensemble that infuses the material with the sense of reality that Hughes's script often misses.

BREAKING AWAY
1979   100m   c   Comedy/Sports   ★★★★
Fox   (U.S.)   PG

Dennis Christopher (*Dave Stohler*), Dennis Quaid (*Mike*), Daniel Stern (*Cyril*), Jackie Earle Haley (*Moocher*), Barbara Barrie (*Mrs. Stohler*), Paul Dooley (*Mr. Stohler*), Robyn Douglass (*Katherine*), Hart Bochner (*Rod*), Amy Wright (*Nancy*), Peter Maloney (*Doctor*)

p, Peter Yates; d, Peter Yates; w, Steve Tesich; ph, Matthew F. Leonetti; ed, Cynthia Scheider; m, Patrick Williams; cos, Betsy Cox

AAN Best Picture; *AAN Best Supporting Actress*: Barbara Barrie; *AAN Best Director*: Peter Yates; *AA Best Original Screenplay*: Steve Tesich; *AAN Best Score*: Patrick Williams

A delightful sleeper. Set in Bloomington, Indiana, and nominated for an Oscar for Best Picture (it lost to KRAMER VS. KRAMER), BREAKING AWAY is a very funny and touching story about love, growing up, bicycle racing, and class consciousness. Dave Stohler (Christopher) and three of his friends (Quaid, Stern, and Haley) are recent high-school graduates. More importantly, in the eyes of nearby Indiana University students, they are "cutters"—declasse Bloomington townies, so named because many of the locals earn their living cutting rock in limestone quarries. For a time, Stohler, an avid bicycle racer, immerses himself in an alternative identity, pretends to be Italian, and does his best to woo a college coed. After a team of real Italian bicycle

racers comes to town and treats Stohler horribly, he discards his false identity but not his desire to prove himself the equal of the college students. He and his cutter buddies (who barely know one end of a racing bicycle from another) enter the university's "Little 500" bicycle race with suspenseful but not-so-surprising results at the film's uplifting finish. Tesich won an Oscar for his amusing screenplay; Barrie, as Christopher's mother, was nominated for Best Supporting Actress; composer Williams and director Yates also received nominations from the Academy. The four young leads all deliver excellent performances, as does Dooley (unjustly overlooked by the Academy) as Dave's father. Cyclists of the world, unite. You have nothing to lose but your chains!

BREAKING THE WAVES
1996   156m   c   Drama   ★★★
Zentropa Entertainment/Trust Films/Liberator   R/18
Productions/Argus/Northern Lights/La Sept/Swedish Television
Drama/Media Investment Club/Nordic Film & Television
Fund/VPRO Television   (Denmark /Sweden /Norway
/Netherlands /Finland /France /U.S. /Iceland)

Emily Watson (*Bess*), Stellan Skarsgard (*Jan*), Katrin Cartlidge (*Dodo*), Jean-Marc Barr (*Terry*), Udo Kier (*Man on the Trawler*), Adrian Rawlins (*Doctor Richardson*), Jonathan Hackett (*The Minister*), Sandra Voe (*Bess' Mother*), Mikkel Gaup (*Pits*), Roef Ragas (*Pim*)

p, Vibeke Windelov, Peter Aalbaek Jensen; d, Lars Von Trier; w, Lars Von Trier, Peter Asmussen; ph, Robby Muller; ed, Anders Refn; m, Joachim Holbek; art d, Karl Juliusson; fx, Morten Jacobsen, Lars Andersen; cos, Manon Rasmussen

AAN Best Actress: Emily Watson

Lars Von Trier's BREAKING THE WAVES is a twisted fable about the miraculous powers of faith, sacrifice, and unconditional love. Despite moments of undeniable brilliance, the film is occasionally sabotaged by an unsettling cinematic technique.

In a tiny, severely puritanical Presbyterian fishing village in 1970s Scotland, Bess (Emily Watson), a seemingly unstable young woman, marries an earthy oil-rigger named Jan (Stellan Skarsgard). Bess is blissfully happy with her husband, but she panics whenever Jan reminds her that he must eventually return to work on the rig, which he soon does. Disconsolate, Bess begs God for his return, promising anything in return. After an accident on the rig sends Jan home paralyzed from the neck down, Bess is convinced that it's her fault. When Jan later suggests that she have sleazy sex with other men so she can pleasure him with the details, she agrees, and begins a degrading descent that ultimately ends in tragedy.

Von Trier has admitted that in the past he "had an almost fetishistic attraction to film technology," and this is certainly true here, where the chosen technique is employed so relentlessly that the film is often literally hard to watch. Celebrated cinematographer Robby Muller intentionally filmed with a shaky hand-held camera, then transferred to video, and then transferred back to film, and then finally into the Super 35 widescreen format. Unfortunately, the result is extremely off-putting and distancing. That said, there is much to admire in BREAKING THE WAVES, particularly Emily Watson's fearless and star-making performance. The ending is impressive and memorable, although it's a bit surprising to see the enfant terrible Von Trier aspiring to achieve a Carl Dreyer-like spiritual epiphany.

BREATHLESS
(A BOUT DE SOUFFLE)
1959   89m   bw   Crime   ★★★★★
Imperia   (France)   /15

Jean-Paul Belmondo (*Michel Poiccard/Laszlo Kovacs*), Jean Seberg (*Patricia Franchini*), Daniel Boulanger (*Police Inspector*), Jean-Pierre Melville (*Parvulesco*), Liliane Robin (*Minouche*), Henri-Jacques Huet (*Antonio Berrutti*), Van Doude (*Journalist*), Claude Mansard (*Claudius Mansard*), Michel Fabre (*Plainclothesman*), Jean-Luc Godard (*Informer*) p, Georges de Beauregard; d, Jean-Luc Godard; w, Jean-Luc Godard (based on an idea by Francois Truffaut); ph, Raoul Coutard; ed, Cecile Decugis, Lila Herman; m, Martial Solal; art d, Claude Chabrol

What Stravinsky's "La Sacre du Printemps" is to 20th-century music or Joyce's *Ulysses* is to the 20th-century novel, Godard's first feature, BREATHLESS, is to film. It stands apart from all that came before and has revolutionized all that followed. Dedicated to the B-movies of Hollywood's Monogram Pictures, the film's structure begins with the conventions of the gangster film and film noir and proceeds to fragment them in a manner which greatly influenced the style of subsequent filmic narration. Michel Poiccard, alias Laszlo Kovacs (Belmondo, not conventionally attractive but giving a very sexy and appealing performance), is an amoral, dangerously careless petty criminal who models himself after Bogart and becomes the subject of a police dragnet when he senselessly guns down a traffic cop. He tries every avenue possible to cash a check endorsed "for deposit only" and hides out in the apartment of young American student Patricia Franchini (Seberg, whose imperfect French and limited acting skills lend something impossibly right to her enigmatic charcter). The couple, especially Michel, seem to be falling fatefully in love, but Godard is not content to merely develop character. During an extended, remarkable bedroom scene, this classic existential pair discusses art and philosophy in a way which prefigures Godard's lengthier and more profound ruminations in later films. Resuming the story, Godard ends his film with several ambiguous twists and an unforgettable closeup of Seberg. Rather than tell his tale in a conventional manner, Godard uses nostalgia, humor, and brutality alike to create the cinematic equivalent of contemporary alienation. Quoting Hollywood affectionately, Godard is nevertheless more concerned with destroying previous film language and employing his own. He "jump cuts" with little concern for continuity and then dollies the camera for long, fluid takes. Some scenes have a documentary feel, while others are pure pulp fiction. As the title implies, Godard's philosophy is to leave the viewer breathless so that he may breathe new life into them. (Look for his cameo as an informer.)

BREATHLESS

1983	100m	c	Crime	★★
ORION	(U.S.)			R/18

Richard Gere *(Jesse)*, Valerie Kaprisky *(Monica)*, Art Metrano *(Birnbaum)*, William Tepper *(Paul)*, John P. Ryan *(Lt. Parmental)*, Lisa Jane Persky *(Salesgirl)*, Garry Goodrow *(Berrutti)*, Robert Dunn *(Sgt. Enright)*, James Hong *(Grocer)*, Eugene Lourie *(Dr. Boudreaux)*

p, Martin Erlichman; d, Jim McBride; w, Jim McBride, L.M. Kit Carson (based on a screenplay by Jean-Luc Godard and a story by Francois Truffaut); ph, Richard H. Kline; ed, Robert Estrin; m, Jack Nitzsche; prod d, Richard Sylbert; cos, J. Allen Highfill

Remaking a movie is always a dicey proposition. Remaking a classic is even dicier. This version of BREATHLESS? No dice. The original burst upon the scene in 1959 and blew us all away, and even though we've become somewhat used to its tricks, it can still suggest its original impact. Godard took big chances then with technique, content, and casting and it paid off in spades. The new BREATHLESS features Gere as the wanton criminal Jesse (the Jean-Paul Belmondo role) and Kaprisky as Monica (Jean Seberg's original part). This version follows Godard and Truffaut's story of Jesse's escalating crimes and his involvement with Monica, but pays far too much attention to it, whereas the point of any Godard film is not *what* is told but *how*. Rather than trying to recapture the France of the late 1950s, the talented director, Jim McBride (DAVID HOLZMAN's DIARY) was probably right to switch locations to 1980s Los Angeles and make both characters American. In an attempt to duplicate Godard's feel for contemporary culture, McBride also adds bizarre colors and more than a dozen pop tunes, but the attempt is only modestly successful. The gradually increasing use of violence is effective in an oddly cartoon-like sort of way, but all involved fail to really impress their own creative slant on the project. Gere gives a flashy and not uninteresting performance and shows off his body a lot; Kaprisky shows hers too, though she fails completely to make her character really compelling. In keeping with the tentativeness of the entire enterprise, the ending is one of the great cop-outs in modern moviedom.

BREWSTER'S MILLIONS

1945	79m	bw	Comedy	★★★★
UA	(U.S.)			/PG

Dennis O'Keefe *(Monty Brewster)*, Helen Walker *(Peggy Gray)*, Eddie "Rochester" Anderson *(Jackson)*, June Havoc *(Trixie Summers)*, Gail Patrick *(Barbara Drew)*, Mischa Auer *(Michael Michaelovich)*, Joe Sawyer *(Hacky Smith)*, Nana Bryant *(Mrs. Gray)*, John Litel *(Swearengen Jones)*, Herbert Rudley *(Nopper Harrison)*

p, Edward Small; d, Allan Dwan; w, Sig Herzig, Charles Rogers, Wilkie Mahoney (based on the novel by George Barr McCutcheon and the play by Winchell Smith and Byron Ongley); ph, Charles Lawton Jr.; ed, Richard Heermance

AAN Best Score: Lou Forbes

Probably the best of the many filmings of the popular novel and stage play. O'Keefe portrays Monty Brewster, the young, handsome, happy-go-lucky soldier returning from the war to his girlfriend Peggy Gray (Walker). Upon arriving home, he is stunned to find that he has inherited an estate worth $8,000,000, with one catch, however: he must spend $1,000,000 in the span of two months or he gets nothing. Brewster promptly embarks on a whirlwind of spending, racing around town in an effort to divest himself of the money by investing in a flop musical show, a bankrupt banker, the stock market, the racetrack, and a jewel-loving society woman. He soon finds out that spending money isn't as easy as it seems. BREWSTER'S MILLIONS is a broad farce and comes across as such, providing laughs throughout. While the opening is somewhat slow and deliberate, once the plot is established this modestly budgeted production rockets along with one climax topping another. The always reliable and appealing Walker and Anderson provide sturdy support, and O'Keefe gives one of his best performances. Previously filmed in 1921 with Fatty Arbuckle, and in a 1935 British production with Jack Buchanan and Lili Damita, the story was resurrected as THREE ON A SPREE with Jack Watling in 1961 and in an abysmal 1985 effort starring Richard Pryor and John Candy under the original title, with Walter Hill directing. In that version Brewster had to spend $30 million in 30 days to collect $300 million. Talk about inflation!

BRIDE OF FRANKENSTEIN, THE

1935	75m	bw	Horror	★★★★★
Universal	(U.S.)			/PG

Boris Karloff *(The Monster)*, Colin Clive *(Henry Frankenstein)*, Valerie Hobson *(Elizabeth Frankenstein)*, Elsa Lanchester *(Mary Shelley/The Bride)*, O.P. Heggie *(The Hermit)*, Una O'Connor *(Minnie)*, Ernest Thesiger *(Dr. Septimus Pretorius)*, Gavin Gordon *(Lord Byron)*, Douglas Walton *(Percy Shelley)*, E.E. Clive *(Burgomaster)*

p, Carl Laemmle Jr.; d, James Whale; w, William Hurlbut, John Balderston (based on the novel by Mary Shelley); ph, John Mescall; ed, Ted J. Kent; m, Franz Waxman; art d, Charles D. Hall; fx, John P. Fulton

One of the seminal achievements of Hollywood cinema, this brilliant sequel to the original FRANKENSTEIN is one of the greatest films of its genre and remains a lasting tribute to the unique genius of director Whale. Asked to continue the tale of the monster and its maker, Mary Shelley (Lanchester) picks up approximately where FRANKENSTEIN left off, with the injured Dr. Frankenstein (Clive) being taken back to his castle to recover, while the monster (Karloff), also alive, wanders the countryside, wreaking havoc in its search for friendship. Enter the eccentric Dr. Pretorius (Thesiger), an alchemist who has also created artificial life. (An utterly delightful scene ensues when he shows off his miniatures.) Pretorius blackmails the reluctant Frankenstein to aid him in creating a bride for the monster, which, in an incredible scene, they do. A splendid combination of gothic horror and impish wit, BRIDE OF FRANKENSTEIN is a Whale masterpiece. The film is an unforgettable visual experience with its expressionistic sets, costumes and makeup; striking special effects; chiaroscuro lighting and bold camerawork. Waxman's magnificent score adds greatly to the overall effect, from the villagers' march to the mock-love theme attending the monstrous couple's "courtship" to the wedding bells pealing as the bride is presented. The performances are equally superb, with Clive again striking just the right note of nervous hysteria, Karloff beautifully injecting a sense of touching humanity into the confused and angry monster, and charcter actors Una O'Connor, O.P. Heggie, Dwight Frye and E.E. Clive lending ace support. Lanchester is quite amazing as both the deceptively demure Mary Shelley and her marvelously appropriate manifestation in her story, the bride. Thesiger, though, really steals the film with his pithy, menacing and hilarious portrait of the waspish Dr. Pretorius. A film whose black humor and sense of self-parody made Mel Brooks's delightful send-up YOUNG FRANKENSTEIN quite unnecessary, BRIDE OF FRANKENSTEIN transcends even the excesses allowed by its genre to become one of the oddest and most memorable films ever made in America.

BRIDGE ON THE RIVER KWAI, THE

1957 161m c War ★★★★½
Columbia (U.S.) /PG

William Holden (Shears), Alec Guinness (Col. Nicholson), Jack Hawkins (Maj. Warden), Sessue Hayakawa (Col. Saito), James Donald (Maj. Clipton), Geoffrey Horne (Lt. Joyce), Andre Morell (Col. Green), Peter Williams (Capt. Reeves), John Boxer (Maj. Hughes), Percy Herbert (Grogan)

p, Sam Spiegel; d, David Lean; w, Carl Foreman (uncredited), Michael Wilson (uncredited, based on the novel by Pierre Boulle); ph, Jack Hildyard; ed, Peter Taylor; m, Malcolm Arnold

AA Best Picture; AA Best Actor: Alec Guinness; AAN Best Supporting Actor: Sessue Hayakawa; AA Best Director: David Lean; AA Best Adapted Screenplay: Pierre Boulle, Michael Wilson, Carl Foreman; AA Best Cinematography: Jack Hildyard; AA Best Editing: Peter Taylor; AA Best Score: Malcolm Arnold

This intelligent and exciting WWII tale, masterfully helmed by Lean (at the start of his "epic" period), features a splendid performance from Guinness as Col. Nicholson, a British officer who has surrendered with his regiment to the Japanese in Burma in 1943. Martinet Nicholson insists that his men conduct themselves by the book and flatly refuses to cooperate with the equally dutiful Japanese commander, Col. Saito (Hayakawa, in an equally marvelous performance). When Saito insists that the British prisoners construct an elaborate bridge over the gorge of the River Kwai, Nicholson refuses to permit his officers to work side-by-side with the enlisted men, citing the Geneva Convention. After a series of incidents including torture and negotiations, Nicholson suddenly becomes determined to build the best bridge possible, thereby restoring his men's morale and providing a shining example of British rectitude. Meanwhile, Shears (Holden), an American, escapes from the prison camp and makes his way to Australia, where he impersonates an officer to obtain the privileges of rank. Major Warden (Hawkins), the British officer in charge of guerrilla operations, uncovers Shears' duplicity and sends him back to the jungle prison to destroy the bridge Nicholson and his men are so frantically attempting to complete. Lean aptly juxtaposes action sequences with a psychological examination of the folly of war, emphasizing its many ironies (brought home most forcefully at the explosive finale). Screenwriters Carl Foreman and Michael Wilson retained Pierre Boulle's terse, tough dialogue, which finds its greatest expression in Holden's cowardly wise-guy character. Foreman and Wilson were denied credit on the film due to blacklisting problems; in 1996, the Writer's Guild of America officially restored their names. Based on fact, the film stands as one of the finest war films ever. Stunningly photographed and featuring a theme guaranteed to keep you whistling, THE BRIDGE ON THE RIVER KWAI won seven Oscars, including Best Picture, Actor (Guinness), and Director, as well as awards for writing, editing, cinematography, and music.

BRIDGE TOO FAR, A

1977 176m c War ★★½
UA (U.K.) PG/15

Dirk Bogarde (Lt. Gen. Browning), James Caan (Sgt. Dohun), Michael Caine (Lt. Col. Vandeleur), Sean Connery (Maj. Gen. Urquhart), Edward Fox (Lt. Gen. Horrocks), Elliott Gould (Col. Stout), Gene Hackman (Maj. Gen. Sosabowski), Anthony Hopkins (Lt. Col. John Frost), Hardy Kruger (Gen. Ludwig), Laurence Olivier (Dr. Spaander)

p, Joseph E. Levine, Richard Levine, Michael Stanley-Evans; d, Richard Attenborough; w, William Goldman (based on the book by Cornelius Ryan); ph, Geoffrey Unsworth; ed, Anthony Gibbs; m, John Addison; cos, Anthony Mendleson

A movie too long. A BRIDGE TOO FAR tells the true story of a WWII military blunder that cost many lives and, in the end, meant little to the war effort. Field Marshal Montgomery and General Eisenhower planned to drop 35,000 Allied troops into Holland to secure the six bridges leading to Germany, after which a British force was to speed through Belgium to the last bridge at Arnhem. From there, the two groups were to smash into the Ruhr area and crush the already damaged factories of the German war effort. Murphy's Law acted up on a massive scale: foul weather, poor judgment, panic, and bad luck all took their toll, and the operation (code-named "Market Garden") was a total disaster. A BRIDGE TOO FAR is not a *total* disaster, but it does suggest that the curses hanging over certain historical debacles should perhaps be heeded by Hollywood filmmakers. Running three squirming hours and casting a dozen top stars in what are in some cases little more than cameos prove effective as sure ways to annoy an audience. (Gould's performance, for instance, comprises little more than his uttering "Shit!" as a bridge is blown up before his eyes.) A thoroughly disappointing and overproduced picture, A BRIDGE TOO FAR is nevertheless technically impressive and its sheer scope may interest hardcore warmongers. Screenwriter Goldman has also injected a handful of character touches which lend an occasional burst of humanity and intimacy to this otherwise overly indulgent behemoth.

BRIDGES AT TOKO-RI, THE

1954 102m c War ★★★★
Paramount (U.S.) /U

William Holden (Lt. Harry Brubaker, USNR), Fredric March (Rear Adm. George Tarrant), Grace Kelly (Nancy Brubaker), Mickey Rooney (Mike Forney), Robert Strauss (Beer Barrel), Charles McGraw (Cmdr. Wayne Lee), Keiko Awaji (Kimiko), Earl Holliman (Nestor Gamidge), Richard Shannon (Lt. Olds), Willis Bouchey (Capt. Evans)

p, William Perlberg; d, Mark Robson; w, Valentine Davies (based on a novel by James Michener); ph, Loyal Griggs; ed, Alma Macrorie; m, Lyn Murray; art d, Hal Pereira, Henry Bumstead; cos, Edith Head

AAN Best Editing: Alma Macrorie; AA Best Visual Effects

A gripping psychological study of war's effects, starring Holden as Lt. Harry Brubaker, a family man called back to active duty who feels he has already done enough for his country in WW II and resents the Korean War's intrusion on his life with wife Nancy (Kelly) and their kids. Still a military man, however, Brubaker heeds the requests of his admiral (March) and doggedly goes about his duty as a pilot, spending long idle stretches aboard a battleship. The narrative drives toward the climactic bombing of the five bridges of Toko-Ri, which span a strategic pass in Korea's interior. Along the way Holden and Kelly share some effective and intimate scenes together, and several enjoyable lighter moments occur in buddy scenes with fellow pilots Mike Forney (Rooney) and Nestor Gamidge (Holliman). Based on the novel by James Michener, this exciting and thoughtful film features excellent acting all around and is visually quite compelling thanks to Oscar-winning special effects in the aerial scenes. Also nominated for Best Film Editing.

BRIDGES OF MADISON COUNTY, THE

1995 135m c Romance/Drama ★★★
Amblin/Malpaso Productions (U.S.) PG-13/12

Clint Eastwood (Robert Kincaid), Meryl Streep (Francesca Johnson), Annie Corley (Carolyn Johnson), Victor Slezak (Michael Johnson), Jim Haynie (Richard Johnson), Sarah Kathryn Schmitt (Young Carolyn), Christopher Kroon (Young Michael), Phyllis Lyons (Betty), Michelle Benes (Lucy Redfield), Alison Wiegert (Child)

p, Clint Eastwood, Kathleen Kennedy; d, Clint Eastwood; w, Richard LaGravenese (based on the novel by Robert James Waller); ph, Jack N. Green; ed, Joel Cox; m, Lennie Niehaus; prod d, Jeannine Oppewall; art d, William Arnold; fx, Steve Riley, John Frazier; cos, Colleen Kelsall

AAN Best Actress: Meryl Streep

Adapted from the best-selling and much-mocked novel, THE BRIDGES OF MADISON COUNTY is a tearjerker, pure and simple, but its warmth, humor, and charm make it an immensely satisfying one. Aptly exploiting the formidable screen presence of leads Clint Eastwood and Meryl Streep, it's a rare mainstream American romance in which two mature adults move from attraction and flirtation to love and passion.

Iowa, 1965. Francesca Johnson (Streep), an Italian woman married to a Midwesterner, looks forward to a week of splendid solitude with her family off at the State Fair. Her plans change when intriguing stranger Robert Kincaid (Eastwood) pulls into her driveway. He's a *National Geographic* photographer on assignment to shoot some of Madison County's historic covered bridges, and he's lost. The attraction between them is immediate. She's enthralled by his romantic style and tales of adventures in far-off places. The next night, she invites him over again, and they make love. Will Francesca abandon home and hearth for this charismatic drifter?

Robert Waller's *The Bridges of Madison County* was an American publishing phenomenon, a best-selling brew of naive poetry, fuzzy philosophizing, and over-ripe prose that was absolutely impervious to critical brickbats. To his credit, director and star Clint Eastwood has manufactured a cinematic silk purse from a literary sow's ear. Telling the story from Francesca's point of view is a smart change: her womanly wisdom—even in intrusive voice-over—is far more appealing than Kincaid's slippery New Age nonsense.

Eastwood brings an air of easy, romantic charm to Kincaid, but BRIDGES is Streep's film. She completely inhabits Francesca, bringing to life both the character's superficial frumpiness and a grace and natural elegance she has almost forgotten she has.

BRIEF ENCOUNTER

1945	86m	bw	Romance	★★★★★
Cineguild/Eagle-Lion (U.K.)				/PG

Celia Johnson (*Laura Jesson*), Trevor Howard (*Alec Harvey*), Cyril Raymond (*Fred Jesson*), Stanley Holloway (*Albert Godby*), Joyce Carey (*Myrtle Bagot*), Everley Gregg (*Dolly Messiter*), Margaret Barton (*Beryl Waters*), Dennis Harkin (*Stanley*), Valentine Dyall (*Stephen Lynn*), Marjorie Mars (*Mary Norton*)

p, Noel Coward; d, David Lean; w, Noel Coward, David Lean, Anthony Havelock-Allan (based on Noel Coward's play "Still Life"); ph, Robert Krasker; ed, Jack Harris; m, Sergei Rachmaninoff

AAN Best Actress: Celia Johnson; AAN Best Director: David Lean; AAN Best Original Screenplay: Anthony Havelock-Allan, David Lean, Ronald Neame

A touching, exquisitely handled film dealing with two ordinary people who accidentally fall in love. BRIEF ENCOUNTER is a unique and sometimes misunderstood film whose very British restraint has not endeared it to all comers, but which if anything makes the film more passionate as a result. The famous use of Rachmaninoff for the musical score, which would seem ridiculous and cliched in later screen romances, is quite perfect here, as overpowering emotions threaten the reliable dullness the leading couple relies upon every day to get by. Krasker's gleaming black-and-white cinematography, at once delicately stylized and the peak of low-key realism, enhances the story of Alec (Howard) and Laura (Johnson), a doctor and housewife respectively, both happily married to others, who journey into town each Thursday on routine business. Alec's removing a cinder from Laura's eye at the train station one week initiates a casual friendship which rapidly grows into something far stronger than either could have expected. The couple share moments of tenderness, gentle confidences and even wry humor (e.g. while watching shlock cinema, surely writer Noel Coward's sly dig at pablum for the masses). Proof positive that director Lean was far better in his small-scale first half-dozen films than in his later overblown epics, BRIEF ENCOUNTER brings Coward's lovingly detailed and observant script to glowing life. The cast is uniformly faultless, from the sharp comic counterpoint of Carey, Holloway, and Gregg to the wonderful gentility Raymond brings to the role of Laura's husband. Center stage, though, properly belongs to the leading couple. In two screen creations to cherish, dashing new-

comer Howard gives a brilliantly nuanced, ardent and touching performance, while the ordinary-looking, carefully mannered Johnson achieves a heartbreaking performance whose beauty ranks with Garbo's CAMILLE.

BRIGADOON

1954	108m	c	Musical	★★
MGM (U.S.)				/U

Gene Kelly (*Tommy Albright*), Van Johnson (*Jeff Douglas*), Cyd Charisse (*Fiona Campbell*), Elaine Stewart (*Jane Ashton*), Barry Jones (*Mr. Lundie*), Hugh Laing (*Harry Beaton*), Albert Sharpe (*Andrew Campbell*), Virginia Bosier (*Jean Campbell*), Jimmie Thompson (*Charlie Crisholm Dalrymple*), Tudor Owen (*Archie Beaton*)

p, Arthur Freed; d, Vincente Minnelli; w, Alan Jay Lerner (based on the musical play by Alan Jay Lerner and Frederick Loewe); ph, Joseph Ruttenberg; ed, Albert Akst; art d, Cedric Gibbons, Preston Ames; chor, Gene Kelly

AAN Best Art Direction: Cedric Gibbons (Art Direction), Preston Ames (Art Direction), Edwin B Willis (Set Decoration), Keogh Gleason (Set Decoration); AAN Best Costume Design: Irene Sharaff; AAN Best Sound: Wesley C Miller (Sound Director)

Possibly Minnelli's worst screen musical. Confined to an MGM soundstage, this adaptation of the Lerner and Loewe Broadway hit desperately needs air, creatively stifled as it is in practically every department. New Yorkers Jeff and Tommy (Johnson and Kelly) get lost in the Scottish highlands and stumble onto the village of Brigadoon on the one day every 100 years that it appears from out of the mists. The villagers, who sport the garb and manners of antiquity, are in a merry mood, and the Americans happily join in their dancing and festivities. Tommy is particularly enchanted when he falls for bonnie lass Fiona (Charisse). He then must decide whether to return to New York or remain with his love in the land of long ago. Tommy and Jeff do go back to their urban existence, but eventually Tommy returns to Scotland, and such is the power of his love that the village materializes long enough for him to join Fiona in fantasyland forever.

One would like to see more dancing in BRIGADOON, though what's there is generally fine (especially a spirited routine to "I'll Go Home with Bonnie Jean"). Praise should also go to Johnson for doing a good job with his cynical, wisecracking role. Other than that, though, the pleasures of BRIGADOON are as fleeting as the village's centennial appearances. The sense of whimsy crucially needed to make this thing fly is nowhere to be found, and Minnelli seems to enjoy the stylized scenes of an obnoxious Manhattan more than the heather of the highlands. Kelly's patented good cheer is meagerly doled out and his exuberant energy seems to vanish into the Scottish ether. The somber, remote Charisse dances exquisitely but otherwise has all the appeal of plywood. Even the legendary score sounds a little flat. Nominated for three Academy Awards: Best Sound Recording, Best Costume Design and, inexplicably, Best Art Direction/Set Decoration.

BRIGHTNESS
(YEELEN)

1987	106m	c	Fantasy	★★★★
Cisse/Government of Mali/CNC-UTA/WDR/Fuji (Mali)				/PG

Issiaka Kane (*Nianankoro*), Aoua Sangare (*Attu*), Niamanto Sanogo (*Soma*), Balla Moussa Keita (*Peul King*), Soumba Traore (*Nianankoro's Mother*), Ismaila Sarr (*Djigui*), Youssouf Tenin Cisse (*Attu's Son*), Koke Sangare (*Komo Chief*), Brehima Doumbia, Seyba M'Baye

p, Souleymane Cisse; d, Souleymane Cisse; w, Souleymane Cisse; ph, Jean-Noel Ferragut; ed, Dounamba Coulibaly, Andre Davanture, Marie-Catherine Miqueau, Jenny Frenck, Seipati N'Xumalo; m, Michel Portal, Salif Keita; fx, Frederic Duru, Nicos Metelopoulos; cos, Kossa Mody Keita

BRIGHTNESS is very likely the most highly praised African film made to date—a reflection both of the film's merit and of the West's lack of critical attention to Third World films. Boosted by a Special Jury Prize at the 1987 Cannes Film Festival and favorable receptions at the Berlin and New York Festivals, BRIGHTNESS fast became *the* film to see in 1988. Whatever artistic merit the film does or doesn't have (and some critics doubt that it is as great as many claim), it found an audience—an audience that, for the most part, left the film completely baffled and profoundly moved. Like the main character, the audience became involved in a search for knowledge and the hope of enlightenment.

The film opens with a complicated written description of various mystical symbols and rituals of the Bambara tribe and a nutshell introduction to *Komo*—a science of the gods based on the elements of "nature" and key to understanding the greater thrust of the film. The story of a man's (Kane) search for his evil, all-powerful shaman father (Sanogo), the seemingly simple, episodic saga takes on elements of fantasy as its young hero acquires talismans which give him increasingly great magical powers. In a classic showdown we see not only the powers of good and evil finally confront each other, but also the inevitable conflict between father and son enacted on a mythic scale. We also see the embodiment of future generations as a young boy (played by producer-director-writer Cisse's son) literally discovers remnants of the conflict and figuratively acquires the knowledge of his ancestors. Marvelously photographed (the image of Kane and Sangare bathing under the waterfall is unforgettable) and perfectly acted by a cast of nonprofessionals (Sanogo, for example, was a real-life shaman), the production of BRIGHTNESS represents both a triumph over incredible odds (bad weather, financial woes, the death of actor Sarr) and a provocative, creative use by Cisse of indigenous folk mythology.

BRIGHTON ROCK

1947   92m   bw   Crime   ★★★½
Boulting Bros.   (U.K.)   /PG

Richard Attenborough *(Pinkie Brown)*, Hermione Baddeley *(Ida Arnold)*, William Hartnell *(Dallow)*, Carol Marsh *(Rose Brown)*, Nigel Stock *(Cubitt)*, Wylie Watson *(Spicer)*, Harcourt Williams *(Prewitt)*, Alan Wheatley *(Fred Hale)*, George Carney *(Phil Corkery)*, Charles Goldner *(Colleoni)*

p, Roy Boulting; d, John Boulting; w, Graham Greene, Terence Rattigan (based on the novel by Graham Greene); ph, Harry Waxman; ed, Frank McNally; m, Hans May

A brutal look at the British underworld—as seen through the amoral eyes of teenaged thug Pinkie Brown, played brilliantly by the 24 year-old Attenborough. In this adaptation of the popular Graham Greene novel, Pinkie heads a race track gang and commits a murder, using a pretty waitress (Marsh) as an alibi. Worried that she still might betray him, he marries the young woman, planning to kill her by driving her to suicide. His scheme eventually backfires in an ending which, though softened somewhat from Greene's original, still drips with cynical irony. A moody, well-acted film (Hartnell and Baddeley are particularly good), notable for bringing a new viciousness to British cinema (e.g. razor blade slashing). Striking handled by the Boulting brothers and still worth a look for its almost palpable sense of dread, the film can't quite recapture the impact it had upon its initial release.

BRIMSTONE AND TREACLE

1982   87m   c   Thriller   ★★★
UA Classics   (U.K.)   R/18

Sting *(Martin Taylor)*, Denholm Elliott *(Thomas Bates)*, Joan Plowright *(Norma Bates)*, Suzanna Hamilton *(Patricia Bates)*, Mary McLeod *(Valerie Holdsworth)*, Benjamin Whitrow *(Businessman)*, Dudley Sutton *(Stroller)*, Tim Preece *(Clergyman)*

p, Kenith Trodd; d, Richard Loncraine; w, Dennis Potter; ph, Peter Hannan; ed, Paul Green; m, Sting

This quirky, disturbing thriller is chiefly of interest as the work of Dennis Potter, author of PENNIES FROM HEAVEN and TV's "The Singing Detective." Pop star Sting stars as Martin Taylor, a con man so charming he can convince almost anyone that he's met them before. Thomas Bates (Elliott) sees through this ploy but falls victim to Taylor's larger schemes involving Bates's disabled daughter (Hamilton). Relying on psychological effect rather than violence, the picture is excruciatingly suspenseful, alternating goose bumps with nervous laughter in the tradition of Hitchcockian horror.

BRING ME THE HEAD OF ALFREDO GARCIA

1974   112m   c   Crime   ★★★★
UA   (U.S.)   R/18

Warren Oates *(Bennie)*, Isela Vega *(Elita)*, Gig Young *(Quill)*, Robert Webber *(Sappensly)*, Helmut Dantine *(Max)*, Emilio Fernandez *(El Jefe)*, Kris Kristofferson *(Paco)*, Chano Urueta *(One-armed Bartender)*, Jorge Russek *(Cueto)*

p, Martin Baum; d, Sam Peckinpah; w, Gordon Dawson, Sam Peckinpah (based on a story by Frank Kowalski); ph, Alex Phillips Jr.; ed, Garth Craven, Robbe Roberts, Sergio Ortega, Dennis Dolan; m, Jerry Fielding

When El Jefe (Fernandez), the head of a prominent Mexican family, learns the identity of the bounder responsible for his daughter's pregnancy, he offers a million dollars to the man who can bring him the head of the culprit, Alfredo Garcia. Two homosexual hit men (Young and Webber) working for Jefe enlist the aid of Bennie (Oates), a sleazy but good-natured bar owner, who convinces the pair that he can find Garcia. Learning from his hooker girlfriend Elita (Vega) that her former client Garcia is already dead, she and Bennie travel to the cemetery where Garcia is supposedly buried to cut off the corpse's head. Bennie successfully kills two motorcycle riders along the way, but a rival Mexican gang appears and kills Elita, knocks Bennie out and steals the head. In a bloody confrontation Bennie massacres his rivals and then turns on his two gay partners and wipes them out too. All that remains is to turn in the prized head, though Bennie's final encounter with El Jefe also goes bloodily awry. One of the cinema's more perversely intriguing experiences, the film is either appreciated as a bizarre minor classic or denounced as a piece of trash. In the only film over which the director says he had complete control, Peckinpah creates a haunting vision of a loser's quest for love and meaning in a harsh, brutal world. Although his "philosophy" and methods do not appeal to everyone and are certainly open to criticism, Peckinpah attempts to use explicit violence as a means for exploring the brutality he sees as inherent in all men. A nihilistic depiction of an existential quest, the film benefits immeasurably from the presence of Oates in the leading role of a man driven obsessively in suicidal pursuit of self-respect and importance. The macabre scenes in the car where Bennie converses with the head as flies buzz around it are funny and telling. BRING ME THE HEAD OF ALFREDO GARCIA does have some sloppy photography, a few unintentionally humorous scenes, and an excess of Peckinpah's signature slow-motion violence, but it stands as one of Peckinpah's more daring films.

BRINGING UP BABY

1938   102m   bw   Comedy   ★★★★★
RKO   (U.S.)   /U

Katharine Hepburn *(Susan Vance)*, Cary Grant *(David Huxley)*, Charlie Ruggles *(Maj. Horace Applegate)*, May Robson *(Aunt Elizabeth)*, Barry Fitzgerald *(Mr. Gogarty)*, Walter Catlett *(Constable Slocum)*, Fritz Feld *(Dr. Fritz Lehman)*, Leona Roberts *(Hannah Gogarty)*, George Irving *(Alexander Peabody)*, Virginia Walker *(Alice Swallow)*

p, Howard Hawks; d, Howard Hawks; w, Dudley Nichols, Hagar Wilde (based on a story by Hagar Wilde); ph, Russell Metty; ed, George Hively; m, Roy Webb; art d, Van Nest Polglase, Perry Ferguson; fx, Vernon L. Walker; cos, Howard Greer

A delightful piece of utter absurdity and one of director Hawks' most inspired lampoons of the battle between the sexes. Hepburn and Grant are superb in this breathlessly funny screwball comedy with a plot that could have been hatched in a mental institution. She plays Susan Vance, an eccentric heiress whose dog (Asta of the "Thin Man" series) steals a bone from absentminded paleontologist David Huxley (Grant), the last he needs to complete his reconstruction of a dinosaur. David follows Susan to her Connecticut farm in search of the relic and runs smack into the authorities, the possible donor of $1 million to his museum, and a leopard named Baby who enjoys being serenaded with "I Can't Give You Anything but Love". Memorable moments abound throughout: Susan insistently playing David's ball at a golf game, which leads him further and further from his playing companion ("I'll be with you in a minute, Mr. Peabody!"); Susan's tricks with olives; Baby's encounter with a chicken coop; David facing Susan's elderly aunt (Robson) while wearing a frilly negligee ("I just decided to go gay all of a sudden!"); David caught in Susan's butterfly net (surely *not* the best way to catch a runaway leopard); Susan's aunt and cowardly big game hunter Maj. Applegate (Ruggles) deciding they need some exercise ("Shall we run?" "Yes, let's!"); Susan's imitation of a gangster's moll ("Hey flatfoot!")—the list could go on and on. Though Hepburn fans might not be used to seeing her essay such an atypically scatterbrained role, her marvelous timing and zany comic elan are wonderfully engaging. Grant, meanwhile, manages the near-impossible feat of being goofy, suave, dimwitted and sexy all at once. Among a brilliant supporting cast, Robson, Ruggles, Catlett, Feld and Fitzgerald are standouts, and the pace never flags for an instant. A barbed satire of masculinity, romance, wealth, psychiatry and authority, BRINGING UP BABY was, not too surprisingly, a box-office flop in its day, probably because it poked fun at the very conventions it employed. Enormously influential on later comedy writing, it is a milestone of film merriment.

BROADCAST NEWS

1987 131m c Comedy/Romance   ★★★½
Fox (U.S.)   R/15

William Hurt *(Tom Grunick)*, Albert Brooks *(Aaron Altman)*, Holly Hunter *(Jane Craig)*, Robert Prosky *(Ernie Merriman)*, Lois Chiles *(Jennifer Mack)*, Joan Cusack *(Blair Litton)*, Peter Hackes *(Paul Moore)*, Jack Nicholson *(Bill Rorich, News Anchor)*, Christina Clemenson *(Bobby)*, Robert Katims *(Martin Klein)*

p, James L. Brooks, Penney Finkelman Cox; d, James L. Brooks; w, James L. Brooks; ph, Michael Ballhaus; ed, Richard Marks; m, Bill Conti; prod d, Charles Rosen; art d, Kristi Zea; cos, Molly Maginnis, Molly Maginnis

AAN Best Picture; AAN Best Actor: William Hurt; *AAN Best Actress:* Holly Hunter; *AAN Best Supporting Actor:* Albert Brooks; *AAN Best Original Screenplay:* James L. Brooks; *AAN Best Cinematography:* Michael Ballhaus; *AAN Best Editing:* Richard Marks

Blessed with a good script, BROADCAST NEWS examines the ethics of modern-day electronic journalism and the often frazzled emotions of a tightly knit group of workaholics who find that their personal and professional lives have become one and the same. Network news producer Jane Craig (Hunter) and her best pal, veteran correspondent Aaron Altman (Brooks), share not only the same high ethical standards, but a warm and goofy sense of humor. Although Jane considers Aaron her best friend, he pines for a more romantic relationship. Enter Tom Grunick (Hurt), a handsome, affable, but somewhat dim newscaster to whom Jane is attracted. Often touching, biting, and funny, BROADCAST NEWS is an entertaining film hoisted by the performances of its three leads. Hurt, in a rather odd change of pace, and newcomer Hunter display verve and skill and overcome the limitations of the somewhat annoying characters they play. In the seemingly lesser role of the one who stands by and suffers, however, Brooks provides the film's soul and many of its laughs to boot. Nicholson contributes a highly potent performance in a matter of moments as a smug, self-important New York anchorman and the rest of the supporting cast is uniformly fine. A more skillful director of actors than the camera, Brooks gives the script its full head and makes crystal clear the satirical point that appearances count for a great deal in the mass media. A film whose "TV movie" feel is at once incredibly appropriate and a notable drawback, BROADCAST NEWS is nevertheless worthy adult entertainment.

BROADWAY DANNY ROSE

1984 86m bw Comedy/Romance   ★★★½
Rollins-Joffe (U.S.)   PG

Woody Allen *(Danny Rose)*, Mia Farrow *(Tina Vitale)*, Nick Apollo Forte *(Lou Canova)*, Sandy Baron, Corbett Monica, Jackie Gayle, Morty Gunty, Will Jordan, Howard Storm, Jack Rollins

p, Robert Greenhut; d, Woody Allen; w, Woody Allen; ph, Gordon Willis; ed, Susan E. Morse; prod d, Mel Bourne; cos, Jeffrey Kurland

AAN Best Director: Woody Allen; *AAN Best Original Screenplay:* Woody Allen (Screenplay)

After making several more ambitious films, writer-director Allen returned to *terra firma* with BROADWAY DANNY ROSE, a charming comedy shot in black and white that mixes several varieties of the New Yorkers that Allen loves so well. The film begins with a group of Broadway types sitting at the Carnegie Delicatessen reminiscing about the career of Danny Rose (Allen), a two-bit agent who specializes in offbeat acts that no other agent will handle. His one regular client is Lou Canova (Forte), a lounge singer who drinks too much, weighs too much, and uses Rose to cover for him when he's off cheating on his wife with girlfriend Tina (an unusually animated performance by Farrow). When Canova gets a chance to perform at a better place than the dives where he's been working, Rose has to pretend to be Tina's boyfriend, a move which gets him into a lot of trouble. Tina is supposedly engaged to a gangland figure, and the other mobsters, thinking that their pal has been cuckolded, begin chasing poor Danny all around the city. Although the film contains many of the great verbal jokes that are Allen's forte, the visual wit and the sentimental drama fall a bit short.

BROADWAY MELODY, THE

1929 102m bw Musical   ★★½
MGM (U.S.)

Anita Page *(Queenie)*, Bessie Love *(Hank)*, Charles King *(Eddie)*, Jed Prouty *(Uncle Bernie)*, Kenneth Thomson *(Jock)*, Edward Dillon *(Stage Manager)*, Mary Doran *(Blonde)*, J. Emmett Beck *(Babe Hatrick)*, Marshall Ruth *(Stew)*, Drew Demarest *(Turpe)*

d, Harry Beaumont; w, Sarah Y. Mason, James Gleason, Norman Houston (based on a story by Edmund Goulding); ph, John Arnold; ed, Sam S. Zimbalist; art d, Cedric Gibbons; chor, George Cunningham; cos, David Cox

AA Best Picture; AAN Best Actress: Bessie Love; *AAN Best Director:* Harry Beaumont

First musical to win Academy Award reeks of mothballs, but is undeniably the basis of perhaps a hundred others. At least there's an old curiosity shoppe charm and a few classic tunes: "You Were Meant for Me" and the title tune (Brown and Freed—Freed would go on to head the musical production unit at MGM, the biggest of all time, and produce all the Garland classics, among many others), plus Cohan's "Give My Regards to Broadway". Surprisingly, a remake, TWO GIRLS ON BROADWAY, was inferior. Some sequences originally filmed in Technicolor, this was the first sound picture shown all over.

BROKEN ARROW

1996 108m c Action/Adventure   ★★★
20th Century Fox/Mark Gordon Company/Metropolis   R/15
Entertainment (U.S.)

John Travolta *(Vic Deakins)*, Christian Slater *(Riley Hale)*, Samantha Mathis *(Terry Carmichael)*, Delroy Lindo *(Colonel Max Wilkins)*, Bob Gunton *(Pritchett)*, Frank Whaley *(Giles Prentice)*, Howie Long *(Kelly)*, Vondie Curtis Hall *(Lt. Colonel Sam Rhodes)*, Jack Thompson *(Chairman, Joint Chief of Staff)*, Vyto Ruginis *(Johnson)*

p, Mark Gordon, Bill Badalato, Terence Chang; d, John Woo; w, Graham Yost; ph, Peter Levy; ed, John Wright, Steve Mirkovich, Joe Hutshing; m, Hans Zimmer; prod d, Holger Gross; art d, William O'Brien; fx, Richard Thompson, Peter Crosman, Don Baker, Jacques Stroweis, Elliot Markman; cos, Mary Malin

BROKEN ARROW's by-the-book mayhem is proof positive that Hong Kong *auteur* John Woo can make a solid, formulaic Hollywood action picture—he could probably make one standing on his head—but why should we want him to? Woo's Hong Kong pictures—which include THE KILLER, HARD BOILED and BULLET IN THE HEAD—are rapturous fusions of eroticized violence and operatic sentiment, enthralling precisely because they do things that mainstream American action pictures can't (or won't) do. BROKEN ARROW, however, is '90s Hollywood through-and-through: expertly constructed, reasonably entertaining, morally unambiguous, and thoroughly trivial.

John Travolta, blue eyes a-glint, plays gleefully against type as a turncoat pilot planning to blackmail the US government with stolen nuclear weapons—"broken arrow," we learn, is the military code for a lost warhead. Christian Slater, his staunchly upright ex-buddy, is out to stop him, and Samantha Mathis plays the feisty young park ranger who gets stuck in the middle. Woo has never done well by female characters, and Mathis's plucky but colorless character is no exception—but that's not necessarily a liability, especially in a picture as insistently homoerotic as this one is. What matters is Travolta and Slater, who clamber all over an impressive array of military hardware, trading bullets, punches, and meaningful glances as a bass guitar vibrates portentously. The vestiges of Woo's achingly romantic style play badly in this can-do context, while the mayhem is never more—and occasionally less—than competent.

BRONX TALE, A

1993   122m   c   Drama   ★★★
Bronx Tale Inc./Tribeca Productions/Gatien Productions   R/18
/Price Entertainment   (U.S.)

Robert De Niro (Lorenzo Anello), Chazz Palminteri (Sonny), Lillo Brancato (Calogero Anello—Age 17), Francis Capra (Calogero Anello—Age 9), Joe Pesci (Carmine), Taral Hicks (Jane), Kathrine Narducci (Rosina Anello), Clem Caserta (Jimmy Whispers), Robert D'Andrea (Tony Toupee), Eddie Montanaro (Eddie Mush)

p, Robert De Niro, Jane Rosenthal, Jon Kilik; d, Robert De Niro; w, Chazz Palminteri (from his play); ph, Reynaldo Villalobos; ed, David Ray, R.Q. Lovett; m, Butch Barbella; prod d, Wynn Thomas; art d, Chris Shriver; fx, Steve Kirschoff; cos, Rita Ryack

Actor Robert De Niro's directing debut is a nostalgic memoir of growing up in New York in the 1960s, and covers much of the same ground as Martin Scorsese's GOODFELLAS. Developed from a one-man show written by and starring Chazz Palminteri, A BRONX TALE is at its best in the details: the swaggering hoods and the local girls with sky-high hair, skinny heels, and tight dresses; the cars and social clubs; the suave jukebox crooners. . .it's all evoked with a reverent clarity and precision that open a window onto one man's memories of the past, as it was and as he'd like it to have been.

Nine-year-old Calogero (Francis Capra) hangs out on his stoop with his friends, watching Sonny (Palminteri) and his henchmen make deals and issue orders. Calogero sees Sonny kill a man but, true to the code of the neighborhood—practiced even by Calogero's hardworking, law-abiding father Lorenzo (De Niro)—he tells the police he saw nothing, and Sonny goes free. Thus begins a relationship that becomes increasingly close as the boy grows older. Despite his father's objections, the teenage Calogero (Lillo Brancato)—or C, as he now prefers to be called—becomes first Sonny's mascot, then his errand boy, as Sonny and Lorenzo battle for C's love and respect.

A BRONX TALE tries to cover too much ground; racial conflict, family drama, first love, the lure of the gangster life, and the joys and tribulation of coming of age in a kinder, gentler New York are all crammed into the slight story. It all feels too familiar to sustain the viewer's interest, but Palminteri's and De Niro's equally compelling performances help give it life.

BROOD, THE

1979   91m   c   Horror   ★★★½
New World   (Canada)   R/18

Oliver Reed (Dr. Raglan), Samantha Eggar (Nola), Art Hindle (Frank), Cindy Hinds (Candice), Nuala Fitzgerald (Julianna), Henry Beckman (Barton Kelly), Susan Hogan (Ruth), Michael McGhee (Inspector Mrazek), Gary McKeehan (Mike Trellan), Bob Silverman (Jan)

p, Claude Heroux; d, David Cronenberg; w, David Cronenberg; ph, Mark Irwin; ed, Alan Collins

Powerful and disturbing on both a physical and mental level, THE BROOD is the first Cronenberg film to use "name" actors, and marked a significant progression in the director's exploration of "biological horror."

Controversial psychotherapist Dr. Raglan (Oliver Reed) teaches mental patients to manifest their subconscious anger physically, as boils and welts on their bodies. One of his patients, Nola (Samantha Eggar),

has actually begun giving birth to a small army of mutant babies—the ultimate projection of her hostilities. She houses her brood in a nearby cabin from which, dressed in their colorful Dr. Dentons, the murderous little creatures venture out and kill the objects of their mother's rage. Eggar's bitter ex-husband, who is trying to discredit Reed's treatments so he can gain custody of their daughter, uncovers the horrible truth.

More personal than earlier Cronenberg films (the director had just gone through a painful divorce at the time of shooting), THE BROOD is a mature, controlled work that finds horror not only in such institutions as hospitals and schools but, more specifically, in the family unit itself. While his previous efforts (THEY CAME FROM WITHIN, RABID) had been rather clinical exercises, Cronenberg presents more complex and genuinely sympathetic characters here, giving the film added resonance. THE BROOD also marks his growing confidence as a visual stylist, with some memorable—if highly gory—realizations of his pet themes.

BROTHER FROM ANOTHER PLANET, THE

1984   110m   c   Fantasy/Science Fiction   ★★★½
A Train   (U.S.)

Joe Morton (The Brother), Daryl Edwards (Fly), Steve James (Odell), Leonard Jackson (Smokey), Bill Cobbs (Walter), Maggie Renzi (Noreen), Tom Wright (Sam), Ren Woods (Bernice), Reggie Rock Bythewood (Rickey), David Strathairn

p, Peggy Rajski, Maggie Renzi; d, John Sayles; w, John Sayles; ph, Ernest Dickerson; ed, John Sayles; m, Mason Daring; prod d, Nora Chavooshian; art d, Stephen J. Lineweaver; cos, Karen Perry

Still John Sayles's most provocative work, THE BROTHER FROM ANOTHER PLANET blends a stock satirical premise—a look at the world through the eyes of an alien—with a runaway slave narrative, rendering a loosely constructed but keenly observed allegory of race and class in America. The Brother (Joe Morton) is an escaped slave from an unnamed planet who crash-lands his space capsule off Ellis Island. Unable to speak, and marked by his ragged clothing and dark complexion, he's taken for a homeless black man; New Yorkers treat him accordingly, with reactions ranging from pity to contempt. After some dispiriting encounters with white people, he makes his way to Harlem and ends up in a local bar. The regular patrons find him odd, to say the least, but set him up with a social worker after they discover that he can repair video games with just a touch of his hand. Hot on the black man's trail are a pair of white aliens (David Strathairn and John Sayles) dressed in black, who aim to recapture the escapee.

Buoyed by Morton's sensitive performance, the film proceeds as a series of vignettes, some of them unforgettable. In a sequence shot on the subway, a child offers to do a magic trick for the Brother: he'll make the white riders disappear. As the train pulls into the 96th Street Station, the whites file out and are replaced by uniformly black passengers headed uptown. It's a remarkable image of de facto racial segregation in urban America.

BROTHERS KARAMAZOV, THE

1958   149m   c   Drama   ★★½
MGM   (U.S.)   /15

Yul Brynner (Dmitri Karamazov), Maria Schell (Grushenka), Claire Bloom (Katya), Lee J. Cobb (Fyodor Karamazov), Richard Basehart (Ivan Karamazov), Albert Salmi (Smerdyakov), William Shatner (Alexey Karamazov), Judith Evelyn (Mme. Anna Hohlakov), Edgar Stehli (Grigory), Harry Townes (Ippoli Kirillov)

p, Pandro S. Berman; d, Richard Brooks; w, Richard Brooks (based on an adaptation by Julius J. and Philip G. Epstein of the novel by Feodor Dostoyevsky); ph, John Alton; ed, John Dunning; m, Bronislau Kaper; cos, Walter Plunkett

AAN Best Supporting Actor: Lee J Cobb

Marilyn Monroe campaigned desperately for Grushenka, the part played by Maria Schell in this film, and it's one of those casting tragedies that she didn't get her way. For while Schell is okay, the problem here is similar to Glenn Close in DANGEROUS LIAISONS—no sex appeal—and typical of the film as a whole—lots of steam, but no heat. Richard Brooks directs like a traffic cop, without sweep or dramatic gesture. As a result, the film feels like "Classics Comics" instead of a classic.

BROWNING VERSION, THE

1951 90m bw Drama ★★★★½
Javelin (U.K.) /U

Michael Redgrave *(Andrew Crocker-Harris)*, Jean Kent *(Millie Crocker-Harris)*, Nigel Patrick *(Frank Hunter)*, Wilfrid Hyde-White *(Frobisher)*, Brian Smith *(Taplow)*, Bill Travers *(Fletcher)*, Ronald Howard *(Gilbert)*, Paul Medland *(Wilson)*, Ivan Samson *(Lord Baxter)*, Josephine Middleton *(Mrs. Frobisher)*

p, Teddy Baird; d, Anthony Asquith; w, Terence Rattigan (based on his play); ph, Desmond Dickinson; ed, John D. Guthridge

Good show! Rattigan adapted his own play for the screen, and it's lovingly directed by Asquith and acted within an inch of the viewer's life by Redgrave and a magnificent small ensemble. Story explores the tragic restriction of a headmaster's retirement and his wretched, unfaithful wife. Redgrave won the Best Actor award and Terence Rattigan the writing prize at the 1951 Cannes Film Festival for this film. Absolutely not to be missed.

BRUBAKER

1980 132m c Prison/Drama ★★★
Fox (U.S.) R/15

Robert Redford *(Henry Brubaker)*, Yaphet Kotto *(Richard "Dickie" Coombes)*, Jane Alexander *(Lillian)*, Murray Hamilton *(Deach)*, David Keith *(Larry Lee Bullen)*, Morgan Freeman *(Walter)*, Matt Clark *(Purcell)*, Tim McIntire *(Huey Rauch)*, Richard Ward *(Abraham)*, Jon Van Ness *(Zaranska)*

p, Ron Silverman; d, Stuart Rosenberg; w, W.D. Richter (based on a story by W.D. Richter, Arthur Ross); ph, Bruno Nuytten; ed, Robert Brown; m, Lalo Schifrin; fx, Al Wright Jr.

AAN Best Original Screenplay: W D Richter (Story), Arthur Ross (Screenplay)

Matinee idol Redford plays the title character, who's arrested and taken to a terrible prison in which he sees evidence of man's inhumanity to man around every corner. Eventually, we learn that Brubaker is not a convict at all; he's the new warden, and has had himself incarcerated so that he can experience prison life from the convict's point of view.

A very tough movie, BRUBAKER is not for the squeamish. Director Stuart Rosenberg, whose spotty career includes credits ranging from MOVE to THE AMITYVILLE HORROR, moved into a higher strata with this one, but no matter who's directing him, one can't escape the feeling that Redford is the man behind the man behind the camera.

BRUTE FORCE

1947 94m bw Prison ★★★★
Universal (U.S.) /A

Burt Lancaster *(Joe Collins)*, Hume Cronyn *(Capt. Munsey)*, Charles Bickford *(Gallagher)*, Yvonne De Carlo *(Gina)*, Ann Blyth *(Ruth)*, Ella Raines *(Cora)*, Anita Colby *(Flossie)*, Sam Levene *(Louis)*, Howard Duff *(Soldier)*, Art Smith *(Dr. Walters)*

p, Mark Hellinger; d, Jules Dassin; w, Richard Brooks (based on a story by Robert Patterson); ph, William Daniels; ed, Edward Curtiss; m, Miklos Rozsa; art d, Bernard Herzbrun, John DeCuir; fx, David S. Horsley; cos, Rosemary Odell

Classic prison melo, BRUTE FORCE followed THE KILLERS, for Burt Lancaster, establishing him as a dangerously sexy lug in the most interesting period of his career. The predictable premise was directed with innovation by Jules Dassin and also featured the debut of Howard Duff, among a stellar cast. Flashbacks lead to actresses as well, and there's an interesting, untypical job by Hume Cronyn. Rozsa's pounding score and a savage climax make BRUTE FORCE first rate all the way.

BUDDY HOLLY STORY, THE

1978 113m c Biography ★★★½
Columbia (U.S.) PG

Gary Busey *(Buddy Holly)*, Don Stroud *(Jesse)*, Charles Martin Smith *(Ray Bob)*, Bill Jordan *(Riley Randolph)*, Maria Richwine *(Maria Elena Holly)*, Conrad Janis *(Ross Turner)*, Albert Popwell *(Eddie Foster)*, Amy Johnston *(Jenny Lou)*, James Beach *(Mr. Wilson)*, John Goff *(T.J.)*

p, Fred Bauer; d, Steve Rash; w, Robert Gittler (based on the book by Joe Coldrosen); ph, Stevan Larner; ed, David Blewitt; prod d, Joel Schiller; fx, Robby Knott; chor, Maggie Rush; cos, Michael Butler

AAN Best Actor: Gary Busey; *AA Best Score:* Joe Renzetti; *AAN Best Sound:* Tex Rudloff, Joel Fein, Curly Thirlwell, Willie Burton

A-okay rockabilly bio captures the energy of early R&R and its amazing influence. Engaging Busey, Stroud, and Smith all do their own singing. Film won an Oscar for best scoring. Quite good fun, indeed.

BUGSY

1991 135m c Crime/Historical/Romance ★★★½
Baltimore Pictures/Mulholland Productions/Desert Vision R/18
Productions (U.S.)

Warren Beatty *(Benjamin "Bugsy" Siegel)*, Annette Bening *(Virginia Hill)*, Harvey Keitel *(Mickey Cohen)*, Ben Kingsley *(Meyer Lansky)*, Elliott Gould *(Harry Greenberg)*, Joe Mantegna *(George Raft)*, Richard Sarafian *(Jack Dragna)*, Bebe Neuwirth *(Countess di Frasso)*, Giancarlo Scandiuzzi *(Count di Frasso)*, Wendy Phillips *(Esta Siegel)*

p, Mark Johnson, Barry Levinson, Warren Beatty; d, Barry Levinson; w, James Toback (from the book "We Only Kill Each Other: The Life and Bad Times of Bugsy Siegel" by Dean Jennings); ph, Allen Daviau; ed, Stu Linder; m, Ennio Morricone; prod d, Dennis Gassner; art d, Leslie McDonald; fx, Clay Pinney, Rob Bottin; cos, Albert Wolsky

AAN Best Picture; AAN Best Actor: Warren Beatty; *AAN Best Supporting Actor:* Harvey Keitel; *AAN Best Supporting Actor:* Ben Kingsley; *AAN Best Director:* Barry Levinson; *AAN Best Original Screenplay:* James Toback; *AAN Best Cinematography:* Allen Daviau; *AAN Best Score:* Ennio Morricone; *AA Best Art Direction:* Dennis Gassner, Nancy Haigh; *AA Best Costume Design:* Albert Wolsky

BUGSY is an elegant, knowing, but ultimately heartless *hommage* to the bygone glamour of Hollywood and Vegas. Director-star Beatty portrays gangster legend Benjamin "Bugsy" Siegel as both a romantic visionary and a psychopathic killer—a raw mass of contradictory impulses.

The film begins with Bugsy arriving in California, charged with taking over the various LA rackets. Seduced by Hollywood's tacky glamour, he is soon romancing starlet Virginia Hill (Bening) and concocting a plan to build a luxury hotel and casino on an unpopulated expanse of Nevada desert—the roots of modern-day Las Vegas. As the cost of building the Flamingo (Virginia's nickname) soars to $6 million—six times the budget originally approved by his partners—Bugsy runs into increasing conflict with his superiors, particularly his mentor, Meyer Lansky (Kingsley).

Levinson's direction is brisk and, for a film largely about the allure of glamour, suitably flashy. Toback's script, if hardly profound, occasionally manages a colorful incident and some spiky dialogue. An impressive array of actors, meanwhile, help out with crisp performances. Standouts are Kingsley and Keitel as level-headed, no-nonsense figures whose dry, sardonic observations serve as a counterpoint to Siegel's unbounded flamboyance. As opposed to the well-played if little-seen supporting characters, however, Siegel, who is everywhere, comes across as a two-dimensional, almost cartoon-like figure—someone it's impossible to really care about. By the time this rambling film finally chunters to its conclusion, the only point Levinson, Toback, and Beatty can make is that Bugsy was right that Las Vegas was a money-making proposition. Quite apart from the fact that the film monkeys around with the facts in a desperate attempt to paint its protagonist as a man of vision, this is one of the biggest who-gives-a-damn finales in the history of filmmaking.

BUGSY MALONE

1976 93m c Children's/Musical ★★★
Paramount (U.K.) PG/U

Scott Baio (Bugsy Malone), Jodie Foster (Tallulah), Florrie Dugger (Blousey), John Cassisi (Fat Sam), Paul Murphy (Leroy), Albin Jenkins (Fizzy), Martin Lev (Dandy Dan), Davidson Knight (Knuckles), Paul Chirelstein (Smolsky), Paul Besterman (Yonkers)

p, Alan Marshall; d, Alan Parker; w, Alan Parker; ph, Michael Seresin, Peter Biziou; ed, Gerry Hambling; m, Paul Williams; chor, Gillian Gregory; cos, Monica Howe

AAN Best Score: Paul Williams (Song Score)

Spoof of 1920s gangster pics with all-kiddie cast is interesting idea that loses steam before the fade. Why? Big problem is parody can only be really amusing played (and cast) pretty straight. Kids lack ability to put sin and sex element across (some scenes feel positively pedophilic); only Foster seems able to bring up the requisite toughness. Things aren't helped by Paul Williams's limp score.

BULL DURHAM

1988 108m c Comedy ★★★½
Mount (U.S.) R/15

Kevin Costner (Crash Davis), Susan Sarandon (Annie Savoy), Tim Robbins (Ebby Calvin "Nuke" LaLoosh), Trey Wilson (Joe "Skip" Riggins), Robert Wuhl (Larry Hockett), Jenny Robertson (Millie), Max Patkin (Himself), William O'Leary (Jimmy), David Neidorf (Bobby), Danny Gans (Deke)

p, Thom Mount, Mark Burg; d, Ron Shelton; w, Ron Shelton; ph, Bobby Byrne; ed, Robert Leighton, Adam Weiss; m, Michael Convertino; prod d, Armin Ganz; cos, Louise Frogley

AAN Best Original Screenplay: Ron Shelton

Smutty, terrific fun. Featuring outstanding lead performances by Kevin Costner, Susan Sarandon, and Tim Robbins; a witty, literate script; and an insider's familiarity with life around minor league baseball—BULL DURHAM is both one of the best films ever made about the national pastime and a charming romantic comedy. As smart as she is sexy, Annie Savoy (Sarandon), the No. 1 fan of the Class A Durham Bulls, chooses one player a year for her student in the art of lovemaking as well as in metaphysics and literature. This summer two players vie for her attentions: Nuke Laloosh (Robbins), a bonus-baby pitcher "with a million-dollar arm and five-cent head" and Crash Davis (Costner), the power-hitting longtime minor-league catcher brought to the club to prepare Nuke for the big leagues. First-time director Ron Shelton (who spent five years in the Baltimore Orioles farm system) suffuses his film with carefully realized bush-league details and evokes laugh after rich laugh. Costner (a former high school shortstop) is wholly convincing as a pro ballplayer, delivering perhaps his best performance to date. Sarandon sizzles, and BULL DURHAM is an extremely sexy movie that uses bared souls rather than bared bodies to turn up the heat. The diamond action was shot at El Toro Field, home of the real Durham Bulls. Max Patkin, "the Clown Prince of Baseball," also appears.

BULLDOG DRUMMOND

1929 90m bw Mystery ★★★½
Goldwyn (U.S.)

Ronald Colman (Bulldog Drummond), Joan Bennett (Phyllis Benton), Lilyan Tashman (Erma Peterson), Montagu Love (Carl Peterson), Lawrence Grant (Doctor Lakington), Wilson Benge (Danny), Claud Allister (Algy Longworth), Adolph Milar (Marcovitch), Charles Sellon (John Travers), Tetsu Komai (Chong)

p, Samuel Goldwyn, F. Richard Jones; d, F. Richard Jones; w, Wallace Smith, Sidney Howard (based on the play by H.C. "Sapper" McNeile, Gerald Du Maurier); ph, Gregg Toland, George Barnes; ed, Viola, Frank Lawrence; art d, William Cameron Menzies

AAN Best Actor: Ronald Colman; *AAN Best Art Direction:* William Cameron Menzies (Art Direction)

Polished to a fine sheen. Colman's first talkie is a witty romp—he's delightfully teamed with Bennett in one of her rich American life-is-art roles. Audiences were delighted to find Colman sounded exactly as they expected. A beautiful film.

BULLDOG DRUMMOND STRIKES BACK

1934 83m bw Mystery ★★★★
UA (U.S.) /A

Ronald Colman (Hugh Drummond), Loretta Young (Lola Field), C. Aubrey Smith (Inspector Nielsen), Charles Butterworth (Algy Longworth), Una Merkel (Gwen), Warner Oland (Prince Achmed), George Regas (Singh), Mischa Auer (Hassan), Kathleen Burke (Jane Sothern), Arthur Hohl (Dr. Sothern)

p, Joseph M. Schenck; d, Roy Del Ruth; w, Henry Lehrman, Nunnally Johnson (based on the novel by H.C. "Sapper" McNeile); ph, Peverell Marley; ed, Allen McNeil; art d, Richard Day; cos, Gwen Wakeling

Colman repeats his 1929 success in the first film he made after refusing to work for Samuel Goldwyn ever again. Fast-moving, smartly produced, laugh-studded melodrama is as incredible as it is engrossing. Drummond tries to convince Scotland Yard of the existence of a kidnapping ring in London, but every time he discovers a witness to prove the point, the witness mysteriously disappears. Colman was delighted to repeat his Drummond role because the improvement in sound and other technical refinements made it possible to portray the character with more polish and bite than the primitive 1929 version had permitted, even though he had received an Academy Award nomination for the earlier performance. Charles Butterworth's portrayal as Drummond's sidekick Algy was also a major factor in the film's success. This movie never lags and has all the plausibility of a well-written mystery novel read in the middle of the night.

BULLETS OVER BROADWAY

1994 99m c Comedy ★★★½
Sweetheart Productions/Sweetland Films (U.S.) R/15

John Cusack (David Shayne), Jack Warden (Julian Marx), Chazz Palminteri (Cheech), Joe Viterelli (Nick Valenti), Jennifer Tilly (Olive Neal), Rob Reiner (Sheldon Flender), Mary-Louise Parker (Ellen), Dianne Wiest (Helen Sinclair), Harvey Fierstein (Sid Loomis), Jim Broadbent (Warner Purcell)

p, Robert Greenhut; d, Woody Allen; w, Woody Allen, Douglas McGrath; ph, Carlo Di Palma; ed, Susan E. Morse; prod d, Santo Loquasto; art d, Tom Warren; cos, Jeffrey Kurland

AA Best Supporting Actress: Dianne Wiest; *AAN Best Supporting Actor:* Chazz Palminteri; *AAN Best Supporting Actress:* Jennifer Tilly; *AAN Best Director:* Woody Allen; *AAN Best Original Screenplay:* Woody Allen, Douglas McGrath; *AAN Best Art Direction:* Santo Loquasto, Susan Bode; *AAN Best Costume Design:* Jeffrey Kurland

In a welcome return to straightforward comedy, erratic auteur Woody Allen laid off the arty melodramas in 1994, directing both an amusing made-for-TV film of his Broadway play, *Don't Drink the Water*, and this deft period farce, his most enjoyable movie in years.

At the height of the Roaring Twenties, Broadway playwright David Shayne (John Cusack) is an honest artist among the Philistines—until his backer, mobster Nicky Valenti (Joe Viterelli), sees Shayne's play as a vehicle for his ditzy showgirl mistress, Olive (Jennifer Tilly). Further concessions are called for by grande dame of the thea-tuh Helen Sinclair (Diane Wiest). But Shayne's most effective critic is dese-and-dose hitman Cheech (Chazz Palminteri), who turns out to be a distinctly dangerous dramaturg.

Arguably, Allen continues his Great Masters series here, on the heels of the Fritz Lang chiaroscuro of SHADOWS AND FOG and the overripe Cassavetes stylings of HUSBANDS AND WIVES. Here he tips his hat to the Algonquin Round Table types he once emulated in his magazine prose—George S. Kaufman, Moss Hart, Thurber, Perelman, even the Marx Brothers' backstage high jinks in A NIGHT AT THE OPERA. After his brush with the tabloids, Allen appears to be making good on his frequent claim that what he desires most from an adoring public is his privacy. This is the first Woody Allen film in which neither he nor one of his romantic partners appears, and he's pruned back the autobiographical excess of several previous films. Moreover, everyone seems to be enjoying themselves, maybe for the first time since ANNIE HALL.

BULLITT

1968 113m c Crime ★★★★
Warner Bros. (U.S.) /15

Steve McQueen *(Bullitt)*, Robert Vaughn *(Chalmers)*, Jacqueline Bisset *(Cathy)*, Don Gordon *(Delgetti)*, Robert Duvall *(Weissberg)*, Simon Oakland *(Capt. Bennett)*, Norman Fell *(Baker)*, Georg Stanford Brown *(Dr. Willard)*, Justin Tarr *(Eddy)*, Carl Reindel *(Stanton)*

p, Philip D'Antoni; d, Peter Yates; w, Alan R. Trustman, Harry Kleiner (based on the novel *Mute Witness* by Robert L. Pike); ph, William A. Fraker; ed, Frank P. Keller; m, Lalo Schifrin; art d, Albert Brenner; cos, Theadora Van Runkle

AA Best Editing: Frank P Keller; *AAN Best Sound:* Seven Arts Studio Sound Department

Expert chase film, breathless and modern, that sent McQueen to the top of the box office heap. He plays the title character, a colorful and unorthodox police lieutenant assigned to protect a government witness scheduled to inform on the national crime syndicate. Climax has McQueen spotting hoodlums and following in one of the most spectacular car chases ever filmed, up and down the hills of San Francisco while hand-held cameras record the perilous pursuit as each car narrowly misses intersecting autos, barriers, and buildings as they squeal, slide, and lurch along the narrow streets.

BULLITT was a return to the old, tough crime movies so expertly played by Bogart and Robinson, but made modern here by great technical advances and McQueen's taciturn, antihero stance. Yates's superb direction presents a fluid, always moving camera. All the performers are top-notch, from sour-faced Norman Fell to a curious bit part played by Robert Duvall as a cab driver who is seen almost entirely through a rear-view mirror. Aside from THE SAND PEBBLES, this fine production stands as McQueen's top achievement in a lamentably short career. The film won an Oscar for Best Film Editing and was nominated for Best Sound.

BUS STOP

1956 94m c Comedy ★★★½
Fox (U.S.)

Marilyn Monroe *(Cherie)*, Don Murray *(Bo)*, Arthur O'Connell *(Virgil)*, Betty Field *(Grace)*, Eileen Heckart *(Vera)*, Robert Bray *(Carl)*, Hope Lange *(Elma)*, Hans Conried *(Life Photographer)*, Max Showalter *(Life Reporter)*, Henry Slate *(Manager of Night Club)*

p, Buddy Adler; d, Joshua Logan; w, George Axelrod (based on the play by William Inge); ph, Milton Krasner; m, Alfred Newman, Cyril J. Mockridge

AAN Best Supporting Actor: Don Murray

Few Marilyn Monroe fans can listen to "That Old Black Magic" without recalling Monroe's tinny, off-key, magically poignant rendition of the standard in BUS STOP. In her energetic and warm portrayal of Cherie, whose dream of Hollywood and Vine is interrupted by the reality of a layover in Phoenix, Monroe exposes her vulnerability without sacrificing any of her radiance—for many viewers, this was the film that proved she could act.

In the Blue Dragon Cafe in Phoenix we meet Bo (Don Murray in his first screen role), a rambunctious cowboy who is in town to take part in a rodeo. He bullies the noisy patrons into a respectful silence during Cherie's big song and is rewarded with an innocent kiss of appreciation. From that moment on, he's determined to make her his wife, in spite of her protestations and the dismay of his loyal sidekick Virgil (Arthur O'Connell). Cherie boards a bus headed out of town to escape him, but Bo follows. The bus is stranded in a snowstorm and the passengers are forced to spend the night in a diner, where a fight involving the bus driver, protecting his passenger, and the cowboy, claiming his woman, leaves Bo defeated and humiliated. By the time the road is cleared the next day, a chastened Bo has begun to realize that he'll get nowhere acting like a brute.

During her year-long absence from the screen, Monroe had diligently pursued her craft under the firm hand of theater legend Lee Strasberg, and it shows. William Inge's rowdy play was adapted by George Axelrod (LORD LOVE A DUCK) with delightful results. The play, which unfolded on a single diner set, is skillfully opened out to include a ranch, a dance hall, a rodeo, and scenes of the countryside. The film is further enhanced by some action-packed rodeo sequences.

BUTCH CASSIDY AND THE SUNDANCE KID

1969 112m c Western ★★★½
Fox (U.S.) /PG

Paul Newman *(Butch Cassidy)*, Robert Redford *(Sundance Kid)*, Katharine Ross *(Etta Place)*, Strother Martin *(Percy Garris)*, Henry Jones *(Bike Salesman)*, Jeff Corey *(Sheriff Bledsoe)*, George Furth *(Woodcock)*, Cloris Leachman *(Agnes)*, Ted Cassidy *(Harvey Logan)*, Kenneth Mars *(Marshal)*

p, Paul Monash, John Foreman; d, George Roy Hill; w, William Goldman; ph, Conrad Hall; ed, John C. Howard, Richard C. Meyer; m, Burt Bacharach; art d, Jack Martin Smith, Philip Jefferies; fx, L.B. Abbott, Art Cruickshank; cos, Edith Head

AAN Best Picture; AAN Best Director: George Roy Hill; *AA Best Adapted Screenplay:* William Goldman; *AA Best Cinematography:* Conrad Hall; *AA Best Score:* Burt Bacharach; *AA Best Song:* Burt Bacharach (Music), Hal David (Lyrics); *AAN Best Sound:* William Edmundson, David Dockendorf

Although much of its freshness has faded, this still-amusing film reinvented the Western for a new generation.

Newman and Redford reimagine the two famous train robbers as a pair of urbane businessmen who go about their work with the easy nonchalance of seasoned professionals. Threatened by determined Pinkertons and rapidly advancing technology, they reconsider their careers, returning to The Kid's native New York City for a brief vacation. But, succumbing to the desire to return to the work they know and love, they strike out for South America to start over. At first successful (despite not speaking a word of Spanish), they soon find the Bolivian government less tolerant and more aggressive than Pinkerton men, and die in a blaze of glory in a gunfight, unaware how seriously outnumbered they are.

BUTCH CASSIDY's winking awareness of its own cinematic nature (from the opening "silent movie" train robbery to the famous closing freeze frame) and witty banter give the story a degree of charm and exuberance, but otherwise it's trapped in its own context, most notably apparent in the (Oscar-winning) Bacharach score that now feels silly and dated. Ross's stiff performance as the Kid's paramour, Etta Place (which later spawned a terrible sequel) is more than offset by the wonderful supporting cast and, especially, the chemistry between the stars. This film revived Newman's flagging career and officially catapulted Redford to stardom (giving him the industry clout to make such personal projects as DOWNHILL RACER, THE CANDIDATE and JEREMIAH JOHNSON).

BUTTERFIELD 8

1960 109m c Drama ★★★
MGM (U.S.) /X

Elizabeth Taylor *(Gloria Wandrous)*, Laurence Harvey *(Weston Liggett)*, Eddie Fisher *(Steve Carpenter)*, Dina Merrill *(Emily Liggett)*, Mildred Dunnock *(Mrs. Wandrous)*, Betty Field *(Mrs. Fanny Thurber)*, Jeffrey Lynn *(Bingham Smith)*, Kay Medford *(Happy)*, Susan Oliver *(Norma)*, George Voskovec *(Dr. Tredman)*

p, Pandro S. Berman; d, Daniel Mann; w, Charles Schnee, John Michael Hayes (based on the novel by John O'Hara); ph, Joseph Ruttenberg; ed, Ralph E. Winters; m, Bronislau Kaper; art d, George W. Davis, Urie McCleary; cos, Helen Rose

AA Best Actress: Elizabeth Taylor; *AAN Best Cinematography:* Joseph Ruttenberg, Charles Harten

Glossy trash with the star at full throttle, it's the quintessential La Liz movie. Loosely based on John O'Hara's novel, loose Gloria Wandrous encompasses the legendary wanton Taylor persona; indeed, Hollywood was so pleased by the cementing of Hurricane Liz's public image they rewarded her with an Oscar. As for Taylor's critical response, when she watched it the first time in a screening room, she threw a high heel at the screen, fled to a john, and promptly threw up. All the more reason to tune in. . .

Liz reluctantly plays Gloria (the very idea—casting Liz in something tawdry and commercial), a "model" searching for understanding, who, like Liz, cannot breathe if she is not in love. Enter married rake, ultimate heel Laurence Harvey, who fancies Liz in a sort of violent bedroom way and we're off to the races. Our fave scenes: that opening, which chronicles a typical La Liz good morning, and the barside "disagreement" she shares with Harvey.

Miss Taylor gives quite a star performance and she's buoyed by a talented supporting cast with two eyesores: the bland Dina Merrill and the blank Eddie Fisher (his appearance was a consolation prize to soothe the star). This was the height of the "I stole Debbie's husband; so what?" scandal, so the public turned out in droves to snoop their chemistry (there was none) and hate Liz en masse. Hate turned to public sympathy when Taylor caught pneumonia in London and nearly died, surviving only when an emergency tracheotomy was performed (and guaranteed Liz a lot of Oscar sympathy votes). This was an important chapter in the Taylor Roadshow and she would next land CLEOPATRA, and celebrate by dumping Fisher. Meanwhile, enjoy BUTTERFIELD 8. It's a rave!

BYE-BYE BRAZIL

1980 100m c Drama   ★★★
Carnaval Unifilm (Brazil)

Jose Wilker *(Lord Gypsy)*, Betty Faria *(Salome)*, Fabio Junior *(Cico)*, Zaira Zambelli *(Dasdo)*, Principe Nabor *(Swallow)*, Jofre Soares *(Ze da Luz)*, Marcus Vinicius *(Gent)*, Jose Maria Lima *(Assistant)*, Emanuel Cavalcanti *(Mayor)*, Jose Marcio Reis *(Smuggler)*

p, Lucy Barreto; d, Carlos Diegues; w, Carlos Diegues; ph, Lauro Escorel Filho; ed, Anisio Medeiros

BYE BYE BRAZIL is a colorful, exotic collection of vignettes about modern Brazil. The film follows a carnival troupe as they travel throughout the country, wandering deep into the Amazonian jungles, in search of new places where they can put on a show. The eccentric group consists of Lord Cigano (Jose Wilker), a magician who organized the troupe; Salome (Betty Faria), his mistress and the show's exotic dancer/prostitute; Cico (Fabio Junior), a young accordionist infatuated with Salome; Dasdo (Zaira Zambelli), Cico's pregnant wife; and Swallow (Principe Nabor), a black, deaf-mute strongman. An insightful and humorous look at two Brazils in conflict—the traditional Brazil versus the progressive Brazil, with its infusions of North American culture.

C

CABARET

1972 124m c Musical/War   ★★★★½
Allied Artists (U.S.)   PG/15

Liza Minnelli *(Sally Bowles)*, Michael York *(Brian Roberts)*, Helmut Griem *(Maximilian von Heune)*, Joel Grey *(Master of Ceremonies)*, Fritz Wepper *(Fritz Wendel)*, Marisa Berenson *(Natalia Landauer)*, Elisabeth Neumann-Viertel *(Fraulein Schneider)*, Sigrid von Richthofen *(Fraulein Maur)*, Helen Vita *(Fraulein Kost)*, Gerd Vespermann *(Bobby)*

p, Cy Feuer; d, Bob Fosse; w, Jay Presson Allen (based on the stage play by Joe Masteroff, the stage play *I Am a Camera* by John Van Druten, and the writings of Christopher Isherwood); ph, Geoffrey Unsworth; ed, David Bretherton; m, Ralph Burns; art d, Jurgen Kiebach, Rolf Zehetbauer; chor, Bob Fosse; cos, Charlotte Flemming

AAN Best Picture; *AA Best Actress:* Liza Minnelli; *AA Best Supporting Actor:* Joel Grey; *AA Best Director:* Bob Fosse; *AAN Best Adapted Screenplay:* Jay Presson Allen; *AA Best Cinematography:* Geoffrey Unsworth; *AA Best Editing:* David Bretherton; *AA Best Score:* Ralph Burns; *AA Best Art Direction:* Rolf Zehetbauer, Jurgen Kiebach, Herbert Strabel; *AA Best Sound:* Robert Knudson, David Hildyard

Chilling Fosse vision of Weimar Berlin, stylishly directed and choreographed, featuring a show-stopping musical performance by Minnelli, Grey's unforgettable emcee and thoughtful acting from Michael York. The screenplay utilizes much of the Broadway musical's book, but also is influenced by both play and screen versions of I AM A CAMERA. Englishman Brian Roberts (York) arrives in Berlin, takes a small flat, and meets a promiscuous, eccentric American, Sally Bowles (Minnelli), who earns her living singing in the seedy Kit Kat Club. Brian, a bisexual, becomes involved with both Sally and a wealthy German playboy (Griem); meanwhile, Nazism is ever more evidently on the rise.

Minnelli's knockout musical delivery tends to obscure the film's finer points, and, because Liza literally becomes a star before our eyes, her enactment of Sally Bowles's tragic mediocrity isn't plausible. Fosse wisely scrapped several weak songs from the original score and songwriters Kander and Ebb added some fine new ones. Everyone raves about "Money," the Grey-Minnelli duet, but the real showstoppers are "Mein Herr," where Liza rivals Dietrich in evoking Weimar-era decadence, and "Tomorrow Belongs to Me," in which a freshfaced German youth is gradually revealed as a Nazi. The final fadeout is extraordinary.

CABIN IN THE SKY

1943 98m bw Musical   ★★★★
MGM (U.S.)   /A

Ethel Waters *(Petunia Jackson)*, Eddie "Rochester" Anderson *(Little Joe)*, Lena Horne *(Georgia Brown)*, Louis Armstrong *(The Trumpeter)*, Rex Ingram *(Lucius/Lucifer, Jr.)*, Kenneth Spencer *(Rev. Green, The General)*, John "Bubbles" Sublett *(Domino)*, Oscar Polk *(The Deacon/Flatfoot)*, Mantan Moreland *(First Idea Man)*, Willie Best *(Second Idea Man)*

p, Arthur Freed; d, Vincente Minnelli; w, Joseph Schrank (based on the play by Lynn Root, John Latouche, Vernon Duke); ph, Sidney Wagner; ed, Harold F. Kress; m, Roger Edens

AAN Best Song: Harold Arlen (Music), E.Y. Harburg (Lyrics)

Vincente Minnelli's debut as a Hollywood director was the first all-black musical since GREEN PASTURES in 1936 and a monument to Ethel Waters in all her glory. Though the film perpetuates racial stereotypes—hardly surprising, given the period in which it was made—it's a fresh, inventive take on the original Broadway production which showcases a number of prodigious talents.

The story focuses on Little Joe (Eddie "Rochester" Anderson), a gambler who is nearly killed in a bar-room brawl and whose soul then becomes the site of a battle (fought in dream sequences) between God's General (Kenneth Spencer) and Lucifer Jr. (Rex Ingram). This tug-of-war is reflected in another, real-life struggle, for Joe's heart, between his devoted wife (Waters) and the alluring Georgia Brown (Lena Horne).

Though shot in sepia, CABIN IN THE SKY offers ample proof of Minnelli's visual flair in several scenes, particularly an early sequence of a church service and a nightclub dance routine (to "Shine") performed by Domino (John "Bubbles" Sublett). The cast is quite exceptional. Anderson makes an engaging, sympathetic rascal, whose moral dilemma is understandable given the siren call of the ravishing Lena Horne. Ethel Waters steals the show, blazing through the picture with sincerity and compassion and handling her songs with unparalleled assurance—"Taking a Chance on Love" and the Oscar-nominated "Happiness Is Just a Thing Called Joe" are standouts.

CABIN was far from plain sailing for Minnelli and MGM. The director was supposedly romancing Horne, leading to tensions between her, Minnelli and Waters which came to a head over the "Honey in the Honeycomb" number. The number was originally slated to be sung by Waters but, during production, plans were changed to accommodate two versions, one to be performed by Waters as a ballad, one as a dance number led by Horne and featuring John "Bubbles." Horne, however, broke her ankle during production, and the two numbers had to be reversed, with Horne singing the ballad (a highlight of the film) and Waters displaying surprising talent as a dancer.

The Duke Ellington Orchestra lends musical pizazz and Louis Armstrong can be seen as one of Lucifer Jr.'s hilarious henchmen—his joyous face almost steals every scene he's in. Only three of the songs and three principals—Minnelli, Waters and Ingram—came from the original Broadway show.

CABLE GUY, THE

1996 91m c Comedy/Thriller ★★½
Bernie Brillstein/Brad Grey/Licht/Mueller PG-13/12
Film Corp. (U.S.)

Jim Carrey (Cable Guy), Matthew Broderick (Steven), Leslie Mann (Robin), Jack Black (Rick), George Segal (Steven's Father), Diane Baker (Steven's Mother), Ben Stiller (Sam Sweet), Eric Roberts (Himself), Janeane Garofalo (Medieval Waitress), Misa Koprova (Heather)

p, Andrew Licht, Jeffrey A. Mueller, Judd Apatow; d, Ben Stiller; w, Lou Holtz Jr.; ph, Robert Brinkmann; ed, Steven Weisberg; m, John Ottman; prod d, Sharon Seymour; art d, Jeff Knipp; fx, Matt Sweeney, Sony Pictures Imageworks; cos, Erica Edell Phillips

Much of this dark farce, about the chaos that erupts when a buttoned-down milksop (Matthew Broderick) slips the Cable Guy (Jim Carrey) 50 bucks for free premium service, verges on the unwatchable. It's an uneasy hybrid of vulgar slapstick and nightmarish comedy-of-mortification, and its modest ambitions are entirely subordinate to Carrey's manic mugging and capering. But it soars above the plebian rudeness of DUMB AND DUMBER by virtue of a few moments of excoriating brilliance.

Carrey's Cable Guy, his personality formed entirely by TV, is the neediest nerd of all time, and his dismantling of Broderick's ordered life is in the classic tradition of anarchic comedy, complete with undercurrents of class-based hostility and homoerotic menace. A cruel clown, Carrey puts the belligerent libido back in the sexless spazz character perfected by Jerry Lewis, and exploits teasing as the socially condoned form of torture it is. In all, about a third of the film is audaciously funny and genuinely disturbing. The rest will sorely test the devotion of Carrey's fans.

Although first-time writer Lou Holtz Jr.'s awkward script could easily have been played for light laughs, director Ben Stiller (REALITY BITES) consistently brings out its darkest implications. One keenly edited sequence intercuts Carrey's vigorously lewd karaoke rendering of Jefferson Airplane's "Somebody to Love" with Broderick's seduction by a wanton young woman (Misa Koprova). At once amusing and appropriately discomfiting, the scene is a perfectly balanced construct that could be toppled by a single false cut, and isn't. Though less unnerving, the sequence involving hokey theme restaurant "Medieval Times"—which features wry comedienne Janeane Garofolo as a sulky serving wench—is also a tour de force.

CADDYSHACK

1980 99m c Comedy ★★½
Orion (U.S.) R/15

Rodney Dangerfield (Al), Ted Knight (Judge), Michael O'Keefe (Danny), Bill Murray (Carl), Sarah Holcomb (Maggie), Scott Colomby (Tony), Cindy Morgan (Lacey), Dan Resin (Dr. Beeper), Henry Wilcoxon (Bishop), Albert Salmi (Noonan)

p, Douglas Kenney; d, Harold Ramis; w, Brian Doyle-Murray, Harold Ramis, Douglas Kenney; ph, Stevan Larner; ed, William Carruth; m, Johnny Mandel; prod d, Stan Jolly; art d, George Szeptycki

A slapstick comedy featuring a host of great clowns, CADDYSHACK boosted the career of "Saturday Night Live" alum Bill Murray and revived the sagging fortunes of the wonderful Rodney Dangerfield, whose opening scenes are some of the funniest on film.

Adorned in garish garb and throwing his money around, the newly wealthy Dangerfield offends the stuffed-shirt members of the swanky country club he has just joined. No one is more put off by Dangerfield than Knight, who considers the club his private fiefdom. Chase is a dissipated but tremendously talented golfer; O'Keefe is a clean-cut caddie trying to make good and snag a college scholarship by winning a tournament; and Murray is the grubby groundskeeper who spends much of his time devising methods to rid the course of a pesky gopher.

Too much time is spent on the forced romance between O'Keefe and Holcomb, an attractive waitress, however, and the slapstick becomes utterly mindless toward the end (as if the producer said, "Okay, it's time for this film to really get out of control!"). Still, the laughs keep coming. Even the film's absurd stereotypes provoke guilty titters. There is a marvelous moment when Wilcoxon, portraying a golf-loving clergyman, begins to play a perfect game in a raging rainstorm. Dropping one hole-in-one after another, laughing hysterically, thanking the Almighty for the greatest game of his life, he lifts his club heavenward and is struck by lightning while a crescendo from the score of THE TEN COMMANDMENTS (in which Wilcoxon played pharoah's general) blares on the soundtrack.

CAESAR AND CLEOPATRA

1945 138m c Biography/Historical ★★★★
Two Cities (U.K.) /U

Vivien Leigh (Cleopatra), Claude Rains (Caesar), Stewart Granger (Apollodorus), Flora Robson (Ftatateeta), Francis L. Sullivan (Pothinus), Basil Sydney (Rufio), Cecil Parker (Britannus), Raymond Lovell (Lucius Septimus), Anthony Eustrel (Achillas), Ernest Thesiger (Theodotus)

p, Gabriel Pascal, J. Arthur Rank; d, Gabriel Pascal; w, George Bernard Shaw, Marjorie Deans (based on the play by George Bernard Shaw); ph, Freddie Young, Robert Krasker, Jack Hildyard, Jack Cardiff; ed, Frederick Wilson; m, Georges Auric; cos, Oliver Messel

AAN Best Art Direction: John Bryan (Art Direction)

Don't be misled. Don't try to convince yourself this is wonderful entertainment, don't second guess your basic instinct. Yes, it's Shaw's acerbic and uncinematic play, but Pascal has slowed it down to a lumbering crawl and puffed it up to VIP dinosaur status. Two finer stars being saddled hopelessly we cannot recall, but this occasion frankly finds Rains dishing up ham too readily, and Leigh sorely lacking in the siren department (the arrival of handsome Stewart Granger barely rates a glance). Indeed, this doom laden production was far more interesting behind the cameras than it was in front of them.

Irascible Shaw became so fond of Leigh that he broke precedent and actually wrote an entirely new scene for her, although he adamantly refused to introduce "a little love interest" into the script as politely requested by producer J. Arthur Rank. Producer-director Pascal went at CAESAR AND CLEOPATRA with a vengeance, intent on proving that the British film industry could rival in scope anything Hollywood could create, particularly in the belt-tightening years of WWII. The result was the most extravagantly expensive film Britain produced up to that time, so opulent that when Shaw first viewed it he expressed annoyance at the lavish sets, the hordes of extras, and spendthrift feel of the overall production.

American distribution was promoted by Rank and United Artists with an enormous budget that initially caused US audiences to flock to see favorites Leigh and Rains; but disappointment soon set in when viewers emerged bored, and the Rank organization sustained staggering losses—some $3 million—that brought it to the very brink of bankruptcy. But from the ranks of the film's over 100 bit players emerged many a star, including Michael Rennie, who plays a Centurion, Kay Kendall, a slave girl, and Jean Simmons, a harpist.

CAINE MUTINY, THE

1954 123m c Drama ★★★★
Columbia (U.S.) /U

Humphrey Bogart (Capt. Philip Francis Queeg), Jose Ferrer (Lt. Barney Greenwald), Van Johnson (Lt. Steve Maryk), Fred MacMurray (Lt. Tom Keefer), Robert Francis (Ens. Willie Keith), May Wynn (May Wynn), Tom Tully (Capt. DeVriess), E.G. Marshall (Lt. Cmdr. Challee), Arthur Franz (Lt. Paynter), Lee Marvin (Meatball)

CALIFORNIA SPLIT

p, Stanley Kramer; d, Edward Dmytryk; w, Stanley Roberts, Michael Blankfort (based on the play and novel by Herman Wouk); ph, Franz Planer; ed, William Lyon, Henry Batista; m, Max Steiner; prod d, Rudolph Sternad; art d, Cary Odell; fx, Lawrence Butler; cos, Jean Louis

AAN Best Picture; AAN Best Actor: Humphrey Bogart; *AAN Best Supporting Actor:* Tom Tully; *AAN Best Original Screenplay:* Stanley Roberts; *AAN Best Editing:* William Lyon, Henry Batista; *AAN Best Score:* Max Steiner; *AAN Best Sound:* John P Livadary (Sound Director)

Complex, atypical Bogie performance is keynote for strong drama from Pulitzer-winning novel and Broadway show. Francis, Johnson, and MacMurray are shipmates early in WWII aboard a destroyer-cum-minesweeper. Bogart, in one of his greatest performances, boards the ship as her new captain and immediately establishes both his power over the men and his neurosis. When he clashes with Johnson, the latter is court-martialed, and Ferrer must defend him.

The scenes with Bogart disintegrating on the witness stand have become part of American film folklore, as he delineates the layers of perfectionism and obsessiveness overlaying an inferiority complex. This is a don't-miss picture, unnecessarily beefed up with a gratuitous, concocted love story between Wynn (using her own name in the film) and Francis. Bogart was later asked how he managed to totally capture the paranoid personality of Queeg. "Simple," growled Bogie, "everybody knows I'm nuts, anyway."

CALIFORNIA SPLIT

1974 108m c Comedy ★★
Columbia (U.S.) R/X

George Segal *(Bill Denny)*, Elliott Gould *(Charlie Walters)*, Ann Prentiss *(Barbara) (Miller)*, Gwen Welles *(Susan Peters)*, Edward Walsh *(Lew)*, Joseph Walsh *(Sparkie)*, Bert Remsen *(Helen Brown)*, Barbara London *(Lady on Bus)*, Barbara Ruick *(Reno Barmaid)*, Jay Fletcher *(Robber)*

p, Robert Altman, Joseph Walsh; d, Robert Altman; w, Joseph Walsh; ph, Paul Lohmann; ed, Lou Lombardo; m, Phyllis Shotwell; art d, Leon Ericksen

Altman has done the almost impossible. He's made a gambling story dull. In his constant striving for "loose-ending" a movie, he has strung together a series of vignettes, some funny, others boring, and has called it a film. Segal and Gould are both excellent as compulsive gamblers in various situations. Several real gamesmen play themselves in the film and the supporting players all contribute fine work but the picture crumbles in its overall concept. Altman, to his credit, is always after something elusive—a sense of realism that is often missing with more structured films. When it works, it's marvelous. Unfortunately for Altman, it hardly ever works. Screenwriter Walsh was a fairly successful young actor, at one point, who gave up acting for writing. This script was not his best effort, but it's not easy to say where the words end and where Altman's improvisational, sketchy technique begins.

CALIFORNIA SUITE

1978 103m c Comedy ★★★½
Columbia (U.S.) PG/15

Alan Alda *(Bill Warren)*, Michael Caine *(Sidney Cochran)*, Bill Cosby *(Dr. Willis Panama)*, Jane Fonda *(Hannah Warren)*, Walter Matthau *(Marvin Michaels)*, Elaine May *(Millie Michaels)*, Richard Pryor *(Dr. Chauncy Gump)*, Maggie Smith *(Diana Barrie)*, Gloria Gifford *(Lola Gump)*, Sheila Frazier *(Bettina Panama)*

p, Ray Stark; d, Herbert Ross; w, Neil Simon (based on his play); ph, David M. Walsh; ed, Michael A. Stevenson; m, Claude Bolling; cos, Ann Roth, Patricia Norris

AA Best Supporting Actress: Maggie Smith; *AAN Best Adapted Screenplay:* Neil Simon; *AAN Best Art Direction:* Albert Brenner, Marvin March

An all-star bitch fest, slickly served, but finally monotonous. The quartet of stories are weaved together more or less, with the Caine/Smith segment the most successful because the actors realize the value of comedic understatement—this kind of wordplay requires

enough assurance to make it look as though you're not working. The Fonda/Alda sketch is interesting only because Fonda's character is such a welcome relief from her usual gung-ho over-achiever. Matthau and May are an acquired taste—your move. And the Cosby/Pryor sketch is so vile, you can't believe it even made it past an editor. Smith won an Oscar for her deft portrayal of an Academy Award nominee. Truly, a mixed bag.

CALL NORTHSIDE 777

1948 111m bw Biography/Crime ★★★★
Fox (U.S.) /A

James Stewart *(McNeal)*, Richard Conte *(Frank Wiecek)*, Lee J. Cobb *(Brian Kelly)*, Helen Walker *(Laura McNeal)*, Betty Garde *(Wanda Skutnik)*, Kasia Orzazewski *(Tillie Wiecek)*, Joanna De Bergh *(Helen Wiecek-Rayska)*, Howard Smith *(Palmer)*, Moroni Olsen *(Parole Board Chairman)*, John McIntire *(Sam Faxon)*

p, Otto Lang; d, Henry Hathaway; w, Jerry Cady, Jay Dratler (adapted by Leonard Hoffman and Quentin Reynolds from articles by James P. McGuire appearing in the *Chicago Times*); ph, Joseph MacDonald; ed, J. Watson Webb; m, Alfred Newman; art d, Lyle Wheeler, Mark-Lee Kirk; fx, Dick Smith, Fred Sersen; cos, Kay Nelson

One of the most impressive semi-documentary noir thrillers, CALL NORTHSIDE 777 was shot on location in Chicago in striking black-and-white by cinematographer Joe MacDonald. Renowned movie nice guy Jimmy Stewart stars in a change-of-pace characterization as a hard-boiled newspaper reporter who evolves from a sceptical news hound to a dedicated crusader when he investigates a decade-old cop killing based on the actual case of Joe Majczek of Chicago who was imprisoned for a crime he did not commit.

Stewart is handed an assignment by editor Cobb: follow up a small ad that appeared in his newspaper offering a $5,000 reward for information leading to the arrest and conviction of the man responsible for killing a policeman years earlier. Stewart learns that the ad was placed by a cleaning woman (Orzazewski) who has slaved for years to earn reward money for anyone able to clear her son of the murder. The cynical Stewart initially believes the convicted Conte is guilty but opts to write a human interest story about the loving mother. When the public reaction proves to be overwhelming, Cobb encourages Stewart to back up his original story with some more digging. As he investigates, Stewart unearths evidence that there was some police coverup in the case and that certain evidence is missing. His interest is piqued.

Stewart effectively plays the part of Jim McGuire, the *Chicago Times* reporter who won the Pulitzer Prize for his investigative efforts, and the rest of the cast turn in fine, realistic performances. For Stewart, this film was a departure from the genial roles (though sometimes dark-tinged) for which he had become famous (IT'S A WONDERFUL LIFE, THE PHILADELPHIA STORY, MAGIC TOWN); this performance paved the way for his more morally ambiguous and gritty characterizations for directors such as Hitchcock and Anthony Mann in the 1950s. Director Hathaway had recently had a resounding success with the Ben Hecht story, KISS OF DEATH, also shot in a grim realistic style. Newman's moody score adds depth and feeling to the emotionally charged story.

CALL OF THE WILD

1935 89m bw Adventure ★★★
20th Century (U.S.) /U

Clark Gable *(Jack Thornton)*, Loretta Young *(Claire Blake)*, Jack Oakie *(Shorty Hoolihan)*, Frank Conroy *(John Blake)*, Reginald Owen *(Smith)*, Sidney Toler *(Groggin)*, Katherine DeMille *(Marie)*, Lalo Encinas *(Kali)*, Charles Stevens *(Francois)*, James Burke *(Ole)*

p, Darryl F. Zanuck; d, William A. Wellman; w, Gene Fowler, Leonard Praskins (based on the novel by Jack London); ph, Charles Rosher; ed, H.T. Fritch; m, Alfred Newman

This epic Alaskan adventure story features Clark Gable as prospector Jack Thornton. After losing his money gambling, Thornton acquires a huge dog, Buck, which is considered too vicious to be a sled dog. Thornton patiently trains the animal, then sets out with his friend Shorty Hoolihan (Jack Oakie) for the wilderness in search of gold. Thereafter they must battle the weather, the wilds, and crooks in their attempts to make their fortunes, and Thornton finds a love interest in the wife of a missing prospector. This hearty film was shot on the snowy slopes of Washington's Mount Baker, at 5,000 feet, where the harsh winter snows forced cast and crew to use snowplows to get to their daily locations. Through the hardships, they created a stirring adventure, loosely based on the writings of Jack London.

CAMILLE

1937 108m bw Romance   ★★★★★
MGM   (U.S.)   /PG

Greta Garbo *(Marguerite)*, Robert Taylor *(Armand)*, Lionel Barrymore *(Duval)*, Elizabeth Allan *(Nichette)*, Jessie Ralph *(Nanine)*, Henry Daniell *(Baron de Varville)*, Lenore Ulric *(Olympe)*, Laura Hope Crews *(Prudence)*, Rex O'Malley *(Gaston)*, Russell Hardie *(Gustave)*

p, Bernard Hyman; d, George Cukor; w, Zoe Akins, Frances Marion, James Hilton (based on the novel and play *La Dame aux Camelias* by Alexander Dumas fils); ph, William Daniels; ed, Margaret Booth; m, Herbert Stothart

AAN Best Actress: Greta Garbo

The great Garbo at her radiant peak, and certainly among the top five most romantic movies ever made. Cukor's renowned "rapport" with actresses is unfailing here. MGM's glamour shows unmistakable care—if it's not the same as style, the luxuriance befits the story of a courtesan. It's a puzzle why Garbo's Marguerite is a whore—she seems too intelligent, too yearning, too serious to have ever considered the demimonde life, yet her acting is so generous, so overcome with the warmth of true love, and so tinged with the irony of the character's circumstances, that she sweeps you away. Her final scene is among the finest ever committed to film, as she signals death with her eyes in a lingering close-up.

Robert Taylor is so beautiful, you can forgive his lack of skill. His earnestness seems consistent with the rash actions of young love, and his ardent awe of Garbo imparts a worshipful aura that is touching. The fact that he looks younger makes the whore component of Garbo's character more believable; it justifies Armand's not immediately grasping his love's circumstances.

This is Daniell's most interesting performance, subtle in his control and villainy. Laura Hope Crews finally is able to utilize her vocal vulgarity; she is by far a better old strumpet than she was an old maid busybody in so many films. Tempestuous Lenore Ulric is a curiosity that works. This former Belasco stage star embodies a disappointed envy of Garbo that Cukor uses to great advantage. Lionel Barrymore, all growling propriety, is the jarring note in the ensemble.

The screenplay was adapted from the Dumas play by Frances Marion, James Hilton, and Zoe Akins. And Adrian's costumes, usually white, for Miss Garbo, contribute to her divination of literature's most beloved dying swan. This was Irving Thalberg's last production; he died while it was being made and it was completed by Bernard Hyman.

CAMILLE CLAUDEL

1988 149m c Biography   ★★½
Christian Fechner/Lilith/Gaumont/A2/D.D.   (France)   R/PG

Isabelle Adjani *(Camille Claudel)*, Gerard Depardieu *(Auguste Rodin)*, Laurent Grevill *(Paul Claudel)*, Alain Cuny *(Louis-Prosper Claudel)*, Madeleine Robinson *(Louise-Athanaise Claudel)*, Katrine Boorman *(Jessie Lipscomb)*, Daniele Lebrun *(Rose Beuret)*, Aurelle Doazan *(Louise Claudel)*, Madeleine Marie *(Victoire)*, Maxime Leroux *(Claude Debussy)*

p, Christian Fechner; d, Bruno Nuytten; w, Bruno Nuytten, Marilyn Goldin (based on the biography by Reine-Marie Paris); ph, Pierre Lhomme; ed, Joelle Hache, Jeanne Kef; m, Gabriel Yared; art d, Bernard Vezat; cos, Dominique Borg

AAN Best Actress: Isabelle Adjani; *AAN Best Foreign Language Film*

This film about the tragic life of French artist Camille Claudel is as dark and unwieldy as one of Claudel's own sculptures. Born in 1864, Claudel (played by Oscar-nominated Isabelle Adjani, who also coproduced) demonstrated talent early. At 20, she met sculptor Auguste Rodin (Gerard Depardieu), who became her mentor and lover. Their 12-year liaison was an artistically fertile time for Claudel, but the affair's

disastrous outcome caused the already high-strung Claudel to deteriorate further emotionally to the point of becoming an impoverished recluse, and in 1913 she was forcibly committed to a psychiatric hospital.

Adjani and director Bruno Nuytten's film is an admiring but emotionally ininvolving and sketchy account of a woman about whom little is actually known. Faced with gaps in the record, they have imagined a life of towering romantic passion and destruction for Claudel, but the plot motivation becomes murky, leaving Adjani to indulge in protracted emotional fireworks that damage her portrayal. On the other hand, Depardieu is amazingly successful in his tricky role as the great Rodin, and ex-cinematographer Nuytten fills his film with memorable images.

His inexperience as a first-time director shows, however, in the film's uncertain pacing and lack of dramatic cohesiveness (the inadequate script is no help). In addition to Adjani's Oscar nomination, the film was also up for Best Foreign Film, but lost to CINEMA PARADISO.

CANDIDATE, THE

1972 109m c Political   ★★★½
Warner Bros.   (U.S.)   /15

Robert Redford *(Bill McKay)*, Peter Boyle *(Luck)*, Don Porter *(Sen. Crocker Jarmon)*, Allen Garfield *(Howard Klein)*, Melvyn Douglas *(John J. McKay)*, Quinn Redeker *(Rich Jenkin)*, Michael Lerner *(Paul Corliss)*, Karen Carlson *(Nancy McKay)*, Morgan Upton *(Henderson)*, Kenneth Tobey *(Starkey)*

p, Walter Coblenz; d, Michael Ritchie; w, Jeremy Larner; ph, Victor J. Kemper, John Korty; ed, Richard A. Harris, Robert Estrin; m, John Rubinstein; cos, Patricia Norris

AA Best Adapted Screenplay: Jeremy Larner; *AAN Best Sound:* Richard Portman, Gene Cantamessa

Handlers, spin-doctors, and the good man they lead astray. Jeremy Larner's Academy Award-winning screenplay provides a voyage into the sea of politics; the result is a fascinating film that sometimes feels like a documentary. Despite minor glitches, this is a prophetic glimpse of politics in the age of TV.

Redford plays an altruistic attorney whose father (Douglas) was California's governor. Having seen all the dirt as a young man, Redford has no interest in politics. Porter is the typical big-state senator—bluff, hearty, and full of bull—there doesn't seem to be anyone who can come close to defeating him in the next election. Boyle asks Redford to run for office. After some soul-searching, Redford agrees—with the proviso that his father be kept out of the campaign and that he, Redford, be allowed to say what he feels with no political tracts being pushed upon him by the party. His candor appeals to the public, and he begins to climb in the opinion polls. With popularity behind him, will he sell out? This, ironically enough, is the film that inspired Dan Quayle to enter politics.

CANDY MOUNTAIN

1987 91m c Drama   ★★★½
Xanadu/Plain-Chant/Vision 4   (Switzerland/Canada/France)   R/15

Kevin J. O'Connor *(Julius Book)*, Harris Yulin *(Elmore Silk)*, Tom Waits *(Al Silk)*, Bulle Ogier *(Cornelia)*, Roberts Blossom *(Archie)*, Leon Redbone *(Huey)*, Dr. John *(Henry)*, Rita MacNeil *(Winnie)*, Joe Strummer *(Mario)*, Laurie Metcalf *(Alice)*

p, Ruth Waldburger; d, Robert Frank, Rudy Wurlitzer; w, Rudy Wurlitzer; ph, Pio Corradi; ed, Jennifer Auge; m, Max Rebennack "Dr. John", David Johansen, Leon Redbone, Rita MacNeil, Tom Waits; fx, Jacques Godbout; cos, Carol Wood

Failed rock 'n' roll musician Julius Book (Kevin J. O'Connor) embarks on a mission to find guitar-maker Elmore Silk (Harris Yulin), a legendary craftsman who, 20 years before, at the height of his fame, dropped out of sight. Elmore's guitars are now worth $20,000 apiece, and Julius is hired by some music-industry big shots to find him. Desperately looking for a way to carve out a career for himself in the music business, Julius, who has never even heard of Elmore, takes the job and learns the hard way that "life ain't no candy mountain."

The product of a reportedly uneasy collaboration between photographer and filmmaker Robert Frank (PULL MY DAISY) and screenwriter Rudy Wurlitzer (TWO LANE BLACKTOP, WALKER), CANDY MOUNTAIN is an excellent road movie detailing the enlightenment of a callow young musician who mistakenly believes that simply pulling off a scam will somehow make him a successful artist. Filled with beautiful imagery, poetic dialogue, sly humor, savvy cameos, and excellent music, the film travels straight north from New York City to "the last town on the last street in North America."

O'Connor is superb as the would-be rock star whose romantic notions persist despite the fact that he is an empty vessel with absolutely nothing to say, and this odd, offbeat film richly deserves the audience it failed to find during its theatrical run.

CANDYMAN

1992 101m c Horror ★★★½
Propaganda Films (U.S.) R/

Virginia Madsen (Helen Lyle), Tony Todd (Candyman), Xander Berkeley (Trevor Lyle), Kasi Lemmons (Bernadette Walsh), Vanessa Williams (Anne-Marie McCoy), DeJuan Guy (Jake), Marianna Eliott (Clara), Ted Raimi (Billy), Ria Pavia (Monica), Mark Daniels (Student)

p, Alan Poul, Sigurjon Sighvatsson, Steve Golin; d, Bernard Rose; w, Bernard Rose (from the short story "The Forbidden" by Clive Barker); ph, Anthony B. Richmond; ed, Dan Rae; m, Philip Glass; prod d, Jane Ann Stewart; art d, David Lazan; fx, Bob Keen; cos, Leonard Pollack

Serious, straightforward cinematic terror is hard to come by these days, but this literate shocker is the scariest film since THE SILENCE OF THE LAMBS, and joins BRAM STOKER'S DRACULA as one of the best supernatural movies in years.

A Chicago-based doctoral student named Helen Lyle (Virginia Madsen) is working on a paper about urban legends. One of the myths she's focusing on concerns a spirit called "Candyman," who supposedly appears before anyone who says his name five times into a mirror—then slaughters them with a hook hand. When Helen learns that a murder in the nearby Cabrini Green housing projects has been attributed by the residents to Candyman, she investigates. Local legend has it that Candyman was originally the son of a slave who had won fame as a painter in the 1800s, before an affair with a white woman led to his gruesome murder by a white mob. Helen is skeptical, and comes to believe that he's just a bogeyman used by local drug dealers to cover their crimes and keep the residents in line. That is until Candyman himself (Tony Todd) appears before her, angrily intoning that he now must shed innocent blood to prove his existence.

It's one of the many strengths of CANDYMAN that its story is actually about something. Derived from Clive Barker's short story "The Forbidden," writer-director Bernard Rose turns the gruesome material into a dark meditation on the nature of urban legends. The way the Cabrini Green residents cling to the myth as a way to rationalize the violence of their daily lives is intriguing, and the film is notable for the way in which it manages to utilize ghetto realities without condescending to its black characters. The acting here is first-rate, with Madsen turning in a forceful performance as the confused but resilient heroine. And special mention must be made of Philip Glass's superlative score, which combines synthesizers, piano, and chorus to haunting effect.

CAPE FEAR

1962 105m bw Thriller ★★★★
Melville/Talbot (U.S.) /X

Gregory Peck (Sam Bowden), Robert Mitchum (Max Cady), Polly Bergen (Peggy Bowden), Lori Martin (Nancy Bowden), Martin Balsam (Mark Dutton), Jack Kruschen (Dave Grafton), Telly Savalas (Charles Sievers), Barrie Chase (Diane Taylor), Paul Comi (Garner), Edward Platt (Judge)

p, Sy Bartlett; d, J. Lee Thompson; w, James R. Webb (based on the novel The Executioners by John D. MacDonald); ph, Sam Leavitt; ed, George Tomasini; m, Bernard Herrmann; art d, Alexander Golitzen, Robert Boyle; cos, Mary Wills

Unforgettable villainy. Suspenseful and very frightening, thanks to Robert Mitchum's lethally threatening performance and the frightened reactions of a pro cast.

Sexual deviate and lethal psychopath Mitchum is released from prison after serving a six-year term for rape and assault. He is bent on revenge against Peck, the witness whose testimony put him there, who is a family man and a lawyer with a private practice in Florida. When Peck learns Mitchum is in town, he goes to Balsam, the sheriff, who tries to make life miserable for Mitchum until a lawyer threatens to file suit on charges of harassment. Peck's dog is poisoned, then Mitchum takes to the phone, calling Bergen, the lawyer's wife, plaguing her with obscene remarks. Though he makes no overt threats, he intimates a dire fate for the family, including their teenage daughter, Martin. Because the police are helpless to jail the lunatic and the calls and oblique threats continue, Peck decides to handle matters himself.

J. Lee Thompson directs at a clip, until the crawl toward the bayou climax, where the minutes feel like hours, and your heart sits in your throat. Peck is careful not to act the fear; he's an interesting foe for Mitchum. Bergen's performance reminds one that she should have been a bigger star, given her beauty and undeniable talent, and Martin recalls an era when teenagers really were innocent. Balsam, Savalas, and Chase contribute effective cameos. The musical score by Bernard Herrmann is a nerve-beater.

CAPE FEAR

1991 128m c Thriller ★★★½
Universal/Cape Fear Inc./Amblin/Cappa Films/Tribeca R/18
Productions (U.S.)

Robert De Niro (Max Cady), Nick Nolte (Sam Bowden), Jessica Lange (Leigh Bowden), Juliette Lewis (Danielle Bowden), Joe Don Baker (Claude Kersek), Robert Mitchum (Lieutenant Elgart), Gregory Peck (Lee Heller), Martin Balsam (Judge), Illeana Douglas (Lori Davis), Fred Dalton Thompson (Tom Broadbent)

p, Barbara De Fina; d, Martin Scorsese; w, Wesley Strick (based on the 1962 screenplay by James R. Webb, from the novel The Executioners by John D. MacDonald); ph, Freddie Francis; ed, Thelma Schoonmaker; m, Bernard Herrmann; prod d, Henry Bumstead; art d, Jack G. Taylor Jr.; fx, J.B. Jones, Derek Meddings, Neal Martz, Stephan Dupuis; cos, Rita Ryack

AAN Best Actor: Robert DeNiro; AAN Best Supporting Actress: Juliette Lewis

Martin Scorsese's loose remake of J. Lee Thompson's 1962 thriller is an exercise in audience manipulation, with every frame designed to stagger the senses. During quiet scenes, the camera is in constant, unsettling motion. During big scenes, shock cuts to weird, menacing angles and reality-bending, high-tech optics accompany dark images of eroticism and violence.

In a telling twist on the original film, Nick Nolte plays lawyer Sam Bowden as a mean-spirited womanizer who has cheated on his burntout, embittered wife Leigh, played by Jessica Lange. (In the 1962 version, the Bowdens were morally pristine, impossibly upright citizens.) Leigh broods at home, venting her bile on teenage daughter Dani (Juliette Lewis), who stumbles through the film pathetically shellshocked and alone.

One of Sam's past professional betrayals comes home to roost. As a public defender, he railroaded client Max Cady (Robert DeNiro) into a 14-year prison sentence for sexual assault by burying a court report attesting to his victim's promiscuity. Now Cady is out and hungry for revenge, having spent his sentence remaking himself into a wily lawyer and con-man psychologist. Cady's plan is to destroy Max's career and family from within. He poisons the family dog, beats up and mutilates Bowden's employee Lori (Illeana Douglas), and comes close to twisting Dani's adolescent frustrations into sympathy with his cause, successfully goading Sam into violence.

There are no heroes in CAPE FEAR, only victims and their tormentors. De Niro rolls through the film like a demented descendant of Popeye the Sailor, his sinewy body awash with jailhouse tattoos (giving Mitchum the film's best line: "I don't know whether to look at him or read him"). Nolte winces, cowers and sweats; even normal activities like brushing his teeth are filmed in extreme close-ups that make him look subhuman. Lange looks pinched and drawn throughout, with the 17-year-old Lewis giving the movie's most impressiveperformance.

Scorsese's contempt for his characters extends to his handling of the scenario, credited to Wesley Strick (TRUE BELIEVER). The death of the Bowden's dog is treated with more genuine gravity than the notably gruesome crime against Lori. Though Scorsese throws in the occasional touch of humor, CAPE FEAR remains an overblown assault on the senses that leaves the viewer feeling physically—and morally—drained.

CAPTAIN BLOOD

1935   119m   bw   Adventure/Historical   ★★★★
Warner Bros.   (U.S.)   /PG

Errol Flynn *(Dr. Peter Blood)*, Olivia de Havilland *(Arabella Bishop)*, Lionel Atwill *(Col. Bishop)*, Basil Rathbone *(Capt. Levasseur)*, Ross Alexander *(Jeremy Pitt)*, Guy Kibbee *(Hagthorpe)*, Henry Stephenson *(Lord Willoughby)*, George Hassell *(Gov. Steed)*, Forrester Harvey *(Honesty Nuttall)*, Frank McGlynn Sr. *(Rev. Ogle)*

p, Harry Joe Brown; d, Michael Curtiz; w, Casey Robinson (based on the novel by Rafael Sabatini); ph, Hal Mohr, Ernest Haller; ed, George Amy; m, Erich Wolfgang Korngold; art d, Anton Grot; fx, Fred Jackman; cos, Milo Anderson

Flynn's star-making swashbuckler is right on target. Based on the novel by Rafael Sabatini, CAPTAIN BLOOD concerns the adventures of a young Brit surgeon who turns buccaneer after unjust persecution. The film had been originally earmarked for Robert Donat whose recurrent asthma convinced Jack Warner to gamble on Flynn. The unknown de Havilland also scored as love interest, and despite a tight budget, Curtiz contributed a lush production. Highlight is the trademark duel between Flynn and Rathbone.

Mindful that his two novice stars might bomb, wily Jack Warner decided not to build full-scale sailing ships for the many action scenes. To represent the bombardments, naval battles, and sinking of ships, technicians built several model ships 18 feet long, with 16-foot masts, and the battles were fought in a studio tank. Even the town of Port Royal was built in miniature. Clips from silent films (First National's 1924 SEA HAWK and Vitagraph's 1923 CAPTAIN BLOOD) were used to show full-scale ships in battle. The main decks of two ships were constructed on a soundstage for the life-size action, and on-location scenes were made along the California coastline.

Almost from the day of CAPTAIN BLOOD's release, Flynn was a Hollywood star, a favorite with a public that would forever see him as the great swashbuckler, a perception that he lived up to in one adventure film after another. BLOOD not only served to introduce Flynn as a stellar lead, but brought critical acclaim as well to lovely 19-year-old de Havilland, who carries off her part with great maturity and sophistication. She and the dashing Flynn eventually appeared together in eight films. Curtiz, the master of adventure films who shot every scene as if it were a cavalry charge, directed a total of nine Flynn epics, and Erich Wolfgang Korngold, whose rich and resonant scores set the musical standard for such spectacular films, composed seven scores for Flynn epics.

CAPTAIN FROM CASTILE

1947   140m   c   Adventure/Historical   ★★★★
Fox   (U.S.)   /A

Tyrone Power *(Pedro De Vargas)*, Jean Peters *(Catana Perez)*, Cesar Romero *(Hernando Cortez)*, Lee J. Cobb *(Juan Garcia)*, John Sutton *(Diego De Silva)*, Antonio Moreno *(Don Francisco)*, Thomas Gomez *(Fr. Bartolome Romero)*, Alan Mowbray *(Prof. Botello)*, Barbara Lawrence *(Luisa De Caravajal)*, George Zucco *(Marquis De Caravajal)*

p, Lamar Trotti; d, Henry King; w, Lamar Trotti (based on the novel by Samuel Shellabarger); ph, Charles Clarke, Arthur E. Arling; ed, Barbara McLean; m, Alfred Newman; art d, Richard Day, James Basevi; fx, Fred Sersen; cos, Charles LeMaire

AAN Best Score: Alfred Newman

A sweeping, majestic spectacle, neatly divided into a double feature: Spanish inquisition and the expedition of Cortez into Mexico. CAPTAIN FROM CASTILE was a major star vehicle for Power, and he's supported in style by Peters (in her film debut; she was discovered as a 20-year-old Ohio State coed), Cobb, Sutton, and especially Romero, as Cortez.

Although the script sometimes stretches credibility, King's panorama is distracting enough to sweep away your suspicions. CASTILE was a return to the old and glorious pageantry of yesteryear Hollywood, a huge $4.5 million production with one of the most memorable and stirring scores ever composed by Newman. The film was a pet project for Zanuck, who bought Princeton professor Samuel Shellabarger's unpublished novel for $100,000 when it was serialized in *Cosmopolitan* magazine.

Henry King, Fox's top action director, loved to scout locations in his small private plane. He had flown over Morales, a province of southern Mexico, as early as 1933 and selected this remote and rugged area as the site for this project. The trek deep into Mexico was similar to Cortez's own march, except that this one involved eight railroad cars packed with dozens of actors and technicians, including a dry cleaning unit for the expensive costumes and a refrigerated car in which the Technicolor film was kept.

Power, a pilot himself, flew 50 cast members down in a large chartered plane. A smoldering volcano near the location constantly threatened to erupt, delaying the shooting schedule which stretched on for almost four months while the budget doubled and Zanuck fumed. The film lost money but it remains as one of Fox's great epics.

CAPTAIN HORATIO HORNBLOWER

1951   116m   c   Adventure   ★★★½
Warner Bros.   (U.K.)   /U

Gregory Peck *(Horatio Hornblower)*, Virginia Mayo *(Lady Barbara Wellesley)*, Robert Beatty *(Lt. William Bush)*, James Robertson Justice *(Quist)*, Denis O'Dea *(Adm. Leighton)*, Terence Morgan *(Lt. Gerard)*, Richard Hearne *(Polwheal)*, James Kenney *(Midshipman Longley)*, Moultrie Kelsall *(Lt. Crystal)*, Michael Dolan *(Gundarson)*

p, Gerry Mitchell; d, Raoul Walsh; w, Ivan Goff, Ben Roberts, Aeneas MacKenzie (based on the novel by C.S. Forester); ph, Guy Green; ed, Jack Harris; m, Robert Farnon

Full of valiant guff. Peck took over for dissipated Errol Flynn, playing title role of 19th-century English hero who outwits the French and Spanish during the Napoleonic wars. Alas, Peck's a touch sober for a credible swashbuckler. In another instance of offbeat casting, Mayo plays Lady Barbara, the Duke of Wellington's sister, and she has a bad fever! Despite miscasting, Walsh's direction has no time to linger. Guy Green's camerawork and Robert Farnon's jolly score are helpful. In the small role of Polwheal is Richard Hearne, who may be remembered as Britain's comic "Mr. Pastry!"—an acrobatic, often hilarious silent comedian whom Ed Sullivan loved.

CAPTAINS COURAGEOUS

1937   115m   bw   Adventure   ★★★★★
MGM   (U.S.)   /U

Freddie Bartholomew *(Harvey)*, Spencer Tracy *(Manuel)*, Lionel Barrymore *(Disko)*, Melvyn Douglas *(Mr. Cheyne)*, Charley Grapewin *(Uncle Salters)*, Mickey Rooney *(Dan)*, John Carradine *("Long Jack")*, Oscar O'Shea *(Cushman)*, Jack LaRue *(Priest)*, Walter Kingsford *(Dr. Finley)*

p, Louis D. Lighton; d, Victor Fleming; w, John Lee Mahin, Marc Connelly, Dale Van Every (based on the novel by Rudyard Kipling); ph, Harold Rosson; ed, Elmo Veron; m, Franz Waxman; art d, Cedric Gibbons

AAN Best Picture; AA Best Actor: Spencer Tracy; *AAN Best Screenplay:* Marc Connolly, John Lee Mahin, Dale Van Every; *AAN Best Editing:* Elmo Veron

For once, a script perfectly suited to its director and star and one of the most lyrical children's classics ever made. Ignore the typical MGM "prestige picture" touches and enjoy the spirited cast performing under man's man director Fleming, who is reverential to the Kipling story. Young Harvey (Freddie Bartholomew), the spoiled-rotten son of a business tycoon, believes he can lie, cheat, and whine his way through life. On a trip to Europe with his father, the young man falls off a posh ocean liner into the sea and is rescued by a boat filled with Portuguese fishermen. One of the sailors is Manuel (Spencer Tracy), a big-hearted veteran of the seas who has a lot to teach the selfish Harvey about life.

CAPTAINS COURAGEOUS is a wonderful sea adventure with a heartwarming drama at its core. Tracy is excellent as the gentle fisherman, turning in a performance that won him a Best Actor Oscar. He reportedly hated his role, however, especially having his hair curled and wrestling with an accent (Tracy loathed externalized acting), but it doesn't show for a moment. The following year, he won the coveted statuette again for BOYS TOWN.

CAPTAIN'S PARADISE, THE

1953 93m bw Comedy   ★★★½
London Films (U.K.)   /U

Alec Guinness *(Capt. Henry St. James)*, Yvonne De Carlo *(Nita)*, Celia Johnson *(Maud)*, Charles Goldner *(Chief Officer Ricco)*, Miles Malleson *(Lawrence St. James)*, Bill Fraser *(Absalom)*, Tutte Lemkow *(Principal Dancer)*, Nicholas Phipps *(The Major)*, Walter Crisham *(Bob)*, Ferdy Mayne *(Sheikh)*

p, Anthony Kimmins; d, Anthony Kimmins; w, Alec Coppel, Nicholas Phipps (based on a story by Alec Coppel); ph, Ted Scaife; ed, Gerald Turney-Smith; m, Malcolm Arnold; art d, Paul Sheriff; chor, Walter Crisham, Tutte Lemkow

AAN Best Original Screenplay: Alec Coppel

Guinness at his conniving best in a droll, consistently funny comedy. He plays the captain of a steamer that sails between Gibraltar and North Africa. Instead of having a girl in every port, Guinness has a wife at either end, each offering him a completely different lifestyle. In Gibraltar it's Johnson, a sedate British housewife who makes him home-cooked meals and is content to stay at home by the fire. In North Africa, it's De Carlo, a sexy, voluptuous woman with whom he does the hot spots, dancing through the exotic nights. (On his ship, Guinness keeps a revolving picture frame that has a photo of Johnson on one side and De Carlo on the other!) In flashback, we watch as Guinness manages to have the best of both worlds, while his chief officer, Goldner, slavishly admires this grand deception and seeks to emulate his captain.

Suspense is sustained throughout THE CAPTAIN'S PARADISE because as the film opens Guinness is about to be shot by a firing squad and the viewer does not become privy to his fate until the very surprising ending. In between, the scheming captain is undone by the women in his life. Guinness's life goes topsy-turvy when Johnson insists on seeking adventure and excitement, while De Carlo suddenly takes up cooking, tiring of night life and desiring domestic tranquility. When Guinness resists these disturbing transformations both women leave him.

Guinness gives a masterful performance, and Johnson and De Carlo are superb in their unpredictable parts. The pace is vigorous under Kimmins's direction, and he manages to relate the subtle and frivolous story with verve, his transitions from scene to scene as smooth as Guinness's own incomparable style. A generous serving of delicious whimsy.

CAR WASH

1976 97m c Comedy   ★★★
Universal (U.S.)   PG

Franklyn Ajaye *(T.C.)*, Sully Boyar *(Mr. B.)*, Richard Brestoff *(Irwin)*, George Carlin *(Taxi Driver)*, Irwin Corey *(Mad Bomber)*, Ivan Dixon *(Lonnie)*, Bill Duke *(Duane)*, Antonio Fargas *(Lindy)*, Michael Fennell *(Calvin)*, Arthur French *(Charlie)*

p, Art Linson, Gary Stromberg; d, Michael Schultz; w, Joel Schumacher; ph, Frank Stanley; ed, Christopher Holmes; m, Norman Whitfield; art d, Robert Clatworthy; cos, Daniel Paredes

Coarse, hilarious comedy detailing a day in the life of an L.A. car wash, featuring an ensemble cast of superb performers. Basically plotless, the film shows the lives, hopes, dreams, ambitions, and foibles of the multiracial employees and customers of Boyar's Car Wash. One of many highlights has Richard Pryor as a fancy-pants preacher who arrives in his flashy car accompanied by the Pointer Sisters. Great musical score by Whitfield is integrated into the movement of the

scenes to give the film a funky rhythm. Director Schultz, one of the first mainstream Black filmmakers, also helmed the spirited inner-city comedy COOLEY HIGH. You won't sit still.

CARAVAGGIO

1986 93m c Biography   ★★★½
British Film Institute/Channel 4 (U.K.)   /18

Nigel Terry *(Caravaggio)*, Sean Bean *(Ranuccio Thomasoni)*, Garry Cooper *(Davide)*, Spencer Leigh *(Jerusaleme)*, Tilda Swinton *(Lena)*, Michael Gough *(Cardinal Del Monte)*, Nigel Davenport *(Marchese Giustiniani)*, Robbie Coltrane *(Cardinal Borghese)*, Jonathan Hyde *(Baglione)*, Dexter Fletcher *(Young Caravaggio)*

p, Sarah Radclyffe; d, Derek Jarman; w, Derek Jarman; ph, Gabriel Beristain; ed, George Akers; m, Simon Fisher Turner, Mary Phillips; prod d, Christopher Hobbs; cos, Sandy Powell

Marrying a painterly aesthetic with a defiantly homosexual sensibility, this ironic biopic is probably the most accessible film of avant-garde British director Derek Jarman (LAST OF ENGLAND, EDWARD II). A fanciful reconstruction of the life of the late Rennaisance master (about which almost nothing is known), CARAVAGGIO dramatizes the painter's need for patronage, his religious beliefs, and his sexuality. Noting Caravaggio's unusually muscle-bound depictions of St. John, Jarman posits a sexual relationship between the painter (Nigel Terry) and Ranuccio Thomasoni (Sean Bean), a street thug who served as his model; Ranuccio's mistress (Tilda Swinton) stands in for Mary Magdalene and the Blessed Virgin in filmic facsimiles of some of the painter's best-known canvasses. Curiously, though Jarman undercuts narrative conventions through his use of obvious anachronisms—typewriters, motorbikes, etc.—the film reiterates one of the oldest cliches of Hollywood biopics (LUST FOR LIFE, MOULIN ROUGE); i.e., that art is little more than immediately recorded experience, "life" thrown directly onto the canvas; the *process* of artistic creation is completely glossed over.

Jarman, a tireless advocate of gay rights, died of AIDS in 1994 at the age of 52. Ironically, while his best work remained unseen outside of festival showings, his influence was profound in the realm of music video. REM's award-winning "Losing My Religion" and Nirvana's "Heart Shaped Box," for example, both draw heavily on THE GARDEN's pastoral and Christian imagery.

CARLITO'S WAY

1993 141m c Crime/Drama   ★★★
Epic Productions/Martin Bregman Productions (U.S.)   R/18

Al Pacino *(Carlito Brigante)*, Sean Penn *(David Kleinfeld)*, Penelope Ann Miller *(Gail)*, John Leguizamo *(Benny Blanco)*, Ingrid Rogers *(Steffie)*, Luis Guzman *(Pachanga)*, James Rebhorn *(Norwalk)*, Joseph Siravo *(Vinnie Taglialucci)*, Viggo Mortensen *(Lalin)*, Richard Foronjy *(Pete Amadesso)*

p, Martin Bregman, Willi Baer, Michael Scott Bregman; d, Brian De Palma; w, David Koepp (from the novels *Carlito's Way* and *After Hours* by Edwin Torres); ph, Stephen H. Burum; ed, Bill Pankow, Kristina Boden; m, Patrick Doyle; prod d, Richard Sylbert; art d, Gregory Bolton; fx, Steven Kirshoff, Pacific Data Images, The Effects House; chor, Jeffrey Hornaday, Debbie Benitez; cos, Aude Bronson-Howard

After the costly, clumsy debacle of BONFIRE OF THE VANITIES and the addled psychosis of RAISING CAIN, Brian De Palma engineered something of a recovery with CARLITO'S WAY, a colorful melodrama set in the Latino mob world of the mid-1970s.

The director is in good company here. Al Pacino gives an urgent, bravura performance as the title character, a former drug boss who's had a lengthy prison sentence cut short thanks to a legal technicality, and now wants to go straight—really. Sean Penn is superbly nerdy as David Kleinfeld, the lawyer who freed Carlito, but whose greed ultimately leads to his and his client's undoing. Standouts among the classy ensemble are John Leguizamo (SUPER MARIO BROS.), as a brutal young hood on his way up through the ranks, and Luis Guzman (Q & A), as Carlito's trusted sidekick.

CARLITO'S WAY has its slow moments (any scenes with the anemic Penelope Ann Miller, who plays Carlito's girlfriend), and its plot weaknesses (we can't quite believe Carlito would be so loyal to

Kleinfeld, who is so transparently devious). But these are far outweighed by the great cast; the lovingly detailed recreation of disco-era New York (the soundtrack, ranging from "Oye Como Va" to "Disco Inferno," was compiled by Jellybean Benitez); the street poetry that slurs its way so convincingly out of Pacino's mouth; and, most of all, some classic De Palma action sequences. For the heart-stopping scenes in the poolroom and at Grand Central Station, the director can be forgiven anything—even BONFIRE OF THE VANITIES.

CARMEN

1983 102m c Drama/Dance/Musical	★★★½
Orion (Spain)	R/15

Antonio Gades *(Antonio)*, Laura del Sol *(Carmen)*, Paco de Lucia *(Paco)*, Christina Hoyos *(Cristina)*, Juan Antonio Jimenez *(Juan)*, Sebastian Moreno *(Escamillo)*, Jose Yepes *(Pepe Giron)*, Pepa Flores *(Pepa Flores)*

p, Emiliano Piedra; d, Carlos Saura; w, Carlos Saura, Antonio Gades (from the opera by Georges Bizet, based on the novel by Prosper Merimee); ph, Teo Escamilla; ed, Pedro del Rey; m, Paco de Lucia, Georges Bizet; chor, Carlos Saura, Antonio Gades; cos, Teresa Nieto

AAN Best Foreign Language Film

This version of the Merimee classic uses rehearsals for a flamenco version of Bizet's opera (not unlike director Saura's previous BLOOD WEDDING) as the setting for an identical, parallel storyline.

Laura del Sol (THE HIT) plays Carmen, a fiery actress-dancer who is slated to play her namesake despite her lack of experience. Antonio Gades (BLOOD WEDDING) is the choreographer who falls in love with her. The dance sequences are superb, as expected, with the added plus of del Sol's eroticism and Christina Hoyos's explosive performance as Carmen's rival. Saura's acclaimed dance trilogy (the third film is EL AMOR BRUJO), abetted by Antonio Gades's incendiary choreography, are must-sees for dance enthusiasts. Others may greet CARMEN with mixed emotions. But meanwhile, what other version measures up?

CARMEN JONES

1954 105m c Opera	★★★
Fox (U.S.)	

Dorothy Dandridge *(Carmen)*, Harry Belafonte *(Joe)*, Olga James *(Cindy Lou)*, Pearl Bailey *(Frankie)*, Diahann Carroll *(Myrt)*, Roy E. Glenn Sr. *(Rum)*, Nick Stewart *(Dink)*, Joe Adams *(Husky Miller)*, Brock Peters *(Sgt. Brown)*, Sandy Lewis *(T-Bone)*

p, Otto Preminger; d, Otto Preminger; w, Harry Kleiner (based on the book by Oscar Hammerstein II); ph, Sam Leavitt; ed, Louis Loeffler; m, Georges Bizet

AAN Best Actress: Dorothy Dandridge; AAN Best Score: Herschel Burke Gilbert

Intermittently successful updating of Bizet's "Carmen" with an all-black cast. Preminger's heavy-handed adaptation of a Broadway triumph combines gorgeous music with risible lyrics by Oscar Hammerstein II; the project is saved by a terrific cast.

Dandridge is a revelation. Even mouthing Marilyn Horne's vocals (not that Dandridge wasn't an accomplished singer; following a brief retirement in the late 1940s, her career was rekindled by a smash engagement at the posh Mocambo nightclub), she is chilling and exactly right, projecting psychological transitions and reflecting clearly the sequences of her thoughts. She's almost matched by Belafonte, and both leads are mesmerizingly beautiful. Considering the waste of Dandridge's career, it is heartening that CARMEN JONES exists as a testament to her beauty and singular talent. She died from a barbiturate overdose in 1965 at age 41.

CARNAL KNOWLEDGE

1971 97m c Drama	★★★½
Avco Embassy (U.S.)	R/X

Jack Nicholson *(Jonathan)*, Candice Bergen *(Susan)*, Art Garfunkel *(Sandy)*, Ann-Margret *(Bobbie)*, Rita Moreno *(Louise)*, Cynthia O'Neal *(Cindy)*, Carol Kane *(Jennifer)*

p, Mike Nichols; d, Mike Nichols; w, Jules Feiffer; ph, Giuseppe Rotunno; ed, Sam O'Steen; prod d, Richard Sylbert; art d, Robert Luthardt; cos, Anthea Sylbert

AAN Best Supporting Actress: Ann-Margret

Deeply felt, somewhat dated critique of middle-class sexual politics, and one of the better films of formerly interesting director Mike Nichols. Jules Feiffer's script is an uneasy, confessional work rooted in the regret and confusion experienced by his generation of Americans—men who reached middle age at a time when the rules governing male-female relationships were undergoing radical change.

The film follows college roommates (Jack Nicholson and Art Garfunkel) from youth through embittered middle age. Nicholson is a manipulative misogynist, apparently incapable of emotional intimacy; Garfunkel is his less confident, more sensitive chum. In the opening segment, set in the 1940s, the two compete for the affections of bewildered coed Candice Bergen. Ten years later, Garfunkel is a bored suburban husband; Nicholson is wrangling with his mistress (Ann-Margret), who senses his contempt for her but still dreams of domesticity. The final segment shows the aging friends, now accompanied by Moreno and Kane (in her debut), attempting to cope with the unfamiliar values of the late 1960s.

Nicholson's performance here did much to consolidate his stardom, while Ann-Margret, previously wasted as a campy sex kitten, used a meaty role to establish herself as a serious actress. An uneven but unusually thoughtful melodrama, CARNAL KNOWLEDGE avoids most of the the trendy excesses that make some other films of its era so difficult to watch today.

CARO DIARIO

1994 100m c Comedy /Drama	★★★
Sacher Film/Banfilm/La Sept/Le Studio Canal Plus (Italy/France)	/15

Nanni Moretti *(Himself)*, Giovanna Bozzolo *(Actress in Italian Film)*, Sebastiano Nardone *(Actor in Italian Film)*, Antonio Petrocelli *(Actor in Italian Film)*, Giulio Base *(Car Driver)*, Italo Spinelli *(On the Wall at Spinaceto)*, Jennifer Beals *(Herself)*, Alexandre Rockwell *(Himself)*, Carlo Mazzacurati *(Film Critic)*, Renato Carpentieri *(Gerardo)*

p, Angelo Barbagallo, Nanni Moretti, Nella Banfi; d, Nanni Moretti; w, Nanni Moretti; ph, Giuseppe Lanci; ed, Mirco Garrone; prod d, Marta Maffucci; cos, Maria Rita Barbera

Unashamedly introspective and unexpectedly poignant, Nanni Moretti's three-part comedy uses a cinematic diary format to explore his beloved homeland and the recesses of his own personality. As himself, Moretti joyrides around Rome on his Vespa, opining about architecture, cinema, and social change; battles writer's block by taking a trip with a scholar pal, Gerardo (Renato Carpentieri); and seeks a cure for a skin rash that is misdiagnosed and mistreated by a staggering number of physicians.

CARO DIARIO (which translates as "Dear Diary") lulls viewers into expecting a light-hearted entertainment, then veers unexpectedly into darker territory with the third segment; the change in tone is so abrupt that it almost feels like a betrayal. Ultimately, however, it's the medical episode that redeems the film. Moretti's exploration of his personal obsessions isn't quite as fascinating as he seems to believe, but his sudden transformation from self-involved artiste to terrified Everyman brings his sympathetic qualities to the fore. Charting a life in transit and barely sidestepping a tragic journey's end, CARO DIARIO proves that you never really know people until you travel with them.

CAROUSEL

1956 128m c Musical	★★★★
Fox (U.S.)	/U

Gordon MacRae *(Billy)*, Shirley Jones *(Julie)*, Cameron Mitchell *(Jigger)*, Barbara Ruick *(Carrie)*, Claramae Turner *(Cousin Nettie)*, Robert Rounseville *(Mr. Snow)*, Gene Lockhart *(Starkeeper)*, Audrey Christie *(Mrs. Mullin)*, Susan Luckey *(Louise)*, William Le Massena *(Heavenly Friend)*

p, Henry Ephron; d, Henry King; w, Phoebe Ephron, Henry Ephron (based on the musical by Richard Rodgers, Oscar Hammerstein II, from the play "Liliom" by Ferenc Molnar); ph, Charles Clarke; ed, William Reynolds; chor, Rod Alexander, Agnes De Mille; cos, Mary Wills

Haunting and poignant; the best of Rodgers and Hammerstein, sans the corn and cotton candy fluff of other works. This remake of the famous stage play and the Fritz Lang and Frank Borzage-directed adaptations of LILIOM emerges as a wonderful and touching fantasy.

It begins with MacRae as a spirit in Heaven who begs the starkeeper for a visit back to Earth to help his teenage daughter understand his death and prepare her for high-school graduation. Seen in flashback, carny barker MacRae, a brash, dishonest young man living in a New England fishing village (changed from Ferenc Molnar's original Budapest setting), falls in love with a mill worker, Jones. They marry, but MacRae's inability to find a job leads him into the bad company of Mitchell and an attempted robbery in which MacRae is killed by Mitchell after having second thoughts and trying to stop the thief.

This sadly resigned fantasy, a commercial failure upon its original release, features some of the greatest musical numbers ever filmed, all R&H classics: "If I Loved You," "What's the Use of Wondrin'?" and the stirring "You'll Never Walk Alone." Jones is lovely and heartfelt as the trusting lover, and MacRae is magnetic in his best musical performance, his fine tenor given a range equalled only in OKLAHOMA! Mitchell and other supporting players are excellent in this richly mounted extravaganza that is superb on all technical points and directed with verve and affection by King.

CARRIE
1976 97m c Horror   ★★★½
UA (U.S.)   R/18

Sissy Spacek (Carrie White), Piper Laurie (Margaret White), Amy Irving (Sue Snell), William Katt (Tommy Ross), John Travolta (Billy Nolan), Nancy Allen (Chris Hargenson), Betty Buckley (Miss Collins), P.J. Soles (Norma Watson), Sydney Lassick (Mr. Fromm), Stefan Gierasch (Principal Morton)

p, Paul Monash; d, Brian De Palma; w, Larry Cohen (based on the novel by Stephen King); ph, Mario Tosi; ed, Paul Hirsch; m, Pino Donaggio; art d, William Kenny, Jack Fisk; fx, Greg Auer, Ken Pepiot; cos, Rosanna Norton

AAN Best Actress: Sissy Spacek; AAN Best Supporting Actress: Piper Laurie

A telekinetic revenge. De Palma's first big hit remains one of his best efforts to date and a landmark film for the horror genre. Spacek, in a stunning performance, stars as Carrie, a troubled, sexually repressed high schooler who slowly realizes that she possesses incredible telekinetic powers. Plagued with problems in school (she feels homely, and nobody likes her) and at home (her mother, Laurie—whose performance is delightfully over the top—is a religious fanatic who hates men and makes her daughter pray in a closet), she struggles to maintain her dignity and sanity. She's finally driven over the edge when cruel classmates conspire to elect her prom queen in an elaborate joke designed to embarrass her.

Based on the best-selling Stephen King novel and cleverly designed to target a teenage audience, CARRIE was the synthesis of De Palma's talent for intense, stylish, visual filmmaking. His techniques—elaborate compositions, daring camera moves, and slow motion—combined with a fairly literate screenplay, make for an interesting and frightening film that successfully deals with the inner rage every teenager feels. The film has a strikingly unsettling mood that enhances its power and gives it an impact that the story would otherwise lack. Much of the credit, though, must go to Spacek, who so convincingly portrays Carrie's pain and her longing for acceptance. The talented ensemble inludes Betty Buckley, Amy Irving, Nancy Allen, and John Travolta.

CARRINGTON
1995 122m c Biography/Historical/Romance   ★★★
PolyGram/Freeway Productions/Shedlo Productions/Dora   R/18
Productions Ltd./Cinea & Orsans/Le Studio Canal Plus/Euston
Films Ltd./European Co-production Fund   (U.K./France)

Emma Thompson (Dora Carrington), Jonathan Pryce (Lytton Strachey), Steven Waddington (Ralph Partridge), Samuel West (Gerald Brenan), Rufus Sewell (Mark Gertler), Penelope Wilton (Lady Ottoline Morrell), Janet McTeer (Vanessa Bell), Peter Blythe (Phillip Morrell), Jeremy Northam (Beacus Penrose), Alex Kingston (Frances Partridge)

p, Ronald Shedlo, John McGrath; d, Christopher Hampton; w, Christopher Hampton (based on the book Lytton Strachey by Michael Holroyd); ph, Denis Lenoir; ed, George Akers; m, Michael Nyman; prod d, Caroline Amies; art d, Frank Walsh; cos, Penny Rose

Oscar-winning screenwriter Christopher Hampton (DANGEROUS LIAISONS) makes an promising debut with this ambitious, closely observed biopic of two notoriously eccentric members of the Bloomsbury group.

Dora Carrington (Emma Thompson) is a young painter who attracts the attention of flamboyant writer Lytton Strachey (Jonathan Pryce) when he initially mistakes her for a "ravishing boy." She is at first repulsed by the scruffy, caustic belletrist, a confirmed homosexual, but eventually the two become extremely close, forming a relationship that stops just short of sexual consummation. For a time, their singular liaison is the calm center of Bloomsbury's emotional tempest, but the incessant games of musical beds, together with her thwarted artistic ambitions, ultimately take a tragic toll on Dora.

Smarter than the average biopic and genuinely moving, this shrewd film deconstructs an obsessive relationship with remarkable sympathy. Viewers hoping for another high-toned, Anglophilic soap opera will be disappointed: Hampton's screenplay is as witty, self-conscious and unclubbable as its tragically hip protagonists. Thompson's neurasthenic mannerisms, which usually drive us batty, are appropriate here; Pryce, who was honored as Best Actor at Cannes, is simply brilliant.

CARRY ON NURSE
1959 86m bw Comedy   ★★½
Anglo-Amalgamated   (U.K.)

Kenneth Connor (Bernie Bishop), Kenneth Williams (Oliver Reckitt), Charles Hawtrey (Hinton), Terence Longdon (Ted York), Bill Owen (Percy Hickson), Leslie Phillips (Jack Bell), Cyril Chamberlain (Bert Able), Brian Oulton (Henry Bray), Wilfrid Hyde-White (Colonel), Hattie Jacques (Matron)

p, Peter Rogers; d, Gerald Thomas; w, Norman Hudis (based on the play "Ring for Catty" by Patrick Cargill and Jack Beale); ph, Reginald Wyer; ed, John Shirley; m, Bruce Montgomery

The second and perhaps best entry in the seeemingly endless "Carry On" series has no real plot, just every cliche and old hospital joke imaginable in this romp through a men's surgical ward. You can see the jokes coming a mile off, and if they still make you laugh, you may want to check out CARRY ON SERGEANT, CARRY ON CABBY, CARRY ON SPYING, and CARRY ON CAMPING.

CARS THAT ATE PARIS, THE
1974 91m c Adventure/Comedy   ★★
Salt-Pan (Australia)   /X

Terry Camilleri (Arthur), John Meillon (Mayor), Melissa Jaffa (Beth), Kevin Miles (Dr. Midland), Max Gillies (Metcalfe), Peter Armstrong (Gorman), Edward Howell (Tringham), Bruce Spence (Charlie), Derek Barnes (Al Smedley), Charles Metcalfe (Clive Smedley)

p, Jim McElroy, Howard McElroy; d, Peter Weir; w, Peter Weir, Keith Gow, Piers Davies; ph, John McLean; ed, Wayne LeClos; m, Bruce Smeaton

Scattered, but typically overrated now that the director is a force to be reckoned with. Weir marked his feature debut with a black comedy that now supposedly anticipates THE ROAD WARRIOR with themes culled from THE WILD ONE and HIGH NOON. Spiked wrecks are driven by adventurous youths through the streets of Paris, Australia, causing an endless string of accidents. These collisions are planned events that serve the vulturous townsfolk in both an economic and medical way. The looters profit by pawning what they can recover, and a town doctor performs questionable medical experiments on the victims. The situation culminates in a youth-townsfolk blood bath. It's a big, wide, wonderful world. Whatever.

CASABLANCA

1942 102m bw Drama/War ★★★★★
Warner Bros. (U.S.) /U

Humphrey Bogart (Richard "Rick" Blaine), Ingrid Bergman (Ilsa Lund Laszlo), Paul Henreid (Victor Laszlo), Claude Rains (Capt. Louis Renault), Conrad Veidt (Maj. Heinrich Strasser), Sydney Greenstreet (Senor Ferrari), Peter Lorre (Ugarte), S.Z. Sakall (Carl, Headwaiter), Madeleine LeBeau (Yvonne), Dooley Wilson (Sam)

p, Hal B. Wallis; d, Michael Curtiz; w, Julius J. Epstein, Philip G. Epstein, Howard Koch (based on the play Everybody Goes to Rick's by Murray Burnett and Joan Alison); ph, Arthur Edeson; ed, Owen Marks; m, Max Steiner; art d, Carl Jules Weyl; fx, Lawrence Butler, Willard Van Enger; cos, Orry-Kelly

AA Best Picture; AAN Best Actor: Humphrey Bogart; AAN Best Supporting Actor: Claude Rains; AA Best Director: Michael Curtiz; AA Best Screenplay: Julius J. Epstein, Philip G. Epstein, Howard Koch; AAN Best Cinematography: Arthur Edeson; AAN Best Editing: Owen Marks; AAN Best Score: Max Steiner

The most romantic picture ever made? The best film to come out of a Hollywood studio ever? More an icon than a work of art, CASAB-LANCA is still thoroughly entertaining romantic melodrama, flawlessly directed, subtly played, lovingly evoking our collective daydreams about lost chances and lost loves and love versus honor; everything about CASABLANCA is just right—it seems to have been filmed under a lucky star.

The familiar plot concerns expatriate American Rick Blaine (Humphrey Bogart), a cynical nightclub owner in Casablanca who discovers that his ex-lover, Ilsa (Ingrid Bergman), who abandoned him years before, has arrived in Casablanca with her husband, Resistance leader Victor Laszlo (Paul Henreid). With the Germans on Victor's trail, Ilsa comes to Casablanca to beg Rick for the precious letters of transit that have come into his possession. The documents would allow Victor to escape Casablanca and continue the fight against fascism.

Since its November 1942 release, CASABLANCA has been the movie, one that perfectly blends a turbulent love story with harrowing intrigue, heroic and evil characters, and the kind of genuine sentiment that makes the heart grow fonder with each viewing. Even upon its initial release, the film appealed to nostalgia for the vanishing, romanticized world between the two great wars, a cafe society crushed by fascism, a civilized, urbane generation in white linen suits, spectator shoes, and wide-brimmed sunhats desperately clinging to values no longer cherished.

Given its turbulent production history—the script was being rewritten almost on a daily basis—CASABLANCA was also most fortunate on all levels. The original leads were to have been Ronald Reagan, Ann Sheridan and Dennis Morgan. Other casting packages included George Raft, Hedy Lamarr and Herbert Marshall. And Lena Horne or Ella Fitzgerald might have crooned "As Time Goes By" instead of Dooley Wilson. Chemistry, that indefinable element, was surely carefully considered by veteran director Michael Curtiz.

So was timing. The film opened on Thanksgiving Day, 1942 at the Hollywood Theater in New York, three weeks after the Allies had landed at Casablanca, and further enjoyed widespread publicity generated by the Casablanca Conference two months later, when the eyes of the free world focused upon its leaders' meeting in the Moroccan city. It propelled Bogart's star to new heights, adding a romantic component to his world-weary persona, and gave Bergman a tragic edge to blend with her healthy radiance, making her seem complex and emotionally fragile. The film received eight Academy Award nominations and won three: Best Picture, Best Screenplay and Best Director.

CASINO

1995 182m c Drama/Crime ★★★
Syalis D.A./Legende Enterprises/Universal (U.S.) R/18

Robert De Niro (Sam "Ace" Rothstein), Sharon Stone (Ginger McKenna), Joe Pesci (Nicky Santoro), James Woods (Lester Diamond), Don Rickles (Billy Sherbert), Alan King (Andy Stone), Kevin Pollak (Phillip Green), L.Q. Jones (Pat Webb), Dick Smothers (Senator), Frank Vincent (Frank Marino)

p, Barbara De Fina; d, Martin Scorsese; w, Nicholas Pileggi, Martin Scorsese (based on the book by Nicholas Pileggi); ph, Robert Richardson; ed, Thelma Schoonmaker; prod d, Dante Ferretti; art d, Jack G. Taylor Jr.; fx, Paul Lombardi, Craig Barron, The Effects House, NY, Matte World Digital; cos, Rita Ryack, John Dunn

AAN Best Actress: Sharon Stone

Martin Scorsese returns to the gangster milieu of GOODFELLAS, and the result is an accomplished film that carries with it the unshakable feeling that we've seen it all before.

Ace Rothstein (Robert De Niro) is a scientific gambler. Looking to get their piece of booming 1960s Las Vegas, the Kansas City Mafia installs him as manager of the Tangiers, where he lives up to his respectful but unaffectionate nickname, "The Golden Jew." The film's first third is a celebration of pre-theme park Vegas, the money-making machine and morality car wash, where the cash flow never dries up and acts that would be criminal anywhere else are the coin of the realm. The serpent in this tawdry Garden of Eden soon appears in the form of Ace's old friend Nicky Santoro (Joe Pesci), who begins busting heads and drawing unwanted attention to the Mafia's pervasive presence. The third point of an ultimately deadly triangle is Ginger McKenna (Sharon Stone) a hooker with a heart of, well . . . stone.

There's nothing really wrong with CASINO. In fact, there are lots of things right with it: the city in the desert has seldom looked so thrillingly sleazy (the grotesquerie of '70s fashions is a delightfully horrifying bonus), and the story delivers its old-fashioned moral (you reap what you sow) with such delirious viciousness that you almost forget what a dreary cliche it is.

Nevertheless, CASINO feels disturbingly predictable, a meticulous and coldly proficient going-over of familiar ground. After MEAN STREETS, GOODFELLAS, THE GODFATHER and countless other examinations of Mafia mores and morals, we don't need to be reminded that the mob-run gambling industry is a microcosm of American capitalism at its most rapacious. We know, we know.

CASINO ROYALE

1967 131m c Adventure/Comedy/Spy ★★
Columbia (U.K.) /PG

Peter Sellers (Evelyn Tremble), Ursula Andress (Vesper Lynd), David Niven (Sir James Bond), Orson Welles (Le Chiffre), Joanna Pettet (Mata Bond), Daliah Lavi (The Detainer), Woody Allen (Jimmy Bond, Dr. Noah), Deborah Kerr (Agent Mimi, Lady Fiona McTarry), William Holden (Ransome), Charles Boyer (Le Grand)

p, Charles K. Feldman, Jerry Bresler; d, John Huston, Ken Hughes, Robert Parrish, Val Guest, Joseph McGrath; w, Wolf Mankowitz, John Law, Michael Sayers, Billy Wilder, Val Guest, Joseph Heller, Ben Hecht, Terry Southern (from the novel by Ian Fleming); ph, John Wilcox, Jack Hildyard, Nicolas Roeg; ed, Bill Lenny; m, Burt Bacharach; art d, John Howell, Ivor Beddoes, Lionel Couch; chor, Tutte Lemkow

AAN Best Song: Burt Bacharach (Music), Hal David (Lyrics)

A mess. CASINO ROYALE is two hours and eleven minutes of non sequitur. David Niven is Sir James Bond. (Author Ian Fleming, a close friend of Niven, always wanted Niven to assay his famous creation.) He's retired, middle-aged, bejowled, and tired. SMERSH is up to no good, so Niven is asked to help when M (John Huston) is slain. He contacts several agents, all of them 007s. These include Andress, Sellers, Terence Cooper, and Pettet (who is Niven's daughter, the result of a liaison with Mata Hari). After more witless, star-loaded vignettes, Niven finally learns that the real villain is none other than his own ineffectual nephew, Woody Allen.

CASINO ROYALE first found life as a one-hour TV show for CBS's "Climax" in 1954, starring Barry Nelson. The film rights were sold in 1955 and eventually acquired by ex-agent Charles Feldman. Almost every actor yukked it up while making this movie, and the result is totally unfocused. Anything with five directors and screenwriters has to rank on anyone's list for sheer chutzpah.

CASUALTIES OF WAR

1989 120m c War ★★★
Columbia (U.S.) R/18

Michael J. Fox (Pfc. Eriksson), Sean Penn (Sgt. Meserve), Don Harvey (Clark), John C. Reilly (Hatcher), John Leguizamo (Diaz), Thuy Thu Le (Oahn), Erik King (Brown, Radio Man), Jack Gwaltney (Rowan), Ving Rhames (Lt. Reilly), Dan Martin (Hawthorne)

p, Art Linson, Fred Caruso; d, Brian De Palma; w, David Rabe (based on the article by Daniel Lang); ph, Stephen H. Burum; ed, Bill Pankow; m, Ennio Morricone; prod d, Wolf Kroeger; art d, Bernard Hydes; cos, Richard Bruno

With this adaptation of Daniel Lang's famous *New Yorker* article, Brian De Palma joins the ranks of Stanley Kubrick, Francis Ford Coppola and Oliver Stone, major directors who have brought their personal visions and styles to bear on the Vietnam War. The result is often hypnotic and perversely gripping, but falls apart during its final reel.

CASUALTIES OF WAR focuses on one patrol, and the inhumane treatment of a young Vietnamese girl at the hands of a calloused, crazed sergeant. Top acting honors go to Penn as the sergeant and Thuy Thu Le as the captive girl. Fox isn't bad at all; one just gets the feeling that the director and screenwriter got caught up in the dramatic situations inherent in the Penn-Thu Le conflict, and left their hero to flounder as best he could. Because Fox is so extraordinarily clean-cut, he seems more than human. This part needed a really average Joe, but one with enough feel of physical gravity to counteract Penn. Fox ends up a mere flyspeck tossed about in a violent whorl of confusion.

CAT AND THE CANARY, THE

1939 72m bw Comedy/Mystery ★★★
Paramount (U.S.) /A

Bob Hope (Wallie Campbell), Paulette Goddard (Joyce Norman), John Beal (Fred Blythe), Douglass Montgomery (Charlie Wilder), Gale Sondergaard (Miss Lu), Elizabeth Patterson (Aunt Susan), Nydia Westman (Cicily), George Zucco (Lawyer Crosby), John Wray (Hendricks), George Regas

p, Arthur Hornblow Jr.; d, Elliott Nugent; w, Walter DeLeon, Lynn Starling (based on the play by John Willard); ph, Charles Lang; ed, Archie Marshek; m, Ernst Toch; art d, Hans Dreier, Robert Usher

The old dark house number, played to the hilt. When an eccentric millionaire dies, lawyer Zucco assembles prospective heirs at the victim's Bayou mansion. Goddard gets all, setting up Hope as straight man for this spooky comic romp. Hope is terrific as the wisecracking but spineless character who attempts to protect Goddard from going insane (if she turns cuckoo she loses the fortune, according to the bizarre will). Director Nugent, who had guided Hope through NEVER SAY DIE and GIVE ME A SAILOR, does a great job in presenting some spine-tingling moments: claw-like hands reach out for the heroine and everyone seems to disappear through swiveling bookcases, sliding doors, and false panels. Lang's camera work is properly moody and supporting player Sondergaard gives a high-camp performance as a spooky, mystic housekeeper dressed in black, with a black cat constantly at her side. This was Goddard's first starring role; following the success of this film, the sly actress with the insinuating voice was teamed with Hope again in THE GHOST BREAKERS.

CAT BALLOU

1965 97m c Comedy/Western ★★★½
Columbia (U.S.) /PG

Jane Fonda (Cat Ballou), Lee Marvin (Kid Shelleen/Tim Strawn), Michael Callan (Clay Boone), Dwayne Hickman (Jed), Tom Nardini (Jackson Two-Bears), John Marley (Frankie Ballou), Reginald Denny (Sir Harry Percival), Jay C. Flippen (Sheriff Cardigan), Arthur Hunnicutt (Butch Cassidy), Bruce Cabot (Sheriff Maledon)

p, Harold Hecht; d, Elliot Silverstein; w, Frank Pierson, Walter Newman (based on the novel by Roy Chanslor); ph, Jack Marta; ed, Charles Nelson; m, Frank DeVol; chor, Miriam Nelson; cos, Bill Thomas

AA Best Actor: Lee Marvin; *AAN Best Adapted Screenplay:* Walter Newman, Frank R. Pierson; *AAN Best Editing:* Charles Nelson; *AAN Best Score:* Frank DeVol; *AAN Best Song:* Jerry Livingston (Music), Mack David (Lyrics)

Funny—but not that funny—western spoof. Fonda employs over-the-hill gunslinger Marvin after his outlaw brother (Marvin again) kills her rancher father. Film is amusing largely due to Marvin's dual hilarity, for which he won an Oscar. It was the beginning of a whole new career as a versatile, middle-aged leading man who could handle drama or comedy with equal finesse. Following several misfires, BALLOU consolidated Fonda's early stardom; while hardly complex, her transformation from prim schoolmarm to sexy gunslinger is utterly charming. Additional diversion is provided by Nat King Cole (in his last film role) and Stubby Kaye, who, as wandering troubadors, break up the screenplay's occasional tedium.

CAT ON A HOT TIN ROOF

1958 108m c Drama ★★★★
MGM (U.S.) /15

Elizabeth Taylor (Maggie Pollitt), Paul Newman (Brick Pollitt), Burl Ives (Big Daddy Pollitt), Jack Carson (Gooper Pollitt), Judith Anderson (Big Mama Pollitt), Madeleine Sherwood (Mae Pollitt), Larry Gates (Dr. Baugh), Vaughn Taylor (Deacon Davis), Patty Ann Gerrity (Dixie Pollitt), Rusty Stevens (Sonny Pollitt)

p, Lawrence Weingarten; d, Richard Brooks; w, Richard Brooks, James Poe (based on the play by Tennessee Williams); ph, William Daniels; ed, Ferris Webster; art d, William A. Horning, Urie McCleary; fx, Lee LeBlanc; cos, Helen Rose

AAN Best Picture; AAN Best Actor: Paul Newman; *AAN Best Actress:* Elizabeth Taylor; *AAN Best Director:* Richard Brooks; *AAN Best Adapted Screenplay:* Richard Brooks, James Poe; *AAN Best Cinematography:* William H Daniels

A southern house divided between patriarchal dominance and hypocrisy, rendered effectively despite censorship and a screenplay that bogs midway. The performances are the thing in this film version of the Tennessee Williams stage triumph, led by Ives, repeating his stage role like a force of nature. Taylor and Newman make a handsomely unhappy husband and wife, with just enough sexual chemistry to justify the union. Mike Todd's plane crashed during filming, and the camera seems to capture Taylor's pent-up energy, but she isn't directed well enough to unleash it. This is fine throughout most of the film, but her catharsis is finally lacking and her little vengeances come off less like a satiated alley cat than a pampered prize kitty. The homosexual overtones are just about laundered out of Newman's role, but his pantherine eyes and profile suggest unplumbed depths between the lines. Jack Carson and Dame Judith Anderson are just right, and Madeleine Sherwood is absolutely definitive as Sister Woman.

CAT PEOPLE

1942 73m bw Horror ★★★★★
RKO (U.S.) /A

Simone Simon (Irena Dubrovna), Kent Smith (Oliver Reed), Tom Conway (Dr. Judd), Jane Randolph (Alice Moore), Jack Holt (Commodore), Alan Napier (Carver), Elizabeth Dunne (Miss Plunkett), Elizabeth Russell (The Cat Woman)

p, Val Lewton; d, Jacques Tourneur; w, DeWitt Bodeen; ph, Nicholas Musuraca; ed, Mark Robson; m, Roy Webb

Significant as the first of the literate, understated horror films Val Lewton produced for RKO in the 1940s, CAT PEOPLE is also notable for playing with audience imagination by refusing to show made-up movie monsters *a la* the Wolfman or Mr. Hyde. Although earlier films had linked horror and sexuality, Tourneur's study of a woman tainted by an ancient Balkan curse was arguably more explicit in this direction than any previous film had been. The result is a haunting and subtle film, filled with desires gone awry and everyday settings turned inexplicably nightmarish.

Immigrant sketch artist Irena Dubrovna (Simon) and all-American architect Oliver Reed (Smith) fall in love and marry after a brief courtship, but Irena won't consummate the union for fear that she will turn into a panther compelled to kill her lover. When Oliver confides in co-worker Alice Moore (Randolph) though, Irena's jealousy proves equally effective in precipitating her "transformation." The disbelief of cynical psychiatrist Dr. Judd (Conway) proves likewise ineffective against the powers unleashed by Irena's psyche.

Beautifully directed by Tourneur and carefully paced by screenwriter Bodeen, the film opens in mundane New York settings, only occasionally hinting that evil is about (e.g. a feline woman at a bar, the reaction of the animals at a pet store to Irena's presence). Once Irena's darker side begins to manifest itself, however, the film's pulse quickens and so does the viewer's. Perhaps most famous are the justly celebrated sequence where Irena stalks Alice along a park path at night (featuring the marvelously jarring cat-like hiss of bus doors) and the brilliant set-piece when Irena surrounds the terrified Alice at a darkened indoor swimming pool with the cries of a ferocious panther.

Superbly acted (with Simon evoking both pity and chills), CAT PEOPLE testifies to the power of suggestion and the priority of imagination over budget in the creation of great cinema. The film was Lewton's biggest hit, its viewers lured in by such bombastic advertising as "Kiss me and I'll claw you to death!"—a line more lurid than anything that ever appeared onscreen. Forty years later Paul Schrader would remake the original, failing to learn any of the lessons which Lewton had taught.

CATCH-22
1970 121m c War ★★½
Paramount (U.S.) R/15

Alan Arkin *(Capt. Yossarian)*, Martin Balsam *(Col. Cathcart)*, Richard Benjamin *(Maj. Danby)*, Art Garfunkel *(Capt. Nately)*, Jack Gilford *(Doc Daneeka)*, Bob Newhart *(Maj. Major)*, Anthony Perkins *(Chaplain Tappman)*, Paula Prentiss *(Nurse Duckett)*, Martin Sheen *(Lt. Dobbs)*, Jon Voight *(Milo Minderbinder)*

p, Martin Ransohoff, John Calley; d, Mike Nichols; w, Buck Henry (based on the novel by Joseph Heller); ph, David Watkin; ed, Sam O'Steen; prod d, Richard Sylbert; art d, Harold Michelson; fx, Lee Vasque; cos, Ernest Adler

This scathing condemnation of war is full of stumbles and rife with misfires. An intermittently interesting adaptation of Joseph Heller's caustic novel, this big-budget, all-star effort was a notorious flop in its day.

Set on a small island just off Italy, circa 1944, the film follows Captain Yossarian (Alan Arkin), an American bombardier who attempts to have himself grounded by claiming he's insane. Unfortunately, as Doc Daneeka (Jack Gilford) informs him, the paradoxical rule of "catch-22" prevents this, since anyone who voluntarily flies on air raids must be crazy, so asking to be grounded indicates that one is sane. As Yossarian becomes increasingly desperate, the inherent madness of the war intensifies.

This film wants to be bleak, nihilistic, and darkly hilarious but CATCH-22 emerges as an exercise in frustration for those unprepared for Nichols's episodic, detached, and surreal treatment of the novel. Like a nightmare, the film shifts from one bizarre episode to another, with Alan Arkin's dazed Yossarian reacting to the madness that surrounds him, but second only to the viewer.

CATERED AFFAIR, THE
1956 92m bw Drama ★★★★
MGM (U.S.)

Bette Davis *(Mrs. Tom Hurley)*, Ernest Borgnine *(Tom Hurley)*, Debbie Reynolds *(Jane Hurley)*, Barry Fitzgerald *(Uncle Jack Conlon)*, Rod Taylor *(Ralph Halloran)*, Robert F. Simon *(Mr. Halloran)*, Madge Kennedy *(Mrs. Halloran)*, Dorothy Stickney *(Mrs. Rafferty)*, Carol Veazie *(Mrs. Casey)*, Joan Camden *(Alice)*

p, Sam Zimbalist; d, Richard Brooks; w, Gore Vidal (based on the teleplay by Paddy Chayefsky); ph, John Alton; ed, Gene Ruggiero, Frank Santillo; m, Andre Previn; art d, Cedric Gibbons, Paul Groesse

Interesting misfire but eminently watchable, this one has divided amateur and pro critics alike. The adaptation by Vidal from Chayefsky's brilliant teleplay concerns a poor Bronx husband and wife wrangling over expenses for their beloved daughter's wedding. Following his triumph in another Chayefsky teleplay-to-screenplay effort, MARTY, the previous year, Borgnine acquits himself honorably as an Irish taxi driver. Davis indeed wrestles with the accent, but she's a mistress at tortured regret getting its own way; even stuck with the rattiest wiglet in showbiz history, when Davis cries on her bed, all our reservations melt away. Reynolds is very touching; it's quite nice to see her away from the sis-boom-bah roles, and a shame she didn't do so more often. But for Barry Fitzgerald, doing his tired old leprechaun bit ten years too late in this attempt at kitchen sink realism, we'd get out the horsewhip in a moment's notice, and we wouldn't spare the steed.

CAVALCADE
1933 110m bw Drama ★★★★
Fox (U.S.) /U

Diana Wynyard *(Jane Marryot)*, Clive Brook *(Robert Marryot)*, Herbert Mundin *(Alfred Bridges)*, Una O'Connor *(Ellen Bridges)*, Ursula Jeans *(Fanny Bridges)*, Beryl Mercer *(Cook)*, Irene Browne *(Margaret Harris)*, Merle Tottenham *(Annie)*, Frank Lawton *(Joe Marryot)*, John Warburton *(Edward Marryot)*

p, Winfield Sheehan; d, Frank Lloyd; w, Reginald Berkeley (based on the play by Noel Coward); ph, Ernest Palmer; ed, Margaret Clancy; fx, William Cameron Menzies

AA Best Picture; AAN Best Actress: Diana Wynyard; *AA Best Director:* Frank Lloyd; *AA Best Art Direction:* William S. Darling

A rare beauty. Noel Coward, in an atypically serious venture, traces 30 years of a British family's life. A big, fine production—little shown or remembered today—CAVALCADE was a sensation at the time of its release, filled as it is with a wistful look at a couple clinging together through years of love. The epochal scenes commence with the Boer War and go on to record the death of Queen Victoria, the sinking of the *Titanic*, WWI, and the birth of jazz. The film won Academy Awards for Best Picture and Best Director while Wynyard was nominated for Best Actress, but lost to Katharine Hepburn for MORNING GLORY.

CEDDO
1978 120m c Drama ★★
Sembene (Nigeria) /A

Tabara Ndiaye *(Princess Dior)*, Moutapha Yade *(Madir Fatim Fall)*, Ismaila Diagne *(The Kidnaper)*, Makoura Dia *(The King)*, Ousmane Sembene *(A Ceddo Renamed Ibrahima)*

d, Ousmane Sembene; w, Ousmane Sembene; ph, Georges Caristan; ed, Florence Eymon; m, Manu Dibango

In turn-of-the century Senegal, the local king becomes a convert to Islam and, under the influence of a Moslem adviser, disbands the little Catholic church in the village of the Ceddo. The people resist this change just as they resisted the Christian missionaries, going to the length of kidnapping the king's daughter. Most of the film consists of meetings between different factions and groups, all conducted according to ancient tribal customs. This film was banned in director Ousmane Sembene's native Senegal not because of its dim view of that country's conversion to Islam, but because the government insists that "Ceddo" is spelled with only one "d."

CELINE AND JULIE GO BOATING
(CELINE ET JULIE VONT EN BATEAU)

1974 193m c Comedy/Fantasy ★★★½
Losange/Films 7/Renn/Saga/Simar/V.M. /AA
/Action/Christian Fachner (France)

Juliet Berto *(Celine)*, Dominique Labourier *(Julie)*, Bulle Ogier *(Camille)*, Marie-France Pisier *(Sophie)*, Barbet Schroeder *(Olivier)*, Philippe Clevenot *(Guliou)*, Nathalie Asnar *(Madlyn)*

d, Jacques Rivette; w, Jacques Rivette, Eduardo de Gregorio, Juliet Berto, Dominique Labourier, Marie-France Pisier; ph, Jacques Renard, Michel Cenet; ed, Nicole Lubtchansky, Chris Tullio-Altan; m, Jean-Marie Senia

Jacques Rivette's CELINE AND JULIE GO BOATING is a witty salute to theater, female bonding, hallucinogenic candy, and those old stand-bys, fantasy and reality. Despite its three-hour-plus length and multi-layered narrative, the film has a devoted cult following, in part because of the surreal humor and delightful lead performances by Juliet Berto and Dominique Labourier.

Celine (Berto), a nightclub magician and fanciful storyteller, meets Julie (Labourier), a shy librarian, somewhere in a Parisian park. After a long game of cat and mouse that takes them through the city streets, Celine and Julie form a fast friendship and move into Julie's apartment, where the women take turns swapping each other's identities and exchanging tall tales. Celine tries to impress Julie with a strange story about a continuous drama taking place in an old, possibly abandoned mansion. Celine not only claims it's true, but that she is also a participant. In the story, two women, Sophie and Camille (Marie-France Pisier, Bulle Ogier), are desperately in love with a widower named Olivier (Barbet Schroeder), who promised his late wife that he would not remarry as long as his ailing young daughter, Madlyn (Nathalie Asnar), was alive. Celine is supposedly the child's nanny who tries to shield the girl from the tension in the house—and possibly murder.

Enigmatic, funny, and engrossing all at once, CELINE AND JULIE GO BOATING is one of Rivette's most playful films. His earlier films were often self-referential, pretentious messes that ran ridiculously long (OUT ONE/SPECTRE is 12 hours long). But, in CELINE AND JULIE, he found a way to temper his excesses, tweak viewer expectation, and toy with the theatrical fourth wall, all in one entertaining movie. It's certainly not always easy to sit through; Rivette's penchant for quirkiness wears thin, and he throws in nonsensical bits that seem geared to his own amusement. Many scenes go on way too long without any payoff, and the ending is abrupt and unsatisfying.

Still, CELINE AND JULIE succeeds at being both entertaining and unconventionally cerebral. Labourier and Berto have a great time playing giddy explorers who take off on a wild spree in the house of fiction, while Schroeder, Pisier, and Ogier hilariously parody dull melodrama with the straightest faces imaginable. Rivette encouraged improvisation and worked with the actors to create their own dialogue, resulting in some truly off-the-wall moments of slapstick humor.

CESAR

1936 117m bw Drama ★★★½
Pagnol (France)

Raimu *(Cesar Olivier)*, Pierre Fresnay *(Marius)*, Orane Demazis *(Fanny)*, Fernand Charpin *(Honore Panisse)*, Andre Fouche *(Cesariot)*, Alida Rouffe *(Honorine Cabinis)*, Milly Mathis *(Aunt Claudine Foulon)*, Robert Vattier *(M. Brun)*, Paul Dullac *(Felix Escartefigue)*, Maupi *(Chauffeur)*

p, Marcel Pagnol; d, Marcel Pagnol; w, Marcel Pagnol; ph, Willy; ed, Suzanne de Troeye, Jeanette Ginestet; m, Vincent Scotto; art d, Galibert

The third part of Marcel Pagnol's "Marseilles Trilogy," CESAR completes the story begun in MARIUS and continued in FANNY.

Cesariot (Andre Fouche) is the 18-year-old son of Marius (Pierre Fresnay) and Fanny (Orane Demazis), but his father disappeared before he was born and he believes the aging Panisse (Fernand Charpin), his stepfather, to be his biological parent. A priest begs Panisse to tell Cesariot about his real father, but he refuses. When Panisse dies, Fanny tells her son about his parentage and he is properly shocked to find that Cesar (Raimu), whom he had always thought to be his godfather, is actually his grandfather. The old man tells Cesariot about his father and where to find him.

Magnificent performances, particularly from Raimu, highlight this fine film—the only one of the three directed by the trilogy's writer and producer, Pagnol. The receptive audiences that made the previous installments such a success did the same for this one, and the fact that the lovers of the first two—Marius and Fanny—were finally reunited after 20 years didn't hurt the box office, either.

CESAR AND ROSALIE
(CESAR ET ROSALIE)

1972 110m c Comedy/Romance ★★★
Fildebroc/U.P.F./Mega/Paramount/Orion R/AA
(France/Italy/West Germany)

Yves Montand *(Cesar)*, Romy Schneider *(Rosalie)*, Sami Frey *(David)*, Umberto Orsini *(Antoine)*, Eva-Maria Meineke *(Lucie)*, Bernard Le Coq *(Michel)*, Gisela Hahn *(Carla)*, Isabelle Huppert *(Marite)*, Henri-Jacques Huet *(Marcel)*, Pippo Merisi *(Albert)*

p, Michelle de Broca; d, Claude Sautet; w, Jean-Loup Dabadie, Claude Sautet, Claude Neron; ph, Jean Boffety; ed, Jacqueline Thiedot; m, Philippe Sarde; art d, Pierre Guffroy; cos, Annalisa Nasilli-Rocca

CESAR AND ROSALIE is an upper-class French romance in which Montand, Schneider, and Frey are the three sides of a love triangle—an arrangement that seems tolerable to all three.

Montand, a likable scrap-metal dealer who lives life to the fullest, is in love with Schneider, who has a young daughter from a previous marriage. When family and friends gather for the wedding of Schneider's mother, an unexpected visitor arrives—Frey, Schneider's former lover, who disappeared from her life after breaking up her marriage. Frey's reappearance shakes Schneider, who still loves him, especially after he admits to Montand that he is still in love with her.

This intelligent and funny romance is directed with Sautet's usual inoffensiveness, especially his all-too-complacent view of bourgeois life. What makes the film (at the time, one of France's top money-makers) worth watching is the interplay among Montand, Schneider, and Frey—and the subtle attraction between Montand and Frey, two very diverse men bonded in their love for the same woman. In a supporting role is 17-year-old Isabelle Huppert, in one of her very first film appearances.

C'EST LA VIE

1990 110m c Drama ★★½
Samuel Goldwyn Company (France) /12

Nathalie Baye *(Lena)*, Richard Berry *(Michel)*, Zabou *(Bella)*, Jean-Pierre Bacri *(Leon)*, Vincent Lindon *(Jean-Claude)*, Valeria Bruni-Tedeschi *(Odette)*, Didier Benureau *(Ruffier)*, Julie Bataille *(Frederique)*, Candice Lefranc *(Sophie)*, Alexis Derlon *(Daniel)*

p, Alexander Arcady, Diane Kurys; d, Diane Kurys; w, Diane Kurys, Alain Le Henry; ph, Gui Feppe Lanci; m, Philippe Sarde

Set in 1958, C'EST LA VIE is the third installment, following the immensely popular PEPPERMINT SODA and ENTRE NOUS, of Diane Kurys' absorbing semi-autobiographical trilogy.

Having decided to divorce her husband Michel (Richard Berry), the beautiful Lena (Nathalie Baye) puts her two daughters on a train in Lyon bound for La Baule Les Pins for a seaside vacation. The summer proves an eventful one, with the girls learning all manner of lessons in living. Lena eventually joins her daughters and engages in what she thinks is a secret affair with a young artist, Leon (Jean-Pierre Bacri), though the children observe her dashing off into the night to meet him. The tranquility of their idyll is shattered by the unexpected arrival of their father.

No one can accuse Kurys of any real depth here; her strength as a director lies primarily in her sense of detail and in her ability to convey a nostalgic atmosphere. In its indolent sensuality and wealth of everyday observation, Kurys's work resembles some of the lighter, summery short stories of Colette. C'EST LA VIE is the merest trifle, but, given its sun-soaked ambience, the film is utterly painless and enjoyable.

Never more glamorous, Baye communicates a slightly neurotic, Jennifer Jones-like quality and makes an appealingly complex heroine. The scene where she first sees her lover on the beach and snakes her way through the cabanas to meet him is dizzyingly romantic. Bacri is properly sexy as Lena's lover, and Berry exudes the right amount of pained anguish as her husband.

Like Truffaut, Kurys has a precious, idealized view of children. They're all angelic, brilliant little paragons. The girls have a woman-in-a-child's-body beauty that is as much of a Gallic cliche as their huskily precocious voices are; the boys are budding artistic geniuses. Still, all of this sweetness and light leaves the viewer yearning for the youthful raunch and anarchy of a film like LIFE IS A LONG QUIET RIVER.

CHAMP, THE

1931 85m bw Sports   ★★★½
MGM (U.S.)   /PG

Wallace Beery *(Champ)*, Jackie Cooper *(Dink)*, Irene Rich *(Linda)*, Roscoe Ates *(Sponge)*, Edward Brophy *(Tim)*, Hale Hamilton *(Tony)*, Jesse Scott *(Jonah)*, Marcia Mae Jones *(Mary Lou)*

p, Harry Rapf; d, King Vidor; w, Leonard Praskins (based on a story by Frances Marion); ph, Gordon Avil; ed, Hugh Wynn

AAN Best Picture; AA Best Actor: Wallace Beery; *AAN Best Director:* King Vidor; *AA Best Original Story:* Frances Marion

Beery won an Oscar for his role as a down-at-heels ex-heavyweight boxing champion who trains for a comeback in Tijuana in between boozing and gambling, egged on by his pipe dreams and those of his young son (Cooper). When he wins some money, the "Champ" buys the boy a racehorse, but promptly loses it in a crap game. The boy's mother (Rich) and her wealthy husband (Hamilton) appear at the track where the boxer works and convince him that the boy would be better off with them. He reluctantly agrees, but the boy later sneaks back to his father's side in time to witness the older man's bout against a much younger opponent.

A famous tearjerker of its day, THE CHAMP is unabashed in its assault upon the audience's emotions. Cynics are advised to keep their distance, but in defense of this extremely sentimental film one should note the genuine rapport between Beery and Cooper and the quiet skill of director Vidor. A film with a lot of heart, unafraid to bare its emotions, THE CHAMP still plays well, its slightly gritty look more effective than the softness Franco Zeffirelli brought to the lesser 1979 remake.

CHAMPAGNE FOR CAESAR

1950 99m bw Comedy   ★★★★
UA (U.S.)   /U

Ronald Colman *(Beauregard Bottomley)*, Celeste Holm *(Flame O'Neil)*, Vincent Price *(Burnbridge Waters)*, Barbara Britton *(Gwenn Bottomley)*, Art Linkletter *(Happy Hogan)*, Gabriel Heatter, George Fisher *(Announcers)*, Byron Foulger *(Gerald)*, Ellye Marshall *(Frosty)*, Vici Raaf *(Waters's Secretary)*

p, George Moskov; d, Richard Whorf; w, Hans Jacoby, Fred Brady; ph, Paul Ivano; ed, Hugh Bennett; m, Dimitri Tiomkin; art d, George Van Marter

An unjustly neglected, extremely funny jab at the media empire and the world of big business. Beauregard Bottomley (Colman) is an unemployed genius who holds a Ph.D., skims the encyclopedia for enjoyment and never forgets a thing he's read. He applies for work at a soap company owned by Burnbridge Waters (Price) but is rebuffed by the suds magnate. Beauregard is so annoyed by the treatment he receives at Waters's hands that he decides to bankrupt the company by becoming a contestant on the popular radio quiz show it sponsors.

Broadly handled but squarely on-target in its satire of the media, CHAMPAGNE FOR CAESAR is nimbly helmed by director Whorf and benefits considerably from its talented cast. Colman's typically understated style meshes nicely with Holm's, and they provide an appropriate foil for Price's deliberate hamminess as the megalomaniacal mogul. Listen for Mel Blanc as the voice of the champagne-loving

parrot, Caesar. Denied a full run upon its initial release and broadcast on television in truncated form, this unexpected if modest delight is likely to halt your late-night channel surfing and leave you howling.

CHAMPION

1949 99m bw Sports   ★★★★½
Screen Plays (U.S.)   /A

Kirk Douglas *(Midge Kelly)*, Marilyn Maxwell *(Grace Diamond)*, Arthur Kennedy *(Connie Kelly)*, Paul Stewart *(Tommy Haley)*, Ruth Roman *(Emma Bryce)*, Lola Albright *(Mrs. Harris)*, Luis Van Rooten *(Jerome Harris)*, John Day *(Johnny Dunne)*, Harry Shannon *(Lew Bryce)*

p, Stanley Kramer; d, Mark Robson; w, Carl Foreman (based on the story by Ring Lardner); ph, Franz Planer; ed, Harry Gerstad; m, Dimitri Tiomkin

AAN Best Actor: Kirk Douglas; *AAN Best Supporting Actor:* Arthur Kennedy; *AAN Best Screenplay:* Carl Foreman; *AAN Best Cinematography:* Frank Planer; *AA Best Editing:* Harry Gerstad; *AAN Best Score:* Dimitri Tiomkin

Released two years after BODY AND SOUL and based on a Ring Lardner short story, CHAMPION is another truly great boxing film. Midge Kelly (Douglas) travels to California with his crippled brother Connie (Kennedy), hoping to buy a diner but ending up working there and falling for the owner's daughter, Emma (Roman), who becomes his shotgun bride. Soon Midge decides to put his boxing skills to use as a professional, and leaves Emma. Managed by Tommy Haley (Stewart), Midge rises through the middleweight ranks until he gets a title shot, which, true to boxing-film formula, he is supposed to throw but doesn't. Nonetheless, he becomes the crime syndicate's boy, growing more corrupt daily.

Douglas' riveting performance as the ruthless fighter earned him an Oscar nomination and made him an overnight sensation, and the gifted supporting cast offers a wide and appropriate variety of foils to the ambitious, amoral character he portrays. Robson's direction is all action, wasting no time in telling this compelling story, and Carl Foreman's script is sharply observant of the boxing milieu.

CHAN IS MISSING

1981 80m bw Crime   ★★★★
Wayne Wang Productions (U.S.)   /15

Wood Moy *(Jo)*, Marc Hayashi *(Steve)*, Laureen Chew *(Amy)*, Judi Nihei *(Lawyer)*, Peter Wang *(Henry, the Cook)*, Presco Tabios *(Presco)*, Frankie Alarcon *(Frankie)*, Ellen Yeung *(Mrs. Chan)*, Emily Yamasaki *(Jenny)*, George Woo *(George)*

p, Wayne Wang; d, Wayne Wang; w, Wayne Wang, Isaac Cronin, Terrel Seltzer; ph, Michael Chin; ed, Wayne Wang; m, Robert Kikuchi

A deliberately modest but genuine delight, full of wicked humor, suspenseful touches, and perceptive insights about the experiences of Chinese immigrants in America. Two San Francisco cab drivers (played by Moy and Hayashi) have their savings stolen by the elusive "Chan Hung" and spend the rest of the film tracking him down. Along the way the film potently considers the problems with the generation gap among Chinese-Americans and conflicts between those Chinese from the mother country and those born in America.

A fine, funny independent production filmed on a minuscule budget in San Francisco's Chinatown by Wayne Wang (DIM SUM and EAT A BOWL OF TEA), CHAN IS MISSING deservedly became a major art-house success. Its cleverness extends even to the film's title, with CHAN suggesting both Charlie Chan (and hence many of the stereotypes commonly held about the Chinese) and "CHinese-americAN".

CHAPLIN

1992 144m c/bw Biography/Drama   ★★½
Carolco/Le Studio Canal Plus/RCS Video/Lambeth   PG-13/12
Productions Ltd. (U.K./U.S.)

Robert Downey Jr. *(Charlie Chaplin)*, Geraldine Chaplin *(Hannah Chaplin)*, Paul Rhys *(Sydney Chaplin)*, John Thaw *(Fred Karno)*, Moira Kelly *(Hetty Kelly/Oona O'Neill)*, Anthony Hopkins *(George*

Hayden), Dan Aykroyd (*Mack Sennett*), Marisa Tomei (*Mabel Normand*), Penelope Ann Miller (*Edna Purviance*), Kevin Kline (*Douglas Fairbanks*)

p, Richard Attenborough, Mario Kassar; d, Richard Attenborough; w, William Boyd, Bryan Forbes, William Goldman (from the story by Diana Hawkins based on the biography *Chaplin: His Life and Art* by David Robinson and *My Autobiography* by Charles Chaplin); ph, Sven Nykvist; ed, Anne V. Coates; m, John Barry; prod d, Stuart Craig; art d, Mark Mansbridge, John King; cos, John Mollo, Ellen Mirojnick

AAN Best Actor: Robert Downey, Jr.; *AAN Best Score:* John Barry; *AAN Best Art Direction:* Stuart Craig, Chris A. Butler

CHAPLIN is the cinematic equivalent of a whistle-stop tour of Europe—the kind that takes you to ten cities in five days at such speed that everything melts into a vaguely entertaining blur. Richard Attenborough's film traces the entire arc of Chaplin's life, including his impoverished childhood in London, his early days as a vaudeville entertainer, his unparalleled success as a star and director of silent films, his enforced exile in Switzerland as a result of his alleged Communist sympathies, and his final, triumphant return to Hollywood in 1972 to accept a special Oscar for his life's work.

That's not to mention the series of young women who punctuated Chaplin's life and who seem to pop up every few minutes throughout the film—the "if this is 1936, that must be Paulette Goddard" school of biography.

Attenborough and his writers fail to impose sufficient dramatic structure on this overabundance of material, and never get to grips with what it was that fueled Chaplin's genius.

Nonetheless, some sections come vividly to life, largely thanks to engaging performances. Robert Downey, Jr., does an impressive job as the title character, perfectly recreating Chaplin's range of English accents (he went from Cockney to genteel as he got more famous) and mimicking, with astonishing precision, the gait and gestures of the Little Tramp.

Downey is ably backed up by a glittering supporting cast, particularly Dan Aykroyd as Keystone Kops mogul Mack Sennett, Kevin Kline as silent screen legend Douglas Fairbanks, and Geraldine Chaplin (the great man's real-life daughter) as Chaplin's mother.

CHARADE

1963 113m c Comedy/Thriller ★★★★
Universal (U.S.) /A

Cary Grant (*Peter Joshua*), Audrey Hepburn (*Regina Lambert*), Walter Matthau (*Hamilton Bartholomew*), James Coburn (*Tex Panthollow*), George Kennedy (*Herman Scobie*), Ned Glass (*Leopold Gideon*), Jacques Marin (*Inspector Edouard Grandpierre*), Paul Bonifas (*Felix*), Dominique Minot (*Sylvie Gaudet*), Thomas Chelimsky (*Jean-Louis Gaudet*)

p, Stanley Donen; d, Stanley Donen; w, Peter Stone (based on the story "The Unsuspecting Wife" by Marc Behm, Peter Stone); ph, Charles Lang; ed, James B. Clark; m, Henry Mancini; art d, Jean d'Eaubonne; cos, Givenchy

AAN Best Song: Henry Mancini (Music), Johnny Mercer (Lyrics)

Charming comedy-romance-thriller pairing Cary Grant and Audrey Hepburn, intelligently scripted by Peter Stone and directed in distinctly Hitchcockian style by Stanley Donen.

Reggie Lambert (Hepburn) returns to Paris from a ski trip in the French Alps to find her house ransacked and her husband dead. His funeral is attended by three curious thugs—played by James Coburn, George Kennedy, and Ned Glass—each of whom make sure that the corpse is indeed dead. Peter (Grant) offers his assistance to Reggie, as does CIA man Bartholomew (Walter Matthau) who informs her that her husband was part of a gang which, during WW II, stole and stashed a quarter of a million dollars. Naturally, everyone thinks—mistakenly—that Reggie knows the whereabouts of the money. Although Reggie finds herself falling in love with Peter, she suspects that he too is after the money, especially given his fondness for aliases—Peter Joshua, Alexander Dyle, Adam Canfield, Brian Cruickshank, etc. As the corpses begin to accumulate, it becomes increasingly important—and difficult—for Reggie to determine who are the good guys and who are the villains.

CHARADE is a finely crafted thriller that has a lot to offer beyond its clever plot. The radiant Hepburn's romance with the suave Grant is delightfully handled; the Oscar-nominated theme song by Henry Mancini and Johnny Mercer is superb; the location photography is exquisite and the rooftop fight scene between Grant and Kennedy is truly harrowing.

CHARGE OF THE LIGHT BRIGADE, THE

1936 115m bw Adventure/War ★★★½
Warner Bros. (U.S.) /U

Errol Flynn (*Maj. Geoffrey Vickers*), Olivia de Havilland (*Elsa Campbell*), Patric Knowles (*Capt. Perry Vickers*), Donald Crisp (*Col. Campbell*), Henry Stephenson (*Sir Charles Macefield*), Nigel Bruce (*Sir Benjamin Warrenton*), David Niven (*Capt. James Randall*), G.P. Huntley Jr. (*Maj. Jowett*), Spring Byington (*Lady Octavia Warrenton*), C. Henry Gordon (*Surat Khan*)

p, Samuel Bischoff; d, Michael Curtiz; w, Michel Jacoby, Rowland Leigh (based on a story by Michel Jacoby inspired by the poem by Alfred, Lord Tennyson); ph, Sol Polito; ed, George Amy; m, Max Steiner; art d, John Hughes; fx, Fred Jackman, H.F. Koenekamp; cos, Milo Anderson

AAN Best Score: Leo Forbstein (Departmental Head), Warner Bros Studio Music Department, Max Steiner (Score); *AAN Best Sound:* Nathan Levinson (Sound)

THE CHARGE OF THE LIGHT BRIGADE is a fine military swashbuckler with some of the most dynamic action sequences ever seen on the screen. Great pains were taken to re-create the 1850s milieu but Warner Bros. typically discarded the actual facts regarding the magnificent military blunder, retaining instead the era's pomp and the stirring lines of Tennyson's famous poem.

The story begins in in 1850 in northwest India during the years leading up to the Crimean War. Major Geoffrey Vickers (Errol Flynn), a dashing British officer of the 27th Lancers, crosses paths with a scheming Indian potentate, Surat Khan (C. Henry Gordon), who is severing ties with the British and allying himself with the Russians in preparation for a revolt. After Surat Khan's murderous betrayal of the British forces, Vickers seeks revenge during a foolhardy but courageous charge on the Russian forces at the Balaclava heights in the Crimea where Surat Khan has fled. Meanwhile Elsa Campbell (Olivia de Havilland), the woman Vickers loves, has secretly fallen in love with his brother, Captain Perry Vickers (Patric Knowles).

As a history lesson, THE CHARGE OF THE LIGHT BRIGADE is wildly inaccurate but a rousing entertainment. History was better served by the 1968 remake by Tony Richardson which exposed more of the truth about the military idiocy that led to the slaughter but movie audiences were largely unmoved.

CHARGE OF THE LIGHT BRIGADE, THE

1968 145m c Historical ★★½
UA (U.K.) /A

Trevor Howard (*Lord Cardigan*), Vanessa Redgrave (*Clarissa*), John Gielgud (*Lord Raglan*), Harry Andrews (*Lord Lucan*), Jill Bennett (*Mrs. Duberly*), David Hemmings (*Capt. Nolan*), Peter Bowles (*Paymaster Duberly*), Mark Burns (*Capt. Morris*), Howard Marion-Crawford (*Sir George Brown*), Mark Dignam (*Airey*)

p, Neil Hartley; d, Tony Richardson; w, Charles Wood; ph, David Watkin; ed, Kevin Brownlow, Hugh Raggett; m, John Addison; art d, Edward Marshall; fx, Robert MacDonald; cos, David Walker

Though well-researched and thought-provoking, this exquisitely made film is ultimately a disappointing drama of events leading up to the British involvement in the Crimean War. Richardson takes a somewhat absurdist approach as he satirizes the snobbishness of the English upper class and its view of the sport of war. He also exposes the soldiers' blind acceptance of the demands of their belittling supervisors. Their much vaunted code of honor turns sour in the wake of the humiliating slaughter of England's Light Brigade. The film completely belittles the undeniable courage that went hand-in-hand with the terrible mistakes it depicts. Dramatic loopholes also diminish the impact of what appears to be intended as a major cinematic statement about war from the 1960s generation.

Nonetheless there are many enjoyable performances, especially those of Gielgud, Hemmings, and Redgrave (the last two previously paired in BLOW UP). Richard Williams provides the clever animation sequences which serve to orient the viewer. Don't look for the spectacular war scenes so sweepingly portrayed in Curtiz's historically inaccurate but crowdpleasing 1936 version; the battle scenes take second place to revisionist satire and political indictment of 19th-century imperialistic England.

CHARIOTS OF FIRE

1981	123m	c	Biography/Sports	★★★
Enigma	(U.K.)			PG/U

Ben Cross (Harold Abrahams), Ian Charleson (Eric Liddell), Nigel Havers (Lord Andrew Lindsay), Nicholas Farrell (Aubrey Montague), Ian Holm (Sam Mussabini), John Gielgud (Master of Trinity), Lindsay Anderson (Master of Caius), Nigel Davenport (Lord Birkenhead), Cheryl Campbell (Jennie Liddell), Alice Krige (Sybil Gordon)

p, David Puttnam; d, Hugh Hudson; w, Colin Welland; ph, David Watkin; ed, Terry Rawlings; m, Vangelis; art d, Roger Hall; cos, Milena Canonero

AA Best Picture; AAN Best Supporting Actor: Ian Holm; AAN Best Director: Hugh Hudson; AAN Best Original Screenplay: Colin Welland; AAN Best Editing: Terry Rawlings; AA Best Score: Vangelis; AA Best Costume Design: Milena Canonero

CHARIOTS OF FIRE is a pleasant, mildly inspirational movie but hardly worthy of all the accolades it received. This true story, based on an original screenplay by Colin Welland, is about what it means to win and what one must do to achieve it. Eric Liddell (Ian Charleson) is a serious Scottish Christian who runs for the glory of Jesus. Harold Abrahams (Ben Cross) is an English Jew who is sensitive to prejudice and whose primary motivation is to be accepted. The movie delineates and crosscuts the lives of both men as they meet and compete at the 1924 Olympics in Paris.

The real-life Liddell became a Christian missionary, went to China, and eventually died in a Japanese prisoner of war camp, true to his faith to the end. Abrahams went on to become the spokesman for English amateur athletics, was knighted, and died a venerated elder statesman in 1978. Few who see the film can forget the lyrically photographed scene of the runners striding through the surf in slow motion to the accompaniment of Vangelis's stirring score, particularly in light of subsequent parodies.

CHARLEY VARRICK

1973	111m	c	Crime	★★★½
Universal	(U.S.)			PG/X

Walter Matthau (Charley Varrick), Joe Don Baker (Molly), Felicia Farr (Sybil Fort), Andy Robinson (Harman Sullivan), John Vernon (Maynard Boyle), Sheree North (Jewell Everett), Norman Fell (Mr. Garfinkle), Benson Fong (Honest John), Woodrow Parfrey (Howard Young), William Schallert (Sheriff Bill Horton)

p, Don Siegel; d, Don Siegel; w, Dean Riesner, Howard Rodman (based on the novel The Looters by John Reese); ph, Michael Butler; ed, Frank Morriss; m, Lalo Schifrin; art d, Fernando Carrere; cos, Helen Colvig

A very well made caper film full of action and rich with character. Directed by genre veteran Don Siegel, the versatile Walter Matthau plays it hard and fast as a small-time thief who robs, with partner Robinson, a tiny New Mexico bank. Instead of the usual loose change, the robbers find $750,000 which turns out to be Mafia money the bank was laundering. It's too risky for the pragmatic Matthau but his avaricious punk partner insists that they keep the money. Matthau warns him that if the loot is not returned, the Mafia will start gunning for them, which is exactly what happens. Hit man Baker begins hunting the pair, destroying everyone and everything in his path—and enjoying it.

Matthau is both shifty and cunning as he evades both the police and the Mafia. Butler's photography is top notch as is Schifrin's score. The whole film is suspenseful and intelligently scripted, thanks to director Siegel (DIRTY HARRY, THE SHOOTIST, ESCAPE FROM ALCATRAZ) and writers Riesner and Rodman. A great B movie of the 1970s.

CHARLEY'S AUNT

1941	80m	bw	Comedy	★★★
Fox	(U.S.)			/U

Jack Benny (Babbs), Kay Francis (Donna Lucia), James Ellison (Jack Chesney), Anne Baxter (Amy Spettigue), Edmund Gwenn (Stephen Spettigue), Reginald Owen (Redcliff), Laird Cregar (Sir Francis Chesney), Arleen Whelan (Kitty Verdun), Richard Haydn (Charley Wyckham), Ernest Cossart (Brasset)

p, William Perlberg; d, Archie Mayo; w, George Seaton (based on the play by Brandon Thomas); ph, Peverell Marley; ed, Robert Bischoff; m, Alfred Newman; art d, Nathan Juran, Richard Day; cos, Travis Banton

This was the third of many screen adaptations of "Charley's Aunt," the beloved 19th-century stage farce. The first starred Sydney Chaplin in 1925 and the second (released in 1930) featured Charlie Ruggles in the lead. Jack Benny stars here as Babbs, an Oxford student who masquerades as his friend Charley Wyckham's (Richard Haydn) aunt from Brazil who will be the chaperon for Charley and Jack (James Ellison) as they court Amy (Anne Baxter) and Kitty (Arleen Whelan). Once Babbs is in drag, however, he must fend off romantic advances from gigolo Sir Francis Chesney (Laird Cregar) and from Stephen Spettigue (Edmund Gwenn), the girl's guardian.

Jack Benny was never better (with the possible exception of his classic TO BE OR NOT TO BE) and carries the film with a top-flight performance. This was his first role of any consequence other than his previous tailor-made parts with radio jokes flying thick and fast around his well-known persona. In CHARLEY'S AUNT, Benny had to play a part totally alien to what he'd done before and he proved more than worthy to the task. Remade as the musical WHERE'S CHARLEY? in 1952.

CHARLIE BUBBLES

1968	89m	c	Drama	★★★
Regional	(U.K.)			/AA

Albert Finney (Charlie Bubbles), Colin Blakely (Smokey Pickles), Billie Whitelaw (Lottie Bubbles), Liza Minnelli (Eliza), Timothy Garland (Jack Bubbles), Richard Pearson (Accountant), John Ronane (Gerry), Nicholas Phipps (Agent), Peter Sallis (Solicitor), Charles Lamb (Mr. Noseworthy)

p, Michael Medwin; d, Albert Finney; w, Shelagh Delaney; ph, Peter Suschitzky; ed, Fergus McDonell; m, Misha Donat; art d, Edward Marshall; cos, Yvonne Blake

Not a great movie but an absorbing one about a writer who becomes suddenly successful, finds it very boring, and has an affair with his secretary. Albert Finney and Liza Minnelli star in a fantasy of escape that remains unique. This was Finney's directorial debut and a romantic touchstone for some in the late Sixties. Billie Whitelaw, as Charlie's estranged wife, won a British Academy award for her role as Best Supporting Actress.

CHARLIE CHAN AT THE OPERA

1936	66m	bw	Mystery	★★★½
Fox	(U.S.)			/A

Warner Oland (Charlie Chan), Boris Karloff (Gravelle), Keye Luke (Lee Chan), Charlotte Henry (Mlle. Kitty), Thomas Beck (Phil Childers), Margaret Irving (Mme. Lilli Rouchelle), Gregory Gaye (Enrico Barelli), Nedda Harrigan (Mme. Lucretia Barelli), Frank Conroy (Mr. Whitely), Guy Usher (Inspector Regan)

p, John Stone; d, H. Bruce Humberstone; w, W. Scott Darling, Charles Belden (based on a story by Bess Meredyth and the character created by Earl Derr Biggers); ph, Lucien Andriot; ed, Alex Troffey

Yes, Charlie Chan is a caricature of the East Asian personality and questions of racism do arise, but in his heyday in the 1930s the character of Chan presented an Oriental hero on the screen in what is perhaps the longest running series in movies. (The first Chan film was made in 1926 and the most recent in 1981.) There's something else going on here besides the caricature. Chan is probably unique in being a family detective and his collaboration with his sons is one of the attractions of the character. As with Nick and Nora Charles in THE THIN MAN movies, we're more interested in the relationship than in the mystery. Of the several actors who have played Chan, Warner Oland, who starred in this one, was generally regarded as the best.

One of the best of the series, this entry has the added attraction of Boris Karloff as Gravelle, an opera star who is presumed dead after being caught in a fire at a theater. He survives as an amnesiac, however, and is admitted unidentified into a mental hospital. When a picture of his opera singer wife appears in the newspaper, Gravelle's memory is spurred and he recalls that it was his unfaithful wife and her lover who set the fire in an attempt to kill him. Seething with a desire for vengeance, Gravelle escapes the mental hospital and heads for the opera house. When several people turn up dead, Charlie Chan is called in to investigate.

Included in the film is the opera *Carnival*, composed especially for the picture by Oscar Levant. This movie was so well made—and holds up so well—that its interest ranges far beyond the usual circle of Chan buffs.

CHARLOTTE'S WEB

1973 94m c Animated/Musical
Paramount (U.S.) G/U

VOICES OF: Debbie Reynolds *(Charlotte)*, Paul Lynde *(Templeton)*, Henry Gibson *(Wilbur)*, Rex Allen *(Narrator)*, Martha Scott *(Mrs. Arable)*, Dave Madden *(Old Sheep)*, Danny Bonaduce *(Avery)*, Don Messick *(Geoffrey)*, Herb Vigran *(Lurvy)*, Agnes Moorehead *(The Goose)*

p, Joseph Barbera, William Hanna; d, Charles A. Nichols, Iwao Takamoto; w, Earl Hamner Jr. (based on the book by E.B. White); ph, Roy Wade, Dick Blundell, Dennis Weaver, Ralph Migliori, George Epperson; ed, Larry Cowan, Pat Foley; m, Richard M. Sherman, Robert B. Sherman; art d, Bob Singer, Paul Julian, Ray Aragon

A charming cartoon adaptation of E.B. White's fantasy. Wilbur is a runt pig who has been raised as the pet of a New England farmer. He is sold to a neighboring farm, where a sheep informs him that he's fated to become what goes with cheese on rye. Wilbur is understandably frightened, until he meets a spider named Charlotte, who devotes her arachnoidal life to saving Wilbur from the fate of most porkers, and who weaves words into her web that convince the superstitious farmer that Wilbur is some sort of miraculous hog. The voices of Reynolds, Lynde, Gibson, and all the rest are perfectly cast, and the songs by the Sherman brothers are solid, although none of them became hits like those they wrote for such Disney movies as MARY POPPINS.

CHARLY

1968 103m c Drama ★
Selmur (U.S.) /PG

Cliff Robertson *(Charly Gordon)*, Claire Bloom *(Alice Kinian)*, Lilia Skala *(Dr. Anna Straus)*, Leon Janney *(Dr. Richard Nemur)*, Dick Van Patten *(Bert)*, William Dwyer *(Joey)*, Ed McNally *(Gimpy)*, Dan Morgan *(Paddy)*, Barney Martin *(Hank)*, Ruth White *(Mrs. Apple)*

p, Ralph Nelson; d, Ralph Nelson; w, Stirling Silliphant (based on the short story and novel *Flowers for Algernon* by Daniel Keyes); ph, Arthur J. Ornitz; ed, Fredric Steinkamp; m, Ravi Shankar; art d, Charles Rosen

AA Best Actor: Cliff Robertson

A strangely compelling mess of a movie which throws in the kitchen sink but forgets the plumbing, CHARLY is at once touching, infuriating and utterly laughable. It's the kind of film that makes you kick yourself for ever taking it seriously.

Based on "Flowers For Algernon," the over-anthologized short story by Daniel Keyes, this mawkish variation on *Pygmalion* casts Robertson as a bakery worker with an IQ of 68 turned into a genius via the marvels of brain surgery. Learning a few new things, he attempts to rape a repressed schoolteacher (Bloom), though of course they later fall in soft-focus love with each other. He also enjoys brief stints as a Hell's Angel and a computer wiz, and one soon realizes that this flick is trying to be a meaningful compilation of 1960s attitudes. (We'll stick with EASY RIDER, thanks.) Naturally, all this intelligence is too good to

last and Charly, upon witnessing the gradual regression of fellow experimentee Algernon the mouse, realizes that he too will soon revert to his former state.

Reeking with its own brand of sleazy sincerity and desperately wanting to be profound about *something*, CHARLY is more than capable of insulting both the mentally handicapped and anyone who cares about them. Part science fiction, part social commentary, part romance, this film is really option D—none of the above. Though he has some very good moments, especially as the enlightened man afraid of losing his newfound perspective, Robertson invests much of his performance with a kind of nutty intensity which should be witnessed at least once.

In all fairness, one doesn't know who could have done much with such cliched, shamelessly manipulative drivel, though heaven knows, the technical incompetence of this baby (including some hilarious use of split screens) doesn't help matters. Then again, maybe it's precisely the helpless frailty of the entire crazed enterprise that seems oddly affecting. Bring plenty of Kleenex, Pepto-Bismol, and hallucinogens.

CHARULATA

1964 117m bw Drama
RDB & Co. (India) /U

Soumitra Chatterjee *(Amal)*, Madhabi Mukherjee *(Charulata)*, Sailen Mukherjee *(Bhupati)*, Syamal Ghosal *(Umapada)*, Gitali Roy *(Mandakini)*, Bholanath Koyal *(Braja)*, Suku Mukherjee *(Nisikanta)*, Dilip Bose *(Sasanka)*, Subrata Sen Sharma *(Motilal)*, Joydeb *(Nilatpal Dey)*

p, R.D. Bansal; d, Satyajit Ray; w, Satyajit Ray (based on the novella *Nastanirh* by Rabindranath Tagore); ph, Subrata Mitra; ed, Dulal Dutta; m, Satyajit Ray; art d, Bansi Chandragupta

Satyajit Ray's fascination with Rabindranath Tagore culminated in CHARULATA, his twelfth film and arguably his greatest achievement. Based on a short story by Tagore, it is a surprisingly modern tale of love, lust, fidelity, and a woman's growing self-awareness against the backdrop of the Bengal Renaissance, a vibrant intellectual awakening in 19th-century India.

Charulata (Madhabi Mukherjee), the childless wife of a wealthy Bengali intellectual, lives in seclusion in her spacious and ornate home in Calcutta, while winds of change are blowing away the cobwebs outside. Her husband, Bhupati (Sailen Mukherjee), inspired by Mill and Bentham, spends his inherited wealth in the pursuit of freedom and equality, by editing an English-language liberal political weekly. But he has no time for Charu, who has little to do in a home run like a well-oiled machine by a fleet of old retainers.

At this point arrives Amal (Soumitra Chatterjee), Bhupati's dynamic young cousin. With Bhupati's encouragement, a close friendship grows between Amal and Charu based on their common interest in literature. Their intellectual sparring, however, hides a deeper attachment and a need which initially neither is fully aware of, and one which society will never sanction.

With its beauty, structural perfection and conceptual purity, CHARULATA remains a triumph of Ray's craftsmanship and cinematic vision. The exquisite interiors created by art director Bansi Chandragupta were among the best of his work, as were the subtle use of lights and the sensitivity of Subrata Mitra's camera. The costumes, the faces, and the detailed structuring of the film created a superbly colourful piece of monochrome cinema. CHARULATA has the quality of a miniature painting, where minute details are revealed by a stroke of the finest brush, and the unspoken is made visual by a mere suggestion.

CHEAPER BY THE DOZEN

1950 85m c Comedy
Fox (U.S.) /U

Clifton Webb *(Frank Bunker Gilbreth)*, Jeanne Crain *(Ann Gilbreth)*, Myrna Loy *(Mrs. Lillian Gilbreth)*, Betty Lynn *(Libby Lancaster)*, Edgar Buchanan *(Dr. Burton)*, Barbara Bates *(Ernestine)*, Mildred Natwick *(Mrs. Mebane)*, Sara Allgood *(Mrs. Monahan)*, Anthony Sydes *(Fred Gilbreth)*, Roddy McCaskill *(Jack Gilbreth)* p, Lamar Trotti; d, Walter Lang; w, Lamar Trotti (based on the novel by Frank B. Gilbreth, Jr. and Ernestine Gilbreth Carey); ph, Leon Shamroy; ed, J. Watson Webb; m, Cyril J. Mockridge

A big hit in its day and a typical Hollywood evocation of a genteel, bygone middle America of the 1920s that never was, this poor man's MEET ME IN ST. LOUIS presents prissy, spinsterish Clifton Webb as the father of twelve. Get real! Though Webb has his fair share of amusing moments, his trademark waspish but kindly crankiness loses its grip here amidst the floodtides of familial fondness. Loy, sadly soft-pedalled in the footage department, is on firmer ground as his devoted wife, a psychologist who uses the tricks of her trade on her efficiency expert husband whenever necessary. The film has no particular driving story but rather is a host of minor family incidents designed to show the closeness of the 14-member clan. Some are amusing, though others cloy in the way that only 20th Century-Fox lollipops can.

Journeyman director Lang is no Vincente Minnelli when it comes to either visuals or mood, and this is the type of film which plays better on television because there's nothing in it which really uses the big screen with any creativity. Honors go to Mildred Natwick as a birth control activist in the film's funniest scene. A true 1950s cultural relic and suitable "family entertainment," the film inspired a modest, quasi-feminist sequel, BELLES ON THEIR TOES.

CHELSEA GIRLS, THE

1966 210m c/bw Experimental ★★★★
Film-makers' Distribution Center (U.S.)

Pepper Davis, Ondine, Ingrid Superstar, Albert Rene Ricard, International Velvet, Brigid Polk, Ed Hood (Ed), Patrick Flemming (Patrick), Mario Montez (Transvestite), Gerard Malanga

p, Andy Warhol; d, Andy Warhol; w, Andy Warhol, Ronald Tavel; ph, Andy Warhol; m, The Velvet Underground

A film whose importance as a 1960s cultural statement outweighs any intrinsic value it may have as a film, CHELSEA GIRLS is nevertheless fascinating, provocative, and hilarious—once you surrender yourself to the totally new way of watching cinema that Andy Warhol films require. Think of it as Antonioni in slow-motion and enjoy the heavy ennui that settles over you. As with most of his other films Warhol simply turned the camera on his camp followers and let them play as they might. A number of his mock-Hollywood "superstars" from the famous Factory crowd are actually born performers. Look for strange and funny moments from Ondine, Ingrid Superstar, Brigid Polk, Ed Hood, Mario Montez, Edie Sedgwick and Nico among others.

CHELSEA GIRLS isn't an easy film to write about and is almost impossible to rank in terms of any "quality" it may possess. Maybe that's why we've given it four stars—because it's one of the purest expressions of how Warhol not only explodes the categories of what art is (remember the famous Campbell's Soup can?) but also that he assaults in revolutionary fashion all the conventions we hold dear. CHELSEA GIRLS is historically notable for requiring two projectors operating side by side (not that the two separate films have any connection!) and for its popular success on the art house circuit, which subsequently opened its doors to other "underground" films. While perhaps not as potent or as clever as more compact masterworks like VINYL, BLOW JOB, BEAUTY #2, MY HUSTLER, NUDE RESTAURANT and LONESOME COWBOYS, CHELSEA GIRLS is probably the ultimate summation of Warhol's cinema. Check it out once. . . if you dare.

CHEYENNE AUTUMN

1964 159m c Western ★★★★
Warner Bros. (U.S.) /U

Richard Widmark (Capt. Thomas Archer), Carroll Baker (Deborah Wright), Karl Malden (Capt. Oscar Wessels), James Stewart (Wyatt Earp), Edward G. Robinson (Carl Schurz), Sal Mineo (Red Shirt), Dolores Del Rio (Spanish Woman), Ricardo Montalban (Little Wolf), Gilbert Roland (Dull Knife), Arthur Kennedy (Doc Holliday)

p, Bernard Smith; d, John Ford; w, James R. Webb (based on the novel by Mari Sandoz); ph, William Clothier; ed, Otho Lovering; m, Alex North; art d, Richard Day; fx, Ralph Webb; cos, Ann Peck, Frank Beetson

AAN Best Cinematography: William H. Clothier

This Ford frontier epic opens in 1887 with the disheartened remnants of the Cheyenne nation waiting for a meeting with government representatives on a wretched Oklahoma reservation—a meeting that never takes place. When they are ignored in their pleas for food and housing, two chiefs (Montalban and Roland) decide to defy the authorities and migrate back to their Wyoming homeland.

Thus begins a heroic and tragic 1,500-mile trek—with a reluctant cavalry captain (Widmark) and his troops in unenthusiastic pursuit, intending to return the 300-strong Cheyenne to their miserable reservation. Moving with the tribe is a white schoolteacher (Baker) who empathizes with their plight. The captain's troops are outfought at every turn by the wily braves, while the press portrays the exodus as another Indian war, and even civilians Wyatt Earp (Stewart) and Doc Holliday (Kennedy) join halfheartedly in a posse to recapture the Native Americans.

Stunningly photographed by William Clothier, the film, in true Fordian fashion, once again makes fine use of that great western icon, Monument Valley. The acting, too, is generally quite good, some of it (Widmark, Robinson, Del Rio) squarely on the mark, some of it (Malden, Baker, Stewart) a trifle off-key at times. No single actor, however, stands out in CHEYENNE AUTUMN: it is ultimately the director's picture, and represents Ford's attitude toward the Native American coming around full circle.

From the nameless vicious hordes of STAGECOACH to the Comanche chief in THE SEARCHERS who is equated with the equally racist white "hero," the Native American has by the time of CHEYENNE AUTUMN become the hero deserving of our sympathy and respect. Flawed on several levels, Ford's perception of a proud people seen through a white man's eyes is ultimately a highly compelling and deeply personal apologia.

CHILDREN OF A LESSER GOD

1986 119m c Romance/Drama ★★★★
Paramount (U.S.) R/15

William Hurt (James Leeds), Marlee Matlin (Sarah Norman), Piper Laurie (Mrs. Norman), Philip Bosco (Dr. Curtis Franklin), Allison Gompf (Lydia), John F. Cleary (Johnny), Philip Holmes (Glen), Georgia Ann Cline (Cheryl), William D. Byrd (Danny), Frank Carter Jr. (Tony)

p, Burt Sugarman, Patrick Palmer; d, Randa Haines; w, Hesper Anderson, Mark Medoff (based on his stage play); ph, John Seale; ed, Lisa Fruchtman; m, Michael Convertino; prod d, Gene Callahan; art d, Barbara Matis; cos, Renee Kalfus

AAN Best Picture; AAN Best Actor: William Hurt; AA Best Actress: Marlee Matlin; AAN Best Supporting Actress: Piper Laurie; AAN Best Adapted Screenplay: Hesper Anderson, Mark Medoff

Nicely helmed by first-time feature director Haines, CHILDREN OF A LESSER GOD is a poignant yet uplifting love story involving a speech teacher and a deaf young woman. James Leeds (Hurt) is a maverick instructor newly arrived at a facility for the hearing impaired, where he meets Sarah Norman (Matlin), a graduate of the school who has chosen to stay and work in a menial job rather than attempt to go out into the world that the school has supposedly taught her to face. He falls in love with her almost instantly, but she resists him at first and also steadfastly refuses to read lips or attempt to talk; she insists on signing. In an attempt to learn why Sarah will not venture out into the world, Leeds visits her mother (Laurie) and discovers the root of Sarah's bitterness.

The major problem with the movie is that the audience is never left to its own interpretive devices. Because Matlin's hearing is severely impaired in real life, Hurt translates everything she signs for the benefit of viewers. Some of this may have been necessary, but Matlin's silent acting is so expressive that we often know exactly what is going through her mind as the emotions flicker across her face, and the translation routine interrupts the flow of the story time and again for no good reason. Nevertheless, despite this flaw, several dramatic lulls, and an aggressive determination to "sparkle," the film often makes for crackling good drama with plenty of leavening humor and magnificent performances by Hurt and newcomer Matlin.

CHILDREN OF PARADISE
(LES ENFANTS DU PARADIS)

1945 195m bw Romance   ★★★★★
S.N. Pathe   (France)   /A

Arletty *(Garance)*, Jean-Louis Barrault *(Baptiste Debureau)*, Pierre Brasseur *(Frederick Lemaitre)*, Marcel Herrand *(Lacenaire)*, Pierre Renoir *(Jericho)*, Maria Casares *(Natalie)*, Etienne Decroux *(Anselme Debureau)*, Fabien Loris *(Avril)*, Leon Larive *(Stage Doorman, "Funambules")*, Pierre Palov *(Stage Manager, "Funambules")*

p, Fred Orain; d, Marcel Carne; w, Jacques Prevert; ph, Roger Hubert, Marc Fossard; ed, Henri Rust, Madeleine Bonin; m, Maurice Thiriet, Joseph Kosma, George Mouque; art d, Leon Barsacq, R. Cabutti, Alexander Trauner

AAN Best Original Screenplay: Jacques Prevert

"Anyone who can resist its flamboyant charm deserves never to see Paris," wrote critic Andrew Sarris of CHILDREN OF PARADISE. It's been called France's answer to GONE WITH THE WIND, the greatest French film ever made, and an overrated bore. Filmed under a plethora of Nazi regulations with a cast peppered with Resistance fighters, the making of this film is almost as interesting as the end result. What is especially fascinating is how Marxist screenwriter Prevert and director Carne were able to pull off a thinly disguised allegory of French resistance under the German occupation.

The story, which takes place in the Paris of the 1820s and 30s, is a complex tale of unrequited love, illicit affairs, jealousy, and romance revolving around the world of theater folk, criminals, and aristocrats. The "children of paradise" are the poor people who inhabit the topmost balconies of the theaters along the Boulevard du Temple, and they are witness to the story of theater mime Baptiste (Barrault) and his true love Garance (Arletty). Along the way we are treated to delightful theater shows, duels, love amidst rain showers, and unfortunate misunderstandings with tragic consequences.

Deliberately theatrical but nevertheless greatly indebted to French poetic realism, CHILDREN OF PARADISE is lovingly handled by director Carne. The entire film is crammed with incident and an intoxicating eye for detail. Trauner's art direction is one of his finest achievements and the music by Kosma, Thiriet, and Mouque both onstage and off is a constant delight. Based on this one performance alone, gifted mime, comic and tragedian Barrault must take his place as one of the century's greatest actors. The raven-haired, fascinating Arletty, meanwhile, was the closest the French ever got to creating their own Marlene Dietrich. Among a superior supporting cast, Brasseur, Herrand, Renoir, Casares, Marker, Salou, and Modot (as a "blind" beggar who can actually see) are particularly outstanding, and the end result is utterly beguiling cinema.

CHILLY SCENES OF WINTER

1979 92m c Drama   ★★★½
UA Classics   (U.S.)   PG/A

John Heard *(Charles)*, Mary Beth Hurt *(Laura)*, Peter Riegert *(Sam)*, Kenneth McMillan *(Pete)*, Gloria Grahame *(Clara)*, Nora Heflin *(Betty)*, Jerry Hardin *(Patterson)*, Tarah Nutter *(Susan)*, Mark Metcalf *(Ox)*, Allen Joseph *(Blind Man)*

p, Mark Metcalf, Amy Robinson, Griffin Dunne; d, Joan Micklin Silver; w, Joan Micklin Silver (based on the novel *Head Over Heels* by Ann Beattie); ph, Bobby Byrne; ed, Cynthia Scheider; m, Ken Lauber; prod d, Peter Jamison

Directed by Joan Micklin Silver (HESTER STREET, CROSSING DELANCEY) and based on a novel by Ann Beattie, CHILLY SCENES OF WINTER focuses on Charles (Heard), an office worker who falls in love with Laura (Hurt) while she is separated from her husband. When Laura returns to her spouse, Charles remains obsessed with her, sitting outside her home in his car watching the lights, even going to visit her *and* her husband, accompanied by his good friend Sam (Riegert). Retaining the mournful tone of Beattie's excellent novel, Silver delivers a slow-moving, occasionally funny, but deeply affecting film blessed with outstanding understated performances by Heard,

Hurt, Riegert, and screen veteran Grahame, on hand in a memorable turn as Charles's suicidal mother. Look for author Beattie in a bit part as a waitress.

CHIMES AT MIDNIGHT
(CAMPANADAS A MEDIANOCHE)

1966 115m bw Drama/War/Historical   ★★★½
Films Espanola/Alpine   (Spain/Switzerland)   /U

Orson Welles *(Sir John "Jack" Falstaff)*, Jeanne Moreau *(Doll Tearsheet)*, Margaret Rutherford *(Hostess Quickly)*, John Gielgud *(King Henry IV)*, Keith Baxter *(Prince Hal—later King Henry V)*, Marina Vlady *(Kate Percy)*, Norman Rodway *(Henry Percy—"Hotspur")*, Alan Webb *(Justice Shallow)*, Walter Chiari *(Mr Silence)*, Michael Aldridge *(Pistol)*

p, Emiliano Piedra; d, Orson Welles; w, Orson Welles (based on the plays *Henry IV Part I, Henry IV Part II, Henry V, Richard II,* and *The Merry Wives of Windsor* by William Shakespeare and *The Chronicles of England* by Raphael Holinshed); ph, Edmond Richard; ed, Fritz Muller; m, Angelo Francesco Lavagnino; prod d, Gustavo Quintana; art d, Jose Antonio de la Guerra; cos, Cornejo Madrid

Orson Welles' brooding, sometimes brilliant art-house film dwells on the tragic side of one of Shakespeare's most famous comic characters. Seamlessly integrating portions of Shakespeare's *Richard II, Henry IV, Henry V,* and *The Merry Wives of Windsor,* along with (in the narration by Ralph Richardson) Raphael Holinshed's *The Chronicles of England,* CHIMES AT MIDNIGHT is one of the finest cinematic translations of the Bard.

Sir John Falstaff (Welles) is the massive, blustering companion to Prince Hal (Baxter), heir to the besieged British throne. Reluctant to assume the duties of kingship, Hal passes his time drinking and carousing with Falstaff. Finally, however, he goes into battle, slaying the honorable, doomed challenger to the crown, Hotspur (Rodway), and he soon thereafter becomes Henry V. Bursting in on the coronation, certain that a high title is forthcoming, Falstaff encounters instead the scorn of the now high-and-mighty Hal.

While not as technically dazzling as CITIZEN KANE (indeed, some are quick to condemn the somewhat confusing editing and murky sound—evidence of the project's haphazard shooting schedule), CHIMES AT MIDNIGHT is the work of a mature artist and proof of Welles's great flair for Shakespearean dramaturgy. Although the film downplays the comic aspects of the Falstaff-Hal relationship, the two lead performances are splendid, with Baxter alternately playful, cunning, icy, and commanding and Welles giving the performance of his career in a part he deeply understands. The moment of Falstaff's rejection is probably the single most moving piece of acting Welles ever committed to film.

Although fans of Moreau and Rutherford may be disappointed by their modestly sized roles, there are compensations, especially in the perfect performance of Gielgud as Henry IV. The film includes one of the best battle scenes ever—a brutal, chaotic affair fought on a mud-soaked field, with the waddling knight Falstaff making every attempt to escape death.

CHINA SYNDROME, THE

1979 122m c Drama   ★★★½
IPC   (U.S.)   PG

Jane Fonda *(Kimberly Wells)*, Jack Lemmon *(Jack Godell)*, Michael Douglas *(Richard Adams)*, Scott Brady *(Herman DeYoung)*, James Hampton *(Bill Gibson)*, Peter Donat *(Don Jacovich)*, Wilford Brimley *(Ted Spindler)*, Richard Herd *(Evan McCormack)*, Daniel Valdez *(Hector Salas)*, Stan Bohrman *(Peter Martin)*

p, Michael Douglas; d, James Bridges; w, Mike Gray, T.S. Cook, James Bridges; ph, James Crabe; ed, David Rawlins; art d, George Jenkins; fx, Henry Millar; cos, Donfeld

AAN Best Actor: Jack Lemmon; *AAN Best Actress:* Jane Fonda; *AAN Best Original Screenplay:* Mike Gray (Story), T S Cook (Story), James Bridges (Story); *AAN Best Art Direction:* George Jenkins (Art Direction), Arthur Jeph Parker (Set Decoration)

Life imitates art. What began as a fanciful premise in the minds of many turned into reality a few weeks after this picture opened when the Three Mile Island nuclear reactor had a dreadful accident.

Fonda plays Kimberly Wells, a television reporter trying to advance from cutesy features to harder news. Douglas is Richard Adams, a freelance cameraman she hires while attempting to do a story on nuclear energy. They're fortuitously present at a power plant when a crisis arises, and a meltdown is narrowly avoided by the quick reactions of engineer Jack Godell (Lemmon). Richard has it all on film and rushes it back to the station, but management won't put it on the air. Godell, meanwhile, is outraged when he learns that the authorities have covered up the incident. He searches the plant and discovers the problem: faulty welding from a cut-rate construction job. He contacts the reporters and gives them X-rays of the offending equipment. But when sound man Hector Salas (Valdez) is murdered while taking the information to a hearing on a proposed nuclear project, Godell realizes that his superiors will stop at nothing to cover up their criminal negligence. Meanwhile, Kimberly's transformation from naif to political activist—a Fonda trademark in 70s films from TOUT VA BIEN to COMING HOME—becomes the real substance of the narrative.

A film more open than most about its political stance, THE CHINA SYNDROME effectively deploys its polemic within the framework of a nightmarish but convincing story. The lack of incidental music adds to the quasi-documentary feel; tight scripting and direction ably maintain suspense during the protracted climax. The sometimes self-conscious and too-earnest Fonda and the occasionally hammy Lemmon both rise beautifully to the occasion, delivering performances that are among their best. In other roles Douglas, Brimley, Hampton, Brady, and Bohrman (an actual reporter who would go on to cover the Three Mile Island incident) offer sterling support. Not a comforting film, but an undeniably potent one.

CHINATOWN

1974   131m   c   Mystery   ★★★★★
Paramount   (U.S.)   /15

Jack Nicholson (*J.J. Gittes*), Faye Dunaway (*Evelyn Mulwray*), John Huston (*Noah Cross*), Perry Lopez (*Escobar*), John Hillerman (*Yelburton*), Darrell Zwerling (*Hollis Mulwray*), Diane Ladd (*Ida Sessions*), Roy Jenson (*Mulvihill*), Roman Polanski (*Man with Knife*), Richard Bakalyan (*Loach*)

p, Robert Evans; d, Roman Polanski; w, Robert Towne; ph, John A. Alonzo; ed, Sam O'Steen; m, Jerry Goldsmith; prod d, Richard Sylbert; art d, Stewart Campbell; fx, Logan Frazee; cos, Anthea Sylbert

AAN Best Picture; AAN Best Actor: Jack Nicholson; AAN Best Actress: Faye Dunaway; AAN Best Director: Roman Polanski; AA Best Original Screenplay: Robert Towne; AAN Best Cinematography: John A. Alonzo; AAN Best Editing: Sam O'Steen; AAN Best Score: Jerry Goldsmith; AAN Best Art Direction: Richard Sylbert, W. Stewart Campbell, Ruby Levitt; AAN Best Costume Design: Anthea Sylbert; AAN Best Sound: Bud Grenzbach, Lawrence Jost

A wonderfully brooding, suspenseful revisitation of the land of film noir, CHINATOWN is not only one of the greatest detective films, but one of the most perfectly constructed of all films. With Polanski's brilliant direction, Towne's intricate screenplay, and Nicholson's and Dunaway's tour de force performances, the film stands as one of the best of the 1970s.

The plot revolves around Gittes (Nicholson), a Chandleresque private eye who specializes in the most distasteful of detective enterprises—snooping after straying spouses. After being duped by a woman purporting to be the wife of the city water commissioner, Gittes meets the man's real wife, Evelyn Mulwray (Dunaway), but before long she ends up a widow. Drawn into these strange goings-on, Gittes follows a jigsaw puzzle of clues that leads to Mulwray's father, Cross (Huston). Cross has involved himself in the "future" of Los Angeles by engineering a plot to divert the city's water supply for his own gain.

Besides telling a gripping story involving incest and political graft, CHINATOWN recaptures the atmosphere of Los Angeles, 1937—the cars, clothes, and buildings, right down to the barber chairs (kudos to production designer Richard Sylbert and costumer Anthea Sylbert). The tone and flavor of this film evoke strong memories of MURDER,

MY SWEET and the original THE BIG SLEEP, yet it stands singularly on its own merits. Even the muted color cinematography (normally antithetical to the tenets of noir) is evocative and appropriate. Interestingly, Towne's script included not a single scene set in Chinatown—initially a metaphorical state of mind rather than a specific place.

Look for director Polanski as the thug who pokes a switchblade up Nicholson's nostril while uttering the infamous line, "You know what happens to nosy fellows? They lose their noses." Another highlight: Dunaway's "sister... daughter... sister... daughter" routine, a camp classic much parodied since. CHINATOWN earned 11 Oscar nominations, including Best Picture, but only Towne took home a statuette for his cynical screenplay.

CHLOE IN THE AFTERNOON
(L'AMOUR L'APRES-MIDI)

1972   97m   c   Drama   ★★★
Losange/Barbet Schroeder   (France)   R/

Bernard Verley (*Frederic*), Zouzou (*Chloe*), Francoise Verley (*Helene*), Daniel Ceccaldi (*Gerard*), Malvina Penne (*Fabienne*), Babette Ferrier (*Martine*), Tina Michelino, Jean-Louis Livi, Pierre Nunzi, Irene Skobline

p, Pierre Cottrell; d, Eric Rohmer; w, Eric Rohmer; ph, Nestor Almendros; ed, Cecile Decugis; m, Arie Dzierlatka; art d, Nicole Rachline

This sixth and final installment of Rohmer's "Six Moral Tales" focuses, for the first time in the series, on the married Frederic (Bernard Verley), a professional who spends very little time with his equally business-minded wife, Helene (Francoise Verley). The first part of the film is essentially a prologue as it carefully sets up the male lead's character. He is a man easily seduced—but only mentally. Frederic imagines what certain women (a wonderful series of cameos by previous Rohmer heroines) are like, concocting romantic adventures with them as they walk down the street. In one telling scene, he purchases a shirt from a pretty saleswoman only because he cannot resist her charms. Having settled into marriage, he dreams only of love in the afternoon (as the original French title translates). Then into Frederic's life walks Chloe (Zouzou), an attractive, sexy mystery woman determined to seduce him.

A fitting close to the series, which finally marries off one of Rohmer's romantic heroes, reunites all his previous heroines, and addresses the basic theme of marital infidelity. To a greater degree than his previous films, Rohmer (to the surprise of those who find his work talky and boring) invests CHLOE IN THE AFTERNOON with a surprising amount of suspense—not the obvious sort, but a variety that is quieter, emotional—with all the tension and conflict occurring inside the character's mind. In this respect Rohmer seems a deserving recipient of the soubriquet "the Henry James of cinema."

CHOCOLATE WAR, THE

1988   100m   c   Drama   ★★★
Management Co. Entertainment   (U.S.)   R/15

John Glover (*Brother Leon*), Ilan M. Mitchell-Smith (*Jerry*), Wally Ward (*Archie*), Doug Hutchison (*Obie*), Adam Baldwin (*Carter*), Brent Fraser (*Emille*), Bud Cort (*Brother Jacques*)

p, Jonathan D. Krane, Simon R. Lewis; d, Keith Gordon; w, Keith Gordon (based on the novel by Robert Cormier); ph, Tom Richmond; ed, Jeff Wishengrad; prod d, David Ensley; cos, Elizabeth Kaye

Keith Gordon, after 10 years of appearing in front of the camera (ALL THAT JAZZ, CHRISTINE), made his directing debut at age 27 with this dark, dazzling film in the tradition of IF... and LORD OF THE FLIES. Working from his own adaptation of Robert Cormier's novel, Gordon uses an inventive narrative technique and stylish visuals to tell the story of a teenager who takes a stand against an oppressive system but, in so doing, ends up playing the system's game.

Set at Trinity, a Catholic boys' high school, the film revolves around 15-year-old Mitchell-Smith, the "new kid." He comes to the attention of Ward and Hutchison, two members of the Vigils, the school's secret society of bullies, and sadistic, pointer-wielding instructor Glover, who moves from the classroom to the principal's office when the school's headmaster takes ill. Glover is also in charge of the school's annual chocolate sale and hopes to impress the board of trustees by selling twice as many boxes of sweets as he did the year before. With assistance from the bullying Vigils, Glover nearly achieves his goal—the only student not fulfilling his quota is Mitchell-Smith, who refuses in order to prove something to himself.

With much of his film's direction dictated by dream logic, Gordon uses an arresting visual style to immerse the viewer in Mitchell-Smith's world. Despite his limited budget, the writer-director presents an array of memorable images. Mitchell-Smith's character is not as well developed as we might want it to be (though much can be inferred from his dreams). Still—aided by strong performances by Adam Baldwin, Ward, and Glover—Gordon has created a deeply involving film. It has much to tell us, not just about a particular adolescent challenge, but also about the difficulty of nonconformity and how easily means and ends become confused.

CHOICE OF ARMS
(LE CHOIX DES ARMES)
1981   135m   c   Crime   ★★★
Sara/Antenne 2/Parafrance/Radio Monte Carlo   (France)

Yves Montand *(Noel Durieux)*, Gerard Depardieu *(Mickey)*, Catherine Deneuve *(Nicole Durieux)*, Michel Galabru *(Bonnardot)*, Gerard Lanvin *(Sarlat)*, Jean-Claude Dauphin *(Ricky)*, Richard Anconina *(Dany)*, Jean Rougerie, Christian Marquand, Etienne Chicot

p, Alain Sarde; d, Alain Corneau; w, Alain Corneau, Michel Grisolia; ph, Pierre-William Glenn; ed, Thierry Derocles; m, Philippe Sarde; art d, Jean-Pierre Kohut-Svelko.

A compelling and superbly directed *policier*, CHOICE OF ARMS pits the new, young breed of criminal—the crazed and disrespectful Mickey (Depardieu)—against an elder, retired underworld hood, the honorable Noel (Montand). Mickey escapes from prison and takes temporary refuge at a ranch owned by Noel and his wife, Nicole (Deneuve). When Mickey refuses to play by Noel's rules, he takes off for Paris. Upon returning, he wrongly assumes that Noel has informed on him and vows to kill both Noel and Nicole. A criminal of the old school—not unlike those who appear in the films of Jean-Pierre Melville—Noel leads a tranquil life but is not beyond violent, angry outbursts. He has fought long and hard to achieve his quiet lifestyle with his loving wife, and now he must fight again.

Although CHOICE OF ARMS does follow certain Hollywood genre expectations, Corneau's direction stamps the film with a crisp, personal style of filmmaking as attentive to the theoretical issues at stake in the conflict as it is to story development or emotional impact. In this respect Corneau merits comparison with his more acclaimed contemporary Bertrand Tavernier. Depardieu turns in a forceful performance as the unpredictable Mickey, and Montand is an explosion waiting to happen as the externally peaceful Noel. Unfortunately, the always beautiful Deneuve is cast here in another role in which she gets little chance to display her considerable acting skills.

CHOOSE ME
1984   106m   c   Romance/Comedy/Drama   ★★★★
Island Alive   (U.S.)   R/15

Keith Carradine *(Mickey)*, Lesley Ann Warren *(Eve)*, Genevieve Bujold *(Ann/Dr. Nancy Lovell)*, Patrick Bauchau *(Zack Antoine)*, Rae Dawn Chong *(Pearl Antoine)*, John Larroquette *(Billy Ace)*, Edward Ruscha *(Ralph Chomsky)*, Gailard Sartain *(Mueller)*, Robert Gould *(Lou)*, John Considine *(Dr. Ernest Greene)*

p, Carolyn Pfeiffer, David Blocker; d, Alan Rudolph; w, Alan Rudolph; ph, Jan Kiesser; ed, Mia Goldman; prod d, Steven Legler; art d, Steven Legler; cos, Tracy Tynan.

Director Alan Rudolph hit his stride with this quirky comedy-drama in which the characterizations outweigh and eventually overwhelm the plot. Ann (Bujold) is a radio psychologist calling herself "Dr. Love" who dispenses advice but is hopelessly maladjusted herself. Eve (Warren), meanwhile, the owner of a small bar, is both blessed and cursed with the ability to attract and capture any man she pleases. But Eve is not the supremely self-confident person she seems; she is actually a frightened woman living on the edge of a breakdown who spends a lot

of time calling Dr. Love. Then Mickey (Carradine), a wayward genius or the world's greatest liar, walks into the bar and into the lives of both Eve and Ann.

This picture is made up of many fine moments and many wonderful verbal insights. There's not much of a story here, but, in typical fashion, director Rudolph wisely allows the film to gently meander in several interesting directions. Lushly photographed and very well acted, with a relaxed, bleary-eyed, 3 a.m. feel to it, this sometimes surprising little film is an intriguing piece of work.

CHRISTMAS IN CONNECTICUT
1945   102m   bw   Comedy   ★★★½
Warner Bros.   (U.S.)   /A

Barbara Stanwyck *(Elisabeth Lane)*, Dennis Morgan *(Jefferson Jones)*, Sydney Greenstreet *(Alexander Yardley)*, Reginald Gardiner *(John Sloan)*, S.Z. Sakall *(Felix Bassenak)*, Robert Shayne *(Dudley Beecham)*, Una O'Connor *(Norah)*, Frank Jenks *(Sinkewicz)*, Joyce Compton *(Mary Lee)*, Dick Elliott *(Judge Crothers)*

p, William Jacobs; d, Peter Godfrey; w, Lionel Houser, Adele Comandini (based on a story by Aileen Hamilton); ph, Carl Guthrie; ed, Frank Magee; m, Frederick Hollander; art d, Stanley Fleischer; cos, Edith Head

A sometimes hilarious farce and a holiday favorite. Stanwyck stars as Elisabeth Lane, a successful but scheming columnist who pretends to be a happy, supercompetent housewife. Compelled to take in Navy hero Jefferson Jones (Morgan) for the holidays as part of a promotion gimmick concocted by her hoodwinked publisher Alexander Yardley (Greenstreet), Elisabeth must deal with the reality that she doesn't own the country home she writes about, can't cook, and isn't married. In desperation, she convinces lounge lizard John Sloan (Gardiner) to play the role of hubby, rents a rustic house, and brings in a world-famous chef (Sakall, genuinely amusing but best taken in small doses) to cover up her own inadequacies.

Director Godfrey's handling of the material is rather mild and not especially creative, but he does keep things lively, and Stanwyck proves her considerable flair for comedy. It's also nice to see a very relaxed Greenstreet in something other than melodrama for a change. The film's endorsement of housewifery over working outside the home is obvious, but to the film's credit its attitude is a heartily self-mocking one.

CHRISTMAS IN JULY
1940   66m   bw   Comedy   ★★★★
Paramount   (U.S.)   /U

Dick Powell *(Jimmy MacDonald)*, Ellen Drew *(Betty Casey)*, Raymond Walburn *(Dr. Maxford)*, Alexander Carr *(Mr. Schindel)*, William Demarest *(Mr. Bildocker)*, Ernest Truex *(Mr. Baxter)*, Franklin Pangborn *(Radio Announcer)*, Harry Hayden *(Mr. Waterbury)*, Rod Cameron *(Dick)*, Adrian Morris *(Tom)*

p, Paul Jones; d, Preston Sturges; w, Preston Sturges; ph, Victor Milner; ed, Ellsworth Hoagland

The great Preston Sturges wrote and directed CHRISTMAS IN JULY, an hysterically funny, short and sweet comedy about a man who goes on a spending spree after he thinks he's won a coffee-slogan contest, only to learn that the whole thing was a practical joke.

Jimmy MacDonald (Dick Powell), a lowly clerk at the Baxter Coffee Company, enters a $25,000 slogan contest for the Maxford House Coffee Company. But on the night the winner is to be announced on the radio, the jury is deadlocked because of an obstinate juror. The next day at work, some pranksters make up a phony telegram and put it on Jimmy's desk, saying that he has won the contest. Jimmy immediately goes to collect his check from Dr. Maxford (Raymond Walburn) and promptly begins spending his newfound wealth.

CHRISTMAS was a little underrated in its time, perhaps because of its very brief running time and seemingly frivolous nature, but in retrospect, it emerges as one of Sturges's funniest and most purely enjoyable films. Sturges's customary frantic pace is even more dizzying than usual, the dialogue is filled with hilarious wisecracks, puns, double-entendres and malapropisms, and in just over an hour, the film manages to encompass slapstick, satire, screwball comedy, pathos, and melodrama. As in all of Sturges's films, the story is really a fable about the pursuit of the American dream, making wry observations about failure and success, and money and happiness.

One of the great pleasures of Sturges's movies was the stock company of superb character actors who were the heart and soul of all his films, and CHRISTMAS is packed with them. Besides the delightful William Demarest as Mr. Bildocker; there's Franklin Pangborn as a prissy radio announcer; Raymond Walburn as the dyspeptic Maxford; and Frank Moran as a boisterous cop. CHRISTMAS IN JULY remains a wonderful present that's perfect for anytime of the year.

CHRISTMAS STORY, A

1983 98m c Comedy ★★★★
MGM (U.S.) PG

Melinda Dillon *(Mother)*, Darren McGavin *(Old Man)*, Peter Billingsley *(Ralphie)*, Ian Petrella *(Randy)*, Scott Schwartz *(Flick)*, R.D. Robb *(Schuartz)*, Tedde Moore *(Miss Shields)*, Yano Anaya *(Grover)*, Zack Ward *(Scot)*, Jeff Gillen *(Santa Claus)*

p, Rene Dupont, Bob Clark; d, Bob Clark; w, Jean Shepherd, Leigh Brown, Bob Clark (based on the novel *In God We Trust, All Others Pay Cash* by Jean Shepherd); ph, Reginald Morris; ed, Stan Cole; m, Carl Zittrer, Paul Zaza; art d, Gavin Mitchell; cos, Mary McLeod

Somehow usually tasteless director Bob Clark, whose specialty was fairly vile exploitation movies (PORKY'S and the even worse PORKY'S II: THE NEXT DAY), managed to make a totally charming and lovable Christmas film.

Based on the short stories of midwestern humorist Jean Shepherd (who also narrates in the first person), A CHRISTMAS STORY is an episodic comedy set in the 1940s about the family life of young Ralphie (Billingsley) as Christmas approaches. The plot loosely revolves around Ralphie's desire for a Red Ryder BB gun for Christmas that his mother (Dillon) has forbidden because she's afraid he'll shoot his eyes out. Among Shepherd's childhood musings are his narrow escapes from the neighborhood bullies, the battles of his old man (McGavin) with the smoke-belching furnace, Mom's attempts to get his little brother (Petrella) to eat, Dad's infatuation with an obnoxious lamp that looks like a woman's leg, and a nightmarish visit with Santa at the local department store.

The cast is wonderful—especially McGavin, Billingsley and Petrella—the laughs are nonstop if rarely subtle, and the whole thing deserves to become a Christmastime classic.

CHRONICLE OF A DEATH FORETOLD
(CRONACA DI UNA MORTE ANNUNCIATA)

1987 109m c Drama ★★★
Italmedia/Soprofilms/Les Films Ariane/FR 3/RAI 2 /15
(France/Italy)

Rupert Everett *(Bayardo San Roman)*, Ornella Muti *(Angela Vicario)*, Gian Maria Volonte *(Dr. Cristo Bedoya)*, Irene Papas *(Angela's Mother)*, Lucia Bose *(Placida Linero)*, Anthony Delon *(Santiago Nasar)*, Alain Cuny *(Widower)*, Sergi Mateu *(Young Cristo Bedoya)*, Carolina Rosi *(Flora Miguel)*, Caroline Lang *(Margot)*

p, Yves Gasser, Francis Von Buren; d, Francesco Rosi; w, Francesco Rosi, Tonino Guerra (based on a novel by Gabriel Garcia Marquez); ph, Pasqualino de Santis; ed, Ruggero Mastroianni; m, Piero Piccioni; art d, Andrea Crisanti; cos, Enrico Sabbatini

As he did in SALVATORE GIULIANO, director Francesco Rosi reconstructs the events which combined to bring about a murder in this Italian-French coproduction based on the novel by Nobel Prize winner Gabriel Garcia Marquez.

Set in a provincial Colombian river town, the story begins in the present as Volonte (THE DEATH OF MARIO RICCI, CHRIST STOPPED AT EBOLI), a doctor in his fifties, returns to his home after nearly 20 years to investigate a murder that occurred just before he left. In flashback, Everett (DANCE WITH A STRANGER, ANOTHER COUNTRY), the son of a wealthy general, visits the town in search of a bride and falls in love with the beautiful Muti. They wed, but soon after the ceremony, Everett discovers that Muti is not a virgin and returns his bride to her shamed family. Muti's father beats her until she names the man who deflowered her, Delon, a brazen young womanizer,

who may or may not have actually compromised Muti. Her twin brothers, Carlos and Rogerio Miranda, are then honor-bound to make Delon pay for his indiscretion.

The film's action is enriched by themes of omnipresent Catholicism, the emptiness of macho stances, and the strength of familial ties. The moody photography increases the languorous mystical aura of the film.

CHUNGKING EXPRESS
(CHONGQING SENLIN)

1994 100m c Drama/Romance/Comedy ★★★★½
Jet Tone (Hong Kong) R/12

Brigitte Lin *(The Drug Dealer)*, Takeshi Kaneshiro *(Ho Chi-wu—Cop #223)*, Tony Leung Chiu-Wai *(Cop #663)*, Faye Wong *(Faye)*, Valerie Chow *(Air Hostess)*, "Piggy" Chan *(Manager of "Midnight Express")*, Guan Lina, Huang Zhiming, Liang Zhen, Zuo Songshen

p, Chan Yi-Kan; d, Wong Kar-Wai; w, Wong Kar-Wai; ph, Christopher Doyle, Lau Wai-Keung; ed, William Chang, Hai Kit-Wai, Kwong Chi-Leung; m, Frankie Chan, Roel A. Garcia, Michael Calasso; prod d, William Chang; art d, Qiu Weiming; fx, Ding Yunda, Deng Weijue, Cheng Xiaolong; cos, Yao Huiming

With its sprung rhythms and pop sensibility, Wong Kar-Wai's genuinely inspired pastiche of early Godard and late Hitchcock could be dismissed as another bit of stylishly pomo navel-gazing—if it weren't so obviously *about* something.

This visually electric film consists of two loosely connected but cleverly rhymed stanzas: Part One traces the intersecting paths of a lovelorn Hong Kong cop (Takeshi Kaneshiro) and a beautiful drug smuggler (HK superstar Brigitte Lin); Part Two is about a slightly cracked counter girl (Faye Wong) in romantic pursuit of a second cop (Tony Leung). It all takes place in and around Chungking House, a sprawling apartment complex-*cum*-shopping mall that houses many of Hong Kong's rootless young professionals. As rendered by Wong, it's a place where distinctions between people and products are rapidly disappearing. Relationships have expiration dates; household objects are cajoled, seduced, and abandoned; interchangeable lovers are identified and valued according to the quality of their packaging. Indeed, like no previous film, CHUNGKING EXPRESS captures the historical moment of capitalism's international triumph: right now, all over the world, you can have anything you're prepared to buy, and none of it is worth having.

CHUSHINGURA

1962 115m c Drama ★★★★
Toho (Japan)

Koshiro Matsumoto *(Kuranosuke Oishi)*, Yuzo Kayama *(Takumi-nokami Asano)*, Chusha Ichikawa *(Kouzuke Kira)*, Toshiro Mifune *(Genba Tawaraboshi)*, Setsuko Hara *(Riku)*, Tatsuya Mihashi *(Yasubei Horibe)*, Yosuke Natsuki *(Kinemon Okano)*, Ichiro Arishima *(Denpachiro Tamon)*, Norihei Miki *(Gayboy Geisha)*

d, Hiroshi Inagaki; w, Toshio Yasumi (based on the Kabuki play cycle *Kanadehon Chushingura* by Izumo Takeda, Senryu Namiki, Shoraku Miyoshi); ph, Kazuo Yamada; m, Akira Ifukube; art d, Kisaku Ito

Kayama plays an honest Japanese noble constantly harassed for bribes by his supervisor (Ichikawa). Goaded beyond endurance, the underling draws his sword and wounds his tormentor. He is consequently ordered to commit *hara kiri*, and, in a gripping scene, he fulfills the command. His 47 samurai retainers (known as ronin), however, swear vengeance and finally, after biding their time and planning carefully for nearly two years, attack the lord's castle. Successful in their revenge and acclaimed as heroes, the ronin are nevertheless arrested and sentenced to death for their actions, but they are able to proudly follow the samurai code and go the way of their master.

Adapted from a popular Kabuki play from the 18th century which was based on historical fact, Inagaki's film is probably the best of dozens of film versions of the story going back to 1913. Leisurely paced but energetically acted and beautifully designed and shot, it stands with SEVEN SAMURAI and THRONE OF BLOOD as the best of the Japanese samurai genre.

CIMARRON

1931 131m bw Western   ★★★½
RKO (U.S.)   /U

Richard Dix *(Yancey Cravat)*, Irene Dunne *(Sabra Cravat)*, Estelle Taylor *(Dixie Lee)*, Nance O'Neil *(Felice Venable)*, William Collier Jr. *(the Kid)*, Roscoe Ates *(Jess Rickey)*, George E. Stone *(Sol Levy)*, Robert McWade *(Louie Heffner)*, Edna May Oliver *(Mrs. Tracy Wyatt)*, Frank Darien *(Mr. Bixby)*

p, William LeBaron; d, Wesley Ruggles; w, Howard Estabrook (based on the novel by Edna Ferber); ph, Edward Cronjager; ed, William Hamilton; art d, Max Ree; cos, Max Ree

AA Best Picture; AAN Best Actor: Richard Dix; *AAN Best Actress:* Irene Dunne; *AAN Best Director:* Wesley Ruggles; *AA Best Adapted Screenplay:* Howard Estabrook; *AAN Best Cinematography:* Edward Cronjager; *AA Best Art Direction:* Max Ree

Edna Ferber's red-blooded western saga. Its biggest scene—the Oklahoma Land Rush—employs thousands of extras racing pell-mell on horseback, in wagons and on foot to stake out claims on the two million acres opened to settlers on April 22, 1889. Among this frenzied horde are Richard Dix and his young wife, Irene Dunne. Much of the film, which covers 40 years from 1889 to 1929, rests upon the considerable talents of the lovely Dunne, whose Sabra Cravat is followed from girlhood until she becomes a grand old woman of the West.

They manage to stake out a prize piece of territory, but scheming Estelle Taylor replaces their marker and takes the land herself. Dix establishes a newspaper, liberally complementing the power of the press with his own quick-draw brand of justice (in one dramatic confrontation, he shoots the earlobe off a bully), but the tough westerner has a big heart. When the same Taylor who robbed him of land is later put on trial for prostitution, Dix defends her in court. But he is also consumed by wanderlust, often leaving Dunne for long periods of time, and the film follows their relationship's inevitble changes.

CIMARRON cost RKO a staggering $1.5 million, the largest budget the studio ever committed to a film up to that time. Though it received across-the-board raves, the film lost more than half a million dollars. Dunne is superb and CIMARRON was considered until the late 1940s the finest Western ever made. Its biggest drawback is Dix, whose performance has dated badly. Still, it holds up surprisingly well today; the 1960 remake of CIMARRON fizzles by comparison.

CINCINNATI KID, THE

1965 102m c Drama   ★★★★
MGM (U.S.)   /AA

Steve McQueen *(The Cincinnati Kid)*, Edward G. Robinson *(Lancey Howard)*, Ann-Margret *(Melba)*, Karl Malden *(Shooter)*, Tuesday Weld *(Christian)*, Joan Blondell *(Lady Fingers)*, Rip Torn *(Slade)*, Jack Weston *(Pig)*, Cab Calloway *(Yeller)*, Jeff Corey *(Hoban)*

p, Martin Ransohoff; d, Norman Jewison; w, Ring Lardner Jr., Terry Southern (based on the novel by Richard Jessup); ph, Philip Lathrop; ed, Hal Ashby; m, Lalo Schifrin; art d, George W. Davis, Edward Carfagno; cos, Donfeld

An attempt to do for poker what THE HUSTLER did for pool, THE CINCINNATI KID succeeds on its own, but it might have been a classic with some more attention paid to the script and, perhaps, a little humor sandwiched in to relieve the suspense.

McQueen is The Kid, a formidable gambler who has built a strong reputation among those in the know. He's in New Orleans hustling small-timers and about to go east to Miami when Robinson rolls into town looking for some action. Robinson is "The Man," acknowledged to be the king of poker. He's visiting town for a private game but isn't averse to a match against McQueen, which is arranged by Malden. Torn had earlier been badly beaten by Robinson and he wants revenge, so he calls in some old debts and forces Malden, who is dealing the game between Robinson and McQueen, to slip some winning cards to The Kid. Once McQueen realizes that's happening, he eases Malden out of the way, determined to win fair and square.

A marathon card game takes place, beautifully directed by Jewison, photographed by Lathrop, and edited by Hal Ashby. Even if you don't understand the game, you'll be biting your nails. Excellent supporting

work is provided by Joan Blondell as Lady Fingers, a blowsy blonde dealer. In his accustomed role as the desk clerk, look for Olan Soule, a small, elderly man with a young voice. Soule, whom Jack Webb used often in his TV series, was "Mr. First Nighter" during the halcyon days of radio.

CINDERELLA

1950 74m c Animated   ★★★★
Walt Disney Productions (U.S.)   /U

VOICES OF: Ilene Woods *(Cinderella)*, William Phipps *(Prince Charming)*, Eleanor Audley *(Stepmother)*, Verna Felton *(Fairy Godmother)*, James MacDonald *(Jacques and Gus-Gus)*, Rhoda Williams *(Anastasia)*, Lucille Bliss *(Drusilla)*, Luis Van Rooten *(King and Grand Duke)*, Don Barclay, Claire DuBrey

p, Walt Disney; d, Wilfred Jackson, Hamilton Luske, Clyde Geronimi; w, Bill Peet, Ted Sears, Homer Brightman, Ken Anderson, Erdman Penner, Winston Hibler, Harry Reeves, Joe Rinaldi (based on the original story by Charles Perrault); ed, Donald Halliday; m, Oliver Wallace, Paul Smith

AAN Best Score: Oliver Wallace, Paul J Smith; *AAN Best Song:* Mack David (Music & Lyrics), Al Hoffman (Music & Lyrics), Jerry Livingston (Lyrics); *AAN Best Sound:* Disney Sound Department (Sound)

Although not originally met with the kind of praise that greeted Disney's SNOW WHITE and PINOCCHIO, CINDERELLA holds up better because the heroine seems timeless in her courage and resourcefulness, a closer cousin to Belle in Disney's BEAUTY AND THE BEAST than to other fairytale protagonists. To expand the simple storyline, the Disney people created a variety of animal characters, led by Jacques and Gus-Gus, two adorable mice and evil chubby charmer, Lucifer, the stepmother's cat. Eleanor Audley, Disney's grande dame of villainy, and Verna Felton, Disney's grande dame of benevolence, lead the company of wonderful voices. Excellent animation, marvelous color, and lovely music make CINDERELLA a delight all the way around.

CINEMA PARADISO
(NUOVO CINEMA PARADISO)

1988 123m c Comedy/Drama   ★★½
Ariane/Cristaldifilm/TFI/RAI-TRE/Forum (Italy/France)   /PG

Jacques Perrin *(Toto as an Adult)*, Salvatore Cascio *(Toto as a Child)*, Marco Leonardi *(Toto as a Teenager)*, Philippe Noiret *(Alfredo)*, Nino Terzo *(Peppino's Father)*, Roberta Lena *(Lia)*, Nicolo di Pinto *(Madman)*, Pupella Maggio *(Older Maria)*, Leopoldo Trieste *(Fr. Adelfio)*, Enzo Cannavale *(Spaccafico)*

p, Franco Cristaldi; d, Giuseppe Tornatore; w, Giuseppe Tornatore; ph, Blasco Giurato; ed, Mario Mora; m, Ennio Morricone, Andrea Morricone; prod d, Andrea Crisanti; cos, Beatrice Bordone

AA Best Foreign Language Film

Successful movie director Salvatore returns to his rural Sicilian village after 30 years to attend the funeral of a dear friend and former mentor who advised him, all those years ago, to forsake his humble origins and journey to Rome to make a life for himself. CINEMA PARADISO wallows in nostalgia for a mythic moviegoing past that it serves up in self-infatuated gobs. No, they don't make movies like they used to and this Oscar-winning Italian-French co-production spends the better part of three hours proving it.

In extended flashback, Salvatore (played by Jacques Perrin as an adult) reviews his postwar childhood and his relationship with the friend—Alfredo (Philippe Noiret), the projectionist at the town's only theater, the Cinema Paradiso. The whole town has been affected by the war and, for many, the Paradiso has become a refuge from the impoverishment and indignity that surrounds them.

A prankish altar boy, Salvatore or Toto for short (played as a boy by Salvatore Cascio) follows the local priest to a private screening at the Paradiso. The priest, also the town censor, registers his disapproval of certain moments in the films that flicker past (it's the kissing scenes that invariably arouse his ire) and Alfredo snips out the offending footage. Toto badgers the projectionist into giving him a strip of discarded celluloid. Naturally, a bond soon grows between them.

That Paradiso is some revival house. Great classics from the likes of Lang, Renoir and Visconti abound and there are enough Anna Magnani classics for a month of screenings at the Museum of Modern Art, but for the folks in this backwater hamlet such stellar fare is as common as going to church each week. Indeed going to the movies is a reverential act, as anyone gazing on those rows of rapt faces can tell. They laugh, they cry, they bliss out on cue.

Director Tornatore (IL CAMORRISTA) pushes every sentimental button—some Felliniesque, some probably personal—but none that hasn't been pushed a dozen times before. The film's censor priest might well approve of the carefully tailored sentimentality. Still, Tornatore's film—shot on location in the director's hometown of Bagheria, Sicily—won a number of film festival accolades, including the Grand Jury prize at Cannes in 1989.

CIRCLE OF DECEIT
(DIE FALSCHUNG)
1981 108m c Drama   ★★★★
Bioskop/Artemis/Argos   (France/West Germany)   /X

Bruno Ganz *(Georg Laschen)*, Hanna Schygulla *(Arianna Nassar)*, Jean Carmet *(Rudnik)*, Jerzy Skolimowski *(Hoffmann)*, Gila von Weitershausen *(Greta Laschen)*, Peter Martin Urtel *(Berger)*, John Munro *(John)*, Fouad Naim *(Excellence Joseph)*, Josette Khalil *(Mrs. Joseph)*, Khaled el Saeid *(Progressive Officer)*

p, Eberhard Junkersdorf; d, Volker Schlondorff; w, Volker Schlondorff, Jean-Claude Carriere, Margarethe von Trotta, Kai Hermann (from a novel by Nicolas Born); ph, Igor Luther; ed, Suzanne Baron; m, Maurice Jarre; art d, Alexandre Riachi, Tannous Zougheib; fx, Paul Trielli, Andre Trielli; cos, Dagmar Niefind

German journalist Bruno Ganz leaves a troubled marriage and questions of self-worth behind him and travels to Beirut to write about the obsessive, violent war raging there. Amid a group of disillusioned reporters who see the fighting in the Middle East as just another sign of the times, Ganz vows to get to the heart of the true story and discover the emotional answer to the ever-present question of "why?" He meets and falls in love with the beautiful Hanna Schygulla, a wealthy German aristocrat still living in a mansion in the middle of bombed-out rubble. When the fighting becomes more intense and the lives of the journalists become threatened, most of the reporters leave Beirut for safer territory. Ganz remains, determined to understand the violence and to report it to the world.

Director Volker Schlondorff, one of the pioneers of the New German Cinema, creates a frightening, effective vision of the nightmarish war in Beirut and the grisly effect it can have on emotions as well as bodies. Ganz is wonderfully powerful as the observant, curious reporter who realizes man always has a way of deceiving himself and others into simple answers for complex questions. Schygulla, the mesmerizing star of many of Fassbinder's films, turns in an exquisite performance as the mysterious woman who courts death as well as men. Shot on location in Beirut, the film's re-created, on-the-street battle sequences are violently intense and realistic.

CITADEL, THE
1938 110m bw Drama   ★★★★½
MGM (U.K.)   /A

Robert Donat *(Andrew Manson)*, Rosalind Russell *(Christine Manson)*, Ralph Richardson *(Denny)*, Rex Harrison *(Dr. Lawford)*, Emlyn Williams *(Owen)*, Penelope Dudley-Ward *(Toppy Leroy)*, Francis L. Sullivan *(Ben Chenkin)*, Mary Clare *(Mrs. Orlando)*, Cecil Parker *(Charles Every)*, Nora Swinburne *(Mrs. Thornton)*

p, Victor Saville; d, King Vidor; w, Ian Dalrymple, Frank Wead, Elizabeth Hill, Emlyn Williams (based on the novel by A.J. Cronin); ph, Harry Stradling; ed, Charles Frend; m, Louis Levy; art d, Lazare Meerson, Alfred Junge

AAN Best Picture; AAN Best Actor: Robert Donat; *AAN Best Director:* King Vidor; *AAN Best Original Screenplay:* Ian Dalrymple, Elizabeth Hill, Frank Wead

A faithful rendering of doctor-turned-author Cronin's semi-autobiographical novel, with the superb Donat toplining as a dedicated doctor who ministers to TB-infected Welsh miners and Russell lending stirring support as his devoted and idealistic wife.

At first, Andrew Manson (Donat) is full of lofty goals as he labors in the slums of a mining town, struggling to save the miserable health of downtrodden workers. Later, though, his noble purpose slowly corrodes when he begins to treat aristocratic, wealthy London patients. Turning to the material pleasures of the "good life," it takes the combined efforts of his wife and a close friend (Richardson) and several dramatic turns of events to convinces Manson that he has lost touch with his true aims in life.

Produced by MGM's British production unit after the studio had met with success in a similar foreign production, A YANK AT OXFORD, THE CITADEL is a gripping portrait of both idealism and its disillusionment, not a mere ode to nobility. It is carefully piloted by director Vidor, who wisely allows the consummate acting skills of Donat, Richardson and a marvelous supporting cast to carry the story forward with sensitivity and relaxed charm. Russell, too, at the cusp of her transition between playing society-matron supporting roles and zany comedic starring parts, artfully combines the gentility of the former and the appeal of the latter.

CITIZEN KANE
1941 119m bw Drama   ★★★★★
Mercury (U.S.)   /U

Orson Welles *(Charles Foster Kane)*, Joseph Cotten *(Jedediah Leland)*, Dorothy Comingore *(Susan Alexander)*, Everett Sloane *(Mr. Bernstein)*, Ray Collins *(Boss J.W. "Big Jim" Gettys)*, George Coulouris *(Walter Parks Thatcher)*, Agnes Moorehead *(Mary Kane)*, Paul Stewart *(Raymond)*, Ruth Warrick *(Emily Norton Kane)*, Erskine Sanford *(Herbert Carter)*

p, Orson Welles; d, Orson Welles; w, Herman J. Mankiewicz, Orson Welles; ph, Gregg Toland; ed, Robert Wise, Mark Robson; m, Bernard Herrmann; art d, Van Nest Polglase, Perry Ferguson; fx, Vernon L. Walker; cos, Edward Stevenson

AAN Best Picture; AAN Best Actor: Orson Welles; *AAN Best Director:* Orson Welles; *AA Best Original Screenplay:* Herman J. Mankiewicz, Orson Welles; *AAN Best Cinematography:* Gregg Toland; *AAN Best Editing:* Robert Wise; *AAN Best Score:* Bernard Herrmann; *AAN Best Art Direction:* Perry Ferguson, Van Nest Polglase, Al Fields, Darrell Silvera; *AAN Best Sound:* John Aalberg

Fading in on an ominous nighttime exterior, the camera slowly focuses on a high wrought-iron fence filigreed with the initial "K." Beyond spreads Xanadu, the vast estate of one of the world's wealthiest men. The camera surveys the grounds—empty gondolas swaying on a private lake, exotic animals penned in a private zoo, manicured lawns and shubbery—all shrouded in fog. Towering above the mist is the top of a man-made mountain on which sits a castle, a single light shining from it. Within is a dying man who clutches a crystal ball enclosing a winter scene and make-believe snow. He utters one word, "Rosebud," and dies, dropping the ball, which breaks into tiny shards.

So begins Orson Welles's legendary CITIZEN KANE. After several projects came to naught, notably an adaptation of Joseph Conrad's *Heart of Darkness*, 25 year-old *wunderkind* Welles, already a sensation in the theater and radio worlds, made what is unquestionably the most stunning debut in the history of film. KANE is a landmark film for myriad reasons, not the least of which is the variety of techniques employed—quick cuts, imaginative dissolves, even the iris device once popular in silent films. Indeed, none of the filmmaking methodology of the past is left unused, but KANE also contributes an array of innovative cinematic devices, most notably Gregg Toland's astonishing deep-focus photography (a technique pioneered by legendary cinematographer James Wong Howe). Visually this is Toland's film, a masterpiece of shadow and sharp contrast that artfully conveys murky moods and occasional moments of gaiety as camera and reporter search for the meaning of a man's life.

Welles took credit for writing most of KANE's superb screenplay, but the bulk of its incisive, witty, and unforgettable scenes and dialogue were most probably scripted by screenwriter Herman Mankiewicz, brother of Joseph, the noted film producer-director-writer. Nonetheless,

Welles's contribution as director-producer remains awe-inspiring: he chronicles Kane's life through a combination of highly dramatic episodes and newsreel-like footage—slices of life that form a compelling patchwork biography. The film is so tightly constructed that every scene counts, filling in a piece of the puzzle, incomplete though it may be after reporter Jerry Thompson (William Alland) traces five accounts of the millionaire's life.

At the film's conclusion, reporters gather at Kane's estate, moving through a warehouse that is being cleared of endless piles of curios, stacks of furniture and countless crates containing Kane's purchases. As they move off into the dark recesses, a high boom shot reveals a staggering collection of toys, paintings and statues. Slowly the camera pans the heaps of Kane's possessions until it comes to a blazing furnace into which workmen throw all items considered to be junk. One of the workers picks up a sled—the very one Kane had as a boy in Colorado—and throws it into the fire. The camera closes in tightly on the top of the sled, and as it catches fire, the name "Rosebud" is revealed before the letters burn away. The scene shifts to the outside of the looming castle, panning upward to the high chimney from which Kane's lost youth curls upward into the night sky. The camera pulls back from the edifice, concluding the film with the shot of the iron fence with which it began.

CITIZEN KANE has influenced countless filmmakers and established the taste of discerning audiences worldwide. It is the epitome of filmmaking, a masterpiece for which Welles, one of the greatest practitioners of the cinematic art, will be forever remembered.

CITIZENS BAND

1977 98m c Comedy   ★★★
Paramount (U.S.)   R/AA

Paul LeMat (Spider/Blaine), Candy Clark (Electra/Pam), Ann Wedgeworth (Joyce Rissley), Bruce McGill (Blood/Dean), Marcia Rodd (Portland Angel/Connie), Charles Napier (Chrome Angel/Harold), Alix Elias (Hot Coffee/Debbie), Roberts Blossom (Papa Thermadyne/Father), Richard Bright (Smilin' Jack/Garage Owner), Ed Begley Jr. (Priest)

p, Freddie Fields; d, Jonathan Demme; w, Paul Brickman; ph, Jordan Cronenweth; ed, John F. Link II; m, Bill Conti; art d, Bill Malley; cos, Jodie Lynn Tillen

AMERICAN GRAFFITI goes redneck. An early and sometimes funny effort by director Demme but the hilarity of the subplots (especially the bigamous Napier) swallows the main storyline. LeMat stars as a decent fellow intent on seeing that the CB airwaves are kept open for emergencies, putting him at odds with an assortment of loony CBers who don't want anybody stopping their fun. LeMat again shows himself to be the closest thing there is to a modern-day Jimmy Stewart, yet he's never snagged that one part that will move him into the star category. Not as good as the sum of its parts, but worth a nod unless redneck humor makes you crazy.

CITY AND THE DOGS, THE
(LA CIUDAD Y LOS PERROS)
1985 144m c Drama   ★★★½
Cinevista (Peru)

Pablo Serra (Poet), Gustavo Bueno (Lt. Gamboa), Juan Manuel Ochoa (Jaguar), Luis Alvarez (Colonel), Liliana Navarro (Teresa), Miguel Iza (Arrospide)

p, Francisco Jose Lombardi; d, Francisco Jose Lombardi; w, Jose Watanabe (based on the novel by Mario Vargas Llosa); ph, Pili Flores Guerra

Based on a novel by Mario Vargas Llosa, this engrossing tale of shifting loyalties and revenge is set in the volatile, rigidly codified world of a boys' military academy. The unofficial leaders among the students are called "The Circle," a powerful unit that trades in contraband. Another boy (Pablo Serra), known as "The Poet," has found his niche, writing love letters and erotic stories for his classmates and is the only confidante—although an untrustworthy one—of "The Slave" (Eduardo Adrianzen), a cowardly scapegoat. When the latter is killed under mysterious circumstances, the stage is set for a confrontation between

The Poet and leader of The Circle (Juan Manuel Ochoa) with dire results for the brutal army official who oversees the boys' activities (Gustavo Bueno).

Producer-director Francisco J. Lombardi's portrayal of the boys' daily discipline is as unflinching as any of the boot camp scenes in FULL METAL JACKET. The film is especially compelling in its examination of the multifaceted nature of honor. Aided by his first-rate ensemble, Lombardi succeeds in giving a strong sense of underlying tension.

CITY FOR CONQUEST

1940 105m bw Sports   ★★★½
Warner Bros. (U.S.)   /PG

James Cagney (Danny Kenny), Ann Sheridan (Peggy Nash), Frank Craven ("Old Timer"), Donald Crisp (Scotty McPherson), Frank Kennedy (Eddie Kenny), Frank McHugh ("Mutt"), George Tobias (Pinky), Blanche Yurka (Mrs. Nash), Elia Kazan ("Googi"), Anthony Quinn (Murray Burns)

p, Anatole Litvak; d, Anatole Litvak; w, John Wexley (based on the novel by Aben Kandel); ph, Sol Polito, James Wong Howe; ed, William Holmes; m, Max Steiner; art d, Robert Haas; fx, Byron Haskin, Rex Wimpy; chor, Robert Vreeland; cos, Howard Shoup

James Cagney is at his dynamic best as a Gotham truck driver who boxes to support his brother, Kennedy (in his film debut), while he tries to make it as a composer. Cagney's girlfriend Sheridan struggles to gain fame as a dancer, though she objects to her partner, unctuously portrayed by Anthony Quinn. CITY FOR CONQUEST is an often heavy melodrama, but it has consistently good dialogue, a sprightly style, and a captivating powerhouse performance by Cagney, who drew on his experience as a longtime fight fan. He was 42 when he made the film and, training like a fighter, shed 30 pounds for the role. His fight scenes are realistically photographed by veteran cameramen Sol Polito and James Wong Howe, and in many cases hard blows were actually exchanged between the actor and his opponents. Director Anatole Litvak and Cagney argued over just about every scene, and most of Cagney's ideas, including much of his fight choreography, were edited out of the final version. Moreover, Cagney felt that the story had been ruined and sent a note of apology to its author, novelist Aben Kandel. But Litvak's careful production overcomes any flaws. Watch out for Elia Kazan as a neighborhood kid gone gangster.

CITY OF HOPE

1991 129m c Drama   ★★★½
Esperanza Productions (U.S.)   R/15

Vincent Spano (Nick Rinaldi), Tony Lo Bianco (Joe Rinaldi), Joe Morton (Wynn), Barbara Williams (Angela), John Sayles (Carl), Anthony John Denison (Rizzo), Bill Raymond (Les), Angela Bassett (Reesha), Chris Cooper (Riggs), Gloria Foster (Jeanette)

p, Sarah Green, Maggie Renzi; d, John Sayles; w, John Sayles; ph, Robert Richardson; ed, John Sayles; m, Mason Daring; prod d, Dan Bishop, Dianna Freas; art d, Charles B. Plummer; cos, John Dunn

A schematic tale of urban corruption in a decaying northeastern town, John Sayles's CITY OF HOPE focuses on the network of greed and influence surrounding an urban development plan and its effects on the innocent and guilty alike.

Nick (Vincent Spano), the son of a successful construction company owner, is not only bored by his sinecure on one of his father's sites but troubled by a large gambling debt. His judgment contorted by drugs, Nick walks off his "no-show" job. Arriving at the car repair shop run by his loan shark, Carl (John Sayles), Nick learns of a plan to rob the local appliance dealer, oddly enough a friend of his father, and agrees to drive the getaway van. Nick's father, Joe (Tony Lo Bianco), is also beset by problems. Not only has he had to hire a number of crime-connected characters, he is also the owner of dilapidated apartment buildings that stand in the way of plans to build a shopping center, plans being pushed by foreign money behind the mayor's and district attorney's offices. Joe laments that he has been prevented from improving the slums he owns by such pressures in the same breath as he complains that the tenants stay on despite lack of heat and services. Nick's part in the planned appliance store robbery soon provides the leverage to solve the renewal dilemma.

A cross between BONFIRE OF THE VANITIES and OUR TOWN, CITY OF HOPE is John Sayles's cluttered elegy for the ruined dreams of one segment of urban American society, intermingling themes of big money—characteristically from Japan—simmering racial tensions and generational conflict. Sayles has posited a small town sensibility where everyone knows a lot about others. High school memories provide both gossip, characterization and motivation. The would-be theft at the appliance store seems almost a boyish prank, while the fire at the slum is seen by all as a clear-cut case of arson for profit. Despite the basic pessimism of the plot, Sayles does supply traces of hopefulness: the friendly chatter between Nick and the watchman on a basketball court and the apology by one of the teens to the professor.

CITY OF WOMEN

1980 140m c Drama   ★★★
Gaumont (Italy/France)   /X

Marcello Mastroianni *(Snaporaz)*, Ettore Manni *(Dr. Xavier Zuberkock)*, Anna Prucnal *(Elena)*, Bernice Stegers *(Woman on Train)*, Donatella Damiani *(Feminist on Roller Skates)*, Sara Tafuri *(Other Dancing Girl)*, Jole Silvani *(Old Woman on Motorcycle)*, Carla Terlizzi *(Dr. Zuberkock's Conquest)*, Katren Gebelein *(Enderbreith Small)*, Dominique Labourier *(Feminist)*

p, Renzo Rossellini; d, Federico Fellini; w, Federico Fellini, Bernardino Zapponi, Brunello Rondi; ph, Giuseppe Rotunno; ed, Ruggero Mastroianni; m, Luis Bacalov; art d, Dante Ferretti; chor, Leonetta Bentivoglio; cos, Gabriella Pescucci

Plotless but undoubtedly Fellini. Federico Fellini's psychedelic exploration of feminine mysteries is another visual tour de force in an elaborate dream framework, with a ponderous tone, typical of Fellini's efforts in the latter stages of his career. The film begins as Snaporaz (Marcello Mastroianni), the threatened male protagonist, finds himself trapped at a feminist convention. Dr. Zuberkock (Ettore Manni) offers him refuge in a villa constructed for sexual pleasure, where a celebration of Zuberkock's 10,000th conquest ends with an invasion of female militia. This is followed by a brief reunion between Snaporaz and his estranged wife, leading into a fantasy sequence. For fans of the master only.

CITY SLICKERS

1991 112m c Comedy/Adventure   ★★★½
Castle Rock/Nelson Entertainment/Face Productions (U.S.)PG-13/12

Billy Crystal *(Mitch Robbins)*, Daniel Stern *(Phil Berquist)*, Bruno Kirby *(Ed Furillo)*, Patricia Wettig *(Barbara Robbins)*, Helen Slater *(Bonnie Rayburn)*, Jack Palance *(Curly)*, Noble Willingham *(Clay Stone)*, Tracey Walter *(Cookie)*, Josh Mostel *(Barry Shalowitz)*, David Paymer *(Ira Shalowitz)*

p, Irby Smith; d, Ron Underwood; w, Lowell Ganz, Babaloo Mandel (from the story by Billy Crystal); ph, Dean Semler; ed, O. Nicholas Brown; m, Marc Shaiman; prod d, Lawrence G. Paull; art d, Mark Mansbridge; fx, Ken Pepiot, Frank Welker; cos, Judy Ruskin

AA Best Supporting Actor: Jack Palance

CITY SLICKERS is a skewed, serio-comic variation on Howard Hawks' classic RED RIVER in which the cattle drive becomes a two-week vacation, Walter Brennan, Montgomery Clift and John Wayne become Daniel Stern, Bruno Kirby and Billy Crystal, and the manifest destiny subtext becomes an inner search for the "child within" and a man's discovery of his smile.

Mitch Robbins (Billy Crystal), the man without a smile, is in the throes of a mid-life crisis, questioning his success and his family's happiness. Joining Mitch are his two best friends, Ed Furillo (Bruno Kirby), a loudmouth womanizer fretful about settling down and raising a family, and Phil Berquist (Daniel Stern), whose life is coming apart after his shrewish wife finds out about an affair he had with a 20-year-old woman. At Mitch's 39th-birthday party, his pals give him their gift—a two-week vacation in the West on a cattle drive from New

Mexico to Colorado. Upon arriving, the three friends demonstrate their lack of cowboy skills but they gradually learn to rope and ride as they discuss their childhood hopes and adult disappointments.

CITY SLICKERS successfully skirts the chance for a cheapshot gag comedy and becomes a friendly, heartfelt celebration of friendship and community, greatly aided by a funny and moving script by Lowell Ganz and Babaloo Mandell (PARENTHOOD, VIBES, SPLASH). Ron Underwood's direction complements the script and, while evoking memories of old Western films and TV shows, never overshadows the acting of a uniformly capable cast. Crystal manages to avoid the schtick that marred his previous film work; Jack Palance as Curly plays his role in an almost frightening evocation as a mythic Western hero. His whisper-growls and godlike demeanor make Palance seem a Disney World automaton. But since Palance's job is to carry with him the weight of 90 years of Western film myth, his performance is finely tuned, without any hint of parody that could throw the film out of whack.

CLAIRE'S KNEE
(LE GENOU DE CLAIRE)

1970 103m c Drama   ★★★½
Losange (France)   GP/PG

Jean-Claude Brialy *(Jerome)*, Aurora Cornu *(Aurora)*, Beatrice Romand *(Laura)*, Laurence de Monaghan *(Claire)*, Michele Montel *(Mme. Walter)*, Gerard Falconetti *(Gilles)*, Fabrice Luchini *(Vincent)*

p, Pierre Cottrell; d, Eric Rohmer; w, Eric Rohmer; ph, Nestor Almendros; ed, Cecile Decugis

A rarefied conversation fest, the fifth of Rohmer's "Moral Tales" stars Jean-Claude Brialy as Jerome, a middle-aged intellectual who feels with his head, not his heart. A French diplomat who is about to be married to a woman he loves, but for whom he feels no passion, Jerome visits the provincial town where he was raised. There he meets Claire (Laurence de Monaghan), a summery 17-year-old who is completely absorbed with her boyfriend. Jerome channels his desire for her into a form of passion that, for him, is much more controllable—he wants only to touch her knee.

One of Rohmer's greatest expressions of male-female relationships, CLAIRE'S KNEE presents a portrait of a man who, under his fairly charming and harmless demeanor, is eroding emotionally, convincing even himself that he can control his desires. In order to do so, he must completely detach his actions from his heart and make a physical gesture completely devoid of romance or emotion. What makes this so poignant is that it is only the audience which understands this.

CLASH BY NIGHT

1952 105m bw Drama   ★★★★
RKO (U.S.)   /A

Barbara Stanwyck *(Mae Doyle)*, Paul Douglas *(Jerry D'Amato)*, Robert Ryan *(Earl Pfeiffer)*, Marilyn Monroe *(Peggy)*, J. Carrol Naish *(Uncle Vince)*, Keith Andes *(Joe Doyle)*, Silvio Minciotti *(Papa)*, Diane Stewart, Deborah Stewart *(Baby Gloria)*, Julius Tannen *(Sad-Eyed Waiter)*

p, Harriet Parsons; d, Fritz Lang; w, Alfred Hayes, David Dortort (based on the play by Clifford Odets); ph, Nicholas Musuraca; ed, George Amy; m, Roy Webb; art d, Albert S. D'Agostino, Carroll Clark; fx, Harold Wellman

A Stanwyck field day, in the kind of role she could do with her eyes closed, but because it's well-directed by Fritz Lang, the actress can let go with the snarls, venom, and wounded savagery we've come to expect and love. CLASH is a California cousin of Williams's STREETCAR but Stanwyck's Mae is tougher than Blanche; she's returned home a fallen woman to lick her big-city wounds, and Stanwyck gives it the commonness that Tallulah Bankhead had been too elegant for on Broadway. The story is essentially an Odets kitchen-sink triangle, with dangerous Ryan as resident trouble—he's terrific—and Douglas as the cuckholded spouse. The latter is the weak part of the triangle, but it still works.

In her first major role, Monroe gives a surprising turn as a young woman who, for the most part, is refreshingly independent. This is the lovely Monroe without the candy floss accoutrements; one watches CLASH sensing her career might have gone in a totally different direction had Fox marketed her in an adult manner. The steam she generates with the muscular Andes when Stanwyck and Ryan aren't clawing at each other's clothes makes CLASH BY NIGHT eminently watchable. And fun besides.

CLEAN AND SOBER

1988 124m c Drama ★★★
Image/Warner Bros. (U.S.) R/18

Michael Keaton (*Daryl Poynter*), Kathy Baker (*Charlie Standers*), Morgan Freeman (*Craig*), M. Emmet Walsh (*Richard Dirks*), Brian Benben (*Martin Laux*), Luca Bercovici (*Lenny*), Tate Donovan (*Donald Towle*), Henry Judd Baker (*Xavier*), Claudia Christian (*Iris*), J. David Krassner (*Tiller*)

p, Tony Ganz, Deborah Blum, Jay Daniel; d, Glenn Gordon Caron; w, Tod Carroll; ph, Jan Kiesser; ed, Richard Chew; m, Gabriel Yared; prod d, Joel Schiller; cos, Robert Turturice

This poignant film, directed by Caron, the creator of TV's fleetingly acclaimed "Moonlighting" series, casts Keaton against type as a sleazy cocaine- and alcohol-addicted real estate hotshot who is forced to come to terms with himself. After "borrowing" $92,000 from his Philadelphia company's escrow account and losing it on a stock market gamble, Keaton awakes one morning to find that his one-night stand has OD'd in his bed. He subsequently checks into a 21-day chemical dependency program that promises anonymity—not because he thinks he has a drug problem but in order to avoid the cops. Even as he undergoes detoxification, Keaton tries to obtain some coke over the phone. Freeman, however, the recovering addict who oversees Poynter's group, is wise to every trick. As the treatment progresses, Keaton falls for Baker, a steelworker who is as addicted to her alternately abusive and whimpering boyfriend as she is to cocaine. Keaton receives some much-needed guidance from Walsh, a worldly patient who helps him readjust to the real world.

Reminiscent of THE DAYS OF WINE AND ROSES, LOST WEEKEND, and PANIC IN NEEDLE PARK—this "problem" film doesn't offer many surprises. Once again the duplicity, self-deception, and pathetic dependency of the addict is meticulously and painfully drawn. Keaton's recovery is predictable, the sympathetic presence of the counselor who's seen it all and the kindly "guardian angel" is dramatically convenient, and the doomed love between the addicts is heart-wrenching but not unexpected. Nonetheless CLEAN AND SOBER is very moving because its outstanding performances make each moment seem real and important.

CLEAR AND PRESENT DANGER

1994 142m c Action/Adventure/War ★★★½
Neufeld/Rehme Productions/Paramount (U.S.) PG-13/12

Harrison Ford (*Jack Ryan*), Willem Dafoe (*CIA Field Contractor Mr. Clark*), Anne Archer (*Dr. Cathy Ryan*), James Earl Jones (*Admiral James Greer*), Joaquim De Almeida (*Felix Cortez*), Henry Czerny (*CIA Deputy Director of Operations Robert Ritter*), Harris Yulin (*National Security Advisor James Cutter*), Donald Moffat (*US President Edward Bennett*), Miguel Sandoval (*Ernesto Escobedo*), Benjamin Bratt (*Captain Ramirez*)

p, Mace Neufeld, Robert Rehme; d, Phillip Noyce; w, Donald Stewart, Steve Zaillian, John Milius (based on the novel by Tom Clancy); ph, Donald M. McAlpine; ed, Neil Travis; m, James Horner; prod d, Terence Marsh; art d, William Cruse; fx, Joe Lombardi, Paul Lombardi, Robert Grasmere; cos, Bernie Pollack

AAN Best Sound: Donald O. Mitchell, Michael Herbick, Frank A. Montano, Arthur Rochester; *AAN Best Sound Effects:* Bruce Stambler, John Leveque

The third screen treatment of Tom Clancy's best-selling Jack Ryan series is a sharp improvement over THE HUNT FOR RED OCTOBER and PATRIOT GAMES. It's a formula film with a typically dubious political message, but the storytelling is livelier and more engaging than previous adaptations of Clancy's turgid techno-thrillers.

This time out, CIA administrator Jack Ryan (Harrison Ford) is pitted against Medellin drug kingpin Escobedo (Miguel Sandoval). Ryan's investigation of a string of assassinations leads him to Colom-

bia, where he teams up with a covert team of American soldiers led by Clark (Willem Dafoe) and runs afoul of the duplicitous President Bennett (Donald Moffat).

CLEAR AND PRESENT DANGER develops a multi-track story line of some substance. A solid screenplay neatly follows Jack's investigation into both the drug cartel and the White House cover-ups, while proficiently depicting Clark's covert war and Escobedo's machinations. Politically speaking, the film presents less of a rightward thrust than the red-baiting OCTOBER or the neo-monarchist PATRIOT GAMES.

For director Phillip Noyce, the film—a smash hit—represents a smart recovery from the disastrous SLIVER. Harrison Ford lends a klutzy charm to the role of Jack Ryan that was missing from his first turn in the role; the best performance, however, comes from Sandoval, who manages to create more sympathy for his character than the film probably intended.

CLEO FROM 5 TO 7
(CLIO DE CINQ A SEPT)

1962 90m bw Drama ★★★
Rome Paris (France) /A

Corinne Marchand (*Cleo*), Antoine Bourseiller (*Antoine*), Dorothee Blanck (*Dorothee*), Michel Legrand (*Bob, the Pianist*), Dominique Davray (*Angele*), Jose-Luis de Vilallonga (*The Lover*), Jean-Claude Brialy, Anna Karina, Eddie Constantine, Sami Frey

p, Georges de Beauregard; d, Agnes Varda; w, Agnes Varda; ph, Jean Rabier; ed, Jeanne Verneau; m, Michel Legrand; prod d, Edith Tertza, Jean-Francois Adam; art d, Bernard Evein; cos, Alyette Samazeuilh

Literally, a slice of life. Agnes Varda's second feature opens with an overhead shot of a table, two pairs of women's hands, and a deck of tarot cards. The woman whose fortune is being read, Cleo (played superbly by Corinne Marchand), is told she has cancer. Cleo is dreading the results of a recent medical test and believes her fortune. The rest of the film is a chronicle of the next 90 minutes in her life. Photographed almost exclusively in the streets of Paris, CLEO FROM 5 TO 7 is a portrait of a woman whose view of life has previously never extended past her own vanity and singing success. Faced with the possibility of death, however, Cleo begins to perceive things differently—finding beauty and life in all things. Curiously, the only one of the film's scenes to fall completely flat is a silent comedy sketch that features Anna Karina, Jean-Luc Godard, Sami Frey, Jean-Claude Brialy, Eddie Constantine, and Yves Robert. One especially nice moment is a song, "Sans Toi" (by Michel Legrand and Varda), which Marchand delivers directly into the camera.

CLEOPATRA

1934 102m bw Historical ★★★★
Paramount (U.S.) /A

Claudette Colbert (*Cleopatra*), Warren William (*Julius Caesar*), Henry Wilcoxon (*Marc Antony*), Gertrude Michael (*Calpurnia*), Joseph Schildkraut (*Herod*), Ian Keith (*Octavian*), C. Aubrey Smith (*Enobarbus*), Ian MacLaren (*Cassius*), Arthur Hohl (*Brutus*), Leonard Mudie (*Pothinos*)

p, Cecil B. DeMille; d, Cecil B. DeMille; w, Waldemar Young, Vincent Lawrence (based on historical material by Bartlett Cormack, Jeanie MacPherson, Finley Peter Dunne, Jr.); ph, Victor Milner; ed, Anne Bauchens; m, Rudolph G. Kopp

AAN Best Picture; AA Best Cinematography: Victor Milner; *AAN Best Editing:* Anne Bauchens; *AAN Best Sound:* Franklin Hansen

Opulent, totally satisfying DeMille, due in no small part to the vocal command and trickery brought to Cleopatra by Colbert, a surprisingly good choice despite her leanness and kittenish reputation. CLEOPATRA sails down the Nile with authority and majesty; it may well be DeMille's best film. William and Wilcoxon almost match Colbert; indeed, there's not a lemon in the entire cast. CLEOPATRA exemplifies DeMille's obsession with historical accuracy in setting and props. In one giant set crammed with hundreds of extras, as shooting was about to begin, he stopped everything when he spotted a small flagon 20 feet away. He walked over and picked it up, holding it aloft with disgust. It was silver-plated and represented an era much later than the setting of the film. But his commercial genius demanded liberal doses of sexual fantasy mixed with the historically faithful set designs.

Nowhere in CLEOPATRA is this so obvious as in the infamous barge scene, where DeMille's rendition makes Shakespeare's description look like TUGBOAT ANNIE. While Wilcoxon and Colbert recline aboard the queen's bordello on the sea, a huge net is drawn up from the sea, holding dozens of squirming almost-naked girls—DeMille's catch of the day—who offer Wilcoxon giant sea shells which spill out priceless gems. Then a veil slowly descends around Colbert and the bedazzled Wilcoxon, and DeMille cuts to a shot of the enormous pleasure barge being rowed by hundreds of slaves into the darkened sea, a drummer beating out the cadence of the oarsmen and suggesting the additional rhythm of the unseen seduction. It is DeMille's carnal poetry in action.

CLEOPATRA was a box-office smash, but the critics tore at DeMille for representing the historical characters as satyrs and nymphomaniacs. Some of his severest critics complained about the abundance of British actors dominating the CLEOPATRA cast, speaking with English accents. Some carped about the slangy dialogue. But DeMille knew his public. To the writers of CLEOPATRA, DeMille specified contemporary, vernacular speech. They gave him just what he wanted, and DeMille kept the film sizzling. That's no history lesson, that's entertainment!

CLEOPATRA

1963 243m c Historical ★★½
Fox (U.S.) /PG

Elizabeth Taylor *(Cleopatra)*, Richard Burton *(Mark Antony)*, Rex Harrison *(Julius Caesar)*, Pamela Brown *(High Priestess)*, George Cole *(Flavius)*, Hume Cronyn *(Sosigenes)*, Cesare Danova *(Apollodorus)*, Kenneth Haigh *(Brutus)*, Andrew Keir *(Agrippa)*, Martin Landau *(Rufio)*

p, Walter Wanger; d, Joseph L. Mankiewicz; w, Joseph L. Mankiewicz, Ranald MacDougall, Sidney Buchman (based on works by Plutarch, Appian, and Suetonius, and the novel *The Life And Times Of Cleopatra* by Carlo Mario Franzero); ph, Leon Shamroy; ed, Dorothy Spencer; m, Alex North; prod d, John De Cuir; art d, Jack Martin Smith, Hilyard Brown, Herman A. Blumenthal, Elven Webb, Maurice Pelling, Boris Juraga; fx, L.B. Abbott, Emil Kosa Jr.; chor, Hermes Pan; cos, Irene Sharaff, Vittorio Nino Novarese

AAN Best Picture; AAN Best Actor: Rex Harrison; *AA Best Cinematography:* Leon Shamroy; *AAN Best Editing:* Dorothy Spencer; *AAN Best Score:* Alex North; *AA Best Art Direction:* John DeCuir, Jack Martin Smith, Hilyard Brown, Herman Blumenthal, Elven Webb, Maurice Pelling, Boris Juraga, Walter M. Scott, Paul S. Fox, Ray Moyer; *AA Best Costume Design:* Irene Sharaff, Vittorio Nino Novarese, Renie; *AAN Best Sound:* James P. Corcoran; *AA Best Visual Effects:* Emil Kosa, Jr.

Chaucer's Wife of Bath plays Cleolizzie, the million-dollar sultana of 60s jetset sirens, in enough eyeliner to resurrect Theda Bara, and ten costumes for every occasion. This is not a film——it's a deal, decorated with extensive publicity, but weighed down by listless direction and lots of nasal talk, talk, talk. Even fans of camp would have to admit what's here is about an hour's worth of television MOW. Taylor brings notoriety and cleavage to her performance as Cleopatra; she's at her best when Cleo makes her entrance into Rome, when Taylor worried that the Catholic extras might riot and kill her. The scene is a triumph of morass over morality. Hurricane Liz conquers Rome! Otherwise, she plays the Egyptian tigress (original choice was Susan Hayward, an expert at tigresses, Biblical and otherwise) as a spewing, mewing, pampered Roman housecat who makes fusses because she can. Would the film have been better with Hayward, Peter Finch and Stephen Boyd, directed by Mamoulian? Perhaps, but at least Harrison, taking over for Finch, strikes a few waspish notes. Otherwise, it's a Vegas-style history lesson, but dammit, a boring one, depriving us of a thousand laughs and cracks.

CLERKS

1994 92m bw Comedy ★★★
View Askew Productions (U.S.) R/18

Brian O'Halloran *(Dante Hicks)*, Jeff Anderson *(Randal)*, Marilyn Ghiglotti *(Veronica)*, Lisa Spoonauer *(Caitlin)*, Jason Mewes *(Jay)*, Kevin Smith *(Silent Bob)*, Scott Schiaffo *(Chewlie's Rep)*, Scott Mosier *(William the Idiot Manchild/Angry Hockey Playing Customer/Angry Mourner)*, Walt Flanagan *(Wooden Cap Smoker/Egg Man/Offended Customer/Cat Admiring Bitter Customer/Angry Mourner)*, Al Berkowitz *(Old Man)*

p, Kevin Smith, Scott Mosier; d, Kevin Smith; w, Kevin Smith; ph, David Klein; ed, Kevin Smith, Scott Mosier; m, Scott Angley

This sourly amusing farce about suburban slackers is a lowball bid on the minimum production values needed to put across an independent first feature. Dante (Brian O'Halloran), who looks like a cranky Charlie Sheen in a Vandyke beard, is the proprietor of a convenience store in Asbury Park, NJ. Make that *inconvenience* store, since Dante's working life, an unending stream of minor atrocities, is a prolonged slow burn. Dante's best friend Randal (Jeff Anderson) mans the video store next door, and spends his time ordering titles like HAPPY SCRAPPY HERO PUP and BEST OF BOTH WORLDS, a compilation of hermaphrodite porn. Their (considerable) downtime is spent in earnest debate over monumentally trivial issues, though a narrative of sorts does eventually unfold in a series of arch blackouts.

Some of the aimless dialogue is very sharp among these lumpen bourgeoisie, who've got wit and intellect to spare, but little in the way of education, ambition, or opportunity. ("There's nothing more exhilarating than pointing out the shortcomings of others, is there?" notes Randal.) Director Kevin Smith billboards his influences, cheekily thanking Hal Hartley, Richard Linklater, Spike Lee, and Jim Jarmusch in the closing crawl. Unlike his models, however, Smith hasn't demonstrated that his sensibility reaches much beyond bathroom humor and meaningless drift. It might have been more accurate to invoke that other Mt. Rushmore of Gen-X taste: Ren, Stimpy, Beavis, and Butt-head.

CLIENT, THE

1994 124m c Crime/Thriller ★★★
Client Productions Inc./New Regency Productio/Alcor Films PG-13/15

Susan Sarandon *(Reggie Love)*, Tommy Lee Jones *("Reverend" Roy Foltrigg)*, Brad Renfro *(Mark Sway)*, Mary-Louise Parker *(Dianne Sway)*, Anthony LaPaglia *(Barry "The Blade" Muldano)*, J.T. Walsh *(McThune)*, Anthony Edwards *(Clint Von Hooser)*, Will Patton *(Sergeant Hardy)*, Bradley Witford *(Thomas Fink)*, Anthony Heald *(Trumann)*

p, Arnon Milchan, Steven Reuther; d, Joel Schumacher; w, Akiva Goldsman, Robert Getchell (based on the novel by John Grisham); ph, Tony Pierce-Roberts; ed, Robert Brown; m, Howard Shore; prod d, Bruno Rubeo; art d, P. Michael Johnston; fx, Larry Fioritto, Wes Mattox; cos, Ingrid Ferrin

AAN Best Actress: Susan Sarandon

Based on the bestseller by John Grisham, THE CLIENT is a slickly packaged thriller wrapped in fashionable paranoia and tied up with an incongruously heartening moral. Susan Sarandon won an Academy Award nomination for her portrayal of anti-establishment lawyer Reggie Love, whose tough surface hides a heart of pure Jell-O.

When young Mark Sway (Brad Renfro) discovers the truth about the murder of a US Senator, he becomes the prey of murderous gangster Barry Muldano (Anthony LaPaglia). In desperate need of help, the boy walks into the office of feisty recovering alcoholic Reggie Love (Sarandon), who can't resist a hopeless case. Her first task is to protect Mark from flamboyant Federal Attorney Roy Foltrigg (Tommy Lee Jones), who tries to trick Mark into revealing what he knows. Unless Love can negotiate certain guarantees of protection before he testifies, her client and his family will be killed.

Though ostensibly a thriller, THE CLIENT is rather short on suspense; the movie's real center is the relationship between brittle professional Reggie Love and the tough, vulnerable boy she wants to protect. Jones puts on a captivating show, playing a swaggering tyrant in an expensive suit who's Bible-thumping one moment and preening for the cameras the next; but it's Sarandon and Renfro, an unusually appealing child actor, who dominate the film.

CLIFFHANGER

1993   112m   c   Action/Thriller   ★★★
Carolco International N.V.   (U.S./Netherlands)   R/15

Sylvester Stallone *(Gabe Walker)*, John Lithgow *(Qualen)*, Michael Rooker *(Hal Tucker)*, Janine Turner *(Jessie Deighan)*, Rex Linn *(Travers)*, Caroline Goodall *(Kristel)*, Leon Robinson *(Kynette)*, Craig Fairbrass *(Delmar)*, Gregory Scott Cummins *(Ryan)*, Denis Forest *(Heldon)*

p, Alan Marshall, Renny Harlin; d, Renny Harlin; w, Michael France, Sylvester Stallone (from a story by France); ph, Alex Thomson, Adam Dale; ed, Frank J. Urioste; m, Trevor Jones; prod d, John Vallone; art d, Aurelio Crugnola, Christiaan Wagener; fx, Neil Krepela, John Bruno; cos, Ellen Mirojnick

AAN Best Sound: Bob Beemer, Tim Cooney, Michael Minkler; *AAN* Best Sound Effects Editing: Gregg Baxter, Wylie Stateman; *AAN* Best Visual Effects: John Bruno, Pamela Easly, Neil Krepela, John Richardson

CLIFFHANGER offers us breathtaking mountain scenery, some occasionally gripping action sequences, and a lot of gags—mostly unintentional and mostly courtesy of Sylvester Stallone. It may go down in screen history as the nail in the coffin of the "Die Hard" sub-genre, in which all the key elements of that blockbuster have been recycled to the point of self-parody.

Stallone plays Gabe Walker, a rescue climber pitted against a gang of hijackers whose plane has crashed on a snow-capped Rocky Mountain peak. Led by Qualen (John Lithgow), whose hammy quips and English accent peg him as a criminal mastermind, the gang is now intent on retrieving three suitcases containing $100 million. But they haven't reckoned on Walker, who can climb thousands of feet of snowy rockface clad only in a T-shirt, outpace a helicopter, and anticipate every move Qualen makes.

When he's not killing bad guys or rescuing his girlfriend, Jessie (Janine Turner), Walker gets to deliver some dialogue that is as spectacular, in its own Stallonesque way, as the scenery. (Qualen: "Walker, you're a real piece of work." Walker: "Yeah, an' you're a real piece of sh. . .")

Audiences who stayed away from Stallone's early 90s comedies, OSCAR and STOP! OR MY MOM WILL SHOOT, may have been wrong. What CLIFFHANGER tells us is that the star *is* a comic actor, after all. From the moment he first opens his mouth, we give up any hope of a suspenseful action drama and settle in, instead, for a ride punctuated alternately by chuckles and groans.

CLOCK, THE

1945   90m   bw   Romance   ★★★★
MGM   (U.S.)

Judy Garland *(Alice Mayberry)*, Robert Walker *(Cpl. Joe Allen)*, James Gleason *(Al Henry)*, Keenan Wynn *(The Drunk)*, Marshall Thompson *(Bill)*, Lucille Gleason *(Mrs. Al Henry)*, Ruth Brady *(Helen)*, Chester Clute *(Michael Henry)*, Dick Elliott *(Friendly Man)*

p, Arthur Freed; d, Vincente Minnelli; w, Robert Nathan, Joseph Schrank (based on a story by Paul and Pauline Gallico); ph, George Folsey; ed, George White; m, George Bassman; art d, Cedric Gibbons, William Ferrari; fx, A. Arnold Gillespie; cos, Irene

A small wartime gem featuring the luminous Garland, directed by her future husband, in a rare nonsinging role. The story is deceptively simple; it is in the subtle touches that the genius of this film lies. Garland and Walker meet under the big clock at Pennsylvania Station in New York. They fall in love and marry within 48 hours. This kind of thing happened often in real life, and Gallico's story feels authentic. So does the incredible rear-screen projection work and the huge sets that would cause any New Yorker to bet serious money that the film was done on location in the Big Apple. Not so. It was a back-lot job and a tribute to the talents of its technicians. Every single bit player is perfectly cast, and special plaudits go to Wynn, who plays a drunken patriot.

This was Minnelli's first straight directing job and he went on to distinguish himself away from musicals with such giants as THE BAD AND THE BEAUTIFUL, FATHER OF THE BRIDE and many others. Looking at the two young, well-scrubbed stars, it's hard to believe that both their lives would end tragically. Walker, only 33 at the time of his death, had been married to Jennifer Jones and John Ford's daughter, Barbara. He'd been institutionalized for alcohol abuse almost a year before returning to work in Alfred Hitchcock's STRANGERS ON A TRAIN. While filming MY SON JOHN in 1951, he died from too many sedatives doctors had prescribed to calm his emotional instability. This is a rare tribute to the acting genius of Garland, who would still have had all the makings of a star, even if she had never sung a note.

CLOCKMAKER, THE
(L'HORLOGER DE SAINT-PAUL)

1973   105m   c   Drama   ★★★½
Lira   (France)

Philippe Noiret *(Michel Descombes)*, Jean Rochefort *(Commissioner Guiboud)*, Jacques Denis *(Antoine)*, William Sabatier *(Lawyer)*, Andree Tainsy *(Madeleine)*, Sylvain Rougerie *(Bernard Descombes)*, Christine Pascal *(Lilliane Terrini)*, Cecile Vassort *(Martine)*, Yves Afonso, Jacques Hilling

d, Bertrand Tavernier; w, Jean Aurenche, Pierre Bost (based on the novel *The Clockmaker of Everton* by Georges Simenon); ph, Pierre-William Glenn; ed, Armand Psenny; m, Philippe Sarde

A first feature from former critic Tavernier, THE CLOCKMAKER stars Noiret as Descombes, a widowed Lyons watchmaker who leads a perfectly orderly life, plays by the rules, and has no intention of ever stepping out of line. His life is thrown into disarray when police inspectors arrive at his shop to report that his only son, Rougerie, is suspected of murdering a hated factory foreman. Although Noiret has what he considers a good relationship with his son, he comes to realize that he really doesn't know Rougerie at all.

Based on a novel by Simenon, THE CLOCKMAKER is an introspective, intelligent, sad, but ultimately positive look, not at murderers and criminal investigations, but at a strong relationship between a father and son. Rather than resort to heavy-handed speechmaking or maudlin sentiment, Tavernier treats his material with the honesty and subtlety it deserves. This exceptional debut clearly marked Tavernier, one of the few realist film directors, as a force to be reckoned with.

CLOCKWISE

1986   96m   c   Comedy   ★★★
Moment   (U.K.)   PG

John Cleese *(Brian Stimpson)*, Alison Steadman *(Gwenda Stimpson)*, Penelope Wilton *(Pat Garden)*, Stephen Moore *(Mr. Jolly)*, Joan Hickson *(Mrs. Trellis)*, Sharon Maiden *(Laura)*, Penny Leatherbarrow *(Teacher)*, Howard Lewis *(Ted)*, Jonathan Bowater *(Clint)*, Mark Bunting *(Studious Boy)*

p, Michael Codron; d, Christopher Morahan; w, Michael Frayn; ph, John Coquillon; ed, Peter Boyle; m, George Fenton; prod d, Roger Murray-Leach; art d, Diana Charnley; cos, Judy Moorcroft

Thin comedy, sometimes transformed by the energy of Monty Python's Cleese as a school headmaster, driven by punctuality. On the way to a speaking engagement at a convention, he keeps getting into all manner of trouble. If you adore Cleese, you'll have a fine time. Otherwise Frayn's script is not meaty enough to sustain viewer interest, nor is there any momentum built by Morahan's direction.

CLOCKWORK ORANGE, A

1971   137m   c   Science Fiction   ★★★★
Warner Bros.   (U.K.)   R/X

Malcolm McDowell *(Alex)*, Patrick Magee *(Mr. Alexander)*, Michael Bates *(Chief Guard)*, Warren Clarke *(Dim)*, John Clive *(Stage Actor)*, Adrienne Corri *(Mrs. Alexander)*, Carl Duering *(Dr. Brodsky)*, Paul Farrell *(Hobo)*, Clive Francis *(Lodger)*, Michael Gover *(Prison Warden)*

p, Stanley Kubrick; d, Stanley Kubrick; w, Stanley Kubrick (based on the novel by Anthony Burgess); ph, John Alcott; ed, Bill Butler; m, Walter Carlos; prod d, John Barry; art d, Russell Hagg, Peter Shields; cos, Milena Canonero

AAN Best Picture; *AAN Best Director*: Stanley Kubrick; *AAN Best Adapted Screenplay*: Stanley Kubrick; *AAN Best Editing*: Bill Butler

Who else but Stanley Kubrick could successfully direct an ultra-stylish, sci-fi cult film about the impossibility of redemption in the absence of freely willed sin? In a shabbily futuristic British welfare state, Alex (Malcolm McDowell) leads a gang of juvenile delinquents through nightly rounds of beatings, rapes and, as they call it, "ultraviolence." The lads wear motley uniforms—jumpsuits fitted with codpieces—and speak in a bizarre patois that combines elements of colloquial Russian with Cockney rhyming slang; Alex hates school but loves Beethoven, whose music he associates with sexual violence. Among their victims is a prominent writer (Patrick Magee); they beat him senseless and gang-rape his wife (Adrienne Corri). After violently suppressing an uprising among his "droogies" (from the Russian for "friends"), Alex is betrayed by them during an attack on another home, knocked senseless and left for the police. In prison, he agrees to undergo horrific experiments in "aversion therapy" in order to shorten his term. Now nauseated by the mere thought of violence—or Beethoven—he's pronounced cured and released into the outside world. There, vengeance of one kind or another is visited upon him by his erstwhile fellow gang-members (now policemen), and by his former victims (including Magee). Victimized by his former victims, he becomes a media celebrity and reaches a cynical accomodation with the parliamentary opposition. "I was cured, all right," Alex observes.

Kubrick's liberal, anti-authoritarian reading of Anthony Burgess's very Catholic allegorical novel is morally confused but tremendously powerful. A CLOCKWORK ORANGE is a visually dazzling, highly unsettling work that revolves around one of the few truly amoral characters in film or literature. It pits a gleefully vicious individual against a blandly inhuman state, leaving the viewer little room for emotional involvement (though McDowell gives such an ebullient, wide-eyed performance as the Beethoven-loving delinquent that it is hard for us not to feel some sympathy toward him). Meanwhile, we're dazzled by Kubrick's directorial pyrotechnics—slow motion, fast motion, fish-eye lenses, etc.; entertained by John Barry's witty, ostentatious sets; and intrigued by dialogue laden with Burgess's specially created slang ("good" is "horrorshow"; sex is "the old inout," etc.). A particularly graphic film for its time, A CLOCKWORK ORANGE continues to divide critics. No serious moviegoer can afford to ignore it.

CLOSE ENCOUNTERS OF THE THIRD KIND

1977 135m c Science Fiction ★★★★★
Columbia (U.S.) PG/A

Richard Dreyfuss *(Roy Neary)*, Francois Truffaut *(Claude Lacombe)*, Teri Garr *(Ronnie Neary)*, Melinda Dillon *(Jillian Guiler)*, Cary Guffey *(Barry Guiler)*, Bob Balaban *(Interpreter Laughlin)*, J. Patrick McNamara *(Project Leader)*, Warren Kemmerling *(Wild Bill)*, Roberts Blossom *(Farmer)*, Philip Dodds *(Jean Claude)*

p, Julia Phillips, Michael Phillips; d, Steven Spielberg; w, Steven Spielberg; ph, Vilmos Zsigmond; ed, Michael Kahn; m, John Williams; prod d, Joe Alves; art d, Dan Lomino; fx, Roy Arbogast, Gregory Jein, Douglas Trumbull, Matthew Yuricich, Richard Yuricich; cos, Jim Linn

AAN Best Supporting Actress: Melinda Dillon; *AAN Best Director*: Steven Spielberg; *AA Best Cinematography*: Vilmos Zsigmond; *AAN Best Editing*: Michael Kahn; *AAN Best Score*: John Williams; *AAN Best Art Direction*: Joe Alves, Dan Lomino, Phil Abramson; *AAN Best Sound*: Robert Knudson, Robert J. Glass, Don MacDougall, Gene S. Cantamessa; *AAN Best Visual Effects*: Roy Arbogast, Douglas Trumbull, Matthew Yuricich, Gregory Jein, Richard Yuricich

Steven Spielberg proves decisively that a special effects-dependent film need not be cold, mechanistic, or simpleminded. Here he presents first contact with an extraterrestrial culture in spirit of near-religious awe in sharp contrast to the dark paranoia of traditional science fiction Cold War parables. CLOSE ENCOUNTERS OF THE THIRD KIND is a humanistic postmodern masterpiece that incorporates much of movie history—images, sounds, and subtle evocations of the works of Walt

Disney, John Ford, Alfred Hitchcock, Cecil B. DeMille, and Chuck Jones—into its revisionist project. Classic Sixties fantasy television fare such as "Star Trek," "Bewitched," and "The Twilight Zone" also figure in the meaningful mosaic of citations. This film shows the power pop-culture imagery exerts over our humdrum lives and the ever present lure of escapism. The movies may set you free, it suggests, but perhaps only at the cost of losing real human relationships.

The story depicts the life-transforming experiences of lineman Roy Neary (Richard Dreyfuss) who is sent out into the night to investigate a mysterious power outage. His truck gets stalled on the road and he's bathed in a brilliant light from above. Thus begins Roy's journey from disinterested spectator to impassioned participant in an otherworldly spectacle. A mysterious vision and five musical notes are imprinted in his mind after he witnesses strange lights in the sky. His family life is devastated by his obsession but he acquires a spiritual surrogate family along the path to enlightenment including the delightful (and delighted) child Cary Guffey who is spirited away from his mother (Melinda Dillon) during the film's only frightening set piece and Francois Truffaut (the beloved director of such French New Wave classics as THE 400 BLOWS, JULES AND JIM and THE WILD CHILD) as Claude Lacombe, the endearingly humane director of the scientific ad hoc "welcome wagon."

Special effects master Douglas Trumbull (the FX wizard of 2001: A SPACE ODYSSEY) created the strikingly beautiful and dreamy visions that set the look of this film apart from the cool razzle dazzle of Industrial Light and Magic projects. John Williams contributes one of his most unusual and memorable scores. This is one for the angels.

CLOSELY WATCHED TRAINS
(OSTRE SLEDOVANE VLAKY)

1966 89m bw Comedy/Drama ★★★★
Barrandov/Ladislav Fikar/Bohumil Smida (Czechoslovakia)

Vaclav Neckar *(Trainee Milos Hrma)*, Jitka Bendova *(Conductor Masa)*, Josef Somr *(Train Dispatcher Hubicka)*, Vladimir Valenta *(Stationmaster Max)*, Vlastimil Brodsky *(Counselor Zednicek)*, Jiri Menzel *(Dr. Brabek)*, Libuse Havelkova *(Max's Wife)*, Alois Vachek *(Novak)*, Jitka Zelenohorska *(Zdenka)*, Ferdinand Kruta *(Masa's Uncle)*

p, Zdenek Oves; d, Jiri Menzel; w, Jiri Menzel, Bohumil Hrabal (based on his novel); ph, Jaromir Sofr; ed, Jirina Lukesova; m, Jiri Sust; art d, Oldrich Bosak; cos, Ruzena Bulickova

AA Best Foreign Language Film

The first feature from the 28-year-old Czech filmmaker Menzel is a comic, humanistic look at a teenage railway trainee, Milos (Neckar), who is sent off to a desolate station in Bohemia during the German occupation of Czechoslovakia. Hidden away from much of the rest of the world, Milos and the very ordinary characters who pass through the station try to live as if they were not caught in the midst of WWII. Milos learns his trade with relative ease, working under the experienced guidance of dispatcher Hubicka (Somr). A bored womanizer, Hubicka also becomes the uneasy boy's mentor in the ways of the world, which are all too quickly being thrust upon him. During the course of the film, Milos turns freedom fighter and experiences a variety of incidents, including sexual initiation, a botched suicide, and an act of heroism.

Possibly the best known and the most commercially successful film of the Czech New Wave of the 1960s during the all-too-brief Prague Spring, CLOSELY WATCHED TRAINS went on to win an Oscar for Best Foreign Film. Comic, tragic, romantic, and realistic, it is a film of great warmth and honesty, photographed in wonderfully stark black and white and cast with an exceptional group of actors.

CLUELESS

1995 97m c Comedy/Romance ★★★★
Robert Lawrence Productions/Paramount (U.S.) PG-13/12

Alicia Silverstone *(Cher Horowitz)*, Stacey Dash *(Dionne)*, Brittany Murphy *(Tai)*, Paul Rudd *(Josh)*, Dan Hedaya *(Mel Hamilton)*, Donald Adeosun Faison *(Murray)*, Elisa Donovan *(Amber)*, Breckin Meyer *(Travis Birkenstock)*, Jeremy Sisto *(Elton)*, Aida Linares *(Lucy)*

p, Robert Lawrence, Scott Rudin; d, Amy Heckerling; w, Amy Heckerling; ph, Bill Pope; ed, Debra Chiate; m, David Kitay; prod d, Steven Jordan; art d, William Hiney; chor, Patrick Romano; cos, Mona May

Bust beneath the bubbly, candy-colored surface of this good-natured fluff about privileged California teens lies a sharply observed comedy of manners with a good deal more to say about family, romance, and friendship in the '90s than mainstream audiences have any right to expect. Like its effortlessly adorable protagonist Cher, CLUELESS is anything but.

Pretty, impeccably groomed Cher Hamilton (Alicia Silverstone) is the most popular girl at Bronson Alcott High School (Beverly Hills High in all but name). Her father (Dan Hedaya) is a successful lawyer who indulges her every whim (her mom died during routine liposuction surgery), and her best friend Dionne (Stacey Dash) shares her preoccupations: music, fitness, and fashion. Cher's perfect life is only slightly disrupted when her ex-step-brother Josh (Paul Rudd)—a *terribly* serious college student—comes to stay. Stung by Josh's exhortations that she should try to do some good in the world, Cher resolves to rescue grunge girl Tai (Brittany Murphy) from a life of social exile. The result, however, is not at all what she anticipates.

Cher (winningly played by Silverstone) is a beautifully packaged bundle of contradictions: superficially sophisticated but deeply ignorant, kind but oblivious, controlling but generous. She's clever without being smart, instinctively perceptive without the discipline that would tell her what to do with her insights. That Heckerling and Silverstone make Cher entirely lovable without glossing over her substantial deficiencies is one of the film's greatest triumphs. The other is its deft use of language. Cher and her friends speak a sleek, allusive patois that's almost Asian in its sensitivity to inflection and poetic in its reliance on convoluted metaphor. Can this remarkable film really be based on Jane Austen's *Emma*? As if!

COAL MINER'S DAUGHTER

1980   125m   c   Biography/Musical   ★★★★
Universal   (U.S.)   PG/A

Sissy Spacek *(Loretta)*, Tommy Lee Jones *(Doolittle "Mooney" Lynn)*, Levon Helm *(Ted Webb)*, Phyllis Boyens *(Clara Webb)*, Bill Anderson Jr., Foister Dickerson, Malla McCown, Pamela McCown, Kevin Salvilla *(Webb Children)*, William Sanderson *(Lee Dollarhide)*

p, Bernard Schwartz; d, Michael Apted; w, Thomas Rickman (based on autobiography by Loretta Lynn with George Vescey); ph, Ralf D. Bode; ed, Arthur Schmidt; m, Owen Bradley; prod d, John W. Corso; cos, Joe I. Tompkins

AAN Best Picture; AA Best Actress: Sissy Spacek; *AAN Best Adapted Screenplay:* Tom Rickman; *AAN Best Cinematography:* Ralf D. Bode; *AAN Best Editing:* Arthur Schmidt; *AAN Best Art Direction:* John W. Corso, John M. Dwyer; *AAN Best Sound:* Richard Portman, Roger Heman, Jim Alexander

The rare expert film bio. COAL MINER'S DAUGHTER features an Oscar-winning performance by Sissy Spacek as country music queen Loretta Lynn. Masterfully directed by Michael Apted, the film traces the famed country singer's life from her beginnings in a tumbledown shack in Butcher Hollow, Kentucky, through her huge success, marital discord, and battle with prescription drugs. The film's early sequences are lyrical, melancholy accounts of mountain life and comprise the film's most poignant, memorable moments. There are outstanding acting jobs by Levon Helm and Phyllis Boyens as Lynn's parents, Tommy Lee Jones as her well-meaning, ne'er-do-well husband, and Beverly D'Angelo in a dazzling turn as the magnificent Patsy Cline. Spacek and D'Angelo do their own warbling quite expertly; after this, it's hard to get worked up over Jessica Lange's lukewarm, lipsynched take on Cline in SWEET DREAMS.

COCA-COLA KID, THE

1985   94m   c   Comedy   ★★★
Smart Egg/Cinecom/Film Gallery   (Australia)   R/15

Eric Roberts *(Becker)*, Greta Scacchi *(Terri)*, Bill Kerr *(T. George McDowell)*, Chris Haywood *(Kim)*, Kris McQuade *(Juliana)*, Max Gilles *(Frank)*, Tony Barry *(Bushman)*, Paul Chubb *(Fred)*, David Slingsby *(Waiter)*, Tim Finn *(Philip)*

p, David Roe, Sylvie Le Clezio; d, Dusan Makavejev; w, Frank Moorhouse (based on the short story collections *The Americans, Baby,* and *The Electrical Experience* by Moorhouse); ph, Dean Semler; ed, John Scott; m, William Motzing; prod d, Graham Walker; cos, Terry Ryan

When Coca-Cola's big bosses suspect that profits could be greater in Australia, they send in Eric Roberts, a quirky wunderkind troubleshooter who, as an ex-Marine, takes pride in the company and views Coca-Cola as a symbol of the US. Arriving at the Australian office, he meets Greta Scacchi, a beautiful young secretary who wanders around the office in her stocking feet, lets her daughter photocopy her face on the office copier, and is nearly raped by her angry estranged husband. After studying a geographical representation of the areas where their product is being sold, Roberts discovers a section of Australia completely devoid of his company's beverage. This region prefers a local soft drink made by eccentric Bill Kerr, an embittered, trigger-happy old man, now determined to keep Coke's imperialists off his land and to continue his operations in a traditional, antiquated, steam-powered plant.

In THE COCA-COLA KID Yugoslavian director Dusan Makavejev has made a truly international picture that, like Coca-Cola, knows no borders, enlisting the contributions of an Australian writer, Frank Moorhouse; an American actor, Roberts; and a British actress, Scacchi. Scacchi, exuding a raw sexuality, makes a lasting impression, but Roberts's handsomeness can't save his ham acting. This is far from Makavejev's finest work (WR: MYSTERIES OF THE ORGANISM and SWEET MOVIE are much more challenging), but it is the film that has spread the director's political message to the widest audience.

COCOANUTS, THE

1929   90m   bw   Comedy   ★★★½
Paramount   (U.S.)

Groucho Marx *(Hammer)*, Harpo Marx *(Harpo)*, Chico Marx *(Chico)*, Zeppo Marx *(Jamison)*, Mary Eaton *(Polly)*, Oscar Shaw *(Bob)*, Kay Francis *(Penelope)*, Margaret Dumont *(Mrs. Potter)*, Cyril Ring *(Yates)*, Basil Ruysdael *(Hennessey)*

p, Monta Bell, James R. Cowan; d, Robert Florey, Joseph Santley; w, Morrie Ryskind (based on the play by George S. Kaufman and Irving Berlin); ph, George Folsey; chor, Joseph Santley, Robert Florey

The greatest of zanies, the Marx Brothers, perform with dizzying speed in this farcical and nearly plotless romp through a Florida hotel, ostensibly dealing with the arrival and departure of would-be millionaires getting richer or poorer during the Florida land boom of the late 1920s. The mayhem is often side-splitting in this "pure" Marx vehicle, where the love story is strictly incidental. While they basically kept to the routines audiences had enjoyed in the original play by George S. Kaufman and Irving Berlin, the boys were given their usual freedom to ad lib; these bits were constantly changing, even during the shooting of the film. Berlin himself cut many tunes that were never sung since the brothers cavalierly changed the material.

This is a crude, shapeless talkie, a technically unsophisticated film in which the sound is static and the camera immobile, with the comedians leaping into the set scenes. Yet the boys are there in all their frenetic glory. Harpo honks his horn for the first time, chasing but never catching a scantily clad cutie; he would pursue her in vain for decades to come, while his brothers chewed up the sets and spat out laughter. THE COCOANUTS was officially the debut of the madcap brothers, although they had appeared in an obscure silent production, HUMOR RISK, which is now an apparently lost film.

COCOON

1985   117m   c   Comedy/Science Fiction   ★★★
Fox   (U.S.)   PG-13/PG

Don Ameche *(Art Selwyn)*, Wilford Brimley *(Ben Luckett)*, Hume Cronyn *(Joe Finley)*, Brian Dennehy *(Walter)*, Jack Gilford *(Bennie Lefkowitz)*, Steve Guttenberg *(Jack Bonner)*, Maureen Stapleton *(Mary Luckett)*, Jessica Tandy *(Alma Finley)*, Gwen Verdon *(Bess McCarthy)*, Herta Ware *(Rose Lefkowitz)* p, Richard D. Zanuck, David Brown, Lili Fini Zanuck; d, Ron Howard; w, Tom Benedek; ph, Don Peterman, Jordan Klein; ed, Michael Hill, Daniel Hanley; m, James Horner; prod d, Jack T. Collis; fx, Greg Cannom, Rick Baker; cos, Aggie Guerard Rodgers, Mort Schwartz

AA Best Supporting Actor: Don Ameche; *AA Best Visual Effects:* Ken Ralston, Ralph McQuarrie, Scott Farrar, David Berry

In this fun, lighthearted comedy, a group of aliens led by Brian Dennehy arrive from the planet Antarea and take on human form so they can go about their work without detection. They land near the heart of geriatric country, St. Petersburg, Florida, and rent a tour boat from Steve Guttenberg. They also rent a nearby home that had been left unattended, thereby enabling some elderly residents at a rest home—Don Ameche, Wilford Brimley, and Hume Cronyn—to sneak in and use its indoor pool. Guttenberg takes the boat to a specified spot in the ocean where Dennehy and his crew pull boulder-like cocoons from the ocean floor, which they store in the swimming pool. Later when Ameche, Brimley, and Cronyn take their usual swim, they notice the curious cocoons and then begin to sense a change in themselves—they are suddenly more youthful and vital.

A gentle and effective heart-tugger, COCOON tries to make its audience feel good, but you can't help but feel uneasy about the vision of old age that director Ron Howard depicts—one in which the young cannot accept the notion of getting old. The derivative special effects feel like leftovers from the infinitely superior CLOSE ENCOUNTERS OF THE THIRD KIND. A number of the performances are superb, including Ameche's, for which he won a Best Supporting Actor Oscar. The film also won an Academy Award for Best Visual Effects.

COLD COMFORT FARM

1995 95m c Drama/Romance/Comedy   ★★★½
BBC Films/Thames International   (U.K.)   PG

Eileen Atkins (*Judith Starkadder*), Kate Beckinsale (*Flora Poste*), Sheila Burrell (*Ada Doom*), Freddie Jones (*Adam Lambsbreath*), Joanna Lumley (*Mrs. Smiling*), Ian McKellen (*Amos Starkadder*), Maria Miles (*Elfine*), Rufus Sewell (*Seth*), Ivan Kaye (*Reuben*), Rupert Penry-Jones (*Dick Hawk-Monitor*)

d, John Schlesinger; w, Malcolm Bradbury (based on the novel by Stella Gibbons); ph, Chris Seager; ed, Mark Day; m, Robert Lockhart; prod d, Malcolm Thornton; art d, Jim Holloway; fx, Mike Kelt, Jeremy King; cos, Amy Roberts

COLD COMFORT FARM, based on the 1932 novel by Stella Gibbons, is a lively satire set in rural 1930s England.

Suddenly orphaned, Flora Poste (Kate Beckinsale) procures an invitation to Cold Comfort Farm, the bleak home of her distant cousins, the Starkadders. When she arrives, she's appalled by the disheveled homestead and its odd inhabitants. Cousin Judith (Eileen Atkins) tells fortunes while bemoaning her fate; her husband Amos (Ian McKellen) preaches fire-and-brimstone sermons at the Church of the Quivering Brethren; their two sons, handsome Seth (Rufus Sewell) dreams of Hollywood stardom, while Reuben (Ivan Kaye) fears Flora has designs on the farm; and fey young Elfine (Maria Miles) is in love with upper-crust Dick Hawk-Monitor (Rupert Penry-Jones). The whole lot are ruled by the tyrannical matriarch Ada Doom (Sheila Burrell), who once "saw something nasty in the woodshed," and forbids her wretched brood ever to leave the farm. Undaunted, Flora immediately sets about straightening up their doom-laden existence, and, with a little help from her London friend Mrs. Smiling (Joanna Lumley), she's a smashing success.

This is your basic "fish out of water" tale, though novelist Malcolm Bradbury's clever adaptation wisely avoids parable. While Gibbons' novel could be dry and earnest, Schlesinger's film is outspoken and robust. Some of the most memorable scenes are those that take place in London, where smart photography and witty production design dazzle the audience. Schlesinger has recruited a very talented cast, with Beckinsale charming as the dogged sophisticate; Atkins endowing Judith with formidable presence; McKellen amusingly homespun; and Lumley delightfully daft as Mrs. Smiling, a London socialite who happens to be a devoted collector of brassieres.

COLONEL REDL
(REDL EZREDES)

1984 144m c Biography/Historical/War   ★★★
Mafilm-Objectiv/Manfred Durniok/ORF/ZDF   R/15
(Hungary/Austria/West Germany)

Klaus Maria Brandauer (*Alfred Redl*), Armin Mueller-Stahl (*Crown Prince Archduke Franz-Josef*), Gudrun Landgrebe (*Katalin Kubinyi*), Jan Niklas (*Kristof Kubinyi*), Hans Christian Blech (*Col. von Roden*), Laszlo Mensaros (*Col. Ruzitska*), Andras Balint (*Dr. Gustav Sonnenschein*), Karoly Eperjes (*Lt. Jaromil Schorm*), Dorottya Udvaros (*Clarissa, Redl's Wife*), Laszlo Galffi (*Alfredo Velocchio*)

p, Joszef Marx; d, Istvan Szabo; w, Istvan Szabo, Peter Dobai (based on the stage play "A Patriot for Me" by John Osborne); ph, Lajos Koltai; ed, Zsuzsa Csakany; m, Robert Schumann, Johann Strauss, Frederic Chopin, Franz Liszt; prod d, Jozsef Romvari; art d, Tibor Szollar; cos, Peter Pabst

AAN Best Foreign Language Film

Istvan Szabo's follow-up to MEPHISTO again stars Klaus Maria Brandauer, here as Colonel Alfred Redl, who became head of the Austro-Hungarian military intelligence bureau in the early 1900s, despite his impoverished origins. His Gatsby-like strivings for upper-class acceptance prove, however, to be his downfall when a czarist agent threatens to expose Redl's homosexual double life.

Though not as richly textured or urgent as MEPHISTO, this is an expertly made historical drama that, while fictionalizing some events, truthfully examines the desire for power and the catalysts of war. The film boasts yet another tour de force performance by Brandauer, as well as an equally strong portrayal by Armin Mueller-Stahl as the ruthless, power-hungry archduke. The film won the Jury Prize at the Cannes Film Festival, and received an Oscar nomination for Best Foreign Film.

COLOR OF DESTINY, THE
(A COR DO SEU DESTINO)

1988 104m c Drama   ★★★½
Nativa   (Brazil)

Guilherme Fontes (*Paulo*), Norma Bengell (*Laura*), Franklin Caicedo (*Victor*), Julia Lemmertz (*Patricia*), Andrea Beltrao (*Helena*), Chico Diaz, Antonio Grassi, Anderson Schereiber, Antonio Ameijeiras, Marcos Palmeira

p, Jorge Duran; d, Jorge Duran; w, Nelson Natotti, Jorge Duran, Jose Joffily (based on a story by Duran); ph, Jose Tadeu Ribeiro; ed, Dominique Paris; m, David Tygel

With THE COLOR OF DESTINY, Brazilian director Jorge Duran has created a sensitive portrayal of adolescent angst.

Paulo (Guilherme Fontes) is a teenager living in Rio de Janeiro with his parents, who have fled Chile for political reasons. After splitting up with his girlfriend, Paulo retreats to the privacy of his bedroom, where he creates experimental works of art. Burdened by the memory of an older brother who was tortured and killed for political activity in Chile, Paulo confronts his late brother in dream sequences, while his parents worry that he will follow in their dead son's footsteps. Word comes from Santiago that Patricia (Julia Lemmertz), Paulo's 18-year-old cousin who was arrested by Chilean authorities during a demonstration, has been freed from prison. She is sent to her relatives in Brazil to recuperate from her experience and is welcomed with open arms by her aunt and uncle. She develops a somewhat antagonistic relationship with Paulo. Paulo can't help but admire his cousin for her fortitude, however, and slowly finds himself falling for her. Eventually he realizes that he must follow his brother's example and become involved in Chile's political turmoil.

What makes THE COLOR OF DESTINY work so well are the natural performances by its teenage leads, allowing us to empathize with their complex struggles and pain. Duran, who directs with great heart, is sympathetic to his characters and is never afraid to show his political leanings. This is his debut feature as a director (following an apprenticeship as a screenwriter in the Brazilian film industry), and his ability to deal with multilayered issues points toward a strong career behind the camera.

COLOR OF MONEY, THE

1986 119m c Drama/Sports ★★★½
Touchstone (U.S.) R/15

Paul Newman (Eddie), Tom Cruise (Vincent), Mary Elizabeth Mastrantonio (Carmen), Helen Shaver (Janelle), John Turturro (Julian), Bill Cobbs (Orvis), Keith McCready (Grady Seasons), Carol Messing (Casino Bar Band Singer/Julian's Flirt), Steve Mizerak (Duke, Eddie's 1st Opponent), Bruce A. Young (Moselle)

p, Irving Axelrad, Barbara De Fina; d, Martin Scorsese; w, Richard Price (based on the novel by Walter Tevis); ph, Michael Ballhaus; ed, Thelma Schoonmaker; m, Robbie Robertson; prod d, Boris Leven; fx, Curt Smith; cos, Richard Bruno

AA Best Actor: Paul Newman; AAN Best Supporting Actress: Mary Elizabeth Mastrantonio; AAN Best Adapted Screenplay: Richard Price; AAN Best Art Direction: Boris Leven, Karen A. O'Hara

Twenty-five years after being banned from big-time pool, THE HUSTLER's "Fast Eddie" Felsen (Paul Newman) resurfaces—older, wiser, and much more cynical—in THE COLOR OF MONEY. Eddie, who no longer plays the game, now peddles whiskey and bankrolls talented pool hustlers for a percentage. He takes young hotshot Vincent (Tom Cruise) and his coolheaded girlfriend (Mary Elizabeth Mastrantonio) on the road, teaching his flamboyant, flaky protege how to "dump," i.e., lose deliberately in order to set up the suckers for the big score ("Sometimes if you lose, you win"). Vincent has trouble learning to lose, Eddie begins to yearn to play again himself, and they part ways, only to meet again in a big tournament in Atlantic City. There the pupil surprises his rehabilitated teacher with how well he's learned his lessons.

Approached by Newman, who felt that "Fast Eddie" was due for renewed exploration, director Martin Scorsese and novelist-screenwriter Richard Price (The Wanderers) came up with a richly nuanced film that retains little more than the title and Eddie Felsen's character from novelist Walter Tevis's sequel to The Hustler. One of Scorsese's most commercial undertakings, THE COLOR OF MONEY relinquishes none of his unique style and vision, using a swooping, gliding camera and countless trick shots to maximum impact. The film also boasts two bravura performances—from Newman, who finally—and deservedly—won an Oscar for Best Actor, and Cruise, who is a joy to behold. Watch for Forest Whittaker and Iggy Pop in colorful bit roles.

COLOR PURPLE, THE

1985 152m c Drama ★★★½
Guber/Peters (U.S.) PG-13/15

Danny Glover (Albert), Whoopi Goldberg (Celie), Margaret Avery (Shug Avery), Oprah Winfrey (Sofia), Willard Pugh (Harpo), Akosua Busia (Nettie), Adolph Caesar (Old Mister), Rae Dawn Chong (Squeak), Desreta Jackson (Young Celie), Dana Ivey (Miss Millie)

p, Steven Spielberg, Kathleen Kennedy, Frank Marshall, Quincy Jones, Jon Peters, Peter Guber; d, Steven Spielberg; w, Menno Meyjes (based on the novel by Alice Walker); ph, Allen Daviau; ed, Michael Kahn; m, Quincy Jones; prod d, J. Michael Riva; art d, Bo Welch; cos, Aggie Guerard Rodgers

AAN Best Picture; AAN Best Actress: Whoopi Goldberg; AAN Best Supporting Actress: Margaret Avery; AAN Best Supporting Actress: Oprah Winfrey; AAN Best Adapted Screenplay: Menno Meyjes (Screenplay); AAN Best Cinematography: Allen Daviau; AAN Best Score: Quincy Jones, Jeremy Lubbock, Rod Temperton, Caiphus Semenya, Andrae Crouch, Chris Boardman, Jorge Calandrelli, Joel Rosenbaum, Fred Steiner, Jack Hayes, Jerry Hey, Randy Kerber; AAN Best Song: Quincy Jones (Music & Lyrics), Rod Temperton (Music & Lyrics), Lionel Richie (Lyrics); AAN Best Art Direction: J Michael Riva (Art Direction), Robert W Welch (Art Direction), Linda DeScenna (Set Decoration); AAN Best Costume Design: Aggie Guerard Rodgers; AAN Best Makeup: Ken Chase

Far worse films than Steven Spielberg's laudable if problematic adaptation of Alice Walker's novel have been treated much less harshly. This film, which introduced Whoopi Goldberg and Oprah Winfrey to national audiences, has been unfairly attacked as an ill-considered and unseemly plea for "serious" consideration from an extremely successful young filmmaker better known for fantasy adventure films. Though a commercial success, this was one of the few major Hollywood dramas to concern itself with the lives of black women. Where are the subsequent black female films? Similarly, it soft-pedals the novel's lesbianism but how many subsequent Hollywood films have done better?

The story begins in 1909 as teenager Celie (Desreta Jackson) gives birth to two children (apparently fathered by her own father) and is married off to Albert (Danny Glover), who hates her and wants her sister, Nettie (Akosua Busia). When Nettie resists his advances, Albert persuades the sisters' father to separate the girls. Celie's children are sold to a local preacher and Nettie leaves. As an adult, Celie (now Whoopi Goldberg) lives a life of servitude to Albert who mistreats her shamelessly. He intercepts Nettie's letters to Celie, not allowing the sisters to communicate. Celie is cut off from all human affection. Celie eventually does receive love and gains self-respect through the timely intervention of an outside force who enters her life in an unexpected manner.

Spielberg lacks his usual intuitive affinity for his story material; consequently the film is a bit clunky at times. There are some unfortunate slapstick comic relief sequences and a few of the characterizations are also much too broad and cartoonish. The film was strongly criticized in some quarters for its negative depiction of black men but, if anything, it is less harsh than the novel. The film deserves praise for its heartwarming, empowering presentation of the strength and nobility of black women. It has also been damned for its gloriously lush cinematography as if the lives of black folk were only meant to be shown in squalid environments. Black people enjoy Hollywood fantasy as much as anyone.

COLORS

1988 120m c Crime ★★½
Orion (U.S.) R/18

Sean Penn (Danny McGavin), Robert Duvall (Bob Hodges), Maria Conchita Alonso (Louisa Gomez), Randy Brooks (Ron Delaney), Grand L. Bush (Larry Sylvester), Don Cheadle (Rocket), Gerardo Mejia (Bird), Glenn Plummer (Clarence Brown, "High Top"), Rudy Ramos (Melindez), Sy Richardson (Bailey)

p, Robert H. Solo; d, Dennis Hopper; w, Michael Schiffer (from a story by Schiffer and Richard DiLello); ph, Haskell Wexler; ed, Robert Estrin; m, Herbie Hancock; prod d, Ron Foreman; chor, Patrick Alan; cos, Nick Scarano

Hopper's controversial directorial reentry into mainstream Hollywood is a disappointingly routine effort that is neither socially irresponsible nor particularly distinguished by any insights or artfulness. The considerable controversy aroused by COLORS centered on Hopper's choice of subject matter—urban youth gangs. Set in the barrios and slums of East Los Angeles, the film is basically an all-too-familiar tale of a confident veteran cop (Duvall) with one more year to go until his retirement and his relationship with his new partner (Penn), a young, cocky, and hot-headed rookie who thinks he has all the answers. Their conflict is played out amid the shocking violence of a bloody war between LA's two most notorious gangs, the Bloods and the Crips. No one should expect a Hollywood movie to address and cure complicated social ills. In COLORS Hopper makes no attempt to provide solutions but merely presents the disturbing reality of the situation as a backdrop for the narrative. Unfortunately the end result is an unfocused hodgepodge of documentary realism, expressionism, TV cop show, liberalmessage movie, and violent action film. None of these elements are handled with in a distinctive manner. In several interviews, Hopper admitted that had he initiated the project himself, he would have preferred to concentrate on the gangs rather than the cops. As it is, COLORS has a tentative, ambivalent feel to it—as if Hopper merely considered himself a hired gun who should avoid imposing too personal a vision on the material.

COLOSSUS: THE FORBIN PROJECT

1970 100m c Science Fiction ★★★
Universal (U.S.)

Eric Braeden *(Dr. Charles Forbin)*, Susan Clark *(Dr. Cleo Markham)*, Gordon Pinsent *(The President)*, William Schallert *(Grauber)*, Leonid Rostoff *(Chairman)*, Georg Stanford Brown *(Fisher)*, Willard Sage *(Blake)*, Alex Rodine *(Dr. Kurpin)*, Martin Brooks *(Johnson)*, Marion Ross *(Angela)*

p, Stanley Chase; d, Joseph Sargent; w, James Bridges; ph, Gene Polito; ed, Folmar Blangsted; m, Michel Colombier; art d, John Lloyd, Alexander Golitzen; fx, Whitey McMahon

Taut, well-made sci-fi thriller about a massive computer, Colossus, which is designed by Braeden to control the entire American missile defense system. Once put into service, however, it takes over and develops a plan of *its* own to safeguard mankind from nuclear disaster. It hooks up with its Russian counterpart, Guardian, and together the two computers hold the world hostage, threatening to destroy the Earth. Braeden is forced to attempt to destroy his creation, but the computer thwarts him at every turn.

COMA

1978 113m c Science Fiction/Thriller ★★½
UA (U.S.) PG/

Genevieve Bujold *(Dr. Susan Wheeler)*, Michael Douglas *(Dr. Mark Bellows)*, Elizabeth Ashley *(Mrs. Emerson)*, Rip Torn *(Dr. George)*, Richard Widmark *(Dr. Harris)*, Lois Chiles *(Nancy Greenly)*, Hari Rhodes *(Dr. Morelind)*, Gary Barton *(Computer Technician)*, Frank Downing *(Kelly)*, Richard Doyle *(Jim)*

p, Martin Erlichman; d, Michael Crichton; w, Michael Crichton (based on the novel by Robin Cook); ph, Victor J. Kemper, Gerald Hirschfeld; ed, David Bretherton; m, Jerry Goldsmith; prod d, Albert Brenner; fx, Joe Day, Ernie Smith; cos, Eddie Marks, Yvonne Kubis

An inquisitive hospital physician (Genevieve Bujold) discovers that unscrupulous higher-ups on the staff are drugging healthy patients into a comatose state, killing them, and selling their organs to rich patients in desperate need of transplants. When she confronts her ambitious doctor lover (Michael Douglas) with the information, he refuses to believe her, and she sets out alone to expose the sinister conspiracy.

Adapted from the best-selling book by Robin Cook, COMA is the second feature directed by doctor-novelist-filmmaker Crichton (the first was the popular WESTWORLD), who later scripted the phenomenal JURASSIC PARK. As a rare attempt to invert some of the gender conventions of the thriller genre—insistently presenting events from a female point-of-view—the film has won favor among some feminist critics. On the whole, however, COMA wastes a superb performance by Bujold on a simplistic, predictable series of cliched suspense scenes, seasoned with some last-minute moralizing about contemporary medicine. Look for Tom Selleck as one of the comatose bodies suspended from the ceiling of a clandestine medical lab—the most memorably eerie image in the film.

COMANCHE STATION

1960 74m c Western ★★★★
Renown (U.S.) /U

Randolph Scott *(Jefferson Cody)*, Nancy Gates *(Mrs. Lowe)*, Claude Akins *(Ben Lane)*, Skip Homeier *(Frank)*, Richard Rust *(Dobie)*, Rand Brooks *(Station Man)*, Dyke Johnson *(Mr. Lowe)*, Foster Hood *(Comanche Lance Bearer)*, Joe Molina *(Comanche Chief)*, Vince St. Cyr *(Warrior)*

p, Harry Joe Brown, Budd Boetticher, Randolph Scott; d, Budd Boetticher; w, Burt Kennedy; ph, Charles Lawton Jr.; ed, Edwin Bryant

This fine, haunting western was the last of the Randolph Scott-Budd Boetticher collaborations. Its predecessors were SEVEN MEN FROM NOW (1956), THE TALL T. (1957), DECISION AT SUNDOWN (1957), BUCHANAN RIDES ALONE (1958), RIDE LONESOME (1959), and WESTBOUND (1959). Together they encapsulate themes that made these films some of the most striking, intelligent, and complex westerns ever made. Boetticher, an often-underrated talent,

created films that dealt with the sadness of independence, the questing impulse, the overpowering forces of nature, and the past's influence on the present.

Interrupting a futile ten-year search for his own wife, who was kidnaped by Indians, Scott agrees to track down a settler's wife, Gates, who has been raped and captured by Comanches. On their way back to her husband, Scott and Gates are met by outlaw Akins and his two adolescent proteges, Homeier and Rust, who inform the couple that they are being trailed by Comanche braves. Akins and the boys, offering to accompany Scott and Gates on their journey, create an atmosphere of tension, with Akins frequently commenting on the cowardice of Gates's husband in sending another man to do his work. It soon becomes apparent that Akins is plotting to get the reward for himself.

As in many of the Renown westerns, Scott is truly a loner in the film, a man whose personal code limits his ability to coexist with others. Adhering to the mythic type of the western hero, Scott remains true to the ideals of honesty, courage, and the responsibility to aid those in need. Boetticher's films are not happy, optimistic westerns in which evil is defeated before the final credits roll. They are sad films that focus on isolated men and the harsh world they exist in, men who strive for things they will probably never attain.

COME AND SEE
(IDI I SMOTRI)

1985 142m c War ★★★½
Byelarusfilm/Mosfilm (U.S.S.R.) /15

Aleksei Kravchenko *(Florya Gaishun)*, Olga Mironova, Lyubomiras Lautsiavitchus, Vladas Bagdonas, Victor Lorentz

d, Elem Klimov; w, Ales Adamovich, Elem Klimov (based on *The Story of Khatyn and Others* by Adamovich); ph, Alexi Rodionov

A highly charged, emotionally exhausting indictment of war and the inhumanity of the Nazis, set in Byelorussia during the 1943 Nazi invasion, COME AND SEE focuses on the experiences of an adolescent transformed, in a matter of days, from naive boy to worn man. Young Florya (Aleksei Kravchenko) finds a rifle and immediately joins the local freedom fighters, despite the desperate pleas of his mother, who wants to lose neither her son nor the only source of protection for her and her two young daughters. Florya is left behind by the makeshift army and tries to return to his mother, but the Germans launch an air raid, which is followed by an invasion of paratroopers before he can get to his village. Only the most insensitive could sit through COME AND SEE without being emotionally devastated. From its opening scene, COME AND SEE descends into a virtual hell on earth that becomes increasingly frightening as it advances to the final horror. This film won the Grand Prix at the Moscow film festival; its director, Elem Klimov, was recently named the head of the Soviet Filmmakers Union.

COME BACK, LITTLE SHEBA

1952 95m bw Drama ★★★★
Paramount (U.S.) /A

Burt Lancaster *(Doc Delaney)*, Shirley Booth *(Lola Delaney)*, Terry Moore *(Marie Buckholder)*, Richard Jaeckel *(Turk Fisher)*, Philip Ober *(Ed Anderson)*, Lisa Golm *(Mrs. Goffman)*, Walter Kelley *(Bruce)*

p, Hal B. Wallis; d, Daniel Mann; w, Ketti Frings (based on the play by William Inge); ph, James Wong Howe; ed, Warren Low; m, Franz Waxman

AA Best Actress: Shirley Booth; *AAN Best Supporting Actress:* Terry Moore; *AAN Best Editing:* Warren Low

Lancaster is Doc Delaney, a mild-mannered alcoholic ex-chiropractor who has been dry for a year. Booth, his frumpy, loquacious wife, lives for the day when her lost dog, little Sheba, will return home. Theirs is a life of quiet desperation until Moore, a vibrant student, rents a room from the tired couple. Lancaster doesn't approve of the intentions of Jaeckel, who has been dating Moore, perhaps because the young man's lust stirs painful memories for Lancaster, whose premarital relationship with Booth resulted in their shotgun wedding. Returning to the bottle, he viciously criticizes his wife.

COME BACK, LITTLE SHEBA opened Christmas week of 1952 in order to qualify for the Academy Awards. The strategy was excellent as Shirley Booth won the Oscar for Best Actress, beating out Joan Crawford (SUDDEN FEAR), Julie Harris (THE MEMBER OF THE WEDDING), Bette Davis (THE STAR) and Susan Hayward (WITH A SONG IN MY HEART). Booth's brilliant work (she originated the role on Broadway) remains etched forever in the memory of anyone who has seen this film. Moore, in her finest performance, also received a nomination for Best Supporting Actress.

COME BACK TO THE 5 & DIME, JIMMY DEAN, JIMMY DEAN

1982   109m   c   Drama   ★★½
Sandcastle 5   (U.S.)   /15

Sandy Dennis *(Mona)*, Cher *(Sissy)*, Karen Black *(Joanne)*, Sudie Bond *(Juanita)*, Marta Heflin *(Edna Louise)*, Kathy Bates *(Stella Mae)*, Mark Patton *(Joe Qualley)*, Caroline Aaron *(Martha)*, Ruth Miller *(Clarissa)*, Gena Ramsel *(Sue Ellen)*

p, Scott Bushnell; d, Robert Altman; w, Ed Graczyck (based on his play); ph, Pierre Mignot; ed, Jason Rosenfield; prod d, David Gropman

Five women who grew up together in a small Texas town idolizing James Dean reunite 20 years later at a local dime store and discuss their lives and loves, illusion and reality. The most touching moment comes when Sandy Dennis, who has deluded herself for years, finally accepts that Dean was not the father of her illegitimate child. Director Robert Altman, turning Super 16mm cameras on the cast that he directed on Broadway in Ed Graczyck's play, captures the vitality of live performances from each of his actors. Using much technical invention, Altman does his best to invest his uncinematic material with a cinematic feel, but if COME BACK TO THE 5 & DIME, JIMMY DEAN, JIMMY DEAN still looks like a filmed play—and not a great play at that—it is nonetheless presented with great sensitivity. Karen Black, Cher, and Dennis contribute especially fine performances to this insightful film that was shot in just 19 days.

COMFORT AND JOY

1984   106m   c   Comedy   ★★★
Kings Road   (U.K.)   PG

Bill Paterson *(Alan "Dickie" Bird)*, Eleanor David *(Maddy)*, C.P. Grogan *(Charlotte)*, Alex Norton *(Trevor)*, Patrick Malahide *(Colin)*, Rikki Fulton *(Hilary)*, Roberto Bernardi *(Mr. McCool)*, George Rossi *(Bruno)*, Peter Rossi *(Paolo)*, Billy McElhaney *(Renato)*

p, Davina Belling, Clive Parsons; d, Bill Forsyth; w, Bill Forsyth; ph, Chris Menges; ed, Michael Ellis; m, Mark Knopfler; prod d, Adrienne Atkinson; art d, Andy Harris; cos, Mary-Jane Reyner, Lindy Hemming

One of a string of first-rate Scottish comedies directed and written by Forsyth, COMFORT AND JOY—though at times rather bittersweet and melancholy—still has plenty of laughs, more than a few insights, and several offbeat characters. Paterson is a popular morning disc jockey in Glasgow. His kooky, kleptomaniac, live-in girlfriend, David, has abruptly walked out of his life, leaving him mired in depression. Paterson's placid existence really goes screwy when he gets involved in a conflict between two rival gangs that are seeking to control the Glasgow ice-cream business. (The two companies are called Mr. Bunny and Mr. McCool.) Paterson, unwilling to see chaos erupt and innocent people hurt, uses his radio show to relay messages between the warring factions. This puts his job at risk and wins him the anger of the ice-cream combatants.

This is an unusual premise for a film. Some of the potentially hilarious situations don't garner as many laughs as they might, but there are many funny moments, and the picture often throws unexpected curve balls at the audience. Although this is one of Forsyth's lesser works, his films are generally impressive and there is more here to laugh at than has been seen in British comedies for some time.

COMFORT OF STRANGERS, THE
(CORTESIE PER GLI OSPITI)

1991   107m   c   Drama   ★★★
Erre Produzioni/Sovereign Pictures/Reteitalia   (Italy/U.K.)   R/18

Christopher Walken *(Robert)*, Natasha Richardson *(Mary)*, Rupert Everett *(Colin)*, Helen Mirren *(Caroline)*, Manfredi Aliquo *(The Concierge)*, David Ford *(Waiter)*, Daniel Franco *(Waiter)*, Rossana Caghiari *(Hotel Maid)*, Fabrizio Castellani *(Bar Manager)*, Giancarlo Previati *(First Policeman)*

p, Angelo Rizzoli; d, Paul Schrader; w, Harold Pinter (from the novel by Ian McEwan); ph, Dante Spinotti; ed, Bill Pankow; m, Angelo Badalamenti; prod d, Gianni Quaranta; art d, Luigi Marchione; cos, Mariolina Bono

Based on the novel by Ian McEwan, with a screenplay by playwright Harold Pinter, THE COMFORT OF STRANGERS is a story of decadence and decay, sexual obsession and violence.

Colin (Rupert Everett) and Mary (Natasha Richardson) are a naive young English couple vacationing in Venice. One night they become lost in the winding streets and encounter Robert (Christopher Walken), a dapper Italian who speaks excellent English and graciously escorts them to his out-of-the-way restaurant. Later, Mary and Colin visit Robert's palatial apartment, where they meet his beautiful crippled wife, Caroline (Helen Mirren). The visit quickly becomes strained: there is something alluring, but disturbingly off-kilter, about the older couple. Before long, the innocents are lured into a bizarre web of sexual gamesmanship and murder.

Former Calvinist and critic Paul Schrader, who has written and/or directed such films as AMERICAN GIGOLO, the remake of CAT PEOPLE and the biopic MISHIMA, is no stranger to provocative subject matter. But depravity is a tricky thing to make concrete, and film is a resolutely literal medium. The risk of looking silly is tremendously high—many films have aspired to decadence and achieved unintended camp. Schrader plunges in fearlessly, attempting to generate a sense of erotic menace through location and such devices as gliding steadicam shots that sweep through sumptuous surroundings, devouring them in every detail without ever pausing. Mirren's and Walken's brittle, mannered performances unquestionably add to the sense that something is ominously wrong, even early on on the film. But overall, THE COMFORT OF STRANGERS seems tremendously overwrought for no good reason.

COMING HOME

1978   126m   c   Drama/War   ★★★½
UA   (U.S.)   R/18

Jane Fonda *(Sally Hyde)*, Jon Voight *(Luke Martin)*, Bruce Dern *(Capt. Bob Hyde)*, Robert Ginty *(Sgt. Dink Mobley)*, Penelope Milford *(Viola Munson)*, Robert Carradine *(Bill Munson)*, Charles Cyphers *(Pee Wee)*, Mary Jackson *(Fleta Wilson)*, Kenneth Augustine *(Ken)*, Tresa Hughes *(Nurse De Groot)*

p, Jerome Hellman; d, Hal Ashby; w, Waldo Salt, Robert C. Jones (based on a story by Nancy Dowd); ph, Haskell Wexler; ed, Don Zimmerman; prod d, Michael Haller; cos, Ann Roth, Michael Hoffman, Silvio Scarano, Jennifer Parsons

AAN Best Picture; AA Best Actor: Jon Voight; AA Best Actress: Jane Fonda; AAN Best Supporting Actor: Bruce Dern; AAN Best Supporting Actress: Penelope Milford; AAN Best Director: Hal Ashby; AA Best Original Screenplay: Nancy Dowd, Waldo Salt, Robert C. Jones; AAN Best Editing: Don Zimmerman

Nominated for eight Academy Awards—and winning for Best Actress (Jane Fonda), Best Actor (Jon Voight), and Best Original Screenplay (THE DEER HUNTER, another Vietnam film, won Best Picture and Best Director)—COMING HOME was one of the first films to deal seriously with the plight of returning Vietnam veterans. Unfortunately, it is marred by some cloying melodramatics and overly preachy politics. The story opens circa 1968, when Bob Hyde (Bruce Dern), a gung-ho Marine captain, is finally going off to Vietnam on active duty. His dutiful wife, Sally (Fonda), wants to do her share and begins volunteer work at a local veterans' hospital, where she meets Luke (Jon Voight), a bitter paraplegic. Within a month Sally and Luke have learned that they went to the same high school, knew many of the same people, and have much more in common than most others at the hospital. Luke's anger begins to subside, although he begins speaking out publicly against the war. The friendship broadens Sally's perspective; soon she is becoming more liberal in her politics, more feminist in her orientation, and comfortable leading a life independent of her husband. Eventually Luke and Sally become lovers (in a R-rated scene). Their relationship is jeopardized, however, when Bob is wounded in the leg and comes home from the war a changed man—taciturn but potentially violent. While COMING HOME has its heart in the right place, the script by Salt and Jones is too pat, and Ashby's direction simply too self-satisfied to be wholly effective. What does work in COMING HOME are the small, human, unguarded moments. The performances, undeniably appealing, were deservedly praised, Dern and Voight coming off best.

COMING TO AMERICA

1988 116m c Comedy/Romance ★★½
Paramount (U.S.) R/15

Eddie Murphy *(Prince Akeem/Clarence the Barber/Saul the Old Jew/Randy Watson the Singer)*, Arsenio Hall *(Semmi/Morris the Barber/Extremely Ugly Girl/Rev. Brown)*, John Amos *(Cleo McDowell)*, James Earl Jones *(King Jaffe Joffer)*, Shari Headley *(Lisa McDowell)*, Madge Sinclair *(Queen Aoleon)*, Eriq LaSalle *(Darryl Jenks)*, Allison Dean *(Patrice McDowell)*, Paul Bates *(Oha)*, Louie Anderson *(Maurice)*

p, George Folsey Jr., Robert D. Wachs; d, John Landis; w, David Sheffield, Barry Blaustein (based on a story by Murphy); ph, Woody Omens; ed, Malcolm Campbell, George Folsey Jr.; m, Nile Rodgers; prod d, Richard MacDonald; fx, Dan Cangemi, Syd Dutton, Rick Baker, Bill Taylor; chor, Paula Abdul; cos, Deborah Nadoolman

AAN Best Costume Design: Deborah Nadoolman; *AAN Best Makeup:* Rick Baker

This light romantic comedy represents a change of pace for the phenomenally successful Murphy. Here he plays a polite, pampered, and fabulously wealthy African prince who comes to America in search of true love. Although the fairy-tale script is as old as the motion picture industry itself, the resourceful cast of COMING TO AMERICA brings freshness to the annoyingly cliched material. Unfortunately, Landis' inelegant direction nearly derails the film. Poorly paced, indifferently shot, and haphazardly edited, the movie lurches unsteadily from scene to scene, undermining the best efforts of its performers. Luckily, Murphy gives his sweetest, most touching, and most genuinely likable performance to date, playing a character who embraces society instead of holding it in contempt. Arsenio Hall, in his first featured role, is also impressive. The film is best remembered in Hollywood as the object of a plagiarism suit brought by columnist Art Buchwald; Paramount allegedly cooked the books to avoid giving Buchwald his court-awarded points, resulting in years of bitter litigation.

COMMITMENTS, THE

1991 120m c Drama/Musical ★★★
Beacon Communications/First Film Co./Dirty Hands Productions/Sovereign Pictures (U.S./U.K.) R/15

Robert Arkins *(Jimmy Rabbitte)*, Michael Aherne *(Steven Clifford)*, Angeline Ball *(Imelda Quirke)*, Maria Doyle *(Natalie Murphy)*, Dave Finnegan *(Mickah Wallace)*, Bronagh Gallagher *(Bernie McGloughlin)*, Felim Gormley *(Dean Fay)*, Glen Hansard *(Outspan Foster)*, Dick Massey *(Billy Mooney)*, Johnny Murphy *(Joey "The Lips" Fagan)*

p, Roger Randall-Cutler, Lynda Myles; d, Alan Parker; w, Ian La-Frenais, Dick Clement, Roddy Doyle (from his novel); ph, Gale Tattersall; ed, Gerry Hambling; prod d, Brian Morris; art d, Mark Geraghty, Arden Gantly; fx, Maurice Foley; cos, Penny Rose

AAN Best Editing: Gerry Hambling

This typically slick but largely enjoyable Alan Parker offering is the story of the rise and demise of a young Irish soul band. As with his earlier film, FAME, Parker has attempted to capture the infectious energy of popular music; and as with his previous feature, MISSIS-

SIPPI BURNING, the director has taken on an alien culture (this time that of the working-class, primarily Catholic North Side of Dublin) and reduced its complexities to a glib, commercial formula.

When Jimmy Rabbitte (Robert Arkins) is asked by two friends to manage a dreadful wedding band, he takes the opportunity to begin building something more ambitious: an authentic soul outfit to be called The Commitments. The newly formed band immerse themselves in the soul classics as they begin struggling their way through rehearsals. Their working-class philosophy is spelled out by Jimmy: "The Irish are the blacks of Europe; Dubliners are the blacks of Ireland; and the North Siders are the blacks of Dublin. So say it loud: I'm black and I'm proud." The Commitments' music improves with predictable, if enjoyable speed. As they begin to develop a following on the pub circuit, the usual tensions start to manifest themselves.

For all its emphasis on working-class integrity, THE COMMITMENTS is really FAME wrapped in streetwise packaging. All the cliches of the star-is-born subgenre are here, from the neatness with which the band members fall into place to the amazing rapidity with which they develop a professional sound (not to mention the implausibility of a group achieving such success by playing straight cover versions of classic soul songs). The whole thing has the feel of an extended sitcom—not surprising given the fact that Dick Clement and Ian La Frenais, veteran English TV writers, helped Roddy Doyle adapt his original novel for the screen. THE SNAPPER, a superior film, is also based on a Doyle novel about the Rabbitte family.

COMPANY OF WOLVES, THE

1984 95m c Horror/Fantasy ★★★★½
Palace (U.K.) R/18

Angela Lansbury *(Granny)*, David Warner *(Father)*, Graham Crowden *(Old Priest)*, Brian Glover *(Amorous Boy's Father)*, Kathryn Pogson *(Young Bride)*, Stephen Rea *(Young Groom)*, Tusse Silberg *(Mother)*, Micha Bergese *(Huntsman)*, Sarah Patterson *(Rosaleen)*, Georgia Slowe *(Alice)*

p, Chris Brown, Stephen Woolley; d, Neil Jordan; w, Angela Carter, Neil Jordan (based on a collection of short stories by Carter); ph, Bryan Loftus; ed, Rodney Holland; m, George Fenton; prod d, Anton Furst; art d, Stuart Rose; fx, Peter MacDonald, Alan Whibley, Rodney Holland, Christopher Tucker; cos, Elizabeth Waller

The most innovative, intelligent, and visually sumptuous horror film of recent years. Not a traditional werewolf movie, this film explores the psychosexual undercurrents of the classic "Little Red Riding Hood" fairy tale.

Taking place almost entirely in the troubled dreams of 13-year-old Rosaleen (Sarah Patterson), the film takes the viewer deep into the archetypal, erotically charged realm of fairy stories. Rosaleen and her parents (David Warner and Tusse Silberg) live in a small village on the outskirts of a dark, forbidding forest. The girl's grandmother (Angela Lansbury) comes to visit and fills the young girl's head with cautionary tales about men who turn into wolves. Nonetheless her interest in men continues to grow. Sometime later a young neighbor boy discovers the ravaged carcass of a farm animal in the woods and warns the adults that a wolf is stalking the area.

THE COMPANY OF WOLVES has a complex and dreamy narrative structure built on intermingled fantasies, myths, and fairy tales. Nearly every scene is compelling and haunting; and the special makeup effects are impressive. Neil Jordan (THE CRYING GAME) is a director with visionary qualities, a distinctive visual stylist who knows how to use his medium to convey complex emotions and simmering sensuality. This is a remarkable movie that plumbs the unconscious netherworld of dreams and fantasy, evoking deeply held fears and desires.

COMPULSION

1959 103m bw Crime ★★★★
Fox (U.S.) /A

Orson Welles *(Jonathan Wilk)*, Diane Varsi *(Ruth Evans)*, Dean Stockwell *(Judd Steiner)*, Bradford Dillman *(Artie Straus)*, E.G. Marshall *(Horn)*, Martin Milner *(Sid)*, Richard Anderson *(Max)*, Robert F. Simon *(Lt. Johnson)*, Edward Binns *(Tom Daly)*, Robert Burton *(Mr. Straus)*

p, Richard D. Zanuck; d, Richard Fleischer; w, Richard Murphy (based on the novel by Meyer Levin); ph, William Mellor; ed, William Reynolds; m, Lionel Newman; cos, Charles LeMaire

Based on the famous 1924 murder trial of Loeb and Leopold, two Chicago homosexual law students who murdered a boy, Bobby Franks, to demonstrate their intellectual superiority, this is a compelling and stylish thriller.

Dillman delivers a strong performance as the mother-dominated, sadistic Loeb, here called Artie Straus, and Stockwell is even more impressive as the submissive, introverted Leopold (renamed Judd Steiner). Of course, Welles is flamboyantly grand as the Clarence Darrow-figure who has the unenviable task of defending the two arrogant unsympathetic killers. They even have the effrontery to offer the police aid in solving the killing (exactly what Loeb did, which led to his arrest and that of Leopold). Raised by wealthy families, Dillman and Stockwell consider themselves superior intellects who are above conventional notions of morality. Their crime was executed without remorse. They offer no defense so, like Clarence Darrow, Welles must come up with a defense of his own.

COMPULSION is full of suspense and electrifying courtroom theatrics, even though the informed viewer knows the story's outcome. Fleischer's direction is taut, and Murphy's script, which takes the narrative almost word-for-word from Meyer Levin's best-selling novel, is terse and telling.

CON AIR
1997 115m c Action ★★½
Jerry Bruckheimer Films/Kouf/Bigelow R/15
Productions/Touchstone (U.S.)

Nicolas Cage (Cameron Poe), John Cusack (US Marshal, Agent Vince Larkin), John Malkovich (Cyrus "The Virus" Grissom), Steve Buscemi (Garland Greene), Ving Rhames (Nathan Jones—aka "Diamond Dog"), Colm Meaney (DEA Agent Duncan Malloy), Mykelti Williamson (Baby-O), Rachel Ticotin (US Marshal, Guard Sally Bishop), Monica Potter (Tricia Poe), David Chappelle ("Pinball" Parker)

p, Jerry Bruckheimer; d, Simon West; w, Scott Rosenberg; ph, David Tattersall; ed, Chris Lebenzon, Steve Mirkovich, Glen Scantlebury; m, Mark Mancina, Trevor Rabin; prod d, Barbara Mesney, Daniel R. Jennings; art d, Edward T. McAvoy, Chas Butcher; fx, Chuck Stewart, David Goldberg, Dream Quest Images; cos, Bobbie Read

The patented Don Simpson-Jerry Bruckheimer formula that produced THE ROCK, BAD BOYS, DAYS OF THUNDER, and TOP GUN sizzles on after Simpson's death.

The vilest criminals the American penal system has to offer are packed into one small plane that is soon navigating some very unfriendly skies. Led by psychopath Cyrus "the Virus" Grissom (John Malkovich) and demented, militant black nationalist Nathan "Diamond Dog" Jones (Ving Rhames), the bad, bad boys—who include pallid serial killer Garland Greene (Steve Buscemi), who's brought on board in full Hannibal Lecter restraints—commander their flying cell block and make a break for freedom. Standing between this airborne crime wave and civilization: quirky federal marshall Vince Larkin (John Cusack), who monitors the disaster-in-progress from the ground, and newly released prisoner Cameron Poe (Nicolas Cage), who once killed a man while defending his wife's honor and now wants nothing more than to get home to her and their angelic little girl.

Ten years ago, who could ever have imagined that awkward, weak-chinned weird boys Cusack and Cage would be able to reinvent themselves as action stars, doing the Sylvester Stallone thing with high-powered weapons and stolen police motorcycles? But their macho antics are no more improbable than anything else about this polished-to-a-high-hard-gloss testosterone attack, a noisy, nasty diversion for adrenaline junkies that's almost worth seeing for the scene in which Cage rescues his daughter's birthday present from some smirking hard-ass or other. "Put . . . the bunny . . . down," Cage intones, voice trembling with suppressed paternal rage, as the plush toy dangles in mid air from an open cargo door. Mega-budget action extravaganzas don't get much sillier.

CONFESSION, THE
(L'AVEU)
1970 135m c Political ★★★½
Corona (France/Italy) /AA

Yves Montand (Gerard), Simone Signoret (Lise), Gabriele Ferzetti (Kohoutek), Michel Vitold (Smola), Jean Bouise (Boss), Laszlo Szabo (Secret Policeman), Monique Chaumette, Guy Mairesse, Marc Eyraud, Gerard Darrieu

p, Robert Dorfmann, Bertrand Javal; d, Constantin Costa-Gavras; w, Jorge Semprun (based on a book by Lise London and Arthur London); ph, Raoul Coutard; ed, Francoise Bonnot; prod d, Claude Hauser; art d, Bernard Evein

Z brought director Costa-Gavras to the public's eye and THE CONFESSION was a respectable follow-up in what has become a career of politically aware movies such as STATE OF SIEGE, SPECIAL SECTION, and MISSING. THE CONFESSION is a searing indictment of the excesses of Stalinism. This film begins in 1951 when Montand is an East European Communist official who notices that he's being followed. During the Spanish Civil War, he had been a Loyalist. He mentions his fears to some friends who also served that cause and they admit that they too are being watched. He is soon arrested and taken to a makeshift jail. His wife, Signoret (in reel and real life), is not told his whereabouts but she is falsely reassured that it will all be over shortly. Meanwhile Montand has not been informed of the reason for his imprisonment and must endure psychological torture from his inquisitors as they try to extract a confession. Montand is a dedicated Communist and takes solace that these men are also Communists and only doing what they feel is right. He eventually finds himself in a well-publicized show trial.

Born in Greece, Costa-Gavras (Konstantin Gavras) is now a naturalized Frenchman and married to daring journalist Michele Ray, who excited the world with her dispatches from Vietnam and her account of being held captive by the Viet Cong.

CONFIDENCE
(BIZALOM)
1979 105m c Drama ★★★½
Mafilm (Hungary) /AA

Ildiko Bansagi (Kata), Peter Andorai (Janos Biro), O. Gombik, Karoly Csaki, Ildiko Kishonti, Lajos Balazsovits, Tamas Dunai, Zoltan Bezeredi, Eva Bartis, Danielle du Tombe

d, Istvan Szabo; w, Istvan Szabo (based on a story by Erika Szanto and Szabo); ph, Lajos Koltai; ed, Zsuzsa Csakany; art d, Jozsef Romvari

AAN Best Foreign Language Film

During WWII, Kata (Bansagi) discovers that her husband has gone underground and that she also must go into hiding. She is told to go to Janos Biro (Andorai) and the two must pretend to be husband and wife. Kata constantly tests Janos, seeing if she will betray him. Eventually the two become lovers, but drift apart into distrust again. The leading performances and the careful buildup of mood and tension are the things to watch here. Beautifully guided by Szabo, long one of Hungary's leading filmmakers and the director of the superb MEPHISTO, CONFIDENCE was nominated by the Academy for Best Foreign-Language Film.

CONFORMIST, THE
(IL CONFORMISTA)
1970 110m c Political ★★★★
Mars/Marianne/Maran (Italy/France/West Germany) R/18

Jean-Louis Trintignant (Marcello Clerici), Stefania Sandrelli (Giulia), Dominique Sanda (Anna Quadri), Pierre Clementi (Lino Seminara), Gastone Moschin (Manganiello), Enzo Tarascio (Prof. Quadri), Jose Quaglio (Italo), Milly (Marcello's Mother), Giuseppe Addobbati (Marcello's Father), Yvonne Sanson (Giulia's Mother) p, Maurizio Lodi-Fe; d, Bernardo Bertolucci; w, Bernardo Bertolucci (based on the novel by Alberto Moravia); ph, Vittorio Storaro; ed, Franco Arcalli; m, Georges Delerue; prod d, Ferdinando Scarfiotti; cos, Gitt Magrini

AAN Best Adapted Screenplay: Bernardo Bertolucci

One of Bertolucci's best films, THE CONFORMIST makes a provocative connection between repressed sexual desires and fascist politics. It's an intriguing, elegantly photographed study of the twisted Italian character of the 1930s.

Plagued by the memory of a traumatic sexual experience during childhood and desperate to demonstrate his "normalcy," Marcello Clerici (Jean-Louis Trintignant) marries the dull, petit-bourgeois Giulia (Stefania Sandrelli). He later joins the Italian Fascist movement, accepting an assignment to travel to Paris and help assassinate Prof. Quadri (Enzo Tarascio), his former mentor. Before the assassination, Marcello becomes attracted to Anna (Dominique Sanda), the professor's seductive, bisexual wife, though she herself is actually more interested in Giulia. Marcello's affiliation with the Fascists eventually self-destructs, as does his own personality.

Here, as in all his best work, Bertolucci addresses the issue of duality—of both sexual and political conflict. Marcello's personal contradictions parallel those of the Italian government, with his own decline taking place at the same time as Mussolini's, in 1943. Visually, THE CONFORMIST is stunning; its gliding camerawork, unusual camera angles and rich color perfectly evoke the baroque decadence of Marcello's world. Bertolucci received an Oscar nomination for Best Adapted Screenplay.

CONNECTICUT YANKEE, A

1931   95m   bw   Comedy/Fantasy   ★★★½
Fox   (U.S.)

Will Rogers *(Hank)*, William Farnum *(King Arthur)*, Myrna Loy *(Queen Morgan Le Fay)*, Maureen O'Sullivan *(Alisande)*, Frank Albertson *(Clarence)*, Mitchell Harris *(Merlin)*, Brandon Hurst *(Sagramor)*
d, David Butler; w, William Conselman, Owen Davis Sr. (based on the novel *A Connecticut Yankee in King Arthur's Court* by Mark Twain); ph, Ernest Palmer; ed, Irene Morra

Will Rogers's fabled charm was well utilized in this excellent adaptation of the popular Mark Twain novel. Rogers, owner of a small-town radio shop, goes to install a battery in the old house of an eccentric character who thinks that he can contact King Arthur by radio. When Rogers is felled by an accidental blow on the head, he dreams his way back to days when knights were bold. The locals soon conclude that the mysterious stranger is a warlock. His only hope of saving himself is to exploit his unique knowledge of the future. Rogers's co-stars provide able support to the satirical proceedings. Myrna Loy plays the villainess and Maureen O'Sullivan is Rogers's love interest. Since the picture was made during the depths of the Depression, much of Rogers's topical humor may be lost on today's audiences but the anachronistic visual gags (for example, Rogers lassoes a Knight of the Round Table in the middle of a joust) remain as fresh and funny as ever.

CONNECTICUT YANKEE IN KING ARTHUR'S COURT, A

1949   106m   c   Science Fiction/Fantasy/Musical   ★★★
Paramount   (U.S.)

Bing Crosby *(Hank Martin)*, William Bendix *(Sir Sagramore)*, Cedric Hardwicke *(King Arthur)*, Rhonda Fleming *(Alisande La Carteloise)*, Murvyn Vye *(Merlin)*, Virginia Field *(Morgan Le Fay)*, Henry Wilcoxon *(Sir Lancelot)*, Richard Webb *(Sir Galahad)*, Joseph Vitale *(Sir Logris)*, Alan Napier *(High Executioner)*
p, Robert Fellows; d, Tay Garnett; w, Edmund Beloin (based on the novel by Mark Twain); ph, Ray Rennahan; ed, Archie Marshek; m, Victor Young; art d, Hans Dreier, Roland Anderson; fx, Farciot Edouart; cos, Edith Head

Mark Twain's popular satirical fantasy is mellowed into an amusingly carefree, lavishly mounted Bing Crosby vehicle, rich in color and pleasant if unmemorable songs. Crosby stars as Hank Martin, a Connecticut blacksmith who is knocked unconscious in a wild rainstorm

and wakes up in King Arthur's Camelot. This production boasts wonderful sets and softly focused color lensing by Ray Rennahan. The famed art director Hans Dreier created a spectacular and authentic medieval castle for the film, with an enormous dining hall for King Arthur's knights, a huge ballroom, lush gardens, courtyards, and jousting grounds. Rhonda Fleming's auburn-haired beauty is lovely in the rich Technicolor process and Tay Garnett's direction is smooth and well paced. It was remade and updated by Disney in 1979 as UNIDENTIFIED FLYING ODDBALL.

CONNECTION, THE

1962   110m   bw   Drama   ★★½
Allen/Clarke   (U.S.)

William Redfield *(Jim Dunn)*, Warren Finnerty *(Leach)*, Garry Goodrow *(Ernie)*, Jerome Raphel *(Solly)*, James Anderson *(Sam)*, Carl Lee *(Cowboy)*, Barbara Winchester *(Sister Salvation)*, Roscoe Lee Browne *(J.J. Burden)*, Henry Proach *(Harry)*, Freddie Redd *(Piano)*
p, Lewis Allen, Shirley Clarke; d, Shirley Clarke; w, Jack Gelber (based on the play by Gelber); ph, Arthur J. Ornitz; ed, Shirley Clarke; m, Freddie Redd; prod d, Richard Sylbert; art d, Albert Brenner; cos, Ruth Morley

Eight drug addicts gather in a Manhattan loft to wait for their connection. To pay for their drugs, they have agreed to allow Dunn, a would-be documentary filmmaker, to photograph them. Film within a film records their conversation, reflections, and an impromptu jam session involving four of the junkies who are musicians. The "connection" arrives with a soldier from the Salvation Army, who suspects the addicts are drinking and beats a hasty retreat. Dunn is then persuaded to try some heroin so that he will have a deeper understanding of the subject of his film, and he becomes violently ill.

This film was considered a tour de force for choreographer-turned-director Clarke, who heretofore had specialized in prize-winning shorts. It is a jolting look at the drug crowd. The characters get laughs with their crisp lingo and wry wit, showing them to be acceptable types one can empathize with. There are no phony dramatics here.

CONTEMPT
(LE MEPRIS)

1963   101m   c   Drama   ★★★★½
Films Concordia/Compagnia/C.C. Champion/Rome-Paris Films   /PG
(France/Italy)

Brigitte Bardot *(Camille Javal)*, Michel Piccoli *(Paul Javal)*, Jack Palance *(Jeremy Prokosh)*, Fritz Lang *(Himself)*, Georgia Moll *(Francesca Vanini)*, Jean-Luc Godard *(Lang's Assistant Director)*, Linda Veras *(Siren)*, Raoul Coutard *(Cameraman)*
p, Georges de Beauregard, Carlo Ponti, Joseph E. Levine; d, Jean-Luc Godard; w, Jean-Luc Godard (based on the novel *Il Disprezzo [A Ghost At Noon]* by Alberto Moravia); ph, Raoul Coutard; ed, Agnes Guillemot, Lila Lakshmanan; m, Georges Delerue; cos, Tanine Autre

A profoundly sad yet beautiful fable about the cinema, CONTEMPT is the story of Paul Javal (Michel Piccoli), a former writer of detective stories who has become a screenwriter of little consequence. He claims that he longs to write for the stage but he believes that his beautiful young wife, Camille (Brigitte Bardot), expects more financial rewards than the theater can offer. Paul is approached by crass American film producer Jeremy Prokosh (Jack Palance) to perform a rewrite on the screenplay for his production of Homer's *Odyssey*. The film is to be directed by the legendary German director Fritz Lang (playing himself). Paul accepts the job, but Camille is disappointed at his lack of conviction in the assignment, even though he ostensibly accepted the job to benefit her. She begins to manifest a profound mistrust of him that is never really explained. After a strained social situation in which Paul acts in a less than noble manner, Camille turns to Prokosh to pursue what appears to be an affair.

An adaptation of Alberto Moravia's novel *A Ghost at Noon*, CONTEMPT concerns itself with the filmmaking process, the nature of film authorship, and the art of adapting a novel for the screen. Godard favors a personal idiosyncratic approach to filmmaking and adaptation as is evidenced in his utilizing Moravia and Homer's work to relate the characters in the film to the people in his own life: Paul, Camille, and

Prokosch evoke Odysseus, Penelope, and Poseidon while also suggesting Godard, his wife (and favored female lead at that time) Anna Karina, and distributor Joseph E. Levine.

The genesis of the project is worth recounting. Approached by Italian producer Carlo Ponti about a possible collaboration, the New Wave auteur suggested an adaptation of the Moravia novel with Kim Novak and Frank Sinatra in the leads. The pair refused. Ponti then suggested Sophia Loren and Marcello Mastroianni. Godard refused. Eventually Bardot was chosen because of the potential financial rewards that could be garnered from revealing her celebrated delectable flesh on screen. However, Godard had the last laugh: the most extensive nudity is in the film's subversively tame opening scene. Committed to a personal cinema, Godard cast himself as Lang's assistant director and used the great auteur as his mouthpiece. CONTEMPT is beautifully photographed in Cinemascope with sun dappled color by Raoul Coutard and Georges Delerue provides the haunting score.

CONTINENTAL DIVIDE

1981 103m c Comedy/Romance ★★½
Amblin (U.S.) PG

John Belushi *(Souchak)*, Blair Brown *(Nell)*, Allen Garfield *(Howard)*, Carlin Glynn *(Sylvia)*, Tony Ganios *(Possum)*, Val Avery *(Yablonowitz)*, Liam Russell *(Deke)*, Everett Smith *(Fiddle)*, Bill Henderson *(Train Conductor)*, Bruce Jarchow *(Hellinger)*

p, Bob Larson; d, Michael Apted; w, Lawrence Kasdan; ph, John Bailey; ed, Dennis Virkler; m, Michael Small; prod d, Peter Jamison; cos, Moss Mabry

Chicago newspaper columnist Souchak (John Belushi, playing a sort of young, overweight Mike Royko) is a true urbanite who enjoys all the goings-on around City Hall and consumes cigarettes, coffee, and whiskey with abandon and little regard for his health. When his series of stories about a crooked politician backfires, Souchak is dispatched to the Rockies to interview wacky ornithologist Nell (Blair Brown) as a pretext to get him out of town. This unlikely love story never really pays off, largely due to Lawrence Kasdan's contrived script. To their credit, a very subdued Belushi and an appealing Brown do their best to add a patina of light charm to this minor effort, and largely they succeed. Michael Apted (COAL MINER'S DAUGHTER), one of the few British directors who can convey a sense of Americana, does a good job of keeping things going, but even his efforts fall short.

CONTRACT

1980 111m c Comedy ★★★½
PRF/Zespol (Poland) /PG

Maja Komorowska, Tadeusz Lomnicki, Magda Jaroszowna, Krzystof Kolberger, Nina Andrycz, Zofia Mrozowska, Beata Tyszkiewicz, Janusz Gajos, Edward Lubaszenko, Leslie Caron

d, Krzysztof Zanussi; w, Krzysztof Zanussi; ph, Slawomir Idziak; ed, Urszula Sliwinska, Ewa Smal; m, Wojciech Kilar; art d, Tadeusz Wybult, Maciej Putowski, Teresa Gruber, Gabriela Allina, Joanna Lelanow

This satirical look at Polish life focuses on the wedding reception of a marriage that did not take place. The couple are pushed into an arranged marriage, and when the bride backs out at the last minute the groom's father decides to have the reception anyway. The reception, which is a celebration of nothing, is filled with drunken altercations, sexual liaisons, and flaring of tempers between the rival families. Leslie Caron is a standout as a kleptomaniac rich woman symbolizing Western decadence. An offbeat, extremely interesting film helmed by one of contemporary Poland's most interesting filmmakers, THE CONTRACT was filmed at the same time as Zanussi's THE CONSTANT FACTOR.

CONVERSATION, THE

1974 113m c Drama ★★★★★
Paramount (U.S.) PG/15

Gene Hackman *(Harry Caul)*, John Cazale *(Stan)*, Allen Garfield *(Bernie Moran)*, Frederic Forrest *(Mark)*, Cindy Williams *(Ann)*, Michael Higgins *(Paul)*, Elizabeth MacRae *(Meredith)*, Teri Garr *(Amy)*, Harrison Ford *(Martin Stett)*, Mark Wheeler *(Receptionist)*

p, Francis Ford Coppola; d, Francis Ford Coppola; w, Francis Ford Coppola; ph, Bill Butler; ed, Walter Murch, Richard Chew; m, David Shire; prod d, Dean Tavoularis

AAN Best Picture; AAN Best Original Screenplay: Francis Ford Coppola; *AAN Best Sound:* Walter Murch (Sound), Arthur Rochester (Sound)

One of Coppola's very best. Harry Caul (Gene Hackman) is a professional surveillance expert, a wire-tapper and industrial spy for hire by anyone—if the price is right. Harry and his assistant Stan (Cazale) use state-of-the-art technical expertise to track a young couple, Ann (Williams) and Mark (Forrest), and record their conversations. The client is a mysterious and powerful businessman, known only as the "director" (Robert Duvall, in an unbilled cameo), whose motives are unclear. After listening to the tapes repeatedly, however, Harry deduces that Ann is the director's wife and that she is having an affair with Mark, one of her husband's employees. To his horror, Harry concludes that his client plans to murder the couple. Plagued by guilt from a previous assignment in which the information he gathered led to the murders of several people, Harry becomes obsessed with preventing the murders of Ann and Mark—for the first time in his career, he decides to get involved—but he gets in over his head.

Following the triumph of THE GODFATHER, writer-director Francis Ford Coppola surprised everyone with this small, intimate, and brilliantly crafted film, which explores the implications of indiscriminate eavesdropping. Gene Hackman is superb as Harry Caul, a painfully lonely, cynical, paranoid, and alienated man whose work has driven him to guard his own privacy zealously, although there is precious little to protect. A year later Hackman would play another eavesdropper named Harry, this time a detective in Arthur Penn's NIGHT MOVES, and the similarities between the two characters were not lost on the actor—NIGHT MOVES could be a prequel to THE CONVERSATION.

The film was released just after the Watergate break-in, but it was written many years before and was already shooting when the news of the break-in appeared. Technically brilliant, THE CONVERSATION does in aural terms what Antonioni's BLOW UP does in visual terms. This is certainly one of the key films of the 1970s.

COOGAN'S BLUFF

1968 93m c Crime/Western ★★★½
Universal (U.S.) /X

Clint Eastwood *(Coogan)*, Lee J. Cobb *(Sheriff McElroy)*, Susan Clark *(Julie)*, Tisha Sterling *(Linny Raven)*, Don Stroud *(Ringerman)*, Betty Field *(Mrs. Ringerman)*, Tom Tully *(Sheriff McCrea)*, Melodie Johnson *(Millie)*, James Edwards *(Jackson)*, Rudy Diaz *(Running Bear)*

p, Don Siegel; d, Don Siegel; w, Herman Miller, Dean Riesner, Howard Rodman (based on a story by Miller); ph, Bud Thackery; ed, Sam E. Waxman; m, Lalo Schifrin; art d, Alexander Golitzen, Robert MacKichan; cos, Helen Colvig

Western myth gets urban update in basis for "McCloud" television series. Arizona deputy arrives in NYC to track killer and teach city cops a thing or three. The interest here is in watching Eastwood, mid-point between spaghetti westerns and assuming his Dirty Harry persona, lock horns with Cobb, who gives a socko performance. Sterling is of passing interest as a female hippie. The first collaboration between Eastwood and Siegel raised the hackles of many a moralist with what was considered needless violence and too much sex. That's one way of saying today it looks tame, but you may get a literal kick out of the poolroom fight scene.

COOK, THE THIEF, HIS WIFE & HER LOVER, THE

1989 124m c Drama ★★★½
Allarts Cook/Erato/Films Inc. (U.K./France) /18

Richard Bohringer *(Richard Borst, the Cook)*, Michael Gambon *(Albert Spica, the Thief)*, Helen Mirren *(Georgina Spica, the Wife)*, Alan Howard *(Michael, the Lover)*, Tim Roth *(Mitchel)*, Ciaran Hinds *(Cory)*, Gary Olsen *(Spangler)*, Ewan Stewart *(Harris)*, Roger Ashton Griffiths *(Turpin)*, Ron Cook *(Mews)*

p, Kees Kasander; d, Peter Greenaway; w, Peter Greenaway; ph, Sacha Vierny; ed, John Wilson; m, Michael Nyman; prod d, Ben Van Os, Jan Roelfs; cos, Jean-Paul Gaultier

Greenaway describes the impulses behind his work as "technical and aesthetic and cerebral and academic." His films have not been developed according to the demands of narrative ("Cinema is much too important to be left to the storytellers," says Greenaway), but by equally deterministic formulas of the director's own devising: formalism, structural symmetry, recurring patterns and symbols, puns and conceits.

At its core a simple tale of adultery, jealousy and revenge, THE COOK, THE THIEF, HIS WIFE & HER LOVER is built around the four characters of the title, the divisions of the restaurant (each room perhaps representing its own historical epoch), the tradition of table painting (a huge Frans Hals reproduction dominates the dining room), and the central metaphysical conceit linking mouth with anus, food with feces, and sex with death.

Greenaway reportedly identifies with the cook: he watches, maintains a dignified distance, but acts decisively on behalf of the lovers. Michael Gambon's Thief and Alan Howard's Lover are diametrical opposites, the one boorish, crude, and ignorant, the other calm, gentle, and cultured. Gambon never stops talking but has little to say; Howard, on the other hand, remains silent for the first 20 minutes of the film but proves thoughtful and wise. Setting out to create an irredeemable monster, Greenaway takes his film to the very limits of screen permissiveness, from graphic torture to cannibalism.

The film has been seen as a vitriolic condemnation of contemporary consumerism and greed, but for all the brutality and physical savagery Greenaway depicts, one suspects his contempt is really aimed at the *nouveaux riches* who do not appreciate the gourmet dishes they can pay for but whose names they cannot pronounce. If there is a connection between this philistine lack of sophistication and Howard's study of the French Revolution, then Gambon is surely representative of the peasants and the Terror—in his resolutely one-dimensional role he embodies every snob or aesthete's nightmare villain. Not surprisingly, his ranting soon becomes repetitive and boring. Greenaway's dialogue cannot sustain our interest, and his lack of humor is the film's biggest drawback. For a lover of games, the director is never remotely playful.

COOL HAND LUKE

1967 126m c Prison ★★★★
Warner Bros. (U.S.) /15

Paul Newman *(Luke)*, George Kennedy *(Dragline)*, J.D. Cannon *(Society Red)*, Lou Antonio *(Koko)*, Robert Drivas *(Loudmouth Steve)*, Strother Martin *(Captain)*, Jo Van Fleet *(Arletta)*, Clifton James *(Carr)*, Morgan Woodward *(Boss Godfrey)*, Luke Askew *(Boss Paul)*

p, Gordon Carroll; d, Stuart Rosenberg; w, Donn Pearce, Frank Pierson (based on a novel by Pearce); ph, Conrad Hall; ed, Sam O'Steen; m, Lalo Schifrin; art d, Cary Odell; cos, Howard Shoup

AAN Best Actor: Paul Newman; *AA Best Supporting Actor:* George Kennedy; *AAN Best Adapted Screenplay:* Donn Pearce, Frank R. Pierson; *AAN Best Score:* Lalo Schifrin

Too cool for words, then switches past midstream into a work of poignancy and power. Not much has changed since Warner Bros in the 1930s, and it's interesting to realize, looking over Newman's career, how many overrated male-bonding, macho-buddy movies he has made. COOL HAND LUKE starts out that way with Newman as irreverent loner put on a chain gang for destroying parking meters. Kennedy won the Best Supporting Actor Oscar as the bastardly convict boss who tries to crack Newman; the comedic part of film is highlighted by a hilarious egg-eating contest, but LUKE gains additional steam thanks to an

unforgettable cameo by Van Fleet and a sharp turn toward tragedy. Newman emerges as a victim more to be pitied than scorned or laughed with, adding a deeper tinge of revelance to the film.

Produced by Jack Lemmon's company for Warner Bros., the movie is set in the South but was actually shot near Stockton, California. Pearce, the author of the original novel, was a reformed safecracker and had served time in such a camp. He does a bit role as Sailor, one of the cons. Also in small roles are Joe Don Baker (WALKING TALL), Wayne Rogers (television's "M*A*S*H"), and Dennis Hopper.

COOL WORLD, THE

1963 125m bw Drama ★★★½
Wiseman (U.S.) /X

Hampton Clayton *(Duke)*, Yolanda Rodriguez *(Luanee)*, Bostic Felton *(Rod)*, Gary Bolling *(Littleman)*, Carl Lee *(Priest)*, Gloria Foster *(Mrs. Custis)*, Georgia Burke *(Grandma)*, Charles Richardson *(Beep Bop)*, Bruce Edwards *(Warrior)*, Teddy McCain *(Saint)*

p, Frederick Wiseman; d, Shirley Clarke; w, Shirley Clarke (based on the novel by Warren Miller and the play by Miller and Robert Rossen); ph, Baird Bryant; ed, Shirley Clarke; m, Mal Waldron

Unfortunately, timeless and not too cool. Deep down, not even the rent is happenin', but on the surface this little alleycat film captures the day-to-day desperation of the ghetto world, mainlining its images with transfusions of eclectic jazz background. We have here a mood piece focusing on Clayton's efforts to rise to authority in his Harlem street gang after hearing a Black Muslim evangelist spouting black supremacy and hatred against whites. An effective look at the mind-set of bored youths who see violence as a way out of poverty, and an indictment of the failings of federal law.

COP

1988 110m c Crime/Mystery ★★★½
Atlantic (U.S.) R/18

James Woods *(Lloyd Hopkins)*, Lesley Ann Warren *(Kathleen McCarthy)*, Charles Durning *(Dutch Pelz)*, Charles Haid *(Whitey Haines)*, Raymond J. Barry *(Fred Gaffney)*, Randi Brooks *(Joanie Pratt)*, Steven Lambert *(Bobby Franco)*, Christopher Wynne *(Jack Gibbs)*, Jan McGill *(Jen Hopkins)*, Vicki Wauchope *(Penny Hopkins)*

p, James B. Harris, James Woods; d, James B. Harris; w, James B. Harris (based on the novel *Blood On The Moon* by James Ellroy); ph, Steve Dubin; ed, Anthony Spano; m, Michel Colombier; prod d, Gene Rudolf; fx, Larry Fioritto, Bill Myer; cos, Gale Parker Smith

Based on James Ellroy's novel *Blood on the Moon*, COP is a grim, modern-day film noir starring James Woods as Lloyd Hopkins, the most obsessive, vile and amoral cop since Ralph Meeker played Mike Hammer in Robert Aldrich's KISS ME DEADLY. Coproduced by Woods, and written and directed by his friend James B. Harris (who produced Stanley Kubrick's THE KILLING, PATHS OF GLORY and LOLITA), COP combines brutal violence with a self-mocking sense of black humor.

Its action is set in a Los Angeles overwhelmed by hypocrisy, cynicism and sleaze, where Woods, an inveterate loner who is one of the LAPD's best detectives, finds himself investigating a murder he believes to have been the work of a serial killer who preys on innocent-looking women. Oppressively seedy and bleak, COP presents a world destroyed by the corruption of romantic notions, and Woods, who understands this warped milieu, is obsessed with the way society fills women's heads with fairy-tale promises of security, decency, justice, and romance. "Innocence kills," he tells his shocked wife. "I see it every day." Although directed and written with a sometimes-unsure hand by Harris, COP is completely absorbing because of Woods's chillingly effective performance.

Few actors can make an amoral, intelligent, sardonic, hyperactive, womanizing, violent and downright warped character as disarmingly appealing as Woods can. As an actor, he juggles complex contradictions with ease, showing an audience the various sides of his character's psyche with the skill of a magician. In COP, Woods takes us on a singularly unpleasant ride, but it is always an insightful and fascinating one. Fueled by his frightening performance, the film rushes headlong into an ending that is so inevitable, yet still so shocking, that it terminates the genre with an irrevocable bang.

CORNERED

1945 102m bw Thriller/War ★★★★
RKO (U.S.) /A

Dick Powell (Gerard), Walter Slezak (Incza), Micheline Cheirel (Mme. Jarnac), Nina Vale (Senora Camargo), Morris Carnovsky (Santana), Edgar Barrier (DuBois), Steven Geray (Senor Camargo), Jack LaRue (Diego), Luther Adler (Marcel Jamac), Gregory Gaye (Perchon)

p, Adrian Scott; d, Edward Dmytryk; w, John Paxton (based on a story by John Wexley and a title by Ben Hecht); ph, Harry Wild; ed, Joseph Noriega; m, Roy Webb; art d, Albert S. D'Agostino, Carroll Clark; cos, Renie

Peak Powell the way we like him, and it's a long way from Ruby Keeler. Canadian flier Powell gets out of a POW camp with his mind set on avenging the death of his French war bride, caused by Vichy officer Jarnac (Adler). Although by all reports Jarnac is dead, Gerard refuses to believe it. He pursues leads through Switzerland and then to Buenos Aires, where he encounters an underground group of Nazi hunters—Carnovsky, Barrier, and LaRue. His quest is further complicated when he finds himself drawn to the attractive Cheirel, who married Adler, without ever having met him, in order to emigrate safely.

Tightly directed by the talented Edward Dmytryk, CORNERED is a terse thriller, with Powell turning in another tough-talking, hardboiled performance as the man seeking vengeance with cold-blooded determination. The script was based on the title of a 20-page Ben Hecht treatment that was, according to Dmytryk, "such poor stuff. . . " that they kept only the title and brought in new writers to shape the film. Well-sculpted.

CORSICAN BROTHERS, THE

1941 111m bw Adventure ★★★½
UA (U.S.) /U

Douglas Fairbanks Jr. (Mario/Lucien), Ruth Warrick (Isabelle), Akim Tamiroff (Colonna), J. Carrol Naish (Lorenzo), H.B. Warner (Dr. Paoli), John Emery (Tomasso), Henry Wilcoxon (Count Franchi), Gloria Holden (Countess Franchi), Walter Kingsford (M. Dupre), Nana Bryant (Mme. Dupre)

p, Edward Small; d, Gregory Ratoff; w, George Bruce (based on an adaptation of the Alexandre Dumas novel by Bruce and Howard Estabrook); ph, Harry Stradling; ed, Grant Whytock, William Claxton; m, Dimitri Tiomkin; fx, Howard Anderson

AAN Best Score: Dimitri Tiomkin

Exciting Dumas tale, which has some basis in fact, brought to the screen with great gusto on the part of Fairbanks whose dashing feats rival the acrobatic antics of his illustrious father. It is the tale of Siamese-twin boys born in Corsica and separated by brilliant doctor Warner just before their parents and relatives are killed by Tamiroff's henchmen in a blood feud. One child is sent to Paris to be raised, the other into the mountains with family retainer Naish. When both grow to manhood they are reunited—Fairbanks skillfully playing both roles—and launch a revenge plan against Tamiroff.

Fairbanks excels in showing how the emotional/intellectual telepathy works on each twin, particularly the agony one feels whenever the other is emotionally upset or physically wounded, and the jealousy one feels when the other falls in love with Warrick. Ratoff's direction is eccentric, but he provides great pace and the script is excellent. The superb Tamiroff plays his evil role with the usual guttural relish, almost as if practicing for his fun bad guy, Pablo, in FOR WHOM THE BELL TOLLS.

COTTON CLUB, THE

1984 127m c Crime/Musical ★★★½
Zoetrope (U.S.) R/15

Richard Gere (Dixie Dwyer), Gregory Hines (Sandman Williams), Diane Lane (Vera Cicero), Lonette McKee (Lila Rose Oliver), James Remar (Dutch Schultz), Nicolas Cage (Vincent Dwyer), Allen Garfield (Abbadabba Berman), Bob Hoskins (Owney Madden), Fred Gwynne (Frenchy Demange), Gwen Verdon (Tish Dwyer)

p, Robert Evans; d, Francis Ford Coppola; w, William Kennedy, Francis Ford Coppola (based on a story by Kennedy, Coppola, Mario Puzo, inspired by a pictorial history by James Haskins); ph, Stephen Goldblatt; ed, Barry Malkin, Robert Q. Lovett; m, John Barry; prod d, Richard Sylbert; art d, David Chapman, Gregory Bolton; fx, Connie Brink; chor, Michael Smuin, Henry LeTang, Gregory Hines, Claudia Asbury, George Faison, Arthur Mitchell, Michael Meachum; cos, Milena Canonero

AAN Best Editing: Barry Malkin, Robert Q Lovett; *AAN Best Art Direction:* Richard Sylbert (Art Direction), George Gaines (Set Decoration), Les Bloom (Set Decoration)

Lavish, interesting, evocative but strained and self-conscious, THE COTTON CLUB is all watchable curiosity. Film doctor Coppola came in at the last minute to salvage a troubled production, but couldn't give it a clear storyline with incisive character motivation. This marriage of gangsters and musicals has many elements of genius, but its biggest flaws are its leads. Gere does his own cornet solos, but his hair oil defines his character. Lane, who can only point to LONESOME DOVE in a career full of big chances, walks right through this one, like she's distracted by a flashing traffic light. Hines does what he can without much material to create around, but Hoskins and Gwynne are terrific gangsters and McKee's rendition of "Ill Wind" is a revelation, defining her own lack of career chances and the ill-fated luck of this production.

The mix of fact and fiction, the show-stopping Ellington music, the heady, poisonous aroma of sinister glamour—COTTON CLUB has much to recommend it before it comes up empty-handed. Yet what success it can muster is discolored by might-have-beens. No doubt a behind-the-scenes documentary would have been wildly successful.

COTTON COMES TO HARLEM

1970 97m c Crime/Comedy ★★★
UA (U.S.) R/X

Raymond St. Jacques (Coffin Ed Johnson), Godfrey Cambridge (Grave Digger Jones), Calvin Lockhart (Rev. Deke O'Malley), Judy Pace (Iris), Redd Foxx (Uncle Budd), John Anderson (Bryce), Emily Yancy (Mabel), J.D. Cannon (Calhoun), Mabel Robinson (Billie), Dick Sabol (Jerema)

p, Samuel Goldwyn Jr.; d, Ossie Davis; w, Ossie Davis, Arnold Perl (based on the novel by Chester Himes); ph, Gerald Hirschfeld; ed, John Carter, Robert Q. Lovett; m, Galt MacDermot; art d, Manny Gerard; fx, Sol Stern; cos, Anna Hill Johnstone

One of the first of a wave of action comedies, not for delicate tastes. Ossie Davis made his directorial debut in this gaudy blaxploitation crime comedy, filmed on location in Harlem. St. Jacques and Cambridge are, respectively, Coffin Ed Johnson and Grave Digger Jones, a pair of Harlem plainclothesmen investigating a "Back to Africa" campaign run by shady preacher Lockhart. A huge success, it inspired an inferior sequel (COME BACK, CHARLESTON BLUE) as well as a new genre for the 1970s.

COUNSELLOR-AT-LAW

1933 80m bw Drama ★★★★★
Universal (U.S.) /A

John Barrymore (George Simon), Bebe Daniels (Regina Gordon), Doris Kenyon (Cora Simon), Onslow Stevens (John P. Tedesco), Isabel Jewell (Bessie Green), Melvyn Douglas (Roy Darwin), Thelma Todd (Lillian La Rue), Marvin Kline (Weinberg), Conway Washburne (Sandler), John Qualen (Breitstein)

p, Carl Laemmle Jr.; d, William Wyler; w, Elmer Rice (based on his play); ph, Norbert Brodine; ed, Daniel Mandell

A monument to acting and direction at peak form. John Barrymore gives one of his finest performances as a Jewish lawyer who works his way to the top of his profession only to have his gentile wife, Doris Kenyon, leave him. Barrymore was the second choice to play the role after Paul Muni, who had played the role on stage but feared being typecast. The film is superbly directed by William Wyler, who discarded a musical score, having music only at the opening and closing credits, so that the dramatic weight fell upon the crisp dialogue and Barrymore's spellbinding delivery.

The film was made at breakneck speed, with lines delivered in the rapid-fire manner that was then popular in the new talkies. Wyler offered a new brand of filmic realism when he kept his cameras inside the lawyer's offices almost through the first reel, jump-cutting from one office to another but focusing on Barrymore and his nerve-center desk, providing urgency and high drama at an electrifying pace. Today the lightning still crackles through this masterful film.

COUNT OF MONTE CRISTO, THE

1934   113m   bw   Adventure   ★★★★
Reliance   (U.S.)

Robert Donat *(Edmond Dantes)*, Elissa Landi *(Mercedes)*, Louis Calhern *(De Villefort, Jr.)*, Sidney Blackmer *(Mondego)*, Raymond Walburn *(Danglars)*, O.P. Heggie *(Abbe Faria)*, William Farnum *(Capt. Leclere)*, Georgia Caine *(Mme. De Rosas)*, Walter Walker *(Morrel)*, Lawrence Grant *(De Villefort, Sr.)*

p, Edward Small; d, Rowland V. Lee; w, Philip Dunne, Dan Totheroh, Rowland V. Lee (based on the novel by Alexandre Dumas); ph, Peverell Marley; ed, Grant Whytock; m, Alfred Newman

The oft-told tale by Alexandre Dumas *pere* was never better served than in this Edward Small production, with Robert Donat giving one of his finest performances. He is the wronged man, sailor Edmond Dantes, who has just received a promotion and is about to marry the beautiful Mercedes (Elissa Landi) when he is framed and imprisoned in the terrible sea-locked Chateau d'If, where he languishes for years. While wasting away in captivity, he meets an imprisoned clergyman (O.P. Heggie) who tells him of a fabulous pirate treasure hidden on the island of Monte Cristo. From that moment on Edmond works to escape from the prison and travel to Monte Cristo, where he will establish a new identity and wreak vengeance on those who imprisoned him.

Donat is captivating as the good-hearted victim and the cool seeker of justice, measuring his vengeance with subtle moves and slow deliberation. Producer Small spared no expense in this lavish, technically top-notch production and director Rowland V. Lee, who aided in the adaptation, lends his usual flair for high drama and action.

COUNTRY

1984   105m   c   Drama   ★★★½
Walt Disney Productions   (U.S.)   PG

Jessica Lange *(Jewell Ivy)*, Sam Shepard *(Gil Ivy)*, Wilford Brimley *(Otis)*, Matt Clark *(Tom McMullen)*, Therese Graham *(Marlene Ivy)*, Levi L. Knebel *(Carlisle Ivy)*, Jim Haynie *(Arlon Brewer)*, Sandra Seacat *(Louise Brewer)*, Alex Harvey *(Fordyce)*, Stephanie-Stacie Poyner *(Missy Ivy)*

p, William D. Wittliff, Jessica Lange, William Beaudine Jr.; d, Richard Pearce; w, William D. Wittliff; ph, David M. Walsh, Roger Shearman; ed, Bill Yahraus; m, Charles Gross; prod d, Ron Hobbs; art d, John B. Mansbridge; cos, Tommy Welsh, Rita Salazar

AAN Best Actress: Jessica Lange

Lange takes the reins as co-producer and tower of matriarchal strength in a terrific movie. COUNTRY details the plight of the 1980s farmer, presenting an Iowan family that stands up to a faceless government bureaucracy that threatens their land. Effective performances and a strong message make this project seem more like a PBS documentary than a staged, rehearsed production—the supreme compliment. Lange received an Academy Award nomination for Best Actress in a year when almost everyone—Lange, Spacek, Field—was on a back-to-the-earth kick.

COUNTRY GIRL, THE

1954   104m   bw   Drama   ★★★½
Paramount   (U.S.)   /A

Bing Crosby *(Frank Elgin)*, Grace Kelly *(Georgie Elgin)*, William Holden *(Bernie Dodd)*, Anthony Ross *(Phil Cook)*, Gene Reynolds *(Larry)*, Jacqueline Fontaine *(Singer)*, Eddie Ryder *(Ed)*, Robert Kent *(Paul Unger)*, John W. Reynolds *(Henry Johnson)*, Frank Scannell *(Bartender)*

p, William Perlberg, George Seaton; d, George Seaton; w, George Seaton (based on the play by Clifford Odets); ph, John F. Warren; ed, Ellsworth Hoagland; m, Victor Young; art d, Hal Pereira, Roland Anderson; fx, John P. Fulton; chor, Robert Alton; cos, Edith Head

AAN Best Picture; AAN Best Actor: Bing Crosby; *AA Best Actress:* Grace Kelly; *AAN Best Director:* George Seaton; *AA Best Original Screenplay:* George Seaton; *AAN Best Cinematography:* John F. Warren; *AAN Best Art Direction:* Hal Pereira, Roland Anderson, Sam Comer, Grace Gregory

Early examination of co-dependency in alcoholic marriages. Adequate in a vague sort of way, which is our way of breaking the news that it's been overrated for a long time. Crosby is a supposedly down-at-the-heels entertainer, trying to keep his comeback up and his compulsive drinking down. Although the dapper Crosby doesn't seem desperate enough, his sober, genial side works to capture the doormat side of the active alcoholic. And given the dark side of Crosby that has been documented by now, we're willing to say he's worth a look; there had to be a lot of fury and tears to sustain a career built on being easy-going.

Kelly, despite the sensible shoes and lack of make-up, is still just too lovely and too reserved to play the gritty wife whose neurotic dependence on her souse husband is as strong as his is on her. She lacks the ability to suggest the complicated levels of a very complicated relationship, and she's totally lacking in passion besides. Odets's character is much more poignant cast against beauty, making her looks almost a dream in the alcoholic's mind. We can imagine maybe a Dorothy Malone, an Eleanor Parker or a Vera Miles pulling it off; we'd be more inclined to say Shelley Winters, Barbara Bel Geddes, or Kim Stanley. But not Princess Grace.

COUNTRY GIRL has a nice backstage feel and Holden gives a strong perfomance as does Anthony Ross, but the film is directed unevenly by Seaton, as if he thought the material was strong enough to do the work by itself.

COUP DE TORCHON

1981   128m   c   Crime   ★★★½
La Tour/Little Bear/A2   (France)   /AA

Philippe Noiret *(Lucien Cordier)*, Isabelle Huppert *(Rose)*, Jean-Pierre Marielle *(Le Peron/His Brother)*, Stephane Audran *(Hughuette Cordier)*, Eddy Mitchell *(Nono)*, Guy Marchand *(Chavasson)*, Irene Skobline *(Anne)*, Michel Beaune *(Vanderbrouck)*, Jean Champion *(Priest)*, Victor Garrivier *(Mercaillou)*

p, Adolphe Viezzi, Henri Lassa; d, Bertrand Tavernier; w, Bertrand Tavernier, Jean Aurenche (based on the novel *Pop. 1280* by Jim Thompson); ph, Pierre-William Glenn; ed, Armand Psenny; m, Philippe Sarde; prod d, Alexander Trauner; cos, Jacqueline Laurent

AAN Best Foreign Language Film

Stylish, twisted black comedy moves setting from the American South of Jim Thompson's pulp novel to a French colonial town in 1938 Africa. There, Noiret is the police chief, a likable, bleary-eyed slob treated like dirt by most everyone he meets. Policing the town with anything but an iron fist, he prefers to turn a blind eye to vice and corruption. Then, having one day decided he's taken enough abuse, Lucien starts killing anyone who crosses him.

COUP DE TORCHON combines black humor at its blackest, with as dead-on an evocation of a torpid, seedy backwater as anyone has achieved on screen. Noiret is an excellent choice in the role, providing a perfect balance between the dangerous and the charming, the moral and the amoral, the killer and the victim. The presence of Isabelle Huppert, as his scruffy but alluring mistress, is an added bonus.

Although his films vary radically from one to the next, director Bertrand Tavernier consistently and adroitly builds on the classical French tradition scorned by New Wave filmmakers. He just might have a point.

COURAGE UNDER FIRE

1996 120m c Drama/War ★★½
Davis Entertainment Company/Fox 2000 Pictures (U.S.) R/15

Denzel Washington (Nat Serling), Meg Ryan (Karen Walden), Lou Diamond Phillips (Monfriez), Michael Moriarty (General Hershberg), Matt Damon (Ilario), Bronson Pinchot (Bruno), Seth Gilliam (Altameyer), Regina Taylor (Meredith Sterling), Zeljko Ivanek (Banacek), Scott Glenn (Gartner)

p, John Davis, Joseph M. Singer, David T. Friendly; d, Edward Zwick; w, Patrick Sheane Duncan; ph, Roger Deakins; ed, Steven Rosenblum; m, James Horner; prod d, John Graysmark; art d, Steve Cooper; fx, Peter Michael Sullivan; cos, Francine Jamison-Tanchuck

Ethical decisions in war and peacetime get a real workout in COURAGE UNDER FIRE, but this film about the investigation into the death of a captain during the 1991 Persian Gulf War ends up romanticized and reactionary.

The film tells two stories simultaneously: the events leading up to the death of Capt. Karen Walden (Meg Ryan) and the struggles of Lt. Col. Nathaniel Serling (Denzel Washington) to uncover the truth about her demise. Serling hears a number of different views of Walden's command: the team's medic claims she died heroically in combat, while the gunner describes her as a scared, ineffectual leader who died in shame. Serling's tenacity takes its toll on him both professionally and personally: his boss threatens to expose a traumatic "friendly fire" incident in which Serling was involved if he doesn't submit his report immediately; and Serling's wife, Meredith (Regina Taylor), threatens to leave him if he doesn't stop his excessive drinking.

Director Edward Zwick (GLORY) and screenwriter Patrick Sheane Duncan would rather address such lofty themes as heroism and truthtelling than shed any light on the Persian Gulf War. The film's plot unfolds in a competent way, but lacks dramatic fire. The RASHOMON-like structure surrounding Walden's death lends suspense to the primary investigation, but as only one of the stories holds any truth, the effect of the subjective point-of-view experiment is negated. Washington strains to make Serling's inner turmoil convincing, but the scenes with his family are sketchy and his liberation from alcohol (thanks to Alka-Seltzer!) seems downright silly. Overall, the film does have its moments, but if Zwick and company wanted to show the moral complexities that occur in war, their film lacks the courage of its own convictions.

COURT JESTER, THE

1956 101m c Adventure/Comedy ★★★
Paramount (U.S.) /U

Danny Kaye (Hawkins), Glynis Johns (Maid Jean), Basil Rathbone (Sir Ravenhurst), Angela Lansbury (Princess Gwendolyn), Cecil Parker (King Roderick), Mildred Natwick (Griselda), Robert Middleton (Sir Griswold), Michael Pate (Sir Locksley), Herbert Rudley (Captain of the Guard), Noel Drayton (Fergus)

p, Norman Panama, Melvin Frank; d, Norman Panama, Melvin Frank; w, Norman Panama, Melvin Frank; ph, Ray June; ed, Tom McAdoo; m, Vic Schoen; chor, James Starbuck; cos, Edith Head, Yvonne Wood

A flawlessly executed, beautifully designed genre parody. Danny Kaye, in his best film, stars as a lowly valet who rises to become the leader of a peasant rebellion aimed at restoring the rightful heir to the throne of England. He disguises himself as a court jester to gain access to evil baron Rathbone, the real power behind the throne, and overthrow his oppressive rule. Genius cast handles the laughs with dash and aplomb, but the real surprise is Rathbone, whose charmingly villainous manner and comedic timing provide the perfect foil for Kaye's antics.

COURT-MARTIAL OF BILLY MITCHELL, THE

1955 100m c Biography/War ★★★
United States (U.S.)

Gary Cooper (Gen. Billy Mitchell), Charles Bickford (Gen. Guthrie), Ralph Bellamy (Congressman Frank Reid), Rod Steiger (Maj. Allan Guillion), Elizabeth Montgomery (Margaret Lansdowne), Fred Clark (Col. Moreland), James Daly (Col. Herbert White), Jack Lord (Cmdr. Zachary Lansdowne), Peter Graves (Capt. Elliott), Darren McGavin (Russ Peters)

p, Milton Sperling; d, Otto Preminger; w, Milton Sperling, Emmet Lavery (based on the story by Milton Sperling, Emmet Lavery); ph, Sam Leavitt; ed, Folmar Blangsted; m, Dimitri Tiomkin; art d, Malcolm Bert; fx, H.F. Koenekamp; cos, Howard Shoup

AAN Best Original Screenplay: Milton Sperling, Emmet Lavery

Yup, low-key and earnest but slow like molasses. Courtroom drama features Coop as the visionary and much-maligned Billy Mitchell who, in 1925, was placed on secret military trial for accusing the Army of being unprepared for invasion and predicting a US bombing by the Japanese. There's not much action aside from the courtroom antics, but the Oscar-nominated Milton Sperling-Emmet Lavery screenplay and the powerful and dignified performance of Cooper might hold you until Steiger's late entrance as a hateful prosecutor sparks proceedings. The many real-life figures—General Douglas MacArthur, Fiorello La Guardia, Admiral William S. Sims, Major Carl Spaatz, President Calvin Coolidge, Major Hap Arnold, General John J. Pershing—are portrayed as walking monuments. Curiously, the film was photographed in CinemaScope, presumably to make the static visuals somehow more cinematic.

COUSIN, COUSINE

1975 95m c Comedy ★★★
Pomereu/Gaumont (France) R/AA

Marie-Christine Barrault (Marthe), Victor Lanoux (Ludovic), Marie-France Pisier (Karine), Guy Marchand (Pascal), Ginette Garcin (Biju), Sybil Maas (Diane), Jean Herbert (Sacy), Pierre Plessis (Gobert), Catherine Verlor (Nelsa), Hubert Gignoux (Thomas)

p, Bertrand Javal; d, Jean-Charles Tacchella; w, Jean-Charles Tacchella, Daniele Thompson; ph, Georges Lendi; ed, Agnes Guillemot; m, Gerard Anfosso; cos, Jeannine Vergne

AAN Best Actress: Marie-Christine Barrault; *AAN Best Original Screenplay:* Jean-Charles Tacchella (Story), Daniele Thompson (Adaptation); *AAN Best Foreign Language Film*

Pleasant diversion, but not brave enough to push into full-fledged farce. A surprising popular success in the US, the film is what is often mistakenly described as "quintessentially French," perhaps because it has so much that one associates with Gallicism (frank sexuality and matter-of-fact adultery, pretty countrysides and city cafes) and that many Americans fondly consider charming.

Two families gather to celebrate their aging parents' marriage. During the festivities, Barrault and Lanoux, cousins by marriage, become friendly and agree to see each other more often. As both are sensible, intelligent, married people, they keep emotions in check, determined to keep their relationship platonic. Soon their spouses are assuming the worst, and inevitably the worst happens.

Much of the film's success comes from the excellent rapport between Barrault and Lanoux in a thoroughly convincing portrayal of the hesitant lovers. Tacchella, however, undermines his film by directing the scenes of bourgeois scandal as acceptably as possible, thereby creating the sort of "art film" guaranteed to offend no one.

COUSINS, THE
(LES COUSINS)

1959 112m bw Drama ★★★★
Ajym (France) /X

Gerard Blain (Charles), Jean-Claude Brialy (Paul), Juliette Mayniel (Florence), Claude Cerval (Clovis), Genevieve Cluny (Genevieve), Michele Meritz (Yvonne), Corrado Guarducci (Italian Count), Guy Decombie (Librarian)

p, Claude Chabrol; d, Claude Chabrol; w, Claude Chabrol, Paul Gegauff; ph, Henri Decae; m, Paul Misraki

Harrowing peer rivalry in the name of love. Claude Chabrol's second feature deals with the contrast between two cousins studying law in Paris. Blain is the country bumpkin at odds with the decadent, city-bred Brialy. They compete for the same girl, and in the end Blain destroys Brialy. A major film of the French New Wave that provides a grim, clear-eyed look at the cynicism of youth, this is not to be missed.

COVER GIRL

1944 105m c Musical/Comedy ★★★★
Columbia (U.S.) /18

Rita Hayworth (Rusty Parker/Maribelle Hicks), Gene Kelly (Danny McGuire), Lee Bowman (Noel Wheaton), Phil Silvers (Genius), Jinx Falkenburg (Jinx), Leslie Brooks (Maurine Martin), Eve Arden (Cornelia Jackson), Otto Kruger (John Coudair), Jess Barker (Coudair as a Young Man), Anita Colby (Anita)

p, Arthur Schwartz; d, Charles Vidor; w, Virginia Van Upp, Marion Parsonnet, Paul Gangelin (based on a story by Erwin Gelsey); ph, Rudolph Mate, Allen Davey; ed, Viola Lawrence; m, Carmen Dragon; art d, Lionel Banks, Cary Odell; chor, Val Raset, Seymour Felix, Gene Kelly, Stanley Donen; cos, Travis Banton, Gwen Wakeling, Muriel King, Kenneth Hopkins

AAN Best Cinematography: Rudy Mate, Allen M. Davey; AA Best Score: Carmen Dragon, Morris Stoloff; AAN Best Song: Jerome Kern (Music), Ira Gershwin (Lyrics); AAN Best Art Direction: Lionel Banks, Cary Odell, Fay Babcock; AAN Best Sound: John Livadary

Triumph of style over substance, Hayworth over all. Charming musical built on a skimpy plot but boasting a score by Jerome Kern and Ira Gershwin that includes some of their best work, notably "Long Ago and Far Away," which even Kelly's reedy pipes couldn't ruin. Kelly saves the best dance for himself, the "Alter Ego" number which is really two dances filmed separately and synchronized together. The other stand-out number is "Make Way for Tomorrow," a roughhouse morning-after number danced by Kelly, Hayworth, and Silvers. COVER GIRL's plot has Hayworth moving from a Brooklyn chorus to become top magazine model, predictable conflict of ambition vs. love. The editorial offices, based on a combination of Conde Nast and Harry Conover (whose beautiful models are seen in the film), lend a 40s-elan and sheen to the film, and the addition of the wise-cracking, always welcome, Eve Arden.

This would be the peak of sweetheart roles for Hayworth, before her shift into dangerous siren territory, and her sumptuous Technicolor candybox beauty was the apotheosis of her era's ideal. She never sang in her musicals—here she is dubbed by Martha Mears—but she danced in an expressive way more akin to acting than athletics. Her passive personality made her a partner equally at home with Astaire or Kelly. She was more of an actress than Cyd Charisse, more elegant in her sensuality, less a traditional tap and ballroom dancer than Ginger Rogers. The sense of longing and abandonment Hayworth brings to her character in COVER GIRL helps her to transcend the formulaic plot; when she dances, it's the only time she looks happy. The film also remains notable for ably incorporating its musical numbers into the storyline.

CRAIG'S WIFE

1936 73m bw Drama ★★★★
Columbia (U.S.) /A

Rosalind Russell (Harriet Craig), John Boles (Walter Craig), Billie Burke (Mrs. Frazier), Jane Darwell (Mrs. Harold), Dorothy Wilson (Ethel Landreth), Alma Kruger (Miss Austen), Thomas Mitchell (Fergus Passmore), Raymond Walburn (Billy Birkmire), Robert Allen (Gene Fredericks), Nydia Westman (Mazie)

p, Edward Chodorov; d, Dorothy Arzner; w, Mary C. McCall Jr. (based on a play by George Kelly); ph, Lucien Ballard; ed, Viola Lawrence

Russell's first step to the bigtime. Obsessive bitch cares more about her spotless museum home than the love of her husband. Roz was only 28 when she undertook the role but her imperious manner, deep voice and matronly looks added a weightiness to the interpretation. George

Kelly's Pulitzer Prize-winning play had been made as a silent in 1928 with Warner Baxter as Craig and Irene Rich as the shrew. Harry Cohn wisely handed over the adaptation chores to Mary McCall who added an Oedipal touch (Kelly objected) to the husband-wife relationship. Dorothy Arzner was given direction chores; therefore the project has a feminist feel that is rare in old Hollywood. Russell's big chance is enhanced by Boles, Burke, Darwell, and Westman, and the production team breathes life into what threatened to remain a stagebound work. In 1950, Joan Crawford would take the role she had been playing most of her life, in HARRIET CRAIG.

CRANES ARE FLYING, THE
(LETYAT ZHURAVLI)

1957 97m bw Romance/War ★★★★
Mosfilm (U.S.S.R.) /U

Tatyana Samoilova (Veronica), Alexei Batalov (Boris), Vasiliy Merkuryev (Fyodor Ivanovich), Alexander Shvorin (Mark), Svetlana Kharitonova (Irina), Konstantine Niktin (Volodya), Valentin Zubkov (Stepan), Anno Bogdanova (Grandmother), B. Kokobkin (Tyernov), E. Kupriyanova (Anna Mikhailovna)

p, Mikhail Kalatozov; d, Mikhail Kalatozov; w, Viktor Rozov (based on his play); ph, Sergei Urusevsky; ed, M. Timofeyeva; m, Moisei Vaynberg

Generally free of the party line one usually associates with Soviet films of its period, THE CRANES ARE FLYING is an antiwar love story, set during WWII, which centers on the romance between pretty young Samoilova and sensitive factory worker Batalov. Boris, like hordes of other patriotic Soviet men, marches off to war, leaving behind the woman he loves. She is eventually told of his death, but refuses to accept the horrible news. Finally, however, she resigns herself to a loveless marriage with Boris's draft-dodger brother, Merkuryev, despite the fact that he raped her during an air raid and although she still loves Boris.

The film gained international attention and was one of the first postwar Soviet features to be seen in the West. A beautiful performance is given by the gorgeous Samoilova, the great-niece of Stanislavsky and daughter of an actor father, Yevgeni Samoilov. The Cannes Film Festival awarded Samoilova the Golden Palm for her electrifying performance, and named the film as Best Picture.

CRASH

1996 98m c Erotic/Drama ★★★½
Alliance Entertainment/Telefilm Canada NC-17/18
/The Movie Network (Canada)

James Spader (James Ballard), Holly Hunter (Dr. Helen Remington), Rosanna Arquette (Gabrielle), Elias Koteas (Vaughan), Deborah Unger (Catherine Ballard), Peter MacNeil (Colin Seagrave)

p, David Cronenberg; d, David Cronenberg; w, David Cronenberg (based on the novel by J. G. Ballard); ph, Peter Suschitzky; ed, Ron Sanders; m, Howard Shore; prod d, Carol Spier; art d, Tamara Deverell; cos, Denise Cronenberg

The term "autoerotica" takes on new meaning as dreamily disaffected couple James and Catherine (James Spader and Deborah Unger) who fuel their own sex life with extramarital escapades, get sucked into a carnal demolition derby. Like almost all Cronenberg's films, CRASH is cold, cold, cold: proof positive that movies about sex aren't always sexy movies, at least by conventional standards.

While driving home from work, James lets his attention wander and smashes headlong into the Remingtons' car, killing the driver and wounding his wife. James and Helen Remington (Holly Hunter) wind up in the same hospital, and are both sought out by the mysterious Vaughan (Elias Koteas). He introduces them to the perverse world of car-collision commandos, including the scarred, crippled Gabrielle (Rosanna Arquette), who wears her elaborate medical brace with the latest in fetish gear. Their idea of fun: re-staging the vehicular demises of stars like Jayne Mansfield and James Dean, an obsessive hobby that can only end badly.

Working from J.G. Ballard's cult novel, itself a dispassionate exegesis of warped desire, Cronenberg assumes an intensely detached tone (think the Normal and their extremely apropos song, "Warm Leatherette"). Nonetheless, the movie is seductive. Its eerie, icy eroticism is embodied in Unger's sneaky sidelong glances—she's always looking at some elusive something off to the side, just out of frame. The weak link is Koteas as the seductive guru of chrome, flesh, and glass. His Vaughan is creepy and insinuating without ever being enticing: Why would anyone want to play "Death of James Dean" with this guy? *This guy?*

CREEPSHOW

1982 129m c Horror ★★
Alpha (U.S.) R/15

Hal Holbrook *(Henry)*, Adrienne Barbeau *(Wilma)*, Fritz Weaver *(Dexter)*, Leslie Nielsen *(Richard)*, Carrie Nye *(Sylvia)*, E.G. Marshall *(Upson)*, Viveca Lindfors *(Aunt Bedelia)*, Ed Harris *(Hank)*, Ted Danson *(Harry)*, Stephen King *(Jordy)*

p, Richard P. Rubinstein; d, George Romero; w, Stephen King; ph, Michael Gornick; ed, Michael Spolan, Pasquale Buba, George Romero, Paul Hirsch; m, John Harrison; prod d, Cletus Anderson; fx, Tom Savini; cos, Barbara Anderson

This collaboration between director George Romero and horror novelist Stephen King is a loving tribute to the E.C. comic books of the 1950s. Unfortunately, it never quite gels. The film starts off on a stormy night with an angry father's discovery that his son has been reading an E.C. comic book, He throws the book into the street, where the wind opens it to the first of five vignettes, a tale about a long-buried corpse that returns on his birthday to wreak havoc.

Each vignette features a cast full of recognizable actors who play the material in an appropriately broad manner. Stylistically, Romero attempts to duplicate the look of an E.C. comic book and relies heavily on exaggerated lighting schemes and angles; however, the trick simply doesn't work, and the film looks ham-handed and juvenile. Moreover, King's stories are nothing special, and with the exception of the final entry, nothing in the film is particulary scary.

Romero is capable of much better, but ironically, CREEPSHOW was his biggest box-office hit The sequel, CREEPSHOW 2, in which Romero adapted more King stories with the directorial chores handed over to CREEPSHOW cinematographer Michael Gornick, is even worse.

CRIA!
(CRIA CUERVOS)

1976 110m c Drama ★★★★
Querejeta (Spain) /AA

Geraldine Chaplin *(Ana as an Adult/Her Mother Maria)*, Ana Torrent *(Ana as a Child)*, Conchita Perez *(Irene)*, Maite Sanchez *(Juana)*, Monica Randall *(Paulina)*, Florinda Chico *(Rosa)*, Hector Alterio *(Anselmo)*, German Cobos *(Nicolas Garontes)*, Mirta Miller *(Amelia Garontes)*, Josefina Diaz *(Abuela)*

p, Carlos Saura; d, Carlos Saura; w, Carlos Saura; ph, Teo Escamilla; ed, Pablo del Amo; m, Federico Mompoll

A quietly haunting family album, CRIA! follows an upper-class Spanish family, specifically a young child, during the years following the Spanish Civil War. As the film opens, nine-year-old Ana (Ana Torrent) comes downstairs in her nightgown, awakened by the sounds of her father (Hector Alterio) making love. Behind his closed door, he gasps for breath and dies. Hurriedly leaving his room is Amelia (Mirta Miller), the wife of his best friend. This is the second death for Ana, her mother, Maria (Geraldine Chaplin), having died a few years earlier. Maria, however, has not left Ana's imagination and continues in this manner to return to her daughter's side, enabling the young girl to resist the attempts of her friendly but stern aunt Paulina (Monica Randall) to raise her and her sisters.

A mesmerizing tale, CRIA! brilliantly weaves the tapestry of time—past and present—into a perfect blend of history. Rather than separate the past from the present, director Carlos Saura layers the two on top of one another. Characters who have died rejoin the living; others, like Ana, exist in any number of generations. Ana is seen not only as a young girl (the brilliant Torrent) and as an adult (Chaplin), but also in the form of Maria (again Chaplin)—all of whom share the

same time and space in the film. A remarkable achievement, which both examines the textures of a once-patriarchal family life and draws a parallel to the end of the Franco regime.

CRIES AND WHISPERS
(VISKNINGAR OCH ROP)

1972 95m c Drama ★★★★½
Cinematograph/Swedish Film Institute (Sweden) R/X

Ingrid Thulin *(Karin)*, Liv Ullmann *(Maria/Her Mother)*, Harriet Andersson *(Agnes)*, Kari Sylwan *(Anna)*, Erland Josephson *(Doctor)*, Georg Arlin *(Fredrik, Karin's Husband)*, Henning Moritzen *(Joakin, Maria's Husband)*, Anders Ek *(Pastor)*, Linn Ullmann *(Maria's Daughter)*, Rosanna Mariano *(Agnes as a Child)*

p, Ingmar Bergman; d, Ingmar Bergman; w, Ingmar Bergman; ph, Sven Nykvist; ed, Siv Lundgren; m, Frederic Chopin, Johann Sebastian Bach; art d, Marik Vos; cos, Greta Johansson

AAN Best Picture; AAN Best Director: Ingmar Bergman; AAN Best Adapted Screenplay: Ingmar Bergman; AA Best Cinematography: Sven Nykvist; AAN Best Costume Design: Marik Vos

Relentlessly discursive and somber, also hauntingly elliptical and exquisitely crafted. CRIES examines three sisters, one of whom is dying, and the robust family retainer who cares for them. Bergman uses the four women as metaphors for humanity, respresenting how we respond to anxiety, death, and the visitations of what appears to be a wrathful rather than benevolent God.

Thulin (the standout in an ensemble of breathtaking performances) is on the brink of suicide and, we learn, once mutilated her own genitalia rather than honor her marital vows. The earthy Ullmann (never more beautiful) once had an affair over which her husband attempted suicide. Sylwan is the glue that holds these Chekhovian sisters together. She can accept God's will and imparts her fatalistic viewpoint to the dying Andersson (Agnes). The former lost a child early in life and has come to terms with death—neither hard nor bad, just a new voyage. Andersson, in terrible pain, cannot fully accept this view; still, she is much closer to the housekeeper than she is to her sisters.

There are many moments in the film during which nothing is said, and the silence is more eloquent than any words might have been. Nonetheless, sound plays a huge role in the movie, as Bergman uses ticking clocks, rustling dresses, sighs, cries and whispers to make his points. Bergman and cinematographer Sven Nykvist move the camera with remarkable fluidity, the beauty of their visuals contrasting pointedly with the almost unbearably stark subject matter.

CRIME OF MONSIEUR LANGE, THE
(LE CRIME DE M. LANGE)

1936 90m bw Comedy/Drama ★★★★
Oberon (France) /PG

Rene Lefevre *(Mons. Amedee Lange)*, Odette Florelle *(Valentine)*, Henri Guisol *(Meunier)*, Marcel Levesque *(Bessard, the Concierge)*, Odette Talazac *(Mme. Bessard)*, Maurice Baquet *(Charles Bessard, their Son)*, Nadia Sibirskaia *(Estelle)*, Jules Berry *(Batala)*, Sylvia Bataille *(Edith)*, Marcel Duhamel

p, Andre Halley des Fontaines; d, Jean Renoir; w, Jean Castanier, Jean Renoir, Jacques Prevert (based on a story by Jean Castanier and Jean Renoir); ph, Jean Bachelet; ed, Marguerite Renoir; m, Jean Wiener; art d, Marcel Blondeau

A clever Renoir film, with a decidedly anti-capitalist message. Lefevre is a meek author of French novels about the American West whose avaricious boss, Berry, cheats him out of his earnings. Berry embezzles the company funds, flees, and is later reported dead in a train wreck. The employees of the publishing house are overjoyed and form a cooperative that achieves great success with Lefevre's "Arizona Jim" series. He falls in love with a woman from a neighboring laundry, but then Berry returns (he survived the wreck and took the clothes of a priest) and demands a share in the company's newfound prosperity. Should Lefevre kill the villain? One of Jean Renoir's best films, THE CRIME OF MONSIEUR LANGE is also one of the most obvious examples of his Front Populaire period of filmmaking—reflecting the social politics of its day and the belief that a collective could effectively overthrow a tyranny. This wonderfully entertaining and sharply scripted film is hampered by its poor sound quality, a result of Renoir's meager production budget.

CRIME WITHOUT PASSION

1934 70m bw Crime ★★★★
Paramount (U.S.) /A

Claude Rains (Lee Gentry), Margo (Carmen Brown), Whitney Bourne (Katy Costello), Stanley Ridges (Eddie White), Paula Trueman (Buster Malloy), Leslie Adams (O'Brien), Greta Granstedt (Della), Esther Dale (Miss Keeley), Charles Kennedy (Lt. Norton), Fuller Mellish (Judge)

p, Ben Hecht, Charles MacArthur; d, Ben Hecht, Charles MacArthur; w, Ben Hecht, Charles MacArthur; ph, Lee Garmes; fx, Slavko Vorkapich

Loosely based on the career of New York City criminal lawyer William J. Fallon, the great "mouthpiece" of the 1920s, this strange drama was the product of Ben Hecht and Charles MacArthur, with Claude Rains as the suave, ever-confident legal wizard. The film opens with Rains successfully defending a killer by snatching up and drinking "Exhibit A," a vial containing poison, and then having his stomach pumped during a recess. Rains attempts to dump Margo, a jealous honky-tonk singer, for hot blonde Whitney Bourne, but Margo inveigles him into shooting her. Thinking her dead, he prepares an elaborate alibi which involves the killing of another man. Margo survives to haunt him in court, and the real killing is finally laid at his door in a surprise ending.

Hecht and MacArthur directed this minor masterpiece and used imaginative techniques in almost every frame. They even appear before the cameras as newsmen interviewing Rains after a legal victory. Fanny Brice and Helen Hayes, MacArthur's wife, appear briefly in a hotel lobby scene. Hayes looks almost directly into the camera which provides a Rains-eye-view as he hurries about establishing an alibi. The opening and closing credits for this film show three female "Furies" darting through the canyons of New York, randomly selecting their victims—those whom they will make mad and upon whom they will visit their evils—a marvelous bit of special effects constructed by Slavko Vorkapich.

CRIMES AND MISDEMEANORS

1989 107m C Drama ★★★½
Orion (U.S.) PG-13/15

Caroline Aaron (Barbara), Alan Alda (Lester), Woody Allen (Cliff Stern), Claire Bloom (Miriam Rosenthal), Mia Farrow (Halley Reed), Joanna Gleason (Wendy Stern), Anjelica Huston (Dolores Paley), Martin Landau (Judah Rosenthal), Jenny Nichols (Jenny), Jerry Orbach (Jack Rosenthal)

p, Robert Greenhut; d, Woody Allen; w, Woody Allen; ph, Sven Nykvist; ed, Susan E. Morse; prod d, Santo Loquasto; art d, Speed Hopkins; cos, Jeffrey Kurland

AAN Best Supporting Actor: Martin Landau; AAN Best Director: Woody Allen; AAN Best Original Screenplay: Woody Allen

Woody Allen tackles morality and murder in CRIMES AND MISDE-MEANORS, starring Martin Landau as Judah Rosenthal, an ophthalmologist esteemed by family, friends and colleagues. Judah has a less admirable secret life: his mistress, Dolores (Anjelica Huston), is determined to reveal their affair to his wife (Claire Bloom), and threatens to expose his past embezzling. Judah decides he has no choice but to have her killed, helped by his underworld-connected brother (Jerry Orbach). Allen also introduces a humorous story line involving a politically committed documentary filmmaker, Cliff Stern (Allen), his egotistical commercial TV director brother-in-law (Alan Alda), and a TV producer (Mia Farrow) with whom Cliff falls in love. Only in the film's dark final scene do Judah and Cliff finally meet, both struggling with their ideas of right and wrong, morality and immorality, crimes and misdemeanors.

Allen is an auteur who often defines his artistic vision in reference to those of other filmmakers, and it becomes increasingly difficult for educated viewers to take his creative borrowings on good faith. In one scene here he restages a sequence from Ingmar Bergman's WILD STRAWBERRIES nearly shot-for-shot, a dubious act of homage.

Nevertheless Allen's expertise is evident everywhere in CRIMES AND MISDEMEANORS, with its fine ensemble acting (Alda and Huston are outstanding), evocative composition and design, intelligent writing, and spritely musical score.

CRIMSON TIDE

1995 116m c War/Thriller/Action ★★★½
Simpson-Bruckheimer Productions
/Hollywood Pictures (U.S.) R/15

Denzel Washington (Lt. Commander Jim Hunter), Gene Hackman (Captain Ramsey), George Dzundza (Cob), Viggo Mortensen (Lt. Peter Ince), Matt Craven (Lt. Roy Zimmer), James Gandolfini (Lt. Bobby Dougherty), Rocky Carroll (Lt. Darik Westergaurd), Jaime Gomez (Ood Mahoney), Lillo Brancato Jr. (Russell Vossler), Michael Milhoan (Hunsicker)

p, Don Simpson, Jerry Bruckheimer; d, Tony Scott; w, Michael Schiffer (from a story by Michael Schiffer and Richard P. Henrick); ph, Dariusz Wolski; ed, Chris Lebenzon; m, Hans Zimmer; prod d, Michael White; art d, James J. Murakami, Dianne Wagner; fx, Alfred A. DiSarro Jr., Hoyt Yeatman, Dream Quest Images; cos, George Little

AAN Best Editing: Chris Lebenzon; AAN Best Sound: Kevin O'Connell, Rick Kline, Gregory H. Watkins, William B. Kaplan; AAN Best Sound Effects: George Watters II

The testosterone really swims when Denzel Washington and Gene Hackman go toe-to-toe in this bombastic submarine thriller from the producers and director of TOP GUN.

Ultra-nationalist rebels in the former Soviet Union have seized a Russian nuclear missile base and are threatening to attack the US. Aboard the USS Alabama, executive officer Ron Hunter (Denzel Washington) is at odds with his captain, Frank Ramsey (Gene Hackman). Hunter, a graduate of Annapolis and Harvard, is the Navy's rising star; grizzled, cigar-chomping Ramsey is a Cold War veteran seasoned by combat. When the Alabama receives orders to launch its nuclear missiles, and the radio fails in the midst of a follow-up emergency message, Hunter must decide whether to relieve his captain of command or risk nuclear disaster.

There's little substance to CRIMSON TIDE, but it sails through its action at a breakneck pace. Director Tony Scott effectively uses the claustrophobic confines of the sub to keep the tension high, while Hackman and Washington face off like the old pros they are. Screenwriter Michael Schiffer has loaded the movie with enough high-tech jargon for verisimilitude, but the script's idiosyncrasies—cockeyed dialogue, pop culture references, and philosophical debates—are presumably the result of uncredited rewrites by Quentin Tarantino and Robert Towne.

CRISS CROSS

1949 87m bw Thriller ★★★½
Universal (U.S.)

Burt Lancaster (Steve Thompson), Yvonne De Carlo (Anna), Dan Duryea (Slim), Stephen McNally (Ramirez), Richard Long (Slade Thompson), Esy Morales (Orchestra Leader), Tom Pedi (Vincent), Percy Helton (Frank), Alan Napier (Finchley), Griff Barnett (Pop)

p, Michel Kraike; d, Robert Siodmak; w, Daniel Fuchs (based on the novel by Don Tracy); ph, Franz Planer; ed, Ted J. Kent; m, Miklos Rozsa; art d, Bernard Herzbrun, Boris Leven; fx, David S. Horsley; cos, Yvonne Wood

A bleak but compelling film noir, CRISS CROSS stars the forceful Burt Lancaster as an honest armored-car guard who takes up again with his ex-wife, De Carlo, now married to sleazy gangster Duryea. When the mobster finds Lancaster with his wife, Lancaster excuses the rendezvous by telling Duryea that they had merely been conducting business, planning to rob the armored car he drives. This lie leads him into a bizarre robbery scheme in which he must work with Duryea and his henchmen while dodging suspicious cop McNally.

De Carlo complicates matters by promising to run off with Lancaster after he completes the robbery, in a double cross of Duryea's gang. During the robbery, Lancaster kills two of his fellow thieves, but is also wounded. It's all downhill from there.

CRISS CROSS is a somber, extremely violent, utterly grim film, with suspense expertly maintained throughout by Robert Siodmak's taut direction—his handling of flashbacks and clever staging of the robbery, stand out. Lancaster is powerful as the love-torn guard, and Yvonne De Carlo smokes up the screen with her earthy portrayal of a money-hungry vamp (a role almost twin to Ava Gardner's slippery siren opposite Lancaster in THE KILLERS). Watch for a very young Tony Curtis as a handsome lounge lizard.

"CROCODILE" DUNDEE

1986 102m c Comedy   ★★★
Rimfire (Australia)   PG-13/15

Paul Hogan (Michael J. "Crocodile" Dundee), Linda Kozlowski (Sue Charlton), John Meillon (Wally Reilly), Mark Blum (Richard Mason), Michael Lombard (Sam Charlton), David Gulpilil (Neville Bell), Irving Metzman (Doorman), Graham Walker (Bellhop), Maggie Blinco (Ida), Steve Rackman (Donk)

p, John Cornell; d, Peter Faiman; w, Paul Hogan, Ken Shadie, John Cornell (based on a story by Paul Hogan); ph, Russell Boyd; ed, David Stiven; m, Peter Best; prod d, Graham Walker

AAN Best Original Screenplay: Paul Hogan (Story), Ken Shadie (Screenplay), John Cornell (Screenplay)

Paul Hogan became an Australian phenomenon whose fame spread worldwide with this amiable, good-natured and often very funny movie. Crocodile hunter shows pretty reporter around Bush Country and then she shows him around equally alien New York City. The film's fish-out-of-water story line is a film comedy standard; what makes the picture work so well is Hogan's cheerful, weatherbeaten appeal.

CROOKLYN

1994 112m c Drama   ★★★
40 Acres and a Mule Filmworks   PG-13/
/Child Hoods Productions (U.S.)

Alfre Woodard (Carolyn Carmichael), Delroy Lindo (Woody Carmichael), David Patrick Kelly (Tony Eyes), Zelda Harris (Troy Carmichael), Carlton Williams (Clinton Carmichael), Sharif Rashid (Wendell Carmichael), Tse-Mach Washington (Joseph Carmichael), Christopher Knowings (Nate Carmichael), Jose Zuniga (Tommy La La), Isaiah Washington (Vic)

p, Spike Lee; d, Spike Lee; w, Spike Lee, Joie Susannah Lee, Cinque Lee (from a story by Joie Susannah Lee); ph, Arthur Jafa; ed, Barry Alexander Brown; m, Terence Blanchard, Donny Hathaway; prod d, Wynn Thomas; art d, Chris Shriver; fx, Steve Kirshoff; cos, Ruth Carter

Spike Lee returns to the Brooklyn neighborhood milieu of DO THE RIGHT THING, setting a semi-autobiographical family drama against the sights and sounds of an early 1970s summer. While Lee fails to impose sufficient structure on his material, expertly drawn performances help vividly to evoke the family and street life of an era untroubled by crack or drive-by shootings.

On a well-kept block in Brooklyn, the Carmichaels, a lower middle-class African-American family, occupy a brownstone amidst a multiracial mix of colorful and eccentric neighbors. As summer beckons, the kids—Clinton (Carlton Williams), Wendell (Sharif Rashid), Nate (Christopher Knowings), Joseph (Tse-Mach Washington), and the only girl, 9-year-old Troy (Zelda Harris)—take to the streets to play games and engage in mischief, while at home they eat, fight, and watch lots of TV. Their parents, musician Woody (Delroy Lindo) and school teacher Carolyn (Alfre Woodard), intervene in the children's squabbles—as well as battling frequently over their own financial troubles—and give them the love and guidance they need to navigate the difficult path to adulthood.

In his seventh feature film Lee for the first time draws primarily on his own family background, though the result is still characterized by his trademark freneticism. Powerhouse performances—notably from Lindo, Woodard, and Harris—help compensate for the lack of dramatic focus. Concentrating on Troy, CROOKLYN explores the coming-of-age process with a candor rarely seen on screen; the script, co-written by Lee with two of his siblings, brother Cinque and sister Joie Susannah, captures all the complexity of this turbulent period in a girl's life.

CROSS CREEK

1983 127m c Drama   ★★
Universal (U.S.)   PG/U

Mary Steenburgen (Marjorie Kinnan Rawlings), Rip Torn (Marsh Turner), Peter Coyote (Norton Baskin), Dana Hill (Ellie Turner), Alfre Woodard (Geechee), Joanna Miles (Mrs. Turner), Ike Eisenmann (Paul), Cary Guffey (Floyd Turner), Toni Hudson (Tim's Wife), Bo Rucker (Leroy)

p, Robert B. Radnitz; d, Martin Ritt; w, Dalene Young (based on the book Cross Creek by Marjorie Kinnan Rawlings); ph, John A. Alonzo; ed, Sidney Levin; m, Leonard Rosenman; prod d, Walter Scott Herndon; cos, Joe I. Tompkins

AAN Best Supporting Actor: Rip Torn; *AAN Best Supporting Actress:* Alfre Woodard; *AAN Best Score:* Leonard Rosenman; *AAN Best Costume Design:* Joe I Tompkins

Marjorie Kinnan Rawlings's memoirs of a sojourn in the Florida backwoods during the 1930s provide the loose basis of this film. Mary Steenburgen plays the author of The Yearling, who retreats to the wilderness to observe the locals and renew herself creatively. Unfortunately, it's all very pretty and pasteurized, though Rip Torn does a decent job as redneck Marsh Turner. Steenburgen's then real-life husband, Malcolm McDowell, is good as famed book editor Maxwell Perkins in a brief part. Alas, this uninspired, perfunctory literary bio isn't saved by its handsome visuals.

CROSS OF IRON

1977 133m c War   ★★★
Avco Embassy (U.K./West Germany)   R/18

James Coburn (Steiner), Maximilian Schell (Stransky), James Mason (Brandt), David Warner (Kiesel), Klaus Lowitsch (Kruger), Vadim Glowna (Kern), Roger Fritz (Triebig), Dieter Schidor (Anselm), Burkhardt Driest (Maag), Fred Stillkraut (Schnurrbart)

p, Wolfgang Hartwig; d, Sam Peckinpah; w, Walter Kelley, James Hamilton, Julius J. Epstein (based on the book Cross of Iron by Willi Heinrich); ph, John Coquillon; ed, Michael Ellis, Tony Lawson, Herbert Taschner; m, Ernest Gold; fx, Richard Richtsfeld

Bleak, unpleasant, and ugly look at men in combat that was almost universally panned by the mainstream press upon its initial release. Its complex and vivid portrayal of the absurdity of war, however, prompted none other than Orson Welles to write Peckinpah and proclaim it the finest antiwar film he had ever seen. Based on a celebrated book by German author Willi Heinrich, the film is set at the Russian front circa 1943, as the Germans are retreating before the Soviet army. We follow corporal Coburn (in what may be his best performance), a German soldier—not a Nazi—who "hates this uniform and everything it stands for." Loyal only to his men, a tight-knit group of soldiers fighting for their survival, Coburn finds his nemesis in his new commander, captain Schell—an arrogant, narcissistic Prussian aristocrat who desperately wants to come home with an Iron Cross, Germany's highest honor for bravery, but who is terrified of battle. Since Coburn comes highly recommended by other commanders and has already been awarded the Iron Cross himself, Schell promotes him to sergeant in the hope of winning an ally. After a siege on their compound in which many brave men die while Schell cowers in his bunker, Coburn learns that the captain has filed a false report claiming that he led the counterattack—a deed certain to earn an Iron Cross. When Coburn refuses to confirm Schell's claims (he also resists calling him a liar, which would indicate reverence for a medal he considers worthless), Schell plots to dispose of the troublesome sergeant and his men.

CROSS OF IRON, which was plagued with production problems (producer Hartwig ran out of money before the final sequence was filmed) and was cut extensively by its American distributor before its US release, is yet another mutilated Peckinpah film but one that holds up exceedingly well nonetheless (the uncut version was restored for home video). From its opening—a brilliant montage of WWII stock footage intercutting Hitler and his armies with shots of Hitler Youth raising a flag on a mountain while a chorus of German children sing—to its bizarre, almost surreal climax, CROSS OF IRON is anything but a standard WWII movie, especially compared to its mythicizing contemporaries. Shot superbly by cinematographer Coquillon, the film shows war as hideously brutal, inglorious, and insane. With its focus on the corruption of moral values and the betrayal of the innocence of children, CROSS OF IRON is an angry film that ends with a bitter quote from Bertolt Brecht: "Do not rejoice in his defeat you men. For though the world has stood up and stopped the bastard, the bitch that bore him is in heat again."

CROSSFIRE

1947 86m bw Crime ★★★★
RKO (U.S.) /PG

Robert Young (Finlay), Robert Mitchum (Keeley), Robert Ryan (Montgomery), Gloria Grahame (Ginny), Paul Kelly (The Man), Sam Levene (Joseph Samuels), Jacqueline White (Mary Mitchell), Steve Brodie (Floyd), George Cooper (Mitchell), William Phipps (Leroy)

p, Adrian Scott; d, Edward Dmytryk; w, John Paxton (based on the novel The Brick Foxhole by Richard Brooks); ph, J. Roy Hunt; ed, Harry Gerstad; m, Roy Webb; art d, Albert S. D'Agostino, Alfred Herman; fx, Russell A. Cully

AAN Best Picture; AAN Best Supporting Actor: Robert Ryan; AAN Best Supporting Actress: Gloria Grahame; AAN Best Director: Edward Dmytryk; AAN Best Original Screenplay: John Paxton

A classic. Anti-Semitism had been unexplored in Hollywood for decades; no studio wanted to take on this social evil until Fox decided to film GENTLEMAN'S AGREEMENT, but RKO beat Fox to the punch by releasing CROSSFIRE first, and the impact was tremendous. It is a simple and chilling story centering on sadistic bully Ryan, who is about to be mustered out of the Army with three buddies, Brodie, Cooper, and Phipps. In a nightclub, the three meet Levene and his girl friend Grahame, then go with the couple to Levene's apartment, where they drink themselves into near collapse. In a drunken rage Ryan, who seethes with hatred for Jews, beats Levene to death. His friends vaguely recall the incident but vanish so they can't be questioned by authorities. Young, a pipe-smoking, introspective detective aided by G.I. Mitchum, begins to investigate and lays a trap for the elusive sadist.

All of the performers contribute fine work, particularly Ryan, who is terrifying as the brutish, bigoted killer—a role the actor was determined to play. Ryan had served in the Marine Corps with Richard Brooks, upon whose novel CROSSFIRE is based, and Ryan had told the author that if his book were made into a film, he wanted to play the part of Montgomery. Ironically, Ryan's performance is so convincing that he would long be associated with the vile character he plays here, and he would be repeatedly cast in vicious, mean-spirited roles throughout a distinguished career that included his extraordinary portrayal of a boxer in THE SET-UP.

In the novel the central issue is not race or religion but sex—a homosexual is beaten to death by other Marines. However, in 1947 this subject matter was still taboo, and producer Scott convinced RKO to buy the book on the proviso that anti-Semitism would replace homophobic intolerance. Dore Schary had just taken over the reins at RKO, and this thriller—which grossed $1,270,000 at the box office, a whopping amount in 1947—was his first production. It was also the last film director Dmytryk and producer Scott, long a duo, would co-create for the studio: after CROSSFIRE's completion, both men were brought before HUAC and became enmeshed in the Communist witchhunt.

CROSSING DELANCEY

1988 97m c Comedy/Romance ★★★
Warner Bros. (U.S.) PG

Amy Irving (Isabelle "Izzy" Grossman), Reizl Bozyk (Bubbie Kantor), Peter Riegert (Sam Posner), Jeroen Krabbe (Anton Maes), Sylvia Miles (Hannah Mandelbaum), Suzzy Roche (Marilyn), George Martin (Lionel), John Bedford Lloyd (Nick), Claudia Silver (Cecilia Monk), David Pierce (Mark)

p, Michael Nozik; d, Joan Micklin Silver; w, Susan Sandler (based on her play); ph, Theo Van de Sande; ed, Rick Shaine; m, Paul Chihara; prod d, Dan Leigh; cos, Rita Ryack

Set partly in New York's Lower East Side, where director Silver's excellent tale of immigrant Jewish life in the 1890s, HESTER STREET, also took place, this gentle romantic comedy is a fairy tale populated with real people. Irving stars as an attractive, intelligent Jewish woman in her early 30s who works in a classy Midtown bookstore. Although she lives on the Upper West Side, she frequently treks down to her old neighborhood south of Delancey Street to visit her grandmother, Bozyk. Appalled that her treasured granddaughter has not found a husband, Bozyk engages matchmaker Miles to find Irving a husband, and Miles comes up with pickle merchant Riegert. Although Riegert proves to be a good-hearted soul, Irving can't see herself spending her life with a guy who sells pickles, and she rebuffs him. The remainder of the film recounts Riegert's efforts to win her. Guided by director Silver's gentle but sure hand and benefiting from strong performances by the leads, this is a sweet, funny movie that doesn't exploit the sentimentality of its story. Silver has nicely captured Lower East Side Jewish life and the conflict between tradition and change while also offering resonant slice-of-life portraits of New York.

CROSSOVER DREAMS

1985 86m c Musical ★★★
Max Mambru/Crossover (U.S.)

Ruben Blades (Rudy Veloz), Shawn Elliott (Orlando), Elizabeth Pena (Liz Garcia), Virgilio Marti (Chico Rabala), Tom Signorelli (Lou Rose), Frank Robles (Ray Soto), Joel Diamond (Neil Silver), Amanda Barber (Radio DJ), John Hammil (Joe, Liz's Husband), Natalie Gentry (Lawyer)

p, Manuel Arce; d, Leon Ichaso; w, Manuel Arce, Leon Ichaso; ph, Claudio Chea; ed, Gary Karr; m, Mauricio Smith; prod d, Octavio Soler; art d, Richard Karnbach

Panamanian salsa singer Ruben Blades made an impressive acting debut in this clever reworking of the old story of a man who rises to fame, forgets about his old friends, and then hits the skids. Blades and his band struggle to earn a living on New York's less-than-lucrative Latino music circuit, but Blades has "crossover dreams," yearning to make it big in the mainstream. His musical mentor, Virgilio Marti, discourages Blades from abandoning his roots, but after Marti's death Blades comes to the attention of slick producer Joel Diamond, who pays him $15,000 to record a pop single. The song becomes a minor hit, and Blades says adios to his old friends and takes to life in the fast lane in a financed fancy car. As his head swells, Blades even drives away his devoted girlfriend, Elizabeth Pena; then the bottom falls out when the album follow-up to his single bombs.

CROSSOVER DREAMS is a simple but effective tale of a talented individual sucked into the void of a sleazy industry. Though director Leon Ichaso deserves much of the credit for the film's success, the real find here is Blades, whose evocative singing comes as no surprise to salsa fans, but whose excellent dramatic performance led to a number of other screen roles, including his excellent work in THE MILAGRO BEANFIELD WAR.

CROW, THE

1994 100m c Horror/Thriller ★★★½
Crowvision Inc./Edward R. Pressman Film Corporation R/
/Dimension Pictures/Jeff Most Productions (U.S.)

Brandon Lee (Eric Draven), Michael Wincott (Top Dollar), Rochelle Davis (Sarah), Ernie Hudson (Albrecht), David Patrick Kelly (T-Bird), Michael Berryman (Skull Cowboy), Angel David (Skank), Bai Ling (Myca), Lawrence Mason (Tin Tin), Michael Massee (Funboy)

p, Edward R. Pressman, Jeff Most; d, Alex Proyas; w, David J. Schow, John Shirley (based on the comic book and comic strip series by James O'Barr); ph, Dariusz Wolski; ed, Dov Hoenig, Scott Smith; m, Graeme Revell; prod d, Alex McDowell; art d, Simon Murton; fx, Andrew Mason, J.B. Jones, James Robert; cos, Arianne Phillips

THE CROW is a gorgeous black valentine that captures the essence of adolescent misery, coupled with a wildly romantic vision of the power of pure love to overcome all obstacles—even the grave. Based on the bleak comic books of James O'Barr, the film scores high on the morbid curiosity scale because star Brandon Lee (son of Bruce Lee) was accidentally killed during production.

The streets are rain-slicked and littered with filth, smokey fires burn in the distance and daylight never seems to shine in the industrial slum where tough little street waif Sarah (Rochelle Davis) lives, and where aspiring rock star Eric Draven (Lee) and his angelic fiancee Shelley

(Sofia Shinas) are brutally slaughtered by hoods in the employ of crime boss/slumlord Top Dollar (Michael Wincott). A year after he and Shelley have been laid to rest, Draven claws his way out of the grave. He's met by a crow perched on his headstone, his guide between the worlds of the living and the dead, and sets about tracking down and killing those responsible for the murders.

THE CROW aims higher than the average revenge tale, but the pallid Lee—all ferocious black hair and scary clown make-up—is almost the whole show. Michael Wincott steals some of the thunder as the Luciferesque Top Dollar; director Alex Proyas and production designer Alex McDowell stay impressively true to the look and feel of the original comic book (which, believe it or not, quotes liberally from Rimbaud).

CRUCIBLE, THE

1996 123m c Drama ★★★½
20th Century Fox   (U.S.) PG-13/12

Daniel Day-Lewis (*John Proctor*), Winona Ryder (*Abigail Williams*), Paul Scofield (*Judge Danforth*), Joan Allen (*Elizabeth Proctor*), Bruce Davison (*Reverend Parris*), Rob Campbell (*Reverend Hale*), Jeffrey Jones (*Thomas Putnam*), Peter Vaughan (*Giles Corey*), Karron Graves (*Mary Warren*), Charlayne Woodard (*Tituba*)

p, Robert A. Miller, David V. Picker; d, Nicholas Hytner; w, Arthur Miller (based on his play); ph, Andrew Dunn; ed, Tariq Anwar; m, George Funton; prod d, Lilly Kilvert; art d, John Warnke; fx, Brian Ricci; cos, Bob Crowley

AAN Best Supporting Actress: Joan Allen; *AAN Best Adapted Screenplay:* Arthur Miller

After more than 40 years, a classic of the American stage comes to the screen with powerful performances and an adaptation penned by playwright Arthur Miller himself.

Salem, Massachusetts, 1692. Respected citizen John Proctor (Daniel Day-Lewis) has committed adultery with his young servant, Abigail Williams (Winona Ryder). After her dismissal by Proctor's prim wife, Elizabeth (Joan Allen), the scorned maid and a dozen other girls convene in the woods for a shamanistic ritual, during which Abigail calls for Elizabeth's demise and the return of Proctor's affections. The "coven" is spied by the passing Reverend Parris (Bruce Davison), and rumors begin to circulate about witchery. Led by Abigail, the girls take the only avenue available: they confess to being influenced by Satan and begin charging other townspeople with being in his league. The recriminations quickly spread to include Elizabeth, and ultimately lead to Proctor's own doom.

The Salem Witch Trials, a moment during which mad authority came cloaked in piety, are a famous metaphor for the McCarthy witch-hunts of the 1940s and '50s. But Miller's play is also a timeless tale of the necessity of taking a principled stand against the ill winds of popular fascism. The notion of someone choosing death over "life with a bad name" may be a head-scratcher in our morally ambiguous culture, but director Nicholas Hytner (THE MADNESS OF KING GEORGE) infuses Miller's spellbinding argument with a passionate kineticism. Day-Lewis, the embodiment of rough-hewn nobility, and Ryder, a dervish of fierce emotionality, head a superb cast, with Allen in particular turning in a remarkably precise, high-strung performance.

CRUEL SEA, THE

1953 120m bw War ★★★★
Ealing   (U.K.) /PG

Jack Hawkins (*Capt. Ericson*), Donald Sinden (*Lockhart*), John Stratton (*Ferraby*), Denholm Elliott (*Morrell*), Stanley Baker (*Bennett*), John Warner (*Baker*), Bruce Seton (*Tallow*), Liam Redmond (*Watts*), Virginia McKenna (*Julie Hallam*), Moira Lister (*Elaine Morell*)

p, Leslie Norman; d, Charles Frend; w, Eric Ambler (based on the novel by Nicholas Monsarrat); ph, Gordon Dines; ed, Peter Tanner; m, Alan Rawsthorne

AAN Best Original Screenplay: Eric Ambler

THE CRUEL SEA is the tough, often gruesome account of British corvette life on the Atlantic during WWII as seen through the tormented consciousness of Lt. Comdr. Ericson (Jack Hawkins). After losing one ship to a U-boat while protecting a convoy, Ericson's ship, *Compass*

Rose, is itself torpedoed; Ericson and a handful of his men barely survive, adrift on a raft. Given a new command on the frigate *Saltash Castle*, Ericson is again at the mercy of the "cruel sea" and must face an impossible choice in risking the lives of his men. The film is shot in documentary style, with harsh black-and-white images, and is based on the wartime exploits depicted in author Nicholas Monsarrat's novel, which was adapted by suspense writer Eric Ambler. The supporting cast appear marginally as crew members in the Royal Navy and in brief flashback and furlough sequences. A top-notch film from Britain's Ealing Studios, with Hawkins turning in an intense, fascinating performance.

CRUMB

1995 120m c Documentary/Biography ★★★★
Superior Pictures   (U.S.) R/15

Robert Crumb (*Himself*), Alice Kominsky (*Herself—Robert's Wife*), Charles Crumb (*Himself—Robert's Older Brother*), Max Crumb (*Himself—Robert's Younger Brother*), Robert Hughes (*Himself—Time Magazine Art Critic*), Martin Muller (*Himself—Owner of Modernism Gallery*), Don Donahue (*Himself—Former Zap Comix Publisher*), Dana Crumb (*Herself—Robert's First Wife*), Trina Robbins (*Herself—Cartoonist*), Spain Rodriguez (*Himself—Cartoonist*)

p, Lynn O'Donnell, Terry Zwigoff; d, Terry Zwigoff; ph, Maryse Alberti; ed, Victor Livingston; m, David Boeddinghaus

A remarkably revealing documentary about Robert Crumb, the auteur of underground comics. Director Terry Zwigoff, an old friend and colleague, links the hilariously rendered and rather peculiar obsessions of Crumb's graphic work to the artist's fantastically dysfunctional family.

A pioneer of the countercultural comic scene that flowered in San Francisco during the 1960s, Crumb is still best known for the ribald adventures of Fritz the Cat and the iconic hipster Mr. Natural. His sometimes puerile, often pornographic, and arguably misogynistic imagery remains controversial, and Zwigoff marshals a roster of cultural gatekeepers to interpret (with varying success) the meanings of Crumb's work and the nature of its appeal. More memorable is the frank portrait of Crumb's family, particularly his brother Charles, a reclusive emotional wreck who was potentially a finer cartoonist than Robert. While some may find the film's implicit psychobiographical "explanation" of Crumb's work too pat, CRUMB succeeds admirably as a documentary portrait of a wilfully perverse American original.

CRY-BABY

1990 85m c Comedy/Musical ★★★½
Imagine Entertainment   (U.S.) PG-13/12

Johnny Depp (*Cry-Baby*), Amy Locane (*Allison*), Susan Tyrrell (*Ramona*), Polly Bergen (*Mrs. Vernon-Williams*), Iggy Pop (*Belvedere*), Ricki Lake (*Pepper*), Traci Lords (*Wanda*), Kim McGuire (*Hatchet-Face*), Darren E. Burrows (*Milton*), Stephen Mailer (*Baldwin*)

p, Rachel Talalay; d, John Waters; w, John Waters; ph, David Insley; ed, Janice Hampton; m, Patrick Williams; prod d, Vincent Peranio; art d, Dolores Deluxe; fx, Steve Kirshoff; chor, Lori Eastside; cos, Van Smith

Revel without a cause. Trashy cult director Waters, now in the mainstream, returns to his Baltimore home turf in this rock 'n' roll take on star-crossed lovers, caught in the cultural tug-of-war between hipsters and squares. The film is high on energy, color and camera movement and, as usual in Waters's world, everything is styled within an inch of its life, capturing all the fun and fever of the 1950s. But underneath the numerous entertaining cameos, not much is going on, and it shows. The film's terrific first half-hour can't sustain itself. Depp is nice to look at, but too diminutive to bring much force to his sexy biker. Locane is well, okay, but she's eclipsed at every turn by the marvelously vulgar Lords, who embraces the genre with the energy and anarchy of the much-missed Divine.

CRY IN THE DARK, A

1988 121m c Docudrama ★★★★
Cannon/Cinema Verity (U.S.) PG-13/15

Meryl Streep (*Lindy Chamberlain*), Sam Neill (*Michael Chamberlain*), Bruce Myles (*Barker*), Charles Tingwell (*Justice Muirhead*), Nick Tate (*Charlwood*), Neil Fitzpatrick (*Phillips*), Maurie Fields (*Barritt*), Lewis Fitz-Gerald (*Tipple*)

p, Verity Lambert; d, Fred Schepisi; w, Robert Caswell, Fred Schepisi (based on the book *Evil Angels* by John Bryson); ph, Ian Baker; ed, Jill Bilcock; m, Bruce Smeaton; prod d, Wendy Dickson, George Liddle; cos, Bruce Finlayson

AAN Best Actress: Meryl Streep

A CRY IN THE DARK tells the true story of Australians Michael and Lindy Chamberlain (Sam Neill and Meryl Streep), the Seventh-Day Adventist minister and his wife whose infant disappeared from their tent during a family outing in 1980. In the film the parents contend their baby was dragged off by a dingo, but authorities don't buy that story. Lindy is indicted for the murder of her daughter, and Michael is charged as an accessory to the crime, beginning a tortuous legal process in which Lindy eventually becomes the center of a storm of controversy that dominates Australian news. Although sometimes slow-moving, A CRY IN THE DARK is a poignant family-in-crisis drama aided by spectacular performances from Streep and Neill. It's based on a nonfiction thriller, *Evil Angels*, written in Lindy's support by a Melbourne barrister who was critical of the prosecution's handling of the case.

CRYING GAME, THE

1992 112m c Drama/Romance/Thriller ★★★★
Palace Pictures (U.K.) R/18

Stephen Rea (*Fergus*), Jaye Davidson (*Dil*), Miranda Richardson (*Jude*), Forest Whitaker (*Jody*), Jim Broadbent (*Col*), Ralph Brown (*Dave*), Adrian Dunbar (*Maguire*), Breffini McKenna (*Tinker*), Joe Savino (*Eddie*), Birdie Sweeney (*Tommy*)

p, Stephen Woolley; d, Neil Jordan; w, Neil Jordan; ph, Ian Wilson; ed, Kant Pan; m, Anne Dudley; prod d, Jim Clay; art d, Chris Seagers; cos, Sandy Powell

AAN Best Picture; AAN Best Actor: Stephen Rea; *AAN Best Supporting Actor:* Jaye Davidson; *AAN Best Director:* Neil Jordan; *AA Best Original Screenplay:* Neil Jordan; *AAN Best Editing:* Kant Pan

A perverse moral tale preaching the oldest of lessons—that love conquers all—THE CRYING GAME was helped by clever marketing to seduce an unexpectedly wide audience.

Fergus (Stephen Rea), an IRA foot soldier, is part of a small group led by ferocious idealogues Jude (Miranda Richardson) and Maguire (Adrian Dunbar). They kidnap a British soldier, Jody (Forest Whitaker), in Northern Ireland and attempt to exchange him for a group of imprisoned IRA members. As the tense and exhausted comrades take turns guarding Jody, a tentative friendship forms between Fergus and the frightened captive. Aware of his colleagues' growing contempt for what they perceive to be a weakness on his part, Fergus pointedly accepts the task of killing their captive when it becomes apparent that British officials will not comply with their demands. As Fergus marches Jody into the woods at gunpoint, the prisoner gets away, only to run into a road and be be run over by a British armored car. Fergus escapes, leaving Maguire and Jude trapped in a hail of gunfire.

Fergus flees Ireland and melts into London's underground of undocumented Irish workers. Haunted by the memory of Jody, he looks up the dead man's lover, Dil (Jaye Davidson). Alternately seductive and petulant, desperately needy and infuriatingly aloof, Dil soon has Fergus bewitched. But Fergus is tormented by his past and, as their relationship grows ever more intimate, tortured by the fact that he has an entire other life of which she is unaware. Still, it's Fergus who's in for the biggest shock, when he learns Dil has an even more surprising secret. Things are further complicated by the unexpected re-appearance of Jude and Maguire, who insist Fergus help them with one last assassination.

THE CRYING GAME's audacity is remarkable, and extends far beyond its "controversial" subject matter. In fact, its utter belief in the power of love to overcome all obstacles may be its boldest conceit.

While a conventional Hollywood romance pretends to place roadblocks in the paths of its lovers, THE CRYING GAME presents Dil and Fergus with a *real* dilemma and refuses to opt for the easy ending.

Thematic issues aside, THE CRYING GAME pulls off a tremendously difficult technical feat; its screenplay contains not one, but two, wrenching twists, each of which could easily derail the narrative in the hands of a lesser storyteller. Viewers are introduced to the story of Fergus's growing friendship with the captive and doomed Jody, then have the rug pulled out from under them when Jody dies barely a third of the way into the film. Fergus's relationship with Dil seems to be proceeding along conventional lines until the moment of revelation, at which point the average film would consider it had done its job and bring things to a swift close. But THE CRYING GAME keeps on going, patiently playing its story out to its appointed, ironic end.

CUBA

1979 122m c Adventure/Political/War ★★★½
UA (U.S.) R/AA

Brooke Adams (*Alexandra Pulido*), Sean Connery (*Maj. Robert Dapes*), Jack Weston (*Gutman*), Hector Elizondo (*Ramirez*), Denholm Elliott (*Skinner*), Martin Balsam (*Gen. Bello*), Chris Sarandon (*Juan Pulido*), Alejandro Rey (*Faustino*), Lonette McKee (*Therese*), Danny De La Paz (*Julio*)

p, Arlene Sellers, Alex Winitsky; d, Richard Lester; w, Charles Wood; ph, David Watkin; ed, John Victor Smith; m, Patrick Williams; prod d, Gil Parrondo; art d, Dennis Gordon-Orr; cos, Shirley Russell

Intelligent, zany satire of Cuban military dictatorships and revolutions from director Richard Lester and screenwriter Charles Wood, who previously collaborated on a number of projects, including HOW I WON THE WAR and the 1968 CHARGE OF THE LIGHT BRIGADE. Connery is a British mercenary enlisted by the Batista regime to come to Havana and help crush Castro's guerrillas. In addition to encountering various scoundrels—including cynical Batista general Balsam, angry would-be revolutionary De La Paz, and grotesque American businessman Weston—Dapes meets former flame Adams, a Cuban tobacco factory manager with a philandering husband (Chris Sarandon). As the Batista government comes tumbling down, the film focuses on how the selfish, corrupt and hypocritical characters respond to the tumultuous events. Filmed in Spain, CUBA was virtually ignored upon its release, but it's an entertaining and well-crafted political satire that is definitely worth a look.

CUL-DE-SAC

1966 111m bw Thriller ★★★½
Sigma (U.K.) /15

Donald Pleasence (*George*), Francoise Dorleac (*Teresa*), Lionel Stander (*Richard*), Jack MacGowran (*Albert*), Iain Quarrier (*Christopher*), Geoffrey Sumner (*His Father*), Renee Houston (*His Mother*), William Franklyn (*Cecil*), Trevor Delaney (*Nicholas*), Marie Kean (*Mrs. Fairweather*)

p, Gene Gutowski; d, Roman Polanski; w, Gerard Brach, Roman Polanski; ph, Gilbert Taylor; ed, Alastair McIntyre; m, Krzysztof Komeda

Neat little chiller with Polanski honing his abilities as a director and standout performances from Pleasence, Stander, and Dorleac. Pleasence, a hermit, lives with his succulent wife, Dorleac, in a large, dank, dark castle on a small island off the northeast coast of Britain. Dorleac is a nympho-in-training who's always looking for someone new to take her mind off her nutty husband. Escaped criminals Stander and MacGowran make their way to this remote outpost, and what we get is Polanski's version of THE DESPERATE HOURS. But the director exhibits such style in his writing and direction that one can forgive the excesses. CUL-DE-SAC is exaggerated, sinister, bleak, and spine-tingling. It is also somewhat thick in the middle and could have used a serious editor to whack away at it. Still, it's well worth seeing for the radiance of Dorleac, who died the following year in an automobile crash. In a tiny speaking part, Jacqueline Bisset is seen for the second time in her career.

CUTTER'S WAY

1981 105m c Mystery ★★★½
UA (U.S.) R/X

Jeff Bridges *(Richard Bone)*, John Heard *(Alex Cutter)*, Lisa Eichhorn *(Mo Cutter)*, Ann Dusenberry *(Valerie Duran)*, Stephen Elliott *(J.J. Cord)*, Arthur Rosenberg *(George Swanson)*, Nina Van Pallandt *(Woman in Hotel)*, Patricia Donahue *(Mrs. Cord)*, Geraldine Baron *(Susie Swanson)*, Katherine Pass *(Toyota Woman)*

p, Paul R. Gurian; d, Ivan Passer; w, Jeffrey Alan Fiskin (based on the novel *Cutter and Bone* by Newton Thornburg); ph, Jordan Cronenweth; ed, Caroline Ferriol; m, Jack Nitzsche; art d, Josan Russo

A fiercely powerful film about heroes, romanticism, and friendship among three initially unlikable characters— Cutter (Heard) a vulgar, crippled Vietnam vet who is an outlaw in a society without commitment or heroes; his best friend Bone (Bridges), a pretty boy with no convictions at all; and the woman who bonds them, Mo (Eichhorn), wife of Cutter but desirous of Bone. After nearly taking the rap for a girl's murder, Bone, while at a parade, thinks he spots the real killer—Elliott, a powerful and arrogant oil tycoon. Cutter lets his imagination run free and comes up with an elaborate conspiracy theory about the night of the murder, devising a plan to blackmail Cord—a plan of which Bone wants no part.

Rapped by the critics on its initial release, it was almost instantly pulled from exhibition. Slowly rave reviews began to surface. After a title change (from the misleading, medically oriented CUTTER AND BONE), it was rereleased, becoming something of a cult movie in the process. An inspiring film, it is constructed like a thriller; but instead of reaching for thrills, it leaves them in the background and concentrates on the complexities of its characters. It may require multiple viewings to appreciate, but it is nonetheless a fascinating picture, and the best of Czech director Ivan Passer's American films. The Jack Nitzsche score is hauntingly effective.

CYCLO
(XICH LO)

1995 127m c Drama ★★★★
Lazennec Productions/Lumiere/La Sept Cinema/Societe /18
Francaise de Production/Soficas Cofimage 5 & 6/Canal
Plus/Centre National de la Cinematographie/Salon Films/Giai
Phong Film Studio (France/Vietnam)

Le Van Loc *(The Cyclo)*, Tony Leung *(The Poet)*, Tran Nu Yen-Khe *(The Sister)*, Nguyen Nhu Quynh *(The Madam)*, Nguyen Hoang Phuc *(Tooth)*, Ngo Vu Quang Hai *(Knife)*, Nguyen Tuyet Ngan *(The Happy Woman)*, Doan Viet Ha *(The Sad Woman)*, Bjuhoang Huy *(The Crazy Son)*, Vo Vinh Phuc *(The Cyclo's Friend)*

p, Christophe Rossignon; d, Tran Anh Hung; w, Tran Anh Hung, Nguyen Trung Bing; ph, Benoit Delhomme; ed, Nicole Dedieu, Claude Ronzeau; m, Ton That Tiet; art d, Benoit Barouh; cos, Henriette Raz

Part neorealist urban drama and part surrealist hallucination, director Tran Anh Hung's second feature—his startling follow-up to the hypnotic SCENT OF GREEN PAPAYA—is an altogether electrifying vision of life in contemporary Vietnam. Tran uses De Sica's THE BICYCLE THIEF as a point of departure, but here the theft of the impoverished young protagonist's bicycle (or more accurately his *cyclo*, a bicycle taxi) sets him on a very different kind of journey, one that takes him deep into a nightmarish netherworld of crime and extreme violence.

Deprived of his livelihood by a rival cyclo gang, the Cyclo (Le Van Loc)—like all the other characters in the film, he's never named—falls under the influence of a brooding gangster (Tony Leung), who, unbeknownst to the Cyclo, is also pimping the boy's sister (Tran Nu Yen-Khe). It's a simple plot, fractured and fragmentary, in which events repeat themselves down through generations and across Ho Chi Minh City with the same inexorable logic as Tran's audacious imagery: the tender flesh of a meaty fruit, sliced open with a razor then splashed with blood; the Cyclo, covered in blue paint (one of several references to Jean-Luc Godard), with a plastic bag over his head and a gun in his hand. Tran's film is a startling achievement: brimming with moments

of exquisite tenderness and shocking brutality—sometimes simultaneously—and each invested with an almost perverse beauty. An extraordinary movie.

CYRANO DE BERGERAC

1950 112m bw Drama ★★★½
UA (U.S.) /U

Jose Ferrer *(Cyrano)*, Mala Powers *(Roxane)*, William Prince *(Christian)*, Morris Carnovsky *(Le Bret)*, Ralph Clanton *(De Guiche)*, Lloyd Corrigan *(Ragueneau)*, Virginia Farmer *(Duenna)*, Edgar Barrier *(Cardinal)*, Elena Verdugo *(Orange Girl)*, Al Cavens *(Valvert)*

p, Stanley Kramer; d, Michael Gordon; w, Carl Foreman (based on the play by Edmond Rostand, translated by Brian Hooker); ph, Franz Planer; ed, Harry Gerstad; m, Dimitri Tiomkin

AA Best Actor: Jose Ferrer

Outstanding performance by Ferrer won him an Oscar and is central feature of film adaptation of Rostand by Brian Hooker. Essentially, the property remains stagebound; it is not well directed, nor does it seem to have had a decent budget. It is hampered by unimaginative backlot settings and lacks the flair color would have helped supply.

For those in need of it, the plot concerns a tragic wit, born with an outrageously long nose, who lends his words to a more handsome man who is wooing the woman that both love. Your opinion of Ferrer's work will depend upon your taste in acting. This is technique work, like Olivier's. The performance feels outward bound, theatrical, expert in that manner. Ferrer never really caught on in films. Undeniably talented, there was something hard-bitten about him, and rumor has it he was not an easy ego to contend with.

CYRANO DE BERGERAC

1990 135m c Romance/Drama ★★★★
Hachette Premiere/Union Generale (France) PG/U

Gerard Depardieu *(Cyrano de Bergerac)*, Anne Brochet *(Roxane)*, Vincent Perez *(Christian de Neuvillette)*, Jacques Weber *(Count DeGuiche)*, Roland Bertin *(Ragueneau)*, Philippe Morier-Genoud *(Le Bret)*, Pierre Maguelon *(Carbon de Castel-Jaloux)*, Josiane Stoleru *(Roxane's Handmaid)*, Anatole Delalande *(The Child)*, Ludivine Sagnier *(The Little Sister)*

p, Rene Cleitman, Michel Seydoux; d, Jean-Paul Rappeneau; w, Jean-Claude Carriere, Jean-Paul Rappeneau (based on the play by Edmond Rostand); ph, Pierre Lhomme; ed, Noelle Boisson; m, Jean-Claude Petit; art d, Ezio Frigerio; cos, Franca Squarciapino

AAN Best Actor: Gerard Depardieu; AAN Best Art Direction: Ezio Frigerio, Jacques Rouxel; AA Best Costume Design: Franca Squarciapino; AAN Best Makeup: Michele Burke, Jean-Pierre Eychenne; AAN Best Foreign Language Film:

A virtuoso update. Gerard Depardieu's Cyrano is nothing short of magnificent. In this version of Edmond Rostand's classic drama of unrequited love, his Cyrano is less physical caricature, more flesh and blood, and a markedly younger, more virile nobleman than the usually avuncular ones of the past. Dealing as it does with universals—that beauty is both in the eye of the beholder and only skin deep—this slightly abbreviated adaptation by director Jean-Paul Rappeneau and Jean-Claude Carriere retains both the panache and poignancy of its source.

As in the play, the film opens in a theater where the lovers first meet and where Cyrano has come to jeer at his enemy, the ham Montfleury (Gabriel Monnet). Cyrano is heard before he is seen, and his voice practically bellows with resonant majesty. When he finally appears, in profile, his nose immediately draws attention. What is interesting here is, unlike other productions where the nose stops just short of Pinocchio's and makes an obvious freak of the character, the producers have gone to pains to see that this Cyrano is not grotesque. It is Depardieu's normal nose in shape, only extended, and by making the character less of a freak, the filmmakers also succeed in making his pain all the more poignant.

The extraordinarily talented Depardieu, who has appeared in more than 70 films, gives his Cyrano a winning combination of grace and gusto, and is a commanding presence, both literally and figuratively

He's unexpectedly fleet of foot during the dueling scenes, recalling Douglas Fairbanks or Burt Lancaster. He brings a welcome vibrancy to the role, which won him the Best Actor award at the Cannes Film Festival. Brochet's Roxane is not shallow, as she is often portrayed, but much a product of her times, impressed with the literary conceits of poseurs of her generation. With its masterful acting, exquisitely muted cinematography, vast complement of extras, extravagant props and scenery, CYRANO DE BERGERAC was, at $20 million, France's most expensive movie production. Though filmed on a grand scale, it does not lose the emotional impact of the play, which had its premiere in Paris in 1898, and has been a mainstay of the legitimate theater ever since.

D

D.O.A.

1950   83m   bw   Mystery   ★★★★½
UA   (U.S.)   /PG

Edmond O'Brien *(Frank Bigelow)*, Pamela Britton *(Paula Gibson)* , Luther Adler *(Majak)*, Beverly Garland *(Miss Foster)*, Lynne Baggett *(Mrs. Philips)*, William Ching *(Holliday)*, Henry Hart *(Stanley Philips)*, Neville Brand *(Chester)*, Laurette Luez *(Marla Rakubian)*, Jess Kirkpatrick *(Sam)*

p, Leo C. Popkin; d, Rudolph Mate; w, Russell Rouse, Clarence Greene; ph, Ernest Laszlo; ed, Arthur H. Nadel; m, Dimitri Tiomkin; art d, Duncan Cramer; cos, Maria Donovan

A clever ruse for suspense. Murder victim O'Brien discovers he has been poisoned and, in his remaining days, tries to track down his own killer. He's a CPA who arrives in San Francisco to get some time away from fiancee Britton but after a night on the town he grows ill and consults a doctor who tells him he has been poisoned and he will be dead in a few days. He then learns that he notarized a shipment of deadly iridium and that he is the only one who can provide proof against a criminal gang. O'Brien is great as the victimized businessman, harassed by the psychopathic Brand and the sinister Ching. Mate's direction suitably increases O'Brien's pace as the story unravels and the plot becomes more hectic, particularly when the bloodthirsty Brand is ordered to take O'Brien out and murder him. Mate also makes spectacular use of exterior locations giving the film a very different feel from most studio-bound entries. The film takes much of its basic story line from Robert Siodmak's 1931 German-made DER MANN, DER SEINEN MORDER SUCHT. The story line was the basis for the 1969 Australian film COLOR ME DEAD. Remade poorly in 1988 with Dennis Quaid and again titled D.O.A.

DADDY LONG LEGS

1931   80m   bw   Comedy/Romance   ★★★★
Fox   (U.S.)   /U

Janet Gaynor *(Judy Abbott)*, Warner Baxter *(Jervis Pendleton)*, Una Merkel *(Sally McBride)*, John Arledge *(Jimmy McBride)*, Claude Gillingwater *(Riggs)*, Kathlyn Williams *(Mrs. Pendleton)*, Louise Closser Hale *(Miss Pritchard)*, Elizabeth Patterson *(Mrs. Lippett)*, Kendall McComas *(Freddie Perkins)*, Sheila Bromley *(Gloria Pendleton)*

d, Alfred Santell; w, Sonya Levien, S.N. Behrman (based on the novel and play by Jean Webster); ph, Lucien Andriot; ed, Ralph Dietrich

A perennial, DADDY LONG LEGS has been done to death. Made in 1919 with Mary Pickford, then in 1935 as CURLY TOP with Shirley Temple, then again in 1955 with Leslie Caron, this 1931 version features Janet Gaynor and Warner Baxter as protagonists in a May-December relationship. It's another variant on the CINDERELLA theme, with perky Gaynor living in an orphanage and bridling under the harsh treatment of matron Elizabeth Patterson. Gaynor is sent to college by mystery man Baxter, a soft-touch millionaire who is a trustee of the orphanage. Matters get complicated when her roommate's (Una Merkel) brother (John Arledge) falls in love with Gaynor. But all ends well when she discovers that the man she loves is also the man who has been her benefactor for all those years. There's enough pathos for two hankies, but spirited cast just manages to keep film from falling into bathos. Gaynor was 25 and Baxter was 40—not quite a May-December romance, more like a June-October—but they suffuse their characters with pro instincts. Patterson was the perfect crotchety old biddy. She didn't get into movies until she was in her fifties, but she made a slew of features and endeared herself to generations of television watchers in her recurring role of Mrs. Trumble on "I Love Lucy."

DADDY LONG LEGS

1955   126m   c   Musical/Romance   ★★★
Fox   (U.S.)   /U

Fred Astaire *(Jervis Pendleton)*, Leslie Caron *(Julie)*, Terry Moore *(Linda)*, Thelma Ritter *(Miss Pritchard)*, Fred Clark *(Griggs)*, Charlotte Austin *(Sally)*, Larry Keating *(Alexander Williamson)*, Kathryn Givney *(Gertrude)*, Kelly Brown *(Jimmy McBride)*, Sara Shane *(Pat)*

p, Samuel G. Engel; d, Jean Negulesco; w, Phoebe Ephron, Henry Ephron (based on the novel and play by Jean Webster); ph, Leon Shamroy; ed, William Reynolds; m, Alfred Newman, Alex North; chor, Roland Petit, David Robel, Fred Astaire

AAN Best Score: Alfred Newman; *AAN Best Song:* Johnny Mercer (Music & Lyrics); *AAN Best Art Direction:* Lyle Wheeler (Art Direction), John DeCuir (Art Direction), Walter M Scott (Set Decoration), Paul S Fox (Set Decoration)

Inert and lengthy version of the old chestnut. The musical numbers, rather than lightening the vehicle, tend to weigh it down. Jean Negulesco helmed this fourth version of Jean Webster's tale about a love affair that has everything going against it but eventually flourishes anyway. Caron is the waif in an orphanage; Astaire is the playboy who finances her from afar. Unless you've been under a rock, you know this means love. Johnny Mercer, writing both music and lyrics for one of the few times in his life, received an Oscar nomination for "Something's Gotta Give," which remains a standard; it's the only foolproof number in the score. Other tunes serve as almost adequate backdrops for Caron and Astaire as they dance their way into our hearts, or at least each other's. The weakest element of the film is Petit's choreography for the dream ballets, which evidences little of the brilliance he'd demonstrated in ANYTHING GOES. Nor does the Astaire-Robel choreography evidence much strenuous innovation. What also hurts is that Astaire and Caron manage to generate considerable rapport together as actors but almost none when they dance together. Both their styles and their bodies are largely incompatible. Ritter occasionally adds verbal snap and Moore supplies that other quality we've come to expect from Hollywood in spades.

DAMAGE

1992   112m   c   Drama/Erotic   ★★★
Nouvelles Editions de Film/Skreba Damage   (France/U.K.)   R/18

Jeremy Irons *(Dr. Stephen Fleming)*, Juliette Binoche *(Anna Barton)*, Miranda Richardson *(Ingrid)*, Rupert Graves *(Martyn)*, Ian Bannen *(Edward Lloyd)*, Leslie Caron *(Elizabeth Prideaux)*, Peter Stormare *(Peter Wetzler)*, Gemma Clark *(Sally)*, Julian Fellowes *(Donald Lyndsaymp)*, Tony Doyle *(Prime Minister)*

p, Louis Malle; d, Louis Malle; w, David Hare (from the novel by Josephine Hart); ph, Peter Biziou; ed, John Bloom; m, Zbigniew Preisner; prod d, Brian Morris; art d, Richard Earl; cos, Milena Canonero

AAN Best Supporting Actress: Miranda Richardson

With DAMAGE, based on the novel by Josephine Hart, acclaimed French director Louis Malle has created one of the most passionless movies about passion ever to hit the screen. Married, successful Member of Parliament Dr. Stephen Fleming (Jeremy Irons) becomes immediately infatuated when he meets Anna Barton (Juliette Binoche), girlfriend of his newspaper editor son, Martyn (Rupert Graves). The two begin an intensely erotic affair that continues even after Martyn announces that he and Anna are to be married. After discovering Anna and his father making love, a stunned Martyn falls to his death from the apartment balcony, setting off a scandal that will leave Stephen's life and career in ruins.

DAMAGE's plot is pure soap opera melodrama, but Malle imbues the material with an almost morbid seriousness that matches David Hare's irony-free screenplay. Strangely enough, the sex scenes are so mechanical that the ratings controversy that colored the film's release now seems ridiculous: no one could possibly find this material erotic. Stephen and Anna's many couplings look cold, clinical and—especially when lit through Venetian blinds—terminally arty. Irons, of course, is excellent.

DAMN YANKEES

1958 110m c Sports/Musical/Comedy ★★★★
Warner Bros. (U.S.) /U

Tab Hunter *(Joe Hardy)*, Gwen Verdon *(Lola)*, Ray Walston *(Applegate)*, Russ Brown *(Van Buren)*, Shannon Bolin *(Meg)*, Nathaniel Frey *(Smokey)*, Jimmie Komack *(Rocky)*, Rae Allen *(Gloria)*, Robert Shafer *(Joe Boyd)*, Jean Stapleton *(Sister)*

p, George Abbott, Stanley Donen; d, George Abbott, Stanley Donen; w, George Abbott (based on the play by George Abbott and Douglas Wallop, from the novel *The Year the Yankees Lost the Pennant* by Wallop); ph, Harold Lipstein; ed, Frank Bracht; m, Jerry Ross, Richard Adler; prod d, William Eckart, Jean Eckart; art d, Stanley Fleischer; chor, Bob Fosse, Pat Ferrier; cos, William Eckart, Jean Eckart

AAN Best Score: Ray Heindorf

Somewhere along the way of opening up the smash stage version, DAMN YANKEES gets saddled with too much plot. It's only 110 minutes long, but you'd never know it. If Hunter is lacking in assurance among all the legit pros, there's nothing distinctly wrong in his performance. A middle-aged Washington Senators fan (Shafer) would give his soul for a long-ball hitter and promptly enough the devil shows up in the form of Walston, to change him into a handsome, athletic 22-year-old (Hunter), who wins a place on the Senators team. Walston is a perfect comic Satan, but gets bogged down in too much superfical action. It's unfortunate that the screenplay depends upon him to tie up all the loose ends. Verdon's eternal Lilith, Lola, is expert, sexy, and hilarious but because she's not a conventional beauty (Monroe had turned down both the Broadway and film versions) the need for Hunter is more than evident. Terrific, Oscar-nominated score by Jerry Ross and Richard Adler is electric, contains "Heart," "Whatever Lola Wants" and "Shoeless Joe from Hannibal Mo." That's Bob Fosse dancing with Verdon on "Who's Got the Pain."

DAMNATION
(KARHOZAT)

1988 116m bw Drama ★★★★
Hungarian Film Institute/Mokep/Hungarian TV (Hungary)

Miklos B. Szekely *(Karrer)*, Vali Kerekes *(The Singer)*, Gyula Pauer *(Willarsky)*, Hedi Temessy *(Cloakroom Attendant)*, Gyorgy Cserhalmi *(Sebestyen)*

p, Jozsef Marx; d, Bela Tarr; w, Laszlo Krasznahorkai, Bela Tarr; ph, Gabor Medvigy; ed, Agnes Hraniczky; m, Mihaly Vig; cos, Gyula Pauer

Photographed in black and white, Tarr's DAMNATION is a slowly paced, deeply pessimistic, yet poetic film set in a grim, featureless industrial area outside Budapest. There, alone and friendless, the unemployed Szekely lives a monotonous existence, making the rounds of the local bars and staring out the window at miner's buckets passing back and forth, suspended on cables. Szekely is "in love" (the term's potential banality emerges when applied to Tarr's alienated characters) with Kerekes, a chanteuse at the Titanic bar who is married to Cserhalmi. She has ended their affair (not—we suspect—for the first time), but Szekely still pursues her, haunting the Titanic and waiting outside Kerekes and Cserhalmi's apartment building, unprotected in the furiously pouring rain, for Cserhalmi to leave. When a barkeeper (Pauer) offers Szekely an opportunity to make some money as the courier in a smuggling expedition, Szekely tips off Cserhalmi to the job, knowing

he is badly in debt, and thereby gets him out of the country for a few days. He and Kerekes then resume their affair, after a fashion, as the two fight violently, have sex, and engage in hopelessly one-sided conversations.

In addition to giving his actors pessimistic, near-monologue dialogue, director-coscreenwriter Tarr emphasizes his characters' despair with a number of visual motifs. The incessant rain is the chief image of several that recur. The buckets passing back and forth, rows of stacked glasses, several views of textural patterns in walls—these, in Tarr and cinematographer Medvigy's static shots, have the nearly abstract compositional beauty of the best black-and-white still photographs, and the film is filled with stunning images of the most mundane objects and scenes. When the camera does move, the director favors slow lateral pans that seem to suit the monotony of his characters' lives. Tarr's uncompromisingly tragic view of the human condition is well supported by a rigorous formal approach, resulting in an austere work of art.

DAMNED, THE
(LA CADUTA DEGLI DEI)

1969 155m c Drama ★★★★
Eichberg/Pegaso/Praesidens (Italy/West Germany) X/18

Dirk Bogarde *(Friedrich Bruckmann)*, Ingrid Thulin *(Baroness Sophie von Essenbeck)*, Helmut Griem *(Aschenbach)*, Helmut Berger *(Martin von Essenbeck)*, Renaud Verley *(Gunther von Essenbeck)*, Umberto Orsini *(Herbert Thallman)*, Rene Kolldehoff *(Baron Konstantin von Essenbeck)*, Albrecht Schoenhals *(Baron Joachim von Essenbeck)*, Charlotte Rampling *(Elisabeth Thallman)*, Florinda Bolkan *(Olga)*

p, Alfredo Levy, Ever Haggiag; d, Luchino Visconti; w, Luchino Visconti, Nicola Badalucco, Enrico Medioli; ph, Armando Nannuzzi, Pasquale De Santis; ed, Ruggero Mastroianni; m, Maurice Jarre

AAN Best Adapted Screenplay: Nicola Badalucco (Story), Enrico Medioli (Screenplay), Luchino Visconti (Screenplay)

Luchino Visconti's epic of decadence, set in Germany during 1933 and 1934, parallels the end of a family of industrialists with the rise of Nazism. The films opens with an extravagant dinner celebrating the retirement of the family patriarch, Baron Joachim von Essenbeck, the magnate of a huge steel enterprise, and his appointment of an outsider, Friedrich Bruckmann (Dirk Bogarde) as temporary head. While at first all seems very respectable and bourgeois, the gathering turns strange when Joachim's grandson, Martin (Helmut Berger) delivers his rendition of Marlene Dietrich's "Falling in Love Again" dressed in drag. Before the party is over, it is announced that the Reichstag has been burned, symbolizing the end of German democracy. Later, as the highly organized SS plots to annihilate the SA (the populist Fascist front), Martin, a bisexual, sadistic, pedophilic drug addict who even rapes his own mother, engineers his plot to stop a takeover attempt by Friedrich and Sophie (Ingrid Thulin), Friedrich's lover and Martin's mother.

THE DAMNED is Visconti at his most operatic (the German title is GOTTERDAMMERUNG, after Wagner), containing baroque sets and costumes, highly melodramatic acting, and orgiastic scenes of violence and sex. While it has been criticized on a number of levels (the equating of perverts and pedophiles with fascists has been done before; its English dialogue is often poor; it indulges in its own distastefulness; it's too long, etc.), the film is a spectacular, meticulously crafted work that cannot fail to elicit some response, be it disgust or appreciation, from its audience.

DANCE WITH A STRANGER

1985 102m c Biography/Crime ★★★★
First Film/Goldcrest/HFFC/4 Intl. (U.K.) R/15

Miranda Richardson *(Ruth Ellis)*, Rupert Everett *(David Blakely)*, Ian Holm *(Desmond Cussen)*, Matthew Carroll *(Andy)*, Tom Chadbon *(Anthony Findlater)*, Jane Bertish *(Carole Findlater)*, David Troughton *(Cliff Davis)*, Paul Mooney *(Clive Gunnell)*, Stratford Johns *(Morrie Conley)*, Joanne Whalley-Kilmer *(Christine)*

p, Roger Randall-Cutler; d, Mike Newell; w, Shelagh Delaney; ph, Peter Hannan; ed, Mick Audsley; m, Richard Hartley; prod d, Andrew Mollo; art d, Adrian Smith; cos, Pip Newberry

Dark, haunting kichen-sink noir, deftly done; the life and death of Ruth Ellis, the last woman to be hanged for murder in England in 1955. The screenplay by Shelagh Delaney takes a few liberties for the sake of dramatic license but by and large keeps close to the real account. Miranda Richardson (playing Ellis), a divorcee and ex-hooker, now a "hostess" in a tawdry nightclub in Soho. Though she lives with Holm, he is more of a pal than a lover and also the surrogate father to her teenage son, Carroll. Richardson falls obsessively in love with upper-class Everett, an immature cad. But the more she wants to be with Everett, the more he pushes her aside, both mentally and physically. Eventually she retaliates and murders him. The real case provided months of lurid reading for the British and several years later, Ellis's son committed suicide.

STRANGER inhabits the seedy milieu beneath the repressed 1950s British surface. Richardson's performance is a knockout; with her birdlike gestures and darting eyes, she's reminiscent of young Bette Davis in her peroxide period. And she challenges two topics the English hesitate to look at—sexual compulsivity and outward expression of nasty emotions; no wonder Ellis got the death sentence.

DANCES WITH WOLVES

1990   183m   c   Western   ★★½
TIG   (U.S.)   PG-13/12

Kevin Costner (Lt. John W. Dunbar), Mary McDonnell (Stands with a Fist), Graham Greene (Kicking Bird), Rodney A. Grant (Wind in his Hair), Floyd Red Crow Westerman (Chief Ten Bears), Tantoo Cardinal (Black Shawl), Robert Pastorelli (Timmons), Charles Rocket (Lt. Elgin), Maury Chaykin (Maj. Fambrough), Jimmy Herman (Stone Calf)

p, Jim Wilson, Kevin Costner; d, Kevin Costner; w, Michael Blake (based on his novel); ph, Dean Semler; ed, Neil Travis; m, John Barry; art d, William L. Skinner; fx, Robbie Knott; cos, Elsa Zamparelli

AA Best Picture; AAN Best Actor: Kevin Costner; AAN Best Supporting Actor: Graham Greene; AAN Best Supporting Actress: Mary McDonnell; AA Best Director: Kevin Costner; AA Best Adapted Screenplay: Michael Blake; AA Best Cinematography: Dean Semler; AA Best Editing: Neil Travis; AA Best Score: John Barry; AAN Best Art Direction: Jeffrey Beecroft, Lisa Dean; AAN Best Costume Design: Elsa Zamparelli; AA Best Sound: Russell Williams, II, Jeffrey Perkins, Bill W. Benton, Greg Watkins

The plodding vanity project of star, director, and co-producer Kevin Costner, this three-hour-plus revisionist western, much of it in subtitled Sioux language, shocked movie-industry observers by becoming a huge hit and garnering 12 Oscar nominations, winning seven, including Best Picture and Best Director. The Sioux gave the film their own rave review by admitting Costner as a full tribal member.

Costner plays Lt. John W. Dunbar, a Union officer during the Civil War who undergoes a conversion experience on the frontier that transforms him into the title character. The film begins with Dunbar wounded, depressed, and suicidal. His suicide attempt is mistaken for an act of heroism and he gets transferred to the post of his choice—an outpost on the frontier far away from white "civilization." After a series of peculiar experiences he finds himself alone in a little shelter on the prairie where he befriends an amiable wolf. Before long he meets his equally amiable Native American neighbors and slowly wins their respect and love as he goes native with a vengeance. Over the course of his unlikely adventures, he trades in his dreary Union duds for some cool Sioux threads, forms a very close friendship with a white woman (McDonnell) who was captured and raised by Indians, and even breaks the "Prime Directive" by giving out rifles and ammunition to his "good" Lakota Sioux pals to battle the mean ol' Pawnees.

Not a great film by any standard, this is a western for people who are completely ignorant about the genre. Costner's direction is barely competent and frequently clumsy. Michael Blake's script, adapted from his novel, is loose and disconnected, rambling about with no real story holding it together, beyond the imminent arrival of the white bad guys to spoil Dunbar's frontier fantasy paradise. Despite its attention to surface details of day-to-day Sioux life, the film shows no genuine curiosity about the larger designs of the Sioux culture. We see little of tribal life through Sioux eyes, and come away having learned nothing at all about Sioux spirituality. Instead, the film renders the Sioux as just average folks.

DANGEROUS LIAISONS

1988   120m   c   Drama   ★★★★
NFH/Lorimar   (U.S.)   R/15

Glenn Close (Marquise de Merteuil), John Malkovich (Vicomte de Valmont), Michelle Pfeiffer (Madame de Tourvel), Swoosie Kurtz (Madame de Volanges), Keanu Reeves (Chevalier Danceny), Mildred Natwick (Madame de Rosemonde), Uma Thurman (Cecile de Volanges), Joe Sheridan, Peter Capaldi

p, Norma Heyman, Hank Moonjean, Christopher Hampton; d, Stephen Frears; w, Christopher Hampton (based on his play and the novel Les Liaisons Dangereuses by Choderlos de Laclos); ph, Philippe Rousselot; ed, Mick Audsley; m, George Fenton; prod d, Stuart Craig; cos, James Acheson

AAN Best Picture; AAN Best Actress: Glenn Close; AAN Best Supporting Actress: Michelle Pfeiffer; AA Best Adapted Screenplay: Christopher Hampton; AAN Best Score: George Fenton; AA Best Art Direction: Stuart Craig, Gerard James; AA Best Costume Design: James Acheson

Choderlos de Laclos reportedly said of his epistolary 1782 novel, Les Liaisons Dangereuses, that he created it with the intent to shock. That novel, on which British director Stephen Frears's first American feature film is based, did much of what Laclos hoped, the first edition becoming the succes de scandale of Paris. Frears's version, a costume drama set in pre-Revolutionary France, isn't precisely shocking, but its classic story of sexual power, depravity, cruelty, and deceit is rendered with force and without compromise.

The Marquise de Merteuil (Glenn Close) and the Vicomte de Valmont (John Malkovich) are monsters of the aristocracy, former lovers who spend their days planning sexual seductions and vengeance. Merteuil makes Valmont a proposition: if he deflowers Cecile (Uma Thurman), the 16-year-old future wife of another of Merteuil's former lovers, she will gratefully reward Valmont with her favors. Valmont instead devotes his attention to the greater challenge of seducing Madame de Tourvel (Michelle Pfeiffer)—a highly moral, married, and convent-bred young woman. Plying his suit with the greatest skill and subtlety, Valmont eventually breaks down Tourvel's reserve. In the meantime, to please Merteuil, he also deflowers Cecile—who, after yielding to Valmont, becomes insatiably sensual. DANGEROUS LIAISONS is less about debauchery and amorality than it is about the sexual and psychological domination of one person by another.

Malkovich and Close take a while before they shift into expert gear, the former lacking the physical grace of a Don Juan, the latter vapid in a Connecticut housewife kind of way. Nor does it help that Close, despite her talent, is utterly devoid of sex appeal. But Pfeiffer is a revelation in her part, almost stealing the film. Her relative stillness, masking internal unrest, makes her character seem more authentically "period" than her co-stars, who have adopted no formal period mannerisms. But its vernacular style allows the film to connect easily with present-day morals, sexual politics, and thirst for power. While not perfect, LIAISONS is miles above Forman's bland VALMONT.

DANGEROUS MOVES
(LA DIAGONALE DU FOU)

1984   95m   c   Thriller   ★★★½
Arthur Cohn   (Switzerland)   /PG

Michel Piccoli (Akiva Liebskind), Alexandre Arbatt (Pavius Fromm), Leslie Caron (Henia Liebskind), Liv Ullmann (Marina), Daniel Olbrychski (Tac-Tac), Michel Aumont (Kerossian), Serge Avedikian (Fadenko), Pierre Michael (Yachvili), Pierre Vial (Anton Heller), Wojciech Pszoniak (Felton)

p, Arthur Cohn; d, Richard Dembo; w, Richard Dembo; ph, Raoul Coutard; ed, Agnes Guillemot; m, Gabriel Yared; art d, Ivan Maussion; cos, Pierre Albert

AA Best Foreign Language Film

This ingenious thriller takes place in the world of chess championships, using the politically neutral Geneva, Switzerland, as its backdrop. The reigning world chess champion, Michel Piccoli, is the pride of the Soviet Union, but his weak heart may mean the end of his reign. His competitor is Alexandre Arbatt, a rebellious young Soviet exile. As the championship begins, Arbatt attempts to disrupt the proceedings, and thereby Piccoli's concentration, by arriving late for his first move. His habitual tardiness and basic contempt for regulations force Piccoli to register a formal complaint with the jury. When Piccoli threatens to withdraw, Arbatt buckles under and writes a formal apology rather than lose his chance to defeat the champion. As a result of their moves away from the chess board, both men begin to deteriorate—Piccoli physically, Arbatt mentally. The chess masters, however, are merely pawns in a larger political game involving the Soviet government and the West.

Director Richard Dembo, in his debut feature, has contrasted skillfully the players' maneuvers with political power plays, yet he avoids pretension. Rather than concentrating too much on the chess matches themselves (a knowledge of chess is helpful in viewing DANGEROUS MOVES, but by no means a requirement), Dembo brings to the screen an emotional battle between two powerful personalities. He also receives support from a solid who's-who of European film, including actors Liv Ullmann, Leslie Caron, Bernhard Wicki, Daniel Olbrychski, and Jean-Hugues Anglade; cameraman Raoul Coutard; and editor Agnes Guillemot.

DANTON

1982   136m   c   Historical/Biography/War   ★★★
TF1/SFPC/Film Polski/Losange/Gaumont   (France/Poland)   PG

Gerard Depardieu *(Georges Danton)*, Wojciech Pszoniak *(Maximillian Robespierre)*, Patrice Chereau *(Camille Desmoulins)*, Angela Winkler *(Lucile Desmoulins)*, Boguslaw Linda *(Saint Just)*, Roland Blanche *(Lacroix)*, Anne Alvaro *(Eleonore Duplay)*, Roger Planchon *(Fouquier Tinville)*, Serge Merlin *(Philippeaux)*, Lucien Melki *(Fabre d'Eglantine)*

p, Margaret Menegoz; d, Andrzej Wajda; w, Jean-Claude Carriere, Andrzej Wajda, Agnieszka Holland, Boleslaw Michalek, Jacek Gasiorowski (based on the play "The Danton Affair" by Stanislawa Przybyszewska); ph, Igor Luther; ed, Halina Prugar; m, Jean Prodromides; art d, Allan Starski, Gilles Vaster; cos, Yvonne Sassinot de Nesle

DANTON is a powerful drama of revolution, set in 1794 France, during the second year of the Republic, that centers on the rivalry between the humanist Georges Danton (the typically memorable Gerard Depardieu) and the ideologue Maximilien de Robespierre (Wojciech Pszoniak), "The Incorruptible." Danton, the most popular of the French revolutionaries, temporarily retired from politics and retreated to the countryside. He returns to Paris now, however, to stop the Reign of Terror led by Robespierre, his former compatriot in the Revolution whose efforts to keep the "pure patriots" in power have turned tyrannical. Although a great freedom fighter and proponent of political, religious, and human rights, Robespierre, with his Committee of Public Safety, has become just as oppressive as the monarchs he fought against. Despite the fact that Danton is a people's hero, Robespierre convinces himself that he must be executed in order to save the Republic.

DANTON is a stirring film on freedom from Andrzej Wajda, in his first directing effort outside of Poland. Criticized by some for being too static and theatrical, the movie takes care to show only the center of the Revolution and its aftermath: the battle between Danton and Robespierre and the unseen fight for liberty that takes place behind closed doors. Wajda disregards the rebellion in the streets in favor of showing us the power in the hands of government—those chosen few who are supposed to be representatives of the people.

DARBY O'GILL AND THE LITTLE PEOPLE

1959   93m   c   Children's/Fantasy   ★★★★½
Walt Disney Productions   (U.S.)   /U

Albert Sharpe *(Darby O'Gill)*, Janet Munro *(Katie)*, Sean Connery *(Michael McBride)*, Jimmy O'Dea *(King Brian)*, Kieron Moore *(Pony Sugrue)*, Estelle Winwood *(Sheelah)*, Walter Fitzgerald *(Lord Fitzpatrick)*, Denis O'Dea *(Fr. Murphy)*, J.G. Devlin *(Tom Kerrigan)*, Jack MacGowran *(Phadrig Oge)*

p, Walt Disney; d, Robert Stevenson; w, Lawrence E. Watkin (based on the Darby O'Gill stories by H.T. Kavanagh); ph, Winton C. Hoch; ed, Stanley Johnson; m, Oliver Wallace; art d, Carroll Clark; fx, Peter Ellenshaw, Eustace Lycett; cos, Chuck Keehne, Gertrude Casey; anim, Joshua Meador

This excellent fantasy romps through the folklore world of Ireland, with Albert Sharpe starring as Darby O'Gill, the aging caretaker of a large estate. He falls into a well and lands in the cavernous realm of the Little People, ruled by King Brian (Jimmy O'Dea, in an unforgettable performance). Following a wild leprechaun celebration, the rock walls open and the king leads his men out on miniature horses to frolic in the Irish countryside. Later, Darby tricks King Brian into granting him three wishes, but quickly learns that one should be careful of what one wishes for.

This wonderful tale is told with a brisk, imaginative pace and the special effects—whereby Darby interacts with the tiny leprechauns—are marvelously executed, and sometimes frightening. Sharp camerawork is enhanced with brilliant colors and the music (by Oliver Wallace and Lawrence E. Watkin) is delightfully and capriciously Irish. Young Sean Connery is a breathtaking feast for the eyes, and Munro makes a fetching colleen. Overall production reflects Walt Disney's perfectionist detail; Disney dreamed of making the film for 20 years and took a trip to Ireland in 1948 to do research. Any child who hasn't seen DARBY O'GILL AND THE LITTLE PEOPLE has missed an important bit of fancy, and that goes for adults too.

DARK CRYSTAL, THE

1982   94m   c   Children's/Science Fiction/Fantasy   ★★★
Associated Film/Universal   (U.K.)   PG

VOICES OF: Stephen Garlick *(Jen)*, Lisa Maxwell *(Kira)*, Billie Whitelaw *(Aughra)*, Percy Edwards *(Fizzgig)*, Barry Dennen *(Chamberlain)*, Michael Kilgarriff *(General)*, Jerry Nelson *(High Priest)*, Steve Whitmire *(Scientist)*, Thick Wilson *(Gourmand)*, Brian Muehl *(Ornamentalist/Dying Master)*

p, Jim Henson, Gary Kurtz; d, Jim Henson, Frank Oz; w, David Odell (based on a story by Henson); ph, Oswald Morris; ed, Ralph Kemplen; m, Trevor Jones; prod d, Harry Lange; art d, Terry Ackland-Snow, Malcolm Stone, Brian Ackland-Snow; fx, Roy Field, Brian Smithies; chor, Jean Pierre Amierl

Once again employing his famous muppets, Jim Henson creates a brilliantly detailed universe with this intriguing fairy-tale adventure revolving around a power struggle between the monstrous Skeksis and the benevolent Mystics. Because the Dark Crystal has been broken, the Skeksis are in ascendance and will remain so unless Jen, one of two remaining Gelflings, is able to heal the crystal, thus fulfilling a prophesy that promises an end to Skeksis rule. Guided by the Mystics' cryptic instructions, and aided by Aughra, a sorceress, and Kira, the other (female) Gelfling, Jen goes about restoring the crystal. Like the children's classics SNOW WHITE AND THE SEVEN DWARFS and SLEEPING BEAUTY, this film has some graphic scenes that may be upsetting for younger kids.

DARK EYES
(OCI CIORNIE)

1987   118m   c   Romance/Comedy   ★★★½
Excelsior/RAI-TV   (Italy)   /PG

Marcello Mastroianni *(Romano)*, Silvana Mangano *(Elisa, Romano's Wife)*, Marthe Keller *(Tina, Romano's Mistress)*, Elena Sofonova *(Anna Sergeyevna, Governor's Wife)*, Vsevolod Larionov *(Pavel,*

Russian Ship Passenger), Innokenty Smoktunovsky (Governor of Sisoiev), Pina Cei (Elisa's Mother), Roberto Herlitzka (Lawyer), Dimitri Zolothukin (Konstantin), Paolo Baroni

p, Silvia D'Amico Bendico, Carlo Cucchi; d, Nikita Mikhalkov; w, Alexander Adabachian, Nikita Mikhalkov, Suso Cecchi D'Amico (based on material from the Anton Chekhov stories "The Lady With the Little Dog," "The Name-Day Party," "Anna Around the Neck" and "My Wife"); ph, Franco Di Giacomo; ed, Enzo Meniconi; m, Francis Lai; art d, Mario Garbuglia, Alexander Adabachian; cos, Carlo Diappi

AAN Best Actor: Marcello Mastroianni

A myriad of emotions, elegantly served. Directed by Nikita Mikhalkov (his first movie outside the USSR), the film brought a Soviet and Italian cast and crew together, and the result was a new, cross-cultural interpretation of the Chekhov stories upon which the film is based.

Set at the turn of the century, the film stars Mastroianni as Romano, a paunchy, alcoholic waiter who works in the dining room of a cruise ship. While voyaging from Greece to Italy, he meets Pavel (Vsevolod Larionov), a jovial Russian on his honeymoon with his much younger wife. Romano begins to reminisce, and the film goes to flashback. As young architecture student, Romano falls in love with Elisa (Silvana Mangano), a wealthy heiress, despite the objections of her high-society family.

He eventually leaves her and retreats to a lavish health spa. He finds willing young ladies to sleep with, pulls an occasional practical joke, watches old women racing through the marble-columned grounds in their wheelchairs, wanders about the beautifully manicured lawns, and eats extravagant meals. He meets Anna Sergeyevna (Elena Sofonova), a timid, lovely, easily embarrassed young woman with dark eyes and a lapdog. Mesmerized by her presence and the magical sparkle of her hat pin, Romano becomes obsessed.

Mastroianni is superb: his performance won the Best Actor prize at the Cannes Film Festival. However, it is not his performance alone that makes DARK EYES so enjoyable; there is also the discovery (for Western audiences) of the lovely Sofonova, a Soviet actress whose combination of fragility and strength is reminiscent of Audrey Hepburn.

DARK MIRROR, THE
1946   85m   bw   Thriller   ★★★★
Universal   (U.S.)   /A

Olivia de Havilland (Terry Collins/Ruth Collins), Lew Ayres (Dr. Scott Elliott), Thomas Mitchell (Detective Stevenson), Richard Long (Rusty), Charles Evans (District Attorney Girard), Garry Owen (Franklin), Lester Allen (George Benson), Lela Bliss (Mrs. Didriksen), Marta Mitrovich (Miss Beade), Amelita Ward (Photo Double)

p, Nunnally Johnson; d, Robert Siodmak; w, Nunnally Johnson (based on the novel by Vladimir Pozner); ph, Milton Krasner; ed, Ernest Nims; m, Dimitri Tiomkin; prod d, Duncan Cramer; fx, Devereaux Jennings, Paul K. Lerpae; cos, Irene Sharaff

AAN Best Original Screenplay: Vladimir Pozner

De Havilland's finest hour, thanks to her underplayed escape from the butter-wouldn't-melt-in-her-mouth moments that flawed some of her finest performances. Here she tackles two roles: identical twins. One is loving and compassionate, the other a calculating killer. After one sister's suitor is found dead, police detective Mitchell rounds up witnesses who pin the blame on good twin Ruth, although she has a concrete alibi. Witnesses, however, cannot tell one twin from the other so psychologist Ayres is brought in to analyze the two women. When both twins fall in love with Ayres, his job becomes even more difficult, personal, and dangerous.

De Havilland is absolutely riveting in her roles—roles which are enriched by special effects wizards J. Devereaux Jennings and Paul Lerpae, whose split-screen technique allows for intimate scenes wherein the actress plays opposite herself. Siodmak's attention to detail creates a mood of psychological disturbance and dark suspense evident from the word go (there's a dynamite opening scene), and typical of the postwar fascination with mental illness.

DARK PASSAGE
1947   106m   bw   Crime   ★★★½
Warner Bros.   (U.S.)   /15

Humphrey Bogart (Vincent Parry), Lauren Bacall (Irene Jansen), Bruce Bennett (Bob), Agnes Moorehead (Madge Rapf), Tom D'Andrea (Sam), Clifton Young (Baker), Douglas Kennedy (Detective), Rory Mallinson (George Fellsinger), Houseley Stevenson (Dr. Walter Coley), Bob Farber

p, Jerry Wald; d, Delmer Daves; w, Delmer Daves (based on the novel by David Goodis); ph, Sid Hickox; ed, David Weisbart; m, Franz Waxman; art d, Charles H. Clarke; fx, H.F. Koenekamp; cos, Bernard Newman

An example of how star power can compensate plot, this is the least electric of the Bogart-Bacall pairings; luckily, there's Agnes Moorehead, the screen's best hornet, to intervene whenever the going gets too lackadasical. She's the only female Bogie ever played opposite he looks scared of.

Bogie escapes from San Quentin, where he has been imprisoned for murdering his wife, and is picked up by Bacall who has long been obsessed with his case. Convinced that he is innocent, Bacall hides him in her San Francisco apartment. On a tip from a friendly cabbie, Vincent visits an underworld plastic surgeon who gives the fugitive a new face—thereby enabling him to dodge the authorities and find his wife's real murderer.

Coming just one year after LADY IN THE LAKE, this mystery likewise employs a subjective camera technique in which the viewer sees the action through Vincent's "eyes." The chief difference, however, is the ability here to integrate the technique into the film's plastic surgery plot twist. The audience does not see Vincent's (Bogart's) face until after the bandages are removed (more than an hour into the film) and, since we haven't seen his face until that point, the switch isn't very interesting. And since the narration up until then has been by Bogie, it's impossible not to imagine you've seen him all through the film. No one else ever inflected like that. At the time of this movie, Bogart was Hollywood's highest paid actor, making more than $450,000 a year.

DARK STAR
1975   83m   c   Science Fiction   ★★½
Jack H. Harris   (U.S.)   G/

Brian Narelle (Doolittle), Andreijah Pahich (Talby), Carl Kuniholm (Boiler), Dan O'Bannon (Pinback), Joe Sanders (Powell)

p, John Carpenter; d, John Carpenter; w, John Carpenter, Dan O'Bannon; ph, Douglas Knapp; ed, Dan O'Bannon; m, John Carpenter; prod d, Dan O'Bannon; fx, Dan O'Bannon, Bill Taylor

John (HALLOWEEN) Carpenter's first directorial effort, an intermittently hilarious satire on 2001—A SPACE ODYSSEY. Carpenter's spaceship is piloted by four goofy astronauts who live like slobs and are bored out of their skulls by their long, uneventful mission. The crew is leaderless because their commander has died during the voyage and is kept in a freezer; somehow he is still able grudgingly to give his men advice when need be. Also in the ship are two talking computers and a pet alien that looks like a red beachball with claws (one of the consistently funny things in the movie). The film is a series of vignettes detailing how the men deal with their boredom, and it eventually sees one of the crew, Narelle, surfing through space on a board-shaped piece of debris. Dan O'Bannon, who would later go on to write ALIEN, cowrote the screenplay and was in charge of the set design and special effects. Carpenter shot half the film on 16mm as his thesis project for the University of Southern California film school. Hoping to get major financing from a studio to expand the film (as George Lucas did with his thesis THX 1138), he dropped out of school and went hunting for investors. Eventually, a Canadian investor gave him enough money to blow up the 16mm footage to 35mm, which led to exploitation distributor Jack Harris financing the rest of the project (which allowed for a modicum of special effects). Unfortunately, Harris' company went broke, and the rights to the film went to Bryanston, who had distributed THE TEXAS CHAINSAW MASSACRE. The film eventually got some bookings, but it never really caught on until it hit the midnight-show circuit.

DARK VICTORY

1939 105m bw Drama ★★★★
Warner Bros. (U.S.) /PG

Bette Davis (*Judith Traherne*), George Brent (*Dr. Frederick Steele*), Humphrey Bogart (*Michael O'Leary*), Geraldine Fitzgerald (*Ann King*), Ronald Reagan (*Alec Hamin*), Henry Travers (*Dr. Parsons*), Cora Witherspoon (*Carrie Spottswood*), Virginia Brissac (*Martha*), Dorothy Peterson (*Miss Wainwright*), Charles Richman (*Colonel Mantle*)

p, David Lewis; d, Edmund Goulding; w, Casey Robinson (based on the play by George Emerson Brewer, Jr. and Bertram Bloch); ph, Ernest Haller; ed, William Holmes; m, Max Steiner; art d, Robert Haas; cos, Orry-Kelly

AAN Best Picture; AAN Best Actress: Bette Davis; AAN Best Score: Max Steiner

Davis is the centerpiece of this film version of the Tallulah Bankhead stage vehicle, faring better early on when she slams through her scenes in her most hyperthyroid manner. She knows it's cliche stuff, and she's determined to wow you anyhow—barking in her most clipped manner, guzzling cocktails with "little Ronnie Reagan" (as Davis always called him), and brandishing her riding crop at miscast stablehand Bogie.

When hedonistic heiress Davis discovers she has a brain tumor, the pace drops to allow romance in the form of George Brent, her doctor. Thank God she stiff-upper-lips it through their short-lived marriage; he's the soggiest newlywed ever, and looks as if his practice consists of trimming his pencil thin mustache. There is a fine assist from lovely newcomer Geraldine Fitzgerald, as Davis's best girlfriend and Edmund Goulding has elevated the form whenever he can. Unfortunately, when Davis climbs the stairs for the last time, composer Max Steiner goes with her. Remade in 1963 as STOLEN HOURS.

DARKMAN

1990 96m c Action/Science Fiction ★★★½
Robert Tapert (U.S.) R/15

Liam Neeson (*Peyton Westlake/Darkman*), Frances McDormand (*Julie Hastings*), Colin Friels (*Louis Strack, Jr.*), Larry Drake (*Robert G. Durant*), Jenny Agutter (*Doctor—uncredited*), Nelson Mashita (*Yakitito*), Jesse Lawrence Ferguson (*Eddie Black*), Rafael H. Robledo (*Rudy Guzman*), Danny Hicks (*Skip*), Theodore Raimi (*Rick*)

p, Robert Tapert; d, Sam Raimi; w, Chuck Pfarrer, Sam Raimi, Ivan Raimi, Daniel Goldin, Joshua Goldin (based on a story by Sam Raimi); ph, Bill Pope; ed, Bud Smith, Scott Smith, David Stiven; m, Danny Elfman; prod d, Randy Ser; art d, Phil Dagort; fx, Introvision Systems International, FourWard Productions, Tony Gardner, Larry Hamlin; cos, Grania Preston; anim, Chiodo Brothers Productions, Kevin Kutchaver, Jammie Friday

DARKMAN is a deliriously energetic comic-book movie from Sam Raimi, the young mastermind behind the uproariously funny and gory EVIL DEAD movies. While the press doted on the likes of David Lynch and the Coen brothers (Joel worked as an assistant editor on THE EVIL DEAD) in 1990, this cutting-edge independent filmmaker came to Hollywood with a relative lack of fanfare to make this ambitious, hallucinatory adventure. Though relatively low budget, the manic cinematic virtuosity on display here would have been welcome in BATMAN. DARKMAN's only weakness is its rather hokey and disjointed screenplay. But why carp? At its best, the film suggests a Universal horror film of the Thirties on LSD.

Peyton Westlake (Liam Neeson) is a scientist working on a formula for artificial skin. Peyton's girl friend, Julie (Frances McDormand), a lawyer working for crooked developer Strack (Colin Friels), stumbles on a memo revealing that Strack is actually an urban megalomaniac bent on taking over the city. Strack sends his thugs to Peyton's lab to find Julie; she's not there, and the thugs blow up Peyton and his lab. Presumed dead by Julie, Peyton is cared for by an odd "doctor" (the uncredited Jenny Agutter). She tries a radical new pain therapy that turns Peyton into a raving, adrenaline-pumped, superhuman schizophrenic. He slips out of the hospital and re-creates his artificial skin lab in an abandoned factory. From there, he plots his revenge and works on winning back Julie while wearing various "masks" of skin.

DARKMAN has much going for it. It boasts the right look and even the right sound, owing to another thundering, mock-operatic score by BATMAN composer Danny Elfman. The film is visually riveting. Melodramatically canted camera angles, audacious shock cuts and eccentric lap dissolves abound. DARKMAN offers bigger-than-life villains, an intriguingly flawed hero, and a tough, appealing heroine—all portrayed by terrific actors. It's a darkly amusing treat.

DARLING

1965 128m bw Drama ★★★
Vic/Appia (U.K.) /15

Laurence Harvey (*Miles Brand*), Dirk Bogarde (*Robert Gold*), Julie Christie (*Diana Scott*), Roland Curram (*Malcolm*), Jose-Luis de Vilallonga (*Cesare*), Alex Scott (*Sean Martin*), Basil Henson (*Alec Prosser-Jones*), Helen Lindsay (*Felicity Prosser-Jones*), Pauline Yates (*Estelle Gold*), Tyler Butterworth (*William Prosser-Jones*)

p, Joseph Janni; d, John Schlesinger; w, Frederic Raphael (based on a story by Raphael, Schlesinger, and Janni); ph, Ken Higgins; ed, James B. Clark; m, John Dankworth; cos, Julie Harris

AAN Best Picture; AA Best Actress: Julie Christie; AAN Best Director: John Schlesinger; AA Best Original Story and Screenplay: Frederic Raphael; AA Best Costume Design: Julie Harris

The British New Wave turns inward and eats itself alive—unwittingly. If the movie is overrated, it's still interesting to watch it collapse upon itself. One decade earlier, the censorship standards would have truncated this film to a point that it would not have made sense. Today it appears nervous and shallow, a metaphor for the empty values it claims to take to task. Julie Christie is the amoral heroine who drifts into success casually, like she's changing panties—she models, does a bit in films, deserts a husband, deceives a lover, drifts through affairs; it takes about 20 minutes to get that she doesn't "feel complete," and we understand, even if we can't pay our bills. Marilyn Monroe and a multitude of others found out fame wasn't what it was cracked up to be. But where a Marilyn differs from The Darling is that the latter is an empty person and always was. She's like Madonna with low blood sugar doing an old Lana Turner script—but cool. She may be miserable, but at least the future is rich with tears, rather than poor.

Christie is the main reason to tune in—she's very beautiful and accomplished in a brittle sort of way. Her performance won awards all over the place, but she can't supply emotions the story and character won't let her have. Its a Best Actress in a Vacuum turn, and we defy you to feel a single thing.

DAS BOOT

1981 150m c War ★★★★
Bavaria Atelier (West Germany) R/15

Jurgen Prochnow (*Captain*), Herbert Gronemeyer (*Lt. Werner/Correspondent*), Klaus Wennemann (*Chief Engineer*), Hubertus Bengsch (*1st Lt./Number One*), Martin Semmelrogge (*2nd Lieutenant*), Bernd Tauber (*Chief Quartermaster*), Erwin Leder (*Johann "The Ghost"*), Martin May (*Midshipman Ullmann*), Heinz Honig (*Hinrich*), U.A. Ochsen (*Chief Bosun*)

p, Gunter Rohrbach; d, Wolfgang Petersen; w, Wolfgang Petersen (based on the novel by Lothar-Gunther Buchheim); ph, Jost Vacano; ed, Hannes Nikel; m, Klaus Doldinger; prod d, Rolf Zehetbauer; art d, Gotz Weidner; fx, Karl Baumgartner; cos, Monika Bauert

AAN Best Director: Wolfgang Petersen; AAN Best Adapted Screenplay: Wolfgang Petersen; AAN Best Cinematography: Jost Vacano; AAN Best Editing: Hannes Nikel; AAN Best Sound: Milan Bor (Sound), Trevor Pyke (Sound), Mike Le-Mare (Sound); AAN Best Sound Effects Editing: Mike Le-Mare

Gripping and authentic; based on the experiences of photographer Lothar-Guenther Buchheim, this superbly filmed action movie chronicles a U-boat voyage in 1941, detailing above- and below-the-surface horrors as well as the mundane hours that characterize time spent at sea. Though most of the footage concentrates on the intense, noble captain, Jurgen Prochnow, the only fully developed "character" in the film is the boat, as it undergoes numerous attacks. Decidedly anti-Nazi in tone, THE BOAT presents the crew as individual warriors upholding their own brand of honor and sneering at Hitler's Reich. The chief attraction of this film, however, is the incredible camerawork. Racing through the sub, squeezing through tiny openings, director Wolfgang Petersen's camera brilliantly evokes the claustrophobia and clamor of undersea battle. A technical marvel, THE BOAT is a breathtaking and powerful portrait of war and death. Though the film was originally released on videocassette as the subtitled DAS BOOT, most copies now available are dubbed into English.

DAUGHTER OF THE NILE
(NI-LO-HO NU-ERH)

1988 91m c Drama   ★★★½
Fu-Film (Taiwan)   /PG

Yang Lin *(Lin Hsiao-yang)*, Kao Jai *(Lin Hsiao-fang, Brother)*, Yang Fan *(Ah-sang)*, Li T'ien-lu *(Grandfather)*, Ts'ui Fu-sheng *(Father)*, Hsing Shu-fen, Yu An-shun, Wu Nien-chen, Huang Ch'iung-yao, Ch'en Chien-wen

p, Lu Wen-jen, Ts'ai Sung-lin; d, Hou Hsiao-hsien; w, Chu T'ien-wen; ph, Ch'en Huai-en; ed, Liao Ch'ing-sung; m, Ch'en Cihyuan, Chang Hung-yi; prod d, Liu Chih-hua, Lin Chu

Another excellent film from Taiwanese director Hou Hsiao-hsien, who, along with Yang, is responsible for the international rise of Taiwanese cinema. A switch from the director's rural dramas, such as A SUMMER AT GRANDPA'S or A TIME TO LIVE AND A TIME TO DIE, the film is set in the heart of the city and focuses on a teenage girl, Yang Lin, and her troubled family. Her brother, Kao Jai, is a small-time thief whose crimes have intensified since the deaths of both their elder brother and their mother. Their father, Ts'ui Fu-sheng, stays away from home for long periods of time, leaving Yang Lin to care for the house, her brother, and her younger sister. Yang Lin's only escape comes in reading a popular comic book called "Daughter of the Nile," which is about a modern girl trapped in ancient Egypt who falls in love with a doomed boy king.

Although DAUGHTER OF THE NILE has more plot than any of Hou Hsiao-hsien's other work, it is still a movie made up of small, subtle moments with no strong narrative impetus. The director's visual style, greatly reminiscent of that of Japan's Yasujiro Ozu, makes use of deep-focus long takes that allow the action to unfold between the actors naturally, without the camera's becoming obtrusive. The film is like a picture puzzle, in which each unconnected piece eventually fits together to form a vivid picture of life in urban Taiwan. The cast is superb, with Taiwanese pop singer Yang Lin turning in a wonderful performance as the put-upon teen, Taipei fashion-boutique owner Kao Jai excellent as the brooding brother, and elderly Li T'ien-lu nearly stealing the film as the chatty old grandfather who constantly worries that the "neighbors will laugh" if his family doesn't behave.

DAVE

1993 110m c Comedy/Political   ★★★½
Shuler-Donner Productions/Ivan Reitman   PG-13/12
Productions (U.S.)

Kevin Kline *(Dave Kovic/President Bill Mitchell)*, Sigourney Weaver *(Ellen Mitchell)*, Frank Langella *(Bob Alexander)*, Kevin Dunn *(Alan Reed)*, Ving Rhames *(Duane Stevenson)*, Ben Kingsley *(Vice President Nance)*, Charles Grodin *(Murray Blum)*, Faoth Prince *(Alice)*, Laura Linney *(Randi)*, Bonnie Hunt *(White House Tour Guide)*

p, Lauren Shuler-Donner, Ivan Reitman; d, Ivan Reitman; w, Gary Ross; ph, Adam Greenberg; ed, Sheldon Kahn; m, James Newton Howard; prod d, J. Michael Riva; art d, David Klassen; fx, Buena Vista Visual Effects, Harrison Ellenshaw, David M. Blitstein; cos, Richard Hornung, Ann Roth

AAN Best Original Screenplay: Gary Ross

A winning blend of MR. SMITH GOES TO WASHINGTON and BEING THERE, DAVE gives Kevin Kline the best comic role of his screen career.

Kline plays the title character, a presidential look-alike asked to double for the Chief Executive for "security" reasons. (As Dave waves to the crowd en route to his limo, the President is taking a very secret meeting with an attractive secretary.) When the Prez suffers a massive

stroke at a rather delicate moment, White House Chief of Staff Bob Alexander (Frank Langella) installs Dave in the Oval Office, rather than allow "boy scout" Vice-President Nance (Ben Kingsley) to assume power.

Gary Ross's script is a perfect showcase for Kline, who gleefully inhabits his dual role as the cynical, sleazy President and his earnest, naive double. He also gets fantastic support: Sigourney Weaver at her most icily bitchy as the First Lady ("Why couldn't you have died from a stroke like everyone else?"); Frank Langella as the suave, Machiavellian Chief of Staff; and Charles Grodin as a small-time accountant who, summoned to the White House by his old friend Dave, trims $650 million off the budget over a bratwurst dinner.

Add a host of cameo appearances by real-life personalities—"Tip" O'Neill applauds the President's new-found energy; J.F.K. director Oliver Stone is convinced the whole thing is a conspiracy—and the result is the funniest, savviest political comedy to come our way in some time.

DAVID AND BATHSHEBA

1951 116m c Religious   ★★★½
Fox (U.S.)   /A

Gregory Peck *(David)*, Susan Hayward *(Bathsheba)*, Raymond Massey *(Nathan)*, Kieron Moore *(Uriah)*, James Robertson Justice *(Abishai)*, Jayne Meadows *(Michal)*, John Sutton *(Ira)*, Dennis Hoey *(Joab)*, Walter Talun *(Goliath)*, Paula Morgan *(Adulteress)*

p, Darryl F. Zanuck; d, Henry King; w, Philip Dunne (based on biblical accounts); ph, Leon Shamroy; ed, Barbara McLean; m, Alfred Newman; art d, Lyle Wheeler, George W. Davis; fx, Fred Sersen; chor, Jack Cole; cos, Edward Stevenson

AAN Best Original Screenplay: Philip Dunne; *AAN Best Cinematography:* Leon Shamroy; *AAN Best Score:* Alfred Newman; *AAN Best Art Direction:* Lyle Wheeler (Art Direction), George W Davis (Art Direction), Thomas Little (Set Decoration), Paul S Fox (Set Decoration); *AAN Best Costume Design:* Charles LeMaire, Edward Stevenson

Big-budget Biblical yucky muck. Peck plays stoic King David, fierce in battle but frail where temptresses trod. Having saved a cuckold in battle, he returns home to nurse a wound, instead nurses a raging. . . torch for the cuckold's wife, tempestuous Susan Hayward, acting within an inch of her insured head of tossing tendrils, whom he spots taking a bath. He, wisely, we say, dumps the first wife of his harem— the shrewish Jayne Meadows—that's right, Jayne Meadows! The cuckold gets sent to war and gets killed, Bathsheba marries David and a baby is born eight months, three-and-a-half weeks, six days and ten seconds later, but dies. The Lord sends Raymond Massey, as the prophet Nathan, to raise hell for their shameless ways and protest the famine that has been wrought upon the land. David sees the error of his ways, improvises the 23rd Psalm and the rains come and wash their sins away!

Typical lavish Hollywood Biblical treatment, but awash with juice, thanks to the force supplied by the three leads. Look for young Gwen Verdon as a specialty dancer. Perfect for a cold, rainy Sunday afternoon.

DAVID AND LISA

1962 95m bw Drama   ★★★½
CONTINENTAL (U.S.)   /X

Keir Dullea *(David)*, Janet Margolin *(Lisa)*, Howard Da Silva *(Dr. Swinford)*, Neva Patterson *(Mrs. Clemens)*, Clifton James *(John)*, Richard McMurray *(Mr. Clemens)*, Nancy Nutter *(Maureen)*, Matthew Anden *(Simon)*, Coni Hudak *(Kate)*, Jaime Sanchez *(Carlos)*

p, Paul M. Heller; d, Frank Perry; w, Eleanor Perry (based on the book by Dr. Theodore Isaac Rubin); ph, Leonard Hirshfield; ed, Irving Oshman; m, Mark Lawrence; art d, Paul M. Heller; cos, Anna Hill Johnstone

AAN Best Director: Frank Perry; *AAN Best Adapted Screenplay:* Eleanor Perry

A big "little" film. Prior to this, there had been many films like THE SNAKE PIT and THE THREE FACES OF EVE, but the understated charm of DAVID AND LISA is what set the movie apart from so many other attempts at depicting the problems of the mentally ill. Dullea is a bright young man who cannot bear to be touched by anyone. His overly protective mother and father, Patterson and McMurray, leave him at the private school with Da Silva, the intelligent doctor who runs the institution which caters to children with mental problems. Margolin is a very troubled schizophrenic who talks in rhyme and is deeply ensconced in her shell. The two meet, and the gradual falling-in-love story is what forms the basis for the film. As they begin to trust each other, Dullea is able to be touched and Margolin feels secure enough to reveal her emotions.

The story was based on a real case history by Dr. T.I. Rubin, and Eleanor Perry handled the screenplay with tact and subtle care that avoids mawkishness. This is a thoughtful, poignant film with a documentary feel; there are enough comic moments and a welcome absence of psychiatric jargon. Frank Perry's direction won an award at the Venice Film Festival in 1962. Margolin and Dullea were honored as best actress and actor at the San Francisco Film Festival.

DAVID COPPERFIELD

1935 133m bw Drama   ★★★★½
MGM (U.S.)   /U

W.C. Fields *(Micawber)*, Lionel Barrymore *(Dan Peggotty)*, Maureen O'Sullivan *(Dora)*, Frank Lawton *(David Copperfield)*, Madge Evans *(Agnes)*, Edna May Oliver *(Aunt Betsey)*, Lewis Stone *(Mr. Wickfield)*, Freddie Bartholomew *(David as Child)*, Elizabeth Allan *(Mrs. Copperfield)*, Roland Young *(Uriah Heep)*

p, David O. Selznick; d, George Cukor; w, Howard Estabrook, Hugh Walpole (based on the novel by Charles Dickens); ph, Oliver T. Marsh; ed, Robert J. Kern; m, Herbert Stothart; art d, Cedric Gibbons; fx, Slavko Vorkapich; cos, Dolly Tree

Directed with restraint and impeccable taste by Cukor, produced by Selznick, DAVID COPPERFIELD is diverse and satisfying intellectually and emotionally, capturing the unparalleled beauty of Dickens's melancholic truths about life's hardships and human survival. The entire cast perform admirably, but of course it is Fields's Micawber which has achieved immortality. Despite the absence of accent, it still appears he was born to play the role, and it's the only time the Great Man allowed any heart to seep through on screen. Dickens died in 1870 at the age of 58, leaving his final work, *The Mystery of Edwin Drood*, unfinished, which didn't stop Universal from making it into a movie also released in 1935. Doubtless, he would have been thrilled at DAVID COPPERFIELD and bored with the latter.

DAVID HOLZMAN'S DIARY

1968 74m bw Drama/Experimental   ★★★★
Paradigm (U.S.)

L.M. Kit Carson *(David Holzman)*, Eileen Dietz *(Penny Wohl)*, Louise Levine *(Sandra)*, Lorenzo Mans *(Pepe)*, Fern McBride *(Girl on the Subway)*, Mike Levine *(Sandra's Boyfriend)*, Bob Lesser *(Max, Penny's Agent)*, Jack Baran *(Cop)*

p, Jim McBride; d, Jim McBride; w, Jim McBride; ph, Michael Wadleigh, Paul Glickman, Paul Goldsmith; ed, Jim McBride

A unique, often brilliant satire on *cinema verite*, this "fake documentary" was shot in only five days on a $2500 budget. Carson plays a young New York filmmaker who decides to get a handle on his life by putting it all down on film. Things don't go entirely as planned, however. His girlfriend leaves him in annoyance because he's constantly filming her, his artist friend Pepe (Mans) tells him that his concept is invalid, and the police punch him for harassing people with his camera. Gradually he grows more desperate as it becomes obvious that his life is only getting more confusing on film. One day he announces to the camera that he has to go to his uncle's funeral in New Jersey. In the next scene we see photographs of David of the type taken by coin-operated booths. His voice on a scratchy record says that he is making this recording in another coin-operated booth and that when he returned from New Jersey that day, he found his apartment broken into and all his equipment stolen. He tries to come to some conclusion about his life and this project but is ultimately unable to do so.

One of cinema's most pointed statements about the impossibility of objectivity in film, DAVID HOLZMAN'S DIARY breaks down the comfortable position audiences usually enjoy while watching most mainstream films. Spectators unfamiliar with experimental cinema often resent being fooled by the documentary style of the film, which highlights the concept that "documentary" is a style of filmmaking more than it is a means of presenting "truth" in some unmediated way. Unafraid to present and implicitly criticize the more unpleasant sides of its "hero," at once witty and strangely touching, this provocative, endlessly self-conscious film today stands as one of the best independent films of the 1960s. How ironically appropriate that semi-underground filmmaker McBride later went mainstream himself, offering us modern revamps of old Hollywood ideas (THE BIG EASY, GREAT BALLS OF FIRE) or attempts to recreate the magic of other innovative landmarks (BREATHLESS).

DAWN OF THE DEAD

1979 125m c Horror   ★★★★
Dawn Associates/Laurel Group (U.S.)   /X

David Emge *(Stephen)*, Ken Foree *(Peter)*, Scott Reininger *(Roger)*, Gaylen Ross *(Francine)*, David Crawford *(Dr. Foster)*, David Early *(Mr. Berman)*, Richard France *(Scientist)*, Howard K. Smith *(Television Commentator)*, James A. Baffico *(Wooley)*, George A. Romero *(Television Director)*

p, Richard P. Rubinstein, Herbert Steinmann, Billy Baxter, Alfredo Cuomo; d, George Romero; w, George Romero; ph, Michael Gornick; ed, George Romero, Kenneth Davidow; m, Dario Argento, Goblin; fx, Gary Zeller, Don Berry; cos, Josie Caruso

One of the key horror films of the 1970s (a particularly fecund period for the genre), George Romero's apocalyptic followup to his classic NIGHT OF THE LIVING DEAD (1968) abandons easy scare tactics in favor of a darkly satirical assault on bourgeois culture, traditional notions of masculinity, and rampant consumerism. Zesty contributions from cinematographer Michael Gornick and special makeup effects mastermind Tom Savini help make this feel like a brightly colored action comic book peppered with gruesome (but not gratuitous) violence. Celebrated Italian horror maestro Dario Argento (SUSPIRIA, DEEP RED) co-produced and provided the lively rock score with his band, Goblin. Though all of the performances are at least adequate, this is not an actor's movie. Believe it or not, this is a film about ideas as well as gore. Nonetheless, this is strong medicine and not for all tastes

In DAWN the recently dead are still returning to life and eating the flesh of the living but the phenomena has spread to nationwide if not worldwide proportions. A brutal police assault on a minority housing project that occurs early in the film expands upon the conclusion of NIGHT. We see that in the eyes of the law, there is little difference between political radicals, innocent bystanders of color, and carnivorous zombies. Ross, an employee of a local television station, and her boyfriend Emge, a traffic helicopter pilot, decide to try to escape the madness in a helicopter accompanied by two SWAT team cops, Reiniger and Foree. They eventually land atop a shopping mall. Once they clear out the zombies, the four decide to remain in this shoppers' paradise where they get to live out their wildest consumer fantasies until they are forced to defend themselves from marauding bikers who want to crash their party.

Romero's films tend to be left of center in outlook: ethnically and sexually integrated, pro-feminist, gay-friendly, anti-macho, and skeptical about capitalism, they represent a progressive aspect of the genre. His "living dead" movies are among the Pittsburgh-based auteur's most personal efforts. So terrifying in their initial incarnation, the zombies in DAWN have become rather pathetic (though still very dangerous) eating machines. Nuns, clowns, and Hare Krishnas number among their ranks as they return to the mall they loved in life. "They are us," one of the characters wryly observes. This independently produced low budget film ($1.5 million) went on to become one of the most profitable "indies" in film history. DAY OF THE DEAD, ostensibly the conclusion of the DEAD series, followed in 1985.

DAWN PATROL, THE

1930 105m bw War   ★★★
First National (U.S.)

Richard Barthelmess *(Dick Courtney)*, Douglas Fairbanks Jr. *(Douglas Scott)*, Neil Hamilton *(Major Brand)*, William Janney *(Gordon Scott)*, James Finlayson *(Field Sergeant)*, Clyde Cook *(Bott)*, Gardner James *(Ralph Hollister)*, Edmund Breon *(Lt. Bathurst)*, Frank McHugh *(Flaherty)*, Jack Ackroyd

p, Robert North; d, Howard Hawks; w, Howard Hawks, Dan Totheroh, Seton I. Miller (based on the story "The Flight Commander" by John Monk Saunders); ph, Ernest Haller; ed, Ray Curtiss; fx, Fred Jackman

AA Best Original Screenplay: John Monk Saunders

The original, but for once, not the best. Director Howard Hawks's first foray into sound cinema shows his typically interesting and exciting visuals, but there is little evidence of his future skill with dialogue in the stilted and overly talky screenplay penned by Totheroh, Miller, and Hawks himself.

The action takes place during WWI, and Richard Barthelmess and Douglas Fairbanks are hot-dog aces of the British air corps who consistently disobey orders to settle disputes of "honor" with the Germans. After German fliers taunt the pair regarding their flying prowess, Barthelmess and Fairbanks jump into their planes and ruthlessly attack a helpless German air squadron, killing many pilots before they can get off the ground. On their return, outraged commanding officer Neil Hamilton vents his fury on the boyish pilots, only to be suddenly handed a message telling him that he has been transferred to another unit. Hamilton delights in telling Barthelmess that he is now in command and perhaps now he will develop a sense of responsibility when he must deal with a group of unruly fliers like himself.

Hawks's film is a strong antiwar statement which illustrates the futility of heroics that only end in death on both sides. The dogfight footage is some of the best aerial fighting photography ever filmed, but the movie suffers from the stagey, stiff dialogue sequences that obviously frustrated Hawks. DAWN PATROL was re-made in 1938 by Edmund Goulding starring Basil Rathbone, Errol Flynn, and David Niven, and it is this version that modern-day audiences find easier to sit through due to the more polished handling of the dialogue sequences.

DAWN PATROL, THE

1938 103m bw War   ★★★★
Warner Bros. (U.S.)   /A

Errol Flynn *(Courtney)*, David Niven *(Scott)*, Basil Rathbone *(Major Brand)*, Donald Crisp *(Phills)*, Melville Cooper *(Watkins)*, Barry Fitzgerald *(Bott)*, Carl Esmond *(Von Mueller)*, Peter Willes *(Hollister)*, Morton Lowry *(Johnnie Scott)*, Michael Brooke *(Squires)*

p, Robert Lord; d, Edmund Goulding; w, Seton I. Miller, Dan Totheroh (based on the story "The Flight Commander" by John Monk Saunders); ph, Tony Gaudio; ed, Ralph Dawson; m, Max Steiner; art d, John Hughes; fx, Edwin DuPar

A superbly-cast remake of Hawks's 1930 picture of the same name, THE DAWN PATROL concerns a dashing, conscience-haunted flight commander, Capt. Courtney (Errol Flynn), of the 59th Squadron in France during WWI. He and his men fly the most dangerous aircraft—a source of Courtney's anger which he attempts to cover with banter and cynical humor—creating unsafe odds for the fliers and contributing to their untimely deaths. The fatalities mount so drastically that raw recruits with little flying experience are sent into the skies to battle without much chance of survival. Between the daily dawn patrols that decimate the command, the fliers face death with stiff upper lips and scotch and sodas at the club bar, where a battered gramophone continually grinds out the plaintive "Poor Butterfly." In another room sits Maj. Brand (Basil Rathbone), the deskbound commander whose job it is to assign fliers to each dawn patrol, mechanically writing their names on a blackboard and methodically erasing those killed each day. Later, when Brand is reassigned, Courtney is called on to replace him; now it is he who must decide which flier will take off to face a certain death. Though the original story of Hawks's film was retained, the dialogue was rewritten and polished to great improvement, chiefly in the rela-

tionship between Courtney and his best pal, Lt. Scott (David Niven). As in the original (or in Hawks's AIR FORCE), the remake is very much concerned with fraternity, loyalty, and courage in the face of death.

DAY AT THE RACES, A

1937 109m c/bw Comedy/Musical   ★★★½
MGM (U.S.)   /U

Groucho Marx *(Dr. Hugo Z. Hackenbush)*, Chico Marx *(Tony)*, Harpo Marx *(Stuffy)*, Allan Jones *(Gil)*, Maureen O'Sullivan *(Judy)*, Margaret Dumont *(Mrs. Upjohn)*, Leonard Ceeley *(Whitmore)*, Douglas Dumbrille *(Morgan)*, Esther Muir *("Flo")*, Sig Rumann *(Dr. Steinberg)*

p, Max Siegel, Sam Wood; d, Sam Wood; w, Robert Pirosh, George Seaton, George Oppenheimer (based on a story by Pirosh and Seaton); ph, Joseph Ruttenberg; ed, Frank E. Hull; m, Bronislau Kaper, Walter Jurmann, Gus Kahn; art d, Cedric Gibbons; chor, Dave Gould

Hugo Z. Hackenbush (Groucho Marx) is a horse doctor who takes over a large sanitarium at the behest of hypochondriac socialite Mrs. Upjohn (Margaret Dumont). The sanitarium is owned by Judy (Maureen O'Sullivan), but she's having trouble paying off the mortgage. With the help of Stuffy (Harpo Marx), Tony (Chico Marx), and a racehorse named Hi-Hat, she is able to save the hospital. Of course, the plot isn't important here; what really counts is the steady stream of wild comedy routines provided by the Marx Brothers who poke fun at everything from the medical profession to high society.

Striving for a worthy follow-up to the magnificent A NIGHT AT THE OPERA, the comedians took their act on the road and performed these routines for live audiences throughout the country. The opulent, though somewhat dull, musical production numbers prevent this from being as mesmerizing as its predecessor, but while dated, A DAY AT THE RACES is, nonetheless, a very entertaining comedy. Producer Irving Thalberg, to whom the Marxes were devoted, died during production.

DAY FOR NIGHT
(LA NUIT AMERICAINE)

1973 120m c Drama   ★★★★★
Carrosse/PECF/PIC (France)   PG/15

Francois Truffaut *(Ferrand)*, Jacqueline Bisset *(Julie Baker)*, Jean-Pierre Leaud *(Alphonse)*, Valentina Cortese *(Severine)*, Jean-Pierre Aumont *(Alexandre)*, Dani *(Lilianna)*, Alexandra Stewart *(Stacey)*, Jean Champion *(Bertrand)*, Nathalie Baye *(Joelle)*, Bernard Menez *(Bernard, the Prop Man)*

p, Marcel Berbert; d, Francois Truffaut; w, Francois Truffaut, Suzanne Schiffman, Jean-Louis Richard; ph, Pierre-William Glenn; ed, Yann Dedet, Martine Barraque; m, Georges Delerue; art d, Damien Lanfranchi; cos, Monique Dury

AAN Best Supporting Actress: Valentina Cortese; *AAN Best Director:* Francois Truffaut; *AAN Best Original Story and Screenplay:* Francois Truffaut, Jean-Louis Richard, Suzanne Schiffman; *AA Best Foreign Language Film:*

One of the best films ever made about the process of shooting a film. Director Truffaut plays director Ferrand, who is in the midst of directing "I Want You to Meet Pamela," a feature being shot in the La Victorine studios in the south of France. His cast includes a temperamental actor, Alphonse (Jean-Pierre Leaud), who wonders aloud, "Are women magic?"; Julie (Jacqueline Bisset), a famous actress recovering from a nervous breakdown; Alexandre (Jean-Pierre Aumont), a veteran actor, "continental lover" and closet homosexual; Severine (Valentina Cortese), a loud, alcoholic Italian actress who once was a great screen lover opposite Alexandre but who now cannot remember even the simplest dialogue; and Stacey (Alexandra Stewart), a bit player whose pregnancy causes terrible scheduling problems. Given equal time is Ferrand's crew—bumbling prop man Bernard (Bernard Menez); flaky makeup girl Odile (Nike Arrighi); script girl Lilianna (Dani), who cares nothing for film and gets the job only because she sleeps with Alphonse; unit manager Lajoie (Gaston Joly); producer Bertrand (Jean Champion); and the all-important production assistant, Joelle (Nathalie Baye).

As one might expect, the characters themselves are more important than the thin plot—Ferrand trying to keep his production on track when his emotionally unstable leads, Alphonse and Julie, make the mistake of sleeping together for just one night. Full of in jokes and cross-references, DAY FOR NIGHT is ample proof that what goes on behind the screen is often of more interest than the film itself. Paradoxically, it is also one of Truffaut's least personal films, as he hides behind his alter ego Ferrand and interacts only on the most superficial levels with his cast and crew. By the film's end, it is Ferrand whom we know least.

DAY OF THE DEAD

1985 102m c Horror   ★★★½
Laurel (U.S.)

Lori Cardille (Sarah), Terry Alexander (John), Joseph Pilato (Capt. Rhodes), Jarlath Conroy (McDermott), Antone DiLeo Jr. (Miguel), Richard Liberty (Dr. Logan), Howard Sherman (Bub), Gary Howard Klar (Steel), Ralph Marrero (Rickles), John Amplas (Fisher)

p, Richard P. Rubinstein; d, George Romero; w, George Romero; ph, Michael Gornick; ed, Pasquale Buba; m, John Harrison; prod d, Cletus Anderson; art d, Bruce Miller; fx, Tom Savini, Steve Kirshoff, Mark Mann; cos, Barbara Anderson

The third, and perhaps last, chapter in George Romero's "Living Dead" series is a claustrophobic character study set almost entirely in a huge underground storage facility that has been converted into a laboratory and barracks. The military has been assigned to protect and assist the group of scientists (Lori Cardille, John Amplas, and Richard Liberty) who are working to develop a solution to the zombie epidemic, experimenting on zombies who have been herded into a holding pen. One scientist, Liberty—nicknamed "Frankenstein" by the soldiers—tries to modify the zombies' behavior so that humans can train them like dogs. One zombie, whom Liberty calls "Bub," seems to be the missing link between animal instinct and civilized human behavior. The operation has taken its toll on the soldiers, however, and their commander, the near-psychotic Joseph Pilato, tries to take over the project and put an end to it.

Fans of the first two films in the series may be a bit dismayed by DAY OF THE DEAD's deemphasis of gory action in favor of characterization, but the need to exploit the horror of the situation has passed and the film works by concentrating instead on its implications and possible solution. The standard 1950s sci-fi/horror film conflict between science and the military is also resurrected here, with distinct political overtones. One thing becomes clear in DAY OF THE DEAD—the zombies are here to stay, and humanity must adapt to them in order to survive. On a psychosocial level, as Robin Wood has persuasively argued, Romero's zombies seem to represent the "return of the repressed"; if so, this final chapter might be read as a plea for a reconciliation between forbidden desires and traditional social strictures. Generally underrated—even by horror-film fans—DAY OF THE DEAD ranks with Romero's best work.

DAY OF THE JACKAL, THE

1973 142m c Thriller   ★★★★
Warwick (U.K./France)   PG/15

Edward Fox ("The Jackal"), Terence Alexander (Lloyd), Michel Auclair (Colonel Rolland), Alan Badel (The Minister), Tony Britton (Inspector Thomas), Denis Carey (Casson), Adrien Cayla-Legrand (The President), Cyril Cusack (Gunsmith), Maurice Denham (General Colbert), Vernon Dobtcheff (Interrogator)

p, John Woolf, David Deutsch, Julien Derode; d, Fred Zinnemann; w, Kenneth Ross (based on the novel by Frederick Forsyth); ph, Jean Tournier; ed, Ralph Kemplen; m, Georges Delerue; art d, Willy Holt, Ernest Archer; fx, Georges Iaconelli, John Richardson; cos, Elizabeth Haffenden, Joan Bridge, Rosine Delamare, Jean Zay, Chanel

AAN Best Editing: Ralph Kemplen

A secret French military organization plans to assassinate President de Gaulle (played by Adrien Cayla-Legrand, an uncanny look-alike), by hiring one of the world's most fearsome professional killers, a man known only as "The Jackal" (Edward Fox). Top French police investigator Lebel (Michel Lonsdale) learns the name "Jackal" from an informer in the plotter's ranks and cleverly pieces together the identity

of the killer-for-hire. What follows is an intricate and meticulous story with a parallel structure that details the Jackal's preparations for the assassination and Lebel's efforts to stop him. Director Zinnemann faithfully follows the Forsyth best-seller, presenting a precise, almost discomfitting reconstruction of the story. Fox is superb as the coldly impassionate killer, and Lonsdale is properly plodding yet magnificently analytical as the detective tracking him down. A taut, suspenseful, and fascinating political thriller.

DAY OF THE LOCUST, THE

1975 144m c Drama   ★★★★
Paramount (U.S.)   R/X

Donald Sutherland (Homer), Karen Black (Faye), Burgess Meredith (Harry), William Atherton (Tod), Geraldine Page (Big Sister), Richard Dysart (Claude Estee), Bo Hopkins (Earle Shoop), Pepe Serna (Miguel), Lelia Goldoni (Mary Dove), Billy Barty (Abe)

p, Jerome Hellman; d, John Schlesinger; w, Waldo Salt (based on the novel by Nathanael West); ph, Conrad Hall; ed, Jim Clark; m, John Barry; prod d, Richard MacDonald; art d, John Lloyd; cos, Ann Roth

AAN Best Supporting Actor: Burgess Meredith; AAN Best Cinematography: Conrad Hall

DAY OF THE LOCUST, like the powerful and incisive Nathanael West novel on which it is based, focuses on the seamy side of the city of dreams in its 1930s heyday—the subculture of losers, misfits, and neurotic fringe characters. Black is a sexy untalented aspiring actress who lives with her father, Meredith, a former vaudevillian, now a down on his luck door-to-door saleman. Recognizing her limited prospects, Black becomes a regular on the casting couch of producers in the hope that she'll rise above her usual walk-ons. She still has dreams of fame and legitimacy. Despite her dubious character, Atherton, an altruistic art director, falls for her but she gives him the cold shoulder—at first. She soon begins amusing herself by toying with him. This is the beginning of a pattern. When she finds herself destitute she moves in with a sensitive but oafish accountant, Sutherland, who loves her from afar. She and all about him use and ridicule him as he lumbers through life; he is particularly vexed by an evil neighborhood child, Haley. Everything comes to a head in the apocalyptic finale of the film, a memorably traumatic spectacle.

This grim conclusion, along with the stark and unsavory story and characters that preceded it, brought shudders to audiences and undoubtedly helped this excellent film fail at the box office. Nevertheless, it accurately captures the intent of West's dark masterpiece. Black is the perfect slattern with movie ambition—cheap, shallow, conniving, and utterly reprehensible. Sutherland gives one of his best performances as the doltish but sensitive outsider whose concern for films is marginal at best. The movie boasts excellent supporting players, such as Atherton as the ethereal art director. He is savvy to Hollywood and gives it back the banal glibness that is the hallmark of its society. Many of the characters are inspired by historical Hollywood figures. DAY OF THE LOCUST exudes authenticity, from the costuming to the cars, from the exotic clothes to the marcelled hair styles.

DAY OF THE TRIFFIDS, THE

1963 93m c Science Fiction/Horror   ★★½
Allied Artists (U.S.)   /15

Howard Keel (Bill Masen), Nicole Maurey (Christine Durrant), Janette Scott (Karen Goodwin), Kieron Moore (Tom Goodwin), Mervyn Johns (Prof. Coker), Janina Faye (Susan), Alison Leggatt (Miss Coker), Ewan Roberts (Dr. Soames), Colette Wilde (Nurse Jamieson), Carole Ann Ford (Bettina)

p, George Pitcher; d, Steve Sekely, Freddie Francis; w, Bernard Gordon (based on the novel by John Wyndham); ph, Ted Moore; ed, Spencer Reeve; m, Ron Goodwin; art d, Cedric Dawe; fx, Wally Veevers

Decent, albeit uneven, British sci-fi/horror film. Keel stars as an American sailor who has escaped being blinded by a sudden meteor shower that has robbed most of the Earth's population of its sight. The mysterious meteor storm has also brought with it alien plant spores which grow into large, carnivorous plants that multiply and threaten to overrun the planet. The man-eating plants are known as "Triffids" and resemble rampaging stalks of broccoli that have an easy time feeding off of the blind humans who can't protect themselves. Keel becomes the leader of a small band of people who have somehow escaped being blinded. Together they plot to make a final stand against the vicious plants. Meanwhile, marine biologist Moore and his wife, Scott (who have been trapped in a lighthouse by the Triffids) search for a scientific solution.

Always interesting but bogged down by lengthy romantic interludes, the film is thought-provoking and scary at times (the Triffids are more effective than they have any right to be). This is the third adaptation from the works of John Wyndham, the first two yielding the superb VILLAGE OF THE DAMNED and CHILDREN OF THE DAMNED. For fans of the once great untrained baritone voice of Keel, it is interesting that in THE DAY OF THE TRIFFIDS he rewrote his own dialogue because he was so displeased by the screenplay. Due to problems with blacklisting, scripter Bernard Gordon was left off the film's credits on its initial release in favor of screenwriter Philip Yordan, who served as a front for Gordon. In 1996, the Writer's Guild of America officially restored Gordon's credit.

DAY OF WRATH
(VREDENS DAG)

1943 97m bw Drama
Palladium   (Denmark) /A

Thirkild Roose *(Absalon Pedersson)*, Lisbeth Movin *(Anne Peders-dotter, His Wife)*, Sigrid Neiiendam *(Meret, His Mother)*, Preben Lerdorff-Rye *(Martin, Son by His First Marriage)*, Albert Hoeberg *(The Bishop)*, Olaf Ussing *(Laurentius)*, Anna Svierkier *(Herlofs Marte)*

p, Carl-Theodor Dreyer; d, Carl-Theodor Dreyer; w, Carl-Theodor Dreyer, Poul Knudsen, Mogens Skot-Hansen (based on the novel by Wiers Jenssens); ph, Carl Anderson; ed, Edith Schlussel, Anne Marie Petersen; m, Poul Schierbeck; art d, Erik Aaes

DAY OF WRATH was the first feature film directed by the great Carl Dreyer after his 1932 masterwork, VAMPYR. In WRATH, Dreyer returns to the witches, religion, and spiritualism that marked his earlier, silent masterpiece, THE PASSION OF JOAN OF ARC (1928).

Set during the throes of a witch hunt in the 17th century, the film centers around a young woman, Anne (Lisbeth Movin), who is married to a much older, puritanical man she hates. She falls in love with his son, with whom she spends idyllic afternoons in the woods. Pressure begins to build, and she is heard to whisper aloud how she hungers for the death of her husband. Soon afterward, the husband dies, and she is accused of being a witch.

The plot is deceptively simple and is barely representative of the film's power, for the film's brilliance lies in Dreyer's direction and the uncanny imagery, which resembles nothing so much as Rembrandt masterworks come to life. At a slow and deliberate pace, he allows the camera to linger, almost erotically, on images, waiting for the "right" look on a face or the correct movement of a hand. A study of good and evil, repression and oppression, sexuality and guilt, DAY OF WRATH is a truly spiritual film.

DAY THE EARTH STOOD STILL, THE

1951 92m bw Science Fiction ★★★★
Fox   (U.S.) /U

Michael Rennie *(Klaatu)*, Patricia Neal *(Helen Benson)*, Hugh Marlowe *(Tom Stevens)*, Sam Jaffe *(Dr. Barnhardt)*, Billy Gray *(Bobby Benson)*, Frances Bavier *(Mrs. Barley)*, Lock Martin *(Gort)*, Drew Pearson *(Himself)*, Frank Conroy *(Harley)*, Fay Roope *(Major General)*

p, Julian Blaustein; d, Robert Wise; w, Edmund H. North (based on a story by Harry Bates); ph, Leo Tover; ed, William Reynolds; m, Bernard Herrmann; art d, Lyle Wheeler, Addison Hehr; fx, Fred Sersen

Working from Edmund H. North's unusually literate adaptation of Harry Bates's short story "Farewell to the Master," Robert Wise created a classic science fiction film with a strong pacifist message.

Sent by a federation of planets to warn the people of Earth to stop nuclear testing before the planet is destroyed, the Christ-like Rennie descends into Washington, D.C., in his spaceship, accompanied by his massive robot, Gort. When an American soldier panics and shoots Rennie, Gort eliminates them. The wounded Rennie stops the robot from destroying the planet by uttering the now-classic phrase, "Klaatu barada nikto." Taken to a military hospital, Rennie escapes and, posing as a normal human, seeks shelter in Neal's boarding house. Here he begins to learn that Earth people really are not so bad. Since he can make no formal contact with the governments of Earth, Rennie arranges a demonstration of his power that justifies the title of the film.

Superb performances by all involved, restrained direction by Wise, and a magnificent and innovative score by Bernard Herrmann help keep this 35-year-old film just as relevant today as it was the day it was released.

DAYBREAK
(LE JOUR SE LEVE)

1939 89m bw Drama/Romance ★★★★
Sigma Productions   (France) /A

Jean Gabin *(Francois)*, Jules Berry *(M. Valentin)*, Jacqueline Laurent *(Francoise)*, Arletty *(Clara)*, Rene Genin *(Concierge)*, Mady Berry *(Concierge's Wife)*, Bernard Blier *(Gaston)*, Marcel Peres *(Paulo)*, Jacques Baumer *(The Inspector)*, Rene Bergeron *(Cafe Proprietor)*

d, Marcel Carne; w, Jacques Prevert, Jacques Viot; ph, Curt Courant; ed, Rene Le Henaff; m, Maurice Jaubert; art d, Alexandre Trauner; cos, Boris Bilinsky

A superb example of French poetic realism, and probably the finest of the several collaborations between director Marcel Carne and screenwriter Jacques Prevert. Jean Gabin is Francois, a tough, romantic loner who barricades himself in his apartment after committing a crime of passion, the murder of the lecherous Valentin (Jules Berry). While police surround his Normandy home, Francois remembers (in flashback) the two women he loved—Francoise (Jacqueline Laurent) and Clara (Arletty)—and Valentin, the man who wooed both. Every facet of the film's production values is expertly realized, but perhaps the most awe-inspiring is the set design of Alexandre Trauner—a re-creation of a city street corner decorated with Dubonnet posters that is one of the most memorable ever filmed. More poetic than realistic, it is very much a film of a mood, but despite the optimism of its ironic title, melancholy and despair predominate. This inherent irony was then mirrored by real-life events as the film was released not long before Paris became an occupied city, and its citizens, like Francois, were left with no way out. Recognizing the similarities, the Vichy government banned the picture as "demoralizing." Remade in Hollywood as THE LONG NIGHT. (In French; English subtitles.)

DAYS OF HEAVEN

1978 95m c Drama ★★★★
Paramount   (U.S.) PG

Richard Gere *(Bill)*, Brooke Adams *(Abby)*, Sam Shepard *(The Farmer)*, Linda Manz *(Linda)*, Bob Wilke *(Farm Foreman)*, Jackie Shultis *(Linda's Friend)*, Stuart Margolin *(Mill Foreman)*, Timothy Scott *(Harvest Hand)*, Gene Bell *(Dancer)*, Doug Kershaw *(Fiddler)*

p, Bert Schneider, Harold Schneider; d, Terrence Malick; w, Terrence Malick; ph, Nestor Almendros; ed, Billy Weber; m, Ennio Morricone; art d, Jack Fisk; fx, John Thomas, Mel Merrells; cos, Patricia Norris

AA Best Cinematography: Nestor Almendros; *AAN Best Score:* Ennio Morricone; *AAN Best Costume Design:* Patricia Norris; *AAN Best Sound:* John K. Wilkinson, Robert W. Glass, Jr., John T. Reitz, Barry Thomas

Set in the postindustrial revolution America of the early 1900s, DAYS OF HEAVEN chronicles the odyssey of a rootless migrant laborer (Gere), his little sister (Manz), and his soulmate (Adams), as they flee the industrial blight of the city for the sanctuary and anonymity of the Heartland. When the impulsive and hot-tempered Gere kills a steel-mill foreman in anger, the three jump a train and head for the plains of Texas, merging with the endless caravan of homeless immigrants looking for work. Their journey brings them to the land of wealthy, self-made wheat farmer Shepard, who offers them employment during the harvest.

An enigmatic figure, Shepard, living alone in a huge Victorian mansion that overlooks his golden empire, is slowly wasting away from some illness. As he watches Adams work in the fields, he grows to love her—as Pharaoh did young Sarah in the Old Testament story—and sees some private salvation in making her his "queen." Gere learns of the farmer's illness and, reasoning that the powerful farmer will be dead soon, contrives like Abraham of old to masquerade with Adams as brother and sister thereby allowing Shepard to marry Adams and plant the seeds of a future inheritance. For a time after the marriage, the four live together as a family in a state of grace and sublime happiness. The scheme goes awry, however, when Adams begins to genuinely care for Shepard. When Shepard realizes the lovers' duplicity, his rage is that of the Old Testament Pharoah, on whose lands Jehovah's wrathful plagues fell. The contest between the two suitors precipitates a holocaust that blows apart the fragile paradise that so briefly flourished.

Director Malick endows this simple, timeless story with the enormous scope and resonance of myth through a clear vision unclouded by sentimentality and by a deft juxtaposition of image, music, and character. Although this is only his second feature film (BADLANDS, made five years earlier, was his first), he demonstrates a mastery of cinematic technique. The story is rich with Biblical and mythical allusions: there are echoes of Genesis, the Wasteland myth, and Greek tragedy. The vast, uncluttered compositions sometimes render the characters as little more than puppets in the hands of fate, reinforcing the universality of the story. Almendros's hyper-realistic cinematography is breathtaking.

The dialogue is sparse and almost incidental, the characters' words insignificant amidst the pervasive whisper of the wheat, the clatter of the threshing machines, and the awful drone of the locust horde that accompanies the final holocaust. The sound alone is astonishing. Morricone's haunting, wistful score adds measurably to the sweep and timelessness of the film.

DAYS OF WINE AND ROSES

1962 117m bw Drama   ★★★★
Warner Bros. (U.S.)   /X

Jack Lemmon (Joe), Lee Remick (Kirsten), Charles Bickford (Arnesen), Jack Klugman (Jim Hungerford), Alan Hewitt (Leland), Tom Palmer (Ballefoy), Debbie Megowan (Debbie), Maxine Stuart (Dottie), Katherine Squire (Mrs. Nolan), Jack Albertson (Trayner)

p, Martin Manulis; d, Blake Edwards; w, J.P. Miller (based on the television play by J.P. Miller); ph, Philip Lathrop; ed, Patrick McCormack; m, Henry Mancini; art d, Joseph C. Wright; fx, Horace L. Hulburd; cos, Don Feld

AAN Best Actor: Jack Lemmon; AAN Best Actress: Lee Remick; AA Best Song: Henry Mancini (Music), Johnny Mercer (Lyrics); AAN Best Art Direction: Joseph Wright, George James Hopkins; AAN Best Costume Design: Don Feld

Former light comedian Jack Lemmon's powerful performance as an alcoholic counts among Hollywood's most memorable depictions of this condition such as Ray Milland in THE LOST WEEKEND and Jimmy Cagney in COME FILL THE CUP. He's a young, bright adman who meets and falls in love with Remick. Early in their relationship, he's just a social drinker and she's a teetotaler. Soon after their marriage, subtle changes begin to occur. Lemmon is stressed out from work and begins drinking daily after work. Remick adores him and soon joins in sharing the bottle. Before long they are immersed in the liquored life and even the birth of their baby daughter fails to slow their descent into the gutter.

The movie features many emotionally shattering scenes and the going sometimes gets rough. Lemmon surprised many with the intensity of his performance. He has a mad spell in a greenhouse and an almost SNAKE PIT-like siege in a hospital ward. This is a long way from frolicking in drag with Marilyn Monroe in SOME LIKE IT HOT! The screenplay was based on J.P. Miller's teleplay, which starred Cliff Robertson on "Playhouse 90." Robertson was not a star at the time, and the decision was made to use Lemmon. Edwards's direction was smooth and neither he nor Miller ever took a stance or moralized. They just showed what it was like to be an alcoholic in the 1960s and let the audience draw its own conclusions.

DAZED AND CONFUSED

1993 97m c Drama   ★★★
Dazed Pictures Corporation (U.S.)   R/

Jason London (Randy "Pink" Floyd), Sasha Jenson (Don Dawson), Rory Cochrane (Slater), Wiley Wiggins (Mitch Kramer), Michelle Burke (Jodi Kramer), Shawn Andrews (Pickford), Anthony Rapp (Tony), Adam Goldberg (Mike), Christin Hinojosa (Sabrina), Parker Posey (Darla)

p, Richard Linklater, Sean Daniel, James Jacks; d, Richard Linklater; w, Richard Linklater; ph, Lee Daniel; ed, Sandra Adair; prod d, John Frick; art d, Jenny C. Patrick; cos, Katherine "K.D." Dover

Director Richard Linklater's follow-up to the 1991 surprise independent hit SLACKER, this is an affectionate but unsentimental recreation of suburban teen culture in the rock- and pot-drenched 70s.

The film follows an ensemble of more than 20 characters through their last day and night of high school in 1976. The kids separate into cliques of familiar character types—jocks and nerds, senior bullies and freshmen weaklings, potheads and eggheads, the cool and the uncool. As quarterback of the high school football team, Randy "Pink" Floyd (Jason London) must decide whether to sign the coach's pledge to remain drug-free or to continue to indulge with his friends; meanwhile, freshman Mitch (Wiley Wiggins) spends the day fleeing from paddle-wielding, abusive hazers while trying to hang with the older gang of cool kids and the girls who find him cute. All parties convene at a huge beer bust in the woods, where fights erupt, romances are consummated, and dazed visions of "what comes next" are hashed out.

A much-praised portrait of 70s youth, DAZED AND CONFUSED expertly captures the details and textures of the time without condescending or lapsing into cheap-shot parody. A classic rock score (Aerosmith, Black Oak Arkansas, Foghat, and other quintessential AOR sounds) combines with smooth camerawork and editing to help create a seamless succession of typical incidents and conversations. The youths so frankly portrayed here lead lives of aimlessness, sloth, and apathy—understandably, given the banality of the choices available to them. Truly dazed and confused, Linklater's characters inhabit a moral universe so murky and enervated that Floyd's willingness to make a stand—any stand—emerges finally as something of a triumph.

DEAD, THE

1987 83m c Drama   ★★★★½
Liffey (U.S.)   PG/U

Anjelica Huston (Gretta Conroy), Donal McCann (Gabriel Conroy, Her Husband), Rachael Dowling (Lily), Cathleen Delany (Aunt Julia Morkan), Helena Carroll (Aunt Kate Morkan), Ingrid Craigie (Mary Jane), Dan O'Herlihy (Mr. Browne), Frank Patterson (Bartell D'Arcy), Donal Donnelly (Freddy Malins), Marie Kean (Mrs. Malins)

p, Wieland Schulz-Keil, Chris Sievernich; d, John Huston; w, Tony Huston (based on the short story from The Dubliners by James Joyce); ph, Fred Murphy; ed, Roberto Silvi; m, Alex North; prod d, Stephen Grimes, J. Dennis Washington; cos, Dorothy Jeakins

AAN Best Adapted Screenplay: Tony Huston; AAN Best Costume Design: Dorothy Jeakins

This sublime adaptation of the last story in James Joyce's Dubliners is John Huston's final film, and it is as beautiful, delicate, and moving an epitaph as any filmmaker could ever desire.

Set in Dublin on the chilly night of January 6, 1904, the feast of the Epiphany, THE DEAD takes place at the home of spinsters Kate (Helena Carroll) and Julia Morkan (Cathleen Delany) during their annual post-holidays party. Their favorite guests are their sophisticated nephew, Gabriel Conroy (Donal McCann), and his beautiful wife, Gretta (Anjelica Huston). After most of the revelers have left, Gretta is struck by the haunting rendition of "The Lass of Aughrim" sung by one of the guests. On the cab ride back to their hotel, Gretta is distant, lost in her thoughts. In their room, a tearful Gretta confesses to Gabriel that the song has stirred long-suppressed memories of a brief and tragic romance from her youth. After hearing her story, Gabriel marvels at the power that the dead hold over the living.

THE DEAD is a breathtakingly beautiful movie, a mature work of a master filmmaker. Huston, a lifelong admirer of Joyce, had wanted to make a film adaptation of "The Dead" since the 1950s, but put the idea on the back burner because of its uncommercial nature. When producer Wieland Schulz-Keil decided the time was right, he hired Huston's eldest son, Tony, to write the screenplay, which is scrupulously faithful to Joyce. The casting is marvelous, and Huston allows all his performers equal screen time until the end when Anjelica Huston and McCann become the focus. The party scene is a flurry of detailed movement, wonderfully choreographed. Huston concentrates on the interaction of the characters—the conversations, the movements, the rituals—and glories in the nuances of human behavior.

The film's most powerful sequence, however, is the scene between husband and wife. Anjelica Huston is superb, striking the perfect balance of emotions. It is a performance of grace and eloquence. Equally excellent is McCann, who somehow manages to convey with a minimum of visible acting the dawning self-awareness described by Joyce. THE DEAD was made by a man who had a deep appreciation for all the arts and how they enrich the human experience.

DEAD AGAIN

1991   107m   c   Mystery/Romance   ★★★
Mirage Enterprises/Paramount   (U.S.)   R/15

Kenneth Branagh *(Mike Church/Roman Strauss)*, Emma Thompson *(Grace/Margaret Strauss)*, Andy Garcia *(Gray Baker)*, Lois Hall *(Sister Constance)*, Richard Easton *(Father Timothy)*, Jo Anderson *(Sister Madeleine/Starlet)*, Patrick Montes *(Pickup Driver)*, Raymond Cruz *(Clerk)*, Robin Williams *(Doctor Cozy Carlisle)*, Wayne Knight *("Piccolo" Pete)*

p, Lindsay Doran, Charles H. Maguire; d, Kenneth Branagh; w, Scott Frank; ph, Matthew F. Leonetti; ed, Peter E. Berger; m, Patrick Doyle; prod d, Tim Harvey; art d, Sydney Z. Litwack; fx, Tom Burman, Bari Burman; cos, Phyllis Dalton

Director Kenneth Branagh and his then real-life wife Emma Thompson both have dual roles in DEAD AGAIN, a complexly plotted mystery that is steeped in a pastiche of Hollywood classics.

Los Angeles. Private detective Mike Church (Branagh), at the behest of the orphanage priest who raised him, rescues an unknown amnesiac (Thompson), who he names Grace and with whom he quickly falls in love. With the aid of hypnotist and antique dealer Franklyn Madson (Derek Jacobi), who appears on the scene, Grace undergoes hypnosis and recounts her past life as Margaret, a British concert pianist married to Roman Strauss, a flamboyant emigre conductor who was imprisoned for her brutal murder. At a second session, she begins to blur the identities of Roman and Mike, and the latter realizes that Grace is remembering a past life in which he plays a part as well. Intrigued, Church undergoes hypnosis himself and discovers just how symbiotic their relationship is: *he* was Margaret and Grace was Roman. Further investigation reveals that in 1949 the Strauss murder case actually transpired, resulting in Roman's execution. As the modern-day and past experiences increasingly overlap, Church fears his romantic attraction to Grace will again end with a violent death.

Scott Frank (PLAIN CLOTHES, LITTLE MAN TATE) has created a screenplay which, at the expense of story and character development, prides itself on its ability to quote liberally from great films of the past. DEAD AGAIN borrows icons, motifs, characters and camera angles from a number of classics, most notably Hitchcock thrillers such as REBECCA, with its gothic mansion and creepy housekeeper, SPELLBOUND, with its hypnosis, psychoanalysis and giant Salvador Dali scissors, and VERTIGO, with its reincarnated doubles and Catholic trappings, but also film noir mysteries and Orson Welles's CITIZEN KANE. However unlikely the twists and turns in this mystery, DEAD AGAIN moves briskly forward, never weighed down by any sense of seriousness. Branagh's transformations between his lightweight, American detective and his heavy, Germanic musician are pure bravado, done for the thrill of watching the Master Thespian assume two wildly different incarnations.

DEAD CALM

1989   96m   c   Horror/Thriller   ★★★½
Kennedy Miller   (Australia)   R/15

Sam Neill *(John Ingram)*, Nicole Kidman *(Rae Ingram)*, Billy Zane *(Hughie Warriner)*, Rod Mullinar *(Russell Bellows)*, Joshua Tilden *(Danny)*, George Shevtsov *(Doctor)*, Michael Long *(Specialist Doctor)*

p, Terry Hayes, Doug Mitchell, George Miller; d, Phillip Noyce; w, Terry Hayes (based on the novel by Charles Williams); ph, Dean Semler; ed, Richard Francis-Bruce; m, Graeme Revell; prod d, Graham Walker; art d, Kimble Hilder; cos, Norma Moriceau

Though it lacks Alfred Hitchcock's wry and macabre sense of humor, DEAD CALM is a cracklingly good, cold-blooded film that never lets up in its truly Hitchcockian suspense. Under the gripping direction of Phillip Noyce, the film sustains tension and power beautifully, right through to its startling conclusion.

Middle-aged surgeon John Ingram (Sam Neill) and his wife Rae (Nicole Kidman) embark on an extended yachting trip after the gruesome death of their little son in a car accident. The trip is intended as a therapeutic measure for the traumatized Rae. Things go well until the couple rescues Hughie Warriner (Billy Zane), the sole survivor from a sinking schooner near the Great Barrier Reef. Warriner claims that all the other passengers died of food poisoning, but Ingram boards the schooner to investigate and makes a nasty discovery that turns their vacation into a nightmare.

Neill and Zane both turn in excellent performances, but Kidman (DAYS OF THUNDER, BILLY BATHGATE) does the most interesting and demanding work as the wife who must snap out of her melancholy distraction to outwit her vile captor. During the film's last half, Kidman convincingly transforms from a vunerable, distraught housewife into a ferocious battler—and it's an electrifying metamorphosis. The taut editing and Noyce's direction are splendid, augmenting Terry Hayes's sharp (though somewhat predictable) script. George Miller, director of the MAD MAX trilogy and former student of Phillip Noyce at Melbourne University, is one of the producers.

DEAD END

1937   93m   bw   Crime   ★★★★
UA   (U.S.)   /PG

Sylvia Sidney *(Drina)*, Joel McCrea *(Dave)*, Humphrey Bogart *(Baby Face Martin)*, Wendy Barrie *(Kay)*, Claire Trevor *(Francie)*, Allen Jenkins *(Hunk)*, Marjorie Main *(Mrs. Martin)*, Billy Halop *(Tommy)*, Huntz Hall *(Dippy)*, Bobby Jordan *(Angel)*

p, Samuel Goldwyn; d, William Wyler; w, Lillian Hellman (based on the play by Sidney Kingsley); ph, Gregg Toland; ed, Daniel Mandell; m, Alfred Newman; art d, Richard Day; fx, James Basevi; cos, Omar Kiam

AAN Best Picture; AAN Best Supporting Actress: Claire Trevor; *AAN Best Cinematography:* Gregg Toland; *AAN Best Art Direction:* Richard Day (Art Direction)

Depression-era poverty, slums and crime provide the themes for DEAD END, Sam Goldwyn's film production of the popular Sidney Kingsley play. Well meaning and once considered hardhitting, this celebrated social drama now seems rather mawkish and quaint. The message is not just that these impoverished surroundings can be a cradle for crime but that good folks may also be brought up on these mean streets.

After ten years of pursuing a criminal career, escalating from robbery to murder, Bogart returns to his old New York City neighborhood. Disguised by extensive plastic surgery, he wants to see his mother (Main) and his old girlfriend (Trevor) while avoiding a nationwide dragnet. DEAD END is also the story of McCrea, a scrupulous and unsuccessful architect struggling to get out of the slum. He thinks he's in love with Barrie, a rich woman living in a nearby luxury apartment building but he is the apple of Sidney's eye. She is a respectable woman living in poverty and struggling to keep her kid brother, Halop, on the straight and narrow. Meanwhile, Bogart begins teaching Halop and the other "Dead End Kids" all the wiseguy tricks he's learned in his misspent life. McCrea, his boyhood chum, warns Bogart that he will take steps against him unless he stops exerting his rotten influence on the impressionable youths.

William Wyler's sterling direction creates a stagey but fairly compelling vision of slum life. The wonderful set by Richard Day is an enlarged duplicate of the Broadway set. Lillian Hellman's script changes little of Kingsley's earthy prose except for the ending. Humphrey Bogart is captivating as the alienated gangster, building upon his success of THE PETRIFIED FOREST a year earlier. He was originally billed beneath Sidney, but, in re-releases of this film, he was given star billing.

DEAD MAN

1996 121m bw Western   ★★★★
12-Gauge Productions/JVC/Newmarket Capital Group/Victor   R/18
Company of Japan/Pandora Film   (U.S./Germany/Japan)

Johnny Depp *(William Blake)*, Gary Farmer *(Nobody)*, Lance Henriksen *(Cole Wilson)*, Gabriel Byrne *(Charlie Dickinson)*, Robert Mitchum *(John Dickinson)*, John Hurt *(John Scholfield)*, Crispin Glover *(The Fireman)*, Michael Wincott *(Conway Twill)*, Eugene Byrd *(Johnny "The Kid" Pickett)*, Mili Avital *(Thel Russell)*

p, Demetra J. MacBride; d, Jim Jarmusch; w, Jim Jarmusch; ph, Robby Muller; ed, Jay Rabinowitz; m, Neil Young; prod d, Bob Ziembicki; art d, Ted Berner; fx, Lou Carlucci, Jon Farhat, R/Greenberg Associates West, Inc.; cos, Marit Allen

This splendid art film in Western clothing marks a departure for director/writer Jim Jarmusch, the hipster auteur best known for quirky, coolly amusing character studies like STRANGER THAN PARADISE and MYSTERY TRAIN. In a town called Machine, mild-mannered accountant Bill Blake (Johnny Depp) turns outlaw after shooting a man in self-defense. Pursued by an unlikely team of gunslingers (Lance Henriksen, Michael Wincott, Eugene Byrd), he heads for the wilderness, finding a partner and spiritual guide in the person of a philosophical Indian called Nobody (Gary Farmer).

Despite appearances, DEAD MAN is no conventional outlaw saga. Just beneath its surface lies a visionary allegory of the soul's progress from physical death to spiritual transcendence, seasoned with references to the life and works of the poet William Blake. (Just for example, John Hurt appears as a toadying clerk called John Scholfield, the name of the vengeful soldier who accused Blake of sedition.) A slow-paced but hypnotically absorbing movie, it's buoyed by Jarmusch's trademark off-key humor and embellished throughout by an electrifying instrumental score, courtesy of Neil Young. On the visual level, it's resplendent: cinematographer Robby Muller works from an exceptionally rich black-and-white palette, and what he does for Jarmusch here is comparable to what Kazuo Miyagawa's camera did for Mizoguchi. DEAD MAN even has star power, in the form of Depp, who gives further evidence of his gallant—to some, inexplicable—commitment to the offbeat.

DEAD MAN WALKING

1995 120m c Drama   ★★★
Working Title Films/Havoc Productions/Polygram (U.S.)   R/15

Susan Sarandon *(Sister Helen Prejean)*, Sean Penn *(Matthew Poncelet)*, Robert Prosky *(Hilton Barber)*, Raymond J. Barry *(Earl Delacroix)*, R. Lee Ermey *(Clyde Percy)*, Celia Weston *(Mary Beth Percy)*, Lois Smith *(Helen's Mother)*, Scott Wilson *(Chaplain Farley)*, Roberta Maxwell *(Lucille Poncelet)*, Margo Martindale *(Sister Colleen)*

p, Jon Kilik, Tim Robbins, Rudd Simmons; d, Tim Robbins; w, Tim Robbins (based on the book by Sister Helen Prejean, C.S.J.); ph, Roger A. Deakins; ed, Lisa Zeno Churgin; m, David Robbins; prod d, Richard Hoover; art d, Tom Warren; cos, Renee Ehrlich Kalfus

AA Best Actress: Susan Sarandon; *AAN Best Actor:* Sean Penn; *AAN Best Director:* Tim Robbins; *AAN Best Original Song:* Bruce Springsteen

DEAD MAN WALKING is an extraordinarily well-made message movie that punks out at the eleventh hour. Tim Robbins's film about the death penalty wants to be perceived as painstakingly balanced and fair to both sides; ultimately, however, it's just unresolved.

Sister Helen (Susan Sarandon), a nun who's abandoned her privileged background to live and work with the poor of New Orleans, is asked to write to a man on death row. Her pen pal, Matthew Poncelet (Sean Penn), asks her to help him file an appeal of his sentence. Though he was convicted of taking part in the rape and murder of a young couple—his partner in crime received a life sentence, apparently for no better reason than that he had a sharper lawyer—Poncelet says he's innocent. Sister Helen is drawn into the case and, as the execution date approaches, she takes on a mission: to get Poncelet to admit to his guilt and regret his actions before he dies.

Boosters of capital punishment hated DEAD MAN WALKING, but so did serious opponents. Although some critics took this as evidence of the film's "even-handed" treatment of the issue, in fact it's proof that DEAD MAN WALKING doesn't treat the issue at all. It's a message movie without a message. The topical movies of Abby Mann or Stanley Kramer have often been assailed as simplistic or crudely moralistic, but at least they had the courage of their makers' convictions.

This ideologically muddled construction rests on a pair of phenomenal performances. In the hands of a lesser actress, pious Sister Helen would be absolutely intolerable, but Sarandon gives her a simple decency and conviction. Sean Penn, meanwhile, is a riveting study in Mephistophelian facial hair and white-trash attitude. His Poncelet is a genuinely bad guy, but one with a distinctly human face.

DEAD MEN DON'T WEAR PLAID

1982 89m bw Comedy/Crime   ★★★★
Universal (U.S.)   PG

Steve Martin *(Rigby Reardon)*, Rachel Ward *(Juliet Forrest)*, Carl Reiner *(Field Marshall Von Kluck)*, Reni Santoni *(Carlos Rodriguez)*, George Gaynes *(Dr. Forrest)*, Frank McCarthy *(Waiter)*, Adrian Ricard *(Mildred)*, Charles Picerni, Gene Labell, George Sawaya *(Hoods)*

p, David V. Picker, William E. McEuen; d, Carl Reiner; w, George Gipe, Carl Reiner, Steve Martin; ph, Michael Chapman; ed, Bud Molin; m, Miklos Rozsa; prod d, John De Cuir; fx, Glen Robinson; cos, Edith Head

A consistently hilarious parody of the noir and detective genres, expertly blending classic archival footage with the action. As an inept private eye, Steve Martin tracks killers, playing opposite old film clips of James Cagney, Alan Ladd, Humphrey Bogart, Charles Laughton, and Ava Gardner, among others; scenes are lifted from, *inter alia*, WHITE HEAT, DOUBLE INDEMNITY, THE KILLERS, THE BIG SLEEP, DARK PASSAGE, IN A LONELY PLACE, SUSPICION and, most notably, THE BRIBE. Some of the cleverer jokes depend on the viewer's knowledge of 1940s movies, but there's enough slapstick to please even the cinematically illiterate. The basic film—what there is of it—is prettily shot in black-and-white by Michael Chapman (RAGING BULL); the continuity between the clips and the rest of the movie is remarkable. Martin is priceless as usual.

DEAD OF NIGHT

1945 104m bw Horror   ★★★★½
Rank (U.K.)   /18

Mervyn Johns *(Walter Craig)*, Roland Culver *(Eliot Foley)*, Mary Merrall *(Mrs. Foley)*, Frederick Valk *(Dr. Van Straaten)*, Renee Gadd *(Mrs. Craig)*, Anthony Baird *(Hugh Grainger)*, Judy Kelly *(Joyce Grainger)*, Miles Malleson *(Hearse Driver)*, Sally Ann Howes *(Sally O'Hara)*, Michael Allan *(Jimmy Watson)*

p, Michael Balcon; d, Alberto Cavalcanti, Basil Dearden, Robert Hamer, Charles Crichton; w, John Baines, Angus Macphail, T.E.B. Clarke (based on stories by H.G. Wells, E.F. Benson, John Baines, and Angus Macphail); ph, Jack Parker, Harold Julius; ed, Charles Hasse; m, Georges Auric; art d, Michael Relph

Perhaps the best horror anthology film ever made, this much-praised film still holds up, but suffers from the variances of pace and mood that inevitably affect all compilation efforts. Architect Walter Craig (Mervyn Johns) is called to Pilgrim's Farm, a country house he has been hired to remodel. Approaching the austere Victorian building in his car, he finds that there is something hauntingly familiar about the house. Once inside, Craig recognizes everyone present and tells them they have all been part of a recurring nightmare he has had, whereupon the guests relate their own nightmares, one by one.

The first tale, "The Hearse Driver," is told by Grainger (Antony Baird). In it he is a racetrack driver who, while recuperating from an accident, has a vision of a hearse from the window of his hospital room. The teen-aged Sally O'Hara (Sally Ann Howes) then reports "The Christmas Story," in which she attends a holiday party and, during a game of hide-and-seek, finds a crying child in a strange room. He is not what he seems. Joan Courtland (Googie Withers), in "The Haunted Mirror," relates a chilling tale in which she is given an antique mirror by her fiance which begins to reflect a Victorian room where a killing once took place. In "The Golfing Story"—the only piece designed for comic relief—two golfers (Basil Radford and Naunton Wayne) vie for the attentions of one woman. One golfer tricks the other into suicide, only to have the deceased return and haunt him as he is about to enjoy his wedding night. The last story, an Expressionistic entry entitled "The Ventriloquist's Dummy," shows a ventriloquist (Michael Redgrave) going mad. He believes that his dummy is assuming his personality while he is becoming the manipulated prop.

With typical disregard for consistency, US distributors thought this excellent British import was too long and cut the golfing sequence (not a bad move, actually) and the Christmas ghost tale, confusing audiences, who could not understand what Howes, Radford, and Wayne were doing in the linking story. The two tales were later reinstated. Of the four directors of the various stories, Robert Hamer is a standout with "The Haunted Mirror" and Alberto Cavalcanti excels with his two chillers, "The Christmas Story" and "The Ventriloquist's Dummy."

DEAD PIGEON ON BEETHOVEN STREET

1972 102m c Mystery ★★★
Bavaria Atelier (West Germany) PG/15

Glenn Corbett *(Sandy)*, Christa Lang *(Christa)*, Sieghardt Rupp *(Kessin)*, Anton Diffring *(Mensur)*, Alex D'Arcy *(Novka)*, Anthony Ching *(Fong)*, Eric P. Caspar *(Charlie)*

d, Samuel Fuller; w, Samuel Fuller; ph, Jerzy Lipman; ed, Liesgret Schmitt-Klink; art d, Lothar Kirchem

American director Fuller answered his cult of European fans by making this bizarre tongue-in-cheek private-eye movie financed by German television. Corbett stars as a detective whose partner is murdered while investigating a gang of drug-dealing extortionists who photograph big-shot international-politico types in compromising situations with the lovely Lang. Corbett goes undercover and joins the ring to get the goods on the group. The film offers typically vigorous camera work but what makes it special is its looney sense of humor. Laden with in-jokes, the film is best approached as a goofy parody of crime thrillers.

DEAD POETS SOCIETY

1989 128m c Drama ★★½
Silver Screen Partners IV/Touchstone (U.S.) PG

Robin Williams *(John Keating)*, Robert Sean Leonard *(Neil Perry)*, Ethan Hawke *(Todd Anderson)*, Josh Charles *(Knox Overstreet)*, Gale Hansen *(Charlie Dalton)*, Dylan Kussman *(Richard Cameron)*, Allelon Ruggiero *(Steven Meeks)*, James Waterson *(Gerard Pitts)*, Norman Lloyd *(Mr. Nolan)*, Kurtwood Smith *(Mr. Perry)*

p, Steven M. Haft, Paul Junger Witt, Tony Thomas; d, Peter Weir; w, Tom Schulman; ph, John Seale; m, Maurice Jarre; prod d, Wendy Stites; art d, Sandy Veneziano; cos, Marilyn Matthews

AAN Best Picture; *AAN Best Actor*: Robin Williams; *AAN Best Director*: Peter Weir; *AA Best Original Screenplay*: Tom Schulman

Tea and empathy. Tinkering with his screen persona, comedian-actor Robin Williams plays it relatively straight as a dedicated teacher at an elite Vermont prep school. The year is 1959, a time of strict adherence to educational goals and teaching methods at Welton, under the no-nonsense stewardship of headmaster Nolan (Norman Lloyd). The academic apple cart teeters, however, when John Keating (Williams) is engaged to teach a class of bright and impressionable young men. An inspirational mentor, Keating ignores conventional teaching procedures and offers his students access to a world of culture, ideas, and

creativity that changes their lives. The role of Keating is a plum assignment for the talented Williams, who largely steers clear of schtick under Peter Weir's direction. Nicely shot with a good youthful cast.

DEAD RINGERS

1988 115m c Horror ★★★★½
Mantle Clinic II (Canada) R/18

Jeremy Irons *(Beverly Mantle/Elliot Mantle)*, Genevieve Bujold *(Claire Niveau)*, Heidi von Palleske *(Cary)*, Barbara Gordon *(Danuta)*, Shirley Douglas *(Laura)*, Stephen Lack *(Anders Wolleck)*, Nick Nichols *(Leo)*, Lynn Cormack *(Arlene)*, Damir Andrei *(Birchall)*, Miriam Newhouse *(Mrs. Bookman)*

p, David Cronenberg, Marc Boyman; d, David Cronenberg; w, David Cronenberg, Norman Snider (based on the book *Twins* by Bari Wood, Jack Geasland); ph, Peter Suschitzky; ed, Ronald Sanders; m, Howard Shore; prod d, Carol Spier; fx, Gordon Smith; cos, Denise Cronenberg

Quietly devastating, DEAD RINGERS offers compelling evidence that David Cronenberg has matured into a truly great filmmaker. Continuing the detailed character study that blossomed in THE FLY and combining it with his fixation on the metaphysical, Cronenberg has vividly created yet another film that is powerful, moving and rich in ideas.

Inspired by the real-life story of respected twin New York City gynecologists Steven and Cyril Marcus (who in 1975 were both found dead in their garbage-strewn Upper East Side apartment, a double suicide brought on by barbiturate addiction), Cronenberg introduces us to Elliot and Beverly Mantle, a pair of brilliant gynecologists who open a state-of-the-art fertility clinic and share an opulent apartment. Although physically identical, the twins possess very different personalities. Elliot is something of a cad—suave, debonair, and self-confident to the point of arrogance—whereas Beverly is shy, studious, and more sensitive. Elliot has always procured women for Beverly—seducing them first, then turning them over to his shy sibling when he was through—unbeknownst to the woman. When a famous actress, Claire Niveau (Genevieve Bujold), arrives at the clinic looking for answers to her infertility, trouble brews between the brothers, for although they both share her physically, Beverly falls in love for the first time, driving a wedge between the twins.

Extremely unsettling, at times amusing, cold yet personal, DEAD RINGERS gradually and deliberately comes to horrify the viewer, rather than shocking outright with such spectacular displays of gore as the exploding heads of SCANNERS, gaping stomach cavities of VIDEODROME, or vomiting Brundleflies of THE FLY. Not your average horror roller-coaster ride, DEAD RINGERS asks some disturbing questions about the nature of individual identity and, within that net, explores such outgrowths as eroticism, narcissism and misogyny. During the last decade, Cronenberg has matured into a filmmaker of remarkable scope, able to convey his obsessions with impeccable skill without sacrificing one iota of his own remarkable individuality. The astonishing Irons receives superb support from Bujold who breathes life into a part that, in other hands, might have been a mere plot device.

DEAD ZONE, THE

1983 103m c Horror ★★★½
Paramount (U.S.) R/

Christopher Walken *(Johnny Smith)*, Brooke Adams *(Sarah Bracknell)*, Tom Skerritt *(Sheriff Bannerman)*, Herbert Lom *(Dr. Sam Weizak)*, Anthony Zerbe *(Roger Stuart)*, Colleen Dewhurst *(Henrietta Dodd)*, Martin Sheen *(Greg Stillson)*, Nicholas Campbell *(Frank Dodd)*, Sean Sullivan *(Herb Smith)*, Jackie Burroughs *(Vera Smith)*

p, Debra Hill; d, David Cronenberg; w, Jeffrey Boam (based on the novel by Stephen King); ph, Mark Irwin; ed, Ronald Sanders; m, Michael Kamen; prod d, Carol Spier; art d, Barbara Dunphy; fx, Jon G. Belyeu

Arguably the best adaptation of a Stephen King novel, THE DEAD ZONE stars Christopher Walken as Johnny Smith, a shy schoolteacher who leaves his fiancee's house one night during a rainstorm and suffers a near-fatal auto accident. Five years later Johnny comes out of a deep coma, his life forever changed. His fiancee has married another man, his mother has become a religious fanatic, and he has developed the power to see people's futures by touching their hands. After helping to solve a murder and saving the life of a child he "saw" drowning in a vision, Johnny attends a political rally. There he shakes hands with local candidate Greg Stillson (Martin Sheen) and has a spontaneous vision: Stillson will become President and precipitate a nuclear war. As the politician gains power and influence through his calculated right-wing populism, Johnny resolves to assassinate him.

David Cronenberg's first mainstream film, THE DEAD ZONE alienated some genre fans who missed the director's trademark gross-out effects (which made an unforgettable reappearance in his 1986 masterpiece, THE FLY). Here, Cronenberg's well-known obsessions with the human body, disease, and aberrant sexuality take a back seat to another very personal theme—social alienation, as expressed through unconventional ways of seeing. It's also an attack on the destructive impulses associated with masculinity: Sheen's aggressively potent Stillson is insistently contrasted with Johnny, a crippled, anemic Cassandra brilliantly embodied by Christopher Walken.

DEADLY AFFAIR, THE

1966   107m   c   Spy   ★★★½
Columbia   (U.K.)   /15

James Mason *(Charles Dobbs)*, Simone Signoret *(Elsa Fennan)*, Maximilian Schell *(Dieter Frey)*, Harriet Andersson *(Ann Dobbs)*, Harry Andrews *(Inspector Mendel)*, Kenneth Haigh *(Bill Appleby)*, Lynn Redgrave *(Virgin)*, Roy Kinnear *(Adam Scarr)*, Max Adrian *(Adviser)*, Robert Flemyng *(Samuel Fennan)*

p, Sidney Lumet; d, Sidney Lumet; w, Paul Dehn (from the novel *Call for the Dead* by John le Carre); ph, Freddie Young; ed, Thelma Connell; m, Quincy Jones; art d, John Howell; cos, Cynthia Tingey

This is a superior John le Carre novel filmed by Sidney Lumet with an interesting international cast: James Mason, Simone Signoret, Maximilian Schell, Harriet Andersson, Harry Andrews, and Lynn Redgrave. The downbeat spy story captures the mood that made TINKER, TAILOR, SOLDIER, SPY so popular 15 years later. It's also of interest technically because Lumet experimented with "flashing" techniques, exposing the film stock before shooting to give it unusually subdued color. These techniques later became common.

This gritty, moody film is a superb but overlooked entry in the spy genre. Charles Dobbs (James Mason) is a security agent who okays clearance for Samuel Fennan (Robert Flemyng), a top-level official who has been accused of communist activities. When Fennan apparently commits suicide, Dobbs checks into the death and grows suspicious of Elsa Fennan (Simone Signoret), the dead man's widow. Before he can probe too deeply, however, he is taken off the case. Rather than bend to pressure from his superiors, Dobbs resigns, enlists the aid of some fellow agents, and sets out to solve Fennan's murder. Complicating matters is the arrival of Dieter Frey (Maximilian Schell), an agent who is a former friend of Dobbs and is preparing to run off with Dobbs's wife Ann (Harriet Andersson). Though Dobbs is weary of the espionage game, he finds himself more thoroughly enmeshed in it than he has ever been.

The complex plot is actually just a structure to support an insightful look into the lives of these characters. Mason is excellent as a man who knows the spy game for what it is, but still finds himself caught in its machinations. He gets admirable support from Schell, Andersson, and especially Signoret. Lumet's taut direction creates a film that is memorably atmospheric. Le Carre specialized in stripping the movie-fed illusion of glitz and glamour away from the world of espionage to reveal a grim unrewarding milieu where there are no heroes and villains, only people trapped in confusing webs of intrigue and turmoil.

DEALING: OR THE BERKELEY-TO-BOSTON FORTY-BRICK LOST-BAG BLUES

1971   88m   c   Comedy   ★★½
Warner Bros.   (U.S.)   R/

Barbara Hershey *(Susan)*, Robert F. Lyons *(Peter)*, Charles Durning *(Murphy)*, Joy Bang *(Sandra)*, John Lithgow *(John)*, Ellen Barber *(Annie)*, Gene Borkan *(Musty)*, Ted Williams *(Receptionist)*, Demond Wilson *(Rupert)*, Herbert Kerr *(Emir)*

p, Edward R. Pressman; d, Paul Williams; w, Paul Williams, David Odell (based on the novel by Michael and Douglas Crichton); ph, Edward Brown; ed, Sidney Katz; m, Michael Small; prod d, Gene Callahan

Paul Williams directed this interesting time-capsule essay on the way people back then lived on the fringe of the drug culture. The lead, Lyons, is fairly ho-hum but future promise can be detected in the performance of Lithgow as a snobby Harvard student who goes to Berkeley to purchase marijuana to transport back to the Ivy League. Hershey plays the hippie with whom he falls in love. Lithgow would go on to glory on Broadway in plays such as *M. BUTTERFLY*, memorable supporting roles in films like THE WORLD ACCORDING TO GARP and TERMS OF ENDEARMENT. Filmed on location in San Francisco and Boston, this film offers an interesting comparison with THE BIG CHILL, which shows us more or less the same folks a decade later.

DEATH AND THE MAIDEN

1994   103m   c   Drama/Political   ★★★½
Electra Film/City Films/Flach Films/Capitol Films   /18
(U.S./France/U.K.)

Sigourney Weaver *(Paulina Escobar)*, Ben Kingsley *(Roberto Miranda)*, Stuart Wilson *(Gerardo Escobar)*

p, Thom Mount, Josh Kramer; d, Roman Polanski; w, Ariel Dorfman, Rafael Yglesias (based on the play by Ariel Dorfman); ph, Tonino Delli Colli; ed, Herve DeLuze; prod d, Pierre Guffroy; art d, Claude Moesching; fx, Gilbert Pieri, Bruno Lefebvre; cos, Milena Canonero

Set in an unnamed South American country, DEATH AND THE MAIDEN layers elements of a melodramatic thriller over a chamber drama with serious moral and political aspirations.

Paulina Escobar (Sigourney Weaver) is a former torture victim now sharing a respectable, upper-middle class lifestyle with her husband, Gerardo (Stuart Wilson). A prominent lawyer, Gerardo has been invited to head a commission investigating human rights violations under the country's former military regime. When Dr. Roberto Miranda (Ben Kingsley) accompanies Gerardo home after having assisted him with a blown tire, Paulina is immediately certain that this is the man who brutalized her years before. Resolving to seek vengeance and the truth, she begins to subject the doctor to some of the same treatment she endured.

Argentinian writer Ariel Dorfman's internationally celebrated play has been adapted by its author together with Rafael Yglesias (FEARLESS). The material is well served by director Roman Polanski, who knows well how to instill a subtle, claustrophobic sense of dread in an audience and has put together a rather elegant potboiler. Despite DEATH's limited physical setting, the audience never feels trapped in a filmed play, thanks to Tonino Delli Colli's beautiful camerawork, Herve De Luze's fluid editing, and Polanski's mastery of atmosphere and emotional nuance. This is particularly true of the lengthy first scene, which superbly conveys much of Paulina's character and condition *sans* dialogue.

Sigourney Weaver begins the film as an enigmatic, emotionally clipped figure, then becomes as fierce as any of her ALIEN incarnations once her fury toward Roberto is unleashed. It's an impressive performance occasionally marred by self-consciousness; there are moments when we feel Ms. Weaver is rather impressed with herself for tackling so *important* a role. Ben Kingsley, meanwhile, hams up his part with relish, making the sweatiest, pulpiest, most obsequious screen victim since Peter Lorre.

DEATH BECOMES HER

1992   105m   c   Comedy/Fantasy   ★★½
Universal   (U.S.)   PG-13/PG

Meryl Streep *(Madeline Ashton)*, Bruce Willis *(Ernest Menville)*, Goldie Hawn *(Helen Sharp)*, Isabella Rossellini *(Lisle Von Rhuman)*, Sydney Pollack *(Doctor)*, Ian Ogilvy *(Chagall)*, Adam Storke *(Dakota)*, Nancy Fish *(Rose)*, Alaina Reed Hall *(Psychologist)*, Michael Caine p, Robert Zemeckis, Steve Starkey; d, Robert Zemeckis; w, Martin Donovan, David Koepp; ph, Dean Cundey; ed, Arthur Schmidt; m, Alan Silvestri; prod d, Rick Carter; art d, Jim Teegarden; fx, Ken Ralston, Doug Chiang,, Tom Woodruff, Doug Smythe; cos, Joanna Johnston

AA Best Visual Effects: Ken Ralston, Doug Chiang, Doug Smythe, Tom Woodruff

Is it a showbiz melodrama about the rivalry between a faded movie star and a successful author? Is it a black comedy about the unforeseen side effects of a mysterious magic potion? Or is it a spoof horror movie complete with detached body parts and walking dead? Be warned: seeing DEATH BECOMES HER will probably *not* help you answer these questions.

This bizarre combination of SUNSET BOULEVARD, ATTACK OF THE KILLER ZOMBIES, and "Laugh In" stars Meryl Streep as Madeline Ashton, a beautiful, manipulative blonde actress whose star is beginning to fade. After stealing plastic surgeon Ernest Menville (Bruce Willis) from her college "friend" and aspiring author Helen Sharp (Goldie Hawn), Madeline proceeds to ruin Ernest's career and drive him to drink. Meanwhile, Helen, after growing to the size of a blimp and being institutionalized, realizes the only way to get even with Madeline is to become a beautiful, manipulative, blonde author. Throw in a Gothic mansion from which the beautiful, manipulative, raven-haired Lisle von Rhuman (Isabella Rossellini) dispenses a magic potion that guarantees eternal youth, and the mix is complete.

DEATH BECOMES HER boasts some sharply funny dialogue and inventive special effects, and a couple of scenes achieve genuine comic lunacy—notably the film's opening, which finds Madeline starring in "Songbird," a Broadway musical version of Tennessee Williams's "Sweet Bird of Youth" complete with gold lame and disco dancers. Bruce Willis does a good job as the bumbling Dr. Menville, and Meryl Streep's performance is flawless (Streep fans will be pleased to note that, in moments of stress, the actress adds an authentic Newark accent to her impressive repertoire.) The end result, though, is a film that tries to do too many things at once and does none of them quite right.

DEATH IN VENICE
(MORTE A VENEZIA)
1971 130m c Drama   ★★★★½
Alfa/Editions Cinegraphiques   (Italy/France)   GP/15

Dirk Bogarde (*Gustav Von Aschenbach*), Bjorn Andresen (*Tadzio*), Silvana Mangano (*Tadzio's Mother*), Marisa Berenson (*Frau Von Aschenbach*), Mark Burns (*Alfred*), Romolo Valli (*Hotel Manager*), Nora Ricci (*Governess*), Carole Andre (*Esmeralda*), Masha Predit (*Singer*), Leslie French (*Travel Agent*)
p, Luchino Visconti; d, Luchino Visconti; w, Luchino Visconti, Nicola Badalucco (based on the novel by Thomas Mann); ph, Pasqualino De Santis; ed, Ruggero Mastroianni; m, Gustav Mahler, Ludwig van Beethoven, Modest Mussorgsky; art d, Ferdinando Scarfiotti; cos, Piero Tosi

AAN Best Costume Design: Piero Tosi

Luchino Visconti's powerful and controversial screen adaptation of Thomas Mann's novella stars Dirk Bogarde as Gustav von Aschenbach, an aging German composer (modeled after Gustav Mahler) who visits Venice while on the verge of a physical and mental breakdown. Plagued by fears that he can no longer feel emotion because he has been avoiding it for so long, he is unfazed by the boorish and obnoxious behavior of the bourgeois creatures around him. Suddenly, he sees a beautiful blond boy named Tadzio (Bjorn Andresen) who is traveling with his mother and sisters. Gustav becomes obsessed with Tadzio and the ideal of classic beauty he represents. He seeks out the boy, who stirs feelings within him he thought he had lost, but refrains from making contact with him, watching as the lad wanders through the dank, decaying city.

Bogarde is superb as the dying composer. The beautiful cinematography combines with Ferdinando Scarfiotti's art direction to produce a powerful remembrance of time and place past. Visconti also makes effective use of Mahler's Third and Fifth symphonies. The music haunts the film, as do the quiet whispers of sound that help create the film's almost surreal environment. The delicacy of the soundtrack evokes the mood of Aschenbach's last days and his obsession with the face of

Tadzio. DEATH IN VENICE was met with almost universal disapproval and misunderstanding when it was first released but, despite the omissions from Mann's text, dependence on flashbacks, and over-wrought arguments about art and music between Aschenbach and a colleague, it remains a film of great beauty.

DEATH OF A BUREAUCRAT
1966 87m bw Comedy   ★★★
Cuban Film Institute   (Cuba)

Salvador Wood (*Nephew*), Silvia Planas (*Aunt*), Manuel Estanillo (*Bureaucrat*), Gaspar de Santelices (*Nephew's Boss*), Carlos Ruiz de la Tejera (*Psychiatrist*), Omar Alfonso (*Cojimar*), Ricardo Suarez (*Tarafa*), Luis Romay (*El Zorro*), Elsa Montero (*Sabor*)
d, Tomas Guttierez Alea; w, Tomas Guttierez Alea, Alfredo del Cueto, Ramon F. Suarez; ph, Ramon Suarez; ed, Mario Gonzalez; m, Leo Brower

When the inventor of a machine to produce busts of Cuban hero Jose Martin dies, he is hailed as a model worker and given a lavish funeral. Among the honors, he is buried with his union card, which his widow needs to collect a pension from the state. She asks her nephew to help, and he is soon entangled in a bureaucracy that won't let him obtain an exhumation permit until the body has been buried for two years. Desperate, he steals the body out of its grave, then finds he can't rebury it until he shows his exhumation permit. Full of homages to silent comedians like Laurel and Hardy and Harold Lloyd, DEATH OF A BUREAUCRAT is both a classic slapstick and a sly satire on the choking bureaucracy of Cuban Communism. Director Guttierez Alea, whose MEMORIES OF UNDERDEVELOPMENT put him among the first rank of Third World filmmakers, did not go unnoticed in his attack on the government; this film was banned in Cuba after a brief release there in 1966.

DEATH OF A SALESMAN
1952 115m bw Drama   ★★★★
Columbia   (U.S.)   /PG

Fredric March (*Willy Loman*), Mildred Dunnock (*Linda Loman*), Kevin McCarthy (*Biff*), Cameron Mitchell (*Happy*), Howard Smith (*Charley*), Royal Beal (*Ben*), Don Keefer (*Bernard*), Jesse White (*Stanley*), Claire Carleton (*Miss Francis*), David Alpert (*Howard Wagner*)
p, Stanley Kramer; d, Laslo Benedek; w, Stanley Roberts (based on the play by Arthur Miller); ph, Franz Planer; ed, William Lyon, Harry Gerstad; m, Alex North; prod d, Rudolph Sternad; art d, Cary Odell

AAN Best Actor: Fredric March; *AAN Best Supporting Actor:* Kevin McCarthy; *AAN Best Supporting Actress:* Mildred Dunnock; *AAN Best Cinematography:* Franz Planer; *AAN Best Score:* Alex North

With Fredric March and Kevin McCarthy, this is a very good record of the classic American stage play. Arthur Miller never fared as well again. His somber stage play retained much of its power in this film version featuring one of March's greatest performances as the end-of-the-line Willy Loman.

Willy is incapable of changing a lifestyle and career that are lost in the past. He is in his early sixties and, after being fired, has nowhere to go, clinging to his petty, mediocre values and looking backward with soul-wrenching agony. He has a long-suffering wife, Linda (Dunnock), and two sons, Biff (McCarthy) and Happy (Mitchell). The older son, Biff, is an average business success but has no spirit. Happy is disillusioned after losing his job and has no motivation to find another. The sons share the spiritual malaise of their father. The film powerfully depicts Willy relentlessly plodding to his doom, looking for redemption inside empty rooms of the past and babbling cliches to the apparition of his long-vanished brother.

Lee J. Cobb gave what many consider the definitive performance as Willy in the original 1949 stage hit, and Dustin Hoffman applied his considerable talent to project a tragic Willy in a 1985 TV presentation, though his portrayal is really a caricature. March is excellent if ultimately inferior to Cobb who reportedly was "reverse blacklisted" for his friendly testimony before HUAC during the McCarthy era. Still March looked, felt, and understood the part completely, bringing the character to life as the playwright envisioned him. Kramer's production and Benedek's direction are equally faithful to Miller's vision. Although DEATH OF A SALESMAN lost money at the box office, it stands as one of the great theatrical classics on film.

DEATH RACE 2000

1975 78m c Action/Science Fiction ★★★
New World (U.S.) R/18

David Carradine (*Frankenstein*), Simone Griffeth (*Annie*), Sylvester Stallone (*Machine Gun Joe Viterbo*), Mary Woronov (*Calamity Jane*), Roberta Collins (*Mathilda the Hun*), Martin Kove (*Nero the Hero*), Louisa Moritz (*Myra*), Don Steele (*Junior Bruce*)

p, Roger Corman; d, Paul Bartel; w, Robert Thom, Charles B. Griffith (based on a story by Ib Melchior); ph, Tak Fujimoto; ed, Tina Hirsch; m, Paul Chihara; art d, Robin Royce, B.B. Neel; fx, Richard MacLean

Superior drive-in exploitation fare, this violent, campy action flick presents Carradine as Frankenstein, a scarred road warrior in black leather suit and cape. He's the formidable defending champion in the nationally televised Transcontinental Death Race in which competitors gain points by running over pedestrians. His challengers include Stallone as sort of a gangster on wheels with a machine gun in his car and Woronov as a western-outlaw Amazon. Carradine's navigator, Griffeth, is actually a revolutionary spy dedicated to sabatating the savage race.

DEATH RACE 2000 boasts nonstop brutally funny comic-book action. Intended as a rip-off of the big-budget ROLLERBALL, this likably ragged knockoff has become a cult favorite, while its bombastic inspiration has been consigned to the junk heap of genre movie history. The success of this film is a testament to producer Roger Corman's shrewd exploitation of promising filmmakers under the aegis of his New World production company. This legendary "B-minus" movie factory was formed in 1970 and attracted bright young filmmakers eager to break into the Guild-controlled industry. As a case in point, the film's director, Paul Bartel (who would later direct EATING RAOUL and SCENES FROM THE CLASS STRUGGLE IN BEVERLY HILLS), was paid $3,500 for his work on this profitable production.

DEATH TAKES A HOLIDAY

1934 79m bw Fantasy/Romance ★★★★
Paramount (U.S.) /A

Fredric March (*Prince Sirki*), Evelyn Venable (*Grazia*), Guy Standing (*Duke Lambert*), Katherine Alexander (*Alda*), Gail Patrick (*Rhoda*), Helen Westley (*Stephanie*), Kathleen Howard (*Princess Maria*), Kent Taylor (*Corrado*), Henry Travers (*Baron Cesarea*), G.P. Huntley Jr. (*Eric*)

p, E. Lloyd Sheldon; d, Mitchell Leisen; w, Maxwell Anderson, Gladys Lehman, Walter Ferris (based on the play by Alberto Casella); ph, Charles Lang; art d, Hans Dreier, Ernst Fegte

Fredric March, as Death, becomes bored with his usual grim-reaping job and is puzzled that humans fear him so. To learn how he is perceived, he takes on human form as a handsome young prince and becomes the houseguest of an Italian nobleman (Guy Standing). Several guests are quickly repelled by the strange, mysterious prince who bluntly talks of their "meeting with Fate," but a lovely, mystical young woman (Evelyn Venable) is drawn to him. Not a living thing dies as Death dallies with love, and so his stay must be brief. But the unusual visitor fears that his new love will be repelled once he reveals his true identity.

March is riveting as Death, and Standing is also fine as the nervous host. Surprisingly, Paramount assigned the direction of this film to Mitchell Leisen, who had only one previous credit, CRADLE SONG. He was given a sumptuous budget and made the most of it. His background as a set designer for Cecil B. DeMille is evident in the magnificent villa in which March frolicked with Venable. Leisen, who would go on to make HOLD BACK THE DAWN and LADY IN THE DARK, rarely equalled the splendor of this film. He let March have his head, and the actor played his part with ironic vigor, wearing a monocle and delivering his lines in a Balkan accent with great arrogance. Of course, March could do almost no wrong, having won an Oscar only two years earlier for his arresting performance in DR. JEKYLL AND

MR. HYDE. (He would win his second for THE BEST YEARS OF OUR LIVES.) The 21-year-old Venable, appearing in her second film, had previously starred in CRADLE SONG.

DEATH WATCH
(LA MORT EN DIRECT)

1980 128m c Science Fiction ★★★½
Selta/Little Bear/Sara/Antenne 2/TV 13/Gaumont R/15
(France/West Germany)

Romy Schneider (*Katherine Mortenhoe*), Harvey Keitel (*Roddy*), Harry Dean Stanton (*Vincent Ferriman*), Therese Liotard (*Tracey*), Max von Sydow (*Gerald Mortenhoe*), Bernhard Wicki, Caroline Langrishe, William Russell

p, Gabriel Boustiani, Janine Rubeiz; d, Bertrand Tavernier; w, David Rayfiel, Bertrand Tavernier (based on the novel *The Continuous Katherine Mortenhoe* by David Compton); ph, Pierre-William Glenn; ed, Armand Psenny, Michael Ellis; m, Antoine Duhamel; art d, Anthony Pratt

For followers of Bertrand Tavernier who know the director only through A SUNDAY IN THE COUNTRY or 'ROUND MIDNIGHT, the very realistic science-fiction film DEATH WATCH may come as a surprise. Set in Glasgow, the film takes place in a not-too-distant future when nearly all diseases have been conquered by medical science, leaving natural causes as society's prime killer. Katherine (Romy Schneider) is an independent, sensitive, and beautiful woman who has contracted a terminal disease; Vincent Ferriman (Harry Dean Stanton) is a crass television producer who finds her imminent demise perfect entertainment for a society that can't get enough of death; and Roddy (Harvey Keitel) is an employee who had a video camera implanted in his head, sending everything he sees back to the TV station for editing and broadcast. As Roddy follows Katherine through the countryside, in effect shooting a narrative film, he finds himself becoming attracted to her.

More than just a simple attack on electronic information in a modern technological society, DEATH WATCH (which can been seen as Tavernier's "Peeping Tom") also addresses the issue of the objectification of women and depersonalization of death via the (implicitly male-oriented) media.

DECLINE OF THE AMERICAN EMPIRE, THE
(LE DECLIN DE L'EMPIRE AMERICAIN)

1986 101m c Drama ★★★½
Malo/Natl. Film Board of Canada/Telefilm Canada/Cinema Du R/18
Quebec (Canada)

Pierre Curzi (*Pierre*), Remy Girard (*Remy*), Yves Jacques (*Claude*), Daniel Briere (*Alain*), Dominique Michel (*Dominique*), Louise Portal (*Diane*), Dorothee Berryman (*Louise*), Genevieve Rioux (*Danielle*), Gabriel Arcand (*Mario*)

p, Rene Malo, Roger Frappier; d, Denys Arcand; w, Denys Arcand; ph, Guy Dufaux; ed, Monique Fortier; m, Francois Dompierre; art d, Gaudeline Sauriol; cos, Denis Sperdouklis

AAN Best Foreign Language Film

Four men swap stories of their sexual escapades while preparing an elaborate dinner. Four women do the same while working out in a gym. When the two groups come together, mutual betrayals come to light and shatter some illusions. On the surface this is all that happens in this fine film, one of the most successful Canadian exports ever, but the sparkling wit of the dialogue and the acutely observed jabs at our eternal preoccupation with sex distinguish THE DECLINE OF THE AMERICAN EMPIRE. The film's philosophy could best be summed up in a line uttered by one of the men: "Love—the kind that makes your heart race—lasts two years at best. Then the compromises begin." Perhaps the most valid criticism of the film is that its questions are too easy, its answers too pat, and its characters too similar. On the other hand, the ensemble performance is impeccable, the technical credits flawless, and the whole thing quite enjoyable.

DEEP COVER

1992 112m c Crime/Thriller ★★★½
New Line/Image Organization (U.S.) R/18

Laurence Fishburne *(Russell Stevens Jr./John Q. Hull)*, Jeff Goldblum *(David Jason)*, Victoria Dillard *(Betty McCutcheon)*, Charles Martin Smith *(Jerry Carver)*, Clarence Williams III *(Ken Taft)*, Gregory Sierra *(Felix Barbosa)*, Rene Assa *(Hector Guzman)*, Alex Colon *(Molto)*, Roger Guenveur Smith *(Eddie)*, Sydney Lassick *(Gopher)*

p, Henry Bean, Pierre David; d, Bill Duke; w, Henry Bean, Michael Tolkin (from his story); ph, Bojan Bazelli; ed, John Carter; m, Michel Colombier; prod d, Pam Warner; art d, Daniel W. Bickel; cos, Arlene Gant

DEEP COVER takes us over a lot of familiar territory, with a plot that reads like a compendium of recent crime movies.

There's an undercover narcotics cop who begins to lose sight of which side he's on (RUSH); a plentiful helping of drugs and violence (NEW JACK CITY); a smuggling ring protected by diplomatic immunity (LETHAL WEAPON 2); and a corrupt political system which greases the wheels of organized crime at the expense of the officer on the street (Q & A).

The pleasant surprise is that DEEP COVER puts a fresh, original spin on its second-hand subject matter. Screenwriters Michael Tolkin (THE PLAYER) and Henry Bean (INTERNAL AFFAIRS) have injected intelligence and wit into the drama, fleshing out the moral dilemma of a man who is forced to kill and deal drugs in the name of justice. ("Am I a cop pretending to be a drug dealer, or a drug dealer pretending to be a cop?") Veteran black director Bill Duke (A RAGE IN HARLEM) has achieved a visual style that is both edgy and lyrical, a fiercely contemporary blend that mirrors the contradictions of his hero's world.

Duke has also drawn outstanding performances from Larry Fishburne, as undercover policeman John Q. Hull; and the incomparable Jeff Goldblum who, as Hull's lawyer partner, develops from an amoral wimp into a greedy, reptilian killer. DEEP COVER has a shaky beginning and a hokey ending but, somewhere in between, it becomes a movie of considerable power—largely thanks to the contrasting styles of its two stars. Fishburne radiates sullen intensity, while Golblum is the essence of superficiality, a man with a witty riposte for almost any occasion. The chemistry between the two creates some of the film's best moments, when tragedy—or, at least, violence—is juxtaposed with high humor in a style reminiscent of GOODFELLAS. It's an unsettling yet compelling blend, and probably one you don't want to think about too much.

DEER HUNTER, THE

1978 183m c War ★★★★½
EMI/Universal (U.S.) R/18

Robert De Niro *(Michael)*, John Cazale *(Stan)*, John Savage *(Steven)*, Christopher Walken *(Nick)*, Meryl Streep *(Linda)*, George Dzundza *(John)*, Chuck Aspegren *(Axel)*, Shirley Stoler *(Steven's Mother)*, Rutanya Alda *(Angela)*, Pierre Segui *(Julien)*

p, Barry Spikings, Michael Deeley, Michael Cimino, John Peverall; d, Michael Cimino; w, Deric Washburn (based on a story by Cimino, Washburn, Louis Garfinkle, and Quinn K. Redeker); ph, Vilmos Zsigmond; ed, Peter Zinner; m, Stanley Myers; art d, Ron Hobbs, Kim Swados; fx, Fred Cramer; cos, Eric Seelig

AA Best Picture; AAN Best Actor: Robert DeNiro; *AA Best Supporting Actor:* Christopher Walken; *AAN Best Supporting Actress:* Meryl Streep; *AA Best Director:* Michael Cimino; *AAN Best Original Screenplay:* Michael Cimino, Deric Washburn, Louis Garfinkle, Quinn K. Redeker; *AAN Best Cinematography:* Vilmos Zsigmond; *AA Best Editing:* Peter Zinner; *AA Best Sound:* Richard Portman, William McCaughey, Aaron Rochin, Darin Knight

Director Michael Cimino's epic look at how the Vietnam War affected a small Pennsylvania steel community was a huge hit at the box office and garnered several awards, including a Best Picture Oscar. Though its emotional power is undeniable, the film has been justifiably criticized for its somewhat thoughtlessly slanted view of the war and its implicitly racist depiction of the Vietnamese.

Three hours long and neatly divided into three acts, the film follows a trio of close friends—Michael (Robert De Niro), Nick (Christopher Walken) and Steven (John Savage)—from the eve of their tour of duty in Vietnam to the resumption of their interrupted lives. Just before their departure, the steelworkers attend Steven's wedding to Angela (Rutanya Alda); later, Michael and Nick go deer hunting with friends Axel (Chuck Aspegren), Stan (John Cazale) and John (George Dzundza). After the hunt, the film rudely cuts to the heat of battle in Vietnam. Michael, Nick and Steven are all taken prisoner by the Viet Cong and are forced to play Russian roulette while their captors make bets on the outcome. When they finally return home, readjustment is difficult. Steven is embittered and disabled. Nick has chosen to remain in Vietnam and has been sending hundreds of dollars to Steven without explanation. Determined to bring his friend back, Michael returns to Vietnam just as Saigon is about to fall.

Brutally memorable, THE DEER HUNTER is an emotionally draining production that draws a vivid portrait of its characters and their milieu—and succeeds in showing the devastating effect of the war on their lives, as well as their brave attempts at renewal. Unfortunately, the film falters when it comes to the larger questions of America's involvement in Vietnam.

DEFENCE OF THE REALM

1985 96m c Political/Thriller ★★★½
Enigma (U.K.) PG

Gabriel Byrne *(Nick Mullen)*, Greta Scacchi *(Nina Beckman)*, Denholm Elliott *(Vernon Bayliss)*, Ian Bannen *(Dennis Markham)*, Fulton Mackay *(Victor Kingsbrook)*, Bill Paterson *(Jack Macleod)*, David Calder *(Harry Champion)*, Frederick Treves *(Arnold Reece)*, Robbie Coltrane *(Leo McAskey)*, Annabel Leventon *(Trudy Markham)*

p, Robin Douet, Lynda Myles; d, David Drury; w, Martin Stellman; ph, Roger Deakins; ed, Michael Bradsell; m, Richard Harvey; prod d, Roger Murray-Leach; art d, Diana Charnley; cos, Louise Frogley

This fascinating conspiracy thriller hinges on two seemingly unrelated occurrences: two teenagers' attempted escape from a reformatory and a political scandal involving Dennis Markham (Ian Bannen), a distinguished member of Parliament. When the papers proclaim that Markham was observed leaving the home of a courtesan who was also cozy with an East German official, his loyalty to his country is questioned and his career ruined. Hack reporter Nick Mullen (Gabriel Byrne) is assigned to the story. When a colleague who is also interested in the story mysteriously dies, Mullen digs deeper and finds evidence of a shocking covert operation. With the help of his late colleague's secretary, Nina Beckman (Greta Scacchi), he battles to bring the truth to light.

An extremely well made film, DEFENCE OF THE REALM features a strong central performance by Byrne (GOTHIC, SIESTA, MILLER'S CROSSING), a typically marvelous turn by Elliott as his besotted elder journalist friend, and the beautiful Scacchi (THE COCA-COLA KID, PRESUMED INNOCENT). The direction and editing are fast and tight, and the script by Martin Stellman (who also cowrote the superb QUADROPHENIA) has intelligent and tight plotting rare in this kind of film.

DEFIANT ONES, THE

1958 97m bw Prison ★★★★
UA (U.S.) /PG

Tony Curtis *(John Jackson)*, Sidney Poitier *(Noah Cullen)*, Theodore Bikel *(Sheriff Max Muller)*, Charles McGraw *(Captain Frank Gibbons)*, Lon Chaney, Jr. *(Big Sam)*, King Donovan *(Solly)*, Claude Akins *(Mac)*, Lawrence Dobkin *(Editor)*, Whit Bissell *(Lou Gans)*, Cara Williams *(The Woman)*

p, Stanley Kramer; d, Stanley Kramer; w, Nedrick Young, Harold Jacob Smith; ph, Sam Leavitt; ed, Frederic Knudtson; m, Ernest Gold; prod d, Rudolph Sternad; art d, Fernando Carrere; fx, Alex Weldon; cos, Joe King

AAN Best Picture; AAN Best Actor: Tony Curtis; *AAN Best Actor:* Sidney Poitier; *AAN Best Supporting Actor:* Theodore Bikel; *AAN Best Supporting Actress:* Cara Williams; *AAN Best Director:* Stanley

Kramer; *AA Best Story and Screenplay:* Nathan E. Douglas, Harold Jacob Smith; *AA Best Cinematography:* Sam Leavitt; *AAN Best Editing:* Frederic Knudtson

Tony Curtis and Sidney Poitier are handcuffed together as white and Black escaped convicts in the South in this classic liberal adventure from Stanley Kramer. Their plight is an all-too-obvious metaphor for American race relations. Though the political lesson drives the movie, the action is also effective as the odd couple flees from their oppressors. This is an engrossing depiction of racial tensions and an oppressive penal system. Both Poitier and Curtis give memorable performances. Curtis's portrayal of a bigoted uneducated Southern "cracker" is probably the best performance and role of his career. This was the film that established Poitier as a star.

DELICATESSEN

1991 97m c Comedy/Fantasy   ★★★★
Constellation Production/Union Generale   R/15
Cinematographique/Hachette Premiere   (France)

Marie-Laure Dougnac *(Julie Clapet)*, Dominique Pinon *(Louison)*, Karin Viard *(Miss Plusse)*, Jean-Claude Dreyfus *(The Butcher)*, Ticky Holgado *(Mr. Tapioca)*, Anne-Marie Pisani *(Mrs. Tapioca)*, Edith Ker *(The Grandmother)*, Mickael Todde *(Lucien)*, Boban Janevski *(Remi)*, Jacques Mathou *(Roger Kube)*

p, Claude Ossard; d, Jean-Pierre Jeunet, Marc Caro; w, Adrien Gilles (screenplay); ph, Darius Khondji; ed, Herve Schneid; m, Carlos D'Alessi; prod d, Jean-Philippe Carp, Kreka Kjnakovic; cos, Valerie Pozzo DiBorgo

Cannibalism serves as a potent metaphor for social oppression in DELICATESSEN, the darkly stylish feature debut by French animators Jean-Pierre Jeunet and Marc Caro.

This surreal, blackly comic fable is set in a run-down apartment building sometime in a dystopian future. The landlord of the building also runs the butcher shop on the ground floor, and keeps his tenants supplied with meat by chopping up hapless applicants for the job of building superintendent. The problem is that the butcher's mousey, nearsighted daughter, Julie Clapet (Marie-Laure Dougnac), keeps falling in love with these sirloins-to-be. In the past, gastronomical necessity has overcome romantic yearning. However, she insists that the newest arrival, Louison (Dominique Pinon, who made such an indelible impression in Jean-Jacques Beineix's DIVA), is different. The butcher doesn't believe her, but something makes him hold off from doing in the newest superintendent until well after the neighbors begin complaining about the lack of meat in their diet.

DELICATESSEN is not as grisly as its premise might suggest. Much of the mayhem and violence takes place offscreen, and the main stylistic influences are Carne, Prevert, Dali and Bunuel, rather than Tobe Hooper. Carno and Jeunet construct a series of vignettes—some hilarious, some grotesque—of the tenants, often as seen through the eyes of two spying little boys. They include an old man who keeps his basement apartment flooded to raise escargots (one of the *slimiest* scenes in screen history); a prim matron who hears mysterious voices—actually a malicious upstairs neighbor speaking through the building vents—telling her to do away with herself (something she attempts, via a series of elaborate Rube Goldberg-style set-ups); and two brothers who support themselves by constructing moo-ing noisemakers. Into this bizarre, painstakingly rendered universe wanders the new superintendent, a former clown still mourning the death of his "partner," a chimpanzee who came to an ugly end when he was eaten by other members of their circus troupe. Though not for all tastes, DELICATESSEN is an ingeniously funny film with a surprisingly sweet romance at its center.

DELIVERANCE

1972 109m c Adventure   ★★★★
Warner Bros. (U.S.)   R/18

Jon Voight *(Ed)*, Burt Reynolds *(Lewis)*, Ned Beatty *(Bobby)*, Ronny Cox *(Drew)*, Bill McKinney *(Mountain Man)*, Herbert "Cowboy" Coward *(Toothless Man)*, James Dickey *(Sheriff Bullard)*, Ed Ramey *(Old Man)*, Billy Redden *(Lonny)*, Seamon Glass *(1st Griner)*

p, John Boorman; d, John Boorman; w, James Dickey (based on his novel); ph, Vilmos Zsigmond; ed, Tom Priestley; m, Eric Weissberg; art d, Fred Harpman; fx, Marcel Vercoutere; cos, Bucky Rous

AAN Best Picture; AAN Best Director: John Boorman; *AAN Best Editing:* Tom Priestley

Morose, shockingly violent yet strangely beautiful, DELIVERANCE is a tale of what happens to civilized values when put to the test in a hostile wilderness environment. Four Atlanta businessmen decide to get back to nature by treking to the Appalachian wilds to canoe, hunt, and fish in an unspoiled environment before it is permanently flooded by a new dam. But what begins as an adventurous vacation becomes a nightmare of survival as they find themselves hunted by vengeful cretinous mountain men. Voight, Reynolds, Beatty, and Cox are the four city dwellers looking to prove their manhood in the wild. Each of their personal values is put to the test in the course of their deadly adventure. What does it mean to be a man? How far will one go to survive?

This is a tough and powerful portrait of men out of their usual environment. Nor is the deplorable squalor of the mountain communities glossed over. This is not a film for the squeamish. Some have accused the film of exploiting rather than exploring the moments of violent drama culled from James Dickey's first novel while deemphasizing its ecological concerns. Others were troubled by the seemingly perverse beauty of the film. All agree, however, that the meeting between the uneasy quartet and a deformed albino mountain child is a highlight. Cox sees that the kid has a banjo, picks up his own, and strums a few notes. The boy answers him. Then the two challenge each other until both go at a frenzied pace banging out a mountain tune. This celebrated "Duelling Banjos" sequence is an eerie moment of grace before the violence begins.

Boorman's direction is gripping if a bit heavy-handed. The rapids scenes in particular are electrifying. Cinematographer Zsigmond presents breathtaking scenes that sear the memory. Reynolds excelled in this rare serious role. Dickey adapted his own novel and appears as a sheriff.

DEMENTIA 13

1963 81m bw Horror   ★★★
Filmgroup (U.S.)

William Campbell *(Richard Haloran)*, Luana Anders *(Louise Haloran)*, Bart Patton *(Billy Haloran)*, Mary Mitchell *(Kane)*, Patrick Magee *(Justin Caleb)*, Eithne Dunne *(Lady Haloran)*, Peter Read *(John Haloran)*, Karl Schanzer *(Simon)*, Ron Perry *(Arthur)*, Derry O'Donovan *(Lillian)*

p, Roger Corman, Charles Hannawalt, R. Wright Campbell; d, Francis Ford Coppola; w, Francis Ford Coppola; ph, Charles Hannawalt; ed, Stuart O'Brien; m, Ronald Stein; art d, Albert Locatelli

Francis Ford Coppola's first mainstream feature (after a few unremarkable skin flicks) is a little gem of gothic horror, stylishly helmed on a shoestring budget. As an eccentric Irish family bickers over a vast inheritance in a lonely mansion, a mysterious axe murderer picks them off one by one.

The film opens with a violent argument between John (Peter Read) and his wife, Louise (Luana Anders), over the disputed will of his eccentric mother (Eithne Dunne). The argument becomes so heated that John is stricken with a heart attack and dies. Desperate to save her share of the inheritance, Louise sinks her husband's body in a nearby lake and conceals his death from other family members. Meanwhile, more relatives have arrived at the estate (Bart Patton, William Campbell, and Mary Mitchell as Campbell's fiancee) to attend a memorial ceremony for their sister, who drowned in the lake eight years before. Louise sees an opportunity to drive her mother-in-law completely bonkers, persuading her that she's made psychic contact with the dead woman. Howver, before Louise can execute her scheme, she's axed to death, and the hunt for the killer is on.

The film that launched Francis Ford Coppola began as an afterthought. While serving as sound man on Corman's THE YOUNG RACERS, Coppola dashed off a screenplay for a quickie gothic chiller and persuaded the producer to finance the film. Corman supplied $22,000 and several of his stars. Though the plot is rather silly and labored, the film rises above the material by virtue of Coppola's clever editing and obvious flair for composition. The film opens with a typical

Corman promotional device: a "psychiatrist" sits in his office and gives the audience a test to determine if they are mentally stable enough to see the movie.

DEMOLITION MAN

1993 115m c Action/Comedy ★★★
Silver Pictures (U.S.) R/15

Sylvester Stallone (Sergeant John Spartan), Wesley Snipes (Simon Phoenix), Sandra Bullock (Lenina Huxley), Nigel Hawthorne (Dr. Raymond Cocteau), Benjamin Bratt (Alfredo Garcia), Bob Gunton (Chief George Earle), Glenn Shadix (Associate Bob), Denis Leary (Edgar Friendly), Grand Bush (Zachary Lamb (Young)), Andre Gregory (Warden William Smithers (Aged))

p, Joel Silver, Michael Levy, Howard Kazanjian; d, Marco Brambilla; w, Daniel Waters, Robert Reneau, Peter M. Lenkov, Jonathan Lemkin (from a story by Reneau and Lenkov); ph, Alex Thomson, Tom Priestley; ed, Stuart Baird; m, Elliot Goldenthal; prod d, David L. Snyder; art d, Walter P. Martishius; fx, Michael McAlister, Kimberly K. Nelson; cos, Bob Ringwood

Tofu-eating proponents of PC can look forward to the future with confidence, at least if they live in Los Angeles. According to DEMOLITION MAN, LA (actually, San Angeles) in the year 2035 will be a place where violence is unheard of, "hello" has been replaced by the phrase "mellow greetings," and everything "bad for you"—cigarettes, alcohol, hamburgers, coffee, sugar—has been outlawed.

Somewhat out of place in this anemic paradise are John Spartan (Sylvester Stallone), a maverick cop, and Simon Phoenix (Wesley Snipes), a superpsychocriminal, both of whom have recently emerged from extended stays in a deep-freeze prison facility. Phoenix has escaped and begun to wreak havoc in a world where the police have no guns; Spartan has been released in a desperate attempt to hunt him down.

The pleasant surprise about DEMOLITION MAN is that both the script, and Stallone, are funny; the film blends big-budget action and tongue-in-cheek humor in the way that LAST ACTION HERO tried, and failed, to do. The future world has been conceived with a gently satirical eye toward the late 20th century, with citizens speaking in CONEHEADS-style euphemisms ("enhance your calm"), admiring the "Hall of Violence" (including a preserved LA city block) at the Museum of History, and referring those interested in studying the past to the President Schwarzenegger Memorial Library. It could never happen here.

DERSU UZALA
(DERUSU USARA)

1975 137m c Adventure ★★★½
Toho/Mosfilm (U.S.S.R./Japan) /U

Maxim Munzuk (Dersu Uzala), Yuri Solomine (Capt. Vladimir Arseniev), Schemeikl Chokmorov (Jan Bao), Vladimir Klemena (Turtwigin), Svetlana Danielchanka (Mrs. Arseniev)

p, Nikolai Sizov, Yoichi Matsue; d, Akira Kurosawa; w, Akira Kurosawa, Yuri Nagibin (based on the journals of Vladimir Arseniev); ph, Asakazu Nakai, Yuri Gantman, Fyodor Dobronavov; m, Isaac Schwalz; prod d, Yuri Raksha

AA Best Foreign Language Film

Captain Vladimir Arseniev (Solomine), leading a topographic expedition deep into the wilds of 19th-century Siberia, meets an old woodsman, Dersu Uzula (Munzuk), who shows him the ways of nature. The two men become close friends over a number of expeditions in which Uzula acts as guide. Each time Arseniev tries to convince the hardy but aging Siberian to return to the city with him, the latter refuses. Finally Uzala does go to the city, but he finds that he cannot readily adapt.

Akira Kurosawa filmed in the USSR with an all-Soviet cast, but a Japanese cinematographer, Asakazu Nakai, photographed the production in 70mm. The first half is wonderful, full of reverence for nature and the man who lives in it. However, it becomes increasingly obvious, literal, and rather ponderous as it progresses. Still these faults cannot detract from DERSU UZALA's magnificence. Like so much of Kurosawa's work, this is a film of great humanism and respect.

DESERT FOX, THE

1951 88m bw War/Biography ★★★½
Fox (U.S.) /PG

James Mason (Erwin Rommel), Cedric Hardwicke (Dr. Karl Strolin), Jessica Tandy (Frau Rommel), Luther Adler (Hitler), Everett Sloane (Gen. Burgdorf), Leo G. Carroll (Field Marshal Von Rundstedt), George Macready (Gen. Fritz Bayerlein), Richard Boone (Aldinger), Eduard Franz (Col. Von Stauffenberg), Desmond Young (Himself)

p, Nunnally Johnson; d, Henry Hathaway; w, Nunnally Johnson (based on the biography by Desmond Young); ph, Norbert Brodine; ed, James B. Clark; m, Daniele Amfitheatrof; art d, Lyle Wheeler, Maurice Ransford; fx, Fred Sersen, Ray Kellogg

The first film that attempted to humanize a WWII German military leader, THE DESERT FOX features a magnetic performance by James Mason as Hitler's greatest field commander, Field Marshal Erwin Rommel—grudgingly respected by his opponents, loyally followed by men of the *Afrika Korps*. Opening with a British commando raid on Rommel's headquarters, the film traces the general's remarkable career from his early success in North Africa to his defeat at El Alamein (where he disregarded Hitler's "victory or death" command and retreated), his later illness, his command of the French coastal defenses, and his role in a failed attempt to assassinate Hitler. This last act led to his high-command-mandated, face-saving suicide.

Though Mason is the main attraction in this fragmentary biopic, the supporting cast is excellent (particularly Luther Adler's unforgettable cameo as Hitler). Henry Hathaway's semi-documentary-style direction is as brisk as a panzer attack and Nunnally Johnson's script is literate and penetrating. Mason's sympathetic portrait of Rommel is in marked contrast with other cinematic treatments of the general: Erich Von Stroheim in FIVE GRAVES TO CAIRO, Albert Lieven in FOXHOLE IN CAIRO, Werner Hinz in THE LONGEST DAY, Gregory Gay in HITLER, Christopher Plummer in THE NIGHT OF THE GENERALS, Wolfgang Preiss in RAID ON ROMMEL, Karl Michael Vogler in PATTON and Mason, once more, in THE DESERT RATS.

DESERT HEARTS

1985 96m c Drama/Erotic ★★★½
Desert Hearts (U.S.) R/18

Helen Shaver (Vivian Bell), Patricia Charbonneau (Cay Rivvers), Audra Lindley (Frances Parker), Andra Akers (Silver), Gwen Welles (Gwen), Dean Butler (Darell), James Staley (Art Warner), Katie La Bourdette (Lucille), Alex McArthur (Walter), Antony Ponzini (Joe Lorenzo)

p, Donna Deitch; d, Donna Deitch; w, Natalie Cooper (based on the novel *Desert of the Heart* by Jane Rule); ph, Robert Elswit; ed, Robert Estrin; prod d, Jeannine Claudia Oppewall

Though not without problems, DESERT HEARTS is a triumph for director Donna Deitch and an inspiration for any independent filmmaker. Determined to develop a feature film depicting a sexual relationship between two women—a topic never done justice in an American commercial release—Deitch adapted Jane Rule's novel *Desert of the Heart*. The story opens in Reno, Nevada, in 1959. Helen Shaver is Vivian Bell, a college professor from New York, staying in Reno temporarily to obtain a divorce. She stays at Frances Parker's (Audra Lindley) small ranch outside of town. Also living there is Cay Rivvers (Patricia Charbonneau), an employee at one of the local casinos, who is more like a daughter to Parker than a tenant. Bell and Rivvers gradually become close friends but, when their relationship changes, others are affected as well.

Deitch deals sensitively with her theme, eliciting fine performances from her two leads. Charbonneau, after a memorable entrance worthy of the coolest of screen male lovers, portrays Rivvers as a fiery natural force. Shavers's portrayal of the repressed college professor with her hair in a tight bun is a model of restraint and latent passion. We know that when this cool lady finally melts, it will be something to see. The film falters a bit with some of the plot development, a reflection, no doubt, of Deitch's budget rather than her talent. DESERT HEARTS unfolds in a format typical for commercial filmmaking, which isn't a detriment, but doesn't allow for some of the more complicated emotions and issues within the story to surface.

DESIRE

1936 89m bw Romance ★★★★
Paramount (U.S.) /A

Marlene Dietrich *(Madeleine de Beaupre)*, Gary Cooper *(Tom Bradley)*, John Halliday *(Carlos Margoli)*, William Frawley *(Mr. Gibson)*, Ernest Cossart *(Aristide Duval)*, Akim Tamiroff *(Police Official)*, Alan Mowbray *(Dr. Edouard Pauquet)*, Zeffie Tilbury *(Aunt Olga)*, Enrique Acosta *(Pedro)*, Stanley Andrews *(Customs Inspector)*

p, Ernst Lubitsch; d, Frank Borzage; w, Edwin Justus Mayer, Waldemar Young, Samuel Hoffenstein (based on an original story by Hans Szekeley and R.A. Stemmle); ph, Charles Lang, Victor Milner; ed, William Shea; m, Frederick Hollander; art d, Hans Dreier, Robert Usher; cos, Travis Banton

Clearly the product of a gilded cocktail shaker. Bearing the stylistic stamps of both producer Lubitsch and director Borzage, this is a sophisticated romantic comedy about a lovely jewel thief, Madeleine de Beaupre (Dietrich), who tricks a gem dealer (Cossart) out of a priceless string of pearls and flees Paris after implicating a stuffy psychiatrist (Mowbray). She drives wildly toward the Spanish border and nearly runs down Tom Bradley (Cooper), a young American engineer on vacation. She uses him as an unwitting accomplice in smuggling the pearls out of the country. Cleared by Spanish customs, he drives off with Madeleine in hot pursuit. The romantic chase is on! What began as mere expediency soon develops into love—with numerous complications along the way, of course.

Successful with the public, DESIRE was one of the most elegantly produced films of the 1930s; the sets, costumes, and decor all shimmer with hot light. Borzage, who also directed the silent classic SEVENTH HEAVEN, added his sweetly romantic warmth to the deft, spicy production plans already laid out by Lubitsch for this wonderful film. Playing with both conviction and wit, Dietrich achieves one of her best performances away from mentor Josef von Sternberg; here she is slightly less exotic and rather more human than in her other films. Cooper, too, in his second pairing with Dietrich (after the memorable MOROCCO) really shows his flair for sophisticated romance with this one. He makes the most of the funny yet impossibly romantic line, "All I know about you is you stole my car and I'm insane about you." The remarkable John Halliday, whose presence graces any film, leads a terrific supporting cast. One of the ultimate expressions of Paramount Studios chic, DESIRE remains one of its desirable star's finest films.

DESPERATE CHARACTERS

1971 87m c Drama ★★★½
ITC (U.S.)

Shirley MacLaine *(Sophie)*, Kenneth Mars *(Otto)*, Gerald S. O'Loughlin *(Charlie)*, Sada Thompson *(Claire)*, Jack Somack *(Leon)*, Chris Gampel *(Mike)*, Mary Alan Hokanson *(Flo)*, Robert Bauer *(Young Man)*, Carol Kane *(Young Girl)*, Michael Higgins *(Francis Early)*

p, Frank D. Gilroy; d, Frank D. Gilroy; w, Frank D. Gilroy (based on the novel by Paula Fox); ph, Urs Furrer; ed, Robert Q. Lovett; m, Lee Konitz, Jim Hall, Ron Carter; art d, Edgar Lansbury; cos, Sally Gifft

This well-written if somewhat stagey character study focuses on a day in the life of an urban proto-yuppie couple, Sophie and Otto (Maclaine and Mars) who reside near the once fashionable but now rundown Brooklyn Heights (this is 1971, before the gentrification boom). Urban violence is breaking out all around them but they are becoming inured to it. Their conversation has deteriorated into banalities. Otto, an attorney, casually remarks that he is ending his partnership with Charlie (O'Loughlin), his long-time associate and best friend. It seems that Charlie has gone liberal and, as such, he is spending altogether too much time with causes and not enough with cases. A street cat paws at their door and MacLaine feeds it some milk. This act of kindness is rewarded by a deep bite on her hand. At a party thrown later that night by psychiatrist Mike (Gampel) and his wife, Flo (Hokanson), the joy of the evening is shattered by a rock that smashes a window. You get the idea? The times they are a'changin'.

MacLaine and Mars were acclaimed for their performances but the public stayed away. This is one of MacLaine's best performances. Mars carved himself a comfortable niche in comedy with a starring role as the Nazi playwright in THE PRODUCERS and several hilarious parts

in various Mel Brooks films. This was the feature directorial debut for playwright turned screenwriter-director Gilroy who had won previously won accolades for his award-winning play, *The Subject Was Roses* and his screenplay for the film version. He went on to write and direct films such as ONCE IN PARIS... , a delightful story of a screenwriter who goes to Paris to write a screenplay which was as at least as interesting as DESPERATE CHARACTERS and, sadly, suffered a similar fate.

DESPERATE HOURS, THE

1955 112m bw Crime ★★★★
Paramount (U.S.) /A

Humphrey Bogart *(Glenn)*, Fredric March *(Dan Hilliard)*, Arthur Kennedy *(Jesse Bard)*, Martha Scott *(Eleanor Hilliard)*, Dewey Martin *(Hal)*, Gig Young *(Chuck)*, Mary Murphy *(Cindy)*, Richard Eyer *(Ralphie)*, Robert Middleton *(Kobish)*, Alan Reed *(Detective)*

p, William Wyler; d, William Wyler; w, Joseph Hayes (based on his novel and play); ph, Lee Garmes; ed, Robert Swink; m, Gail Kubik; art d, Hal Pereira, Joseph MacMillan Johnson; fx, John P. Fulton, Farciot Edouart; cos, Edith Head

In his second-to-last film, Humphrey Bogart comes full circle, playing a character nearly identical to his pivotal role in THE PETRIFIED FOREST, the 1936 film that catapulted him to stardom. Bogart undertakes his reprise with a vengeance. As the film opens, Glenn (Bogart) breaks out of prison with his kid brother (Martin) and a mentally deficient behemoth (Middleton). They take refuge in the middle-class home of Dan Hilliard (March) where they terrorize his family as Glenn waits for a call from his sweetheart. Her assignment was to dig up some long-buried loot and then rendezvous with the escapees. However, the call doesn't come and Glenn grows increasingly desperate, brutalizing Hilliard, his wife (Scott), his attractive daughter (Murphy), and his feisty young son (Eyer).

Here William Wyler has expertly directed a taut suspenseful thriller. Joseph Hayes has also done a marvelous job in adapting his own novel for the screen. Two old pros who get the maximum impact out of every line, Fredric March and Bogart give spellbinding performances as two strong personalities engaged in a mortal showdown. Bogart reportedly had some reservations about this film, worrying that he might be too old to play a convincingly menacing hoodlum but his qualms never show on screen. The story had also been a successful stage play with the much-younger Paul Newman in Bogart's role, but the part was purposely "aged" by Hayes to suit Bogie's 55 years, each of which shows on his wonderful, craggy face. Among the supporting performers, Gig Young, Mary Murphy, and Richard Eyer are all fine, and Martha Scott is a standout as the hero's wife.

DESPERATELY SEEKING SUSAN

1985 104m c Romance/Comedy ★★★½
Orion (U.S.) PG-13/15

Rosanna Arquette *(Roberta Glass)*, Madonna *(Susan)*, Aidan Quinn *(Dez)*, Mark Blum *(Gary)*, Robert Joy *(Jim)*, Laurie Metcalf *(Leslie)*, Anna Levine *(Crystal)*, Bill Patton *(Nolan)*, Peter Maloney *(Ian)*, Steven Wright *(Larry)*

p, Sarah Pillsbury, Midge Sanford; d, Susan Seidelman; w, Leora Barish; ph, Ed Lachman; ed, Andrew Mondshein; m, Thomas Newman; prod d, Santo Loquasto; art d, Speed Hopkins; cos, Santo Loquasto

This is one of the most charming low-budget films in years, a freewheeling, light-hearted farce that gives some new twists to old plot devices. Rosanna Arquette is Roberta, a bored New Jersey housewife married to swimming pool magnate, Gary (Mark Blum). To spice up her bland life, Roberta takes to reading the personal ads and becomes intrigued by a periodically recurring notice headlined "Desperately Seeking Susan." On a whim, she goes off to New York City and eventually finds the mysterious Susan (Madonna). She follows Susan around the city and watches as the wildly garbed woman sells her leather jacket at a used clothing store. Roberta buys the jacket, not realizing it contains Egyptian earrings Susan has stolen from a murdered mobster. The plot twists are fairly simple, but that really doesn't matter in this energetic and well-acted comedy. Director Susan Seidelman guides her cast with a light, enthusiastic touch, never making more out of her frothy material than need be.

DESTRY RIDES AGAIN

1939   94m   bw   Western   ★★★★
Universal   (U.S.)

Marlene Dietrich *(Frenchy)*, James Stewart *(Tom Destry)*, Mischa Auer *(Boris Callahan)*, Charles Winninger *("Wash" Dimsdale)*, Brian Donlevy *(Kent)*, Allen Jenkins *(Bugs Watson)*, Warren Hymer *(Gyp Watson)*, Irene Hervey *(Janice Tyndall)*, Una Merkel *(Lily Belle Callahan)*, Tom Fadden *(Lem Claggett)*

p, Joe Pasternak; d, George Marshall; w, Felix Jackson, Henry Myers, Gertrude Purcell (based on the novel by Max Brand); ph, Hal Mohr; ed, Milton Carruth; m, Frank Skinner; art d, Jack Otterson; cos, Vera West

A classic sendup of western heroism starring James Stewart and—of all people—Marlene Dietrich. Stewart is the lawman who takes control of his town without shooting it up. Dietrich is the chantoosie who sings "See What the Boys in the Back Room Will Have." The son of a brave lawman gone to his reward, Tom Destry (Stewart) appears to be anything but a two-fisted fighter for justice. He refuses to wear guns, and, when he steps up to the bar, he orders milk. Soft-spoken and mild-mannered, he becomes the butt of jokes when he shows up in Bottleneck where Kent (Donlevy) runs the wildest saloon in town and lords it over the populace. His girlfriend and star attraction is the famous Frenchy (Dietrich), arguably the *real* power in town. Destry has arrived in Bottleneck to be deputy to "Wash" Dimmsdale (Winninger), the former deputy turned town drunk who has been made sheriff by Kent as a joke. Sheriff Dimmsdale is mortified when he learns that the young Destry does not carry a gun. "You shoot it out with them, and, for some reason, they get to look like heroes," Destry reasons. " You put 'em behind bars, and they look little and cheap, like they are."

Dietrich's career was in free fall prior to this movie. She had left the protective wing of her directorial mentor Josef von Sternberg in 1935, and most of her subsequent movies were not popular. After appearing in ANGEL, an uncommon failure for Ernst Lubitsch, Dietrich was considered "box office poison" by exhibitors. For three years, she made no films of consequence, and, when Paramount dropped her contract in 1937, she was considered washed up. She fled to Europe believing that American film audiences were through with her. Then she got a transatlantic call in the middle of the night from producer Joe Pasternak who wanted her for his new film at Universal—a western! One of the screen's most glamorous women, renowned for romances, melodramas, and sophisticated comedy, playing a saloon hussy in a crude oater? But Dietrich took it and she was appropriately bawdy, tempestuous, and wicked but with a heart of gold. The public responded and her star shot up again, higher than before.

Under the sure directorial hand of genre veteran Marshall, DESTRY RIDES AGAIN is a well-paced western that seamlessly combines humor, romance, suspense and action. Stewart's performance is rendered in his usual low-key manner and provides the perfect counterpoint to Dietrich's bold and brassy character. All the great character actors in this film are superb as well. DESTRY was filmed three times following the publication of the Max Brand novel in 1930, first as a Tom Mix standard in 1932, again in the 1939 Dietrich/Stewart classic, and in 1954 as a routine western with Audie Murphy.

DETECTIVE, THE

1968   114m   c   Crime   ★★★½
Fox   (U.S.)   /X

Frank Sinatra *(Joe Leland)*, Lee Remick *(Karen Leland)*, Ralph Meeker *(Lt. Curran)*, Jack Klugman *(Dave Schoenstein)*, Horace MacMahon *(Farrell)*, Lloyd Bochner *(Dr. Roberts)*, William Windom *(Colin MacIver)*, Jacqueline Bisset *(Norma MacIver)*, Tony Musante *(Felix)*, James Inman *(Teddy Leikman)*

p, Aaron Rosenberg; d, Gordon Douglas; w, Abby Mann (based on the novel by Roderick Thorp); ph, Joseph Biroc; ed, Robert Simpson; m, Jerry Goldsmith; art d, Jack Martin Smith, William Creber; fx, L.B. Abbott, Art Cruickshank; cos, Moss Mabry

Joe Leland (Sinatra) is a top New York City detective investigating the mutilation and murder of a homosexual (Inman). He arrests the victim's former roommate (Musante) for the crime, and the suspect is tried, convicted and executed. But the case haunts Sinatra because he allowed himself to blindly railroad Musante into a confession for the sake of a promotion. Ironically, another case leads Sinatra to the real killer, and he soon finds himself embroiled in a political scandal that could rock New York City. Now somewhat dated because of its misguidedly "enlightened" attitude toward homosexuality, this film is engrossing nonetheless because of its superb cast. Screenwriter Abby Mann took a few liberties with Thorp's trashy novel, but the changes were an improvement. Look for Robert Duvall in a small role.

DETECTIVE STORY

1951   105m   bw   Crime   ★★★★
Paramount   (U.S.)   /X

Kirk Douglas *(Jim McLeod)*, Eleanor Parker *(Mary McLeod)*, William Bendix *(Lou Brody)*, Cathy O'Donnell *(Susan Carmichael)*, George Macready *(Karl Schneider)*, Horace MacMahon *(Lt. Monahan)*, Gladys George *(Miss Hatch)*, Joseph Wiseman *(Charles Gennini)*, Lee Grant *(Shoplifter)*, Gerald Mohr *(Tami Giacoppetti)*

p, William Wyler; d, William Wyler; w, Philip Yordan, Robert Wyler (based on the play by Sidney Kingsley); ph, Lee Garmes; ed, Robert Swink; art d, Hal Pereira, Earl Hedrick; cos, Edith Head

AAN Best Actress: Eleanor Parker; *AAN Best Supporting Actress:* Lee Grant; *AAN Best Director:* William Wyler; *AAN Best Original Screenplay:* Philip Yordan, Robert Wyler

Kirk Douglas gives one of his best performances in this seminal cop film, directed by William Wyler. The plot is thin, but the drama is fleshed out with interesting characters. Chief among these is Jim McLeod (Douglas), a hardboiled, dedicated, by-the-book detective proud of his untarnished record in a one-man war against crime. Douglas is tough on all the lawbreakers he drags in to police headquarters, particularly an unscrupulous doctor (Macready), whom he beats up in a police van before delivering him to the lock-up. Lieutenant Monahan (MacMahon) becomes suspicious of McLeod's brutal treatment of the crooked physician, investigates further, and finds out that the abortionist has a surprising link to the detective.

Douglas is intense and electrifying as the altruistic yet narrow-minded Jim McLeod. Like DEAD END the source material for the film is a Sidney Kingsley morality play. Once again director Wyler deftly handles this potentially stagey material. And, as in DEAD END, one of the film's most outstanding features is an impressive set. This stark creation by Hal Pereira and Earl Hedrick is comprised of little more than floorboards, desks, unaccommodating tables, and ancient file cabinets. It suggests a precinct office with no frills or comforts, physical or spiritual.

Though confined to this one set, ace cinematographer Lee Garmes provides fluid camera movement as our eye is smoothly directed from one character to another. DETECTIVE STORY is methodical in its depiction of the sometimes traumatic events of one day in a precinct but the marvelous quirks and shadings of these characters create highly exciting drama.

DETOUR

1945   67m   bw   Crime   ★★★★
Producers Releasing Corp.   (U.S.)   /A

Tom Neal *(Al Roberts)*, Ann Savage *(Vera)*, Claudia Drake *(Sue)*, Edmund MacDonald *(Charles Haskell, Jr.)*, Tim Ryan *(Diner Proprietor)*, Esther Howard *(Hedy)*, Roger Clark *(Dillon)*, Pat Gleason *(Man)*, Don Brodie *(Used Car Salesman)*

p, Leon Fromkess; d, Edgar G. Ulmer; w, Martin Goldsmith; ph, Benjamin Kline; ed, George McGuire; m, Leo Erdody; art d, Edward C. Jewell; cos, Mona Barry

DETOUR puts the noir in film noir. Utilizing "night-for-night" cinematography, this amazingly dark genre landmark unfolds with the logic of a nightmare as Al Roberts (Tom Neal) recounts in voice-over the unlikely chain of events that landed him in a purgatorial diner in the middle of nowhere. A triumph of talent and inspiration over budget, it was made on the cheap by a Poverty Row studio in just six days. This road picture was filmed almost entirely in the studio, but director Edgar Ulmer transforms limitations into virtues. The sleazy look somehow feels right for DETOUR's self-consciously Freudian allegory of Oedipal rage and misogyny.

Roberts is a piano player at a chintzy joint in New York City. Sue (Claudia Drake), his fiancee, is a singer who dreams of stardom. She goes off to Hollywood, leaving him to his embittered reveries. He decides to marry her and hits the road with outstretched thumb. Al gets a ride from Haskell (MacDonald), a drug-addled businessman who buys him a meal and regales him with the story of how he got his scars. Haskell inexplicably dies on the road; Roberts, fearing he'll be blamed, buries the body and takes the car. When Roberts meets Vera (Ann Savage), a castrating harpy who knows his secrets and how to exploit them, things go from bad to worse.

DETOUR is a film that must be seen to be (dis)believed. Today it enjoys a richly deserved cult-film status. The wooden Neal is just right as the fatalistic protagonist and Savage is one of the most memorably off-kilter vixens in movie history.

DEVIL AND DANIEL WEBSTER, THE

1941 107m bw Science Fiction/Fantasy ★★★★
RKO (U.S.)

Edward Arnold (Daniel Webster), Walter Huston (Mr. Scratch), James Craig (Jabez Stome), Jane Darwell (Ma Stone), Simone Simon (Belle), Gene Lockhart (Squire Slossum), John Qualen (Miser Stevens), Frank Conlan (Sheriff), Lindy Wade (Daniel Stone), George Cleveland (Cy Bibber)

p, William Dieterle; d, William Dieterle; w, Dan Totheroh (based on the story "The Devil and Daniel Webster" by Stephen Vincent Benet); ph, Joseph August; ed, Robert Wise; m, Bernard Herrmann; fx, Vernon L. Walker

AAN Best Actor: Walter Huston; *AA Best Score:* Bernard Herrmann

Two fascinating stalwarts, Arnold and Huston, have a go at each other in this witty fantasy based on the O. Henry Prize-winning Stephen Vincent Benet short story. The author reportedly had a hand in the film version with Dan Totheroh. Jabez Stone (Craig) is a New England farmer having a difficult time making a living. When he casually swears that he would sell his soul for enough money to make life easier, up pops Huston as Mr. Scratch. This charming devil purchases Stone's soul in return for seven years of good luck. At first Stone thinks it's all an elaborate joke but then the money starts rolling in. Sudden success transforms the simple, good-hearted Stone into a venal, cold-blooded businessman who now cheats his neighbors, ignores his wife (Shirley) and their new-born child, refuses to listen to his mother (Darwell), and even gives up going to church on Sundays, opting to play poker instead. His phenomenal luck makes the entire farming community suspicious. The situation worsens on the homefront when Mr. Scratch's temptingly beautiful emissary (Simon), an odd servant girl, comes to live with Stone's family. Stone builds a grand mansion and gives an elegant ball, inviting everyone, including the famous Daniel Webster (Arnold). But everything goes wrong. Strange, crude people arrive and eat savagely at the banquet tables, and an equally strange band plays eerie music. All the guests, it seems, are people who have struck bargains with the Devil. The scene terrifies Stone and he flees, following his family whom he has run out of the mansion. He catches up with them on the road and his wife promises help. She goes to Webster, begging him to plead her husband's case. The great lawyer agrees to save his fellow New Englander if he can.

Arnold, though appearing only intermittently, is at his stentorian best and Huston steals the film as a roguish Devil full of snap, crackle and pop. Huston was nominated for an Oscar for his performance and the film won a richly deserved Oscar for Bernard Herrmann's lively and eerie score. Director Dieterle does one of his finest ever jobs of directing with the telling of this picturesque tale, and August's camerawork is masterful.

DEVIL AND MISS JONES, THE

1941 92m bw Comedy ★★★½
RKO (U.S.) /U

Jean Arthur (Mary Jones), Robert Cummings (Joe O'Brien), Charles Coburn (John P. Merrick), Edmund Gwenn (Hooper), Spring Byington (Elizabeth Ellis), S.Z. Sakall (George), William Demarest (1st Detective), Walter Kingsford (Allison), Montagu Love (Harrison), Richard Carle (Oliver)

p, Frank Ross, Norman Krasna; d, Sam Wood; w, Norman Krasna; ph, Harry Stradling; ed, Sherman Todd; m, Roy Webb; prod d, William Cameron Menzies; fx, Vernon L. Walker

AAN Best Supporting Actor: Charles Coburn; *AAN Best Original Screenplay:* Norman Krasna

Fun, but one wishes it were better. John P. Merrick (Coburn), the world's richest man, decides to infiltrate one of his holdings, a department store, to ferret out union organizers who have targeted him as responsible for the miserable working conditions of his employees. He is subjected to many indignities by the management, finally ending up in the shoe department alongside Mary Jones (Arthur). She thinks him destitute and takes pity on him, showing him the intricacies of the department. He attends union meetings and carefully notes everybody there, but as the abuse from the store's management becomes more intolerable and as Merrick himself becomes romantically interested in Elizabeth Ellis (Byington), he has a change of heart, eventually sacking the management and marrying Ellis. This comedy is enhanced by the Capraesque presence of Arthur, but what it really needed is Capra himself.

DEVIL DOLL, THE

1936 79m bw Horror/Fantasy ★★★★
MGM (U.S.) /A

Lionel Barrymore (Paul Lavond/Madame Mandelip), Maureen O'Sullivan (Lorraine Lavond), Frank Lawton (Toto), Robert Greig (Emil Coulvet), Lucy Beaumont (Mme. Lavond), Henry B. Walthall (Marcel), Grace Ford (Lachna), Pedro de Cordoba (Charles Matin), Arthur Hohl (Victor Radin), Rafaela Ottiano (Malita)

p, Edward J. Mannix; d, Tod Browning; w, Garrett Fort, Guy Endore, Erich von Stroheim, Tod Browning (based on the novel *Burn, Witch, Burn!* by Abraham Merritt); ph, Leonard Smith; ed, Frederick Y. Smith; m, Franz Waxman; art d, Cedric Gibbons; cos, Dolly Tree

Tiny people, and we don't mean Munchkins. Another Tod Browning foray into the macabre, THE DEVIL DOLL stars Lionel Barrymore as Paul Lavond, a wrongly convicted prisoner who escapes Devil's Island with mad scientist Marcel (Walthall). They take refuge in Marcel's old laboratory, where he demonstrates his miraculous invention, a serum that reduces all living things to miniature size. Before dying, the ailing Marcel passes his secret formula on to Lavond, who decides to seek vengeance on the three men who framed him. Disguised as an old woman who runs a doll shop, Lavond manages to reduce two of his enemies, but begins to lose control of the scheme because of his crazed assistant, Ottiano, who is so spellbound by the miniaturizing process that she refuses to stop, at one point hissing, "We'll make the *whole world* small!"

While THE DEVIL DOLL is no FREAKS, director Tod Browning, in his second-to-last film, adds a sinister edge to what is basically a morality play. The special effects still impress today; the oversized sets and props are expertly done, with much attention given to detail; and the film is excellently photographed by Leonard Smith. Erich Von Stroheim is credited with co-writing the screenplay, but the exact nature of his contributions has never been made clear. Cast is generally expert, with the exception of veddy-British Lawton, who is too refined for his assignment.

DEVIL IN A BLUE DRESS

1995 102m c Crime/Mystery/Drama ★★★★
Clinica Estetico/Mundy Lane Entertainment (U.S.) R/15

Denzel Washington (*Easy Rawlins*), Tom Sizemore (*Dewitt Albright*), Jennifer Beals (*Daphne Monet*), Don Cheadle (*Mouse*), Maury Chaykin (*Matthew Terell*), Terry Kinney (*Todd Carter*), Mel Winkler (*Joppy*), Albert Hall (*Odell*), Lisa Nicole Carson (*Coretta James*), Jernard Burks (*Dupree Brouchard*)

p, Jesse Beaton, Gary Goetzman; d, Carl Franklin; w, Carl Franklin (based on the novel by Walter Mosley); ph, Tak Fujimoto; ed, Carole Kravetz; m, Elmer Bernstein; prod d, Gary Frutkoff; art d, Dan Webster; fx, Tom Ward; cos, Sharen Davis

In this marvelously realized adaptation of Walter Mosley's hard-boiled detective novel, private investigator Ezekiel "Easy" Rawlins (Denzel Washington) isn't so much solving a puzzle as negotiating a minefield, hoping to find his way out without losing his skin. And because he's black in an overtly racist town, his skin is always an issue.

Los Angeles, 1948. Rawlins has lost his job and desperately needs cash to make a mortgage payment on his little bungalow-style piece of the American Dream. A local barkeep hooks him up with grinning, blue-eyed reptile Dewitt Albright (Tom Sizemore), who commissions him to find a white woman, Daphne (Jennifer Beals), who's known to "enjoy the company of Negroes." Her fiance, rich mayoral candidate Todd Carter (Terry Kinney), wants her back. Rawlins is no detective, but he doesn't have to be — all he has to do is show his face in some colored dives, ask some questions, and report back. Naturally, it's not that easy. Hard-boiled narrative complications develop in short order, but director Carl Franklin isn't particularly concerned with the machinations of mystery plots. Nor is he seduced by the temptations of noir visual style (although Tak Fujimoto's camera work is plenty stylish). Instead, he's interested in the faces behind the swirling cigarette smoke and the emotions beneath the chic period clothes.

Franklin explores the racial realities of a Los Angeles in which no one even *pretends* to be surprised that cops use the word "nigger" and routinely frame non-white suspects. But the film is no polemic; rather, it's a stunningly successful recreation of a time and place largely ignored by the (white) cultural mainstream, and a deliberate rehabilitation of the idea of African-American community and continuity. Moreover, unlike many neo-noir narratives, DEVIL IN A BLUE DRESS truly is a moral journey. Rawlins starts out an innocent man and ends up compromised. When he announces he's given up on honest factory work and intends to become a full-time private investigator, it's a sad moment. He's destined to develop a cynical skin and a knowing manner, doomed to become a more conventional character than he needs to be.

DEVIL IN THE FLESH, THE
(LE DIABLE AU CORPS)

1946 110m bw Romance ★★★★
TRC (France) /18

Micheline Presle (*Marthe Graingier*), Gerard Philipe (*Francois Jaubert*), Jean Debucourt (*M. Jaubert*), Denise Grey (*Mme. Grangier*), Pierre Palau (*M. Marin*), Jean Varas (*Jacques Lacombe*), Jeanne Perez (*Mme. Marin*), Germaine Ledoyen (*Mme. Jaubert*), Maurice Lagrenee (*Doctor*), Richard Francoeur (*Headwaiter*)

p, Paul Graetz; d, Claude Autant-Lara; w, Jean Aurenche, Pierre Bost (based on the novel by Raymond Radiguet); ph, Michel Kelber; ed, Madeleine Gug; m, Rene Cloerec

A scandalous picture in its day, DEVIL IN THE FLESH tells the tale of a 17-year-old (Philipe) in love with a married older woman (Presle) whose soldier husband has been assigned to the front. The story is told through the boy's eyes, in a flashback structure that points out the doomed nature of the affair. Many contemporary viewers were furious at the way the soldier—a man risking his life for his country—was deceived, and petitions were sent to the French government urging that the film be banned. (Canada agreed to the ban, and New York state censors would show it only after certain cuts were made.) This touching story now seems quite harmless, but it still works extremely well as drama, hoisted by the wonderful Presle and Philipe and the helming of

director Autant-Lara. It was poorly remade as an X-rated film in 1986 by Marco Bellocchio. Based on the novel by Raymond Radiguet, who wrote his tale of romance at the age of 18, two years before his death.

DEVIL, PROBABLY, THE
(LE DIABLE, PROBABLEMENT)

1977 95m c Drama ★★★★
Sunchild/GMF/Gaumont (France) /X

Antoine Monnier (*Charles*), Tina Irissari (*Alberte*), Henri De Maublanc (*Michel*), Laelita Carcano (*Edwige*), Regis Hanrion (*Dr. Mime*), Nicolas Deguy (*Valentin*), Geoffrey Gaussen (*Bookseller*), Robert Honorat (*Commissioner*)

p, Stephane Tcholgdjieff; d, Robert Bresson; w, Robert Bresson; ph, Pasqualino De Santis; ed, Germaine Lany; m, Philippe Sarde

Another rigorous—and unusually watchable—exercise in cinematic discipline by Bresson, the master of the minimal. The story, the end of which Bresson reveals immediately, depicts young Monnier drifting through politics, religion, and finally to suicide. The actors are all nonprofessionals who don't so much act as move around and blankly state their lines to the director's intricate commands. The best introduction (along with LANCELOT DU LAC) to the work of one of film's greatest thinkers.

DEVIL'S OWN, THE

1997 107m c Action/Drama ★★½
Devil's Own Productions/Lawrence Gordon R/15
Productions/Columbia (U.S.)

Harrison Ford (*Sgt. Tom O'Meara*), Brad Pitt (*Rory Devaney—Francis "Frankie" McGuire*), Margaret Colin (*Sheila O'Meara*), Ruben Blades (*Edwin Diaz*), Treat Williams (*Billy Burke*), George Hearn (*Judge Peter Fitzsimmons*), Natascha McElhone (*Megan Doherty*), Paul Ronan (*Sean Phelan*), Simon Jones (*Harry Sloan*), Julia Stiles (*Bridget O'Meara*)

p, Lawrence Gordon, Robert F. Colesberry; d, Alan J. Pakula; w, David Aaron Cohen, Vincent Patrick, Kevin Jarre (based on a story by Kevin Jarre); ph, Gordon Willis; ed, Tom Rolf, Dennis Virkler; m, James Horner; prod d, Jane Musky; art d, Robert Guerra; fx, Philip Cory, Steve Riley, Steve Kirshoff, Robert Kirshoff, Andrew McDade; cos, Bernie Pollack

An earnest, surprisingly well-written drama about guilt and betrayal that dares to defy the juvenile, wham-bam-thank-you-ma'am aesthetics that have turned mainstream action pictures into feature-length video games.

IRA foot soldier Frankie McGuire (Pitt) is sent to New York City with a false name, Rory Devaney, and a mad mission to buy Stinger missiles. He's placed with the family of cop Tom O'Meara (Ford), whose Irishness doesn't extend much beyond an appreciation of Guinness, corned beef and step-dancing. Surrounded by a wife and three daughters, O'Meara takes to the polite Irish lad, who in turn sees in O'Meara the benevolent father he lost to the violence at home when he was a child. But violence inevitably follows Frankie and endangers his substitute family, leading to a schematic showdown.

Given the number of writers and the widely-reported clashes that marred production, it's a wonder THE DEVIL'S OWN turned out as well as it did. Pitt does fine work here (proving, among other things, that Hollywood hunks can learn accents if they try), and Ford lets painful slivers of vulnerability show through the sober shell he has spent the better part of the decade constructing. The movie's look is pure glum, deglamorized 1970s—PRINCE OF THE CITY springs to mind, and not just because Treat Williams is on hand as Irish-American gunrunner Billy Burke—which suits the subject matter, though it's a little hard to stomach the fact that this kind of low-rent grit now costs $90 million. And despite Frankie's frequent reminders that "this isn't an American story, it's an Irish story," it *is* a mainstream American movie, marred by a certain moral smugness and the need to tie up loose ends, whether or not it makes any dramatic sense.

DIABOLIQUE
(LES DIABOLIQUES)
1955 107m bw Thriller ★★★★½
Filmsonor (France)

Simone Signoret (*Nicole Horner*), Vera Clouzot (*Christina Delasalle*), Paul Meurisse (*Michel Delasalle*), Charles Vanel (*Inspector Fichet*), Jean Brochard (*Plantiveau*), Noel Roquevert (*Herboux*), Therese Dorny (*Mme. Herboux*), Pierre Larquey (*Drain*), Michel Serrault (*Raymond*), Yves-Marc Maurin (*Moinet*)

p, Henri-Georges Clouzot; d, Henri-Georges Clouzot; w, Henri-Georges Clouzot, Jerome Geronimi, Frederic Grendel, Rene Masson (from the novel *Celle Qui N'etait Pas* by Pierre Boileau, Thomas Narcejac); ph, Armand Thirard; ed, Madeleine Gug; m, Georges Van Parys; art d, Leon Barsacq

A bitter chiller. One of the most suspenseful films ever made, DIABOLIQUE revolves around a callous schoolmaster, Meurisse, his heiress wife, Clouzot, and his mistress, Signoret. The latter, a cold-blooded murderess, helps Christina poison and drown her husband. They dump the corpse in the pool of Michel's boarding school, but Christina grows increasingly fearful that Michel is still alive. An investigation of the schoolmaster's death proceeds, but when the pool is drained no body is found. Adding to the mystery is the testimony of schoolchildren who insist they've seen Michel.

Director Henri-Georges Clouzot keeps the viewer guessing to the final frames. The picture received great critical acclaim, sharing the prestigious New York Film Critics Award for Best Foreign Film with Vittorio de Sica's UMBERTO D. The frightened wife of the "dead" man, Vera Clouzot, is the real-life Mrs. Clouzot. Authors Pierre Boileau and Thomas Narcejac, upon learning that Alfred Hitchcock was interested in acquiring the rights to *Celle Qui N'Etait Pas* (upon which DIABOLIQUE was based), set out to pen another novel that would surely interest Hitch—*D'Entre Les Mortes,* which later became VERTIGO.

DIABOLIQUE also includes one of the most effective "eyeball scenes" in filmmaking (second only to that in Bunuel and Dali's UN CHIEN ANDALOU) when the "dead" man rises from the bathtub. Rumor has it Clouzot's films were always shot in an atmosphere of antagonism, and the camera here seems to be observing in a merciless way. The last 15 minutes are as suspenseful as anything ever put on film.

DIAL M FOR MURDER
1954 105m c Thriller ★★★½
Warner Bros. (U.S.) /PG

Ray Milland (*Tony Wendice*), Grace Kelly (*Margot Wendice*), Robert Cummings (*Mark Halliday*), John Williams (*Chief Inspector Hubbard*), Anthony Dawson (*Captain Swan Lesgate*), Leo Britt (*The Narrator*), Patrick Allen (*Pearson*), George Leigh (*William*), George Alderson (*The Detective*), Robin Hughes (*Police Sergeant*)

p, Alfred Hitchcock; d, Alfred Hitchcock; w, Frederick Knott (based on his play); ph, Robert Burks; ed, Rudi Fehr; m, Dimitri Tiomkin; art d, Edward Carrere, George James Hopkins; cos, Moss Mabry

Lower case Hitch, but diverting and sleek, with the climax early on. Milland is a playboy whose wealth has come entirely through his marriage to chic heiress Kelly. When he fears he'll lose her riches to American mystery writer Cummings, he plots her unfortunate demise. Milland contacts Dawson, an old chum who now operates in the underworld, and blackmails him into killing Kelly while he is conveniently away. Milland's plan misfires, however, when the murder plans go awry, leading to a thorough round of questioning from the crafty inspector Williams.

Based on the successful play by Frederick Knott, this adaptation was essentially treated as an assignment by Hitchcock, who had already begun to work on REAR WINDOW. Shackled by Jack Warner's insistence on filming the picture in 3D (with its terribly immobile cameras), Hitchcock focused his attention on his new favorite actress, Kelly, with whom he would work again on his next two films, REAR WINDOW and TO CATCH A THIEF.

Repeating his stage role as the Scotland Yard inspector is John Williams, who excells among the cast. Although the 3D version has hardly been seen, it does contain one of the best, least gimmicky, uses of the added dimension as Kelly, while being attacked, reaches "into the audience," desperately searching for a weapon to defend herself. The opening credit sequence of a finger dialing "M" on a telephone is, because of the problems of achieving close focus with 3D cameras, actually a giant dial and a large wooden finger which Hitchcock had specially constructed.

DIAMONDS ARE FOREVER
1971 118m c Spy ★★★
Eon/Danjaq (U.K.) GP/PG

Sean Connery (*James Bond*), Jill St. John (*Tiffany Case*), Charles Gray (*Blofeld*), Lana Wood (*Plenty O'Toole*), Jimmy Dean (*Willard Whyte*), Bruce Cabot (*Saxby*), Bruce Glover (*Wint*), Putter Smith (*Kidd*), Norman Burton (*Felix Leiter*), Joseph Furst (*Metz*)

p, Harry Saltzman, Albert R. Broccoli; d, Guy Hamilton; w, Richard Maibaum, Tom Mankiewicz (based on the novel by Ian Fleming); ph, Ted Moore; ed, Bert Bates; m, John Barry; prod d, Ken Adam; art d, Jack Maxsted, Bill Kenney; fx, Les Hillman, Albert Whitlock, Wally Veevers, Whitey McMahon; cos, Elsa Fennell, Ted Tetrick, Donfeld

AAN Best Sound: Gordon K McCallum (Sound), John Mitchell (Sound), Alfred J Overton (Sound)

Next door to glass, but aided by the return of Connery (George Lazenby had undertaken the role of Bond in ON HER MAJESTY'S SECRET SERVICE) teamed with Jill St. John, instead of the usual parade of faceless Bond girls. The Las Vegas locations sizzle and the script at least has the good sense not to take itself too seriously. The producers had by now decided that Connery, not Bond, was their big attraction and lured him back into the fold with an offer he couldn't refuse—1.25 million, a percentage of the profits on the film, and an agreement to back two films of Connery's choice, which he could either star in or direct. Connery accepted the offer, but was not to be persuaded to do the role again until NEVER SAY NEVER AGAIN in 1983. Shirley Bassey, who sang the title song from GOLDFINGER, returned here to sing the title song written by Barry Don Black. Two karate-kicking girls initiate Bond into sexual equality, but the genre was beginning to look shopworn by now. That's Lana Wood, Natalie's sister, as Plenty O'Toole. But no amount of frou-frou can distract us from wondering why no arch villain just shot old 007.

DIARY OF A CHAMBERMAID
(LE JOURNAL D'UNE FEMME DE CHAMBRE)
1964 97m bw Drama ★★★★
Speva/Cine Alliance/FS/Dear (France/Italy) /15

Jeanne Moreau (*Celestine*), Georges Geret (*Joseph*), Michel Piccoli (*Mons. Monteil*), Francoise Lugagne (*Mme. Monteil*), Jean Ozenne (*Mons. Rabour*), Daniel Ivernel (*Capt. Mauger*), Jean-Claude Carriere (*Cure*), Gilberte Geniat (*Rose*), Bernard Musson (*Sacristan*), Muni (*Marianne*)

p, Serge Silberman, Michel Safra; d, Luis Bunuel; w, Luis Bunuel, Jean-Claude Carriere (based on the novel *A Chambermaid's Diary* by Octave Mirbeau); ph, Roger Fellous; ed, Louisette Hautecoeur; art d, Georges Wakhevitch; cos, Georges Wakhevitch

A wonderfully vulgar film from the masterful Spanish director Luis Bunuel, DIARY OF A CHAMBERMAID is an adaptation in spirit of Octave Mirbeau's novel and Jean Renoir's 1946 film. Moreau is a Parisian chambermaid who takes a new job in the country at the estate of a bourgeois womanizer, Piccoli, his frigid wife Lugagne, and her likeable, foot-fetishist father, Ozenne. Sexual vices are not limited to the bourgeoisie, however, as Geret, the filthy, fascist longtime servant, is found to be a sadistic rapist and murderer.

Although Bunuel would regularly attack societal institutions, this film is one of his most overtly political. Set in the late 1920s, this chambermaid's diary sets up the social conditions of both political and sexual aggression that made the rise of fascism not only possible but—as Bunuel makes clear in the film's final shot of the stormy heavens—inevitable. His statement is a Surrealist one, presented in the most realistic of styles (which may surprise viewers who have only a peripheral familiarity with Bunuel's work).

The director's wicked humor and unforgettable visual sense are perhaps best illustrated in his filming the rape and murder of an innocent young girl. Instead of narrating the attack in detail, Bunuel uses three shots—a wild boar running through the forest, a frightened rabbit, and the corpse's legs covered with the live snails she had been collecting.

DIARY OF A COUNTRY PRIEST
(LE JOURNAL D'UN CURE DE CAMPAGNE)
1950 120m bw Religious   ★★★★½
UGC (France)   /U

Claude Laydu (Priest of Ambricourt), Jean Riveyre (Count), Andre Guibert (Priest of Torcy), Nicole Maurey (Louise), Nicole Ladmiral (Chantal), Marie-Monique Arkell (Countess), Martine Lemaire (Seraphita), Antoine Balpetre (Dr. Delbende), Jean Danet (Olivier), Gaston Severin (Canon)

p, Leon Carre; d, Robert Bresson; w, Robert Bresson (based on the novel by George Bernanos); ph, L.H. Burel; ed, Paulette Robert; m, Jean-Jacques Grunenwald; art d, Pierre Charbonnier

A frail, unnamed priest (Laydu, an untrained actor) is assigned to his first parish—Ambricourt, a small and only somewhat religious town. He does as saintly priests are known to do—simply accepting the people around him as they are and attempting to strengthen their faith, while himself living a life of poverty, with bread and wine the only food he can eat without falling ill. His major achievement is bringing a withdrawn countess out of her hatred for God and into a state of peacefulness.

Robert Bresson, returning to the screen after a five-year absence, succeeds in capturing the literary spirit of George Bernanos' book and retelling it in a cinematic language. It is a brilliant adaptation, remaining faithful to Bernanos without resorting to harmful omissions or additions, allowing its audience to enjoy the identical spiritual experience as the reader of the novel. DIARY OF A COUNTRY PRIEST shared the top prize at the Venice Film Fest with Kurosawa's RASHOMON. It is definitely not a film for everyone's tastes—Bresson's work is known for its slow, meditative pace—but a brilliant picture all the same.

DIARY OF A MAD HOUSEWIFE
1970 95m c Comedy/Drama   ★★★½
Universal (U.S.)   R/X

Richard Benjamin (Jonathan Balser), Frank Langella (George Prager), Carrie Snodgress (Tina Balser), Lorraine Cullen (Sylvie Balser), Frannie Michel (Liz Balser), Lee Addams (Mrs. Prinz), Peter Dohanos (Samuel Keefer), Katherine Meskill (Charlotte Rady), Leonard Elliott (Mon. Henri), Valma (Margo)

p, Frank Perry; d, Frank Perry; w, Eleanor Perry (based on the novel by Sue Kaufman); ph, Gerald Hirschfeld; ed, Sidney Katz; prod d, Peter Dohanos; cos, Ruth Morley, Flo Transfield, James Hagerman

AAN Best Actress: Carrie Snodgress

The angst of yuppiedom. Benjamin, one of the great film twits of our time, portrays a money-mad attorney who bullies his wife, Snodgress, to the point where she takes a lover, Langella. Soon enough Snodgress discovers Langella is every bit the twit Benjamin is, just a different sort of twit. Langella is self-centered and will play only with committed women because he is unable to commit himself. The plot takes Snodgress into several diverting episodes and culminates when she divests herself of both husband and lover and seeks solace in group therapy, only to learn that happiness doesn't reside in psychiatry, either.

The three leads are excellent. Benjamin has been seen in many films as the consummate ass: THE MARRIAGE OF A YOUNG STOCK-BROKER, THE SUNSHINE BOYS, LOVE AT FIRST BITE, THE STEAGLE, and as the ultimate nerd in PORTNOY'S COMPLAINT. Langella played the cad in a few more films and eventually the lead in John Badham's DRACULA. Snodgress was nominated for an Oscar for her role in this film, the highpoint of her career and the only nomination this rather slight picture received.

DIARY OF ANNE FRANK, THE
1959 170m bw Drama/War   ★★★★
Fox (U.S.)   /U

Millie Perkins (Anne Frank), Joseph Schildkraut (Otto Frank), Shelley Winters (Mrs. Van Daan), Richard Beymer (Peter Van Daan), Gusti Huber (Edith Frank), Lou Jacobi (Mr. Van Daan), Diane Baker (Margot Frank), Douglas Spencer (Kraler), Dody Heath (Miep), Ed Wynn (Albert Dussell)

p, George Stevens; d, George Stevens; w, Frances Goodrich, Albert Hackett (based on their play and the autobiography, Anne Frank: Diary of a Young Girl); ph, William Mellor, Jack Cardiff; ed, Robert Swink, William Mace, David Bretherton; m, Alfred Newman; art d, Lyle Wheeler, George W. Davis; fx, L.B. Abbott

AAN Best Picture; AAN Best Supporting Actor: Ed Wynn; AA Best Supporting Actress: Shelley Winters; AAN Best Director: George Stevens; AA Best Cinematography: William C. Mellor; AAN Best Score: Alfred Newman; AA Best Art Direction: Lyle R. Wheeler, George W. Davis, Walter M. Scott, Stuart A. Reiss; AAN Best Costume Design: Charles LeMaire, Mary Wills

Millie Perkins seems too mature and too flat for the pivotal role in this touching film, based on the famous WWII diary of the young Anne Frank. Skillfully directed by George Stevens (who photographed much of the famous concentration camp footage after Germany's defeat), the film is told in flashback, as Anne's father Schildkraut, a camp survivor, returns to the warehouse attic in Amsterdam where his Jewish family hid from the "Green Police" (the Dutch Gestapo) for two years.

Cramped in uncomfortable quarters, Schildkraut, his wife Huber, and their two daughters, Baker and Perkins, are sheltered through the kindness and courage of two Gentile shop owners. Also sharing the tiny living space are husband and wife Jacobi and Winters (in the first of her character parts), their teenage son Beymer, and the aging dentist Wynn. As the atrocities rage outside their hideaway, Anne concerns herself with many of the usual teenage problems—parental relationships, her affection for Peter, her jealousy towards her older sister—and records them in her diary. There are a number of close calls, surprise searches, and suspenseful moments that terrify the hidden inhabitants, who, when they are finally discovered, are carted off to a concentration camp.

Only Otto Frank survives, returning to the attic to find Anne's written reflections. He is moved to tears and shamed when he reads Anne's famous line: "In spite of everything, I still believe that people are really good at heart." A vivid and carefully produced work of poignancy and loss.

DICK TRACY
1990 103m c Adventure/Comedy   ★★★½
Silver Screen Partners IV/Touchstone (U.S.)   PG

Warren Beatty (Dick Tracy), Charlie Korsmo (Kid), Glenne Headly (Tess Trueheart), Madonna (Breathless Mahoney), Al Pacino (Big Boy Caprice), Dustin Hoffman (Mumbles), William Forsythe (Flattop), Charles Durning (Chief Brandon), Mandy Patinkin (88 Keys), Paul Sorvino (Lips Manlis)

p, Warren Beatty; d, Warren Beatty; w, Jim Cash, Jack Epps Jr. (based on characters created by Chester Gould); ph, Vittorio Storaro; ed, Richard Marks; m, Danny Elfman; prod d, Richard Sylbert; art d, Harold Michelson; fx, Buena Vista Visual Effects Group, John Caglione Jr., Doug Drexler; chor, Jeffrey Hornaday; cos, Milena Canonero; anim, Allen Gonzales, Samuel Recinos

AAN Best Supporting Actor: Al Pacino; AAN Best Cinematography: Vittorio Storaro; AA Best Song: Stephen Sondheim; AA Best Art Direction: Richard Sylbert, Rick Simpson; AAN Best Costume Design: Milena Canonero; AAN Best Sound: Thomas Causey, Chris Jenkins, David E. Campbell, D.M. Hemphill; AA Best Makeup: John Caglione, Jr., Doug Drexler

In sheer visual terms, this is the most convincing of the comic book movies that have been popular for the last decade or so. Surprisingly sweet and good-natured, DICK TRACY is a highly stylized piece of fluff that's easier to digest than the ponderous pretensions of the equally over-hyped BATMAN. Producer/director/star Warren Beatty looks great in his yellow fedora and trench coat though his jaw is never as sharp as Chester Gould's celebrated comic strip cop.

This old-fashioned story takes place in a strikingly stylized comic-strip city of the 1930s. Handsome, hardworking detective Dick Tracy is hot on the trail of crime boss Big Boy Caprice (played with gusto by a nearly unrecognizable Al Pacino) who has taken the entire underworld syndicate of the city away from Lips Manlis (Paul Sorvino). After disposing of Lips, taking over his nightclub, and stealing his girl, Breathless Mahoney (Madonna), Big Boy comes up with the idea of uniting all the villains in town under his leadership, thereby running the city. This is a job for Dick Tracy!

From the opening shot of the famous fedora and badge to the wildly extravagant long sweeps of the matte-painted comic-book city, DICK TRACY has a gorgeous but hollow look. It's the first film to transfer successfully the look of a comic book to the screen (kudos to Vittorio Storaro, whose striking photography makes striking use of primary colors) in an entirely cinematic way.

The performances are all fairly interesting. Hoffman's cameo as Mumbles is creepy and surprisingly funny, Headly and Korsmo are terrific, and Beatty is mesmerizingly hollow. The true star of this film, however, is Pacino, who provides a wildly over-the-top performance as Big Boy—in many ways he out-Jokers Jack Nicholson's Joker in BATMAN.

DIE HARD

1988   131m   c   Action   ★★★
Gordon/Silver   (U.S.)   R/18

Bruce Willis (John McClane), Bonnie Bedelia (Holly Gennaro McClane), Reginald Veljohnson (Sgt. Al Powell), Paul Gleason (Dwayne T. Robinson), De'voreaux White (Argyle), William Atherton (Thornburg), Hart Bochner (Ellis), James Shigeta (Takagi), Alan Rickman (Hans Gruber), Alexander Godunov (Karl)

p, Lawrence Gordon, Joel Silver; d, John McTiernan; w, Jeb Stuart, Steven E. de Souza (based on the novel by Roderick Thorp); ph, Jan De Bont; ed, Frank J. Urioste, John F. Link II; m, Michael Kamen; prod d, Jackson DeGovia; fx, Richard Edlund, Al Di Sarro; cos, Marilyn Vance-Straker

AAN Best Editing: Frank J Urioste, John F Link; AAN Best Sound: Don Bassman, Kevin F Cleary, Richard Overton, Al Overton; AAN Best Visual Effects: Richard Edlund, Al DiSarro, Brent Boates, Thaine Morris; AAN Best Sound Effects Editing: Stephen H Flick, Richard Shorr

The pumped-up, high tech surprise hit of 1988; a triumph of slick direction and lowbrow thrills, marred but not spoiled by a sour aftertaste.

On Christmas Eve, a New York cop (Willis) arrives in Los Angeles to spend the holidays with his estranged wife (Bedelia) and their two young children. The couple separated after the Japanese corporation Bedelia works for promoted her to a powerful position in their brand-new Los Angeles headquarters, an imposing state-of-the-art office building in Century City. Willis now meets her at a Christmas party thrown on the building's 30th floor. While he is washing up in his wife's executive bathroom, a group of international terrorists seizes the building and takes everyone at the party hostage, in an attempt to break into the company safe and steal $670 million in negotiable bonds. Barefoot and wearing only a T-shirt and slacks, Willis escapes the terrorists and makes his way to the unfinished upper floors of the building, where he wages a one-man war against the intruders.

Tautly directed by McTiernan (PREDATOR), DIE HARD is skillfully shot and consistently thrilling throughout its lengthy running time. The high-rise location, in particular, is cleverly employed to provide an array of unusual and breathtaking action scenes. Unfortunately, the film's script panders to the audience's worst fears and resentments—suggesting that foreigners are not to be trusted and feminism has destroyed the fabric of the American family, and so on. Despite this distasteful subtext, however, DIE HARD is a well-made, exciting film. A beefed-up Willis fares well in a breezy mode, but looks uncomfortable when the emoting turns heavy. The talented Bedelia is wasted, while Rickman, as the chief villain, gives an impeccably evil performance which put him on the international map.

DIE HARD WITH A VENGEANCE

1995   128m   c   Action/Adventure/Crime   ★★½
Cinergi Productions/20th Century Fox   (U.S.)   R/15

Bruce Willis (John McClane), Jeremy Irons (Simon), Samuel L. Jackson (Zeus), Graham Greene (Joe Lambert), Colleen Camp (Connie Kowalski), Larry Bryggman (Arthur Cobb), Anthony Peck (Ricky Walsh), Nick Wyman (Targo), Sam Phillips (Katya), Kevin Chamberlin (Charles Weiss)

p, John McTiernan, Michael Tadross; d, John McTiernan; w, Jonathan Hensleigh (based on characters created by Roderick Thorp); ph, Peter Menzies; ed, John Wright; m, Michael Kamen; prod d, Jackson DeGovia; art d, John R. Jensen, Woods Mackintosh; fx, Phil Cory, Conrad F. Brink, John E. Sullivan, Mass. Illusion; cos, Joseph G. Aulisi

The third DIE HARD movie is easily the most spectacular, featuring an exploding subway train and a manic car chase through the congested streets of New York that rivals THE FRENCH CONNECTION. Indeed, for the first hour or so—as long as the action is confined to Manhattan—the film's inexorable action-pic logic is as compelling as that of SPEED. Unfortunately, as soon as the Nazi-esque villain makes his appearance, the whole thing turns into an overblown Bond film with a working-class hero, if that's not a contradiction in terms.

Bruce Willis, reprising his role as unruly but resourceful policeman John McClane, hooks up with a black nationalist sidekick (Samuel L. Jackson), who's shoehorned into the plot as the occasion for some queasy racial humor (and perhaps to ameliorate some of the nastier implications of the series' blatant appeal to white male resentment). Jeremy Irons is suitably reptilian as the criminal mastermind, but Bonnie Bedelia, McClane's long-suffering wife in the first two films, is sorely missed. DIE HARD WITH A VENGEANCE supplies the requisite number of thrills—and then some—but it's at least 20 minutes too long and stretches a worn concept to its breaking point.

DIM SUM: A LITTLE BIT OF HEART

1985   88m   c   Comedy   ★★★½
CIM   (U.S.)   PG/U

Laureen Chew (Geraldine Tam), Kim Chew (Mrs. Tam), Victor Wong (Uncle Tam), Ida F.O. Chung (Auntie Mary), Cora Miao (Julia), John Nishio (Richard), Amy Hill (Amy Tam), Keith Choy (Kevin Tam), Elsa Cruz Pearson (Eliza), Helen Chew (Linda Tam)

p, Tom Sternberg, Wayne Wang, Danny Yung; d, Wayne Wang; w, Terrel Seltzer (based on an idea by Laureen Chew, Seltzer, Wang); ph, Michael Chin; ed, Ralph Wikke, David Lindblom; m, Todd Boekelheide; art d, Christopher P. Lee, Lydia Tanji; cos, Lydia Tanji

Appealing if uneventful. This humanistic story involves an old Chinese widow who resides in San Francisco with her 30-year-old daughter. Though she has lived for many years in America, the widow is proud of her Chinese heritage and refuses to assimilate into American culture. She loves her daughter but feels the time has come for her, like her brother and sister, to be wed. Her daughter is torn between wanting to marry her boyfriend, a Los Angeles doctor, and the duty she feels toward her mother. When the mother learns from a fortune teller that she is approaching her time to die, the old woman must make some drastic changes in her attitudes. DIM SUM: A LITTLE BIT OF HEART is composed of small moments commenting in ways both broad and subtle on assimilation. Director Wayne Wang understands these problems, allowing scenes to build slowly and letting the audience get to know the characters. The universality of this comedy's subject matter makes it a gentle pleasure.

DINER

1982   110m   c   Comedy/Drama   ★★★★
MGM-UA   (U.S.)   R/15

Steve Guttenberg (Eddie), Daniel Stern (Shrevie), Mickey Rourke (Boogie), Kevin Bacon (Fenwick), Timothy Daly (Billy), Ellen Barkin (Beth), Paul Reiser (Modell), Kathryn Dowling (Barbara), Michael Tucker (Bagel), Jessica James (Mrs. Simmons)

p, Jerry Weintraub; d, Barry Levinson; w, Barry Levinson; ph, Peter Sova; ed, Stu Linder; m, Bruce Brody, Ivan Kral, Joe Tuley; art d, Leon Harris; cos, Gloria Gresham

AAN Best Original Screenplay: Barry Levinson (Screenplay)

A thoughtful, charming sleeper. Writer-director Barry Levinson's debut takes us back to the late-1950s Baltimore of his youth, brilliantly evoking that era through carefully drawn characters. Five pals meet at their favorite diner in between problems with women, gambling, and all the woes attendant upon being twentysomething in 1959. Steve Guttenberg, who has been dragging his feet on the way to the altar, forces his fiancee to pass the world's toughest Baltimore Colts quiz to qualify for marriage; Daniel Stern, who is already married, would rather spend time with the guys than with the wife he thinks doesn't understand him; Timothy Daly has a pregnant girlfriend who doesn't want to get married; Kevin Bacon is rich, bright, and usually bombed; and Mickey Rourke is a rebellious hairdresser and law student who spends most of his spare time chasing women.

The prominent rock 'n' roll soundtrack keeps the film firmly grounded in its period, but Levinson's masterly script, filled with funny, realistic dialogue (especially in the diner scenes), transcends time and place even as the film so richly conveys both. Featuring excellent performances by a host of actors who've gone on to prominent careers, to say nothing of Ellen Barkin's wistful turn as Stern's neglected wife, DINER is an often hilarious, frequently touching film.

DINNER AT EIGHT

1933 113m bw Comedy/Drama   ★★★★★
MGM (U.S.)   /PG

Marie Dressler *(Carlotta Vance)*, John Barrymore *(Larry Renault)*, Wallace Beery *(Dan Packard)*, Jean Harlow *(Kitty Packard)*, Lionel Barrymore *(Oliver Jordan)*, Lee Tracy *(Max Kane)*, Edmund Lowe *(Dr. Wayne Talbot)*, Billie Burke *(Mrs. Oliver Jordan)*, Madge Evans *(Paula Jordan)*, Jean Hersholt *(Joe Stengel)*

p, David O. Selznick; d, George Cukor; w, Frances Marion, Herman J. Mankiewicz, Donald Ogden Stewart (based on the play by George S. Kaufman and Edna Ferber); ph, William Daniels; ed, Ben Lewis; art d, Cedric Gibbons; cos, Adrian

A gorgeous, high-gloss deco mosaic, overloaded with star power, and a curious triumph over all by the electroplated Venus, Jean Harlow. DINNER AT EIGHT was the second all-star vehicle from MGM (after GRAND HOTEL) and did much to establish Selznick as a producer to be reckoned with. The script, expertly adapted from the Kaufman-Ferber stage play by Frances Marion, Herman Mankiewicz, and Donald Ogden Stewart, polished the comedy elements of the original to further balance the existing melodrama. The MGM constellations twinkle as Gotham strata of society are invited to dine by Lionel Barrymore and Billie Burke. Underneath the patina of luxe, hearts break, plans go up in smoke, dreams are dashed.

This is the beginning of the end for John Barrymore, playing a has-been that had been patterned after him; it's a bitchy casting idea, chilling to watch. Other good parts would follow but DINNER AT EIGHT would mark the point where he began careening into parody. Burke and Barrymore turn in definitive portrayals of their star personas. Dressler's shrewd grande dame in decline (based on Mrs. Patrick Campbell) is a textbook of brilliant comic business, and Beery turns in his usual workmanlike despisable grizzly.

But it's Jean Harlow who elevates herself to the big guns here. Her gold-digging, amoral little hussy, spitting out the chocolates she doesn't like back into her fancy candybox, is just as self-centered as the others. But despite the whinny voice, rock candy cosmetology and bratty manipulation, she still manages to infuse heart into her characterization. Cukor, who expertly directed, claimed she did it on her own; it's proof positive that the legendary sex symbols always have an undeniable element of humanity. (It may have helped that she and Beery hated each other's guts.) Madge Evans plays the ingenue, a role Joan Crawford pulled out of at the last minute, wisely, given the Harlow victory. Devotees of Hollywood costume design should enjoy the platinum blonde's outrageous costumes, the last word in Adrian vulgarity.

The Breen Office took exception to DINNER AT EIGHT (Joseph I. Breen being the West Coast assistant to Will Hays, who headed the censorship board affixing production codes to films at the time). Breen told Selznick that he seemed to have a predilection for suicide in his movies, citing such films as ANNA KARENINA and WHAT PRICE HOLLYWOOD. To calm the censors, the scene where John Barrymore

actually turns on the gas was cut. The producer would remain forever proud of this film, taking particular delight that the chic set decorations of the movie (especially Harlow's bedroom set) helped popularize art deco in the early 1930s.

DIRTY DANCING

1987 97m c Dance   ★★★
Vestron (U.S.)   PG-13/15

Jennifer Grey *(Frances "Baby" Houseman)*, Patrick Swayze *(Johnny Castle)*, Jerry Orbach *(Dr. Jake Houseman)*, Cynthia Rhodes *(Penny Johnson)*, Jack Weston *(Max Kellerman)*, Jane Brucker *(Lisa Houseman)*, Kelly Bishop *(Marjorie Houseman)*, Lonny Price *(Neil Kellerman)*, Max Cantor *(Robbie Gould)*, Charles "Honi" Coles *(Tito Suarez)*

p, Linda Gottlieb, Eleanor Bergstein; d, Emile Ardolino; w, Eleanor Bergstein; ph, Jeff Jur; ed, Peter C. Frank; m, John Morris; prod d, David Chapman; art d, Mark Haack, Stephen J. Lineweaver; chor, Kenny Ortega; cos, Hilary Rosenfeld

AA Best Song: Franke Previte (Music & Lyrics), John DeNicola (Music), Donald Markowitz (Music)

Teenage titillation for girls, circa 1963. Orbach is a New York doctor visiting a Catskill Mountains resort hotel with his wife Bishop and two daughters, Grey—known as Baby—and Brucker. Baby, a teenage activist, is soon bored and goes to the off-limits employees' area, where the hotel staff are engaging in "dirty dancing"—bodies rubbing and undulating around each other to pulsating music. There she meets the hotel's resident swain, Patrick Swayze, who with his partner, Cynthia Rhodes, gives dancing lessons to the guests. Although they come from two different worlds, the two fall in love.

Grey is Joel Grey's daughter and she acquits herself adequately. Swayze is a sexy dancer who can be sweet, suggest macho, and act a little. Of particular interest is Rhodes. Her part isn't large, but she is believable as an actress and spectacular as a dancer. One problem with the film is that it does nothing to endear the Catskill social setting to an audience; the inhabitants seem to be competing for awards in obnoxiousness. DIRTY DANCING produced a top-selling soundtrack album and the hit single "(I've Had) The Time of My Life."

DIRTY DOZEN, THE

1967 149m c War   ★★★★
MGM (U.K.)   /15

Lee Marvin *(Maj. Reisman)*, Ernest Borgnine *(Gen. Worden)*, Charles Bronson *(Joseph Wladislaw)*, Jim Brown *(Robert Jefferson)*, John Cassavetes *(Victor Franko)*, Richard Jaeckel *(Sgt. Bowren)*, George Kennedy *(Maj. Max Armbruster)*, Trini Lopez *(Pedro Jiminez)*, Ralph Meeker *(Capt. Stuart Kinder)*, Robert Ryan *(Col. Everett Dasher-Breed)*

p, Kenneth Hyman; d, Robert Aldrich; w, Lukas Heller, Nunnally Johnson (based on the novel by E.M. Nathanson); ph, Ted Scaife; ed, Michael Luciano; m, Frank DeVol; art d, William Hutchinson; fx, Cliff Richardson

AAN Best Supporting Actor: John Cassavetes; *AAN Best Editing:* Michael Luciano; *AAN Best Sound:* Metro-Goldwyn-Mayer Studio Sound Department; *AA Best Sound Effects Editing:* John Poyner

Robert Aldrich's anti-everything-except-explosives war movie, presented as an all-star game. The film follows nonconformist Major Reisman (Lee Marvin) in his assigned task of assembling a suicide squad of military felons (murderers, rapists, thieves) to infiltrate and destroy a chateau in occupied France at which the Nazi top brass congregate during WWII. Since the cast is presented as bad guys without stories, it's impossible to get emotionally involved. Aided by his assistant, Jaeckel, Marvin recruits 12 men: Cassavetes, Savalas, Bronson, Sutherland, Brown, Walker, Lopez, Mancini, Cooper, Carruthers, Busby, and Maitland, ranging from the merely dim-witted to the overtly psychotic, to form his "dirty dozen," then subjects them to brutal training designed to mold them into an efficient fighting force. After the lengthy, but wholly entertaining training session which climaxes in a war game pitting Reisman's troops against a crack unit, the dirty dozen and their leaders parachute into France to begin a mission that most of them will not survive.

Slambang funny, and extremely violent for its time, THE DIRTY DOZEN was a box-office smash that continues to be popular to this day, despite hundreds of showings on television (and two made-for-television sequels in the 1980s). Boasting excellent performances from a stellar cast, this is the ultimate macho action movie. Yet it calls into question the morals of the *Americans*, not the Germans: the instigators of the mission smugly sip sherry and smoke cigars, content that it was accomplished and that some of their most troublesome recruits died in carrying it out. Aldrich was a master at presenting his distinctly cynical outlook in the context of crowd-pleasing entertainment, and THE DIRTY DOZEN is one of his most effective and lasting efforts.

DIRTY HARRY

1971 102m c Crime   ★★★½
Malpaso/Warner Bros. (U.S.)   R/18

Clint Eastwood *(Harry Callahan)*, Reni Santoni *(Chico)*, Harry Guardino *(Bressler)*, Andy Robinson *(Scorpio)*, John Mitchum *(De-Georgio)*, John Larch *(Chief)*, John Vernon *(Mayor)*, Mae Mercer *(Mrs. Russell)*, Lyn Edgington *(Norma)*, Ruth Kobart *(Bus Driver)*

p, Don Siegel; d, Don Siegel; w, Harry Julian Fink, Rita M. Fink, John Milius (uncredited), Dean Riesner (based on an unpublished story by Rita M. and Harry Julian Fink); ph, Bruce Surtees; ed, Carl Pingitore; m, Lalo Schifrin; art d, Dale Hennesy; cos, Glenn Wright

A fascist film, or a film about a fascist cop? Either way, this is suspenseful, energetic stuff, directed with urgency and style by *Cahiers du Cinema* favorite Don Siegel; embellished with some of Lalo Schifrin's coolest electro-jazz confections; and driven by the inimitable Clint as Detective "Dirty" Harry Callahan, last line of defence against the assorted hippie liberal types who, in the early 70s, threatened the very fabric of Western civilization.

Maverick San Francisco cop Harry Callahan (Clint Eastwood) is ordered by the city mayor (John Vernon) to stop the serial killer who calls himself Scorpio (Andy Robinson). The psycho wants $100,000, or he will continue his bloody work. The mayor and others are willing to give in, but Eastwood disagrees, sensing it would be just the first payment. Eastwood bristles when teamed with young Chico (Reni Santoni) against his wishes (Chico fails Callahan on three counts, by being new to the force, Mexican-American, and, perhaps worst of all, college-educated); but he reluctantly begins to accept the junior partner. Scorpio says he's buried a teenage girl somewhere in the city and will let her die unless the town comes up with $200,000. Eastwood gets the job of delivering the money (backed up by Chico), but eventually pursues his own, extralegal route to nail Scorpio.

DIRTY HARRY proved popular, controversial, and influential. With uncredited screenplay contributions by John Milius, the film represented, via its title character, the apotheosis of the maverick cop figure that Siegel had portrayed in films from HELL IS FOR HEROES through MADIGAN. Harry Callahan is both more openly scornful of the law—his nailing of Scorpio is basically a critique of the concept of "criminal rights"—and, thanks to Eastwood's perfectly calibrated performance, more compelling an individual, than Siegel's earlier neo-vigilantes. The film propelled Eastwood to his second round of stardom, left its mark on countless urban cop dramas to come, and marked the beginning of one of the most celebrated director/star relationships in American cinema—one movingly recalled by Eastwood-as-director in the joint dedication of his 1992 masterpiece, UNFORGIVEN, "to Sergio and Don." Sequels: MAGNUM FORCE, THE ENFORCER, SUDDEN IMPACT, and THE DEAD POOL.

DISCLOSURE

1994 127m c Drama/Mystery/Thriller   ★★★
Baltimore Pictures/Constant c (U.S.)   R/18

Michael Douglas *(Tom Sanders)*, Demi Moore *(Meredith Johnson)*, Donald Sutherland *(Bob Garvin)*, Roma Maffia *(Catherine Alvarez)*, Caroline Goodall *(Susan Hendler)*, Dennis Miller *(Mark Lewyn)*, Dylan Baker *(Philip Blackburn)*, Nicholas Sadler *(Don Cherry)*, Allan Rich *(Ben Heller)*, Rosemary Forsyth *(Stephanie Kaplan)*

p, Barry Levinson, Michael Crichton; d, Barry Levinson; w, Paul Attanasio (based on the novel by Michael Crichton); ph, Tony Pierce-Roberts; ed, Stu Linder; m, Ennio Morricone; prod d, Neil Spisak; art d, Richard Yanez-Toyon, Charles William Breen; fx, Eric Brevig, Industrial Light & Magic; cos, Gloria Gresham

It's no great surprise that Hollywood's first attempt to grapple with sexual harassment hinges on the ludicrous notion that it's something done by women to men. What *is* surprising is that producer-director Barry Levinson has resisted what must have been considerable pressure to contrive another FATAL ATTRACTION, turning Michael Crichton's best-selling corporate thriller into a quietly efficient entertainment gizmo that eschews cathartic violence in favor of lurking paranoia.

Michael Douglas plays Tom Sanders, a married computer exec who believes he's in line for a promotion; instead, he's crushed to discover that his unctuous boss (Donald Sutherland) has passed him over for Meredith Johnson (Demi Moore), a coolly competent number-cruncher and, coincidentally, an old flame. When she seduces him during a private meeting, Tom suffers a last-minute attack of conscience and breaks things off mid-tryst, and an enraged Meredith threatens to destroy him. The next morning, he discovers that he's been charged with sexual harassment. In the course of a tense campaign to clear his name and save his marriage, Tom hires a hard-bitten feminist attorney (Roma Maffia), ponders the import of a series of cryptic e-mail messages, and makes use of the company's latest invention—a snazzy virtual-reality filing system.

The screenplay, by Paul Attanasio (QUIZ SHOW), is a distinct improvement on Crichton's one-dimensional source potboiler. Besides adding some cleverly positioned laugh lines, Attanasio complicates the hero's motives and moral standing—the seduction scene is now considerably more ambiguous than it was in the book, and Tom is pointedly shown to have engaged in some borderline sexual harassment of his own. Levinson adds a couple of interesting touches—the camera lingers significantly on a succession of Asian-American nannies, cleaning women, and secretaries, suggesting the ever-growing dependence of American high-tech playthings on a pool of cheap Third World labor—but fans of the director's "serious" work will look in vain for any trace of what used to be called personal filmmaking.

In the end, the movie comes closest to thematic coherence, and the popular mood, in its depiction of something nearly everyone can relate to: the office from hell. In a time when job insecurity tops the list of American anxieties, DISCLOSURE's paradigmatic 90s workplace—a ruthless, conspiratorial, profit-driven nightmare—will speak to viewers much more clearly than its fatuous take on sexual harassment.

DISCREET CHARM OF THE BOURGEOISIE, THE
(LE CHARME DISCRET DE LA BOURGEOISIE)

1972 100m c Comedy/Drama   ★★★½
Greenwich/Jet/Dean (France/Italy/Spain)   PG/AA

Fernando Rey *(Ambassador Raphael Acosta)*, Delphine Seyrig *(Mme Simone Thevenot)*, Stephane Audran *(Mme Alice Senechal)*, Bulle Ogier *(Florence)*, Jean-Pierre Cassel *(M. Henri Senechal)*, Paul Frankeur *(M. Francois Thevenot)*, Julien Bertheau *(Bishop Dufour)*, Claude Pieplu *(Colonel)*, Michel Piccoli *(Home Secretary)*, Muni *(Peasant Girl)*

p, Serge Silberman; d, Luis Bunuel; w, Luis Bunuel, Jean-Claude Carriere; ph, Edmond Richard; ed, Helene Plemiannikov; m, Galaxie Musique; art d, Pierre Guffroy; cos, Jacqueline Guyot

AA Best Foreign Language Film ; AAN Best Adapted Screenplay: Luis Bunuel, Jean-Claude Carriere

A finely barbed Surrealist attack on the mores of the upper class, the clergy, the military and politicians. THE DISCREET CHARM OF THE BOURGEOISIE is so couth that even many of Bunuel's fans mistakenly misread this brilliant joke as a sign that the then-72-year-old Spanish director had lost his bite. It is, however, every bit as wicked as Bunuel's long-banned 1930 classic, L'AGE D'OR—just a little more "refined."

The plot, which does no justice to a reading of the film, concerns the efforts of a group of middle-aged members of the bourgeoisie to sit down together for a dinner party. Sometimes they meet on the wrong evening, or they gather at a restaurant only to find the corpse of the recently deceased owner, or they are told that all beverages except water are out of stock, or they discover that they are not at a dinner party at all, but on stage in front of an angry audience. These doomed meetings—which, it is suggested, may all be dreams—are interspersed with scenes which reveal the main characters to be involved in such decorous pursuits as drug smuggling, fascism and torture. In a recurring sequence, the friends are seen walking along a country road, their destination—if they have one—unknown to the audience.

A subversively witty film, THE DISCREET CHARM was in some ways a return to the playful irrationality of Bunuel's early Surrealist classics. Despite its coruscating, if sophisticated, attacks on the establishment, it was nominated for Best Original Screenplay and won the Oscar as Best Foreign Language Film—a perfect punch line to Bunuel's joke.

DISRAELI

1929 90m bw Biography   ★★★½
Warner Bros. (U.S.)

George Arliss (Disraeli), Joan Bennett (Lady Clarissa Pevensey), Florence Arliss (Lady Mary Beaconsfield), Anthony Bushell (Charles/Lord Deeford), David Torrence (Sir Michael/Lord Probert), Ivan Simpson (Hugh Meyers), Doris Lloyd (Mrs. Agatha Travers), Gwendolyn Logan (Duchess of Glastonbury), Charles E. Evans (Potter), Cosmo Kyrle Bellew (Mr. Terle),

d, Alfred E. Green; w, Julian Josephson (based on the play by Louis Napoleon Parker); ph, Lee Garmes; ed, Owen Marks; m, Louis Silvers

AAN Best Picture; AA Best Actor: George Arliss; AAN Best Screenplay: Julian Josephson

Arliss is a fine centerpiece for one of the earliest of the Warner Bros. biographies; DISRAELI sets high standards for biopics to come. It marked the film debut of aging George Arliss, and showed America a style of acting it had seen little of in the silent years. Arliss was stage-trained and able to make the switch from stage to silents and then sound with no difficulty. Rather than attempt a long picture about the Jew who converted to Christianity and was Queen Victoria's closest ally, the film deals with a brief slice of Disraeli's life, focusing on his attempt to outwit the Russians in the rush to purchase the Suez Canal. Along the way, we get the opportunity to observe his wit, his amours, his geniality, and his brilliance.

Florence Arliss played his screen wife, and their ability to play off each other lent sparkle to both performances. Arliss would come to specialize in historical figures, playing Rothschild, Richelieu, Wellington, Alexander Hamilton, and others. He had played Disraeli in a 1921 silent film first, but this is the definitive performance.

DISTANT VOICES, STILL LIVES

1988 85m c Drama   ★★★½
British Film Institute/Film Four/Channel 4/ZDF (U.K.)   PG-13/15

Freda Dowie (Mother), Pete Postlethwaite (Father), Angela Walsh (Eileen), Lorraine Ashbourne (Maisie), Dean Williams (Tony), Sally Davies (Eileen as a child), Nathan Walsh (Tony as a child), Susan Flanagan (Maisie as a Child), Michael Starke (Dave), Vincent Maguire (George)

p, Jennifer Howarth; d, Terence Davies; w, Terence Davies; ph, William Diver, Patrick Duval; ed, William Diver; art d, Miki van Zwanenberg, Jocelyn James; cos, Monica Howe

Part nostalgia, part nightmare, the autobiographical DISTANT VOICES, STILL LIVES is writer-director Terence Davies's bittersweet look back at his working-class upbringing in postwar Liverpool. While it's beautifully photographed, Davies's portrait of a house divided by a near-psychotic father (Pete Postlethwaite)—loving one moment, brutal the next—is not a pretty sight. All of the familial warts and blemishes are visible as Davies avoids any romanticizing of the past whatsoever. In this highly stylized, cinematic portrait of his family, there is no enhancement, no glitz, not even much of a plot. Rather, Davies leaves us with a series of impressions, presented non-chronologically, that evoke memories of his basically repressive Catholic childhood in the 1950s.

Told in flashback, the film begins and ends with family weddings held several years apart as the grown children reflect on their father and his mostly negative influence upon their lives. Despite Davies' often harsh, brutal focus, this is no gloom-and-doom period piece. Remarkably, all his sensitively drawn, subtle observations coalesce, forming an emotionally compelling whole that visually and vividly recalls a traditional way of life. Static as their lives may be, his people are never dull. In this very personal portrait, Davies, the artist, has re-created universal experiences—familiar passions and needs—that draw us to his family's humanity.

DIVA

1981 123m c Crime/Romance   ★★★★½
Galaxie/Greenwich (France)   /15

Frederic Andrei (Jules), Wilhelmenia Wiggins Fernandez (Cynthia Hawkins), Richard Bohringer (Gorodish), Thuy An Luu (Alba), Jacques Fabbri (Saporta), Chantal Deruaz (Nadia), Roland Bertin (Weinstadt), Gerard Darmon (L'Antillais), Dominique Pinon (Le Cure), Jean-Jacques Moreau (Krantz)

p, Irene Silberman; d, Jean-Jacques Beineix; w, Jean-Jacques Beineix, Jean Van Hamme (based on a novel by Delacorta); ph, Philippe Rousselot; ed, Marie-Josephe Yoyotte, Monique Prim; m, Vladimir Cosma; art d, Hilton McConnico

A lady prone to technique but dazzling nonetheless, DIVA is visually astonishing film fare. The complex plot concerns Andrei, a young Parisian mail carrier, and his love for Fernandez, a famous black American opera singer. Andrei attends a performance by the diva, recording it secretly while a sinister Taiwanese man watches him. In a separate incident a dazed girl walking through the Paris metro is murdered by two thugs—the greasy Darmon and the punkish, bald Pinon. As the girl dies she slips an audiocassette into Andrei's mailpouch. Andrei now finds himself unwittingly caught in two plots: that of Taiwanese record pirates who want his recording of the diva and that of pimps and drug runners who want the incriminating tape left in his mailpouch.

The debut film from Jean-Jacques Beineix, DIVA is perhaps the most picturesque film to come out of France in years. Together with art director Hilton McConnico and cameraman Philippe Rousselot, Beineix creates awesome shot after awesome shot, so much so that many felt the film was too stylish. At times the sensibility is very "New Wave" (as in fashion and music, not the film movement); at other times, Beineix is intensely Impressionistic. These qualities are even further enhanced by a perfect musical score, contributed by Vladimir Cosma, who has used Act I of Alfredo Catalani's opera *La Wally*.

DIVORCE, ITALIAN STYLE
(DIVORZIO ALL'ITALIANA)

1962 108m bw Comedy   ★★★★
Lux (Italy)   /A

Marcello Mastroianni (Ferdinando), Daniela Rocca (Rosalia), Stefania Sandrelli (Angela), Leopoldo Trieste (Carmelo Patane), Odoardo Spadaro (Don Gaetano), Margherita Girelli (Sisina), Angela Cardile (Agnese), Bianca Castagnetta (Donna Matilde), Lando Buzzanca (Rosario Mule), Pietro Tordi (Attorney DeMarzi)

p, Franco Cristaldi; d, Pietro Germi; w, Ennio De Concini, Alfredo Giannetti, Pietro Germi; ph, Leonida Barboni; ed, Roberto Cinquini; m, Carlo Rustichelli; cos, Dina Di Bari

AAN Best Actor: Marcello Mastroianni; AAN Best Director: Pietro Germi; AA Best Original Story and Screenplay: Ennio DeConcini, Alfredo Giannetti, Pietro Germi

To die laughing for. Rocca is a whining sex-crazed Sicilian wife who drives husband Mastroianni to consider divorce. Unfortunately for Rocca it is easier to murder in Italy than it is to divorce. And that's precisely what is done. The scheming Mastroianni then goes on to marry the proverbial nymphet next door after his wife is out of the picture. A brilliant comic performance from Mastroianni which has been compared to the deadpan style of Keaton. It earned him an Oscar nomination for Best Actor, as well as Best Actor accolades from the Golden Globes and the British Film Academy. Considered by some to be one of the greatest modern comedies.

DIVORCEE, THE
1930 83m bw Drama ★★★½
MGM (U.S.)

Norma Shearer (Jerry), Chester Morris (Ted), Conrad Nagel (Paul), Robert Montgomery (Don), Florence Eldridge (Helen), Helene Millard (Mary), Robert Elliott (Bill), Mary Doran (Janice), Tyler Brooke (Hank), Zelda Sears (Hannah)

p, Robert Z. Leonard; d, Robert Z. Leonard; w, Nick Grinde, Zelda Sears, John Meehan (based on the novel Ex-Wife by Ursula Parrott); ph, Norbert Brodine; ed, Hugh Wynn, Truman K. Wood; art d, Cedric Gibbons; cos, Adrian

AAN Best Picture; AA Best Actress: Norma Shearer; AAN Best Director: Robert Leonard; AAN Best Screenplay: John Meehan

Norma Shearer, in an Oscar-winning role, tries daringly to confront the double standard, but not upset her legion of fans (or the censors) who wouldn't approve of her really letting loose. Thankfully, something always gets in the way. The plot is a trifle: her husband (Morris) cheats on her, but won't hear of her doing the same. They divorce, and since Jerry (Shearer) is supposedly liberated from the shackles of matrimony, she flirts with several men (Montgomery and Nagel) before the requisite New Year's Eve reconciliation with her ex.

Based on Ursula Parrott's then-steamy novel Ex-Wife, much of the spirit has been laundered out here. (Things would become much worse, though, after the 1934 Production Code clampdown, so enjoy the spice that survives.) Shearer turns in a fine performance of the silken suffering which was her pre-Code specialty. While never in the same league, beauty-wise, with Garbo and Crawford, the other two of MGM's big three, she had a definite image advantage for many prestige pictures. Seemingly American (she was Canadian), she could play the moderns Garbo could not, but in more ladylike turns than Crawford. Being the pope's wife—she was married to production genius Irving Thalberg—never hurt her, either. (In all fairness, however, she was a star before she and Thalberg tied the knot, and audiences genuinely liked her as well.) Whether or not you like Shearer and THE DIVORCEE depends on how you respond to this particular "tease" variety of soap opera, but this enjoyable film stands as an index to the sexual politics of an era.

DO THE RIGHT THING
1989 120m c Comedy/Drama ★★★★½
40 Acres and a Mule Filmworks (U.S.) R/18

Danny Aiello (Sal), Ossie Davis (Da Mayor), Ruby Dee (Mother Sister), Richard Edson (Vito), Giancarlo Esposito (Buggin Out), Spike Lee (Mookie), Bill Nunn (Radio Raheem), John Turturro (Pino), Rosie Perez (Tina), Paul Benjamin (ML)

p, Spike Lee, Monty Ross; d, Spike Lee; w, Spike Lee; ph, Ernest Dickerson; ed, Barry Alexander Brown; m, Bill Lee; prod d, Wynn Thomas; chor, Rosie Perez, Otis Sallid; cos, Ruth Carter

AAN Best Supporting Actor: Danny Aiello; AAN Best Original Screenplay: Spike Lee

DO THE RIGHT THING has been hailed as the most insightful view of race relations ever to hit US screens and condemned as dangerous agitprop, but its timeliness—and its ability to touch a nerve in the culture at large—was never in question.

The story is set in Brooklyn's Bedford-Stuyvesant neighborhood on a broiling hot Saturday. Blacks and Latinos inhabit the area, but the local eatery, Sal's Famous Pizzeria, is owned and managed by Italian-American Sal (Danny Aiello) who commutes to work with his two sons, the embittered, bigoted Pino (John Turturro) and the mild-mannered and sympathetic Vito (Richard Edson). Also working at Sal's is Mookie (writer-director Spike Lee), the deliveryman, who tries to do as little work as possible in his dead-end job. On the hottest day of the year, tensions rise when the self-styled local activist Buggin Out (Giancarlo Esposito), upset by the absence of black faces on Sal's "Wall of Fame," attempts to organize a boycott of the pizzeria. This apparently trivial incident sparks the explosion which climaxes the film.

Lee has crafted a film of astonishing power and originality. Cinematographer Ernest Dickerson shows signs of genius as he provides brightly colored images so hot they make you sweat with excitement.

No currently working lensman is better at lighting black actors. The large ensemble cast is excellent. Aiello makes Sal a likable guy despite his unconscious paternalism. Turturro is frighteningly believable as the volatile Pino, but he's no cardboard villain. Ossie Davis and Ruby Dee, two stalwarts of the black theater, serve with special distinction as both a vivid reminder of past glories of black culture and an inspiration for the future.

Lee has promoted himself as a political activist filmmaker working with a conscious agenda: to tell black stories that have traditionally been ignored by Hollywood. Indeed his success has opened the doors for a new generation of black filmmakers. DO THE RIGHT THING, his breakthrough film, is no blunt work of propaganda; it is a subtle and humane entertainment with a refreshingly serious view of the world. There are no absolute heroes or villains. There are no easy answers to the questions that this film poses with such artistry and grace.

DOCTOR DOLITTLE
1967 152m c Musical ★½
Fox (U.S.) /U

Rex Harrison (Dr. John Dolittle), Anthony Newley (Matthew Mugg), Peter Bull (Gen. Bellowes), William Dix (Tommy Stubbins), Portia Nelson (Sarah Dolittle), Samantha Eggar (Emma Fairfax), Richard Attenborough (Albert Blossom), Muriel Landers (Mrs. Blossom), Geoffrey Holder (Willie Shakespeare), Norma Varden (Lady Petherington)

p, Arthur P. Jacobs; d, Richard Fleischer; w, Leslie Bricusse (based on stories by Hugh Lofting); ph, Robert Surtees; ed, Samuel E. Beetley, Marjorie Fowler; prod d, Mario Chiari; art d, Jack Martin Smith, Ed Graves; fx, L.B. Abbott, Art Cruickshank, Emil Kosa Jr., Howard Lydecker; chor, Herbert Ross; cos, Ray Aghayan

AAN Best Picture; AAN Best Cinematography: Robert Surtees; AAN Best Editing: Samuel E. Beetley, Marjorie Fowler; AAN Best Score: Leslie Bricusse; AAN Best Score: Lionel Newman, Alexander Courage; AA Best Song: Leslie Bricusse; AAN Best Art Direction: Mario Chiari, Jack Martin Smith, Ed Graves, Walter M. Scott, Stuart A. Reiss; AAN Best Sound: 20th Century-Fox Studio Sound Department; AA Best Visual Effects: L.B. Abbott

Does little. As a matter of fact, a huge, stillborn dinosaur in quicksand, this one almost bankrupted its studio. Doctor Dolittle (Rex Harrison) is considered a nut by his neighbors. After this nuttiness leads to his arrest, Dolittle decides to avoid people and devote his life to animals since, as one who can speak all the animal tongues (he was taught 498 different languages by his parrot, Polynesia), he serves as a unique link between human and beast. With Anthony Newley, the most irritating man in show business, and the vapid Samantha Eggar at his side, the doctor sails off to find the elusive Great Pink Sea Snail and the Giant Lunar Moth in the South Seas, but no box office.

Problems on the set were many, especially with the use of so many live animals—more than 1,500. Alan Jay Lerner, originally set to write the book and lyrics, attempted to write for over a year but finally gave up, whereupon Harrison wanted to leave as well. Harrison hadn't wanted to star in a children's film in the first place, and only the involvement of prestigious author-lyricist Lerner attracted him to the project. The songs by Lerner's replacement, Leslie Bricusse, pleased Harrison, so he stayed with the production. Will put the kids to sleep, but may kill you.

DR. EHRLICH'S MAGIC BULLET
1940 103m bw Biography ★★★★
Warner Bros. (U.S.) /A

Edward G. Robinson (Dr. Paul Ehrlich), Ruth Gordon (Mrs. Ehrlich), Otto Kruger (Dr. Emil von Behring), Donald Crisp (Minister Althoff), Maria Ouspenskaya (Franziska Speyer), Montagu Love (Prof. Hartmann), Sig Rumann (Dr. Hans Wolfert), Donald Meek (Mittlemeyer), Henry O'Neill (Dr. Lentz), Albert Basserman (Dr. Robert Koch)

p, Wolfgang Reinhardt; d, William Dieterle; w, John Huston, Heinz Herald, Norman Burnside (based on a story by Burnside from letters and notes owned by the Ehrlich family); ph, James Wong Howe; ed, Warren Low; m, Max Steiner; art d, Carl Jules Weyl; fx, Robert Burks

AAN Best Original Screenplay: Norman Burnside, Heinz Herald, John Huston

Another entry in the superb series of Warner Bros. historical biographies, and alongside the same director's THE LIFE OF EMILE ZOLA, the best of them. By even mentioning the subject of venereal disease, this splendid saga also merits pride of place in any history of Hollywood.

Robinson is positively electric in a role quite unlike the types he usually played, that of gentle yet determined research scientist Dr. Paul Ehrlich. Unable to fit into the conservative routine of a Berlin hospital, painfully honest with his patients, Dr. Ehrlich finally finds his niche on the staff of respected physician Dr. Robert Koch (Basserman). Although his experiments cause him to contract TB, Ehrlich's ever-fertile mind first grasps a theory of poison immunity while he recovers from his illness in Egypt. Returning to Germany, Ehrlich must face short-sighted grant agencies and even a court of law while implementing his treatments for syphillis and childhood diphtheria, but the good doctor's steadfastness eventually wins the day.

Beautifully directed by ace studio craftsman Dieterle, the detailed, Oscar-nominated screenplay (using information from Ehrlich's family) manages to turn meticulous scientific research into absorbing subject matter. Robinson convincingly ages over 35 years during the film, bringing warmth and idiosyncrasy to a challenging role. Among a great supporting cast, Kruger and Basserman are particularly fine. Gordon, however, though sweet and likable as Ehrlich's supportive wife, brings little to the role which suggests her legendary stage reputation.

DOCTOR IN THE HOUSE

1954 92m c Comedy ★★★★
General Films (U.K.) /U

Dirk Bogarde *(Simon)*, Muriel Pavlow *(Joy)*, Kenneth More *(Grimsdyke)*, Donald Sinden *(Benskin)*, Kay Kendall *(Isobel)*, James Robertson Justice *(Sir Lancelot)*, Donald Houston *(Taffy)*, Suzanne Cloutier *(Stella)*, Geoffrey Keen *(Dean)*, George Coulouris *(Briggs)*

p, Betty E. Box; d, Ralph Thomas; w, Richard Gordon, Ronald Wilkinson, Nicholas Phipps (based on the novel by Gordon); ph, Ernest Steward; ed, Gerald Thomas; m, Bruce Montgomery; art d, Carmen Dillon; cos, Yvonne Caffin

The original "Doctor" comedy that spawned an entire series of films and a popular television sitcom, DOCTOR IN THE HOUSE is certainly the best of the lot. Simon Sparrow (Bogarde) begins his five long years of medical school and is immediately taken over by three student repeaters, all of whom failed their preliminary exams. Bogarde (like almost everyone else in the cast) is a bit too old for his role, but his appeal is undeniable and the film is notable for confirming his status as Britain's leading matinee idol of the 1950s. Shot with the appropriate lighthearted touch in bright, shiny color, with fine performances all around (Kenneth More is particularly good), this sometimes hilarious film started the series off on a high note.

DR. JEKYLL AND MR. HYDE

1932 90m bw Horror ★★★★½
Paramount (U.S.) /15

Fredric March *(Dr. Henry Jekyll/Mr. Hyde)*, Miriam Hopkins *(Ivy Pearson)*, Rose Hobart *(Muriel Carew)*, Holmes Herbert *(Dr. Lanyon)*, Edgar Norton *(Poole)*, Halliwell Hobbes *(Brig-Gen. Carew)*, Arnold Lucy *(Utterson)*, Tempe Pigott *(Mrs. Hawkins)*, Col. G.L. McDonnell *(Hobson)*, Eric Wilton *(Briggs)*

p, Rouben Mamoulian; d, Rouben Mamoulian; w, Samuel Hoffenstein, Percy Heath (based on the novel *The Strange Case of Dr. Jekyll and Mr. Hyde* by Robert Louis Stevenson); ph, Karl Struss; ed, William Shea; art d, Hans Dreier; cos, Travis Banton

AA Best Actor: Fredric March; *AAN Best Adapted Screenplay:* Percy Heath, Samuel Hoffenstein; *AAN Best Cinematography:* Karl Struss

Easily the best of the many versions of the Stevenson horror classic. Although heavily made up as a jagged-toothed simian, March is memory-scarring with his weird body language and fierce posturing as Hyde, in stark contrast to the upright if simpering Jekyll. As Jekyll, courting his unattainable fiancee (Hobart) or tampering with nature and chemistry to create the evil side of his nature in living form, March embodies the essence of gentility. As Hyde, March is truly frightening in his hideous alter ego who taunts and brutalizes a promiscuous barmaid (Hopkins). The film reaches its exciting finale as the law confronts the grotesque Hyde, locked out of his laboratory, only to discover that he is also the respectable Dr. Jekyll.

March deservedly won an Oscar for his astonishing "dual" role (shared with Wallace Beery for THE CHAMP), but perhaps the real star of the film is director Mamoulian, whose audacious use of symbolism and careful pacing increase the mystique of this strange story. His heavy use of point-of-view editing is entirely appropriate to the story, and Struss's outstanding photography is a marvel to behold.

Made before the Production Code clampdown in 1934, DR. JEKYLL AND MR. HYDE not only uses violence to great effect but also does not shy away from the links between horror and sexuality. During the first transformation scene Mamoulian includes a montage which makes it clear that Hyde represents Jekyll's id, the socially and sexually repressed side of the doctor's psyche. The highly charged scenes between March and Hopkins (who's marvelous as Ivy) are the film's highlights, while those between March and the suitably demure Hobart pale by comparison.

DR. NO

1962 110m c Spy ★★★½
UA (U.K.) /PG

Sean Connery *(James Bond)*, Jack Lord *(Felix Leiter)*, Joseph Wiseman *(Dr. No)*, Ursula Andress *(Honey)*, Zena Marshall *(Miss Taro)*, Eunice Gayson *(Sylvia)*, Lois Maxwell *(Miss Moneypenny)*, Margaret LeWars *(Photographer)*, John Kitzmiller *(Quarrel)*, Bernard Lee *("M")*

p, Harry Saltzman, Albert R. Broccoli; d, Terence Young; w, Richard Maibaum, Johanna Harwood, Berkely Mather (based on the novel by Ian Fleming); ph, Ted Moore; ed, Peter Hunt; m, John Barry, Monty Norman; prod d, Ken Adam; art d, Syd Cain; fx, Frank George

The first entry in what was to become the most profitable movie series of all time is a solid, surprisingly modest spy thriller, enlivened by Sean Connery's screen charisma and occasional hints of the extravagance to come. James Bond (Sean Connery) is sent by his Secret Service superior, "M" (Bernard Lee), to investigate the murder of another agent in Jamaica. There he learns of Dr. No (Joseph Wiseman), a mysterious Eurasian who's up to something sinister on his private island, Crab Key.

In the service of SPECTRE—the Special Executive for Counterintelligence, Terrorism, Revenge and Extortion—Dr. No has built a device that can alter the flight paths of rockets launched from Cape Canaveral. Bond survives several attempts on his life—notably a skin-crawling encounter with a poisonous spider—and makes his way to Crab Key, where he meets knife-toting, bikini-clad Honey Rider (Ursula Andress) and does battle with a flame-throwing armored vehicle. After Bond and Honey become the evil scientist's prisoners, 007 must defeat a private army single-handed.

In DR. NO, the Bond formula is not yet graven in stone, and viewers may be surprised by the absence of favorite conventions—e.g., the standard title sequence, with silhouetted nude bodies floating in space to the tune of a lush pop ballad. Still, under director Young's sure hand, the performances are amusing and the plotline suitably enthralling. To play Bond, producers Albert "Cubby" Broccoli and Harry Saltzman required a relative unknown with just the right combination of ruggedness, suavity, and sex appeal. Connery fit the profile and instantly made the role his own (to the chagrin of Roger Moore and other later Bond impersonators). Dr. NO is also notable for introducing John Barry's famous James Bond theme music (although the featured song, a forgettable piece of *faux* calypso called "Underneath the Mango Tree," is repeated at least once too often).

DR. STRANGELOVE OR: HOW I LEARNED TO STOP WORRYING AND LOVE THE BOMB

1963 102m bw Science Fiction/Comedy/War ★★★★★
Columbia (U.K.) /PG

Peter Sellers *(Group Capt. Lionel Mandrake/President Merkin Muffley/Dr. Strangelove)*, George C. Scott *(Gen. "Buck" Turgidson)*, Sterling Hayden *(Gen. Jack D. Ripper)*, Keenan Wynn *(Col. "Bat" Guano)*,

Slim Pickens *(Maj. T.J. "King" Kong)*, Peter Bull *(Ambassador de Sadesky)*, Tracy Reed *(Miss Scott)*, James Earl Jones *(Lt. Lothar Zogg)*, Jack Creley *(Mr. Staines)*, Frank Berry *(Lt. H.R. Dietrich)*

p, Stanley Kubrick; d, Stanley Kubrick; w, Stanley Kubrick, Terry Southern, Peter George (based on the novel *Red Alert* by Peter George); ph, Gilbert Taylor; ed, Anthony Harvey; m, Laurie Johnson; prod d, Ken Adam; art d, Peter Murton; fx, Wally Veevers; cos, Bridget Sellers

AAN Best Picture; AAN Best Actor: Peter Sellers; *AAN Best Director:* Stanley Kubrick; *AAN Best Adapted Screenplay:* Stanley Kubrick, Peter George, Terry Southern

Easily the funniest movie ever made about global thermonuclear holocaust, DR. STRANGELOVE seems to grow more relevant with each passing year. Obsessed with the idea that Communists are trying to rob Americans of their "precious bodily fluids," General Jack D. Ripper (Hayden), commander of Burpelson Air Force Base, goes completely mad and sends his bomber wing to attack the USSR. US President Muffley (Sellers) meets desperately with his advisors, including blustery Gen. "Buck" Turgidson (Scott) and wheelchair-bound ex-Nazi scientist Dr. Strangelove (also played by Sellers). Left with little choice, the powers that be formulate a plan to have the Russians shoot down the American bombers. However, the Soviet ambassador (Bull), informs the president that the Soviet Union has constructed a "Doomsday Device" which will automatically trigger buried nuclear weapons if their country is hit. Meanwhile, British officer Lionel Mandrake (also Sellers) busies himself with trying to trick Gen. Ripper into revealing the code that will recall the bombers. Eventually, all of them are shot down or recalled, except for one flown by Major T.J. "King" Kong (Pickens), a crafty pilot who manages to evade Russian fighters and missiles as he heads for his target deep inside the USSR. One of the film's final images, that of Kong riding the phallic bomb like a bucking bronco, is unforgettable.

Expertly directed by Kubrick, who deftly intercuts the events at Burpelson with the War Room conference and the action on Kong's B-52, DR. STRANGELOVE is the ultimate black comedy, one that makes unthinkable horror unbearably funny. The film is a model of barely controlled hysteria in which the absurdity of hypermasculine Cold War posturing becomes devastatingly funny—and at the same time nightmarishly frightening in its accuracy. (The Burpelson motto, "Peace Is Our Profession," is not so absurd; consider the labeling of the Strategic Defense Initiative as a "Peace Shield.") While at times Kubrick seems to strive a bit too hard for laughs (Keenan Wynn's being sprayed in the face after shooting a Coca-Cola machine comes to mind), other effects, especially the cinematography and Adam's brilliant production design, potently enhance the film's satirical vision.

STRANGELOVE also contains some truly remarkable comic performances, especially from Sellers in his triple role and Hayden as the mad general, and genuinely priceless dialogue ("Gentlemen, you can't fight in here. This is the War Room!"). A prophetic look at the insanity of superpower politics which, like George Orwell's *1984*, has entered the lexicon of modern political discourse.

DOCTOR X

1932 77m c/bw Horror   ★★★★
First National (U.S.)   /A

Lionel Atwill *(Doctor Xavier, Head of Research Laboratory)*, Lee Tracy *(Lee, a Newspaper Reporter)*, Fay Wray *(Joanne, Dr. X's Daughter)*, Preston Foster *(Dr. Wells)*, Arthur Edmund Carewe *(Dr. Rowitz)*, John Wray *(Dr. Haines)*, Harry Beresford *(Dr. Duke)*, George Rosener *(Otto, Dr. X's Butler)*, Leila Bennett *(Mamie, Dr. X's Housekeeper)*, Robert Warwick *(Police Commissioner Stevens)*

d, Michael Curtiz; w, Robert Tasker, Earl Baldwin (based on a play by Howard Warren Comstock and Allen C. Miller); ph, Ray Rennahan, Richard Towers; ed, George Amy; art d, Anton Grot

A rare excursion into horror for First National (later Warner Bros.), DR. X became one of the great "lost" films after its initial release and developed a reputation as a masterpiece of early talkie horror during the 30 years it went unseen. When a black-and-white print of this two-color Technicolor landmark was finally discovered, however, some

found the film a disappointment. Now that enough time has passed and viewers can forget all those long-cherished expectations, the film proves to be a delightful product of its period.

The story is set in a spooky old mansion atop the cliffs at Blackstone Shoals on Long Island. Atwill plays the sinister Dr. Xavier, who runs the research laboratory where most of the action takes place. It seems that a member of his staff has discovered a synthetic flesh substitute which imbues its wearer with abnormal powers and this transformed monster has been strangling people during full moons. Much of the film involves a recreation of the murders designed to expose the killer, but all does not go quite as planned.

Talented studio craftsman Curtiz (CASABLANCA) shapes the material well, showing particular flair in his semi-expressionistic handling of the haunted house trappings of the story. If he doesn't have quite the flair for grotesquerie or black humor of James Whale, he does use the wisecracking of Tracy and the glowering of Atwill to good effect. Atwill especially shines when called upon to casually discuss topics from cannibalism to depravity. Several scenes, from the unexpected animation of a skeleton to the recreation of the final murder, where the killer puts in an unexpected guest appearance, are genuinely eerie. Fay Wray, as Dr. Xavier's daughter, also gets to scream as only she can.

Finally, the two-color Technicolor techniques (involving the processing of two negatives rather than the three which became standard after 1935) are extremely effective. The rather slack and hokey 1939 film, THE RETURN OF DOCTOR X, is not a sequel, but it does contain Humphrey Bogart's only horror movie appearance.

DOCTOR ZHIVAGO

1965 197m c Drama/War   ★★★★
MGM (U.S.)   /15

Geraldine Chaplin *(Tonya)*, Julie Christie *(Lara)*, Tom Courtenay *(Pasha/Strelnikoff)*, Alec Guinness *(Yevgraf)*, Siobhan McKenna *(Anna)*, Ralph Richardson *(Alexander)*, Omar Sharif *(Yuri)*, Rod Steiger *(Komarovsky)*, Rita Tushingham *(The Girl)*, Adrienne Corri *(Amelia)*

p, Carlo Ponti; d, David Lean; w, Robert Bolt (based on the novel by Boris Pasternak); ph, Freddie Young; ed, Norman Savage; m, Maurice Jarre; prod d, John Box; art d, Terence Marsh; fx, Eddie Fowlie; cos, Phyllis Dalton

AAN Best Picture; AAN Best Supporting Actor: Tom Courtenay; *AAN Best Director:* David Lean; *AA Best Adapted Screenplay:* Robert Bolt; *AA Best Cinematography:* Freddie Young; *AAN Best Editing:* Norman Savage; *AA Best Score:* Maurice Jarre; *AA Best Art Direction:* John Box, Terry Marsh, Dario Simoni; *AA Best Costume Design:* Phyllis Dalton; *AAN Best Sound:* A.W. Watkins, Franklin E. Milton

Lumpy if sometimes sinfully rich borscht. This sprawling adaptation of Pasternak's epic novel of the Russian Revolution was director Lean's follow-up to his masterful LAWRENCE OF ARABIA. Told in flashback, the film follows Yuri Zhivago (Sharif) and Tonya Gromeko (Chaplin), who meet as youths when the orphaned Yuri is taken in by Tonya's parents. Eventually Yuri becomes a physician and marries Tonya, but several times during WWI he crosses paths with Lara (Christie), the beautiful daughter of a dressmaker, and the two fall into a passionate affair that is disrupted by the Bolshevik Revolution.

Unable to maintain a consistent level of interest through its seat-squirmingly long running time, this typically overblown Lean epic is not as exciting or as powerful as LAWRENCE OF ARABIA or THE BRIDGE ON THE RIVER KWAI. Bolt's choppy screenplay leaves out great chunks of Pasternak's novel, turning the narrative in a bumpy, who-gives-a-damn roller coaster ride in the film's last half. Equally regrettable is the miscasting of Sharif, who had done quite well in LAWRENCE but here contributes a performance with all the sparkle of sawdust. Christie, Steiger, and (to a lesser extent) Guinness, however, imbue their parts with passion and intensity, and the huge supporting cast is generally fine.

As always, Lean's handling of the purely physical aspects of the material is spectacular, with the scenes of revolution, the harsh Russian winters, and Zhivago's trek across the steppes simply unforgettable. Filmed mostly in Spain and Finland, the cinematography is often stunning even when the effects are pretentious (e.g. Lean's screen-filling closeup of the inside of a flower). Jarre's jarring score, though much praised at the time for the lilting "Lara's Theme," now seems repetitive and grating enough to make one want to sabotage balalaika factories everywhere.

DODGE CITY

1939 104m c Western ★★★★
Warner Bros. (U.S.) /PG

Errol Flynn (*Wade Hatton*), Olivia de Havilland (*Abbie Irving*), Ann Sheridan (*Ruby Gilman*), Bruce Cabot (*Jeff Surrett*), Frank McHugh (*Joe Clemens*), Alan Hale (*Rusty Hart*), John Litel (*Matt Cole*), Victor Jory (*Yancy*), Henry Travers (*Dr. Irving*), Henry O'Neill (*Col. Dodge*)

p, Robert Lord; d, Michael Curtiz; w, Robert Buckner; ph, Ray Rennahan, Sol Polito; ed, George Amy; m, Max Steiner; art d, Ted Smith; fx, Byron Haskin, Rex Wimpy; cos, Milo Anderson

This great action Western, Flynn's first, has the intrepid adventurer enter Dodge City, a notorious, wide-open range town, as cattle buyer Wade Hatton. He leads lawmen to rustler Jeff Surrett (Cabot) and his henchmen (Jory and Fowley) before leading a covered wagon train with his pals (Hale and Guinn "Big Boy" Williams) en route to Dodge City. Attracted to spirited Abbie Irving (de Havilland), he draws only her scorn after she blames him for the death of her brother (Lundigan), a hellion crushed in a stampede he himself started. Once at Dodge City, Wade finds that Surrett now runs the town and, after being pushed far enough, takes the sheriff's badge and cleans up the hellhole. Although he has a brief flirtation with saloon gal Ruby Gilman (Sheridan), his heart belongs to Abbie, and she soon comes to respect Wade's heroic endeavors.

DODGE CITY is top-flight action directed with verve and invention by Warner Bros. workhorse Curtiz. In a year with plenty of worthy Western competition, this expensively mounted film nevertheless found a wide and appreciative public. Polito's camerawork, highlighted by the rich use of color, is sweeping and fluid, and Steiner's score is vigorous and effective. A sequence involving a burning runaway train is handled well and the saloon brawl midway through the film, used time and again by the studio as stock footage, is magnificently staged and remains a classic of its kind. Not too surprisingly, de Havilland hated her rather standardized role, and Sheridan, in a more colorful part, unfortunately doesn't get as much footage as she deserves. This film belongs to the men, especially Flynn, who attacks the part with gusto and suitably adapts his British veneer to the code of the Old West. Flynn would make seven more Westerns, but DODGE CITY remains his best outing in the genre. The story line for BLAZING SADDLES was taken from this film.

DODSWORTH

1936 90m bw Romance ★★★★★
UA (U.S.) /PG

Walter Huston (*Sam Dodsworth*), Ruth Chatterton (*Fran Dodsworth*), Paul Lukas (*Arnold Iselin*), Mary Astor (*Edith Cortright*), David Niven (*Lockert*), Gregory Gaye (*Kurt von Obersdorf*), Maria Ouspenskaya (*Baroness von Obersdorf*), Odette Myrtil (*Mme. de Penable*), Kathryn Marlowe (*Emily*), Spring Byington (*Matey Pearson*)

p, Samuel Goldwyn; d, William Wyler; w, Sidney Howard (based on his play, adapted from the novel by Sinclair Lewis); ph, Rudolph Mate; ed, Daniel Mandell; m, Alfred Newman; art d, Richard Day; fx, Ray Binger; cos, Omar Kiam

AAN Best Picture; AAN Best Actor: Walter Huston; AAN Best Supporting Actress: Maria Ouspenskaya; AAN Best Director: William Wyler; AAN Best Screenplay: Sidney Howard; AA Best Art Direction: Richard Day; AAN Best Sound: Oscar Lagerstrom

A film of maturity, intelligence, and understanding. Huston, repeating his popular stage role, plays reserved auto mogul Sam Dodsworth, who retires to enjoy his middle age at the prompting of his wife Fran (Chatterton). Traveling in Europe, the unsophisticated Midwesterners have completely opposite reactions to the Continental milieu: while Sam soon gets bored, Fran aspires to become a woman of the world. Embarrassed by her flirtation with a roue (Niven) and hurt by her encounter with a more subtle adventurer (Lukas), Fran doesn't learn from her failures. She finally asks Sam for a divorce in order to marry

a young but mother-dominated baron (Gaye). Sam, meanwhile, meets a kindly widow (Astor) with whom he finds he might salvage his happiness. But the longtime romance of Sam and Fran must be dealt with first.

The direction of the autocratic Wyler sensitively plots a tale of marital problems, middle age, and the Ugly American abroad. Huston was never better than in this magnificent performance of a simple man whose blissful world disintegrates. His effortless acting was so splendidly moving that he was voted Best Actor by the NY Film Critics. (With their typical fondness for showy acting, however, Oscar voters cited Paul Muni in THE STORY OF LOUIS PASTEUR.) Chatterton, too, is superb in a role she wanted to play as a total heavy. Wyler, though, was wisely able to temper this portrait of a selfish, shallow woman with great insight. Chatterton's sometimes theatrical emoting perfectly suits her rich study of a woman playacting her way through life. The low-key scenes between Huston and Chatterton are warm and tender, while their arguments are positively blistering. The support includes gems from Lukas, Niven, Gaye, Ouspenskaya, Myrtil, and Byington, but it is really Astor who equals the stars with a performance of consummate artistry.

DOG DAY AFTERNOON

1975 130m c Crime ★★★★★
Artists Entertainment (U.S.) R/15

Al Pacino (*Sonny*), John Cazale (*Sal*), Charles Durning (*Moretti*), Chris Sarandon (*Leon*), Sully Boyar (*Mulvaney*), Penny Allen (*Sylvia*), James Broderick (*Sheldon*), Carol Kane (*Jenny*), Susan Peretz (*Angie*), Beulah Garrick (*Margaret*)

p, Martin Bregman, Martin Elfand; d, Sidney Lumet; w, Frank Pierson (based on a magazine article by P.F. Kluge, Thomas Moore); ph, Victor J. Kemper; ed, Dede Allen; prod d, Charles Bailey; art d, Douglas Higgins; cos, Anna Hill Johnstone

AAN Best Picture; AAN Best Actor: Al Pacino; AAN Best Supporting Actor: Chris Sarandon; AAN Best Director: Sidney Lumet; AA Best Original Screenplay: Frank Pierson; AAN Best Editing: Dede Allen

One of the finest films of the 1970s. A bisexual man, Sonny (Pacino), to finance a sex-change operation for his transvestite lover (Sarandon), robs the First Savings Bank of Brooklyn with his moronic friend Sal (Cazale). Police, headed by Moretti (Durning), surround the bank and hold the thieves inside who, in turn, hold employees and customers as hostages. Through it all Sonny carries on endless phone conversations with his obese wife (Peretz), his lover, and assorted police and FBI officials. At one point, while releasing a female hostage, Sonny notices the large crowds outside, watching from behind barriers as if at a carnival. To enlist mob sympathy he begins to shout "Attica! Attica!" (the name of the New York prison where authorities inflicted heavy casualties on rioting prisoners). The crowd picks up the chant, decidedly favoring the bank robbers. Ultimately, however, Sonny threatens to begin shooting hostages unless he and Sal are given $1 million and taken to the airport where they will be flown to a distant country. (When Sonny asks his dim friend what country he wants to go to, the *non compos mentis* thief replies, "Wyoming.") Sonny and Sal's getaway attempt brings this remarkable film to its simmering finale.

DOG DAY AFTERNOON benefits immeasurably from a cast and crew doing some of the finest work of their careers. In a role based on actual incident, Pacino is both funny and tragic as the uneducated, passionate street tough over his head in a lethal situation of his own making. In difficult roles, Cazale and Sarandon are similarly superb, and even those actors on more familiar ground (Durning, Broderick, Peretz) contribute sterling support. The taut script and Lumet's exceptionally disciplined and insightful direction highlight both the suspense and the absurdity of the situation beautifully. The heavy use of off-color language and scorching violence if anything adds to the ultimate sympathy this memorable film successfully evokes.

$ (DOLLARS)

1971 119m c Crime/Comedy ★★★½
Columbia (U.S.) R/15

Warren Beatty *(Joe Collins)*, Goldie Hawn *(Dawn Divine)*, Gert Frobe *(Mr. Kessel)*, Robert Webber *(Attorney)*, Scott Brady *(Sarge)*, Arthur Brauss *(Candy Man)*, Robert Stiles *(Major)*, Wolfgang Kieling *(Granich)*, Robert Herron *(Bodyguard)*, Christiane Maybach *(Helga)*

p, M.J. Frankovich; d, Richard Brooks; w, Richard Brooks; ph, Petrus Schloemp; ed, George Grenville; m, Quincy Jones; art d, Guy Sheppard, Olaf Ivens

$ (DOLLARS) is a pleasant, somewhat underrated chase movie which was written and directed by Richard Brooks, in a significant departure from the heavy dramas (IN COLD BLOOD, THE BROTHERS KARAMAZOV, THE BLACKBOARD JUNGLE, and CAT ON A HOT TIN ROOF) he was usually associated with.

Joe Collins (Beatty) is a security expert employed in Hamburg who plans to rob three safety deposit boxes which he knows are rented by criminals, and Dawn Divine (Hawn) is a prostitute whom he enlists to help him in the endeavor. Their targets are a crooked US Army sergeant (Brady) who scammed money from service clubs, a drug dealer (Brauss) and a courier (Webber) who's been double-dealing the mob. Employed at their bank to install a security system, Collins arranges to be placed inside the vault after a bomb scare. Timing his moves perfectly so as to go unnoticed by surveillance cameras, he stashes the loot in Dawn's safety deposit box so she can blithely collect it later.

An exercise in triviality, and, like most of Brooks's films, not particulary original, $ is nevertheless quite entertaining. Beatty and Hawn play extremely well together and Frobe is outstanding as the bank manager. Running rather longer than one might like, $ benefits from Brooks's lively handling and Quincy Jones's sparse but effective musical score.

DON QUIXOTE
(DON QUICHOTTE)

1933 73m bw Musical ★★★★
Nelson/Vandor (U.K./France) /U

Feodor Chaliapin *(Don Quixote)*, George Robey *(Sancho Panza)*, Sidney Fox *(The Niece)*, Miles Mander *(The Duke)*, Oscar Asche *(Police Captain)*, Dannio *(Carrasco)*, Emily Fitzroy *(Sancho's Wife)*, Renee Valliers *(Dulcinea)*, Frank Stanmore *(Priest)*, Wally Patch *(Gypsy King)*

p, G.W. Pabst; d, G.W. Pabst; w, Paul Morand, Alexandre Arnoux (based on the novel *Don Quixote De La Mancha* by Miguel de Cervantes); ph, Nicolas Farkas; m, Jacques Ibert

Save only the denouement—an allegory added by director Pabst and the French adaptors—this is a fairly faithful rendition of the 300-year-old tale of "The Knight of the Mournful Countenance." Chaliapin, as famed for his striking acting as for his operatic basso, plays Don Quixote, the man immersed for years in the library of chivalric romances for which he has mortgaged his estates. Venturing forth on his bony nag Rocinante, the quiet country gentleman elects to redress the wrongs of the world. He enlists the aid of Sancho Panza (Robey) as his squire, promising him great future rewards in return for faithful service. He pronounces Dulcinea (Valliers), a slatternly milkmaid, to be the fair and pure maiden whose honor he is pledged to protect. Taking windmills for giants and flocks of sheep for armies, he battles them with vigor but invariably suffers defeat.

Many viewers saw in this film an allegorical reference to the Nazi bookburnings of the 1930s, as Pabst's ending departs completely from Cervantes's original, in which the disillusioned Don Quixote renounces his books of knightly lore. Pabst's liberal political orientation had been demonstrated in many of his earlier films, such as KAMERADSCHAFT and THE THREEPENNY OPERA (both 1931). Regardless of the director's political convictions (he later made films under the Nazi regime and, later still, produced a number of anti-fascist films), this telling of the tale benefits from a memorable windmill sequence and its stunning star turn by Chaliapin.

DON QUIXOTE
(DON-KIKHOT)

1957 110m c Drama ★★★★
Lenfilm (U.S.S.R.) /U

Nikolai Cherkassov *(Don Quixote)*, Yuri Tolubeyev *(Sancho Panza)*, T. Agamirova *(Altisidora)*, V. Freindlich *(Duke)*, L. Vertinskaya *(Duchess)*, Georgiy Vitsin *(Carrasco)*, L. Kasyanova *(Aldonsa)*, O. Viklandt *(Peasant Girl)*, Serafima Birman *(Housekeeper)*, A. Beniaminov *(Shepherd)*

d, Gregory Kozintsev; w, Yevgeniy Shvarts (based on the novel by Miguel de Cervantes); ph, Andrey Moskvin, Apollinariy Dudko; ed, Ye. Makhankova; m, Kara Karayev; art d, Yevgeniy Yeney

The final Soviet film to reach the US under a joint cultural exchange program halted due to bad relations between the administrations of President Kennedy and Premier Khrushchev, this is an excellent and faithful adaptation of the Cervantes novel. Cherkassov, the USSR's best-known actor, on screen since 1927 in roles such as ALEXANDER NEVSKY and the two-part IVAN THE TERRIBLE, brings to the knight the same level of demented dignity possessed by Chaliapin in G.W. Pabst's 1935 version. Tolubeyev's Sancho Panza, with his field smarts, is a fine match for Cherkassov's chivalric Don Quixote. Technically adept, in wide screen and color, the film reflects the long-time collaboration of director Kozintsev and cameraman Moskvin, both active in FEX (Factory of Eccentric Actors). The English dubbing is wonderfully handled; the English-language actors' voices are well suited to the roles. Location scenes, resembling the Iberian plain, were shot in the Crimea.

DONA FLOR AND HER TWO HUSBANDS
(DONA FLOR E SEUS DOIS MARIDOS)

1976 106m c Erotic/Comedy ★★★
Coline/Gaumont (Brazil) R/X

Sonia Braga *(Dona Flor)*, Jose Wilker *(Vadhino)*, Mauro Mendonca *(Teodoro)*, Dinorah Brillanti *(Rozilda)*, Nelson Xavier *(Mirandao)*, Arthur Costa Filho *(Carlinhos)*, Rui Rezende *(Cazuza)*, Mario Gusmao

p, Luis Carlos Barreto, Newton Rique, Cia Serrador; d, Bruno Barreto; w, Bruno Barreto (based on a novel by Jorge Amado); ph, Maurilo Salles; ed, Raimundo Higino; m, Chico Buarque; art d, Anisio Medeiros

This wonderfully sexy and funny comedy, a variation on BLITHE SPIRIT, shattered Brazilian box-office records and proved very popular worldwide, chiefly because of Braga's tremendously sensual presence. She plays a beautiful woman whose gambling, whoring husband drops dead after an all-night carousal. Deciding to marry again, she chooses a boring, devout, middle-aged pharmacist who rarely wants to make love. One night, as she lies in bed next to her sleeping spouse, the ghost of her first husband appears, nude, in the room. She tries to get rid of him, but he refuses. She finally succumbs to his blandishments and takes the ghost to bed with her, while the second husband continues to sleep.

This entertaining and erotic picture, while perhaps not the most challenging film to come out of Brazil in the 1970s, is nevertheless enjoyable. At times, though, the creative personalities involved seem to want to play it both ways and make it "art cinema" as well as "commercial cinema" simply because it was aimed at the international market. Director Barreto and Braga teamed up again in in GABRIELA, costarring Marcello Mastroianni. Remade in 1982 as KISS ME GOODBYE with—are you ready for this?—Sally Field in the lead role.

DONA HERLINDA AND HER SON
(DONA HERLINDA Y SU HIJO)

1986 90m c Comedy ★★★★½
Cinevista (Mexico) /15

Guadalupe Del Toro *(Dona Herlinda)*, Arturo Meza *(Ramon)*, Marco Antonio Trevino *(Rodolfo)*, Leticia Lupersio *(Olga)*, Guillermina Alba

p, Manuel Barbachano Ponce; d, Jaime Humberto Hermosillo; w, Jaime Humberto Hermosillo (based on a novel by Jorge Lopez Paez); ph, Miguel Ehrenberg; ed, Luis Kelly

A sex comedy usually succeeds when it gives a fresh twist to old expectations, something the satirical DONA HERLINDA AND HER SON does with unrelenting zest. Dona Herlinda (Del Toro) is the wealthy mother of Rodolfo (Trevino), a closeted gay doctor involved in a relationship with Ramon (Meza), a music student. The two men are in desperate need of some privacy to carry on their affair, a problem which seems to be solved when Dona Herlinda invites Ramon to move in with her and her son. This is more than an act of charity, though, for this particular doting mother has an involved plan to keep her son both happy and respectable, bringing in Olga (Lupersio) to become Rodolfo's heterosexual wife. Disappointed with his lover's acceptance of this plan and jealous of Olga, Ramon goes out for a romp, but is unable to forget the traitorous mama's boy he loves.

Marvelously funny, DONA HERLINDA AND HER SON develops its unusual plot line in a simple, matter-of-fact style, and the final twists arrive at the end of considerable comic momentum. What is most amazing is not only Dona Herlinda's orchestration of personality and situation, but what also seems to be her determined blindness to her son's homosexuality. Each of the characters is mindfully etched, with performances that make the viewer honestly care about these people. Sexual situations, be they homosexual or heterosexual, are wisely presented without judgment, simply becoming a part of the hilarious comic tableau. Director Hermosillo skillfully evolves a pointed yet gentle satire of mothering and traditional family structures while managing to produce a highly engaging entertainment at the same time.

DONNIE BRASCO
1997   121m   c   Crime   ★★★½
Mandalay Entertainment/Baltimore Pictures   (U.S.)   R/18

Al Pacino *(Lefty Ruggiero)*, Johnny Depp *(Donnie Brasco/Joe Pistone)*, Michael Madsen *(Sonny)*, Bruno Kirby *(Nicky)*, James Russo *(Paulie)*, Anne Heche *(Maggie Pistone)*, Zeljko Ivanek *(Tim Curley)*, Gerry Becker *(Dean Blandford)*, Zach Grenier *(Dr. Berger)*, Brian Tarantina *(Bruno)*

p, Mark Johnson, Barry Levinson, Louis DiGiaimo, Gail Mutrux; d, Mike Newell; w, Paul Attanasio (based on the book *Donnie Brasco: My Undercover Life in the Mafia*, by Joseph D. Pistone with Richard Woodley); ph, Peter Sova; ed, Jon Gregory; m, Patrick Doyle; prod d, Donald Graham Burt; art d, Jefferson Sage; fx, Ronald Ottesen Jr.; cos, Aude Bronson-Howard, David Robinson

Perhaps the freshest gangster movie since THE GODFATHER, PART II, as well as the glummest. FBI agent Joe Pistone (Johnny Depp) infiltrates the mob via a disgruntled, middle-aged, low-level Mafioso named Lefty (Al Pacino), who sees the son he wishes he had in Pistone's undercover persona—orphan Donnie Brasco, a shrewd but honest operator with heart. Pistone learns the organization inside out, eventually burrowing in so deep that the danger of being unmasked takes a back seat to the danger of being killed by rival mobsters for his organized crime alliances. With acceptance comes the inevitable crisis of conscience, as Pistone drifts further and further away from his so-called real life: his wife and kids become strangers, and the uptight FBI higher-ups don't understand the toll that living a day-in, day-out lie takes on a man's sense of self. You know he'll get out somehow—the movie's based on the memoirs of the real-life Pistone, who lived to tell—but the suspense of wondering how, and who will be hurt in the process, is excruciating. The most striking thing about Mike Newell's approach is how clear it is that the whole American mythology of the Mafia leaves him cold. There's no sense of exhilaration in putting one over on the law, no warmth in the *familiga*, no real honor among hoods and no hopped-up intensity in violence: it's all dangerous and arbitrary and ugly, even before it all goes wrong. Depp's tight, guarded performance is almost painful to watch, and Newell seems to have reined in the flamboyant Pacino, whose portrait of the mobster as a grumpy old woman may be his best work in years.

DON'S PARTY
1976   90m   c   Comedy   ★★★★
Double Head   (Australia)   /X

Ray Barrett *(Mal)*, Claire Binney *(Susan)*, Pat Bishop *(Jenny)*, Graeme Blundell *(Simon)*, Jeanie Drynan *(Kath)*, John Gorton *(Himself)*, John Hargreaves *(Don)*, Harold Hopkins *(Cooley)*, Graham Kennedy *(Mack)*, Veronica Lang *(Jody)*

p, Phillip Adams; d, Bruce Beresford; w, David Williamson (based on his play); ph, Don McAlpine; ed, Bill Anderson; m, Leos Janacek; art d, Rhoisin Harrison; cos, Anna Senior

Excellent drama from Down Under concerns a group of friends in the suburbs that gathers to watch election results on television. As the party wears on and everyone's tongue is loosened by alcohol, the veneer of camaraderie drops away, and the men reveal themselves to be a set of back-biting boors, verbally attacking each other like characters straight out of WHO'S AFRAID OF VIRGINIA WOOLF. Extremely well directed by Beresford (BREAKER MORANT), with sharp dialogue and terrific performances all around. American audiences won't catch all of the slang expressions and will need to get used to the thick accents, but the effort of immersing oneself into this black comedy-drama is well worth it.

DON'T LOOK NOW
1973   110m   c   Mystery   ★★★★½
Casey/Eldorado   (U.K./Italy)   R/18

Julie Christie *(Laura Baxter)*, Donald Sutherland *(John Baxter)*, Hilary Mason *(Heather)*, Clelia Matania *(Wendy)*, Massimo Serato *(Bishop)*, Renato Scarpa *(Inspector Longhi)*, Giorgio Trestini *(Workman)*, Leopoldo Trieste *(Hotel Manager)*, David Tree *(Anthony Babbage)*, Ann Rye *(Mandy Babbage)*

p, Peter Katz; d, Nicolas Roeg; w, Allan Scott, Chris Bryant (based on a short story by Daphne du Maurier); ph, Anthony Richmond; ed, Graeme Clifford; m, Pino Donaggio; art d, Giovanni Soccol

A truly eerie film, based on a story by Daphne du Maurier. John Baxter (Sutherland) travels to Venice with his wife, Laura (Christie), after the accidental drowning death in England of their young daughter. While completing restoration work on a church, Baxter discovers he has certain psychic abilities—abilities nourished by two very strange sisters, Wendy (Matania) and Heather (Mason), who have visions of the couple's dead daughter. Baxter refuses to believe in his powers, but he begins to relent when he sees a small figure darting around Venice dressed in the same red raincoat that his daughter wore. These sightings, coupled with his haunting visions of a funeral boat drifting down a Venetian canal, make for a puzzling and mysterious atmosphere in which "nothing is what it seems."

Making wonderful use of Venice locales and boasting two fine performances from Sutherland and Christie (including one of the most convincing lovemaking scenes ever), DON'T LOOK NOW is one of director Roeg's finest and most accessible films. Among many memorable scenes, Baxter's near-fall in the church and his final encounter with the red-cloaked figure are particularly memorable. While the vagueness of the plot may frustrate viewers at first, the payoff is considerable for patient audiences. A film which more than gets by on its directorial style, unforgettable imagery, and striking music alone, DON'T LOOK NOW also manages to be a haunting meditation on fear, death and the beyond.

DOUBLE INDEMNITY
1944   106m   bw   Crime   ★★★★★
Paramount   (U.S.)   /PG

Fred MacMurray *(Walter Neff)*, Barbara Stanwyck *(Phyllis Dietrichson)*, Edward G. Robinson *(Barton Keyes)*, Porter Hall *(Mr. Jackson)*, Jean Heather *(Lola Dietrichson)*, Tom Powers *(Mr. Dietrichson)*, Gig Young *(Nino Zachette)*, Richard Gaines *(Mr. Norton)*, Fortunio Bonanova *(Sam Gorlopis)*, John Philliber *(Joe Pete)*

p, Joseph Sistrom; d, Billy Wilder; w, Raymond Chandler, Billy Wilder (based on a short story in the book *Three of A Kind* by James M. Cain); ph, John Seitz; ed, Doane Harrison; m, Miklos Rozsa, Cesar Franck; art d, Hans Dreier, Hal Pereira; cos, Edith Head

DOUBLE LIFE, A

AAN Best Picture; *AAN Best Actress:* Barbara Stanwyck; *AAN Best Director:* Billy Wilder; *AAN Best Original Screenplay:* Raymond Chandler, Billy Wilder; *AAN Best Cinematography:* John Seitz; *AAN Best Score:* Miklos Rozsa; *AAN Best Sound:* Loren Ryder (Sound)

A seminal work in the emergence of film noir as an explosive movement in American film. Based on the notorious Snyder-Gray case of 1927, DOUBLE INDEMNITY is both a starkly realistic and a carefully stylized masterpiece of murder.

Walter Neff (MacMurray), bleeding from a bullet wound, staggers into an office building. As he speaks into his dictating machine, we learn in flashback that he is an insurance salesman who becomes involved with the sleek Phyllis Dietrichson (Stanwyck). Phyllis convinces Walter not only to help her take out a life insurance policy on her husband (Powers) without his knowledge, but also to help her murder him in order to collect on it. Staging an unlikely accident in order to qualify for the "double indemnity" clause in the contract, the deadly duo must next face claims adjustor Barton Keyes (Robinson), whose instinct tells him that something suspicious is afoot. Their faith in their story and each other sorely tested, Walter and Phyllis finally square off in a fatal game of cat and mouse.

Wilder's typically passionless direction fits beautifully with this sinister story. On his first studio assignment, screenwriter Chandler peppered the dialogue from Cain's original with his distinctive brand of hardboiled cynicism. The results, as when Phyllis and Walter flirt by using the extended metaphor of a speeding motorist, are terrific. Rosza contributes a typically edgy score and Seitz's cinematography makes great use of such noir trademarks as sharp camera angles, heavy, sculpted shadows and light slatted by venetian blinds. But it is really the starring trio which lends bite to this compelling crime classic. Stanwyck, in a deliberately phony blonde wig, remade her career with her striking portrayal of an icy woman whose boredom and desire fuel a plot of murder and intrigue. MacMurray, in a great change of pace, gives the performance of his career as the shifty loner excited by a challenge and a deadly dame's anklet. Robinson, meanwhile, beautifully gives the film its heart. His speech about death statistics, rattled off at top speed, is one of the film's highlights. Lifelessly remade for television in 1954 and 1973.

DOUBLE LIFE, A

1947 103m bw Crime   ★★★★
Kanin (U.S.)   /A

Ronald Colman *(Anthony John)*, Signe Hasso *(Brita)*, Edmond O'Brien *(Bill Friend)*, Shelley Winters *(Pat Kroll)*, Ray Collins *(Victor Donlan)*, Philip Loeb *(Max Lasker)*, Millard Mitchell *(Al Cooley)*, Joe Sawyer *(Pete Bonner)*, Charles La Torre *(Stellini)*, Whit Bissell *(Dr. Stauffer)*

p, Michael Kanin; d, George Cukor; w, Ruth Gordon, Garson Kanin (based on the play "Othello" by William Shakespeare); ph, Milton Krasner; ed, Robert Parrish; m, Miklos Rozsa; prod d, Harry Horner; art d, Bernard Herzbrun, Harvey T. Gillett; fx, David S. Horsley; cos, Yvonne Wood, Travis Banton

AA Best Actor: Ronald Colman; *AAN Best Director:* George Cukor; *AAN Best Original Screenplay:* Ruth Gordon, Garson Kanin; *AA Best Score:* Miklos Rozsa

A fine film overall, if a wee bit pretentious, A DOUBLE LIFE explores the schizoid personality of a gifted stage actor whose despair and murderous moods come during his portrayal of Othello. Colman is a much-respected gentleman actor who specializes in classical drama. His courtly manners and winning charm endear him to one and all, including his ex-wife, Hasso, who loves him but fears that his cruel streak will once again take over his otherwise stable personality. Winters, a buxom, steamy waitress, is attracted to Colman but soon learns that he is capable of violence. Losing all touch with reality, Colman believes he is actually the terrible Moor he is portraying on stage, so he strangles Winters and returns to his apartment, blocking out the hideous act. O'Brien, an enterprising publicity agent for the play, picks up on the strangulation and tries to link the murder with the play to entice audiences. This blatant sensationalism causes Colman to explode; he attacks O'Brien, who now believes the actor is mad. O'Brien sets up Colman for the police, arranging for a waitress who is almost Winters's twin to wait on him in a restaurant. Her appearance

so alarms Colman that police are convinced he is the killer. Detectives decide to arrest him following the final performance of "Othello." The actor realizes he is exposed and the tragedy takes its final turn.

Colman's performance is riveting and deservedly won him an Oscar, as well as universal applause from critics and public alike. His genteel manners and mellifluous voice set up audiences for a huge shock when Colman turns into a lethal lunatic, a transformation that is simply amazing to witness. He is a man obsessed, one who can no longer differentiate between his theatrical and everyday personalities. Colman is mesmerizing, brilliant, and even horrific in his role. Kanin and Gordon's script is both literate and packed with suspense, interweaving the dialogue of classical theater and that of the street. Cukor's direction is as properly mannered and carefully constructed as the script is, and he draws the complex portrayal out of Colman with great care.

This was Winters' first film break after stage appearances and it established her as a movie star. Harry Cohn, head of Columbia Studios, originally bought the script for A DOUBLE LIFE years earlier but later reneged, refusing to pay for it or produce it. Kanin was so angry that he vowed never to talk to Cohn again. He would take his vengeance on a literary level, using Cohn as the role model for the brutish Broderick Crawford part in BORN YESTERDAY.

DOUBLE LIFE OF VERONIQUE, THE
(LA DOUBLE VIE DE VERONIQUE)

1991 90m c Fantasy/Drama   ★★½
Sideral Productions/Studio Tor/Canal Plus   (France/Poland)   /15

Irene Jacob *(Veronique/Veronika)*, Halina Gryglaszewska *(Aunt)*, Kalina Jedrusik *(Gaudy Woman)*, Aleksander Bardini *(Orchestra Conductor)*, Wladyslaw Kowalski *(Veronika's Father)*, Jerzy Gudejko *(Antek)*, Jan Sterninski *(Lawyer)*, Philippe Volter *(Alexandre Fabbri)*, Sandrine Dumas *(Catherine)*, Louis Ducreux *(Professor)*

p, Leonardo De La Fuente; d, Krzysztof Kieslowski; w, Krzysztof Kieslowski, Krzysztof Piesiewicz; ph, Slawomir Idziak; ed, Jacques Witta; m, Zbigniew Preisner; prod d, Patrice Mercier, Halina Dobrowolska; art d, Krzysztof Zanussi; cos, Laurence Brignon, Claudy Fellous, Elzbieta Radke

THE DOUBLE LIFE OF VERONIQUE is a slight, lyrical fable that benefits enormously from the charm of its star, Cannes award-winner Irene Jacob.

The film introduces us to two women, both played by Jacob. Polish Veronika leaves her provincial home town and family for the city of Krakow, where she is offered a place to study singing at a prestigious music school; after suffering chest pains, she is stricken and dies onstage during her first public performance. The action then shifts to Paris, where the French Veronique abruptly, and without explanation, abandons her own ambitions of becoming a professional singer to pursue a more modest career as an elementary school teacher, and enjoys a romantic liaison with a charming puppeteer. (Like Veronika, Veronique also has a weak heart, but she goes for regular check-ups with a cardiologist.)

An opaque, if stylish, film, THE DOUBLE LIFE OF VERONIQUE plays like an enigmatic warning on the dangers of excessive ambition. Though pleasing to the eye, it's not everything we would have hoped for from Kieslowski, who confirmed his status as a major contemporary filmmaker with 1988's DEKALOG, a series of 10 hour-long works funded by Polish TV and based on the 10 Commandments. In the same year, he expanded segments five and six into two features, A SHORT FILM ABOUT KILLING and A SHORT FILM ABOUT LOVE, both of which are far more substantial than this Polish-French co-production.

DOUBLE TEAM

1997 90m c Action   ★★★
Moshe Diamant Productions/One Story Pictures/Mandalay   R/
Entertainment/Signature Films   (U.S.)

Jean-Claude Van Damme *(Quinn)*, Dennis Rodman *(Yaz)*, Paul Freeman *(Goldsmythe)*, Mickey Rourke *(Stavros)*, Natacha Lindinger *(Kath)*, Valeria Cavalli *(Dr. Maria Trifioli)*, Jay Benedict *(Brandon)*, Joelle Devaux-Vullion *(Stavros's Girlfriend)*, Bruno Bilotta *(Kofi)*, Mario Opinato *(James)* p, Moshe Diamant; d, Tsui Hark; w, Don Jakoby, Paul Mones (based on the story by Don Jakoby); ph, Peter Pau; ed, Bill Pankow; m, Gary Chang; prod d, Marek Dobrowolski; art d, Damien Lanfranchi; fx, Bruno Van Zeebroeck; cos, Magali Guidasci

Vietnamese-born producer-director Tsui Hark gives his US debut a densely layered, nightmarish, and utterly chaotic look that will be familiar to Hong Kong action buffs.

Quinn (Jean-Claude Van Damme) is a former crack anti-terrorist agent, now living a quiet life with his pregnant wife. Stavros (Mickey Rourke) is a terrorist head case, and Quinn is brought out of retirement to take him down. Quinn fails to get his man (though he does kill Stavros' small son) and is seriously injured. When he recovers, he's in the Colony—an isolated prison where "retired" agents are kept until their dangerous smarts are needed (shades of TV's "The Prisoner")—from which he must escape and rescue his wife and soon-to-be-born son from the nutty Stavros.

Plot is hardly the point here: DOUBLE TEAM's selling points are scary amusement parks, Dennis Rodman selling high-tech weapons out of a sex shop in Antwerp, tigers, Jean-Claude Van Damme's thighs, captive super-spies on a tropical island, and bald Chinese dervishes holding switchblades between their toes. The angles are canted, the close-ups are disorienting, the colors are supersaturated, and the action never stops. Making a Van Damme picture appears to have become a rite of passage for Hong Kong directors looking to break into the American mainstream market (remember Ringo Lam's MAXIMUM RISK and John Woo's HARD TARGET?) and Hong Kong neophytes may be baffled by the film's weirdly sentimental streak—remember, the vendetta that drives Quinn and Stavros is all about *babies*. But by the time the black leather-clad Stavros has mined the Coliseum and sicced a Bengal tiger on Quinn, wise viewers are just sitting back and enjoying the show.

DOWN AND DIRTY
(BRUTTI, SPORCHI E CATTIVI)
1976   115m   c   Comedy/Drama   ★★★½
C.C. Champion   (Italy)

Nino Manfredi *(Giacinto)*, Francisci Anniballi *(Domizio)*, Maria Bosco *(Gaetana)*, Giselda Castrini *(Lisetta)*, Alfredo D'Ippolito *(Plinio)*, Giancarlo Fanelli *(Paride)*, Marian Fasoli *(Maria Lobera)*, Ettore Garofolo *(Camilio)*, Marco Marsili *(Vittoriano)*, Franco Merli *(Fernando)*

d, Ettore Scola; w, Ettore Scola, Ruggero Maccari; ph, Dario Di Palma; ed, Raimondo Crociani; m, Armando Trovaioli

A mean, nasty, vile, ugly, and wickedly funny look at the inhabitants of a squatters' slum outside of Rome, where the subproletariat lives a miserable existence, DOWN AND DIRTY focuses on Giacinto (Nino Manfredi), a brutal animal of a man who has won a million lira insurance settlement after losing an eye. Driven by greed and selfishness, Giacinto sleeps with a shotgun for fear that someone will steal his fortune. He refuses to spend even a small portion of his stash on his family—which consists of at least 20 people, all of whom live, eat, sleep, fight, and have sex in the same one-room shanty. He beats and stabs his wife, humiliates his children, drinks himself into a stupor, and gropes the local women. When he takes an obese, huge-chested whore (Maria Luisa Santella) as a mistress, lets her live under the same roof as his family, and then generously squanders his money on gifts for her, his relatives plot to murder him. An amazing picture from Ettore Scola, DOWN AND DIRTY presents an endless stream of human indignities (people living with rats, a drag queen seducing his sister-in-law, a proud mother displaying her daughter's nude centerfold, children spending the day locked in a cage that serves as a day-care center) with such a curious, crude sense of humor one cannot be sure whether to look away in horror or laugh. What is sure is that you cannot ignore these people, or their unfathomable living conditions—and this is Scola's intent. Shooting on location, with Manfredi as his only professional actor, Scola in DOWN AND DIRTY pays tribute to the Neo-Realist tradition in Italy and produces a film worthy of Rossellini or De Sica.

DOWN AND OUT IN BEVERLY HILLS
1986   103m   c   Comedy   ★★★½
Touchstone   (U.S.)   R/15

Nick Nolte *(Jerry Baskin)*, Richard Dreyfuss *(Dave Whiteman)*, Bette Midler *(Barbara Whiteman)*, Little Richard *(Orvis Goodnight)*, Tracy Nelson *(Jenny Whiteman)*, Elizabeth Pena *(Carmen)*, Evan Richards *(Max Whiteman)*, Mike the Dog *(Matisse)*, Donald Muhich *(Dr. Von Zimmer)*, Paul Mazursky *(Sidney Waxman)*

p, Paul Mazursky; d, Paul Mazursky; w, Paul Mazursky, Leon Capetanos (based on the play *Boudu Sauve Des Eaux* by Rene Fauchois); ph, Don McAlpine; ed, Richard Halsey; m, Andy Summers; prod d, Pato Guzman; art d, Todd Hallowell; fx, Ken Speed; cos, Albert Wolsky

This very first R-rated picture ever to come out of that bastion of squeaky-cleanness, Walt Disney Studios (under the aegis of their subsidiary Touchstone), is a howl from start to finish. Dave Whiteman (Dreyfuss) has made it big in the coat hanger business. He and wife Barbara (Midler) live in a huge house in Beverly Hills with their children, Jenny (Nelson), an anorexic college student, and Max (Richards), an androgynous budding filmmaker. Barbara is the ultimate yenta who spends her days having her hair and nails done, shopping, and going to classes. Also living in the house are Carmen (Pena), a seductive Latino maid with whom Dave is having an affair, and Matisse (Mike), the family dog who refuses to eat despite regular visits to a doggie psychiatrist. When tramp Jerry Baskin (Nolte) enters their lives after attempting to drown himself in the Whiteman swimming pool, Dave saves his life and invites him to become part of the family, a decision that has some very comic results.

A sometimes extremely funny revamping of Jean Renoir's classic black comedy BOUDU SAVED FROM DROWNING, Mazursky's film also works as a broad but scathing satire of upper-class California culture. Although the ending is softened from Renoir's original, this garishly colored film succeeds quite well on its own terms. The film is full of moments both surprising (Jerry showing Matisse that his dog food is eminently eatable) and entertainingly predictable (Jerry getting intimately involved with several family members; an "everyone into the pool" sequence). The cast is entirely up to the comic hysteria Mazursky requires of them, though Mike the dog steals whatever scene he is in. Look for Mazursky in a bit part as an accountant.

DOWN BY LAW
1986   106m   bw   Comedy   ★★★
Black Snake/Grokenberger   (U.S.)   R/15

Tom Waits *(Zack)*, John Lurie *(Jack)*, Roberto Benigni *(Roberto)*, Nicoletta Braschi *(Nicoletta)*, Ellen Barkin *(Laurette)*, Billie Neal *(Bobbie)*, Rockets Redglare *(Gig)*, Vernel Bagneris *(Preston)*, Timothea *(Julie)*, L.C. Drane *(L.C.)*

p, Alan Kleinberg; d, Jim Jarmusch; w, Jim Jarmusch; ph, Robby Muller; ed, Melody London; m, John Lurie; cos, Carol Wood

Set in New Orleans, DOWN BY LAW begins as down-on-his-luck disc jockey Zack (Waits) tries to make some quick bucks by driving a stolen car across town. Unfortunately he gets pulled over by the police and is thrown into jail when a body is found in the car's trunk. In the meantime a pimp, Jack (Lurie), has been set up by an enemy and fellow procurer, and he too is carted off by police and thrown into Orleans Parish Prison, where he becomes Zack's cellmate. Three may be a crowd, but soon they are joined in their small cell by Roberto (Benigni), a confused and likable Italian who knows only a few phrases of English, which he keeps written in a pocket notebook. Eventually the three escape into the Louisiana bayous, where they're soon hungry, tired and lost.

Director-writer Jarmusch's characters are insignificant antiheroes adrift in an America that is both sad and beautiful. Jarmusch has a powerful visual sense, but he is weaker in the realm of content. The jazzy relationship between Lurie and Waits never quite clicks. As a result DOWN BY LAW merely reiterates the ideas about people and American life that Jarmusch had already stated more richly in STRANGER THAN PARADISE. The only sign of life in the film is in Benigni, who works wonders.

DOWNHILL RACER

1969 101m c Sports ★★★★
Wildwood   (U.S.)   M/PG

Robert Redford (*Davis Chappellet*), Gene Hackman (*Eugene Claire*), Camilla Sparv (*Carole Stahl*), Karl Michael Vogler (*Machet*), James McMullan (*Creech*), Christian Doermer (*Brumm*), Kathleen Crowley (*American Newspaperwoman*), Dabney Coleman (*Mayo*), Kenneth Kirk (*D.K. Bryan*), Oren Stevens (*Kipsmith*)

p, Richard Gregson; d, Michael Ritchie; w, James Salter (based on the novel *The Downhill Racers* by Oakley Hall); ph, Brian Probyn; ed, Nick Archer; m, Kenyon Hopkins; art d, Ian Whittaker; cos, Cynthia May

An influential and extremely well-done sports film, worth watching even if you don't normally enjoy films of this type. Documentarian in style, DOWNHILL RACER is a strangely dispassionate but captivating look behind the glamorous facade of international ski racing. Redford, who did much of his own skiing, stars as Davis Chappellet, a self-centered, success-hungry skier from Colorado who is summoned to Europe when a member of the US team is injured. Over the next two racing seasons he proves himself to be one of the sport's most promising newcomers, dueling with a famous teammate (McMullan) for the spotlight and clashing with his strong-willed coach (Hackman). In the process of chasing Olympic gold in the downhill, he fails to win approval from his father and is unable to maintain a relationship with a beautiful ski manufacturer's assistant (Sparv).

Redford, who was determined to make a skiing film, went to great lengths to sell the project: soliciting a screenplay from James Salter, enlisting a team of ski bums and photographers to shoot 20,000 feet of action on the sly at the 1968 Grenoble Olympics, and giving Michael Ritchie, who provides a sure directorial hand, his first feature film assignment. As with a number of later Ritchie films, the focus here is on the price paid in pursuit of what seems to be victory. The acting is fine all around, with kudos to Redford for being unafraid to make his character dislikable at the core. Many of the downhill scenes were filmed by skier Joe Jay Jalbert, who raced behind Redford with a camera, adding to the film's realism and excitement. DOWNHILL RACER is fascinating viewing, even if the closest you've gotten to a ski slope is "Wide World of Sports."

DRACULA

1931 84m bw Horror ★★★
Universal   (U.S.)   /PG

Bela Lugosi (*Count Dracula*), Helen Chandler (*Mina Seward*), David Manners (*Jonathan Harker*), Dwight Frye (*Renfield*), Edward Van Sloan (*Dr. Van Helsing*), Herbert Bunston (*Dr. Seward*), Frances Dade (*Lucy Weston*), Charles Gerrard (*Martin*), Joan Standing (*Maid*), Moon Carroll (*Briggs*)

p, Carl Laemmle Jr.; d, Tod Browning; w, Tod Browning, Garrett Fort (based on the novel by Bram Stoker and the 1927 stage play by Hamilton Deane and John Lloyd Balderston); ph, Karl Freund; ed, Milton Carruth, Maurice Pivar; m, Peter Ilich Tchaikovsky, Richard Wagner; art d, Charles D. Hall; cos, Ed Ware, Vera West

Creak. The grandaddy of 'em all and ready for mothballs to be put in the coffins. An atmospheric opening is the best part—moody and full of sinister potential. After that, it's stilted drawing-room talk, variably acted, except for the cultish over-the-top dementia of Dwight Frye. Still, DRACULA is the film that started the 1930s horror cycle, secured Universal's position as *the* horror studio, and made Hungarian actor Bela Lugosi a worldwide curiosity.

Following the successful stage play more than Bram Stoker's classic novel, the film opens in Transylvania, where Renfield (Dwight Frye), a British real estate salesman, arrives to arrange the sale of a deserted English manor house to a strange nobleman, Count Dracula (Lugosi). The mysterious count turns out to be a 500-year-old vampire, and Renfield is bitten and made his slave. Arriving in London, Dracula becomes smitten with Mina Seward (Helen Chandler) and attempts to make her his bride, but her fiance, John Harker (David Manners), and vampire expert Prof. Van Helsing (Edward Van Sloan) try and put a stop to the undead count. While the first part of the film is quite cinematic, mainly due to the brilliant cinematography of Karl Freund, the movie bogs down once it gets to England, after which it appears that director Tod Browning was intent on making a documentary of the stage play. More likely, he lacked the creativity of James Whale, who directed FRANKENSTEIN. While the incidental music (mostly snippets from Tchaikovsky's *Swan Lake*) is kept to a minimum, the sound effects are showing age, with the creaking of coffin lids, opening and slamming of doors, thudding footsteps, actors' voices, and howling of wolves beginning to seem like something out of a Bob Hope spoof. Studio heads felt that the film would do well abroad, so a Spanish-language version starring Carlos Villarias in the Dracula role and featuring a completely new all-Spanish cast, directed by George Melford, was produced with the same sets only days after the English version was completed. Reports have it that this version is even better than the Browning-Lugosi film. We should hope so. A remarkable sequel, DRACULA'S DAUGHTER, followed, featuring the stranger-than-true Gloria Holden.

DRAGNET

1954 89m c Crime ★★½
Mark VII   (U.S.)   /PG

Jack Webb (*Sgt. Joe Friday*), Ben Alexander (*Officer Frank Smith*), Richard Boone (*Capt. Hamilton*), Ann Robinson (*Grace Downey*), Stacy Harris (*Max Troy*), Virginia Gregg (*Ethel Marie Starkie*), Vic Perrin (*Adolph Alexander*), Georgia Ellis (*Belle Davitt*), James Griffith (*Jesse Quinn*), Dick Cathcart (*Roy Cleaver*)

p, Stanley Meyer; d, Jack Webb; w, Richard Breen; ph, Edward Colman; ed, Robert M. Leeds; m, Walter Schumann

Big-screen spin-off of the immensely successful radio-TV "Dragnet" show has L.A. cops Sgt. Joe Friday (Webb) and Officer Frank Smith (Alexander) investigating the murder of a former syndicate member. Webb's direction is spotty, notably when the screenplay bogs down into the tedium of cop life, or during a fight scene unwittingly designed to provoke yuks. Acting honors go to Virginia Gregg's sodden syndicate widow. Webb is his usual deadpan cop, with Alexander as his dronelike sidekick (later replaced in a 1969 TV film by Harry Morgan as Joe Gannon—a better choice). Based on actual L.A. police files, the film manages to still deliver plenty of suspense. The theme beat for the series and this film—"dum-de-dum-dum"—was first used in Robert Siodmak's marvelous THE KILLERS (1946).

DRAGON: THE BRUCE LEE STORY

1993 114m c Biography/Romance/Martial Arts ★★★½
Old Code Productions Ltd.   (U.S.)   PG-13/15

Jason Scott Lee (*Bruce Lee*), Lauren Holly (*Linda Lee*), Robert J. Wagner (*Bill Krieger*), Michael Learned (*Vivian Emery*), Nancy Kwan (*Gussie Yang*), Kay Tong Lim (*Philip Tan*), Ric Young (*Bruce's Father*), Luoyong Wang (*Yip Man*), Sterling Macer (*Jerome Sprout*), Sven-Ole Thorsen (*The Demon*)

p, Raffaella De Laurentiis, Charles Wang; d, Rob Cohen; w, Edward Khmara, John Raffo, Rob Cohen (from the book *Bruce Lee: The Man Only I Knew* by Linda Lee Cadwell); ph, David Eggby; ed, Peter Amundson; m, Randy Edelman; prod d, Robert Ziembicki; art d, Ted Berner; fx, Kevin O'Neill, William H. Schirmer, Peter Bohanna; cos, Carol Ramsey

DRAGON: THE BRUCE LEE STORY dares to be corny and gets away with it, thanks to sensitive scripting and direction, cleverly staged kung-fu sequences (fight co-ordinator John Cheung has worked with Hong Kong martial arts star Jackie Chan), and an inspirational performance by Jason Scott Lee. (No relation to Bruce: in fact, Bruce Lee's son, Brandon, was accidentally killed during production of THE CROW just a few weeks before DRAGON was released.)

DRAGON traces Lee's life from his Hong Kong childhood to international success and early, mysterious death. Born in San Francisco while his father, an actor, was on tour, Bruce returns as a young man. He works as a dishwasher/delivery boy, goes to college and begins giving kung-fu lessons leavened with philosophy. At the urging of his beautiful, white girlfriend Linda (Lauren Holly)—they date despite widespread disapproval—he opens a kung-fu school. They marry, and Bruce is cast as sidekick Kato in "The Green Hornet," but he moves his family to Hong Kong after he's passed over in favor of white actor

David Carradine for "Kung Fu," which he helped develop as a starring vehicle for himself. With ENTER THE DRAGON, a Hollywood picture to be shot in Hong Kong, Bruce is poised for international success, but fate intervenes.

Director/co-screenwriter Rob Cohen shrewdly opts for a three-tiered approach to the biographical material, making DRAGON a poignant interracial love story, a thrilling kung-fu flick, and a surreal fantasy in the which the hero literally confronts his inner demons. Jason Scott Lee captures his subject perfectly, and his handling of the action scenes is particularly impressive. The result is one of the most purely enjoyable American films in recent years.

DRAGONSLAYER

1981 108m c Adventure/Fantasy		★★★½
Walt Disney Productions (U.S.)		PG

Peter MacNicol (Galen), Caitlin Clarke (Valerian), Ralph Richardson (Ulrich), John Hallam (Tyrian), Peter Eyre (Casidorus Rex), Albert Salmi (Greil), Sydney Bromley (Hodge), Chloe Salaman (Princess Elspeth), Emrys James (Simon), Roger Kemp (Horsrik)

p, Hal Barwood; d, Matthew Robbins; w, Hal Barwood, Matthew Robbins; ph, Derek Vanlint; ed, Tony Lawson; m, Alex North; prod d, Elliot Scott; art d, Alan Cassie; fx, Brian Johnson, Dennis Muren, Industrial Light & Magic; chor, Peggy Dixon; cos, Anthony Mendleson

AAN Best Score: Alex North; AAN Best Visual Effects: Dennis Muren, Phil Tippett, Ken Ralston, Brian Johnson

An Arthurian-type legend is marvelously re-created when Galen (Peter MacNicol), sorcerer's apprentice to Ulrich (Ralph Richardson), a great wizard, bungles his way to ridding the kingdom of a monstrous, fire-spitting dragon. King Tyrian (John Hallam) has made an evil pact whereby he will sacrifice the virgins of his land to the dragon if it will leave the kingdom in relative peace. When Princess Elspeth (Chloe Salaman), his brave daughter, volunteers her own life, Ulrich and Galen attempt to save her, even though the wizard is dying and his magic fading. Like EXCALIBUR, this film has smoky atmosphere, medieval sets, and rugged terrain strange enough to suggest far-off mythic lands; moreover, its special effects are positively staggering. The giant computerized dragon alone is worth viewing. But DRAGONSLAYER profits from spirited direction and camera work plus the expert Richardson at its nucleus. Failing to capture the fancy of either the teenage market or adult action-fantasy fans, however, DRAGONSLAYER was a major disappointment at the box office, returning just $6 million on an $18 million investment. With terror prevalent and gory violence in spots, this fable is not for young viewers.

DRAUGHTSMAN'S CONTRACT, THE

1982 108m c Comedy/Historical/Mystery		★★★★
British Film Institute (U.K.)		R/15

Anthony Higgins (Mr. Neville), Janet Suzman (Mrs. Herbert), Anne Louise Lambert (Mrs. Talmann), Hugh Fraser (Mr. Talmann), Neil Cunningham (Mr. Noyles), Dave Hill (Mr. Herbert), David Gant (Mr. Seymour), David Meyer, Tony Meyer (The Poulenas), Nicholas Amer (Mr. Parkes)

p, David Payne; d, Peter Greenaway; w, Peter Greenaway; ph, Curtis Clark; ed, John Wilson; m, Michael Nyman; art d, Bob Ringwood; cos, Sue Blane

Peter Greenaway's dark comedy about power games between the classes is one of his easiest films to enjoy on a surface level. Those unfamiliar with Greenaway's work should be warned, however, that although THE DRAUGHTSMAN S CONTRACT looks like a period mystery, it really isn't: if you spend too much time worrying about who done it, you'll miss the movie's real pleasures.

England, 1694. Ambitious artist Mr. Neville (Anthony Higgins) is offered a commission by Mrs. Herbert (Janet Suzman), who wants twelve drawings of her husband's estate, to be done while he is away. Neville accepts, on the condition that his payment includes the sexual use of his hostess. Mrs. Herbert reluctantly agrees. Mrs. Talmann (Anne Louise Lambert), the Herberts' only child, hints to Neville that certain oddities in his drawings can be construed as clues to a plot involving her father, who is missing. Aware of the sexual contract between Neville

and her mother, she proposes a similar contract in exchange for her silence. Heedless but amused, Neville agrees. Soon after, Mr. Herbert's body is found in the estate's moat: he has been murdered.

That we never find out who killed Mr. Herbert, or even why, is central to THE DRAUGHTSMAN'S CONTRACT's theme of social power. Neville thinks he has the upper hand over his hosts and the other local gentry; it isn't until it s too late, however, that he realizes he hasn't got a clue as to what's really going on. We the viewers do have clues, but not much more: we learn just enough to put us a step ahead of Neville, but in the long run are as ignorant (and therefore as powerless) as he.

Despite having been filmed on a limited budget, THE DRAUGHTS-MAN'S CONTRACT is as sumptuous to the eye as it is to the ear. Most shots are designed as tableaux in which the actors move only minimally against elegant backgrounds (there is little camera movement or cross-cutting). Even if you don't share Greenaway's formalist interests, THE DRAUGHTSMAN'S CONTRACT makes for compelling viewing.

DREAMS

1990 119m c Fantasy		★★★½
Akira Kurosawa USA (Japan/U.S.)		/PG

Akira Terao ("I"), SUNSHINE THROUGH THE RAIN: Mitsuko Baisho (Mother of "I"), Toshihiko Nakano ("I" as a Young Child), THE PEACH ORCHARD: Mitsunori Isaki ("I" as a Boy), Mie Suzuki ("I's" Sister), THE BLIZZARD: Mieko Harada (The Snow Fairy), Masayuki Yui, Shu Nakajima, Sakae Kimura (Members of the Climbing Team), THE TUNNEL: Yoshitaka Zushi (Pvt. Noguchi)

p, Hisao Kurosawa, Mike Y. Inoue; d, Akira Kurosawa; w, Akira Kurosawa; ph, Takao Saito, Masahuro Ueda; ed, Tome Minami; m, Shinichiro Ikebe; art d, Yoshiro Muraki, Akira Sakuragi; fx, Industrial Light & Magic; chor, Michiyo Hata; cos, Emi Wada

DREAMS is a mixed bag from one of the Old Masters of world cinema. One the one hand, it overflows with heavy-handed messages on topics ranging from ecology to pacifism as it scolds the audience for their wanton ways. On the other, it's a glorious triumph of style over content.

Kurosawa is best known as a director of epic action dramas such as THE SEVEN SAMURAI, YOJIMBO, and THE HIDDEN FORTRESS. DREAMS also has its moments of spectacle but it springs from the side of Kurosawa that produced IKIRU, DODES'KA-DEN, THE MOST BEAUTIFUL, and other films with which American audiences are less familiar and which lack the presence of Toshiro Mifune or samurai swordplay. These are intimate dramas focusing on everyday people searching for the right path to follow in life.

Beginning with a wedding that looks more like a funeral and ending with a funeral that seems more like a wedding, DREAMS is made up of eight vignettes, thematically united by their concern with Man's relationship to nature, mystery and his fellow man. In "Sunshine Through the Rain," a little boy disobeys his mother, running into a forest during a sunlit rainstorm to witness a gravely magical wedding procession of foxes. "The Peach Orchard" focuses on a boy who is made to understand what his parents have lost by cutting down a peach orchard on their property when the spirits of the downed trees appear to him. In "The Blizzard," the weary leader of a mountain expedition is tempted by Death in the form of a beautiful snow demoness. "The Tunnel" concerns a military officer who is tormented by the ghosts of the soldiers who were killed in combat under his command. In "Crows," an aspiring artist enters a Vincent Van Gogh painting to learn the artist's secrets from the painter himself (played with appropriate intensity by director Martin Scorsese). In "Mt. Fuji in Red," Japan's most famous landmark is destroyed in a nuclear power-plant meltdown. "The Weeping Demon" shows the torture of the damned following a conflagration that has left the earth a scorched ruin. Concluding the film is "Village of the Watermills," in which a traveller, passing through the title village, joins a 99-year-old man as he buries his 103-year-old "sweetheart" who never returned his love.

None of the vignettes have much narrative beyond their rudimentary premises and when they do, they are left eerily unresolved. Some of the action is staged in stylized, excruciating slow motion. Though the film certainly has some nightmarish moments, it also has a wry sense of humor which often bubbles up when least expected. At other times,

DREAMS is almost dismayingly mundane, especially in its scripting. Nonetheless this is clearly the work of a master filmmaker, even if his DREAMS are as unpredictable and uneven as our own.

DRESSED TO KILL

1980 105m c Thriller   ★★★½
Samuel Z. Arkoff (U.S.)   R/18

Michael Caine *(Dr. Robert Elliott)*, Angie Dickinson *(Kate Miller)*, Nancy Allen *(Liz Blake)*, Keith Gordon *(Peter Miller)*, Dennis Franz *(Detective Marino)*, David Margulies *(Dr. Levy)*, Kenny Baker *(Warren Lockman)*, Brandon Maggart *(Cleveland Sam)*, Susanna Clemm *(Bobbi)*, Fred Weber *(Mike Miller)*

p, George Litto; d, Brian De Palma; w, Brian De Palma; ph, Ralf D. Bode; ed, Jerry Greenberg; m, Pino Donaggio; prod d, Gary Weist; cos, Ann Roth, Gary Jones

All dressed up with no script to go, but a feverish nerve jangler nonetheless. Kate (Dickinson) is a sexually dissatisfied middle-aged housewife who fantasizes about erotic encounters while in the shower. Kate's sympathetic psychiatrist (Caine) advises her to indulge in an extra-marital affair. Immediately after her first tryst, however, Kate is cornered in an elevator and murdered by a leather-clad blonde wielding a straight razor. Now it is up to Kate's son (Gordon) to solve the murder with the help of the prostitute (Allen) who discovered his mom's corpse. Although heavily indebted to Alfred Hitchcock, Mario Bava, and Dario Argento, De Palma infused this film with enough sex, blood, and visual panache to make it a big hit at the box office. Gushingly praised by some critics at the time of its release, it now seems a definite case of cinematic style over substance. A slightly longer and more explicit version was released in Europe, mainly for fans of Angie Dickinson's stand-in. But it's probably Dickinson's best work, and Caine is fine indeed. Best surprises: between subway cars, and that nurse's shoe!

DRESSER, THE

1983 118m c Drama   ★★★★
Goldcrest/World Film (U.K.)   PG

Albert Finney *(Sir)*, Tom Courtenay *(Norman)*, Edward Fox *(Oxenby)*, Zena Walker *(Her Ladyship)*, Eileen Atkins *(Madge)*, Michael Gough *(Frank Carrington)*, Cathryn Harrison *(Irene)*, Betty Marsden *(Violet Manning)*, Sheila Reid *(Lydia Gibson)*, Lockwood West *(Geoffrey Thornton)*

p, Peter Yates; d, Peter Yates; w, Ronald Harwood (based on his play); ph, Kelvin Pike; ed, Ray Lovejoy; m, James Horner; prod d, Stephen Grimes; art d, Colin Grimes; cos, H. Nathan, L. Nathan

AAN Best Picture; AAN Best Actor: Tom Courtenay; AAN Best Actor: Albert Finney; AAN Best Director: Peter Yates; AAN Best Adapted Screenplay: Ronald Harwood (Screenplay)

The head of a Shakespearean acting troupe touring England during WWII, "Sir" (Albert Finney) is a senile boozer who is looked after by his gay dresser, Norman (Tom Courtenay). In episodic fashion, the film reveals Norman's devotion to his employer and the complexities of the relationship between the two men of the theater. This adaptation of Ronald Harwood's very successful play reveals its staginess, but the film is saved by dynamic direction, its feel of authenticity, and the two stars' performances that veer close to haminess without actually entering the terrain. Interesting, then, that Eileen Atkins steals the film out from under both as a pathetic stage-manager.

DREYFUS CASE, THE

1931 90m bw Biography   ★★★★
British Intl. (U.K.)   /U

Cedric Hardwicke *(Capt. Alfred Dreyfus)*, Charles Carson *(Col. Picquart)*, George Merritt *(Emile Zola)*, Sam Livesey *(Labori)*, Beatrix Thomson *(Lucie Dreyfus)*, Garry Marsh *(Maj. Esterhazy)*, Randle Ayrton *(President, Court-Martial)*, Henry Caine *(Col. Henry)*, Reginald Dance *(President, Zola Trial)*, George Skillan *(Maj. Paty du Clam)*

p, F.W. Kraemer; d, F.W. Kraemer, Milton Rosmer; w, Reginald Berkeley, Walter C. Mycroft (based on the play by Wilhelm Herzog and Hans Rehfisch); ph, Willy Winterstein, Walter Harvey, Horace Wheddon; ed, Langford Reed, Betty Spiers

Stately and underplayed, with more plot animation than many British films of this time. A true-to-life rendition of the infamous case that shook France in the late 1800s, THE DREYFUS CASE stars Cedric Hardwicke as Alfred Dreyfus, the only Jew on the French general staff. When treason is discovered, blame is laid at his feet, and he is sent to Devil's Island. One of the greatest writers of his time, Emile Zola (George Merritt), feels that Dreyfus has been railroaded. He engages Georges Clemenceau, and they succeed in getting the former soldier a new trial. Although serious doubt is cast on the justice of Dreyfus's conviction, they still lose the case, and Dreyfus is remanded to Devil's Island. After several more years of imprisonment, the duplicity is uncovered, and Dreyfus, vindicated, returns to his first love, the army. The exceptional Merritt and Hardwicke lead a talented cast, and producer Kraemer and the reliable Rosmer do a decent job of directing here.

DRILLER KILLER

1979 90m c Horror   ★★½
Navaron Films (U.S.)   R/

Abel Ferrara *(Reno)*, Carolyn Marz *(Carol)*, Baybi Day *(Pamela)*, Harry Schultz *(Dalton Briggs)*, Alan Wynroth *(Landlord)*, Maria Helhoski *(Nun)*, James O'Hara *(Man in Church)*, Richard Howorth *(Carol's Husband)*, Tommy Santora *(Attacker)*, Rita Gooding *(TV Spot Actress)*

p, Rochelle Weisberg; d, Abel Ferrara; w, Nicholas St. John; ph, Ken Kelsch; m, Joseph Delia

The ultra-low budget feature debut of the remarkable Abel Ferrara is disturbing and powerful, evincing the promise that would be fulfilled in MS. 45 (1981). Hiding behind the pseudonym "Jimmy Laine," Ferrara stars as Reno, an alienated Manhattan painter who lives in terror of winding up like his derelict father. Suffering from hallucinations in which his paintings whisper to him, and driven to distraction by a raucous punk band that rehearses downstairs, Reno vents his frustrations by taking to the streets and murdering bums with a power drill. As his rage spirals out of control, Reno moves from killing derelicts to slaying those in his own life who have angered him—namely girlfriend Carol (Carolyn Marz) and libidinous art dealer Dalton Briggs (Harry Schultz). A bleak, often repugnant rumination on the harsh realities of urban life, DRILLER KILLER will offend tender sensibilities. But Ferrara is already a distinctive and conscientious talent behind the camera, unmistakably concerned with more than gore-filled exploitation. Turning budget restrictions to his advantage, he and cinematographer Ken Kelsch shot much of the film with a hand-held camera, giving the picture an immediate, documentary urgency.

DRIVER, THE

1978 91m c Crime   ★★★★
Fox (U.S.)   R/15

Ryan O'Neal *(The Driver)*, Bruce Dern *(The Detective)*, Isabelle Adjani *(The Player)*, Ronee Blakley *(The Connection)*, Matt Clark *(Red Plainclothesman)*, Felice Orlandi *(Gold Plainclothesman)*, Joseph Walsh *(Glasses)*, Rudy Ramos *(Teeth)*, Denny Macko *(Exchange Man)*, Frank Bruno *(The Kid)*

p, Lawrence Gordon; d, Walter Hill; w, Walter Hill; ph, Philip Lathrop; ed, Tina Hirsch, Robert K. Lambert; m, Michael Small; prod d, Harry Horner; art d, David M. Haber; fx, Charles Spurgeon

A curiosity. Hill's second feature is a bare-bones, existential *film noir.* O'Neal is The Driver, a top getaway driver for a gang of crooks, and Dern is The Detective (nobody in the film has a proper name) obsessed with arresting him. The sparse story of the struggle of the two men with their obsessions, and with each other, skillfully creates a mood that is hard to shake after the ending credits. The car chases are breathtaking.

DRIVING MISS DAISY

1989 99m c Comedy/Drama ★★★½
Zanuck (U.S.) PG/U

Jessica Tandy *(Miss Daisy Werthan)*, Morgan Freeman *(Hoke Colburn)*, Dan Aykroyd *(Boolie Werthan)*, Patti LuPone *(Florine Werthan)*, Esther Rolle *(Idella)*, Joann Havrilla *(Miss McClatchey)*, William Hall Jr. *(Oscar)*, Alvin M. Sugarman *(Dr. Weil)*, Clarice F. Geigerman *(Nonie)*, Muriel Moore *(Miriam)*

p, Richard D. Zanuck, Lili Fini Zanuck; d, Bruce Beresford; w, Alfred Uhry (based on his play); ph, Peter James; ed, Mark Warner; m, Hans Zimmer; prod d, Bruno Rubeo; art d, Victor Kempster; cos, Elizabeth McBride

AA Best Picture; AAN Best Actor: Morgan Freeman; *AA Best Actress:* Jessica Tandy; *AAN Best Supporting Actor:* Dan Aykroyd; *AA Best Adapted Screenplay:* Alfred Uhry; *AAN Best Editing:* Mark Warner; *AAN Best Art Direction:* Bruno Rubeo, Crispian Sallis; *AAN Best Costume Design:* Elizabeth McBride; *AA Best Makeup:* Manlio Rocchetti, Lynn Barber, Kevin Haney

Driving Us Crazy that this flick won all those Oscars—but then what do you expect? In all fairness, Australian director Bruce Beresford (BREAKER MORANT; TENDER MERCIES) successfully translates playwright-screenwriter Alfred Uhry's loosely autobiographical, Pulitzer Prize-winning play of the same name to the screen. The simple but compelling story opens in 1948, when Miss Daisy (Jessica Tandy), a wealthy 72-year-old southern Jewish matron who lives in quiet dignity, accidentally backs her Packard into her neighbor's prized garden. Miss Daisy's already frustrated son, Boolie (Dan Aykroyd), insists that his mother employ the services of a chauffeur. Reluctantly, she hires Hoke (Morgan Freeman), a Black gentleman, thus beginning a friendship that blossoms over the next quarter century until, in her mid-90s, after many years of really getting to know and appreciate Hoke, the eccentric Miss Daisy at last concedes that the respectful yet forceful driver is indeed her very best friend. Set in a small community near Atlanta, DRIVING MISS DAISY covers 25 years (1948-73) in a changing South, and the manner in which the momentous and turbulent events of the civil rights movement affect Hoke and Daisy personally is the film's true subject. Directed and written with a pleasant simplicity and clarity, DRIVING MISS DAISY is a blandly liberal if touching and dignified depiction of decent human beings who must live their everyday lives amid the turmoil of historical events. Chief among the film's rewards are the extraordinary performances of its trio of stars, Freeman, Tandy, and Aykroyd—all of whom received Oscar nominations. Tandy won the Oscar for Best Actress.

DROWNING BY NUMBERS

1987 118 minm c Drama ★★½
Film Four International/Elsevier Vendex Film/Allarts/VPRO Television (U.K./Netherlands) R/18

Joan Plowright *(1st Cissie Colpitts)*, Juliet Stevenson *(2nd Cissie Colpitts)*, Joely Richardson *(3rd Cissie Colpitts)*, Bernard Hill *(Henry Madgett)*, Jason Edwards *(Smut)*, Bryan Pringle *(Jake)*, Trevor Cooper *(Hardy)*, David Morrissey *(Bellamy)*, John Rogan *(Gregory)*, Paul Mooney *(Teigan)*

p, Kees Kasander, Denis Wigman, Bill Stephens; d, Peter Greenaway; w, Peter Greenaway; ph, Sacha Vierny; ed, John Wilson; m, Michael Nyman; prod d, Ben Van Os, Jan Roelfs; cos, Dien Van Stralen

Another typical Greenaway outing, in which plot and character take second place to those favorite thematic concerns of formal symmetry and physical decomposition.

Against a backdrop of the autumnal Suffolk seaside, three generations of women, each named Cissie Colpitts—60-year-old mother Joan Plowright, 34-year-old daughter Juliet Stevenson and 19-year-old granddaughter Joely Richardson, murder their unsatisfactory husbands by drowning—respectively, Jake (Bryan Pringle), in a bathtub; Hardy (Trevor Cooper), while swimming in the sea; and Bellamy (David Morrissey), in a swimming pool. In return for promised sexual favors, which the women ultimately withhold, the local coroner Henry Madgett (Bernard Hill) agrees to certify the deaths as accidental, although a small but steadily growing crowd of witnesses and relatives

put pressure on him, as well as on Madgett's adolescent son Smut (Jason Edwards), who is obsessed with death and collects animal and insect corpses. True to Madgett's—and the film's—own obsession with games, to decide the issue he sets up a tug-of-war across a river, with him and Smut joining the Cissies against their detractors.

As the "story" of DROWNING unfolds, the filmmaker literally counts sequentially from 1 to 100, the numerals appearing somewhere within the frame, whether painted on trees, walls or dead cows, or as laundry marks, cricket scores, etc. For good measure, Greenaway also adds the dying words of historical figures like Gainsborough and Lord Nelson, and he works in the names of 100 stars—the celestial kind. Then there's a circumcision by scissors, a continual revulsion for food and flesh, and some fairly nauseating scenes of bodily decay and corruption.

DROWNING BY NUMBERS is an amoral tale told morally, with a strong feminist undertone—almost all the male characters die via the unbeatable Cissies' conspiracy—reflecting, as Greenaway himself has stated, that "the good do not get rewarded, the wicked are rarely punished, and the innocent are always abused."

DRUGSTORE COWBOY

1989 100m c Drama ★★★★½
Avenue (U.S.) R/18

Matt Dillon *(Bob)*, Kelly Lynch *(Dianne)*, James LeGros *(Rick)*, Heather Graham *(Nadine)*, James Remar *(Gentry)*, William S. Burroughs *(Tom the Priest)*, Grace Zabriskie *(Bob's Mother)*, Max Perlich *(David)*, Beah Richards *(Drug Counselor)*

p, Nick Wechsler, Karen Murphy; d, Gus Van Sant; w, Gus Van Sant Jr., Daniel Yost (based on a novel by James Fogle); ph, Robert Yeoman; ed, Curtiss Clayton; m, Elliot Goldenthal; prod d, David Brisbin; art d, Eve Cauley; cos, Beatrix Aruna Pasztor

A darkly funny, stylish, and realistic look at the world of drug addiction in 1971, DRUGSTORE COWBOY focuses on Bob (Matt Dillon) as the leader of a bedraggled quartet of addicts who get what they need by robbing drugstore pharmacy departments in the Pacific Northwest. His crew consists of his wife Dianne (Kelly Lynch), Bob's sluggish lieutenant, Rick (James Le Gros), and his underage girl friend, Nadine (Heather Graham). After one particularly fruitful heist, Bob devises a scheme whereby they can all stay constantly high, for a while, by sending their stash of drugs ahead of them via Greyhound bus as they migrate through the region. Hot on their trail is Gentry (James Remar), a cop bent on nailing Bob. Gus Van Sant's direction here is supremely confident, fusing witty camerawork, neat editing, and a jazz-oriented score to make DRUGSTORE COWBOY an exhilaratingly bumpy ride. DRUGSTORE COWBOY presents a rare insider's view of the drug lifestyle that is all the more refreshing for its lack of facile moralizing or apologies. It's a true comedy of desperation. After many photogenic but unchallenging roles, Dillon is a wonder here, portraying his antihero with an empathy that recalls James Cagney, Marlon Brando, James Dean, and Robert De Niro. The film's producers anticipated that DRUGSTORE COWBOY might receive an X rating for its explicit depiction of drug paraphernalia and use. Luckily, their fears proved wrong, allowing this honest, genuinely independent film to reach the broad audience it deserves.

DRUMS

1938 96m c Adventure/War ★★★★
Korda/London Films (U.K.)

Sabu *(Prince Azim)*, Raymond Massey *(Prince Ghul)*, Valerie Hobson *(Mrs. Carruthers)*, Roger Livesey *(Capt. Carruthers)*, Desmond Tester *(Bill Holder)*, Martin Walker *(Herrick)*, David Tree *(Lt. Escott)*, Francis L. Sullivan *(Governor)*, Roy Emerton *(Wafadar)*, Edward Lexy *(Sgt. Maj. Kernel)*

p, Alexander Korda; d, Zoltan Korda; w, Arthur Wimperis, Patrick Kirwan, Hugh Gray (based on Lajos Biro's adaptation of the novel by A.E.W. Mason); ph, Georges Perinal, Osmond Borradaile, Robert Krasker, Christopher Challis, Geoffrey Unsworth; ed, William Hornbeck, Henry Cornelius; m, John Greenwood; prod d, Vincent Korda; fx, Edward Cohen

Set in northwest India at the height of the British presence there, DRUMS finds the treacherous Indian Prince Ghul (Raymond Massey) usurping his brother's kingdom by murdering his sibling and forcing his nephew and the heir apparent, Prince Azim (Sabu), into hiding. The boy finds refuge at the British garrison, where the commander, Captain Carruthers (Roger Livesey), and his wife (Valerie Hobson) treat him with kindness. Azim learns the regulations of the British Army and how to beat military cadence on a drum, a skill he uses later to warn the garrison that it is about to be attacked by Ghul and his evil followers. The spectacle is excellent, the direction and beautiful color cinematography superb. Sabu is wonderful as the innocent, wide-eyed royal youth, a role that earned him 100 fan letters a day, and Livesey is a great match for the wily Massey, a villain minus a decent bone in his body. Needless to say, it's an unabashed apology for imperialism.

DRUMS ALONG THE MOHAWK

1939   103m   c   Historical/Adventure/War   ★★★★
Fox   (U.S.)

Claudette Colbert (Lana "Magdelana" Martin), Henry Fonda (Gil Martin), Edna May Oliver (Mrs. Sarah McKlennar), Eddie Collins (Christian Reall), John Carradine (Caldwell), Dorris Bowdon (Mary Reall), Jessie Ralph (Mrs. Weaver), Arthur Shields (Rev. Rosenkrantz), Robert Lowery (John Weaver), Roger Imhof (Gen. Nicholas Herkimer).

p, Raymond Griffith; d, John Ford; w, Lamar Trotti, Sonya Levien (based on the novel by Walter D. Edmonds); ph, Bert Glennon, Ray Rennahan; ed, Robert Simpson; m, Alfred Newman; art d, Richard Day, Mark-Lee Kirk; cos, Gwen Wakeling

AAN Best Supporting Actress: Edna May Oliver

A sentimental beauty. This richly directed and acted colonial epic concerns Fonda and Colbert, young newlyweds starting out on the frontier of the Mohawk Valley just before the outbreak of the Revolutionary War. Their transition from a life of privilege to that of the rugged frontier proves an exercise in stamina. To help fend off Indian attacks engineered by the British, Gil joins the militia and goes off to fight; finally, after many battles and hardships, the future of the new Americans begins to look bright. This historical chronicle directed by John Ford is made believable through its attention to small details, presenting a mosaic of frontier life. One of Ford's biggest problems in making the spectacular film was the unavailability of necessary props and costumes; Fox had not specialized in costume or historical films, particularly those with 18th-century settings, and almost everything had to be made from scratch at great cost. The ancient flintlock muskets brandished by scores of extras were the real weapons of the era, however, not reproductions. A Fox prop man chased the flintlocks down in Ethiopia—where they had actually seen combat in the mid-1930s, when they were used by Ethiopian soldiers against Mussolini's armies. This was Ford's first color film, his cameras recording the lush forests and valleys of northern Utah. So rich and verdant is the color in this film that it later provided stock footage for several Fox productions, including BUFFALO BILL (1944) and MOHAWK (1956).

DRUNKEN ANGEL
(YOIDORE TENSHI)

1948   102m   bw   Drama   ★★★★
Toho   (Japan)

Toshiro Mifune (Matsunaga), Takashi Shimura (Dr. Sanada), Reisaburo Yamamoto (Okada), Michiyo Kogure (Nanse), Chieko Nakakita (Miyo), Noriko Sengoku (Gin), Eitaro Shindo (Takahama), Choko Iida (Old Maid Servant)

p, Sojiro Motoki; d, Akira Kurosawa; w, Keinosuke Uegusa, Akira Kurosawa; ph, Takeo Ito; m, Fumio Hayasaka; art d, So Matsuyama

Akira Kurosawa's DRUNKEN ANGEL captures the mood of postwar Japan in the same way the neorealist films of Italy did in that country. In a war-scarred town controlled by the Yakuza (Japanese gangsters), an alcoholic doctor runs a small clinic. A young gangster, Matsunaga (Toshiro Mifune), comes to have a bullet removed from his hand and is treated by Dr. Sanada (Takashi Shimura), who hates the Yakuza. Sanada discovers that Matsunaga has tuberculosis and, after arguments and fistfights, convinces Matsunaga to let him treat the illness, creating

a love-hate relationship between the two. This was the first film on which Kurosawa had creative control and, although he had directed other pictures, it is the one in which his personal voice is first clearly heard. It was also the first starring role for Mifune, who, like his costar Shimura, turns in a mesmerizing performance. What makes the film so powerful is the characters' dependence on one another—Matsunaga's need for medical treatment and emotional support when faced with an incurable disease, and the humanist urge that compels Sanada to treat the gangster despite the fact that he hates everything the Yakuza represents.

DRY WHITE SEASON, A

1989   97m   c   Drama   ★★★
MGM-UA   (U.S.)   R/15

Donald Sutherland (Ben du Toit), Winston Ntshona (Gordon Ngubene), Susan Sarandon (Melanie Bruwer), Janet Suzman (Susan du Toit), Marlon Brando (Ian McKenzie), Zakes Mokae (Stanley), Jurgen Prochnow (Capt. Stolz), Thoko Ntshinga (Emily Ngubene), Susannah Harker (Suzette du Toit), Leonard Maguire (Mr. Bruwer)

p, Paula Weinstein; d, Euzhan Palcy; w, Euzhan Palcy, Colin Welland (based on the novel by Andre Brink); ph, Kelvin Pike, Pierre-William Glenn; ed, Sam O'Steen, Glenn Cunningham; m, Dave Grusin; prod d, John Fenner; art d, Alan Tomkins, Mike Phillips

AAN Best Supporting Actor: Marlon Brando

A polemic against South African apartheid, this may not meet criteria for "great" filmmaking, but director Euzhan Palcy's film succeeds in being significant. History teacher Ben du Toit (Donald Sutherland), an Afrikaner, lives a comfortable middle-class existence with wife Susan (Janet Suzman) and their children in Johannesburg in the 1970s. He finds all of his personal and political ties thrown into question, however, following the event that sparked the Soweto uprising of 1976, when a peaceful protest march by black schoolchildren demanding better education was put down in a bloody massacre. When his longtime gardener (Winston Ntshona), in the process of trying to recover his son's body, is himself arrested, then brutally tortured and murdered, du Toit's liberal consciousness is raised. A DRY WHITE SEASON is worth watching for the (sometimes painful) force of its truths and its perspective, which shows the effects of racism from both white *and* black standpoints. This is the first full-length feature to be directed by a black woman for a major US studio. Adding to this already significant achievement, Palcy, in what amounts to the casting coup of the year, enlisted the reclusive Brando to make his brief but memorable cameo appearance—his first film role since 1980—for union scale. His performance alone is worth the price of admission to this earnest, somewhat predictable, but moving and significant film. Brando's cameo earned him an Oscar nomination for Best Supporting Actor.

DUCK SOUP

1933   70m   bw   Comedy/War   ★★★★★
Paramount   (U.S.)   /U

Groucho Marx (Rufus T. Firefly), Chico Marx (Chicolini), Harpo Marx (Pinky), Zeppo Marx (Bob Rolland), Raquel Torres (Vera Marcal), Louis Calhern (Ambassador Trentino), Margaret Dumont (Mrs. Teasdale), Verna Hillie (Secretary), Leonid Kinskey (Agitator), Edmund Breese (Zander)

p, Herman Mankiewicz; d, Leo McCarey; w, Bert Kalmar, Harry Ruby, Arthur Sheekman, Nat Perrin; ph, Henry Sharp; ed, LeRoy Stone; art d, Hans Dreier, Wiard B. Ihnen

A masterpiece. Fast-moving, irreverent, almost anarchic in style, DUCK SOUP is considered by many to be the Marx Brothers' greatest achievement,though it was not a hit upon its release. The story, if one can call it that, concerns Mrs. Teasdale (Margaret Dumont), a dowager millionairess who will donate $20 million to the destitute duchy of Freedonia if it will agree to make Rufus T. Firefly (Groucho) its dictator. Firefly woos Mrs. Teasdale and spends his spare time insulting Trentino (Louis Calhern), the ambassador from neighboring Sylvania; Trentino hires the sultry Vera Marcal (Raquel Torres) to vamp Firefly so that Trentino can move in on Mrs. Teasdale, marry her, and get control of Freedonia. To aid his chicanery, Trentino hires Chicolini (Chico), a peanut salesman, and his friend Pinky (Harpo) as spies. Eventually war breaks out and, after much manic double-crossing and side-switching, Freedonia emerges victorious.

DUCK SOUP is perhaps the best, and funniest, depiction of the absurdities of war ever committed to celluloid. The Marxes' depiction of two-bit dictators destroying their own countries was a slap at the rising fascists, so much so that Mussolini considered it a direct insult and banned the film in Italy. The Marx Brothers were thrilled to hear that. Best gag among what seems like hundreds: the mirror sequence.

DUEL IN THE SUN

1946 138m c Western   ★★★½
Selznick (U.S.)   /PG

Jennifer Jones *(Pearl Chavez)*, Joseph Cotten *(Jesse McCanles)*, Gregory Peck *(Lewt McCanles)*, Lionel Barrymore *(Sen. McCanles)*, Lillian Gish *(Laura Belle McCanles)*, Walter Huston *(The Sin Killer)*, Herbert Marshall *(Scott Chavez)*, Charles Bickford *(Sam Pierce)*, Joan Tetzel *(Helen Langford)*, Harry Carey *(Lem Smoot)*

p, David O. Selznick; d, King Vidor; w, Oliver H.P. Garrett, David O. Selznick (based on the novel by Niven Busch); ph, Lee Garmes, Harold Rosson, Ray Rennahan, Charles P. Boyle, Allen Davey; ed, Hal C. Kern, William Ziegler, John Faure, Charles Freeman; m, Dimitri Tiomkin; prod d, J. McMillan Johnson; art d, James Basevi, John Ewing; fx, Clarence Slifer, Jack Cosgrove; chor, Tilly Losch, Lloyd Shaw; cos, Walter Plunkett

AAN Best Actress: Jennifer Jones; *AAN Best Supporting Actress:* Lillian Gish

An enormous, lumbering horse opera, done up like an oversexed prize-winning bronco but revealing itself as a florid cartoon nag. DUEL is full of grand spectacle, steamy sensualism, and a storyline that could have snaked only out of Hollywood; it was Selznick's hymn to the allure of Jennifer Jones (in for Hedy Lamarr and, unbelievably, Teresa Wright—both were pregnant) and her failing entry into the Jane Russell/OUTLAW sex-goddess sweepstakes. Gregory Peck actually plays the studly bully who loves her (original choice when the project began in 1944 was John Wayne, but the dubious sex angle made him squeamish), and lightning blazes when they kiss. How to criticize a climax with two lovers orgasmically shooting each other to smithereens? The unforgettable supporting cast includes Walter Huston, having one whale of a good time as a hellfire preacher, Butterfly McQueen caricaturing her GWTW role (!) and Lillian Gish and Joseph Cotten as bastions of restraint. This is undeniable hooey, but it's also candybox entertainment. Can you really afford to miss Peck taming a sex-crazed stallion? Or Jones crawling for miles, spouting blood and words of love for her surly beau? We think not.

DUEL's accent on sex, heavy-handed and often repugnant, caused jocular critics of the day to dub the film "Lust in the Dust." The budget for the film soared beyond $6 million before it was over and an additional $2 million was used to scandalously promote the sex angle. A storm of protest from Catholic and Protestant leaders alike thunderclapped over Selznick's head. All over America local authorities competed with each other to ban the film. It was censored in Memphis and kicked out of Hartford, Connecticut. Certain scenes had to be edited before DUEL IN THE SUN opened in Philadelphia and other major cities. The publicity was enormous, and the public ignored the universal drubbing the film received from critics, flocking to see it and returning $12 million to the Selznick coffers. The film was begun in 1944, with John Wayne originally set to play the bad cowboy, but he veered away from the film after reading the dubious script.

DUELLISTS, THE

1977 95m c Historical/War   ★★★
Paramount (U.K.)   PG

Keith Carradine *(D'Hubert)*, Harvey Keitel *(Feraud)*, Albert Finney *(Fouche)*, Edward Fox *(Col. Reynard)*, Cristina Raines *(Adele)*, Robert Stephens *(Gen. Treillard)*, Tom Conti *(Jacquin)*, John McEnery *(2nd Major)*, Diana Quick *(Laura)*, Alun Armstrong *(Lacourbe)*

p, David Puttnam; d, Ridley Scott; w, Gerald Vaughan-Hughes (based on the story "The Duel" by Joseph Conrad); ph, Frank Tidy; ed, Pamela Powers; m, Howard Blake; art d, Bryan Graves

Competent feature debut of director Ridley Scott, who would go on to make the popular science-fiction films ALIEN and BLADE RUNNER, THE DUELLISTS is a beautifully photographed adaptation of a Joseph Conrad story in which two officers in Napoleon's army, Carradine and Keitel, fall out and proceed to engage in an obsessive series of duels for the next 30 years. The film's outstanding beauty is not enough to compensate its slim story, which remains preoccupied with the duellists' insane obsession with military codes of conduct and personal honor.

The leads are often remarkable, but neither of them seems quite fitting to a period setting. Therefore the burden of authenticity falls to those in supporting roles, including Finney as the Napoleonic head of the Paris police. Scott's approach to his material seems essentially a stylistic one; it imposes itself upon the story rather than visa-versa, giving an account of the Napoleonic wars that lacks passion and depth, despite the expert visuals.

DUMB & DUMBER

1994 106m c Comedy   ★★★
New Line/Motion Picture Corporation of America (U.S.) PG-13/12

Jim Carrey *(Lloyd Christmas)*, Jeff Daniels *(Harry)*, Lauren Holly *(Mary Swanson)*, Mike Starr *(Joe Mentalino)*, Karen Duffy *(J.P. Shay)*, Charles Rocket *(Nicholas Andre)*, Joe Baker *(Barnard)*, Hank Brandt *(Karl Swanson)*, Teri Garr *(Helen Swanson)*, Brady Bluhm *(Billy)*

p, Charles B. Wessler, Brad Krevoy, Steve Stabler; d, Peter Farrelly; w, Peter Farrelly, Bennett Yellin, Bobby Farrelly; ph, Mark Irwin; ed, Christopher Greenbury; m, Todd Rundgren; prod d, Sidney J. Bartholomew Jr.; art d, Arian Jay Vetter; fx, Frank Ceglia; cos, Mary Zophres

In the tradition of American slapstick, DUMB AND DUMBER exploits the comic possibilities of a pair of imbeciles who can complicate any imaginable situation through their propensity for infantile, anarchic folly. The film's commercial success, despite the coolness of critics, is proof that there is still pleasure to be found in pure and simple buffoonery, and that basic bodily functions remain a resonant subject for comedy.

Limousine driver Lloyd Christmas (Jim Carrey) has a bowl haircut, a chipped tooth, and a dangerously low IQ. Smitten by beautiful heiress Mary Swanson (Lauren Holly), he pursues her to Aspen in a fur-covered van driven by recently fired dog-groomer Harry (Jeff Daniels), Lloyd's best buddy and intellectual equal. Our heroes are oblivious to the fact that they have inadvertently taken possession of a suitcase full of ransom money, and are being pursued by a gang of criminals.

Every gross childhood gag and indiscretion makes an appearance somewhere in this picture, with eating and excretion given special prominence. Underlying the slapstick, however, is an extravagant parody of American culture—bad taste, bad manners, the gushing sentimentality of Lloyd's daydreams, or the classic westward road trip, complete with diner scenes and archetypal rednecks. This gleefully lowbrow film is best enjoyed by the young, and by those who can still laugh at the passing of gas. There's little here for Merchant-Ivory fans, but devotees of Bunuel—e.g., the notorious dinner party sequence in THE PHANTOM OF LIBERTY—may not be entirely disappointed.

DUMBO

1941 64m c Animated   ★★★★½
Walt Disney Productions (U.S.)   /U

VOICES OF: Edward Brophy *(Timothy Mouse)*, Herman Bing *(Ringmaster)*, Verna Felton *(Elephant)*, Sterling Holloway *(Stork)*, Cliff Edwards *(Jim Crow)*

p, Walt Disney; d, Ben Sharpsteen, Norman Ferguson, Wilfred Jackson, Bill Roberts, Jack Kinney, Sam Armstrong; w, Joe Grant, Dick Huemer (based on a book by Helen Aberson and Harold Pearl); art d, Herb Ryman, Kenneth O'Connor, Terrell Stapp, Donald Da Gradi, Al Zinnen, Ernest Nordli, Dick Kelsey,

Charles Payzant; anim, Wolfgang Reitherman, Arthur Babbitt, Walt Kelly, John Lounsbery, Ward Kimball, Fred Moore, Cy Young, Vladimir Tytla

AA Best Score: Frank Churchill, Oliver Wallace; *AAN Best Song:* Frank Churchill (Music), Ned Washington (Lyrics)

One of Disney's finest films, this simple tale is set in a circus and spotlights a baby elephant, Dumbo, who is mocked and ridiculed because his ears are too big. With the help of his best friend Timothy the mouse and some very hip crows, Dumbo discovers that he can use his gigantic ears to fly and becomes the hit of the circus. The message of the film is spoken by Timothy as he declares to his doubting friend, "The very things that held you down will carry you up and up and up!"

A small, flawless gem, DUMBO is one of the shortest animated features Disney ever made and inexpensive to boot, costing less than $1 million (whereas more ambitious films like BAMBI shot well beyond the $2 million mark). A masterpiece of visual story-telling, the film contains relatively little dialogue and Dumbo never speaks; his mother only speaks to him in the song "Baby Mine." Humans are shown in shadows and silhouettes, the animals taking center stage. As with all his major feature-length animation films, Disney made sure that none of the scenes were flat, that blades of grass rippled in the wind and leaves fluttered in the trees. A delight from beginning to end, the film's absolute highlight is the "Pink Elephants on Parade" sequence in which Dumbo and Timothy hallucinate after accidentally drinking liquor.

It took the resourceful Disney craftsman a year and a half to design and execute this stunning achievement of animation art. This was time well spent. The result was an experience—alternately hilarious, thrilling, and heartbreaking—that will appeal to every child in the world and every adult who can still recall the happy world of childhood fantasies and fables. The film won an Oscar for its score and received a nomination for Best Song ("Baby Mine"). Warning to parents: the film contains some objectionable racial caricatures.

E.T. THE EXTRA-TERRESTRIAL
1982 115m c Science Fiction/Fantasy ★★★★
Universal (U.S.) PG/U

Dee Wallace Stone *(Mary)*, Henry Thomas *(Elliott)*, Peter Coyote *(Keys)*, Robert MacNaughton *(Michael)*, Drew Barrymore *(Gertie)*, K.C. Martel *(Greg)*, Sean Frye *(Steve)*, Tom Howell *(Tyler)*, Erika Eleniak *(Pretty Girl)*, David O'Dell *(Schoolboy)*

p, Steven Spielberg, Kathleen Kennedy; d, Steven Spielberg; w, Melissa Mathison; ph, Allen Daviau; ed, Carol Littleton; m, John Williams; prod d, James D. Bissell; fx, Industrial Light & Magic; cos, Deborah L. Scott, Carlo Rambaldi

One of the most popular movies ever made, E.T. translates religious myth into cute, familiar terrain with its story of a lovable alien stranded in suburbia.

Elliott (Henry Thomas) finds E.T., a visitor from another planet left stranded on Earth, hiding in his backyard and, like any kid who finds a stray, decides to keep him. Hiding the alien from his mother, Thomas and the neighborhood kids befriend the creature. Though E.T. becomes attached to Elliott and his friends, he wants to get back to his own planet; meanwhile, the children must save him from some government types who are trying to capture and study him.

A major hit at the box office which also spawned an extremely profitable merchandising campaign, E.T. was embraced by audiences worldwide and instantly became absorbed into popular culture. Though the story feels standard, the fun comes from the meticulously realized

details that director Steven Spielberg and associate producer-writer Melissa Mathison have injected into the material. From E.T.'s too-cute encounters with suburban living to the undeniable exhilaration felt when Thomas's bicycle magically soars into the air, the film bears witness to the undeniable powers of one of cinema's most skillful craftsmen. The film won Oscars for Best Original Score and Best Visual Effects.

EARRINGS OF MADAME DE ... , THE
(MADAME DE . . .)
1953 105m bw Drama ★★★★★
Franco London/Indusfilms/Rizzoli (France/Italy)

Danielle Darrieux *(Countess Louise de . . .)*, Charles Boyer *(Gen. Andre de . . .)*, Vittorio De Sica *(Baron Fabrizio Donati)*, Mireille Perrey *(Mme de . . .'s Nurse)*, Jean Debucourt *(M Remy)*, Serge Lecointe *(Jerome)*, Lia di Leo *(Lola)*, Jean Galland *(M de Bernac)*, Hubert Noel *(Henri de Maleville)*, Leon Walther *(Theater Manager)*

p, H. Baum, Ralph Baum; d, Max Ophuls; w, Marcel Achard, Annette Wademant, Max Ophuls (based on the novel by Louise de Vilmorin); ph, Christian Matras; ed, Borys Lewin; m, Oscar Straus, Georges Van Parys; cos, Georges Annenkov, Rosine Delamare

AAN Best Costume Design: Georges Annenkov, Rosine Delamare

For the five-year period from 1950-55 (shortly before he died), Max Ophuls was arguably the world's greatest filmmaker, creating LA RONDE, LE PLAISIR, LOLA MONTES, and this masterful study of a tragic, three-cornered romance.

THE EARRINGS OF MADAME DE. . . opens brilliantly as the Countess Louise de. . . (Darrieux; her character's last name is obscured throughout the story) searches through her belongings for something to sell. The camera glides along as she examines furs, a necklace, a cross, and finally a pair of diamond earrings she received as a wedding present from her husband, General Andre de. . . (Boyer). When she pretends that the earrings have been stolen, the general begins a search, eventually recovering them discreetly from the jeweler to whom his wife sold them. The general gives the earrings to his mistress (di Leo), who later loses them while gambling with Baron Donati (De Sica). Upon returning to Paris, the Baron falls in love with the Countess, giving her a gift meant to express his deepest affection. . . .

EARRINGS is masterfully told in both verbal and visual terms. The genteel, brittle dialogue traces an elliptical path to tragedy while the relentlessly mobile camera dollies and pans around the stiflingly ornate rooms that Ophuls's characters inhabit. The star trio of Darrieux, Boyer and De Sica have rarely been better, playing characters whose narcissism deepens to obsession and, ultimately, desperation. The film's lush visual style is a perfect, ironic backdrop for the superficialities of the society explored, particularly in the famous ballroom sequence where the Countess and the Baron first become aware of their ill-fated love.

EAST OF EDEN
1955 115m c Drama ★★★★½
Warner Bros. (U.S.) /PG

Julie Harris *(Abra)*, James Dean *(Cal Trask)*, Raymond Massey *(Adam Trask)*, Richard Davalos *(Aron Trask)*, Burl Ives *(Sam)*, Jo Van Fleet *(Kate)*, Albert Dekker *(Will)*, Lois Smith *(Ann)*, Harold Gordon *(Mr. Albrecht)*, Timothy Carey *(Joe)*

p, Elia Kazan; d, Elia Kazan; w, Paul Osborn (based on the novel by John Steinbeck); ph, Ted McCord; ed, Owen Marks; m, Leonard Rosenman; art d, James Basevi, Malcolm Bert; cos, Anna Hill Johnstone

AAN Best Actor: James Dean; *AA Best Supporting Actress:* Jo Van Fleet; *AAN Best Director:* Elia Kazan; *AAN Best Screenplay:* Paul Osborn

Overwrought, often splendid Kazan version of the Steinbeck novel. The movie's chief distinction is the amazing debut of rebellious, romantic James Dean, who in this and his next film, REBEL WITHOUT A CAUSE, would enshrine the misunderstood teen, and become a tragic icon in his own right. Dean plays the neurotic son of Massey, a devoutly religious lettuce farmer whose vast acreage stretches through the rich Salinas Valley of California. Dean's twin brother (Davalos, also making a powerful film debut) is well adjusted and upstanding, involved in a stable relationship with girlfriend Harris and diligently pursuing the development of his father's lands. Dean is his brother's opposite: troubled and troublesome, he challenges all authority, including his father's, and mistakenly believes that Davalos is the favored son. It's the Cain and Abel story, circa 1917, and the rush from stability to destruction and tragedy is swift, as Dean seeks to undo his brother and himself.

A powerful film whose influence can be seen in HUD and most other antihero films, EAST OF EDEN is masterfully directed by Kazan. All the principals give riveting performances, but it was Dean who emerged as an overnight sensation. EDEN also features a quintessentially hard-bitten performance from Van Fleet, who won an Oscar for her pains.

EASTER PARADE

1948 107m c Musical/Comedy ★★★½
MGM (U.S.) /U

Judy Garland (Hannah Brown), Fred Astaire (Don Hewes), Peter Lawford (Jonathan Harrow III), Ann Miller (Nadine Gale), Jules Munshin (Francois, Headwaiter), Clinton Sundberg (Mike, the Bartender), Jeni le Gon (Essie), Richard Beavers (Singer), Richard Simmons (Al, Ziegfeld's Stage Manager), Jimmie Bates (Boy with Astaire in "Drum Crazy" Musical Number)

p, Arthur Freed; d, Charles Walters; w, Frances Goodrich, Albert Hackett, Sidney Sheldon, Guy Bolton (based on a story by Frances Goodrich and Albert Hackett); ph, Harry Stradling; ed, Albert Akst; art d, Cedric Gibbons, Jack Martin Smith; fx, Warren Newcombe; chor, Robert Alton; cos, Irene, Valles

AA Best Score: Johnny Green, Roger Edens

Pretty, deft, and tuneful but, given the top-rate talent involved, not particularly inspired. Between Easter 1911 and Easter 1912, Astaire gets dumped by dance partner Miller and vows revenge by grooming unknown chorus girl Garland for stardom.

Gene Kelly was originally slated to play the lead, but injured his ankle playing volleyball, so he suggested to producer Arthur Freed that they prevail on Astaire to come out of his "retirement" for the role. Astaire had announced he was done after BLUE SKIES, but jumped at the opportunity and gave yet another classic performance. Garland was beginning to tire of the formula of her films, and the horrendous pace of her filming schedule, but Astaire apparently helped coax her through the production despite her exhaustion. Look for cameos from Lola Albright, as a hat model, and a two-and-a-half-year-old Liza Minnelli in the finale. Irving Berlin wrote 17 of the film's tunes, and Johnny Green and Roger Edens won an Oscar for their musical adaptation. The standout number is the delightful "A Couple of Swells."

EASY LIVING

1937 88m bw Comedy ★★★½
Paramount Pictures (U.S.) /PG

Jean Arthur (Mary Smith), Edward Arnold (J.B. Ball), Ray Milland (John Ball, Jr.), Luis Alberni (Mr. Louis Louis), Mary Nash (Mrs. Jennie Ball), Franklin Pangborn (Van Buren), Barlowe Borland (Mr. Gurney), William Demarest (Wallace Whistling), Andrew Tombes (E.F. Hulgar), Esther Dale (Lillian)

p, Arthur Hornblow Jr.; d, Mitchell Leisen; w, Preston Sturges (based on a story by Vera Caspary); ph, Ted Tetzlaff; ed, Doane Harrison; art d, Hans Dreier, Ernst Fegte; fx, Farciot Edouart; cos, Travis Banton

Preston Sturges wrote the screenplay for this hilarious screwball comedy about a working girl whose life is turned upside down by a millionaire and his son.

Millionaire banker J.B. Ball (Edward Arnold) lectures his son John Ball Jr. (Ray Milland) for being a lazy spendthrift, then discovers that his wife has bought a $58,000 sable coat. He throws it off the roof of their penthouse and it lands on Mary Smith (Jean Arthur), ruining her hat. Ball tells her she can keep the coat, and also buys her a new hat, but when she shows up at work late, she's fired. Mr. Louis Louis (Luis Alberni) is told by Ball that he has one week to pay the back mortgage on the Hotel Louis or Ball will foreclose, but Louis is told by a milliner (Franklin Pangborn) that Mary is Ball's mistress, so Louis gives her the most lavish suite in the hotel to appease Ball. Mary goes to eat at the automat, where she unwittingly meets John Ball Jr. who's taken a job as a busboy to impress his father. John goes with Mary back to her suite and spends the night there, and the elder Ball also checks into the hotel after his wife leaves him. In the morning, the hotel suddenly becomes fashionable after a gossip columnist (William Demarest) reports that Mary is Ball's mistress and is staying there.

Preston Sturges's imaginative script is one of his best, adroitly mixing his customary satire of capitalism and the class system with some dazzling dialogue and hilarious slapstick. The entire cast is perfection, from the tyrannical Edward Arnold, to the charming Jean Arthur, to the insouciant Ray Milland, and of course, the usual Paramount stock company of superb character actors, particularly Franklin Pangborn as the prissy milliner. Everyone throws dignity out the window and even the stars have a great time indulging in broad slapstick, including some hysterical fistfights and pratfalls. Leisen's direction is, as always, smooth and elegant, although the film is sometimes slowly paced and deliberate, lacking the mad whirl of frantic craziness that Sturges later brought to his own films as a director.

EASY RIDER

1969 94m c Drama ★★★★
Pando/Raybert (U.S.) R/18

Peter Fonda (Wyatt), Dennis Hopper (Billy), Antonio Mendoza (Jesus), Phil Spector (Connection), Mac Mashourian (Bodyguard), Warren Finnerty (Rancher), Tita Colorado (Rancher's Wife), Luke Askew (Stranger), Luana Anders (Lisa), Sabrina Scharf (Sarah)

p, Peter Fonda; d, Dennis Hopper; w, Peter Fonda, Dennis Hopper, Terry Southern; ph, Laszlo Kovacs; ed, Donn Cambern; art d, Jerry Kay; fx, Steve Karkus

AAN Best Supporting Actor: Jack Nicholson; AAN Best Adapted Screenplay: Peter Fonda, Dennis Hopper, Terry Southern

A must-see, if only once. More notable as a document of its times than as a piece of cinema, EASY RIDER is slack but powerful, sentimental yet scathing, experimental but predictable.

A tale of two men searching for a freedom they can never attain, the film features Fonda and Hopper as Wyatt and Billy, a pair of hippie bikers who journey to New Orleans, hoping to arrive in time for Mardi Gras. On the way, the duo encounter rebuffs at various motels because of their way-out appearance, a hitchhiker who takes them back to the sun-drenched revels of his commune, and a squeaky-clean Texas parade. Arrested for joining the latter, the pair meets up with drunken civil-rights lawyer George Hanson (Jack Nicholson, enjoying the film's most well-rounded part and giving its best performance, one which earned him an Oscar nomination and finally made him a star). Now a trio, the men suffer beatings from local rednecks, but Hanson also gets to enjoy his first joint, which prompts one of the film's most memorable moments—Hanson's tongue-in-cheek theory that Venusians have already landed on Earth and occupy several important posts. Billy and Wyatt finally make it to New Orleans and find that their journey to the freewheeling world of Fat Tuesday (including an LSD-laced jaunt to a cemetery) has not brought them any happiness or sense of direction. The animosity the pair have dealt with throughout reaches its peak at the film's famous ending, as the film attempts to martyr its quasi-religious antiheroes.

A finely observed film but insufficiently developed as a satire of middle America, EASY RIDER seemed the paragon of hip rebellion at the time of its release; in retrospect, its worldview seems closer to whining self-pity.

EAT A BOWL OF TEA

1990 102m c Romance ★★★½
American Playhouse (U.S.) PG-13/12

Cora Miao (Mei Oi), Russell Wong (Ben Loy), Victor Wong (Wah Gay), Lee Sau Kee (Bok Fat), Eric Tsiang Chi Wai (Ah Song), Law Lan (Aunt Gim), Lau Siu Ming (Lee Gong)

p, Tom Sternberg; d, Wayne Wang; w, Judith Rascoe (based on the novel by Louis Chu); ph, Amir Mokri; ed, Richard Candib; m, Mark Adler; prod d, Bob Ziembicki; art d, Timmy Yip; cos, Marit Allen

This engaging comedy-drama set in New York's Chinatown examines an intriguing post-WWII American phenomenon: after years of strict immigration laws and forced separation of spouses, Chinese immigrants were finally able to bring their mates to the US. For longtime residents of Chinatown, it was too late to effect conjugal reunions, but many older Chinese-American men wanted their sons to provide them with grandchildren by finding brides in China.

Director Wang (CHAN IS MISSING, DIM SUM) and screenwriter Rascoe have fashioned a graceful movie powered by deliciously eccentric characters, bringing to the screen a slice of American life unfamiliar to many. Abounding in magical moments (like the scene in which the two young leads fall in love in front of an outdoor screen on which LOST HORIZON is playing), the film cleverly parallels the difficulties of adjusting to a foreign culture with those of adjusting to a new marriage. The result is both a perceptive historical document and a captivating love story.

EAT DRINK MAN WOMAN

1994 120m c Comedy/Drama   ★★★½
Central Motion Pictures Co./Good Machine Inc.   /PG
(U.S./Taiwan)

Sihung Lung *(Mr. Chu)*, Kuei-Mai Yang *(Jia-Jen)*, Chien-Lien Wu *(Jia-Chien)*, Yu-Wen Wang *(Jia-Ning)*, Sylvia Chang *(Jin-Rong)*, Winston Chao *(Li Kai)*, Chao-Jung Chen *(Guo Lun)*, Lester Chen *(Raymond)*, Yu Chen *(Rachel)*, Ah-Leh Gua *(Mrs. Liang)*

p, Li-Kong Hsy; d, Ang Lee; w, Ang Lee, Hui Ling Wang, James Schamus; ph, Jong Lin; ed, Tim Squyres; m, Mader; prod d, Fu-Hsiung Lee

AAN Best Foreign Language Film

A remarkably assured comedy-drama of domestic life in Taiwan, Ang Lee's EAT DRINK MAN WOMAN explores how families use meals and other rituals to appease their hunger for love in stressful times.

Widower Mr. Chu (Sihung Lung), one of Taipei's leading chefs, laboriously prepares gourmet meals each night for his three unmarried daughters: Jia-Jen (Kuei-Mai Yang), a high school teacher and recent convert to Christianity, Jia-Chien (Chien-Lien Wu), an ambitious airline executive and a talented chef in her own right, and Jia-Ning (Yu-Wen Wang), the youngest, a cheerful student who works part-time in a fast food restaurant. The harmony of this close-knit family is soon disrupted by romance, as the daughters cope with the blandishments of three very different men and Mr. Chu commences a relationship of his own.

Writer-director Ang Lee has described this film as "the last in my 'Father Knows Best' trilogy." Whereas PUSHING HANDS (1991) and THE WEDDING BANQUET (1993) focus on children who disappoint their more traditional parents, EAT DRINK MAN WOMAN is about parents who fail to measure up to the expectations of their offspring. At its best, the film echoes and parodies the characteristic themes, if not the stylistic rigor, of Japanese director Yasujiro Ozu. Lee's more playful sensibility comments on changing Taiwanese values through ironic juxtapositions and detailed scenes of food preparation. With Western influences (Christianity, classical music, interracial marriages) and modernity (technology, sexual liberation, divorce) constantly intruding on family life, elaborate dinners become the last surviving group ritual.

EATING RAOUL

1982 90m c Comedy   ★★★
Bartel (U.S.)   R/18

Mary Woronov *(Mary Bland)*, Paul Bartel *(Paul Bland)*, Robert Beltran *(Raoul)*, Buck Henry *(Mr. Leech)*, Richard Paul *(Mr. Kray)*, Susan Saiger *(Doris, the Dominatrix)*, Ed Begley Jr. *(Hippy)*, Dan Barrows *(Bobbie R.)*, Dick Blackburn *(James)*, Ralph Brannen *(Paco)*

p, Anne Kimmel; d, Paul Bartel; w, Paul Bartel, Richard Blackburn; ph, Gary Thieltges; ed, Alan Toomayan; m, Arlon Ober; prod d, Robert Schulenberg

Bon appetit? This sometimes hilarious black comedy has gained quite a cult following over the years, and it remains writer-director-star Bartel's best effort yet. Set in Los Angeles, the story follows a straight-laced couple, Mary and Paul Bland (Bartel and the galvanizingly odd Woronov), who dream of someday opening their own gourmet restaurant. Since Mary is a nurse and Paul has just been fired from his job at a liquor store, realizing their dream soon seems unlikely. Fate knocks, however, when a drunken reveler stumbles into their apartment and begins mauling Mary. Paul kills the intruder and discovers a large wad of cash on the dead man. Inspired, the couple place an ad in a swingers' newspaper to lure victims into their home, where they will be killed for their money (something the ultra-conservative couple feels they deserve anyway).

With Bartel and Woronov giving wonderfully funny deadpan performances, EATING RAOUL is a terrifically droll satire on both horror movies and American middle-class values. Despite the subject matter, our hero and heroine emerge as genuinely sympathetic characters, which ultimately makes one wonder where the film's true sympathies lie. Working independently, Bartel scraped together financing from family and friends and shot the film in piecemeal fashion when he could afford it. The resulting film, despite its lulls, is probably the better for it. Beltran, in the title role, brings along some much-needed energy, so enjoy his performance. . . while it lasts.

ECSTASY
(EXTASE)

1933 82m bw Drama/Erotic   ★★★
Elekta (Czechoslovakia)   /18

Hedy Lamarr *(Eva)*, Zvonimir Rogoz *(Emile)*, Aribert Mog *(Adam)*, Leopold Kramer *(Eva's Father)*

p, Frantisek Horky, Moriz Grunhut; d, Gustav Machaty; w, Gustav Machaty, Frantisek Horky, Vitezslav Nezval, Jacques A. Koerpel; ph, Jan Stallich, Hans Androschin; m, Giuseppe Becce; art d, Bohumil Hes

A once-daring gander at nude pre-MGM Hedy Lamarr (then Hedy Kiesler). Promoted in its day as "the most whispered-about film in the world" (in fact, everyone was talking about it out loud, and L.B. Mayer was roaring) and the "stark naked truth of a woman's desire for love," it's tame stuff, even for the good old days.

Kiesler plays a child bride whose husband ignores her on her wedding night. In frustration, she has a sexual tryst in a hut with a roadway engineer. When her horse wanders away with her clothes as she takes a swim, Eva gives chase, bumping into the engineer who hands over her clothes like a gentleman. She arranges to go away with him but leaves him after her former husband commits suicide. She subsequently appears with a baby, the offspring of this illicit affair, happy and fulfilled.

The simple story is told with invention by director Gustav Machaty, who seems especially influenced by the editing techniques of Eisenstein. The big deal back then was really not the nudity but the close-ups of Hedy during her tryst. Machaty couldn't elicit the facial responses he wanted from the young actress, until he got under the table she lay on and started pricking her with a pin. The film was released in the US in 1940.

ED WOOD

1994 127m bw Biography/Comedy/Drama   ★★★½
Touchstone/Burton-DiNovi/Casual Pictures Inc. (U.S.) R/

Johnny Depp *(Ed Wood)*, Martin Landau *(Bela Lugosi)*, Sarah Jessica Parker *(Dolores Fuller)*, Patricia Arquette *(Kathy O'Hara)*, Jeffrey Jones *(Criswell)*, G.D. Spradlin *(Reverend Lemon)*, Vincent D'Onofrio *(Orson Welles)*, Bill Murray *(John "Bunny" Breckinridge)*, Mike Starr *(Georgie Weiss)*, Max Casella *(Paul Marco)*

p, Denise DiNovi, Tim Burton; d, Tim Burton; w, Scott Alexander, Larry Karaszewski; ph, Stefan Czapsky; ed, Chris Lebenzon; m, Howard Shore; prod d, Tom Duffield; art d, Okowita; fx, Howard Jensen, Kevin J. Pike, Paul Boyington; cos, Colleen Atwood

AA Best Supporting Actor: Martin Landau; AA Best Makeup:

It's ironic that one of the best films of 1994 told the story of one of the worst filmmakers of all time. Tim Burton's ED WOOD is a delightful, off-the-wall, and ultimately moving portrait of a young man trying to claw his way up into Hollywood from the bottom.

Ed Wood (Johnny Depp) produces awful plays in LA with various friends and hangers-on, including his girlfriend, Dolores Fuller (Sarah Jessica Parker), and transsexual wannabe Bunny Breckinridge (Bill Murray). Ed himself is a secret cross-dresser, and when he learns that schlock producer George Weiss (Mike Starr) intends to make a film based on notorious transsexual Christine Jorgensen, he pitches himself as the best man for the job. A chance encounter with his idol, Bela Lugosi (Martin Landau), leads Ed to cast the now drug-addicted actor in his picture, and a deep friendship begins to develop between the two.

Typically, Burton's storytelling is sometimes erratic, but his emphasis on humanizing marginal characters—a project that seems central to his artistic agenda—is as strong as ever. Wood and his entourage may be bizarre, but they're sympathetic and likable; one roots for Wood to succeed despite his evidently complete lack of talent. Indeed, Burton, a true devotee of bargain-basement pop culture, probably intends to question whether "talent" is not just a cultural shibboleth, as misleading and overdetermined as "taste," or even "art."

EDISON, THE MAN

1940 104m bw Biography   ★★★½
MGM   (U.S.)

Spencer Tracy (*Thomas Alva Edison*), Rita Johnson (*Mary Stilwell*), Lynne Overman (*Bunt Cavatt*), Charles Coburn (*Gen. Powell*), Gene Lockhart (*Mr. Taggart*), Henry Travers (*Ben Els*), Felix Bressart (*Michael Simon*), Peter Godfrey (*Ashton*), Frank Faylen (*Galbreath*), Byron Foulger (*Edwin Hall*)

p, John W. Considine Jr., Orville O. Dull; d, Clarence Brown; w, Talbot Jennings, Bradbury Foote (based on a story by Dore Schary and Hugo Butler); ph, Harold Rosson; ed, Frederick Y. Smith; m, Herbert Stothart; art d, Cedric Gibbons, John S. Detlie; cos, Dolly Tree, Gile Steele

AAN Best Original Story: Hugo Butler, Dore Schary

A warm, watchable whitewash. MGM went all out for Thomas Alva Edison in 1940, producing two films on his life. YOUNG TOM EDISON was a box-office flop despite Mickey Rooney's energetic portrayal; EDISON, THE MAN was a much more lavish and popular production, with Tracy giving a dutiful but dynamic performance as the famous inventor. The film opens as Edison, at age 82, is about to be honored on the 50th anniversary of his invention of the incandescent light. He is being interviewed by two youths and begins to relate the story of his early manhood. It then goes into flashback and chronicles Edison's most productive years, from age 25 to 35, when he produced the phonograph, the dictaphone, and the electric light.

A little too old for the part, Tracy nevertheless immersed himself in the details of Edison's life, trying to capture the flavor of his personality as well as the words of the script. The result is a much more interesting performance than the one he gave in MGM's similar canonization of Father Flanagan in BOYS TOWN—energetic and committed, but not over-earnest. Tracy was ably backed up by a fine cast, particularly Rita Johnson, and directed with a sure feel for Americana by Clarence Brown. What's missing is a sense of the "difficult" side of his personality, which could have made this more of a well-rounded biography than a one-note song of tribute.

EDUCATING RITA

1983 110m c Drama   ★★★
Acorn   (U.K.)   PG/15

Michael Caine (*Dr. Frank Bryant*), Julie Walters (*Rita*), Michael Williams (*Brian*), Maureen Lipman (*Trish*), Jeananne Crowley (*Julia*), Malcolm Douglas (*Denny*), Godfrey Quigley (*Rita's Father*), Dearbhla Molloy (*Elaine*), Pat Daly (*Bursar*), Kim Fortune (*Collins*)

p, Lewis Gilbert; d, Lewis Gilbert; w, Willy Russell (based on his play); ph, Frank Watts; ed, Garth Craven; m, David Hentschel; art d, Maurice Fowler

AAN Best Actor: Michael Caine; *AAN Best Actress:* Julie Walters; *AAN Best Adapted Screenplay:* Willy Russell (Screenplay)

Julie Walters plays Rita, a working-class hairdresser who signs on for adult education classes and chooses alcoholic hack Frank Bryant (Michael Caine) as her tutor. As Rita's intellectual horizons expand, she becomes torn between her stifling home life and the alluring, but pretentious, world of her amorous professor. Adapted by Willy Russell from his stage play, this is a poignant if predictable take on the English class system, buoyed by an effervescent performance from Walters (though Caine gets the best line: "Life is such a rich and frantic form that I need the drink to help me step delicately through it"). Caine, Walters, and Russell were all nominated for Academy Awards for their work.

EDWARD SCISSORHANDS

1990 100m c Fantasy/Romance   ★★★½
Fox   (U.S.)   PG-13/PG

Johnny Depp (*Edward Scissorhands*), Winona Ryder (*Kim Boggs*), Dianne Wiest (*Peg Boggs*), Anthony Michael Hall (*Jim*), Kathy Baker (*Joyce*), Robert Oliveri (*Kevin*), Conchata Ferrell (*Helen*), Caroline Aaron (*Marge*), Dick Anthony Williams (*Officer Allen*), O-Lan Jones (*Esmeralda*)

p, Tim Burton, Denise DiNovi; d, Tim Burton; w, Caroline Thompson, Tim Burton; ph, Stefan Czapsky; ed, Richard Halsey; m, Danny Elfman; prod d, Bo Welch; art d, Tom Duffield; fx, Stan Winston, Michael Wood; cos, Colleen Atwood

AAN Best Makeup: Ve Neill, Stan Winston

A poignant, personal fairy tale from the director of PEE-WEE'S BIG ADVENTURE, BEETLEJUICE and BATMAN.

Edward (Johnny Depp) is the creation of an inventor (Vincent Price) who dies before his work is completed, leaving his otherwise perfect progeny with pointed metal shards for hands. When Avon Lady Peg (Dianne Wiest) comes calling at Edward's Gothic castle one day, she takes a shine to the creature and persuades him to go back with her to the picture-perfect, pastel-colored suburb where she lives. The initially terrified Edward becomes an object of great curiosity among Peg's neighbors, and soon gains minor celebrity status with his unique talents for hedge trimming and hair styling. But Edward's newfound happiness is threatened when the suburban residents come to believe he is guilty of a crime.

Drawing upon influences that range from FRANKENSTEIN to BEING THERE, Burton creates a satire/allegory that is both funny and moving. The theme—that just beyond the edge of the perfectly normal lies the truly bizarre—is realized with intelligence and visual flair. In one particularly charming sequence, Edward creates a beautiful sculpture from a slab of ice, as Kim dances in the frozen flakes which rain down from his flying metallic fingers. Fine performances all around, particularly from Depp and the immensely sympathetic Wiest.

EFFECT OF GAMMA RAYS ON MAN-IN-THE-MOON MARIGOLDS, THE

1972 100m c Drama   ★★★½
Fox   (U.S.)   PG/AA

Joanne Woodward (*Beatrice*), Nell Potts (*Matilda*), Roberta Wallach (*Ruth*), Judith Lowry (*Nanny Annie*), Richard Venture (*Floyd*), Estelle Omens (*Floyd's Wife*), Carolyn Coates (*Granny's Daughter*), Will Hare (*Junk Man*), Jess Osuna (*Sonny*), David Spielberg (*Mr. Goodman*)

p, Paul Newman; d, Paul Newman; w, Alvin Sargent (based on the play by Paul Zindel); ph, Adam Holender; ed, Evan Lottman; m, Maurice Jarre; prod d, Gene Callahan; cos, Anna Hill Johnstone

Joanne Woodward is superb in this film adaptation of Paul Zindel's Pulitzer Prize-winning play, directed for the screen by her husband, Paul Newman. Woodward plays an embittered and overbearing widow who is struggling to raise her two very different daughters, Ruth (Roberta Wallach, daughter of actors Eli Wallach and Anne Jackson) and Matilda (Nell Potts, Newman and Woodward's real-life daughter). Wallach is loud and outgoing, Potts withdrawn and shy. Woodward makes ends meet by boarding elderly people and making phone sales for a dance studio. She is spiteful and distrusting of all men, including Potts's science teacher (Spielberg), whom she accuses of endangering her child's life by exposing her to gamma rays in order to grow marigolds for a school project. The widow's bitter outlook on life and grim view of men slowly work their way into her daughters' consciousness, but the blooming marigolds become a symbol of hope for a less stunted life.

EFFI BRIEST

1974 135m bw Drama   ★★★★½
Tango-Film (West Germany)   /U

Hanna Schygulla (Effi Briest), Wolfgang Schenck (Baron Geert von Instetten), Ulli Lommel (Major Crampas), Lilo Pempeit (Frau Briest), Herbert Steinmetz (Herr Briest), Mark Bohm (Gieshubler), Ursula Stratz (Roswitha), Irm Hermann (Johanna), Karl Scheydt (Kruse), Karl-Heinz Bohm (Wullersdorf)

p, Rainer Werner Fassbinder; d, Rainer Werner Fassbinder; w, Rainer Werner Fassbinder (based on the novel by Theodor Fontane); ph, Jurgen Jurges, Dietrich Lohmann; ed, Thea Eymesz; m, Camille Saint-Saens; art d, Kurt Raab; cos, Barbara Baum

One of the finest films to come out of postwar Germany, EFFI BRIEST marked the 16th feature in five years for the prolific Fassbinder. In 19th-century Germany, a 17-year-old girl (Schygulla) is forced into an unhappy marriage with a much older count (Schenck), and then falls into a short-lived relationship with an army major (Lommel). When, years after it has ended, the count discovers their affair, he kills the man in a duel and abandons his disgraced wife.

Schygulla, one of the finest actresses working in Germany today, carries the film with a truly astonishing performance, painting a moving picture of a woman exploited by everyone around her and powerless to fight back. Schygulla's professional relationship with Fassbinder—whose tyrannical working methods have been well documented—dissolved with this picture but, unlike most of the actors in the director's informal stock company, she went on to pursue a successful independent career. Schygulla would eventually work with Fassbinder again, in THE MARRIAGE OF MARIA BRAUN, BERLIN ALEXANDERPLATZ (a 15-hour miniseries for German television), and LILI MARLEEN.

EGG AND I, THE

1947 108m bw Comedy   ★★★½
Universal (U.S.)   /U

Claudette Colbert (Betty MacDonald), Fred MacMurray (Bob MacDonald), Marjorie Main (Ma Kettle), Louise Allbritton (Harriet Putnam), Percy Kilbride (Pa Kettle), Richard Long (Tom Kettle), Billy House (Billy Reed), Ida Moore (Old Lady), Donald MacBride (Mr. Henty), Samuel S. Hinds (Sheriff)

p, Chester Erskine, Fred Finklehoffe; d, Chester Erskine; w, Chester Erskine (based on the novel by Betty MacDonald); ph, Milton Krasner; ed, Russell Schoengarth; m, Frank Skinner; prod d, Bernard Herzbrun

AAN Best Supporting Actress: Marjorie Main

Amusing if slightly bland comedy in which Colbert and MacMurray uproot themselves from city living after MacMurray decides he can't stand the brokerage business. They buy a ramshackle farm, intending to raise chickens and live a leisurely rural existence. Instead, they face one problem after another, watching their bank account dwindle as Kilbride, the most unhandy handyman on record, fritters away their hard-earned dollars on building and landscaping materials. Complications develop when MacMurray becomes fascinated with the mechanized farm owned by Allbritton, a wealthy widow who tries to court him away from Colbert.

THE EGG AND I has many a laugh-filled scene—Colbert attempting to carry water in a bottomless bucket, MacMurray beaming with pride as he chops down a bothersome tree which crashes onto the roof of the henhouse—and was a success at the box office, bringing in $5.5 million. Colbert is suitably arch as the cultured, city-bred lady trying to cope with rural life, and MacMurray deftly deadpans his way through one disaster after another. This was the first appearance of Kilbride and Main as Ma and Pa Kettle and they would continue playing these lovable hick roles through a very successful series.

8 1/2
(OTTO E MEZZO)

1963 140m bw Drama   ★★★★★
Cineriz/Francinex (Italy)   /15

Marcello Mastroianni (Guido Anselmi), Claudia Cardinale (Claudia), Anouk Aimee (Luisa Anselmi), Sandra Milo (Carla), Rossella Falk (Rossella), Barbara Steele (Gloria Morin), Mario Pisu (Mezzabotta), Guido Alberti (Producer), Madeleine LeBeau (French Actress), Jean Rougeul (Writer)

p, Angelo Rizzoli; d, Federico Fellini; w, Federico Fellini, Tullio Pinelli, Ennio Flaiano, Brunello Rondi (based on a story by Federico Fellini and Ennio Flaiano); ph, Gianni Di Venanzo; ed, Leo Catozzo; m, Nino Rota; art d, Piero Gherardi; cos, Piero Gherardi

AA Best Foreign Language Film ; AAN Best Director: Federico Fellini; AAN Best Original Screenplay: Federico Fellini, Ennio Flaiano, Tullio Pinelli, Brunello Rondi; AAN Best Art Direction: Piero Gherardi; AA Best Costume Design: Piero Gherardi

After having directed six feature films, co-directed one (THE WHITE SHEIK), and directed two short episodes of anthology movies, Federico Fellini had made, according to his count, seven and a half films—hence the title of this brilliant, sumptuous semi-autobiographical account of the creative process.

Marcello Mastroianni plays Fellini-like figure Guido Anselmi, a director coming off a big hit. He needs rest and goes to a spa to regain his strength. He cannot recuperate, however, being interrupted instead by his producer (Guido Alberti), his screenwriter (Jean Rougeul), his wife (Anouk Aimee), and his mistress (Sandra Milo), all of whom want details from the director about his new sci-fi film. Hundreds of people are waiting in the wings, but Guido finds himself creatively blocked and fends off the inquiries of his actors, reporters, and especially his persistent screenwriter, in between lapsing into fantasy visions of past, present, and future.

8 1/2 is a grab-bag of Felliniesque delights, with stunning photography by Di Venanzo, superb performances, a haunting score from Nino Rota, and a labyrinthine structure that keeps the viewer in a pleasurable state of confusion. It received an Academy Award for Best Foreign-Language Film.

EIGHT MEN OUT

1988 119m c Sports/Drama   ★★★
Orion (U.S.)   PG

Jace Alexander (Dickie Kerr), John Cusack (Buck Weaver), Gordon Clapp (Ray Schalk), Don Harvey (Swede Risberg), Bill Irwin (Eddie Collins), Perry Lang (Fred McMullin), John Mahoney (Kid Gleason), James Read (Lefty Williams), Michael Rooker (Chick Gandil), Charlie Sheen (Hap Felsch)

p, Sarah Pillsbury, Midge Sanford; d, John Sayles; w, John Sayles (based on the book by Eliot Asinof); ph, Robert Richardson; ed, John Tintori; m, Mason Daring; prod d, Nora Chavooshian; cos, Cynthia Flynt

Gripping account of the 1919 "Black Sox" baseball scandal, when eight members of the Chicago White Sox were accused of "fixing" the World Series. Working from one-time Philadelphia Phillies farmhand Asinof's assiduously researched book, writer-director Sayles has fashioned a convincing account of the scandal, underlaid with an unconventional (by Hollywood standards) workers-vs.-owners critique.

Sayles not only depicts the circumstances that led to the fix (most notably Sox owner Charles Comiskey's legendary tightfistedness), but he also re-creates the games in great detail, making the best possible use of an athletic cast tutored by former White Sox outfielder Ken Berry. Among the players Sayles concentrates on are: pitcher Eddie Cicotte (David Strathairn); third baseman Buck Weaver (Cusack), who spent the rest of his life protesting his innocence; and the legendary "Shoeless" Joe Jackson (D.B. Sweeney, whose own baseball career was ended by a motorcycle accident and who spent five weeks with the minor-league Kenosha Twins learning to bat left-handed for the role). The fine ensemble cast also includes Chicago journalist Studs Terkel, as sportswriter Hugh Fullerton, and Sayles himself, as Ring Lardner.

84 CHARING CROSS ROAD

1987 97m c Drama   ★★★
Brooksfilms (U.S.)   PG/U

Anne Bancroft *(Helene Hanff)*, Anthony Hopkins *(Frank Doel)*, Judi Dench *(Nora Doel)*, Jean De Baer *(Maxine Bellamy)*, Maurice Denham *(George Martin)*, Eleanor David *(Cecily Farr)*, Mercedes Ruehl *(Kay)*, Daniel Gerroll *(Brian)*, Wendy Morgan *(Megan Wells)*, Ian McNeice *(Bill Humphries)*

p, Geoffrey Helman; d, David Jones; w, Hugh Whitemore (based on the book by Helene Hanff); ph, Brian West; ed, Christopher Wimble; m, George Fenton; prod d, Eileen Diss, Edward Pisoni; cos, Jane Greenwood, Lindy Hemming

Charming, understated story of a love affair between two people who never meet. The "affair" begins in 1949 when Helene Hanff (Anne Bancroft), a struggling New York writer with a love of fine old books, responds to an ad placed by an antiquarian bookshop at 84 Charing Cross Road in London. Her letter is answered by Frank Doel (Anthony Hopkins), who runs the overseas department of the store, beginning a 20-year correspondence between the assertive, sometimes acerbic spinster and the dry, reserved man with two children, a plain wife, and a sparse home. Though literate and intelligent, CHARING CROSS ROAD never shakes free of its origins as a stage adaptation of Helene Hanff's novel; clearly, the subject matter is more suited to the page, or the stage, than the screen. Fine performances and a generous measure of humor still make this an absorbing drama.

EL

1952 100m bw Drama   ★★★★½
Tepeyac (Mexico)   /A

Arturo de Cordova *(Don Francisco)*, Delia Garces *(Gloria)*, Luis Beristain *(Raul)*, Manuel Donde *(Pablo)*, Carlos Martinez Baena *(Padre Velasco)*, Fernando Casanova *(Beltran)*, Aurora Walker *(Mother)*, Rafael Banquells *(Ricardo)*

p, Oscar Dancigers; d, Luis Bunuel; w, Luis Bunuel, Luis Alcorzia (based on the novel *Pensamientos* by Mercedes Pinto); ph, Gabriel Figueroa; ed, Carlos Savage, Alberto Valenzuela; m, Luis Hernandez Breton; art d, Edward Fitzgerald, Pedro Galvan

Bunuel's fascinating study of a married man's obsession with his wife's virtue. Middle-aged, church-going Francisco (de Cordova) has abstained from sex his entire life. One day, while helping the local priest wash the feet of parishioners, he notices the delicate feet of a woman and looks up to see the hauntingly beautiful Gloria (Garces), of whom he is instantly enamored. He lures Gloria away from her architect lover and they marry, but on their wedding night Francisco reveals a jealous nature of obsessional proportions. In what is far from the film's most deranged moment, he pokes a knitting-needle through the keyhole of the bedroom door, convinced that his wife's ex-lover is spying on them.

EL is a compelling indictment of religious repression and sexual obsession. By pushing the macho concern with female chastity to an absurd extreme, Bunuel reveals its inherently ridiculous nature. The film is one of the best from the director's Mexican period, though, like others from that time, its production values leave something to be desired.

EL AMOR BRUJO

1986 100m c Dance   ★★★
Emiliano Piedra (Spain)   PG

Antonio Gades *(Carmelo)*, Christina Hoyos *(Candela)*, Laura Del Sol *(Lucia)*, Juan Antonio Jimenez *(Jose)*, Emma Penella *(Aunt Rosario)*, La Polaca *(Pastora)*, Gomez de Jerez *(El Lobo)*, Enrique Ortega *(Jose's Father)*, Diego Pantoja *(Candela's Father)*, Giovana *(Rocio)*

p, Emiliano Piedra; d, Carlos Saura; w, Carlos Saura, Antonio Gades (based on the ballet by Manuel de Falla); ph, Teo Escamilla; ed, Pedro del Rey; m, Manuel de Falla; fx, Basilio Cortijo; chor, Carlos Saura, Antonio Gades; cos, Garardo Vera

EL AMOR BRUJO is the third entry in Spanish director Saura's flamenco dance trilogy, preceded in 1981 by BLOOD WEDDING and in 1983 by CARMEN. This time Saura and his choreographer, Gades, have turned to the Manuel de Falla opera for their source of inspiration.

Using much of the cast from CARMEN—Del Sol has here been relegated to a supporting role, and Hoyos has been given the lead—Saura has set the film on an exotically colored and stylishly designed studio set of a Madrid shantytown. Jimenez and Hoyos are gypsies who have been betrothed since childhood—when their fathers, having drunk too much wine, confirmed the arrangement. Early in the film a splendid wedding takes place, but we learn that each partner has another love interest. Gades admires Hoyos from a distance, while Jimenez is having an affair with the gorgeous Del Sol.

Following the critical and commercial success of CARMEN, which became one of Spain's highest-grossing pictures and received an Academy Award nomination as Best Foreign Film, EL AMOR BRUJO has been considerably less appreciated by critics and audiences alike, perhaps because the general audience is more familiar with Bizet's *Carmen* than with de Falla's *El Amor Brujo*. BRUJO is somewhat more stylized that its two predecessors, with some wonderfully fluid camera moves to highlight the cinematography. The dancing is equally astounding and, according to some enthusiasts, benefits from Hoyos' having taken over the lead from Del Sol.

EL CID

1961 180m c Biography/War   ★★★
Bronston/Rank (U.S./Italy)   /U

Sophia Loren *(Chimene)*, Charlton Heston *(Rodrigo Diaz de Bivar/El Cid)*, John Fraser *(King Alfonso)*, Raf Vallone *(Count Ordonez)*, Genevieve Page *(Queen Urraca)*, Gary Raymond *(King Sancho)*, Herbert Lom *(Ben Yussef)*, Massimo Serato *(Fanez)*, Douglas Wilmer *(Moutamin)*, Frank Thring *(Al Kadir)*

p, Samuel Bronston, Anthony Mann; d, Anthony Mann; w, Philip Yordan, Fredric M. Frank; ph, Robert Krasker; ed, Robert Lawrence; m, Miklos Rozsa; prod d, Veniero Colasanti, John Moore; fx, Alex Weldon, Jack Erickson; cos, Veniero Colasanti, John Moore

AAN Best Score: Miklos Rozsa; *AAN Best Song:* Miklos Rozsa (Music), Paul Francis Webster (Lyrics); *AAN Best Art Direction:* Veniero Colasanti (Art Direction), John Moore (Set Decoration)

Director Anthony Mann's first and finest venture into big-budget epic terrain, with Charlton Heston as the 11-century Spanish leader.

EL CID becomes estranged from his fiancee, Chimene (Sophia Loren), after he kills her father (Andrew Cruickshank), who has unjustly accused him of treason. El Cid and Chimene are married but never enjoy a wedding night; she plots against him and, when her intrigues come to naught, enters a convent. Upon the death of King Ferdinand (Ralph Truman), Spain, which is continually besieged by the Islamic Moors, is further divided by the deceased ruler's warring offspring. Meanwhile, Chimene realizes that her husband is an honorable man and they reconcile, eventually having children. The family retreats to a monastery while El Cid lays siege to Valencia, the last outpost of the Moorish usurpers.

Eleventh-century Spain has been lavishly recreated by Mann and producer Samuel Bronston. The photography by Robert Krasker is spectacular, as are the battle scenes, filmed with the help of veteran stuntman Yakima Canutt as second-unit director. Canutt staged the siege of Valencia brilliantly, employing the ancient walled city of Pensacola, 5,000 Spanish army troops, and a Moorish battle fleet of 35 lifesize reconstructed ships. What gets lost is Mann's signature focus on psychological conflict. The sheer size of the production dwarfs such issues, and Heston is far better at conveying righteous authority than moral doubt.

EL DORADO

1967 125m c Western   ★★★½
Paramount (U.S.)   /U

John Wayne (Cole Thornton), Robert Mitchum (J.P. Harrah), James Caan (Alan "Mississippi" Bourdillon Traherne), Charlene Holt (Maudie), Michele Carey (Joey MacDonald), Arthur Hunnicutt (Bull Harris), R.G. Armstrong (Kevin MacDonald), Edward Asner (Bart Jason), Paul Fix (Doc Miller), Christopher George (Nelse McLeod)

p, Howard Hawks; d, Howard Hawks; w, Leigh Brackett (based on the novel The Stars in Their Courses by Harry Brown); ph, Harold Rosson; ed, John Woodcock; m, Nelson Riddle; art d, Carl Anderson, Hal Pereira; fx, Paul K. Lerpae; cos, Edith Head

Sly, leisurely-paced western from Howard Hawks, with a script by Leigh Brackett ensuring a few laughs. EL DORADO addresses the standard Hawks themes of group loyalty and professionalism, but is also a poignant meditation on the passing of the old and the coming of the new.

Wayne plays an aging, wounded gunfighter and Mitchum a drunken sheriff; with the help of "Mississippi" (Caan) and Bull Harris (Hunnicutt), they take on ruthless cattle baron Bart Jason (Asner), who is using extortion to gain water rights to some land. The finale sees an attack on the bad guys by a crippled quartet of Mitchum (on crutches), Wayne (partially paralyzed and unable to shoot a revolver), Caan (wounded in the head), and Hunnicutt (armed with a bow and arrow). DORADO forms part of a loose trilogy with RIO BRAVO and RIO LOBO, also scripted by Brackett.

EL MARIACHI

1993 80m c Action   ★★★½
Los Hooligans (U.S.)   R/15

Carlos Gallardo (El Mariachi), Consuelo Gomez (Domino), Jaime DeHoyos (Bigoton), Peter Marquardt (Mauricio [Moco]), Reinol Martinez (Azul), Ramiro Gomez (Cantinero), Jesus Lopez (Viejo Clerk), Luis Baro (Domino's Assistant), Oscar Fabila (The Boy), Poncho Ramon (Azul's Rat)

p, Robert Rodriguez, Carlos Gallardo; d, Robert Rodriguez; w, Robert Rodriguez; ph, Robert Rodriguez; ed, Robert Rodriguez; m, Eric Guthrie; fx, Robert Rodriguez, Carlos Gallardo

23-year-old Robert Rodriguez's feature debut combines the premise of Hitchcock's THE WRONG MAN with the frenetic pace of THE ROAD WARRIOR and the tongue-in-cheek style of a spaghetti western. Originally intended for the Spanish-language video market, EL MARIACHI so impressed Hollywood that after some post-production upgrading far in excess of production costs, it was showcased at festivals and released in theaters.

The title character, an unemployed singer/guitarist (Carlos Gallardo), wanders into a small Mexican town and is mistaken for vicious hitman Azul (Reinol Martinez), who has just broken out of prison, since they both wear black and carry guitar cases. After several close calls, the innocent musician receives help from the woman who runs a local tavern. He charms her and convinces her he isn't the hunted criminal; she hires him to perform in her club and they become lovers. Azul, seeking revenge on his former partner, Moco (Peter Marquardt), terrorizes the town; things come to a head when Moco abducts the woman and the mariachi must come to the rescue.

EL MARIACHI's genius lies not in its complexity or innovation but in its ability to create an engaging action picture from bare-bones resources. Mexican-American Rodriguez (the film's director/writer/producer/cinematographer/editor/sound recordist) turned out a fun, stylish, action-packed movie on a ridiculously low budget of $7,000. The unrelenting tempo is bolstered by Rodriguez's camera work and editing: nearly every frame seems to have been shot with a careening, handheld camera, and they're cut together in a skillful, fluid fashion that enhances the tension and pace of the 80-minute chase.

EL NORTE

1983 139m c Drama   ★★★★
Independent Productions (U.S.)   R/15

Zaide Silvia Gutierrez (Rosa Xuncax), David Villalpando (Enrique Xuncax), Ernesto Gomez Cruz (Arturo Xuncax), Alicia Del Lago (Lupe Xuncax), Eraclio Zepeda (Pedro), Stella Quan (Josefita), Rodrigo Puebla (Puma), Trinidad Silva (Monty), Abel Franco (Raimundo), Mike Gomez (Jaime)

p, Anna Thomas; d, Gregory Nava; w, Anna Thomas, Gregory Nava; ph, James Glennon; ed, Betsy Blankett; m, Gustav Mahler, Samuel Barber, Giuseppe Verdi, The Folkloristas, Melecio Martinez, Emil Richards, Linda O'Brien

AAN Best Original Screenplay: Gregory Nava (Screenplay), Anna Thomas (Screenplay)

A Spanish-language American film produced independently in association with the PBS TV series "American Playhouse," EL NORTE is an effective and moving drama about the strength of the human spirit and the will to survive. Brother and sister Enrique and Rosa Xuncax (David Villalpando and Zaide Silvia Gutierrez) are Guatemalan Indians forced to flee their village when their politically active father is murdered. They decide to make a new life in el Norte ("the North," i.e. the US) but, as difficult and demeaning as the illegal trek across the border is, it is not nearly so rough as the struggle to make a living in Los Angeles. EL NORTE's style alternates between straightforward, almost documentary-like exposition and surreal sequences that take place in the characters' dreams. The film has a political message, but it is a subtle and compelling one that allows situations and characters to speak for themselves.

ELEPHANT MAN, THE

1980 125m bw Biography   ★★★★
Paramount (U.K.)   PG

Anthony Hopkins (Dr. Frederick Treves), John Hurt (John Merrick), Anne Bancroft (Mrs. Kendal), John Gielgud (Carr Gomm), Wendy Hiller (Mothershead), Freddie Jones (Bytes), Michael Elphick (Night Porter), Hannah Gordon (Mrs. Treves), Helen Ryan (Princess Alex), John Standing (Fox)

p, Jonathan Sanger; d, David Lynch; w, Christopher DeVore, Eric Bergren, David Lynch (based on The Elephant Man, A Study in Human Dignity by Ashley Montagu and The Elephant Man and Other Reminiscences by Sir Frederick Treves); ph, Freddie Francis; ed, Anne V. Coates; m, John Morris, Samuel Barber; prod d, Stuart Craig; art d, Robert Cartwright; cos, Patricia Norris

AAN Best Picture; AAN Best Actor: John Hurt; AAN Best Director: David Lynch; AAN Best Adapted Screenplay: Christopher DeVore (Screenplay), Eric Bergren (Screenplay), David Lynch (Screenplay); AAN Best Editing: Anne V Coates; AAN Best Score: John Morris; AAN Best Art Direction: Stuart Craig (Art Direction), Bob Cartwright (Art Direction), Hugh Scaife (Set Decoration); AAN Best Costume Design: Patricia Norris

THE ELEPHANT MAN features an Academy Award-nominated performance by John Hurt as John Merrick, the victim of a disease that has left him so grotesquely deformed, he's spent most of his life as a carnival-show freak. In time, Merrick comes under the care of Dr. Treves (brilliantly played by Anthony Hopkins), who installs the "Elephant Man" in a hospital, where he studies him, helps him to overcome a seemingly insurmountable speech impediment, and—for a time—gives him back some human dignity. As word gets out about Merrick's existence and the press once again turns him into a freak, the film raises the question of Treves's motivation: has he helped Merrick out of decency, in the name of medical science, or to enhance his own reputation?

A moving, faithful retelling of a bizarre true story, THE ELEPHANT MAN was nominated for eight Oscars (though it won none), including a Best Direction nod for David Lynch. The black-and-white cinematography of Freddie Francis wonderfully evokes 19th-century England and Hurt gives a tour de force performance, masterfully conveying emotions while unable to use his face or even much of his voice.

ELMER GANTRY

1960 146m c Drama ★★★★
UA (U.S.) /PG

Burt Lancaster (*Elmer Gantry*), Jean Simmons (*Sister Sharon Falconer*), Arthur Kennedy (*Jim Lefferts*), Shirley Jones (*Lulu Bains*), Dean Jagger (*William L. Morgan*), Patti Page (*Sister Rachel*), Edward Andrews (*George Babbitt*), John McIntire (*Rev. Pengilly*), Joe Maross (*Pete*), Everett Glass (*Rev. Brown*)

p, Bernard Smith; d, Richard Brooks; w, Richard Brooks (based on the novel by Sinclair Lewis); ph, John Alton; ed, Marjorie Fowler; m, Andre Previn; cos, Dorothy Jeakins

AAN Best Picture; *AA Best Actor:* Burt Lancaster; *AA Best Supporting Actress:* Shirley Jones; *AA Best Adapted Screenplay:* Richard Brooks; *AAN Best Score:* Andre Previn

Lancaster pulls out all the stops in one of his most memorable roles as the lustful, ambitious charlatan of Sinclair Lewis's powerful novel. Elmer Gantry (Lancaster) first appears on the screen, roaring drunk, trying to mooch drinks while selling his own distinctive take on scripture with his remarkable gift of gab. He encounters evangelist Sister Sharon Falconer (Simmons)—a role no doubt intended by Lewis to suggest Aimee Semple McPherson. Gantry appeals to her vanity and joins her entourage. Together they become rich and famous enough for Sister Falconer to build her own huge seaside temple. She falls in love with Gantry who loves life and every woman he meets; he had once been with a preacher's daughter, Lulu Baines (Shirley Jones, in a standout, Oscar-winning performance), now a prostitute hungry for revenge.

Writer-director Brooks made a few revisions in the novel's story. Gantry is no longer the ordained minister fallen from grace as depicted in the novel but now a traveling salesman for the Lord. Kennedy as Jim Lefferts, his empathic friend, is transformed from another seminary dropout in the novel into a cynical, savvy newsman in the H.L. Mencken tradition. Nonetheless the integrity of the characterizations is maintained in a script that is both literate and ironic. Brooks later sarcastically commented that "ELMER GANTRY is the story of a man who wants what everyone is supposed to want—money, sex, and religion. He's the All-American boy."

ELVIRA MADIGAN

1967 90m c Romance ★★★
Europa/Janco (Sweden) PG/A

Pia Degermark (*Elvira*), Thommy Berggren (*Sixten Sparre*), Lennart Malmer (*Friend*), Nina Widerberg (*Little Girl*), Cleo Jensen (*Cook*)

d, Bo Widerberg; w, Bo Widerberg (based on a ballad by Johan Lindstrom Saxon); ph, Jorgen Persson; ed, Bo Widerberg; m, Ulf Bjorlin, Wolfgang Amadeus Mozart, Antonio Vivaldi

In 19th-century Sweden, a tightrope performer (Pia Degermark) and an army lieutenant (Thommy Berggren) give up their previous lives—he leaves his wife and children, and she deserts the circus troupe of which she is the top attraction—to find a new freedom for themselves. Their romance appears perfect, but, as the story progresses, they realize that their idyllic state cannot continue. . . .

This was a very popular film at the time and—whatever else it did—made Mozart acceptable for the world's teenagers. It's a rather silly love story of two adolescents, but prettily photographed and, although we don't like to admit it, even grownups occasionally like to watch this sort of jejeune adolescent romantic fantasy. Those were legitimate feelings when we were 15, and there's nothing wrong with reliving them for an hour or two. A decade later a whole genre was spawned on this model—THE BLUE LAGOON for example—bringing the level down to proto-kiddy-porn.

Sixteen-year-old Degermark was named Best Actress at the Cannes Film Festival for her performance as the title character. Additional music by Mozart and Vivaldi is ideally suited to the film.

EMERALD FOREST, THE

1985 113m c Adventure ★★★★
Christel (U.K.) R/15

Powers Boothe (*Bill Markham*), Meg Foster (*Jean Markham*), William Rodriquez (*Young Tommy*), Yara Vaneau (*Young Heather*), Estee Chandler (*Heather*), Charley Boorman (*Tomme*), Dira Paes (*Kachiri*), Eduardo Conde (*Uwe Werner*), Ariel Coelho (*Padre Leduc*), Peter Marinker (*Perreira*)

p, John Boorman, Michael Dryhurst; d, John Boorman; w, Rospo Pallenberg; ph, Philippe Rousselot; ed, Ian Crafford; m, Junior Homrich, Brian Gascoigne; prod d, Simon Holland; art d, Marcos Flacksman, Terry Pritchard; fx, Raph Salis; chor, Jose Possi; cos, Christel Boorman, Clovis Bueno

In October 1972 an account written by Leonard Greenwood appeared in the *Los Angeles Times*. It told of a Peruvian engineer whose son had been kidnapped by a band of Indians and of the man's successful search to locate the child. Screenwriter Rospo Pallenberg saw the news item and took it to producer-director John Boorman. The result was this amazing, beautiful and sometimes fanciful film. Powers Boothe is Bill Markham, a US engineer working on a dam project in Brazil where he lives with his wife, Jean (Meg Foster), and his small children. One day while the family is picnicking at the edge of the rain forest, some painted Indians swiftly and silently kidnap young Tommy (William Rodriguez). The only clue left is an arrow stuck in a tree, and Boothe uses it in his ten-year search for his son.

The film is a powerful meditation on the clash between two civilizations. Charley Boorman (the director's son) is outstanding as the grown Tomme and Boothe also gives a powerful performance. The film has many opportunities to tip over into the ludicrous and become a parody of traditional jungle action pictures. But director Boorman keeps matters on an even keel, deftly balancing the mystical elements with reality to produce a memorable film that is enthralling throughout and never heavy-handed.

EMIGRANTS, THE
(UTVANDRARNA)

1971 151m c Drama ★★★★
Svensk (Sweden) PG/AA

Max von Sydow (*Karl Oskar*), Liv Ullmann (*Kristina*), Eddie Axberg (*Robert*), Svenolof Bern (*Nils*), Aina Alfredsson (*Marta*), Allan Edwall (*Danjel*), Monica Zetterlund (*Ulrika*), Pierre Lindstedt (*Arvid*), Hans Alfredson (*Jonas Petter*), Ulla Smidje (*Danjel's Wife*)

p, Bengt Forslund; d, Jan Troell; w, Jan Troell, Bengt Forslund (based on the novels of Vilhelm Moberg); ph, Jan Troell; ed, Jan Troell; m, Erik Nordgren; art d, P.A. Lundgren, Berndt Fritiof; cos, Ulla-Britt Soderlund

AAN Best Foreign Language Film ; *AAN Best Picture*; *AAN Best Actress:* Liv Ullmann; *AAN Best Adapted Screenplay:* Jan Troell, Bengt Forslund

An engaging, well-crafted film about a group of Swedish peasants who migrate to America in the mid-19th century. One of the best films to show the tribulations, bravery and faith of the people who helped build this country. The film is split into three parts: the departure from Sweden, the voyage over and the journey to Minnesota. The acting is superb by all cast members, but some might be put off by the film's length. The tone is lyrical, and the photography (by director Troell) gives an added dimension. Nominated by the Academy for Best Foreign Film of 1971, it also earned nominations for Best Picture, Best Actress, Best Direction and Best Screenplay in 1972. The sequel is THE NEW LAND.

EMMA

1996 120m c Romance/Historical/Comedy   ★★★½
Matchmaker Films/Haft Entertainment/Miramax   PG/U
(U.K./U.S.)

Gwyneth Paltrow (*Emma Woodhouse*), Toni Collette (*Harriet Smith*), Alan Cumming (*Mr. Elton*), Jeremy Northam (*Mr. Knightley*), Ewan McGregor (*Frank Churchill*), Greta Scacchi (*Mrs. Weston*), Juliet Stevenson (*Mrs. Elton*), Polly Walker (*Jane Fairfax*), Sophie Thompson (*Miss Bates*), Edward Woodall (*Robert Martin*)

p, Patrick Cassavetti, Steven Haft; d, Douglas McGrath; w, Douglas McGrath (based on the novel by Jane Austen); ph, Ian Wilson; ed, Lesley Walker; m, Rachel Portman; prod d, Michael Howells; art d, Sam Riley, Joshua Meath Baker; fx, Effects Associates; chor, Sue Lefton; cos, Ruth Myers

AA Best Original Musical or Comedy Score: Rachel Portman; AAN Best Costume Design: Ruth Myers

This third adaptation of a Jane Austen novel to reach the big screen within a year's passage can rightly be considered "the Americanization of *Emma*." With a wonderfully comic cast featuring Gwyneth Paltrow, EMMA has plenty of humor and charm, but will pique Austen's ardent fans.

In the village of Highbury, Emma Woodhouse (Paltrow) is the pretty and wealthy mistress of her domain, an insular world of strict social etiquette. Kind-hearted Emma bestows her charity on the town's poor, but in the opinion of Mr. Knightley (Jeremy Northam), her brother-in-law, Emma is a meddling know-it-all because she fancies herself a matchmaker without peer. Emma convinces her friend, Harriet Smith (Toni Collette), to refuse the proposal of one Robert Martin (Edward Woodall), a humble but kind farmer, and set her sights on the Reverend Elton (Alan Cumming). Unbeknownst to Emma, the Reverend has his sights set on *her*. Meanwhile, Emma finds herself attracted to the dashing Frank Churchill (Ewan McGregor), who pays altogether too much attention to Jane Fairfax (Polly Walker). When Harriet becomes infatuated with Mr. Knightley, it arouses such jealousy in Emma that she realizes her *own* love for the gentleman.

Writer and first-time director Douglas McGrath (who co-wrote 1994's BULLETS OVER BROADWAY) empasizes *Emma's* humor and downplays the darker motifs of folly and pain arising from class and gender oppression. The elaborate dance of Austen's narrative becomes mere fodder for a high-minded date movie. The luminous Paltrow nevertheless deserves praise for her excellent performance. Her Emma is at once innocent and poised, elegant and funny. Unfortunately, McGrath omits the politely destructive hubris that gives complexity to Emma's character and depth to Austen's novel.

EMMANUELLE

1974 105m c Erotic/Drama   ★★½
Trinacre/Orphee (France)   R/18

Sylvia Kristel (*Emmanuelle*), Alain Cuny (*Marco*), Daniel Sarky (*Jean*), Jeanne Colletin (*Ariane*), Marika Green (*Bee*), Christine Boisson (*Marie-Ange*)

p, Yves Rousset-Rouard; d, Just Jaeckin; w, Jean-Louis Richard (based on the book by Emmanuelle Arsan); ph, Richard Suzuki; ed, Claudine Bouche

One of the classics of soft-core erotic cinema, EMMANUELLE stars Sylvia Kristel as the title creature, the pretty wife of a French ambassador in Bangkok. It's not long before Emmanuelle discovers a burning sexual passion she has heretofore repressed. With the help of an attractive young teenager, Emmanuelle is exposed (literally) to the joys of eroticism. Although the film takes itself far too seriously and engages in much of the usual naughty Victoriana, it is a relatively well-made picture that became an international hit because of its appeal to both men and women. Many sequels followed (the first being EMMANUELLE 2, released in the U.S. as EMMANUELLE—THE JOYS OF A WOMAN) with Mia Nygren taking over the lead in 1984's EMMANUELLE 4. The Kristel-Nygren EMMANUELLE series (spelled with two "m"s) should not be confused with Laura Gemser's EMANUELLE (with one "m") films.

EMPEROR JONES, THE

1933 80m bw Drama   ★★★★
Krimsky/Cochran (U.S.)   /18

Paul Robeson (*Brutus Jones*), Dudley Digges (*Smithers*), Frank C. Wilson (*Jeff*), Fredi Washington (*Undine*), Ruby Elzy (*Dolly*), George Haymid Stamper (*Lem*), Jackie Mayble (*Marcella*), Blueboy O'Connor (*Treasurer*), Brandon Evans (*Carrington*), Taylor Gordon (*Stick-Man*)

p, John Krimsky, Gifford Cochran; d, Dudley Murphy; w, DuBose Heyward (based on the play by Eugene O'Neill); ph, Ernest Haller; ed, Grant Whytock; m, Frank Tours, J. Rosamond Johnson; art d, Herman Rosse

This fascinating—if rather stiff—production of the brooding Eugene O'Neill play showcases Paul Robeson as Brutus Jones, his most forceful and memorable film role.

Jones, a newly hired railroad porter, is first shown admiring himself before a mirror in his new uniform. His rich baritone voice makes him stand out as he booms out a moving hymn in church. Jones is clearly a man who thinks very highly of himself. This false pride proves to be his undoing. He goes on to cheat on his fiancee and fool around with his best friend's girlfriend. He deserts her and later enters a crap game where he stabs his friend to death. He gets sentenced to a chain gang for life.

He escapes and eventually ends up in Haiti where he meets Smithers (Dudley Digges), an unscrupulous trader who uses Jones to keep the natives in line. Jones is so feared by the natives, whom he has fooled into believing that he is immortal, that he becomes rich as Smithers's partner. In a short time, he unseats the native king and declares himself emperor, ruling the land with an iron fist.

Robeson is the main attraction here and he is well supported by the sleazy Digges (the only white actor in an otherwise all-black cast). Robeson's powerful presence, particularly through his wonderful, mellifluous voice, dominates each scene. There was never any doubt about Robeson playing the role of the vainglorious Jones; a distinguished athlete and Columbia Law School graduate, he deferred his entry into the New York bar when O'Neill himself persuaded Robeson to star in a production of *The Emperor Jones*.

EMPIRE OF THE SUN

1987 152m c War   ★★★½
Amblin (U.S.)   PG

Christian Bale (*Jim Graham*), John Malkovich (*Basie*), Miranda Richardson (*Mrs. Victor*), Nigel Havers (*Dr. Rawlins*), Joe Pantoliano (*Frank Demerest*), Leslie Phillips (*Maxton*), Masato Ibu (*Sgt. Nagata*), Emily Richard (*Jim's Mother*), Rupert Frazer (*Jim's Father*), Peter Gale (*Mr. Victor*)

p, Steven Spielberg, Kathleen Kennedy, Frank Marshall; d, Steven Spielberg; w, Menno Meyjes (uncredited), Tom Stoppard (based on the novel by J.G. Ballard); ph, Allen Daviau; ed, Michael Kahn; m, John Williams; prod d, Norman Reynolds; art d, Charles Bishop, Fred Hole, Maurice Fowler, Huang Qia Gui, Norman Dorme; fx, Kit West, David Watkins, Ye Mao Gen, Antonio Parra, Industrial Light & Magic

AAN Best Cinematography: Allen Daviau; AAN Best Editing: Michael Kahn; AAN Best Score: John T Williams; AAN Best Art Direction: Norman Reynolds (Art Direction), Harry Cordwell (Set Decoration); AAN Best Costume Design: Bob Ringwood; AAN Best Sound: Robert Knudson, Don Digirolamo, John Boyde, Tony Dawe

This adaptation of J.G. Ballard's quasi-autobiographical novel witnesses WWII through a child's eyes, and does so through a visual means more akin to silent than to modern filmmaking. Spielberg's vision is no longer one of innocent wonderment; instead, EMPIRE OF THE SUN concerns the end of innocence—a young boy thrown into adulthood and an entire generation thrown into an atomic age.

The film opens just before the Japanese attack on Pearl Harbor in 1941. Jim Graham (Christian Bale) is a nine-year-old English brat who has lived all his life in Shanghai with his aristocratic parents. Although adventurous, he is also wholly dependent on his parents and servants. Later, as the Japanese conquer Shanghai and the war intensifies, he is separated from his parents and meets Basie (John

Malkovich), an opportunistic merchant seaman reminiscent of Dickens's Fagin, who somewhat reluctantly takes Jim under his wing and teaches him the most Darwinian methods of survival—lessons that help Jim endure a lengthy stay in a Japanese prison camp.

The most emotionally complex film of Steven Spielberg's career, EMPIRE OF THE SUN is not a traditional blockbuster. In fact, with its unknown lead, barely known supporting cast and near-plotlessness, it breaks Hollywood's rules. Further, Spielberg has adapted an admired but little-read novel, set it in far-off Shanghai, and made his lead character a Briton who idolizes the Japanese. As Jim, Bale delivers a stunning performance; he appears in virtually every frame and truly seems to grow over the course of the film from a coddled rich child to a calculating, almost feral creature who will ally himself with whoever wields the most power in a given situation.

Working on a grand canvas in the tradition of the David Lean epics, Spielberg includes several of his own distinctive visual epiphanies but the usual sense of wonder threatens to slide into madness. Spielberg also displays a progressive and sophisticated awareness of issues of class and race that may be viewed as an apology for the casual imperialist and racist assumptions of his INDIANA JONES series.

EMPIRE STRIKES BACK, THE

1980   124m   c   Science Fiction   ★★★★
Fox   (U.S.)   PG/U

Mark Hamill (*Luke Skywalker*), Harrison Ford (*Han Solo*), Carrie Fisher (*Princess Leia*), Billy Dee Williams (*Lando Calrissian*), Anthony Daniels (*C-3PO*), David Prowse (*Darth Vader*), Peter Mayhew (*Chewbacca*), Kenny Baker (*R2-D2*), Frank Oz (*Yoda*), Alec Guinness (*Ben Kenobi*)

p, Gary Kurtz; d, Irvin Kershner; w, Leigh Brackett, Lawrence Kasdan (based on a story by George Lucas); ph, Peter Suschitzky; ed, Paul Hirsch; m, John Williams; prod d, Norman Reynolds; art d, Leslie Dilley, Harry Lange, Alan Tomkins; fx, Brian Johnson, Richard Edlund, Dennis Muren, Bruce Nicholson; cos, John Mollo

AAN Best Score: John Williams; *AAN Best Art Direction:* Norman Reynolds, Leslie Dilley, Harry Lange, Alan Tomkins, Michael Ford; *AA Best Sound:* Bill Varney, Steve Maslow, Gregg Landaker, Peter Sutton

Considered by many the best entry in the series, the second chapter of the STAR WARS trilogy finds the evil Darth Vader (David Prowse and the voice of James Earl Jones) aiding the emperor in his attempts to crush the rebellion dedicated to halting the Empire's domination of the universe. The rebel forces are on the ice planet Hoth and the evil empire sends troops to wipe them out. Forced to flee, Han Solo (Harrison Ford) and Princess Leia (Carrie Fisher) regroup in Cloud City, which is run by the roguish Lando Calrissian (Billy Dee Williams). Meanwhile, Luke Skywalker (Mark Hamill) searches for and finds Yoda (the voice of Frank Oz), a wise little creature who teaches him the finer points of the Force. The whole thing climaxes in a showdown between Luke and Darth Vader, the revelation of some surprising plot twists, and a cliffhanger ending.

After the phenomenal success of STAR WARS, creator George Lucas retired from directing and hired veteran Kershner to direct and the great Leigh Brackett (THE BIG SLEEP, RIO BRAVO, EL DORADO, THE LONG GOODBYE) to write the screenplay with an assist from a new kid on the block, Lawrence Kasdan. Financially, Lucas could afford to push the special effects envelope even further this time. The result is a darker, richer, and more elaborate film than the original; it suffers most from being just what it is: a middle chapter with no real ending. The film's final cliffhanger may prove upsetting to youngsters, since the dark side of the Force has the upper hand, but it's dramatically correct, setting the stage for the triumphant return of Good in part three, RETURN OF THE JEDI.

ENCHANTED APRIL

1991   101m   c   Romance/Comedy   ★★½
Miramax   (U.K.)   PG/U

Josie Lawrence (*Lottie Wilkins*), Miranda Richardson (*Rose Arbuthnot*), Joan Plowright (*Mrs. Fisher*), Polly Walker (*Lady Caroline Dester*), Alfred Molina (*Mellersh Wilkins*), Jim Broadbent (*Frederick Arbuthnot*), Michael Kitchen (*George Briggs*), Neville Phillips (*Vicar*), Stephen Beckett (*Jonathan*), Mathew Radford (*Patrick*)

p, Ann Scott; d, Mike Newell; w, Peter Barnes (based on the novel by Elizabeth Von Arnim); ph, Rex Maidment; ed, Dick Allen; m, Richard Rodney Bennett; prod d, Malcolm Thornton; cos, Sheena Napier

AAN Best Supporting Actress: Joan Plowright; *AAN Best Adapted Screenplay:* Peter Barnes; *AAN Best Costume Design:* Sheena Napier

ENCHANTED APRIL sets out to celebrate the liberating effects of an Italian vacation on four troubled English women—a gentle, low-budget blend of A ROOM WITH A VIEW and THELMA & LOUISE. But this paper-thin drama, directed by Mike Newell (DANCE WITH A STRANGER) and adapted from the 1921 novel by Elizabeth von Arnim, fails to achieve the sense of magical transformation for which it strives.

Lottie Wilkins (Josie Lawrence) is a downtrodden middle-class wife with a vaguely mystical ability to "see *into* people." Captivated by a newspaper ad offering a month in an Italian villa, she senses that her neighbor Rose Arbuthnot (Miranda Richardson) is equally in need of a getaway and—though the two have never before spoken—enlists her as a traveling partner. To save money, they bring along haughty widow Mrs. Fisher (Joan Plowright) and society beauty Lady Caroline Dester (Polly Walker). Once ensconced by the sea in the admittedly charming villa, these four women undergo transformations as unconvincing as they are predictable.

Everything about ENCHANTED APRIL is half-baked, from its stock characters, to its occasional gestures toward slapstick and farce, to its throwaway mysticism. The whole thing seems like it was dreamed up during a sleepy afternoon by the Italian seaside, and is guaranteed to put viewers into a similarly soporific state.

ENCHANTED COTTAGE, THE

1945   91m   bw   Romance   ★★★½
RKO   (U.S.)   /U

Dorothy McGuire (*Laura Pennington*), Robert Young (*Oliver Bradford*), Herbert Marshall (*John Hillgrave*), Mildred Natwick (*Abigail Minnett*), Spring Byington (*Violet Price*), Richard Gaines (*Frederick*), Hillary Brooke (*Beatrice Alexander*), Alec Englander (*Danny*), Mary Worth (*Mrs. Stanton*), Josephine Whittell (*Canteen Manager*)

p, Harriet Parsons; d, John Cromwell; w, DeWitt Bodeen, Herman J. Mankiewicz (based on the play by Arthur Wing Pinero); ph, Ted Tetzlaff; ed, Joseph Noriega; m, Roy Webb; art d, Albert S. D'Agostino, Carroll Clark; fx, Vernon L. Walker; cos, Edward Stevenson

AAN Best Score: Roy Webb

This sensitive, touching film, based on the classic romance play by Pinero, is beautifully enacted by McGuire and Young as the uncommon lovers. Oliver (Young) is the embittered, disfigured WWI veteran obsessed with suicide, the only alternative, he feels, to coping with an ugliness that repels everyone. He meets the shy and plain Laura (McGuire), a woman also shunned by society. They marry and move into seclusion inside a small New England cottage, all that's left of a great estate which burned down years earlier. As a honeymoon cottage scores of happy lovers have carved their initials on its windowpanes; its owner (Natwick) knows well the legend of its wonderful spell. Slowly Oliver regains his handsome countenance and Laura blossoms into a beautiful young woman. It is, of course, their mutual love which has brought about these astounding transformations, images shattered by mindless friends.

An unforgettable fable for all who have found beauty in another person, the film does a remarkable job of sidestepping the maudlin and convincingly argues that "beauty is in the eye of the beholder." Pinero's intent, to write about the triumph of love over adversity, is as fully preserved in this version as it was in its original 1922 stage production and 1924 silent film, starring Richard Barthelmess and May McAvoy. Young and McGuire underplay roles that would doubtless have been more histrionically delivered in less able hands. This 1945 remake also benefits from subtle makeup, a stirring score by Webb, innovative lensing by Tetzlaff and a literate screenplay by Mankiewicz and Bodeen.

ENFORCER, THE

1951 87m bw Crime   ★★★½
United States   (U.S.)   /18

Humphrey Bogart *(Martin Ferguson)*, Zero Mostel *(Big Babe Lazich)*, Ted de Corsia *(Joseph Rico)*, Everett Sloane *(Albert Mendoza)*, Roy Roberts *(Capt. Frank Nelson)*, Lawrence Tolan *(Duke Malloy)*, King Donovan *(Sgt. Whitlow)*, Bob Steele *(Herman)*, Adelaide Klein *(Olga Kirshen)*, Don Beddoe *(Thomas O'Hara)*.

p, Milton Sperling; d, Bretaigne Windust; w, Martin Rackin; ph, Robert Burks; ed, Fred Allen; m, David Buttolph; art d, Charles H. Clarke

Based on the 1940 revelations of Abe Reles regarding the existence of an organized crime group called Murder Inc., but inspired by the Kefauver Committee investigations of 1950, this raw drama can be viewed as a key transitional film between the noir ethos of the 1940s and crime syndicate obsessed 1950s. Reveling in the lingo of the murder business with its talk of "contracts," "hits" and "fingers," this was the first film to deal with the mysterious structures of organized crime.

The film begins with a brief prologue by Senator Estes Kefauver, the head of the crime investigation committee, explaining the burning need to bring criminals to justice. Joseph Rico (De Corsia), head of the syndicate's professional murder squad, has been brought in and put under protective custody after agreeing to testify against crime czar Albert Mendoza (Sloane). Martin Ferguson (Bogart), the district attorney, has spent four years building his case against Mendoza and, with Rico's testimony, he'll be able to send him to the electric chair for mass murder. However, Rico, in terror, escapes and falls to his death. Ferguson seeks to find some tiny clue in the bulk of evidence so as to save his case.

This powerful crime drama was shot in stark black and white by frequent Hitchcock collaborator Robert Burks and directed in a quick, crisp style by Windust. Reportedly some of the film's footage had to be restaged by action veteran Raoul Walsh. Though he is uncredited, Walsh's imprint is apparent as he establishes the semidocumentary approach that proved so successful in his WHITE HEAT. Rackin's script is tough, even brutal, in depicting the slaughterhouse deeds of the worst gang of killers ever to intimidate America.

ENGLISH PATIENT, THE

1996 162m c Romance/Drama   ★★★
Saul Zaentz/Miramax   (U.K./U.S./Italy)   R/15

Ralph Fiennes *(Almasy)*, Juliette Binoche *(Hana)*, Willem Dafoe *(Caravaggio)*, Kristin Scott Thomas *(Katharine Clifton)*, Naveen Andrews *(Kip)*, Colin Firth *(Geoffrey Clifton)*, Julian Wadham *(Madox)*, Kevin Whately *(Hardy)*, Clive Merrison *(Fenelon-Barnes)*, Nino Castelnuovo *(D'Agostino)*.

p, Saul Zaentz; d, Anthony Minghella; w, Anthony Minghella (based on the novel by Michael Ondaatje); ph, John Seale; ed, Walter Murch; m, Gabriel Yared; prod d, Stuart Craig; art d, Aurelio Crugnola; fx, Richard Conway, Dennis Lowe; cos, Ann Roth

AA Best Picture; *AA Best Director*: Anthony Minghella; *AA Best Supporting Actress*: Juliette Binoche; *AA Best Art Direction*: Stuart Craig, Stephenie McMillan; *AA Best Cinematography*: John Seale; *AA Best Sound*: Walter Murch, Mark Berger, David Parker, Chris Newman; *AA Best Original Dramatic Score*: Gabriel Yared; *AA Best Costume Design*: Ann Roth; *AA Best Film Editing*: Walter Murch; *AAN Best Actor*: Ralph Fiennes; *AAN Best Actress*: Kristin Scott Thomas; *AAN Best Adapted Screenplay*: Anthony Minghella

THE ENGLISH PATIENT, winner of nine Academy Awards, is a sweeping story of love, war, and adultery set in Italy and North Africa.

In 1938, a cartographic expedition to the Sahara Desert includes Hungarian Count Laszlo Almasy (Ralph Fiennes) and English newlyweds Katharine (Kristin Scott Thomas) and Geoffrey Clifton (Colin

Firth). Almasy and Katharine begin a torrid affair. After war has erupted, Geoffrey learns of their liaison and tries to kill them all by crashing his plane. He dies and Katherine is badly injured, but Almasy is able to carry her to a cave and promises to return. By the time he does, Katharine has died; he flies off with her body, but is shot down by military fire. Horribly burned and near death, Almasy is placed by the Allies in a ruined Italian monastery where he is cared for by Hana (Juliette Binoche), a Canadian nurse. Sharing the monastery are Kip (Naveen Andrews), a Sikh British army lieutenant, and Caravaggio (Willem Dafoe), a former thief and Allied spy.

Rather than telling its story chronologically, THE ENGLISH PATIENT jumps back and forth from the present to the past. While this keeps the story from flagging, it never really soars either, mainly because its principal characters are so passive: things happen to them. The supporting roles suffer too, from Caravaggio's anticlimactic decision to abort his mission, to Hana and Kip's aimless romance, which simply peters out. Ralph Fiennes displays some of the sly wit of late Olivier in his portrayal of the mortally burned Count. To some extent, THE ENGLISH PATIENT is a victim of its own good taste. Apart from the crystalline photography of John Seale, an appealing turn by Andrews, and Juliette Binoche's exquisite complexion, the picture doesn't give its viewers much to remember.

ENTER LAUGHING

1967 112m c Comedy   ★★½
Columbia   (U.S.)   /U

Jose Ferrer *(Mr. Marlowe)*, Shelley Winters *(Mrs. Kolowitz)*, Elaine May *(Angela)*, Jack Gilford *(Mr. Foreman)*, Reni Santoni *(David Kolowitz)*, Janet Margolin *(Wanda)*, David Opatoshu *(Mr. Kolowitz)*, Michael J. Pollard *(Marvin)*, Don Rickles *(Harry Hamburger)*, Richard Deacon *(Pike)*.

p, Carl Reiner, Joseph Stein; d, Carl Reiner; w, Joseph Stein, Carl Reiner (based on a play by Joseph Stein); ph, Joseph Biroc; ed, Charles Nelson; m, Quincy Jones

Stagestruck David Kolowitz (Santoni) leaves his job as a machinist's apprentice and gets work at a decrepit theater run by Mr. Marlowe (Ferrer), a drunken old ham. Mrs. Kolowitz (Winters), David's mother, objects to his choice of careers, wanting her son to go to school and become a pharmacist. Based on Carl Reiner's recollections of his beginnings, *Enter Laughing* made a star out of Alan Arkin on Broadway, but Santoni is hopeless in the lead, lacking both the charm and the wit to pull it off.

ENTER THE DRAGON

1973 98m c Action/Martial Arts   ★★★
Concord   (U.S.)   R/18

Bruce Lee *(Lee)*, John Saxon *(Roper)*, Jim Kelly *(Williams)*, Shih Kien *(Han)*, Bob Wall *(Oharra)*, Anna Capri *(Tania)*, Angela Mao Ying *(Su-Lin)*, Betty Chung *(Mei Ling)*, Geoffrey Weeks *(Braithwaite)*, Yang Sze *(Bolo)*.

p, Fred Weintraub, Paul M. Heller; d, Robert Clouse; w, Michael Allin; ph, Gil Hubbs; ed, Kurt Hirschler, George Watters; m, Lalo Schifrin; art d, James Wong Sun

If you have a yen for spectacular chopsocky action, this is as good a flick to start with as any. The legendary Bruce Lee is showcased in his most lavish adventure—though, as this was made in Hong Kong after all, it still feels like a low-rent James Bond thriller crossed with Fu Manchu.

The plot barely rates relating but here goes: Lee (Bruce Lee) is recruited by a government agent, Braithwaite (Weeks), to enter a martial arts contest on the island fortress of Han (Shih), a particularly vicious chap with a nasty iron claw who is believed to be involved in drug smuggling and prostitution. Lee agrees because he knows that Han's right-hand man, Oharra (Wall), is responsible for his sister's death (she committed suicide rather than be raped by him).

On the island he meets Roper (Saxon) and Williams (Kelly), ex-army buddies from the US, on the run, respectively, from the mob and the law. Lee tries to infiltrate Han's underground chamber but fails, beating up a number of guards in the process. The next morning Han orders the men who let the intruder escape to fight Bolo (Sze), who kills them all easily. But enough plot. . . let it suffice to say that the only compelling reason to sit through this film is to see the greatest martial arts star of all time.

Lee proves why he is still the dominant legend in the genre more than a decade after his death. During one fight scene, Lee performed a flying kick so fast it couldn't be captured on film at 24 frames a second. The cameraman had to film the sequence in slow motion to get it to look like it wasn't faked. Nobody shows much evidence of acting ability, and the script is full of holes. Nonstop action is what these films are about, and that's what you get here.

ENTERTAINER, THE

| 1960 | 96m | bw | Drama | ★★★★ |
| Woodfall | (U.K.) | | | /X |

Laurence Olivier (Archie Rice), Brenda de Banzie (Phoebe Rice), Joan Plowright (Jean), Roger Livesey (Billy), Alan Bates (Frank), Daniel Massey (Graham), Albert Finney (Mick Rice), Miriam Karlin (Soubrette), Shirley Ann Field (Tina), Thora Hird (Mrs. Lapford)

p, Harry Saltzman; d, Tony Richardson; w, John Osborne, Nigel Kneale (based on the play by Osborne); ph, Oswald Morris; ed, Alan Osbiston; m, John Addison; art d, Ralph Brinton, Ted Marshall; cos, Barbara Gillett

AAN Best Actor: Laurence Olivier

"Life is a beastly mess," states the great Olivier in this bleak drama of moral stagnation. He's Archie Rice, a third-rate vaudevillian who, in garish makeup, delivers his creaky song and dance routines before increasingly scarce and indifferent audiences. Rice's home life is as shabby as his stage career. Phoebe (De Banzie), his loyal wife, has been driven to alcoholism and fits of hysteria by her husband's selfishness and infidelities. His father, Billy (Livesey, the star of THE LIFE AND DEATH OF COLONEL BLIMP), a once famous entertainer, is dying, yet Archie prevails upon him to back just one more tawdry musical revue. Only Jean (Plowright), his protective daughter, tries to meet Olivier's emotional needs but at the cost of her own professional and personal fulfilment. Archie is an incorrigible liar and self-promoter whose raging ego demands that he be admired by one and all even if it means destroying the lives of those around him.

This depressing but fascinating film is another Olivier tour de force; he later claimed this role, which he had perfected on the London stage, really reflected his own personality, telling an interviewer that "it had the advantage of being a complete break from the other sort of work and that made it much more refreshing than tormenting oneself through these punishing roles of Shakespeare. I have an affinity with Archie Rice. It's what I really am. I'm not like Hamlet."

The rest of the cast is stunning, particularly newcomer Plowright and veteran De Banzie (HOBSON'S CHOICE), though Albert Finney and Alan Bates are also memorable as Archie's sons. Scripters Osborne and Kneale present a gloomy and penetrating adaptation of Osborne's play. Richardson's direction of this unhappy little gem gives off the appropriate dull glimmer while being economical and inventive.

ENTERTAINING MR. SLOANE

| 1969 | 94m | c | Comedy | ★★★★ |
| Canterbury | (U.K.) | | | /15 |

Beryl Reid (Kath), Peter McEnery (Mr. Sloane), Harry Andrews (Ed), Alan Webb (Dada Kemp)

p, Douglas Kentish; d, Douglas Hickox; w, Clive Exton (based on the play by Joe Orton); ph, Wolfgang Suschitzky; ed, John Trumper; m, Georgie Fame; prod d, Michael Seymour; cos, Emma Porteous

Entertaining Mr. Audience. You can tell something offbeat is taking place right at the start, with the hefty, garishly dressed Kath (Reid) licking a popsicle while observing a funeral. Spotting the handsome, blonde Mr. Sloane (McEnery) sunning himself on a nearby tombstone, she asks him to move into her home and sets about seducing him. Her brother Ed (Andrews), a closeted homosexual, entertains similar notions, outfitting his new chauffeur stud in leather from head to toe. Their father (Webb), a retired grave-digger, recognizes Sloane as the man who killed his former boss, a pornographer. Dada accuses the enigmatic youth of murder and Sloane calmly kicks him to death. Ed and Kath,

now pregnant, threaten to tell the police what happened unless Sloane swears eternal allegiance to them. The film ends with three remarkable ceremonies all rolled into one.

Adapted from Joe Orton's hilarious play, which won the London Drama Critics Award in 1964 but which folded on Broadway after only 13 performances, ENTERTAINING MR. SLOANE is full of morbid humor and grotesque touches. In other words, the film is an almost constant delight, going out of its way to shock whenever possible. The tiny cast achieves a remarkable range of complex emotions and diverse moods, with Reid and Andrews especially superb. Not a film for everybody, granted, but a fine one nonetheless.

ENTRE NOUS
(COUP DE FOUDRE)

| 1983 | 110m | c | Drama | ★★★★½ |
| Partner's/Alexandre/Hachette Premiere/A2/SFPC | (France) | | | /15 |

Miou-Miou (Madeleine), Isabelle Huppert (Lena), Jean-Pierre Bacri (Costa), Guy Marchand (Michel), Robin Renucci (Raymond), Patrick Bauchau (Carlier), Guy Alric (Monsieur Vernier), Jacqueline Doyen (Madame Vernier), Patricia Champane (Florence), Saga Blanchard (Sophie)

p, Ariel Zeitoun; d, Diane Kurys; w, Diane Kurys, Alain Henry (from the book by Kurys, Olivier Cohen); ph, Bernard Lutic; ed, Joele Van Effenterre; m, Luis Bacalov; prod d, Jacques Bufnoir; cos, Mic Cheminal

AAN Best Foreign Language Film

This autobiographical work from French director Diane Kurys serves as a prequel to PEPPERMINT SODA, her superb 1977 feature debut.

The film opens during the German occupation of France. Lena (Isabelle Huppert), a young Russian Jew, escapes from a prison camp by marrying a stranger, Michel (Guy Marchand). Meanwhile, in Paris, art student Madeleine (Miou-Miou) must start life anew when her husband is brutally gunned down before her. The scene then shifts to Lyons, 1952, for a chance meeting between these two women. Lena is still wed to Michel and is the mother of two children, while Madeleine has remarried. They come to realize that they can only find support from each other and not from their boorish husbands.

A resounding art-house success in the US and Oscar nominee for Best Foreign Film, ENTRE NOUS is an excellent examination of the bond of friendship. Like very few films before it, ENTRE NOUS focuses—with subtle but distinct lesbian undertones—on a female friendship instead of the usual male "buddy" formula. Based in part on the experiences of the director's own mother, this fictionalized account is one of great emotional truth. The relationships between Lena and Madeleine and between the women and their respective families are written, directed, and acted with a touch usually seen only in the films of Renoir, Pagnol or Truffaut. The picture's chief weakness is its sometimes uninvolving episodic structure, beginning with the rocky 1940s prologue that opens the movie. Still, ENTRE NOUS is intelligent, adult cinema.

EQUUS

| 1977 | 137m | c | Drama | ★★★ |
| UA | (U.K.) | | | R/15 |

Richard Burton (Dr. Martin Dysart), Peter Firth (Alan Strang), Colin Blakely (Frank Strang), Joan Plowright (Dora Strang), Harry Andrews (Harry Dalton), Eileen Atkins (Magistrate Hesther Saloman), Jenny Agutter (Jill Mason), John Wyman (The Horseman), Kate Reid (Margaret Dysart), Ken James (Mr. Pearce)

p, Lester Persky, Elliott Kastner; d, Sidney Lumet; w, Peter Shaffer (based on his play); ph, Oswald Morris; ed, John Victor-Smith; m, Richard Rodney Bennett; prod d, Tony Walton; art d, Simon Holland; cos, Tony Walton, Patti Unger, Brenda Dabbs

AAN Best Actor: Richard Burton; AAN Best Supporting Actor: Peter Firth; AAN Best Adapted Screenplay: Peter Shaffer

A reverential and somewhat bumpy film adaptation. Shaffer adapted his own gripping play about a young man, Alan Strang (Firth), who is inexplicably compelled to blind horses. Burton is Dr. Martin Dysart, the psychiatrist who realizes that Alan's religious fervor is the key to the mystery. Alan's devout mother, Dora Strang (Plowright), has supplied the confused youth with a thwarted view of life that has resulted in his behavior. The court appoints Dr. Dysart to get to the bottom of the reasons for Alan's deeds and he learns much about himself in the process.

This is a fairly convincing rendition of a real psychiatrist-patient relationship. Burton confirms his status as a master thespian as he begins to take stock of his own life in the pressure-cooker of his work with Firth. He's extremely intense albeit in a particularly actorly way. Firth's performance is technically flawless but it is periodically interrupted by scenes in which the dumbfounded camera simply observes him nude. Veteran director Lumet's work here is earnest yet unimaginative. He does his best with what is still essentially a filmed play. Shaffer's words are often smart and incisive but the film could have done with a few less of them.

ERASERHEAD

1976 89m bw Fantasy/Horror   ★★★★
AFI (U.S.)   /18

Jack Nance (*Henry Spencer*), Charlotte Stewart (*Mary X*), Allen Joseph (*Mr. X*), Jeanne Bates (*Mrs. X*), Judith Anna Roberts (*Beautiful Girl Across the Hall*), Laurel Near (*Lady in the Radiator*), V. Phipps-Wilson (*Landlady*), Jack Fisk (*Man in the Planet*), Jean Lange (*Grandmother*), Thomas Coulson (*The Boy*)

p, David Lynch; d, David Lynch; w, David Lynch; ph, Frederick Elmes, Herbert Cardwell; ed, David Lynch; m, Peter Ivers; prod d, David Lynch; fx, David Lynch

Disturbing, repulsive, hilarious, frightening, sensitive and challenging, David Lynch's ERASERHEAD has been aptly described by its creator as a "dream of dark and troubling things," namely fatherhood.

A young man, Henry Spencer (Nance), living in a dilapidated apartment building in an industrialized city learns that his girlfriend, Mary X (Stewart), is pregnant. Leaving his room, which seems to be inhabited by spermlike creatures, he visits Mary and her parents—a hyperactive father with a passion for synthetic meat and a mother obsessed with her daughter's sexuality. Grandmother sits in the kitchen, stonelike, maybe dead. Mary moves in with Henry and they begin to take care of their "baby"—a deformed, constantly crying mass of tissue and bandages that looks something like a skinned lamb. The infant is repulsive yet fascinating, as well as sad. Its constant whining drives Mary out of the apartment, leaving Henry alone with the baby. After an accidental tragedy, Henry is hurled into the nightmarish world that has existed on the fringes of his "real" world since the beginning of the film.

Five years in the making, ERASERHEAD is not just a film about a man who has nasty dreams. It's a creepily sensuous film that suggests that the "dark and troubling things" we like to repress inhabit dresser drawers, live behind the radiator or lie under the bed. They are part of the environment. This is a nightmare about a man's horror of commitment, sexuality, and adult responsibility. This was the first feature directed by Lynch, a former painter, and it proudly displays its roots in past avant-garde film movements—surrealism and expressionism in particular—while tipping its hat to classic horror films. Lynch has since gone on to become what could be described somewhat paradoxically as the modern Hollywood equivalent of an avant-garde filmmaker but his subsequent career has not lived up to the promise of this extraordinary debut.

ESCAPE FROM ALCATRAZ

1979 112m c Prison   ★★★½
Paramount (U.S.)   PG/15

Clint Eastwood (*Frank Morris*), Patrick McGoohan (*Warden*), Roberts Blossom (*Doc*), Jack Thibeau (*Clarence Anglin*), Fred Ward (*John Anglin*), Paul Benjamin (*English*), Larry Hankin (*Charley Butts*), Bruce M. Fischer (*Wolf*), Frank Ronzio (*Litmus*), Fred Stuthman (*Johnson*)

p, Don Siegel; d, Don Siegel; w, Richard Tuggle (based on the book by J. Campbell Bruce); ph, Bruce Surtees; ed, Ferris Webster; prod d, Allen Smith

Veteran genre director Don Siegel directed this simple and gripping story about an actual escape from the supposedly escape-proof Alcatraz. Siegel is extremely good at this sort of thing (see his 1954 genre classic, RIOT IN CELL BLOCK 11) and if you like to watch people doing a job, you won't find it done better elsewhere.

The escape-proof "Rock" was designed in the early 1930s to hold the most infamous, incorrigible and escape-prone inmates in the federal prison system. Located in the dead center of San Francisco Bay, Alcatraz played host to Al Capone and Doc Barker, among others, and was considered by J. Edgar Hoover and other federal executives to be the only American prison from which no inmate could ever escape. In 1962, however, Frank Morris and the Anglin brothers did escape, resulting in the institution's closure.

This film is the story of that escape, convincingly enacted by Eastwood as mastermind Morris, a taciturn, calculating man with nerves of steel. Upon Morris's arrival at Alcatraz, he is met by a vain, smug warden (McGoohan) who informs him that he can forget about escaping; it has never been done and never will be done. But as an inmate who has escaped from other prisons, Morris's attitude remains unchanged.

The pace of this movie is a bit slow, but Siegel's deliberate, sparse direction works to the benefit of a film where time is all his characters have. Surprisingly, there are few exciting set pieces and relatively little violence, yet ESCAPE is relentlessly tense. This production marked the fifth time Eastwood worked with Siegel, his directorial mentor.

ESCAPE FROM NEW YORK

1981 99m c Action/Science Fiction   ★★★
Avco Embassy (U.S.)   R/

Kurt Russell (*Snake Plissken*), Lee Van Cleef (*Bob Hauk*), Ernest Borgnine (*Cabby*), Donald Pleasence (*The President*), Isaac Hayes (*Duke of New York*), Season Hubley (*Girl in Chock Full O'Nuts*), Harry Dean Stanton (*Brain*), Adrienne Barbeau (*Maggie*), Tom Atkins (*Rehme*), Charles Cyphers (*Secretary of State*)

p, Debra Hill, Larry Franco; d, John Carpenter; w, John Carpenter, Nick Castle; ph, Dean Cundey; ed, Todd Ramsay; m, John Carpenter, Alan Howarth; prod d, Joe Alves; cos, Stephen Loomis

A futuristic thriller set in 1997, John Carpenter's ESCAPE FROM NEW YORK finds Snake Plissken (Kurt Russell)—an ex-war hero, now convict—forced to rescue the President (Donald Pleasence) from a plane crash in New York City. The US is now a police state, and Manhattan has become one vast prison in which convicts are summarily dumped and left to fend for themselves. If Snake fails to find the President in time, he'll be atomized by a time bomb implanted in his neck by ruthless Bob Hauk (Lee Van Cleef). Snake sallies forth into this dark world and experiences violent battles, narrow escapes, and white-knuckle adventures, enlisting an anachronistic cabbie (Ernest Borgine) in his struggle to outwit a criminal mastermind played by Isaac Hayes. A generally gripping actioner, the film can also be read as a percipient satire of a society irreparably split along lines of class and race. Carpenter's clever premise has since become fodder for innumerable straight-to-video cheapies. A "director's edition," featuring some 15 minutes of footage cut from the original theatrical release, appeared on video in 1994.

EUROPA, EUROPA

1991 110m c Biography/War/Historical   ★★★★
Les Films du Losange/CCC Filmkunst/Perspektywa Unit   R/15
(France/Germany)

Marco Hofschneider (*Young Solomon Perel*), Julie Delpy (*Leni*), Andre Wilms (*Robert Kellerman*), Solomon Perel (*Himself*), Aschley Wanninger (*Eric*), Rene Hofschneider (*Isaak Perel*), Piotr Kozlowski (*David Perel [Solomon's Brother]*), Klaus Abramowsky (*Solly's Father*), Michele Gleizer (*Solly's Mother*), Marta Sandrowicz (*Berta [Solomon's Sister]*)

p, Margaret Menegoz, Artur Brauner; d, Agnieszka Holland; w, Agnieszka Holland, Paul Hengge (from the book *Memoires* by Solomon Perel); ph, Jacek Petrycki; ed, Ewa Smal, Isabelle Lorente; m, Zbigniew Preisner; prod d, Allan Starski; fx, Jacek Jelinski; cos, Wieslawa Starska, Malgorzata Stefaniak

AAN Best Adapted Screenplay: Agnieszka Holland

Agnieszka Holland's fascinating, richly realized EUROPA, EUROPA is based on the real-life story of Solomon Perel, one of a handful of Jews who ironically managed to survive the Nazi terror by masquerading as Aryans.

Solomon Perel (Marco Hofschneider) was born in Germany, near Braunschweig, to German-speaking Polish-Jewish parents in 1925. (He shares a birthday—April 20th—with Adolf Hitler.) In the opening scene, the baby Solomon is circumcized—an ironic beginning to a story that will revolve around Solomon's attempts to conceal his lack of a foreskin. Solly grows up to be a handsome, engaging youth who does not look particularly Jewish. On the eve of Solomon's bar mitzvah, his family's home is attacked by a Nazi mob. Solly saves himself by diving from the bathroom window and hiding in an empty barrel. The family then flee to Poland, where they are separated during the German invasion of September 1939.

Solly makes his way into Soviet-occupied Poland and winds up in an orphanage near Grodno, where he undergoes a seemingly painless transformation into a Young Pioneer. Although there are hints of the Stalinist terror, they are eclipsed by the German attack on Russia, during which Solly is picked up by the invaders. By virtue of his impeccable German and his claim to be among Poland's ethnic German minority, the Volksdeutsche, Solly escapes the winnowing out of Communist Party members and Jews being conducted by German troops. Since he also speaks Russian, Solly is immediately adopted by an advance Wehrmacht squad as their translator, under his false name of Josef Peters, or "Jupp."

Solly's inner tension is expressed in the form of wonderfully surreal dreams, where Stalin and Hitler waltz together and a fellow orphan appears as a crucified Christ. In one nightmare he hides in a closet with Hitler, whose pose suggests he, too, is concealing the same secret that Solly does. Holland, a frequent collaborator of Andrzej Wajda (she wrote the screenplays for DANTON, A LOVE IN GERMANY and KORCZAK), also directed BITTER HARVEST and TO KILL A PRIEST. Her screenplay covers much of the range of anti-Semitism in Hitler's Germany, whether the airy intellectual sort or the bloody-minded kind. Also familiar with the love-hate relations between Poles and Russians, Holland has not skirted the harmful effects of the Soviet occupation. The most poignant sequence is a recreation of the Warsaw ghetto familiar to viewers from Nazi newsreels, glimpsed by Solly through a chink in the white-washed window of a tram that passes through this forbidden zone.

EUROPA, EUROPA is a compelling story told with intelligence and wit. Holland's direction, and the acting by the ensemble cast, are superb. The real-life Solomon Perel makes an appearance as himself in the present day.

EVERY MAN FOR HIMSELF
(SAUVE QUI PEUT—LA VIE)
1980 87m c Drama   ★★★
Sonimage/Sara/MK2/Saga (France)

Isabelle Huppert *(Isabelle Riviere)*, Jacques Dutronc *(Paul Godard)*, Nathalie Baye *(Denise Rimbaud)*, Anna Baldaccini *(Isabelle's Sister)*, Fred Personne *(1st Costumer)*, Roland Amstutz *(2nd Costumer)*, Nicole Jaquet *(Woman)*, Dore DeRosa *(Elevator Attendant)*, Monique Barscha *(Opera Singer)*, Cecile Tanner *(Paul's Daughter)*

p, Alain Sarde, Jean-Luc Godard; d, Jean-Luc Godard; w, Jean-Claude Carriere, Anne-Marie Mieville; ph, William Lubtchansky, Renato Berta; ed, Marie Mieville, Jean-Luc Godard; m, Gabriel Yared; art d, Romain Goupil

After years of Maoist polemics and made-for-TV obscurities, Jean-Luc Godard marked his return to relatively accessible cinema with a film that explores money, prostitution, masculine violence, and the relationship between sound and image—all familiar Godardian concerns. For the first time since 1972's TOUT VA BIEN (which featured Yves Montand and Jane Fonda), Godard elected to use stars in his film, casting Isabelle Huppert as a high-priced Swiss hooker who caters to some notably bizarre tastes. An especially memorable scene shows Huppert servicing her businessman clients in an elaborate sexual daisy chain—a kind of Rube Goldberg sex machine that figures the mechanization of desire under capitalism. One of the film's alternate titles,

SLOW MOTION, is derived from Godard's recurrent use of stretch-printed/freeze-framed images. At this point in Godard's career, his desire to use stars in ways critical of stardom coincided aptly with his choice of subject matter, especially in the never-made THE STORY, a gangster film about Hollywood that was to have been shot at Coppola's Zoetrope Studios with Robert De Niro, Diane Keaton, and Marlon Brando. Unfortunately, this never made it past the storyboard stage.

EVERY MAN FOR HIMSELF AND GOD AGAINST ALL
(JEDER FUR SICH UND GOTT GEGEN ALLE)
1975 110m c Biography   ★★★★
ZDF/Werner Herzog (West Germany)

Bruno S. *(Kaspar Hauser)*, Walter Ladengast *(Daumer)*, Brigitte Mira *(Kathe)*, Hans Musaus *(Unknown Man)*, Willy Semmelrogge *(Circus Director)*, Michael Kroecher *(Lord Stanhope)*, Henry van Lyck *(Calvary Captain)*, Enno Patalas *(Pastor Fuhrmann)*, Elis Pilgrim *(Pastor)*, Volker Prechtel *(Hiltel, the Prison Guard)*

p, Werner Herzog; d, Werner Herzog; w, Werner Herzog; ph, Jorg Schmidt-Reitwein; ed, Beate Mainka-Jellinghaus; m, Johann Pachelbel, Tomaso Albinoni, Orlando DiLasso, Wolfgang Amadeus Mozart; prod d, Henning V. Gierke; cos, Gisela Storch, Ann Poppel

The winner of the Grand Jury Award at the 1975 Cannes Film Festival, this haunting and, at times, disconcertingly whimsical film helped to propel the self-styled visionary New German filmmaker, Werner Herzog, to international prominence.

Herzog's slow and meditative films are fairly unique in contemporary narrative cinema. Landscapes and music are at least as important as the human characters in his work. His protagonists tend to be obsessive dreamers compelled to action by the power of their visions—with consequences that are sometimes transcendental, sometimes disastrous. At their most excessive, Herzog's films can be regressive, reactionary, self-indulgent and naively romantic; at their best, they are dreamily hypnotic, mystical and awe-inspiring in their beauty. EVERY MAN FOR HIMSELF AND GOD AGAINST ALL happily falls in the latter category.

The film is based on the documented story of a young man, Kaspar Hauser (Bruno S.), who, after living in a cellar for years with only a pet rocking horse, is abandoned by his protector and provider, the mysterious Man in Black. Having been isolated from all humans except his godlike "father," Kaspar is suddenly thrust into civilization. Though at first he can barely walk and cannot speak, he is expected to readily adapt to 19th-century society. His past remains a mystery to the townspeople, as does his purpose. Some teach him the mannerisms of the civilized, while others spy on his every move attempting to uncover some hidden identity. Untainted by society, Kaspar functions as a natural man in this repressed and repressive society. His very existence calls their assumptions into question.

Many consider this, along with AGUIRRE: THE WRATH OF GOD, to be Herzog's best film. Bruno S. is of particular interest here. A non-professional actor, Mr. S. is an eccentric German street performer who spent much of his childhood in mental institutions. He also stars in Herzog's STROSZEK.

EVERYONE SAYS I LOVE YOU
1996 97m c Musical/Comedy   ★★½
Sweetland Films (U.S.)   R/12

Woody Allen *(Joe)*, Julia Roberts *(Von)*, Goldie Hawn *(Steffi)*, Tim Roth *(Charles Ferry)*, Alan Alda *(Bob)*, David Ogden Stiers *(Holden's Father)*, Drew Barrymore *(Skylar)*, Lukas Haas *(Scott)*, Natasha Lyonne *(DJ)*, Edward Norton *(Holden)*

p, Robert Greenhut; d, Woody Allen; w, Woody Allen; ph, Carlo Di Palma; ed, Susan E. Morse; prod d, Santo Loquasto; art d, Tom Warren; fx, Connie Brink; chor, Graciela Daniele; cos, Jeffrey Kurland

Woody Allen pays tribute to 1930s Hollywood musicals in this story of romance among New York City's upper crust. What should be a special treat, however, is just another Woody Allen movie with songs thrown in.

DJ (Natasha Lyonne) narrates this tale of her wealthy, extended family—headed by Bob (Alan Alda) and Steffi (Goldie Hawn)—and their life on the Upper East Side of New York City. Her half sister Skylar

(Drew Barrymore) gets engaged to mild-mannered Holden (Edward Norton) but finds more romantic interest in Charles (Tim Roth), a lascivious ex-con. While on vacation in Venice, DJ escapes her family's travails and helps her biological father, Joe (Woody Allen), woo Von (Julia Roberts), an unhappily married woman. After much plotting to win her affections, Joe convinces Von to live with him in his garret in Paris.

A flawed, uneven attempt to reproduce Hollywood musical magic, EVERYONE SAYS I LOVE YOU references some of the earliest, most conventional sound musicals, rather than the more experimental MGM pictures of the later "Golden Age." Indeed, the only creative energy comes from the idea of everyday characters breaking into song-and-dance at the drop of a hat—a notion that was used to greater effect in Dennis Potter's "Pennies from Heaven." Old musicals allowed viewers to imagine they could sing and dance like Astaire and Kelly, but no one in this cast would inspire anyone with their tone-deaf renditions of the classic numbers. Allen assembles a talented group of actors only to waste most of them, and he himself seems grafted onto the proceedings. Occasionally, the director comes up with a well-timed gag but mostly passes up the chance to revise or tinker with old forms.

EVIL DEAD, THE

1983 85m c Horror   ★★★½
Renaissance (U.S.)   /18

Bruce Campbell *(Ash)*, Ellen Sandweiss *(Cheryl)*, Betsy Baker *(Linda)*, Hal Delrich *(Scott)*, Sarah York *(Shelly)*

p, Robert G. Tapert; d, Sam Raimi; w, Sam Raimi; ph, Tim Philo, Joshua M. Becker; ed, Edna Ruth Paul; m, Joseph LoDuca; fx, Tom Sullivan, Bar Pierce

Self-promoted as "The Ultimate Experience in Grueling Terror," THE EVIL DEAD marks the directorial debut of what may be the next great practitioner of this eternally disreputable form. Writer-director Sam Raimi and his college pals took the genre by storm with this amazingly assured and exhilarating horror exercise in which narrative and characterization take a backseat to sheer cinematic panache.

Five college students take shelter in an abandoned cabin deep in the woods, where they find a strange book along with a tape explaining that the book is an ancient Sumerian Book of the Dead. The tape translates some of the incantations in the book, and giant demons are unleashed in the woods. One by one the teenagers are taken over by the demons, until only Ash (Bruce Campbell) is left to fight the evil.

Shot in 16mm (and blown up to grainy 35mm) on location in Tennessee and Michigan on a tiny budget of under $400,000, this film has some undeniable technical limitations—and the acting is less than professional—but Raimi's wildly creative filmmaking turns these limitations into virtues that make THE EVIL DEAD a landmark in recent American horror films.

While it set new standards in outlandish screen gore, it's never really too disturbing due to its old fashioned funhouse feel. Raimi does not aspire to dark satirical social commentary like Romero nor to psychosexual insights like Cronenberg; some boys just wanna have fun. Though genuinely shocking and spooky, the movie has enough sick black humor and deliciously bad special effects to keep all the nightmarish imagery from getting too oppressive. Not for the faint of heart or those uninitiated in the ways of modern horror, it's a hoot for fans of the genre.

EVIL DEAD 2: DEAD BY DAWN

1987 85m c Horror   ★★★½
Renaissance (U.S.)   /18

Bruce Campbell *(Ash)*, Sarah Berry *(Annie)*, Dan Hicks *(Jake)*, Kassie Wesley *(Bobby Joe)*, Theodore Raimi *(Possessed Henrietta)*, Denise Bixler *(Linda)*, Richard Domeier *(Ed)*, John Peaks *(Prof. Raymond Knowby)*, Lou Hancock *(Henrietta)*

p, Robert G. Tapert; d, Sam Raimi; w, Sam Raimi, Scott Spiegel; ph, Peter Deming; ed, Kaye Davis; m, Joseph LoDuca; art d, Philip Duffin, Randy Bennett; fx, Mark Shostrom, Vern Hyde, Doug Beswick Productions, Tom Sullivan, Rick Catizone; chor, Susan Labatt, Andrea Brown, Tam G. Warner

Less than a sequel than a remake; Ash (Bruce Campbell), the sole survivor of THE EVIL DEAD, seems to have no memory of that film's events. After a high-speed recap and continuation of first film's ending, Ash ventures out to that same lonely cabin for a romantic weekend with his girlfriend (Denise Bixler). There he discovers that darn tape recorder again. When the voice reads a translation of the "Book of the Dead," a vicious evil force awakens in the woods and rushes into the house, and all hell breaks loose once more.

A deliriously cinematic experience for those with a taste for Grand Guignol, this is a relentlessly energetic nightmare world where quite literally *anything* can happen—and does. By pushing the events to an absurd extreme, the film frequently leaves the realm of horror and becomes a cartoon gone mad. Animation director Tex Avery is a stronger influence here than the German Expressionists or modern masters of horror. Campbell's admirably straightfaced performance suggests a modern-day Harold Lloyd trapped in a splatter film spinning madly out of control. He gamely tries to cope with everything the evil spirits hurl at him including bleeding walls, scary monsters, flying eyeballs, a possessed hand, and all manner of bad craziness.

To keep things interesting, the then 26-year-old director employs a myriad of expressive movie tricks including stop-motion animation, impossible point-of-view shots, portentous crane shots, shaky handheld camera sequences, rotating sets, rear projection, distorting anamorphic lenses, weird sound effects and good old-fashioned dramatic lighting. The film is a breathless celebration of the possibilities of the medium. "Good" dramatic narrative values hold little interest for Raimi. The setting and story are merely functional, and most of the dialogue is perfunctory. Maximum visceral impact is what this film is all about—and it delivers.

EVITA

1996 135m c Musical/Biography   ★★★
Cinergi Productions/Dirty Hands Productions/Hollywood   PG
Pictures (U.S.)

Madonna *(Eva "Evita" Peron)*, Antonio Banderas *(Che Guevara)*, Jonathan Pryce *(General Juan Domingo Peron)*, Jimmy Nail *(Agustin Magaldi)*, Victoria Sus *(Dona Juana)*, Julian Littman *(Brother Juan)*, Olga Merediz *(Blanca)*, Laura Pallas *(Elisa)*, Julia Worsley *(Erminda)*, Maria Lujan Hidalgo *(Young Eva)*

p, Robert Stigwood, Alan Parker, Andrew G. Vajna; d, Alan Parker; w, Alan Parker, Oliver Stone (based on the musical play *Evita*, lyrics by Tim Rice and music by Andrew Lloyd Webber); ph, Darius Khondji; ed, Gerry Hambling; m, Andrew Lloyd Webber; prod d, Brian Morris; art d, Jean-Michel Hugon, Richard Earl; fx, Yves De Bono; chor, Vincent Paterson; cos, Penny Rose

AA Best Original Song: Andrew Lloyd Webber (music), Tim Rice (lyrics); AAN Best Art Direction: Brian Morris, Philippe Turlure; AAN Best Cinematography: Darius Khondji; AAN Best Film Editing: Gerry Hambling; AAN Best Sound: Andy Nelson, Anna Behlmer, Ken Weston

Yes, Madonna *is* Eva Peron. Alan Parker's breathlessly paced film version of Andrew Lloyd Webber and Tim Rice's rock-opera bio is all sound and fury, with an admittedly dazzling array of visual treats.

During the 1930s, a young Eva Duarte arrives in Buenos Aires, determined to transcend the dull poverty of her provincial youth. Using whatever connections her increasingly powerful parade of lovers can provide, Eva becomes a successful actress and is soon introduced to the equally ambitious politician Juan Peron (Jonathan Pryce), whom she marries. Eva uses her popularity and poor background to seduce the lower classes and helps Juan secure the presidency, but her efforts to improve living conditions for *los descamisados* are plagued by corruption. Her splashy life-style alongside a penchant for self-aggrandizement help earn her considerable hostility both at home and abroad, and "Santa Evita" remains a controversial figure until her death in 1952. Throughout the film, on-screen narrator Che (Antonio Banderas) explicates events and acts as a one-man vox pop, providing the film with its moral point of view.

After two decades of fits and starts, EVITA finally landed in the hands of Alan Parker, one of the few contemporary directors with any musical experience (FAME). Parker is responsible for the film's spectacular look and cunning casting, but his commitments to character and coherent storytelling are comparatively weak. Madonna, however, is just fine: she handles vulnerable ballads like "Another Suitcase in Another Hall" with surprising delicacy and braves some of the somewhat dated score's more ridiculous moments. But despite the film's ample pleasures, it cannot be forgotten that this story is based in fact. Can the rise of fascism be obliterated or even glorified by magnificent set design? It obviously makes little difference to Parker, Webber, and Rice.

EXCALIBUR

1981 140m c Action/Fantasy	★★★
Orion (U.S.)	R/15

Nigel Terry *(King Arthur)*, Nicol Williamson *(Merlin)*, Nicholas Clay *(Lancelot)*, Helen Mirren *(Morgana)*, Cherie Lunghi *(Guenevere)*, Paul Geoffrey *(Perceval)*, Robert Addie *(Mordred)*, Gabriel Byrne *(Uther)*, Liam Neeson *(Gawain)*, Corin Redgrave *(Cornwall)*

p, John Boorman; d, John Boorman; w, Rospo Pallenberg, John Boorman (based on *Le Morte D'Arthur* by Thomas Malory); ph, Alex Thomson; ed, John Merritt; m, Trevor Jones; prod d, Anthony Pratt; art d, Tim Hutchinson; fx, Peter Hutchinson, Alan Whibley; cos, Bob Ringwood

AAN Best Cinematography: Alex Thomson

EXCALIBUR is a grand, clanky, brooding fantasy following Arthurian legend from the young king's anonymous background to his rise as ruler of ancient Britain. Nigel Terry is excellent as a naive, altruistic Arthur; Nicol Williamson camps it up amusingly as Merlin; Guenevere (Cherie Lunghi) and Lancelot (Nicholas Clay) provide a couple of steamy moments. Excessive but occasionally inspired, EXCALIBUR gives us grimy lumbering knights, gloomy castles, slithering dragons, mesmerizing magic, and (of course) the struggle between good and evil. Excellent makeup and costuming, as well as convincingly rustic Irish location work. Williamson and Helen Mirren, who plays Morgana, seem to understand that the film takes itself a bit too seriously, and do a lot of nudging and winking.

EXECUTIVE SUITE

1954 104m bw Drama	★★★★½
MGM (U.S.)	/U

William Holden *(McDonald Walling)*, June Allyson *(Mary Blemond Walling)*, Barbara Stanwyck *(Julia O. Tredway)*, Fredric March *(Loren Phineas Shaw)*, Walter Pidgeon *(Frederick Y. Alderson)*, Shelley Winters *(Eva Bardeman)*, Paul Douglas *(Josiah Walter Dudley)*, Louis Calhern *(George Nyle Caswell)*, Dean Jagger *(Jesse W. Grimm)*, Nina Foch *(Erica Martin)*

p, John Houseman; d, Robert Wise; w, Ernest Lehman (based on the novel by Cameron Hawley); ph, George Folsey; ed, Ralph E. Winters; art d, Cedric Gibbons, Edward Carfagno; fx, A. Arnold Gillespie; cos, Helen Rose

AAN Best Supporting Actress: Nina Foch; *AAN Best Cinematography:* George Folsey; *AAN Best Art Direction:* Cedric Gibbons (Art Direction), Edward C Carfagno (Art Direction), Edwin B Willis (Set Decoration), Emile Kuri (Set Decoration); *AAN Best Costume Design:* Helen Rose

A spectacular array of MGM superstars shine in this slick fascinating drama of corporate intrigue. The death of the president of a gigantic furniture firm prompts a series of power plays among the company's executives, all vying for the vacated top position. The jockeying vice presidents are Loren Phineas Shaw (March), Josiah Walter Dudley (Douglas), Frederick Y. Alderson (Pidgeon), George Nyle Caswell (Calhern), and a junior executive, McDonald Walling (Holden). Surveying the candidates is Julia O. Tredway (Stanwyck), the daughter of the manufacturing firm's founder and the mistress of the recently deceased company head. As the chief stockholder as well, her decision will tip the scales.

Director Wise intercuts among the many characters but this strategy actually serves to unify the story and action rather than fragmenting the tale. The drama unfolds from a sparkling, witty, and provocative screenplay by Ernest Lehman adapted from the Cameron Hawley novel. Holden, March, Douglas, Stanwyck, Calhern, Jagger, Foch and

Pidgeon are riveting in their parts, even though some, like Stanwyck, are only on camera occasionally. Holden, still building a great career, was reunited with Stanwyck on screen for the first time in 15 years—their last previous work together was in GOLDEN BOY. Critics universally and correctly singled out March as the most impressive performer in the awesome cast. His obsessive villain hasn't a single virtue, only the relentless drive to win at all costs while mouthing the predictable rationale that he is merely practicing "good business." Foch, as the suicidal secretary to the deceased boss, gained an Oscar nomination as Best Supporting Actress.

This was one of the first major films to eschew a continuous musical score; producer Houseman elected to incorporate the sounds of the business world throughout such as when the bells of a Wall Street clock are heard while the cast names roll up on the screen.

EXODUS

1960 212m c Historical	★★★★
Preminger (U.S.)	/PG

Paul Newman *(Ari Ben Canaan)*, Eva Marie Saint *(Kitty Fremont)*, Ralph Richardson *(Gen. Sutherland)*, Peter Lawford *(Maj. Caldwell)*, Lee J. Cobb *(Barak Ben Canaan)*, Sal Mineo *(Dov Landau)*, John Derek *(Taha)*, Hugh Griffith *(Mandria)*, Gregory Ratoff *(Lakavitch)*, Felix Aylmer *(Dr. Lieberman)*

p, Otto Preminger; d, Otto Preminger; w, Dalton Trumbo (based on the novel by Leon Uris); ph, Sam Leavitt; ed, Louis Loeffler; m, Ernest Gold; art d, Richard Day, Bill Hutchinson; fx, Win Ryder; cos, Joe King, May Walding, Margo Slater, Rudi Gernreich, Hope Bryce

AAN Best Supporting Actor: Sal Mineo; *AAN Best Cinematography:* Sam Leavitt; *AA Best Score:* Ernest Gold

A stirring chronicle of Israel's struggle for independence in 1947, EXODUS focuses on Newman as Ben Canaan, the leader of the Haganah, whose affair with Kitty Fremont (Saint) is engulfed by the conflict. The film tackles the independence movement as a whole, dealing with various factions involved in the internecine struggle between the moderate Haganah and the radical terrorist Irgun. Interspersed throughout are segments showing the migration of European Jews to the new nation, paying special attention to the ragged survivors of Nazi death camps on board the vessel *Exodus*, blockaded in a Cyprus harbor by British warships. The film also depicts the struggle of the Jews in Palestine to gain partition, then profiles the main characters after the partition, fighting to continue as the nation of Israel.

Under the direction of Otto Preminger, EXODUS boasts strong performances and many memorable sequences including the bombing of the King David Hotel, the capture and subsequent rescue of the Irgun leaders, masterfully handled crowd scenes, and Canaan's moving final speech. Preminger is generally faithful to history and to Leon Uris's best-selling novel; Uris himself was dismissed as the film's screenwriter (Preminger thought he had no gift for screen dialogue), and the filmmakers were necessarily forced to abridge the story to make it cinematically feasible. Though the film is overlong, the story is movingly told, the production values are high, and Ernest Gold's Oscar-nominated score is considered a classic.

EXORCIST, THE

1973 121m c Horror	★★★½
Warner Bros. (U.S.)	R/18

Ellen Burstyn *(Mrs. MacNeil)*, Max von Sydow *(Father Merrin)*, Jason Miller *(Father Karras)*, Lee J. Cobb *(Lt. Kinderman)*, Jack MacGowran *(Burke)*, Kitty Winn *(Sharon)*, Linda Blair *(Regan)*, Vasiliki Maliaros *(Mother Karras)*, Wallace Rooney *(Bishop)*, Titos Vandis *(Karras's Uncle)*

p, William Peter Blatty; d, William Friedkin; w, William Peter Blatty; ph, Owen Roizman, Billy Williams; ed, Norman Gay, Jordan Leondopoulos, Evan Lottman, Bud Smith; m, Jack Nitzsche; prod d, Bill Malley

AAN Best Picture; *AAN Best Actress:* Ellen Burstyn; *AAN Best Supporting Actor:* Jason Miller; *AAN Best Supporting Actress:* Linda Blair; *AAN Best Director:* William Friedkin; *AA Best Adapted Screenplay:* William Peter Blatty; *AAN Best Cinematography:* Owen

Roizman; *AAN Best Editing:* Jordan Leondopoulos, Bud Smith, Evan Lottman, Norman Gay; *AAN Best Art Direction:* Bill Malley, Jerry Wunderlich; *AA Best Sound:* Robert Knudson, Chris Newman

Extremely controversial at the time of its release, THE EXORCIST kicked off intense debate among critics, community leaders, and even religious leaders—spurring the public, of course, to make it one of the most financially successful horror films ever made.

Regan (Linda Blair), the 12-year-old daughter of a famous stage actress (Ellen Burstyn), begins to suffer unexplainable fits and bouts of bizarre behavior. The girl is brought to doctors, but examinations fail to pinpoint a physical or psychiatric ailment. Regan's condition grows worse, and she begins to transform physically, taking on an ugly, demonic appearance. In desperation, Regan's mother asks the help of a young priest, Father Karras (Jason Miller). Realizing that Regan is possessed by the Devil and knowing that his own faith is too weak for him to deal successfully with the problem himself, Karras turns to Father Merrin (Max von Sydow), an elderly priest who specializes in exorcisms.

Based on William Peter Blatty's runaway best seller (which itself was based upon a reported exorcism in 1949) THE EXORCIST shrewdly exploits the fears and frustrations of parents while disturbing religious implications merely provide portentous window dressing. The film is an intense rollercoaster ride, a marvel of audience manipulation, with director William Friedkin pushing all the right buttons to make this a genre landmark. The movie balances its then-state-of-the-art special effects with good old-fashioned atmospheric horror to produce an excruciating—though shallow—two hours of dread and unease. It's too bad the film failed to get further inside its characters.

EXOTICA

1995 104m c Mystery/Drama   ★★½
Alliance/Communication Corp./Ego Films/Telefilm   R/18
Canada/Ontario Film Development Corp. (Canada)

Bruce Greenwood *(Francis)*, Mia Kirshner *(Christina)*, Don McKellar *(Thomas)*, Arsinee Khanjian *(Zoe)*, Elias Koteas *(Eric)*, Sarah Polley *(Tracey)*, Victor Garber *(Harold)*, Calvin Green *(Customs Officer)*, David Hemblen *(Customs Inspector)*, Peter Krantz *(Man in Taxi)*

p, Atom Egoyan, Camelia Frieberg; d, Atom Egoyan; w, Atom Egoyan; ph, Paul Sarossy; ed, Susan Shipton; m, Mychael Danna; prod d, Linda Del Rosario, Richard Paris; fx, Michael Kavanagh; chor, Claudia Moore; cos, Linda Muir

EXOTICA is the Egoyan movie for people who feel faintly guilty about never having seen one: it may be Art, but at least it's set in a strip club, albeit the most portentous strip club in North America.

Pet shop owner Thomas (Don McKellar), arrives at the airport with a clutch of smuggled macaw eggs in tow. Sharing a cab with a stranger, he winds up at Exotica, an upscale girlie club with a wildly artificial jungle motif and a high-tech sound system that blasts disco versions of Urdu *ghazals*. Its star stripper is Christina (Mia Kirshner), who exploits her pedophilic allure by dressing in a schoolgirl's uniform. Two men are obsessed with her: longhaired DJ Eric (Elias Koteas) and tax auditor Francis (Bruce Greenwood). Zoe (Arsinee Khanjian), the hugely pregnant owner of Exotica, has befriended the troubled Christina; she's also paid Eric to father her child. All the principal characters are drawn together when Francis begins an audit of Thomas's pet store, and we finally learn what has drawn them into their tortured relationship.

EXOTICA sounds terrifically lurid and interesting, but like most Egoyan films, it's far more interesting in the telling than in the watching. It's easy to defend Egoyan as a serious and provocative filmmaker, since all his liabilities can be made to sound like the results of his rigorous intellectual defiance of mainstream norms. His characters are opaque because they're meant to defy bourgeois psychological conventions. His plots are unconvincing because they explore modes of storytelling that challenge received notions of good narrative structure. His movies are dull because he rejects the audience's Pavlovian desire for familiar scene structure and easy narrative resolution. Egoyan is a phenomenally successful filmmaker on his own terms. But he's still a pretentious bore.

EXTERMINATING ANGEL, THE
(EL ANGEL EXTERMINADOR)

1962 91m bw Comedy/Drama   ★★★★★
Uninci/S.A. Films 59   (Mexico)   /X

Silvia Pinal *(Letitia, the Valkyrie)*, Jacqueline Andere *(Senora Alicia Roc)*, Jose Baviera *(Leandro)*, Augusto Benedico *(Doctor)*, Antonio Bravo *(Russell)*, Xavier Masse *(Eduardo)*, Ofelia Montesco *(Beatriz)*, Nadia Haro Oliva *(Ana Maynar)*, Javier Loya *(Francisco Avila)*, Ofelia Guilmain *(Juana Avila)*

p, Gustavo Alatriste; d, Luis Bunuel; w, Luis Bunuel, Luis Alcoriza (based on the play *Los Naufragos de la Calle de la Providentia* by Jose Bergamin); ph, Gabriel Figueroa; ed, Carlos Savage; m, Alessandro Scarlatti, Pietro Domenico Paradisi; art d, Jesus Bracho; fx, Juan Munoz Ravelo; cos, Georgette Somohano

One of the greatest masterworks of a giant of cinema. A brilliantly pointed blitzkrieg on bourgeois values and organized religion from the master of iconoclastic assault, Luis Bunuel, this deceptively simple film works with consummate artistry and uncompromising irony.

The allegorical story tells of a group of upper-class dinner guests who, for no apparent reason, find themselves incapable of leaving the sitting room at the end of the party. Days and days pass, and their well-mannered facades are torn down by the animalistic qualities they harbor inside themselves. One guest (Bravo) dies and is irreverently stuffed into a cupboard; a pair of lovers (Masse and Montesco) commit suicide; a believer in witchcraft (Oliva) hallucinates and brings forth demons; an incestuous brother and sister (Loya and Guilmain) steal morphine from a cancer-ridden guest. Making mincemeat of a stray sheep at one point, they later contemplate cannibalism to stay alive. After memorable encounters with a bear and a child, they do escape, but Bunuel has similar fun in store at a cathedral.

The theme of entrapment in a hell of our own making—one fashioned largely of social conventions and traditions—is a familiar one in literature, but it has never been more successfully rendered in visual terms. Bunuel's subjective, surreal imagery recalls the outspoken savagery of L'AGE D'OR 30 years earlier. Like no other director, Bunuel has continually aimed at the faces of the bourgeois the swiftest of blows, and in this film he is in top form. Lacking the softness of his similar Oscar-winning THE DISCREET CHARM OF THE BOURGEOISIE, THE EXTERMINATING ANGEL brandishes a bitter hilarity almost unequalled in the history of cinema.

ALI, FEAR EATS THE SOUL
(ANGST ESSEN SEELE AUF)

1974 89m c Drama/Romance   ★★★★
Tango Film/Autorn   (West Germany)   /AA

Brigitte Mira *(Emmi)*, El Hedi Ben Salem *(Ali)*, Barbara Valentin *(Barbara)*, Irm Hermann *(Krista)*, Peter Gauhe *(Bruno)*, Rainer Werner Fassbinder *(Eugen)*, Karl Scheydt *(Albert)*, Elma Karlowa *(Mrs. Kargus)*, Anita Bucher *(Mrs. Ellis)*, Walter Sedlmayr *(Grocer)*; d, Rainer Werner Fassbinder; w, Rainer Werner Fassbinder; ph, Jurgen Jurges; ed, Thea Eymesz; prod d, Rainer Werner Fassbinder

ALI, FEAR EATS THE SOUL is one of Rainer Werner Fassbinder's finest films, a mordant satire that's also a touching romance and a powerful indictment of prejudice.

60-year-old German charwoman Emmi (Brigitte Mira) goes into a Munich bar frequented by Arab immigrants and dances with a 40-year-old Moroccan named Ali (El Hedi Ben Salem). Ali walks her home and spends the night at her apartment, then moves in with her, much to the chagrin of her neighbors and grown children. Emmi is shunned by her fellow cleaning-women and quarrels with her grocer (Walter Sedlmayr) after he refuses to serve Ali. Ali and Emmi decide to take a vacation, and when they return, suddenly everyone is nice to them. The problem: the lovers themselves begin to have their own reservations about the relationship.

Taking Douglas Sirk's classic 1955 melodrama ALL THAT HEAVEN ALLOWS as a starting point, Fassbinder expands on its theme of social prejudice by making his protagonists different races as well. In Fassbinder's hands, however, ALI, FEAR EATS THE SOUL is not simply an anti-racism polemic. The suffering that Emmi and Ali go through is symptomatic of the pain that all people inflict upon each other. From the first scene—a *tableau vivant* of the patrons in the Arab bar contemptuously staring at Emmi—the characters are all depicted as alienated outsiders, trapped in their own private hells.

Influenced by Sirk's cinematic style, Fassbinder uses saturated colors to create split compositions, and constantly shoots through doorways, windows, and staircases to create frames-within-frames which isolate his characters. Despite Fassbinder's emotional detachment, the film contains a large degree of deadpan humor and some incredibly poignant moments, including the bittersweet finale.

FABULOUS BAKER BOYS, THE

1989	114m	c	Comedy/Drama	★★½
Gladden/Mirage	(U.S.)			R/15

Jeff Bridges *(Jack Baker)*, Beau Bridges *(Frank Baker)*, Michelle Pfeiffer *(Susie Diamond)*, Ellie Raab *(Nina)*, Xander Berkeley *(Lloyd)*, Dakin Matthews *(Charlie)*, Ken Lerner *(Ray)*, Albert Hall *(Henry)*, Terri Treas *(Girl in Bed)*, Gregory Itzin *(Vince Nancy)*

p, Paula Weinstein, Mark Rosenberg, William Finnegan; d, Steve Kloves; w, Steve Kloves; ph, Michael Ballhaus; ed, William Steinkamp; m, Dave Grusin; prod d, Jeffrey Townsend; chor, Peggy Holmes; cos, Lisa Jensen

AAN Best Actress: Michelle Pfeiffer; *AAN Best Cinematography:* Michael Ballhaus; *AAN Best Editing:* William Steinkamp; *AAN Best Score:* David Grusin

Though full of atmosphere, mood, and attitude, THE FABULOUS BAKER BOYS is all dressed up with no place to go. Jeff and Beau Bridges play brothers Jack and Frank Baker, a musical duo whose act consists of dueling piano arrangements of lounge songs. Frank decides to bring in a female singer, and the nod finally goes to Susie Diamond (Michelle Pfeiffer). Her professional experience has been limited to an extended engagement as an escort service, but to say she knows how to sell a song is an understatement. Tensions rise when womanizing Jack embarks on a professionally dangerous liaison with Susie.

Early in the film, THE FABULOUS BAKER BOYS crackles with smart talk and smooth moves from writer-director Steve Kloves (who makes his directing debut here and who wrote the equally off-center RACING WITH THE MOON) and later in the film, Pfeiffer continues to captivate. When it comes to plot and characters, however, THE FABULOUS BAKER BOYS is purely superficial and the three principals become less interesting as the action grinds on. Though the Bridges boys give typically solid performances, it's Pfeiffer who deserves the most credit. Her Susie is an original—smart, hard-headed, and unsentimental. Pfeiffer's sultry rendition of "Makin' Whoopee" is one of the film's highlights. Photographed by the gifted Michael Ballhaus, THE FABULOUS BAKER BOYS unfortunately fails to base its evocative style on real substance, and thus fails to emerge from the run of the mill.

FACE IN THE CROWD, A

1957	125m	bw	Drama	★★★★
Warner Bros.	(U.S.)			/A

Andy Griffith *(Lonesome Rhodes)*, Patricia Neal *(Marcia Jeffries)*, Anthony Franciosa *(Joey Kiely)*, Walter Matthau *(Mel Miller)*, Lee Remick *(Betty Lou Fleckum)*, Percy Waram *(Colonel Hollister)*, Rod Brasfield *(Beanie)*, Charles Irving *(Mr. Luffler)*, Howard Smith *(J.B. Jeffries)*, Paul McGrath *(Macey)*

p, Elia Kazan; d, Elia Kazan; w, Budd Schulberg (based on his short story "The Arkansas Traveler"); ph, Harry Stradling, Gayne Rescher; m, Tom Glazer; cos, Anna Hill Johnstone

Andy Griffith made an unforgettable screen debut in this film as Lonesome Rhodes, a cracker-barrel philosopher discovered by Marcia Jeffries (Neal), who puts him on her local television station in Arkansas. His down-home wit and backwater jokes soon gain a wide audience, after which one of the state's largest stations picks up his show, followed by a network, until his face is seen throughout the land and his homespun wisdom becomes the creed of large numbers of Americans. But Jeffries and her assistant, Mel Miller (Matthau), soon realize that good old "Lonesome Rhodes" is not the kindly rural savant he appears to be.

Director Elia Kazan and writer Budd Schulberg, who collaborated so effectively in ON THE WATERFRONT, again proved their ability to produce a raw, penetrating, and terrifying portrait of humanity in A FACE IN THE CROWD. Griffith, who had made a name for himself on Broadway with *No Time for Sergeants*, skyrocketed to fame after his performance as the vicious but fascinating Lonesome Rhodes—capturing the character so well it would take him some time to live the role down. Neal is superb as the tough but vulnerable television producer snared by the hillbilly philosopher, and Matthau plays his cynical newsman to the hilt.

FACE/OFF

1997	115m	c	Action/Thriller	★★★½
Douglas/Reuther Productions/Constellation Films/WCG Entertainment/Permut Presentations	(U.S.)			R/

John Travolta *(Sean Archer)*, Nicolas Cage *(Castor Troy)*, Joan Allen *(Eve Archer)*, Alessandro Nivola *(Pollux Troy)*, Gina Gershon *(Sasha Hassler)*, Dominique Swain *(Jamie Archer)*, Nick Cassavetes *(Dietrich Hassler)*, Harve Presnell *(Victor Lazzaro)*, Colm Feore *(Dr. Malcom Walsh)*, John Carroll Lynch *(Prison Guard Walton)*

p, David Permut, Barrie M. Osborne, Terence Chang, Christopher Godsick; d, John Woo; w, Mike Werb, Michael Colleary; ph, Oliver Wood; ed, Christian Wagner, Steven Kemper; m, John Powell; prod d, Neil Spisak; art d, Steve Arnold; fx, Lawrence Cavanaugh; cos, Ellen Mirojnik

Hong Kong action auteur John Woo finally finds the balance between the excesses of his Hong Kong movie making background and the demands of US mainstream filmmaking in this preposterous, high-octane tale of an FBI agent and a psychotic terrorist who quite literally swap faces.

Sean Archer (John Travolta) is a driven man: six years ago, lethal nut job Castor Troy (Nicolas Cage) tried to assassinate him, and wound up killing Archer's five-year-old son instead. When Archer finally brings in Castor and his even loonier brother, Pollux (Alessandro Nivola), it looks as though he can finally put it all behind him and start patching up his relationship with long-suffering wife Eve (Joan Allen) and rebellious daughter Jamie (Dominique Swaim). The curve ball: the Troys have planted a nerve gas bomb somewhere in LA. Castor is in an apparently irreversible coma, and Pollux—now an inmate in a hellish, high tech prison—won't talk. Now, if he thought he were talking to his *brother*... A bit of EYES WITHOUT A FACE-style plastic surgery later, Archer is shipped off to jail to get the information and save the day. But wouldn't you just know that there's wicked life in Castor yet, and that this whole trading places thing is going to take a turn for the very, very nasty?

Unlike Woo's successful but rather disappointingly conventional BROKEN ARROW, this brutal, stunningly choreographed spectacle weaves together lyrical beauty, casual blasphemy, sadistic cruelty, and grotesque sentimentality with breathtakingly smooth assurance. Which is to say, it's everything fans love in Woo's Hong Kong films. Come to think of it, he lifts more than a little from THE KILLER and skillfully tailors it for US cast and locales. A treat for Woo aficionados, and a great introduction to Hong Kong-style action for others.

FACE TO FACE
(ANSIKTE MOT ANSIKTE)
1976 136m c Drama ★★★★
DEG (Sweden) R/X

Liv Ullmann *(Dr. Jenny Isaksson)*, Erland Josephson *(Dr. Tomas Jacobi)*, Gunnar Bjornstrand *(Grandpa)*, Aino Taube *(Grandma)*, Kari Sylwan *(Maria)*, Siv Ruud *(Mrs. Elizabeth Wankel)*, Sven Lindberg *(Dr. Erik Isaksson)*, Tore Segelcke *(The Lady)*, Ulf Johansson *(Dr. Helmuth Wankel)*, Kristina Adolphsson *(Veronica)*

p, Ingmar Bergman; d, Ingmar Bergman; w, Ingmar Bergman; ph, Sven Nykvist; ed, Siv Lundgren; m, Wolfgang Amadeus Mozart; prod d, Anne Hagegard

AAN Best Actress: Liv Ullmann; *AAN Best Director:* Ingmar Bergman

Bergman originally filmed FACE TO FACE for Swedish television as a four-part series. While appropriate for the more liberal television codes of Sweden, it was unlikely fare for US consumption. He edited it down to a length that would permit distribution as a feature film. Despite the snipping, it remains a potent representative of Bergman's psychodrama cycle that began with CRIES AND WHISPERS and ended with AUTUMN SONATA.

The film depicts the slow and painful nervous breakdown of a successful psychiatrist. Ullmann is Dr. Jenny Isaksson, a psychiatrist vacationing at her grandparents' gloomy home in the country—alone because her husband, Dr. Erik Isaksson (Lindberg)—also a shrink—is away. She soon begins hallucinating about an old woman. This leads to depression and a feeling of helplessness as she is overwhelmed by memories of the past.

FACE TO FACE is an extremely intense experience from start to finish, due in large part to Ullmann's performance as she powerfully expresses a range of emotions seldom seen in American films. Bergman's frequent collaborator, cinematographer Sven Nykvist, enhances the film's harrowing mood with his stark imagery.

FACES
1968 130m bw Drama ★★★★
Continental Distributing (U.S.) /X

John Marley *(Richard Forst)*, Gena Rowlands *(Jeannie Rapp)*, Lynn Carlin *(Maria Forst)*, Fred Draper *(Freddie)*, Seymour Cassel *(Chet)*, Val Avery *(McCarthy)*, Dorothy Gulliver *(Florence)*, Joanne Moore Jordan *(Louise)*, Darlene Conley *(Billy Mae)*, Gene Darfler *(Jackson)*

p, Maurice McEndree; d, John Cassavetes; w, John Cassavetes; ph, Al Ruban; ed, Maurice McEndree, Al Ruban, John Cassavetes; m, Jack Ackerman; art d, Phedon Papamichael

AAN Best Supporting Actor: Seymour Cassel; *AAN Best Supporting Actress:* Lynn Carlin; *AAN Best Original Screenplay:* John Cassavetes

Like SHADOWS before it, FACES was hailed at the time as a great accomplishment of American independent cinema. John Cassavetes, his friends, and family took several years to shoot and edit the film on very grainy 16mm black-and-white stock. As would become usual for Cassavetes, it's about marriages and the war between men and women. He would do better in the 1970s with films like HUSBANDS, made with a little more money, but FACES remains a landmark cultural document of the late 60s.

FACES is a rudimentary study of a husband and wife, disenchanted after 14 years of marriage, who drift apart. Richard Forst (Marley), the husband, spends an evening with a prostitute, Jennie Rapp (Rowlands), while his wife, Maria (Carlin), and her girlfriends go out to a disco looking for a little excitement. She finds it in the form of Chet (Cassel), a handsome hippie whom she takes home to bed. The illusions of the night before look very different the next morning for both husband and wife.

The original cut ran nearly six hours, making it an inevitable victim of severe editing. (The original version exists only in the form of a published screenplay.) In a sense, FACES can be seen as a reaction to Cassavetes's previous directorial outing, A CHILD IS WAITING, which he disowned after it was recut by producer Stanley Kramer. Cassavetes became wary of the major companies and turned independent. Upon its release, FACES was hailed by most critics but tepidly

received by the moviegoers. Though it is sometimes a tedious viewing experience, its improvisational and documentary techniques are rewarding.

FAHRENHEIT 451
1966 112m c Science Fiction ★★★★
Vineyard/Rank/Anglo-Amalgamated (U.K.) /A

Oskar Werner *(Montag)*, Julie Christie *(Linda/Clarisse)*, Cyril Cusack *(Captain)*, Anton Diffring *(Fabian)*, Jeremy Spenser *(Man with Apple)*, Bee Duffell *(Book Woman)*, Gillian Lewis *(TV Announcer)*, Ann Bell *(Doris)*, Caroline Hunt *(Helen)*, Anna Palk *(Jackie)*

p, Lewis Allen; d, Francois Truffaut; w, Francois Truffaut, Jean-Louis Richard, David Rudkin, Helen Scott (based on the novel by Ray Bradbury); ph, Nicolas Roeg; ed, Thom Noble; m, Bernard Herrmann; prod d, Tony Walton; art d, Syd Cain; fx, Charles Staffel, Bowie Films; cos, Tony Walton

Throughout much of his brilliant career, Francois Truffaut was criticized for not making explicitly political films. However, he did tackle political themes in two films: FAHRENHEIT 451, an indictment of totalitarianism and book-burning, and THE LAST METRO, which dealt with the German occupation of France. These films address the suppression of two media of deep personal significance for Truffaut—literature and the theater, respectively. The former is the most restrained and elegaic of science fiction films, full of poignant moments: a paean to the physical importance of books.

FAHRENHEIT 451 (the title refers to the temperature at which paper burns) is set sometime in the future and follows Montag (Oskar Werner), a devoted and obedient "fireman" who excels in ferreting out books in the most obscure hiding places. One day, after watching a woman sacrifice her life for her forbidden library, he decides to keep a volume for himself, curious to learn why these tomes are deemed so threatening. Soon he must choose between his life as a civil servant—in which he follows orders and lives with a listless, television-addicted wife, Linda (Julie Christie)—and his desire to live as a free thinking man in a free society, inspired by subversive schoolteacher Clarisse (Christie again).

Severely underrated and misunderstood by critics who wanted Truffaut to continue making films like his early French New Wave classics THE 400 BLOWS and JULES AND JIM, FAHRENHEIT 451 is a marvelously courageous personal statement that becomes more fascinating with time. This was Truffaut's first color film. The cool crisp cinematography is provided by future director Nicolas Roeg. The great Bernard Herrmann supplied the memorable score.

FAIL SAFE
1964 111m bw Drama/War ★★★½
Columbia (U.S.) /PG

Dan O'Herlihy *(Gen. Black)*, Walter Matthau *(Groeteschele)*, Frank Overton *(Gen. Bogan)*, Edward Binns *(Col. Grady)*, Fritz Weaver *(Col. Cascio)*, Henry Fonda *(The President)*, Larry Hagman *(Buck)*, William Hansen *(Secretary Swenson)*, Russell Hardie *(Gen. Stark)*, Russell Collins *(Knapp)*

p, Max E. Youngstein; d, Sidney Lumet; w, Walter Bernstein (based on the novel by Eugene Burdick and Harvey Wheeler); ph, Gerald Hirschfeld; ed, Ralph Rosenblum; art d, Albert Brenner; fx, Storyboard, Inc.; cos, Anna Hill Johnstone

Released only seven months after DR. STRANGELOVE by the very same studio, the virtually identical, albeit totally serious, FAIL SAFE was a relative failure at the box office. Kubrick went to Columbia's top brass and threatened a plagiarism lawsuit. (His film was based on Peter George's almost unknown novel *Red Alert*.) Since Columbia was distributing both DR. STRANGELOVE and FAIL SAFE, it appeased Kubrick by releasing his film first, and, of course, that cult classic captured the lion's share of viewers, leaving FAIL SAFE to appear as a serious, comparatively dreary rehash.

In it, a squadron of SAC bombers flies off to drop nuclear bombs on Moscow after a faulty transmission of orders that cannot be reversed through normal channels. The US military tries everything to stop them, but the bombers fly beyond "fail safe" and the president (Henry Fonda) is alerted. He goes to his bomb-proof bunker deep beneath the White

House, where, in a simple, sterile room, he tries to inform Soviet leaders of the terrible blunder. Meanwhile, his cabinet and advisers meet in the War Room, keeping him informed of fast-developing events and channeling messages from the Omaha command center. After several attempts to recall or shoot down the planes, it becomes obvious that one of the bombers will deliver its load on Moscow. In a desperate effort to prevent a retaliatory attack by the Soviets that would result in all-out nuclear war, the president must resort to a horrifying compromise.

Grim, bleak and highly claustrophobic, FAIL SAFE is very much like director Sidney Lumet's previous film, 12 ANGRY MEN, in that it concentrates almost exclusively on the actors' performances and is shot mainly in tight close-ups. While this is a wonderful showcase for some fine acting—notably by Fonda—it is not great filmmaking, and one may be left wishing for the biting, off-the-wall satire of DR. STRANGELOVE.

FALCON AND THE SNOWMAN, THE

1985   131m   c   Spy   ★★★
Orion   (U.S.)   R/15

Timothy Hutton (Christopher Boyce), Sean Penn (Daulton Lee), Pat Hingle (Mr. Boyce), Richard Dysart (Dr. Lee), Lori Singer (Lana), David Suchet (Alex), Dorian Harewood (Gene), Priscilla Pointer (Mrs. Lee), Nicholas Pryor (Eddie), Sam Ingraffia (Kenny Kahn)

p, Gabriel Katzka, John Schlesinger; d, John Schlesinger; w, Steve Zaillian (based on the book The Falcon and the Snowman by Robert Lindsey); ph, Allen Daviau; ed, Richard Marden; m, Pat Metheny, Lyle Mays; prod d, James D. Bissell; cos, Albert Wolsky

Based on fact, this absorbing film tells the story of Christopher Boyce and Daulton Lee, two young upper-middle-class southern Californians who were convicted of selling secrets to the Soviet Union in 1977.

Boyce (Timothy Hutton), the more introspective of the pair and the son of a former FBI man (Pat Hingle), works for a company that does top-secret work for the CIA. Already disillusioned by the American experience in Vietnam, the idealistic Hutton completely loses faith in his government when he learns the CIA has been meddling in the internal affairs of Australia, and decides to become a traitor. He enlists the help of his directionless friend Lee (Sean Penn), who has been in and out of trouble with the law, but who continues using and dealing drugs. The security at Hutton's company is astonishingly lax, and he easily steals sensitive documents, which Penn delivers to the Soviet Embassy in Mexico City.

Directed by John Schlesinger, THE FALCON AND THE SNOWMAN is both a spy drama and an intriguing character study. Penn invests his "Snowman" with fascinating eccentricity and is the more interesting of the pair, though Hutton delivers an estimable performance as the sullen young falconer.

FALLEN ANGEL

1945   98m   bw   Mystery   ★★★½
Fox   (U.S.)   /15

Alice Faye (June Mills), Dana Andrews (Eric Stanton), Linda Darnell (Stella), Charles Bickford (Mark Judd), Anne Revere (Clara Mills), Bruce Cabot (Dave Atkins), John Carradine (Prof. Madley), Percy Kilbride (Pop), Olin Howlin (Joe Ellis), Hal Taliaferro (Johnson)

p, Otto Preminger; d, Otto Preminger; w, Harry Kleiner (based on the novel by Marty Holland); ph, Joseph La Shelle; ed, Harry Reynolds; m, David Raksin; art d, Lyle Wheeler, Leland Fuller; fx, Fred Sersen; cos, Bonnie Cashin

Eric Stanton, a press agent down on his luck, drifts into a small coastal town in California and meets June Mills (Faye), a reclusive rich woman, and a sultry waitress named Stella (Darnell). In love with Stella but broke, Eric decides to marry June, steal her fortune, divorce her, and wed Stella. However Stella turns up murdered and suspicion falls on Eric. In order to clear his name, Eric launches his own investigation to find the real killer.

Director Preminger hoped to have another LAURA with this film, but it fell short due to some loose ends in the script and disjointed points of view as the director shifts the focus of the story erratically from one character to another, a blatant red herring to mislead the viewer from guessing the killer's identity. The overall mood, lighting, and pace of the film, nevertheless, are top, hardboiled film noir.

Faye, who had been a Fox superstar for many years, had been promised a meaty and significant part; she had rejected almost three dozen scripts before accepting the lead in FALLEN ANGEL but her role was slowly chiseled away by Preminger, who played up Darnell during the production, giving her more and more scenes. Faye felt that some of her best scenes had been chopped and considered herself betrayed. She retired on the spot, so bitter that it would be 16 years before she returned to the screen.

FALLEN IDOL, THE

1948   94m   bw   Thriller   ★★★★
London Films   (U.K.)   /A

Ralph Richardson (Baines), Michele Morgan (Julie), Bobby Henrey (Felipe), Sonia Dresdel (Mrs. Baines), Denis O'Dea (Inspector Crowe), Walter Fitzgerald (Dr. Fenton), Karel Stepanek (1st Secretary), Joan Young (Mrs. Barrow), Dandy Nichols (Mrs. Patterson), Bernard Lee (Detective Hart)

p, David O. Selznick, Carol Reed; d, Carol Reed; w, Graham Greene, Lesley Storm, William Templeton (based on the short story "The Basement Room" by Greene); ph, Georges Perinal; ed, Oswald Hafenrichter; m, William Alwyn; prod d, Vincent Korda, James Sawyer, John Hawkesworth; fx, W. Percy Day; cos, Ivy Baker

AAN Best Director: Carol Reed; AAN Best Original Screenplay: Graham Greene

Told from a child's point of view, THE FALLEN IDOL is a subdued thriller set in a foreign embassy in London. The ambassador departs and leaves his precocious, imaginative son, Felipe (Henrey), with the butler, Baines (Richardson), and Baines's wife (Dresdel). The boy idolizes the kindly, considerate Baines but dislikes the butler's shrewish, vicious wife. Baines and embassy typist Julie (Morgan) have been having an affair and Felipe overhears them agreeing to end the relationship. This information is later wheedled out of Felipe by Mrs. Baines, who then has a violent argument with her husband. In her jealous rage, Mrs. Baines accidentally falls down a flight of stairs to her death. Her demise is heard but not wholly witnessed by the boy. When police begin a routine investigation, Felipe fears that his idol will be arrested.

Director Carol Reed skillfully blends elegant camera movement, expressive angles, stylized lighting, and sterling performances into a fascinating and suspenseful motion picture. Richardson is superb as the innocent butler. His tender treatment of the boy, his cultured bearing, and his gentlemanly demeanor convey a supreme nobility that belies his working-class position. Henrey is even more exciting in his wonderful portrayal of a jittery and intelligent child. Reed's direction of Henrey gave him a reputation as a great director of children, which was further confirmed by the engaging performances he drew from children in A KID FOR TWO FARTHINGS and OLIVER! THE FALLEN IDOL received a British Best Film award, and Reed was honored as Best Director by the New York Film Critics.

FALLING DOWN

1993   115m   c   Drama/Comedy   ★★★
Arnold Kopelson Productions   (U.S.)   R/18

Michael Douglas (D-Fens), Robert Duvall (Det. Martin Prendergast), Barbara Hershey (Beth), Rachel Ticotin (Sandra), Tuesday Weld (Mrs. Prendergast), Frederic Forrest (Surplus Store Owner), Joey Hope Singer (Adele (Beth's Child)), Lois Smith (D-Fens' Mother), Ebbe Roe Smith (Guy on Freeway), Michael Paul Chan (Mr. Lee)

p, Arnold Kopelson, Timothy Harris, Herschel Weingrod; d, Joel Schumacher; w, Ebbe Roe Smith; ph, Andrzej Bartkowiak; ed, Paul Hirsch; prod d, Barbara Ling; art d, Larry Fulton; fx, Bob Stoker, Matt Sweeney, James Schwalm, Lucinda Strub; cos, Marlene Stewart

FALLING DOWN opens with a scene of a nightmarish L.A. traffic jam in which drivers are driven to distraction by boredom, frustration, noise and heat. If you manage to sit through this film, you will know just how they feel.

Stuck in that jam is a disgruntled defense worker (Michael Douglas) suffering the combined pressures of unemployment, divorce, and a haircut someone must have given him as an April Fool's joke. As the tension is ham-fistedly turned up, it becomes clear that something is very wrong. A bead of sweat runs down Douglas's face; a fly lands on his neck; perhaps, off-camera, someone makes a joke about his buttock-baring scene in BASIC INSTINCT.

That does it! Douglas is off, abandoning his car for a cross-town hike across L.A.'s seediest neighborhoods, en route to a showdown with his ex-wife (Barbara Hershey) and child. Along the way, he has a series of encounters that tread an uncomfortable line between black comedy and clumsy social criticism. He trashes a Korean grocery store because the prices are too high; provokes a drive-by gang shooting in which several innocent people die; and laughs as he gives a rich white golfer a fatal heart attack.

These adventures would be offensive if you could take them seriously, so it's probably good that you can't. Despite a nicely understated performance from Robert Duvall as a cop on Douglas's trail, FALLING DOWN fails to convince on any level.

FAME

1980   134m   c   Musical   ★★★
MGM   (U.S.)   PG/15

Ed Barth (Angelo), Irene Cara (Coco), Lee Curreri (Bruno), Laura Dean (Lisa), Antonia Franceschi (Hilary), Boyd Gaines (Michael), Albert Hague (Shorofsky), Tresa Hughes (Mrs. Finsecker), Steve Inwood (Francois Lafete), Paul McCrane (Montgomery)

p, David DeSilva, Alan Marshall; d, Alan Parker; w, Christopher Gore; ph, Michael Seresin; ed, Gerry Hambling; m, Michael Gore; prod d, Geoffrey Kirkland; art d, Ed Wittstein; chor, Louis Falco; cos, Kristi Zea

AAN Best Original Screenplay: Christopher Gore; AAN Best Editing: Gerry Hambling; AA Best Score: Michael Gore; AA Best Song: Michael Gore (Music), Dean Pitchford (Lyrics); AAN Best Song: Michael Gore (Music), Lesley Gore (Lyrics); AAN Best Sound: Michael J. Kohut, Aaron Rochin, Jay M. Harding, Chris Newman

This is a wonderfully simple idea that succeeds very well indeed: take a bunch of kids from New York's High School of Performing Arts and let them strut their stuff. A lot of music, a few desultory plotlines, and you've got the contemporary version of the Mickey Rooney/Judy Garland "Hey kids, let's put on a show!" vehicle. FAME shows us how much life there still is in moribund genres like the musical.

It focuses on five episodes—set during auditions and successive academic years through to graduation—featuring various struggling young hopefuls, among them Coco (Irene Cara), a gifted, determined singer; Montgomery (Paul McCrane), a sensitive, gay actor; Leroy (Gene Anthony Ray), a talented, illiterate dancer; Bruno (Lee Curreri), a synthesizer player; and Ralph (Barry Miller), a Puerto Rican who is ashamed of his background. However, Parker's interest lies mainly in lavish production numbers, rather than in more intimate subtleties. (The real High School of the Performing Arts refused to let Parker film inside the building; perhaps they too disapproved of his sensationalism.)

The subject's treatment here was best suited for the television show it launched, but FAME's score and title song did win Academy Awards. Cara, who shines as Coco, was the only one of the aforementioned young leads to actually achieve fame (McCrane and Miller are respected stage, film and TV actors), racking up a couple of hit singles.

FAMILY, THE
(LA FAMIGLIA)

1987   127m   c   Comedy   ★★★½
Maasfilm/Cinecitta/RAI-TV/Ariane   (Italy/France)

Vittorio Gassman (Carlo), Fanny Ardant (Adriana), Stefania Sandrelli (Beatrice), Andrea Occhipinti (Young Carlo), Jo Ciampa (Young Adriana), Alberto Gimignani, Massimo Dapporto, Carlo Dapporto, Cecilia Dazzi, Ottavia Piccolo

p, Franco Committeri; d, Ettore Scola; w, Ruggero Maccari, Furio Scarpelli, Ettore Scola; ph, Ricardo Aronovich; ed, Ettore Scola; m, Armando Trovajoli; art d, Luciano Ricceri

AAN Best Foreign Language Film

After venturing into pedestrian comedy in his previous film, MACARONI, director Ettore Scola returned to the single set limitations of his LE BAL for this pleasant drama which covers 80 years in the life of one Italian family. The film opens in 1906 as the clan gathers in a large Rome apartment for a group photograph. A narrator, Carlo (Vittorio Gassman), points himself out in the picture—an infant who has just been baptized. Carlo narrates the entire film as time passes, Scola never showing the characters outside of their apartment. In addition to Carlo, the family includes his brother, his parents, the maid, his three matronly aunts, his wife, Beatrice (Stefania Sandrelli), and Beatrice's older and more worldly sister, Adriana (Fanny Ardant), whom Carlo really loves.

Like many of the films of Ingmar Bergman or Woody Allen, THE FAMILY goes to great lengths to recreate a family portrait album. Scola gives his audience a collection of characters, each with qualities and idiosyncracies that change and develop over the course of time. As a unifying stylistic thread, Scola uses a recurring dolly shot through the apartment's empty hall that symbolizes the passing of time. Filled with humor, sadness, and anger, the film also manages to encompass nearly all the major political and social events of 20th-century Italy.

FAMILY PLOT

1976   120m   c   Thriller/Comedy   ★★★½
Universal   (U.S.)   PG

Karen Black (Fran), Bruce Dern (Lumley), Barbara Harris (Blanche), William Devane (Adamson), Ed Lauter (Maloney), Cathleen Nesbitt (Julia Rainbird), Katherine Helmond (Mrs. Maloney), Warren J. Kemmerling (Grandison), Edith Atwater (Mrs. Clay), William Prince (Bishop)

p, Alfred Hitchcock; d, Alfred Hitchcock; w, Ernest Lehman (from the novel The Rainbird Pattern by Victor Canning); ph, Leonard South; ed, J. Terry Williams; m, John Williams; art d, Henry Bumstead; fx, Frank Brendel, Albert Whitlock; cos, Edith Head

With two parallel plots running throughout, Alfred Hitchcock's final film is a brilliantly constructed mystery-thriller. Hired by elderly Miss Rainbird (Nesbitt) to locate a long-lost heir, phoney medium Blanche Tyler (Harris) and her cabbie boy friend George Lumley (Dern)—amiable frauds— begin their search with very few clues. Meanwhile another more sinister couple, jeweler Arthur Adamson (Devane) and his girlfriend Fran (Black) are engineering a kidnapping scheme in which the ransom is to be paid in valuable diamonds. The paths of all of these characters and their respective "plots" eventually cross, in a comical directorial move, at a cemetery. Just when the mystery ends, however, the thrills begin—the most harrowing of which takes place along a curving mountainside road.

The film is a dense but extremely entertaining collection of symmetric patterns, doubles, and rhymes. The performances are first-rate (finally free of the casting constraints, Hitchcock displayed—in 1972's FRENZY as well—a deliciously offbeat taste in performers) and the screenplay by Ernest Lehman (NORTH BY NORTHWEST) is a witty model of construction. The humor is more obvious and subversive than any of Hitchcock's films since THE TROUBLE WITH HARRY. Hitch's final, tongue-in-cheek wink at his audience was one of his most memorable cameos—a broad shadow obscured behind a glass door on which may be read "Registrar of Births and Deaths." Based on a British novel by Victor Canning, the film was scripted under the title "One Plus One Equals One," and went into production as "Deceit," before a studio worker hit on the final title.

FAN, THE

1996   120m   c   Thriller   ★★
Wendy Finerman Productions/Scott Free Productions   R/15
/Mandalay Entertainment/TriStar   (U.S.)

Robert De Niro *(Gil Renard)*, Wesley Snipes *(Bobby Rayburn)*, Ellen Barkin *(Jewel Stern)*, John Leguizamo *(Manny)*, Benicio Del Toro *(Juan Primo)*, Patti D'Arbanville *(Ellen Renard)*, Chris Mulkey *(Tim)*, Andrew J. Ferchland *(Richie Renard)*, Brandon Hammond *(Sean Rayburn)*, Charles Hallahan *(Coop)*

p, Wendy Finerman; d, Tony Scott; w, Phoef Sutton (based on the novel by Peter Abrahams); ph, Dariusz Wolski; ed, Christian Wagner, Claire Simpson; m, Hans Zimmer; prod d, Ida Random; art d, Mayne Berke; fx, Joe Ramsey; cos, Rita Ryack, Daniel Orlandi

This slick, stylish tale of a baseball fan's obsession with a star player promises to be a film noir thriller for the '90s, but strikes out with bases loaded

Gil Renard (Robert De Niro) is "the fan," a wild supporter of celebrated centerfielder Bobby Rayburn (Wesley Snipes). Rayburn seems to have it all: he's a four-time League RBI player with a .310 lifetime batting average and a $40 million annual paycheck. Renard excitedly greets his hero's arrival in San Francisco on a radio call-in show hosted by Jewel Stern (Ellen Barkin). When Rayburn is injured, his rival, Juan Primo (Benicio Del Toro), becomes the new golden boy, a development that does sit well with Rayburn's number one fan. The increasingly deranged Renard kills Primo, enabling Rayburn to reclaim his former star status. When Renard finally meets his hero, he's disappointed with Rayburn's ingratitude. Seeking revenge, Renard kidnaps and threatens to kill Rayburn's son (Brandon Hammond)—unless he hits a home run during the next game.

Director Tony Scott takes Phoef Sutton's screenplay (based on Peter Abrahams's novel) all too seriously. Scott's penchant for rain and smoke effects gives THE FAN more atmosphere than thrills, and the frequent use of slow motion and close-ups weighs down what could have been a tense, exciting movie. A series of loud rock songs and several continuity errors also are distracting. As usual, De Niro makes his psychotic case study believable, but it's an act we've seen before—and better. The other performers are well cast but not well used, including John Leguizamo as Rayburn's fast-talking agent.

FANNY

1932   125m   bw   Drama   ★★★½
Pagnol   (France)

Raimu *(Cesar Olivier)*, Orane Demazis *(Fanny)*, Pierre Fresnay *(Marius)*, Fernand Charpin *(Honore Panisse)*, Alida Rouffe *(Honorine Cabanis)*, Robert Vattier *(M. Brun)*, Auguste Mouries *(Felix Escartefigue)*, Milly Mathis *(Aunt Claudine Foulon)*, Maupi *(Chauffeur)*, Edouard Delmont *(Dr. Felicien Venelle)*

p, Marcel Pagnol; d, Marc Allegret; w, Marcel Pagnol (based on his play); ph, Nicolas Toporkoff, Andre Dantan, Roger Hubert, Georges Benoit, Coutelain; ed, Raymond Lamy; m, Vincent Scotto

The second installment of Marcel Pagnol's "Marseilles Trilogy" picks up just a short while after the end of MARIUS. After Marius (Pierre Fresnay) has gone to sea, it is learned that the girl he loves, Fanny (Orane Demazis), is pregnant. Because she has her reputation to think of, Fanny is persuaded by her family to marry the older, widowed sailmaker Panisse (Fernand Charpin), despite the fact that she is still deeply in love with Marius. After a year at sea, Marius returns and tries to convince the woman he loves to leave Marseilles with him. However, she must consider the consequences and the feelings of Panisse, who has grown to love not only Fanny but the child as well.

Pagnol's warm, touching tale has been a success wherever it has played, attesting to the story's universal truthfulness. Written and produced by Pagnol and starring his troupe of actors, FANNY was filmed under the direction of Marc Allegret. MARIUS was directed by Alexander Korda, and the concluding film CESAR was directed by Pagnol himself.

FANNY AND ALEXANDER
(FANNY OCH ALEXANDER)

1982   188m   c   Drama   ★★★★½
Cinematograph/Swedish Film Institute/Swedish TV   R/15
One/Gaumont/Persona/Tobis   (France/West Germany/Sweden)

Gunn Wallgren *(Helena Ekdahl)*, Boerje Ahlstedt *(Prof. Carl Ekdahl)*, Christina Schollin *(Lydia Ekdahl)*, Allan Edwall *(Oscar Ekdahl)*, Ewa Froeling *(Emilie Ekdahl)*, Pernilla Allwin *(Fanny Ekdahl)*, Bertil Guve *(Alexander Ekdahl)*, Jarl Kulle *(Gustav-Adolph Ekdahl)*, Mona Malm *(Alma Ekdahl)*, Pernilla Wallgren *(Maj)*

d, Ingmar Bergman; w, Ingmar Bergman; ph, Sven Nykvist; ed, Sylvia Ingemarsson; m, Daniel Bell, Benjamin Britten, Frans Helmerson, Robert Schumson, Marianne Jacobs; art d, Anna Asp, Susanne Lingheim; cos, Marik Vos

Steering away from the pain, neuroses, and heavy metaphysical questions showcased in his earlier work, Ingmar Bergman created this film based on childhood memories of the turn of the century.

FANNY AND ALEXANDER begins with the Ekdahl family's Christmas celebration, their large home serving as the meeting place for a merry celebration by family members and servants who dance about heedless of social constraints. Late that night, ten-year-old Alexander (Bertil Guve) is tucked in by the buxom maid, who apologizes for being unable to spend the night with him because she has other obligations—namely bedding down with his kindly Uncle Carl (Boerje Ahlstedt), a married man with children of his own, whose wise wife graciously tolerates his infidelities. Alexander's charmed life is suddenly shattered when his actor-manager father suffers a heart attack and dies, leaving the widow Ekdahl (Ewa Froeling) to be calmed by an understanding bishop (Jan Malmsjoe) whom she eventually marries. She takes her two children, Fanny (Pernilla Allwin) and Alexander, away from their warm family into the cold, strict world of the clergyman.

Not only does Bergman manage in FANNY AND ALEXANDER to capture the flavor and atmosphere of a Swedish town circa 1907, he also expertly reveals events as seen through the eyes of a child and, without any wordy dissertations on doctrines, makes a powerful statement against religious zealotry. The results are quite frightening and far superior to the lengthy gloom and doom that fill many earlier Bergman films. A magical movie, FANNY AND ALEXANDER is likely to be the achievement for which Bergman will be most remembered.

FANTASIA

1940   120m   c   Animated   ★★★★
Walt Disney Productions   (U.S.)   /U

Deems Taylor *(Himself)*, Leopold Stokowski *(Himself)*, The Philadelphia Symphony Orchestra

p, Walt Disney; d, Samuel Armstrong, James Algar, Bill Roberts, Paul Satterfield, Hamilton Luske, Jim Handley, Ford Beebe, Walt Disney, Norman Ferguson, Wilfred Jackson; w, Lee Blair, Elmer Plummer, Phil Dike, Sylvia Moberly-Holland, Norman Wright, Albert Heath, Bianca Majolie, Graham Keid, Paul Pearse, Carl Fallberg, Leo Thiele, Robert Sterner, John Fraser McLeish, Otto Englander, Webb Smith, Erdman Penner, Joseph Sabo, Bill Peet, George Stallings; m, Johann Sebastian Bach, Peter Ilich Tchaikovsky, Igor Stravinsky, Ludwig van Beethoven, Modest Mussorgsky, Franz Schubert

The most ambitious animated feature ever to come out of the Disney studios, FANTASIA integrates famous works of classical music with wildly uneven but extraordinarily imaginative visuals that run the gamut from dancing hippos to the purely abstract. It's like a feature-length compilation of elaborate Silly Symphonies. This impressive attempt to combine high art with mass culture was a financial debacle initially but in subsequent years it has become one of the studio's perennial cash cows.

Among the wonderfully kitschy combinations of sight and sound are J.S. Bach's "Toccata and Fugue in D Minor" (a rare exercise in abstraction for the Disney artists); Tchaikovsky's "Nutcracker Suite" (danced by fairies, mushrooms, flower petals, fish, thistles, and orchids); Stravinsky's "Rite of Spring" (illustrated as the genesis of the planet); Mussorgsky's "Night on Bald Mountain" (some key imagery is lifted from the opening scenes of F.W. Murnau's silent German Expressionist version of FAUST with Emil Jannings as Mephistopheles looming over a village; the fearsome "Black God" was pantomimed by Bela Lugosi as an animation guide for the Disney artists); and Schubert's "Ave Maria" (a subdued Impressionistic sequence of villagers walking through the woods to church).

Beethoven's "Pastoral Symphony" proved to be the most controversial segment, raising the hackles of music critics who didn't approve of the cartoon Bacchus, nymphs, and li'l' centaurs who accompanied it. (Reportedly, after screening the completed segment for the first time, a tearful Walt Disney declared "This will *make* Beethoven!" Stravinsky also cried after seeing the film, but for very different reasons.) The film's most famous segment, Paul Dukas's "Sorcerer's Apprentice," stars Mickey Mouse (voiced by Walt himself for the final time) as the ambitious assistant who gets in way over his head when he uses his boss's magic hat to put a broom to work doing his chores. Originally intended as a short, "The Sorcerer's Apprentice" brought together Walt Disney and famed conductor Leopold Stokowski but when the production ran over budget, Disney decided that the only way to recoup his investment would be to incorporate the segment into a feature.

The film began to appear in limited roadshow engagements in 1940, but due to wartime difficulties in getting the materials for the sound system that had to be installed in each theater, it was not until 1942 that it received general release. In the late 1960s FANTASIA re-emerged as a drug culture favorite and it continues to delight both children and adults today.

FANTASTIC VOYAGE

1966   100m   c   Science Fiction   ★★★½
Fox   (U.S.)   /U

Stephen Boyd (Grant), Raquel Welch (Cora Peterson), Edmond O'Brien (Gen. Carter), Donald Pleasence (Dr. Michaels), Arthur O'Connell (Col. Donald Reid), William Redfield (Capt. Bill Owens), Arthur Kennedy (Dr. Duval), Jean Del Val (Jan Benes), Barry Coe (Communications Aide), Ken Scott (Secret Serviceman)

p, Saul David; d, Richard Fleischer; w, Harry Kleiner, David Duncan (adapted from the novel by Otto Klement and Jay Lewis Bixby); ph, Ernest Laszlo; ed, William B. Murphy; m, Leonard Rosenman; art d, Jack Martin Smith, Dale Hennesy; fx, L.B. Abbott, Art Cruickshank, Emil Kosa Jr.

AAN Best Cinematography: Ernest Laszlo; AAN Best Editing: William B. Murphy; AA Best Art Direction: Jack Martin Smith, Dale Hennesy, Walter M. Scott, Stuart A. Reiss; AA Best Visual Effects: Art Cruickshank; AAN Best Sound Effects Editing: Walter Rossi

A medical crew (Stephen Boyd, Raquel Welch, William Redfield, Arthur Kennedy, and Donald Pleasence) and a submarine are miniaturized to remove a blood clot from the brain of a Czech scientist who was shot while defecting. Once shrunk and inside the body, the crew battle white corpuscles while the heart and lungs also make their journey rougher. Early on, it becomes apparent that one of the crew members is a double agent, and matters become even more complex as they race against the clock to complete their mission before returning to normal size.

Their voyage through the body's bloodstream past assorted organs was created by inventive special effects that make this one of the more visually interesting science fiction films of its era. FANTASTIC VOYAGE won Oscars for Best Color Art Direction and Best Visual Effects. It was also nominated for Best Cinematography and Best Film Editing. Joe Dante's INNERSPACE is an amusing variation of the same idea.

FAR COUNTRY, THE

1955   96m   c   Western   ★★★★
Universal   (U.S.)   /U

James Stewart (Jeff), Ruth Roman (Ronda), Corinne Calvet (Renee), Walter Brennan (Ben), John McIntire (Mr. Gannon), Jay C. Flippen (Rube), Harry Morgan (Ketchum), Steve Brodie (Ives), Royal Dano (Luke), Gregg Barton (Rounds)

p, Aaron Rosenberg; d, Anthony Mann; w, Borden Chase; ph, William Daniels; ed, Russell Schoengarth; m, Joseph Gershenson; art d, Bernard Herzbrun, Alexander Golitzen

A strange, almost self-conscious, Western from one of the greatest practioners of the form. Like other Mann efforts , THE FAR COUNTRY is noteworthy for the parable starkness of its story and its flawless command of landscape photography. His films also have the most articulated moments of combat in the cinema: issues of honor, betrayal, violence, and death figure prominently.

Partners Jeff (Stewart) and Ben (Brennan) travel north from Wyoming to the Oregon Territory with a herd of cattle, planning to sell the steers for a fortune in the gold-boom towns. They arrive in the town of Skagway, where the self-appointed judge, Mr. Gannon (McIntire), takes the herd from them. Jeff steals his cattle back, and goes to the town of Dawson, where he is befriended by a saloonkeeper, Ronda (Roman). She decides to help him against Mr. Gannon and his men, who will stop at nothing to get the herd back.

One of the most engrossing and original Westerns made in the 1950s, THE FAR COUNTRY was the fifth collaboration of producer Aaron Rosenberg, director Anthony Mann, and James Stewart. The film benefits greatly from the presence of James Stewart and his barely suppressed malevolence as the hero. Mann's strong and thoughtful direction, the sturdy script by Borden Chase, and the beautiful cinematography of the northern wilderness all contribute to make this an outstanding film.

FAR FROM THE MADDING CROWD

1967   168m   c   Drama   ★★½
MGM   (U.K.)   /U

Julie Christie (Bathsheba Everdene), Terence Stamp (Sgt. Troy), Peter Finch (William Boldwood), Alan Bates (Gabriel Oak), Prunella Ransome (Fanny Robin), Fiona Walker (Liddy), Paul Dawkins (Henery Fray), Andrew Robertson (Andrew Randle), John Barrett (Joseph Poorgrass), Julian Somers (Jan Coggan)

p, Joseph Janni; d, John Schlesinger; w, Frederic Raphael (adapted from the novel by Thomas Hardy); ph, Nicolas Roeg; ed, Malcolm Cooke; m, Richard Rodney Bennett; art d, Roy Forge Smith; cos, Alan Barrett

AAN Best Score: Richard Rodney Bennett

Director Schlesinger makes the best of a script that adheres to Thomas Hardy's novel almost page for page. Set in 1874, Bathsheba Everdene (Christie) is in love with (and feels superior to) three men, Sergeant Troy (Stamp), William Boldwood (Finch), and Gabriel Oak (Bates). Who will she choose?

This is a predictable story that Schlesinger struggles to keep fresh and moving. The actors have a difficult time with the flat characters but, at times, are able to breath life into them. Nicolas Roeg's cinematography is stunning.

FAREWELL, MY LOVELY

1975   97m   c   Mystery   ★★★
EK/ITC   (U.S.)   R/15

Robert Mitchum (Philip Marlowe), Charlotte Rampling (Mrs. Velma Grayle), John Ireland (Lt. Nulty), Sylvia Miles (Mrs. Jessie Florian), Jack O'Halloran (Moose Malloy), Anthony Zerbe (Laird Burnette), Harry Dean Stanton (Billy Rolfe), Jim Thompson (Judge Grayle), John O'Leary (Lindsay Marriott), Kate Murtagh (Frances Amthor)

p, George Pappas, Jerry Bruckheimer; d, Dick Richards; w, David Zelag Goodman (based on the novel by Raymond Chandler); ph, John A. Alonzo; ed, Walter Thompson, Joel Cox; m, David Shire; prod d, Dean Tavoularis; art d, Angelo Graham; fx, Chuck Gaspar; cos, Tony Scarano

AAN Best Supporting Actress: Sylvia Miles

Mitchum, as the intrepid private eye Marlowe, is hired by Moose Malloy (O'Halloran), a giant thug recently released from prison, to find his girlfriend. Mitchum takes on a second case when the fey Lindsay Marriott (O'Leary) seeks his assistance in buying back a valuable jade necklace held for ransom after being stolen from the sultry Velma

Grayle (Rampling). Investigating both cases simultaneously, Marlowe discovers that the two cases are really one and the same—a puzzle involving false identity, hidden loot, and murder.

An affectionate adaptation of Raymond Chandler's novel that beautifully evokes the seamy side of 1940s Los Angeles via superb production design and the same period atmosphere cinematographer Alonzo previously evoked for CHINATOWN. Interestingly, Mitchum's appeal here has more to do with his own exalted status as a noir icon rather than any particularly inspired interpretation of Marlowe. The novel was adapted for the screen twice before, as a vehicle for George Sanders in RKO's THE FALCON TAKES OVER and the superb MURDER, MY SWEET. A moderate hit at the box office, FAREWELL MY LOVELY spawned a fatally flawed remake of THE BIG SLEEP that abandons 1940s Los Angeles in favor of modern-day London.

FAREWELL TO ARMS, A

1932 90m bw Romance/War ★★★★
Paramount (U.S.) /15

Helen Hayes (Catherine Barkley), Gary Cooper (Lt. Frederic Henry), Adolphe Menjou (Maj. Rinaldi), Mary Philips (Helen Ferguson), Jack LaRue (the Priest), Blanche Frederici (Head Nurse), Henry Armetta (Bonello), George Humbert (Piani), Fred Malatesta (Manera), Mary Forbes (Miss Van Campen)

d, Frank Borzage; w, Benjamin Glazer, Oliver H.P. Garrett (based on the novel by Ernest Hemingway); ph, Charles Lang; ed, Otho Lovering; m, Ralph Rainger, John Leipold, Bernhard Kaun, Paul Marquardt, Herman Hand, W. Franke Harling; art d, Hans Dreier, Roland Anderson; cos, Travis Banton

AAN Best Picture; AA Best Cinematography: Charles Bryant Lang, Jr.; *AAN Best Art Direction:* Hans Dreier, Roland Anderson; *AA Best Sound:* Harold C. Lewis

Frank Borzage's masterful adaptation of Ernest Hemingway's celebrated novel stars Gary Cooper as Lt. Frederic Henry, an American adventurer serving in the Italian ambulance corps during WWI, and Helen Hayes as Catherine Barkley, the beautiful English nurse with whom he falls madly in love. When Lt. Henry returns to the front, his jealous friend and superior, Maj. Rinaldi (Adolphe Menjou), intervenes to disrupt their budding romance. Nonetheless the two share a blissful interlude in Milan before Henry returns to the war and Catherine travels to Switzerland to have their baby. Henry knows that someday he will return to her but he must endure many hardships along the way.

Despite Hemingway's reported disgust with the film's comparatively optimistic ending, A FAREWELL TO ARMS is generally faithful to his novel. Director Borzage is at his best here as he utilizes light and movement like brushstrokes to paint a beautifully romantic melodrama with the aid of cinematographer Charles Lang. Borzage's focus is on the love story, but his sweeping battle scenes, loaded with armies of extras, smack of war-torn reality, especially the famous retreat from Caporetto, brilliantly captured in montage. And the performances, while a trifle overblown by modern standards, are so powerful that the film retains its emotional jolt. Hayes was never more appealing, Menjou is at his manipulative best, Cooper displays tremendous depth of feeling, and the supporting work is equally accomplished.

The story is drawn from Hemingway's WWI experiences, his battlefield injury, and his love affair with Agnes von Kurowsky. A Farewell to Arms was adapted for the screen twice more: in 1950 as FORCE OF ARMS with William Holden and Nancy Olsen, and under the original title in 1957 with Rock Hudson and Jennifer Jones.

FAREWELL, MY CONCUBINE
(BA WANG BIE JI)

1993 170m c Historical/Drama ★★★½
Tomson Films/China Film Co-production Corp. R/15
(China/Hong Kong)

Leslie Cheung (Cheng Dieyi), Zhang Fengyi (Duan Xiaolou), Gong Li (Juxian), Lu Qi (Guan Jifa), Ying Da (Na Kun), Ge You (Master Yuan), Li Chun (Xiao Si (teenager)), Lei Ha Man-zhang (Xiao Si (adult)), Tong Di (Xiao Si (adult)), Ma Mingwei (Douzi (child))

p, Hsu Feng; d, Chen Kaige; w, Lilian Lee, Lu Wei (from the novel by Lilian Lee); ph, Gu Changwei; ed, Pei Xiaonan; m, Zhao Jiping; art d, Chen Huaikai; cos, Chen Changmin

AAN Best Foreign Language Film ; AAN Best Cinematography: Gu Changwei

This adaptation of Lilian Lee's novel, co-written by the author and directed by Chinese "Fifth Generation" filmmaker Chen Kaige (YELLOW EARTH), favorably compares to the best films of David Lean, and won the 1993 Cannes *Palme d'Or.* FAREWELL, MY CONCUBINE brings a balance of psychological intimacy and epic sweep to its story of an insoluble love triangle that plays itself out over 50 tumultuous years of Chinese history.

CONCUBINE revolves around Duan Xiaolou (Zhang Fengyi) and Cheng Dieyi (Leslie Cheung), friends since their childhood schooling in the 1920s at the Peking Opera Academy. The story begins in 1977, as the two are about to reprise their most famous roles—King Chu and his loyal concubine Yu Ji—in the classic opera *Farewell to My Concubine.* The story flashes back to their first meeting: tormented because of his effeminacy and inability to memorize lines, Cheng comes under the protection of the more virile Duan. Cheng is trained to play female roles while Duan learns to play heroes, and their interpretation of *Concubine* makes them both opera superstars. Their friendship is shattered when Duan marries prostitute Juxian (Gong Li), and the film follows their separate destinies, each filled with betrayal and heartbreak.

Chen Kaige's tragic vision contrasts sharply with the more socially slanted films of Zhang Yimou, the only other "Fifth Generation" filmmaker whose works have had much Western exposure. Chen eloquently equates Cheng's tragic disconnection from reality with China's inability to strike a political balance between individual freedom and national unity; there are no heroes in this view of Chinese history, only varying degrees of bad luck. Chen and his players bring passion and intelligence to the story, making CONCUBINE the best kind of spectacle—one whose scale is always human, despite its vastness and ambition.

FARGO

1996 98m c Crime/Drama/Comedy ★★★½
Working Title Films/PolyGram (U.S.) R/18

Frances McDormand (Marge Gunderson), Steve Buscemi (Carl Showalter), William H. Macy (Jerry Lundegaard), Peter Stormare (Gaear Grimsrud), Harve Presnell (Wade Gustafson), John Carroll Lynch (Norm Gunderson), Kristin Rudrud (Jean Lundegaard), Tony Denman (Scotty Lundegaard), Steve Park (Mike Yanagita), Steven Reevis (Shep Proudfoot)

p, Ethan Coen; d, Joel Coen; w, Ethan Coen, Joel Coen; ph, Roger Deakins; ed, Roderick Jaynes; m, Carter Burwell; prod d, Rick Heinrichs; art d, Thomas P. Wilkins; fx, Paul Murphy; cos, Mary Zophres

AA Best Actress: Frances McDormand; *AA Best Original Screenplay:* Ethan Coen, Joel Coen; *AAN Best Picture; AAN Best Supporting Actor:* William H. Macy; *AAN Best Director:* Joel Coen; *AAN Best Cinematography:* Roger Deakins; *AAN Best Film Editing:* Roderick Jaynes

The erratic Coen Brothers hit their stride again with this comically violent crime saga, set in the Great American Midwest and enlivened by its surprisingly sympathetic portraits of quirky, relentlessly cheery locals.

In the icy heart of snow-blanketed Minnesota, a dumb-as-dirt car salesman (William H. Macy) hatches a plan to wipe out his personal debts. He'll hire a pair of small-time, out-of-town crooks (Steve Buscemi and Peter Stormare) to kidnap his wife (Kristin Rudrud), then collect the ransom from her dad (Harve Presnell), a wealthy tightwad. Naturally, things go horribly wrong.

Briskly plotted and filmed with surpassing competence, this snappy black comedy comes as a relief after a recent onslaught of less-than-inspired Tarantino imitations. With the exception of the brooding MILLER'S CROSSING, this may be the warmest movie the Coens have ever made. There's something unmistakably human beneath the oh-so-clever surface, and Frances McDormand's hugely pregnant local cop Marge Gunderson—who waddles implacably from bloody crime scene to even bloodier crime scene—radiates solid decency instead of the synthetic perkiness that too often passes for character. Granted, just about everyone here is a borderline moron with an annoying accent, but this isn't a case of big-city contempt for small-town mores: born and raised in Minnesota, the Coens know their targets well and generally hit them squarely.

FARMER'S DAUGHTER, THE

1947 96m bw Political/Comedy ★★★½
RKO (U.S.) /A

Loretta Young *(Katrin Holstrom)*, Joseph Cotten *(Glenn Morley)*, Ethel Barrymore *(Mrs. Morley)*, Charles Bickford *(Clancy)*, Rose Hobart *(Virginia)*, Rhys Williams *(Adolph)*, Harry Davenport *(Dr. Mathew Sutven)*, Tom Powers *(Nordick)*, William Harrigan *(Ward Hughes)*, Lex Barker *(Olaf Holstrom)*

p, Dore Schary; d, H.C. Potter; w, Allen Rivkin, Laura Kerr (from the play "Hulda, Daughter of Parliament" by Juhni Tervataa); ph, Milton Krasner; ed, Harry Marker; m, Leigh Harline

AA Best Actress: Loretta Young; *AAN Best Supporting Actor:* Charles Bickford

This winning Capraesque romantic comedy features Loretta Young as Katrin Holstrom, a Swedish farmer's daughter who comes to the capital in search of a nursing job but eventually becomes the maid for Congressman Glenn Morley (Joseph Cotten) and his powerful politico mother (Ethel Barrymore). Katrin is the perfect housekeeper in almost every way, but when the Morleys try to promote the congressional candidacy of a man Katrin can't abide, she speaks out publicly and ends up as the rival party's candidate for the office. Young won an Academy Award for her delightful performance and Charles Bickford received a Best Supporting Actor Oscar nomination for his role as the butler who shows Katrin the ropes.

FAST TIMES AT RIDGEMONT HIGH

1982 92m c Comedy ★★★
Universal (U.S.) R/18

Sean Penn *(Jeff Spicoli)*, Jennifer Jason Leigh *(Stacy Hamilton)*, Judge Reinhold *(Brad Hamilton)*, Robert Romanus *(Mike Damone)*, Brian Backer *(Mark "Rat" Ratner)*, Phoebe Cates *(Linda Barrett)*, Ray Walston *(Mr. Hand)*, Scott Thomson *(Arnold)*, Vincent Schiavelli *(Mr. Vargas)*, Amanda Wyss *(Lisa)*

p, Art Linson, Irving Azoff; d, Amy Heckerling; w, Cameron Crowe (adapted from his book); ph, Matthew F. Leonetti; ed, Eric Jenkins; m, Joe Walsh; art d, Dan Lomino

At age 22, writer Cameron Crowe returned to high school, posing as a student, and wrote a book about his experiences. In adapting the book, director Amy Heckerling created a brashly funny yet sensitive comedy that has become a cult favorite.

Chronicling a year in the lives of a group of California teenagers, the film follows the fortunes of Ridgemont High senior Brad Hamilton (Judge Reinhold) and his freshman sister Stacy (Jennifer Jason Leigh). Brad's popularity wanes when he loses his "good" fast-food job, and Stacy is introduced to the wonders of boys by Linda (Phoebe Cates). Mark "Rat" Ratner (Brian Backer) has a big crush on Stacy, but it's oily Mike Damone (Robert Romanus) who initiates her into the world of sex. The film's most memorable character is the perpetually stoned surfer played by Sean Penn. His confrontations with Mr. Hand (Ray Walston), a draconian history teacher, provide the film's finest moments.

In addition to adapting his novel for this film, onetime rock critic Crowe also wrote the screenplay for the less successful teenage comedy THE WILD LIFE before making his directorial debut with the extraordinary SAY ANYTHING. Forest Whitaker (GOOD MORNING VIETNAM, BIRD), Anthony Edwards (MR. NORTH, TOP GUN), and Eric Stoltz (MASK, MEMPHIS BELLE) made their film debuts in this superior teen comedy.

FASTER, PUSSYCAT, KILL! KILL!

1966 84m bw Erotic/Action ★★★
Eve Productions, Inc. (U.S.)

Tura Satana, Haji, Lori Williams, Susan Bernard, Stuart Lancaster, Paul Trinka

p, Russ Meyer; d, Russ Meyer; w, Jack Moran; ph, Walter Schenk; ed, Russ Meyer; m, Paul Sawtelle

Gleefully sordid, violent, good-humored exploitation from Russ Meyer, the thinking person's skin-flick director. A trio of exotic dancers, led by the impossibly bosomy Tura Satana, cruises through the deserts of Southern California on a lust-driven quest for kicks, wreaking death on a series of salivating, treacherous males. Technically impressive, especially at a budget of $40,000, the film amply evidences the director's (somewhat uncomprehending) fascination with female anatomy, hipster attitude, and West Coast youth culture. Probably the most lighthearted and enjoyable of Meyer's films, FASTER PUSSYCAT was embraced by a new generation during its art-house re-release in 1994; many viewers detected a feminist subtext beneath its extravagantly campy surface.

FAT CITY

1972 100m c Drama/Sports ★★★★
Columbia (U.S.) PG/AA

Stacy Keach *(Billy Tully)*, Jeff Bridges *(Ernie Munger)*, Susan Tyrrell *(Oma)*, Candy Clark *(Faye)*, Nicholas Colasanto *(Ruben)*, Art Aragon *(Babe)*, Curtis Cokes *(Earl)*, Sixto Rodriguez *(Lucero)*, Billy Walker *(Wes)*, Wayne Mahan *(Buford)*

p, Ray Stark; d, John Huston; w, Leonard Gardner (based on his novel); ph, Conrad Hall; ed, Margaret Booth; m, Marvin Hamlisch; prod d, Richard Sylbert; fx, Paul Stewart; cos, Dorothy Jeakins

AAN Best Supporting Actress: Susan Tyrrell

Set in Stockton, California, against a backdrop of run-down bars, cheap apartments and half-empty second rate gyms, FAT CITY is a grim story of hope and despair among life's losers.

Billy Tully (Stacy Keach), a 29-year-old one-time boxing contender, contemplates a comeback after nearly two years of alcoholism brought about by the loss of both his wife and the biggest fight of his career. He meets Ernie Munger (Jeff Bridges), a promising 19-year-old, and encourages him to hook up with Billy's old manager (Nicholas Colasanto). This Ernie does and so begins his own boxing career. Billy, however, continues boozing and his personal and professional lives continue their downward trajectory.

Adapted by Leonard Gardner from his own novel and brilliantly directed by John Huston, who was himself once an amateur champion, FAT CITY is both an extraordinarily realistic look at the bottom rungs of the fight game and a moving exploration of the human condition. Keach, Bridges, Tyrrell (who received an Oscar nomination for her portrayal of the alcoholic Oma, Billy's temporary girlfriend), and all the supporting players give first-rate performances. All in all, this strong downbeat film, which makes appropriate use of Kris Kristofferson's "Help Me Make It through the Night," is never less than captivating.

FATAL ATTRACTION

1987 119m c Thriller/Romance ★★★
Paramount (U.S.) R/18

Michael Douglas *(Dan Gallagher)*, Glenn Close *(Alex Forrest)*, Anne Archer *(Beth Gallagher)*, Ellen Hamilton Latzen *(Ellen Gallagher)*, Stuart Pankin *(Jimmy)*, Ellen Foley *(Hildy)*, Fred Gwynne *(Arthur)*, Meg Mundy *(Joan Rogerson)*, Tom Brennan *(Howard Rogerson)*, Lois Smith *(Martha)*

p, Stanley R. Jaffe, Sherry Lansing; d, Adrian Lyne; w, James Dearden; ph, Howard Atherton; ed, Michael Kahn, Peter E. Berger; m, Maurice Jarre; prod d, Mel Bourne; art d, Jack Blackman; cos, Ellen Mirojnick

AAN Best Picture; AAN Best Actress: Glenn Close; *AAN Best Supporting Actress:* Anne Archer; *AAN Best Director:* Adrian Lyne; *AAN Best Adapted Screenplay:* James Dearden; *AAN Best Editing:* Michael Kahn, Peter E Berger

FATAL ATTRACTION was more than a box-office smash; it was a cultural phenomenon. This story of an extramarital fling that turns into a nightmare begins as a well-crafted psychological thriller but degenerates into a misogynistic thrill-fest in its closing moments.

Dan Gallagher (Michael Douglas) is a Manhattan lawyer with a gorgeous wife (Anne Archer) and a six-year-old daughter. When he first meets Alex (Glenn Close), he is intrigued, but unavailable. On another weekend, though, a chance meeting brings Dan and Alex together for a passionate two-night stand in her apartment. When Dan tries to say his final goodbye and return to his family, he gets the first hint that Alex is not entirely rational and has become obsessed with him. That obsession soon turns life into an escalating nightmare for Dan and his family.

Screenwriter James Dearden has created a set of initially believable characters, placed them in a familiar situation, and then drastically upped the stakes. Unfortunately, motivations and psychological concerns are thrown out the window in the final reel. The blame for this doesn't rest entirely with Dearden or director Adrian Lyne; the producers tested the original ending (Alex commits suicide, but not before implicating Dan as her murderer) and preview audiences found it less than satisfying. The thrill-a-minute conclusion was then shot and substituted.

Notwithstanding the ending, the performances are excellent. Playing against type, Close is overtly libidinous, while at the same time making her obsession and slide into madness convincing and pathetic. Douglas also gives a performance of reasonable depth, and Archer does a nice turn as his implicitly frigid but alluring wife.

FATHER GOOSE

1964 115m c War/Comedy	★★★
Universal (U.S.)	/U

Cary Grant *(Walter Eckland)*, Leslie Caron *(Catherine Freneau)*, Trevor Howard *(Commodore Frank Houghton)*, Jack Good *(Lt. Stebbins)*, Verina Greenlaw *(Christine)*, Pip Sparke *(Anne)*, Jennifer Berrington *(Harriet)*, Stephanie Berrington *(Elizabeth)*, Laurelle Felsette *(Angelique)*, Nicole Felsette *(Dominique)*

p, Robert Arthur; d, Ralph Nelson; w, Frank Tarloff, Peter Stone (based on the story "A Place Of Dragons" by S.H. Barnett); ph, Charles Lang; ed, Ted J. Kent; m, Cy Coleman; art d, Alexander Golitzen, Henry Bumstead; cos, Ray Aghayan

AA Best Original Story and Screenplay: S.H. Barnett, Peter Stone, Frank Tarloff; *AAN Best Editing:* Ted J. Kent; *AAN Best Sound:* Waldon O. Watson

Playing against his sophisticated image, Cary Grant is Walter Eckland, a drunken beach bum who sits out WWII on a South Seas island until he is coerced by an Australian naval officer (Trevor Howard) into monitoring Japanese air activity. When Eckland travels to a nearby island to rescue another plane watcher, he finds the observer dead, but schoolteacher Catherine Freneau (Leslie Caron) and her seven young female charges are very much alive after being marooned when their plane went down. They return with Eckland and clean up his act while he and Freneau fall in love. Danger looms, however, as the Japanese forces close in. Grant's penultimate film (WALK, DON'T RUN was his last), this romantic comedy won Best Screenplay Oscars for Frank Tarloff and Peter Stone, who worked on the screenplay separately but were awarded a shared credit by a Writers Guild arbitration.

FATHER OF THE BRIDE

1950 92m bw Comedy	★★★★
MGM (U.S.)	/U

Spencer Tracy *(Stanley T. Banks)*, Joan Bennett *(Ellie Banks)*, Elizabeth Taylor *(Kay Banks)*, Don Taylor *(Buckley Dunstan)*, Billie Burke *(Doris Dunstan)*, Leo G. Carroll *(Mr. Massoula)*, Moroni Olsen *(Herbert Dunstan)*, Melville Cooper *(Mr. Tringle)*, Taylor Holmes *(Warner)*, Paul Harvey *(Rev. Galsworthy)*

p, Pandro S. Berman; d, Vincente Minnelli; w, Frances Goodrich, Albert Hackett (based on the novel by Edward Streeter); ph, John Alton; ed, Ferris Webster; m, Adolph Deutsch; art d, Cedric Gibbons, Leonid Vasian; cos, Helen Rose, Walter Plunkett

AAN Best Picture; AAN Best Actor: Spencer Tracy; *AAN Best Original Screenplay:* Frances Goodrich, Albert Hackett

Nowadays remembered primarily as the first of many walks La Liz was to take down the aisle, FATHER OF THE BRIDE is also one of the best comedies MGM made in the 1950s. Although Taylor perfectly embodies an idealized vision of the demure but spirited young bride, this fine film is foremost a showcase for the supple comic drollery of Spencer Tracy. As Stanley Banks, the harassed father who must cope with the business of marrying his daughter off, Tracy finds a marvelous vehicle for his expressive but low-key style.

The movie begins as the exhausted Banks looks over the debris and chaos in his home after the wedding, then turns to the audience to relate his story. The problems and responsibilities of marrying off a daughter are legion: there's the heart-to-heart talk with the suitor; meeting the in-laws; selecting the honeymoon site; and, of course, the near-ruinous financial expense.

Although continually skimming the edge of bland sitcom land, this satiric look at the American Family, circa 1950, still packs a gentle punch. The screenplay, if occasionally contrived, is witty and incisive and Minnelli's assured direction keeps the proceedings from disintegrating into indulgent slapstick. As the bride's mother, Joan Bennett is excellent in her first film for MGM, and the supporting performances are all good, with especially fine work from Moroni Olsen and Billie Burke as the parents of the groom. The last is played with charm and the perfect touch of dullness by Don Taylor, who later traded acting for the director's chair. The film inspired a sequel, FATHER'S LITTLE DIVIDEND, and a mediocre 1991 remake.

FEAR AND DESIRE

1953 68m bw War	★★★
Kubrick (U.S.)	

Frank Silvera *(Mac)*, Kenneth Harp *(Lt. Corby)*, Paul Mazursky *(Sidney)*, Steve Coit *(Fletcher)*, Virginia Leith *(Girl)*, David Allen *(Narrator)*

p, Stanley Kubrick; d, Stanley Kubrick; w, Howard Sackler, Stanley Kubrick; ph, Stanley Kubrick; ed, Stanley Kubrick; m, Gerald Fried

Notable as Stanley Kubrick's first film, produced when he was 22 years old on a budget of $40,000. A modest effort, FEAR AND DESIRE nonetheless displays the preoccupation with the pressures and absurdities of war which would later mark many of Kubrick's later films. Not only did he produce and direct, but he also shot and edited this story of four soldiers caught behind enemy lines in an abstractly depicted war.

Trying to move back to their own side, they kill several enemy soldiers and capture a young woman (Leith). One of the men, Sidney (Mazursky, making his film debut), is left to guard her as the other three (Silvera, Harp and Coit) go to a river to build a raft. Wanting to seduce the girl, Sidney unties her from a tree, and when she runs away, he kills her and then goes insane. Returning from the river, the three soldiers discover an enemy outpost holding a general and his aide. The confrontation between the three enterprising soldiers and the enemy climaxes this highly promising first effort by one of America's premiere filmmakers.

FEAR STRIKES OUT

1957 100m bw Biography/Sports	★★★★
Paramount (U.S.)	/A

Anthony Perkins *(Jimmy Piersall)*, Karl Malden *(John Piersall)*, Norma Moore *(Mary Teevan)*, Adam Williams *(Dr. Brown)*, Peter Votrian *(Jimmy Piersall as a Boy)*, Perry Wilson *(Mrs. John Piersall)*, Dennis McMullen *(Phil)*, Gail Land *(Alice)*, Brian Hutton *(Bernie Sherwill)*, Bart Burns *(Joe Cronin)*

p, Alan J. Pakula; d, Robert Mulligan; w, Ted Berkman, Raphael Blau (based on the autobiography by James A. Piersall, with Albert S. Hirshberg); ph, Haskell Boggs; ed, Aaron Stell; m, Elmer Bernstein; fx, John P. Fulton; cos, Edith Head

Perkins portrays Jimmy Piersall in this well-done biopic of one of baseball's most colorful characters, who, from boyhood, was relentlessly driven by his father (Malden) to make it in the major leagues. Nothing the talented Jimmy does is good enough for his dad, and, after finally making the Boston Red Sox, he breaks down, maniacally climbing the backstop after hitting a home run—one of the best-remembered scenes in any sports film. Jimmy is then admitted to Westborough State Hospital, where he gradually recovers under the supervision of Dr. Brown (Williams), eventually returning to his wife, his repentant father, and the Red Sox lineup.

The physically awkward Perkins may seem an unlikely candidate to portray a professional athlete, however, in a dry run of his performance in PSYCHO, he delivers a powerful portrayal of a young man undergoing tremendous emotional turmoil; in the final analysis, the film's psychological impact far outweighs how Perkins looks throwing a baseball back into the infield. Based on Piersall's autobiography, this directorial debut for Mulligan also boasts an extremely effective, typically full-volume performance by Malden as Piersall's demanding but loving father.

FEARLESS

1993 122m c Drama   ★★★½
Spring Creek Productions   (U.S.)   R/15

Jeff Bridges *(Max Klein)*, Isabella Rossellini *(Laura Klein)*, Rosie Perez *(Carla Rodrigo)*, Tom Hulce *(Brillstein)*, John Turturro *(Bill Perlman)*, Benicio Del Toro *(Manny Rodrigo)*, Deirdre O'Connell *(Nan Gordon)*, John DeLancie *(Jeff Gordon)*, Spencer Vrooman *(Jonah Klein)*, Daniel Cerny *(Byron Hummel)*

p, Mark Rosenberg, Paula Weinstein; d, Peter Weir; w, Rafael Yglesias (from his novel); ph, Allen Daviau, Tom Cannole; ed, William Anderson, Armen Minasian, Lee Smith; m, Maurice Jarre; prod d, John Stoddart; art d, Christopher Burian-Mohr; fx, Ken Pepiot, Gintar Repecka, Peter Albiez, Robert L. Olmstead, Gary L. Karas, Kelly Kirby, William Mesa; cos, Marilyn Matthews

AAN Best Supporting Actress: Rosie Perez

By Hollywood standards, FEARLESS is a brave attempt to grapple with some Big Issues—life, death, faith, guilt, stuff like that. At times, it crashes to the ground in a blaze of heavy-handed symbolism, but "Fearless" also achieves some haunting, hallucinatory flights of beauty.

Jeff Bridges plays Max Klein, a San Francisco architect psychologically transformed by an appalling plane crash. In the moments before impact, Max realizes he is not afraid of dying. Until now a nervous, harried figure, he discovers a heroic calm that helps him save several passengers, but also makes his entire previous existence seem foreign and irrelevant. The only person the new Max can relate to is fellow survivor Carla (Rosie Perez), a working-class Hispanic mother stricken with guilt over her failure to save her son during the crash.

If Max's beautiful, adoring wife (Isabella Rossellini) has a hard time understanding her husband's almost mystical attraction to Carla, so does the audience. Perez's performance undoes the film's delicate chemistry, with her shrill delivery sabotaging many key scenes. Bridges, by contrast, is a marvel—even as he strides through the physical world, he somehow makes us believe he has transcended it. Rossellini is superb as his wife, Tom Hulce is funny as a venal attorney, and John Turturro makes a quietly effective therapist. It's a shame that not all of the crew can fly at the same altitude.

FELLINI SATYRICON

1969 128m c Historical   ★★★★
P.E.A./Artistes   (France/Italy)   /18

Martin Potter *(Encolpius)*, Hiram Keller *(Ascyltus)*, Max Born *(Giton)*, Capucine *(Tryphaena)*, Salvo Randone *(Eumolpus)*, Magali Noel *(Fortunata)*, Alain Cuny *(Lichas)*, Lucia Bose *(Suicide Wife)*, Tanya Lopert *(Caesar)*, Gordon Mitchell *(Robber)*

p, Alberto Grimaldi; d, Federico Fellini; w, Federico Fellini, Bernardino Zapponi, Brunello Rondi (based on the fragment "Satyricon" by Gaius Petronius); ph, Giuseppe Rotunno; ed, Ruggero Mastroianni; m, Nino Rota, Ilhan Mimaroglu, Tod Dockstader, Andrew Rudin; prod d, Danilo Donati; art d, Luigi Scaccianoce, Giorgio Giovannini; fx, Adriano Pischiutta; cos, Danilo Donati

AAN Best Director: Federico Fellini

Orgy, anyone? The bizarre characters and situations that had filled the films of Federico Fellini since his early VARIETY LIGHTS found their ultimate expression in this dreamy, hallucinatory depiction of ancient Rome. Based on the 1st century A.D. fragment of a drama by Gaius Petronius (with added inspiration from other writings of the period), this film strips away all the glamor and honor associated with the early Romans to expose a society in which conventional morality has little or no significance. But Fellini's desire was not to criticize Rome, nor was it to set the history books straight; rather, he found the perfect setting with which to parallel the youth culture of the 1960s.

Encolpius (Potter) and Ascyltus (Keller) are two students whose adventures in a hotbed of decadence are the excuse for the threadbare plot that holds this extraordinary spectacle together. Their sole aim is the pursuit of hedonistic desires, and hedonism is just what Fellini gives us—there are concubines, nymphomaniacs, hermaphrodites (in the form of an albino infant with magical healing powers), sadism, masochism, and no doubt a few more "isms" as well amidst all the group sex going on.

The odd thing is that the excess seems visual and mythical rather than really sexual. (For one thing we *see* very little sex.) The masterful cinematography and stunning use of color, achieved through the use of deliberately artificial light sources, lend the film an almost hypnotic sheen. Even if you can't recall particular images, the look of the film is likely to linger in your memory.

FELLINI'S ROMA

1972 119m c Drama   ★★½
Ultra/Artistes   (Italy/France)   R/

Federico Fellini *(Himself)*, Peter Gonzales *(Fellini, Age 18)*, Stefano Majore *(Fellini As a Child)*, Pia De Doses *(Princess)*, Renato Giovanneli *(Cardinal Ottaviani)*, Fiona Florence *(Young Prostitute)*, Marne Maitland *(Underground Guide)*, Galliano Sbarra *(Music Hall Compere)*, Alvaro Vitali *(Tap Dancer Imitating Fred Astaire)*, Britta Barnes

p, Turi Vasile; d, Federico Fellini; w, Federico Fellini, Bernardino Zapponi; ph, Giuseppe Rotunno; ed, Ruggero Mastroianni; m, Nino Rota; prod d, Danilo Donati; fx, Adriano Pischiutta; chor, Gino Landi; cos, Danilo Donati

ROMA, a confounding and confused semi-documentary, tried the patience of even the most devoted Fellini fans. The story, such as it is, begins in the small town where young Fellini, played by Majore, is born. Majore wants desperately to live in Rome and finally moves there in 1938, just before war breaks out. Majore gives way to Gonzales as a teenaged Fellini, living in a tenement where he observes the rich, noisy lives of his neighbours.

Jump to the early 1970s and Fellini, as himself, is now a renowned director making a picture. He's shooting a scene in a traffic jam during a heavy rainstorm, and his memory is jogged back to his early days in the city when he attended a vaudeville show during the war. Back in the present, "Fellini" is shooting the construction of the subway that has been being built for decades: wherever workers dig, they make an archaeological find and the area becomes off-limits to the builders. We visit bordellos, a perverse clerical fashion show, and a street festival where cops besiege radical youths. Amid further reveries, Fellini begins interviewing people on camera: Anna Magnani, Gore Vidal, Alberto Sordi, and Marcello Mastroianni, among others. (The latter two were cut from the US print.) Darkness descends, the city begins to snore, and the silence is overwhelmed by a horde of motorcyclists careening through the city past the old relics and winding up at the Colosseum.

What does it all mean? Who knows? Fellini had already made two movies about directorial alter egos with creative block, LA DOLCE VITA and 8 1/2. Here, however, the director himself is blocked: he recycles familiar themes and ideas, with the result that ROMA often feels like a remake. Episodic and enigmatic, it's almost a parody of Fellini's other movies. Two versions were released, in English and with subtitles; the dubbed version is unobjectionable. Many laughs and just as many winces.

FERRIS BUELLER'S DAY OFF

1986 103m c Comedy ★★
Paramount (U.S.) PG-13/15

Matthew Broderick *(Ferris Bueller)*, Alan Ruck *(Cameron Frye)*, Mia Sara *(Sloane Peterson)*, Jeffrey Jones *(Ed Rooney)*, Jennifer Grey *(Jeanie Bueller)*, Cindy Pickett *(Katie Bueller)*, Lyman Ward *(Tom Bueller)*, Edie McClurg *(School Secretary)*, Charlie Sheen *(Boy in Police Station)*, Ben Stein *(Economics Teacher)*

p, John Hughes; d, John Hughes; w, John Hughes; ph, Tak Fujimoto; ed, Paul Hirsch; m, Ira Newborn, Arthur Baker, John Robie; prod d, John W. Corso; chor, Kenny Ortega; cos, Marilyn Vance

Well, it would have made a great television sitcom pilot. Broderick plays the title role, a popular high school student living in a well-to-do Chicago suburb. After convincing his parents that he is truly sick, Ferris calls on his friend Cameron (Ruck) to join him for a day off from school. Cameron agrees, reluctantly, because it means taking his father's prized classic 1961 red Ferrari 250 GT convertible. They pick up Ferris's girlfriend (Sara) and head for downtown Chicago, but our plucky hero's nemesis, the high school's dean of students (Jones), has caught on to the scheme and is determined to catch the boy in the act.

Considering that the story and pacing of this offbeat comedy wear thin after the first 20 minutes, FERRIS BUELLER'S DAY OFF has more funny moments than most bad teenage comedies, primarily because Broderick brings some real charm and chutzpah to the part. Unfortunately, the wonderfully clever promise of the film's opening is never fulfilled. Hughes, directing from his own screenplay, starts off well but pushes his premise too far and ultimately kills the joke. Where Hughes really succeeds is in his obviously affectionate lensing of Chicago locations.

FEW GOOD MEN, A

1992 138m c Drama ★★★
Manhattan Project/Castle Rock (U.S.) R/15

Tom Cruise *(Lt. J.G. Daniel Kaffee)*, Jack Nicholson *(Col. Nathan R. Jessep)*, Demi Moore *(Lt. Cmdr. JoAnne Galloway)*, Kevin Bacon *(Capt. Jack Ross)*, Kiefer Sutherland *(Lt. Jonathan Kendrick)*, Kevin Pollak *(Lt. Sam Weinberg)*, James Marshall *(PFC Louden Downey)*, J.T. Walsh *(Lt. Col. Matthew Markinson)*, Christopher Guest *(Dr. Stone)*, Wolfgang Bodison *(Lance Corp. Harold W. Dawson)*

p, David Brown, Rob Reiner, Andrew Scheinman; d, Rob Reiner; w, Aaron Sorkin (from his play); ph, Robert Richardson; ed, Robert Leighton; m, Marc Shaiman; prod d, J. Michael Riva; art d, David Klassen; cos, Gloria Gresham

AAN Best Picture; AAN Best Supporting Actor: Jack Nicholson; *AAN Best Editing:* Robert Leighton; *AAN Best Sound:* Kevin O'Connell, Rick Kline, Bob Eber

Directed by Rob Reiner and adapted from Aaron Sorkin's hit Broadway play, A FEW GOOD MEN starts out by treading some very familiar ground.

Tom Cruise plays Lt. J.G. Daniel Kaffee, a second-generation lawyer who lives in the shadow of his late, revered father. When he's handed a case involving the death of a young Marine during an unofficial disciplinary procedure, Kaffee does what comes naturally: he works out a quick, clever plea bargain with the prosecuting officer (Kevin Bacon) and then goes back to softball practice.

Not so fast! Here comes Lt. Cdr. Joanne Galloway (Demi Moore), an earnest, uncompromising colleague who's convinced there's more to this case than meets even the most beady military eye. Galloway despises Kaffee's glib opportunism, but also recognizes that he's a potentially great lawyer—the only one good enough, in fact, to get to the bottom of the case and topple the man behind it all, His Extreme Scariness Col. Nathan R. Jessep (Jack Nicholson).

It looks for a while as though this might get tedious, with Galloway woodenly haranguing Kaffee as he slugs away with his beloved baseball bat, doing the Tom Cruise callow youth routine. But once Kaffee decides to go to trial, confronting his own oedipal hang-ups and taking on the might of the Naval heirarchy, he becomes winningly believable. The final scene, when Kaffee locks horns with Jessep, more than makes up for the predictability of what's come before.

FIDDLER ON THE ROOF

1971 180m c Comedy/Musical ★★★½
Mirisch (U.S.) G/U

Topol *(Tevye)*, Norma Crane *(Golde)*, Leonard Frey *(Motel)*, Molly Picon *(Yente)*, Paul Mann *(Lazar Wolf)*, Rosalind Harris *(Tzeitel)*, Michele Marsh *(Hodel)*, Neva Small *(Chava)*, Paul Michael Glaser *(Perchik)*, Raymond Lovelock *(Fyedka)*

p, Norman Jewison; d, Norman Jewison; w, Joseph Stein (from the book of the musical, based on stories by Sholem Aleichem); ph, Oswald Morris; ed, Antony Gibbs, Robert Lawrence; art d, Michael Stringer; chor, Tom Abbott, Sam Bayes; cos, Elizabeth Haffenden, Joan Bridge

AAN Best Picture; AAN Best Actor: Topol; *AAN Best Supporting Actor:* Leonard Frey; *AAN Best Director:* Norman Jewison; *AA Best Cinematography:* Oswald Morris; *AA Best Score:* John Williams; *AAN Best Art Direction:* Robert Boyle, Michael Stringer, Peter Lamont; *AA Best Sound:* Gordon K. McCallum, David Hildyard

Fiddlesticks. Although scenarist Stein closely adapted the book of his long-running Broadway smash, FIDDLER ON THE ROOF is simply not up to the original's standard, suffering from excessive length and dim photography. Set in the Ukraine in the early 1900s and based on several tales by Sholem Aleichem, the overly sentimental story focuses on Tevye (Topol), his long-suffering wife (Crane), and their three dissimilar daughters, Hodel (Marsh), Tzeitel (Harris), and Chava (Small). Each of the girls finds a potential husband, though Tevye disapproves of all three matches. Meanwhile, the Jewish community faces harassment from the Czar and neighboring Cossacks which culminates in a pogrom, with the survivors left to pick up the pieces of their lives.

The film's strengths lie in the careful detailing of life in pre-Bolshevik Jewish Russia, and the often rough-hewn, open-air quality the film achieves. These same qualities pervade the zestful yet touching performance of Topol, who justly received an Oscar nomination for his fine work. What a pity that no one else in the cast makes a similar impression. An even greater pity lies in director Jewison's pacing and visual style.

Apart from several lovely shots of twilight vistas, Jewison proves yet again that he does not know what to do with a camera. The rhythm is not so much leisurely as it is slack, and the pogrom sequence is not nearly as powerful as it should be. The most obvious victim of the choppy cutting is the choreography, all but destroyed by the editor's handiwork. Finally, as handled here, the famous score reveals its major defect: almost every decent song is in the movie's first half. What could have been a brilliant film experience, expanding on the stage version as only film can, ends up instead as a series of wonderful bits and pieces.

FIELD OF DREAMS

1989 107m c Sports ★★★
Gordon (U.S.) PG

Kevin Costner *(Ray Kinsella)*, Amy Madigan *(Annie Kinsella)*, Gaby Hoffman *(Karin Kinsella)*, Ray Liotta *(Shoeless Joe Jackson)*, Timothy Busfield *(Mark)*, James Earl Jones *(Terence Mann)*, Burt Lancaster *(Dr. "Moonlight" Graham)*, Frank Whaley *(Archie Graham)*, Dwier Brown *(John Kinsella)*, James Andelin *(Feed Store Farmer)*

p, Lawrence Gordon, Charles Gordon; d, Phil Alden Robinson; w, Phil Alden Robinson (based on the book *Shoeless Joe* by W.P. Kinsella); ph, John Lindley; ed, Ian Crafford; m, James Horner; prod d, Dennis Gassner; art d, Leslie McDonald; cos, Linda Bass

AAN Best Picture; AAN Best Adapted Screenplay: Phil Alden Robinson; *AAN Best Score:* James Horner

A rare choke-up movie for guys and one of 1989's biggest hits, Phil Alden Robinson's FIELD OF DREAMS made stiff but sensitive Kevin Costner a superstar. Based on the W.P. Kinsella's oddball fantasy novel *Shoeless Joe*—in which the protagonist kidnaps novelist J.D. Salinger—the film is a canny blend of myth, dreams, and baseball which (some viewers of good faith believe) actually skirts the sentimental and obvious.

At the urging of a mysterious voice, Iowa farmer Ray Kinsella (Costner) comes to believe that if he carves a baseball field out of his cornfield, his late father's hero, long-dead baseball great Shoeless Joe Jackson, will return to play. Supported by his wife, Annie (Amy Madigan), he plows away his family's livelihood and constructs a baseball field—complete with lights! His neighbors think he's crazy but—would you believe it?—Jackson (an unintentionally sinister-looking Ray Liotta) does indeed appear as the harbinger of an incredible assemblage of ghosts of all-stars past. However, nobody but Kinsella and his family can see these baseball greats. With his farm threatened by bankruptcy, Kinsella is mysteriously led to Boston's Fenway Park, and to a burned-out radical novelist (James Earl Jones) who may hold the key to the mystery.

If any movie of its decade begged to be called Capraesque, it is FIELD OF DREAMS, a sappy, good-naturedly dopey paean to traditional family values and nostalgia for innocent pleasures. The most powerful element of the movie is its trendy exploitation of men's yearning to bond with their fathers. For many people, particularly at the peak of the late-80s "Men's Movement," this was irresistible stuff; others were left cold by its manipulative, "Twilight Zone"-style fabulism. Ultimately, the film relies too heavily on consensual acceptance of baseball iconography as some kind of symbolic shorthand for all kinds of American values. These days, most of us prefer the NBA.

FIERCE CREATURES
1997 93m c Comedy ★★
Fish Productions/Jersey Films/Prominent Features PG-13/PG
(U.S./U.K.)

John Cleese (Rollo Lee), Jamie Lee Curtis (Willa Weston), Kevin Kline (Vince McCain/Rod McCain), Michael Palin (Adrian "Bugsy" Malone), Ronnie Corbett (Reggie Sealions), Carey Lowell (Cub Felines), Robert Lindsay (Sidney Small Mammals), Bille Brown (Neville Coltrane), Derek Griffiths (Gerry Ungulates), Cynthia Cleese (Pip Small Mammals)

p, Michael Shamberg, John Cleese; d, Robert Young, Fred Schepisi; w, John Cleese, Iain Johnstone (partially based on "The Fierce Animal Policy" by Terry Jones and Michael Palin); ph, Adrian Biddle, Ian Baker; ed, Robert Gibson; m, Jerry Goldsmith; prod d, Roger Murray-Leach; art d, David Allday, Kevin Phipps; fx, Effects Associates Ltd., Animated Extras, Asylum Models; cos, Hazel Pethig

A lame, sort-of sequel to 1988's A FISH CALLED WANDA, in which a corporate takeover of a zoo sparks a comedy of errors driven by the clash between greedy Kiwis, brazen Yanks, and uptight Brits.

The predatory Octopus Corporation, headed up by vulgar, rapacious New Zealand billionaire Rod McCain (Kevin Kline), buys a small English zoo and puts former cop Rollo Lee (John Cleese) in charge. Rollo declares that since people only come to zoos to see fierce creatures, all the cute ones must go, occasioning much distress among the animal-loving zookeepers. Meanwhile, American can-do gal Willa Weston (Jamie Lee Curtis) volunteers to make the zoo profitable, and McCain's lecherous, conniving ninny of a son, Vince (Kline again), joins the new management team with an eye to getting into Willa's pants. While Vince's pursuit of corporate sponsorships and marketing tie-ins turn the once-tranquil place into a gaudy travesty of advertisements and celebrity endorsements, Willa and Rollo come around to the zookeepers' point of view and team up to save the zoo.

The WANDA team of Cleese, Curtis, Kline, and Michael Palin goes through very similar paces to considerably less comic effect, though the movie's occasional highlights recall the earlier film's tone of inspired lunacy. The notoriously troubled production was extensively reworked after disastrous previews—hence the second director, the famously funny Fred Schepisi—but laughs are still few and far between. The funniest scenes come early, as desperately inventive zookeepers misrepresent a variety of adorable, mild-mannered herbivores as killer beasts of unparalleled savagery. But things quickly degenerate into a series of juvenile jokes about flatulence and bosoms, and by the end the cast is reduced to frantically manhandling a corpse for laughs.

FIFTH ELEMENT, THE
(LE CINQUIEME ELEMENT)
1997 127m c Science Fiction ★★★
Gaumont (France) PG-13/PG

Bruce Willis (Korben Dallas), Gary Oldman (Zorg), Milla Jovovich (Leeloo), Ian Holm (Cornelius), Chris Tucker (Ruby Rhod), Luke Perry (Billy), Brion James (General Munro), Tommy "Tiny" Lister Jr. (President Lindberg), Lee Evans (Fog), Tricky (Right Arm)

p, Patrice Ledoux; d, Luc Besson; w, Luc Besson, Robert Mark Kamen (based on a story by Luc Besson); ph, Thierry Arbogast; ed, Sylvie Landra; m, Eric Serra; prod d, Dan Weil; art d, Jim Morahan, Kevin Phipps, Michael Lamont; fx, Mark Stetson, Nick Dudman, Nick Allder, Neil Corbould, Norman Baillie, Digital Domain; cos, Jean-Paul Gaultier, Vin Burnham

Brash, silly, often very beautiful, and art-directed within an inch of its life. This juvenile fantasy-adventure was first conceived by writer-director Luc Besson (LA FEMME NIKITA) as an adolescent, and it shows.

In the future, New York City is one big 60-story traffic jam; interstellar airline stewardesses dress in belly-baring Gaultier; shape-shifting Mangalors (rubber, bulldog-like aliens) prowl the streets carrying automatic weapons; and a planet-sized ball o' badness is hurtling toward the Earth at unimaginable speed. The only one who can stop it is fetching waif Leeloo (Milla Jovovich), whose "I dreamed I went walking in my Maidenform bra of the future" scene should insure her a place in the hearts of 14-year-old boys of all ages. THE FIFTH ELEMENT pits Leeloo and crack starfighter-turned-taxi driver Korben Dallas (Bruce Willis) against evil capitalist Zorg (Gary Oldman), and the fate of the Earth hangs on a quartet of ancient stones. The fun is in Besson's vision, which draws deeply on European graphic novel traditions with a bit of BLADE RUNNER tossed in for good measure: the giant alien diva (Maiwenn Le Besco) behind her shimmering chador, the flying cars, the friendly Mondoshawan (turtle-like aliens with great bronze shells), the efficiency apartment of tomorrow, the floating junk that delivers Chinese food, and much, much more. It's all densely imagined and more than a little goofy: Besson's "All You Need is Love" message doesn't entirely jibe with the high-powered fire-fights, which don't mix awfully well with the silly humor. The supporting cast, which includes POSSE's Tiny Lister as the President, BLADE RUNNER's Brion James as the President's military adviser, and ALIEN's Ian Holm as Father Cornelius, keeper of the ancient wisdom, is a genre fan's delight.

FIGHTING 69TH, THE
1940 90m bw War ★★★★
Warner Bros. (U.S.) /PG

James Cagney (Jerry Plunkett), Pat O'Brien (Father Duffy), George Brent (Wild Bill Donovan), Jeffrey Lynn (Joyce Kilmer), Alan Hale (Sgt. Big Mike Wynn), Frank McHugh ("Crepe Hanger" Burke), Dennis Morgan (Lt. Ames), William Lundigan (Timmy Wynn), Dick Foran (John Wynn), Guinn "Big Boy" Williams (Paddy Dolan)

p, Louis F. Edelman; d, William Keighley; w, Norman Reilly Raine, Fred Niblo Jr., Dean Franklin; ph, Tony Gaudio; ed, Owen Marks; m, Adolph Deutsch; art d, Ted Smith; fx, Byron Haskin, Rex Wimpy

Enough fighting Irish blarney for a dozen St. Patrick's Days. A showcase for the wisecracking, swaggering antics of Cagney, playing a would-be hero from Brooklyn who joins the all-Irish 69th New York Regiment after the US enters WWI.

Jerry Plunkett (Cagney) is a street-corner brawler who couldn't care less about the illustrious military tradition embodied in the old 69th and who snubs feisty Father Duffy (O'Brien, who else?) when he finds out that Duffy is a priest. ("I don't go in for that Holy Joe stuff," as he puts it.) Throughout his training, which he regards as a waste of time, Jerry defies his superiors, including a tough old sergeant (Hale) and his commanding officer, "Wild Bill" Donovan (Brent). Actual combat, however, proves to be too much for the obnoxious recruit, who first accidentally gives away his company's position and whose later cowardice results in the death of dozens of doughboys. Sentenced to death,

Plunkett is inadvertantly given a chance to redeem himself when a bomb destroys his prison, and the stage is set for the action-packed finale.

One of the rare Hollywood films without any women or romantic angles whatsoever, THE FIGHTING 69TH was, not too surprisingly, an enormous hit with an American public about to enter WWII. Cagney gives such a galvanizing performance that one almost doesn't care that the film's one-note patriotism and Irish sentiment are as high as the corn in late summer. O'Brien fares less well as yet another priestly paragon of virtue, but the supporting cast is extremely proficient, Keighley's direction very zippy, and the technical merit of the enterprise quite exhilarating.

FIRE OVER ENGLAND

1937 92m bw Adventure/Historical/War   ★★★★
Mayflower/Pendennis/Korda/London Films (U.K.)   /U

Laurence Olivier *(Michael Ingolby)*, Flora Robson *(Queen Elizabeth)*, Leslie Banks *(Earl of Leicester)*, Raymond Massey *(Philip of Spain)*, Vivien Leigh *(Cynthia)*, Tamara Desni *(Elena)*, Morton Selten *(Burleigh)*, Lyn Harding *(Sir Richard)*, George Thirlwell *(Gregory)*, Henry Oscar *(Spanish Ambassador)*

p, Erich Pommer; d, William K. Howard; w, Clemence Dane, Sergei Nolbandov (based on the novel by A.E.W. Mason); ph, James Wong Howe; ed, Jack Dennis; m, Richard Addinsell; art d, Lazare Meerson; fx, Ned Mann, Lawrence Butler, Edward Cohen; cos, Rene Hubert

A rare example of a film that succeeds superbly both as a swashbuckler and as historical drama. Michael Ingolby (Olivier) is a young British naval officer whose father is burned to death for heresy by the Spanish Inquisition. He seeks revenge and finds his opportunity in the court of the tempestuous Queen Elizabeth I (a scene-stealing Robson). Elizabeth knows she is surrounded by traitors in league with her archenemy, Philip of Spain (Massey), who plans to invade England. Thus, when Michael offers to infiltrate Philip's court and learn the details of the invasion, Elizabeth seizes the chance. The queen is also romantically inclined toward the handsome officer, and vexed at the attentions he shows his childhood sweetheart who is her lady-in-waiting, Cynthia (Leigh). Michael soon learns of Philip's plans, escapes to England and helps lead the British ships into battle against the Spanish Armada.

A bit slow getting started, and typically glossy in its treatment of details (e.g. the softening of Elizabeth's character), FIRE OVER ENGLAND nevertheless conveys a certain historical grandeur amidst all the showmanship. It succeeds through the combined talents of many great names: Alexander Korda's sponsorship, Pommer's production, Howard's masterful direction, Wong Howe's superb photography, Meerson's grand sets, and the acting of Olivier, Robson and Leigh. A host of versatile supporting players add to the depth of FIRE OVER ENGLAND, not the least of whom are Banks, Selten, and Massey (as the darkly brooding, expansionist King Philip). Look for a bearded James Mason in a small role as an envoy.

FIREMAN'S BALL, THE
(HORI MA PANENKO)

1967 73m c Comedy   ★★★½
Barrandov (Czechoslovakia)

Vaclav Stockel *(Fire Brigade Commander)*, Josef Svet *(Old Man)*, Josef Kolb *(Josef)*, Jan Vostrcil *(Committee Chairman)*, Frantisek Debelka *(1st Committee Member)*, Josef Sebanek *(2nd Committee Member)*, Karel Valnoha *(3rd Committee Member)*, Josef Rehorek *(4th Committee Member)*, Marie Jezkova *(Josef's Wife)*, Anina Lipoldva

d, Milos Forman; w, Milos Forman, Ivan Passer, Jaroslav Papousek; ph, Miroslav Ondricek; ed, Miroslav Hajek; m, Karel Mares

AAN Best Foreign Language Film

This ingratiating farce is perhaps the last noteworthy film of the Czech renaissance before the political crackdown forced most filmmakers, director Forman and co-screenwriter Passer included, into exile. It's a more thorough realization of the same kinds of themes that directors like Forman and Passer developed in several films in the mid-1960s:

invigorating essays in everyday life. THE FIREMAN'S BALL uses a small, local event—in this case a retirement ball and a beauty contest—to examine larger social and political problems.

Promised the presentation of a ceremonial hatchet at a ball given upon his retirement, a cancer-stricken, 86-year-old retired commander of a fire brigade sits helplessly as all hell breaks loose around him. A beauty contest organized as part of the evening's events fizzles. The tension is broken by a fire alarm which tears the fire company away from the festivities to a fire that is destroying another old man's home. Unfortunately things seem to keep going wrong.

The New York Times reported that 40,000 Czech firemen resigned when the government released the film in their homeland. They returned to their posts when Forman let it be known the film might be allegorical. The film received an Academy Award nomination for Best Foreign Film in 1968 but lost to WAR AND PEACE.

FIRM, THE

1993 153m c Thriller   ★★★
Mirage Enterprises (U.S.)   R/15

Tom Cruise *(Mitch McDeere)*, Jeanne Tripplehorn *(Abby McDeere)*, Gene Hackman *(Avery Tolar)*, Hal Holbrook *(Oliver Lambert)*, Terry Kinney *(Lamar Quinn)*, Wilford Brimley *(William Devasher)*, Ed Harris *(Wayne Tarrance)*, Holly Hunter *(Tammy Hemphill)*, David Strathairn *(Ray McDeere)*, Gary Busey *(Eddie Lomax)*

p, Scott Rudin, John A. Davis, Michael Hausman, Sydney Pollack; d, Sydney Pollack; w, David Rabe, Robert Towne, David Rayfiel (from the novel by John Grisham); ph, John Seale; ed, William Steinkamp, Fredric Steinkamp; m, Dave Grusin; prod d, Richard MacDonald; art d, John Willett; fx, Ken Estes; cos, Ruth Myers

AAN Best Supporting Actress: Holly Hunter; *AAN Best Original Score:* Dave Grusin

If stuffy, prestigious law firms were in the business of making thrillers, the results would probably look something like THE FIRM. This is a professional machine of a movie that compresses huge amounts of information into its two and a half hours of screen time. But it's so weighed down by detail, it fails to generate any real suspense.

Directed by Sydney Pollack and adapted from John Grisham's best-seller, THE FIRM pleads the case of Mitch McDeere (Tom Cruise), a hungry, hot-shot Harvard Law School grad who's tempted into a lucrative job with an exclusive Memphis legal practice. The drawback? The firm is a front for the mob, and the only way to escape its grip is by dying, either naturally or otherwise.

Pollack and his screenwriters have made a heroic, but unsuccessful, attempt to boil Grisham's massive book down into a cinematic thriller. Much of the novel's elaborate set-up has been efficiently tailored for the screen, but the ending—which deviates quite drastically from Grisham's—is more confusing than satisfying. It's like spending months cramming for a bar exam, only to finally be given an I.Q. test instead.

Tom Cruise and Jeanne Tripplehorn, as McDeere's wife Abby, give solid if hardly explosive performances, leaving it to the supporting cast to liven things up; standouts are Gene Hackman, as McDeere's criminal mentor; Holly Hunter, as a secretary who helps Mitch out of his jam; and a shaven-headed Ed Harris, as an FBI agent whose temper is quicker than his wit.

FIRST NAME: CARMEN
(PRENOM: CARMEN)

1983 93m c Drama   ★★★½
Sara/Jean-Luc Godard/A2 (France)   /18

Maruschka Detmers *(Carmen X)*, Jacques Bonnaffe *(Joseph Bonnaffe)*, Myriem Roussel *(Claire)*, Christophe Odent *(The Boss)*, Jean-Luc Godard *(Uncle Jean)*, Hyppolite Girardot *(Fred)*, Bertrand Liebert *(Carmen's Bodyguard)*, Alain Bastien-Thiry *(Hotel Worker)*, Pierre-Alain Chapuis, Odile Roire

p, Alain Sarde; d, Jean-Luc Godard; w, Anne-Marie Mieville (based on the novel *Carmen* by Prosper Merimee); ph, Raoul Coutard; ed, Suzanne Lang-Willar; m, Ludwig van Beethoven; cos, Renee Renard

Director Jean-Luc Godard has taken a less than reverent approach to the famed opera *Carmen*. Godard chose to depart substantially from the original Merimee novel and, to the horror of Bizet fans, replaced the composer's score with Beethoven violin concertos and a ballad called "Ruby's Arms" by the gruff-voiced Tom Waits.

Here Carmen (Maruschka Detmers) is a *femme fatale* who concocts a daring plan to rob a bank while pretending to shoot a movie. Luckily she has an uncle (Godard) who was once a brilliant movie director and is now a resident at the local mental hospital. He jumps at the chance to "direct" Carmen's film of the robbery. While staging the robbery, she is nearly apprehended by a police officer (Jacques Bonnaffe), but the two fall in love instead. It appears that Carmen is in complete control of the relationship.

Not only is FIRST NAME: CARMEN optimistic, it is also relatively linear in its narrative structure, making it perhaps Godard's most accessible film. What's more, FIRST NAME: CARMEN is Godard's first comedy, although not in the customary sense. This comes as no surprise as his gangster films, war movies, musicals and dramas are hardly typical of their genres. Godard's films have always had their funny moments but this is his first step in the direction of the great comedians. The film is spiced with passion, philosophy, eroticism, and technical innovation, and while its ideas are relatively accessible, they still do not make for "easy" viewing.

FIRST WIVES CLUB, THE

1996   105m   c   Comedy   ★★
Scott Rudin Productions/Paramount   (U.S.)   PG

Bette Midler (*Brenda Morelli Cushman*), Goldie Hawn (*Elise Elliot Atchison*), Diane Keaton (*Annie MacDuggan Paradise*), Maggie Smith (*Gunilla Garson Goldberg*), Sarah Jessica Parker (*Shelly*), Dan Hedaya (*Morty Cushman*), Bronson Pinchot (*Duarto Feliz*), Jennifer Dundas (*Chris Paradise*), Eileen Heckart (*Catherine MacDuggan*), Stephen Collins (*Aaron Paradise*)

p, Scott Rudin; d, Hugh Wilson; w, Robert Harling (based on the novel by Olivia Goldsmith); ph, Donald Thorin; ed, John Bloom; m, Marc Shaiman; prod d, Peter Larkin; art d, Charley Beal; fx, Matt Vogel, VIFX; cos, Theoni V. Aldredge

AAN Best Original Musical or Comedy Score: Marc Shaiman

THE FIRST WIVES' CLUB drearily proves that a sound comic premise and a dream cast don't guarantee a heavenly farce.

When Cynthia Griffin (Stockard Channing) commits suicide after being deserted by her husband, her three best friends feel her pain: middle-class Brenda (Bette Midler) has been dumped by her husband, Morty (Dan Hedaya), for a beautiful but vulgar bimbo (Sarah Jessica Parker); rich Upper East Side matron Annie (Diane Keaton) has learned that her husband (Stephen Collins) has been having an affair with his therapist (Marcia Gay Harden); and Elise (Goldie Hawn), a fading movie star, has been given the heave-ho by her producer-husband (Victor Garber), who looks to fresher, more nubile talent (Elizabeth Berkley). The three ladies meet up at Cynthia's funeral, get drunk, and plot their revenge: to financially ruin their no-good husbands.

As was the case with the very similar 9 TO 5, the fun is all in the set-up; after the first half hour or so, the film bogs down in petty bitchery and unrelenting vengefulness. The women scream and sneer and slap so much that your sympathy very nearly goes out to their beleaguered victims. Director Hugh Wilson throws pace, nuance, and logic to the wind, and the actresses don't bring anything fresh or exciting to their flatly drawn roles. Midler, as a wistful, struggling single mom, seems totally out of her element; when she breaks out with a catty line it's a welcome relief, but out of character. Hawn seems to be enjoying herself as the epitome of an aerobicized, mindlessly determined careerist, but we've seen her do the funny-shallow-vain bit already. Surprisingly, Keaton is the real embarrassment here: WASP-y repression and spinster-like nervousness have sadly become her stock-in-trade.

FISH CALLED WANDA, A

1988   108m   c   Comedy/Crime/Romance   ★★★
MGM   (U.S.)   R/15

John Cleese (*Archie Leach*), Jamie Lee Curtis (*Wanda Gerschwitz*), Kevin Kline (*Otto*), Michael Palin (*Ken*), Maria Aitken (*Wendy Leach*), Tom Georgeson (*George*), Patricia Hayes (*Mrs. Coady*), Geoffrey Palmer (*Judge*), Cynthia Caylor (*Portia*), Mark Elwes (*Shop Customer*)

p, Michael Shamberg; d, Charles Crichton; w, John Cleese (based on a story by Cleese and Charles Crichton); ph, Alan Hume; ed, John Jympson; m, John Du Prez; prod d, Roger Murray-Leach; fx, George Gibbs; cos, Hazel Pethig

AA Best Supporting Actor: Kevin Kline; *AAN Best Director:* Charles Crichton; *AAN Best Original Screenplay:* John Cleese, Charles Crichton

Combining the talents of Monty Python stalwart John Cleese and Ealing Studios veteran Charles Crichton (THE LAVENDER HILL MOB, THE TITFIELD THUNDERBOLT), this hilariously offbeat post-caper comedy benefits from two of British film comedy's most accomplished traditions.

Cleese, who wrote the screenplay, stars as Archie Leach, an emotionally and sexually repressed English barrister whose life is thrown into upheaval by the appearance of Wanda—not the fish of the title, but a sexy American thief played by Jamie Lee Curtis. She and her gang—Cockney tough guy George (Tom Georgeson), stuttering animal rights advocate, Ken (Michael Palin), and ex-CIA assassin, Otto (Kevin Kline)—pull off a well-executed jewel heist but in the thieves' subsequent rush to double-cross one another and grab all the loot, George ends up in jail and the booty hidden in a safety deposit box, the location of which is known only to him. Deciding that the best way to learn the whereabouts of the jewels is through George's barrister (Cleese), Wanda sets out to seduce the information out of him.

With British-American culture clash as its dominant theme, A FISH CALLED WANDA bristles with wit, enlivened by delightfully over-the-top ensemble acting. Cleese's screenplay uses a farcical framework to send up both British inhibition and formality and American intuitiveness and lack of sophistication. Although filled with clever twists and double-crosses, the film's storyline is less important than the opportunities it gives the actors to exploit their goofy characterizations, especially in the case of Kline who won a Best Supporting Actor Academy Award for his outlandish performance.

FISHER KING, THE

1991   137m   c   Drama/Fantasy/Comedy   ★★½
TriStar/Hill/Obst Productions   (U.S.)   R/15

Robin Williams (*Parry*), Jeff Bridges (*Jack Lucas*), Mercedes Ruehl (*Anne Napolitano*), Amanda Plummer (*Lydia*), Adam Bryant (*Radio Engineer*), Paul Lombardi (*Radio Engineer*), David Pierce (*Lou Rosen*), Ted Ross (*Limo Bum*), Lara Harris (*Sondra*), Warren Olney (*TV Anchorman*)

p, Debra Hill, Lynda Obst; d, Terry Gilliam; w, Richard LaGravenese; ph, Roger Pratt; ed, Lesley Walker; m, George Fenton; prod d, Mel Bourne; art d, P. Michael Johnston; fx, Robert E. McCarthy, Dennis Dion; chor, Robin Horness; cos, Beatrix Pasztor

AAN Best Actor: Robin Williams; *AA Best Supporting Actress:* Mercedes Ruehl; *AAN Best Original Screenplay:* Richard LaGravenese; *AAN Best Score:* George Fenton; *AAN Best Art Direction:* Mel Bourne, Cindy Carr

Terry Gilliam's first project as a directorial "hired gun" is a grandiose, overblown attempt to fuse the medieval myth of the Fisher King with a story of alienation and redemption in contemporary Manhattan.

Jack Lucas (Jeff Bridges) is a cynical disc jockey whose radio talk show attracts the lonely and frustrated. When one of his frequent callers, Edwin (Christian Clemenson), confides he's just met a beautiful girl at Babbitts, a trendy bar, Jack goes off on a vitriolic tirade against the yuppies who frequent the place. He ends by saying: "Edwin, they have to be stopped before it's too late. It's us or them." Taking Jack's words at face value, Edwin goes on a shooting spree inside the restaurant, slaughtering several patrons.

Three years later Jack has reached a nadir of despair and self-loathing. Although involved in a relationship with Anne (Mercedes Ruehl), the supportive owner of a video store, he has lost his will to live. Drunk, he decides to end it all by jumping off a pier into the river. Before he can do this, though, he is attacked by two homicidal teenagers, and then rescued by Parry (Robin Williams), who appears to be some kind of vagrant with a mystical turn of phrase. It turns out that Parry is a former professor of medieval history who is now engaged on a quest for the Holy Grail. Parry is convinced he's spotted the Grail in a magazine (it's actually a silver trophy belonging to a billionaire), and that Jack is the ideal candidate to retrieve it from its owner's castellated Fifth Avenue apartment building.

THE FISHER KING's problems begin with Richard LaGravenese's screenplay and are amplified by Gilliam's showy direction and an unbearably fey performance by Robin Williams. The idea, apparently, was to give an explicitly mythical dimensional to a modern-day story of sin and redemption. Unfortunately, though, the script never resolves the different levels on which it tries to operate, and also throws in too many loose ends which never get cleared up. The tone of the film, largely set by Williams's "Please feel sorry for me" performance, is unremittingly cloying, with an impossibly cute, feel-good ending that adds insult to injury.

There *are* redeeming factors; a scene in which bustling commuters in Grand Central Station are suddenly transformed into waltzing couples has undeniable magic, and Bridges and Ruehl give gritty, unaffected performances that sometimes threaten to make the whole thing believable. For the most part, though, THE FISHER KING is awash in the kind of neo-mythical whimsy that Gilliam helped to puncture in the far more enjoyable MONTY PYTHON AND THE HOLY GRAIL.

FIST IN HIS POCKET
(I PUGNI IN TASCA)
1966 105m bw Drama   ★★★½
Peppercorn/Wormser (Italy)

Lou Castel *(Alessandro)*, Paola Pitagora *(Giulia)*, Marino Mase *(Augusto)*, Liliana Gerace *(Mother)*, Pier Luigi Troglio *(Leone)*, Jennie MacNeil *(Lucia)*, Mauro Martini *(the Boy)*, Gianni Schicchi *(Tonino)*, Alfredo Filippazzi *(Doctor)*, Gianfranco Cella *(Young Man at the Party)*
p, Ezio Passadore; d, Marco Bellocchio; w, Marco Bellocchio; ph, Alberto Marrama; ed, Aurelio Mangiarotti; m, Ennio Morricone; art d, Gisella Longo

This amazing debut film from director Marco Bellochio is an unusual tragicomedy about a family of crazy epileptics—with a blind mother. The plot synopsis suggests a particularly peverse soap opera. Augusto (Mase) is the one healthy member of a family whose manifold problems threaten to stifle his life. He wants to marry but feels he cannot as long as his family is around to bedevil him. His younger brother, Alessandro (Castel), empathizes with his sibling so he decides to kill off the rest of the family so that Augusto can use the resulting inheritance to begin a new life.

Bellochio's exhilaratingly cool and assured direction charges the film with temperament. The savage material—matricide, fratricide, and incest—is never as funny as it seems intended to be; the actors are directed with such verve and passion that audiences are often left too breathless to laugh. Lou Castel's performance seethes with a hateful energy rarely seen on the screen.

FISTFUL OF DOLLARS, A
(PER UN PUGNO DI DOLLARI)
1964 100m c Western   ★★★
Jolly (Italy/Spain/West Germany)   /15

Clint Eastwood *(The Man with No Name)*, Marianne Koch *(Marisol)*, Gian Maria Volonte *(Ramon Rojo)*, Jose Calvo *(Silvanito)*, Wolfgang Lukschy *(John Baxter)*, Sieghardt Rupp *(Esteban Rojo)*, Antonio Prieto *(Benito Rojo)*, Margarita Lozano *(Consuela Baxter)*, Daniel Martin *(Julian)*, Bruno Carotenuto *(Antonio Baxter)*
p, Arrigo Colombo; Giorgio Papi; d, Sergio Leone; w, Sergio Leone, Duccio Tessari, Victor A. Catena, G. Schock (based on the film YOJIMBO by Akira Kurosawa); ph, Massimo Dallamano; ed, Roberto Cinquini; m, Ennio Morricone

A landmark Western that established the Clint Eastwood persona and revitalized the genre. The plot is deceptively simple—and it's lifted from Japanese director Akira Kurosawa's 1961 classic YOJIMBO. Eastwood, the mysterious Man with No Name, rides into a small town embroiled in a struggle for power between two families. Eastwood hires himself out as a mercenary, first to one faction and then to the other, with no regard for honor or morality. He eventually destroys both, leaving the town to the bartender, coffin-maker, and bell ringer as he rides off into the desert from whence he came.

The plot is simple and the Italian performances verge on the operatic, but Leone revitalizes the Western through a unique and complex visual style. The film is full of brilliant spatial relationships (extreme close-ups in the foreground, with detailed compositions visible in the background) combined with Ennio Morricone's vastly creative musical score full of grunts, wails, groans, and bizarre-sounding instruments. Aural and visual elements together give a wholly original perspective on the West and its myths.

Eastwood had a heavy hand in the interpretation of his role, stripping his part of most of its dialogue. His character is wholly amoral, a mystery man with no past who relies on his skill with a gun and his cleverness. This image, which he would hone to perfection in the subsequent Leone movies (and one the actor continues to examine and sometimes criticize, especially in the films in which he directs himself) transformed Eastwood into a cultural icon of almost mythic proportions. Though far from perfected in this film, Leone's style would mature through his next two films and peak with his masterpiece ONCE UPON A TIME IN THE WEST.

FITZCARRALDO
1982 157m c Drama   ★★★★
New World (West Germany)   /PG

Klaus Kinski *(Brian Sweeney Fitzgerald/Fitzcarraldo)*, Claudia Cardinale *(Molly)*, Jose Lewgoy *(Don Aquilino)*, Miguel Angel Fuentes *(Cholo, the Mechanic)*, Paul Hittscher *(Capt. Orinoco Paul)*, Huerequeque Enrique Bohorquez *(Cook)*, Grande Othelo *(Station Master)*, Peter Berling *(Opera Manager)*, David Perez Espinosa *(Chief of the Campa Indians)*, Milton Nascimento *(Black Man at Opera House)*

p, Werner Herzog, Lucki Stipetic; d, Werner Herzog; w, Werner Herzog; ph, Thomas Mauch; ed, Beate Mainka-Jellinghaus; m, Popol Vuh; art d, Henning von Gierke, Ulrich Bergfelder; cos, Gisela Storch

A major filmmaking accomplishment that only Werner Herzog would have the looney audacity to attempt, FITZCARRALDO stars Klaus Kinski as the title character, a dreamer who plans to bring opera and Enrico Caruso to the South American jungles. With limited funding he decides to finance the opera house by capitalizing on South America's rubber industry. He discovers a hidden forest of rubber trees well protected by rapids but the only way to get them is via a river on the other side of a small group of mountains. Fitzcarraldo has a bizarre inspiration: he'll hire local natives to pull his steamship over the mountain—320 tons up a 40-degree incline.

The hauling of the boat is the poetic and symbolic heart of the movie and no camera trickery is used in its filming. This is a real steamship being hauled over a real mountain—all at the command of Herzog, a man as crazed in his way as his most obsessed heroes. The insurmountability of this labor of filmmaking parallels the character's determination to bring Caruso to the jungles, and herein lies the attraction of FITZCARRALDO—it is an artistic achievement that one watches for the drama of the film and of the filmmaking.

Jason Robards was originally set to play the lead but was forced to quit the film after catching a jungle illness. The resulting schedule delays also forced Mick Jagger, who was cast as Robards's sidekick, to drop out. Herzog was quoted as saying, "If I should abandon this film I should be a man without dreams. . . I live my life or end my life with this project." An excellent companion piece is Les Blank's BURDEN OF DREAMS, a documentary about the making of FITZCARRALDO.

FIVE EASY PIECES

1970 96m c Drama ★★★★
BBS (U.S.) R/AA

Jack Nicholson *(Robert Eroica Dupea)*, Karen Black *(Rayette Dipesto)*, Billy "Green" Bush *(Elton)*, Fannie Flagg *(Stoney)*, Sally Struthers *(Betty)*, Marlena MacGuire *(Twinky)*, Richard Stahl *(Recording Engineer)*, William Challee *(Nicholas)*, Helena Kallianiotes *(Palm Apodaca)*, Toni Basil *(Terry Grouse)*

p, Bob Rafelson, Richard Wechsler; d, Bob Rafelson; w, Adrien Joyce (from a story by Joyce and Rafelson); ph, Laszlo Kovacs; ed, Gerald Shepard, Christopher Holmes; m, Johann Sebastian Bach, Wolfgang Amadeus Mozart, Frederic Chopin; cos, Bucky Rous

AAN Best Picture; AAN Best Actor: Jack Nicholson; *AAN Best Supporting Actress:* Karen Black; *AAN Best Adapted Screenplay:* Bob Rafelson (Story), Adrien Joyce (Story)

This episodic character study is one of the key American films of its era. Nicholson, in an early major performance, appears to be a redneck oilrigger in a California oil field. He and his best friend, Bush, when not working together, spend most of their time bowling, downing beers, and just hanging out. This lifestyle is actually a charade. Nicholson hails from a well-to-do family of musicians. He's a brilliant classical pianist who's given up the instrument in favor of another life.

When Black, his witless waitress girlfriend, announces she's pregnant, he leaves his job and heads for Los Angeles to visit Smith, his sister, who is also a pianist and about to record an album. Smith tells Nicholson that their father, Challee, has suffered a pair of strokes back at their home on Puget Sound and he should visit the old man before he dies. Black talks him into taking her along. They bid Bush and his wife, Flagg, goodbye and begin the drive to Washington. What follows is a probing examination of the upper middle class American way of life.

Nicholson delivers a brilliant, edgy and complex characterization and Black won the 1970 New York Film Critics Award for her courageous performance as well as an Oscar nomination. Deceptively simple, PIECES is one of the most complex pictures of the 1970s.

FIVE FINGERS

1952 108m bw Thriller/Spy ★★★★
Fox (U.S.) /U

James Mason *(Cicero)*, Danielle Darrieux *(Anna)*, Michael Rennie *(George Travers)*, Walter Hampden *(Sir Frederic)*, Oscar Karlweis *(Moyzisch)*, Herbert Berghof *(Col. von Richter)*, John Wengraf *(Von Papen)*, Ben Astar *(Siebert)*, Roger Plowden *(MacFadden)*, Michael Pate *(Morrison)*

p, Otto Lang; d, Joseph L. Mankiewicz; w, Michael Wilson (based on the book *Operation Cicero* by L.C. Moyzisch); ph, Norbert Brodine; ed, James B. Clark; m, Bernard Herrmann; art d, Lyle Wheeler, George W. Davis; fx, Fred Sersen

AAN Best Director: Joseph L Mankiewicz; *AAN Best Original Screenplay:* Michael Wilson

Five fingers, yes; five stars, not quite. In a heavily ironic story based, amazingly, on fact, Mason plays a valet working for Sir Frederic (Hampden), the British ambassador in WWII Ankara. Using the pseudonym Cicero, he uses his position to sell military secrets to the Germans. The scheming servant sets up Countess Anna (Darrieux), a down-and-out noblewoman, in a mansion and uses it to meet with Nazi agents. The Germans pay handsomely for Cicero's information even though the Nazi high command considers the secrets—including the real time and date of the invasion in Europe—too incredible to be believed. They are afraid, however, to shut off the flow of information and keep purchasing Cicero's documents. The British finally discover a leak in the embassy, and George Travers (Rennie) leads a team of agents to unearth the spy.

Director Mankiewicz, who also contributed some uncredited dialogue, provides the skillful if somewhat cold direction and holds suspense from beginning to end. Also noteworthy is the fine work of cinematographer Brodine. Although the film never gets us close to any of the characters, Mason is nonetheless a suave wonder to behold as

the shifty, ever-alert Albanian valet who outwits British intelligence. In real life Cicero managed to sell German intelligence 35 top-secret documents. The Nazis never acted on any of them.

FIVE GRAVES TO CAIRO

1943 96m bw Spy ★★★★½
Paramount (U.S.) /A

Franchot Tone *(John J. Bramble)*, Anne Baxter *(Mouche)*, Akim Tamiroff *(Farid)*, Erich von Stroheim *(Field Marshal Rommel)*, Peter Van Eyck *(Lt. Schwegler)*, Fortunio Bonanova *(Gen. Sebastiano)*, Konstantin Shayne *(Maj. von Buelow)*, Fred Nurney *(Maj. Lamprecht)*, Miles Mander *(British Colonel)*, Leslie Denison *(British Captain)*

p, Charles Brackett; d, Billy Wilder; w, Charles Brackett, Billy Wilder (based on the play "Hotel Imperial" by Lajos Biro); ph, John Seitz; ed, Doane Harrison; m, Miklos Rozsa; art d, Hans Dreier, Ernst Fegte; cos, Edith Head

AAN Best Cinematography: John Seitz; *AAN Best Editing:* Doane Harrison; *AAN Best Art Direction:* Hans Dreier (Art Direction), Ernst Fegte (Art Direction), Bertram Granger (Interior Decoration)

Notable as an early example of Wilder's talent for turning headlines into storylines. This tense WWII espionage film stars Tone as John Bramble, a British soldier stranded in a desert town which suddenly fills with German troops. Assuming the role of a dead servant at a hotel run by Farid (Tamiroff), Bramble gradually gains the confidence of French housekeeper Mouche (Baxter), a woman deeply resentful of the British for leaving French troops, including her brother, behind at Dunkirk. After the hotel becomes Rommel's temporary headquarters, Bramble realizes that his impersonation is even more hazardous than he had envisioned: the dead man was really an agent working for the Germans. Convincing the Nazis that he is indeed the spy in their employ, he is instructed to go to Cairo to prepare for a German invasion.

Although the devilishly clever plotting of the film is one of its more obvious merits, FIVE GRAVES TO CAIRO scores on every level. The dialogue is by turns crisp, witty and stinging, and this cast is fully capable of making the most of it. Tone's gift for lending depth to his characters through understatement rarely found such a worthy vehicle. Baxter (in a moving turn and sporting a decent French accent), Tamiroff, Mander, Van Eyck (as a sleazy Nazi aide), and Bonanova (as an opera-loving Italian general) are all in fine form as well.

But of course a large share of the praise must go to that master scene-stealer Von Stroheim. Alternately brutal and civilized, arrogant and quiet, Rommel emerges as a complex military genius in this marvelous performer's hands. Wilder introduces him with a close-up of the back of his creased neck bursting over a high military collar, a technique Von Stroheim used in silent days when he profiled the evil Huns of WWI.

FIVE PENNIES, THE

1959 117m c Musical/Biography ★★★
Paramount (U.S.) /U

Danny Kaye *(Loring "Red" Nichols)*, Barbara Bel Geddes *(Bobbie Meredith)*, Louis Armstrong *(Himself)*, Bob Crosby *(Wil Paradise)*, Harry Guardino *(Tony Valani)*, Susan Gordon *(Dorothy Nichols at 6)*, Tuesday Weld *(Dorothy at 12 to 14)*, Valerie Allen *(Tommye Eden)*, Ray Anthony *(Jimmy Dorsey)*, Shelly Manne *(Dave Tough)*

p, Jack Rose; d, Melville Shavelson; w, Melville Shavelson, Jack Rose (based on a story by Robert Smith, suggested by the life of Loring "Red" Nichols); ph, Daniel Fapp; ed, Frank P. Keller; m, Leith Stevens; art d, Hal Pereira, Tambi Larsen; fx, John P. Fulton

AAN Best Cinematography: Daniel L Fapp; *AAN Best Score:* Leith Stevens; *AAN Best Song:* Sylvia Fine (Music & Lyrics); *AAN Best Costume Design:* Edith Head

All that jazz. A schmaltz-laden biopic, THE FIVE PENNIES is nevertheless a jazz lover's movie, chock full of good old Dixieland tunes. Kaye plays Loring "Red" Nichols, who migrates to New York, where his cornet playing gains him acclaim with the Wil Paradise Band. He meets singer Bobbie Meredith (Bel Geddes, her vocals dubbed by Eileen Wilson); they later marry and have a baby girl. When Red and Paradise (Crosby) disagree over the latter's conservative repertoire, the flaming Red finally gets axed. Coming back with a new group, "The Five Pennies," however, he soon becomes a jazz legend as a leading purveyor of Dixieland.

Decent enough as entertainment, THE FIVE PENNIES doesn't always manage to avoid slipping on its own soap. The film unfortunately gets a mite laughable as it equates, in true repressed 1950s fashion, Red's inability to hit a high note on his horn with sexual impotence. (See Kirk Douglas in YOUNG MAN WITH A HORN for another example of this phenomenon.) Otherwise, Kaye, as aggressively eager to please as ever, is pretty believable as the ambitious jazzman who rolls with some tough punches. Bel Geddes brings warmth if not excitement to her role as his loyal wife, and 15 year-old Weld, in her film debut as Red's daughter, gives evidence of her future success. Jazz fans will be most delighted, however, by the duet by Nichols (who actually plays Kaye's solos) and Louis Armstrong; other jazzmen in the film include Ray Anthony, Bobby Troup, Shelly Manne and Ray Daley.

5,000 FINGERS OF DR. T., THE

1953   89m   c   Children's/Fantasy/Musical   ★★★★½
Columbia   (U.S.)   /U

Peter Lind Hayes (Zabladowski), Mary Healy (Mrs. Collins), Hans Conried (Dr. Terwilliker), Tommy Rettig (Bart), John Heasley (Uncle Whitney), Robert Heasley (Uncle Judson), Noel Cravat (Sgt. Lunk), Henry Kulky (Stroogo)

p, Stanley Kramer; d, Roy Rowland; w, Ted Geisel, Allan Scott; ph, Franz Planer; ed, Al Clark; m, Frederick Hollander; prod d, Rudolph Sternad; art d, Cary Odell; chor, Eugene Loring

AAN Best Score: Frederick Hollander, Morris Stoloff

Hollywood films just don't get any weirder than this underappreciated 1950s classic. This surrealistic children's film (cowritten by Ted Geisel, better known as Dr. Seuss), features Tommy Rettig of TV's "Lassie" as Bart Collins, a young boy who would rather play baseball than take piano lessons with the eccentric and tyrannical Dr. Terwilliker (Conried).

Falling asleep at his piano, Bart dreams he's being chased by weird creatures with butterfly nets through a land of fog, cylinders, and odd-shaped mounds. Here he stumbles upon the castle of Dr. T, who runs a piano school for captive boys. The film's key image is the massive winding double-decker piano keyboard with 500 seats, one for each student. 500 boys, 5000 fingers—get it? Kept in the dungeon are pitiful creatures imprisoned as punishment for playing instruments other than the piano. The prisoners have built musical instruments out of odd materials and, in the film's most elaborate sequence, perform a strange ballet. Bart's widowed mom (Mary Healy) is second-in-command at this terrible school but she is hypnotized by Dr. T. Eventually Bart teams up with Mr. Zabladowski (Hayes), a resourceful plumber and reluctant surrogate father, to topple Dr. T's evil empire.

THE 5,000 FINGERS OF DR T. is one of the best fantasy films ever produced by Hollywood. Adults will find it every bit as diverting and intriguing as children as it explicitly connects dreams, surrealism and psychoanaysis. The dreamy sets succeed in making this film look like a Dr. Seuss book brought to life. Rettig and Hayes are delightful and Healy's OK but Conried gives what may be the performance of his estimable career as the dastardly fop. Though at times deliriously perverse, particularly in the context of conformist 1950s filmmaking, the film is also quite moving. Essential viewing for any potentially cool kids.

FLAMINGO KID, THE

1984   100m   c   Comedy/Drama   ★★★½
Mercury/ABC   (U.S.)   PG-13/15

Matt Dillon (Jeffrey Willis), Hector Elizondo (Arthur Willis), Molly McCarthy (Ruth Willis), Martha Gehman (Nikki Willis), Richard Crenna (Phil Brody), Jessica Walter (Phyllis Brody), Carole Davis (Joyce Brody), Janet Jones (Carla Samson), Brian McNamara (Steve Dawkins), Fisher Stevens (Hawk Ganz)

p, Michael Phillips; d, Garry Marshall; w, Garry Marshall, Neal Marshall (based on his story); ph, James A. Contner; ed, Priscilla Nedd; prod d, Lawrence Miller; art d, Duke Durfee; cos, Ellen Mirojnick

A touching account of a working-class teenager tempted to reject his honorable ambitions in favor of a life of easy luxury.

Jeffrey Willis (Dillon) is an 18-year-old Brooklyn kid who joins some friends on a jaunt to "El Flamingo," a ritzy beachside club for affluent Long Islanders. There he observes Phil Brody (Crenna), a wealthy car dealer and the club's champion gin player, effectively demolishing his competition at the card table. Jeffrey is hired by the club for the summer, and slowly a romance develops between him and Brody's niece, Carla (Jones). Brody also takes a liking to Jeffrey and helps him get a promotion. After a talk with his new mentor, Jeffrey decides to become a car salesman too. His father (Elizondo), who dreams of his son's going to college, is dead set against this idea.

There's not a single bad performance here, and director Marshall wisely builds his film on small moments, realized with sympathy and intelligence.

FLASH GORDON

1936   97m   bw   Science Fiction   ★★★★
Universal   (U.S.)   /PG

Buster Crabbe (Flash Gordon), Jean Rogers (Dale Arden), Charles Middleton (Ming, the Merciless), Priscilla Lawson (Princess Aura), Jack Lipson (King Vultan), Richard Alexander (Prince Barin), Frank Shannon (Dr. Zarkov), Duke York Jr. (King Kala), Earl Askam (Officer Torch), George Cleveland (Prof. Hensley)

p, Henry MacRae; d, Frederick Stephani; w, Frederick Stephani, George Plympton, Basil Dickey, Ella O'Neill (based on the comic strip by Alex Raymond); ph, Jerome Ash, Richard Fryer; m, Franz Waxman; art d, Ralph Berger; fx, Norman Drewes

The one, the only, the original, and the best, this film was initially released as a 13-part serial based on a King Features comic strip.

Flash Gordon (Crabbe), his companion, Dr. Zarkov (Shannon), and sweetheart Dale Arden (Rogers) blast off for the planet Mongo, trying to stop it from a collision course with Earth. In a flash, Flash encounters evil Ming the Merciless (the unforgettable Middleton) along with assorted hawk men, shark men, dinosaurs, horned gorillas, giant lobsters, space ships (hanging from decidedly visible wires) and some mighty nifty costumes. Ming lusts wantonly for Dale, and Princess Aura (Lawson), Ming's equally lustful daughter, has a heavy crush on Flash.

A film whose naive, eager-to-please energy is almost as transporting as Flash's rocketship, FLASH GORDON is likely to delight even the fussiest audiences. The music and some of the sets were borrowed from THE BRIDE OF FRANKENSTEIN, and several sequels were to borrow heavily from this film. Not to be missed.

FLASH OF GREEN, A

1984   131m   c   Drama   ★★★½
Spectrafilm   (U.S.)

Ed Harris (Jimmy Wing), Blair Brown (Kate Hubble), Richard Jordan (Elmo Bliss), George Coe (Brian Haas), Joan Goodfellow (Mitchie), Jean De Baer (Jackie Halley), Helen Stenborg (Aunt Middie), William Mooney (Leroy Shannard), Isa Thomas (Doris Rohl), John Glover (Ross Halley)

p, Richard Jordan; d, Victor Nunez; w, Victor Nunez (based on the novel by John D. MacDonald); ph, Victor Nunez; ed, Victor Nunez; m, Charles Engstrom; art d, Carlos Asse; cos, Marilyn Wall-Asse, Dana Moser

Adapted and directed by Victor Nunez, A FLASH OF GREEN is a sure-handed look at corruption in Florida, with all the richly observed characterizations found in John D. MacDonald's novel.

In the mythical town of Palm City, we first meet Jimmy Wing (Harris), a likable reporter for the local paper. Elmo Bliss (Jordan), the local county commissioner, has been a pal of Jimmy's since they were in school together years before. Elmo is very ambitious and comes to Jimmy with a bribe offer. Elmo and his buddies want to gain control of some publicly owned land for development but are stymied by a group of ecological do-gooders known as the "SOBs" (Save Our Bay). The would-be developers mean to get that opposition out of the way, and things start to get pretty ugly before it's all over.

A complex story with no easy answers, A FLASH OF GREEN is beautifully acted, and one of the few adaptations of a MacDonald novel that sticks closely to the intent of the original. Where it falls apart is in failing to provide a sustained story line for the audience. Too many side issues detract from the story, and the uncertain editing doesn't help. But the film is moody, steamy and provocative enough to warrant your attention.

FLESH

1968   105m   c   Drama   ★★★
Andy Warhol Productions   (U.S.)

Joe Dallesandro *(Joe)*, Geraldine Smith *(Gerry)*, John Christian *(Young Man)*, Maurice Bardell *(Artist)*, Harry Brown *(Boy on Street)*, Candy Darling *(Blonde on Sofa)*, Jackie Curtis *(Redhead on Sofa)*, Geri Miller *(Terry)*, Louis Waldon *(David)*, Patti D'Arbanville *(Gerry's Girlfriend)*

p, Andy Warhol; d, Paul Morrisey; w, Paul Morrisey; ph, Paul Morrisey; ed, Paul Morrisey

As Andy Warhol recuperated from gunshot wounds inflicted by Valerie Solanis, his Factory associate Paul Morrisey directed this drowsy, picaresque tale of a henpecked Manhattan hustler, the first of several "Warhol" films that are actually part of Morrisey's equally interesting *oeuvre*. Joe (Joe Dallesandro), a virtually affectless but oddly charming creature of the East Village, drags himself out of bed to hustle tricks on 33rd Street; his girlfriend Gerry (Geraldine Smith) has demanded cash to pay for an abortion. During a long day of entrepreneurial improvisation, Joe encounters a variety of Warhol regulars, including legendary transvestites Jackie Curtis and Candy Darling (who, along with Dallesandro, were later immortalized in Lou Reed's "Walk On The Wild Side"). Although FLESH displays many of the hallmarks of Warhol's non-narrative house style (endless takes, speed-fueled improvisation, casually amateurish lighting and sound), Morrisey is already experimenting with the kind of traditional filmmaking techniques that Warhol pretended to disdain—at least until Morrisey's increasingly polished movies began turning handsome profits.

FLIGHT OF THE PHOENIX, THE

1965   149m   c   Adventure   ★★★★
Fox   (U.S.)   /A

James Stewart *(Frank Towns)*, Richard Attenborough *(Lew Moran)*, Peter Finch *(Capt. Harris)*, Hardy Kruger *(Heinrich Dorfmann)*, Ernest Borgnine *(Trucker Cobb)*, Ian Bannen *(Crow)*, Ronald Fraser *(Sgt. Watson)*, Christian Marquand *(Dr. Renaud)*, Dan Duryea *(Standish)*, George Kennedy *(Bellamy)*

p, Robert Aldrich; d, Robert Aldrich; w, Lukas Heller (based on a novel by Elleston Trevor); ph, Joseph Biroc; ed, Michael Luciano; m, Frank DeVol; art d, William Glasgow; fx, L.B. Abbott, Howard Lydecker; cos, Norma Koch

AAN Best Supporting Actor: Ian Bannen; *AAN Best Editing:* Michael Luciano

A riveting survival film in which Stewart and his cohorts give power-packed performances as a downed pilot and passengers awaiting death in the Sahara desert.

At first pilot Frank Towns (Stewart) assumes the blame for the crash landing, although it's clearly the fault of alcoholic navigator Lew Moran (Attenborough). For a while, the men await rescue in the broiling sun, conserving their water. British officer Capt. Harris (Finch), however, decides to seek help from a passing caravan, but he gets more than he bargains for from the hostile Arabs. All seems hopeless until Heinrich Dorfmann (Kruger) announces that he can design a working single-engined plane from the wreck.

The crux of this gripping drama ultimately becomes the antagonism between pilot Towns and scientist Dorfmann, and Stewart and Kruger handle their encounters superbly—particularly in the scene where Towns learns that Dorfmann is a designer of *model* airplanes. Finch is convincing as the stoic British officer, and Borgnine, Marquand, and Duryea give fine performances as stranded men. Aldrich's direction is sharp and well paced, and Heller's screenplay absorbing and authentic.

FLINTSTONES, THE

1994   92m   c   Comedy/Fantasy/Children's   ★★½
Amblin   (U.S.)   PG/

John Goodman *(Fred Flintstone)*, Elizabeth Perkins *(Wilma Flintstone)*, Rick Moranis *(Barney Rubble)*, Rosie O'Donnell *(Betty Rubble)*, Kyle MacLachlan *(Cliff Vandercave)*, Halle Berry *(Miss Rosetta Stone)*, Elizabeth Taylor *(Pearl Slaghoople)*, Dann Florek *(Mr. Slate)*, Richard Moll *(Hoagie)*, Irwin Keyes *(Joe Rockhead)*

p, Bruce Cohen; d, Brian Levant; w, Tom S. Parker, Jim Jennewein, Steven E. de Souza (based on the animated series from Hanna-Barbera Productions); ph, Dean Cundey; ed, Kent Beyda, David Tanaka; m, David Newman; prod d, William Sandell; art d, Jim Teegarden, Nancy Patton, Christopher Burian-Mohr; fx, Industrial Light & Magic, Mark Dippe, Michael Lantieri; chor, Adam M. Shankman; cos, Rosanna Norton, Monique Brown

THE FLINTSTONES is the most faithful of all the film recreations of 60s TV shows, but is fidelity to a cartoon knock-off of "The Honeymooners" really a virtue? Rarely has more high-powered movie technology been deployed to achieve such frivolous ends. Kids seem to love it, while sophisticated viewers may find it enchanting, appalling, or both.

Smarmy executive Cliff Vandercave (Kyle MacLachlan) plans to embezzle big bucks from the Slate Gravel Company by framing a gullible working stiff promoted from the gravel pit. Engagingly oafish Fred Flintstone (John Goodman) fits the bill. He becomes a V.P. and has to fire his pal Barney Rubble (Rick Moranis), a new adoptive father. Subsequently, he is tricked into laying off all of his former co-workers in the gravel pit. Fred's life falls apart at home and at the office, but we're never worried that it won't all work out for the best.

THE FLINTSTONES is about as good as it could possibly be. The spirit of the TV cartoon sitcom is obsessively recreated with the genuine love of an ardent fan. The silly puns are delivered with conviction; the sets, costumes, and critters look great; and Goodman is a stroke of casting genius. (The sole innovation here is a PC view of a BC society; this Bedrock is thoroughly integrated.) Not many belly laughs, but constant smiles of recognition for the sympathetically inclined.

FLIRTING

1990   96m   c   Drama/Romance   ★★★½
Kennedy-Miller Productions   (Australia)   R/PG

Noah Taylor *(Danny Embling)*, Thandie Newton *(Thandiwe Adjewa)*, Nicole Kidman *(Nicola Radcliffe)*, Bartholomew Rose *("Gilby" Fryer)*, Felix Nobis *(Jock Blair)*, Josh Picker *("Baka" Bourke)*, Kiri Paramore *("Slag" Green)*, Marc Gray *(Christopher Laidlaw)*, Greg Palmer *(Colin Proudfoot)*, Joshua Marshall *("Cheddar" Fedderson)*

p, George Miller, Terry Hayes, Doug Mitchell; d, John Duigan; w, John Duigan; ph, Geoff Burton; ed, Robert Gibson; prod d, Roger Ford

This sequel to writer-director John Duigan's acclaimed THE YEAR MY VOICE BROKE is an intelligently written and marvelously acted coming-of-age tale set in rural Australia in the 1960s.

Danny Embling (Noah Taylor) is a bright, sensitive boarding school student who falls in love with Thandiwe Adjewa (Thandie Newton), the only black pupil at the girl's school which sits tantalizingly across the lake from Danny's college. Despite the interference of authoritarian teachers and bigoted school bullies, the two embark on an extremely charming relationship that is ended when political events force Thandiwe's family to return to Uganda.

FLIRTING is a rather more serious film than its name implies. Duigan's main focus is on the teenage love story, yet he gives his tale a broader dramatic context through succinct, telling allusions to bigger events taking place in the world at large. Aided by a literate screenplay and fine performances from his ensemble cast, Duigan brings a sense of universality to his treatment of first love, while still filtering in a keen sense of time and place.

Taylor, as young outsider Danny, is flawless in his interpretation of the character, displaying an uncanny depth seldom found in juvenile actors. The exceptionally pretty Newton is graceful and charming as Thandiwe and Nicole Kidman (DEAD CALM, FAR AND AWAY)

contributes a fine turn in the underwritten role of Nicola Radcliffe, an initially snobbish upperclassman who becomes a firm friend of Thandiwe's.

FLOWER OF MY SECRET, THE
(LA FLOR DE MI SECRETO)

1995   107m   c   Drama/Romance   ★★★½
CiBy 2000/El Deseo SA   (Spain/France)   R/15

Marisa Paredes (Leo Macias), Juan Echanove (Angel), Imanol Arias (Paco), Carmen Elias (Betty), Rossy de Palma (Rosa), Chus Lampreave (Mother), Joaquin Cortes (Antonio), Manuela Vargas (Blanca), Kiti Manver, Gloria Munoz

p, Esther Garcia; d, Pedro Almodovar; w, Pedro Almodovar; ph, Affonso Beato; ed, Jose Salcedo; m, Alberto Iglesias; art d, Wolfgang Burmann; fx, Molina; cos, Hugo Mezcua, Marisa Paredes, Juan Echanove

In THE FLOWER OF MY SECRET, the usually comedic filmmaker Pedro Almodovar opts for melodrama rather than farce as he follows a romance novelist who conducts her personal life as if she were one of her own compulsive heroines.

Best-selling author Leo (Marisa Paredes) is intent on resuscitating her already-dead marriage to Paco (Imanol Arias), a NATO officer who is often away from home. Although unable to extricate herself from her unrequited love, she jump-starts her professional life by taking a critic's post at El Pais, a newspaper run by the portly Angel (Juan Echanove). Absorbed in heartache, Leo doesn't realize that Angel has more than an editorial interest in her.

Fluidly directed, this wittily conceived exploration of loving well but unwisely parallels serious scenes and pastel parodies. Perhaps this clever film signifies Almodovar's own acceptance of his unique gifts as soap opera jester. But there's nothing more serious than the aspects of love he deals with, and the film's comedy doesn't diminish its sentimental impact. Paredes is a superb dramatic actress, who meshes beautifully with the melancholy of this Almodovar offering. Through this vibrant actress, Almodovar counsels inveterate sufferers that, by working through their pain, they can reach a future that flowers more sublimely than any unfulfilled romantic past. This bracing comedy-drama holds out a hand to anyone who has ever despaired of finding love a second or third time around.

FLOWERS OF ST. FRANCIS, THE
(FRANCESCO, GIULLARE DI DIO)

1950   75m   bw   Religious   ★★★★★
Cineriz/Rizzoli   (Italy)

Aldo Fabrizi (Nicolaio, the Tyrant), Arabella Lemaire (Saint Clair), Brother Nazario Gerardi (Saint Francis)

p, Giuseppe Amato; d, Roberto Rossellini; w, Roberto Rossellini, Federico Fellini, Fr. Felix Morion, Fr. Antonio Lisandrini (based on the life of Fioretti di San Francesco); ph, Otello Martelli; ed, Jolando Benvenuti; m, Renzo Rossellini, Fr. Enrico Buondonno

A film of great harmony and natural beauty, this short historical feature from the celebrated Italian noerealist Roberto Rossellini is a tone poem comprised of physical gestures. Performed, with the exception of Aldo Fabrizi, by nonprofessionals (all of whom are real-life Franciscan monks), the film captures the brothers' purity and their desire to live in harmony with nature. More striking than the film's grand themes—man and nature, God and man, peace and defiance, love and hate, generosity and greed—Rossellini sensitively captures the monks' expressive physical movements. Illustrating one character's line of dialogue, "Souls are won over by examples, not words," Rossellini does not show us speeches or have us listen to readings from scripture. Instead we see the hands and faces of these monks, their wonder, their peace, their simplicity. As these monks can say so much with their eyes, so too can Rossellini speak volumes with a single shot.

FLY, THE

1986   100m   c   Horror   ★★★★½
Brooksfilms   (U.S.)   R/18

Jeff Goldblum (Seth Brundle), Geena Davis (Veronica Quaife), John Getz (Stathis Borans), Joy Boushel (Tawny), Les Carlson (Dr. Cheevers), George Chuvalo (Marky), Michael Copeman (Man in Bar), David Cronenberg (Gynecologist), Carol Lazare (Nurse), Shawn Hewitt (Clerk)

p, Stuart Cornfeld; d, David Cronenberg; w, Charles Pogue, David Cronenberg (based on a story by George Langelaan); ph, Mark Irwin; ed, Ronald Sanders; m, Howard Shore; prod d, Carol Spier; art d, Rolf Harvey; fx, Louis Craig, Ted Ross; cos, Denise Cronenberg

AA Best Makeup: Chris Walas, Stephan Dupuis

Obsessed with the horrifying implications of a combination of science, technology and the powerful potentials of the human mind, body and sexuality, Cronenberg had created several highly personal films over the previous 15 years. While the concepts of these films are interesting and unique, the films themselves were quite uneven. Slapdash, poorly cast, underbudgeted, and sometimes incoherent, there was also insufficient attention paid to the development of characters as complex, emotional human beings. With his decision to remake the 1958 classic THE FLY, Cronenberg found the perfect outlet for his obsessions, producing his most controlled, mature and insightful work to date.

Enhanced by a more complex personal relationship between the protagonists, the new version of THE FLY pairs a young science-magazine reporter, Veronica Quaife (Geena Davis), and a somewhat shy, awkward scientist, Seth Brundle (Jeff Goldblum), who is involved in a secret experiment to transport matter that will "change life as we know it." Although brilliant intellectually, Brundle lacks social graces and his endearingly clumsy efforts to seduce Veronica look like a high school nerd trying to impress the prom queen with his science project. The pair gradually fall in love, and they make a heartwarming couple. Brundle continues his experiments, trying to advance from transporting objects to transporting living beings. Eventually, he is driven to transport himself but fails to notice the little fly that has traveled through space with him.

THE FLY succeeds on many levels. Cronenberg has never elicited better performances from his players. Goldblum is sublime in a rare leading role. Davis is also in top form. As a couple, they are so convincing and appealing that one regrets knowing that their love story will soon become a tragic horror movie. As a remake, THE FLY transcends the original, taking it in new directions and exploring its underutilized potential. Whereas the original degenerated into a campy fly hunt, the remake opts for a slow metamorphosis from man to fly that develops as a disease might. This gives Cronenberg time to examine the implications of such a process, meditating upon our fear of disease, death and change.

FLY AWAY HOME

1996   110m   c   Children's/Drama   ★★★½
Branti Film Productions/Sandollar Productions   (U.S.)   PG/U

Jeff Daniels (Thomas Alden), Anna Paquin (Amy Alden), Dana Delany (Susan Barnes), Terry Kinney (David Alden), Holter Graham (Barry Stickland), Jeremy Ratchford (Glen Seifert), Deborah Verginella (Amy's Mother), Michael J. Reynolds (General), David Hemblen (Dr. Killian), Ken James (Developer)

p, John Veitch, Carol Baum; d, Carroll Ballard; w, Robert Rodat, Vince McKewin (based on the autobiography by Bill Lishman); ph, Caleb Deschanel; ed, Nicholas C. Smith; m, Mark Isham; prod d, Seamus Flannery; fx, Martin Malivoire, John Mariella, C.O.R.E. Digital Pictures; cos, Marie-Sylvie Deveau

AAN Best Cinematography: Caleb Deschanel

An incredible journey in the air becomes a voyage of self-discovery for a young girl in this touching tale directed by Carroll Ballard (THE BLACK STALLION).

After her mother's death, 13-year-old Amy Alden (Anna Paquin, THE PIANO) is uprooted from her New Zealand home and sent to Canada to live with a father she doesn't remember. Tom Alden (Jeff Daniels) is an eccentric artist, inventor, and flying enthusiast who hasn't a clue about how to reach out to the brooding Amy. When nearby woods are clear-cut by developers, Amy discovers an abandoned nest of goose eggs, which she secretly adopts. When the goslings hatch, they imprint on Amy as their mother goose. As the birds mature, the Aldens face a dilemma: by law, domesticated geese must be pinioned, but the orphaned flock doesn't know how to migrate. Tom hatches a crazy scheme: he will fly the migration route with Amy following him in her own plane, and the geese following behind her.

One of the best "family films" of 1996, FLY AWAY HOME was nonetheless largely overlooked by audiences who clamor for such offerings from Hollywood. Though a reading of the film's plot rings like a knock-off of FREE WILLY, the film, based on a true incident, is a resonant and affecting work. Ballard and cinematographer Caleb Deschanel rely largely on beautiful and poetic imagery to tell Amy's story and effectively reign in any potentially hokey melodrama. Paquin gives a nicely modulated, understated performance that allows viewers to indentify with Amy. And so, in the end, when she soars through the clouds with the white ocean shoals below, Ballard has correctly calculated how to make the viewer's spirit soar as well.

FLYING DOWN TO RIO

1933 89m bw Musical   ★★★★
RKO (U.S.)   /U

Dolores Del Rio *(Belinha de Rezende)*, Gene Raymond *(Roger Bond)*, Raul Roulien *(Julio Rubeiro)*, Ginger Rogers *(Honey Hale)*, Fred Astaire *(Fred Ayres)*, Blanche Frederici *(Dona Elena)*, Walter Walker *(Senor de Rezende)*, Etta Moten *(Black Singer)*, Roy D'Arcy, Maurice Black

p, Lou Brock; d, Thornton Freeland; w, Cyril Hume, H.W. Hanemann, Erwin Gelsey (based on a play by Anne Caldwell from an original story by Brock); ph, J. Roy Hunt; ed, Jack Kitchin; m, Vincent Youmans; art d, Van Nest Polglase, Carroll Clark; fx, Vernon L. Walker; chor, Dave Gould; cos, Walter Plunkett

AAN Best Song: Vincent Youmans (Music), Edward Eliscu (Lyrics), Gus Kahn (Lyrics)

Highway robbery, Astaire-Rogers style. Whoever failed to see that the brilliantly talented and engaging Astaire and the playful, gifted Rogers were ideal star material must have been wearing airplane goggles throughout the making of FLYING DOWN TO RIO. Billed fourth and fifth, playing a sassy band singer and the accordionist pal of romantic lead Raymond, Rogers and Astaire positively shimmer with high spirits in this whoops-a-daisy extravaganza.

RKO's bid to cash in on the new breed of musical introduced by the Busby Berkeley tunefests over at Warner Bros. FLYING DOWN TO RIO toplines gorgeous, dark Del Rio and gorgeous, white-blonde Raymond in a silly romantic triangle alongside likable crooner Roulien. Although the lead trio does well enough, the presence of cinema's greatest musical comedy team fairly blasts the screen lovers into orbit whenever either or both of them are onscreen.

Astaire and Rogers both have a great flair for comedy; perhaps only Joan Blondell and Eve Arden can equal Rogers's way with a wisecrack. Working more apart than together in this initial venture, Ginger and Fred all but monopolize the delightful Youmans score. The 18-minute showpiece, "The Carioca," though it gives the dynamic duo but a few moments together on the dance floor, already represents the start of a beautiful conspiracy.

The only major production number not to spotlight Rogers and Astaire is the title tune, a bizarre attempt to outdo Busby's bodacious ballets with chorines strapped to airplane wings. Despite this lollapalooza's tuneful terror tactics, the film's most memorable image is the last one: Fred and Ginger bantering before the end titles. They are *more* than ready to be stars on their own. A kooky Depression-era delight.

FOLLOW THE BOYS

1944 122m bw Musical/Comedy   ★★★½
Universal (U.S.)   /U

George Raft *(Tony West)*, Vera Zorina *(Gloria Vance)*, Grace McDonald *(Kitty West)*, Charley Grapewin *(Nick West)*, Charles Butterworth *(Louie Fairweather)*, Ramsay Ames *(Laura)*, Elizabeth Patterson *(Annie)*, Regis Toomey *(Dr. Jim Henderson)*, George Macready *(Walter Bruce)*, Spooks the Dog *(Junior)*

p, Charles K. Feldman; d, A. Edward Sutherland; w, Lou Breslow, Gertrude Purcell; ph, David Abel; ed, Fred R. Feitshans Jr.; art d, John B. Goodman, Harold MacArthur; fx, John P. Fulton; chor, George Hale; cos, Vera West, Howard Greer

AAN Best Song: Jule Styne (Music), Sammy Cahn (Lyrics)

Forget about the penny-dreadful's worth of plot and just sit back and enjoy the star cameos. A long wartime rouser, FOLLOW THE BOYS begins with the closing of New York's Palace Theater and the demise of vaudeville. Tony (Raft), Kitty (McDonald), and Nick West (Grapewin), a brother-sister-father trio, have just finished doing their turkey of an act at the Palace in New York, and Tony suggests that they try their luck in Hollywood. Once there, Tony soon hits it big, teaming with Gloria Vance (Zorina) in several hit movies. They fall in love and marry, but WWII drives them apart as Tony, refused induction because of a bad knee, takes on the task of organizing entertainment for the fighting men going overseas.

It's perhaps unfair to criticize FOLLOW THE BOYS for its hackneyed storyline, considering that the real purpose of the film is to show off the assortment of legendary performers herein assembled. The odd collection consists largely of established talent on its way down or notable personalities on their way up, but one cherishes the film for what it records for posterity. Jeanette MacDonald reprises one of her earliest song hits, "Beyond the Blue Horizon" and Sophie Tucker is on hand to belt out her signature "Some of These Days." W.C. Fields, meanwhile, though clearly not in the best of health, commits another performance of his famous pool routine to celluloid, and the Andrews Sisters do a fun medley of several of their hits.

Perhaps most priceless of all, however, is Orson Welles, who, assisted by Marlene Dietrich, does a marvelous six-minute magic act. Follow the boys? Sure, why not!

FOLLOW THE FLEET

1936 110m bw Musical/Comedy   ★★★★½
RKO (U.S.)   /U

Fred Astaire *(Bake Baker)*, Ginger Rogers *(Sherry Martin)*, Randolph Scott *(Bilge Smith)*, Harriet Hilliard *(Connie Martin)*, Astrid Allwyn *(Iris Manning)*, Harry Beresford *(Capt. Ezra Hickey)*, Russell Hicks *(Jim Nolan)*, Brooks Benedict *(Sullivan, Nolan's Assistant)*, Ray Mayer *(Dopey Williams)*, Lucille Ball *(Kitty Collins)*

p, Pandro S. Berman; d, Mark Sandrich; w, Dwight Taylor, Allan Scott (based on the play "Shore Leave" by Hubert Osborne); ph, David Abel; ed, Henry Berman; art d, Van Nest Polglase, Carroll Clark; fx, Vernon L. Walker; chor, Hermes Pan, Fred Astaire; cos, Bernard Newman

Often regarded as one of the best of the legendary Astaire-Rogers musicals, FOLLOW THE FLEET really isn't up to TOP HAT, SWING TIME or ROBERTA, the wonder films of the series. The main reason is the bland plot, which, though similar to that of several of their other films, grinds along at a rather poky pace. Astaire and Scott play sailor buddies on leave, and Rogers and Hilliard are cast as sisters with whom they become involved.

Essentially consigned to second-lead status, Rogers and Astaire fittingly play the couple who already know each other, and they banter their way through their dialogue with great rapport. Their range and talent as dancers is also on prominent display here, from their explosive romp to "Let Yourself Go" to Astaire's blazing nautical tap to "I'd Rather Lead a Band" to Roger's delightful solo, her first in the series.

They are hilariously out of sync with each other in a comic cut-up routine to "I'm Putting All My Eggs in One Basket" and resume their trademark after-dinner elegance for a stunning turn to "Let's Face the Music and Dance." Performed as part of a melodramatic playlet onstage, this glamorous number is the closest they ever got to playing Garbo, replete with sumptuous poses and an unforgettable finale. Occasional lumps notwithstanding, FOLLOW THE FLEET is great entertainment. All aboard!

FOOTLIGHT PARADE

1933 102m bw Musical ★★★★★
Warner Bros. (U.S.) /U

James Cagney *(Chester Kent)*, Joan Blondell *(Nan Prescott)*, Ruby Keeler *(Bea Thorn)*, Dick Powell *(Scotty Blair)*, Guy Kibbee *(Silas Gould)*, Ruth Donnelly *(Harriet Bowers Gould)*, Claire Dodd *(Vivian Rich)*, Hugh Herbert *(Charlie Bowers)*, Frank McHugh *(Francis)*, Arthur Hohl *(Al Frazer)*

p, Robert Lord; d, Lloyd Bacon, William Keighley, Busby Berkeley; w, Manuel Seff, James Seymour; ph, George Barnes; ed, George Amy; art d, Anton Grot; chor, Busby Berkeley; cos, Milo Anderson

Following its success with the blockbuster backstage musicals 42ND STREET and GOLD DIGGERS OF 1933, Warner Bros. launched this lavish production, with Cagney marvelous in the lead. He plays Chester Kent, a theatrical producer who finds himself unemployed after the advent of the Depression and talking pictures. The dogged Kent, however, sells his backers (Kibbee and Hohl) on the idea of doing "prologues," short but stunning stage musical numbers designed to precede the showing of feature films. Two-thirds of the movie deals with Chester's behind-the-scenes efforts to put together the prologues; the final third is devoted to the prologues themselves and to a suitable wrap-up.

Seemingly schizophrenic in form, with a gritty, backstage saga yielding to three flights of Busby Berkeley fantasy, FOOTLIGHT PARADE is actually an amazing cultural index of the Depression. All the wisecracking, all the struggle, all the buildup find a remarkable payoff when the film shifts gears into la-la land. The "Honeymoon Hotel" number is standard risque fare, but "By a Waterfall," with Berkeley doing a "wet run" for his later Esther Williams spectaculars, is an astounding surrealistic kaleidoscope. "Shanghai Lil," meanwhile, adds a Warner Bros. toughness to Paramount's Shanghai Lily (Marlene Dietrich in SHANGHAI EXPRESS) of the year before.

Cagney is in great acting, comic and dancing form throughout and Blondell, as Kent's devoted secretary, proves that she has few peers at wisecracking or conveying low-key warmth. A great supporting cast and Bacon's well-judged direction help make FOOTLIGHT PARADE one of the greatest of the Berkeley extravaganzas.

FOR A FEW DOLLARS MORE
(PER QUALCHE DOLLARO IN PIU)

1965 130m c Western ★★★★
Europee/Arturo Gonzales/Constantin /15
(Italy/Spain/West Germany)

Clint Eastwood *(The Man With No Name)*, Lee Van Cleef *(Col. Douglas Mortimer)*, Gian Maria Volonte *(Indio)*, Josef Egger *(Old Man Over Railway)*, Rosemarie Dexter *(Colonel's Sister)*, Mara Krup *(Hotel Manager's Wife)*, Klaus Kinski *(Hunchback)*, Mario Brega, Aldo Sambrelli, Luigi Pistilli

p, Alberto Grimaldi; d, Sergio Leone; w, Luciano Vincenzoni, Sergio Leone (based on a story by Leone and Fulvio Morsella); ph, Massimo Dallamano; ed, Giorgio Ferralonga, Eugenio Alabiso; m, Ennio Morricone; art d, Carlo Simi; cos, Carlo Simi

The second film in Leone's "Dollar" trilogy (THE GOOD, THE BAD, AND THE UGLY would follow) finds the Italian director in better form than in A FISTFUL OF DOLLARS. FOR A FEW DOLLARS MORE has better writing, superior production values, and more characters who aptly complement Eastwood's stoic Man with No Name.

In this installment, the mysterious drifter is locked in combat with rival bounty hunter Colonel Mortimer (Van Cleef) to collect the reward for killing psychopathic bandit Indio (Volonte). At first, the men attempt to capture the crook separately, without success. The pair form an uneasy alliance, and Mortimer eventually guns Indio down in a shootout as No Name watches from the sidelines. It turns out, though, that Mortimer is not interested in money after all.

By introducing the character of Mortimer, Leone is able to counterpoint Eastwood's cold, amoral gunslinger with a man who has a past and a purpose. A more *human* character with which the audience can more readily identify makes Eastwood's role all the more mythic. Once again, Morricone's music is superbly appropriate, with each character's own theme (and one for the flashbacks too) bursting into this epic at just the right moment.

In FOR A FEW DOLLARS MORE, Leone's thematic concerns about the civilizing influence of the family and the hypocrisy of the Church are now richly in focus. His tone of self-parody and his portrait of an unrelenting landscape where men suddenly appear and vanish are all more detailed than before. We are also given the sense that the Man with No Name has been somewhat humanized by his encounter with Mortimer, a suspicion that would be confirmed in the final chapter of the trilogy.

FOR ME AND MY GAL

1942 104m bw Musical ★★★½
MGM (U.S.) /U

Judy Garland *(Jo Hayden)*, George Murphy *(Jimmy K. Metcalf)*, Gene Kelly *(Harry Palmer)*, Marta Eggerth *(Eve Minard)*, Ben Blue *(Sid Simms)*, Richard Quine *(Danny Hayden)*, Keenan Wynn *(Eddie Milton)*, Stephen McNally *(Mr. Waring)*, Lucille Norman *(Lily Duncan)*, Betty Wells

p, Arthur Freed; d, Busby Berkeley; w, Richard Sherman, Fred Finklehoffe, Sid Silvers, Jack McGowan, Irving Brecher (based on the story "The Big Time" by Howard Emmett Rogers); ph, William Daniels; ed, Ben Lewis; art d, Cedric Gibbons, Gabriel Scognamillo; chor, Bobby Connolly, Gene Kelly; cos, Robert Kalloch, Gile Steele

AAN Best Score: Roger Edens, Georgie Stoll

A delightful and nostalgic return to the fun-filled pre-WWI days of vaudeville. Jo Hayden (Garland) troops the boards with Jimmy Metcalf (Murphy), Sid Simms (Blue), and Lily Duncan (Norman). Though she loves the hardscrabble life of the stage, Jo's main career motive is to send her kid brother (Quine) to medical school. When smoothie Harry Palmer (Kelly) advises Jo that she could do much better in his song-and-dance act, she, with Jimmy's blessing, teams up with him. They struggle along for two years; meanwhile, Jimmy and Sid hit the big time. Harry, meanwhile, becomes infatuated with a singing star (Eggerth), even though Jo is the one who truly loves him. When WWI threatens to halt his burgeoning success, Harry compounds his sins by dodging the draft, causing Jo to leave him—until he redeems himself in heroic style.

The story is pure hokum, but this warm film is more than buoyed by the many old tunes and the superb production numbers—staged, surprisingly, not by specialist Berkeley, who directed, but by Bobby Connolly. The dynamic Kelly, in his film debut, exhibits star quality in spades, while at the same time hinting at the darker side to his persona in the scene where he maims his hand to avoid the draft. He and Garland play beautifully off each other, and of course their performance of the title standard is a highlight of the film.

FOR WHOM THE BELL TOLLS

1943 170m c Adventure/War ★★★
Paramount (U.S.) /U

Gary Cooper *(Robert Jordan)*, Ingrid Bergman *(Maria)*, Akim Tamiroff *(Pablo)*, Arturo de Cordova *(Agustin)*, Vladimir Sokoloff *(Anselmo)*, Mikhail Rasumny *(Rafael)*, Fortunio Bonanova *(Fernando)*, Eric Feldary *(Andres)*, Victor Varconi *(Primitivo)*, Katina Paxinou *(Pilar)*

p, Sam Wood; d, Sam Wood; w, Dudley Nichols (based on the novel by Ernest Hemingway); ph, Ray Rennahan; ed, Sherman Todd, John F. Link; m, Victor Young; prod d, William Cameron Menzies; art d, Hans Dreier, Haldane Douglas; fx, Gordon Jennings

AAN Best Picture; AAN Best Actor: Gary Cooper; *AAN Best Actress:* Ingrid Bergman; *AAN Best Supporting Actor:* Akim Tamiroff; *AA Best Supporting Actress:* Katina Paxinou; *AAN Best Cinematography:* Ray Rennahan; *AAN Best Editing:* Sherman Todd, John Link; *AAN Best Score:* Victor Young; *AAN Best Art Direction:* Hans Dreier, Haldane Douglas, Bertram Granger

FOR YOUR EYES ONLY

A bowdlerized version of one of Hemingway's most famous works, FOR WHOM THE BELL TOLLS makes its most overtly political move by cutting Ingrid Bergman's hair so short. Otherwise, it's pretty much of a yawner, with people (in Spain, right?) doing something or other to fight some kind of oppression. At one point during the film's three agonizing hours someone hints at fascism, but since that's *such* a difficult concept, HUAC "friendly witness" Wood and his writers largely drop it in favor of boy meets girl. Butch Bergman meets stoic Cooper and we're off!

Even more taciturn than usual, Cooper is in many ways a perfect Hemingway hero (as he showed in the romanticized but lovely A FAREWELL TO ARMS). He has his moments, but otherwise seems a bit too respectful of the whole noble undertaking. Obviously remembering her luminous Ilsa from CASABLANCA, Bergman strives mightily to endow the film with romantic resonance, but she's treading on tenuous ground. The famous "I would kiss you but where do the noses go" is, depending on your mood, either the most dauntingly romantic moment this side of CASABLANCA's "Is that cannon fire or my heart pounding" or it's completely laughable. Cast mostly with Russians in all the Hispanic roles, this glamourfest is Hollywood politics at its most apolitical, lacking even the energy of a good B movie.

When critics with an interest in reality accused Paramount of fence-sitting (reports claimed that Franco's envoys and the Catholic Church pressured the studio into a nonpartisan stand), studio chief Adolph Zukor came back with one of the great double-edged truths about commercial cinema: "It's a great picture, without political significance. We are not for or against anybody."

FOR YOUR EYES ONLY

1981   127m   c   Spy/Adventure   ★★★½
UA   (U.K.)   PG

Roger Moore *(James Bond)*, Carole Bouquet *(Melina)*, Topol *(Columbo)*, Lynn-Holly Johnson *(Bibi)*, Julian Glover *(Kristatos)*, Cassandra Harris *(Lisl)*, Jill Bennett *(Brink)*, Michael Gothard *(Locque)*, John Wyman *(Kriegler)*, Jack Hedley *(Havelock)*

p, Albert R. Broccoli; d, John Glen; w, Richard Maibaum, Michael G. Wilson (based on the short stories "For Your Eyes Only" and "Risico" by Ian Fleming); ph, Alan Hume; ed, John Grover; m, Bill Conti; prod d, Peter Lamont; art d, John Fenner; fx, Derek Meddings; cos, Elizabeth Waller

AAN Best Song: Bill Conti (Music), Mick Leeson (Lyrics)

After returning to Earth from his MOONRAKER fiasco, Roger Moore resumes his role as James Bond without the excessive technical gadgetry. Against a sea-and-ski Greek backdrop, Bond and the obligatory beauty, Melina (Bouquet), lovely but lifeless, race Soviet agents for a device lost in a shipwreck that transmits the "fire" order to missile-carrying British submarines. The same Soviet agents killed Melina's parents, motivating her to seek Elektra-like revenge. One fast-paced chase follows another, and a slightly more vulnerable Bond gets his share of knocks along the way.

The success of this picture (perhaps Moore's best in the Bond series) can be attributed to the marvelous direction of Glen, who had previously worked as a second-unit director on earlier Bond movies. Not surprisingly, the stunts are some of the best in the series. Lynn-Holly Johnson is decidedly annoying in the unnecessary role of a horny young skater, but Topol helps offset this gaffe with his engaging presence. Very pleasant, unforced, throwaway entertainment, though Moore is clearly getting a mite too old for all this.

FORBIDDEN GAMES
(LES JEUX INTERDITS)

1952   102m   bw   War/Drama   ★★★★★
Silver   (France)

Brigitte Fossey *(Paulette)*, Georges Poujouly *(Michel Dolle)*, Lucien Hubert *(Dolle, the Father)*, Suzanne Courtal *(Mme Dolle)*, Jacques Marin *(Georges Dolle)*, Laurence Badie *(Berthe Dolle)*, Andre Wasley *(Gouard, the Father)*, Amedee *(Francis Gouard)*, Denise Pereonne *(Jeanne Gouard)*, Louis Sainteve *(Priest)*

p, Robert Dorfmann; d, Rene Clement; w, Rene Clement, Jean Aurenche, Pierre Bost (based on the novel *Les Jeux Inconnus* by Francois Boyer); ph, Robert Juillard; ed, Roger Dwyre; m, Narciso Yepes; art d, Paul Bertrand

One of the best films ever about war and its effects, FORBIDDEN GAMES also speaks beautifully to the need of children to construct their own fantasy world away from adult supervision.

Director Clement's most famous film carefully begins with its one action highlight, as refugees flee WWII Paris in the face of a Nazi attack. At a bottleneck on a bridge, German planes swoop down in perfect formation and strafe the confused column. Paulette (Fossey) is seen standing alone on the bridge, her parents and dog dead. When someone throws the dog over the bridge, she goes after it and meets Michel (Poujouly), the 11 year-old son of peasants (Hubert and Courtal). The boy takes the girl home with him, and his parents take her in. When Paulette sees her parents buried, she decides that her dog also needs to be buried in a grave with a cross. She and Michel steal a cross from the hearse carrying his older brother. He and Paulette begin to expand their secret animal cemetery to include moles, chickens, and even insects, all given elaborate memorial services with stolen crosses. The eventual discovery of the children's secret and their future together make for a moving climax.

FORBIDDEN GAMES derives most of its power from Clement's painstakingly methodical direction and the remarkable performances of the two child leads. Poujouly and the amazing five year-old Fossey are highly expressive actors who give this stunning film its emotional core. The visual and narrative style is a potent blend of stark documentary, pastoral realism and film noir. Seeing war through the eyes of children who cope with its atrocities by constructing their own little game of death was a brilliant move—it seems morbid and grotesque to all the adults, but the problem is that *they* are the ones who really lack understanding and respect.

FORBIDDEN PLANET

1956   98m   c   Science Fiction   ★★★★
MGM   (U.S.)   /U

Walter Pidgeon *(Dr. Morbius)*, Anne Francis *(Altaira)*, Leslie Nielsen *(Cmdr. Adams)*, Warren Stevens *(Lt. "Doc" Ostrow)*, Jack Kelly *(Lt. Farman)*, Richard Anderson *(Chief Quinn)*, Earl Holliman *(Cook)*, George Wallace *(Bosun)*, Bob Dix *(Grey)*, Jimmie Thompson *(Youngerford)*

p, Nicholas Nayfack; d, Fred M. Wilcox; w, Cyril Hume (based on a story by Irving Block, Allen Adler); ph, George Folsey; ed, Ferris Webster; m, Louis Barron, Bebe Barron; art d, Cedric Gibbons, Arthur Lonergan; fx, A. Arnold Gillespie, Warren Newcombe, Irving G. Reis, Joshua Meador; cos, Helen Rose, Walter Plunkett

AAN Best Visual Effects: A. Arnold Gillespie, Irving Ries, Wesley C. Miller

A superb sci-fi flick, FORBIDDEN PLANET offers an unusually intelligent script, exciting direction by Wilcox and generally good acting from a decent if rather dull cast.

It is 2200 A.D. when Commander Adams (Nielsen) lands his United Planets Cruiser on Altair-4, which features a green sky, pink sand, and two moons. He had been warned not to do so by Dr. Morbius (Pidgeon), a member of a missing Earth colony sent to the planet 20 years earlier. Adams and crew are greeted by Robby the Robot, a benign and astounding creation fluent in 88 languages and capable of any task, including producing an endless supply of bourbon at the behest of the crew's mischievous cook (Holliman). The robot drives Adams and his senior officers to the home of Morbius and his daughter Altaira (Francis, failing entirely to transcend her ill-conceived, camp classic role). Morbius explains that he and his glamorous love-spawn are the only survivors of attacks by an invisible monster prowling the planet. After the viewer is treated to scenes like Altaira's kissing lesson (the poor lusty darling has gone man-less, just imagine!), the invisible terror begins killing again.

FORBIDDEN PLANET is really a futuristic version of Shakespeare's *The Tempest*, with Morbius doubling for the wizard Prospero, Altaira a substitute Miranda, Robby the Robot serving as the spirit Ariel, and the Id monster being Caliban the witch-child. The first sci-fi film to cost $1 million, FORBIDDEN PLANET benefits immeasurably from its astounding technical prowess. The deadpan, all-purpose Robby the Robot is the film's most delightful creation, and it's not surprising that he later appeared in THE INVISIBLE BOY and scores of television shows.

While the spacemen are all likably heroic and Francis and Holliman can be forgiven for the enjoyable excesses of their roles, it is really Pidgeon who gives the drama flair and majesty. All in all, a splendid fantasy achievement that wears its age well.

FORCE OF EVIL

1948 78m bw Crime	★★★★½
Enterprise (U.S.)	/A

John Garfield *(Joe Morse)*, Beatrice Pearson *(Doris Lowry)*, Thomas Gomez *(Leo Morse)*, Howland Chamberlin *(Freddy Bauer)*, Roy Roberts *(Ben Tucker)*, Marie Windsor *(Edna Tucker)*, Paul McVey *(Hobe Wheelock)*, Tim Ryan *(Johnson)*, Sid Tomack *("Two & Two" Taylor)*, Georgia Backus *(Sylvia Morse)*

p, Bob Roberts; d, Abraham Polonsky; w, Abraham Polonsky, Ira Wolfert (based on his novel, *Tucker's People*); ph, George Barnes; ed, Walter Thompson, Arthur Seid; m, David Raksin; art d, Richard Day; cos, Louise Wilson

Garfield is Joe Morse, a slick, self-centered lawyer who knows the law but feels he's above it. He practices on Wall Street and has his eyes on millions, working on retainer for racketeer Ben Tucker (Roberts). The policy czar plans to have the number 776 come up on July 4; knowing that most people will bet on it, Tucker hopes to bankrupt and take over most of the city's smaller numbers operations. Without spilling the beans, Joe attempts to get his kindly brother Leo (Gomez) to shut down for one day, but the stubborn older man feels obligated to let his regulars take their holiday chances. Joe arranges for a police raid to break his brother's spirit, but to no avail. After Tucker achieves his expected success on the Fourth, Leo's people, including bookkeeper Doris (Pearson), become nervous about the gangsters suddenly in their midst.

Dark and brooding, FORCE OF EVIL offers one of Garfield's greatest performances as the cynical, hard-as-nails lawyer. Pearson, in her first of only two films, doesn't really register in a role that could use Shelley Winters or Ida Lupino rather than a June Allyson clone. Her presence is more than offset, however, by Gomez's marvelous performance and that of the suitably slimy Roberts. A tour de force for gifted writer Polonsky, FORCE was the only film he directed before he was blacklisted for being an uncooperative witness before HUAC in 1951; he didn't direct another feature for 21 years. At its best, FORCE achieves a style at once brutal and poetic, documentarian and noir.

FOREIGN CORRESPONDENT

1940 120m bw Spy/War	★★★★★
UA (U.S.)	/PG

Joel McCrea *(Johnny Jones/Huntley Haverstock)*, Laraine Day *(Carol Fisher)*, Herbert Marshall *(Stephen Fisher)*, George Sanders *(Scott Ffolliott)*, Albert Basserman *(Van Meer)*, Robert Benchley *(Stebbins)*, Edmund Gwenn *(Rowley)*, Eduardo Ciannelli *(Krug)*, Martin Kosleck *(Tramp)*, Harry Davenport *(Mr. Powers)*

p, Walter Wanger; d, Alfred Hitchcock; w, Charles Bennett, Joan Harrison, James Hilton, Robert Benchley; ph, Rudolph Mate; ed, Otho Lovering, Dorothy Spencer; m, Alfred Newman; art d, Alexander Golitzen; fx, Lee Zavitz

AAN Best Picture; AAN Best Supporting Actor: Albert Bassermann; *AAN Best Original Screenplay:* Charles Bennett, Joan Harrison; *AAN Best Cinematography:* Rudolph Mate; *AAN Best Art Direction:* Alexander Golitzen (Art Direction); *AAN Best Visual Effects:* Paul Eagler (Special Effects-Photographic), Thomas T Moulton (Special Effects-Sound)

One of the great espionage films, tautly handled by the stellar Hitchcock, FOREIGN CORRESPONDENT gleams with suspense, atmosphere and sharp dialogue. Johnny Jones (McCrea) is a top American crime reporter reassigned as a foreign correspondent to Western Europe. Ordered to find the most provocative stories swirling in the political cauldron just prior to WWII, he meets Stephen Fisher (Marshall), head of a peace organization, and Fisher's attractive daughter

Carol (Day). Before long, Johnny gets entangled in international intrigue involving the kidnaping of Van Meer (Basserman), a Dutch diplomat carrying vital information.

One of Hitchcock's greatest entertainments, FOREIGN CORRESPONDENT is also a stirring propaganda piece which clearly indicts the Nazi regime. This fact was recognized by no less than Nazi propaganda minister Josef Goebbels, who nonetheless hailed the film as a masterpiece, calling it "a first-class production, a criminological bang-up hit, which no doubt will make a certain impression upon the broad masses of the people in enemy countries." FOREIGN CORRESPONDENT also boasts some of the finest production design of its time—a huge windmill set was built to simulate a Dutch location, and a square in Amsterdam was reconstructed on a 10-acre set—a testament to the talents of Golitzen and Menzies. The acting is uniformly excellent, with McCrea an ideal Hitchcock hero and Marshall, Sanders, Gwenn, and especially Basserman stealing the supporting honors.

FOREIGN CORRESPONDENT is perhaps best remembered for its splendid set pieces, which include an assassination in the rain with umbrellas bobbing everywhere and terrific moments atop Westminster Cathedral, inside the windmill, and especially aboard a plane crashing into the ocean. Viewers are not likely to forget the struggle of the passengers as their air supply is slowly cut off. Not one of the director's more profound meditations on voyeurism and sexuality, FOREIGN CORRESPONDENT aims at something simpler than REAR WINDOW or VERTIGO; it shows him going through his playful paces at his professional best.

FORREST GUMP

1994 142m c Drama/Comedy/Historical	★★★
Tisch Company (U.S.)	PG-13/12

Tom Hanks *(Forrest Gump)*, Gary Sinise *(Lieutenant Dan Taylor)*, Robin Wright *(Jenny Curran)*, Sally Field *(Mrs. Gump)*, Mykelti Williamson *(Benjamin Buford Blue—"Bubba")*, Rebecca Williams *(Nurse at the Park Bench)*, Michael Conner Humphreys *(Young Forrest)*, Harold Herthum *(Doctor)*, George Kelly *(Barber)*, Bob Penny *(Crony)*

p, Wendy Finerman, Steve Tisch, Steve Starkey; d, Robert Zemeckis; w, Eric Roth (based on the novel by Winston Groom); ph, Don Burgess; ed, Arthur Schmidt; m, Alan Silvestri; prod d, Rick Carter; art d, Leslie McDonald, Jim Teegarden; fx, Ken Ralston, George Murphy, Stephen Rosenbaum, Allen Hall, Industrial Light & Magic; cos, Joanna Johnston

AA Best Picture; AA Best Actor: Tom Hanks; *AA Best Director:* Robert Zemeckis; *AA Best Adapted Screenplay:* Eric Roth; *AA Best Editing:* Arthur Schmidt; *AA Best Visual Effects:* Ken Ralston, George Murphy, Stephen Rosenbaum, Allen Hall; *AAN Best Supporting Actor:* Gary Sinise; *AAN Best Art Direction:* Rick Carter, Nancy Haigh; *AAN Best Cinematography:* Don Burgess; *AAN Best Makeup:* Daniel C. Striepeke, Hallie D'Amore, Judith A. Cory; *AAN Best Original Score:* Alan Silvestri; *AAN Best Sound:* Randy Thom, Tom Johnson, Dennis Sands, William B. Kaplan; *AAN Best Sound Effects:* Gloria S. Borders, Randy Thom

By the time FORREST GUMP swept most of the major 1994 Academy Awards, it had already become the third highest-grossing film of all time, as well as a ubiquitous pop phenomenon embracing best-selling books, gnomic catch phrases, and reams of commentary on the editorial pages of magazines and newspapers throughout the world. Clearly a great event, FORREST GUMP is not, however, a great film. It has the form of an epic without real depth or resonance; the trappings of satire without a coherent attitude; and the semblance of historical revisionism without a critical sensibility. To paraphrase the screenplay, FORREST GUMP is not a smart film, but it knows what love is—its dim-witted protagonist, as expertly portrayed by Tom Hanks, captured the love of millions.

As he waits for a bus in Savannah, Georgia, good-natured simpleton Forrest Gump (Hanks) tells his story to anyone who will listen. In flashbacks, punctuated by ZELIG-style special effects that graft Hanks onto famous pieces of archival footage, we learn that Gump has led a remarkably successful and adventurous life despite his low IQ. As football star, decorated war hero, Ping-Pong champion, and business magnate, he's crossed paths with most of the important historical figures of the American post-war era. Throughout, his destiny has been intertwined with those of crippled Vietnam veteran Lt. Dan (Gary Sinise) and his childhood friend and sometime lover, Jenny (Robin Wright).

Vague in its attitude toward the events it depicts, FORREST GUMP was embraced by several national figures in the Republican party as a celebration of traditional values and a condemnation of the 1960s counterculture. In many ways, however, the film represents old-fashioned Hollywood liberalism: racists are wrong, war is hell, assassinations are bad, and it's good to be nice. This is a film that dares not offend anyone too much. It's good—and profitable—to be comforting.

In order to achieve its considerable emotional power, FORREST GUMP draws upon some of the less savory elements of the American character—most obviously, a distrust of intellectualism and a naive belief in the redemptive power of innocence. Frank Capra once fared well promoting similar values, but his films were far darker, conflicted, and ambiguous. Zemeckis's film has lots of heart but little in the way of guts or brains.

FORT APACHE

1948   127m   bw   Western/War   ★★★★½
Argosy   (U.S.)   /U

Henry Fonda (Lt. Col. Owen Thursday), John Wayne (Capt. Kirby York), Shirley Temple (Philadelphia Thursday), Ward Bond (Sgt. Maj. Michael O'Rourke), John Agar (Lt. Michael "Mickey" O'Rourke), George O'Brien (Capt. Sam Collingwood), Irene Rich (Mrs. Mary O'Rourke), Victor McLaglen (Sgt. Festus Mulcahy), Anna Lee (Mrs. Emily Collingwood), Pedro Armendariz (Sgt. Beaufort)

p, John Ford, Merian C. Cooper; d, John Ford; w, Frank S. Nugent (based on the story "Massacre" by James Warner Bellah); ph, Archie Stout; ed, Jack Murray; m, Richard Hageman; art d, James Basevi; fx, David Koehler; chor, Kenny Williams; cos, Michael Meyers, Ann Peck

Philadelphia Thursday—sounds like an itinerary entry, right? No, it's the character played by teen-aged Shirley Temple in FORT APACHE, and you want nothing so much as to edit her part and that of husband John Agar (a really bad actor) right out of the damn picture. Apart from this irritation, FORT APACHE is a marvelous film, the first of director John Ford's US Cavalry trilogy.

The awesome exterior scenes reflect Ford's early training as a painter and provide a remarkable backdrop for the irony which unfolds. Lt. Col. Owen Thursday (Fonda) is a martinet commander bitter over having been sent to fight "digger" Indians instead of being assigned a glory post. He foolishly leads his men to disaster, but the press later presents him as a hero for the sake of the military's image.

FORT APACHE is rich beyond its wonderful action scenes and the outdoor panoramas so dear to Ford's heart. The film expertly depicts the social affairs of a far-flung military outpost, the struggle of the women to maintain civility, and the routines of the men in their daily military chores. More importantly, though, it exposes the sham behind public and national conceptions of "the hero." APACHE is one of the earliest films of Ford's final period, in which he questioned noisy, patriotic bravado and the white man's treatment of the Native American.

Wayne gives a solid performance, and such stalwarts as McLaglen, Bond, O'Brien, Foran, Armendariz, and Kibbee lend the film its humor and heart. But you find yourself watching Fonda transcend the possible critic's charge of "miscasting" as the permapressed, power-bloated commander. Of course, Fonda's character and the doomed route he pursues are based on the massacre of George Armstrong Custer's 7th Cavalry at Little Big Horn, and this if anything lends weight to Ford's elegiac reconsideration of "the American spirit."

FORTUNE, THE

1975   88m   c   Comedy   ★★★★
Columbia   (U.S.)   PG/AA

Warren Beatty (Nicky), Jack Nicholson (Oscar), Stockard Channing (Freddie), Florence Stanley (Landlady), Richard B. Shull (Chief Detective), Thomas Newman (John the Barber), John Fiedler (Police Photographer), Scatman Crothers (Fisherman), Dub Taylor (Rattlesnake Tom), Ian Wolfe (Justice of the Peace)

p, Mike Nichols, Don Devlin; d, Mike Nichols; w, Adrien Joyce; ph, John A. Alonzo; ed, Stu Linder; m, David Shire; prod d, Richard Sylbert; art d, Stewart Campbell

An offbeat but often hilarious comedy where Beatty and Nicholson play Nicky and Oscar, two competing confidence men trying to bilk heiress Freddie (Channing) out of her fortune. The source of this wealth is Freddie's father, a manufacturer of sanitary napkins (which naturally results in plenty of tacky humor). Though she is in love with the married Nicky, Freddie plans to marry the slippery Oscar and then carry on an affair with the man she wants. Oscar, a failed embezzler, has no intention of playing the cuckolded hubby; he means to have his carnal share of the attractive heiress. When she learns that the two con men are up to something, Freddie tells them her plans to give her fortune to charity. Alarmed, they conclude that their only course of action is murder, and the rest of the film is a series of black comedy sketches of plans gone awry and misplaced guilt.

A catalogue of slapstick errors, THE FORTUNE works well through the fine performances of the leads and the superb timing of director Nichols. Beatty nervously twitches through his part but is quickly outdone by the easy-going Nicholson and the marvelous Channing. LUCKY LADY, a similar type of love triangle also set in the 1920s (with Gene Hackman, Liza Minnelli and Burt Reynolds), was made the same year but nowhere approaches the style and wit on display here. Full of period and period-sounding music, THE FORTUNE is cold to the core—agreeably disagreeable amusement.

FORTUNE COOKIE, THE

1966   125m   bw   Comedy/Sports   ★★★½
Mirisch   (U.S.)   /U

Jack Lemmon (Harry Hinkle), Walter Matthau (Willie Gingrich), Ron Rich (Luther "Boom Boom" Jackson), Cliff Osmond (Mr. Purkey), Judi West (Sandy Hinkle), Lurene Tuttle (Mother Hinkle), Harry Holcombe (O'Brien), Les Tremayne (Thompson), Marge Redmond (Charlotte Gingrich), Noam Pitlik (Max)

p, Billy Wilder; d, Billy Wilder; w, Billy Wilder, I.A.L. Diamond; ph, Joseph La Shelle; ed, Daniel Mandell; m, Andre Previn; art d, Robert Luthardt; fx, Sass Bedig; cos, Charles Arrico, Paula Giokaris

AA Best Supporting Actor: Walter Matthau; AAN Best Original Screenplay: Billy Wilder, I.A.L. Diamond; AAN Best Cinematography: Joseph LaShelle; AAN Best Art Direction: Robert Luthardt, Edward G. Boyle

A very funny film, this morality tale is a deft mixture of cynicism, wit and idealism as only writer-director Wilder could do it. The only problem is that morality tales can get moralizing.

While working the sidelines during a Browns-Vikings game, cameraman Harry Hinkle (Lemmon) is flattened by Browns running back Luther "Boom Boom" Jackson (Rich) and rushed to the hospital. Although Harry is fine, his shyster brother-in-law, "Whiplash" Willie Gingrich (Matthau), convinces him to fake an injury and sue the Browns, CBS and Municipal Stadium for $1 million. Pretending to be paralyzed from the neck down and relying on an old spinal injury for X-ray proof, Harry fools a team of doctors and, under Willie's supervision, continues to deceive private investigator Purkey (Osmond). In the meantime, Harry's wife, Sandy (West), a would-be singer who ran off with another guy, returns, anxious to get in on the gravy train.

Lemmon and especially Matthau—who deservedly won a Best Supporting Actor Oscar for his role—are superb; this first teaming together more than justified later reunions. The screenplay by Wilder and Diamond sparkles with the dark satiric cynicism for which they are famous and LaShelle's frankly unattractive cinematography is entirely appropriate to the unsavory goings-on. Rich's Boom Boom is a bit too noble, but his relationship with Harry is still touching. In fact, toward the end the film goes perhaps a little too soft. Despite some minor flaws, THE FORTUNE COOKIE is a very satisfying film.

48 HRS.

1982 96m c Comedy/Crime ★★★½
Paramount (U.S.) R/18

Nick Nolte *(Jack Cates)*, Eddie Murphy *(Reggie Hammond)*, Annette O'Toole *(Elaine)*, Frank McRae *(Haden)*, James Remar *(Ganz)*, David Patrick Kelly *(Luther)*, Sonny Landham *(Billy Bear)*, Brion James *(Kehoe)*, Kerry Sherman *(Rosalie)*, Jonathan Banks *(Algren)*

p, Lawrence Gordon, Joel Silver; d, Walter Hill; w, Walter Hill, Larry Gross, Steven E. de Souza; ph, Ric Waite; ed, Freeman Davies, Mark Warner, Billy Weber; m, James Horner; prod d, John Vallone; cos, Marilyn Vance

A big box-office hit, this action film casts Nolte as Jack Cates, a hard-as-granite cop, and Murphy as Reggie Hammond, a glib convict who is released from prison in Cates's custody for 48 hours. Hammond's job is to help Cates track down a pair of maniacal cop killers (Landham and Remar) who happen to be his former associates. Together Cates and Hammond take a thrill-a-minute trip through the San Francisco underworld and along the way develop one of the 1980s' more interesting cinematic buddy pairings.

In this, his first film, comedian Murphy turned in a marvelous performance, setting the stage for his enormously popular Axel Foley character in the BEVERLY HILLS COP films. Nolte, however, always threatens to steal the film in his customary quiet way as Murphy's rough and gruff partner. Director Hill (THE LONG RIDERS, SOUTHERN COMFORT, RED HEAT) pushes the film along at his traditional rapid pace, aided by Waite's excellent cinematography. In the film's most poignant moment Cates gives Hammond a badge and sends him into a rowdy country-western bar for a role-reversal confrontation with a passel of rednecks. Hang on for the ride.

42ND STREET

1933 98m bw Musical ★★★★★
Warner Bros. (U.S.) /U

Warner Baxter *(Julian Marsh)*, Bebe Daniels *(Dorothy Brock)*, George Brent *(Pat Denning)*, Una Merkel *(Lorraine Fleming)*, Ruby Keeler *(Peggy Sawyer)*, Guy Kibbee *(Abner Dillon)*, Dick Powell *(Billy Lawler)*, Ginger Rogers *(Ann Lowell/Anytime Annie)*, George E. Stone *(Andy Lee)*, Robert McWade *(Al Jones)*

p, Hal B. Wallis; d, Lloyd Bacon; w, James Seymour, Rian James (based on the novel by Bradford Ropes); ph, Sol Polito; ed, Thomas Pratt; art d, Jack Okey; chor, Busby Berkeley; cos, Orry-Kelly

AAN Best Picture; AAN Best Sound: Nathan Levinson (Sound)

Hear the beat of dancing feet! The film that revived public interest in musicals after many early talkie bombs sabotaged the genre, 42ND STREET was the first real glimpse of the surreal artistry of choreographer Busby Berkeley. The film also highlighted two fresh-faced new stars, the likably cornball crooner Dick Powell and the endearingly untalented Ruby Keeler.

The familiar plot concerns Broadway director Julian Marsh's (Warner Baxter) desire for one more hit so he can retire and recover his health. Abner Dillon (Guy Kibbee) is his wealthy backer, Dorothy Brock (Bebe Daniels) his temperamental star, Peggy Sawyer (Keeler) a hopeful chorine, and Billy Lawler (Powell) a singer with the hots for Peggy. As Julian struggles with the show, promises and hearts are broken, but that's nothing compared to the crisis created when Dorothy's ankle is broken on the eve of the show's premiere. Understudy Peggy has to go on in her place, giving Baxter the chance to say the immortal line, "You're going out a youngster, but you've got to come back a star!"

42ND STREET's charm and fascination lie in director Bacon's fast-paced and vivid backstage atmosphere, crammed with exhausted chorus kids and sudden hysterics. The great cast is in fine fettle: Baxter brings real edge to what could have been a standardized part; fading star Daniels is eerily appropriate as the performer who gets replaced; Una Merkel makes the most of her wisecracks; and when Ginger Rogers enters sporting a monocle and an Erich von Stroheim shtick, you oddly sense that a star is almost ready to be born.

The real star, though, is the master of kaleidoscopic imagery, Busby Berkeley. Backed by the ebullient songs of Harry Warren and Al Dubin, Buzz unleashed his startling creations on an escapism-hungry public. The dizzying combination of sexuality and abstraction in such numbers as "Young and Healthy," "Shuffle Off to Buffalo," and the title tune remains potent to this day. A film that returned it's $400,000 investment ten times over, inspired dozens of imitations and a Broadway reprise in the 1970s, 42ND STREET, "that avenue I'm takin' you to," remains hard to beat.

49TH PARALLEL

1941 105m bw War ★★★★½
General Films (U.K.)

Leslie Howard *(Philip Armstrong Scott)*, Raymond Massey *(Andy Brock)*, Laurence Olivier *(Johnnie)*, Anton Walbrook *(Peter)*, Eric Portman *(Lt. Hirth)*, Glynis Johns *(Anna)*, Niall MacGinnis *(Vogel)*, Finlay Currie *(Factor)*, Raymond Lovell *(Lt. Kuhnecke)*, John Chandos *(Lohrmann)*

p, Michael Powell, John Sutro; d, Michael Powell; w, Rodney Ackland, Emeric Pressburger (based on a story by Pressburger); ph, Freddie Young; ed, David Lean; m, Ralph Vaughan Williams; art d, David Rawnsley

AAN Best Picture; AA Best Original Story: Emeric Pressburger; *AAN Best Screenplay:* Rodney Ackland, Emeric Pressburger

THE INVADERS (49TH PARALLEL in the UK) is an excellent war drama from British director Powell, co-scripted by his longtime collaborator Pressburger. Filmed mostly in Canada, the film opens as a U-37 German submarine surfaces in the Gulf of St. Lawrence. It is obliterated by RCAF bombers, but six Germans survive and march to a Hudson Bay trading post. Constructed in episodic fashion, the story shows them wandering through Canada to avoid detection. Along the way, they meet Johnnie (Olivier), a trapper filled with contempt for the Nazis; a group of German Hutterites living on a Christian collective headed by Peter (Walbrook); and Philip Armstrong Scott (Howard), a decadent novelist living in a teepee while writing about the Blackfoot Indians. With each meeting, the number of "invaders" diminishes; some are captured, others killed, and a decent one (MacGinnis) tries to remain with the Hutterites. Finally, the last to elude death or capture (Portman) meets Andy Brock (Massey), an AWOL Canadian soldier who complains about democracy while stowing away on a freight train bound for the US. The wily Andy shows his true colors, though, when he must confront Nazism incarnate.

The anti-Fascist message here is extremely eloquent, the Oscar-winning script witty and intelligent, and the photography handsome and atypical for a war film. Powell beautifully ties it all together in a directorial style that is part war adventure, part Robert Flaherty-influenced documentary, taking just as much time with action sequences as he does with Hutterite communal living, Eskimo culture, or Indian rituals. The acting is almost uniformly excellent, with Walbrook his usual superb self, and marvelous work from Johns, MacGinnis, Currie, Howard and Massey. With his gravelly voice and incisive manner, Portman makes an electrifying villain, and he became a major British star with this film. Unfortunately Olivier lowers this high standard with a rather hammy performance, replete with variable French-Canadian accent. The British release runs nearly 20 minutes longer than the version generally seen in America.

FOUR DAUGHTERS

1938 90m bw Romance ★★★★
Warner Bros. (U.S.) /U

Claude Rains *(Adam Lemp)*, May Robson *(Aunt Etta)*, Priscilla Lane *(Ann Lemp)*, Lola Lane *(Thea Lemp)*, Rosemary Lane *(Kay Lemp)*, Gale Page *(Emma Lemp)*, Dick Foran *(Ernest)*, Jeffrey Lynn *(Felix Deitz)*, Frank McHugh *(Ben Crowley)*, John Garfield *(Mickey Borden)*

p, Henry Blanke; d, Michael Curtiz; w, Julius J. Epstein, Lenore Coffee (based on the novel *Sister Act* by Fannie Hurst); ph, Ernest Haller; ed, Ralph Dawson; m, Max Steiner; art d, John Hughes

AAN Best Picture; AAN Best Supporting Actor: John Garfield; *AAN Best Director:* Michael Curtiz; *AAN Best Original Screenplay:* Lenore Coffee, Julius J Epstein; *AAN Best Sound:* Nathan Levinson (Sound)

An engrossing film which both endorses and questions a vision of small-town American romance. When Felix Deitz (Lynn) arrives at Adam Lemp's (Rains) house to board, the music professor's four daughters all fall in love with him. Ann (Priscilla Lane) becomes engaged to him but later finds out from the cynical Mickey Borden (Garfield) that one of her sisters is devastated by the impending marriage. In a great act of sibling generosity, she gives up Felix and runs off with the embittered Mickey. Felix departs, however, and the sister falls in love with another man. The tough, indolent Mickey realizes that he's breaking Ann's heart and decides to engineer her reunion with Felix.

A fun tearjerker, this film is saved from its own candybox prettiness by the scorching presence of Garfield in the seemingly tailor-made role that brought him stardom. His Mickey Borden is a rebellious, surly, disillusioned young man from the big city, where poverty has scarred his otherwise brilliant mind. His rare smiles are wry grins, and his laughter is ironic. His character at once shouts defiance and defeat. His remarks to the kindly small-town folks who take him in reflect both their naivete and his jaded worldliness.

Further help is offered by director Curtiz, whose sense of pace and proportion never gives this cottage cheese a chance to curdle. Although the Lane sisters and Page are simply *too* cute for words, they, Rains, and Robson do evoke something idealistically cozy when you let your guard down. Several sequels followed, including the superior DAUGHTERS COURAGEOUS, as well as a mediocre remake, YOUNG AT HEART.

FOUR FEATHERS, THE

1939 130m c Adventure/War   ★★★★★
Korda/London Films   (U.K.)   /U

John Clements *(Harry Faversham)*, Ralph Richardson *(Capt. John Durrance)*, C. Aubrey Smith *(Gen. Burroughs)*, June Duprez *(Ethne Burroughs)*, Allan Jeayes *(Gen. Faversham)*, Jack Allen *(Lt. Willoughby)*, Donald Gray *(Peter Burroughs)*, Frederick Culley *(Dr. Sutton)*, Amid Taftazani *(Karaga Pasha)*, Henry Oscar *(Dr. Harraz)*

p, Alexander Korda; d, Zoltan Korda; w, R.C. Sherriff, Lajos Biro, Arthur Wimperis (based on the novel by A.E.W. Mason); ph, Georges Perinal, Osmond Borradaile, Jack Cardiff; ed, William Hornbeck, Henry Cornelius; m, Miklos Rozsa; prod d, Vincent Korda; cos, Godfrey Brennan, Rene Hubert

One of the all-time great adventure films. THE FOUR FEATHERS is based on the 1902 tale of cowardice and courage by A.E.W. Mason, filmed at least six times but never as well as in this marvelous production.

The tale of empire, battle, and redemption begins when Harry Faversham (Clements), the son of a brigadier general, refuses to follow family tradition and join the army, choosing instead to settle down and wed Ethne Burroughs (Duprez). He resigns his commission just before his regiment leaves for the 1898 Sudan campaign conducted by Lord Kitchener, and his friends—John Durrance (Richardson), Peter Burroughs (Gray), and Tom Willoughby (Allen)—present him three white feathers symbolizing cowardice. Also disgusted by his actions is Ethne, who gives him the fourth feather. Determined to prove his courage, Faversham leaves for Egypt alone and disguises himself as a native, his skin stained and an "S" branded on his forehead to mark him as a Sangali tribe member with his tongue cut out by enemies. Eventually Faversham is able to redeem himself in the eyes of those he loves.

One of the great British films of the 1930s and one of producer Alexander Korda's finest achievements, THE FOUR FEATHERS is directed by Alexander's brother, Zoltan, with the elan demanded by the action-packed story. His talent is evident in the magnificent battle scenes, particularly the awesome attack of the "Fuzzi Wuzzies" against the British lines, shown in wide panorama by cameras mounted high on hilltops overlooking the battlefield.

The acting is distinguished throughout, with Clements a sensitive and dashing nonconformist, Richardson superb as a man who must reconsider a friendship, and Smith equally good as a crusty career officer whose hypocrisy is revealed. A film unafraid to question those traditions it celebrates, THE FOUR FEATHERS balances its highly impressive spectacle with a drama of substance and intelligence.

FOUR HUNDRED BLOWS, THE
(LES QUATRES CENTS COUPS)

1959 93m bw Drama   ★★★★★
Carosse   (France)   /A

Jean-Pierre Leaud *(Antoine Doinel)*, Claire Maurier *(Mme Doinel)*, Albert Remy *(M Doinel)*, Guy Decombie *(Teacher)*, Patrick Auffay *(Rene Bigey)*, Georges Flament *(M Bigey)*, Yvonne Claudie *(Mme Bigey)*, Robert Beauvais *(Director of the School)*, Claude Mansard *(Examining Magistrate)*, Jacques Monod *(Commissioner)*

p, Francois Truffaut; d, Francois Truffaut; w, Francois Truffaut, Marcel Moussy (story by Truffaut); ph, Henri Decae; ed, Marie-Josephe Yoyotte; m, Jean Constantin; art d, Bernard Evein

AAN Best Original Screenplay: Francois Truffaut, Marcel Moussy

This extraordinary film was the first feature from Francois Truffaut, who was, until its release, best known as a hell-raising critic from the journal *Cahiers du Cinema*. THE 400 BLOWS is not only one of the foremost films of the French New Wave, but also the first in a Truffaut series that included "Antoine and Colette" (an episode from LOVE AT TWENTY), STOLEN KISSES, BED AND BOARD, and LOVE ON THE RUN.

These films all starred the remarkable Leaud as Truffaut's alter ego Antoine Doinel and span 20 years in this semiautobiographical character's life. Here Leaud beautifully embodies Doinel at age 12, a child more or less left to his own devices by his mother (Maurier) and father (Remy). He gets into trouble at school, runs away from home, and eventually ends up in an observation center for juvenile delinquents.

THE 400 BLOWS—an idiomatic French expression for the limit of what anyone can bear—is a nonjudgmental film about injustice, pain, and the events in a young boy's life that make him the person he is. Neither good nor bad, Antoine is treated with warmth and compassion by Truffaut as a child caught up in a maelstrom not of his own making. The grace and perfection of THE 400 BLOWS has made it the standard against which all films on the subject of youth are judged, and Leaud's portrayal that to which all young performers' are compared.

The film also features Decae's poetic black-and-white photography, and together he and Truffaut offer a glimpse of the freedom that Antoine's life never really affords. Images such as a line of schoolboys snaking their way through the streets linger like pages from a mental yearbook of schooldays. Best of all, though, is the film's famous final freeze frame, in which Truffaut conveys both promise and sadness, and demonstrates that the cinema offers no easy answers to the problems of living.

FOUR MUSKETEERS, THE

1975 108m c Adventure/Historical   ★★★½
Fox   (U.S.)   PG

Michael York *(D'Artagnan)*, Oliver Reed *(Athos)*, Richard Chamberlain *(Aramis)*, Frank Finlay *(Porthos)*, Raquel Welch *(Mme. Constance Bonacieux)*, Christopher Lee *(Rochefort)*, Faye Dunaway *(Milady)*, Jean-Pierre Cassel *(Louis XIII)*, Geraldine Chaplin *(Queen Anne of Austria)*, Simon Ward *(Duke of Buckingham)*

p, Alexander Salkind; d, Richard Lester; w, George MacDonald Fraser (from *The Three Musketeers* by Alexandre Dumas); ph, David Watkin; ed, John Victor Smith; m, Lalo Schifrin; prod d, Brian Eatwell

AAN Best Costume Design: Yvonne Blake, Ron Talsky

A sequel to THE THREE MUSKETEERS. Both pictures were originally supposed to have been one huge 3 1/2-hour epic, but the producers decided to release them as two films—and lawsuits followed immediately from a cast and crew who wanted to be paid for making two films. That aside, this sequel is a worthy follow-up to the original.

In this installment, Milady DeWinter (Dunaway) plans to wreak revenge on D'Artagnan (York), his cohorts (Chamberlain, Finlay, and Reed), his "lady fair" Constance (Welch), and the Duke (Ward) for foiling her plans in the first film. Milady attempts seduction and later allows herself to be arrested so as to manipulate a religious-fanatic jailer into assassinating the Duke. She also kidnaps Constance, a move certain to bring the swashbuckling quartet into the picture.

Much of the film is played for merry comedy, and the cast makes a good job of it. Welch, for example, handles both the physical and the verbal comedy with the same brio which marked her work in the earlier film. Dunaway, on the other hand, does not make the pivotal role of Milady DeWinter *quite* as fascinating as one would like. Although there is less slapstick than in THE THREE MUSKETEERS, the lightness of the enterprise stays constant until the swashbuckling climax and dramatic resolution. What is especially notable in this sequel is Lester's determination to deglamorize life in the 1620s, and his film is amply populated with mercenaries, boors and slobs.

FOUR NIGHTS OF A DREAMER
(QUATRE NUITS D'UN REVEUR)

1971 87m c Drama   ★★★★
Victoria/Albina/Del Orso (France)   /AA

Isabelle Weingarten *(Marthe)*, Guillaume Des Forets *(Jacques)*, Maurice Monnoyer *(Lover)*

d, Robert Bresson; w, Robert Bresson (based on the story "White Nights" by Feodor Dostoyevsky); ph, Pierre Lhomme

This fascinating feature by master director Bresson adapts Dostoyevsky's story "White Nights" and puts it in Paris in the modern age.

Jacques (Des Forets) is a young artist living a life of daydreams who meets Marthe (Weingarten) on a bridge one night while she is contemplating suicide. They talk and arrange to meet there the next night. They speak of their lives—he of his painting and his fantasies, she of the man she loves and his leaving her with the promise to meet her on the bridge one year later. It is because he hasn't kept the rendezvous that she has thought to kill herself. Jacques falls in love with the enigmatic woman, walking around Paris with a tape recorder against his heart that just plays a recording of him repeating her name. For four nights they meet on the bridge and talk, but on the last night the missing lover returns.

Bresson's spare, totally restrained style has seldom been used to such effect. With its highly deliberate editing and elegant use of color, the film emerges a delicate if sad paean to young love. Mystical and erotic but also dispassionate, FOUR NIGHTS OF A DREAMER is an important film by one of the cinema's most important figures. It makes for fascinating comparison with Visconti's memorable WHITE NIGHTS, an earlier adaptation of the same story.

FOUR WEDDINGS AND A FUNERAL

1994 116m c Romance/Comedy   ★★★½
Working Title/Channel Four (United Kingdom)   R/15

Hugh Grant *(Charles)*, James Fleet *(Tom)*, Simon Callow *(Gareth)*, John Hannah *(Matthew)*, Kristin Scott Thomas *(Fiona)*, David Bower *(David)*, Charlotte Coleman *(Scarlett)*, Andie MacDowell *(Carrie)*, Timothy Walker *(Angus the Groom)*, Sara Crowe *(Laura the Bride)*

p, Duncan Kenworthy; d, Mike Newell; w, Richard Curtis; ph, Michael Coulter; ed, Jon Gregory; m, Richard Rodney Bennett; prod d, Maggie Gray; fx, Ian Wingrove; cos, Lindy Hemming

AAN Best Picture; *AAN Best Original Screenplay*: Richard Curtis

A witty romantic comedy with a sardonic edge, FOUR WEDDINGS AND A FUNERAL follows the engaging Hugh Grant and his friends as they search for love in a whirlwind of nuptials.

Always a guest, never a groom (he's Best Man once, but forgets the rings), handsome, timid Charles (Grant) meets Carrie (Andie MacDowell) at a wedding and falls instantly in love with her. She returns to America, and the next time he sees her—at another wedding—she's got a wealthy fiance in tow. He's devastated, she's oblivious, tongues wag. Can once in a lifetime, bolt-from-the-blue love survive bad timing, comically misunderstood intentions and the well-meaning interference of friends? Charles finds out—two weddings (one of them his own) and a funeral later—but not before things come to some very sticky passes.

Casting is everything in FOUR WEDDINGS AND A FUNERAL; the more one falls for Grant's ineffectual-but-adorable upper-middle-class schtick, the more charming everything seems. MacDowell is the weak link in a fine ensemble that includes the splendid Kristin Scott-Thomas (A HANDFUL OF DUST) and Simon Callow (A ROOM WITH A VIEW); among the film's highlights is a fairly devastating reading of W.H. Auden's *Funeral Blues*.

FOXES

1980 106m c Drama   ★★½
UA (U.S.)   R/15

Jodie Foster *(Jeanie)*, Scott Baio *(Brad)*, Sally Kellerman *(Mary)*, Randy Quaid *(Jay)*, Lois Smith *(Mrs. Axman)*, Adam Faith *(Bryan)*, Cherie Currie *(Annie)*, Marilyn Kagan *(Madge)*, Kandice Stroh *(Deirdre)*, Jon Sloan *(Loser)*

p, David Puttnam, Gerald Ayres; d, Adrian Lyne; w, Gerald Ayres; ph, Paul Ryan; ed, James Coblentz; m, Giorgio Moroder; art d, Michel Levesque

Guided by former TV commercial director Lyne in his feature debut, this exploration of the lives of four teenage girls is weakly scripted but engaging nonetheless. In a fine performance, Foster plays the steadiest of the quartet, Jeanie, who finds herself dealing with the problems of her three friends: Annie (Currie, onetime member of the rock group the Runaways), a burnt-out hooker trying to escape her crazed father; overweight, unpopular Madge (Kagan), who is determined to free herself from her parents' pampering; and Deirdre (Stroh), a flirtatious, compulsive liar. Although FOXES's attempt to delve into the problems of modern-day teenagers is admirable, its screenplay is frequently trite, lacks any leavening humor, and too easily ties together its plentiful loose ends with a contrived plot device.

FRANKENHOOKER

1990 90m c Comedy/Horror   ★★★
Ievins-Henenlotter Production (U.S.)   /15

James Lorinz *(Jeffrey Franken)*, Patty Mullen *(Elizabeth)*, Charlotte Helmkamp *(Honey)*, Shirley Stoler *(Spike)*, Louise Lasser *(Jeffrey's Mom)*, Joseph Gonzalez *(Zorro)*, Lia Chang *(Crystal)*, Jennifer Delora *(Angel)*, Vicki Darnell *(Sugar)*, Kimberly Taylor *(Amber)*

p, Edgar Ievins; d, Frank Henenlotter; w, Robert Martin, Frank Henenlotter; ph, Robert M. Baldwin; ed, Kevin Tent; m, Joe Renzetti; fx, Gabe Bartalos

The most accomplished effort to date from writer-director Frank Henenlotter (BASKET CASE), one of the prime movers of the moribund midnight movie movement. Though the weak-hearted and taste-conscious should approach with extreme caution, the predisposed will find it a funny, stylish, stunningly gross black comedy that boasts surprisingly effective performances from its unknown leads.

Jeffrey Franken (James Lorinz), a resident of Hohokus, New Jersey, works in a power-plant and plays mad scientist in his spare time. His fiancee, Elizabeth (Patty Mullen), has a tragic lawn-care-related accident but resourceful Jeff manages to save her head. He schemes to construct a new body for his betrothed with remnants of expired ladies of the evening. To aid the body-part harvest, he takes a power drill to his own brain centers to boost his IQ and proceeds to concoct some "super crack," a drug so powerful that it causes its users to explode. After the smoke clears he gathers the most appealing limbs and such, sews them back together, attaches Elizabeth's head, and waits for an electrical storm. It isn't long before his "Frankenhooker" is staggering up 42nd Street, wreaking late-night havoc and frying johns with her lethal high-voltage love.

Granted this is tasteless shlock, but in Henenlotter's capable hands it manages to be quite funny. Until now, Henenlotter's ideas have tended to be better than their execution; miniscule budgets and compromised casting have kept style and wit in short supply. No more. Lorinz's acting style—as wildly funny as it is wanly low-key—eerily recalls Preston Sturges-stalwart Eddie Bracken's whiny plaintiveness filtered through a Jersey drawl.

Lorinz's performance is more than matched by former *Penthouse* Pet of the Year Mullen. A genuine find as Frankenhooker, Mullen pays fond, funny tribute to Elsa Lanchester's BRIDE OF FRANKENSTEIN with her remarkably refined comic performance. It's a lot of fun but leave the kids at home.

FRANKENSTEIN

1931 71m bw Horror/Science Fiction ★★★★★
Universal (U.S.) /PG

Colin Clive (*Henry Frankenstein*), Mae Clarke (*Elizabeth*), John Boles (*Victor Moritz*), Boris Karloff (*the Monster*), Edward Van Sloan (*Dr. Waldman*), Dwight Frye (*Fritz, the Dwarf*), Frederick Kerr (*Baron Frankenstein*), Lionel Belmore (*Herr Vogel, Burgomaster*), Michael Mark (*Ludwig, Peasant Father*), Marilyn Harris (*Maria the Child*)

p, Carl Laemmle Jr.; d, James Whale; w, Garrett Fort, Francis Edwards Faragoh, John Balderston, Robert Florey (based on the novel by Mary Shelley and the play by Peggy Webling); ph, Arthur Edeson; ed, Maurice Pivar, Clarence Kolster; m, David Broekman; art d, Charles D. Hall; fx, John P. Fulton

Six decades since its premiere, this early sound chiller is still a great film of its genre. Immeasurably superior to Tod Browning's DRACULA, which preceded it by a mere ten months, it shows how quickly Hollywood mastered the art of sound. FRANKENSTEIN also illustrates why James Whale is still—Cronenberg notwithstanding—*the* greatest director of horror films.

The story doesn't quite follow Mary Shelley's original, but it still milks the tragic tale of the inspired doctor and his piecemeal creation for all it's worth. Dr. Frankenstein (Clive) and the hunchbacked Fritz (Frye) steal bodies from their graves to assemble a "man" (Karloff) breathed into life with electricity. Unfortunately, Fritz's mistreatment of the bewildered being and the criminal brain mistakenly implanted in its skull combine to produce a killer, with grim consequences for all involved.

Still new to films, Whale displays astonishing technical mastery of the medium, as well as the imagination to break rules where appropriate. His innate theatricality makes a memorable moment of the monster's introduction. Karloff backs in from a doorway as our curiosity peaks. He slowly turns and Whale brilliantly cuts along an unchanging axis to increasingly tight close-ups of Karloff's face. Jack Pierce's marvelous make-up perfectly suits the film's blend of fantasy and science, and still manages to highlight Karloff's beautifully expressive face. This role made the gentle British character actor a star and a legend almost instantly. At once terrifying and pathetic, his monster is a moving study of alienation and primitive anger.

The film lacks the campy humor of later Whale; except for the delightful doddering of Kerr as Frankenstein's father, the wit is subdued in favor of a stark, dank tone. The result is a touching, cathartic sobriety seen at its best in the monster's encounter with an eight-year-old girl (Harris) who sees no reason to be afraid of the scarred creature before her. Universal backed down from including Clive's line, "Now I know what it feels like to be God," and they added a rather quaint disclaimer (featuring Van Sloan) warning viewers of the terror to follow, but nothing can detract from the power of the most influential monster movie ever made.

FRANTIC

1988 120m c Thriller ★★★★
Mount (U.S.) R/15

Harrison Ford (*Dr. Richard Walker*), Emmanuelle Seigner (*Michelle*), Betty Buckley (*Sondra Walker*), John Mahoney (*Williams*), Jimmy Ray Weeks (*Shaap*), Yorgo Voyagis (*The Kidnaper*), David Huddleston (*Peter*), Gerard Klein (*Gaillard*), Jacques Ciron (*Hotel Manager*), Dominique Pinon (*Wino*)

p, Thom Mount, Tim Hampton; d, Roman Polanski; w, Roman Polanski, Gerard Brach; ph, Witold Sobocinski; ed, Sam O'Steen; m, Ennio Morricone; prod d, Pierre Guffroy; cos, Anthony Powell

One of Roman Polanski's best, and too often overlooked. FRANTIC is a dreamy, tense thriller set against a stylishly reimagined Paris and featuring the performance of Harrison Ford's career. Dr. Richard Walker (Ford), a San Francisco surgeon, arrives in Paris with his wife (Betty Buckley), intending to deliver a medical paper and hoping to revitalize their relationship (they'd honeymooned in Paris 20 years earlier). Walker speaks no French and cannot even make a phone call without his wife's help. The Walkers arrive at the posh Le Grand Hotel and begin to unpack, only to discover they have the wrong suitcase. Later, while Dr. Walker showers, Sondra disappears without a trace.

Initially baffled and annoyed, Walker soon becomes deeply concerned and finally frantic as he realizes that the police won't help him in this alien environment. Acting alone, he locates the owner of the mysterious suitcase, Michelle (Emmanuelle Seigner), an alluring Parisian who draws him further into a web of intrigue.

Director Polanski, a master of movie atmospherics (e.g., CHINATOWN, ROSEMARY'S BABY), here creates a hauntingly foreign, forbiddingly stylish Paris that seems to move to the oneiric disco stylings of Grace Jones. Harrison Ford, outstanding as an American innocent abroad, moves persuasively from complacency to confusion, rage, and paranoid desperation in a performance comparable to James Stewart's best work for Hitchcock.

FREAKS

1932 64m bw Horror ★★★★
MGM (U.S.) /X

Wallace Ford (*Phroso*), Leila Hyams (*Venus*), Olga Baclanova (*Cleopatra*), Roscoe Ates (*Roscoe*), Henry Victor (*Hercules*), Harry Earles (*Hans*), Daisy Earles (*Frieda*), Rose Dione (*Madame Tetrallini*), Daisy Hilton, Violet Hilton (*Siamese Twins*)

p, Tod Browning, Irving Thalberg; d, Tod Browning; w, Willis Goldbeck, Leon Gordon, Edgar Allan Woolf, Al Boasberg (based on the short story "Spurs" by Clarence Aaron "Tod" Robbins); ph, Merritt B. Gerstad; ed, Basil Wrangell; art d, Cedric Gibbons, Merrill Pye

Long unseen, FREAKS was MGM's answer to Universal's popular FRANKENSTEIN and DRACULA, but public and critical revulsion to the use of actual circus freaks soon forced the movie from distribution. Dwain Esper (of MANIAC fame) later gave it road shows in tents and burlesque houses, further adding to this cult classic's notorious reputation.

The story follows Cleopatra (Baclanova), a beautiful but avaricious trapeze artist who seduces and marries midget circus owner Hans (Earles) to get at his money. In one of the film's most memorable scenes, the close-knit society of "freaks" warmly welcomes her into their family at the wedding reception as "one of us, one of us." Cleopatra shrinks back in disgust, however, telling them all that she will never be grotesque, while her secret lover, Hercules the strongman (Victor), howls with laughter. She humiliates her smitten husband by openly kissing the lecherous Hercules and the community soon realizes a threat is in their presence. When Hans falls ill, the group figures out that Cleopatra and Hercules have been slowly poisoning him, and so they plan a horrible, ironic revenge.

Although the suspenseful, brilliantly handled final scenes suggest an exploitation of the film's handicapped players, by then we have actually come to identify more with them than with the "normal" Cleopatra and Hans. The final revenge is thus not so much an attempt to turn melodrama into horror as it is the resolution of an old-fashioned morality play. Possibly Browning's warmest film, FREAKS is a compassionate study of how physically deformed people manage on their own. We see how they bond to each other and to those (Ford and Hyams) who love them as they are.

Some of the film's best moments are those unburdened by the plot, as we visit circus members—the bearded lady; the bird girl; the hermaphrodite; the human skeleton; the pinheads; and the Siamese twins—to see how they move, how they feel, how they love. Although slow-moving and uneven, FREAKS is one of Browning's more consistently fine films, a landmark still worth seeing.

FREE SOUL, A

1931 91m bw Drama ★★★½
MGM (U.S.) /A

Norma Shearer (*Jan Ashe*), Leslie Howard (*Dwight Winthrop*), Lionel Barrymore (*Stephen Ashe*), Clark Gable (*Ace Wilfong*), James Gleason (*Eddie*), Lucy Beaumont (*Grandma Ashe*), Claire Whitney (*Aunt Helen*), Frank Sheridan (*Prosecuting Attorney*), E. Alyn Warren (*Bottomley, Ace's Chinese Boy*), George Irving (*Defense Atty. Johnson*)

d, Clarence Brown; w, John Meehan (based on the novel by Adela Rogers St. Johns and the play by Willard Mack); ph, William Daniels; ed, Hugh Wynn; m, William Axt; art d, Cedric Gibbons; cos, Adrian

AA Best Actor: Lionel Barrymore; *AAN Best Actress:* Norma Shearer; *AAN Best Director:* Clarence Brown

"A new kind of man, a new kind of world". This is how lusty Jan Ashe (Shearer) describes sinister stud Ace Wilfong (Gable). She might have been describing Gable himself who, still in his first year in movies, became a star in this hard-breathing melodrama of the old school.

Shearer plays a spoiled, high-powered filly whose alcoholic barrister dad (Barrymore) has encouraged her to follow his indulgent lead. Her desires configure around gangster Gable, who was terrified that in one scene he actually had to push around one of MGM's most prestigious divas. Women fans of the time loved it. The hormones flow freely in A FREE SOUL, and the film's best moments are when Shearer and Gable make raunchy yet silken sinning a fine art.

Of course, all this horniness is too good to last and there's a lot of redemption involved at the end. Eventually, Papa has to rouse himself sufficiently to give a killer-diller courtroom speech which proves to be a killer indeed. Yes, that's right. When Stephen Ashe is ready to let "the defense rest," he "rests" permanently, keeling over right in the courtroom. Totally fabulous, huh? Damn right it is.

Remade without spark as THE GIRL WHO HAD EVERYTHING. La Liz is theoretically well cast, but the film simply hasn't the foolish bravado of the original.

FREE WILLY

1993   112m   c   Children's/Adventure/Drama   ★★½
Donner-Shuler-Donner/Le Studio Canal Plus/Regency   PG/U
Enterprises/Alcor Films   (U.S.)

Jason James Richter *(Jesse)*, Lori Petty *(Rae Lindley)*, Jayne Atkinson *(Annie Greenwood)*, August Schellenberg *(Randolph Johnson)*, Michael Madsen *(Glen Greenwood)*, Michael Ironside *(Dial)*, Richard Riehle *(Wade)*, Mykel T. Williamson *(Dwight Mercer)*, Michael Bacall *(Perry)*, Danielle Harris *(Gwenie)*

p, Lauren Shuler-Donner, Jennie Lew Tugend; d, Simon Wincer; w, Keith A. Walker, Corey Blechman, Tom Benedek (from a story by Keith A. Walker); ph, Robbie Greenberg, Pete Romano; ed, O. Nicholas Brown; m, Basil Poledouris; prod d, Charles Rosen; art d, Diane Yates, Chas Butcher, Theresa Wachter; fx, Tom Ward, Robert S. Henderson, Wayne W. Rose; cos, April Ferry

This modest boy-and-his-killer-whale story was a surprising, if carefully orchestrated, summer success. FREE WILLY's ads asked, "How far would you go for a friend?" but a more probing query to parents would be "How much will you sit through for your kid?" Shamelessly manipulative and heavyhanded, it may be an endurance test for those not absolutely entranced by large aquatic mammals.

A killer whale is separated from his family, shipped to an amusement park, christened Willy and expected to entertain. Meanwhile, runaway Jesse (Jason James Richter) survives on the streets by stealing and begging. Jesse finds new foster parents and must clean up the graffiti he sprayed at the park: the moment the surly, uncooperative youngster lays eyes on the equally cantankerous whale, they bond. Trouble looms in the form of Park owner Dial (Michael Ironside), who fears Willy was a bad investment and plots to kill the whale for the insurance.

FREE WILLY is dopey and schematic—Michael Ironside lets us know he's a bad guy by scowling and muttering "I hate that whale!"—but things pick up a bit whenever kid and whale interact. Keiko is a very talented animal, making it ironic that he plays a whale with performance anxiety, and even jaded viewers may experience some artificial uplift at the end. Michael Jackson sings the amazingly overwrought theme song "Will You Be There" over the credits. And you thought "Ben" was a bit odd!

FREEZE—DIE—COME TO LIFE
(ZAMRI OUMI VOSKRESNI)

1990   105m   bw   Drama   ★★★½
Lenfilm   (U.S.S.R.)

Dinara Drukarova *(Galiya)*, Pavel Nazarov *(Valerka)*, Yelena Popova *(Valerka's Mother)*, Vyacheslav Bambushek *(Vitka)*, Vadim Ermolayev *(School Principal)*

p, Valentina Tarasova; d, Vitaly Kanevski; w, Vitaly Kanevski; ph, Vladimir Brylyakov; ed, Galina Kornilova; m, Sergei Banevich; cos, Tatyana Kochergina, Natalya Milliant

Vitaly Kanevski's FREEZE-DIE-COME TO LIFE is a grim, wrenching, beautifully realized story of a trouble-prone boy growing up in a postwar gulag town in Soviet Asia.

Valerka (Pavel Nazarov) lives in a decrepit block of flats with his mother (Yelena Popova), a prostitute and dance-hall bartender who is struggling to build a good life for her son. Valerka is an irrepressible prankster at school. His antics provide him with a much-needed release from the dreary reality of his existence; it is his street-smarts and wit that keep him from becoming one of the walking dead that inhabit his town. Valerka is also enterprising, and he goes into competition with his friend Galiya (Dinara Drukarova) as a tea seller. As an aspiring capitalist, Valerka tries to scare away Galiya's customers by claiming that her water is rusty and that her kettle has very recently been a home to cockroaches. He also makes false grand claims for his own tea. Valerka and Galiya are never protected from the harsh realities of the adult world.

Shot in a grim black-and-white that creates a sense of a world of perpetual grays, FREEZE-DIE-COME TO LIFE is a movingly authentic document that recalls the best of neorealism. Moreover it captures the indomitability of Valerka's and Galiya's spirits even under the most hopeless circumstances. The performances, particularly Nazarov and Drukarova, are compelling and spontaneous. Kanevski's direction is impressive and his screenplay is unsparing and touched with humor.

FRENCH CANCAN

1955   93m   c   Musical   ★★★★
Franco-London/Jolly   (France)   /A

Jean Gabin *(Danglard)*, Maria Felix *(La Belle Abesse)*, Francoise Arnoul *(Nini)*, Jean-Roger Caussimon *(Baron Walter)*, Gianni Esposito *(Prince Alexandre)*, Philippe Clay *(Casimir)*, Michel Piccoli *(Valorgueil)*, Jean Paredes *(Coudrier)*, Lydia Johnson *(Guibole)*, Max Dalban *(Manager of The Reine Blanche)*

p, Louis Wipf; d, Jean Renoir; w, Jean Renoir (based on an idea by Andre-Paul Antoine); ph, Michel Kelber; ed, Borys Lewin; m, Georges Van Parys; art d, Max Douy; chor, G. Grandjean; cos, Rosine Delamare

After a 15-year hiatus from filmmaking in France, Jean Renoir returned with this high-spirited celebration of color and movement. FRENCH CANCAN vibrantly brings to life the dawning days of the Moulin Rouge, complete with high-kicking choristers flaunting their frills. Gabin turns in one of his most memorable performances as Danglard, an aging theater impresario known for his ability to take common women and transform them into dancehall sensations—he also succeeds in seducing them. Before long, he becomes captivated with Montmartre laundress Nini (Arnoul) and he ignores a previous love to devote his energies into making her a star.

A deceptively simple picture, FRENCH CANCAN lets us relive an era previously vivid only in the painted art of Toulouse-Lautrec and Jean's father Auguste Renoir. Renoir, whose films have consistently served as training grounds for a number of prominent directors (Jacques Becker on LA CHIENNE, Yves Allegret and Luchino Visconti on the short A DAY IN THE COUNTRY, and Robert Aldrich on THE SOUTHERNER), also gave a start to Jacques Rivette in this picture by letting him serve as a directorial trainee.

FRENCH CONNECTION, THE

1971   104m   c   Crime   ★★★★½
Fox   (U.S.)   R/18

Gene Hackman *(Jimmy "Popeye" Doyle)*, Fernando Rey *(Alain Charnier)*, Roy Scheider *(Buddy Russo)*, Tony Lo Bianco *(Sal Boca)*, Marcel Bozzufi *(Pierre Nicoli)*, Frederic de Pasquale *(Devereaux)*, Bill Hickman *(Mulderig)*, Ann Rebbot *(Marie Charnier)*, Harold Gary *(Weinstock)*, Sonny Grosso *(Klein)*

p, Philip D'Antoni; d, William Friedkin; w, Ernest Tidyman (based on the book by Robin Moore); ph, Owen Roizman; ed, Jerry Greenberg; m, Don Ellis; art d, Ben Kazaskow; fx, Sass Bedig; cos, Joseph Fretwell

FRENCH LIEUTENANT'S WOMAN, THE

AA Best Picture; AA Best Actor: Gene Hackman; *AAN Best Supporting Actor:* Roy Scheider; *AA Best Director:* William Friedkin; *AA Best Adapted Screenplay:* Ernest Tidyman; *AAN Best Cinematography:* Owen Roizman; *AAN Best Editing:* Jerry Greenberg; *AAN Best Sound:* Theodore Soderberg, Christopher Newman

This tough, brilliant crime film features Hackman as the indefatigable Popeye Doyle, who passionately hates drug pushers. Professional hit man Bozzuffi kills a French detective in Marseilles while Hackman and his partner Scheider roust a drug dealer in a vacant lot in Brooklyn. Later that night, Hackman and Scheider spot a group of mobsters celebrating and tail Lo Bianco and his wife. This leads to a massive surveillance of a large US drug ring on which Hackman and Scheider are ordered to work with federal agents Hickman and Grosso. Hackman and Hickman have a long-standing feud which begins to boil to the surface. Meanwhile, Rey, the mastermind of the French drug traffic, stashes 120 pounds of heroin in the Lincoln Continental car of television actor de Pasquale, who unwittingly escorts the shipment to New York. Rey contacts Lo Bianco in Manhattan to arrange for the sale of the heroin, but is spotted by Hackman who has staked out Lo Bianco and trailed the pair to a hotel. Hackman follows Rey, who is aware that he is being tailed, and the wiley Frenchman outwits the detective, escaping on a subway train, smugly waving goodbye as the cop is left standing on the platform. Enraged, Hackman hijacks a car and gives chase.

Young director Friedkin produced a suspenseful and utterly absorbing film which incorporated thrills with street humor and routine police work with highly dramatic scenes. The chase scene, an incredible, hair-raising sequence, was shot from Hackman's car with cameras mounted in the back seat and on the front fenders. The police are portrayed as being almost as brutal as the criminals, with Hackman shown to be a near-maniac who will stop at nothing to corral drug offenders. Hackman won an Oscar for his riveting portrayal, as did the film, Friedkin, Tidyman's screenplay and Greenberg's editing.

FRENCH LIEUTENANT'S WOMAN, THE

1981 127m c Romance ★★★½
UA (U.K.) /15

Meryl Streep *(Sarah/Anna)*, Jeremy Irons *(Charles/Mike)*, Hilton McRae *(Sam)*, Emily Morgan *(Mary)*, Charlotte Mitchell *(Mrs. Tranter)*, Lynsey Baxter *(Ernestina)*, Jean Faulds *(Cook)*, Peter Vaughan *(Mr. Freeman)*, Colin Jeavons *(Vicar)*, Liz Smith *(Mrs. Fairley)*

p, Leon Clore; d, Karel Reisz; w, Harold Pinter (based on the novel by John Fowles); ph, Freddie Francis; ed, John Bloom; m, Carl Davis; prod d, Assheton Gorton; art d, Norman Dorme, Terry Pritchard, Allan Cameron; cos, Tom Rand

AAN Best Actress: Meryl Streep; *AAN Best Adapted Screenplay:* Harold Pinter (Screenplay); *AAN Best Editing:* John Bloom; *AAN Best Art Direction:* Assheton Gorton (Art Direction), Ann Mollo (Set Decoration); *AAN Best Costume Design:* Tom Rand

Translating John Fowles' complex novel to the screen was a formidable task, previously attempted—then abandoned—by the likes of Fred Zinnemann, Richard Lester and Mike Nichols. Undaunted, director Karel Reisz joined forces with esteemed playwright Harold Pinter to convey the essence of Fowles' epic romance.

In a technically flawless performance, Meryl Streep plays Sarah Woodruff, a mysterious pariah in mourning who has been dishonored after an affair with a French army officer in Victorian England. In his first starring role, Jeremy Irons portrays Charles Smithson, the wealthy young man of principle who finds her and falls hopelessly in love. Pinter's screenplay shrewdly incorporates both the novel's 19th-century point of view, and underscoring the oppressive constraints of Victorian society, a contemporary tale featuring Streep and Irons as Anna and Mike, the sophisticated actors playing Sarah and Charles in a film adaptation of *The French Lieutenant's Woman* who casually embark on their own affair—with decidedly different results.

Though occasionally jarring, the intercutting between the parallel stories, aided immeasurably by Streep's disparate characterizations, succeeds in conveying the complexity of Fowles' novel.

FRENCH, THEY ARE A FUNNY RACE, THE
(LES CARNETS DU MAJOR THOMPSON)

1955 105m bw Comedy ★★★
Continental/Gaumont (France)

Jack Buchanan *(Major Thompson)*, Martine Carol *(Martine)*, Noel-Noel *(Taupin)*, Totti Truman Taylor *(Nurse)*, Andre Luguet *(Editor)*, Genevieve Brunet *(Secretary)*, Catherine Boyle *(Wife)*

p, Paul Wagner, Alain Poire; d, Preston Sturges; w, Preston Sturges (based on the book *The Notebooks of Major Thompson* by Pierre Daninos); ph, Maurice Barry, Christian Matras; ed, Raymond Lanny

Notable as Preston Sturges's last film, made in France after an absence of six years. Based on essays allegedly written by an English major about his adjustment to carefree French life, the film is anecdotal and often amusing, but the overwhelming feeling is one of sadness as we watch the greatest comic talent of the 1940s straining along shortly before he died in exile.

Jack Buchanan, that former effervescent musical comedy star, also makes his final appearance as Major Thompson, who resides in Paris with his air-headed but beautiful French wife (Carol, likable but underused); the two appear to have nothing better to do than argue over how to raise their child. Boyle appears as the major's English wife, whose conjugal outlook stems from her mother's advice to her on her wedding night: "My dear, it's utterly unbearable, but just close your eyes and think of England." Sturges does effectively lampoon both English and French lifestyles as he sees them, and the contrasts are sometimes evocative of his earlier sophistication. Still, the visuals are drab and the energy is low, making this a far cry from such brilliant earlier Sturges works as THE MIRACLE OF MORGAN CREEK and SULLIVAN'S TRAVELS, both masterpieces of satirical wit.

FRENZY

1972 116m c Thriller ★★★★
Universal (U.K.) R/18

Jon Finch *(Richard Blaney)*, Barry Foster *(Robert Rusk)*, Barbara Leigh-Hunt *(Brenda Blaney)*, Anna Massey *(Babs Milligan)*, Alec McCowen *(Chief Inspector Oxford)*, Vivien Merchant *(Mrs. Oxford)*, Billie Whitelaw *(Hetty Porter)*, Clive Swift *(Johnny Porter)*, Bernard Cribbins *(Felix Forsythe)*, Michael Bates *(Sgt. Spearman)*

p, Alfred Hitchcock; d, Alfred Hitchcock; w, Anthony Shaffer (from the novel *Goodbye Piccadilly, Farewell Leicester Square* by Arthur LaBern); ph, Gilbert Taylor; ed, John Jympson; m, Ron Goodwin; prod d, Syd Cain; art d, Robert Laing

Hitchcock's first British film in almost two decades marked a smashing return to his earlier form after the dull TORN CURTAIN and TOPAZ. Although not a mystery (we know the killer's identity early on), the film is intensely suspenseful, at times forcing the audience to identify with the murderer. Richard Blaney (Finch) is accused of murdering his ex-wife Brenda (Leigh-Hunt) and his girlfriend (Massey), both of whom have been strangled with neckties. The real "Necktie Murderer," however, remains at large.

There's more explicit sex and violence in this movie than is usual for Hitchcock. His famous touches still abound, however, juxtaposing some screamingly funny bits involving Scotland Yard Inspector Oxford (McCowen) with brutal rape-strangulation scenes. The first murder is particularly well done, and expect a jolt when a body falls off a truck. FRENZY also contains perhaps the most wicked of Hitchcock's scenes—the killer searching through a stack of potato sacks in order to find his missing monogrammed tie pin, which a nude corpse clutches in her death grip.

FRESH

1994 112m c Drama/Thriller ★★★★
Fresh Productions/A Band Apart Productions/Lawrence Bender R/
Productions/Lumiere (U.S./France)

Sean Nelson *(Fresh)*, Giancarlo Esposito *(Esteban)*, Samuel L. Jackson *(Sam)*, N'Bushe Wright *(Nicole)*, Ron Brice *(Corky)*, Jean Claude Lamarre *(Jake)*, Jose Zuniga *(Lt. Perez)*, Luis Lantigua *(Chuckie)*, Yul Vasquez *(Chillie)*, Cheryl Freeman *(Aunt Frances)*

p, Randy Ostrow, Lawrence Bender; d, Boaz Yakin; w, Boaz Yakin; ph, Adam Holender; ed, Dorian Harris; m, Stewart Copeland; prod d, Dan Leigh; cos, Ellen Lutter

FRESH sounds like another slice of low-life, a study of an intelligent but fatally disadvantaged ghetto child's inexorable descent into criminality. But if the situations are (at first) familiar, the characters aren't; they may look like the same old junkies and dealers and whores and gangsters, but first-time director Boaz Yakin invests all of them—particularly Fresh (Sean Nelson)—with a subtle, complex life that's both painful and exhilarating.

On the mean streets of New York City, 12-year-old Fresh works as a courier for Esteban (Giancarlo Esposito), a drug dealer who functions as a surrogate father. His real father (Samuel L. Jackson), unemployed and embittered, has channelled a lifetime of frustration into mastering the game of chess, in which he periodically instructs his son. Yakin's tightly plotted character study seems poised to follow a well-worn path: promising ghetto youth, desperate family, bad companions, violence and death, capped off with the usual dose of pat moralizing. Instead, FRESH offers a welcome departure from well-worn themes and plot developments, as the title character launches a cold-blooded, intricately plotted scheme to rescue himself and the remnants of his family from the depredations of ghetto life.

FRESH stands on young Sean Nelson's performance, and he is so good it's hard to believe. Fresh is a complex and contradictory character, a boy who's simultaneously sophisticated and callow, naive enough to think life can be played like a board game and smart enough to do it and win, though at a disturbing price. Yakin deserves special praise for endowing his characters with intellect—a quality that blacks are rarely allowed to display in Hollywood films—and for resisting the temptation to mar his quietly intelligent film with a commercially desirable hip-hop soundtrack.

FRESHMAN, THE

1990 102m c Comedy ★★★
Lobell-Bergman (U.S.) PG

Marlon Brando (Carmine Sabatini), Matthew Broderick (Clark Kellogg), Bruno Kirby (Victor Ray), Penelope Ann Miller (Tina Sabatini), Frank Whaley (Steve Bushak), Jon Polito (Chuck Greenwald), Paul Benedict (Arthur Fleeber), Richard Gant (Lloyd Simpson), Kenneth Welsh (Dwight Armstrong), Pamela Payton-Wright (Liz Armstrong)

p, Mike Lobell; d, Andrew Bergman; w, Andrew Bergman; ph, William A. Fraker; ed, Barry Malkin; m, David Newman; prod d, Ken Adam; art d, Alicia Keywan; fx, Neil Tifunovich; cos, Julie Weiss

Matthew Broderick stars as Clark Kellogg, a freshman from Vermont who comes to the Big Apple to study film at New York University. His most flamboyant professor is Arthur Fleeber (a scene-stealing turn by Paul Benedict, best known as Mr. Bentley of television's "The Jeffersons") who has committed every moment from THE GODFATHER PART II to memory. The great man assigns $700 worth of his own publications as required reading for his course. Kellogg gets an education in New York street life before he even gets to school, as he is robbed shortly upon hitting town by a con man, Victor Ray (Bruno Kirby). Kellogg eventually tracks Ray down but, instead of returning his stuff, the slick character offers to introduce the freshman to a real Godfather, his Uncle Carmine (Marlon Brando), an "importer-exporter" who can provide Kellogg with a high-paying, "totally legitimate" job.

There's not much to THE FRESHMAN beyond the spectacle of Brando gently spoofing his most famous role, but that's a pretty sizeable asset. Broderick is his usual charming self, and there are occasional moments of inspired whimsy or absurdity: Brando on ice skates, Bert Parks delivering a rousing rendition of Bob Dylan's "Maggie's Farm."

FRIED GREEN TOMATOES

1991 130m c Drama/Comedy ★★★½
Avnet/Kerner Company/Electric Shadow PG-13/12
Productions/Act III Communications (U.S.)

Kathy Bates (Evelyn Couch), Jessica Tandy (Ninny Threadgoode), Mary Stuart Masterson (Idgie Threadgoode), Mary-Louise Parker (Ruth Jamison), Nick Searcy (Frank Bennett), Cicely Tyson (Sipsey), Chris O'Donnell (Buddy Threadgoode), Stan Shaw (Big George), Gailard Sartain (Ed Couch), Tim Scott (Smokey Lonesome)

p, Jon Avnet, Jordan Kerner; d, Jon Avnet; w, Fannie Flagg, Carol Sobieski (from the novel Fried Green Tomatoes at the Whistle Stop Cafe by Flagg); ph, Geoffrey Simpson; ed, Debra Neil; m, Thomas Newman; prod d, Barbara Ling; art d, Larry Fulton; fx, Larry Reid; cos, Elizabeth McBride

AAN Best Supporting Actress: Jessica Tandy; AAN Best Adapted Screenplay: Fannie Flagg, Carol Sobieski

Past and present are winningly blended in the "sleeper" hit FRIED GREEN TOMATOES, a gentle comedy based on Fannie Flagg's novel, Fried Green Tomatoes at the Whistle Stop Cafe.

Evelyn Couch (Kathy Bates), an overweight, repressed housewife, meets and befriends—or is befriended by—Ninny Threadgoode (Jessica Tandy), a remarkable octogenarian and firstrate storyteller. Ninny is a permanent resident, though she won't admit it, at a rest home for the aged where Evelyn accompanies her husband Ed (Gailard Sartain) on his weekly visits to his gruff aunt. The aunt detests Evelyn and will not allow her into the room, thus giving Evelyn ample time to spend with Ninny. The aged Alabaman begins to enthrall Evelyn with the fascinating life story—seen in flashback—of one of her relatives, Idgie Threadgoode.

An early proto-feminist, Idgie (Mary Stuart Masterson) owns and operates the local cafe in Whistle Stop, Alabama. Traumatized as a girl by the gory death of a beloved older brother, Idgie has remained a tomboy loner all her life, taking to the trees when the world around her gets to be too much. As such, she does none of the things respectable Southern women of the Depression Era 1930s are expected to do—like stay home and cook for the men. Idgie literally rescues her best friend, Ruth Jamison (Mary-Louise Parker), from Ruth's marriage to the abusive Frank Bennett (Nick Searcy). Bringing her young baby with her, Ruth moves in with Idgie and the two women soon have a thriving business at the cafe, with Ruth doing the cooking and Idgie handling the bookwork. They are aided in their endeavors by Sipsey (Cicely Tyson), a black seamstress, and Sipsey's handyman son, Big George (Stan Shaw). All goes well until Frank reappears, in an attempt to retrieve his child. Idgie and Ruth are not around, so it is left to Sipsey and Big George to protect the baby—with the end result that no-one ever sees Frank again.

During the weeks it takes Ninny to finish telling Evelyn the story, the younger woman undergoes a gradual transformation. Evelyn works hard at improving her appearance through diet and exercise, and learns how to begin asserting herself and building her self-esteem. Inspired by the tale of Idgie and Ruth and increasingly drawn to Ninny, she asks the older woman to move out of the rest home and to come and live with her and her husband. Ninny delightedly accepts and, in the last scene, it is strongly hinted that Ninny and the "Idgie" of her stories are one and the same.

FRIED GREEN TOMATOES is an engaging if sentimental tale, charmingly handled by producer-turned-director Jon Avnet (RISKY BUSINESS) and flawlessly acted by its four female stars. Plaudits must also go to Geoffrey Simpson, for his splendid cinematography, and to Thomas Newman for his drama-enhancing musical score.

FRIENDLY PERSUASION

1956 137m c Drama ★★★★
Allied Artists (U.S.) /U

Gary Cooper (Jess Birdwell), Dorothy McGuire (Eliza Birdwell), Marjorie Main (Widow Hudspeth), Anthony Perkins (Josh Birdwell), Richard Eyer (Little Jess), Phyllis Love (Mattie Birdwell), Robert Middleton (Sam Jordan), Mark Richman (Gard Jordan), Walter Catlett (Professor Quigley), Richard Hale (Elder Purdy)

FRIENDS OF EDDIE COYLE, THE

p, William Wyler; d, William Wyler; w, Michael Wilson (uncredited, based on the novel *The Friendly Persuasion* by Jessamyn West); ph, Ellsworth Fredricks; ed, Robert Swink, Edward A. Biery, Robert Belcher; m, Dimitri Tiomkin; art d, Ted Haworth; cos, Dorothy Jeakins, Bert Henrikson

AAN Best Picture; *AAN Best Supporting Actor:* Anthony Perkins; *AAN Best Director:* William Wyler; *AAN Best Adapted Screenplay:* Michael Wilson; *AAN Best Song:* Dimitri Tiomkin (Music), Paul Francis Webster (Lyrics); *AAN Best Sound:* Gordon R Glennan (Westrex Sound Services Inc), Gordon Sawyer (Samuel Goldwyn Studio Sound Department)

Long and a tad preachy, FRIENDLY PERSUASION recounts the story of a peaceful Quaker family in Indiana whose sanctity is disturbed by the Civil War in 1862.

Cooper and McGuire play the parents of Josh (Perkins), who listens to a Union officer make a plea for young men to take up the Blue cudgel. Although morally opposed to war, Josh fears that he's using his religion to mask a cowardly streak. When the news comes that the Southern band known as Morgan's Raiders is nearing his town, Josh joins the local militia and prepares to fight. He is hurt in battle, and his father goes into the war zone to save his son and find a pal (Middleton) who's been ambushed.

There's humor galore in this picture, especially in a scene with Main and her three lonesome daughters. There are many tearful moments too and several incisive looks into the lives of the "Society of Friends." Aiming for a collage effect, director Wyler deals lovingly with McGuire's ongoing battles with Samantha the goose as well as a little boy who suddenly yells "God is love" in a crowded church. A shorter running time would have helped but, as it is, FRIENDLY PERSUASION ranks as one of Wyler's best comedy-dramas.

FRIENDS OF EDDIE COYLE, THE

1973 102m c Crime	★★★½
Paramount (U.S.)	R/X

Robert Mitchum *(Eddie Coyle)*, Peter Boyle *(Dillon)*, Richard Jordan *(Dave Foley)*, Steven Keats *(Jackie Brown)*, Alex Rocco *(Scalise)*, Joe Santos *(Artie Van)*, Mitchell Ryan *(Waters)*, Helena Carroll *(Sheila Coyle)*, Peter MacLean *(Partridge)*, Kevin O'Morrison *(Manager of 2nd Bank)*

p, Paul Monash; d, Peter Yates; w, Paul Monash (based on the novel by George V. Higgins); ph, Victor J. Kemper; ed, Patricia Jaffe; m, Dave Grusin; prod d, Gene Callahan; art d, Gene Callahan; cos, Eric Seelig

Mitchum is Eddie Coyle, a three-time loser. One more offense and he goes to prison for life—no parole, no hope. Police learn of an impending Boston bank robbery and go to Coyle, telling him that they know he earns a living for his destitute family by running illegal goods across state lines. They will put him away unless he squeals on the robbery gang. He reluctantly agrees to help and, after selling the gang some guns, contacts detectives, who tell him his information is insufficient. He must go on being a permanent informer and is ordered to help capture gang boss Scalise (Rocco). Before Eddie can move, however, Scalise is arrested. Coyle's underworld friends point the finger at him, ordering him murdered.

THE FRIENDS OF EDDIE COYLE is a tough look at the world of petty crooks and the sleazy side of the underworld. Mitchum is surprisingly effective as the down-and-out thief, as if worn out over the decades from earlier film noir escapades in THE RACKET and OUT OF THE PAST. Boyle is terrific as the thug who goes in for synthetic friendships, willing to sell out his own mother for survival in a system he knows will destroy him anyway. Yates's direction is grimly taut, and Monash's screenplay pulls no punches. A bit gruesome, but potent viewing nonetheless.

FRIGHT NIGHT

1985 106m c Horror	★★★½
Columbia (U.S.)	R/18

Chris Sarandon *(Jerry Dandridge)*, William Ragsdale *(Charley Brewster)*, Amanda Bearse *(Amy Peterson)*, Roddy McDowall *(Peter Vincent)*, Stephen Geoffreys *(Evil Ed)*, Jonathan Stark *(Billy Cole)*, Dorothy Fielding *(Judy Brewster)*, Art Evans *(Detective Lennox)*, Stewart Stern *(Cook)*, Nick Savage

p, Herb Jaffe; d, Tom Holland; w, Tom Holland; ph, Jan Kiesser; ed, Kent Beyda; m, Brad Fiedel; prod d, John De Cuir; fx, Richard Edlund, Michael Lantieri, Darrell D. Prichett, Clay Pinney, Albert Lannutti; cos, Robert Fletcher

A minor classic of the genre, this is a memorable addition to the vampire tradition in the horror film. FRIGHT NIGHT depicts the plight of Charley Brewster (Ragsdale), a fatherless teenager tottering on the brink of manhood, as he becomes obsessed with the charming new man next door, Jerry Dandridge (Sarandon). He is convinced that his neighbor is actually a vampire and responsible for a series of local murders. Charley alerts the local authorities but they dismiss him as a crank. His mom (Dorothy Fielding) won't listen to him and even his best buddy, Evil Ed (Geoffreys), and his devoted girlfriend, Amy Peterson (Bearse), think he's crazy. Desperate, Charley turns to the only vampire expert he can find, Peter Vincent (McDowall), an aging washed-up horror movie ham. Though at first he only humors the boy, Vincent soon realizes that Charley is telling the truth.

This film is the feature directing debut of Tom Holland who was previously known for his smart genre screenplays— CLASS OF 1984, CLOAK AND DAGGER and PSYCHO II. Like his earlier scripts, FRIGHT NIGHT is a clever amalgam; this teen-oriented vampire movie deftly combines Hitchcockian themes, Hammer horror trappings, a subversive gay subtext and a John Hughes milieu into a genuinely scary horror movie that is comfortably old-fashioned yet cool.

Holland, a former actor, elicits much better than average performances from his teen actors. Stephen Geoffreys is particularly enjoyable in a crazed Jack Nicholson turn as Evil Ed. The more seasoned players deliver outstanding performances. Chris Sarandon is stunning as the sensually handsome—yet deadly—new neighbor. Roddy McDowall is also in fine form in his best role in years as the cynical has-been who must become a true hero. FRIGHT NIGHT may not be great art but it *is* great fun.

FROM DUSK TILL DAWN

1996 108m c Horror/Crime/Comedy	★★
A Band Apart Productions/Les Hooligans Productions/Miramax (U.S.)	R/18

Harvey Keitel *(Jacob Fuller)*, George Clooney *(Seth Gecko)*, Quentin Tarantino *(Richard Gecko)*, Juliette Lewis *(Kate Fuller)*, Ernest Liu *(Scott Fuller)*, Cheech Marin *(Border Guard/Chet Pussy/Carlos)*, Fred Williamson *(Frost)*, Salma Hayek *(Santanico Pandemonium)*, Marc Lawrence *(Old Timer)*, Michael Parks *(Texas Ranger Earl McGraw)*

p, Gianni Nunnari, Meir Teper; d, Robert Rodriguez; w, Quentin Tarantino (from a story by Robert Kurtzman); ph, Guillermo Navarro; ed, Robert Rodriguez; m, Graeme Revell; prod d, Cecilia Montiel; art d, Mayne Schuyler Berke; fx, Daniel A. Fort, Diana Dru Botsford, T. "Brooklyn" Belissimo, Charles Belardinelli, Bellisimo/Belardinelli Effects Inc.; cos, Graciela Mazon

Two of the more promising creative talents in contemporary genre filmmaking (Robert Rodriguez and Quentin Tarantino), some marquee-value, and several cult icons conspired to produce this prodigious waste of time. Though not without entertainment value, the film is a mindless addition to an over-populated sub-genre of the horror film.

The Gecko brothers are on the lam after a string of violent bank robberies in the American Southwest. Seth (George Clooney) is a smooth professional thief, while Richie (Quentin Tarantino) is a nerdy-looking psycho. Bound for sanctuary south of the border, the Geckos take a female hostage to a cheap motel, where they cross paths with lapsed minister Jacob Fuller (Harvey Keitel) and his teenaged children, Kate (Juliette Lewis) and Scott (Ernest Liu). When Richie rapes and murders their hostage, the Geckos kidnap the Fullers and commandeer their vehicle to Mexico. The make a stop at the Titty Twister, a rollicking roadhouse bar, unaware that the bar's staff and clientele are all vampires. Soon all hell breaks loose as the Geckos, the Fullers, and several human customers join forces to battle the rapacious horde of bloodsuckers.

FROM DUSK TILL DAWN offers the pleasures of excess, but little ingenuity, and the film's lack of a consistent tone is further aggravated by mediocre dialogue. The filmmakers trot out second-string '70s genre figures (Fred Williamson, John Saxon) as if their mere presence might help elevate the tiresome proceedings. Clooney makes a credible action anti-hero, and even Tarantino is surprisingly restrained and inoffensive. Keitel, however, seems to have wandered in from another movie. Hype notwithstanding, one has come to expect a bit more from the creators of PULP FICTION and EL MARIACHI.

FROM HERE TO ETERNITY

1953   118m   bw   Drama/War   ★★★★★
Columbia   (U.S.)   /PG

Burt Lancaster *(Sgt. Milton Warden)*, Deborah Kerr *(Karen Holmes)*, Montgomery Clift *(Robert E. Lee Prewitt)*, Frank Sinatra *(Angelo Maggio)*, Donna Reed *(Alma Lorene)*, Ernest Borgnine *(Sgt. "Fatso" Judson)*, Philip Ober *(Capt. Dana Holmes)*, Jack Warden *(Cpl. Buckley)*, Mickey Shaughnessy *(Sgt. Leva)*, Harry Bellaver *(Mazzioli)*

p, Buddy Adler; d, Fred Zinnemann; w, Daniel Taradash (based on the novel by James Jones); ph, Burnett Guffey; ed, William Lyon; m, George Duning; art d, Cary Odell; cos, Jean Louis

AA Best Picture; *AAN Best Actor:* Montgomery Clift; *AAN Best Actor:* Burt Lancaster; *AAN Best Actress:* Deborah Kerr; *AA Best Supporting Actor:* Frank Sinatra; *AA Best Supporting Actress:* Donna Reed; *AA Best Director:* Fred Zinnemann; *AA Best Screenplay:* Daniel Taradash; *AA Best Cinematography:* Burnett Guffey; *AA Best Editing:* William Lyon; *AAN Best Score:* Morris Stoloff, George Duning; *AAN Best Costume Design:* Jean Louis; *AA Best Sound:* John P. Livadary

The massive James Jones novel, deemed impossible to put onscreen because of its strong sexual content and language, finally emerged as a lavish, star-studded spectacle, much bowdlerized but redeemed by a slew of fine performances.

The film opens as Robert E. Lee Prewitt (Montgomery Clift), a soldier with a reputation as both a fine boxer and bugler, arrives at Schofield Barracks at Pearl Harbor. His new commander, the brutal, philandering Captain Holmes (Philip Ober), promises Prewitt that if he boxes on the company team he will be rewarded with the post of bugler—a job Prewitt covets. But Prewitt refuses, haunted by a previous ugly experience in the ring. For Prewitt's obstinacy, Holmes orders Sgt. Warden (Burt Lancaster) to give the soldier every dirty detail in the company. As it turns out, Warden is about to begin a torrid affair with Holmes's wife Karen (Deborah Kerr). Meanwhile, Prewitt's suffering is eased by his newly established relationship with Lorene (Donna Reed), a nightclub hostess. Prewitt's only other friend, Maggio (Frank Sinatra), a wisecracking enlisted man, commits several small offenses and draws repeated punishment—especially from a sadistic Italian-hating sergeant named Fatso (Ernest Borgnine).

FROM HERE TO ETERNITY was an uphill battle all the way for director Zinnemann. Most of his war was with Columbia's dictator, Harry Cohn, who had purchased the novel for $82,000 and was determined to retain its seamy story, raw language, and violence, rejecting one adaptation after another. The Army was not happy with Jones's fierce indictment of its system and refused to allow the use of Schofield Barracks unless some major concessions were made. One chief point involved the role of Captain Holmes. In the novel he gets away with everything and is even promoted to major, but in the film he is cashiered for his cruelty and malfeasance.

The featured roles were also difficult to cast under Cohn's capricious supervision. Zinnemann had to fight to cast Clift, who gave one of his greatest performances; ditto Sinatra, whose faltering career received a much-needed boost here. He had to beg Cohn for the part of Maggio and ended up playing it for practically nothing (this episode was exaggerated and fictionalized by Mario Puzo in *The Godfather*). Joan Crawford was to have played the straying wife, but the icy-turned-passionate Kerr helped keep the famous lovemaking scene on the beach more realistic and low-key. Reed's part, on the other hand, was softened somewhat, her occupation being changed from prostitute to "hostess."

FROM RUSSIA WITH LOVE

1963   110m   c   Spy   ★★★★
UA   (U.K.)   /PG

Sean Connery *(James Bond)*, Daniela Bianchi *(Tatiana Romanova)*, Pedro Armendariz *(Kerim Bey)*, Lotte Lenya *(Rosa Klebb)*, Robert Shaw *(Red Grant)*, Bernard Lee *("M")*, Eunice Gayson *(Sylvia)*, Walter Gotell *(Morzeny)*, Francis de Wolff *(Vavra)*, George Pastell *(Train Conductor)*

p, Harry Saltzman, Albert R. Broccoli; d, Terence Young; w, Richard Maibaum, Johanna Harwood (based on the novel by Ian Fleming); ph, Ted Moore; ed, Peter Hunt; m, John Barry; art d, Syd Cain; fx, John Stears; cos, Jocelyn Rickards

The second James Bond movie, and the first to sport the lavish production values that characterized all subsequent entries in the series, FROM RUSSIA WITH LOVE sends Secret Agent 007 (Sean Connery) to mysterious Istanbul to grab a top-secret Russian decoding machine. There, he falls for Tatiana Romanova (Daniela Bianchi), a Soviet Embassy clerk who is an unwitting pawn of SPECTRE. Bond is pursued by ruthlessly butch East German agent Rosa Klebb (Lotte Lenya, lots of fun here) who carries a poisonous switchblade in her shoe. He also has to fend off Robert Shaw, sporting a fabulously bogus blond dye job, who plays a psychopathic trained assassin posing as a British agent (Bond spots him as a fraud when he orders red wine with fish). The highlight of the film is a terrific battle to the death on the Orient Express between Connery and Shaw.

Written with enough self-consciously campy humor to defuse the paranoid ideologies running rampant here, FROM RUSSIA WITH LOVE is also acted with tongues held firmly in cheek. Thankfully, the film displays little evidence of the excessive gadgetry that would plague later Bond flicks. One of the best of the Bond films, featuring Matt Monro singing the decidedly unmemorable Lionel Bart-penned title tune.

FRONT PAGE, THE

1931   101m   bw   Drama/Comedy   ★★★★½
Caddo   (U.S.)   /A

Adolphe Menjou *(Walter Burns)*, Pat O'Brien *(Hildy Johnson)*, Mary Brian *(Peggy)*, Edward Everett Horton *(Bensinger)*, Walter Catlett *(Murphy)*, George E. Stone *(Earl Williams)*, Mae Clarke *(Molly)*, Slim Summerville *(Pincus)*, Matt Moore *(Kruger)*, Frank McHugh *(McCue)*

p, Howard Hughes; d, Lewis Milestone; w, Bartlett Cormack, Ben Hecht (uncredited), Charles Lederer (based on the play by Ben Hecht and Charles MacArthur); ph, Glen MacWilliams, Hal Mohr, Tony Gaudio; ed, Duncan Mansfield; art d, Richard Day

AAN Best Picture; *AAN Best Actor:* Adolphe Menjou; *AAN Best Director:* Lewis Milestone

A vigorous, manic drama, this Lewis Milestone classic about newspapers and newsmen wonderfully preserves a host of Depression-era attitudes and a glorious headline era.

O'Brien, in his film debut, is the fast-talking Hildy Johnson, sensation-hunting star of the Chicago press. His shifty editor Walter Burns (Menjou) is trying to prevent his star reporter from quitting the business and moving to a New York advertising job with his wife-to-be Peggy (Brian). He hates everything about the sleazy tabloid world that has made Hildy famous, and she pressures him to finish his last day's work so they can flee to New York. In his farewell visit to the press room, however, Hildy gets caught up in the escape of an anarchist (Stone) scheduled for execution.

THE FRONT PAGE is an excellent production with a superior performance from novice O'Brien in a role better than many he later got to play. Menjou is marvelous too as a wily and sophisticated rascal, with a brilliant flair for dialogue. Howard Hughes let Milestone have his creative way with the film, and it shows in the film's no-holds-barred action and witty repartee. Hughes did make two decisions regarding the film, though, vetoing Milestone's first two choices for O'Brien's role: James Cagney and Clark Gable.

All of the character actors shine in the reporter roles, from the cynical Catlett and McHugh to the fussy, hygiene-obsessed Horton, who believes himself to be a poet. The play's lines were kept almost intact, with all the wild newspaper argot, glib quips and slurs delivered rapid-fire by the actors. Remade as HIS GIRL FRIDAY by Howard Hawks.

FRONT PAGE, THE

1974 105m c Drama/Comedy ★★½
Universal (U.S.) PG/AA

Jack Lemmon *(Hildy Johnson)*, Walter Matthau *(Walter Burns)*, Carol Burnett *(Mollie Malloy)*, Susan Sarandon *(Peggy Grant)*, Vincent Gardenia *(Sheriff)*, David Wayne *(Bensinger)*, Allen Garfield *(Kruger)*, Austin Pendleton *(Earl Williams)*, Charles Durning *(Murphy)*, Herb Edelman *(Schwartz)*

p, Paul Monash; d, Billy Wilder; w, Billy Wilder, I.A.L. Diamond (based on the play by Ben Hecht and Charles MacArthur); ph, Jordan S. Cronenweth; ed, Ralph E. Winters; m, Billy May; art d, Henry Bumstead; cos, Burton Miller

Wanted: a better remake of Lewis Milestone's classic original and Howard Hawks' revamp, HIS GIRL FRIDAY. This slick remake of the ebullient original falls short of being the film it could have been, despite the presence of master filmmaker Wilder and his engaging costars.

Hildy Johnson (Lemmon) is bound for New York with Peggy Grant (Sarandon) to begin a new life, but Walter Burns (Matthau) uses the escape of anarchist Earl Williams (Pendleton) to hold him on the job. Along the way they pointedly ignore the pleas of prostitute Mollie Malloy (Burnett), who is in love with the condemned man. The hide-and-seek game the newsmen play with authorities in covering up the wanted man's whereabouts is forced, but Martin Gabel, as the balmy psychiatrist, gives a hilarious performance. Durning is too vicious for the newsman role he plays, as is Garfield; Hecht and MacArthur drew their characters as jocular, not sadistic, personalities. The posturing, no doubt Wilder's doing, mars the impact of his satirical cynicism. It overpowers the screenplay and even the good performances of the leads.

Despite the obvious charismatic interaction between Lemmon and Matthau, the film is oddly stilted. In an overly emphatic turn, the miscast Burnett easily gives the most awful performance of her career. She projects only one emotion—a gratingly annoying hysteria. One never enjoys the film so much as when her character throws herself out of a window. Wilder was much more effective with Lemmon and Matthau in THE FORTUNE COOKIE and THE ODD COUPLE. This one just doesn't have the big story at press time.

FUGITIVE, THE

1947 104m bw Drama ★★★★
RKO (U.S.) /A

Henry Fonda *(The Fugitive)*, Dolores Del Rio *(Mexican Woman)*, Pedro Armendariz *(Police Lieutenant)*, Ward Bond *(El Gringo)*, Leo Carrillo *(Chief of Police)*, J. Carrol Naish *(Police Spy)*, Robert Armstrong *(Police Sergeant)*, John Qualen *(Doctor)*, Fortunio Bonanova *(Governor's Cousin)*, Chris-Pin Martin *(Organ Player)*

p, John Ford, Merian C. Cooper; d, John Ford; w, Dudley Nichols (based on the novel *The Labyrinthine Ways* and *The Power and the Glory* by Graham Greene); ph, Gabriel Figueroa; ed, Jack Murray; m, Richard Hageman; art d, Alfred Ybarra; fx, Fred Sersen

One of John Ford's favorite films; he sometimes considered it his masterpiece. It's hardly that, just as its companion piece, THE INFORMER, isn't quite the masterpiece everyone once thought it was. A powerful passion play set in a modern, fictitious south-of-the-border country, THE FUGITIVE is hauntingly photographed by Figueroa and boasts a highly effective performance from Fonda in which an intensely warm and likable saintliness largely replaces a three-dimensional character.

Much of this stems from Ford's influence on Nichols's screenplay, which changed the complex, sinful "whiskey priest" of Greene's original novel into a man whose main fear is that he's not sacrificing enough. The fugitive (Fonda) is hunted by a revolutionary government attempting to eliminate all traces of the Catholic religion. He hides in a small village and, passing as a peasant, performs secret rites for the locals. He even baptizes the bastard child a woman (the impossibly gorgeous Del Rio) has borne to a savage police lieutenant (Armendariz). He also

comforts an American criminal on the run (Bond) before escaping to a country without religious persecution. An encounter with a half-breed police spy (Naish) and the call to duty, though, lure him back to his hostile native terrain.

As with much of Ford, THE FUGITIVE is often sentimental and very Catholic, blunting Greene's political edge in favor of Ford's preference for lyric poetry. Here Fonda is the true Ford hero: quiet, contemplative, nonviolent and capable of superhuman sacrifice. Naive in some ways and full of portentous, obvious yet admittedly striking symbolism, THE FUGITIVE is nevertheless true to its own convictions.

FUGITIVE, THE

1993 127m c/bw Action/Thriller/Drama ★★★½
Keith Barish Productions/Arnold Kopelson
Productions (U.S.) PG-13/12

Harrison Ford *(Dr. Richard Kimble)*, Tommy Lee Jones *(Deputy US Marshal Samuel Gerard)*, Sela Ward *(Helen Kimble)*, Julianne Moore *(Dr. Ann Eastman)*, Joe Pantoliano *(Cosmo Renfro)*, Andreas Katsulas *(Sykes—"The One-Armed Man")*, Jeroen Krabbe *(Dr. Charles Nichols)*, Daniel Roebuck *(Biggs)*, L. Scott Caldwell *(Poole)*, Tom Wood *(Newman)*

p, Arnold Kopelson; d, Andrew Davis; w, Jeb Stuart, David Twohy (from a story by Twohy); ph, Michael Chapman; ed, Dennis Virkler, David Finfer, Dean Goodhill, Don Brochu, Richard Nord, Dov Hoenig; m, James Newton Howard; prod d, Dennis Washington; art d, Maher Ahmad, Charles Wood; fx, Roy Arbogast; cos, Aggie Guerard Rodgers

AA Best Supporting Actor: Tommy Lee Jones; *AAN Best Picture*Arnold Kopelson; *AAN Best Cinematography:* Michael Chapman; *AAN Best Editing:* Don Brochu, David Finfer, Dean Goodhill, Dov Hoenig, Richard Nord, Dennis Virkler; *AAN Best Original Score:* James Newton Howard; *AAN Best Sound:* Michael Herbick, Donald O. Mitchell, Frank A. Montano, Scott D. Smith; *AAN Best Sound Effects Editing:* John Leveque, Bruce Stambler

Lacking the dinos of JURASSIC PARK, the three-dimensional hero of IN THE LINE OF FIRE, or the seductive slickness of RISING SUN, THE FUGITIVE nevertheless emerged as one of the biggest hits of the 1993 summer season, proving Harrison Ford's virtual indestructibility at the box office and vindicating the trend of turning TV shows into movies.

Building on the premise of the 60s TV series, THE FUGITIVE opens with Dr. Richard Kimble (Harrison Ford) being convicted of killing his wife, despite his claims that he witnessed a one-armed man commit the murder. A bungled escape attempt by fellow convicts allows Kimble to get away and start a hunt for the real killer, while he himself is doggedly tracked by US Marshal Sam Gerard (Tommy Lee Jones). Though the film tries to grow into a conspiracy thriller involving a corrupt pharmaceutical company, that's one of its weaker points. The story is really just an excuse to put the two men through an ingenious series of chases, in settings ranging from a maze of flood drains to a St. Patrick's Day parade.

The action varies from a show-stopping train/bus wreck of Schwarzeneggerian proportions, to some more ironically staged pursuits which throw a welcome dash of "Tom and Jerry" into the mix. As the not-so-bad bad guy, Tommy Lee Jones gets all the best lines and delivers them superbly. Harrison Ford mostly just runs and fights, but that's O.K. Running, after all, is what fugitives are supposed to do.

FULL METAL JACKET

1987 116m c War ★★★★
Natant (U.K.) R/18

Matthew Modine *(Pvt. Joker)*, Adam Baldwin *(Animal Mother)*, Vincent D'Onofrio *(Leonard Lawrence, Pvt. Gomer Pyle)*, R. Lee Ermey *(Gunnery Sgt. Hartman)*, Dorian Harewood *(Eightball)*, Arliss Howard *(Pvt. Cowboy)*, Kevyn Major Howard *(Rafterman)*, Ed O'Ross *(Walter J. Schinoski, Lt. Touchdown)*, Jon Stafford *(Doc Jay)*, John Terry *(Lt. Lockhart)* p, Stanley Kubrick; d, Stanley Kubrick; w, Stanley Kubrick, Michael Herr, Gustav Hasford (based on the novel *The Short-Timers* by Gustav Hasford); ph, Douglas Milsome; ed, Martin Hunter; m, Abigail Mead; prod d, Anton Furst; art d, Rod Stratford, Leslie Tomkins, Keith Pain; fx, John Evans; cos, Keith Denny

AAN Best Adapted Screenplay: Stanley Kubrick, Michael Herr, Gustav Hasford

An uncompromisingly bleak film, as cold and distant as they come, Kubrick's FULL METAL JACKET is a perversely fascinating movie—one that answers no questions, offers no hope and has little meaning. In a way this is perfect for what the film has to say about war, but you find yourself numbed and apathetic as the film progresses. What one is left with is a remarkable display of the resources of cinema and a bludgeoning use of extreme violence which ironically undermines Kubrick's good intentions.

Highly structured, the film is presented in two parts: the first details the training of a group of Marines at the hands of the sadistic, foul-mouthed DI, Gunnery Sergeant Hartman (Ermey); and the second follows one of the recruits, "Joker" (Modine), a reporter for *Stars and Stripes* who finds himself in combat at the height of the Tet Offensive. There are no characterization and no heroics in FULL METAL JACKET; instead, Kubrick coolly shows the systematic dehumanization required to turn men into killing machines, then sits back and watches as they perform their assigned task.

From the shaving of the recruits' heads, the assignment of generic nicknames, and the profane bellowing that replaces conversation, to the orderly, ritualized existence of camp training is designed to drain all traces of individuality and humanity from soldiers and replace them with a cold hatred that can be directed at the enemy without hesitation. With his sarcastic humor and contradictory nature, Joker is the only character who retains a modicum of personality. Kubrick, however, dangles him before the viewer and then pulls him away slowly until Joker, too, is drained of his humanity.

Technically, FULL METAL JACKET is as flawless as any other meticulously designed Kubrick work and boasts superb cinematography by Milsome. Filming entirely in England, Kubrick found a military barracks outside London that doubles for Parris Island in the film. He also used a vast, deserted gasworks in London's East End, a plant area that had been bombed to ruination during WWII, and further destroyed the area to great effect.

FULL MOON IN PARIS
(LES NUITS DE LA PLEINE LUNE)
1984 101m c Drama   ★★★½
Losange/Ariane (France)   R/15

Pascale Ogier *(Louise)*, Fabrice Luchini *(Octave)*, Tcheky Karyo *(Remi)*, Christian Vadim *(Bastien)*, Virginie Thevenet *(Camille)*, Anne-Severine Liotard *(Marianne)*, Laszlo Szabo *(Painter at Cafe)*, Lisa Garneri *(Tina, the Babysitter)*, Mathieu Schiffman *(Louise's Decorator Friend)*, Herve Grandsart *(Remi's Friend Bertrand)*

p, Margaret Menegoz; d, Eric Rohmer; w, Eric Rohmer; ph, Renato Berta; ed, Cecile Decugis; m, Elli et Jacno; art d, Pascale Ogier; cos, Pascale Ogier

This fourth entry in Eric Rohmer's "Comedies and Proverbs" series begins with the proverb, "He who has two women loses his soul. He who has two houses loses his mind." The remarkably effervescent Pascale Ogier stars as the quintessential Rohmer woman, loved and admired by the men around her but desperately confused about the meaning of love.

A trainee at an interior-design firm, Louise (Ogier) lives with her architect-tennis player lover, Remi (Karyo), in a plastic suburb outside Paris. He wants to marry and settle down, but Louise is still young and enjoys dancing at parties until dawn. Remi's pressure proves too much for Louise, and she takes an apartment in Paris in order "to experience loneliness." Ostensibly, she will spend her late party nights in Paris, sleep in her new apartment, and return to the suburbs the following afternoon. While in Paris, she spends a great deal of time with Octave (Luchini) a likable writer who's tortured by Louise's refusal to sleep with him. At one fateful party, Louise meets Bastien (Vadim, son of

Roger Vadim and Catherine Deneuve) and takes him back to her Paris apartment. Soon, however, she regrets her mistake and reconsiders her affection for Remi. But several things have changed since back when.

What Rohmer has done in this film—and has done so successfully in the past—is to take a brief, intelligent, comic look at a young Frenchwoman and her ideas of love. Ogier (the 24-year-old daughter of actress Bulle Ogier) delivers her lines with animation rarely captured on film, and she knows how to dance on screen as well. Her performance justly earned her a Best Actress award at the Venice Film Festival, but her career was tragically cut short by a fatal heart attack.

FUNERAL, THE
(OSOSHIKI)
1984 124m c Comedy   ★★★
Itami/New Century (Japan)   /18

Nobuko Miyamoto *(Chizuko Amamiya)*, Tsutomu Yamazaki *(Wabisuke Inoue)*, Kin Sugai *(Kikue Amamiya)*, Chishu Ryu *(The Priest)*, Shuji Otaki *(Shokichi Amamiya)*, Ichiro Zaitsu *(Satomi)*, Kiminobu Okumura *(Shinkichi Amamiya)*, Haruna Takaso *(Yoshiko Saito)*

p, Yasushi Tamaoki, Yutaka Okada; d, Juzo Itami; w, Juzo Itami; ph, Akira Suzuki; ed, Joji Yuasa

The first feature from Juzo Itami (TAMPOPO, A TAXING WOMAN), this is a black comedy that pokes fun at solemn traditional Japanese funeral rites. When a patriarch dies suddenly, his family—including his actress daughter (Nobuko Miyamato), her actor husband (Tsutomu Yamazaki), and their manager (Ichiro Zaitsu)—comes together for the three-day Buddhist ceremony for the former brothel owner. Many of the scenes that ensue will be familiar to viewers of similarly structured films but the Japanese setting is revelatory to Western eyes. While THE FUNERAL is not as loopy as TAMPOPO, a wildly appetizing comedy about food, it is still very energetic and inventive.

FUNERAL IN BERLIN
1966 102m c Spy   ★★★½
Paramount (U.K.)   /PG

Michael Caine *(Harry Palmer)*, Paul Hubschmid *(Johnny Vulkan)*, Oscar Homolka *(Col. Stok)*, Eva Renzi *(Samantha Steel)*, Guy Doleman *(Ross)*, Rachel Gurney *(Mrs. Ross)*, Hugh Burden *(Hallam)*, Thomas Holtzmann *(Reinhart)*, Gunter Meisner *(Kreutzmann)*, Heinz Schubert *(Aaron Levine)*

p, Harry Saltzman, Charles Kasher; d, Guy Hamilton; w, Evan Jones (based on the novel by Len Deighton); ph, Otto Heller; ed, John Bloom; m, Konrad Elfers; prod d, Ken Adam; art d, Peter Murton

Caine, repeating his role from THE IPCRESS FILE, stars as Harry Palmer, the bespectacled British soldier forced to become a counterspy. This time Palmer is sent back to Germany, where his espionage career began, to contact Colonel Stok (Homolka), the Russian head of security for the Berlin Wall. Stok is anxious to defect, and Palmer arranges his escape only to be double-crossed by everyone and his brother. A bit poky, the film isn't quite up to the original, but it's rather better than most sequels of this kind. Featuring a fine cast (Homolka is *always* worth watching), FUNERAL IN BERLIN provides an excellent look at the spy business and an interesting view of postwar Berlin. One more sequel (and the weakest of the three), BILLION DOLLAR BRAIN, followed.

FUNNY BONES
1994 128m c Comedy/Drama   ★★★★
Sun Trust Ltd./Hollywood Pictures (U.K.)   R/15

Oliver Platt *(Tommy Fawkes)*, Jerry Lewis *(George Fawkes)*, Lee Evans *(Jack Parker)*, Leslie Caron *(Katie Parker)*, Richard Griffiths *(Jim Minty)*, Oliver Reed *(Dolly Hopkins)*, George Carl *(Thomas Parker)*, Freddie Davis *(Bruno Parker)*, Ian McNeice *(Stanley Sharkey)*, Christopher Greet *(Lawrence Berger)*

p, Simon Fields, Peter Chelsom; d, Peter Chelsom; w, Peter Chelsom, Peter Flannery; ph, Eduardo Serra; ed, Martin Walsh; m, John Altman; prod d, Caroline Hanania; art d, Andrew Munro; fx, Tom Harris; cos, Lindy Hemming

This postmodern tragicomedy is an eccentric, exhilarating film that couldn't find an audience. It's a mesmerizing exploration of the dangerous essence of comedy; at the same time, it's an adventure film about smuggling, a heart-breaker about children and their parents' expectations, a back-handed fable about immortality, and a bracingly hilarious take on the desperation of performance.

Aging Beverly Hills brat Tommy Fawkes (Oliver Platt) is the son of America's undisputed King of Comedy, George Fawkes (Jerry Lewis). Refusing to admit he hasn't inherited his dad's "funny bones," Tommy flies to Blackpool, England, and attempts to purchase bits of physical comedy he can import for an act in the States. Meanwhile, troubled young performer Jack Parker (Lee Evans) is the convenient fall-guy for bent policeman Stanley Sharkey (Ian McNeice). Sharkey needs a patsy for the illegal activities of a group of French adventurers who are selling stolen life-extending power nestled inside golden eggs. Sharkey's scheme, Tommy's ambitions, and numerous other plot threads are gradually woven together in unexpected ways, culminating in a fanciful, spectacular climax.

In FUNNY BONES, reality mirrors theater art in the most deliriously invigorating way since CABARET. Screenwriters Peter Chelsom and Peter Flannery inventively explore what makes some lost souls hilarious while other wannabees toil at comedy like day-laborers. Each Pirandellian element rings true, enhanced by some visual correlative in Chelsom's direction. Every frame is packed with symbolic resonance and the hoariest of show-biz cliches are revitalized—suffice it to say that "I died on stage" takes on new meaning here.

FUNNY FACE

| 1957 | 103m | c | Musical | | ★★★★½ |
| Paramount | (U.S.) | | | | /U |

Audrey Hepburn *(Jo Stockton)*, Fred Astaire *(Dick Avery)*, Kay Thompson *(Maggie Prescott)*, Michel Auclair *(Prof. Emile Flostre)*, Robert Flemyng *(Paul Duval)*, Dovima *(Marion)*, Virginia Gibson *(Babs)*, Suzy Parker, Sunny Harnett, Don Powell

p, Roger Edens; d, Stanley Donen; w, Leonard Gershe (based on "Wedding Day," an unproduced musical libretto by Gershe); ph, Ray June; ed, Frank Bracht; m, George Gershwin, Ira Gershwin, Roger Edens, Leonard Gershe; art d, George W. Davis, Hal Pereira; fx, John P. Fulton; chor, Fred Astaire, Eugene Loring; cos, Edith Head, Givenchy

AAN Best Original Screenplay: Leonard Gershe; *AAN Best Cinematography:* Ray June; *AAN Best Art Direction:* Hal Pereira (Art Direction), George W Davis (Art Direction), Sam Comer (Set Decoration), Ray Moyer (Set Decoration); *AAN Best Costume Design:* Edith Head, Hubert DeGivenchy

A film crucial to understanding Hepburn's glorious gamine appeal and one of Astaire's best musicals of the 1950s. A satire of both the fashion world and the fashionable pretensions of beatnik life and existentialism, FUNNY FACE concerns the May-December romance between Greenwich Village bookseller Jo Stockton (Hepburn) and Madison Avenue fashion photographer Dick Avery (Astaire). Dick discovers the sweet, young Jo and plays Henry Higgins to her Eliza, turning her into a top model in Paris.

That's all that need be said about the story, since this film exists only for its glamorous visuals, gorgeous Gershwin music, and the dancing choreographed by Astaire and Eugene Loring. Thompson, in a fabulous turn as a fashion editor, commands her underlings to "Think Pink" and the screen bursts with pink furniture, pink toothpaste and pink pets. "Bonjour Paris" is a whirlwind tour of the city, and "He Loves and She Loves" is a soft-focus fairy tale romance. Hepburn, who does remarkably well singing "How Long Has This Been Going On?" in her own voice, is exquisitely appealing and the byplay between her and the mellow, supple Astaire is enchanting.

As a dancer, Hepburn manages quite well in a satiric cafe number with two fellow mods, but shows her limitations in a climactic duet with Astaire set in the woods. (Maybe she had trouble with her heels in all that grass.) Astaire, meanwhile, displays his uncanny way with a song and enjoys one angular solo dance with his raincoat and umbrella. Real-life model superstars Suzy Parker and Dovima appear, but the

most unforgettable fashion moment features Hepburn at her most "Givenchy" descending a flight of stairs in a stunning red gown. Beautifully helmed by Donen.

FUNNY GIRL

| 1968 | 151m | c | Musical/Biography | ★★★★ |
| Rastar | (U.S.) | | | G/U |

Barbra Streisand *(Fanny Brice)*, Omar Sharif *(Nick Arnstein)*, Kay Medford *(Rose Brice)*, Anne Francis *(Georgia James)*, Walter Pidgeon *(Florenz Ziegfeld)*, Lee Allen *(Eddie Ryan)*, Mae Questel *(Mrs. Strakosh)*, Gerald Mohr *(Branca)*, Frank Faylen *(Keeney)*, Mittie Lawrence *(Emma)*

p, Ray Stark; d, William Wyler; w, Isobel Lennart (based on the musical by Jule Styne, Bob Merrill, Lennart); ph, Harry Stradling; ed, Maury Winetrobe, William Sands; prod d, Gene Callahan; art d, Robert Luthardt; chor, Herbert Ross; cos, Irene Sharaff

AAN Best Picture; AA Best Actress: Barbra Streisand; *AAN Best Supporting Actress:* Kay Medford; *AAN Best Cinematography:* Harry Stradling; *AAN Best Editing:* Robert Swink, Maury Winetrobe, William Sands; *AAN Best Score:* Walter Scharf; *AAN Best Song:* Jule Styne (Music), Bob Merrill (Lyrics); *AAN Best Sound:* Columbia Studio Sound Department

Few film debuts in the 1960s were more auspicious than that of Barbra Streisand in FUNNY GIRL. Already a legit and recording star, she shot to superstardom and nabbed an Academy Award for best actress in the bargain. William Wyler's musical debut is less assured than one would have liked, but no matter; La Babs had played musical-comedy star Fanny Brice on Broadway and had the role down pat by the time director Wyler brought the story to the screen.

In the early 1900s in New York City, young Fanny, an ugly duckling with an unstoppable ambition to be a star, is determined to get out of the Lower East Side. Her big break comes when she's spotted by handsome gambler Nicky Arnstein (Sharif), who helps her catch the eye of Florenz Ziegfeld (Pidgeon). Ziegfeld hires her for his new Follies presentation, where her subversive comic style proves extraordinarily popular; soon she is one of the Follies' biggest stars. The remainder of the picture—which, despite its real-life subject, tells a formulaic story—recounts her steady rise to national celebrity and her tumultuous marriage to Arnstein.

The oddly cast Sharif is better than usual, but Streisand, of course, is most of the show, belting out songs, pulling heartstrings, alternating between raucous slapstick and dramatic power, and generally demonstrating that she has *arrived* in a big way. The memorable Broadway score was augmented for the screen with several tunes from Brice's life, including her signature, "My Man."

FUNNY THING HAPPENED ON THE WAY TO THE FORUM, A

| 1966 | 99m | c | Comedy | ★★★ |
| UA | (U.S.) | | | /PG |

Zero Mostel *(Pseudolus)*, Phil Silvers *(Lycus)*, Jack Gilford *(Hysterium)*, Buster Keaton *(Erronius)*, Michael Crawford *(Hero)*, Michael Hordern *(Senex)*, Annette Andre *(Philia)*, Patricia Jessel *(Domina)*, Leon Greene *(Miles Gloriosus)*, Inga Neilsen *(Gymnasia)*

p, Melvin Frank; d, Richard Lester; w, Melvin Frank, Michael Pertwee (based on the book by Burt Shevelove, Larry Gelbart); ph, Nicolas Roeg; ed, John Victor Smith; prod d, Tony Walton; fx, Cliff Richardson; chor, Ethel Martin, George Martin; cos, Tony Walton

AA Best Score: Ken Thorne

Typical hit-and-miss filmmaking by the relentlessly antsy Richard Lester, but lots of fun all the same. Based on the smash Broadway musical, the film toplines Mostel as a Roman slave desperately trying to win his freedom and Gilford as his unwitting accomplice. Plot complications involve Silvers as a brothel owner, Andre and Crawford as young lovers, and Keaton searching for his lost children. Lester's direction is full of the flashy technique which worked better in his Beatles movies. Sometimes he would have done better to just let some of the farcical set-pieces alone. His sense of timing is sometimes off, and laughs are lost as a result. The songs are quite delightful, but somehow the production numbers don't quite fly as they should and just end up bogging down the story. To his credit, however, Lester does add a certain energy and spirit to many scenes, and some great comic moments result. Also, the overall performances make this film well worth watching—Gilford in particular is a gem. FUNNY THING now seems one of the more enjoyable of the many overcooked musical adaptations Hollywood was desperately cranking out during the 1960s.

FURY

1936 90m bw Crime ★★★★½
MGM (U.S.) /18

Spencer Tracy *(Joe Wheeler)*, Sylvia Sidney *(Katherine Grant)*, Walter Abel *(District Attorney)*, Edward Ellis *(Sheriff)*, Walter Brennan *(Buggs Meyers)*, Bruce Cabot *(Bubbles Dawson)*, George Walcott *(Tom)*, Frank Albertson *(Charlie)*, Arthur Stone *(Durkin)*, Morgan Wallace *(Fred Garrett)*

p, Joseph L. Mankiewicz; d, Fritz Lang; w, Bartlett Cormack, Fritz Lang (based on the story "Mob Rule" by Norman Krasna); ph, Joseph Ruttenberg; ed, Frank Sullivan; m, Franz Waxman; art d, Cedric Gibbons, William A. Horning, Edwin B. Willis; cos, Dolly Tree

AAN Best Original Screenplay: Norman Krasna

An uncharacteristically trenchant indictment of mob rule for the usually family-oriented MGM. Despite studio interference, Fritz Lang, in his first Hollywood outing, succeeded in making a penetrating study of injustice and inhumanity with Spencer Tracy delivering a memorable performance as an innocent man who's wrongly accused of a sensational crime and transformed into a malevolent force of vengeance.

Spencer Tracy is Joe Wheeler, a honest guy trying to earn enough money to get married to his devoted fiancee, Katherine Grant (Sylvia Sidney). While driving to meet up with Katherine, Joe gets picked up by the cops. Arrested as a suspected kidnaper, he is imprisoned in a small-town jail pending trial. He is damned by circumstantial evidence and rampant rumours. A mob gathers and heads for the jail. The sheriff gets nervous and calls the governor begging him to put the National Guard on alert as he does not have enough guards to withstand a full-scale assault on his small jail. However, the governor's advisers steer him away from the potentially controversial situation. Meanwhile, back at the jail, things quickly get out of hand.

Lang brings striking expressionist touches to the social problem picture with expressive shadowplay and stylized subjective fantasy sequences. This was his favorite American film and rightfully so, for it demonstrates his directorial genius in wasting not a frame of film, telling his story with sharp cross-cutting between victim and tormentors, while unraveling the mindless and murderous passion of a mob out of control.

F/X

1986 107m c Thriller ★★★
Orion (U.S.) R/15

Bryan Brown *(Rollie Tyler)*, Brian Dennehy *(Leo McCarthy)*, Diane Venora *(Ellen)*, Cliff De Young *(Lipton)*, Mason Adams *(Col. Mason)*, Jerry Orbach *(Nicholas DeFranco)*, Joe Grifasi *(Mickey)*, Martha Gehman *(Andy)*, Roscoe Orman *(Capt. Wallenger)*, Trey Wilson *(Lt. Murdoch)*

p, Dodi Fayed, Jack Wiener; d, Robert Mandel; w, Robert T. Megginson, Gregory Fleeman; ph, Miroslav Ondricek; ed, Terry Rawlings; m, Bill Conti; prod d, Mel Bourne; art d, Speed Hopkins; fx, Carl Fullerton, John Stears; cos, Julie Weiss

Rollie Tyler (Brown) is an ace New York-based special-effects man who specializes in doing the gore effects for horror films. Between pictures he is approached by government agent Lipton (De Young) from the Justice Department's Witness Protection Program. Lipton wants to hire Brown to fake the assassination of Mafia kingpin Nicholas DeFranco (Orbach), who is about to testify against members of his gang. If the gang thinks DeFranco is dead, it will make it easier for the Justice Department to protect him from potential mob "hits" until he has the chance to squeal in court. Although apprehensive, Rollie takes the challenge and concocts an elaborate plan for "assassinating" the mobster. Unfortunately, soon after the deed is done, Rollie realizes that the whole thing was a set-up, and now his employers want him dead.

This is a slick little thriller that benefits greatly from its clever use of special effects. Australian actor Bryan Brown is fine as the effects man who finds himself embroiled in an often-confusing plot, and Brian Dennehy lends his usual solid support as the New York cop trying to make sense of it all. Director Robert Mandel has a nice flair for light comedy and never hesitates to go for a laugh when the absurdities of the script call for it. The action sequences are well staged and the twists and turns of the convoluted plot will keep viewers guessing. A competent and unpretentious entertainment.

G

GALLIPOLI

1981 110m c War ★★★★
Paramount (Australia) PG

Mark Lee *(Archy)*, Bill Kerr *(Jack)*, Mel Gibson *(Frank Dunne)*, Ronnie Graham *(Wallace Hamilton)*, Harold Hopkins *(Les McCann)*, Charles Yunupingu *(Zac)*, Heath Harris *(Stockman)*, Gerda Nicolson *(Rose Hamilton)*, Robert Grubb *(Billy)*, Tim McKenzie *(Barney)*

p, Robert Stigwood, Patricia Lovell; d, Peter Weir; w, David Williamson (based on a story by Weir); ph, Russell Boyd; ed, William Anderson; m, Brian May; prod d, Wendy Weir; art d, Herbert Pinter

Focusing on two fleet-footed young Australians, Peter Weir's extraordinarily moving antiwar film examines the disastrous WWI invasion of Gallipoli by the Australian-New Zealand Army Corps.

Archy (Mark Lee) and Frank (Mel Gibson) come from different backgrounds, but they share a love of king, country and life—never more apparent than when the two sprinters race each other. Together, they join the army and become part of the ill-fated campaign to wrest control of the Dardanelles from the Ottoman Turks. Meeting heavy resistance from the well-entrenched Turks and their German allies, the ANZAC offensive bogs down on the beachhead. Poor generalship and worse communication eventually lead to a suicidal assault and a tremendous waste of young lives.

Director Weir (PICNIC AT HANGING ROCK, THE YEAR OF LIVING DANGEROUSLY) and cinematographer Russell Boyd's recreation of the invasion and battle action is stunning, but what makes GALLIPOLI such an affecting film is its intimate presentation of the friendship between Archy and Frank (wonderfully essayed by Lee and Gibson). Weir uses the first part of the film to establish the vibrant optimism of their lives down under, then he demonstrates how quickly and pointlessly such young lives can be snuffed out.

Not always easy to watch, GALLIPOLI is both a fitting testimony to the courage of the thousands of Australians and New Zealanders who died fighting for their country and one of the most powerful cinematic examinations of the futility and tragic cost of war.

GANDHI

1982 188m c Biography ★★★
Intl. Film Investors/Goldcrest/Indo-British Films/Natl. Film PG
Development (U.K./India)

Ben Kingsley *(Mahatma Gandhi)*, Candice Bergen *(Margaret Bourke-White)*, Edward Fox *(Gen. Dyer)*, John Gielgud *(Lord Irwin)*, Trevor Howard *(Judge Broomfield)*, John Mills *(The Viceroy)*, Martin Sheen *(Walker)*, Rohini Hattangady *(Kasturba Gandhi)*, Ian Charleson *(Charlie Andrews)*, Athol Fugard *(Gen. Smuts)*

p, Richard Attenborough; d, Richard Attenborough; w, John Briley; ph, Billy Williams, Ronnie Taylor; ed, John Bloom; m, Ravi Shankar, George Fenton; prod d, Stuart Craig; art d, Robert Laing, Ram Yedekar, Norman Dorme; fx, David Hathaway; cos, John Mollo, Bhanu Athaiya

AA Best Picture; AA Best Actor: Ben Kingsley; *AA Best Director:* Richard Attenborough; *AA Best Original Screenplay:* John Briley; *AA Best Cinematography:* Billy Williams, Ronnie Taylor; *AA Best Editing:* John Bloom; *AAN Best Score:* Ravi Shankar, George Fenton; *AA Best Art Direction:* Stuart Craig, Bob Laing, Michael Seirton; *AA Best Costume Design:* John Mollo, Bhanu Athaiya; *AAN Best Sound:* Gerry Humphreys, Robin O'Donoughue, Jonathan Bates, Simon Kaye; *AAN Best Makeup:* Tom Smith

Despite an intelligent title performance by Ben Kingsley and impressive cinematography in the manner of David Lean, this huge, clunky biopic offers less than meets the eye. Director Attenborough seeks not to understand but to canonize his subject; as a result, both Gandhi's teachings and the complexities of Indian political history are distorted and trivialized. The film spans decades, opening in South Africa where Mohandas Gandhi (Kingsley) is a struggling attorney victimized by that country's racial policies. Returning to India, he develops a strategy of non-violent civil disobedience that proves more effective than armed struggle in throwing off British imperial rule. The film is at its best in its several melodramatic, large-scale "epic" sequences (Salt March, post-Partition riots, assassination), but Gandhi remains a saintly cipher; other major figures are even more carelessly drawn; e.g., Nehru, who appears as a colorless Gandhi disciple (he was anything but), and Pakistan founder Jinnah, who comes off as a Muslim Darth Vader. African playwright Athol Fugard (*Master Harold and the Boys*) appears as General Smuts; Candice Bergen is fun in a cameo as American photographer Margaret Bourke-White.

GANG'S ALL HERE, THE

1943 103m c Musical   ★★★
Fox   (U.S.)   /A

Alice Faye (*Eadie Allen*), Carmen Miranda (*Dorita*), Phil Baker (*Himself*), Benny Goodman and His Orchestra (*Themselves*), Eugene Pallette (*Mr. Mason, Sr.*), Charlotte Greenwood (*Mrs. Peyton Potter*), Edward Everett Horton (*Peyton Potter*), Tony DeMarco (*Himself*), James Ellison (*Andy Mason*), Sheila Ryan (*Vivian*)

p, William LeBaron; d, Busby Berkeley; w, Walter Bullock (from a story by Nancy Winter, George Root, Jr., and Tom Bridges); ph, Edward Cronjager; ed, Ray Curtiss; art d, James Basevi, Joseph C. Wright; fx, Fred Sersen; chor, Busby Berkeley; cos, Yvonne Wood

AAN Best Art Direction: James Basevi (Art Direction), Joseph C Wright (Art Direction), Thomas Little (Interior Decoration)

A camp classic. If you consider Berkeley a genius, this is the highpoint of his career. It's his first in color, and filtering his kaleidoscope cuties through the garish mixmaster of 1940's Fox Technicolor is like a male hairdresser's acid trip: chorines dissolve into artichokes; Carmen Miranda arrives in an overloaded fruit wagon, more animated than any character at Disney, and cha-chas down a boulevard of strawberries. Alice Faye, in her big-budget musical swan song, swoons some sanity into the proceedings with "No Love, No Nothing" and "Journey to a Star," but she's overwhelmed introducing the "Polka-Dot Polka" ballet, a description of which wouldn't do full justice to it anyway. By the time Berkeley's chorus girls wave huge phallic bananas in rhythmic waves, you'll swear you're lost in a giant fruit cocktail. The film enhanced the stardom of Miranda but because of those *big* bananas, THE GANG'S ALL HERE was never released in her native Brazil.

GANJA AND HESS

1973 110m c Horror   ★★★★½
Kelly/Jordan   (U.S.)   R/

Duane Jones (*Dr. Hess Green*), Marlene Clark (*Ganja*), Bill Gunn (*George*), Sam Waymon (*Rev. Williams*), Leonard Jackson (*Archie*), Candece Tarpley (*Girl in Bar*), Richard Harrow (*Dinner Guest*), John Hoffmeister (*Jack*), Betty Barney (*Singer*), Mabel King (*Queen of Myrthia*)

p, Chiz Schultz; d, Bill Gunn; w, Bill Gunn; ph, James E. Hinton; ed, Victor Kanefsky; m, Sam Waymon; prod d, Tom H. John; cos, Scott Barrie

One of the best black-oriented movies to come out of Hollywood in the 1970s, GANJA AND HESS stars the late Duane Jones (NIGHT OF THE LIVING DEAD) as a New York anthropologist embroiled in a study of the lost ancient African culture of Myrthia, a nation that died out from a communicable parasite that fed on human blood. During his research, Jones is stabbed with a jewel-encrusted Myrthian dagger by his crazed assistant (played by director Bill Gunn) and finds that he has become infected with the virus, turning him into a vampirelike creature addicted to blood. He fancies himself an invincible African god and turns his wife, Clark, into a vampire as well.

This is a fascinating picture, managing both to subvert its commercial horror angle and to explore the contrasts between Western and African cultures—the former represented as repressive and puritanical, the latter as more virile and liberating. The late Gunn, who was also an accomplished novelist, playwright and painter, imbues the film with a cultural richness little seen in black-targeted films. Impressionistic, vibrant, and rhythmic (the original soundtrack used both American spirituals and African traditional music), GANJA AND HESS is a memorable and haunting film.

Tragically, it was recut by its distributors for theatrical release. Most of the thematic lushness wound up on the floor, but the most heinous change was the removal of the African soundtrack in favor of bland American soul music.

GARDEN OF THE FINZI-CONTINIS, THE
(IL GIARDINO DEL FINZI-CONTINI)

1971 103m c War/Drama   ★★★★
Documento/CCC   (Italy/West Germany)   R/A

Dominique Sanda (*Micol*), Lino Capolicchio (*Giorgio*), Helmut Berger (*Alberto*), Fabio Testi (*Malnate*), Romolo Valli (*Giorgio's Father*), Raffaele Curi (*Ernesto*), Camillo Angelini-Rota (*Micol's Father*), Katina Viglietti (*Micol's Mother*), Ina Alexeiff (*Micol's Grandmother*), Barbara Pilavin

p, Arthur Cohn, Gianni Hecht Lucari; d, Vittorio De Sica; w, Cesare Zavattini, Vittorio Bonicelli, Ugo Pirro (based on the novel by Giorgio Bassani); ph, Ennio Guarnieri; ed, Adriana Novelli; m, Manuel De Sica; art d, Giancarlo Bartolini Salimbeni; cos, Antonio Randaccio

AA Best Foreign Language Film ; *AAN Best Adapted Screenplay:* Ugo Pirro, Vittorio Bonicelli

Lyrical and melancholy, and a surprising contrast to much of De Sica's earlier work. Although the director spent a good part of the latter half of his career acting in other director's works (Roberto Rossellini's GENERAL DELLA ROVERE, for example), THE GARDEN OF THE FINZI-CONTINIS is proof he had not lost his touch.

Set in Ferrara, Italy, during WWII, this story of love and culture unfolds effortlessly, albeit a trifle slowly. The Finzi-Continis are an aristocratic Jewish-Italian family who cannot believe that the war will ever invade their hallowed garden walls. Rather than flee, they stay on in the false hope that they will not be betrayed, but they eventually come to realize that Fascism is not going to go away and that they must join the fight against it. THE GARDEN OF THE FINZI-CONTINIS is one of the few films in which flashbacks are absolutely necessary; they provide the historical perspective the characters lack.

This film bears very little resemblance to De Sica's early work. Like all previously state-funded filmmakers, he suddenly needed to concern himself with his films' commercial potential. But the movie is still directed with the familiar De Sica skill. His handling of the unknowns in the cast is exceptional, as is his direction of the wonderful Dominique Sanda.

GAS FOOD LODGING

1992 100m c Drama   ★★★★
Cineville Partners II/Seth Willenson Inc.   (U.S.)   R/15

Brooke Adams (*Nora*), Ione Skye (*Trudi*), Fairuza Balk (*Shade*), James Brolin (*John Evans*), Robert Knepper (*Dank*), David Landsbury (*Hamlet*), Jacob Vargas (*Javier*), Donovan Leitch (*Darius*), Chris Mulkey (*Raymond*), Laurie O'Brien (*Thelma*)

p, Daniel Hassid, William Ewart, Seth M. Willenson; d, Allison Anders; w, Allison Anders (from the novel *Don't Look and It Won't Hurt* by Richard Peck); ph, Dean Lent; ed, Tracy S. Granger; m, J. Mascis; prod d, Jane Ann Stewart; art d, Lisa Denker, Carla Weber; cos, Susan Bertram

Bleak and beautiful, GAS FOOD LODGING is a richly evocative look at lives in waiting.

Nora (Brooke Adams) is a divorced truck stop waitress in Laramie, New Mexico, the kind of place people barely notice unless they need to fill up one way or the other. Her older daughter, the beautiful Trudi (Ione Skye), is bored and rebellious, fast becoming the town tramp; her younger daughter, Shade (Fairuza Balk), is immersed in the fantasy world of Mexican exploitation movies. During the course of the film, all three women find various degrees of emotional satisfaction, Trudi with the offbeat Dank (Robert Knepper), an English geologist; Shade with a Mexican neighbor, Javier (Jacob Vargas); and Nora with the man who comes to install their satellite dish.

Based on Richard Peck's *Don't Look and It Won't Hurt*, GAS FOOD LODGING is a film about women—and, to a lesser degree, men—whose lives are so circumscribed that every dust mote and heat ripple over the blacktop is charged with significance. Nora, Trudi, and Shade each react to the painful emptiness of their world differently, but are united by their single-minded determination to force meaning into their lives. Through these three women, Anders examines racism, economic oppression and the numbing effect of the infinite highway—America's favorite "boy" metaphor for existence—on the lives of those who wait by the roadside.

Anders has a fine eye for detail: a near-empty movie theater, cave walls turned by ultraviolet light into a shimmering fantasy of glowing colors, a box of buttons and other worthless treasures carefully hidden beneath a bed. She has also coaxed fine performances from Adams, Skye and, especially, Balk (RETURN TO OZ, VALMONT), who miraculously delineates the prickly world of the awkwardly bright adolescent without ever becoming cloying.

GASLIGHT

1940 88m bw Thriller ★★★★★
BNP (U.K.)

Anton Walbrook *(Paul Mallen)*, Diana Wynyard *(Bella Mallen)*, Frank Pettingell *(Rough)*, Cathleen Cordell *(Nancy)*, Robert Newton *(Vincent Ullswater)*, Jimmy Hanley *(Cobb)*, Minnie Rayner *(Elizabeth)*, Mary Hinton *(Lady Winterbourne)*, Marie Wright *(Alice Barlow)*, Jack Barty *(Chairman)*

p, John Corfield; d, Thorold Dickinson; w, A.R. Rawlinson, Bridget Boland (based on the play by Patrick Hamilton); ph, Bernard Knowles; ed, Sidney Cole; m, Richard Addinsell

A lost black pearl, better than Mayer's sugar-coated 1944 version. This British psychological thriller is truly a forgotten masterpiece due to the machinations of MGM's Louis B. Mayer.

In one of her finest roles, Wynyard is a wealthy patrician lady who marries the urbane but calculating Walbrook. They move into an 1880 mansion, her ancestral London home, where Cordell is the ever-present brazen maid. Before long, Wynard notices the gaslight in her rooms flickers downward nightly and comes to believe that this is a hallucination. Meanwhile, through clever, subtle measures, Walbrook slowly drives her to the brink of insanity, convincing her that she is losing her memory. Pettingell, a kindly and perceptive Scotland Yard detective, meets Wynyard socially and begins paying attention to her and Walbrook—too much attention from the latter's point of view.

Columbia purchased the rights to the film in 1941, intending an American remake with Irene Dunne in the lead. Then MGM bought the property for Hedy Lamarr who unwisely turned it down. When the Ingrid Bergman-Charles Boyer production was shot in 1944, Mayer ordered his minions to track down all the prints of the original GASLIGHT and destroy them, so it would never compete with his lavish production. Fortunately, prints survived. It's one of the most stylish British films to be made before WWII and one of director Dickinson's most polished works, each scene carefully set up as the tension mounts brilliantly, frame by frame. Walbrook is magnificent as the arch villain, his extravagant Middle-European acting style bordering on the flamboyant, his dark charm shrouding his evil purposes.

GASLIGHT

1944 114m bw Thriller ★★★★
MGM (U.S.)

Charles Boyer *(Gregory Anton)*, Ingrid Bergman *(Paula Alquist)*, Joseph Cotten *(Brian Cameron)*, Dame May Whitty *(Miss Thwaites)*, Angela Lansbury *(Nancy Oliver)*, Barbara Everest *(Elizabeth Tompkins)*, Eustace Wyatt *(Budge)*, Emil Rameau *(Mario Gordi)*, Edmund Breon *(Gen. Huddleston)*, Halliwell Hobbes *(Mr. Mufflin)*

p, Arthur Hornblow Jr.; d, George Cukor; w, John Van Druten, Walter Reisch, John Balderston (based on the play "Angel Street" by Patrick Hamilton); ph, Joseph Ruttenberg; ed, Ralph E. Winters; m, Bronislau Kaper; art d, Cedric Gibbons, William Ferrari; fx, Warren Newcombe

AAN Best Picture; AAN Best Actor: Charles Boyer; *AA Best Actress:* Ingrid Bergman; *AAN Best Supporting Actress:* Angela Lansbury; *AAN Best Screenplay:* John L. Balderston, Walter Reisch, John Van Druten; *AAN Best Cinematography:* Joseph Ruttenberg; *AA Best Art Direction:* Cedric Gibbons, William Ferrari, Edwin B. Willis, Paul Huldschinsky

Lusher, ornate version of *Angel Street*, without the telling chill of the 1940 Diana Wynward GASLIGHT, but satisfactorily directed all the same. Bergman is deeply sympathetic as the wealthy socialite married to Boyer, who turns into an insidious monster in his attempt to drive his ravishing wife mad. But the lengthy Italian honeymoon starts the picture on too sunny a disposition, and Bergman's victim does look as healthy as a horse. Boyer nearly steals the picture, aided and abetted by the stunning debut of Angela Lansbury as a hardbitten servant—only 18, she grabbed the role and chewed it to bits. The climax is a workmanlike rise of psychological terror, but the whole exercise looks self-consciously careful.

GATE OF HELL
(JIGOKUMON)

1953 89m c Historical/War ★★★★
Daiei (Japan) /A

Machiko Kyo *(Lady Kesa)*, Kazuo Hasegawa *(Moritoh)*, Isao Yamagata *(Wataru)*, Koreya Senda *(Kiyomori)*, Yataro Kurokawa *(Shigemori)*, Kikue Mohri *(Sawa)*, Kotaro Bando *(Rokuroh)*, Jun Tazaki *(Kogenta)*, Tatsuya Ishiguro *(Yachuta)*, Kenjiro Uemura *(Masanaka)*

p, Masaichi Nagata; d, Teinosuke Kinugasa; w, Teinosuke Kinugasa (based on a play by Kan Kikuchi); ph, Kohei Sugiyama; m, Yasushi Akutagawa; cos, Sanzo Wada

AA Best Costume Design: Sanzo Wada

Set in the 12th century, GATE OF HELL is the dazzlingly beautiful and simple Japanese tale centering on a heroic samurai, Moritoh (matinee idol Kazuo Hasegawa), who is to be rewarded for his bravery with anything he desires by his country's ruler. What he most desires is the beautiful Lady Kesa (Machiko Kyo), though she is already married. Attempts are made to persuade Kesa to leave her husband (Isao Yamagata), but her devotion to him is great, and Moritoh is left with no other choice than to murder his rival. Less revered today than RASHOMON or UGETSU, both of which also starred the gorgeous Kyo, GATE OF HELL was the first color Japanese film to reach US shores and helped build an international reputation for Japanese cinema.

GAY DIVORCEE, THE

1934 107m bw Musical/Comedy ★★★★
RKO (U.S.) /U

Fred Astaire *(Guy Holden)*, Ginger Rogers *(Mimi Glossop)*, Alice Brady *(Hortense Ditherwell)*, Edward Everett Horton *(Egbert Fitzgerald)*, Erik Rhodes *(Rodolfo Tonetti)*, Eric Blore *(Waiter)*, Lillian Miles *(Hotel Guest)*, Charles Coleman *(Valet)*, William Austin *(Cyril Glossop)*, Betty Grable *(Hotel Guest)*

p, Pandro S. Berman; d, Mark Sandrich; w, George Marion Jr., Dorothy Yost, Edward Kaufman (based on the musical play "The Gay Divorce" by Dwight Taylor and Cole Porter); ph, David Abel; ed, William Hamilton; art d, Van Nest Polglase, Carroll Clark; fx, Vernon L. Walker; chor, Fred Astaire, Hermes Pan; cos, Walter Plunkett

AAN Best Picture; AAN Best Score: Max Steiner, RKO Radio Studio Music Department, Kenneth Webb, Samuel Hoffenstein; *AA Best Song:* Con Conrad (Music), Herb Magidson (Lyrics); *AAN Best Art Direction:* Van Nest Polglase, Carroll Clark; *AAN Best Sound:* Carl Dreher

One of the best examples of Depression-era musicals. After a brief twirl together in FLYING DOWN TO RIO, Fred Astaire and Ginger Rogers hooked up again, and so captivated filmgoers that this costarring vehicle would be only the first of many for cinema's most famous dance team.

Modern gal Mimi Glossop (Rogers) wants a divorce, but to get it she must venture to an English seaside resort where her lawyer (Horton) has arranged for her to be witnessed having an assignation with a professional correspondent, thus providing the necessary grounds for her divorce—infidelity. Matters become confused, however, when Mimi mistakes Guy Holden (Astaire), an American dancer who has taken a serious interest in her, for the correspondent and treats him disdainfully. Several songs and cases of mistaken identity later, Guy and Mimi end up in each other's arms for good.

Although in hindsight it seems incredible, the producers of THE GAY DIVORCEE weren't certain that Astaire and Rogers could carry the movie on their own, so they "insured" the success of the film by including several of the best second bananas around—Horton and Eric Blore among them. As a result the film is loaded with laughs and energetic performances. Moreover, its sets are superb, Max Steiner's orchestrations are a marvel, and the choreography by Dave Gould is excellent. If Astaire and Rogers had never danced a lick after the frustrated seduction of "Night and Day", they still would have been screen immortals.

GENERAL DELLA ROVERE
(IL GENERALE DELLA ROVERE)
1959   130m   bw   War/Drama   ★★★★
Zebra/SNE Gaumont   (Italy/France)

Vittorio De Sica *(Victorio Emanuele Bardone/Grimaldi)*, Hannes Messemer *(Col. Mueller)*, Vittorio Caprioli *(Banchelli)*, Guiseppe Rossetti *(Pietro Valeri)*, Ivo Garrani *(Fabrizio)*, Sandra Milo *(Valeira)*, Giovanna Ralli *(Olga)*, Anne Vernon *(Chiara Fassio)*, Baronessa Barzani *(Contessa della Rovere)*, Kurt Polter *(German Officer)*

p, Moris Ergas; d, Roberto Rossellini; w, Roberto Rossellini, Sergio Amidei, Diego Fabbri, Indro Montanelli (based on a story by Montanelli); ph, Carlo Carlini; ed, Anna Maria Montanari, Cesare Cavagna; m, Renzo Rossellini; art d, Piero Zuffi

AAN Best Original Screenplay: Sergio Amidei, Diego Fabbri, Indro Montanelli

GENERAL DELLA ROVERE was the film that returned director Roberto Rossellini to international favor after he ended his filmmaking collaboration with Ingrid Bergman and explored documentary filmmaking with INDIA. Although Rossellini, who took on this film as a survival project, looked upon GENERAL DELLA ROVERE with shame, it is one of his great achievements, the story of a man who discovers his own morality by imitating another's.

Revolving around this essentially Christian theme, the film is set during the German occupation of Genoa during the winter of 1943-44. After Resistance leader Gen. della Rovere is accidentally murdered by Gestapo troops, the local Nazi commandant "persuades" Bardone (Vittorio De Sica), an amoral, low-life swindler, to impersonate the general. In this guise, Bardone is sent to the Milan jail, where he is supposed to find and identify a partisan leader whom della Rovere had planned to meet before his death. Bardone, however, gradually begins to identify with his fellow prisoners and assumes the moral stance, if not the full being, of the Resistance leader.

Recalling OPEN CITY and PAISAN, Rossellini's great early achievements, GENERAL DELLA ROVERE is a powerful, beautifully acted picture, which—and this is the source of Rossellini's discontent with the work—retreads the ideas and forms of his past successes. While it may have been a step backwards in the development of this great filmmaker, this cannot diminish the film's undeniable strength.

GENEVIEVE
1953   86m   c   Comedy   ★★★★½
Sirius   (U.K.)   /U

John Gregson *(Alan McKim)*, Dinah Sheridan *(Wendy McKim)*, Kenneth More *(Ambrose Claverhouse)*, Kay Kendall *(Rosalind Peters)*, Geoffrey Keen *(1st Speed Cop)*, Harold Siddons *(2nd Speed Cop)*, Reginald Beckwith *(J.C. Callahan)*, Arthur Wontner *(Elderly Gentleman)*, Joyce Grenfell *(Hotel Proprietress)*, Leslie Mitchell *(Himself)*

p, Henry Cornelius; d, Henry Cornelius; w, William Rose; ph, Christopher Challis; ed, Clive Donner; m, Larry Adler; chor, Eric Rogers

AAN Best Original Screenplay: William Rose; *AAN Best Score:* Muir Mathieson

As smooth as custard. A wonderful British comedy about two couples, classic-car enthusiasts, who participate in the annual London-to-Brighton rally. The title comes from the 1904 roadster owned by Alan and Wendy McKim (John Gregson and Dinah Sheridan) who, on the return trip, challenge their friends Ambrose (Kenneth More) and Rosalind (Kay Kendall) to a friendly race. Their playfulness becomes increasingly intense as they speed to the Westminster Bridge finish line.

The screenplay is marvelous, the film is full of the fresh air of the English countryside, the color is appealing and the famous harmonica score by Larry Adler is perfect. The four leads are wonderful in the roles that clinched stardom for them all. From Kay Kendall's trumpet solo to Kenneth More's ongoing battle with his girlfriend's dog, each one has at least a few priceless bits of character business. That old stalwart Arthur Wontner has a lovely, touching bit at the finale, and the whole film is so good it makes you regret that Henry Cornelius didn't make more films than he did.

GENTLE CREATURE, A
(UNE FEMME DOUCE)
1969   88m   c   Drama   ★★★★
Parc/Marianne   (France)   /AA

Dominique Sanda *(She)*, Guy Frangin *(He)*, Jane Lobre *(Anna)*

p, Mag Bodard; d, Robert Bresson; w, Robert Bresson (based on the novella *A Gentle Creature* by Feodor Dostoyevsky); ph, Ghislain Cloquet; ed, Raymond Lamy; m, Jean Wiener; art d, Pierre Charbonnier

A hauntingly simple film about a young wife (Sanda) who commits suicide, leaving no explanation for her obsessively dominant husband (Frangin). Shattered, he recounts their first meeting—she's a free spirit who visits his pawnshop. They marry, but the woman must adapt her life style to his, being subjected to his accusations and jealousies. She toys with murdering him, pointing a gun at his head, but lacks the ability to pull the trigger. When she falls ill, the man finally realizes his love for her. He takes a positive outlook on the marriage and plans for a future together, only to have her shut the door on his hopes. Bresson's first film in color, and only his ninth in 26 years, A GENTLE CREATURE marked the film debut of former model Sanda, who would the same year be seen in Bertolucci's THE CONFORMIST.

GENTLEMAN JIM
1942   104m   bw   Sports   ★★★★
Warner Bros./First National   (U.S.)   /U

Errol Flynn *(James J. Corbett)*, Alexis Smith *(Victoria Ware)*, Jack Carson *(Walter Lowrie)*, Alan Hale *(Pat Corbett)*, John Loder *(Carlton DeWitt)*, William Frawley *(Billy Delaney)*, Minor Watson *(Buck Ware)*, Ward Bond *(John L. Sullivan)*, Madeleine LeBeau *(Anna Held)*, Rhys Williams *(Harry Watson)*

p, Robert Buckner; d, Raoul Walsh; w, Vincent Lawrence, Horace McCoy (based on the autobiography *The Roar of the Crowd* by James J. Corbett); ph, Sid Hickox; ed, Jack Killifer; m, Heinz Roemheld; art d, Ted Smith; cos, Milo Anderson

One of the best sports biopics ever. Historically inaccurate, but a directorial field day for director Raoul Walsh, who excelled at action direction and also period nostalgia. Errol Flynn's colorful temperament, capricious moods, and daring nature were perfect for the role of James J. Corbett, the brash Irish bank clerk from San Francisco who went on to defeat John L. Sullivan (nicely essayed by Ward Bond) for the heavyweight championship of the world in New Orleans in 1892. As Gentleman Jim's reputation grows, so does his ego, but in the fine scene wherein Sullivan presents Corbett with the championship belt, Corbett displays a heretofore unseen humility that finally wins the heart of the patrician woman he loves (Alexis Smith). The bout in which Corbett matches his "scientific" boxing techniques against the toe-to-toe slugging of Sullivan is particularly winning but Walsh is firmly in control throughout.

GENTLEMAN'S AGREEMENT

1947   118m   bw   Drama   ★★★★
Fox   (U.S.)   /A

Gregory Peck (*Phil Green*), Dorothy McGuire (*Kathy*), John Garfield (*Dave*), Celeste Holm (*Anne*), Anne Revere (*Mrs. Green*), June Havoc (*Miss Wales*), Albert Dekker (*John Minify*), Jane Wyatt (*Jane*), Dean Stockwell (*Tommy*), Sam Jaffe (*Prof. Lieberman*)

p, Darryl F. Zanuck; d, Elia Kazan; w, Moss Hart (based on the novel by Laura Z. Hobson); ph, Arthur Miller; ed, Harmon Jones; m, Alfred Newman; art d, Lyle Wheeler, Mark-Lee Kirk

AA Best Picture; AAN Best Actor: Gregory Peck; AAN Best Actress: Dorothy McGuire; AA Best Supporting Actress: Celeste Holm; AAN Best Supporting Actress: Anne Revere; AA Best Director: Elia Kazan; AAN Best Screenplay: Moss Hart; AAN Best Editing: Harmon Jones

Today, it looks like a heart on a sleeve, but GENTLEMAN'S AGREEMENT is a landmark film—Hollywood's first major attack on anti-Semitism.

Peck, in a convincing portrayal, is a magazine writer who decides to write a series of exposes on anti-Semitism. After failing to achieve an in-depth grasp of the problem, he pretends to be Jewish in order to experience the hostility of bigots first-hand. AGREEMENT surprised audiences of 1947, and it was a heroic endeavor personally sponsored by producer Zanuck (who, ironically, was one of the few Hollywood moguls who was not Jewish; in fact his 20th Century-Fox was known, in filmdom's argot, as "the goyim studio").

Garfield initially debated accepting such a small part, but on David Niven's advice, he took the role; his powerful performance shows the commitment he obviously developed during production. Despite the excellence of Peck and Garfield, though, today the finest work seems that of Holm and, in perhaps the film's most difficult part, McGuire. Shot mostly on location in New York, GENTLEMAN'S AGREEMENT remains a classic crusading film.

GENTLEMEN PREFER BLONDES

1953   91m   c   Musical   ★★★★
Fox   (U.S.)   /U

Jane Russell (*Dorothy*), Marilyn Monroe (*Lorelei*), Charles Coburn (*Sir Francis Beekman*), Elliott Reid (*Malone*), Tommy Noonan (*Gus Esmond*), George "Foghorn" Winslow (*Henry Spofford III*), Marcel Dalio (*Magistrate*), Taylor Holmes (*Gus Esmond, Sr.*), Norma Varden (*Lady Beekman*), Howard Wendell (*Watson*)

p, Sol C. Siegel; d, Howard Hawks; w, Charles Lederer (based on the play by Anita Loos, Joseph Fields); ph, Harry Wild; ed, Hugh S. Fowler; art d, Lyle Wheeler, Joseph C. Wright; fx, Ray Kellogg; chor, Jack Cole; cos, Travilla

Garish good fun. The film version of Anita Loos's Broadway musical has scrapped the 1920s plot and most of the songs. If the plot of vacationing showgirls—one out for money, the other for love—sometimes lags in director Hawks's hands, it's compensated by a genuine sentiment and sweetness, the ironic and witty use of sex-symbol stereotypes, and the reduction of males to foils for the affectionate wisecracks traded by the femme leads. Both Jane Russell and Marilyn Monroe act with the confidence of whales; it's the last time in Monroe's career you feel sure watching her work. In a way Russell steals BLONDES. She's certainly more at home in gaudy territory, and her Dorothy is loving and supervisory of Monroe's Lorelei at the same time. Certainly, BLONDES proves Russell's knockout instinct for deadpan sarcasm, rare among pin-up girls. BLONDES exploits her

whole sex-symbol-as-earth-mom persona more than any of her films. An inferior sequel, GENTLEMEN MARRY BRUNETTES followed in 1955.

GEORGIA

1995   117m   c   Drama/Musical   ★★★½
Georgia Film Corporation/CiBy 2000/Miramax   (U.S./France)   R/

Jennifer Jason Leigh (*Sadie*), Mare Winningham (*Georgia*), Ted Levine (*Jake*), Max Perlich (*Axel*), John Doe (*Bobby*), John C. Reilly (*Herman*), Jimmy Witherspoon (*Trucker*), Jason Carter (*Chasman*), Tom Bower (*Erwin Flood*), Smokey Hormel (*Leland*)

p, Ulu Grosbard, Barbara Turner, Jennifer Jason Leigh; d, Ulu Grosbard; w, Barbara Turner; ph, Jan Kiesser; ed, Elizabeth Kling; prod d, Lester Cohen; fx, Don Dumas; cos, Carol Oditz

Harrowing and heartfelt, with knockout performances by a pair of fine actresses.

It's about two siblings, both singers. Sadie (Jennifer Jason Leigh) is hugely ambitious, wildly self-destructive, and all but unknown outside of small-time punk clubs. Georgia (Mare Winningham) is stable and successful, an accomplished folk artist with a husband and two beautiful children. Is Sadie a legend in her own mind, too deluded to see that her talents don't measure up to her aspirations? Is Georgia a hypocritical hausfrau blessed with talent she's too smug to share? This rare study of the relationship between two sisters (scripted by Leigh's mother, Barbara Turner) doesn't offer any easy answers. It's keenly observed, judiciously balanced, and deftly helmed by Ulu Grosbard (TRUE CONFESSIONS, STRAIGHT TIME).

Although Sadie is the film's main character, Grosbard claims he called his film GEORGIA because Sadie longs to be like her sister. But does she? We're never quite sure whether Sadie is just selfish and irresponsible by nature, or whether her sister's apparently effortless success drove Sadie to drink and drugs. At one point Georgia implies that Sadie was always like this, and if that's the case it's amazing Georgia has put up with her for so long. The film's most affecting scene—which is also the scene many viewers find intolerable—is Leigh's startling, painful and brave eight-minute rendition of Van Morrison's "Take Me Back," a song whose longing for the past is made sharper by Leigh's alternately angry and sad delivery. It appears to have been done in one bravura take, and it says more about Sadie than the rest of the film.

GEORGY GIRL

1966   100m   bw   Comedy/Drama   ★★★★
Everglades   (U.K.)   /15

James Mason (*James Leamington*), Alan Bates (*Jos*), Lynn Redgrave (*Georgy*), Charlotte Rampling (*Meredith*), Bill Owen (*Ted*), Clare Kelly (*Doris*), Rachel Kempson (*Ellen*), Denise Coffey (*Peg*), Dorothy Alison (*Health Visitor*), Peggy Thorpe-Bates (*Hospital Sister*)

p, Otto Plaschkes, Robert A. Goldston; d, Silvio Narizzano; w, Margaret Forster, Peter Nichols (based on the novel by Forster); ph, Ken Higgins; ed, John Bloom; m, Alexander Faris; art d, Tony Woollard; chor, Marjory Sigley; cos, Mary Quant

AAN Best Actress: Lynn Redgrave; AAN Best Supporting Actor: James Mason; AAN Best Cinematography: Ken Higgins; AAN Best Song: Tom Springfield (Music), Jim Dale (Lyrics)

A heart-tugger. Redgrave is Georgy, a chubby virgin in her early 20s suffering from a lack of self-esteem. Her parents are servants employed by Mason, a well-to-do married man who never sired any children. Through the years Mason has treated Redgrave like a daughter, but as she grows older his affection changes, and he eventually asks her to become his mistress. Rampling, Redgrave's sensual but patronizing roommate, announces she's pregnant by her new lover, Bates. Redgrave and Bates meet and fall in love, which spurs Rampling to declare she's going to give up the child for adoption. Redgrave will not hear of this and becomes the baby's surrogate mother. By picture's end, Redgrave is impaled on the horns of a dilemma: should she marry Bates, should she just keep the baby, or should she marry the conveniently widowed Mason and keep the baby?

Mason is wonderful as the older man, harried by a nagging, sickly wife. Redgrave shot to stardom in this role, and rightly so. She shows her range as she grows from a self-conscious, uncertain waif to a woman with responsibilities. A charming movie that aided the careers of all concerned, GEORGY GIRL was also helped by the Oscar-nominated title song, which became a hit for the Seekers on two continents.

GET ON THE BUS

1996   122m   c   Drama   ★★★
40 Acres and a Mule Filmworks   (U.S.)   R/15

Richard Belzer (Rick), DeAundre Bonds (Junior), Andre Braugher (Flip), Thomas Jefferson Byrd (Evan Thomas, Sr.), Gabriel Casseus (Jamal), Albert Hall (Craig), Hill Harper (Xavier), Harry Lennix (Randall), Roger Guenveur Smith (Gary), Isaiah Washington (Kyle)

p, Reuben Cannon, Bill Borden, Barry Rosenbush; d, Spike Lee; w, Reggie Rock Bythewood; ph, Elliot Davis; ed, Leander T. Sales; m, Terence Blanchard; prod d, Ina Mayhew; cos, Sandra Hernandez

A small-scale, low-budget commemoration of 1995's Million Man March in Washington, DC, GET ON THE BUS is a thumbnail encapsulation of the issues that informed the march.

George (Charles S. Dutton) has arranged for a bus to take passengers from LA to Washington, DC, for the Million Man March, called by Nation of Islam leader Minister Louis Farrakhan. The 15 black male riders include Flip (Andre Braugher), an aspiring actor; Gary (Roger Guenveur Smith), the son of a murdered black cop and a white woman; Jamal (Gabriel Casseus), a gangbanger turned Muslim; Xavier (Hill Harper), a film student videotaping the ride; Randall (Harry Lennix) and Kyle (Isaiah Washington), a gay couple; Evan Thomas (Thomas Jefferson Byrd) and his son, Junior (DeAundre Bonds), who are chained together by a court order; and Jeremiah (Ossie Davis), the group elder, a laid-off factory worker. En route, the men discuss family relationships, the treatment of women, economic troubles, and racial identity.

Director Spike Lee turns in his most focused and compelling film yet, thanks to a handful of well-etched characters, a concise script by Reggie Rock Bythewood, and a strong cast. Although its characters tend to sheechify and launch into personal discussions of issues, the film remains a joyous, moving, and highly cinematic celebration of black male camaraderie at a time when such images are rare in mainstream films. If there is a flaw, it lies in the narrow scope of black viewpoints presented and the script's insistence on political correctness. Explicity crediting Farrakhan as the catalyst behind the historic march, GET ON THE BUS does stop short of endorsing the controversial figure. Unfortunately, it pays only lip service to a criticism of Farrakhan's oft-cited anti-Semitism.

GET OUT YOUR HANDKERCHIEFS
(PREPAREZ VOS MOUCHOIRS)

1978   108m   c   Comedy   ★★★½
Ariane/C.A.P.A.C./Belga/SODEP   (France/Belgium)   R/X

Gerard Depardieu (Raoul), Patrick Dewaere (Stephane), Carole Laure (Solange), Riton (Christian Beloeil), Michel Serrault (Neighbor), Eleonore Hirt (Mrs. Beloeil), Sylvie Joly (Passerby), Jean Rougerie (Mr. Beloeil), Liliane Rovere, Michel Beaune

p, Paul Claudon; d, Bertrand Blier; w, Bertrand Blier; ph, Jean Penzer; ed, Claudine Merlin; m, Georges Delerue, Wolfgang Amadeus Mozart, Franz Schubert; art d, Eric Moulard; cos, Michele Cerf

AA Best Foreign Language Film

A more civilized, less offensive version of GOING PLACES, Blier's earlier film, GET OUT YOUR HANDKERCHIEFS again pairs Depardieu and Dewaere, as childlike men who are completely emasculated by the mysterious woman in their lives.

Frustrated by his inability to make his wife (Laure) happy, Depardieu asks a complete stranger (Dewaere) to give it a try. All Laure seems to do is knit sweaters with a completely expressionless face. Dewaere is equally impotent, however, and succeeds only in establishing a close friendship with Depardieu. It takes a third "man"—Riton, a 13-year-old genius the threesome meets at the boys' summer camp that Dewaere runs—to fulfill the unhappy woman. Laure, who has been unable to have a child with Depardieu or Dewaere, finally finds someone to love and care for, even though he is only 13.

Besides Blier's sharp direction and screenplay, the film is memorable for the performances of Depardieu and Dewaere. These two superb actors seem so in tune with one another that one must judge their performance as a synthesized whole.

GET SHORTY

1995   105m   c   Comedy/Crime   ★★★
Jersey Films/MGM   (U.S.)   R/15

John Travolta (Chili Palmer), Gene Hackman (Harry Zimm), Rene Russo (Karen Flores), Danny DeVito (Martin Weir), Dennis Farina (Ray "Bones" Barboni), Delroy Lindo (Bo Catlett), James Gandolfini (Bear), Jon Gries (Ronnie Wingate), Renee Props (Nicki), David Paymer (Leo Devoe)

p, Danny DeVito, Michael Shamberg, Stacey Sher; d, Barry Sonnenfeld; w, Scott Frank (based on the novel by Elmore Leonard); ph, Don Peterman; ed, Jim Miller; m, John Lurie; prod d, Peter Larkin; art d, Steve Arnold; fx, Danny Gill, Gary Bierend, Michael McAlister; cos, Betsy Heimann

Based on a gracefully self-reflexive crime novel by Elmore Leonard, this lighthanded black comedy consolidated John Travolta's much-vaunted comeback in the wake of PULP FICTION.

Chili Palmer (Travolta), a Miami-based loan collector with mafia connections and a thing for movies, arrives in Hollywood to collect an outstanding debt from washed-up schlock film producer Harry Zimm (Gene Hackman). Chili becomes intrigued with the business and soon finds himself producing a script for egomanical actor Martin Weir (Danny DeVito). The problem: Harry is hip deep in debt to Bo Catlett (Delroy Lindo), a slick drug dealer who sees Harry as his ticket into the producing business, where "the real money" is. With the help of former B-movie queen—and the former Mrs. Martin Weir—Karen Flores (Rene Russo), Chili brings his underworld skills to bear on moguls and mobsters alike.

With its expertly executed mixture of snappy dialogue, dark humor, and first-rate performances, GET SHORTY is a tremendously entertaining film. While every major performer is perfectly cast and capably used, Travolta—effortlessly outflanking the perils of typecasting—creates an attractive, fully realized character in Chili Palmer, whom no one will confuse with PULP FICTION's smack-shooting Vincent Vega. Of course, much of GET SHORTY's success can be credited to director and executive producer Barry Sonnenfeld (THE ADDAMS FAMILY, THROW MOMMA FROM THE TRAIN). Using quirky camera moves and angles to survey the wiseguys, Sonnenfeld never allows the tone to become too heavy, even when the characters are doing things that are downright despicable. The slinky jazz soundtrack by John Lurie and others puts just the right spring in SHORTY's step.

GETAWAY, THE

1972   122m   c   Crime   ★★★½
Solar/First Artists   (U.S.)   PG/18

Steve McQueen (Doc McCoy), Ali MacGraw (Carol McCoy), Ben Johnson (Jack Benyon), Sally Struthers (Fran Clinton), Al Lettieri (Rudy Butler), Slim Pickens (Cowboy), Richard Bright (Thief), Jack Dodson (Harold Clinton), Dub Taylor (Laughlin), Bo Hopkins (Frank Jackson)

p, David Foster, Mitchell Brower; d, Sam Peckinpah; w, Walter Hill (based on the novel by Jim Thompson); ph, Lucien Ballard; ed, Robert Wolfe; m, Quincy Jones; art d, Ted Haworth, Angelo Graham; fx, Bud Hulburd; cos, Ray Summers

Peckinpah does Peckinpah. In one of his most hard-bitten roles, taciturn McQueen is released on a parole arranged for by his wife, MacGraw, who slept with Johnson to get the political big shot to pull the strings. He wants McQueen to lead a group of professional thieves on a bank raid, so McQueen organizes the small band, including MacGraw as a getaway driver and cocky Lettieri and Hopkins as gun-happy goons.

Through an elaborate plan, McQueen and cohorts successfully rob the Southwestern bank of $500,000, but Hopkins spoils the caper by panicking and killing a guard. When the thieves rendezvous, McQueen learns that Lettieri has murdered Hopkins. The gunman tells him, "He didn't make it. . . neither did you," as he draws a gun. McQueen has anticipated the double cross and is quicker, however, blasting several shots into Lettieri's chest. McQueen now realizes that Johnson has set him up.

This violent film, typical of Peckinpah's slam-bang action movies, relentlessly depicts ruthless robbery and murder, not to mention adultery, kidnaping, bribery, extortion, and general mayhem. The vivid direction and lightning pace, however, make the film completely fascinating as the culprits attempt to destroy each other, and the viewer finds himself actually rooting for McQueen and MacGraw, thieves though they are, hoping they'll get away. No one in this film is honorable or attractive, emphatically symbolized in one cynical Peckinpah scene in which, to escape detection, McQueen and MacGraw hide in a garbage truck and are dumped, along with their stolen loot, in a vast waste area.

Lettieri gives a wonderful study in evil, and Struthers is the ultimate repugnant tramp, obsessed with the gunman's guns and menacing manner, encouraging him to murder her husband. MacGraw is just a waste of time, having no acting ability at all and projecting the attitude of a spoiled rich girl whose Neiman-Marcus charge card has been taken away. But in retrospect, perhaps her blankness deserves another look.

GETTING STRAIGHT

1970 126m c Drama ★★★½
Columbia (U.S.) R/15

Elliott Gould (Harry Bailey), Candice Bergen (Jan), Jeff Corey (Dr. Willhunt), Max Julien (Ellis), Robert F. Lyons (Nick), Cecil Kellaway (Dr. Kasper), Jon Lormer (Vandenburg), Leonard Stone (Lysander), William Bramley (Wade Linden), Jeannie Berlin (Judy Kramer)

p, Richard Rush; d, Richard Rush; w, Bob Kaufman (based on the novel by Ken Kolb); ph, Laszlo Kovacs; ed, Maury Winetrobe; m, Ronald Stein; art d, Sydney Z. Litwack; fx, Ira Anderson; cos, Gene Ashman

In 1970, Hollywood's attempt to capitalize on student rebellion looked trivial in comparison to real events (the shootings at Kent State occured in the same year), but GETTING STRAIGHT, buoyed by Gould's eccentric screen presence and Kovacs' stylish camerawork, holds up surprisingly well. Gould, a returning Vietnam vet, goes back to school to secure a graduate degree and inevitably becomes involved in the lives of his students, many of whom are 10 years younger than he is and light-years more naive. Corey, the department head, forces smart-aleck Gould to teach remedial English, a job he hates. Gould looks at teaching as a calling, but Corey sees it as a job; their differences culminate in an oral examination straight out of every Ph.D candidate's nightmares. Meanwhile, when student protestors attempt to take over the university, Gould is called upon to act as mediator between them and the administration, forcing a choice between career and principle. Director Richard Rush (FREEBIE AND THE BEAN, THE STUNT MAN) is something of a cult favorite.

GHOST

1990 128m c Fantasy/Romance ★★★
Howard W. Koch (U.S.) PG-13/15

Patrick Swayze (Sam Wheat), Demi Moore (Molly Jensen), Whoopi Goldberg (Oda Mae Brown), Tony Goldwyn (Carl Brunner), Rick Aviles (Willie Lopez), Gail Boggs (Louise Brown), Armelia McQueen (Clara Brown), Vincent Schiavelli (Subway Ghost)

p, Lisa Weinstein; d, Jerry Zucker; w, Bruce Joel Rubin; ph, Adam Greenberg; ed, Walter Murch; m, Maurice Jarre; prod d, Jane Musky; fx, Industrial Light & Magic, Richard Edlund; cos, Ruth Morley

AAN Best Picture; AA Best Supporting Actress: Whoopi Goldberg; AA Best Original Screenplay: Bruce Joel Rubin; AAN Best Editing: Walter Murch; AAN Best Score: Maurice Jarre

A big sweet hit, tingly and glycerined in a phony way, but diverting. This sometimes spooky mystery-thriller-comedy-fantasy-romance focuses on loved ones who die suddenly, only to linger in spirit form, helping the mortals they have left behind. Specifically, when have-it-all yuppies Sam and Molly (Patrick Swayze and Demi Moore) are held up, sentimental bank executive Swayze gets shot. But he finally figures out—we've seen smarter ghosts in "Casper" cartoons—that vulnerable,

adorable Moore is in danger from his corrupt co-worker (Tony Goldwyn). He solicits fake medium Goldberg to help him communicate, and she discovers she's a bonafide psychic after all.

GHOST manages to work despite the constant distractions of writer Bruce Joel Rubin's mishmash screenplay and Jerry Zucker's uneven direction. Zucker makes his solo debut here after co-directing AIRPLANE!, TOP SECRET, and RUTHLESS PEOPLE with brother David Zucker and Jim Abrahams. His work here isn't the embarrassment that often results when a comedy director turns serious; on the contrary, Zucker shows great potential. But instead of packing GHOST with every possible gag—the hallmark of his comedy collaborations—he fills it with an array of clashing movie styles that never harmonize into a compelling whole.

Still, viewers will find it hard not to reach for their hankies at the moment when Sam finally reveals himself in spirit form to Molly, proving that, however cluttered by extraneous characters and subplots, the theme of romantic love reaching beyond the grave, and into eternity, remains potent and pure as a cinematic conceit. Or maybe what makes this movie so appealing are all of those romantic notions *plus* a shirtless Patrick Swayze and a nude Demi Moore.

GHOST AND MRS. MUIR, THE

1947 104m bw Romance/Science Fiction/Fantasy ★★★★
Fox (U.S.) /A

Gene Tierney (Lucy), Rex Harrison (The Ghost of Capt. Daniel Gregg), George Sanders (Miles Fairley), Edna Best (Martha), Vanessa Brown (Anna), Anna Lee (Mrs. Fairley), Robert Coote (Coombe), Natalie Wood (Anna as a Child), Isobel Elsom (Angelica), Victoria Horne (Eva)

p, Fred Kohlmar; d, Joseph L. Mankiewicz; w, Philip Dunne (based on the novel by R.A. Dick); ph, Charles Lang; ed, Dorothy Spencer; m, Bernard Herrmann; art d, Richard Day, George W. Davis; fx, Fred Sersen; cos, Oleg Cassini

AAN Best Cinematography: Charles Lang Jr

Wonderful fantasy-romance, in which beautiful widow Lucy (Gene Tierney) buys a remote coastal home that was once occupied by a dashing merchant captain. Shortly after Lucy moves in with her little daughter, Anna (Natalie Wood), she encounters some strange doings, but is not alarmed even though her neighbors have already warned the headstrong woman that the cottage is haunted. Lucy is more curious than apprehensive and she demands that the ghost (Rex Harrison) reveal himself. He does, in all his handsome, bearded glory, and not only befriends Lucy and her daughter, but falls in love with the lovely lady.

This fragile story would immediately collapse into implausibility were it not for the wonderful chemistry between Harrison and Tierney. In this, his second American film, Harrison is superb as the sharp-tongued, affectionate ghost and Tierney shines as his earthbound object of love. Bernard Herrmann's score is both whimsical and full of otherworldly lyricism. Remade in 1955 as STRANGER IN THE NIGHT.

GHOST GOES WEST, THE

1936 85m bw Science Fiction/Fantasy/Comedy ★★★★
London Films (U.K.) /U

Robert Donat (Murdoch/Donald Glourie), Jean Parker (Peggy Martin), Eugene Pallette (Joe Martin), Elsa Lanchester (Lady Shepperton), Ralph Bunker (Ed Bigelow), Patricia Hilliard (Shepherdess), Everley Gregg (Gladys Martin), Morton Selten (Gavin Glourie), Dorothy "Chili" Bouchier (Cleopatra), Mark Daly (Groom)

p, Alexander Korda; d, Rene Clair; w, Robert E. Sherwood, Rene Clair, Geoffrey Kerr (based on the story "Sir Tristram Goes West" by Eric Keown); ph, Harold Rosson; ed, Harold Earle-Fishbacher, Henry Cornelius; m, Mischa Spoliansky; prod d, Vincent Korda; fx, Ned Mann; cos, Rene Hubert, John Armstrong

This was the first English-language film for French master director Rene Clair, and it proved a winner. The story begins in 18th-century Scotland where Robert Donat, as the head of a clan, is insulted by another laird but dies before he can remedy the stain upon his stiff honor. His modern-day descendant, also played by Donat, is trying to maintain the sprawling family castle but is going broke, his creditors waiting for him behind every door. Salvation arrives in the form of loud, acquisitive Eugene Pallette, whose pretty daughter Jean Parker immediately falls for Donat. Pallette has the castle transported to the US and rebuilds it stone by stone on his vast Florida estate. Parker and Donat—he goes along with the castle as caretaker—are eyeing the altar, but matters become complicated when it's discovered that the ghost of Donat's lookalike ancestor has also made the journey to Florida and is haunting everyone in sight.

Clair's light comedic touch is everywhere in a film loaded with the screwball comedy which was so popular in the 1930s. At one point Clair considered removing his name from the credits—producer Korda frequently interrupted the shooting of the film to make changes—but enough of his imprint remained to cause him to reconsider. US audiences took the stereotype of American materialism good-naturedly and made the film a hit.

GHOSTBUSTERS

1984 107m c Comedy/Science Fiction   ★★★½
Columbia (U.S.)   PG

Bill Murray (*Dr. Peter Venkman*), Dan Aykroyd (*Dr. Raymond Stantz*), Sigourney Weaver (*Dana Barrett*), Harold Ramis (*Dr. Egon Spenler*), Rick Moranis (*Louis Tully*), Annie Potts (*Janine Melnitz*), William Atherton (*Walter Peck*), Ernie Hudson (*Winston Zeddmore*), David Margulies (*Mayor*), Steven Tash (*Student*)

p, Ivan Reitman; d, Ivan Reitman; w, Dan Aykroyd, Harold Ramis; ph, Laszlo Kovacs, Herb Wagreitch; ed, Sheldon Kahn, David Blewitt; m, Elmer Bernstein; prod d, John De Cuir; art d, John De Cuir Jr., John J. Moore; fx, Richard Edlund, John Bruno, Mark Vargo, Chuck Gaspar; cos, Theoni V. Aldredge

AAN Best Song: Ray Parker Jr (Music & Lyrics); AAN Best Visual Effects: Richard Edlund, John Bruno, Mark Vargo, Chuck Gaspar

An enormously successful movie that owes much to many less successful ones that preceded it, GHOSTBUSTERS is an all-star big-budget hybrid of pictures as diverse as SPOOK CHASERS, SPOOK BUSTERS, GHOST CATCHERS and countless others. The difference between those films and GHOSTBUSTERS is that the latter had a huge special-effects budget and the presence of Bill Murray, whose irreverent personality makes the whole thing work.

Murray, Dan Aykroyd, and Harold Ramis play a trio of New York City parapsychologists who set up their own "ghost-busting" shop—not unlike exterminators—in a downtown building, complete with a bored secretary (Annie Potts). For a fee, the trio will rid homes or places of business of supernatural residents. They are hired by Dana Barrett (Sigourney Weaver), a symphony cellist who lives in a spectacular apartment above Central Park where strange things have been happening. After capturing a large, gooey, green ghost and experiencing several other weird occurrences, the busters determine that the apartment building was built by a Sumerian devil cult and that the site is actually the doorway to the spirit world.

Originally planned as an Aykroyd-John Belushi vehicle, the picture was rewritten after Belushi's untimely death, giving Murray's character the emphasis—and it is Murray's movie all the way. With his deadpan delivery and snide quips, Murray more than holds his own amid the myriad state-of-the-art special effects. An inferior sequel, GHOST-BUSTERS II, was released in 1989.

GIANT

1956 201m c Drama   ★★★★
Warner Bros. (U.S.)   /PG

Elizabeth Taylor (*Leslie Benedict*), Rock Hudson (*Bick Benedict*), James Dean (*Jett Rink*), Carroll Baker (*Luz Benedict II*), Jane Withers (*Vashti Snythe*), Chill Wills (*Uncle Bawley*), Mercedes McCambridge (*Luz Benedict*), Sal Mineo (*Angel Obregon II*), Dennis Hopper (*Jordan Benedict III*), Judith Evelyn (*Mrs. Horace Lynnton*)

p, George Stevens, Henry Ginsberg; d, George Stevens; w, Fred Guiol, Ivan Moffat (based on the novel by Edna Ferber); ph, William Mellor; ed, William Hornbeck, Fred Bohanan, Philip W. Anderson; m, Dimitri Tiomkin; prod d, Boris Leven; cos, Marjorie Best, Moss Mabry

AAN Best Picture; AAN Best Actor: James Dean; AAN Best Actor: Rock Hudson; AAN Best Supporting Actress: Mercedes McCambridge; AA Best Director: George Stevens; AAN Best Adapted Screenplay: Fred Guiol, Ivan Moffat; AAN Best Editing: William Hornbeck, Philip W. Anderson, Fred Bohanan; AAN Best Score: Dimitri Tiomkin; AAN Best Art Direction: Boris Leven, Ralph S. Hurst; AAN Best Costume Design: Moss Mabry, Marjorie Best

Like the title says. Based on Edna Ferber's sprawling novel, GIANT covers two generations of Texas rivalry, spear-headed by Hudson, in his best performance, and Dean, in a performance that defies description. Hudson marries Virginia belle Taylor and transplants her to Texas, where she must learn to adapt herself to the harsher culture of her husband's huge cattle empire. Dean is an outcast who strikes oil and whose financial empire grows to rival Hudson's, even as he nurses a lifelong broken heart over Taylor.

This was the last role in Dean's all-too-brief career—he was dead when the film was released—and his presence ran away with the film. He performs his role in the overwrought method manner of the era, and the rest of the cast seems to be split between awe of his talent and disgust over his indulgence. He's a strange spectacle indeed as he ages, like a Howard Hughes burlesque that doesn't quite come off. Still he works well early on opposite Taylor, as does Hudson, who more or less leads the rest of the cast in the conventional style of presentational acting. GIANT confirms Taylor's skills as an actress; she's entirely believable even when she ages by just having her hair greyed.

Director Stevens encouraged a feeling for animosity between Dean and Hudson and irritated Taylor with his endless retakes and chatter about how he wished original choice Grace Kelly had been available; this made for lively filming. The result strains for prestige but considering its length moves along at a considerable clip, due to Ferber's narrative prowess more than anything else.

GIDGET

1959 95m c Comedy   ★★½
Columbia (U.S.)   /U

Sandra Dee (*Francie*), James Darren (*Moondoggie*), Cliff Robertson (*Kahoona*), Arthur O'Connell (*Russell Lawrence*), Mary LaRoche (*Dorothy Lawrence*), Joby Baker (*Stinky*), Tom Laughlin (*Lover Boy*), Sue George (*B.L.*), Robert Ellis (*Hot Shot*), Jo Morrow (*Mary Lou*)

p, Lewis J. Rachmil; d, Paul Wendkos; w, Gabrielle Upton (based on the novel by Frederick Kohner); ph, Burnett Guffey; ed, William Lyon; m, M.W. Stoloff; art d, Ross Bellah

Watch at risk. Sugar-posioning, with the unctous Dee, as the all-American pertly perky happy-go-brainless model for countless teenagers in the late 1950s—today that seems scary. Dee plays Gidget (a nickname meaning "girl midget"), a whiny youngster who doesn't quite measure up to the chesty, bikinied girls on the beach. Her mom's reassurances come true when the two grooviest surfers in town, Moondoggie (James Darren) and Kahoona (Cliff Robertson), start paying Gidget some attention. Dee had just appeared in Douglas Sirk's IMITATION OF LIFE, and Robertson had turned in a commendable performance in AUTUMN LEAVES. Also hanging ten was Tom Laughlin, who much later made BILLY JACK. Inbred sequels followed, and two horrifying television series.

GIGI

1958 116m c Musical   ★★★½
MGM (U.S.)   /PG

Leslie Caron (*Gigi*), Maurice Chevalier (*Honore Lachaille*), Louis Jourdan (*Gaston Lachaille*), Hermione Gingold (*Mme Alvarez*), Eva Gabor (*Liane D'Exelmans*), Jacques Bergerac (*Sandomir*), Isabel Jeans (*Aunt Alicia*), John Abbott (*Manuel*), Monique Van Vooren (*Showgirl*), Lydia Stevens (*Simone*)

p, Arthur Freed; d, Vincente Minnelli; w, Alan Jay Lerner (based on the play *Gigi* by Anita Loos, from the novel by Colette); ph, Joseph Ruttenberg, Ray June; ed, Adrienne Fazan; m, Frederick Loewe; prod d, Cecil Beaton; art d, William A. Horning, Preston Ames; cos, Cecil Beaton

AA Best Picture; *AA Best Director:* Vincente Minnelli; *AA Best Adapted Screenplay:* Alan Jay Lerner; *AA Best Cinematography:* Joseph Ruttenberg; *AA Best Editing:* Adrienne Fazan; *AA Best Score:* Andre Previn; *AA Best Song:* Frederick Loewe (Music), Alan Jay Lerner (Lyrics); *AA Best Art Direction:* William A Horning (Art Direction), Preston Ames (Art Direction), Henry Grace (Set Decoration), Keogh Gleason (Set Decoration); *AA Best Costume Design:* Cecil Beaton

Overbaked but enjoyable, and a banquet for the eyes, thanks to the visual wonder of the Minnelli-Beaton teaming. But contemporary critics have long objected that Frederick Loewe and Alan Jay Lerner simply reworked their milestone *My Fair Lady*. To an extent, that's true; certainly the score is a rather vapid one. Based on the Colette novel, GIGI followed in the footsteps of a 1950 French film adaptation of the story and a 1951 straight dramatic production that starred Audrey Hepburn on Broadway.

The story concerns a waif (Leslie Caron), who lives in turn-of-the-century Paris with her grandmother, Mme Alvarez (Hermione Gingold), who, along with Gigi's Aunt Alicia (Isabel Jeans), seeks to transform the young woman into a courtesan so she can become the mistress of Gaston Lachaille (Louis Jourdan), wealthy heir to a sugar fortune. At first, Gaston is content to accept Gigi as his mistress; then he realizes he truly loves the beauty and is determined to marry her, throwing Mme Alvarez for a loop since the family tradition is to be a kept woman, not a wife. Ultimately, however, Mme Alvarez, who was once the mistress of Gaston's uncle, Honore (Maurice Chevalier), agrees to allow her granddaughter to marry.

Caron—never the most effortless of waifs—had played the role of Gigi in the London production of the straight stageplay, and here leads the cast (she's dubbed by Betty Wand) in a contest to see who can be the most French. The winner is Chevalier, in a performance that makes one feel as if you're gagging on pastry. The exceptions: Gingold and Jeans. Perhaps if the sweetness of GIGI was contrasted with elements of honest vulgarity, the picture could balance itself out. Considering the aspects of the courtesan life, the opportunity is there, but as it is we are left to make do with Eva Gabor's continental suggestions; she's too docile to inhabit her role.

Ten minutes into the movie, you've resolved the plot and are left to wallow in lovely frou-frou. Produced in the City of Light, GIGI makes wonderful use of the usual Parisian landmarks, and benefits from extraordinary period costumes and sets.

GILDA

1946 110m bw Drama   ★★★★
Columbia (U.S.)   /PG

Rita Hayworth *(Gilda)*, Glenn Ford *(Johnny Farrell)*, George Macready *(Ballin Mundson)*, Joseph Calleia *(Obregon)*, Steven Geray *(Uncle Pio)*, Joe Sawyer *(Casey)*, Gerald Mohr *(Capt. Delgado)*, Robert Scott *(Gabe Evans)*, Ludwig Donath *(German)*, Don Douglas *(Thomas Langford)*

p, Virginia Van Upp; d, Charles Vidor; w, Marion Parsonnet (based on Jo Eisinger's adaptation of E.A. Ellington's original story); ph, Rudolph Mate; ed, Charles Nelson; m, Hugo Friedhofer; art d, Stephen Goosson, Van Nest Polglase; chor, Jack Cole; cos, Jean Louis

Hayworth at her peak. Rita is the main reason to see GILDA, bringing her blue-moon beauty and star presence to Hollywood's definitive kept-woman role. GILDA proves Hayworth had a neat line: she wasn't as erotic as Dietrich or Ava Gardner, nor as suggestive as Harlow and Monroe. What she was, specifically, was provocative like no actress before or since.

The torrid, turgid plot of this myth of misogyny needn't be dwelled on in depth. Ford gets hired to play goon by Teutonic casino owner Macready. His duties include bringing to heel the duplicitous Hayworth, even to slapping her around. The triangle becomes a sicko menage a trois; surely Ford's character is the most sexually ambiguous leading man ever. He's only interested in asserting dominance and muscle, and both Hayworth and Macready enjoy taunting him—GILDA's dialogue fairly snakes with euphemism and innuendo. Critics remained indifferent to the film, but returning GIs flocked with their wives and sweethearts to see Columbia's "love goddess," who accented her role with such lines as: "If I had been a ranch they would have called me the Bar *Nothing!*" When Hayworth reprises a few bars of "Put the Blame on Mame," is she herself singing or not? This remains a famous guessing game with film buffs. Otherwise she's amazingly dubbed by Anita Ellis.

Cohn spared no expense in the production, and choreographer Cole lavished Hayworth with dances patterned after those of a professional stripper he had known. These numbers were brought into the production long after director Vidor began shooting, which indicates the haphazard fashion in which this film was shaped. It was Hayworth's film from the beginning; Vidor began shooting the story before Ford was actually signed and joined the production. The original story was written exclusively for Hayworth by producer Van Upp, named to oversee the production by Cohn himself.

Van Upp was later blamed by Hayworth for establishing a sex goddess no woman could ever hope to be in reality. When she had problems with Aly Khan, Hayworth told Van Upp: "It's all your fault. You wrote GILDA. And every man I've known has fallen in love with Gilda and wakened with me." GILDA is an erotic landmark to be especially considered today, when erotic thrillers dominate the boxoffice and television screens.

GIRL CRAZY

1943 97m bw Musical/Comedy   ★★★★
MGM (U.S.)   /U

Mickey Rooney *(Danny Churchill, Jr.)*, Judy Garland *(Ginger Gray)*, Gil Stratton *(Bud Livermore)*, Robert Strickland *(Henry Lathrop)*, Rags Ragland *(Rags)*, June Allyson *(Specialty)*, Nancy Walker *(Polly Williams)*, Guy Kibbee *(Dean Phineas Armour)*, Tommy Dorsey and His Band *(Themselves)*, Frances Rafferty *(Marjorie Tait)*

p, Arthur Freed; d, Norman Taurog; w, Fred Finklehoffe, Dorothy Kingsley, Sid Silvers, William Ludwig (based on the play by George Gershwin, Ira Gershwin, Guy Bolton, Jack McGowan); ph, William Daniels, Robert Planck; ed, Albert Akst; art d, Cedric Gibbons; chor, Charles Walters, Busby Berkeley

Irresistible entertainment, based on the play by Guy Bolton and Jack McGowan, with music by George and Ira Gershwin. Rooney stars as Danny Churchill, Jr., the rich son of a newspaper publisher (Henry O'Neill). He's sent to an all-boys mining school where wake-up time is 6 a.m., which is usually the hour he goes to sleep. Stuck out in the desert, Danny finds it hard to exercise his girl-craziness, until he meets Ginger Gray (Garland, looking quite delectable), the granddaughter of the school's dean (Guy Kibbee). Although Danny originally hates the school, his love for Ginger eventually prompts him to help save the financially imperiled institution with a musical rodeo.

The movie was originally to be directed by Busby Berkeley, but he and MGM musical maven Roger Edens didn't get along. And Garland's loathing of him was monumental; it stands to reason his power would be compromised as she ascended to queen of the MGM lot. But since *Girl Crazy* had been a big hit for Ethel Merman on Broadway, Berkeley was brought in to stage Garland's white-buckskinned finale of "I Got Rhythm," Merman's big hit. The rest of the musical work went to Charles Walters. Other songs included are "Embraceable You," "Fascinating Rhythm" and the sadly beautiful "But Not for Me," all by the Gershwins, and Edens's "Happy Birthday, Ginger."

GIRL WITH GREEN EYES

1964 91m bw Drama   ★★★½
Woodfall (U.K.)   /PG

Peter Finch *(Eugene Gaillard)*, Rita Tushingham *(Kate Brady)*, Lynn Redgrave *(Baba Brenan)*, Marie Kean *(Josie Hannigan)*, Arthur O'Sullivan *(Mr. Brady)*, Julian Glover *(Malachi Sullivan)*, T.P. McKenna *(Priest)*, Lislott Goettinger *(Joanna)*, Patrick Laffan *(Bertie Counihan)*, Eileen Crowe *(Mrs. Byrne)*

p, Oscar Lewenstein; d, Desmond Davis; w, Edna O'Brien (based on her novel *The Lonely Girl*); ph, Manny Wynn; ed, Antony Gibbs, Brian Smedley-Aston; m, John Addison; art d, Ted Marshall

Memorable and sentimental "women's picture" adapted by Edna O'Brien from her own novel. Filmed in and around Dublin, GIRL WITH GREEN EYES tells the story of a young woman, Rita Tushingham, who leaves her father's barren farm in County Clare to come to

Dublin where she gets a job in a grocery and shares a flat with Redgrave, an old pal from Catholic school. She meets Finch, a divorced writer many years older than she. She pursues him, they become friends, and she moves into his home.

Despite their propinquity and the underlying attraction, she remains chaste due to a combination of youth, shyness and her religious upbringing. When her father, O'Sullivan, learns that she's living with a man, he forces her to return home. Her priest, McKenna, rebukes her for her lax behavior, and she leaves home again and goes to Finch's place. She's tailed by O'Sullivan and a horde of his besotted buddies. They break into Finch's house, only to flee when Finch points his aged shotgun at them. Tushingham finally relents and sleeps with Finch.

Originally titled "Once Upon A Summer," the film featured several of the best Irish actors. All the roles were well played, and the dialogue smacked of Irish reality, though occasionally it is a trifle stilted for the American ear. There is lots to recommend this film, including first-time direction by Desmond Davis and the debut photography of Manny Wynn. Turner, Finch's real-life wife, does an excellent cameo as a bitch. It was Redgrave's second film for Richardson, the first having been TOM JONES. Lovingly made, it's a fine introduction to the Ireland of lyrical romance, rather than the strife-torn area we see so often.

GIRLFRIENDS

1978 86m c Comedy/Drama ★★★
Cyclops (U.S.) PG/AA

Melanie Mayron (*Susan Weinblatt*), Anita Skinner (*Anne Munroe*), Eli Wallach (*Rabbi Gold*), Christopher Guest (*Eric*), Bob Balaban (*Martin*), Gina Rogak (*Julie*), Amy Wright (*Ceil*), Viveca Lindfors (*Beatrice*), Mike Kellin (*Abe*), Jean De Baer (*Terry*)

p, Claudia Weill, Jan Saunders; d, Claudia Weill; w, Vicki Polon (based on a story by Polon and Weill); ph, Fred Murphy; ed, Suzanne Pettit; m, Michael Small; art d, Patrizia von Brandenstein

A refreshing little film that marked the directorial debut of Weill, GIRLFRIENDS strips away the pretentiousness of so many small movies and offers us a real look at real people. Weill spent many years as a documentarian; she uses her experience and her ear and eye for realism to present us with an episodic story that mixes comedy and poignancy with excellent results.

Mayron is a chubby Jewish photographer whose roommate, Skinner, is leaving to get married. Mayron must now go it alone and contemplates her life, new insecurities, and cellulite. Mayron is so good in the role that she seems closer to "being" her part than acting it. Not unlike SHEILA LEVINE IS DEAD AND LIVING IN NEW YORK, this character study of a certain type of urban Jewish woman never hits a false note. As Mayron's boyfriend, Balaban is depicted as likable and believable, an honest human being with honest problems. Mayron flirts with Wallach, a rabbi, and almost has a fling with him, but she winds up as the house photographer doing weddings and bar mitzvahs. It's unsentimental, emotional, and made with great affection.

GLASS KEY, THE

1942 85m bw Mystery/Political ★★★★
Paramount (U.S.) /A

Brian Donlevy (*Paul Madvig*), Veronica Lake (*Janet Henry*), Alan Ladd (*Ed Beaumont*), Bonita Granville (*Opal Madvig*), Richard Denning (*Taylor Henry*), Joseph Calleia (*Nick Vama*), William Bendix (*Jeff*), Frances Gifford (*Nurse*), Donald MacBride (*Farr*), Margaret Hayes (*Eloise Matthews*)

p, Fred Kohlmar; d, Stuart Heisler; w, Jonathan Latimer (based on the novel by Dashiell Hammett); ph, Theodor Sparkuhl; ed, Archie Marshek; m, Victor Young; art d, Hans Dreier, Haldane Douglas

This film of Dashiell Hammett's tale of political corruption and murder is slightly better than the 1935 version, profiting from a bigger budget, stellar casting, and a zippier pace, thanks to Johnathan Latimer's taut screenplay.

Donlevy is accused of murder, solicits aid of henchman Ladd to clear his name. Memorable, chilling sado-masochism of Bendix repeatedly beating Ladd is typical of the unorthodox undertow of sexual currents snaking through the plot. Ladd's character seems equally committed to Donlevy and the mysterious, cyclopean Lake, at one point

confiding he'd let the latter hang if it served his purpose. Despite the copout ending, Ladd's deadpan toughens his character up, serving up partial compensation. As usual, the Ladd-Lake slow-burn chemistry, deceptive in it's offhandedness, is a pleasurable contrast to all the overstoked new wave *noir* interpretations currently flourishing.

This film was put into production before the release of THIS GUN FOR HIRE, which featured an electric performance from Ladd and made him Paramount's newest star. But Bendix nearly steals the film as the scary but pathetic henchman whose only joy in life is to administer sadistic beatings. According to Beverly Linet in *Ladd: A Hollywood Tragedy*, in one scene calling for Bendix's character to beat up Ladd's, the the rugged six-footer slipped and struck the 5-foot-5-inch Ladd square on the jaw, knocking him out. Director Heisler, never one to let a convincing scene go unrecorded, ordered the shot printed and it appears in the film.

GLASS MENAGERIE, THE

1987 135m c Drama ★★★★
Aspetuck Productions, Ltd./Columbia (U.S.) PG

Joanne Woodward (*Amanda Wingfield*), John Malkovich (*Tom Wingfield*), Karen Allen (*Laura Wingfield*), James Naughton (*Gentleman Caller—Jim O'Connor*)

p, Burtt Harris; d, Paul Newman; w, Tennessee Williams; ph, Michael Ballhaus; ed, David Ray; m, Henry Mancini, Paul Bowles; prod d, Tony Walton; art d, John Kasarda; cos, Tony Walton

The third and best of the filmed versions of martyrs and dead magnolias. Directed by Paul Newman, the Tennessee Williams classic is painstakingly faithful to the play and features extraordinary performances from all the actors. Tom (John Malkovich) is the story's narrator and sets the scene for the "memory play" by introducing the characters. Tom himself is a poet who works in a warehouse to support his family but who longs for escape. Amanda (Joanne Woodward) is his mother, a Southern belle who forsook her genteel background to marry a telephone man who eventually left his family. Laura (Karen Allen) is his sister, the victim of a childhood disease that left one leg shorter than the other, though she is even more crippled by shyness. Finally, there is the gentleman caller (James Naughton), Tom's coworker at the warehouse. While Laura is engrossed in the world of the fragile glass figurines that she collects, Amanda is concerned with finding a husband for her and asks Tom's help.

Newman has said that he approached THE GLASS MENAGERIE less as a filmmaker than as an archivist, and his version is, in essence, a filmed stage play. It is something of a cliche to give a filmed play a claustrophobic feel, but THE GLASS MENAGERIE and its trapped characters cry out for such a treatment and Newman has effectively evoked it. Newman lets the actors and Williams's poetic language do the work. All of the performances are superb. Woodward's delightful Amanda is full of contradictions and Malkovich's Tom is a product of frustration, romantic dreams and guilt. Allen is a surprising revelation, as her previous film roles have asked so little of her. Here she plumbs emotions of considerable depth, and is entirely capable of rationalizing her character's retreat from reality.

GLENGARRY GLEN ROSS

1992 100m c Drama ★★★★
Zupnik Enterprises Inc. (U.S.) R/15

Al Pacino (*Ricky Roma*), Jack Lemmon (*Shelley "The Machine" Levine*), Alec Baldwin (*Blake*), Ed Harris (*Dave Moss*), Alan Arkin (*George Aaronow*), Kevin Spacey (*John Williamson*), Jonathan Pryce (*James Lingk*), Bruce Altman (*Mr. Spaniel*), Jude Ciccolella (*Detective*), Paul Butler (*Policeman*)

p, Jerry Tokofsky, Stanley R. Zupnik; d, James Foley; w, David Mamet (from his play); ph, Juan Ruiz-Anchia; ed, Howard Smith; m, James Newton Howard; prod d, Jane Musky; art d, Robert K. Shaw Jr., Bill Barclay; fx, Mike Maggi; cos, Jane Greenwood

AAN Best Supporting Actor: Al Pacino

Another seamy slice of life from acclaimed playwright David Mamet, GLENGARRY GLEN ROSS is a searing showcase for a remarkable ensemble cast.

This foul-mouthed drama revolves around a phony real estate operation, Premiere Properties, which gets a royal shaking up in the very first scene from consulting supersalesman Blake (Alec Baldwin). Blake's motivation strategy is brutally simple—sell or get out—and his ultimatum sets up a mad scramble in the office. Veteran supersalesman Shelley "The Machine" Levine (Jack Lemmon) trained the office's current sales leader, Ricky Roma (Al Pacino). But Levine is now a desperate man, his selling skills thwarted by stale leads and his situation complicated by a hospitalized daughter. His frustrated colleague Moss (Ed Harris) draws fellow salesman Aaronow (Alan Arkin) into a plot to burgle the office, steal the leads and sell them to a rival company. Aaronow isn't too thrilled, but there's another conspirator who is already set up to take the fall for the burglary. What drama there is hinges on whether the third party is Levine or Roma, himself driven to desperation when his "locked-in" deal with a henpecked prospect (Jonathan Pryce) unravels.

Whereas most films would focus on the details of the theft itself, Mamet's screenplay doesn't reveal exactly what happened, and it's clear that he's not particularly interested. Instead, GLENGARRY GLEN ROSS focuses on the dilemmas of the various salesmen as they sustain themselves by reliving past glories in the desiccated present. Lemmon is superb here in the type of role he's justly renowned for, a downtrodden individual who, in previous incarnations, has always found some form of salvation through self-knowledge. (In this instance, that solution is not forthcoming.) Pacino starts cocky and confident as Roma, only to shrink before our eyes as his miserable "prospect" flees to report him to the authorities. Arkin is wonderfully cagy and Harris brings real acid to his role as the most coldly cynical of the group. Director James Foley turns the screenplay's staginess into an asset, creating a claustrophobic vision of hell as a place where we're all fighting for survival, clutching a sweat-stained, dog-eared pile of bad leads.

GLENN MILLER STORY, THE

1953 115m c Musical/Biography ★★★★
Universal (U.S.) /U

James Stewart *(Glenn Miller)*, June Allyson *(Helen Burger Miller)*, Charles Drake *(Don Haynes)*, George Tobias *(Si Schribman)*, Harry Morgan *(Chummy MacGregor)*, Marion Ross *(Polly Haynes)*, Irving Bacon *(Mr. Miller)*, Kathleen Lockhart *(Mrs. Miller)*, Barton MacLane *(Gen. Arnold)*, Sig Rumann *(Mr. Krantz)*

p, Aaron Rosenberg; d, Anthony Mann; w, Valentine Davies, Oscar Brodney; ph, William Daniels; ed, Russell Schoengarth; m, Joseph Gershenson; chor, Kenny Williams

AAN Best Story and Screenplay: Valentine Davies, Oscar Brodney; *AAN Best Score:* Joseph Gershenson, Henry Mancini; *AA Best Sound:* Leslie I. Carey

Unlike so many film bios, this is an honest, intelligent depiction of one of America's greatest musical influences and doesn't merely string together a series of hit tunes and gratuitous scenes. But oh, what music!

James Stewart is Glenn Miller, a bright young man with a love for the trombone and a desire to create music. At the University of Colorado he falls for Helen Burger (June Allyson, at her charming best, and a perfect match for Stewart); then, after graduation, he goes to work for Ben Pollack (playing himself) and later has a gig in the pit of a Broadway show. On their wedding night, Helen is shocked to find her husband in a jam session in Harlem with Gene Krupa and Louis Armstrong. Later, in Boston, at the dance hall run by Si Schribman (George Tobias), Miller refines his art, stumbling upon his signature sound when his trumpet player splits his lip, forcing the clarinetist to play lead on "Moonlight Serenade."

Although Stewart learned how to handle the trombone, the actual playing was dubbed by Murray MacEachern and Joe Yukl, who are great on such Miller classics as "In the Mood," "Tuxedo Junction" and "Little Brown Jug." All that's missing from this well-crafted film is Tex Beneke, the "boy singer" for Miller's band, who went on to lead it after his mentor's death. Look for the great Frances Langford really doing her thing.

GLORIA

1980 123m c Crime ★★★½
Columbia (U.S.) R/PG

Gena Rowlands *(Gloria Swenson)*, Juan Adames *(Philip Dawn)*, Buck Henry *(Jack Dawn)*, Julie Carmen *(Jeri Dawn)*, Lupe Guarnica *(Margarita Vargas)*, Jessica Castillo *(Joan Dawn)*, Tony Knesich *(1st Man/Gangster)*, Filomena Spagnuolo *(Old Lady)*, Tom Noonan *(2nd Man/Gangster)*, Gregory Cleghorne *(Kid in Elevator)*

p, John Cassavetes; d, John Cassavetes; w, John Cassavetes; ph, Fred Schuler; ed, Jack McSweeney; m, Bill Conti; prod d, Rene D'Auriac, Fred Schuler; cos, Peggy Farrell

AAN Best Actress: Gena Rowlands

Under the masterful direction of husband John Cassavetes, Gena Rowlands delivers a gutsy, spellbinding performance in this excellent crime film.

Rowlands is the title character, a woman in her 40s who lives alone with her cats and her savings, compiled by turning tricks with high-placed mobsters. Her life is thrown into turmoil when her neighbor, Mafia accountant Jack Dawn (Buck Henry), and his family are exterminated by the mob. Their eight-year-old son Philip (Juan Adames), whom the Dawns left in Gloria's care, is the only survivor and it's then up to Gloria to protect the boy from mob hit men.

Rowlands is brilliant as the apprehensive woman who finds in herself the courage to defy an evil system and fight it to a bloody standstill. Adames contributes a fascinating portrayal of the boy who becomes uncannily adult in the pressurized situation. Cassavetes's direction is incisive while maintaining a chillingly brisk pace, marvelously supported by cinematographer Fred Schuler's fluid camerawork and penetrating closeups of the hunted pair. Too long by far, but still one sustained, frenetic gulp of a film.

GLORY

1989 122m c Historical/War ★★★★
Tri-Star (U.S.) R/15

Matthew Broderick *(Col. Robert Gould Shaw)*, Denzel Washington *(Trip)*, Cary Elwes *(Cabot Forbes)*, Morgan Freeman *(John Rawlins)*, Jihmi Kennedy *(Sharts)*, Andre Braugher *(Searles)*, John Finn *(Sgt. Mulcahy)*, Donovan Leitch *(Morse)*, John David Cullum *(Russell)*, Alan North *(Gov. Andrew)*

p, Freddie Fields; d, Edward Zwick; w, Kevin Jarre (based on the books *Lay This Laurel* by Lincoln Kirstein, *One Gallant Rush* by Peter Burchard, and the letters of Robert Gould Shaw); ph, Freddie Francis; ed, Steven Rosenblum; m, James Horner; prod d, Norman Garwood; art d, Keith Pain, Dan Webster; fx, Kevin Yagher, Carl Fullerton; cos, Francine Jamison-Tanchuck

AA Best Supporting Actor: Denzel Washington; *AA Best Cinematography:* Freddie Francis; *AAN Best Editing:* Steven Rosenblum; *AAN Best Art Direction:* Norman Garwood, Garrett Lewis; *AA Best Sound:* Donald O. Mitchell, Gregg C. Rudloff, Elliot Tyson, Russell Williams, II

Never self-serving, this glorious film tells the hitherto shamefully uncelebrated story of the 54th Regiment of Massachusetts Volunteer Infantry, the first unit of black troops raised by the Union to fight in the Civil War.

Commanded by Colonel Robert Shaw (Matthew Broderick), the 25-year-old son of abolitionist Boston Brahmins, the ragtag assemblage includes Rawlins (Morgan Freeman), a gravedigger who is the regiment's anchor and voice of reason; Trip (Denzel Washington), an embittered, bullying, but tough-as-steel runaway slave; Searles (Andre Braugher), a bespectacled Emerson scholar; and Sharts (Jihmi Kennedy), a shy, stuttering former field slave. While undergoing relentless training, the black troops are subjected to the racism of white enlistees and officers, denied shoes and uniforms, and offered less than standard wages, which, with Shaw's support, they refuse to accept. Finally given a chance to enter combat, the 54th acquit themselves heroically, then make a brave suicidal assault against an impregnable harbor fortification—South Carolina's Fort Wagner.

Based partly on the real Robert Gould Shaw's letters, GLORY is remarkable in its fidelity to history. Director Edward Zwick (ABOUT LAST NIGHT, television's "thirtysomething") re-creates the period with remarkable accuracy, both in the observation of small details and in the truly harrowing battle scenes. Though essentially an ensemble piece, GLORY also contains especially compelling performances by Broderick, Washington, and Freeman. Richly plotted, alternately inspiring and horrifying, GLORY is an enlightening and entertaining tribute to heroes too long forgotten.

GO-BETWEEN, THE

1971 118m c Drama ★★★★
MGM/EMI (U.K.) PG

Julie Christie *(Marian Maudsley)*, Alan Bates *(Ted Burgess)*, Dominic Guard *(Leo Colston)*, Margaret Leighton *(Mrs. Maudsley)*, Michael Redgrave *(The Older Leo)*, Michael Gough *(Mr. Maudsley)*, Edward Fox *(Hugh Trimingham)*, Richard Gibson *(Marcus Maudsley)*, Simon Hume-Kendall *(Denys)*, Amaryllis Garnett *(Kate)*

p, John Heyman, Norman Priggen; d, Joseph Losey; w, Harold Pinter (based on the novel by L.P. Hartley); ph, Gerry Fisher; ed, Reginald Beck; m, Michel Legrand; art d, Carmen Dillon; cos, John Furniss

AAN Best Supporting Actress: Margaret Leighton

Stylish look back into an old man's memories, courtesy of Harold Pinter, who wrote the screenplay adaptation of L.P. Hartley's novel. Redgrave reviews his life in painstaking and sometimes dizzying detail under Losey's deft direction. Julie Christie is engaged to Edward Fox, a member of the British aristocracy, but she is in love with Bates, a lowly farmer. Guard is Redgrave as a young man, hired as the go-between for Christie and Bates. This assignment gives the youth his first taste of love: he falls for Christie too. In fact, he never marries, and we are given to believe it was this feeling for Christie that kept him a bachelor for seven decades.

Set in Norfolk in the 1900s, the film flashes forward and backward with several twists and such attention to fine shadings that you cannot watch this movie without giving it your utmost attention. The cover for the affair is blown when Christie's mother, Leighton, forces young Guard to take her to where Christie and Bates are trysting. Several shocking incidents, including Bates shooting himself, keep this film constantly surprising. The ending, in which an aged Christie asks the aged Redgrave to once more act as a go-between, is a smashing climax to a superb film.

GO TELL THE SPARTANS

1978 114m c War ★★★½
Spartan (U.S.) R/15

Burt Lancaster *(Maj. Asa Barker)*, Craig Wasson *(Cpl. Stephen Courcey)*, Jonathan Goldsmith *(Sgt. Oleonowski)*, Marc Singer *(Capt. Al Olivetti)*, Joe Unger *(Lt. Raymond Hamilton)*, Dennis Howard *(Cpl. Abraham Lincoln)*, David Clennon *(Lt. Finley Wattsberg)*, Evan Kim *(Cowboy)*, John Megna *(Cpl. Ackley)*, Hilly Hicks *(Signalman Coffee)*

p, Allan F. Bodoh, Mitchell Cannold; d, Ted Post; w, Wendell Mayes (based on the novel *Incident at Muc Wa* by Daniel Ford); ph, Harry Stradling Jr.; ed, Millie Moore; m, Dick Halligan; art d, Jack Senter; cos, Ron Dawson

Lost in the shuffle between THE DEER HUNTER and APOCALYPSE NOW, this neat little war movie tells of the US presence in Vietnam in 1964, with advisor Lancaster commanding a small group of combat "advisors." Lancaster is ordered to send a platoon of Vietnamese militia (old men with shotguns, commanded by Communist-hating mercenary Kim) and a squad of Americans under green lieutenant Unger to garrison an old French stronghold. A veteran of three wars, Lancaster argues that the site is of no value and that all putting troops there will accomplish is enticing the Viet Cong to mass for an attack. He is overruled on the grounds that the French abandoned the spot and lost the war, "and we don't want to make the same mistake the French did." Lancaster is proved right, though, and before long the Viet Cong have besieged the isolated outpost.

The film features a typically fine performance by Lancaster, who wonders, through most of the film, why a draftee like Wasson would volunteer for combat duty. When Wasson explains that he wanted to

know what a war was like, Lancaster exclaims, "I should have known it—you're a tourist!" Even at this point in the war, the film makes it obvious that we don't belong there; the US Army command is portrayed as greedy and stupid, while the South Vietnamese appear to be thoroughly corrupt (Lancaster has to bribe the local warlord to give the battle some air support). The title derives from the inscription above the French cemetery, quoting the doomed Spartans at Thermopylae: "Stranger, go tell the Spartans how we lie; loyal to their laws, here we die."

GOALIE'S ANXIETY AT THE PENALTY KICK, THE
(DIE ANGST DES TORMANNS BEIM ELFMETER)

1971 101m c Crime ★★★½
Autoren/Osterreichischen (West Germany) /PG

Arthur Brauss *(Joseph Bloch)*, Kai Fischer *(Hertha Gabler)*, Erika Pluhar *(Gloria)*, Libgart Schwartz *(Maid)*, Marie Bardeschewski *(Waitress)*, Michael Troost *(Salesman)*, Bert Fortell *(Customs Officer)*, Edda Koechl *(Girl in Vienna)*, Mario Kranz *(School Janitor)*, Ernst Meister *(Tax Inspector)*

p, Peter Genee; d, Wim Wenders; w, Wim Wenders, Peter Handke based on the novel by Handke; ph, Robby Muller; ed, Peter Przygodda; m, Jurgen Knieper

Haunting. Wim Wenders's second feature film and his first collaboration with the Austrian novelist-poet-playwright Peter Handke is an adaptation of Handke's short novel about a soccer goalie driven to murder.

From the start of Wenders's film, the personality of the goalie, Josef Bloch (Arthur Brauss), is evident. While the game's action take place at one end of the field, Bloch waits at his net at the opposite end. As play nears, he takes little notice, walks in front of his net, and stands completely still as the ball is kicked past him. Bloch is a character who considers it pointless to try to evade or outwit the course of events. He leaves the team (whose popularity has taken them around the world) and begins to wander. He visits movie theaters, plays American songs on jukeboxes, drinks, encounters people, and observes life as it passes him by. After he meets a cinema cashier named Gloria (Erika Pluhar)—which, as she reminds him, is spelled G-L-O-R-I-A as in the rock 'n' roll song by Them—Bloch returns with her to her apartment and, eventually, strangles her for no apparent reason.

Wenders, who has long professed his fascination with America, its films, and its music, cannot make an American-style picture. Instead, he presents a meditative, fragmentary reconstruction of the killer's mind, his distorted perceptions, his personal morality, and the otherwise unimportant events in his daily existence. While most directors insist on sensationalizing acts of violence and perpetuating the myth of the outlaw hero, Wenders, in this portrait of a killer, delivers one of cinema's most truthful depictions of the criminal.

GOD IS MY WITNESS
(KHUDA GAWAH)

1992 192m c Action/Romance/Musical ★★★★
Headliner Productions, Inc./Glamour Films (India)

Amitabh Bachchan *(Badshah Khan)*, Sridevi *(Benazir/Mehndi)*, Danny Denzongpa *(Khuda Baksh)*, Nagarjuna *(Raja)*, Shilpa Shirodkar *(Henna)*, Kiran Kumar, Vikram Gokhale

p, Manoj Desai, Nazir Ahmed; d, Mukul S. Anand; w, Santosh Saroj; ph, W.B. Rao; ed, R. Rajendran; m, Laxmikant Pyarelal; chor, Saroj Khan

One of the finest recent specimens of Indian commercial cinema, GOD IS MY WITNESS is a far cry from the stereotypical *masala* film — supposedly a shoddy assemblage of action cliches, "wet sari" numbers, kitschy dialogue, and witless plot contrivances. This is a sweeping melodrama of genuine emotional resonance and, in its best moments, a fulfillment of the operatic aspirations of classic Hollywood musicals, weaving song and dance into the very fabric of the narrative.

A wide-screen "curry western," GOD IS MY WITNESS takes place in an imaginary Afghanistan, a world of muscular, saber-wielding Pathan horsemen that seems to co-exist with contemporary India while only rarely intersecting with any form of modernity. Dominating the plot-heavy scenario is Badshah Khan, a Pathan chieftain and paragon of cocky masculinity played by Bombay superstar Amitabh Bachchan. During a game of *buzkashi* — a traditional Afghan test of manhood described as "a sport in name only; more like a terrible battle" — Badshah encounters the ravishing woman warrior Benazir (Sridevi) and is instantly smitten. But Benazir won't marry him until he brings her the head of Habibullah, the man who murdered her father. Badshah sets out on an arduous horseback journey to India, where he eventually finds and kills Habibullah — thereby incurring the wrath of a twisted bandit king called Pasha — only to be placed under arrest. While Badshah languishes in an Indian prison, Benazir quietly goes mad. Subsequent developments include several murders, a smuggling subplot with a gratifying car chase, a quest for truth conducted by Badshah's grown daughter, Mehndi (also played by Sridevi), various revelations of identity and tests of loyalty, and a final confrontation with vengeful Pasha.

GOD IS MY WITNESS may not strike the average American as a "good movie," at least in the Siskel & Ebert sense. It isn't at all concerned with character psychology or historical plausibility. It disdains naturalism, particularly where acting is concerned. Its deliberately excessive style will elicit laughter at times.

But it's no more overwrought than Hollywood melodramas of the 1950s, and, like those movies, it is best understood as a broadly symbolic "acting out" of cultural values in conflict. By the film's end, the hero is made to confront the inadequacies of his traditionalist logic, and the tensions of Indian masculinity — passion vs. duty, freedom vs. domesticity — are exposed according to conventions that American genre fans will immediately recognize.

The sweeping story line and fabulous setting provide an excuse for a first-rate production team — including Bombay's leading set decorators, costume designers, choreographers, and composers — to create an opulent mise-en-scene punctuated by exhilarating, delightfully ersatz "traditional" song-and-dance sequences. Meanwhile, the heightened rhetoric and heroic conventions of India's Moghul-period romances are unblushingly deployed right alongside leitmotifs borrowed from Sergio Leone. Directed with sophistication and visual panache by Mukul S. Anand, GOD IS MY WITNESS is the perfect introduction to the richly entertaining and often startling norms of Indian commercial film.

GODFATHER, THE

1972   175m   c   Crime   ★★★★★
Paramount   (U.S.)   R/18

Marlon Brando *(Don Vito Corleone)*, Al Pacino *(Michael Corleone)*, James Caan *(Sonny Corleone)*, Richard Castellano *(Clemenza)*, Robert Duvall *(Tom Hagen)*, Sterling Hayden *(McCluskey)*, John Marley *(Jack Woltz)*, Richard Conte *(Barzini)*, Diane Keaton *(Kay Adams)*, Al Lettieri *(Sollozzo)*

p, Albert S. Ruddy; d, Francis Ford Coppola; w, Mario Puzo, Francis Ford Coppola (based on the novel by Mario Puzo); ph, Gordon Willis; ed, William Reynolds, Peter Zinner, Marc Laub, Murray Solomon; m, Nino Rota; prod d, Dean Tavoularis; art d, Warren Clymer; fx, A. D. Flowers, Joe Lombardi, Dick Smith, Sass Bedig; cos, Anna Hill Johnstone

AA Best Picture; AA Best Actor: Marlon Brando; AAN Best Supporting Actor: James Caan; AAN Best Supporting Actor: Robert Duvall; AAN Best Supporting Actor: Al Pacino; AAN Best Director: Francis Ford Coppola; AA Best Adapted Screenplay: Mario Puzo, Francis Ford Coppola; AAN Best Editing: William Reynolds, Peter Zinner; AAN Best Costume Design: Anna Hill Johnstone; AAN Best Sound: Bud Grenzbach, Richard Portman, Christopher Newman

One of the central American movies of the last 25 years, and one of very few to succed as both popular entertainment and high art. THE GODFATHER changed forever the popular perception of organized crime, implying strong parallels between the workings of the Mafia and those of any other profit-making corporation, and imparting operatic gravity to its liberal doses of violence.

The film opens with the wedding of Don Vito Corleone's (Marlon Brando) daughter Connie (Talia Shire) to Carlo Rizzi (Gianni Russo), a small-time bookie. Present at the ceremony is Brando's second son, Michael (Al Pacino), a much-decorated Marine captain who has just returned from WWII. College-educated, sensitive and perceptive, Mi-

chael is unlike almost all the other guests except Kay (Diane Keaton), his WASP sweetheart. Pacino points out gangster luminaries to Kay as a small boy might see heroes in a baseball park.

Problems for the Corleone family arise with the appearance of Sollozzo (Al Lettieri), a maverick gangster who has the backing of a rival Mafia family. In a meeting with the Corleones, Sollozzo informs the family that he intends to establish wide-scale heroin sales in NYC, but requires the permission of Don Vito to do so. Corleone, an old-school Mafia don, sends Sollozzo packing, saying that he is disgusted by the thought of narcotics and is content with his gambling, prostitution and protection rackets. (In fact, he is reluctant to jeopardize his political contacts by venturing into this controversial new terrain.) The refusal leads to a gang war in which the Godfather is wounded, but not killed, in an assassination attempt.

Sonny (James Caan) temporarily takes over control of the family from the injured don, as Michael opts to kill Sollozzo and a corrupt police captain in revenge for the attack on Vito. After Michael goes into hiding in Sicily, the volatile Sonny beats up Carlo for having assaulted Connie and is then killed in an ambush that Carlo helped set up.

While in hiding, Michael takes a young Sicilian wife, only to lose her in a botched assassination attempt that was aimed at him by a rival family. Newly hardened, he returns to America to take control of the family from Don Vito who, now recuperated from his injuries, is retiring.

Great movies aren't usually planned as such; they happen through an unusual confluence of talents and qualities. THE GODFATHER is no exception. Coppola had set out simply to redeem a faltering career when he started to shoot the popular Mario Puzo mafia novel. His talent brought him luck. He collected an extraordinary number of the great actors who made American filmmaking interesting during the 70s and 80s: Marlon Brando, James Caan, Al Pacino, Diane Keaton, Robert Duvall. Then he spiced the mixture with some accomplished character actors: John Marley, Al Lettieri, Sterling Hayden, and Coppola's sister, Talia Shire. Coppola also had the eminent good sense—or good luck—to get Nino Rota to write his last great score. He got a finely crafted script from author Puzo, and then worked obsessively to push all involved to the limits of their abilities, and sometimes beyond.

Puzo's novel (which also redeemed a faltering career) provided not one, but several mythic elements that Coppola was canny enough to reinforce in the film. THE GODFATHER is a generational saga; it's also an action film; but above all, it catches the imagination of audiences because it suggests that the career of a gangster is not so very different from the career of a businessman or a politician. This had important resonance for the generation of the early 70s.

The film is dark—Coppola had cinematographer Gordon Willis deliberately underlight each scene; the mood is dark; and the climax, in which Michael indulges in an orgy of blood vengeance, would simply be horrific, were it not for the ironic melodies of the Rota score, which underline the humane sensibilities of the storyteller and keep us at an appropriate distance. And this points to Coppola's greatest achievement with THE GODFATHER: he simultaneously presents us with two views of the Corleone family. We see it from within, sympathizing with the motives and dilemmas of these very real, attractive and charismatic individuals; and we see it from without, in a state of suspended disgust at a moral code that knows only greed and blood.

GODFATHER, PART II, THE

1974   200m   c   Crime   ★★★★★
Paramount   (U.S.)   R/18

Al Pacino *(Michael)*, Robert Duvall *(Tom Hagen)*, Diane Keaton *(Kay)*, Robert De Niro *(Vito Corleone)*, Talia Shire *(Connie)*, John Cazale *(Fredo)*, Lee Strasberg *(Hyman Roth)*, G.D. Spradlin *(Senator Geary)*, Michael V. Gazzo *(Frank Pentangeli)*, Richard Bright *(Al Neri)*

p, Francis Ford Coppola, Gray Frederickson, Fred Roos; d, Francis Ford Coppola; w, Francis Ford Coppola, Mario Puzo (based on characters from his novel); ph, Gordon Willis; ed, Peter Zinner, Barry Malkin, Richard Marks; m, Nino Rota, Carmine Coppola; prod d, Dean Tavoularis; art d, Angelo Graham; fx, A.D. Flowers, Joe Lombardi; cos, Theodora Van Runkle

AA Best Picture; *AAN Best Actor:* Al Pacino; *AA Best Supporting Actor:* Robert DeNiro; *AAN Best Supporting Actor:* Michael V. Gazzo; *AAN Best Supporting Actor:* Lee Strasberg; *AAN Best Supporting Actress:* Talia Shire; *AAN Best Director:* Francis Ford Coppola; *AA Best Adapted Screenplay:* Francis Ford Coppola, Mario Puzo; *AA Best Score:* Nino Rota, Carmine Coppola; *AA Best Art Direction:* Dean Tavoularis, Angelo Graham, George R. Nelson; *AAN Best Costume Design:* Theadora Van Runkle

Sequels were beginning to become all the rage in the early seventies, so it's not surprising that a film as popular as THE GODFATHER gave birth to what could easily have been just a followup exploitation. What is remakable, perhaps unique, is that THE GODFATHER, PART II actually expands upon and amplifies its predecessor. This is in fact both a sequel and a "prequel," intercutting the reign of Don Michael Corleone (Al Pacino) with the early story of his father, Vito, here brilliantly played by Robert De Niro.

Coppola was given a free hand with this sequel, and his deft directorial touches are everywhere, particularly in the earlier historical sequences. Cinematographer Willis superbly captures the turn-of-the-century period, applying a seriographic tint to flashback scenes for a softer, richer look than the sharp image of the ongoing contemporary story.

GODFATHER, PART III, THE

1990 161m c Crime ★★½
Zoetrope (U.S.) R/15

Al Pacino *(Michael Corleone)*, Diane Keaton *(Kay Adams)*, Talia Shire *(Connie Corleone)*, Andy Garcia *(Vincent Mancini)*, Eli Wallach *(Don Altobello)*, Joe Mantegna *(Joey Zasa)*, George Hamilton *(B.J. Harrison)*, Bridget Fonda *(Grace Hamilton)*, Sofia Coppola *(Mary Corleone)*, Raf Vallone *(Cardinal Lamberto)*

p, Gray Frederickson, Fred Roos, Francis Ford Coppola, Charles Mulvehill; d, Francis Ford Coppola; w, Mario Puzo, Francis Ford Coppola; ph, Gordon Willis; ed, Barry Malkin, Lisa Fruchtman, Walter Murch; m, Carmine Coppola, Nino Rota; prod d, Dean Tavoularis; art d, Alex Tavoularis; fx, Lawrence J. Cavanaugh, R. Bruce Steinheimer; cos, Milena Canonero

AAN Best Picture; *AAN Best Supporting Actor:* Andy Garcia; *AAN Best Director:* Francis Ford Coppola; *AAN Best Cinematography:* Gordon Willis; *AAN Best Editing:* Barry Malkin, Lisa Fruchtman, Walter Murch; *AAN Best Song:* Carmine Coppola (Music), John Bettis (Lyrics); *AAN Best Art Direction:* Dean Tavoularis (Art Direction), Gary Fettis (Set Decoration)

The sequel that was never meant to be, and one that, ultimately, few of the original players could refuse. Out of the resulting confusion—budget excesses, creative clashes, last-second rewrites, cast dissension, a breakneck pace—emerged one of the most frustrating films of 1990, an epic without epic scope, a muted, strained, unnatural affair that never comes into dramatic focus. Coppola's wisest move in PART III was to not try to take the Corleone saga in a radically different direction. Instead, the third part becomes an extended coda to the ending of PART II, as Michael continues to fulfill his tragic legacy, doing his best for his family, only to destroy it in the process. Much of the critical drubbing the movie received centered on Coppola's ill-advised casting of his daughter, Sofia, in the crucial role of Michael's daughter, Mary.

GODS MUST BE CRAZY, THE

1981 109m c Comedy ★★★★
Mimosa (Botswana) PG

Marius Weyers *(Andrew Steyn)*, Sandra Prinsloo *(Kate Thompson)*, Louw Verwey *(Sam Boga)*, Nixau *(Xi)*, Jamie Uys *(The Reverend)*, Michael Thys *(Mpudi)*, Nic De Jager *(Jack Hind)*, Fanyana H. Sidumo *(1st Card Player)*, Joe Seakatsie *(2nd Card Player)*, Ken Gampu *(President)*

p, Jamie Uys; d, Jamie Uys; w, Jamie Uys; ph, Buster Reynolds, Robert Lewis, Jamie Uys; ed, Jamie Uys; m, John Boshoff; art d, Caroline Burls; cos, Gail Grobbelaar, Mij Reynolds

A hoot from South Africa and a brilliantly funny throwback to the days of slapstick silent comedy.

It begins as a *National Geographic* sort of documentary about the Kalahari Bushmen, an uncivilized African tribe that knows no violence, is thoroughly self-contained, and holds no material possessions. One day a small plane overhead drops a Coke bottle in the tribe's midst. Assuming that the bottle is a gift from the gods, the members begin to make use of it—and they discover that it has not one but many uses: mashing meal, flattening skins, playing music, making patterns. Since it is such a valuable tool, the tribesmen soon become possessive of it. This leads to greed, greed leads to anger, and anger leads to violence. Xi (Nixau, an actual Bushman), being the tribal leader, is elected to rid his people of the bottle by taking it to the end of the earth and throwing it off.

Writer-director Jamie Uys resurrects a familiar, long-forgotten style of sight gags and traditional comic techniques in this delightful comedy that succeeds as both entertainment and nostalgic homage to the earliest days of film.

GOING MY WAY

1944 130m bw Religious/Musical ★★★★
Paramount (U.S.) /U

Bing Crosby *(Father Chuck O'Malley)*, Rise Stevens *(Genevieve Linden)*, Barry Fitzgerald *(Father Fitzgibbon)*, Frank McHugh *(Father Timothy O'Dowd)*, Gene Lockhart *(Ted Haines, Sr.)*, William Frawley *(Max Dolan)*, James Brown *(Ted Haines, Jr.)*, Jean Heather *(Carol James)*, Porter Hall *(Mr. Belknap)*, Fortunio Bonanova *(Tomasso Bozzani)*

p, Leo McCarey; d, Leo McCarey; w, Frank Butler, Frank Cavett (based on a story by McCarey); ph, Lionel Lindon; ed, LeRoy Stone; art d, Hans Dreier, William Flannery; fx, Gordon Jennings; cos, Edith Head

AA Best Picture; *AA Best Actor:* Bing Crosby; *AAN Best Actor:* Barry Fitzgerald; *AA Best Supporting Actor:* Barry Fitzgerald; *AA Best Director:* Leo McCarey; *AA Best Original Story:* Leo McCarey; *AA Best Screenplay:* Frank Butler, Frank Cavett; *AAN Best Cinematography:* Lionel Lindon; *AAN Best Editing:* Leroy Stone; *AA Best Song:* James Van Heusen (Music), Johnny Burke (Lyrics)

A warm and moving sleeper hit. Father Chuck O'Malley (Bing Crosby) is an easy-going, trouble-shooting priest who arrives at St. Dominic's Church, a Catholic institution that has seen better days, as has its curate, the elderly Father Fitzgibbon (Barry Fitzgerald). The old and stubborn priest has led the parish for 45 years, but recently the church has gotten heavily in to debt, disillusioning even the parishioners. Through the magic of music, however, Father O'Malley brings Father Fitzgibbon out of the doldrums and saves the parish.

Leo McCarey's direction is masterful, stopping the sentiment just short of the maudlin. It all works like magic, especially the unbeatable chemistry between Crosby and Fitzgerald. The film was box-office dynamite and swept the Oscars, winning for Best Picture, Best Director, Best Screenplay, Best Actor and Best Supporting Actor. GOING MY WAY and its sequel, THE BELLS OF ST. MARY'S, were also popular with the Catholic Church and Pope Pius XII, who later gave a private audience to Crosby in thanks for the latter's priestly portrayal.

GOING PLACES
(LES VALSEUSES)

1974 117m c Comedy/Drama ★★★
C.A.P.A.C./U.P.F./SN (France) R/

Gerard Depardieu *(Jean-Claude)*, Patrick Dewaere *(Pierrot)*, Miou-Miou *(Marie-Ange)*, Jeanne Moreau *(Jeanne Pirolle)*, Jacques Chailleux *(Jacques Pirolle)*, Michel Peyrelon *(Surgeon)*, Brigitte Fossey *(Young Mother)*, Isabelle Huppert *(Jacqueline)*, Christiane Muller *(Jacqueline's Mother)*, Christian Alers *(Jacqueline's Father)*

p, Paul Claudon; d, Bertrand Blier; w, Bertrand Blier, Philippe Dumarcay (based on the novel by Blier); ph, Bruno Nuytten; ed, Kenout Peltier; m, Stephane Grappelli

Disagreeable but fascinating examination of youth constructed as a buddy-road movie. GOING PLACES revolves around the friendship between Depardieu and Dewaere, a couple of long-haired, disheveled petty thieves in their mid-20s. As the film begins, the duo is terrorizing a middle-aged woman—grabbing her ample behind, blowing kisses on her neck, and finally stealing her purse. So begins a spree—which, as crime sprees go, is relatively harmless. Along the way, the two steal cars, break into stores, insult people, seduce some semi-willing women, and even have sex with each other when no one else is available. They seem, however, to have no profound effect on anyone.

After returning a stolen car Dewaere is shot, and superficially wounded in one testicle, by the angry owner. His fear that he'll never have sex again proves groundless, however, when the thieves meet Miou-Miou, a flighty young woman who doesn't mind disrobing for, or having sex with, the fellows—but who doesn't seem to enjoy it either—which infuriates these two macho men who are convinced they can make any woman melt in their arms.

The first major film from Bertrand Blier (son of actor Bernard), GOING PLACES is an ugly and brutal, yet somehow charming, look at two young men who are wholly worthless as human beings. They have no future; and, despite the fact that they travel from one side of France to the other, they never get anywhere. They just go—fast and furiously. The most significant moment in their lives is their meeting with Moreau, an older woman just released from prison, who laments her lost youth. She who has nothing is even worse off than Depardieu and Dewaere, who have youth, at least. The alluring Moreau appears only briefly but gives one of her most glowing performances.

GOLD DIGGERS OF 1933

1933 94m bw Musical ★★★★★
Warner Bros. (U.S.) /A

Warren William (*J. Lawrence Bradford*), Joan Blondell (*Carol King*), Aline MacMahon (*Trixie Lorraine*), Ruby Keeler (*Polly Parker*), Dick Powell (*Brad Roberts/Robert Treat Bradford*), Guy Kibbee (*Faneuil H. Peabody*), Ned Sparks (*Barney Hopkins*), Ginger Rogers (*Fay Fortune*), Clarence Nordstrom (*Gordon*), Robert Agnew (*Dance Director*)

p, Robert Lord; d, Mervyn LeRoy; w, Erwin Gelsey, James Seymour, David Boehm, Ben Markson (based on the play "Gold Diggers of Broadway" by Avery Hopwood); ph, Sol Polito; ed, George Amy; art d, Anton Grot; chor, Busby Berkeley; cos, Orry-Kelly

AAN Best Sound: Nathan Levinson (Sound)

Pure depression gold. After their success with 42ND STREET, Warner Bros. threw this film together quickly, sensing that they were on to something with movie musicals. Based on 1929's *Gold Diggers of Broadway* by Avery Hopwood, this Mervyn LeRoy-directed extravaganza not only became a hit but spawned several more films of its ilk.

Joan Blondell, Aline MacMahon and Ruby Keeler play a trio of unemployed showgirls who are thrilled when producer Barney Hopkins (Ned Sparks) informs them he's about to start a new show. The problem is that he doesn't have a penny, but Brad Roberts (Dick Powell), a songwriter who is mad for Polly (Keeler) does, and lends Sparks $15,000 to get "Forgotten Melody" off the ground. The show goes into rehearsal, with Brad taking one of the roles, but the girls wonder if his money is clean, except for Polly, who *just knows* he's legit. Of course he is. In fact, he's the scion of a wealthy Beacon Hill family; however, his brother, J. Lawrence (Warren William), and a lawyer, Faneuil Hall Peabody (Guy Kibbee), arrive from Boston to put an end to Brad's frivolousness.

Harry Warren and Al Dubin wrote the excellent songs, and Busby Berkeley did the startling choreography, including a Ginger Rogers-led chorus dressed in gold coin costumes in the extravagant rendition of "We're in the Money" (which Ginger does in pig latin). The picture is loaded with inside jokes, including cameo appearances by famed agent Louis Schurr and Berkeley as the "Call-Boy" (that's the correct term). If you have but one 1930s Warner Bros. musical to see, make it this one. Remade as PAINTING THE CLOUDS WITH SUNSHINE.

GOLD DIGGERS OF 1935

1935 95m bw Musical ★★★½
Warner Bros./First National (U.S.) /U

Dick Powell (*Dick Curtis*), Gloria Stuart (*Amy Prentiss*), Adolphe Menjou (*Nicoleff*), Glenda Farrell (*Betty Hawes*), Grant Mitchell (*Louis Lamson*), Dorothy Dare (*Arline Davis*), Alice Brady (*Mrs. Mathilda Prentiss*), Frank McHugh (*Humboldt Prentiss*), Hugh Herbert (*T. Mosely Thorpe*), Winifred Shaw (*Winny*)

p, Robert Lord; d, Busby Berkeley; w, Manuel Seff, Peter Milne (based on a story by Milne, Robert Lord); ph, George Barnes; ed, George Amy; art d, Anton Grot

AA Best Song: Harry Warren (Music), Al Dubin (Lyrics)

Gold-plated good fun. A minor plot is mangled in a major fashion by Busby Berkeley, but his choreography and the score assure us of delirious delight. The scene is a summer resort in a New England town, the story revolving around a number of romantic pairings. The inn's employees include Dick Powell as a desk clerk studying to be a doctor, Adolphe Menjou as the somewhat dishonest owner of the hotel, Gloria Stuart as the attractive ingenue, and Frank McHugh as the ne'er-do-well comedy relief.

The key to all the fun is the Harry Warren-Al Dubin score which features the remarkable "Lullaby of Broadway" (a song reprised from their score for FORTY SECOND STREET) as well as "I'm Going Shopping With You" and "The Words Are In My Heart." Around these tunes Berkeley devised what was, to some, the apex of his choreographic career. The highlight is a production number done for a charity show at the hotel, featuring the aforementioned "Lullaby of Broadway" in a sequence that shows the last day in the life of a "Broadway Baby" before she falls out of a window to her death. The number uses more than 100 dancers, seen from evey possible angle and doing some of the most precise dancing ever put on celluloid.

GOLD OF NAPLES
(L'ORO DI NAPOLI)

1954 74m bw Drama/Comedy ★★★
Ponti/DEG/Gala (Italy) /A

THE RACKETEER: Lianella Carrell (*The Wife*), Toto (*The Husband*), Pasquale Cennamo (*The Racketeer*), PIZZA ON CREDIT: Sophia Loren (*The Wife*), Giacomo Furia (*The Husband*), Alberto Farnese (*The Lover*), Paolo Stoppa (*The Widower*), THE GAMBLER: Vittorio De Sica (*The Count*), Mario Passante (*His Valet*), Irene Montalto (*The Countess*)

p, Dino De Laurentiis, Carlo Ponti; d, Vittorio De Sica; w, Cesare Zavattini, Dino De Sica, Giuseppe Marotta (based on the novel by Marotta); ph, Otello Martelli; ed, Eraldo Da Roma; m, Alessandro Cicognini

By turns melancholy and very witty, in the beloved vignette format of the greatest Italian filmmakers. The stories include (two of the film's six episodes were cut before US release) "The Racketeer," in which pantomimist Toto outwits and undoes a bullying friend who has intruded into his home as a permanent guest. "Pizza on Credit" shows Loren as a cheating wife who loses her wedding ring while trysting with Farnese, which causes husband Furia to become suspicious and necessitates a frantic search for the ring (returned by the lover at the last moment).

De Sica, the director, plays the lead role in "The Gambler," an inveterate gamester who has squandered away every dime his family ever had, but who continues to believe he is a grand sharper. In this, the best of the vignettes, De Sica has a marvelous scene playing cards with the young son of the doorman where he resides, Piero Bilancioni, who wearily wins every hand, cleaning out the old man once again. In "Theresa," Silvana Mangano is an alluring prostitute who marries a mentally unbalanced young man and has to apply her own brand of psychology to straighten out their relationship.

Though the acting is generally above average here, GOLD OF NAPLES is not 14 karat, mostly because of the erratic story lines and the lack of logical transition between vignettes. This film marked one of Loren's earliest appearances. The segment with Loren as the pizza-maker's lusty spouse is very close to the French movie, THE BAKER'S WIFE, but the scene of her walking is as classic as Monroe's in NIAGARA.

GOLDEN BOY

1939 99m bw Sports ★★★★
Columbia (U.S.) /A

Barbara Stanwyck (*Lorna Moon*), Adolphe Menjou (*Tom Moody*), William Holden (*Joe Bonaparte*), Lee J. Cobb (*Mr. Bonaparte*), Joseph Calleia (*Eddie Fuseli*), Sam Levene (*Siggie*), Edward Brophy (*Roxy Lewis*), Beatrice Blinn (*Anna*), William H. Strauss (*Mr. Carp*), Don Beddoe (*Borneo*)

p, William Perlberg; d, Rouben Mamoulian; w, Lewis Meltzer, Daniel Taradash, Sarah Y. Mason, Victor Heerman (based on the play by Clifford Odets); ph, Nicholas Musuraca, Karl Freund; ed, Otto Meyer; m, Victor Young; art d, Lionel Banks; cos, Robert Kalloch

AAN Best Score: Victor Young

Not strictly faithful to Odets, but GOLDEN BOY nonetheless captures his drama's spirit of proletarian angst, propelled by the extraordinary performances of Barbara Stanwyck and William Holden in his first major role.

Joe Bonaparte (Holden), a gifted violinist, is forced by poverty to enter the ring, where he proves to be a talented boxer even though he seemingly pulls his punches, afraid of damaging his musician's hands and ending the dream for which his immigrant father (Lee J. Cobb) has sacrificed so much. Lorna Moon (Stanwyck), the girlfriend of Joe's manager (Adolphe Menjou), is given the task of persuading Joe to give up his musical aspirations. After falling in love with Lorna and then feeling betrayed by her duplicity, Joe returns to the ring, with tragic results.

The film manages to reveal a silver-lined ending that is far more upbeat than Odets's suicide finale. Just the same, Rouben Mamoulian does a wonderful job of retaining the essential story and basic character, building beautifully upon both through his careful scenes; his direction of the brutal but realistic fight scenes adds much to the film's power. Menjou and Cobb offer excellent support, but this film belongs to Stanwyck and to Holden, the 21-year-old unknown who was chosen for the part over John Garfield who created the role in the original Group Theater production.

GOLDEN COACH, THE
(LE CARROSSE D'OR)

1952 105m c Drama ★★★★
Panaria/Hoche (France/Italy) /U

Anna Magnani (*Camilla*), Odoardo Spadaro (*Don Antonio*), Nada Fiorelli (*Isabella*), Dante (*Harlequin*), Duncan Lamont (*Viceroy*), George Higgins (*Martinez*), Ralph Truman (*Duke of Castro*), Gisella Mathews (*Marquise Altamirano*), Raf de la Torre (*Chief Justice*), Elena Altieri (*Duchess of Castro*)

p, Francesco Alliata; d, Jean Renoir; w, Jean Renoir, Renzo Avanzo, Jack Kirkland, Ginette Doynel, Giulio Macchi (based on the play "La Carrosse du Saint-Sacrement" by Prosper Merimee); ph, Claude Renoir; ed, Mario Serandrei, David Hawkins; m, Antonio Vivaldi; cos, Maria De Matteis

Belatedly hailed as one of the great films about acting; certainly, a stunning visual example of the use of color. Marking Jean Renoir's return to France after his decade in Hollywood and his short period in India filming THE RIVER, THE GOLDEN COACH has often been seen as the key to understanding all the director's work.

Filmed in English at Rome's Cinecitta studios, the film stars Anna Magnani as Camilla, a *commedia dell'arte* performer who, with her ragtag troupe, arrives in Peru to open a new theater. Already pursued by Felipe (Paul Campbell), Camilla captures the hearts of the vain bullfighter Ramon (Riccardo Rioli) and the Viceroy (Duncan Lamont). Swept away by Camilla's charms and attracted to the vulgar manner that is so alien to his aristocratic experience, the Viceroy presents her with his prized golden coach, a beautifully crafted vehicle that had been used solely for royal business. As the drama rolls on and Camilla struggles to differentiate between reality and the stage, all three of her suitors vie for her love—the Viceroy learning to feel "common" emotions; Ramon impressing her with his manliness; and Felipe inviting her to live with him in the wilderness among the "noble savages."

Opening and closing with a stage curtain, THE GOLDEN COACH is Jean Renoir's invitation to sit back and enjoy the colorful, romantic, humorous spectacle that is real life. While artists have often addressed the confusion of reality and fiction, few have done it with as much grace and love as Renoir. Much of the film's success, however, is due to the brilliant Magnani. THE GOLDEN COACH does not so much star Magnani as it exists because of her. It is her film and everything in it thrives because of the life she breathes into it.

GOLDEN VOYAGE OF SINBAD, THE

1973 105m c Fantasy/Adventure ★★★½
Columbia (U.K.) G/U

John Phillip Law (*Sinbad*), Caroline Munro (*Margiana*), Tom Baker (*Koura*), Douglas Wilmer (*Vizier*), Martin Shaw (*Rachid*), Gregoire Aslan (*Hakim*), Kurt Christian (*Haroun*), Takis Emmanuel (*Achmed*), John David Garfield (*Abdul*), Aldo Sambrell (*Omar*)

p, Charles H. Schneer, Ray Harryhausen; d, Gordon Hessler; w, Brian Clemens; ph, Ted Moore; ed, Roy Watts; m, Miklos Rozsa; prod d, John Stoll; art d, Fernando Gonzalez; fx, Ray Harryhausen

This sequel to the terrific THE SEVENTH VOYAGE OF SINBAD, is great fun—with a minimum of plot and a maximum of wonderful Ray Harryhausen special effects. John Phillip Law is the famed sailor here, in search of a gold tablet that will restore a deposed ruler (Douglas Wilmer) to the throne. En route Sinbad encounters a one-eyed centaur, a winged griffin, a six-armed statue and a host of other fantastic creatures. Fast-paced and exciting, the film features some of Harryhausen's best stop-motion animation work. Tom (television's "Dr. Who") Baker makes a marvelous villain. The surprising box-office success of THE GOLDEN VOYAGE OF SINBAD led to yet another sequel, the relatively disappointing SINBAD AND THE EYE OF THE TIGER.

GOLDENEYE

1995 130m c Action/Spy/Thriller ★★★
Eon Productions Ltd./Danjaq Inc./United Artists (U.S.) PG-13/12

Pierce Brosnan (*James Bond*), Sean Bean (*Alec Trevelyan*), Izabella Scorupco (*Natalya Simonova*), Famke Janssen (*Xenia Onatopp*), Joe Don Baker (*Jack Wade*), Judi Dench (*M*), Robbie Coltrane (*Valentin Zukovsky*), Tcheky Karyo (*Dmitiri Mishkin*), Gottfried John (*General Ourumov*), Alan Cumming (*Boris Grishenko*)

p, Michael G. Wilson, Barbara Broccoli; d, Martin Campbell; w, Jeffrey Caine, Bruce Feirstein (from a story by Michael France, based on characters created by Ian Fleming); ph, Phil Meheux; ed, Terry Rawlings; m, Eric Serra; prod d, Peter Lamont; art d, Neil Lamont; fx, Chris Corbould, Mara Bryan, Derek Meddings; cos, Lindy Hemming

By 1995, had the longest-running franchise in film history finally run its course, done in by changing politics, sexual mores, and audience tastes? In a word, no. GOLDENEYE, starring Pierce Brosnan as Bond No. 5, should appeal equally to die-hard Bond fans and bonded DIE HARD fans.

The plot is along the usual lines, involving a Russian satellite, code-named GoldenEye, that comes under the control of supervillains Alec Trevelyan (Sean Bean) and General Ourumov (Gottfried John). GoldenEye has the power to destroy anything containing an electrical circuit, up to and including an entire city, and the villains plan to decimate London while also making themselves super-rich.

Lean, dark and graceful, Brosnan wraps his perfectly calculated accent around all the standard phrases without making us hear quotation marks. He's a worthy Bond, glib and convincingly athletic, and ought to last a good half-dozen films before his waist thickens and his solid good looks begin to slide. And although GOLDENEYE is the first Bond film that owes nothing to Ian Fleming but 007 himself, that's no particular drawback. The Bond movies, particularly the later ones, were less about plot than trappings: cool gear, perverted bad guys, gorgeous girls and exotic locations. The writers get the mix just about right, and first-time Bond director Martin Campbell moves things along fairly briskly.

More importantly, let's talk about girls, beginning with the new M, Judi Dench. She plays M as a steely schoolmarm who coolly tells her underlings that if she wants sarcasm, she'll talk to her children. Famke Janssen, as the ultravixenish Xenia Onatopp, is all wide, devouring mouth and rolling eyes: that she kills men by scissoring them between her thighs strikes at least some of them as a reasonable exchange.

GOLDFINGER

1964 112m c Spy/Adventure   ★★★★½
UA (U.K.)   /PG

Sean Connery *(James Bond)*, Gert Frobe *(Goldfinger)*, Honor Blackman *(Pussy Galore)*, Shirley Eaton *(Jill Masterson)*, Tania Mallett *(Tilly Masterson)*, Harold Sakata *(Oddjob)*, Bernard Lee *("M")*, Martin Benson *(Solo)*, Cec Linder *(Felix Leiter)*, Lois Maxwell *(Moneypenny)*

p, Harry Saltzman, Albert R. Broccoli; d, Guy Hamilton; w, Richard Maibaum, Paul Dehn (based on the novel by Ian Fleming); ph, Ted Moore; ed, Peter Hunt; m, John Barry; prod d, Ken Adam; art d, Peter Murton; fx, John Stears

AA Best Sound Effects Editing: Norman Wanstall

Probably the best of the gadget-filled 007 extravaganzas, GOLDFINGER represents the consolidation of the wildly profitable Bond formula. For the first time, the well-loved conventions of the series are all in place, and they jell perfectly—perhaps for the last time.

This third Bond movie pits the hero (Sean Connery) against one of his more memorable adversaries, Goldfinger (Gert Frobe), a gold-hoarding, power-hungry maniac who plans to detonate a small atomic device inside Fort Knox, contaminating its huge gold supply with deadly radiation and making him the richest man in the world. Bond's attempts to foil Goldfinger's plans take him from Miami to Europe to Kentucky and force him to confront Goldfinger's hare-lipped Korean assistant, Oddjob (Harold Sakata), who kills his victims with a razor-edged bowler hat. Bond also battles and eventually woos martial arts expert and pilot Pussy Galore (Honor Blackman, who abandoned her spot on the highly successful television series "The Avengers" for this role).

GOLDFINGER contains more crowd-pleasing moments than any other Bond film, including Oddjob's flying bowler, a laser beam that almost emasculates Bond, the lavishly accessorized Aston Martin DB5, and the bizarre murder of Goldfinger's secretary (Shirley Eaton): she's gilded to death. It also features Shirley Bassey's terrific rendition of the Leslie Bricusse-Anthony Newley title song. Much credit is due director Guy Hamilton, who was able to juggle all the gadgets, wild characters, and strange locations long enough to produce a perfectly balanced, entertaining film that stands on its own. Later Bond films were to rely too heavily on campy one-liners, expensive sets, and gimmicky effects.

GONE WITH THE WIND

1939 220m c Drama/Historical/Romance   ★★★★★
Selznick (U.S.)   /PG

Clark Gable *(Rhett Butler)*, Vivien Leigh *(Scarlett O'Hara)*, Hattie McDaniel *(Mammy)*, Leslie Howard *(Ashley Wilkes)*, Olivia De Havilland *(Melanie Hamilton)*, Butterfly McQueen *(Prissy)*, Everett Brown *(Big Sam)*, Zack Williams *(Elijah)*, Oscar Polk *(Pork)*, Thomas Mitchell *(Gerald O'Hara)*

p, David O. Selznick; d, Victor Fleming, George Cukor, Sam Wood; w, Sidney Howard, Jo Swerling, Charles MacArthur, Ben Hecht, John Lee Mahin, John Van Druten, Oliver H.P. Garrett, Winston Miller, John Balderston, Michael Foster, Edwin Justus Mayer, F. Scott Fitzgerald, David O. Selznick (based on the novel by Margaret Mitchell); ph, Ernest Haller, Ray Rennahan, Lee Garmes; ed, Hal C. Kern, James E. Newcom; m, Max Steiner; prod d, William Cameron Menzies; art d, Lyle Wheeler, Hobe Erwin; fx, Jack Cosgrove, Lee Zavitz, Arthur Johns, Fred Albin; chor, Frank Floyd, Eddie Prinz; cos, Walter Plunkett

AA Best Picture; AAN Best Actor: Clark Gable; *AA Best Actress:* Vivien Leigh; *AA Best Supporting Actress:* Hattie McDaniel; *AAN Best Supporting Actress:* Olivia De Havilland; *AA Best Director:* Victor Fleming; *AA Best Screenplay:* Sidney Howard; *AA Best Cinematography:* Ernest Haller, Ray Rennahan; *AA Best Editing:* Hal C. Kern,

James E. Newcom; *AAN Best Score:* Max Steiner; *AA Best Art Direction:* Lyle Wheeler; *AAN Best Sound:* Thomas T. Moulton; *AAN Best Visual Effects:* John R. Cosgrove, Fred Albin, Arthur Johns

The best remembered and most publicized film in Hollywood's flamboyant history, the biggest of David O. Selznick's grand obsessions, and quite probably the most beloved movie of all time.

This star-studded Civil War epic, based on Margaret Mitchell's immensely popular novel, is nearly as powerful and moving today as when first released in 1939. Beneath the surface of a lavish and sometimes awe-inspiring production lies a deftly handled story about an endlessly fascinating—if not always attractive—heroine. Though she's frequently dismissed as a simpering Southern belle, Scarlett O'Hara (Vivien Leigh) is a resilient, resourceful protagonist, equal to acts of real heroism but incapable of cliched nobility. And for many of us, there's a lesson in her story—that buying into romantic obsession almost certainly guarantees that we'll end up with the last person we need.

Leigh won the the most coveted role in film history from a field that included Paulette Goddard, Norma Shearer, Bette Davis, Joan Crawford, Miriam Hopkins, Jean Harlow, Carole Lombard, Tallulah Bankhead, Claudette Colbert, Jean Arthur, Joan Bennett, and Irene Dunne, among some 2,000 women tested in a much-ballyhooed two-year talent search. She's nothing short of perfection. As Rhett Butler, co-star Clark Gable likewise couldn't be bettered. The only player among the majors who disappoints is Leslie Howard—he just isn't handsome or vigorous enough to motivate so much of Scarlett's energy. Supporting performances are generally of a high order, though McDaniel's heart-tugging Mammy and Ona Munson's bittersweet trollop are rather cloying. If Butterfly McQueen's character is an alarming stereotype, her perfectly modulated comic hysteria is brilliantly entertaining; the actress can hardly be faulted for doing her best in the context of the film's essentially racist discourse.

From a directorial standpoint, the sequences shot by "women's director" George Cukor are the best. His style is more lyrical, and more attentive to the literary qualities of the source material, than that of Victor Fleming. Nowhere is this more evident than the barbecue at Twelve Oaks and the announcement of war—possibly the best sequence in the piece. Later, GWTW under Fleming seems to settle into itself and just tell the story. Despite some excellent sequences—Scarlett's attempt to get Dr. Meade to leave the railroad station springs immediately to mind—many of the film's purely narrative sequences verge on the mundane. Cukor began at the film's helm but was replaced by Fleming (whose WIZARD OF OZ was also released in 1939), reportedly because the former had shifted the focus of the film too much to Scarlett and Melanie (to say nothing of leading man Gable's open disdain for Cukor). During the course of the production Fleming suffered a nervous breakdown and Sam Wood stepped in until Fleming was well enough to return.

Although its "historical" set-pieces (e.g., the burning of Atlanta) are brilliantly realized, GWTW should not be mistaken for history—it romanticizes the slave-owning south and caricatures Reconstruction. Still, it's the peak example of the collaborative artistic achievement for which Hollywood's Golden Age is justly celebrated. To quote Olivia De Havilland, "Everytime I see it, I find something fresh, some shade of meaning I hadn't noticed before. . . How fortunate that so many gifted people found immortality in GONE WITH THE WIND."

GOOD EARTH, THE

1937 138m bw Drama   ★★★★★
MGM (U.S.)   /A

Paul Muni *(Wang Lung)*, Luise Rainer *(O-Lan)*, Walter Connolly *(Uncle)*, Tilly Losch *(Lotus)*, Charley Grapewin *(Old Father)*, Jessie Ralph *(Cuckoo)*, Soo Yong *(Aunt)*, Keye Luke *(Elder Son)*, Roland Got *(Younger Son)*, Ching Wah Lee *(Ching)*

p, Irving Thalberg, Albert Lewin; d, Sidney Franklin; w, Talbot Jennings, Tess Slesinger, Frances Marion (uncredited), Claudine West (based on the novel by Pearl S. Buck); ph, Karl Freund; ed, Basil Wrangell; m, Herbert Stothart; art d, Cedric Gibbons, Harry Oliver, Arnold Gillespie; cos, Dolly Tree

AAN Best Picture; AA Best Actress: Luise Rainer; *AAN Best Director:* Sidney Franklin; *AA Best Cinematography:* Karl Freund; *AAN Best Editing:* Basil Wrangell

Classic melodrama. Muni, in a powerful role—another marvelous offbeat characterization—is a simple rice farmer who weds Rainer, a kitchen slave, in an arranged marriage. Through incredible labor, Muni and Rainer make their little farm into a success, allowing Muni to buy many more rice fields and to prosper. They produce three children, and all seems promising until severe drought turns the land into an unyielding crust. When famine sets in, the family begins to starve, forcing Rainer to feed her children cooked earth. Through a stroke of Rainer's good luck, the family's fortunes are turned around, but their lives are ruined by Muni's greed. Too late, the stoic Muni learns the magnificent qualities of his loving wife.

Rainer is overwhelming as the self-sacrificing O-lan and deservedly won an Oscar for Best Actress, beating out Greta Garbo in CAMILLE and accomplishing the seemingly impossible task of winning back-to-back statuettes, having received the same award the previous year for THE GREAT ZEIGFELD.

This superlative adaptation of the Pulitzer Prize-winning Pearl Buck novel was three years in the making; it was Thalberg's last production, which he personally oversaw. He had never taken a film credit and died before THE GOOD EARTH was completed; to honor this young, driving force, who was responsible for a string of majestic films, Mayer had the following inserted in the credits of THE GOOD EARTH: "To the memory of Irving Grant Thalberg we dedicate this picture, his last great achievement."

Thalberg sent George Hill, a talented but alcoholic director, to China to get background footage and gather important props. Hill's wife, Frances Marion, went along to do research since she was originally slated to write the screenplay. Hill and Marion returned with more than two million feet of background footage, some of which was used in the released film. Victor Fleming, who replaced Hill, grew ill during production and had to be hospitalized. (The same thing happened to Fleming when he was at work on GONE WITH THE WIND three years later.) With costs mounting, Thalberg brought in Sidney Franklin to replace Fleming.

There are several great sequences in THE GOOD EARTH, not the least of which are the terrifying mob scenes in which the palace is ransacked. The most astounding scene, however, is the invasion of the locusts. Hundreds of extras, Muni, Rainer, and family in the lead, took to the jeopardized fields to combat the pests which blackened the sky, frantically digging fire lanes, disorienting the insects by banging gongs, then beating them with shovels, feet, and hands. Every known photographic gimmick up to that time was employed in the locust invasion scene. The Chinese location footage was used as a backdrop, closeups of the locusts on a miniature soundstage were intercut, and special effects paintings were inserted on the film to produce a startling montage of the menace.

GOOD MORNING, VIETNAM

1987 119m c Comedy/Drama/War ★★★½
Touchstone/Silver Partners III (U.S.) R/15

Robin Williams *(Adrian Cronauer)*, Forest Whitaker *(Edward Garlick)*, Tung Thanh Tran *(Tuan)*, Chintara Sukapatana *(Trinh)*, Bruno Kirby *(Lt. Steven Hauk)*, Robert Wuhl *(Marty Lee Dreiwitz)*, J.T. Walsh *(Sgt. Major Dickerson)*, Noble Willingham *(Gen. Taylor)*, Richard Edson *(Pvt. Abersold)*, Juney Smith *(Phil McPherson, Radio Engineer)*

p, Mark Johnson, Larry Brezner, Ben Moses, Harry Benn; d, Barry Levinson; w, Mitch Markowitz; ph, Peter Sova; ed, Stu Linder; m, Alex North; prod d, Roy Walker; art d, Steve Spence; fx, Fred Cramer; cos, Keith Denny

AAN Best Actor: Robin Williams

Robin Williams was finally given a showcase for his extraordinary improvisational skills in this, the first comedy set in Vietnam.

Based on the story of real-life Armed Forces Radio disc jockey Adrian Cronauer, GOOD MORNING, VIETNAM begins in 1965, as Cronauer (Williams) arrives in Saigon, imported because his comedic broadcasts have proven a huge morale-booster elsewhere. At the AFR's Saigon station, Cronauer incurs the wrath of superiors who resent his intrusion in their programming, with its dull announcers, health and safety tips, censored news, and geriatric playlist. Cronauer changes all that, knocking listening troops out of their stupor with his howling salutation—"Goooood morning, Vietnammmm!"—hip song selection, and comedic improvisation, poking wild fun at any and all sacred cows.

GOOD MORNING, VIETNAM stumbles whenever Williams isn't behind the mike, placing him in melodramatic, hackneyed situations that become increasingly predictable and preposterous, and director Barry Levinson's seemingly endless reaction shots of listeners grooving to the DJ's antics become irritating. Levinson manages, however, to be one of the few filmmakers to show the Vietnamese as complex, cultured people, rather than as helpless victims or the faceless enemy.

Forrest Whitaker (BIRD) does wonders with his thankless role as Cronauer's loyal aide, Sukapatana—as Williams's Vietnamese love interest—is impressive, and Bruno Kirby, as Cronauer's nemesis, comes as close as any actor could to walking off with a film dominated by Williams at his best.

GOOD, THE BAD, AND THE UGLY, THE
(IL BUONO, IL BRUTTO, IL CATTIVO)

1966 161m c Western ★★★★
Europee (Italy/Spain) R/18

Clint Eastwood *(Joe)*, Eli Wallach *(Tuco)*, Lee Van Cleef *(Setenza)*, Aldo Giuffre, Chelo Alonso, Mario Brega, Luigi Pistilli, Rada Rassimov, Enzo Petito, Claudio Scarchilli

p, Alberto Grimaldi; d, Sergio Leone; w, Luciano Vincenzoni, Sergio Leone (based on a story by Agenore Incrocci, Furio Scarpelli, Vincenzoni, and Leone); ph, Tonino Delli Colli; ed, Nino Baragli, Eugenio Alabiso; m, Ennio Morricone; art d, Carlo Simi; fx, Eros Bacciucchi; cos, Carlo Simi

The definitive spaghetti western. Director Sergio Leone's epic end to the Clint Eastwood "Dollars" trilogy is a stunning, panoramic view of the West during the Civil War. THE GOOD, THE BAD, AND THE UGLY is a deceptively simple story detailing the efforts of three drifters, the "Good" (Eastwood), the "Bad" (Lee Van Cleef), and the "Ugly" (Eli Wallach), to find a fortune hidden in the unmarked grave of a man named Bill Carson.

Leone's narrative structure is incredibly complex: the characters' paths intersect and intertwine repeatedly until the Civil War impinges upon their lives and dwarfs their petty crimes. The war eventually involves Eastwood and Wallach in a massive battle for an unimportant bridge in which hundreds of soldiers march to pointless doom. The scale of violence shocks these two violent men; Eastwood, whose character begins to show a humanity only hinted at in the previous two films, states that he has never "seen so many men wasted so badly."

This is Leone's most violent film, but also one of his most compassionate. One of its most memorable scenes shows the Union troops organizing an orchestra of Confederate prisoner-musicians to play in order to cover the noise as Van Cleef tortures his prisoners. The effect is haunting, and recalls stories of similar incidents in Nazi death camps. A touching moment occurs when Eastwood comes across a dying young soldier, covers the shivering man with his duster, and helps him smoke his final cigarette.

Though not up to the standards of Leone's masterpiece ONCE UPON A TIME IN THE WEST, in which the director synthesizes scale, narrative, casting, and style, THE GOOD, THE BAD, AND THE UGLY is a massive, many-faceted film that continues to hold up, viewing after viewing. It also features one of Ennio Morricone's finest scores.

GOODBYE GIRL, THE

1977 110m c Romance/Comedy ★★★★
MGM (U.S.) PG

Richard Dreyfuss *(Elliott Garfield)*, Marsha Mason *(Paula McFadden)*, Quinn Cummings *(Lucy McFadden)*, Paul Benedict *(Mark Morgenweiss)*, Barbara Rhoades *(Donna Douglas)*, Theresa Merritt *(Mrs. Crosby)*, Michael Shawn *(Ronnie)*, Patricia Pearcy *(Rhonda Fontana)*, Gene Castle *(Assistant Choreographer)*, Daniel Levans *(Dance Instructor)* p, Ray Stark; d, Herbert Ross; w, Neil Simon; ph, David M. Walsh; ed, John F. Burnett; m, Dave Grusin; prod d, Albert Brenner; fx, Al Griswold; cos, Ann Roth

AAN Best Picture; AA Best Actor: Richard Dreyfuss; AAN Best Actress: Marsha Mason; AAN Best Supporting Actress: Quinn Cummings; AAN Best Original Screenplay: Neil Simon

A rarity for Neil Simon's screen efforts, THE GOODBYE GIRL perfectly blends humor, sentiment, and romance on a level so pleasant it's almost suspicious.

Mason is a divorced ex-Broadway dancer in her thirties living with her precocious daughter in an apartment suddenly subleased by aspiring actor Dreyfuss, who arrives to take possession in the middle of the night. This is shocking news to Mason who thus learns that her departed lover, also an actor, has not only made her and daughter Cummings homeless but also has jilted her without notice. Dreyfuss makes it easy on Mason by offering to share the apartment, provided she pays half the rent. She agrees out of desperation, and the two strike up an uneasy truce that gradually blossoms into love.

This is a superb lighthearted comedy deftly directed by Ross, who helmed such hits as PLAY IT AGAIN, SAM and THE TURNING POINT. Mason is wonderfully warm and sensitive in a precarious role, while Dreyfuss, in a trademark performance, is nothing short of sensational. Cummings is a charming little girl whose premature sophistication provides some good humor. Next to THE SUNSHINE BOYS, this may be Simon's best original screenplay.

GOODBYE MR. CHIPS

1939 114m bw Drama   ★★★★½
MGM (U.K.)   /PG

Robert Donat *(Charles Chipping)*, Greer Garson *(Katherine Ellis)*, Terry Kilburn *(John/Peter Colley)*, John Mills *(Peter Colley as a young man)*, Paul Henreid *(Max Staefel)*, Judith Furse *(Flora)*, Lyn Harding *(Dr. Wetherby)*, Milton Rosmer *(Charteris)*, Frederick Leister *(Marsham)*, Louise Hampton *(Mrs. Wickett)*

p, Victor Saville; d, Sam Wood; w, R.C. Sherriff, Claudine West, Eric Maschwitz, Sidney Franklin (based on the novella by James Hilton); ph, Freddie Young; ed, Charles Frend; m, Richard Addinsell; art d, Alfred Junge; cos, Julie Harris

AAN Best Picture; AA Best Actor: Robert Donat; AAN Best Actress: Greer Garson; AAN Best Director: Sam Wood; AAN Best Screenplay: Eric Maschwitz, R.C. Sherriff, Claudine West; AAN Best Editing: Charles Frend; AAN Best Sound: A.W. Watkins

Robert Donat gives a poignant performance in this superlative production as the shy, retiring British schoolteacher who guides several generations of young boys to manhood. Set at Brookfield Boys School in the late 1800s, the film follows the career of Charles Chipping, nicknamed "Mr. Chips," from his first days as an unpopular novice instructor through the marriage that brings him out of his shell to his final years as the school's beloved elder statesman.

So moving was Donat's performance that he beat out the most popular American candidate for the Best Actor Oscar, Clark Gable, who was nominated for his work in GONE WITH THE WIND. Greer Garson, as Mrs. Chips, also shines in the film that introduced her to American audiences. The screenplay is bright and the direction gentle, but it is Donat who elevates this bittersweet, affectionate tribute. (The great James Hilton wrote the original story as a novella in four days to meet a 1934 magazine deadline.) Skip the 1969 musical remake starring Peter O'Toole; despite his rightness in the role, he can't salvage a lumbering horror show.

GOODFELLAS

1990 148m c Crime/Drama   ★★★★
Irwin Winkler (U.S.)   R/18

Robert De Niro *(James Conway)*, Ray Liotta *(Henry Hill)*, Joe Pesci *(Tommy DeVito)*, Lorraine Bracco *(Karen Hill)*, Paul Sorvino *(Paul Cicero)*, Frank Sivero *(Frankie Carbone)*, Tony Darrow *(Sonny Bunz)*, Mike Starr *(Frenchy)*, Frank Vincent *(Billy Batts)*, Chuck Low *(Morris Kessler)*

p, Irwin Winkler; d, Martin Scorsese; w, Nicholas Pileggi, Martin Scorsese (based on the book *Wiseguy* by Pileggi); ph, Michael Ballhaus; ed, Thelma Schoonmaker; prod d, Kristi Zea; art d, Maher Ahmad; fx, Connie Brink; cos, Susan O'Donnell, Thomas Lee Keller

AAN Best Picture; AA Best Supporting Actor: Joe Pesci; AAN Best Supporting Actress: Lorraine Bracco; AAN Best Director: Martin Scorsese; AAN Best Adapted Screenplay: Nicholas Pileggi, Martin Scorsese; AAN Best Editing: Thelma Schoonmaker

Based on journalist Nicholas Pileggi's nonfiction book *Wiseguy*, GOODFELLAS revolves around the career of low-level gangster Henry Hill (Ray Liotta), who became part of the federal witness protection program after testifying against his erstwhile partners in crime. At the center of the book is Hill's insider account of the $6 million robbery of a Lufthansa cargo facility at New York's Idlewild Airport. Scorsese doesn't show the heist itself; instead, he focuses on its bloody aftermath, in which all the participants are brutally murdered by Henry's partners, the lethally paranoid Jimmy Conway (Robert De Niro) and the psychotic Tommy De Vito (Joe Pesci).

Generally, GOODFELLAS is concerned with Tommy and Jimmy's climb up the mob ladder and its effects on Henry, but Scorsese's rich tapestry is both broader in scope and more detailed than a mere recounting of the events in the trio's life of crime. Because Scorsese is equally concerned with the minutiae of his main characters' world and with the grand design that appears to underlie that world, the downfall of Henry and his associates seems fated.

Many of the seemingly peripheral subplots are showstoppers. Focusing on the one-woman war Henry's wife Karen (wonderfully played by Lorraine Bracco) fights against his mistress, Scorsese casts Henry's homelife as a raucous parody of the domineering husbands and quiet wives of THE GODFATHER.

Karen, so fiercely self-possessed early in the film, is cowed and exhausted by the movie's hellish climax, during which Henry has gone from a trim mob dandy to a coked-up, misshapen mess. His subsequent arrest and induction into the witness protection program leads to the film's final, and most disturbing image—a suburbanized Henry appearing at the front door of his new tract home to bring in the morning paper.

GORILLAS IN THE MIST

1988 129m c Biography   ★★★
Peters/Arnold Glimcher/Guber (U.S.)   PG-13/15

Sigourney Weaver *(Dian Fossey)*, Bryan Brown *(Bob Campbell)*, Julie Harris *(Roz Carr)*, John Omirah Miluwi *(Sembagare)*, Iain Cuthbertson *(Dr. Louis Leakey)*, Constantin Alexandrov *(Van Vecten)*, Waigwa Wachira *(Mukara)*, Iain Glenn *(Brendan)*, David Lansbury *(Larry)*, Maggie O'Neill *(Kim)*

p, Arnold Glimcher, Terence Clegg, Robert Nixon, Judy Kessler; d, Michael Apted; w, Anna Hamilton Phelan (based on the story by Harold T.P. Hayes); ph, John Seale, Alan Root; ed, Stuart Baird; m, Maurice Jarre; prod d, John Graysmark; fx, Rick Baker, David Harris; cos, Catherine Leterrier

AAN Best Actress: Sigourney Weaver; AAN Best Adapted Screenplay: Anna Hamilton Phelan (screenplay), Tab Murphy (story); AAN Best Editing: Stuart Baird; AAN Best Score: Maurice Jarre; AAN Best Sound: Andy Nelson, Brian Saunders, Peter Handford

Well-done monkey business, but an abrupt, uncentered screenplay, cluttered by unfocused direction, poor music and obligatory romance.

During the 1970s, Dian Fossey journeyed to Africa, where she closely studied the mountain gorilla, work later chronicled in a popular *National Geographic* television special. In this biopic Weaver portrays the late, controversial Fossey, beginning with her 1963 meeting with anthropologist Louis Leakey (Cuthbertson). He agrees to let her accompany him to Africa, and that begins her lifelong commitment to the study of gorillas. The film shows how this passion gains her fame but also leads to her fatal obsession with protecting her subjects as she grows increasingly irrational in dealing with those she feels pose a threat to the gorillas.

Although the film offers no real insights into Fossey's courage and obsessions, Weaver has some riveting moments. But because the screenplay doesn't penetrate the gradual shift Fossey made from animal activist to crank, she's forced to dredge it up from nowhere. There's terrific footage of the gorillas and the African setting is stunning. But the real star is Baker, who created the gorilla costumes donned by human beings for many scenes. His work is so well done that it is impossible to tell the real gorillas from the guys in the suits.

GORKY PARK

1983 103m c Mystery ★★★
Orion (U.S.) R/15

William Hurt (Arkady Renko), Lee Marvin (Jack Osborne), Brian Dennehy (William Kirwill), Ian Bannen (Iamskoy), Joanna Pacula (Irina), Michael Elphick (Pasha), Richard Griffiths (Anton), Rikki Fulton (Pribluda), Alexander Knox (General), Alexei Sayle (Golodkin)

p, Gene Kirkwood, Howard W. Koch Jr.; d, Michael Apted; w, Dennis Potter (based on the novel by Martin Cruz Smith); ph, Ralf D. Bode; ed, Dennis Virkler; m, James Horner; prod d, Paul Sylbert; cos, Richard Bruno

Uneven but sometimes fascinating murder mystery. Three bodies are found in Moscow's Gorky Park, stripped of their faces and fingertips, making identification nearly impossible. William Hurt, in a highly polished performance, plays the Moscow police inspector assigned to the case. His trail leads to an American fur trader (Lee Marvin) who has all of Moscow at his disposal. A young dissident (Joanna Pacula), who was a friend of one of the victims, also gets caught in the intrigue. Though a little confusing at times, this mystery, based on the Martin Cruz Smith bestseller, has some great twists and gives a harshly realistic picture of the average man's life behind the Iron Curtain. GORKY suffers from the miscasting of Marvin, an unrealistic romance and, most unfortunately, a plodding climax. It was filmed in Helsinki, since the Soviets refused permission to shoot in Moscow.

GOSPEL ACCORDING TO ST. MATTHEW, THE
(IL VANGELO SECONDO MATTEO)

1964 136m bw Religious ★★★★
L'Arco/C.C.F. Lux (France/Italy) /U

Enrique Irazoqui (Jesus Christ), Margherita Caruso (Mary, as a Girl), Susanna Pasolini (Mary, as a Woman), Marcello Morante (Joseph), Mario Socrate (John the Baptist), Settimo Di Porto (Peter), Otello Sestili (Judas), Ferruccio Nuzzo (Matthew), Giacomo Morante (John), Alfonso Gatto (Andrew)

p, Alfredo Bini; d, Pier Paolo Pasolini; w, Pier Paolo Pasolini (based on the gospel according to Saint Matthew); ph, Tonino Delli Colli; ed, Nino Baragli; m, Luis Bacalov, Johann Sebastian Bach, Wolfgang Amadeus Mozart, Sergei Prokofiev, Anton Webern; art d, Luigi Scaccianoce; fx, Ettore Catallucci; cos, Danilo Donati

Unconventional and very moving. Pier Paolo Pasolini's epic film, a Special Jury Prize-winner at the Venice Film Festival, tells the life story of Jesus in a semi-documentary style using nonprofessional actors, including the director's mother as the Virgin Mary. Hailed by many as the greatest adaptation of the life of Christ, this picture was dedicated to Pope John XXIII, who brought the Catholic Church into the 20th century. It may come as a surprise to those who see this film that Pasolini was not only an atheist, but a homosexual and Marxist as well. As if to underline the unorthodox nature of the film, Pasolini has included on his soundtrack the American spiritual "Sometimes I Feel Like a Motherless Child," sung by Odetta.

GRADUATE, THE

1967 105m c Drama/Comedy ★★★★½
Lawrence Turman/Embassy (U.S.) /15

Anne Bancroft (Mrs. Robinson), Dustin Hoffman (Ben Braddock), Katharine Ross (Elaine Robinson), William Daniels (Mr. Braddock), Murray Hamilton (Mr. Robinson), Elizabeth Wilson (Mrs. Braddock), Brian Avery (Carl Smith), Walter Brooke (Mr. Maguire), Norman Fell (Mr. McCleery), Elisabeth Fraser (Lady)

p, Lawrence Turman; d, Mike Nichols; w, Calder Willingham, Buck Henry (based on the novel by Charles Webb); ph, Robert Surtees; ed, Sam O'Steen; m, Dave Grusin; prod d, Richard Sylbert; cos, Patricia Zipprodt

AAN Best Picture; AAN Best Actor: Dustin Hoffman; AAN Best Actress: Anne Bancroft; AAN Best Supporting Actress: Katharine Ross; AA Best Director: Mike Nichols; AAN Best Adapted Screenplay: Calder Willingham, Buck Henry; AAN Best Cinematography: Robert Surtees

A social force of cinema that influenced the generation gap, THE GRADUATE was a tour de force for newcomer Hoffman and made him an overnight sensation.

Hoffman plays Ben Braddock, a pensive and somewhat shy youth of wealthy Southern California suburbia. Upon completion of his college studies, he's pressured by family and friends to "get going" with his life, encouraged at every turn to find a job, marry, and become a clone of his parents. Bancroft seduces Hoffman who cannot believe the older, married woman—she and her husband Hamilton are his parents' best friends—is pursuing him. Hoffman falls in love with her daughter Ross, and is put in the exhausting position of maintaining relationships with mother and daughter. He finally decides that Ross will be his wife, although Bancroft is wholly opposed to the union.

This comedy is wonderfully crafted by director Nichols who presents a half-dozen hilarious scenes, including Hoffman escaping badgering advice by submerging himself in the family pool in scuba gear and Bancroft's sudden shift from respectable matron to predatory tease, hiking her skirts lasciviously and purring promises of smoldering sex which almost put Hoffman into a comatose state. Nichols was to declare: "I think Benjamin and Elaine will end up exactly like their parents; that's what I was trying to say in the last scene." Yet the well-to-do younger audiences of the day interpreted this sequence of blatant heroics as a wonderful act of defiance by two young people whose destinies were being manipulated by their parents.

The film was an enormous hit, turning Nichols, who'd already scored heavily with WHO'S AFRAID OF VIRGINIA WOOLF?, into one of Hollywood's most important directors. However much of the credit for the innovative and fluid graphics in the film must go to cameraman Surtees, who was allowed a free hand to experiment widely. For example, the telescopic shot of Hoffman running to prevent the wedding causes him to appear not to be getting anywhere, almost as if he is running in place. All in all, THE GRADUATE is a flawlessly acted and produced film. Look fast for Richard Dreyfuss in his film debut as a college student.

GRAND CANYON

1991 134m c Drama ★★★½
Fox (U.S.) R/15

Danny Glover (Simon), Kevin Kline (Mack), Steve Martin (Davis), Mary McDonnell (Claire), Mary-Louise Parker (Dee), Alfre Woodard (Jane), Jeremy Sisto (Roberto), Tina Lifford (Deborah), Patrick Malone (Otis), Randle Mell (The Alley Baron)

p, Lawrence Kasdan, Charles Okun, Michael Grillo; d, Lawrence Kasdan; w, Lawrence Kasdan, Meg Kasdan; ph, Owen Roizman; ed, Carol Littleton; m, James Newton Howard; prod d, Bo Welch; art d, Tom Duffield; fx, Burt Dalton; cos, Aggie Guerard Rodgers

AAN Best Original Screenplay: Lawrence Kasdan, Meg Kasdan

GRAND CANYON is the cinematic equivalent of Planet Hollywood, the New York nightspot where ordinary people can supposedly rub shoulders with the rich and famous. In Lawrence Kasdan's movie, co-written by his wife Meg, big, dramatic events—deaths, shootings, etc.—take place alongside mundane things like cutting your finger while chopping vegetables or learning how to make a left turn in Los Angeles traffic. The film invites us into the lives of a wide cross-section of people, painting a densely textured portrait of a sprawling, modern city.

Mack (Kevin Kline), a successful immigration attorney, catches an L.A. Lakers game with his best friend Davis (Steve Martin), a self-absorbed, self-righteous film producer who specializes in blood 'n' guts exploitation fare and whose license plates read "GRSS PNTS." As he is driving back from the game, Mack's car konks out on an unlit street somewhere in Inglewood. He manages to call for a tow truck but becomes the target of a gang of hoods who threaten to take his car and maybe his life. Luckily, the tow truck arrives, driven by a man whose composure and quiet authority convince the gang to lay off. An eloquently thankful Mack rides back to the garage with his saviour, Simon (Danny Glover), and the episode marks the beginning of a friendship between the two men.

GRAND CANYON successfully recreates the random, haphazard ways in which individual lives intersect, and captures the sense of menace and disintegration that permeate contemporary urban life. It's much less convincing, though, when it tries to turn its characters into spokespeople. Kline, in particular, gets too many speeches that should be accompanied by a blinking subtitle reading "MESSAGE." Similarly, the Kasdans' attempt to bring the various strands of the story together through the metaphor of the Grand Canyon (it's wide, like the gulfs between different sections of society, but it can also bring us together in awe of its size and beauty) is unconvincing.

GRAND HOTEL

1932 115m bw Drama ★★★★★
MGM (U.S.) /U

Greta Garbo *(Grusinskaya)*, John Barrymore *(Baron Felix von Gaigern)*, Joan Crawford *(Flaemmchen)*, Wallace Beery *(General Director Preysing)*, Lionel Barrymore *(Otto Kringelein)*, Jean Hersholt *(Senf)*, Robert McWade *(Meierheim)*, Purnell Pratt *(Zinnowitz)*, Ferdinand Gottschalk *(Pimenov)*, Rafaela Ottiano *(Suzette)*

d, Edmund Goulding; w, William A. Drake (based on Drake's stage adaptation of the novel *Menschen im Hotel* by Vicki Baum); ph, William Daniels; ed, Blanche Sewell; art d, Cedric Gibbons; cos, Adrian

AA Best Picture

Gleaming deco dinosaur, Thalberg's pet, and the most legendary all-star movie ever made; a tribute to all that "stars" and glamour used to be in Hollywood's vanished Golden Age.

This omnibus blockbuster chronicles the interwining lives of the denizens of GRAND HOTEL: Garbo, the lonely ballerina; John Barrymore, the noble thief; Crawford, the ambitious stenographer; Lionel Barrymore, the dying man on a last fling, and Beery, the ruthless industrialist. Lewis Stone and Hersholt exist to supervise and comment upon the others. If DINNER AT EIGHT, made a year later, has held up far better as a picture because it comments upon the rich and famous, HOTEL set the standard of those who don't achieve the twin pinnacles. Don't expect a particularly lucid screenplay or even acting of a high order; this masterpiece is hopelessly dated, directed by Goulding in the grand manner, and supported by Gibbons's, Daniels's, and Adrian's opulent work.

Revival house audiences laugh today at Garbo, with her permanently furrowed brow and her weird little bobby pin that holds back her hair. But striding through the hotel's lobby, swathed in chinchilla, remote in her fabled Swedish melancholy, "acting" hope swirling above a heavy heart, she really is the most extraordinary *monstre sacre* the screen will ever know.

Secondly, there's a surprisingly warm vixen by the name of Joan Crawford, who steals GRAND HOTEL. Even though her face looks like a deco statue's—perhaps the most beautiful eyes and nose ever photographed—she's brimming like a livewire of ambitious current. She's a legend, too—the chorus girl who became a great star. Here she wants top-rung stardom badly, and it shows. Today, with her little black dresses and casual hair, she looks almost modern. Curious that she holds up better than anyone else and only bears a passing resemblance to the bitch goddess people insist on remembering her as. She's marvelously in awe of John Barrymore, and very good indeed reaching out to Lionel. It's a part that exploits Crawford's most likable quality—her loyalty.

John Barrymore is all continental matinee-idol charm. If it seems hammy and somewhat affected today—though Barrymore is never effete—just guffaw through the current Broadway revival to be reminded of the sadness of this vanishing breed. Lionel's performance may be his best—this was before the scenery chewing of later years. But for scenery chewing, Wallace Beery is on hand. He's so thoroughly disagreeable and dense that it somehow works.

GRAND HOTEL remains a classic of its kind. MGM shrewdly marketed this film by withholding its general release for many months after its Hollywood premiere, allowing a tremendous word-of-mouth campaign to heighten expectation from viewers and critics alike. And

the critics cheered, along with the Academy of Motion Picture Arts and Sciences, which voted the film an Oscar for Best Picture. The enormous success of GRAND HOTEL set the stage for many all-star films to come. In 1945, GRAND HOTEL was remade as the lightweight WEEKEND AT THE WALDORF with Ginger Rogers, Lana Turner, Walter Pidgeon, Van Johnson, and Edward Arnold in the lead roles.

GRAND ILLUSION
(LA GRANDE ILLUSION)

1937 95m bw War/Prison ★★★★★
R.A.C. (France) /PG

Jean Gabin *(Marechal)*, Pierre Fresnay *(Capt. de Boeldieu)*, Erich von Stroheim *(Von Rauffenstein)*, Marcel Dalio *(Rosenthal)*, Dita Parlo *(Elsa, Farm Woman)*, Julien Carette *(Cartier)*, Gaston Modot *(Surveyor)*, Georges Peclet *(Soldier)*, Edouard Daste *(Teacher)*, Sylvain Itkine *(Demolder)*

p, Raymond Blondy; d, Jean Renoir; w, Jean Renoir, Charles Spaak; ph, Christian Matras; ed, Marguerite Renoir; m, Joseph Kosma; art d, Eugene Lourie; cos, Decrais

AAN Best Picture

One of the undeniably great films in the history of world cinema, Jean Renoir's GRAND ILLUSION is an eloquent commentary on the borders that divide people, classes, armies and countries.

The film opens during WWI, as Marechal (Jean Gabin) and Boeldieu (Pierre Fresnay) are shot down by German ace Von Rauffenstein (Erich von Stroheim). The two survive the crash and are invited to lunch by Rauffenstein before ground troops arrive to cart the French officers off to a POW camp. Although Marechal and Boeldieu are compatriots, the latter has more in common with Von Rauffenstein, both of them being members of the white-gloved aristocracy. After lunch the Frenchmen are placed in barracks, where French officer Rosenthal (Marcel Dalio), a Jew, befriends them, along with several British officers who have also been taken prisoner. The newcomers join the others in working on an escape tunnel beneath the barracks, but a French victory on the Western Front is a sign that the war is turning against the Germans, and Marechal, Boeldieu, and the rest of the French prisoners are transferred to another prison, where they are reunited with Von Rauffenstein.

Now confined to a neck brace after a combat injury, the Commandant warmly welcomes the Frenchmen, pointing out that his prison, Wintersborn, is escape-proof. He treats his prisoners with great deference, having them to dinner and extending what meager courtesies he can, talking with Boeldieu about how this war will bring to an end the gentlemanly class of officers, dispensing with the honor and dignity of their rank and bloodlines. Caught someplace in between his loyalty to a member of his class (Von Rauffenstein) and to his country, Boeldieu once again agrees to assist his fellow prisoners in their escape attempts.

Directed with patience and care by Renoir, the film was banned in Germany by Nazi Propaganda Minister Josef Goebbels, who labeled it "Cinematographic Enemy No. 1" and compelled his Italian counterpart to have the film banned in that country, although the 1937 Venice Film Festival gave the film a "Best Artistic Ensemble" award. It was thought that all European prints of the film were destroyed by the Nazis, but American troops uncovered a negative in Munich in 1945 (preserved, strangely, by the Germans themselves), leading to the truncated film's reconstruction. Gabin, Fresnay, Dalio, and Stroheim all give impressive performances in this beautifully directed and written film.

GRAND PRIX

1966 179m c Sports ★★½
Douglas & Lewis (U.S.) /A

James Garner *(Pete Aron)*, Eva Marie Saint *(Louise Frederickson)*, Yves Montand *(Jean-Pierre Sarti)*, Toshiro Mifune *(Izo Yamura)*, Brian Bedford *(Scott Stoddard)*, Jessica Walter *(Pat)*, Antonio Sabato *(Nino Barlini)*, Francoise Hardy *(Lisa)*, Adolfo Celi *(Agostini Manetta)*, Claude Dauphin *(Hugo Simon)*

p, Edward Lewis; d, John Frankenheimer; w, Robert Alan Aurthur, William Hanley; ph, Lionel Lindon; ed, Fredric Steinkamp; m, Maurice Jarre; prod d, Richard Sylbert; fx, Milt Rice; cos, Sydney Guilaroff

AA Best Editing: Fredric Steinkamp, Henry Berman, Stewart Linder, Frank Santillo; *AA Best Sound:* Franklin E Milton (Metro-Goldwyn-Mayer Studio Sound Department); *AA Best Sound Effects Editing:* Gordon Daniel

The personal lives and loves of four professional auto racers—played by James Garner, Antonio Sabato, Brian Bedford, and Yves Montand—are mingled with impressively photographed racing footage in this stylistically inventive but narratively tedious effort directed by John Frankenheimer. The film follows the drivers through a number of important European competitions, including Monte Carlo, England's Brand's Hatch, and Italy's Monza, while their off-the-track affairs involve Eva Marie Saint, Jessica Walter, Francoise Hardy, and Toshiro Mifune, who plays Garner's corporate sponsor.

Frankenheimer pulls out all the stops to lend excitement to the racing footage—splitting the screen into ever smaller increments, mounting cameras to the cars to get shots taken inches above the track, and using slow motion—but ultimately his obsession with technique becomes wearying, and the plot is simply not interesting enough to stand on its own.

GRAPES OF WRATH, THE

1940 129m bw Drama ★★★★★
Fox (U.S.) /PG

Henry Fonda *(Tom Joad)*, Jane Darwell *(Ma Joad)*, John Carradine *(Casey)*, Charley Grapewin *(Grandpa Joad)*, Dorris Bowdon *(Rosaharn)*, Russell Simpson *(Pa Joad)*, O.Z. Whitehead *(Al)*, John Qualen *(Muley Graves)*, Eddie Quillan *(Connie Rivers)*, Zeffie Tilbury *(Grandma Joad)*

p, Darryl F. Zanuck; d, John Ford; w, Nunnally Johnson (based on the novel by John Steinbeck); ph, Gregg Toland; ed, Robert Simpson; art d, Richard Day, Mark-Lee Kirk; cos, Gwen Wakeling

AAN Best Picture; *AAN Best Actor:* Henry Fonda; *AA Best Supporting Actress:* Jane Darwell; *AA Best Director:* John Ford; *AAN Best Screenplay:* Nunnally Johnson; *AAN Best Editing:* Robert E. Simpson; *AAN Best Sound:* E.H. Hansen.

THE GRAPES OF WRATH is not only one of John Ford's greatest films, it documents an American social tragedy, giving the victims a voice through art. Based on the classic John Steinbeck novel, the film recounts the painful, poignant odyssey of the Joad family, Steinbeck's Depression-era tenant farmers from Dust Bowl Oklahoma, whose story has come to represent the plight of the "Okies" for generations of readers—and, through Ford's masterpiece, generations of moviegoers too.

As the film opens, Tom (Henry Fonda, in possibly the greatest performance of his career), eldest of the Joad sons, hitchhikes home to the family farm through the desolate Oklahoma landscape, having completed a four-year prison term for manslaughter. After getting a short ride from a suspicious trucker, Tom hoofs it to a clearing where he meets the slightly mad Casey (John Carradine), a former preacher who's "lost the call" and no longer ministers to the spiritual needs of the local farmers. The two walk to the Joad farm but find it abandoned except for Muley (John Qualen), who's even more mentally unbalanced than Casey and is hiding in the house. Muley tells them that sheriff's deputies working for banks and farming combines have been looking for him ever since he knocked one of them unconscious. Muley tells Tom that the Joad family, too, has moved on, the victims of foreclosure. Tom and Casey head for the farm of Tom's Uncle John (Frank Darien), where all the Joads have gathered, preparing to head westward to California in search of jobs advertised in a handbill Pa Joad (Russell Simpson) received. Ma (Jane Darwell) joyously greets her eldest son, and the next morning the whole family piles into a broken-down truck overloaded with their belongings and sets out in search of a better future.

Ford's visualization of Steinbeck's novel is so emotionally gripping that viewers have little time to collect themselves from one powerful scene to the next. Shooting mainly in California in the migrant camps around Pomona, with a second unit filming some backgrounds in Oklahoma, the director framed his shots to show that vast, almost barren landscapes, overcast skies, and bleak exteriors are omnipresent, giving a pervasive sense of the harshness of the displaced Okies' lives.

The sense of doom is dispelled, however, with the film's optimistic turn after the Joads find the government camp and its guardian (Grant Mitchell), a benevolent figure representing security, who, not coincidentally, bears a resemblance to Franklin D. Roosevelt. Though Ford does not hesitate to show the banks and the companies which took advantage of the farmers as land-grabbers without conscience, he also turns the Okies' bleak tale into one of hope by showing the Joads to be more than victims. Physically displaced, but not emotionally or spiritually defeated, they come to embody faith in the future and in the American people, and therein lies the film's greatness.

It took considerable courage to make THE GRAPES OF WRATH at a time when the Hollywood studios, on guard against unionization and attempts to challenge their monopoly, were in no mood to indulge its indictment of capitalism. In 1989, when it was named among the first movies included in the National Film Registry, the picture had lost none of its power as a social document, a historical testimony, or a work of cinematic art.

GREASE

1978 110m c Musical/Comedy ★★½
Paramount (U.S.) PG

John Travolta *(Danny)*, Olivia Newton-John *(Sandy)*, Stockard Channing *(Rizzo)*, Jeff Conaway *(Kenickie)*, Didi Conn *(Frenchy)*, Jamie Donnelly *(Jan)*, Dinah Manoff *(Marty)*, Barry Pearl *(Doody)*, Michael Tucci *(Sonny)*, Kelly Ward *(Putzie)*

p, Robert Stigwood, Allan Carr; d, Randal Kleiser; w, Bronte Woodard, Allan Carr (adapted by Carr from the musical by Jim Jacobs, Warren Casey); ph, Bill Butler; ed, John F. Burnett; prod d, Philip Jefferies; chor, Patricia Birch; cos, Albert Wolsky

AAN Best Song: John Farrar (Music & Lyrics)

Mousse. Disappointing, opportunistic nostalgia dirtied up by 1978's permissive standards and originally thrown up to an audience too young to really identify. Randall Kleiser's flat rendition of the long-running Broadway musical reaped huge rewards at the box office, among the highest grosses ever captured by a film musical. Set in the 1950s at Rydell High, it attempts a nostalgic look at young love, with plot turns not really important—the usual misunderstandings; a satire of teachers; a car race between rivals. At the center of the film are John Travolta as Danny, the ultimate cool dude, and Olivia Newton-John as Sandy, the junior miss who aches to have their summer romance continue into the school year. Channing's the standout, but all of the performers had long since departed high school when the film was made, and there's not enough to enjoy to warrant suspension of belief.

GREAT DICTATOR, THE

1940 127m bw Comedy/War ★★★★½
UA (U.S.) /U

Charles Chaplin *(Hynkel, Dictator of Tomania/A Jewish Barber)*, Paulette Goddard *(Hannah)*, Jack Oakie *(Napaloni, Dictator of Bacteria)*, Reginald Gardiner *(Schultz)*, Henry Daniell *(Garbitsch)*, Billy Gilbert *(Herring)*, Maurice Moscovich *(Mr. Jaeckel)*, Emma Dunn *(Mrs. Jaeckel)*, Grace Hayle *(Mme. Napaloni)*, Carter DeHaven *(Bacterian Ambassador)*

p, Charles Chaplin; d, Charles Chaplin; w, Charles Chaplin; ph, Roland Totheroh, Karl Struss; ed, Willard Nico; m, Meredith Willson; art d, J. Russell Spencer

AAN Best Picture; *AAN Best Actor:* Charles Chaplin; *AAN Best Supporting Actor:* Jack Oakie; *AAN Best Original Screenplay:* Charles Chaplin; *AAN Best Score:* Meredith Willson

Chaplin's first complete talkie and it's fascinating to see the way the structures of his silent films are translated into a unique blend of slapstick, wordplay, parody, and pointed political commentary. This is Chaplin's brilliant and heartfelt plea for world peace in an era of rising fascism and mass annihilation.

Chaplin, well aware of the ironic physical similarity between his sweet Little Tramp and Adolf Hitler, casts himself in a dual role as a nameless Jewish barber and as Adenoid Hynkel, Dictator of Tomania. The barber, a soldier for the German Army in WWI, awakens from a state of amnesia to learn that Hynkel, the country's new dictator, is calling for the persecution of all Jews. The barber's friend, Hannah (Paulette Goddard), is forced to flee the country; his barber shop is defaced and burned and he is arrested and sent to a concentration camp for sheltering an old friend, Schultz (Reginald Gardiner).

Filled with equal parts of humanity, outrage, and comedy, THE GREAT DICTATOR contains some of Chaplin's finest moments, including the famous upside-down flying sequence in which the barber doesn't even realize that he's not flying upright, Hynkel's fiery speech, delivered in an unintelligible German-English gibberish, and the film's scene of great genius, Hynkel's "ballet" with an air-filled globe of the world—tossing it, kicking it, adoring it, and, finally, destroying it as only a dictator dreaming of world domination could. The power of this strangely haunting film is enhanced by the realization that the extremes of human nature in the first half of this century were personified by these two mustached figures—Hitler and the Little Tramp.

GREAT ESCAPE, THE

1963 169m c Prison/War ★★★★
UA (U.S.) /PG

Steve McQueen ("Cooler King" Hilts), James Garner ("The Scrounger" Hendley), Richard Attenborough ("Big X" Bartlett), James Donald (Senior Officer Ramsey), Charles Bronson (Danny Velinski), Donald Pleasence ("The Forger" Blythe), James Coburn ("The Manufacturer" Sedgwick), David McCallum (Ashley-Pitt), Gordon Jackson (MacDonald), John Leyton (Willie)

p, John Sturges; d, John Sturges; w, James Clavell, W.R. Burnett (based on the book by Paul Brickhill); ph, Daniel Fapp; ed, Ferris Webster; m, Elmer Bernstein; art d, Fernando Carrere; cos, Bert Henrikson

AAN Best Editing: Ferris Webster

Expertly directed and written with an infectious undercurrent of wry humor, this classic WWII POW escape yarn features an all-star cast of hardened Allied prisoners who the Germans have thrown together in a special "escape-proof" camp. Naturally, the first thing they set about doing is planning their escape—not just any escape, but one so massive that thousands of German troops will be kept away from the front in the effort to track them down.

The prime instigators include "Big X" (Richard Attenborough), the British master planner; a Polish tunnel-digging expert (Charles Bronson); a forger of passports and papers (Donald Pleasence); and two Americans, "The Scrounger" (James Garner), in charge of assembling needed supplies, and Hilts (Steve McQueen), "The Cooler King," who has his own ideas about how to get out. When those ideas fail, he uses a baseball and mitt to while away his days in solitary confinement. The prisoners ingeniously go about digging three tunnels, and though one of them is discovered, the big breakout still takes place. The film follows the principals as they try to make their way to safety—some successfully, others meeting tragic ends, but all providing great excitement.

Based on a book detailing a real-life mass escape of Allied troops in 1942, producer-director John Sturges's film is involving throughout, due mainly to the excellent performances of its stellar cast, particularly McQueen in a breakthrough performance. Elmer Bernstein's exhilarating score is perfectly suited to the film's nonstop tension. A hit with the critics and at the box office. THE GREAT ESCAPE is for many *the* great "escape" film.

GREAT EXPECTATIONS

1946 118m bw Drama ★★★★★
Cineguild (U.K.) /PG

John Mills (Pip Pirrip), Valerie Hobson (Estella/Her Mother), Bernard Miles (Joe Gargery), Francis L. Sullivan (Jaggers), Martita Hunt (Miss Havisham), Finlay Currie (Abel Magwitch), Anthony Wager (Pip as Child), Jean Simmons (Estella as Child), Alec Guinness (Herbert Pocket), Ivor Barnard (Wemmick)

p, Ronald Neame; d, David Lean; w, David Lean, Ronald Neame, Anthony Havelock-Allan, Cecil McGivern, Kay Walsh (from the novel by Charles Dickens); ph, Guy Green; ed, Jack Harris; m, Walter Goehr; prod d, John Bryan; art d, Wilfred Shingleton; cos, Sophia Harris

AAN Best Picture; AAN Best Director: David Lean; *AAN Best Screenplay:* David Lean, Ronald Neame, Anthony Havelock-Allan; *AA Best Cinematography:* Guy Green; *AA Best Art Direction:* John Bryan, Wilfred Shingleton

A masterful realization of Charles Dickens's novel, this may be the best cinematic translation of the author's work, as well as director David Lean's greatest achievement. Beginning in 1830, the film follows the life of orphan Pip Pirrip (Anthony Wager as a child, John Mills as an adult), from his humble beginnings as a blacksmith's apprentice to his days as the wealthy beneficiary of an escaped convict (Finlay Currie) he once helped. Wonderfully directed by Lean—especially the childhood passages—GREAT EXPECTATIONS is brimming with unforgettable images and characters. Although admirers of the novel may bemoan the absence of several characters, the film captures the spirit of Dickens, translating his prose into flawless cinema. Cinematographer Guy Green and production designer John Bryan were awarded Academy Awards for their memorable work. A must see.

GREAT GATSBY, THE

1949 92m bw Drama ★★★½
Paramount (U.S.) /PG

Alan Ladd (Jay Gatsby), Betty Field (Daisy Buchanan), Macdonald Carey (Nick Carraway), Ruth Hussey (Jordan Baker), Barry Sullivan (Tom Buchanan), Howard da Silva (Wilson), Shelley Winters (Myrtle Wilson), Henry Hull (Dan Cody), Carole Mathews (Ella Cody), Ed Begley (Myron Lupus)

p, Richard Maibaum; d, Elliott Nugent; w, Cyril Hume, Richard Maibaum (based on the novel by F. Scott Fitzgerald and the play by Owen Davis, Sr.); ph, John Seitz; ed, Ellsworth Hoagland; m, Robert Emmett Dolan; art d, Hans Dreier, Roland Anderson; cos, Edith Head

The first sound adaptation of F. Scott Fitzgerald's classic Jazz Age novel, this version is far superior to its silent predecessor and the botched 1974 remake with Robert Redford in the title role. A large part of what makes this version work is the glacial central presence of Alan Ladd, who's quite convincing as a man with a mysterious past. Ladd is the enigmatic Jay Gatsby, a fabulous bootlegger who has used his relentless drive to amass a fortune. That mission accomplished, he turns his attention to wooing back a woman he lost many years earlier to a wealthy man.

Ladd is quite appropriate for Fitzgerald's hero. Embodying youthful disillusionment, false hope, and tragic nobility, he captures Gatsby's melancholy, mythic persona. Interestingly, the film ultimately feels more like a 1940s film noir than a 20s costume drama due to the moody monochrome cinematography of John F. Seitz.

GREAT MCGINTY, THE

1940 81m bw Political/Comedy ★★★★
Paramount (U.S.)

Brian Donlevy (Dan McGinty), Muriel Angelus (Catherine McGinty), Akim Tamiroff (The Boss), Allyn Joslyn (George), William Demarest (The Politician), Louis Jean Heydt (Thompson), Harry Rosenthal (Louis, the Bodyguard), Arthur Hoyt (Mayor Tillinghast), Libby Taylor (Bessie), Thurston Hall (Mr. Moxwell)

p, Paul Jones; d, Preston Sturges; w, Preston Sturges; ph, William Mellor; ed, Hugh Bennett; m, Frederick Hollander; art d, Hans Dreier, Earl Hedrick; cos, Edith Head

AA Best Original Screenplay: Preston Sturges

A hilarious spoof of American politics, this film marked the directorial debut of the mercurial and brilliant Preston Sturges, one of the best writer-directors of the 1940s. While this film never reaches the giddy heights of some of his subsequent films, THE GREAT MCGINTY was a favorable harbinger of the therapeutic madness to come.

The film opens in a smoky banana-republic bar largely patronized, it seems, by Americans on the lam. One such denizen, Thompson (Heydt), is a one-time chief cashier of a major bank turned embezzler. Now dejected from hiding out in this steamy exile, he attempts suicide in the men's room but he's stopped by the bartender, Dan McGinty (Donlevy). McGinty has an even more ignominious tale to tell: he used to be governor of a state! His strange story unravels in flashback.

McGinty begins as a seedy hobo looking for a quick buck. During an election in a major city, he's hired by a slick politician (Demarest) to vote repeatedly using the names of dead citizens. He proves to be an overzealous participant in the democratic process, voting dozens of times at an expected $2 per vote but the politico is unable to come across with the dough. McGinty remains persistent. He's taken to the party hall where The Boss (Tamiroff) is so taken with the bum's moxie that he appoints him a collector of funds in his protection racket. McGinty proves himself a born collector and he continues moving up the ladder of crime until he is finally ready for the big time—politics.

Donlevy, in an early starring role, gives a marvelous performance as a dim-witted bum who's transformed into a polished politician. The flamboyant Tamiroff's rendering of the boss is a comic delight. Demarest is colorful and full of street savvy and wit, once remarking: "If you didn't have graft, you'd have a lower class of people in politics!" This terrific satire was the brainchild of screenwriter Sturges, who, by the time he penned this script, was the highest-paid writer in Hollywood, having written films such as EASY LIVING and DIAMOND JIM.

GREAT NORTHFIELD, MINNESOTA RAID, THE

1972 91m c Biography/Western ★★★
Universal (U.S.) PG/X

Cliff Robertson *(Cole Younger)*, Robert Duvall *(Jesse James)*, Luke Askew *(Jim Younger)*, R.G. Armstrong *(Clell Miller)*, Dana Elcar *(Allen)*, Donald Moffat *(Manning)*, John Pearce *(Frank James)*, Matt Clark *(Bob Younger)*, Wayne Sutherlin *(Charley Pitts)*, Robert H. Harris *(Wilcox)*

p, Jennings Lang; d, Philip Kaufman; w, Philip Kaufman; ph, Bruce Surtees; ed, Douglas Stewart; m, Dave Grusin; art d, Alexander Golitzen, George Webb; cos, Helen Colvig

An offbeat, ragged but totally absorbing Western, this film profiles the infamous yet celebrated James-Younger gang in relatively realistic terms, showing them for the murderous and desperate men they probably were while offering a refreshingly sophisticated and cynical political analysis of their situation. Though it borrows heavily from late 1960s-early 1970s genre landmarks such as BONNIE AND CLYDE and McCABE AND MRS. MILLER, it remains interesting for its depiction of how exploitive capitalism—the railroads in this case—compels somewhat simpleminded farmers into outlaw lives.

The Missouri legislature is preparing to vote on granting amnesty to those notorious outlaws, Jesse James (Duvall) and Cole Younger (Robertson). Some enlightened members argue that these men and their followers were driven into crime by powerful behind-the-scenes interests that appropriated their lands. Cole is willing to accept the amnesty and return to farming, but James argues that nothing will change, the railroads will continue to steal their land and their persecution will never stop. He's right. After the amnesty motion is ruled out of order, James plans to take the gang from their native Missouri to rob the big bank in Northfield, Minnesota, after reading a newspaper account about its financial standing as the biggest bank west of the Mississippi. Things go wrong.

Although director-writer Kaufman claimed to have researched the real tale of the James-Younger gang while studying history at the University of Chicago, many of his details are inaccurate and some scenes are outright fabrications. However, the awkward, crude, unsophisticated dialogue is appropriate to the period, region, and characters. Duvall delivers an interesting interpretation of Jesse James as a borderline psychotic. Robertson credibly portrays Cole Younger as a cunning, intelligent and even sensitive person. The supporting players also are all believable, and the well mounted production seems clearly authentic. One of the best profiles of the James-Younger gang yet made, although Walter Hill's THE LONG RIDERS more aptly captures the character of the gang.

GREAT SANTINI, THE

1979 115m c Drama/War ★★★½
Orion (U.S.) PG

Robert Duvall *(Bull Meechum)*, Blythe Danner *(Lillian Meechum)*, Michael O'Keefe *(Ben Meechum)*, Lisa Jane Persky *(Mary Anne Meechum)*, Julie Anne Haddock *(Karen Meechum)*, Brian Andrews *(Matthew Meechum)*, Stan Shaw *(Toomer Smalls)*, Theresa Merritt *(Arrabelle Smalls)*, David Keith *(Red Pettus)*, Paul Mantee *(Col. Hedgepath)*

p, Charles A. Pratt; d, Lewis John Carlino; w, Lewis John Carlino (based on the novel by Pat Conroy); ph, Ralph Woolsey; ed, Houseley Stevenson; m, Elmer Bernstein; prod d, Jack Poplin

AAN Best Actor: Robert Duvall; *AAN Best Supporting Actor:* Michael O'Keefe

Robert Duvall received an Academy Award nomination for his forceful performance as a warrior without a war in this touching, well-crafted drama based on the novel by Pat Conroy.

As Marine pilot Bull Meechum, he rules his family with military discipline, setting impossibly high standards for his four children (Julie Anne Haddock, Brian Andrews, Lisa Jane Persky, and Michael O'Keefe). When Bull's harsh manner becomes too oppressive for his offspring, they know that their mother, Lillian (Blythe Danner), is there to provide an understanding shoulder to cry on, especially the sensitive Ben (O'Keefe), whose battle to earn his father's respect is most tellingly played out in one-on-one basketball games that force Bull to play dirty to win. Although Bull's kids are never able to reach their father, they do offer him the kind of stoic tribute that would have made him proud when tragedy strikes.

Deftly scripted, beautifully shot—making good use of its South Carolina locations—and magnificently acted, The Great Santini garnered Academy nominations for both Duvall and O'Keefe. Though its emotions are big, the performances are so nicely nuanced that sentiment never overwhelms the story's emotional realism. In addition to Duvall's tour-de-force performance, Danner is outstanding as the nurturing mother, and O'Keefe's heartfelt portrayal of the tortured son earned him an Oscar nomination as Best Supporting Actor.

GREAT WHITE HOPE, THE

1970 102m c Sports ★★★½
Fox (U.S.) GP/15

James Earl Jones *(Jack Jefferson)*, Jane Alexander *(Eleanor)*, Lou Gilbert *(Goldie)*, Joel Fluellen *(Tick)*, Chester Morris *(Pop Weaver)*, Robert Webber *(Dixon)*, Marlene Warfield *(Clara)*, R.G. Armstrong *(Cap'n Dan)*, Hal Holbrook *(Cameron)*, Beah Richards *(Mama Tiny)*

p, Lawrence Turman; d, Martin Ritt; w, Howard Sackler (based on his play); ph, Burnett Guffey; ed, William Reynolds; m, Lionel Newman; prod d, John De Cuir; art d, Jack Martin Smith; chor, Donald McKayle; cos, Irene Sharaff

AAN Best Actor: James Earl Jones; *AAN Best Actress:* Jane Alexander

Adapted by Howard Sackler from his own Broadway hit, this excellent period drama is a thinly veiled depiction of the life of the first black heavyweight champion of the world, Jack Johnson.

By winning the title Johnson (James Earl Jones, who played the role on Broadway) incurs the wrath of the white world. His troubles begin in earnest when he takes up with Eleanor (Alexander), a white divorcee. He's convicted of breaking the Mann Act and gets sent to prison. After Jefferson escapes, he and Alexander begin an itinerant exile that takes them to Canada, England (where he's refused a boxing license), France and Germany. Few are willing to take on the great champion but he is determined to fight again. THE GREAT WHITE HOPE persuasively recreates the climate of the time and generally avoids the preachiness for which director Ritt is sometimes known. The love story between Alexander and Jones is touchingly portrayed. Sackler's screenplay is written in free verse, but you'd never know it.

GREAT ZIEGFELD, THE

1936 170m bw Musical/Biography ★★★
MGM (U.S.) /U

William Powell (*Florenz Ziegfeld*), Luise Rainer (*Anna Held*), Myrna Loy (*Billie Burke*), Frank Morgan (*Billings*), Reginald Owen (*Sampson*), Nat Pendleton (*Sandow*), Virginia Bruce (*Audrey Lane*), Ernest Cossart (*Sidney*), Robert Greig (*Joe*), Raymond Walburn (*Sage*)

p, Hunt Stromberg; d, Robert Z. Leonard; w, William Anthony McGuire; ph, Ray June, Oliver T. Marsh, Karl Freund, Merritt Gerstad, George Folsey; ed, William S. Gray; art d, Cedric Gibbons; chor, Seymour Felix; cos, Adrian

AA Best Picture; *AA Best Actress:* Luise Rainer; *AAN Best Director:* Robert Z. Leonard; *AAN Best Original Screenplay:* William Anthony McGuire; *AAN Best Editing:* William S. Gray; *AAN Best Art Direction:* Cedric Gibbons, Eddie Imazu, Edwin B. Willis

How appropriate that this ode to an ambitious, amiable shyster featured future First Lady Pat Nixon as an extra. Incredibly, THE GREAT ZIEGFELD, three hours of lumpy, overcooked pudding, took Best Picture at the 1936 Oscars. But then, the film is *big*, and it's an ode to lavish showmanship—what better pat on the back could Hollywood give itself?

The details of the whitewashed story aren't worth dwelling on in detail. Flo (Powell) begins as a sideshow barker and eventually becomes Broadway impresario extraordinaire. Along the way he marries temperamental actress-singer Anna Held (Rainer) but their oh-so-turbulent relationship just doesn't make it. He later weds actress Billie Burke (Loy) and, after enduring his darkest hours, stuns Broadway with four simultaneous hits.

Oddly enough, the film does have enough thrust to keep rigor mortis from setting in. Powell can't give his shallow role much depth beyond a consideration of Ziegfeld's incredible ambition and ego, but he does give it energy and rascally charm. Loy would have been foolish to copy the inimitable twittering of Billie Burke and wisely she doesn't try. What she's left with are a new hair color, uxorial devotion and relatively little footage.

The latter applies to Rainer as well, though we mind that less. She does have a delicate appeal onstage and also in the "legendary" telephone scene in which Anna, still in love, calls Flo to congratulate him on his second marriage. Still, Rainer's fluttery performance did *not* deserve an Oscar for Best Actress and today stands as a glass menagerie relic just waiting to be dropped on the floor. Ray Bolger adds a few delightful moments, but a pre-WIZARD OF OZ Frank Morgan is way overboard and Fanny Brice is ditched right in the middle of singing "My Man"!! What can you do with a movie like this? Surrender, I guess.

GREATEST SHOW ON EARTH, THE

1952 153m c Drama ★★★★
Paramount (U.S.) /U

Betty Hutton (*Holly*), Cornel Wilde (*Sebastian*), Charlton Heston (*Brad*), Dorothy Lamour (*Phyllis*), Gloria Grahame (*Angel*), James Stewart (*Buttons, a Clown*), Henry Wilcoxon (*Detective*), Lyle Bettger (*Klaus*), Lawrence Tierney (*Henderson*), John Kellogg (*Harry*)

p, Cecil B. DeMille; d, Cecil B. DeMille; w, Fredric M. Frank, Barre Lyndon, Theodore St. John (based on a story by Frank, St. John, Frank Cavett); ph, George Barnes, Peverell Marley, W. Wallace Kelley; ed, Anne Bauchens; m, Victor Young; art d, Hal Pereira, Walter Tyler; fx, Gordon Jennings, Paul K. Lerpae, Devereaux Jennings; chor, Richard Barstow; cos, Miles White, Edith Head, Dorothy Jeakins

AA Best Picture; *AAN Best Director:* Cecil B. DeMille; *AA Best Story:* Fredric M. Frank, Theodore St. John, Frank Cavett; *AAN Best Editing:* Anne Bauchens; *AAN Best Costume Design:* Edith Head, Dorothy Jeakins, Miles White

It's big, it's garish, it's loud, and most of all, it's wonderful. This is Cecil B. DeMille's superlative salute to the circus world, and all its glamour and flashy hoopla suits perfectly the director whose middle name was epic. An episodic soap opera set under the big top, the film is almost like a documentary in its meticulous detailing of circus life. Charlton Heston plays the head of the sprawling ensemble and the entire cast is

outstanding, particularly James Stewart as the clown hiding from his past. Since the early 1920s, DeMille had planned on producing a spectacular circus film, but his biblical epics got in the way. Finally, in 1949, after Paramount paid Ringling Brothers $250,000 for the right to use the circus' name, equipment, and talent, DeMille began elaborate preparations. The film is authentic and awesome and earned an Oscar as Best Picture.

GREEN DOLPHIN STREET

1947 140m bw Adventure/Romance ★★½
MGM (U.S.) /A

Lana Turner (*Marianne Patourel*), Van Heflin (*Timothy Haslam*), Donna Reed (*Marguerite Patourel*), Richard Hart (*William Ozanne*), Frank Morgan (*Dr. Edmund Ozanne*), Edmund Gwenn (*Octavius Patourel*), Dame May Whitty (*Mother Superior*), Reginald Owen (*Capt. O'Hara*), Gladys Cooper (*Sophie Patourel*), Moyna MacGill (*Mrs. Metivier*)

p, Carey Wilson; d, Victor Saville; w, Samson Raphaelson (based on the novel by Elizabeth Goudge); ph, George Folsey; ed, George White; m, Bronislau Kaper; art d, Cedric Gibbons, Malcolm Brown; fx, Warren Newcombe, A. Arnold Gillespie; cos, Walter Plunkett, Valles

AAN Best Cinematography: George Folsey; *AAN Best Editing:* George White; *AAN Best Sound:* Metro-Goldwyn-Mayer Sound Department; *AA Best Visual Effects:* A. Arnold Gillespie, Warren Newcombe, Douglas Shearer, Michael Steinore

Lana Turner's bid for the sweep of epic skirts, her GWTW as it were, and a classic egg-layer. You can swallow this clinker whole if you can stomach one plot turn: Richard Hart's New Zealand army deserter who gets loaded and writes a love letter to Turner, even though it's little sis Donna Reed he really cares for; the poor lad has the names confused. When Turner blows in, he marries her rather than admit his mistake and all karmic hell breaks loose. Here Saville's direction rises to the fore, with giant trees falling over and the earth belching and shivering in a killer earthquake sequence. Just when things seem tame there's a Maori uprising. Meanwhile, spurned sis Reed takes the nun's vow.

Without murderous acts of passion, Lana's out of her element; but not to worry. Natural disasters and aboriginal riots take no toll on Turner's visage—a strand of hair displaced here, a streak of dirt there. Brunette haircolor and a possible acting chore deter her not one whit from her goal of genus: star.

GREEN FOR DANGER

1946 91m bw Mystery/Comedy ★★★★★
Individual Picture (U.K.) /A

Sally Gray (*Nurse Linley*), Trevor Howard (*Dr. Barney Barnes*), Rosamund John (*Esther Sanson*), Alistair Sim (*Inspector Cockrill*), Leo Genn (*Mr. Eden*), Judy Campbell (*Marion Bates*), Megs Jenkins (*Nurse Woods*), Moore Marriott (*Joe Higgins*), Henry Edwards (*Mr. Purdy*), Ronald Adam (*Dr. White*)

p, Frank Launder, Sidney Gilliat; d, Sidney Gilliat; w, Sidney Gilliat, Claude Guerney (based on a novel by Christianna Brand); ph, Wilkie Cooper; ed, Thelma Myers; m, William Alwyn; prod d, Peter Proud

Green for go! An unfairly overlooked delight in the annals of British film history, GREEN FOR DANGER is one of the most enjoyable films ever produced by those masters of comic entertainment, Launder and Gilliat.

Inspector Cockrill (Sim), an unorthodox detective, investigates a strange double murder that takes place in a British emergency hospital during WWII. A postman who has been slightly wounded by a buzz bomb dies on the operating table, and, when nurse Marion Bates (Campbell) discovers that he was murdered, she's stabbed to death. Cockrill discovers that everyone present during the operation had a motive, and, with an odd sense of amusement, he sets about exposing the surprising culprit.

Though most US audiences remember Sim primarily for his flawless performance as Scrooge, his use of his droopy features, lugubrious yet fruity intonations and impeccable timing make this role one of his best. Gray, Howard and John are appealing as always, and a marvelous supporting cast gives fine moments to Genn, Jenkins, Marriott, Edwards and others. Still, it's the remarkable Sim (unlikely star material only at first glance) and the smooth, feather-light scripting and direction of Gilliat that makes watching this film like sitting up late on a stormy night reading your first Agatha Christie novel.

GREEN MAN, THE

1956 80m bw Comedy   ★★★★
Grenadier (U.K.)   /PG

Alastair Sim *(Hawkins)*, George Cole *(William Blake)*, Jill Adams *(Ann Vincent)*, Avril Angers *(Marigold)*, Terry-Thomas *(Boughtflower)*, John Chandos *(McKecknie)*, Dora Bryan *(Lily)*, Colin Gordon *(Reginald)*, Eileen Moore *(Joan Wood)*, Raymond Huntley *(Sir Gregory Upshoot)*

p, Sidney Gilliat, Frank Launder; d, Robert Day; w, Sidney Gilliat, Frank Launder (based on their play *Meet a Body*); ph, Gerald Gibbs; ed, Bernard Gribble; m, Cedric Thorpe Davie

This hilarious comedy stars Alastair Sim as Hawkins, a professional assassin who has long been out of action. He comes out of his retirement when he is hired to do away with Sir Gregory Upshoot (Huntley), a pompous politician. Hawkins tracks his quarry to a decrepit seaside hotel called the Green Man, and waits there to spring his trap, disguising himself as a simple clockmaker. As such he puts up with a bevy of dowagers at the resort, joining in the staid teas, conversations, and musical diversions. Meanwhile, a bomb he has planted is ready to explode upon Sir Upshoot's arrival. But it seems as if the victim will never appear! Alastair Sim is a delight as the assassin with the soul of an aesthete. Terry-Thomas is also very funny in this underrated little gem.

GREEN PASTURES

1936 93m bw Religious   ★★★½
Warner Bros. (U.S.)   /U

Rex Ingram *(De Lawd, Adam/Hezdrel)*, Oscar Polk *(Gabriel)*, Eddie "Rochester" Anderson *(Noah)*, Frank C. Wilson *(Moses)*, George Reed *(Mr. Deshee)*, Abraham Gleaves *(Archangel)*, Myrtle Anderson *(Eve)*, Al Stokes *(Cain)*, Edna Mae Harris *(Zeba)*, James Fuller *(Cain the Sixth)*

p, Henry Blanke; d, Marc Connelly, William Keighley; w, Marc Connelly, Sheridan Gibney (from the play by Connelly, suggested by Roark Bradford's *Ol' Man Adam an' His Chillun*); ph, Hal Mohr; m, Hall Johnson; art d, Allen Saalburg, Stanley Fleischer

Based on the Pulitzer Prize-winning play, this is The Gospel According To Marc—Connelly, that is. Using a series of brief sketches by Roark Bradford, Connelly and coscreenwriter Gibney fashioned an interesting—though grossly racially stereotyped—account of the Bible using an all-Black cast.

The film takes place in a sunday school where the teacher begins telling biblical stories from the Old Testament. As he speaks, all of the characters come to life, portrayed by notable Black actors of the period. On the stage, De Lawd was played by Richard Berry Harrison but he passed away before the film was shot and his role was undertaken by Ingram, who also played Adam and Hezdrel. All of the dialogue is done in archaic Southern Black colloquialisms with much talk of ten cent "seegars" and fish-fries and expressions like "Gangway for de Lawd God Jehovah." We see the tales of Joshua at Jericho, Abraham, Isaac and Jacob, Noah, Adam and Eve, Moses, and even Gabriel (whom De Lawd God refers to as "Gabe").

In many ways, this is one of the best biblical films ever done. Mostly because it doesn't preach, just entertains, and in doing that, puts its lessons across with a minimum of effort. One of the best elements of the movie is the music by the Hall Johnson Choir, which functions as sort of a Greek Chorus, singing tunes like "When the Saints Go Marching In," "Let My People Go," "Joshua Fit de Battle of Jericho" and many more.

GREEN ROOM, THE
(LA CHAMBRE VERTE)

1978 94m c Drama/War   ★★★½
Carrosse/UA (France)   PG/A

Francois Truffaut *(Julien Davenne)*, Nathalie Baye *(Cecilia Mandel)*, Jean Daste *(Bernard Humbert)*, Jean-Pierre Moulin *(Gerard Mazet)*, Antoine Vitez *(Bishop's Secretary)*, Jane Lobre *(Mazet's Second Wife)*, Monique Dury *(Monique, Editorial Secretary)*, Laurence Ragon *(Julie Davenne)*, Marcel Berbert *(Dr. Jardine)*, Christian Lentretian *(Orator in Cemetery)*

d, Francois Truffaut; w, Francois Truffaut, Jean Gruault (based on themes in the writings of Henry James); ph, Nestor Almendros; ed, Martine Barraque; m, Maurice Jaubert; art d, Jean-Pierre Kohut-Svelko

Francois Truffaut's testimony of obsession, THE GREEN ROOM, is perhaps the most unheralded film of his career, and surely one of his most personal.

Truffaut himself plays Julien Davenne, a secretive man who excels at writing obituaries for a fading journal and who's stubbornly obsessed with death, believing that the deceased are not given the love and attention they deserve. His reverence is inspired both by his guilt over returning from WWI unharmed, while everyone he knew was killed or injured, and by the sudden death of his newlywed wife. In her memory, he constructs a shrine, complete with a frightening, life-size wax figurine. At the cemetary where she's buried he discovers an old chapel in need of restoration and remodels it as an elaborate temple for the dead, filling it with photos of dead friends and acquaintances killed in the trenches.

On the surface, THE GREEN ROOM is an excessively depressing and strange portrait of a man who values death over life, but underneath it runs the study of a man driven by his obsessions. An interesting and atmospheric counterpoint to the numerous war films that pay tribute to those who died for their country, THE GREEN ROOM concerns a man who lived through war, is tormented by survivor's guilt, and is driven to actively remember the dead.

GREETINGS

1968 88m c Comedy/Drama   ★★★½
West End Films (U.S.)   R/

Robert De Niro *(Jon Rubin)*, Jonathan Warden *(Paul Shaw)*, Gerrit Graham *(Lloyd Clay)*, Richard Hamilton *(Pop Artist)*, Megan McCormick *(Marina)*, Bettina Kugel *(Tina)*, Allen Garfield *(Smut Peddler)*, Roz Kelly *(Photographer)*, Jack Cowley *(Photographer)*, Jane Lee Salmons *(Model)*

p, Charles Hirsch; d, Brian De Palma; w, Brian De Palma, Charles Hirsch; ph, Robert Flore; ed, Brian De Palma; m, The Children of Paradise

Brian De Palma's breezy, Godardian first feature distills the heady atmosphere of Greenwich Village in an era of countercultural experimentation and anti-war protest. Irrepressibly libidinous Paul (Jonathan Warden) receives a draft notice and schemes to avoid induction with the aid of Lloyd (Gerrit Graham), a trendy paranoiac who's obsessed with the Kennedy assassination, and Jon (Robert De Niro), a De Palma alter ego who channels his voyeurism through filmmaking. Shot in two weeks on a budget of $43,000, the film took in over a million dollars, bringing its 28-year-old director to the attention of Hollywood. Like much of De Palma's later work, GREETINGS is primarily concerned with the process, conventions, and political meanings of cinema. Nevertheless, it's funny, vulgar, and outrageously politically incorrect—as when Jon, ostensibly documenting the Vietnam War, allows his obsessions to get the better of him and implores a Vietnamese woman to strip for the camera.

GREGORY'S GIRL

1981 91m c Romance/Comedy ★★★½
Lake (U.K.) PG/A

Gordon John Sinclair *(Gregory)*, Dee Hepburn *(Dorothy)*, Jake D'Arcy *(Phil Menzies)*, Clare Grogan *(Susan)*, Robert Buchanan *(Andy)*, Billy Greenlees *(Steve)*, Alan Love *(Eric)*, Caroline Guthrie *(Carol)*, Carol Macartney *(Margo)*, Douglas Sannachan *(Billy)*

p, Clive Parsons, Davina Belling; d, Bill Forsyth; w, Bill Forsyth; ph, Michael Coulter; ed, John Gow; m, Colin Tully; art d, Adrienne Atkinson

A funny and touching teen romance from Scottish director Bill Forsyth. Gordon John Sinclair stars as an awkward teen who develops a major crush on the new girl in school, soccer star Dorothy (Dee Hepburn). Sinclair successfully portrays the uneasy quandary most adolescent boys go through when suffering from painful shyness coupled with the outrageous hormonal imbalance that drives them to do ridiculous things to get the attention of a pretty girl. While the plot is a straight, simple romance, the true charm of the film comes from its quirky characters, its general air of tolerance and good will and some irrepressible and delightfully absurd touches that creep (or waddle) along the periphery of the narrative. With this unpretentious little film, Forsyth decisively demonstrates that there was still life in the classic British comedy more than 30 years after its heyday.

GREMLINS 2: THE NEW BATCH

1990 105m c Comedy/Horror ★★★★
Mike Finnell/Amblin (U.S.) PG-13/12

Zach Galligan *(Billy Peltzer)*, Phoebe Cates *(Kate Beringer)*, John Glover *(Daniel Clamp)*, Robert Prosky *(Grandpa Fred)*, Howie Mandel *(Voice of Gizmo)*, Tony Randall *(Voice of "Brain" Gremlin)*, Robert Picardo *(Forster)*, Christopher Lee *(Dr. Catheter)*, Haviland Morris *(Marla Bloodstone)*, Dick Miller *(Murray Futterman)*

p, Michael Finnell; d, Joe Dante; w, Charlie Haas (based on characters created by Chris Columbus); ph, John Hora; ed, Kent Beyda; m, Jerry Goldsmith; prod d, James Spencer; art d, Joe Lucky; fx, Rick Baker; cos, Rosanna Norton; anim, Chuck Jones

GREMLINS 2: THE NEW BATCH is surprisingly sympathetic towards the title menace and surprisingly thought-provoking in its use of the gremlins to make an extended commentary on modern life and morality. That the beasties should wind up the tragically ill-fated good guys should come as no surprise to director Joe Dante's admirers; he's an enthusiastic fan of classic Hollywood kitsch, especially those monster movies, in which the saddest scene is the one in which the monster dies.

With GREMLINS 2, Dante has come up with what may be his best film yet—a dizzying, no-holds-barred satirical spectacle that will please fans of the original and anyone else lucky enough to drop by. This is no lifeless retread, even though every big scene from the first film has its equivalent here. (Dante still seems especially concerned about the safe use of microwave ovens.) And even if the filmmakers' apparent intent was to make a movie that feels wildly out of control, GREMLINS 2 rarely loses sight of its objectives. Almost every plot twist, stunt, and sight gag elaborates the movie's basic theme: the metaphysical price paid for plundering a rich human past to build a dubious, impoverished, and inhumane future, of which the gremlins are merely an unnatural byproduct.

This theme is mainly suggested by Clamp's urgency in tearing down New York landmarks (such as *all* of Chinatown), to construct cold, high-tech, soulless structures in their place, but it is echoed everywhere—from the Splice of Life lab, dedicated to developing new and "improved" life forms, to the romantic subplot, in which Billy is tempted to throw away his long-term romance with Kate to further his career with Clamp.

Still, no one who makes movies as thoroughly modernist and as full of high-tech special effects as Dante does can ever make a sincere claim to yearning for gentler, simpler times. As a result, the film exhibits an oddly compelling ambivalence toward the gremlins throughout. But it doesn't stop us from feeling a little sad for the gremlins after they meet

their sticky end. They may be nasty, but they know how to party, particularly when they spontaneously mount a lavish musical number inspired by the Kander and Ebb classic "New York, New York."

GREY FOX, THE

1982 92m c Biography/Western ★★★★
Mercury (Canada) PG

Richard Farnsworth *(Bill Miner)*, Jackie Burroughs *(Kate Flynn)*, Wayne Robson *(Shorty)*, Ken Pogue *(Jack Budd)*, Timothy Webber *(Fernie)*, Gary Reineke *(Detective Seavey)*, David Petersen *(Louis Colquhoun)*, Don Mackay *(Al Sims)*, Samantha Langevin *(Jenny)*, Tom Heaton *(Tom)*

p, Peter O'Brian; d, Phillip Borsos; w, John Hunter; ph, Frank Tidy; ed, Frank Irvine; m, Michael Conway Baker, The Chieftains; art d, William Brodie

This charming "art" Western is a great example of what can be done with a small budget and a terrific idea. Richard Farnsworth plays real-life train robber Bill Miner, released from prison after 30 years. The old West that he knew has disappeared, but knowing no other trade, he goes back to train robbing.

An ex-stuntman and character actor who was suggested for the part by Francis Ford Coppola, Farnsworth is dignified and charismatic in his first starring role as the Gentleman Bandit. No young pretty boy, Farnsworth has a leathery face that looks well lived in, but his beautiful blue eyes, sparkling impishly over his snow white handlebar moustache, help make him the most appealing old codger in modern movies.

Phillip Borsos's direction is fine in his first feature, after a career as a documentary filmmaker. The marvelous photography of the unspoiled Canadian landscape is by Frank Tidy, who also did the moody lensing on Ridley Scott's underrated THE DUELLISTS.

GREYSTOKE: THE LEGEND OF TARZAN, LORD OF THE APES

1984 129m c Adventure ★★★½
Warner Bros. (U.K.) PG

Ralph Richardson *(The 6th Lord of Greystoke)*, Ian Holm *(Capt. Phillippe D'Arnot)*, Christopher Lambert *(John Clayton/Tarzan)*, Andie MacDowell *(Jane Porter)*, James Fox *(Lord Esker)*, Ian Charleson *(Jefferson Brown)*, Nigel Davenport *(Maj. Jack Downing)*, Paul Geoffrey *(Lord Jack Clayton)*, Cheryl Campbell *(Lady Alice Clayton)*, Nicholas Farrell *(Sir Hugh Belcher)*

p, Hugh Hudson, Stanley S. Canter; d, Hugh Hudson; w, Robert Towne, Michael Austin (based on the novel *Tarzan of the Apes* by Edgar Rice Burroughs); ph, John Alcott; ed, Anne V. Coates; m, John Scott; prod d, Stuart Craig; art d, Simon Holland, Norman Dorme; fx, Albert Whitlock; chor, Peter Elliot; cos, John Mollo, Shirley Russell

AAN Best Supporting Actor: Ralph Richardson; *AAN Best Adapted Screenplay:* P.H. Vazak, Michael Austin; *AAN Best Makeup:* Rick Baker, Paul Engelen

The most intelligent and perhaps the best filmic treatment of Edgar Rice Burroughs's classic pulp novels about Tarzan, the white child of noble blood raised by apes in the jungle, since Elmo Lincoln first brought the character to the screen in 1918.

The film opens with the shipwreck that casts Lord Jack Clayton (Paul Geoffrey) and his pregnant wife Lady Alice (Cheryl Campbell) on the wild coast of Africa. They build a hut in the jungle, she bears a son, and shortly thereafter they both die. The infant is adopted by a clan of apes, with whom he grows to manhood, after which his ape mother is killed by pygmies. They also wipe out the first white men that Tarzan (Christopher Lambert) has ever seen, a party of hunters. He saves one of them, a wounded Belgian, Captain Phillippe D'Arnot (Ian Holm), who teaches him to speak English. Eventually Tarzan returns to civilization with D'Arnot and goes to his ancestral home in Scotland, Greystoke Manor. There, his grandfather, the Sixth Lord of Greystoke (Sir Ralph Richardson), tries to integrate his heir into upper-crust society.

The film is beautifully photographed and marvelously acted, with Lambert showing remarkable subtlety and emotion. Richardson, in his final film role, is even better; he carries much of the second half of the film when the story starts to sag. The special-effects costuming by Rick

Baker is superb and his actor-apes are so expressive and natural that it is almost impossible to tell them from the real apes that appear in the scenes with them. Nominated by the Academy for Best Supporting Actor (Richardson), Best Screenplay (co-writer Robert Towne writing under the pseudonym P.H. Vasak), and Best Makeup.

GRIFTERS, THE
1990　113m　c　Crime　　★★★★
Grifters Inc./Scorsese Productions　(U.S.)　R/18

John Cusack (*Roy Dillon*), Anjelica Huston (*Lilly Dillon*), Annette Bening (*Myra Langtry*), Pat Hingle (*Bobo Justus*), J.T. Walsh (*Cole Langtry*), Henry Jones (*The Desk Clerk*), Michael Laskin (*Irv*), Eddie Jones (*Mints*), Charles Napier (*Hebbing*), Jan Munroe (*Guy at Bar*)

p, Martin Scorsese, Robert A. Harris, James Painten; d, Stephen Frears; w, Donald E. Westlake (based on the novel by Jim Thompson); ph, Oliver Stapleton; ed, Mick Audsley; m, Elmer Bernstein; prod d, Dennis Gassner; art d, Leslie McDonald; cos, Richard Hornung

AAN Best Actress: Anjelica Huston; AAN Best Supporting Actress: Annette Bening; AAN Best Director: Stephen Frears; AAN Best Adapted Screenplay: Donald E. Westlake

THE GRIFTERS has the mastery and hallucinatory, all-involving feel of an instant classic. Stephen Frears, a fearlessly diverse director, has immersed himself in the Los Angeles world of film noir and emerged with a movie that can easily stand alongside such classics of the genre as THE MALTESE FALCON, THE BIG SLEEP and OUT OF THE PAST.

The tale is spun of three "grifters," con artists forever on the lookout for an easy hustle. Lily (Anjelica Huston) is an ultra-experienced pro who specializes in racetrack odds altering. Her son, Roy (John Cusack), is basically small-time, hustling sailors and bartenders with loaded dice and sleight-of-hand tricks. His inamorata, Myra (Annette Bening), likes corporate action, a field she is easily able to ply with her siren's body and wardrobe of Chanel suits. Lily had Roy when she was but a girl herself, and the two have mostly gone their separate ways. They meet up again in California, where Lily takes an immediate dislike to Myra. Her ill feeling is met and matched by Roy, who has never resolved his filial feelings for her, as well as by Myra, who, having been wholly rebuffed by Lily, resolves to take her down. The climax, involving Lily and Roy, is swift, ugly, cathartic and ultimately elegiac all at once.

Adapted from modish tough-guy writer Jim Thompson's novel, Donald Westlake's screenplay has the right combination of vivid characters, mordant wit and avaricious savagery which distinguishes the best noir. The characters speak in a faintly disconcerting 1950s argot right out of the book, adding an authentic flavor to the simmeringly suggestive stew Frears has concocted.

GROOVE TUBE, THE
1974　75m　c　Comedy　　★★★
Levitt/Pickman　(U.S.)　R/X

Buzzy Linhart (*The Hitchhiker*), Richmond Baier (*The Hitchhiker*), Ken Shapiro (*Koko the Clown/Kramp TV Kitchen/The Dealer/Newscaster/Sex Olympias*), Paul Norman (*Mouth Appeal*), Victoria Medlin (*Mouth Appeal*), Chevy Chase (*Geritan/Four Leaf Clover*), Jennifer Welles (*Geritan*), Richard Belzer (*The Dealers/President*), Bill Kemmill (*Butz Beer*), Alex Stephens (*Butz Beer*)

p, Ken Shapiro; d, Ken Shapiro; w, Ken Shapiro, Lane Sarasohn; ph, Bob Bailin; anim, Linda Taylor, Pat O'Neill

A sometimes humorous satire of modern television that leaves no aspect of television programming unscathed, nailing everything from commercials to kiddie programming. Made up of dozens of sketches and vignettes, THE GROOVE TUBE was a legitimate theater venture that ran off-Broadway and toured other US cities for five years. This film was first rated X, but was later trimmed to an R rating. Vulgar, which isn't really bothersome, but trivial, which is.

GROSSE POINTE BLANK
1997　107m　c　Crime/Thriller/Comedy　　★★★½
Roth/Arnold Productions/New Crime Productions　R/
/Caravan Pictures　(U.S.)

John Cusack (*Martin Q. Blank*), Minnie Driver (*Debi Newberry*), Dan Aykroyd (*Grocer*), Alan Arkin (*Dr. Oatman*), Joan Cusack (*Marcella*), Jeremy Piven (*Paul Spericki*), Hank Azaria (*Lardner*), Barbara Harris (*Mary Blank*), K. Todd Freeman (*McCullers*), Mitchell Ryan (*Mr. Newberry*)

p, Susan Arnold, Donna Arkoff Roth, Roger Birnbaum; d, George Armitage; w, Tom Jankiewicz, D. V. DeVincentis, Steve Pink, John Cusack (based on a story by Tom Jankiewicz); ph, Jamie Anderson; ed, Brian Berdan; m, Joe Strummer; prod d, Stephen Altman; art d, Scott Meehan; fx, Ron Trost; cos, Eugenie Bafaloukos

A slick, mannered, and frequently very clever comedy about yuppie hit man Martin Blank (John Cusack), who decides to mix business and pleasure by doing a job and attending his 10-year high school reunion over the same weekend. Awaiting him in Grosse Pointe, MI are the sweetheart he stood up on prom night (Minnie Driver) and a raft of old friends who get a real charge out of Martin's forthright answer to the inevitable, "So, what do you do?" He just slays 'em. Eccentric director George Armitage (MIAMI BLUES) takes what could easily have been a second-rate exercise in PULP FICTION attitude and gives it a clean, vivid look, wasting little time on the mercenary metaphors (making a killing in business, and so on) and keeping Martin's misbegotten, near-surreal sentimental journey moving along briskly. Propelled by a hippest-hits of the '80s soundtrack and Cusack's deceptively subtle performance, this potentially queasy mix of John Hughes-style high school nostalgia and Tarantino-esque cool gets past the gags and ventures into some surprisingly poignant territory without ever losing its brittle edge. Blank's relationship with his unwilling therapist (Alan Arkin) is particularly bracing, and even the bloated Dan Aykroyd (playing a fellow professional killer who's hell-bent on unionizing) manages not to spoil things.

GROUNDHOG DAY
1993　103m　c　Comedy　　★★★½
Columbia　(U.S.)　PG

Bill Murray (*Phil*), Andie MacDowell (*Rita*), Chris Elliott (*Larry*), Stephen Tobolowsky (*Ned*), Brian Doyle-Murray (*Buster*), Marita Geraghty (*Nancy*), Angela Paton (*Mrs. Lancaster*), Rick Ducommun (*Gus*), Rick Overton (*Ralph*), Robin Duke (*Doris the Waitress*)

p, Trevor Albert, Harold Ramis; d, Harold Ramis; w, Danny Rubin, Harold Ramis (from the story by Rubin); ph, John Bailey, James Blanford, George Kohut; ed, Pembroke J. Herring; m, George Fenton; prod d, David Nichols; art d, Peter Lansdown Smith; fx, Tom Ryba; cos, Jennifer Butler

GROUNDHOG DAY is an amiable comedy with a respectable laugh quotient—more than NATIONAL LAMPOON'S LOADED WEAPON 1, but not as many as "Michael Jackson Talks . . . to Oprah."

Bill Murray stars as Phil, a TV weatherman sent to Punxsutawney, PA, to cover the Groundhog Day festival. A grinch who disdains all things provincial, Phil is predictably peeved when a blizzard forces him, his producer Rita (Andie MacDowell) and cameraman Larry (Chris Elliott) to spend a second night in the picture-postcard town.

Peeved doesn't even begin to approach how he feels next morning, when he wakes up and discovers that it's Groundhog Day—again. Stuck in a time loop, Phil seems doomed to spend the rest of his life repeating the same day over and over. Whatever he does—from getting thrown in jail to committing several varieties of suicide—he invariably wakes up at 6:00 the next morning in his guest-house bed, with "I Got You, Babe" blaring from his radio alarm.

What do you do when you're sentenced to re-live one day in your life for eternity? Phil starts out trivial (he memorizes all the answers to "Jeopardy"); then decides to better himself (piano lessons); and finally searches for true love, coming up with some ingenious ways of wooing Rita in less than 24 hours. (However far he gets each day, he's always back to square one in the morning.)

With Bill Murray being his usual self and Andie McDowell injecting a high charm factor, GROUNDHOG DAY makes a pretty entertaining couple of hours. Seeing it once is fine, but seeing it every day for the rest of your life is not recommended.

GUARDSMAN, THE

1931 89m bw Comedy ★★★★
MGM (U.S.) /A

Alfred Lunt *(the Actor)*, Lynn Fontanne *(the Actress)*, Roland Young *(the Critic)*, ZaSu Pitts *(Liesl)*, Maude Eburne *(Mama)*, Herman Bing *(a Creditor)*, Ann Dvorak *(a Fan)*

p, Irving Thalberg, Albert Lewin; d, Sidney Franklin; w, Ernest Vajda, Claudine West (based on the play by Ferenc Molnar); ph, Norbert Brodine; ed, Conrad A. Nervig

AAN Best Actor: Alfred Lunt; *AAN Best Actress:* Lynn Fontanne

A tattered, irresistible Valentine, more like a photographed stage play than a film, but a souvenir of lyrical, happy talent. French playwright Ferenc Molnar's clever marital comedy was never better performed than by the illustrious stars of American theater, Alfred Lunt and Lynn Fontanne, who had made the play a Broadway hit in 1924.

This bubbling sex farce begins when Lunt, watching Fontanne dreamily playing Chopin on the piano, suspects that her mind is on another. He quickly determines to resolve this doubt by a dangerous charade. Impersonating his imagined rival—a Russian guardsman with mustache and broad accent—he seduces his wife, who turns the tables on him the next morning, telling him "I knew it was you all along." Or is this just a clever attempt to preserve her marriage?

It took the supreme talents of Lunt and Fontanne to make this delicate stage material work. Although the public did not respond well to the sophisticated comedy, the film was a smashing critical success. Except for cameo roles in STAGE DOOR CANTEEN, this would be the only sound film the couple made in their illustrious careers, although Hollywood had previously wooed them into silents. MGM's Irving Thalberg managed to convince the famous pair to leave Broadway for THE GUARDSMAN, but it took a *lot* of convincing. To them the movies were merely cloudy mirrors of their own live theater reputations, reflections they did not appreciate. But in all fairness to their undeniable talent, it is said both realized they didn't photograph worth a damn.

GUELWAAR

1993 115m c Drama ★★★½
Film Domireew/Galatee Film/FR3 Film Production (Senegal)

Omar Seck *(Gora)*, Ndiawar Diop *(Barthelemy)*, Mame Ndoumbe Diop *(Nogoy Marie Thioune)*, Isseu Niang *(Veronique)*, Myriam Niang *(Helene)*, Mustapha Diop *(Aloys)*, Thierno Ndiaye *(Pierre Henri Thioune (Guelwaar))*, Marie-Augustine Diatta *(Sophie)*, Joseph Sane *(Father Leon)*, Samba Wane *(Gor Mag)*

p, Ousmane Sembene, Jacques Perrin; d, Ousmane Sembene; w, Ousmane Sembene; ph, Dominique Gentil; ed, Marie Aimee; m, Baba Mall; prod d, Francois Laurent Sulva

With the release of GUELWAAR, his seventh feature and first outing since 1987's CAMP DE THIAROYE, the renowned Senegalese filmmaker Ousmane Sembene reconfirms his stature both as a master storyteller and a distinctively humanitarian artist.

Pierre Henri Thioune (Thierno Ndiaye), called Guelwaar—or Noble One—by his family and friends, has died under mysterious circumstances, leaving behind his grieving wife, Nogoy Marie (Mame Ndoumbe Diop); their daughter Sophie (Marie-Augustine Diatta), who toils as a prostitute in Dakar; and their two sons, Barthelemy (Ndiawar Diop) and Aloys (Mustapha Diop). Funeral proceedings are delayed, however, by the unaccountable disappearance of Guelwaar's corpse from the local morgue. When policeman Gora (Omar Seck) goes in search of the missing body, he finds himself in the midst of a bitter dispute between local Christians and Muslims.

Despite its languorous pace and folkloric quality, GUELWAAR reflects a hugely sophisticated sensibility, frequently diverging from the central story to include illuminating flashbacks, digressions, and soliloquies. Among the many contemporary issues Sembene touches

upon—the loss of traditions, AIDS, the spread of corruption—the film offers a scathing indictment of the neocolonialism that permeates West African society.

GUESS WHO'S COMING TO DINNER

1967 108m c Drama ★★½
Columbia (U.S.) /PG

Spencer Tracy *(Matt Drayton)*, Sidney Poitier *(John Prentice)*, Katharine Hepburn *(Christina Drayton)*, Katharine Houghton *(Joey Drayton)*, Cecil Kellaway *(Monsignor Ryan)*, Roy E. Glenn Sr. *(Mr. Prentice)*, Beah Richards *(Mrs. Prentice)*, Isabel Sanford *(Tillie)*, Virginia Christine *(Hilary St. George)*, Alexandra Hay *(Car Hop)*

p, Stanley Kramer; d, Stanley Kramer; w, William Rose; ph, Sam Leavitt; ed, Robert C. Jones; m, Frank DeVol; prod d, Robert Clatworthy; fx, Geza Gaspar; cos, Jean Louis, Joe King

AAN Best Picture; AAN Best Actor: Spencer Tracy; *AA Best Actress:* Katharine Hepburn; *AAN Best Supporting Actor:* Cecil Kellaway; *AAN Best Supporting Actress:* Beah Richards; *AAN Best Director:* Stanley Kramer; *AA Best Original Story and Screenplay:* William Rose; *AAN Best Editing:* Robert C. Jones; *AAN Best Score:* Frank DeVol; *AAN Best Art Direction:* Robert Clatworthy, Frank Tuttle

William Rose, with a stilted screenplay, and Stanley Kramer, who literally makes this dinner hour stand still—say we're not in. Big deal in its day, but really safe, lame melodrama, and an unfitting finale to the Tracy-Hepburn screen partnership.

Bland little Houghton arrives home after a Hawaiian vacation to announce to parents Tracy and Hepburn that she is about to wed a brilliant research physician, Poitier, who is Black. This creates considerable social turmoil for the upper-middle-class family. Poitier tells the parents that unless they give their unreserved consent he will not marry their daughter, thereby putting the responsibility for the interracial marriage squarely upon their shoulders. After some soul-searching and breaking with friends who oppose miscegenation, the parents back up the young couple.

Tracy looks tired in this draggy production; he died soon afterward, and it's infuriating to watch him sweat to inject fire into such pap. Hepburn, with her blithely resolute air and great, watering eyes, is magnanimous as always; watching her watch Tracy during his big speech is one of the film's two great Moments. The other? Hepburn in the driveway, banishing an ex-friend: "Don't say anything, Hillary, just—go."

GUMSHOE

1971 88m c Crime/Comedy ★★★½
Memorial (U.K.) PG/15

Albert Finney *(Eddie Ginley)*, Billie Whitelaw *(Ellen)*, Frank Finlay *(William)*, Janice Rule *(Mrs. Blankerscoon)*, Carolyn Seymour *(Alison Wyatt)*, Fulton Mackay *(Straker)*, George Innes *(Bookshop Proprietor)*, George Silver *(Jacob De Fries)*, Billy Dean *(Tommy)*, Wendy Richard *(Anne Scott)*

p, Michael Medwin; d, Stephen Frears; w, Neville Smith; ph, Chris Menges; ed, Fergus McDonell, Charles Rees; m, Andrew Lloyd Webber; prod d, Michael Seymour; art d, Richard Rambaut; fx, Bowie Films; cos, Daphne Dare

This offbeat feature debut from director Stephen Frears (MY BEAUTIFUL LAUNDRETTE, DANGEROUS LIAISONS, THE GRIFTERS) cleverly satirizes the detective films of the past, particularly those featuring the hardboiled private eyes created by Dashiell Hammett and Raymond Chandler.

Finney, a bingo caller in a seedy Liverpool nightclub who envisions himself as a tough detective *a la* Humphrey Bogart, advertises his sleuthing services and is hired by a mysterious fat man (Silver). After receiving a package containing a photo of a young woman (Seymour), a gun and a thousand pounds—but no instructions—Finney becomes enmeshed in an extraordinarily convoluted affair that involves heroin smuggling, gun running and African politics.

Produced by Finney's own company, GUMSHOE is packed with witty, if absurd, dialogue and plenty of action, all harking back to the film noir days of the tough detective and made even funnier by Finney's struggles through the awkward transition from British commoner to the image of a hard-as-nails American-type sleuth. Great fun.

GUNFIGHT AT THE O.K. CORRAL

1957 122m c Western ★★★★
Paramount (U.S.) /PG

Burt Lancaster (Wyatt Earp), Kirk Douglas (John H. "Doc" Holliday), Rhonda Fleming (Laura Denbow), Jo Van Fleet (Kate Fisher), John Ireland (Johnny Ringo), Lyle Bettger (Ike Clanton), Frank Faylen (Cotton Wilson), Earl Holliman (Charles Bassett), Ted de Corsia (Abel Head "Shanghai Pierce"), Dennis Hopper (Billy Clanton)

p, Hal B. Wallis; d, John Sturges; w, Leon Uris (based on the magazine article "The Killer" by George Scullin); ph, Charles Lang; ed, Warren Low; m, Dimitri Tiomkin; art d, Hal Pereira, Walter Tyler; fx, John P. Fulton; cos, Edith Head

AAN Best Editing: Warren Low; AAN Best Sound: George Dutton (Paramount Studio Sound Department)

Solid, expert "town" Western, but lacking the fuel of passion. Still it's a landmark Western—more than any other of its era, it gave the genre major film status. The story is legend: strong, resolute, and stoic, Lancaster is the famed Marshal Wyatt Earp, and Douglas is his closest friend, the deadly gunfighter "Doc" Holliday.

It's an interesting acting exercise: these two have been called "the two terrible-tempered twins"; they're like Davis and Crawford, in a way. People confuse their roles, claim one's a better actor, the other a bigger star, but unlike the aforementioned ladies, the two opinions offered flip back and forth on the respective men. Curious—but predictable—that GUNFIGHT is exactly the same. It's a stand-off between bravura egos, supported mightily by Van Cleef, Ireland, and the other men, with Van Fleet and Fleming doing definitive western turns as frontier whore and gambling hall floozie. But the film might have profited more from reverse casting in the leads (Lancaster's flamboyance seeming more suited to a gunman than a sheriff). And Sturges's direction lacks the bite of Anthony Mann's Jimmy Stewart oaters.

Yet GUNFIGHT, written—with generous dashes of dramatic license—by Leon Uris and beautifully photographed by Charles Lang, is truly a classic Western, one which thoroughly revitalized the genre. Its big-budget production and tremendous box-office success sent the making of B Westerns into decline; they all but vanished in the 1960s. The legendary gunfight has been filmed many other times, first in FRONTIER MARSHAL, then in John Ford's magnificent MY DARLING CLEMENTINE, again in Sturges's impressive sequel to this film, HOUR OF THE GUN, and in the introspective DOC.

GUNFIGHTER, THE

1950 84m bw Western ★★★★
Fox (U.S.) /A

Gregory Peck (Jimmy Ringo), Helen Westcott (Peggy Walsh), Millard Mitchell (Sheriff Mark Strett), Jean Parker (Molly), Karl Malden (Mac), Skip Homeier (Hunt Bromley), Anthony Ross (Charlie), Verna Felton (Mrs. Pennyfeather), Ellen Corby (Mrs. Devlin), Richard Jaeckel (Eddie)

p, Nunnally Johnson; d, Henry King; w, William Bowers, William Sellers, Nunnally Johnson, Andre De Toth (based on a story by Bowers); ph, Arthur Miller; ed, Barbara McLean; m, Alfred Newman; art d, Lyle Wheeler, Richard Irvine

AAN Best Original Screenplay: Andre DeToth, William Bowers

An arresting, superbly produced and downbeat Western photographed in stark black and white, THE GUNFIGHTER presents an unglorified view of the Old West as a grim, dirty and decidedly desperate place.

Peck stars as an alienated gunfighter who's feeling his age and beginning to look back more often than forward. Entering a saloon one night, he finds that his notorious reputation has preceded him. Loud-mouthed punk Jaeckel picks a fight with him, calling Peck names. Peck tries to beg off, asking anyone in the bar to talk the brash and foolish youth out of going for his gun. But Jaeckel reaches and Peck beats him,

shooting and killing the aspiring gunslinger. After being informed that despite justification in defending himself, it won't matter to Jaeckel's three older brothers, the seasoned gunfighter leaves hastily and moves on to his original destination, taking a room in a nearby town where he hopes to be reunited with his young son. Meanwhile, Jaeckel's blood-thirsty siblings follow close behind.

Generally tough and humorless, THE GUNFIGHTER is a grim portrait of a man whose time and historical role have run out, and he knows it. Peck is dazzling as the doomed and haunted gunfighter, a man desperately trying to escape his own past and identity, but knowing all along that hope is false and that there is only a bullet in his future. Henry King's direction is outstanding, keeping the action tautly drawn, while Arthur Miller's high-contrast cinematography is highly suggestive as it documents Peck's inexorable movement toward death. Preceding HIGH NOON by two years, THE GUNFIGHTER was a seminal film in the western's movement away from action cliches toward more psychological depth.

GUNGA DIN

1939 117m bw Adventure/War ★★★★★
RKO (U.S.) /U

Cary Grant (Sgt. Cutter), Victor McLaglen (Sgt. MacChesney), Douglas Fairbanks Jr. (Sgt. Ballantine), Sam Jaffe (Gunga Din), Eduardo Ciannelli (Guru), Joan Fontaine (Emmy Stebbins), Montagu Love (Col. Weed), Robert Coote (Higginbotham), Abner Biberman (Chota), Lumsden Hare (Maj. Mitchell)

p, George Stevens; d, George Stevens; w, Fred Guiol (based on the story by Ben Hecht, Charles MacArthur, William Faulkner from the poem by Rudyard Kipling); ph, Joseph August, John Lockert; m, Alfred Newman; art d, Van Nest Polglase, Perry Ferguson; fx, Vernon L. Walker; cos, Edward Stevenson

The GONE WITH THE WIND of the comic action-adventure genre, GUNGA DIN has a bit of everything—humor, suspense, spectacle, action and a heavy dose of racism, imperialism and xenophobia.

Based on a story by Ben Hecht and Charles MacArthur (it's the same friendly rivals plot of THE FRONT PAGE) and the moving Rudyard Kipling poem, this rousing adventure opens as a remote, mountainous British outpost in India is raided by a band of rebel natives. Three of the Army's most reliable frontier veterans—Sergeants Cutter (Cary Grant), MacChesney (Victor McLaglen) and Ballantine (Douglas Fairbanks Jr.)—are sent to the now-silent outpost. Accompanying them is a small contingent of Indian troops and water-carriers, or bhistis, including Gunga Din (Sam Jaffe), whose only ambition in life is to become a soldier. The sergeants then receive their orders—to annihilate the murderous Thugs, a violent and mystical sect previously thought extinct.

A $2 million production that wowed them at the box office, GUNGA DIN is an undeniably rousing adventure tale. The performances and direction are a great deal of fun—part Three Musketeers, part Laurel and Hardy (Stevens began his career directing the duo's comedy shorts)—but it's difficult to overlook the blatantly racist nature of the proceedings, which endorse British imperialism and the violence inflicted on the Indian people.

GUNS OF NAVARONE, THE

1961 157m c Adventure/War ★★★½
Open Road (U.S./U.K.) /PG

Gregory Peck (Capt. Mallory), David Niven (Cpl. Miller), Anthony Quinn (Col. Andrea Stavros), Stanley Baker (CPO Brown), Anthony Quayle (Maj. Franklin), Irene Papas (Maria), Gia Scala (Anna), James Darren (Pvt. Pappadimos), James Robertson Justice (Jensen), Richard Harris (Barnsby)

d, J. Lee Thompson; w, Carl Foreman (based on the novel Guns of Navarone by Alistair MacLean); ph, Oswald Morris; ed, Alan Osbiston; m, Dimitri Tiomkin; prod d, Geoffrey Drake; art d, Geoffrey Drake; fx, Bill Warrington, Wally Veevers; cos, Monty Berman, Olga Lehmann

AAN Best Picture; AAN Best Director: J. Lee Thompson; AAN Best Adapted Screenplay: Carl Foreman,; AAN Best Editing: Alan Osbiston; AAN Best Score: Dimitri Tiomkin; AAN Best Sound: John Cox; AA Best Visual Effects: Bill Warrington, Vivian C. Greenham

This WWII spectacle, with its cliched story, hackneyed characters, and triumph-over-impossible-odds finale, could only have been born in a Hollywood dream tank; nevertheless, it's great adventure.

British intelligence learns that two enormous guns have been installed on the Aegean island of Navarone. The long-range field pieces are capable of destroying any British fleet trying to sail to Kheros, near Turkey, where a large British force is facing annihilation unless it is evacuated. It's the job of Captain Mallory (Gregory Peck) and a handful of men to land secretly on Navarone and dismantle the guns. The group includes killers Private Pappadimos (James Darren) and CPO Brown (Stanley Baker), explosives expert Corporal Miller (David Niven), and tough Greek patriot Andrea Stavros (Anthony Quinn). Meeting the men along the way are resistance leader Maria (Irene Papas) and Anna (Gia Scala), a beautiful Greek girl who was reportedly tortured by the Germans.

There are a few subplots in this stirring spectacle—Miller's dislike for Mallory's dispassionate procedures, Stavros's grudge against Mallory for an old disservice—but the destruction of the guns is the constant theme. It's handled well by veteran director J. Lee Thompson, with strong cast support and excellent production values that make it all lavish, rich, and often breathtaking. A sequel starring Harrison Ford, FORCE 10 FROM NAVARONE, appeared 17 years later.

GUY NAMED JOE, A

1944   120m   bw   War/Romance/Fantasy   ★★★
MGM   (U.S.)   /A

Spencer Tracy *(Pete Sandidge)*, Irene Dunne *(Dorinda Durston)*, Van Johnson *(Ted Randall)*, Ward Bond *(Al Yackey)*, James Gleason *(Col. "Nails" Kilpatrick)*, Lionel Barrymore *(The General)*, Barry Nelson *(Dick Rumney)*, Esther Williams *(Ellen Bright)*, Henry O'Neill *(Col. Sykes)*, Don DeFore *("Powerhouse" James J. Rourke)*

p, Everett Riskin; d, Victor Fleming; w, Dalton Trumbo (based on a story by Chandler Sprague, David Boehm, Frederick Hazlitt Brennan); ph, George Folsey, Karl Freund; ed, Frank Sullivan; m, Herbert Stothart; art d, Cedric Gibbons, Lyle Wheeler; fx, A. Arnold Gillespie, Donald Jahraus, Warren Newcombe; cos, Irene

AAN Best Original Screenplay: David Boehm, Chandler Sprague

A sticky, tear-jerking fantasy, A GUY NAMED JOE was one of the most popular movies during WWII, combining the considerable talents of Spencer Tracy, Irene Dunne, and Van Johnson in a big-scale production.

Pete Sandidge (Tracy), a daredevil bomber pilot, dies when he crashes his plane into a German aircraft carrier (though, in fact, there were none in WWII), leaving his devoted girlfriend, Dorinda (Irene Dunne), who is also a pilot, heartbroken. In heaven, Pete receives a new assignment: he is to become the guardian angel for Ted Randall (Van Johnson), a young Army flyer. Invisibly, Pete guides Ted through flight school and into combat, but the ectoplasmic mentor's tolerance is tested when Ted falls for Dorinda. Ultimately, however, Pete not only comes to terms with their relationship but also acts as Dorinda's copilot when she undertakes a dangerous bombing raid, so that Ted won't have to.

The film goes in too many directions at the same time, trying to combine its romantic fantasy line and a grim war outlook. But Dalton Trumbo's script is verbally wry—with the best lines going to wisecracking Tracy. Alas, Fleming was probably the wrong director for JOE; despite Arnold Gillespie's special effects, the Fleming-Tracy-Johnson chemistry feels as heavy as combat boots. Incidentally, there is no character in the film named "Joe"; the title is derived from the Army Air Corps practice of calling a "right fellow" Joe. Remade by Steven Spielberg in 1989 as ALWAYS.

GYPSY

1962   149m   c   Musical/Biography   ★★★½
Warner Bros.   (U.S.)   /A

Rosalind Russell *(Rose)*, Natalie Wood *(Louise "Gypsy")*, Karl Malden *(Herbie Sommers)*, Paul Wallace *(Tulsa No. 2)*, Betty Bruce *(Tessie Tura)*, Parley Baer *(Mr. Kringelein)*, Harry Shannon *(Grandpa)*, Morgan Brittany *("Baby" June)*, Ann Jillian *("Dainty" June)*, Diane Pace *("Baby" Louise)*

p, Mervyn LeRoy; d, Mervyn LeRoy; w, Leonard Spigelgass (based on the musical play by Arthur Laurents and the book *Gypsy, A Memoir* by Gypsy Rose Lee); ph, Harry Stradling; ed, Philip W. Anderson; art d, John Beckman; chor, Robert Tucker; cos, Orry-Kelly, Howard Shoup, Bill Gaskin

AAN Best Cinematography: Harry Stradling Sr; *AAN Best Score:* Frank Perkins; *AAN Best Costume Design:* Orry-Kelly

The original casting package for this blockbuster no doubt would have created motion picture history, with Miss Show Business herself, Judy Garland taking on the Ethel Merman legend, and the steamy Ann-Margret re-creating the strips of famed burlesque queen Gypsy Rose Lee. We love Roz, and her comic business as quintessential stage ma Rose Hovick is terrific; her moments of pathos don't disappoint, either, but she's just not the cyclonic force of nature that made Merman immortal in the annals of show business history. With her mother-resentments, and grueling vaudeville childhood, the thought of Garland is a chilling one indeed, for GYPSY is a musical about child abuse and frustrated ambition, though sometimes funny it may be.

As Gypsy, Natalie Wood lacks the latent sex appeal that needs to come to life when Rose's ambitions land the act she manages into lowlife burlesque, where the "untalented" Louise finds her niche at last. Though expertly coached by the original herself, Wood resembles a plastic wind-up doll strutting the runway, and that her cleavage was the result of extensive adhesive tape has passed into Hollywood lore long ago.

Mervyn LeRoy, sans any brass in casting, directs with an abrasive hand, as if coarse treatment can make up for what's missing. But Karl Malden, Ann Jillian (Dainty June), and Morgan Brittany (Baby June) are just right, and as three healthy surrogate stripper moms, Faith Dane, Roxanne Arlen, and especially Betty Bruce are perfection, playing dames actresses today don't know how to approach. The script's guts have been torn out; Leonard Spiegelgass prettied up Arthur Laurents's perfect work, presumably to throw sympathy to the star. There is an atmospheric strip montage that captures the spirit of Minsky and some great costumes, but Tucker's choreography has been largely snatched from Jerome Robbins.

The score, with music by Jule Styne and lyrics by Stephen Sondheim, is so perfect, so joyous, it's worth watching just to hear it aloud. Alas, "Together, Wherever We Go" was cut before the release, and the score's only blight, "Little Lamb," was left in to give Wood a big moment while we're waiting for the flesh. She's dubbed of course, and although, as we said, we love Roz, she lied that she did all her own singing—they spliced her voice in with the pipes of Lisa Kirk. The effect is brisk without carrying much conviction, although Russell's conviction in the finale is thoroughly satisfactory. Watch anyway.

H

HAIL, MARY
(JE VOUS SALUE, MARIE)

1985   86m   c   Religious   ★★★★
Pegase/JLG/Sara/SSR/Channel 4/Gaumont   /18
(France/Switzerland/U.K.)

Myriem Roussel *(Mary)*, Thierry Rode *(Joseph)*, Philippe Lacoste *(Angel)*, Juliette Binoche *(Juliette)*, Manon Anderson *(Girl)*, Malachi Jara Kohan *(Jesus)*, Johan Leysen *(Professor)*, Anne Gauthier *(Eva)*

d, Jean-Luc Godard; w, Jean-Luc Godard; ph, Jean-Bernard Menoud, Jacques Frimann; m, Johann Sebastian Bach, Anton Dvorak, John Coltrane

Ever since his first film, BREATHLESS, Jean-Luc Godard has subverted the conventions of cinema and caused critical outrage in the process. Remaining true to form, Godard, some 26 years later, again whipped the public into a frenzy with HAIL MARY. By updating the story of the Virgin Mary, Godard produced, as the critics billed it, "the most controversial film of our time," and for once the advertisements exaggerated only slightly.

Myriem Roussel is Mary, a young woman who pumps gas, plays basketball, and has a taxi driver boyfriend named Joseph (Thierry Rode). Though another woman is anxious to sleep with Rode, he chooses instead to chase the chaste Roussel. One day Roussel learns she is to give birth to the Son of God; Rode, however, cannot believe that Roussel is pregnant and a virgin. But after they are wed Roussel teaches Rode to love her from a distance, revering her without touching her—Godard's personal definition of faith.

Sight unseen, HAIL MARY was protested in many cities throughout the world and banned in others, including Rome, where Pope John Paul II officially condemned the film. Curiously, Godard had originally intended to make a film about incest—planning to concentrate on a man's impossible love for his unattainable daughter—but as the film evolved, it became the story of Joseph's love for his unattainable Mary. Since BREATHLESS, Godard has been fascinated with the idea of a man becoming obsessed with a woman he cannot attain or possess, and HAIL, MARY takes this preoccupation to the extreme.

HAIL THE CONQUERING HERO

1944   101m   bw   Comedy   ★★★★
Paramount   (U.S.)   /U

Eddie Bracken (Woodrow Lafayette Pershing Truesmith), Ella Raines (Libby), Bill Edwards (Forrest Noble), Raymond Walburn (Mayor Noble), William Demarest (Sergeant), Jimmie Dundee (Corporal), Georgia Caine (Mrs. Truesmith), Alan Bridge (Political Boss), James Damore (Jonesy), Freddie Steele (Bugsy)

p, Preston Sturges; d, Preston Sturges; w, Preston Sturges; ph, John Seitz; ed, Stuart Gilmore; m, Werner R. Heymann; art d, Hans Dreier

AAN Best Original Screenplay: Preston Sturges

The premier comedy writer-director of 1940s Hollywood strikes again! Preston Sturges satirizes home-front American patriotism run amuck during WWII. All the sacred cows of the era—heroic fathers, loving moms, battle fatigue—are milked for laughs in this fastpaced comedy.

Sad sack Woodrow Lafayette Pershing Truesmith (Bracken) desperately wants to live up to the reputation of his Marine dad who died a war hero in WWI. Truesmith enlists to carry on the family honor at the outbreak of WWII but he's classified 4-F due to severe chronic hay fever. Ashamed to return home, he takes a job in a shipyard and, with the help of friends in the Marine Corps, sends letters from the Pacific to his mother (Caine) and his sweetheart Libby (Raines). To avoid telling the truth, Bracken breaks up with Libby through the mail. Some genuine Marine heroes returning from Guadalcanal find Truesmith drowning his sorrows in a saloon. Bugsy (Steele), a shell-shocked vet who values motherhood above all else, calls Mrs. Truesmith and tells her that her son has returned from the war. To complete the charade, the crusty Sergeant (Demarest) and the others convince the reluctant wash-out to put on a uniform, slip back home to Oakridge, and make his mother happy. He can then put his uniform in the closet and resume his life of obscurity. Truesmith agrees and takes the train back home with his new Marine friends. To their astonishment, the entire town has turned out with two brass bands to greet the conquering hero.

Who else but this brilliant iconoclast would have dared to make this kind of counter-heroic comedy very near the end of World WarII? Supporting the very funny Bracken is a cast composed mostly of Sturges's stock people—Demarest, Pangborn, Walburn and others—all of them outstanding. HAIL THE CONQUERING HERO was nominated for an Oscar for Best Original Screenplay, putting Sturges in competition with himself for the award since he was also nominated for his script for THE MIRACLE OF MORGAN'S CREEK.

HAIR

1979   118m   c   Musical   ★★★★
UA   (U.S.)   PG/15

John Savage (Claude), Treat Williams (Berger), Beverly D'Angelo (Sheila), Annie Golden (Jeannie), Dorsey Wright (Hud), Don Dacus (Woof), Cheryl Barnes (Hud's Fiancee), Richard Bright (Fenton), Nicholas Ray (The General), Charlotte Rae (Party Guest)

p, Lester Persky, Michael Butler; d, Milos Forman; w, Michael Weller (based on the musical play by Gerome Ragni, James Rado, and Galt MacDermot); ph, Miroslav Ondricek; ed, Lynzee Klingman; m, Galt MacDermot; prod d, Stuart Wurtzel; fx, Al Griswold; chor, Twyla Tharp; cos, Ann Roth

Milos Forman had already proven his talent with TAKING OFF and the multiple-Oscar-winning ONE FLEW OVER THE CUCKOO'S NEXT, but when the Czech director was chosen to make this very American film, based on the long-running Broadway play, some wondered about the combination. They needn't have worried.

Savage plays a square draftee from Oklahoma on his way to Vietnam via New York City. There, he is adopted by a group of flower children who guide him through a series of euphoric countercultural adventures, including an introduction to marijuana and an encounter with a slightly batty debutante (D'Angelo). Along the way, there are many excellent songs and some of the most inventive choreography (by the ingenious Twyla Tharp) ever seen, including a "horse ballet" by mounted police in Central Park where they have been assigned to observe a "be-in."

There is much to recommend in this film, and sheer energy pours off the screen in every frame. Forman and scenarist Michael Weller deftly synthesized the pastiche of sketches and tunes that comprised the stage musical into a compelling screen entertainment. Unfortunately, the movie was not a hit, perhaps because HAIR was made almost 12 years after the play opened and, while dated, was not quite ready to be enjoyed nostalgically.

HAIRDRESSER'S HUSBAND, THE
(MARI DE LA COIFFEUSE, LA)

1992   84m   c   Romance/Drama   ★★★★
Lambart Productions/TF1 Films Production/PAC   (France)   R/15

Jean Rochefort (Antoine), Anna Galiena (Mathilde), Roland Bertin (Antoine's Father), Maurice Chevit (Agopian), Philippe Clevenot (Morvoisieux), Jacques Mathou (Mr. Chardon), Claude Aufaure (Gay Customer), Albert Delpy (Donecker), Henry Hocking (Antoine—Age 12), Ticky Holgado (Morvoisieux Son-in-Law)

p, Thierry DeGanay; d, Patrice Leconte; w, Patrice Leconte, Claude Klotz (from the story by Leconte); ph, Eduardo Serra; ed, Joelle Hache; m, Michael Nyman; prod d, Ivan Maussion

THE HAIRDRESSER'S HUSBAND is another tale of obsessive love from director Patrice Leconte (MONSIEUR HIRE).

Ever since an erotic childhood experience with his barber, Antoine (Jean Rochefort) has had a single ambition in life: to marry a hairdresser. He finally meets the shampoo girl of his dreams, Mathilde (Anna Galiena), who centers her life entirely around a barber shop she has inherited. The two marry and live in a state of erotic bliss, until Mathilde's obsessive fear of losing Antoine's love begins to unravel the relationship.

THE HAIRDRESSER'S HUSBAND is a realistically told fable, creating a tension between style and content that grows as Mathilde's initial romanticism begins to seem more like a phobic fear of the world outside her shop. Never has love-soaked indolence seemed so attractive in a movie as it does here. Rochefort's Antoine is an avid devourer of the minutiae of life, while Galiena's Mathilde is like the answer to a sensualist's prayer—a woman of dark, earthy beauty living only to be loved, and living in terror of the day when she might be loved no more. Leconte understands the intoxicating powers of love, but he also understands what happens when we wake from our erotic reveries. And that is what makes a film as slight as this seem like a story for the ages, a rapturous epic of the heart that is gripping and unforgettable.

HAIRSPRAY
1988 90m c Comedy ★★★½
New Line (U.S.) PG

Sonny Bono (Franklin Von Tussle), Ruth Brown (Motormouth Maybell), Divine (Edna Turnblad/Arvin Hodgepile), Colleen Fitzpatrick (Amber Von Tussle), Michael St. Gerard (Link Larkin), Deborah Harry (Velma Von Tussle), Ricki Lake (Tracy Turnblad), Leslie Ann Powers (Penny Pingleton), Clayton Prince (Seaweed), Jerry Stiller (Wilbur Turnblad)

p, Rachel Talalay, Stanley F. Buchthal, John Waters; d, John Waters; w, John Waters; ph, David Insley; ed, Janice Hampton; chor, Edward Love; cos, Van Smith

Set in Baltimore circa 1962, HAIRSPRAY joyously details the last days of 50s-era American naivete, as the country moves from postwar complacency to massive social upheaval. Cult filmmaker John Waters enters the mainstream with surprisingly little fuss.

Caught up in all this is the "Corny Collins Show," a wildly popular Baltimore television dance program. The show's queen is the spoiled and snobbish Fitzpatrick, whose father, Bono, owns the "Tilted Acres" amusement park. Lake, an obese working-class teen, auditions for a spot on the show, against the wishes of her mother, Divine, and she earns it because of her sensational dancing. The socially progressive teen begins to cause trouble, however, when she demands the segregated program be opened up to include the black teenagers of Baltimore.

Controversial filmmaker John Waters finally hits his commercial stride in this film, parlaying his keen social observation and great compassion for society's outsiders into a colorful and engaging comedy full of dancing, music and heartfelt nostalgia. Unfortunately, what should have been a celebration turned into sadness when Waters's longtime friend and collaborator Divine, who was poised on the edge of stardom, died of a heart attack a mere two weeks after HAIRSPRAY opened nationwide.

HALLELUJAH
1929 100m bw Drama ★★★★
MGM (U.S.)

Daniel Haynes (Zeke), Nina Mae McKinney (Chick), William E. Fontaine (Hot Shot), Harry Gray (Parson), Fannie Belle DeKnight (Mammy), Everett McGarrity (Spunk), Victoria Spivey (Missy Rose), Milton Dickerson, Robert Couch, Walter Tait (Johnson Kids)

p, King Vidor; d, King Vidor; w, Wanda Tuchock, Ransom Rideout (based on a story by King Vidor); ph, Gordon Avil; ed, Hugh Wynn, Anson Stevenson; m, Irving Berlin; art d, Cedric Gibbons

AAN Best Director: King Vidor

This was the first all-black feature film and one of the boldest pictures ever made, especially since MGM knew the film would not get much of a release in the deep South. King Vidor was a man vitally interested in social issues (witness his work on THE BIG PARADE and THE CROWD), and he wanted to show the rest of America what black people were going through. Daniel Haynes plays Zeke, an innocent young man who is very close to his mother (Fannie Belle DeKnight), and to his brother, Spunk (Everett McGarrity), whom he accidentally kills. Zeke turns to religion to ease his grief.

With a cast that included many amateurs (Harry Gray had been a janitor at a Harlem newspaper, and Nina Mae McKinney, the female lead, had never been in front of a camera), Vidor elicited performances from the group as good as any you might see in a seasoned troupe. Even today, more than half a century later, this film is not dated. Shot on location in Tennessee, HALLELUJAH is redolent with authenticity. The treatment of some scenes tends toward the melodramatic, notably the revival meetings, a wake, and various scenes on the plantation; but the film is filled with humanity and insight into black experience at the time. Irving Thalberg, the young chief of production at MGM, known and remembered as a man of integrity, gave Vidor the green light to make HALLELUJAH. This was the director's first talkie, but the film was shot as a silent, with the sound added in post-production.

HALLELUJAH THE HILLS
1963 88m bw Experimental/Comedy ★★★½
Vermont (U.S.) /A

Peter H. Beard (Jack), Martin Greenbaum (Leo), Sheila Finn (Jack's Vera in Winter), Peggy Steffans (Leo's Vera in Summer), Jerome Raphel (Father), Blanche Dee (Mother)

p, David C. Stone; d, Adolfas Mekas; w, Adolfas Mekas; ph, Ed Emshwiller; ed, Adolfas Mekas; m, Meyer Kupferman

Once upon a time in the early 1960s, there was a movement known as the New American Cinema. Jonas Mekas was its prophet in a weekly column in the Village Voice. He and his brother, Adolfas, who directed HALLELUJAH, THE HILLS, were among its practitioners. Most of this underground cinema consisted of arty shorts. (Perhaps Kenneth Anger's SCORPIO RISING was the best known of these.) The Mekas brothers produced more traditional feature-length films. This one is an interesting confluence of Hollywood structures and home-movie techniques: a document of its time, in part.

This delightful comedy for film buffs begins as an enthusiastic send-up of early French New Wave techniques. The thin story line has to do with a pair of young men, Jack (Beard) and Leo (Greenbaum), pursuing the same young lady (shades of Truffaut's JULES AND JIM) at different times of the year. Thus she is played by two actresses: one for winter (Finn) and one for summer (Steffans). The girl's parents are also featured: a wisecracking father and a no-nonsense mother. Ultimately, the question of just who will win Vera's love takes a backseat to the giddy celebration of movie magic.

The film plays around with time, space, character, and the history of the cinema and achieves a remarkable freshness. Adolfas Mekas shows a remarkable flair for visuals, using his forest settings well. The film is packed full of gags and silliness, having a good time with itself and movie cliches. The ending juxtaposes the characters of this film with the actual ending from Griffith's classic silent WAY DOWN EAST with Lillian Gish and Richard Barthelmess. HALLELUJAH THE HILLS is a personable and fun bit of filmmaking; its enthusiasm is infectious.

HALLOWEEN
1978 93m c Horror ★★★★
Falcon (U.S.) R/18

Donald Pleasence (Loomis), Jamie Lee Curtis (Laurie), Nancy Loomis (Annie), P.J. Soles (Lynda), Charles Cyphers (Brackett), Kyle Richards (Lindsey), Brian Andrews (Tommy), John Michael Graham (Bob), Nancy Stephens (Marion), Arthur Malet (Graveyard Keeper)

p, Debra Hill; d, John Carpenter; w, Debra Hill, John Carpenter; ph, Dean Cundey; ed, Tommy Lee Wallace, Charles Burnstein; m, John Carpenter; prod d, Tommy Lee Wallace

A modern horror classic. On Halloween night in 1963, a six-year-old boy in a Halloween mask inexplicably stabs his sister and her boyfriend to death while they are making love. He's institutionalized—until, exactly 15 years later, he escapes and returns to his small Illinois hometown once more to wreak Halloween havoc. His psychiatrist Dr. Loomis (Donald Pleasence) proclaims "The Evil is loose!" and is in hot pursuit with the authorities. Meanwhile Laurie (Jamie Lee Curtis) seems to be the only girl in town without a date for Halloween. All her high school friends seem to have hot dates scheduled but bright, bookish Laurie must settle for a quiet evening of babysitting, fending off trick-or-treaters, and watching old science fiction movies on television. Just another boring evening? Hardly.

There's nary a drop of blood on screen in this rollicking funhouse of a movie but there is enough sheer cinematic ingenuity on display to coax screams out of the most jaded gorehound. Cheap thrills—often accompanied by a joybuzzer noise on the soundtrack—lurk on the periphery of nearly every frame and film history allusions abound. Fans the moving camera also have reason to cheer as the Steadicam prowls the suburban streets unexpectedly turning into ominous point-of-view shots accompanied by creepy piano music (composed by the resourceful Carpenter). The performances are also far better than average for this kind of fare. Pleasence is a hoot as he gnaws on the scenery and the pleasingly equine beauty of Jamie Lee Curtis—at the beginning of the fondly remembered Queen of the B's stage of her career—enhances her sensitive performance.

HALLOWEEN was the surprise hit of the 1978 Chicago Film Festival. Some over-enthusiastic critics even compared it with Hitchcock's classic PSYCHO (which starred Curtis's mother, Janet Leigh) but such comparisons are silly and groundless; HALLOWEEN is just a superbly made unpretentious thriller whereas one can make higher claims for Carpenter. Furthermore Carpenter's clean, economical style owes a much greater debt to another master craftsman—Howard Hawks. From the opening—a long Steadicam point-of-view shot seen from behind a Halloween mask—to the climactic battle in which Curtis fends off the maniac time after time, only to have him rise again, Carpenter displays an astounding stylistic assurance for a young director working with a low budget.

Made for less than half a million dollars, HALLOWEEN grossed well over $50 million on its initial release making it the single most successful independent feature of all time. Two sequels, both produced by Carpenter, were woefully inferior to the original, but a third—released in 1988—wasn't too bad.

HAMBURGER HILL

1987 110m c War	★★★½
RKO (U.S.)	/18

Anthony Barrile *(Langulli)*, Michael Boatman *(Motown)*, Don Cheadle *(Washburn)*, Michael Dolan *(Murphy)*, Don James *(McDaniel)*, Dylan McDermott *(Sgt. Frantz)*, M.A. Nickles *(Galvin)*, Harry O'Reilly *(Duffy)*, Daniel O'Shea *(Gaigin)*, Tim Quill *(Beletsky)*

p, Marcia Nasatir, Jim Carabatsos; d, John Irvin; w, Jim Carabatsos; ph, Peter MacDonald; ed, Peter Tanner; m, Philip Glass; prod d, Austin Spriggs; art d, Toto Castillo; fx, Joe Lombardi

Instead of trying to match the hallucinatory bombast of APOCALYPSE NOW, the surreal metaphysics of PLATOON, or the studied idiosyncrasy of FULL METAL JACKET, director John Irvin reaches back to such classic combat films as THE SANDS OF IWO JIMA and PORK CHOP HILL for his inspiration here. So straightforward as to be old-fashioned, HAMBURGER HILL becomes unique by virtue of its unwillingness to participate in the current cycle of war-as-philosophical-metaphor Vietnam films and instead goes for a more conventional approach.

Realistic almost to a fault, Irvin's film is an account of the Third Squad, First Platoon, Bravo Company of the 101st Airborne Division and its battle to secure Hill 937 in the Ashau Valley, Vietnam, 1969. Short on plot, the film derives its power from isolated moments: letters from home, chats, arguments, visits to a brothel, and, of course, intense combat—all performed with vigor by an almost faceless ensemble of unknown actors spouting a nearly incomprehensible stream of GI lingo.

Shot in an unfussy, realistic manner by cinematographer Peter MacDonald, the visuals emphasize wide angles and deep focus, bombarding the senses without resorting to the kind of hallucinatory imagery found in most Vietnam films. The battle for the hill is exhausting to watch as the soldiers struggle upwards in the mud, clinging to exposed roots, tree stumps, and each other in a desperate effort to advance. Irvin rarely allows a glimpse of the top of the hill, further preventing the viewer from thinking ahead, instead forcing him to concentrate on climbing the few feet visible before him right along with the GIs.

Although it was underrated at the time of its release, time will eventually reveal that HAMBURGER HILL is one of the best and most realistic films made about the Vietnam War.

HAMLET

1948 155m bw Drama	★★★★
Two Cities/Rank (U.K.)	/U

Laurence Olivier *(Hamlet)*, Eileen Herlie *(Queen Gertrude)*, Basil Sydney *(King Claudius)*, Jean Simmons *(Ophelia)*, Norman Wooland *(Horatio)*, Felix Aylmer *(Polonius)*, Terence Morgan *(Laertes)*, Peter Cushing *(Osric)*, Stanley Holloway *(Gravedigger)*, John Laurie *(Francisco)*

p, Laurence Olivier; d, Laurence Olivier; w, Alan Dent (based on the play by William Shakespeare); ph, Desmond Dickinson; ed, Helga Cranston; m, William Walton; prod d, Roger Furse; art d, Carmen Dillon; fx, Paul Sheriff, Henry Harris, Jack Whitehead; cos, Elizabeth Hennings

AA Best Picture; *AA Best Actor:* Laurence Olivier; *AAN Best Supporting Actress:* Jean Simmons; *AAN Best Director:* Laurence Olivier; *AAN Best Score:* William Walton; *AA Best Art Direction:* Roger K. Furse, Carmen Dillon; *AA Best Costume Design:* Roger K. Furse

At 155 minutes, this screen adaptation of Shakespeare's most celebrated play bears scars from deep cuts in the text. Hamlet swears to his father's ghost that he will wreak revenge for the man's murder by taking the life of Claudius, who is now married to Hamlet's mother, Gertrude. By cutting the text, Olivier has fashioned a tighter, albeit abridged, version of the famed play. One of its flaws is that, in directing, Olivier should have concentrated more on performances; he had apparently fallen in love with the camera and employed many visual tricks instead of sticking to the lines. However, Olivier always felt that each different Hamlet is an essay, subject to the individual's interpretation.

HENRY V had been done in color, and many wondered why Olivier chose black and white for HAMLET. His reasons were the mood of the piece and various technical problems that arose while doing deep-focus photography. Olivier dyed his hair blonde so no one would feel that it was him playing the melancholy Dane. Rather, he wanted them to feel that what they were seeing was Hamlet himself. What they got was a mannered, overrated performance in a film with a similarly inflated reputation. Jean Simmons goes properly mad as Ophelia, and a very youthful Anthony Quayle makes his debut in a speaking role.

HAMLET

1969 119m c Drama	★★★½
Woodfall/Filmways (U.K.)	G/U

Nicol Williamson *(Hamlet)*, Gordon Jackson *(Horatio)*, Anthony Hopkins *(Claudius)*, Judy Parfitt *(Gertrude)*, Mark Dignam *(Polonius)*, Michael Pennington *(Laertes)*, Marianne Faithfull *(Ophelia)*, Ben Aris *(Rosencrantz)*, Clive Graham *(Guildenstern)*, Peter Gale *(Osric)*

p, Neil Hartley; d, Tony Richardson; w, (based on the play by William Shakespeare); ph, Gerry Fisher; ed, Charles Rees; m, Patrick Gowers; prod d, Jocelyn Herbert

A key figure in the British Free Cinema movement, director Richardson (LOOK BACK IN ANGER, A TASTE OF HONEY, TOM JONES) filmed his interpretation of Shakespeare's most celebrated play in London's Round House theatre, where he had previously staged the play. Richardson concentrates on the faces of his performers, privileging the spoken word above all else.

HAMLET

1996 242m c Drama	★★½
Castle Rock Entertainment/Fishmonger Films Ltd. (U.S.)	PG-13/PG

Kenneth Branagh *(Hamlet)*, Derek Jacobi *(Claudius)*, Julie Christie *(Gertrude)*, Richard Briers *(Polonius)*, Kate Winslet *(Ophelia)*, Nicholas Farrell *(Horatio)*, Michael Maloney *(Laertes)*, Billy Crystal *(First Gravedigger—uncredited)*, Robin Williams *(Osric—uncredited)*, Brian Blessed *(Ghost)*

p, David Barron; d, Kenneth Branagh; w, Kenneth Branagh (based on the play *The Tragedy of Hamlet, Prince of Denmark* by William Shakespeare); ph, Alex Thomson; ed, Neil Farrell; m, Patrick Doyle; prod d, Tim Harvey; art d, Desmond Crowe; fx, Josh Williams; cos, Alexandra Byrne

AAN Best Art Direction: Tim Harvey; *AAN Best Costume Design:* Alexandra Byrne; *AAN Best Original Dramatic Score:* Patrick Doyle; *AAN Best Adapted Screenplay:* Kenneth Branagh

Whatever Kenneth Branagh's motives for filming *Hamlet* in its entirety—recouping his somewhat tarnished reputation as the next Olivier, perhaps—he's managed to pull off a considerable *coup de cinema*, and the result is by turns brilliant, sumptuous, garish, and awful.

Updated to 19th century, Branagh himself stars as the Danish prince with revenge on his fevered brain after the ghost of his father, the late King (Brian Blessed), appears to tell him of his murder at the hands of his own brother, Claudius (Derek Jacobi), and demand justice be served. Branagh has jettisoned yesterday's impotent brooder in favor of Hamlet the manic, peroxide-blond showman, and despite the sumptuous production design and Alex Thomson's masterful cinematography, the whole thing feels gauche. One of the more peculiar things about Branagh is that while he thinks he wants to challenge his audience—and a four-hour, unabridged *Hamlet* is certainly a challenge—he continues to pander to the groundlings, hamming it up while downplaying the text's subtitles as if he's uncertain of the Bard's continuing appeal. Or is it the viewer's intelligence he doubts? Scenes are crushed under a barrage of visual detritus—unnecessary expository flashbacks abound—and too often the immortal dialogue is either ridiculously dramatized or overwhelmed by the aggressively stirring soundtrack. The film, however, is simply gorgeous to look at, and a number of the performances are outstanding, particularly Derek Jacobi as Claudius, Richard Briers as a not-so-nice Polonious, and Kate Winslet, whose Ophelia is wondrously affecting.

HAMMETT

1982　100m　c　Mystery　★★★★
Orion　(U.S.)　　　　　　　　　　PG/AA

Frederic Forrest *(Hammett)*, Peter Boyle *(Jimmy Ryan)*, Marilu Henner *(Kit Conger/Sue Alabama)*, Roy Kinnear *(English Eddie Hagedorn)*, Elisha Cook Jr. *(Eli, the Taxi Driver)*, Lydia Lei *(Crystal Ling)*, R.G. Armstrong *(Lt. O'Mara)*, Richard Bradford *(Detective Bradford)*, Michael Chow *(Fong)*, David Patrick Kelly *(Punk)*
p, Fred Roos, Ronald Colby, Don Guest; d, Wim Wenders; w, Ross Thomas, Dennis O'Flaherty, Thomas Pope (based on the book by Joe Gores); ph, Philip Lathrop, Joseph Biroc; ed, Barry Malkin, Marc Laub, Robert Q. Lovett, Randy Roberts; m, John Barry; prod d, Dean Tavoularis, Eugene Lee; art d, Angelo Graham, Leon Ericksen; cos, Ruth Morley

Impressed by Wim Wenders's obvious talent, Francis Coppola invited the German director to come to America and make a Hollywood film. The project chosen was a highly fictionalized account of the exploits of famed detective novelist Dashiell Hammett.

Set in 1920s San Francisco, the film follows Hammett (Frederic Forrest) as he leaves the Pinkerton Detective Agency to devote himself to writing. His former Pinkerton boss, Jimmy Ryan (Peter Boyle), recruits him to help crack a particularly tough case involving a Chinese prostitute. The cinematography and performances are terrific and highly stylized in this moody thriller, and Wenders directs the film well, but the story is a pastiche of many Hammett tales and is at times so splintered as to be confusing. Like THE AMERICAN FRIEND, Wenders's previous meditation on American genres, HAMMETT is less concerned with its storyline than it is with focusing on an American myth. As such it is not to be missed.

In between HAMMETT's production delays, Wenders made the low-budget black-and-white THE STATE OF THINGS, a film about the difficulties of filmmaking and the elusiveness of an American film producer. Rumor has it that much of HAMMETT was reshot by Coppola but the end result looks seamless.

HAND THAT ROCKS THE CRADLE, THE

1992　110m　c　Thriller　★★★½
Interscope/Rockin' Cradle Productions/Hollywood　　R/15
Pictures　(U.S.)

Annabella Sciorra *(Claire Bartel)*, Rebecca De Mornay *(Peyton Flanders)*, Matt McCoy *(Michael Bartel)*, Ernie Hudson *(Solomon)*, Julianne Moore *(Marlene)*, Madeline Zima *(Emma Bartel)*, John de Lancie *(Doctor Mott)*, Kevin Skousen *(Marty)*, Mitchell Laurance *(Lawyer)*, Justin Zaremby *(Schoolyard Bully)*
p, David Madden; d, Curtis Hanson; w, Amanda Silver; ph, Robert Elswit; ed, John F. Link; m, Graeme Revell; prod d, Edward Pisoni; art d, Mark Zuelzke; fx, Bob Riggs, Craig Reardon; cos, Jennifer Von Mayrhauser

This jovially sinister, middle-class morality tale-cum-horror show is predictable, implausible and fiendishly entertaining.

Claire and Michael Bartel (Annabella Sciorra and Matt McCoy) are a prosperous suburban couple with one young daughter, Emma (Madeline Zima), and a baby boy on the way. After being sexually abused by her gynecologist, Claire files charges, leading other patients to come forward with similar complaints. The doctor commits suicide, leaving his pregnant wife Peyton (Rebecca De Mornay) broke and homeless, and contributing to her miscarriage. While recovering, Peyton becomes obsessed with Claire and, after her release, charms her way into the Bartel household as a live-in nanny. There, she begins to implement a systematic strategy of revenge on the woman she feels has ruined her life.

At the climax, Peyton learns too late what villains of her ilk always learn too late: don't mess with the nuclear family! Up to that point, though, director Curtis Hanson and screenwriter Amanda Silver (the latter making an auspicious debut) have an awful lot of unwholesome fun letting her try. Hanson, a skilled craftsman and Hitchcock imitator, moves things along with finely crafted momentum, barrelling through the manifest plot implausibilities to create a tense psychological conflict between a deranged but sympathetic villainess and a likable but flawed heroine.

HANGIN' WITH THE HOMEBOYS

1991　88m　c　Drama　★★★½
Juno Pix/New Line　(U.S.)　　　　　　　R/15

Doug E. Doug *(Willie)*, Mario Joyner *(Tom)*, John Leguizamo *(Johnny)*, Nestor Serrano *(Vinny)*, Kimberly Russell *(Vanessa)*, Mary B. Ward *(Luna)*, Reggie Montgomery *(Rasta)*, Christine Claravall *(Daria)*, Rosemary Jackson *(Lila)*, Steven Randazzo *(Pedro)*
p, Richard Brick; d, Joseph B. Vasquez; w, Joseph B. Vasquez; ph, Anghel Decca; ed, Michael Schweitzer; art d, Isabel Bau Madden; fx, Steve Kirschoff; cos, Mary Jane Fort

The third feature, following STREET STORY and THE BRONX WAR, by New York-based filmmaker Joseph B. Vasquez, HANGIN' WITH THE HOMEBOYS is a remarkable film, a character study that is by turns funny, biting and melancholy.

Tom (Mario Joyner), Willie (Doug E. Doug), Johnny (John Leguizamo) and Vinnie (Nestor Serrano) are buddies—two black, two Puerto Rican—who grew up together in the Bronx. Though their lives have developed along very different lines, they remain friends. Tom is an aspiring actor, though he's selling magazine subscriptions to pay the rent. Johnny works in a supermarket; he's been encouraged to go to college, but he's afraid to take the first step—filling out a scholarship application. Vinnie is a smooth-talking layabout who hides his Puerto Rican heritage behind the fiction that he's Italian and lets his many girlfriends pay his way. And Willie is unemployed and unemployable, convinced that he's oppressed by racial prejudice. His furious mantra is, "It's because I'm black, right?" On a typical Friday night they get together to cruise and have a good time.

Vasquez's first film to be widely distributed, HANGIN' WITH THE HOMEBOYS opens with a beautifully written and performed sequence that sets the tone for the entire picture. On a crowded subway train, riders stare at their newspapers and try to ignore four boisterous minority youths who enter the car gesticulating and arguing loudly. Two of them come to blows, and the riders shrink back in their seats. Suddenly, all the young men—Willie, Tom, Johnny and Vinnie—begin to laugh and clown around: it's all been a joke, impromptu "street theater." The scene establishes relationships between the four, while setting them within the larger context of contemporary New York. It's funny, scary and feels absolutely authentic.

HANGMEN ALSO DIE

1943　131m　bw　War　★★★½
UA　(U.S.)　　　　　　　　　　/A

Brian Donlevy *(Dr. Franz Svoboda)*, Walter Brennan *(Prof. Novotny)*, Anna Lee *(Mascha Novotny)*, Gene Lockhart *(Emil Czaka)*, Dennis O'Keefe *(Jan Horek)*, Alexander Granach *(Alois Gruber)*, Margaret Wycherly *(Aunt Ludmilla Novotny)*, Nana Bryant *(Mrs. Novotny)*, Billy Roy *(Beda Novotny)*, Hans von Twardowski *(Reinhard Heydrich)* p, Fritz Lang; d, Fritz Lang; w, John Wexley (based on a story by Fritz Lang and Bertolt Brecht); ph, James Wong Howe; ed, Gene Fowler Jr.; m, Hanns Eisler; art d, William Darling; cos, Julie Heron

AAN Best Score: Hanns Eisler; *AAN Best Sound:* Jack Whitney (Sound Service Inc)

In Czechoslovakia during WWII, Deputy Reich Protector Reinhard Heydrich (von Twardowski), Nazi-appointed "governor" of Prague, gathers prominent citizens and voices his displeasure at insidious acts of sabotage in the factories. Not only are the Czech acts of defiance holding up vital production for the Third Reich, they are also endangering the lives of the civic leaders assembled, Heydrich says, adding that stern measures will be taken unless production increases. After leaving the meeting, Heydrich is assassinated by a member of the Czech resistance, Svoboda (Donlevy). On the run, Svoboda is given shelter by kindly Professor Novotny (Brennan) and his daughter Mascha (Lee). Though Heydrich's death becomes a hopeful symbol for the Czechoslovakian people and improves their morale, the Nazis demand revenge and the Gestapo begin to round up hundreds of innocent Czech citizens suspected of subversion and complicity, and kill them off one by one until the killer is handed over.

While HANGMEN ALSO DIE is a much better than average American WWII propaganda film, it is a bit of a disappointment in the impressive career of master director Fritz Lang. Beyond a precious few scenes containing some stunning Lang visuals, the film is overlong and the characters haphazardly developed. The tension is occasionally interrupted by impassioned patriotic speeches that comment didactically and intelligently on the proceedings in a Brechtian fashion. As well they should, since this was the first Hollywood screenplay collaborated on by that celebrated German playwright. (Brecht was, however, denied co-screenwriting credit following a Guild arbitration.) Visually the film's atmosphere is marvelously dark and oppressive due to the moody lensing of the great cinematographer James Wong Howe.

HANNAH AND HER SISTERS

1986   106m   c   Comedy/Drama ★★★★
Orion   (U.S.) PG-13/15

Woody Allen *(Mickey)*, Michael Caine *(Elliot)*, Mia Farrow *(Hannah)*, Carrie Fisher *(April)*, Barbara Hershey *(Lee)*, Lloyd Nolan *(Hannah's Father)*, Maureen O'Sullivan *(Hannah's Mother)*, Daniel Stern *(Dusty)*, Max von Sydow *(Frederick)*, Dianne Wiest *(Holly)*

p, Robert Greenhut; d, Woody Allen; w, Woody Allen; ph, Carlo Di Palma; ed, Susan E. Morse; prod d, Stuart Wurtzel; cos, Jeffrey Kurland

AAN Best Picture; *AA Best Supporting Actor:* Michael Caine; *AA Best Supporting Actress:* Dianne Wiest; *AAN Best Director:* Woody Allen; *AA Best Original Screenplay:* Woody Allen; *AAN Best Editing:* Susan E. Morse; *AAN Best Art Direction:* Stuart Wurtzel, Carol Joffe

Essentially three separate tales that intertwine at times, HANNAH AND HER SISTERS is one of writer-director Woody Allen's most complex films and the first one in which his neurotic character is given a happy ending.

The picture takes place over a couple of years, framed by Thanksgiving dinners. Hannah (Mia Farrow) is married to Elliot (Michael Caine), a business manager for rock stars. She used to be married to Mickey (Allen), a TV producer. Hannah's sisters are Lee (Barbara Hershey)—who's living with Frederick (Max von Sydow), a witty, bitter SoHo artist—and Holly (Dianne Wiest), an actress who's a bundle of nerves. Elliot harbors a passion for Lee and eventually makes it known to her. She succumbs, guilt-ridden for betraying Hannah. Holly, a former cocaine addict, can no longer contain her envy of Hannah—the oldest, "perfect" sister, who has what appears to be a blissful existence.

The plot could easily have been an afternoon soap opera, but Allen has infused it with wit, a superb cast and his usual "the best direction is the least direction" style, so that the camera never calls attention to itself.

HANS CHRISTIAN ANDERSEN

1952   120m   c   Biography ★★★
RKO   (U.S.) /U

Danny Kaye *(Hans Christian Andersen)*, Farley Granger *(Niels)*, Zizi Jeanmaire *(Doro)*, Joseph Walsh *(Peter)*, Philip Tonge *(Otto)*, Erik Bruhn *(Hussar)*, Roland Petit *(Prince)*, John Brown *(Schoolmaster)*, John Qualen *(Burgomaster)*, Jeanne Lafayette *(Celine)*

p, Samuel Goldwyn; d, Charles Vidor; w, Moss Hart (based on a story by Myles Connolly); ph, Harry Stradling; ed, Daniel Mandell; m, Frank Loesser; art d, Richard Day, Antoni Clave; chor, Roland Petit; cos, Antoni Clave, Mary Wills, Barbara Karinska

AAN Best Cinematography: Harry Stradling; *AAN Best Score:* Walter Scharf; *AAN Best Song:* Frank Loesser (Music & Lyrics); *AAN Best Art Direction:* Richard Day (Art Direction), Clave (Art Direction), Howard Bristol (Set Decoration); *AAN Best Costume Design:* Clave, Mary Wills, Madame Karinska; *AAN Best Sound:* Gordon Sawyer (Goldwyn Sound Department)

This glossy children's musical stars Danny Kaye as the beloved Danish author of fairy tales whose rise to literary prominence is detailed here in a totally fabricated manner. Most adults will squirm during the syrupy proceedings but kids seem to like it just fine.

This movie was something of an obsession for producer Samuel Goldwyn, who had been announcing production of the project for nearly 15 years, only to have it delayed time and time again. After paying a king's ransom for 16 different screenplays, Goldwyn finally found one he liked, and production began. Luckily, Goldwyn's dream paid off big at the box office, as HANS CHRISTIAN ANDERSEN grossed $6 million and eventually ranked as Goldwyn's third biggest moneymaker (behind THE BEST YEARS OF OUR LIVES and GUYS AND DOLLS). Kaye is wonderful and the enjoyable songs include "Inchworm" and "Wonderful Wonderful Copenhagen."

HARD DAY'S NIGHT, A

1964   83m   bw   Musical/Comedy ★★★★½
UA   (U.K.) G/U

John Lennon *(John)*, Paul McCartney *(Paul)*, George Harrison *(George)*, Ringo Starr *(Ringo)*, Wilfrid Brambell *(Grandfather)*, Norman Rossington *(Norm)*, Victor Spinetti *(TV Director)*, John Junkin *(Shake)*, Deryck Guyler *(Police Inspector)*, Anna Quayle *(Millie)*

p, Walter Shenson; d, Richard Lester; w, Alun Owen; ph, Gilbert Taylor; ed, John Jympson; m, John Lennon, Paul McCartney; art d, Ray Simm; cos, Dougie Millings & Son, Julie Harris

AAN Best Original Screenplay: Alun Owen; *AAN Best Score:* George Martin

Refreshing, innovative and immensely funny, A HARD DAY'S NIGHT tells the story of 36 hours in the lives of the Beatles in a quirky fashion that has everyone laughing from the first moment.

Besieged by their frenzied fans, John, Paul, George, and Ringo board a train for London, where they are to do a live television appearance. They are accompanied by Norm (Rossington), their manager (a parody of Brian Epstein), his aide, Shake (John Junkin), and Paul's grandfather (Wilfrid Brambell), a "clean old man" who proves to be a mischievous old coot. In London, the boys cavort at a swinging nightspot before going in search of Grandfather, whom they find chatting up a buxom bird at a casino, and drag him back to the hotel over his angry protests. At the television studio the next day, Grandfather convinces Ringo that he is unappreciated by the rest of the group, and the dejected drummer disappears into the city streets. But how can the lads go on television without Ringo?

Producer Walt Shenson thought he would rush this into production and take advantage of the Beatles' immense popularity before their celebrity waned. Made in only seven weeks for just over half a million dollars, A HARD DAY'S NIGHT returned many times its cost. Its sequel, HELP (also directed by Richard Lester), cost almost three times as much, wasn't as good, and won't be remembered as long as this anarchistic, Marx Brothers-like romp. Combining surrealistic imagery and cinema verite techniques, borrowing from Fellini, Godard, Keaton, and even Busby Berkeley, Lester arrives at his own dazzling style and creates one of the most inventive pictures of the era. Alun Owen's wonderful screenplay is full of witty surprises, delivered as only the Beatles could, and a number of their classics are well integrated into the narrative.

HARD-BOILED
(LASHOU SHENTAN)
1992 126m c Crime/Action/Drama ★★★½
Milestone Pictures (Hong Kong)

Chow Yun-fat *(Inspector Tequila Yuen)*, Leung Chiu-Wai *(Tony)*, Teresa Mo *(Teresa)*, Philip Chan *(Pang)*, Anthony Wong *(Johnny Wong)*, Bowie Lam *(Yuen's Partner)*, Kwan Hoi-shan *(Mr. Hoi)*, Cheung Jue-lin *(Mad Dog)*, Philip Kwok, Tung Wai *(Little Ko)*

p, Linda Kuk, Terence Chang; d, John Woo; w, Barry Wong (from the story by John Woo); ph, Wang Wing-heng; ed, David Wu, Kai Kit-wai; m, Michael Gibbs; prod d, James Leung; art d, Joel Chong

Released in the US just as director John Woo was himself venturing to Hollywood, HARD-BOILED takes Woo's signature gunplay to even more hyperbolic extremes than he had previously achieved. HARD-BOILED doesn't have quite the melodramatic kick of THE KILLER, but the same themes of loyalty, honor and violence are explored to nearly the same impact.

Woo's perennial leading man Chow Yun-fat stars as police inspector Yuen, nicknamed "Tequila," who is first seen moonlighting as a jazz musician in a Hong Kong club. We're soon plunged into the more violent side of Tequila's world, as he and his partner (Bowie Lam) battle a gang of gunrunners in a restaurant. His partner is killed, and Tequila is subsequently browbeaten by his commander, Pang (Philip Chan), who has become increasingly frustrated with Tequila's overly violent tactics. Meanwhile, Tequila is trying to rekindle a relationship with coworker Teresa (Teresa Mo), who has been receiving frequent gifts of white roses. As it happens, the flowers come with coded messages from an undercover gangland source that Teresa passes on to Pang. The usual complications, and elaborately choreographed battles, ensue. . .

In a sort of reverse move on THE KILLER, this time it's Chow Yun-fat who plays the cop while his costar is the hitman but, as before, the lines are not so easily defined. Tequila, like many American cop heroes, disdains the rules that keep him from doing his job effectively, while Tony is actually a policeman who finds himself increasingly unable to cope with the violent demands of his undercover work. (Reportedly, the cop angle of his character was not originally part of the film as planned, but was added in deference to actor Leung's pop-idol status in Hong Kong.)

The incredible action sequences in HARD-BOILED leave no doubt that Woo is in top form. The opening gunfight in the restaurant is worthy of the climax of any American actioner, and the entire last 40 minutes of the film is one long, breathtaking set piece in the hospital, with one tense confrontation and shootout after another. There's one Steadicam shot, following Tequila and Tony from one floor of the hospital, into an elevator, onto another floor and into another gunfight, that's truly stunning.

The cut of HARD-BOILED that played Chinese-language theaters in America is a slightly trimmed version of Woo's original director's cut (shown at the 1992 Toronto Festival of Festivals), shorn of several minutes for violence and running-time concerns.

HARDCORE
1979 105m c Drama ★★★
Columbia (U.S.) R/18

George C. Scott *(Jake Van Dorn)*, Peter Boyle *(Andy Mast)*, Season Hubley *(Niki)*, Dick Sargent *(Wes DeJong)*, Leonard Gaines *(Ramada)*, David Nichols *(Kurt)*, Gary Graham *(Tod)*, Larry Block *(Detective Burrows)*, Marc Alaimo *(Ratan)*, Leslie Ackerman *(Felice)*

p, Buzz Feitshans; d, Paul Schrader; w, Paul Schrader; ph, Michael Chapman; ed, Tom Rolf; m, Jack Nitzsche; prod d, Paul Sylbert; art d, Edwin O'Donovan

"Oh my God, it's my daughter!" wails George C. Scott in the most celebrated scene in HARDCORE, an inconsistent but challenging film from writer-director Paul Schrader (BLUE COLLAR, AMERICAN GIGOLO, CAT PEOPLE, MISHIMA).

Scott (in a performance that ranges from completely over-the-top to downright heartbreaking) plays Jake Van Dorn, a devoutly religious Calvinist from Grand Rapids, Michigan, whose teenaged daughter, Kristen (Davis), disappears during a church trip to California. Van Dorn ventures out to sinful California to find his missing child. He hires sleazy private detective Andy Mast (Boyle) to look for her and then returns to his virtuous life back in Michigan. Soon he gets a call from Mast, now in Grand Rapids, telling him to meet him in town. The cheap detective takes Van Dorn to a porno theater where they watch a film in which the devout spots his daughter. Mast returns to LA to continue the hunt but Van Dorn can no longer stand by as an observer. He flies to California himself to begin his own search in LA's X-rated underworld.

Realistic one minute, unbelievable the next, HARDCORE is a truly schizophrenic film. A somber, serious moment is followed by a tongue-in-cheek parody or a flat-out joke. Every scene involving the porno film industry is played strictly for laughs, with wildly exaggerated characters. Scott's performance is similarly divided. He's completely serious during the scenes in which he shows the desperation of the parent of a lost child, but becomes loud and terribly unconvincing as he wanders through the peep shows and massage parlors. He even poses as a porn producer to look for leads to his daughter's whereabouts. Whatever its flaws, this is one of very few American films to deal with fundamentalist beliefs about predestination, faith, and sin with empathy and intellectual acuity.

HARDER THEY COME, THE
1973 98m c Drama ★★★½
International Films (Jamaica) R/15

Jimmy Cliff *(Ivan)*, Carl Bradshaw *(Jose)*, Janet Bartley *(Elsa)*, Ras Daniel Hartman *(Pedro)*, Basil Keane *(Preacher)*, Bob Charlton *(Hilton)*, Winston Stona *(Detective)*

p, Perry Henzell; d, Perry Henzell; w, Perry Henzell, Trevor D. Rhone; ph, Peter Jessop, David McDonald; ed, John Victor Smith, Seicland Anderson, Richard White; m, Jimmy Cliff, Desmond Dekker, The Slickers

This outstanding Jamaican feature became a major cult favorite in the US and did much to popularize reggae with its fabulous musical score.

Reggae star Jimmy Cliff plays Ivan, a young aspiring singer from the country who arrives in Kingston with high hopes of becoming a recording star. Work is hard to come by, however, and after a rude awakening on the city streets, Ivan becomes a handyman for a local preacher. When an argument over a bicycle escalates into a knife fight, Ivan is sent to jail. After his release he moves in with the preacher's ward, Elsa (Bartley), and pursues the island's biggest record producer, Hilton (Charlton). Eventually he gets the chance to record "The Harder They Come." However Ivan balks when Hilton offers him a paltry $20 for the song. The producer retaliates by releasing the record without any promotion. Penniless, Ivan has no choice but to get involved in the lucrative but dangerous marijuana trade. As his criminal notoriety grows so do his record sales.

THE HARDER THEY COME is a gritty, realistic view of urban Jamaica that reveals the squalor of shantytowns tourists never see. Cliff delivers a charismatic and memorable performance as a young man who is determined to become famous, mirroring his own real-life ascendence to worldwide fame as a reggae artist. Despite the ostensible show-business plot, this film most resembles a 1930s gangster film with its relentless depiction of regrettable social conditions, police corruption and the lure of illicit cash. The filmmaking is a bit crude at times but it packs an emotional wallop.

HARDER THEY FALL, THE
1956 109m bw Sports ★★★★
Columbia (U.S.) /15

Humphrey Bogart *(Eddie Willis)*, Rod Steiger *(Nick Benko)*, Jan Sterling *(Beth Willis)*, Mike Lane *(Toro Moreno)*, Max Baer *(Buddy Brannen)*, Jersey Joe Walcott *(George)*, Edward Andrews *(Jim Weyerhause)*, Harold J. Stone *(Art Leavitt)*, Carlos Montalban *(Luis Agrandi)*, Nehemiah Persoff *(Leo)*

HAROLD AND MAUDE

p, Philip Yordan; d, Mark Robson; w, Philip Yordan (based on the novel by Budd Schulberg); ph, Burnett Guffey; ed, Jerome Thoms; m, Hugo Friedhofer; art d, William Flannery

AAN Best Cinematography: Burnett Guffey

One of the most scathing indictments of professional boxing ever committed to film, THE HARDER THEY FALL presents Humphrey Bogart as Eddie Willis, a once-scrupulous sportswriter, now working for Nick Benko (Rod Steiger), a shady mob-connected promoter. Eddie is handling the publicity for Benko's new find, Toro Moreno (Mike Lane), a giant Argentine boxer with a powder-puff punch and a glass jaw. But Benko fixes one fight after another and soon the towering heavyweight, who thinks he's doing it on his own, faces Gus Dundee (Pat Comiskey), a top contender who was so battered by the current champ, Buddy Brannen (one-time heavyweight title holder Max Baer), that even Toro's feeble punches are enough to bring about a brain hemorrhage that kills him. This is the beginning of a moral crisis for Eddie.

Scripted by producer Philip Yordan from the novel by Budd Schulberg, THE HARDER THEY FALL was similar enough to the real-life story of heavyweight Primo Carnera (who lost his title to Baer) that he sued Columbia. Nothing about it is pretty, with director Mark Robson (who'd already helmed the powerful CHAMPION) moving the story along at a frenetic pace and Burnett Guffey's stark black-and-white photography lending a grim feel to the movie. All of the performers are excellent, especially Bogart, in what would be his final screen appearance.

HAROLD AND MAUDE

1971 90m c Comedy   ★★★½
Paramount (U.S.)   GP/15

Ruth Gordon *(Maude)*, Bud Cort *(Harold)*, Vivian Pickles *(Mrs. Chasen)*, Cyril Cusack *(Sculptor)*, Charles Tyner *(Uncle Victor)*, Ellen Geer *(Sunshine)*, Eric Christmas *(Priest)*, G. Wood *(Psychiatrist)*, Judy Engles *(Candy Gulf)*, Shari Summers *(Edith Fern)*
p, Charles B. Mulvehill, Colin Higgins; d, Hal Ashby; w, Colin Higgins; ph, John A. Alonzo; ed, William A. Sawyer, Edward Warschilka; m, Cat Stevens; prod d, Michael Haller; art d, Michael Haller; fx, A.D. Flowers; cos, William Ware Theiss

HAROLD AND MAUDE got lost in the holiday shuffle when first released in late 1971, but there's much in this oddball film to recommend, including superb performances from the three leads. Harold (Cort) is the son of Mrs. Chasen (Pickles), a wealthy woman who pays little attention to him. His frequent depressions and lack of friends motivate him to stage increasingly elaborate mock suicides, none of which impress his distracted mother. Fascinated by death and all its trappings, Harold has an old hearse which he drives to funerals at various cemeteries around town. At two successive services, he meets Maude (Gordon), a 79-year-old concentration camp survivor who is as thrilled with life as he is with death. A classic free spirit, she is the polar opposite of the solemn Harold. Nonetheless they become great pals, and she instills in him a desire to live, to spread his wings, to enjoy his brief time on earth. As time passes, they share several wacky adventures and their friendship blossoms into love—much to the alarm of Harold's mother.

This is a doggedly eccentric film which some will reject out of hand. Others will find it profoundly moving and life affirming. Not surprisingly it became one of the major cult films on college campuses in the 1970s. This film was originated as a 20-minute script written as a graduate thesis by UCLA student Higgins. He later showed it to his landlady, Lewis, the wife of a film producer, and the two formed their own production company to make the film. Higgins went on to become a writer-director best known for films such as FOUL PLAY, NINE TO FIVE, and THE BEST LITTLE WHOREHOUSE IN TEXAS. He died in 1988 from AIDS complications.

HARPER

1966 121m c Mystery   ★★★
Warner Bros. (U.S.)   /A

Paul Newman *(Harper)*, Lauren Bacall *(Mrs. Sampson)*, Julie Harris *(Betty Fraley)*, Arthur Hill *(Albert Graves)*, Janet Leigh *(Susan Harper)*, Pamela Tiffin *(Miranda Sampson)*, Robert Wagner *(Alan Traggert)*, Robert Webber *(Dwight Troy)*, Shelley Winters *(Fay Estabrook)*, Harold Gould *(Sheriff Spanner)*

p, Elliott Kastner, Jerry Gershwin; d, Jack Smight; w, William Goldman (based on the novel *The Moving Target* by Ross MacDonald); ph, Conrad Hall; ed, Stefan Arnsten; m, Johnny Mandel; art d, Alfred Sweeney; cos, Sally Edwards, William Smith

Based on Ross MacDonald's novel *The Moving Target*, HARPER showcases Paul Newman in the role of Lew Harper, a down-on-his-luck but ultra hip Los Angeles private eye hired by the cynical Mrs. Sampson (Bacall) to track down her missing and very wealthy husband. The trail leading to Mr. Sampson is laden with strange characters and brings more than a few bumps and bruises Harper's way. His snooping takes him from an over-the-hill actress (Winters) to a junkie nightclub chanteuse (Harris) and from a religious zealot (Martin) to a smuggling operation. William Goldman's adaptation of MacDonald's novel—his first solo screenwriting credit—is full of rapid-fire dialogue but some of the characterizations are thin. Despite all the big names involved, HARPER doesn't begin to approach the big leagues of hard-boiled detective films. Nonetheless, Newman gives a convincing performance in a role he would repeat nearly ten years later in THE DROWNING POOL.

HARRY AND TONTO

1974 115m c Drama   ★★★
Fox (U.S.)   R/A

Art Carney *(Harry Coombs)*, Ellen Burstyn *(Shirley)*, Chief Dan George *(Sam Two Feathers)*, Geraldine Fitzgerald *(Jessie)*, Larry Hagman *(Eddie)*, Arthur Hunnicutt *(Wade)*, Philip Bruns *(Burt)*, Josh Mostel *(Norman)*, Melanie Mayron *(Ginger)*, Dolly Jonah *(Elaine)*
p, Paul Mazursky; d, Paul Mazursky; w, Paul Mazursky, Josh Greenfeld; ph, Michael Butler; ed, Richard Halsey; m, Bill Conti; prod d, Ted Haworth; cos, Albert Wolsky

AA Best Actor: Art Carney; *AAN Best Original Screenplay:* Paul Mazursky, Josh Greenfeld

When his comfortable New York City apartment building is torn down, 72-year-old widower and retired college professor Harry (Carney) temporarily moves in with his eldest son but finds his daughter-in-law less than enthusiastic. Perhaps inspired by his grandson, Norman (Mostel, son of Zero), who is currently immersed in Zen philosophy, Harry decides to postpone his search for new lodgings to fulfill a lifelong ambition to travel across the country to California. With his beloved cat Tonto, Harry hits the road, planning to stop and visit his other children—Shirley (Burstyn), a daughter who lives in Chicago, and youngest son, Eddie (Hagman), who lives on the West Coast. During his journey, Harry encounters several situations that cause him to examine what life means to him.

HARRY AND TONTO is a sweet, sentimental road movie that draws force and relevance from Carney's touching and subtle performance. Incredibly, after nearly 25 years on television, this was the actor's first major feature film role. In HARRY AND TONTO writer-director Mazursky shows the innocence of youth and the disappointment of middle age but offers solace in old age if the internal energy that once produced ambition is rediscovered and prompts us to hope for better things to come.

HARVEY

1950 104m bw Comedy   ★★★★
Universal (U.S.)   /U

James Stewart *(Elwood P. Dowd)*, Josephine Hull *(Veta Louise Simmons)*, Peggy Dow *(Miss Kelly)*, Charles Drake *(Dr. Sanderson)*, Cecil Kellaway *(Dr. Chumley)*, Victoria Horne *(Myrtle Mae)*, Jesse White *(Wilson)*, William Lynn *(Judge Gaffney)*, Wallace Ford *(Lofgren)*, Nana Bryant *(Mrs. Chumley)*
p, John Beck; d, Henry Koster; w, Mary Chase, Oscar Brodney (based on a play by Chase); ph, William Daniels; ed, Ralph Dawson; m, Frank Skinner; art d, Nathan Juran, Bernard Herzbrun

AAN Best Actor: James Stewart; *AA Best Supporting Actress:* Josephine Hull

Elwood P. Dowd (Jimmy Stewart) is the whimsical inebriate whose kindness spills over into the lives of all around him as he tries to help those in need. Elwood lurches home one night to see a six-foot rabbit named Harvey leaning against a lamppost. This invisible "Pooka" becomes his friend and follows him everywhere, much to the chagrin of Elwood's social-climbing family, who think he has finally flipped and should be put in an asylum. Faithfully adapted by Mary Chase from her popular Broadway play, HARVEY is a delightful comedy-fantasy. Jimmy Stewart, in one of his best-loved roles, is wonderful as the gentle, sweet soul who befriends the invisible rabbit. His performance earned him an Oscar nomination, and the priceless Josephine Hull, as Stewart's harried sister, was honored as Best Supporting Actress. The supporting cast features wonderful work from Dow (who retired far too soon), Drake, Kellaway, Horne, and White. Henry Koster's direction is sharp and moves along at a rapid clip. This is a happy movie and leaves a long, lingering warm glow.

HATE
(LA HAINE)
1995 98m bw Drama ★★½
Les Productions Lazennec/Le Studio Canal+/La Sept Cinema/Kaso /15 Inc. Productions (France)

Vincent Cassel *(Vinz)*, Hubert Kounde *(Hubert)*, Said Taghmaoui *(Said)*, Karim Belkhadra *(Samir)*, Edouard Montoute *(Darty)*, Francois Levantal *(Asterix)*, Solo Dicko *(Santo)*, Marc Duret *(Inspector "Notre Dame")*, Heloise Rauth *(Sarah)*, Rywka Wajsbrot *(Vinz's Grandmother)*

p, Christophe Rossignon; d, Mathieu Kassovitz; w, Mathieu Kassovitz; ph, Pierre Aim; ed, Mathieu Kassovitz, Scott Stevenson; art d, Giuseppe Ponturo; fx, Pierre Foury; cos, Virginie Montel

A bitter melange of Scorsese, Godard, and Spike Lee, HATE tries to bridge the gap between European art film and American pop, and succeeds to a surprising extent. This second feature from young Mathieu Kassovitz (his first was released in the US in 1994 under the title CAFE AU LAIT) is set in a public housing project outside Paris, where a trio of angry young men drift, dance, brood, flirt with violence, and chatter ceaselessly in gutter French.

As the film opens, the interracial residents of a grim working-class suburb have stormed the local police station and torched cars in protest of the arrest and beating of a young Arab. Vinz (Vincent Cassel) is a violence-prone Jew who has a fanatical hatred of cops. Hubert (Hubert Kounde) is a black part-time drug dealer who dreams of going straight and becoming a professional boxer. Said (Said Taghmaoui), an Arab, is something of a follower, more confused than the others and deeply affected by the racial strife. During the riot, Vince pockets a policeman's lost gun and vows to kill a cop if the victimized Arab dies of his injuries. HATE follows the three young men through the next 24 hours, offering a rare glimpse into a vibrant lumpen subculture that partakes equally of American television and European multicult. Exquisitely shot, culturally savvy, and intermittently thrilling, it easily transcends the American ghetto pictures it emulates.

HAUNTING, THE
1963 112m bw Horror ★★★½
Argyle (U.S./U.K.) /X

Julie Harris *(Eleanor Vance)*, Claire Bloom *(Theodora)*, Richard Johnson *(Dr. John Markway)*, Russ Tamblyn *(Luke Sanderson)*, Lois Maxwell *(Grace Markway)*, Fay Compton *(Mrs. Sanderson)*, Valentine Dyall *(Mr. Dudley)*, Rosalie Crutchley *(Mrs. Dudley)*, Diane Clare *(Carrie Fredericks)*, Ronald Adam *(Eldridge Harper)*

p, Robert Wise; d, Robert Wise; w, Nelson Gidding (based on the novel *The Haunting of Hill House* by Shirley Jackson); ph, Davis Boulton; ed, Ernest Walter; m, Humphrey Searle; prod d, Elliot Scott; fx, Tom Howard; cos, Mary Quant, Maude Churchill

A bit overrated upon its initial release, THE HAUNTING is, nonetheless, an undeniably effective adaptation of the Shirley Jackson novel and remains one of the best haunted-house movies.

Dr. Markway (Richard Johnson) is a professor of anthropology experimenting with ESP and other forms of psychic phenomena. He arrives at Hill House, a New England mansion that is reputed to be crammed with demons and ghosts and the home of everything evil. Along with Markway is Eleanor (Julie Harris), a slim spinster who, until recently, has spent her life caring for her aged mother, and Theodora (Claire Bloom), a lesbian. Both women have experienced

extra-sensory occurrences, and Markway has enlisted their aid in his quest for knowledge on the subject. Luke (Russ Tamblyn), who is the heir to the house and hopes to sell it at a great profit, goes along for a ride he will regret. Once inside, the quartet is besieged by terror—noises, yowls, and eerie events pour off the screen until Eleanor is convinced that Hill House is alive and wants her to stay there.

Director Robert Wise, who began his directorial career under the tutelage of Val Lewton, takes the lessons learned there to a bit of an extreme, overplaying his hand through the use of extremely exaggerated angles and distorting lenses. But the politically incorrect and oversimplified notion that Eleanor's repressed lesbianism is the cause of her downfall, was outdated even when the film was made. THE HAUNTING spends too much time setting up the idea that it will scientifically shed light on psychic phenomena and then withdraws from us. All said, the high order of acting seems wasted.

HE WALKED BY NIGHT
1948 79m bw Crime ★★★★
Bryan Foy/Eagle-Lion (U.S.) /A

Richard Basehart *(Davis Morgan)*, Scott Brady *(Sgt. Marty Brennan)*, Roy Roberts *(Capt. Breen)*, Whit Bissell *(Reeves)*, James Cardwell *(Chuck Jones)*, Jack Webb *(Lee)*, Robert Bice *(Detective Steno)*, Reed Hadley *(Narrator)*, Chief Bradley *(Himself)*, John McGuire *(Rawlins)*

p, Robert T. Kane; d, Alfred Werker, Anthony Mann; w, John C. Higgins, Crane Wilbur, Harry Essex (uncredited), Beck Murray (based on a story by Crane Wilbur); ph, John Alton; ed, Al DeGaetano; m, Leonid Raab; art d, Edward L. Ilou; fx, George J. Teague, Jack Rabin

This is a smashing film noir entry with Basehart as Davis Morgan, a brilliant, cold-hearted thief with underlying psychopathic tendencies that chill the viewer to the bone. Morgan is an electronics wizard who robs stores and warehouses to obtain electrical equipment which he modifies and then rents out to Reeves (Bissell). The Los Angeles police are in a quandary about this successful burglar since Morgan listens in on their radio network and cleverly alters his *modus operandi* so that his work appears to be that of another burglar. With cops Brennan (Brady) and Breen (Roberts) hot on his trail, Morgan attempts to escape into the vast sewer system beneath Los Angeles.

Director Werker (with an uncredited assist from Anthony Mann) does a fine job in maintaining the hectic pace, and Basehart is gripping as the lone, loveless thief who even sacrifices his dog when the going gets tough. His role is based on the career of thief and cop-killer Erwin Walker, a WWII hero turned burglar who terrorized LA in 1946. This film marked the first time the huge drainage system canals in Los Angeles were employed in a film; they would later be put to heavy use in THEM!, GREASE, and a number of other productions. Jack Webb drew the inspiration for his long-running documentary-style television series "Dragnet" from this film, in which he played a featured role.

HEAD
1968 85m c Musical/Comedy ★★★
Raybert (U.S.) G/

Peter Tork, David Jones, Micky Dolenz, Michael Nesmith *(Monkees)*, Annette Funicello *(Minnie)*, Timothy Carey *(Lord High 'n' Low)*, Logan Ramsey *(Officer Faye Lapid)*, Abraham Sofaer *(Swami)*, Vito Scotti *(I. Vittelloni)*, Charles Macaulay *(Inspector Shrink)*

p, Bob Rafelson, Jack Nicholson; d, Bob Rafelson; w, Bob Rafelson, Jack Nicholson; ph, Michel Hugo; ed, Mike Pozen; m, Ken Thorne; art d, Sydney Z. Litwack; fx, Butler-Glouner, Inc., Chuck Gaspar, Burton Gershfield, Bruce Lane; chor, Toni Basil; cos, Gene Ashman

After the demise of their TV show, the Monkees brought their particular brand of musical madness to the screen under the direction of Bob Rafelson (FIVE EASY PIECES; THE KING OF MARVIN GARDENS; BLACK WIDOW), who also played a key role in putting the group together for television and, with Jack Nicholson, cowrote the script for this quasi-underground film. The result is a visually daring cinematic game that is virtually plotless and better off for being so. Rafelson takes the Monkees through a variety of adventures both on location and on movie lots, where he and the Prefab Four satirize a variety of movie genres. Among the plentiful guest stars are Victor

Mature, whose hair the mini-Monkees invest with dandruff; ex-heavy-weight boxing champ Sonny Liston as an extra who climbs into the ring with Jones; Annette Funicello, Frank Zappa, former Green Bay Packer linebacker Ray Nitschke, famed San Francisco stripper Carol Doda, and the then-unknown Teri Garr. A fun collection of old movie clips is also included, featuring Ronald Reagan, Bela Lugosi, Charles Laughton, Ann Miller, and Rita Hayworth. The Monkees deliver the songs, "Circle Sky" (Michael Nesmith), "Can You Dig It," "Long Title: Do I Have to Do This All Over Again" (Peter Tork), "Daddy's Song" (Nilsson), "As We Go Along" (Carole King, Toni Stern), and "The Porpoise Song" (Carole King, Gerry Goffin).

HEAR MY SONG

1991 113m c Comedy/Drama   ★★★
Limelight Ltd./Film Four International/Windmill Lane   R/15
Productions/Vision Investments   (U.K./Ireland)

Ned Beatty (*Josef Locke*), Adrian Dunbar (*Micky O'Neill*), Shirley Anne Field (*Cathleen Doyle*), Tara Fitzgerald (*Nancy Doyle*), William Hootkins (*Mr. X*), Harold Berens (*Benny Rose*), David McCallum (*Jim Abbott*), John Dair (*Derek*), Stephen Marcus (*Gordon*), Britta Smith (*Kitty Ryan*)

p, Alison Owen; d, Peter Chelsom; w, Peter Chelsom, Adrian Dunbar (from the story by Chelsom); ph, Sue Gibson; ed, Martin Walsh; m, John Altman; prod d, Caroline Hanania; art d, Katharine Naylor; cos, Lindy Hemming

The lilt of Irish laughter and wit fills the screen in Peter Chelsom's romantic comedy HEAR MY SONG, and its blarney is irresistible. Micky O'Neill (Adrian Dunbar) runs a nightclub, Heartly's, that caters to Liverpool's Irish community. He's engaged to Nancy Doyle (Tara Fitzgerald), the best girl in town, and all is right with his world. His only problem, it seems, is booking talent for his venue and he usually wheels and deals in order to find "names" that will bring in the masses. He even hires one, a Franc Cinatra (Joe Cuddy), hoping that the public won't notice that this one is spelled with two "C's". Alas, Franc is the world's worst Sinatra impersonator and Micky is soon in danger of losing his clientele.

Then Mickey hits on a scheme. He'll bring back the notorious "Mr. X" and hints broadly that this is the legendary and much loved Josef Locke. When that tenor sang, it's widely bruited, "women wept." But Locke is a wanted man because of massive tax evasion. He fled to Ireland some 30 years earlier and hasn't been heard from since. The intrepid Micky convinces "Mr. X" to make an appearance because he's sure it will be a sold-out event. "Mr. X" (William Hootkins), not surprisingly, is a fraud. He might fool the masses but not the elegant Cathleen Doyle (Shirley Anne Field) who fell in love with the real Locke when he crowned her Miss Dairy Wholesomeness of 1958. Nor does this "Mr. X" fool Jim Abbott (David McCallum), the local police chief. As a result of his wheeling and dealing, Micky loses Heartly's. He also loses Nancy, who's Cathleen's daughter and feels especially conned by the imposter. So Micky has no alternative. He returns to Ireland, determined to find the real Josef Locke and somehow get him to risk arrest and return to Liverpool for a special appearance.

HEAR MY SONG is based on an incident in the life of the world-famous Irish tenor Josef Locke, who really did flee Britain due to tax difficulties. Former stage actor Peter Chelsom, who makes an auspicious feature directorial debut and also co-wrote the screenplay with Adrian Dunbar, remembers the real Josef Locke from his own youth in Blackpool. The celebrated Irish tenor, played by Ned Beatty with enormous ebullience and charm, sang for 19 seasons at the seaside resort which gave him his *nom de chanson*, Mr. Blackpool.

The film is structured in three segments. Early scenes center around Heartly's nightclub and Micky's office. The lush landscape of Ireland's scenic west country comprises the middle section, while the end returns to the city, where Heartly's is being demolished. Production designer Caroline Hanania has succeeded in giving each segment a unique feel, from harsh big city to small picturesque town to the fantastical elements in Heartly's demise, all of which has provided splendid opportunities for cinematographer Sue Gibson.

One of the film's themes, how dreams can be distorted, intrigues Chelsom. "There's a phrase in the film spoken by Grandma Ryan which is the key: "You close your eyes. You cast your mind back 30 years and

you see and hear what you want to see and hear." Dreams and longing and cravings for something more fundamental in a very transient world are what HEAR MY SONG is all about.

HEART LIKE A WHEEL

1983 113m c Biography   ★★★
Aurora   (U.S.)   PG

Bonnie Bedelia (*Shirley Muldowney*), Beau Bridges (*Connie Kalitta*), Leo Rossi (*Jack Muldowney*), Hoyt Axton (*Tex Roque*), Bill McKinney ("*Big Daddy*" *Don Garlits*), Anthony Edwards (*John Muldowney, Age 15-23*), Dean Paul Martin (*Sonny Rigotti*), Paul Bartel (*Chef Paul*), Missy Basile (*Angela*), Michael Cavanaugh (*NHRA Boss*)

p, Charles Roven; d, Jonathan Kaplan; w, Ken Friedman; ph, Tak Fujimoto; ed, O. Nicholas Brown; m, Laurence Rosenthal; prod d, James William Newport; cos, William Ware Theiss

AAN Best Costume Design: William Ware Theiss

This insightful biography of drag-racing champ Shirley "Cha-Cha" Muldowney (the underrated Bonnie Bedelia) begins with the foreshadowing image of little Shirley driving her father's sedan and continues with her first race in 1966. Meeting with the usual sexism, she surprises all by breaking the track record on her qualifying run. Her career soars, but her marriage to mechanic Jack Muldowney (Leo Rossi) ends in divorce when he realizes that he can't handle his wife's success. Shirley then turns to banned driver Connie Kalitta (Beau Bridges, who also appears in the similarly themed GREASED LIGHTING, the story of black NASCAR driver Wendell Scott's triumph over racial prejudice) for support and love as she goes on to win the National Hot Rod Association World Championship three times.

The film is marred by a lackluster narrative, failing to inspire or move us in any way, but there's no denying Bedelia's beautifully nuanced performance. She's deserving of projects that are the equivalent of the forthright intelligence she brings to everything she does.

HEARTBREAK KID, THE

1972 104m c Comedy   ★★½
Palomar   (U.S.)   PG

Charles Grodin (*Lenny Cantrow*), Jeannie Berlin (*Lila Kolodny*), Cybill Shepherd (*Kelly Corcoran*), Eddie Albert (*Mr. Corcoran*), Audra Lindley (*Mrs. Corcoran*), William Prince (*Colorado Man*), Mitchell Jason (*Cousin Ralph*), Augusta Dabney (*Colorado Woman*), Art Metrano (*Entertainer*), Marilyn Putnam (*Mrs. Kolodny*)

p, Edgar J. Scherick; d, Elaine May; w, Neil Simon (based on a story by Bruce Jay Friedman); ph, Owen Roizman; ed, John Carter; m, Garry Sherman; art d, Richard Sylbert; cos, Anthea Sylbert

AAN Best Supporting Actor: Eddie Albert; *AAN Best Supporting Actress:* Jeannie Berlin

Neil Simon's comedy, based on the Bruce Jay Friedman story, is a film you'll either find funny or disgusting. It's been broadly directed by May and concerns a Jewish bridegroom dumping whiny princess wife Berlin (May's real life daughter) to pursue WASP Shepherd. Although engagingly played, the film cannot find a voice or climax. What is this exercise in self-loathing all about? Are all Jewish women irritating? Are all WASPS cold featherbrains? HEARTBREAK doesn't end; it just runs out of steam.

HEARTBREAK RIDGE

1986 130m c Drama/War   ★★★★
Malpaso/Jay Weston   (U.S.)   R/15

Clint Eastwood (*Tom Highway*), Marsha Mason (*Aggie*), Everett McGill (*Maj. Powers*), Moses Gunn (*Sgt. Webster*), Eileen Heckart (*Little Mary*), Bo Svenson (*Roy Jennings*), Boyd Gaines (*Lt. Ring*), Mario Van Peebles (*Stitch*), Arlen Dean Snyder (*Choozoo*), Vincent Irizarry (*Fragetti*)

p, Clint Eastwood; d, Clint Eastwood; w, James Karabatsos; ph, Jack N. Green; ed, Joel Cox; m, Lennie Niehaus; prod d, Edward Carfagno; cos, Glenn Wright

AAN Best Sound: Les Fresholtz, Dick Alexander, Vern Poore, William Nelson

Further exploring and expanding his iconic screen persona, producer-director-actor Clint Eastwood stars as Tom Highway, a gruff, foul-mouthed anachronism of the old Marine Corps who drinks too much and is constantly getting in trouble. Nearing retirement age, having alienated most of his superiors, Highway asks to end his career where it began and is transferred to perform gunnery sergeant duties in his old outfit. There, the small reconnaissance platoon he is to train proves to be a group of lazy malcontents who feel that they've been duped by the slick military advertising on television. Earning the admiration of these young hotshots by besting them physically and mentally at every turn, Highway proceeds to whip them into a self-respecting fighting unit that knows how to work as a team. This newfound purpose is tested when Highway and his men are sent off to a small Caribbean island none of them has ever heard of—Grenada—to rescue American medical students from a hostile Marxist government backed by Cuban troops.

HEARTBREAK RIDGE has drawn flak from those who think Eastwood somehow endorsed the Grenada invasion by refusing to overtly criticize it. But Eastwood isn't interested in the political meaning of the action; what concerns him is how it defines his characters, who only want to survive, not analyze, the conflict. The strengths and foibles of human beings are what this film—and all of Eastwood's directorial efforts—is all about, and his Tom Highway is one of the most vividly etched male characters seen onscreen in years. Eastwood makes no apologies for this man who knows only how to train men to kill, but he does understand him. Highway knows he's an anachronism and that he will soon have to leave the only role in which he feels confident; he's made the Marines his family, but now that family is rejecting him in favor of a much more glamorous image.

Eastwood believes that people can change, that contact with others can enlighten, and that attempting to understand one another is extremely valuable, but his characters are close-mouthed, wary, and afraid of appearing vulnerable, simply because they *are* vulnerable. He proves that it is still possible to infuse an "entertainment" with greater relevance. Eastwood fans who choose to simply watch and root for the "good guys" will not be disappointed by HEARTBREAK RIDGE, but neither will those looking for insights into the human condition.

HEARTS OF THE WEST

1975 102m c Western   ★★★½
MGM (U.S.)   PG

Jeff Bridges *(Lewis Tater)*, Andy Griffith *(Howard Pike)*, Donald Pleasence *(A.J. Nietz)*, Blythe Danner *(Miss Trout)*, Alan Arkin *(Kessler)*, Richard B. Shull *(Stout Crook)*, Herb Edelman *(Polo)*, Alex Rocco *(Earl, Assistant Director)*, Frank Cady *(Pa Tater)*, Anthony James *(Lean Crook)*

p, Tony Bill; d, Howard Zieff; w, Rob Thompson; ph, Mario Tosi; ed, Edward Warschilka; m, Ken Lauber; art d, Robert Luthardt

An homage to the B westerns of the 1930s and 1940s that stars Bridges as an aspiring young pulp writer in the fashion of Zane Grey. He heads for Hollywood, first making a stop in Nevada where he discovers that his correspondence school is a crooked operation. He accidentally takes the swindled cash and retreats to the desert; he's then "rescued" by a film crew led by Arkin and joins the bunch as they head back to the studio, falling in love with Arkin's secretary, Danner, and becoming pals with elder stuntman Griffith. The crooks pursue but are stopped when Griffith, convincingly dressed as an oater star, outwits them with a prop gun.

A charming film that takes the conventions and simplicity of early western serials and treats them in a careful and artistic manner. HEARTS is also a fine film about filmmaking, but experienced box-office failure. In keeping with tradition, the old black-and-white Metro lion logo opens the film by delivering his famous three roars.

HEAT

1995 160m c Crime/Drama   ★★★★
Forward Pass Productions/New Regency   R/15
Productions (U.S.)

Al Pacino *(Vincent Hanna)*, Robert De Niro *(Neil McCauley)*, Val Kilmer *(Chris Shiherlis)*, Jon Voight *(Nate)*, Tom Sizemore *(Michael Cheritto)*, Diane Venora *(Justine)*, Amy Brenneman *(Eady)*, Ashley Judd *(Charlene)*, Mykelti Williamson *(Drucker)*, Wes Studi *(Casals)*

p, Art Linson, Michael Mann; d, Michael Mann; w, Michael Mann; ph, Dante Spinotti; ed, Dov Hoenig, Pasquale Buba, William Goldenberg, Tom Rolf; m, Elliot Goldenthal; prod d, Neil Spisak; art d, Margie Stone McShirley; fx, Terry Frazee, Neil Krepela; cos, Deborah L. Scott

A preening, self-dramatizing cop (Al Pacino) pursues a tight-lipped criminal mastermind (Robert De Niro) around L.A. for three hours. It didn't sound like fun to us, either, but we were wrong; HEAT scores on many fronts.

The pairing of Pacino and De Niro (the first time they've shared a bill since THE GODFATHER, PART II in 1974) is HEAT's drawing card, but the real star of a Michael Mann film is always the visuals. HEAT has style to burn. Again working with the brilliant cinematographer Dante Spinotti, Mann turns the city itself into HEAT's major player. A shot of the cityscape at night quotes MY DARLING CLEMENTINE, but where John Ford viewed the open spaces of the Old West with optimistism, Mann presents the urban wasteland as the realization of a cynical, soulless culture. Tellingly, he sets one of his violent set pieces in the void of an abandoned drive-in.

Throughout, style is backed up with real substance. The plot, though it seems to ramble, builds suspense with deft precision, and the action set pieces are triumphs. HEAT also gets us deeply involved in the messy lives of both cops and robbers, via some richly textured domestic scenes only occasionally sabotaged by psychobabble. The result is that we actually *care* about these characters, which just might make this an Important Movie. Why? It's one of a handful of films since THE GODFATHER to successfully portray a criminal fraternity from within and without at the same time. When a bad guy's loved one risks her future to ensure his freedom, we root for the both of them; but when an ex-con who's been making a valiant effort to go straight gets sucked into the "crew," we're crushed. What more can you ask?

HEAT AND DUST

1983 133m c Drama   ★★½
Merchant Ivory (U.K.)   R/15

Julie Christie *(Anne)*, Greta Scacchi *(Olivia)*, Christopher Cazenove *(Douglas Rivers)*, Julian Glover *(Crawford)*, Susan Fleetwood *(Mrs. Crawford)*, Shashi Kapoor *(The Nawab)*, Madhur Jaffrey *(The Begum, His Mother)*, Nickolas Grace *(Harry)*, Zakir Hussain *(Inder Lal)*, Barry Foster *(Maj. Minnies)*

p, Ismail Merchant; d, James Ivory; w, Ruth Prawer Jhabvala (based on her novel); ph, Walter Lassally; ed, Humphrey Dixon; m, Richard Robbins; prod d, Wilfred Shingleton; art d, Maurice Fowler, Ram Yadekar; cos, Barbara Lane

Here's HEAT AND DUST—less heat than dust. Julie Christie is cast as Anne, grandniece of Olivia (Greta Scacchi), an Englishwoman living in India 60 years earlier. Anne follows in Olivia's footsteps in an attempt to discover why her great-aunt was the subject of a scandal in the 1920s. The stories of the two women are intercut, inter-weaving the different time periods. Olivia traveled to India, married an Indian, and became pregnant by him. The local population objected, especially when she decided to abort the child—a Western custom. Anne's personal history parallels that of her aunt in many respects. What could have been an interesting exploration of the mystical and seductive atmosphere of India is never realized; the film concerns itself with propriety more than exotic culture. It's a waste of the striking talents of these two lovely actresses, particularly the highly selective Christie.

HEATHERS

1989 102m c Comedy/Fantasy   ★★★½
Cinemarque (U.S.)   R/18

Winona Ryder *(Veronica Sawyer)*, Christian Slater *(J.D.)*, Shannen Doherty *(Heather Duke)*, Lisanne Falk *(Heather McNamara)*, Kim Walker *(Heather Chandler)*, Penelope Milford *(Pauline Fleming)*, Glenn Shadix *(Fr. Ripper)*, Lance Fenton *(Kurt Kelly)*, Patrick Laborteaux *(Ram)*, Jeremy Applegate *(Peter Dawson)*

p, Denise Di Novi; d, Daniel Waters; w, Daniel Waters; ph, Francis Kenny; ed, Norman Hollyn; m, David Newman; prod d, Jon Hutman; art d, Kara Lindstrom; cos, Rudy Dillon

HEAVEN CAN WAIT

The near-surreal world of high-school *popularity* is imaginatively probed in this black comedy revolving around teenage suicide. With scenes and dialogue sure to offend many, HEATHERS is, nevertheless, a film of startling originality and verve.

The eponymous Heathers (Shannen Doherty, Lisanne Falk, Kim Walker), the most exclusive clique at Westerburg High, routinely drop insufficiently cool friends and humiliate poor Martha "Dumptruck" Dunnstock (Carrie Lynn). Veronica (Winona Ryder), a relatively recent addition to their clique, demonstrates her independence by taking up with J.D. (Christian Slater), a motorcycle-riding misfit, becoming his mostly unwilling accomplice as he murders three of the school's most popular, albeit piggish, students, leaving behind heartrending suicide notes. But what begins as a lark for Veronica becomes a nightmare as she realizes that her mischievous fantasies are diabolical realities for the increasingly psychotic J.D.

HEATHERS might have been a moronic teen gross-out film were it not for the immediacy and careful observation of the surprisingly rich script by Daniel Walters, Michael Lehmann's clever direction, and the extraordinary performances of Ryder and, to a lesser extent, Slater (who does an appropriately creepy, raspy-voiced Jack Nicholson imitation). Dark, cynical, but deliciously funny, HEATHERS is a fascinating look not just at high school but at the way we look at high school.

HEAVEN CAN WAIT

1943 112m c Comedy   ★★★½
Fox (U.S.)   /A

Gene Tierney *(Martha)*, Don Ameche *(Henry Van Cleve)*, Charles Coburn *(Hugo Van Cleve)*, Marjorie Main *(Mrs. Strabel)*, Laird Cregar *(His Excellency)*, Spring Byington *(Bertha Van Cleve)*, Allyn Joslyn *(Albert Van Cleve)*, Eugene Pallette *(Mr. Strabel)*, Signe Hasso *(Mademoiselle)*, Louis Calhern *(Randolph Van Cleve)*

p, Ernst Lubitsch; d, Ernst Lubitsch; w, Samson Raphaelson (based on the play *Birthdays* by Ladislaus Bus-Fekete); ph, Edward Cronjager; ed, Dorothy Spencer; m, Alfred Newman; art d, James Basevi, Leland Fuller; cos, Rene Hubert

AAN Best Picture; *AAN Best Director:* Ernst Lubitsch; *AAN Best Cinematography:* Edward Cronjager

Astute salute to a charming rake, deceptive satire disguised as a bubble. This movie has Ameche as an innocent Casanova, shown from infancy to his death at age 70. The film opens with a deceased Ameche standing before the Devil, Cregar, requesting his passport to Hell. Cregar studies his newest applicant and then reviews Ameche's carefree and often careless life. Based on the Hungarian play *Birthdays* by Ladislaus Bus-Fekete, with additional bromides from Samson Raphaelson. But Ameche is short on charm and too hapless for the role; he can't get any real chemistry cooking with Tierney. Still, it's compensated by a supporting cast of pros, and Lubitsch's deft direction. This was Lubitsch's first color film; the Basevi-Fuller Hell is a fabulous sight to see.

HEAVEN CAN WAIT

1978 101m c Comedy/Fantasy   ★★½
Paramount (U.S.)   PG/A

Warren Beatty *(Joe Pendleton)*, Julie Christie *(Betty Logan)*, James Mason *(Mr. Jordan)*, Dyan Cannon *(Julia Farnsworth)*, Charles Grodin *(Tony Abbott)*, Jack Warden *(Max Corkle)*, Buck Henry *(The Escort)*, Vincent Gardenia *(Lt. Krim)*, Joseph Maher *(Sisk)*, Hamilton Camp *(Bentley)*

p, Warren Beatty; d, Warren Beatty, Buck Henry; w, Warren Beatty, Elaine May (based on the play by Harry Segall); ph, William A. Fraker; ed, Robert C. Jones, Don Zimmerman; m, Dave Grusin; prod d, Paul Sylbert; art d, Edwin O'Donovan; fx, Robert MacDonald; cos, Theadora Van Runkle, Richard Bruno

AAN Best Picture; *AAN Best Actor:* Warren Beatty; *AAN Best Supporting Actor:* Jack Warden; *AAN Best Supporting Actress:* Dyan Cannon; *AAN Best Director:* Warren Beatty, Buck Henry; *AAN Best Adapted Screenplay:* Elaine May, Warren Beatty; *AAN Best Cinematography:* William A. Fraker; *AAN Best Score:* Dave Grusin; *AA Best Art Direction:* Paul Sylbert, Edwin O'Donovan, George Gaines

Beatty's ballgame, an unecessary remake of HERE COMES MR. JORDAN—he produced, co-directed, co-wrote (with Elaine May) and starred as Joe Pendleton, a Los Angeles Rams quarterback who is prematurely ushered to heaven by a bumbling celestial messenger (co-director Henry) after an auto accident. An archangel, Mr. Jordan (Mason), tries to redress this error by restoring Joe to life in the body of a wealthy industrialist moments after he's murdered by his adulterous wife (Cannon) and the industrialist's nitwit secretary (Grodin). Determined to play in the Super Bowl, Beatty buys the Rams and hires his old coach (Warden) to help him train, convincing Warden that Beatty has been reincarnated. Beatty also meets and falls in love with Christie, an English environmental activist, but just when it looks as though everything is going to work out, Cannon and Grodin try again.

The title comes from the Harry Segall play, upon which the 1941 JORDAN was based. There are a few laughs from Grodin and Cannon, but Beatty and Christie are like 400-pound gorillas chasing a milkweed seed. The more Beatty concentrates, the more glazed and distracted he looks. The film won an Oscar for Art Direction—presumably for Beatty's expensive bathrobes, Cannon's mane and the clipped hedges and boxwoods of a California estate.

HEAVENLY CREATURES

1994 98m c Drama   ★★★★
Wingnut Films/Fontana Film Productions (New Zealand)   R/18

Melanie Lynskey *(Pauline Parker)*, Kate Winslet *(Juliet Hulme)*, Sarah Peirse *(Honora Parker)*, Diana Kent *(Hilda Hulme)*, Clive Merrison *(Henry Hulme)*, Simon O'Connor *(Herbert Rieper)*, Jed Brophy *(John/Nicholas)*, Peter Elliot *(Bill Perry)*, Gilbert Goldie *(Dr. Bennett)*, Geoffrey Heath *(Reverend Norris)*

p, Jim Booth; d, Peter Jackson; w, Peter Jackson, Frances Walsh; ph, Alun Bollinger; ed, Jamie Selkirk; m, Peter Dasent; prod d, Grant Major; art d, Jill Cormack; fx, Richard Taylor; cos, Ngila Dickson

AAN Best Original Screenplay: Frances Walsh, Peter Jackson

A disturbing, boldly conceived story of two teenaged New Zealand girls whose obsessive friendship leads to murder, HEAVENLY CREATURES is equal parts psychodrama and dark fairy tale. Its flamboyant style evokes the fantasy world in which the girls lose themselves, and its breathless, childishly hyperbolic voice-over narration perfectly captures the dangerous passions of insular youth.

Pauline Parker (Melanie Lynskey) is plump, smart, plain, and painfully insecure; Juliet Hulme (Kate Winslet) is a dream walking, sleekly blonde and sophisticated beyond her years. To everyone's surprise, the two girls become friends, united by their feverish imaginations. Together, Juliet and Pauline spin a candy-colored imaginary universe of tremendous depth and complexity, pieced together from movies, novels, fairy tales, and their own lurid and strangely naive imaginings. When their parents sense that the relationship is unnaturally close, they attempt to separate the girls, with results that prove deadly.

Based on an actual murder committed in 1954, HEAVENLY CREATURES is the story of a *folie a deux*, a relationship born in innocuous mutual interests (movies, celebrities, popular music) that blossoms into a lethally insular us-against-them (adults, society, the world) alliance. But HEAVENLY CREATURES breaks the pattern of films as diverse as Alfred Hitchcock's ROPE, Arthur Penn's BONNIE AND CLYDE, and even Tom Kalin's SWOON, by taking rebellious, hormonally raging boys out of the equation. Pauline and Juliet are quintessential adolescent girls; their longings are precise, if wildly fanciful—not inchoate yearnings to be free and seek excitement. Their fantasies are rooted less in restlessness and the desire to make a mark on the world, than the need to find all-enveloping romance and a place to hide.

HEAVENLY CREATURES excited extensive press coverage when it was revealed that in real life, Juliet Hulme had changed her name to Anne Perry and made a successful career as a mystery writer. Perry refused to see the film, but insisted that it distorted her relationship with Pauline, and was particularly disturbed that the filmmakers strongly suggested a lesbian relationship between the girls.

HEAVEN'S GATE

1980 217m c/bw Western ★★½
Partisan Productions (U.S.) R/18

Kris Kristofferson *(Marshal James Averill)*, Christopher Walken *(Nathan D. Champion)*, John Hurt *(Billy Irvine)*, Isabelle Huppert *(Ella Watson)*, Sam Waterston *(Frank Canton)*, Jeff Bridges *(John H. Bridges)*, Joseph Cotten *("The Reverend Doctor")*, Roseanne Vela *(Beautiful Girl)*, Ronnie Hawkins *(Wolcott)*, Geoffrey Lewis *(Trapper)*

p, Joann Carelli; d, Michael Cimino; w, Michael Cimino; ph, Vilmos Zsigmond; ed, Tom Rolf, William Reynolds, Lisa Fruchtman, Gerald Greenberg; m, David Mansfield; art d, Tambi Larsen, Spencer Deverill, Maurice Fowler; fx, Paul Stewart, Ken Pepiot, Stan Parks, Sam Price, Jim Camomile, Kevin Quibell; chor, Eleanor Fazan; cos, J. Allen Highfill

AAN Best Art Direction: Tambi Larsen (Art Direction), Jim Berkey (Set Decoration)

This beautiful but notoriously disappointing film is one of the most overblown epic Westerns of any decade. The story allegedly relates the events of the bloody 1892 Johnson County wars in Wyoming, pitting cattlemen against immigrant settlers. James Averill (Kris Kristofferson) becomes marshal and must hold the county's combatants in check. Nathan D. Champion (Christopher Walken) is a gunfighter hired by the ranchers. Both men share the sexual favors of prostitute Ella "Cattle Kate" Watson (Isabelle Huppert). Through various slice-of-life episodes without a unifying thread, writer-director Michael Cimino tries to depict the lifestyles of the ranchers and the settlers, and the differences that lead to all-out war between the factions.

Kristofferson is wooden, Walken far too remote, and no one else in the cast stands out. Cimino's financial excesses included having trains completely rebuilt, providing infinitely detailed costumes for extras, and planting miles of sod on a battle field that would be blown up. The film's final cost was estimated to be $35 million, though some reports went as high as $50 million. Cimino's sins might have been forgiven in Hollywood had the film made a positive statement; but it derides the American Dream as a history of moral compromise——this in lieu of a story—and the American press took off after it in droves; the public's reaction to the truncated version released was to reject it instantly. The director's cut, available on cassette, is regarded as a masterpiece in Europe where Cimino's star shines brighter.

HEAVY METAL

1981 91m c Animated/Science Fiction ★★
Columbia (Canada) R/AA

VOICES OF: Roger Bumpass, Jackie Burroughs, John Candy, Joe Flaherty, Don Francks, Martin Lavut, Eugene Levy, Marilyn Lightstone, Alice Playten, Harold Ramis

p, Ivan Reitman; d, Gerald Potterton; w, Dan Goldberg, Len Blum (based on work and stories by Richard Corben, Angus McKie, Dan O'Bannon, Thomas Warkentin, and Berni Wrightson); ed, Janice Brown; m, Elmer Bernstein; prod d, Michael Gross; anim, Thomas Warkentin, Angus McKie, Dab O'Bannon, Richard Corben, Juan Gimenez, Lee Mishkin

Although the concept for this animated film is derived from the adult fantasy magazine of the same name, HEAVY METAL is clearly targeted for a teen audience. Divided into a number of episodes, the film is held together by the Loc-Nar, a sinister, glowing jewel that catapults characters into weird, threatening confrontations. In one of the better episodes, a New York City cab driver becomes involved with a sexy but greedy woman who is being chased by criminals. In another, a young bookworm (voiced by John Candy) is transformed into a brawny, heroic stud and saves a maiden from being sacrificed to the jewel. Otherwise, it's a mixed bag, but successful in a mindless, adolescent way. The spirited, energetic music is contributed by a variety of rock performers, including Blue Oyster Cult, Black Sabbath and Nazareth.

HEIMAT

1984 924m c/bw Drama ★★★½
Reitz/WDR/SFB (West Germany) /15

Marita Breuer *(Maria)*, Willi Burger, Gertrud Bredel, Rudiger Weigang, Karin Rasenack, Dieter Schaad, Michael Lesch, Peter Harting, Jorg Richter, Johannes Lobewein

p, Edgar Reitz, Joachim von Mengershausen, Hans Kwiet; d, Edgar Reitz; w, Edgar Reitz, Peter Steinbach; ph, Gernot Roll; ed, Heidi Handorf; m, Nikos Mamangakis; art d, Franz Bauer

Though HEIMAT runs an imposing 15-and-a-half hours, this epic work, chronicling life in a German village from 1919 to 1982, rarely fails to capture the viewer within its immense visionary scope. The events of the period—Germany's post-WWI depression, the rise of Nazism, WWII, and postwar recovery—are seen not through the eyes of Germany's leaders, politicians, and artists, but through the eyes of the common people in the fictional village of Schabbach. At the center of the events is Breuer, who gives a remarkable performance. Using makeup, costumes and her gifted acting talents, Breuer gives HEIMAT a heartfelt anchor, playing her character from childhood to old age.

Director Edgar Reitz's film, which is usually shown in four successive screenings, is both in color and black and white. The black-and-white sequences go from the 1920s to the early 1950s, with color encompassing the rest of the film, though at times Reitz intercuts the two processes to give emphasis within a scene. Reitz's original plan was to rediscover his own background, so he began writing down the stories of his family and the people from his rural village. He had planned to turn this story into an epic novel, but at the urging of television producer Joachim von Mengershausen, Reitz decided to put this project before the cameras. After writing a 2,000-page script with Peter Steinbach, Reitz shot a documentary dealing with a similar subject.

Production on HEIMAT finally began in 1981, but Reitz was forced to put everything on hold after four months because funding ran out. Though he started again two months later, the shooting was halted for financial reasons a second time. Reitz finally completed the lensing in late 1982, then took 18 months to edit the enormous amount of footage he had created. All told, HEIMAT took five years and four months to create from conception to final cut.

HEIRESS, THE

1949 115m bw Drama ★★★★★
Paramount (U.S.) /U

Olivia de Havilland *(Catherine Sloper)*, Montgomery Clift *(Morris Townsend)*, Ralph Richardson *(Dr. Austin Sloper)*, Miriam Hopkins *(Lavinia Penniman)*, Vanessa Brown *(Maria)*, Mona Freeman *(Marian Almond)*, Ray Collins *(Jefferson Almond)*, Betty Linley *(Mrs. Montgomery)*, Selena Royle *(Elizabeth Almond)*, Paul Lees *(Arthur Townsend)*

p, William Wyler; d, William Wyler; w, Ruth Goetz, Augustus Goetz (based on their play and the novel *Washington Square* by Henry James); ph, Leo Tover; ed, William Hornbeck; m, Aaron Copland; art d, John Meehan, Harry Horner; fx, Gordon Jennings; cos, Edith Head, Gile Steele

AAN Best Picture; AA Best Actress: Olivia DeHavilland; *AAN Best Supporting Actor:* Ralph Richardson; *AAN Best Director:* William Wyler; *AAN Best Cinematography:* Leo Tover; *AA Best Score:* Aaron Copland; *AA Best Art Direction:* John Meehan, Harry Horner, Emile Kuri; *AA Best Costume Design:* Edith Head, Gile Steele

This powerful and compelling drama, based on Henry James's 1881 novel *Washington Square* and the successful Broadway play by Ruth and Augustus Goetz, owes its triumph to the deft hand of director William Wyler and a remarkable lead performance by Olivia de Havilland.

Set circa 1850, the film casts de Havilland as the plain-looking daughter of wealthy, widowed doctor Richardson, with whom she lives at their home at 16 Washington Square. Life is uneventful. Richardson is a tyrant at home, dictating his daughter's every move and cruelly telling her that she bears no resemblance to his dear departed wife, who was beautiful and charming. Suitors shun de Havilland—who is awkward in her movements, conversation, and manners—until she receives some unexpected attention from Clift at a ball. He flatters her and asks to call on her, news that is derisively greeted by Richardson, who tells de Havilland that Clift must be a fortune hunter, and will break her heart.

This was one of de Havilland's greatest roles; Wyler finally breaks her of her habit of sweet smiles (she'd later revert) and her transformation from docile emotional victim to rational, resolved adult is a masterpiece of acting. Ralph Richardson is equally good, injecting a majestic presence into his portrait of a hateful man who is really so fearful for his daughter's future that he will incur her permanent loathing to protect that future. Miriam Hopkins is fine, too, as the one eternally bright spot in de Havilland's life, but Clift is surprisingly weak.

Wyler worked hard to produce this masterpiece. He had requested Gregg Toland (with whom he had collaborated memorably on films like WUTHERING HEIGHTS, THE BEST YEARS OF OUR LIVES and THE LITTLE FOXES) for his cinematographer, and instead got Leo Tover. When Wyler asked for a setup calling for deep focus, Tover took half a day to make preparations, where Toland would have achieved the setup in an hour. The director did score a coup, however, when he secured Aaron Copeland's services as the film's composer. Copeland had written memorable music for such films as OF MICE AND MEN, OUR TOWN and NORTH STAR but had gained a "Red" taint as a result of his involvement in the last and, in the suspicious climate of 1949, Wyler had to argue heavily with Paramount executives to retain Copeland who came through with a haunting, telling score.

HELLO, DOLLY!

1969 129m c Musical/Comedy ★★★
Chenault (U.S.) G/U

Barbra Streisand (Dolly Levi), Walter Matthau (Horace Vandergelder), Michael Crawford (Cornelius Hackl), Louis Armstrong (Orchestra Leader), Marianne McAndrew (Irene Molloy), E.J. Peaker (Minnie Fay), Danny Lockin (Barnaby Tucker), Joyce Ames (Ermengarde), Tommy Tune (Ambrose Kemper), Judy Knaiz (Gussie Granger)

p, Ernest Lehman; d, Gene Kelly; w, Ernest Lehman (based on the play The Matchmaker by Thornton Wilder); ph, Harry Stradling; ed, William Reynolds; m, Jerry Herman, Lennie Hayton, Lionel Newman; prod d, John De Cuir; art d, Jack Martin Smith, Herman A. Blumenthal; fx, L.B. Abbott, Art Cruickshank, Emil Kosa Jr.; chor, Michael Kidd; cos, Irene Sharaff

AAN Best Picture; AAN Best Cinematography: Harry Stadling; AAN Best Editing: William Reynolds; AA Best Score: Lennie Hayton, Lionel Newman; AA Best Art Direction: John DeCuir, Jack Martin Smith, Herman Blumenthal, Walter M. Scott, George James Hopkins, Raphael Bretton; AAN Best Costume Design: Irene Sharaff; AA Best Sound: Jack Solomon, Murray Spivack

Here's the film that, joined by DOCTOR DOOLITTLE and STAR!, sounded the death knell for the film musical, a stroke it still hasn't recovered from. It's also the film where Striesand allegedly slapped Matthau, and he slapped her back. But she had no problem bullying director Kelly: it's an exercise in star turns, surrounded by elephantine blandness. The supporting cast look, and act, like refugees from Disney or Oral Roberts University, handpicked not to ruffle the star. Whatever terrific future lay ahead for Tune and Crawford, you've no inkling of it from all the too cute mugging here. Not only is Striesand far too young (and it makes one weep to think of all the marvelous ladies who should have been considered), but her Dolly Levi arouses no affection. Without the dose of healthy sentiment the character arouses to balance her machinations, she's just a nasty bitch on the make. Furthermore, this exposes how pallid Thornton Wilder's The Matchmaker (the play on which the musical is based) really is. There are two good songs in Jerry Herman's score: "Before the Parade Passes By" and the title tune, here an exercise in star wrestling between Striesand and the irrepressible Louis Armstrong, who connect not one whit.

HELLRAISER

1987 90m c Horror ★★½
Cinemarque/Film Futures/New World (U.K.) R/18

Andrew Robinson (Larry Cotton), Clare Higgins (Julia Cotton), Ashley Laurence (Kirsty Swanson), Sean Chapman (Frank Cotton), Oliver Smith (Frank the Monster), Robert Hines (Steve), Leon Davis (2nd Victim), Mike Cassidy (3rd Victim), Frank Baker (Derelict), Kenneth Nelson (Bill)

p, Christopher Figg; d, Clive Barker; w, Clive Barker (based on his novella "The Hellbound Heart"); ph, Robin Vidgeon; ed, Richard Marden; m, Christopher Young; prod d, Mike Buchanan; art d, Jocelyn James; fx, Bob Keen; cos, Joanna Johnston

Somewhat disappointing directorial debut of the man called the "future of horror fiction" by Stephen King, Clive Barker, based on his own novella The Hell-Bound Heart.

Frank (Sean Chapman), a sexual adventurer in search of new carnal pleasures, purchases a mysterious Chinese puzzle box while visiting an unnamed Third World country. Back home in England, he opens the box only to discover that he has unlocked the door to hell. Frank is pulled into another dimension, whose inhabitants, known as Cenobites, push him over the fine line between pleasure and pain by ripping him apart with tiny fish hooks. Years later, Frank's brother, Larry (Andrew Robinson), moves his family into the house—to which, through some blood spilled on the attic floor, Frank returns in near-skeletal form. With the help of sister-in-law Julia (Clare Higgins)—with whom he once had an affair—Frank begins sucking the life out of bodies in order to regenerate to his old form. Meanwhile, Larry's daughter from a previous marriage, Kirsty (Ashley Laurence), begins to suspect her hated stepmother of having an affair, and to her horror becomes involved with Frank, the puzzle box and the Cenobites.

Undoubtedly head and shoulders above average horror fare thematically, HELLRAISER is, however, extremely graphic, badly paced, and, with few exceptions, poorly acted. As a director, Barker does possess a striking visual sensibility; the film literally drips with horrific ambience. However, while the author's cinematic sense is a pleasant surprise, his narrative is shockingly haphazard, and the film lurches from one set piece to the next with little dramatic rhythm. While Barker does a respectable job of developing the characters of Julia and Frank and the lustful ties that bind them, the writer-director is clearly less interested in victims Larry and Kirsty. The film never gets a handle on these characters and never provides enough characterization so that the viewer cares about their fate.

HELL'S ANGELS

1930 135m c/bw War ★★★½
Caddo (U.S.)

Ben Lyon (Monte Rutledge), James Hall (Roy Rutledge), Jean Harlow (Helen), John Darrow (Karl Arnstedt), Lucien Prival (Baron von Kranz), Frank Clark (Lt. von Bruen), Roy Wilson (Baldy), Douglas Gilmore (Capt. Redfield), Jane Winton (Baroness von Kranz), Evelyn Hall (Lady Randolph)

p, Howard Hughes; d, Howard Hughes, James Whale, Marshall Neilan, Luther Reed; w, Harry Behn, Howard Estabrook, Joseph Moncure March (based on a story by Marshall Neilan, Joseph Moncure March); ph, Tony Gaudio, Paul Perry, E. Burton Steene, Elmer Dyer, Harry Zeck, Dewey Wrigley; ed, Douglas Biggs, Perry Hollingsworth, Frank Lawrence; m, Hugo Riesenfeld; art d, Julian Boone Fleming, Carroll Clark

AAN Best Cinematography: Gaetano Gaudio, Harry Perry

And hell's memorable belle, here and there among the aerial sequences. The film looks dated and the story seems to have been written in crayon by Hughes; it's a testimony to his two great loves—wings and breasts, about good brother and bad brother, and the blonde who comes between them. Beside Hughes, it was directed by Marshall Neilan, Luther Reed, and sometimes James Whale (credited as dialogue director, but he also wrote much of the script). There is a bang-up aerial dogfight and a solid zeppelin sequence; many believe these moments have never been surpassed. Hughes worked them out on blackboards and with model planes before he shot. When the zeppelin moves through the clouds and we see London below, we feel *inside* the camera.

The plot was corn in 1930—it feels very much like a silent picture—and eighteen year-old Harlow hasn't the foggiest notion what she's supposed to do. Her take on the British Helen is undeniably piggy, but clad in a velvet evening gown with beaded straps, she's like no one the camera had ever photographed when she turns her bare back to us. And audiences stopped laughing when she inquired, "Would you be shocked if I put on something more comfortable?"

Launched in 1927 as the first major effort of Hughes's Caddo Productions, the ANGELS was so long in the making that sound came into being, and much of the film, which had been shot as a silent, had to be redone. Both Lyon and Hall had good "sound" voices, but the female lead, Greta Nissen, had a pronounced Norwegian accent, and, though Hughes had paid her handsomely, he scrapped her performance completely and began searching for a new actress who could handle the role's vocal chores. Among the candidates was Harlow, then an 18-year-old, blue-eyed platinum blonde with a voluptuous shape. Although Hughes was unimpressed with her screen test, Harlow's agent, Arthur Landau, talked the millionaire playboy into letting his client play the part. Her debut caused Hughes endless arguments with the censors. After the film, Hughes inexplicably ignored the new star he had created, though he had the presence of mind to put her under permanent contract. Nevertheless, he sold her contract for a mere $60,000 to MGM, for whom she would make millions as the reigning sex queen of the cinema until her death in 1937.

The film's staggering $3.8 million budget made HELL'S ANGELS the cinema's most expensive film to date, and Hughes, determined to get his money back, employed the kind of hoopla for which he later became notorious, arranging for a squadron of planes to buzz Grauman's Chinese Theater at the film's premiere while parachutists descended on Hollywood Boulevard. Trying to orchestrate a similarly flashy stunt in New York, Hughes offered the owners of the dirigible *Graf Zeppelin* $100,000 to sail over Broadway and 42nd Street, where *two* theaters were premiering the film, but the owners refused. Despite his best efforts, Hughes took a bath on the film, losing more than $1.5 million, although, at first, he claimed to have made $2 million. It is said that he later admitted that the film would have been better and cost less had he allowed someone else to direct it.

HELLZAPOPPIN'

1941   84m   bw   Comedy   ★★★
Universal   (U.S.)   /U

Ole Olsen *(Ole)*, Chic Johnson *(Chic)*, Robert Paige *(Jeff Hunter)*, Jane Frazee *(Kitty Rand)*, Lewis Howard *(Woody Tyler)*, Martha Raye *(Betty Johnson)*, Clarence Kolb *(Mr. Rand)*, Nella Walker *(Mrs. Rand)*, Mischa Auer *(Pepi)*, Richard Lane *(Director)*

p, Jules Levy; d, H.C. Potter; w, Nat Perrin, Warren Wilson (based on the play by Nat Perrin); ph, Elwood Bredell; ed, Milton Carruth; fx, John P. Fulton; chor, Nick Castle, Eddie Prinz; cos, Vera West

AAN Best Song: Gene DePaul (Music), Don Raye (Music)

Crazy as hell, at 100 miles an hour, loaded with sight gags that sometimes work and sometimes fall as flat as a burned pancake; but the feeling is surprisingly contemporary. The story begins in Purgatory, with Olsen and Johnson jumping in and out of a story that's barely there, basically a trite romance tale of poor boy meets rich girl and wins her heart after putting on the traditional show. O. and J. constantly argue with the film's director and cameraman on camera about the restraints put upon them while mindless mayhem ensues—someone constantly yelling "Jones!" for no good reason; Auer, a rich count, chasing Martha Raye about madly, and vice versa. At one point a film director, Lane, tells the madcaps Olson and Johnson: "This is Hollywood; we change everything here. We've *got* to!" If it's not as immortal as the Marx Brothers' best work, it's definitely admirable in its cutting edge risk.

HELP!

1965   92m   c   Musical/Comedy   ★★★½
Walter Shenson/Subafilms   (U.K.)   G/U

John Lennon *(John)*, Paul McCartney *(Paul)*, Ringo Starr *(Ringo)*, George Harrison *(George)*, Leo McKern *(Clang)*, Eleanor Bron *(Ahme)*, Victor Spinetti *(Foot)*, Roy Kinnear *(Algernon)*, John Bluthal *(Bhuta)*, Patrick Cargill *(Superintendent)*

p, Walter Shenson; d, Richard Lester; w, Marc Behm, Charles Wood (based on an original story by Behm); ph, David Watkin; ed, John Victor Smith; m, Ken Thorne; art d, Ray Simm; fx, Cliff Richardson, Roy Whybrow; cos, Julie Harris, Dinah Greet, Arthur Newman

Shot on location in the Bahamas, Austria, and on Salisbury Plain, HELP!, the second Beatles film, is nonsensical fun.

Filled as it is with wonderful music and enlivened by the Fab Four's engaging screen presence, the story revolves around the crazed efforts of a pair of Eastern religious zealots, Clang (Leo McKern) and Ahme (the ravishing, underrated Eleanor Bron), to get hold of a sacred ring that has been given to Ringo by a fan and which he can't get off his finger. Foot (Victor Spinetti), the scientist Ringo approaches for help, comes to believe that the ring will allow him to control the world, and he and his assistant (Roy Kinnear) join the scramble to wrest the ring from Ringo. Antics aplenty ensue as Ringo and the other Beatles lead their pursuers on a madcap, globe-trotting chase.

Silly at its worst and brilliant at its best, HELP! picks up where the joyous insouciance of A HARD DAY'S NIGHT—director Richard Lester's first collaboration with the Fab Four—left off. McKern, Bron, Kinnear and Spinetti display fine comedic timing, and the Beatles make a reasonable stab at being a modern-day version of the Marx Brothers.

HENRY & JUNE

1990   136m   c   Drama/Erotic   ★★½
Walrus & Associates   (U.S.)   NC-17/18

Fred Ward *(Henry Miller)*, Uma Thurman *(June Miller)*, Maria de Medeiros *(Anais Nin)*, Richard E. Grant *(Hugo)*, Kevin Spacey *(Osborn)*, Jean-Philippe Ecoffey *(Eduardo)*, Bruce Myers *(Jack)*, Jean-Louis Bunuel *(Editor-Publisher)*, Feodor Atkine *(Spanish Dance Instructor)*, Sylvie Huguel *(Emilia)*

p, Peter Kaufman; d, Philip Kaufman; w, Philip Kaufman, Rose Kaufman (based on the diaries of Anais Nin); ph, Philippe Rousselot; ed, Vivien Hillgrove, William S. Scharf, Dede Allen; prod d, Guy-Claude Francois; art d, Georges Glon; chor, Nathalie Erlbaum; cos, Yvonne Sassinot de Nesle

AAN Best Cinematography: Philippe Rousselot

A second excursion into literary erotica from Philip Kaufman (THE UNBEARABLE LIGHTNESS OF BEING), this is notable as the first film to be released with the MPAA's NC-17 rating, created in 1990 to distinguish steamy-but-serious movies from hardcore porn. The film isn't nearly sexy enough to merit the new rating or the ensuing controversy.

Novelist Henry Miller (Fred Ward) has been sent to France by his wife, June (Uma Thurman), a former taxi dancer who has been supporting his career on her earnings as another man's mistress. The purpose of the trip is twofold: to get Henry away from distractions in New York so he can finish the novel, and to allow June, a bisexual, more freedom to frolic with a new girlfriend. The film actually opens not with Henry or June, but with Miller's lover, lifelong friend, and literary advocate Anais Nin (Maria de Medeiros), upon whose diaries the screenplay is based. Legendary *poseur* Anais is hot to trot; when a college professor stiffly kisses and fondles her during a meeting, she transforms the mild indiscretion into a full-blown seduction in her diary, which she hides from bland, likable middle-class husband Hugo (Richard E. Grant). Anais generally chafes at her mundane existence and yearns for a more bohemian social life and, especially, for a big, swarthy lover. Enter big and swarthy Henry, brought to Anais's house by her husband, who is friends with Henry's eccentric roommate (Kevin Spacey). Initially, Anais and Henry are tentative friends, providing each other with support for their respective writing projects. And though

Anais has polite erotic palpitations when she is around the earthy but cultured Henry, it is June, briefly in Paris to check up on Henry, who brings Anais's passions to a furious boil.

The couplings in HENRY AND JUNE are as explicit as any to be found in mainstream American cinema; still, the sex here seems mild compared to the erotic imaginings of Almodovar, Bertolucci, Imamura, Oshima, and many others. Kaufman tries to project a kind of professorial sobriety, hoping his film will seem classy and serious instead of raunchy. We think it could've used *more* raunch, and we're sure Henry Miller (whose favorite film was L'AGE D'OR) would have agreed.

HENRY: PORTRAIT OF A SERIAL KILLER

1989 83m c Crime/Horror   ★★★★
Maljack (U.S.)   /18

Michael Rooker (*Henry*), Tom Towles (*Otis*), Tracy Arnold (*Becky*), Ray Atherton (*Fence*), David Katz (*Henry's Boss*), Eric Young (*Parole Officer*), Mary Demas (*Hooker #1/Dead Prostitute/Dead Woman*), Kristin Finger (*Hooker #2*), Anne Bartoletti (*Waitress*), Erzsebet Sziky (*Hitchiker*)

p, Lisa Dedmond, Steven A. Jones, John McNaughton; d, John McNaughton; w, Richard Fire, John McNaughton; ph, Charlie Lieberman; ed, Elena Maganini; m, Robert McNaughton, Ken Hale, Steven A. Jones; art d, Rick Paul; cos, Patricia Hart

HENRY: PORTRAIT OF A SERIAL KILLER surely ranks as one of the most frightening and disturbing films ever made. An angry and raw independent feature, HENRY begins with a creepy montage of shots of dead bodies. The corpses are the victims of Henry (Michael Rooker), a lowlife drifter who looks for victims while driving around in his green Impala. Rooker murders with knives, guns, rope, even his hands—he has no preferred method or pattern.

Rooker lives with Towles, a degenerate he met while in prison (for killing his mother) who now works in a gas station and sells drugs on the side. When Towles's sister (Arnold) comes to Chicago, she stays with Towles and Rooker while she looks for a job; meanwhile, Rooker, who works as a bug sprayer, and Towle continue to murder people at random, videotaping every detail, until they start to get on each other's nerves. When Rooker can no longer stand Towles's stupidity and sloppiness, the two argue; meanwhile, Arnold quits her job in a hair salon and asks Rooker to move away with her.

A stunning feature debut from director John McNaughton, HENRY tells its horrible story with chilling straightforwardness. Presenting his sick characters nonjudgmentally and without shrinking from gory details, McNaughton creates a world in which there is no good to counterbalance evil, where incest and rape are permitted and murder is an acceptable way to relieve tension. Providing no "good" characters to identify with—not even a cop to offer us hope—and ending on a bitter, ugly note, HENRY leaves viewers emotionally drained and deeply, deeply disturbed. McNaughton succeeds in showing just how vulnerable anyone can be to someone like Henry, a frightening reality few will want to contemplate.

No film in recent memory has tapped into primal, visceral fear as HENRY does, with its vision of a depraved world that seems at once too horrible to exist and too realistic to be denied. Hard to watch (though at times it's bizarrely and blackly funny) and definitely not for the squeamish, HENRY will prove unforgettable for the brave souls who do see it. A major achievement in independent filmmaking, HENRY: PORTRAIT OF A SERIAL KILLER is a horror masterpiece.

HENRY V

1944 127m c Drama/War   ★★★★★
Two Cities (U.K.)   /U

Laurence Olivier (*King Henry V*), Robert Newton (*Ancient Pistol*), Leslie Banks (*Chorus*), Renee Asherson (*Princess Katherine*), Esmond Knight (*Fluellen*), Leo Genn (*Constable of France*), Felix Aylmer (*Archbishop of Canterbury*), Ralph Truman (*Mountjoy*), Harcourt Williams (*King Charles VI of France*), Ivy St. Helier (*Alice. Lady in Waiting*)

p, Laurence Olivier, Filippo Del Giudice; d, Laurence Olivier, Reginald Beck; w, Alan Dent, Laurence Olivier (based on the play by William Shakespeare); ph, Robert Krasker; ed, Reginald Beck; m, William Walton; art d, Paul Sheriff; cos, Roger Furse

AAN Best Picture; AAN Best Actor: Laurence Olivier; *AAN Best Score:* William Walton; *AAN Best Art Direction:* Paul Sheriff (Art Direction), Carmen Dillon (Art Direction)

Made at the height of the German blitz, this dazzling British adaptation of Shakespeare's classic tale of victory in the face of overwhelming odds brought new hope and resolve to embattled Britons who saw it in 1944. Filippo del Giudice, an Italian lawyer who had fled Mussolini's rule, persuaded Laurence Olivier to undertake the project, and when William Wyler, Carol Reed, and Terence Young were unable to helm the film, Olivier not only took on the title role but the director's mantle, performing both roles magnificently.

Innovatively structured, the film begins with a 17th-century staging of Shakespeare's play at the Globe Theatre; then, gradually, the proscenium disappears as the film moves toward a more realistic presentation of the story, with stylized sets giving way to the real-life scenery of the impressive re-creation of the Battle of Agincourt. Finally, Olivier brings the film full circle, back to the stage of the Globe.

Set in 1415, HENRY V chronicles the invasion of France undertaken by the 28-year-old English king in an attempt to consolidate his power at home. After a number of costly victories drastically deplete Henry's army, it is besieged by French forces that outnumber it nearly five to one. Under the king's courageous leadership, however, the English triumph at Agincourt.

Olivier, who was mustered out of the navy to make the film, collaborated with movie critic Alan Dent on the adaptation, and editor Reginald Beck helped with direction chores when Olivier the star was in front of the cameras. Though given a large budget considering the wartime circumstances, the production was continually forced to cut corners, and its wonderfully realized costumes and sets are testaments to the ingenuity of the film's designers.

HENRY V

1989 138m c Drama/Historical   ★★★★
BBC/Curzon/Renaissance (U.K.)   PG

Kenneth Branagh (*King Henry V*), Derek Jacobi (*Chorus*), Simon Shepherd (*Duke of Gloucester*), James Larkin (*Bedford*), Brian Blessed (*Duke of Exeter*), James Simmons (*York*), Paul Gregory (*Earl of Westmoreland*), Charles Kay (*Archbishop of Canterbury*), Alec McCowen (*Bishop of Ely*), Fabian Cartwright (*Cambridge*)

p, Bruce Sharman; d, Kenneth Branagh; w, Kenneth Branagh; ph, Kenneth MacMillan; ed, Michael Bradsell; m, Pat Doyle; prod d, Tim Harvey; art d, Norman Dorme; cos, Phyllis Dalton

AAN Best Actor: Kenneth Branagh; *AAN Best Director:* Kenneth Branagh; *AA Best Costume Design:* Phyllis Dalton

Straightforward, energetic, updated Bard. 28-year-old star-director-adapter Kenneth Branagh's spellbinding version of Shakespeare's *Henry* isn't superior to Olivier's 1944 version—it's different, and complementary to it.

Filmed mostly in medium and close-up shots, Branagh's more intimate version discards the pageantry of Olivier's grand spectacle; focusing on carnage and casualties, Branagh's film is strongly antiwar whereas Olivier's vision, filmed as a paean to England's greatness, was a morale builder for his countrymen embroiled in a world war. Branagh's HENRY V is also a visceral coming-of-age film, following a young playboy prince as he is forced to grow up quickly and assume the responsibilities of leadership. Throughout the film, Branagh uses flashbacks, excerpted from the earlier *Henry IV* plays to clarify events, and though he has pruned the 400-year-old play, all of its most memorable moments are in place and brilliantly conveyed: from the seige of Harfleur and Henry's stirring exhortation to his small army to go "Once more unto the breach," to the dramatic victory at Agincourt.

In addition to his own extraordinary performance as King Henry, Branagh elicits brilliant work from a stellar cast, including Derek Jacobi as the chorus, Paul Scofield as the French king, Ian Holm as Fluellen, Robbie Coltrane as Falstaff and Judi Dench as Mistress Quickly.

HERCULES

1997 80m c Children's/Animated/Musical ★★★
Walt Disney (U.S.) G/

VOICES OF: Tate Donovan (Adult Hercules—"Herc"), Joshua Keaton (Young Hercules—Speaking), Roger Bart (Young Hercules—Singing), Danny DeVito (Philoctetes—"Phil"), James Woods (Hades), Susan Egan (Megara—"Meg"), Rip Torn (Zeus), Samantha Eggar (Hera), Bobcat Goldthwait (Pain), Charlton Heston (Narrator)

p, John Musker, Ron Clements, Alice Dewey; d, John Musker, Ron Clements; w, John Musker, Ron Clements, Bob Shaw, Donald McEnery, Irene Mecchi, Barry Johnson (story supervisor); ed, Tom Finan, Jeff Jones; m, Alan Menken; prod d, Gerald Scarfe; art d, Andy Gaskill; anim, Roger L. Gould, Andreas Deja, Randy H. Haycock, Eric Goldberg, Nik Ranieri, Ken Duncan, Ellen Woodbury, Anthony DeRosa, Michael Show, James Lopez, Brian Ferguson, Dominique Monfery, Richard Bazley, Nancy Beiman, Oscar Urretabizkaia

It's no BEAUTY AND THE BEAST, but it's fun for the kids and peppered with jokes designed to keep grown-ups from squirming too desperately.

On orders from the villainous Hades (James Woods), the infant Hercules is stolen from his loving parents, Zeus and Hera (Rip Torn and Samantha Eggar). Hades knows that an adult Hercules could bring his plans to rule the classical world to a grinding halt. A kindly, childless farm couple adopt the stronger-than-strong babe, who grows up a lonely outcast. But after learning of his Olympian heritage, Hercules (Tate Donovan) finds the gruff old satyr (Danny De Vito) who trained history's other peerless champions, and sets out to become the greatest hero the world has ever known.

This child-friendly retelling of the Greek myth takes a few liberties with a story originally chockablock with sex, violence, and general sordid behavior. Passed through the Disney wringer, Hercules emerges a sanitized, blandly blond, and none-too-bright muscle-boy. Both "Greek" and the "mythology" are pretty much tossed away with the washing-up water, making way for rousing, up-tempo songs and a high-profile voice cast that also includes Hal Holbrook, Amanda Plummer, and comedian Bobcat Goldthwait. The hand of ferocious illustrator Gerald Scarfe (PINK FLOYD — THE WALL), a surprising addition to the Disney design line-up, isn't always evident in the movie's brightly colored milieu, but it's all over the snaggle-fanged Hades, whose feet are shrouded in smoke and whose head glows with perpetual flame. He's one of the best things in the picture: a conniving, angle-figuring, glad-handing Prince of Darkness — the Devil as Hollywood agent.

HERE COMES MR. JORDAN

1941 93m bw Science Fiction/Fantasy ★★★★
Columbia (U.S.) /A

Robert Montgomery (Joe Pendleton), Evelyn Keyes (Bette Logan), Claude Rains (Mr. Jordan), Rita Johnson (Julia Farnsworth), Edward Everett Horton (Messenger No. 7013), James Gleason (Max Corkle), John Emery (Tony Abbott), Donald MacBride (Inspector Williams), Don Costello (Lefty), Halliwell Hobbes (Sisk)

p, Everett Riskin; d, Alexander Hall; w, Sidney Buchman, Seton I. Miller (based on the play Heaven Can Wait by Harry Segall); ph, Joseph Walker; ed, Viola Lawrence; m, Frederick Hollander; art d, Lionel Banks; cos, Edith Head

AAN Best Picture; AAN Best Actor: Robert Montgomery; AAN Best Supporting Actor: James Gleason; AAN Best Director: Alexander Hall; AA Best Original Story: Harry Segall; AA Best Screenplay: Sidney Buchman, Seton I. Miller; AAN Best Cinematography: Joseph Walker

Full of hilarious plot twists and blessed with brilliant performances from a stellar cast, HERE COMES MR. JORDAN is a thoroughly beguiling fantasy with a boxing subplot. Joe Pendleton (Robert Montgomery), a saxophone-playing up-and-coming prizefighter, crashes while flying his single-engine plane, and his spirit is plucked up by an anxious heavenly messenger (Edward Everett Horton) who learns later that Joe was supposed to have lived for another 50 years and was destined to be the world heavyweight champion. It's up to the messenger's superior, Mr. Jordan (Claude Rains, amusingly sinister and atypical for this kind of role), to help Joe find another body in which to finish his life. JORDAN suffers from being too talky and the extraneous romance, but has remained an audience perennial. A weak nonsports sequel, DOWN TO EARTH, followed in 1947, and the story was remade with a football backdrop in 1978 as the pallid HEAVEN CAN WAIT.

HERE WE GO ROUND THE MULBERRY BUSH

1967 94m c Comedy ★★★
UA (U.K.) /X

Barry Evans (Jamie McGregor), Judy Geeson (Mary Gloucester), Angela Scoular (Caroline Beauchamp), Sheila White (Paula), Adrienne Posta (Linda), Vanessa Howard (Audrey), Diane Keen (Claire), Moyra Fraser (Mrs. McGregor), Michael Bates (Mr. McGregor), Maxine Audley (Mrs. Beauchamp)

p, Clive Donner; d, Clive Donner; w, Hunter Davies (based on the novel by Hunter Davies); ph, Alex Thomson; ed, Fergus McDonell; m, Spencer Davis Group, Stevie Winwood, Traffic

Teenybop hop of Evans's final year at high school when he attempts to lose his virginity. He takes one girl to the church dance but all they do is hold hands in the dark. With another girl he can't unzip her zippers and gets involved in a sexual square dance with her parents. Finally, he spends a weekend with the best-looking girl in the school but they end up arguing most of the time. This is a humorous look at the awkwardness of teenage sexuality that remains above exploitation.

HESTER STREET

1975 90m bw Drama ★★★½
Midwest (U.S.) PG

Steven Keats (Jake), Carol Kane (Gitl), Mel Howard (Bernstein), Dorrie Kavanaugh (Mamie), Doris Roberts (Kavarsky), Stephen Strimpell (Joe Peltner), Lauren Frost (Fanny), Paul Freedman (Joey), Zvee Scooler (Rabbi), Eda Reiss Merin (Rabbi's Wife)

p, Raphael D. Silver; d, Joan Micklin Silver; w, Joan Micklin Silver (based on the story "Yekl" by Abraham Cahan); ph, Kenneth Van Sickle; ed, Katherine Wenning; m, William Bolcom

AAN Best Actress: Carol Kane

Neglected piece of history receives atmospheric examination as old customs are replaced by assimilation. Keats is a young Jewish immigrant living on the title street while his wife Kane and their child are waiting back in the Old World. While trying to earn the money to bring them to the US, he becomes increasingly Americanized. He soon becomes involved with a fast-moving socialite who gives him some cash, which he in turn sends to his wife. Kane arrives but only shames Keats with her old-fashioned ways. They divorce and Keats goes off with his other woman, while Kane falls in love with a family friend. An engagingly simple first feature written and directed by Joan Micklin Silver, which earned an Academy Award nomination for Kane, whose acting is quite fine indeed. Unfortunately, other roles suffer from being poorly cast.

HEY BABU RIBA
(BAL NA VODI)

1986 112m c Drama ★★★½
Avala/Inex (Yugoslavia)

Gala Videnovic (Miriana/Esther), Milan Strljic (Ristic), Dragan Bjelogrlic (Young Sasha), Goran Radakovic (Young Pop), Relja Basic (Glen), Nebojsa Bakocevic (Young Glen), Marko Todorovic (Sacha), Milos Zutic (Kicha), Srdjan Todorovic (Young Kicha), Djordje Nenadovic (Pop)

p, George Zecevic, Dragoljub Popovic, Nikola Popovic; d, Jovan Acin; w, Jovan Acin (based on memories of Petar Jankovic, George Zecevic, and Jovan Acin); ph, Tomislav Pinter; ed, Shezana Ivanovic; m, Zoran Simjanovic; art d, Sava Acin

An appealing look at adolescence in 1950s Yugoslavia, HEY BABU RIBA is a bittersweet tale of four teenage boys who grow up loving the same girl, hating the same political system and dancing to the same American music.

As the film opens the boys are now middle-aged men who have returned to Belgrade from homes in New York, London, Paris and Milan for the funeral of the girl. At the grave site, they approach the dead woman's daughter who believes that one of them must be her father. The foursome then agree to have a drink with a fifth mourner, a former Communist who is the actual father. They reflect on their youth which leads to a flashback in which the boys (Bakocevic, Bjelogrlic, Todorovic and Radakovic) are members of a rowing team and their coxswain is Miriana (Videnovic), the teenage girl they all once desired. They love Glenn Miller, Levis, Marlboros, and American films, especially the 1944 Esther Williams picture BATHING BEAUTY.

Although the political climate under Marshal Tito makes everyone's life difficult, the foursome survive on the strength of their friendship. Their bond is threatened, however, as each boy declares his love for Miriana, who is determined to keep her relationship with them platonic. Each of the lads is feeling the pressures of puberty, so each finds an older woman who will take him into her bed. The day following each boy's ascent to manhood, he appears, wearing blue jeans and smoking cigarettes. The naive Miriana makes no connection between this behavior and their loss of virginity. She is still more concerned with friendship than sexual relations. Things begin to change for her when she is courted by Ristic (Strljic), the Communist. One morning, she is seen smoking a cigarette. Then she learns that she's pregnant.

A semi-autobiographical account of life in Yugoslavia, HEY BABU RIBA is the work of three lifelong friends who, like the characters in the film, have all gone on to highly successful careers outside of their native country. The second feature from director Jovan Acin (his first, THE CONCRETE ROSE led to his leaving the country), HEY BABU RIBA originated during a yearly reunion between Acin and the film's two producers—George Zecevic and Petar Jankovic. Finding a delicate balance between politics and daily life, director Acin has made a picture which is universal in its appeal. The performances all capture a certain adolescent honesty, with the stunning 16-year-old Videnovic photographing beautifully. It is unfortunate that her underdeveloped character lacks the depth and complexity to match her lovely face.

HI, MOM!

1970 87m c/bw Comedy   ★★
West End (U.S.)   R/15

Robert De Niro (Jon Rubin), Charles Durning (Superintendent), Allen Garfield (Joe Banner), Abraham Goren (Pervert in Theater), Lara Parker (Jeannie Mitchell), Jennifer Salt (Judy Bishop), Gerrit Graham (Gerrit Wood), Nelson Peltz (Playboy), Peter Maloney (Pharmacist), William Daley (Co-op Neighbor)

p, Charles Hirsch; d, Brian De Palma; w, Brian De Palma (based on a story by Brian De Palma, Charles Hirsch); ph, Robert Elfstrom; ed, Paul Hirsch; m, Eric Katz; art d, Peter Bocour

Curiously interesting early effort from Brian De Palma and Robert De Niro is which De Niro plays a porno filmmaker. He leases a ratty apartment in New York, across the street from an expensive co-op where Garfield, a wealthy producer of "adult" films, lives. The benevolent Garfield takes De Niro under his wing and gives him advice about how to make these sleazy movies. He spies comely neighbor Salt and wants to sleep with her—for his own benefit and the camera's. He promptly sets up his camera on his window sill, goes across the street, and proceeds to seduce her, but his camera falls and he misses his opportunity to immortalize the encounter on film.

De Niro then gets a job as an actor in an off-Broadway revue called "Be Black, Baby!" The actors all walk out in whiteface and begin to blacken the faces of the white audience, then abuse them both verbally and physically. Meanwhile, a gang of urban guerrillas, raid the huge apartment building, but they are all cut down by machine-gun fire. A young businessman in the high-rise just happens to have a 50-millimeter gun in his apartment. Salt and De Niro marry; she gets pregnant and becomes an instant nag, pestering him with her dreams of having a

dishwasher. De Niro calmly goes to the building's basement and tosses a huge charge of dynamite into the clothes washer which levels the entire building.

De Niro, before he became a major star, made a fine living playing weird types (GREETINGS, BLOODY MAMA), and his role here is no exception. Partially filmed in 16mm black and white, HI, MOM! is an original, often inventive picture, though it is also disjointed and sometimes painfully slow-moving. When it's on the money, the satire is very funny, particularly in its lampooning of the "touchy-feely" theater which had some popularity in the late 1960s and early 1970s. Most of the time, however, the film misses its targets and comes off as simply amateurish.

HIDDEN, THE

1987 96m c Science Fiction/Thriller   ★★★
New Line/Heron (U.S.)   R/18

Michael Nouri (Tom Beck), Kyle MacLachlan (Lloyd Gallagher), Ed O'Ross (Cliff Willis), Clu Gulager (Ed Flynn), Claudia Christian (Brenda Lee), Clarence Felder (John Masterson), Bill Boyett, Richard Brooks, Catherine Cannon, Larry Cedar

p, Robert Shaye, Gerald T. Olson, Michael Meltzer; d, Jack Sholder; w, Bob Hunt; ph, Jacques Haitkin; ed, Michael Knue; m, Michael Convertino; prod d, C.J. Strawn, Mick Strawn

An exciting mix of science fiction, cop thriller, and buddy film, THE HIDDEN is one of the most exciting and unique genre hybrids.

The movie opens with an action sequence in which a young stock-broker with a strange glint in his eye robs a bank, steals a Ferarri, and drives non-stop through several police blockades while listening to pounding rock music. Finally the police force the car into a fiery crash that sends the critically injured stockbroker to the hospital. Later that day a mysterious young FBI officer, Lloyd Gallagher (Kyle MacLachlan), arrives at police headquarters to enlist the aid of veteran detective Tom Beck (Michael Nouri) in finding a fugitive—the stockbroker. In the meantime, the stockbroker dies but a slimy alien creature crawls out of his mouth and into the body of another patient. Soon the madness begins anew.

Bob Hunt's screenplay and Jack Sholder's direction combine to create a sci-fi action yarn replete with exciting chases, well-staged shootouts and some extremely funny black humor. Nouri and MacLachlan turn in superior performances as does the rest of the large cast. In retrospect, MacLachlan's character feels like an audition for Agent Cooper of "Twin Peaks." This is an outstanding buddy film with a smart extraterrestrial twist.

HIDDEN FORTRESS, THE
(KAKUSHI TORIDE NO SAN AKUNIN)

1958 137m bw Adventure   ★★★★
Toho (Japan)   /A

Toshiro Mifune (Rokurota), Misa Uehara (Lady Yukihime), Minoru Chiaki (Tahei), Kamatari Fujiwara (Matashichi), Susumu Fujita (The Grateful Soldier), Takashi Shimura (The Old General), Eiko Miyoshi (The Old Woman), Toshiko Higuchi (The Farmer's Daughter), Kichijiro Ueda (Girl-Dealer)

d, Akira Kurosawa; w, Ryuzo Kikushima, Hideo Oguni, Shinobu Hashimoto, Akira Kurosawa; ph, Kazuo Yamazaki; m, Masaru Sato

A film that might very likely change the consciousness of those who dislike foregin films. Two unlikely looking soldiers, Tahei (Minoru Chiaki) and Matashichi (Kamatari Fujiwara), flee following the defeat of their army. They stumble across a gold bar hidden in some firewood, but before they can take it, Rokurota (Toshiro Mifune), a general, appears. He enlists the two to help him take a wagon load of gold—plus deposed princess Lady Yukihime (Misa Uehara)—to safety in the next province.

One of Akira Kurosawa's best works—with an odd mix of periods, from medieval to modern—HIDDEN FORTRESS is filled with humor and excitement, owing more to Hollywood adventure films than to the Japanese tradition. George Lucas claimed that this film was the chief inspiration for STAR WARS, and it is easy to see the resemblance, especially in Chiaki and Fujiwara, who were copied in metal to make

R2-D2 and C-3PO. Originally released in the US in a truncated 90-minute print, THE HIDDEN FORTRESS quickly disappeared and was not released in a full-length version until 1983.

HIGH AND LOW
(TENGOKU TO-JIGOKU)

1963 142m c/bw Crime ★★★★
Toho (Japan) /A

Toshiro Mifune *(Kingo Gondo)*, Tatsuya Nakadai *(Inspector Tokura)*, Kyoko Kagawa *(Reiko, Gondo's Wife)*, Tatsuya Mihashi *(Kawanishi)*, Yutaka Sada *(Aoki)*, Kenjiro Ishiyama *(Detective Taguchi)*, Tsutomu Yamazaki *(Ginji Takeuchi)*, Takashi Shimura *(Director)*, Susumu Fujita *(Commissioner)*, Ko Kimura *(Detective Arai)*

p, Tomoyuki Tanaka, Ryuzo Kikushima; d, Akira Kurosawa; w, Akira Kurosawa, Hideo Oguni, Ryuzo Kikushima, Eijiro Hisaita (based on the novel *King's Ransom* by Ed McBain); ph, Choichi Nakai, Takao Saito; m, Masaru Sato; art d, Yoshiro Muraki

Based on a crime novel by Ed McBain, this brilliant Kurosawa film stars Toshiro Mifune as Kingo Gondo, a rich industrialist who receives word that his son has been kidnapped by a madman demanding an outrageous ransom that will ruin Gondo financially if he pays it. Before Gondo can make a decision, his son enters the house, and we learn that it is his playmate, the chauffeur's son, who has been kidnapped. Gondo is then faced with a tough moral decision: is his chauffeur's son worth as much as his own? When the kidnapper calls and admits his mistake, but demands payment anyway, Gondo initially refuses, but is conscience stricken.

In HIGH AND LOW Kurosawa succeeds in developing a highly visual structural style within the wide-screen format. The first half of the film takes place in the living room of Gondo's hilltop house and is characterized by static shots that hold for several minutes on a single composition. Time transitions are handled by wipes, creating a charged atmosphere. This steadiness is broken suddenly for the second half of the film, involving the criminal manhunt, shot with a normal amount of motion and cutting—its pace frenetic in comparison with the first half of the film.

HIGH AND THE MIGHTY, THE

1954 147m c Disaster ★★★½
Wayne/Fellows (U.S.) /U

John Wayne *(Dan Roman)*, Claire Trevor *(May Hoist)*, Laraine Day *(Lydia Rice)*, Robert Stack *(Sullivan)*, Jan Sterling *(Sally McKee)*, Phil Harris *(Ed Joseph)*, Robert Newton *(Gustave Pardee)*, David Brian *(Ken Childs)*, Paul Kelly *(Flaherty)*, Sidney Blackmer *(Humphrey Agnew)*

p, Robert Fellows, John Wayne; d, William A. Wellman; w, Ernest K. Gann (based on the novel by Gann); ph, Archie Stout, William Clothier; ed, Ralph Dawson; m, Dimitri Tiomkin; art d, Alfred Ybarra; cos, Gwen Wakeling

AAN Best Supporting Actress: Jan Sterling; *AAN Best Supporting Actress:* Claire Trevor; *AAN Best Director:* William Wellman; *AAN Best Editing:* Ralph Dawson; *AA Best Score:* Dimitri Tiomkin; *AAN Best Song:* Dimitri Tiomkin (Music), Ned Washington (Lyrics)

Cliche-bound but boosted by taut direction, memorable music and, for once, just right for CinemaScope. Wayne is a has-been pilot—"an ancient pelican" according to airline executive Toomey—now copiloting under the command of cocky Stack. Also on board is an inept navigator, Brown, and an apprentice pilot, Campbell, who constantly derides Wayne, even bringing up a terrible crash occurring years earlier which Wayne survived but in which his wife and young child were killed.

Beautiful, statuesque, and cool stewardess Doe Avedon makes 22 passengers comfortable as the airliner leaves Honolulu for San Francisco. Her passengers: divorce-seeking Day and Howard; shady mail-order bride Sterling; wacko theatrical impresario Newton; jaded, bitter Trevor; pompous playboy Brian who is being stalked by vengeful Blackmer; oblivious newlyweds Smith and Sharpe; guilty nuclear scientist Kelly; and second honeymooners Doran and Harris. Then, all hell breaks loose, forcing everyone to face each other, "reality," and a competitive race for acting honors.

Wellman does a dynamite job directing air traffic; though characters are drawn only briefly, they are tellingly etched with pathos and melodrama. Wayne's performance as the one fixed and reliable point in a collapsing world got him voted number one box-office attraction, replacing Gary Cooper. Oddly, Wayne, who coproduced the film, intended to have Spencer Tracy play the pioneer pilot role but when that venerable actor turned down the part Wayne took it over himself. The haunting title song became so closely associated with Wayne that when this giant died it was this score that was played during his funeral.

HIGH ANXIETY

1977 94m c Comedy ★★★
Fox (U.S.) PG/15

Mel Brooks *(Richard Thorndyke)*, Madeline Kahn *(Victoria Brisbane)*, Cloris Leachman *(Nurse Diesel)*, Harvey Korman *(Dr. Charles Montague)*, Ron Carey *(Brophy)*, Howard Morris *(Prof. Lilloman)*, Dick Van Patten *(Dr. Wentworth)*, Jack Riley *(Desk Clerk)*, Charlie Callas *(Cocker Spaniel)*, Ron Clark *(Zachary Cartwright)*

p, Mel Brooks; d, Mel Brooks; w, Mel Brooks, Ron Clark, Rudy DeLuca, Barry Levinson; ph, Paul Lohmann; ed, John C. Howard; m, John Morris; prod d, Peter Wooley; fx, Albert Whitlock; cos, Patricia Morris

Mel Brooks's so-so feat of Hitchcockian tribute: he stars, produces, directs, cowrites, and sings the title song (and he has a much better singing voice than you might imagine). Whereas men like Brian De Palma and Colin Higgins will make movies reminiscent of Hitchcock without citing that director, Brooks is patently spoofing the rotund master with HIGH ANXIETY. Even if you don't know the original work, this film indicates its inspiration fairly well. The head of the Institute for the Very Very Nervous is found murdered, and Brooks, a man who fears heights so badly that he won't wear elevator shoes, takes over as psychiatrist-in-charge. Assistant Korman and nurse Leachman have been spinning a plot to keep the patients captive while bilking them out of their money, and they fear that Brooks will put an end to that. Parody is a tricky business, but Brooks sometimes succeeds in paying homage to SPELLBOUND, VERTIGO, PSYCHO, and THE BIRDS with all of the usual middle-cut Hitchcock formulae: innocent man accused of something he didn't do, reluctant heroine (Kahn) who helps, etc. Many familiar scenes come out of Hitchcock with the standouts being prowling camera work and Hitch's use of musical scores. Audiences flocked to theaters and made this movie a hit. Some interesting sidelights in casting include famed matte artist Albert Whitlock as Brisbane, successful commercials actors Bob Ridgely and Jack Riley, and co-writer Levinson as the bellboy. Levinson went on to become highly regarded as a director with DINER and THE NATURAL. Morris was for years one of Sid Ceasar's second bananas on TV and now earns his living as a director and sometimes cartoon voice ("The Paw-Paws" for Hanna-Barbera, among others). Callas is a busy nightclub comic, and Richard Stahl is one of the best comedy character men in the business. Assistant director Sanger stayed with Brooks and eventually became a producer.

HIGH HOPES

1988 110m c Comedy/Drama ★★★★
Portman/Film Four (U.K.) PG/15

Philip Davis *(Cyril Bender)*, Ruth Sheen *(Shirley)*, Edna Dore *(Mrs. Bender)*, Philip Jackson *(Martin Burke)*, Heather Tobias *(Valerie Burke)*, Lesley Manville *(Laetitia Boothe-Braine)*, David Bamber *(Rupert Boothe-Braine)*, Jason Watkins *(Wayne)*, Judith Scott *(Suzi)*, Cheryl Prime *(Martin's Girl Friend)*

p, Simon Channing-Williams, Victor Glynn; d, Mike Leigh; w, Mike Leigh; ph, Roger Pratt; ed, John Gregory; m, Andrew Dixon; prod d, Diana Charnley; art d, Andrew Rothschild; cos, Lindy Hemming

Mike Leigh's funny and deeply touching HIGH HOPES is yet another inventive cinematic reaction to Margaret Thatcher's overhaul of British society. Employing an episodic structure and a semi-improvisational approach, Leigh (BLEAK MOMENTS) presents three couples and an elderly woman as a microcosm of modern-day Britain.

Cyril (Philip Davis), a 35-year-old motorcycle messenger, and Shirley (Ruth Sheen), his companion of ten years, are children of the working class who have embraced a countercultural lifestyle that once included a passionate faith in revolutionary ideology. Although they can't agree to have a child of their own, they spend plenty of time parenting Davis's aging mother (Dore), who lives in the last council-owned house on a gentrified street, where an impossibly snooty yuppie couple, the Boothe-Braines (Lesley Manville and David Bamber), are her neighbors. Rounding out the cast are Cyril's shrill, nouveau riche sister (Heather Tobias) and her philandering used-car-salesman husband (Philip Jackson). Alternately silly, serious, and poignant, HIGH HOPES uses its players as political symbols, without subordinating character to the demands of allegory. . . well, almost.

Leigh's approach is most realistic when dealing with Cyril's mother, Cyril, and Shirley, and the bedtime conversations between the last two are certainly among cinema's most privileged moments. Because of the care Leigh takes with these three characters, HIGH HOPES is not just an indictment of Thatcher-engendered inequity; it is also a survival primer for those who have lost faith in the Left's traditional grand solutions yet refused to succumb to "compassion fatigue."

HIGH NOON

1952 85m bw Western ★★★★★
UA (U.S.) /U

Gary Cooper (Will Kane), Grace Kelly (Amy Kane), Thomas Mitchell (Jonas Henderson), Lloyd Bridges (Harvey Pell), Katy Jurado (Helen Ramirez), Otto Kruger (Percy Mettrick), Lon Chaney Jr. (Martin Howe), Harry Morgan (William Fuller), Ian MacDonald (Frank Miller), Eve McVeagh (Mildred Fuller)

p, Stanley Kramer; d, Fred Zinnemann; w, Carl Foreman (based on the story "The Tin Star" by John W. Cunningham); ph, Floyd Crosby; ed, Elmo Williams, Harry Gerstad; m, Dimitri Tiomkin; prod d, Rudolph Sternad; art d, Ben Hayne

AAN Best Picture; AA Best Actor: Gary Cooper; AAN Best Director: Fred Zinnemann; AAN Best Screenplay: Carl Foreman; AA Best Editing: Elmo Williams, Harry Gerstad; AA Best Score: Dimitri Tiomkin; AA Best Song: Dimitri Tiomkin (Music), Ned Washington (Lyrics)

Not a frame is wasted in this taut, superbly directed, masterfully acted film, the first so-called "adult Western," in which the traditional and predictable elements of action, song and minimal romance give way to a swift, intense unraveling of a situation and complex character development. HIGH NOON is also the story of a western town, Hadleyville, and its sometimes stouthearted citizenry, the most prominent of whom is the stoic, heroic Will Kane (Gary Cooper), a lawman surrounded by friends and admirers at the start, deserted and doomed at the finish.

Just married, Will and his beautiful blonde Quaker bride, Amy (Grace Kelly), are about to leave town forever, intending to put peacemaking behind them to settle down to ranch life. However, news comes that a fierce killer, Frank Miller (Ian MacDonald), is about to arrive and take vengeance against Will and the town for sending him to prison years earlier. Miller's brother (Sheb Wooley) and two gunslingers (Bob Wilke and Lee Van Cleef) are already at the depot, waiting for the train carrying Miller, which is due to arrive at high noon. In a moment of panic, urged on by his friends, Will races his buckboard and bride out of town and down the road into the open prairie, but he suddenly pulls up. When Amy asks him why he is stopping, Will tells her that he has to go back, that it's his duty to return.

A landmark Western in every sense, HIGH NOON was shot by cinematographer Floyd Crosby in high contrast, an approach director Fred Zinnemann used to bring documentarylike authenticity to the film. Zinnemann's outstanding economical direction is in full force here, every minute pertinent and packed with suspense. Significantly, the film takes almost as much time to unreel as Will Kane takes in the story to prepare for the gun battle.

For Cooper, this was a tour de force, a film wherein his mere presence overwhelms the viewer and carries a story that is believable only through his actions. He utters no long speeches, yet his expressions and movements are those of a man resolute in his lonely duty and resigned to his own doom. Every confrontation with the unresponsive townspeople causes him to suffer; in truth, Cooper was in real agony

during the production, enduring a bleeding ulcer and an injured hip. After finishing the film, he said, "I'm all acted out." Cooper's exhaustion is evident in his onscreen appearance, but reportedly an appropriately haggard-looking Will Kane was just what Zinnemann was after, despite Hollywood's proclivity for dashing leading men.

Though Kramer later claimed that the project was entirely his own creation, writer Carl Foreman contended neither Kramer nor his associates had any interest in the film from the outset. Kramer did, however, view the first showing with concern. Believing that it had a lot of dead spots, he ordered a series of closeups showing the anxiety lining Cooper's face, and included many quick cuts to clocks ticking relentlessly toward the doom of high noon.

To further heighten the tension Kramer asked Dmitri Tiomkin to write a ballad that could be interwoven with the action. Though the composer protested that he only wrote scores, he and Ned Washington produced the wonderful "High Noon (Do Not Forsake Me)", sung by Tex Ritter. The song has since become a classic, along with Tiomkin's memorable score.

HIGH PLAINS DRIFTER

1973 105m c Western ★★★½
Malpaso (U.S.) R/18

Clint Eastwood (The Stranger), Verna Bloom (Sarah Belding), Marianna Hill (Callie Travers), Mitchell Ryan (Dave Drake), Jack Ging (Morgan Allen), Stefan Gierasch (Mayor Jason Hobart), Ted Hartley (Lewis Belding), Billy Curtis (Mordecai), Geoffrey Lewis (Stacey Bridges), Scott Walker (Bill Borders)

p, Robert Daley; d, Clint Eastwood; w, Ernest Tidyman; ph, Bruce Surtees; ed, Ferris Webster; m, Dee Barton; art d, Henry Bumstead

Eastwood directs his first Western, and it's a knockout. HIGH PLAINS DRIFTER is a morality tale carved out of the harsh Western desert and directed with a panache that synthesized the styles of Sergio Leone and Don Siegel, two directors who had worked with Eastwood frequently. The result is one of the best Westerns of the 1970s.

The story begins as a mysterious stranger (Eastwood) materializes out of the desert heat. He rides into the small town of Lagos, where his presence is considered a threat by the mean and cowardly populace. Before too long, he is attacked by three gunmen, and Eastwood kills them all coolly and efficiently. The stranger then rents a hotel room, and the town dwarf, Curtis (who is also disenfranchised in town due to his size), attends to his needs. At night, Eastwood's dreams are plagued by a recurring nightmare of a helpless man being whipped to death in the street by three sadistic criminals while the townsfolk stand by and do nothing to stop it.

Meanwhile, the town council debates how to handle the impending threat created by a group of escaped convicts who are out to return to Lagos (where they committed their crimes) and destroy it. Desperate, the town's leaders cautiously approach Eastwood and plead with him to save their town from the criminals. Eastwood agrees to help them, but then proceeds to turn the town on its head by teaching self-defense and requesting all sorts of strange things from the townsfolk, including having them paint the town red and rename it "Hell."

An eerie, supernatural western that takes the avenging man-with-no-name character created by Eastwood and Leone to its most logical extreme. Eastwood would later bury the character completely in his own OUTLAW JOSEY WALES only to have him rise like the Phoenix, redefined as a much more human, compassionate and caring hero.

HIGH SIERRA

1941 100m bw Crime ★★★★
Warner Bros. (U.S.) /PG

Ida Lupino (Marie Garson), Humphrey Bogart (Roy Earle), Alan Curtis (Babe Kozak), Arthur Kennedy (Red Hattery), Joan Leslie (Velma), Henry Hull (Doc Banton), Barton MacLane (Jake Kranmer), Henry Travers (Pa), Elisabeth Risdon (Ma), Cornel Wilde (Louis Mendoza)

p, Mark Hellinger; d, Raoul Walsh; w, John Huston, W.R. Burnett (based on the novel by W.R. Burnett); ph, Tony Gaudio; ed, Jack Killifer; m, Adolph Deutsch; art d, Ted Smith; fx, Byron Haskin, H.F. Koenekamp; cos, Milo Anderson

With exception of WHITE HEAT, this was the movie gangster's last stand. Bogart plays a graying criminal who's had it, and is in pursuit of one last caper in a changing world. He hooks up with Kennedy, Curtis, and informer Wilde to pull of the job, and becomes sympathetic to the plight of Curtis's moll Lupino, while also obsessing about young Leslie, a lame girl. HIGH SIERRA romanticizes the Bogie character as much as possible within hardbitten guidelines and, with the exception of the always overeager Leslie, it's acted within an inch of its classic life, especially by Bogie, Lupino and a mongrel dog in the gut-wrenching climax. And that fadeout. . . .

HIGH SIERRA is a landmark crime film in many ways. It was Bogart's first solid role as a sympathetic lead, a good-bad guy out of his element and beyond his time. As was the case with his first gangster role—Duke Mantee, in THE PETRIFIED FOREST—Bogart is made up to look like John Dillinger, to whom he bore an amazing resemblance. Bogart, who was second-billed under Lupino, showed his ability to play sensitive scenes with depth, and the public responded enthusiastically. He would never again play second fiddle to Cagney or anyone else.

Director Walsh does a superb job in keeping a nonstop action pace, succinctly freeing up Bogart setups in which his character is revealed, a masterful balance of movement and repose. Walsh, more than any one else, was responsible for Bogart's big break in getting the part, suggesting him to Jack Warner when others turned down the role. This was also an important film for screenwriter John Huston; his career took a sharp turn upward following HIGH SIERRA, after which he began his own distinguished directing career. Reworked by Walsh himself as COLORADO TERRITORY.

HIGH SOCIETY

1956   107m   c   Musical/Comedy   ★★★
MGM   (U.S.)   /U

Bing Crosby (C.K. Dexter-Haven), Grace Kelly (Tracy Lord), Frank Sinatra (Mike Connor), Celeste Holm (Liz Imbrie), John Lund (George Kittredge), Louis Calhern (Uncle Willie), Sidney Blackmer (Seth Lord), Louis Armstrong (Himself), Margalo Gillmore (Mrs. Seth Lord), Lydia Reed (Caroline Lord)

p, Sol C. Siegel; d, Charles Walters; w, John Patrick (based on the play The Philadelphia Story by Philip Barry); ph, Paul C. Vogel; ed, Ralph E. Winters; m, Johnny Green, Saul Chaplin; art d, Cedric Gibbons, Hans Peters; fx, A. Arnold Gillespie; chor, Charles Walters; cos, Helen Rose

AAN Best Original Screenplay: Edward Bernds, Elwood Ullman; AAN Best Score: Johnny Green, Saul Chaplin; AAN Best Song: Cole Porter (Music & Lyrics)

Written with all the bite of a distinctly middle-class church social, this musical re-working of THE PHILADELPHIA STORY feels distant. Cole Porter's score sits on it like a champagne bubble in a vat of flat beer.

Tracy Lord (Grace Kelly, in her last film before marrying Prince Ranier of Monaco) lives in Newport and has a trio of men encircling her: her ex-husband, C.K. Dexter-Haven (Bing Crosby), with whom she is still on fairly good terms; her fiance, George Kittredge (John Lund), a professional prig; and Mike Connor (Frank Sinatra), a breezy reporter sent to cover the wedding by a Life magazine-like periodical. The rest of the cast includes Celeste Holm as Connor's photographer; Sidney Blackmer as Tracy's skirt-chasing father; Margalo Gillmore as her mother; and Louis Calhern as her uncle.

The leads are all too laconic for the movie's own good. Crosby is far too old for his role—he looks like a piece of walking beef jerky. Sinatra comes off more like a gate-crashing taxi-driver than a reporter. He can't muster the energy to get past his own phony "hip" persona. And Kelly seems preoccupied by another wedding, or perhaps wallpaper choices for the palace. Still, there are a few diverting moments seeing Bing work out with Frank and the ever-welcome Satchmo. Re the score: the only song not written for the movie was "Well, Did You Evah!" which was first sung by Betty Grable in Cole Porter's 1939 Broadway musical Du Barry Was a Lady.

HILLS HAVE EYES, THE

1978   89m   c   Horror   ★★★½
Blood Relations   (U.S.)   R/18

Susan Lanier (Brenda Carter), Robert Houston (Bobby Carter), Virginia Vincent (Ethel Carter), Russ Grieve (Bob Carter), Dee Wallace Stone (Lynne Wood), Martin Speer (Doug Wood), Brenda Marinoff (Katie Wood), Flora the Dog (Beauty), Stricker the Dog (The Beast), James Whitmore (Jupiter)

p, Peter Locke; d, Wes Craven; w, Wes Craven; ph, Eric Saarinen; ed, Wes Craven; m, Don Peake; art d, Robert Burns

With this film and A NIGHTMARE ON ELM STREET, former English professor Wes Craven assured himself a place in the history of the horror film as an important modern filmmaker whose work has had an immense influence on the genre.

THE HILLS HAVE EYES opens as the Carters, an ostensibly typical middle-class suburban family, drive through the desert in their mobile home headed for California. The family consists of Dad (Russ Grieve), a recently retired cop; Mom (Virginia Vincent); big sister Lynne (Dee Wallace); her husband (Martin Speer); their baby; brother and sister, Brenda (Susan Lanier) and Bobby (Robert Houston); and dogs Beauty and the Beast. Trouble starts when the vehicle's axle breaks and the travelers are left stranded in the desert, miles from help. Unfortunately, they've accidentally trespassed on the domain of another family, a brutal, almost atavistic, clan of cannibals who live on the desert mesas.

This family is headed by patriarch Jupiter (James Whitmore), who was abandoned as a baby to die in the wasteland after he was born mutated. His wife (Cordy Clark), a former prostitute "no one would miss," was kidnapped by Jupiter and brought to the desert for companionship. They have four offspring, now fully grown. The boys, Pluto (Michael Berryman), Mars (Lance Gordon) and Mercury (Arthur King), all assist their father in protecting their territory (aided by walkie-talkies and rifles that somehow found their way into the family's possession) and gathering whatever food they can come across. The daughter, Ruby (Janus Blythe), has seen civilization and longs to escape her savage family. Soon the rival families collide with the twisted desert clan attacking the "all-American" suburban clan to loot, kill the men, rape the women, and eat the tasty looking baby.

Though not particularly bloody, THE HILLS HAVE EYES is an extremely intense and disturbing film. As is the case with Sam Peckinpah's classic, STRAW DOGS, it becomes oddly and distressingly exhilarating to watch the nice family become increasingly savage in their efforts to survive. Not for the squeamish, this low-budget potboiler is one of the prime examples of the what was so fascinating about American horror films in the 1970s. It can be profitably read as the kind of thematically rich and insightful meditation on the dark side of the American family that could only be done in the exploitation horror genre. A must-see for those who care about such matters.

HIRED HAND, THE

1971   90m   c   Western   ★★½
Pando   (U.S.)   GP/15

Peter Fonda (Harry Collings), Warren Oates (Arch Harris), Verna Bloom (Hannah Collings), Robert Pratt (Dan Griffin), Severn Darden (McVey), Ted Markland (Luke), Owen Orr (Mace), Gray Johnson (Will), Rita Rogers (Mexican Woman), Al Hopson (Bartender)

p, William Hayward; d, Peter Fonda; w, Alan Sharp; ph, Vilmos Zsigmond; ed, Frank Mazzola; m, Bruce Langhorne; art d, Lawrence G. Paull; cos, Richard Bruno

Peter Fonda's first directorial effort was this scattered, pretentious Western that tried to offer a realistic depiction of the Old West.

The story is about Fonda, who deserted his wife, Bloom, to drift with Oates. After seven years of drifting, Pratt, a fellow wanderer and friend of the duo, is murdered by Darden's men. Fonda and Oates exact revenge on the killers and Fonda decides to go back to his wife, but she is only willing to accept him as a hired hand. Their romance is rekindled, but Fonda is soon off to rescue Oates, who has been captured by the evil Darden. Fonda is killed during the rescue, but Oates goes back to Bloom and takes Fonda's place.

Zsigmond's superb photography conveys much of the lyrical quality of the story but the screenplay by Sharp (NIGHT MOVES) falls short by comparison. Fonda's lack of expertise cannot compensate directorially; the cliches of the genre require a more artful hand, and his dual commitments keep him from developing a sympathetic hero that justifies audience focus.

HIRELING, THE

1973 95m c Drama ★★★½
World Film/Champion (U.K.) PG

Robert Shaw (*Leadbetter*), Sarah Miles (*Lady Franklin*), Peter Egan (*Cantrip*), Elizabeth Sellars (*Mother*), Caroline Mortimer (*Connie*), Patricia Lawrence (*Mrs. Hansen*), Petra Markham (*Edith*), Ian Hogg (*Davis*), Christine Hargreaves (*Doreen*), Lyndon Brook

p, Ben Arbeid; d, Alan Bridges; w, Wolf Mankowitz (based on a novel by L.P. Hartley); ph, Michael Reed; ed, Peter Weatherley; m, Marc Wilkinson; prod d, Natasha Kroll; cos, Phyllis Dalton

A fine British drama that insightfully examines class barriers in England, adapted from the L.P. Hartley novel.

The story is set in 1923 and details the close relationship of a wealthy young widow, Miles, and her hired chauffeur, Shaw. Shaw drives Miles home from a clinic where she has been convalescing from a nervous breakdown. In her fragile state of mind, she starts a love affair with Shaw, and he believes the class barriers are down. However, after she begins to recover her mental stability, the barriers rise once again. She no longer considers Shaw her equal, and when he confesses his love for her, Miles makes it clear that their relationship is an impossibility. Enraged and frustrated, Shaw attacks her expensive car, which has become the symbol of their doomed romance.

Shaw is utterly convincing as he at first reluctantly and then wholeheartedly gets involved with Miles, only to have his love spurned and his dreams dashed. He's ably matched by Miles as the dual-natured lady.

HIROSHIMA, MON AMOUR

1959 88m bw Drama/War ★★★★★
Argos/Como/Daiei/Pathe (France/Japan) /X

Emmanuelle Riva (*Elle*), Eiji Okada (*Lui*), Stella Dassas (*Mother*), Pierre Barbaud (*Father*), Bernard Fresson (*German Lover*)

p, Samy Halfon; d, Alain Resnais; w, Marguerite Duras; ph, Sacha Vierny, Michio Takahashi; ed, Henri Colpi, Jasmine Chasney, Anne Sarraute; m, Georges Delerue, Giovanni Fusco; prod d, Esaka, Mayo, Petri

AAN Best Original Screenplay: Marguerite Duras

It is often, and quite legitimately, said that HIROSHIMA, MON AMOUR has been as important in the development of film art as CITIZEN KANE. The first feature from Alain Resnais, previously well-known for his incredibly moving documentaries, the film is adapted from a script by the French writer Marguerite Duras, one of the greatest writers of the 20th century, and the combination of Duras's text and Resnais's blend of sound and image makes for a film that is completely modern.

The story, which manages to be both complex (in its manipulation of past and present) and simple (it focuses on a very brief love affair), concerns a married Japanese architect (Eiji Okada) and a married French actress (Emmanuelle Riva) who have a two-day affair in Hiroshima. The pain that "She" (their names are never used) feels for the dead of Hiroshima reminds her of a loss she suffered in the past, when the young German soldier whom she loved in Nevers was killed on the day that town was liberated. Castigated by her family, she was imprisoned in a dark cellar, in disgrace for having loved the enemy. Now, she projects the entire city—the bomb, the death, the suffering, and physical mutilation—onto her Japanese lover, whom she calls "Hiroshima," but knows that someday she will forget him.

Interweaving sound and image, brutal documentary footage and tender shots of lovemaking, past and present, past and remembered past, city and individual, passion and despair, Resnais creates a breathtaking picture that, like so many great works of art, can never be entirely appreciated or understood. HIROSHIMA, MON AMOUR must be

felt—combining the soft loving caresses of two intertwined bodies with the burnt, blistering, peeling flesh of a dying victim of atomic warfare—and the feelings it evokes defy understanding or explanation.

HIS GIRL FRIDAY

1940 92m bw Comedy ★★★★★
Columbia (U.S.)

Cary Grant (*Walter Burns*), Rosalind Russell (*Hildy Johnson*), Ralph Bellamy (*Bruce Baldwin*), Gene Lockhart (*Sheriff Hartwell*), Helen Mack (*Mollie Malloy*), Porter Hall (*Murphy*), Ernest Truex (*Roy Bensinger*), Cliff Edwards (*Endicott*), Clarence Kolb (*Mayor*), Roscoe Karns (*McCue*)

p, Howard Hawks; d, Howard Hawks; w, Charles Lederer (based on the play by Ben Hecht, Charles MacArthur); ph, Joseph Walker; ed, Gene Havlick; m, M.W. Stoloff; art d, Lionel Banks; cos, Robert Kalloch

Perfection and possibly the fastest comedy on record. This hilarious re-working of THE FRONT PAGE by Hecht and MacArthur sees Grant as the savage editor and, in a switch, the reporter played by a scheming Russell. Instead of merely having the editor doing all in his power to keep his most brilliant reporter on staff, this version adds the twin lures of sex and romance, since Russell is Grant's ex-wife. She intends to marry again and her intended is the blatheringly innocent Bellamy, here in the quintessential Bellamy second lead. When convicted killer Qualen escapes his cell the night before he is to hang and hides in the news room of the jail—inside a rolltop desk—Grant uses the incident to entice Russell back to work. She is to write the scoop of the break, but Grant's deeper motive is to keep Russell near him so he can somehow woo her back.

The machine gun dialogue is by Charlie Lederer, Hecht's friend and sometime collaborator: Biberman, a thug working for Grant, defends his new girlfriend by saying: "She's not an albino; she was born right here in this country!" Russell calls in a report to the city desk: "Shot him right in the classified ads. . . No, 'ads'!" And there are many inside jokes. Grant criticizes Bellamy to Russell, saying he "looks like that actor. . . Ralph Bellamy!" Grant again grins as he says: "The last man that said that to me was Archie Leach just a week before he cut his throat." (Archie Leach was Grant's real name.)

The film moves at whirlwind speed, as Hawks instructed his actors to overlap their lines, so much so that at times everyone seems to be talking at once. One archivist actually timed the hurricane delivery of the actors at 240 words per minute, so fast that the dialogue is just discernible, the actors speaking about 130 words per minute above average delivery. Hawks also had his cast move at twice normal speed so the whole thing was frantic from scene to scene, thus conveying the urgency of the news world he was depicting.

HIS GIRL FRIDAY is distinctly Hawksian, bearing his trademark of madcap comedy, also brilliantly shown in BRINGING UP BABY and I WAS A MALE WAR BRIDE, both starring Grant. But FRIDAY presents Grant in a no-holds-barred comedy-bully performance. This time he's the aggressor, the persecutor as he cajoles, aggravates, intimidates, lies—sometimes he even resorts to noises in this hilariously self-centered performance. It's his greatest comedic role, proving once again the amazing versatility of this fine actor.

Russell is at her peak, too—demonstrating her own brittle breakneck speed with comedy lines and instilling an ungainly charm into Hildy's physicality. Katharine Hepburn, Jean Arthur, Margaret Sullavan, Irene Dunne, Claudette Colbert and Carole Lombard were all offered the role, but turned it down. Russell leapt at the chance to play the screwball role and it turned out to be her greatest comedy part, one which assured her immortality. The supporting cast is a Who's Who of willing comedy loons.

HIT, THE

1984 100m c Drama ★★★½
Zenith (U.K.) R/18

Terence Stamp (*Willie Parker*), John Hurt (*Braddock*), Tim Roth (*Myron*), Laura del Sol (*Maggie*), Bill Hunter (*Harry*), Fernando Rey (*Chief Inspector*), Carlos Lucena (*Uniformed Officer*), Freddie Stuart, Ralph Brown, A.J. Clarke (*Government Agents*)

p, Jeremy Thomas; d, Stephen Frears; w, Peter Prince; ph, Mike Molloy; ed, Mick Audsley; m, Paco de Lucia, Eric Clapton; prod d, Andrew Sanders; art d, Julio Molina; fx, Alan Whibley, Reyes Abades; cos, Marit Allen

Stephen Frears' second feature as a director (after his debut, 1971's GUMSHOE, he had worked in TV for 13 years) is an offbeat, existential crime drama buoyed by fine performances; nicely turned dialogue; and an evocative soundtrack and theme song from Paco di Lucia and Eric Clapton, respectively.

The story begins in 1973 at a criminal trial where former mob operative Willie Parker (Terence Stamp) testifies against his sometime cronies. After turning state's evidence, he is released. Cut to a quiet Spanish village ten years later. Parker, having enjoyed a quiet, contemplative period of exile following his turning state's evidence, is flushed out of his house by a gang of thugs and handed over to Braddock (John Hurt), a veteran hit man, and his volatile young assistant, Myron (Tim Roth). Parker is hustled into their car, to be taken to Paris and executed by a mob chieftain for his testimony of ten years before. Stamp, however, doesn't seem in the least bit frightened; in fact, he seems to enjoy what is happening. . .

In THE HIT, director Stephen Frears works against all genre conventions—the hit man becomes emotionally involved with his prey, while the victim accepts his fate with equanimity and grace. The characters are not genre stereotypes, but fully rounded individuals riddled with insecurities and doubts. Besides having a superb screenplay, Frears is blessed, here, with an unparalleled cast. Both Hurt and Stamp are as good as they've ever been, while the very young Tim Roth makes a very promising debut. Reviewed well in the US, THE HIT made very little impression at the box office.

HOBSON'S CHOICE

1954 107m bw Comedy ★★★★
London Films (U.K.) /U

Charles Laughton (Henry Horatio Hobson), John Mills (Willie Mossop), Brenda de Banzie (Maggie Hobson), Daphne Anderson (Alice Hobson), Prunella Scales (Vicky Hobson), Richard Wattis (Albert Prosser), Derek Blomfield (Freddy Beenstock), Helen Haye (Mrs. Hepworth), Joseph Tomelty (Jim Heeler), Julien Mitchell (Sam Minns)

p, David Lean; d, David Lean; w, David Lean, Norman Spencer, Wynyard Browne (based on the play by Harold Brighouse); ph, Jack Hildyard; ed, Peter Taylor; m, Malcolm Arnold; prod d, Wilfred Shingleton; cos, John Armstrong

Laughton is marvelous in this wry comedy as the crusty old curmudgeon who rules his profitable boot shop and his three unmarried daughters with an iron hand. He hypocritically downs his pints of ale at the local pub and cries out against the inhumanity of life at leaving him a widower. His eldest daughter, de Banzie, is 30 and, in Laughton's words, "on the shelf." Undaunted, she finds herself a husband in the form of the self-effacing, illiterate, and ambitionless Mills, Laughton's assistant and chief bootmaker for the firm.

Mills is a bit dumbfounded when being led to the altar and even more puzzled when de Banzie sets him up in his own bootmaking business after Laughton refuses to award de Banzie a dowry. With de Banzie brainstorming the business, Mills's shop grows and he prospers, so much so that he begins to make inroads into Laughton's once dominant operation.

This is a fully developed comedy of human foibles and follies with Laughton rendering a masterful, sly performance, beautifully supported by de Banzie and Mills. Laughton, who played the role on stage years earlier, was reputedly unhappy on the set; he developed a dislike for de Banzie (who, incredibly, almost upstages Laughton, himself a consummate upstager) and he didn't care for Mills in the role of Willie Mossop, a part he'd wanted Robert Donat to play. Lean's direction is careful and properly mannered as he draws forth one poignant scene after another, some painful, others full of mirth.

Arnold's inventive score adds considerable charm to this best of three versions of Harold Brighouse's 1915 stage comedy (filmed in 1920 as a silent with Arthur Pitt and Joan Ritz, and again as a talkie in 1931 with James Harcourt and Viola Lyel). This film rightly won the Best British Film Award in 1954.

HOLD BACK THE DAWN

1941 115m bw Romance ★★★★
Paramount (U.S.) /A

Charles Boyer (Georges Iscovescu), Olivia de Havilland (Emmy Brown), Paulette Goddard (Anita Dixon), Victor Francen (Van Den Luecken), Walter Abel (Inspector Hammock), Curt Bois (Bonbois), Rosemary DeCamp (Berta Kurz), Eric Feldary (Josef Kurz), Nestor Paiva (Flores), Eva Puig (Lupita)

p, Arthur Hornblow Jr.; d, Mitchell Leisen; w, Charles Brackett, Billy Wilder (based on a story by Ketti Frings); ph, Leo Tover; ed, Doane Harrison; m, Victor Young; art d, Hans Dreier, Robert Usher; cos, Edith Head

AAN Best Picture; AAN Best Actress: Olivia DeHavilland; AAN Best Original Screenplay: Charles Brackett, Billy Wilder; AAN Best Cinematography: Leo Tover; AAN Best Score: Victor Young; AAN Best Art Direction: Hans Dreier (Art Direction), Robert Usher (Art Direction), Sam Comer (Interior Decoration)

A touching and memorable film, this brilliant romance offers evocative performances by Boyer and de Havilland. It opens with a typical Wilder twist: Leisen, shown on the set of I WANTED WINGS, directing a scene with Brian Donlevy and Veronica Lake, is approached by Romanian gigolo Boyer, a one-time European dancer and ladies' escort. Boyer wants to sell movie director Leisen a story for $500. He then fascinates the director with the tale that is HOLD BACK THE DAWN, played out in flashback.

Boyer, stranded in a Mexican border town, lives in a rundown hotel, the Esperanza, which houses all manner of human driftwood from Europe, refugees from Nazi oppression, not the least of whom is Francen, a Dutch professor who acts as a sort of father confessor to the disenfranchised. One pathetic emigre is Rosemary DeCamp, a pregnant refugee who slips across the border to have her child in the US. Visiting the area with her students is American schoolteacher de Havilland, who becomes Boyer's easy victim in a matrimonial-immigration scam suggested by vixen Goddard.

Unabashed soppy soaper, but Leisen's pro touch and sensitive direction keep it from ever becoming maudlin. DAWN exploits the darkly sexy side of Boyer and the mechanistic side of Goddard quite well; the screenplay by Brackett and Wilder is beautifully written, covering for any loopholes in the de Havilland role. The characters were drawn from the life of story writer Frings and her struggle to get her immigrant husband Kurt into the US via Mexico. There is much here that calls to mind ARCH OF TRIUMPH, also starring Boyer, who always felt that HOLD BACK THE DAWN was one of his best films.

HOLIDAY INN

1942 100m bw Musical/Comedy ★★★
Paramount (U.S.) /U

Bing Crosby (Jim Hardy), Fred Astaire (Ted Hanover), Marjorie Reynolds (Linda Mason), Virginia Dale (Lila Dixon), Walter Abel (Danny Reid), Louise Beavers (Mamie), John Gallaudet (Parker), James Bell (Dunbar), Irving Bacon (Gus), Shelby Bacon (Vanderbilt)

p, Mark Sandrich; d, Mark Sandrich; w, Claude Binyon, Elmer Rice (based on an idea by Irving Berlin); ph, David Abel; ed, Ellsworth Hoagland; art d, eans Dreier, Roland Anderson; chor, Danny Dare; cos, Edith Head

AAN Best Original Story: Irving Berlin; AAN Best Score: Robert Emmett Dolan; AA Best Song: Irving Berlin

Dowdy and thin. Based on an idea by Irving Berlin, this is a small musical about a song-and-dance man, Jim Hardy (Bing Crosby), who retires from the biz to become a gentleman farmer in New England, finds country life more demanding than he thought, and tries to have best of both worlds when he turns his farm into a very special hostelry that's only open to the public on national holidays. The film's highlight is a bang-up July 4th "Let's Say It with Firecrackers" that finds Astaire in fine form, Crosby sings "White Christmas" for the first time, and the score includes "Easter Parade." But the girls are duds and the film lacks festivity, showbiz pizzazz, flash. Decidedly improved upon as 1954's WHITE CHRISTMAS.

HOLLYWOOD BOULEVARD

1976 83m c Comedy ★★★
New World (U.S.) R/18

Candice Rialson (*Candy Wednesday*), Mary Woronov (*Mary McQueen*), Rita George (*Bobbi Quackenbush*), Jeffrey Kramer (*Patrick Hobby*), Dick Miller (*Walter Paisley*), Richard Doran (*Producer*), Tara Strohmeier (*Jill McBain*), Paul Bartel (*Erich Von Leppe*), John Kramer (*Duke Mantee*), Jonathan Kaplan (*Scotty*)

p, Jon Davison; d, Joe Dante, Allan Arkush; w, Patrick Hobby; ph, Jamie Anderson; ed, Amy Jones, Allan Arkush, Joe Dante; m, Andrew Stein; art d, Jack DeWolfe; fx, Roger George; cos, Jane Rum

Totally shameless but self-accepting parody of the schlock movie business and Roger Corman's B-factory, New World Pictures. Rialson is a would-be actress who wants stardom. Her agent, Miller, sends her to Miracle Pictures, where she lands a role in the studio's latest epic, MACHETE MAIDENS OF MARATAU. But actress Woronov doesn't like competition, and suddenly there is a series of murders. The film ends with a shootout atop the famous Hollywood sign. HOLLYWOOD BOULEVARD is that rarest of creatures: a parody of a parody that actually is funny and works well. Not to be missed by camp fans.

HOLLYWOOD CANTEEN

1944 124m bw Musical/Comedy ★★★
Warner Bros. (U.S.) /U

Robert Hutton (*Slim*), Dane Clark (*Sergeant*), Janis Paige (*Angela*), Jonathan Hale (*Mr. Brodel*), Barbara Brown (*Mrs. Brodel*), Mark Stevens, Richard Erdman (*Soldiers on Deck*), James Flavin (*Marine Sergeant*), Eddie Marr (*Dance Director*), Theodore von Eltz (*Director*)

p, Alex Gottlieb; d, Delmer Daves; w, Delmer Daves; ph, Bert Glennon; ed, Christian Nyby; m, Ray Heindorf; art d, Leo K. Kuter; chor, LeRoy Prinz; cos, Milo Anderson

AAN Best Score: Ray Heindorf; AAN Best Song: M.K. Jerome (Music), Ted Koehler (Lyrics); AAN Best Sound: Nathan Levinson

Patriotic pap, but so what? Director Daves had a smash with STAGE DOOR CANTEEN and followed it quickly with this film, one of those patriotic displays of self-congratulation WWII Hollywood was so good at.

The plot lies like a feather. After being wounded fighting in the Pacific, Hutton, a young soldier, returns to the US on leave and visits the Hollywood Canteen with his best pal (Dane Clark). The Canteen is tended by John Garfield, Bette Davis, and a host of other stars playing themselves, and when some of them learn of Hutton's crush on actress Joan Leslie, a phony raffle is arranged and Hutton wins first prize—a kiss from Leslie. Later Hutton really hits the jackpot when he is counted the one-millionth serviceman to enter the Canteen. His prize is a night in Hollywood with any actress he wants. On the big night, Leslie doesn't show up; however, she appears at Union Station, where Hutton prepares to leave for reassignment, explaining that she ran out of gas, professing her love for the young GI, and promising that she'll await his return.

The movie is overloaded with talent, much of it ill-used, with a list of songs almost as long as the cast. Best bits: Jack Benny, Greenstreet and Lorre, and the unflappably cheery Andrews Sisters, singing patriotic-bounce ballads like "Gettin' Corns for My Country." Anyway, good-natured as all get out.

HOME ALONE

1990 98m c Comedy ★★½
Hughes (U.S.) PG

Macaulay Culkin (*Kevin McCallister*), Joe Pesci (*Harry*), Daniel Stern (*Marv*), John Heard (*Peter*), Roberts Blossom (*Marley*), Catherine O'Hara (*Kate*), Angela Goethals (*Linnie*), Devin Rattray (*Buzz*), Gerry Bamman (*Uncle Frank*), Hillary Wolf (*Megan*)

p, John Hughes; d, Chris Columbus; w, John Hughes; ph, Julio Macat; ed, Raja Gosnell; m, John Williams; prod d, John Muto; art d, Dan Webster; fx, Bill Purcell; cos, Jay Hurley

AAN Best Score: John Williams; AAN Best Song: John Williams (Music), Leslie Bricusse (Lyrics)

STRAW DOGS Lite. HOME ALONE, a surprisingly violent, paranoid fantasy for kids, became the highest grossing comedy of all time. It also made a star out of a funny-looking kid named Macaulay Culkin.

Eight-year-old Kevin McCallister (Culkin) feels slighted by his large, obnoxious family and throws a temper tantrum on the eve of a vacation trip to Europe. Exiled to his room by his mother (Catherine O'Hara), Kevin fatefully wishes that his family would disappear. The next morning, he awakens to find himself all alone in the house. Scared at first, he soon proves adept at fending for himself. As his guilt-stricken mom begins an arduous journey back from Europe to rescue her son, Kevin elaborately defends the house against a pair of menacing but comically inept burglars (Daniel Stern and Joe Pesci).

The first half of HOME ALONE features the sugar-coated sentimentality that can usually be found in a Hughes film, while the second half is full of unanticipated sadism (a close-up of Stern's bare foot slipping slowly down a six-inch nail is the film's most ghastly image). As directed by Chris Columbus (HEARTBREAK HOTEL), the film's slapstick falls flat and only the pain remains. Yet the film's message seems even more disturbing than its violence. This could be the first comedy—it's certainly the first holiday film—which focuses on child abuse. As Kevin shoots pellets into the intruders and takes a blowtorch to their heads, he's directing the hostility he feels toward his neglectful parents at these two guys. The only really likable thing about this film is Culkin (UNCLE BUCK, JACOB'S LADDER). He's an uncommonly natural child actor, but even he doesn't always survive the tiresome gags (the aftershave bit is funny once; three times is tedious).

HOME AND THE WORLD, THE
(GHARE BAIRE)

1984 140m c Drama ★★★
Natl. Film Dev. Corp. of India (India) /U

Soumitra Chatterjee (*Sandip Mukherjee*), Victor Banerjee (*Nikhilesh Choudhury*), Swatilekha Chatterjee (*Bimala Choudhury*), Manoj Mitra (*Headmaster*), Indrapramit Roy (*Amulya*), Bimala Chatterjee (*Kulada*)

d, Satyajit Ray; w, Satyajit Ray (based on the novel by Rabindranath Tagore); ph, Soumendu Roy; ed, Dulal Dutta; m, Satyajit Ray; art d, Ashoke Bose

This graceful film by Ray is as much a tragic love story as an examination of political turmoil in 1908 India. Banerjee stars as a Westernized Hindu maharajah who lives with his wife, Swatilekha Chatterjee, in colonial Bengal. Political tension grows when Lord Curzon, the British governor-general of India, enacts a plan to "divide and rule" Hindus and Muslims through the partition of Bengal. Because of the resulting unrest, Soumitra Chatterjee, a fiery rebel and friend of Banerjee, pays a visit to the town. Not convinced that his wife truly loves him, Banerjee encourages his wife to come out of purdah (orthodox seclusion) to meet other men, namely his rebellious friend. If she remains faithful after having met others, Banerjee reasons, he can be certain of her love. His plan backfires, however, when his wife falls in love with the rebel.

What's more, political differences arise between the two men. Based on a novel by Nobel Prize-winning author Tagore, THE HOME AND THE WORLD was to have come to the screen 30 years earlier as Ray's first film. Tagore, a friend of Ray's family, had published his book in 1919 to much acclaim; Ray read the book as a youth and wrote a screenplay based on it. It wasn't until 1980, however, that the great Indian filmmaker returned to the project.

HOME OF THE BRAVE

1949 88m bw Drama/War ★★★
Screen Plays (U.S.)

Douglas Dick (*Maj. Robinson*), Steve Brodie (*T.J.*), Jeff Corey (*Doctor*), Lloyd Bridges (*Finch*), Frank Lovejoy (*Mingo*), James Edwards (*Moss*), Cliff Clark (*Colonel*)

p, Stanley Kramer; d, Mark Robson; w, Carl Foreman (based on the play by Arthur Laurents); ph, Robert de Grasse; ed, Harry Gerstad; m, Dimitri Tiomkin; art d, Rudolph Sternad; fx, Jack Rabin

Set against the backdrop of the war in the Pacific, this provocative (for its time) Stanley Kramer-produced message film deals with a black GI's psychosomatic paralysis. Moss (James Edwards) and four white comrades—including his boyhood friend (Lloyd Bridges) and a bigoted corporal (Steve Brodie)—are sent on a reconnaissance mission to a Japanese-held island. In the wake of a terrifying experience on the island and in response to prejudice he has encountered throughout his life, Moss becomes paralyzed from the waist down and is sent to a hospital where a psychiatrist (Jeff Corey) helps him get to the root of his pain. Originally produced on Broadway as an exploration of anti-Semitism, HOME OF THE BRAVE is commendable for its examination of the WW II experience of a black soldier at a time when Hollywood so steadfastly ignoring the concerns of African-Americans. Edwards gives a sensitive performance, and Mark Robson's direction never condescends or makes him an object of bleeding-heart pity.

HOMECOMING, THE

1973   111m   c   Drama   ★★★★
American Film Theatre   (U.S.)   PG/AA

Cyril Cusack *(Sam)*, Ian Holm *(Lenny)*, Michael Jayston *(Teddy)*, Vivien Merchant *(Ruth)*, Terence Rigby *(Joey)*, Paul Rogers *(Max)*

p, Ely A. Landau; d, Peter Hall; w, Harold Pinter (based on his play); ph, David Watkin; ed, Rex Pike; prod d, John Bury; art d, Jack Stevens; cos, Elizabeth Haffenden, Joan Bridge

Excellent adaptation of the Pinter play for the American Film Theatre series of the early 1970s. The simple plot features Jayston returning to his childhood home with wife Merchant. There he sees his father (Rogers), uncle (Cusack), and his brothers (Holm and Rigby), who are a pimp and boxer, respectively. The small family is held together by volatile fighting, boredom, and ultimate dependency on one another. Each performance is a gem. The individual quirks of each character are well- executed and utterly believable. Hall's direction is sensitive to Pinter's script and to the acting of the ensemble (who all played in the original 1965 stage production). There is a magical chemistry within every frame of this powerful, unforgettable film.

HOMICIDE

1991   102m   c   Crime/Drama   ★★★½
Cinehaus Inc./Edward R. Pressman Corporation   (U.S.)   R/15

Joe Mantegna *(Bobby Gold)*, William H. Macy *(Tim Sullivan)*, Natalija Nogulich *(Chava)*, Ving Rhames *(Randolph)*, Rebecca Pidgeon *(Miss Klein)*, Vincent Guastaferro *(Lt. Senna)*, Lionel Mark Smith *(Charlie Olcott)*, Jack Wallace *(Frank)*, J.J. Johnston *(Curren)*, Paul Butler *(Deputy Mayor Walker)*

p, Michael Hausman, Edward R. Pressman; d, David Mamet; w, David Mamet; ph, Roger Deakins; ed, Barbara Tulliver; m, Alaric Jans; prod d, Michael Merritt; art d, Susan Kaufman; fx, Kenny Estes; cos, Nan Cibula

HOMICIDE starts out as a tense, superbly acted police drama, but degenerates fast when it starts dabbling in anti-Semitic conspiracy theories and questions of identity and ethnicity.

Joe Mantegna is superb in the role of Bobby Gold, a tough Chicago cop known as "the orator" for to his ability to sweet-talk villains into deals with the law. He regards himself as a cop first and a Jew hardly at all, and reacts with annoyance when the well-connected family of a murdered elderly Jewish woman pull strings to ensure that he is assigned the case. The dead woman's beautiful granddaughter (Rebecca Pidgeon) shames Gold into reconsidering his sneering attitude toward his own race, and soon he is hot on an increasingly unconvincing trail that involves cryptic Hebrew scholars, underground Zionist groups, and an overnight transformation for our hero from cynical cop to militant Jewish activist.

It's sad that HOMICIDE goes so drastically off the rails, because the first half of the film is a positive joy. Writer-director David Mamet does a brilliant job of capturing the camaraderie among Gold's colleagues, with his trademark staccato, repetitious dialogue building to some hilarious exchanges. The action sequences are cleverly and even humorously handled. But the later, "conspiracy" scenes are as unconvincing and somber as the earlier "cop" sequences are concretely realized and funny—a structural problem that is particularly disappointing in the light of Mamet's superbly crafted earlier films, HOUSE

OF GAMES and THINGS CHANGE. Not even Mantegna can make us believe the conversion his character is supposed to undergo; things change, but not that fast, and not with so little explanation.

HONEY, I SHRUNK THE KIDS

1989   86m   c   Children's/Science Fiction   ★★★
Walt Disney Productions   (U.S.)   PG/U

Rick Moranis *(Prof. Wayne Szalinski)*, Matt Frewer *(Big Russ Thompson)*, Marcia Strassman *(Diane Szalinski)*, Kristine Sutherland *(Mae Thompson)*, Thomas Brown *(Little Russ Thompson)*, Jared Rushton *(Ron Thompson)*, Amy O'Neill *(Amy Szalinski)*, Robert Oliveri *(Nick Szalinski)*, Carl Steven *(Tommy Pervis)*, Mark L. Taylor *(Don Forrester)*

p, Penney Finkelman Cox, Brian Yuzna, Jon Landau; d, Joe Johnston; w, Ed Naha, Tom Schulman (based on a story by Stuart Gordon, Yuzna, Naha); ph, Hiro Narita; ed, Michael A. Stevenson; m, James Horner; prod d, Gregg Fonseca; art d, John Iacovelli, Dorree Cooper; cos, Carol Brolaski

Reminiscent of earlier Disney live-action classics like THE ABSENT-MINDED PROFESSOR and SON OF FLUBBER, HONEY, I SHRUNK THE KIDS provides a wonderful blend of thrills, character, and humor that will keep both children and adults charmed and engaged throughout.

Rick Moranis stars as Prof. Wayne Szalinski, a nutty inventor who is trying to create a machine that will shrink living things. When the professor's kids—teenage daughter Amy (Amy O'Neil) and little brother Nick (Robert Oliveri)—and two of their friends (Thomas Brown, Jared Rushton) accidentally activate the machine, they are all shrunk to quarter-inch size. So begins their dangerous adventure from the trash can, where the professor has unknowingly put them, through the seemingly gargantuan back yard, to what they hope will be the safety of the house.

Based on a story by Stuart Gordon (RE-ANIMATOR), Brian Yuzna and Ed Naha, HONEY, I SHRUNK THE KIDS was to have been directed by Gordon, but, after conflicts with the studio, he was replaced by special-effects man Joe Johnston (making his directorial debut). Espousing values of decency and tolerance between its terrific action sequences, HONEY harkens back to Disney's past. Consistently exciting, inventive and fun, the film is a rollicking good adventure, with enough bravura effects to keep the most hyperactive youngster interested. Fittingly, Buena Vista's best release since WHO FRAMED ROGER RABBIT? was coupled with a brand new Roger Rabbit cartoon short, TUMMY TROUBLE, the first animated short produced by the Disney studio in over 25 years.

HONEYMOON IN VEGAS

1992   95m   c   Romance/Comedy   ★★★½
Castle Rock/Lobell/Bergman Productions   (U.S.)   PG-13/12

James Caan *(Tommy Korman)*, Nicolas Cage *(Jack Singer)*, Sarah Jessica Parker *(Betsy/Donna)*, Pat Morita *(Mahi)*, Peter Boyle *(Chief Orman)*, Anne Bancroft *(Bea Singer)*, Seymour Cassel *(Tony Cataracts)*, Johnny Williams *(Johnny Sandwich)*, John Capodice *(Sally Molars)*, Robert Costanzo *(Sidney Tomashefsky)*

p, Mike Lobell; d, Andrew Bergman; w, Andrew Bergman; ph, William A. Fraker; ed, Barry Malkin; m, David Newman; prod d, William A. Elliott; art d, John Warnke; cos, Julie Weiss

An amiable, if instantly forgettable, comedy, saved from oblivion by Nicolas Cage in medium-wacky mode.

Cage plays Jack Singer, a New York private detective haunted by his late mother's deathbed plea that he never marry. When, after years of procrastination, he finally pops the question to his schoolteacher girlfriend Betsy (Sarah Jessica Parker), she can't believe he's serious. "I must be serious," he replies, as his immobile car halts an angry line of traffic—"My legs are paralyzed."

Jack comes up against more than commitment angst when the couple fly to Vegas to tie the knot. He takes time out for a few rounds of poker before the ceremony and ends up losing big to Tommy (James Caan), a pro gambler who's willing to accept a weekend with Betsy in lieu of the $65,000 Jack owes him. Tommy's dastardly plan is to whisk Betsy (who's a dead ringer for his late wife) off to Hawaii for a romantic weekend that will convince her *he's* the man she needs.

HONEYMOON IN VEGAS has its fair share of snappy one-liners and a goofy visual sense that fits the material, with Bergman getting a lot of mileage out of an Elvis look-alike convention taking place in the couple's hotel. Sarah Jessica Parker does what little she's asked to do with style, and James Caan is clearly at home playing a lizard who *nearly* has you thinking he's a nice guy. It's Nicolas Cage, though, who walks off with the show, thanks to his trademark blend of the sentimental and absurd. The final scene has him returning to Vegas in a desperate bid to save his loved one. Only Cage could make that return via parachute, wearing an illuminated Elvis costume, and still seem believable. Viva Las Vegas.

HONEYMOON KILLERS, THE

1969 115m bw Crime   ★★★½
Roxanne (U.S.)   R/18

Shirley Stoler *(Martha Beck)*, Tony Lo Bianco *(Ray Fernandez)*, Mary Jane Higby *(Janet Fay)*, Doris Roberts *(Bunny)*, Kip McArdle *(Delphine Downing)*, Marilyn Chris *(Myrtle Young)*, Dortha Duckworth *(Mrs. Beck)*, Barbara Cason *(Evelyn Long)*, Ann Harris *(Doris)*, Mary Breen *(Rainelle Downing)*

p, Warren Steibel; d, Leonard Kastle; w, Leonard Kastle; ph, Oliver Wood; ed, Stanley Warnow, Richard Brophy; m, Gustav Mahler

A remarkable low-budget film that offers a chilling portrait of a pair of cold-blooded murderers. Stoler is a lonely, sexually frustrated, 200-pound nurse at a Mobile, Alabama, hospital. She lives alone with her mother, which only adds to her frustration. In desperation she joins a lonelyhearts correspondence club and soon begins receiving torrid love letters from Lo Bianco, a Spanish immigrant in New York. When he comes to visit Stoler, she quickly falls in love with him.

When he steals money from her and leaves, she tracks him down and finds that he makes his living stealing from love-starved women he finds through the correspondence clubs. She loves him nonetheless, and after she is fired from her job, she puts her mother in a nursing home and heads off with Lo Bianco in search of new victims. Stoler poses as Lo Bianco's sister while he woos lonely women and then flees with their money. But when Lo Bianco marries Chris to give her baby a father, a jealous Stoler turns to murder.

Based on an actual case that got much press in the late 1940s, THE HONEYMOON KILLERS is shot in stark black-and-white documentary style and the music of Mahler is effective in counterpointing the action. The acting is second to none: the two leads are frighteningly good in their psychotic roles and supporting characters are also well dileneated. But there are some technical problems with the film, notably too much shadow in the frame, several highly visible microphones and the choppy editing, which jumbles the story at times.

Still, the straightforwardness of the telling is not totally destroyed. To their credit the filmmakers have refused to romanticize the brutality of the criminals at the heart of the film. Lo Bianco went on to star in other pictures; Stoler's other major role was as the brutal Nazi prison camp commandant in Lina Wertmuller's marvelous SEVEN BEAUTIES.

HOOK

1991 144m c Fantasy/Adventure   ★★★
Hook Productions/Amblin (U.S.)   PG/U

Dustin Hoffman *(Captain James Hook)*, Robin Williams *(Peter Banning/Peter Pan)*, Julia Roberts *(Tinkerbell)*, Bob Hoskins *(Smee)*, Maggie Smith *(Granny Wendy Darling)*, Caroline Goodall *(Moira Banning)*, Charlie Korsmo *(Jack Banning)*, Amber Scott *(Maggie Banning)*, Laurel Cronin *(Liza)*, Phil Collins *(Inspector Good)*

p, Kathleen Kennedy, Frank Marshall, Gerald R. Molen; d, Steven Spielberg; w, Jim V. Hart, Malia Scotch Marmo (from the story by Hart and Nick Castle, adapted from the original stage play and books by Sir James M. Barrie); ph, Dean Cundey; ed, Michael Kahn; m, John Williams; prod d, Norman Garwood; art d, Andrew Precht, Thomas E. Sanders; fx, Michael Lantieri; chor, Vince Paterson; cos, Anthony Powell

AAN Best Song: John Williams (Music), Leslie Bricusse (Lyrics); *AAN Best Art Direction:* Norman Garwood (Art Direction), Garrett Lewis (Set Decoration); *AAN Best Costume Design:* Anthony Powell; *AAN Best Visual Effects:* Eric Brevig, Harley Jessup, Mark Sullivan, Michael Lantieri; *AAN Best Makeup:* Christina Smith, Montague Westmore, Greg Cannom

On paper, HOOK looked promising. It boasted the high-concept idea of a grown-up Peter Pan, directed by Hollywood's perennial child-man Steven Spielberg. And thanks to a lucrative deal brokered by Creative Artists Agency, the film featured a cast of truly stellar proportions; Dustin Hoffman, Robin Williams, and Julia Roberts. It all seemed too good to be true. Well, it was.

Peter Banning (Williams) is a hard-nosed workaholic merger and buyout king. He cares about his wife, Moira (Caroline Goodall), and family, but is too consumed by his career to pay enough attention to them, missing his son Jack's (Charlie Korsmo) important baseball game and his daughter Maggie's (Amber Scott) appearance in a school production of *Peter Pan*. However, he takes time to make a Christmas trip with his family to visit his wife's grandmother, Granny Wendy Darling (Maggie Smith), in London, where she's being honored for her work with the Great Ormond Street Children's Hospital. His children are excited by the prospect of meeting her, as they know she was the Wendy on whom J.M. Barrie based the heroine of *Peter Pan*. Peter spends all his time there on the phone, trying to supervise a buyout, but matters are dramatically interrupted when his children are kidnapped, with only a rip along the wallpaper and a strange parchment as clues. That night, Peter is visited by Tinkerbell (Roberts) who tries to convince Peter that he is—or used to be—Peter Pan and that his children have been kidnapped by the evil Captain Hook (Hoffman). This seven-inch-fairy also insists that he has no choice but to return with her to Neverland to reclaim them.

One of the most eagerly awaited—and expensively hyped—releases of 1991, HOOK is not entirely devoid of entertainment value. Yet it's impossible to walk away from the film without a feeling of regret that this talented group of artists couldn't have accomplished more. The problems begin with the screenplay, a clumsy attempt to meld reality and fantasy which leaves too many issues unresolved and repeatedly assaults the viewer with wishy-washy, New Age philosophy about the importance of preserving the "inner child."

The casting also has its flaws. Hoffman turns in a casually goofy performance as the captain, but Roberts is seriously out of place playing a pixie. Williams, too, seems a bland presence, having played far more genuinely free-spirited roles in many other movies. Hoskins' hammy performance as Smee shows how much he learned from his animated co-stars in WHO FRAMED ROGER RABBIT.

The biggest disappointment, though, is Spielberg's direction; instead of youthful ebullience, we get lots of cutesy slapstick violence. And though the Neverland sets are among the most spectacular ever built, the onscreen bustle is inadequately choreographed. Our eyes are confounded, rather than delighted, by the constant, chaotic activity. As top-heavy as Captain Hook's ornate, immobile ship, this lavish, elaborate production ultimately collapses under its own weight.

HOOP DREAMS

1994 171m c Documentary/Sports   ★★★★½
Kartemquin Films/KCTA-TV (St. Paul   PG-13/12
/Minneapolis) (U.S.)

William Gates *(Himself)*, Arthur Agee *(Himself)*, Emma Gates *(Herself—William's Mother)*, Curtis Gates *(Himself—William's Brother)*, Sheila Agee *(Herself—Arthur's Mother)*, Arthur "Bo" Agee *(Himself—Arthur's Father)*, Earl Smith *(Himself—Talent Scout)*, Gene Pingatore *(Himself—St. Joseph High School Basketball Coach)*, Isiah Thomas *(Himself—Detroit Piston Basketball Player)*, Sister Marilyn Hopewell *(Herself—St. Joseph Guidance Counselor)*

p, Frederick Marx, Steve James, Peter Gilbert; d, Steve James; ph, Peter Gilbert; ed, Frederick Marx, Steve James, Bill Haugse

AAN Best Editing: Frederick Marx, Steve James, Bill Haugse

One of the most widely discussed and well-received documentaries of the decade, HOOP DREAMS is a powerful and moving film that intimately chronicles the lives of two Chicago teenagers as they struggle with the pressures of potential basketball stardom. For five years, independent filmmakers Steve James, Frederick Marx, and Peter Gilbert recorded both the private moments and public experiences of Arthur Agee and William Gates. The result is both a sympathetic portrait of two human beings and a stunning expose of the system that exploits "student-athletes."

The film begins in 1986, with a talent scout discovering Arthur and William as 14-year-old stars of the playground. Lured by the "hoop dreams" of college and NBA careers, both accept athletic scholarships to St. Joseph High School—introducing the film's central conflict, as young black men shuttle back and forth between their economically marginalized families in the city and a wealthy, predominantly white prep school in the suburbs. The film follows the successes and failures of four seasons of high school hoops and four years of personal growth, frustration, and tragedy.

Although HOOP DREAMS skillfully edits together exciting basketball highlights, the Agee and Gates families are its true subjects. Presumably because the cameras became such a fixture in these homes over time, they capture, in the best cinema verite tradition, compelling and revelatory moments of family dynamics. Despite the harshness of their lives, members of both families are shown to be supportive, hard-working, and (perhaps unreasonably) optimistic. Their image offers a refreshingly complicated and humane look at underclass life that puts the lie to media stereotypes of the welfare mother and the gang banger. On the other hand, the film admirably refuses to elide aspects of its subjects' lives that conflict with the old liberal myth of long-suffering, impossibly noble poor blacks.

The triumph of HOOP DREAMS is that it celebrates the game of basketball while critiquing its corporate and social underpinnings. Like Arthur and William and the culture they come from, the Chicago-based filmmakers love basketball too much not to get caught up in the excitement of the boys' final state tournament. And to some extent the film concludes with a different message than than that of its first two hours. However briefly, Arthur Agee and William Gates *do* get out of the ghetto. Their path is inglorious, their success tenuous, but this pair of likable, reluctant heroes are shown as completing a bittersweet journey.

While HOOP DREAMS was named as one of the year's best movies by virtually every prominent critic in the US, it failed to win Oscar nominations for Best Picture and Best Documentary Feature, giving rise to widespread criticism of the arcane and complicated process by which the Academy reviews documentary films.

HOOSIERS

1986   114m   c   Sports   ★★★½
Hemdale   (U.S.)   PG

Gene Hackman (*Coach Norman Dale*), Barbara Hershey (*Myra Fleener*), Dennis Hopper (*Shooter*), Sheb Wooley (*Cletus*), Fern Persons (*Opal Fleener*), Brad Boyle (*Whit*), Steve Hollar (*Rade*), Brad Long (*Strap*), David Neidorf (*Everett*), Kent Poole (*Merle*)

p, Carter DeHaven, Angelo Pizzo; d, David Anspaugh; w, Angelo Pizzo; ph, Fred Murphy; ed, C. Timothy O'Meara; m, Jerry Goldsmith; prod d, David Nichols; art d, David Lubin; cos, Jane E. Anderson

AAN Best Supporting Actor: Dennis Hopper; *AAN Best Score:* Jerry Goldsmith

It should come as little surprise that this solid, sentimental movie about basketball is set in Indiana, where babies are given roundballs before they get rattles. Loosely based on the true story of the team from tiny Milan High School (164 students), which won the 1954 Indiana state championship, this uplifting film, set in 1951, follows Norman Dale (Gene Hackman), a big-time college coach who has fallen from grace, in his leadership of the Hickory, Indiana, high-school basketball team to victory. Jimmy (Maris Valanis), the town's most gifted player, is so disturbed by the death of the previous coach that he declines to join the team, but Norman refuses to pressure him into doing so, earning the reluctant respect of Myra Fleener (Barbara Hershey), the acting principal.

Norman also remains determined to run the team *his* way, despite the animosity of the townspeople, who in the past have felt free to offer advice. With the expert help of Shooter (Dennis Hopper, in an Oscar-

nominated performance that is one of the finest of his career), the alcoholic father of one of the players, Norman perseveres, and Jimmy decides to play after all.

Bursting with emotion and full of exhilarating game action, HOOSIERS captures the ambience of small-town Indiana basketball. David Anspaugh's direction is assured, Fred Murphy's cinematography and Jerry Goldsmith's score masterful, and the performances uniformly strong. However, the film clearly functions as wish-fulfillment for the kind of people who are nostalgic about all-white basketball, leaving a nasty aftertaste.

HOPALONG CASSIDY

1935   60m   bw   Western   ★★★
Paramount   (U.S.)

William Boyd (*Bill Cassidy*), James Ellison (*Johnny Nelson*), Paula Stone (*Mary Meeker*), Robert Warwick (*Jim Meeker*), Charles Middleton (*Buck Peters*), Frank McGlynn Jr. (*Red Connors*), Kenneth Thomson (*Pecos Jack Anthony*), George "Gabby" Hayes (*Uncle Ben*), James Mason (*Tom Shaw*), Frank Campeau (*Frisco*)

p, Harry Sherman; d, Howard Bretherton; w, Doris Schroeder, Harrison Jacobs (based on a story by Clarence E. Mulford); ph, Archie Stout; ed, Edward Schroeder

The first of the HOPALONG CASSIDY oaters in what became one of the longest-running series of Westerns in the history of movies and made an international star of the nearly washed-up silent actor William Boyd.

Boyd, youngster Ellison, and McGlynn, Jr. try to prevent a range war between two cattlemen which is instigated by an evil ranch foreman who plays both sides against the middle and helps an outlaw gang snatch the cattle. The scheme succeeds because each side blames the other for the missing stock. Eventually, with Boyd's help, both ranchers wise up, and they combine their efforts, sending a small army of cowboys into the gang's mountain hideout where justice eventually triumphs.

Independent producer Sherman bought the rights to Clarence E. Mulford's series of "Bar 20" western novels which featured a grizzled, tough-talking, hard-drinking, slightly crippled old cowboy named Hopalong Cassidy. When producer Sherman asked Boyd to play the ranch foreman, he refused but agreed to play Cassidy if the character was rewritten to be a clean-living, noble hero. (The limp was also abandoned after the first few movies, leaving the name "Hopalong" something of a mystery years later.) The result was a seemingly unending string of Westerns. After 50 films, Sherman sold out his ownership to Boyd, who saw the series to its eventual conclusion and its 1950s TV craze.

HOPE AND GLORY

1987   113m   c   Comedy/Drama/War   ★★★★½
Columbia   (U.K.)   PG-13/15

Sebastian Rice-Edwards (*Bill Rohan*), Geraldine Muir (*Sue Rohan*), Sarah Miles (*Grace Rohan*), David Hayman (*Clive Rohan*), Sammi Davis (*Dawn Rohan*), Derrick O'Connor (*Mac*), Susan Wooldridge (*Molly*), Jean-Marc Barr (*Cpl. Bruce Carey*), Ian Bannen (*George*), Annie Leon (*Bill's Grandmother*)

p, John Boorman, Michael Dryhurst; d, John Boorman; w, John Boorman; ph, Philippe Rousselot, John Harris; ed, Ian Crafford; m, Peter Martin; prod d, Anthony Pratt; art d, Don Dossett; fx, Rodney Fuller, Michael Collins, Phil Stokes; chor, Anthony Van Laast; cos, Shirley Russell

AAN Best Picture; AAN Best Director: John Boorman; *AAN Best Original Screenplay:* John Boorman; *AAN Best Cinematography:* Philippe Rousselot; *AAN Best Art Direction:* Anthony Pratt (Art Direction), Joan Woollard (Set Decoration)

HOPE AND GLORY is a wonderful film, an intelligent, heartfelt, personal and, marvelously entertaining look at what it was like to grow up in wartorn England.

A semiautobiographical project from British director John Boorman, the film depicts nine-year-old Bill (Sebastian Rice-Edwards) as he experiences the wonders of WWII from his suburban London home. While Americans may find it somewhat disconcerting to see the Blitz and its horrors made the setting for a nostalgic comedy, for Boorman's young boy the war was a particularly exciting and vivid time, and a joyous feeling permeates the film. The total upheaval of the staid family order, the lack of normal restrictions and discipline, and the liberating effect the war had on women are all brilliantly conveyed by Boorman, because he views the war from a child's perspective.

Told in a series of vignettes, HOPE AND GLORY unfolds in a surprisingly nonchalant manner, dispensing its vividly realized observations at every turn. Boorman skillfully combines nuggets of truth with moments of mirth and is always prepared to surprise and amuse without sentimentalizing.

HOPSCOTCH

1980 104m c Comedy/Spy   ★★★½
Avco Embassy (U.S.)   R/15

Walter Matthau (*Miles Kendig*), Glenda Jackson (*Isobel von Schmidt*), Sam Waterston (*Cutter*), Ned Beatty (*Myerson*), Herbert Lom (*Mikhail Yaskov*), David Matthau (*Ross*), George Baker (*Westlake*), Ivor Roberts (*Ludlum*), Lucy Saroyan (*Carla*), Severn Darden (*Maddox*)

p, Edie Landau, Ely Landau; d, Ronald Neame; w, Brian Garfield, Bryan Forbes (based on the novel by Garfield); ph, Arthur Ibbetson; ed, Carl Kress; m, Ian Fraser; prod d, William J. Creber

This well-crafted comedy concerns top-drawer CIA agent Miles Kendig (Walter Matthau), who is demoted to managing the office files by his bureaucratic boss (Ned Beatty). Miles takes off for Europe and meets Mikhail Yaskov (Herbert Lom), an old friend and Soviet agent, who suggests Miles write his memoirs. Taken with the idea, Miles flies off to Salzburg and meets Isobel von Schmidt (Glenda Jackson), an old flame who is also a former agent. She provides support as he begins writing a book that will expose the secrets of world espionage.

A thoroughly entertaining picture, HOPSCOTCH is based on a serious spy novel. The casting of Matthau, however, changed that premise, and the film's most enjoyable aspect is his character's playfulness as he turns the CIA on its head. An unlikely pair, Matthau and Jackson build on the interesting chemistry they developed in HOUSE CALLS. If it's a classically styled throwback to Hollywood espionage films of the 1940s and 1950s you're looking for, HOPSCOTCH is it.

HORROR OF DRACULA

1958 82m c Horror   ★★★★
Hammer (U.K.)

Peter Cushing (*Van Helsing*), Michael Gough (*Arthur Holmwood*), Melissa Stribling (*Mina Holmwood*), Christopher Lee (*Count Dracula*), Carol Marsh (*Lucy*), John Van Eyssen (*Jonathan Harker*), Miles Malleson (*Marx, the Undertaker*), Valerie Gaunt (*Vampire Woman*), Charles Lloyd Pack (*Dr. Seward*), Janina Faye (*Tania*)

p, Anthony Hinds; d, Terence Fisher; w, Jimmy Sangster; ph, Jack Asher; ed, Bill Lenny; m, James Bernard; art d, Bernard Robinson; cos, Molly Arbuthnot

Bloody well done. Hammer finally gave the Dracula legend the treatment it deserved here, entrusting it to the brilliant director of THE CURSE OF FRANKENSTEIN, Terence Fisher, who injected glorious life into the familiar material.

English librarian Jonathan Harker (John Van Eyssen) travels to Transylvania, where he is employed by the mysterious Count Dracula (Christopher Lee). Eventually, Harker learns that his employer is a vampire, one of the undead who must suck the blood of the living to survive, and he becomes one of Dracula's victims. Dracula then travels to London and tracks down Harker's fiancee, Lucy (Carol Marsh), and transforms her into one of the undead. Enter Dr. Van Helsing (played with zest by Peter Cushing) and the battle lines are drawn.

Fisher's version of the Dracula legend brought with it many innovative (and, yes, subsequently overdone) approaches to the genre. The film moves quickly and forcefully from one scene to the next, keeping the audience on their seat edges. Lush sets, rousing musical score, spirited acting and a direct attitude toward undead sensuality heighten the vampiric illusion. The result is a terrific combination of the intellectual and visceral that continues to work today. Followed by DRACULA - PRINCE OF DARKNESS and five more sequels.

HORSE FEATHERS

1932 70m bw Comedy   ★★★★
Paramount (U.S.)   /U

Groucho Marx (*Professor Wagstaff*), Harpo Marx (*Harpo*), Chico Marx (*Chico*), Zeppo Marx (*Zeppo*), Thelma Todd (*Connie Bailey*), David Landau (*Jennings*), Florine McKinney (*Peggy Carrington*), Jim Pierce (*Mullens*), Nat Pendleton (*McCarthy*), Reginald Barlow (*President of College*)

d, Norman Z. McLeod; w, Bert Kalmar, Harry Ruby, S.J. Perelman; ph, Ray June

Not a masterpiece but divine all the same. The Marx Brothers bring their special brand of anarchy to the world of college football in this wonderfully madcap comedy.

Prof. Quincy Adams Wagstaff (Groucho) is named president of Huxley College, which hasn't won a football game since its founding in 1888. Acting on the advice of his son (Zeppo), Wagstaff attempts to recruit a pair of pro players, but a mixup at a speakeasy leads him to mistake a dog catcher (Harpo) and bootlegging iceman (Chico) for football players. Just the same, Wagstaff sends them to kidnap arch rival Darwin College's ringers; unfortunately, they fail. Meanwhile, college widow Connie Bailey (Thelma Todd), who is in cahoots with Darwin's Jennings, tries to wheedle the Huxley "signals" out of Groucho.

Although there are many funny moments preceding it, the film's big payoff comes in the Huxley-Darwin game, in which Harpo, Chico and Groucho all contribute to a zany comeback victory brought about through the use of banana peels, an elastic band, a chariot, and a surplus of footballs. Perhaps the most freewheeling film the Brothers Marx ever made, this fast-paced laugh fest was directed by Norman Z. McLeod and written by the great humorist S.J. Perelman with help from Bert Kalmar and Harry Ruby. With the delectable, unappreciated Thelma Todd, a spun-sugar confection from the Lombard sorority, and a marvelous foil for Groucho.

HORSE SOLDIERS, THE

1959 119m c Western/War   ★★★
Mirisch (U.S.)   /PG

John Wayne (*Col. John Marlowe*), William Holden (*Maj. Henry Kendall*), Constance Towers (*Hannah Hunter*), Althea Gibson (*Lukey*), Hoot Gibson (*Brown*), Anna Lee (*Mrs. Buford*), Russell Simpson (*Sheriff*), Stan Jones (*Gen. U.S. Grant*), Carleton Young (*Col. Jonathan Miles*), Basil Ruysdael (*Boys School Commandant*)

p, John Lee Mahin, Martin Rackin; d, John Ford; w, John Lee Mahin, Martin Rackin (based on the novel by Harold Sinclair); ph, William Clothier; ed, Jack Murray; m, David Buttolph; art d, Frank Hotaling; fx, Augie Lohman; cos, Frank Beetson, Ann Peck

With the exception of the Civil War segment in HOW THE WEST WAS WON, THE HORSE SOLDIERS was director John Ford's only film dealing with the War Between the States. The film is gorgeously photographed and contains many memorable images (the opening credits and breathtaking final shot) and moving scenes (one in which a Southern military school is forced to send its cadets—all children—into battle against the Union forces is a stunner), but this is not one of Ford's best efforts, suffering from a weak script and an overwrought performance from its female lead, Constance Towers.

Based on an actual mission known as Grierson's Raid, the film takes place in the spring of 1863 and finds Union general U.S. Grant (Stan Jones) frustrated by his inability to take Vicksburg. Taking drastic action, Grant decides to send a cavalry unit to Newton Station, Mississippi, deep in Confederate territory, to cut enemy supply lines to Vicksburg. The man selected to lead this daring raid is tough, no-nonsense Col. Marlowe (John Wayne), a citizen soldier who designed railroads before the war. With him goes a bevy of officers with mixed motives, including Col. Secord (Willis Bouchey), whose political ambitions dictate his every action, and Maj. Kendall (William Holden), a conscientious physician who sees no glory in war—only suffering and death. En route to Newton Station, the cavalry bivouacs at a plantation owned by Hannah (Towers), a Southern belle devoted to the Confederate cause. Caught spying on Marlowe and his commanders as they plan strategy, Hannah and her slave, Lukey (Althea Gibson), are taken along on the mission, lest they reveal the top-secret plans to the rebels.

While minor Ford is still head-and-shoulders above the best of most others, THE HORSE SOLDIERS is a mostly workmanlike effort in which the great director struggles against a poorly written script, with sketchy characters and overly explicit dialogue in which deep feelings and motivations come tumbling out in succinct speeches. Such pat character development invariably lends a superficial feel to the conflicts and relationships among the principals, and the viewer never really feels very deeply for the protagonists. Ford is such a master of his craft that he injects enough personal spark into the material to nearly override the script's deficiencies, but there's no denying that THE HORSE SOLDIERS is the work of a distracted, tired, and somewhat bored artist. Indeed, in his famous interview with Peter Bogdanovich, the director couldn't recall whether or not he had even seen the final cut.

HORSE'S MOUTH, THE

1958 95m c Comedy   ★★★½
UA (U.K.)   /U

Alec Guinness (Gulley Jimson), Kay Walsh (Coker), Renee Houston (Sarah), Mike Morgan (Nosey), Robert Coote (Sir William Beeder), Arthur Macrae (Alabaster), Veronica Turleigh (Lady Beeder), Reginald Beckwith (Capt. Jones), Michael Gough (Abel), Ernest Thesiger (Hickson)

p, John Bryan; d, Ronald Neame; w, Alec Guinness (based on the novel by Joyce Carey); ph, Arthur Ibbetson; ed, Anne V. Coates; m, Ken Jones

AAN Best Adapted Screenplay: Alec Guinness

Hugely enjoyable comedy about the anti-social nature of the true artist. Guinness plays Gulley Jimson, a marvelous creation of Joyce Cary's that the author loosely based on his friend Dylan Thomas. Guinness adapted the screenplay himself—a personal labor of love—and breathes fantastic life into the part of a basket-case painter who lives like a bum but produces brilliant, unorthodox work.

Released from prison after serving time as a vagrant, Guinness returns to his wife and becomes enraged when he realizes that she has been surviving by selling off his paintings. He learns that a wealthy collector, Coote, is interested in his work, and he goes to see the man but finds that he is out of town. Guinness looks about Coote's enormous flat and decides that he will simply move in and affix his latest masterpieces (actually the work of English artist John Bratby) to the walls.

Guinness first saw the film in Mexico City, where it was being shown at a film festival without the benefit of either dubbing or subtitles. Although most of the audience could not understand the dialogue, the vast majority roared their approval at the end, even though a faction who considered the film an insult to artists started a fight, which developed into a riot. Guinness, accompanied by the British Ambassador and his wife, escaped unnoticed in the fleeing crowd.

HOSPITAL, THE

1971 103m c Comedy/Drama   ★★★½
Gottfried/Chayefsky (U.S.)   GP/15

George C. Scott (Dr. Herbert Bock), Diana Rigg (Barbara Drummond), Barnard Hughes (Drummond), Richard Dysart (Dr. Welbeck), Andrew Duncan (William Mead), Nancy Marchand (Mrs. Christie, Head Nurse), Stephen Elliott (Sunstrom), Donald Harron (Milton Mead), Roberts Blossom (Guernsey), Tresa Hughes (Mrs. Donovan)

p, Howard Gottfried; d, Arthur Hiller; w, Paddy Chayefsky; ph, Victor J. Kemper; ed, Eric Albertson; m, Morris Surdin; prod d, Gene Rudolf; cos, Frank Thompson

AAN Best Actor: George C. Scott; *AA Best Adapted Screenplay:* Paddy Chayefsky

Satire at its darkest. Scott in fine, hammy form (for once a part that takes advantage of his overblown core) as a N.Y. medical center's chief surgeon whose personal life has driven him to the brink of suicide. The busy hospital is being torn apart by a string of inexplicable murders of staff members. The laughs are sardonic, and the reality of Chayefsky's

heavy-handed message (i.e., hospitals treat their patients badly) eats away at the viewer. But even when it falls flat, it's still an interesting watch.

HOT SHOTS!

1991 84m c Action/Comedy   ★★★
Treadwell Enterprises/Pap Inc/Fox (U.S.)   PG-13/12

Charlie Sheen (Sean "Topper" Harley/Rhett Butler/Superman), Cary Elwes (Kent Gregory), Valeria Golino (Ramada Thompson/Scarlett O'Hara/Lois Lane), Lloyd Bridges (Admiral "Tug" Benson), Kevin Dunn (Lieutenant Commander James Block), Jon Cryer (Jim "Washout" Pfaffenbach), William O'Leary (Pete "Dead Meat" Thompson), Kristy Swanson (Dawn Kowalski), Efrem Zimbalist Jr. (Wilson), Bill Irwin (Buzz Harley)

p, Bill Badalato; d, Jim Abrahams; w, Pat Proft, Jim Abrahams; ph, Bill Butler; ed, Jane Kurson, Eric Sears; m, Sylvester Levay; prod d, William A. Elliott; art d, Greg Papalia; fx, Phil Cory; cos, Mary Malin

HOT SHOTS! spoofs not only flyboy films in general, but kids the pants off at least a half-dozen famous movies, including the likes of GONE WITH THE WIND, DANCES WITH WOLVES, THE FABULOUS BAKER BOYS, DINER and even the infamous 9 1/2 WEEKS. At its core, however, HOT SHOTS! is a blatant sendup of the Tom Cruise smash TOP GUN and the names of the various ace flyboy characters help to set the mood for the off-the-wall humor to come.

There's the obviously ill-fated Pete "Dead Meat" Thompson (William O'Leary) and an ace pilot suffering from a malady known as "walleye vision" named Jim "Wash Out" Pfaffenbach (Jon Cryer). The major "hot shot" is Sean "Topper" Harley (Charlie Sheen), while his nemesis—both in matters of the heart and in the air—is ace narcissist Kent Gregory (Cary Elwes), the very model of military perfection—or so he likes to think. The flyboys are rousingly led by blustery multi-war veteran, Admiral "Tug" Benson (Lloyd Bridges), a pratfall-prone, "Damn the torpedoes. . . " type leader who, through the years, has had just about every part of his body replaced, due to a spectacular series of inept combat injuries.

When Topper and Kent aren't snarling at each other through clenched teeth in the air, they're snarling at each other with clenched fists on the ground. Kent blames Topper's ace pilot father for causing the death of his own dad years before in a freak airplane accident. Kent is also Topper's chief rival for the affections of the alluring base psychiatrist, equestrienne, sculptor and torch singer, Ramada Thompson (Valeria Golino).

While the slapstick comedy antics are frequently amusing and, on rare occasions, even hilarious, HOT SHOTS!, like so many other cinematic parodies before it, tends to lose sight—or control—of the plot, such as it is, in favor of more jokes, more visual gags and more dialogue puns—all hurled at the audience at a rapid-fire pace.

HOT SHOTS! PART DEUX

1993 89m c Comedy   ★★★
Fox (U.S.)   PG-13/12

Charlie Sheen (Topper Harley), Lloyd Bridges (Tug Benson), Valeria Golino (Ramada Rodham Hayman), Richard Crenna (Colonel Denton Walters), Brenda Bakke (Michelle Rodham Huddleston), Miguel Ferrer (Harbinger), Rowan Atkinson (Dexter Hayman), Jerry Haleva (Saddam Hussein), David Wohl (Gerou), Mitchell Ryan (Gray Edwards)

p, Bill Badalato; d, Jim Abrahams; w, Jim Abrahams, Pat Proft; ph, John R. Leonetti; ed, Malcolm Campbell; m, Basil Poledouris; prod d, William A. Elliott; art d, Greg Papalia; fx, Erik Henry, John Frazier, David Simmons; chor, Lester Wilson, Carol Tong; cos, Mary Malin

The following is an exclusive interview granted to the *Virgin Film Guide* by the real-life Topper Harley, the reclusive, "Rambo"-style commando played by Charlie Sheen in HOT SHOTS! PART DEUX.

VFG: Topper, how does it feel to be portrayed as a figure of ridicule in a movie that spoofs everything from RAMBO through BASIC INSTINCT, APOCALYPSE NOW, LADY AND THE TRAMP, "American Gladiators" and the Energizer bunny?

TH: What do you mean? I didn't catch any of those references.

VFG: You must be joking!

TH: No—if I were joking, I would say "A horse walks into a bar, and the bartender asks him, 'Why the long face?'"

VFG: This is a highly patriotic film in which you rescue a bunch of American hostages from one of Saddam Hussein's prison camps. How do you feel, though, about the way the US President (Lloyd Bridges) is played? I mean, if he's not throwing up in the Japanese President's lap during dinner, he's listing all the body parts he's had replaced because of war wounds. He claims to have the tongue of a Bassett Hound, for instance?

TH: Yeah, but at the end, he gets into hand-to-hand combat with Saddam, and he kicks the guy's butt! I love that part.

VFG: For me, one of the funniest lines comes when you're reunited with your old love, Ramada (Valeria Golino), and you say, "I never forgot you; your face was always on the tip of my tongue." How did you say that without laughing?

TH: It's not a funny line. It's beautiful.

VFG: You must be joking!

VFG: No—if I were joking, I would say "A priest, a rabbi and a minister go into a bar . . . "

HOUND OF THE BASKERVILLES, THE
1939   80m   bw   Mystery   ★★★★
Fox   (U.S.)

Richard Greene *(Sir Henry Baskerville)*, Basil Rathbone *(Sherlock Holmes)*, Wendy Barrie *(Beryl Stapleton)*, Nigel Bruce *(Dr. Watson)*, Lionel Atwill *(James Mortimer, M.D.)*, John Carradine *(Barryman)*, Barlowe Borland *(Frankland)*, Beryl Mercer *(Mrs. Jenifer Mortimer)*, Morton Lowry *(John Stapleton)*, Ralph Forbes *(Sir Hugo Baskerville)*

p, Gene Markey; d, Sidney Lanfield; w, Ernest Pascal (based on the story by Arthur Conan Doyle); ph, Peverell Marley; ed, Robert Simpson; art d, Richard Day, Hans Peters; cos, Gwen Wakeling

This was the first time that Rathbone and Bruce were cast as Holmes and Watson and their superlative performances resulted in the delightful series that followed this excellent mystery. A faithful adaptation of the Doyle novel, the film is set in the 1880s period of gaslit London with all its wet cobblestone streets, billowing fog, and eerie atmosphere. The young heir to the Baskerville estate (Greene) fears for his life and calls in the great Sherlock Holmes to help solve the mysterious curse that has killed every Baskerville master since 1650.

This version of THE HOUND OF THE BASKERVILLES was an enormous success immediately upon release, and it proved to be the best of the series. Rathbone was the perfect Holmes, his well-modulated voice, his sharply-honed features, his lanky figure all conforming to the public's image of the great detective as Sidney Paget first drew his imagined likeness in *Strand Magazine* in 1889 when Doyle created the character. He had earned the role and would keep it for life as Bruce would claim the amiable character of Dr. Watson, the two becoming a beloved screen team.

Lanfield's direction is solid and careful as he unfolds the sinister tale. Carradine, Lowry, and particularly Atwill are all superb in their supporting roles. THE HOUND OF THE BASKERVILLES was always Rathbone's favorite film, even though he considered it "a negative from which I merely continued to produce endless positives of the same photograph." Rathbone would go on to appear in 16 films as Sherlock Holmes and more than 200 radio shows dealing with the indefatigable sleuth between 1939 and 1946.

HOUR OF THE WOLF, THE
(VARGTIMMEN)
1968   88m   bw   Drama   ★★★
Svensk   (Sweden)   /X

Liv Ullmann *(Alma Borg)*, Max von Sydow *(Johan Borg)*, Erland Josephson *(Baron von Merkens)*, Gertrud Fridh *(Corinne von Merkens)*, Gudrun Brost *(Gamla Fru von Merkens)*, Bertil Anderberg *(Ernst von Merkens)*, Georg Rydeberg *(Arkivarie Lindhorst)*, Ulf Johansson *(Kurator Heerbrand)*, Naima Wifstrand *(Old Lady with Hat)*, Ingrid Thulin *(Veronica Vogler)*

d, Ingmar Bergman; w, Ingmar Bergman; ph, Sven Nykvist; ed, Ulla Ryghe; m, Lars-Johan Werle, Wolfgang Amadeus Mozart, Johann Sebastian Bach; art d, Marik Vos-Lundh; fx, Evald Andersson; cos, Mago

Fine acting exercise. This Bergman discourse on the nature of art and the artist's relation to society is shrouded in the trappings of gothic horror and stars Max von Sydow as Johan Borg, a painter haunted by bad dreams and apparitions while secluded on an island with his pregnant wife, Alma (Liv Ullmann). Both of them experience a series of haunting visions: Johan sees a beautiful boy, a ghost able to walk on walls, and an ancient woman who tears off her face; Alma is approached by a woman (who may or may not be an apparition) who instructs her to read her husband's diary. There she learns of Johan's love affair. Generally considered one of Bergman's lesser pictures, THE HOUR OF THE WOLF was originally to be shot before PERSONA, in 1965, as "The Cannibals."

HOUSE OF GAMES
1987   102m   c   Crime   ★★★★
Filmhaus   (U.S.)   R/15

Lindsay Crouse *(Dr. Margaret Ford)*, Joe Mantegna *(Mike)*, Mike Nussbaum *(Joey)*, Lilia Skala *(Dr. Littauer)*, J.T. Walsh *(Businessman)*, Willo Hausman *(Girl with Book)*, Karen Kohlhaas *(Prison Ward Patient)*, Steve Goldstein *(Billy Hahn)*, Jack Wallace *(Bartender, "House of Games")*, Ben Blakeman *(Bartender, "Charlie's Tavern")*

p, Michael Hausman; d, David Mamet; w, David Mamet; ph, Juan Ruiz-Anchia; ed, Trudy Ship; m, Alaric Jans; prod d, Michael Merritt; fx, Robert Willard; cos, Nan Cibula

The extraordinary first film from Pulitzer Prize-winning playwright David Mamet, HOUSE OF GAMES is a stylish cinematic puzzle. Dr. Margaret Ford (Lindsay Crouse), a psychologist and best-selling author of a book on obsessive behavior, ventures into the world of confidence games to try to help out a patient whose gambling has gotten him in over his head. Her excursion brings her in contact with Mike (Joe Mantegna), a con man who engineers a back-room hustle that almost leaves Margaret $6,000 poorer. Instead of being angry, she is attracted to this streetwise philosopher and his world and returns to get to know him and it better. In the process she becomes involved in an elaborate con game revolving around a suitcase full of cash supposedly borrowed from the mob. The plot grows increasingly convoluted until Margaret—and the audience—no longer knows who is conning whom—that is, until the shocking climax.

Mamet has created a suspenseful, psychologically complex film that constantly plays tricks on the viewer as it draws him into its milieu of insightful deceit. Crouse and Mantegna are outstanding, and the supporting performances are all first rate. In the tradition of Alfred Hitchcock, Mamet worked from his own storyboards, and he and cinematographer Juan Ruiz Anchia have created a visually stunning film that is the equal of his airtight screenplay.

HOUSE OF ROTHSCHILD, THE
1934   94m   c/bw   Biography   ★★★★
20th Century   (U.S.)

George Arliss *(Mayer Rothschild/Nathan Rothschild)*, Boris Karloff *(Count Ledrantz)*, Loretta Young *(Julie Rothschild)*, Robert Young *(Capt. Fitzroy)*, C. Aubrey Smith *(Duke of Wellington)*, A.S. Byron *(Baring)*, Helen Westley *(Gudula Rothschild)*, Reginald Owen *(Herries)*, Florence Arliss *(Hannah Rothschild)*, Alan Mowbray *(Metternich)*

p, Darryl F. Zanuck; d, Alfred Werker; w, Nunnally Johnson (based on the play by George Humbert Westley); ph, Peverell Marley; ed, Allen McNeil, Barbara McLean; m, Alfred Newman

AAN Best Picture

An outstanding historical account of the Rothschild financial dynasty during the Napoleonic wars, THE HOUSE OF ROTHSCHILD was the ambitious brainchild of Darryl F. Zanuck, who had left Warner Bros. to form Twentieth Century Productions, which would later merge with Fox.

George Arliss, who plays a dual role, is first seen as the patriarch of the German-Jewish ghetto family. On his deathbed, he urges his five sons to travel to the capitals of Europe and establish powerful banking firms. Led by their brother (Arliss's other role), the Rothschilds slowly build the most powerful banking conglomerate in Europe. The Rothschild banks secretly lend money to England, Austria, Italy, and Prussia to defeat Napoleon. Once Napoleon is in exile, however, Boris Karloff, the anti-Semitic Prussian ambassador to England, refuses Arliss's offer of money to rebuild France. Outraged, the banker creates financial havoc in the bond markets, but this only results in Karloff's launching violent and bloody pogroms. Fate intervenes when Napoleon escapes from exile and rises again to threaten Europe.

A potent, adult film, handsomely produced (the final sequence was shot in early three-strip Technicolor) and cast, and a memorable showcase for the effective "old school" acting of the unique Arliss.

HOUSE OF USHER

1960 79m c Horror   ★★★½
AIP (U.S.)   /18

Vincent Price (Roderick Usher), Mark Damon (Philip Winthrop), Myrna Fahey (Madeline Usher), Harry Ellerbe (Bristol), Bill Borzage, Mike Jordan, Nadajan, Ruth Oklander, George Paul, David Andar

p, Roger Corman; d, Roger Corman; w, Richard Matheson

A real coup for Roger Corman and AIP, HOUSE OF USHER was the first of their horror films that had a decent budget ($350,000), boasted a shooting schedule of more than 10 days (they were allowed 15), was shot in color and CinemaScope, and was "inspired" by Edgar Allen Poe. The gamble paid off and the film was a critical and commercial hit that unleashed scads of other films based on the works of Poe.

The wonderful Vincent Price stars as Roderick Usher, the creepy, white-haired owner of the mysterious house of Usher, who lives in seclusion in the creaking old house with his sister, Madeline (Myrna Fahey). When Madeline announces her engagement to Philip (Mark Damon), Roderick will have none of it and informs her betrothed that he and his sister are the last of the Ushers and they suffer from a bizarre madness that must not be transmitted to another generation. When Philip refuses to leave the spooky house despite this warning, strange accidents befall him, and he is nearly killed. Meanwhile, Madeline falls ill, and soon after, Roderick informs Philip that she has died of a heart attack and entombs her in the family chapel. The butler, however, informs Philip that his fiancee has suffered from periodic blackouts and that she may have been buried alive.

Moody, atmospheric, and effective, HOUSE OF USHER succeeds in making the house a "monster," which a desperate Corman had to make clear to skeptical executive producer Sam Arkoff when he questioned the film's lack of a menacing creature. Corman's savvy use of color, musty cobwebs, and creaking and groaning sound effects combine to make the *house* appear to be the cause of all the madness. Price is wonderful as the spooky owner, but the other three players are merely adequate. But still a superlative Corman/AIP effort and a great beginning to a varying but always interesting series of horror films.

HOUSE OF WAX

1953 90m c Horror   ★★★
Warner Bros. (U.S.)   GP/PG

Vincent Price (Prof. Henry Jarrod), Frank Lovejoy (Lt. Tom Brennan), Phyllis Kirk (Sue Allen), Carolyn Jones (Cathy Gray), Paul Picerni (Scott Andrews), Roy Roberts (Matthew Burke), Angela Clarke (Mrs. Andrews), Paul Cavanagh (Sidney Wallace), Dabbs Greer (Sgt. Jim Shane), Charles Bronson (Igor)

p, Bryan Foy; d, Andre de Toth; w, Crane Wilbur (based on a play by Charles Welden); ph, Bert Glennon, Peverell Marley; ed, Rudi Fehr; m, David Buttolph; art d, Stanley Fleischer

Paddleball anyone? This fine remake of the classic THE MYSTERY OF THE WAX MUSEUM was filmed in 3-D and employed "WarnerPhonic Sound," a forerunner to stereo that utilized a number of speakers.

Vincent Price plays Professor Henry Jarrod, a wax sculptor in New York at the turn of the century who presides over a wax museum that is floundering because of his pursuit of beauty rather than sensationalism. When Jarrod again refuses partner Burke's (Roy

Roberts)request to create more horrifying pieces, Burke sets fire to the museum, intent on collecting the insurance money. It is presumed that Jarrod died with his creations, but he returns, horribly scarred, and strangles Burke. Years later, Jarrod, feigning a wheelchair-confining back injury, opens a new wax museum with even more lifelike displays. Because his hands have been horribly burned, he employs two assistants to do the sculpting under his supervision (one of whom is played by Charles Bronson, then billed as Buchinsky). In reality, however, Jarrod's mad sculpting is accomplished by pouring wax over people he has murdered.

HOUSE OF WAX was stunningly directed by Andre de Toth who used the new 3-D process to its fullest potential without bogging down the narrative with too many "gee-look-what-I-can-do" tricks. Ironically, this man who saw the potential of 3-D and who directed one of the most effective movies ever shot in that process had only one eye, which hampered his depth perception. Price is magnificent as usual and manages to steal the role of Professor Jarrod from its creator, Lionel Atwill. Although it is now extremely difficult to see in its original format, HOUSE OF WAX is still well worth viewing in flat prints or on video. The line that kills 'em in revival houses: "You never see things like this in Provincetown." Oh, but you do.

HOUSE ON 92ND STREET, THE

1945 88m bw Spy   ★★★★
Fox (U.S.)   /U

William Eythe (Bill Dietrich), Lloyd Nolan (Inspector George A. Briggs), Signe Hasso (Elsa Gebhardt), Gene Lockhart (Charles Ogden Roper), Leo G. Carroll (Col. Hammersohn), Lydia St. Clair (Johanna Schmedt), Reed Hadley (Narrator), William Post Jr. (Walker), Harry Bellaver (Max Coburg), Bruno Wick (Adolphe Lange)

p, Louis de Rochemont; d, Henry Hathaway; w, Barre Lyndon, Charles G. Booth, John Monks Jr. (based on the story by Booth); ph, Norbert Brodine; ed, Harmon Jones; m, David Buttolph; art d, Lyle Wheeler, Lewis Creber; fx, Fred Sersen; cos, Bonnie Cashin

AA Best Original Screenplay: Charles G Booth

Suspense-packed espionage yarn, approached from a documentary angle, has Nolan as a no-nonsense federal investigator who is sought out by German-American Eythe, a brilliant student. He has been contacted by Nazi spies, he tells Nolan, and asked to work with them. Nolan encourages Eythe to accept the offer and work as a double agent, reporting all Nazi activities to the FBI. Slowly, Eythe ingratiates himself with several Nazi agents and is assigned, as a technician, to transmit messages to Germany via short-wave radio. He establishes a remote radio hideout and begins sending messages, really to FBI headquarters, and its operators pass on fake information to Germany. Through this system Eythe is able to learn that Nazi agents are after data concerning the development of the atomic bomb (referred to here as "Process 97"), identifying Lockhart, one of the scientists working on the apparatus, as a Nazi agent.

Hathaway's direction is quick and uses the newsreel style made famous by producer de Rochemont, who produced the MARCH OF TIME series. The film was shot on location in New York and other points where actual spy cases from FBI files really occurred. The semi-documentary style gave sharp authenticity to the film as did the use of nonprofessional actors (many of whom were FBI agents and technical personnel). The stentorian narration provided by Hadley, who made a handsome living in films narrating such stories, further convinced viewers that they were watching the real thing. In some instances they were; Hathaway incorporated newsreel shots of real German spies being rounded up at the beginning of WWII, along with telephotos of the German consulate in New York and its real life spies coming and going. The tremendous atmospherics gave birth to a series of films adopting the same semi-documentary approach, notably T-MEN, THE NAKED CITY, and WALK A CROOKED MILE. Hasso is incomparable as the Nazi ringleader in this, her most impressive film.

HOUSE PARTY

1990 100m c Comedy   ★★★
(U.S.)   R/15

Christopher Reid *(Kid)*, Robin Harris *(Pop)*, Christopher Martin *(Play)*, Martin Lawrence *(Bilal)*, Tisha Campbell *(Sidney)*, A.J. Johnson *(Sharane)*, Paul Anthony *(Stab)*, Bowlegged Lou *(Pee-Wee)*, B. Fine *(Zilla)*, Edith Fields *(Principal)*

p, Warrington Hudlin; d, Reginald Hudlin; w, Reginald Hudlin; ph, Peter Deming; ed, Earl Watson; m, Marcus Miller; prod d, Bryan Jones; art d, Susan Richardson; chor, A.J. Johnson, Kid 'N' Play, Tisha Campbell; cos, Harold Evans

Crude and cartoony but hypnotic in its infectious energy, an auspicious debut from brothers Reginald and Warrington Hudlin. With Reggie directing and Warrington producing, the Hudlins have collaborated to expand Reggie's Harvard thesis film from a short into a feature, and the result is HOUSE PARTY, a low-budget comedy that is a seriously funny look at a night in the lives of some black teenagers.

The film is more of a portrait than a story. Kid (Christopher Reid, one half of the rap duo Kid 'N' Play) is dying to go to a party hosted by his buddy Play (Christopher Martin, the other half). Unfortunately, Kid has gotten into some trouble with the local bullies (played by three members of the hiphop band Full Force) at school and, after a note from the principal's office arrives at home, he's grounded by his strict father (the late, great Robin Harris). Determined to go to Play's party, especially since two of the prettiest girls in school are going to be there, Kid risks life and limb to sneak out of the house while Pop dozes in front of the television. He makes it to the party and gets to know the girls, one of whom has a crush on him, while dancing up a storm. The evening, however, is not without its complications.

Deceptively simple on the surface, HOUSE PARTY is a realistic depiction of black teenagers. Though its main purpose is obviously to provoke laughter, it also provokes thought by dealing honestly with a variety of subjects, including safe sex, teen drinking, class prejudice, and, in a roundabout way, racism. Reginald Hudlin has given his wide assortment of characters a great deal of intelligence, much more than usual for this kind of film, allowing each room to breathe and establish a personality. Stars Kid 'N' Play make a strong film debut, creating a fun, light image for themselves without sacrificing the edge of their music; their rap-duel scene is fast and funky. Kid, with his foot-high fade haircut (one character refers to him as "Eraserhead") and freckle-faced grin, handles the duties of "leading man" extremely well, giving a supremely likable performance.

Aside from its likable performances and message, HOUSE PARTY is a film that *moves* in every way possible. From the opening dream sequence to the final sight gag, the film sways to a funky contagious rhythm that will have most viewers rocking in their seats. The dance sequences are directed with such lively timing and slick camera movements that one can't help but bounce along. Reginald Hudlin is a terrific filmmaker who has a wonderfully assured feel for the camera. With HOUSE PARTY, Hudlin has created one of the flat-out funniest films in a long time, marred only by the homophobic and cruel jailhouse rap.

HOUSEKEEPING

1987 116m c Drama   ★★★½
Columbia (U.S.)   PG

Christine Lahti *(Sylvie)*, Sara Walker *(Ruth)*, Andrea Burchill *(Lucille)*, Anne Pitoniak *(Lily)*, Barbara Reese *(Nona)*, Bill Smillie *(Sheriff)*, Wayne Robson *(Mr. French)*, Margot Pinvidic *(Helen)*

p, Robert F. Colesberry; d, Bill Forsyth; w, Bill Forsyth (based on the novel by Marilynne Robinson); ph, Michael Coulter; ed, Michael Ellis; m, Michael Gibbs; prod d, Adrienne Atkinson; cos, Mary-Jane Reyner

Offbeat but absorbing. Set in the 1950s and based on a Marilynne Robinson novel, this is the first American film from Scottish director Bill Forsyth.

After the suicide of their mother, two young girls, Ruth (Sara Walker) and Lucille (Andrea Burchill), are brought up by their grandmother in a small Idaho town. When she dies, a pair of elderly great-aunts persuade Ruth and Lucille's itinerant aunt, Sylvie (Christine Lahti), to look after her two nieces, who are now approaching adolescence. Sylvie, who has spent most of her life riding the rails and

sleeping on benches, sets up housekeeping in her own fashion and goes about child-rearing in an unorthodox manner. Lucille, more concerned with appearances than her sister, begins to be embarrassed by Sylvie's refusal to abide by society's conventions.

HOUSEKEEPING is a reversal of the formula that has brought director Forsyth, a master of character development and storytelling, so much success. Instead of weaving dramatic moments into capricious comedy, he leavens this heartwarming drama with laughter. Playing against type and avoiding what could have been a paint-by-numbers portrayal, Lahti plays Sylvie as loving and ingenuous, but with a half-glimpsed sense of tragedy and disappointment. Walker and Burchill also turn in fine performances.

HOW GREEN WAS MY VALLEY

1941 118m bw Drama   ★★★★★
Fox (U.S.)   /U

Walter Pidgeon *(Mr. Gruffydd)*, Maureen O'Hara *(Angharad)*, Donald Crisp *(Mr. Morgan)*, Anna Lee *(Bronwyn)*, Roddy McDowall *(Huw Morgan)*, John Loder *(Ianto Morgan)*, Sara Allgood *(Mrs. Morgan)*, Barry Fitzgerald *(Cyfartha)*, Patric Knowles *(Ivor Morgan)*, Morton Lowry *(Mr. Jonas)*

p, Darryl F. Zanuck; d, John Ford; w, Philip Dunne (based on the novel by Richard Llewellyn); ph, Arthur Miller; ed, James B. Clark; m, Alfred Newman; art d, Richard Day, Nathan Juran; cos, Gwen Wakeling

AA Best Picture; AA Best Supporting Actor: Donald Crisp; *AAN Best Supporting Actress:* Sara Allgood; *AA Best Director:* John Ford; *AAN Best Screenplay:* Philip Dunne; *AA Best Cinematography:* Arthur Miller; *AAN Best Editing:* James B. Clark; *AAN Best Score:* Alfred Newman; *AA Best Art Direction:* Richard Day, Nathan Juran, Thomas Little; *AAN Best Sound:* E.H. Hansen.

Emotionally majestic and spiritually moving , this is one of John Ford's undisputed masterpieces, a film that neither fades nor fails after repeated viewings.

The mining area in South Wales and its hard-working miners and their families are seen through the eyes of Huw (Roddy McDowall), the youngest of six children in a family headed by a stern father (Donald Crisp) and loving mother (Sara Allgood). Set at the turn of the century and told in flashback, the film shows an unspoiled valley, full of love and warmth, wherein the trials and hardships of the community are told through a series of moving vignettes.

Everything about this film is touching; master director John Ford builds one simple scene upon another with very little plot, using incidents in the life of one family to tell the general tale, demonstrating changes and recording milestones. Beautifully assisted by cameraman Arthur Miller, Ford received strong support from studio chief Darryl Zanuck, who personally produced the film. The superlative cast is a Who's Who of Hollywood's Irish community, with a noble assist from Welsh singers.

HOW I WON THE WAR

1967 109m c Comedy/War   ★★★
UA (U.K.)   /X

Michael Crawford *(Lt. Ernest Goodbody)*, John Lennon *(Gripweed)*, Roy Kinnear *(Clapper)*, Lee Montague *(Sgt. Transom)*, Jack MacGowran *(Juniper)*, Michael Hordern *(Grapple)*, Jack Hedley *(Melancholy Musketeer)*, Karl Michael Vogler *(Odlebog)*, Ronald Lacey *(Spool)*, James Cossins *(Drogue)*

p, Richard Lester; d, Richard Lester; w, Charles Wood (based on the novel by Patrick Ryan); ph, David Watkin; ed, John Victor Smith; m, Ken Thorne; art d, Philip Harrison, John Stoll; fx, Eddie Fowlie; cos, Dinah Greet

Richard Lester, director of the hit Beatles movies A HARD DAY'S NIGHT and HELP!, intended this black comedy as a stinging condemnation of war, but occasionally he fails even as he succeeds, eliciting such plentiful laughs that he blunts the impact of his message.

Revolving around the rose-colored reminiscences of a middle-aged British WWII veteran whose wartime career was actually a disaster, HOW I WON THE WAR follows the inept Lt. Goodbody (Michael Crawford) as he leads his men from North Africa to France. Among his unfortunate misfit charges are the overweight Clapper (Roy Kinnear), who is obsessed with his wife's infidelity; Juniper (Jack MacGowran), a music-hall comic; and Gripweed (then-Beatle John Lennon, whose billing is considerably more prominent than his presence in the film). Transom (Lee Montague), the only competent military man in the bunch, tries in vain to correct his superior's command blunders, but so ill-prepared to lead is Goodbody that he eventually causes the deaths of all of his men save one, the Melancholy Musketeer (Jack Hedley).

Based on a novel by Patrick Ryan, Lester's film offers both hilarious moments of satire (of war and war movies) and grim, bloody depictions of the awful reality of combat. This seemingly incongruous mixture will work for some viewers, and, though the seriousness of Lester's intent may not be appreciated by everyone, most should at least find something here to make them laugh.

HOW THE WEST WAS WON

1963   165m   c   Western   ★★★½
MGM   (U.S.)   /PG

Spencer Tracy (Narrator), Carroll Baker (Eve Prescott), Lee J. Cobb (Lou Ramsey), Henry Fonda (Jethro Stuart), Karl Malden (Zebulon Prescott), Gregory Peck (Cleve Van Valen), George Peppard (Zeb Rawlings), Robert Preston (Roger Morgan), Debbie Reynolds (Lilith Prescott), James Stewart (Linus Rawlings)

p, Bernard Smith; d, Henry Hathaway, John Ford, George Marshall, Richard Thorpe; w, James R. Webb (based on articles in Life magazine); ph, Joseph La Shelle, Charles Lang, William Daniels, Milton Krasner, Harold Wellman; ed, Harold F. Kress; m, Alfred Newman, Ken Darby; art d, George W. Davis, William Ferrari, Addison Hehr; fx, A. Arnold Gillespie, Robert R. Hoag; cos, Walter Plunkett

AAN Best Picture; AA Best Original Story and Screenplay: James R. Webb; AAN Best Cinematography: William H. Daniels, Milton Krasner, Charles Lang, Jr., Joseph LaShelle; AA Best Editing: Harold F. Kress; AAN Best Score: Alfred Newman, Ken Darby; AAN Best Art Direction: George W. Davis, William Ferrari, Addison Hehr, Henry Grace, Don Greenwood, Jr., Jack Mills; AAN Best Costume Design: Walter Plunkett; AA Best Sound: Franklin E. Milton

Dense and episodic western omelet, tries to condense the evolution of the American west by channeling it through one family's experiences, over three generations. The film is split between four directors with Hathaway's sequences clearly the most cohesive and colorful. This is an all-star guessing-game cast that adults can have fun with, and there's enough history lesson to validate it for children. The acting alternates between star turn, cute, and storybook portmanteau. It's a big-budget fastfood history lesson with Debbie Reynolds as brash schoolmarm. Spencer Tracy narrates, and was probably grateful for the relative safety.

HOW TO GET AHEAD IN ADVERTISING

1989   95m   c   Comedy   ★★★½
HandMade   (U.K.)   R/15

Richard E. Grant (Dennis Bagley), Rachel Ward (Julia Bagley), Richard Wilson (Bristol), Jacqueline Tong (Penny Wheelstock), John Shrapnel (Psychiatrist), Susan Wooldridge (Monica), Mick Ford (Richard), Jacqueline Pearce (Maud), Roddy Maude-Roxby (Dr. Gatty), Pauline Melville (Mrs. Wallace)

p, David Wimbury, Ray Cooper; d, Bruce Robinson; w, Bruce Robinson; ph, Peter Hannan; ed, Alan Strachan; m, David Dundas, Rick Wentworth; prod d, Michael Pickwoad; art d, Henry Harris; chor, David Toguri; cos, Andrea Galer

More satire than comedy, and aimed at a sophisticated audience that can appreciate its barbs at the business of "creating need," HOW TO GET AHEAD IN ADVERTISING is a movie of extremes, both in plot and characterizations.

Dennis Bagley (Richard E. Grant), a veteran advertising executive who has all the perks of success—an attractive wife (Rachel Ward), a country home, and an expensive car—undergoes a drastic change of heart when a creative block prevents him from coming up with an ad campaign for pimple cream. Quitting his job and embarking on an "anti-advertising" campaign, Dennis is soon plagued by a huge boil on

the side of his neck that takes on a human visage and becomes Dennis's alter ego. Eventually, the boil, an unprincipled proponent of a "buyer beware" philosophy, even takes possession of Dennis's being.

In asking the audience to decide which is the real Dennis Bagley, writer-director Bruce Robinson is not only concerned with the moral implications of advertising but with those of capitalism in general. Clearly, he has stacked his deck, allowing Grant (who starred in Robinson's wonderful WITHNAIL AND I) to push his character to the outer limits. More subtlety or quiet introspection might have lent greater credibility to the role, though Grant and Robinson unquestionably have made their point.

HOW TO MURDER YOUR WIFE

1965   118m   c   Comedy   ★★★½
UA   (U.S.)   /PG

Jack Lemmon (Stanley Ford), Virna Lisi (Mrs. Ford), Terry-Thomas (Charles), Eddie Mayehoff (Harold Lampson), Claire Trevor (Edna), Sidney Blackmer (Judge Blackstone), Max Showalter (Tobey Rawlins), Jack Albertson (Dr. Bentley), Alan Hewitt (District Attorney), Mary Wickes (Harold's Secretary)

p, George Axelrod; d, Richard Quine; w, George Axelrod; ph, Harry Stradling; ed, David Wages; m, Neal Hefti; prod d, Richard Sylbert; chor, Robert Sidney; cos, Moss Mabry

Daft sexist comedy stars Lemmon as a successful cartoonist who loathes the idea of marriage. His widely syndicated cartoon strip about secret agent "Bash Brannigan" has earned him a fortune and a lifestyle the envy of his devout bachelor. But Bash has become a kind of alter ego, and Lemmon has begun to act out aspects of his comic character's life. Into Lemmon's well-organized life comes Italian blonde bombshell Lisi, as sexy and sensuous a woman ever to pop out of a stag party cake. In fact, that's when Lemmon sees and falls in love with her. He's drunk, she snakes out of the cake, and he wakes up the next morning with Lisi beside him. She wears a wedding ring and he realizes to his horror that he's gotten married to someone he doesn't even know.

This dated comedy is saved by Lemmon's comedic genius which eschews macho. There is solid support from Mayehoff and Trevor, and Lisi is gorgeous to behold.

HOW TO SUCCEED IN BUSINESS WITHOUT REALLY TRYING

1967   121m   c   Musical/Comedy   ★★★★
Mirisch   (U.S.)   /U

Robert Morse (J. Pierpont Finch), Michele Lee (Rosemary Pilkington), Rudy Vallee (J.B. Biggley), Anthony Teague (Bud Frump), Maureen Arthur (Hedy LaRue), Murray Matheson (Benjamin Ovington), Kay Reynolds (Smitty), Sammy Smith (Mr. Twimble/Wally Womper), John Myhers (Bratt), Jeff DeBenning (Gatch)

p, David Swift; d, David Swift; w, David Swift (based on the musical book by Abe Burrows, Willie Gilbert, and Jack Weinstock, and the novel by Shepherd Mead); ph, Burnett Guffey; ed, Ralph E. Winters, Allan Jacobs; m, Nelson Riddle; art d, Robert Boyle; chor, Dale Moreda; cos, Micheline

David Swift produced, directed, adapted, and even played a small role in this scathing musical satire. The film is based on Shepherd Mead's novel which had been brought to the stage by Loesser and Burrows, who co-wrote the stage book with Gilbert and Weinstock.

Morse is an elfin, yet aggressive, window washer who buys a copy of Mead's book on his way to work and decides to put it to work immediately. He walks into the office of World Wide Wickets, a huge conglomerate, and enchants Lee, a pretty secretary, who introduces him to the chief of personnel. That achieved, he convinces the man that he is a great pal of Vallee, who heads the company. This bit of trickery gets him as far as the mailroom. It isn't long before he finagles, cajoles, and charms his way into a junior executive position and endears himself to all the women in the company, but incurs the enmity of Teague, Vallee's insidious nephew. Soon after, Morse is made chief of an advertising department where many heads have rolled. Teague knows that Vallee absolutely despises television giveaway shows, so he tells Morse the opposite, thinking that when Morse presents the idea to Vallee, he will be rewarded with a pink slip.

The film is cartoonlike, its characters caricatures, as befits the story. The lion's share of the acting kudos goes to Morse, in a role that is perfect for him, and Lee, a refreshing, attractive actress who went on to national fame. But Vallee's fussy boss is definitely memorable. Veteran television panelist Robert Q. Lewis plays a small role as an executive and proves to be a much better actor than anyone realized. Myhers does his usual hammy job, but it isn't out of place here. Producer-director-writer-actor Swift was the man responsible for one of television's most beloved early shows, "Mr. Peepers." Good fun.

HOWARDS END

1992 140m c Drama/Historical   ★★★½
Merchant Ivory/Nippon Herald Films/Channel Four (U.K.)   PG

Anthony Hopkins *(Henry Wilcox)*, Emma Thompson *(Margaret Schlegel)*, Vanessa Redgrave *(Ruth Wilcox)*, Helena Bonham Carter *(Helen Schlegel)*, Sam West *(Leonard Bast)*, Prunella Scales *(Aunt Juley)*, Joseph Bennett *(Paul Wilcox)*, Adrian Ross-Magenty *(Tibby Schlegel)*, Jo Kendall *(Annie)*, James Wilby *(Charles Wilcox)*

p, Ismail Merchant; d, James Ivory; w, Ruth Prawer Jhabvala (from the novel by E.M. Forster); ph, Tony Pierce-Roberts; ed, Andrew Marcus; m, Richard Robbins; prod d, Luciana Arrighi; art d, John Ralph; cos, Jenny Beavan, John Bright

AAN Best Picture; AA Best Actress: Emma Thompson; AAN Best Supporting Actress: Vanessa Redgrave; AAN Best Director: James Ivory; AA Best Adapted Screenplay: Ruth Prawer Jhabvala; AAN Best Cinematography: Tony Pierce-Roberts; AAN Best Score: Richard Robbins; AA Best Art Direction: Luciana Arrighi, Ian Whittaker; AAN Best Costume Design: Jenny Beavan, John Bright

An elegant, if bland reworking of Forster's classic 1910 novel, from the acclaimed filmmaking team of James Ivory (director), Ismail Merchant (producer) and Ruth Prawer Jhabvala (screenwriter).

HOWARDS END takes its name from a country house belonging to Ruth Wilcox (Vanessa Redgrave). Though married to Henry Wilcox (Anthony Hopkins), a pillar of wealth and tradition, Ruth is a slightly other-worldly figure who feels a mystic bond with the house where she was born. In the later stages of a terminal illness, Ruth strikes up a friendship with Margaret Schlegel (Emma Thompson), a cultured, free-thinking woman who lives with her like-minded sister, Helen (Helena Bonham Carter).

Before she dies, Ruth makes out an informal will leaving Howards End to Margaret, but her note is destroyed by the Wilcoxes. The two families nevertheless remain involved, as the widowed Henry begins to take a (well-concealed) romantic interest in Margaret. HOWARDS END goes on to flesh out the relations between the materialistic Wilcoxes and the emancipated Schlegels—relations which build to a tragic climax in the person of Leonard Bast (Sam West), a sensitive clerk who is befriended by Margaret and Helen but ulimately undone by Henry.

Forster's novel has been adapted with such emphasis on good taste that other, more crucial elements have been neglected. The filmmakers have allowed themselves an overlong 140 minutes in order to preserve as much of the plot as possible, but they have bypassed many of the novel's key ideas and ironies. And though the film *looks* marvelous, it lacks the zest—the conflict and the passion—that informed the team's earlier hit, A ROOM WITH A VIEW. There are times when it feels as though the major literary influence at work is not E.M. Forster, but *House and Garden* magazine.

HOWLING, THE

1981 91m c Horror   ★★★½
Avco Embassy (U.S.)   R/18

Dee Wallace Stone *(Karen White)*, Patrick Macnee *(Dr. George Waggner)*, Dennis Dugan *(Chris)*, Christopher Stone *(R. William "Bill" Neill)*, Belinda Balaski *(Terry Fisher)*, Kevin McCarthy *(Fred Francis)*, John Carradine *(Erle Kenton)*, Slim Pickens *(Sam Newfield)*, Elisabeth Brooks *(Marsha)*, Robert Picardo *(Eddie)*

p, Michael Finnell, Jack Conrad; d, Joe Dante; w, John Sayles, Terence H. Winkless (based on the novel by Gary Brandner); ph, John Hora; ed, Mark Goldblatt, Joe Dante; m, Pino Donaggio; art d, Robert Burns; fx, Rob Bottin, Roger George

A wonderful combination of horror, laughs, and state-of-the-art special effects from director and Roger Corman alumnus Joe Dante (PIRANHA, GREMLINS, EXPLORERS), screenwriter (now screenwriter-director) John Sayles (PIRANHA, RETURN OF THE SECAUCUS SEVEN, BROTHER FROM ANOTHER PLANET), and makeup artist Rob Bottin.

Wallace plays a television anchorwoman who, after being severely traumatized while investigating a story, decides to venture to Macnee's ultra-exclusive California transcendental meditation spa with husband Stone. Unfortunately, the members of Macnee's cult are all werewolves. The transformation scenes are incredible—the highlight being when sexy siren Brooks seduces Stone and they make love under the moonlight while turning into werewolves. Dante fills the film with hysterical cameos from Corman (at a phone booth) and Sayles (a morgue attendant), among others, and demonstrates a subtle wit and a flair for horror. A must-see for horror fans, with more than one viewing recommended. Unfortunately, a slew of really awful sequels followed.

HUCKSTERS, THE

1947 115m bw Drama   ★★★½
MGM (U.S.)   /A

Clark Gable *(Victor Albee Norman)*, Deborah Kerr *(Kay Dorrance)*, Sydney Greenstreet *(Evan Llewellyn Evans)*, Adolphe Menjou *(Mr. Kimberly)*, Ava Gardner *(Jean Ogilvie)*, Keenan Wynn *(Buddy Hare)*, Edward Arnold *(Dave Lash)*, Aubrey Mather *(Valet)*, Richard Gaines *(Cooke)*, Frank Albertson *(Max Herman)*

p, Arthur Hornblow Jr.; d, Jack Conway; w, Luther Davis, Edward Chodorov, George Wells (based on the novel by Frederic Wakeman); ph, Harold Rosson; ed, Frank Sullivan; m, Lennie Hayton; art d, Cedric Gibbons, Urie McCleary; fx, Warren Newcombe, A. Arnold Gillespie

Madison Avenue ad agencies, radio commercials, and bigshot businessmen all got a lashing in this glossy drama. Gable plays a predictable rabble-rouser, Kerr the genteel society girl, Gardner the showbiz siren. It's all fairly predictable, a notch above MGM formula stuff, stolen by the expansive Greenstreet's egomania. Gable at first was not interested in doing this film but MGM toned down the hard-hitting best-seller by Wakeman and softened Gable's character to the point where he maintained some scruples at the finish. He approved of both his leading ladies and was particularly fond of Gardner. Kerr had been in films for about six years; this was touted as her first American film by MGM. Although effective in her role, few thought she would ever reach the superstar status that would come with later films such as FROM HERE TO ETERNITY. MGM mogul Louis B. Mayer was convinced Kerr would make it to the top and it was he who suggested a line the studio used in its advertisements for THE HUCKSTERS when listing her name: "Deborah Kerr (rhymes with 'star')."

HUD

1963 112m bw Western   ★★★½
Paramount (U.S.)   /A

Paul Newman *(Hud Bannon)*, Melvyn Douglas *(Homer Bannon)*, Patricia Neal *(Alma Brown)*, Brandon de Wilde *(Lon Bannon)*, Whit Bissell *(Burris)*, John Ashley *(Hermy)*, Crahan Denton *(Jesse)*, Val Avery *(Jose)*, Sheldon Allman *(Thompson)*, Pitt Herbert *(Larker)*

p, Martin Ritt, Irving Ravetch; d, Martin Ritt; w, Irving Ravetch, Harriet Frank Jr. (based on the novel *Horseman, Pass By* by Larry McMurtry); ph, James Wong Howe; ed, Frank Bracht; m, Elmer Bernstein; art d, Hal Pereira, Tambi Larsen; fx, Paul K. Lerpae; cos, Edith Head

AAN Best Actor: Paul Newman; AA Best Actress: Patricia Neal; AA Best Supporting Actor: Melvyn Douglas; AAN Best Director: Martin Ritt; AAN Best Adapted Screenplay: Irving Ravetch, Harriet Frank, Jr.; AA Best Cinematography: James Wong Howe; AAN Best Art Direction: Hal Pereira, Tambi Larsen, Sam Comer, Robert Benton

A blistering adult western which broke ground in its depiction of an unglamorous West and in the decidedly anti-heroic nature of its lead.

The charismatic Newman is the title character, an immoral Texas heel—insensitive, crude, avaricious, and irresponsible. He has a stormy relationship with his father, Douglas, an extremely decent but rigid old man who long ago rejected his son. Somewhere in between them is the innocent de Wilde, whose attraction to Newman is almost as strong as that of salty housekeeper Neal. Newman does as little as possible around the ranch his father owns; ignoring the proud past, he is concerned only with having a good ol' time.

HUD belongs to a group of "anti-westerns" which includes LONELY ARE THE BRAVE, THE MISFITS, THE LUSTY MEN and JUNIOR BONNER. It's almost impossible to sympathize with Newman's character, presented cynically by director Ritt in an approach typical of many 60s filmmakers. Newman's performance, though, is unquestionably the best thing about this brutal portrait of humanity.

HUDSUCKER PROXY, THE

1994 115m c Comedy/Drama ★★★
Silver Pictures/Working Title (U.S.) PG

Tim Robbins (Norville Barnes), Jennifer Jason Leigh (Amy Archer), Paul Newman (Sidney J. Mussburger), Charles Durning (Waring Hudsucker), John Mahoney (Chief), Jim True (Buzz), William Cobbs (Moses), Bruce Campbell (Smitty), Harry Bugin (Aloysius), John Seitz (Benny)

p, Ethan Coen; d, Joel Coen; w, Ethan Coen, Joel Coen, Sam Raimi; ph, Roger Deakins; ed, Thom Noble; m, Carter Burwell; prod d, Dennis Gassner; art d, Leslie McDonald; fx, Michael McAlister, Peter M. Chesney; cos, Richard Hornung

A lavish parody of/homage to Hollywood big business comedies, THE HUDSUCKER PROXY is gorgeous but lifeless, a very small joke writ very large by the talented but perversely insular Coen brothers.

Guileless but ambitious hick Norville Barnes (Tim Robbins) comes to the big city to make his fortune, and gets a job in the mailroom of Hudsucker Industries. When CEO Waring Hudsucker (Charles Durning) commits suicide, the Board of Directors—led by ruthless Sidney J. Mussberger (Paul Newman)—decides to make a killing by installing an idiot in his place, then taking advantage of lowered stock price. Barnes is the unwitting idiot, Amy Archer (Jennifer Jason Leigh) the fast-talking, crackerjack columnist who lies her way into his life, hoping to get the big scoop, but falls in love instead. When Barnes' tenure proves a surprise success, Mussberger will stop at nothing to get rid of him.

Beautifully designed and costumed, THE HUDSUCKER PROXY is a curiously arid movie, clever without being witty. One could blame the performances, which are almost all too broad, but the real trouble lies elsewhere: the Coens are often accused of heartlessness, and HUDSUCKER is the proof. It is, however, an impressive technical achievement—the period New York sets are to die for—and its version of the invention of the hula-hoop is a comic highlight.

HUNCHBACK OF NOTRE DAME, THE

1939 115m bw Horror ★★★★★
RKO (U.S.)

Charles Laughton (The Hunchback), Cedric Hardwicke (Frollo), Thomas Mitchell (Clopin), Maureen O'Hara (Esmeralda), Edmond O'Brien (Gringoire), Alan Marshal (Proebus), Walter Hampden (Claude), Harry Davenport (Louis XI), Katherine Alexander (Mme. De Lys), George Zucco (Procurator)

p, Pandro S. Berman; d, William Dieterle; w, Sonya Levien, Bruno Frank (based on the novel by Victor Hugo); ph, Joseph August; ed, William Hamilton, Robert Wise; m, Alfred Newman; art d, Van Nest Polglase; fx, Vernon L. Walker

AAN Best Score: Alfred Newman; AAN Best Sound: John Aalberg (Sound)

With its lavish production and superb cast, a brilliant performance by Charles Laughton, and moody, atmospheric direction from German expatriate William Dieterle, this is easily the best film version of Victor Hugo's classic novel.

Laughton is the pathetic, lonely, misshapen bellringer of Notre Dame who falls in love with the beautiful gypsy Esmeralda (Maureen O'Hara). In addition to gorgeous sets by Van Nest Polglase and breathtaking photography by Joseph H. August, the film benefits from a script that is a vast improvement over the 1923 version. Bringing Hugo's social and political concerns to the forefront, screenwriters Sonya Levien and Bruno Frank make the corrupt machinations of the church almost as important as Quasimodo's tragic love. Laughton, whom some

have accused of overplaying the role's pathos, is magnificent here in one of his greatest roles. His makeup, created by George and R. Gordon Bau, is at least the equal of Lon Chaney's, with modern foam latex technology allowing for a subtler and, therefore, more jarring visage.

RKO spent more than $2 million on this production—one of the most expensive films ever made by the studio—and was rewarded with both critical and financial success. This was the US film debut of the breathtaking O'Hara and a fine film debut for Edmond O'Brien. Superior, gripping filmmaking, well worth revisiting for Dieterle's marvelous command of detail.

HUNCHBACK OF NOTRE DAME, THE

1996 95m c Animated/Romance/Musical ★★★
Walt Disney Pictures (U.S.) G/U

VOICES OF: Tom Hulce (Quasimodo), Demi Moore (Esmeralda), Tony Jay (Frollo), Kevin Kline (Phoebus), Paul Kandel (Clopin), Jason Alexander (Hugo), Charles Kimbrough (Victor), Mary Wickes (Laverne), David Ogden Stiers (Archdeacon), Mary Kay Bergman (Quasimodo's Mother)

p, Don Hahn; d, Gary Trousdale, Kirk Wise; w, Tab Murphy, Irene Mecchi, Bob Tzudiker, Noni White, Jonathan Roberts (from a story by Tab Murphy, based on the novel Notre Dame de Paris by Victor Hugo); ed, Ellen Keneshea; m, Alan Menken; art d, David Goetz; fx, Christopher Jenkins; anim, James Baxter, Tony Fucile, Kathy Zielinski, Russ Edmonds, Danny Galieote, David Pruiksma, Will Finn, Ron Husband, Dave Burgess, Gregory Griffith, Mike "Moe" Merell

AAN Best Musical or Comedy Score: Alan Menken (music, orchestral score), Stephen Schwartz (lyrics)

Considering that Disney couldn't help but trash Victor Hugo's novel in the process of reforming it for tender young sensibilities, this animated adaptation of his Notre Dame de Paris is pricklier and more disturbing than we had any right to expect. The story is still driven by cruelty, intolerance, and lust, and while Quasimodo (voiced by Tom Hulce) has been given a makeover by Uncle Walt's art department, he's still a drooling grotesque with a big hairy hump. His best friends are three adorably peppy stone gargoyles whose irreverent cheer can't entirely obscure the fact that they have no lower bodies and must hop around on their stumps. Then there's that uplifting message: syrupy sentiments about inner beauty notwithstanding, comely (and buxom) gypsy Esmeralda (voiced by Demi Moore) and hunky Phoebus, captain of the guards (voiced by Kevin Kline), go off together, while ugly but supremely virtuous Quasimodo creeps back to his drafty bell tower and his concrete friends. Kids won't fail to get the point. As for the rest, the songs are undistinguished and the background animation is breathtaking. The most arresting set piece illustrates the temptation of the pious hypocrite Frollo (voiced by Tony Jay) with a guilt-fueled fantasia of shimmying flames and red-cloaked inquisitors. Smokin'!

HUNT, THE
(LA CAZA)

1966 93m bw Drama ★★★★
Elias Querejeta (Spain)

Ismael Merlo (Jose), Alfredo Mayo (Paco), Jose Maria Prada (Luis), Emilio Gutierrez Caba (Enrique), Fernando Sanchez Polack (Juan), Violetta Garcia (Nina), Maria Sanchez Arosa

p, Elias Querejeta; d, Carlos Saura; w, Carlos Saura, Angelino Fons (based on a story by Saura); ph, Luis Cuadrado; ed, Pablo del Amo; m, Luis de Pablo; art d, Carlos Ochoa

Brutal, excellent moral tale, dealing with four rabbit hunters. Three Spanish Civil War veterans return to an old battleground that is now filled with rabbits. Merlo, the outing organizer, hopes to borrow some money from his war buddy, Mayo, now a rich businessman. The tensions between the two build with frightening force, and old angers and rivalries are taken out on the rabbits with frightening brutality. Mayo is killed by an accidental shot from Merlo's gun. Prada, believing the shot intentional, drives his jeep head on towards Merlo, who shoots him in the face. Caba, Mayo's teenage brother-in-law, stares numbly at the bloodied corpses. The tensions are well realized by the ensemble. In pitting friend against friend in senseless slaughter, Saura has created a fine allegory for the Spanish Civil War.

HUNT FOR RED OCTOBER, THE

1990 134m c Thriller ★★½
Mace Neufeld-Jerry Sherlock (U.S.) PG

Sean Connery (Capt. Marko Ramius), Alec Baldwin (Jack Ryan), Scott Glenn (Capt. Bart Mancuso), Sam Neill (Capt. Vasily Borodin), James Earl Jones (Admiral James Greer), Joss Ackland (Andrei Lysenko), Richard Jordan (Jeffrey Pelt), Peter Firth (Ivan Putin), Tim Curry (Dr. Petrov), Courtney B. Vance (Seaman Jones)

p, Mace Neufeld; d, John McTiernan; w, Larry Ferguson, Donald Stewart (based on the book by Tom Clancy); ph, Jan De Bont; ed, Dennis Virkler, John Wright; m, Basil Poledouris; prod d, Terence Marsh; art d, Dianne Wager, Donald Woodruff, William Cruse; fx, Scott Squires; cos, James Tyson; anim, Eric Swenson, Christopher Dierdorff, Pat Meyers, Charlie Canfield

AAN Best Editing: Dennis Virkler, John Wright; AAN Best Sound: Richard Bryce Goodman, Richard Overton, Kevin F. Cleary, Don Bassman; AA Best Sound Effects Editing: Cecelia Hall, George Watters, II

In spite of the high level of talent on board and at the helm, THE HUNT FOR RED OCTOBER is a heavy-duty mediocrity, sluggish, unwieldy, and instantly forgettable. The plot revolves around Marko Ramius (Sean Connery), a veteran Soviet sub commander who is guiding the new, super-advanced Red October submarine on its maiden mission. Abruptly, Ramius murders the onboard political officer and burns his orders. Red October is supposed to participate in war games meant to showcase its ability to evade sonar detection and deliver a full load of nuclear missiles to major American targets. Ramius instead tells his crew that they will approach the US coastline to embarrass the American military. In fact, he has something very different in mind. When Ramius goes off course, factions within the US military and government suspect a sneak attack. Guided by CIA analyst Dr. Jack Ryan (Alec Baldwin), who happens to be an expert on Ramius, the American security brain trust has to decide whether the Russians are telling the truth. Then they must choose the appropriate response—either help the Russians sink Red October (the FAIL SAFE scenario) or help Ramius defect.

Tom Clancy's exciting (albeit instantly dated) Cold War bestseller served as the basis for the film. But on the screen, RED OCTOBER suffers from a bad case of bloated scenario, lacking unities of place and action. In simpler terms, it should have stayed put, either above the surface or in the briny depths. Instead, the two major plots—two different movies, really—wind up neutralizing each other. Each time McTiernan cuts from one setting to the other, he's forced to start from scratch in rebuilding tension and involvement. Moreover, Larry Ferguson's adaptation doesn't bother to supply motivation for its stock, square-jawed characters. Ryan is so short of substance viewers may find it hard to remember that he's the movie's hero. While James Earl Jones reprised his role in subsequent Clancy-based pictures (PATRIOT GAMES, CLEAR AND PRESENT DANGER), notoriously obstreperous Baldwin lost the Ryan role to Harrison Ford after a contract dispute.

HURRICANE, THE

1937 110m bw Disaster ★★★★
Goldwyn (U.S.) /PG

Dorothy Lamour (Marama), Jon Hall (Terangi), Mary Astor (Madame Germaine De Laage), C. Aubrey Smith (Father Paul), Thomas Mitchell (Dr. Kersaint), Raymond Massey (Governor Eugene De Laage), John Carradine (Jailer), Jerome Cowan (Capt. Nagle), Al Kikume (Chief Mehevi), Kuulei DeClercq (Tita)

p, Samuel Goldwyn; d, John Ford, Stuart Heisler; w, Dudley Nichols, Oliver H.P. Garrett (based on the novel by Charles Nordhoff and James Norman Hall); ph, Bert Glennon; ed, Lloyd Nosler; art d, Richard Day, Alexander Golitzen; fx, James Basevi; cos, Omar Kiam

AAN Best Supporting Actor: Thomas Mitchell; AAN Best Score: Alfred Newman, Samuel Goldwyn Studio Music Department; AA Best Sound: Thomas Moulton

A stunning big blowout; this South Seas spectacular from the great John Ford is a rare perennial. The story is pretty much hooey with a dollop of tropical glamour on top, but anyway, marvelously self-serving. The beauteous Lamour is in love with barrel-chested Hall, whose hot temper lands him in hot water with corrupt island governor Massey. There's a fine assist from Astor, Mitchell, Cowan, Carradine, and Smith. Then the hurricane comes—a real lulu—and steals everyone's thunder. These scenes are terrifyingly spectacular, done on actual and miniature scales so cleverly edited that it is next to impossible to discern where one leaves off and the other takes over.

Hall and Lamour, two relatively unknown actors, became big deals in their roles as scantily clad natives. Lamour, a $75-a-week bit player at Paramount with only four films to her credit, was borrowed by Goldwyn from that studio. Goldwyn originally wanted Howard Hawks to direct this film, but they had argued violently over the making of COME AND GET IT, so Goldwyn turned to John Ford to direct THE HURRICANE. The mogul had also intended Joel McCrea to enact the part of the persecuted native Terangi, but McCrea convinced Ford that he was not right for the role, so Ford came up with Hall, a handsome, virile-looking actor Ford had spotted in a minor production at the Hollywood Playhouse.

Hall would have a checkered career after THE HURRICANE, coming to prominence in the early 1940s in a series of adventure and fantasy tales with exotic co-star Maria Montez. Lamour's star would rise even higher, especially after parlaying her sarong to fame—she first wore it in THE JUNGLE PRINCESS—and she would wear it through many a Bob Hope-Bing Crosby road film.

HUSBANDS

1970 154m c Drama/Comedy ★★★½
Faces Music (U.S.) PG/X

Ben Gazzara (Harry), Peter Falk (Archie), John Cassavetes (Gus), Jenny Runacre (Mary Tynan), Jenny Lee Wright (Pearl Billingham), Noelle Kao (Julie), Leola Harlow (Leola), Meta Shaw (Annie), John Kullers (Red), Delores Delmar (Countess)

p, Al Ruban; d, John Cassavetes; w, John Cassavetes; ph, Victor J. Kemper; ed, Peter Tanner; art d, Rene D'Auriac; cos, Louis Brown

John Cassavetes, Peter Falk, and Ben Gazzara give outstanding performances in HUSBANDS, Cassavetes's seriocomic improvisatory marathon about three men who go on a wild binge after the sudden death of one of their friends.

Harry (Ben Gazzara), Archie (Peter Falk) and Gus (John Cassavetes), three best friends in their mid-30s who live in suburban, middle-class Long Island with their families, are shocked when their friend Stuart Jackson (David Rowlands) suddenly dies of a heart attack. After attending the funeral, the men go into Manhattan and get drunk, then stay up all night and play basketball, followed by some more bar-hopping. When they finally go home two days later, Harry has a violent fight with his wife, who tells him she wants a divorce, then goes with Gus and Archie into Manhattan to go to work. Archie accompanies Gus to his dental practice, and talks him into leaving, and they meet Harry, who is fed up with his job. The trio decide to take a weekend trip to London where they check into a fancy hotel and gamble at a casino, then pick up three women and take them back to their rooms.

Most of Cassavetes's cinema verite films as a director are invariably accused (and with some justification) of being rambling, self-indulgent, and unfocused, but it is precisely those elements that make his best work so affecting and memorable, and HUSBANDS, though deeply flawed, is one of the finest examples of that. It originally ran 154 minutes when it premiered at the San Francisco Film Festival in 1970, then was cut by 16 minutes for general release, but even in the shortened version, many of its scenes go on far too long after they've made their point, while others seem totally unnecessary. The film's subtitle is "A comedy about life, death and freedom," and although there isn't much plot in the conventional sense, the basic premise allows for a penetrating look at the dreams and frustrations of disillusioned average men who have reached a mid-life crisis and are searching for some meaning and a reason to go on living. It's about basic things like what it means to have a family, hold a job, make compromises, and be responsible (or not), and treats these issues in an honest and probing manner, catching some revealing glimpses of life.

HUSBANDS AND WIVES

1992 107m c Comedy/Drama ★★★★
TriStar (U.S.) R/15

Woody Allen (Gabe Roth), Mia Farrow (Judy Roth), Judy Davis (Sally), Juliette Lewis (Rain), Liam Neeson (Michael), Sydney Pollack (Jack), Lysette Anthony (Sam), Nick Metropolis (TV Scientist), Cristi Conaway (Shawn Grainger), Timothy Jerome (Paul)

p, Robert Greenhut; d, Woody Allen; w, Woody Allen; ph, Carlo Di Palma; ed, Susan E. Morse; prod d, Santo Loquasto; art d, Speed Hopkins; cos, Jeffrey Kurland

AAN Best Supporting Actress: Judy Davis; AAN Best Original Screenplay: Woody Allen

This is one of Woody Allen's best films to date, combining some of his finest serious writing about relationships, in the style of HANNAH AND HER SISTERS, with humor that's all the more effective thanks to its dark, edgy context.

Allen has rounded up all the usual suspects for his latest look at the foibles, romantic and otherwise, of a group of privileged Manhattanites. They include Gabe Roth (Allen), a distinguished novelist and writing professor; his wife Judy (Mia Farrow), an editor at a prestigious art magazine; Jack (real-life film director Sydney Pollack), a chronically unfaithful businessman; and his wife Sally (Judy Davis), a woman so fiercely critical of everything that she is literally never satisfied. HUSBANDS AND WIVES leads us through the break-up of both marriages, via a trio of passionate infatuations—Jack with his aerobics instructor (Lysette Anthony), Gabe with a 21-year-old student (Juliette Lewis), and Sally with a colleague (Liam Neeson) of Judy's. It ends with one of the couples attempting a reconciliation, chastened by the realization that everlasting romantic love is a misleading, befuddling myth.

The film is greatly indebted to the improvisatory, pseudo-verite style of John Cassavetes, with a hand-held camera either dodging and wheeling around the characters, or sitting stationary as they volunteer information directly to the screen. The effect is of an artless, spontaneous attempt to capture life in the raw, but it belies a cannily crafted structure which uses both flashbacks and ellipses to lay bare the lives of its subjects. The acting is flawless throughout, with top honors going to Davis, who blazes through the picture with devastating intensity and honesty. It's an urgent, unsettling performance, perfectly complemented by Pollack, who projects quiet ease and authenticity in this, his first major role.

HUSH . . . HUSH, SWEET CHARLOTTE

1964 134m bw Thriller ★★★½
Fox (U.S.) /15

Bette Davis (Charlotte), Olivia de Havilland (Miriam), Joseph Cotten (Drew), Agnes Moorehead (Velma), Cecil Kellaway (Harry), Victor Buono (Big Sam), Mary Astor (Jewel Mayhew), Wesley Addy (Sheriff), William Campbell (Paul Marchand), Bruce Dern (John Mayhew)

p, Robert Aldrich; d, Robert Aldrich; w, Henry Farrell, Lukas Heller; ph, Joseph Biroc; ed, Michael Luciano; m, Frank DeVol; art d, William Glasgow; chor, Alex Ruiz; cos, Norma Koch

AAN Best Supporting Actress: Agnes Moorehead; AAN Best Cinematography: Joseph Biroc; AAN Best Editing: Michael Luciano; AAN Best Score: Frank DeVol; AAN Best Song: Frank DeVol (Music), Mack David (Lyrics); AAN Best Art Direction: William Glasgow (Art Direction), Raphael Bretton (Set Decoration); AAN Best Costume Design: Norma Koch

A Grand Guignol Southern Gothic cauldron. . . the next dish preferred by Aldrich and Davis after the success of WHATEVER HAPPENED TO BABY JANE? CHARLOTTE was originally planned as Crawford's revenge—Davis is the victim here, a loopy loon living in a moldy mansion in Louisiana, with hair like Spanish moss, skin like a lichen and a hobby of shooting at land developers.

She's haunted by an Electra complex and memories of a murdered beau she may have chopped up. Her nocturnal ramblings are interrupted, then encouraged, by the arrival of her prissbitch cousin from Virginia, de Havilland, finally getting a chance to give Davis hell and

act out the dark side of Melanie Wilkes. Cotten is the corrupt ole boy family doctor, Agnes Moorehead the Broomhilda housekeeper and the great Mary Astor (as a favor to Davis) in a swansong cameo.

Davis has some authentic, poignant moments, before all hell breaks loose. She seems to be making up for her lost chances on Tennessee Williams territory (she had wanted MENAGERIE and STREETCAR), and there's one kabuki lioness flip-out on a stairway that's a must-see. She's matched by Moorehead's perfect, obscure portrayal. The best line goes to de Havilland: "You just can't keep the hogs away from the trough."

Next to this, JANE looks like Masterpiece Theatre—it's the mutilation aspect that saddles the proceedings (both films were from Henry Farrell novels). Victor Buono (who received an Academy Award nomination for BABY JANE) is back for more as young Charlotte's father, and Dern is the lover who gets the axe. The tacky title song was a camp hit for Patti Page.

HUSTLE

1975 120m c Crime/Mystery ★★★½
Paramount (U.S.) R/15

Burt Reynolds (Lt. Phil Gaines), Catherine Deneuve (Nicole Britton), Ben Johnson (Marty Hollinger), Paul Winfield (Sgt. Louis Belgrave), Eileen Brennan (Paula Hollinger), Eddie Albert (Leo Sellers), Ernest Borgnine (Santoro), Catherine Bach (Peggy Summers), Jack Carter (Herbie Dalitz), James Hampton (Bus Driver)

p, Robert Aldrich; d, Robert Aldrich; w, Steve Shagan; ph, Joseph Biroc; ed, Michael Luciano; m, Frank DeVol; art d, Hilyard Brown; fx, Henry Miller Jr.; chor, Alex Romero; cos, Oscar Rodriguez, Betsy Cox

A disturbing and grim modern film noir directed by Aldrich, who was a master of the genre in the early 1950s. Reynolds stars as Phil Gaines, a bitter, cynical cop who finds the body of a young girl washed up on the beach and launches an investigation to determine her identity. After she is identified as a small-time hooker and porno actress, Gaines calls in the girl's parents, Marty (Johnson, in a superb performance) and Paula (Brennan), to identify the body. Soon Gaines finds himself competing with the headstrong Marty to solve a crime that turns out to have grave personal implications for them both.

Director Aldrich (KISS ME DEADLY) offers an unrelentingly diseased portrait of modern society in HUSTLE. Reynolds is trapped in this disgusting, seedy world from the opening of the film when his pleasant day off is intruded upon by the washed-up corpse, forcing him back into the underworld. There is no way out. HUSTLE is one of the few examples of true modern film noir. But director and screenwriter cannot resolve their different approaches. The script's humanistic, if depressing, angle gets battered by Aldrich's approach. An interesting mixed bag.

HUSTLER, THE

1961 134m bw Sports ★★★★½
Fox (U.S.) /15

Paul Newman ("Fast" Eddie Felson), Jackie Gleason (Minnesota Fats), Piper Laurie (Sarah Packard), George C. Scott (Bert Gordon), Myron McCormick (Charlie Bums), Murray Hamilton (Findlay), Michael Constantine (Big John), Stefan Gierasch (Preacher), Jake LaMotta (Bartender), Gordon B. Clarke (Cashier)

p, Robert Rossen; d, Robert Rossen; w, Sidney Carroll, Robert Rossen (based on the novel by Walter Tevis); ph, Eugene Schuftan; ed, Dede Allen; m, Kenyon Hopkins; prod d, Harry Horner, Albert Brenner, Harry Horner; cos, Ruth Morley

AAN Best Picture; AAN Best Actor: Paul Newman; AAN Best Actress: Piper Laurie; AAN Best Supporting Actor: Jackie Gleason; AAN Best Supporting Actor: George C. Scott; AAN Best Director: Robert Rossen; AAN Best Adapted Screenplay: Sidney Carroll, Robert Rossen; AA Best Cinematography: Eugen Shuftan; AA Best Art Direction: Harry Horner, Gene Callahan

This dark stunner, based on Walter Tevis's novel, boasts Paul Newman in the role that made him an overnight superstar. The treatment feels like a cross between Hemingway and Odets and there are some affectations with dialogue. But Rossen knows how to frame his story and give his actors room to breathe, eliciting terrific performances from everyone.

"Fast" Eddie Felson is a pool shark who hustles his way across the country to Ames Billiard Parlor in New York, where he challenges the unbeatable Minnesota Fats (Jackie Gleason). Penniless and alone, Eddie falls in love with Sarah Packard (Piper Laurie), an alcoholic cripple; then, after a return to small-time hustling that leads to two thug-administered broken thumbs, Eddie teams up with gambler Bert Gordon (George C. Scott), who becomes his backer but also personifies a vision of evil.

With the help of Gene Shufton's Oscar-winning black-and-white cinematography, producer-writer-director Robert Rossen offers a grim world where the only bright spot is the top of the pool table, yet his characters maintain a shabby nobility and grace. Gleason is brilliantly detached, witty, and charming as Fats; sexy, waifish Laurie offers some of the best work of her career; Scott is evil incarnate; and Newman is simply unforgettable in his Oscar-nominated role (he would have to play Fast Eddie again 25 years later in the excellent sequel, THE COLOR OF MONEY, to actually win his first Academy Award). The great pool player Willie Mosconi coached Gleason and Newman in their shots. Not to be missed.

I

I AM A CAMERA
1955 98m bw Drama/Comedy   ★★½
Romulus/Remus (U.K.)   /X

Julie Harris (Sally Bowles), Laurence Harvey (Christopher Isherwood), Shelley Winters (Natalia Landauer), Ron Randell (Clive), Lea Seidl (Fraulein Schneider), Anton Diffring (Fritz), Ina De La Haye (Herr Landauer), Jean Gargoet (Pierre), Stanley Maxted (American Editor), Alexis Bobrinskoy (Proprietor)

p, Jack Clayton; d, Henry Cornelius; w, John Collier (based on the play by John Van Druten from the "Berlin Stories" by Christopher Isherwood); ph, Guy Green; ed, Clive Donner; m, Malcolm Arnold; art d, William Kellner

In the beginning there were Christopher Isherwood's "Berlin Stories." From them came the award-winning play that provided the basis for both I AM A CAMERA and CABARET. Despite an intelligent adaptation and cast, this version is little more than an erratically filmed stage play. The action is static and the plot developed mostly through dialogue, which takes a far lighter tone than CABARET. The comedy deals with the episodic adventures of Harvey, a poor, struggling writer, and the effervescent Harris, a nightclub chanteuse—roommates caught up in the swirl of pre-WWII Berlin. Winters is a German girl who begins to experience the anti-Semitism of the Nazi regime.

I AM A FUGITIVE FROM A CHAIN GANG
1932 93m bw Prison   ★★★★★
Warner Bros. (U.S.)   /A

Paul Muni (James Allen), Glenda Farrell (Marie Woods), Helen Vinson (Helen), Preston Foster (Pete), Allen Jenkins (Barney Sykes), Edward Ellis (Bomber Wells), John Wray (Nordine), Hale Hamilton (Rev. Robert Clinton Allen), Harry Woods (Guard), David Landau

p, Hal B. Wallis; d, Mervyn LeRoy; w, Howard J. Green, Brown Holmes, Sheridan Gibney (based on the autobiography I Am a Fugitive from a Georgia Chain Gang by Robert E. Burns); ph, Sol Polito; ed, William Holmes; art d, Jack Okey; cos, Orry-Kelly

AAN Best Picture; AAN Best Actor: Paul Muni; AAN Best Sound: Nathan Levinson

One of the toughest movies ever made, an uncompromising and frightening film that lays bare the inhuman conditions of the penal system in post-WWI Georgia.

Based on a collection of writings by Robert Elliot Burns, who escaped from a chain gang to become a successful magazine editor but lived with the continual threat of being recaptured, the film tells the story of James Allen (Paul Muni), who is framed for the robbery of a hamburger stand and sentenced to ten years' hard labor. Every ounce of his strength and dignity is stripped away until he resolves to escape.

The reputation of socially conscious director Mervyn LeRoy is identified perhaps more with this film than with any other. Here the director of LITTLE CAESAR and THEY WON'T FORGET (which explored the horrors of lynching) pulls no punches, with every scene of I AM A FUGITIVE an expression of social outrage. Much of the film's story and technique would influence later prison movies, especially those dealing with prison farm systems. The escape through the swamps was duplicated by Edward G. Robinson in BLACKMAIL; the escape by truck was employed by Paul Newman in COOL HAND LUKE. Muni's captivating performance marked one of the highlights of his career.

Though the film specifically excluded the word "Georgia" from its title and never mentioned the state in the entire film, the indictment of that state's cruel chain-gang system was clear. The film was banned in Georgia and the state filed a libel suit against the studio. Two prison wardens in Georgia also filed unsuccessful million-dollar suits against Warner Brothers. Georgia was also relentless in its attempts to recapture Burns, whom Warner Bros. asked to travel to Hollywood to serve as an advisor on the project. Burns smuggled himself into Los Angeles using an assumed name and, reportedly, not only suggested ideas for the script but helped write dialogue before nervously fleeing after a few weeks.

I KNOW WHERE I'M GOING!
1945 91m bw Romance/Comedy   ★★★★½
Archers (U.K.)   /U

Roger Livesey (Torquil MacNeil), Wendy Hiller (Joan Webster), Pamela Brown (Catriona Potts), Nancy Price (Mrs. Crozier), Finlay Currie (Ruairidh Mur), John Laurie (John Campbell), George Carney (Mr. Webster), Walter Hudd (Hunter), Murdo Morrison (Kenny), Margot Fitzsimmons (Bridie)

p, Michael Powell, Emeric Pressburger; d, Michael Powell, Emeric Pressburger; w, Michael Powell, Emeric Pressburger; ph, Erwin Hillier; ed, John Seabourne; m, Allan Gray; art d, Alfred Junge

Wendy Hiller gives an ebullient and charming performance as a headstrong young British woman in I KNOW WHERE I'M GOING!, a mystical, lyrical romance by the great writer-producer-director team of Michael Powell and Emeric Pressburger, known as the Archers.

25-year-old Joan Webster (Wendy Hiller) announces to her father (George Carney) that she's engaged to Sir Robert Bellinger, the elderly owner of the chemical plant where she works, and one of the richest men in England. The two are to be married on the Scottish island of Kiloran in the Hebrides, which Bellinger has rented. Joan travels to the Isle of Mull, where she's supposed to catch a boat to Kiloran, but a storm prevents her from leaving, and she's forced to stay on the mainland. There, she meets a young naval officer on leave named Torquil MacNeil (Roger Livesy) who's also trying to get to Kiloran, and the two of them spend the night at the home of one of Torquil's friends. In the days following, Torquil exposes Joan to some intriguing Scottish traditions, and makes her question her decision to marry.

One of the most low-key of all the great Powell-Pressburger productions, I KNOW WHERE I'M GOING! is an absolute delight from beginning to end, combining romance, comedy, fantasy, and folklore to create a unique style that can only be described as "magical realism." Hiller brilliantly captures Joan's intelligence and determination without turning her into a stereotype, and makes her transformation totally believable. Roger Livesy is excellent as Torquil, although amazingly, all of his exterior scenes were filmed with a double, since he was unavailable when the company went to Scotland. The rest of the cast is amusingly filled with the usual assortment of Archers eccentrics, most notably Captain C.W.R. Knight as the falconer Colonel Barnstaple, and a pre-teen Petula Clark. Erwin Hillier's superb, high-contrast photography creates some stunning romantic images and awesome sights, such as the blanket of black mist swirling across the sea, and the incredible shot of the tiny boat about to be swallowed up by the whirlpool. I KNOW WHERE I'M GOING! is a beautiful film about the profound effects of nature on people, and that fact that the universe can be a wondrous and magical place if one keeps oneself open to its vast mysteries.

I LOVE YOU, ALICE B. TOKLAS!

1968 92m c Comedy   ★★
Warner Bros. (U.S.)   /X

Peter Sellers *(Harold)*, Jo Van Fleet *(Mother)*, Leigh Taylor-Young *(Nancy)*, Joyce Van Patten *(Joyce)*, David Arkin *(Herbie)*, Herb Edelman *(Murray)*, Salem Ludwig *(Father)*, Louis Gottlieb *(Guru)*, Grady Sutton *(Funeral Director)*, Janet E. Clark *(Mrs. Foley)*

p, Charles Maguire; d, Hy Averback; w, Paul Mazursky, Larry Tucker; ph, Philip Lathrop; ed, Robert C. Jones; m, Elmer Bernstein; prod d, Pato Guzman; cos, Theadora Van Runkle

An inspired performance by Sellers cannot redeem this giddy satire of 60s hippie culture, in which he plays a neurotic, asthmatic, fortyish attorney who discovers pot and the counter-culture. Van Fleet plays his mother, Van Patten the boring blonde his parents wish he would marry, and Arkin his hippy brother. Mazursky and Tucker, who came from TV's "Monkees," wrote in enough laughs to make this a hit at the time, but from the point that Sellers grows his hair and drops out, the embarassment factor becomes too much to take. Look for Grady Sutton, the butt of so many W.C. Fields jokes, effective in a small role.

I MARRIED A WITCH

1942 82m bw Science Fiction/Comedy   ★★★★½
Paramount (U.S.)   /A

Fredric March *(Wallace Wooley)*, Veronica Lake *(Jennifer)*, Robert Benchley *(Dr. Dudley White)*, Susan Hayward *(Estelle Masterson)*, Cecil Kellaway *(Daniel)*, Elizabeth Patterson *(Margaret)*, Robert Warwick *(J.B. Masterson)*, Eily Malyon *(Tabitha Wooley)*, Nora Cecil *(Harriet)*, Emory Parnell *(Allen)*

p, Preston Sturges; d, Rene Clair; w, Robert Pirosh, Marc Connelly, Dalton Trumbo (based on the novel *The Passionate Witch* by Thorne Smith and Norman Matson); ph, Ted Tetzlaff; ed, Eda Warren; m, Roy Webb; art d, Hans Dreier, Ernst Fegte; fx, Gordon Jennings; cos, Edith Head

AAN Best Score: Roy Webb

Although Clair is famous for his experimental French silents and several early talkies, here's the master at a later peak in, yes, Hollywood, USA. An accomplished confection, WITCH is required Halloween viewing.

Kellaway and his daughter Lake are branded witches in 1690 and burned at the stake, but not before putting a curse on their persecutors, the Wooley family. They threaten that no male member of the family will find happiness, and the curse is shown taking effect as misfortune befalls Wooley males (all played by March) through the ages, up to 1942 where March is shown to be a stuffed shirt with a snobbish fiancee, Hayward. He's running for governor of the state with backing from Hayward's filthy rich father, Warwick, an influential publisher. A storm comes up and lightning splits the ancient tree under which Kellaway and Lake were buried over 250 years before. They are freed, emerging as a rotund, booze-loving fellow and a blonde siren. From that point on, Lake does all in her power to make March fall in love with her. Yet her powers seem unable to sway him, as his plans to wed Hayward remain unchanged.

Lake, who had only been in films for a year, is wonderfully effective. Released from the sustained tension of film noir material, she demonstrates a quirky sense of comedy. Her line readings tingle with malice and hoydenish longing. WITCH also presents a lighter, warmer, more likable March than ever before—his chemistry with Lake is very engaging.

This is one of the rare instances where the "other woman" measures up to the lead in beauty and presence. Despite having her own beautiful hair chignoned to play up Lake's, Hayward's career took a major step here, snagging her a series of hard-bitten second leads that prepared her for the Davis-Crawford-Stanwyck roles that would establish her

later as a great star. And WITCH finds Kellaway in peak form—it's his most three-dimensional role. Look out, too, for humorist Robert Benchley as March's confused political advisor.

This film, with its wonderful special effects, was in the hilarious tradition of TOPPER and THE GHOST GOES WEST. Clair's direction is swift and sure, producing a livelier, more cohesive effort than his first Hollywood production, THE FLAME OF NEW ORLEANS, which fizzled at the box office. This Thorne Smith tale, taken from an incomplete novel, worked so well onscreen that it inspired the popular sitcom, "Bewitched."

I NEVER PROMISED YOU A ROSE GARDEN

1977 96m c Drama   ★★★½
Imorh (U.S.)   R/18

Bibi Andersson *(Dr. Fried)*, Kathleen Quinlan *(Deborah Blake)*, Ben Piazza *(Mr. Blake)*, Lorraine Gary *(Mrs. Blake)*, Darlene Craviotto *(Carla)*, Reni Santoni *(Hobbs)*, Susan Tyrrell *(Lee)*, Signe Hasso *(Helene)*, Norman Alden *(McPherson)*, Martine Bartlett *(Secret Wife of Henry VIII)*

p, Terence F. Deane, Michael Hausman, Daniel H. Blatt; d, Anthony Page; w, Lewis John Carlino, Gavin Lambert (based on the novel by Joanne Greenberg); ph, Bruce Logan; ed, Garth Craven; m, Paul Chihara; prod d, Toby Rafelson; cos, Jane Ruhm

AAN Best Adapted Screenplay: Gavin Lambert, Lewis John Carlino

A compelling drama about the terrors of schizophrenia, I NEVER PROMISED YOU A ROSE GARDEN is almost, but not quite, a female version of ONE FLEW OVER THE CUCKOO'S NEST. Quinlan is a certified mental case who is taken to a new and what appears to be tranquil hospital by her parents, Gary and Piazza. The similarity between this film and CUCKOO'S NEST ends in the fact that most of the patients in that one are only mildly afflicted and the ward becomes a microcosm of society. In ROSE GARDEN, there is no question of the horrors taking place inside the brains of the inmates. Quinlan is counseled by psychiatrist Andersson, and the bulk of the film deals with exorcising her various demons.

ROSE GARDEN falls short in its simplistic analysis of Quinlan's problem. Nor do we ever know much about her interaction with her family except for a brief indication of some resentment toward her brother. Most of our interest is sustained by the relationship between Quinlan and Andersson. Some casting sidelights include the great Sylvia Sidney as a patient who opts to come back to the hospital after being released; Hasso, who made her name playing what everyone thought was a man in THE HOUSE ON 92ND STREET; horror diva Barbara Steele; and Jeff Conaway, who later became popular on TV's "Taxi."

I NEVER SANG FOR MY FATHER

1970 92m c Drama   ★★★½
Columbia (U.S.)   GP/A

Melvyn Douglas *(Tom Garrison)*, Gene Hackman *(Gene Garrison)*, Dorothy Stickney *(Margaret Garrison)*, Estelle Parsons *(Alice)*, Elizabeth Hubbard *(Peggy)*, Lovelady Powell *(Norma)*, Daniel Keyes *(Dr. Mayberry)*, Conrad Bain *(Rev. Pell)*, Jon Richards *(Marvin Scott)*, Nikki Counselman *(Waitress)*

p, Gilbert Cates; d, Gilbert Cates; w, Robert W. Anderson (based on his play); ph, Morris Hartzband, George Stoetzel; ed, Angelo Ross; m, Barry Mann, Al Gorgoni; art d, Hank Aldrich; cos, Theoni V. Aldredge

AAN Best Actor: Melvyn Douglas; *AAN Best Supporting Actor:* Gene Hackman; *AAN Best Adapted Screenplay:* Robert Anderson

Honest, powerful and never sloppy, I NEVER SANG is a virtuoso acting exercise reined in by Cates, a terrific actors' director. The screenplay, adapted by Robert Anderson from his own play, feels drawn from real life.

Hackman is a fortyish New York professor who tells his aging parents, Douglas and Stickney, he is planning to change his life by marrying Hubbard, a divorced doctor, and moving to California. Stickney understands Hackman's need to break away but warns him that moving that far away may have a deleterious effect on Douglas. Just before the wedding, Stickney dies of heart failure. Parsons, Hackman's sister, has been disowned by Douglas for marrying a Jewish man. While at the funeral of their mother, Parsons advises Hackman not to allow himself to be manipulated by the old man and to live his life for himself.

Douglas is truly brilliant here—it's one of those performances that captures you so strongly that you are purged emotionally, yet equally enjoy the sureness of the talent at work. Hackman is able to personify the struggle of a conscience choosing between self or family.

I REMEMBER MAMA

1948   134m   bw   Drama   ★★★★
RKO   (U.S.)   /U

Irene Dunne *(Mama)*, Barbara Bel Geddes *(Katrin)*, Oscar Homolka *(Uncle Chris)*, Philip Dorn *(Papa)*, Cedric Hardwicke *(Mr. Hyde)*, Edgar Bergen *(Mr. Thorkelson)*, Rudy Vallee *(Dr. Johnson)*, Barbara O'Neil *(Jessie Brown)*, Florence Bates *(Florence Dana Moorhead)*, Peggy McIntyre *(Christine)*

p, Harriet Parsons; d, George Stevens; w, DeWitt Bodeen (based on the play by John Van Druten and the novel *Mama's Bank Account* by Kathryn Forbes); ph, Nicholas Musuraca; ed, Robert Swink, Tholen Gladden; m, Roy Webb; art d, Albert S. D'Agostino, Carroll Clark; fx, Russell A. Cully, Kenneth Peach; cos, Edward Stevenson, Gile Steele

AAN Best Actress: Irene Dunne; *AAN Best Supporting Actor:* Oscar Homolka; *AAN Best Supporting Actress:* Barbara Bel Geddes; *AAN Best Supporting Actress:* Ellen Corby; *AAN Best Cinematography:* Nicholas Musuraca

A delicate charmer, sometimes precious, but nonetheless fine. Based on Kathryn Forbes's collection of autobiographical short stories *Mama's Bank Account*, this meticulously directed George Stevens film tells the heartwarming story of a Norwegian immigrant family making a go of it in turn-of-the-century San Francisco. Katrin (Barbara Bel Geddes), one of the daughters, narrates from her diary as the family's trials, tribulations, and triumphs are shown in flashback. At the center of the proceedings is the indefatigable Mama (Irene Dunne, giving one of her finest performances), keeping the house and her head while a dizzying parade of offbeat relatives and friends come and go, including Oscar Homolka (overacting), Cedric Hardwicke (wonderful indeed), Rudy Vallee, Edgar Bergen, and Philip Dorn as Papa. Forbes's nostalgic tale had earlier been brought to Broadway by Richard Rodgers and Oscar Hammerstein II (adapted by John Van Druten), and Peggy Wood later appeared in a long-running (1946-57) TV series based on the story.

I SHOT ANDY WARHOL

1996   103m   c   Docudrama/Biography/Drama   ★★★
Playhouse International Pictures/BBC Arena/Orion   (U.S.)   R/18

Lili Taylor *(Valerie Solanas)*, Jared Harris *(Andy Warhol)*, Stephen Dorff *(Candy Darling)*, Martha Plimpton *(Stevie)*, Danny Morgenstern *(Jeremiah)*, Lothaire Bluteau *(Maurice Girodias)*, Michael Imperioli *(Ondine)*, Reg Rogers *(Paul Morrissey)*, Coco McPherson *(Brigid Berlin)*, Donovan Leitch *(Gerard Malanga)*

p, Tom Kalin, Christine Vachon; d, Mary Harron; w, Mary Harron, Daniel Minahan; ph, Ellen Kuras; ed, Keith Reamer; m, John Cale; prod d, Therese Deprez; art d, John Bruce; cos, David Robinson

Propelled by an ensemble of manic and mannered performances, I SHOT ANDY WARHOL follows quintessential outsider Valerie Solanas from obscure feminist writer to Warhol Factory hanger-on to would-be assassin. Filmmaker Mary Harron's stylish debut feature is a slick verite tour through the Factory and its margins that ultimately falls short of real insight into her characters.

In the 1960s, Valerie Solanas (Lili Taylor) moves to New York City where, despite her ostensible feminist separatism, she works as a prostitute. While writing plays based on her radical sexual politics, she becomes determined to meet Andy Warhol (Jared Harris) and eventually does, but her pleas that he produce one of her plays go unanswered. Eventually, Warhol does take an interest in her—whether out of pity or affection is unclear. As Valerie's friend, transvestite Candy Darling (Stephen Dorff), rises in popularity among the Factory's denizens, Solanas's modicum of acceptance fades. Finally, her rage boils over

and she steals a gun from a member of a revolutionary street-theater troupe. On June 3, 1968, she enters the new Factory office and shoots Warhol at point-blank range.

While Harron has neatly constructed a biographical film on a woman about whom little is actually known, I SHOT ANDY WARHOL fails to tell us much more than the facts. Despite an astute eye for detail and astounding production design by Therese Deprez, the film remains as cynical and detached as the Factory crowd itself. The people around Warhol are colorfully portrayed as a band of arrogant and paranoid posers, each with a peculiar magnetism that offsets other less-than-attractive qualities. Whether or not the film's one-dimensionality simply reflects its subject matter, it certainly portrays enough of the spirit of the milieu explored—if not its innermost emotions—to warrant a serious look.

I SHOT JESSE JAMES

1949   81m   bw   Western   ★★½
Lippert   (U.S.)   /U

Preston Foster *(John Kelley)*, Barbara Britton *(Cynthy Waters)*, John Ireland *(Bob Ford)*, Reed Hadley *(Jesse James)*, J. Edward Bromberg *(Kane)*, Victor Kilian *(Soapy)*, Barbara Woodell *(Mrs. Zee James)*, Tom Tyler *(Frank James)*, Tommy Noonan *(Charles Ford)*, Byron Foulger *(Room Clerk)*

p, Carl K. Hittleman; d, Samuel Fuller; w, Samuel Fuller (based on an article by Homer Croy); ph, Ernest Miller; ed, Paul Landres; m, Albert Glasser; art d, Frank Hotaling

Fuller's first directorial effort made evident the great talent he possessed as a filmmaker. Ireland plays the man who guns down Jesse James (Hadley), but Fuller avoids the obvious route and concentrates on what compels Ireland to kill his onetime friend. Ireland has a childhood sweetheart, Britton, whom he hopes to marry after he has carried out the shooting and received a pardon and reward money. But once the killing is over, Britton will have nothing to do with Ireland. Fuller uses effective close-ups in this stylish western, giving a fresh psychological twist to familiar narrative ground.

I, THE JURY

1953   87m   bw   Crime   ★★★
UA   (U.S.)   /18

Biff Elliot *(Mike Hammer)*, Preston Foster *(Capt. Pat Chambers)*, Peggie Castle *(Charlotte Manning)*, Margaret Sheridan *(Velda)*, Alan Reed *(George Kalecki)*, Frances Osborne *(Myrna)*, Bob Cunningham *(Hal Kines)*, Elisha Cook Jr. *(Bobo)*, Paul Dubov *(Marty)*, Mary Anderson *(Eileen Vickers)*

p, Victor Saville; d, Harry Essex; w, Harry Essex (based on the novel by Mickey Spillane); ph, John Alton; ed, Frederick Y. Smith; m, Franz Waxman; art d, Wiard Ihnen

The first film adaptation of Mickey Spillane's trashy best seller was written and directed by Harry Essex, the screenwriter of two of the best science fiction-horror films of the 1950s—IT CAME FROM OUTER SPACE and CREATURE FROM THE BLACK LAGOON—both originally released in 3-D, as was I, THE JURY.

As the film opens we hear "Hark the Herald Angels Sing," but the Yuletide spirit is shattered by a gunman, shrouded in darkness, brutally shooting Jack Williams (Robert Swanger), an amputee, several times. Still alive, Williams painfully crawls towards his own gun. The mysterious killer allows the dying man a chance at the weapon and then finishes him off before he can retaliate. Enter Mike Hammer (Elliot), a private detective and friend of the victim. Williams had saved Hammer's life during WWII, and now the detective is determined to avenge his death. Warned against breaking the law by police detective Foster, he begins to dig for clues. What he finds is a seedy world populated by junkies, nymphomaniacs, and drug dealers. Hammer swaggers through the sleaze, and a number of bodies complicate the case.

The opening and closing scenes of I, THE JURY are stunningly brutal and skillfully executed. The murder of the amputee while "Hark the Herald Angels Sing" plays in the background is profoundly chilling, as is the unexpected finale. Unfortunately, the film's center suffers from Elliot's feeble performance as Spillane's brutish detective. Audiences would have to wait two years for Ralph Meeker to deliver the definitive Mike Hammer performance in Robert Aldrich's incredible KISS ME DEADLY.

I WALK THE LINE

1970 95m c Drama ★★★½
Frankenheimer/Lewis (U.S.) GP/15

Gregory Peck (Sheriff Henry Tawes), Tuesday Weld (Alma McCain), Estelle Parsons (Ellen Haney), Ralph Meeker (Carl McCain), Lonny Chapman (Bascomb), Charles Durning (Hunnicutt), Jeff Dalton (Clay McCain), Freddie McCloud (Buddy McCain), Jane Rose (Elsie), J.C. Evans (Grandpa Tawes)

p, Harold D. Cohen; d, John Frankenheimer; w, Alvin Sargent (based on the novel An Exile by Madison Jones); ph, David M. Walsh; ed, Henry Berman; art d, Albert Brenner; cos, Louis Brown

Too downbeat for its own good, I WALK THE LINE forgets it needs an audience. The one reason to watch is the astonishing, unsung Weld, the modern Louise Brooks, who can suggest amorality, skewed innocence and ageless sensuality—she played nymphets through her thirties with infinite ease—that makes Bardot pale. Her tragedy is that she never chose a commercially successful script.

I WALK THE LINE presents haggard but handsome Peck as a backwoods Tennessee sheriff who falls in love with teenager Weld. Her father, Meeker, is a moonshiner, and Peck becomes involved in the illicit operations, making sure his men and federal agents stay clear of the stills. When deputy Durning stumbles upon the still, Meeker kills him, and Peck becomes an accomplice to the crime.

Frankenheimer does an apt job of creating the bleak mood, but the film doesn't seem to have anywhere it wants to go. There are five songs, including the title track, from the inimitable Johnny Cash that help capture the strangely compelling mountain mood.

I WALKED WITH A ZOMBIE

1943 69m bw Horror ★★★★★
RKO (U.S.) /A

James Ellison (Wesley Rand), Frances Dee (Betsy), Tom Conway (Paul Holland), Edith Barrett (Mrs. Rand), James Bell (Dr. Maxwell), Christine Gordon (Jessica Holland), Theresa Harris (Alma), Sir Lancelot (Calypso Singer), Darby Jones (Carre Four), Jeni le Gon (Dancer)

p, Val Lewton; d, Jacques Tourneur; w, Curt Siodmak, Ardel Wray (based on an original story by Inez Wallace); ph, J. Roy Hunt; ed, Mark Robson; m, Roy Webb; art d, Albert S. D'Agostino, Walter E. Keller

I WALKED WITH A ZOMBIE was the second in the series of thought-provoking, literate horror films produced by Val Lewton in the 1940s (the first was THE CAT PEOPLE), and, under the masterful direction of Jacques Tourneur, it is an unqualified horror masterpiece. The story idea and title were borrowed from a series of newspaper articles that detailed voodoo and witchcraft practices in Haiti, hung on an off-the-wall adaptation of Jane Eyre!

Betsy (Dee) is a young nurse sent to Haiti by rich American planter Paul Holland (Conway) to take care of his catatonic wife, Jessica (Gordon). Paul thinks his wife has gone insane, and is ridden with guilt that he may have caused it. The locals suspect, however, that Jessica has become a zombie—one of the living dead. Betsy, who makes little progress with Jessica, meets Paul's mother (Barrett), a contradictory woman torn between her strong beliefs in the Christian church and in voodoo, and his brother, Wesley (Ellison), who is slowly drinking himself to death as he watches his brother's mistreatment of Jessica, whom he has always secretly loved. To make matters worse, Betsy and her employer begin to fall in love. Their desire to marry is intense, but impossible as long as Jessica lives. Not wanting to lose Paul, nor to see him torture himself, Betsy attempts to cure Jessica by taking her to a voodoo ceremony, in hopes that the experience will shock her back to "life."

Lewton's horror was based on the suggested, the psychological—not the visceral, tangible "monsters" that characterized the Universal horror series in the 1930s and 40s. The terror was presented in a shadowy, low-key atmosphere that allowed the audience to imagine

and feel the unease instead of showing it to them, making the chills much more effective. The most outstanding example of this approach here is director Tourneur's beautiful realization of the lengthy, haunting, and elegiac sequence in which Betsy walks through the sugar cane fields with the silent Jessica to the voodoo ceremony. The scene is played in silence, save for the distant sound of drums and the gentle rustling of the wind. Visually, it is filled with gentle, floating movements—of Jessica's white gown, of the sugar cane in the wind—that are abruptly halted with the appearance of the massive zombie guard (Jones) whose presence signals the women's arrival at their destination. This scene is unforgettable, as is the entire film. Essential viewing.

I WANT TO LIVE!

1958 120m bw Crime/Biography ★★★★½
Figaro (U.S.) /X

Susan Hayward (Barbara Graham), Simon Oakland (Ed Montgomery), Virginia Vincent (Peg), Theodore Bikel (Carl Palmberg), Wesley Lau (Henry Graham), Philip Coolidge (Emmett Perkins), Lou Krugman (Jack Santo), James Philbrook (Bruce King), Bartlett Robinson (District Attorney), Gage Clark (Richard Tibrow)

p, Walter Wanger; d, Robert Wise; w, Nelson Gidding, Don Mankiewicz (based on newspaper articles by Ed Montgomery and the letters of Barbara Graham); ph, Lionel Lindon; ed, William Hornbeck; m, Johnny Mandel; art d, Ted Haworth

AA Best Actress: Susan Hayward; AAN Best Director: Robert Wise; AAN Best Adapted Screenplay: Nelson Gidding, Don Mankiewicz; AAN Best Cinematography: Lionel Lindon; AAN Best Editing: William Hornbeck; AAN Best Sound: Gordon Sawyer

Unswerving, uneasy, unbeatable crime melodrama with a shattering Susan Hayward gathering all her glory into a performance without one false note. For devotees of Miss Hayward, this is the one to study; it feels and looks like life.

The nasty plot has Hayward playing real-life Barbara Graham, whose sensational trial brought her a conviction and death sentence that made her a nationwide cause celebre. The film depicts Graham, the product of a broken home, as a classic bad girl: perjurer, prostitute, thief. She arrives in San Francisco and is quickly sent to prison for falsely testifying to help out a friend. When released, she contacts two gamblers on the recommendation of fellow inmates. The gamblers, Coolidge and Krugman, use her as a shill; Hayward steers gullible suckers into their crooked card games and begins to make big money. With a bank account, Hayward decides to go straight, but she makes the mistake of marrying corrupt Lau—one of Coolidge's associates—and he introduces her to drugs. By the time she has a baby, she is an addict and her husband takes her last $10 for a fix. She leaves him and goes back to work for Coolidge and Krugman, with tragic results.

Hayward's performance is so intense, and the film so grim, it's exhausting watching her suffer through one agony after another. Wise directs with the perspective that Hayward/Graham was innocent all along, although the film offers little evidence to support this claim (the most insistent being Graham's repeated and vociferous insistence of her innocence), a stance that brought universal criticism from law enforcement agencies. For the most part, the hapless heroine is convincingly portrayed as a social victim. Hayward had been denied the Oscar for many deserving performances in the past—SMASH-UP, THE STORY OF A WOMAN, MY FOOLISH HEART, I'LL CRY TOMORROW—but this time the Academy could not ignore her bravura. The ensemble cast is uniformly excellent and believable. Wise's direction is relentlessly gloomy and swift, telling Graham's story in adroitly crafted scenes; mention should also be made of Gerry Mulligan's fine rendering of Johnny Mandel's classic jazz soundtrack.

ICEMAN COMETH, THE

1973 239m c Drama ★★★
American Film Theatre (U.S.) PG/

Lee Marvin (Hickey), Fredric March (Harry Hope), Robert Ryan (Larry Slade), Jeff Bridges (Don Parritt), Bradford Dillman (Willie Oban), Sorrell Booke (Hugo Kalmar), Hildy Brooks (Margie), Juno Dawson (Pearl), Evans Evans (Cora), Martyn Green (The Captain/Cecil Lewis)

p, Ely A. Landau; d, John Frankenheimer; w, Thomas Quinn Curtiss (based on the play by Eugene O'Neill); ph, Ralph Woolsey; ed, Harold F. Kress; prod d, Jack Martin Smith; cos, Dorothy Jeakins

Though some consider this one of Eugene O'Neill's finest plays, THE ICEMAN COMETH does not translate well to the screen. No matter what Frankenheimer pulled from his bag of directorial tricks, the work remains stagey and talky on celluloid; even the majestic talent of March cannot turn it around.

March runs a saloon peopled by has-beens and drunks. All their lives, including March's, have been lived and lost; only their memories remain, voiced despairingly through bitter nostalgia. The only meager salvation for this bevy of forlorn creatures is the expected arrival of Marvin, a hardware salesman who drops by once a year to regale the customers with his forced humor and tired stories about his wife and the iceman. When Marvin does arrive, it's a letdown, even though this realistic actor tries hard to walk O'Neill's tightrope between nimble-witted charm and blunt hectoring. March is superb in his last film, and Bridges is good as the despondent young man wanting more than promises out of life. Dillman delivers his cynical wisecracks with aplomb, but Booke's role is delivered with such lunacy that the intended fear is replaced with black humor. The scene-stealer is Robert Ryan, one of cinema's forgotten great actors. He delivers a superlative performance as the radical with dark reason and fearful purpose, bringing a new, almost heroic dimension to the character.

IDENTIFICATION OF A WOMAN
(IDENTIFICAZIONE DI UNA DONNA)
1982 130m c Drama ★★★
Gaumont (Italy) /18

Tomas Mllan (Niccolo), Daniela Silverio (Mavi), Christine Boisson (Ida), Veronica Lazar (Carla), Sandra Monteleoni, Giampaolo Saccarola, Alessandro Ruspoli, Giada Gerini, Sergio Tardioli, Paola Dominguin

p, Giorgio Nocella, Antonio Macri; d, Michelangelo Antonioni; w, Michelangelo Antonioni, Tonino Guerra, Gerard Brach; ph, Carlo Di Palma; ed, Michaelangelo Antonioni; m, John Foxx; art d, Andrea Crisanti

Antonioni's first Italian film in nearly two decades (he did, however, shoot THE MYSTERY AT OBERWALD for video in 1979), offers his familiar treatment of the relationship between a man and a woman—or, in this case, a man and two women. Milian is a middle-aged film director (not unlike Antonioni) who gets involved with Silverio, an upper-class woman. He receives anonymous threats to terminate the relationship, which he ignores. Before long, Silverio moves away without telling Milian. He then starts seeing avant-garde stage actress Boisson, but this relationship also ends after she informs him that she is pregnant by another man.

This is a respectable return by Antonioni to familiar thematic ground—the impossibility of maintaining relationships in the contemporary world—helped by a fine ironic underpinning and smoothly assured visuals.

IDOLMAKER, THE
1980 107m c Drama ★★★½
UA (U.S.) PG/15

Ray Sharkey (Vincent Vacarri), Tovah Feldshuh (Brenda Roberts), Peter Gallagher (Caesare), Paul Land (Tommy Dee), Joe Pantoliano (Gino Pilato), Maureen McCormick (Ellen Fields), John Aprea (Paul Vacarri), Richard Bright (Uncle Tony), Olympia Dukakis (Mrs. Vacarri), Steven Apostlee Peck (Mr. Vacarri)

p, Gene Kirkwood, Howard W. Koch Jr.; d, Taylor Hackford; w, Edward Di Lorenzo; ph, Adam Holender; ed, Neil Travis; m, Jeff Barry; art d, David L. Snyder; chor, Deney Terrio; cos, Rita Riggs

Ray Sharkey gives a dynamic performance here as the hustling Vincent Vacarri (a thinly veiled version of technical adviser Bob Marcucci, mentor of Frankie Avalon and Fabian), who promotes the careers of rock 'n' roll singers Tommy Dee (Paul Land) and Caesare (Peter Gallagher)—managing their every move, calling in favors here and making payoffs there, making sure his charges have the best clothes

and backup bands, etc.—in the late 50s and early 60s. Brenda Roberts (Tovah Feldshuh) is an editor of a fan magazine who has a fling with Vincent and uses her influence to help make his boys into stars. THE IDOLMAKER takes itself too seriously, but is nonetheless one of the best and most energetic film treatments of the early days of rock 'n' roll and a fine depiction of how performers are groomed for stardom (far superior to THE ROSE). In his directorial debut, Taylor Hackford (AN OFFICER AND A GENTLEMAN, 1982; WHITE NIGHTS, 1985) shows a solid command of the medium. The anachronistic music by Jeff Barry is a problem, however; its too-contemporary sound presumably stems from the producers' desire to get airplay for the film's score.

IF...
1968 110m c/bw Drama ★★★★½
Memorial (U.K.) R/18

Malcolm McDowell (Mick Travers), David Wood (Johnny), Richard Warwick (Wallace), Christine Noonan (the Girl), Rupert Webster (Bobby Philips), Robert Swann (Rowntree), Hugh Thomas (Denson), Peter Jeffrey (Headmaster), Mona Washbourne (Matron), Arthur Lowe (Mr. Kemp, Housemaster)

p, Michael Medwin, Lindsay Anderson; d, Lindsay Anderson; w, David Sherwin (based on a script by Sherwin, John Howlett, entitled "The Crusaders"); ph, Miroslav Ondricek; ed, David Gladwell; m, Marc Wilkinson; prod d, Jocelyn Herbert; art d, Brian Eatwell

A furious, exhilarating assault on the mores of contemporary Britain, sited in a microcosmic boarding school. With LA CHINOISE and THE BATTLE OF ALGIERS, IF. . . instantly became one of the key texts of 60s revolutionary sentiment; decades later, it retains most of its considerable impact.

Having spent the summer absorbing London's burgeoning counter-culture, a quietly simmering Mick Travis (Malcolm McDowell) returns to his public school—a nightmarishly oppressive institution in which privilege is based on rank, intellectual achievement is despised, and cynical upper classmen routinely extort sexual favors from younger boys. The school's systematic brutality is condoned by an ineffectual headmaster whose "modern" views clash ludicrously with the medieval environment. With three close friends, Mick indulges in petty rebellions—a forbidden excursion into town, a late-night drinking party—until he runs afoul of the sadistic head of house (Robert Swann), who administers a vicious ritual beating in the name of school spirit. Thereafter, Mick and his comrades declare war, and an increasingly surreal chain of events leads to a violent finale in which a guerrilla band disrupts Founder's Day ceremonies with automatic weapons and grenade launchers.

Strikingly orginal and breathlessly entertaining, IF . . . (the title refers ironically to Kipling's jingoistic poem) can profitably be read on several levels simultaneously. On one hand, it's a critique of schoolboys' adventure stories, the ideologically overdetermined, peculiarly British genre that was memorably parodied in Michael Palin's TV series "Ripping Yarns." On another—particularly in its palpable atmosphere of sexual repression and sublimation—it bears a striking resemblance to Jean Vigo's innovative ZERO DE CONDUITE. (The film is also unmistakably concerned with the Vietnam War and its ideological underpinnings.) Throughout, director Lindsay Anderson (THIS SPORTING LIFE) aims to keep the viewer off-balance, switching deftly from the formal conventions of British realism to dreamily erotic flights of fancy.

IF. . . was conceived in 1958 and scripted in 1960 under the title THE CRUSADERS. At the time of its release, the film's putative call-to-arms was a subject of some controversy. Promotional material depicted a group of youths armed with machine guns and hand grenades, asking "Which side are you on?" Originally envisioned as a more violent REBEL WITHOUT A CAUSE, the picture was first offered to Nicholas Ray, who suggested it would be best served by a British director. Some scenes of this color film were shot in black-and-white, prompting much critical speculation upon its release. Only later did director Lindsay Anderson explain that the production ran out of money toward the end of the shoot and couldn't afford to buy any more color stock. The highly effective music includes the "Sanctus" from "Missa Luba."

IF I HAD A MILLION

1932 88m bw Comedy/Drama ★★★★
Paramount (U.S.)

Gary Cooper *(Gallagher)*, George Raft *(Eddie Jackson)*, Wynne Gibson *(Violet)*, Charles Laughton *(The Clerk)*, Jack Oakie *(Mulligan)*, Frances Dee *(Mary Wallace)*, Charlie Ruggles *(Henry Peabody)*, Alison Skipworth *(Emily)*, W.C. Fields *(Rollo)*, Mary Boland *(Mrs. Peabody)*

p, Louis D. Lighton; d, Ernst Lubitsch, Norman Taurog, Stephen Roberts, James Cruze, William A. Seiter, H. Bruce Humberstone, Lothar Mendes; w, Claude Binyon, Whitney Bolton, Malcolm Stuart Boylan, John Bright, Sidney Buchanan, Lester Cole, Isabel Dawn, Boyce DeGaw, Walter DeLeon, Oliver H.P. Garrett, Harvey Gates, Grover Jones, Ernst Lubitsch, Lawton Mackall, Joseph L. Mankiewicz, William Slavens McNutt, Seton I. Miller, Robert Sparks, Tiffany Thayer (based on the novel *Windfall* by Robert D. Andrews)

For once, an episodic film that holds together, and the link that holds it is lots of money: millions, in fact. Richard Bennett plays a multimillionaire who is disgusted with his dollar-clutching relatives. When told by his doctors that he is dying, Bennett decides to pick out total strangers and give each $1 million, mostly to see what they will do with the money. He closes his eyes and picks a name from the phone book. Eight sketches follow that depict the results of Bennett's largesse. In "The China Shop," directed by James Cruze, Charles Ruggles is a spineless clerk who is forever hiding from shrewish wife Mary Boland and is terrified at work of dropping a piece of china, the cost of which will be deducted from his salary. With Bennett's check for $1 million in hand, Ruggles proceeds to tell off Boland for good and go on a china-smashing binge. In the next segment, "The Streetwalker," directed by Ernst Lubitsch, $1 million goes to Wynne Gibson, a prostitute, who immediately abandons her street corner and rents a lavish penthouse apartment, determined to make up for lost sleep between silk sheets. Stephen Roberts directs the next segment, "The Forger," which profiles a slick George Raft who is so notorious that his photo is in every bank where he might cash his check. After failing to cash the check, the hysterical Raft goes to a flophouse and begs the owner to take the $1 million check for a bed. As he dozes off, the owner lights his cigar with the burning check and then calls the police to come and arrest the wanted forger. The next sequence, "The Auto" or "Rollo and the Road Hogs," is directed by Norman Taurog. Alison Skipworth receives the check at her little teashop where she and newly acquired hubby W.C. Fields, a worn-out vaudeville juggler, reside, harboring a bone-deep hatred for roadhogs, especially since their new car has just been wrecked by a bevy of these very people. With the $1 million, Fields and Skipworth go to a new car dealership and begin buying one new car after another, taking to the streets as roadhog vigilantes! Bruce Humberstone directs "The Condemned Man." Gene Raymond is about to go to the electric chair when he receives the $1 million. He is dragged to the chair hysterically crying and laughing over the ironic twist of fate. "The Clerk," also directed by Lubitsch, has Charles Laughton as a meek, harassed clerical worker. When he receives his $1 million check, he stands up quietly, and then walks into the resplendent office of the firm's president. As the man looks up, Laughton gives the boss a loud Bronx cheer, slams the door, and goes into unperturbed retirement. In "The Three Marines," directed by Norman McLeod, $1 million goes to Gary Cooper, a fun-loving Marine. He and his buddies, Jack Oakie and Roscoe Karns, are in the brig for fighting; when they get out, they rush to a lunchwagon to see pretty Joyce Compton. Knowing cook Lucien Littlefield cannot read, Cooper passes off the check for $10 in cash and takes Compton to a carnival that night where he and his buddies get into another fight and wind up behind bars once more. Cooper looks through the barred window of his cell and sees Littlefield getting into a limousine. "Old Ladies' Home" is directed by William A. Seiter and profiles May Robson, a resident at a home for retired old ladies, where the women are treated like prison inmates by the overbearing director. When Robson's check arrives, she buys the home and compels the directors to sit back silently and watch all the old ladies pursue their hobbies and enjoy life for a change.

Most of these stories are well-told, expertly acted, and brilliantly directed. Paramount poured out its best acting and technical talent for this enormous production, the Laughton and Fields segments considered strongest. Us? We'll go with W.C., the Great One himself. MILLION inspired a popular radio and later a TV series, "The Millionaire."

IKIRU

1952 140m bw Drama ★★★★
Toho (Japan) /A

Takashi Shimura *(Kanji Watanabe)*, Nobuo Kaneko *(Mitsuo Watanabe)*, Kyoko Seki *(Kazue Watanabe)*, Miki Odagiri *(Toyo)*, Kamatari Fujiwara *(Ono)*, Makoto Koburi *(Kiichi Watanabe)*, Kumeko Urabe *(Tatsu Watanabe)*, Yoshie Minami *(Hayoshi, the Maid)*, Nobuo Nakamura *(Deputy Mayor)*, Minosuke Yamada *(Saito)*

d, Akira Kurosawa; w, Akira Kurosawa, Hideo Oguni, Shinobu Hashimoto; ph, Asakazu Nakai; m, Fumio Hayasaka; art d, So Matsuyama

In IKIRU, Akira Kurosawa has created a subtle and moving account of a man who searches for meaning in the final days of his shallow existence. Kanji Watanabe (Takashi Shimura) is a clerk in a government office who discovers that he has cancer and, at most, only a year to live. Up to this point he has lived a highly structured life, rarely varying from routines. He has two children who offer him no comfort, and he decides he must find something to make him feel that his life has not been a total waste. The movement of IKIRU is extremely low key, and the overall emotional impact is quite powerful, with the character of Kanji serving as a metaphor for postwar Japan. A beautiful and unusually quiet film from one of the world's greatest living directors.

I'LL CRY TOMORROW

1955 117m bw Biography ★★★★
MGM (U.S.) /X

Susan Hayward *(Lillian Roth)*, Richard Conte *(Tony Bardeman)*, Eddie Albert *(Burt McGuire)*, Jo Van Fleet *(Katie Roth)*, Don Taylor *(Wallie)*, Ray Danton *(David Tredman)*, Margo *(Selma)*, Virginia Gregg *(Ellen)*, Don "Red" Barry *(Jerry)*, David Kasday *(David as a Child)*

p, Lawrence Weingarten; d, Daniel Mann; w, Helen Deutsch, Jay Richard Kennedy (based on the book by Lillian Roth, Mike Connolly and Gerold Frank); ph, Arthur E. Arling; ed, Harold F. Kress; m, Alex North; art d, Cedric Gibbons, Malcolm Brown; fx, Warren Newcombe; cos, Helen Rose

AAN Best Actress: Susan Hayward; *AAN Best Cinematography:* Arthur E. Arling; *AAN Best Art Direction:* Cedric Gibbons, Malcolm Brown, Edwin B. Willis, Hugh Hunt; *AA Best Costume Design:* Helen Rose

Hayward stars as Lillian Roth (based on Roth's autobiography of the same name), Broadway and Hollywood singing sensation, who let success slide through her fingers as she reached for the next drink.

As a child, Lillian is driven unmercifully by her ambitious stage mother (Jo Van Fleet) and has already begun appearing on Broadway and being the breadwinner by the time she is a teenager. As an adult, Roth (Susan Hayward) falls in love with an old friend (Ray Danton) who dies unexpectedly, precipitating a lengthy downward spiral.

Although the script doesn't capture much sense of period or time passing, Mann establishes enough strong moments to keep the viewer enthralled. There's a fine child performance by Carole Ann Campbell, who looks like the real Roth, and scores strongly in a post-audition scene that is painful to watch. Indeed, the film dotes on an uneasy sense of dread, daring you not to look away. Hayward doesn't suggest much of what audiences saw in the real Roth. Instead she uses her own sexy, hellcat persona when performing, saving contemplation for her big offstage scenes. The scene in which Hayward deserts her mother is one of Hollywood's grittiest examinations of the love-hate relationship between parent and child, the cross-purposes of both characters wrenching to behold. Both actresses seem to be defining their boundaries and crossing each other's at the same time, using the hyper-emotional 50s genre in a devastatingly successful way.

Roth made a successful nightclub and theatrical comeback after the film's release, and published a second memoir, *Beyond My Worth*, but, tragically, her bouts with alcohol were far from finished. Hayward won the Cannes Film Festival Best Actress Award for TOMORROW and Helen Rose grabbed an Oscar for her gorgeous costumes.

I'M ALL RIGHT, JACK

1959 105m bw Comedy   ★★★★
Boulting Bros. (U.K.)   /U

Ian Carmichael *(Stanley Windrush)*, Peter Sellers *(Fred Kite)*, Terry-Thomas *(Maj. Hitchcock)*, Richard Attenborough *(Sidney de Vere Cox)*, Dennis Price *(Bertram Tracepurcel)*, Margaret Rutherford *(Aunt Dolly)*, Irene Handl *(Mrs. Kite)*, Liz Fraser *(Cynthia Kite)*, Miles Malleson *(Windrush Sr.)*, Marne Maitland *(Mr. Mohammed)*

p, Roy Boulting; d, John Boulting; w, Frank Harvey, Alan Hackney, John Boulting (based on Hackney's novel *Private Life*); ph, Mutz Greenbaum; ed, Anthony Harvey; m, Ken Hare, Ron Goodwin

Hilarious satire of British trade unionism. Carmichael is an addled but earnest young man who has just finished his army service and now seeks a career in industry. He visits his uncle, Price, who is in cahoots with Attenborough in a most interesting scheme; they would like to arrange a strike at Price's factory so that Attenborough's factory can take over the contracts and do the work at inflated prices. Price gives Carmichael a job as an unskilled laborer, and his intelligence soon detects several ways to streamline the factory's operation and reap larger profits. This, of course, angers the union shop steward, Sellers. Carmichael figures out a way to load and unload deliveries and suggests that a new schedule be printed and that the workers live up to it instead of taking tea breaks every other hour. Sellers is livid and calls a strike, which delights Price. But the laborers at Attenborough's plant go out in sympathy, thus tossing Price and Attenborough's plans into a cocked hat. Things get progressively more ludicrous from there on in.

A sharp screenplay and expert farceurs in every role make this one of the great British comedies of the 1950s and 1960s. Many of the "Carry On" players are here, including Rutherford and her husband, Davis. Even Punch editor Muggeridge takes a turn as the moderator of the TV show. It's subtlety and slapstick mixed perfectly in a refreshing glace. BAFTA Awards (British Oscars) went to Sellers and to the screenplay.

I'M GONNA GIT YOU SUCKA

1988 88m c Comedy   ★★★
Ivory Way (U.S.)   R/15

Keenen Ivory Wayans *(Jack Spade)*, Bernie Casey *(John Slade)*, Antonio Fargas *(Flyguy)*, Steve James *(Kung Fu Joe)*, Isaac Hayes *(Hammer)*, Jim Brown *(Slammer)*, Ja'Net DuBois *(Ma Bell)*, Dawn Lewis *(Cheryl)*, John Vernon *(Mr. Big)*, Clu Gulager *(Lt. Baker)*

p, Peter McCarthy, Carl Craig; d, Keenen Ivory Wayans; w, Keenen Ivory Wayans; ph, Tom Richmond; ed, Michael R. Miller; m, David Frank; prod d, Melba Farquhar, Catherine Hardwicke

Wayans wrote and directed this very funny satire of the black-oriented exploitation films of the 1970s. Set in "Any Ghetto, USA," I'M GONNA GIT YOU SUCKA opens as upstanding young Army veteran Jack Spade (Wayans) returns home to avenge the death of his brother, who died because he wore too many gold chains. Wayans vows to shut down the business of a ruthless gold-chain pusher known only as Mr. Big (Vernon). Because his experience in the armed forces is mostly bureaucratic, however, Jack seeks the help of his childhood hero, John Slade (Casey) in this endeavor. An extremely funny movie that presents a torrent of insightful gags at breakneck pace, I'M GONNA GIT YOU SUCKA features many of the stars of the old "blaxploitation" movies, adding weight and authenticity to Wayan's film. In offering up this affectionate parody of the old movies, Wayans also turns a satiric eye on black culture in general—but in an inoffensive, lighthearted manner.

I'M NO ANGEL

1933 87m bw Comedy   ★★★½
Paramount (U.S.)

Mae West *(Tira)*, Cary Grant *(Jack Clayton)*, Gregory Ratoff *(Benny Pinkowitz)*, Edward Arnold *(Big Bill Barton)*, Ralf Harolde *(Slick Wiley)*, Kent Taylor *(Kirk Lawrence)*, Gertrude Michael *(Alicia Hatton)*, Russell Hopton *(Flea Madigan, the Barker)*, Dorothy Peterson *(Thelma)*, William B. Davidson *(Ernest Brown, the Chump)*

p, William LeBaron; d, Wesley Ruggles; w, Mae West, Harlan Thompson (based on "The Lady and the Lions," an unproduced screenplay by Lowell Brentano); ph, Leo Tover; ed, Otho Lovering; m, Harvey Brooks; art d, Hans Dreier, Bernard Herzbrun

The best of the West. Mae is a Depression-era angel of mercy, dispensing quips and songs like fallout in one of the funniest films ever lensed. On camera 95% of the time, West's screenplay traces her climb from sideshow carnival hootchie-kootchie girl to international circus star. In true lady Leo form, she even gets to realize her own biggest fantasy on camera: taming lions. Obviously, West was being rewarded with total creative control, a power seldom given by the studios, but the success of her previous film, SHE DONE HIM WRONG, had gone a long way toward keeping Paramount from declaring bankruptcy. She is surrounded by a slick supporting cast working at comedic fever pitch, but West never breaks a sweat, parading through her promenades, amazed by her own dazzle, savoring every star turn, thrilled with her own reflection in each costar's eyes.

Indeed, I'M NO ANGEL is a monument to the Westian ego; never has fullblown female narcissism been explored in such an utterly unselfconcious way, yet it's tempered by West at her most self-mocking. Each time you're convinced that it's all parody, West suddenly plays it straight. . . but so you'll laugh out loud. She's a textbook of historic comic technique and diva timing—historic because West embraces every great bygone tradition of show business: vaudeville, burlesque, legit and speakeasy. And ANGEL is highlighted by a lesson in diva plotline no other star can equal, because only West would dare defend herself in court. Crammed into the 87 minutes of running time are numerous other unforgettable moments. Watch for West's record collection, her weird lion tamer boots (designed to hide her platforms), her midway rendition of "They Call Me Sister Honky-Tonk", her spider wing dress sleeves. This was the second time West used Cary Grant as her leading man, and he later said she was the most difficult person he ever played opposite, yet she taught him more about comedy than anyone else he ever worked with. ANGEL came after the beauticians had perfected West's visual star persona and before the moral bluenoses took to laundering her work—it's the peak of her stardom. Certainly we feel rewarded by this flawless comedy classic and enriched by the legacy of West herself: a legend of legends, a figure of American folklore that stands alone in the cinematic pantheon.

IMITATION OF LIFE

1934 106m bw Drama   ★★★½
Universal (U.S.)

Claudette Colbert *(Beatrice Pullman)*, Warren William *(Stephen Archer)*, Ned Sparks *(Elmer)*, Louise Beavers *(Delilah Johnson)*, Juanita Quigley *(Jessie Pullman, Age 3)*, Marilyn Knowlden *(Jessie, Age 8)*, Rochelle Hudson *(Jessie, Age 18)*, Sebie Hendricks *(Peola Johnson, Age 4)*, Dorothy Black *(Peola, Age 9)*, Fredi Washington *(Peola, Age 19)*

p, Carl Laemmle; d, John M. Stahl; w, William Hurlbut (based on the novel by Fannie Hurst); ph, Merritt Gerstad; ed, Philip Cahn

AAN Best Picture; AAN Best Sound: Gilbert Kurland

Highly sentimental social soaper, subtly crafted by director Stahl.

In this adaptation of Fannie Hurst's melodramatic novel, Colbert ages 15 years—quite believably—as a widow raising her daughter alone. (The daughter is played first by Juanita Quigley, then by Marilyn Knowlden, and as a young woman by Rochelle Hudson.) When Colbert decides to join forces with her maid, Louise Beavers, and open a small pancake parlor, Beavers, who also has a young daughter (played by Sebie Hendricks, by Dorothy Black, and primarily the largely forgotten, beautiful Fredi Washington), becomes Colbert's full partner in the business, which proves highly successful. As the enterprise flourishes, however, the women's family lives become fraught with conflict. Washington, whose light complexion enables her to pass for Caucasian, finds herself unable to live in both the white and black worlds, and as a result breaks off relations with Beavers and runs away from school, hoping to live as a white woman. Colbert, meanwhile, is shocked to learn that the 18-year-old Hudson is in love with the man Colbert herself wants to marry, Warren William.

Audiences didn't seem to mind the rather downbeat ending of IMITATION OF LIFE (remade successfully in 1959, with Lana Turner starring under Douglas Sirk's direction), but there was a great deal of controversy over the basic elements of the narrative. Some white southern viewers disapproved of Colbert's character going into business with her black maid (despite the fact that it's the latter's recipe that makes both women rich); Black critics, on the other hand, felt that Beavers should have been shown establishing her own residence, rather than staying on with Colbert and continuing to function as household help. At one point, Stahl makes an explicit visual social comment: a masterful camera shot of a staircase that divides upstairs from down, with Beavers catering upstairs and Colbert hostessing downstairs, revealing the hypocrisy of the entire exercise. Beavers' interpretation has dated badly; she's either jolly or resigned and does not suggest the transitions from one emotion to another.

IMITATION OF LIFE

1959 125m c Drama   ★★★★
Universal (U.S.)   /U

Lana Turner (Lora Meredith), John Gavin (Steve Archer), Sandra Dee (Susie, Age 16), Dan O'Herlihy (David Edwards), Susan Kohner (Sarah Jane, Age 18), Robert Alda (Allen Loomis), Juanita Moore (Annie Johnson), Mahalia Jackson (Herself), Karen Dicker (Sarah Jane, Age 8), Terry Burnham (Suzie, Age 6)

p, Ross Hunter; d, Douglas Sirk; w, Eleanore Griffin, Allan Scott (based on the novel by Fannie Hurst); ph, Russell Metty; ed, Milton Carruth; m, Frank Skinner; art d, Alexander Golitzen, Richard H. Riedel; fx, Clifford Stine; cos, Jean Louis, Bill Thomas

AAN Best Supporting Actress: Susan Kohner; *AAN Best Supporting Actress:* Juanita Moore

Plush and overblown, the last Hollywood hurrah for Sirk, and the resurrection of the weepie by producer Ross Hunter. A string of similar sudsers followed (several with Turner), but this one is the pick of the litter, thanks to Sirk. It's a bizarre, Byzantine, calculatingly depressed and cold affair, with Miss Big Chill herself, Lana Turner, breathing dry ice into the role originally played by Claudette Colbert (and trading Colbert's dignity for helplessness and pearls). The central theme remains the same, but the major tension that exists is 1950s materialism versus the disentegration of the nuclear family, tinged with gut-wrenching racism. If Sirk exploits the material for all it's worth and seems to be sardonically allowing the artifical genre to devour itself as he sits back and watches, at the same time the weepie aspect is so melodramatic as to tear the sobs from your throat.

Lana Turner, playing a successful actress, is not so much acting as parodying herself; Juanita Moore, as the black maid who shares her life, plays the part so haltingly and straight that it feels like ironic commentary. Susan Kohner, as Moore's light-skinned daughter who passes for white, is a noir revelation, giving her character a restless, dangerous sensuality. When she turns the malice of that energy on Turner, it's one of the great standoffs in Hollywood history. And it's magnificently undercut later, when Turner is crying over Moore's deathbed, with Kohner's photograph smiling out from the wall behind them. Oh, and be prepared for the all-stops-out cinematic funeral, complete with Mahalia Jackson singing "Trouble of the World." You'll be horrified at how this hokum manipulates you, but the best strategy is to just surrender and enjoy it.

IMPORTANCE OF BEING EARNEST, THE

1952 95m c Comedy   ★★★★½
Two Cities/Javelin British/Asquith (U.K.)   /U

Michael Redgrave (Jack Worthing), Michael Denison (Algernon Moncrieff), Edith Evans (Lady Bracknell), Joan Greenwood (Gwendolen Fairfax), Dorothy Tutin (Cecily Cardew), Margaret Rutherford (Miss Prism), Miles Malleson (Canon Chasuble), Richard Wattis (Seton), Aubrey Mather (Merriman), Walter Hudd (Lane)

p, Teddy Baird; d, Anthony Asquith; w, Anthony Asquith (based on the play by Oscar Wilde); ph, Desmond Dickinson; ed, John D. Guthridge; m, Benjamin Frankel; art d, Carmen Dillon; cos, Beatrice Dawson

Wilde's wittiest play took 57 years to make it to the screen but was well worth the wait. Director-writer Asquith made absolutely no attempt to "open up" this repertory standard in order to make it more cinematic. The film does of course benefit from close-ups and such, but Asquith goes so far as to have a couple enter a stage box and sit down before a curtain rises at the start. This is meant to be theater first and foremost, and it's a valuable record of a great performance. Stylish, sunny, and as nonsensical as any work can be (at least, on the surface), THE IMPORTANCE OF BEING EARNEST takes well-aimed potshots at the social pretentions of the 1890s. The satire goes down like punch because the artful Wilde has cloaked it in badinage containing some of his best epigrams and *bon mots*. The decor and costumes are charmingly detailed, the perfect setting for this hilarious jewel.

This comedy classic tells of Jack and Algy, two well-to-do bachelors (Redgrave and Dennison) enamored of two women (Greenwood and Tutin) who both have an incredible fixation about falling in love with men named Ernest. Of course neither man is "earnest" about his real name—not that Jack is sure of his. Bring in dragon Lady Bracknell (Evans), a dizzy tutor (Rutherford) and an amorous reverend (Malleson) and the identity search is on. This marvelous cast makes each pearl of dialogue shine. Redgrave and Dennison are impossibly smooth, Tutin is delightfully pert and Greenwood uses her inimitable voice and crisp acting style to delightful effect. The role of the anxious, garrulous Miss Prism is perfect for Rutherford and Malleson makes an ideal foil. Perhaps the best of them all is Edith Evans, in a role she made her own. "Do you smoke," she asks the nervous Jack. "Yes I do," he tentatively responds. "Good," she notes, "a man should have an occupation of some sort." Best of all, though, is her legendary multi-octave reading of the simple line "Handbag?". It doesn't get much better than this.

IMPROMPTU

1990 107m c Biography/Romance   ★★★½
Governor/Ariane (U.K.)   PG-13/12

Judy Davis (George Sand), Hugh Grant (Frederic Chopin), Mandy Patinkin (Alfred DeMusset), Bernadette Peters (Marie d'Agoult), Julian Sands (Franz Liszt), Ralph Brown (Eugene Delacroix), Georges Corraface (Felicien Mallefille), Anton Rodgers (Duke d'Antan), Emma Thompson (Duchess d'Antan), Anna Massey (George Sand's Mother)

p, Stuart Oken, Daniel A. Sherkow; d, James Lapine; w, Sarah Kernochan; ph, Bruno de Keyzer; ed, Michael Ellis; m, Frederic Chopin, Franz Liszt; art d, Gerard Daoudal; fx, Gilbert Pieri; cos, Jenny Beavan

The life and many loves of French novelist George Sand (1804-67), as depicted in James Lapine's IMPROMPTU, has the feel of a contemporary romantic comedy. This feature debut for Pulitzer Prize-winning stage director Lapine (*Sunday in the Park with George*) is distinguished by a fine cast, including Judy Davis as the truly liberated Sand, a woman whose vacillation with respect to men is exceeded only by her passion for them.

The film introduces viewers to Sand's circle of friends, including the painter Eugene Delacroix (Ralph Brown), poet and one-time lover Alfred DeMusset (Mandy Patinkin), and composers Franz Liszt (Julian Sands) and Frederic Chopin (Hugh Grant). It is Chopin who captures Sand's heart and is the object of her determined affection throughout the film. An unassuming man, in continual ill-health, Chopin first encounters the brazen Sand when she steals into his room, hides under his piano, and revels in his music. This takes place during the summer of 1835 at the country estate of the Duke and Duchess d'Antan (Anton

Rodgers and Emma Thompson), where Chopin, Liszt, Delacroix and DeMusset have been invited to enrich the lives of their culture-starved hosts. Sand has quite candidly invited herself and her two young children.

The gathering also includes Liszt's mistress, Marie d'Agoult (Bernadette Peters), and Sand's newly jilted lover, Felicien Mallefille (Georges Corraface), her children's tutor. Consumed with jealousy, Mallefille spends his time threatening any man who looks at Sand, and instigating a duel with DeMusset. Sand, meanwhile, enlists Marie's help in delivering a note to Chopin. Envious of Sand and feeling neglected by Liszt, Marie passes on the note, but not before removing Sand's name and substituting her own. The fortnight holiday soon comes to an end and Sand, unsuccessful in her efforts to seduce Chopin but determined win his affection, departs with her children and Mallefille.

Favored by Sarah Kernochan's character-driven screenplay and its elegant French locations, IMPROMPTU gives its actors ample room in which to play. Davis shines as Sand, balancing her decided independence with her desire for heady companionship. Grant's Chopin is a bit overplayed, making him seem too prudish. Patinkin is credible as the volatile DeMusset, as are Sands as Liszt, Brown as Delacroix, and Corraface as Mallefille. Peters is well-cast as the manipulative, everpregnant Marie and Thompson is hilarious as the duchess—a woman with far too much free time. Those performances, along with the fine music and costumes, help to make this an appealingly offbeat period piece.

IN A LONELY PLACE
1950 94m bw Drama   ★★★★★
Santana (U.S.)   /PG

Humphrey Bogart (Dixon Steele), Gloria Grahame (Laurel Gray), Frank Lovejoy (Brub Nicolai), Carl Benton Reid (Capt. Lochner), Art Smith (Mel Lippman), Jeff Donnell (Sylvia Nicolai), Martha Stewart (Mildred Atkinson), Robert Warwick (Charlie Waterman), Morris Ankrum (Lloyd Barnes), William Ching (Ted Barton)

p, Robert Lord, Henry S. Kesler; d, Nicholas Ray; w, Andrew Solt (based on a story by Edmund H. North, from the novel by Dorothy B. Hughes); ph, Burnett Guffey; ed, Viola Lawrence; m, George Antheil; art d, Robert Peterson; cos, Jean Louis

Superb film noir, brilliantly directed by the gifted Ray with Bogart as a talented but volatile Hollywood screenwriter.

Because of his heavy drinking and truculent nature, Bogart is not much in demand among the film studios but his dogged, devoted agent, Smith, manages to get him a writing assignment, to adapt a celebrated romance novel for the screen. They meet in a Hollywood bar-restaurant (a thinly disguised Chasen's) where Bogart argues with Ankrum, the director of the proposed film, accusing him of making the same film over and over again. His one friend in the bar is a broken down actor, Warwick, and when a strutting, bragging producer, Howard (perhaps modeled on Carl Laemmle, Jr.), insults the actor, Bogart knocks Howard about and has to be restrained. Smith urges him to go home and read the novel he must adapt, but Bogart knows it's a potboiler and is reluctant. Then the hatcheck girl at the club, Stewart, who has read and loves the novel, offers to tell Bogart the tale. He takes her home to his bungalow (in a complex that smacks of the famous Garden of Allah, owned and operated by Ali Nazimova, a haven for actors and writers such as Robert Benchley and F. Scott Fitzgerald). Watching Bogart and Stewart enter the bungalow from across the courtyard is lovely Grahame, a new neighbor. As Stewart rattles on about the story, Bogart slips into his bathrobe, pours himself a drink, and tries to calm Stewart down when she begins histrionically enacting scenes from the novel, which brings Grahame to her upstairs window again to watch the couple through open windows. Finally, Bogart has had enough. He's tired, he explains. He gives Stewart cab fare and sends her home. The next day, Stewart's viciously disfigured body is found and Bogart, thought to be the last person to see her alive, is brought in for questioning by the police.

LONELY PLACE epitomizes star-crossed lovers incapable of escaping environment and circumstances no matter how hard they try. The entire cast is excellent, with Bogart giving an electrifying portrait of a man in torment. Grahame, never more beautiful, is captivating as

a woman who has been kept too many times and now has one last chance for real love. Ray's helmsmanship here is superb as he runs the story to a quick conclusion, dwelling upon loving and frightening scenes with the skilled balance of a master juggler, keeping the viewer doubting and believing in Bogart from scene to scene. Many thought the film's central relationship reflected on Ray's unraveling marriage to Grahame. They split when filming was over, and the offbeat Grahame went on to marry Ray's son by a previous marriage, causing shockwaves in the 50s fanzines.

IN COLD BLOOD
1967 134m bw Biography/Crime   ★★★½
Pax (U.S.)   R/X

Robert Blake (Perry Smith), Scott Wilson (Dick Hickock), John Forsythe (Alvin Dewey), Paul Stewart (Reporter), Gerald S. O'Loughlin (Harold Nye), Jeff Corey (Hickock's Father), John Gallaudet (Roy Church), James Flavin (Clarence Duntz), Charles McGraw (Smith's Father), Jim Lantz (Officer Rohleder)

p, Richard Brooks; d, Richard Brooks; w, Richard Brooks (based on the book by Truman Capote); ph, Conrad Hall; ed, Peter Zinner; m, Quincy Jones; art d, Robert Boyle; fx, Geza Gaspar; cos, Jack Martell

AAN Best Director: Richard Brooks; AAN Best Adapted Screenplay: Richard Brooks; AAN Best Cinematography: Conrad Hall; AAN Best Score: Quincy Jones

Like the title says. IN COLD BLOOD dramatizes actual events and people in a realistic, technically well-crafted fashion, based upon Truman Capote's "nonficton" novel. Capote seized upon the real-life November 15, 1959 mass murder of the Clutter family in Holcomb, Kansas, by two psychopathic killers, and turned the grisly tale into a bestseller. In making the movie, director Brooks avoids further analysis, laying out the story of Smith and Hickock as faithful docudrama.

Vagrants Blake and Wilson desperately cast about for ways to make an illegal buck, having been cell mates in state prison. Wilson has learned from another inmate that the Clutters keep $10,000 in their farm house, so the pair invades the home, terrorizing, then savagely slaughtering, the family; they leave with little loot since there is no $10,000 to be found. The killers are shown running to Mexico, then back to the US, leaving a trail of bad checks which federal agents follow until they're apprehended in Las Vegas. Brooks then spends half the film displaying Blake and Wilson in the Kansas State Penitentiary at Lansing waiting to be hanged. He emphasizes the state's brutality in taking their lives on the gallows on April 14, 1965, after endless appeals, stays, and agonizing soul-searching on the part of the culprits.

The facts described, what's it all about? Brooks avoids all the pitfalls of cliche, but shouldn't an in-depth docudrama have presented the aftermath of the murders on the Clutter's community and relatives? For those familiar with the case, the leads do bear a resemblance to the two real-life murderers, but Brooks's examination is decidedly one-sided. Exquisitely photographed in wide-screen black-and-white by Conrad Hall.

IN OLD CHICAGO
1938 115m bw Historical/Disaster   ★★★
Fox (U.S.)

Tyrone Power (Dion O'Leary), Alice Faye (Belle Fawcett), Don Ameche (Jack O'Leary), Alice Brady (Molly O'Leary), Andy Devine (Pickle Bixby), Brian Donlevy (Gil Warren), Phyllis Brooks (Ann Colby), Tom Brown (Bob O'Leary), Sidney Blackmer (Gen. Phil Sheridan), Berton Churchill (Sen. Colby)

p, Kenneth MacGowan; d, Henry King, Robert D. Webb; w, Lamar Trotti, Sonya Levien (based on a story "We the O'Learys" by Niven Busch); ph, Peverell Marley; ed, Barbara McLean; art d, William Darling, Rudolph Sternad; fx, Fred Sersen, Ralph Hammeras, Louis J. White; cos, Royer

AAN Best Picture; AA Best Supporting Actress: Alice Brady; AAN Best Original Screenplay: Niven Busch; AAN Best Score: Louis Silvers, 20th Century-Fox Studio Music Department; AAN Best Sound: E.H. Hansen

In old Zanuck's studio, a big-budget, mediocre cash-in on MGM's SAN FRANCISCO, minus the male star-charisma of the latter.

All the biggest Fox stars of the time were assembled for this nearly $2 million production: Alice Brady won a supporting actress Oscar for her role as Mrs. O'Leary, the woman who supports her family after the death of her husband by taking in washing. She manages to raise her sons into a handsome rake and political schemer (Power); a crusading lawyer (Ameche); and a young man with no ambitions other than to marry his sweetheart and have babies (Brown). Alice Faye gets to do her saloon singer bit, parading her legs in $1500 jeweled stockings and swooning her way through nostalgic sentiments with that deep, honeyed voice. There's a lot of political intrigue involving Power, Ameche and crooked mayor Donlevy, but it's all just a build-up to the fire, sparked by a well-placed kick from one of Mrs. O'Leary's cows. Director King's specialty—spectacle—gets a workout, and he has a blast staging teeming city crowds, brawling saloons, police platoons dismantling riots, runaway horses, stampeding cattle and all the drama the rise of Irish tempers will allow.

CHICAGO makes up in atmosphere and color what it lacks in historical accuracy; the screenplay was based on Niven Busch's *We the O'Learys*. The fire itself propelled production costs to $1,800,000, and runs for twenty minutes. (Assistant director Robert Webb won an Oscar for his work on the sequence.) Worth a view along with the great disaster epics of the 1930s, the aforementioned SAN FRANCISCO, THE HURRICANE, and THE RAINS COME.

IN THE HEAT OF THE NIGHT

1967   109m   c   Crime   ★★★★
Mirisch   (U.S.)   /15

Sidney Poitier (Virgil Tibbs), Rod Steiger (Bill Gillespie), Warren Oates (Sam Wood), Quentin Dean (Delores Purdy), James Patterson (Purdy), William Schallert (Webb Schubert), Jack Teter (Philip Colbert), Lee Grant (Mrs. Leslie Colbert), Scott Wilson (Harvey Oberst), Matt Clark (Packy Harrison)

p, Walter Mirisch; d, Norman Jewison; w, Stirling Silliphant (based on the novel by John Ball); ph, Haskell Wexler; ed, Hal Ashby; m, Quincy Jones; art d, Paul Groesse; cos, Alan Levine

AA Best Picture; AA Best Actor: Rod Steiger; AAN Best Director: Norman Jewison; AA Best Adapted Screenplay: Stirling Silliphant; AA Best Editing: Hal Ashby; AA Best Sound: Samuel Goldwyn Studio Sound Department; AAN Best Sound Effects Editing: James A. Richard

Superb thriller starring Rod Steiger in an Oscar-winning role as Bill Gillespie, a shrewd southern sheriff, and Sidney Poitier as Virgil Tibbs, a sensitive, intellectual detective from the big city. When a wealthy industrialist is murdered in the little town of Sparta, Mississippi, a well-dressed black stranger is arrested while waiting at the train station. The stranger, Tibbs, identifies himself as a Philadelphia policeman, and, under orders from his superiors up north, assists Gillespie in his investigation. Gillespie grudgingly accepts his assistance and protects him from brutal attacks by local rednecks, and the two grow to admire each other as they confront red herrings and racism en route to identifying the killer.

IN THE HEAT OF THE NIGHT was carefully directed by Norman Jewison, who avoids sentimentality and all the racial cliches that could have crept into almost every scene. As a result, his film won the Academy's Best Picture Award, shocking many when it was chosen over BONNIE AND CLYDE and THE GRADUATE. Steiger's performance is subtle, funny, sad, and fascinating, and Poitier demonstrates the same superb talent he would bring to THEY CALL ME MR. TIBBS and THE ORGANIZATION. Lee Grant is also good as the hysterical widow. The film was shot in Illinois and Tennessee, the latter standing in for Mississippi.

IN THE LINE OF FIRE

1993   123m   c   Thriller   ★★★½
Apple/Rose Productions/Castle Rock   (U.S.)   R/15

Clint Eastwood (Frank Horrigan), John Malkovich (Mitch Leary), Rene Russo (Lilly Raines), Dylan McDermott (Al D'Andrea), Gary Cole (Bill Watts), Fred Dalton Thompson (Harry Sargent), John Mahoney (Sam Campagna), Gregory Alan-Williams (Matt Wilder), Jim Curley (President), Sally Hughes (First Lady)

p, Jeff Apple; d, Wolfgang Petersen; w, Jeff Maguire; ph, John Bailey; ed, Anne V. Coates; m, Ennio Morricone; prod d, Lilly Kilvert; art d, John Warnke; fx, Rocky Gehr, John Nelson, R. Greenberg Associates West Inc., Bruno George; cos, Erica Edell Phillips

AAN Best Supporting Actor: John Malkovich; AAN Best Editing: Anne V. Coates; AAN Best Original Screenplay: Jeff Maguire

It seems postal workers are not the only government employees likely to go on a vengeful rampage as a response to being fired. IN THE LINE OF FIRE pits Secret Service Agent Frank Horrigan (Clint Eastwood) against Mitch Leary (John Malkovich), a top CIA hit man until the agency cancelled his contract. Leary plans to get even by undertaking a suicide-mission assassination of the President. The twist is that Horrigan was present at J.F.K.'s assassination 30 years ago, and is ridden with guilt at having failed to take the fatal bullet. Leary is ready to trade his life for that of the Prez; if the situation requires it, is Horrigan equally willing to give up *his* life to save the Chief Executive?

IN THE LINE OF FIRE explores this intriguing premise with subtlety and suspense, particularly during several phone conversations between a gloating, you-can't-stop-me Leary and a visibly shaken Horrigan. Eastwood plays the agent in a style you could call "Unforgiven Lite," as a physical and emotional burnout who seems no match for his criminal mastermind adversary. (His age, though, doesn't stop Horrigan from romancing an initially disdainful fellow agent, played by Rene Russo.) As Leary, Malkovich has fun donning a wide array of disguises and dispatching human obstacles with Hannibal Lecter-like precision. The result is a finely tuned suspense thriller, though executives who have recently laid off trained killers may experience some discomfort.

IN THE NAME OF THE FATHER

1993   127m   c   Drama/Historical/Political   ★★★½
Hell's Kitchen Ltd.   (U.S.)   R/15

Daniel Day-Lewis (Gerald Conlon), Pete Postlethwaite (Guiseppe Conlon), Emma Thompson (Gareth Peirce), John Lynch (Paul Hill), Joanna Irvine (Ann Conlon), Beatie Edney (Carole Richardson), Britta Smith (Anne Maguire), Don Baker (Joe McAndrew), Corin Redgrave (Robert Dixon), Gerard McSorley (Belfast Detective Pavis)

p, Jim Sheridan; d, Jim Sheridan; w, Terry George, Jim Sheridan (from the autobiography Proved Innocent by Gerry Conlon); ph, Peter Biziou; ed, Gerry Hambling; m, Trevor Jones; prod d, Caroline Amies; art d, Rick Butler, Tom Brown; fx, Joss Williams; cos, Joan Bergin

AAN Best Picture; AAN Best Actor: Daniel Day-Lewis; AAN Best Supporting Actor: Pete Postlethwaite; AAN Best Supporting Actress: Emma Thompson; AAN Best Director: Jim Sheridan; AAN Best Editing: Gerry Hambling; AAN Best Adapted Screenplay: Terry George, Jim Sheridan

Based on the true story of accused IRA bomber Gerry Conlon, Jim Sheridan's IN THE NAME OF THE FATHER is the powerful saga of an unlikely Irish martyr wrongfully imprisoned by the British government. Sheridan takes a controversial subject and gives it wider appeal by focusing on the family drama of two men who are also political prisoners.

In 1974, the Irish Republican Army bombs a pub in Guildford, England, killing five people. British police detain a number of suspects, including Gerry Conlon (Daniel Day-Lewis)—who has recently moved to London from Belfast—and his friend Paul. Gerry returns to his family in Belfast, and the police arrest him and three of his commune friends. The Guildford Four are ruthlessly interrogated for seven days until they each sign bogus confessions; Gerry's relatives—including his father Giuseppe

(PetePostlethwaite)—are unjustly charged with abetting the IRA and given harsh sentences. Father and son are imprisoned together; Giuseppe dies after years of cruel confinement, and Gerry pours his energy into exonerating his family, helped by English solicitor Gareth Peirce (Emma Thompson).

Sheridan explores a controversial, real-life political injustice, complete with police interrogations, courtroom antics, and prison confrontations, but his real interest is Gerry's relationship with his dad. Sheridan demonizes both the British police and the IRA, leaving the Guildford Four as symbols of injustice, with no specific national, political, or ethnic affiliation. Though the facts have been manipulated in the interests of drama—Gerry and Giuseppe were never imprisoned together, etc.—this has been done in a brave and responsible way, shedding light on an important episode in recent history.

IN THE REALM OF THE SENSES
(AI NO CORRIDA)

1976 105m c Erotic/Drama ★★★
Argos Films/Oceanic/Oshima Productions/Shibata /18
Organization Inc.   (France/Japan)

Tatsuya Fuji (Kichizo), Eiko Matsuda (Sada), Aoi Nakajima (Toku), Maika Seri (Matsuko—Maid), Taiji Tonoyama (Old Beggar), Hiroko Fuji (Tsune—Maid), Naomi Shiraishi (Yaeji—Geisha), Kyoko Okada (Hangyoku), Kikuhei Matsunoya (Hohkan), Yasuko Matsui (Manageress of Inn)

p, Anatole Dauman; d, Nagisa Oshima; w, Nagisa Oshima; ph, Hideo Ito, Kenichi Okamoto; ed, Keiichi Uraoka, Patrick Sauvion; m, Minoru Miki; art d, Jusho Toda; fx, Isao Nishimura, Terumi Hosoishi; cos, Jusho Toda

Based on a true case involving a woman in 1936 who was found wandering the streets of Tokyo carrying her dead lover's severed penis, Nagisa Oshima's sexually graphic, and extremely disturbing, IN THE REALM OF THE SENSES, became notorious when it was seized by U.S. Customs officials in 1976, postponing its showing at the New York Film Festival.

In 1936 Japan, a nymphomaniac ex-prostitute named Sada (Eiko Matsuda) goes to work at an inn owned by Kichizo (Tatsuya Fuji) and his wife. Sada and Kichizo begin an affair and he eventually leaves his wife and runs away with Sada. They move into a geisha house in the red-light district, where their frequent bouts of sex, often outdoors and in front of others, shocks even the other prostitutes. Needing money, Sada has sex with an ex-client, an elderly man who was her school principal, and Kichizo has sex with the geisha house's fat maid (Kazue Tomiyama) while Sada is gone. As their sexual practices become increasingly intense and bizarre, the couple begin experimenting with partial strangulation as a method of sexual stimulation.

The iconoclastic Oshima made IN THE REALM OF THE SENSES with the intention to shock and shatter taboos. With its explicit and graphic shots of actual penetration and fellatio, there is no doubt that the film is pornographic in the broadest definition of the term, although whether it was made with the intention to arouse sexual desire is quite doubtful. It's certainly a completely honest film, fearlessly showing what others whose subject is sex, only hint at, but whether or not the photographic depiction of real sex can be transformed into art by a distinguished filmmaker, by placing it into the context of a metaphorical story of obsession and domination, is highly debatable. There is no doubt that Oshima is a serious and talented artist, as evidenced by many of his other films, and in the surreal qualities of certain scenes here. On a traditional level, the film is visually quite beautiful, with delicate and sensitive use of color, composition, decor, and music, and as the lovers, Tatsuya Fuji and Eiko Matsuda give remarkably natural performances, under the circumstances, but the repeated scenes of them having sex become numbing and eventually laughable, and the horrifying ending is almost impossible to watch.

IN WHICH WE SERVE

1942 115m bw War ★★★½
Two Cities (U.K.) /U

Noel Coward (Capt. Kinross), John Mills (Shorty Blake), Bernard Miles (Walter Hardy), Celia Johnson (Alix Kinross), Kay Walsh (Freda Lewis), Joyce Carey (Kath Hardy), Michael Wilding (Flags), Penelope-Dudley Ward (Maureen Fenwick), Philip Friend (Torps), Derek Elphinstone (No. One)

p, Noel Coward; d, Noel Coward, David Lean; w, Noel Coward (based on the experiences of Lord Louis Mountbatten); ph, Ronald Neame; ed, Thelma Myers, David Lean; m, Noel Coward

AAN Best Picture; AAN Best Original Screenplay: Noel Coward

Noel Coward performed with unexpected brilliance here as co-director, writer, musical composer, and star of this stirring WWII drama. Presented in a series of poignant and revealing vignettes, the film tells the story of the British destroyer *Torrin* and its crew, commanded by Capt. Kinross (Coward), a father figure for his stalwart men. Constructed like a documentary, IN WHICH WE SERVE is also narrated by Coward, who recounts the ship's heroic actions: hit by torpedoes, it survives and is towed back to England, later participating in the Dunkirk evacuation and in naval battles off Crete, where it is dive-bombed and sinks. Kinross and his crew cling to a raft for hours, and while waiting for rescue, remember their loved ones in a series of flashbacks.

Regarded as noble and understated at the time, IN WHICH WE SERVE now comes across as patronizing and riven with class condescension. But to Coward's credit (he recieved a special Oscar "for his outstanding production achievement"), he had the good sense to choose the most distinguished film editor in England at the time, David Lean, to assist with the production; and so impressive was Lean's work that, halfway through the picture, Coward handed him the directorial reins. Out of respect, Lean's next three productions—THIS HAPPY BREED; BLITHE SPIRIT; and BRIEF ENCOUNTER—were adaptations of Coward's writing. SERVE marked the film debuts of Johnson, Massey and baby Mills.

INCREDIBLE SHRINKING MAN, THE

1957 81m bw Science Fiction ★★★
Universal (U.S.) /A

Grant Williams (Scott Carey), Randy Stuart (Louise Carey), April Kent (Clarice), Paul Langton (Charlie Carey), Raymond Bailey (Dr. Thomas Silver), William Schallert (Dr. Arthur Bramson), Frank Scannell (Barker), Helene Marshall, Diana Darrin (Nurses), Billy Curtis (Midget)

p, Albert Zugsmith; d, Jack Arnold; w, Richard Matheson (based on his novel The Shrinking Man); ph, Ellis W. Carter; ed, Al Joseph; m, Fred Carling, Elliot Lawrence; art d, Alexander Golitzen, Robert Clatworthy; fx, Clifford Stine, Roswell A. Hoffmann, Everett H. Broussard; cos, Jay A. Morley Jr.

Pulp sci-fi classic about a man who starts to shrink after being enveloped by a strange atomic cloud while on holiday. Notable for its relatively intelligent script (adapted by Richard Matheson from his novel), for some imaginatively amusing special effects, and for an existential streak which finally has our (tiny) hero pondering the meaning of existence. (Matheson sold his novel on the condition that he be allowed to write the script. His first novel, *I Am Legend*, had been badly butchered, and he had no wish to see that happen again. Eventually, *I Am Legend* was filmed as L'ULTIMO UOMO DELLA TERRA from another writer's screenplay.) Source for a promising, but largely unsuccessful remake, THE INCREDIBLE SHRINKING WOMAN, in 1981.

INDECENT PROPOSAL

1993 118m c Romance/Drama ★★★
Sherry Lansing Productions (U.S.) R/15

Robert Redford (John Gage), Demi Moore (Diana Murphy), Woody Harrelson (David Murphy), Seymour Cassel (Mr. Shackelford), Oliver Platt (Jeremy), Billy Bob Thornton (Day Tripper), Rip Taylor (Mr. Langford), Billy Connolly (Auction Emcee), Joel Brooks (Realtor), Pierre Epstein (Van Buren) p, Sherry Lansing; d, Adrian Lyne; w, Amy Holden Jones (from the novel by Jack Englehard); ph, Howard Atherton; ed, Joe Hutshing; m, John Barry; prod d, Mel Bourne; art d, Gae Buckley; fx, David Kelsey; cos, Bobbi Read, Bernie Pollack, Beatrix Aruna Pasztor

A huge commercial hit in theaters, INDECENT PROPOSAL should be able to crack two markets in the home video realm: as a feature film, and as an anthology of romantic screen cliches.

David (Woody Harrelson) and Diana Murphy (Demi Moore) are a devoted, financially strapped young couple faced with an unusual way out of their fiscal dilemma; a rich gambler (Robert Redford) offers $1,000,000 for a night of passion with the beautiful wife. If the premise is mildly intriguing, the execution is preposterous. This becomes clear after the first thirty seconds of soft-focus cinematography, over which we hear the following two lines of voiceover: Woody—"Losing Diana was like losing a part of me." Demi—"Someone once said that if you really love something, you should set it free." It's all downhill from there.

Director Adrian Lyne wastes no opportunity to show off Ms. Moore's pneumatic physique, which is the most noticeable feature of her performance. Robert Redford, meanwhile, seems fresh from the embalmer's studio—which at least puts his "young" rival Woody's receding hairline into flattering perspective. INDECENT PROPOSAL is as relentlessly entertaining as it is silly—so shamelessly over the top that you watch in a mixture of horror and delight as the drama unfolds toward a climax that is truly mind-boggling.

INDEPENDENCE DAY

1996 146m c Science Fiction/Thriller/Action ★★½
Centropolis Entertainment/20th Century Fox (U.S.) PG-13/12

Will Smith (Captain Steve Hiller), Bill Pullman (President Thomas J. Whitmore), Jeff Goldblum (David Levinson), Mary McDonnell (Marilyn Whitmore), Judd Hirsch (Julius Levinson), Robert Loggia (General William Grey), Randy Quaid (Russell Casse), Margaret Colin (Constance Spano), James Rebhorn (Albert Nimziki), Harvey Fierstein (Marty Gilbert)

p, Dean Devlin; d, Roland Emmerich; w, Dean Devlin, Roland Emmerich; ph, Karl Walter Lindenlaub; ed, David Brenner; m, David Arnold; prod d, Patrick Tatopoulos, Oliver Scholl; art d, Jim Teegarden; fx, Clay Pinney, Volker Engel, Douglas Smith, Joseph Viskocil; cos, Joseph Porro

AA Best Visual Effects: Volker Engel, Douglas Smith, Clay Pinney, Joseph Viskocil; AAN Best Sound: Chris Carpenter, Bill W. Benton, Bob Beemer, Jeff Wexler

In technical terms, INDEPENDENCE DAY—one of the highest grossing films in history—is a masterpiece. As entertainment, it's effective in a bustling, bullying way, but sorely lacking in wonder, surprise, and eccentricity.

US President Thomas J. Whitmore (Bill Pullman) tackles an apocalyptic crisis that no other world leader has ever faced—invasion from outer space. In spaceships so huge they shadow entire cities, the mysterious visitors make their intentions deadly obvious by unleashing global destruction. Out to save the world with good-old American chutzpah and a lot of firepower are New York physicist David Levinson (Jeff Goldblum), fighter-pilot Steve Hiller (Will Smith), and Russell Casse (Randy Quaid), the alcoholic survivor of a close encounter many years before.

In INDEPENDENCE DAY, the moviemaking team of director Roland Emmerich and screenwriter Dean Devlin (STARGATE) invent a state-of-the-art weapon that shoots satiric holes in sci-fi formulas, while at the same time asking viewers to surrender to the film's dramatic weight. At hairpin turns of the narrative, viewers are expected to be moved by events that the filmmakers themselves take lightly. One-dimensional characters defined only by ethnic shtick and no real emotional stakes mar the perfect course of annihilation that the film maps out. Viewed as a gung-ho flick extolling xenophobia, the film does acquire some snap, crackle, and pop, zapping spectators on a thrill-ride of inventive effects. INDEPENDENCE DAY can be enjoyed as a feel-good, Earthman's pep rally, but the science fiction is really just a sideshow to the main carnival celebrating Uncle Sam's destructive know-how and Hollywood's ever-bigger bang. Sadly, it is also the most benign movie ever made about the end of our universe.

INDIAN IN THE CUPBOARD, THE

1995 96m c Children's/Fantasy/Adventure ★★★½
Kennedy/Marshall Company/Scholastic PG
Productions/Paramount/Columbia (U.S.)

Hal Scardino (Omri), Litefoot (Little Bear), Lindsay Crouse (Jane), Richard Jenkins (Victor), Rishi Bhat (Patrick), Steve Coogan (Tommy), David Keith (Boone), Sakina Jaffrey (Lucy), Vincent Kartheiser (Gillon), Nestor Serrano (Teacher)

p, Kathleen Kennedy, Frank Marshall, Jane Startz; d, Frank Oz; w, Melissa Mathison (based on the novel by Lynne Reid Banks); ph, Russell Carpenter; ed, Ian Crafford; m, Randy Edelman; prod d, Leslie McDonald; art d, Tony Fanning; fx, Eric Brevig, David Blitstein, Michael Lanteri, Ginger Theisen, Anne Calanchini, Industrial Light & Magic; cos, Deborah L. Scott

bThis exemplary work of political correctness boasts strong performances, low-key direction, and an intelligent screenplay. The film champions the validity of unfamiliar cultures and the importance of empathy without preaching.

Omri (Hal Scardino) lives with his family in New York, where he celebrates his ninth birthday. His presents include an old wooden cupboard, salvaged by older brother Gillon (Vincent Kartheiser), and a plastic figurine of an American Indian brave, a gift from Omri's best friend, Patrick (Rishi Bhat). Omri's mother (Lindsay Crouse) gives him an old key for the cupboard door. He places the plastic Indian inside, locks the door, and goes to sleep. Awakened by a sound from the cupboard, Omri finds that the Indian, an Iroquois named Little Bear (Litefoot), has come to life. Omri initially treats him like a pet, but he learns to respect him as he learns about Native American culture.

Adapted from the acclaimed children's book by Lynn Reid Banks, THE INDIAN IN THE CUPBOARD marks the return of screenwriter Melissa Mathison (aka Mrs. Harrison Ford) to movies. Best known for scripting E.T. THE EXTRA-TERRESTRIAL, Mathison excels at conjuring the private world of young boys. Director Frank Oz opts for solid story-telling over action set-pieces and star power. The special effects—though first-rate—fondly recall the quaint kiddie fantasies of yesteryear. The film's best aspects include the tender love of Omri's parents; the boy's quiet alliance with his mother; and the comparisons drawn between the lives of children, women, the elderly, and figures of Otherness. The buck-toothed, beguiling Scardino is a welcome alternative to the standard cute kid star, and Litefoot is properly strong and dignified.

INDIANA JONES AND THE LAST CRUSADE

1989 127m c Adventure ★★½
Lucasfilm (U.S.) PG-13/PG

Harrison Ford (Indiana Jones), Sean Connery (Dr. Henry Jones), Denholm Elliott (Marcus Brody), Alison Doody (Dr. Elsa Schneider), John Rhys-Davies (Sallah), Julian Glover (Walter Donovan), River Phoenix (Young Indy), Michael Byrne (Vogel), Kevork Malikyan (Kazim), Robert Eddison (Grail Knight)

p, Robert Watts; d, Steven Spielberg; w, Jeffrey Boam (based on a story by George Lucas, Menno Meyjes, and characters created by Lucas, Philip Kaufman); ph, Douglas Slocombe, Paul Beeson, Robert Stevens; ed, Michael Kahn; m, John Williams; prod d, Elliot Scott; art d, Fred Hole, Stephen Scott, Richard Berger, Benjamin Fernandez, Guido Salsilli; cos, Anthony Powell, Joanna Johnston

AAN Best Score: John Williams; AAN Best Sound: Ben Burtt, Gary Summers, Shawn Murphy, Tony Dawe; AA Best Sound Effects Editing: Ben Burtt, Richard Hymns

We're over it. The third and mercifully, final installment in Steven Spielberg and George Lucas's INDIANA JONES series sends the intrepid adventurer out with more bucks than bang. This time Indy (Harrison Ford) has a sidekick in his archaeologist father, Dr. Henry Jones (Sean Connery), a relationship involving not a little Oedipal tension. Together, the Joneses embark on a quest to find the Holy Grail, hoping to keep it from the evil Nazis (who want it because it gives eternal life), and falling afoul of a beautiful spy (Alison Doody) along the way.

INDIANA JONES AND THE TEMPLE OF DOOM

Proceeding with considerably less blood, energy or danger than either RAIDERS OF THE LOST ARK or INDIANA JONES AND THE TEMPLE OF DOOM, THE LAST CRUSADE hearkens more purely back to the series's sources—the fairly innocuous weekly cliff-hangers of days gone by. The film offers some thrills and chills, but does so with such sanitized filmcraft that it's difficult to get excited about them. Despite strong acting (the slapstick energy between Ford and Connery is wasted), obligatory chases and stunts and splendid art direction, the virtuoso technique evident in every frame remains formulaic—unaccompanied by revelation, epiphany or surprise.

INDIANA JONES AND THE TEMPLE OF DOOM

1984 118m c Adventure   ★★★
Lucasfilm (U.S.)   PG

Harrison Ford (*Indiana Jones*), Kate Capshaw (*Willie Scott*), Ke Huy Quan (*Short Round*), Amrish Puri (*Mola Ram*), Roshan Seth (*Chattar Lal*), Philip Stone (*Capt. Blumburtt*), Roy Chiao (*Lao Che*), David Yip (*Wu Han*), Ric Young (*Kao Kan*), Chua Kah Joo (*Chen*)

p, Robert Watts; d, Steven Spielberg; w, Willard Huyck, Gloria Katz (based on a story by George Lucas and on characters from RAIDERS OF THE LOST ARK); ph, Douglas Slocombe; ed, Michael Kahn; m, John Williams; prod d, Elliot Scott; art d, Alan Cassie, Roger Cain, Joe Johnston, Errol Kelly; fx, Dennis Muren; chor, Danny Daniels; cos, Anthony Powell

AAN Best Score: John Williams; *AA Best Visual Effects:* Dennis Muren, Michael McAlister, Lorne Peterson, George Gibbs

After the release of director Steven Spielberg's RAIDERS OF THE LOST ARK, the question on almost everyone's lips was "How can he top this?" The answer won't be found in the $25 million sequel INDIANA JONES AND THE TEMPLE OF DOOM, a breakneck adventure that moves at twice the pace of the original but has only half the creative strength. The film opens with one of the decade's most purely entertaining scenes, a Busby Berkeley-style dance number to Cole Porter's "Anything Goes" (perhaps a clue to the line of logic the filmmakers were to follow). The setting is a swanky Shanghai nightclub in 1935 where heroic archaeologist Indiana Jones (Harrison Ford) has a run-in with some bad guys and is forced to make his getaway with singer Willie Scott (Kate Capshaw). Moments later they meet up with a 12-year-old named Short Round (Ke Huy Quan). The trio ends up in a primitive Indian village, where Jones is beckoned to retrieve a sacred stone from a heavily guarded palace and encounters a sanguinary Khali cult lifted from GUNGA DIN.

Director Spielberg has crammed ceaseless special effects, chases, and gross-outs into the film's nearly two hours. The nonstop pace may eventually numb viewers to the thrills, although Spielberg must be congratulated for adding some shades of character to his archetypal action hero this time around. The film is not helped by a xenophobia that sometimes verges on racism, or by its surprisingly graphic violence. A gruesome scene in which a beating heart is ripped from the chest of a sacrificial victim stirred controversy and prompted the MPAA to create the PG-13 rating.

INDISCREET

1958 100m c Romance/Comedy   ★★★½
Grandon (U.K.)   /PG

Cary Grant (*Philip Adams*), Ingrid Bergman (*Anna Kalman*), Cecil Parker (*Alfred Munson*), Phyllis Calvert (*Margaret Munson*), David Kossoff (*Carl Banks*), Megs Jenkins (*Doris Banks*), Oliver Johnston (*Mr. Finleigh*), Michael Anthony (*Oscar*), Middleton Woods (*Finleigh's Clerk*), Frank Hawkins

p, Stanley Donen; d, Stanley Donen; w, Norman Krasna (based on his play "Kind Sir"); ph, Freddie Young; ed, Jack Harris; m, Richard Rodney Bennett, Ken Jones; art d, Don Ashton; cos, Quintino

One of those rare movies that is far better than the play from which it was adapted. Based on Norman Krasna's Broadway flop, "Kind Sir," the movie is a frothy, often funny, diversion. Bergman, who proved her expertise in comedy with this performance, is a rich actress living in regal London luxury. Her sister, Calvert, and brother-in-law, Parker, introduce her to Grant, a financial genius who has come to London for a NATO dinner. Grant is a lifelong bachelor who masquerades as a

married man to keep his single status secure. Grant tells Bergman that he's married, wich is fine with her. She has no interest in getting married and no compunctions about having an affair with a man who claims that he's separated and whose wife won't grant him freedom. Grant takes a job with NATO in Paris and their romance thrives as he comes to visit Bergman in London every weekend. When Grant is told he must transfer to New York for as long as five months, Bergman is at first heartbroken, then plans to quit the play she's appearing in and head for the US herself. But Calvert, who has learned the truth about Grant's marital status, lets Bergman in on the secret. Hurt and angry, Bergman plots to arouse Grant's jealousy by feigning an affair with a former lover.

The play starred Charles Boyer and Mary Martin, and, as good as they were, Grant and Bergman eclipsed them in the movie. This was a throwback to the Philip Barry school of drawing room comedy, and both Grant and Bergman were up to the challenge of re-creating the kind of movie that had been popular 20 years before. (Many of those, after all, had starred Grant.) This was the second pairing of Bergman and Grant (the first was in Alfred Hitchcock's NOTORIOUS in 1946) and they make a wonderful screen team, both adroitly handling the film's humor. Not to be missed is Grant's impromptu dance at a proper London club. INDISCREET is the perfect film to watch when you just want to lean back and smile, knowing full well what the outcome will be. The only surprise in the picture is how deft a comedienne Bergman could be.

INFORMER, THE

1935 91m bw Drama   ★★★★
RKO (U.S.)

Victor McLaglen (*Gypo Nolan*), Heather Angel (*Mary McPhillip*), Preston Foster (*Dan Gallagher*), Margot Grahame (*Katie Madden*), Wallace Ford (*Frankie McPhillip*), Una O'Connor (*Mrs. McPhillip*), J.M. Kerrigan (*Terry*), Joe Sawyer (*Bartley Mulholland*), Neil Fitzgerald (*Tommy Conner*), Donald Meek (*Pat Mulligan*)

p, Cliff Reid; d, John Ford; w, Dudley Nichols (based on the novel by Liam O'Flaherty); ph, Joseph August; ed, George Hively; m, Max Steiner; art d, Van Nest Polglase, Charles Kirk; cos, Walter Plunkett

AAN Best Picture; AA Best Actor: Victor McLaglen; *AA Best Director:* John Ford; *AA Best Screenplay:* Dudley Nichols; *AA Best Score:* Max Steiner, RKO Radio Studio Music Department; *AAN Best Editing:* George Hively

Victor McLaglen gave the performance of his life as the scar-faced betrayer, Gypo Nolan, in this telling adaptation of Liam O'Flaherty's novel, directed by John Ford. The film gleaned top honors from the Academy, winning Oscars for McLaglen as Best Actor, Dudley Nichols for Best Adaptation, Max Steiner for Best Musical Score, and Ford for Best Director (he also won the New York Critics Best Director award).

Ford's tale of a hard-drinking brute who informs on one of his friends in order to collect a reward during the Irish Civil War of 1922 was made for a mere $243,000, and stands as one of the director's finer 1930s films. Joseph August's photography is superb, with its atmospheric shadows and light; the studio sets are brilliant representations of a fog-bound 1920s Dublin, complete with wet cobblestones and sweating walls. Through this mythic setting Ford moves his characters stoically to their grim fates. His selection of Victor McLaglen, who had starred in his other memorable talkie, THE LOST PATROL, was a masterstroke. Barrel-chested, with a thunderous voice and ox-like shoulders, McLaglen was the perfect Gypo Nolan, his battered face jutting pugnaciously into the camera (he had once been Heavyweight Champion of Great Britain). McLaglen never again reached such heights, although he appeared in around 150 films.

The first of three features Ford did for RKO, THE INFORMER became the studio's most prestigious production for years. Writer Nichols, one of Ford's favorite collaborators, wrote the script in six days, and Ford shot the entire film within another 17 days. THE INFORMER marked a turning point both for Ford, just entering into his most productive period, and composer Steiner, whose marvelous score perfectly fits every scene, from thundering patriotic cadences to lyrical and evocative motifs. The O'Flaherty novel had previously been filmed by British International as a silent; a remake with an all-Black cast, directed by Jules Dassin under the title UPTIGHT!, appeared in 1968.

INHERIT THE WIND

1960 127m bw Drama ★★★★
UA (U.S.) /A

Fredric March (Matthew Harrison Brady), Spencer Tracy (Henry Drummond), Gene Kelly (E.K. Hornbeck), Florence Eldridge (Mrs. Brady), Dick York (Bertram T. Cates), Donna Anderson (Rachel Brown), Harry Morgan (Judge), Elliott Reid (Davenport), Philip Coolidge (Mayor), Claude Akins (Rev. Brown)

p, Stanley Kramer; d, Stanley Kramer; w, Nedrick Young, Harold Jacob Smith (based on the play by Jerome Lawrence and Robert E. Lee); ph, Ernest Laszlo; ed, Frederic Knudtson; m, Ernest Gold; prod d, Rudolph Sternad; art d, Rudolph Sternad; cos, Joe King

AAN Best Actor: Spencer Tracy; AAN Best Adapted Screenplay: Nathan E Douglas, Harold Jacob Smith; AAN Best Cinematography: Ernest Laszlo; AAN Best Editing: Frederic Knudtson

Absorbing, if long-winded courtroom drama bolstered by two fine central performances from Tracy and March.

In the summer of 1925 the sovereign state of Tennessee played host to one of the most spectacular and ludicrous court trials in the history of American jurisprudence. A teacher named John T. Scopes had been arrested for teaching Darwin's theories of evolution in a public school, thus violating a state law. Prosecuting Scopes was the Rock of Ages fundamentalist, William Jennings Bryan, and defending him was the champion of liberal thinking, Clarence Darrow.

Producer-director Kramer used this high-voltage "Monkey Trial," as it came to be known, as the basis for one of his best film efforts. The names of the historical figures were all changed for the film, but their characters remain clearly recognizable. York plays the meek teacher, imprisoned for daring to teach Darwin in tiny Hillsboro. His girl friend is the daughter of fundamentalist preacher Akins, who agonizes over his daughter's affection for the religious infidel and sends for March to prosecute the young teacher. Tracy plays March's liberal opposite number, and song-and-dance man Kelly is inadequate as cynical journalist E.K. Hornbeck (based on H.L. Mencken).

INHERIT THE WIND acutely captures the farcical Monkey Trial and offers the awesome talents of two double-Oscar winners, Tracy and March, in their only film together. March's real wife, Florence Eldridge, plays his onscreen spouse, and Harry Morgan turns in a fine performance as the judge caught between heavyweights. Much of the dialog is lifted from the successful Broadway play by Lawrence and Lee and first starring Paul Muni and Ed Begley.

INNOCENCE UNPROTECTED
(NEVINOST BEZ ZASTITE)

1968 75m c/bw Drama ★★★★
Avala (Yugoslavia) /U

Dragoljub Aleksic (Acrobat Aleksic), Ana Milosavljevic (Nada The Orphan), Vera Jovanovic (The Wicked Stepmother), Bratoljub Gligorijevic (Mr. Petrovic), Ivan Zivkovic (Aleksic's Brother), Pera Milosavljevic (Servant)

d, Dusan Makavejev; w, Dusan Makavejev; ph, Branko Perak, Stevan Miskovic; ed, Ivanka Vukasovic; m, Vojislav Dostic

In 1942, Aleksic, a Yugoslavian gymnast and stunt man, wrote, produced, directed, and starred in a film titled INNOCENCE UNPROTECTED. Its simple plot concerns an acrobat with a pure heart rescuing young Milosavljevic from the clutches of her evil stepmother, Jovanovic. The final production was subsequently confiscated by the Nazis, fading into cinema obscurity. Aleksic himself was accused (but later exonerated) of collaborating with the enemy. In 1968 Yugoslavian director Dusan Makavejev discovered the long-forgotten movie and reworked it into a film collage, a technique Makavejev further explored in WR: MYSTERIES OF THE ORGANISM. He hand-tinted some of the original footage and edited in newsreels of Nazi-occupied Yugoslavia. To this was added vintage documentary footage of Aleksic performing various stunts and new scenes with surviving members of the original film's cast and crew. The result is a wonderful and highly

unusual film experience. Makavejev called it "a montage of attractions," an investigation of reality and illusion. The film is often confusing but full of ironies and biting humor, with a youthful exuberance emanating from both the director and Aleksic. A real love for the film medium irradiates the production.

INNOCENTS, THE

1961 99m bw Horror ★★★★½
Fox/Achilles (U.S./U.K.) /X

Deborah Kerr (Miss Giddens), Michael Redgrave (The Uncle), Peter Wyngarde (Peter Quint), Megs Jenkins (Mrs. Grose), Martin Stephens (Miles), Pamela Franklin (Flora), Clytie Jessop (Miss Jessel), Isla Cameron (Anna), Eric Woodburn (Coachman)

p, Jack Clayton; d, Jack Clayton; w, William Archibald, Truman Capote, John Mortimer (based on the novel The Turn of the Screw by Henry James); ph, Freddie Francis; ed, James B. Clark; m, Georges Auric; prod d, Wilfred Shingleton; art d, Wilfred Shingleton; cos, Sophie Devine, Motley

Based on Henry James' The Turn of the Screw, THE INNOCENTS is a fine chiller that builds suspense slowly, subtly, and inexorably. Kerr is on top form here, enacting a role that takes perfect advantage of her respectable facade wrestling with unspeakable turbulence beneath the surface.

In Victorian England, Kerr arrives at the country estate of Redgrave, who has hired her to serve as the governess of his young niece and nephew, Franklin and Stephens. The housekeeper, Jenkins, introduces her to Franklin, an angelic little child with a beguiling smile who appears to have a mysterious foreknowledge of her brother's imminent arrival, though he is not expected. Soon a letter arrives from Stephens' school, informing the household that the boy has been expelled because he is a corrupting influence on his schoolmates. However, when Stephens arrives, he proves to be every bit as innocent and entrancing as his sister, and Kerr decides that the school officials must have been mistaken. Though the estate is a beautiful refuge, there is also an air of eeriness about the place. Kerr thinks she sees a man atop the house, is temporarily blinded by the sun, and then discovers Stephens feeding pigeons where she thought the man was. Feeling that her eyes must have played tricks on her, she calms down; later, however, she sees the specter of a woman at a window, and then sees the man again, getting a glimpse of his twisted face. When she describes these apparitions to Jenkins, she is told that the descriptions match those of the estate's late manager and his dead lover, the woman who preceded Kerr as governess. Kerr learns further that the deceased lovers had a sadomasochistic relationship, and that they had a considerable influence on the children. Are the children possessed by evil, earthbound spirits or is Kerr going mad?

Filmed at Sheffield Park in Sussex, this literate and elegant gothic horror, co-scripted by Truman Capote and John Mortimer, is fairly faithful to the James original. THE INNOCENTS manipulates the viewer's imagination as few films can, with Kerr and Redgrave doing a masterful job of creating a sense of repressed hysteria.

INSIDE DAISY CLOVER

1965 128m c Drama ★★
Warner Bros. (U.S.) /X

Natalie Wood (Daisy Clover), Christopher Plummer (Raymond Swan), Robert Redford (Wade Lewis), Roddy McDowall (Walter Baines), Ruth Gordon (The Dealer), Katharine Bard (Melora Swan), Betty Harford (Gloria Goslett), John Hale (Harry Goslett), Harold Gould (Cop), Ottola Nesmith (Old Lady in Hospital)

p, Alan J. Pakula, Robert Mulligan; d, Robert Mulligan; w, Gavin Lambert (based on his own novel); ph, Charles Lang; ed, Aaron Stell; m, Andre Previn; prod d, Robert Clatworthy; art d, Dean Tavoularis; chor, Herbert Ross; cos, Bill Thomas, Edith Head

AAN Best Supporting Actress: Ruth Gordon; AAN Best Art Direction: Robert Clatworthy (Art Direction), George James Hopkins (Set Decoration); AAN Best Costume Design: Bill Thomas, Edith Head

Too much, too soon, for Daisy and for us. Gothic Hollywood-insider account of a Garland-like waif-star suffers from weak characters and minimalist (to say the least) plot. Gavin Lambert's screenplay (from his novel), throws us one big, hammy campfest scene, followed by another that expects us to take it seriously. Wood's teen star comes close to conjuring up Mickey Rooney in his show-in-the-barn phase; Ruth Gordon is abominable as a sort of Gladys Baker (Marilyn Monroe's mother) character; and Christopher Plummer plays his scenes like he's trying to run through a swimming pool. It's only Redford's narcissistic gay star that holds interest. (He won a Golden Globe as "Star of Tommorrow" for the role.) The songs by Andre and Dory Previn are, amazingly, musical ciphers, which is both disappointing and surprising. Most songwriters would give their eyeteeth for an excuse to write rich, full-blooded Golden Era showbiz songs.

INTERIORS

1978 93m c Drama   ★★★½
UA (U.S.)   PG/15

Kristin Griffith *(Flyn)*, Mary Beth Hurt *(Joey)*, Richard Jordan *(Frederick)*, Diane Keaton *(Renata)*, E.G. Marshall *(Arthur)*, Geraldine Page *(Eve)*, Maureen Stapleton *(Pearl)*, Sam Waterston *(Mike)*, Henderson Forsythe *(Judge Bartel)*

p, Charles H. Joffe; d, Woody Allen; w, Woody Allen; ph, Gordon Willis; ed, Ralph Rosenblum; prod d, Mel Bourne; cos, Joel Schumacher

AAN Best Actress: Geraldine Page; *AAN Best Supporting Actress:* Maureen Stapleton; *AAN Best Director:* Woody Allen; *AAN Best Original Screenplay:* Woody Allen (Story); *AAN Best Art Direction:* Mel Bourne (Art Direction), Daniel Robert (Art Direction)

Allen fans didn't like this stark examination of love, life, and death because they kept expecting it to turn funny and it never did. INTERIORS nevertheless represented an important and impressive change of direction for Allen, who here pays explicit homage to one of his acknowledged mentors, Ingmar Bergman—he even goes as far as to employ some of the master's best-known techniques, photographing the principals against blank walls and having them speak directly into the camera.

Wealthy Arthur (Marshall) and mentally disturbed Eve (Page) are the parents of three sisters. Arthur announces one day that he is leaving his wife to marry Pearl (Stapleton, in a role that gives the film its heart). The news causes Eve to disintegrate, and the daughters rush to their mother's side to help her through the crisis, even though they are having problems of their own. Renata (Keaton) is a poet married to a hack novelist (Jordan). Joey (Hurt), the most talented of the trio, seems incapable of focusing her abilities. Flyn (Griffith), meanwhile, a TV actress, is intensely self-centered. How the family deals with its problems forms the core of the film. The acting is outstanding all around, with special mention going to Hurt, Marshall, Page and Stapleton. Nominated for Oscars for writing, direction, actress (Page, inexplicably defeated by Jane Fonda in COMING HOME) and supporting actress.

INTERMEZZO: A LOVE STORY

1939 70m bw Romance   ★★★½
Selznick (U.S.)   /A

Leslie Howard *(Holger Brandt)*, Ingrid Bergman *(Anita Hoffman)*, Edna Best *(Margit Brandt)*, John Halliday *(Thomas Stenborg)*, Cecil Kellaway *(Charles Moler)*, Enid Bennett *(Greta Stenborg)*, Ann Todd *(Ann Marie Brandt)*, Douglas Scott *(Eric Brandt)*, Eleanor Wesselhoeft *(Emma)*, Marie Flynn *(Marianne)*

p, David O. Selznick; d, Gregory Ratoff; w, George O'Neil (based on a story by Gosta Stevens and Gustaf Molander); ph, Gregg Toland; ed, Hal C. Kern, Francis D. Lyon; m, Heinz Provost; art d, Lyle Wheeler; fx, Jack Cosgrove; cos, Irene, Travis Banton

AAN Best Score: Lou Forbes

Bergman made her American debut in this somewhat saccharine romance, becoming a star of the first magnitude almost overnight. An established actress in her native Sweden, she had appeared in a Swedish production of the same story in 1937, but it lacked the rich production values Selznick and Howard (who coproduced and starred) infused into this version.

Howard plays Holger Brandt, a brilliant, aging violinst weary of his great fame. After a successful tour, he returns to Sweden to the arms of his wife Margit (Best) and adoring children (Todd and Scott). Deeply attracted to the fresh-faced, bright-eyed Anita (Bergman), the children's piano teacher, he joins her in an impromptu recital before the family. Soon the pair discover that they are in love and Holger asks Margit for his freedom. She still loves him, though, and asks him to take time to reconsider. Holger and Anita travel abroad and she becomes his accompanist, to considerable acclaim. But Anita notices how Holger dotes on other people's children, and she decides that happiness is not built on the sadness of others.

Appealingly Continental in look and style, INTERMEZZO continually verges on soap, but is redeemed by carefully calibrated performances and Ratoff's loving direction. Beautifully photographed, the film won Toland an Oscar nomination (he lost to himself for his work on WUTHERING HEIGHTS). The memorable theme music, "Intermezzo" (composed by Heinz Provost), became a tremendously popular hit.

INTERNAL AFFAIRS

1990 115m c Crime/Thriller   ★½
Frank Mancuso, Jr./Pierre David (U.S.)   R/18

Richard Gere *(Dennis Peck)*, Andy Garcia *(Sgt. Raymond Avila)*, Nancy Travis *(Kathleen Avila)*, Laurie Metcalf *(Sgt. Amy Wallace)*, Richard Bradford *(Lt. Sgt. Grieb)*, William Baldwin *(Van Stretch)*, Michael Beach *(Dorian)*, Ron Vawter *(Comdr. Oakes)*, John Getz *(Teeters)*, Faye Grant *(Penny Stretch)*

p, Frank Mancuso Jr., Pierre David; d, Mike Figgis; w, Henry Bean; ph, John A. Alonzo; ed, Robert Estrin; m, Michael Figgis, Anthony Marinelli, Brian Banks; prod d, Waldemar Kalinowski

How many ridiculous movies can an actor's career endure? Richard Gere explores the possibilities with his appearance in this solemnly silly thriller helmed by Michael Figgis. In the wake of STORMY MONDAY, his critically acclaimed debut, this outing also represents a professional stumble for Mike Figgis. Figgis again aims for sensual moodiness, but so many clashing tones clamor for the viewer's attention that the result is a noisy mishmash.

Gere plays Dennis Peck, a star cop in one of the ritzier precincts of LA's San Fernando Valley. In his spare time, Peck is also a master criminal, running a vast empire of corruption out of that notorious breeding ground for vice, the Sherman Oaks Galleria shopping mall. Taking a bribery cut out of most of the vice in the Valley, Peck launders his ill-gotten fortunes through his four ex-wives, making them all tycoons on paper. (All we see them doing, though, is making breakfast and doing laundry for Peck and his passel of kids.)

Peck also has a unique method of keeping his criminal operatives under control: he turns their wives into his pliant sex slaves by introducing them to the joys of kinky sex during his free afternoons—which he seems to have ten days a week. In fact, we rarely see Peck doing anything so mundane and legit as actually arresting people; nonetheless, when internal affairs investigator Raymond Avila (Garcia) tries to unravel Peck's web of corruption, he meets a wall of resistance from his superiors for going after one of the force's most "productive" cops. Instead, Avila is called in to investigate Peck's partner, Stretch (Baldwin), an old friend of Avila's who has apparently been stretched to the breaking point as Peck's right-hand man.

Enough. The plot is, to say the least, mindlessly complex, with little room left to develop any kind of consistent mood, much less to develop characters beyond the sum of their cliches. Moreover, as LETHAL WEAPON and its spin-offs have indicated, today's high-impact cop thriller is no place for subtlety anyway. When in doubt, LETHAL WEAPON damned the critics to plunge full-speed ahead into boom-boom cartoon action, giving audiences a wild roller-coaster movie ride in lieu of compelling drama. Figgis tries to have it both ways, creating an ersatz aura of worldly cynicism for the art-house crowd, while providing plenty of sleazy sex and blood-pellet violence for those in the cheaper seats. The result is yet another goofy credit in Gere's already overloaded resume of embarrassment—although some may consider this one of those movies that's so silly it's good.

INTERNATIONAL HOUSE

1933 70m bw Comedy ★★★★
Paramount (U.S.)

Peggy Hopkins Joyce *(Herself)*, W.C. Fields *(Prof. Quail)*, Stuart Erwin *(Tommy Nash)*, Sari Maritza *(Carol Fortescue)*, George Burns *(Dr. Burns)*, Gracie Allen *(Nurse Allen)*, Bela Lugosi *(Gen. Petronovich)*, Edmund Breese *(Dr. Wong)*, Lumsden Hare *(Sir Mortimer Fortescue)*, Franklin Pangborn *(Hotel Manager)*

d, A. Edward Sutherland; w, Francis Martin, Walter DeLeon (based on a story by Lou Heifetz, Neil Brant); ph, Ernest Haller; cos, Travis Banton

Manic, ragtag W.C. Fields vehicle, full of the usual lunacy and laughter.

Breese plays Dr. Wong, an eccentric inventor who intends to exhibit his early version of television in Wuhu, China before a group of international buyers. Foremost of these is a Russian general (Lugosi) who arrives at the hotel to be greeted by his golddigging ex-wife. Arriving later is Dr. Quail (Fields), who has flown in from Mexico in an autogyro, dropping beer bottles en route and injuring countless victims below. At least so say the reports read by Dr. Burns and Nurse Allen (George and Gracie) of the International House's hotel staff. Meanwhile, American envoy Tommy Nash (Erwin) is busy trying to woo Carol Fortescue (Maritza), while evading the Russian's predatory ex. Finally, all the players gather to view Wong's new invention. Tommy ends up buying the device mostly to escape the hotel, quarantined with the measles. During the last demonstrations, Wong manages to pick up on transmissions of Baby Rose Marie warbling a torch song, then tunes in to Cab Calloway singing a song called "Reefer Man," which later became a camp classic. (This number is invariably cut from the prints shown on television.) Before the cast escapes the madhouse, there are several big musical production numbers on a Busby Berkeley scale, as well as numerous romantic pairings, including one for Dr. Quail.

In INTERNATIONAL HOUSE, director Sutherland wisely let Fields do practically whatever he wanted, inserting gags and routines that caught the public's fancy and boosted his stardom even higher. Pangborn, Burns, Allen, and Lugosi are all hilarious, but this near-surreal spoof of GRAND HOTEL ultimately belongs to Fields.

INTERVIEW WITH THE VAMPIRE

1994 122m c Horror/Drama ★★★
Geffen Pictures (U.S./United Kingdom) R/18

Tom Cruise *(Lestat de Lioncourt)*, Brad Pitt *(Louis Pointe du Lac)*, Antonio Banderas *(Armand)*, Stephen Rea *(Santiago)*, Christian Slater *(Daniel Malloy—The Interviewer)*, Kirsten Dunst *(Claudia)*, Domiziana Giordano *(Madeleine)*, Thandie Newton *(Yvette)*, Virginia McCollam *(Whore on Waterfront)*, John McConnell *(Gambler)*

p, Stephen Woolley, David Geffen; d, Neil Jordan; w, Anne Rice (based on her novel); ph, Philippe Rousselot; ed, Mick Audsley, Joke Van Wijk; m, Elliot Goldenthal; prod d, Dante Ferretti; art d, Malcolm Middleton, Alan Tomkins, Jean-Michel Ducourty; fx, Rob Legato, Yves De Bono, Cari Thomas; cos, Sandy Powell, John Scott, Deirdre Williams

AAN Best Art Direction: Dante Ferretti, Francesca Lo Schiavo; *AAN Best Original Score:* Elliot Goldenthal

This darkly effective horror drama holds plenty of interest, even for those who find Anne Rice's gothic cult novels unreadable.

In contemporary San Francisco, young interviewer Daniel Malloy (Christian Slater) is approached by Louis (Brad Pitt), who claims to be a vampire and tells Daniel his story. A flashback to late 18th-century Louisiana shows Louis as a 24-year-old plantation owner who sinks into a depression after the deaths of his wife and child. He meets the roguish vampire Lestat (Tom Cruise), who grants him eternal life in death. But while Lestat delights in draining his youthful victims, Louis cannot bring himself to do murder and subsists on animals. When he breaks down and attacks a young girl, Claudia (Kirsten Dunst), Lestat brings her back to life, and she becomes Louis's close companion.

Nearly two decades after the publication of Anne Rice's novel, the news that *Interview With the Vampire* was finally coming to the screen no doubt warmed the hearts of Rice's fans. Yet they were outraged when Cruise was announced for the Lestat role, and Rice herself repeatedly blasted the choice in interviews. After viewing the movie, however, Rice had a two-page retraction printed in national periodicals, and it's not hard to see why. INTERVIEW WITH THE VAMPIRE is a dark, lush, and reasonably faithful adaptation of Rice's novel. Cruise is masterful; his Lestat is a devilishly appealing but convincingly dangerous creature of the night. Throughout, director Neil Jordan recalls the haunting mix of dark psychodrama and visceral horror he brought to 1984's THE COMPANY OF WOLVES.

VAMPIRE's best (and funniest) moments chart the dynamics of a decidedly non-traditional family unit, with Louis and Lestat playing proud papas to the precocious Claudia. Lestat's desperate assertions of paternal authority—"Never [kill] in the house!"—make for subversive domestic comedy that's only heightened by contrast with the film's predominantly grim (and very gory) tone.

INTRUDER IN THE DUST

1949 87m bw Drama ★★★★
MGM (U.S.) /A

David Brian *(John Gavin Stevens)*, Claude Jarman Jr. *(Chick Mallison)*, Juano Hernandez *(Lucas Beauchamp)*, Porter Hall *(Nub Gowrie)*, Elizabeth Patterson *(Miss Habersham)*, Charles Kemper *(Crawford Gowrie)*, Will Geer *(Sheriff Hampton)*, David Clarke *(Vinson Gowrie)*, Elzie Emanuel *(Aleck)*, Lela Bliss *(Mrs. Mallison)*

p, Clarence Brown; d, Clarence Brown; w, Ben Maddow (based on the novel by William Faulkner); ph, Robert Surtees; ed, Robert J. Kern; m, Adolph Deutsch; art d, Cedric Gibbons, Randall Duell

The lack of big name stars is, if anything, a plus in making this one of the most powerful movies ever made about racism. Based on Faulkner's novel and filmed on location near the writer's native Oxford, MI, Brown's film features more than 500 people, only a small portion of whom were professional actors. Hernandez plays Lucas Beauchamp, an elderly black man who owns his own property, something the locals resent. The police arrest him for the murder of a townsman because he was discovered near the body and the revolver he carried had just been fired. On the way to jail he spots Chick (Jarman), a young white lad with whom he is friendly. He asks Chick to get Stevens (Brian), the boy's attorney uncle, to come to the jail. Despite Chick's pleas, Stevens resists the idea of defending Lucas, knowing he'll be ostracized by the townspeople if he does. Crawford Gowrie (Kemper), brother of the dead man, spreads the word, and the lawyer becomes a pariah as Gowrie rouses the rabble to lynch Beauchamp. The jailed man, though, has his story, which involves a beating he suffered at the hands of the victim. Lucas' supporters grow as Chick and Miss Habersham (Patterson) help dig up the dead man's coffin to prove that Lucas' gun was not the murder weapon. When the corpse is found instead in a quicksand swamp, even the dead man's father (Hall) has his doubts. Finally the canny Sheriff Hampton (Geer) uses a ruse to catch the real killer and the lynch-hungry mob is confronted with its own bigotry.

The most chilling scene in the movie is a lengthy sequence which cuts from the people of Oxford gleefully assembling (not unlike the crowd to see the man trapped below ground in THE BIG CARNIVAL) at the jail for a lynching to shots of music playing and kids eating ice cream. Everyone is in a jolly mood, in direct contrast to the grisly plans they have for the prisoner. This is not a pretty story and it does not exactly feature the people of Mississippi in a flattering light. Brown must have had a silver tongue to convince so many locals to play in the film, when one considers how they are portrayed. After many years of seeing stereotyped blacks on screen, Hernandez's role was a revelation as he stood up to the charges with pride and dignity. Patterson is equally marvelous in one of the finest roles of her lengthy career.

INVASION OF THE BODY SNATCHERS

1956 80m bw Science Fiction ★★★★
Allied Artists (U.S.) /PG

Kevin McCarthy *(Miles Bennel)*, Dana Wynter *(Becky Driscoll)*, Larry Gates *(Dr. Dan Kauffmann)*, King Donovan *(Jack)*, Carolyn Jones *(Theodora)*, Jean Willes *(Sally)*, Ralph Dumke *(Nick Grivett)*, Virginia Christine *(Wilma Lentz)*, Tom Fadden *(Uncle Ira Lentz)*, Kenneth Patterson *(Driscoll)* p, Walter Wanger; d, Don Siegel; w, Geoffrey Homes (based on the novel *The Body Snatchers* by Jack Finney); ph, Ellsworth Fredricks; ed, Robert S. Eisen; m, Carmen Dragon; prod d, Joseph Kish; art d, Ted Haworth; fx, Milt Rice

A superbly crafted film by innovative director Siegel, this low-budget science fiction tale became one of the great cult classics of the genre.

Miles (McCarthy), a doctor from the small town of Santa Mira, arrives in San Francisco in hysterical condition; he raves that his community has been invaded by aliens who have literally taken over the bodies of his friends and relatives. He's a candidate for the lunatic asylum, most agree, but they hear him out, and the story unfolds in flashback. Miles has returned home from a medical convention to find that many people have been complaining that their loved ones somehow don't appear to be the same people as before. He also runs into Becky (Wynter), an old girlfriend and recent divorcee, and they both note how odd it is that all the complaints seem to be suddenly vanishing. Miles and Becky have dinner with two friends (Donovan and Jones) and, to their horror, the quartet discover enormous pods growing in the couple's greenhouse which open to reveal exact physical reproductions of each of them. Miles and Becky run for their lives; half the population of the town, including the police, has been replaced. The phone system is also in the alien grip: when Miles tries to call federal authorities, operators tell him that all the lines to Washington are tied up. Miles and Becky later witness the police directing locals to drive their pod-filled cars to neighboring towns, and they realize that the whole world is in great danger. The local psychiatrist (Gates) catches them and arranges for two pods to be placed in the next room. The sinister shrink explains that all Miles and Becky have to do is go to sleep; they will awaken as one of the new creatures and will never again know pain, hate, or worry. Miles counters that they will also be without joy or love, and he and Becky attempt to escape.

This film was originally conceived by producer Wanger as standard B fare, but Siegel made much more of it, with writer Mainwaring injecting an element of subtle humor. It's since come to seem typical of 50s paranoia about everything from the Red Scare to nuclear warfare. INVASION spawned an adequate remake, starring Donald Sutherland, in 1978.

INVASION OF THE BODY SNATCHERS

1978 115m c Science Fiction   ★★½
UA (U.S.)   PG/15

Donald Sutherland *(Matthew Bennell)*, Brooke Adams *(Elizabeth Driscoll)*, Leonard Nimoy *(Dr. David Kibner)*, Veronica Cartwright *(Nancy Bellicec)*, Art Hindle *(Geoffrey)*, Lelia Goldoni *(Katherine)*, Kevin McCarthy *(Running Man)*, Jeff Goldblum *(Jack Bellicec)*, Don Siegel *(Cab Driver)*

p, Robert H. Solo; d, Philip Kaufman; w, W.D. Richter (based on the novel by Jack Finney); ph, Michael Chapman; ed, Douglas Stewart; m, Denny Zeitlin; prod d, Charles Rosen; fx, Dell Rheaume, Russ Hessey

Colorful and expensive remake of the 1956 sci-fi classic, with mopey, sleepy-eyed Sutherland playing the part originated by Kevin McCarthy, a health inspector giving a hard time to San Francisco restaurant owners when he finds rat droppings in their kitchens. Instead of the original setting, a little town in California, the setting here is the sprawling city of San Francisco, now under alien attack by the mysterious pods (with Nimoy as the psychiatrist advocating the takeover). The film collapses midway—because of unsure and sloppy direction, splintered story continuity, and the overacting of Adams, Cartwright, and others. The battle between Sutherland and the aliens in the "pod factory" at the end is simply absurd and sophomoric. In a nod to the earlier classic, McCarthy appears at the beginning of the film, shouting hysterical warnings to motorists until he is struck and killed by a car. A great number of shots show the Transamerica pyramid building in downtown San Francisco, a subtle plug for the distributor of the movie, whose corporate offices are housed there.

INVESTIGATION OF A CITIZEN ABOVE SUSPICION
(INDAGINE SU UN CITTADINO AL DI SOPRA DI OGNI SOSPETTO)

1970 112m c Crime   ★★★★
Vera (Italy)   R/18

Gian Maria Volonte *(Police Inspector)*, Florinda Bolkan *(Augusta Terzi)*, Salvo Randone *(Plumber)*, Gianni Santuccio *(Police Commissioner)*, Arturo Dominici *(Mangani)*, Orazio Orlando *(Biglia)*, Sergio Tramonti *(Antonio Pace)*, Massimo Foschi *(Augusta's Husband)*, Aldo Rendine *(Homicide Functionary)*, Aleka Paizi

p, Daniele Senatore; d, Elio Petri; w, Ugo Pirro, Elio Petri; ph, Luigi Kuveiller; ed, Ruggero Mastroianni; m, Ennio Morricone; prod d, Romano Cardarelli; cos, Angela Sammaciccia, Mayer

AA Best Foreign Language Film ; *AAN Best Adapted Screenplay:* Elio Petri, Ugo Pirro

The winner of 1970's foreign film Oscar, this jarring and potent Italian film tells the story of a recently promoted Fascist police inspector (Volonte) who one Sunday afternoon slits his mistress's throat. He then plants phony evidence and makes an anonymous call to report the crime. The police unearth clues that point to the inspector, but ignore them because of his standing. The killer eventually writes a confession and awaits his capture, while planning to receive an acquittal.

An excellent look into the mind of a murderer, INVESTIGATION features a fine performance from Volonte in the leading role. Director Petri has made an antifascist statement that is both pointed and poignant, full of eerie, unsettling moods abetted by Morricone's score. A piercing satire of Italian investigative techniques, and an interesting meditation on the relationship between class and guilt.

INVISIBLE MAN, THE

1933 71m bw Science Fiction   ★★★★½
Universal (U.S.)

Claude Rains *(Jack Griffin/The Invisible One)*, Gloria Stuart *(Flora Cranley)*, William Harrigan *(Doctor Kemp)*, Henry Travers *(Dr. Cranley)*, Una O'Connor *(Mrs. Jenny Hall)*, Forrester Harvey *(Mr. Herbert Hall)*, Holmes Herbert *(Chief of Police)*, E.E. Clive *(Jaffers)*, Dudley Digges *(Chief of Detectives)*, Harry Stubbs *(Inspector Bird)*

p, Carl Laemmle Jr.; d, James Whale; w, Philip Wylie (uncredited), R.C. Sherriff (based on the novel by H.G. Wells); ph, Arthur Edeson; m, W. Franke Harling; art d, Charles D. Hall; fx, John P. Fulton, John Mescall

Few debuts have been as impressive or odd as that made by the voice of Claude Rains in this macabre classic based on the novel by H.G. Wells. (Actually, there's a glimpse of the rest of Rains, too, but not until the very end.)

Jack Griffin (Rains) is an English scientist who has been experimenting with a drug called monocaine which, he finds, has made his entire body invisible. He goes to the small village of Ipping, wrapped in bandages and wearing dark glasses, and takes a room at the local inn to continue his research in secret. This subsequently arouses the curiosity of the nosy locals. As Griffin continues his experiments, he begins to suffer from drug-induced megalomania, which eventually becomes full-blown madness. He begins to terrorize the countryside—first playing pranks, and then turning to murder.

Memorable moments and lines of dialogue pepper this striking fantasy: Griffin informing his terrified, unwilling assistant Kemp, "We'll start with a few murders. Small men. Great men. Just to show we make no distinction"; any of the scenes involving the priceless Una O'Connor as the innkeeper's flighty wife; the farmer's discovery of breathing in his barn. Whale was always fascinated by the inconveniences of being a monster and Griffin tells us how it's hard to walk down steps when you can't see your feet. Best of all, though, is the scene where the enraged scientist first takes of his disguise and to the amazement of the locals reveals . . . nothing. Fine acting all around, especially from Rains, great camera work and effects from Edeson and Fulton (who used black velvet-clad actors filmed before black backgrounds to achieve the needed effects), and brilliantly judged direction from Whale make this film hard to beat. The dialogue by Wylie and Sherriff is by turns hilarious, haunting and horrific.

INVITATION, THE
(L'INVITATION)

1973 100m c Comedy/Drama ★★★★
Citel/Group 5/Swiss TV/Planfilm (France/Switzerland) /AA

Jean-Luc Bideau (*Maurice*), Francois Simon (*Emile*), Jean Champion (*Alfred*), Corinne Coderey (*Simone*), Michel Robin (*Remy*), Cecile Vassort (*Aline*), Rosina Rochette (*Helene*), Jacques Rispal (*Rene*), Neige Dolsky (*Emma*), Pierre Collet (*Pierre*)

d, Claude Goretta; w, Claude Goretta, Michel Viala; ph, Jean Zeller; ed, Joele Van Effenterre; m, Patrick Moraz

One of the most impressive works to come out of Switzerland in the past decade or two (along with the films of Alain Tanner), THE INVITATION was nominated for an Academy Award for Best Foreign Film. The subtle, naturalistic story unfolds during an office party. As with all parties of this sort, the workers get out of hand and reveal facets of themselves that they usually keep hidden from 9 to 5. The affair, thrown by a meek dullard (Robin), comes to life when the office stud (Bideau) begins his conquests of women. It is up to a cultured, patient butler (Simon) to keep things in order—a seemingly futile task. Writer-director Claude Goretta has wrought an uncluttered, worthy piece of adult entertainment blessed with acting and dialogue that are completely convincing.

IPCRESS FILE, THE

1965 109m c Spy ★★★½
Lowndes/Steven (U.K.) /PG

Michael Caine (*Harry Palmer*), Nigel Green (*Dalby*), Guy Doleman (*Maj. Ross*), Sue Lloyd (*Jean*), Gordon Jackson (*Jock Carswell*), Aubrey Richards (*Radcliffe*), Frank Gatliff (*Bluejay*), Thomas Baptiste (*Barney*), Oliver MacGreevy (*Housemartin*), Freda Bamford (*Alice*)

p, Harry Saltzman; d, Sidney J. Furie; w, Bill Canaway, James Doran (based on the novel by Len Deighton); ph, Otto Heller; ed, Peter Hunt; m, John Barry; prod d, Ken Adam; art d, Peter Murton

Based on the first and the best of Len Deighton's novels about myopic, flabby antihero Harry Palmer, THE IPCRESS FILE is a witty, fast-paced espionage film. Palmer, a British army sergeant stationed in Berlin, is nabbed for black marketeering but told that he can do his penance by serving as a counterintelligence agent. When Radcliffe (Richards), the latest in a string of scientists to be kidnaped, disappears along with a top secret file, Palmer is put on the case. During the investigation, a mysterious tape turns up with "Ipcress" written on it, and just when it appears that the case is about to be cracked, an agent is murdered and Palmer is confronted by the real—and surprising—enemy.

The best part of the film is Caine's characterization. Hardly a superhero, Harry Palmer is an ordinary chap tossed into a maelstrom in much the same way Alfred Hitchcock placed people in situations beyond their scope and then let them triumph over seemingly unbeatable odds. Canadian-born Sidney J. Furie seems determined to be a flashy director here, but if his restless camera and kooky *mise en scene* are sometimes just plain weird, they are also sometimes stylishly suited to the foolishness of the entire undertaking. Look for a scene in which Harry makes coffee in his elegant *caffetiere*, a very chic device at the time. (It's that kind of movie.) Produced by Harry Saltzman, the coproducer of many James Bond films, THE IPCRESS FILE gave rise to two sequels, FUNERAL IN BERLIN and BILLION DOLLAR BRAIN, both of which starred Caine. Neither was as exciting or enjoyable as this one, however.

IRMA LA DOUCE

1963 147m c Comedy ★★★
Mirisch/Phalanx/Alperson (U.S.) /15

Jack Lemmon (*Nestor*), Shirley MacLaine (*Irma La Douce*), Lou Jacobi (*Moustache*), Bruce Yarnell (*Hippolyte*), Herschel Bernardi (*Inspector LeFevre*), Hope Holiday (*Lolita*), Joan Shawlee (*Amazon Annie*), Grace Lee Whitney (*Kiki the Cossack*), Tura Satana (*Suzette Wong*), Harriette Young (*Mimi the MauMau*)

p, Billy Wilder; d, Billy Wilder; w, Billy Wilder, I.A.L. Diamond (based on the play by Alexandre Breffort); ph, Joseph La Shelle; ed, Daniel Mandell; m, Andre Previn; art d, Alexander Trauner; fx, Milt Rice; chor, Wally Green; cos, Orry-Kelly

AAN Best Actress: Shirley MacLaine; *AAN Best Cinematography:* Joseph LaShelle; *AA Best Score:* Andre Previn

IRMA LA DOUCE has a curious history: a French musical in 1956, an American adaptation in 1960, then this nonmusical film in 1963. Far too long for a lighthearted farce, with dull patches that outnumber the high spots, the film is really about Maclaine and Lemmon striving to rise above the fat Diamond-Wilder script and Wilder's lethargic direction.

Wilder was the logical choice to adapt this type of film, but it still misses. MacLaine is Irma, a Paris streetwalker whose money goes to her handsome pimp Hippolyte (Yarnell). Enter Nestor (Lemmon), a cop who antedates Clouseau in his bumbling but sincere ineptitude. Nestor cannot believe all the women plying their trade, and seeks to reform the area by raiding a local bistro run by Moustache (Jacobi). The chief police inspector (Bernardi) is arrested in the raid and Nestor is promptly sacked. Nestor and Irma become an item and she fires Hippolyte, making Nestor her "protector".

Previn won an Oscar, and MacLaine and La Shelle were nominated, but this was less than a complete success. The movie was filmed on a 360-degree set so shooting could be done in any direction. You can't help but wonder what the film might have been with a half hour cut, or with the Broadway score retained.

IS PARIS BURNING?
(PARIS BRULE-T-IL?)

1966 173m c/bw War ★★½
Transcontinental/Marianne (U.S./France) /A

Jean-Paul Belmondo (*Morandat*), Charles Boyer (*Monod*), Leslie Caron (*Francoise Labe*), Jean-Pierre Cassel (*Lt. Henri Karcher*), George Chakiris (*GI in Tank*), Claude Dauphin (*Lebel*), Alain Delon (*Jacques Chaban-Delmas*), Kirk Douglas (*Gen. George Patton*), Glenn Ford (*Gen. Omar Bradley*), Gert Frobe (*Gen. Dietrich von Choltitz*)

p, Paul Graetz; d, Rene Clement; w, Gore Vidal, Francis Ford Coppola, Jean Aurenche, Pierre Bost, Claude Brule, Marcel Moussy, Beate von Molo; ph, Marcel Grignon; ed, Robert Lawrence; m, Maurice Jarre; art d, Willy Holt; fx, Robert MacDonald, Paul Pollard; cos, Jean Zay, Pierre Nourry

AAN Best Cinematography: Marcel Grignon; *AAN Best Art Direction:* Willy Holt (Art Direction), Marc Frederix (Art Direction), Pierre Guffroy (Art Direction)

Is it any wonder that a film with writers from Aurenche and Bost to Francis Ford Coppola to Gore Vidal would be a bit rambling? Is it any surprise that a film featuring two dozen movie stars is a bit of a mess?

Full of dramatically unwieldy crosscutting between the Allies and Germans during the 1944 liberation, IS PARIS BURNING? is a fairly entertaining, action-packed film which seems continually in danger of collapsing under the weight of its own pageantry.

The plot basically deals with the Germans' attempts to torch Paris before having to pull out because they're losing the war. Frobe is the German general assigned to light the match; Caron is the wife of a political prisoner; Welles—desperate as always for money to finance his own films—is a Swedish consul; Belmondo is a resistance fighter who takes over police headquarters; Vaneck is a Free French officer trying to enlist Allied aide in saving gay Paree; Signoret owns a cafe; Stack, Douglas, Ford and Rich compare square jawlines as four (what else?) generals; and Montand and Perkins, of course, encounter bad luck on film yet again.

Producer Graetz underwent innumerable headaches in assembling vintage props for the film and in expanding the script every time another movie star became available. Director Clement, expert at documentary and low-key realism, does a fine job of mixing period footage with the stuff he shot, though continuity suffers somewhat during this extravaganza. A favorite: Frobe and another general speak English en route to

Hitler's office, but once in the Fuhrer's presence we get German with English subtitles. There's plenty of fun to be had here if you don't mind (or if you have a perverse fascination with) that kind of thing.

ISHTAR

1987 107m c Comedy   ★★
Delphi V/Columbia (U.S.)   PG-13/PG

Warren Beatty (*Lyle Rogers*), Dustin Hoffman (*Chuck Clarke*), Isabelle Adjani (*Shirra Assel*), Charles Grodin (*Jim Harrison*), Jack Weston (*Marty Freed*), Tess Harper (*Willa*), Carol Kane (*Carol*), Aharon Ipale (*Emir Yousef*), Fijad Hageb (*Abdul*), David Margulies (*Mr. Clarke*)

p, Warren Beatty; d, Elaine May; w, Elaine May; ph, Vittorio Storaro; ed, Stephen A. Rotter, William Reynolds, Richard Cirincione; m, Bahjawa; prod d, Paul Sylbert; art d, Bill Groom, Vicki Paul, Peter Childs, Tony Reading; cos, Anthony Powell

It's inevitable that when a film costs upwards of $40 million, stars two of the biggest names in Hollywood (Hoffman and Beatty), and is directed by a person (May) notorious for her wasteful shooting methods, the result will be savaged by industry insiders and film critics. An incredible box office loser and, to be frank, far from great, ISHTAR is still not nearly as awful as many would have it.

Struggling songwriters Chuck Clarke (Hoffman) and Lyle Rogers (Beatty) have known each other for only a few months but have formed a strong bond. Despite the pathetic but honestly expressive songs they bang out, entertainment agent Marty Freed (Weston) offers them a booking—in Morocco. On their way, they get mixed up in a civil war in the fictitious "Ishtar" and become involved with a goofy CIA agent (Grodin).

For all the bad press ISHTAR received, it does have a certain odd charm. Cast against type, Beatty and Hoffman do their darndest to mimic Hope and Crosby. The biggest problem is that any attempted subtlety is swamped by May's bid to turn the film into an epic adventure story. The talented Adjani doesn't help much, doing little more than float around in loose-fitting garments. The hopelessly banal lyrics to the songs written by the Beatty and Hoffman characters can be hilarious if you're in the mood. ("Telling the truth is a dangerous business/Honest and popular don't go hand-in-hand/If you admit that you play the accordian/You'll never make it a rock and roll band.") Yes, it's that kind of movie.

ISLAND OF LOST SOULS

1933 67m bw Science Fiction/Horror   ★★★★½
Paramount (U.S.)

Charles Laughton (*Dr. Moreau*), Bela Lugosi (*Sayer of the Law*), Richard Arlen (*Edward Parker*), Leila Hyams (*Ruth Walker*), Kathleen Burke (*Lota, the Panther Woman*), Arthur Hohl (*Montgomery*), Stanley Fields (*Capt. Davies*), Bob Kortman (*Hogan*), Tetsu Komai (*M'Ling*), Hans Steinke (*Ouran*)

d, Erle C. Kenton; w, Philip Wylie, Waldemar Young (based on the novel *The Island of Dr. Moreau* by H.G. Wells); ph, Karl Struss; fx, Gordon Jennings

There's not a wasted frame in this chilling horror film that was banned in England upon its first release. Laughton is Dr. Moreau, a smiling, benign-seeming man who welcomes shipwrecked Edward Parker (Arlen) to his own private island. While waiting for the next passing freighter, Parker learns that the "natives" who serve Moreau are really animals who have been transformed into semi-humans by the doctor's experiments in an area known as "The House of Pain." The only woman around, Lota (Burke), becomes involved with Parker but she too conceals a terrible secret. When Edward's fiancee Ruth (Hyams) arrives with a search expedition, the two women vie for his affections while Moreau makes his own attempts to deal with the new intruders. Unfortunately for him he makes a crucial error which goes against the lessons in "humanity" and "civility" he has browbeaten into his creations. The famous, controversial climax is still a shocker.

H.G. Wells, from whose novel the screenplay was written, hated the picture from the start because he felt the makers missed his point about a man playing God and opted for the easy way out. The film is steeped in atmosphere and foreboding, and much of the terror was hinted at rather than shown graphically. Struss' cinematography is stunning, especially in the "lesson" scenes Moreau administers. "Are we not men?" and "What is the law?" are lines chanted by the half-human denizens of Moreau's isle, led by Bela Lugosi in an amazingly small yet very effective performance, that will stick in your memory. Burke's appearance is striking but her acting less so; Laughton, on the other hand, is unfailingly marvelous. So many countries (as well as many midwestern states) banned the movie that it took a while to recoup the cost, but ISLAND OF LOST SOULS remains, to this day, a classic chiller which holds up better than many others from its period. Remade in 1959 as TERROR IS A MAN and in 1978 (with Burt Lancaster and Michael York) as THE ISLAND OF DR. MOREAU. Neither version was quite up to the original.

IT CAME FROM OUTER SPACE

1953 80m bw Science Fiction   ★★★½
Universal (U.S.)   /PG

Richard Carlson (*John Putnam*), Barbara Rush (*Ellen Fields*), Charles Drake (*Sheriff Matt Warren*), Russell Johnson (*George*), Kathleen Hughes (*Jane*), Joe Sawyer (*Frank Daylon*), Dave Willock (*Pete Davis*), Alan Dexter (*Dave Loring*), George Eldredge (*Dr. Snell*), Brad Jackson (*Snell's Assistant*)

p, William Alland; d, Jack Arnold; w, Harry Essex (based on the story "The Meteor" by Ray Bradbury); ph, Clifford Stine; ed, Paul Weatherwax; m, Herman Stein; art d, Bernard Herzbrun, Robert Boyle; fx, David S. Horsley

One of the better science-fiction films to come out of the Cold War 50s, this one must be counted among the anti-McCarthy statements. Not just passively anti-conformist like the original INVASION OF THE BODY SNATCHERS, it actively supports the right of any being to be different. Unusually restrained and sober in tone for its time, IT CAME FROM OUTER SPACE is a film noir variant on the sci-fi genre.

Carlson is John Putnam, an astronomer who lives alone out in the desert. The folks in town find him eccentric and distrust his intellectualism. One night he sees what he thinks is a meteor blaze across the sky and crash in the desert. As it turns out, the UFO is actually an alien spacecraft. The creatures, cloaked with invisibility, replace the locals with alien doubles, thereby making it difficult for Putnam to prove they exist. He tells the townspeople but no one wants to believe him. Once he makes contact with the aliens, he learns that their intentions are not really threatening but, by that time, the townspeople are finally starting to panic.

Inspired by a Ray Bradbury story, this film had the added bonus of being photographed in 3-D, and it was worth putting up with the annoying glasses to view Arnold's creepy deep-focus compositions. This was director Arnold's first science fiction work, a genre in which he was to make quite a mark, directing such films as THIS ISLAND EARTH, TARANTULA, and his classic, THE INCREDIBLE SHRINKING MAN.

IT HAPPENED HERE

1963 99m bw Drama   ★★★★
Rath (U.K.)   /A

Pauline Murray (*Pauline*), Sebastian Shaw (*Dr. Richard Fletcher*), Fiona Leland (*Helen Fletcher*), Honor Fehrson (*Honor Hutton*), Col. Percy Binns (*Immediate Action Commandant*), Frank Bennett (*IA Political Leader*), Bill Thomas (*IA Group Leader*), Reginald Marsh (*IA Medical Officer*), Rex Collett (*IA NCO*), Nicolette Bernard (*IA Woman Commandant*)

p, Kevin Brownlow, Andrew Mollo; d, Kevin Brownlow, Andrew Mollo; w, Kevin Brownlow, Andrew Mollo (based on an idea by Kevin Brownlow); ph, Peter Suschitzky, Kevin Brownlow; ed, Kevin Brownlow; m, Jack Beaver, Anton Bruckner; art d, Andrew Mollo, Jim Nicolson

Reminiscent in title and theme of Sinclair Lewis' terrifying novel *It Can't Happen Here*, this intensely fascinating effort from film historians Kevin Brownlow and Andrew Mollo speculates about what could have happened in WWII England if the Germans had successfully invaded. Murray stars as a British nurse employed by the Fascist government. Shocked to discover that Russian and Polish hospital patients are being killed, she raises loud protests, is arrested, and eventually joins the resistance. Made on a miniscule budget of only $20,000, the production—partly filmed in 16mm—took 10 years to complete. It has a remarkable documentary look and feel, and the direction by Brownlow and Mollo is amazingly assured. A very disturbing and compelling film, it makes an incisive point about politics and nationality: the British would have gotten along quite nicely under Nazi rule, just as the French did.

IT HAPPENED ONE NIGHT

1934 105m bw Romance/Comedy ★★★★★
Columbia (U.S.) /U

Claudette Colbert *(Ellie Andrews)*, Clark Gable *(Peter Warne)*, Roscoe Karns *(Oscar Shapeley)*, Henry Wadsworth *(Drunk Boy)*, Claire McDowell *(Mother)*, Walter Connolly *(Alexander Andrews)*, Alan Hale *(Danker)*, Arthur Hoyt *(Zeke)*, Blanche Frederici *(Zeke's Wife)*, Jameson Thomas *(King Westley)*

p, Harry Cohn; d, Frank Capra; w, Robert Riskin (based on the story "Night Bus" by Samuel Hopkins Adams); ph, Joseph Walker; ed, Gene Havlick; art d, Stephen Goosson; cos, Robert Kalloch

AA Best Picture; AA Best Actor: Clark Gable; *AA Best Actress:* Claudette Colbert; *AA Best Director:* Frank Capra; *AA Best Adapted Screenplay:* Robert Riskin

It happened one night in 1934, and it happens every time we watch this utterly beguiling film. A rather modest effort which brought Capra into the spotlight, we frankly prefer it to many of the more "important" films he made later. It also clinched for good the stardom of Gable and Colbert. (What a pity that their only other teaming was the dismal BOOM TOWN.)

The familiar story, a prototype for many screwball comedies to follow, opens with headstrong heiress Ellie Andrews (Colbert) fleeing her father (Connolly). Trying to make it to her washout fiance (Thomas) on her own, she soon encounters errant reporter Peter Warne (Gable). He agrees to help her make it from Florida to New York in exchange for her story, which will square him with his disgruntled boss. Over the course of several nights, the inevitable happens.

What really distinguishes IT HAPPENED ONE NIGHT from so many other films are Capra's handling of the individual comic and romantic setpieces, Riskin's way with a line, and the marvelous cast. Every viewer has his or her favorite scenes. Consider the "wall of Jericho" (a blanket) Peter sets up between himself and Ellie before bedding down for the night, a sly dig at Production Code prudery just then being enforced. Or what about Peter's famous lessons in how to dunk a donut or how a man undresses? (We all recall, of course, how Ellie shows him up in the memorable hitchhiking lesson.) For romance, there's some lovely bedside dreaming and even a scene in the hay. There's also Ellie's wonderful wedding gown near the end, the lengthy veil providing a visual exclamation point to rival Elsa Lanchester's hair in BRIDE OF FRANKENSTEIN. The splendidly cast actors, too, make their bits of business their own, from Karns' mildly lecherous salesperson ("Shapeley's the name and that's the way I like 'em") turned scared rabbit to Hale's aggressively cheering but deceptive singing motorist. The best support, though, comes from the unfailingly marvelous Connolly in a role he made his own. Gable and Colbert's screen personas were firmly established here, his tongue-in-cheek machismo and her witty, supple sophistication mixing like gin and tonic.

IT HAPPENED ONE NIGHT won the top five Oscars (Picture, Director, Actor, Actress, Screenplay), a feat only duplicated twice since. Watch it again and you'll remember why.

IT SHOULD HAPPEN TO YOU

1954 86m bw Comedy ★★★★
Columbia (U.S.) /U

Judy Holliday *(Gladys Glover)*, Jack Lemmon *(Pete Sheppard)*, Peter Lawford *(Evan Adams III)*, Michael O'Shea *(Brod Clinton)*, Connie Gilchrist *(Mrs. Riker)*, Vaughn Taylor *(Entrikin)*, Heywood Hale Broun *(Sour Man in Central Park)*, Rex Evans *(Con Cooley)*, Art Gilmore *(Don Toddman)*, Whit Bissell *(Robert Grau)*

p, Fred Kohlmar; d, George Cukor; w, Garson Kanin; ph, Charles Lang; ed, Charles Nelson; m, Frederick Hollander; art d, John Meehan; cos, Jean Louis

AAN Best Costume Design: Jean Louis

Charming satire in which Lemmon made a winning debut opposite the flawless Holliday.

Holliday is Gladys Glover (a name you'll never forget once you've seen the film), a poor model from Binghampton who has come to New York. She's spotted by film documentarian Pete Sheppard (Lemmon), who is roaming Central Park with his camera. When Gladys looks up and sees an empty billboard, she promptly uses all her money to have her name painted there in huge letters. Suddenly, all of New York is wondering who she is and why she's done this. Lawford plays Evan Adams III, an executive for a huge soap company who wants the billboard for his products, making a deal with Gladys whereby he gives her several other billboards in return for the big one. Gladys and Pete become lovers, but he doesn't like what is transpiring. He thinks his feckless love is cheapening herself, and he wishes she would stop the campaign and settle in with him. Fame follows her, however, and she becomes a celebrity, appearing on talk shows and doing commercials. Pete leaves her in disgust, but that's just until they get back together for a customary happy ending.

IT SHOULD HAPPEN TO YOU benefits from fine performances from some wonderful farceurs, a witty Kanin script, and Cukor's light-hearted direction. Melvine Cooper, Wendy Barrie, Constance Bennett, and Ilka Chase spoof the inanities of TV talk shows perfectly, and Lemmon and Holliday also get a chance to sing with "Let's Fall in Love," which had been written (by Harold Arlen and Ted Koehler) almost 20 years earlier. In a tiny role, John Saxon is the young man who watches the argument in the park. Jean Louis' costumes were nominated for an Oscar.

IT'S A GIFT

1934 73m bw Comedy ★★★★★
Paramount (U.S.)

W.C. Fields *(Harold Bissonette)*, Jean Rouverol *(Mildred Bissonette)*, Julian Madison *(John Durston)*, Kathleen Howard *(Amelia Bissonette)*, Tommy Bupp *(Norman Bissonette)*, Tammany Young *(Everett Ricks)*, Baby LeRoy *(Baby Ellwood Dunk)*, Morgan Wallace *(Jasper Fitchmueller)*, Charles Sellon *(Mr. Muckle/Blind Man/House Detective)*, Josephine Whittell *(Mrs. Dunk)*

p, William LeBaron; d, Norman Z. McLeod; w, Jack Cunningham, W.C. Fields (based on the play *The Comic Supplement* by J.P. McEvoy and a story by Charles Bogle); ph, Henry Sharp; art d, Hans Dreier, John B. Goodman

Never was a film so well titled. Along with THE BANK DICK this is the finest, funniest movie W.C. Fields ever made. It's also a rollicking spoof of middle-class marriage and mainstream ambitions.

Fields appears as Harold Bissonette, a small-town shopowner with selfish children and a nagging wife. When his family isn't making his life miserable, his customers and neighbors are. He dreams of the good life and a California orange grove he's purchased with an inheritance, but the hostile world won't even let him get a decent night's sleep. (In a memorable scene poor Harold copes with a noisy milkman, a grape-wielding baby, a porch swing chain and an obnoxious saleman looking for one "Karl La Fong".) When Harold and family finally make it to California, they learn he's been swindled, but, predictably, he gets the last laugh.

IT'S A GIFT is almost nonstop laughter, loaded with Fields' patented sight gags, slapstick, and dialogue uttered out of the corner of his mouth. Fields resurrected much of this material from other sources, such as his silent film IT'S THE OLD ARMY GAME and the 1925 play *The Comic Supplement*. He also drew on his memories as the son of a Philadelphia pushcart vendor for some of the story, which he wrote under the name of Charles Bogle. Though Norman McLeod was the nominal director, Fields picked his own cast and essentially ran the film, and his wonderful, caustic humor comes through on every frame.

IT'S A MAD, MAD, MAD, MAD WORLD

1963   192m   c   Comedy   ★★★
Casey   (U.S.)   /U

Spencer Tracy *(Capt. C.G. Culpepper)*, Milton Berle *(J. Russell Finch)*, Sid Caesar *(Melville Crump)*, Buddy Hackett *(Benjy Benjamin)*, Ethel Merman *(Mrs. Marcus)*, Mickey Rooney *(Ding Bell)*, Dick Shawn *(Sylvester Marcus)*, Phil Silvers *(Otto Meyer)*, Terry-Thomas *(J. Algernon Hawthorne)*, Jonathan Winters *(Lennie Pike)*

p, Stanley Kramer; d, Stanley Kramer; w, William Rose, Tania Rose; ph, Ernest Laszlo; ed, Frederic Knudtson, Robert C. Jones, Gene Fowler Jr.; m, Ernest Gold; prod d, Rudolph Sternad; art d, Gordon Gurnell; fx, Danny Lee, Linwood Dunn; cos, Bill Thomas

AAN Best Cinematography: Ernest Laszlo; AAN Best Editing: Frederic Knudtson, Robert C. Jones, Gene Fowler, Jr.; AAN Best Score: Ernest Gold; AAN Best Song: Ernest Gold (Music), Mack David (Lyrics); AAN Best Sound: Gordon E. Sawyer; AA Best Sound Effects Editing: Walter G. Elliott

Overkill, the CLEOPATRA of the funnybone. This comic extravaganza starts off funny, but exhausts rather than delights. Designed to be the biggest, most lavish comedy ever made, IT'S A MAD, MAD, MAD, MAD WORLD is a coarse, star-studded pageant of Keystone Kops-style slapstick.

With his dying breath, a gangster (Jimmy Durante) recently released from prison tells the motorists who come upon him after an auto accident that $350,000 is buried under "the Big W," instigating a greedy, madcap dash for the cash. Among the lunatic treasure seekers who will stop at nothing to get to the loot first are Milton Berle, Dorothy Provine, Ethel Merman (who, curiously, steals the film from under everyone else's talented nose), Sid Caesar, Edie Adams, Buddy Hackett, Mickey Rooney, and Jonathan Winters. Phil Silvers, Terry-Thomas, Peter Falk, Dick Shawn, and Spencer Tracy also become involved, and the film is a who's who of Hollywood comedians in cameo appearances.

Director-producer Kramer spared no expense (tame today, the $7 million price tag was a hefty one at the time) on the spectacular stunts, using 39 stunt men and paying them $252,000 for some of the most incredible feats on film. But at 154 minutes of running time, it's way too long for what it is. Watching it at home with breaks may be the best way to analyze individual comic takes; certainly it's the most painless.

IT'S A WONDERFUL LIFE

1946   129m   bw   Drama   ★★★★★
Liberty   (U.S.)   /U

James Stewart *(George Bailey)*, Donna Reed *(Mary Hatch)*, Lionel Barrymore *(Mr. Potter)*, Thomas Mitchell *(Uncle Billy)*, Henry Travers *(Clarence)*, Beulah Bondi *(Mrs. Bailey)*, Frank Faylen *(Ernie)*, Ward Bond *(Bert)*, Gloria Grahame *(Violet Bick)*, H.B. Warner *(Mr. Gower)*

p, Frank Capra; d, Frank Capra; w, Frances Goodrich, Albert Hackett, Frank Capra, Jo Swerling (based on the story "The Greatest Gift" by Philip Van Doren Stern); ph, Joseph Walker, Joseph Biroc; ed, William Hornbeck; m, Dimitri Tiomkin; art d, Jack Okey; fx, Russell A. Cully; cos, Edward Stevenson

AAN Best Picture; AAN Best Actor: James Stewart; AAN Best Director: Frank Capra; AAN Best Editing: William Hornbeck; AAN Best Sound: John Aalberg (Sound)

The holiday gift for all time. This heartwarming fantasy, one of the most popular films ever made, begins as angels discuss George Bailey (James Stewart), a small-town resident so beset with problems that he contemplates a Christmastime suicide.

In flashback, we review George's life, learning that he has always wanted to leave his hometown to see the world, but that circumstances and his own good heart have kept him in Bedford Falls, sacrificing his own education for his brother's, keeping the family-run savings and loan afloat, protecting the town from the avarice of banker Potter (Lionel Barrymore), marrying his childhood sweetheart (Donna Reed), and raising a family. Back in the present, George prepares to jump from a bridge, but ends up rescuing his guardian angel, Clarence Oddbody (Henry Travers), who has come to earn his wings. Clarence shows him how badly Bedford Falls would have turned out without George and

his good deeds. Filled with renewed joy in life, George goes home to his loving family and friends, who pitch in to put his worries behind him.

Few filmmakers have rivaled director Frank Capra when it comes to examining the human heart, and IT'S A WONDERFUL LIFE is a masterfully crafted exercise in sentiment, augmented by Capra's undying faith in community. Reed and Barrymore give excellent performances, as does a superb cast of character players, but this is Stewart's film—heart-stirring as the dreamer who sacrifices all for his fellow man. The bright, funny screenplay is based on "The Greatest Gift," a story that Philip Van Dorn Stren originally sent to his friends as a Christmas card.

IT'S ALIVE

1974   90m   c   Horror   ★★
Larco   (U.S.)   PG/

John P. Ryan *(Frank Davies)*, Sharon Farrell *(Lenore Davies)*, Andrew Duggan *(The Professor)*, Guy Stockwell *(Clayton)*, James Dixon *(Lt. Perkins)*, Michael Ansara *(The Captain)*, Robert Emhardt *(The Executive)*, William Wellman Jr. *(Charlie)*, Daniel Holzman *(Chris Davies)*, Shamus Locke *(Doctor)*

p, Larry Cohen; d, Larry Cohen; w, Larry Cohen; ph, Fenton Hamilton; ed, Peter Honess; m, Bernard Herrmann; fx, Rick Baker

The film that put maverick producer-writer-director Larry Cohen on the map, IT'S ALIVE is a justifiably praised low-budget effort that delves into the dark side of American family life from a horror-movie perspective. The film opens as proud parents Frank and Lenore Davies (John P. Ryan and Sharon Farrell) enter the hospital to deliver their new child. Suddenly all hell breaks loose in the delivery room, as Lenore gives birth to a monstrous baby that kills several hospital personnel before scurrying off into the night. (The mutation may have been caused by a new fertility drug pushed on mothers by the pharmaceutical industry.) The horrified parents are torn: while Lenore feels strong maternal instincts for the child, Frank resolves to hunt it down and kill it. He assists the police in their search for the monster, but as the hunt gets warmer, he too begins to feel instinctive affection for the creature and finally attempts to save his child. Part visceral horror flick and part Oedipal allegory, IT'S ALIVE explores a widely repressed but crucial element of family life—parents' ambivalence toward their children—and satirizes society's cavalier treatment of its youngest members, prefiguring the mean social policies of the American 90s. Cohen turned this rich and terrifying concept into a trilogy: IT LIVES AGAIN and IT'S ALIVE III: ISLAND OF THE ALIVE followed.

IT'S ALWAYS FAIR WEATHER

1955   102m   c   Musical/Comedy   ★★★★
MGM   (U.S.)   /U

Gene Kelly *(Ted Riley)*, Dan Dailey *(Doug Hallerton)*, Cyd Charisse *(Jackie Leighton)*, Dolores Gray *(Madeline Bradville)*, Michael Kidd *(Angie Valentine)*, David Burns *(Tim)*, Jay C. Flippen *(Charles Z. Culloran)*, Steve Mitchell *(Kid Mariacchi)*, Hal March *(Rocky Lazar)*, Paul Maxey *(Mr. Fielding)*

p, Arthur Freed; d, Stanley Donen, Gene Kelly; w, Betty Comden, Adolph Green; ph, Robert Bronner; ed, Adrienne Fazan; art d, Cedric Gibbons, Arthur Lonergan; fx, Irving G. Reis, Warren Newcombe; chor, Stanley Donen, Gene Kelly; cos, Helen Rose

AAN Best Original Screenplay: Betty Comden, Adolph Green; AAN Best Score: Andre Previn

A scathing satire of television and advertising is only one element in this cynical musical, which masks the seriousness of its theme with many excellent numbers.

In 1945, soldiers Ted (Gene Kelly), Doug (Dan Dailey), and Angie (Michael Kidd) come home from WWII to dance in the streets (in the celebrated trash-can cover number) and drink their way across New York, then decide to meet in a decade. After a montage of news headlines to indicate time's passage, the trio return to the bar in which they last saw one another. Mutually disappointed by how their lives turned out, the men soon realize they have little in common anymore, and the evening disintegrates into perfunctory nostalgia. The film continues with a sour examination of their present-day lives.

FAIR WEATHER is stolen by Dailey's disillusioned advertising man (he has the best routine in the film); here was a musical comedy actor ahead of his time, a specialist in world-weary characters who just happen to be song and dance men. Delores Gray is dazzling in her female pirhana way, and Cyd Charisse is her novocained, scowling self—until she goes into her dance surrounded by uglies at Stillman's gym.

Directors Kelly and Stanley Donen make wonderful use of the CinemaScope screen, splitting it to achieve a previously unattainable intimacy. The songs have little to do with the plot, a lack of integration that may have prevented this ambitious, innovative picture from getting the audiences it deserved. But many film buffs find FAIR WEATHER more authentically deserving of praise than its predictable precursor, ON THE TOWN.

IT'S LOVE I'M AFTER

1937 90m bw Comedy   ★★★½
Warner Bros./First National (U.S.)

Leslie Howard *(Basil Underwood)*, Bette Davis *(Joyce Arden)*, Olivia de Havilland *(Marcia West)*, Eric Blore *(Digges)*, Patric Knowles *(Henry Grant)*, George Barbier *(William West)*, Spring Byington *(Aunt Ella Paisley)*, Bonita Granville *(Gracie Kane)*, E.E. Clive *(Butler)*, Veda Ann Borg *(Elsie)*

p, Harry Joe Brown; d, Archie Mayo; w, Casey Robinson (based on the story "Gentleman After Midnight" by Maurice Hanline); ph, James Van Trees; ed, Owen Marks, Tony Martinelli; m, Heinz Roemheld; art d, Carl Jules Weyl; cos, Orry-Kelly

A hammy romp, dated and with energy petering out after a while, but furiously acted by costars Davis and Howard. He's an egocentric matinee idol engaged to Davis, his battle-axe leading lady.

They have called off their marriage 11 times because, as loving as they are on stage, they constantly bicker off stage. Howard revels in the adoration of his stage-door Janies, which Davis can't stand. The most blatant swooner is de Havilland, who comes to every performance and sits there starry-eyed and almost salivating. being engaged to Knowles doesn't stop her from visiting the backstage dressing room and declaring her love to Howard. Later, Knowles confronts Howard and pleads with him to turn de Havilland away so he can marry the girl. Howard sees this as a chance to help Knowles and have some fun at the bothersome de Havilland's expense. It backfires, of course, and Howard, desperate to get the beautiful deb out of his life, asks Davis to pose as his wife. She agrees, but has some malicious fun of her own.

The film is better before it bogs down in too many in staples of 1930's comedy: de Havilland's execrable heiress and the country house of stultifying wasps. LOVE begins with a spoof of the tomb scene from *Romeo and Juliet*, and there are some funny bits backstage between dressing rooms, played by the leads. There's one hilarious performance once they get stuck in the country: Eric Blore's loony manservant. What a strange and welcome egg he is.

IVAN THE TERRIBLE, PARTS I & II
(IVAN GROZNYI)

1958 96m c/bw Biography/War   ★★★★★
Central Cinema/Alma-Ata Film Studio/Mosfilm   /PG
Studio (U.S.S.R.)

Nikolai Cherkasov *(Czar Ivan IV—Ivan the Terrible)*, Ludmila Tselikovskaya *(Anastasia Romanovna—the Czarina)*, Serafima Birman *(Euphrosyne Staritsky—the Czar's Aunt)*, Pavel Kadochnikov *(Vladimir Staritsky—her Son)*, Mikhail Nazvanov *(Prince Andrew Kurbsky)*, Andrei Abrikosov *(Boyar Fyodor Kolychev—Philip, Metropolitan of Moscow)*, Alexander Mgebrov *(Pimen, Archbishop of Novgorod—sometime Metropolitan of Moscow)*, Vladimir Balachov *(Peter Volynets—his Acolyte)*, Mikhail Zharov *(Malyuta Skuratof)*, Amvrosy Buchma *(Alexey Basmanov)*

p, Sergei Eisenstein; d, Sergei Eisenstein; w, Sergei Eisenstein; ph, Edward Tisse, Andrei Moskvin; ed, Sergei Eisenstein; m, Sergei Prokofiev; prod d, Isaac Shpinel; cos, Leonid Naumova

These are the first two parts of Sergei Eisenstein's intended trilogy about the 16th-century Russian hero Czar Ivan IV. Part I, completed in 1945, chronicles the ruler's coronation, his marriage, his illness and

sudden unexplained recovery, the poisoning of his wife, and his battles against conspirators. By the end, he declares his intention of returning from Alexandrov to Moscow at the will of his people. Part II (subtitled "The Revolt of the Boyars"), filmed shortly after Part I but not released until 1958, follows Czar Ivan on his return, and depicts his confrontations with his enemies, the poisoning of his mother, and his discovery of an assassination plot. The heretofore black-and-white film ends with a brilliantly colored banquet scene.

Although the scenario for Part III ("The Battles of Ivan") was approved by Stalin (oddly enough, since Stalin censored Part II because of its negative portrayal of Ivan's secret police), Eisenstein, who died in 1948, never completed the project. Viewers familiar only with Eisenstein's BATTLESHIP POTEMKIN will find the shift from that film's revolutionary editing style to IVAN's emphasis on composition and lighting quite a surprise. A vast, important, and occasionally difficult historical effort that closed Eisenstein's legendary career, IVAN THE TERRIBLE includes a remarkable score by Sergei Prokofiev.

IVANHOE

1952 106m c Historical   ★★★½
MGM (U.K.)   /U

Robert Taylor *(Ivanhoe)*, Elizabeth Taylor *(Rebecca)*, Joan Fontaine *(Rowena)*, George Sanders *(De Bois-Guilbert)*, Emlyn Williams *(Wamba)*, Robert Douglas *(Sir Hugh De Bracy)*, Finlay Currie *(Cedric)*, Felix Aylmer *(Isaac)*, Francis de Wolff *(Font De Boeuf)*, Guy Rolfe *(Prince John)*

p, Pandro S. Berman; d, Richard Thorpe; w, Noel Langley (based on the novel by Sir Walter Scott); ph, Freddie Young; ed, Frank Clarke; m, Miklos Rozsa; art d, Alfred Junge; fx, Tom Howard; cos, Roger Furse

AAN Best Picture; AAN Best Cinematography: Fred A Young; AAN Best Score: Miklos Rozsa

Luxe MGM historical ransacking, locationed to the nines, beautiful to look upon, but with energy lapses in the soggy script of Sir Walter Scott's epic classic. It is 1190 and Robert Taylor, as the brave Sir Wilfred of Ivanhoe, returns secretly to England from the Crusades. He has served England's King Richard the Lionhearted well in the Third Crusade, but the king has been captured and is held for ransom in Austria. It's Taylor's job to raise an enormous sum to free Richard (Wooland). Taylor is a Saxon knight, son of lord Currie, who more or less disowned his son when he went to fight for Richard, a Norman king.

Taylor encounters three Norman knights, Sanders, Douglas and de Wolff, who are in league with Prince John (Rolfe), who intends to usurp his missing brother, Richard. Taylor tells the knights that Currie's castle is nearby should they wish to seek shelter for the night, and he escorts them to his father's estate. Watching this encounter is Warrender (Robin Hood), and his men who were about to kill the hated Norman knights. But, seeing Taylor with the Normans, Warrender holds his men back, telling them he will wait to see what Taylor is up to.

The Norman knights are given a cool reception by Currie, but they are nevertheless extended the hospitality of the day. At dinner, these knights meet Currie's ward, the beautiful Fontaine, whom Douglas immediately covets. Sitting at the end of the table is Taylor, Fontaine's true love, who is recognized by his father when he toasts King Richard, but Currie refuses immediately to talk to his errant son. He later communicates with Taylor through his servant-fool, Williams.

After Taylor leaves the castle with Williams as his newly appointed squire, he rescues a rich Jew, Aylmer, from the anti-Semitic Normans and is later given jewels by Aylmer's grateful daughter, Elizabeth Taylor, so he can buy horse and armor to enter the jousting tournament at Ashby and win more money to ransom Richard.

The film is certainly rousing, with a particularly grisly bout between Taylor and Sanders and the Taylor-Fontaine-Taylor triangle adequate for romantic spectacle. Though undeniably waspy as Rebecca, Elizabeth Taylor's early beauty has a way of making you forget anything, including your name. IVANHOE is filled with majestic sets, brilliantly constructed by Junge. The costuming was painstakingly created by Furse. MGM spared no expense in making IVANHOE; this became the costliest epic ever produced in England. The truth is that the studio had no choice. MGM had accumulated millions of dollars in British banks but was restrained from taking this money out of the country.

J

J'ACCUSE
1939 95m bw War   ★★★½
Forrester/Parant   (France)

Victor Francen *(Jean Diaz)*, Jean Max *(Henri Chimay)*, Delaitre *(Francois Laurin)*, Renee Devillers *(Helene)*, Line Noro *(Edith)*, Marie Lou *(Flo)*, Georges Saillard *(Giles Tenant)*, Paul Amiot *(Captain)*, Andre Nox *(Leotard)*, Georges Rollin *(Pierre Fonds)*

p, Abel Gance; d, Abel Gance; w, Abel Gance, Steve Passeur; ph, Roger Hubert; m, Henri Verdun

An excellent antiwar film, J'ACCUSE is all the more poignant considering it was produced and released in France shortly before the Occupation. Francen invents a device he believes will stop war forever, only to see it used by his government as a defense measure against the enemy. Driven mad by this exploitation, Francen decides only the war dead marching through the streets will stop the people's thirst for an upcoming war. In his delusion, bodies rise from their graves, and the sight of war's actual horrors so terrifies the patriotic countrymen that all thoughts of war are abandoned. Gance's plot is a simple one, but told with enormous power and passion for the theme. The ravaged faces of the dead are disturbing, powerful images that are not soon forgotten. The message is conveyed clearly, without preaching, and with a sensitivity toward pacifism. Like so many films of this nature, its message was considered unsuitable by Nazi Germany, and the film was banned in that country.

JACK
1996 104m c Comedy   ★★
American Zoetrope/Hollywood Pictures   (U.S.)   PG-13/PG

Robin Williams *(Jack Powell)*, Diane Lane *(Karen Powell)*, Brian Kerwin *(Brian Powell)*, Jennifer Lopez *(Miss Marquez)*, Bill Cosby *(Lawrence Woodruff)*, Fran Drescher *(Dolores Durante)*, Adam Zolotin *(Louis Durante)*, Todd Bosley *(Edward)*, Seth Smith *(John-John)*, Mario Yedidia *(George)*

p, Richard Mestres, Fred Fuchs, Francis Ford Coppola; d, Francis Ford Coppola; w, James DeMonaco, Gary Nadeau; ph, John Toll; ed, Barry Malkin; m, Michael Kamen; prod d, Dean Tavoularis; art d, Angelo Graham; fx, John McLeod, Gary Gutierrez; cos, Aggie Guerard Rodgers

JACK offers a twist on the premise of BIG, with Robin Williams as a boy in a man's body trying to fit in with the lunchbox set. Director Francis Ford Coppola strives a little too earnestly for bittersweet, and crosses the line into melancholia.

Due to a mysterious medical condition that causes his body to age at four times the normal rate, 10-year-old Jack (Williams) has the appearance of a 40-year-old man. Jack's protective parents (Diane Lane and Brian Kerwin) have kept him secluded at home, but Jack longs to be around other kids his age, so he enters the fifth grade. At first, the other kids tease him, but they soon come around when they discover that Jack can pass for an adult. A convenient situation, but one which gets him into a sticky situation when the randy mother (Fran Drescher) of Jack's new best friend takes a shine to him.

The concept of Williams as a 10-year-old is a pitchman's dream, and JACK was sold easily to audiences with advertising that emphasized its star's special appeal to children. The film's first half provides some genuinely touching and funny moments, with Williams cavorting amidst his young co-stars. But Jack's accelerated growth also means

an accelerated mortality, and once Jack has his own end in his sights, the comedy becomes a fairly maudlin affair. Known for directing decidedly adult dramas like THE GODFATHER and APOCALYPSE NOW, Coppola was drawn to this Disney project because his own short-lived "shooting star," his son Giancarlo (to whom he dedicates the film), died at the age of 22. And while no one would question the heartfelt sincerity with which Coppola means to deliver JACK's "carpe diem" message, one might view it as unintentionally ironic, considering the film's juvenile and often downright libidinous humor.

JACKNIFE
1989 102m c Drama   ★★★
Kings Road/Sandollar-Schaffel   (U.S.)   R/15

Robert De Niro *(Joseph "Megs" Megessey)*, Ed Harris *(Dave)*, Kathy Baker *(Martha)*, Charles Dutton *(Jake)*, Loudon Wainwright III *(Ferretti)*, Elizabeth Franz, Tom Isbell, Sloane Shelton, Walter Massey, Jordan Lund

p, Robert Schaffel, Carol Baum; d, David Jones; w, Stephen Metcalfe (based on the play "Strange Snow" by Stephen Metcalfe); ph, Brian West; ed, John Bloom; m, Bruce Broughton; prod d, Edward Pisoni

This modest but compelling drama received only a brief theatrical release; it's a must-see on video—for it's acting, not the predictable story. Robert De Niro stars as "Megs" Megessey, nicknamed "Jacknife" in Vietnam because of his fondness for wrecking vehicles. Back Stateside, with the war long over, Megs is still a bit strange, and tends to irritate his war buddy Dave (Ed Harris)—who would just as soon forget both Vietnam and Megs. When Megs unexpectedly arrives at the house Dave shares with his sister, Martha (Kathy Baker), and subsequently begins a romance with her, Dave is forced to face some uncomfortable truths about himself, his memories, and his relationships with Megs and with Martha. Though it's stage origins show (adapted from Stephen Metcalfe's *Strange Show*), and we're cooked on 'Nam sigificance (with the flasbacks here particular eyesores), all three leads are splendid in their roles.

JACOB'S LADDER
1990 115m c Horror   ★★★½
Carolco   (U.S.)   R/18

Tim Robbins *(Jacob Singer)*, Elizabeth Pena *(Jezzie)*, Danny Aiello *(Louis)*, Matt Craven *(Michael)*, Pruitt Taylor Vince *(Paul)*, Jason Alexander *(Geary)*, Patricia Kalember *(Sarah)*, Eriq La Salle *(Frank)*, Ving Rhames *(George)*, Brian Tarantina *(Doug)*

p, Alan Marshall; d, Adrian Lyne; w, Bruce Joel Rubin; ph, Jeffrey Kimball; ed, Tom Rolf; m, Maurice Jarre; prod d, Brian Morris; art d, Jeremy Conway; fx, FXSMITH Inc., Gordon J. Smith, Connie Brink, Steven Dewey, Musikwerks; cos, Ellen Mirojnick @DESC = Director Adrian Lyne followed his trashy smash FATAL ATTRACTION with this arresting oddity, an arty, terrifying psychological thriller. Scripted by Bruce Joel Rubin (GHOST) and produced at a cost of $40 million, the film failed at the box office, probably due to a twist ending that almost everyone perceived as a cop-out.

JACOB'S LADDER stars Tim Robbins as Jacob, a divorced Vietnam veteran who lives in New York with his girlfriend Jezzie (a smoldering Elizabeth Pena) and works as a mailman. Jacob is haunted by painful memories of his dead son (a mysteriously unbilled Macaulay Culkin, star of 1990's monster hit HOME ALONE) and of his Vietnam experience when he was nearly killed by a soldier with a bayonet. As the film progresses, Jacob also begins to see weird creatures and startling visions. Suddenly, there are monsters roaming through the streets of New York; closed subway stations take on a creepy life of their own; a crowded party turns into a room full of winged demons; a train full of strangers look as though they have sprouted tails and horns. Are these the visions of a madman or have demons actually come to get Jacob Singer? While trying desperately to cling to his sanity, Jacob enlists the help of his ex-wife (Patricia Kalember), a mysterious stranger (Matt Craven), and an angelic chiropractor (Danny Aiello) to help solve the mystery.

The much-touted screenplay for JACOB'S LADDER circulated in Hollywood for almost a decade, and in a 1983 *American Film* article, Rubin's screenplay was listed among the ten best unproduced scripts.

(In our view, Lyne improved on the screenplay by heightening its ambiguities and jettisoning much fabular preachiness.) Truly frightening and visually unique, this messy, challenging film is anchored by Tim Robbins' remarkable performance.

JAGGED EDGE

1985 108m c Mystery/Thriller ★★★
Columbia (U.S.) R/18

Glenn Close (*Teddy Barnes*), Jeff Bridges (*Jack Forrester*), Peter Coyote (*Thomas Krasny*), Robert Loggia (*Sam Ransom*), John Dehner (*Judge Carrigan*), Karen Austin (*Julie Jensen*), Guy Boyd (*Matthew Barnes*), Marshall Colt (*Bobby Slade*), Louis Giambalvo (*Fabrizi*), Ben Hammer (*Dr. Goldman*)

p, Martin Ransohoff; d, Richard Marquand; w, Joe Eszterhas; ph, Matthew F. Leonetti; ed, Sean Barton, Conrad Buff; m, John Barry; prod d, Gene Callahan; art d, Peter Lansdown Smith; cos, Ann Roth, Michael Dennison, Elizabeth Pine

AAN Best Supporting Actor: Robert Loggia

No cutting edge, but does keep you guessing. It's one of the oldest of Hollywood chestnuts—a socialite is murdered, her husband is suspected by a crafty district attorney, and the female lawyer who defends the accused falls in love with her client—but it still works thanks to Richard Marquand's adroit direction and a tightly knit screenplay from Joe Eszterhas.

Jeff Bridges is one of the beautiful people—possessor of money, luxury, looks and power. When his wife is savagely murdered by an assailant with a jagged-edged knife, Peter Coyote, a tough, sleazy DA, refuses to believe Bridges' innocence. One person who does believe the accused is Glenn Close, a disillusioned lawyer who is sick of Coyote's methods and decides to defend Bridges, falling in love with him in the process.

This film's ending received a great deal of discussion because it purposely obscures the killer's identity, leaving the exiting audience with an uneasy feeling of doubt. It's slick, romantic, funny (Close has a great rapport with her beer-guzzling, foul-mouthed mentor, Robert Loggia), intriguing, and filled with excellent performances.

JAILHOUSE ROCK

1957 96m bw Musical ★★★½
MGM (U.S.) /U

Elvis Presley (*Vince Everett*), Judy Tyler (*Peggy Van Alden*), Mickey Shaughnessy (*Hunk Houghton*), Jennifer Holden (*Sherry Wilson*), Dean Jones (*Teddy Talbot*), Anne Neyland (*Laury Jackson*), Hugh Sanders (*Warden*), Vaughn Taylor (*Mr. Shores*), Mike Stoller (*Pianist*), Grandon Rhodes (*Prof. August Van Alden*)

p, Pandro S. Berman; d, Richard Thorpe; w, Guy Trosper (based on a story by Ned Young); ph, Robert Bronner; ed, Ralph E. Winters; art d, William A. Horning, Randall Duell; fx, A. Arnold Gillespie

All shook up and enjoyably bad, JAILHOUSE ROCK captures early Elvis in all his leg-quivering, nostril-flaring, lip-snarling teen idol glory.

This hot black-and-white number was Elvis Presley's third (after LOVE ME TENDER and LOVING YOU) and set the standard for the rest of his movie outings—too bad the the others omitted the dangerous element of his character presented here. Elvis comes across like a white-trash musical genius version of James Dean, playing Vince Everett, a surly good ole boy who accidentally kills a man while defending a lady's honor. . . in a bar. This heroism gets him sent up for manslaughter, sharing his prison cell with Hunk Houghton (Mickey Shaughnessy), an ex-singer who convinces him to perform in the slammer's convict show. After Vince is freed, he meets Peggy Van Alden (Judy Tyler), with whom he forms a record company, and in no time he is a national star on his way to Hollywood. Peggy, however, sees that Vince is turning into an egomaniac, and she can't stand it.

There's little surprise but JAILHOUSE really rocks, establishing pre-Army Elvis, the rockabilly elemental force, when he was really something. The steamy songs are mostly by Lieber and Stoller; the latter can be seen as the pianist in the famous "Jailhouse Rock" sequence (which the young King choreographed). The title song sold two million records within two weeks, and the picture, in turn, grossed

several million, with Presley receiving 50 percent of the profits. Other tunes include "Treat Me Nice," "Baby, I Don't Care" and "Young and Beautiful."

JANE EYRE

1944 97m bw Romance ★★★½
Fox (U.S.) /PG

Orson Welles (*Edward Rochester*), Joan Fontaine (*Jane Eyre*), Margaret O'Brien (*Adele*), Peggy Ann Garner (*Jane as a Child*), John Sutton (*Dr. Rivers*), Sara Allgood (*Bessie*), Henry Daniell (*Brockelhurst*), Agnes Moorehead (*Mrs. Reed*), Elizabeth Taylor (*Helen Burns*), Aubrey Mather (*Col. Dent*)

p, William Goetz; d, Robert Stevenson; w, Aldous Huxley, Robert Stevenson, John Houseman (based on the book by Charlotte Bronte); ph, George Barnes; ed, Walter Thompson; m, Bernard Herrmann; art d, James Basevi, Wiard Ihnen; fx, Fred Sersen; cos, Rene Hubert

A touch too plodding, but an atmospheric reduction of Bronte. This was the fifth time around for the doughty English lady: In 1913 Irving Cummings and Ethel Grand did it. In 1915 it was Alan Hale and Louise Vale. Mabel Ballin and Norman Trevor tried again in 1921; then Virginia Bruce and Colin Clive made the first talkie version in 1934. Although shot on the West Los Angeles sound stages of 20th Century-Fox, Barnes's eerie cinematography truly evokes the bleakness of the novel.

Fontaine is Jane Eyre, an orphan girl who has been tossed about by fate and managed to survive a sordid upbringing. (In the early scenes the role is touchingly played by Peggy Ann Garner.) Fontaine takes a job as governess to Yorkshireman Welles's ward, O'Brien. They live on the Yorkshire moors in a huge house called Thornfield Hall. Fontaine appears as though she'll remain a spinster for the rest of her days, but there is an attraction growing between her and Welles. He is a troubled man, brooding and enigmatic, yet Fontaine has come to love him; a wedding is planned, but it fails to take place.

This is Bronte as gothic paperback romance, and the music, by longtime Welles associate Bernard Herrmann, richly slathers over discrepancies between Welles's and Fontaine's acting styles (after Welles makes his entrance, everything seems to swirl about him—or at least out of his way). In the original book Jane was the protagonist and Rochester was more of a large supporting part. To accommodate Welles, who was emerging as one of the country's most popular actors, the male role was expanded and he received billing above Fontaine.

The Peggy Ann Garner sequences are the best in the film, with Jane's dismal schooling realized very well. You can bet there wasn't a dry eye in the house when strange, beautiful little Helen Burns (Elizabeth Taylor), dies from gross neglect. Later, in 1957, it was done with Patrick Macnee and Joan Elan and then again in 1971 with George C. Scott and Susannah York, both of these versions for television.

JASON AND THE ARGONAUTS

1963 104m c Fantasy/Adventure ★★★½
Columbia (U.K.) /U

Todd Armstrong (*Jason*), Nancy Kovack (*Medea*), Gary Raymond (*Acastus*), Laurence Naismith (*Argus*), Niall MacGinnis (*Zeus*), Michael Gwynn (*Hermes*), Douglas Wilmer (*Pelias*), Jack Gwillim (*King Aeetes*), Honor Blackman (*Hera*), John Cairney (*Hylas*)

p, Charles H. Schneer; d, Don Chaffey; w, Jan Reed, Beverley Cross; ph, Wilkie Cooper; ed, Maurice Rootes; m, Bernard Herrmann; prod d, Geoffrey Drake; art d, Herbert Smith, Jack Maxsted, Toni Sarzi-Braga; fx, Ray Harryhausen

What a blast! This film, along with THE SEVENTH VOYAGE OF SINBAD, contains special-effects master Ray Harryhausen's finest work, evoking a world of dragons, living statues, harpies and gods. Pelias (Douglas Wilmer) murders the king of Thessaly and steals his throne, but the infant prince, Jason, survives.

Years later, aided by the goddess Hera (Honor Blackman), Jason (Todd Armstrong) begins a search for the Golden Fleece, which will finally instate him as rightful king. With a crew of brave men (including Hercules, in a fine performance by Nigel Green), he sets out on his glorious quest in his ship, the *Argo*. At one point, the *Argo* is menaced by a giant living statue, but Jason defeats it. After further adventures in which Jason battles harpies, encounters the gigantic Neptune, and discovers Medea (Nancy Kovack) on an empty ship, the crew finally find the fleece. They kill the seven-headed hydra that guards it but are halted again when the hydra's teeth grow into seven sword-brandishing living skeletons. In a stunning display of technical wizardry, the Argonauts fight the skeletons to the death.

Harryhausen is at his most creative and brilliant (except for the disappointing bronze Titan), the film is well directed by Don Chaffey and adequately acted as these things go. Featuring gorgeous Mediterranean photography and a rousing Bernard Herrmann score, making this a great film for kids that will also please adult viewers. A must-see.

JAWS

1975 124m c Horror ★★★★
Universal (U.S.) PG

Roy Scheider (*Police Chief Martin Brody*), Robert Shaw (*Quint*), Richard Dreyfuss (*Matt Hooper*), Lorraine Gary (*Ellen Brody*), Murray Hamilton (*Mayor Larry Vaughn*), Carl Gottlieb (*Meadows*), Jeffrey Kramer (*Deputy Hendricks*), Susan Backlinie (*Chrissie Watkins*), Jonathan Filley (*Cassidy*), Ted Grossman (*Estuary Victim*)

p, Richard D. Zanuck, David Brown; d, Steven Spielberg; w, Peter Benchley, Carl Gottlieb, Howard Sackler (uncredited, based on the novel by Benchley); ph, Bill Butler; ed, Verna Fields; m, John Williams; prod d, Joe Alves; fx, Robert A. Mattey

AAN Best Picture; AA Best Editing: Verna Fields; *AA Best Score:* John Williams; *AA Best Sound:* Robert L. Hoyt, Roger Heman, Earl Madery, John Carter

A looming, terrifying catch of the day, JAWS was the summer mega-hit that established Steven Spielberg. This is the most cynically manipulative movie he's ever made (although it's deepened by some telling points about the tensions of contemporary masculinity), and it must be seen for its unexpected editing, driving score, and careful build toward shock images so big they feel like they're jumping into your lap.

An East Coast resort, Amity Island, is plagued by attacks on swimmers by a 28-foot great white shark. Although the mayor (Murray Hamilton) would like to keep the whole thing quiet—he doesn't want to ruin the summer tourist season—the brutal attacks soon cannot be ignored, so police chief Martin Brody (Roy Scheider), marine biologist Matt Hooper (Richard Dreyfuss), and grizzled old shark hunter Quint (Robert Shaw) go after the monstrous creature, winding up in a desperate fight for their lives.

The film that put Steven Spielberg on the cinematic map, JAWS was phenomenally successful at the box office and seemed to tap into a universal fear of what lies beneath the sea. The director's vision of *Moby Dick*, with Quint as Ahab, finally digs a grave for macho, exposing it as a foolhardy joke; it's high time. Spielberg's direction turns the material into a nerve-jangling *tour de force*. From the outrageously frightening opening—in which a beautiful young woman skinny-dipping in the moonlight is devoured by the unseen shark—to the claustrophobic climax aboard Quint's fishing boat, Spielberg has us in his grip and rarely lets go (although the film does bog down momentarily in some soap-opera scenes of Brody's family life).

Because the film tapped into a common fear and played on it so skillfully, it was a worldwide hit and entered international popular culture. JAWS has been endlessly parodied by comedians and filmmakers alike, and John Williams's effective score has now become a cliche. Three vastly inferior sequels followed. Now, everybody into the pool!

JE T'AIME, JE T'AIME

1968 91m c Science Fiction ★★★
Parc/Fox Europa (France/Sweden) /A

Claude Rich (*Claude Ridder*), Olga Georges-Picot (*Catrine*), Anouk Ferjac (*Wiana Lust*), Marie-Blanche Vergnes (*Young Woman*), Dominique Rozan (*Dr. Haesserts*), Van Doude (*Jan Rouffer*), Annie Fargue (*Agnes de Smet*), Bernard Fresson (*Bernard Hannecart*), Yvette Etievant (*Germaine Coster*), Irene Tunc (*Marcelle Hannecart*)

p, Mag Bodard; d, Alain Resnais; w, Alain Resnais, Jacques Sternberg; ph, Jean Boffety; ed, Albert Jurgenson, Colette Leloup; m, Krzysztof Penderecki, Jean-Claude Pelletier, Jean Dandeny; art d, Jacques Dugied, Auguste Pace

Resnais continues exploring the relation of time and memory to individual perceptions and feelings, the pervasive theme in his work since HIROSHIMA, MON AMOUR. This time he conducts his investigations in a science fiction environment. Rich plays a man recovering from a suicide attempt who is able to go back in time and become involved once more in the love affair that drove him to attempt suicide. Although he eventually returns to normal time strictures, Rich's mind is still unable to transcend past events. A tight collaboration between Resnais and screenwriter Sternberg has woven complex thematic content into a film more accessible than any of Resnais's earlier works.

JEAN DE FLORETTE

1986 122m c Drama ★★★½
Renn/RAI-TV/D.D./A2 (France) PG

Yves Montand (*Cesar Soubeyran/"Le Papet"*), Gerard Depardieu (*Jean de Florette/Cadoret*), Daniel Auteuil (*Ugolin Soubeyran/"Galignette"*), Elisabeth Depardieu (*Aimee Cadoret*), Ernestine Mazurowna (*Manon Cadoret*), Marcel Champel (*Pique-Bouffigue*), Armand Meffre (*Philoxene*), Andre Dupon (*Pamphile*), Pierre Nougaro (*Casimir*), Marc Betton (*Martial*)

p, Pierre Grunstein; d, Claude Berri; w, Claude Berri, Gerard Brach (based on the novel by Marcel Pagnol); ph, Bruno Nuytten; ed, Arlette Langmann, Herve de Luze, Noelle Boisson; m, Jean-Claude Petit; prod d, Bernard Vezat; cos, Sylvie Gautrelet

The most talked-about French production in many years, this picture and its sequel, MANON OF THE SPRING (MANON DES SOURCES), were completed at a combined record-breaking budget of $17 million (about eight times the cost of the average French picture). Shot back to back with its successor, JEAN DE FLORETTE is set in a French farming village tucked into a picturesque hillside.

Le Papet (Yves Montand), an imperious and unscrupulous local landowner, welcomes the return to the village of his nephew, Ugolin (Daniel Auteuil). An unappealing social misfit, Ugolin dreams of making his fortune by growing carnations. Carnations, however, need a great deal of water—a sparse commodity in the village. When Le Papet realizes that Ugolin's idea is potentially profitable, he sets his sights on a neighboring farm that has an untapped natural spring. But the farm is owned by Jean Cadoret (Gerard Depardieu), a hunchbacked ex-tax collector who has bid farewell to the city and proves to be a tenacious convert to the farming life.

Directed by Claude Berri, JEAN DE FLORETTE is based on Marcel Pagnol's two-part novel *L'Eau des Collines* (The Water of the Hills), which, in turn, was based on an unsuccessful 1952 film Pagnol directed. A throwback to the pre-New Wave days of French cinema, the film offers complex characterizations, careful scripting, and lyrically pastoral images.

JEREMIAH JOHNSON

1972 108m c Western/Adventure ★★★½
Warner Bros. (U.S.) PG

Robert Redford (*Jeremiah Johnson*), Will Geer (*Bear Claw*), Stefan Gierasch (*Del Gue*), Allyn Ann McLerie (*Crazy Woman*), Charles Tyner (*Robidoux*), Josh Albee (*Caleb*), Joaquin Martinez (*Paints His Shirt Red*), Paul Benedict (*Reverend*), Matt Clark (*Qualen*), Richard Angarola (*Lebeaux*)

p, Joe Wizan; d, Sydney Pollack; w, John Milius, Edward Anhalt (based on the novel *Mountain Man* by Vardis Fisher, and the story "Crow Killer" by Raymond W. Thorp and Robert Bunker); ph, Andrew Duke Callaghan; ed, Thomas Stanford; m, John Rubenstein, Tim McIntire; art d, Ted Haworth

Slow as molasses. Redford stars as a lone wolf who dislikes civilization. He moves into the Rocky Mountains in the 1830s but is barely managing to stay alive when trapper Geer meets him and takes him under his wing. For a year Redford learns all the basic skills of survival in the wilderness, and then he's off on his own. When he comes upon a settlement that has been wiped out by marauding Indians who have left only a woman, now deranged, and her son alive, he buries the dead, transports the woman to a ferry, and adopts the boy. Later, he finds another rugged trapper, bald Gierasch (who shaves his head so that the Indians will not attempt to scalp him), left buried up to his neck. Redford rescues him and later when they raid an Indian camp, Gierasch scalps several of his victims. When they are again on the trail, Gierasch spots advancing Indians and puts the scalps into Redford's pack. The Indians are not hostile, however, and when they discover the scalps of their enemy in Redford's possession, he is hailed as a great warrior.

These Flathead Indians insist that the chief's daughter, Swan (Delle Bolton), be given as a wife to Redford. Rather than risk insulting the tribe and losing his own scalp, the young trapper takes the Indian woman with him. They all form a bond of deep affection as they carve out a cabin and clearing in the wilderness. All is tranquil until a US Cavalry unit arrives and asks Redford to guide the troopers through the mountains to a stranded wagon train of settlers. He does, reluctantly leading the soldiers through the sacred Crow Indian burial grounds.

Beautifully photographed in the wilds of Utah, this film unfortunately doesn't know when to stop; it feels consumed by a self-concious desire to be arty, and offers a treatment too cool for its subject matter. The dialogue, by John Milius and Edward Anhalt, is full of homespun homilies that undercut the attempted seriousness. Of the small cast, Will Geer steals the film. The story is purportedly based on the experiences of a real trapper known as "Liver-Eatin' Johnson," so called because of how he disposed of his victims. Not until the very end of the shooting did Pollack decide how Redford would meet his fate. "Pollack wanted me to freeze to death," Redford was later quoted, "but I preferred to leave Johnson's fate up to the audience's imagination by having him disappear into the mountains." That ambiguous fate is exactly what happened to the real Johnson, and it's one that befalls Redford in the film.

JERRY MAGUIRE

1996 135m c Comedy/Drama   ★★★½
Gracie Films (U.S.)   R/15

Tom Cruise (Jerry Maguire), Cuba Gooding Jr. (Rod Tidwell), Renee Zellweger (Dorothy Boyd), Kelly Preston (Avery Bishop), Bonnie Hunt (Laurel Boyd), Jerry O'Connell (Frank Cushman), Jay Mohr (Bob Sugar), Regina King (Marcee Tidwell), Jonathan Lipnicki (Ray Boyd), Todd Louiso (Chad the Nanny)

p, James L. Brooks, Laurence Mark, Richard Sakai, Cameron Crowe; d, Cameron Crowe; w, Cameron Crowe; ph, Janusz Kaminski; ed, Joe Hutshing; m, Nancy Wilson; prod d, Stephen Lineweaver; art d, Virginia Randolph, Clayton Hartley; fx, Paul Haines; cos, Betsy Heimann

AA Best Supporting Actor: Cuba Gooding Jr.; AAN Best Picture; AAN Best Actor: Tom Cruise; AAN Best Film Editing: Joe Hutshing; AAN Best Original Screenplay: Cameron Crowe

Cameron Crowe's popular romantic comedy features standout performances by Tom Cruise and Oscar winner Cuba Gooding Jr., as well as impressive turns by Renee Zellweger and Jonathan Lipnicki.

Jerry Maguire (Tom Cruise) is a sports agent who wins salaries and endorsements for his clients that are so overinflated that they repel fans. During a fit of guilt, he writes a memo outlining how sports agencies ought to lessen their concern with the almighty dollar. He is subsequently fired and, in an effort to stay in the game, convinces one of his clients—Rod Tidwell (Cuba Gooding Jr.), a receiver for the Arizona Cardinals—to stick with him as he builds a solo career. As Jerry packs up his desk and leaves, he implores his co-workers to follow him. The only one who agrees is Dorothy Boyd (Renee Zellweger), an accountant who has been secretly attracted to Jerry for some time. Jerry busily hypes Rod as a sputtering romance begins between him and Dorothy.

Like 1989's SAY ANYTHING, JERRY MAGUIRE displays Cameron Crowe's ability to create romantic relationships that ring true. Crowe also nimbly avoids the stereotype traps that characters like Jerry Maguire and Rod Tidwell often place in a writer's path. Though JERRY MAGUIRE's happy ending is a bit too neat, the overall package is well worth the price of admission. JERRY MAGUIRE also gives audiences a rare look at Cruise's underappreciated comic side. He displays deft comic timing and a surprising aptitude

for physical comedy. The film's other pleasant surprise is the performance of Gooding, who easily holds his own against Cruise. He even manages to steal a few scenes from the star, and scored himself an Oscar in the process.

JESSE JAMES

1939 105m c Western   ★★★★
Fox (U.S.)   /U

Tyrone Power (Jesse James), Henry Fonda (Frank James), Nancy Kelly (Zee), Randolph Scott (Will Wright), Henry Hull (Major Rufus Cobb), Brian Donlevy (Barshee), John Carradine (Bob Ford), Jane Darwell (Mrs. Samuels), Donald Meek (McCoy), Slim Summerville (Jailer)

p, Nunnally Johnson; d, Henry King; w, Nunnally Johnson (based on historical data assembled by Rosalind Schaeffer and Jo Frances James); ph, W. Howard Greene, George Barnes; ed, Barbara McLean; m, Louis Silvers; art d, William Darling, George Dudley

This classic Western unfolds the legendary saga of the notorious James boys, notably Jesse Woodson James (1847-1882). Director King directed this blockbuster that captures the image and era of the infamous outlaw, if not the reality of his character.

Until this film the 24-year-old Power had been an attractive matinee idol, but here he proved that he could really act. Though Fonda has fewer scenes, he renders his stalwart, prosaic character so effectively that Fox cast him in the successful sequel, THE RETURN OF FRANK JAMES. JESSE JAMES was the film that made Fonda a star.

Both King and Johnson had been eager to do a film on the legendary outlaw. Johnson researched Jesse James in Missouri, drawing most of his historic notions from the *Sedalia Gazette*, a strongly pro-James paper which promoted the idea that the notorious lawlessness of the James boys was caused by railroad and Union Army persecution following the Civil War. In the beginning this was true, but even Missouri residents grew tired of this excuse as the James-Younger gang went on looting for almost two decades; in fact, Jesse James was at large for eighteen years before being gunned down by Bob Ford on April 3, 1882. Screenwriter Johnson opted for nostalgia and legend and left out much of the outlaw's grim career. Jo Frances James, granddaughter of Jesse James, was hired as a consultant to the production, but she was later disappointed with the film, commenting: "I don't know what happened to the history part of it. It seemed to me the story was fiction from beginning to end. About the only connection it had with fact was that there once was a man named James and he did ride a horse."

The old Technicolor process has never been more richly reproduced than in JESSE JAMES, which offers spellbinding hues of deep green, brown, and gold, giving the countryside portrayed the soft appearance of mellow history. There have been many films dealing with America's most celebrated outlaw, but this is the best.

JESUS OF MONTREAL
(JESUS DE MONTREAL)

1989 120m c Drama   ★★★½
Max/Gerard Mital (Canada/France)   R/18

Lothaire Bluteau (Daniel), Catherine Wilkening (Mireille), Johanne-Marie Tremblay (Constance), Remy Girard (Martin), Robert Lepage (Rene), Gilles Pelletier (Fr. Leclerc), Yves Jacques (Richard Cardinal), Denys Arcand (The Judge)

p, Roger Frappier; d, Denys Arcand; w, Denys Arcand; ph, Guy Dufaux; ed, Isabelle Dedieu; m, Yves Laferriere; prod d, Francois Seguin

AAN Best Foreign Language Film

Denys Arcand's JESUS OF MONTREAL is a modern Passion Play that takes aim at organized religion and the superficial values of our media-saturated society, yet suggests salvation through technology. Thoughtful without being didactic, this is a strong, provocative film.

The story begins as Daniel (Bluteau) is hired to stage the annual Summer Passion Play in a park overlooking the skyline of Montreal. From the start, Daniel's production—which he is to direct, as well as to star in as Jesus—is not entirely conventional. His ensemble cast comprises fellow actor friends forced to get along by dubbing porn movies and modeling for sleazy commercials. Mireille (Wilkening) is the Passion Play's (as well as the film's) Mary Magdalene. At first, she drifts aimlessly and almost amorally through life, but ultimately finds meaning in her devotion to Daniel and the play. Daniel becomes fascinated with some of the more unorthodox theories that he encounters in his research of Jesus' life, including questions of Jesus' true parentage, and these details go into the play. When the play is finally staged, it emerges as an avant-garde performance piece, with audiences ushered to the various installations representing the events in Jesus' life. The resulting drama doesn't adhere to standard biblical interpretations, but it truly moves and inspires the audience, and the revisionist Passion Play, its cast, and particularly Daniel become the toast of the town, cooed over by critics and culture vultures. Soon, life begins to imitate art, as church officials decide to discontinue the play because of questions about its possibly blasphemous content.

Arcand's excellent screenplay invests his vision of this spiritual parable with scathing satire and social commentary. The superb cast includes Bluteau as Daniel, his quiet brooding erupting into indignant rage; Girard as Martin, the most down-to-earth character in the film; and Wilkening as Mireille, who represents the modern-day lost soul's search for meaning. However, in drawing parallels between Daniel and Jesus, Arcand paints himself into a corner. The too-literal quality of these comparisons threatens to diminish the film's overall impact. The final resurrection sequence should be extraordinarily powerful as well as clinically probing; instead it is more of the latter than the former. But despite these weaknesses, the handsomely produced JESUS OF MONTREAL remains fresh, intelligent, and fascinating.

JEZEBEL

1938 104m bw Drama   ★★★★
Warner Bros. (U.S.)   /U

Bette Davis (Julie Morrison), Henry Fonda (Preston Dillard), George Brent (Buck Cantrell), Margaret Lindsay (Amy Bradford Dillard), Fay Bainter (Aunt Belle Massey), Richard Cromwell (Ted Dillard), Donald Crisp (Dr. Livingstone), Henry O'Neill (Gen. Theopholus Bogardus), John Litel (Jean LeCour), Gordon Oliver (Dick Allen)

p, Henry Blanke; d, William Wyler; w, Clements Ripley, Abem Finkel, John Huston, Robert Buckner (based on the play by Owen Davis, Sr.); ph, Ernest Haller; ed, Warren Low; m, Max Steiner; art d, Robert Haas; cos, Orry-Kelly

AAN Best Picture; AA Best Actress: Bette Davis; AA Best Supporting Actress: Fay Bainter; AAN Best Cinematography: Ernest Haller; AAN Best Score: Max Stiner

Our favorite magnolia. A mesmerizing romantic melodrama with "Popeye the Magnificent" playing a southern belle so peverse she ruins her own chances, as well as shaking up the Olde South. Without Davis, who snared her second Oscar for the role—JEZEBEL was her consolation prize for losing the plum role in GONE WITH THE WIND, and there was a rush to get it into theaters first—this would seem mildewed indeed. But because her nervy, edgy performance conveys so much rage it leads convincingly into the film's second half where raging fires and fever sweep through New Orleans.

We may never really know if Davis and director Wyler had a great, doomed love affair, but the film looks like they did. Especially when Davis's Julie wrecks a great ball, and her own life, by wearing a flaming red gown when unmarried women are expected to wear pristine white. It's an outrageously great moment. Wyler's camera (abetted by the gifted cinematographer Ernest Haller) bores down on Davis, with her large, guilty eyes darting about to Max Steiner's swooping waltz—she's in too far to turn back. And the scene captures a quality in Fonda rarely exploited—his stubbornness—which may account for the longevity of his career. GONE WITH THE WIND may not have a single moment quite as incredible as this one, but then, that film didn't have Wyler who also gives Davis her other all-stops-out moment—her apology to Fonda, going to her knees in a white gown of breathtaking proportions. Davis gives the scene an overwhelmingly hushed sense of sexual urgency and surrender. JEZEBEL is indeed Wyler's love letter to Davis. (THE LETTER represents the souring of their collaboration; THE LITTLE FOXES, its death).

The screenplay by Clements Ripley, Abem Finkel and John Huston was based on the Owen Davis, Sr. play that lasted about five minutes on Broadway with Miriam Hopkins replacing the ailing Tallulah Bank-

head ("It was dreadful," said Tallulah. "Had I played the part it might have run two weeks."). The casting of Davis fanned the flames of her feuds with both of these southern belles, who hailed from Georgia and Alabama respectively.

Fonda had made a deal with the studio that his work on the film be completed by early December, so he could fly back to New York where his wife was awaiting their first child (Jane, born on December 21st). Although they tried to rush things, Wyler's perfectionism put the film behind schedule. As a result, Davis had to do her closeups and inserts without Fonda on the set. JEZEBEL features two songs: the title tune and "Raise a Ruckus." The film cost slightly over $1 million but made a bundle for everyone involved and got the country in an antebellum mood that went into overdrive with the release of Selznick's greatest work.

JFK

1991 189m c Historical/Drama   ★★★½
Camelot Productions/Warner Bros./New Regency Films/Canal   R/15
Plus/Ixtlan (U.S.)

Kevin Costner (Jim Garrison), Sissy Spacek (Liz Garrison), Joe Pesci (David Ferrie), Tommy Lee Jones (Clay Shaw), Gary Oldman (Lee Harvey Oswald), Jay O. Sanders (Lou Ivon), Michael Rooker (Bill Broussard), Laurie Metcalf (Susie Cox), Gary Grubbs (Al Oser), John Candy (Dean Andrews)

p, A. Kitman Ho, Oliver Stone; d, Oliver Stone; w, Oliver Stone, Zachary Sklar (from the books On the Trail of the Assassins by Jim Garrison and Crossfire: The Plot That Killed Kennedy by Jim Marrs); ph, Robert Richardson; ed, Joe Hutshing, Pietro Scalia; m, John Williams; prod d, Victor Kempster; art d, Derek R. Hill, Alan R. Tomkins; cos, Marlene Stewart

AAN Best Picture; AAN Best Supporting Actor: Tommy Lee Jones; AAN Best Director: Oliver Stone; AAN Best Adapted Screenplay: Oliver Stone, Zachary Sklar; AA Best Cinematography: Robert Richardson; AA Best Editing: Joe Hutshing, Pietro Scalia; AAN Best Score: John Williams; AAN Best Sound: Michael Minkler, Gregg Landaker, Tod A. Maitland

Director and co-screenwriter Oliver Stone pulls off an amazing filmmaking feat with JFK, transforming the dry minutiae of every John F. Kennedy assassination conspiracy theory of the past three decades into riveting screen material.

Stone's story revolves around New Orleans District Attorney Jim Garrison's (Kevin Costner) unsuccessful 1967 prosecution of local businessman Clay Shaw (Tommy Lee Jones) for complicity in Kennedy's murder. Shaw's exact connection, even in the film, is hazy at best. But Garrison uses Shaw's trial mostly as a pretext to advance his own theory that Lee Harvey Oswald (Gary Oldman) was only one of several gunmen involved in the assassination and that he probably, as he claimed at the time of his arrest, never fired a single shot.

It's a measure of Stone's forcefulness as a filmmaker that he struck raw nerves across the political spectrum with a film that, in substance, did little more than dust off an accretion of well-worn conspiracy theories, most of which have been in circulation since the days following the assassination itself. Partly as a result of the film's impact, legislation was introduced into Congress in March of 1992 in an attempt to secure the release of FBI, CIA, and government files relating to the assassination which had previously been ordered sealed until 2029. That, however, is far from the most extraordinary thing about JFK.

Imagine a three-hour-plus epic that jettisons any recognizable dramatic structure, as JFK does, in favor of almost non-stop dialogue exposition and ends, not with a bang, but with an extended courtroom monologue and the hero's inglorious defeat, and you would normally have a surefire formula for failure. But JFK succeeds, partly thanks to a taut and intelligent script, and partly because the central investigation is spiced up by a series of key witnesses, each of whom injects the film with color and life; Pesci, Jones, and Kevin Bacon give particularly good performances. Stone's rapid-fire recreations and dramatizations of possible events also help keep things moving. But it is the director's evident passion to expose the deepest, darkest elements at work in society that really makes JFK come alive.

JIM THORPE—ALL AMERICAN
1951   107m   bw   Biography/Sports   ★★★
Warner Bros.   (U.S.)

Burt Lancaster *(Jim Thorpe)*, Charles Bickford *(Glenn S. "Pop" Warner)*, Steve Cochran *(Peter Allendine)*, Phyllis Thaxter *(Margaret Miller)*, Dick Wesson *(Ed Guyac)*, Jack Big Head *(Little Boy)*, Suni Warcloud *(Wally Denny)*, Al Mejia *(Louis Tewanema)*, Hubie Kerns *(Tom Ashenbrunner)*, Nestor Paiva *(Hiram Thorpe)*

p, Everett Freeman; d, Michael Curtiz; w, Douglas Morrow, Frank Davis, Everett Freeman (based on the story "Bright Path" by Morrow and Vincent X. Flaherty, from the biography by Russell Birdwell and James Thorpe); ph, Ernest Haller; ed, Folmar Blangsted; m, Max Steiner; art d, Edward Carrere; cos, Milo Anderson

Sports and big teeth. Burt Lancaster sets his jaw and plays one of America's greatest athletes, the wondrous Jim Thorpe, a Native American who captured gold medals in the pentathlon and decathlon at the 1912 Stockholm Olympics, only to be stripped of them because he had played semiprofessional baseball, violating his amateur status.

This biopic begins with Billy Gray portraying Thorpe as a youth on an Oklahoma reservation. Lancaster takes over as Thorpe matriculates to the all-Indian college at Carlisle, Pennsylvania, where he begins playing football to impress Margaret Miller (Phyllis Thaxter), his college sweetheart and future wife. Coached by the legendary Glenn "Pop" Warner (Charles Bickford), he captures All-American honors, then goes on to glory and disappointment in Stockholm, followed by an illustrious career in professional baseball and football. When his young son dies, Thorpe's spirit is broken, and he turns to the bottle, losing Margaret.

Thorpe was actually enshrined in the Pro Football Hall of Fame and his Olympic medals have been posthumously restored. As usual, Lancaster did most of his own athletic feats. Unfortunately some of his performances tend to confuse bravura with thoughtful interpretation. Curtiz tries hard to infuse the predictability with life, but the formula is the real champ here. Adequate.

JOE HILL
1971   114m   c   Biography   ★★½
Sagittarius (U.S./Sweden)   GP/AA

Thommy Berggren *(Joe Hill)*, Anja Schmidt *(Lucia)*, Kelvin Malave *(Fox)*, Evert Anderson *(Blackie)*, Cathy Smith *(Cathy)*, Hasse Persson *(Paul)*, David Moritz *(David)*, Wendy Geier *(Elizabeth)*, Franco Molinari *(Tenor)*, Richard Weber *(Richard)*

p, Bo Widerberg; d, Bo Widerberg; w, Bo Widerberg, Richard Weber, Steve Hopkins; ph, Petter Davidsson, Jorgen Persson; ed, Bo Widerberg; m, Stefan Grossman; art d, Ulf Axen

Somewhat fictionalized biography of the famed labor leader, served up with striking imagery. After immigrating to America from Sweden, Hill (Thommy Berggren) tramps around the U.S. until getting involved with the Industrial Workers of the World (the famed Wobblies). He quickly learns his way around the union and, with his ever-present banjo, begins writing labor songs. After achieving some success and power within the Wobblies he goes to Utah where, to protect a girl he loves, he takes the rap for a murder and gets executed.

Politically simplistic and sentimental, JOE HILL never succeeds in evoking the tone of moral outrage that the film would have needed to really succeed. The Wobblies are presented as two-dimensional symbols rather than fully rounded characters.

JOHN CARPENTER'S ESCAPE FROM L.A.
1996   102m   c   Action/Science Fiction   ★★½
Debra Hill Productions/Rysher Entertainment/Paramount   (U.S.)R/15

Kurt Russell *(Snake Plissken)*, A.J. Langer *(Utopia)*, Steve Buscemi *(Map to the Stars Eddie)*, George Corraface *(Cuervo Jones)*, Stacy Keach *(Malloy)*, Michelle Forbes *(Brazen)*, Pam Grier *(Hershe)*, Jeff Imada *(Saigon Shadow)*, Cliff Robertson *(President)*, Valeria Golino *(Taslima)*

p, Debra Hill, Kurt Russell; d, John Carpenter; w, John Carpenter, Debra Hill, Kurt Russell (based on characters created by John Carpenter and Nick Castle); ph, Gary B. Kibbe; ed, Edward A.

Warschilka; m, Shirley Walker, John Carpenter; prod d, Lawrence G. Paull; art d, Bruce Crone; fx, Kimberly K. Nelson, Marty Bresin, Dale Ettema, Michael Lessa, Juliette Yager, Buena Vista Visual Effects; cos, Robin Michel Bush

It's meant to be a sequel, but in reality JOHN CARPENTER'S ESCAPE FROM L.A. is a big-budget remake of Carpenter's 1981 cult hit ESCAPE FROM NEW YORK (1981), with Kurt Russell reprising his role of S.D. "Snake" Plissken.

The year is 2013, and United States is a fundamentalist, theocratic police state where all "moral aberrants" are deported to the prison island of Los Angeles, separated from the mainland by an earthquake. War-hero-turned-outlaw Snake Plissken, who 16 years ago rescued a president from the Manhattan Island Penitentiary, gets an offer he can't refuse: LA's rebel chieftain Cuervo Jones (George Corraface) has the controls to the US's Satellite Defense System, and Snake's been given just eight hours to retrieve them. His life and the future of the world depend on his success.

ESCAPE FROM L.A. isn't just a remake with a change of locale; it's a complete refit and upgrade, with a hard-driving rock soundtrack and pointlessy huge explosions. The problem is that, having seen their "ESCAPE FROM. . ." formula reworked over and over in films from DIE HARD to THE ROCK, the trio who wrote the screenplay (Carpenter, Russell, and producer Debra Hill) can't resist placing their tongues squarely in their cheeks. While this may be the only viable option left for this kind of film, by the end it's all gone so far over the top that one can't take the stakes involved very seriously. Some of what ESCAPE FROM L.A. aims for was achieved with greater success in DEMOLITION MAN, where the humor meshes with a sunnier vision of LA's future. Here, the right black-comic tone is never struck to balance the lighthearted air with the bleakness of the film's atmosphere.

JOHNNY BELINDA
1948   102m   bw   Drama   ★★★★½
Warner Bros.   (U.S.)   /A

Jane Wyman *(Belinda McDonald)*, Lew Ayres *(Dr. Robert Richardson)*, Charles Bickford *(Black McDonald)*, Agnes Moorehead *(Aggie McDonald)*, Stephen McNally *(Locky McCormick)*, Jan Sterling *(Stella McGuire)*, Rosalind Ivan *(Mrs. Peggety)*, Dan Seymour *(Pacquet)*, Mabel Paige *(Mrs. Lutz)*, Ida Moore *(Mrs. McKee)*

p, Jerry Wald; d, Jean Negulesco; w, Irmgard Von Cube, Allen Vincent (based on the play by Elmer Harris); ph, Ted McCord; ed, David Weisbart; m, Max Steiner; art d, Robert Haas; fx, William McGann, Edwin DuPar; cos, Milo Anderson

AAN Best Picture; AAN Best Actor: Lew Ayres; *AA Best Actress:* Jane Wyman; *AAN Best Supporting Actor:* Charles Bickford; *AAN Best Supporting Actress:* Agnes Moorehead; *AAN Best Director:* Jean Negulesco; *AAN Best Screenplay:* Irmgard Von Cube, Allen Vincent; *AAN Best Cinematography:* Ted McCord; *AAN Best Editing:* David Weisbart; *AAN Best Score:* Max Stiner; *AAN Best Art Direction:* Robert Haas, William Wallace; *AAN Best Sound:* Warner Bros Sound Department

After 15 years of hoofing her way through Warner Bros. films as a chorus girl and the second-fiddle friend of female leads, Jane Wyman finally got her dream part as the sensitive deaf-mute in this screen adaptation of the play by Elmer Harris. Thanks to Jean Negulesco's careful crafting, the result is admirably restrained, a triumph of atmosphere over potential tearjerking.

As the forlorn Belinda, Wyman is the unwanted daughter of Bickford, a stoic, iron-willed New England farmer who has blames the girl for her mother's having died while giving her birth. Ayres, a kindly doctor practicing in the nearby town, befriends Wyman and teaches her sign language, chastising all in the community who cruelly refer to her as "The Dummy." Slowly, Wyman's sweet and loving nature emerges and attracts the attention of brutish McNally, the local bully. Drunk one night, he attacks and rapes Wyman. She delivers a child which everyone believes has been fathered by Ayres, a situation which later forces him to leave the community in disgrace.

Wyman's performance is a marvel of beauty and innocence. Preparing for the most important role of her career thus far, Wyman studied the behavior of the hearing impaired and labored for weeks to capture an "anticipation light," as she called the look of eager curiosity of deaf people who want to learn and understand. Still Wyman felt an element was absent in her performance, that she was not accurately portraying the world of the deaf. She huddled with director Negulesco, who suggested she stuff her ears with wax. She did so, sealing off all sounds except loud percussions. This induced deafness made it difficult for her to pick up cue lines from other actors, but the very faltering and groping appearance Wyman projected made her all the more convincing.

Since the story was originally set on the dank and forbidding New England coast, Negulesco, along with the cast and crew, traveled to the rough, jagged coastal area near Mendocino, about 200 miles north of San Francisco. Here cinematographer McCord beautifully captured the deep fog, heavy rain, and driving winds, all of which further dramatized an already dynamic story. None of the special handling of this film impressed Jack Warner, head of the studio, who objected vociferously to the bills for location shooting, expressing disbelief that anyone would want to see a picture "where the leading lady doesn't say a word." But the world did want to see this film and Wyman in it; audiences marveled at a performance that thoroughly merited the Oscar it received. Wyman had been strong in THE LOST WEEKEND, but in JOHNNY BELINDA she was exceptional, joining the ranks of Hollywood's leading actresses.

JOHNNY EAGER
1942 107m bw Crime   ★★★★
MGM (U.S.)   /A

Robert Taylor *(Johnny Eager)*, Lana Turner *(Lisbeth Bard)*, Edward Arnold *(John Benson Farrell)*, Van Heflin *(Jeff Hartnett)*, Robert Sterling *(Jimmy Lanthrop)*, Patricia Dane *(Garnet)*, Glenda Farrell *(Mae Blythe)*, Barry Nelson *(Lew Rankin)*, Henry O'Neill *(A.J. Verne)*, Charles Dingle *(A. Frazier Marco)*

p, John W. Considine Jr.; d, Mervyn LeRoy; w, John Lee Mahin, James Edward Grant (based on a story by James Edward Grant); ph, Harold Rosson; ed, Albert Akst; m, Bronislau Kaper; art d, Cedric Gibbons, Stan Rogers; cos, Robert Kalloch

AA Best Supporting Actor: Van Heflin

Here's a glossy world of crime wrapped in white fox and expensive leather where one sinks into deep armchairs and drinks imported Scotch. This is the crooked cafe society world of callow, sexy Taylor who abuses callow, sexy Turner. They're made for each other, see? Each acts in a highly stylized mode of tragic glamour that is most evident in the swooning vortex of their love scenes. Casting them together was inspired—they give each other extra resonance and depth.

Taylor is the rottenly handsome title character, hiding the tenderness of his pretty face behind a gigolo's pencil mustache. At the opening, he misleads viewers. He wears a cab driver's hat and reports to his fatherly parole officer, O'Neil, explaining how diligently he drives his hack, and stays on the straight and narrow. O'Neil introduces the slick Taylor to two earnest, pretty sociology students, Turner and Diana Lewis. Turner thinks he's anything but what he pretends to be. Her instincts are right, even though her heart takes her in another direction. Taylor dutifully gets into his cab after meeting with O'Neil and charming Lewis and Turner. Then he drives to an unopened dog track, reports to the front desk, goes into the inner offices without seeking approval, then into even posher living quarters where he discards his cab driver's outfit and dons expensive tie and suitcoat. As he begins barking orders to his minions, it becomes apparent that Taylor is not only back in the rackets but that he's running them.

Later that night, Taylor exposes his real nature and status when he confronts Nelson in his nightclub, making threats about what will happen to the club owner if he fails to do as he is told. This is witnessed by Turner whom he escorts home to father Arnold, the same prosecuting attorney who sent him to prison. Arnold explodes when he sees Taylor with Turner, threatening to return him to prison if he ever sees them together again. Taylor backs off but hatches a plan to take revenge on Arnold, seduce Turner, and guarantee the opening of his dog track without interference from the authorities. He inveigles Turner to his lavish apartment where he stages an attack by a vicious hoodlum, Stewart. Stewart is about to kill Taylor, or so it seems to Turner, and she grabs a convenient gun and ostensibly kills Stewart.

JOHNNY EAGER is an lavish candy box film in which Taylor wholly abandons his male ingenue image and becomes a believable bad guy whose sliver of human compassion causes his undoing; its one of his best early roles. Although there's a synthetic element to JOHNNY EAGER, the crime melodrama aspect is so well handled by LeRoy and the chemistry between Taylor and the luscious 21-year-old Turner so strong that it's wholly satisfying. Taylor and Turner made only this film together and more's the pity. Their penthouse balcony scene is definitive Hollywood passion, all glossy open lips, eye lash shadows and whispered urgency—the latter a Turner specialty.

Throughout, Heflin is the presence that gives depth to the film as the drunken conscience of cold-hearted Taylor. The homoerotic content of the film is unusual for staid MGM. Heflin acts like Taylor's domesticated, kept house pet and he won an Oscar for Best Supporting Actor for his effort.

JOHNNY GUITAR
1954 110m c Western   ★★★★
Republic (U.S.)   /PG

Joan Crawford *(Vienna)*, Sterling Hayden *(Johnny "Guitar" Logan)*, Mercedes McCambridge *(Emma Small)*, Scott Brady *(Dancin' Kid)*, Ward Bond *(John McIvers)*, Ben Cooper *(Turkey Ralston)*, Ernest Borgnine *(Bart Lonergan)*, John Carradine *(Old Tom)*, Royal Dano *(Corey)*, Frank Ferguson *(Marshal Williams)*

p, Herbert J. Yates; d, Nicholas Ray; w, Philip Yordan (based on the novel by Roy Chanslor); ph, Harry Stradling; ed, Richard L. Van Enger; m, Victor Young; art d, James Sullivan; fx, Howard Lydecker, Theodore Lydecker; cos, Sheila O'Brien

JOHNNY GUITAR has been called everything from a feminist statement to a gay camp-classic to an anti-McCarthyism allegory. While it certainly is all of these—and more—it's about time it was acclaimed for it what it really is: a genuine western film classic.

Johnny Guitar (Sterling Hayden) travels to a saloon owned by his former lover, Vienna (Joan Crawford). Emma Small (Mercedes McCambridge), a vindictive woman who has designs on Vienna's land, joins with a posse, headed by John McIvers (Ward Bond), to accuse Vienna of being in on a stagecoach job with a gang led by the Dancin' Kid. Both Vienna and the Dancin' Kid (Scott Brady) deny they had anything to do with the robbery, but Emma urges the Marshal to arrest them anyway. McIvers gives Vienna and the gang 24 hours to get out of town. The Dancin' Kid and his gang decide to head out, but Vienna tells Johnny she's staying. The next morning, Vienna goes to the bank to close her account, and finds herself in the middle of a heist engineered by the Kid and his gang. Emma insists that Vienna was behind the job. After one of the Kid's gang members is coerced into testifying that Vienna did participate, she is set to hang for a crime she did not commit.

When it was first released in 1954, most critics dismissed JOHNNY GUITAR as being nothing more than a ridiculous Republic potboiler, which isn't surprising given that it was probably the first western to be set in the land of the imagination. It took critics such as Jean-Luc Godard and Francois Truffaut (who called the film "beautiful and profound") to recognize that Nicholas Ray's film was a dreamlike and deliriously stylized piece masquerading as a typical shoot-em-up. Ray called the novel by Roy Chanslor (who later wrote *Cat Ballou*) "completely valueless," and he and writer Philip Yordan used the plot's bare bones to create a baroque, operatic and symbolic tale of *l'amour fou* and Freudian psychology.

The much maligned Crawford actually acquits herself quite well—all bulging black eyes, thick red lips and steel jaw. As her nemesis, McCambridge is brilliant, portraying Emma as a sexually frustrated butch lesbian who trembles with orgasmic glee watching Vienna's place burn down. And as the laconic Johnny, Hayden is magnificent, playing the role with tongue in check but never condescendingly so. With its twisted sexual dynamics, surreal color photography, expressionistic Frank Lloyd Wright-like sets, and haunting score by Victor Young, JOHNNY GUITAR is a one-of-a-kind experience.

JOLSON STORY, THE

1946 128m c Musical/Biography ★★★★
Columbia (U.S.) /U

Larry Parks *(Al Jolson)*, Evelyn Keyes *(Julie Benson)*, William Demarest *(Steve Martin)*, Bill Goodwin *(Tom Baron)*, Ludwig Donath *(Cantor Yoelson)*, Tamara Shayne *(Mrs. Yoelson)*, John Alexander *(Lew Dockstader)*, Jo-Carroll Dennison *(Ann Murray)*, Ernest Cossart *(Father McGee)*, Scotty Beckett *(Jolson as a Boy)*

p, Sidney Skolsky; d, Alfred E. Green; w, Stephen Longstreet, Harry Chandlee, Andrew Solt; ph, Joseph Walker; ed, William Lyon; art d, Stephen Goosson, Walter Holscher; chor, Jack Cole, Joseph H. Lewis; cos, Jean Louis

AAN Best Actor: Larry Parks; *AAN Best Supporting Actor:* William Demarest; *AAN Best Cinematography:* Joseph Walker; *AAN Best Editing:* William Lyon; *AA Best Score:* Morris Stoloff; *AA Best Sound:* John Livadary

A standout of the musical film-bio genre, THE JOLSON STORY was a box office smash, despite the fact that it contained just about every show business cliche imaginable. It's a highly idealized portrait of Jolson, remembered by everyone who knew him to have been as personally difficult as he was professionally talented. Jolson was Larry Park's first big role after five years of strictly small-time work, and he took full advantage of the opportunity, delivering a top-caliber performance.

Jolson's real story—a mixture of joy, anger, bitterness, and super-stardom—is mixed with JAZZ SINGER-inspired fictionalization, charting his youth in vaudeville, his parents's desire that he follow another career, and his eventual rise to the top. Coached by Jolson himself (who dubs Parks' singing voice), Parks perfectly captures the entertainer's famous mannerisms, including his whistling and deliberate interruptions in the middle of a show to stop and banter with the audience. Ruby Keeler, Jolson's third wife (of four), refused to allow her name to be used in the film (her character here is renamed Julie Benson). The musical numbers were pleasingly staged by Joseph H. Lewis.

JONAH WHO WILL BE 25 IN THE YEAR 2000
(JONAS—QUI AURA 25 ANS EN L'AN 2000)

1976 116m c Comedy ★★★½
Action/Citel/Societe Francaise/SSR Swiss TV (Switzerland) /X

Jean-Luc Bideau *(Max Stigny)*, Myriam Boyer *(Mathilde Vernier)*, Myriam Mziere *(Madeleine)*, Jacques Denis *(Marco Perly)*, Roger Jendly *(Marcel Certoux)*, Dominique Labourier *(Marguerite)*, Miou-Miou *(Marie)*, Raymond Bussieres *(Old Charles)*, Rufus *(Mathieu Vernier)*, Jonas *(Himself)*

p, Yves Gasser, Yves Peyrot; d, Alain Tanner; w, John Berger, Alain Tanner; ph, Renato Berta; ed, Brigitte Sousselier, Marc Blavet; m, Jean-Marie Senia

Unlike most films that seem to dwell on the lost ideals of the children of the 1960s, JONAH is an exhilarating film with characters that are filled with life and who refuse to become trapped in endless dreams that can never come true. Although each of these people stops short of achieving some desire, the failure doesn't result in a personal deterioration or self-pity. Perhaps this is a function of the beliefs fought for in the 1960s: goals that were never quite reached but offered the consolation of an effort well made. Whatever the case, all of these characters are extremely likable, uplifting the film with energy that is easily transmitted to the viewer. Prime among them are Miou-Miou, a grocery clerk who steals food for a retired engineer (Bussieres), and Denis, a teacher who can't keep a steady job. It would be a miscarriage of justice to limit the credit to just these two, however; every one of the characters is a joy. Tanner subtly interweaves the roles and knows when to turn off their exhilaration to allow his own themes to take over.

JOUR DE FETE

1949 90m bw Comedy ★★★★
Francinex/Cady (France) /U

Jacques Tati *(Francois)*, Guy Decombie *(Roger)*, Paul Frankeur *(Marcel)*, Santa Relli *(Roger's Wife)*, Maine Vallee *(Jeanette)*, Roger Rafal *(Barber)*, Beauvais *(Cafe Proprietor)*, Delcassan *(Cinema Operator)*

p, Fred Orain; d, Jacques Tati; w, Jacques Tati, Rene Wheeler, Henri Marquet; ph, Jacques Mercanton; ed, Marcel Morreau; m, Jean Yatove; art d, Rene Moullaert

Quite clever. The first feature film by Jacques Tati was actually a lengthened version of his short L'ECOLE DES FACTEURS, and helped gain Tati an international reputation as one of the best film comics to come out of France. Also starring in JOUR DE FETE, Tati plays the postman of a small sleepy village who becomes obsessed with applying the methods of the American postal system, as seen in a short educational film, to his job. This simple premise provides an abundance of opportunities for Tati to engage in some spectacular jokes. The emphasis of Tati's style was always aimed at the visual, music and dialog being used only to enhance what was being seen. The results were quite successful in producing laughter from cinema patrons in almost every country, and had a large impact upon the editing techniques later to be used by Jean-Luc Godard and Francois Truffaut.

JOURNEY INTO FEAR

1942 71m bw Spy ★★★★
Mercury (U.S.) /A

Joseph Cotten *(Graham)*, Dolores Del Rio *(Josette)*, Ruth Warrick *(Stephanie)*, Agnes Moorehead *(Mme. Mathews)*, Jack Durant *(Gogo)*, Everett Sloane *(Kopeikin)*, Eustace Wyatt *(Haller)*, Frank Readick *(Mathews)*, Edgar Barrier *(Kuvetli)*, Jack Moss *(Banat)*

p, Orson Welles; d, Norman Foster; w, Orson Welles, Joseph Cotten (based on a novel by Eric Ambler); ph, Karl Struss; ed, Mark Robson; m, Roy Webb; art d, Albert S. D'Agostino, Mark-Lee Kirk; fx, Vernon L. Walker; cos, Edward Stevenson

Sure it says "directed by Norman Foster," but don't let that fool you, this is an Orson Welles film all the way. Welles is listed as producer, his Mercury Players fill the cast, his then-companion Del Rio is in the lead, and he cowrote the screenplay with Joseph Cotten. The result is a strange, obsessive and often brilliant film, much of which takes place aboard a dilapidated freighter.

Howard Graham (Cotten) is a US Navy engineer who is to return to the US with his beautiful wife Stephanie (Warrick) after a business conference in Istanbul. Graham soon realizes that someone is trying to kill him and is taken by Turkish agent Kopeikin (Sloane) to secret police headquarters where intelligence chief Haki (Welles) explains that Nazi agents are after him.

JOURNEY INTO FEAR is a wonderfully murky study of espionage, realistically portrayed in all its mayhem and confusion, one spy not really knowing what the other spy is up to, but operating on instinct to get results. Cotten's quiet, unassuming part is so well played that the viewer gets frustrated at his inability to either act or even think clearly. A visually arresting film with a nod to the quirky that just can't be beat in terms of the bizarre.

JOURNEY TO THE CENTER OF THE EARTH

1959 132m c Science Fiction ★★★½
Fox (U.S.) G/U

Pat Boone *(Alec McEwen)*, James Mason *(Prof. Oliver Lindenbrook)*, Arlene Dahl *(Carla)*, Diane Baker *(Jenny)*, Thayer David *(Count Saknussemm)*, Peter Ronson *(Hans)*, Robert Adler *(Groom)*, Alan Napier *(Dean)*, Alex Finlayson *(Prof. Bayle)*, Ben Wright *(Paisley)*

p, Charles Brackett; d, Henry Levin; w, Charles Brackett, Walter Reisch (based on the novel *Journey to the Center of the Earth* by Jules Verne); ph, Leo Tover; ed, Stuart Gilmore, Jack W. Holmes; m, Bernard Herrmann; art d, Lyle Wheeler, Franz Bachelin, Herman A. Blumenthal; fx, L.B. Abbott, James B. Gordon, Emil Kosa Jr.; cos, David Ffolkes

AAN Best Art Direction: Lyle R Wheeler (Art Direction), Franz Bachelin (Art Direction), Herman A Blumenthal (Art Direction), Walter M Scott (Set Decoration), Joseph Kish (Set Decoration); *AAN Best Sound:* Carl Faulkner (20th Century-Fox Studio Sound Department); *AAN Best Visual Effects:* L B Abbott (Special Effects-Visual), James B Gordon (Special Effects-Visual), Carl Faulkner (Special Effects-Audible)

An excellent combination of witty scripting and fine acting resulting in grand adventure.

James Mason plays Oliver Lindenbrook, an Edinburgh geologist who travels with student Alec McEwen (Pat Boone) to Iceland as part of a planned descent to the center of the earth via volcano. There, they meet Carla (Arlene Dahl), whose husband has been killed in a similar attempt. She joins the expedition, along with a young Icelander (Peter Ronson) and his pet duck. They begin the descent, imperiled by prehistoric beasts, rock slides, and the evil Count Saknussemm (Thayer David), who murdered Carla's husband and is determined to be the first to reach the earth's core.

A well-photographed film, with location footage shot in Carlsbad Caverns, featuring great special effects and a Bernard Herrmann score that heightens the excitement. Mason is charming, caustic and debonair, and the whole affair is captivating, silly fun. Watch for some sly sexual lampooning.

JOY LUCK CLUB, THE

1993 135m c Drama   ★★★
Hollywood Pictures/Joy Luck Company/Ixtlan (U.S.)   R/15

Kieu Chinh *(Suyuan)*, Tsai Chin *(Lindo)*, France Nuyen *(Ying Ying)*, Lisa Lu *(An Mei)*, Ming-Na Wen *(June)*, Tamlyn Tomita *(Waverly)*, Lauren Tom *(Lena)*, Rosalind Chao *(Rose)*, Chao-Li Chi *(June's Father)*, Melanie Chang *(June—Age 9)*

p, Wayne Wang, Amy Tan, Ronald Bass, Patrick Markey; d, Wayne Wang; w, Amy Tan, Ronald Bass (from the book by Amy Tan); ph, Amir Mokri; ed, Maysie Hoy; m, Rachel Portman; prod d, Donald Graham Burt; art d, Diana Kunce, Kwan Kit 'Eddy' Kwok, Jian Jun Li; fx, Frank W. Tarantino; chor, Michael Smuin; cos, Lydia Tanji, Shu Lan Ding

As irresistibly sentimental as TERMS OF ENDEARMENT and nearly as complex as JFK, THE JOY LUCK CLUB unravels the web of relationships linking four Chinese-born mothers to their American daughters. Wayne Wang's sleek, intelligent adaptation of Amy Tan's celebrated novel is too long and, ultimately, too soapy, but he and his screenwriters (Tan herself, together with RAIN MAN writer Ronald Bass) have injected just enough irony into the proceedings to save the day.

Wang's biggest achievement is navigating the narrative maze of the novel in such a way that the audience doesn't get hopelessly lost. Most of the drama happens in flashback, with several actresses stepping in to play each character during different stages of her life. The segments set in China, dealing with the early lives of the mothers, are the most eventful, encompassing generous doses of lust, betrayal, suicide, murder, and more. It's pure melodrama, but stylishly done, with finely tuned performances played out against meticulously realized settings. The American episodes, dealing with the more mundane domestic dramas of the daughters, are equally well acted, but overconcerned with spelling out the glib moral ("never let your spirit die") that links all the segments.

Thankfully, some of the elder women have been blessed with acidly witty tongues; as well as making us laugh, they insure brief, tear-free episodes during which audience members can load up on fresh Kleenex.

JU DOU

1989 95m c Drama/Romance/Historical   ★★★★
Tokuma Shoten Publishing Company/Tokuma   PG-13/15
Communications Company/China Film Coproduction
Corporation/China Film Export & Import Corporation
/Xi-an Film Studio (Japan/China)

Gong Li *(Ju Dou)*, Li Bao-tian *(Yang Tian-qing)*, Li Wei *(Yang Jin-shan)*, Zhang Yi *(Yang Tian-bai—as a Child)*, Zheng Ji-an *(Yang Tian-bai—as a Youth)*

p, Zhang Wenze, Hu Jian, Yasuyoshi Yokuma; d, Zhang Yimou; w, Lui Heng; ph, Gu Changwei, Yang Lun; ed, Du Yuan; m, Xia Ru-jin; art d, Fei Jiupeng, Xia Ru-jin; cos, Zhi-an Zhang

AAN Best Foreign Language Film

Acclaimed "Fifth Generation" filmmaker Zhang Yimou, of RED SORGHUM fame, delves once more into the past for JU DOU, his second feature, a haunting story of illicit love set in 1920s China.

Ju Dou (Gong Li), a virginal beauty, is purchased by old and rich Yang Jin-shan (Li Wei) to be his bride. When, due to his impotence, she fails to bear him the son he craves, Jin-shan vents his rage against his wife, bringing her to the brink of suicide.

Yang Tian-qing (Li Bao-tian) is the solitary worker in the textile dyeing factory that Jin-shan owns. He is a distant relative of his employer but treated like a slave nonetheless. Tian-qing, aware of the beatings and abuse that Ju Dou suffers at the hands of her husband, reaches out to console her and quickly becomes her only solace. They meet clandestinely whenever they can and one fateful night, when Jin-shan is away, they become lovers. When Ju Dou becomes pregnant, the son that Jin-shan desires is finally on its way, but he's clearly not the father. Then, in a strange twist of fate, the old man is paralyzed in an accident and left unable to walk. When the townspeople congratulate him on his newborn son, Jin-shan must accept or lose face. He is left at the mercy of Ju Dou and her lover, who pursue their illicit relationship to a tragic conclusion.

The "Fifth Generation" filmmakers began a new wave in Chinese cinema by emphasizing the visual and aural qualities of film rather than traditional dramatic and literary elements. JU DOU is no exception to this trend. The cinematography by Gu Changwei and Yang Lun highlights and accentuates the unfolding drama; a painter's palette of color emerges in images that act as counterpoints to the story. By displaying the ancient processes still in use for dyeing cloth, Yimou makes full use of his early background in a textile factory; the splashes of colored fabric and the dyeing process itself are an integral part of the film's beauty. The screenplay, written by Lui Heng, is spare and constant. JU DOU tantalizes all the senses as the story of the ill-fated lovers unfolds with hypnotic logic.

JUAREZ

1939 132m bw Biography   ★★★½
Warner Bros. (U.S.)   /U

Paul Muni *(Benito Pablo Juarez)*, Bette Davis *(Empress Carlotta von Habsburg)*, Brian Aherne *(Maximilian von Habsburg)*, Claude Rains *(Louis Napoleon)*, John Garfield *(Porfirio Diaz)*, Donald Crisp *(Marechal Bazaine)*, Gale Sondergaard *(Empress Eugenie)*, Joseph Calleia *(Alejandro Uradi)*, Gilbert Roland *(Col. Miguel Lopez)*, Henry O'Neill *(Miguel Miramon)*

p, Henry Blanke; d, William Dieterle; w, John Huston, Wolfgang Reinhardt, Aeneas MacKenzie (based on the novel *The Phantom Crown* by Bertita Harding and the play *Juarez & Maximillian* by Franz Werfel); ph, Tony Gaudio; ed, Warren Low; m, Erich Wolfgang Korngold; art d, Anton F. Grot; cos, Orry-Kelly

AAN Best Supporting Actor: Brian Aherne

Weighs a ton, thanks to meddling Muni's obsessive hand in the screenplay. The effective casting lacks spark, save two firebrand ladies: Davis and Sondergaard, the latter stoking the cauldron and the former jumping in. Benito Pablo Juarez was to Mexico what Abraham Lincoln was to the United States. Both of them lived at the same time, and Juarez was profoundly influenced by the North American president. Like Lincoln, Juarez was physically homely, yet full of wisdom and spiritual clarity that was irresistible to his people.

The film opens with Rains, playing the evil Napoleon III, appointing Aherne (Archduke Maximilian von Habsburg of Austria) emperor of Mexico. Through his agents in Mexico, Rains has set up a fake election by which Aherne has been chosen the monarch of a people he has never seen. Aherne and wife Davis (Carlotta) journey to Mexico, escorted by an army commanded by Crisp. Meeting the royal couple are thousands of jubilant peasants in Mexico City, but the royal couple is again deceived by the insidious French, who have staged the reception.

The duly elected president of Mexico, Muni (Juarez), leads his people in revolt against the monarchs imposed upon Mexico by Rains. To mollify the people Aherne offers Muni the powerful position of Secretary of State, but he rejects it. Undaunted, Aherne believes that he can unite the Mexican people by adopting a native prince in an elaborate ceremony. Yet, when they take their new son to the balcony of their palace to show to their ostensibly adoring subjects, a tremendous explosion rocks the area. *Juaristas* have just blown up a huge ammunition dump of the French army. So enraged by this "slap" is Aherne that he signs the shoot-to-kill order for those found with weapons. Wholesale executions ensue, and soon even those who have paid homage to Aherne and Davis turn against the monarchy. A full-scale revolution breaks out, with the US ordering the French army to leave Mexico under the Monroe Doctrine.

JUAREZ was unique in that it was shot as two separate films—first the Aherne-Davis story, then the Muni portion; both stories were then edited together. Muni only meets Aherne when viewing his corpse, and even this scene is spliced together. Muni had the benefit of viewing the edited first portion of the film before going in front of the cameras to play Juarez and, to offset the Davis histrionics, he underplayed his role almost down to a whisper. Muni was afforded the privilege since he was then the most important actor on the Warner lot. But despite studying hundreds of books, documents and photographs of his subject, and spending six weeks visiting the areas where Juarez lived, worked and administered to his infant republic, the resulting portrayal proved unsuitable to a long epic film, slowing the ponderous drama to a crawl.

Davis has only a small role but one she coveted when the project was first begun in 1937. She knew she would have one fantastic scene where Carlotta goes mad after confronting the scheming Rains and she played it to the hilt; this sequence is a classic, and Davis's descent from the emperor is like watching a candle dim, flicker and go out. She is matched by Sondergaard's velvety villainy and this meeting portends their eventual collaboration on THE LETTER.

JUDE

1996 123m c Drama   ★★★
Revolution Films (U.K.)   R/15

Christopher Eccleston (*Jude Fawley*), Kate Winslet (*Sue Bridehead*), Liam Cunningham (*Richard Phillotson*), Rachel Griffiths (*Arabella*), June Whitfield (*Aunt Drusilla*), Ross Colvin Turnbull (*Little Jude*), James Daley (*Jude as a Boy*), Berwick Kaler (*Farmer Troutham*), Sean McKenzie (*1st Stonemason*), Richard Albrecht (*2nd Stonemason*)

p, Andrew Eaton; d, Michael Winterbottom; w, Hossein Amini (based on the novel *Jude the Obscure* by Thomas Hardy); ph, Eduardo Serra; ed, Trevor Waite; m, Adrian Johnston; prod d, Joseph Bennett; art d, Andrew Rothschild; fx, John Markwell; cos, Janty Yates

This faithful and engaging adaptation of Thomas Hardy's classic novel, *Jude the Obscure,* features powerful performances, a rich atmosphere, and good writing, making it well worth the often harrowing ordeal of watching love struggle helplessly against poverty and social injustice.

Jude Fawley (Christopher Eccleston) dreams of escaping his impoverished rural life through education. As a child, his teacher, Phillotson (Liam Cunningham), encourages him to pursue a university education in nearby Christminster. Arabella (Pamela Griffiths), the daughter of a local pig-farmer, seduces Jude, but runs away to Australia as soon as they are married. Moving to Christminster to continue his studies, Jude meets his beautiful and sophisticated cousin, Sue Bridehead (Kate Winslet), and falls in love with her. The couple endures a series of wrenching setbacks, tempered by brief moments of simple happiness, before the ultimate tragedy strikes.

The film's muted colors underscore Jude and Sue's ultimate inability to transcend the constraints that their society has placed upon them and their class. JUDE feels very contemporary, in part due to the language (though in fact much of Hardy's dialogue is preserved in the script), and to the style of the camerawork and editing, which is more athletic than one expects. But the credit goes mostly to Michael Winterbottom's direction and the performances from Eccleston, Winslet, Cunningham, and Griffiths, who convincingly own their characters. Any adaptation of such a beloved novel is likely to elicit accusations of infidelity, and

indeed JUDE falls short of Hardy's psychological complexity, but it ultimately adheres to the paramount virtues of the novel: its themes of injustice and the collision of hope with destiny and reality.

JUDGMENT AT NUREMBERG

1961 190m bw Historical/War   ★★★★
Roxlom (U.S.)   /PG

Spencer Tracy (*Judge Dan Haywood*), Burt Lancaster (*Ernst Janning*), Richard Widmark (*Col. Tad Lawson*), Marlene Dietrich (*Mme. Bertholt*), Maximilian Schell (*Hans Rolfe*), Judy Garland (*Irene Hoffman*), Montgomery Clift (*Rudolph Petersen*), William Shatner (*Capt. Harrison Byers*), Edward Binns (*Sen. Burkette*), Kenneth MacKenna (*Judge Kenneth Norris*)

p, Stanley Kramer; d, Stanley Kramer; w, Abby Mann; ph, Ernest Laszlo; ed, Frederic Knudtson; m, Ernest Gold; prod d, Rudolph Sternad; cos, Joe King

AAN Best Picture; *AA Best Actor:* Maximilian Schell; *AAN Best Actor:* Spencer Tracy; *AAN Best Supporting Actor:* Montgomery Clift; *AAN Best Supporting Actress:* Judy Garland; *AAN Best Director:* Stanley Kramer; *AA Best Adapted Screenplay:* Abby Mann; *AAN Best Cinematography:* Ernest Laszlo; *AAN Best Editing:* Frederic Knudtson; *AAN Best Art Direction:* Rudolph Sternad, George Milo; *AAN Best Costume Design:* Jean Louis

For the patient starwatcher, a revelation. In its day, JUDGMENT AT NUREMBERG was a sensation—the first film to deal seriously with the trials of Nazi war criminals. The chief Allied judge, Dan Haywood (Spencer Tracy), has been sent to Germany after failing to be reelected to the bench in New England, a political payoff that does not go unnoticed by his adversaries. Prosecuting attorney Tad Lawson (Richard Widmark), an Army colonel, indicts several Germans who have committed war crimes in enforcing Hitler's mad mandates. Defense attorney Hans Rolfe (Maximilian Schell) roars that his clients were merely upholding Hitler's laws, and that to place them on trial is to judge all of Germany. Meanwhile, Haywood, in his off hours, wanders the ancient city of Nuremberg trying to understand what went wrong with a whole people and a great culture.

The rest of the cast in this three-hour-plus picture is equally distinguished: Marlene Dietrich is the widow of a German general who was executed for ordering the slaughter of captured American soldiers at Malmedy; Burt Lancaster is an intellectual German judge who unwillingly aided the Nazis; Montgomery Clift is a dim-witted victim of sterilization who testifies for the prosecution; and Judy Garland is a woman who "polluted the Aryan race" by having sex with a Jew.

Though unrelentingly bleak, JUDGMENT AT NUREMBERG is absorbing from beginning to end. Dietrich and Tracy contribute polished, seemingly effortless work; at the other end of the thespian spectrum are Clift and Garland, who turn in harrowing, nakedly emotional perfomances. These are star turns, to be sure, but the Hollywood-style interplay between image, portrayal, and reality is fascinating to behold.

JUGGERNAUT

1974 109m c Thriller   ★★★½
UA (U.S.)   PG

Richard Harris (*Fallon*), Omar Sharif (*Capt. Brunel*), David Hemmings (*Charlie Braddock*), Anthony Hopkins (*Supt. John McCleod*), Shirley Knight (*Barbara Banister*), Ian Holm (*Nicholas Porter*), Clifton James (*Mr. Corrigan*), Roy Kinnear (*Social Director Curain*), Caroline Mortimer (*Susan McCleod*), Freddie Jones (*Mr. Buckland*)

p, Richard DeKoker; d, Richard Lester; w, Richard DeKoker, Alan Plater; ph, Gerry Fisher; ed, Anthony Gibbs; m, Ken Thorne; prod d, Terence Marsh; art d, Alan Tomkins; fx, John Richardson

Jolly well done. Sharif plays the captain of an ocean liner upon which several bombs have been planted by Jones, a demolitions expert who demands a ransom not to blow up the ship at sea. Back on shore, the superintendent in charge of the case (Hopkins) brings extra concern to his work on the crisis because his wife, Mortimer, is one of the hostages. A team of experts, including Harris and Hemmings, is dispatched to the ship by helicopter to defuse the bombs. The rest of the film is a tense battle between the bomb experts and Jones, who stays on the telephone to taunt the crisis-intervention team with details about his plot.

Lester, known mainly for his comedy work (A HARD DAY'S NIGHT), does a good job of keeping viewers on the edge of their seats. And JUGGERNAUT, far more than a disaster picture, is a telling statement about England's troubles, the country neatly symbolized by the liner itself. The film captures perfecly the atmosphere of an over-hyped "luxury" liner. Harris gives a terrific performance and this is the best work ever done by Sharif, thanks to apt casting as the slimy ship captain.

JUGGLER, THE

1953 84m bw Drama	★★★½
Columbia (U.S.)	/A

Kirk Douglas *(Hans Muller)*, Milly Vitale *(Ya'El)*, Paul Stewart *(Detective Karni)*, Joseph Walsh *(Yehoshua Bresler)*, Alf Kjellin *(Daniel)*, Beverly Washburn *(Susy)*, Charles Lane *(Rosenberg)*, John Banner *(Emile Halevy)*, Richard Benedict *(Kogan)*, Oscar Karlweis *(Willy Schmidt)*

p, Stanley Kramer; d, Edward Dmytryk; w, Michael Blankfort (based on the novel by Michael Blankfort); ph, J. Roy Hunt; ed, Aaron Stell; m, George Antheil; art d, Robert Peterson

A tight little sleeper. Douglas is a German Jew who survived the Nazi concentration camps but lost his wife and children. He was a famous juggler before the war and now finds himself with thousands of other displaced persons in Israel.

When he arrives in a temporary camp, his actions are odd enough to merit notice by the camp psychiatrist. He runs away on his first night and is followed by Benedict, an Israeli cop, who finally stops him and wants to see his papers. Douglas immediately flashes back to when a Nazi asked the same thing, and he knocks Benedict out, then flees. Douglas escapes Haifa and makes his way to Mount Carmel where he spends the night. In the morning Douglas, now pursued by detective Stewart, is discovered by several children whom he tells he is an American tourist. Walsh, one of the young boys, is traveling to a kibbutz near Syria and Douglas joins him. Douglas wants to get to Egypt where he has some friends who he feels will help him.

A terrific movie in many ways, THE JUGGLER is a small-scale, almost intimate film that quietly depicts the sadness of a man looking for a home and a purpose following the war. The main character is not a heroic figure, but a deeply troubled man trying to make some sense out of life. Douglas, in one of his most restrained performances, is quite good at conveying the man's torment and confusion. Paul Stewart, one of the original Mercury Players on radio who made his film debut in CITIZEN KANE, is also good as the compassionate detective who does his best to reassure Douglas. Young Walsh nicely complements Douglas and their scenes together are often touching without being overly sentimental. Walsh went on to become a writer, scripting such films as BON VOYAGE and CALIFORNIA SPLIT.

JULES AND JIM
(JULES ET JIM)

1962 110m bw Drama	★★★★★
Carosse (France)	/15

Jeanne Moreau *(Catherine)*, Oskar Werner *(Jules)*, Henri Serre *(Jim)*, Marie Dubois *(Therese)*, Vanna Urbino *(Gilberte)*, Sabine Haudepin *(Sabine)*, Boris Bassiak *(Albert)*, Kate Noelle *(Birgitta)*, Anny Nelsen *(Lucie)*, Christiane Wagner *(Helga)*

p, Marcel Berbert; d, Francois Truffaut; w, Francois Truffaut, Jean Gruault (based on the novel by Henri-Pierre Roche); ph, Raoul Coutard; ed, Claudine Bouche; m, Georges Delerue; cos, Fred Capel

Francois Truffaut's greatest achievement, JULES AND JIM is a shrine to lovers who have known obsession and been destroyed by it.

The film begins in Paris in 1912 when two writers—Jules (Oskar Werner), a shy German, and Jim (Henri Serre), a dark-haired Parisian—become obsessed with an ancient stone carving of a woman. Their life changes when they meet Catherine (Jeanne Moreau), the personification of the stone goddess, whose smile enchants both men. Jules begins to court her, but only with Jim's blessing.

The three become great friends, though Catherine's unpredictability flares whenever she feels she is being ignored. (At one point, she jumps into the Seine when Jules and Jim's heated discussion of a Strindberg play does not include her.) Although Catherine gives Jules a child, Sabine (the adorable, bespectacled Sabine Haudepin), her ever-changing moods are not those of a mother or a wife, and she begins an affair with Jim. Jules, however, refuses to leave her, or even to get angry—he only wants to be near her and his friend.

The film is a celebration both of love and cinema, as Truffaut directs with equal concern for his characters and for film technique—one never overshadowing the other. Scripted from Henri-Pierre Roche's novel, the screenplay has not a wasted word or gesture, with every element working together perfectly to create three unique and interdependent characters. As much in love with Catherine as Jules and Jim are, Truffaut photographs her with the greatest love and admiration. Just as Jules and Jim respond lovingly to Catherine's every move, and just as the camera swirls and dollies around the ancient stone carving in the film's early scenes, so too does Truffaut's filmmaking revolve around the great Moreau, who returns the compliment with one of the most memorable performances in screen history.

JULIA

1977 116m c Biography	★★★
Fox (U.S.)	PG/A

Jane Fonda *(Lillian Hellman)*, Vanessa Redgrave *(Julia)*, Jason Robards Jr. *(Dashiell Hammett)*, Maximilian Schell *(Johann)*, Hal Holbrook *(Alan Campbell)*, Rosemary Murphy *(Dorothy Parker)*, Meryl Streep *(Anne Marie)*, Dora Doll, Elisabeth Mortensen *(Train Passengers)*, John Glover *(Sammy)*

p, Richard Roth; d, Fred Zinnemann; w, Alvin Sargent (based on the story in the book *Pentimento* by Lillian Hellman); ph, Douglas Slocombe; ed, Walter Murch, Marcel Durham; m, Georges Delerue; prod d, Willy Holt, Gene Callahan, Carmen Dillon; cos, Anthea Sylbert, Joan Bridge, Annalisa Nasilli-Rocca, John Apperson, Colette Baudot

AAN Best Picture; AAN Best Actress: Jane Fonda; *AA Best Supporting Actor:* Jason Robards; *AAN Best Supporting Actor:* Maximilian Schell; *AA Best Supporting Actress:* Vanessa Redgrave; *AAN Best Director:* Fred Zinnemann; *AA Best Adapted Screenplay:* Alvin Sargent; *AAN Best Cinematography:* Douglas Slocombe; *AAN Best Editing:* Walter Murch; *AAN Best Score:* Georges Delerue; *AAN Best Costume Design:* Anthea Sylbert

Beautifully crafted, nominated for nine Academy Awards, a big hit at the box office—and a dramatic dud. Based on an episode from Lillian Hellman's bestselling memoirs, the film takes place in the 1930s as Fonda, playing the author, lives with Robards in a beach house. She's writing her first play and turns to famed writer Robards for his helpful (and sometimes cruel) criticism.

When it's done and produced successfully, Fonda decides to visit a childhood friend, Redgrave, with whom she shared some wonderful moments in their youth (shown in flashbacks with Pelikan and Jones as the girls). Redgrave moved to Austria to study medicine with Freud and became a crusader in social matters, joining the antifascists. She was injured in a battle with the Hitler Youth and is now in a hospital in Vienna. Fonda visits Redgrave as she is recovering. Later, on a trip to Moscow, Fonda is asked by Schell, a pal of Redgrave's, if she will smuggle a large sum of money from Russia to Germany where it will be used to aid the effort against the Nazis.

If you like red nail polish, faux-cynicism, painfully brave smiles and European train stations, JULIA may be your kind of cocktail. But Redgrave plays Julia as a noble martyr in sensible shoes, and Zinneman fails to communicate the sense of danger that her political commitment entailed. Fonda's Hellman is a prig with writer's block and low self-esteem. Her relationship with Hammett and Julia, too, looks like hero-worship. The script, the direction and finally, Fonda's acting choices capture nothing of what made Hellman a true piss-and-vinegar original.

JULIET OF THE SPIRITS
(GIULIETTA DEGLI SPIRITI)
1965   148m   c   Drama   ★★★½
Federiz/Francoriz/Rizzoli/Eichberg   (France/Italy/West Germany) /18

Giulietta Masina *(Juliet)*, Alba Cancellieri *(Juliet as a Child)*, Mario Pisu *(Giorgio)*, Caterina Boratto *(Juliet's Mother)*, Luisa Della Noce *(Adele)*, Sylva Koscina *(Sylva)*, Sabrina Gigli, Rosella di Sepio *(Granddaughters)*, Lou Gilbert *(Grandfather)*, Valentina Cortese *(Valentina)*

p, Angelo Rizzoli; d, Federico Fellini; w, Federico Fellini, Tullio Pinelli, Ennio Flaiano, Brunello Rondi (based on a story by Fellini, Pinelli); ph, Gianni De Venanzo; ed, Ruggero Mastroianni; m, Nino Rota; art d, Piero Gherardi; cos, Piero Gherardi

AAN Best Art Direction: Piero Gherardi (Art Direction); *AAN Best Costume Design:* Piero Gherardi

Gaudy, more integrated than later Fellini, but this take on feminine psyche lacks vision. Juliet's fantasies might have been culled from Hollywood back lots, suggesting women have colorful imaginations, but not much in the brain department.

Juliet (Giulietta Masina) is a married woman in her mid-30s, more or less resigned to a dull life with her dull husband, Giorgio (Mario Pisu), who pays her little attention. At first she thinks it's just the pressures of business that cause him to be so indifferent, but soon she begins to wonder if he may have someone else. One night, Giorgio and some friends hold a seance, and Juliet discovers that she can conjure up various spirits. These wraiths tell her that she deserves some enjoyment in life and should give herself a treat. To see if her suspicions about Giorgio are correct, Juliet hires a sleuth who corroborates her worst fears, causing her to change her lifestyle and move out from the shadow of her unloving husband.

A feminized version of 8 1/2—both Masina's and Pisu's characters drift in and out of fantasy in order to come to grips with reality—JULIET OF THE SPIRITS will likely appeal to fans of that previous Fellini picture. This was his first color feature, and the results are spectacular and festive.

JULIUS CAESAR
1953   120m   bw   Historical   ★★★★½
MGM   (U.S.)   /U

Marlon Brando *(Marc Antony)*, Louis Calhern *(Julius Caesar)*, John Gielgud *(Cassius)*, Edmond O'Brien *(Casca)*, Greer Garson *(Calpurnia)*, Deborah Kerr *(Portia)*, George Macready *(Marullus)*, Michael Pate *(Flavius)*, Richard Hale *(Sooothsayer)*, Alan Napier *(Cicero)*

p, John Houseman; d, Joseph L. Mankiewicz; w, Joseph L. Mankiewicz (based on the play by William Shakespeare); ph, Joseph Ruttenberg; ed, John Dunning; m, Miklos Rozsa; art d, Cedric Gibbons, Edward Carfagno; fx, Warren Newcombe; cos, Herschel McCoy

AAN Best Picture; AAN Best Actor: Marlon Brando; *AAN Best Cinematography:* Joseph Ruttenberg; *AAN Best Score:* Miklos Rozsa; *AA Best Art Direction:* Cedric Gibbons, Edward C. Carfagno, Edwin B. Willis, Hugh Hunt

Lavish, starstruck and for the most part, splendid. When John Houseman and Joseph Mankiewicz, brother of Herman, decided to film Shakespeare's *Julius Caesar*, they picked an elegant and distinguished cast—Mason, Gielgud, Calhern, O'Brien—but they also shocked the industry and not a few literary scholars by selecting Brando to play Marc Antony. He was then still known as "The Mumbler" and "The Slob," for his brutish performance as Stanley Kowalski in A STREETCAR NAMED DESIRE. But Brando turned that opinion about in a startling performance.

JULIUS CAESAR was the brainchild of Houseman and Mankiewicz, the producer having worked with Orson Welles and the Mercury Players on the 1937 version of *Caesar*. Houseman, who had been lobbying to make the film for years, heard that the property was seriously being considered and contacted studio boss Dore Schary, saying that if he were not named the director he would leave MGM. The studio reluctantly agreed, but did not expect much from this production. Films based on the works of the immortal Bard had been

box-office poison at best, especially ROMEO AND JULIET, produced by MGM in 1936, starring Leslie Howard and Norma Shearer, a pet project of then-production chief Irving Thalberg. But this film surprisingly turned in a considerable profit, much of which was due to the astounding performance of Brando as Marc Antony, a role first intended for Paul Scofield, and then for Leo Genn or Charlton Heston. Performances aside, this is clearly Mankiewicz's film, expertly crafted from every angle, with the mob and murder scenes adroitly staged.

JUMANJI
1995   100m   c   Children's/Fantasy/Adventure   ★★½
Interscope Communications/Teitler Films/TriStar   (U.S.)   PG

Robin Williams *(Alan Parrish)*, Jonathan Hyde *(Van Pelt/Sam Parrish)*, Kirsten Dunst *(Judy)*, Bradley Pierce *(Peter)*, Bonnie Hunt *(Sarah)*, Bebe Neuwirth *(Nora)*, David Alan Grier *(Bentley)*, Patricia Clarkson *(Carol Parrish)*, Adam Hann-Byrd *(Young Alan)*, Laura Bell Bundy *(Young Sarah)*

p, Scott Kroopf, William Teitler; d, Joe Johnston; w, Jonathan Hensleigh, Greg Taylor, Jim Strain (from a story by Greg Taylor, Jim Strain, and Chris Van Allsburg, based on the book by Chris Van Allsburg); ph, Thomas Ackerman; ed, Robert Dalva; m, James Horner; prod d, James Bissell; art d, David Willson, Glen Pearson; fx, Stan Parks, Rory Cutler, Stephen L. Price, Ken Ralston, Industrial Light & Magic; cos, Martha Wynne Snetsinger

Not recommended for the Robin Williams-intolerant, JUMANJI is an in-your-face kiddie spectacular with plenty of noise, hectic activity, and dizzying special effects.

It's about a mysterious board game that unleashes both Williams and the sinister forces of the jungle to wreak havoc on a sleepy suburb. Kids love it — it's as relentlessly brash and colorful as a 32-bit video game — and adults won't be bored, although a handful of Tylenols may come in handy. Regrettably, however, the weird elegance of Chris Van Allsburg's much-praised picture book has been all but lost in translation. Director Joe Johnston (HONEY, I SHRUNK THE KIDS) handles the action scenes with cliff-hanger gusto—these, presumably, were what made the film a US box-office smash—although dim lighting (to hide the seams from the computer-generated animals) is a drawback. But screenwriters Jonathan Hensleigh (A FAR OFF PLACE), Greg Taylor (PRANCER), and Jim Strain (BINGO) have taken the story far too seriously, infusing it with another ersatz nuclear family metaphor that puts too much pressure on what was originally a goofy fantasy about confronting fear. By compelling JUMANJI to be more than a game, they take all the fun out of it. Just like grown-ups!

JUNGLE BOOK, THE
1967   78m   c   Children's/Animated   ★★★½
Walt Disney Productions   (U.S.)   G/U

VOICES OF: Phil Harris *(Baloo the Bear)*, Sebastian Cabot *(Bagheera the Panther)*, Louis Prima *(King Louie of the Apes)*, George Sanders *(Shere Khan the Tiger)*, Sterling Holloway *(Kaa the Snake)*, J. Pat O'Malley *(Col. Hathi the Elephant)*, Bruce Reitherman *(Mowgli the Man Cub)*, Verna Felton, Clint Howard *(Elephants)*, Chad Stuart Lord

p, Walt Disney; d, Wolfgang Reitherman; w, Larry Clemmons, Ralph Wright, Ken Anderson, Vance Gerry (based on the "Mowgli" stories in *The Jungle Book* by Rudyard Kipling); ed, Tom Acosta, Norman Carlisle; m, George Bruns; anim, Milt Kahl, Franklin Thomas, Oliver M. Johnston Jr., John Lounsbery

AAN Best Song: Terry Gilkyson (Music & Lyrics)

A witty animated feature from Disney based on the famous Rudyard Kipling stories. Abandoned as a child, Mowgli is raised by wolves, then befriended by a panther who attempts to return him to civilization until the beast realizes that the wolf-boy doesn't want to leave the jungle. Mowgli's happy-go-lucky trail leads to a meeting with a lazy bear, a kidnapping by monkeys, and an encounter with a fire-fearing tiger. In the finale, Mowgli sees a beautiful young girl with whom he falls in love, finally forsaking jungle life to be with her.

The last animated film to be directly overseen by Walt Disney himself, JUNGLE BOOK contains some great visual laughs and is low on sticky sentiment, but the sketchy animation style strains to be modern and looks careless instead. Well-known personalities are particularly effective in providing the voices, notably Phil Harris, Louis Prima, and especially George Sanders. Released ten months after Disney's death, the film went on to be one of the studio's most successful pictures.

JUNGLE BOOK, THE

1942 108m c Adventure   ★★★★
UA (U.S.)   /U

Sabu (Mowgli), Joseph Calleia (Buldeo), John Qualen (The Barber), Frank Puglia (The Pundit), Rosemary DeCamp (Messua), Patricia O'Rourke (Mahala), Ralph Byrd (Durga), John Mather (Rao), Faith Brook (English Girl), Noble Johnson (Sikh)

p, Alexander Korda; d, Zoltan Korda; w, Laurence Stallings (based on the books by Rudyard Kipling); ph, Lee Garmes; ed, William Hornbeck; m, Miklos Rozsa; prod d, Vincent Korda; fx, Lawrence Butler

AAN Best Cinematography: W Howard Green; AAN Best Score: Miklos Rozsa; AAN Best Art Direction: Vincent Korda (Art Direction), Julia Heron (Interior Decoration); AAN Best Visual Effects: Lawrence Butler (Special Effects-Photographic), William H Wilmarth (Special Effects-Sound)

Colorful Korda production, fine family fare. This loose adaptation of Rudyard Kipling's Jungle Books stars Sabu as Mowgli, a young man raised by wolves who returns to his native village with no idea of human language or customs.

Once he acquires speech, he captivates Mahala (Patricia O'Rourke), the daughter of the aged Buldeo (Joseph Calleia), with tales of the jungle and his animal friends. Mowgli and Mahala trek into the jungle and discover ruins of a lost civilization, filled with treasures. When Mahala returns to the village with a gold coin, her father tries to get Mowgli to divulge the gold's location, but the boy refuses, fearing the village will be corrupted. Buldeo then turns others against the lad, who is sentenced to be burned at the nearest convenient stake.

Shot outside Los Angeles, the film features dazzling photography, expressive animals and a brilliant Miklos Rozsa score, with individual themes for each animal. An enchanting film for viewers of all ages.

JUNIOR BONNER

1972 100m c Western/Sports   ★★★½
ABC (U.S.)   PG/A

Steve McQueen (Junior Bonner), Robert Preston (Ace Bonner), Ida Lupino (Elvira Bonner), Ben Johnson (Buck Roan), Joe Don Baker (Curly Bonner), Barbara Leigh (Charmagne), Mary Murphy (Ruth Bonner), Bill McKinney (Red Terwiliger), Sandra Deel (Nurse Arlis), Don "Red" Barry (Homer Rutledge)

p, Joe Wizan; d, Sam Peckinpah; w, Jeb Rosebrook; ph, Lucien Ballard; ed, Robert Wolfe; m, Jerry Fielding; art d, Ted Haworth

A trifle clumsy, but affecting nonetheless. Steve McQueen stars in this Sam Peckinpah-directed film as the title character, an aging rodeo cowboy who returns to his small hometown of Prescott, Arizona, and learns that nothing stays the same. Saddened to discover that his parents (Lupino and Preston) have split and that his brother (Baker) is getting rich selling off parcels of his father's land, Junior tries to regain his self-esteem by staying on a previously unrideable bull at the town's annual Fourth of July rodeo.

There's much to recommend here, including some fine rodeo footage, winning characterizations from Johnson as the man who supplies the livestock for the rodeo and from Taylor as the owner of the bar, and an especially strong performance by McQueen as the cowboy who realizes that he can't go home on the range again. Lupino and Preston are especially fine among a good supporting cast. But the territory covered is similar to Nick Ray's earlier, superior THE LUSTY MEN.

JURASSIC PARK

1993 127m c Adventure/Science Fiction/Thriller   ★★★½
Universal/Amblin (U.S.)   PG-13/PG

Sam Neill (Dr. Alan Grant), Laura Dern (Dr. Ellie Sattler), Jeff Goldblum (Ian Malcolm), Richard Attenborough (Dr. John Hammond), Bob Peck (Robert Muldoon), Martin Ferrero (Donald Gennaro), B.D. Wong (Dr. Wu), Joseph Mazzello (Tim), Ariana Richards (Lex), Samuel L. Jackson (Arnold)

p, Kathleen Kennedy, Gerald R. Molen; d, Steven Spielberg; w, David Koepp, Michael Crichton, Malia Scotch Marmo (adapted from the novel by Michael Crichton); ph, Dean Cundey; ed, Michael Kahn, David Tanaka; m, John Williams; prod d, Rick Carter; art d, Jim Teegarden, John Bell; fx, Stan Winston, Dennis Muren, Phil Tippett, Michael Lantieri

AA Best Sound: Ron Judkins, Shawn Murphy, Gary Rydstrom, Gary Summers; AA Best Sound Effects Editing: Richard Hymns, Gary Rydstrom; AA Best Visual Effects: Michael Lantieri, Dennis Muren, Phil Tippett, Stan Winston

Like DIE HARD and BATMAN, JURASSIC PARK is not so much a dramatic story as a theme-park ride through spectacular special effects and action sequences.

These being the post-modern 90s, this is a theme-park ride about a theme park—an exclusive, as-yet-unopened island resort where dinosaurs have been cloned from DNA deposits. Such a scientific feat would be only a little more impressive than what's been accomplished for this film, which brings prehistoric beasts convincingly back to life through a combination of sophisticated models and computer-generated animation. Director Steven Spielberg does a masterful job of putting the beasts through their paces in some scenes that will have even the most jaded observers clutching the edges of their seats.

"Jurassic" is not without its flaws. Michael Crichton's novel has been clumsily condensed and his nastier characters unnecessarily whitewashed. Some of the actors—Sam Neill and Laura Dern as paleontologists, Richard Attenborough as the park's creator—give performances that seem also to have been achieved by computer animation. (The biggest exception here is the ever-quirky Jeff Goldblum, playing a gonzo mathematician with a quip for every occasion: "I wonder if this will be part of the tour," he muses, as he lies wounded in the back of a speeding jeep with a T. rex in hot pursuit.)

If these sound like quibbles, they are. This is an exhilarating, sometimes terrifying monster of a movie that, once it gets you in its clutches, won't put you down again until the closing credits start to roll.

JUST A GIGOLO

1978 98m c Drama   ★★★
Leguan (West Germany)   R/15

David Bowie (Paul), Sydne Rome (Cilly), Kim Novak (Helga), David Hemmings (Capt. Kraft), Marlene Dietrich (Baroness von Semering), Maria Schell (Mutti), Curt Jurgens (Prince), Erika Pluhar (Eva), Rudolf Schundler (Gustav), Hilde Weissner (Aunt Hilda)

d, David Hemmings; w, Joshua Sinclair, Ennio De Concini; ph, Charly Steinberger; ed, Susan Jaeger, Fred Srp, Maxine Julius; m, Gunther Fischer; art d, Peter Rothe; chor, Herbert F. Schubert; cos, Ingrid Zore

Tragically, a misfire. This interesting (if only for its cast) tale of a Prussian WWI veteran who returns to Berlin, torn between wealthy, older women and homosexual Nazis, cannot find itself. Is it farce or melodrama? Bowie has some startling moments, but his overall performance languishes in uncertainty.

The underrated Rome provides a definite energy lift to the proceedings, but everyone else is reduced to doing star turns. It's surprising to find Hemmings photographed in such a singularly unflattering manner in his own movie. Perhaps he exhausted all his resources filming Miss Dietrich's cameo: she's a grande dame madam who wanders on long enough, veiled and diffused to the max, to croak the title song, before adding Bowie to her stable. It's a hypnotic swansong—visually and vocally—a fitting farewell to the last of the golden age goddesses.

Another goddess from another era, the still-lucious Novak, turns in a commanding portrayal of a lusty widow. The period mood, soundtrack and use of color are never less than first-rate. Yet the film, reduced from its original 147-minute running length, flounders badly.

JUST BEFORE NIGHTFALL
(JUSTE AVANT LA NUIT)

1971 100m c Crime   ★★
Boetie/Cinegai/Columbia (France/Italy)   PG/X

Stephane Audran (*Helen*), Michel Bouquet (*Charles*), Francois Perier (*Francois*), Jean Carmet (*Jeannot*), Dominique Zardi (*Prince*), Henri Attal (*Cavanna*), Paul Temps (*Bardin*), Marina Ninchi (*Ginette*), Clelia Matania (*Mme. Masson*), Anna Douking (*Laura*)

p, Andre Genoves; d, Claude Chabrol; w, Claude Chabrol (based on the novel *The Thin Line* by Edouard Atiyah); ph, Jean Rabier; ed, Jacques Gaillard; m, Pierre Jansen; art d, Guy Littaye

A surburban crime melodrama from French New Wave director Chabrol that opens as Parisian advertising man Bouquet strangles his mistress, the wife of his best friend, Perier. His guilt goes undetected by the police, but he cannot live with his crime.

He pitifully tells his wife, Audran, of his affair and the subsequent murder. She accepts the news with surprising calm, talking him out of turning himself in. He then confesses to Perier, who also accepts the news as if he were just told a weather report. Bouquet reveals that his relationship with Perier's wife was a sadomasochistic one, with his act of punishment being carried a bit too far. It is now his turn to be punished, but his confessions only bring solace. One evening (the nightfall of the title representing death) Bouquet quietly dies after taking an overdose of sleeping medicine that his wife has prepared.

As interesting as the plot may seem, JUST BEFORE NIGHTFALL is more concerned with its poke at the middle class than with characterization or pacing. The result is an incredibly slow-moving picture, which is as ugly visually (the modernized, split-level, glassy house they live in is colored with putrid oranges and greens) as the film's psychological themes are. One wishes that Bouquet had strangled Perier, who designed the house, instead of his wife.

K

KAGEMUSHA

1980 179m c Drama/War   ★★★★
Toho/Kurosawa (Japan)   PG

Tatsuya Nakadai (*Shingen Takeda/Kagemusha*), Tsutomu Yamazaki (*Nobukado Takeda*), Kenichi Hagiwara (*Katsuyori Takeda*), Kota Yui (*Takemaru*), Shuji Otaki (*Yamagata*), Hideo Murata (*Baba*), Daisuke Ryu (*Oda*), Kaori Momoi (*Otsuyanokata*)

p, Akira Kurosawa; d, Akira Kurosawa; w, Akira Kurosawa, Masato Ide; ph, Takao Saito, Shoji Ueda, Kazuo Miyagawa, Asaichi Nakai; m, Shinichiro Ikebe; art d, Yoshiro Muraki

AAN Best Foreign Language Film ; AAN Best Art Direction: Yoshiro Muraki (Art Direction)

After a long period of inactivity, Akira Kurosawa returned to the genre of which he is the unparalleled master, the samurai film.

Tatsuya Nakadai plays a 16th-century warlord, Shingen Takeda, who uses doubles for himself on the battlefield, instilling confidence and fear through his constant presence while his clan fights to establish dominance in Japan. When Shingen is killed, his current "shadow warrior" or *kagemusha*—in actuality a petty thief (again powerfully played by Tatsuya Nakadai)—must take over so that the army's morale

will not die. Trained in secret by Shingen's assistants, the double genuinely begins to acquire some of his master's attributes, but the masquerade becomes increasingly difficult to maintain.

Kurosawa's epic is alive with color, the spectacular visuals overlying a somber exploration of traditionalism, honor loyalty, and identity, played out against a sumptuous tapestry of political intrigue and the 16th-century clan warfare that came to an end with the Tokugawa *shogunate*. The massive battle scenes rank with the director's best, using brilliant color, contrasting light, and the enormous cast to great advantage. Kurosawa also alternates compelling scenes of near hypnotic stillness with scenes of rousing action. Sadly the film's score is a noisy irritant.

Made and distributed with the financial aid and clout of George Lucas and Francis Ford Coppola, KAGEMUSHA prefigured and paved the way for the great RAN, Kurosawa's epic adaptation of *King Lear*.

KAMERADSCHAFT
(LA TRAGEDIE DE LA MINE)

1931 93m bw Drama   ★★★★
Nero/Gaumont/Franco-Film-Aubert (Germany)

Fritz Kampers (*Wilderer*), Gustav Puttjer (*Kaplan*), Alexander Granach (*Kaspers*), Andree Ducret (*Francoise*), Georges Charlia (*Jean*), Ernst Busch (*Wittkopp*), Daniel Mandaille (*Emile*), Pierre Louis (*Georges*), Alex Bernard (*Grandfather*)

p, Seymour Nebenzal; d, G.W. Pabst; w, Karl Otten, Peter Martin Lampel, Ladislas Vajda; ph, Fritz Arno Wagner, Robert Baberske; ed, Hans Oser

This stirring plea for peace and internationalism was the highpoint of German socialist filmmaking in this period. KAMERADSCHAFT, a German-French co-production set in the Lorraine mining region on the French-German border in the aftermath of WWI, was inspired by an actual 1906 mining disaster that claimed 1,200 lives.

Combining elements of classic German expressionism and and Soviet Socialist realism, German director G.W. Pabst (STREET OF SORROW, PANDORA'S BOX, THE THREEPENNY OPERA) introduces the viewer to the German and French miners. Separated by mine walls and metal bars below and by armed border patrols above, they have little contact with one another. But when a series of explosions causes a cave-in on the French side, the hearts of the Germans go out to them. Wittkopp (Ernst Busch) appeals to his bosses to send a rescue team while, underground, a trio of German miners breaks through a set of steel bars that marks the 1919 border. Meanwhile, on the French side, an elderly retired miner (Alex Bernard) sneaks into the shaft, hoping to rescue his young grandson, Georges (Pierre Louis).

Although occasionally overly sentimental, Pabst's plea for a peaceful future is sincere and compelling. His direction of the heartbreak and devastation is enhanced by the brilliant photography of Fritz Arno Wagner and Robert Baberske and the alarmingly authentic set design is provided by Erno Metzner and Karl Vollbrecht.

KANAL

1956 96m bw War   ★★★
Film Polski (Poland)   /X

Teresa Izewska (*Daisy Stokrotka*), Tadeusz Janczar (*Corporal Korab*), Wienczyslaw Glinski (*Lieutenant Zadra*), Tadeusz Gwiadowski (*Sergeant Kula*), Stanislaw Mikulski (*Smulky*), Wladyslaw Sheybal (*Composer*), Emil Karewicz (*Madry*), Teresa Berezowska (*Halinka*), Adam Pawlikowski (*German Officer*), Zofia Lindorf

p, Stanislaw Adler; d, Andrzej Wajda; w, Jerzy Stefan Stawinski (based on his short story); ph, Jerzy Lipman; ed, Halina Nawrocka; m, Jan Krenz; art d, Roman Mann; cos, Jerzy Szeski

This extremely intense and relentlessly graphic second feature from Polish filmmaker Andrzej Wajda takes place during the final days of the Warsaw Uprising in 1944. Three groups of Poles, no longer able to hold off the enemy, retreat to the city's *kanaly*, or sewer system. The viewer is told from the very start to "watch them closely; these are the last hours of their lives." With this pessimistic tone established, we observe them as they try to escape and live an underground existence free from the oppression and lost ideals of their lives above ground. Although we know that death awaits them, we also know that freedom from the sewers is only a relative freedom.

Wajda spares the viewer nothing, showing death, betrayal, suffering, suicide, capture, and despair. Still the Poles fight on in the hope that they will see sunlight pouring into the sewer, even if it is filtered through a metal grate.

KANSAS CITY

1996 110m c Crime/Drama ★★★½
Sandcastle 5/CiBy 2000 (U.S.) R/15

Jennifer Jason Leigh *(Blondie O'Hara)*, Miranda Richardson *(Carolyn Stilton)*, Harry Belafonte *(Seldom Seen)*, Michael Murphy *(Henry Stilton)*, Dermot Mulroney *(Johnny O'Hara)*, Steve Buscemi *(Johnny Flynn)*, Brooke Smith *(Babe Flynn)*, Jane Adams *(Nettie Bolt)*, Jeff Feringa *(Addie Parker)*, A.C. Smith *(Sheepshan Red)*

p, Robert Altman; d, Robert Altman; w, Robert Altman, Frank Barhydt; ph, Oliver Stapleton; ed, Geraldine Peroni; m, Hal Willner; prod d, Stephen Altman; art d, Richard L. Johnson; cos, Dona Granata

Robert Altman's hometown of Kansas City, MO is the setting for this atmospheric period piece about a hopelessly misconceived kidnapping. As always with Altman, the milieu is richly textured, and the characters' weaknesses inform the story line.

Expecting her manicurist for a home appointment, laudanum-addicted Carol Stilton (Miranda Richardson) is surprised by a substitute—a tough-talking Jean Harlow wanna-be who calls herself Blondie (Jennifer Jason Leigh) and has come to kidnap her. Blondie has chosen to abduct Carol in order to force her politico husband (Michael Murphy) to help Blondie's hoodlum husband, Johnny O'Hara (Dermot Mulroney), out of a jam. Johnny has foolishly robbed a high-rolling client of the Hey Hey Club, a jazz club and gambling den, and is awaiting execution by the club's owner, a ruthless gangster named Seldom Seen (Harry Belafonte). Over the course of 24 hours, Blondie drags the hapless Carol across Kansas City in a desperate attempt to get her Johnny back.

After a trio of densely-populated "tapestry" films that placed him back in the Hollywood mainstream (THE PLAYER, SHORT CUTS, READY TO WEAR), Altman reaffirms his status as a master storyteller with this small, dark character study. KANSAS CITY supplies vivid period detail spotlighting various early 1930s phenomena: the consolidation of jazz styles; the corrupt political "machines" that ran certain cities; and rabid movie fandom. But the film's central theme remains one that Altman has explored in most of his major works: love relationships. Altman's strong point is his direction of actors, and KANSAS CITY offers three excellent lead performances. Jennifer Jason Leigh delivers another extraordinarily nuanced turn as the hard-boiled Blondie, Richardson supplies a nice balance as the socially proper but very stoned Carol, and, offering the film a strong backbone, Belafonte is superlative as the ominously verbose Seldom.

KARATE KID, THE

1984 126m c Martial Arts/Sports ★★★
Columbia (U.S.) PG/15

Ralph Macchio *(Daniel)*, Noriyuki "Pat" Morita *(Miyagi)*, Elisabeth Shue *(Ali)*, Martin Kove *(Kreese)*, Randee Heller *(Lucille)*, William Zabka *(Johnny)*, Ron Thomas *(Bobby)*, Rob Garrison *(Tommy)*, Chad McQueen *(Dutch)*, Tony O'Dell *(Jimmy)*

p, Jerry Weintraub; d, John G. Avildsen; w, Robert Mark Kamen; ph, James Crabe; ed, Bud Smith, Walt Mulconery, John G. Avildsen; m, Bill Conti; prod d, William J. Cassidy; fx, Frank Toro; chor, Pat E. Johnson; cos, Richard Bruno, Aida Swenson

AAN Best Supporting Actor: Noriyuki 'Pat' Morita

Derivative and sentimental, THE KARATE KID treads the same path as ROCKY, and with good reason—it was directed by John Avildsen, who also directed Sylvester Stallone's star-making vehicle.

Daniel (Ralph Macchio) and his mother (Randee Heller) move from Newark, New Jersey, to southern California, where the whole world seems blond and brutal to this hapless ethnic kid. Daniel is immediately set upon by bullies, led by a Hitler Youth-type, Johnny (William Zabka). Daniel's new life grows increasingly unpleasant until he meets Miyagi

(Pat Morita), a friendly aged Japanese janitor. Miyagi takes the kid under his wing and begins to teach him about life and karate while getting him to do some chores around the house.

Made for a relative pittance, the way the first ROCKY was, THE KARATE KID reaped a bonanza at the box office. Though shamelessly manipulative, it is undeniably effective. It offers some genuine moments of warmth, humor and excitement. Of course it all leads up to a big tournament where Fair Play has a showdown with Dirty Tricks. Guess who wins. This is the kind of movie where you find yourself cheering even though you know you're being hoodwinked. Naturally the movie gave birth to two sequels and, not surprisingly, neither measures up to the original.

KENNEL MURDER CASE, THE

1933 73m bw Mystery ★★★★½
Warner Bros. (U.S.)

William Powell *(Philo Vance)*, Mary Astor *(Hilda Lake)*, Eugene Pallette *(Sgt. Heath)*, Ralph Morgan *(Raymond Wrede)*, Jack LaRue *(Eduardo Grassi)*, Helen Vinson *(Doris Delafield)*, Paul Cavanagh *(Sir Bruce MacDonald)*, Robert Barrat *(Archer Coe)*, Arthur Hohl *(Gamble)*, Robert McWade *(District Attorney John F.X. Markham)*

p, Robert Presnell; d, Michael Curtiz; w, Robert N. Lee, Peter Milne, Robert Presnell (based on the novel *The Return of Philo Vance* by S.S. Van Dine); ph, William Rees; ed, Ed N. McLarnin; art d, Jack Okey; cos, Orry-Kelly

Justifiably a cult favorite, and a damn fine film in the bargain. Certainly the best of the Philo Vance series, THE KENNEL MURDER CASE stars the inimitable Powell for the fourth time as the debonair detective.

Here the mystery involves the members of a Long Island kennel club, and Philo, with the assistance of his Scottie and a prize-winning Doberman, solves a double murder. The plot is full of interesting twists and is eminently serviceable. But the real appeal of this amazing little film is Powell's delightful flair for repartee; it's a pleasure to sit back and let him purr. Astor, too, brings her own special brand of warmth, conviction and appeal to almost everything she does.

The real star of the film, however, is director Michael Curtiz, who races through this flick like a piranha breaking a fast. His exposure to German expressionism pays off handsomely here, and the film is chock full of bizarre compositions, flashy editing, inventive camera angles and memorable camerawork. Fast, foolish, engrossing and unique, this breathtaking little gem is a tribute to both Curtiz's craftsmanship and his fiery temperament. Remade by William Clemens as CALLING PHILO VANCE.

KENTUCKY FRIED MOVIE, THE

1977 90m c/bw Comedy ★★★
Kentucky Fried Theatre (U.S.) R/18

Marilyn Joi *(Cleopatra)*, Saul Kahan *(Schwartz)*, Marcy Goldman *(Housewife)*, Joe Medalis *(Paul)*, Barry Dennen *(Claude)*, Rich Gates *(Boy)*, Tara Strohmeier *(Girl)*, Neil Thompson *(Newscaster)*, George Lazenby *(Architect)*, Henry Gibson

p, Robert K. Weiss; d, John Landis; w, David Zucker, Jerry Zucker, Jim Abrahams; ph, Stephen Katz; ed, George Folsey Jr.; art d, Rich Harvel; cos, Deborah Nadoolman, Joyce Unruh

A vulgar and uproariously funny college party movie made up of a series of comedy sketches from the Kentucky Fried Theater, a fresh young satirical group formed at the University of Wisconsin at Madison in the early 1970s.

Depending on one's mood, or level of sobriety, it can be a hysterical picture that pokes good natured fun at American movies, TV and commercials. The gags are hurled forth in a fast and furious manner; if you don't like one—fear not—another will be along any second. Memorable segments include "Catholic High School Girls in Trouble," "Cleopatra Schwartz" and "That's Armageddon!" but the most outstanding episode is "A Fistful of Yen," a lengthy kung-fu parody that casts two actual martial arts experts in a surprisingly lavish environment.

Landis has rarely done better work than in this modest early effort. Writers Zucker, Zucker, and Abrahams went on to make the gleefully absurd AIRPLANE and THE NAKED GUN films.

KES

1969 112m c Drama   ★★★★
Woodfall/Kestrel (U.K.)   GP/PG

David Bradley *(Billy Casper)*, Colin Welland *(Mr. Farthing)*, Lynne
Perrie *(Mrs. Casper)*, Freddie Fletcher *(Jud)*, Brian Glover *(Mr. Sug-
den)*, Bob Bowes *(Mr. Gryce)*, Trevor Hasketh *(Mr. Crossley)*, Eric
Bolderson *(Farmer)*, Geoffrey Banks *(Mathematics Teacher)*, Zoe
Sutherland *(Librarian)*

p, Tony Garnett; d, Kenneth Loach; w, Kenneth Loach, Tony Garnett,
Barry Hines (based on the novel *A Kestrel for a Knave* by Barry
Hines); ph, Chris Menges; ed, Roy Watts; m, John Cameron; art d,
William McCrow

Imagine THE 400 BLOWS reconfigured around a working class English boy living in a grimy industrial town and you get some idea of the
emotional power of this bleakly realistic film adapted from a novel by
Barry Hines.

Billy Casper (Bradley) is the product of a broken home and the
victim of school bullies. He takes refuge in his comic books and
shoplifting. One day he finds a baby kestrel (a small falcon) and
becomes determined to raise the bird. He names it "Kes" and promptly
steals a book on falconry. He becomes quite adept at his newfound skills
and catches the eye of his teacher, Mr. Farthing (Welland). However
his relationship with the beautiful bird cannot ameliorate his depressing
home life with his brutish older brother, Jud (Fletcher). Nor does it
change the fact that his future options are severely limited by lack of
class status, money, or family stability and support.

Though it's a sensitive and heartfelt film, KES never lapses into the
sentimentality that often attends these "a boy and his pet" pictures. Ken
Loach's low key, clear-eyed direction makes this a fairly unique "children's film." It is aided immeasurably by Chris Menges's naturalistic
yet evocative cinematography.

KEY LARGO

1948 101m bw Crime   ★★★★
Warner Bros. (U.S.)   /PG

Humphrey Bogart *(Frank McCloud)*, Edward G. Robinson *(Johnny
Rocco)*, Lauren Bacall *(Nora Temple)*, Lionel Barrymore *(James
Temple)*, Claire Trevor *(Gaye Dawn)*, Thomas Gomez *(Curley)*, Harry
Lewis *(Toots)*, John Rodney *(Deputy Clyde Sawyer)*, Marc Lawrence
(Ziggy), Dan Seymour *(Angel Garcia)*

p, Jerry Wald; d, John Huston; w, Richard Brooks (based on the play
by Maxwell Anderson); ph, Karl Freund; ed, Rudi Fehr; m, Max
Steiner; art d, Leo K. Kuter; fx, William McGann, Robert Burks; cos,
Leah Rhodes

AA Best Supporting Actress: Claire Trevor

With superb casting and performances, a sharp and resonant screenplay, John Huston's taut direction and Karl Freund's deep-focus photography, KEY LARGO transcends the windy allegories of its
theatrical origins to become a suspenseful and entertaining minor
classic of 1940s Hollywood.

Based on the play by Maxwell Anderson, Bogart stars as Frank
McCloud, a disillusioned WW II veteran who travels to a run-down
hotel in Key Largo, Florida, to pay his respects to the family of a buddy
who was killed in the war. The hotel is operated by the father of the
deceased, James Temple (Barrymore), and the widowed Nora Temple
(Bacall). McCloud arrives to find the hotel full of seedy, threatening
characters. He can only visit briefly with Nora and Mr. Temple before
they must begin preparing for a huge storm which is coming their way.

Soon a group of Seminole Indians arrives in small boats, seeking
shelter. Among them are John and Tom Osceola (Silverheels and
Redwing), brothers who recently escaped from prison. Sheriff Wade
(Blue) and Deputy Sawyer (Rodney) had visited the hotel earlier
searching for the fugitives. John tells Nora that he and his brother are
ready to give themselves over to the authorities. Meanwhile the massive
storm grows closer and closer. McCloud, Nora, and Mr. Temple head
inside the hotel where it quickly becomes apparent that the tough-look-
ing "guests" are all criminals. They have waylaid the deputy and are
now holding him prisoner in one of the guest rooms. No one will be
allowed to leave the premises until they finish their "business."

While all these introductions were being made, the gang's leader
has been taking a bath. When the aging gangster finally makes his
entrance he is immediately recognized by McCloud as Johnny Rocco,
an infamous gangster who had run a huge mob empire until he was
deported. He has arrived from Cuba by a ship anchored just off shore.
The last major character arrives for the festivities: Gaye Dawn (Trevor),
an alcoholic ex-entertainer who is now the girlfriend of the gangster. The
storm can finally begin in earnest.

In a film of outstanding performances—Claire Trevor won an Oscar
for Best Supporting Actress—Edward G. Robinson deserves special
praise. As the fallen crime czar longing for a return to an earlier lawless
time, Robinson is spellbinding in a portrayal that echoes his own iconic
status in movie history. Though Robinson had at one point grown weary
of endlessly repeating the gangster persona he established in LITTLE
CAESAR, even parodying the role in BROTHER ORCHID, he resurrected his gangster image here as his final major statement on the genre
that brought him stardom.

KID FOR TWO FARTHINGS, A

1955 91m c Comedy/Fantasy   ★★★★
Big Ben/London Films (U.K.)   /U

Celia Johnson *(Joanne)*, Diana Dors *(Sonia)*, David Kossoff *(Kand-
insky)*, Joe Robinson *(Sam)*, Jonathan Ashmore *(Joe)*, Brenda de
Banzie *("Lady" Ruby)*, Vera Day *(Mimi)*, Primo Carnera *(Python
Macklin)*, Sydney Tafler *(Mme. Rita)*, Sidney James *(Ice Berg)*

p, Carol Reed; d, Carol Reed; w, Wolf Mankowitz (based on his novel);
ph, Ted Scaife; ed, Bert Bates; m, Benjamin Frankel; art d, Wilfred
Shingleton; cos, Anna Duse

An absolutely charming comedy-fantasy set against the Jewish trades-
men's life in London's Petticoat Lane. Based on the novel by Mankowitz, it's the story of a young boy, Joe (Ashmore), who has been told
stories about a unicorn by tailor Kadinsky (Kossoff). When the boy
buys a goat with only one horn, he is convinced that he has purchased
a unicorn, because "magical" things begin to happen to the denizens of
the area.

Kadinsky has one great desire—to own his own steam press. Sonia
(Dors) is a buxom blonde who has been waiting for many years to marry
muscular Sam (Robinson). She gets her wish when he enters the ring
and wins enough money for them to wed. Celia Johnson plays Joanne,
Joe's mother, but she doesn't have enough to do to merit her casting.
Tafler, a terrific comic actor (MAKE MINE MINK), is again shown to
good advantage as a storekeeper, and Canadian character actor Lou
Jacobi makes one of his earliest appearances as a wrestling promoter.
Naturally, all of the miracles are logically explained, but, to the boy, it's
the unicorn that has brought all the happiness to Petticoat Lane.

This is a delightful film, and Reed, working for the first time in color,
shows how well he deals with children. He used this ability before in
THE FALLEN IDOL and later with the musical version of OLIVER!.

KID FROM SPAIN, THE

1932 118m bw Musical/Comedy   ★★★★
Goldwyn (U.S.)   /U

Eddie Cantor *(Eddie Williams)*, Lyda Roberti *(Rosalie)*, Robert Young
(Ricardo), Ruth Hall *(Anita Gomez)*, John Miljan *(Pancho)*, Noah
Beery Sr. *(Alonzo Gomez)*, J. Carrol Naish *(Pedro)*, Robert Emmett
O'Connor *(Detective Crawford)*, Stanley Fields *(Jose)*, Paul Porcasi
(Gonzales, Border Guard)

p, Samuel Goldwyn; d, Leo McCarey; w, William Anthony McGuire,
Bert Kalmar, Harry Ruby; ph, Gregg Toland; ed, Stuart Heisler; art d,
Richard Day; chor, Busby Berkeley; cos, Milo Anderson

A lavish musical vehicle for the immensely popular comic genius Eddie
Cantor, THE KID FROM SPAIN is directed by the brilliant Leo
McCarey (DUCK SOUP, THE AWFUL TRUTH, RUGGLES OF RED
GAP, MAKE WAY FOR TOMORROW) and boasts choreography by
the legendary Busby Berkeley just before he hit his hallucinatory stride
(42ND STREET, GOLD DIGGERS OF 1933, DAMES). This is Eddie
Cantor at his best!

After being tossed out of school, Ricardo (Robert Young) invites his
college roommate, Eddie (Eddie Cantor), to his home in Mexico. Their
trip becomes a necessity when bank robbers mistake Eddie for their

getaway driver, the only person who can identify them. Once they are south of the border, mistaken identity strikes again. This time Eddie is thought to be the offspring of a legendary matador and is forced into the bull ring, though Ricardo has arranged for him to face a tame animal that will stop its charge upon command. However, a rough character involved in one of the story's many subplots substitutes a considerably less docile bull and hilarity results as Eddie does his best not to get gored.

THE KID FROM SPAIN is chock-full of laughs and boasts some fine songs, written mostly by Bert Kalmar and Harry Ruby who co-wrote the screenplay.

KID GALAHAD

1937 101m bw Sports   ★★★½
Warner Bros. (U.S.)   /PG

Edward G. Robinson (Nick Donati), Bette Davis (Louise "Fluff" Phillips), Humphrey Bogart (Turkey Morgan), Wayne Morris (Kid Galahad/Ward Guisenberry), Jane Bryan (Marie Donati), Harry Carey (Silver Jackson), William Haade (Chuck McGraw), Soledad Jiminez (Mrs. Donati), Joe Cunningham (Joe Taylor), Ben Welden (Buzz Stevens)

p, Samuel Bischoff; d, Michael Curtiz; w, Seton I. Miller (based on the novel by Francis Wallace); ph, Tony Gaudio; ed, George Amy; m, Heinz Roemheld, Max Steiner; art d, Carl Jules Weyl; fx, James Gibbons, Edwin DuPar; cos, Orry-Kelly

Edward G. Robinson and Humphrey Bogart play rival fight managers in this memorable indictment of corruption in the boxing ring with Wayne Morris in the title role, the first of his three turns as a pugilist (THE KID COMES BACK and THE KID FROM KOKOMO).

When a bellhop (Morris) knocks out highly touted heavyweight Chuck McGraw (William Haade) in defense of the honor of "Fluff" Phillips (Bette Davis), she dubs him Kid Galahad. Her boyfriend, Nick Donati (Robinson), decides to make the young man into a prizefighter. Jealous because both Fluff and her sister appear interested in Kid, Nick arranges a bout with McGraw that he is so certain his fighter will lose that he assures the rival manager Turkey Morgan of the same. Of course, things don't work out as planned. . . .

A solid story with good characterizations and sensational prizefight footage, KID GALAHAD was remade as THE WAGONS ROLL AT NIGHT, with the story switched to a circus, then made again as a fight film with Elvis Presley. To avoid confusion with the Presley movie, the title has been changed to THE BATTLING BELLHOP for television.

KIDNAPPED

1971 100m c Adventure   ★★★
Omnibus (U.K.)   G/U

Michael Caine (Alan Breck), Trevor Howard (Lord Advocate Grant), Jack Hawkins (Capt. Hoseason), Donald Pleasence (Ebenezer Balfour), Gordon Jackson (Charles Stewart), Vivien Heilbron (Catriona Stewart), Lawrence Douglas (David Balfour), Freddie Jones (Cluny Macpherson), Andrew McCulloch (Andrew), Eric Woodburn (Doctor)

p, Frederick H. Brogger; d, Delbert Mann; w, Jack Pulman (based on the novels Kidnapped and Catriona by Robert Louis Stevenson); ph, Paul Beeson; ed, Peter Boita; m, Roy Budd; art d, Alex Vetchinsky; fx, Cliff Culley; cos, Olga Lehmann

Originally released in 1938 with Warner Baxter and Freddie Bartholomew in the leads, KIDNAPPED was remade in 1948 with Roddy McDowall and Dan O'Herlihy, then again with James MacArthur and Peter Finch in 1960. This fourth version of Robert Louis Stevenson's novel was a rare, relatively classy project for American International Pictures (AIP), the prolific producer of "classic" teen-oriented drive-in fodder during the 1950s and 1960s. This screenplay offers the audience more bang for its buck by including material from Stevenson's less well known sequel, Catriona.

In the final years of the 18th century, the British are brutally ravaging the Scottish forces of the Jacobite Rebellion. David Balfour (Douglas) is an orphan boy who comes to the home of his wicked uncle, Ebenezer Balfour (Pleasence), unaware that he is actually the rightful heir to the family fortune. Ebenezer hires Captain Hoseason (Hawkins), a ruthless sea captain, to force the boy into service on a ship prior to selling him

into slavery in the New World. On its way to the Carolinas, Hoseason's ship rams a small boat, sinking it and drowning every hand aboard save Alan Breck (Caine), a rebel on his way to France to raise money to continue the war against the Crown. Breck and young Balfour hit it off immediately and join forces to battle the cutthroat crew. However, a storm hits and the ship is wrecked. Here their high adventure begins in earnest.

Rather than use their well worn matte paintings, AIP splurged and went to England and Scotland to find the proper settings. The photography that resulted is splendid. After a decade of "Beach Party" films, AIP decided to remake classics and foisted some dreadful ones upon the public, WUTHERING HEIGHTS and JULIUS CAESAR among them. This is the best of the lot, although it has so much plot that it may be difficult for youngsters to follow. Caine shows his costume mettle in this role, a welcome change from the spies and cads he'd played until making KIDNAPPED. A little too much talk and not enough action, but it's still fun.

KIDS

1995 90m c Drama   ★★★
Independent Pictures/The Guys Upstairs (U.S.)   /18

Leo Fitzpatrick (Telly), Justin Pierce (Casper), Chloe Sevigny (Jennie), Sarah Henderson (Girl No. 1), Rosario Dawson (Ruby), Harold Hunter (Harold), Yakira Peguero (Darcy), Joseph Knofelmacher (Taxi Driver), Joseph Chan (Ball Owner), Jonathan S. Kim (Korean Guy)

p, Cary Woods; d, Larry Clark; w, Harmony Korine (from an original story treatment by Larry Clark, Jim Lewis, Leo Fitzpatrick, and Justin Pierce); ph, Eric Alan Edwards; ed, Chris Tellefsen; m, Lou Barlow, John Davis; prod d, Kevin Thompson; cos, Kim Druce

Though it promised to be 1995's most scandalous indie release, this edgy, downbeat film emerged as little more than REEFER MADNESS for the Age of AIDS. Disney sought to hide its financial interest in KIDS by forcing its subsidiary, Miramax, to release the film under a corporate pseudonym, but it needn't have bothered. Director Larry Clark, famous for his arty, voyeuristic still photos of adolescents, cleverly seeds his titillating subject matter—teen sex and drug abuse—with enough fear, loathing, and cautionary finger-wagging to keep the most reactionary would-be censors at bay.

KIDS follows a crowd of bored, unblushingly aimless New York teenagers through a day of hanging out, getting stoned, kicking ass, and having sex; each of these activities is depicted in sometimes excruciating verite detail. The narrative center and moral focus of the piece is Telly (Leo Fitzpatrick), a thoroughgoing scumbag with a taste for deflowering and abandoning girls. When one of his conquests, Jennie (Chloe Sevigny), discovers she's HIV-positive, she resolves to find him before he passes on the virus to another innocent girl.

The screenplay, by 21-year-old skateboard enthusiast Harmony Korine, pays apparently clever—though possibly unwitting—homage to Arthur Schnitzler's classic Reigen, which follows the liaisons of a daisy-chain of sex partners. Unlike Schnitzler, however, Korine fails to root his characters in a plausible social context: these kids may be going nowhere, but that's no excuse for neglecting to tell us where they come from. Anyone who has grown up in New York City will detect something irredeemably bogus in the way Korine's characters mingle and match, regardless of class, race, ethnicity, or neighborhood loyalties. Clark's visually trendy rendering of events is generally effective but eventually wears out its welcome: one yearns for a simple, steady tripod shot and release from the tangential glances at homeless people that suggest a Profound Statement in the making.

KIKA

1993 115m c Comedy/Drama   ★★
El Deseo/CiBy 2000 (Spain/France)   NC-17/

Veronica Forque (Kika), Peter Coyote (Nicholas), Victoria Abril (Andrea Scarface), Alex Casanovas (Ramon), Rossy DePalma (Juana), Santiago Lajusticla (Pablo), Anabel Alonso (Amparo), Bibi Andersen (Susana), Jesus Bonilla (Policia 1), Karra Elejalde (Policia 2)

d, Pedro Almodovar; w, Pedro Almodovar; ph, Alfredo Mayo; ed, Pepe Salcedo; cos, Jose Maria Cossia, Gianni Versace

Pedro Almodovar upholds his reputation for controversy with this candy-colored burlesque. Unfortunately, Almodovar's peculiar vision is more repellent than risque here, particularly in his farcical depiction of rape.

Kika (Veronica Forque) is a flirtatious make-up artist who gets involved with several odd characters in modern-day Madrid, including Nicholas (Peter Coyote), a penniless American writer whose wife has just died under suspicious circumstances, and his stepson Ramon (Alex Casanovas), who literally rises from the dead while Kika prepares him for his funeral. After Ramon's "resurrection," he and Kika move in together. Complications include Ramon's sexual quirks; their lesbian maid, Juana (Rossy de Palma), who has a crush on Kika; Juana's mentally retarded, sex-mad, ex-porno star brother Pablo (Santiago Lajusticia), who rapes Kika; Andrea Scarface (Victoria Abril), host of the tabloid TV show "Today's Worst," who shows a videotape of Kika's ordeal on her program; and the fact that Kika is having an affair with Nicholas, who has a very scary secret life.

Despite the presence of some talented and charismatic actresses, KIKA is much closer in spirit to Almodovar's more disturbing recent films (TIE ME UP! TIE ME DOWN! 1989, HIGH HEELS 1991) than WOMEN ON THE VERGE OF A NERVOUS BREAKDOWN (1987), the witty ensemble comedy that put him on the international map. Almodovar's color design is as bright as ever, but his vision is at its ugliest, and many viewers may be put off by his freewheeling, screwball approach to violence against women. That KIKA isn't thoroughly offensive is a tribute to the cast, especially Forque and the striking Abril, a vision in Gaultier and Versace.

KILLER OF SHEEP

1978 80m bw Drama/Comedy ★★★★★
(U.S.)

Henry Gayle Sanders (Stan), Kaycee Moore (Stan's Wife), Charles Bracy (Bracy), Angela Burnett (Stan's Daughter), Eugene Cherry (Eugene), Jack Drummond (Stan's Son)

p, Charles Burnett; d, Charles Burnett; w, Charles Burnett; ph, Charles Burnett; ed, Charles Burnett

Milieu is the main character in Charles Burnett's KILLER OF SHEEP, an essentially plotless look at everyday life in a semi-suburban black neighborhood. The film is probably the most perceptive and poetic study ever done of Americans existing one level above poverty. Produced for a mere $10,000 with an amateur cast, it was one of fewer than 100 pictures proclaimed "national treasures" by the National Film Registry of the Library of Congress in 1990.

Stan (Henry Gayle Sanders), a slaughterhouse worker, complains to a friend about his hard life. When his son (Jack Drummond) persists in teasing his sister (Angela Burnett), he chases the boy out of the house. Stan's wife (Kaycee Moore) attempts to talk to him about his increasing melancholy and lethargy, but he is unresponsive. Two of Stan's friends try to convince him to join them in a murder plot. He refuses and his wife, who has overheard, berates Stan's friends. Stan and his friend, Eugene (Eugene Cherry), visit a man with an old car motor for sale. Minutes after they purchase it, it falls out of the back of Eugene's pickup and is ruined. Stan and his wife share a romantic dance in their parlor but, when she initiates further intimacy, he does not respond and leaves her unhappily alone.

Burnett filmed KILLER OF SHEEP in Watts—the mostly black, largely poor area of Los Angeles where he grew up—and populated it with friends and acquaintances. The movie, which served as his master's thesis at UCLA, took five years to complete. It is a great film and a unique one. Rarely on the screen has authenticity been so artistic, or (relentless) irony so free of cynicism. The squalid settings, gritty black-and-white cinematography, and innate modesty of Burnett's sensibility and temperance of his voice tend at first to mask his enormous gifts. Burnett's overall reluctance to play on audience sympathy does not, however, prevent him from framing many affecting images. KILLER OF SHEEP is everything an independent film should be: artistically ambitious yet accessible; narrowly focused yet suggestive of larger ramifications; and free of obligation to formula, genre, or the star system. Brilliantly conceived, imaginatively structured, superbly written, stylishly composed and photographed, and very often wryly funny, KILLER OF SHEEP lives up to its official designation as a national treasure.

KILLER, THE
(DIE XUE SHUANG XIONG)

1989 110m c Action/Crime ★★★★
Film Workshop/Golden Princess/Magnum (Hong Kong)

Chow Yun-fat (Jeffrey Chow), Sally Yeh (Jennie), Danny Lee (Detective "Eagle" Lee), Kenneth Tsang (Sergeant Randy Chung), Chu Kong (Sydney Fung), Lam Chung (Willie Tsang), Shing Fui-on (Johnny Wang), Ye Rongzu (Tony Weng), Yi Fanwei (Frankie Feng), Huang Guangliang (Wong Tong)

p, Tsui Hark; d, John Woo; w, John Woo; ph, Wong Wing-hang, Peter Pao; ed, Fan Kung-ming; m, Lowell Lowe; art d, Luk Man-wah; cos, Shirley Chan

In the world of John Woo's over-the-top action movies, it seems there's no problem that can't be solved by a hail of bullets. Don't be fooled; THE KILLER is far more than the sum of its plot elements.

Jeffrey Chow (Chow Yun-fat) is a professional killer with his own code of ethics and a lethal two-handed draw. Detective "Eagle" Lee (Danny Lee) is a cop at odds with the system: he'd rather get the scum off the streets than play departmental politics. Sydney Fung (Chu Kong), a hit man past his prime, is Jeff's only friend. Jennie (Sally Yeh) is a nightclub singer caught in the crossfire and blinded when Jeff slaughters a room full of gangsters. Guilt-stricken, Jeff befriends and then falls in love with the blind woman. But when Sydney hires him to kill Tony Weng (Ye Rongzu)—the one last job that will allow him to leave the life of a killer forever—the hit doesn't go off as cleanly as it should, and Lee vows to hunt him down, using Jennie as bait.

THE KILLER rings a genuinely delirious set of changes on American movie themes, careening between brutality and mawkish sentiment without missing a beat. In the days before Quentin Tarantino brought HK stylings to the American screen, Western audiences were almost literally stunned by the extravagance of this film: the insistent visual and narrative symmetry, the barely repressed homoeroticism, the pathetic comedy of blind Jennie—unaware of the gunplay going on around her—trying to serve tea. One moment Woo's heroes are .44 magnum dervishes, the next they're spinning some outrageous fiction about childhood friendship and their nicknames for one another—"Mickey Mouse" and "Dumbo."

And the bullets . . . the bullets. They fly freely at the drop of a hat, splatter bad guys all over the walls while missing the protagonists (special credit to the sightless Jennie, who shows a particular flare for dodging speeding projectiles), and generally make the world go round. For Western viewers unfamiliar with Hong Kong gangster films, there's no better introduction.

KILLERS, THE

1946 102m bw Crime ★★★★★
Universal (U.S.) /A

Burt Lancaster (Swede), Ava Gardner (Kitty Collins), Edmond O'Brien (Jim Reardon), Albert Dekker (Big Jim Colfax), Sam Levene (Lt. Sam Lubinsky), Virginia Christine (Lilly Lubinsky), John Miljan (Jake), Vince Barnett (Charleston), Charles D. Brown (Packy Robinson), Donald MacBride (Kenyon)

p, Mark Hellinger; d, Robert Siodmak; w, Anthony Veiller, John Huston (based on the story by Ernest Hemingway); ph, Elwood Bredell; ed, Arthur Hilton; m, Miklos Rozsa; art d, Jack Otterson, Martin Obzina; fx, David S. Horsley; cos, Vera West

AAN Best Director: Robert Siodmak; AAN Best Original Screenplay: Anthony Veiller; AAN Best Editing: Arthur Hilton; AAN Best Score: Miklos Rozsa

The first Universal production supervised by Hellinger, a one-time reporter turned film producer, this definitive film noir is at least as powerful as his earlier crime movies, THE ROARING TWENTIES and HIGH SIERRA. THE KILLERS, which features a now famous musical score (later used in the "Dragnet" TV series) by Miklos Rosza, is also notable as Burt Lancaster's film debut. The ace crime director Siodmak uses the bare bones of Hemingway's terse story to build a taut and fascinating tale of murder, robbery, and betrayal. It also features one of the genre's most celebrated femme fatales.

It opens with the killers of the Hemingway story (Charles McGraw and William Conrad) entering the diner in search of the Swede (Lancaster). They have a murder contract to fulfill, they learn that he will soon be coming in for dinner. Nick Adams (Phil Brown) overhears the killer's intent and runs to a boarding house to warn the Swede. He listens, but remains indifferently on his bed, explaining simply "I did something wrong... once". With that he quietly awaits his fate. The Hemingway story ends about there, but this is only the beginning of the film. Edmond O'Brien is Jim Reardon, an energetic insurance investigator whose company has to pay off on the Swede's death. By interviewing the Swede's associates, Rearden begins the laborious process of reconstructing the dead man's turbulent life, a process we see through a series of extended flashbacks.

We first see him as a young boxer who gets thrust into the posh and corrupt world of organized crime, overlorded by boss Big Jim Colfax (Dekker). He becomes enamored of the sultry Kitty Collins (Gardner), Colfax's girlfriend. She entices the big, handsome boxer with the promise that she will leave the boss for him if he helps the gang in an elaborate armored car robbery. Kitty and the Swede would then take the loot, double-cross Big Jim, and flee to a life of their own. This sounds too good to be true. It is.

The cast is excellent and Siodmak's direction is hard-edged and moody. Lancaster's personality amazed viewers seeing him for the first time, and he soon reached star status with BRUTE FORCE, I WALK ALONE, ALL MY SONS and other heavyweight films. Lancaster, a former circus acrobat, began his career here at age 32 but looked much younger. THE KILLERS was also the first important dramatic role for Gardner. Hemingway admired Gardner's portrayal of the eternal vixen and they became lifelong friends. She appeared in other Hemingway vehicles, notably THE SNOWS OF KILIMANJARO and THE SUN ALSO RISES.

KILLERS, THE
1964 93m c Crime   ★★★
Revue   (U.S.)

Lee Marvin (*Charlie*), Angie Dickinson (*Sheila Farr*), John Cassavetes (*Johnny North*), Ronald Reagan (*Browning*), Clu Gulager (*Lee*), Claude Akins (*Earl Sylvester*), Norman Fell (*Mickey*), Virginia Christine (*Miss Watson*), Don Haggerty (*Mail Truck Driver*), Robert Phillips (*George*)

p, Don Siegel; d, Don Siegel; w, Gene L. Coon (based on the story by Ernest Hemingway); ph, Richard L. Rawlings; ed, Richard Belding; m, John Williams; art d, Frank Arrigo, George Chan, George O'Connell; cos, Helen Colvig

Hit men Charlie (Marvin) and Lee (Gulager) are ordered to go to a school for the blind and kill Johnny North (Cassavetes), one of the teachers there, who puts up no resistance. They wonder why he accepted his death so passively and who ordered him killed. The killers connect him to an armored car heist several years before from which the money was never recovered. They learn that North was a race car driver in love with Sheila Farr (Dickinson), the mistress of crime czar Browning (Reagan). She had persuaded him to drive the getaway car in the armored car job and they planned to double-cross Browning. But things did not work out that way. As they learn more about the story of the man they killed, the killers develop their own interest in its ultimate outcome.

This was Reagan's final film, and the only one in which he's the villain. THE KILLERS was originally produced for TV by NBC but censors determined it was too violent for that medium, so it was released in theaters. Reagan was reluctant to play the heavy, but the head of Universal at the time, Reagan's former agent, talked him into accepting the part, a decision Reagan still regrets. Though the film does not stand up to the 1946 version with Burt Lancaster, it has its own pleasures, including Marvin's rather likable role of an assassin, the exciting robbery sequence, and, of course, the villainous Reagan getting his just desserts. Two years later he was elected governor of California. And the rest is history.

KILLER'S KISS
1955 67m bw Thriller   ★★★½
Minotaur   (U.S.)   /A

Frank Silvera (*Vincent Rapallo*), Jamie Smith (*Davy Gordon*), Irene Kane (*Gloria Price*), Jerry Jarret (*Albert, the Fight Manager*), Mike Dana, Felice Orlandi, Ralph Roberts, Phil Stevenson (*Gangsters*), Julius Adelman (*Owner of the Mannequin Factory*), David Vaughan
p, Stanley Kubrick; d, Stanley Kubrick; w, Stanley Kubrick, Howard Sackler (based on a story by Kubrick); ph, Stanley Kubrick; ed, Stanley Kubrick; m, Gerald Fried; chor, David Vaughan

The second film directed by future master filmmaker Stanley Kubrick, KILLER'S KISS is no one's idea of a great film but it displays much evidence of future brilliance. The story is nothing more than B-movie film noir fodder, but some of the images and set pieces are indelible.

Davy Gordon (Smith) is a second-rate prizefighter who gets romantically involved with Gloria Price (Kane), a young dancer who lives across the courtyard in his apartment building. Returning home one night after another lost fight, he sees Price fending off a rapist. The assailant is Vincent Rapallo (Silvera), Price's boss at the nightclub where she dances. Gordon rescues her and they decide to flee the city. But Rapallo plans a murderous revenge. ...

This modest thriller was financed for $75,000 by various friends and relatives of the neophyte filmmaker. He served not only as director, writer and producer but also filmed and edited the project. Though the screenplay is undistinguished (and gives no hint of what Kubrick's future ability as a writer), he makes some interesting choices as a director.

The vivid flashbacks and surrealistic nightmare sequences are memorable. The nightmares are represented on negative film stock, an interesting and effective choice. Other idiosyncratic touches include the disorienting contrast created by showing a bloody boxing match on a television screen while an equally violent near-rape and struggle occurs between the nominal viewers, and the surreal effect achieved by using of the dismembered limbs of female mannequins as weapons during a brutal fight sequence in a factory.

All in all, it's hardly Kubrick's best work, but is a revealing early look at a visual style that soon ripened to maturity to produce such film classics as PATHS OF GLORY, SPARTACUS, DR. STRANGELOVE, 2001: A SPACE ODYSSEY, and A CLOCKWORK ORANGE. This film was also the inspiration for Matthew Chapman's film, STRANGER'S KISS.

KILLING, THE
1956 83m bw Crime   ★★★★½
UA   (U.S.)   /A

Sterling Hayden (*Johnny Clay*), Coleen Gray (*Fay*), Vince Edwards (*Val Cannon*), Jay C. Flippen (*Marvin Unger*), Marie Windsor (*Sherry Peatty*), Ted de Corsia (*Randy Kennan*), Elisha Cook Jr. (*George Peatty*), Joe Sawyer (*Mike O'Reilly*), Timothy Carey (*Nikki Arane*), Jay Adler (*Leo*)
p, James B. Harris; d, Stanley Kubrick; w, Stanley Kubrick, Jim Thompson (based on the novel *Clean Break* by Lionel White); ph, Lucien Ballard; ed, Betty Steinberg; m, Gerald Fried; art d, Ruth Sobotka Kubrick; cos, Rudy Harrington

Hardboiled early Kubrick. This lean, mean genre film is similar in mood and structure to John Huston's earlier THE ASPHALT JUNGLE, but many of Kubrick's characteristic obsessions are already firmly in place: fatally flawed humans, complicated interlocking timetables and meticulous plans gone awry.

Johnny Clay (Hayden) is an ex-con who tells his childhood sweetheart, Fay (Gray), that he and a few others are going to make a "big score" that will be his last caper. During a race at the local racetrack he intends to rob the money room where the betting take is kept, while Nikki Arane (Carey), a professional killer, shoots one of the horses on the far turn to create a diversion. Clay assembles a group of associates for the job, each with some problem that is getting too big for him to handle: Marvin Unger (Flippen), a retired friend; Randy Kennan (de Corsia), a cop who owes the syndicate money; Mike O'Reilly (Sawyer), a bartender at the racetrack who needs money for his sick wife; and George Peatty (Cook), a cashier at the track with a money-grubbing wife (Windsor). They are all ordinary men "with a touch of larceny in their souls." Everything is planned down to the smallest detail but things go terribly wrong.

THE KILLING brought Kubrick to the attention of the industry as a major directorial talent even though this film was produced on a small budget of $320,000—and it shows. The sets are like cardboard but Kubrick emphasizes that fact, panning his camera from one room to another, showing partitions, devising every conceivable angle from which to shoot, so that the space in which his actors move appears as it really is, confining, cramped, and claustrophobic, reflecting the attitudes of his characters. The film's semi-documentary feel is only enhanced by its meticulous intersecting flashback structure. Time becomes a palpable presence in this fatalistic film.

Hayden gives a stoical top drawer performance as the nominal leader of this unprofessional gang of thieves. Cook gives one of the best performances of his career as the henpecked little man who suffers an avalanche of insults from his wretched wife, Windsor, whose own performance is spectacular.

KILLING FIELDS, THE

1984   141m   c   Drama/War   ★★★½
Enigma/Goldcrest   (U.K.)   R/15

Sam Waterston (*Sydney Schanberg*), Haing S. Ngor (*Dith Pran*), John Malkovich (*Al Rockoff*), Julian Sands (*Jon Swain*), Craig T. Nelson (*Military Attache*), Spalding Gray (*US Consul*), Bill Paterson (*Dr. Macentire*), Athol Fugard (*Dr. Sundesval*), Graham Kennedy (*Dougal*), Katherine Krapum Chey (*Ser Moeun*)

p, David Puttnam; d, Roland Joffe; w, Bruce Robinson (based on the magazine article "The Death and Life of Dith Pran," by Sydney Schanberg); ph, Chris Menges; ed, Jim Clark; m, Mike Oldfield; prod d, Roy Walker; art d, Roger Murray Leach, Steve Spence; fx, Fred Cramer; cos, Judy Moorcroft

AAN Best Picture; AAN Best Actor: Sam Waterston; AA Best Supporting Actor: Haing S. Ngor; AAN Best Director: Roland Joffe; AAN Best Adapted Screenplay: Bruce Robinson; AA Best Cinematography: Chris Menges; AA Best Editing: Jim Clark

A deeply moving film, THE KILLING FIELDS is the somewhat-fictionalized story of *New York Times* reporter Sydney Schanberg (Sam Waterston) and his efforts to find his friend Dith Pran (Haing S. Ngor) after the Cambodian translator falls into the hands of the brutal Khmer Rouge. Although Dith's family is evacuated with the last US personnel to leave Phnom Penh, Schanberg persuades his translator to remain behind with him; and when Khmer Rouge troops enter the city, Dith convinces them that Schanberg and his photographer (John Malkovich) are French.

Regrettably, Schanberg is unable to return the favor later, and Dith is sent off to a rural reeducation camp, which he barely survives but eventually escapes. While undertaking the arduous journey to safety, he comes across the horrifying remains of some of the three million people who died at the hands of the Khmer Rouge. Meanwhile, racked with guilt, Schanberg, who has received a Pulitzer Prize for "international reporting at great risk," does everything he can to locate his friend.

THE KILLING FIELDS wisely emphasizes the human element of its story, concentrating on Schanberg and Dith's friendship, and lets the political situation speak for itself. Haing S. Ngor, the Cambodian physician whose real-life experiences were similar to those of the character he plays, gives a sincere, heartrending performance that is the film's emotional core. Although Waterston is less effective, he too contributes a believable performance, as does Malkovich in an impressive film debut. Aided by Chris Menges' spectacular Oscar winning cinematography, director Roland Joffe's first feature is a significant achievement, its sequences unfolding with precision as the emotions mount.

KIND HEARTS AND CORONETS

1949   105m   bw   Comedy   ★★★★★
Ealing   (U.K.)   /U

Dennis Price (*Louis Mazzini*), Valerie Hobson (*Edith D'Ascoyne*), Joan Greenwood (*Sibella*), Alec Guinness (*Duke/Banker/ Parson etc.*), Audrey Fildes (*Mama*), Miles Malleson (*The Hangman*), Clive Morton (*Prison Governor*), John Penrose (*Lionel*), Cecil Ramage (*Crown Counsel*), Hugh Griffith (*Lord High Steward*)

p, Michael Balcon; d, Robert Hamer; w, Robert Hamer, John Dighton (based on a novel by Roy Horniman); ph, Douglas Slocombe; ed, Peter Tanner; m, Wolfgang Amadeus Mozart; art d, William Kellner

Coming on the heels of GREAT EXPECTATIONS and OLIVER TWIST, this was the film that made Alec Guinness an international star. Although Dennis Price has the largest single role in the picture (and plays it beautifully), Guinness took the lion's share of the credit for its success with a *tour de force* performance as no less than eight characters, all members of the same family. A black comedy about mass murder, KIND HEARTS AND CORONETS is one of the British film industry's funniest movies, as well as one of the most memorable and notorious.

The action is set around 1900. Price is in line to a dukedom, but is treated as a pariah because of his mother's unfortunate marriage. Seething with class resentment, he decides to remove all the obstacles in his way. While conducting an affair with the married Greenwood, he begins knocking off his relatives in various fanciful ways. Matters are complicated when he falls in love with Hobson, the widow of one of his victims. But after Price ascends to the dukedom and marries Hobson, fate catches up: he's arrested for a murder he did *not* commit.

The film is full of bright dialogue and quotable quotes ("Revenge is the dish which people of taste prefer to eat cold!"). Robert Hamer (who also directed) and John Dighton loosely based the story on Roy Horniman's turn-of-the-century novel *Israel Rank,* dispensing with all but the core of the book to write the sharp screenplay. The result, KIND HEARTS AND CORONETS, is one of those films that can be seen repeatedly and still offer surprises. As a combination of rollicking black humor and satirical pokes at the English upper crust, nothing else comes close.

KIND OF LOVING, A

1962   112m   bw   Drama   ★★★★
Vic/Waterhall   (U.K.)   /15

Alan Bates (*Vic Brown*), June Ritchie (*Ingrid Rothwell*), Thora Hird (*Mrs. Rothwell*), Bert Palmer (*Mr. Brown*), Gwen Nelson (*Mrs. Brown*), Malcolm Patton (*Jim Brown*), Pat Keen (*Christine*), David Mahlowe (*David*), Jack Smethurst (*Conroy*), James Bolam (*Jeff*)

p, Joseph Janni; d, John Schlesinger; w, Willis Hall, Keith Waterhouse (based on the novel by Stan Barstow); ph, Denys Coop; ed, Roger Cherrill; m, Ron Grainer; art d, Ray Simm; cos, Laura Nightingale

A kind of marvelous. One of the greatest achievements of the marriage between "angry young man" drama and the Free Cinema movement in Britain in the early 1960s, this was Schlesinger's first feature after a successful sojourn in commercials.

Bates stars as Vic Brown, a draftsman in a Lancashire factory attracted to Ingrid Rothwell (Ritchie), a typist at the plant. They sleep together at her place when her mother (Hird) is out of town and though Ingrid falls hard for Vic, he soon loses interest in her. Her pregnancy, however, leads to marriage and life with the domineering, snobbish Mrs. Rothwell. After Ingrid has a miscarriage Vic regrets having said "I do" and goes off on a bender. The film comes to its sober conclusion as the confused young couple sort through their relationship and wonder if "a kind of loving" is possible.

It's not much of a story when summarized, but that's part of the film's beauty, and the script and direction elevate this film far beyond the norm. Shot almost like a documentary, this low-key production reveals, as few have, the power of realism as a style.

Other than Bates, who was fairly recognizable to film audiences, many of the actors were newcomers with little or no film experience. This lack of movie stars works to the film's advantage, as Bates and Ritchie are simply superb as a young pair who act first and think later. Schlesinger is unafraid to expose the unsympathetic qualities of his characters, and the result is a remarkably rounded drama.

KING AND COUNTRY

That seasoned veteran Thora Hird is at or near her greatest, and the casting throughout is well-nigh perfect. There's not a false note in the picture, and Schlesinger's supple control and Waterhouse and Hall's moving screenplay deserve much of the credit. Despite the grimy surroundings and downbeat theme, A KIND OF LOVING is filled with humor, insight and intelligence which make it an unjustly overlooked landmark in British cinema.

KING AND COUNTRY

1964 86m bw War ★★★★½
BHE (U.K.) /PG

Dirk Bogarde (*Capt. Hargreaves*), Tom Courtenay (*Pvt. Arthur Hamp*), Leo McKern (*Capt. O'Sullivan*), Barry Foster (*Lt. Webb*), James Villiers (*Capt. Midgley*), Peter Copley (*Colonel*), Barry Justice (*Lt. Prescott*), Vivian Matalon (*Padre*), Jeremy Spenser (*Pvt. Sparrow*), James Hunter (*Pvt. Sykes*)

p, Joseph Losey, Norman Priggen; d, Joseph Losey; w, Evan Jones (based on the play *Hamp* by John Wilson, from an episode in the novel *Return to the Wood* by James Lansdale Hodson); ph, Denys Coop; ed, Reginald Mills; m, Larry Adler; prod d, Richard MacDonald; art d, Peter Mullins; cos, Roy Ponting

This brutally frank, thoughtful anti-war tract contains no battle scenes and little gunfire. Bogarde is a British captain assigned to defend a slow-witted soldier, Courtenay, who has been accused of desertion. Highly educated and a strict military disciplinarian, Bogarde approaches this assignment with distaste. Consequently, he accepts his superior's expedient suggestion that he ignore Courtenay's shell-shocked state and push for a quick conviction. While interviewing his client, Bogarde learns that Courtenay enlisted in the army on a dare from friends. Three years later, the uneducated soldier—having learned of his wife's infidelity and emerging from a battle as the sole survivor of his unit—falls victim to what we now call "post traumatic stress syndrome." Fed up and very very tired, Courtenay simply wanted to "go for a walk". Twenty four hours later, he's still walking along the road when he's taken into custody. During the testimony Bogarde begins to feel sympathy for the obviously sincere and somewhat confused Courtenay. For the first time in his military career, Bogarde begins to question the army's methods and attitudes toward its men.

KING AND COUNTRY is a grim indictment of the arrogant, simple-minded mentality of the men who send their fellow citizens off to war. A good army is driven by discipline and devotion to duty, but director Losey shows us that things are not that simple. Bogarde's character is a cold, unblinking automaton, and therefore quite successful in the military. His interviews with Courtenay change all that. KING AND COUNTRY is an extremely claustrophobic film that takes place in dark, dirty, rat-infested interiors; shot mostly in long, deep-focus takes, they effectively portray the situation of all concerned as both physically and morally cramped. Tom Courtenay won the best actor award at the Venice film festival for his performance.

KING AND I, THE

1956 133m c Musical ★★★★
Fox (U.S.) G/U

Deborah Kerr (*Anna Leonowens*), Yul Brynner (*The King*), Rita Moreno (*Tuptim*), Martin Benson (*Kralahome*), Terry Saunders (*Lady Thiang*), Rex Thompson (*Louis Leonowens*), Carlos Rivas (*Lun Tha*), Patrick Adiarte (*Prince Chulalongkorn*), Alan Mowbray (*British Ambassador*), Geoffrey Toone (*Ramsay*)

p, Charles Brackett; d, Walter Lang; w, Ernest Lehman (based on the musical by Oscar Hammerstein II and Richard Rodgers, from the book *Anna and The King of Siam* by Margaret Landon); ph, Leon Shamroy; ed, Robert Simpson; m, Richard Rodgers; art d, Lyle Wheeler, John De Cuir; chor, Jerome Robbins; cos, Irene Sharaff

AAN Best Picture; AA Best Actor: Yul Brynner; *AAN Best Actress:* Deborah Kerr; *AAN Best Director:* Walter Lang; *AAN Best Cinematography:* Leon Shamroy; *AA Best Score:* Alfred Newman, Ken Darby; *AA Best Art Direction:* Lyle R. Wheeler, John DeCuir, Walter M. Scott, Paul S. Fox; *AA Best Costume Design:* Irene Sharaff; *AA Best Sound:* Carl Faulkner

Starring Yul Brynner in the part he seemed born to play, this is a fine if slightly stage-bound example of the 1950s Hollywood musical spectacular.

Deborah Kerr is an English schoolteacher who journeys to Siam with her son, Thompson. She has been hired by the king (Brynner) to teach his many children about the world outside their kingdom. Arrogant and chauvinistic, the King is very comfortable as the unchallenged ruler of his land. Kerr herself is a very strong woman, and it isn't long before the two are at odds, mainly because Brynner is stunned by her unwillingness to bend to his every whim. In a series of vignettes, Kerr is shown teaching the children, dealing with problems within the household (one of which involves persuading Brynner to let Moreno, one of his wives, leave because she loves another), and verbally sparring with the king. Eventually, Kerr wins Brynner's respect and his love.

Even without the music, this well-written story would be a splendid entertainment. But it's the music, that wonderful score written by Rodgers and Hammerstein, that makes this movie as beloved as it is. Kerr's voice was looped by that most ubiquitous of song loopers, Marni Nixon (wife of music composer Ernest Gold), who did the singing for, among others, Audrey Hepburn in MY FAIR LADY and Natalie Wood in WEST SIDE STORY. Brynner, of course, is marvelous in the role of the supreme ruler who slowly comes to realize he's behind the times. He won an Oscar for his portrayal, and continued to do the play on the stage. At the time of his death in 1985, he had played the king in more than 4,000 performances. The screenplay by Ernest Lehman, who went on to write the adaptation of Rogers and Hammerstein's THE SOUND OF MUSIC, is faithful to the play, and even improves on it somewhat.

KING KONG

1933 100m bw Science Fiction/Adventure/Fantasy ★★★★½
RKO (U.S.) /PG

Fay Wray (*Ann Darrow*), Robert Armstrong (*Carl Denham*), Bruce Cabot (*John Driscoll*), Frank Reicher (*Capt. Englehorn*), Sam Hardy (*Charles Weston*), Noble Johnson (*Native Chief*), Steve Clemente (*Witch King*), James Flavin (*2nd Mate Briggs*), Victor Wong (*Charley*), Paul Porcasi (*Socrates*)

p, Merian C. Cooper, Ernest B. Schoedsack; d, Merian C. Cooper, Ernest B. Schoedsack; w, James Ashmore Creelman, Ruth Rose (based on a story by Cooper and Edgar Wallace); ph, Eddie Linden, Vernon Walker, J.O. Taylor; ed, Ted Cheesman; m, Max Steiner; art d, Carroll Clark, Al Herman, Van Nest Polglase; fx, Willis O'Brien, E.B. Gibson, Marcel Delgado, Fred Reese, Orville Goldner, Carroll L. Shepphird, Mario Larrinaga, Byron L. Crabbe

The ultimate monster movie and one of the grandest and most beloved adventure films ever made, KING KONG is a film that has given us one of the most enduring icons of American popular culture—a massively destructive but curiously sympathetic giant gorilla whose rampage through New York City suggests, on a psychological level, the re-emergence of repressed desire. While Kong is, in most scenes, only an 18-inch studio model, the stop motion special effects are so intelligently accomplished and lovingly detailed that the animated gorilla often appears more expressive than the human actors.

Hollywood filmmaker Carl Denham (Robert Armstrong) takes starlet Ann Darrow (Fay Wray) to a mysterious prehistoric island in search of the legendary King Kong, a giant ape worshipped as a god by the local natives. "Bet they've never seen a blonde before!" some wag observes. They find the giant beast and it falls in love with Ann. Denham manages to capture the monster and bring it back to New York City for display, but Kong breaks loose and wreaks havoc on Manhattan in his search for his beloved Ann.

As a monster, Kong is akin to Boris Karloff's interpretation of the Frankenstein monster—more victim than victimizer. Of course, Kong was a fearful monster who killed with abandon and could destroy entire cities given a chance, but the beast had desires, a temper, needs and fears, and could feel emotions that audiences to this day identify with. No man in an ape suit could convey such a complex variety of emotions—only a fine actor or a master in the art of stop-motion animation, such as Willis O'Brien, who was able to create one of the cinema's most unique and memorable characters from an inanimate 18-inch stop-motion model.

On its initial release, at the height of the Great Depression, KING KONG grossed $1,761,000 and by itself saved the studio that produced it from bankruptcy. In 1938, the studio decided to re-release its classic, but took several steps to tone it down. The film had been made before 1934 when the Production Code began to be vigorously enforced. In accordance with the revised rules of the game, cut were the scenes of Kong chewing and crushing human beings. Gone was the scene in which a curious Kong strips Fay Wray of her clothing. In fact, RKO made the new release prints several shades darker in an effort to tone down the incredible detail of O'Brien's work (dying dinosaurs bleeding, etc.) that made everything seem so realistic.

This travesty practically obliterated the steps O'Brien took to ensure that his creations would *live* onscreen. Generations of moviegoers and television watchers were thus denied the true, uncut brilliance of the vision of Merian C. Cooper, Ernest B. Schoedsack, and O'Brien, until recently, when restored prints of KING KONG began to circulate both in revival houses and on home video. It's probably best, for your viewing pleasure if not for your conscience, if you don't think too hard about the racist subtext.

KING LEAR

1988   90m   c   Drama/Experimental   ★★★★
Cannon   (U.S./France)   /15

Burgess Meredith *(Don Learo)*, Peter Sellars *(William Shakespeare, Jr., V)*, Molly Ringwald *(Cordelia)*, Jean-Luc Godard *(Professor)*, Woody Allen *(Mr. Alien)*, Norman Mailer *(Himself)*, Kate Mailer *(Herself)*, Leos Carax *(Edgar)*

p, Menahem Golan, Yoram Globus; d, Jean-Luc Godard; w, Jean-Luc Godard (based on the play by William Shakespeare); ph, Sophie Maintigneux

It should come as no surprise that in this film version of Shakespeare's play, director Jean-Luc Godard shows very little concern for plot, or that—as with every addition to the Godard canon—KING LEAR further considers his previous ideas, preoccupations, and experiments. Though many will cry foul at this adaptation of Shakespeare, KING LEAR, in an odd sense, does more with the original than any number of faithful, literary adaptations by allowing the material to transcend its medium and find new power in a modern time. As usual, Godard is also interested in self-consciously exploring his own position as a filmmaker.

The film opens with Godard and producer Menahem Golem discussing the making of the film, and throughout we see shots of famous deceased directors. The rest is full of audacious experiments in sound, and bizarre casting with lots of established, movie star types (the weirdest of all being Molly Ringwald). Godard casts himself, in Rastafarian dreadlocks as the Fool in this often heady convergence of high camp, solemn philosophy, Fellini's 8 1/2, and someone's drug trip. A challenge, as with all Godard, but not quite his most rewarding one.

KING OF COMEDY, THE

1983   108m   c   Comedy/Drama   ★★★★½
20th Century Fox   (U.S.)   PG

Robert De Niro *(Rupert Pupkin)*, Jerry Lewis *(Jerry Langford)*, Diahnne Abbott *(Rita)*, Sandra Bernhard *(Masha)*, Ed Herlihy *(Himself)*, Louis Brown *(Bandleader)*, Whitey Ryan *(Stage Door Guard)*, Doc Lawless *(Chauffeur)*, Marta Heflin *(Young Girl)*, Katherine Wallach

p, Arnon Milchan; d, Martin Scorsese; w, Paul Zimmerman; ph, Fred Schuler; ed, Thelma Schoonmaker; m, Robbie Robertson; prod d, Boris Leven; art d, Edward Pisoni, Lawrence Miller; cos, Richard Bruno

Martin Scorsese and Robert DeNiro must be the most celebrated director/star collaborators in recent American film history. Together they have produced some of the most powerful films of the last several decades—MEAN STREETS, TAXI DRIVER, RAGING BULL, GOODFELLAS—but here they tried something a little different and the result is a chilling black comedy.

Robert De Niro is tragic, goofy and crazy as Rupert Pupkin, a grown man working as a messenger and living in his parents' basement. (Scorsese's own mother is the off-screen voice of the unseen Mrs.

Pupkin.) Pupkin is a Times Square hangabout who dogs celebrities for autographs but imagines himself the greatest comic in the world, patterning himself on his hero, funnyman talk-show host Jerry Langford (Jerry Lewis in a part written for the erstwhile King of Late Night, Johnny Carson). His dream is that he will appear on Langford's show, perform his comedy routine, and then take his rightful place among the stars. He'll have none of that nonsense about learning his craft and working his way up the ladder of success; he wants it *now*.

At the beginning of the film, Pupkin ingratiates himself with Langford by helping him fend off some particularly manic autograph seekers. Slipping into the car with Langford, he introduces himself as a yet-undiscovered great comedian who has written some terrific material. Initially Langford encourages him, but eventually Pupkin becomes a major nuisance. At first he hangs around the network offices for a followup meeting until he must be physically thrown out. Eventually he works up to calling on Mr. Langford at his fabulous country retreat. He resorts, at last, to even more drastic measures to get his big break on television.

De Niro gives a miraculous character performance, much different from the intense brooding loners for which he is renowned. He seems to disappear into this oddball, somewhat repulsive, but ultimately rather touching character. Sandra Bernhard, in her film debut, is nearly as memorable as Rupert's outrageous partner in crime. As a thoroughly demented, poor little rich girl who yearns to physically possess her favorite celebrity, Bernhard is simultaneously frightening, unconventionally sexy and *very* funny. THE KING OF COMEDY was a huge flop upon its release. Let's hope that future generations will hail it as the classic it truly is.

KING OF HEARTS
(LE ROI DE COEUR)

1966   100m   c   Comedy/Drama/War   ★★★½
Artistes Associes/Montoro/Fildebroc   (France/Italy)   /A

Alan Bates *(Pvt. Charles Plumpick)*, Pierre Brasseur *(Gen. Geranium)*, Jean-Claude Brialy *(The Duke—Le Duc de Trefle)*, Genevieve Bujold *(Coquelicot)*, Adolfo Celi *(Col. Alexander MacBibenbrook)*, Micheline Presle *(Mme. Eglantine)*, Francoise Christophe *(The Duchess)*, Julien Guiomar *(Bishop Daisy—Monseigneur Marguerite)*, Michel Serrault *(The Crazy Barber)*, Marc Dudicourt *(Lt. Hamburger)*

p, Philippe de Broca; d, Philippe de Broca; w, Daniel Boulanger (based on an idea by Maurice Bessy); ph, Pierre Lhomme; ed, Francoise Javet; m, Georges Delerue; art d, Francois de Lamothe; cos, Jacques Fonteray

Breathing new life into old themes, Philippe de Broca's charming antiwar fable KING OF HEARTS has been a perennial favorite on college campuses since it first reached the screen at the height of the Vietnam War.

Set during WWI, the occupying Germans retreat from the town of Marville, France, but not before leaving behind a time bomb. The fleeing townspeople tell the approaching British forces about the hidden explosives, and Pvt. Charles Plumpick (Bates, quite appealing), a poetry-loving Scotsman, is dispatched to locate the bomb. To avoid the German rear guard, Plumpick ducks into Marville's insane asylum, and the inmates hail him as the "King of Hearts" before retaking the town and resuming their former lives in a decidedly loony fashion.

While trying to find and defuse the bomb, Plumpick comes to love the crazy citizens, especially Coquelicot (Bujold). In time, the Germans and British clash in Marville, littering the town with bodies, and, when the townspeople return, Plumpick is left with a choice: go back to soldiering or join the "crazy" folks in the asylum. The film's last shot is justifiably famous.

In addition to its strong antiwar message, KING OF HEARTS ponders the old question of who's crazier, the people who accept life's brutality or those who reject it. Some have said that de Broca states his case with a heavy hand—and he does—but for those willing to open themselves to a lighthearted treatment of this all-too-serious subject, KING OF HEARTS will be both touching and life-affirming.

KING OF KINGS

1961 168m c Religious/Biography ★★★½
MGM (U.S.) /U

Jeffrey Hunter (*Jesus Christ*), Siobhan McKenna (*Mary*), Hurd Hatfield (*Pontius Pilate*), Ron Randell (*Lucius, the Centurion*), Viveca Lindfors (*Claudia*), Rita Gam (*Herodias*), Carmen Sevilla (*Mary Magdalene*), Brigid Bazlen (*Salome*), Harry Guardino (*Barabbas*), Rip Torn (*Judas*)

p, Samuel Bronston; d, Nicholas Ray; w, Philip Yordan; ph, Franz Planer, Milton Krasner, Manuel Berenguer; ed, Harold F. Kress, Renee Lichtig; m, Miklos Rozsa; fx, Alex Weldon, Lee LeBlanc; chor, Betty Utey; cos, Georges Wakhevitch

This excellent biblical epic was produced by the legendary Samuel Bronston and directed with a skillful mix of spiritual reverence and cinematic imagination by Nicholas Ray. The film covers the 33 years from Jesus Christ's birth in Bethlehem through the Crucifixion, Resurrection and Ascension. Included are His relationship with John, the 40 days in the desert, the choosing of the Apostles, the Sermon on the Mount, and Judas's betrayal at the Passover seder that was Jesus's Last Supper.

Although Ray Bradbury is not credited, he reportedly wrote the narration spoken by Orson Welles, whose incredible voice and delivery would add dignity and import to dirty limericks. Jeffrey Hunter, not really a major actor, is much more effective than one would expect as Jesus, and Robert Ryan is excellent as John. Hurd Hatfield, though, who sadly never recovered from his initial amazing impression in THE PICTURE OF DORIAN GRAY, goes a bit over the top as Pilate. Other outstanding performances are contributed by Royal Dano, Harry Guardino, Viveca Lindfors and Rip Torn.

KING OF KINGS is an epic of considerable scope, filled with broad vistas, yet there are enough intimate moments to give audience a chance to engage with the characters rather than just admire their pontificating. This is a film where people sweat and labor, and the film, though hardly great, is much better for it. Credit reasonable and restrained writing by Yordan and Ray's sense of judgment for this one.

KING OF MARVIN GARDENS, THE

1972 103m c Drama ★★½
BBS (U.S.) R/X

Jack Nicholson (*David Staebler*), Bruce Dern (*Jason Staebler*), Ellen Burstyn (*Sally*), Julia Robinson (*Jessica*), Scatman Crothers (*Lewis*), Charles Lavine (*Grandfather*), Arnold Williams (*Rosko*), John Ryan (*Surtees*), Sully Boyar (*Lebowitz*), Josh Mostel (*Frank*)

p, Bob Rafelson; d, Bob Rafelson; w, Jacob Brackman (based on a story by Jacob Brackman and Bob Rafelson); ph, Laszlo Kovacs; ed, John F. Link II; art d, Toby Rafelson; cos, Tony Scarano

Alternately dreary and fascinating, THE KING OF MARVIN GARDENS is half of a terrific film, but director Rafelson didn't know which half. After the success of FIVE EASY PIECES, Rafelson attempted to create something as different as possible, but his quest for uniqueness is what did him in.

Nicholson plays David Staebler, a long-winded FM talk jockey on a Philadelphia radio station. Instead of playing records, he waxes on about his brother Jason (Dern) and the things they did as children. He dubs Jason "The King of Marvin Gardens," in reference to the Monopoly board game landmark and the actual place in Atlantic City. David goes back to Atlantic City to visit Jason, now working for Lewis (Crothers), head of a black crime syndicate.

Jason is in jail on a "grand theft auto" charge and is released on bail. He and David have a happy reunion, and Jason introduces his baby brother to Sally (Burstyn), a fading ex-beauty queen, and her step-daughter (Robinson). Jason tells David of his pipe dream to buy a small island near Hawaii and the others, humoring him, help him stage a beauty contest spoof. Things get hairy when David realizes Jason intends to use Lewis' money to buy his dream island.

Much of the film has been deliberately confused (or so it seems) by Rafelson and Brackman in order to flatten the crease between fantasy and reality. For all its faults, THE KING OF MARVIN GARDENS has some merit and many of the individual scenes linger in the memory. It appeared to be a melange of the 1960s mentality of FIVE EASY

PIECES with a 1940s-type plot of irony and surprise. The weakest part of the film was the repetitious, indulgent dialogue credited to Brackman, but one wonders how much of that was in the script and how much Rafelson and his actors improvised. The film is a fairly daring if rather pretentious attempt at originality, but this type of intimate narrative generally requires that one be given the pleasure of caring about the characters.

KING OF NEW YORK

1990 103m c Crime ★★★
Augusto Caminito (Italy/U.S.) R/18

Christopher Walken (*Frank White*), David Caruso (*Dennis Gilley*), Laurence Fishburne (*Jimmy Jump*), Victor Argo (*Roy Bishop*), Wesley Snipes (*Thomas Flannigan*), Janet Julian (*Jennifer Poe*), Joey Chin (*Larry Wong*), Giancarlo Esposito (*Lance*), Paul Calderon (*Joey Dalesio*), Steve Buscemi

p, Mary Kane; d, Abel Ferrara; w, Nicholas St. John; ph, Bojan Bazelli; ed, Anthony Redman; m, Joe Delia; prod d, Alex Tavoularis; art d, Stephanie Ziemer; fx, Matt Vogel; cos, Carol Ramsey

Frank White (Walken), a middle-aged drug lord, is released from prison to find that the streets of New York are tougher and less forgiving than they were when he went in. Still, his gang remains loyal, and his enemies—police and thieves alike—are as hostile as ever. Frank, though, has changed, and decides to make a positive mark on society. Countless hurdles, however, stand in the way of his civic-minded ambitions, which revolve around raising the money needed to keep a public hospital open in a poverty-stricken neighborhood. For starters, he has made a bad name for himself in virtually every ethnic enclave in the city. Nevertheless, White decides to team with Lance Wong (Chin), a young Chinatown dealer who has a huge shipment of drugs to move. Wong's lack of altruism ("If I wanted socialized medicine, I'd have stayed in the Peking province") is a problem, as is the hostility of the Mafia, which is horrified by White's interracial operation. Further complicating White's efforts are some frustrated Brooklyn cops willing to use any means necessary to put an end to White's plans. Hot-headed Dennis Gilley (Caruso), in particular, persuades his fellow officers that the system favors the criminal, and that if anything is to be done about White, it won't be done by the book. Doomed from the start, White's plan precipitates a wave of violence.

Ferrara and St. John's vision of New York is jittery, complex, and defined by juxtapositions of wealth and poverty, legal and illegal commerce, politics and crime, business and recreation that are so extreme as to verge on the ludicrous. Their New York is the biggest, glossiest, most high-tech banana republic conceivable, a jungle of steel and concrete animated by atavistic rhythms and primitive, clannish conceptions of loyalty. Ferrara's great gift as a director is his ferocious sense of place: New York's boroughs, ethnic neighborhoods, subways, hotels, landmarks, bars and fast-food joints are all convincingly rendered here.

KING SOLOMON'S MINES

1937 80m bw Adventure ★★★½
Gaumont (U.K.) /U

Paul Robeson (*Umbopa*), Cedric Hardwicke (*Allan Quartermaine*), Roland Young (*Cmdr. Good*), John Loder (*Henry Curtis*), Anna Lee (*Kathy O'Brien*), Sydney Fairbrother (*Gagool*), Majabalo Hiubi (*Kapsie*), Ecce Homo Toto (*Infadoos*), Robert Adams (*Twala*), Frederick Leister (*Wholesaler*)

d, Robert Stevenson; w, A.R. Rawlinson, Charles Bennett, Ralph Spence (based on the novel by H. Rider Haggard); ph, Bernard Knowles

Memorable version of H. Rider Haggard's oft-filmed novel which boasts superior production values and an excellent performance from Robeson. Spunky Irishwoman Kathy O'Brien (Lee) becomes determined to search for her father, who has disappeared deep in the African jungles while searching for the fabled diamond cache known as King Solomon's Mines. She is accompanied by three explorers (Hardwicke, Young, and Loder) and is guided through the treacherous territory by dignified African native Umbopa (Robeson). After hacking their way through desert and jungle, the small party finally arrives at an encampment of natives who look to the white explorers as gods. The tribe is run by an evil king who had stolen the throne from Umbopa years ago with the help of the witch Gagool (Fairbrother). Sensing a threat to their reign, the king and Gagool plot to kill the newcomers. The explorers manage to defend themselves, though, by capitalizing on a soon-to-arrive solar eclipse to prove that their magic is more powerful than Gagool's. Refusing to give up, the deposed king leads an attack by rival warriors. A final battle, the discovery of the mine and an ill-timed volcano bring the story to its thundering close.

Robeson almost singlehandedly undermines the racism in this classic adventure tale. It's a shame he had to go to England to become a movie star and even then (with occasional exceptions like PROUD VALLEY) he was generally cast as semi-articulate but sweet African natives. In this respect his very American singing interludes throw the entire film out of kilter, but he's so good that one really doesn't care.

He, Hardwicke, Fairbrother and Young are the standouts in KING SOLOMON'S MINES, which does less well by its romantic lead roles. Kathy and Henry are not choice parts, and the generally reliable Loder and the less-than-reliable Lee don't come off so well. Their love scenes tend to put a damper on the film between action highlights. The script is decent and director Stevenson shows the promise he would later (sometimes) get to display in Hollywood.

KING SOLOMON'S MINES

1950 102m c Adventure ★★★★
MGM (U.S.) /U

Deborah Kerr *(Elizabeth Curtis)*, Stewart Granger *(Allan Quartermain)*, Richard Carlson *(John Goode)*, Hugo Haas *(Van Brun)*, Lowell Gilmore *(Eric Masters)*, Kimursi *(Khiva)*, Siriaque *(Umbopa)*, Sekaryongo *(Chief Gagool)*, Baziga *(King Twala)*, Munto Anampio *(Chief Bilu)*

p, Sam Zimbalist; d, Compton Bennett, Andrew Marton; w, Helen Deutsch (based on the novel by H. Rider Haggard); ph, Robert Surtees; ed, Ralph E. Winters, Conrad A. Nervig; art d, Cedric Gibbons, Conrad A. Nervig; cos, Walter Plunkett

AAN Best Picture; AA Best Cinematography: Robert Surtees; AA Best Editing: Ralph E. Winters, Conrad A. Nervig

For those who love thrilling, large-scale adventure films loaded with action and exotic scenery, KING SOLOMON'S MINES is your cup of colonialist tea. MGM spent $3.5 million—a fortune in those days—in producing this highly engaging old-fashioned entertainment.

Great white hunter Allan Quartermain (Granger) is hired by the beautiful Elizabeth (Kerr) and her brother (Carlson) to help find Elizabeth's husband, who disappeared while searching for the fabled diamond mines of King Solomon. Their party goes through swamps and forests, over mountains and deserts, and flees nasty natives and stampeding animals in their search.

One of the most majestically filmed adventure tales ever put on celluloid, the film copped cinematographer Surtees a deserved Oscar for his efforts. The production went first to Nairobi and then, via specially built trucks and airplanes, to Tanganyika and the Belgian Congo, covering more than 14,000 miles and contending with temperatures soaring between 140 and 152 degrees and a wide variety of exotic diseases, snakes and flies. The footage of African natives (e.g. a Watusi dance) is fascinating and persuasive, and some efforts were made to portray the dignity of African tribal life. The imperialism of it all might get you hot under the collar, but don't despair entirely—the Africans are the most interesting characters in the film.

To be fair, the Hollywoodians are pretty decent and throw themselves into the bracing if silly spirit of the whole enterprise. Granger isn't sexy enough but he *is* stalwart, and Kerr expertly plays another one of those prim but horny types she was assigned to do every so often. So much excess quality footage of Africa was left over that MGM went on a recurrent diet of jungle epics, using the stuff in, among others, WATUSI, TARZAN THE APE MAN, DRUMS OF AFRICA, TRADER HORN, and even the 1977 remake of KING SOLOMON'S MINES.

KINGDOM, THE
(RIGET)

1994 271m c Drama/Horror ★★★★
Zentropa Entertainment/Danmarks Radio/Swedish R/U
Television/Westdeutscher Rundfunk/ARTE/The Coproduction
Office (Denmark)

Ernst-Hugo Jaregard *(Stig Helmer)*, Kirsten Rolffes *(Mrs. Drusse)*, Ghita Norby *(Rigmor)*, Soren Pilmark *(Krogen)*, Holger Juul Hansen *(Dr. Moesgaard)*, Annevig Schelde Ebbe *(Mary)*, Jens Okking *(Bulder)*, Otto Brandenburg *(Porter Hansen)*, Baard Owe *(Bondo)*, Solbjorg Hojfeldt *(Camilla)*

p, Ole Reim; d, Lars von Trier; w, Lars von Trier, Tomas Gislason (from a story by Lars von Trier and Niels Vorsel); ph, Eric Kress; ed, Jacob Thuesen, Molly Marlene Stensgaard; m, Joachim Holbek; art d, Jette Lehmann; fx, Niels Skovgaard, Niels Fly

Made for Danish television, THE KINGDOM is four episodes of an entertainingly cracked medical soap opera-*cum*-ghost story, strung together and released in the US as a theatrical film. The closest thing to it in recent memory is the David Lynch-produced television series "Twin Peaks," but THE KINGDOM works as a theatrical release, despite the segment breaks, episodic story development, and wildly unresolved cliff-hanger ending.

The Kingdom is the name of a huge, crumbling hospital, built on sinister marshland and home to a diverse and eccentric crew of doctors and patients. It's also the backdrop for an immensely complex storyline involving, *inter alia*, ghostly little girls, doomed romance, haunted ambulances, exorcism, medical malpractice, mongoloid seers, demon dogs, severed heads in lockers, and unearthly pregnancy.

Prior to THE KINGDOM, director Lars von Trier (ZENTROPA) had distinguished himself primarily for his flamboyant visual style and singular humorlessness. So the great and pleasant surprise of THE KINGDOM is how blackly funny it is. At the same time von Trier manages to work up some real scares: a little girl's first appearance, crouched in a high corner of the elevator shaft and ringing a tiny bell is chilling, as is the scene in which a medium questions a newly dead friend by having her make the buzzing fluorescent lights dim—once for yes, twice for no. The 271-minute running time, so daunting when spelled out—four-and-a-half hours!—seems like nothing in the unfolding.

KINGS OF THE ROAD
(IM LAUF DER ZEIT)

1976 176m bw Drama ★★★★★
Filmverlag der Autoren (West Germany) /18

Rudiger Vogler *(Bruno)*, Hanns Zischler *(Robert)*, Lisa Kreuzer *(Cashier)*, Rudolf Schuendler *(Robert's Father)*, Marquard Bohm *(Man Who Lost His Wife)*

p, Wim Wenders; d, Wim Wenders; w, Wim Wenders; ph, Robby Muller, Martin Schafer, Peter Przygodda; m, Axel Linstadt

One of the seminal films of New German cinema, KINGS OF THE ROAD is, along with WINGS OF DESIRE, one of Wim Wenders' greatest achievements to date. The ultimate road movie, this lengthy but never dull picture traces the small adventures of two men as they wander along the back roads of Germany, moving from one small town to the next.

One morning Bruno (Vogler), a motion-picture-projector repairman who lives in his van, sees a Volkswagen plunge off a dock and into the Elbe River, a natural border between East and West Germany. Out of the water comes Robert (Zischler), a linguist who has just made a half-hearted suicide attempt. Robert accepts a ride from Bruno—and, as they travel across the country on Bruno's repair route, a strong friendship develops. The two drink, meet people, wander the streets, and sing along to American songs, especially Roger Miller's "King of the Road."

The story is simple and told in the main without much dialogue (Wenders and crew set out with an itinerary but no script), and the core of the film eschews narrative. Instead, as the translated title tells us, it is "the course of time" that holds Wenders' interest. The changes that occur throughout history (symbolized by crumbling small-town movie houses) are the film's central concern and justify its length. Scenes are filmed in real time, as we watch the characters shave, wash, think, talk, and even defecate. This last moment is something that you not only don't mind, you find it entirely fitting amid the ordinariness of it all.

KINGS OF THE ROAD becomes an even more revealing entry in Wenders' canon when one views it in light of WINGS OF DESIRE. Both films examine the walls that exist between people, between past and present, and between East and West Germany. Both films also tellingly highlight the imbrication of American pop culture on European sensibilities. No reference to this film should fail to mention the power of the naturally lit, black-and-white images beautifully captured by Robby Muller. A terrific and thoughtful film.

KINGS ROW

1942 127m bw Drama ★★★★½
Warner Bros. (U.S.) /A

Ann Sheridan (Randy Monoghan), Robert Cummings (Parris Mitchell), Ronald Reagan (Drake McHugh), Betty Field (Cassandra Tower), Charles Coburn (Dr. Henry Gordon), Claude Rains (Dr. Alexander Tower), Judith Anderson (Mrs. Harriet Gordon), Nancy Coleman (Louise Gordon), Kaaren Verne (Elise Sandor), Maria Ouspenskaya (Mme. Von Eln)

p, David Lewis; d, Sam Wood; w, Casey Robinson (based on the novel by Henry Bellamann); ph, James Wong Howe; ed, Ralph Dawson; m, Erich Wolfgang Korngold; prod d, William Cameron Menzies; art d, Carl Jules Weyl

"Where's the rest of me?" Too bad Ronnie never found the answer. Containing what is easily the future President's finest performance, KINGS ROW was a startling film for its day, portraying a small town not with the poignancy and little joys of Thorton Wilder's Our Town, but rather in grim, often tragic tones.

The film begins with its main characters as children. Playful Drake, tomboyish Randy and uppity Louise are among the friends of the sensitive Parris. He, meanwhile, befriends the strange, lonely Cassandra, but her psychiatrist father, Dr. Tower (Rains) soon removes her from school to be tutored at home. We advance in time to the grown Parris (Cummings), now a brilliant medical student who studies with Dr. Tower and still sees the increasingly quirky Cassandra (Field) occasionally. The feisty Randy loves both Parris and the rakish Drake (Reagan), but Louise (Coleman) remains sheltered by her strict parents.

Trouble brews when Louise becomes jealous of Randy's involvement with Drake, and Cassandra begins to go off the deep end and wants to go to Vienna with Parris. Ultimately, two very different fathers, the kindly Dr. Tower and Louise's avaricious dad, Dr. Gordon (Coburn), take brutal action in their misguided attempts to protect their daughters.

KINGS ROW remains one of director Wood's finest films, but one wonders how much he relied on his ace support. Robinson did a fine job of adapting Bellamann's rich novel, even if he cut out a death from cancer, deleted a mercy killing, and toned down the narrative's homosexual angle. Korngold's rich score is haunting and the detailed sets by Menzies quite stunning. Howe's gorgeous cinematography, meanwhile, maintains in deep focus many layers of drama, as befits this brooding tapestry. An uneven film in spots, but one of the most memorable melodramas of its day, compelling and unusual for early WWII.

KISS BEFORE DYING, A

1956 94m c Mystery ★★★
UA (U.S.) /18

Robert Wagner (Bud Corliss), Jeffrey Hunter (Gordon Grant), Virginia Leith (Ellen Kingship), Joanne Woodward (Dorothy Kingship), Mary Astor (Mrs. Corliss), George Macready (Leo Kingship), Robert Quarry (Dwight Powell), Howard Petrie (Chesser), Bill Walker (Butler), Mollie McCart (Annabelle)

p, Robert L. Jacks; d, Gerd Oswald; w, Lawrence Roman (based on the novel by Ira Levin); ph, Lucien Ballard; ed, George Gittens; m, Lionel Newman; art d, Addison Hehr; cos, Henry Helfman, Evelyn Carruth

Wagner plays Bud Corliss, a money-hungry youth who kills his girlfriend Dorothy (Woodward), when her pregnancy threatens his chances of being accepted by her wealthy family. Her sister Ellen (Leith) refuses to believe the police report that the death was a suicide, and does some investigating on her own. She runs into Bud, ignorant of his relationship with Dorothy, and a romance between the two begins. When Ellen discovers Bud's involvement with her sister, the stage is set for the final showdown. An excellent screenplay (unoriginal but full of tension), subtle direction by the overlooked and underutilized Oswald, and good photography help gloss over any weaknesses in the performances.

KISS ME DEADLY

1955 105m bw Crime ★★★★★
Parklane (U.S.) /15

Ralph Meeker (Mike Hammer), Albert Dekker (Dr. Soberin), Paul Stewart (Carl Evello), Maxine Cooper (Velda), Gaby Rodgers (Gabrielle/Lily Carver), Wesley Addy (Pat Chambers), Juano Hernandez (Eddie Yeager), Nick Dennis (Nick), Cloris Leachman (Christina Bailey/Berga Torn), Marian Carr (Friday)

p, Robert Aldrich; d, Robert Aldrich; w, A.I. Bezzerides (based on the novel by Mickey Spillane); ph, Ernest Laszlo; ed, Michael Luciano; m, Frank DeVol; art d, William Glasgow

Private eye Mike Hammer (Meeker) is driving his convertible on a dark highway when he sees the almost naked Christina Bailey (Leachman) running down the middle of the road. He picks her up, but is soon forced off the road. Hammer is knocked unconscious, and Christina is killed. Both of them are put back in his car, which is then pushed off a cliff. Surviving, Hammer investigates, his curiosity aroused by an FBI warning to stay away. He finds Christina's roommate (Rodgers) and also meets a powerful gangster (Stewart) whose strings are being pulled by a mysterious higher power. Hammer knows he's on to something when his mechanic friend (Dennis) is killed and his secretary (Cooper) kidnapped. Hammer himself is kidnapped but manages to escape, killing his tormentors. He eventually figures out that Christina swallowed a key that will lead to the "great Whatsit." Convincing a morgue attendant (by slamming the man's fingers in a drawer) to give him the key, Hammer later uses similar charm at a health club to acquire the box the key opens. In the end, we meet the chief villain, see another side to the mysterious roommate, and discover the contents of the box. The results are, to put it mildly, explosive.

One of the most brutal films ever made, KISS ME DEADLY enjoys a huge cult following. There's not a single really likable character to be found; everyone wants something, and the neanderthal Hammer barely gives people a chance to say no before he starts beating them up. Aldrich's direction heightens the script's misanthropy, shooting with extreme close-ups and at disorienting angles. Christina's murder is achieved with a pair of pliers, and all we see are a pair of bare legs dangling in midair. The murder of the mechanic is similarly jarring, the camera swooping in on his screaming face as a set of hydraulic jacks do their work. Hammer himself is knocked out no less than six times, only to strut down those mean streets yet again. Aldrich was so concerned about possible reactions to all the violence that he wrote a defense of the film in the New York Herald Tribune.

KISS ME DEADLY is shot in an unforgettably harsh fashion, visually underlining the paranoia and existential funk of the film noir world view as few other films have done. Aldrich's greatest directorial effort, this important film takes a number of noir elements to their most nihilistic extremes, leaving us in the violent, atomically threatened world we encounter upon leaving the theater.

KISS ME KATE

1953 109m c Musical/Comedy ★★★★
MGM (U.S.) /U

Kathryn Grayson (Lilli Vanessi/Katherine), Howard Keel (Fred Graham/Petruchio), Ann Miller (Lois Lane/Bianca), Tommy Rall (Bill Calhoun/Lucentio), Bobby Van (Gremio), Keenan Wynn (Lippy), James Whitmore (Slug), Kurt Kasznar (Baptista), Bob Fosse (Hortensio), Ron Randell (Cole Porter)

p, Jack Cummings; d, George Sidney; w, Dorothy Kingsley (based on the play by Cole Porter, Sam Spewack, Bella Spewack, from the play The Taming of the Shrew by William Shakespeare); ph, Charles Rosher; ed, Ralph E. Winters; art d, Cedric Gibbons, Urie McCleary; fx, Warren Newcombe; chor, Hermes Pan; cos, Walter Plunkett

AAN Best Score: Andre Previn, Saul Chaplin

KISS ME KATE is almost, but not quite, a classic cinematic version of the hit Broadway musical. Filmed in 3-D, it was largely released "flat" when the 3-D craze began to wane. Boasting an intelligent and highly amusing book, this tunefest features parallel tales of a musical production of *The Taming of the Shrew* and simultaneously occurring events in the lives of its cast.

Actor-director Fred Graham (Keel) and Cole Porter (Randell) are working together to musicalize the Bard's comedy, and both feel that the only woman to play the shrew Katherine is Fred's ex-wife, Lilli Vanessi (Grayson). Trouble brews when Fred's current flame, Lois Lane (Miller), is set to play Bianca, Katherine's younger sister. Fred, playing Petruchio, enjoys needling his ex, while Lois' dancing partner (Rall) turns out to be a compulsive gambler who has signed Fred's name on an IOU for several thousand dollars. On opening night, two gangsters (Wynn and Whitmore) arrive to collect the debt; how this overlaps with Fred and Lilli's love-hate affair insures plenty of comic bickering until the finale.

KISS ME KATE makes for delightful entertainment, though it does have its drawbacks. Among them is director Sidney, as smooth and professional as ever, but still lacking real flair and imagination. The same might be said for Grayson, who is at or near her best here. Admittedly, Hollywood didn't really have any operetta stars then who could both hit high C and eat the camera whole. Keel, ever a braggadocio, is fun; his best song is "Where Is the Life That Late I Led?". Miller is in great form, too, her loud charm quite amusing. She sparkles in one of her patented pneumatic tap numbers, absolutely blazing away with "Too Darn Hot". Much of the later dancing, though, is of the Gene Kelly/Bob Fosse type and it does tax her range, limiting her to high kicks and lots of spins. Rall and Randell are appealing, too, though the latter is a very whitewashed version of what we *know* the real Cole Porter was like.

Actually, since we brought up Bob Fosse, we should note that he is one of the onstage dancers. He enters (literally) with a screech and later does a backflip, effortlessly upstaging the struggling Bobby Van. (Look for a pre-*Pajame Game* Carol Haney, too.) The score, of course, is witty and tuneful, and one just waits for each classic to come bouncing along in this extremely enjoyable if less than brilliant musical.

KISS OF DEATH

1947   98m   bw   Crime   ★★★★½
Fox   (U.S.)   /A

Victor Mature (*Nick Bianco*), Brian Donlevy (*D'Angelo*), Coleen Gray (*Nettie*), Richard Widmark (*Tom Udo*), Karl Malden (*Sgt. William Cullen*), Taylor Holmes (*Earl Howser*), Howard Smith (*Warden*), Anthony Ross (*Williams*), Mildred Dunnock (*Ma Rizzo*), Millard Mitchell (*Max Schulte*)

p, Fred Kohlmar; d, Henry Hathaway; w, Ben Hecht, Charles Lederer (based on a story by Eleazar Lipsky); ph, Norbert Brodine; ed, J. Watson Webb; m, David Buttolph; art d, Lyle Wheeler, Leland Fuller; fx, Fred Sersen; cos, Charles LeMaire

AAN Best Supporting Actor: Richard Widmark; AAN Best Original Screenplay: Eleazar Lipsky

A hard-hitting, often frightening crime drama from the Hecht-Lederer typewriter, KISS OF DEATH has a grimly realistic look and feel, mostly because expert helmsman Hathaway insisted upon shooting the whole film in New York. The movie pulls no punches as it represents life on the seamy side of the street. It also introduced an electric personality to the screen, Richard Widmark, in an unforgettable role. Narrating the film is Nettie (Gray), second wife of Nick Bianco (Mature). Recounting his tough life, she tells how he is the one member of a gang who was caught robbing a jewelry store at Christmastime. Later to by the gang's crooked lawyer (Holmes) lies to him assuring him that his family will be looked after. In prison, Nick learns that his first wife has committed suicide out of poverty and that his two little girls have been placed in an orphanage. In a rage, he makes a deal with district attorney D'Angelo (Donlevy): in exchange for his parole, he will inform on his old gang. D'Angelo particularly wants to send sadistic gang boss Tommy Udo (Widmark) to prison. Nick ingratiates himself with the perverted murderer, listening to his big talk and going with him to bars and bordellos. Meanwhile, Nick falls for and marries

Nettie, moving his family into a new home. When Nick's cover is blown and D'Angelo forces him to testify against Tommy, Nick becomes a marked man. Unable to stand waiting, Nick decides to push Udo to the point of murder.

Hathaway's New York locations give KISS OF DEATH a style reminiscent of other crime films employing a documentary-like approach, including CALL NORTHSIDE 777 and THE NAKED CITY. Mature is exceptional as the reluctant squealer, Gray appealingly low-key as his wife, and Donlevy solid as the crusading attorney. Widmark, however, with his maniacal smile, falsetto baby talk, and hyena-like laughter, really captured the public's imagination with his riveting performance. KISS OF DEATH features the famous scene where Udo murders a wheelchair-bound old woman by pushing her down a flight of stairs. An overnight sensation, Widmark was signed to a long-term contract by Fox. The Hecht-Lederer script is taut and clever, more literate than many gangster films, with well-developed characters and a starkly believable plot line. The story was later be used for the shlock cult film THE FIEND WHO WALKED THE WEST.

KISS OF DEATH

1995   101m   c   Crime/Drama   ★★★½
20th Century Fox   (U.S.)   R/18

David Caruso (*Jimmy Kilmartin*), Samuel L. Jackson (*Calvin*), Nicolas Cage (*Little Junior*), Helen Hunt (*Bev*), Kathryn Erbe (*Rosie*), Stanley Tucci (*Frank Zioli*), Michael Rapaport (*Ronnie*), Ving Rhames (*Omar*), Philip Baker Hall (*Big Junior*), Anthony Heald (*Jack Gold*)

p, Barbet Schroeder, Susan Hoffman; d, Barbet Schroeder; w, Richard Price (based on the 1947 screenplay by Ben Hecht and Charles Lederer from a story by Eleazar Lipsky); ph, Luciano Tovoli; ed, Lee Percy; m, Trevor Jones; prod d, Mel Bourne; fx, Steve Kirshoff; cos, Theadora Van Runkle

Loosely based on the 1947 film of the same name, this solid crime drama marks TV star David Caruso's big-screen debut in a leading role, though Nicolas Cage dominates the proceedings as an eccentric crime lord.

Caruso plays smalltime ex-con Jimmy Kilmartin, a family man who, despite his best efforts to go straight, is drawn into the world of volatile, asthmatic Junior Brown (Cage). Part monster, part cornball New Age philosopher, the pumped-up, track-suited Brown runs the criminal empire bequeathed him by his dad from a strip club in Queens. While serving a second prison term following a bungled car theft operation, Jimmy is approached by the D.A. (Stanley Tucci) and a hardnosed police detective (Samuel L. Jackson), who persuade him to infiltrate Junior's gang. When the Feds get involved, Jimmy realizes that he's become a pawn in an extremely dangerous game.

KISS OF DEATH has the right tone for this noir-ish examination of petty criminals and their world: Barbet Schroeder has shot much of it at night, using auto junkyards and other unglamorous locales, and screenwriter Richard Price has a well-known flair for grungy atmosphere. As Junior (a character only vaguely suggested by Richard Widmark's fiendish turn in the original), Cage dispenses with his customary mumbling lethargy to give an electric performance, alternately menacing and pitiable.

KISS OF THE SPIDER WOMAN

1985   119m   c/bw   Prison   ★★★★
HB   (U.S./Brazil)   R/15

William Hurt (*Luis Molina*), Raul Julia (*Valentin Arregui*), Sonia Braga (*Leni Lamaison/Marta/Spider Woman*), Jose Lewgoy (*Warden*), Milton Goncalves (*Pedro*), Miriam Pires (*Mother*), Nuno Leal Maia (*Gabriel*), Fernando Torres (*Americo*), Patricio Bisso (*Greta*), Herson Capri (*Werner*)

p, David Weisman; d, Hector Babenco; w, Leonard Schrader (based on the novel by Manuel Puig); ph, Rodolfo Sanchez; ed, Mauro Alice, Lee Percy; m, John Neschling, Wally Badarou; art d, Clovis Bueno; cos, Patricio Bisso

AAN Best Picture; AA Best Actor: William Hurt; AAN Best Director: Hector Babenco; AAN Best Adapted Screenplay: Leonard Schrader

Based on Manuel Puig's novel of the same name, KISS OF THE SPIDER WOMAN treats its unusual premise with an often lyrical grace. In a South American country, Luis Molina, a flamboyant gay man jailed for taking liberties with a minor, shares a cell with Valentin Arregui (Julia), a political prisoner. Though the revolutionary initially dislikes Luis, he is gradually drawn in by the latter's retelling of films, including a Nazi propaganda piece about a cabaret singer, and a B picture featuring the "Spider Woman" (both "starring" Braga).

The two men develop a deep friendship wherein Luis learns the importance of political convictions and Valentin discovers the power of fantasy. He becomes able to withstand the tortures he endures by dreaming of his lover outside (Braga again). Luis falls in love with his cellmate and, shortly before Luis's release, Valentin agree to share a night of lovemaking with his smitten friend. Luis soon returns the favor by getting involved in Valentin's dangerous political efforts on the outside.

Hurt does a fine job with this difficult role, even if a self-conscious quality not entirely befitting the character does creep in; he seems to want to go out of his way to make it a showy performance, but he deserves credit for pursuing the challenge. Julia, while admittedly on much safer ground, really gives the performance to watch, however. His tenderness is as compelling as his rage, and he never strikes a false note. The impact of the entire film rests on the relationship these actors construct, and both Hurt and Julia succeed brilliantly.

Braga does a good job differentiating among her essentially thankless roles, but she's not entirely into the camp spirit of the movie sequences. Babenco's fine direction is a masterwork of detailed camera choreography, and the films-within-a-film episodes aptly complement the prisoners's relationship.

KITTY FOYLE

1940 105m bw Drama ★★★★
RKO (U.S.) /A

Ginger Rogers *(Kitty Foyle)*, Dennis Morgan *(Wyn Strafford)*, James Craig *(Mark)*, Eduardo Ciannelli *(Giono)*, Ernest Cossart *(Pop)*, Gladys Cooper *(Mrs. Strafford)*, Odette Myrtil *(Delphine Detaille)*, Mary Treen *(Pat)*, K.T. Stevens *(Molly)*, Walter Kingsford *(Mr. Kennett)*

p, David Hempstead; d, Sam Wood; w, Dalton Trumbo, Donald Ogden Stewart (based on the novel by Christopher Morley); ph, Robert de Grasse; ed, Henry Berman; m, Roy Webb; art d, Van Nest Polglase, Mark-Lee Kirk; fx, Vernon L. Walker; cos, Renie

AAN Best Picture; *AA Best Actress:* Ginger Rogers; *AAN Best Director:* Sam Wood; *AAN Best Screenplay:* Dalton Trumbo; *AAN Best Sound:* John Aalberg

In a dramatic role right after the Astaire years, Ginger Rogers proved yet again that she had more than enough star quality herself to carry major films. A minor classic and a very typical "woman's picture" of its day, KITTY FOYLE details its feisty heroine's romances with two men. Wyn (Morgan) is the embodiment of the society scions Kitty has watched entering Philadelphia's classiest ball every year. The two fall in love when she becomes his secretary, but his social obligations continually tear them apart, even to the point where he marries another woman. Kitty later begins a sincere if casual romance with Mark (Craig), a struggling young doctor. Eventually accepting his marriage proposal, Kitty has a big choice to make when Wyn sweeps back into her life.

Highly sentimental, KITTY FOYLE features typically variable direction by Wood and includes an unnecessary prologue showing how the treatment of women supposedly changed through the years. Despite these drawbacks, this film makes no apologies for being a romantic tearjerker. The humor and warmth are real, and the film maintains admirable restraint even amid Kitty's most sorrowful travails. Best of all, Rogers offers a performance of considerable dexterity and poignancy. This proletariat Cinderella is a showcase part and she makes the most of it, whether wisecracking with her cronies or during a very cheap first date with Mark, telling off Wyn's snobbish family in fine style, or in her several moving encounters with children. Rogers's Oscar win has always been slightly controversial, given the stiff competition that year (Bette Davis, Katharine Hepburn, Joan Fontaine and Martha Scott). If, however, one considers her equally fine work in the same year's excellent but controversial PRIMROSE PATH and realizes that

Academy Awards are often given for a good *year's* work, then maybe it's entirely fitting to say that Ginger Rogers *was* the Best Actress of 1940.

KLUTE

1971 114m c Crime ★★★★
Warner Bros. (U.S.) R/18

Jane Fonda *(Bree Daniels)*, Donald Sutherland *(John Klute)*, Charles Cioffi *(Peter Cable)*, Roy Scheider *(Frank Ligourin)*, Dorothy Tristan *(Arlyn Page)*, Rita Gam *(Trina)*, Vivian Nathan *(Psychiatrist)*, Nathan George *(Lt. Trask)*, Morris Strassberg *(Mr. Goldfarb)*, Jean Stapleton *(Goldfarb's Secretary)*

p, Alan J. Pakula, David Lang; d, Alan J. Pakula; w, Andy Lewis, Dave Lewis; ph, Gordon Willis; ed, Carl Lerner; m, Michael Small; art d, George Jenkins; cos, Ann Roth

AA Best Actress: Jane Fonda; *AAN Best Adapted Screenplay:* Andy Lewis, Dave Lewis

Along with BARBARELLA and THEY SHOOT HORSES, DON'T THEY?, one of the best things the highly variable Jane Fonda has ever done.

When a research scientist turns up missing, his best friend, John Klute (Sutherland), a small-town police detective, goes to New York City in search of Bree Daniels (Fonda), a prostitute to whom the missing man had written letters. Bree, who is trying to switch professions, tells Klute that she has been getting threatening phone calls from a violent former client who she also thinks has been following her. In the process of his investigation, Klute falls for Bree, though she has difficulty returning his affection. After another prostitute who had contact with the sadistic caller is murdered, Bree finds herself alone in a dark warehouse in the exciting finale.

The film's predictable plotting is not its strong point, nor is Pakula's uneven direction. The strictly thriller aspects of the film vary from the artfully constructed to the showy but shallow. It's as if Pakula feels compelled to indulge all the conventions of the genre, but without quite knowing why. On the other hand, he does ably highlight some of the more provocative and complex aspects of Andy and Dave Lewis's often fine screenplay. We see Bree calmly look at her watch while simulating passionate sex, and she develops a sentimental attachment to the lonely old man who simply likes to look at her nude. Bree can, with perfect professionalism, explain that certain sex acts will cost clients more, but she also cowers from an awareness of her own vulnerability and realizes the painful contradictions in her life.

Sutherland is either an excellent sounding board for this nuanced portrait or he's a big zero, probably both. Fonda, however, transcends her limitations, making the most of her often forced quality as an actress. Bree emerges as likably strong yet dangerously weak, refreshingly intelligent yet searching and confused.

KNACK...AND HOW TO GET IT, THE

1965 84m bw Comedy ★★★★
Woodfall (U.K.) /X

Rita Tushingham *(Nancy Jones)*, Ray Brooks *(Tolen)*, Michael Crawford *(Colin)*, Donal Donnelly *(Tom)*, William Dexter *(Dress Shop Owner)*, Charles Dyer *(Man in Photo Booth)*, Margot Thomas *(Female Teacher)*, John Bluthal *(Father)*, Wensley Pithey *(Teacher)*, Helen Lennox *(Blonde in Photo Booth)*

p, Oscar Lewenstein; d, Richard Lester; w, Charles Wood (from the play by Ann Jellicoe); ph, David Watkin; ed, Anthony Gibbs; m, John Barry; art d, Assheton Gorton; cos, Jocelyn Rickards

Director Lester continued to defy convention as he had with A HARD DAY'S NIGHT in this, his follow-up feature. The style is extremely fast paced; the characters are nonstop talkers who move about incessantly. Essentially created in the cutting room, Lester's films rely upon techniques which have been commonly employed throughout commercial film history, but which are combined in a unusual and flamboyant, if not always successful manner.

Tolen's (Brooks) luck with women ("the knack") baffles his schoolteacher landlord Colin (Crawford). This resident stud takes the eager but shy man under his wing and advises him to buy a new brass bed. After finding an appropriate model, they roll it through London streets to their digs, causing traffic jams and general hysteria. Along the way, they meet Nancy (Tushingham), who is new to London and is trying to find a place to stay. She accompanies them on their trek home, and Colin gets a yen for her. Back at the boarding house, however, Tolen takes control and runs off with her on his motorbike. Colin follows in hot pursuit, only to find the couple in a park, where Nancy is loudly accusing Tolen of rape. Losing his patience with this unusually (but justifiably) uncooperative woman, Tolen makes room for Colin.

The characters are deliberately little more than cardboard types. They talk all the time, but never say much of anything. They do, however, convey quite a bit of personality, which can be attributed to Lester's not over-dramatizing any situations and his reliance upon semi-improvisational material. Such an endlessly tricksy style does miss occasionally, but what often emerges is a genuinely energetic celebration of 1960s youth. A film of sunshiny, horny dreams and determinedly chic comic anarchy, this manic display remains a zingy if slightly dated adaptation of Ann Jellicoe's fascinating original play.

KNIFE IN THE HEAD
(MESSER IM KOPF)

| 1978 | 113m | c | Drama/Thriller/Political | ★★★★ |
| Biskop Film/Hallelujah-Film | (West Germany) | | | /AA |

Bruno Ganz (Dr. Berthold Hoffmann), Angela Winkler (Ann Hoffmann), Hans Christian Blech (Scholz), Udo Samel (Schurig), Eike Gallwitz (Dr. Groeske), Carla Egerer (Nurse Angelika Mueller), Gabriele Dossi (Nurse Emmilie), Hans Fuchs (Head Doctor), Erich Kleiber (Herr Arnold)

p, Eberhard Junkersdorf; d, Reinhard Hauff; w, Peter Schneider; ph, Frank Bruhne

A dark, ambiguous political thriller relecting the paranoia of Germany's Baader-Meinhof era. Bruno Ganz, in a moving and meticulously conceived performance, plays an apolitical scientist who is shot in the head during a clash between leftist students and a quasi-totalitarian police force. His tortuous recovery from aphasia figures both an Oedipal journey and a search for political certainty. Angela Winkler (THE TIN DRUM) is a standout as Ganz's chilly, faithless wife. Director Hauff's vision of an alienated, ultra-modern Germany is well served by Frank Bruhne's cool cinematography.

KNIFE IN THE WATER
(NOZ W WODZIE)

| 1962 | 94m | bw | Drama | ★★★★ |
| Film Polski | (Poland) | | | /X |

Leon Niemczyk (Andrzej), Jolanta Umecka (Christine), Zygmunt Malanowicz (The Young Man)

p, Stanislaw Zylewicz; d, Roman Polanski; w, Roman Polanski, Jerzy Skolimowski, Jakub Goldberg; ph, Jerzy Lipman; m, Krzysztof Komeda

AAN Best Foreign Language Film

Roman Polanski's first feature immediately established him as a filmmaker to be reckoned with, winning top honors at the Venice Film Festival, a Best Foreign Film Oscar nomination, and a place on the cover of *Time* in conjunction with the first New York Film Festival. Polanski's career-long fascination with human cruelty and violence is already evident, as is his intense interest in exploring the complex tensions involved in close relations.

When Andrzej (Niemczyk), a successful sportswriter on holiday with his wife, Christine (Umecka), picks up a hitchhiker (Malanowicz), the couple asks the young man (nameless throughout) to join them on a short boating excursion. Jealous of the blonde boy's youth and looks, Andrzej boasts of his physical prowess, faulting his guest's inexperience at sea. Tension between the men intensifies, with the pocket knife that represents the hitchhiker's particular skills lending a continual suggestion of violence and sexuality to the goings-on. Things eventually do get violent.

Filmed in black and white, this film is extremely assured, concise, and telling in its characterizations. KNIFE IN THE WATER is also notable in the career of another Polish filmmaker, coscenarist Jerzy Skolimowski, who had already begun to direct, but emerged interna-

tionally in 1982 with the offbeat MOONLIGHTING. Some would argue that KNIFE IN THE WATER is a more interesting movie than any Polanski made in the west after leaving his native land. Brilliantly told and well-acted, Polanski's half tongue-in-cheek, lugubrious and sinister filmic style seemed quite refreshing at the time.

KNOCK ON ANY DOOR

| 1949 | 100m | bw | Crime | ★★★½ |
| Santana | (U.S.) | | | /A |

Humphrey Bogart (Andrew Morton), John Derek (Nick Romano), George Macready (District Attorney Kerman), Allene Roberts (Emma), Susan Perry (Adele), Mickey Knox (Vito), Barry Kelley (Judge Drake), Dooley Wilson (Piano Player), Cara Williams (Nelly), Jimmy Conlin (Kid Fingers)

p, Robert Lord; d, Nicholas Ray; w, Daniel Taradash, John Monks Jr. (based on the novel by Willard Motley); ph, Burnett Guffey; ed, Viola Lawrence; m, George Antheil; art d, Robert Peterson; cos, Jean Louis

"Live fast, die young, and have a good-looking corpse." This hard-hitting crime melodrama offers excellent direction from the always interesting Nicholas Ray and a fine performance from Bogart as Andrew Morton a crusading attorney.

Morton's latest crusade involves saving Nick Romano (Derek), an embittered slum youth, from the electric chair. Piecing together the young man's story in flashback, Morton describes Nick's crooked early life and his brief happiness with Emma (Roberts). Already having difficulty holding down a job, Nick really cracks when Emma tells him she's pregnant. His return to thievery gets worse after Emma commits suicide, and Nick's crime spree climaxes with his murder of a policeman. An expert liar who makes the most of his boyish good looks, Nick has convinced Morton of his innocence, only to crack when district attorney Kerman (Macready) asks about Emma.

Ray really makes us feel the oppressive filth and poverty of slum life, conjuring considerable sympathy for the distinctly dislikable Nick Romano. A problem even he couldn't surmount, however, was John Derek. Making his film debut here, pretty boy Derek constructs his dull performance with scissors, cardboard and library paste. The role could have ignited the screen, but Derek's high-school histrionics make for a pretty wet blanket. Bogart, on the other hand, does quite well, even if principled attorney Morton recalls the actor's fledgling days in MARKED WOMAN more than any of the classic Bogie roles. Straightforward virtue was never his strong suit, but Bogart nevertheless does a great job with his long climactic courtroom speech.

Not as memorable as Bogart's other collaboration with director Ray, the haunting IN A LONELY PLACE, this film still makes for absorbing viewing. Sequel: LET NO MAN WRITE MY EPITAPH.

KNOCK ON WOOD

| 1954 | 103m | c | Spy/Thriller/Comedy | ★★★ |
| Dena | (U.S.) | | | /U |

Danny Kaye (Jerry), Mai Zetterling (Ilse Nordstrom), Torin Thatcher (Langston), David Burns (Marty Brown), Leon Askin (Gromeck), Abner Biberman (Papinek), Gavin Gordon (Car Salesman), Otto Waldis (Brodnik), Steven Geray (Dr. Kreuger), Diana Adams (Princess)

p, Norman Panama, Melvin Frank; d, Norman Panama, Melvin Frank; w, Norman Panama, Melvin Frank; ph, Daniel Fapp; ed, Alma Macrorie; chor, Michael Kidd

AAN Best Original Screenplay: Norman Panama, Melvin Frank

An often funny, sight gag variation on Hitchcock's "wrong man" thrillers. Danny Kaye plays Jerry, a ventriloquist with a dummy that talks when he doesn't want it to and insults the customers. His manager (Burns) suggests he see a psychiatrist (Zetterling). Meanwhile, the the plans for a new weapon have been stolen and two rival groups are after them. The blueprints are placed in, you guessed it, the dummy. The spies begin chasing Jerry all over creation and that's where most of the comedy happens.

The entire premise is all an excuse for several of Kaye's best comic set pieces, including his dancing with a Russian ballet troupe to avoid being found by the spies. (Alfred Hitchcock did something similar in THE 39 STEPS when Robert Donat steps in front of a political rally and masquerades as a speaker while the spies look on.) The chase also leads Kaye into a convention of Irishmen, where he sings "The Drastic, Livid History of Monahan O'Han," penned by Kaye's wife, the writer, Sylvia Fine. The versatile Kaye gets the chance to wear several disguises, to sing a few tunes (including a nice ballad "All About You"), and, in general, to do what Danny Kaye does best. It's just that sometimes he's more manic than funny and he often doesn't know when to quit.

KNUTE ROCKNE—ALL AMERICAN
1940 98m bw Biography/Sports   ★★½
Warner Bros. (U.S.)   /U

Pat O'Brien *(Knute Rockne)*, Gale Page *(Bonnie Skiles Rockne)*, Ronald Reagan *(George Gipp)*, Donald Crisp *(Father John Callahan)*, Albert Basserman *(Father Julius Nieuwland)*, John Litel *(Committee Chairman)*, Henry O'Neill *(Doctor)*, Owen Davis Jr. *(Gus Dorais)*, John Qualen *(Lars Knutson Rockne)*, Dorothy Tree *(Martha Rockne)*

p, Robert Fellows; d, Lloyd Bacon; w, Robert Buckner (based on the private papers of Mrs. Knute Rockne); ph, Tony Gaudio; ed, Ralph Dawson; m, Ray Heindorf; art d, Robert Haas; fx, Byron Haskin, Rex Wimpy; cos, Milo Anderson

Corn doesn't grow any higher than this male bonding tribute to testosterone. Pat O'Brien gives a gung-ho performance as the great Notre Dame football coach Knute Rockne in this bland biography that features Reagan as Rockne's most famous player, George Gipp. The film follows Rockne from his Norwegian immigrant beginnings through his playing days at Notre Dame (when he helped invent the forward pass) and on to his glory days as head coach at his alma mater. With the support of Father Callahan (Donald Crisp), Rockne rises from assistant coach and chemistry teacher to the top spot, and revolutionizes the game as he turns out winning team after winning team, blessed with great players like the "Four Horseman" and Gipp, who dies young of pneumonia and provides the inspiration for Rockne's famed "win one for the Gipper" pep talk! Along the way, Rockne even finds time to romance and marry Bonnie Skilles (Gale Page). Four of Rockne's contemporaries play themselves—the grandfather of all coaches, Amos Alonzo Stagg, Howard Jones of USC, William Spaulding, and "Pop" Warner—and much of the football action is culled from newsreel footage. For legal reasons, some of the big scenes—such as the pep talk O'Brien gives in the locker room and the "for the Gipper" speech are missing on television. But it's all there in the home video, sitting in the cobwebs on your video store shelf.

KRAMER VS. KRAMER
1979 105m c Drama   ★★★★
Columbia (U.S.)   PG

Dustin Hoffman *(Ted Kramer)*, Meryl Streep *(Joanna Kramer)*, Jane Alexander *(Margaret Phelps)*, Justin Henry *(Billy Kramer)*, Howard Duff *(John Shaunessy)*, George Coe *(Jim O'Connor)*, JoBeth Williams *(Phyllis Bernard)*, Bill Moor *(Gressen)*, Howland Chamberlin *(Judge Atkins)*, Jack Ramage *(Spencer)*

p, Stanley R. Jaffe; d, Robert Benton; w, Robert Benton (based on the novel by Avery Corman); ph, Nestor Almendros; ed, Jerry Greenberg; m, Henry Purcell, Antonio Vivaldi; prod d, Paul Sylbert; cos, Ruth Morley

AA Best Picture; AA Best Actor: Dustin Hoffman; AAN Best Supporting Actor: Justin Henry; AA Best Supporting Actress: Meryl Streep; AAN Best Supporting Actress: Jane Alexander; AA Best Director: Robert Benton; AA Best Adapted Screenplay: Robert Benton; AAN Best Cinematography: Nestor Almendros; AAN Best Editing: Jerry Greenberg

For weepie fans, a high class divorce, finely played. KRAMER VS. KRAMER is, essentially, a television movie that was raised into the feature category by the excellence of the execution. With Robert Reed in the Hoffman role and Suzanne Pleshette as his wife, it would have been a typical CBS entry.

Based on a novel by Avery Corman, the story takes place in New York City and shows Streep, an independent woman, leaving husband Hoffman, an art director in an ad agency, for no other reason than that

she wants to "find herself." Hoffman is left to care for their young son, Henry. The extra strain of having to be both father and mother to Henry causes Hoffman to make some mistakes at work and lose a major account, which results in his getting fired. On top of that, Streep surfaces and is suing for custody of the child she's abandoned. Streep now has an excellent job and can afford day care for Henry, so she wants him back.

It's the old wash, but so well done that we can overlook Benton's manipulations of our emotions and let our feelings flow. Movies about divorce and the wrenching apart of families have been part of the motion picture scene since the silents. They will always work, however, if the writing is honest and if the acting is sincere.

KWAIDAN
(KAIDAN)
1964 125m c Horror   ★★★★
Toho (Japan)   /X

Rentaro Mikuni *(Samurai)*, Michiyo Aratama *(1st Wife)*, Misako Watanabe *(2nd Wife)*, Katsuo Nakamura *(Hoichi)*, Ganjiro Nakamura *(Head Priest)*, Takashi Shimura *(Priest)*, Joichi Hayashi *(Yoshitsune)*, Ganemon Nakamura *(Kannai)*, Noboru Nakaya *(Heinai)*, Tetsuro Tamba

d, Masaki Kobayashi; w, Yoko Mizuki (based on the stories of Lafcadio Hearn); ph, Yoshio Miyajima; m, Toru Takemitsu; art d, Shigemasa Toda

AAN Best Foreign Language Film

Four short supernatural stories based on the tales of Lafcadio Hearn, an American who settled in Japan in 1890 and eventually became a citizen of that country, comprise KWAIDAN. Directed with an eerie visual sense by Masaki Kobayashi and containing some spectacular art direction by Shigemasa Toda, the stories each involve an encounter with a ghost—in Hearn's tales a supernatural being who appears to be corporeal but is actually one of the dear departed left to wander aimlessly through the real world. "Black Hair" is the tale of a samurai (Rentaro Mikuni) who returns to the wife he deserted years before and, after sleeping with her, discovers her skeletal remains and long black tresses in his bed. "The Woman of the Snow" is a story cut from the US release about a young woodcutter (Tatsuya Nakadai) saved from death by a mysterious snow maiden who swears to kill him should he ever reveal what has occurred. "Hoichi, the Earless" is about a blind musician (Katsuo Nakamura) whose ears are cut off as he sings at the request of a samurai ghost. "In a Cup of Tea" features a guard (Ganemon Nakamura) who sees a samurai's face in his teacup and absorbs the ghost's soul into his body after drinking the tea. A celebration of the marvelous from director Kobayashi, KWAIDAN's haunting poetry is conveyed not only in its beautiful color images, but also through the chilling soundtrack.

L

L-SHAPED ROOM, THE
1962 142m bw Drama   ★★★★
Romulus (U.K.)   /15

Leslie Caron *(Jane Fosset)*, Anthony Booth *(Youth in Street)*, Avis Bunnage *(Doris)*, Patricia Phoenix *(Sonia)*, Verity Edmett *(Jane II)*, Tom Bell *(Toby)*, Cicely Courtneidge *(Mavis)*, Harry Locke *(News Agent)*, Ellen Dryden *(Girl in News Agent's)*, Emlyn Williams *(Dr. Weaver)*

p, James Woolf, Richard Attenborough; d, Bryan Forbes; w, Bryan Forbes (based on the novel by Lynne Reid Banks); ph, Douglas Slocombe; ed, Anthony Harvey; m, John Barry; art d, Ray Simm; cos, Beatrice Dawson.

AAN Best Actress: Leslie Caron

An excellent, albeit talky, drama with enough comedy to leaven the heaviness. Caron is a French woman in her late twenties who departs her home in the provinces and moves to London. She gets pregnant but, rather than have an abortion, she decides to have the baby after meeting a money-hungry gynecologist (Williams) in Harley Street. By this time, she's moved to a sleazy boarding house in Notting Hill Gate and occupies the small L-shaped room of the title.

The house is filled with characters, and she soon falls for Bell, an out-of-work writer. Since everyone in the small hotel knows everyone else, Caron and Bell's affair is the main topic of conversation, and the tenants are thrilled by what's transpiring. The other people who live there, actresses, hookers, et al., are sentimental about the love that's flourishing, but Bell's best friend, Brock Peters, is incensed. He's a jazz musician with a conservative streak, and when he learns that Caron is pregnant, he tells Bell in an attempt to split the two.

Bell is angered and leaves Caron, who responds by taking some "abortion pills" given to her by Courtneidge, an aging actress who occupies a room below Caron's. The pills fail to work and Caron is actually relieved. Bell returns but cannot accept the fact that Caron is having someone else's baby. Caron goes to the hospital to have the child, and Bell arrives with a copy of a story he's written about their situation. It's called "The L-Shaped Room." Caron returns to France and leaves the story in Bell's room with a note attached to it saying, "It's a lovely story but it has no end." That's basically what's wrong with the movie, though Forbes and co. do a good job of making these characters sympathetic and involving.

LA BALANCE
1982 102m c Crime ★★★
Ariane/Spectrafilm/A2 (France) R/

Nathalie Baye *(Nicole)*, Philippe Leotard *(Dede)*, Richard Berry *(Palouzi)*, Christophe Malavoy *(Tintin)*, Jean-Paul Connart *(Le Belge)*, Bernard Freyd *(Le Capitaine)*, Albert Dray *(Carlini)*, Florent Pagny *(Simoni)*, Jean-Daniel Laval *(Arnaud)*, Luc-Antoine Diquero *(Picard)*

p, Georges Dancigers, Alexandre Mnouchkine; d, Bob Swaim; w, Bob Swaim, M. Fabiani; ph, Bernard Zitzermann; ed, Francoise Javet; m, Roland Bocquet; art d, Eric Moulard; cos, Catherine Meurisse

American expatriate director Bob Swaim puts a decidedly Parisian spin on Hollywood gangster conventions. One-time mobster Dede (Philippe Leotard) and prostitute Nicole (Nathalie Baye) play a power game with sleazy cops who are pressuring them to turn snitch. The couple are trying to live quietly on the money she earns from the street, but cop Palouzi (Richard Berry) is less concerned with their struggles than he is with busting a crime ring headed by a former associate of Dede's. If Dede cooperates, the police will leave him and Nicole alone. Unfortunately for Dede, he doesn't like the idea of being a stoolie or winding up dead. There are some nice moments here—the colorful opening sequence and an unlikely traffic jam shootout that results in a cop's Walkman stopping a bullet—but it all adds up to reasonably stylish pulp without much thought behind it. Warmly received by French audiences, LA BALANCE garnered a number of Cesars, including one for Best Picture.

LA BAMBA
1987 108m c Biography ★★½
New Visions (U.S.) PG-13/15

Lou Diamond Phillips *(Ritchie Valens)*, Esai Morales *(Bob Morales)*, Rosana DeSoto *(Connie Valenzuela)*, Elizabeth Pena *(Rosie Morales)*, Danielle von Zerneck *(Donna Ludwig)*, Joe Pantoliano *(Bob Keene)*, Rick Dees *(Ted Quillin)*, Marshall Crenshaw *(Buddy Holly)*, Howard Huntsberry *(Jackie Wilson)*, Brian Setzer *(Eddie Cochran)*

p, Taylor Hackford, Bill Borden; d, Luis Valdez; w, Luis Valdez; ph, Adam Greenberg; ed, Sheldon Kahn, Don Bruchu; m, Carlos Santana, Miles Goodman; prod d, Vincent Cresciman; cos, Sylvia Vega-Vasquez

Cliched melodrama about rock 'n' roll pioneer Ritchie Valens, notable as one of the first Mexican-Americans to achieve pop stardom. Beginning with his teenage days as a poor barrio resident in California, the film follows Valens (Lou Diamond Phillips) as he meets Donna Ludwig (Danielle von Zerneck), the love of his life and later the inspiration for his song "Donna," while living with his adoring mother (Rosana De Soto) and irresponsible, violent half-brother, Bob (Esai Morales). Ritchie's natural talent soon makes him the star of the small band he's joined, though his personal popularity causes friction with his jealous sibling. Soon, a record producer spots Ritchie, leading to his recording "Donna" and "La Bamba," which top the charts. At the peak of success, Valens loses his life in the plane crash made famous by Don McLean as "The Day the Music Died." The film is rich with period flavor, and Phillips is superb as Valens, but the rags-to-riches story (even if true) is maudlin and overfamiliar. Los Lobos does an excellent job of re-creating Valens' tunes and Carlos Santana provides a top-notch score.

LA BETE HUMAINE
1938 105m bw Drama ★★★½
Paris (France) /PG

Jean Gabin *(Jacques Lantier)*, Simone Simon *(Severine)*, Fernand Ledoux *(Roubaud, Severine's Husband)*, Julien Carette *(Pecqueux)*, Blanchette Brunoy *(Flore)*, Jean Renoir *(Cabuche, the Poacher)*, Gerard Landry *(Dauvergne's Son)*, Jenny Helia *(Philomene)*, Colette Regis *(Victoire)*, Jacques Berlioz *(Grand-Morin)*

p, Robert Hakim, Raymond Hakim; d, Jean Renoir; w, Jean Renoir (based on the novel by Emile Zola); ph, Curt Courant; ed, Marguerite Renoir, Suzanne de Troeye; m, Joseph Kosma

Locomotive engineer Jacques Lantier (Jean Gabin) is infatuated with Severin (Simone Simon), the beautiful but dangerous young wife of assistant stationmaster Roubaud (Fernand Ledoux). When Roubaud learns that Severin secured his job by sleeping with his superior, he goes mad with jealousy. With the aid of Severin, he kills his superior, an act blamed on an innocent poacher but witnessed by Lantier. Roubaud then sends his wife to Lantier as a means of ensuring the engineer's silence. Again Severin's bedroom prowess secures a lover's loyalty, resulting in a romance between the pair, whereupon Severin tries to persuade Lantier to kill Roubaud.

Based on the novel by Emile Zola (whose *Nana* was also adapted by Jean Renoir in 1926), LA BETE HUMAINE features one of Jean Gabin's greatest performances—one with even more force than the locomotive he powers. The catlike Simon is perfect as the persuasive beauty who drives both of the men in her life to their destructive deeds, her unattainable love their tragic downfall. This picture was remade by Fritz Lang as HUMAN DESIRE, Lang's second remake of a Renoir film. The first was SCARLET STREET, a remake of LA CHIENNE.

LA CAGE AUX FOLLES
1978 103m c Comedy ★★★½
Artistes/Da.Ma. (France/Italy) R/15

Ugo Tognazzi *(Renato)*, Michel Serrault *(Albin/"Zaza")*, Michel Galabru *(Charrier)*, Claire Maurier *(Simone)*, Remi Laurent *(Laurent)*, Benny Luke *(Jacob)*, Carmen Scarpitta *(Madame Charrier)*, Luisa Maneri *(Andrea)*

p, Marcello Danon; d, Edouard Molinaro; w, Marcello Danon, Edouard Molinaro, Francis Veber, Jean Poiret (based on his play); ph, Armando Nannuzzi; ed, Robert Isnardon, Monique Isnardon; m, Ennio Morricone; art d, Mario Garbuglia; cos, Piero Tosi, Ambra Danon

AAN Best Director: Edouard Molinaro; *AAN Best Adapted Screenplay:* Francis Veber (Screenplay), Edouard Molinaro (Screenplay), Marcello Danon (Screenplay), Jean Poiret (Screenplay); *AAN Best Costume Design:* Piero Tosi, Ambra Danon

LA COLLECTIONNEUSE

In less assured hands, this could have wound up as a disaster, but director Edouard Molinaro was skillfully able to film the long-running play and wring every drop of humor from it. Renato (Ugo Tognazzi) and Albin (Michel Serrault) have been lovers for more than 20 years. Albin is the lead "drag queen" of La Cage aux Folles, a Saint-Tropez nightclub, and Renato, the more masculine of the two, runs the day-to-day operations of the boite. Many years before, Renato stepped out of his gay lifestyle long enough to father Laurent (Remi Laurent) in a one-night stand, and since then both men have raised the boy. Now, Laurent comes home from college with the news that he is engaged to Andrea (Luisa Maneri), whose father, Charrier (Michel Galabru), is the secretary of the blue-nosed Union of Moral Order. As a result, Laurent has lied about his parentage and told his future father-in-law that his father is a cultural attache. From this set-up alone, one can guess that the situations that follow—revolving around Charrier's meeting with Renato—lead to some riotous results. Despite the apparent risk of making a movie with two gay leads, LA CAGE AUX FOLLES is basically an old-fashioned bedroom farce—and tamer than most, at that. Nonetheless, it was a huge international hit, spawning a pair of dreadful sequels and a fabulously successful stage musical.

LA COLLECTIONNEUSE

1967 88m c Drama ★★★
Losange/Rome Paris (France) /X

Patrick Bauchau (Adrien), Haydee Politoff (Haydee), Daniel Pommereulle (Daniel), Alain Jouffroy (Writer), Mijanou Bardot (Carole), Eugene Archer (Sam), Annik Morice (Carole's Friend), Denis Berry (Charlie), Brian Belshaw (Haydee's Lover), Donald Cammell (Boy At St. Tropez)

p, Georges Beauregard, Barbet Schroeder; d, Eric Rohmer; w, Eric Rohmer, Patrick Bauchau, Haydee Polltoff, Daniel Pommereulle; ph, Nestor Almendros; ed, Jackie Raynal; m, Blossom Toes, Giorgio Gomelsky

This film is the third in a series by Rohmer, "Six Moral Tales." Adrien (Bachau) is the handsome young man faced with the problem of whether to sleep with Haydee (Politoff), the pretty temptress who is staying at the same boarding house during his vacation in St. Tropez. Listening to her carry on with a number of different men, he attempts to purify himself, avoiding sex and other pleasurable pursuits.

The figure of Woman here provides a vehicle for Rohmer to question notions of moral correctness. The narrative structure follows a pattern that resembles Rohmer's other films, a presentation of a threatened moral stance in which the male always opts out of taking chances for a more secure existence. Bauchau could be criticized for being much too haughty and self-possessed to be very likable, but he is otherwise a perfect subject for Rohmer's experiment. The beautiful temptress played by Politoff is not really required to do much beyond looking nice; the camera does all the work. Almendros captures the beauty of Politoff and the scenery with an acute sense of detail. COLLECTIONEUSE was released belatedly in the US following the tremendous success of MY NIGHT AT MAUD'S, the fourth entry in Romer's series.

LA DOLCE VITA

1960 180m bw Drama ★★★½
Riama/Pathe/Gray (Italy/France) /X

Marcello Mastroianni (Marcello Rubini), Anita Ekberg (Sylvia), Anouk Aimee (Maddalena), Yvonne Furneaux (Emma), Magali Noel (Fanny), Alain Cuny (Steiner), Nadia Gray (Nadia), Lex Barker (Robert), Annibale Ninchi (Marcello's Father), Walter Santesso (Paparazzo)

p, Giuseppe Amato, Angelo Rizzoli; d, Federico Fellini; w, Federico Fellini, Ennio Flaiano, Tullio Pinelli, Brunello Rondi (based on a story by Federico Fellini, Tullio Pinelli, Ennio Flaiano, Tullio Pinelli); ph, Otello Martelli; ed, Leo Catozzo; m, Nino Rota; art d, Piero Gherardi; cos, Piero Gherardi

AAN Best Director: Federico Fellini; AAN Best Original Story and Screenplay: Federico Fellini, Tullio Pinelli, Ennio Flaiano, Brunello Rondi; AAN Best Art Direction: Piero Gherardi; AA Best Costume Design: Piero Gherardi

After what we've seen of decadence during the past three decades or so, LA DOLCE VITA now seems tame, but people wasting time in nightclubs, dancing in the fountains of Rome, and just generally hanging out seemed a bit of a shock in 1960.

The picture begins as Romans are shocked by seeing a large statue of Jesus being carried over the city by a helicopter. Following in a second chopper is Mastroianni, a gossip writer for the local scandal sheets. He aspires to serious writing but never gets beyond what he churns out for lire. While visiting a local nightspot, Mastroianni meets Aimee, a wealthy heiress suffering from a huge case of ennui. Everything bores her, and she is constantly on the lookout for new thrills. Together, they pick up hooker Moneta and spend the night as a menage a trois in the prostitute's room. When Mastroianni gets home, he finds his regular mistress, Furneaux, has taken an overdose of sleeping pills. He rushes her to the hospital, where he is assured that she'll recover, then races off to cover the arrival of Hollywood starlet Ekberg at the airport. He is soon infatuated with the buxom blonde and takes her for a tour around his Rome, including all the usual spots—Trevi, St. Peter's, the Caracalla Baths, etc. The tour is interrupted violently when Mastroianni is attacked by Ekberg's fiance Barker (who was her husband in real life). Things continue in this mode as Mastroianni takes in a fake vision of the Blessed Virgin by two young children, a visit from his quiet-living father, an infatuation with an innocent young waitress, etc. His crisis about the meaninglessness of his life comes to a head when Cuny, a bohemian intellectual whom he idolizes and envies, inexplicably commits suicide and takes the lives of his two children. True to the spirit of the film, Mastroianni still fails to act on his feelings, continuing with his hollow, glamorous life.

Episodic yet engrossing, LA DOLCE VITA is still worth a look, primarily for the window it offers onto the early days of the jet-set lifestyle. After nearly three hours, though, Fellini's relentlessly enigmatic, non-committal approach leaves you wishing for something more than poignant imagery and moody, self-obsessed characters.

LA FEMME INFIDELE

1969 98m c Thriller ★★★★
Les Films La Boetie/Cinegai (France/Italy) R/AA

Stephane Audran (Helene Desvallees), Michel Bouquet (Charles Desvallees), Maurice Ronet (Victor Pegala), Serge Bento (Bignon), Michel Duchaussoy (Police Officer Duval), Guy Marly (Police Officer Gobet), Stephane Di Napoli (Michel Desvallees), Louise Chevalier (Maid), Louise Rioton (Mother-in-Law), Henri Marteau (Paul)

p, Andre Genoves; d, Claude Chabrol; w, Claude Chabrol; ph, Jean Rabier; ed, Jacques Gaillard; m, Pierre Jansen; art d, Guy Littaye; cos, Maurice Albray

Michel Bouquet and Stephane Audran give superb performances in Claude Chabrol's LA FEMME INFIDELE, a gripping and stylishly made suspense tale.

Charles Desvallees (Michel Bouquet), a wealthy, mild-mannered insurance broker suspects that his wife Helene (Stephane Audran) is cheating on him. The detective reports that Helene spends her afternoons in the apartment of a divorced writer named Victor Pegala (Maurice Ronet). Charles visits Victor and sees Helene s cigarette lighter, and so questions him. As Victor starts to brag about their affair, Charles picks up a statuette and hits him over the head with it, killing him. He then calmly cleans up the blood, puts Victor's corpse into a sack and dumps it into a pond, then returns home to his son's birthday party. Helene is mystified by her lover's disappearance, but when the police interrogate her, she lies about their relationship. Subsequently, Helene finds a picture of Victor in Charles's coat pocket that would incriminate him in Victor's murder, but instead of informing the police, she burns it. Ironically, Helene develops a newfound love and respect for Charles, although neither of them lets the other know what they've done.

LE FEMME INFIDELE is arguably the best of Chabrol's superb, Hitchcockian studies of guilt, love, and murder among the French elite. His masterful, elegantly detached direction and trenchant psychological insight create moments of almost unbearable tension and suspense, aided by Jean Rabier's subtly sinister camera movements. Michel Bouquet and Stephane Audran (who was Chabrol's real-life wife at the time), give perhaps the finest performances of their careers. The two stars perfectly capture the deluded sensibility of their privileged characters in a satirical way without resorting to ridicule. Chabrol has stated that he makes films about the bourgeoisie because "I am one myself—I know them and I hate them, especially their extraordinary egoism." In Charles and Helene's complacent world of decorum and insincere emotions, nothing must be allowed to intrude to upset the balance and niceties of daily life, even murder.

LA FEMME NIKITA
(NIKITA)

1990 115m c Action/Drama ★★★
Films du Loup/Cecchi Gori Group/Tiger Cinematografica/Gaumont Production (France/Italy) R/18

Anne Parillaud *(Nikita)*, Jean-Hugues Anglade *(Marco)*, Tcheky Karyo *(Bob)*, Jeanne Moreau *(Amande)*, Jean Reno *(Nikita's Partner)*, Jean Bouise *(Cabinet Chief)*, Philippe DuJanerand *(Ambassador)*, Roland Blanche *(Police Investigator)*, Phillipe Leroy-Beaulieu *(Commander Grosmann)*, Marc Duret *(Rico)*

d, Luc Besson; w, Luc Besson; ph, Thierry Arbogast; ed, Olivier Mauffroy; m, Eric Serra; prod d, Dan Weil

A high-gloss thriller from director-writer Luc Besson about the transformation of a sociopathic punk into a beautiful, enigmatic spy.

After casually shooting a policeman during a bungled robbery attempt, Nikita (Parillaud) is tried and sentenced to death. Her nihilism lands her the chance to forego her sentence, in return for agreeing to work as an undercover government agent/hit-person. During several years of training in a mysterious high-tech compound, Nikita begins by exuding attitude—i.e. biting the ear of her karate instructor—but finally shapes up as an operative and is "released" into the world for a series of sleek, if farfetched assignments.

In the tradition of NOTORIOUS and DISHONORED, LA FEMME NIKITA features a morally questionable beauty burnished by a master spy, only to be converted from the secret trade by both a lover and the harsher elements of spycraft. LA FEMME NIKITA has far less substance than either of those films, offering little in the way of character development or verisimilitude. We are never given a rationale for Nikita's missions, and the screenplay never even begins to explain her behavior. Jeanne Moreau's cameo as a woman who instructs our heroine in the art of femininity borders on the ludicrous. For fans of Besson (SUBWAY, THE BIG BLUE), though, that's hardly the point. The director has turned out a supremely slick piece of entertainment where style triumphs over substance. The beautiful Parillaud leads us on a high-tech rollercoaster ride which, if you don't mind the stylized ultra-violence and throwaway plot, can be a lot of fun.

LA GUERRE EST FINIE
(KRIGETAR SLUT)

1966 121m bw Drama ★★★★
Sofracima/Europa (France/Sweden) /X

Yves Montand *(Diego)*, Ingrid Thulin *(Marianne)*, Genevieve Bujold *(Nadine Sallanches)*, Jean Daste *(Chief)*, Jorge Semprun *(Narrator)*, Dominique Rozan *(Jude)*, Jean-Francois Remi *(Juan)*, Marie Mergey *(Madame Lopez)*, Jacques Wallet *(CRS Policeman)*, Michel Piccoli *(1st Customs Inspector)*

p, Catherine Winter, Gisele Rebillon; d, Alain Resnais; w, Jorge Semprun; ph, Sacha Vierny; ed, Eric Pluet; m, Giovanni Fusco; cos, Marie Martine

AAN Best Original Screenplay: Jorge Semprun

Montand is Diego, a longtime revolutionary who lives in Paris. He has been active against the Spanish government and is now returning from Madrid carrying a false passport. The *Guardia Civil* stops him at the border and tries to determine his real identity, but a call to his Paris phone number turns up Nadine (Bujold), a student in the revolutionary movement who corroborates his papers. Diego returns to Paris to learn that his pals have been captured in Madrid and that his local contact, Juan (Remi), went back to Spain at the same time he was returning to France. Diego wants to help Juan, but has difficulties enlisting any aid for the mission.

He turns briefly to Nadine for love, but soon goes back to his former mistress Marianne (Thulin), a divorcee who is raising a son on her own. Diego still yearns to go to Madrid to aid the cause, but others in his group forbid their well-known colleague from going and send another (Jean Bouise) in his place. Diego must also contend with the plans of Nadine and her student comrades to terrorize tourists in Spain in order to publicize their political beliefs. Ultimately, though, Diego does head for Madrid, where things go awry almost instantly.

This picture has more tension than action, which is typical of director Resnais, who gave us the endlessly teasing LAST YEAR AT MARIENBAD. Filmed in and around Paris, LA GUERRE EST FINIE never did much at the box office and sank into the sunset all too quickly. Not Resnais' greatest effort, but a provocative portrait of political rebels and a challenging anti-war film just the same.

LA NOTTE

1961 122m bw Drama ★★★
Nepi/Silver/Sofitedip (France/Italy) /X

Marcello Mastroianni *(Giovanni)*, Jeanne Moreau *(Lidia)*, Monica Vitti *(Valentina Gherardini)*, Bernhard Wicki *(Tommaso)*, Maria Pia Luzi *(Patient)*, Rosy Mazzacurati *(Resy)*, Guido A. Marsan *(Fanti)*, Gitt Magrini *(Signora Gherardini)*, Vincenzo Corbella *(Gherardini)*, Giorgio Negro *(Roberto)*

p, Emanuele Cassuto; d, Michelangelo Antonioni; w, Michelangelo Antonioni, Tonino Guerra, Ennio Flaiano (based on a story by Michelangelo Antonioni); ph, Gianni Di Venanzo; ed, Eraldo Da Roma; m, Giorgio Gaslini

Marcello Mastroianni and Jeanne Moreau play husband and wife in Antonioni's study of emptiness and sterility in modern life and relationships.

It opens with their visit to a hospitalized friend dying of cancer. They are on their way to a party for the publication of Giovanni's (Mastroianni) new novel, but the celebration is cut short when Lidia (Moreau) informs him, en route, that he disgusts her and she no longer wants to live with him. She leaves the party and wanders the barren streets for the remainder of the night, while Giovanni chases after Valentina (Vitti), the young daughter of an industrialist who has offered him a job. When Lidia and Giovanni confront one another at home later, the news of a friend's death that night draws them together once again.

Much of Antonioni's greatness is evident in this picture—the seemingly hopeless relationship between a man and a woman, the overwhelming environment which is devoid of emotion, and the quietly observant camerawork. But at the same time Antonioni is sometimes painfully obvious with his use of symbolism. One of the film's major faults lies in its casting of Mastroianni, who simply doesn't fit his role. This problematic film serves more as a transition for Antonioni than anything else, and seems to make even less sense when screened without having seen his previous film, the masterful L'AVVENTURA.

LA NUIT DE VARENNES

1982 135m c Historical/Comedy ★★★★
Gaumont/Columbia (France/Italy) R/15

Marcello Mastroianni *(Casanova)*, Jean-Louis Barrault *(Nicolas Edme Restif)*, Hanna Schygulla *(Countess Sophie de la Borde)*, Harvey Keitel *(Thomas Paine)*, Jean-Claude Brialy *(M. Jacob)*, Daniel Gelin *(De Wendel)*, Jean-Louis Trintignant *(M. Sauce)*, Michel Piccoli *(King Louis XVI)*, Eleonore Hirt *(Queen Marie-Antoinette)*, Andrea Ferreol *(Mme. Adelaide Gagnon)*

p, Renzo Rossellini; d, Ettore Scola; w, Ettore Scola, Sergio Amidei; ph, Armando Nannuzzi; ed, Raimondo Crociani; m, Armando Travajoi; art d, Dante Ferretti; cos, Gabriella Pescucci

This fine, often bizarre, historical drama begins with a basis in fact and runs wild with imaginative possibilities. King Louis XVI (Michel Piccoli) and his queen (Eleonore Hirt) flee Paris for the safety of Varennes at the height of the French Revolution. Close behind in a pursuing coach, bickering about life and politics, are Casanova (Marcello Mastroianni, in an excellent performance) and American revolutionary Thomas Paine (Harvey Keitel). All the while, the revolution spreads like wildfire. As with other recent films by Italian director

LA RONDE

Ettore Scola—LE BAL, MACARONI, THE FAMILY—the exploration of the past becomes a vehicle for understanding today's problems and those of the future.

Besides the benefits of the lush photography and elegant costumes, Scola again works with an excellent cast that reads as a virtual Who's Who of European cinema, including Jean-Louis Barrault, Hanna Schygulla, Jean-Claude Brialy, Jean-Louis Trintignant, Andrea Ferreol and Daniel Gelin. A feast of a film in many ways.

LA RONDE

1950 97m bw Drama ★★★★★
Commercial (France) /X

Anton Walbrook *(Raconteur)*, Simone Signoret *(Leocadie, the Prostitute)*, Serge Reggiani *(Franz, the Soldier)*, Simone Simon *(Marie, the Maid)*, Daniel Gelin *(Alfred)*, Danielle Darrieux *(Emma Breitkopf)*, Fernand Gravet *(Charles, Emma's Husband)*, Odette Joyeux *(The Grisette)*, Jean-Louis Barrault *(Robert Kuhlenkampf)*, Isa Miranda *(The Actress)*

p, Sacha Gordine; d, Max Ophuls; w, Max Ophuls, Jacques Natanson (based on the play *Der Reigen* by Arthur Schnitzler); ph, Christian Matras; ed, Leonide Azar; m, Oscar Straus

AAN Best Original Screenplay: Jacques Natanson, Max Ophuls; *AAN Best Art Direction:* D'Eaubonne (Art Direction)

Released in Paris in 1950, LA RONDE, though quickly hailed as one of Max Ophuls' greatest achievements, was kept from US shores for four years thanks to a judgment of "immoral" by the New York State censorship board. A merry-go-round of romance is detailed in episodic fashion as characters drift from sequence to sequence, switching lovers as they go.

A young prostitute (Signoret) meets a soldier (Reggiani), who leaves her for a maid (Simon). The maid, however, soon meets another (Gelin), who seduces a wealthy married woman (Darrieux), whose husband is involved with a young worker (Joyeux). This woman in turn loves a poet (Barrault) in love with an actress (Miranda). The actress, however, loves an officer (Philipe). Love comes around full circle when he calls on the prostitute from the first episode. Each segment is delightfully introduced by a master of ceremonies (Walbrook), who appears with the metaphorical carousel in each of his scenes.

Originally Ophuls had planned to adapt a novel by Balzac with Greta Garbo in a lead role, but instead he turned his attentions to the heralded Arthur Schnitzler play, which in his hands emphasized the follies of love over the concerns about syphillis the play explored. One of four masterworks Ophuls dashed off in the 1950s before his untimely death, LA RONDE explores his recurrent obsession with circles to dizzying effect. The humor is beguiling, the satire on target, Ophuls legendary camerawork is in fine and restless form, and the acting of a very high order.

Signoret is particularly good, but stealing the show, unexpectedly, is the marvelous Walbrook. Indulging the gentle sentiment of the whole undertaking to just the right degree, he is dapper and alert. The moment where one story is interrupted as he quickly reassembles the broken film is perfection. You're not likely to forget Walbrook's song—a round, of course.

L.A. STORY

1991 95m c Comedy/Romance ★★½
Carolco/IndieProd Company/L.A. Films (U.S.) PG-13/15

Steve Martin *(Harris K. Telemacher)*, Victoria Tennant *(Sara)*, Richard E. Grant *(Roland)*, Marilu Henner *(Trudi)*, Sarah Jessica Parker *(SanDeE*)*, Susan Forristal *(Ariel)*, Kevin Pollak *(Frank Swan)*, Sam McMurray *(Morris Frost)*, Patrick Stewart *(Maitre d' at l'Idiot)*, Andrew Amador *(Male News Reporter)*

p, Daniel Melnick, Michael Rachmil; d, Mick Jackson; w, Steve Martin (from his story); ph, Andrew Dunn; ed, Richard A. Harris; m, Peter Melnick; prod d, Lawrence Miller; art d, Charles Breen; cos, Rudy Dillon

In its dream-like sweetness and fairy tale romanticism, L.A. STORY resembles another film written by and starring Steve Martin, ROXANNE. But the comic romance that was that film's *raison d'etre* is not much in evidence here.

The film unfolds from the clear-eyed gaze of Harris K. Telemacher (Martin), who immediately reveals his peculiar malaise by confiding to us: "I was deeply unhappy but I didn't know it because I was happy all the time." As a TV news program's wacky weekend weatherman, Telemacher predicts the predictable, propagating a heaven-on-earth Los Angeles of perfect sunshine and a perpetual temperature of 72 degrees. But pockets of unease quietly begin to undermine his complacency, culminating in an outdoor luncheon with his testy girlfriend Trudi (Henner) and a group of shallow acquaintances. Arriving late is unconventional British reporter Sara (Tennant), to whom Harris is curiously attracted. Shortly afterward, Harris has an epiphany on the Los Angeles Freeway, and his life is turned upside down.

In L.A. STORY, the romance assumes a supporting role beside the mystical, apocalyptic aura evoked by the city itself. The characters in the film have no past, no future, and are in the grip of the off-balance life of L.A. Unlike Woody Allen's New York City, which becomes a staging area for character angst and transformation, Martin's L.A. stifles the characters, and neither they, screenwriter Martin or director Jackson seem to be aware of it. Instead, Harris and Sara find themselves put through the paces of a Spielbergian fantasy landscape as they gaze upward at the divine white aura of a Hollywood sign before the final clinch. And it is a sad loss, for the filmmakers squandered the opportunity to produce a satiric West Coast MANHATTAN.

LA STRADA

1954 115m bw Drama ★★★★★
Trans-Lux (Italy) /PG

Giulietta Masina *(Gelsomina)*, Richard Basehart *(Matto "The Fool")*, Aldo Silvani *(Columbiani)*, Marcella Rovere *(La Vedova)*, Livia Venturini *(La Suorina)*

p, Carlo Ponti, Dino De Laurentiis; d, Federico Fellini; w, Federico Fellini, Tullio Pinelli, Ennio Flaiano (based on a story by Federico Fellini and Tullio Pinelli); ph, Otello Martelli; ed, Leo Catozzo, Lina Caterini; m, Nino Rota; art d, Mario Ravasco, E. Cervelli

AA Best Foreign Language Film

Federico Fellini was at the top of his form here, as was his wife and frequent star, Giulietta Masina, whose pantomime in LA STRADA caused her to be dubbed a female Chaplin. She *is* marvelous.

Zampano (Anthony Quinn), a traveling strongman, "buys" the dim-witted but pure of heart Gelsomina (Masina) to help him with his act. The two travel together, with her beating the drum and playing a trumpet to herald his act, and serving as his mistress and slave. Eventually, the pair join a tiny circus and meet il Matto ("The Fool," played by Richard Basehart), a clown and high-wire artist who treats Gelsomina kindly. When the ethereal Fool is accidentally killed by the brutish Zampano, she is devastated and suffers an emotional breakdown, and the strongman abandons her. Many years later, still traveling, Zampano learns of Gelsomina's fate and belatedly realizes his need for her.

Perhaps the simplest and certainly one of the most powerful of Fellini's films, LA STRADA established his international fame while marking a distinct break from neorealism in its poetic, deeply personal imagery (especially the "Felliniesque" circus motif), and religious symbolism. While Masina's unforgettable performance, perfectly combining comedy and pathos, caused the greatest stir, Quinn and Basehart are also excellent, and Nino Rota's music became famous worldwide.

LA TERRA TREMA

1947 160m bw Drama ★★★★★
Universalia (Italy)

Luchino Visconti, Antonio Pietrangeli *(Narrators)*, Antonio Arcidiacono
p, Salvo D'Angelo; d, Luchino Visconti; w, Luchino Visconti (based on the novel *I Malavoglia* by Giovanni Verga); ph, G.R. Aldo; ed, Mario Serandrei

With a lyrical, even operatic quality that subtly combines photographic beauty with the cruel plight of its subjects, LA TERRA TREMA is one of the greatest films to emerge from the Italian neorealist movement.

Set in Aci-Trezza, a small Sicilian fishing village, with the entire cast consisting of locals—their weather-beaten faces lending a sense of realism—the film involves the villagers' victimization by the entrepreneurs who control the fishing market. One young man, 'Ntoni (Antonio Arcidiacono), returns home from WWII convinced that the villagers need no longer be subject to such unfairness, that by pulling together they can alter the system and eventually overcome their imposed poverty.

LA TERRA TREMA is a powerful picture that exposes the injustice inherent in a society where the privileged are allowed to ride roughshod over their inferiors. Despite its social import, the film was a terrible failure at the Italian theaters. Its historical significance, however, is immense. The use of non-professional actors, deep-focus cinematography, natural light, and direct sound recording, while rarely seen in Italian films of the day, were all integral to LA TERRA TREMA—products undoubtedly of Visconti's work with Jean Renoir.

Serving as assistant directors on this picture were Francesco Rosi and Franco Zeffirelli, both of whom would eventually become leading directors. LA TERRA TREMA today stands as one of the most brilliant combinations of the realistic with the stylized that Visconti ever achieved.

LA TRAVIATA

1982 105m c Opera ★★★★
Accent/RA-1 (Italy) G/U

Teresa Stratas (Violetta Valery), Placido Domingo (Alfredo Germont), Cornell MacNeil (Giorgio Germont), Alan Monk (Baron), Axelle Gall (Flora Betvoix), Pina Cei (Annina), Maurizio Barbacini (Gastone), Robert Sommer (Doctor Grenvil), Ricardo Oneto (Marquis d'Obigny), Luciano Brizi (Giuseppe)

p, Tarak Ben Ammar; d, Franco Zeffirelli; w, Franco Zeffirelli (based on the libretto by Francesco Maria Piave from the novel The Lady of the Camelias by Alexandre Dumas); ph, Ennio Guarnieri; ed, Peter Taylor, Franca Sylvi; m, Giuseppe Verdi; prod d, Franco Zeffirelli; art d, Gianni Quaranta; chor, Alberto Testa; cos, Piero Tosi

AAN Best Art Direction: Franco Zeffirelli (Art Direction), Gianni Quaranta (Set Decoration); AAN Best Costume Design: Piero Tosi

Franco Zeffirelli's version of the classic Verdi opera stars Teresa Stratas as Violetta and Placido Domingo as her lover, Alfredo. Zeffirelli outdoes himself this time, offering no less than one of cinema's finest opera adaptations. LA TRAVIATA boasts not only the presence of Domingo and the electrifying Stratas but some truly amazing camerawork. The camera dollies, zooms, cranes and pans relentlessly showcase the gigantic, elaborately constructed set. Indeed, cinematographer Ennio Guarnieri and art designer Gianni Quaranta have joined forces with Zeffirelli to present a feast for the eyes—a worthy accompaniment to the brilliant score.

LABYRINTH OF PASSION
(LABERINTO DE PASIONES)

1982 100m c Comedy ★★★★
Alphaville (Spain)

Cecilia Roth (Sexilia), Luis Ciges (Her Father), Imanol Arias (Riza Niro), Antonio Banderas (Sadeq), Helga Line (Toraya), Marta Fernandez-Muro (Queti), Angel Alcazar (Eusebio), Agustin Almodovar (Hassan), Pedro Almodovar (Performer)

d, Pedro Almodovar; w, Pedro Almodovar; ph, Angel L. Fernandez; ed, Jose Salcedo; prod d, Pedro Almodovar

Made in 1982, but released in the US in 1990 following the success of WOMEN ON THE VERGE OF A NERVOUS BREAKDOWN, Pedro Almodovar's LABYRINTH OF PASSION is a screwball sex comedy set in a world of unorthodox and baroquely intertwined personal relationships in Madrid. Predicated on mistaken identity and misinterpreted motives, the plot is a tangle that defies simple summary.

Among the some 50 characters is Sexilia (Cecilia Roth), "Sexi" for short, a carefree, heliophobic nymphomaniac whose father (Luis Ciges) is a repressed, world-famous fertility specialist. Hoping to exorcise her fear of sunlight, Sexi consults a therapist, who announces that Sexi's trouble is incestuous attraction to her father. The therapist then confesses her own determination to seduce the fertility expert, whose patients include the manipulative, aristocratic Toraya (Helga Line). Toraya, in turn, has designs on Riza Niro (Imanol Arias), the gay son of the deposed ruler of the Arab nation of Tyran. Riza, who just wants to cruise the Spanish bars and docks incognito, has difficulty maintaining a low profile. Scandal sheets speculate about his activities, revolutionary student terrorists hope to kidnap him, and Toraya is determined

to find and seduce him as part of a plot to avenge herself on his father. Blithely unaware of these goings-on, Riza meets Sexi in a discotheque, and they fall head over heels for one another. Needless to say, the course of their love—true though it is—does not run smooth.

What gives the film its revolutionary twist is the breadth of its definition of love. LABYRINTH OF PASSION's sexual landscape is a virtual catalogue of erotic possibility, a pop paean to a multiplicity of forms and desires. Old and young, fat and thin, beautiful and homely pair off and break up according to the whims of outrageous fortune, paying little, if any, attention to conventional notions of appropriate coupling. And in the end, all's well that ends well—an optimistic message delivered with sophisticated, satirical bite.

LACEMAKER, THE
(LA DENTELLIERE)

1977 108m c Romance ★★★½
Citel/FR-3/Action/Janus (France) R/AA

Isabelle Huppert (Beatrice, "Pomme"), Yves Beneyton (Francois), Florence Giorgetti (Marylene), Christian Baltauss (Gerard), Renata Schroeter (Marianne), Annemarie Duringer (Beatrice's Mother), Michel de Re (Painter), Monique Chaumette (Francois' Mother), Jean Obe (Francois' Father), Odile Poisson (Cashier)

d, Claude Goretta; w, Claude Goretta, Pascal Laine (based on the novel by Laine); ph, Jean Boffety; ed, Joele Van Effenterre; m, Pierre Jansen

As carefully spun as fine lace. Huppert plays Beatrice, a shy and passive young woman nicknamed "Pomme" ("Apple") who travels to the Normandy coast with her best friend Marylene (Giorgetti) and meets Francois (Beneyton), a middle-class literature student. He is attracted to the sheepish, freckle-faced Beatrice even though there is an obvious difference in class and education.

They become lovers and get an apartment together in Paris. They are genuinely in love, but their differences begin to surface. Marylene tries to convince Beatrice to do more with her life than be a beautician. She is content, however, with simply loving Francois. When he brings her home to meet the family, he realizes that he should be with a woman who shares his interests in journalism. They soon drift apart, and finally he asks her to leave. Beatrice becomes ill and soon is admitted to a mental hospital. Her mother writes to Francois, asking him to pay her daughter a visit. At the urging of his friends, he agrees. Their bittersweet reunion leads the film to its conclusion.

A delicately wrought yet devastating look at the pain of love, THE LACEMAKER boasts one of the earliest major performances from the 22-year-old Huppert, who has gone on to become one of Europe's most breathtakingly prolific actresses, appearing in ENTRE NOUS and two Godard films, EVERY MAN FOR HIMSELF and PASSION.

LACOMBE, LUCIEN

1974 141m c Drama/War ★★★★
Fox (U.S.) R/

Pierre Blaise (Lucien), Aurore Clement (France), Holger Lowenadler (Albert Horn), Therese Gieshe (Bella Horn), Stephane Bouy (Jean Bernard), Loumi Iacobesco (Betty Beaulieu), Rene Bouloc (Faure), Pierre Decazes (Aubert), Jean Rougerie (Tonin), Gilberte Rivet (Mme. Lacombe)

p, Louis Malle; d, Louis Malle; w, Louis Malle, Patrick Modiano; ph, Tonino Delli Colli; ed, Suzanne Baron; m, Django Reinhardt, Andre Claveau, Irene de Trebert; art d, Ghislain Uhry

AAN Best Foreign Language Film

A masterful job. Director Louis Malle directs his intellectual focus at the Occupation this time around. Blaise plays Lucien, a young farm boy who tries to join the French Resistance but is rejected because of his youth. The Gestapo, however, is happy to have the boy and treats him royally, supplying him with liquor and anything else he requests. He then makes the mistake of falling in love with a Jewish girl, France (Clement), resulting in her father's deportation. With France and her mother in tow, Lucien sets out for Spain with the Resistance out to kill him.

LACOMBE, LUCIEN represents a turn for the better for Malle, whose sometimes tends to shroud audience sympathy in underdeveloped intellectualizing. Much of Malle's motivation came from his own experiences growing up in France during the German Occupation. Even so, his fellow countrymen did not care very much for this cutting portrayal of the Resistance. Their vocal indictments inspired Malle to migrate to America, where he made such films as ATLANTIC CITY and PRETTY BABY. A great score by Reinhardt helps flesh out this moving, carefully handled film.

LADY AND THE TRAMP

1955 75m c Animated ★★★½
Walt Disney Productions (U.S.) /U

VOICES OF: Peggy Lee (Darling/Peg/Si/Am), Barbara Luddy (Lady), Larry Roberts (Tramp), Bill Thompson (Jock/Bull/Dachsie), Bill Baucon (Trusty), Stan Freberg (Beaver), Verna Felton (Aunt Sarah), Alan Reed (Boris), George Givot (Tony), Dal McKennon (Toughy/Professor)

p, Walt Disney; d, Hamilton Luske, Clyde Geronimi, Wilfred Jackson; w, Erdman Penner, Joe Rinaldi, Ralph Wright, Don DaGradi (based on the novel by Ward Greene); ed, Donald Halliday; m, Oliver Wallace; anim, Milt Kahl, Franklin Thomas, Oliver M. Johnston, John Lounsbery, Wolfgang Reitherman, Eric Larson, Hal King, Les Clark

This animated Disney classic tells the tale of Lady, a prim and proper cocker spaniel who falls in love with Tramp, a ragged mutt. When Lady runs away from her owner and is pursued by tough dogs in a bad neighborhood, Tramp rescues her. The two dogs spend a night on the town, which includes the memorable spaghetti-eating scene in which both Lady and Tramp eat the same strand, their mouths drawn closer and closer until at last they kiss. Lady is furious with Tramp when they end up in the pound after being caught raiding a chicken coup, but by the finale they are happily raising their own litter of pups. Disney's first CinemaScope cartoon, LADY AND THE TRAMP cost $4,000,000 and took three years to complete, but it grossed over $25,000,000, making more money than any other film from the 1950s except THE TEN COMMANDMENTS and BEN-HUR.

LADY EVE, THE

1941 97m bw Comedy/Romance ★★★★★
Paramount (U.S.) /U

Barbara Stanwyck (Jean Harrington), Henry Fonda (Charles Pike), Charles Coburn ("Colonel" Harry Harrington), Eugene Pallette (Mr. Pike), William Demarest (Muggsy-Ambrose Murgatroyd), Eric Blore (Sir Alfred McGlennan Keith), Melville Cooper (Gerald), Martha O'Driscoll (Martha), Janet Beecher (Mrs. Pike), Robert Greig (Burrows)

p, Paul Jones; d, Preston Sturges; w, Preston Sturges (based on the story "The Faithful Heart" by Monckton Hoffe); ph, Victor Milner; ed, Stuart Gilmore; art d, Hans Dreier, Ernst Fegte; cos, Edith Head

AAN Best Original Screenplay: Monckton Hoffe

Sturges's chic, sly little masterpiece of comic seduction. Fonda, who is the son of a wealthy brewer (Pallette, whose slogan is "Pike's Pale, the Ale That Won for Yale"), is a rather shy and backward young man whose main interest is in snakes. As the film opens, he has just spent a year with a scientific expedition on the Amazon, looking for undiscovered species of reptiles. He and his bodyguard, Demarest, board a ship in the Atlantic which will take them back to New York. Of course, Fonda, being young, handsome, and the heir to a vast fortune, attracts the attention of virtually every female on the ship, but he shows no interest in the opposite sex.

Also on board is a team of card sharps, father and daughter Stanwyck and Coburn, and Cooper, posing as their butler. They figure Fonda would make an excellent pigeon, and Stanwyck conspires to gain his trust, which she does. Fonda is quickly smitten with her, and sits down to play some cards with her and her father. He considers himself to be quite the card player, but is embarrassed when he wins $600 from these nice people. Of course, he's only being set up to lose; but before the cons can reel in their prey, they hit a snag. Stanwyck has genuinely fallen in love with the man, much to the disgust of her associates.

THE LADY EVE is one of Sturges' best romantic comedies, with just the right blend of satire and slapstick, the laughs coming mostly from his clever, often inspired comedic lines. His direction is flawless, and the cast, from stars to stock players, performs beautifully. Stanwyck, is particular, is an effortless comedienne. She pitches much of her performance into a kind of hushed, urgent, intimate whisper.

When she talks to Fonda, she's constantly toying with him, touching him like a fetish, and she's always in his face, often looking at his lips. Then out snakes a sexy leg—a very sexy leg—and over he topples. There's an unparalleled moment early on, when she narrates his movements, taking his part and every woman's who attempts to trap him in conversation, while watching the action backwards in her compact mirror. It's a daring, roguish display of her talent; one can't imagine any comedienne—even Colbert or Russell—bringing it off as she does. Sturges, who began as a contract scriptwriter for Paramount, promised Stanwyck that he would write a great comedy for her some day, and she got it.

LADY FROM SHANGHAI, THE

1948 87m bw Crime ★★★★½
Columbia (U.S.) /A

Rita Hayworth (Elsa Bannister), Orson Welles (Michael O'Hara), Everett Sloane (Arthur Bannister), Glenn Anders (George Grisby), Ted de Corsia (Sidney Broome), Erskine Sanford (Judge), Gus Schilling (Goldie), Carl Frank (District Attorney), Lou Merrill (Jake), Evelyn Ellis (Bessie)

p, Orson Welles; d, Orson Welles; w, Orson Welles (based on the novel by [Raymond] Sherwood King); ed, Viola Lawrence; m, Heinz Roemheld; art d, Stephen Goosson, Sturges Carne; fx, Lawrence Butler; cos, Jean Louis

This remarkably inventive if decidedly confusing film noir stars Welles as a wandering Irishman named Michael O'Hara. One evening he saves Elsa Bannister (Hayworth) from a couple of thugs and, as a result, she is drawn to him like a shark to a swimmer. Her husband, famed lawyer Arthur Bannister (Sloane), offers to hire O'Hara as a deckhand for an upcoming cruise. O'Hara—who begins the film by saying, "When I start out to make a fool of myself, there's very little can stop me!"—accepts the offer, trying not to succumb to Elsa's advances along the way. Pretty soon O'Hara is on his way to making an A-1 fool out of himself, entering into an agreement with Bannister's goony, sweat-stained friend George Grisby (Anders), who offers O'Hara a sum of money to stage Grisby's own murder. When things start to misfire, O'Hara becomes, in fatalistic noir fashion, a puppet under the reckless control of everyone around him.

Replete with humorous self-deprecating narration, marvelous performances, and typically Wellesian visuals, THE LADY FROM SHANGHAI dazzles as much as it obfuscates. The most amazing visual effect is the climactic Crazy House/Hall of Mirrors location, which is a wonder of surrealistic set design. With its complex and occasionally incoherent narrative, the film will stump many of those viewers who think they can easily decipher a mystery. Fans of Rita Hayworth, then Welles's wife, were shocked—as was studio mogul Harry Cohn—when they saw her long, luxuriant russet hair cut into a blonde bob. The yacht on which the characters sail belonged to Welles's friend Errol Flynn, and it is Flynn (unseen) who is sailing the vessel during the trip. An uneven film, perhaps, but one which only seems to improve with age.

LADY IN THE DARK

1944 100m c Musical ★★★
Paramount (U.S.) /U

Ginger Rogers (Liza Elliott), Ray Milland (Charley Johnson), Jon Hall (Randy Curtis), Warner Baxter (Kendall Nesbitt), Barry Sullivan (Dr. Brooks), Mischa Auer (Russell Paxton), Mary Philips (Maggie Grant), Phyllis Brooks (Allison DuBois), Edward Fielding (Dr. Carlton), Don Loper (Adams)

p, Richard Blumenthal; d, Mitchell Leisen; w, Frances Goodrich, Albert Hackett (based on the play by Moss Hart, Kurt Weill, Ira Gershwin); ph, Ray Rennahan, Farciot Edouart; ed, Alma Macrorie; m, Robert Emmett Dolan; art d, Hans Dreier, Raoul Pene du Bois; fx, Gordon Jennings, Paul K. Lerpae; chor, Billy Daniels, Don Loper; cos, Edith Head, Mitchell Leisen, Babs Wilomez, Raoul Pene Du Bois

AAN Best Cinematography: Ray Rennahan; AAN Best Score: Robert Emmett Dolan; AAN Best Art Direction: Hans Dreier (Art Direction), Raoul Pene DuBois (Art Direction), Ray Moyer (Interior Decoration)

LADY IN THE DARK seemed like a breakthrough on Broadway, where it featured Danny Kaye and Victor Mature in support of Gertrude Lawrence. Unfortunately, none of these suitably cast players made it to the screen version, and the loss is evident. Also regrettable is the excising of several wonderful Weill-Gershwin tunes from the play in favor of new songs that don't enhance the plot. As if all this weren't enough, even the original's book doesn't seem quite as good as its reputation would suggest.

Ginger Rogers (in her first color film) is Liza Elliott, a magazine editor who's on the verge of a nervous breakdown, partly because she has too many men in her life. She seeks help from a psychiatrist (Sullivan), and her sessions with him and some dream sequences provide the material for the film's production numbers. Vying for Liza's attention and threatening her job security are Charley Johnson (Milland), the advertising manager for her magazine; recently divorced Kendall Nesbitt (Baxter); and handsome hunk Randy Curtis (Hall).

This expensive film made a lot of money upon its 1944 release, when audiences were clamoring for something light to relieve wartime anxieties. The story was unusual then, dealing as it did with Liza's position in a high-pressured man's world, her precarious emotional state (presented in Freudian terms that were still fairly novel for most moviegoers), and her inability to make a decision. It's all lavishly presented with glamorous style, but it's almost as if director Leisen cared more about the look of the film than its content.

Rogers has a good (if too distantly filmed) dance number with Don Loper, and she does a fine job singing the amusing "The Saga of Jenny", but her performance is uneven. The same goes for most of the cast, and even the storyline, missing the crucial song "My Ship" (from the heroine's childhood), seems a little out of kilter in retrospect. The result is a glitzy but superficial marriage of musical comedy and pop psychology.

LADY IN THE LAKE

1947   105m   bw   Mystery   ★★★½
MGM   (U.S.)   /A

Robert Montgomery (Philip Marlowe), Lloyd Nolan (Lt. DeGarmot), Audrey Totter (Adrienne Fromsett), Tom Tully (Capt. Kane), Leon Ames (Derace Kingsby), Jayne Meadows (Mildred Havelend), Morris Ankrum (Eugene Grayson), Lila Leeds (Receptionist), Richard Simmons (Chris Lavery), Ellen Ross (Elevator Girl)

p, George Haight; d, Robert Montgomery; w, Steve Fisher, Raymond Chandler (based on the novel by Chandler, uncredited); ph, Paul C. Vogel; ed, Gene Ruggiero; m, David Snell; art d, Cedric Gibbons, Preston Ames; fx, A. Arnold Gillespie; cos, Irene

"YOU accept an invitation to a blonde's apartment! YOU get socked in the jaw by a murder suspect!" That's how ads promoted this inventive if not entirely successful film noir, the first to employ a subjective camera. Under star Montgomery's direction, the viewer is in the film, so to speak, with all the action and characters addressing the camera, which tells the story from the point of view of Raymond Chandler's incorruptible private eye, Philip Marlowe.

The film opens as Marlowe begins to relate the "Lady in the Lake" caper. The subjective camera takes over, the story unfolding in flashback. Tired of sleuthing for a living, Marlowe has taken up writing and produced a number of detective stories that he has submitted to Kingsby Publications. Having read his most recent story, editor Adrienne Fromsett (Totter) asks that he come to see her. When he arrives in the magazine office, Marlowe learns that Adrienne is not really interested in his story; instead she plans to wed Kingsby (Ames), and she wants the detective to find his missing wife so she can have her man. The first step in Marlowe's investigation is a visit to Lavery (Simmons), a wealthy, musclebound gigolo. At first, Montgomery is welcomed by the handsome young rake, but when the detective asks one sensitive question too many, he is suddenly punched silly.

Marlowe wakes up in the Bay City jail, where Lt. DeGarmot (Nolan) tells him that he was picked up for drunk driving. Marlowe claims that he was framed—averring that he was knocked out and had booze poured over him before he was thrown into his car, which was then sent careening down the street. Marlowe returns to Adrienne's office and informs her that he's dropping the case. Then comes a report that the wife of the caretaker of Kingsby's retreat at Little Fawn Lake has been murdered, her body found floating in the lake. Believing that the caretaker's wife was murdered by Kingsby's wife, Adrienne asks Marlowe to prove her theory so that the wife can be prosecuted for murder. The more Marlowe discovers about the lady in the lake, the more determined he is to stay with the case.

The cast is uniformly good, with Totter and Nolan real standouts. Appearing onscreen only in the introduction and conclusion (or when Marlowe looks into a mirror), Montgomery has deliberately and effectively soured his pre-war playboy image. Yet Chandler not only disliked Montgomery's performance but hated the film itself, perhaps because of the hard time he had attempting to adapt his novel. (This was the only time Chandler was ever paid to create a screenplay from one of his original works.)

LADY JANE

1985   142m   c   Biography   ★★½
Paramount   (U.K.)   PG-13/PG

Helena Bonham Carter (Lady Jane Grey), Cary Elwes (Guilford Dudley), John Wood (John Dudley, Duke of Northumberland), Michael Hordern (Dr. Feckenham), Jill Bennett (Mrs. Ellen), Jane Lapotaire (Princess Mary), Sara Kestelman (Frances Grey, Duchess of Suffolk), Patrick Stewart (Henry Grey, Duke of Suffolk), Warren Saire (King Edward VI), Joss Ackland (Sir John Bridges)

p, Peter Snell; d, Trevor Nunn; w, David Edgar (based on a story by Chris Bryant); ph, Douglas Slocombe; ed, Anne V. Coates; m, Stephen Oliver; prod d, Allan Cameron; art d, Fred Carter, Martyn Hebert; chor, Geraldine Stephenson, Sheila Falconer; cos, Sue Blane, David Perry

Talented Helena Bonham Carter stars in this look at the life of Lady Jane Grey, the 15-year-old Queen of England whose reign lasted a scant nine days. Despite Trevor Nunn's direction, this gorgeously photographed travesty of history doesn't omit a single cliche of the costume genre and feels even longer than its 142-minute running time. Fans of RSC-style scenery-chewing will not, however, be disappointed.

LADY SINGS THE BLUES

1972   144m   c   Biography/Musical   ★★★
Motown/Weston/Furie   (U.S.)   R/X

Diana Ross (Billie Holiday), Billy Dee Williams (Louis McKay), Richard Pryor (Piano Man), James Callahan (Reg Hanley), Paul Hampton (Harry), Sid Melton (Jerry), Virginia Capers (Mama Holiday), Yvonne Fair (Yvonne), Scatman Crothers (Big Ben), Robert L. Gordy (Hawk)

p, Jay Weston, James S. White; d, Sidney J. Furie; w, Terence McCloy, Chris Clark, Suzanne DePasse (based on the book by Billie Holiday, William Dufty); ph, John A. Alonzo; ed, Argyle Nelson; m, Michel Legrand; prod d, Carl Anderson; cos, Bob Mackie, Ray Aghayan, Norma Koch

AAN Best Actress: Diana Ross; AAN Best Adapted Screenplay: Terence McCloy, Chris Clark, Suzanne DePasse; AAN Best Score: Gil Askey (Adaptation); AAN Best Art Direction: Carl Anderson (Art Direction), Reg Allen (Set Decoration); AAN Best Costume Design: Bob Mackie, Ray Aghayan, Norma Koch

View this film about Billie Holiday as a completely fictional story, and you'll enjoy it far more than you would otherwise. Ostensibly based on Holiday's autobiography, LADY SINGS THE BLUES begins in the early 1930s in Baltimore, where the teenaged Billie (Diana Ross) is raped and then sent to New York to stay with a friend of her mother's. In Harlem she works first as a maid, and later as a whore, in a brothel. With the encouragement of the brothel's "piano man" (Richard Pryor), she begins singing professionally and eventually becomes the lover of gambler Louis McKay (Billy Dee Williams)—actually Holiday's third husband but the sole romantic interest in the film.

"Lady Day's" inimitable style begins to win her notice on the club circuit, and she is invited to tour the South with a band led by white musicians. On tour she's devastated by racist treatment and turns to drugs, becoming an addict—a habit which threatens both her professional and personal success. Things get worse when her mother dies, and Holiday enters a sanitarium in an attempt to get clean. Although she later begins a new life with McKay, her triumph is short-lived, and the film closes by glancing over her remaining, troubled days until her death at age 44.

Perhaps because Holiday's true life story is so well documented, the filmmakers felt they had to alter the facts in order to interest audiences. The dramatized results angered many; jazz critic Leonard Feather, for one, noted that the film made no mention of Lester Young, Jimmy Monroe (to whom Holiday was married), John Hammond, Benny Goodman, Count Basie, Artie Shaw and Teddy Wilson—all important associations for Holiday during the period covered in the film. Taken as pure fiction, however, LADY SINGS THE BLUES is an overdirected but fairly watchable movie, aided by a good if not quite good enough performance by Ross in her dramatic screen debut. Ross's renderings of Holiday's songs, however, are travesties.

LADY VANISHES, THE

1938 97m bw Mystery/Spy ★★★★★
Gaumont (U.K.) /U

Margaret Lockwood (*Iris Henderson*), Michael Redgrave (*Gilbert Redman*), Paul Lukas (*Dr. Hartz*), Dame May Whitty (*Miss Froy*), Cecil Parker (*Eric Todhunter*), Linden Travers (*Margaret Todhunter*), Mary Clare (*Baroness*), Naunton Wayne (*Caldicott*), Basil Radford (*Charters*), Emile Boreo (*Hotel Manager*)

p, Edward Black; d, Alfred Hitchcock; w, Alma Reville, Sidney Gilliat, Frank Launder (based on the novel *The Wheel Spins* by Ethel Lina White); ph, Jack Cox; ed, Alfred Roome, R.E. Dearing; m, Louis Levy

Flabbergasting peak suspense, civilized but breathlessly fast. This is one of Hitchcock's finest British films, a classic mystery that manages to combine humor with a genuine sense of menace—not to mention the kinds of characters that everyone dreams of meeting on a Central European train journey.

The film is set into motion when a seemingly innocuous old woman, Miss Froy (Whitty), disappears while on board a train bound for England. An acquaintance, Iris (Lockwood), becomes concerned and sets out to find her. Despite the fact that there are only so many places to hide on a speeding train, Whitty cannot be found. Even more mysteriously, no one else seems convinced that she ever really existed. Each time that Lockwood thinks she has proof of what happened, that proof itself evaporates; and each time she begins to doubt her own memory, some objective fact re-alerts her suspicions. After a series of ingenious developments, Lockwood finally uncovers the truth with the help of music scholar Gilbert (Redgrave).

THE LADY VANISHES begins slowly but picks up speed as it goes along, finally steaming toward a suspenseful denouement. The film was extremely popular in the US and laid the tracks for the great British director's new career in Hollywood. After striking a deal with David O. Selznick, Hitchcock completed one more British picture, JAMAICA INN, and began a love affair with America, returning to England just once more, some 30 years later, for FRENZY.

LADYHAWKE

1985 121m c Fantasy/Adventure ★★★½
Warner Bros. (U.S.) PG-13/PG

Matthew Broderick (*Phillipe Gaston*), Rutger Hauer (*Navarre*), Michelle Pfeiffer (*Isabeau*), Leo McKern (*Imperius*), John Wood (*Bishop*), Ken Hutchison (*Marquet*), Alfred Molina (*Cezar*), Loris Loddi (*Jehan*), Alessandro Serra (*Mr. Pitou*), Charles Borromel (*Insane Prisoner*)

p, Richard Donner, Lauren Shuler; d, Richard Donner; w, Edward Khmara, Michael Thomas, Tom Mankiewicz (based on a story by Edward Khmara); ph, Vittorio Storaro; ed, Stuart Baird; m, Andrew Powell; prod d, Wolf Kroeger; art d, Giovanni Natalucci, Ken Court; fx, John Richardson; cos, Nana Cecchi

AAN Best Sound: Les Fresholtz (Sound), Dick Alexander (Sound), Vern Poore (Sound), Bud Alper (Sound); *AAN Best Sound Effects Editing:* Bob Henderson, Alan Murray

Phillipe (Matthew Broderick), a pickpocket in 13th-century France, is thrown into a dungeon, but escapes and tries to elude the palace guards in the thick of a nearby forest. Rescued by Navarre (Rutger Hauer), a mysterious knight, Phillipe is eager to be on his way, but the knight refuses to set him free, eventually filling him in on his secret. Navarre, the former chief guard for an evil bishop (John Wood), was involved in a romance with the bishop's mistress Isabeau (Michelle Pfeiffer). When

the bishop learned of the affair, he appealed to the gods and had the lovers cursed. As a result the two take on different forms—Navarre, a wolf by night, and Isabeau, a hawk by day—never again able to embrace each other as humans.

Majestically photographed, LADYHAWKE is a joy to look at, employing some beautiful techniques to capture the transformations. Unfortunately, the synthesized soundtrack is drastically out of place and out of character. Hauer, playing a more gentle role than usual, is excellent, but Pfeiffer, who looks stunning, isn't given much to do. While not without faults, LADYHAWKE is much more striking than many of Donner's other films. A poetic, mythic tale of impossible love that was one of the overlooked films of 1985.

LADYKILLERS, THE

1955 96m c Comedy/Crime ★★★★½
Ealing (U.K.) /U

Alec Guinness (*Professor Marcus*), Cecil Parker (*The Mayor*), Herbert Lom (*Louis*), Peter Sellers (*Harry*), Danny Green (*One-Round*), Jack Warner (*Police Superintendent*), Katie Johnson (*Mrs. Wilberforce*), Philip Stainton (*Police Sergeant*), Frankie Howerd (*Barrow Boy*), Fred Griffiths (*The Junkman*)

p, Seth Holt; d, Alexander Mackendrick; w, William Rose (based on his story); ph, Otto Heller; ed, Jack Harris; m, Tristram Cary; art d, Jim Morahan

AAN Best Original Screenplay: William Rose

The last of the comedies produced by the Ealing Studios, and one of the finest, with a supremely dark tone which makes a climactic series of murders as hilarious as they are grotesque.

THE LADYKILLERS pits an implacably dotty landlady (Katie Johnson) against a criminal gang which includes Alec Guinness, as a "mastermind" with hideous teeth; Cecil Parker, as a bumbling military type; Herbert Lom, as an American-style gangster; Peter Sellers, as an inept teddy boy; and Danny Green, as a kind-hearted thug. The gang are using Johnson's house as a base from which to plan an elaborate robbery, but their combined talents evaporate in the face of their landlady's blithe command of her own, idiosyncratic world. In one scene, they are forced to halt their attempted getaway in order to take tea with Johnson and her friends and join in a sing-song around the harmonium!

THE LADYKILLERS was the last comedy produced by Ealing, which was in the process of closing down at the time of the film's release in 1955. Johnson, who was to die two years later, won a British Film Academy Award for her role. Shortly after the film's completion, director Mackendrick left England for the US, where he scored another triumph with SWEET SMELL OF SUCCESS.

L'AGE D'OR

1930 60m bw Drama ★★★★★
Corinth (France) /AA

Lya Lys (*The Woman*), Gaston Modot (*The Man*), Max Ernst (*Bandit Chief*), Pierre Prevert (*Bandit*), Caridad de Laberdesque, Lionel Salem, Madame Noizet, Jose Artigas, Jacques Brunius

p, Le Vicomte de Noailles; d, Luis Bunuel; w, Luis Bunuel, Salvador Dali; ph, Albert Duverger; ed, Luis Bunuel; m, Richard Wagner, Felix Mendelssohn, Ludwig van Beethoven, Claude Debussy

One of the most controversial films of all time, L'AGE D'OR is a surreal inquiry into the traditions and standards of modern culture that have kept true passion and instinct from being freely expressed.

Modot and Lys, simply called the Man and the Woman, are the lovers who allow nothing to prevent them from demonstrating their feelings for each other. They want to make love, but must first overcome a number of seemingly insurmountable obstacles: the church, bourgeois social etiquette, and their own psychological handicaps. This love is demonstrated through surreal images that are both hilarious (a cow lying on a bed, a frustrated man kicking a socialite's obnoxious poodle into the air) and disturbing (a helpless boy being brutally shot to death), but the overall impact suggests love's transcendent power.

L'AGE D'OR, like many other surrealist and Dadaist works, is more than a piece of art—it is a manifesto. It is not an entertainment but a display of the iconoclasm, rage, wit and passion which Bunuel, Salvador Dali and their contemporaries wanted humanity to embrace. L'AGE D'OR is full of incredible moments: the opening documentary on the savagery of scorpions, Lys obsessively sucking the toes of a statue, the pompous clerics on the rocks. The accompanying program for the film read, "It is LOVE that brings about the transition from pessimism to action: Love, denounced in the bourgeois demonology as the root of all evil. For love demands the sacrifice of every other value: status, family, and honor."

During one of the film's initial showings in Paris, a minor riot broke out as people destroyed paintings by such artists as Man Ray, Max Ernst and Dali. L'AGE D'OR was subsequently banned and became the subject of heated debate in both left- and right-wing newspapers. Although Dali was involved, this film more properly belongs to Bunuel. Many of the themes appearing in his later works are evident here for the first time, though less tempered with his later occasional gentleness.

LAMERICA

1994   120m   c   Drama/Political   ★★★★
Cecchi Gori Group/Tiger Cinematografica/Arena Films/Alia Film
(Italy/France)

Enrico Lo Verso (Gino), Michele Placido (Fiore), Carmelo Di Mazzarelli (Spiro), Piro Milkani (Selimi), Elida Janushi (Selimi's Cousin), Sefer Pema (Prison Warden), Nikolin Elezi (Boy Who Dies), Artan Marina (Ismail), Besim Kurti (Policeman), Esmerald Ara (Little Girl)

p, Mario Cecchi Gori, Vittorio Cecchi Gori; d, Gianni Amelio; w, Gianni Amelio, Andrea Porporati, Alessandro Sermoneta; ph, Luca Bigazzi; ed, Simona Paggi; m, Franco Piersanti; prod d, Giuseppe M. Gaudino, Nicola Rubertelli; cos, Liliana Sotira, Claudia Tenaglia

LAMERICA is a boldly chilling portrait of post-Communist Europe in moral eclipse, directed with passion and singular grace by Italian Gianni Amelio (STOLEN CHILDREN).

A pair of cynical Italian capitalists, Gino and Fiore (Enrico Lo Verso and Michele Placido) need an Albanian — any Albanian — to serve as front man for a business scheme. They find him in Spiro (Carmelo Di Mazzarelli), an addled old man who has spent 50 years in a Communist prison. When Spiro disappears, Gino sets out in pursuit across the nightmarish landscape of contemporary Albania. Amelio's genuinely moving film deservedly won the European Felix Award and Italy's equivalent of the Oscar (it was also the Italian entry for the 1995 Academy Awards). Its near-hallucinatory portrayal of the chaotic plight of Albania in the grip of a singularly ruthless brand of capitalism is trenchant and unforgettable. LAMERICA's central theme, however, is the timeless hope of the migrant—a dubious dream of spiritual renewal in a real or imagined "Lamerica." Beautifully structured despite an episodic plot, the film is also brilliantly acted, especially by Lo Verso, one of the most gifted actors of his generation.

LANCELOT OF THE LAKE
(LE GRAAL)

1974   80m   c   Historical/Drama   ★★★★
Mara-Films/Laser Productions/ORTF/Gerico Sound   (France)   /A

Luc Simon (Lancelot), Laura Duke Condominas (Queen Guinevere), Humbert Balsan (Gawain), Vladimir Antolek-Oresek (King Arthur), Patrick Bernard (Modrick), Arthur De Montalambert (Lionel)

p, Jean-Pierre Rassam, Jean Yanne, Francois Rochas; d, Robert Bresson; w, Robert Bresson; ph, Pasqualino de Santis; ed, Germaine Lamy; m, Philippe Sarde; prod d, Pierre Charbonnier; cos, Gres

In 1974, the most austere of the major filmmakers, Robert Bresson, released his version of the tale of Lancelot and Guinevere. Not surprisingly, Bresson's stripped-to-the-bone adaptation eschews the traditionally heroic, spectacular, fabulous, and exaltedly romantic aspects of the legendary saga in order to lay bare the confusion and pain within the human soul.

The knights of the round table have returned empty-handed from their quest for the Holy Grail. Lancelot (Luc Simon) the knight and young Queen Guinevere (Laura Duke Condominas) continue to carry on a clandestine affair behind the back of King Arthur (Vladimir Antolek-Oresek). Urged by Arthur to cultivate the friendship of the other nights, Lancelot offers his hand to the devious Modrick (Patrick Bernard) but is rebuffed. Gawain (Humbert Balsan), Arthur's nephew,

urges his friend and ally to fight Modrick, but Lancelot declines, even though he is told that the other knights are shifting their allegiance from him to Modrick. Though he announces that he will not participate in an upcoming tournament, Lancelot appears there in disguise, and proceeds to win the jousting events. En route to the contest, Modrick tells Arthur that Guinevere and Lancelot are lovers. After Lancelot, wounded from the jousts, disappears into the forest, the other knights presume he is dead. Guinevere, however, believes that her lover is alive and will return to rescue her, possibly from execution as an adulteress.

Bresson's unrelenting minimalism carries over into every aspect of the production, most conspicuously in the flat, emotionless line readings of his amateur performers, the profusion of low-angled shots, and a modest soundtrack, heightened by the almost total absence of background music. This is one of the few film of its kind that never stoops to vulgarity and refuses to honor the genre's most cherished supposition: that all medieval people were animals. Though unwilling to render his characters as superhuman or godlike, Bresson never wallows in the mud he photographs. In exchange for all the pomp and pageantry of the old tradition and the phlegm and flatulence of the new tradition (pioneered by Monty Python), Bresson has given moviegoers something more valuable: a sober rendition of an oft told tale, freshened and renewed by the unique, almost aberrant sensibility of its narrator.

LAND BEFORE TIME, THE

1988   70m   c   Animated/Children's   ★★★½
Sullivan-Bluth/Amblin   (U.S.)   G/U

VOICES OF: Pat Hingle (Narrator/Rooter), Helen Shaver (Littlefoot's Mother), Gabriel Damon (Littlefoot), Candice Houston (Cera), Burker Barnes (Daddy Topps), Judith Barsi (Ducky), Will Ryan (Petrie)

p, Don Bluth, Gary Goldman, John Pomeroy; d, Don Bluth; w, Stu Krieger (based on a story by Judy Freudberg, Tony Geiss); ed, Dan Molina, John K. Carr; m, James Horner; prod d, Don Bluth; fx, D.A. Lanpher; anim, John Pomeroy, Linda Miller, Ralph Zondag, Dan Kuenster, Lorna Pomeroy, Dick Zondag

In THE LAND BEFORE TIME, created under the tutelage of George Lucas and Steven Spielberg, Don Bluth capitalizes on the renewed interest in dinosaurs among children, setting his tale millions of years ago and creating what has been called a prehistoric BAMBI.

An orphaned brontosaurus named Littlefoot (voiced by Gabriel Damon) is forced to make his way through desolation in order to find the Great Valley, which is lush and green but very far away. Joining Littlefoot on his adventure are a feisty baby triceratops named Cera (Candice Houston); a restless, chatty anatosaurus named Ducky (Judith Barsi); a pterodactyl named Petrie (Will Ryan); and a mute, dull-witted stegosaurus named Spike. A gorgeous production from beginning to end, THE LAND BEFORE TIME contains all the essential elements missing from most of Disney's recent efforts. Bluth, a former Disney animator, understands that the greatest Disney films take us on an emotional journey in which all our hopes and fears are played out in a vivid fantasy world where anything can happen. THE LAND BEFORE TIME continues that great tradition.

LANDLORD, THE

1970   112m   c   Drama/Comedy   ★★★½
Mirisch   (U.S.)   R/X

Beau Bridges (Elgar Enders), Pearl Bailey (Marge), Diana Sands (Fanny), Louis Gossett Jr. (Copee), Lee Grant (Mrs. Enders), Douglas Grant (Walter Gee), Mel Stewart (Prof. Duboise), Walter Brooke (Mr. Enders), Susan Anspach (Susan), Robert Klein (Peter)

p, Norman Jewison; d, Hal Ashby; w, Bill Gunn (based on the novel by Kristin Hunter); ph, Gordon Willis; ed, William A. Sawyer, Edward Warschilka; m, Al Kooper; prod d, Robert Boyle; cos, Domingo Rodriguez

AAN Best Supporting Actress: Lee Grant

This satiric look at racial tensions has sheltered rich kid Elgar Enders (Beau Bridges) buying a ghetto tenement with the intention of kicking the tenants out and remodeling it for his own use. His plans change when he grows attached to the people living in the building—an interesting assortment who spark emotions in Elgar that he never knew he possessed. He falls in love with Lanie (Marki Bey), a black art student, and decides to marry her, but their plans are postponed when he discovers he has gotten his neighbor Fanny (Diana Sands) pregnant. The film offers some fine performances (Lee Grant was nominated for Best Supporting Actress), and Ashby's quirky but skillful direction allows the individual personalities of the characters to shine through. The script has a few uneven moments, none of which damage the overall quality of the film, and Willis captures the atmosphere of both rich and poor New York lifestyles with an impressive visual style.

L'ARGENT

1983 90m c Crime ★★★★★
Marion's/FR3/EOS (France/Switzerland) /PG

Christian Patey *(Yvon Targe)*, Sylvie van den Elsen *(Old Woman)*, Michel Briguet *(The Woman's Father)*, Caroline Lang *(Elise Targe)*, Vincent Risterucci *(Lucien)*, Beatrice Tabourin *(Woman Photographer)*, Didier Baussy *(Man Photographer)*, Marc Ernest Fourneau *(Norbert)*, Brune Lapeyre *(Martial)*, Andre Cler *(Norbert's Father)*

p, Jean-Marc Henchoz; d, Robert Bresson; w, Robert Bresson (based on the story "The False Note" by Leo Tolstoy); ph, Emmanuel Machuel, Pasqualino De Santis; ed, Jean Francois Naudon; m, Johann Sebastian Bach; art d, Pierre Guffroy; cos, Monique Dury

Writer-director Robert Bresson's 13th film in 40 years, L'ARGENT is, like so many of his other films, a work of true cinematic genius that stands head and shoulders above most other pictures and seems to defy critical judgment. L'ARGENT begins with young schoolboy Norbert's (Marc Ernest Fourneau) trying unsuccessfully to get money from his parents. An enterprising classmate gives him some counterfeit bills, which Norbert passes on to a worker in a photographic shop. The shop owner (Didier Baussy) is determined to get rid of the phony bills and palms them off to an unsuspecting deliveryman (Christian Patey), who innocently pays a cafe bill with the forged notes and is promptly arrested. The schoolboy's mother pays the shop owner to keep silent about her son's involvement. Throughout the first half-hour of the film (before we are certain that Patey is the leading player), money is the central character. It changes hands from one person to another in extreme close-ups and carries us from one scene to the next, one location to the next. The bills are recognizable, whereas the people passing them are not. The power of money and the effects of one person's impositions upon another eventually lead the feckless deliveryman along an increasingly harrowing life's path to the film's stunning conclusion. Bresson justly won acclaim for this piercing film from the Cannes Film Festival, which voted him Best Director.

LASSIE COME HOME

1943 90m c Adventure/Children's ★★★★
MGM (U.S.) /U

Roddy McDowall *(Joe Carraclough)*, Donald Crisp *(Sam Carraclough)*, Edmund Gwenn *(Rowlie)*, Dame May Whitty *(Dolly)*, Nigel Bruce *(Duke of Rudling)*, Elsa Lanchester *(Mrs. Carraclough)*, Elizabeth Taylor *(Priscilla)*, J. Pat O'Malley *(Hynes)*, Ben Webster *(Dan'l Fadden)*, Alec Craig *(Snickers)*

p, Samuel Marx; d, Fred M. Wilcox; w, Hugo Butler (based on the novel by Eric Knight); ph, Leonard Smith; ed, Ben Lewis; m, Daniele Amfitheatrof; art d, Cedric Gibbons, Paul Groesse; fx, Warren Newcombe

AAN Best Cinematography: Leonard Smith

This low-budget effort wasn't expected to do much at the box office, but moviegoers fell in love with the title collie, and many sequels, a radio program, and a long-running TV show followed. In Yorkshire in the dark days after WWI, young Joe Carraclough (Roddy McDowall) is forced to give up Lassie when his parents (Donald Crisp and Elsa Lanchester) can no longer afford to keep the dog. After escaping once from her new owner, the Duke of Rudling (Nigel Bruce), Lassie is taken by him to Scotland, and, freed by the duke's sympathetic granddaughter (Elizabeth Taylor), makes a long, eventful journey back to Joe.

This Lassie, actually a male dog named Pal, was bought for $10 by trainer Rudd Weatherwax, who had worked for MGM training animals for PECK'S BAD BOY and THE CHAMP. The studio wanted a female dog and Weatherwax was chosen to find a good one, but when shooting began the female shed heavily and was replaced by Pal. Contrary to

popular belief, this was not Taylor's first film. She had been signed to a brief contract by Universal and appeared in THERE'S ONE BORN EVERY MINUTE the year before. Even more than costar Roddy McDowall, the seductive Taylor has that uncanny quality some child actors possess of looking and sometimes acting quite like an adult, even at a pre-adolescent age. The presence of these kids, and that of the well-trained pooch, quite upstage the endearing and highly professional actors surrounding them. Still, this film is a fairly well-balanced effort, and if you're in the mood for an evening of obvious sentiment, this boy-and-his-dog film works quite well.

LAST ACTION HERO

1993 122m c Action/Adventure/Comedy ★★
Steve Roth Productions/Columbia (U.S.) PG-13/15

Arnold Schwarzenegger *(Sergeant Jack Slater)*, Austin O'Brien *(Danny Madigan)*, Mercedes Ruehl *(Ilene Madigan)*, Bridgette Wilson *(Whitney/Meredith)*, Charles Dance *(Benedict)*, Tom Noonan *(Ripper)*, Robert Prosky *(Nick)*, F. Murray Abraham *(John Practice)*, Art Carney *(Frank)*, Frank McRae *(Dekker)*

p, Steve Roth, John McTiernan; d, John McTiernan; w, Zak Penn, Adam Leff, Shane Black, David Arnott, William Goldman (from the story by Penn and Leff); ph, Dean Semler, David B. Nowell; ed, John Wright, Frank J. Urioste, Richard A. Harris; m, Michael Kamen; prod d, Eugenio Zanetti; art d, Marek Dobrowolski, Rick Heinrichs, John Wright Stevens; fx, Tommy Fisher, John Sullivan, Neil Krepela, Gene Warren Jr., Kevin O'Neil; cos, Gloria Gresham

Forget JURASSIC PARK. If you're fascinated by life-forms destined for extinction, look no further than Arnold Schwarzenegger, as presented in LAST ACTION HERO.

HERO claims to be a gentle, playful parody of the action/adventure genre, but comes off as a mercenary attempt to cash in on summer moviegoing habits. Action films pull in large audiences, mostly comprised of young men; non-violent films clean up in the family market. How to combine the two? Make an action movie in which the violence has no edge, since it takes place in a fictional world, and team your macho star with a young, fatherless child (Austin O'Brien) and a struggling single mom (Mercedes Ruehl).

If this sounds like naked calculation, it is. LAST ACTION HERO is a marketing idea with no real film to back it up. The central premise—that people can cross over from the real world into the world of moviedom and back—is borrowed from PURPLE ROSE OF CAIRO and mercilessly flogged to death. The relentless in-jokes and filmic references suggest, not a joyful homage to earlier movie feats, but a self-congratulatory smugness. Mr. O'Brien is an almost entirely charmless young man, but at least he's human; Schwarzenegger's performance, on the other hand, could easily have been computer-generated. Perhaps one day it will be.

The final irony is that HERO fails to parody a form that has already become a parody of itself. Without even meaning to, LETHAL WEAPON 3 or CLIFFHANGER generate bigger laughs than this clunking, joyless monolith of a movie.

LAST AMERICAN HERO, THE

1973 95m c Sports ★★★
Fox (U.S.) PG/AA

Jeff Bridges *(Elroy Jackson Jr.)*, Valerie Perrine *(Marge)*, Geraldine Fitzgerald *(Mrs. Jackson)*, Ned Beatty *(Hackel)*, Gary Busey *(Wayne Jackson)*, Art Lund *(Elroy Jackson Sr.)*, Ed Lauter *(Burton Colt)*, William Smith II *(Kyle Kingman)*, Gregory Walcott *(Morley)*, Tom Ligon *(Lamar)*

p, William Roberts, John Cutts; d, Lamont Johnson; w, William Roberts (based on articles by Tom Wolfe); ph, George Silano; ed, Tom Rolf, Robbe Roberts; m, Charles Fox; art d, Lawrence G. Paull

Based on an *Esquire* article by Tom Wolfe, this well-crafted film tells the story of real-life stock car driver Junior Jackson, who served as THE LAST AMERICAN HERO's technical adviser. As a North Carolina youth, Jackson (Jeff Bridges) is a hot-rodding, small-time hoodlum until his father is busted for moonshining and hauled off to prison. He then decides to put his ability behind the wheel to good use, becoming a professional stock car racer to raise money for his father's defense.

Starting at a local track, Bridges begins a rise to the stock car big time, where his stubborn independence runs up against the realities of corporate sponsorship. Well written and subtly directed, THE LAST AMERICAN HERO concentrates on the human elements of the story without becoming overly sentimental. Its performances—including Ned Beatty as the local promoter and Valerie Perrine a trackside groupie—are also excellent.

LAST DAYS OF CHEZ NOUS, THE

1993 96m c Drama   ★★★
Jan Chapman Productions   (Australia)   R/15

Lisa Harrow *(Beth)*, Bruno Ganz *(J.P.)*, Kerry Fox *(Vicki)*, Miranda Otto *(Annie)*, Kiri Paramore *(Tim)*, Bill Hunter *(Beth's Father)*, Lex Marinos *(Angelo)*, Mickey Camilleri *(Sally)*, Lynne Murphy *(Beth's Mother)*, Clair Haywood *(Janet)*

p, Jan Chapman; d, Gillian Armstrong; w, Helen Garner; ph, Geoffrey Simpson; ed, Nicholas Beauman; m, Paul Grabowsky; prod d, Janet Patterson; cos, Janet Patterson

Australian director Gillian Armstrong (MY BRILLIANT CAREER) offers up an exquisite entertainment about a family upset by the return of a prodigal sister.

A novelist, Beth (Lisa Harrow) is accused by her effete French husband JP (Bruno Ganz) of viewing the world through rose-colored glasses in her work, evidenced in an over-tidiness in her novel's resolutions. Recovering from a failed relationship that has left her pregnant and alone, Beth's younger sister Vicki (Kerry Fox) at first irritates JP with her slovenliness and refusal to perform household duties. Shortly after helping her younger sister obtain an abortion that further upsets her emotional equilibrium, Beth takes her crusty, disagreeable father (Bill Hunter) on an extended motoring vacation through the outback. JP's efforts to comfort Vicki lead to an affair that escalates into a serious relationship, and threatens the delicate emotional connections betwene all the family members.

It's not surprising that Hollywood never quite figured out what to do with Gillian Armstrong: in CHEZ NOUS the accents are thick, crucial dialog is sometimes tossed away and there's no conventional "spine" to the story. There is a sense throughout CHEZ NOUS of the family as a state of contained anarchy that could also describe the film itself. Yet something is always happening, from the foreground to the edges of the screen, to the extent that you can literally blink and miss something important. The result feels oddly and warmly familiar throughout, and if it's sometimes baffling and annoying, it deserves to be cherished over the course of repeated viewings.

LAST DETAIL, THE

1973 103m c Drama   ★★★★
Columbia   (U.S.)   R/18

Jack Nicholson *(Buddusky SM1)*, Otis Young *(Mulhall GM1)*, Randy Quaid *(Meadows SN)*, Clifton James *(Chief Master-at-Arms)*, Michael Moriarty *(Marine Duty Officer)*, Carol Kane *(Young Whore)*, Luana Anders *(Donna)*, Kathleen Miller *(Kathleen)*, Nancy Allen *(Nancy)*, Gerry Salsberg *(Henry)*

p, Gerald Ayres; d, Hal Ashby; w, Robert Towne (based on the novel by Darryl Ponicsan); ph, Michael Chapman; ed, Robert C. Jones; m, Johnny Mandel; prod d, Michael Haller; cos, Ted Parvin

AAN Best Actor: Jack Nicholson; *AAN Best Supporting Actor:* Randy Quaid; *AAN Best Adapted Screenplay:* Robert Towne

A grim yet very touching portrait of a trip taken by three men, one of whom is to lose his freedom by journey's end. Two career sailors, Nicholson and Young, are randomly selected to escort Quaid from their West Virginia base to a prison in Massachusetts. Quaid was caught stealing from the polio charity box; since that was the favorite charity of the admiral's wife, he is sentenced to eight years in jail, or a year for every five dollars. Nicholson and Young got a lot more than they bargained for when they were assigned this detail. At first, they think it's just another shore leave with liberty to be enjoyed and lots of carousing. The two hardened sailors are soon won over, however, by Quaid's bumbling ways and the difficulty of his plight. This causes them to take a paternal attitude toward him as they travel from one dim location to another. Only the characters in the film look alive, as

everywhere they go appears to have been filtered by pale grays and yellows. Nicholson and Young try to show Quaid a good time before his long stay in the brig. They encounter Anders, who brings them to a Nicheren Shoshu meeting where religious zealots (including Gilda Radner before she became a TV star) chant "Nam-Myoho-Renge-Kyo" and dance happily in their scented environment. Anders next takes Quaid to her room when she learns of his bleak future and tells him that she's going to do something that will be very important. The naive Quaid thinks she's about to seduce him; instead, she begins to chant, which confuses him at first, then leads to a poignant scene later. Nicholson and Young can't make any time with Anders's pals, so it's off to another adventure—this time to a brothel where they offer Quaid a good time with Kane, which they'll pay for. Quaid unsuccessfully tries to escape (while chanting the liturgy Anders taught him), but after an agonizing chase across a frozen park, Nicholson and Young capture him and deliver him to prison. We get the feeling that Nicholson and Young, if their naval careers did not depend on it, would have taken off with Quaid. They try hard not to be emotional as Quaid is escorted up a small staircase to the room where he will spend the rest of his youth.

THE LAST DETAIL is a gritty look at the military life and the people who are attracted to it. It is dark in its message and gray to the eye. Locations are all washed out as though there were a thin membrane of filth spread across everything except the leads, who pop out colorfully like three strawberries in a bowl of Cream of Wheat. This is Nicholson's best work since FIVE EASY PIECES, perhaps because his character seems to be an extension of that film's Bobby DuPea. Ashby's direction is superlative, as is his use of music to help secure the mood. Ashby was able to get Nicholson's least-mannered performance in many a day, after bombs with THE KING OF MARVIN GARDENS; A SAFE PLACE; and DRIVE, HE SAID. Ponicsan also wrote the naval-based novel, *Cinderella Liberty,* which was made into a film the same year. THE LAST DETAIL won no Oscars but did get nominations for Quaid, Nicholson (who lost to Jack Lemmon for SAVE THE TIGER), and Robert Towne for his screenplay.

LAST EMPEROR, THE

1987 160m c Historical/Biography   ★★★★½
Columbia   (U.S.)   PG-13/15

John Lone *(Aisin-Gioro "Henry" Pu Yi as an Adult)*, Joan Chen *(Wan Jung, "Elizabeth")*, Peter O'Toole *(Reginald Johnston)*, Ying Ruocheng *(The Governor)*, Victor Wong *(Chen Pao Shen)*, Dennis Dun *(Big Li)*, Ryuichi Sakamoto *(Masahiko Amakasu)*, Maggie Han *(Eastern Jewel)*, Ric Young *(Interrogator)*, Wu Jun Mei *(Wen Hsiu)*

p, Jeremy Thomas; d, Bernardo Bertolucci; w, Mark Peploe, Bernardo Bertolucci, Enzo Ungari (based on *From Emperor To Citizen,* the autobiography of Pu Yi); ph, Vittorio Storaro; ed, Gabriella Cristiani; m, Ryuichi Sakamoto, David Byrne, Cong Su; prod d, Ferdinando Scarfiotti; art d, Gianni Giovagnoni, Gianni Silvestri, earia Teresa Barbasso; fx, Gianetto De Rossi, Fabrizio Martinelli; cos, James Acheson

AA Best Picture; AA Best Director: Bernardo Bertolucci; *AA Best Adapted Screenplay:* Mark Peploe, Bernardo Bertolucci; *AA Best Cinematography:* Vittorio Storaro; *AA Best Editing:* Gabriella Cristiani; *AA Best Score:* Ryuichi Sakamoto, David Byrne, Cong Su; *AA Best Art Direction:* Ferdinando Scarfiotti (Art Direction), Bruno Cesari (Set Decoration); *AA Best Costume Design:* James Acheson; *AA Best Sound:* Bill Rowe, Ivan Sharrock

Fascinating but passive pageantry, due to an inactive protagonist. But where else can you get some of *these* visuals. After a six-year absence, Italian director Bernardo Bertolucci returned to the screen with this grand and powerful biography of Aisin-Gioro "Henry" Pu Yi, who in 1908, at the age of three, was named emperor of China and by the end of his life was quietly working as a gardener at Peking's Botanical Gardens. Told in an intricate flashback/flashforward narrative that uses Pu Yi's communist "remolding" period as its fulcrum, the film opens in 1950 as Pu Yi, and thousands of others, are returned to their now-communist homeland to face rehabilitation. From that point the story moves to Pu Yi's childhood, his imprisonment in the Forbidden City, his term as Japan's puppet emperor of Manchukuo, and his release into the population of China in 1959. Combining the command of the historical epic he displayed in 1900 with the political intrigue and melodrama of THE CONFORMIST, Bertolucci has, in THE LAST EMPEROR, constructed a beautiful film about the transformation of both a man and a country. A storyteller and not a historian, Bertolucci offers two tales in THE LAST EMPEROR—that of China's change, told through a selective sampling of events; and that of Pu Yi's change, told with an emphasis on myth rather than on fact. Moreover, Vittorio Storaro's carefully constructed lighting schemes and moving camera are unmatched by any cinematographer working today. Lone, as the adult Pu Yi, is wholly credible, and Wu Tao, as the adolescent Pu Yi, is every bit his equal. Both actors convey the emperor's innocence, ignorance, and veiled sadistic streak. Chen demonstrates her skill by playing both a radiant teen bride and a rotting opium addict. O'Toole shows more restraint than usual and simply becomes his character, as if he, like Reginald Johnston, would have made an excellent tutor for the emperor. Also worthy of note is the film's score, which combines lush romanticism with traditional Chinese melodies and was written chiefly by Ryuichi Sakamoto (who also scored MERRY CHRIST-MAS, MR. LAWRENCE) and David Byrne (of Talking Heads fame). How we wish the film had used a more red-blooded attack on its commentary on blue-blooded privilege.

LAST EXIT TO BROOKLYN

1989 102m c Drama   ★★★½
Neue Constantin   (West Germany)   /18

Stephen Lang *(Harry Black)*, Jennifer Jason Leigh *(Tralala)*, Burt Young *(Big Joe)*, Peter Dobson *(Vinnie)*, Jerry Orbach *(Boyce)*, Stephen Baldwin *(Sal)*, Jason Andrews *(Tony)*, James Lorenz *(Freddy)*, Maia Danziger *(Mary Black)*, Cameron Johann *(Spook)*

p, Bernd Eichinger; d, Uli Edel; w, Desmond Nakano (based on the novel by Hubert Selby Jr.); ph, Stefan Czapsky; ed, Peter Przygodda; m, Mark Knopfler; art d, Mark Haack; cos, Carol Oditz

Red Hook, Brooklyn, 1952: Korea-bound conscripts, sadistic teenage gangs, and despondent strikers eke out their desolate existences amidst a frenzied mixture of prostitutes, psychos, winos, and junkies. Based on a collection of short stories by Hubert Selby Jr., which unleashed a storm of controversy upon their publication in 1964, German director Uli Edel's film is a relentlessly bleak account of life in the neighborhood during a brief period in the summer of '52.

The stories of a cross-section of characters is recounted in episodic fashion. Tralala (Jennifer Jason Leigh) is a prostitute who picks up tricks in sleazy bars and lures them to rubble-strewn vacant lots where they are mugged by ex-convict Vinnie (Peter Dobson) and his gang of thugs. Harry (Stephen Lang) is in charge of the local strike office, enjoying his position of power, but troubled by his awakening homosexuality. Georgette (Alexis Arquette) is an effeminate, tormented gay who lusts after Vinnie. Big Joe (Burt Young) is a striking worker who is upset over the pregnancy of his unmarried daughter Donna (Ricki Lake), while his motorcycle-obsessed son Spook (Cameron Johann) pines for Tralala.

In blending the personal worlds of these characters into a complete cosmology of the abyss, director Uli Edel (CHRISTIANE F.) and scriptwriter Desmond Nakano have transformed Selby's episodic book into an aesthetic whole that is greater than the sum of its parts. Moreover, Edel's and Nakano's efforts are just part of what was clearly the engaged teamwork of a group of gifted people committed to doing justice to Selby's uncompromising vision. Lang and, especially, Jason Leigh, are standouts in a terrific ensemble cast.

LAST HOUSE ON THE LEFT

1972 91m c Crime   ★★★
Hallmark   (U.S.)   R/

David Hess *(Krug)*, Lucy Grantham *(Phyllis)*, Sandra Cassel *(Mari Collingwood)*, Marc Sheffler *(Junior)*, Jeramie Rain *(Sadie)*, Fred Lincoln *(Weasel)*, Gaylord St. James *(Dr. Collingwood)*, Cynthia Carr *(Mrs. Collingwood)*, Ada Washington *(Truck Driver)*

p, Sean S. Cunningham; d, Wes Craven; w, Wes Craven; ph, Victor Hurwitz; ed, Wes Craven; m, Steve Chapin, David Hess

An ugly, disturbing, passionately conceived cult favorite, LAST HOUSE ON THE LEFT is much more complex (albeit crudely made) than its controversial reputation would suggest. Loosely based on

Ingmar Bergman's THE VIRGIN SPRING, Wes Craven's film depicts the atrocities committed by a makeshift family of rootless criminals who kidnap, rape, and murder two teenaged girls on their way to a rock concert. After hiding the bodies, the convicts make their way through the dense New Jersey woods and take refuge with a suburban couple, posing as a family whose car has broken down. Little do the killers know that the house they have picked for their refuge is owned by Dr. and Mrs. Collingwood, the parents of one of their victims. After discovering the truth, the nice middle-class couple exact savage revenge on the killers.

Expertly made on a tiny budget, this drive-in exploitation flick decisively transcends its genre. The extremely graphic violence is never played for thrills; indeed, Craven has said he wanted to resensitize Americans to the reality of violence in the wake of the Vietnam war. Craven—who would go on to polish his themes in the slicker THE HILLS HAVE EYES—never for a moment allows the viewer to sympathize with the killers, but he does provide a window of understanding into how seemingly senseless acts of violence occur. The killers initially toy with the girls, as if playing a game; but when the game gets out of hand and the girls wind up dead, the killers look at their corpses with saddened confusion, like children who have broken a favorite doll. Some have seen the film as a critique of the nuclear family, exploring the threat of patriarchal violence that lies beneath traditional structures of domestic authority. Undeniably, the good Dr. Collingwood's behavior, from his surreptitious appraisal of his daughter's figure to his spectacularly gory revenge, is hardly a model of benign fatherhood.

LAST HURRAH, THE

1958 121m bw Political   ★★½
Columbia   (U.S.)   /U

Spencer Tracy *(Frank Skeffington)*, Jeffrey Hunter *(Adam Caulfield)*, Dianne Foster *(Maeve Caulfield)*, Pat O'Brien *(John Gorman)*, Basil Rathbone *(Norman Cass, Sr.)*, Donald Crisp *(The Cardinal)*, James Gleason *(Duke Gillen)*, Edward Brophy *(Ditto Boland)*, John Carradine *(Amos Force)*, Willis Bouchey *(Roger Sugrue)*

p, John Ford; d, John Ford; w, Frank S. Nugent (based on the novel by Edwin O'Connor); ph, Charles Lawton Jr.; ed, Jack Murray; art d, Robert Peterson

One of John Ford's weakest films. Spencer Tracy breezes through this cliched, sentimental study of a political boss like a college student showing off when asked to recite his multiplication tables. Frank Skeffington (Tracy) rises each morning to put a rose beneath the portrait of his deceased wife. His son (Arthur Walsh), an empty-headed good-for-nothing, does nothing but play jazz and chase women. Though surrounded by cronies and political associates, Skeffington is essentially friendless, except for his young and idealistic nephew Adam (Hunter). Adam works as a reporter for an opposition newspaper run by Amos Force (Carradine), leader of the patrician class which has always been at odds with Skeffington and his minions. Skeffington seeks a loan from banker Cass (Rathbone) to back a new housing project. Cass refuses, and Frank retaliates by making Cass' retarded son (O.Z. Whitehead) acting fire commissioner. Rather than see his childlike son disgrace the family, Cass grants the loan but takes his revenge by financially backing the opposition. Adam records Frank's last political campaign, his "last hurrah" for the city's mayoralty, which is packed with old-time street marches, slogans, and banners. The venerable politico loses, however, and soon after dies in bed after his political pals (Pat O'Brien, James Gleason, Edward Brophy and Frank McHugh among them) make their final farewells.

For Ford, Tracy and most of the veteran cast, this film was like old home week, and Tracy considered making it his final film. It did turn out to be the last film made by veteran character actor Brophy, here giving the film's best performance. The rest of the cast, Tracy included, turn in enjoyably effortless if not particularly inspired work; the heavily sentimental atmosphere seemed to get the better of the cast and crew. Ford's approach here is rather tedious and somber, despite the comedic aspects of the script, placing emphasis on death; his scenes are deeply shadowed, and there is a pervasive gloom in almost every scene, heralding Tracy's demise. Some of the humor works well, though the comedy milked at the expense of the mentally retarded Cass Jr. today seems in bad taste.

LAST METRO, THE
(LE DERNIER METRO)
1980 133m c War/Romance ★★★½
Carrosse/TF-1 (France) R/PG

Catherine Deneuve *(Marion Steiner)*, Gerard Depardieu *(Bernard Granger)*, Jean Poiret *(Jean-Loup Cottins)*, Heinz Bennent *(Lucas Steiner)*, Andrea Ferreol *(Arlette Guillaume)*, Paulette Dubost *(Germaine Fabre)*, Sabine Haudepin *(Nadine Marsac)*, Jean-Louis Richard *(Daxiat)*, Maurice Risch *(Raymond, the Stage Manager)*, Marcel Berbert *(Merlin)*

d, Francois Truffaut; w, Francois Truffaut, Suzanne Schiffman, Jean-Claude Grumberg (based on a story by Truffaut, Schiffman); ph, Nestor Almendros; ed, Martine Barraque; m, Georges Delerue; art d, Jean-Pierre Kohut-Svelko; cos, Lisele Roos

AAN Best Foreign Language Film

Truffaut's oblique, microcosmic look at the German occupation of France is set almost entirely in a theater building. Marion Steiner (Deneuve, in an arresting performance) is the wife of top stage director Lucas Steiner (Bennent), who is forced to go underground in order to avoid Nazi persecution. Instead of fleeing Paris, Lucas hides in the cellar of the theater, eavesdropping on the rehearsals of his new play, which costars Marion and Bernard Granger (Depardieu). Time passes and the lives of the theater personnel become strained, particulary as Marion and Bernard try to resist a growing mutual attraction.

Politics and romance are placed on parallel tracks in this film through the figure of Marion, who tries to remain as loyal to her husband as she is to her countrymen. Often scolded for not addressing political issues in his pictures, director Francois Truffaut finally found a suitable vehicle in THE LAST METRO, which filters the Nazi occupation through a love story and recognizes the complexities of the situation with a dual, on- and off-stage ending. Truffaut's vision of 1940s Paris is more influenced by mythicized images of the city in films of the period than by historical reality, but the social commentary is vivid nonetheless.

LAST MOVIE, THE
1971 108m c Drama ★★½
Universal (U.S.) R/X

Julie Adams *(Mrs. Anderson)*, Dennis Hopper *(Kansas)*, Daniel Ades *(Thomas Mercado)*, Rod Cameron *(Pat)*, John Alderman *(Jonathan)*, Michael Anderson Jr. *(Mayor's Son)*, Rich Aguilar *(Gaffer)*, Donna Baccala *(Miss Anderson)*, Tom Baker *(Member of Billy's Gang)*, Toni Basil *(Rose)*

p, Paul Lewis; d, Dennis Hopper; w, Stewart Stern (based on a story by Dennis Hopper and Stewart Stern); ph, Laszlo Kovacs; ed, Dennis Hopper, David Berlatsky, Antranig Mahakian; m, Kris Kristofferson, John Buck Wilkin, Chabuca Granda, Severn Darden, The Villagers of Chinchero, Peru; art d, Leon Ericksen; fx, Milt Rice; cos, Jerry Alpert

After the success of EASY RIDER, Dennis Hopper was given $1 million by Universal to make a film, and came back with more than 40 hours worth of footage. His final cut, after more than a year of editing, was incomprehensible to the studio and to most of the people who saw the film, except for those at the Venice Film Festival, who gave it an award. Take a look at the cast list and you'll see that Hopper called in many of his pals to do cameos, but all that talent couldn't help. The picture is supposedly based on some experiences Hopper had while filming THE SONS OF KATIE ELDER in Mexico. He'd hoped to shoot this in Mexico but was refused, so he took the entire company to Peru. The movie begins at the end, flashes back to the beginning, and winds up somewhere in the middle. Hopper plays Kansas, a movie stunt man who stays behind on a film location after the company has moved off. He takes up with a local whore (Stella Garcia) then goes off to find gold with his friend Neville (Don Gordon) who, inexplicably, commits suicide. The local priest (Tomas Milian), meanwhile, makes trouble by blaming movies for the introduction of death and destruction to his naive villagers. Kansas is adopted by the local Peruvian Indians who

have made some abandoned movie equipment part of their religion. In the end, the Indians plan to crucify Kansas, as they have cast him as Billy The Kid in their production.

THE LAST MOVIE is filled with such distancing devices as blank frames and inserts that read "Scene Missing." It is also overly pretentious. Cinematographer Kovacs can usually make anything look good, but he comes a cropper in this case. Hopper, to this day, thinks that his film is a masterpiece, and while the film's self-conscious play with the medium of filmmaking does generate some interest, there probably aren't many people out there who agree with the director's evaluation.

LAST OF SHEILA, THE
1973 120m c Mystery ★★★½
Warner Bros. (U.S.) PG/AA

Richard Benjamin *(Tom)*, Dyan Cannon *(Christine)*, James Coburn *(Clinton)*, Joan Hackett *(Lee)*, James Mason *(Philip)*, Ian McShane *(Anthony)*, Raquel Welch *(Alice)*, Yvonne Romain *(Sheila)*, Pierro Rosso *(Vittorio)*, Serge Citon *(Guido)*

p, Herbert Ross; d, Herbert Ross; w, Anthony Perkins, Stephen Sondheim; ph, Gerry Turpin; ed, Edward Warschilka; m, Billy Goldenberg; prod d, Ken Adam; art d, Tony Roman

THE LAST OF SHEILA is a superb murder mystery and something of a curio in film history, thanks to a script (by Anthony Perkins and Stephen Sondheim) that is written in the style of a British crossword puzzle. A wealthy Hollywood producer (Coburn) whose wife was killed by a hit-and-run driver at a party a year before, invites six people, all suspects, to his yacht in the south of France, hoping to uncover the culprit. He engages the six—a failed screenwriter (Benjamin); his rich, neurotic wife (Hackett); a movie star (Welch); her manager-husband (McShane); an aging film director (Mason); and a high-powered agent (Cannon)—in a psychological game designed to provoke the murderer into revealing his or her identity. The producer actually succeeds in getting murdered himself, and another death follows before the mystery is solved. If you enjoy puns, anagrams, and wordplay, you will find THE LAST OF SHEILA a positive Joycean delight. Listen for Bette Midler singing "Friends" on the soundtrack.

LAST OF THE MOHICANS, THE
1936 91m bw Historical/Adventure/War ★★★★
Small (U.S.)

Randolph Scott *(Hawkeye)*, Binnie Barnes *(Alice Munro)*, Heather Angel *(Cora Munro)*, Hugh Buckler *(Col. Munro)*, Henry Wilcoxon *(Maj. Duncan Heyward)*, Bruce Cabot *(Magua)*, Robert Barrat *(Chingachgook)*, Philip Reed *(Uncas)*, Willard Robertson *(Capt. Winthrop)*, Frank McGlynn Sr. *(David Gamut)*

p, Edward Small, Harry M. Goetz; d, George B. Seitz; w, Philip Dunne, John Balderston, Paul Perez, Daniel Moore (based on the novel by James Fenimore Cooper); ph, Robert Planck; ed, Jack Dennis, Harry Marker; art d, John DuCasse Schulze; cos, Franc Smith

Arguably the finest film version of James Fenimore Cooper's classic adventure tale, THE LAST OF THE MOHICANS benefits from fine performances by Randolph Scott as Hawkeye, Henry Wilcoxon as Maj. Duncan Heyward, and Bruce Cabot as the vicious, lascivious Huron Indian, Magua, one of the most hateful roles in film history. During the height of the French and Indian War, Hawkeye escorts Maj. Heyward, Alice (Binnie Barnes), and Cora Munro (Heather Angel), the daughters of the commander of Ft. William Henry, through hostile lines, accompanied by Chingachgook (Robert Barrat) and his son, Uncas (Philip Reed), who are the last survivors of the Mohican tribe, wiped out by the French-allied Hurons. During the course of their dangerous trek to the fort, Alice becomes enamored of Hawkeye, Cora and Uncas fall in love, and Magua makes life miserable for everyone. Before Chingachgook sends Magua to the happy hunting ground, the sadistic Huron brings about the deaths of both Cora and Uncas. What's more, the British are routed at Ft. William Henry and Hawkeye is taken prisoner and tied to a stake by the Hurons before Maj. Heyward comes to his rescue.

Packed with excitement and well-staged battle scenes, this superbly crafted adventure film was masterfully directed by George B. Seitz and magnificently lensed in California's High Sierras by Robert Planck.

LAST OF THE MOHICANS, THE

Cooper's famous tale has been brought to the screen a number of times (including two 1911 one-reelers; Maurice Tourneur and Clarence Brown's smashing 1922 feature-length silent with Wallace Beery as Magua; a ten-chapter 1924 serial version called LEATHERSTOCK-ING; Mascot Films's 1932 12-chapter serial with Harry Carey; and a 1947 Columbia version, THE LAST OF THE REDMEN, starring Jon Hall, Evelyn Ankers, and Buster Crabbe as Uncas), but none of these other versions matches the scope and wonderful performances of this extraordinary film. The film earned an Oscar nomination for Clem Beauchamp for Best Assistant Director, losing to Jack Sullivan for THE CHARGE OF THE LIGHT BRIGADE.

LAST OF THE MOHICANS, THE

1992	122m	c	Action/Adventure/Historical	★★★
Forward Pass Productions/Fox		(U.S.)		R/12

Daniel Day-Lewis (Nathaniel Poe/Hawkeye), Madeleine Stowe (Cora Munro), Russell Means (Chingachgook), Eric Schweig (Uncas), Jodhi May (Alice Munro), Steven Waddington (Major Duncan Heyward), Wes Studi (Magua), Maurice Roeves (Colonel Munro), Patrice Chereau (General Montcalm), Edward Blatchford (Jack Winthrop)

p, Michael Mann, Hunt Lowry; d, Michael Mann; w, Michael Mann, Christopher Crowe, Philip Dunne (from his screenplay, based on the adaptations by John L. Balderston, Paul Perez and Daniel Moore of the novel by James Fenimore Cooper); ph, Dante Spinotti; ed, Dov Hoenig, Arthur Schmidt; m, Trevor Jones, Randy Edelman; prod d, Wolf Kroeger; art d, Richard Holland, Robert Guerra

AA Best Sound: Chris Jenkins, Doug Hemphill, Mark Smith, Simon Kaye

Michael Mann's version of the creaky Fenimore Cooper classic takes place in a wilderness America circa 1757, where British colonists in New York state have become pawns in a power struggle between England and France during the French and Indian War. The principal characters are Hawkeye (Day-Lewis), a frontier woodsman more at home with his adopted Mohican father, Chingachgook (Native American activist Russell Means), and brother, Uncas (Eric Schweig), than the white British colonials; Cora (Madeleine Stowe) and Alice Munro (Jodhi May), comely daughters of a British colonel (Maurice Roeves); the insufferable Major Duncan Heyward (Steven Waddington), who has set his sights on marrying Cora; and the hateful Huron brave Magua (Wes Studi), who has sworn revenge on Munro for the Colonel's earlier anti-Indian exploits.

Mann, best known for TV's "Miami Vice," here eschews his customary hip, urban locales in favor of the breathtaking colonial wilderness. THE LAST OF THE MOHICANS offers some of the most spectular landscapes ever seen on screen, as well as some lavish, if confusingly staged, battle scenes. Given the two-dimensionality of the characters, the performances are all creditable, with Daniel Day-Lewis making a successful leap from art-house favorite to running, jumping, shooting box-office hero. Thanks to a hackneyed screenplay that also makes the historical background seem very confusing, these formulaic characters never stray too far from expectations, and indulge in dialogue that occasionally verges on self-parody ("What are you looking at, Sir?" "I'm looking at you, Miss"). Mann, however, successfully overcomes the weak script by dint of sheer directorial bravura, delivering Fenimore Cooper into the 1990s with roaring cannons and whizzing tomahawks.

LAST PICTURE SHOW, THE

1971	118m	bw	Drama	★★★★½
BBS		(U.S.)		R/X

Timothy Bottoms (Sonny Crawford), Jeff Bridges (Duane Jackson), Cybill Shepherd (Jacy Farrow), Ben Johnson (Sam the Lion), Cloris Leachman (Ruth Popper), Ellen Burstyn (Lois Farrow), Eileen Brennan (Genevieve), Clu Gulager (Abilene), Sam Bottoms (Billy), Sharon Taggart (Charlene Duggs)

p, Stephen Friedman; d, Peter Bogdanovich; w, Peter Bogdanovich, Larry McMurtry (based on the novel by McMurtry); ph, Robert Surtees; ed, Donn Cambern; prod d, Polly Platt; art d, Walter Scott Herndon

AAN Best Picture; AA Best Supporting Actor: Ben Johnson; AAN Best Supporting Actor: Jeff Bridges; AA Best Supporting Actress: Cloris Leachman; AAN Best Supporting Actress: Ellen Burstyn; AAN Best Director: Peter Bogdanovich; AAN Best Adapted Screenplay: Larry McMurtry, Peter Bogdanovich; AAN Best Cinematography: Robert Surtees

Bogdanovich's finest effort; bleak and beguiling. None of his other films ranks with THE LAST PICTURE SHOW when it comes to dramatic flair and authenticity. He seems comfortable doing period pieces, but, in this, his second feature (preceded by TARGETS), he captures the era so accurately that the viewer can feel the hopelessness of living in a dying Texas town. Bridges and Timothy Bottoms are the stars of the lackluster local high school football team. Bridges is the aggressive one, and Timothy Bottoms provides the contrasting sensitivity; they are best friends. The story unfolds seamlessly, detailing relationships in a small town. Sam Bottoms is a retarded boy (he got the part after he showed up to watch brother Tim's first day of shooting) who is the butt of cruel jokes by the denizens of the cafe-pool hall-theater owned by Johnson, a one-time cowboy who seems to be every boy's idol and surrogate father. Tim Bottoms takes up the cudgel as Sam Bottom's protector and is soon befriended, then bedded by Leachman, the lonely wife of the school's basketball coach, Thurman. The affair continues for most of the picture, heating up and cooling down a few times. To keep it up, Tim Bottoms ceases dating his regular girl friend, Taggart. Bridges continues dating his girl, Shepherd, but is not happy about her self-centered behavior. She attends a nude bathing party in order to meet the rich Brockette. Her mother, Burstyn, wants her daughter to marry well. Brockette rejects Shepherd because he doesn't want to be bothered with a virgin. Bridges and Tim Bottoms take a short and wild trip to Mexico, and when they return they are saddened to learn that Johnson has died.

THE LAST PICTURE SHOW is a refreshing look backward. While others were outfoxing themselves with multiscreen techniques, Bogdanovich made a movie that could have been shot years before and the result was critically and financially rewarding. The director is an admirer of Ford and Hawks and this is a homage to their styles, as opposed to the kind of ripoffs Colin Higgins and Brian De Palma have done with Hitchcock. The only element that separates this from an early film is the use of frontal nudity and the frank treatment accorded the adult themes. Bogdanovich was hailed as another Orson Welles (another of the director's mentors and friends). This episodic, human story lives and breathes with more power than any Darth Vader or Rocky. There was a time when Bogdanovich considered Jimmy Stewart, among others, for a part in the film. However, he wisely opted against using established stars. Johnson and Leachman each won Oscars, and the entire cast is quite fine (especially Ellen Burstyn, seen here like she's never been, before or since). Look for "Magnum's" John Hillerman in a small role as a teacher. THE LAST PICTURE SHOW could have been a tawdry, sleazy soap opera, but the 31-year-old former film critic kept a light, compassionate touch that elevated the story and presented it as a slice of a life that has all but disappeared.

LAST SEDUCTION, THE

1994	110m	c	Thriller	★★★½
Oakwood Films Inc./DBA Kroy Pictures Inc.		(U.S.)		R/18

Linda Fiorentino (Bridget Gregory), Peter Berg (Mike Swale), J.T. Walsh (Frank Griffith), Bill Nunn (Harlan), Bill Pullman (Clay Gregory), Jack Shearer (Public Defender), Michael Raysses (Phone Sales Rep), Zack Phifer (Gas Station Attendant), Brien Varady (Chris), Donna Wilson (Stacy)

p, Jonathan Shestak; d, John Dahl; w, Steve Barancik; ph, Jeff Jur; ed, Eric L. Beason; m, Joseph Vitarelli; prod d, Linda Pearl; art d, Dina Lipton; fx, John Hartigan; cos, Terry Dresbach

An updated noir thriller that decisively puts the *fatale* back into *femme fatale*, THE LAST SEDUCTION is a dark, expertly contrived display of paranoid nastiness; it's so gleefully mean that only the most tender-hearted viewer could resist going along for the ride.

Ambitious Bridget Gregory (Linda Fiorentino) and her malleable husband Clay (Bill Pullman), a doctor, have just pulled off a drug deal that's left them with $700,000, which Clay intends to use to pay off his gambling debts. While Clay's in the shower, she coolly takes the money and runs, ending up in a friendly little town called Beston. There she sizes up local stud Mike (Peter Berg) in a bar and, having deemed him adequate to her purposes, rocks his world and sets about guaranteeing her future with deadly precision.

Released theatrically after limited airings on the HBO cable channel, John Dahl's THE LAST SEDUCTION joined a growing handful of films—including Tamra Davis's GUNCRAZY and Dahl's previous picture, RED ROCK WEST (both 1993)—to have transcended the stigma attached to made-for-TV movies. Unlike such bloated erotic thrillers as BASIC INSTINCT, which wallow in their own excesses, THE LAST SEDUCTION gets straight to the cold heart of classic noir: life is a stacked deck and only the most twisted, cunning, and ruthless stand a chance of survival. Jeffrey Jur's photography is excellent, dark and smoky at night, crisp and misleadingly clear during the day, and the production design is a marvel of smoky bars and bland suburban houses. But what really makes THE LAST SEDUCTION cook is the performances, especially Linda Fiorentino's praying-mantis-in-lace turn as the amoral Bridget. Though the film made many critics' Ten Best lists and Fiorentino was frequently singled out as an Oscar candidate, THE LAST SEDUCTION could not be included on Academy Awards nomination ballots because it debuted on television.

LAST TANGO IN PARIS
(L'ULTIMO TANGO A PARIGI)

1972 129m c Drama/Erotic		★★★★
PEA/Les Artistes Associes (France/Italy)		X/18

Marlon Brando (Paul), Maria Schneider (Jeanne), Jean-Pierre Leaud (Tom), Massimo Girotti (Marcel), Maria Michi (Rosa's Mother), Veronica Lazare (Rosa), Gitt Magrini (Jeanne's Mother), Darling Legitimus (Concierge), Catherine Sola (TV Script Girl), Mauro Marchetti (TV Cameraman)

p, Alberto Grimaldi; d, Bernardo Bertolucci; w, Bernardo Bertolucci, Franco Arcalli, Agnes Varda (based on a story by Bertolucci); ph, Vittorio Storaro; ed, Franco Arcalli; m, Gato Barbieri; prod d, Ferdinando Scarfiotti; cos, Gitt Magrini

AAN Best Actor: Marlon Brando; AAN Best Director: Bernardo Bertolucci

Shattering social and sexual conventions, LAST TANGO IN PARIS stands as one of Bernardo Bertolucci's finer achievements. Marlon Brando plays Paul, a confused middle-aged American living in Paris whose wife has just, inexplicably, committed suicide. Paul is obsessed with the thought that his wife's death, and her whole life, is a mystery to him. He knew nothing about her, and nothing of the secret affair she carried on for years with Marcel (Massimo Girotti).

Maria Schneider plays Jeanne, a 20-year-old from a wealthy Parisian family who is engaged to Tom (Jean-Pierre Leaud), a New Wave filmmaker who documents his fiancee's life in an attempt to discover the truth about her. While hunting for an apartment, Jeanne meets Paul. Moments later, the two strangers are making passionate love on the floor of the empty apartment. When they meet again, it is under Paul's ground rules: "You and I are going to meet here without knowing anything that goes on outside here. We are going to forget everything we knew—everything." If the psychosexual dynamics and existential maunderings of the screenplay are sometimes less than plausible, the remaining elements are perfectly synthesized in this landmark erotic film—Bertolucci's direction; the raw, brave performances of Brando and Schneider; Storaro's lush camerawork. Not to be missed.

LAST TEMPTATION OF CHRIST, THE

1988 164m c Religious		★★★★
Cineplex Odeon (U.S.)		R/18

Willem Dafoe (Jesus Christ), Harvey Keitel (Judas Iscariot), Barbara Hershey (Mary Magdalene), Harry Dean Stanton (Saul/Paul), David Bowie (Pontius Pilate), Verna Bloom (Mary, Mother of Jesus), Andre Gregory (John the Baptist), Juliette Caton (Girl Angel), Roberts Blossom (Aged Master), Irvin Kershner (Zebedee)

p, Barbara De Fina; d, Martin Scorsese; w, Paul Schrader (based on the novel by Nikos Kazantzakis); ph, Michael Ballhaus; ed, Thelma Schoonmaker; m, Peter Gabriel; fx, Gino Galliani, Iginio Fiorentini; chor, Lahcen Zinoune

AAN Best Director: Martin Scorsese

Martin Scorsese's adaptation of Nikos Kazantzakis's controversial novel The Last Temptation of Christ seeks to emphasize the human aspects of Jesus Christ, a figure described in the Bible as both fully God and fully man. The film opens with the carpenter Jesus of Nazareth (Willem Dafoe) making crosses upon which the Romans crucify rebellious Jews; it closes with the controversial last-temptation sequence, depicting the human love and gratifications Jesus sacrificed to fulfill his destiny as the savior of humankind. Between these powerful and affecting scenes is a fresh and vivid retelling of the Gospel's familiar events—the assembly of the disciples, the miracles, and so forth. Striving for historical accuracy, Scorsese presents Jerusalem as a flat, arid, harsh land suffering under the oppressive thumb of Roman rule. Cinematographer Michael Ballhaus's and production designer John Beard's evocative vision of the Holy Land combines with Peter Gabriel's musical score (derived mostly from traditional and contemporary Arabic rhythms) to vividly convey Christ's world and time—and it is not the lush, picturesque, sanitized Hollywood version popularized by Cecil B. DeMille. Powerful, haunting, and at times very moving, THE LAST TEMPTATION OF CHRIST presents its account of the events and conflicts of Christ's life with a depth of dramatized feeling and motivation that renders them freshly compelling.

LAST WAVE, THE

1977 106m c Thriller		★★★★
Ayer/South Australian/Australian Film Commission (Australia)		PG/AA

Richard Chamberlain (David Burton), Olivia Hamnett (Anne Burton), David Gulpilil (Chris Lee), Frederick Parslow (Rev. Burton), Vivean Gray (Dr. Whitburn), Nanjiwarra Amagula (Charlie), Walter Amagula (Gerry Lee), Roy Bara (Larry), Cedric Lalara (Lindsey), Morris Lalara (Jacko)

p, Hal McElroy, James McElroy; d, Peter Weir; w, Peter Weir, Tony Morphett, Peter Popescu; ph, Russell Boyd; ed, Max Lemon; m, Charles Wain; art d, Neil Angwin; fx, Neil Angwin, Monty Fieguth; cos, Annie Bleakley

A powerful, yet subtle, picture from Australian director Weir, who has demonstrated quite a flair for mystical themes. Like his earlier work, PICNIC AT HANGING ROCK, this picture involves inexplicable events and their connection with the aboriginal world and the ancient Australian landscape. The picture opens as a raging thunderstorm from a clear blue sky drenches a small desert settlement, and then flashes quickly to Sydney, which is also in the midst of a torrential downpour. A voice over the radio unconvincingly attempts to explain the phenomenon as a reaction to cold winds from the Antarctic. An earlier shot of an aborigine painting on a cave wall lets the viewer know there is something at work here that transcends scientific explanation, setting the mood for the rest of the film. The contrast between the Western viewpoint, which attributes geophysical results to scientific reason, and the aboriginal perspective of a cosmos beyond the grasp of conscious thought, creates a tension that is carried throughout the film. Chamberlain plays a Sydney lawyer who becomes involved in defending a group of aborigines accused of murder (despite his lack of experience with both aborigines and criminal law).

Weir does a fine job of weaving real events with dream sequences, as well as capturing the aboriginal perspective—this is one of few films that does not portray the aborigines as a defeated people, entirely subjugated by white settlers. Chamberlain is convincing as a wealthy lawyer and family man who becomes possessed by a vision beyond his grasp. Although the plot falters in a few instances, it maintains a high level of overall suspense.

LAST YEAR AT MARIENBAD
(L'ANNEE DERNIERE A MARIENBAD)

1961 94m bw Drama		★★★★★
Terra/Cormoran/Precitel/Como/Tamara /Silver-Cineriz (France/Italy)		/U

Delphine Seyrig (A/Woman), Giorgio Albertazzi (X/Stranger), Sacha Pitoeff (M/Escort/Husband), Francoise Bertin, Luce Garcia-Ville, Helena Kornel, Francois Spira, Karin Toeche-Mittler, Pierre Barbaud, Wilhelm von Deek

L'ATALANTE

p, Pierre Courau, Raymond Froment; d, Alain Resnais; w, Alain Robbe-Grillet; ph, Sacha Vierny; ed, Henri Colpi, Jasmine Chasney; m, Francis Seyrig; art d, Jacques Saulnier; cos, Bernard Evein, Chanel

AAN Best Original Screenplay: Alain Robbe-Grillet

The cinematic equivalent of the *nouveau roman* ("new novel") and a true landmark in film history. One of the most formally inventive of all feature films, LAST YEAR AT MARIENBAD stretches the limits of film language to the extreme. Scripted by Robbe-Grillet, the movie introduces us to four main characters—A (Seyrig), a lovely, well-dressed woman; X (Albertazzi), a handsome stranger; M (Pitoeff), a man who might be A's husband; and a luxurious estate (important enough to be considered a character) with long, sterile hallways and perfectly manicured grounds. The "plot", if you can call it one, focuses on X's attempt to convince A that they met, possibly last year, at a resort hotel, perhaps in Marienbad, where she may have promised to run away with him this year. A, however, has no recollection of the meeting. . . or else is being coy. . . or dares not recognize X. . . or whatever you care to make of it. The viewer is kept in perpetual doubt as to whether the meeting ever took place, whether it has not yet taken place, or whether it's a hopeful fantasy X has made up. Frustrated? You should be.

LAST YEAR AT MARIENBAD was hailed as a masterpiece at the time of its release, largely thanks to Robbe-Grillet and director Resnais's manipulation of time—past, present, and future—in relation to the subjective realities of the film's characters. Easy to read as a parody of Hollywood love triangles, MARIENBAD also mocks classical cinema's tendency to be redundant by repeating lines, indeed entire scenes, over and over again. All the characters are flat, often nothing but statues in a well-kept mausoleum. This is precisely how they appear in the film's most famous shot, in which the tiny figures amid the large sculpture garden cast shadows, but the starkly groomed bushes do not. A true cinematic puzzle, stunningly shot, MARIENBAD decenters the human subject from its place of primacy in most narrative cinema, and the result is a provocative study of alienation.

L'ATALANTE
(LE CHALAND QUI PASSE)
1934 89m bw Romance   ★★★★★
J.L. Nounez (France)   /PG

Michel Simon *(Pere Jules)*, Jean Daste *(Jean)*, Dita Parlo *(Juliette)*, Gilles Margaritis *(Peddler)*, Louis Lefebvre *(Cabin Boy)*, Fanny Clar *(Juliette's Mother)*, Raphael Diligent *(Juliette's Father)*, Maurice Gilles *(Office Manager)*, Rene Bleck *(Best Man)*, Charles Goldblatt *(Thief)*

p, Jacques-Louis Nounez; d, Jean Vigo; w, Jean Vigo, Albert Riera (based on a scenario by R. de Guichen); ph, Boris Kaufman, Louis Berger; ed, Louis Chavance

Jean Vigo's poetic tale centers on Jean (Daste), captain of the barge L'Atalante, who marries Juliette (Parlo), a young woman from the country. (The early scenes leading up to and including their wedding are marvelous.) Bored with life on the barge, Juliette longs to see the bright lights of Paris. Jean finally gives in to his wife's request and takes her to a Paris cabaret, where a peddler flirts with the young woman. The next day, an angry and jealous Jean leaves the ship without his wife. She is visited by the peddler, who entertains her and then is promptly thrown off the barge upon Jean's return. Juliette then sneaks off to Paris, and Jean purposefully sets sail without his wife, leaving his penniless wife to take a job in town. The film then concentrates on the lovers' pain before L'Atalante again sails on.

Vigo made only four films (A PROPOS DE NICE, TARIS CHAMPION DE NATATION, ZERO DE CONDUITE, and L'ATALANTE) before his untimely death at age 29. In L'ATALANTE, he treats his simple story both realistically and surrealistically, combining and contrasting styles. Thus, in one scene, Jean dives into the water and sees an image of a smiling Juliette swimming in her wedding gown; in another, a seaman played by Michel Simon (in possibly the greatest role of his distinguished career) displays his odd collection of curios, including a pair of severed hands in a jar. (Surrealist poet Jacques Prevert and his brother, filmmaker Pierre, also make cameo appearances.) L'ATALANTE was poorly received at its initial 1934 screening,

prompting its distributors to insert a popular song and re-edit nearly all the scenes. The result was a box-office disaster, and three weeks later Vigo was dead.

Years later, a complete version was finally constructed thanks to the Cinematheque Francais and Henri Langlois. Less iconoclastic and experimental than his earlier films, L'ATALANTE is nonetheless brilliantly idiosyncratic and insightful, the warmest film of this great director's career.

LATE AUTUMN
(AKIBIYORI)
1960 127m c Drama   ★★★
New Yorker (Japan)

Setsuko Hara *(The Mother)*, Yoko Tsukasa *(The Daughter)*, Chishu Ryu *(The Uncle)*, Mariko Okada *(The Daughter's Friend)*, Keiji Sada *(The Young Man)*

d, Yasujiro Ozu; w, Kogo Noda, Yasujiro Ozu; ph, Yushun Atsuta; m, Takanobu Saito; art d, Tatsuo Hamada

One of the final efforts from one of the great masters of Japanese cinema, LATE AUTUMN was originally made in 1960 but not brought to the US until ten years after Ozu's death. Tsukasa plays the daughter of Hara, a recently widowed woman who finds that her late husband's friends are taking an extreme interest in seeing her remarried. Hara herself is not so keen on walking down the aisle quite yet, something that shocks men raised in a tradition that has little place for an unattached woman. Eventually Hara does agree to marry, out of a desire to please the insistent elders, but her ideas of marriage still seem quite obscure to the traditionalists.

Ozu made 54 films in his long career, most marked by a subtle, distinctive directorial style featuring a stationary camera placed only a few feet above the floor. The latter portion of his career saw Ozu extremely concerned about the effects of Westernization upon traditional Japan; in LATE AUTUMN this is reflected in the consternation caused in the elders by Hara's "unorthodox" views.

LATE SHOW, THE
1977 94m c Crime   ★★★½
Lion's Gate (U.S.)   PG/15

Art Carney *(Ira Wells)*, Lily Tomlin *(Margo Sperling)*, Bill Macy *(Charlie Hatter)*, Eugene Roche *(Ron Birdwell)*, Joanna Cassidy *(Laura Birdwell)*, John Considine *(Lamar)*, Ruth Nelson *(Mrs. Schmidt)*, John Davey *(Sgt. Dayton)*, Howard Duff *(Harry Regan)*

p, Robert Altman; d, Robert Benton; w, Robert Benton; ph, Charles Rosher Jr.; ed, Lou Lombardo, Peter Appleton; m, Ken Wannberg

AAN Best Original Screenplay: Robert Benton (Story)

This fine, overlooked film stars Carney as Ira Wells, an aging private eye whose former partner, Harry Regan (Duff), is murdered while tracking down a missing cat for Margo Sperling (Tomlin). A sometime dealer in stolen goods, she suspects her pet has been nabbed by an associate whom she's failed to pay. At the urging of Charlie Hatter (Macy), Ira picks up where Regan left off, and he and Margo do a Nick and Nora Charles number as they piece together the complex clues that lead to the cat and climax of this intriguing mystery. Along the way, Margo begins to find herself attracted to Ira, but he doesn't return her affection—at least at first.

THE LATE SHOW was director Benton's second outing, and he showed immense sensitivity and the ability to spin a good yarn. Tomlin, in her second film after NASHVILLE, and Carney, in his return to the screen after his Oscar-winning performance in HARRY AND TONTO, work wonderfully together. Carney's portrayal of a man whose body is beginning to betray him but whose spirit won't throw in the towel is nothing short of elegant.

LAUGHTER

1930 85m bw Comedy/Drama ★★★½
Paramount (U.S.)

Fredric March (*Paul Lockridge*), Nancy Carroll (*Peggy Gibson*), Frank Morgan (*C. Mortimer Gibson*), Glenn Anders (*Ralph Le Saint*), Diane Ellis (*Marjorie Gibson*), Leonard Carey (*Benham*), Ollie Burgoyne (*Pearl*)

d, Harry d'Abbadie D'Arrast; w, Donald Ogden Stewart (based on a story by Douglas Doty, Harry d'Abbadie D'Arrast); ph, George Folsey; ed, Helene Turner

AAN Best Original Screenplay: Harry D'Abbadie D'Arrast, Douglas Doty, Donald Ogden Stewart

Absolutely enchanting, and an important precursor to the romantic comedies of the 1930s. Director and cowriter Harry d'Abbadie D'Arrast had a brief film career that included a stint with Charlie Chaplin, but had he done nothing but work on LAUGHTER, his place in film history would be secure. This undated film is ahead of its time in content and style. Nancy Carroll is Peggy, a Follies dancer surrounded by amorous stage-door Johnnies. When she falls for wealthy C. Mortimer Gibson (Morgan) Peggy gives up all her old suitors, including Paul (March), a free-spirited composer who travels to Paris to forget his rejection. Neglected by her business-obsessed husband, Peggy occasionally revisits her bohemian past when she drops in on another former beau, Ralph (Anders), a Greenwich Village sculptor. She also befriends her stepdaughter Marjorie (Ellis), who is close to her own age. Trouble begins when Paul returns from Paris and when Ralph woos Marjorie because he can't have Peggy.

LAUGHTER could have been as soapy as a tubful of Tide, but D'Abbadie D'Arrast lends his fast-paced comedy-drama the deft sophisticated touch that would become Ernst Lubitsch's trademark. The characters relate to each other in a moving, adult, intimate manner, and even the film's melodramatic moments are beautifully underplayed. The script crackles with wit, and Carroll (the real centerpiece here), March and Morgan lead a cast shimmering with conviction.

LAURA

1944 88m bw Mystery ★★★★★
Fox (U.S.) /U

Gene Tierney (*Laura Hunt*), Dana Andrews (*Mark McPherson*), Clifton Webb (*Waldo Lydecker*), Vincent Price (*Shelby Carpenter*), Judith Anderson (*Ann Treadwell*), Dorothy Adams (*Bessie Clary*), James Flavin (*McAvity*), Clyde Fillmore (*Bullitt*), Ralph Dunn (*Fred Callahan*), Grant Mitchell (*Corey*)

p, Otto Preminger; d, Otto Preminger; w, Jay Dratler, Samuel Hoffenstein, Elizabeth Reinhardt, Ring Lardner Jr., Jerry Cady (based on the novel by Vera Caspary); ph, Joseph La Shelle; ed, Louis Loeffler; m, David Raksin; prod d, Thomas Little, Paul S. Fox; art d, Lyle Wheeler, Leland Fuller; fx, Fred Sersen; cos, Bonnie Cashin

AAN Best Supporting Actor: Clifton Webb; *AAN Best Director:* Otto Preminger; *AAN Best Screenplay:* Jay Dratler, Samuel Hoffenstein, Betty Reinhardt; *AA Best Cinematography:* Joseph LaShelle; *AAN Best Art Direction:* Lyle Wheeler, Leland Fuller, Thomas Little

The sleekest of *Noirs*, the chicest of murders, and deliciously twisted—the detective is a necrophilliac, two of the title character's suitors seem gay, and the Laura all the men are vying for is a corpse with no face. Indeed LAURA, goes the genre one further by taking apart the conventions, then putting them back together, and diving wholeheartedly into them for the finale—a cocktail party denouement to name the killer.

LAURA, based on the novel by Vera Caspary, revolves around the murder of the title character (Tierney)—a shotgun blast completely obliterating the corpse's once-lovely face. Homicide detective Mark McPherson (Andrews) has a trio of suspects—newspaper critic Waldo Lydecker (Webb), who "created" Laura; playboy/parasite and fiance Shelby Carpenter (Price); and Anne Treadwell (Anderson), Laura's socialite aunt who has been carrying on with Shelby. Just as Mark is beginning to fall in love with a vision of the deceased woman—in the form of an oil portrait—in walks the *real* Laura . . .

LAURA is a truly haunting study of obsession, with suitably poignant music provided by David Raksin (lyrics by Johnny Mercer). Originally, Otto Preminger was assigned only as producer, with studio chieftain Darryl Zanuck offering the directing chore to Rouben Mamoulian. Part of the way into production, however, Zanuck fired Mamoulian and handed the reins over to Preminger. Preminger reshot Mamoulian's footage, replaced cinematographer Lucian Ballard with Joseph La Shelle (who won an Academy Award), and scrapped the Mamoulian costumes and sets—including a portrait of Laura which Mamoulian's wife had painted.

LAVENDER HILL MOB, THE

1951 82m bw Crime/Comedy ★★★★½
Ealing (U.K.) /U

Alec Guinness (*Henry Holland*), Stanley Holloway (*Pendlebury*), Sidney James (*Lackery*), Alfie Bass (*Shorty*), Marjorie Fielding (*Mrs. Chalk*), John Gregson (*Farrow*), Edie Martin (*Miss Evesham*), Clive Morton (*Station Sergeant*), Ronald Adam (*Turner*), Sydney Tafler (*Clayton*)

p, Michael Balcon; d, Charles Crichton; w, T.E.B. Clarke; ph, Douglas Slocombe; ed, Seth Holt; m, Georges Auric; art d, William Kellner

AAN Best Actor: Alec Guinness; *AA Best Story and Screenplay:* T.E.B. Clarke

A hilarious tongue-in-cheek crime comedy, one of the finest to come out of the Ealing Studios during their most prolific years. Guinness stars as a mild-mannered transporter of gold bullion who, after 20 years of faithful service, blithely decides to steal one million pounds' worth. He enlists Holloway, an old pal who is a paperweight manufacturer and a bit of a sculptor. They team up with James and Bass, two cockney professional crooks, and the scheme is launched. After a successful hijack, they melt down their booty, mold it into small, souvenir Eiffel Towers, and ship it off to Paris. Guinness and Holloway follow the gold, only to learn that six of the Eiffel Towers have been purchased by a group of daytripping English schoolgirls . . . Much hilarity follows, including a superlative chase scene in which Guinness and Holloway, driving a stolen police car, thwart their pursuers by issuing contradictory messages over the police radio, which ends by broadcasting "Old MacDonald Had a Farm" to all cars! The film had begun, however, with Guinness telling this story to a man in a swank Rio restaurant. The camera returns there for the conclusion, and we see that Guinness is not only having a drink with the other chap—he's handcuffed to him.

Guinness is winning as the last man on earth you'd suspect of being a criminal (he was nominated for an Oscar but lost to Gary Cooper, for HIGH NOON). Clarke's screenplay quite rightly won the award. Many of England's best comic actors are seen in small roles, including Sidney Tafler, Peter Bull, and John Gregson. In a tiny role, you may notice James Fox (brother of Edward), still being billed as William. And in the opening sequence, Guinness hands a cute young woman some money and tells her to buy a little gift. You'll have to look fast to recognize Audrey Hepburn as the little girl.

L'AVVENTURA

1959 145m bw Drama ★★★★★
Cino del Duca/Produzioni Cinematografiche Europee/Societe /X
Cinematographique Lyre (Italy/France)

Monica Vitti (*Claudia*), Gabriele Ferzetti (*Sandro*), Lea Massari (*Anna*), Dominique Blanchar (*Giulia*), James Addams (*Corrado*), Renzo Ricci (*Anna's Father*), Esmeralda Ruspoli (*Patrizia*), Lelio Luttazzi (*Raimondo*), Dorothy De Poliolo (*Gloria Perkins*), Giovanni Petrucci (*Young Prince*)

p, Amato Pennasilico; d, Michelangelo Antonioni; w, Michelangelo Antonioni, Elio Bartolini, Tonino Guerra (based on the story by Antonioni); ph, Aldo Scavarda; ed, Eraldo da Roma; m, Giovanni Fusco; art d, Piero Poletto; cos, Adriana Berselli

The title translates as "The Adventure" and this *is* an adventure, if you're willing to take it. A group of wealthy Italians goes yachting to a rocky island near Sicily. After arriving, they notice that Anna (Massari) is missing, and everyone searches for her amidst the endless crevices and wave-battered cliffs. Her best friend, Claudia (Vitti), teams with Anna's lover, Sandro (Ferzetti), in the search, which is eventually abandoned in the hope that Anna simply left the island. Inquiries are made in town as to her whereabouts, and several people claim to have seen her. In the process, Sandro becomes increasingly involved with Claudia, who becomes his lover and substitute for Anna.

L'AVVENTURA is one of Antonioni's finest films, and a landmark in the devlopment of cinematic narrative. The seemingly pressing question raised by the film's opening—"What happened to Anna?"—becomes increasingly irrelevant as we learn that there is no "adventure" of this type, just a shifting, unsettling meditation on contemporary alienation and the opacity of all human relationships. The acting is appropriately minimalist and the blank-faced, passive Vitti is marvelouly Garboesque in the role that deservedly made her an international star. One character will be in deep focus at the "back" of the image, seemingly ready to call out to the person in the foreground, but communication is all but impossible. Even sex is a feeble attempt to escape the oddly charged ennui of this milieu. As with all Antonioni, the cinematography and composition are unsurpassed. He scatters his existential characters over the landscape, brilliantly emphasizing empty space over the trappings of plot. Photographed largely outdoors, shooting took months to complete and sent the original production company, Imeria, into debt. Cino Del Duca came to Antonioni's aid and filming continued, though many of the summer shots actually took place in the winter. Some four months later, the Cannes Film Festival audience greeted the picture with an unparalleled assault of hisses and boos. Several months later, though, L'AVVENTURA set box-office records in Paris; by the time it hit America, it had received a "condemned" rating from the National League of Decency—always a good sign.

LAWRENCE OF ARABIA

1962 220m c Biography/Adventure/War ★★★★★
Horizon (U.K.) /PG

Peter O'Toole (*T.E. Lawrence*), Alec Guinness (*Prince Feisal*), Anthony Quinn (*Auda Abu Tayi*), Jack Hawkins (*Gen. Allenby*), Jose Ferrer (*Turkish Bey*), Anthony Quayle (*Col. Harry Brighton*), Claude Rains (*Mr. Dryden*), Arthur Kennedy (*Jackson Bentley*), Donald Wolfit (*Gen. Murray*), Omar Sharif (*Sherif Ali Ibn El Kharish*)

p, Sam Spiegel, David Lean; d, David Lean; w, Robert Bolt, Michael Wilson (based on *The Seven Pillars of Wisdom* by T.E. Lawrence); ph, Freddie Young; ed, Anne V. Coates; m, Maurice Jarre; prod d, John Box; art d, John Stoll; cos, Phyllis Dalton

AA Best Picture; AAN Best Actor: Peter O'Toole; AAN Best Supporting Actor: Omar Sharif; AA Best Director: David Lean; AAN Best Adapted Screenplay: Robert Bolt; AA Best Cinematography: Fred A. Young; AA Best Editing: Anne Coates; AA Best Score: Maurice Jarre; AA Best Art Direction: John Box, John Stoll, Dario Simoni; AA Best Sound: John Cox

David Lean's splendid biography of the enigmatic T.E. Lawrence paints a complex portrait of the desert-loving Englishman who united Arab tribes in battle against the Ottoman Turks during WWI. At the center of Lean's superbly sun-drenched, 70mm canvas is Peter O'Toole's eccentric but magnificent portrayal of the erudite, Oxford-educated lieutenant, who wangles an assignment as an observer with Prince Feisal (Alec Guinness), the leader of the Arab revolt against the Turks. Feisal is resigned to allowing his tribal army to become just another branch of the British forces, but the messianic Lawrence, determined to prevent the Arabs from falling under British colonial domination, undertakes a military miracle. He, Sherif Ali (Omar Sharif)—whom Lean introduces as a tiny dot on the desert horizon that steadily enlarges, in one of the film's most striking scenes—and 50 men traverse the "uncrossable" Nefud Desert; join forces with their traditional tribal enemies, led by Auda Abu Tayi (Anthony Quinn), and rout the Turks at the strategic port city of Aqaba. Given the go-ahead by Gen. Allenby (Jack Hawkins), worshiped by the Arabs he has brought together, and cloaked in their flowing white robes, "El Aurens" leads the Arabs in a brutal guerrilla war that is as much about establishing Arab sovereignty as it is about defeating the Turks. His thrilling exploits are glorified by the Lowell Thomas-like American journalist Jackson Bentley (Arthur Kennedy). In time, however, Lawrence's legions dwindle, he begins to revel sadistically in violence, his grand attempt at overseeing the formation of a united Arab Council in Damascus collapses, and he returns to Britain exhausted. Lean's film is best appreciated on the big

screen, and in 1989 a carefully restored version of LAWRENCE was released that reinstated 20 minutes cut for the original roadshow release and another 15 minutes trimmed when it was rereleased in 1970. Moreover, Lean and his original editor, Anne V. Coates, were finally given the chance to do a "fine cut" on the film, now 216 memorable minutes long.

LAWS OF GRAVITY

1992 100m c Drama ★★★½
Meistrich Corporation (U.S.) R/18

Peter Greene (*Jimmy*), Edie Falco (*Denise*), Paul Schulzie (*Frankie*), Tony Fernandez (*Tommy*), James McCauley (*Kenny*), Anibal Lierras (*Ray*), Miguel Sierra (*Vasquez*), Adam Trese (*Jon*), Arabella Field (*Celia*), Saul Stein (*Sal*)

p, Larry Meistrich, Bob Gosse; d, Nick Gomez; w, Nick Gomez; ph, Jean DeSegonzac; ed, Nick Gomez, Tom McArdle; prod d, Monica Bretherton

A gritty take on the day-to-day life of petty thugs on the mean streets of Brooklyn, LAWS OF GRAVITY captures this violent and volatile world without without being exploitative or sensationalist.

Jimmy (Peter Greene) and his lifelong friend Jon (Adam Trese) are two neighborhood punks who spend their days stealing, fighting and hanging out. Jimmy, at least, is in a stable domestic relationship with Denise (Edie Falco), and is beginning to question his lot in life; Jon, a few years younger, runs on a very short fuse and is only one step ahead of the police, who have issued a summons for his arrest; this doesn't stop him from picking fights with virtually anyone who looks in the direction of his girlfriend Celia (Arabella Field). The endless cycle of stealing, brawling and drinking takes on new dimensions when another local, Frankie (Paul Schultzie), returns home from Florida. A sociopath with boy-next-door looks, Frankie has brought with him a cache of stolen handguns which he convinces Jon and Jimmy to help him "move." The presence of the weapons only serves to escalate the tensions within the group, leading to an appropriately violent conclusion.

LAWS OF GRAVITY's shoestring budget (reputedly only $38 thousand) forced some interesting choices on writer-director Nick Gomez. The use of a hand-held camera (masterfully employed by Jean De Segonzac), and frequent lack of master shots, gives the film a compelling *cinema verite* feel. This is complemented by the improvisational quality of the dialogue and the realistically drawn characters. Gomez's keen eye for casting is one of the film's strongest attributes, with an entire group of virtual unknowns turning in uniformly credible performances.

LE BEAU MARIAGE

1982 97m c Drama/Comedy ★★★★
Losanger/Carosse (France) PG/

Beatrice Romand (*Sabine*), Andre Dussollier (*Edmond*), Feodor Atkine (*Simon*), Huguette Faget (*Antique Dealer*), Arielle Dombasle (*Clarisse*), Thamila Mezbah (*Mother*), Sophie Renoir (*Lise*), Herve Duhamel (*Frederic*), Pascal Greggory (*Nicolas*), Virginie Thevenet (*The Bride*)

p, Margaret Menegoz; d, Eric Rohmer; w, Eric Rohmer; ph, Bernard Lutic, Romain Winding, Nicolas Brunet; ed, Cecile Decugis, Lisa Heredia; m, Ronan Gure, Simon Des Innocents

The second installment in Eric Rohmer's "Comedies and Proverbs" series, LE BEAU MARIAGE is the charming tale of Sabine (Beatrice Romand), a university student with a Paris flat who decides one day, quite arbitrarily, to get married. All she is lacking is a husband, a minor detail. She leaves her painter boyfriend, quits her antique-store job, and begins pursuing Edmond (Andre Dussollier), a busy lawyer who is friendly to Sabine but clearly not interested in romancing her. This thoroughly enjoyable picture is carried by the spunky, idiosyncratic performance of Romand, who appeared 12 years earlier in Rohmer's "Moral Tale," CLAIRE'S KNEE. Two of her costars in this film would also be rewarded with lead roles in subsequent Rohmer films—Arielle Dombasle, who appears in PAULINE AT THE BEACH, and Sophie Renoir (cast here as Romand's pesty little sister), who stars in Rohmer's final "Comedies and Proverbs" entry, BOYFRIENDS AND GIRL-

FRIENDS. There's also a fine synthesized pop score that you may find yourself humming long after the film's end. In French with English subtitles.

LE BEAU SERGE

1958 97m bw Drama   ★★★½
United Motion Picture   (France)   /X

Gerard Blain *(Serge)*, Jean-Claude Brialy *(Francois)*, Bernadette Lafont *(Marie)*, Edmond Beauchamp *(Glomaud)*, Michele Meritz *(Yvonne)*, Jeanne Perez, Claude Cerval, Andre Dino

d, Claude Chabrol; w, Claude Chabrol; ph, Henri Decae; ed, Jacques Gaillard; m, Emile Delpierre

Generally considered the film that put the French New Wave in the history books (though Jacques Rivette's PARIS BELONGS TO US was the first to go into production), LE BEAU SERGE received overwhelming critical approval of its use of non-professional actors, raw black-and-white photography (masterfully executed by Henri Decae), and personal vision. It is the tale of two old friends, Francois (Jean-Claude Brialy), a city dweller who returns to the provincial French village of his childhood, and Serge (Gerard Blain), a successful architect-turned-drunkard. After the birth of a malformed son, Serge's life and marriage go into a tailspin as he collapses under the weight of tremendous guilt. Unfortunately, the film is cluttered with Catholicism, which director Claude Chabrol had the good sense to deemphasize as his career developed. Though highly acclaimed, LE BEAU SERGE was quickly overshadowed by the subsequent success of Francois Truffaut's 400 BLOWS, Jean-Luc Godard's BREATHLESS, and Alain Resnais's HIROSHIMA MON AMOUR. LES COUSINS, a companion piece to LE BEAU SERGE that also starred Brialy and Blain, appeared the following year to an equally enthusiastic reception.

LE BOUCHER

1969 93m c Thriller   ★★★★
La Boetie/Euro Intl.   (France/Italy)   GP/18

Stephane Audran *(Helene)*, Jean Yanne *(Popaul)*, Antonio Passalia *(Angelo)*, Mario Beccaria *(Leon Hamel)*, Pasquale Ferone *(Pere Cahrpy)*, Roger Rudel *(Police Inspector Grumbach)*, William Guerault *(Charles)*

p, Andre Genoves; d, Claude Chabrol; w, Claude Chabrol; ph, Jean Rabier; ed, Jacques Gaillard; m, Pierre Jansen; cos, Joseph Poulard

A calculated, slow-paced thriller set in the French countryside, where schoolteacher Audran begins a new assignment. She is soon romanced by the village butcher, Yanne, though she seems more concerned with her schoolwork than with finding a lover. In the meantime, the village is stricken with random murders. Audran finds herself directly involved when a young girl's body is found near the schoolyard. During a school outing, she and the children take a lunch break and eat their sandwiches outdoors. One girl, who is sitting next to a cliff, suddenly finds blood dripping onto her bread. Above her is discovered yet another butchered body. Audran's suspicions are raised when she finds Yanne's cigarette lighter next to the body, but the clever, deranged killer is one step ahead of her and buys an identical lighter. By the finale, Audran's concern has turned into deadly fear as she barricades herself inside her house.

LE BOUCHER is a compelling psychological thriller that occasionally gets bogged down and fails to reach the level of suspense that could have been achieved. Like the psychopathic killer of little girls in Fritz Lang's M, Yanne's character is presented in a manner which is calculated to stir a measure of audience sympathy: he is a man with good qualities who is unable to help himself. Audran, the real-life wife of director Chabrol and star of three of his films, gives a compelling performance, but she is simply too sophisticated to come across as a country schoolteacher.

LE GAI SAVOIR

1968 95m c Drama   ★★★★
O.R.T.F./Anouchka/Bavaria Atelier   (France)   /X

Juliet Berto *(Patricia Lumumba)*, Jean-Pierre Leaud *(Emile Rousseau)*

d, Jean-Luc Godard; w, Jean-Luc Godard (based on "Emile" by Jean Jacques Rousseau); ph, Georges Leclerc; ed, Germaine Cohen

A fascinating film from the master of cinematic discourse, Jean-Luc Godard, in which he makes a profound attempt to dissolve narrative structure to its most basic elements: sound and image. Commissioned by the French government as a television adaptation of Jean Jacques Rousseau's "Emile," LE GAI SAVOIR instead turned out to be a study of language, or, more precisely, film language. It is completely absent of plot and leaves Berto and Leaud (two of the most prominent acting figures in the French New Wave) sitting in the black void of a sound stage, lit only by a single light. Not surprisingly the French government was furious with Godard for his failure to deliver an "acceptable" movie and refused to televise it, allowing him to buy back the rights. What results is a wealth of philosophy relating to Godard's radical thoughts on filmmaking, delivered in the form of a conversation between Leaud and Berto. Intercut with their thoughts are some compelling word association tests which further exemplify Godard's love of language. It's no CASABLANCA, but for those with adventurous tastes and an interest in questioning the status quo, LE GAI SAVOIR's language deserves the same consideration as the literature of such contemporaries as Jean-Paul Sartre.

LE PETIT THEATRE DE JEAN RENOIR

1969 100m c Drama   ★★★★
Son et Lumiere/ORTF   (France)   /U

THE LAST NEW YEAR'S EVE: Nino Fornicola *(The Bum)*, Minny Monti *(The Female Bum)*, Roger Trapp *(Max Vialle)*, Roland Martin, Frederic Santaya, Pierre Gulda, THE ELECTRIC FLOOR WAXER: Marguerite Cassan *(Isabelle)*, Pierre Olaf *(The Husband)*, Jacques Dynam *(The 2nd Husband)*, Jean-Louis Tristan *(Agent)*

p, Pierre Long; d, Jean Renoir; w, Jean Renoir; ph, Georges Leclerc; ed, Genevieve Winding; m, Joseph Kosma, Jean Wiener; prod d, Gilbert Margerie

An exceptional coda to the long and magnificent career of Renoir, which sums up his world in a personal manner. Divided into four parts, each introduced by the charming 75-year-old director himself, the picture moves from the artificially theatrical to the naturally realistic. The first episode, "The Last New Year's Eve," has Fornicola, a ragged and seemingly lonely bum, standing outside the window of an upper-class restaurant. One of the rich people inside pays to have the bum watch them eat from the outside. Of course, the diners lose their appetites, and as a consolation they have the food given to the bum. One of the rich women also gives her coat to the man. He is then seen returning to his riverside shelter, where he is greeted by his equally ragged wife. Together, during the night, they peacefully die. The segment was shot entirely on a stage, with Renoir paying homage in his narration to Hans Christian Andersen. The second episode, "The Electric Floor Waxer," is an odd little piece for those familiar with Renoir (and for anyone else, for that matter). Based on an earlier project, "It's Revolution," this tale is a satirical opera complete with singing choruses of office workers rising up from the lower depths of the Metro station. They sing repetitive refrains about their offices and their jobs. One woman (Cassan) goes through life obsessed with giving the floor a good waxing, causing heartache among her successive husbands. Dynam, her second, finally saves Cassan from waxing by throwing the vibrating, whirling machine out the window. As it crashes to the ground below, Cassan leaps from the window to join her electric lover. The third episode is hardly an episode at all; in one long dolly in-dolly out Jeanne Moreau sings a little tune called "When Love Dies" (Oscar Cremieux). It is included, as Renoir puts it, to "take us for a little while outside our century of sleazy progress." The fourth episode, "The King of Yvetot," is the most purely realistic, shot entirely on location. At the introduction Renoir shows us his little theater (a miniature model of a stage) and briefly explains the sport of petanque, the values and the rules of this game. He takes a tiny metal ball and rolls it along the little stage, and with one quick edit, we are transported into the world of cinema as a large petanque ball rolls along the ground. An old man is seen playing, then his young wife, and then her younger lover. The conflicts of this triangle are resolved peacefully and with respect to set morals in a final game of petanque, which Renoir "firmly believes to be an instrument of peace." The film's finale is also the end of Renoir's little theater; the members of the cast come out for a closing bow. The actors thank us for watching, and we cannot help but feel thanks for Renoir's humble presentation. What way could be more appropriate for one of filmdom's greatest directors (and probably the greatest in Europe) to wrap up his truly profound career? Originally made for French television in 1969.

LEADBELLY

1976   126m   c   Musical/Biography   ★★★½
Paramount   (U.S.)   PG/AA

Roger E. Mosley (*Huddie Ledbetter*), Paul Benjamin (*Wes Ledbetter*), Madge Sinclair (*Miss Eula*), Alan Manson (*Prison Chief Guard*), Albert Hall (*Dicklicker*), Art Evans (*Blind Lemon Jefferson*), James E. Brodhead (*John Lomax*), John Henry Faulk (*Governor Neff*), Vivian Bonnell (*Old Lady*), Dana Manno (*Margaret Judd*)

p, Marc Merson; d, Gordon Parks Sr.; w, Ernest Kinoy; ph, Bruce Surtees; ed, Harry Howard; m, Fred Karlin; prod d, Robert Boyle

Fine biopic of famed black blues/folk singer Huddie Ledbetter, known as Leadbelly, who wrote or adapted such classics as "Goodnight, Irene," "The Midnight Special," "Rock Island Line," and "The Bourgeois Blues." Ledbetter's hard life is related in flashback from his early teens to his last term in prison (he also served twice on chain gangs). The film shows how he he was victimized by racism but does not minimize the complexity of his erratic personality—often manifested in outbursts of violence. Though several of his songs are rendered well here by HiTide Harris, backed by Sonny Terry, Brownie McGhee, David Cohen, and Dick Rosmini, LEADBELLY focuses less on the man's musical artistry than one would wish. Still, this is a very informative film, beautifully photographed by Bruce Surtees, with fine performances by almost everyone in the cast, especially Robert E. Mosley in the title role.

LEAGUE OF THEIR OWN, A

1992   128m   c   Comedy/Sports   ★★½
Parkway Productions/Columbia   (U.S.)   PG

Tom Hanks (*Jimmy Dugan*), Geena Davis (*Dottie Hinson*), Lori Petty (*Kit Keller*), Madonna (*Mae Mordabito*), Rosie O'Donnell (*Doris Murphy*), Megan Cavanagh (*Marla Hooch*), David Strathairn (*Ira Lowenstein*), Garry Marshall (*Walter Harvey*), Jon Lovitz (*Ernie Capadino*), Bill Pullman (*Bob Hinson*)

p, Elliot Abbott, Robert Greenhut; d, Penny Marshall; w, Lowell Ganz, Babaloo Mandel (from the story by Kim Wilson and Kelly Candaele); ph, Miroslav Ondricek; ed, George Bowers; m, Hans Zimmer; prod d, Bill Groom; art d, Tim Galvin; cos, Cynthia Flynt

As uneven as an amateur baseball game, A LEAGUE OF THEIR OWN has a degree of charm which is all but drowned out by sentimental overkill.

Dottie Hinson (Geena Davis) and Kit Keller (Lori Petty) are two sisters recruited to play in the first all-womens' baseball league, formed during World War II to keep the sport alive while much of the male population—including Dottie's husband—are off at war. The sisters are assigned to the "Rockford Peaches," where their teammates include Marla Hooch (Megan Cavanagh), a slugger whose plain looks are the butt for some of the film's weakest jokes; and Mae Mordabito, a former dance-hall hostess who comes across like a 1940s version of Madonna (not much of a surprise, since that's who plays her). Tom Hanks plays the team's coach, Jimmy Dugan, a pro player turned pro drinker.

Directed by Penny Marshall (BIG), A LEAGUE OF THEIR OWN sports some fine performances and well-staged ball scenes, but also suffers from serious miscasting and sophomoric humor. It occasionally strives for a kind of gentle feminism in the style of FRIED GREEN TOMATOES, but never follows through on these half-hearted gestures.

LEARNING TREE, THE

1969   107m   c   Drama   ★★★
Winger Enterprises   (U.S.)   M/AA

Kyle Johnson (*Newt Winger*), Alex Clarke (*Marcus Savage*), Estelle Evans (*Sarah Winger*), Dana Elcar (*Sheriff Kirky*), Mira Waters (*Arcella Jefferson*), Joel Fluellen (*Uncle Rob*), Malcolm Atterbury (*Silas Newhall*), Richard Ward (*Booker Savage*), Russell Thorson (*Judge Cavanaugh*), Peggy Rea (*Miss McClintock*)

p, Gordon Parks Sr.; d, Gordon Parks Sr.; w, Gordon Parks (based on his novel); ph, Burnett Guffey; ed, George Rohrs; m, Gordon Parks; art d, Edward Engoron; fx, Albert Whitlock

Undoubtedly the biggest surprise among the first 25 films selected in 1989 for inclusion in the National Film Registry, this visually beautiful and moving, if somewhat melodramatic, story of a black teenager growing up in Kansas in the 1920s was the first feature film by a black director to be financed by a major Hollywood studio. Gordon Parks directed, produced, wrote, and composed the score of this adaptation of his semi-autobiographical novel *The Learning Tree* (1963) after a highly successful, 20-year career as an acclaimed photojournalist for *Life* magazine.

Essentially a coming-of-age tale, the film focuses on smalltown Kansas denizen Newt Winger (Johnson). Like many other movie teens, Newt is shown learning about sex (from a prostitute) and death, encountering the latter after discovering the corpse of a black gambler who was murdered by the local sheriff, Kirby (Elcar). Newt's nemesis is Marcus Savage (Clarke), an embittered young black saddled with an absent mother and a negligent, angry father. Newt, by contrast, is supported by his hard-working, understanding mother (Evans), who has kept her son on the square despite the hardships and racism he must face, advising him to put life's ups and downs to beneficial use as a "learning tree". The strength of his tree's roots is tested when Newt experiences heartbreak and later witnesses the murder of his benign white employer Kiner (George Mitchell) by Marcus's father (Ward) and a white drunkard (Atterbury).

In tracing the encounters that make up Newt's moral and practical education, Parks depicts the ambiguous racial attitudes of blacks and whites in the Kansas town with an ironic complexity rarely found in earlier films about racism. The callous white seducer of Newt's girlfriend, for instance, also advocates desegregation, while the local judge, though part of a system of unequal justice for whites and blacks, angrily denounces his fellow whites' lynch-mob thirst for "justice." In another scene, Newt's highschool principal criticizes a teacher for discouraging the young man's dreams of college, though he himself will not or cannot dare to allow blacks to play on the school's sports teams. Newt's struggle to adhere to absolutes of justice and and morality is, therefore, by no means easy or clear-cut.

The fact that he does hold to that standard, however, places THE LEARNING TREE far more in the mainstream thematically than Parks's strikingly different second feature, SHAFT, the hugely successful, angry, urban action film that set the tone for the 70s blaxploitation movies. THE LEARNING TREE's potential openness to criticism as a naive, old-fashioned tale is made greater by its sentimental characterizations, occasional sermonizing, leisurely pace, and melodrama, as when the film nears its closing. On the other hand, Parks and cinematographer Guffey, who filmed on location in the director's native Fort Scott, beautifully capture the feel of 1920s Kansas, and Johnson's performance (if none of the others) is very fine.

LEATHER BOYS, THE

1963   108m   bw   Drama   ★★★
Raymond Stross   (U.K.)   /15

Rita Tushingham (*Dot*), Colin Campbell (*Reggie*), Dudley Sutton (*Pete*), Gladys Henson (*Gran*), Avice Landone (*Reggie's Mother*), Lockwood West (*Reggie's Father*), Betty Marsden (*Dot's Mother*), Martin Matthews (*Uncle Arthur*), Johnny Briggs (*Boy Friend*), James Chase (*Les*)

p, Raymond Stross; d, Sidney J. Furie; w, Gillian Freeman (based on the novel by Eliot George); ph, Gerald Gibbs; ed, Reginald Beck; m, Bill McGuffie; art d, Arthur Lawson

Dot (Tushingham) marries motorcycle buff Reggie (Campbell) to escape from her parents, but the relationship never gets off the ground. She doesn't do any housework, and only cooks cans of beans. Reggie moves out and goes to live with his friend Pete (Sutton), whom Reggie begins to suspect is gay. He moves back when he hears that Dot is pregnant but discovers that she's sleeping with another man. He and Pete decide to run off to sea, but a few realities about their relationship must be settled first. Not the greatest of Britain's "angry young man" films of the period, but it benefits from good acting, Furie's evocation of "kitchen sink" realism and an attempt to be adult about hasty marriages and gay themes.

LEAVING LAS VEGAS

1995   112m   c   Drama   ★★★
United Artists/Lumiere Pictures   (U.S.)   R/18

Nicolas Cage (Ben Sanderson), Elisabeth Shue (Sera), Julian Sands (Yuri), Richard Lewis (Peter), Valeria Golino (Terri), Steven Weber (Marc Nussbaum), Kim Adams (Sheila), Emily Procter (Debbie), Graham Beckel (L.A. Bartender), R. Lee Ermey (Conventioneer)

p, Lila Cazes, Annie Stewart; d, Mike Figgis; w, Mike Figgis (based on the novel by John O'Brien); ph, Declan Quinn; ed, John Smith; m, Mike Figgis; prod d, Waldemar Kalinowski; art d, Barry M. Kingston; fx, William Harrison; cos, Laura Goldsmith, Vivienne Westwood

AA Best Actor: Nicolas Cage; AAN Best Actress: Elisabeth Shue; AAN Best Director: Mike Figgis; AAN Best Adapted Screenplay: Mike Figgis

One of the most highly praised films of 1995, LEAVING LAS VEGAS is as obsessive, but not so well written, as LAST TANGO IN PARIS or JULES AND JIM, films that are also far more cinematically imaginative. The critical consensus on Mike Figgis's romantic downer hinged on its universal theme—"It's about unconditional love, don't you see?"—suggesting that certain overwhelmed critics really should get out more, and not just to the movies.

When we first meet Ben (Nicolas Cage), he's careening through the aisles of a liquor store, blissfully filling up his cart with bottles. Ben is systematically divesting himself of everything most people care about—his family, his possessions, his job—and intends to blow his severance pay on a final, fatal alcoholic binge in Las Vegas. While driving drunkenly along the Strip, he meets clean-scrubbed prostitute Sera (Elisabeth Shue), takes her back to his room and promptly passes out. This, perhaps needless to say, is only the beginning of a beautiful and damned relationship.

Figgis gives the film his trademark velvet-noir look—a remarkable, if not necessarily laudable achievement, given that it was shot for a pittance on Super 16 film—which belies the grittily nihilistic, verite intentions he professed. The busy jazz score was composed by Renaissance Man Figgis, and features the distinctive and wholly inappropriate vocal stylings of Sting. Cage, who has proved an effective comedian in RAISING ARIZONA, MOONSTRUCK, and VAMPIRE'S KISS, won an Academy Award for his monotonously doomed performance. His weird, San Fernando Valley-boy inflections merely emphasize the thudding banality of Figgis's would-be mordant lines, like "I kept running out of booze, and the store would be closed because I kept forgetting to look at my watch." Shue works like the dickens, but she's never convincing as a streetwalker: her Sera is too perfectly groomed, aerobicized, and dressed. What draws her to Ben is, like his inner torment, a complete mystery.

LEFT-HANDED GUN, THE

1958   102m   bw   Biography/Western   ★★★½
Warner Bros.   (U.S.)   /PG

Paul Newman (Billy Bonney), Lita Milan (Celsa), John Dehner (Pat Garrett), Hurd Hatfield (Moultrie), James Congdon (Charlie Boudre), James Best (Tom Folliard), Colin Keith-Johnston (Tunstall), John Dierkes (McSween), Robert Anderson (Hill), Wally Brown (Moon)

p, Fred Coe; d, Arthur Penn; w, Leslie Stevens (based on the teleplay "The Death of Billy the Kid" by Gore Vidal); ph, Peverell Marley; ed, Folmar Blangsted; m, Alexander Courage; art d, Art Loel; cos, Marjorie Best

A good but disturbing psychological western, well directed by Penn and acted in a strangely fascinating style by Newman. Penn demythologizes Billy the Kid, and Newman plays him more honestly than anyone else ever has. He was a slow-witted illiterate with a streak of sadistic bloodlust in him, fiercely loyal to his few friends and deadly to all who became his enemy. Newman is nothing but a western guttersnipe until John Tunstall (Keith-Johnston), a kindly rancher whom Billy had known in real life, treats him with understanding. Newman reacts as would any loveless human, becoming fanatically devoted to the rancher. When the unarmed Keith-Johnston is shot to death by a deputy and three others in a range war, Newman and his equally empty-headed saddlemates, Best and Congdon, track down the killers and murder them one by one. Pat Garrett (Dehner), the famous lawman who was the harsh, real-life father figure for Billy, vows revenge on the Kid after Newman kills one of the guests—the last of the foursome sought for Keith-Johnston's death—at Dehner's wedding party. Newman is arrested and jailed, but he escapes, murdering his guards in the process. The relentless Dehner then tracks him down and kills the unarmed outlaw with a single shot. Flitting in and out of Newman's life is a neurotic pulp writer, Hatfield, who creates the myth of Billy the Kid and then condemns the outlaw for not living up to his lies. This first film by director Penn stems from Gore Vidal's wacky, self-serving teleplay, "The Death of Billy the Kid," which was helmed by Penn for TV in 1955. Penn toned down Vidal's portrait of the Kid as a rampant homosexual which reflected the author's interests perhaps more than the facts of history. Newman, as he had in SOMEBODY UP THERE LIKES ME, took a role here which was originally coveted by James Dean, who died prematurely in a car accident, but he does a masterful job in portraying the ruthless killer whose reputation existed only beyond the grave.

LEGENDS OF THE FALL

1994   133m   c   Western/Historical/Drama   ★★½
TriStar   (U.S.)   R/

Brad Pitt (Tristan Ludlow), Anthony Hopkins (Colonel William Ludlow), Aidan Quinn (Alfred Ludlow), Julia Ormond (Susannah Finncannon), Henry Thomas (Samuel Ludlow), Karina Lombard (Isabel Two), Tantoo Cardinal (Pet), Gordon Tootoosis (One Stab), Paul Desmond (Decker), Christina Pickles (Isabel)

p, Edward Zwick, Bill Wittliff, Marshall Herskovitz; d, Edward Zwick; w, Susan Shilliday, Bill Wittliff (based on the novella by Jim Harrison); ph, John Toll; ed, Steven Rosenblum; m, James Horner; prod d, Lilly Kilvert; art d, Rick Roberts, Andrew Precht; fx, Mike Vezina; cos, Deborah Scott

AA Best Cinematography: John Toll; AAN Best Art Direction: Lilly Kilvert, Dorree Cooper; AAN Best Sound: Paul Massey, David Campbell, Christopher David, Douglas Ganton

The golden shadows of the waning Old West are thrown across the big screen with full reverential treatment in this solid, unsurprising rendition of Jim Harrison's widely praised novella. Director Edward Zwick manages the requisite epic sweep, and most of the performances are on the money, but LEGENDS OF THE FALL succeeded at the box office largely thanks to freshly-minted screen superstar Brad Pitt.

Colonel Ludlow (Anthony Hopkins), an ex-cavalry officer living in the Montana wilderness, is left to raise three sons by himself when his wife leaves for the winter and never returns. The oldest, Alfred (Aidan Quinn), is sensible, with a head for business and politics. Hotheaded Samuel (Henry Thomas), the youngest, is always ready to subscribe to the latest political enthusiasm. The Colonel reserves a special fondness for the middle son, Tristan (Pitt). When Samuel returns from college with his fiancee, Susannah (Julia Ormond), all the men are smitten, stumbling over one another to teach her how to ride, rope, and shoot. But the close-knit family soon disintegrates, sundered by romantic rivalry and the outbreak of WWI.

Although Zwick's grand, even monumental, presentation is reminiscent of his Civil War opus GLORY, the picture belongs to the golden-maned Pitt, who is afforded no less than three princely entrances on horseback. A performer with more charisma than intelligence, he nevertheless easily dominates the ensemble and, with a big assist from Oscar-winning cinematographer John Toll, sometimes casts such a saintly, beatific sheen over the proceedings that he seems to glow from within. Newcomer Julia Ormond hits her mark as the sort of storybook British beauty for whom civilizations topple.

LENNY

1974 111m bw Biography   ★★★
UA (U.S.)   R/18

Dustin Hoffman (Lenny Bruce), Valerie Perrine (Honey Bruce), Jan Miner (Sally Marr), Stanley Beck (Artie Silver), Gary Morton (Sherman Hart), Rashel Novikoff (Aunt Mema), Guy Rennie (Jack Goldstein), Frankie Man (Baltimore Strip Club MC), Mark Harris (San Francisco Defense Attorney), Lee Sandman (San Francisco Judge)

p, Marvin Worth; d, Bob Fosse; w, Julian Barry (based on the play by Julian Barry); ph, Bruce Surtees; ed, Alan Heim; prod d, Joel Schiller; cos, Albert Wolsky

AAN Best Picture; AAN Best Actor: Dustin Hoffman; AAN Best Actress: Valerie Perrine; AAN Best Director: Bob Fosse; AAN Best Adapted Screenplay: Julian Barry; AAN Best Cinematography: Bruce Surtees

Harsh, funny, grim, and, like all Bob Fosse's films, primarily concerned with the intersection of life and showbiz. Fosse's followup to the masterly CABARET, LENNY proves that it's not easy to be ahead of your time. By today's standards, much of what Lenny Bruce said on stage would be unremarkable, and it's still debatable whether the comedian was crushed for his irrepressible foul mouth or his subversive (if not exactly profound) social commentary. Either way, his customary mode of agonized self-analysis was irresistible to director Fosse, who was to use similar techniques in filming the story of his own life, ALL THAT JAZZ.

The film begins with Lenny's courtship of his wife Honey (Perrine), a stripper with a surprising amount of class and smarts (at least as Perrine plays her). His overpowering love for Honey suggests a problem with his personality: he never seems to know how to let go of anything. On the brink of mainstream success, he refuses, literally, to clean up his act, resulting in a series of arrests for obscenity; a heroin addiction brings further trouble with the law. He becomes preoccupied with his legal battles and begins to see himself as a martyr for artistic freedom. Finally, his obsession with death overrides all others.

A series of flashbacks prompted by pseudo-verite interviews (conducted by an unseen Fosse) LENNY is structured like a patchwork quilt a la CITIZEN KANE. Perrine, never considered much of an actress before this movie, is quite solid as Honey, as is Miner in a rendition of Bruce's actress-manager mom Sally Marr. Hoffman, generally successful in abrasive roles, never loses one's sympathy here, and is especially good in the courtroom scenes. Towards the end, one wonders whether the film's sexual and thanatological obsessions have more to do with Bruce or with Fosse (the menage-a-trois scene, for instance, has no known basis in the comedian's life, but it was familiar territory for the director). In ALL THAT JAZZ, Fosse's alter ego is shown editing a film very like LENNY; it features Cliff Gorman as a death-obsessed comedian. Gorman had played Lenny Bruce on Broadway; his role in ALL THAT JAZZ was Fosse's apology for failing to use him in LENNY. Visually striking, due mostly to Surtees' beautifully shaded black-and-white cinematography.

LEOPARD, THE
(IL GATTOPARDO)

1963 165m c Historical   ★★★★½
Titanus (Italy)   PG

Burt Lancaster (Prince Don Fabrizio Salina), Alain Delon (Tancredi), Claudia Cardinale (Angelica Sedara/Bertiana), Rina Morelli (Maria Stella), Paolo Stoppa (Don Calogero Sedara), Romolo Valli (Father Pirrone), Lucilla Morlacchi (Concetta), Serge Reggiani (Don Ciccio Tumeo), Ida Galli (Carolina), Ottavia Piccolo (Caterina)

p, Goffredo Lombardo; d, Luchino Visconti; w, Luchino Visconti, Suso Cecchi D'Amico, Pasquale Festa Campanile, Enrico Medioli, Massimo Franciosa (based on the novel Il Gattopardo by Giuseppe Tomasi di Lampedusa); ph, Giuseppe Rotunno; ed, Mario Serandrei; m, Nino Rota, Giuseppe Verdi; art d, Mario Garbuglia; cos, Piero Tosi, Reanda, Sartoria Safas

AAN Best Costume Design: Piero Tosi

Superb, sumptuous epic based on Giuseppe di Lampedusa's novel about the decline of the Italian aristocracy and the rise to power of the bourgeoisie. Financed by 20th Century-Fox and released to critical acclaim in Europe, THE LEOPARD was butchered for its initial, inauspicious U.S. release, finally earning the acclaim it deserved when a restored version was presented in 1983.

Burt Lancaster plays an elderly prince struggling to come to terms with the rapidly changing Italian social structure of the 1860s. He arranges for his nephew, Tancredi (Alain Delon), to marry Angela (Claudia Cardinale), the daughter of a rich merchant, in an attempt to shore up his status and lifestyle and, during a nearly hour-long ball scene with which the film closes, ruminates on his own past and present as well as that of his social class.

This is a gorgeous, fascinating account of the interplay between the personal and the social, directed with the kind of insight that only an aristocrat-turned-Marxist like Visconti could afford. (Lancaster claimed that he actually based his performance on Visconti's character.) The ball scene, at which the aristocrats come to accept that power has passed into the hands of the nouveau riches, is justly regarded as one of the finest set pieces in film history. THE LEOPARD took the Golden Palm as Best Film at Cannes.

LES BICHES

1968 104m c Drama   ★★★½
Boetie/Alexandra (Italy/France)   R/X

Stephane Audran (Frederique), Jacqueline Sassard (Why), Jean-Louis Trintignant (Paul Thomas), Nane Germon (Violetta), Serge Bento (Bookseller), Dominique Zardi (Riais), Henri Attal (Robeque), Claude Chabrol (Filmmaker), Henri Frances

p, Andre Genoves; d, Claude Chabrol; w, Paul Gegauff, Claude Chabrol; ph, Jean Rabier; ed, Jacques Gaillard; m, Pierre Jansen; cos, Maurice Albray

Claude Chabrol's suspenseful and erotic story of two lesbian lovers—Frederique (Stephane Audran), a wealthy and elegant woman, and Why (Jaqueline Sassard), a young bohemian who earns a living making charcoal drawings on the sidewalks of Paris. Frederique, who has already seduced Why and dragged her off to a lovely St. Tropez villa, upsets the balance when she next seduces architect Paul (Jean-Louis Trintignant). Why loves them both and cannot bear the thought of being left behind when Frederique and Paul run off to Paris together. One of the few Chabrol films available on videotape (under the title BAD GIRLS), LES BICHES features the director's favorite lead actress, Audran (then his wife), in yet another situation of suspense that, while Hitchcockian at its root, is pure Chabrol. The setup is a familiar one—a love triangle—but Chabrol's delicate treatment and highly controlled direction make this one of his finest efforts.

LES COMPERES

1983 92m c Comedy/Drama   ★★★½
Fideline/Efve/D.D. (France)   PG/

Pierre Richard (Francois Pignon), Gerard Depardieu (Jean Lucas), Anne Duperey (Christine Martin), Michel Aumont (Paul Martin), Stephane Bierry (Tristan Martin), Jean-Jacques Scheffer (Ralph), Philippe Khorsand (Milan), Roland Blanche (Jeannot), Jacques Frantz (Verdier), Maurice Barrier (Raffart)

d, Francis Veber; w, Francis Veber (based on his story); ph, Claude Agostini; ed, Marie-Sophie Dubus; m, Vladimir Cosma; prod d, Gerard Daoudal; cos, Corinne Jorry

Tristan Martin (Stephane Bierry) is a 16-year-old runaway who leaves Paris and hitchhikes to Nice with Michele (Florence Moreau), a tough young girl who hangs out with degenerate bikers. Tristan's middle-class parents (Anne Duperey and Michel Aumont) inform the authorities but receive only the feeble assurance that their son will turn up sooner or later, "like a stolen car." Tristan's mother decides to phone newspaperman and old flame Jean (Gerard Depardieu), convincing him that he is Tristan's real father, in the hope that he will offer to find the boy. When he refuses, she tries the same scheme on another past lover, Francois (Pierre Richard), a suicidal manic-depressive who is thrilled by the request and agrees to help. In the meantime, Jean has reconsidered.

Both men eventually meet and discover they have a mutual interest—finding a missing son—but it takes a while for them to realize that they are both looking for the same son. Naturally, the question of the boy's real parentage is at issue, with both men claiming to be the father. A delightful film, LES COMPERES combines healthy doses of comedy, drama, and crime with three superbly sketched characters. Jean's and Francois's reactions to the possibility of fatherhood are fascinating, as is the interaction between the two. LES COMPERES is a film that depends on the chemistry among the actors, and fortunately this doesn't fail for a moment. Depardieu and Richard are both superb, reminiscent of Laurel and Hardy—the hulkish Depardieu playing Hardy to Richard's whimpering Laurel—in their affectionate dislike for each other. The result is a thoroughly enjoyable, entertaining, funny, and touching celebration of fatherhood.

LES ENFANTS TERRIBLES

1950 107m bw Drama ★★★
Melville (France) /X

Nicole Stephane *(Elisabeth)*, Edouard Dermit *(Paul)*, Jacques Bernard *(Gerard)*, Renee Cosima *(Dargelos/Agathe)*, Roger Gaillard *(Gerard's Uncle)*, Melvyn Martin *(Michael)*, Maurice Revel *(Doctor)*, Adeline Aucoc *(Mariette)*, Maria Cyliakus *(The Mother)*, Jean-Marie Robain *(Headmaster)*

p, Jean-Pierre Melville; d, Jean-Pierre Melville; w, Jean-Pierre Melville, Jean Cocteau (based on the novel by Jean Cocteau); ph, Henri Decae; ed, Monique Bonnot; m, Johann Sebastian Bach, Antonio Vivaldi

Two seemingly disparate filmmakers—Jean-Pierre Melville, best known for his dark black-and-white ventures into the criminal underworld, and Jean Cocteau, the poet of the mythical underworld—came together to bring Cocteau's celebrated play of love, death, and incest to the screen. Paul (Edouard Dermit), a young Parisian, is severely injured when hit by a snowball thrown by Dargelos (Renee Cosima), the school bully whom he idolizes. He is cared for by his sister Elisabeth (Nicole Stephane), with whom he shares a bedroom, though both are in their teens. The near-incestuous pair are brought closer together by the death of their ailing mother and are joined by Paul's friend Gerard (Jacques Bernard), who is infatuated with Elisabeth. The trio eventually becomes a quartet when Paul meets his sister's friend Agathe (Cosima, in a dual, cross-gender role). As the relationships intertwine, Elisabeth is forced to admit her attraction to her brother. Melville, who was given the chance to direct this prestigious property after Cocteau saw one of his early 16mm films, shot LES ENFANTS TERRIBLES in his own apartment, which he rented with the intention of using it as a location. The film also unmistakably bears Cocteau's stamp, and he even directed one scene (at the beach) when Melville fell ill.

LES GIRLS

1957 114m c Musical/Comedy ★★★
MGM (U.S.) /A

Gene Kelly *(Barry Nichols)*, Mitzi Gaynor *(Joy Henderson)*, Kay Kendall *(Lady Wren)*, Taina Elg *(Angele Ducros)*, Jacques Bergerac *(Pierre Ducros)*, Leslie Phillips *(Sir Gerald Wren)*, Henry Daniell *(Judge)*, Patrick Macnee *(Sir Percy)*, Stephen Vercoe *(Mr. Outward)*, Philip Tonge *(Associate Judge)*

p, Sol C. Siegel; d, George Cukor; w, John Patrick (based on a story by Vera Caspary); ph, Robert Surtees; ed, Ferris Webster; m, Cole Porter; art d, William A. Horning, Gene Allen; chor, Jack Cole; cos, Orry-Kelly

AAN Best Art Direction: William A. Horning, Gene Allen, Edwin B. Willis, Richard Pefferle; *AA Best Costume Design:* Orry-Kelly; *AAN Best Sound:* Dr. Wesley C. Miller

Attempting to carry on the tradition of their great musicals of the 1930s and 40s, MGM released this relatively minor effort employing some of the studio's finest creative talents in 1957. Barry (Gene Kelly), Angele (Taina Elg), Joy (Mitzi Gaynor), and Sybil (Kay Kendall) are the former members of "Barry Nichols and Les Girls," a popular European cabaret act. Years after the group has dissolved, Sybil, now Lady Wren, publishes her all-too-candid recollections of what went on romantically behind the scenes among Barry and his partners. Angele is outraged by

the revelations and sues Sybil for defamation of character, the case is tried in court, and the picture becomes a musical RASHOMON, with each of the principals telling the story of the act as they remember it—none lying, but all recalling matters very differently. Not surprisingly, Barry (now married to Joy) gives the key testimony, and the picture ends with resumed good relations among the group, after all have had their say and a host of musical numbers have been performed. The script is more complicated than witty and can't sustain what's meant to be a breezy paean to the great MGM musicals; Kelly (in his last MGM appearance before THAT'S ENTERTAINMENT) never quite musters the energy needed for his role; and Cole Porter's last Hollywood score is not one of his best. LES GIRLS's failure to make big money signaled the end of the "original musical" for Hollywood. The tunes include a delicious satire of Brando's THE WILD ONE entitled "Why Am I So Gone (About That Gal)?"

LES LIAISONS DANGEREUSES
(RELAZIONI PERICOLOSE)

1959 106m bw Drama ★★
Marceau/Cocinor/Laetitia (France/Italy) /X

Gerard Philipe *(Valmont de Merteuil)*, Jeanne Moreau *(Juliette de Merteuil)*, Jeanne Valerie *(Cecile Volanges)*, Annette Vadim *(Marianne Tourvel)*, Simone Renant *(Mme. Volanges)*, Jean-Louis Trintignant *(Danceny)*, Nicolas Vogel *(Court)*, Boris Vian *(Prevan)*, Frederic O'Brady, Gillian Hills

d, Roger Vadim; w, Roger Vadim, Roger Vailland, Claude Brule (based on the novel by Choderlos de Laclos); ph, Marcel Grignon; ed, Victoria Mercanton; m, Thelonius Monk, Jack Murray

Philipe and Moreau are a married couple who thrive on extramarital affairs. When Philipe finds himself emotionally involved with Vadim (nee Stroyberg, director Vadim's wife after Brigitte Bardot), his relationship with Moreau falls apart. Eventually Philipe is killed and Moreau disfigured in a fire that she set to burn her husband's incriminating letters.

LES MISERABLES

1935 108m bw Drama ★★★★
20th Century (U.S.) /A

Fredric March *(Jean Valjean)*, Charles Laughton *(Javert)*, Cedric Hardwicke *(Bishop Bienvenu)*, Rochelle Hudson *(Big Cosette)*, Marilyn Knowlden *(Little Cosette)*, Frances Drake *(Eponine)*, John Beal *(Marius)*, Jessie Ralph *(Mme. Magloire)*, Florence Eldridge *(Fantine)*, Ferdinand Gottschalk *(Thenardier)*

p, Darryl F. Zanuck; d, Richard Boleslawski; w, W.P. Lipscomb (based on the novel by Victor Hugo); ph, Gregg Toland; ed, Barbara McLean

Fredric March gives a superb performance as the sensitive, persecuted Jean Valjean who steals a loaf of bread to survive, is captured, and given ten years' hard labor. When he finally escapes the prison galley, March is a hardbitten, unsympathetic character, all compassion hammered out of him by the rigors of confinement. He is taken in by Bishop Bienvenu, played by Cedric Hardwicke, who refuses to prosecute him for stealing two silver candlesticks. Through Hardwicke's kindness and understanding, March regains his sensitive nature and is reformed. He builds a new life for himself under an assumed name and adopts a young child as his own. He becomes a well-to-do businessman, and, moving to another town, becomes so widely liked and respected that he is elected mayor, an office which helps him devote his life to benefiting others. Charles Laughton, as Javert, the town's chief of police, is a cold, unimpassioned official, single-minded in his view that the law is to be upheld and enforced at all costs, with no mercy shown to anyone committing the slightest infraction. Laughton and March clash repeatedly over the interpretation of the law, and the policeman becomes incensed when March intercedes on behalf of a social pariah (Florence Eldridge, March's real-life wife). One day March sees a villager trapped beneath a heavy wagon, and, with what seems to be superhuman strength, he puts his back to the wagon and lifts it so the man can be saved. Laughton watches this feat and is reminded of a galley prisoner he once encountered. He investigates March's past and identifies March as Jean Valjean, the wanted criminal. He is then confused when another prisoner is found, a mindless inmate who amazingly resembles March and who claims to be Jean Valjean. The impostor is put on trial, but the honorable March (who plays both parts) admits that he is the real Jean Valjean. Before he can be jailed, he again escapes with his daughter (Frances Drake) to Paris where he assumes yet another identity. His daughter falls in love with John Beal, a young radical who works for prison reform. Laughton arrives in Paris and is assigned to watch the revolutionaries. He gets onto March's trail once more as March becomes more and more involved with Beal and his revolutionary friends. When Drake comes to her father with the news that Beal has been injured in the fighting, March goes to the barricades. With Laughton on his heels, he escapes into the Paris sewers, carrying the injured young man through treacherous chest-high waters and delivering him to Drake. Once Beal and Drake are reunited, March goes to surrender to Laughton. But having witnessed March's selfless sacrifice, the policeman begins to feel compassion, an emotion that so confuses and vexes him that he is almost willing to break the law to allow the noble March his freedom. Laughton solves his dilemma by hurling himself into the Seine and drowning himself. March is free to rejoin his daughter and Beal and to live out his life with those who love him.

This lavish production is full of meticulous detail, and, with the exception of the ending, faithful to Victor Hugo's novel. (Valjean dies in the original tale.) Richard Boleslawski (RASPUTIN AND THE EMPRESS, THE PAINTED VEIL), a largely forgotten director today, was masterful in his handling of LES MISERABLES, adhering closely to Hugo's scenes and working diligently from W.P. Lipscomb's compact 108-minute script, which is literate and moving. March gives one of his greatest performances as the hunted victim Jean Valjean, far superior to the rendering of the character in a French version in 1936, or in the crude 1918 silent version (also made by Fox, and starring William Farnum). The film was remade in 1952 with Michael Rennie as Jean Valjean and Robert Newton as Javert, the policeman, but this later version is a pale imitation of the 1935 classic. A number of other actors, including Richard Jordan in a British remake of the film in 1979, portrayed Hugo's great fictional character. But no one has ever approached March's profound performance.

LES PARENTS TERRIBLES

1948 105m bw Drama   ★★★★
Ariane (France)   /A

Jean Marais (*Michel*), Yvonne de Bray (*Yvonne-Sophie*), Gabrielle Dorziat (*Aunt Leo*), Marcel Andre (*Georges*), Josette Day (*Madeleine*), Jean Cocteau (*Narrator*)

d, Jean Cocteau; w, Jean Cocteau (based on the play by Jean Cocteau); ph, Michel Kelber; ed, Jacqueline Sadoul; m, Georges Auric; art d, Christian Berard, Guy de Gastyne

Cocteau's brilliant domestic drama which many, including Cocteau himself, consider to be his greatest achievement. Based on his stage play (performed ten years earlier with much the same cast) it casts de Bray as the dangerously possessive mother who is wed to Andre, a weak and defeated man. De Bray opposes the marriage of her young son Marais to the beautiful Day. It turns out that Day is the mistress of Andre, who happens to be the object of Marais's aunt's (Dorziat's) desires. When the tangled affairs come into the open, de Bray commits suicide, unable to accept the loss of her magnetic hold over her family. Set in only two locations—de Bray's family's apartment and Day's apartment—the film is, as Cocteau said, a record "of the acting of an incomparable cast." Georges Auric's score is a prime example of sound in perfect unity with the picture. A far-inferior remake, INTIMATE RELATIONS, was released in Britain in 1953. Various lengths exist, with both a 98m and 86m cut being shown in the US.

LETHAL WEAPON

1987 110m c Action/Adventure/Comedy   ★★★½
Warner Bros. (U.S.)   R/18

Mel Gibson (*Martin Riggs*), Danny Glover (*Roger Murtaugh*), Gary Busey (*Joshua*), Mitchell Ryan (*The General*), Tom Atkins (*Michael Hunsaker*), Darlene Love (*Trish Murtaugh*), Traci Wolfe (*Rianne Murtaugh*), Jackie Swanson (*Amanda Hunsaker*), Damon Hines (*Nick Murtaugh*), Ebonie Smith (*Carrie Murtaugh*)

p, Richard Donner, Joel Silver; d, Richard Donner; w, Shane Black; ph, Stephen Goldblatt; ed, Stuart Baird; m, Michael Kamen, Eric Clapton; prod d, J. Michael Riva; fx, Chuck Gaspar; cos, Mary Malin

AAN Best Sound: Les Fresholtz, Dick Alexander, Vern Poore, Bill Nelson

It's drugs again, this time in southern California with cop partners Mel Gibson and Danny Glover chasing sleazy dope dealers in a nonstop crime actioner. Roger Murtaugh (Glover), who is about to turn 50, exercises the kind of life-preserving caution that Martin Riggs (Gibson) has discarded. Riggs's wife has been killed in an accident, and he doesn't care whether he lives or dies, just so long as he can take all the bad guys with him. Murtaugh has a hard time surviving with such a self-destructive partner as they investigate "The General" (Mitchell Ryan), head of an extensive drug smuggling operation. The acceleration of this film, which has a brisk pace at the start, is dizzying at the finale and is accomplished mostly through fantastic editing. It's an effective if not obvious ploy to blind the viewer to the fact that there is not much plot or character development in the predictable script. Gibson is truly frightening as the cop about to go into orbit, and Glover is a standout as the down-to-earth lawman with very much to lose. Director Richard Donner, whose previous efforts include the first SUPERMAN and LADYHAWKE, had another hit with LETHAL WEAPON, which grossed more than $60 million at the box office within three months after its release. A less entertaining sequel, LETHAL WEAPON II, appeared in 1989.

LETHAL WEAPON 2

1989 113m c Comedy/Action/Adventure   ★★★
Silver (U.S.)   R/15

Mel Gibson (*Martin Riggs*), Danny Glover (*Roger Murtaugh*), Joe Pesci (*Leo Getz*), Joss Ackland (*Arjen Rudd*), Derrick O'Connor (*Pieter Vorstedt*), Patsy Kensit (*Rika van den Haas*), Darlene Love (*Trish Murtaugh*), Traci Wolfe (*Rianne Murtaugh*), Steve Kahan (*Capt. Murphy*), Mark Rolston (*Hans*)

p, Richard Donner, Joel Silver, Steve Perry, Jennie Lew Tugend; d, Richard Donner; w, Jeffrey Boam (based on a story by Shane Black, Warren Murphy and on the characters created by Black); ph, Stephen Goldblatt; ed, Stuart Baird; m, Michael Kamen, Eric Clapton, David Sanborn; prod d, J. Michael Riva; art d, Virginia Randolph, Richard Berger; cos, Barry Delaney

AAN Best Sound Effects Editing: Robert Henderson, Alan Robert Murray

A sequel that stands on its own, LETHAL WEAPON 2 is a well-crafted, rousingly fast-paced action thriller with a first-rate cast. Los Angeles cops Roger Murtaugh (Danny Glover) and Martin Riggs (Mel Gibson) are in hot pursuit of a red BMW as the film gets off to a fender-bending start. After much property destruction, the cops capture the red car, but lose the driver. However, they discover a fortune in South African gold Krugerrands in the trunk. Determined to keep the two hyperactive cops out of further high-priced mayhem, their superior puts them in charge of guarding a government witness in a drug-money laundering case. But when the witness (Joe Pesci) reveals he was laundering for South Africans, Murtaugh and Riggs spring back into action. Those stopping to think about such things may find more than a few holes in LETHAL WEAPON 2's plot. But to question is to quibble in this case; LETHAL WEAPON 2's pluses easily outweigh its minuses. If anything, Gibson and Glover are even better here than they were the first time out. Jeffrey Boam's script polishes and improves their characters. Returning director Richard Donner seems to have smoothed over the few stylistic rough edges remaining from the earlier film to deliver here two hours of pure, breathless, high-impact entertainment.

LET'S TALK ABOUT WOMEN
(SE PERMETTETE)

1964 108m bw Comedy   ★★★
Fair/CON (France/Italy)

Vittorio Gassman (*Stranger/Practical Joker/Client/Lover/Impatient Lover/Waiter/Timid Brother/Ragman/Prisoner*), FIRST EPISODE: Maria Fiore (*Fearful Wife*), SECOND EPISODE: Donatella Mauro

(His Wife), Mario Lucidi *(Son)*, Giovanna Ralli *(Prostitute)*, Umberto D'Orsi *(Old Friend)*, FOURTH EPISODE: Antonella Lualdi *(Fiancee)*, FIFTH EPISODE: Sylva Koscina *(Reluctant Girl)*, Edda Ferronao *(Willing Maid)*, SIXTH EPISODE: Heidi Stroh *(Pick-Up)*

p, Mario Cecchi Gori; d, Ettore Scola; w, Ettore Scola, Ruggero Maccari; ph, Sandro D'Eva; ed, Marcello Malvestiti; m, Armando Trovajoli; art d, Arrigo Breschi

A captivating Italian comedy made up of nine episodes about Gassman's encounters with various women. One of the better skits has Gassman visiting a hooker and recognizing a picture of her husband as an old chum. She brings him back to her house for a reunion, during which the husband refuses to let Gassman pay for the wife-hooker's services. In another episode, Gassman is a rag dealer who pays a visit to a wealthy and promiscuous woman, wanting to buy her rag collection. She tries instead to give him her body, but he declines, stating that he prefers material goods.

LETTER, THE

1940 95m bw Drama ★★★★
Warner Bros. (U.S.) /PG

Bette Davis *(Leslie Crosbie)*, Herbert Marshall *(Robert Crosbie)*, James Stephenson *(Howard Joyce)*, Gale Sondergaard *(Mrs. Hammond)*, Bruce Lester *(John Withers)*, Elizabeth Inglis *(Adele Ainsworth)*, Cecil Kellaway *(Prescott)*, Victor Sen Yung *(Ong Chi Seng)*, Doris Lloyd *(Mrs. Cooper)*, Willie Fung *(Chung Hi)*

p, Robert Lord; d, William Wyler; w, Howard Koch (based on the story by W. Somerset Maugham); ph, Tony Gaudio; ed, George Amy; m, Max Steiner; art d, Carl Jules Weyl; cos, Orry-Kelly

AAN Best Picture; AAN Best Actress: Bette Davis; AAN Best Supporting Actor: James Stephenson; AAN Best Director: William Wyler; AAN Best Cinematography: Gaetano Gaudio; AAN Best Editing: Warren Low; AAN Best Score: Max Steiner

As THE LETTER opens, David Newell visits Davis's Malayan rubber plantation while her husband, Marshall, is away on business. Davis shoots him to death, and later claims that Newell, an old family friend, tried to attack her and that she killed him in self-defense. Marshall, ever faithful, believes her absolutely and asks Stephenson, a respected lawyer, to defend her. Stephenson then receives word that Newell's Eurasian widow, Sondergaard, has in her possession a letter Davis wrote to Newell, asking him to come to visit her at the plantation on the night he was killed. When confronted with this information, Davis coldly admits that she murdered Newell and that he was her lover. Taking pity on her, Stephenson agrees to buy the letter for $10,000—Sondergaard's blackmail price—telling Marshall there will be some extra expenses in preparing Davis' case, but not how much money is involved. Sondergaard insists that she will not turn the letter over unless Davis claims it personally, leading to a dramatic scene in which Davis must kneel at her feet to pick up the incriminating document. After Davis is deemed innocent of the murder charge in court and returns home to Marshall, the husband discovers that all his savings have been spent to buy the letter and demands to be told what it contains. Davis admits everything, but the always forgiving Marshall—now an emotional shambles—tells her he loves her still. As Davis walks into the garden, Sondergaard appears with a henchman and stabs Davis to death. Police stop them when they try to flee.

Though W. Somerset Maugham's story could easily have been filmed as a turgid melodrama, director William Wyler's magnificent handling of the material and Bette Davis's taut and calculated performance converted it into enduring cinematic art. THE LETTER is as good today as it seemed upon its first release. Though Davis's strong performance is the film's center, Herbert Marshall (who had played the lover in an earlier version of the story) is excellent as the long-suffering husband, and James Stephenson actually manages to steal scenes from his costars as the honest lawyer who puts his career in jeopardy for a friend. Jack Warner asked Wyler to test Stephenson for the role, but when Wyler (to his own surprise) recognized the superiority of Stephenson's acting and cast him, the unpredictable Warner balked at the move, worrying about the stock player's lack of name recognition. Wyler insisted upon keeping Stephenson, putting him in the odd position of having to fight to cast an actor Warner had originally suggested.

LETTER FROM AN UNKNOWN WOMAN

1948 86m bw Drama ★★★★★
Rampart (U.S.) /A

Joan Fontaine *(Lisa Berndle)*, Louis Jourdan *(Stefan Brand)*, Mady Christians *(Frau Berndle)*, Marcel Journet *(Johann Stauffer)*, John Good *(Lt. Leopold von Kaltnegger)*, Leo B. Pessin *(Stefan, Jr.)*, Art Smith *(John)*, Carol Yorke *(Marie)*, Howard Freeman *(Herr Kastner)*, Erskine Sanford *(Porter)*

p, John Houseman; d, Max Ophuls; w, Howard Koch (based on the novel *Brief Einer Unbekannten* by Stefan Zweig); ph, Franz Planer; ed, Ted J. Kent; m, Daniele Amfitheatrof; art d, Alexander Golitzen; cos, Travis Banton

An intense and lush romantic film made by the incomparable Ophuls during his often trying sojourn in America in the WWII and immediate postwar years. Fontaine plays Lisa, who has a brief encounter with and falls for her pianist neighbor Stefan (Jourdan). As he heads off on a concert tour, Stefan promises to return for her, but that doesn't happen. Lisa holds out as long as possible but is forced to marry another man when she discovers that she's pregnant with Stefan's child. She meets the pianist some time later, but he doesn't remember her and sets about seducing her all over again. The story is told in flashbacks as Stefan reads a letter from Lisa as she is suffering from typhus, and he finally learns her entire story.

The first film from the production company formed by Fontaine and William Dozier, LETTER FROM AN UNKNOWN WOMAN has an unusually persuasive Continental look to it. Its lyrical, sweet sadness and incredibly lovely *mise en scene* are typical of Ophuls at his best. His meaningful, highly deliberate camera wanderings beautifully capture the sorrows of Lisa's entrapment by cultural norms. The direction and Koch's well-judged screenplay admirably manage to retain an ironic edge despite the potent romanticism of it all. Fontaine has never looked lovelier and gives what is probably the greatest performance of her career. The dashing and persuasive Jourdan and a fine cast ably support her, as does the incredible camerawork of regular Ophuls collaborator Franz Planer. Although CAUGHT and THE RECKLESS MOMENT are films of considerable merit, LETTER is almost certainly Ophuls' greatest American film. Watching it is like finding a locket you thought you had lost, one which contains the picture of someone who once broke your heart.

LETTER TO BREZHNEV

1985 94m c Romance/Comedy ★★★½
Yeardream/Film Four/Palace (U.K.) R/15

Alfred Molina *(Sergei)*, Peter Firth *(Peter)*, Margi Clarke *(Teresa)*, Tracy Lea *(Tracy)*, Alexandra Pigg *(Elaine)*, Susan Dempsey *(Girl in Yellow Pedal Pushers)*, Ted Wood *(Mick)*, Carl Chase *(Taxi Driver)*, Robbie Dee *(Charlie)*, Sharon Power *(Charlie's Girlfriend)*

p, Janet Goddard, Caroline Spack; d, Chris Bernard; w, Frank Clarke; ph, Bruce McGowan; ed, Lesley Walker; m, Alan Gill; prod d, Lez Brothrston, Nick Englefield, Jonathan Swain; cos, Mark Reynolds

LETTER TO BREZHNEV is a low-budget gem. Teresa (Margi Clarke) and Elaine (Alexandra Pigg) are best pals. Teresa works in a frozen-chicken factory and Elaine is unemployed, as are many thousands in the depressed area of Liverpool. One night the two decide to go out on the town. At a local spot Teresa steals a wallet, and the friends head for an upscale disco where they meet Peter (Peter Firth) and Sergei (Alfred Molina), two Russian sailors in Liverpool for some R&R. With the money she stole, Teresa rents a pair of hotel rooms and drags Sergei into hers. The sweeter, gentler Elaine spends the evening talking to Peter. Both are terminally romantic; and in the course of nonstop conversation, they decide that they are in love and would like to get married. This is a simple story on the surface, but the details are many and the individual moments joyous. It's a mature picture (there is no stinting on the raunchy and often-incomprehensible Liverpudlian dialogue), unabashedly romantic but not sentimental. There are amateurish moments here and there, and one wishes that the production values were better, but all the flaws pale in light of the overall impact of the love story.

LETTER TO THREE WIVES, A

1948 103m bw Drama ★★★★
Fox (U.S.) /U

Jeanne Crain (*Deborah Bishop*), Linda Darnell (*Lora May Hollingsway*), Ann Sothern (*Rita Phipps*), Kirk Douglas (*George Phipps*), Paul Douglas (*Porter Hollingsway*), Barbara Lawrence (*Babe*), Jeffrey Lynn (*Brad Bishop*), Connie Gilchrist (*Mrs. Finney*), Florence Bates (*Mrs. Manleigh*), Hobart Cavanaugh (*Mr. Manleigh*)

p, Sol C. Siegel; d, Joseph L. Mankiewicz; w, Joseph L. Mankiewicz, Vera Caspary (based on the novel by John Klempner); ph, Arthur Miller; ed, J. Watson Webb; m, Alfred Newman; art d, Lyle Wheeler, J. Russell Spencer; fx, Fred Sersen; cos, Kay Nelson

AAN Best Picture; AA Best Director: Joseph L. Mankiewicz; *AA Best Screenplay:* Joseph L. Mankiewicz

Delicious bites of suburbia, with lucious Darnell a surprising prize plum. This ingeniously constructed film is one of the finest movies ever made about marriage. It focuses on the doubts, fears and recriminations of three lovely wives who believe they are soon to lose their husbands to another woman. Crain, Darnell, and Sothern are about to leave on a boat trip along the Hudson River, escorting a group of youngsters, when a messenger delivers a letter to each of them, all from the same woman, Addie Ross, never shown and played only as an off-screen voice by Holm. Holm has written the same message to all three wives; she has run off with *one* of their husbands but she does not mention which one, leaving them to figure out who has lost out, and subjecting all three to subtle emotional torture. The three wives live in comfortable homes in the Hudson Valley and have ostensibly happy marriages, but the letters cause them to frantically review their relationships.

The acting of the six leading players here is outstanding, with the aforementioned Darnell in particular giving the finest performance of her career (in the film's best sketch) as the supposedly hardhearted lady with only wealth on her mind (Top line—when Thelma Ritter cracks Darnell should dress up, wear beads, Linda retorts, "What I got don't need beads!"). Both Douglases, Ann Southern, the Gilchrist and Ritter team, Florence Bates and Jeanne Crain all rise to the occasion. The sharp piquancy of the dialog earned Mankiewicz an Oscar for his script, another for his deft direction. Originally, Zanuck wanted Ernst Lubitsch to direct the film, and gave producer Siegel a fight before he would accept Mankiewicz. The film was a landmark achievement for Mankiewicz, who, on the strength of it, became the darling of the Fox lot, earning profound resentment from Zanuck. Years later, Zanuck blamed Mankiewicz personally for almost destroying Fox with his hugely expensive production of CLEOPATRA.

LIANNA

1983 110m c Drama ★★★
Winwood (U.S.) R/18

Linda Griffiths (*Lianna*), Jane Hallaren (*Ruth*), Jo Henderson (*Sandy*), Jessica MacDonald (*Theda*), Jesse Solomon (*Spencer*), John Sayles (*Jerry*), Stephen Mendillo (*Bob*), Betsy Julia Robinson (*Cindy*), Nancy Mette (*Kim*)

p, Jeffrey Nelson, Maggie Renzi; d, John Sayles; w, John Sayles; ph, Austin de Besche; ed, John Sayles; m, Mason Daring; art d, Jeanne McDonnell; chor, Marta Renzi; cos, Louise Martinez

Lianna (Linda Griffiths) is the unsure wife of a domineering college professor (Jon DeVries). He ridicules her decision to return to school, but she continues to pursue her degree anyway. Ruth (Jane Hallaren), one of her teachers, helps Lianna to cope with her internal struggles. The two women gradually grow closer until their friendship blossoms into a love affair. This is a restrained and caring film that never lapses into preachiness about its lesbian theme. Director-writer John Sayles was noted for writing such films as THE HOWLING and ALLIGATOR, so he could finance his own independent features. The direction and dialog appear completely natural, allowing the characters to tell the story; not a moment in the film seems false or contrived. The two female leads give sensitive performances, and DeVries handles his character's sexual confusions and anger convincingly. There are some technical problems, symptomatic of a low budget, but they don't much hamper this otherwise fine and intelligently told story.

LIAR LIAR

1997 86m c Comedy ★★
Imagine Entertainment (U.S.) PG-13/12

Jim Carrey (*Fletcher Reede*), Maura Tierney (*Audrey Reede*), Jennifer Tilly (*Samantha Cole*), Swoosie Kurtz (*Dana Appleton*), Amanda Donohoe (*Miranda*), Jason Bernard (*Judge Marshall Stevens*), Mitchell Ryan (*Mr. Allan*), Anne Haney (*Greta*), Justin Cooper (*Max Reede*), Cary Elwes (*Jerry*)

p, Brian Grazer; d, Tom Shadyac; w, Paul Guay, Stephen Mazur; ph, Russell Boyd; ed, Don Zimmerman; m, John Debney, James Newton Howard; prod d, Linda DeScenna; art d, Richard A. Toyon; fx, Burt Dalton, Jon Farhat; cos, Judy L. Ruskin

A sickly, soft-swirl confection of low laughs and smarmy sentiment, this message comedy returns Jim Carrey to the form his fans know and love: a one-man whirlwind of pratfalls, silly faces, rude sounds, and anarchic *epater le bourgeoisieI schtick. And there's an important lesson in there, too: nothing in this crazy old world is more important than a little boy's love for his dad.*

Lies are the air workaholic lawyer Fletcher Reede (Carey) breathes, both on the job and off. His ex-wife (Maura Tierney) is sick to death of him, and his adoring son Max (Justin Cooper) lives in a state of perpetual disappointment. When Fletcher breaks his promise to attend the child's 5th birthday party, Max makes a special birthday wish: that Fletcher will have to tell the truth for 24 hours. Wacky complications ensue, as Fletcher tells the whole truth and nothing but to family, acquaintances, and colleagues in the office and—even worse—the courtroom.

You'd be wrong to imagine that just because this movie's premise involves words, it is a verbal comedy: compulsive truth-teller Carrey spends most of his time mugging, contorting himself, and quite literally bouncing off walls. The evidence is irrefutable—he is the modern-day Jerry Lewis, a creepy blend of the infantile, the manic, and the deeply hostile. Fans put off by THE CABLE GUY's edgy shifts of tone should be mollified by this picture's consistent self-satisfaction: it is simultaneously all touchy-feely about the beauty of paternal love and contemptuous of women, who are all frumps, sex bombs, martyrs, bitches, and ugly cows who say stupid things like "Real beauty comes from the inside."

LIBELED LADY

1936 98m bw Comedy ★★★★
MGM (U.S.) /A

William Powell (*Bill Chandler*), Myrna Loy (*Connie Allenbury*), Jean Harlow (*Gladys Benton*), Spencer Tracy (*Warren Haggerty*), Walter Connolly (*James B. Allenbury*), Charley Grapewin (*Hollis Bane*), Cora Witherspoon (*Mrs. Burns-Norvell*), E.E. Clive (*Evans, the Fishing Instructor*), Bunny Beatty (*Babs Burns-Norvell*), Otto Yamaoka (*Ching*)

p, Lawrence Weingarten; d, Jack Conway; w, Maurine Watkins, Howard Emmett Rogers, George Oppenheimer (based on a story by Wallace Sullivan); ph, Norbert Brodine; ed, Frederick Y. Smith; m, William Axt; art d, Cedric Gibbons, William A. Horning; cos, Dolly Tree

AAN Best Picture

A sparkler from the days when they knew how to do screwball comedy. Tracy plays Warren Haggerty, the managing editor of a newspaper which erroneously prints a story saying that wealthy Connie Allenbury (Loy) is busy nabbing another woman's husband, a British peer. She sues the paper for $5 million. Warren is about to marry Gladys Benton (Harlow), a woman he's left at the altar several times. Now the festivities have to be postponed once again, because Warren must get to the bottom of the story and defuse the lawsuit which could cost him his job. He hires Bill Chandler (Powell), a former co-worker who doesn't like him but needs a job. The task is to marry Gladys (in name only), thus clearing the way for Bill to woo Connie. If that works, Gladys can sue the heiress for alienation of affection, and then agree to drop that suit if Connie drops hers. What goes wrong in all this confusion is that Connie isn't entirely crazy about being used like this and Bill and Connie really do start falling in love. (What else would you expect from William Powell and Myrna Loy?) The complications are fast and furious before the expected two-pair finale.

LIBELED LADY combines the talents of four first-rate farceurs with a crackling script and ace direction. They all have a chance to shine, but we give the slightest of edges to Harlow, who shifts into high wisecracking gear for this one. Don't try to make any sense of the plot; you'll find yourself following its daffy logic just fine. Simply relax and enjoy the merry meanderings of a cast that seemed to be having a bang-up time making this movie. The laughs come rolling off the screen in just about every sequence, but Powell's attempt at fishing and the "bride kisses the best man" bit at one wedding are two highlights. Jack Conway, a good director of many fine films, isn't quite a Leo McCarey or a Howard Hawks, and this film doesn't quite equal THE AWFUL TRUTH or BRINGING UP BABY. Still, LIBELED LADY stands as one of the better "screwball" comedies of the 1930s. It earned an Academy Award nomination for Best Picture, but lost to THE GREAT ZIEGFELD.

LIFE AND DEATH OF COLONEL BLIMP, THE

1943 163m c Drama/War   ★★★★½
The Archers (U.K.)   /U

Roger Livesey *(Clive Candy)*, Deborah Kerr *(Edith Hunter/Barbara Wynne/Johnny Cannon)*, Anton Walbrook *(Theo Kretschmar-Schuldorff)*, Roland Culver *(Col. Betteridge)*, James McKechnie *(Spud Wilson)*, Albert Lieven *(Von Ritter)*, Arthur Wontner *(Embassy Counsellor)*, David Hutcheson *(Hoppy)*, Ursula Jeans *(Frau von Kalteneck)*, John Laurie *(Murdoch)*

p, Michael Powell, Emeric Pressburger; d, Michael Powell; w, Michael Powell, Emeric Pressburger; ph, Jack Cardiff, Georges Perinal; ed, John Seabourne; m, Allan Gray

One of the most celebrated films from the extraordinary director-writer partnership of Michael Powell and Emeric Pressburger, THE LIFE AND DEATH OF COLONEL BLIMP is a warm and wise work that displays extraordinary generosity of spirit. It tells the story of Clive Candy (Roger Livesey), a stuffy British soldier whose life is shown in episodes that range from 1902, when he had a dashing career as a young officer in the Boer War, to 1943, when he creaks crankily about in the London blitz, remembering his lost youth and loves. Not at all a war film in any conventional sense, but a character study that lingers with the viewer long after it's over.

Roger Livesey ably portrays a character with a long and complex life as he is transformed by time and experience from the dashing young firebrand of the 1890s to the anachronistic old codger of the World War II era. The great old British warrior virtues of fair play and chivalry become quaint and inappropriate when faced with the modern horrors of war. Deborah Kerr is a joy to watch as she plays three different roles from different eras in the great man's life. Anton Walbrook (who would be even better a few years later in Powell and Pressburger's THE RED SHOES) is splendid as Theo Kretschmar-Schuldorff, the charming Prussian officer whom Clive fights in a duel and who far exceeds the young Briton in sensitivity and understanding.

The title comes from the satiric character created by cartoonist David Low in the *London Evening Standard*, by which members of Britain's pompous and stiff military upper-crust came to be known as "Colonel Blimps." Churchill illegally prohibited the film's exportation for two years, citing its portrayal of a Colonel Blimp as "detrimental to the morale of the Army." Refusing to heed the advice of the Ministry of Information (which felt his position would do more harm than good), Churchill lifted the ban only after the film became such a smash commercial hit in England that its export could no longer be thwarted. Initially released in America in a butchered 93-minute version, the film was restored to its full length in 1986 by Britain's National Film Archive.

LIFE AND NOTHING BUT
(LA VIE EST RIEN D'AUTRE)

1990 135m c Drama   ★★★½
Hachette Premiere/Little Bear/A2 (France)   PG

Philippe Noiret *(Maj. Dellaplanne)*, Sabine Azema *(Irene de Courtil)*, Pascale Vignal *(Alice)*, Maurice Barrier *(Mercadot)*, Francois Perrot *(Perrin)*, Jean-Pol Dubois *(Andre)*, Daniel Russo *(Lt. Trevise)*, Michel Duchaussoy *(Gen. Villerieux)*, Arlette Gilbert *(Valentine)*, Louis Lyonnet *(Valentin)*

p, Rene Cleitman, Albert Prevost; d, Bertrand Tavernier; w, Bertrand Tavernier, Jean Cosmos; ph, Bruno de Keyzer; ed, Armand Psenny; m, Oswald d'Andrea; prod d, Guy-Claude Francois; cos, Jacqueline Moreau

A compelling successor to such antiwar movies as Stanley Kubrick's PATHS OF GLORY and Lewis Milestone's ALL QUIET ON THE WESTERN FRONT, focusing, like these earlier films, on WWI. Instead of detailing the ongoing carnage of life in the trenches, however, Tavernier paints a grim portrait of devastation after the fact. The year is 1920 (almost two years after the Armistice), and the massive task of counting corpses and identifying the missing among the French soldiers remains. Supervising these efforts is Major Dellaplane (Noiret), a career soldier obsessed with detail who turns his responsibility into a personal crusade to justify the sacrifice made by the dead men, believing that by naming the unidentified and humanizing the statistics, he can somehow make sense of the horror that has occurred. Dellaplane's quest to tie up war's loose ends is interwoven with the tale of another officer's mission to locate a suitable unknown soldier for ceremonial enshrinement in the Arc de Triomphe, and with vignettes concerning families seeking information about the fate of loved ones.

Cowritten by Tavernier and Jean Cosmos (a playwright and TV scenarist making his screenwriting debut), LIFE AND NOTHING BUT is a carefully wrought drama about the emotionally shell-shocked survivors of WWI. Somber, handsome, exquisitely produced, with a towering performance by Noiret in what is reportedly his 100th screen role, Tavernier's elegy strikes no false notes. With an extraordinary talent for conveying the bustle of life amidst the stasis of death, Tavernier employs his sweeping camera and his skill in relating characters to their widescreen environment to create an unforgettable *mise-en-scene*. Despite its brilliant technical accomplishment and its seamless blend of gallows humor and intriguing drama, however, Tavernier's examination of lives held in check by the fortunes of war lacks the full-throttle emotionalism that might have made it a classic pacifist epic. Visually, Tavernier's work with the superb de Keyzer couldn't be improved upon (as in the haunting final shot), but one does wish it were a little less calculated, a little more reckless.

LIFE BEGINS FOR ANDY HARDY

1941 100m bw Drama   ★★★½
MGM (U.S.)   /U

Mickey Rooney *(Andy Hardy)*, Lewis Stone *(Judge Hardy)*, Judy Garland *(Betsy Booth)*, Fay Holden *(Mrs. Hardy)*, Ann Rutherford *(Polly Benedict)*, Sara Haden *(Aunt Milly)*, Patricia Dane *(Jennitt Hicks)*, Ray McDonald *(Jimmy Frobisher)*, George Breakston *(Beezy)*, Pierre Watkin *(Dr. Waggoner)*

d, George B. Seitz; w, Agnes Christine Johnston (based on characters created by Aurania Rouverol); ph, Lester White; ed, Elmo Veron; art d, Cedric Gibbons; cos, Robert Kalloch

A serious departure in MGM's highly successful "Andy Hardy" series finds Rooney as the prodigal. The recent high school graduate has a heart-to-heart discussion with his father, Stone, about his future. Not wanting to follow immediately in his father's footsteps, Rooney's ambition is to go off to New York and "find himself." Though they don't agree with him, the Hardys let their son go off to New York City. There he joins his long-suffering friend Garland (in her third and last film in the "Hardy" series, though she continued to work onscreen with Rooney in other films). After much difficulty, Rooney finds a job as an office boy for the paltry sum of $10 a week. He meets McDonald, a struggling dancer, and sneaks the penniless, homeless young man into his hotel room. But Rooney is startled one evening when he comes home to find his new friend dead of a heart attack. He gets a loan on his jalopy so McDonald can have a decent funeral rather than a pauper's grave. Rooney has befriended Dane, an older divorcee—the receptionist in his employer's office—who invites the young man up to her apartment for an evening. The offer is tempting, but Rooney's homespun value system—along with the arrival of his father in the big city—cause him to decline. Looking over the events that have happened since his arrival in New York, Rooney decides that his home town and college are his real future and he returns to Carvel with Stone. Though the critics attacked the film as too much of a departure from the "Andy Hardy" series's normal vein, this is a fine addition. Rooney and Garland both show great maturity with their characters. Garland is a fine counterbalance for Rooney, constantly watching over him like a loving mother and calling his father when things look dark. Though she truly wants to be in love with him, she can circumvent her feelings to help the skittish young man when he really needs her. The National Legion of Decency surprised everyone in the film world by rating this film A-2, an objectional film for children. They felt that Rooney's heart-to-heart talks with Stone were too "daring" for children, to say nothing of his scenes with Dane.

LIFE IS A BED OF ROSES
(LA VIE EST UN ROMAN)
1983 111m c Fantasy   ★★★
Soprofilm/A2/Fideline/Ariane/Filmedi s   (France)   PG

Vittorio Gassman *(Walter)*, Ruggero Raimondi *(Count Michel Forbek)*, Geraldine Chaplin *(Nora)*, Fanny Ardant *(Livia)*, Pierre Arditi *(Robert)*, Sabine Azema *(Elizabeth)*, Robert Manuel *(Georges)*, Martine Kelly *(Claudine)*, Samson Fainsilber *(Zoltan)*, Nathalie Holberg *(Veronique)*

p, Philippe Dussart; d, Alain Resnais; w, Jean Gruault; ph, Bruno Nuytten; ed, Albert Jurgenson, Jean-Pierre Besnard; m, M . Philippe-Gerard; art d, Jacques Saulnier, Enki Bilal; cos, Catherine Leterrier

A unique and funny film from intellectual French director Resnais that combines a three-part narrative structure with fantasy, comedy, and musical elements. Raimondi is a wealthy turn-of-the-century eccentric who designs a "temple of happiness," in which people who visit revert to a state of infancy. To create a Utopian aura, Raimondi's guests are exposed to only positive sensations—strains of harmonious music fill the air, and blindfolds keep out unpleasant sights—while they lie blissfully in oversized cribs. Raimondi's plan goes awry when Ardant, who never drank the assigned potion, discovers that one of her friends accidentally died because of negligence. The arrival of WW I, however, puts an end to the temple of happiness and to Raimondi's dreams. Intercut with this episode is a present-day symposium on the methods of Raimondi and the possibility of achieving Utopia, attended by teachers, philosophers, anthropologists, and city planners. The gist of the symposium is that the imagination must be nurtured and developed in order for lives to improve. This theory quickly leads to a difference of opinion among those in attendance and results in a flurry of heated arguments. The third tale, which is intercut with the others and is related through the imaginations of a group of children in a forest, is a medieval one in which a warrior must battle a diabolical king. As usual with Resnais, the audience can comprehend part of the film but not another (usually greater) portion, which seems completely out of reach. Instead of simply filming a story, Resnais films a puzzle. The viewer has the choice of whether or not to unravel Resnais's tightly woven structure. Unless one possesses a genius level IQ, it is probably best (for sanity's sake) just to sit back and be bewildered by LIFE IS A BED OF ROSES.

LIFE IS SWEET
1991 102m c Drama/Comedy   ★★★½
Thin Man Films   (U.K.)   /15

Alison Steadman *(Wendy)*, Jim Broadbent *(Andy)*, Timothy Spall *(Aubrey)*, Claire Skinner *(Natalie)*, Jane Horrocks *(Nicola)*, David Thewlis *(Nicola's Lover)*, Moya Brady *(Paula)*, Stephen Rea *(Patsy)*, David Neilson *(Steve)*, Jack Thorpe Baker *(Nigel)*

d, Mike Leigh; w, Mike Leigh; ph, Dick Pope; ed, John Gregory; m, Rachel Portman; prod d, Alison Chitty; art d, Sophie Becher; cos, Lindy Hemming

Between HIGH HOPES (1988), a grimly humorous portrait of Thatcherite London, and the apocalyptic NAKED (1993), came this sometimes unsettling but essentially sweet-tempered feature from acclaimed British director Mike Leigh.

The film concerns a lower-middle-class family of more or less lovable eccentrics living in outer London. The woman of the house, Wendy (Alison Steadman), is perpetually busy and compulsively optimistic. Her husband, Andy (Jim Broadbent), is a chef employed in a large institutional kitchen. He's a laid-back sort, inclined to tinker but never completing any of his initially ambitious projects. Wendy and Andy have twin daughters, Natalie (Claire Skinner) and Nicola (Jane

Horrocks). Natalie is quiet, subdued and focused, an apprentice plumber. The bulimic Nicola, by contrast, is a sullen university dropout intent on letting everyone within earshot know how awful life is and how much she hates living.

While hardly plot-driven, LIFE IS SWEET has its share of small events: Andy, intent on finally becoming his own boss, unwisely purchases a dilapidated mobile food stand; Nicola's disgusted lover (David Thewlis, soon to become famous as NAKED's mad anti-hero) walks out on her; Natalie quietly makes plans for a trip to America; Aubrey (Timothy Spall), a farcically drawn friend of the family, makes last-minute preparations for the opening of his small restaurant; Andy suffers an accident at work which, if only temporarily, brings the family together.

A creative force on London's fringe theater scene since the 1960s, Mike Leigh made his feature directorial debut with the acclaimed BLEAK MOMENTS in 1971. This was followed by a 17-year hiatus, during which Leigh focused on TV and stage work, notably *Abigail's Party* and the BBC telemovies HARD LABOUR, HOME SWEET HOME and FOUR DAYS IN JULY. While not to everyone's taste, Leigh's films have been hailed as a kind of "neo-Marxist Dickens." Not surprisingly, his forte is chronicling, with grace and economy, the vicissitudes of daily life among Britain's downtrodden. The well-rounded characters who populate his films stem from extensive one-on-one collaborations with his actors, followed by group improv sessions from which his precisely structured scripts emerge.

LIFE OF EMILE ZOLA, THE
1937 123m bw Biography   ★★★★½
Warner Bros.   (U.S.)

Paul Muni *(Emile Zola)*, Gale Sondergaard *(Lucie Dreyfus)*, Joseph Schildkraut *(Capt. Alfred Dreyfus)*, Gloria Holden *(Alexandrine Zola)*, Donald Crisp *(Maitre Labori)*, Erin O'Brien-Moore *(Nana)*, John Litel *(Charpentier)*, Henry O'Neill *(Col. Picquart)*, Morris Carnovsky *(Anatole France)*, Louis Calhern *(Maj. Dort)*

p, Henry Blanke; d, William Dieterle; w, Norman Reilly Raine, Heinz Herald, Geza Herczeg (based on the story by Heinz Herald and Geza Herczeg); ph, Tony Gaudio; ed, Warren Low; m, Max Steiner; art d, Anton Grot; cos, Milo Anderson, Ali Hubert

AA Best Picture; AAN Best Actor: Paul Muni; *AA Best Supporting Actor:* Joseph Schildkraut; *AAN Best Director:* William Dieterle; *AA Best Screenplay:* Heinz Herald, Geza Herczeg, Norman Reilly Raine; *AAN Best Original Story:* Heinz Herald, Geza Herczeg; *AAN Best Score:* Leo Forbstein, Warner Bros Studio Music Department, Max Steiner; *AAN Best Art Direction:* Anton Grot; *AAN Best Sound:* Nathan Levinson

Along with George Arliss, Paul Muni was Hollywood's designated portrayer of Great Men. He appeared as Louis Pasteur (an Oscar-winning role), as Benito Juarez, as French explorer Pierre Radisson, as Chopin's teacher Joseph Elsner, and as Napoleon and Schubert (among others) in SEVEN FACES. So it's no surprise to find him playing Emile Zola—and wonderfully—in this fine film. Literate and powerful, THE LIFE OF EMILE ZOLA was a huge box-office success, although its subject matter—the French novelist's part in the Dreyfus Affair—hardly seemed promising in that regard. The film introduces an anguished Zola censured by the French government and public for his frank treatment of squalid life and social problems in his novel *Nana* (based on his own experiences with a prostitute, played by O'Brien-Moore). As time passes, though, he is increasingly heralded as France's greatest writer and as the champion of those who cannot speak for themselves during France's Second Empire. Zola's greatest challenge comes when he fights for the freedom of the framed Jewish officer Alfred Dreyfus (Schildkraut). Pen in hand, Zola writes, "J'accuse. . ."

The film's script was originally shown to Ernst Lubitsch at Paramount, who liked it but felt he had no actor in his stable who could do justice to the main character. He generously passed it on to producer Henry Blanke of Warners, which had the services of Muni, Lubitsch's choice for the part. As on so many other occasions, Lubitsch was right; Muni triumphs completely in this demanding role. As was his custom, Muni steeped himself in his character, reading all of Zola's works, extensively researching the Dreyfus case, and attempting many different makeup variations before settling on his final choice. The other actors are equally fine, with Holden in particular a warm glow as Zola's wife. It's nice to see Sondergaard in a rare sympathetic part and, as her husband, the center of the controversy, Schildkraut rivals Muni in effectiveness. Scene after scene of the nervous and later numbed Dreyfus being stripped of his honor haunt this film and Schildkraut was the only possible choice for the year's Supporting Actor Oscar. The movie itself, though it deviates from the facts a bit, is basically faithful to history and well scripted, without extraneous characters or plot lines. The period details are all authentic, with no expense spared to recreate the settings. Director Dieterle, one of Hollywood's best, handles the script beautifully, especially in the brilliant courtroom scenes, and the anti-Semitic nature of Dreyfus's persecution is also conveyed potently, though circumspectly. (We never hear the word *Jew*.) Skip the 1958 remake, I ACCUSE.

LIFE OF OHARU, THE
(SAIKAKU ICHIDAI ONNA)

1952 146m bw Drama ★★★½
Shin Toho (Japan) /A

Kinuyo Tanaka *(Oharu)*, Tsukie Matsura *(Tomo, Oharu's Mother)*, Ichiro Sugai *(Shonzaemon, Oharu's Father)*, Toshiro Mifune *(Katsunosuke)*, Toshiaki Konoe *(Lord Tokitaka Matsudaira)*, Hisako Yamane *(Lady Matsudaira)*, Jukichi Uno *(Yakichi Senya)*, Eitaro Shindo *(Kohei Sasaya)*, Akira Oizumi *(Fumikichi, Sasaya's Friend)*, Masao Shimizu *(Kikuno Koji)*

d, Kenji Mizoguchi; w, Yoshikata Yoda, Kenji Mizoguchi (based on the novel *Koshuku Ichidai Onna* by Saikaku Ibara); ph, Yoshimi Kono, Yoshimi Hirano; ed, Toshio Goto; m, Ichiro Saito; art d, Hiroshi Mizutani

LIFE OF OHARU is a later film in the long and brilliant career of masterful director Kenji Mizoguchi. The plot details the painful life of Oharu (Kinuyo Tanaka), a 50-year-old, 17th-century prostitute. In flashback, Oharu's life unfolds, beginning when she, the young daughter of a samurai, falls in love with a lower-class man, Katsunosuke (Toshiro Mifune). As punishment, her lover is decapitated and her family banished from Kyoto. After a failed suicide, Oharu becomes the mistress of a prince, who sends her away after she bears him a son. She is then sold by her father and put to work as a prostitute. A wealthy client buys her, but he is discovered to be a criminal, and she is again forced to sell herself. In time, Oharu meets and marries a merchant and lives with him until his death. Once again, at age 50, she is forced to turn to prostitution. In LIFE OF OHARU, Mizoguchi concentrates on the formal style he developed so successfully in his earlier work—extremely long takes of meticulously composed shots with a minimal amount of cutting. Kinuyo Tanaka is superb as the prostitute whose unceasing degradation Mizoguchi uses to criticize feudal Japan and its treatment of women. The winner of the Silver Lion at the Venice Film Festival.

LIFE ON A STRING
(BIAN ZHOU BIAN CHANG)

1992 110m c Drama ★★★
Serene Productions/Pandora Film/Beijing Film Studio/China /PG
Film/Diva Film (China/U.K./Germany)

Liu Zhongyuan *(The Saint)*, Huang Lei *(Shitou)*, Xu Qing *(Lanxiu)*, Ma Ling *(Noodleshop Owner's Wife)*, Zhang Zhenguan, Yao Jingou

p, Don Ranvaud; d, Chen Kaige; w, Chen Kaige (from the short story by Shi Tiesheng); ph, Gu Changwei; ed, Pei Xiaonan; m, Qu Xiaosong; art d, Shao Ruigang

A film—at least ostensibly—about blindness, LIFE ON A STRING contains some of the most stunning images in recent screen history, beautifully capturing the thundering waterfalls, sparkling mountain ranges and mistfallen crags of China's Shaanxi Province.

The setting is feudal China, where a sightless old musician, known simply as the Saint (Liu Zhongyuan), wanders purposefully with his young, equally blind apprentice, Shitou (Huang Lei). As a youth the Saint was disciple to Grand Master, who told him that if he spent his days in ceaseless practice on the *sanxian* (a long-necked banjo), his blindness would end. All the Saint had to do was break 1,000 strings in the course of playing. That task has consumed 60 years, and the count

has reached the 990s. Meanwhile, Shitou yearns for earthier pleasures, mainly in the form of a peasant girl named Lanxiu (Xu Qing). The Saint disapproves, but is ultimately forced to reconsider his own, unquestioning faith in the rigid moral code by which he has lived.

LIFE ON A STRING presents itself as an epic fable whose precise moral has been lost to the ages, allowing many meanings to be read into its dense spectacle. Kaige composes each frame with an artisan's care. He restricts his camera movements to slow, formal pans and lengthy takes that slow down the narrative, but impart a mythic quality to the material. Most impressive is a lyrical series of long shots in which the Saint stops a war between two clans by hobbling into the midst of opposing armies and singing about peace and brotherhood. As the legendary minstrel's frail voice fills the soundtrack, the warriors unite around him to form a single, mighty procession. Though at times ponderous and obscure, LIFE ON A STRING leaves a lasting impression on the eye.

LIFE WITH FATHER

1947 118m c Comedy ★★★★
Warner Bros. (U.S.) /A

William Powell *(Clarence Day)*, Irene Dunne *(Vinnie Day)*, Elizabeth Taylor *(Mary)*, Edmund Gwenn *(Rev. Dr. Lloyd)*, ZaSu Pitts *(Cora)*, James Lydon *(Clarence)*, Emma Dunn *(Margaret)*, Moroni Olsen *(Dr. Humphries)*, Elisabeth Risdon *(Mrs. Whitehead)*, Derek Scott *(Harlan)*

p, Robert Buckner; d, Michael Curtiz; w, Donald Ogden Stewart (based on the play by Howard Lindsay, Russel Crouse and the book by Clarence Day Jr.); ph, Peverell Marley, William V. Skall; ed, George Amy; m, Max Steiner; art d, Robert Haas; fx, Ray Foster, William McGann; cos, Milo Anderson

AAN Best Actor: William Powell; *AAN Best Cinematography:* Peverell Marley, William V Skall; *AAN Best Score:* Max Steiner; *AAN Best Art Direction:* Robert M Haas (Art Direction), George James Hopkins (Set Decoration)

Based on an autobiographical book by Clarence Day, Jr., and a play that ran for 3,224 performances on Broadway (a total that was eclipsed only by "Fiddler on the Roof"), LIFE WITH FATHER is a son's fond remembrance of his Victorian youth spent in the home of his authoritarian but lovable father (William Powell). There's really not much of a plot, just a lot of alternately quiet and raucous moments of love and laughter as the family goes about its urban, urbane life. Irene Dunne, playing the mother of the red-headed Day clan, is frequently rankled by Father's sexist ways, but, like the rest of the family, she loves dear old Dad anyway.

Powell is nothing less than magnificent as the mustached philosophizing patriarch, and Dunne casts a warm glow beside him. Elizabeth Taylor, Martin Milner, Jimmy Lydon, and Edmund Gwenn all contribute strong supporting performances; Michael Curtiz (CASABLANCA; YANKEE DOODLE DANDY; THE ADVENTURES OF ROBIN HOOD) provides his usual sure-handed direction. There was an attempt at a sequel, LIFE WITH MOTHER, but it doesn't hold a candle to this. Day's story also inspired a brief TV series in 1955. Look for a very young and beautiful Arlene Dahl in a scene at Delmonico's Restaurant. Older TV fans will also recognize singer Russell Arms as the stock quotation operator.

LIFEBOAT

1944 96m bw Drama/War ★★★★½
Fox (U.S.) /PG

Tallulah Bankhead *(Connie Porter)*, William Bendix *(Gus)*, Walter Slezak *(The German)*, Mary Anderson *(Alice)*, John Hodiak *(Kovak)*, Henry Hull *(Rittenhouse)*, Heather Angel *(Mrs. Higgins)*, Hume Cronyn *(Stanley Garrett)*, Canada Lee *(Joe)*, William Yetter Jr. *(German Sailor)*

p, Kenneth MacGowan; d, Alfred Hitchcock; w, Jo Swerling (based on the story by John Steinbeck); ph, Glen MacWilliams; ed, Dorothy Spencer; m, Hugo Friedhofer; art d, James Basevi, Maurice Ransford; fx, Fred Sersen

AAN Best Director: Alfred Hitchcock; *AAN Best Original Screenplay:* John Steinbeck; *AAN Best Cinematography:* Glen MacWilliams

Alfred Hitchcock's taut wartime thriller concerns a handful of survivors who climb into a lifeboat after their ship is torpedoed by a German U-boat. The captain (Walter Slezak) of the U-boat, which has also sunk, swims to the already crowded boat and is taken aboard by the kind-hearted survivors. Since he is the only man capable of handling the craft in rough weather and navigating it to a safe harbor, he is elected helmsman. The survivors are an odd lot—fashion writer Connie Porter (Tallulah Bankhead), industrial tycoon Rittenhouse (Henry Hull), socially conscious seaman Kovak (John Hodiak), wounded stoker Gus (William Bendix), meek radio operator Stanley Garrett (Hume Cronyn), bewildered nurse Alice (Mary Anderson), a mother in shock (Heather Angel), cradling her child who had just died, and black steward Joe (Canada Lee). Slowly, and with insidious cleverness, the German steers a course not for land, but to a secret rendezvous with a German mother ship. The entire cast is superb, but the standouts are Bankhead, as the spoiled, wealthy dilettante writer whose expensive furs and jewelry are worth more to her than the lives of her fellow survivors, and Bendix, as the compassionate but not-too-bright stoker whose gangrenous leg poses a threat to his dreams of returning home to dance with his sweetheart. John Steinbeck, on whose original story the film was based, was first assigned to pen the script, but reportedly felt too restricted by the film's single set (the lifeboat). Jo Swerling eventually wrote the script, but, as was customary with Hitchcock, the talented Ben Hecht was brought in at the last moment to tighten up scenes and sharpen dialogue.

LIFEGUARD
1976 96m c Drama   ★★★
Paramount (U.S.)   PG/15

Sam Elliott *(Rick Carlson)*, Anne Archer *(Cathy)*, Stephen Young *(Larry)*, Parker Stevenson *(Chris)*, Kathleen Quinlan *(Wendy)*, Steve Burns *(Machine Gun)*, Sharon Weber *(Tina)*, Mark Hall, Scott Lichtig
p, Ron Silverman; d, Daniel Petrie; w, Ron Koslow; ph, Ralph Woolsey; ed, Argyle Nelson; m, Dale Menten

This quickie is a real surprise: a sensitive, thought-provoking story involving a man forced to look at himself as youth gives way to middle age. Elliott is outstanding as the title character, an old-timer in the profession at age 30. Although he enjoys his work, pressure from his parents and peers force Elliott to realize that beach life can't go on forever. His performance is intelligent, with some good support by Archer as Elliott's high school sweetheart and Quinlan as a young girl with a crush on him. Unfortunately, this was marketed as nothing more than another beach movie and consequently had little box office success.

LIGHT THAT FAILED, THE
1939 97m bw Drama   ★★★★
Paramount (U.S.)   /A

Ronald Colman *(Dick Heldar)*, Walter Huston *(Terpenhow)*, Muriel Angelus *(Maisie)*, Ida Lupino *(Bessie Broke)*, Dudley Digges *(The Nilghai)*, Ernest Cossart *(Beeton)*, Ferike Boros *(Mme. Binat)*, Pedro de Cordoba *(M. Binat)*, Colin Tapley *(Gardner)*, Fay Helm *(Red-Haired Girl)*
p, William A. Wellman; d, William A. Wellman; w, Robert Carson (based on the novel by Rudyard Kipling); ph, Theodor Sparkuhl; ed, Thomas Scott; m, Victor Young; art d, Hans Dreier, Robert Odell

This tragic Kipling tale, from his first novel, displays Wellman's consummate directorial skills in following the story faithfully, unlike earlier versions in which sugar-coated endings are supplied. Colman is a gifted artist who receives a sabre cut during a battle. He returns to England where he becomes a famous painter; his masterpiece is a portrait of a London prostitute, Lupino. She is driven half-mad with desire for him, a part so intensely played that it brought her to stardom. Realizing that her station in life will prevent her from ever having him, she viciously destroys the painting. The old wound has caused him to slowly go blind. In a shattering scene, Colman proudly displays the portrait to his devoted friend Huston, not realizing that Lupino has slashed it. His sight almost gone, Colman bids goodbye to his childhood sweetheart and returns to the Sudan with friend Huston. At the first sound of battle, Colman begs Huston to put him into the fight, and he

is sent blindly charging on his white stallion to his death. This moving, haunting film reinforces Kipling's love of honor, male friendship, and nobility of spirit. Wellman handles the story and gaslight era with great care, developing his characters with incisive scenes. This was no easy task for Wellman since he and Colman argued throughout the film, the director refusing Colman's perfectionist demands for endless takes and ignoring the actor's insistence that Vivien Leigh play the slatternly Bessie. Lupino got that emotion-charged part by barging into Wellman's office to tell him that no other woman in the world could play Bessie as well as she and providing an impromptu interpretation right then and there. She got the role, and audiences around the world were stunned by her marvelous portrayal. Of Colman, the director would later comment: "Ronald Colman and Wellman, an odd combination to say the least. He didn't like me; I didn't like him—the only two things we agreed fully on. [He has] the most beautiful voice in the whole motion picture business."

LIKE WATER FOR CHOCOLATE
(COMO AGUA PARA CHOCOLATE)
1992 114m c Drama/Romance/Fantasy   ★★★½
Arau Films International/Mexican National Council for Culture   /15
and the Arts/Mexican Institute of Cinematography/Mexican
Ministry of Tourism/Mexican National Fund for the
Development of Tourism (Mexico)

Marco Leonardi *(Pedro Muzquiz)*, Lumi Cavazos *(Tita de la Garza)*, Regina Torne *(Mama Elena)*, Mario Ivan Martinez *(John Brown)*, Ada Carrasco *(Nacha)*, Yareli Arizmendi *(Rosaura)*, Claudette Maille *(Gertrudis)*, Pilar Aranda *(Chencha)*, Farnesio DiBernal *(Priest)*, Joaquin Garrido *(Sergeant Trevino)*
p, Alfonso Arau; d, Alfonso Arau; w, Laura Esquivel (from her Novel); ph, Emmanuel Lubezki, Steve Bernstein; ed, Carlos Bolado, Francisco Chiu; m, Leo Brower; art d, Marco Antonio Arteaga, Mauricio DeAguinaco, Denise Pizzini; fx, Raul Falomir; chor, Farnesio DeBernal

Alfonso Arau's LIKE WATER FOR CHOCOLATE proved a tremendous hit with American movie audiences, becoming the highest-grossing foreign-language feature ever released in the US.

Mexico, 1910. Tita (Lumi Cavazos) lives cursed by a cruel family tradition; as the youngest daughter, she is to take care of Mama Elena (Regina Torne) in her old age, and is forbidden to wed. Tita falls in love with Pedro (Marco Leonardi), and when Mama Elena refuses to let them marry, he agrees to take older daughter Rosaura's (Yareli Arizmendi) hand, thinking he will at least be close to his true love. Forced to bake their wedding cake, Tita moistens the cake batter with her heartbroken tears. Upon eating the cake, the wedding guests are overcome with an unbearable sadness and begin uncontrollably crying and throwing up. Thus begins Tita's special magic with food; resigned to her fate as family cook, she will impart her feelings to the dishes she prepares, with results that range from amusing to truly shocking.

An adult fairy tale, LIKE WATER FOR CHOCOLATE has evil family members, a prince charming, numerous trials, and a happy ending—sort of. It proved an international breakthrough for Arau, a character actor and filmmaker who previously specialized in political comedies. The real auteur of the piece, though, is novelist Laura Esquivel, a writer in the magic realist tradition, and her screenplay largely succeeds in translating the appeal of her book to the screen. Though one wonders if Arau couldn't have found more visual parallels for Esquivel's narrative, overall the film is a witty, charming diversion that struck a chord with audiences.

LILI
1953 81m c Drama   ★★★½
MGM (U.S.)   /U

Leslie Caron *(Lili Daurier)*, Mel Ferrer *(Paul Berthalet)*, Jean-Pierre Aumont *(Marc)*, Zsa Zsa Gabor *(Rosalie)*, Kurt Kasznar *(Jacquot)*, Amanda Blake *(Peach Lips)*, Alex Gerry *(Proprietor)*, Ralph Dumke *(M. Corvier)*, Wilton Graff *(M. Tonit)*, George Baxter *(M. Enrique)* p, Edwin H. Knopf; d, Charles Walters; w, Helen Deutsch (based on the story by Paul Gallico); ph, Robert Planck; ed, Ferris Webster; m, Bronislau Kaper; art d, Cedric Gibbons, Paul Groesse; fx, Warren Newcombe; chor, Charles Walters, Dorothy Jarnac; cos, Mary Ann Nyberg

AAN Best Actress: Leslie Caron; *AAN Best Director:* Charles Walters; *AAN Best Screenplay:* Helen Deutsch; *AAN Best Cinematography:* Robert Planck; *AA Best Score:* Bronislau Kaper; *AAN Best Art Direction:* Cedric Gibbons, Paul Groesse, Edwin B. Willis, Arthur Krams

Leslie Caron plays the title role in this charming film. Sixteen-year-old Lili Daurier runs off to work as a waitress with a carnival and falls in love with Marc (Jean Pierre Aumont), a magician who is more amused by the young innocent than anything else. Fired for paying too much attention to Marc, Lili is comforted by a group of puppets operated by Paul Berthalet (Mel Ferrer), a bitter ex-dancer crippled by a war injury. Though Paul is insanely jealous of Lili's affection for Marc, he is only able to show his tender side through his puppets (in the film's nicest moment, as Lili and the dancing figures sing the famous "Hi-Lili, Hi-Lo"), and Lili thinks of him as a cruel man. When Lili learns that Rosalie (Zsa Zsa Gabor, in a surprisingly good performance) is Marc's wife as well as his assistant, she packs her bags to leave, but love wins out in the end, though it's not the magician who has the final trick up his sleeve. Caron is wonderful as Lili, Ferrer and Aumont provide handsome support, and the whole look of the film is just right. LILI was the basis for a hit Broadway musical in 1961 called "Carnival," with Anna Maria Alberghetti in the Caron role.

LILI MARLEEN

1981 120m c Drama/War   ★★
Roxy/CIP/Rialto (West Germany)   R/15

Hanna Schygulla *(Wilkie Bunterberg)*, Giancarlo Giannini *(Robert Mendelsson)*, Mel Ferrer *(David Mendelsson)*, Karl-Heinz von Hassel *(Henkel)*, Christine Kaufmann *(Miriam)*, Hark Bohm *(Tascher)*, Karin Baal *(Anna Lederer)*, Udo Kier *(Drewitz)*, Erik Schumann *(Von Strehlow)*, Gottfried John *(Aaron)*

p, Luggi Waldleitner, Enzo Peri; d, Rainer Werner Fassbinder; w, Manfred Purzer, Joshua Sinclair, Rainer Werner Fassbinder (based on the song by Lale Andersen); ph, Xaver Schwarzenberger; ed, Franz Walsch, Juliane Lorenz; m, Peer Raben; prod d, Rolf Zehetbauer; art d, Herbert Stravel; fx, Joachim Schulz; chor, Dr. Dieter Gackstetter; cos, Barbara Baum

Fassbinder was surely one of the world's most prolific filmmakers, producing an enormous body of work before his early death, which ironically occurred as he was editing film. With such a large output there were bound to be a few pictures that fell short of the director's normally high quality, LILI MARLEEN being an example. "The story of a song!" claimed the advertising copy, which is more or less truth in advertising. "Lili Marleen" was a song made famous in Germany by Lale Andersen and later Marlene Dietrich. It was very popular with the German forces during WWII. However, Fassbinder's film has little to do with the true story of the song. The film opens in 1938 with the lovely and accomplished Schygulla, a cabaret singer in Zurich. She discovers that boyfriend Giannini, a Swiss Jew, is not only a musical composer but also a member of the underground resistance movement. During a trip to Germany, her song becomes a hit, and no less than the Fuhrer himself wants to meet her. She becomes a big star, while Giannini's father blocks her return to Switzerland. Giannini sneaks into Berlin and meets once more with his now-famous lover. She becomes blacklisted and is forced to leave the country while Giannini is arrested. After the war, they meet once more, but he is now married and well on his way to success. Though Fassbinder's camerawork is excellent, including some allusions to the famous German studio UFA, his themes are never really developed. The political and social messages so often found in his work give way to more melodramatic storytelling. Schygulla, who is usually a shining performer, is spotty here. Her singing makes one wonder how the song got to be such a hit.

LILIES OF THE FIELD

1963 94m bw Drama   ★★★½
Rainbow (U.S.)   /U

Sidney Poitier *(Homer Smith)*, Lilia Skala *(Mother Maria)*, Lisa Mann *(Sister Gertrude)*, Isa Crino *(Sister Agnes)*, Francesca Jarvis *(Sister Albertine)*, Pamela Branch *(Sister Elizabeth)*, Stanley Adams *(Juan)*, Dan Frazer *(Father Murphy)*, Ralph Nelson *(Mr. Ashton)*

p, Ralph Nelson; d, Ralph Nelson; w, James Poe (based on the novel by William E. Barrett); ph, Ernest Haller; ed, John McCafferty; m, Jerry Goldsmith

AAN Best Picture; AA Best Actor: Sidney Poitier; *AAN Best Supporting Actress:* Lilia Skala; *AAN Best Adapted Screenplay:* James Poe; *AAN Best Cinematography:* Ernest Haller

LILIES OF THE FIELD is a "feel-good" movie that blazed new trails in the motion picture world. Not that it had any particular special effects or innovations in movies. It had no spectacular action or dance sequences and surely no violence. But it was a trendsetter in that it marked the first time that the Academy of Motion Picture Arts and Sciences ever awarded an Oscar to a black actor, Poitier. Poitier is an ex-GI roaming around the Southwest, taking odd jobs and seeing what there is to see when he stops at a small farm to refill his car radiator. The farm is run by five German nuns who immediately set upon him to help them with their manual labors. They are new to these shores and don't speak much English but the Mother Superior, Skala, convinces Poitier to stay a while and help work the farm that was willed to them. He fixes their leaky roof and they send up prayers in honor of the man whom "God has sent." Now, Skala asks if he will stay on to help with some other chores. Poitier is a little tired of his aimless wanderings and not much convincing is necessary, even though they prevail on him to do a major project—the building of a chapel. Poitier agrees, as long as they will supply the needed materials. He teams up with Nelson (doing double chores as director and actor), a contractor, and they start to build the chapel. Meanwhile, he donates his small salary back to the nuns to buy food and spends his spare time teaching them how to speak English. When building materials for the chapel run out, Poitier disappears and the nuns think he's abandoned them, but he returns a few weeks later to complete the job he started for the nuns he has come to love. Now, however, he is finally assisted by the local townspeople who refused to help him the first time around. On the night before the sanctification of the chapel, Poitier leaves as little fanfare as when he first arrived. This was a small, low-budget picture that went straight for the heart and succeeded critically as well as financially.

LIMELIGHT

1952 145m bw Drama/Comedy   ★★★★
Chaplin (U.S.)   G/U

Charles Chaplin *(Calvero)*, Claire Bloom *(Terry, a Ballet Dancer)*, Sydney Chaplin *(Neville, a Composer)*, Andre Eglevsky *(Harlequin)*, Melissa Hayden *(Columbine)*, Charles Chaplin Jr., Wheeler Dryden *(Clowns)*, Nigel Bruce *(Postant, an Impresario)*, Norman Lloyd *(Stage Manager)*, Buster Keaton *(Piano Accompanist)*

p, Charles Chaplin; d, Charles Chaplin; w, Charles Chaplin; ph, Karl Struss; ed, Joe Inge; m, Charles Chaplin; art d, Eugene Laurie; chor, Charles Chaplin, Andre Eglevsky, Melissa Hayden

AA Best Score: Charles Chaplin, Raymond Rasch, Larry Russell

Chaplin, as usual, is the whole show, superb in this swansong statement about his own career and the old-style entertainment he best represented. He is a one-time great of the British music halls at the turn of the century (which is exactly where Chaplin himself began), who finds a young dancer, Bloom, depressed over setbacks, attempting suicide in their cheap boarding house. He takes her in, nurses her back to health, and supports her efforts to become a success. As her star rises, his fades, but he bows out with magnificent aplomb in the place he most loves, the theater. Chaplin plays comic and dramatic scenes with great skill. He is simply wonderful in his pantomime routines, particularly so when he tames a flea and when he imagines himself a great lion tamer. Chaplin is a delight as he teaches Bloom his "laughter therapy." He ends his career—and his life—with a hilarious routine with the great comic Keaton, collapsing from exhaustion, falling into the orchestra pit and getting wedged in a large drum, commenting: "Ladies and gentlemen, I would like to say something, but I am stuck." He dies happy, believing that Bloom is in love, not with him, but with a young composer, played by Chaplin's real-life son, Sydney. Other children, from his marriage with Oona O'Neill (daughter of the great American playwright), appear as street urchins. The overlong film is extraordinary in that Chaplin produced, directed, wrote the script, and helped compose the haunting, Oscar winning score (In an unusual occurance, the composers won the Award, not in 1952, but in 1972, which was the first year the picture was ever shown in a Los Angeles theatre). The film's main love theme, "Eternally," became a popular ballad. LIMELIGHT is a direct comment on Chaplin's own fabulous career, one which saw the triumph and decline of physical comedy. He had fallen out of favor with a public that believed him to be a wild-eyed leftist radical, if not an outright communist, and LIMELIGHT suffered as a result, yielding little profit at the box office. LIMELIGHT pays homage to a past in which simple, nuance-free entertainment gave joy and laughter to millions. Bloom, at age 19, became an overnight star with her appearance in the film. (She had debuted in THE BLIND GODDESS at age 16.) She later recalled in her memoirs, *Limelight and After*: "Chaplin was the most exacting director, not because he expected you to produce wonders on your own, but because he expected you to follow unquestioningly his every instruction. I was surprised at how old-fashioned much of what he prescribed seemed—rather theatrical effects that I didn't associate with the modern cinema."

LION IN WINTER, THE

1968 134m c Historical   ★★★★
Haworth (U.K.)   PG/15

Peter O'Toole *(King Henry II)*, Katharine Hepburn *(Queen Eleanor of Aquitaine)*, Jane Merrow *(Princess Alais)*, John Castle *(Prince Geoffrey)*, Timothy Dalton *(King Philip of France)*, Anthony Hopkins *(Prince Richard the Lion-Hearted)*, Nigel Stock *(William Marshall)*, Nigel Terry *(Prince John)*, Kenneth Griffith *(Strolling Player)*, O.Z. Whitehead *(Bishop of Durham)*

p, Martin Poll; d, Anthony Harvey; w, James Goldman (based on the play by Goldman); ph, Douglas Slocombe; ed, John Bloom; m, John Barry; art d, Peter Murton, Gilbert Margerie; cos, Margaret Furse

AAN Best Picture; AAN Best Actor: Peter O'Toole; *AA Best Actress:* Katharine Hepburn; *AAN Best Director:* Anthony Harvey; *AA Best Adapted Screenplay:* James Goldman; *AA Best Score:* John Barry; *AAN Best Costume Design:* Margaret Furse

O'Toole, the all-powerful Henry II, summons his politically ambitious family to a reunion in 1183. This includes his wife, Hepburn, whom he has kept in a remote castle to keep her from meddling with his empire. His three sons—all coveting his wide kingdom—Castle, Terry, and Hopkins are also present, along with O'Toole's mistress Merrow and her brother Dalton, playing King Philip of France. The members of this tempestuous family jockey for position and brutally squabble among each other, rekindling every injury suffered and adding new, Homeric insults to their already bruised reputations.

Hepburn is simply wonderful as the scheming and shrewd Eleanor of Aquitaine. Her verbal duels with the equally impressive O'Toole (here playing a man of 50 behind a beard and heavy makeup) are spellbinding. Hepburn won her third Oscar for this superlative performance, becoming the first actress in history to do so (her previous Oscars were for MORNING GLORY and GUESS WHO'S COMING TO DINNER). O'Toole holds his own with the magnificent Hepburn in a witty, literate, and inventive script. The claim that costume dramas are never successful was mightily disproved by this film, which enjoyed a booming box-office business and the wide respect of the public. Shot on location in Ireland, Wales, and France.

LION KING, THE

1994 87m c Animated/Children's/Musical   ★★★
Walt Disney Productions (U.S.)   G/U

VOICES OF: Jonathan Taylor Thomas *(Young Simba)*, Matthew Broderick *(Adult Simba)*, James Earl Jones *(Mufasa)*, Jeremy Irons *(Scar)*, Moira Kelly *(Adult Nala)*, Niketa Calame *(Young Nala)*, Ernie Sabella *(Pumbaa)*, Nathan Lane *(Timon)*, Robert Guillaume *(Rafiki)*, Rowan Atkinson *(Zazu)*

p, Don Hahn; d, Roger Allers, Robert Minkoff; w, Irene Mecchi, Jonathan Roberts, Linda Woolverton; ed, Tom Finan, John Carnochan, Lisa M. Smith, Ivan Bilancio, Beth Stegmaier, Kat Connolly; m, Hans Zimmer; prod d, Chris Sanders; art d, Andy Gaskill; fx, Scott Santoro, Jeff Dutton

AA Best Original Score: Hans Zimmer; *AA Best Original Song:* Elton John (Music), Tim Rice (Lyrics); *AAN Best Original Song:* Elton John (Music), Tim Rice (Lyrics); *AAN Best Original Song:* Elton John (Music), Tim Rice (Lyrics)

The 1994 installment in a series of animated musical blockbusters from Disney, THE LION KING boasts animation as spectacular as any the studio has ever produced, and earned an extraordinary $300 million-plus at the box office. However, this tale of a lion cub's coming of age in the African veldt offers a less memorable song score than did the previous hits, and a hasty, unsatisfying dramatic resolution.

As son and heir of the Lion King Mufasa (voice of James Earl Jones), young Simba (Jonathan Taylor Thomas) expects to inherit dominion over the jungle kingdom called Prideland. But the machinations of Mufasa's jealous brother, Scar (Jeremy Irons), result in Simba's banishment. Near death from exhaustion in the desert, Simba is rescued by Timon (Nathan Lane), a meerkat, and Pumbaa (Ernie Sabella), a warthog, who take him to a jungle paradise, where they sing the praises of "Hakuna Matata" (a carefree life). With their advice and assistance, Simba grows to maturity and prepares to confront Scar and reclaim his throne.

An "original" story—reportedly devised by then-production head Jeffrey Katzenberg—THE LION KING obviously draws on several previous Disney hits. The real inspiration for the film's oddly anachronistic story line, however, seems to lie in Shakespeare's histories; in particular, the extended meditation on the nature and responsibilities of kingship found in *Henry V* and the two parts of *Henry IV*. Like many recent Hollywood epics of fatherhood (FIELD OF DREAMS, LEGENDS OF THE FALL), THE LION KING makes the most sense as an attempted redemption of patriarchy—a call upon contemporary males to resume their "natural" role as all-wise, all-powerful guarantors of the social order.

The film has some of Disney's most spectacular animation yet—particularly in the wildebeest stampede—and strong vocal performances, especially by skilled Broadway comedian Nathan Lane. However, it suffers from a curiously undeveloped story line: the climactic confrontation with Scar has few surprises and is disposed of rather quickly in the final minutes of the film. The events leading up to it, however, are well-told, exciting, and suspenseful, set against a series of exquisitely detailed background tapestries.

LIQUID SKY

1982 118m c Science Fiction   ★★★½
Z Films (U.S.)   R/18

Anne Carlisle *(Margaret/Jimmy)*, Paula Sheppard *(Adrian)*, Susan Doukas *(Sylvia)*, Otto von Wernherr *(Johann)*, Bob Brady *(Owen)*, Elaine C. Grove *(Katherine)*, Stanley Knapp *(Paul)*, Lloyd Ziff *(Lester)*, Harry Lum *(Deliveryman)*, Roy MacArthur *(Jack)*

p, Slava Tsukerman; d, Slava Tsukerman; w, Slava Tsukerman, Anne Carlisle, Nina V. Kerova; ph, Yuri Neyman; ed, Sharyn L. Ross; m, Slava Tsukerman, Brenda I. Hutchinson, Clive Smith; prod d, Marina Levikova; fx, Yuri Neyman; cos, Marina Levikova

Outrageous fun, this film is New Wave chic, satire, self-parody, science fiction, and certainly one of the more accessible independent features ever made. Aliens are after the heroin-like substance produced by the human brain at the point of orgasm. Anne Carlisle, who cowrote the screenplay, plays a lesbian punk model *and* a male homosexual punk model. As a woman, Carlisle discovers a special sexual power. At orgasm she can make her lover disappear into thin air, courtesy of some wonderful special effects. A subplot involves Otto von Wernherr, a government scientist investigating the UFO on Carlisle's roof. He holes up across the street in the apartment of a horny and hysterically funny socialite, Susan Doukas, whose very vocal expressions of frustration he balances with a great low-key performance. This offbeat film was directed by Slava Tsukerman, a classically trained Soviet-born filmmaker. His observations of modern America, as well as the beautiful New York City photography, are right on the money. LIQUID SKY won a cult following shortly after its release.

LITTLE BIG MAN

1970 147m c Western/War   ★★★★½
National General (U.S.)   PG/15

Dustin Hoffman *(Jack Crabb)*, Faye Dunaway *(Mrs. Pendrake)*, Martin Balsam *(Allardyce T. Merriweather)*, Richard Mulligan *(Gen. George A. Custer)*, Chief Dan George *(Old Lodge Skins)*, Jeff Corey *(Wild Bill Hickok)*, Aimee Eccles *(Sunshine)*, Kelly Jean Peters *(Olga)*, Carol Androsky *(Caroline)*, Robert Little Star *(Little Horse)*

p, Stuart Millar; d, Arthur Penn; w, Calder Willingham (based on the novel by Thomas Berger); ph, Harry Stradling Jr.; ed, Dede Allen; m, John Hammond; prod d, Dean Tavoularis; art d, Angelo Graham; fx, Dick Smith, Logan Frazee; cos, Dorothy Jeakins

AAN Best Supporting Actor: Chief Dan George

One of the most unconventional westerns ever made. This startling (if occasionally heavy-handed) revisionist tale is recounted in flashback by 121-year-old Jack Crabb (Dustin Hoffman), who claims to be the only survivor of the massacre at the Little Big Horn. As a boy, Jack is taken in by Cheyenne Indians and raised by Old Lodge Skins (Chief Dan George), but later he protests that he is white when his tribe is attacked by the cavalry, beginning a pattern of cultural fence-hopping that dominates the rest of his life. Over the course of a century or so, Jack earns the name Little Big Man for his bravery in battle; is taken in by a preacher and his randy wife (Faye Dunaway); becomes both an assistant to a cure-all-peddling drummer (Martin Balsam) and a less-than-successful gunfighter; nearly dies when Custer (Richard Mulligan) and his troops attack his tribe at the Washita River; turns to alcohol; and guides the Seventh Cavalry into the Little Big Horn massacre.

Shot twenty years before Kevin Costner's smugly pro-Indian DANCES WITH WOLVES, Arthur Penn's epic western brilliantly retells American history from the viewpoint of its victims. Based on the Thomas Berger novel, LITTLE BIG MAN retains much of Berger's wit but invests the material with a passionate indignation inspired by Vietnam—a quality most obvious in the film's recreation of the Washita massacre, with its unmistakable overtones of My Lai (note Penn's use of Asian-American extras in this scene). Even with Vietnam fast receding from the national consciousness, Penn's movie remains fascinating; cultural studies types will note its handling of, *inter alia*, racial/cultural identity (Crabb defines himself as Indian or white as convenience dictates, but he can't control how others define *him*) and the ideology of the American past (compare Penn's treatment of the traditional "captivity narrative" with THE SEARCHERS).

Hoffman is uncharacteristically charming in a demanding role; the supporting cast is uniformly excellent, particularly Chief Dan George as a befuddled patriarch who takes the supernatural as a matter of course. Like all wide-screen westerns, the film loses a lot on television.

LITTLE CAESAR

1931 80m bw Crime   ★★★★
First National (U.S.)   /PG

Edward G. Robinson *(Cesare Enrico Bandello/"Little Caesar")*, Douglas Fairbanks Jr. *(Joe Massara)*, Glenda Farrell *(Olga Strassoff)*, William Collier Jr. *(Tony Passa)*, Ralph Ince *(Diamond Pete Montana)*, George E. Stone *(Otero)*, Thomas Jackson *(Lt. Tom Flaherty)*, Stanley Fields *(Sam Vettori)*, Armand Kaliz *(DeVoss)*, Sidney Blackmer *(The Big Boy)*

p, Hal B. Wallis; d, Mervyn LeRoy; w, Robert N. Lee, Darryl F. Zanuck (uncredited), Francis Edwards Faragoh (uncredited), Robert Lord (based on the novel by W.R. Burnett); ph, Tony Gaudio; ed, Ray Curtiss; art d, Anton Grot; cos, Earl Luick

AAN Best Adapted Screenplay: Francis Faragoh, Robert N. Lee

LITTLE CAESAR now seems a bit dated and inelegant, but it is an indisputable landmark. Though not the first gangster film, it spawned the immensely popular gangster cycle of the 1930s and launched the career of one of the greatest icons of the genre—Edward G. Robinson.

This tough film still packs a considerable wallop largely due to the mesmerizing performance of Robinson as the thoroughly vicious Rico Bandello.

Rico Bandello is a dedicated killer and thief right from the opening scene. He disappears into a gas station and, after a flash of gunfire, emerges with the money from the till. His driver, Joe Massara (Douglas Fairbanks, Jr.), nervously wheels the coupe into the darkness. Later, Rico and Joe are in a diner, ordering "spaghetti and coffee for two," telegraphing their ethnicity to the audience. After reading in the newspaper about underworld big shots, Rico informs Joe of his ambition to become a rackets czar. He declares that he's not "just another mug." Rico is a man with a mission. He quickly goes about making his criminal dreams come true.

LITTLE CAESAR was one of the first sound films to portray the American gangster outside of prison walls, coming after such early prison stories as THE LAST MILE, THE BIG HOUSE, and NUMBERED MEN. Robinson's character is as ruthless as Al Capone, the real-life gangster upon whom Chicago author W.R. Burnett based the novel from which the film is adapted. Made for a then-hefty $700,000, the film was a box-office smash and typecast Robinson in the role of the gangster. Given free rein by Zanuck, director Mervyn LeRoy produced a fast-paced film that kept up with its lightning-fast star. Oddly, LITTLE CAESAR contains a minimum of explicit violence, although murderous intent is always lurking in Robinson's menacing face. The 37-year-old Robinson was not new to films; he had been acting in movies since 1923, though he was largely unnoticed. Wallis assigned Robinson the lead, but the sensitive actor found it difficult to adjust to the role of the killer, blinking wildly every time he had to fire a gun. LeRoy solved the problem by affixing little transparent bands of tape to Robinson's upper eyelids, so that when he did blast away, his eyes remained wide open; this trick had the added benefit of giving Robinson an even more menacing, heartless appearance.

LITTLE DORRIT

1988 360m c Comedy/Drama   ★★★★
Sands/Cannon (U.K.)   G/U

Alec Guinness *(William Dorrit)*, Derek Jacobi *(Arthur Clennam)*, Cyril Cusack *(Frederick Dorrit)*, Sarah Pickering *(Little Dorrit)*, Joan Greenwood *(Mrs. Clennam)*, Max Wall *(Flintwinch)*, Amelda Brown *(Fanny Dorrit)*, Daniel Chatto *(Tip Dorrit)*, Miriam Margolyes *(Flora Finching)*, Bill Fraser *(Mr. Casby)*

p, John Brabourne, Richard Goodwin; d, Christine Edzard; w, Christine Edzard (based on the novel by Charles Dickens); ph, Bruno de Keyzer; ed, Olivier Stockman, Fraser Maclean; m, Giuseppe Verdi; cos, Barbara Sonnex, Judith Loom, Joyce Carter, Jackie Smith, Sally Neale, Claudie Gastine, Danielle Garderes

AAN Best Supporting Actor: Alec Guinness; *AAN Best Adapted Screenplay:* Christine Edzard (screenplay)

Little Dorrit is one of Charles Dickens's greatest and least-read novels, and this massive, six-hour version by director-screenwriter Christine Edzard, essentially faithful to the work, is one of the finest of all Dickens screen adaptations. The film plays in two three-hour parts. Part I, "Nobody's Fault" (Dickens' original title), is told from the point of view of Jacobi, a middle-aged bachelor returning home to London after 20 years in China. Jacobi becomes interested in the case of Guinness, a man who has been locked in a debtors' prison for the last 25 years, and in his daughter, Pickering, a seamstress who works for Jacobi's forbidding mother. Impressed by their sad story, Jacobi sets out to help the man and his daughter to reclaim a fortune. Part II, "Little Dorrit's Story," told from the seamstress's point of view, begins with her birth in prison and follows her as she assumes the role of mother to her selfish family. When Jacobi arrives in England, she falls in love with him, though she knows he loves another. LITTLE DORRIT is *one* film in two feature-length parts. Part II is necessarily the stronger, developing themes and filling out the plot, but the two halves are interdependent. In Edzard's version, Dickens' Little Dorrit character takes on a much more forceful consciousness; she becomes, in a sense, the Dickensian conscience provided by the novel's third-person narration. Boasting a 211-member cast, LITTLE DORRIT is packed with fine performances—and best of all is veteran Dickensian Alec Guinness (GREAT EXPECTATIONS, OLIVER TWIST, SCROOGE).

LITTLE FOXES, THE

1941 115m bw Drama   ★★★½
RKO (U.S.)   /PG

Bette Davis (*Regina Hubbard Giddens*), Herbert Marshall (*Horace Giddens*), Teresa Wright (*Alexandra Giddens*), Richard Carlson (*David Hewitt*), Patricia Collinge (*Birdie Hubbard*), Dan Duryea (*Leo Hubbard*), Charles Dingle (*Ben Hubbard*), Carl Benton Reid (*Oscar Hubbard*), Jessie Grayson (*Addie*), John Marriott (*Cal*)

p, Samuel Goldwyn; d, William Wyler; w, Lillian Hellman, Arthur Kober, Dorothy Parker, Alan Campbell (based on a play by Lillian Hellman); ph, Gregg Toland; ed, Daniel Mandell; m, Meredith Willson; art d, Stephen Goosson; cos, Orry-Kelly

AAN Best Picture; AAN Best Actress: Bette Davis; AAN Best Supporting Actress: Patricia Collinge; AAN Best Supporting Actress: Teresa Wright; AAN Best Director: William Wyler; AAN Best Original Screenplay: Lillian Hellman; AAN Best Editing: Daniel Mandell; AAN Best Score: Meredith Willson; AAN Best Art Direction: Stephen Goosson (Art Direction), Howard Bristol (Interior Decoration)

Time has proven Bette Davis right—no-one could top Tallulah Bankhead's Broadway portrayal of the vituperative Regina Giddens, the central figure of Lillian Hellman's now creaking, but still compelling Deep South potboiler. During filming, William Wyler was often heard to say, "We'll have to get Bankhead." Would that he had. Davis, in an impulsive stampede to make the role her own, took an opposite track to the character. Or perhaps Wyler did; every Davis bio tells it differently. Either way, it's wrong. In her rice powder, with her mouth drawn into a tiny, hard line (it makes her look more beaked and birdlike than ever) she loses the hothouse-flower sensuality that Bankhead brought to her manipulations. And it was precisely *that* certain quality that justified Regina's ability to manipulate men to high heaven in the turn of the century South.

FOXES tells the story of the Hubbards (whose exploits are also detailed in ANOTHER PART OF THE FOREST [1948], from Hellman's prequel), as greedy a bunch as ever drank mint juleps. Regina's brothers (Dingle and Reid) ask her to persuade her husband Horace (Marshall) to supply the rest of the cash they need to build a cotton mill. Milking her position for all the leverage possible, Regina sends her daughter (Wright) to fetch Horace, recovering from a heart attack at a Baltimore sanitarium. The weakened man, however, proves a bigger hurdle than anyone had bargained for.

This is the third and last time Davis worked with Wyler, following the triumphs of JEZEBEL and THE LETTER. The furious battles enacted by the two on FOXES are Hollywood legend—a sad farewell to a legendary collaboration. Perhaps the rest of the principals didn't cotton to Davis's tantrums (having grown accustomed to Bankhead's); except for Wright, in her film debut, they look like wolves successfully moving in on her acting territory. Collinge, in fact, almost steals the movie. The other newcomer, Duryea, does move in; it's overkill that needed slapping down.

We are not, however, discounting FOXES's impressive technical achievement. Many of the sequences directed by Wyler and shot by cinematographer Toland (famed for his deep-focus work in CITIZEN KANE) have been hailed by film scholars, especially during the memorable murder scene (featuring Davis's Kabuki look). Orry-Kelly's costumes for Davis are either great or wrong. Somehow FOXES feels embalmed instead of lived; still we enjoy the drama done aloud.

LITTLE GIRL WHO LIVES DOWN THE LANE, THE

1976 91m c Thriller   ★★★½
Rank (Canada)   PG/AA

Jodie Foster (*Rynn Jacobs*), Martin Sheen (*Frank Hallet*), Alexis Smith (*Mrs. Hallet*), Mort Shuman (*Officer Miglioriti*), Scott Jacoby (*Mario Podesta*), Clesson Goodhue (*Bank Manager*), Hubert Noel, Jacques Famery (*Bank Clerks*), Mary Morter, Judie Wildman (*Tellers*)

p, Zev Braun; d, Nicolas Gessner; w, Laird Koenig (based on novel by Koenig); ph, Rene Verzier; ed, Yves Langlois; m, Christian Gaubert; art d, Robert Prevost; cos, Denis Sperdouklis, Valentino

This Canadian-made film, a star vehicle for the then 13-year-old Jodie Foster, is a disturbing, wonderfully acted, well-scripted, and suspenseful study of a murderous 13-year-old girl, Rynn (Foster). Living alone in her father's home, Rynn makes up stories that her father is away when in fact he is dead. She handles the bills, the upkeep, and her own survival, admirably putting into practice what her father taught her. When a snooping neighbor makes a nuisance of herself, Rynn knocks her down the stairs. Matter-of-factly, Rynn lets the cellar door close and gets back to her work. Soon the creepy Frank (Martin Sheen) is making a pest of himself, wanting both answers to his suspicions and Rynn's barely pubescent body. Meanwhile, Rynn becomes genuinely attracted to Mario (Scott Jacoby), a youngster her own age. Frank, knowing that something is odd about Rynn's situation, presses her for answers about her father, his insistence threatening to ruin the private, self-sustaining, child-as-adult world she has created with Mario. This leads to a fatal game of cat-and-mouse between Rynn and Frank. Tautly directed by Nicolas Gessner, the film is a showcase for the young Foster and she does not disappoint, turning in a slyly nuanced performance that is downright creepy and at the same time oddly innocent.

LITTLE MERMAID, THE

1989 82m c Animated/Children's/Musical   ★★★
Walt Disney Productions/Silver Screen Partners IV (U.S.) G/U

VOICES OF: Rene Auberjonois (*Louis*), Christopher Daniel Barnes (*Eric*), Jodi Benson (*Ariel*), Pat Carroll (*Ursula*), Paddi Edwards (*Flotsam & Jetsam*), Buddy Hackett (*Scuttle*), Jason Marin (*Flounder*), Kenneth Mars (*King Triton*), Edie McClurg (*Carlotta*), Will Ryan (*Seahorse*)

p, Howard Ashman, John Musker; d, John Musker, Ron Clements; w, John Musker, Ron Clements (based on the fairy tale by Hans Christian Andersen); ed, Mark Hester, John Carnochan ; m, Robby Merkin, Alan Menken; prod d, Maureen Donley; art d, Michael A. Peraza Jr., Donald A. Towns; fx, Mark Dindal; anim, Mark Henn, Glen Keane, Duncan Marjoribanks, Ruben Aquino, Andreas Deja, Matthew O'Callaghan

AA Best Score: Alan Menken; AA Best Song: Alan Menken (Music), Howard Ashman (Lyrics); AAN Best Song: Alan Menken (Music), Howard Ashman (Lyrics)

THE LITTLE MERMAID, Disney's 28th feature-length cartoon, is a lushly animated musical, very loosely based on the Hans Christian Andersen fairy tale, that was a smash hit at the box-office and features an Oscar-winning score by Alan Menken.

Princess Ariel lives in Mermaid City with her father, King Triton. Ariel is fascinated by human beings. Attracted by a fireworks display on a ship, Ariel sneaks aboard and falls in love at first sight with the handsome Prince Eric. When a violent storm destroys the ship, Ariel saves Eric's life, and he is smitten with her beautiful singing voice. The court composer, a crab named Sebastian, accidentally tells King Triton that Ariel is in love with a human, and Triton destroys all of her human possessions and forbids her to see Eric again. An evil seawitch named Ursula, who has been banished from Mermaid City by Triton, lures Ariel into a deal whereby she will be given human form, but will have to give Ursula her voice in return. If, after three days, Ariel cannot get Eric to bestow upon her a kiss, she will belong to Ursula.

THE LITTLE MERMAID was the first of Disney's new generation of animated musical-features (which would be quickly followed by BEAUTY AND THE BEAST and others) that marked a return to the studio's former glory days, at least in the eyes of the public, and most critics. The film features some undeniably impressive animation, particularly in the frightening scenes that Disney artists have always excelled at—the violent storms filled with swirling winds, lightning, and crashing waves. But just as undeniably, it also suffers from overly broad and juvenile humor, some sappy songs, and the "wide-eyed human" syndrome, wherein all the humans have huge saucer-eyes and the same constantly startled expression. Eric looks like a hunky fashion-model, while Ariel is drawn as a big-haired, denatured, Barbie-doll, despite her hourglass figure and skimpy seashell brassiere. As usual with Disney, the non-humans are much more interesting, and the various undersea creatures are quite amusing and very well-drawn, as is the whole underwater milieu. Overall, it's an enjoyable film, thankfully free of the computerized look of later Disney cartoons, but it really can't compare to the real Disney classics (which appealed equally to both kids and adults).

LITTLE PRINCESS, A

1995 97m c Children's/Drama ★★★
Baltimore Pictures/Mark Johnson Productions (U.S.) G/U

Eleanor Bron (*Miss Minchin*), Liam Cunningham (*Captain Crewe/Prince Rama*), Liesel Matthews (*Sara Crewe*), Rusty Schwimmer (*Amelia Minchin*), Arthur Malet (*Charles Randolph*), Vanessa Lee Chester (*Becky*), Errol Sitahal (*Ram Dass*), Heather DeLoach (*Ermengarde*), Taylor Fry (*Lavinia*), Darcie Bradford (*Jesse*)

p, Mark Johnson; d, Alfonso Cuaron; w, Richard LaGravenese, Elizabeth Chandler (based on the novel *Sara Crewe* by Frances Hodgson Burnett); ph, Emmanuel Lubezki; ed, Steven Weisberg; m, Patrick Doyle; prod d, Bo Welch; art d, Tom Duffield; fx, Alan E. Lorimer; cos, Judianna Makovsky

AAN Best Art Direction: Bo Welch (art direction), Cheryl Carasik (set decoration); *AAN Best Cinematography:* Emmanuel Lubezki

This new version of Frances Hodgson Burnett's children's classic boasts first-rate production values and a political sensitivity befitting the '90s, but it doesn't quite capture the magic of the 1939 Shirley Temple vehicle.

1914, Simla, India: Imaginative 10-year-old Sara Crewe (Liesel Matthews) lives with her wealthy, widowed father (Liam Cunningham), a British Army captain. Sara enjoys her life in exotic India, but the coming of the Great War destroys the tranquillity of Sara's life. Her father must rejoin his regiment, and places Sara in Miss Minchin's School for Girls in New York City. Stern headmistress Miss Minchin (Eleanor Bron) hates the girl, and when Sara's father is reported killed in battle, she launches a campaign to crush the Sara's resilient spirit.

A LITTLE PRINCESS is adapted respectably by screenwriters Richard LaGravenese and Elizabeth Chandler, meticulously produced, opulently designed—particularly in the colorful fantasy sequences—elegantly photographed by cinematographer Emmanuel Lubezki and adequately (in the case of Eleanor Bron, more than adequately) acted. While Shirley Temple is a more appealing youngster than newcomer Liesel Matthews, Matthews is both sassy and unabashedly emotional. And though the new LITTLE PRINCESS is a far darker affair than the 1939 version, Mexican-born director Alfonso Cuaron doesn't make it anywhere near as drab and moody as Agnieszka Holland's more artistically and commercially successful THE SECRET GARDEN.

LITTLE SHOP OF HORRORS

1986 88m c Comedy/Horror/Musical ★★★
Warner Bros. (U.S.) PG-13/PG

Rick Moranis (*Seymour Krelboin*), Ellen Greene (*Audrey*), Vincent Gardenia (*Mushnik*), Steve Martin (*Orin Scrivello*), Tichina Arnold (*Crystal*), Tisha Campbell (*Chiffon*), Michelle Weeks (*Ronette*), James Belushi (*Patrick Martin*), John Candy (*Wink Wilkinson*), Christopher Guest (*1st Customer*)

p, David Geffen; d, Frank Oz; w, Howard Ashman (based on the musical stage play by Howard Ashman); ph, Robert Paynter; ed, John Jympson; m, Alan Menken, Miles Goodman; prod d, Roy Walker; art d, Steve Spence; fx, Bran Ferren; chor, Pat Garrett; cos, Marit Allen

AAN Best Song: Alan Menken (Music), Howard Ashman (Lyrics); *AAN Best Visual Effects:* Lyle Conway, Bran Ferren, Martin Gutteridge

This is the multimillion-dollar movie version of the off-Broadway musical, which was based in turn on an old movie conceived and shot in a matter of days by Roger Corman. Although the plots (in which a carnivorous plant feeds on human flesh, causing its creator to kill to satisfy it) are virtually identical, much of the edge was taken off of the material in its transition from screen to stage to screen. The killer plant has been transformed into a being from outer space (rather than a warped hybrid created by the dimwitted Seymour in his basement). Big-budget and bloated, the film has none of the shabby charm of Corman's effort and is memorable only for a couple of decent tunes, a

parade of star cameos, some impressive special effects, and a wonderful performance from Greene as Audrey. Conway's special effects involved several generations of Audrey II, from a potted plant to a mammoth 12.5-foot-tall creature that takes over the entire florist shop. It weighed, at the close, more than 2,000 pounds and used almost 12 miles of cable. The most remarkable aspect of the device were the lips, perfectly in sync with the singing and dialogue. Although an impressive technical achievement, the film itself is a rather overblown and overhyped affair—which, for all its expensive excess, fails to recapture the spirit of the original.

LITTLE SHOP OF HORRORS, THE

1961 70m bw Comedy/Horror ★★★
Filmgroup (U.S.) /PG

Jonathan Haze (*Seymour Krelboin*), Jackie Joseph (*Audrey*), Mel Welles (*Gravis Mushnick*), Jack Nicholson (*Wilbur Force*), Dick Miller (*Fouch*), Myrtle Vail (*Winifred Krelboin*), Laiola Wendorf (*Mrs. Shiva*)

p, Roger Corman; d, Roger Corman; w, Charles B. Griffith; ph, Arch R. Dalzell; ed, Marshall Neilan Jr.; m, Fred Katz; art d, Daniel Haller

This is the ultimate Roger Corman super-low-budget cult favorite, also one of the funniest black comedies ever made. The plot details the sorry existence of a dim-witted schlepp, Haze, who works in Welles's Skid Row flower shop. To impress his girl, Joseph, Haze invents a flower he names Audrey, Jr. Soon the plant is all the rage among botanists. The only problem is that the little flower needs human blood to grow. After discovering this gruesome detail, and the fact that the plant can talk (when it's hungry it yells, "Feed me!"), Haze becomes slowly possessed by the flora and commits several murders in order to stop his plant's tummy from growling. With these feedings comes the plant's rapid growth; it soon overgrows the whole flower shop while bellowing "Feeeed meee!" in a monstrously loud and obnoxious voice. Poor Haze finds he can no longer handle his creation. While its story doesn't make for very funny reading, LITTLE SHOP OF HORRORS is a hilarious (and yes, quite silly) film filled to the brim with enough little vignettes and character quirks to sustain laughter throughout its brief 70-minute running time. Shot in two days by Corman, who was challenged by a studio employee to come up with a script and shoot a movie in the brief time remaining before the storefront set was torn down (it had been left standing from another production), LITTLE SHOP OF HORRORS is surprisingly well shot and performed. Corman contacted screenwriter Chuck Griffith from his other camp hit, A BUCKET OF BLOOD, and together they hacked out the killer plant story in less than a week. Aided by on-the-set inspiration, Corman, his crew, and the cast (including a very young Jack Nicholson in a side-splitting cameo as a masochistic dental patient begging for more pain) threw together a small masterpiece of taut, economical filmmaking. The story was revived in the 1980s as a very successful Off-Broadway musical, and a film version of the musical was released in 1986.

LITTLE WOMEN

1994 115m c Drama/Historical/Romance ★★★½
Di Novi Pictures/Columbia (U.S.) PG/U

Winona Ryder (*Jo March*), Susan Sarandon (*Marmee March*), Gabriel Byrne (*Professor Friedrich Baer*), Eric Stoltz (*John Brooke*), Samantha Mathis (*Amy as 16-Year-Old*), Trini Alvarado (*Meg*), Kirsten Dunst (*Amy as 12-Year-Old*), Claire Danes (*Beth*), Christian Bale (*Laurie*), Mary Wickes (*Aunt March*)

p, Denise DiNovi; d, Gillian Armstrong; w, Robin Swicord (based on the novel by Louisa May Alcott); ph, Geoffrey Simpson; ed, Nicholas Beauman; m, Thomas Newman; prod d, Jan Roelfs; art d, Richard Hudolin; cos, Colleen Atwood

AAN Best Actress: Winona Ryder; *AAN Best Costume Design:* Colleen Atwood; *AAN Best Original Score:* Thomas Newman

Director Gillian Armstrong's feminist spin on classic material retains the moving humanity of Louisa May Alcott's novel while reworking it with welcome freshness.

LITTLE WOMEN introduces us to the March family, a struggling, close-knit clan living in Concord, Massachusetts, at the time of the Civil War. The eldest daughter, Meg (Trini Alvarado), is pretty, conventional, and vain. Jo (Winona Ryder) is a hot-tempered tomboy who chafes against Victorian restraints on young women and dreams of a great literary career. Beth (Claire Danes) is musical and pathologically shy, a saint on earth. Amy (Kirsten Dunst, then Samantha Mathis) is artistic and amusingly selfish. Their beloved Marmee (Susan Sarandon) is the anchor that stabilizes the family while her husband is away fighting in the Civil War. The Marches have seen better days financially, but the spirit and invention of the girls are unquenchable as they struggle towards adulthood and overcome their individual weaknesses.

Robin Swicord's screenplay adaptation is very free, adding details of Alcott's life to the familiar events of the novel. At times, the overriding political correctness is a bit heavy-handed (one doesn't recall the Marches being *quite* so taken up with the cause of the "blacks," as they are anachronistically referred to here, or with women's suffrage). Quibbles aside, Armstrong can only be praised for her firm control over the material, steadfast refusal to slip into bathos, and acute visual and emotional sense. The strength of her vision overrides some acting weaknesses as well as the superfluous revisionism; visually, it is easily one of the most beautiful movies of the year. Geoffrey Simpson's camera records the four seasons with remarkable vividness, and the production is appropriately rich, full of dark wood surfaces, comforting quilts, and gleaming cook pots and china.

LITTLE WOMEN

1933   117m   bw   Drama   ★★★★½
RKO   (U.S.)   /U

Katharine Hepburn *(Jo)*, Joan Bennett *(Amy)*, Paul Lukas *(Prof. Fritz Bhaer)*, Edna May Oliver *(Aunt March)*, Jean Parker *(Beth)*, Frances Dee *(Meg)*, Henry Stephenson *(Mr. Laurence)*, Douglass Montgomery *(Laurie)*, John Lodge *(Brooke)*, Spring Byington *(Marmee)*

p, Kenneth MacGowan; d, George Cukor; w, Sarah Y. Mason, Victor Heerman (based on the novel by Louisa May Alcott); ph, Henry Gerrard; ed, Jack Kitchin; m, Max Steiner; art d, Van Nest Polglase; fx, Harry Redmond; cos, Walter Plunkett

AAN Best Picture; *AAN Best Director*: George Cukor; *AA Best Adapted Screenplay*: Victor Heerman, Sarah Y. Mason

This unabashedly sentimental adaptation of Louisa May Alcott's novel remains, to this day, an example of Hollywood's best filmmaking, as it tells the captivating Civil War-era story of four independent New England sisters—Jo (Katharine Hepburn), Amy (Joan Bennett), Meg (Frances Dee), and Beth (Jean Parker) March. Jo, who wants to leave home and become a writer, stays on for the good of the family, but when Meg plans to marry, Jo leaves for New York, fearing that the family will disintegrate. There she meets a professor who helps her with both her anger and her writing. Meanwhile, Amy falls in love with and marries Jo's old sweetheart (Douglass Montgomery). Beth, however, is dying, and Jo returns to be with her during her last days.

Sarah Mason and Victor Heerman's script called for great production values, and RKO provided them, foreshadowing David O. Selznick's opulent treatment of life on the Southern side of the Civil War, GONE WITH THE WIND. The sets, costumes, lighting, and direction by George Cukor all contribute greatly to this magnificent film, but the performances, especially Hepburn's, are what make the simple story so moving. There are laughs and tears aplenty in this movie, which presents a slice of American history in a way that children will find palatable. Released during the depths of the Depression, LITTLE WOMEN buoyed Americans' spirits. It still does.

LIVES OF A BENGAL LANCER, THE

1935   109m   bw   Adventure/War   ★★★★
Paramount   (U.S.)   /U

Gary Cooper *(Lt. Alan McGregor)*, Franchot Tone *(Lt. John Forsythe)*, Richard Cromwell *(Lt. Donald Stone)*, Guy Standing *(Col. Stone)*, C. Aubrey Smith *(Maj. Hamilton)*, Monte Blue *(Hamzulia Khan)*, Kathleen Burke *(Tania Volkanskaya)*, Colin Tapley *(Lt. Barrett)*, Douglas Dumbrille *(Mohammed Khan)*, Akim Tamiroff *(Emir)*

p, Louis D. Lighton; d, Henry Hathaway; w, Waldemar Young, John Balderston, Achmed Abdullah, Grover Jones, William Slavens McNutt (based on the novel by Maj. Francis Yeats-Brown); ph, Charles

Lang, Ernest B. Schoedsack; ed, Ellsworth Hoagland; m, Milan Roder; art d, Hans Dreier, Roland Anderson; chor, LeRoy Prinz; cos, Travis Banton

AAN Best Picture; *AAN Best Director*: Henry Hathaway; *AAN Best Screenplay*: Achmed Abdullah, John L. Balderston, Grover Jones, William Slavens McNutt, Waldemar Young; *AAN Best Editing*: Ellsworth Hoagland; *AAN Art Direction*: Hans Dreier, Roland Anderson; *AAN Best Sound*: Franklin Hansen

Set in northwest India, this rousing adventure film was hailed by many as the greatest war movie ever made at the time of its release. Under Henry Hathaway's adroit direction, Gary Cooper stars as 41st Bengal Lancers member Lt. McGregor, a seasoned frontier fighter who doesn't hesitate to speak his mind or violate orders—a man first and a soldier second. His commanding officer, Col. Stone (Sir Guy Standing), is his very opposite, a total military man who will soon be retiring. In order to keep alive the name of Stone in the regiment, a fellow officer, Maj. Hamilton (C. Aubrey Smith), has Stone's son (Richard Cromwell) transferred into the unit, along with another new officer, Lt. Forsythe (Franchot Tone). The two new arrivals get a quick initiation, as Col. Stone and British intelligence try to prevent a planned Indian uprising by blocking a local chieftain's attempt to steal two million rounds of ammunition from the friendly Emir of Gopal (Akim Tamiroff).

The script is filled with plenty of humor and builds two strong, honest friendships—McGregor and Forsythe have a great buddy rapport while the cold and stubborn Col. Stone opens up to his cub soldier son. The Indian atmosphere is lovingly captured by Hathaway's direction (his love of the exotic appears to have been heavily influenced by his association with Josef von Sternberg) and by Charles Lang and Ernest B. Schoedsack's photography (incorporating some stock footage previously shot by Schoedsack). While the glorification of British imperialism hangs over the picture, the portrayal of the Indians is fortunately less offensive than in other Hollywood films such as 1939's GUNGA DIN.

LIVING DAYLIGHTS, THE

1987   130m   c   Spy   ★★★½
Eon/UA   (U.K.)   PG

Timothy Dalton *(James Bond)*, Maryam D'Abo *(Kara Malovy)*, Jeroen Krabbe *(Gen. Georgi Koskov)*, Joe Don Baker *(Brad Whitaker)*, John Rhys-Davies *(Gen. Leonid Pushkin)*, Art Malik *(Kamran Shah)*, Andreas Wisniewski *(Necros)*, Thomas Wheatley *(Saunders)*, Desmond Llewelyn *(Q)*, Robert Brown *(M)*

p, Albert R. Broccoli, Michael G. Wilson; d, John Glen; w, Richard Maibaum, Michael G. Wilson (based on a story by Ian Fleming); ph, Alec Mills; ed, John Grover, Peter Davies; m, John Barry; prod d, Peter Lamont; art d, Terry Ackland-Snow; fx, John Richardson; cos, Emma Porteous

Celebrating the 25th year of the Bond series, THE LIVING DAYLIGHTS introduces the fourth actor to take on the role of 007, Timothy Dalton, a 40-year-old veteran of the English stage whose Bond is more human and serious than that of the wry Sean Connery and the droll Roger Moore. Scripters Richard Maibaum and Michael G. Wilson have also shifted the emphasis away from glitz and gadgetry and back to the business of spying. Bond is sent to Czechoslovakia to assist with the defection of Gen. Georgi Koskov (Jeroen Krabbe), a KGB higher-up, whose escape is accomplished in a specially designed vehicle that whisks him through the trans-Siberian natural gas pipeline to Austria. Meanwhile, Bond falls for the beautiful Kara Malovy (Maryam d'Abo), a cellist who is a victim of KGB intrigue, and later he helps her make a breathtaking escape, ultimately using her priceless cello as a sled. Once in the West, Koskov is seemingly abducted by the KGB, but Bond suspects otherwise and eventually learns that the Soviet is in cahoots with Brad Whitaker (Joe Don Baker), a psychopathic American arms dealer who, unlike the standard Bond villain, is interested in becoming fabulously wealthy but not in ruling the world. Bond's danger-filled attempts to put an end to Whitaker's scheming take him and Kara from Vienna to Tangier and eventually into the middle of the war in Afghanistan. Made for $30 million, this feast for the eyes has more action than any of the other Bond films and is certainly one of the best of them. Dalton is an engaging Bond, d'Abo is coolly alluring, and Krabbe is the epitome of the double-dealing spy master. Only Baker disappoints, hamming up his villain. Director John Glen is an old hand at James Bond films, having worked on three other 007 movies. He knows this popular spy well and does him great service in this well-paced film.

LOCAL HERO

1983 111m c Comedy	★★★★½
Enigma/Goldcrest (U.K.)	PG

Burt Lancaster *(Happer)*, Peter Riegert *(Mac)*, Fulton Mackay *(Ben)*, Denis Lawson *(Urquhart)*, Norman Chancer *(Moritz)*, Peter Capaldi *(Oldsen)*, Rikki Fulton *(Geddes)*, Alex Norton *(Watt)*, Jenny Seagrove *(Marina)*, Jennifer Black *(Stella)*

p, David Puttnam; d, Bill Forsyth; w, Bill Forsyth; ph, Chris Menges; ed, Michael Bradsell; m, Mark Knopfler; prod d, Roger Murray-Leach; art d, Richard James, Adrienne Atkinson, Frank Walsh, Ian Watson; fx, Wally Veevers

Charming, whimsical, and practically perfect, LOCAL HERO reminds us of the great pleasures that British comedy used to routinely provide. This is the greatest Ealing comedy never made: a quirky character comedy with a skillful use of location that is sweetly reminiscent of WHISKEY GALORE!. A discerning eye may even spot a wee bit of the magical Powell-Pressburger ethos as expressed in I KNOW WHERE I'M GOING. However the offbeat sensibility on display here is ultimately distinctively that of Scottish filmmaker Bill Forsyth (GREGORY'S GIRL, THAT SINKING FEELING, COMFORT AND JOY, HOUSEKEEPING).

Burt Lancaster gets star billing as the loony head of a huge oil company in Texas, a tycoon so ambivalent about his success that he has a psychiatrist (Norman Chancer) come in regularly and insult him. Bored with business success, astronomy has become his great passion. The true protagonist of the film is Mac (Peter Riegert), an ambitious young executive of the oil company, who is dispatched to Scotland to buy an entire town so the company can drill for North Sea oil. An important side mission is to keep watching the sky for anything interesting. The utterly charming remote little coastal town is largely controlled by Urquhart (Dennis Lawson), a sharp but good-natured lawyer-innkeeper. Victor (Christopher Rozycki), a Soviet trawler captain, makes regular stops at the village, where Urquhart conducts sundry investments for him in real estate and securities. The obvious plot turn would be to show the Americans as nasty and rapacious, but it turns out that the Scots would be only too happy to depart the area if the price were right. Throughout the film, nothing is quite what it seems to Mac, and the denouement is wonderfully unexpected.

The Scottish landscape is gorgeous, soothing, and handsomely shot. The casting, down to the smallest role, is just right. Lancaster gives one of his best performances in a parody of the role he's played straight so many times before—the blustering industrial mogul. Scottish writer-director Bill Forsyth has outdone himself with this funny, touching, and original film. Don't miss this magical treat. (Incidentally this film served as a MAJOR source of inspiration for the hit CBS television series, "Northern Exposure.")

LODGER, THE

1944 84m bw Thriller	★★★★
Fox (U.S.)	/A

Merle Oberon *(Kitty)*, George Sanders *(John Garrick)*, Laird Cregar *(The Lodger)*, Cedric Hardwicke *(Robert Burton)*, Sara Allgood *(Ellen)*, Aubrey Mather *(Supt. Sutherland)*, Queenie Leonard *(Daisy)*, David Clyde *(Sgt. Bates)*, Helena Pickard *(Anne Rowley)*, Lumsden Hare *(Dr. Sheridan)*

p, Robert Bassler; d, John Brahm; w, Barre Lyndon (based on the novel by Marie Belloc Lowndes); ph, Lucien Ballard; ed, J. Watson Webb; m, Hugo Friedhofer; art d, James Basevi, John Ewing; fx, Fred Sersen; chor, Kenny Williams

Cregar is absolutely chilling in this Jack the Ripper tale, perhaps the best film made about Bloody Jack. THE LODGER's re-creation of Victorian London is soaked with fog, with cobblestones sweating and

gaslights flickering as blood-chilling screams pierce the night air and a dark figure goes running. Oberon is a beautiful singer whose parents, Allgood and Hardwicke, rent a room to Cregar. The mysterious lodger tells them he won't be joining them for breakfast, lunch, or dinner, because he works at night. During the night, Cregar slips out into the fog carrying a little black bag; in the early hours, he can be heard pacing back and forth in his rooms—which are always kept locked, and where he performs what he terms "experiments." Cregar eyes Oberon and fences with her friend Sanders, a Scotland Yard inspector developing new criminology techniques, but, in the end, he cannot resist killing the lovely Oberon, as he has killed so many others. Before he can murder her, however, the police and Sanders interrupt the attack and chase Cregar wildly through a theater. Trapped like a bear, salivating and maniacal, Cregar hurls himself through a huge window and into the Thames to drown rather than surrender.

This ending is not in keeping with that of the film's source material, the superlative novel written by Marie Belloc Lowndes. In addition, THE LODGER, unlike the novel, leaves no doubt that Cregar's character is Jack the Ripper. The huge actor is superb in this grand *film noir*; he and Sanders would almost repeat their parts in the similar HANGOVER SQUARE, also directed by John Brahm. (Only 28 at the time, Cregar longed to be a matinee idol and, shortly after the release of this film, went on a crash water diet and literally starved himself to death.) THE LODGER remakes the Alfred Hitchcock silent film starring Ivor Novello, and is probably better. Brahm's directs with a taut rein, the script is brilliant, the photography by Lucien Ballard (Oberon's husband-to-be) is a marvel of fluid action, and the whole is mightily enhanced by Hugo Friedhofer's strange and unnerving score.

LOLA
(DONNA DI VITA)

1961 90m bw Drama	★★★
Rome-Paris-Euro Intl. (France/Italy)	/X

Anouk Aimee *(Lola)*, Marc Michel *(Roland)*, Elina Labourdette *(Mme. Desnoyers)*, Alan Scott *(Frankie)*, Annie Duperoux *(Cecile)*, Jacques Harden *(Michel)*, Margo Lion *(Jeanne, Michel's Mother)*, Catherine Lutz *(Claire, the Waitress)*, Corinne Marchand *(Daisy)*, Yvette Anziani *(Mme. Frederique)*

p, Carlo Ponti, Georges de Beauregard; d, Jacques Demy; w, Jacques Demy; ph, Raoul Coutard; ed, Anne-Marie Cotret, Monique Teisseire; m, Michel Legrand, Johann Sebastian Bach, Wolfgang Amadeus Mozart, Carl Maria von Weber; art d, Bernard Evein

Free-flowing debut feature from French director Jacques Demy who, with his wife, director Agnes Varda, flourished during the New Wave. Because of its abundance of sweeping camera movement (superbly engineered by Raoul Coutard), the film has often been called a musical without music. (Demy would later go to Hollywood and make a real musical with Gene Kelly.) Aimee plays the title role, a cabaret singer who awaits the return of Harden, her husband who has been away for seven years. In the meantime she has a few affairs, her strongest affections going to childhood friend Michel. Michel has dreams of settling down with Aimee, but those are shattered when Harden returns and sweeps Aimee away in his glaring white Cadillac. The picture is filled with cinematic allusions (a fondness of French New Wave directors) to Robert Bresson, Gary Cooper, Max Ophuls (especially his camerawork), and Josef von Sternberg. Demy received a helping hand from Jean-Luc Godard, who offered his talents as a production consultant.

LOLA MONTES

1955 110m c Drama	★★★★★
Gamma/Florida/Union (France/West Germany)	/A

Martine Carol *(Lola Montes)*, Peter Ustinov *(Circus Master)*, Anton Walbrook *(Ludwig I, King of Bavaria)*, Ivan Desny *(Lt. James)*, Will Quadflieg *(Franz Liszt)*, Oskar Werner *(Student)*, Lise Delamare *(Mrs. Craigie)*, Henri Guisol *(Maurice)*, Paulette Dubost *(Josephine)*, Helena Manson *(James' Sister)* d, Max Ophuls; w, Max Ophuls, Jacques Natanson, Franz Geiger, Annette Wademant (based on the unpublished novel *La Vie Extraordinaire de Lola Montes* by Cecil Saint-Laurent); ph, Christian Matras; ed, Madeleine Gug; m, Georges Auric; art d, Jean d'Eaubonne, Willy Schatz; cos, Georges Annenkov, Marcel Escoffier

Andrew Sarris in 1963 dubbed this film the greatest ever made, and although he's noted for his quirky opinions, he's no fool. A masterpiece, LOLA MONTES is certainly director Max Ophuls' greatest achievement. In flashback, we take a fascinating look at the life of the passionate yet oddly passive title character (Carol, more perfect in the part than she could possibly have fathomed). Introduced by a New Orleans circus master (Ustinov), the aging Lola answers (or has answered for her) personal questions from the audience for a small fee. The ringmaster tells of her many romances throughout Europe, including one with Franz Liszt (Quadflieg) and another with the king of Bavaria (Walbrook). In the last scene, Lola (who throughout has been made to perform various acts like a well-trained seal) stands atop a high platform, preparing for a dangerous jump. Her health is as precarious as her position, yet the ringmaster removes the safety net. The finale is unforgettable.

Along with Michael Powell's BLACK NARCISSUS, this is one of the most gorgeous films ever shot in color. Eastmancolor generally pales beside Technicolor; leave it to Ophuls to make the most of it. Ditto the use of CinemaScope, which Ophuls didn't want and tried to negate by using pillars and curtains at the edges of the frame. The effect is to frame the whole affair as a performance, and Ophuls' innate visual flair makes shot after shot (e.g. the descending chandeliers at the opening) a stunning use of widescreen. He even knows when to ditch both resources, as Lola's most intimate moments are signaled with a ghostly blue monochrome and a tight closeup with most of the frame in black. His customary genius with the camera has rarely been on better display, as he dizzyingly dollies 360 degrees around the trapped, immobile Lola while the exploitative ringmaster spins her platform. Never cutting when camera movement will do, Ophuls tilts, tracks and cranes magnificently, embodying Lola's flashback motto, "For me, life is movement." By contrast, the overwhelmingly cluttered *mise en scene* of the circus all but smothers the degraded courtesan.

Carol doesn't appear young enough as the teen-aged Lola nor does she look really ravaged at the finale, but her masklike quality allows Ophuls a great chance to project, indulging the French fondness for casting Woman *as* Cinema. Wolbrook is quietly heartrending as the aging monarch, and Werner, as a young student and sex interlude for Lola, displays the promise he would later fulfill so well. Top honors, though, go to the magnificent Ustinov, who, two Oscars elsewhere notwithstanding, has never done anything better. Both heartless and tender to Lola, abusive and always on the verge of falling in love, his rueful expression and biting wit speak volumes that otherwise never surface. A film whose power is in the image itself, the endlessly amazing LOLA MONTES explores the magic (and the cost) of illusion as few films have ever done.

LOLITA

1962 152m bw Drama ★★★★
Seven Arts/A.A./Anya/Trans World (U.S./U.K.) /X

James Mason *(Humbert Humbert)*, Sue Lyon *(Lolita Haze)*, Shelley Winters *(Charlotte Haze)*, Peter Sellers *(Clare Quilty)*, Marianne Stone *(Vivian Darkbloom)*, Diana Decker *(Jean Farlow)*, Jerry Stovin *(John Farlow)*, Gary Cockrell *(Dick)*, Suzanne Gibbs *(Mona Farlow)*, Roberta Shore *(Lorna)*
p, James B. Harris; d, Stanley Kubrick; w, Vladimir Nabokov (based on the novel by Nabokov); ph, Oswald Morris; ed, Anthony Harvey; m, Nelson Riddle; art d, Bill Andrews; cos, Gene Coffin

AAN Best Adapted Screenplay: Vladimir Nabokov

A fascinating if problematic early film from Stanley Kubrick, perhaps the most obsessive of the great auteurs of the 1960s, made just on the cusp of a run of cinematic masterpieces. Here Vladimir Nabakov adapts his own controversial satirical novel about the obsessive love a British middle aged professor develops for a 12-year-old girl. While the novel outraged many bluenoses, the film advances the age of the "nymphet" to about 15 thereby neutralizing much of of the controversy. It's quite long—too long—possibly as a result of having Nabokov do his own screen adaptation. Nabakov's novels are so intensely concerned with

language that one would expect that they would be particularly difficult to translate to the screen. LOLITA, a great grey comedy of the 1950s, succeeds in carefully setting up and knocking down the shibboleths of the silent generation.

James Mason is the smitten professor, Humbert Humbert, in love with the American girl, Lolita (Sue Lyon). Shelly Winters is the vulgar mother with misguided intellectual aspirations who is attracted to Humbert. The ever resourceful Peter Sellers, with a great American accent and a succession of disguises, is a standout as Quilty. The scene in which he explains himself to Mason is a small masterpiece of the acting art. Mason and Winters are less showy but equally impressive while the young Lyons, sadly, is only barely adequate.

The film is not particularly shocking or titillating; the most erotic scene in the film is a pedicure. Kubrick exhibited great subtlety (he had to, or they'd have given this one a hard time in the theaters)—perhaps too much subtlety. The script was nominated for an Oscar.

LONE STAR

1996 138m c Drama ★★★★
Rio Dulce, Inc./Castle Rock Entertainment (U.S.) R/

Chris Cooper *(Sam Deeds)*, Elizabeth Pena *(Pilar Cruz)*, Joe Morton *(Delmore Payne)*, Miriam Colon *(Mercedes Cruz)*, Clifton James *(Mayor Hollis Pogue)*, Kris Kristofferson *(Sheriff Charley Wade)*, Ron Canada *(Otis Payne)*, Matthew McConaughey *(Buddy Deeds)*, Frances McDormand *(Bunny)*, Eddie Robinson *(Chet Payne)*
p, R. Paul Miller, Maggie Renzi; d, John Sayles; w, John Sayles; ph, Stuart Dryburgh; ed, John Sayles; m, Mason Daring; prod d, Dan Bishop; art d, Kyler Black; fx, Jack Bennett; cos, Shay Cunliffe

AAN Best Original Screenplay: John Sayles

From stubbornly independent writer/director John Sayles, an attempted Great American Epic that falls only slightly short of its immoderate ambitions.

Nearly 40 years after the mysterious disappearance of brutal Sheriff Charley Wade (Kris Kristofferson), his skeletal remains are unearthed outside the tiny border town of Frontera, Texas. Rio County's latest sheriff, Sam Deeds (Chris Cooper), begins to suspect not only that Wade was murdered, but also that he died at the hands of the late Sheriff Buddy Deeds (Matthew McConaughey), a local hero and Sam's own father. This Oedipal mystery serves as the pretext for a much broader investigation of the substance of the American past. In what is easily his most accomplished film to date, Sayles aims to show how authority uses history to construct the borders that separate countries, communities, and individuals. The film stumbles a bit towards the end (some deeply rooted conflicts are implausibly resolved), but terrific performances from a large cast—particularly Elizabeth Pena as Sam's childhood sweetheart—smooth over the rough spots.

LONELINESS OF THE LONG DISTANCE RUNNER, THE

1962 104m bw Drama ★★★★
Woodfall/Bryanston/Seven Arts (U.K.) /15

Tom Courtenay *(Colin Smith)*, Michael Redgrave *(The Governor)*, Avis Bunnage *(Mrs. Smith)*, Peter Madden *(Mr. Smith)*, James Bolam *(Mike)*, Julia Foster *(Gladys)*, Topsy Jane *(Audrey)*, Dervis Ward *(Detective)*, Raymond Dyer *(Gordon)*, Alec McCowen *(Brown)*
p, Tony Richardson; d, Tony Richardson; w, Alan Sillitoe (based on his story); ph, Walter Lassally; ed, Anthony Gibbs; m, John Addison; prod d, Ralph Brinton; art d, Ted Marshall; cos, Sophie Harris

It was considered chic among cinephiles in the 1960s to denigrate British stage and film director Tony Richardson, but on balance he was responsible for as many important British films in these years as anyone else. One of the best of the British Angry Young Man films, THE LONELINESS OF THE LONG DISTANCE RUNNER concerns Courtenay, an ill-educated youth who is sentenced to a reformatory after robbing a bakery. The borstal's governor, Redgrave, a great believer in the rehabilitative powers of sports, is delighted to learn that Courtenay is a natural distance runner and encourages him to train for a big meet with a local public school, promising him special privileges in exchange for a victory. Most of the film is taken up with Courtenay's training, during which he flashes back to the events and relationships that have brought him to this point in his life. When the big race finally arrives, Courtenay easily outclasses his competitors, but at the finish line he shocks the governor with an unexpected act of defiance. Adapted by Alan Sillitoe from his own short story and masterfully directed by Richardson, this poignant film was also the auspicious film debut of Courtenay, whose excellent performance earned him the British Academy's Most Promising Newcomer award.

LONELY ARE THE BRAVE

1962 107m bw Western   ★★★★
Universal (U.S.)   /A

Kirk Douglas *(Jack Burns)*, Gena Rowlands *(Jerri Bondi)*, Walter Matthau *(Sheriff Johnson)*, Michael Kane *(Paul Bondi)*, Carroll O'Connor *(Hinton)*, William Schallert *(Harry)*, Karl Swenson *(Rev. Hoskins)*, George Kennedy *(Guitierrez)*, Dan Sheridan *(Deputy Glynn)*, Bill Raisch *("One Arm")*

p, Edward Lewis; d, David Miller; w, Dalton Trumbo (based on the novel *Brave Cowboy* by Edward Abbey); ph, Philip Lathrop; ed, Leon Barsha, Edward Mann; m, Jerry Goldsmith; art d, Alexander Golitzen, Robert E. Smith

Dalton Trumbo wrote this elegy to the western. Kirk Douglas gives one of his finest performances as an out-of-place cowboy in the modern west—almost like a time traveller. The theme of the film is eloquently set up by the opening of the film in which we see Douglas reclining beneath a clear and spacious western sky. The peace and quiet is suddenly disrupted by the sound of a jet plane passing overhead. This brings a wry smile to the old cowboy's face. He rides his horse into Albuquerque to visit friends Kane and Rowlands. Rowlands tells him that her husband has been jailed for helping Mexicans enter the US illegally. Douglas starts a brawl in a saloon to get put into jail; there Douglas offers his friend Kane help in breaking out, but Kane tells Douglas that he wants to serve his brief time, intends to play out his hand with the law, and refuses to become a fugitive. Douglas is hurt but undaunted. He breaks out himself and heads for the hills, pursued by the compassionate technocrat sheriff Matthau and a posse.

Douglas is superb as the cowboy who will not yield to the modern world. Miller's direction is excellent, this being the finest film in his generally ineven career. Matthau is also convincing as the understanding sheriff who tries his best to capture a man he does not want to see locked up. Lathrop's sharp black-and-white photography and Goldsmith's evocative score add measurably to this outstanding production. There is one particularly memorable scene as Douglas and his good old horse attempt to cross a busy highway with the eighteen wheelers barrelling by. It will stay with you forever.

LONG DAY CLOSES, THE

1992 82m c Biography/Drama   ★★★★
British Film Institute/Film Four International (U.K.)   PG/

Marjorie Yates *(Mother)*, Leigh McCormack *(Bud)*, Anthony Watson *(Kevin)*, Nick Lamont *(John)*, Ayse Owens *(Helen)*, Tina Malone *(Edna)*, Jimmy Wilde *(Curly)*, Robin Polley *(Mr. Nicholls)*, Peter Ivatts *(Mr. Bushell)*, Joy Blakeman *(Frances)*

p, Olivia Stewart; d, Terence Davies; w, Terence Davies; ph, Michael Coulter; ed, William Diver; m, Bob Last, Robert Lockhart; prod d, Christopher Hobbs; art d, Kave Naylor; cos, Monica Howe

THE LONG DAY CLOSES vividly demonstrates the redemptive power of alternative modes of cinematic storytelling, even as it celebrates the glories of classical Hollywood movies.

Without a plot in any conventional sense, or traditionally articulated characters, this resonant slice of British family life in the 50s is infinitely more affecting than most conventional domestic dramas. Ironically, the film achieves some of its most sublime effects while depicting its young protagonist listening to American pop songs, watching his family taking part in group singalongs at the local pub, and—most importantly—in rapt contemplation of movies. The filmmaker's alter ego is the fey, lonely Bud (Leigh McCormack), an 11-year-old boy whose drab life is immeasurably more enriched by

going to the movies than by attending school or church. Rarely has the mere act of spectatorship been so convincingly rendered as to suggest spiritual transfiguration.

Director Terence Davies effectively evokes the sounds and textures of post-WWII working-class life in England's Liverpool. At times, looking at THE LONG DAY CLOSES feels like leafing through someone else's old family album—indeed, much of the striking imagery has the quality of period photographs. This is due to an expressive deployment of long and often static takes, shadowy sculptural lighting, and a rich yet muted color scheme that suggests old three-strip Technicolor. Both this film and Davies's 1988 DISTANT VOICES, STILL LIVES are loosely autobiographical: whereas the earlier film was a very dark, impressionistic chronicle of Davies' family life in the 40s, before his birth and during his early childhood, the more sanguine follow-up covers the quiet period in the mid-50s when he became a dedicated moviegoer.

LONG DAY'S JOURNEY INTO NIGHT

1962 174m bw Drama   ★★★★★
Landau (U.S.)   /A

Katharine Hepburn *(Mary Tyrone)*, Ralph Richardson *(James Tyrone, Sr.)*, Jason Robards Jr. *(James Tyrone, Jr.)*, Dean Stockwell *(Edmund Tyrone)*, Jeanne Barr *(Cathleen)*

p, Ely Landau, Jack J. Dreyfus Jr.; d, Sidney Lumet; w, (based on the play by Eugene O'Neill); ph, Boris Kaufman; ed, Ralph Rosenblum; m, Andre Previn; prod d, Richard Sylbert; art d, Richard Sylbert; cos, Motley

AAN Best Actress: Katharine Hepburn

O'Neill's greatest play is brought to the screen with an overpowering wealth of talent: Hepburn, Richardson, and Robards give magnificent, once-in-a-lifetime performances as members of the doomed Tyrone family. The playwright described his autobiographical work as "a play of old sorrow, written in tears and blood."

The setting is one long, long day and night in the year 1912 at the Tyrone summer home in New London, Connecticut. The stingy senior Tyrone, James (Richardson), an impoverished youth turned fine Shakespearean actor, has spent years playing the same role over and over again in a commercial play simply for the money. His wife Mary (Hepburn) has just returned from a sanitarium. She is all lady, an Irish Catholic with strong moral principles, but she is also strangely withdrawn, partly as a result of the drug addiction which began when she was treated by cheap quack doctors. Elder son Jamie (Robards) has attempted to follow his father into the acting profession but, failing miserably, takes solace in drink, becoming a cynic who would rather destroy all around him than show his true feelings. Younger son Edmund (Stockwell), a budding writer, is recovering from tuberculosis and has spent time in a second-rate institution that his tightwad father sent him to in order to save money. As the day wears on, painful truths and long-buried resentments overwhelm them all.

Of the cast, Hepburn takes it. Where she takes it is in her transistion points, from girlish coquette remembering her apple-blossom youth to maddened dope fiend, from loving mother to mindless creature groping for identity. This is where Hepburn departed once and for all from delicious comedienne into legendary tragedienne. Richardson's performance is just right: his spareness as an actor incredibly personifies a miser. For once the camera captures Robards's wildness, his lunging danger, before alcohol crabbed him into permanent grit. There's nothing wrong with Stockwell's performance. It's just that we know he's O'Neill, a heavy task for a young actor. Obviously, it's a part for an older performer who looks younger. We can't help but brood that Montgomery Clift was too prematurely old and ruined for the role.

The screen version followed the superb play almost word for word. According to O'Neill's will, the play was not to be produced until 25 years after his death in 1951, but his widow, Carlotta, only waited until 1956 to let it be staged with Fredric March, Florence Eldridge, Robards and Bradford Dillman. Make sure you see the uncut 174-minute film, and not the shortened 136-minute version.

LONG GOOD FRIDAY, THE

1980 105m c Crime/Drama   ★★★½
Calendar/Black Lion (U.K.)   R/18

Bob Hoskins *(Harold)*, Helen Mirren *(Victoria)*, Eddie Constantine *(Charlie)*, Dave King *(Parky)*, Bryan Marshall *(Harris)*, George Coulouris *(Gus)*, Derek Thompson *(Jeff)*, Pierce Brosnan *(1st Irishman)*, Charles Cork *(Eric)*, Billy Cornelius *(Pete)*

p, Barry Hanson; d, John Mackenzie; w, Barrie Keeffe; ph, Phil Meheux; ed, Mike Taylor; m, Francis Monkman; art d, Vic Symonds

A smooth and efficient film about some pretty rough characters, THE LONG GOOD FRIDAY deserves its status a modern-day crime classic. Though not quite in the league of some other entries in the genre, the story of a crime boss and people out to get him delivers the expected goods.

On "Good Friday" in early 1980s London, Harold (Bob Hoskins) learns that a unknown rival gang is killing off his henchmen. Harold fears less about his safety and more about his honor, however, and seeks to find out the culprit behind the murder of his men. Harold is especially eager to secure a deal with Charlie (Eddie Constantine), a Mafia don visiting from New Jersey, and worries that the murders will scare the money-man away. Harold and his men interrogate a number of underworld suspects, but they get few leads to the identity of the killers. After a near-fatal bomb attack on his American visitors, Harold steps up the pressure on his suspects to talk. Meanwhile, Harold's wife, Victoria (Helen Mirren), entertains Charlie and his lawyer at a restaurant, where they threaten to pull out of the deal unless she tells them what is going on. They then give Harold 24 hours to solve the mystery and stop the murders.

THE LONG GOOD FRIDAY compares well to the American gangster films of the 1930s (SCARFACE, LITTLE CAESAR), which also documented the way tough, fearless working-class thugs could rise and fall as infamous criminals. Screenwriter's Barrie Keeffe's well-rounded, almost Shakespearean, characters serve the genre well, his plot gets involved but not overly perplexing, and John Mackenzie's direction possesses a sure touch. In some ways, THE LONG GOOD FRIDAY presages Peter Greenaway's extraordinary THE COOK, THE THIEF, HIS WIFE AND HER LOVER (1989), which also starred Helen Mirren as a criminal's trophy wife (or "moll"). Both films suggest a criticism of Margaret Thatcher's ^nouveau riche world order. Unfortunately, THE LONG GOOD FRIDAY makes Harold's antihero a bit too cuddly and likable to compete with the thoroughly reprehensible thief (Michael Gambon) in the Greenaway picture. Thus, THE LONG GOOD FRIDAY stops short of brilliant revisionism, but acquits itself admirably in most other ways.

LONG GOODBYE, THE

1973 112m c Crime   ★★★★
UA (U.S.)   R/18

Elliott Gould *(Philip Marlowe)*, Nina Van Pallandt *(Eileen Wade)*, Sterling Hayden *(Roger Wade)*, Mark Rydell *(Marty Augustine)*, Henry Gibson *(Dr. Verringer)*, David Arkin *(Harry)*, Jim Bouton *(Terry Lennox)*, Warren Berlinger *(Morgan)*, Jo Ann Brody *(Jo Ann Eggenweiler)*, Jack Knight *(Hood)*

p, Jerry Bick; d, Robert Altman; w, Leigh Brackett (based on the novel by Raymond Chandler); ph, Vilmos Zsigmond; ed, Lou Lombardo; m, John Williams; cos, Kent James, Marjorie Wahl

The detective film to end all detective films. Director Robert Altman offended the fans of Raymond Chandler's Philip Marlowe character by completely subverting the role here. Elliott Gould plays the usually hard-boiled detective as something of a well-meaning bumbler, and while it may not be Chandler, it is a moody and entertaining film. The film is set in Los Angeles where Gould's troubles begin when he gives his friend, Bouton (a former baseball pitcher), a ride to Tijuana. Upon his return, he learns that Bouton is wanted by police for the brutal murder of his wife. Convinced of his friend's innocence, Gould begins his own investigation of the crime. His inquiry first leads him to the beautiful Van Pallandt, with whom Bouton was having an affair. Her husband, Hayden, is a once-successful author who is suffering a severe case of writer's block, which has turned him into an alcoholic. Somewhat batty and insanely jealous regarding his wife, Hayden becomes Gould's

prime suspect in the killing. Fueling his suspicion is the bizarre relationship Hayden has with the sinister Gibson, an alleged psychologist who has been treating him. The case is complicated further by vicious hood Rydell, to whom Boulton owed a large amount of cash. Rydell is certain Gould has the cash and goes to great lengths to show the detective he better fork it over if he does have it. As Gould sifts through the clues, he is sure he has solved the case—but his instincts are wrong, and the trail leads to a suprising and somewhat improbable conclusion.

Certainly Gould shatters the Marlowe mold in this film, playing the detective as a wisecracking, disheveled eccentric, much the same character he portrayed in other Altman films, M*A*S*H and CALIFORNIA SPLIT. From that viewpoint, Chandler's fans had reason to be upset, but Altman's approach to the film noir crime drama is not without its good points. Gould's persona is an amusing counterpoint to the traditional tough-guy detective who always knew exactly what to say and do and who never ran across a situation he couldn't handle. Gould's Marlowe is an often bewildered investigator, who nevertheless maintains the character's strong sense of morality in the midst of a cruel world. Look for Arnold Schwarzenegger (billed as "Arnold Strong") in a small role as one of Rydell's hoods.

LONG RIDERS, THE

1980 99m c Western   ★★★★
UA (U.S.)   R/18

David Carradine *(Cole Younger)*, Keith Carradine *(Jim Younger)*, Robert Carradine *(Bob Younger)*, James Keach *(Jesse James)*, Stacy Keach *(Frank James)*, Dennis Quaid *(Ed Miller)*, Randy Quaid *(Clell Miller)*, Kevin Brophy *(John Younger)*, Harry Carey Jr. *(George Arthur)*, Christopher Guest *(Charlie Ford)*

p, Tim Zinnemann; d, Walter Hill; w, Bill Bryden, Steven Phillip Smith, James Keach, Stacy Keach; ph, Ric Waite; ed, David Holden; m, Ry Cooder; prod d, Jack T. Collis; art d, Peter Romero; chor, Katina Sawidis; cos, Bobbie Mannix

THE LONG RIDERS is a superb, nitty-gritty retelling of the story of the James-Younger gang, the most notorious American bandits of the 19th century. In a unique bit of casting, the Younger, James, Miller, and Ford brothers are played by the brothers Carradine, Keach, Quaid, and Guest. The film opens with the band led by Jesse James (James Keach) and Cole Younger (David Carradine) robbing a bank. In episodic fashion, it then follows the various gang members as they go their separate ways, reuniting later for a disastrous attempt to rob a bank in Northfield, Minnesota. THE LONG RIDERS is one of the last great westerns made in America, directed tautly by Walter Hill from an excellent, well-researched script. The cinematography by Ric Waite is magnificent, the period is beautifully captured, and Ry Cooder's outstanding score nicely incorporates folk music of the era. The whole feeling of this film is one of antiquity, an atmosphere marvelously created by Hill and enhanced by a superb cast. James Keach realistically plays Jesse James; Stacy Keach is perfect as the puzzled, puritanical, but loyal Frank; David Carradine is excellent as the confident, bold Cole Younger; Keith and Robert Carradine are very good as the other Younger brothers; and Nicholas and Christopher Guest epitomize the treacherous Ford siblings. Though THE LONG RIDERS does not spare the violence, this is a must for any adult western fan.

LONG VOYAGE HOME, THE

1940 105m bw Drama   ★★★★★
Argosy (U.S.)   /A

John Wayne *(Ole Olsen)*, Thomas Mitchell *(Aloysius Driscoll)*, Ian Hunter *(Smitty)*, Barry Fitzgerald *(Cocky)*, Wilfrid Lawson *(Captain)*, Mildred Natwick *(Freda)*, John Qualen *(Axel Swanson)*, Ward Bond *(Yank)*, Joe Sawyer *(Davis)*, Arthur Shields *(Donkeyman)*

p, Walter Wanger; d, John Ford; w, Dudley Nichols (based on the plays "The Moon of the Caribbees," "In the Zone," "Bound East for Cardiff," "The Long Voyage Home," by Eugene O'Neill); ph, Gregg Toland; ed, Sherman Todd; m, Richard Hageman; art d, James Basevi; fx, Ray Binger, R.T. Layton

AAN Best Picture; AAN Best Original Screenplay: Dudley Nichols; AAN Best Cinematography: Gregg Toland; AAN Best Editing: Sherman Todd; AAN Best Score: Richard Hageman; AAN Best Visual Effects: R. T. Layton (Photographic), R. O. Binger (Photographic), Thomas T. Moulton (Sound)

Based on four one-act plays by Eugene O'Neill, THE LONG VOYAGE HOME is a powerful saga of merchant seamen, their hardscrabble lives, and their hopes for the future. Ford's film is a magnificent portrayal of the struggle not only to survive, but also to remain civilized, during the early days of WWII. As the film opens, the crew of the tramp freighter SS Glencairn is enjoying a last night of liberty on a Caribbean island, attending a party that ends in a brawl before they stagger back to the freighter. Among the crew is Ole Olsen (Wayne), a good-hearted young Swede who only wants to make enough money to settle down with his family on a small farm, and Smitty (Hunter), who doesn't participate in the drunken on-shore revels and whose painful secret causes suspicion among the crew. In Baltimore, the ship takes on a load of dynamite to be delivered to England, and the film details the hazards of raging storms, German fighter planes, and scheming barroom wharf rats. Though several are killed, the men eventually pull together to help one crew member escape a life at sea.

THE LONG VOYAGE HOME is a Ford masterwork—grim, touching, and startlingly well-photographed. Toland's high contrast lighting and shot compositions cast a vivid aura over both sea and land. As Wayne told biographer Maurice Zolotow, "Usually it would be Mr. Ford who helped the cinematographer get his compositions for maximum effect. . . but in this case it was Gregg Toland who helped Mr. Ford. LONG VOYAGE is about as beautifully photographed a movie as there ever has been."

Wayne himself initially resisted Ford's instruction that he play his character with a Swedish accent, fearing he would appear comic. But he had actress Osa Massen (who was Danish) help him with the accent, and when he first employed it he was congratulated by Ford for getting it right. His work as a naive, simple but not simple-minded man is surprisingly reserved and very effective, not dominating the action the way he usually did. Mitchell, Bond, Fitzgerald, and Qualen are wonderful as various old salts, and Hunter is moving as the tortured seaman who has ruined his life on land. There is a pervasive air of gloom about THE LONG VOYAGE HOME: death lurks on land and at sea, and though the seamen yearn for their long-lost homes, most of them know that they will sail on until they are buried beneath the waves. THE LONG VOYAGE HOME was playwright O'Neill's favorite film; Ford gave him a print of it and he and he ran it over and over again until he wore it out.

LONGEST DAY, THE

1962   180m   bw   War   ★★★★
Fox   (U.S.)   G/PG

John Wayne (Col. Benjamin Vandervoort), Robert Mitchum (Brig. Gen. Norman Cota), Henry Fonda (Brig. Gen. Theodore Roosevelt), Robert Ryan (Brig. Gen. James Gavin), Rod Steiger (Destroyer Commander), Robert Wagner, Fabian, Paul Anka, Tommy Sands (US Rangers), Richard Beymer (Schultz)

p, Darryl F. Zanuck; d, Andrew Marton, Ken Annakin, Bernhard Wicki, Gerd Oswald; w, Cornelius Ryan, Romain Gary, James Jones, David Pursall, Jack Seddon (based on the novel by Cornelius Ryan); ph, Jean Bourgoin, Henri Persin, Walter Wottitz, Guy Tabary; ed, Samuel E. Beetley; m, Maurice Jarre; art d, Ted Haworth, Leon Barsacq, Vincent Korda; fx, Karl Helmer, Karl Baumgartner, Augie Lohman, Robert MacDonald, Alex Weldon

AAN Best Picture; AA Best Cinematography: Jean Bourgoin, Walter Wottitz; AAN Best Editing: Samuel E. Beetley; AAN Best Art Direction: Ted Haworth, Leon Barsacq, Vincent Korda, Gabriel Bechir; AA Best Visual Effects: Robert MacDonald, Jacques Maumont

One of the most ambitious war films ever undertaken, this star-studded depiction of the D-Day invasion was long the pet project of Fox Studios boss Darryl Zanuck, who spared no expense in bringing THE LONGEST DAY breathtaking scope and authenticity, going so far as to insist that the shooting be done only in weather conditions that matched those of the actual event. Based on Cornelius Ryan's compilation of interviews with D-Day survivors, the film is presented in three segments,

the first detailing the Allied preparation for the invasion and the wait for the weather to break; the second re-creating the movement of the massive armada across the English Channel and the preliminary, behind-the-lines sallies of paratroops and glider-transported commandos; and the last depicting the assaults on the Normandy beaches. Intercut with the portrayal of the Allied side of the momentous invasion is the German (subtitled) response, including the report to headquarters of the first German officer to spot the armada: "Those thousands of ships you say the Allies don't have—well, they have them!" The work of three credited directors (reportedly, Zanuck helmed all the American and British interiors himself) and no less than eight cameramen, THE LONGEST DAY is visually stunning—its extraordinary camera movement and Cinemascope photography brilliantly augmenting the meticulously reenacted battle scenes. The only thing bigger than the film's scope are its stars, including John Wayne (who received $250,000 for four days' work) as Lt. Col. Benjamin Vandervoort of the 82nd Paratroop Division; Henry Fonda as Brig. Gen. Theodore Roosevelt, Jr.; Robert Mitchum as Brig. Gen. Norman Cota, who finally moves his hard-pressed men off bloody Omaha Beach, where they are being slaughtered by German crossfire; Red Buttons as a paratrooper; Rod Steiger as the captain of one of the armada ships; Peter Lawford as the flamboyant commando leader Lord Lovat (who was present at the shoot); Richard Burton as a wounded pilot; and Curt Jurgens as German general Blumentritt. Made for $10 million, this magnificent film was the most expensive black-and-white production to its date.

LONGEST YARD, THE

1974   121m   c   Sports/Comedy   ★★★½
Paramount   (U.S.)   R/X

Burt Reynolds (Paul Crewe), Eddie Albert (Warden Hazen), Ed Lauter (Capt. Knauer), Michael Conrad (Nate Scarboro), James Hampton (Caretaker), Harry Caesar (Granville), John Steadman (Pop), Charles Tyner (Unger), Mike Henry (Rassmeusen), Bernadette Peters (Warden's Secretary)

p, Albert S. Ruddy; d, Robert Aldrich; w, Tracy Keenan Wynn (based on a story by Ruddy); ph, Joseph Biroc; ed, Michael Luciano, Frank Capacchione, Allan Jacobs, George Hively; m, Frank DeVol; prod d, James Vance

AAN Best Editing: Michael Luciano

Part prison film, part football film, this violent but outstanding comedy-drama by gifted action director Robert Aldrich (BIG LEAGUER, ALL THE MARBLES) explores the brutality inherent in both the American penal system and football. Burt Reynolds gives one of his best performances as Paul Crewe, a former pro who tires of being a kept man, steals his lover's car, and ends up in the prison ruled by Warden Hazen (Eddie Albert). Hazen compels Crewe to put together a team of prisoners to face the crack guard team, offering him parole in exchange for a lopsided loss. Crewe assembles the "Mean Machine" and then does his best to throw the game (which takes up 47 minutes of screen time), leaving it early with an "injury" but returning later to lead the Machine's comeback when the guards' savagery continues unabated. Deftly employing split-screen and slow-motion techniques, Aldrich makes the most of Tracy Keenan Wynn's incisive script, aided by fine cinematography and tight Oscar-nominated editing. Both sides of the line of scrimmage feature former gridiron stars: the guards boast one-time Viking quarterback Joe Kapp and Packer Hall of Famer Ray Nitschke, while among the prisoners are Ernie Wheelwright, Pervis Atkins, and the University of Washington's legendary QB Sonny Sixkiller. No stranger to football himself, Reynolds, an All-Southern Conference halfback at Florida State, also played a pigskin hero in SEMI-TOUGH.

LOOK BACK IN ANGER

1959   115m   bw   Drama   ★★★
Pathe/Associated British   (U.K.)   /PG

Richard Burton (Jimmy Porter), Claire Bloom (Helena Charles), Mary Ure (Alison Porter), Edith Evans (Mrs. Tanner), Gary Raymond (Cliff Lewis), Glen Byam Shaw (Cpl. Redfern), Phyllis Neilson-Terry (Mrs. Redfern), Donald Pleasence (Hurst), Jane Eccles (Miss Drury), S.P. Kapoor (Kapoor)

p, Harry Saltzman; d, Tony Richardson; w, Nigel Kneale, John Osborne (based on the play by Osborne); ph, Oswald Morris; ed, Richard Best; m, Chris Barber; art d, Peter Glazier; cos, Jocelyn Richards

In the late 1950s and early 1960s, several films by "Angry Young Men" were written and produced. Osborne, a forerunner of the genre, wrote the play on which this film is based and which had enormous success in London and New York. This lensing was faithful to the original, but it lost a bit in the translation from the intimacy of the stage to the screen. Canadian Harry Saltzman, who made his fortune in England, produced the picture before he decided to make films that had more commercial possibilities (i.e., the James Bond series which he did with Albert Broccoli). He is to be congratulated for taking a chance with an iffy property. Burton, in a no-holds-barred performance, is a university-educated malcontent who currently earns his keep by running a candy stall in a large market run by Pleasence, in yet another of his fine roles. Burton seems to love his wife, Ure, but can't help verbally mistreating her. (She repeats the part she played on the stage. This was one of her very few film appearances. She had been married to playwright Osborne, then married playwright-actor Robert Shaw. She died at 42 after mixing whiskey with barbiturates.) Ure takes about as much as anyone can stand, then leaves Burton when her best friend, Bloom, persuades her that she must to save her sanity. Burton is now alone, with nobody to insult, and he takes up with Bloom, a woman he has despised for most of the first few reels. Ure has been pregnant all along but didn't tell Burton. When she loses the baby, she returns to Burton, and Bloom figures it's time for her to leave. Evans is a sweet old lady who helps Burton set up his business, and Kapoor has a few good scenes as an Indian trader, but most of the picture belongs to Burton's bravura performance.

The major problem of the picture is that Osborne seems to have concocted the slight plot for one reason only: to vent his spleen against the church, society, the rich, the government, and whatever irked him at the time. The dialogue at times is endless and much too flip in the wrong situations. It's as though the author attempted to be a modern-day Oscar Wilde, but with a social conscience, and his message is heard loud, clear, and far too often. Although Burton has the range to be kind, funny, earthy, noble, and passionate, he is given little opportunity to get beyond letting that memorable voice of his bellow and roar. Still, for all the obvious drawbacks, LOOK BACK IN ANGER should be seen by anyone who is interested in learning about the England of that era. Burton had been making films for ten years and had starred as Alexander in ALEXANDER THE GREAT and as Edwin Booth in PRINCE OF PLAYERS. This seamy role, however, was the one that brought him to the attention of many who thought that he could act only when dressed in Biblical clothes, as in THE ROBE, or in doublet and hose. He was only 34 at the time this was made, but the ravages of high living were already beginning to show on his rugged Welsh face.

LOOK WHO'S TALKING

1989 93m c Comedy ★★★
Tri-Star (U.S.) PG-13/12

John Travolta (James), Kirstie Alley (Mollie), Olympia Dukakis (Rosie), George Segal (Albert), Abe Vigoda (Grandpa), Bruce Willis (Voice of Mikey), Twink Caplan (Rona), Jason Schaller, Jaryd Waterhouse, Jacob Haines

p, Jonathan D. Krane; d, Amy Heckerling; w, Amy Heckerling; ph, Thomas Del Ruth; ed, Debra Chiate; m, David Kitay; art d, Reuben Freed; chor, Mary Ann Kellogg; cos, Molly Maginnis

The voice of Bruce Willis is the "who" in LOOK WHO'S TALKING, a mildly amusing comedy buoyed by a voiceover gimmick. With trademark irony, Willis supplies dialogue for an infant, whose jaundiced view of the adult word provides the laughs. Mollie (Kirstie Alley) is an accountant who's been sleeping with Albert (George Segal), a married client who can't bring himself to leave his wife. Even Mollie's pregnancy doesn't change his mind. But when Mollie goes into labor, she meets an interesting taxi driver (John Travolta).

Writer-director Amy Heckerling takes a clever idea and conveys it superbly. The voiceover works well because the filmmakers use the device for all it's worth, with Willis providing a voice for the child when it's a sperm, a fetus, and a baby. With his sarcastic delivery, Willis has the ideal voice for the part. Alley and Travolta are affable enough, but

the story itself is ordinary and merely passes time. Thanks to the ingenious voiceover, however, LOOK WHO'S TALKING is a genial, entertaining film, the enormous popularity of which led to two more mediocre installments, in 1990 and 1993.

LOOKING FOR MR. GOODBAR

1977 135m c Drama ★★½
Paramount (U.S.) R/18

Diane Keaton (Theresa Dunn), Tuesday Weld (Katherine Dunn), William Atherton (James Morrissey), Richard Kiley (Mr. Dunn), Richard Gere (Tony Lopanto), Alan Feinstein (Professor Engle), Tom Berenger (Gary Cooper White), Priscilla Pointer (Mrs. Dunn), Laurie Prange (Brigid Dunn), Joel Fabiani (Barney)

p, Freddie Fields; d, Richard Brooks; w, Richard Brooks (based on the novel by Judith Rosner); ph, William A. Fraker; ed, George Grenville; m, Artie Kane; art d, Edward Carfagno; cos, Jodie Tillen

AAN Best Supporting Actress: Tuesday Weld; AAN Best Cinematography: William A Fraker

Brooks, hardly a great director, doesn't quite pull off this adaptation of the Rossner novel. Keaton is a repressed teacher of deaf-and-dumb children who lives under the thumb of her macho father, Kiley, and her let's-make-everything-nice mother, Pointer. She would love to be free of them, so she sets out to find "Mr. Right" but in all the wrong places. She haunts the singles bars and goes on a sexual voyage, sleeping with Atherton, a befuddled, sweet guy who loves her; Gere, a stud with sadistic tendencies that thrill her; and finally, Berenger, the insane bisexual who eventually takes her life. Keaton is shown existing in two worlds: the safety of school and home versus the madcap life of the swingers who stay up late, drowning their loneliness in stingers and sex. This is the other side of Hoffman and Farrow's JOHN AND MARY; we kept looking hard at the bar scenes to see if Dustin and Mia were in the background. There are many erotic scenes, but they are handled fairly well. Imagine Brian DePalma with the same script, and you'll realize how disgusting it could have been. Feinstein is excellent as Keaton's first lover, and Weld is sensational as Keaton's slightly dippy sister who is happy following whatever trend is au courant. LOOKING FOR MR. GOODBAR made lots of money and showed that Keaton, who had just scored in ANNIE HALL, could get out from under Woody Allen's wing and be a star on her own. An added plus is the score by Artie Kane, which evokes the solitude of living in a city with millions of people but still not having anyone with whom to really talk.

LOOKS AND SMILES

1982 104m bw Drama ★★★
Black Lion/Kestrel/MK2 (U.K.) /15

Phil Askham, Pam Darrell, Graham Greene, Tracey Goodlad, Stuart Golland, Patti Nichols, Tony Pitts, Arthur Davies, Cilla Mason, Carolyn Nicholson

p, Irving Teitelbaum; d, Kenneth Loach; w, Barry Hines; ph, Chris Menges; ed, Stephen Singleton; m, Marc Wilkinson, Richard & The Taxmen; art d, Martin Johnson

Powerful, gritty drama shot in a documentary style about two high school dropouts who are faced with the choice of going into the military or going on public aid. One of the boys enlists and finds himself in Belfast, where he begins terrorizing Catholics; the other stays home and becomes increasingly destitute as he tries to find work. The cast members are all amateurs, and the visual style is stunningly realistic.

LORD JIM

1965 154m c Adventure ★★★★
Columbia (U.K.) /PG

Peter O'Toole (Lord Jim), James Mason (Gentleman Brown), Curt Jurgens (Cornelius), Eli Wallach (The General), Jack Hawkins (Marlow), Paul Lukas (Stein), Akim Tamiroff (Schomberg), Daliah Lavi (The Girl), Ichizo Itami (Waris), Tatsuo Saito (Chief Du-Ramin)

p, Richard Brooks; d, Richard Brooks; w, Richard Brooks (based on the novel by Joseph Conrad); ph, Freddie Young; ed, Alan Osbiston; m, Bronislau Kaper; prod d, Geoffrey Drake; art d, Bill Hutchinson, Ernest Archer; fx, Cliff Richardson; cos, Phyllis Dalton

This stunningly exotic film of Conrad's classic features O'Toole in the title role. He serves an apprenticeship at sea under the protective eye of Hawkins and later graduates to first officer of a tramp liner, the *Patna*, which carries religious passengers on an awful passage in which the ship is mercilessly lashed by a hurricane. In a moment of desperation, the idealistic O'Toole abandons the ship and leaves its passengers to their fate. The craft survives, although many of its passengers are drowned, and O'Toole loses his license and sinks into waterfront obscurity. To redeem himself, O'Toole agrees to take a shipment of dynamite from Lukas and deliver it to a tribe of natives in uncharted territory. The tribe is in bondage to oppressive warlord Wallach. Surviving ambushes and treachery from his own crew members, O'Toole manages to get the explosives to the settlement and hide the barrels, exploding one to make Wallach and his henchmen believe that the entire shipment has been destroyed. Wallach captures O'Toole and tortures him, but native girl Lavi helps him escape. He joins the natives and organizes an attack on the fortress, a seesaw battle that finally sees O'Toole and the natives triumph and Wallach killed. Jurgens, however, escapes to join river pirate Mason, and they muster their forces to return to the fortress to obtain Wallach's fabulous cache of jewels stolen from the natives. O'Toole greets the thieves with a cannon shot that decimates them, but the son of the native chief is killed in the encounter and, to make up for the death, O'Toole nobly sacrifices his own life at the finish. Beautifully photographed by Young and tightly directed by Brooks, LORD JIM is moving and suspenseful. Shot on location in Cambodia and Hong Kong.

LORD LOVE A DUCK

1966 105m bw Comedy   ★★★
Charleston (U.S.)   /A

Roddy McDowall (Alan "Mollymauk" Musgrave), Tuesday Weld (Barbara Ann Greene), Lola Albright (Marie Green), Martin West (Bob Barnard), Ruth Gordon (Stella Barnard), Harvey Korman (Weldon Emmett), Sarah Marshall (Miss Schwartz), Lynn Carey (Sally Grace), Max Showalter (Howard Greene), Donald Murphy (Phil Neuhauser)

p, George Axelrod; d, George Axelrod; w, George Axelrod, Larry H. Johnson (based on a novel by Al Hine); ph, Daniel Fapp; ed, William Lyon; m, Neal Hefti; art d, Malcolm Brown; fx, Herman Townsley; cos, Paula Giokaris

A wacky satire/black comedy with high school senior McDowall helping schoolmate Weld get whatever she desires. McDowall's IQ is so high he knows what everyone wants before they speak. He gets Weld into the sorority of her choice and ensures she will get good grades by getting her a secretarial job with the high school principal, Korman. She meets West, a rich college senior, at a sex seminar at a drive-in church. Weld is tested for a beach party movie with West's help, but problems arise when West's mother, Gordon, doesn't approve of Weld. McDowall fixes that by introducing Gordon to booze. Weld's mother, Albright, kills herself when she thinks she has ruined her daughter's relationship and life. Weld and West marry and he becomes a marriage counselor. When he objects to his wife's movie career, McDowall decides to get rid of him. His attempts fail until he runs him over at the high school graduation with a bulldozer (killing everyone on the speaker's platform as well). The film is told in flashback with McDowall in the prison psychiatric wing telling his story to a tape recorder. Directed by the man who wrote THE SEVEN YEAR ITCH and WILL SUCCESS SPOIL ROCK HUNTER?

LORD OF THE FLIES

1963 90m bw Science Fiction/Drama   ★★½
Allen/Hogdon/Two Arts (U.K.)   /PG

James Aubrey (Ralph), Tom Chapin (Jack), Hugh Edwards (Piggy), Roger Elwin (Roger), Tom Gaman (Simon), The Surtees Twins (Sam and Eric), Roger Allen, David Brunjes, Peter Davy, Kent Fletcher

p, Lewis Allen; d, Peter Brook; w, Peter Brook (based on the novel by William Golding); ph, Tom Hollyman; ed, Peter Brook, Gerald Feil, Jean-Claude Lubtchansky; m, Raymond Leppard

Swat! A disappointing rendition of the Golding novel, routinely directed by Brook. With a war about to erupt, a plane carrying some wealthy British schoolboys is flown to the supposed safety of the South Pacific. The plane crashes on a remote island (the film was shot in Puerto Rico and Vieques in the Caribbean), none of the adults makes it to shore, and forty boys are left to fend for themselves. Since you all read the book in high school, you know that the boys split into two gangs and quickly descend to superstitious rituals and murder. Golding's haunting ruminations about the fine line between civilization and savagery are not done justice here. There are some vicious highlights, but the acting is wildly variable, and the film manages to be both overwrought and dull.

LORDS OF FLATBUSH, THE

1974 86m c Drama   ★★★
Columbia (U.S.)   PG/15

Perry King (Chico), Sylvester Stallone (Stanley Rosiello), Henry Winkler (Butchey Weinstein), Paul Mace (Wimpy Murgalo), Susan Blakely (Jane Bradshaw), Maria Smith (Frannie Malincanico), Renee Paris (Annie Yuckamanelli), Paul Jabara (Crazy Cohen), Bruce Reed (Mike), Frank Steifel (Arnie)

p, Stephen Verona; d, Stephen Verona, Martin Davidson; w, Stephen Verona, Martin Davidson; ph, Joseph Mangine, Ed Lachman; ed, Stan Siegel, Muffie Meyer; m, Joe Brooks, Paul Jabara, Joseph Nicholas; art d, Glenda Miller

Anyone who grew up in the Brooklyn of the 1950s will recognize the essential honesty of this picture, but it might as well be taking place in Korea for everyone else. The rambling movie with a good mix of drama and comedy served to introduce several actors who went on to much greater fame in other movies. The Lords of Flatbush is the name of a tough street gang but not one of those groups that pillage and vandalize. Rather, it is a social club, one of thousands that once were found in Brooklyn. (The small area of Coney Island alone had at least a dozen, including The Mariners, The Acwans [A Club without a Name acronym], the Emanons [Nonames backwards], et al). Stallone and King are best pals in Brooklyn's Flatbush area (and is there an uglier name for a neighborhood?). Codirector Verona must like the area because he used it for BRIGHTON BEACH. Stallone gets his girlfriend, Smith, pregnant and then takes her to a local jewelry shop to buy a ring. King's girlfriend is Blakely (while she was still "Susie" and not Susan), but she eventually dumps him. Several small but compelling incidents serve truly to represent life in Brooklyn. The film is a character piece that wanders from place to place with no single impetus, although one gets the feeling that this technique is intentional. The actors who distinguished themselves later include Blakely; Winkler ("Happy Days"); Armand Assante (I, THE JURY); Ray Sharkey (THE IDOLMAKER); Dolph Sweet ("Gimme a Break"); Jabara (who became a songwriter and won an Oscar); and, of course, Stallone, who was making his leading-man debut after an unbilled bit in Woody Allen's BANANAS and a few roles in films that will never reach a Saturday matinee for kids. Codirector Verona eventually became one of the prime movers of music video as well as a best-selling artist in his own right. Brooks did the music with some help from Nicholas and Jabara. Brooks will be best remembered (or forgotten) for scripting, producing, directing, and writing the song for YOU LIGHT UP MY LIFE.

LORENZO'S OIL

1992 135m c Drama   ★★★½
Kennedy-Miller Productions (U.S.)   PG-13/12

Nick Nolte (Augusto Odone), Susan Sarandon (Michaela Odone), Peter Ustinov (Professor Nikolais), Zack O'Malley Greenburg (Lorenzo), Kathleen Wilhoite (Deirdre Murphy), Gerry Bamman (Doctor Judalon), Margo Martindale (Wendy Gimble), James Rebhorn (Ellard Muscatine), Ann Hearn (Loretta Muscatine), Maduka Steady (Omouri)

LOS OLVIDADOS

p, George Miller, Doug Mitchell; d, George Miller; w, George Miller, Nick Enright; ph, John Seale; ed, Richard Francis-Bruce, Marcus D'Arcy, Lee Smith; prod d, Kristi Zea; art d, Dennis Bradford; cos, Colleen Atwood

AAN Best Actress: Susan Sarandon; *AAN Best Original Screenplay:* George Miller

An unusual piece of work that combines almost thriller-style suspense with an intelligent, neo-documentary approach to its harrowing subject.

The film is based on the true story of Augusto and Michaela Odone (Nick Nolte and Susan Sarandon), whose five-year-old child, Lorenzo, is diagnosed as having a rare, fatal disease that is literally eating away his brain. Rather than accept the medical verdict, Lorenzo's parents become amateur research scientists, devoting their lives to finding a way of keeping him alive.

The film's highest achievement is its honest, uncompromising presentation of unconditional love. In the later stages of Lorenzo's disease, when he seems to have lost any grip on the world outside, Augusto hesitantly suggests that his son may no longer have a "soul": his brain has deteriorated so far that he is no longer capable of thought or emotion. Isn't there a point, we ask ourselves, when a person ceases to be a person, and we should stop feeling for them as we once did? For Lorenzo's mother, the question does not even bear consideration. She condemns anyone who fails to share her zeal to some lower moral plane, banishing not only two capable nurses, but her own sister, from the house when they question the unqualified ardor of her crusade.

Sarandon makes Mrs. Odone compelling, yet largely unsympathetic. We don't just applaud as she and her husband take on, and defeat, the bureaucracy of the medical establishment; we also recoil from her pious, pedantic self-righteousness. It's a brave, complex performance, and the centerpiece of an emotionally searing film.

LOS OLVIDADOS

1950   88m   bw   Drama   ★★★★★
Tepeyac   (Mexico)   /X

Estela Inda *(The Mother),* Alfonso Mejia *(Pedro),* Roberto Cobo *(Jaibo),* Jesus Navarro *(The Lost Boy),* Miguel Inclan *(The Blind Man),* Alma Fuentas *(The Young Girl),* Francisco Jambrino *(The Principal),* Hector Portillo, Salvador Quiros, Victor Manuel Mendoza

p, Oscar Dancigers; d, Luis Bunuel; w, Luis Bunuel, Luis Alcoriza; ph, Gabriel Figueroa; ed, Carlos Savage; m, Gustavo Pittaluga

After a strange interlude of nearly two decades of critical obscurity, one of the great masters of the cinema returned to the public eye with this gripping combination of gritty realism and disorienting surrealism. Set in the slums of Mexico City, this is Luis Bunuel's brutally clear-eyed account of "The Forgotten Ones", the reckless youth whose dismal marginal existence has become a deadly web from which they cannot extract themselves. Bunuel adopts many of the trappings of the popular form of the liberal social problem drama to tell his story but his goals are different. Rather than blaming all of the misery of these young people on their grim social conditions, he utilizes surrealism to expose the psychological underpinnings of their condition as he zeroes in on their dreams and sexuality. The result is a film that is realistic yet dreamy, heartrendingly sad yet subversively funny. There are no easy heroes or villains in this tough film. Bunuel also deftly avoids the sentimentalism that often afflicts this form.

At the film's core is the relationship between Pedro (Alfonso Mejia) and Jaibo (Roberto Cobo), two youths who live in Mexico's most disease-ridden urban slum. Jaibo, the older of the two, is already set in his ways, his selfish, vicious nature leading him to take advantage of those less fortunate than himself. As the film opens, he has just been released from jail and immediately returns to take control of the gang of boys who hang out in the streets and commit senseless acts of violence—not for money but for the pleasure of seeing the less fortunate suffer. The boy most eager to follow and please Jaibo is the childlike Pedro, whose innocent eyes reveal a spark of goodness lacking in the others.

The roots of this film extend back to LAS HURDES, Bunuel's devastating (yet also peversely amusing) 1932 documentary about the wretched living conditions in Spain's poorest region. There is also a vigorous nod to the Italian neo-realists; LOS OLVIDADOS is, as celebrated French critic Andre Bazin called it, "a film that lashes the

mind like a red-hot iron and leaves one's conscience no opportunity for rest." Rarely have such squalor and savagery been displayed so unsentimentally, for Bunuel, who has a deep love for his characters, refuses to judge or pity them. Bunuel was named Best Director at the 1951 Cannes Film Festival, an award richly deserved.

LOST HIGHWAY

1997   135m   c   Horror/Crime   ★★
Lost Highway Productions/Asymmetrical Features/CiBy 2000   R/
(U.S./France)

Bill Pullman *(Fred Madison),* Patricia Arquette *(Renee Madison/Alice Wakefield),* Balthazar Getty *(Pete Dayton),* Robert Blake *(Mystery Man),* Natasha Gregson Wagner *(Sheila),* Robert Loggia *(Mr. Eddy/Dick Laurent),* Gary Busey *(Bill Dayton),* Richard Pryor *(Arnie),* John Roselius *(Al),* Lou Eppolito *(Ed)*

p, Deepak Nayar, Tom Sternberg, Mary Sweeney; d, David Lynch; w, David Lynch, Barry Gifford; ph, Peter Deming; ed, Mary Sweeney; m, Angelo Badalamenti, Barry Adamson; prod d, Patricia Norris; fx, Ann Kroeber-Splet; cos, Patricia Norris

A lavishly beautiful, eerily violent, feature-length "Twilight Zone" episode, filtered—not entirely successfully—though the sensibilities of director David Lynch and his WILD AT HEART collaborator, Barry Gifford.

Sax player Fred Madison (Bill Pullman) and his slinky, auburn-tressed wife Renee (Patricia Arquette) are stalked by a video camera-carrying creepy-crawler who prowls through their house and films them in their sleep, then deposits the tapes on their doorstep. All very mysterious—until Madison gets sent to death row for killing Renee and changes inexplicably into someone named Pete Dayton (Balthazar Getty). Pete begins an affair with noir-ish, blue-nailed gangster's slut Alice Wakefield (Arquette again), and the whole thing spins off into some sort of chic, "isn't this *decadent?*" spookshow. This time, it's not the Devil who's in the details (he's prowling around in the person of Robert Blake in chalky, CABARET-era Joel Grey whiteface): it's the fun. Lovecraftian shadows on the wall; NATURAL BORN KILLERS-style montages, featuring shock-rockers Marilyn Manson and Twiggy Ramirez writhing in the neon slime; a just-plain-horrifying cameo by the wheelchair-bound Richard Pryor; the late Jack Nance; John Waters's gutter-diva Mink Stole; and tattooed rock-boy Henry Rollins. The look is to die for and the soundtrack is drop-dead cool, but there's something distastefully synthetic (as well as a bit sophomoric) about the proceedings. As to the story, it goes off-road the moment Pullman is transformed into the sullen Getty and it never comes back. Ultimately it's hypnotic but frustrating, much like Lynch's previous feature, TWIN PEAKS: FIRE WALK WITH ME.

LOST HONOR OF KATHARINA BLUM, THE
(DIE VERLORENE EHRE DER KATHARINA BLUM)

1975   104m   c   Drama   ★★★★
Orion/WDR/Bioskop/Paramount   (West Germany)   R/AA

Angela Winkler *(Katharina Blum),* Mario Adorf *(Beizmenne),* Dieter Laser *(Werner Toetgess),* Heinz Bennent *(Dr. Blorna),* Hannelore Hoger *(Trude Blorna),* Harald Kuhlmann *(Moeding),* Karl Heinz Vosgerau *(Alois Straubleder),* Jurgen Prochnow *(Ludwig Goetten),* Rolf Becker *(Hach),* Regine Lutz *(Else Woltersheim)*

p, Eberhard Junkersdorf; d, Volker Schlondorff, Margarethe von Trotta; w, Volker Schlondorff, Margarethe von Trotta (based on the novel by Heinrich Boll); ph, Jost Vacano; ed, Peter Przygodda; m, Hans Werner Henze

A riveting adaptation of Heinrich Boll's novel, co-directed by Volker Schlondorff and Margarethe von Trotta. The title character (Angela Winkler), a waitress and model citizen, finds herself the victim of an unorthodox police investigation and media assault after a brief affair with a man wanted by the police because of his political affiliations. Before her troubles began, Katharina had been respected by her employers for her efficiency, and by her friends for her level head. Her calm and uneventful life is made a shambles, however, by one particularly ruthless reporter who stops at nothing (including a grueling interview with her sickly mother) to dig up dirt, and labels her a Communist conspirator. The story unfolds as a series of small revelations about the suspect, providing various conflicting viewpoints of her character. While this method may be too cold and distancing to evoke much audience empathy, it is effective in creating the oppressive atmosphere the story requires. Winkler's performance is equally cool, as a woman who seems incapable of revealing her emotions.

LOST HORIZON

1937 138m bw Science Fiction/Fantasy/Adventure   ★★★★
Columbia (U.S.)   /U

Ronald Colman *(Robert Conway)*, Jane Wyatt *(Sondra)*, Edward Everett Horton *(Alexander P. Lovett)*, John Howard *(George Conway)*, Thomas Mitchell *(Henry Barnard)*, Margo *(Maria)*, Isabel Jewell *(Gloria Stone)*, H.B. Warner *(Chang)*, Sam Jaffe *(High Lama)*, Hugh Buckler *(Lord Gainsford)*

p, Frank Capra; d, Frank Capra; w, Robert Riskin (based on the novel by James Hilton); ph, Joseph Walker; ed, Gene Havlick, Gene Milford; m, Dimitri Tiomkin; art d, Stephen Goosson; fx, Roy Davidson, Ganahl Carson; cos, Ernest Dryden

AAN Best Picture; AAN Best Supporting Actor: H.B. Warner; *AA Best Editing:* Gene Havlick, Gene Milford; *AAN Best Score:* Morris Stoloff, Columbia Studio Music Department, Dimitri Tiomkin; *AA Best Art Direction:* Stephen Goosson; *AAN Best Sound:* John Livadary

Frank Capra's classic romantic fantasy leaves the standard "Capraesque" middle-class milieu of most of his most beloved masterpieces for a vividly realized world of strange adventure and fantasy. Faithfully adapted from James Hilton's popular novel, the film opens as Robert Conway (Colman), a gallant but world-weary British diplomat, author and Far Eastern historian, comes to the aid of some refugees from a Chinese revolution. The group takes off in a small passenger plane, the motley collection including Conway's younger, impressionable brother (Howard); a swindler on the lam (Mitchell); a tubercular prostitute (Jewell); and a fussy, fossil-hunting scientist (Horton). Conway notices that the plane is not headed for safety but climbing into the snow-topped Himalayas and into Tibet, "the Roof of the World." Moreover, the passengers discover that the pilot is not the European they had believed him to be, but an Asian. The plane crashes and the passengers struggle out of it, but awaiting them is the beautiful, snowless, sun-filled world known as the Valley of the Blue Moon, looking down upon the majestic landscapes that make up the lamasery of Shangri-La. Taken to a magnificent structure and given luxurious rooms, the Europeans soon discover the marvelous tranquility of this hidden, unknown land where nothing is known of greed, war, hatred or crime.

LOST HORIZON came to epitomize its audience's image of Utopia. Capra's paradise on earth—with its pure air, bright sun and untroubled centuries of blissful life—became so entrenched in the public imagination that *Shangri-La* became a household word. Though Hilton wrote the novel (published in 1933) in six weeks, Capra took two years to transfer the tale to celluloid. The magnificent Shangri-La set constructed by art designer Stephen Goosson was the largest ever built in Hollywood. For two months, 150 workmen labored to build the 1,000-foot-long, 500-foot-wide lamasery, with its deep flights of marbled stairs and huge patio, broad terraces, rich gardens, lily-coated pools, and main building influenced by art deco and Frank Lloyd Wright. Little Columbia Studios and its tough boss, Harry Cohn, staggered under the burden of the film's $2.5 million cost, which amounted to half of the company's entire yearly budget.

All of the painstaking care Capra took with LOST HORIZON shows; the film is directed with swift pace, inventive shots, and splendid acting. Capra was at a high point in his career. Two reels were eliminated after a problematic preview screening. LOST HORIZON was released in a cut version at 118 minutes to universal applause. Columbia had itself a box-office blockbuster which returned many millions to its depleted coffers and remained popular in re-release for decades. Everything about LOST HORIZON reflects quality work, from Robert Riskin's bright and literate script to Dimitri Tiomkin's stirring music, the outstanding special effects and Joseph Walker's evocative soft-focus photography.

LOST IN AMERICA

1985 91m c Comedy   ★★½
Geffen (U.S.)   R/15

Albert Brooks *(David Howard)*, Julie Hagerty *(Linda Howard)*, Tom Tarpey *(Brad Tooley)*, Gary K. Marshall *(Casino Manager)*, Maggie Roswell *(Patty)*, Ernie Brown *(Pharmacist)*, Art Frankel *(Employment Agent)*, Joey Coleman *(Skippy)*, Donald Gibb *(Ex-Convict)*, Sylvia Farrel *(Receptionist)*

p, Marty Katz; d, Albert Brooks; w, Albert Brooks, Monica Johnson; ph, Eric Saarinen; ed, David Finfer; m, Arthur B. Rubinstein; prod d, Richard Sawyer; fx, Richard Albain Jr.; cos, Cynthia Bales

Just when it seemed Albert Brooks had gotten his creative energies under control, along comes this intermittently funny, often overdone comedy that could have been a classic. Brooks is an ad man expecting to get a senior VP stripe. His main worries are how to furnish the new $450,000 house he is about to occupy and how to satisfy his wife, Julie Hagerty, who is complaining that she is bored with the regimentation of their lives. Brooks is shocked when his boss tells him the veep job has gone to someone else and that Brooks will, instead, be transferred to New York. Brooks storms out of the office and then persuades Hagerty to quit her job. They have no children, and they have money saved up; this is their chance to do what everyone wants to do, get lost in America and have a grand time. They sell everything, buy a huge motor home, and leave. It would be a perfect trip except that they get romantically remarried in Las Vegas, and that is the beginning of the end. If a moral exists here, it's that you can't win. Brooks and Hagerty are excellent, and it's good to see Brooks giving someone else a few moments on the screen. Somewhere, underneath all of the indulgence, beats the heart of a filmmaker.

LOST PATROL, THE

1934 74m bw War   ★★★½
RKO (U.S.)   /A

Victor McLaglen *(The Sergeant)*, Boris Karloff *(Sanders)*, Wallace Ford *(Morelli)*, Reginald Denny *(George Brown)*, J.M. Kerrigan *(Quincannon)*, Billy Bevan *(Herbert Hale)*, Alan Hale *(Cook)*, Brandon Hurst *(Bell)*, Douglas Walton *(Pearson)*, Sammy Stein *(Abelson)*

p, Cliff Reid; d, John Ford; w, Dudley Nichols, Garrett Fort (based on the novel *Patrol* by Philip MacDonald); ph, Harold Wenstrom; ed, Paul Weatherwax; m, Max Steiner; art d, Van Nest Polglase, Sidney Ullman

AAN Best Score: Max Steiner (Score), RKO Radio Studio Music Department

A strange and fascinating film, John Ford's THE LOST PATROL gives a sense of impending doom from frame to frame, but is nevertheless an absorbing adventure drama. The story concerns a British cavalry patrol in the Mesopotamian desert during WWI. A single shot rings out and their leader, an officer, falls dead from his horse, his face buried in the sand. With him goes the knowledge of their mission's purpose and even the direction in which the patrol is traveling. The unnamed sergeant (Victor McLaglen) who takes over finds nothing in the officer's map case to indicate where they are, and tells his men that the officer kept everything in his head. He leads the group to an oasis, but the men find themselves under occasional sniper fire from the Arabs who have surrounded them and lie in wait, out of sight in the stretching dunes. The soldiers—except for the sergeant—never see the Arabs, and this insidious enemy takes on an almost mythic character as, one by one, the British are picked off until only the sergeant, Morelli (Wallace Ford), and Sanders (Boris Karloff) are left, desperately trying to stay alive. Shot on location in the desert around Yuma, Arizona, THE LOST PATROL is a much superior remake of a like-titled 1929 British silent film that featured Agnew McMaster in Karloff's role and Cyril McLaglen, Victor's brother, as the sergeant.

LOST WEEKEND, THE

1945 101m bw Drama ★★★★½
Paramount (U.S.) /A

Ray Milland *(Don Birnam)*, Jane Wyman *(Helen St. James)*, Phillip Terry *(Nick Birnam)*, Howard Da Silva *(Nat the Bartender)*, Doris Dowling *(Gloria)*, Frank Faylen *(Bim)*, Mary Young *(Mrs. Deveridge)*, Anita Sharp Bolster *(Mrs. Foley)*, Lilian Fontaine *(Mrs. St. James)*, Lewis L. Russell *(Charles St. James)*

p, Charles Brackett; d, Billy Wilder; w, Charles Brackett, Billy Wilder (based on the novel by Charles R. Jackson); ph, John Seitz; ed, Doane Harrison; m, Miklos Rozsa, Giuseppe Verdi; art d, Hans Dreier, Earl Hedrick; fx, Gordon Jennings; cos, Edith Head

AA Best Picture; AA Best Actor: Ray Milland; *AA Best Director:* Billy Wilder; *AA Best Screenplay:* Charles Brackett, Billy Wilder; *AAN Best Cinematography:* John F. Seitz; *AAN Best Editing:* Doane Herrison; *AAN Best Score:* Miklos Rozsa

One of the most justly celebrated "problem films" of the 1940s. Though hailed in its time as a great advance in screen seriousness, this film just barely missed being shelved. The script by the noted team of Wilder and Brackett is dispassionate and unrelenting but also occasionally poetic. The film's emotional power is greatly abetted by Seitz's evocative black-and-white cinematography, ranging from unvarnished realism to delirious Expressionism. Finally, Milland's virtuoso work as the hopeless alcoholic is surprising, shocking and utterly riveting.

Don (Milland) is a struggling writer who waters down his writer's block with booze. The film opens with the camera zooming through the window of a New York apartment building which Don shares with his responsible brother Nick (Terry, Mr. Joan Crawford No. 3), who is about to go away for the weekend. Nick is somewhat worried about leaving his brother alone, but Don assures him that he will be settling down to do some serious writing. It's all downhill from there.

THE LAST WEEKEND is candid and brilliantly conceived from shot to shot. Wilder builds his film slowly and utilizes low-key lighting and deep-focus photography to emphasize objects that suggest the menace of alcohol, with scenes photographed through shot-glasses and bottles. A likable lead of light comedy and romance, Milland initially felt unequipped to handle such a serious role, but his wife encouraged him to try it. He was also encouraged by the fact that Wilder and Brackett had never had a flop. Faylen, though only onscreen for a few moments, makes an indelible impact as a bitchy male nurse in the sanitarium. Wyman forever escaped dumb blonde roles with her work here, and da Silva is excellent as a conscientious bartender.

Oddly, Paramount executives took one look at the finished film and told Wilder they were seriously considering not releasing it. They had received an avalanche of protest from temperance advocates who felt the film would *encourage* drinking. Powerful lobbyists for the liquor industry offered as much as $5 million for the negative of the film so it could be destroyed. But, at Wilder's urgings, Paramount released the film on a limited engagement in New York City, and the critics fell all over themselves praising it. It eventually became one of Paramount's biggest hits of 1945.

LOST WORLD: JURASSIC PARK, THE

1997 134m c Action/Fantasy ★★★
Amblin Entertainment/Universal (U.S.) PG-13/

Jeff Goldblum *(Dr. Ian Malcolm)*, Julianne Moore *(Dr. Sarah Harding)*, Pete Postlethwaite *(Roland Tembo)*, Arliss Howard *(Peter Ludlow)*, Richard Attenborough *(John Hammond)*, Vince Vaughn *(Nick Van Owen)*, Vanessa Lee Chester *(Kelly Curtis)*, Peter Stormare *(Dieter Stark)*, Harvey Jason *(Ajay Sidhu)*, Richard Schiff *(Eddie Carr)*

p, Gerald R. Molen, Colin Wilson; d, Steven Spielberg; w, David Koepp (based on the novel *The Lost World*, by Michael Crichton); ph, Janusz Kaminski; ed, Michael Kahn; m, John Williams; prod d, Rick Carter; art d, Jim Teegarden, Lauren Polizzi, Paul Sonski; fx, Dennis Muren, Stan Winston, Michael Lantieri, Ned Gorman, Industrial Light & Magic, Kevin Rafferty, Vicki L. Engel; cos, Sue Moore

"It always starts this way," mutters Dr. Ian Malcolm (Jeff Goldblum) darkly, as his companions ooh and ahh at the sight of real live dinosaurs. "Then there's running and there's screaming." THE LOST WORLD gets right to the running and the screaming.

Twinkly-eyed old capitalist John Hammond (Richard Attenborough) summons Malcolm to tell him that, contrary to what he may have thought, the dinosaurs aren't all dead. There's another island, and—miracle of miracles—nature has found a way around that inbred lysine deficiency that was supposed to ground the genetically engineered colossi. Hammond has sent Malcolm's girlfriend (Julianne Moore) to see how they're doing, and would like Malcolm to take a small crew to check up on her. But Hammond's renegade relative, Peter Ludlow (Arliss Howard), is planning a corporate killing and has brought his own band of mercenaries, led by Great White Hunter Roland Tembo (Pete Postlethwaite), to round up some dinos. Naturally, it all goes terribly, terribly wrong.

The sequel features many more dinosaurs than the first film, and most of its narrative effort is channeled into getting the cast into the proper place from which to be plucked by one scaly set of jaws after another. To that end, seasoned hunters must venture far, far from the group to urinate and, after explaining how the Tyrannosaurus Rex can pick up a scent 10 miles away, brilliant scientists must then traipse through the jungle wearing clothing saturated with blood. "That is the worst idea ever in the sorry history of bad ideas," Malcolm says only once, but the sentiment hangs over many plot developments—not the least of which is the plan to take a very large prehistoric predator to California. Didn't *any* of these guys see KING KONG?

LOVE AFFAIR

1939 87m bw Comedy/Romance ★★★★
RKO (U.S.) /U

Irene Dunne *(Terry McKay)*, Charles Boyer *(Michel Marnet)*, Maria Ouspenskaya *(Grandmother Janou)*, Lee Bowman *(Kenneth Bradley)*, Astrid Allwyn *(Lois Clarke)*, Maurice Moscovich *(Maurice Cobert)*, Scotty Beckett *(Boy on Ship)*, Bess Flowers, Harold Miller *(Couple on Deck)*, Joan Leslie *(Autograph Seeker)*

p, Leo McCarey; d, Leo McCarey; w, Delmer Daves, Donald Ogden Stewart (based on a story by McCarey, Daves, Mildred Cram); ph, Rudolph Mate; ed, Edward Dmytryk, George Hively; m, Roy Webb; art d, Van Nest Polglase, Al Herman; fx, Vernon L. Walker; cos, Howard Greer, Edward Stevenson

AAN Best Picture; AAN Best Actress: Irene Dunne; *AAN Best Supporting Actress:* Maria Ouspenskaya; *AAN Best Original Screenplay:* Mildred Cram, Leo McCarey; *AAN Best Song:* Buddy DeSylva (Music & Lyrics); *AAN Best Art Direction:* Van Nest Polglase (Art Direction), Al Herman (Art Direction)

A superb romance, the film deftly mixes humor with pathos and passion, and takes us on an emotional voyage that never fails to please. Michel (Boyer) is engaged to Lois (Allwyn), and Terry (Dunne) is engaged to Ken (Bowman) when the two meet onboard ship, but their mutual attraction is instant. The two flirt, but soon realize that this is not merely a shipboard fling; there is much more to their feelings about each other. They resolve to meet in six months at the top of the Empire State Building if they still feel the same way about each other. Tragedy strikes Terry on her way to meet Michel, but don't worry—"wishing will make it so."

There are many wonderful moments in the picture, both comedic and touching. As the couple takes its leave of Michel's grandmother (the magnificent Ouspenskaya), Terry suddenly rushes back to embrace the old woman, and Michel can't help but fall in love with her. As the "other man" and "other woman," Bowman and Allwyn are refreshingly adult and sympathetic, and Boyer and Dunne play beautifully together. The first half of the picture is breezy, witty and chic, but, while the second has a decidedly more serious tone, we never have the feeling that they are divided. Reportedly, the writers were scripting new pages every day. If that's true, more power to director McCarey who brought spontaneity rather than jumpiness to his direction. Look for veteran TV actor Gerald Mohr in a tiny extra bit and Joan Leslie, in her fourth film, at the age of 14. Decently remade as AN AFFAIR TO REMEMBER, with Deborah Kerr and Cary Grant.

LOVE AND DEATH

1975 85m c Comedy/War ★★★★
UA (U.S.) PG

Woody Allen *(Boris Dimitrovich Grushenko)*, Diane Keaton *(Sonja)*, Georges Adet *(Old Nehamkin)*, Frank Adu *(Drill Sergeant)*, Edmond Ardisson *(Priest)*, Feodor Atkine *(Mikhail)*, Albert Augier *(Waiter)*, Yves Barsacq *(Rimsky)*, Lloyd Battista *(Don Francisco)*, Jack Berard *(Gen. Lecoq)*

p, Charles H. Joffe; d, Woody Allen; w, Woody Allen; ph, Ghislain Cloquet; ed, Ron Kalish, Ralph Rosenblum; m, Sergei Prokofiev; art d, Willy Holt; cos, Gladys DeSegonzac

LOVE AND DEATH, Woody Allen's hilarious satire of classic Russian literature, might properly be described as Tolstoy meets the Marx Bros., as he and Diane Keaton get caught up in an uproariously funny plot to assassinate Napoleon in 1812.

In 19th-century Russia, Boris Grushenko (Woody Allen) falls in love with his beautiful cousin Sonja (Diane Keaton), but she's in love with his brother Ivan (Henry Czarniak). When Ivan announces his engagement to another woman, Sonja marries an elderly herring merchant, and Boris reluctantly joins the Russian army to fight Napoleon. Boris becomes an accidental hero after hiding in a cannon which destroys the enemy camp. Meanwhile, Sonja's husband dies and Boris proposes to her. Sonja accepts, believing Boris will surely be killed in an upcoming duel, but he survives and the two are married. Sonja eventually comes to love Boris, but when Napoleon again invades Russia, Sonja talks Boris into assassinating him. Disguised as the Spanish ambassador and his sister, Sonja and Boris manage to arrange an audience with Napoleon (James Tolkan), but are unaware that he is actually a double who has been substituted to protect the real Emperor.

LOVE AND DEATH was the first film which truly marked Woody Allen's growth from a stand-up comic and talented, but amateur, filmmaker, to a mature and original comedic director. It was a transitional film, coming between earlier shtick-filled movies such as BANANAS (1971) and his later, adult-oriented ones like ANNIE HALL (1977) and MANHATTAN (1979). LOVE AND DEATH successfully synthesizes Allen's penchant for inspired lunatic gags with his desire to broaden the scope of his films, by parodying the entire school of gloomy and portentous Russian novels with sophisticated wit and style. He also mixes in some priceless Groucho-esque wisecracks, along with other artistic and cultural references, including homages to Sergei Eisenstein (utilizing Prokofiev's score from ALEXANDER NEVSKY; quoting an image from THE BATTLESHIP POTEMKIN), and the Bob Hope costume-drama parodies which Allen has acknowledged as inspiration (particularly MONSIEUR BEAUCAIRE). Technically, the film is one of Allen's most accomplished, handsomely filmed in Hungary and France by Ghislain Cloquet, (who had shot a number of Robert Bresson's films), which helps make the hysterical anachronistic sight gags stand out even more.

LOVE AT TWENTY
(L'AMOUR A VINGT ANS)

1962 110m bw Drama ★★★
Ulysse/Unitec/Toho/Cinescolo/Towa/Kamera/Film Polski/Beta /X
(France/Italy/Poland/West Germany/Japan)

FRANCE: Jean-Pierre Leaud *(Antoine Doinel)*, Marie-France Pisier *(Colette)*, Francois Darbon *(Colette's Father)*, Rosy Varte *(Colette's Mother)*, Patrick Auffay *(Rene)*, Jean-Francois Adam *(Albert Tazzi)*, ITALY: Eleonora Rossi-Drago *(Valentina)*, Cristina Gajoni *(Christina)*, Geronimo Meynier *(Leonardo)*, JAPAN: Koji Furuhata *(Hiroshi)*

p, Pierre Roustang; d, Francois Truffaut, Renzo Rossellini, Shintaro Ishihara, Marcel Ophuls, Andrzej Wajda; w, Yvon Samuel, Francois Truffaut, Renzo Rossellini, Shintaro Ishihara, Marcel Ophuls, Jerzy Stefan Stawinski; ph, Raoul Coutard, Mario Montuori, Shigeo Hayashida, Wolf Wirth, Jerzy Lipman; ed, Claudine Bouche; m, Georges Delerue, Toru Takemitsu, Jerzy Matuszkiewicz

An international compilation film best known for its Truffaut episode, "Antoine and Colette," the second installment of his "Antoine Doinel" series begun in THE 400 BLOWS. Conceived by French producer Roustang, the film is built on the theme of being 20 years old or, as he

would put it, "the inscrutable youth of the atomic age and technological civilization." Five young filmmakers contributed: Francois Truffaut (France), Renzo Rossellini (Italy), Shintaro Ishihara (Japan), Marcel Ophuls (West Germany), and Andrzej Wajda (Poland). Truffaut's episode has Leaud relocate to across the street from the girl he loves only to discover that her parents like him more than she does. In Rossellini's segment a young man juggles relationships with a young woman and an older one. Ishihara's piece has a love-maddened, working-class lad kill his girlfriend—but fail, because of class differences, to win the wealthy girl he loves. Ophuls' segment is far more optimistic. A photographer on a stopover in Munich gets a girl pregnant. After arriving home he learns what has happened and returns, marries the girl, and soon falls in love with her. Wajda's episode differs from the others; it is told from an older person's point of view (not surprising, considering that at age 35 he was the eldest of the directors). A middle-aged man saves a young girl who has slipped into a polar bear pit in a zoo. Later, at a party to which he is invited by two teenage witnesses, he relates an account of his past as a resistance fighter. The party-goers get him drunk, tease him, and sing him a song about a "sleepy old bear" before they kick him out.

LOVE FROM A STRANGER

1937 86m bw Thriller ★★★★
Trafalgar (U.K.) /A

Ann Harding *(Carol Howard)*, Basil Rathbone *(Gerald Lovell)*, Binnie Hale *(Kate Meadows)*, Bruce Seton *(Ronald Bruce)*, Jean Cadell *(Aunt Lou)*, Bryan Powley *(Dr. Gribble)*, Joan Hickson *(Emmy)*, Donald Calthrop *(Hobson)*, Eugene Leahy *(Mr. Tuttle)*

p, Max Schach; d, Rowland V. Lee; w, Frances Marion (based on the short story by Agatha Christie and the play by Frank Vosper); ph, Philip Tannura; ed, Howard O'Neill; cos, Samuel Lange

This top-notch thriller provides some brilliantly theatrical acting by Harding and Rathbone, who parry and thrust in a game of deadly wits. Carol Howard (Harding) is a sweet, unsuspecting lady of beauty and refinement who wins a lottery while on a European vacation. A short time later, she encounters the suave and charming Gerald Lovell (Rathbone) who walks her to the altar. Gerald uses some of Carol's money to buy a luxurious home in the country, and all seems blissful until he quite casually asks Carol to sign a document, claiming it is a mortgage transfer. The document, if signed, would turn over her entire fortune to her husband. It's cat and mouse time.

Rathbone is both charming and frightening in his sophisticated role, and this film remains one of his finest. Harding is also excellent as the victim desperate to preserve her life. This was the American actress's first British film after eight years of Hollywood stardom. All the vagaries and nuances of the original Agatha Christie story remain intact, and Lee's direction and Marion's script shine.

LOVE ME OR LEAVE ME

1955 122m c Musical/Biography ★★★★
MGM (U.S.) /A

Doris Day *(Ruth Etting)*, James Cagney *(Martin "The Gimp" Snyder)*, Cameron Mitchell *(Johnny Alderman)*, Robert Keith *(Bernard V. Loomis)*, Tom Tully *(Frobisher)*, Harry Bellaver *(Georgie)*, Richard Gaines *(Paul Hunter)*, Peter Leeds *(Fred Taylor)*, Claude Stroud *(Eddie Fulton)*, Audrey Young *(Jingle Girl)*

p, Joe Pasternak; d, Charles Vidor; w, Daniel Fuchs, Isobel Lennart (based on the story by Fuchs); ph, Arthur E. Arling; ed, Ralph E. Winters; m, Percy Faith; art d, Cedric Gibbons, Urie McCleary; fx, Warren Newcombe; chor, Alex Romero; cos, Helen Rose

AAN Best Actor: James Cagney; *AA Best Story:* Daniel Fuchs; *AAN Best Screenplay:* Daniel Fuchs, Isobel Lennart; *AAN Best Score:* Percy Faith, George Stoll; *AAN Best Song:* Nicholas Brodszky (Music), Sammy Cahn (Lyrics); *AAN Best Sound:* Wesley C. Miller

Unlike many musical bios of the day, LOVE ME OR LEAVE ME provides a hard-edged love story, augmented with Jazz Age tunes, chronicling the life and times of Prohibition-era torch singer Ruth Etting. This was a once-in-a-lifetime role for Doris Day, who is terrific as Etting in a part unlike any other she played, calling for her to be alternately sizzling in performance and naive offstage. James Cagney is equally sensational as Marty "The Gimp" Snyder, the ruthless gangster who was her Svengali, and normally lightweight Cameron Mitchell excels as Harry Myrl Alderman (called Johnny in the film), Etting's true love. Snyder, a powerful Chicago racketeer, sees Etting at a dime-a-dance club. She wants to be a singer, so Marty pushes the owner into giving her a small singing bit. Club pianist Alderman helps her develop her talents, and, with Snyder's aid, Etting eventually becomes a headliner, going on to radio and a spot in the Ziegfeld Follies in New York. When Etting grows increasingly independent of Snyder, however, he tears up her Ziegfeld contract and takes her on tour, then to movie stardom in Hollywood. There, Alderman resumes subtly courting her, but Snyder has manipulated her into marrying him, and Etting takes to drink over having to live with a man she does not love.

The chemistry between Cagney and Day is electric, Charles Vidor's direction is lively and inventive, and the overall production lavishly and accurately reproduces the 1920s era. The Jazz Age music is outstanding, superbly performed by Day. (Our favorite? "Ten Cents a Dance".) MGM paid $50,000 for the song rights alone, as well as hefty sums to Etting, Alderman, and Snyder for the rights to film their lives. Etting later noted that "they took a lot of liberties with my life, but I guess they usually do with that kind of thing". Metro made back the money upon the film's release, however, when it was enthusiastically received by both critics and audiences.

LOVE ME TONIGHT
(MAREZ-MOI CE SOIR!)

1932 104m bw Musical/Comedy ★★★★★
Paramount (U.S.) /A

Maurice Chevalier *(Maurice Courtelin)*, Jeanette MacDonald *(Princess Jeanette)*, Charlie Ruggles *(Vicomte Gilbert de Vareze)*, Charles Butterworth *(Count de Savignac)*, Myrna Loy *(Countess Vantine)*, C. Aubrey Smith *(The Duke)*, Elizabeth Patterson, Ethel Griffies, Blanche Frederici *(Aunts)*, Joseph Cawthorn *(Dr. Armand de Fontinac)*

p, Rouben Mamoulian; d, Rouben Mamoulian; w, Samuel Hoffenstein, Waldemar Young, George Marion Jr. (based on the play "Tailor in the Chateau" by Leopold Marchand, Paul Armont); ph, Victor Milner; ed, William Shea; art d, Hans Dreier; cos, Edith Head, Travis Banton

Love it forever. Along with SWING TIME and perhaps one of Busby Berkeley's best, this film stands as the greatest musical of the 1930s and one of the finest ever. Although the film seems very much in a Lubitsch vein, Rouben Mamoulian directed it, and he is perhaps most responsible for its stunning appeal. His earliest period in film (1929-34) was certainly his greatest and in this film he displays such audacity in playing with sound and image that it's no wonder he frightened everyone in Hollywood.

The tale of a romance between Princess Jeanette (MacDonald) and Maurice the tailor (Chevalier), LOVE ME TONIGHT is effervescent frippery to be sure, but it's so inventive as to be downright eerie. The slow-motion retreat from the lovers' cottage still astounds and Jeanette's final ride on horseback to stop a train is dramatically quite striking. One is not likely to forget the dark shadows of Chevalier's "I'm an Apache" number or the cutting and framing of both the title duet and the witty "The Son of a Gun Is Nothing But a Tailor". Jeanette's three worrisome aunts could almost be comic variants of the witches in MACBETH and, at one point, they sound like a kennel in an uproar. The film mocks those very conventions the genre employs, from the famous traveling rendition of "Isn't It Romantic?" to the sudden thud of a ladder which ends Jeanette's balcony reverie.

The cast, too, is quite remarkable, and they make the most of the saucy pre-Code antics. Ruggles's mad dash in his underwear and Butterworth's "I fell flat on my flute" demonstrate comic diffidence of the highest caliber. In what is almost certainly her most memorable role before achieving stardom, Loy plies her smooth comic touch and gets to add a naughtiness she usually wasn't allowed later. Her man-crazy Vantine displays a freshness partly inspired by Mamoulian and Loy's creating the part as they went along. When someone is ill and she is asked, "Could you go for a doctor?" she instantly replies, "Oh, yes, send him in." The starring duo, meanwhile, enjoy one of their greatest partnerings here. Though we like some of her later films with Nelson

Eddy, the genial, risque tension between Chevalier and MacDonald works as deliciously as vodka in orange juice. MacDonald is not sufficiently appreciated for her wonderful comic flair and Mamoulian is bold enough to simply toss off her spirited rendition of "Lover" in long shot, knowing that her play with both an uncooperative horse and the ending of the verses will be funnier that way. She matches the winking Frenchman innuendo for innuendo and her carefully stylized, sexy performance fits perfectly within the film's magnificent sense of hyperbole. Finally, the incomparable Chevalier knows exactly what he's up to as well here. Not conventional leading man material, he's both beautifully tongue-in-cheek and utterly sincere. His naughtiness avoids the puerile and the nasty, yet he can get more out of his signature song "Mimi" than any lyricist can write.

LOVE ON THE RUN
(L'AMOUR EN FUITE)

1979 94m c Drama/Comedy ★★★½
Carosse (France) PG/15

Jean-Pierre Leaud *(Antoine Doinel)*, Marie-France Pisier *(Colette)*, Claude Jade *(Christine)*, Dani *(Liliane)*, Dorothee *(Sabine)*, Rosy Varte *(Colette's Mother)*, Marie Henriau *(Divorce Judge)*, Daniel Mesguich *(Xavier the Librarian)*, Julien Bertheau *(M. Lucien)*, Jean-Pierre Ducos *(Christine's Lawyer)*

d, Francois Truffaut; w, Francois Truffaut, Marie-France Pisier, Jean Aurel, Suzanne Schiffman; ph, Nestor Almendros; ed, Martine Barraque; m, Georges Delerue; art d, Jean-Pierre Kohut-Svelko

LOVE ON THE RUN is the fifth and final entry in Francois Truffaut's "Antoine Doinel" series, which began in 1959 with THE 400 BLOWS. By now the young, unpredictable Antoine (Jean-Pierre Leaud) has grown into a man of 34, able to reminisce about his past loves and put them into his new book. The picture opens with the unshaven Antoine and his newest love, Sabine (Dorothee, in a wonderful debut performance), awakening to a sunny morning—the morning that he is to get a divorce from his wife, Christine (Claude Jade, from 1971's BED AND BOARD). Before the day is over Antoine also encounters his first love, Colette (Marie-France Pisier, who appeared years before in Truffaut's episode of LOVE AT TWENTY). There is actually very little in LOVE ON THE RUN that resembles a story. Its chief purpose is simply to look back at the women Antoine has loved. Like so many of Truffaut's characters, Antoine is obsessed with the desire to love, and here he tells how he found a ripped-up, discarded picture of Sabine in a phone booth and set out to find her. In the process, clips are shown from THE 400 BLOWS; LOVE AT TWENTY; STOLEN KISSES; and BED AND BOARD, amounting to an overview of the life of Doinel (as well as those of both Leaud and Truffaut). For those who haven't seen any of the previous "Doinel" pictures, LOVE ON THE RUN will probably be a difficult picture to sit through, but for those who have followed the growth of these characters, the film is a true charmer. In keeping with other Truffaut films, LOVE ON THE RUN includes a superb score from Georges Delerue and a perfectly hummable title song from Alain Souchon.

LOVE PARADE, THE
(PARADE D'AMOUR)

1929 107m bw Musical/Comedy ★★★½
Paramount (U.S.)

Maurice Chevalier *(Count Alfred Renard)*, Jeanette MacDonald *(Queen Louise)*, Lupino Lane *(Jacques)*, Lillian Roth *(Lulu)*, Edgar Norton *(Major Domo)*, Lionel Belmore *(Prime Minister)*, Albert Roccardi *(Foreign Minister)*, Carl Stockdale *(Admiral)*, Eugene Pallette *(Minister of War)*, E.H. Calvert *(Sylvanian Ambassador)*

p, Ernst Lubitsch; d, Ernst Lubitsch; w, Ernest Vajda, Guy Bolton (based on the play "The Prince Consort" by Leon Xanrof, Jules Chancel); ph, Victor Milner; ed, Merrill White; art d, Hans Dreier

AAN Best Picture; AAN Best Actor: Maurice Chevalier; AAN Best Director: Ernst Lubitsch; AAN Best Cinematography: Victor Milner; AAN Best Art Direction: Hans Dreier (Art Direction); AAN Best Sound: Franklin Hansen (Sound)

Students of film lore will find much to enjoy in THE LOVE PARADE. It was Ernst Lubitsch's first sound film, Jeanette MacDonald's debut, Maurice Chevalier's second picture, and the first of three that the director made with these leads. (The others were ONE HOUR WITH YOU, THE MERRY WIDOW.) The featherweight story takes place in mythical Sylvania, where Queen Louise (MacDonald) is desperately lonely for male companionship. Count Alfred Renard (Chevalier), her emissary to France, has been cavorting so conspicuously that she has recalled him to Sylvania. Summoned to Louise's bedchamber so she can check out what endears him to so many women, Alfred is quickly wedded to his Queen. Problems arise when the chauvinistic Count finds his role as consort intolerable, and the battle for the throne is on.

Lubitsch adapted to the requirements of sound film with ease, and the execution of the frail plot is insouciant and bubbly. The film's sexual politics are typical of its era, though a great deal of satiric ribbing takes place before the inevitable finale. The film differed from the many backstage musicals of the day in that its musical numbers advanced, rather than stopped, the action. Chevalier and MacDonald, both expert at risque material, play beautifully together, and are in fine voice as well. Their singing highlights include his "Paris, Stay the Same" and the amusing soliloquy "Nobody's Using It Now" and her rendition of "Dream Lover". The priceless Lupino Lane and Lillian Roth steal many scenes as palace servants, and team up for the delightful "Let's Be Common". Look for the scene where Chevalier ends up showing his "collection" of guns and garters.

LOVE STORY

1970 99m c Romance ★★
Paramount (U.S.) GP/PG

Ali MacGraw (*Jenny Cavilleri*), Ryan O'Neal (*Oliver Barrett IV*), Ray Milland (*Oliver Barrett III*), Katharine Balfour (*Mrs. Oliver Barrett III*), John Marley (*Phil Cavilleri*), Russell Nype (*Dean Thompson*), Sydney Walker (*Dr. Shapely*), Robert Modica (*Dr. Addison*), Walker Daniels (*Ray*), Tommy Lee Jones (*Hank*)

p, Howard G. Minsky; d, Arthur Hiller; w, Erich Segal (based on the novel by Erich Segal); ph, Dick Kratina; ed, Robert C. Jones; m, Francis Lai; art d, Robert Gundlach; cos, Alice Manougian Martin, Pearl Somner

AAN Best Picture; AAN Best Actor: Ryan O'Neal; *AAN Best Actress:* Ali MacGraw; *AAN Best Supporting Actor:* John Marley; *AAN Best Director:* Arthur Hiller; *AAN Best Adapted Screenplay:* Erich Segal; *AA Best Score:* Francis Lai

"Love means never having to say you're sorry" was the catch phrase that helped make this a huge grosser, but we're sorry anyone ever fell in love with this script. LOVE STORY is actually better than Segal's previously released best-seller (written from his screenplay in order to promote the film). But then that's not saying much.

Wistful Oliver (O'Neal) is at Harvard (of course) in his final pre-law year, when he meets and falls for tragic Jenny (MacGraw), a music student at Radcliffe (where else?). She's a rude mite from a lower-class family, and he is one of the Boston Brahmins. You can guess the rest. O'Neal and MacGraw go together like applesauce spread on sandpaper, and the rest of the cast (except John Marley) comes across as a series of caricatures. Milland, in particular, as Oliver's snotty father, acts like a billiard ball in a business suit. By the time O'Neal gets around to intoning the famous tag line, you'll be so sick of hearing Francis Lai's love theme that you'll want to strangle the projectionist. Too bad MacGraw's already bitten the dust. Paging DARK VICTORY.

LOVE STREAMS

1984 141m c Drama ★★★★
MGM (U.S.) PG-13/15

Gena Rowlands (*Sarah Lawson*), John Cassavetes (*Robert Harmon*), Diahnne Abbott (*Susan*), Seymour Cassel (*Jack Lawson*), Margaret Abbott (*Margarita*), Jakob Shaw (*Albie Swanson*), Michele Conway (*Agnes Swanson*), Eddy Donno (*Stepfather Swanson*), Joan Foley (*Judge Dunbar*), Al Ruban (*Milton Kravitz*)

p, Menahem Golan, Yoram Globus; d, John Cassavetes; w, Ted Allan, John Cassavetes (based on the play by Allan); ph, Al Ruban; ed, George Villasenor; m, Bo Harwood; art d, Phedon Papamichael; cos, Jennifer Smith-Ashley

With Israeli filmmakers Golan and Globus watching over him, director John Cassavetes was guilty of less self-indulgence than usual, and the result is one of his best movies ever. Appearing for the first time in a movie that he also directed, Cassavetes and real-life spouse Gena Rowlands team up as a brother and sister, Robert Harmon and Sarah Lawson. The screen exudes their intensity; and despite their apparently different personalities, a oneness of spirit unites them. Robert is a well-known author, who is researching a book on prostitution and becomes the den father to some lively ladies of the evening. His research takes him on nightly forays to the underbelly of town. Sarah is a delicate creature in the throes of a divorce and custody battle against her husband, Jack (Seymour Cassel). The intercutting of the two stories contrasts the tawdriness of Robert's life to the exemplariness of Sarah's. For half the movie we see their separate lives and wonder when and if they will get together. Rowlands is wonderfully convincing in her many opportunities to play unusual scenes. Cassavetes also has his moments. More an amalgam of telling bits and pieces than a real story, this movie (like so many of Cassavetes' works) goes on too long. This time, however, it all seems to work.

LOVE WITH THE PROPER STRANGER

1963 102m bw Comedy/Drama ★★★★
Boardwalk/Rona (U.S.) /X

Natalie Wood (*Angie Rossini*), Steve McQueen (*Rocky Papasano*), Edie Adams (*Barbie, Barbara of Seville*), Herschel Bernardi (*Dominick Rossini*), Tom Bosley (*Anthony Colombo*), Harvey Lembeck (*Julio Rossini*), Penny Santon (*Mama Rossini*), Virginia Vincent (*Anna*), Nick Alexander (*Guido Rossini*), Augusta Ciolli (*Mrs. Papasano*)

p, Alan J. Pakula; d, Robert Mulligan; w, Arnold Schulman; ph, Milton Krasner; ed, Aaron Stell; m, Elmer Bernstein; art d, Hal Pereira, Roland Anderson; cos, Edith Head

AAN Best Actress: Natalie Wood; *AAN Best Original Screenplay:* Arnold Schulman; *AAN Best Cinematography:* Milton Krasner; *AAN Best Art Direction:* Hal Pereira (Art Direction), Roland Anderson (Art Direction), Sam Comer (Set Decoration), Grace Gregory (Set Decoration); *AAN Best Costume Design:* Edith Head

Wood plays a sort of female Marty in this role that netted the actress her third Oscar nomination. She is a quiet, well-brought-up Italian girl in a situation that is more than she can handle. She is so quiet, well-brought-up, and Italian, in fact, that it's hard to imagine how she got into this mess! How does a sweet, traditional type manage to find herself pregnant after a one-night stand with McQueen? And what do you do when the father-to-be has a girlfriend and the expectant mother's unknowing family keep pushing her to marry another man?

The theme of unmarried pregnancy had been seen often before (e.g., in BLUE DENIM) but was not usually handled so deftly as in this picture, which not only dares to deal with the subject of abortion but has lots of down-to-earth, Italian humor from Bosley, Lembeck, and Bernardi. Adams is outstanding as McQueen's stripper girlfriend. She always had a way with comedy and showed it early when playing the foil for her genius husband, Ernie Kovacs. In small roles, look for Richard Mulligan, Arlene Golonka, Vic Tayback, and Richard Dysart, all of whom later achieved success on TV. Not perfect, but touching and adult; with fine work from the two leads, this is one of Mulligan's better films.

LOVED ONE, THE

1965 116m bw Comedy ★★★★
MGM (U.S.) /X

Robert Morse (*Dennis Barlow*), Jonathan Winters (*Wilbur Glenworthy/Harry Glenworthy*), Anjanette Comer (*Aimee Thanatogenos*), Rod Steiger (*Mr. Joyboy*), Dana Andrews (*Gen. Brinkman*), Milton Berle (*Mr. Kenton*), James Coburn (*Immigration Officer*), John Gielgud (*Sir Francis Hinsley*), Tab Hunter (*Guide*), Margaret Leighton (*Mrs. Kenton*) p, John Calley, Haskell Wexler; d, Tony Richardson; w, Terry Southern, Christopher Isherwood (based on the novel by Evelyn Waugh); ph, Haskell Wexler; ed, Anthony Gibbs; m, John Addison; prod d, Rouben Ter-Arutunian; art d, Sydney Z. Litwack; fx, Geza Gaspar; cos, Nat Tolmach, Rouben Ter-Arutunian, James Kelly, Marie T. Harris

This spoof of morticians and funerals captures much of the macabre hilarity in the Waugh novel but failed to impress critics at the time of release. It often sinks into broad burlesque due to Southern and Isherwood's heavy-handed script, but the laughs are still there. Morse, a naive, rather gawky character from England, visits his uncle, Gielgud, an aging, fussy art director living in a dilapidated Hollywood mansion. When his studio fires him, Gielgud hangs himself. Robert Morley, head of the British community of Hollywood talent, arrives and instructs Morse to arrange to have Gielgud buried at Whispering Glades Memorial Park (the real-life Forest Lawn), the most resplendant funeral grounds in America, run by Winters. In the process of contacting morticians, Morse obtains a job at a pet cemetery run by Winters' twin brother (also played by Winters), and the various schemes, scams, and lack of concern by morticians for both humans and pets are revealed in all their callous glories. A host of bizarre characters then parade through Morse's life, including Comer, a sultry, naive beauty he covets and who is lusted after by Winters (the one running the high-class mortuary) and Steiger, a crackpot cosmetologist who works with her. Comer is repelled by Steiger's obese and gluttonous mother and is almost won over by Morse who reads poetry (stolen from Steiger) to her. Then Comer's ideals are smashed by Winters, head of Whispering Glades, when he tries to seduce her, and she commits suicide by injecting herself with embalming fluid. A further plot develops when Morse discovers that Winters, in collusion with Andrews, an Air Force general, plans to get rid of all the bodies on his property by sending them into space, so he can transform his cemetery into a luxurious spa for retirees, making even more millions. He is foiled by Morse who replaces the body of a dead astronaut, the first to be shot into space, with Comer's comely corpse. Having exposed Winters and sent him to ruin, Morse returns to England to try to forget his morbid, morose, and strange experience in America. Morse is unappealing, but the supporting players, especially Winters, and bits performed by Stander, Coburn, and Hunter are very funny.

LOVERS, THE
(LES AMANTS)

1959 90m bw Drama   ★★★
Nouvelle Editions des Films (France)   /X

Jeanne Moreau (Jeanne Tournier), Alain Cuny (Henri Tournier), Jean-Marc Bory (Bernard Dubois-Lambert), Judith Magre (Maggy Thiebaut-Leroy), Jose-Luis de Vilallonga (Raoul Flores), Gaston Modot (Coudray), Patricia Garcin (Catherine, Jeanne's Daughter), Claude Mansard (Marcelot), Georgette Lobbe (Marthe)

d, Louis Malle; w, Louis Malle, Louise de Vilmorin (based on the novel Point de Lendemain by Dominique Vivant); ph, Henri Decae; ed, Leonide Azar; m, Johannes Brahms, Alain de Rosnay; prod d, Bernard Evein, Jacques Saulnier

Notorious for its extended seminude love-making scene when first released in 1959, Louis Malle's THE LOVERS seems tame today when compared with average "R" rated films of the decades following it. The film tells the simple tale of Moreau, a bored mother and wife, who meets, falls in love with, and sleeps with young archaeologist Bory—all in the course of one evening. The next morning she abandons her family and runs off with her new lover to an uncertain future. The film was vastly overrated due to the censorship it incurred overseas and in the US. (A suburban Cleveland theater manager was prosecuted for showing an obscene film. The case went to the Supreme Court and was eventually thrown out.) The film is a solid but not great examination of female mid-life crisis, with Moreau in typically fine form.

LOVES OF A BLONDE
(LASKY JEDNE PLAVOVLASKY)

1965 88m bw Comedy   ★★★½
Barrandov/Ceskoslovensky (Czechoslovakia)

Hana Brejchova (Andula), Vladimir Pucholt (Milda), Vladimir Mensik (Vacovsky), Ivan Kheil (Manas), Jiri Hruby (Burda), Milada Jezkova (Milda's Mother), Josef Sebanek (Milda's Father), Marie Salacova (Marie), Jana Novakova (Jana), Jana Crkalova (Jaruska)

d, Milos Forman; w, Jaroslav Papousek, Ivan Passer, Milos Forman, Vaclav Sasek; ph, Miroslav Ondricek; ed, Miroslav Hajek; m, Evzen Illin; art d, Karel Cerny

AAN Best Foreign Language Film

This charming and frequently touching romantic comedy, directed by Milos Forman, concerns a young woman, Brejchova, who works in a shoe factory and dreams of love. Dissatisfied with the men in her town, she is forced to suffer the attentions of Blazejovsky, an ardent admirer, but less than what she perceives to be her ideal man. When a dance is held in honor of soldiers stationed in the town, Brejchova looks forward to meeting a handsome military man. To her disappointment, however, the soldiers all turn out to be middle-aged reserves, so she sets her sights on the piano player, Pucholt. After some uneasy introductions, Brejchova spends the night with Pucholt. Now in love, she travels to his parents' home in Prague, where her stay is anything but blissful. An international success, LOVES OF A BLONDE was an important film not only in the career of Forman (who would go to America and direct ONE FLEW OVER THE CUCKOO'S NEST), but also as one of the films (along with THE SHOP ON MAIN STREET and CLOSELY WATCHED TRAINS) that helped give Czech cinema worldwide attention. It received an Oscar nomination for Best Foreign Film, but lost to A MAN AND A WOMAN.

LUCK OF GINGER COFFEY, THE

1964 100m c Drama   ★★★
Roth/Kershner/Crawley (U.S./Canada)   /A

Robert Shaw (Ginger Coffey), Mary Ure (Vera), Liam Redmond (MacGregor), Tom Harvey (Joe McGlade), Libby McClintock (Paulie), Leo Leyden (Brott), Powys Thomas (Fox), Tom Kneebone (Kenny), Leslie Yeo (Stan Melton), Vern Chapman (Hawkins)

p, Leon Roth; d, Irvin Kershner; w, Brian Moore (based on his novel); ph, Manny Wynn; ed, Anthony Gibbs; m, Bernardo Segall; prod d, Harry Horner; art d, Albert Brenner

A well-intentioned, noncommercial Canadian-based film starring real-life husband and wife Shaw and Ure as a husband and wife. Shaw is pushing forty and can't hold a job in Dublin, so he and his family emigrate to Montreal in the hope of a new life. His teenage daughter, McClintock, doesn't like the move, but Shaw and Ure hope she'll adjust. Shaw has little success in Canada, and his family asks to return to Ireland. They've had a nest egg for the trip home, but Shaw has spent it, and now they must stay. Ure leaves him, taking McClintock, but soon the girl returns to live with her father. Shaw has apparently settled down and is working as a proofreader at a newspaper under hardhearted Redmond and as a laundry delivery man by day. Shaw thinks he may get a better job as a reporter, so he jettisons his delivery job, despite getting a good offer from the folks who run the laundry. For no apparent reason, he is fired from the newspaper, but it's too late to get back into the laundry. He talks Ure into coming home to help him control McClintock. Shaw can't find work and winds up a drunk. He's soon arrested and tossed in the clink. Kindly judge Legare lets him out with a rap on the knuckles, and Shaw is heartened to see that Ure is standing outside the court waiting for him, open-armed. A nice picture with an interesting look at immigrants who have no language problem, it's about little people in a big predicament and succeeds on its own terms; however, we are left with the thought that if we'd seen another two hours of this, Shaw would have wound up beating his wife and daughter, then stealing a car, and driving drunkenly off a bridge.

LUST FOR LIFE

1956 122m c Biography ★★★★½
MGM (U.S.) /A

Kirk Douglas (Vincent Van Gogh), Anthony Quinn (Paul Gauguin), James Donald (Theo Van Gogh), Pamela Brown (Christine), Everett Sloane (Dr. Gachet), Niall MacGinnis (Roulin), Noel Purcell (Anton Mauve), Henry Daniell (Theodorus Van Gogh), Madge Kennedy (Anna Cornelia Van Gogh), Jill Bennett (Willemien)

p, John Houseman; d, Vincente Minnelli; w, Norman Corwin (based on the novel by Irving Stone); ph, Freddie Young, Russell Harlan; ed, Adrienne Fazan; m, Miklos Rozsa; art d, Cedric Gibbons, Hans Peters, Preston Ames; cos, Walter Plunkett

AAN Best Actor: Kirk Douglas; AA Best Supporting Actor: Anthony Quinn; AAN Best Adapted Screenplay: Norman Corwin; AAN Best Art Direction: Cedric Gibbons, Hans Peters, Preston Ames, Edwin B. Willis, Keogh Gleason

Lust for Life was optioned by MGM in 1947, but it took almost nine years before the studio finally filmed Irving Stone's immensely popular fictionalized biography of Vincent Van Gogh. Douglas plays the Dutch painter, who, as the film opens, leaves Holland to give religious instruction to coal miners in a Belgian province in 1878. There, full of pity for the impoverished workers, Van Gogh gives away not only his own worldly goods, but also those belonging to the church. Censured by his superiors in the church, he denounces them as hypocrites, abandons his evangelical activities, and suffers an emotional and physical decline.

Found living in squalor by his brother, Theo (Donald), Van Gogh is persuaded to return to Holland and recuperate, but his burgeoning interest in painting upsets the whole household, and his sister asks him to leave. In the Hague, Douglas sets up house with Christine (Brown), a prostitute who becomes his model and mistress. Anton Mauve (Purcell), a successful painter and relative of Van Gogh, tries to help him, but the fiercely independent Van Gogh soon rejects Mauve's advice and alienates the better-known painter, losing his economic support and friendship.

After the death of their father, Van Gogh joins Theo in Paris (where Theo is an art dealer), and meets the great artists of the Impressionist movement, befriending Paul Gauguin (Quinn). Gauguin is nearly as eccentric as Van Gogh, but the Dutchman's volatile nature endangers his closest friendship yet and precipitates another decline.

LUST FOR LIFE tells a tragic story, but the portrait of Van Gogh's uncompromised genius is also inspiring. Douglas gives an appropriately fiery star turn as Van Gogh, delivering some of the best work of his career. With typical dedication, Douglas even went so far as to take extensive painting lessons for the role. Quinn, in a relatively small part, is also excellent as the moody Gauguin, who attempts to befriend his fellow genius.

Director Vincente Minnelli fought in vain against using CinemaScope for this film, feeling that "the dimensions of the wider screen [bore] little relation to the conventional shape of paintings." Minnelli also felt that the candybox Eastmancolor MGM used did not offer the soft tones he needed to reproduce Van Gogh's world and art. He described the color process as being "a brilliant mixture of blues, reds, and yellows that resembled neither life nor art." With producer Houseman's support, Minnelli hounded MGM executives into buying up all the remaining film stock from the discontinued Ansco process, and the company responded by opening a special laboratory to process his footage. Houseman and Minnelli also searched out surviving contemporaries of the great artist, visited locales when Van Gogh lived and worked, and managed to film 200 of the painter's masterworks (located around the world) without subjecting them to the dangers of standard movie lighting.

LUSTY MEN, THE

1952 113m bw Sports/Western ★★★★
RKO (U.S.) /U

Susan Hayward (Louise Merritt), Robert Mitchum (Jeff McCloud), Arthur Kennedy (Wes Merritt), Arthur Hunnicutt (Booker Davis), Frank Faylen (Al Dawson), Walter Coy (Buster Burgess), Carol Nugent (Rusty Davis), Maria Hart (Rosemary Maddox), Lorna Thayer (Grace Burgess), Burt Mustin (Jeremiah)

p, Jerry Wald, Norman Krasna; d, Nicholas Ray; w, Horace McCoy, David Dortort (based on a story by Claude Stanush); ph, Lee Garmes; ed, Ralph Dawson; m, Roy Webb; art d, Albert S. D'Agostino, Alfred Herman; cos, Michael Woulfe

Director Nicholas Ray was a master of the offbeat film, and this brilliant contemporary western, easily the best movie ever made about rodeo (see also JUNIOR BONNER, J.W. COOP and RODEO), is no exception. Washed-up rodeo champion Jeff McCloud (Robert Mitchum) takes a job on the ranch of Wes and Louise Merritt (Arthur Kennedy and Susan Hayward) and, with his guidance, Wes becomes a rodeo star. Meanwhile, Louise leads on the infatuated Jeff to insure his continued training of her husband, but, when Wes gets too big for his britches, Jeff goes head to swelled head with him in rodeo competition, with tragic results. THE LUSTY MEN is full of action and dangerous stunts, photographed beautifully by master cinematographer Lee Garmes. Ray's direction is superb, and all three leads give bravura performances. Based on a Life magazine story by Claude Stanush, and coscripted by cowboy David Dortort, its screenplay presents classical situations, full of poetry and destiny. In his search for realism, Ray took his cameras on location, filming rodeos in Tucson, Arizona, Spokane, Washington, Pendleton, Oregon, and Livermore, California, using a host of real rodeo stars such as Gerald Roberts, Jerry Ambler, and Les Sanborn.

M

(MORDER UNTER UNS)

1931 117m bw Crime/Horror ★★★★★
Nero (Germany) /PG

Peter Lorre (Franz Becker), Otto Wernicke (Inspector Karl Lohmann), Gustaf Grundgens (Schraenker), Theo Lingen (Bauernfaenger), Theodor Loos (Police Commissioner Groeber), Georg John (Blind Peddler), Ellen Widmann (Mme. Becker), Inge Landgut (Elsie), Ernst Stahl-Nachbaur (Police Chief), Paul Kemp (Pickpocket)

p, Seymour Nebenzal; d, Fritz Lang; w, Fritz Lang, Thea von Harbou, Paul Falkenberg, Adolf Jansen, Karl Vash (based on an article by Egon Jacobson); ph, Fritz Arno Wagner; ed, Paul Falkenberg; m, Edvard Grieg; art d, Emil Hasler, Karl Vollbrecht

Fritz Lang's first sound film, his most chilling and provocative work, features Peter Lorre's greatest performance as a child molester and murderer. As the film opens, Berlin is gripped by terror: a child molester is killing little girls, while the police's frantic search has so far turned up no clues to his identity. Frenzied citizens inform on their neighbors; police raids net scores of criminals, but none that can be linked to the killings. To stop this trend, the underworld's leading members resolve to catch the killer themselves, ordering the criminal community to find the murderer and bring him to a tribunal—and the trap to catch the desperate man is set in thrilling motion. Lang tells his grim tale in murky, expressive shadow, and (keeping the murders offscreen) achieves chilling effects through brilliant cinematic strategies: distorted camera angles; expressive shadows; innovative use of sound; and meticulously designed claustrophobic sets. Lang succeeds in conveying the increasing frenzy of various strata of Berlin life as he cross-cuts between wildly different environments to suggest their mutual fear. One particularly interesting and effective manuever was Lang's decision to visually link the police search for the killer with that of the criminals, thereby suggesting a parallel between the two. Lang also makes inspired use of the city of Berlin, its antiquity and squalor, to suggest a deep-seated corruption.

While M offers a truly creepy image of its psychopathic killer, it is all the more effective for its psychological subtlety as it conveys his guilt, despair and compulsiveness. At that point in his life, Lorre was a rather roly-poly fellow; his plump child-like features add a poignancy and pathos to the character. The child murderer appears to be a child himself. Lorre was so effective in this role that he would be cast as grotesque psychopaths for the bulk of his long career.

MACBETH

1971 140m c Drama   ★★★★
Playboy (U.K.)   R/AA

Jon Finch *(Macbeth)*, Francesca Annis *(Lady Macbeth)*, Martin Shaw *(Banquo)*, Nicholas Selby *(Duncan)*, John Stride *(Ross)*, Stephan Chase *(Malcolm)*, Paul Shelley *(Donalbain)*, Terence Bayler *(Macduff)*, Andrew Laurence *(Lennox)*, Frank Wylie *(Mentieth)*

p, Andrew Braunsberg, Roman Polanski; d, Roman Polanski; w, Roman Polanski, Kenneth Tynan (based on the play by William Shakespeare); ph, Gilbert Taylor; ed, Alastair McIntyre; m, The Third Ear Band; prod d, Wilfred Shingleton; art d, Fred Carter; fx, Ted Samuels; chor, Sally Gilpin; cos, Anthony Mendleson

Roman Polanski's controversial version of the classic Shakespeare play casts Jon Finch and Francesca Annis as the murderously obsessed couple who utilize witchcraft and prophecies as stepping stones to power. Polanski's first film after the murder of his wife, Sharon Tate, by the Manson family, this graphically violent MACBETH could be read as an attempt to exorcise real-life demons. In any case, this version, if not the best Shakespearean adaptation, is certainly the most inspired in its recreation of the cold barbaric spirit of the play's original setting. The vulgarity and gore on the screen is neither exploitative nor irresponsible, but a thoughtful interpretation that is less beholden to conventional theatrical techniques of the time. In accordance with this approach, Polanski elicited naturalistic understated performances from his actors which bolstered the play's realism while bringing the poetry down to earth. Some would argue he brought it too far down.

While Annis's nude sleepwalking scene has been criticized as evidence of Playboy Enterprises' involvement (in fact, the script was written before Playboy agreed to produce the film), it is true to the period. The project was originally offered to Allied Artists and then to Universal but both deals fell through. *Playboy* publisher Hugh Hefner, who was anxious to diversify into film production, felt this would be an ideal project for the growing Playboy Enterprises. However it turned out to be his first major failure. Polanski originally intended to cast Tuesday Weld as Lady Macbeth, but she declined after learning about the nude scene. Photographed in Wales during incessant downpours and fog, the picture was completed way behind schedule and lost about $3.5 million dollars. The original cut received an "X" rating.

MAD DOG AND GLORY

1993 97m c Drama/Romance   ★★★
Mad Dog Productions/Scorsese Productions/Universal (U.S.)   R/15

Robert De Niro *(Wayne "Mad Dog" Dobie)*, Uma Thurman *(Glory)*, Bill Murray *(Frank Milo)*, David Caruso *(Mike)*, Mike Starr *(Harold)*, Tom Towles *(Andrew)*, Kathy Baker *(Lee)*, Derek Anunciation *(Shooter)*, Doug Hara *(Driver)*, Evan Lionel *(Dealer in Car)*

p, Barbara DeFina, Martin Scorsese; d, John McNaughton; w, Richard Price; ph, Robby Muller; ed, Craig McKay, Elena Maganini; m, Elmer Bernstein; prod d, David Chapman; art d, Mark Haack; fx, Edward Drohan; cos, Rita Ryack

MAD DOG AND GLORY is an edgy romantic drama that never quite jells, but has enough moments of humor and/or charm to make it worth seeing.

The most intriguing aspect of this story—about a shy cop who is "given" a young woman for a week as a reward for saving a mobster's life—is the reverse casting. Robert De Niro, celebrated for a string of violent, volatile types in films from TAXI DRIVER to CAPE FEAR, plays the timid, ineffectual cop; Bill Murray, not exactly known for his hard-man roles, plays the mafioso—albeit a wise-cracking mafioso who moonlights as a stand-up comic. In a slightly more predictable assignment, Uma Thurman plays the lovely young barmaid over whom the two men eventually come to blows.

MAD DOG is stylishly shot and comes with some great macho confrontation scenes, courtesy of screenwriter Richard Price (SEA OF LOVE, THE COLOR OF MONEY). These are handled with humor, as well as real menace, by De Niro's partner (David Caruso, before he became America's first officially hunky redhead as the star of TV's "NYPD Blue") and Murray's lumbering henchman (Mike Starr). Good supporting players, though, tend to draw attention to what's wrong with the leads. De Niro's mumbling, inarticulate delivery is too close to the actor's real-life persona to really qualify as a performance, and Murray can't make the funny/sinister combination work. His comic schtick undercuts the power of his threats ("Have you ever heard of botulism? We can kill her with soup!"), while his nastiness makes it hard to laugh at some of the gags.

MAD LOVE

1935 83m bw Horror   ★★★★½
MGM (U.S.)

Peter Lorre *(Dr. Gogol)*, Colin Clive *(Stephen Orlac)*, Frances Drake *(Yvonne Orlac)*, Ted Healy *(Reagan)*, Edward Brophy *(Rollo)*, Sara Haden *(Marie)*, Henry Kolker *(Prefect Rosset)*, May Beatty *(Francoise)*, Keye Luke *(Dr. Wong)*, Isabel Jewell *(Marianne)*

p, John W. Considine Jr.; d, Karl Freund; w, Guy Endore, P.J. Wolfson, John Balderston (based on the novel *Les Mains d'Orlac* by Maurice Renard); ph, Chester Lyons, Gregg Toland; ed, Hugh Wynn; m, Dimitri Tiomkin

Mad about it. Combining Grand Guignol, surrealism and comedy to great effect, MAD LOVE remains to this day a chilling film. Peter Lorre is Gogol, a doctor who adores Yvonne Orlac (Drake), star of the Parisian Horror Theatre. Although she rebuffs him, Gogol buys a life-size replica of Yvonne that stood in the theater's lobby, harboring a secret wish that perhaps he can bring it to life as Pygmalion did Galatea. Yvonne's husband (Clive), a famous pianist, loses his hands in a railway accident; she goes to Gogol, a brilliant surgeon, and pleads with him to help. The love-crazed doctor grafts the hands of Reagan (Brophy), a recently executed knife-wielding murderer, onto Orlac's stumps. The initially grateful patient finds, though, that while he can't play the piano, he can throw knives only too well. When Gogol kills Orlac's stepfather, the mad doctor brainwashes Orlac into thinking that he did it. Things get even eerier when the dead Reagan ostensibly shows up, claiming that Gogol has sewn his head back on and that he wants his hands back! The truth behind this, as well as how Orlac's new hands ironically help him save his wife from Gogol's clutches, make for an improbable but brilliantly fitting climax.

Three excellent, distinctive cameramen were employed on the film, and the results show it. Director Karl Freund had been behind the lens on many films, and his bringing in Gregg Toland and Chester Lyons adds to the rich mixture of stark semi-Expressionism and dreamy near-surrealism that marks this film. One memorable shot shows Lorre's shaved head half in bright light and half in dark shadow, a striking visual rendering of his psychotic state. Casting the likable Brophy as the killer was admittedly a mistake, although it may have been done because Brophy was the only actor around who somewhat resembled the odd-looking Lorre and was about the same diminutive size. The comic relief by Ted Healy (who used to headline with The Three Stooges) is sometimes unwelcome as it takes too much edge off the film's scare tactics. At other points, though, it provided a much-needed punctuation to the ever-building suspense. Lorre, meanwhile, gives a top-notch performance in his well-written role. His doctor is no mad scientist of the Lugosi-Karloff school, but a man driven crazy by his lust. His character displays recognizable motivations throughout, no matter how bizarre his activities. Though the film is really Lorre's show, Colin Clive deserves praise for pulling off nervousness as few actors can, and Frances Drake brings serenity and vulnerability to the part of the heroine. A film which had a palpable influence on CITIZEN KANE (which Toland shot), MAD LOVE stands today as one of the most compelling horror films of its time.

MAD MAX

1979 90m c Action/Science Fiction ★★★½
Mad Max (Australia) R/18

Mel Gibson (Max), Joanne Samuel (Jessie), Hugh Keays-Byrne (the Toecutter), Steve Bisley (Jim Goose), Roger Ward (Fifi Macaffee), Vincent Gil (Nightrider), Tim Burns (Johnny the Boy), Geoff Parry (Bubba Zanetti), Paul Johnstone (Cundalini), John Ley (Charlie)

p, Byron Kennedy; d, George Miller; w, George Miller, James McCausland (based on a story by George Miller, Byron Kennedy); ph, David Eggby; ed, Tony Paterson, Clifford Hayes; m, Brian May; art d, Jon Dowding; fx, Chris Murray; cos, Clare Griffin

Australia exported this creative, original, exciting, low-budget genre landmark which gave the young Mel Gibson his first starring role. Set in the near future, MAD MAX presents a society descending into chaos. The forces of law and order are barely holding their own. The highways are terrorized by packs of lunatic speed demons. Gibson plays Max, a good cop who's fed up with his job. After chasing crazed criminals for years and seeing so many of his buddies killed in action, he just wants to retire and spend the rest of his days with his wife and child. His chief tries to bribe him with a new, faster police car ("the last of the V-8s"). He attempts to flatter him by telling him that he's the last of the heroes but Max isn't buying. The boss tells him to take a vacation and he does. Spending an idyllic week with his family on the beach, he decides to put away his badge and uniform for good. But this is not to be. A psychotic gang of road rats kills Gibson's wife and child in revenge for the death of one of their members. Left with nothing to live for, Gibson turns avenger, dons his black leather uniform, fuels up his V-8, and hits the road.

Though the plot is that of a simple revenge western, director George Miller infuses the film with a kinetic combination of visual style, amazing stunt work, creative costume design, and eccentric, detailed characterizations that practically jump out of the screen and grab the viewer by the throat. Miller, whose inspiration was comic books, serials, and B westerns, has created some of the most stunning car-chase/crash-and-burn scenes ever put on film. At this point in his career, Miller is a filmmaker who seems to have just discovered the exciting possibilities of composition, camera movement, and editing, and uses them to their most powerful effect, bringing movement back to the movies. Done independently with a laughably small budget (Miller edited most of the film in his bedroom), MAD MAX went on to make more money in Australia than George Lucas's STAR WARS. The American distributors, however, didn't quite know what to do with the film and stupidly dubbed lousy American-sounding voices over the Australians'. An even better sequel, THE ROAD WARRIOR (MAD MAX II in Australia), followed, and a third film, MAD MAX BEYOND THUNDERDOME, was released four years later.

MAD WEDNESDAY

1950 79m bw Comedy ★★★½
California (U.S.) /U

Harold Lloyd (Harold Diddlebock), Frances Ramsden (Miss Otis), Jimmy Conlin (Wormy), Raymond Walburn (E.J. Waggleberry), Edgar Kennedy (Jake, the Bartender), Arline Judge (Manicurist), Franklin Pangborn (Formfit Franklin), Lionel Stander (Max), Margaret Hamilton (Flora), Alan Bridge (Wild Bill Hitchcock)

p, Howard Hughes; d, Preston Sturges; w, Preston Sturges; ph, Robert Pittack; ed, Thomas Neff; m, Werner R. Heymann, Harry Rosenthal; art d, Robert Usher; fx, John P. Fulton

Far from Sturges's best, but intermittently hilarious. The film follows Harold Diddlebock, hero of Lloyd's classic silent THE FRESHMAN, into middle age. Harold is now a frumpy, office-bound bookkeeper with his glory days behind him. Fired from his job after two decades of toil, he goes on a drunken spree, and, in as unlikely a series of events as you'll ever see, wakes up the owner of a moth-eaten and bankrupt circus. Eventually Lloyd winds up reprising the silent comedy scene from SAFETY LAST for which he is perhaps most famous—hanging from a tall building, this time with a huge lion menacing him.

The idea of combining comic aces Lloyd and Sturges sounds highly promising, but both men's careers were on the wane, and the effort they make to milk laughs sometimes shows a bit too much. MAD

WEDNESDAY was financed by, of all people, Howard Hughes, a man not usually known for his sense of humor. It includes several excellent character bits by some of Hollywood's best second bananas: Kennedy (master of the slow burn), Stander (who left movies for years due to Red-baiting, then came back as a TV star), Hamilton (the ultimate witch), and Pangborn, who elevated prissiness to an art form. If you can hang on through the long, dead scenes and wait for Lloyd to get going, you'll probably end up satisfied by at least some of the frantic slapstick which transpires. As with many films Hughes made, several versions of this film exist, the 89-minute version going under the title of THE SIN OF HAROLD DIDDLEBOCK.

MADAME CURIE

1943 124m bw Biography ★★★★
MGM (U.S.) /U

Greer Garson (Mme. Marie Curie), Walter Pidgeon (Pierre Curie), Robert Walker (David LeGros), Dame May Whitty (Mme. Eugene Curie), Henry Travers (Eugene Curie), C. Aubrey Smith (Lord Kelvin), Albert Basserman (Prof. Jean Perot), Victor Francen (President of University), Reginald Owen (Dr. Henri Becquerel), Van Johnson (Reporter)

p, Sidney Franklin; d, Mervyn LeRoy; w, Paul Osborn, Paul H. Rameau (based on the book by Eve Curie); ph, Joseph Ruttenberg; ed, Harold F. Kress; m, Herbert Stothart; art d, Cedric Gibbons, Paul Groesse; fx, Warren Newcombe; cos, Irene Sharaff, Gile Steele

AAN Best Picture; AAN Best Actor: Walter Pidgeon; AAN Best Actress: Greer Garson; AAN Best Cinematography: Joseph Ruttenberg; AAN Best Score: Herbert Stothart; AAN Best Art Direction: Cedric Gibbons, Paul Groesse, Edwin B. Willis, Hugh Hunt; AAN Best Sound: Douglas Shearer

This fine film stirs the heart and stays closer to the facts of its subject's life than might be expected for its time. Greer Garson plays Marie, a Polish student studying in Paris near the turn of the century, who shares a lab with scientist Pierre Curie (Walter Pidgeon). The shy Pierre grows not only to respect Marie's scientific knowledge, but also falls in love with her, and the two soon marry. Together they observe the odd behavior of certain samples of pitchblende, eventually leading, after five years of study, to Marie's discovery of radium. Years pass as the Curies struggle to continue financing their work, until finally they extract one decigram of radium from thousands of pounds of pitchblende. The breakthrough makes the couple famous, but tragedy awaits them as well.

MADAME CURIE maintains its dignity throughout and, if this occasionally weighs down the picture a bit, it also lends a certain low-key intensity to scientific research which proves quite gripping. Garson and Pidgeon are fully into the spirit of the film, and their teaming here is much more satisfying than in the more acclaimed MRS. MINIVER.

MADAME ROSA
(LA VIE DEVANT SOI)

1977 105m c Drama ★★★½
Lira (France) PG/A

Simone Signoret (Mme. Rosa), Claude Dauphin (Dr. Katz), Samy Ben Youb (Mohammed "Momo"), Gabriel Jabbour (Mr. Hamil), Michal Bat Adam (Nadine), Constantin Costa-Gavras (Ramon), Stella Anicette (Mme. Lola), Bernard Lajarrige (Mr. Charmette), Mohammed Zineth (Kadir Youssef), Genevieve Fontanel (Maryse)

p, Jean Bolary; d, Moshe Mizrahi; w, Moshe Mizrahi (based on the novel Momo by Romain Gary); ph, Nestor Almendros; ed, Sophie Coussein; m, Philippe Sarde, Dabket Loubna

AA Best Foreign Language Film

An aging survivor of Auschwitz, Madame Rosa (Simone Signoret) is a Parisian ex-streetwalker who cares for prostitutes' children in the city's poor Arab-Jewish section. Although she is slowly losing her memory, she is still able to care for her charges, especially Momo (Samy Ben Youb), an unruly Arab Muslim boy who, although he tends to be rebellious, reciprocates her love. When Madame Rosa has delusions that the Gestapo is coming for her and makes the boy promise to hide her, he does so, sending a doctor away and maintaining that the dying woman has gone to Israel.

MADAME ROSA handles its underlying conflicts—between Arabs and Jews, between Nazis and Jews—well, and explores its mixed racial and cultural milieu with grace, sensitivity, and subtlety. The film is the first pairing of director-writer Moshe Mizrahi, a Moroccan-born Israeli, and the great Simone Signoret, who won a Cesar for her marvelous and unglamorous performance here. The two would team again for the bittersweet 1981 drama I SENT A LETTER TO MY LOVE. Film director Costa-Gavras has a supporting role.

MADAME SOUSATZKA

1988 122m c Drama ★★★
Sousatzka/Cineplex Odeon (U.K.) PG-13/15

Shirley MacLaine (Mme. Irina Sousatzka), Navin Chowdhry (Manek Sen), Peggy Ashcroft (Lady Emily), Twiggy (Jenny), Shabana Azmi (Sushila Sen), Leigh Lawson (Ronnie Blum), Lee Montague (Vincent Pick), Robert Rietty (Leo Milev), Jeremy Sinden (Woodford), Roger Hammond (Lefranc)

p, Robin Dalton; d, John Schlesinger; w, Ruth Prawer Jhabvala, John Schlesinger (based on a novel by Bernice Rubens); ph, Nat Crosby; ed, Peter Honess; m, Gerald Gouriet; prod d, Luciana Arrighi; cos, Amy Roberts

A fiery, autocratic piano teacher, Madame Sousatzka (Shirley MacLaine) has spent the last 30 years living in a London boardinghouse when she meets Manek Sen (Navin Chowdhry), a gifted 15-year-old Indian pianist. She believes she can turn him into a brilliant musician, starting from scratch and molding him into a new whole. "I teach not only how to play the piano, but how to live," she claims. MADAME SOUSATZKA features a cast good enough to sidestep being sunk by the film's pedestrian script and direction. Five years after her Oscar-winning performance in TERMS OF ENDEARMENT, MacLaine attempts to deliver another tour de force here, and while she's often quite good, too often the showiness of her star turn sabotages the sentiment. Newcomer Chowdhry turns in a strong, believable performance as the musical prodigy on the verge of a major breakthrough. The movie's chief fault is its uninspired handling of the classic themes of change versus tradition, commerce versus art, and the general destruction of history and values. MADAME SOUSATZKA is not the great or important film that it tries to be; rather, it is a warm and touching human drama, made so by the often exceptional acting.

MADIGAN

1968 101m c Crime ★★★½
Universal (U.S.) /X

Richard Widmark (Detective Daniel Madigan), Henry Fonda (Commissioner Anthony X. Russell), Inger Stevens (Julia Madigan), Harry Guardino (Detective Rocco Bonaro), James Whitmore (Chief Inspector Charles Kane), Susan Clark (Tricia Bentley), Michael Dunn (Midget Castiglione), Steve Ihnat (Barney Benesch), Don Stroud (Hughie), Sheree North (Jonesy)

p, Frank P. Rosenberg; d, Don Siegel; w, Howard Rodman, Abraham Polonsky, Harry Kleiner (based on the novel The Commissioner by Richard Dougherty); ph, Russell Metty; ed, Milton Shifman; m, Don Costa; art d, Alexander Golitzen, George Webb

Action-packed cops-and-robbers film cowritten by longtime television vet Howard Rodman, who evidently didn't like the way it turned out (he used his pseudonym, Henri Simoun). In the Spanish Harlem section of Manhattan, detectives Madigan and Bonaro (Widmark and Guardino) arrest Barney Benesch (Ihnat), a wanted hoodlum who is hiding out in a tacky flat to avoid an indictment by the Brooklyn courts. Benesch is in bed with a naked woman when they break in, which distracts the two cops from their quarry long enough for him to pull a gun on them and escape. Police commissioner Russell (Fonda) dresses the two men down for allowing Benesch to get away in such an inglorious manner and gives them 72 hours to nail the killer. Russell has a lot of other woes as well: he's having an affair with a married woman (Clark), his colleague (Whitmore) has accepted bribes to keep a brothel operating, and he must contend with a black minister (St.

Jacques) whose activist son was badly beaten by racist cops. Aggravating this hornet's nest for Madigan is his socialite wife (Stevens), who urges him to give up his career in law enforcement. Although Benesch proves an even more painful thorn for the detectives after he kills two police officers with Madigan's gun, the duo eventually track him down again in Spanish Harlem. A standoff ensues until an enraged Madigan gets fed up. The film ends with a consideration of whether Madigan is "just another lousy cop."

Very documentarian in approach, MADIGAN successfully reworks standard genre material into a realistic, hard-hitting portrait which deliberately sticks pins in the police department hierarchy. Writer Polonsky had been blacklisted in the 1950s and his partner Rodman kept his status active with a local construction union even while working in the Hollywood community. The acting is good throughout, with many fine character sketches of urban types.

MADNESS OF KING GEORGE, THE

1994 107m c Historical/Drama ★★★½
Samuel Goldwyn Company/Channel Four/Close Call /PG
Films (U.K./U.S.)

Nigel Hawthorne (King George III), Helen Mirren (Queen Charlotte), Amanda Donohoe (Lady Pembroke), Rupert Everett (The Prince of Wales), Rupert Graves (Greville), Ian Holm (Willis), Julian Wadham (Prime Minister Pitt), Anthony Calf (Fitzroy), John Wood (Thurlow), Jim Carter (Fox)

p, Stephen Evans, David Parfitt; d, Nicholas Hytner; w, Alan Bennett (based on his play The Madness of George III); ph, Andrew Dunn; ed, Tariq Anwar; m, George Fenton; prod d, Ken Adam; art d, Martin Childs; cos, Mark Thompson

AA Best Art Direction: Ken Adam, Carolyn Scott; AAN Best Actor: Nigel Hawthorne; AAN Best Supporting Actress: Helen Mirren; AAN Best Adapted Screenplay: Alan Bennett

Adapted by screenwriter Alan Bennett from his play, THE MADNESS OF KING GEORGE recounts a remarkable episode in the life of George III, who in 1788 experienced temporary insanity as a result of a metabolic imbalance known as porphyria. Despite an Oscar-nominated performance by Nigel Hawthorne, Bennett's theatrical triumph proves curiously flat on the screen.

England is in political turmoil: the unpopular King George III (Nigel Hawthorne) has antagonized his dissolute son, the Prince of Wales (Rupert Everett), while Prime Minister Pitt (Julian Wadham) is in the midst of a power struggle with Whig leader Fox (Jim Carter). Meanwhile, George's behavior is becoming increasingly erratic. Doctors are called in to treat him and the robust, roaringly confident monarch soon becomes a babbling, foul-mouthed, hyperactive mess. Then Queen Charlotte (Helen Mirren) learns of Dr. Willis (Ian Holm), whose innovative methods have proven remarkably successful in curing madness. With Pitt's help, she arranges to have George treated by the decidedly independent physician.

Acclaimed stage director Nicholas Hytner was obviously determined to make his cinematic debut a memorable one. He doesn't just open up the play; he scatters it across sun-drenched country fields, seemingly all of London, and every nook and cranny of the royal residence. Despite the talents involved, however, the effect is surprisingly static and unexciting, probably because the source material is the kind of talky tour de force that is best carried off on the stage. Even so, Hawthorne's performance is tremendously intelligent and affecting. He manages to strike a difficult and necessary balance between comedy and pathos throughout, energetically attacking Bennett's best scenes, in which the spectacularly vulgar symptoms of the King's condition subvert the bloodless, artificial refinement of aristocratic manners.

MAEDCHEN IN UNIFORM

1931 110m bw Drama ★★★★★
Deutsch/Gemeinschaft (Germany) /A

Emilia Unda (The Principal), Dorothea Wieck (Fraulein von Bernburg), Hedwig Schlichter (Fraulein von Kesten), Hertha Thiele (Manuela von Meinhardie), Ellen Schwannecke (Ilse von Westhagen)

p, Carl Froehlich; d, Leontine Sagan; w, Christa Winsloe, F.D. Andam (based on the play "Gestern und Heute" by Christa Winsloe)

Late Weimar Germany produced a number of fine anti-authoritarian films, perhaps the best of which was MAEDCHEN IN UNIFORM, the story of a girl's struggles within the rigid discipline of a boarding school for daughters of poor military officers. New student Manuela (Thiele) is homesick, introspective, and alienated. The headmistress (Unda) disapproves of such individualism, and rules her students with the proto-Nazi dictum: "Through discipline and hunger, hunger and discipline, we shall rise again." Manuela becomes attached to one teacher (Wieck), who sees in the sensitive new student a reflection of her former, nonconformist self. But Manuela's dependence on her mentor grows into obsessive love, testing the headmistress' tolerance.

Though MAEDCHEN IN UNIFORM's symbolism can seem heavy-handed (like Murnau's THE LAST LAUGH, it invests much in the uniform as an image of German social consciousness), this film displays remarkable emotional, narrative, and visual assurance. It is particularly insightful in its treatment of female bonding, lesbian love, and the perverse interplay of sexuality and power. Written (by Christa Winsloe and F.D. Andam, from the former's play) and directed (Leontine Sagan) by women, with an all-female cast, MAEDCHEN IN UNIFORM suggested for future generations of aspiring women filmmakers the cinematic potential of a woman's point of view.

MAGIC BOX, THE
1951 118m c Biography   ★★★★
Festival (U.K.)   /U

Renee Asherson (Miss Tagg), Richard Attenborough (Jack Carter), Robert Beatty (Lord Beaverbrook), Martin Boddey (Sitter in Bath Studio), Edward Chapman (Father in Family Group), John Charlesworth (Graham Friese-Greene), Maurice Colbourne (Bride's Father at Wedding), Roland Culver (1st Company Promoter), John Howard Davies (Maurice Friese-Greene), Michael Denison (Connaught Rooms Reporter)

p, Ronald Neame; d, John Boulting; w, Eric Ambler (based on the book Friese-Greene, Close-Up of an Inventor by Ray Allister); ph, Jack Cardiff; ed, Richard Best; m, William Alwyn; prod d, John Bryan; art d, Hopewell Ash; cos, Julia Squire

Nearly every actor who ever appeared in British movies worked in this feature. Robert Donat plays William Friese-Greene, the pioneer who patented the first motion picture camera. The film shows his beginnings as a photographer's assistant and his days as a society lenser in London, spending all his resources on his new invention (patented two years before Edison's). His first wife (Maria Schell) shares his triumphs while his second wife (Margaret Johnston) shares his failures. In between, viewers are treated to the sight of at least 50 of England's finest actors, all playing tiny bits. (Laurence Olivier, for example, is quite amusing as a police officer who is an early witness to the moving pictures.) Friese-Greene is hardly remembered now and had already been dead more than 30 years when THE MAGIC BOX was made, but the filmmakers' conviction that his story should be told convinced all of the actors (who agreed to alphabetical billing) to devote their talents to this good-looking, well-directed film. Donat is excellent, holding his own among the industry's finest.

MAGICIAN, THE
(ANSIKTET)
1958 102m bw Drama   ★★★★½
Svensk (Sweden)   /X

Max von Sydow (Vogler), Ingrid Thulin (Manda Aman), Gunnar Bjornstrand (Vergerus), Naima Wifstrand (Grandmother), Bengt Ekerot (Spegel), Bibi Andersson (Sara), Gertrud Fridh (Ottilia), Lars Ekborg (Simson), Toivo Pawlo (Starbeck), Erland Josephson (Egerman)

d, Ingmar Bergman; w, Ingmar Bergman; ph, Gunnar Fischer, Rolf Halmquist; ed, Oscar Rosander; m, Erik Nordgren; art d, P.A. Lundgren

In THE MAGICIAN, Ingmar Bergman takes two favorite motifs—masks and magic—and explores them on a number of different levels. Albert Emanuel Vogler (Max von Sydow), a 19-century magician, brings a troupe of traveling illusionists to a small Swedish town where the people don't believe in magic. Led by Vogler, the troupe

proceeds to play with the townspeople's minds, and director Bergman, in turn, makes imaginative use of editing, lighting, and special effects to toy with audience expectations. Things are never quite what they seem, either narratively or cinematically. The film's mysterious nature is further enhanced by the dark, rich, gothic look of Bergman's mise-en-scene. Though at times the story is overwhelmed by its theme and symbols (especially in its final third), THE MAGICIAN is still fascinating, presenting a myriad of challenging ideas about magic, reality, and the nature of film itself. The acting, as in typical in Bergman, is exceptionally good, with Bjornstrand a standout. The videocassette is available in both dubbed and subtitled (Swedish into English) versions.

MAGNIFICENT AMBERSONS, THE
1942 88m bw Drama   ★★★★★
Mercury Theatre (U.S.)   /U

Joseph Cotten (Eugene Morgan), Dolores Costello (Isabel Amberson Minafer), Anne Baxter (Lucy Morgan), Tim Holt (George Amberson Minafer), Agnes Moorehead (Fanny Amberson), Ray Collins (Jack Amberson), Richard Bennett (Maj. Amberson), Erskine Sanford (Benson), J. Louis Johnson (Sam the Butler), Donald Dillaway (Wilbur Minafer)

p, Orson Welles; d, Orson Welles, Freddie Fleck, Robert Wise; w, Orson Welles (based on the novel by Booth Tarkington); ph, Stanley Cortez, Russell Metty, Harry Wild; ed, Robert Wise, Jack Moss, Mark Robson; m, Bernard Herrmann, Roy Webb; art d, Mark-Lee Kirk; fx, Vernon L. Walker; cos, Edward Stevenson

AAN Best Picture; AAN Best Supporting Actress: Agnes Moorehead; AAN Best Cinematography: Stanley Cortez; AAN Best Art Direction: Albert S. D'Agostino, Al Fields, Darrell Silvera

Though mutilated by studio cuts and misunderstood at the time of its release, THE MAGNIFICENT AMBERSONS, based on the Tarkington novel and set during the twilight of the 19th century, remains Welles's second great masterpiece.

Young George Amberson (Holt), the spoiled, insufferable scion of the wealthy Amberson family, is first seen, to the consternation of his neighbors, whipping his buggy horse through the streets of Indianapolis. Eugene Morgan (Cotten) is a struggling inventor who loves George's mother Isabel (Costello), but loses her to the wealthy Wilbur Minafer (Dillaway). After an absence of several years, Eugene returns, now successful, having invented an automobile, an instrument of the future that many of the old school find repulsive, especially the haughty George. Wilbur dies, and Eugene, a widower with an attractive daughter, Lucy (Baxter), attempts to rekindle his love affair with Isabel, but George interferes. This affects not only George's romance with Lucy, but also the fading Amberson fortunes.

Though more controlled, subtle and cinematically exciting than CITIZEN KANE, Welles's earlier masterpiece, it's a wonder that AMBERSONS survived at all. Alarmed by the negative reaction at the film's premiere, RKO president George Schaefer instructed then-editor Robert Wise to shorten the film drastically. Welles had already cut it from 148 minutes to 131, but Wise hacked it down to 88, and a more optimistic ending was tacked on by a nameless studio writer and directed by Freddie Fleck. This presumptuous, dictatorial savaging of the film, according to Welles, destroyed "the whole heart of the picture, really." Luckily, that's not quite true.

The film is so rich in innovative technique that it takes several viewings to note even the most essential elements. The "Welles sound" permeates every frame, with overlapping dialogue and a subtle control of volume and texture giving a natural feel to the words spoken (sometimes improvised in group scenes) and sounds heard. In crowd scenes he allows a host of gossips to function as a Greek chorus in estimating the worth of the Amberson and Morgan families. At times the voices of the characters boom and bellow, while, at others, they are so hushed as to be barely discernible.

Many of the ideas initally used in CITIZEN KANE are refined in AMBERSONS, showing in split-second frames his people reflected in mirrors, highly glossed furniture, sometimes in a glare of light, most in half-shadow, as if the blackness of time were shutting out the light of the living. Through his great visual gifts, Welles was able to express the true nature of the characters through their actions: Fanny (Moorehead, in the performance of a lifetime) peering over a railing to eavesdrop on those far below; George methodically spooning down strawberry shortcake in the famous kitchen scene, indifferently listening to Aunt Fanny pour out her heart; a stunned Eugene at the front door of the Amberson mansion, which has been closed in his face by George, who stands behind the frosted glass panes; a dark shot of the dying, incoherent Major (Bennett); Fanny slumping against a long-unused heater ("It's not hot!").

The look of AMBERSONS was modeled on the low-key lighting used by photographers at the turn-of-the-century, and Cortez's deep-focus lensing is arresting, dwelling upon scenes only Welles could have framed—notably, ten-minute soliloquies saved from tedium by the unique framing. Dolly and truck shots keep the film fluid, and some crane shots capture the changing architecture from Victorian to modern, from resplendent to mundane, as Welles eloquently shows the passing of an age.

MAGNIFICENT OBSESSION

1954 107m c Drama   ★★★½
Universal (U.S.)   /U

Jane Wyman (Helen Phillips), Rock Hudson (Bob Merrick), Barbara Rush (Joyce Phillips), Agnes Moorehead (Nancy Ashford), Otto Kruger (Rudolph), Gregg Palmer (Tom Masterson), Sara Shane (Valerie), Paul Cavanagh (Dr. Giraud), Judy Nugent (Judy), George Lynn (Williams)

p, Ross Hunter; d, Douglas Sirk; w, Robert Blees, Wells Root (based on the novel by Lloyd C. Douglas and the screenplay by Sarah Y. Mason, Finley Peter Dunne, Jr., Victor Heerman); ph, Russell Metty; ed, Milton Carruth; m, Frank Skinner; art d, Bernard Herzbrun, Emrich Nicholson; fx, David S. Harsley; cos, Bill Thomas

AAN Best Actress: Jane Wyman

Not quite as heart-wrenching as the original version, this remake is still pretty good and does benefit from being filmed in color. Wyman is Helen Phillips, a blind woman, and Hudson is Bob Merrick, the cad who becomes her savior. Merrick is partly responsible for the accidental death of Helen's husband, a man who was revered in the community as a combination of Dr. Kildare, Ben Casey, and every other angel of mercy ever seen. After the doctor's demise, Bob attempts to apologize, and Helen, avoiding him, is blinded in an accident. With Rudolph (Kruger), a friend of the late, great physician, egging him on, Bob forsakes his wastrel ways and decides to dedicate himself to medicine. Without revealing his true identity, he contacts Helen, and their relationship soon becomes a loving one. When she finds out who he is, she departs. Much later, though, Bob is given an incredible opportunity to save Helen and redeem himself for his past peccadilloes.

A film requiring as many Kleenex as you can spare, this unabashed appeal to the tear ducts does not fail in its efforts. Director Douglas Sirk made only a few more films before retiring to Munich in 1959, just before he turned 60. He brings to this effort the same combination of overblown, indulgent melodramatics and distanced perspective which would mark his masterpiece, IMITATION OF LIFE. Notable also as the film which really put Rock Hudson on top and gave the first inklings that he might be able to act if sufficiently prodded, MAGNIFICENT OBSESSION really relies on Wyman's womanly, Oscar-nominated assurance to put this stuff over.

MAGNIFICENT SEVEN, THE

1960 128m c Western   ★★★★
Mirisch/Alpha (U.S.)   R/PG

Yul Brynner (Chris), Eli Wallach (Calvera), Steve McQueen (Vin), Horst Buchholz (Chico), Charles Bronson (O'Reilly), Robert Vaughn (Lee), Brad Dexter (Harry Luck), James Coburn (Britt), Vladimir Sokoloff (Old Man), Rosenda Monteros (Petra)

p, John Sturges; d, John Sturges; w, William Roberts, Walter Newman, Walter Bernstein (based on THE SEVEN SAMURAI); ph, Charles Lang; ed, Ferris Webster; m, Elmer Bernstein; art d, Edward Fitzgerald; fx, Milt Rice

AAN Best Score: Elmer Bernstein

Very nearly a classic, this Americanization of Akira Kurosawa's THE SEVEN SAMURAI does a good job of mirroring the major themes and attitudes of the original while re-creating that monumental film in an occidental setting. However, Sturges's film fails to present its heroes with the style, grace, and dignity that Kurosawa accords his samurai warriors. Nevertheless THE MAGNIFICENT SEVEN is an excellent film and deserves the accolades it has received through the years. A small Mexican village is pillaged regularly by Wallach and his cutthroats. The quaking townsfolk don't have the courage to take on Wallach and his desperadoes so they decide to hire seven of the toughest hombres on that side of the Rio Grande: Brynner, McQueen, Bronson, Vaughn, Dexter, Coburn, and Buchholz. The Seven train the fearful townspeople to fight alongside them and set a trap for the wily Wallach and his group.

There's not a weak performance in the film but that's to be expected with this cast, although Brynner, who had already won an Oscar for THE KING AND I, was the only "name" at the time the film was made. Although Coburn has little dialogue, his presence is strongly felt. It wouldn't be long before screenwriters were giving him plenty to say. In fact, the only member of the Seven who didn't rise in the acting ranks after this film was Dexter, who made a few more movies, then retired from the biz.

Sturges's direction is the key to the film's quality. Just as he did in BAD DAY AT BLACK ROCK and THE GREAT ESCAPE, Sturges assembled a superb cast and skillfully put them through their paces. Bernstein's score also plays a major role in the film's success, and his main theme became an even more familiar part of American popular culture as the signature music for Marlboro cigarettes. The film spawned a number of sequels: RETURN OF THE MAGNIFICENT SEVEN; GUNS OF THE MAGNIFICENT SEVEN; and THE MAGNIFICENT SEVEN RIDE. Perhaps the ultimate testimony to the excellence of THE MAGNIFICENT SEVEN is the sword that Kurosawa presented to Sturges after seeing the film.

MAJOR AND THE MINOR, THE

1942 100m bw Comedy   ★★★★½
Paramount (U.S.)   /U

Ginger Rogers (Susan Applegate), Ray Milland (Maj. Kirby), Rita Johnson (Pamela Hill), Robert Benchley (Mr. Osborne), Diana Lynn (Lucy Hill), Edward Fielding (Col. Hill), Frankie Thomas (Cadet Osborne), Raymond Roe (Cadet Wigton), Charles Smith (Cadet Korner), Larry Nunn (Cadet Babcock)

p, Arthur Hornblow Jr.; d, Billy Wilder; w, Billy Wilder, Charles Brackett (based on the play "Connie Goes Home" by Edward Childs Carpenter and the story "Sunny Goes Home" by Fannie Kilbourne); ph, Leo Tover; ed, Doane Harrison; m, Robert Emmett Dolan; art d, Hans Dreier, Roland Anderson; cos, Edith Head

The LOLITA of the 1940s, and just as sexy. A sparkling farce that marked Wilder's American directorial debut after years of writing witty screenplays for other directors, THE MAJOR AND THE MINOR sails along breezily from its very first scenes until its romantic ending. The scintillating dialogue is very risque and punches out the laughs in rapid-fire succession. Ginger Rogers plays Susan, a working girl who has had it with New York and is eager to return home to the Midwest. When she finds that prices have gone up at the train station, the budget-conscious Susan dresses up as a child and manages to get on for half-fare. ("She looks kind of filled out for twelve," notes one of the lunkheaded conductors.) Caught smoking on board, Susan takes refuge with Maj. Kirby (Milland), en route to a military academy. The major and his cadets are soon at a loss to understand their attraction to such a young girl.

Algonquin Round Table member Robert Benchley is his terrifically wry self in the early scenes. Rogers gives him a hilarious egg shampoo and he also gets the film's most famous line, "Why don't you step out of that wet coat and into a dry martini?" Milland, too, is excellent in a successful invasion of Cary Grant territory. The film, though, really belongs to Rogers, giving one of her greatest performances in a role you can't imagine any other actress pulling off. She seemed to have inherited Mary Pickford's gift for playing children without seeming too ridiculous or coy—except here Wilder takes it one better. Relying on Rogers's formidable talent for mimicry, he has her playing someone who plays someone. Almost as wonderful is Lynn, her pert wisecracking almost an adolescent version of Rogers's style. Featuring the famous "Maginot Line" sequence, THE MAJOR AND THE MINOR retains its sharpness even amidst today's rather more heavy-handed approaches to sex farce. Wilder was a great director from the start, and Ginger proves that she'd have her place in the pantheon even if she'd never even heard of Fred Astaire. Dully remade as YOU'RE NEVER TOO YOUNG.

MAJOR BARBARA

1941 121m bw Comedy   ★★★★½
Pascal/Rank (U.K.)   /A

Wendy Hiller *(Maj. Barbara Undershaft)*, Rex Harrison *(Adolphus Cusins)*, Robert Morley *(Andrew Undershaft)*, Emlyn Williams *(Snobby Price)*, Robert Newton *(Bill Walker)*, Sybil Thorndike *(The General)*, Deborah Kerr *(Jenny Hill)*, David Tree *(Charles Lomax)*, Penelope-Dudley Ward *(Sarah Undershaft)*, Marie Lohr *(Lady Brittomart)*

p, Gabriel Pascal; d, Gabriel Pascal, Harold French, David Lean; w, Anatole de Grunwald, George Bernard Shaw (based on his play); ph, Ronald Neame; ed, Charles Frend; m, William Walton; prod d, Vincent Korda

What price salvation? One of Shaw's most amusing comedies, excitingly performed by a brilliant cast, though Shaw's monologues sometimes get boggy with verbiage and the direction (largely by Pascal) isn't very spritely. Hiller plays the idealistic title character, a major in the Salvation Army who despises her munitions magnate father (Morley). Adolphus Cusins (Harrison), a young professor of Greek history and literature, is hopelessly in love with the major, but she's too busy saving souls. Pop Undershaft believes that benevolent industrial management, not charity and moral uplift, is the way to help the poor. He sets out to show that intellectual Cusins and spiritual Barbara can both be bought, with surprising consequences.

Shaw's 1905 social comedy was brought to the screen by Pascal, who had talked the curmudgeonly playwright into allowing him in 1938 to film (with great success) PYGMALION, starring Hiller and Leslie Howard. MAJOR BARBARA, however, was not as well received by audiences, who found it too sophisticated and couldn't relate to its eccentric Fabian socialism. The cast is uniformly marvelous, with the dry radiance of Hiller (reminiscent of Katharine Hepburn's, but uniquely her own) firing scene after scene. Harrison has a great way with flip dialogue, yet still manages to convey his passion for Barbara. Newton is delightfully wicked as a money-grubbing slum dweller. The rest of the cast reads like a who's who of British character actors; they keep the rather stodgy, unimaginative direction constantly on the go. Special mention must go to the touching Kerr, just starting her career, and the wonderful Morley. (You almost have to look twice to recognize him behind that beard.) The 32-year-old actor is not only convincing as the father of the 28-year-old Hiller but also a worthy and likable mouthpiece for many of Shaw's ideas. Valuable as a fine performance of an important and delightful play, MAJOR BARBARA makes for bracingly intelligent cinema.

MALCOLM X

1992 201m c Biography/Historical/Drama   ★★★★
40 Acres and a Mule Filmworks/Marvin Worth Productions   PG-13/15

Denzel Washington *(Malcolm X)*, Angela Bassett *(Betty Shabazz)*, Albert Hall *(Baines)*, Al Freeman Jr. *(Elijah Muhammad)*, Delroy Lindo *(West Indian Archie)*, Spike Lee *(Shorty)*, Theresa Randle *(Laura)*, Kate Vernon *(Sophia)*, Lonette McKee *(Louise Little)*, Tommy Hollis *(Earl Little)*

p, Marvin Worth, Spike Lee; d, Spike Lee; w, Spike Lee, Arnold Perl, James Baldwin; ph, Ernest Dickerson; ed, Barry Alexander Brown; m, Terence Blanchard; prod d, Wynn Thomas; art d, Tom Warren; fx, Randall Balsmeyer, Steven Kirshoff; chor, Otis Sallid; cos, Ruth Carter

AAN Best Actor: Denzel Washington; *AAN Best Costume Design:* Ruth E. Carter

MALCOLM X opens with a pair of intercut, highly polemical images: the notorious video footage of unarmed black motorist Rodney King being beaten by white L.A. policemen; and an American flag burning down into the shape of an "X." Yet this is one of only a few times in the film where director Spike Lee wears his politics on his sleeve. Lee's biography of the slain civil rights leader treats Malcolm, not as a political rallying point, but as a fully rounded individual whose life defies reduction to symbolic status. The movie begins during WWII, when Malcolm Little (Denzel Washington) and his friend Shorty (Lee) are hustlers in Boston's Black Roxbury section. We then follow Malcolm's progress as he joins a numbers gang in Harlem; ends up in Charleston State Prison, where fellow inmate Baines (Albert Hall) introduces him to the Islamic religion and the teachings of Elijah Muhammad (Al Freeman, Jr.); adopts the name Malcolm X; meets Elijah Muhammad and becomes a spokesman for the Nation of Islam; marries Betty Shabazz (Angela Bassett), a Muslim nurse; has his differences with the Nation crystallized by a pilgrimage to Mecca; and is finally assassinated, presumably by members of the Nation.

It is Lee's willingness to present all sides of Malcolm's character that makes MALCOLM X so persuasive as a biography. Paradoxically, though, this evenhandedness occasionally seems to blunt the film's power; the anger that drove DO THE RIGHT THING is reduced here. There is no denying, however, the passion in Denzel Washington's performance, a superlative job of acting that transcends impersonation. Washington impressively brings across Malcolm's power as an orator, whether he's making a fiery outdoor speech to black followers or calmly, forcefully addressing a white collegiate audience. The rest of the cast is equally fine, particularly Al Freeman, Jr., who does just as persuasive a job of portraying the aging Elijah Muhammad. Lee keeps the film moving at a clip; although it feels long, it's never boring.

MALTESE FALCON, THE

1941 100m bw Mystery   ★★★★★
Warner Bros. (U.S.)   /PG

Humphrey Bogart *(Sam Spade)*, Mary Astor *(Brigid O'Shaughnessy)*, Gladys George *(Iva Archer)*, Peter Lorre *(Joel Cairo)*, Barton MacLane *(Detective Lt. Dundy)*, Lee Patrick *(Effie Perine)*, Sydney Greenstreet *(Kasper Gutman the Fat Man)*, Ward Bond *(Detective Tom Polhaus)*, Jerome Cowan *(Miles Archer)*, Elisha Cook Jr. *(Wilmer Cook)*

p, Henry Blanke; d, John Huston; w, John Huston (based on the novel by Dashiell Hammett); ph, Arthur Edeson; ed, Thomas Richards; m, Adolph Deutsch; art d, Robert Haas; cos, Orry-Kelly

AAN Best Picture; AAN Best Supporting Actor: Sydney Greenstreet; *AAN Best Original Screenplay:* John Huston

A rare bird, the prized one and only. This third film version of the Dashiell Hammett novel was propelled into the ranks of popular classic by a stunning directorial debut from screenwriter John Huston. This was also Bogart's big chance as a star/leading man and he is peerless as private eye Sam Spade, a cynical rebel-hero entangled in a mass of hissing vipers.

While trying to investigate the murder of his partner, Miles Archer (Cowan), Spade finds himself surrounded by a number of eccentric characters: the mysterious Brigid O'Shaughnessy (Astor), the effeminate Joel Cairo (Lorre), the huge Kasper Gutman (Greenstreet), and Gutman's psychotic gunsel Wilmer (Cook)—all greedily fighting for possession of a statue of a falcon containing priceless jewels. From the superb casting (it was the 61-year-old Greenstreet's film debut) to the textbook perfect direction, every aspect of THE MALTESE FALCON revealed the surprisingly assured hand of its novice director. A seminal moment in the development of what would come to be known as film noir, Huston's faithful adaptation helped establish the cynicism, corruption, and moral ambiguity that would mark the genre, while his visuals—although not nearly as dark as what would follow—showed a cramped, stifling, claustrophobic world from which there was no escape. Huston has a field day laughing at greedy corruption and treating the plot with amused insolence; often it's funny to us, too. Lorre's gardenia-scented little crook versus Cook's would-be tough guy, obsequious sugar daddy (to Cook) Greenstreet meeting Bogie's snarls—these make us laugh. Mary Astor has one howler bit when she kicks Lorre, but otherwise she embodies the plot's dark, bottomless center. Piling lie on top of lie, Astor's portrayal keeps us guessing right up to the end. Gladys George is the classic noir widow—you've seen this bit parodied countless times—here's the real thing. Ditto Patrick's doggedly devoted secretary (it's nice to see her playing a dame that's not cheap for once). And that's Walter Huston, John's distinguished father, who delivers the bird to Bogie.

MAMMA ROMA

1962   110m   bw   Drama   ★★★★
Arco Film   (Italy)   /X

Anna Magnani *(Mamma Roma)*, Ettore Garofalo *(Ettore)*, Franco Citti *(Carmine)*, Silvana Corsini *(Bruna)*, Luisa Loiano *(Blancofiore)*, Paolo Volponi *(Priest)*, Luciano Gonini *(Zacaria)*, Vittorio La Paglia *(Signor Pellissier)*, Piero Morgia *(Piero)*

p, Alfredo Bini; d, Pier Paolo Pasolini; w, Pier Paolo Pasolini; ph, Tonino delli Colli; ed, Nino Baragli; m, Carlo Rustichelli

Pasolini's second film after ACCATTONE (1961) stars Magnani as a prostitute who tries to start a new life. She and her son (Garofalo) move to a different part of town where she tries to make a living legitimately, but her past keeps popping up. She is eventually forced to occasionally go back to the red-light district when money becomes scarce. Her son becomes a thief and soon things go from bad to worse for the pair.

   The mood of this film is grim throughout and lingers long after the closing credits roll. Bolstered by yet another powerhouse performance from Magnani, MAMMA ROMA is strongly realistic and remains one of Pasolini's most accessible if not most important films.

MAN AND A WOMAN, A
(UN HOMME ET UNE FEMME)

1966   102m   c/bw   Drama   ★★★½
Films 13   (France)   /X

Anouk Aimee *(Anne Gauthier)*, Jean-Louis Trintignant *(Jean-Louis Duroc)*, Pierre Barouh *(Pierre Gauthier)*, Valerie Lagrange *(Valerie Duroc)*, Simone Paris *(Head Mistress)*, Antoine Sire *(Antoine Duroc)*, Souad Amidou *(Francoise Gauthier)*, Yane Barry *(Mistress of Jean-Louis)*, Paul Le Person *(Garage Man)*, Henri Chemin *(Jean-Louis' Codriver)*

p, Claude Lelouch; d, Claude Lelouch; w, Claude Lelouch, Pierre Uytterhoeven (based on a story by Claude Lelouch); ph, Claude Lelouch; ed, Claude Lelouch, G. Boisser, Claude Barrois; m, Francis Lai; art d, Robert Luchaire

AA Best Foreign Language Film ; *AAN Best Actress:* Anouk Aimee; *AAN Best Director:* Claude Lelouche; *AA Best Original Story and Screenplay:* Claude Lelouche, Pierre Uytterhoeven

Effusively romantic, visually stunning, slightly bland. A MAN AND A WOMAN has been condemned by some as an exercise in style for style's sake and by others for its lack of emotional complexity. Yet for many viewers this Claude Lelouch-directed film is as magical a love story as any brought to the screen. Widowed film studio script girl Anne Gauthier (Aimee, lovely) and auto racer Jean-Louis Duroc (Trintignant), whose wife has committed suicide, meet at the boarding school attended by his son and her daughter. When Jean-Louis gives Anne a ride back to Paris, friendship and then love blossom, though the specter of her much-loved late husband confuses their romance. At one point it looks like the end, but Lelouch still has a dazzling scene on the beach at Deauville up his sleeve.

   Pulling out all the stops, Lelouch employs a wide variety of film-making techniques (swirling cameras, slow motion, switches from color to black and white, flashforwards and flashbacks) to tell his simple but effective love story. Although not the equal of the work of Lelouch's French contemporaries, A MAN AND A WOMAN demonstrated that a wide American audience was interested in stylish films, provided their stories hit home.

MAN ESCAPED, A
(UN CONDAMNE A MORT S'EST ECHAPPE)

1956   102m   bw   Drama   ★★★★★
Gaumont   (France)   /U

Francois Leterrier *(Lt. Fontaine)*, Charles Le Clainche *(Francois Jost)*, Roland Monod *(De Leiris the Pastor)*, Maurice Beerblock *(Blanchet)*, Jacques Ertaud *(Orsini)*, Roger Treherne *(Terry)*, Jean-Paul Delhumeau *(Hebrard)*, Jean-Philippe Delamare *(Prisoner No. 110)*, Jacques Oerlemans *(Chief Warder)*, Klaus Detlef Grevenhorst *(German Intelligence Officer)*

p, Jean Thuillier, Alain Poire; d, Robert Bresson; w, Robert Bresson (based on articles by Andre Devigny); ph, L.H. Burel; ed, Raymond Lamy; m, Wolfgang Amadeus Mozart; art d, Pierre Charbonnier

One of the most important films from a cinema giant. The very spare plot features Leterrier playing a Resistance hero captured by the Nazis and imprisoned in Fort Montluc. Most of the film shows him and his cellmate (Le Clainche) attempting to successfully scale the prison walls and escape. Based on a published account of Andre Devigny, a Resistance fighter who was sentenced to be executed in 1943, A MAN ESCAPED is one of Bresson's finest works, particularly notable for his creative use of sound. Even after the success of THE DIARY OF A COUNTRY PRIEST, Bresson had to wait five years to get this project underway. The two films have in common a faith in God which is made most obvious in this picture's alternate title, THE WIND BLOWETH WHERE IT LISTETH, and in the music (Mozart's "Mass in C Minor"). As in many of Bresson's films, the cast is made up of non-professionals such as Leterrier, a philosophy graduate and a lieutenant in the military. Bresson's experience as a POW at the start of WWII, Devigny's contribution as a technical adviser, and the use of his actual cell for the location make for an grippingly authentic and detailed account. In an unanimous decision, Bresson received the "Best Director" prize from the Cannes Film Festival in 1957 for this film. In a surprisingly similar, but less successful manner, Don Siegel detailed a prison break in ESCAPE FROM ALCATRAZ, with Clint Eastwood in the starring role.

MAN FACING SOUTHEAST
(HOMBRE MIRANDO AL SUDESTE)

1986   105m   c   Science Fiction/Drama   ★★★★½
Cinequanon   (Argentina)   R/

Lorenzo Quinteros *(Dr. Dennis)*, Hugo Soto *(Rantes)*, Ines Vernengo *(Beatriz)*, Cristina Scaramuzza *(Nurse)*, Rubens W. Correa *(Dr. Prieto)*, David Edery, Rodolfo Rodas, Jean Pierre Requeraz

p, Lujan Pflaum; d, Eliseo Subiela; w, Eliseo Subiela; ph, Ricardo de Angelis; ed, Luis Cesar D'Angiolillo; m, Pedro Aznar; art d, Abel Facello

Argentine director Eliseo Subiela takes an allegorical approach to the story of Christ in this enigmatic parable. A jaded mental asylum psychiatrist, Dr. Dennis (Lorenzo Quinteros), becomes fascinated with Rantes (Hugo Soto), who suddenly appears in his ward. Upon questioning, Rantes explains he is a holographic being from another planet, which transmits to him from the southeast. As the two men grow closer, it begins to appear that Rantes' mission is something beyond an intergalactic visit; eventually, his inexplicable influence on the other patients incurs the displeasure of authorities who demand that Dennis take severe measures to counteract his friend and patient's delirium.

   Writer-director Subiela incorporates a wide variety of influences to create a fascinating, multifaceted work of art. The reworking of the Gospels is evident, but the biblical references are a basis for convincing contemporary characters and open questions, with the film clearly participating in and reconsidering the mystical tradition in Latin American literature. Subiela also incorporates a variety of references to paintings in the film's design. Soto's performance is remarkable, with Quinteros proving an excellent counterpart. Their natural, often affectionate, and unique relationship becomes the heart of this profound and highly personal film.

MAN FOR ALL SEASONS, A

1966 120m c Drama ★★★★
Highland (U.K.) /U

Paul Scofield *(Sir Thomas More)*, Wendy Hiller *(Alice More)*, Leo McKern *(Thomas Cromwell)*, Robert Shaw *(King Henry VIII)*, Orson Welles *(Cardinal Wolsey)*, Susannah York *(Margaret More)*, Nigel Davenport *(Duke of Norfolk)*, John Hurt *(Richard Rich)*, Corin Redgrave *(William Roper)*, Colin Blakely *(Matthew)*

p, Fred Zinnemann; d, Fred Zinnemann; w, Robert Bolt, Constance Willis (based on the play by Robert Bolt); ph, Ted Moore; ed, Ralph Kemplen; m, Georges Delerue; prod d, John Box; art d, Terence Marsh; cos, Elizabeth Haffenden, Joan Bridge

AA Best Picture; AA Best Actor: Paul Scofield; *AAN Best Supporting Actor:* Robert Shaw; *AAN Best Supporting Actress:* Wendy Hiller; *AA Best Director:* Fred Zinnemann; *AA Best Adapted Screenplay:* Robert Bolt; *AA Best Cinematography:* Ted Moore; *AA Best Costume Design:* Elizabeth Haffenden, Joan Bridge

This adaptation of Robert Bolt's hit play proved to be both prestigious and commercial. Studio executives were unsure whether folks would turn out for the story of Sir Thomas More, a Catholic statesman in England who rebelled against Henry VIII's self-proclaimed status as the head of the Church of England and paid for his beliefs with his life.

More (Scofield) is appointed to succeed Cardinal Wolsey (Welles) as Lord Chancellor. He comes to grips with Shaw, as Henry VIII, who wants to divorce his barren wife and take a new bride. Henry needs a male heir, but Rome (for reasons both political and spiritual) won't grant an annulment. Henry breaks with the Pope, declaring himself spiritual ruler of the new Church of England, and demands More's endorsement. More is torn between loyalty to his monarch and concern for his immortal soul; a lawyer, he at first hopes to survive through ethical hairsplitting. But the king's rage, and the machinations of Thomas Cromwell (Leo McKern), force his hand.

Scofield is magnificent in his first major film role; Shaw stands out as an energetic, youthfully impetuous Henry. Director Zinnemann never allows his primarily stage-trained actors to indulge in theatrical over-emoting. This absorbing film features inventive camerawork and superior production values. Winner of six Oscars, the film won the exact same awards (and Best British Film as well) from the British Film Academy.

MAN FROM LARAMIE, THE

1955 104m c Western ★★★★
Columbia (U.S.) /U

James Stewart *(Will Lockhart)*, Arthur Kennedy *(Vic Hansbro)*, Donald Crisp *(Alec Waggoman)*, Cathy O'Donnell *(Barbara Waggoman)*, Alex Nicol *(Dave Waggoman)*, Aline MacMahon *(Kate Canaday)*, Wallace Ford *(Charley O'Leary)*, Jack Elam *(Chris Boldt)*, John War Eagle *(Frank Darrah)*, James Millican *(Tom Quigby)*

p, William Goetz; d, Anthony Mann; w, Philip Yordan, Frank Burt (based on a *Saturday Evening Post* story by Thomas T. Flynn); ph, Charles Lang; ed, William Lyon; m, George Duning; art d, Cary Odell

Mann's westerns revitalized the genre in the 1950s because they were derived from classic struggles inspired by such works as the Bible and Shakespeare. His westerns weren't just action-packed chases; they were adult dramas which illustrated the psychological and moral dilemmas regarding the family, hatred, revenge, the land, and the nature of savagery versus civilization. In addition to being skillfully shot, acted, and scripted, Mann's westerns have an intelligence and a brutal conviction which compares well even with those by John Ford.

Will Lockhart (Stewart) leaves his home in Laramie, Wyoming, on a mission to find the men responsible for selling automatic rifles to the Apaches who killed his brother. He enters the town of Coronado, New Mexico, and soon learns that most of the territory is ruled by Alec Waggoman (Crisp), a megalomaniacal rancher who has been waging war against rival female rancher Kate Canaday (MacMahon). The aging Waggoman must decide whether to leave his empire to his smart adopted son and ranch foreman Vic (Kennedy) or his crazed, vicious blood heir Dave (Nicol). While digging for clues, Will comes between not only rival ranchers but also rival sons. Nobody gets out unscathed.

At the time of his death in 1967, director Mann had announced his plan to adapt Shakespeare's King Lear as a western (much the same way Japanese director Akira Kurosawa did in RAN). One can see that THE MAN FROM LARAMIE was something of a dress rehearsal for this project. Crisp, as Lear, frets over the continuation of his empire and is blind to the fact that it is Kennedy who loves him most. His guilt over his ruthless life (and having turned his former lover into an enemy) cloud his mind and move him to make bad decisions that ensure his downfall. Violent but compelling stuff.

MAN FROM SNOWY RIVER, THE

1982 102m c Western/Adventure ★★★
Hoyts/Cambridge (Australia) R/PG

Kirk Douglas *(Harrison/Spur)*, Jack Thompson *(Clancy)*, Tom Burlinson *(Jim Craig)*, Terence Donovan *(Henry Craig)*, Tommy Dysart *(Mountain Man)*, Bruce Kerr *(Man in Street)*, David Bradshaw *(A. B. "Banjo" Paterson)*, Sigrid Thornton *(Jessica)*, Tony Bonner *(Kane)*, June Jago *(Mrs. Bailey)*

p, Geoff Burrowes; d, George Miller; w, John Dixon, Fred Cullen (based on the poem by A.B. "Banjo" Paterson); ph, Keith Wagstaff; ed, Adrian Carr; m, Bruce Rowland; art d, Leslie Binns; cos, Robin Hall

Kirk Douglas plays two brothers, the one, Harrison, an aristocratic landowner, the other, Spur, a one-legged, scraggly prospector. The pair experience a falling out, though this is not addressed until the latter half of the picture. More important than the plot are the characters of the brothers. The film was one of Australia's top-grossing pictures, though the producers took a chance in casting an American in the roles. (Robert Mitchum and Burt Lancaster also were considered.) A fine directorial debut from George Miller, who, not surprisingly, tends to be confused with the director of MAD MAX and THE ROAD WARRIOR, also named George Miller.

MAN HUNT

1941 105m bw Spy ★★★★½
Fox (U.S.) /A

Walter Pidgeon *(Capt. Thorndike)*, Joan Bennett *(Jerry)*, George Sanders *(Quive-Smith)*, John Carradine *(Mr. Jones)*, Roddy McDowall *(Vaner the Cabin Boy)*, Ludwig Stossel *(Doctor)*, Heather Thatcher *(Lady Risborough)*, Frederic Worlock *(Lord Risborough)*, Roger Imhof *(Capt. Jensen)*, Egon Brecher *(Whiskers)*

p, Kenneth MacGowan; d, Fritz Lang; w, Dudley Nichols (based on the novel *Rogue Male* by Geoffrey Household); ph, Arthur Miller; ed, Allen McNeil; m, Alfred Newman; art d, Richard Day, Wiard Ihnen; cos, Travis Banton

One of the best-loved of Lang's spy dramas, MAN HUNT is a superbly exciting, tightly constructed picture which stars Pidgeon, terrific as Thorndike, a big-game hunter in the Bavarian Alps who accidentally discovers that he has a chance to assassinate Hitler. Apprehended by Gestapo leader Quive-Smith (Sanders), he refuses to sign a confession and is beaten and left for dead. With the help of a friendly youngster (McDowall), Thorndike stows away on a Danish steamer. Also on board, however, is the mysterious, umbrella-wielding Mr. Jones (Carradine), who has Thorndike's passport and has taken his identity. Befriended by a friendly cockney prostitute (Bennett, rarely better) in London, Thorndike eventually has a memorable showdown with Jones in a subway tunnel. Our dashing hero isn't out of danger yet, though; Quive-Smith threatens as well, and it's up to a hatpin to save the day.

Based on the best-selling novel, *Rogue Male*, MAN HUNT was scripted by the immensely talented Dudley Nichols and intended as a John Ford picture. Ford, however, disliked the subject matter and the film was offered, by Darryl Zanuck, to Lang. Lang encountered, as he often did, some problems on the set involving both the Hays Code and budget constraints by Zanuck. A great lover of complex female characters, Lang had cast Bennett as a compassionate woman who happened to be a prostitute. The Hays Code, however, which would just as soon have denied the existence of prostitution, required some rewrites. According to Lang, "We had to prominently show a sewing machine in her apartment; thus she was not a whore, she was a 'seamstress.' Talk about authenticity!" Most objectionable to Zanuck was the parting scene between Pidgeon and Bennett which was to take place on London Bridge. Zanuck was distressed by the fact that a "decent" girl had to play the whore in front of the man she loved, and so refused to allow any money in the budget for this essential scene. As Lang tells it, he cinematographer Miller and unit manager Benny Silvi found a single bridge railing in the props department. Two were needed, however, so Lang spent $40 to have a second one constructed. Without the aid of studio workers (whose unions would not allow such defiance), the threesome stole into the studio at 4 a.m. They painted the backdrop, hung light bulbs in a manner of diminishing perspective to create depth, and then obscured the whole thing in a blanket of fog. The result was a beautifully atmospheric set.

MAN IN THE GRAY FLANNEL SUIT, THE

1956   152m   c   Drama   ★★★
Fox   (U.S.)   /A

Gregory Peck (Tom Rath), Jennifer Jones (Betsy Rath), Fredric March (Ralph Hopkins), Marisa Pavan (Maria), Ann Harding (Mrs. Hopkins), Lee J. Cobb (Judge Bernstein), Keenan Wynn (Caesar Gardella), Gene Lockhart (Hawthorne), Gigi Perreau (Susan Hopkins), Portland Mason (Janie)

p, Darryl F. Zanuck; d, Nunnally Johnson; w, Nunnally Johnson (based on the novel by Sloan Wilson); ph, Charles Clarke; ed, Dorothy Spencer; m, Bernard Herrmann; art d, Lyle Wheeler, Jack Martin Smith; fx, Ray Kellogg; cos, Charles LeMaire

Middle-class middle-America. . . the inside story? Hardly, but nonetheless a surprisingly engrossing, if shallow and overlong, Hollywood vision of 1950s thirtysomethings, with Peck turning in a dignified title role.

Tom Rath has a $10K mortgage, three brats and psycho-Betsy (Jones). Fun. He also has bad memories of WWII, where he knifed a German during a freezing winter for his coat, had a fling with wistful peasant Maria (Pavan), and threw a grenade which accidentally killed his best friend. Oops. Acquiring a new, lucrative position writing speeches for avuncular company president Ralph (March), Tom must choose between working overtime on the job or on his relationship with psycho-Betsy. Hmm. And what about his grandmother's estate? And that kid he fathered during the war? My! Don't worry—Lee J. Cobb is on hand to tell us at the finale that "God's in His heaven and all's right with the world." Whew.

Totally hollow trash, with a hysteria-prone Jennifer Jones displaying an odd crease down the middle of her face. So slickly dished up, though, you can feel yourself sliding around on the sofa. Nice to see Ann Harding.

MAN IN THE IRON MASK, THE

1939   110m   bw   Historical/Adventure   ★★★★
UA   (U.S.)   /PG

Louis Hayward (Louis XIV/Philippe), Joan Bennett (Maria Theresa), Warren William (D'Artagnan), Joseph Schildkraut (Fouquet), Alan Hale (Porthos), Miles Mander (Aramis), Bert Roach (Athos), Walter Kingsford (Colbert), Marion Martin (Mlle. de la Valliere), Montagu Love (Spanish Ambassador)

p, Edward Small; d, James Whale; w, George Bruce (based on the novel by Alexandre Dumas); ph, Robert Planck; ed, Grant Whytock; m, Lucien Moraweck; art d, John DuCasse Schulze; fx, Howard Anderson

AAN Best Score: Lud Gluskin, Lucien Moraweck

James Whale's high quality version of Dumas's classic tale of twin brothers, one the king of France and the other a prisoner at Isle St. Marguerite (Hayward, very fine in a dual role). William, as musketeer D'Artagnan, comes to the aid of the imprisoned brother, who is mercilessly forced to wear an iron mask to prevent anyone from realizing he is heir to the throne. Whale directed this elaborately costumed adventure with the greatest of verve and flair, though his career came to a halt in 1941. (Aging and frail, the master director committed suicide 16 years later.) This film also marked the first screen appearance of Peter Cushing.

MAN IN THE WHITE SUIT, THE

1951   85m   bw   Comedy   ★★★★★
Ealing   (U.K.)   /U

Alec Guinness (Sidney Stratton), Joan Greenwood (Daphne Birnley), Cecil Parker (Alan Birnley), Michael Gough (Michael Corland), Ernest Thesiger (Sir John Kierlaw), Howard Marion-Crawford (Cranford), Duncan Lamont (Harry), Henry Mollison (Hoskins), Vida Hope (Bertha), Patric Doonan (Frank)

p, Michael Balcon; d, Alexander Mackendrick; w, Roger MacDougall, John Dighton, Alexander Mackendrick (based on the play by Roger MacDougall); ph, Douglas Slocombe; ed, Bernard Gribble; m, Benjamin Frankel; art d, Jim Morahan; fx, Sydney Pearson, Geoffrey Dickinson; cos, Anthony Mendleson

AAN Best Original Screenplay: Roger MacDougall, John Dighton, Alexander Mackendrick

A sharp satirical comedy about the social contradictions of technology, THE MAN IN THE WHITE SUIT offers a tour de force by master comic Guinness. He plays Sidney Stratton, an eccentric inventor believed crazy by most except for Daphne Birnley (Greenwood), daughter of a millionaire textile king (Parker). Stratton manages to finagle access to Birnley's elaborate development laboratory, supplied with all the chemicals and equipment he requires. Although Birnley and his associates have to deal with lab explosions and the eerie gurgling of Stratton's setup, Sidney eventually comes through, creating a fabric that never wears out and which repels dirt completely. He fashions a pristine white suit of the material and is as first hailed as a genius. Soon enough, though, the problems with the miracle material become evident. Labor dislikes poor Sidney because they'll all be put out of work once people buy enough of these wonder suits, and management changes its attitudes when they realize they'll be put out of business by Sidney's new fashion line. Although the two opposing forces do seem to get the better of Sidney in the memorable finale, his last-second knowing smile suggests an even greater discovery just around the corner.

THE MAN IN THE WHITE SUIT, besides offering consistent humor and often hilarious scenes, is another minor masterpiece of acting on Guinness' part: he shows marvelous restraint that gives way to brief hysteria, emphasizing again the versatility of this astounding actor. Greenwood, meanwhile, with her striking eyes, haughty yet vaguely haunted manner and that one-of-a-kind voice, is at her peak, parrying comic thrusts with great aplomb. The reliable Parker shines yet again as the worried capitalist and, on the proletarian side, the forceful Hope and the adorable Edie Martin are especially outstanding. Special mention should also be made of Thesiger, that unique comic talent from several James Whale masterworks of the 1930s. He is wonderful here as the decrepit but all-powerful industrial czar who decrees Sidney's fate for the sake of business. In addition to the laughs, this film also indicts the ruthless and manipulative ways of businessmen. The acerbic social criticism lacing the film, however, does not exclude union representatives either, and the result is an intelligently rounded satire. Mackendrick's formidable gifts as both director and screenwriter are on vivid display here.

MAN OF A THOUSAND FACES

1957   122m   bw   Biography   ★★★½
Universal   (U.S.)   /A

James Cagney (Lon Chaney), Dorothy Malone (Cleva Creighton Chaney), Jane Greer (Hazel Bennet), Marjorie Rambeau (Gert), Jim Backus (Clarence Logan), Robert Evans (Irving Thalberg), Celia Lovsky (Mrs. Chaney), Jeanne Cagney (Carrie Chaney), Jack Albertson (Dr. J. Wilson Shields), Roger Smith (Creighton Chaney at Age 21)

p, Robert Arthur; d, Joseph Pevney; w, R. Wright Campbell, Ivan Goff, Ben Roberts (based on a story by Ralph Wheelwright); ph, Russell Metty; ed, Ted J. Kent; m, Frank Skinner; art d, Alexander Golitzen, Eric Orbom; fx, Clifford Stine; cos, Bill Thomas

AAN Best Original Screenplay: Ralph Wheelright, R. Wright Campbell, Ivan Goff, Ben Roberts

Few silent screen stars approached the status of Lon Chaney. A makeup genius, he was the heart of horror during the 1920s, and Cagney's respectful rendering of this great artist is spectacular. Born the son of deaf-mute parents, Chaney becomes a successful vaudeville entertainer, creating many distinctive characters through inventive makeup and skilled mime. He meets and marries beautiful but neurotic fellow performer Cleva Creighton (melodramatic Malone) but when he introcuces her to his parents, she becomes hysterical at the thought that their children might be born with congenital deafness. When baby Creighton (later Lon Chaney Jr.) is born without these afflictions, all seems well until Cleva begins to resent her husband's popularity. She abandons her family, whereupon Chaney goes to Hollywood and, in true movie bio fashion, works his way up to film star status. He also marries the supportive Hazel Bennet (Greer, good but a trifle wasted) and Chaney's compelling characterizations in THE PHANTOM OF THE OPERA and THE HUNCHBACK OF NOTRE DAME thrill his ever-growing following. But, as might be expected, Cleva returns to the scene, threatening the relationship between Chaney and his now-grown son (Smith).

Cagney is riveting as Chaney (who died in 1930 at the age of 47), enacting the many great roles the silent star made famous in startling cameo performances. Many of Chaney's makeup secrets died with him, but experts Bud Westmore and Jack Kevan did a good job in coming close.

Lovsky is excellent as Chaney's mother, but newcomer Evans is unconvincing as MGM mogul Irving Thalberg. Thalberg's widow, retired film star Norma Shearer, did a good job in picking a handsome young man who resembled her "boy genius" husband, but that does not an actor make. Ironically, Evans later became a real-life mogul, heading Paramount from 1966 to 1976. Smith, playing the 21-year-old Creighton Chaney, is rather stoical, suggesting little of Chaney Jr's anguish.

MAN OF FLOWERS

1984 91m c Drama   ★★★½
Flowers (Australia)   /18

Norman Kaye (Charles Bremer), Alyson Best (Lisa), Chris Haywood (David), Sara Walker (Jane), Julia Blake (Art Teacher), Bob Ellis (Psychiatrist), Barry Dickins (Postman), Patrick Cook (Coppershop Man), Victoria Eagger (Angela), Werner Herzog (Father)

p, Jane Ballantyne, Paul Cox; d, Paul Cox; w, Paul Cox, Bob Ellis; ph, Yuri Sokol; ed, Tim Lewis; m, Gaetano Donizetti; art d, Asher Bilu; cos, Lirit Bilu

Charles Bremer (Norman Kaye) is a sexually repressed, middle-aged artist who sublimates his desires into paintings of flowers and impassioned organ playing. He hires artist's model Lisa (Alyson Best) for $100 a week to come to his house and take off her clothes for him on a makeshift altar while he plays "The Love Duet" from Donizetti's "Lucia di Lammermoor," after which he rushes to church and vents his emotions on a pipe organ. Charles finally goes to a psychiatrist, who, in the tradition of movie shrinks, is kinkier than his patients.

An interesting, sometimes funny film about loneliness and emotional isolation, MAN OF FLOWERS boasts a literate script, a lush, sensual texture and, best of all, a silent cameo by German director Werner Herzog as Bremer's domineering father.

MAN OF IRON
(CZLOWIEK Z ZELAZA)

1980 140m c Historical   ★★★★
Film Polski/Film Unit X (Poland)   PG/A

Jerzy Radziwilowicz (Tomczyk), Krystyna Janda (Agnieszka), Marian Opania (Winkiel), Irene Byrska (Anna Hulewicz' Mother), Boguslaw Linda (Radio-TV Technician Dzidek), Wieslawa Kosmalska (Anna), Andrzej Seweryn (Capt. Wirski), Krzysztof Janczar (Kryszka), Boguslaw Sobczuk (TV Editor), Franciszek Trzeciak (Badecki)

d, Andrzej Wajda; w, Aleksander Scibor-Rylski; ph, Edward Klosinski, Janusz Kalicinski; ed, Halina Prugar; m, Andrzej Korzynski; art d, Allan Starski, Maja Chrolowska; cos, Wieslawa Starska

AAN Best Foreign Language Film

Andrzej Wajda's sequel to MAN OF MARBLE uses the same scriptwriter and leading players and again traces its story through interviews. This film is a realistic portrayal of Gdansk from the student reform movement of 1968 to the Solidarity strikes in 1980. Strike leader Tomczyk (Jerzy Radziwilowicz) is harassed by the government and by

a journalist (Marian Opania). The latter conducts a smear campaign against the young labor activist, but his own loyalties are tested during the strike. Wajda's superb amalgam of fictional characters and historical fact not only entertains but also documents a tense period in Polish history. Solidarity leader Walesa is among the real-life figures who appear. Made under intense political pressure shortly before an authoritarian crackdown, MAN OF IRON was finished only hours before its premiere at the Cannes Film Festival, where it won top honors.

MAN OF MARBLE
(CZLOWIEK Z MARMURU)

1977 160m c Drama   ★★★★½
Enterprise de Realization/Ensemble X   (Poland)   /U

Jerzy Radziwilowicz (Mateusz Birkut/His Son Maciek Tomczyk), Michal Tarkowski (Wincenty Witek), Krystyna Zachwatowicz (Hanka Tomczyk), Piotr Cieslak (Michalak), Wieslaw Wojcik (Jodia), Krystyna Janda (Agnieszka), Tadeusz Lomnicki (Jerzy Burski), Jacek Lomnicki (Young Burski), Leonard Zajaczkowski (Leonard Frybos), Jacek Domanski (Sound Man)

p, Andrzej Wajda; d, Andrzej Wajda; w, Aleksander Scibor-Rylski; ph, Edward Klosinski; ed, Halina Pugarana, Maria Kalinciska; m, Andrzej Korzynski; prod d, Allan Starski, Wojciech Majda, Maria Osiecka-Kuminek; cos, Lidia Rzeszewska, Wieslawa Konopelska

A fine example of political art. The events which culminated in the workers' revolt and eventual martial law crackdown in Poland in 1982 are foreshadowed by one of Poland's highest-ranking directors in this black satire. Director Wajda follows film student Janda who wants to make a documentary about a former worker as her graduation requirement. Radziwilowicz is to be her subject, a man who had been lauded for his brick-laying skills before vanishing into total obscurity. Previously the subject of a film that showed what a great worker he was, Radziwilowicz became something of a star. But when he began believing the publicity himself and started interfering in worker politics, the government quickly stifled him, disgracing his name, and banishing him into historical obscurity. This is the story Janda discovers through interviews with Radziwilowicz's contemporaries and family and through old newsreels. Using an expository style similar to that of CITIZEN KANE, Wajda has fashioned a sophisticated indictment of Poland's communist regime, with all of its warts clearly exposed. Wajda followed this with MAN OF IRON, using similar storytelling methods to portray the rise of Poland's Solidarity movement and its leader Lech Walesa.

MAN OF THE WEST

1958 100m c Western   ★★★★★
UA (U.S.)   /A

Gary Cooper (Link Jones), Julie London (Billie Ellis), Lee J. Cobb (Dock Tobin), Arthur O'Connell (Sam Beasley), Jack Lord (Coaley), John Dehner (Claude), Royal Dano (Trout), Bob Wilke (Ponch), Jack Williams (Alcutt), Guy Wilkerson (Conductor)

p, Walter M. Mirisch; d, Anthony Mann; w, Reginald Rose (based on the novel The Border Jumpers by Will C. Brown); ph, Ernest Haller; ed, Richard Heermance; m, Leigh Harline; art d, Hilyard Brown; cos, Yvonne Wood

Mann's last western, and his most disturbing foray into the genre. Working here with Cooper instead of Jimmy Stewart, Mann again tells a tale of Shakespearean proportions in which complicated men struggle against their own worst instincts. The film opens as Link (Cooper), a seemingly guileless Texas bumpkin, leaves his wife and children and boards a train to hire a schoolteacher from Fort Worth. Enlisted by con man Sam Beasley (O'Connell) to scam Link, saloon singer Billie Ellis (London) almost succeeds when the psychotic Tobin gang holds up the train. Stranded, Link leads Billie and Beasley to the Tobins's nearby cabin, where it is revealed that he is a former gang member and nephew of its leader (Cobb). While Uncle Dock is happy to see his former right-hand man, his cousins are less than thrilled by his presence but more than thrilled by Billie's. Plans to rob a bank in a former boomtown turned ghost town spearhead family rivalries and the ugly nature of Link's past.

As in Mann's other westerns, there is an air of epic tragedy to MAN OF THE WEST. Link's accidental reentry into the gang causes his base instincts to once again boil to the surface after years of conformity, but, better than the rest of the gang, he realizes that a way of life is passing. In some ways it is Dock rather than Link who plays the title character. Mann's heroes and villains do not wear white and black hats to separate good from evil; they are real people who suffer from anxiety, guilt, hatred, and doubt. Some succumb to lust, others to change, but a few achieve a transcendent grace. Excellent acting all around (even if casting the decade-older Cooper as Cobb's nephew doesn't quite wash), with a gun battle between Cooper and Dehner and a different sort of encounter between Cooper and London as highlights.

MAN ON THE EIFFEL TOWER, THE

1949 97m c Mystery   ★★★★
RKO (U.S.)   /A

Charles Laughton (Inspector Maigret), Franchot Tone (Radek), Burgess Meredith (Huertin), Robert Hutton (Bill Kirby), Jean Wallace (Edna Wallace), Patricia Roc (Helen Kirby), Belita (Gisella), George Thorpe (Comelieu), William Phipps (Janvier), William Cottrell (Moers)

p, Irving Allen; d, Burgess Meredith; w, Harry Brown (based on the story "A Battle of Nerves" by Georges Simenon); ph, Stanley Cortez; ed, Louis Sackin; m, Michel Michelet; art d, Rene Renoux

Georges Simenon's famous sleuth, Inspector Maigret, was never better enacted than by the shrewd, slow, and sure Charles Laughton, who pursues a thrill killer-for-hire in this superb film noir production. The nephew of a rich woman hires Radek (Tone) to kill his aunt, and Maigret investigates. After dismissing a blind knife-grinder (Meredith, who also directed) as too obvious a suspect, Maigret unearths Radek, a psychopathic murderer who enjoys killing and baiting the police. Cop and killer play an intense cat-and-mouse game until one of them finally cracks under the psychological strain, with a superb chase up the Eiffel Tower as the exciting finale. The acting is outstanding in this film, and Franchot Tone actually overcomes Laughton's masterful mannerisms in their scenes together. Burgess Meredith both adroitly performs his red-herring role and directs with a sure hand. The lensing by Stanley Cortez, in rich Ansco color, lovingly shows a majestic Paris while sharply capturing the thrilling story. Michelet's score is also exceptional.

MAN ON THE FLYING TRAPEZE, THE

1935 65m bw Comedy   ★★★★
Paramount (U.S.)   /A

W.C. Fields (Ambrose Wolfinger), Mary Brian (Hope Wolfinger), Kathleen Howard (Leona Wolfinger), Grady Sutton (Claude Neselrode), Vera Lewis (Mrs. Cordelia Neselrode), Lucien Littlefield (Mr. Peabody), Oscar Apfel (President Malloy), Lew Kelly (Adolph Berg), Tammany Young ("Willie" the Weasel), Walter Brennan ("Legs" Garnett)

p, William LeBaron; d, Clyde Bruckman; w, Ray Harris, Sam Hardy, Jack Cunningham, Bobby Vernon (based on a story by Sam Hardy and Charles Bogle); ph, Alfred Gilks; ed, Richard Currier

There's no circus, no flying trapeze, but lots of laughs generated by the myriad frustrations and barely controlled rage of "the man" in this great W.C. Fields vehicle. A deft sketch of the potentially nightmarish qualities of small town America, it still has an edge.

Ambrose Wolfinger (Fields) dawdles over brushing his teeth and gargling in the bathroom until his shrewish wife, Leona (Howard) complains about the noise. Trundling to bed, he falls asleep snoring, only to be awakened when his wife improbably hears sounds of burglars singing. Gun in hand, Wolfinger creeps out of his bedroom to investigate, but the weapon accidentally discharges, bringing his horrendous mother-in-law, Mrs. Cordelia Neselrode (Lewis), and sponging stepson Claude (Sutton), on the run. Fortunately Wolfinger's good-hearted daughter, Hope (Brian) also appears to offer moral support. Wolfinger finds that two burglars "Legs" Garnett (Brennan) and "Willie" the Weasel (Young) have broken into his barrel of applejack whiskey. Soon they are all drinking and singing together. Ambrose Wolfinger's rebellion against the demands of his overbearing family and dead-end job has just begun.

One of Fields's most entertaining movies, THE MAN ON THE FLYING TRAPEZE features a series of ordinary mishaps that escalate into hilarious physical disasters. Directed by Clyde Bruckman (who worked on Buster Keaton's classic THE GENERAL), the film is more than a showcase for its star. Kathleen Howard, a former Metropolitan Opera singer and fashion writer, was Fields's favorite on-screen wife, and he never tired of telling reporters what an accomplished actress she was. Brian, Fields's neighbor, was no longer a star, but she was still charming. Less well known that IT'S A GIFT or THE BANK DICK, this is still an excellent comic outing. Check out that filing system!

MAN WHO CAME TO DINNER, THE

1942 112m bw Comedy   ★★★★
Warner Bros. (U.S.)   /U

Bette Davis (Maggie Cutler), Ann Sheridan (Lorraine Sheldon), Monty Woolley (Sheridan Whiteside), Richard Travis (Bert Jefferson), Jimmy Durante (Banjo), Reginald Gardiner (Beverly Carlton), Billie Burke (Mrs. Stanley), Elisabeth Fraser (June Stanley), Grant Mitchell (Ernest Stanley), George Barbier (Dr. Bradley)

p, Jerry Wald, Jack Saper; d, William Keighley; w, Julius J. Epstein, Philip G. Epstein (based on the play by George S. Kaufman, Moss Hart); ph, Tony Gaudio; ed, Jack Killifer; m, Frederick Hollander; art d, Robert Haas; cos, Orry-Kelly

This hit Broadway comedy became a comparably popular film thanks to a smart adaptation, strong performances, and the fortunate retention of the play's star, Monty Woolley. The celebrated John Barrymore had been slated for the role but he had trouble with the dialogue. Luckily, another genuine movie star—Bette Davis—was eager to take a secondary role in this fanciful account of some thinly veiled real celebrities in an unlikely situation. Theater critics Alexander Woollcott, Harpo Marx and Noel Coward were among the brainy wits who met regularly at the Algonquin Hotel to exchange witticisms over lunch. Resourceful playwrights George S. Kaufman and Moss Hart utilized what they knew of the luncheers, placed them in a "fish out of water" setting, and crafted a funny, acerbic play and film.

Sheridan Whiteside (Woolley as Woollcott), a popular acid-tongued radio host, is traveling cross-country on a lecture tour with Maggie Cutler (Davis), his tolerant secretary. They stop in a small town in Ohio and accept a dinner invitation from Mr. and Mrs. Ernest Stanley (Mitchell and Burke), a prominent local family. Whiteside slips on a patch of ice in front of the Stanley house and gets carried inside spewing insults and threats of lawsuits. The Stanleys—who embody the kind of old-fashioned Middle American values that the intellectual Whiteside abhors—are terrified by the prospect of scandal, so they do their best to keep their "guest from hell" comfortable while he throws their household into chaos, advising the Stanley children to flee the social constraints of Ohio. The plot thickens when Maggie falls for local newsman-playwright Bert Jefferson (Travis). Fearing that he may lose his loyal employee, Whiteside schemes to break up the relationship.

Cynically witty lines, top-notch characterizations (Ann Sheridan is a delight), and welcome guest appearances by Jimmy Durante (as a Harpo Marx figure) and Reginald Gardner (doing a take on Noel Coward) make for classic comedy.

MAN WHO FELL TO EARTH, THE

1976 140m c Science Fiction   ★★★½
Cinema 5 (U.K.)   R/18

David Bowie (Thomas Jerome Newton), Rip Torn (Nathan Bryce), Candy Clark (Mary-Lou), Buck Henry (Oliver Farnsworth), Bernie Casey (Peters), Jackson D. Kane (Prof. Canutti), Rick Riccardo (Trevor), Tony Mascia (Arthur), Linda Hutton (Elaine), Hilary Holland (Jill)

p, Michael Deeley, Barry Spikings; d, Nicolas Roeg; w, Paul Mayersberg (based on the novel by Walter Tevis); ph, Anthony Richmond; ed, Graeme Clifford; fx, Paul Ellenshaw

Nicolas Roeg's cult classic about an alien (Bowie) who arrives on Earth in search of water for his drought-stricken planet, where his wife and children are dying of thirst. The alien takes the name of Thomas Jerome Newton, arrives at the office of patent attorney Farnsworth (Buck Henry), and offers him a number of innovative designs with which they can make a great deal of money—enough for Newton to build a vehicle that will return him to his home planet. Newton and Farnsworth are soon running a huge financial empire, but Newton's plans are threatened both by an inquisitive chemistry professer (Rip Torn), and by his own descent into earthly ways.

Roeg began his career as a cameraman (he worked second-unit on LAWRENCE OF ARABIA) and progressed to become a director of photography (THE MASQUE OF THE RED DEATH, A FUNNY THING HAPPENED ON THE WAY TO THE FORUM, FAHRENHEIT 451). Here, he has come up with some memorable imagery, as well as coaxing a suitably enigmatic performance out of Bowie. Originally released at 140 minutes, the US distributor, Cinema 5, edited the film down to versions of 117, 120, and 125 minutes, before restoring it to its original length in 1980.

MAN WHO KNEW TOO MUCH, THE

1934 75m bw Mystery   ★★★★
Gaumont (U.K.)

Leslie Banks (Bob Lawrence), Edna Best (Jill Lawrence), Peter Lorre (Abbott), Frank Vosper (Ramon Levine), Hugh Wakefield (Clive), Nova Pilbeam (Betty Lawrence), Pierre Fresnay (Louis Bernard), Cicely Oates (Nurse Agnes), D.A. Clarke-Smith (Binstead), George Curzon (Gibson)

p, Michael Balcon; d, Alfred Hitchcock; w, A.R. Rawlinson, Charles Bennett, D.B. Wyndham-Lewis, Emlyn Williams, Edwin Greenwood (based on a story by Charles Bennett and D.B. Wyndham-Lewis); ph, Curt Courant; ed, Hugh Stewart; m, Arthur Benjamin; art d, Alfred Junge, Peter Proud

Married couple Bob and Jill Lawrence (Banks and Best) are vacationing in Switzerland with daughter Betty (Pilbeam), when Louis Bernard (Fresnay), a Frenchman who befriends them, is found murdered. Before dying, however, Louis Bernard whispers a secret—that a diplomat will be assassinated at great embarrassment to the British government. To keep Bob's lips sealed, Betty is kidnapped—to be held until after the assassination by hired killer Abbott (Lorre), scheduled to take place during a concert at London's Albert Hall. Bob must follow his duty as an Englishman and prevent the assassination, but at the same time he must do all in his power to insure the safety of his child. It is in this film that Hitchcock showed his development of a theme he would repeat in films to come—the innocent victim suddenly caught up in a terrifying situation with apparently no way out, coupled with breathless chases in popular public places. This was Lorre's first English-speaking part; he had been brought to England at Hitchcock's request after the director saw him in Fritz Lang's impressive M. Hitchcock, who was not known to favor child actors, got along so well with the young Pilbeam that he gave her her first adult leading role in his film YOUNG AND INNOCENT, three years later.

MAN WHO KNEW TOO MUCH, THE

1956 120m c Mystery   ★★★★
Paramount (U.S.)   PG/A

James Stewart (Dr. Ben McKenna), Doris Day (Jo McKenna), Brenda de Banzie (Mrs. Drayton), Bernard Miles (Mr. Drayton), Ralph Truman (Buchanan), Daniel Gelin (Louis Bernard), Mogens Wieth (Ambassador), Alan Mowbray (Val Parnell), Hillary Brooke (Jan Peterson), Christopher Olsen (Hank McKenna)

p, Alfred Hitchcock; d, Alfred Hitchcock; w, John Michael Hayes, Angus Macphail (based on a story by Charles Bennett, D.B. Wyndham-Lewis); ph, Richard Mueller; ed, George Tomasini; m, Bernard Herrmann; art d, Hal Pereira, Henry Bumstead; fx, John P. Fulton; cos, Edith Head

AA Best Song: Jay Livingston, Ray Evans

The original version of this film so appealed to Hitchcock that he felt it could take a remake and survive. He also believed that he could improve upon it—an opinion open to debate. Though the director altered some locales (Switzerland became Morocco), he kept the original story fairly much intact, enhanced the production values, and added 45 minutes to its running time. Dr. Ben and Jo McKenna (Stewart and Day) are sweetly innocent and unsuspecting tourists whose vacation in French Morocco turns into a nightmare. Traveling with their son

Hank (Olsen) they are enjoying their holiday when they meet Mr. and Mrs. Drayton (Miles and de Banzie), a friendly British couple, and Louis Bernard (Gelin), a suspicious but friendly Frenchman. Later, while Ben and Jo are shopping in the bazaar, an Arab runs frantically up to them, having been stabbed in the back. Ben grabs the man as he falls and finds, to his horror, that it is Louis Bernard in disguise. Before he dies, Louis Bernard whispers something to Ben, thereby tossing him into a tangle of international intrigue that only he can unravel. Though there is obviously more polish and a lavish budget in this remake, the 1956 version of THE MAN WHO KNEW TOO MUCH has no more or less impact than the first version. Again, Hitchcock's scenes are beautifully framed and tautly directed—especially the double climax of the assassination attempt at the Albert Hall and the Embassy search for the kidnapped Hank. Day delivers a song, "Que Sera, Sera," which became a smash hit. Hitchcock makes his customary cameo, as does his composer Bernard Herrmann.

MAN WHO LOVED WOMEN, THE
(L'HOMME QUI AIMAIT LES FEMMES)

1977 119m c Drama/Comedy   ★★★
Carrosse/Artistes (France)   /X

Charles Denner (Bertrand Morane), Brigitte Fossey (Genevieve Bigey), Nelly Borgeaud (Delphine Grezel), Leslie Caron (Vera), Genevieve Fontanel (Helene), Nathalie Baye (Martine Desdoits), Sabine Glaser (Bernadette), Valerie Bonnier (Fabienne), Martine Chassing (Denise), Roselyne Puyo (Nicole)

d, Francois Truffaut; w, Francois Truffaut, Michel Fermaud, Suzanne Schiffman; ph, Nestor Almendros; ed, Martine Barraque; m, Maurice Jaubert

Truffaut's swiftly paced, light-hearted exercise concerns a man whose very existence is devoted to women—a man perhaps not unlike Truffaut himself. Denner is the amorous title male, a well-off researcher who is surely one of the most woman-crazy men ever to appear on film. He can't keep his mind off women; a mere glance at one femme dressed in black silk stockings sends him on a long journey toward love. All the while that Denner chases skirts, he remains charming and innocent, never believing he is doing anything wrong or harmful. Unlike those men who abuse women, Denner adores them—all of them. THE MAN WHO LOVED WOMEN is filled with Truffaut's ironic sense of humor, always charming, and never in any way offending. As in all of Truffaut's romantic comedies, what appears as flippant and sugary is actually a cover for some very complex statements about the nature of love, Truffaut himself, and the cinema. In this sense THE MAN WHO LOVED WOMEN can be viewed, along with THE STORY OF ADELE H. and THE GREEN ROOM, as part of a trilogy about unrequited love and frustrating obsessions. A Hollywood remake of this film appeared in 1983, directed by Blake Edwards and starring Burt Reynolds.

MAN WHO SHOT LIBERTY VALANCE, THE

1962 123m bw Western   ★★★½
Ford (U.S.)   /U

James Stewart (Ransom Stoddard), John Wayne (Tom Doniphon), Vera Miles (Hallie Stoddard), Lee Marvin (Liberty Valance), Edmond O'Brien (Dutton Peabody), Andy Devine (Link Appleyard), Ken Murray (Doc Willoughby), John Carradine (Maj. Cassius Starbuckle), Jeanette Nolan (Nora Ericson), John Qualen (Peter Ericson)

p, Willis Goldbeck; d, John Ford; w, Willis Goldbeck, James Warner Bellah (based on a story by Dorothy M. Johnson); ph, William Clothier; ed, Otho Lovering; m, Cyril J. Mockridge, Alfred Newman; art d, Hal Pereira, Eddie Imazu; cos, Edith Head

AAN Best Costume Design: Edith Head

A solid, if overrated, Ford western, one with its share of cliches and predictability. It's still fascinating to watch Wayne and Stewart deal with hellion Marvin in a changing West. The movie opens after the story is all over, when Sen. Ransom Stoddard (Stewart) and his wife (Miles) return to the western town of Shinbone in 1910. They have unexpectedly come to the funeral of Tom Doniphon (Wayne), which piques the interest of a local reporter. Ransom begins to tell how he came to know Tom, as the movie flashes back to Shinbone's wild and woolly days. A fledgling lawyer, Ransom must contend with local nasty Liberty Valance (Marvin). He is waylaid by Valance and his men just as he enters the territory; working for a group of powerful businessmen, they believe he is an agitator for statehood, exactly what the powerful locals don't want. Beaten up and left for dead by Valance, Ransom is found by Tom, who takes him to town, helps him find work, and supports his eventual bid for elected office. He even tries to teach the awkward lawyer the art of gunfighting, because Valance must still be dealt with. The truth behind the killing of the no-good varmint gradually comes out, but, as the reporter notes: "It ain't news. This is the West. When the legend becomes the fact, print the legend."

Starkly photographed and often heavily screened for nighttime shots, Ford's picture of the West here is a gloomy one, often pitch black when the only thing that comes out of it is the beastly Marvin. Many cliches and stereotypes people the film; the crusading newspaper editor, for example, had been used in many an earlier western, notably DODGE CITY. Oddly Ford, the master of great western exterior scenes, shot the entire film on two Paramount sound stages. Auteur critics have found much worth in this elegiac film, though in some ways it revisits the themes of Ford's earlier FORT APACHE. The movie is certainly above average, thanks to the performances by Stewart and Wayne, but Marvin is so flamboyant a badman that he is simply a caricature, even more so than in his outlandish Oscar-winning turn in CAT BALLOU.

MAN WHO WOULD BE KING, THE

1975 129m c Adventure   ★★★★
Allied Artists (U.K.)   PG

Sean Connery (*Daniel Dravot*), Michael Caine (*Peachy Carnehan*), Christopher Plummer (*Rudyard Kipling*), Saeed Jaffrey (*Billy Fish*), Karroum Ben Bouih (*Kafu-Selim*), Jack May (*District Commissioner*), Doghmi Larbi (*Ootah*), Shakira Caine (*Roxanne*), Mohammed Shamsi (*Babu*), Paul Antrim (*Mulvaney*)

p, John Foreman; d, John Huston; w, John Huston, Gladys Hill (based on the story by Rudyard Kipling); ph, Oswald Morris; ed, Russell Lloyd; m, Maurice Jarre; prod d, Alexander Trauner; art d, Tony Inglis; cos, Edith Head

AAN Best Adapted Screenplay: John Huston, Gladys Hill; *AAN Best Editing:* Russell Lloyd; *AAN Best Art Direction:* Alexander Trauner, Tony Inglis, Peter James; *AAN Best Costume Design:* Edith Head

This was writer-director John Huston's dream project for decades. He originally wanted to film the Rudyard Kipling short story in the 1940s with Clark Gable and Humphrey Bogart. Later he envisioned Richard Burton and Peter O'Toole. However the long wait paid off: Michael Caine, Sean Connery, and Christopher Plummer deliver outstanding performances in a classic adventure that delivers thrills even as it meditates on issues of power and imperialism.

Kipling (Plummer) is working in his office in Lahore, India when an aged beggar enters and begins to spin an amazing tale that fascinates the writer. We flashback to Kipling's office many years earlier when a young, vibrant, if somewhat boorish Peachy Carnehan (Caine) and his dashing friend Daniel Dravot (Connery) ask the writer to witness some "official" document. Stationed in India, these British army officers have been supplementing their salaries with various scams. Down on their luck after squandering their money on vice, they have concocted a new scheme: they will sojourn into the hills of Kafiristan (a province in eastern Afghanistan now called Nuristan) where they will set themselves up as rulers. Intrigued by these brazen soldiers-of-fortune, Kipling secures them an appointment with the District Commissioner (May). However the official sees their true colors and sends them packing. Dravot and Carnehan endure assorted hardships as they trek through the storied Khyber Pass, and although Dravot gets mistaken for a god at one point, things don't quite work out as planned.

This is a grand adventure tale that does not stint on characterization. Connery and Caine join the ranks of Huston's classic overachievers, most notably Bogart's Fred C. Dobbs in THE TREASURE OF SIERRA MADRE. Caine may have gone a wee bit over-the-top but that helped the audience distinguish between the the natures of the two men. The film was shot on location in Morocco because of the costs and dangers of working in Afghanistan. Unfortunately, the score by the

celebrated Jarre (LAWRENCE OF ARABIA) failed to match the evocative power of the setting. However these are minor flaws in a delightful and memorable film.

MAN WITH THE GOLDEN ARM, THE

1955 119m bw Drama   ★★★½
Carlyle (U.S.)   /15

Frank Sinatra (*Frankie Machine*), Kim Novak (*Molly*), Eleanor Parker (*Zosch Machine*), Arnold Stang (*Sparrow*), Darren McGavin (*Louie*), Robert Strauss (*Schwiefka*), George Mathews (*Williams*), John Conte (*Drunky*), Doro Merande (*Vi*), George E. Stone (*Sam Markette*)

p, Otto Preminger; d, Otto Preminger; w, Walter Newman, Lewis Meltzer (based on the novel by Nelson Algren); ph, Sam Leavitt; ed, Louis Loeffler; m, Elmer Bernstein; prod d, Joseph C. Wright; cos, Mary Ann Nyberg

AAN Best Actor: Frank Sinatra; *AAN Best Score:* Elmer Bernstein; *AAN Best Art Direction:* Joseph C. Wright, Darrell Silvera

Otto Preminger defied the Code with this pioneering look at drug addiction, featuring a stylish rendering of the post-war hipster milieu, a crisp jazz soundtrack, and a remarkable Sinatra.

Crooked card dealer Frankie Machine (Sinatra), a junkie trying to stay clean, is back in town after six months in rehab. He wants to try his luck as a jazz drummer, but his resentful, crippled wife Zosch (Parker) demands that he return to his old job. Frankie later falls hard for B-girl Molly (Novak), and pursues his musical dreams in secret at her place. Finally securing an audition, he attempts to leave his old racket, but his boss (Strauss) prevails upon him to handle one last rigged marathon poker game. Professional and personal tensions only make the recurring offers of a drug pusher (McGavin) more tempting.

To some extent, Preminger's slickness clashes with the gritty realism of the screenplay, based on Nelson Algren's best-selling novel. Stang, in a rare dramatic outing for a man who usually played the comic flunky (beginning with Henry Morgan's radio show in the 1940s), is a standout as Frankie's slightly retarded pal. The typically stiff Novak has little to do except look pretty and act concerned, while the over-the-top Parker never hits the right mix of self-hatred and pity. Sinatra, by contrast, is superb, especially in a harrowing withdrawal scene. It's his movie. . . all the way.

MAN WITH TWO BRAINS, THE

1983 93m c Science Fiction/Comedy   ★★★½
Aspen (U.S.)   R/15

Steve Martin (*Dr. Michael Hfuhruhurr*), Kathleen Turner (*Dolores Benedict*), David Warner (*Dr. Necessiter*), Paul Benedict (*Butler*), Richard Brestoff (*Dr. Pasteur*), James Cromwell (*Realtor*), George Furth (*Timon*), Peter Hobbs (*Dr. Brandon*), Earl Boen (*Dr. Conrad*), Bernie Hern (*Gun Seller*)

p, David V. Picker, William E. McEuen; d, Carl Reiner; w, Carl Reiner, Steve Martin, George Gipe; ph, Michael Chapman; ed, Bud Molin; m, Joel Goldsmith; prod d, Polly Platt; art d, Mark Mansbridge; fx, Allen Hall, Clay Pinney, Robert Willard; cos, Kevin Brennan

Following their triumphant parody of film noir, DEAD MEN DON'T WEAR PLAID (1982), comedian Steve Martin and director Carl Reiner took on the mad-scientist films of the 1940s, with hilarious results. Dr. Michael Hfuhruhurr (Martin), a famed neurosurgeon, travels to Vienna with his beautiful-but-frigid wife, Dolores (deliciously vixenish Kathleen Turner), in an attempt to revive their romance. There he meets fellow scientist Dr. Alfred Necessiter (David Warner), who has devised a method to keep disembodied brains alive. Hfuhruhurr begins to communicate telepathically with a brain in a jar; the brain is that of a sweet, sympathetic woman (the voice of Sissy Spacek) with whom he falls hopelessly in love. Desperate to consummate his love, Hfuhruhurr decides to plant the brain in the body of a beautiful woman—but where to find a fresh corpse? Enter the dreaded Elevator Killer.

Carl Reiner, once known chiefly as Mel Brooks' second banana, has stepped in to fill a gap that opened when the formerly able Brooks lost his comic touch. THE MAN WITH TWO BRAINS, which never ceases to amuse, is at its best when most outrageous—as when Hfuhruhurr and his beloved brain enjoy their first kiss (he applies a pair of wax lips to the jar), or when Martin mimes the effects of prolonged sexual abstinence—and wait till you find out who the Elevator Killer is!

MANCHURIAN CANDIDATE, THE

1962 126m bw Political/Thriller ★★★★½
MC/Essex (U.S.) /PG

Frank Sinatra *(Bennett Marco)*, Laurence Harvey *(Raymond Shaw)*, Janet Leigh *(Rosie)*, Angela Lansbury *(Raymond's Mother)*, Henry Silva *(Chunjim)*, James Gregory *(Sen. John Iselin)*, Leslie Parrish *(Jocie Jordon)*, John McGiver *(Sen. Thomas Jordon)*, Khigh Dhiegh *(Yen Lo)*, James Edwards *(Cpl. Melvin)*

p, George Axelrod, John Frankenheimer; d, John Frankenheimer; w, George Axelrod (based on the novel by Richard Condon); ph, Lionel Lindon; ed, Ferris Webster; m, David Amram; prod d, Richard Sylbert; art d, Richard Sylbert, Philip Jefferies; fx, Paul Pollard; cos, Moss Mabry

AAN Best Supporting Actress: Angela Lansbury; *AAN Best Editing:* Ferris Webster

A nerve-beating masterpiece, and more timely now than then. Frankenheimer's tightrope walk between campy political satire and suspense is flawlessly rendered. Based on Richard Condon's paranoid novel.

Harvey returns from the Korean War a superhero and holder of the Congressional Medal of Honor, but those in his platoon—including his own commanding officer, Sinatra—are vague about what Harvey actually did to win the medal. When Sinatra begins to have recurring nightmares about Korea, he decides to investigate. Piece by sinister piece, Sinatra and others put the story together. It turns out that and the entire platoon was captured by North Koreans and brainwashed to think Harvey was a hero when, in truth, he had been programmed as a killer. But whom is he to kill? Upon his return from service Harvey leaves his overly protective mother (Lansbury) and her husband (Gregory), a right-wing senator. Harvey goes to work as a journalist, but when his control contacts him with the code, he kills without mercy or memory; a liberal columnist-publisher is his first victim. Harvey, now married, is next sent to kill his own wife and his father-in-law, a liberal senator. Sinatra discovers the truth: Harvey's controller is Lansbury, the top Communist spy in the US. She orders her robotlike son to kill the presidential nominee; her husband, who is the vice-presidential running mate, will then take control of the White House. Can Sinatra foil the plot?

THE MANCHURIAN CANDIDATE takes aim at both the Left and the Right, rendering them both dangerous fraternal twins—an outrageous, terrifying premise to contend with. The entire cast is first-rate. This is Harvey's best work—for once the unlovable quality he built a career on emerges sympathetically. But it is Angela Lansbury's incestuous, power-mad mother who makes your blood run cold. This was the peak of the first part of her career, which depended upon these hardbitten kind of characters. Forget Hitchcock—here's the monster mother of all time. THE MANCHURIAN CANDIDATE is political fiction—we hope—at its finest, certainly at its most forceful on the screen. It earned distinction as one of the first of a genre that mixed reality, symbolism, and the fantastic, alternating caprice and grim fact so that the view is jarred from one scene to the next as it would be riding on a speeding train constantly being rerouted. Have a wild ride.

MANHATTAN

1979 96m bw Comedy/Romance ★★★★½
UA (U.S.) R/15

Woody Allen *(Isaac Davis)*, Diane Keaton *(Mary Wilke)*, Michael Murphy *(Yale)*, Mariel Hemingway *(Tracy)*, Meryl Streep *(Jill)*, Anne Byrne *(Emily)*, Karen Ludwig *(Connie)*, Michael O'Donoghue *(Dennis)*, Victor Truro, Tisa Farrow

p, Charles H. Joffe; d, Woody Allen; w, Woody Allen, Marshall Brickman; ph, Gordon Willis; ed, Susan E. Morse; m, George Gershwin; prod d, Mel Bourne; cos, Albert Wolsky, Ralph Lauren

AAN Best Supporting Actress: Mariel Hemingway; *AAN Best Original Screenplay:* Woody Allen, Marshall Brickman

Deft comedy set in a neurotic town. People may argue about the relative merits of ANNIE HALL (which took Oscars for Best Picture, Direction, Actress, and Screenplay) vis-a-vis MANHATTAN, which won nothing but is a better and more fully realized film. By this time Allen had forsworn the glib one-liner and spent more time developing well-rounded characters. Allen is Isaac, a well-known TV scribe fed up with the medium who wants to use his talent to amuse in another fashion. He knows how to make people laugh, but can he move them? Isaac sometimes lives with teenaged drama student Tracy (Hemingway), but feelings of guilt over their age difference lead him to try to end their relationship. He commiserates with best friend Yale (Murphy), who is cheating on his own wife Emily (Byrne) with Mary (Keaton). Yale introduces Isaac to Mary, and though he finds her annoying and aggressive, Isaac is also fascinated by her. He comes to realize that her pseudo-intellectual behavior is all a sham and that she's actually a lovely person playing the role of a "Manhattanite" a bit too well. Before Isaac begins having an affair with Mary himself, though, he must deal with his lesbian ex-wife (Streep) book about their marriage and divorce entitled *Marriage, Divorce, and Selfhood*. Isaac tries to persuade her not to publish it, but she does and it's a huge hit; everyone in America now knows how weird Isaac is.

MANHATTAN is funny, though not as funny as some of Allen's earlier work. But it makes his earlier films seem shallow by comparison. Gershwin's music is the perfect accompaniment for the film. Gordon Willis' beautiful black-and-white cinematography reflects a sweet nostalgic sadness in keeping with both Isaac's gloom and Allen's romance with New York. Among the actors, MANHATTAN is stolen, rather surprisingly, by the appealing and assured Hemingway. In a small role, note Wallace Shawn, who has since distinguished himself as a writer for the stage and screen (MY DINNER WITH ANDRE) as well as an actor in several other films (ATLANTIC CITY). The producers petitioned to change the "R" rating to a "PG" but were turned down, mostly because of the content concerning the older man and the teenage girl.

MANHATTAN MELODRAMA

1934 93m bw Crime ★★★★
Cosmpolitan (U.S.) /A

Clark Gable *(Blackie Gallagher)*, William Powell *(Jim Wade)*, Myrna Loy *(Eleanor)*, Leo Carrillo *(Father Joe)*, Nat Pendleton *(Spud)*, George Sidney *(Poppa Rosen)*, Isabel Jewell *(Anabelle)*, Muriel Evans *(Tootsie Malone)*, Claudelle Kaye *(Miss Adams)*, Frank Conroy *(Blackie's Attorney)*

p, David O. Selznick; d, W.S. Van Dyke II; w, Oliver H.P. Garrett, Joseph L. Mankiewicz (based on the story "Three Men" by Arthur Caesar); ph, James Wong Howe; ed, Ben Lewis; art d, Cedric Gibbons, Joseph C. Wright; fx, Slavko Vorkapich; cos, Dolly Tree

AA Best Original Screenplay: Arthur Caesar

A splendid example of 1930s hardboiled melodrama, notable historically for two very different reasons: it marked the first of 14 pairings of the legendary team of William Powell and Myrna Loy, and it also reportedly marked legendary gangster John Dillinger for death—literally. A big Myrna Loy fan, Dillinger sneaked into the Biograph Theatre on July 22, 1934 to watch her in this film. He was spotted, the police were called, and he was gunned down after the picture was over.

Two boys (played by Jimmy Butler and a pre-stardom Mickey Rooney) are saved from a fire on a tour boat which claims the lives of their parents. Taken in by the kindly Jewish merchant Papa Rosen (Sidney), the boys become fast pals even though Jim (Butler) is upstanding and studious and Blackie (Rooney) regularly cuts school to shoot craps. Years later, Blackie (Gable) has, as might be expected, become New York's biggest gambler and racketeer and Jim (Powell) has, as might be expected, become a crusading prosecuting attorney for the Big Apple. Loy enters the picture as Blackie's girlfriend Eleanor, an educated woman who doesn't believe her man is really bad at heart. Will Blackie end up going to the electric chair for murder? Will Jim end up in the governor's mansion? Will Eleanor end up in Jim's arms? Considering all the THIN MAN movies that followed, it's not hard to answer the third question, but the twisty variations wreaked on the admittedly unoriginal plot premise make the ride worthwhile.

MANHATTAN MURDER MYSTERY

Director W.S. ("Woody") Van Dyke II directs with all the breezy assurance which distinguished so many of his films, and the screenplay by Garrett and Mankiewicz is fully of tasty one-liners. Gable (as the most sympathetic crook imaginable) and Powell (virtue never looked so good) perform the male-bonding routine with gusto, and Loy has great rapport with both her co-stars. (Don't forget that she made seven films with Gable.) The plot would go on to inspire such other well-remembered efforts as ANGELS WITH DIRTY FACES, but this early rendition is still well worth catching.

MANHATTAN MURDER MYSTERY

1993 108m c Comedy/Crime	★★½
Manhattan Productions (U.S.)	PG

Woody Allen *(Larry Lipton)*, Diane Keaton *(Carol Lipton)*, Alan Alda *(Ted)*, Anjelica Huston *(Marcia Fox)*, Jerry Adler *(Paul House)*, Lynn Cohen *(Lillian House)*, Ron Rifkin *(Sy)*, Joy Behar *(Marilyn)*, William Addy *(Jack the Super)*, John Doumanian *(Neighbor)*

p, Robert Greenhut; d, Woody Allen; w, Woody Allen, Marshall Brickman; ph, Carlo Di Palma; ed, Susan E. Morse; prod d, Santo Loquasto; art d, Speed Hopkins; cos, Jeffrey Kurland

Woody Allen's first film following the tabloid scandals that emerged during the breakup of his relationship with Mia Farrow, MANHATTAN MURDER MYSTERY is a light confection, whipped up from bits of old movies and toothless domestic banter.

Larry and Carol Lipton (Allen, Diane Keaton) are middle-aged New Yorkers whose lives are too good to be true and too dull to be fiction. He's a book editor and she's thinking about opening a restaurant. Larry is deflecting the advances of exotic writer Marcia Fox (Anjelica Huston), while Carol flirts half-heartedly with longtime friend Ted (Alan Alda). The death of an elderly neighbor, Lillian House (Lynn Cohen), provides the excitement Carol has been yearning for: she suspects Paul House (Jerry Adler) of murder, drawing Ted, Marcia, and even the skeptical Larry into her clumsy snooping. The mystery is resolved in a climax lifted straight from Orson Welles' THE LADY FROM SHANGHAI.

Though MANHATTAN MURDER MYSTERY seems intended as a straightforward comedy, a frothy homage to old movies featuring amateur sleuths and clever repartee, its tone is surprisingly curdled; when Larry mutters that there's nothing wrong with Carol that Prozac and a whack with a polo mallet wouldn't cure, the remark feels too sour for the situation. The film's nervous, gritty style is woefully out of sync with its broadly whimsical tone. Woody Allen is an acquired taste, and MANHATTAN MURDER MYSTERY is a movie for his steadfast fans only.

MANHUNTER

1986 119m c Crime/Thriller	★★★
DEG (U.S.)	R/18

William Petersen *(Will Graham)*, Kim Greist *(Molly Graham)*, Joan Allen *(Reba)*, Brian Cox *(Dr. Lektor)*, Dennis Farina *(Jack Crawford)*, Stephen Lang *(Freddie Lounds)*, Tom Noonan *(Francis Dollarhyde)*, David Seaman *(Kevin Graham)*, Benjamin Hendrickson *(Dr. Chilton)*, Michael Talbott *(Geehan)*

p, Richard Roth, d, Michael Mann; w, Michael Mann (based on the book *Red Dragon* by Thomas Harris); ph, Dante Spinotti; ed, Dov Hoenig; m, The Reds, Michel Rubini; prod d, Mel Bourne; art d, Jack Blackman; fx, Joseph DiGaetano II; cos, Colleen Atwood

A grim stylish thriller from the creator of television's "Miami Vice." Based on Thomas Harris's gripping novel *Red Dragon*, MANHUNTER introduces us to the Behavioral Science Unit of the FBI and its top agent, Will Graham (William Petersen). The secret of Graham's success is his uncanny ability to duplicate the twisted thought processes of serial killers and thereby predict their actions. Brought out of early retirement by his friend and colleague Jack (Dennis Farina), Graham launches an investigation of a serial killer who operates on a "lunar cycle," killing entire families only when the moon is full. Graham's peculiar talent of adopting a criminal's mindset extracts a heavy emotional toll and nearly destroyed him on his last case when he captured Dr. Hannibal Lektor (Brian Cox), a brilliant psychiatrist turned brutal killer. Lektor is in prison and though Graham clearly still fears him, he visits him in an effort to get insights on his new case. He only succeeds in putting himself and his family in great danger.

Writer-director Michael Mann wrote a superior script and assembled an incredible cast for MANHUNTER making one of the most underrated outstanding thrillers of the 1980s. Mann knows how to construct an intense movie. As in his earlier THIEF, he presents the viewer with a fascinating amount of procedural detail—both law-enforcement and criminal. Petersen is superb as the obsessive investigator who risks madness each time he takes on a case, and Tom Noonan is absolutely chilling as the psycho killer. Cox is also frightening as the complex Lektor, a character who would be memorably embodied by Anthony Hopkins in Jonathan Demme's adaptation of Harris's quasi-sequel, THE SILENCE OF THE LAMBS (where the doctor's name is spelled "Lecter," as it is in the novels).

MANON OF THE SPRING
(MANON DES SOURCES)

1986 113m c Drama	★★★½
Renn/RAI-TV/DEG/A2 (France)	R/PG

Yves Montand *(Cesar "Le Papet" Soubeyran)*, Daniel Auteuil *(Ugolin Soubeyran)*, Emmanuelle Beart *(Manon Cadoret)*, Hyppolite Girardot *(Bernard Olivier)*, Elisabeth Depardieu *(Aimee Cadoret)*, Gabriel Bacquier *(Victor)*, Armand Meffre *(Philoxene)*, Andre Dupon *(Pamphile)*, Pierre Nougaro *(Casimir)*, Jean Maurel *(Anglade)*

p, Pierre Grunstein; d, Claude Berri; w, Claude Berri, Gerard Brach (based on the novel by Marcel Pagnol); ph, Bruno Nuytten; ed, Genevieve Louveau, Herve de Luze; m, Jean-Claude Petit, Giuseppe Verdi; prod d, Bernard Vezat; cos, Sylvie Gautrelet

The continuation of JEAN DE FLORETTE resumes the story and follows its characters to their fates. Ten years have passed, and Manon (played by newcomer Emmanuelle Beart), the daughter of the hunch-backed farmer Jean (Gerard Depardieu in Part I), has grown into a beautiful young shepherdess who tends her flock deep in the hills of Provence. In the years since Jean's death, Le Papet (Yves Montand) and his nephew, Ugolin (Daniel Auteuil), have worked Jean's land into a profitable carnation farm by unplugging the underground spring they had kept secret from the hard-working farmer. Ugolin's vibrant red carnations now blossom in full glory, enabling him to save a small fortune. Le Papet, now old and withered, pushes his nephew toward marriage. Unless Ugolin takes a wife and begins a family, the name of Soubeyran (once the most powerful family in the region) will cease to exist. Ugolin, however, has no desire to marry—until, one day, he sees Manon bathing in a small spring and falls instantly in love.

Like its predecessor, MANON OF THE SPRING is filled with marvelous photography, gorgeous rolling landscapes, and spectacular performances. While Part I favors Depardieu's character and his struggles against both man and nature, Part II concentrates on the tragic end of Montand and his final reconciliation with the higher forces of fate. Montand, always brilliant, turns in a performance that ranks with his best work; Auteuil is also excellent as the manipulated young fool. Beart, while easy on the eyes, is given very little to do besides play the object of desire. This is an admirable though traditional piece of entertainment. MANON surpasses JEAN DE FLORETTE in its portrayal of the villagers, a marvelous element virtually absent from the earlier picture. Together JEAN DE FLORETTE and MANON OF THE SPRING earned a total of eight Cesars (the French Oscar): Best Film, Best Director, Best Actor (Auteuil), Best Actress, Best Screenplay, Best Score, Best Cinematography, and Best Sound (Pierre Gamet, Dominique Hennequin).

MAN'S FAVORITE SPORT?

1964 120m c Comedy	★★½
Universal (U.S.)	/U

Rock Hudson *(Roger Willoughby)*, Paula Prentiss *(Abigail Page)*, Maria Perschy *(Isolde "Easy" Mueller)*, Charlene Holt *(Tex Connors)*, John McGiver *(William Cadwalader)*, Roscoe Karns *(Maj. Phipps)*, Forrest Lewis *(Skaggs)*, Regis Toomey *(Bagley)*, Norman Alden *(John Screaming Eagle)*, Don Allen *(Tom)* p, Howard Hawks; d, Howard Hawks; w, John Fenton Murray, Steve McNeil (based on the story "The Girl Who Almost Got Away" by Pat Frank); ph, Russell Harlan; ed, Stuart Gilmore; m, Henry Mancini; art d, Alexander Golitzen, Tambi Larsen; fx, Ben McMahon; cos, Edith Head

Director-producer Hawks here returned to the comic formulas that worked so well for him in BRINGING UP BABY and I WAS A MALE WAR BRIDE but achieved only limited success. Cary Grant had been able to carry the earlier films with a characteristic charm that leading man Hudson was unable to match. Hudson is the star fishing-supplies salesman of a large sporting goods store, but he knows nothing about fishing. Publicity agent Prentiss convinces Hudson's boss, McGiver, that Hudson should enter a fishing contest. With a little luck and assistance from a bear, Hudson wins. Acknowledging that his win is a fluke, he forfeits the prize and subsequently gets fired. In the end, Hudson gets his job back and lands Prentiss as well. Hawks delivers his usual heavy-handed direction, but the film's premise is too flimsy to spread over two hours. The script is marred by tired comic routines and slow pacing. The cast, though, with the exception of Hudson, offers very good performances—Prentiss in particular.

MAN'S HOPE
(SIERRA DE TERUEL)
1947 78m bw War   ★★★★
Lopert (Spain)

Majuto (Capt. Munoz), Nicolas Rodriguez (Pilot Marquez), Jose Lado (The Peasant)

p, Andre Malraux; d, Andre Malraux; w, Andre Malraux (based on the novel Espoir by Andre Malraux); ph, Louis Page; m, Darius Milhaud

This film was shot in Spain during the Spanish Civil War and later smuggled into Occupied France, where screening was postponed until after the Liberation. As a result, it was eight years before the public was allowed to view MAN'S HOPE. When the film finally was screened, it received the Louis Delluc Award, one of the highest honors the French could bestow on a film. In adapting his own novel for the screen, Andre Malraux creates a powerful, sweepingly realistic film through the use of actual combat footage. The story focuses on a Loyalist air squadron's attempt to destroy a bridge. To succeed, the Loyalists must neutralize a new airfield. The only one who can locate the field is a peasant who can't read a map, so he is taken along on the air raid. Although the narrative structure of MAN'S HOPE is unconventional and the film is otherwise flawed, these problems pale next to the overwhelming realism of Malraux's depiction of life during wartime.

MARAT/SADE (THE PERSECUTION AND ASSASSINATION OF JEAN-PAUL MARAT AS PERFORMED BY THE INMATES OF THE ASYLUM OF CHARENTON UNDER THE DIRECTION OF THE MARQUIS DE SADE)
1966 115m c Historical   ★★★
Marat Sade (U.K.)   /X

Patrick Magee (Marquis de Sade), Ian Richardson (Jean-Paul Marat), Glenda Jackson (Charlotte Corday), Clifford Rose (M. Coulmier), Brenda Kempner (Mme. Coulmier), Ruth Baker (Mlle. Coulmier), Michael Williams (Herald), Freddie Jones (Cucurucu), Hugh Sullivan (Kokol), Jonathan Burn (Polpoch)

p, Michael Birkett; d, Peter Brook; w, Peter Weiss, Geoffrey Skelton, Adrian Mitchell (based on the play by Peter Weiss); ph, David Watkin; ed, Tom Priestley; m, Richard Peaslee; prod d, Sally Jacobs; art d, Ted Marshall; chor, Malcolm Goddard; cos, Gunilla Palmstierna Weiss

Peter Brook directed this film of his seminal stage production of the play-within-a-play by Peter Weiss. (It's actually a musical, with more than a dozen songs.) In combining Brechtian techniques with some of the lessons of theatrical philosopher Antonin Artaud, Weiss's play was a landmark of the 60s that seemed to be exploiting everything the theater could do that film could not. Brecht suggested distancing audiences; Artaud demanded the opposite—total involvement. Many fans of the play went to see the film only to prove that this stuff couldn't work on celluloid. It does.

MARAT/SADE takes as its starting point a Parisian custom of the early 1800s, when it was the fashion for sophisticated audiences to attend theatrical performances acted out by the inmates of mental hospitals as part of their therapy. In Weiss's play, an audience arrives at Charenton to see a piece written by the Marquis de Sade (Magee), a patient at the hospital. De Sade has dramatized the bathtub assassination of French Revolutionary leader Jean-Paul Marat (Richardson) by Charlotte Corday (Jackson), using the historical event to anchor an imaginary debate between him and Marat on the relations between politics, sexuality and violence. After the performance, de Sade explains to the audience that his drama was intended to stimulate thought about these thorny issues; meanwhile, though, the patient-actors, carried away by the play's rhetoric, rise up in violent revolt.

Geoffrey Skelton and Adrian Mitchell translated Weiss's play, which opened in Berlin in April 1964. The members of the Royal Shakespeare Company, who did the London stage production, are used again here. Brook is a filmmaker as well as a master of the modern theater and he, perhaps uniquely, understood how to translate something so stagey and theatrical onto the screen. The result is an important—and eminently watchable—record of a turning point in western theater.

MARATHON MAN
1976 125m c Spy/Thriller/War   ★★★★
Paramount (U.S.)   R/18

Dustin Hoffman (Babe Levy), Laurence Olivier (Szell), Roy Scheider (Doc Levy), William Devane (Janeway), Marthe Keller (Elsa), Fritz Weaver (Prof. Biesenthal), Richard Bright (Karl), Marc Lawrence (Erhard), Allen Joseph (Babe's Father), Tito Goya (Melendez)

p, Robert Evans, Sidney Beckerman; d, John Schlesinger; w, William Goldman (based on his novel); ph, Conrad Hall; ed, Jim Clark; m, Michael Small; prod d, Richard MacDonald; art d, Jack DeShields; fx, Richard E. Johnson, Dick Smith, Charles Spurgeon; cos, Robert de Mora

AAN Best Supporting Actor: Laurence Olivier

A truly harrowing film, MARATHON MAN is a clever series of accidents that produce a nightmare thriller with an unrelenting attack on the viewer's nerves. Babe Levy (Dustin Hoffman), a Columbia University graduate student who runs whenever possible, dreaming of the Olympic marathon, is haunted by the memory of his father's suicide, brought about by the McCarthy witchhunts. Babe's brother, Doc (Roy Scheider), an American secret agent, helps sneak Szell (Laurence Olivier), an old Nazi, into the US from South America. Szell's brother, who has watched over a fortune in jewels taken from Jewish concentration camp victims, has died, and Szell has come to New York to collect the booty. After killing Doc, Szell uses the tools of his dentist's trade to torture Babe for information the student doesn't possess. Putting his marathon training to use, Babe escapes Szell, and eventually the pursuer becomes the pursued. Hoffman is excellent as the crazed Szell's victim, and Olivier is the essence of evil, his sadistic acts so expertly enacted that the film has a deeply disturbing quality. John Schlesinger's direction is highly stylized and more than effective, jammed with action and offering unforgettably terrifying scenes. Scheider is good as the errant older brother, and William Devane is his usual tricky self as the double-dealing intelligence chief. William Goldman's script, based on his novel, is morally confused but literate and full of surprises.

MARIANNE AND JULIANE
(DIE BLEIERNE ZEIT)
1981 103m c Drama/Political   ★★★½
Bioskop Film/Sender Fries (West Germany)

Jutta Lampe (Juliane), Barbara Sukowa (Marianne), Rudiger Vogler (Wolfgang), Doris Schade (Mother), Verenice Rudolph, Luc Bondy (Werner), Franz Rudnick (Father), Julia Biedermann (Marianne—Age 16), Ina Robinski (Juliane—Age 17), Patrick Estrada-Pox (Jan—Age 10)

p, Eberhard Junkersdorf; d, Margarethe von Trotta; w, Margarethe von Trotta; ph, Franz Rath; ed, Dagmar Hirtz; m, Nicolas Economou; art d, Barbara Kloth; cos, Monica Hasse, Jorge Jara

Rigorously composed and devoid of easy sentiment, MARIANNE AND JULIANE may be director Margarethe von Trotta's most accessible film. It chronicles the lives of two German sisters for whom character truly is destiny.

Marianne (Barbara Sukowa), radicalized by the events of the mid-70s, joins a terrorist cell and asks sister Juliane (Jutta Lampe) to adopt her four-year-old son. Because of commitments to her lover Wolfgang (Rudiger Vogler) and to her writing career, Juliane reluctantly refuses, and her decision has terrible results: Marianne's ex-husband kills himself and the boy becomes a ward of the state. When the steely Marianne reappears with two comrades, she not only uses Juliane as a convenience but also disparages her lifestyle and part-time activism. While Juliane questions the government in print, militant Marianne attacks it through commando crimes, including bank robbery. Later, when Marianne dies mysteriously in jail, Juliane is overwhelmed with guilt and sets out to prove that her sister was officially silenced.

During the shooting of the movie GERMANY IN AUTUMN, director von Trotta met magazine editor Christine Ensslin, whose sister Gudrun died in Stammheim Prison under suspicious circumstances in 1977. Von Trotta's film uses this footnote to German history as a springboard for meditations on feminism, political activism, jingoism, and family psychology. It's a kind of treatise on the roots of political conscience, but the human element never suffers: the sisters' love-hate relationship is delineated with singular eloquence and subtlety. The film played briefly in US art houses under the title THE GERMAN SISTERS.

MARIE

1985   112m   c   Biography/Political   ★★★½
DEG   (U.S.)   PG-13/15

Sissy Spacek (Marie Ragghianti), Jeff Daniels (Eddie Sisk), Keith Szarabajka (Kevin McCormack), Morgan Freeman (Charles Traughber), Lisa Banes (Toni Greer), Fred Thompson (Himself), Trey Wilson (FBI Agent), John Collum (Deputy Attorney General), Don Hood (Gov. Blanton), Graham Beckel (Charlie Benson)

p, Frank Capra Jr.; d, Roger Donaldson; w, John Briley (based on the book Marie, A True Story by Peter Maas); ph, Chris Menges; ed, Neil Travis; m, Francis Lai; art d, Ron Foreman; cos, Joe I. Tompkins

The true story of Marie Ragghianti, a woman who fought corruption in Tennessee, is a powerful film from a book by Peter Maas with a screenplay by Oscar-winner John Briley and a first US assignment for New Zealand director Roger Donaldson. Marie (Sissy Spacek) leaves home in 1968 after being brutalized by her husband. A mother of three, she must struggle as she stays at her mother's home, works as a waitress, and puts herself through Vanderbilt University. An old pal, Eddie Sisk (Jeff Daniels), helps her get a job with the state. He's the governor's legal counsel and not without power in the hierarchy, so her job as extradition director is an excellent first rung for her. It's not long before she rises in the state bureaucracy and becomes a member of the parole board and finally the chairperson of that board. It's not too long before Marie realizes that the governor (Don Hood) is using his influence to get some powerful criminals released. The movie could have become a cliched investigatory picture, as did so many after Watergate. Director Donaldson keeps matters moving. Spacek is superb and so is Daniels, unaccustomed as he is to the villain's role. But the acting surprise is the work of Fred Thompson, playing himself as the real-life attorney who handled the case for Marie Ragghianti.

MARIE ANTOINETTE

1938   160m   bw   Biography/Historical/Romance   ★★★★
MGM   (U.S.)   /A

Norma Shearer (Marie Antoinette), Tyrone Power (Count Axel de Fersen), John Barrymore (King Louis XV), Gladys George (Mme. Du Barry), Robert Morley (King Louis XVI), Anita Louise (Princess DeLamballe), Joseph Schildkraut (Duke of Orleans), Henry Stephenson (Count Mercey), Reginald Gardiner (Artois), Peter Bull (Gamin)

p, Hunt Stromberg; d, W.S. Van Dyke II, Julien Duvivier; w, Claudine West, Donald Ogden Stewart, Ernest Vajda, F. Scott Fitzgerald (based on a book by Stefan Zweig); ph, William Daniels; ed, Robert J. Kern; m, Herbert Stothart; art d, Cedric Gibbons, William A. Horning; fx, Slavko Vorkapich; chor, Albertina Rasch; cos, Adrian, Gile Steele

AAN Best Actress: Norma Shearer; AAN Best Supporting Actor: Robert Morley; AAN Best Score: Herbert Stothart; AAN Best Art Direction: Cedric Gibbons

Although it has its admirers, this lengthy but consistently gripping film remains an underrated biopic done in the grand Hollywood manner. It's also an eerily apt showcase for Norma Shearer, and along with PRIVATE LIVES, SMILIN' THROUGH and THE WOMEN, stands as one of the best things she ever did. Shearer, long MGM's queen, was on the verge of a decline, like Marie's, linked to her husband's death. True, Marie Antoinette was executed and Shearer lost interest in her career and retired a wealthy woman, but the parallels between the lives of the two women permeate the film. Planned as early as 1933 by Shearer's husband, "boy genius" Irving Thalberg, but halted in 1936 when he died, it's amazing just how well the project turned out.

Marie is married off to Louis Auguste (Morley), heir to the throne, by her mother, Empress of Austria (Alma Kruger), but is repelled by her first meeting with the dullwitted, unattractive Dauphin. (Shearer and Morley share an excellent scene as Louis hints at his impotence—an adult, well-handled scene for the Hollywood of the day.) Further distressing Marie are the sneering, sickly King Louis XV and his conspiratorial mistress, Mme. Du Barry (George). Du Barry, feeling threatened by the future queen, forms intrigues against her, and Marie quickly becomes a pariah at court. She takes Orleans's (Schildkraut) advice and gains solace from fast living, beginning an affair with Count Axel de Fersen (Power). Marie is almost sent back to Austria in disgrace after humiliating the bitchy Du Barry at a ball, but the king dies suddenly and Marie becomes Queen. Fersen tells her that her duties must come before their love, and he sails off to America. Marie develops an affectionate relationship with Louis, who also gathers his wits enough to produce two children. Orleans, however, who had denied Marie help at her low ebb, is now an outcast at court and incites the people to revolt. The guillotine beckons.

After Thalberg's death, MGM mogul Louis B. Mayer tried to make a flat settlement with his estate. Shearer, however, held the studio to an agreement giving Thalberg's estate a percentage of all the profits MGM had made since its 1924 consolidation. The handling of MARIE ANTOINETTE ended up being not only an attempt to control costs on one of the studio's priciest pictures ever, but also perhaps a subtle revenge on the victorious Shearer. Mayer replaced original director Sidney Franklin with Woody Van Dyke, a no-nonsense helmsman who didn't cotton to La Norma's requests for more takes.

Gibbons's magnificent sets, crammed with authentic French antiques, outdid Versailles, and costumers Adrian and Steele used 500 yards of silk on one of Shearer's gowns alone. Daniels's camerawork is exceptional, and Van Dyke makes this long film move like a short one. The flash of Barrymore and Schildkraut (with a great makeup job) steals many scenes, but top supporting honors go to the gifted Morley, who somehow lost an Oscar to Walter Brennan in KENTUCKY. Above all, though, the film showcases the regal qualities fans loved in La Norma. While some scenes show her fluttering or hamming it up a bit much, there's a lot of excellent stuff here, especially as Marie awaits death. The overall result is ornate and satisfying, typical of MGM at its production zenith.

MARIUS

1931   103m   bw   Drama   ★★★★
Joinville/Paramount   (France)

Raimu (Cesar Olivier), Orane Demazis (Fanny), Pierre Fresnay (Marius), Fernand Charpin (Honore Panisse), Alida Rouffe (Honorine Cabanis), Robert Vattier (Mon. Brun), Paul Dullac (Felix Escartefigue), Alexandre Mihalesco (Piquoiseau), Edouard Delmont (2nd Mate), Milly Mathis (Aunt Claudine Foulon)

p, Marcel Pagnol; d, Alexander Korda; w, Marcel Pagnol (based on the play by Marcel Pagnol); ph, Ted Pahle; ed, Roger Mercanton; m, Francis Gromon; prod d, Alfred Junge, Vincent Korda

Faithfully adapted from the enormously popular (over 1,000 performances) stage play by Marcel Pagnol, MARIUS was the first in a trilogy of films evoking, in richly sentimental and gently satirical style, waterfront life in Marseilles in the late 1920s and early 30s. Though still open to the criticism leveled at the time, that this was little more than canned theater, it's vastly enjoyable nonetheless, with the great Raimu stealing the show in the role (reprised from the stage version) of cafe owner Cesar. Cesar's son Marius (Pierre Fresnay) works at his father's Bar de la Marine and loves fish-stall worker Fanny (Orane Demazis, Pagnol's longtime companion and leading lady) just a little less than he does the sea. Cesar spends most of his time in amiably idle conversation with his patrons—the wealthy Panisse (Fernand Charpin), ferry captain Felix Escartefigue (Paul Dullac), and customs inspector Brun (Robert Vattier). When the elderly Panisse asks for Fanny's hand, she sees this as her opportunity to work on Marius' jealousy and force him to choose her over a life at sea, but she finally acknowledges the greater power of his wanderlust in a hugely touching gesture of self-denial. The joys of MARIUS are the joys of the stage play—a fantastic cast, many drawn, like Raimu, from the Marseilles music hall; authentic, unpretentious dialogue peppered with richly provincial idioms; and fully realized, un-glamorous characters drawn with loving detail. Director Alexander Korda brought relatively little of his own to this screen adaptation; writer/producer Pagnol watched the proceedings carefully, hired Marc Allegret to direct the same cast in the next installment, FANNY, and took over the reigns himself for CESAR. This last was an oddity, in that the film preceded the stage play, but entirely in line with Pagnol's belief that the theater was dead and that talking pictures represented a new pinnacle of dramatic art.

MARK OF ZORRO, THE

1940 93m bw Adventure ★★★★
Fox (U.S.) /U

Tyrone Power (Zorro/Don Diego Vega), Linda Darnell (Lolita Quintero), Basil Rathbone (Capt. Esteban Pasquale), Gale Sondergaard (Inez Quintero), Eugene Pallette (Fra Felipe), J. Edward Bromberg (Don Luis Quintero), Montagu Love (Don Alejandro Vega), Janet Beecher (Senora Isabella Vega), Robert Lowery (Rodrigo), Chris-Pin Martin (Turnkey)

p, Raymond Griffith; d, Rouben Mamoulian; w, John Taintor Foote, Garrett Fort, Bess Meredyth (based on the novel The Curse of Capistrano by Johnston McCulley); ph, Arthur Miller; ed, Robert Bischoff; m, Alfred Newman; art d, Richard Day, Joseph C. Wright; cos, Travis Banton

AAN Best Score: Alfred Newman

A smashing remake of the Douglas Fairbanks silent swashbuckler, this remarkable action film owes everything to inventive director Mamoulian. This was Fox's answer to Warner's THE ADVENTURES OF ROBIN HOOD, with some of THE SCARLET PIMPERNEL thrown in for good measure.

In a role that perfectly combines his feyness and machismo, Power is marvelous as the fop by day and brave avenger by night. Returning to 19th-century Los Angeles, Don Diego (Power) finds that his father Don Alejandro (Love) has been replaced as governor by the slimy Don Luis Quintero (Bromberg) and the cruel Capt. Pasquale (Rathbone). Shortly after the mincing Don Diego has convinced the powers that be that he's nothing to worry about, the dashing, heroic but mysterious Zorro begins righting wrongs left and right, leaving his mark (literally) on everything. . . and everyone. Who says the pen is mightier than the sword?

Power cuts a stylish and convincing Zorro, vigorously playing the brilliant swordsman, although his more strenuous routines are performed by stunt double Albert Cavens. Mamoulian cleverly cuts in and out of his terse scenes to suggest more action than really occurs. The final deadly confrontation between Rathbone and Power is a thrilling duel no less exciting than the final contretemps between Errol Flynn and Rathbone in THE ADVENTURES OF ROBIN HOOD. Rathbone is terrific as the villain, always fondling his sword, prepared at any moment to draw blood for sport or sadistic amusement. "Most men have objects they play with," Rathbone remarks in one scene. "Churchmen have their beads; I toy with a sword." Love is as sturdy as ever, the paunchy Bromberg and the sleek Sondergaard are a delight as the

sleazy rulers, and the unique Palette gets to reprise his performance as Friar Tuck from ROBIN HOOD. Darnell doesn't get to do much more than glow in soft focus, but she does show lush promise beneath the prim dictates of her role.

Skilled swordsman Rathbone paid Power a supreme compliment: "Power was the most agile man with a sword I've ever faced before a camera. Tyrone could have fenced Errol Flynn into a cocked hat." There have been other Zorros, of course. Yakima Canutt, the great stuntman, played the role in 1937 in ZORRO RIDES AGAIN; Frank Langella had a swipe at the part in a middling 1974 TV-movie; and George Hamilton overplayed the double-sided nature of the tale's hero to the point of cheap homophobic caricature in ZORRO, THE GAY BLADE. But none would ever equal Power. He looked and acted like a man who could, with bold acts and brave heart, change the course of history. And, of course, for the burgeoning coffers of Fox, he did.

MARNIE

1964 120m c Thriller/Romance ★★★★
Universal (U.S.) PG/X

Tippi Hedren (Marnie Edgar), Sean Connery (Mark Rutland), Diane Baker (Lil Mainwaring), Martin Gabel (Sidney Strutt), Louise Latham (Bernice Edgar), Bob Sweeney (Cousin Bob), Milton Selzer (Man at the Track), Alan Napier (Mr. Rutland), Henry Beckman (1st Detective), Edith Evanson (Rita)

p, Alfred Hitchcock; d, Alfred Hitchcock; w, Jay Presson Allen (based on the novel by Winston Graham); ph, Robert Burks; ed, George Tomasini; m, Bernard Herrmann; prod d, Robert Boyle; cos, Edith Head

Hitchcock's most liberated and poetic film, MARNIE is a masterpiece of psychological mystery that encompasses all of the director's obsessions—the unleashing of suppressed female sexuality, duplicitous personalities and false identities, childhood trauma leading to a disturbed and warped reality in adulthood, and the director's own love of cool-looking blondes and "pure cinema." Its characters are possessed by psychological demons similar to those in VERTIGO or PSYCHO. Hedren plays a kleptomaniac whose compulsion to steal springs from her need to be loved. Using various identities and disguises, she moves from one job to the next, each time running off with a cache of cash and leaving behind no clues. Connery, a business associate of one of Marnie's previous victims, recognizes Marnie when she comes to work for him, and confronts her with his information. Rather than turn her in, however, Mark blackmails her into marriage—discovering her deep-seated fears of men, sex, thunderstorms, and the color red. Met with a less-than-enthusiastic response, MARNIE was one of Hitchcock's 1960s films (THE BIRDS, TORN CURTAIN, and TOPAZ were the others) that raised suspicions among some critics of the master's having lost his touch, unable to adjust to the times. In retrospect, MARNIE emerges as prime Hitchcock—its tone and subtext as revealing as that of VERTIGO, although more desperate and disquieting (perhaps because of Hitchcock's deep obsession with Hedren during production). Of interest is Hitchcock's uncharacteristic use of a technique that makes the audience actually *feel* Hedren's traumas. Seeing Hedren against abstract backdrops and "poor" rear-screen projections makes her world seem disturbingly unreal. The ever-changing weather conditions, in which thunderstorms conveniently brew and night changes rapidly to day, and the use of a few frames of red shock the audience into experiencing Hedren's fear (a technique Hitchcock had attempted as early as 1935 in SECRET AGENT).

MARRIAGE OF MARIA BRAUN, THE
(DIE EHE DER MARIA BRAUN)

1978 120m c Drama/War ★★★★
Albatros/Trio/Westdeutscher/Autoren (West Germany) R/15

Hanna Schygulla (Maria Braun), Klaus Lowitsch (Hermann Braun), Ivan Desny (Oswald), Gottfried John (Willi), Gisela Uhlen (Mother), Gunter Lamprecht (Hans), Hark Bohm (Senkenberg), George Byrd (Bill), Elisabeth Trissenaar (Betti), Rainer Werner Fassbinder (Peddler)

p, Michael Fengler; d, Rainer Werner Fassbinder; w, Peter Marthesheimer, Pia Frohlich, Rainer Werner Fassbinder (based on an idea by Rainer Werner Fassbinder); ph, Michael Ballhaus; ed,

Juliane Lorenz, Franz Walsch; m, Peer Raben; art d, Norbert Scherer, Helga Ballhaus, Claud Kottmann, Georg Borgel; cos, Barbara Baum, Susi Reichel, George Kuhn, Ingeborg Proller

She eludes you, even if she does start—and finish—with a bang. The first in Rainer Werner Fassbinder's trilogy about women in post-WWII Germany (followed by VERONIKA VOSS and LOLA), this was also the film that solidified Fassbinder's reputation abroad and in Germany. In the opening sequence, a German city is being torn apart by Allied bombs while Maria (Hanna Schygulla) and her soldier fiance, Hermann Braun (Klaus Lowitsch), are getting married. Immediately afterwards, the new husband is sent to the Russian front, leaving Maria with her mother and sister, impoverished and waiting for her husband, visiting the train station every day with the hope of hearing news about him. After receiving word that he has died, Maria takes work as a barmaid in a cafe that caters to American soldiers. There she meets Bill (George Byrd), a hefty black soldier who, despite the fact the they can barely converse, becomes her lover. Just when she has nearly forgotten about her husband, however, the starving and emasculated Hermann turns up while Maria and Bill are beginning to make love. The highly stylized, deliberate structure of THE MARRIAGE OF MARIA BRAUN owes much to such Douglas Sirk 1950s Hollywood melodramas as IMITATION OF LIFE and WRITTEN ON THE WIND. For both Sirk and Fassbinder, the director remains distanced from the heart-wrenching dramatics of the story in order to comment on certain societal ills, but Fassbinder is even further removed from his material—a product of the alienation prominent in a postwar Germany striving to rebuild itself into an industrial power, yet failing to account for the human bonds that make a society healthy. The effect is one of helplessness; we can only watch as the beautiful, young Maria Braun places herself in an emotional vacuum.

Schygulla is quite powerful in perhaps the best role of her career, remaining cold and aloof, yet evoking a strong sense of pity. Though THE MARRIAGE OF MARIA BRAUN is not always an easy film to understand, the stark atmosphere, icy performances, and poignant revelations make it one of the most important films to emerge from Germany in the 1970s, and one of Fassbinder's best.

MARRIED TO THE MOB

| 1988 103m c Comedy/Crime | ★★★½ |
| Mysterious Arts (U.S.) | R/15 |

Michelle Pfeiffer *(Angela Demarco)*, Matthew Modine *(Mike Downey)*, Dean Stockwell *(Tony "The Tiger" Russo)*, Mercedes Ruehl *(Connie Russo)*, Oliver Platt *(Ed Benitez)*, Alec Baldwin *(Frank "The Cucumber" DeMarco)*, Anthony J. Nici *(Joey DeMarco)*, Sister Carol East *(Rita Harcourt)*, Paul Lazar *(Tommy Boyle)*, Trey Wilson *(Franklin)*

p, Kenneth Utt, Edward Saxon; d, Jonathan Demme; w, Barry Strugatz, Mark R. Burns; ph, Tak Fujimoto; ed, Craig McKay; m, David Byrne; prod d, Kristi Zea; fx, Efex Specialists, Inc.; cos, Colleen Atwood

AAN Best Supporting Actor: Dean Stockwell

A pleasant trifle. Lacking the disturbing edge of director Demme's previous effort SOMETHING WILD, MARRIED TO THE MOB is a gangster film with a twist and the idiosyncratic Demme touch. There is plenty to amuse and delight here, including fine performances from Michelle Pfeiffer, Matthew Modine, and Dean Stockwell.

The movie begins on Long Island, where the homes are full of gilded Mediterranean furniture, the men dress in pin-striped suits, and the women spend most of their time getting their hair teased at the local beauty salon. Angela DeMarco (Pfeiffer), wife of up-and-coming hit man Frank "The Cucumber" DeMarco (Alec Baldwin), is tired of the criminal mentality of everyone around her and wants out. After Frank is caught by his boss, Mafia don Tony "The Tiger" Russo (Stockwell), with the boss's mistress and "iced," a couple of FBI agents (Modine and Oliver Platt) assume that Angela and Tony are lovers. Angela packs up with her son (Anthony J. Nici) and moves into a seedy apartment on Manhattan's Lower East Side, only to have the Feds follow and keep her embroiled in the mob's doings. Of course, romance eventually blooms between Angela and agent Mike Downey (Modine).

The wonderfully tacky production design by Kristi Zea, the bizarre costumes by Colleen Atwood, the clash of musical styles in the score by David Byrne, and the eccentric performances of the entire cast combine to create a dizzying array of forces swirling around Pfeiffer. She plays her part fairly straight, thus making everyone else seem that much more bizarre. Stockwell in particular is wonderful as the tyrannical hood. This was the last film appearance for veteran character actor Joe Spinell (TAXI DRIVER, ROCKY, NIGHT SHIFT), who has a small role as one of Stockwell's henchmen. He appeared in 40 films in the 70s and 80s before his death in 1989.

MARRIED WOMAN, THE
(UNE FEMME MARIEE)

| 1964 94m bw Drama | ★★★★★ |
| Anouchka/Orsay (France) | |

Macha Meril *(Charlotte)*, Bernard Noel *(Robert, the Lover)*, Philippe Leroy *(Pierre, the Husband)*, Rita Maiden *(Mme. Celine)*, Margaret Le Van, Veronique Duval *(Girls in Swimming Pool)*, Chris Tophe *(Nicolas)*, Georges Liron *(The Physician)*, Roger Leenhardt *(Himself)*, Jean-Luc Godard *(Narrator)*

d, Jean-Luc Godard; w, Jean-Luc Godard; ph, Raoul Coutard; ed, Agnes Guillemot, Francoise Collin; m, Claude Nougaro; art d, Henri Nogaret; cos, Laurence Clairval

Meril plays a Parisian housewife with both an airline pilot husband (Leroy) and a lover (Noel). When she becomes pregnant, she realizes either man could be the father. She debates whether she should stay with her husband or leave him for her lover; she gets no help from either in making her decision.

Subtitled "Fragments of a film made in 1964," THE MARRIED WOMAN is a fragmented, distanced film that dissects Meril's character and morally situates her between the two men in her life. Even at the film's opening, Meril is represented as a disembodied figure—in separate shots we are shown, against a white bed sheet, her hands, legs, feet, torso. Taking place over a 24-hour period, even THE MARRIED WOMAN's time frame is cut apart into almost Resnaisian divisions. Heavily under the influence of Brecht, director Jean-Luc Godard makes brilliant use of the written word, magazine advertisements and billboards, allusions to other artists (Racine, Apollinaire, Hitchcock, Resnais, Beethoven), visual references to film technique (the use of negative film images), and interviews in a *cinema-verite* mode. The result is one of his most important and provocative dissections of modern life.

MARS ATTACKS!

| 1996 105m c Science Fiction/Comedy | ★★★ |
| Warner Bros. (U.S.) | PG-13/12 |

Jack Nicholson *(President James Dale/Art Land)*, Glenn Close *(First Lady Marsha Dale)*, Annette Bening *(Mrs. Barbara Land)*, Pierce Brosnan *(Professor Donald Kessler)*, Martin Short *(Press Secretary Jerry Ross)*, Sarah Jessica Parker *(Nathalie Lake)*, Michael J. Fox *(Jason Stone)*, Tom Jones *(Himself)*, Lukas Haas *(Richie Norris)*, Jim Brown *(Bryon Williams)*

p, Tim Burton, Larry Franco; d, Tim Burton; w, Jonathan Gems (from his story, based on the Topps trading-card series); ph, Peter Suschitzky; ed, Christopher Lebenzon; m, Danny Elfman; prod d, Wynn Thomas; art d, John Dexter; fx, Michael Lantieri, James Mitchell, Industrial Light & Magic, Warner Digital Studios; cos, Colleen Atwood

A childlike sense of malicious fun pervades MARS ATTACKS!, a film inspired by an infamous set of Topps trading cards so graphically violent for their era (1962) that protests from parents caused them to be withdrawn.

After a televised message from the Martian Ambassador is interpreted to have a friendly tone, the shallow but telegenic President of the United States (Jack Nicholson) schedules an event to welcome them. Unfortunately, the Martian soldiers open fire and kill dozens of humans. The Martian Ambassador sends a formal apology to the President, who schedules a second meeting in Congress. Once again, the Martians kill dozens of the assembled and kidnap key Presidential advisor Donald Kessler (Pierce Brosnan), who winds up having an unusual fliration on their spaceship with another kidnapped Earthling, vain TV news anchor Nathalie Lake (Sarah Jessica Parker). With major US cities in ruin and the Martians on the warpath, certain heroes begin to emerge: an alienated Kansas teen (Lukas Haas); an ex-heavyweight champion (Jim Brown); a spacey follower of New Age philosophy (Annette Bening); and singer Tom Jones (playing himself) are among them.

MARS ATTACKS! stands as one of the better contemporary evocations of the low-budget alien invasion movies of the 1950s. Burton's affection for those films is apparent as this one bounces quickly and energetically from location to location. Several of the leads give wonderful performances, including Nicholson, Bening, Brown, Pam Grier, and gawky Haas, who functions well as Burton's ever-present misfit-protagonist. But despite the notable cast, it's the Martians who steal the show. These small, computer-generated creatures provoke laughs as they chatter and waddle along. Any time the film seems in danger of becoming irretrievably cute, however, Burton returns to the element that made the "Mars Attacks" cards so controversial (and attractive to youngsters)—violence and gore with no apologies.

MARTIN

1978   95m   c   Horror   ★★★★
Laurel   (U.S.)   R/X

John Amplas *(Martin)*, Lincoln Maazel *(Cuda)*, Christine Forrest *(Christina)*, Elayne Nadeau *(Mrs. Santini)*, Tom Savini *(Arthur)*, Sarah Venable *(Housewife Victim)*, Fran Middleton *(Train Victim)*, Al Levitsky *(Lewis)*

p, Richard P. Rubinstein; d, George Romero; w, George Romero; ph, Michael Gornick; ed, George Romero; m, Donald Rubinstein; fx, Tom Savini

Considered by many to be George Romero's greatest work, MARTIN is a shocking, thoughtful reworking of the vampire myth set in a dying American steel town. Martin (John Amplas) is a shy, alienated 17-year-old who thinks he may be a vampire—a theory which seems to be confirmed by the opening scene. Aboard a Pittsburgh-bound train, Martin waylays a female passenger, injects her with sodium pentothal, and, while she is in a stupor, violates her. Lacking fangs, he then cuts her wrist with a razor blade and drinks her blood. (The gruesomely realistic special makeup effects are by Tom Savini, here working on the first of his many films for Romero.) When Martin arrives in Pittsburgh, he is confronted with his elderly Old World cousin, Tata Cuda (Lincoln Maazel), a religious zealot who is convinced the boy is an 84-year-old vampire, the product of a family curse. Calling Martin "Nosferatu," Tata Cuda is determined both to save the boy's soul and to destroy him. Martin has no friends in his new life; he only gets to experience a sense of community by becoming a regular caller to a radio talk show. He spills his guts (figuratively) over the air but the host assumes he's just another colorful kook. However Martin becomes popular and earns a playful nickname: "The Count."

Writer-director Romero leaves Martin's true status up in the air. At times the boy is convinced that he is the monster Tata Cuda believes him to be, seeing himself in sepia flashbacks as a Count Dracula-like vampire eluding angry villagers. Other times he seems able to differentiate fantasy from reality, as when he tells his grandfather "There's no magic." For the most part, Martin is shown to be a severely troubled teenager with deadly psychosexual problems, a nightmare version of the kid next door whose only way of relating to attractive women is by drinking their blood. At times, Martin's condition is compared to drug addiction, though the horror of vampirism is shown to pale by comparison to the brutality of a police raid on a den of drug dealers.

Combining the well-worn elements of countless horror films with the harsh realities of life in a depressed contemporary industrial city, Romero creates a resonant, multifaceted, and, at times, surprisingly lyrical film that works both as insightful social commentary and as a fascinating rumination on the conventions of the genre. Well worth a look for anyone with even a passing interest in horror, and essential viewing for serious fright fans. Romero himself appears as a priest and Savini plays the fiance of Martin's cousin.

MARTY

1955   91m   bw   Drama   ★★★★
UA   (U.S.)   /U

Ernest Borgnine *(Marty)*, Betsy Blair *(Clara)*, Esther Minciotti *(Mrs. Pilletti)*, Karen Steele *(Virginia)*, Jerry Paris *(Thomas)*, Frank Sutton *(Ralph)*, Walter Kelley *(the Kid)*, Robin Morse *(Joe)*, Augusta Ciolli *(Catherine)*, Joe Mantell *(Angie)*

p, Harold Hecht; d, Delbert Mann; w, Paddy Chayefsky (based on a television play by Chayefsky); ph, Joseph La Shelle; ed, Alan Crosland Jr.; m, Roy Webb; art d, Ted Haworth, Walter M. Simonds; cos, Norma

AA Best Picture; AA Best Actor: Ernest Borgnine; *AAN Best Supporting Actor:* Joe Mantell; *AAN Best Supporting Actress:* Betsy Blair; *AA Best Director:* Delbert Mann; *AA Best Screenplay:* Paddy Chayefsky; *AAN Best Cinematography:* Joseph LaShelle; *AAN Best Art Direction:* Edward S. Haworth, Walter Simonds, Robert Priestley

Dowdy but winning and poignant, and Ernie's Oscar. Borgnine is a burly, lonely, good-natured man living with his mother, with no prospects for any other kind of future. The heavy-set Bronx butcher lives in a small world populated by his Italian relatives and fast-aging male friends, chiefly Mantell. When Borgnine and Mantell meet after work, they stand about mindlessly thinking of ways to fill their lives with something interesting to do. Their soon predictable, groping interchange never varies: "So, what do you wanna do tonight, Marty?" "I dunno, Angie. What do you wanna do?" At home, Borgnine is totally dominated by his love-smothering mother, Minciotti, who fusses and worries over him. When Borgnine attempts to step outside of his world he's roundly rejected as a bumbling, unattractive person. He attends a dance with Mantell and others and tries to pick up some girls but strikes out. Then he spots homely Blair, a schoolteacher whose life is excruciatingly similar to his, dull, hopeless, inching into loveless middle-age. Borgnine asks Blair to dance, and not long afterward they begin to date. But Borgnine runs into a brick wall when he introduces Blair to his mother and male friends. His pals call her a "dog," and Minciotti is downright hostile to her, considering Blair a threat to her life with her son. Borgnine, not a courageous man, backs away from Blair. He doesn't call her as he promised, leaving her to sit miserably at home alone watching TV, while he agonizes over ignoring the woman he has grown to love.

MARTY, coming in the mid-1950s, in an era of epics and extravagant films designed to stifle upstart television, was all the more startling in that it was a movie expanded from an original television drama (with Rod Steiger in the lead), written brilliantly by Chayefsky, one of the leaders of what came to be known as "kitchen sink" or "clothesline" dramas. Besides Borgnine, Oscars also went to Chayefsky for Best Screenplay and to Mann for Best Direction, and it was named Best Picture.

Before doing this film Borgnine was nothing more than an uninteresting heavy. But here he showed the world the great depths of his own character. Mantell also gives a solid performance as the pal addicted to the more bloody passages of Mickey Spillane, constantly asserting: "Boy, he sure can write." Blair is less effective, and Minciotti is not much more than a prop mother. UA executives were not enthusiastic about the production and almost cancelled the movie; they, along with the rest of Hollywood's elite, were amazed at the movie's universal success, and MARTY soon set a trend toward the small-budgeted, prosaic films to come.

MARY POPPINS

1964   140m   c   Musical/Comedy   ★★★★
Walt Disney Productions   (U.S.)   /U

Julie Andrews *(Mary Poppins)*, Dick Van Dyke *(Bert/Mr. Dawes, Sr.)*, David Tomlinson *(Mr. Banks)*, Glynis Johns *(Mrs. Banks)*, Hermione Baddeley *(Ellen)*, Reta Shaw *(Mrs. Brill)*, Karen Dotrice *(Jane Banks)*, Matthew Garber *(Michael Banks)*, Elsa Lanchester *(Katie Nanna)*, Arthur Treacher *(Constable Jones)*

p, Walt Disney, Bill Walsh; d, Robert Stevenson; w, Bill Walsh, Don DaGradi (based on the *Mary Poppins* books by P.L. Travers); ph, Edward Colman; ed, Cotton Warburton; m, Irwin Kostal; art d, Carroll Clark, William H. Tuntke; fx, Peter Ellenshaw, Eustace Lycett, Robert

MASCULINE FEMININE

A. Mattey; chor, Marc Breaux, Dee Dee Wood; cos, Tony Walton; anim, Milt Kahl, Oliver M. Johnston Jr., John Lounsbery, Hal Ambro, Franklin Thomas, Ward Kimball, Eric Larson, Cliff Nordberg, Hamilton Luske

---

AAN Best Picture; *AA Best Actress:* Julie Andrews; *AAN Best Director:* Robert Stevenson; *AAN Best Adapted Screenplay:* Bill Walsh, Don DaGradi; *AAN Best Cinematography:* Edward Colman; *AA Best Editing:* Cotton Warburton; *AA Best Score:* Richard M. Sherman, Robert B. Sherman; *AAN Best Score:* Irwin Kostal; *AA Best Song:* Richard M. Sherman, Robert B. Sherman; *AAN Best Art Direction:* Carroll Clark, William H. Tuntke, Emile Kuri, Hal Gausman; *AAN Best Costume Design:* Tony Walton; *AAN Best Sound:* Robert O. Cook; *AA Best Visual Effects:* Peter Ellenshaw, Hamilton Luske, Eustace Lycett

---

One of the greatest children's films ever, MARY POPPINS is as perfect and inventive a musical as anyone could see, with a timeless story, strong performances, a flawless blend of live action and animation, wonderful songs, and a sterling script with all the charm of the P.L. Travers books upon which it is based. The film begins when a remote father and mother (Tomlinson and Johns) decide to advertise for a nanny to care for their rowdy children, Michael and Jane Banks (Garber and Dotrice). The children write their own ad, and when their father tears it up and burns it in the fireplace, the pieces miraculously reassemble and go up the flue. Next day, Mary Poppins (Andrews) appears, gliding down from on high with an umbrella as her parachute. This is no ordinary nanny, the children soon learn, as she leads them on a series of delightful escapades, all the while teaching them lessons in proper behavior. Among the wonderful new friends Mary introduces the children to are Bert the chimney sweep (Van Dyke). He accompanies them on holiday to a world inhabited by animated penguins, who serve them tea on a carousel having strangely willful horses, and Uncle Albert (Wynn), whose infectious laughter leads to strange consequences. In retrospect, we consider Andrews a trifle young for the role; she lacks the wisdom of, say, an Irene Dunne, our ideal vision of the role. Look for the magnificent Jane Darwell, as the Bird Lady, in her final role. The movie won Academy Awards for Best Actress, Best Film Editing, Best Original Score, Best Song, and Best Special Visual Effect. MARY POPPINS was producer Walt Disney's crowning achievement in a career that had earned him more Oscars than anyone else. The memorable songs by Disney writers Richard and Robert Sherman include "Supercalifragilisticexpialidocious," "Chim Chim Cheree," and "A Spoonful of Sugar."

MASCULINE FEMININE
(MASCULIN FEMININ)

1966   103m   bw   Drama   ★★★★
Anouchka/Argos/Svensk/Sandrews   (France/Sweden)   /X

Jean-Pierre Leaud *(Paul)*, Chantal Goya *(Madeleine)*, Marlene Jobert *(Elisabeth)*, Michel Deborb *(Robert)*, Catherine Duport *(Catherine)*, Eva-Britt Strandberg *(Lavinia)*, Birger Malmsten *(Actor)*, Elsa Leroy *(Miss 19)*, Francoise Hardy *(Woman with the American Officer)*, Chantal Darget *(Woman on Metro)*

d, Jean-Luc Godard; w, Jean-Luc Godard (based on the stories "The Signal" and "Paul's Mistress" by Guy de Maupassant); ph, Willy Kurant; ed, Agnes Guillemot, Marguerite Renoir; m, Francis Lai, Jean-Jacques Debout

---

Jean-Luc Godard visited the world of young folk to create his most humane film. This is Godard's fifteen-point inquiry into the generation he refers to as the "children of Marx and Coca-Cola," the 1960s youth culture. Paul (Jean-Pierre Leaud), a confused young romantic in search of perfect love, meets pop singer Madeleine (Chantal Goya) in a cafe and eventually moves in with her. Paul copes with his changing views by taking a job for a market research firm, gathering data, and interviewing people (including a young woman voted "Miss Nineteen"). While Madeleine pursues her career, Paul tries to coexist with her and her two roommates, Elisabeth and Catherine (Marlene Jobert and Catherine-Isabelle Duport). Leaud's character—practically an extension of the Antoine Doinel character he played for Francois Truffaut (he even adopts the name Doinel at one point in the film)—wants to live for love, but the ideal becomes problematic in a detached and increasingly consumer-oriented society.

With MASCULINE FEMININE, Godard began a string of increasingly political pictures, leading eventually to his self-imposed exile from commercial cinema. His interest in the synthesis of fiction and documentary is already in full evidence here, with long static shots of people being interviewed included as a means of bringing to the screen an everyday chronicle of Parisian youth in the winter of 1965. (Contrary to the director's intentions, the picture was banned in France for those under 18.) Charming, innovative, provocative, and prophetic, MASCULINE FEMININE is a Godard film that even appeals to people who think they don't like Godard films. One of Godard's masterpieces.

M*A*S*H

1970   116m   c   Comedy/War   ★★★★½
Aspen   (U.S.)   R/15

Donald Sutherland *(Hawkeye Pierce)*, Elliott Gould *(Trapper John McIntyre)*, Tom Skerritt *(Duke Forrest)*, Sally Kellerman *(Maj. Hot Lips Houlihan)*, Robert Duvall *(Maj. Frank Burns)*, Jo Ann Pflug *(Lt. Hot Dish)*, Rene Auberjonois *(Dago Red)*, Roger Bowen *(Col. Henry Blake)*, Gary Burghoff *(Radar O'Reilly)*, David Arkin *(Sgt. Major Vollmer)*

p, Ingo Preminger; d, Robert Altman; w, Ring Lardner Jr. (based on the novel by Richard Hooker); ph, Harold Stine; ed, Danford B. Greene; m, Johnny Mandel; art d, Jack Martin Smith, Arthur Lonergan; fx, L.B. Abbott, Art Cruickshank

---

AAN Best Picture; *AAN Best Supporting Actress:* Sally Kellerman; *AAN Best Director:* Robert Altman; *AA Best Adapted Screenplay:* Ring Lardner, Jr.; *AAN Best Editing:* Danford B. Greene

---

Set during the Korean War but made at the height of the war in Vietnam, Robert Altman's exceptional antiwar comedy-drama follows the fortunes of a MASH (Mobile Army Surgical Hospital) unit. Hawkeye Pierce (Sutherland), Trapper John (Gould), and Duke Forrest (Skerritt) are the martini-swilling, prank-playing, but compassionate and capable battlefield surgeons who make life miserable for chief nurse Hot Lips Houlihan (Kellerman) and fellow surgeon Maj. Frank Burns (Duvall), a by-the-book prig. Among the terrible trio's shenanigans are the broadcast of a Burns-Houlihan lovemaking session over the camp public address system and the collapse of the women's shower to reveal the naked Maj. Houlihan. At the root of all this foolishness, however, is the attempt to mitigate the otherwise overwhelming bleakness of the war, to distract the doctors and nurses from the terrible waste of life they witness. The film's climactic football game, one of Hollywood's funniest (featuring a number of onetime pro players), pits the MASH unit against a crack team brought in by a general who has been investigating the unit.

Clever camera setups, Altman's patented overlapping dialogue, wonderful sight gags and situations, and universally fine ensemble performances combine to make this one the most enjoyable war-themed films ever. What makes M*A*S*H so extraordinary, however, is that beyond its hilarious antics and rich characters, the film offers a poignant portrait of the madness of war. This film was Altman's first major hit; the strength of this film made his subsequent career over the next decade possible.

MASK OF DIMITRIOS, THE

1944   95m   bw   Crime/Spy   ★★★★★
Warner Bros.   (U.S.)   /A

Sydney Greenstreet *(Mr. Peters)*, Zachary Scott *(Dimitrios)*, Faye Emerson *(Irana Preveza)*, Peter Lorre *(Cornelius Latimer Leyden)*, George Tobias *(Fedor Muishkin)*, Victor Francen *(Wladislaw Grodek)*, Steven Geray *(Bulic)*, Florence Bates *(Mme. Chavez)*, Eduardo Ciannelli *(Marukakis)*, Kurt Katch *(Col. Haki)*

p, Henry Blanke; d, Jean Negulesco; w, Frank Gruber (based on the novel *A Coffin For Dimitrios* by Eric Ambler); ph, Arthur Edeson; ed, Frederick Richards; m, Adolph Deutsch; art d, Ted Smith

---

One of the great film noir classics to come out of the 1940s, THE MASK OF DIMITRIOS boasts no superstars, just uniformly fine talents, a terrific script full of subtle intrigue and surprises, and Negulesco's exciting direction. It's an edge-of-the-seater all the way.

Lorre is Leyden, a Dutch mystery writer vacationing in Istanbul. At a party he meets one of his most ardent fans, Col. Haki (Katch), head of the secret police, who tells him that the body of arch criminal Dimitrios Makropoulous (Scott), has washed up on the nearby beach, murdered, stabbed to death. What fascinates Leyden is Haki's obsession with Makropoulos, a man who practiced "murder, treason, and betrayal" as a way of life. After a visit to the morgue to view the body, Leyden decides to write a novel about the sinister man and begins to delve into his past. What he encounters is a heady, complexly plotted brew of blackmail, seduction, spy intrigues, assassination and suicide.

Other than Ambler's American title for his novel and the fact that the mystery-detective writer is English rather than Dutch (an attempt to explain Lorre's slight accent), almost nothing was changed from the original novel. Ambler's despicable antihero is most certainly based upon the early career of one of the world's greatest intriguers, billionaire munitions king Basil Zaharoff. Though Lorre performs one of his few sympathetic roles with fascinating aplomb, Greenstreet, whom Lorre affectionately called "the old man" after they had become close friends while making THE MALTESE FALCON, dominates their scenes together. The entire film fits with the murky intrigue of the era, its stylized sets, low-key lighting, and a literate, witty script working to enchance the wonderful character actors in their segmented roles. Francen is particularly effective as the suave master spy, and impressive, handsome newcomer Scott is a properly loathsome creature without remorse or compassion for his myriad victims. Emerson, as a deserted tart, is also very good, as is Geray as a hapless, trusting government clerk. This film, under Negulesco's superb guidance, remains a superlative espionage yarn that artfully blends fact with fiction.

MASK, THE

1994   101m   c   Comedy/Action   ★★½
New Line/Dark Horse Entertainment   (U.S.)   PG-13/PG

Jim Carrey (Stanley Ipkiss/The Mask), Cameron Diaz (Tina Carlyle), Peter Riegert (Lieutenant Kellaway), Peter Greene (Dorian Tyrel), Amy Yasbeck (Peggy Brandt), Richard Jeni (Charlie Shumacher), Orestes Matacena (Niko), Tim Bagley (Irv), Nancy Fish (Mrs. Peeman), Johnny Williams (Burt)

p, Bob Engelman; d, Chuck Russell; w, Mike Werb (from a story by Michael Fallon and Mark Verheiden based on the Dark Horse Comics strip); ph, John R. Leonetti; ed, Arthur Coburn; m, Randy Edelman; prod d, Craig Stearns; art d, Randy Moore; fx, Scott Squires, Steve Williams, Tom Bertino, Jon Farhat, Robert Staad, Dream Quest Images, Industrial Light & Magic; chor, Jerry Evans; cos, Ha Nguyen

AAN Best Visual Effects: Scott Squires, Steve Williams, Tom Bertino, John Farhat

THE MASK, a live-action cartoon featuring a thoroughly unrestrained performance by Jim Carrey, has a story so slight that it wouldn't be worth telling if it weren't tricked out with the best special effects money can buy, at least in 1994. The effects are show-stopping, but the film's hollowness makes the overall result curiously depressing.

Nebbishy bank clerk Stanley Ipkiss (Jim Carrey) is one of life's perpetual losers. The highlight of his day comes when curvaceous bombshell Tina Carlyle (Cameron Diaz) wants to open a bank account, and declares that only Stanley's help will do. Unbeknownst to him, she's the girlfriend of brutal gangster Dorian Tyrel (Peter Greene), and she's only cuddling up to Stanley so she can secretly photograph the bank's vault. Everything changes when Stanley fishes a funny-looking mask out of the river. When he puts it on, he's transformed into a cackling lime green id in a canary zoot suit, a living cartoon with gleaming tombstone teeth who can go anywhere, do anything, suffer any punishment, and pop up unharmed. Stanley Ipkiss has become The Mask.

There's no denying that THE MASK's special effects are spectacular and lavish; there's scarcely a scene in which something eye-popping (once, literally) is happening, and those few moments of quiet are strangely dead. It's a pachinko machine of a movie: lights flash, bells ring, buzzers buzz, and things spin all over the place, but to no apparent end. Though the story has a certain universal appeal—who hasn't felt like a useless jerk and wished to wake up capable of anything?—the execution is oddly sour and distasteful. Nevertheless, presumably on the basis of Jim Carrey's appeal, the film was a smash success; the

combined domestic grosses of THE MASK, ACE VENTURA, and DUMB AND DUMBER made Carrey the second biggest star attraction of 1994, just behind Tom Hanks.

MASQUE OF THE RED DEATH, THE

1964   86m   c   Horror   ★★★★
Alta Vista/Anglo-Amalgamated   (U.S./U.K.)   /15

Vincent Price (Prince Prospero), Hazel Court (Juliana), Jane Asher (Francesca), David Weston (Gino), Patrick Magee (Alfredo), Nigel Green (Ludovico), Skip Martin (Hop Toad), John Westbrook (Man in Red), Gaye Brown (Senora Escobar), Julian Burton (Senor Veronese)

p, Roger Corman; d, Roger Corman; w, Charles Beaumont, R. Wright Campbell (based on "The Masque of the Red Death" and "Hop-Frog, or the Eight Chained Orang-outangs" by Edgar Allan Poe); ph, Nicolas Roeg; ed, Ann Chegwidden; m, David Lee; prod d, Daniel Haller; art d, Robert Jones; fx, George Blackwell; chor, Jack Carter; cos, Laura Nightingale

One of the best and most ambitious of the Roger Corman Edgar Allan Poe series, this is a colorful symphony of the macabre loosely based on two Poe stories. It boasts a magnificent performance from the always wonderful (and often hammy) Vincent Price. Price is Prince Prospero, a 12th-century Italian despot who lives for his one true love. . . Satan! After jailing two locals, Ludovico (Nigel Green) and Gino (David Weston) for defying his harsh tax laws, Prospero meets the beautiful Francesca (Jane Asher), daughter of Ludovico and the fiancee of Gino. She comes to him to plead for mercy. Prospero tells her that only one will be spared and toys with her emotions for his private amusement. When Prospero learns that the Red Death is sweeping the village, he locks himself and his followers in his castle where they continue their decadent parties. Soon a mysterious figure dressed in red robes arrives but he bides his time outside the castle, playing solitaire in the graveyard.

Weird and extremely downbeat, this is Corman's most sustained attempt at producing an Art Film. It even selfconsciously echoes the work of Ingmar Bergman and Luis Bunuel—two directors Corman greatly admires. The script by Charles Beaumont and R. Wright Campbell is among the most intelligent and literate of the Poe series. With photography by future director Nicolas Roeg (DON'T LOOK NOW, THE MAN WHO FELL TO EARTH), the film is also one of Corman's best-looking. It features incredible sets and costumes and a brilliant use of color. Best of all, however, is Price's inspired performance as the wicked Prospero. While Corman may veer dangerously close to pretention, his crisp staging and confident visual style keep the film from collapsing under its own weight.

MATA HARI

1931   91m   bw   Romance/Biography/Spy   ★★★½
MGM   (U.S.)   /A

Greta Garbo (Mata Hari), Ramon Novarro (Lt. Alexis Rosanoff), Lionel Barrymore (Gen. Serge Shubin), Lewis Stone (Andriani), C. Henry Gordon (Dubois), Karen Morley (Carlotta), Alec B. Francis (Caron), Blanche Frederici (Sister Angelica), Edmund Breese (Warden), Helen Jerome Eddy (Sister Genevieve)

p, Irving Thalberg; d, George Fitzmaurice; w, Benjamin Glazer, Leo Birinski, Doris Anderson, Gilbert Emery; ph, William Daniels; ed, Frank Sullivan

The subject of Mata Hari, the WWI Javanese-Dutch spy, was not new to film, but when Garbo agreed to play the role of the beautiful exotic dancer who traded sex for secrets, it was not only news but also cause for MGM to produce a lavish and memorable film. We first see the German spy in Paris, posing as a dancer. Her spymaster, Stone, directs her to intercept certain Russian messages involving Allied troop movements. For some time Garbo has been having an affair with Barrymore, an indiscreet general, but she meets Novarro, a lowly lieutenant, and truly falls in love with him. Then she learns that Novarro has the messages she is seeking and she betrays her love for him to serve her country, taking him to bed while her associates copy his messages. Barrymore learns of the tryst and explodes, threatening to turn Garbo in as an agent and implicate Novarro. To save herself and her unwitting lover, Garbo shoots and kills Barrymore. When Novarro begins to seek out Barrymore, Garbo compels him to leave. The pilot flies to Russia where he is shot down and blinded. Learning of this, Garbo follows her passion rather than her military orders and goes to Novarro to tell him of her devotion to him. Stone orders an agent to kill her, but the man is foiled by local police. Garbo is then unmasked and brought to trial.

Garbo is stunning, full of her special mystique as the exotic dancer-spy, in one scene wearing a revealing costume and snaking her body around a lascivious-looking, many-armed statue in an odd interpretive dance. Fitzmaurice directs with great style here and makes the most of the lavish production techniques available to him. Both Garbo and Novarro had accents that later caused some critics to sneer, particularly at one of Novarro's lines which sounded like "What's the mata, Mata?" Of course, little shown here is based on real events. The historical figure, Gertrud Margarete Zelle MacLeod (1876-1917), danced in Paris and stole secrets from the French for the Germans, low-level secrets at that, until she was uncovered as a spy and shot, not in Russia, but at Saint-Lazare in France on October 15, 1917.

MATCH FACTORY GIRL, THE
(TULITIKKUTEHTAAN TYTTO)
1990 70m c Drama/Comedy ★★★½
Villealfa/Svenska Filminstitutet   (Finland/Sweden)

Kati Outinen (Iris), Elina Salo (Iris's Mother), Esko Nikkari (Iris's Stepfather), Vesa Vierikko (Man in Dancehall), Reijo Taipale (Singer), Silu Seppala (Brother), Outi Maenpaa (Workmate), Marja Packalen (Doctor), Richard Reitinger (Man in Bar), Helga Viljanen (Office Employee)

p, Aki Kaurismaki; d, Aki Kaurismaki; w, Aki Kaurismaki; ph, Timo Salminen; ed, Aki Kaurismaki; cos, Tuula Hilkamo

A darkly humorous fable, THE MATCH FACTORY GIRL chronicles, in extreme minimalist fashion, the transformation of an ugly duckling into a killer tigress. Utilizing perhaps only a half-dozen lines of dialogue, Finnish filmmaker Aki Kaurismaki relies instead on the lyrics of about a dozen songs to comment on the action. Like some industrial documentary, the film opens with close-ups of the machinery used in making wooden matches, from the skinning of a section of tree trunk to the packaging and labeling of the bundles. Iris (Kati Outinen) has the deadeningly routine job of making sure the labels are properly stuck to the cartons. Her home life is as dreary as her job, since she lives in a shabby apartment with her mother (Elina Salo) and stepfather (Esko Nikkari), whom she supports with her meager earnings. All this changes when, one pay day, Iris sees and buys a red floral print dress; the dress helps her attract a middle-class man (Vesa Vierikko) who, after a one-night stand, wants nothing more to do with her. His callous response when Iris later finds out she is pregnant moves her to exact a deadly, deadpan revenge on him and everyone else who has contributed to the unleavened misery of her existence.

The final installment in Kaurismaki's acclaimed "proletarian trilogy" (the others being SHADOWS IN PARADISE and ARIEL), THE MATCH FACTORY GIRL is a wondrous antidote to the sentimentality of most mainstream films. Kaurismaki's presentation of Helsinki is characteristically grim and anonymous, either modern and bare or old and shabby. The director, writer, producer and editor of the film, Kaurismaki has described it both as his "revenge on Robert Bresson" as well as a "piece of junk." He has also stated that he is not interested in middle-class family values, but in "losers."

MATEWAN
1987 132m c Drama ★★★★
Red Dog (U.S.) PG-13/15

Chris Cooper (Joe Kenehan), Will Oldham (Danny Radnor), Jace Alexander (Hillard), Ken Jenkins (Sephus Purcell), Bob Gunton (C.E. Lively), Gary McCleery (Ludie), Kevin Tighe (Hickey), Gordon Clapp (Griggs), Mary McDonnell (Elma Radnor), James Earl Jones ("Few Clothes" Johnson)

p, Peggy Rajski, Maggie Renzi; d, John Sayles; w, John Sayles; ph, Haskell Wexler; ed, Sonya Polonsky; m, Mason Daring; prod d, Nora Chavooshian; art d, Dan Bishop; cos, Cynthia Flynt

AAN Best Cinematography: Haskell Wexler

Made for $4 million but looking as if it cost three times that, this is an excellent offering from one of America's best-known independent filmmakers, John Sayles (THE BROTHER FROM ANOTHER PLANET; EIGHT MEN OUT). As the film opens, Danny Radnor (Will Oldham), a 15-year-old coal miner, spreads the news that the Stone Mountain Coal Company of Matewan, West Virginia, has decided to lower the tonnage rate paid the miners—again. A strike is called. Joe Kenehan (Chris Cooper), a pacifist and former Wobbly, is sent by the United Mine Workers to coordinate the action and to keep it from becoming violent; however, a group of Italian immigrants continues to work, as do the black miners whom the company has brought from Alabama. A battle seems inevitable; but slowly the three factions grow into a community, and the strike spreads like wildfire. In MATEWAN Sayles captures the feel of a 1930s Popular Front film but grounds it in the complex reality of a world that refuses to present easy choices. With Oscar winner Haskell Wexler acting as cinematographer, MATEWAN is beautifully shot, and there is not a weak performance in the film. Jones is a tower of dignity; Cooper is the epitome of quiet strength; and Oldham glows with the passion of a zealot, first for God, then for the union.

MATINEE
1993 98m c Comedy/Drama/Science Fiction ★★★
Renfield/Matinee Inc./Falcon Film Finance Ltd./Pandora PG/
Cinema   (U.S.)

John Goodman (Lawrence Woolsey), Cathy Moriarty (Ruth Corday), Simon Fenton (Gene Loomis), Omri Katz (Stan), Lisa Jakub (Sandra), Kellie Martin (Sherry), Jesse Lee (Dennis Loomis), Lucinda Jenney (Anne Loomis), James Villemaire (Harvey Starkweather), Robert Picardo (Howard the Theater Manager)

p, Michael Finnell; d, Joe Dante; w, Charlie Haas (from a story by Charlie Haas and Jerico Stone); ph, John Hora; ed, Marshall Harvey; m, Jerry Goldsmith; prod d, Steven Legler; art d, Nanci B. Roberts; fx, Dennis Michelson; cos, Isis Mussenden

A genuine love for B cinema informs all the work of director Joe Dante, from his own Roger Corman-produced cheapies through the GREMLINS films. This affection finds its purest expression in MATINEE, an affectionate homage to the "creature features" of the 50s and 60s.

The story is set in Key West, Florida, in October 1962, just before and during the Cuban missile crisis. Teenager Gene Loomis (Simon Fenton) lives with his mother (Lucinda Jenney) and brother Dennis (Jesse Lee) on a Naval base; his dad is serving on one of the US ships blockading Cuba. Mass destruction looms, but Gene's preoccupied with the imminent arrival in town of his idol, horror filmmaker Lawrence Woolsey (John Goodman). A master showman, Woolsey plans to hold a preview in Key West of his new chiller, MANT ("Half Man, Half Ant, All Terror!"), in Atomo-Vision and Rumble-Rama.

MATINEE succeeds above all as an enjoyable tribute to the monster movies of yesteryear, not only in the way its young characters are enthralled by the promise of MANT's terrors, but in the clips of MANT itself that appear throughout the film. Cast with numerous (sadly uncredited) '50s creature-feature veterans like Kenneth Tobey and William Schallert, MANT is a perfect evocation of those cheesy science fiction thrillers in which atomic radiation turned humans into insectoid mutants. MATINEE has a surfeit of characters and climaxes, but these are compensated by many great moments and a terrific central theme: the juxtaposition of the real-life terrors of the Cold War with the cinematic horrors that reduced the nuclear threat to something outlandish and thus safely entertaining.

MAVERICK
1994 129m c Comedy/Western ★★½
ICON Productions/Donner/Shuler-Donner Productions   (U.S.) PG/

Mel Gibson (Bret Maverick), Jodie Foster (Annabelle Bransford), James Garner (Zane Cooper), Graham Greene (Joseph), Alfred Molina (Angel), James Coburn (Commodore), Dub Taylor (Room Clerk), Geoffrey Lewis (Matthew Wicker), Paul L. Smith (Archduke), Dan Hedaya (Twitchy)

p, Richard Donner, Bruce Davey; d, Richard Donner; w, William Goldman; ph, Vilmos Zsigmond; ed, Stuart Baird, Mike Kelly; m, Randy Newman; prod d, Thomas Sanders; art d, Daniel Dorrance; fx, Matt Sweeney, Industrial Light & Magic, Steve Price; cos, April Ferry

AAN Best Costume Design: April Ferry

Cynical and bloated, MAVERICK is a comic western whose high-powered cast does very little but looks damned fine doing it. Even fans of the vintage TV show may find it trying.

Bret Maverick (Mel Gibson) is a fancy man who's down on his luck and needs some quick cash so he can play in a high-stakes riverboat poker game. Annabelle Bransford (Jodie Foster) is a scheming con artist with a flirty manner, and a pretty fair hand at cards herself. Zane Cooper (James Garner) is a weatherbeaten lawman with a sneaky smile and an irresistibly gracious manner. After a memorable stagecoach ride—the driver dies and it's almost too late before anyone notices—the mismatched trio shoot, gamble, lie, and wisecrack their way across the old West, and finally wind up together on the lavish Lauren Belle, where the Commodore (James Coburn) is playing host to the best gamblers alive.

Based on the 1950s TV series starring James Garner, MAVERICK—a summer hit by-the-numbers—relies shamelessly on the nostalgia factor; it's noisy and filled with twists and turns, but it never seems like a real movie, because the characters are all written in shorthand. Garner and Gibson deliver lazy performances: Garner is charming and gallant, Gibson flashes his winning smile and widens his baby blues. Foster—by far the best of the bunch—seems oddly out of place by comparison; Annabelle is all fluff, and Foster doesn't fluff well: she always seems slightly embarrassed. Formula Hollywood filmmaking at its shallowest.

MAYERLING

1936   96m   bw   Historical/Romance   ★★★★★
Concordea   (France)   /15

Charles Boyer (Archduke Rudolph of Austria), Danielle Darrieux (Marie Vetsera), Suzy Prim (Countess Larisch), Jean Dax (Emperor Franz Joseph), Gabrielle Dorziat (Empress Elizabeth), Jean Debucourt (Count Taafe), Marthe Regnier (Baroness Vetsera/Helene), Yolande Laffon (Stephanie), Vladimir Sokoloff (Chief of Police), Andre Dubosc (Loschek, the Valet)

d, Anatole Litvak; w, Joseph Kessel, Irma Von Cube (based on the novel Idyl's End by Claude Anet); ph, Armand Thirard; ed, Henri Rust; m, Arthur Honegger

MAYERLING is one of the greatest love stories ever brought to the screen, the bittersweet, painfully poignant romance between the star-crossed Crown Prince Rudolph of Austria and his adoring mistress, Marie Vetsera. Charles Boyer, in a riveting performance, is Rudolph, son of the powerful Franz Joseph, Emperor of Austria-Hungary. A free spirit who associates with radicals and gypsies, Rudolph is also a prisoner of his royal blood. Everywhere there are court spies assigned to track and trail the errant heir to the throne. Eluding his followers at a fair, he meets 17-year-old Marie Vetsera (Danielle Darrieux), and it's love at first sight, although Marie has no idea that he is the prince as the couple enjoys such little pleasures as tossing rings around a swan's neck and watching a puppet show. The following night, Marie attends the opera and is startled to see the handsome young man from the fair sitting in the royal box. Though she comes from an aristocratic family, she has no hope of reaching so high. Instead, Rudolph reaches out to her, meeting secretly with the beautiful young woman. Only in Marie's presence does Rudolph find joy and peace; she responds to him with an innocence he has never encountered. When their liaison is discovered, however, the lovers must depart to a country hunting lodge from which they will never return. Based on fact, this story of an impossible love is told on a grand, exquisite scale by Anatole Litvak, and represents one of the high points of the director's spotty career. Filled with dreamy dissolves and fluid, nearly waltzlike camera movements, the film is a brilliant technical achievement, further enhanced by the wonderful performances of the two leads—the debonair Boyer and the ravishing Darrieux, who was then just 21 years old.

MAYTIME

1937   132m   bw   Romance/Musical   ★★★★½
MGM   (U.S.)   /U

Jeanette MacDonald (Marcia Morney/Miss Morrison), Nelson Eddy (Paul Allison), John Barrymore (Nicolai Nazaroff), Herman Bing (August Archipenko), Tom Brown (Kip Stuart), Lynne Carver (Barbara Roberts), Rafaela Ottiano (Ellen), Charles Judels (Cabby), Paul Porcasi (Composer Trentini), Sig Rumann (Fanchon)

p, Hunt Stromberg; d, Robert Z. Leonard; w, Noel Langley (based on the operetta by Rida Johnson Young, Sigmund Romberg); ph, Oliver T. Marsh; ed, Conrad A. Nervig; art d, Cedric Gibbons, Frederic Hope; chor, William von Wymetal, Val Raset; cos, Adrian

AAN Best Score: Nat W. Finston, Herbert Stothart, Metro-Goldwyn-Mayer Studio Music Department; AAN Best Sound: Douglas Shearer

A very fragile lace valentine, admittedly, but performed with the conviction and style to make it work. Based on a Sigmund Romberg-Rida Johnson Young operetta that was so popular that two productions of it ran simultaneously on Broadway in 1917, MAYTIME returned its $1.5 million price tag five time en route to becoming the 1937 box-office champion. The third Nelson Eddy-Jeanette MacDonald pairing, it was also reputedly the actress's personal favorite, because the famed duo had so much more to do than sing and were finally able to prove their depth as actors. At a May Day celebration in 1906, Miss Morrison (MacDonald), an aged woman, meets Kip (Brown), whose fiancee, Barbara (Carver), yearns for a singing career. The elderly woman explains that she was once a famous opera star, and the film flashes back to France, 1865, where Marcia Mornay (MacDonald) accepts a marriage proposal from Nicolai Nazaroff (Barrymore, very potent here), the architect of her success. Later, she is swept off her feet by Paul Allison (Eddy), a handsome young American singer, but remains true to her promise to marry Nazaroff. Several years pass, and when Marcia and Paul costar in an American production, their love is rekindled. What advice will Miss Morrison give to Kip and Barbara? Get ready for the umpteenth reprise of "Will You Remember?"

Perhaps MAYTIME's most intriguing sidelight is the faked opera "Czaritza," written from Tchaikovsky music with French lyrics by Giles Guilbert, created in the tradition of such other great phony movie operas as CITIZEN KANE's "Salammbo," and CHARLIE CHAN AT THE OPERA's "Carnival." The staging is surprisingly intense, as is the entire film.

MCCABE AND MRS. MILLER

1971   120m   c   Western   ★★★★½
Warner Bros.   (U.S.)   R/X

Warren Beatty (John McCabe), Rene Auberjonois (Sheehan), John Schuck (Smalley), Bert Remsen (Bart Coyle), Keith Carradine (Cowboy), Julie Christie (Constance Miller), William Devane (The Lawyer), Corey Fischer (Mr. Elliott), Shelley Duvall (Ida Coyle), Michael Murphy (Sears)

p, David Foster, Mitchell Brower; d, Robert Altman; w, Robert Altman, Brian McKay (based on the novel McCabe by Edmund Naughton); ph, Vilmos Zsigmond; ed, Lou Lombardo; m, Leonard Cohen; prod d, Leon Ericksen; art d, Philip Thomas, Albert J. Locatelli; fx, Marcel Vercoutere; cos, Erickson

AAN Best Actress: Julie Christie

A grim and dirty slice of bleak frontier life rendered with extraordinary beauty. Robert Altman cast a decidedly deglamourized Warren Beatty and Julie Christie together with his stock company in this richly textured anti-Western, with the stated intent of destroying "the myths of heroism in the Old West." The result is an atmospheric and resonant exploration of a small northwestern settlement in the middle of winter, with Christie as the thoroughly modern madam of a bordello and Beatty as the smaller-than-life hero.

Shortly after the turn of the century McCabe (Beatty), a man with a mysterious past, rides into a raw snow-covered northwestern wilderness settlement called Presbyterian Church. Here he gambles his way to some winnings and then establishes the community's first whorehouse. Initially a slapdash collection of tents, it becomes a smoothly running business when the feisty Mrs. Miller (Christie) comes aboard as the madam and chief prostitute. She uses McCabe's money to construct a whorehouse that becomes the communal center of the growing town. Miners pour into the brothel-bathhouse, and McCabe's success does not go unnoticed by the region's mining operators, who offer him $6,250 to sell out. McCabe, a business neophyte grown cocky with commercial triumph, refuses their offer. He's holding out for $15,000. Mrs. Miller warns her smart-talking partner that the company employs hired guns to get its way but he intends to settle before things reach that state. This turns out to be a tragic miscalculation.

MCCABE AND MRS. MILLER is a sad and beautiful film that sides with the losers and dreamers. Beatty, in a courageous anti-star turn, is bearded, blustery and ignorant, but ultimately endearing. Christie is at least as good as the tough-talking, opium-smoking lady from the Continent who's smart enough to know the real score. Altman makes extensive and effective use of Leonard Cohen's haunting ballads throughout the film and Vilmos Zsigmond provides sublime muted images of icy landscapes and warm interiors. Christie received a Best Actress Oscar nomination, but she lost to Jane Fonda for KLUTE. Not an easy film to watch, but almost undoubtedly a great one.

MEAN STREETS

1973 110m c Crime   ★★★★½
TPS (U.S.)   R/X

Harvey Keitel (Charlie), Robert De Niro (Johnny Boy), Amy Robinson (Teresa), David Proval (Tony), Richard Romanus (Michael), Cesare Danova (Giovanni), Victor Argo (Mario), George Memmoli (Joey Catucci), Lenny Scaletta (Jimmy), Jeannie Bell (Diane)

p, Jonathan T. Taplin; d, Martin Scorsese; w, Martin Scorsese, Mardik Martin; ph, Kent Wakeford; ed, Sidney Levin

After making the interesting WHO'S THAT KNOCKING AT MY DOOR? and working for Roger Corman on BOXCAR BERTHA, Scorsese exploded onto the scene with this remarkable low-budgeter about the lives of small-time hoods in New York's Little Italy. The film centers on four guys who aspire to hit it big in business or crime. Tony (Proval), the big friendly one, runs the neighborhood bar; Mike (Romanus) likes to rip off naive teenagers from Brooklyn; Johnny Boy (De Niro) has a penchant for blowing up mailboxes and borrowing money from loan sharks he never intends to repay; and Charlie (Keitel), nephew of the local mafia boss (Danova), wants nothing more than to run his own restaurant. Charlie is torn between the life of the streets and the life his uncle can give him. He is also deeply religious, patterning himself after St. Francis of Assisi—testing his faith and seeking penitence for his sins on the streets. This testing takes the form of trying to "save" Johnny Boy and being kind to his crazed pal's epileptic sister Teresa (Robinson), neither of whom his uncle likes.

MEAN STREETS is a brilliantly made film—terrifically acted, sharply photographed and crisply edited. Stand-out moments include an extended fight scene in a pool hall (the fight starts amusingly enough, over someone being called a "mook"—the guys aren't quite sure what it means, but they fight anyway), in which Scorsese uses long takes to emphasize the chaos and a wild tracking shot to follow a pair fighting throughout the room. Other highlights include Charlie's drunk scene at a party; the guys at a movie theater watching THE SEARCHERS; Johnny Boy shooting a gun from a roof; and the scene when Teresa has an epileptic fit and Charlie chooses to chase after Johnny instead of staying with his girlfriend (he leaves her in the care of an elderly woman played by Scorsese's mother). The hilarious scene in which Charlie and Johnny Boy argue about Johnny Boy's debts in the backroom of a bar (a scene that was improvised) is alone worth the price of admission.

MEDIUM COOL

1969 110m c Political   ★★★½
H and J (U.S.)   R/X

Robert Forster (John Cassellis), Verna Bloom (Eileen Horton), Peter Bonerz (Gus), Marianna Hill (Ruth), Harold Blankenship (Harold Horton), Sid McCoy (Frank Baker), Christine Bergstrom (Dede), Robert McAndrew (Pennybaker), William Sickinger (News Director Karlin), Beverly Younger (Rich Lady)

p, Jerrold Wexler, Haskell Wexler, Tully Friedman; d, Haskell Wexler; w, Haskell Wexler (based on the novel The Concrete Wilderness by Jack Couffer); ph, Haskell Wexler; ed, Verna Fields; m, Mike Bloomfield; art d, Leon Ericksen

This minor classic from the 60s time capsule is a self-conscious essay on the meaning of the media and the nature of political commitment. During the summer of 1968, with anti-war sentiment growing daily, a host of hippies, Yippies, and other countercultural types descended on Chicago for the Democratic Convention, an event marked by all-out battles between police and demonstrators in parks and on the streets. Celebrated left-wing cinematographer Haskell Wexler directed much of MEDIUM COOL while on location there, blending documentary footage with a fictional narrative.

John (Robert Forster) is a television cameraman, Gus (Peter Bonerz) his soundman, Eileen (Verna Bloom) a poor woman from the Kentucky hills who has recently moved to Chicago with her son, Harold (Harold Blankenship). John is initially presented as the archetypal artist divorced from society ("God, I love to shoot film"), but gradually becomes involved in the political process through his growing relationship with Eileen and Harold. Everything comes to a sticky end reminiscent of the finale of Godard's CONTEMPT. Finally, a very solemn-looking Wexler literally turns his camera on us: we're responsible, too, for what we've just seen on screen.

The noted photographer of such films as THE THOMAS CROWN AFFAIR and IN THE HEAT OF THE NIGHT, Wexler took on directorial duties for the first time here, something he would not do again until 1985's LATINO. Interestingly, it's Wexler's skills as a visual storyteller that give MEDIUM COOL its lasting power. While the more explicitly political scenes—any, in fact, that feature substantial dialogue—seem awkward and dated, the long, impressionistic sequences in which Wexler establishes character and locale almost exclusively with image and sound are hauntingly effective. One scene in particular, in which John and a girlfriend lounge, then romp around his spacious apartment, is as exhilarating a piece of camerawork as any we've seen.

MEET JOHN DOE

1941 135m bw Political   ★★★★
Warner Bros. (U.S.)   /U

Gary Cooper ("John Doe"/Long John Willoughby), Barbara Stanwyck (Ann Mitchell), Edward Arnold (D.B. Norton), Walter Brennan (Colonel), James Gleason (Henry Connell), Spring Byington (Mrs. Mitchell), Gene Lockhart (Mayor Lovett), Rod La Rocque (Ted Sheldon), Irving Bacon (Beany), Regis Toomey (Bert Hansen)

p, Frank Capra; d, Frank Capra; w, Robert Riskin (based on a story "The Life and Death of John Doe" by Robert Presnell, Richard Connell); ph, George Barnes; ed, Daniel Mandell; m, Dimitri Tiomkin; art d, Stephen Goosson; fx, Jack Cosgrove; cos, Natalie Visart

AAN Best Original Screenplay: Richard Connell, Robert Presnell

Dark, oddball Capra, but a worthwhile watch with a tail ending wagging the dog. The film opens as Stanwyck, a struggling journalist, is fired from her job when a new managing editor, Gleason, takes over her newspaper. She angrily writes her last piece about a mythical idealist she calls John Doe and through him rants about the little guy being punished and mistreated by tycoons, moguls, magnates and captains of industry. To make good his protest, Doe states, in Stanwyck's fabricated letter to the paper, that he will leap off the top of City Hall on Christmas Eve. The public response is enormous, and Gleason demands that Stanwyck turn over the letter she has received from this so-called John Doe. She confesses that there is no letter, that she made up the whole story. But then, to keep the job she values above all else, Stanwyck suggests they find a phony hero from the ranks of the great unemployed and continue the story to sell more papers. When another paper jeeringly labels the story a fraud, Gleason, to save his newspaper's image, orders Stanwyck to pick out a stewbum and make him into her real-life John Doe. Enter Gary Cooper as Long John Willoughby, a onetime minor league pitcher with a bad arm and a shortage of cash.

MEET JOHN DOE was Capra's first independent film production done away from his home studio, Columbia, and beyond the tyrannical reach of its boss, Harry Cohn. It's basically an attack on the fascist elements then in America, notably the pro-Nazi German-American Bund. Capra wanted to warn Americans about the powerful fascist influences in their midst and did so mightily with this film. Though MEET JOHN DOE reportedly profited Capra and Riskin's independent company $900,000 on its initial release, Capra later reported that the tax bite was so heavy that he dissolved the company after a few months. So great had Capra's reputation become that all the leading players in MEET JOHN DOE agreed to do the film without reading the script.

MEET ME IN ST. LOUIS

1944 113m c Musical ★★★★★
MGM (U.S.) /U

Judy Garland *(Esther Smith)*, Margaret O'Brien *("Tootie" Smith)*, Mary Astor *(Mrs. Anne Smith)*, Lucille Bremer *(Rose Smith)*, June Lockhart *(Lucille Ballard)*, Tom Drake *(John Truett)*, Marjorie Main *(Katie)*, Harry Davenport *(Grandpa)*, Leon Ames *(Mr. Alonzo Smith)*, Hank Daniels *(Lon Smith, Jr.)*

p, Arthur Freed; d, Vincente Minnelli; w, Irving Brecher, Fred Finkle-hoffe (based on the stories by Sally Benson); ph, George Folsey; ed, Albert Akst; art d, Cedric Gibbons, Lemuel Ayers; chor, Charles Walters; cos, Irene Sharaff

AAN Best Original Screenplay: Irving Brecher, Fred F. Finkelhoffe; *AAN Best Cinematography:* George Folsey; *AAN Best Score:* Georgie Stoll; *AAN Best Song:* Ralph Blane, Hugh Martin

A Valentine to the good old days, and all they stood for. Near-peak Judy Garland under the stylish direction of her future husband, Vincente Minnelli, in this wonderful period musical. It opens in 1903 in St. Louis, where Alonzo Smith (Leon Ames), a well-to-do businessman, lives with his wife (Mary Astor), daughters (Garland, Lucille Bremer, Joan Carroll, and Margaret O'Brien), son (Hank Daniels), capricious Grandpa (Harry Davenport), and maid (Marjorie Main). Daughter Rose (Bremer) is courted by one beau at home and corresponds with another away at college, while Esther (Garland) becomes engaged to the new boy next door. Little sisters Agnes (Joan Carroll) and Tootie (Margaret O'Brien) represent the timeless mischief of childhood. Trouble arises when Alonzo is promoted and ordered to New York, a move no one in the family wants to make.

This is a peerless portrayal of America at the turn of the century and one family's struggles to deal with progress, symbolized by the 1904 World's Fair in St. Louis (beautifully re-created for the film). Minnelli proves his eye for detail and captures the era and its values in richly colored, gentle images, displaying a startling balance of emotions from scene to scene, song to song. Among the songs included in this triumph of Americana are "The Boy Next Door," "Meet Me in St. Louis," the marvelous production number "The Trolley Song," and Garland's evergreen "Have Yourself a Merry Little Christmas". An almost unbeatable musical. Note Garland's beauty in this film: a tribute to the overhaul given her by Dottie Pondell, whose services Garland had snatched from under the noses of every major star in Hollywood, upon the death of Carole Lombard.

MELO

1986 110m c Romance ★★★★★
MK2/CNC/A2 (France) /PG

Sabine Azema *(Romaine Belcroix)*, Pierre Arditi *(Pierre Belcroix)*, Andre Dussollier *(Marcel Blanc)*, Fanny Ardant *(Christiane Levesque)*, Jacques Dacqmine *(Dr. Remy)*, Hubert Gignoux *(Priest)*, Catherine Arditi *(Yvonne)*

p, Marin Karmitz; d, Alain Resnais; w, Alain Resnais (based on the play "Melo" by Henri Bernstein); ph, Charlie Van Damme; ed, Albert Jurgenson; m, Johannes Brahms, Johann Sebastian Bach, Philippe Gerard; prod d, Jacques Saulnier; cos, Catherine Leterrier

Since his brilliant HIROSHIMA, MON AMOUR, Alain Resnais's experiments with nonlinear structure and the relationship between memory and the past have placed him among the ranks of the greatest directors. In light of these experiments, MELO comes as a shock, a traditionally constructed linear narrative adapted from a 1929 Parisian stage melodrama written by Henry Bernstein. Deceptively simple in appearance, MELO is the story of two musicians, Marcel Blanc and Pierre Belcroix (Andre Dussollier and Pierre Arditi), whose friendship dates back to their days at the conservatory. Marcel has gone on to international fame as a soloist while Pierre has settled down in a

Parisian suburb to lead a simple life with his wife, Romaine (Sabine Azema). After a quiet evening of drink and reminiscence, Marcel and Romaine begin a passionate affair. Romaine plots to gradually poison the unsuspecting and good-natured Pierre. Masterfully directed, MELO is both an entertaining romantic melodrama and an extension of Resnais's ideas about memory and imagination, reality and fiction. As in HIROSHIMA, MON AMOUR, Resnais gives us characters whose present is haunted by the past. Only rarely is a film this simple *and* this complex.

MELVIN AND HOWARD

1980 93m c Biography/Comedy ★★★½
Universal (U.S.) R/AA

Jason Robards Jr. *(Howard Hughes)*, Paul LeMat *(Melvin Dummar)*, Elizabeth Cheshire *(Darcy Dummar)*, Mary Steenburgen *(Lynda Dummar)*, Chip Taylor *(Clark Taylor)*, Melvin E. Dummar *(Bus Depot Counterman)*, Michael J. Pollard *(Little Red)*, Denise Galik *(Lucy)*, Gloria Grahame *(Mrs. Sisk)*, Pamela Reed *(Bonnie Dummar)*

p, Art Linson, Don Phillips; d, Jonathan Demme; w, Bo Goldman; ph, Tak Fujimoto; ed, Craig McKay; m, Bruce Langhorne; prod d, Toby Rafelson; art d, Richard Sawyer

AAN Best Supporting Actor: Jason Robards; *AA Best Supporting Actress:* Mary Steenburgen; *AA Best Original Screenplay:* Bo Goldman

After churning out CAGED HEAT and CRAZY MAMA for Roger Corman's New World Pictures, Jonathan Demme (STOP MAKING SENSE, SOMETHING WILD, THE SILENCE OF THE LAMBS) finally broke through the ranks of B-movie directors with this pungent fable about the elusiveness of the American Dream.

Based on a real-life incident, Melvin Dummar (Paul LeMat) is an amiable milkman and perpetual also-ran who, while driving along a lonesome stretch of Nevada highway early one morning, picks up a grizzled tramp (Jason Robards) headed for Las Vegas. He's nice to the eccentric codger, who claims to be Howard Hughes, and even gives him two bits at the end of the ride.

Melvin quickly dismisses the incident and goes about his life, remarrying his ex-wife, Lynda (Mary Steenburgen), and chasing success with typically poor results. Even when Lynda wins $10,000 tap dancing to the Rolling Stones's "Satisfaction" on a television game show, the Dummars are unable to turn the situation to their advantage. Life remains a struggle for the embattled couple until Melvin discovers that the bum he befriended earlier really was Howard Hughes—and that the recently deceased billionaire has made him the beneficiary of $156 million via the so-called Morman will.

Like the earlier, underrated HANDLE WITH CARE, Demme displays an affinity for Preston Sturges-like tales that portray a system which places a premium on material success, but MELVIN AND HOWARD never quite lives up to its satiric or dramatic potential, suffering from a somewhat sidelong approach to Melvin's odyssey that renders the film more engaging than truly compelling.

MEMBER OF THE WEDDING, THE

1952 91m bw Drama ★★★
Columbia (U.S.) /A

Ethel Waters *(Berenice Sadie Brown)*, Julie Harris *(Frankie Addams)*, Brandon de Wilde *(John Henry)*, Arthur Franz *(Jarvis)*, Nancy Gates *(Janice)*, William Hansen *(Mr. Addams)*, James Edwards *(Honey Camden Brown)*, Harry Bolden *(T. T. Williams)*, Dickie Moore *(Soldier)*, Danny Mummert *(Barney MacKean)*

p, Stanley Kramer; d, Fred Zinnemann; w, Edna Anhalt, Edward Anhalt (based on the novel and play by Carson McCullers); ph, Hal Mohr; ed, Harry Gerstad, William Lyon; m, Alex North; prod d, Rudolph Sternad; art d, Cary Odell

AAN Best Actress: Julie Harris

An overly static adaptation of Carson McCullers' 1950 Broadway hit about the end of adolescence, saved by the playwright's dialogue; the presence of Ethel Waters; and the work of veteran photographer Hal Mohr, who lovingly captures life in a sleepy Georgia town.

The then 26-year-old Julie Harris plays Frankie, a motherless 12-year-old tomboy who imagines herself a member of her brother's wedding party, then tries to tag along for the honeymoon. Dejected at being refused, she runs away, but returns home after a brush with a drunken soldier. It's the beginning of the end of her childhood, as well as of the two relationships that have defined her life thus far: with Berenice (Waters), her cook and ersatz mother; and with her much put-upon playmate and cousin, John Henry (Brandon de Wilde).

Zinneman's distant, respectful direction fails, unsurprisingly, to capture the ironies and complexities of his source material. MEMBER was still, nonetheless, considered confusing by audiences, with many allegedly thinking Frankie was a boy until the end of the film. In an effort to address complaints that it was "slow-moving," Columbia cut about 20 minutes of footage, restoring it some twenty years later. Cameraman Mohr, approaching the end of his long career, had previously shot such films as THE JAZZ SINGER, THE WEDDING MARCH, A MIDSUMMER NIGHT'S DREAM, and RANCHO NOTORIOUS. Five people from the award-winning theater production (Harris, Waters, de Wilde, Hansen, and Bolden) reprise their roles here. Harris had become a star with the Broadway show, and cemented her rise with an Oscar nomination for the film; de Wilde had made his debut in the play, becoming the first child actor to win Broadway's prestigious Donaldson Award in the process, and would become an Oscar-nominated star the following year in George Stevens' SHANE.

MEN, THE

1950 85m bw Drama/War ★★★★
Kramer (U.S.) /PG

Marlon Brando (Ken), Teresa Wright (Ellen), Everett Sloane (Dr. Brock), Jack Webb (Norm), Richard Erdman (Leo), Arthur Jurado (Angel), Virginia Farmer (Nurse Robbins), Dorothy Tree (Ellen's Mother), Howard St. John (Ellen's Father), Nita Hunter (Dolores)

p, Stanley Kramer; d, Fred Zinnemann; w, Carl Foreman; ph, Robert de Grasse; ed, Harry Gerstad; m, Dimitri Tiomkin; prod d, Rudolph Sternad

AAN Best Original Screenplay: Carl Foreman

This was Marlon Brando's film debut and, as such, set standards not only for his fellow actors but for himself. Brando gives a tremendous performance as Ken, a WWII veteran who has been left a paraplegic as a result of a sniper's bullet in the lower back. In the hospital, Ken is angry, resentful, and uncooperative with his doctors and nurses. His girlfriend, Ellen (Teresa Wright), visits him, but the embittered Ken turns her away. Dr. Brock (Everett Sloane) slowly breaks through Ken's mental wall, however, convincing him to begin his exercise program, through which Ken strengthens his upper torso, later learning to expertly manipulate his wheelchair and to drive a specially equipped auto. Ellen will not give up on him and soon Ken agrees to marry her, but despite the progress he has made, the vet is still consumed with doubt, anger, and self-pity. Producer Stanley Kramer earlier produced such message-filled films as CHAMPION and HOME OF THE BRAVE, the first concerning the corruption of the blood sport of prizefighting, the second dealing with racism and bigotry. Here Kramer, aided by the steady direction of Fred Zinnemann, studies the adjustment of severely wounded men with little hope of complete recovery. Zinnemann rarely steps over the line into mawkishness or bathos, and Carl Foreman's witty, sensitive script was the reason Brando agreed to step off the stage to appear in this film. Brando worked hard at his role, actually moving into a 32-bed ward with real paraplegics and observing their day-to-day agonies, research that resulted in a finely nuanced performance.

MEN...
(MANNER)

1985 99m c Comedy ★★★½
Olga/Second German TV (West Germany) /15

Heiner Lauterbach (Julius Armbrust), Uwe Ochsenknecht (Stefan Lachner), Ulrike Kriener (Paula Armbrust), Janna Marangosoff (Angelika), Marie-Charlott Schuler (Marita Strass), Dietmar Bar (Lothar), Edith Volkmann (Frau Lennert)

d, Doris Dorrie; w, Doris Dorrie; ph, Helge Weindler; ed, Jorg Neumann; m, Claus Bantzer

Taking an age-old situation and turning it on its head, this wonderful farce is brimming with unique twists, wit, and style. Julius Armbrust (Heiner Lauterbach) is an advertising executive about to celebrate his 12th year of wedded bliss with wife Paula (Ulrike Kriener). His world suddenly falls apart, however, when he discovers she has been cheating on him with Stefan Lachner (Uwe Ochsenknecht), a young, long-haired bohemian who meanders about town on his bicycle. Julius decides on revenge, not through blackmail or murder but in a manner he knows will bring Paula back to him. After ingratiating himself with Stefan on the sly, Julius begins work on his scheme, transforming Paula's artist-lover into a carbon copy of himself. MEN is a sharp satire, playing off gender roles and male bonding with some real insight. Made by female director Doris Dorrie, the film wisely carries no obtrusive social message that might undermine the wonderful humor. Dorrie does rely rather heavily on slapstick (there is a silly bit involving a gorilla suit), but fortunately her inventive storytelling overcomes the film's lesser elements. Shot in 25 days on a budget of only $360,000, MEN grossed in excess of $15 million in international box-office receipts.

MEN IN BLACK

1997 98m c ★★★½
Amblin Entertainment/MacDonald/Parkes PG-13/
Productions (U.S.)

Tommy Lee Jones (Agent K), Will Smith (Agent J), Linda Fiorentino (Dr. Laurel Weaver), Vincent D'Onofrio (Edgar), Rip Torn (Agent Zed), Tony Shalhoub (Jeebs), Siobhan Fallon (Beatrice), Mike Nussbaum (Gentle Rosenberg), Jon Gries (Van Driver), Sergio Calderon (Jose)

p, Walter F. Parkes, Laurie MacDonald; d, Barry Sonnenfeld; w, Ed Solomon (based on the Malibu Comic "The Men in Black" by Lowell Cunningham); ph, Don Peterman; ed, Jim Miller; m, Danny Elfman; prod d, Bo Welch; art d, Thomas Duffield; fx, Peter M. Chesney, Kyle Ross Collinsworth, Eric Brevig, Industrial Light & Magic, K.N.B. EFX Group, ME*FX, XFX; cos, Mary E. Vogt

GHOSTBUSTERS meets "The X-Files." Slick, directed with all the considerable panache Barry Sonnenfeld (THE ADDAMS FAMILY) can muster, and very clever in a deeply shallow sort of way. This sci-fi action comedy posits that all those paranoid UFO nuts babbling about the government sending mysterious "Men in Black" to cover up evidence of alien visitations are right on the money.

Since the late 1950s, displaced BEMs have been taking on human form and quietly settling into new lives, mostly alongside the rest of the huddled masses yearning to breathe free in New York City. "It's like Casablanca," says MIB Agent K (Tommy Lee Jones), the old alien hand, "but without the Nazis." The shadowy Men in Black license and monitor the intergalactic out-of-towners, and take care of the bad apples from outer space who try to spoil it for everyone. Following his longtime partner's retirement, K teams up with hotshot new kid Agent J (Will Smith) to stop an alien assassin (Vincent D'Onofrio) who's hell-bent on starting an interstellar war that will spell bad times for this island Earth.

Extravagant special effects notwithstanding, this is really a triumph of casting: the aplomb with which Jones plays wry straight man to Smith's street-smart wiseacre is terrifically enjoyable. Ed Solomon's script (based on the *Men in Black* comic-book series) offers deadpan riffs on everything from the 1963 World's Fair, supermarket tabloids, and Dennis Rodman to velcro and microwaves (products of alien technology, don't you know), and Smith and Jones work them for all they're worth.

MENACE II SOCIETY

1993 90m c Crime/Drama ★★★
New Line (U.S.) R/18

Tyrin Turner (Caine), Larenz Tate (O-Dog), Samuel L. Jackson (Tat Lawson), Glenn Plummer (Pernell), Khandi Alexander (Karen Lawson), Jada Pinkett (Ronnie), Vonte Sweet (Sharif), Bill Duke (Detective), Charles S. Dutton (Mr. Butler), June Kyoko-Lu (Grocery Store Woman)

p, Darin Scott; d, Allen Hughes, Albert Hughes; w, Tyger Williams (from a story by Williams and Allen and Albert Hughes); ph, Lisa Rinzler; ed, Christopher Koefoed; m, QD III; prod d, Penny Barrett; fx, Frank Ceglia; cos, Sylvia Vega-Vasquez;

An impressive first feature from the 21-year-old twin brother directing team of Albert and Allen Hughes, MENACE II SOCIETY is a gritty, uncompromising take on life in the Watts section of Los Angeles. MENACE chronicles the short, hopeless life of Caine (Tyrin Turner), a small-time drug dealer with a vague, barely articulated desire to escape his surroundings. The son of a dealer (Samuel L. Jackson) and an addict, both now dead, Tyrin's hope of escape is thwarted by a culture in which macho one-upmanship, combined with a liberal supply of guns, makes life little more than a cycle of revenge killings.

Although MENACE has invited comparisons to BOYZ N THE HOOD, it's not as good a film as John Singleton's breakthrough hit. It's edgier and savvier, and probably achieves a more accurate feel for life in a gun-crazy urban crucible. But it lacks the vision, and the fully defined characters, of BOYZ. Tyrin never becomes more than the sum of his conflicting impulses—he's a composite sample of a social group rather than a fully-fledged individual. The story, too, tries to cover too many bases, finally abandoning its urgent, streetwise edge in favor of B-movie melodrama. Nonetheless, MENACE is a compelling, visceral piece of work. Its most disturbing subplot—in which Tyrin's friend O-Dog (Larenz Tate) shoots a Korean store owner, and then watches the act over and over on the videotape taken from the store's security camera—has a horrifying, unforgettable ring of truth.

MEPHISTO

1981 144m c War/Drama   ★★★★
Mafilm/Objectiv/Manfred Durniok/Analysis (Hungary/West   /15
Germany)

Klaus Maria Brandauer *(Hendrik Hofgen)*, Krystyna Janda *(Barbara Bruckner)*, Ildiko Bansagi *(Nicoletta Von Niebuhr)*, Karin Boyd *(Juliette Martens)*, Rolf Hoppe *(The General)*, Christine Harbort *(Lotte Lindenthal)*, Gyorgy Cserhalmi *(Hans Miklas)*, Christiane Graskoff *(Cesar Von Muck)*, Peter Andorai *(Otto Ulrichs)*, Ildiko Kishonti *(Dora Martin)*

p, Manfred Durniok; d, Istvan Szabo; w, Istvan Szabo, Peter Dobai (based on the novel by Klaus Mann); ph, Lajos Koltai; ed, Zsuzsa Csakany; m, Zdenko Tamassy; art d, Jozsef Romvari

AA Best Foreign Language Film

The winner of 1981's Academy Award for Best Foreign Language Film, MEPHISTO is an inspired update of the Faust legend featuring a tour de force performance by Klaus Maria Brandauer. Critically acclaimed stage actor Hendrik Hofgen (Brandauer) tires of the "entertaining" theatrical forms and attempts something more revolutionary, more Brechtian. Despite his ground-breaking ideas, he does not rise to fame—they cannot even spell his name correctly on posters. Desperate, Hendrik sells his soul—not to the Devil, but to the Nazis—his desire for fame more urgent than his hatred of the oppressor. It is only later, after he is indebted to the Third Reich, that he realizes his mistake. Based on a novel by Klaus Mann (son of Thomas) and exquisitely photographed, MEPHISTO bubbles over with the energy of Brandauer's bravura performance, which quickly attracted the attention of Hollywood. Brandauer and director Istvan Szabo would team again to make COLONEL REDL and HANUSSEN.

MERRY CHRISTMAS, MR. LAWRENCE

1983 124m c Prison/War   ★★★★
Recorded Picture/Cineventure TV/Asashi/Oshima   R/15
(U.K./Japan)

David Bowie *(Celliers)*, Tom Conti *(Col. John Lawrence)*, Ryuichi Sakamoto *(Capt. Yoni)*, Takeshi Kitano *(Sgt. Hara)*, Jack Thompson *(Hicksley-Ellis)*, Johnny Okura *(Kanemoto)*, Alistair Browning *(De-Jong)*, James Malcolm *(Celliers' Brother)*, Christopher Brown *(Celliers at Age 12)*, Yuya Uchida

p, Jeremy Thomas; d, Nagisa Oshima; w, Nagisa Oshima, Paul Mayersberg (based on the novel *The Seed and the Sower* by Laurens Van Der Post); ph, Toichiro Narushima; ed, Tomoyo Oshima; m, Ryuichi Sakamoto; prod d, Shigemasa Toda; art d, Andrew Sanders

Japanese director Nagisa Oshima's first film in English stars Tom Conti as the title character, a British colonel in a Japanese-run POW camp during WWII.

Colonel Lawrence is an astute observer of the cultural codes of his captors and even forms a friendship of sorts with one Japanese officer (Takeshi). He is also witness to the strange dynamics between new camp commandant Yoni (Ryuichi Sakamoto) and a new prisoner, Jack Celliers (David Bowie), with whom Lawrence served in Libya. Yoni is fascinated by Celliers, and plans to make him the prisoners' CO, replacing Hicksley-Ellis (Jack Thompson).

Oshima's ambitious film is not without faults, but these are overshadowed by its emotional power. Many of the characters' actions and impulses are apparently contradictory, but their motivation can generally be found buried in Oshima's complex story. (The Yoni-Celliers relationship, which needs greater development, is a notable exception). Fine performances by Conti, Takeshi (brilliant in his first dramatic role), Sakamoto (a Japanese pop star in his film acting debut who also contributed the memorable score), and Bowie enhance this provocative film.

MERRY WIDOW, THE

1934 99m bw Musical/Comedy   ★★★★★
MGM (U.S.)   /A

Maurice Chevalier *(Prince Danilo)*, Jeanette MacDonald *(Sonia)*, Edward Everett Horton *(Ambassador Popoff)*, Una Merkel *(Queen Dolores)*, George Barbier *(King Achmed)*, Minna Gombell *(Marcelle)*, Ruth Channing *(Lulu)*, Sterling Holloway *(Mischka)*, Henry Armetta *(Turk)*, Barbara Leonard *(Maid)*

p, Irving Thalberg; d, Ernst Lubitsch; w, Samson Raphaelson, Ernest Vajda (based on the operetta "Die Lustique Witwe" by Franz Lehar, Victor Leon, Leo Stein); ph, Oliver T. Marsh; ed, Frances Marsh; m, Franz Lehar; art d, Cedric Gibbons, Frederic Hope; chor, Albertina Rasch; cos, Adrian, Ali Hubert

AA Best Art Direction: Cedric Gibbons, Frederic Hope

One of the greatest of the screen operattas. After a smashing debut in Austria, Franz Lehar's operetta "The Merry Widow" was brought to the US in 1907, became a silent two-reeler in 1912, then, in 1925, Erich von Stroheim directed Mae Murray and John Gilbert in an opulent, controversial version in which Clark Gable appeared as an extra. This version, however, is by far the best of the lot. Jeanette MacDonald, at the peak of her career, is Sonia, an immensely wealthy widow whose spending keeps the small country of Marshovia afloat economically. When she decides to move to Paris to find a suitable husband, the king (George Barbier) dispatches Danilo (Maurice Chevalier), whom he has caught dallying with Queen Dolores (Una Merkel), to the City of Light to woo the widow and bring her home. Failing to recognize Sonia in a cafe, Danilo falls in love with her, then tries to persuade her that his affection is real when she learns the nature of his mission. Unable to convince her, Danilo is called back to Marshovia and put on trial; however, Sonia becomes the star witness for the defense, the two are trapped in a jail cell, and matters end happily and romantically.

The best musical helmed by the great Ernst Lubitsch, THE MERRY WIDOW is frothy, funny, and tuneful from start to finish. MacDonald more than holds her own in the comedy department, snapping off lines with Carole Lombard-like expertise. Star Chevalier had played with newcomer MacDonald at Paramount, and though he reputedly never liked her, their pairing here is near perfection. The dancing, choreographed by Albertina Rasch, is as good as it comes and the huge waltz in the embassy ball ranks among the best large ensemble pieces ever filmed. Enjoy the opening sequence where Marshovia is found on the map or the "There's a limit to every widow" scene. "The Merry Widow" is one of 30 operettas penned by Lehar, and here his music was given new lyrics by Lorenz Hart, Gus Kahn, and an uncredited Richard Rodgers.

METROPOLITAN

1990 98m c Comedy   ★★★★
Westerly Film (U.S.)   /15

Carolyn Farina (*Audrey Rouget*), Edward Clements (*Tom Townsend*), Christopher Eigeman (*Nick Smith*), Taylor Nichols (*Charlie Black*), Allison Rutledge-Parisi (*Jane Clarke*), Dylan Hundley (*Sally Fowler*), Isabel Gillies (*Cynthia McClean*), Bryan Leder (*Fred Neff*), Will Kempe (*Rick Von Sloneker*), Elizabeth Thompson (*Serena Slocum*)

p, Whit Stillman, Brian Greenbaum, Peter Wentworth; d, Whit Stillman; w, Whit Stillman; ph, John Thomas; ed, Chris Tellefsen; m, Mark Suozzo; cos, Mary Jane Fort

AAN Best Original Screenplay: Whit Stillman

Thanks to taut direction, urbane writing and beguiling performances by a number of new actors, the young, privileged Manhattanites at the heart of this film are surprisingly disarming. It's the Christmas season in Manhattan, and our principal characters are swallowed up in the heady round of debutante balls and swank receptions. This determinedly proper crew, the self-dubbed SFRP (Sally Fowler Rat Pack), includes Nick (Christopher Eigeman), its arrogantly dissolute leader; Audrey (Carolyn Farina), a sweet young thing single-handedly trying to uphold the ideals of Jane Austen; Charlie (Taylor Nichols), an uptight stutterer paralyzed by his love for Audrey; Cynthia (Isabel Gillies), a *femme fatale*-in-training; and pudgy, narcoleptic Fred (Bryan Leder). One snowy eve, Tom Townsend (Edward Clements) stumbles into their exalted midst from truly alien territory—the West Side. With Nick as his Mephistophelian guide, Tom gradually becomes caught up in such life-and-death matters as whether to buy his tux from Brooks Brothers or Paul Stuart. Although Audrey is infatuated with Tom, he is still weathering the after-effects of a fatal crush on the notorious heart-breaker Serena Slocum (Elizabeth Thompson). Also threatening the welfare and happiness of the clique is Nick's special enemy, Rick von Sloneker (Will Kempe), a pony-tailed Lothario over whom an alarming number of debs have committed suicide. The film climaxes with a pursuit and rescue of virtue in Southampton and ends on a sweet note of comradeship.

Exhibiting a prodigy's control over his cleverly devised material, Whit Stillman has made an updated drawing-room comedy that takes place largely at deb-party postmortems, with the SFRP endlessly jawing about honor and position. Only occasionally does METROPOLITAN indulge in more earthy pursuits involving Truth games, mescaline and strip poker. Surprisingly, the film is so adroitly written and played that there is nothing claustrophobic about the proceedings—who wants to leave the room with such stimulating talk going on?

METROPOLITAN is a party-night dream vision of New York, with roots in Astaire-Rogers musicals, screwball comedies, and Woody Allen films. But most notably, it brings to mind George Cukor's elegant masterpiece, HOLIDAY. Like Cary Grant's outsider in that film, Tom wins the heart of an aristocratic rebel, and Christopher Eigeman invests his Nick with some of the pixilated omniscience of Lew Ayres' character in the 1938 film. In the process, Nick emerges as the most engaging of METROPOLITAN's characters, with his easy hypocrisy in carnal matters and propensity for spreading scandalous stories about his rivals. "When you are an egotist, none of the harm you do is intentional. . . I'm about to go upstate to a stepmother of untrammeled malevolence," he explains, with aplomb worthy of Clifton Webb or George Sanders. Epigrams like these and visual touches like the silly Lester Lanin hats the boys wear in one scene should give some idea of the real joy of METROPOLITAN. Stillman is a careful observer with an obvious love of language, and his wonderful, fresh cast handles the script with ease, conveying just the right measure of deadpan, *jejune* super-seriousness.

MICHAEL

1996 105m c Fantasy/Comedy/Drama   ★★½
Alphaville Productions/Turner Pictures (U.S.)   PG

John Travolta (*Michael*), William Hurt (*Frank Quinlan*), Andie MacDowell (*Dorothy Winters*), Robert Pastorelli (*Huey Driscoll*), Jean Stapleton (*Pansy Milbank*), Bob Hoskins (*Vartan Malt*), Teri Garr (*Judge Esther Newberg*), Wallace Langham (*Bruce Craddock*), Joey Lauren Adams (*Anita*), Carla Gugino (*Bride*)

p, Sean Daniel, Nora Ephron, James Jacks; d, Nora Ephron; w, Nora Ephron, Delia Ephron, Pete Dexter, Jim Quinlan; ph, John Lindley; ed, Geraldine Peroni; m, Randy Newman; prod d, Dan Davis; art d, James Tocci; fx, David Blitstein; cos, Elizabeth McBride

John Travolta's charms carry MICHAEL, a comedy-fantasy about a naughty angel and the three jaded humans he helps during a Midwestern road trip. This New Age WIZARD OF OZ fable contains some pleasant moments, but also a few awkward ones.

Michael (Travolta) is a lewd, crude, and heaven-sent angel whose miraculous assistance to an Iowa motel owner, Pansy (Jean Stapleton), inspires the elderly woman to write to Frank Quinlan (William Hurt), the lead reporter at a Chicago tabloid. Frank travels to Iowa with angel "expert" Dorothy Winters (Andie MacDowell), and Huey Driscoll (Robert Pastorelli), another reporter. Each believes the angel story is phony—that is, until they arrive at the motel and meet Michael, with his huge wings and slovenly appearance.

While angel movies may go way back to such classics as ANGEL ON MY SHOULDER, IT'S A WONDERFUL LIFE, and THE BISHOP'S WIFE, what makes MICHAEL unique is the appearance of a good angel who's not a saint, and Travolta makes Michael a perfectly raunchy one. But director Nora Ephron seems more interested in funny or touching bits than in making sense of the whole, and that keeps MICHAEL from achieving any great heights. Ephron makes some of the same mistakes that kept her SLEEPLESS IN SEATTLE so uncomfortably calculated: too many cute moments too much music bridging the scenes and montages of a bumpy plot. But how can anyone be unkind to a movie about angels and the power of believing? So accept MICHAEL the movie like Michael the angel, flaws and all.

MICHAEL COLLINS

1996 117m c Biography   ★★★½
Evergreen Entertainment/Geffen Pictures (U.S./U.K.)   R/15

Liam Neeson (*Michael Collins*), Aidan Quinn (*Harry Boland*), Stephen Rea (*Ned Broy*), Alan Rickman (*Eamon De Valera*), Julia Roberts (*Kitty Kiernan*), Charles Dance (*Soames*), Ian Hart (*Joe O'Reilly*), Richard Ingram (*British Officer*), John Kenny (*Patrick Pearse*), Roman McCairbe (*Thomas McDonagh*)

p, Stephen Woolley; d, Neil Jordan; w, Neil Jordan; ph, Chris Menges; ed, J. Patrick Duffner, Tony Lawson; m, Elliot Goldenthal; prod d, Anthony Pratt; art d, Arden Gantly, Jonathan McKinstry, Cliff Robinson; fx, Yves De Bono, Gerry Johnston; cos, Sandy Powell

AAN Best Cinematography: Chris Menges; AAN Best Original Dramatic Score: Elliot Goldenthal

Clearly a labor of love, Irish writer-director Neil Jordan's biography of Michael Collins is an admirable tribute to his country's beloved patriot that sometimes verges on hagiography.

Arrested after the brutally suppressed Easter Uprising of 1916, Irishmen Michael Collins (Liam Neeson), Harry Boland (Aidan Quinn), and Eamon De Valera (Alan Rickman) are released from jail two years later. The three men come into escalating conflict in pursuit of the common goal of an independent Irish republic. While organizing his fellow guerrilla warriors, Collins becomes intrigued with Boland's girlfriend, Kitty Kiernan (Julia Roberts), and they become intimate after "Dev" and Boland go to America to drum up support for the movement. When they return, Dev sends Collins to represent the Irish in negotiations with the British over a peace settlement. Collins returns with a treaty establishing the Irish Free State, a government which is independent but still answerable to the King. Dev is furious over the compromise. Joined by Boland, he vows to fight Collins, sparking a civil war in Ireland.

History can be messy, particularly when it's the history of a man to whom, it can (and will) be argued, the words *terrorist* and *freedom fighter* are equally applicable. Jordan cannily sidesteps the troubling issue by presenting Collins as the hero of what amounts to a briskly paced, beautifully executed espionage thriller—complete with daring escapes, exploding cars, and a beautiful woman (Roberts). Neeson has the charisma needed to portray Collins, and Rickman has rarely been better. But while the film is unflinching in its depiction of the brutality of both the English and the Irish, Jordan pointedly dissociates his hero from any actual ugliness. He may have been the architect, but Collins is never shown with blood on his hands.

MICROCOSMOS
(MICROCOSMOS LE PEUPLE DE L'HERBE)
1996 77m c Documentary   ★★
Galatee Films   (France/Switzerland/Italy)   G/U

Kristin Scott Thomas *(Narrator)*

p, Jacques Perrin, Christophe Barratier, Yvette Mallet; d, Claude Nuridsany, Marie Perennou; w, Claude Nuridsany, Marie Perennou; ph, Claude Nuridsany, Marie Perennou, Hughes Ryffel, Thierry Machado; ed, Marie-Josephe Yoyotte, Florence Ricard; m, Bruno Coulais

The miracle of microphotography brings nature at its buggiest to the big screen. Snail sex. Mosquito Kabuki dancing. Ladybug frolics. Ants at the watering hole. A caterpillar death march. The victory of one small beetle over a twig and a ball of dung. Though they keep voice-over narration to a minimum, French filmmakers Claude Nuridsany and Marie Perennou don't exactly avoid the trap of anthropomorphization: you can't help but imagine those snails are caressing one another when their slimy coitus is enacted to the accompaniment of an operatic aria. But never mind—the spectacle is absolutely enthralling, and even a bit frightening. Buzzing bees recall helicopters, sparkling spider webs look like steel cables, and a pair of battling beetles resemble warring tanks. Take the kids, but tell them those amorous snails are only playing patty-cake.

MIDNIGHT
1939 94m bw Comedy   ★★★★★
Paramount   (U.S.)   /A

Claudette Colbert *(Eve Peabody/"Baroness Czerny")*, Don Ameche *(Tibor Czerny)*, John Barrymore *(George Flammarion)*, Francis Lederer *(Jacques Picot)*, Mary Astor *(Helene Flammarion)*, Elaine Barrie *(Simone)*, Hedda Hopper *(Stephanie)*, Rex O'Malley *(Marcel)*, Monty Woolley *(Judge)*, Armand Kaliz *(Lebon)*

p, Arthur Hornblow Jr.; d, Mitchell Leisen; w, Charles Brackett, Billy Wilder (based on a story by Edwin Justus Mayer, Franz Shulz); ph, Charles Lang; ed, Doane Harrison; m, Frederick Hollander; art d, Hans Dreier, Robert Usher; fx, Farciot Edouart; cos, Irene

An extremely witty, well-paced comedy which plays beautifully today. The story is set in Paris where Colbert is a struggling showgirl. Wealthy Barrymore believes gigolo Lederer is paying too much attention to his wife Astor, so he hires Colbert to keep Lederer occupied. Ameche plays a taxi driver who has fallen in love with Colbert. When the group goes to Barrymore's chateau in Versailles, Colbert is constantly in danger of being exposed, and the plot is further complicated when Ameche arrives, posing as her husband. Colbert was never better; ditto most of the cast. Leisen's direction (along with KITTY his finest effort) and the cynical Brackett and Wilder script complete one of the masterworks of 30s romantic comedy.

MIDNIGHT CLEAR, A
1992 107m c War/Drama   ★★★½
A&M Films/Tamrose Productions/Beacon   R/15
Communications   (U.S.)

Peter Berg *(Bud Miller)*, Kevin Dillon *(Mel Avakian)*, Arye Gross *(Stan Shutzer)*, Ethan Hawke *(Will Knott)*, Gary Sinise *("Mother" Wilkins)*, Frank Whaley *("Father" Mundy)*, John C. McGinley *(Major Griffin)*, Larry Joshua *(Lieutenant Ware)*, Curt Lowens *(German Soldier)*, Rachel Griffin *(Janice)*

p, Bill Borden, Dale Pollock; d, Keith Gordon; w, Keith Gordon (from the novel by William Wharton); ph, Tom Richmond; ed, Donald Brochu; m, Mark Isham; prod d, David Nichols; art d, David Lubin; cos, Barbara Tfank

Like all the best war movies, A MIDNIGHT CLEAR looks at its subject on a human scale, bringing home the tragedy of armed conflict by showing its effects on a small group of individuals. Made with intelligence and wit, the film combines moments of lyrical beauty with a bitterly ironic sense of the absurdity of war. Adapted from William Wharton's autobiographical novel by actor-turned-director Keith Gordon (THE CHOCOLATE WAR), A MIDNIGHT CLEAR follows the

misadventures of an infantry intelligence patrol somewhere in the Ardennes forest in 1944. Selected for reconnaissance work because of their high I.Q. ratings ("I guess if we're intelligent, we must be good at intelligence"), the group includes Will Knott (Ethan Hawke), a newly promoted sergeant who just can't get around to sewing on his stripes; "Mother" Wilkins (Gary Sinise), named for his attempts to enforce neatness among the squad members; "Father" Mundy (Frank Whaley), a former seminarian; and Mel Avakian (Kevin Dillon), the group's most—perhaps only—competent soldier. Shortly before Christmas, the group is sent by their sadistic commanding officer to commandeer an abandoned house and use it as a lookout to report on enemy troop movements. They do encounter some Germans, but of the kind that shatter their preconceptions about the "enemy." These Germans shout goodnight messages to their American counterparts, attack them with snowballs rather than bullets, and end up exchanging gifts with them around a makeshift Christmas tree. When these peaceful overtures end in bloodshed the effect is doubly moving, since we have come to know those on both sides as real people.

Though it hits an occasional false note, A MIDNIGHT CLEAR is well written and sensitively directed. The pristine, snowbound setting gives the film a still, other-worldly quality, and makes for some arresting images, particularly that of a German and an American corpse frozen in a posthumous embrace.

MIDNIGHT COWBOY
1969 119m c Drama   ★★★★
UA   (U.S.)   R/18

Dustin Hoffman *(Enrico "Ratso" Rizzo)*, Jon Voight *(Joe Buck)*, Sylvia Miles *(Cass)*, John McGiver *(Mr. O'Daniel)*, Brenda Vaccaro *(Shirley)*, Barnard Hughes *(Towny)*, Ruth White *(Sally Buck)*, Jennifer Salt *(Annie)*, Gil Rankin *(Woodsy Niles)*, Gary Owens

p, Jerome Hellman; d, John Schlesinger; w, Waldo Salt (based on the novel by James Leo Herlihy); ph, Adam Holender; ed, Hugh A. Robertson; m, John Barry; prod d, John Robert Lloyd; fx, Dick Smith; cos, Ann Roth

AA Best Picture; AAN Best Actor: Dustin Hoffman; *AAN Best Actor:* Jon Voight; *AAN Best Supporting Actress:* Sylvia Miles; *AA Best Director:* John Schlesinger; *AA Best Adapted Screenplay:* Waldo Salt; *AAN Best Editing:* Hugh A. Robertson

MIDNIGHT COWBOY was the only "X"-rated picture ever to win an Oscar as Best Picture. The rating was later changed to an "R" and, by today's standards, might almost be considered a "PG-13." The film presents New York at its seamiest and, though it includes one very funny parody of a bohemian party, it's mostly pretty downbeat stuff.

Joe Buck (Voight), a restless dishwasher in a tiny Texas burg, is convinced that he can use his sexual prowess to satisfy all of the rich New York women who don't know what real loving is like. He bids farewell to his Lone Star pals (including Salt, the screenwriter's daughter) and heads for the Big Apple. Arriving in New York, he picks up and beds down with a blowsy blonde (Miles), but she doesn't have any money. Soon, tubercular street hustler "Ratso" Rizzo (Hoffman) convinces Joe that what he needs is a manager. Although Joe isn't crazy about having to service a closeted gay Christian (McGiver), he and Rizzo soon become as close as George and Lenny in OF MICE AND MEN, talking about how they're going to move to Florida once they've hit it big.

After the success of THE GRADUATE and the disaster of MADIGAN'S MILLIONS, Hoffman was very picky about his roles and refused several parts that were not unlike the young man who was seduced by Mrs. Robinson. He wanted a part that was unique, and certainly found it in the role of Rizzo. Voight had appeared on Broadway in "The Sound of Music" and a couple of forgettable films (HOUR OF THE GUN, FEARLESS FRANK, OUT OF IT) before achieving acclaim with this role. Talented Englishman Schlesinger had an unerring eye for capturing the grimy reality of New York, even if his directorial style is more jittery than is really necessary. In a small role as one of the partygoers, notice songwriter Paul Jabara, who later won an Oscar for "Last Dance" for the forgettable THANK GOD IT'S FRIDAY. Good work by jazz harmonicist Jean "Toots" Theilemans helps the mood immensely. Several songs provided background, and one of them—"Everybody's Talking" (Fred Neil, sung by Harry Nilsson)—was a hit.

MIDNIGHT EXPRESS

1978 120m c Prison/Biography ★★★★
Casablanca (U.K.) R/18

Brad Davis (*Billy Hayes*), Randy Quaid (*Jimmy Booth*), Bo Hopkins (*Tex*), John Hurt (*Max*), Paul Smith (*Hamidou*), Mike Kellin (*Mr. Hayes*), Norbert Weisser (*Erich*), Irene Miracle (*Susan*), Paolo Bonacelli (*Rifki*), Michael Ensign (*Stanley Daniels*)

p, David Puttnam, Alan Marshall; d, Alan Parker; w, Oliver Stone (based on the book by Billy Hayes, William Hoffer); ph, Michael Seresin; ed, Gerry Hambling; m, Giorgio Moroder; prod d, Geoffrey Kirkland; art d, Evan Hercules; cos, Milena Canonero, Bobby Lavender

AAN Best Picture; AAN Best Supporting Actor: John Hurt; AAN Best Director: Alan Parker; AA Best Adapted Screenplay: Oliver Stone; AAN Best Editing: Gerry Hambling; AA Best Score: Giorgio Moroder

Riveting from the word go. The acting is superb, the direction is excellent, and Moroder's score is exhilarating. Based on the true life story of Billy Hayes (who later became an actor), it begins as he (played by Davis) and girlfriend Susan (Miracle) are about to leave for home after a trip to Turkey. On the alert for drug smugglers, officials at the airport catch Hayes with blocks of hashish taped to his body. In a brilliantly tense scene he is herded at gunpoint to a room where he is stripped and interrogated, then taken to a fierce Turkish prison. Here comfort means a night when someone isn't brutally raped or beaten. Hayes meets many of the other inmates, including a few Westerners in there for the same drug raps: American Jimmy (Quaid), Englishman Max (Hurt), and Scandinavian Erich (Weisser), a gay man with whom Hayes has a brief sexual liason. Billy's father (Kellin) attempts to get his son out of jail, but the Turkish legal system is bent on making an example to other potential smugglers. In a sensational courtroom scene Hayes berates his captors with an obscene lambasting of the judges, most of whom don't speak English and have no idea what he's saying. He is sentenced to more years than he thought he'd get and, once remanded to the jail, makes plans to take the "midnight express," i.e. escape.

All the performances are top-notch. Quaid's portrayal of the slightly deranged American is outstanding; Hurt, as the addicted Englishman, is a study in understatement; Weisser is totally believable; and Smith must rank a close second to Hume Cronyn's Captain Munsey in BRUTE FORCE for sheer evil in a prison official. But the standout is Davis, who is given the task of displaying just about every emotion known to man. MIDNIGHT EXPRESS is occasionally a bit too stylish for its own good, something that may have been an indulgence on the part of director Parker. He is nonetheless, a talent to be reckoned with, and both he and editor Hambling both won British Film Academy Awards for their work.

MIDNIGHT RUN

1988 122m c Comedy/Crime ★★★½
City Lights (U.S.) R/15

Robert De Niro (*Jack Walsh*), Charles Grodin (*Jonathan Mardukas*), Yaphet Kotto (*Alonzo Mosely*), John Ashton (*Marvin Dorfler*), Dennis Farina (*Jimmy Serrano*), Joe Pantoliano (*Eddie Moscone*), Richard Foronjy (*Tony Darvo*), Robert Miranda (*Joey*), Jack Kehoe (*Jerry Geisler*), Wendy Phillips (*Gail*)

p, Martin Brest; d, Martin Brest; w, George Gallo; ph, Donald Thorin; ed, Billy Weber, Chris Lebenzon, Michael Tronick; m, Danny Elfman; prod d, Angelo Graham; fx, Roy Arbogast; cos, Gloria Gresham

A thoroughly engaging action film, MIDNIGHT RUN boasts a superb cast that transforms its rather mundane story line into something memorable, funny, and moving. Tough, foul-mouthed bounty hunter Jack Walsh (Robert De Niro) is hired by bail bondsman Eddie Moscone (Joe Pantoliano) to bring back Mafia accountant Jonathan Mardukas (Charles Grodin), who has embezzled $15 million from the Los Angeles mob, given the money to charity, and skipped bail. In an extended cross-country chase, Walsh, flat broke, drags Mardukas on board nearly every modern mode of transportation available in an effort to avoid their pursuers and get back to LA so Walsh can collect his money. As the plot takes a series of complicated twists and turns, the two men's

personalities and relationship develop. BEVERLY HILLS COP director Martin Brest has allowed the actors to improvise, and their resulting interaction is more realistic, funny, and surprising than that of any buddy film released in the last several years. The characters in MIDNIGHT RUN feel real—not only as if they existed before we met them, but also as if they will continue after the movie ends.

MIDSUMMER NIGHT'S DREAM, A

1935 132m bw Fantasy/Comedy ★★★
Warner Bros. (U.S.) /U

James Cagney (*Bottom*), Dick Powell (*Lysander*), Joe E. Brown (*Flute*), Jean Muir (*Helena*), Hugh Herbert (*Snout*), Ian Hunter (*Theseus*), Frank McHugh (*Quince*), Victor Jory (*Oberon*), Olivia de Havilland (*Hermia*), Ross Alexander (*Demetrius*)

p, Max Reinhardt; d, Max Reinhardt, William Dieterle; w, Charles Kenyon, Mary C. McCall Jr. (based on the play by William Shakespeare); ph, Hal Mohr; ed, Ralph Dawson; m, Felix Mendelssohn; art d, Anton Grot; fx, Fred Jackman, Byron Haskin, H.F. Koenekamp; chor, Bronislava Nijinska, Nini Theilade; cos, Max Ree

AAN Best Picture; AA Best Cinematography: Hal Mohr; AA Best Editing: Ralph Dawson

Cigar-chomping Jack Warner does Shakespeare? What fools these mortals be! Theatrical genius Max Reinhardt had successfully staged the play in Europe and felt that A MIDSUMMER NIGHT'S DREAM was ideal for film, because the fairy sequences offered the proper magic for celluloid. Reinhardt, though, had no idea how to shoot this masterpiece, and blurry rushes of several forest scenes suggested that entrusting him with $1.5 million was unwise. So experienced Hollywood man Dieterle and a new cinematographer were added; Hal Mohr's lensing of the film (the only time a write-in ever won an Oscar) turned out to be its one real triumph. Years later, Powell would claim that he never really understood his lines. While such a remark may be after-the-fact cynicism, it does speak to the generally strained acting from a cast of Hollywoodians unschooled in blank verse. Above all else, this play needs inspiration to fly; the acting *must* be daringly effortless, clownishly gossamer, and if there's one thing Cagney and pals are not, it's gossamer. One would think that de Havilland, who had played Hermia onstage, would steal it, but she's too new to films to have refined her technique, and her emoting seems as heavy as everyone else's. Rooney is one of the few who really looks like he's having fun, but he's having *too* much fun and it begins to grate. (Life imitates art: the high-flying youngster broke his leg tobogganing during a production break and had to be wheeled around on an unseen bicycle for much of the shoot.) Cagney, Muir and Brown have their moments, but only Hunter and a few others with classical backgrounds work against the private school class play feel to the film. Typical Warners touch: the delicate original ballet sequences by Bronislava Nijinska and Nini Theilade (the lead ballerina in the film) were cut and re-choreographed in the Busby Berkeley mold.

MIDSUMMER NIGHT'S SEX COMEDY, A

1982 88m c Comedy ★★½
Orion (U.S.) PG/15

Woody Allen (*Andrew*), Mia Farrow (*Ariel*), Jose Ferrer (*Leopold*), Julie Hagerty (*Dulcy*), Tony Roberts (*Maxwell*), Mary Steenburgen (*Adrian*), Adam Redfield (*Student Foxx*), Moishe Rosenfeld (*Mr. Hayes*), Timothy Jenkins (*Mr. Thompson*), Michael Higgins (*Reynolds*)

p, Robert Greenhut; d, Woody Allen; w, Woody Allen; ph, Gordon Willis; ed, Susan E. Morse; m, Felix Mendelssohn; prod d, Mel Bourne; art d, Speed Hopkins; cos, Santo Loquasto

Woody Allen is among a very few people in the history of film who have provided audiences with really intelligent humor. But even Homer nods, and never has Allen more obviously fallen down on the job than in A MIDSUMMER NIGHT'S SEX COMEDY, a trifle that owes much to Ingmar Bergman in style and to Groucho Marx in content. The setting is a weekend houseparty at a farmhouse in upstate New York at the turn of the century. Andrew (Allen) and his wife, Adrian (Mary Steenburgen), are joined by Leopold (Jose Ferrer), a pretentious intellectual, and his promiscuous fiancee, Ariel (Mia Farrow); the party is completed by

Maxwell (Tony Roberts), a womanizing doctor, and his current fling, Dulcy (Julie Hagerty). Andrew is preoccupied with trying to get his sexually unavailable wife to bed him; his frustration is exacerbated by the presence of Ariel, with whom he had a chaste relationship in the past, and who he now realizes to his chagrin was among the most sexually accessible of women. The stage is set for comedy, but the film doesn't have the wallop, the belly-laughs, or the wry comments usually found in Allen's work. While *bons mots* pepper the screenplay, Allen is prevented by the period setting from exercising his wit on contemporary sexual mores, which have always provided one of his richest comic sources. The pastoral setting is beautifully photographed by Gordon Willis.

MIDWINTER'S TALE, A

1996 98m bw Comedy   ★★★
Midwinter Films/Kenneth Branagh Limited   (U.K.)   R/15

Richard Briers (*Henry Wakefield*), Hetta Charnley (*Molly*), Joan Collins (*Margaretta D'Arcy*), Nicholas Farrell (*Tom Newman*), Mark Hadfield (*Vernon Spatch*), Gerard Horan (*Carnforth Greville*), Celia Imrie (*Fadge*), Michael Maloney (*Joe Harper*), Jennifer Saunders (*Nancy Crawford*), Julia Sawalha (*Nina*)

p, David Barron; d, Kenneth Branagh; w, Kenneth Branagh; ph, Roger Lanser; ed, Neil Farrell; m, Jimmy Yuill; prod d, Tim Harvey; cos, Caroline Harris

Kenneth Branagh has written and directed, but chosen not to star in this cozy variation on the old "Brotherhood of Actors/Thespian Happy Families" theme.

Struggling actor Joe Harper (Michael Maloney) is determined to direct and star in a production of *Hamlet*. With the reluctant help of his more commercially minded agent, Margaretta D'Arcy (Joan Collins), he puts together the most motley crew imaginable. Air-headed Nina (Julia Sawalha) is to be his Ophelia; veteran hack Henry (Richard Briers) is Claudius; intense Method monster Tom (Nicholas Farrel) essays a myriad of roles, including Laertes and Fortinbras; drunken, lovable Carnforth (Gerard Horan) is Rosencranz and Guildenstern; and campy Terry du Bois (John Sessions) will do Gertrude . . . in drag. On a shoestring budget, they descend upon a small English village and begin rehearsals in the local church. The characters, of course, bring their own considerable personal agendas with them, and the rehearsal process is marked by all manner of fits, starts, and stormy blow-ups.

Branagh's way with comedic direction could best be described as unsubtle. His love for the profession of acting is, however, always evident as the performers are given every opportunity to shine, some more so than others. Briers makes a funny old curmudgeon, and Collins is cheekily assured as a hustling ten-percenter, yakking numbers on a cell phone while keeping her own figure in tip-top shape on an exercise machine. There's nothing really new or inordinately hilarious in the cartoonish black-and-white proceedings, but Branagh directs at a whiz-bang pace that keeps this likeable comedy bumping along over the script's many weak spots, clunky punchlines, and cliches.

MIGHTY APHRODITE

1995 95m c Comedy   ★★★
Sweetland Films   (U.S.)   R/15

Woody Allen (*Lenny*), Helena Bonham Carter (*Amanda*), F. Murray Abraham (*Leader*), Claire Bloom (*Amanda's Mother*), Olympia Dukakis (*Jocasta*), Michael Rapaport (*Kevin*), Mira Sorvino (*Linda Ash*), David Ogden Stiers (*Laius*), Jack Warden (*Tiresias*), Peter Weller (*Jerry Bender*)

p, Robert Greenhut; d, Woody Allen; w, Woody Allen; ph, Carlo Di Palma; ed, Susan E. Morse; m, Dick Hyman; prod d, Santo Loquasto; art d, Tom Warren; chor, Graciela Daniele; cos, Jeffrey Kurland

AA Best Supporting Actress: Mira Sorvino; *AAN Best Original Screenplay:* Woody Allen

In MIGHTY APHRODITE, a nerd's revenge fantasy — yet again — from putative genius Woody Allen, our hero pits his romantic sensibilities against feckless women and crass consumerism. Yet again. And lest we forget how *serious* he is deep down, he gives us a Greek chorus.

We know they're The Chorus because they look like tag-sale statuary (if you can overlook the distinctly post-Classical schnozzes sported by F. Murray Abraham and Olympia Dukakis), and they mill around in a boulder-strewn sandpit spouting strophes — or what might pass for strophes in the Borscht Belt. Meanwhile, pity poor Lenny (Allen). He's not a writer but a *sports*writer. And a scrawny one who just happens to be followed around by this Greek chorus that comments on his disagreeable life. Tragedy and humiliation lurk down every alley. His marriage is coming apart. But when his wife, Amanda (Helena Bonham Caretr), isn't preoccupied with the blandishments of suave art-meister Jerry (Peter Weller), she demands a baby. A baby! Lenny doesn't want a baby. They're both too busy to deal with a pregnancy. And when Amanda suggests adoption, Lenny's offended. Nevertheless, he relents, and years later goes in search of the baby's mother, whom he finds in the person of hooker and occasional porno star Linda Ash, aka Judy Cum, a latter-day Irma La Douce played by Mira Sorvino.

The good news is that MIGHTY APHRODITE comes alive when Sorvino is onscreen. Her Linda is the largest cute woman on Earth, a six-foot Minnie Mouse with a closetful of wigs and high heels who voices her comic suspicions about Lenny in a voice that sounds like it was dubbed by Kukla. The bad news? As Woody/Lenny dallies with this conspicuously younger woman, making his case for dumb, beautiful, and innocent, it's impossible not to remember details of Allen's private life that we'd all rather forget. Though he's done two films since the Mia/Soon Yi fiasco, only now has the production cycle caught up with Woody's world. Inevitably, this movie plays like an invitation to hear the story, at long last, *his* way.

MIKEY AND NICKY

1976 119m c Drama   ★★½
Paramount   (U.S.)   R/15

Peter Falk (*Mikey*), John Cassavetes (*Nicky*), Ned Beatty (*Kinney*), Rose Arrick (*Annie*), Carol Grace (*Nell*), William Hickey (*Sid Fine*), Sanford Meisner (*Dave Resnick*), Joyce Van Patten (*Jan*), M. Emmet Walsh (*Bus Driver*), Sy Travers (*Hotel Clerk*)

p, Michael Hausman; d, Elaine May; w, Elaine May; ph, Victor J. Kemper; ed, John Carter, Sheldon Kahn; m, Johann Strauss; prod d, Paul Sylbert

There is much to enjoy in this movie, but just as much to yawn over. One has the feeling that this was a play that was never produced on stage but went directly to the screen from the typewriter. Since so much of it is dialogue with very little cinematic action, it just feels stagebound. Cassavetes and Falk are two small-time thugs who have been friends since their youth. Cassavetes is going to be killed by Beatty, the unlikely hit man in the service of boss Meisner (who was just about everyone's acting coach in New York at one time). Cassavetes gets in touch with Falk after trying to get help from his estranged wife, Van Patten, and his current amour, Grace. Falk is apparently going to help Cassavetes get away from the potential assassin, though we are often struck by Falk's words and actions and not sure if he is friend or foe. Some very touching scenes punctuate the camaraderie, but the film is essentially far too long, self-indulgent, and talky to elicit much emotional response. It's a character study that would be at home in an East Village theater. It's hard to say where the script ends and the improvisation begins, as in so many of Cassavetes' films. The executive producer was veteran TV executive Bud Austin, who had run Paramount Television before moving into feature production. Very foul language and some painful sequences make this hardly fit for anyone with a priggish attitude. This was the third film directed by May and the most experimental. Her first two were A NEW LEAF (which she also wrote and costarred in) and THE HEARTBREAK KID, with a script by Neil Simon and some terrific performances by Jeannie Berlin, Charles Grodin, and Cybill Shepherd.

MILDRED PIERCE

1945 111m bw Drama ★★★★★
Warner Bros. (U.S.) /A

Joan Crawford *(Mildred Pierce)*, Jack Carson *(Wally Fay)*, Zachary Scott *(Monte Beragon)*, Eve Arden *(Ida)*, Ann Blyth *(Veda Pierce)*, Bruce Bennett *(Bert Pierce)*, George Tobias *(Mr. Chris)*, Lee Patrick *(Maggie Binderhof)*, Moroni Olsen *(Inspector Peterson)*, Jo Ann Marlowe *(Kay Pierce)*

p, Jerry Wald; d, Michael Curtiz; w, Ranald MacDougall (based on the novel by James M. Cain); ph, Ernest Haller; ed, David Weisbart; m, Max Steiner; art d, Anton Grot; fx, Willard Van Enger; cos, Milo Anderson

AAN Best Picture; AA Best Actress: Joan Crawford; *AAN Best Supporting Actress:* Eve Arden; *AAN Best Supporting Actress:* Ann Blyth; *AAN Best Screenplay:* Ranald MacDougall; *AAN Best Cinematography:* Ernest Haller

Impeccable, bleak gloss, with the supreme Crawford engineering the greatest comeback of them all. MILDRED PIERCE is one of the finest noir soap operas ever, with the queen of pathos shouldering the storm alone; her efforts snagged the golden statuette as 1945's Best Actress. To begin with, MILDRED was leftovers: Barbara Stanwyck, Bette Davis and Ann Sheridan turned down the role, but producer Wald gambled on MGM-bounced Crawford, and the film swept the box offices, returning $5 million to Warners and putting Crawford back on top as the hottest star in town.

Mildred's marriage to Bert (Bennett) has gone sour. While she dotes on their two daughters, chiefly the older Veda (Blyth), Bert finds pleasant company with Mrs. Biederhof (Patrick). Leaving Bert, Mildred finds work as a waitress to misguidedly keep the vicious, snobbish Veda in fancy duds. Ever ambitious, Mildred slaves her way up to a chain of successful restaurants and takes up with classy playboy Monte Beragon (Scott). She mistakenly weds him, and he goes through her fortune like a plague of locusts. The crushing blow comes when Mildred learns that Monte has been having an affair with Veda behind her back.

Everything about MILDRED PIERCE is first-rate, from stellar production values to Curtiz's marvelously paced direction, which refuses to allow sentiment to rule the story. The MacDougall script, adapted from Cain's terse novel, is adult and literate, with plenty of sharp dialogue. The Curtiz string-pulling is greatly aided by Grot's imposing sets, Haller's moody photography and Steiner's haunting score. Bravely cresting the waves of disaster is a mature Crawford in a real tour de force, defying the industry to write her off as washed up. She's matched every slap of the way by Blyth, here giving the performance of *her* career.

The support in MILDRED is, without exception, expertly handled. Scott is an exceptionally attractive snake and Arden turned in a definitive job as Crawford's wisecracking pal. Two peak scenes among aficionados of Saint Joan: Veda smacks Mildred; Mildred calls the police. Unforgettable.

MILKY WAY, THE
(LA VIA LATTEA)

1969 105m c Religious ★★★½
Greenwich/Fraia (France/Italy) PG/A

Paul Frankeur *(Pierre)*, Laurent Terzieff *(Jean)*, Alain Cuny *(Man with Cape)*, Edith Scob *(Virgin Mary)*, Bernard Verley *(Jesus)*, Francois Maistre *(French Priest)*, Claude Cerval *(Brigadier)*, Muni *(Mother Superior)*, Julien Bertheau *(Maitre d'Hotel)*, Ellen Bahl *(Mme. Garnier)*

p, Serge Silberman; d, Luis Bunuel; w, Luis Bunuel, Jean-Claude Carriere; ph, Christian Matras; ed, Louisette Hautecoeur; m, Luis Bunuel; art d, Pierre Guffroy; cos, Jacqueline Guyot, Francoise Tournafond

The most overtly religious film in Luis Bunuel's *oeuvre*, THE MILKY WAY is an allegorical journey through the history of Catholicism that follows a pair of travelers—the somewhat pious Pierre (Paul Frankeur) and the younger, more skeptical Jean (Laurent Terzieff)—as they undertake a pilgrimage across Spain to the tomb of Saint James. En route, they meet any number of religious figures, including a caped, God-like figure (Alain Cuny) with a midget, the Virgin Mary (Edith Scob), Jesus (Bernard Verley), a bishop (Jean-Claude Carriere, Bunuel's screenwriting collaborator), a sadistic Marquis (Michel Piccoli), a prostitute (Delphine Seyrig), and even the Devil (Pierre Clementi). This comical film will make any viewer question his beliefs—from religious fanatic to rabid atheist. While it may seem strange that Bunuel, a lifetime surrealist and professed atheist, would produce such a work, the filmmaker remarked in his autobiography, *My Last Sigh*, that THE MILKY WAY "evokes the search for truth, as well as the necessity of abandoning it as soon as you've found it." If that doesn't shed some light on Bunuel's intent, then perhaps his most famously ambiguous statement will: "Thank God I'm an atheist."

MILLER'S CROSSING

1990 115m c Crime ★★★½
Circle Films/Ted and Jim Pedas-Ben Berenholtz-Bill R/18
Durkin (U.S.)

Gabriel Byrne *(Tom Reagan)*, Marcia Gay Harden *(Verna)*, John Turturro *(Bernie Bernbaum)*, Jon Polito *(Johnny Caspar)*, J.E. Freeman *(Eddie Dane)*, Albert Finney *(Leo)*, Mike Starr *(Frankie)*, Al Mancini *(Tic-Tac)*, Richard Woods *(Mayor Dale Levander)*, Thomas Toner *(O'Doole)*

p, Ethan Coen; d, Joel Coen; w, Joel Coen, Ethan Coen; ph, Barry Sonnenfeld; ed, Michael R. Miller; m, Carter Burwell; prod d, Dennis Gassner; art d, Leslie McDonald; fx, Image Engineering, Peter Chesney; cos, Richard Hornung

Guns, booze, fast women—timeworn gangster film cliches given a fresh twist in this, the third offering from Joel and Ethan Coen. A gang war is brewing in the anonymous town run by Leo (Finney), a tough but sentimental Irishman, and his acerbic right-hand man, Tom Reagan (Byrne). The Italians are the new kids on the block, and they're sensitive about it. Johnny Caspar (Polito) is particularly thin-skinned, and he's mad as hell because small-time chiseler Bernie Bernbaum (Turturro) is cutting in on his gambling action. Caspar wants Bernie murdered, but Leo won't hear of it; he's promised Bernie's tough-as-nails sister, Verna (Harden), that he'll look out for her brother. Verna is the love of Leo's life, but she's also sleeping with Tom. Meanwhile, Tom, a drinker and gambler, is deeply in debt to his bookie, who's putting the screws to him. When Leo and Tom have a falling out over Verna, Tom offers his services to Caspar. Forced to prove his loyalty by killing Bernie, Tom fakes the murder, only to have Bernie turn around and attempt to blackmail him.

Surprisingly, the Coens resisted the Hollywood dictum that the protagonist must be sympathetic. Byrne's Tom is a man of principles—smart, loyal and willing to gratify his own ambitions through Leo. But he's also a drunk and a gambler. What's more, he sleeps with Verna and murders her brother. Tom has his reasons, and they're quite reasonable, but what's remarkable is that the Coens trust their audience to understand him.

While BLOOD SIMPLE paid homage to film noir, and RAISING ARIZONA put a wacky, post-modernist spin on the screwball comedy, MILLER'S CROSSING attempts to both sum up, and revivify, the gangster genre. It takes place in an artificial world constructed largely from the mythology of other movies, and, though it's both seamless and stylish, some find it a little too self-conscious for its own good.

MILLION, THE
(LE MILLION)

1931 83m bw Comedy ★★★★★
Tobis (France)

Annabella *(Beatrice)*, Rene Lefevre *(Michel)*, Paul Olivier *("Father Tulipe" Crochard, a Gangster)*, Louis Allibert *(Prosper)*, Constantin Stroesco *(Sopranelli)*, Odette Talazac *(La Chanteuse)*, Vanda Greville *(Vanda)*, Raymond Cordy *(Taxi Driver)*

d, Rene Clair; w, Rene Clair (based on a musical play by Georges Berr, M. Guillemaud); ph, Georges Perinal, Georges Raulet; m, Armand Bernard, Philippe Pares, Georges Van Parys; art d, Lazare Meerson

Perhaps Rene Clair's most appealing film, and an extremely inventive one in the bargain. One of the string of superb films this fine French director made in the 1920s and 1930s, this is a nonstop comic chase through a studio set of Paris (designed by Clair's collaborator Lazare Meerson) to find a winning lottery ticket left in the pocket of a discarded jacket. Generally considered Clair's masterpiece (though A NOUS LA LIBERTE also has its supporters), the film is a sustained comic delight. As in the previous UNDER THE ROOFS OF PARIS and his subsequent A NOUS LA LIBERTE, Clair creates a wholly original world of song and sound that completely defies realism. He also manages quite a few satiric touches which belie his background in the Surrealist and Dada movements of the 1920s. Although such uses of sound effects as the noise of a football game dubbed in over one particularly frantic chase have since been repeated, they still enchant today. The camerawork too, is amazingly supple for a period in which bulky sound recording devices turned so many films into stagy bores, and the story simply floats along as a result. Annabella and Rene Lefevre are immensely winning in the leading roles, and are backed by a solid supporting cast. One of the truly great early sound films, it was an international success with both critics and public.

MIN AND BILL

1930 66m bw Drama/Comedy ★★★★
MGM (U.S.)

Marie Dressler *(Min Divot)*, Wallace Beery *(Bill)*, Dorothy Jordan *(Nancy Smith)*, Marjorie Rambeau *(Bella Pringle)*, Donald Dillaway *(Dick Cameron)*, DeWitt Jennings *(Groot)*, Russell Hopton *(Alec Johnson)*, Frank McGlynn Sr. *(Mr. Southard)*, Gretta Gould *(Mrs. Southard)*, Jack Pennick *(Merchant Seaman)*

d, George Hill; w, Frances Marion, Marion Jackson (based on the novel *Dark Star* by Lorna Moon); ph, Harold Wenstrom; ed, Basil Wrangell; art d, Cedric Gibbons; cos, Rene Hubert

AA Best Actress: Marie Dressler

One of the most unlikely romantic duos ever to stroll across a screen was the pairing of 62-year-old bulldog Marie Dressler and big-bellied, 55-year-old Wallace Beery. Yet they made such a lovable couple in MIN AND BILL that they were teamed again in TUGBOAT ANNIE in 1933. Although MIN AND BILL is a heartfelt drama, most viewers recall its hilarious comedy sequences and the noisy relationship between Min (Dressler) and Bill (Beery). Min is the rough-and-tumble owner of a cheap waterfront hotel on the California coast; Bill is the local fisherman who is the object of her affections when she isn't doting on Nancy (Jordan), a sweet young girl whose mother deserted her several years previously. Nevertheless truant officers want Nancy living in a better environment and attending school regularly. Furthermore, local prohibition officers have been observing the cafe and appear ready to close it up. In a tearful scene, Nancy reluctantly leaves Min to live with the school's principal (McGlynn) and his wife (Gould). To make matters worse, Nancy's drunken, slatternly mother (Rambeau) appears on the scene, threatening Nancy's chance at happiness with the wealthy Dick Cameron Dillaway, in his film debut). Min to the rescue.

A legendary star of the stage and vaudeville, Dressler watched her silent screen stardom of the 1910s wane until she made a triumphant return in ANNA CHRISTIE earlier in 1930. As a result of her immense popular success in MIN AND BILL and half a dozen follow-up vehicles, she was to spend her last years as MGM's (indeed, the industry's) biggest star before her death from cancer in 1934. She'd still make any list of the ten most huggable stars in film history.

MINISTRY OF FEAR

1945 84m bw Mystery/Spy ★★★★
Paramount (U.S.)

Ray Milland *(Stephen Neale)*, Marjorie Reynolds *(Carla Hilfe)*, Carl Esmond *(Willi Hilfe)*, Hillary Brooke *(Mrs. Bellane)*, Percy Waram *(Inspector Prentice)*, Dan Duryea *(Cost/Travers)*, Alan Napier *(Dr. Forrester)*, Erskine Sanford *(Mr. Rennit)*, Thomas Louden *(Mr. Newland)*, Aminta Dyne *(1st Mrs. Bellaire)*

p, Seton I. Miller; d, Fritz Lang; w, Seton I. Miller (based on the novel by Graham Greene); ph, Henry Sharp; ed, Archie Marshek; m, Victor Young; art d, Hans Dreier, Hal Pereira

Uncertainty and fear of the unknown are the hallmarks of this classic film noir by master director Lang, which, until the last revelation, is guaranteed to puzzle and chill the viewer. The suspense in this thriller is terrific as Lang, ever the careful craftsman, shows only what is necessary to the confusing plot. The low-key lighting and Sharp's moody cinematography are perfectly suited to the film's elaborate, Kafkaesque approach wherein shadow, silence and normally pedestrian movements, taken out of context, take on an air of evil and doom. Milland gives a spellbinding performance as a man who, ostensibly having murdered his wife, is released from an insane asylum after two years. She was ill, and he brought poison home to perform euthanasia but could not bring himself to go through with it; while his back was turned she took the fatal dose and he was convicted nevertheless. The terrors of the asylum, though, are nothing compared to the Nazi spies of the wartime England into which Milland steps. Lang, screenwriter-producer Seton Miller and Graham Greene (author of the source novel) have in store for Milland (and us) a succession of sinister seances, sinister suits, sinister scissors, sinister blind men and, best of all, a sinister cake. Eat at your own delicious risk.

MINNIE AND MOSKOWITZ

1971 114m c Drama/Comedy ★★★½
Universal (U.S.) PG/

Gena Rowlands *(Minnie Moore)*, Seymour Cassel *(Seymour Moskowitz)*, Val Avery *(Zelmo Swift)*, Tom Carey *(Morgan Morgan)*, Katherine Cassavetes *(Sheba Moskowitz)*, Elizabeth Deering *(Girl)*, Elsie Ames *(Florence)*, Lady Rowlands *(Georgia Moore)*, Holly Near *(Irish)*, Judith Roberts *(Wife)*

p, Al Ruban; d, John Cassavetes; w, John Cassavetes; ph, Arthur J. Ornitz, Alric Edens, Michael D. Margulies; ed, Robert Heffernan, Frederic Knudtson; cos, Helen Colvig

Having provided a starring vehicle for himself and colleagues Peter Falk and Ben Gazzara in 1970's HUSBANDS, director John Cassavetes showcased both his talented wife, Gena Rowlands, and frequent collaborator Seymour Cassel in MINNIE AND MOSKOWITZ the following year.

Minnie Moore (Rowlands) is a lonely former prom queen who's about to turn 40. She's been having an unsatisfactory affair with Jim (John Cassavetes), a married man, and spends the rest of her spare time time with Florence (Elsie Ames), her best friend and movie-going companion. Jim is cruel to Minnie, but she puts up with it until Jim's wife threatens suicide and he's forced to end the affair. They meet for a last time at the museum where Minnie works; he's brought his two kids with him, at the request of his wife, to corroborate the cessation of the affair.

Minnie, lonely and desperate for male companionship, accepts a blind date with Zelmo Swift (Val Avery), a noisy boor who never once notices Minnie's delicate condition. They have lunch at a restaurant, and Zelmo proposes marriage but Minnie, realizing that he's mentally unbalanced, demurs and tries to get away. In the parking lot Zelmo begins to harass Minnie, but this is witnessed by Seymour Moskowitz (Cassel), a thirtyish, aging hippy and parking lot attendant, who comes to her rescue. He gets Zelmo out of the picture, then gets Minnie into his pickup truck and rides away with her. In less than a minute, Moskowitz decides that he is madly in love with Minnie. She leaps out of the pickup truck, but Moskowitz follows her until she agrees to go on a date.

For 35 years, John Cassavetes held a unique position in American film, maintaining dual careers as a highly regarded actor in mainstream features and as a director of independent films which themselves explored the art of acting. With MINNIE AND MOSKOWITZ, Cassavetes took a break from the decidedly somber mood of FACES and HUSBANDS. Unfortunately, although the scenes of Rowlands and Cassel wandering from hot dog stand to hot dog stand are touching and funny, the film ultimately suffers from narrative aimlessness.

MIRACLE IN MILAN
(MIRACOLO A MILANO)
1951 100m bw Fantasy   ★★★★
ENIC   (Italy)

Branduani Gianni (*Little Toto at Age 11*), Francesco Golisano (*Good Toto*), Paolo Stoppa (*Bad Rappi*), Emma Gramatica (*Old Lolatta*), Guglielmo Barnabo (*Mobbi, the Rich Man*), Brunella Bovo (*Little Edvige*), Anna Carena (*Signora Marta Altezzosa*), Alba Arnova (*The Statue*), Flora Cambi (*Unhappy Sweetheart*), Virgilio Riento (*Sergeant*)

p, Vittorio De Sica; d, Vittorio De Sica; w, Cesare Zavattini, Vittorio De Sica, Suso Cecchi D'Amico, Mario Chiari, Adolfo Franci (based on the story "Toto Il Buono" by Cesare Zavattini); ph, Aldo Graziati; ed, Eraldo Da Roma; m, Alessandro Cicognini; art d, Guido Fiorini; fx, Ned Mann

The writing-directing team of Cesare Zavattini and Vittorio De Sica produced this picture shortly after they received international acclaim for THE BICYCLE THIEF. Though not as popular as that masterwork, MIRACLE IN MILAN is an equally touching look into human nature that concentrates on the plight of the poor in post-WWII Italy. The story is essentially a fairy tale, packed with a strong moral implications. The Good Toto (Francesco Golisano), a young orphan, finds refuge in a colony of beggars and helps to organize them, generating happiness among the otherwise distressed members of the group. When a wealthy landowner decides to kick the beggars off his land, Toto is given a magic dove by a fairy. Not only are the landowner's attempts thwarted, but the magical powers of the dove also allow Toto to grant wishes to the beggars. Unable to deny them anything, he grants their greedy requests, until eventually the dove is stolen. As in other neo-realist films, the performers in MIRACLE IN MILAN are a combination of professional actors and actual denizens of the street, and all the players give realistic and humane portrayals. De Sica handles his fantastic material subtly and with simplicity, yielding an original mix of sharp satire and poetic fable that extended the limits of the neo-realist style.

MIRACLE OF MORGAN'S CREEK, THE
1944 99m bw Comedy   ★★★★★
Paramount   (U.S.)   /A

Eddie Bracken (*Norval Jones*), Betty Hutton (*Trudy Kockenlocker*), Diana Lynn (*Emmy Kockenlocker*), William Demarest (*Officer Kockenlocker*), Brian Donlevy (*Governor McGinty*), Akim Tamiroff (*The Boss*), Porter Hall (*Justice of the Peace*), Emory Parnell (*Mr. Tuerck*), Alan Bridge (*Mr. Johnson*), Julius Tannen (*Mr. Rafferty*)

p, Preston Sturges; d, Preston Sturges; w, Preston Sturges; ph, John Seitz; ed, Stuart Gilmore; m, Leo Shuken, Charles Bradshaw; art d, Hans Dreier, Ernst Fegte; cos, Edith Head

AAN Best Original Screenplay: Preston Sturges

Miraculously mad masterpiece. The marvel of THE MIRACLE OF MORGAN'S CREEK is how the film ever got made in the first place. This onslaught against American morals in small towns, against the wartime romances of servicemen, against just about everything that the country held sacred during WWII was reckless, exaggerated, and very funny. Sturges was at his irreverent best with his screenplay and direction of this most unlikely story. Hutton is Trudy Kockenlocker, a man-crazy blonde who lives with her bitchy sister Emmy (Lynn) and her policeman father (Demarest). She gets drunk during one wild, passionate night with a soldier, whom she thinks she may have married, and becomes pregnant. The soldier, who she recalls is named something like "Ratsky-Watsky," vanishes, and since being pregnant in a small town without being married is the worst thing that can happen in a girl's life, Trudy's sometime bank clerk boyfriend Norval (Bracken) is tapped to be the father of her child. In one mix-up after another, Novral winds up being sought by authorities for impersonating a soldier, forgery, corrupting the morals of a minor, kidnapping and robbery. It looks bad for the young couple, and the only thing that can save them is a miracle. It does.

Every role is handled with deftness, and Sturges even gets in a few holdovers from an earlier success, THE GREAT McGINTY, by having Brian Donlevy and Akim Tamiroff stop by for a few well-chosen words.

The idea of having squeaky-clean Hutton shown as a (shudder) girl with loose morals was a sensation that somehow eluded the censor's scissors. Some say that the plot managed to escape snipping because the picture was so funny that no one could take it seriously, but the truth is that this movie kept a tight grip on reality and that's what made it so hilarious. The manic Hutton, always an acquired taste, here gets a hilarious part that requires the frantic energy of a whirling dervish on speed. She was never better, and the same goes for the nervous Bracken, the grouchy Demarest and the wisecracking Lynn. Sturges, having begun his uninterrupted string of comic masterpieces in 1940 with MCGINTY, reached a peak in satirical zaniness with this one. Remade (sort of) in 1958 as ROCK-A-BYE BABY.

MIRACLE ON 34TH STREET
1947 96m bw Fantasy   ★★★½
Fox   (U.S.)   /U

Maureen O'Hara (*Doris Walker*), John Payne (*Fred Gailey*), Edmund Gwenn (*Kris Kringle*), Gene Lockhart (*Judge Henry X. Harper*), Natalie Wood (*Susan Walker*), Porter Hall (*Mr. Sawyer*), William Frawley (*Charles Halloran*), Jerome Cowan (*Thomas Mara*), Philip Tonge (*Mr. Shellhammer*), James Seay (*Dr. Pierce*)

p, William Perlberg; d, George Seaton; w, George Seaton (based on a story by Valentine Davies); ph, Charles Clarke, Lloyd Ahern; ed, Robert Simpson; m, Cyril J. Mockridge; art d, Richard Day, Richard Irvine; fx, Fred Sersen

AAN Best Picture; AA Best Supporting Actor: Edmund Gwenn; *AA Best Original Story:* Valentine Davies; *AA Best Screenplay:* George Seaton

A touch labored but lovable. THE MIRACLE ON 34TH STREET opens during Manhattan's Christmas Parade as Macy's executive Doris Walker (Maureen O'Hara) finds the Santa Claus for the store float so drunk he can't stand up. Chiding Doris for employing such a derelict is a kindly, white-bearded man who, when she asks his name, tells her it's "Kris Kringle." Ignoring this, she pleads with him to replace the drunk, and he proves such a crowd-pleaser that she hires him as Macy's resident Santa for the holiday rush. This sets in motion a series of events in which Kris touches the lives of many, teaching them a lot about faith and the true meaning of Christmas. Among those touched are Doris, her sophisticated little girl, Susan (Natalie Wood), who thinks the very idea of Santa Claus is ridiculous, Doris's suitor Fred Gailey (John Payne), and dozens of Macy's customers who are pleasantly surprised when Kris directs them to competitors to get the gifts they seek. Unfortunately all are not smitten with this kindly man, particularly the store's amateur psychologist whose contention that Kris is unbalanced leads to a trial in which the court must decide the weighty matter of whether or not there is a Santa Claus. Gwenn won an Oscar for his role, and for many, his charming, endearing performance has been identified with the spirit of the Christmas season ever since the completion of this sentimental production. Wood is wonderful in MIRACLE; it's interesting to ponder what happened along the way to transform her into a usually synthetic actress.

MIRACLE WOMAN, THE
1931 90m bw Religious   ★★★½
Columbia   (U.S.)

Barbara Stanwyck (*Florence "Faith" Fallon*), David Manners (*John Carson*), Sam Hardy (*Bob Hornsby*), Beryl Mercer (*Mrs. Higgins*), Russell Hopton (*Sam Welford*), Charles Middleton (*Simpson*), Eddie Boland (*Collins*), Thelma Hill (*Gussie*), Aileen Carlyle (*Violet*), Al Stewart (*Brown*)

p, Harry Cohn; d, Frank Capra; w, Dorothy Howell, Jo Swerling (based on the play "Bless You Sister" by John Meehan, Robert Riskin); ph, Joseph Walker; ed, Maurice Wright; art d, Max Parker

The subject of phony evangelists is a tricky one, entailing the risk of offending believers. Barbara Stanwyck is convincing as the daughter of a pastor who has just been discharged from his parish and, as a result, has died of a broken heart. Stanwyck goes in front of the congregation and delivers a stinging denunciation of their hypocrisy. Sam Hardy, a two-bit promoter and con man, realizing that Stanwyck is mighty handy with her mouth, talks her into becoming an evangelist. Soon she is one of the most important pulpit pounders in the land, and, caught up in the furor of phony cripples "healed" and testifying to the pigeons, Stanwyck is too successful to stop. David Manners, a blind ex-pilot who is about to kill himself by leaping out a window, hears Stanwyck preaching on the radio and decides that she might be able to cure him. He goes to the tent and volunteers to step inside a lion's cage. His faith brings him closer to Stanwyck, and she is soon in love with him. Russell Hopton, the press agent for the group, wants a larger piece of the spoils, but Hardy won't hear of it and knocks Hopton off. Helped by his love for Stanwyck, Manners overcomes his shyness enough to declare himself through his ventriloquist's dummy. When Hardy sees that Manners and Stanwyck are getting close, he arranges a trip to the Holy Land to get her away from the blind lad. Stanwyck is beginning to understand that her faith healing is a lot of nonsense and that the people whom she has really healed just needed something—anything—to believe in. All of her ravings don't help Manners recover his sight. (To the credit of the authors and director, there is no miracle recovery for the blind man.) Hardy sets the tent ablaze as Stanwyck is about to confess to all that she is a sham. Later Stanwyck, who has become a member of the Salvation Army, receives a wire from Manners, opening the possibility that the two young people will get together. Riskin, who became Frank Capra's favorite screenwriter, went on to write such classics as IT HAPPENED ONE NIGHT, MR. DEEDS GOES TO TOWN, LOST HORIZON, YOU CAN'T TAKE IT WITH YOU and and MEET JOHN DOE. THE MIRACLE WOMAN was an expensive film for its day, and every penny shows on the screen. There's hardly a wasted word or frame of film in the movie. It is a fine film, although it would have been even better had Capra and the writers had the freedom to attack their subject with sabers instead of pins.

MIRACLE WORKER, THE

1962   106m   bw   Biography   ★★★★½
Playfilms   (U.S.)   /X

Anne Bancroft (Annie Sullivan), Patty Duke (Helen Keller), Victor Jory (Capt. Keller), Inga Swenson (Kate Keller), Andrew Prine (James Keller), Kathleen Comegys (Aunt Ev), Beah Richards (Viney), Jack Hollander (Mr. Anagnos), Peggy Burke (Helen at Age 7), Mindy Sherwood (Helen at Age 5)

p, Fred Coe; d, Arthur Penn; w, William Gibson (based on the play by William Gibson and the book The Story of My Life by Helen Keller); ph, Ernesto Caparros; ed, Aram Avakian; m, Laurence Rosenthal; art d, George Jenkins, Mel Bourne; cos, Ruth Morley

AA Best Actress: Anne Bancroft; AA Best Supporting Actress: Patty Duke; AAN Best Director: Arthur Penn; AAN Best Adapted Screenplay: William Gibson; AAN Best Costume Design: Ruth Morley

Excellent work, with Arthur Penn repeating his Broadway triumph directing Duke and Bancroft, the two stage leads. This remarkable story of Helen Keller began as then became a William Gibson play that premiered on Broadway in 1959. When the time came to make the film, Penn, Gibson, and producer Coe insisted that Bancroft and Duke be retained, with resulting Oscars for both stars. Duke had riveted Broadway audiences with the role as Keller, and, at age 16, became the youngest recipient of the Best Supporting Actress Oscar. (In 1973, Tatum O'Neal eclipsed her by winning the award at age 10 for PAPER MOON.)

THE MIRACLE WORKER is a powerful picture, even as the credits roll. Keller (Duke) is groping, lost and angry in her silent world when Annie Sullivan (Bancroft) arrives in Tuscumbia, Alabama, on a mission to teach the girl how to communicate through sign language. The task seems impossible, since Helen is blind as well as deaf. Annie, we learn, was blind at birth and still must wear very thick glasses in order to see images. Her own life had been brutalized by many years in institutions and the loss of the one person she cared about, a crippled brother who died young. Bancroft senses that the only way she can make any progress with Duke is to separate the child from her doting mother, Swenson, and her overbearing father, Jory.

The film is a harrowing, painfully honest, sometimes violent journey, astonishingly acted and rendered. Penn and cinematographer Caparros use short dissolves to great advantage, and Rosenthal's score heightens every nuance of the drama. The interiors were shot in New York and the exteriors in New Jersey, which doubled for Alabama. The

eight-minute sequence featuring a physical fight between Bancroft and Duke as the teacher attempts to teach the pupil some manners stands as one of the most electrifying and honest ever committed to film.

MISERY

1990   107m   c   Horror   ★★★
Castle Rock/Nelson   (U.S.)   R/18

James Caan (Paul Sheldon), Kathy Bates (Annie Wilkes), Richard Farnsworth (Buster, Sheriff), Frances Sternhagen (Virginia), Lauren Bacall (Marcia Sindell), Graham Jarvis (Libby), Jerry Potter (Pete), Tom Brunelle (Anchorman), June Christopher (Anchorwoman), Wendy Bowers (Waitress)

p, Rob Reiner, Andrew Scheinman, Steve Nicolaides, Jeffrey Stott; d, Rob Reiner; w, William Goldman (based on the novel by Stephen King); ph, Barry Sonnenfeld; ed, Robert Leighton; m, Marc Shaiman; prod d, Norman Garwood; art d, Mark Mansbridge; fx, Phil Cory, K.N.B. EFX Group; cos, Gloria Gresham

AA Best Actress: Kathy Bates

In the "Kill the Bitch" tradition of FATAL ATTRACTION, this adaptation of Stephen King's misogynist fable about a "serious" (male) author trapped by his own "frivolous" (female) commercial creation isn't quite satisfying either as a flat-out horror screamer or a psychological thriller.

Paul Sheldon (Caan), the creator of the fabulously successful romance-novel heroine Misery Chastain, has a fan in Annie Wilkes (Bates) who is willing to die for him. The trouble is, after she discovers Sheldon has killed off his series of "Misery" novels in order to write "serious" fiction, Annie wants to take him with her.

Director Rob Reiner is clearly more comfortable with the humor and humanity than the gory horror in King's grisly tale. William Goldman's script is similarly at its strongest early on when Sheldon faces off in a test of artistic mettle against Wilkes, the toughest editor of his life. When the horror comes, it feels forced and derivative. The climactic battle between Sheldon and Annie degenerates into yet another recycling of the unkillable movie killer gimmick of "Friday the 13th." Ironically, it is Bates's Oscar-winning work that subverts MISERY as a horror tale. She gives the role a subtle mixture of wit, energy, and psychological realism that undermines the pat, bloodthirsty resolution.

MISFITS, THE

1961   124m   bw   Western   ★★★½
Seven Arts   (U.S.)   /15

Clark Gable (Gay Langland), Marilyn Monroe (Roslyn Taber), Montgomery Clift (Perce Howland), Thelma Ritter (Isabelle Steers), Eli Wallach (Guido), James Barton (Old Man in the Bar), Estelle Winwood (Church Lady), Kevin McCarthy (Raymond Taber), Denis Shaw (Young Boy in Bar), Philip Mitchell (Charles Steers)

p, Frank E. Taylor; d, John Huston; w, Arthur Miller; ph, Russell Metty; ed, George Tomasini; m, Alex North; art d, Stephen Grimes, William Newberry; fx, Cline Jones; cos, Jesse Munden

A disturbing but captivating film about modern cowboys who have lost their purpose in a world that has robbed them of the West into which they were born. THE MISFITS was Gable's and Monroe's last film. Whether or not the strenuous stunts and bronc-busting feats he performed killed Gable is still in debate, but he certainly gave one of the finest performances of his career for the fade-out.

Gay (Gable) and sidekicks Guido (Wallach) and Perce (Clift) are cowboys without saddles, driving a pickup about the West in search of odd jobs. Their talk is laced with thin bravado, and they have more of the past to discuss than the future. In Reno, they meet recently divorced blond voluptuary Roslyn Taber (Monroe), who has left her successful businessman husband. She is a one-time stripper who is seeking truth and a meaningful relationship with anyone who can relate to her idealistic notions. Gay is twice Roslyn's age, has no noble purpose, and intends to round up "misfit" horses, those wild mustangs too small for rodeo or ranch work, so they can be ground up for dog food. They tentatively begin a romance, but these "misfits" have a few things to prove to themselves and to each other first.

This is an awkward film, even though it has many fine moments, most of them Gable's—when he gets drunk and begins calling for his long-lost children, his spirited horse-breaking scenes (he did not employ a double), and some of his nostalgic scenes with Monroe. Gable had his misgivings about what he called the "arty" qualities of Miller's script, but he eventually did more with his introspective role than the playwright could have expected. Monroe has her moments (e.g. screaming in the middle of the desert while she watches Gay and his buddies fighting one particularly spirited mustang), but is often weak and directionless in her part. She tries adopting Actor's Studio methods and deadpanning her scenes while belying her altruistic lines with a jiggling, tight-skirted image. Miller's presence at the on-location scenes in Reno and Dayton, Nevada, undoubtedly inhibited director Huston, who fails to develop anyone's character except Gable's. Huston could not control Monroe, who was taking various drugs and seemed to be on the verge of a nervous breakdown; when she did show up for work, she couldn't remember her lines without heavy coaching. Somewhat surprisingly, Gable treated her and the similarly distraught, alcoholic Clift with great consideration and kindness. He got on less well with Wallach, though, regularly referring to the "boiled ham" he planned to have for lunch, while the studious, showy Method actor would retort, "Hey, king, can you lower my taxes?" The film was finally completed on November 24, 1960, eight days after Gable's death from a heart attack and several months before his fifth wife Kay gave birth to his only child. Monroe's death from a sleeping-pill overdose would soon follow, and Clift would be dead within five years as well. Many have called this film a brilliant mood piece of a dying Old West; that doesn't make it a masterpiece, but the ghosts of its cast do still haunt one's viewing experience.

MISHIMA

1985 120m c Biography   ★★★½
Zoetrope/Filmlink/Lucasfilm (U.S.)   R/15

Ken Ogata (*Yukio Mishima*), Masayuki Shionoya (*Morita*), Hiroshi Mikami (*Cadet No. 1*), Junya Fukuda (*Cadet No. 2*), Shigeto Tachihara (*Cadet No. 3*), Junkichi Orimoto (*Gen. Mashita*), Eimei Exumi (*Ichigaya Aide-de-Camp*), Minoru Hodaka (*Ichigaya Colonel*), Go Riju (*Mishima, Age 18-19*), Yuki Nagahara (*Mishima, Age 5*)

p, Mata Yamamoto, Tom Luddy; d, Paul Schrader; w, Paul Schrader, Leonard Schrader (conceived in collaboration with Jun Shiragi, literary executor of the Mishima estate); ph, John Bailey; ed, Michael Chandler, Tomoyo Oshima; m, Philip Glass; prod d, Eiko Ishioka; art d, Kazuo Takenaka; cos, Etsuko Yagyu

"Never in physical action had I discovered the chilling satisfaction of words. Never in words had I experienced the hot darkness of action. Somewhere there must be a higher principle which reconciles art and action. That principle, it occurred to me, was death." These words, written by Japanese author Yukio Mishima and spoken in a voice-over narration by Roy Scheider, eloquently state what writer-director Paul Schrader tried to convey in this ambitious, unique undertaking. Though MISHIMA contains much biographical material, it doesn't claim to be a definitive biography of the controversial writer. Instead, the film concentrates on Mishima's art, attempting to piece together a complicated puzzle by examining his work and its relation to his personal obsessions. Perhaps Japan's best-known author, Mishima wrote 35 novels, 25 plays, 200 short stories, and 8 volumes of essays before his ritual suicide at age 45. One of his driving concerns was his perception of Japan's post-WWII rejection of its rich history of tradition, ritual, honor, and religion in favor of the Western world's pursuit of money. He formed his own private army, called the Shield Society, whose purpose was to restore Japan to the emperor. Schrader approaches his subject with taste and intelligence, juxtaposing Mishima's suicide with flashbacks from his life and dramatizations of his novels *Temple of the Golden Pavilion*, *Kyoko's House*, and *Runaway Horses*. Separated into four chapters ("Beauty," "Art," "Action," and "Harmony of Pen and Sword"), the film skillfully integrates the novels and real events, slowly dissecting Mishima's obsessions. MISHIMA's most stunning aspect is the visual style employed in the dramatizations of the novels. With colorful, theatrical sets by famed Japanese designer Eiko Ishioka, the

sequences are quite unique and impressive in their own right, and the entire film is photographed beautifully by John Bailey. The visuals are enhanced by Philip Glass's haunting score.

MISSING

1982 122m c Drama/War   ★★★★
Polygram (U.S.)   PG/15

Jack Lemmon (*Ed Horman*), Sissy Spacek (*Beth Horman*), Melanie Mayron (*Terry Simon*), John Shea (*Charles Horman*), Charles Cioffi (*Capt. Ray Tower*), David Clennon (*Consul Phil Putnam*), Richard Venture (*US Ambassador*), Jerry Hardin (*Col. Sean Patrick*), Richard Bradford (*Carter Babcock*), Joe Regalbuto (*Frank Teruggi*)

p, Edward Lewis, Mildred Lewis; d, Constantin Costa-Gavras; w, Donald Stewart, Constantin Costa-Gavras (based on *The Execution of Charles Horman* by Thomas Hauser); ph, Ricardo Aronovich; ed, Francoise Bonnot; m, Vangelis; prod d, Peter Jamison; art d, Agustin Ytuarte, Luceoro Isaac; fx, Albert Whitlock; cos, Joe I. Tompkins

AAN Best Picture; AAN Best Actor: Jack Lemmon; *AAN Best Actress:* Sissy Spacek; *AA Best Adapted Screenplay:* Constantine Costa-Gavras, Donald Stewart

With MISSING, Costa-Gavras (Z; STATE OF SEIGE; THE CONFESSION), one of cinema's most political filmmakers, turned his attention to the alleged US involvement in the coup that led to the death of socialist Chilean president Salvador Allende in 1973. Based on Thomas Hauser's *The Execution of Charles Horman*, Costa-Gavras's first Hollywood-produced film presents an only slightly fictionalized account of the disappearance of American expatriate writer Charles Horman (John Shea) in Santiago (though neither the city nor Chile are ever mentioned) just after a military coup. His wife, Beth (Sissy Spacek), and his conservative father, Ed (Jack Lemmon), who has traveled from the US, become a political odd couple as they search for Charles, growing closer as they run into the official stonewalling of American embassy and Chilean authorities who insist there is no trace of Charles. Costa-Gavras pulled so few punches in this powerful, provocative thriller that then-Secretary of State Alexander Haig felt compelled to issue categorical denials of the film's allegations. Few films fuse the personal and the political as successfully as MISSING, and Lemmon and Spacek bring tremendous feeling to their portrayals. Though Costa-Gavras clearly has a political axe to grind, he manages to do so without haranguing the viewer, keeping the film's focus on his characters and masterfully building tension as the story moves toward its stinging resolution.

MISSION, THE

1986 126m c Historical   ★★★
Enigma/Goldcrest/Kingsmere (U.K.)   PG

Robert De Niro (*Mendoza*), Jeremy Irons (*Gabriel*), Ray McAnally (*Altamirano*), Liam Neeson (*Fielding*), Aidan Quinn (*Felipe*), Ronald Pickup (*Hontar*), Charles Low (*Cabeza*), Cherie Lunghi (*Carlotta*), Bercelio Moya (*Indian Boy*), Sigifredo Ismare (*Witch Doctor*)

p, Fernando Ghia, David Puttnam; d, Roland Joffe; w, Robert Bolt; ph, Chris Menges; ed, Jim Clark; m, Ennio Morricone; prod d, Stuart Craig; art d, George Richardson, John King; fx, Peter Hutchinson; cos, Enrico Sabbatini

AAN Best Picture; AAN Best Director: Roland Joffe; *AA Best Cinematography:* Chris Menges; *AAN Best Editing:* Jim Clark; *AAN Best Score:* Ennio Morricone; *AAN Best Art Direction:* Stuart Craig, Jack Stephens; *AAN Best Costume Design:* Enrico Sabbatini

In South America, circa 1750, Gabriel (Irons) is a Jesuit priest sent to build a mission for the Guarani Indians. There he encounters Mendoza (De Niro), a ruthless slave trader who kills several Guaranis and captures many more, taking them back to town as slaves. Mendoza also kills his handsome young brother Felipe (Quinn) in a duel over Mendoza's fiancee, but because he is an aristocrat, he isn't punished for his crime. But the slave trader has a conscience and feels that he must do penance; accordingly, Gabriel arranges for Mendoza to join him back at the mission where Mendoza committed so many sins. In time, the mission faces serious trouble, brought on by a dispute among Spain, Portugal, and the Church. Ambitious, moving, and visually stunning,

THE MISSION falls right in step with other high-quality British historical epics, but also fails to escape the pitfalls that typically plague such projects. While an impressive production, THE MISSION tries to do so much that little is explored fully. Irons's character is really more an icon than a man, as is De Niro's. Perhaps most distressing is the fact that THE MISSION is yet another film made by Europeans or Americans that, while sympathetic to the plight of South American Indians, portrays them as an indistinguishable mass of childlike innocents just waiting to be exploited by outsiders.

MISSION: IMPOSSIBLE

1996   110m   c   Thriller/Spy/Action   ★★★
CW Productions/Paramount British Pictures   (U.S.)   PG-13/PG

Tom Cruise (Ethan Hunt), Jon Voight (Jim Phelps), Emmanuelle Beart (Claire), Henry Czerny (Kittridge), Jean Reno (Krieger), Ving Rhames (Luther), Kristin Scott Thomas (Sarah Davies), Vanessa Redgrave (Max), Emilio Estevez (Jack Harmon—uncredited), Dale Dye (Frank Barnes)

p, Tom Cruise, Paula Wagner; d, Brian De Palma; w, David Koepp, Robert Towne (from a story by David Koepp and Steven Zaillian, based on the television series created by Bruce Geller); ph, Stephen H. Burum; ed, Paul Hirsch; m, Danny Elfman, Lalo Schifrin; prod d, Norman Reynolds; art d, Frederick Hole; fx, John Knoll, Richard Yuricich, Lyn Nicholson, Industrial Light & Magic; cos, Penny Rose

Brian De Palma's eagerly awaited big-screen adaptation of the classic TV series is a gutsy attempt to reconfigure the timeworn espionage formula. Although this presold blockbuster is far from a complete success on De Palma's terms—it doesn't subvert the genre but gives it a surprisingly gentle goose—it's a nimble, expertly contrived summer entertainment that doesn't insult the intelligence.

Tom Cruise stars as Ethan Hunt, member of the elite Impossible Mission Force led by grizzled patriarch Jim Phelps (Jon Voight). After most of his team is ruthlessly sacrificed during what turns out to be a decoy operation, Hunt turns renegade. He assembles his own crack but highly suspect team of fellow "disavowed" agents (Ving Rhames and Jean Reno) and goes after a mysterious arms dealer called Max (Vanessa Redgrave).

De Palma and screenwriters David Koepp and Robert Towne boldly reduce much of what made the series so popular (gadgets, international supervillains, even the conceit of the seemingly impossible mission) down to a bare minimum. The result is a gracefully plotted spy film in the classic mode, with just enough self-consciousness to keep things interesting.

The pleasures of MISSION: IMPOSSIBLE are mostly conventional—star/producer Cruise reportedly kept his adventurous director on a short leash—but there are moments when De Palma's distinctive obsessions and lyrical sensibility shine through. A parallel between spycraft and stagecraft is cleverly sustained throughout, and the elaborately imagined scenes of video surveillance are in keeping with the director's celebrated critique of vision, technology, and power.

MISSISSIPPI BURNING

1988   128m   c   Historical   ★★
Frederick Zollo   (U.S.)   R/18

Gene Hackman (Rupert Anderson), Willem Dafoe (Alan Ward), Frances McDormand (Mrs. Pell), Brad Dourif (Deputy Pell), R. Lee Ermey (Mayor Tilman), Gailard Sartain (Sheriff Stuckey), Stephen Tobolowsky (Townley), Michael Rooker (Frank Bailey), Pruitt Taylor Vince (Lester Cowens), Badja Djola (Agent Monk)

p, Frederick Zollo, Robert F. Colesberry; d, Alan Parker; w, Chris Gerolmo; ph, Peter Biziou; ed, Gerry Hambling; m, Trevor Jones; prod d, Geoffrey Kirkland, Philip Harrison; fx, Stan Parks; cos, Aude Bronson Howard

AAN Best Picture; AAN Best Actor: Gene Hackman; AAN Best Supporting Actress: Frances McDormand; AAN Best Director: Alan Parker; AA Best Cinematography: Peter Biziou; AAN Best Editing: Gerry Hambling; AAN Best Sound: Robert Litt, Elliot Tyson, Richard C. Kline, Danny Michael

Using the shocking murders of three civil rights workers by the Ku Klux Klan in Mississippi on June 21, 1964, as its inspiration, MISSISSIPPI BURNING presents a grotesquely fictionalized version of the events and turns them into another cop-buddy movie. Alan Ward and Rupert Anderson (Dafoe and Hackman) are two very different FBI agents sent to Mississippi to investigate the disappearance of the young men. Ward is morally outraged by the racism he finds in the South and is determined to do something about it, while Anderson wanders the streets like a good ol' boy, chatting with the townsfolk to ferret out clues. MISSISSIPPI BURNING is visually splendid. From the sets, costumes, props, and Mississippi locations to the gorgeous cinematography of Peter Biziou, director Parker and his crew have created a film that is unquestionably watchable. As a history lesson, however, it's laughable: the FBI were far from heroes to civil rights activists, and insofar as the struggle succeeded, it was because American blacks took their own destiny in hand, not because they were rescued by paternalistic white authority figures.

MISSISSIPPI MASALA

1992   118m   c   Drama/Romance   ★★★½
Mira Nair Films/SCS Films/Palace Pictures/Film   R/15
Four International   (U.S./U.K.)

Denzel Washington (Demetrius), Sarita Choudhury (Mina), Roshan Seth (Jay), Sharmila Tagore (Kinnu), Charles S. Dutton (Tyrone), Joe Seneca (Williben), Ranjit Chowdhry (Anil), Mohan Gokhale (Pontiac), Mohan Agashe (Kanti Napkin), Tico Wells (Dexter)

p, Michael Nozik, Mira Nair; d, Mira Nair; w, Sooni Taraporevala; ph, Edward Lachman; ed, Roberto Silvi; m, L. Subramaniam; prod d, Mitch Epstein; art d, Jefferson Sage; cos, Hope Hanafin

"Masala" refers to a mix of varied spices, and one of the strengths of MISSISSIPPI MASALA is its own collection of colorful characters. While its ostensible focus is on an interracial romance, the film's dramatic scope is wide enough to encompass not only those around the couple, and their reactions to the affair, but the events and forces that led to their coming together in the first place. The lovers are Demetrius (Denzel Washington), a young black man who runs a carpet-cleaning business in Mississippi, and Mina (Sarita Choudhury), whose parents Jay (Roshan Seth) and Kinnu (Sharmila Tagore) run a local liquor store. (Like many of their friends, Mina and her family are Indians who were expelled from Uganda in 1972 by Idi Amin.) After Mina accidentally crashes a car into Demetrius's truck, the two become attracted to each other and begin a romance that stirs the ire of Mina's family.

Indian director Mira Nair, a Harvard graduate and former documentarian (INDIA CABARET) whose first narrative feature, SALAAM BOMBAY!, received widespread acclaim, does a fine job of exploring the complex relations at play here. Sooni Taraporevala's screenplay avoids easy polemics about race, and is as much about the outside forces and past events that influence the central love affair as it is about the affair itself.

In one of his first true romantic leads, Washington proves immensely charming as a man who resists, without being blind to, the social pressures working against the affair. Newcomer Choudhury is excellent as the rebellious Mina, effectively playing the nonconformist side of her character without ever losing sympathy. There's real romantic chemistry between the two, and their love scene in a Biloxi motel room generates real heat without indulging in the sultry silliness of so many recent "erotic" dramas.

MISSISSIPPI MERMAID
(LA SIRENE DU MISSISSIPPI)

1969   123m   c   Mystery   ★★★½
Carrosse/Artistes/Delphos   (France/Italy)   GP/AA

Jean-Paul Belmondo (Louis Mahe), Catherine Deneuve (Julie Roussel/Marion), Michel Bouquet (Comolli), Nelly Borgeaud (Berthe Roussel), Marcel Berbert (Jardine), Martine Ferriere (Landlady), Roland Thenot (Richard), Yves Drouhet

p, Marcel Berbert; d, Francois Truffaut; w, Francois Truffaut (based on the novel Waltz into Darkness by Cornell Woolrich); ph, Denys Clerval; ed, Agnes Guillemot; m, Antoine Duhamel; art d, Claude Pignot

Belmondo is a millionaire tobacco planter who becomes engaged to Deneuve through a personal column. He is taken by her beauty and they soon marry, but she leaves with his bank account. He hires a private detective to track her down, but eventually discovers her himself, or so he thinks. The girl he finds is not his wife, but bears an uncanny resemblance to her (not surprising, since Deneuve plays both roles). Eventually Belmondo learns that his new companion is trying to kill him. As he is about to be poisoned, he professes his love for Deneuve, who promptly knocks the cup from his hand and shamefully vows to love him forever. This is Truffaut's most successful attempt to blend a complex, Hitchcockian genre film with his own personality. It was also his first chance to work with superstars, ensuring success at the box office. The film is full of references to cinema—a clip from LA MARSEILLAISE (the picture is dedicated to Jean Renoir, whose film LA CARROSSE D'OR [THE GOLDEN COACH] was the inspiration for the name of Truffaut's production company), and homages to Humphrey Bogart, Nick Ray, Honore de Balzac, Jean Cocteau, and a *Cahiers Du Cinema* editor who bore the same name as this film's detective, Comolli.

MISSOURI BREAKS, THE

1976 126m c Western   ★★★
UA (U.S.)   PG/15

Marlon Brando (*Lee Clayton*), Jack Nicholson (*Tom Logan*), Randy Quaid (*Little Tod*), Kathleen Lloyd (*Jane Braxton*), Frederic Forrest (*Cary*), Harry Dean Stanton (*Calvin*), John McLiam (*David Braxton*), John Ryan (*Si*), Sam Gilman (*Hank Rate*), Steve Franken (*Lonesome Kid*)

p, Elliott Kastner, Robert M. Sherman; d, Arthur Penn; w, Thomas McGuane; ph, Michael Butler; ed, Jerry Greenberg, Stephen A. Rotter, Dede Allen; m, John Williams; prod d, Albert Brenner; art d, Steve Berger; cos, Patricia Norris

In the 1970s westerns started to come a little weird, and this one was downright eccentric, although Brando, as a nutty gunfighter, and Nicholson, as a leader of rustlers, are fascinating to watch, if not believable in their disjointed roles. The film opens as a rustler, on ranch baron McLiam's orders, is hanged, no little example for Nicholson, who heads a gang of vicious horse thieves. The hanged man, Hunter Von Leer, was Nicholson's friend, and Nicholson intends to avenge the death; but he falls for Lloyd, daughter of the cattle baron, and somehow is persuaded to settle down to the mundane chores of farming, much to the disgust of his gang. The rustlers carry on without Nicholson's help, raiding McLiam's herds and driving the cattle baron half crazy. He sends for a top gun bounty hunter, Brando, who turns out to be the most unpredictable and outright strangest creature to ever visit a western movie. To capture one outlaw he takes to wearing a bonnet and dress, and when Nicholson goes to kill him he finds Brando taking a bubble bath, a sight that so jars him that he misses his opportunity to kill him. Brando continues his rampage, destroying all the rustlers except Nicholson, who manages to finish off the weirdo in the end. The whole thing, script, acting, and especially Penn's heavy-handed direction, is bizarre. Yet there's a perverse joy in watching Brando and Nicholson try to compete with each other in mugging, switching accents, and mannerisms that could only be found elsewhere in institutions like the Bellevue Insane Asylum. The erratic and exotic behavior of the stars is infectious, with Quaid, Forrest, Stanton, and others mimicking them with slavish devotion.

MR. BLANDINGS BUILDS HIS DREAM HOUSE

1948 94m bw Comedy   ★★★½
RKO (U.S.)   /U

Cary Grant (*Jim Blandings*), Myrna Loy (*Muriel Blandings*), Melvyn Douglas (*Bill Cole*), Reginald Denny (*Simms*), Sharyn Moffett (*Joan Blandings*), Connie Marshall (*Betsy Blandings*), Louise Beavers (*Gussie*), Harry Shannon (*W.D. Tesander*), Ian Wolfe (*Smith*), Tito Vuolo (*Mr. Zucca*)

p, Norman Panama, Melvin Frank; d, H.C. Potter; w, Norman Panama, Melvin Frank (based on the novel by Eric Hodgins); ph, James Wong Howe; ed, Harry Marker; m, Leigh Harline; art d, Albert S. D'Agostino, Carroll Clark; fx, Russell A. Cully; cos, Robert Kalloch

Nice and easy. The novel upon which this film was based was very funny and timely. This movie suffered a bit in the translation to the screen, but it still had more than enough humor to make it a hit. This was the third duet for Grant and Loy, and a triangular plot-turn with Douglas was written in to add some spice. Jim and Muriel Blandings are married Manhattanites who must give up their apartment and find new lodgings for themselves and their daughters (Moffett and Marshall). Jim in particular is seduced by the dream of owning a suburban home in the greenery of the country. Dreaming, though, is much easier than building.

Timely in 1948 in light of postwar housing problems, BLANDINGS survives now primarily by the grace of its cast. Loy proves that she didn't need William Powell to be the "perfect wife", and she has two wonderful moments telling off her jealous husband and explaining the color scheme for her house to a laconic painter. Grant handles more of the film's farcical elements, yet he still retains the warm sophistication he's so justly famous for. Douglas is as wry as ever, and the fine supporting cast includes gems from Denny and Shannon. There's little originality here—gags are borrowed from radio's "Fibber McGee and Molly", and much here would be reprised on TV's "Green Acres," but serve up the "Wham" anyway, Gussie!

MR. DEEDS GOES TO TOWN

1936 115m bw Comedy   ★★★★★
Columbia (U.S.)   /U

Gary Cooper (*Longfellow Deeds*), Jean Arthur (*Babe Bennett*), George Bancroft (*MacWade*), Lionel Stander (*Cornelius Cobb*), Douglas Dumbrille (*John Cedar*), Raymond Walburn (*Walter*), Margaret Matzenauer (*Madame Pomponi*), H.B. Warner (*Judge Walker*), Warren Hymer (*Bodyguard*), Muriel Evans (*Theresa*)

p, Frank Capra; d, Frank Capra; w, Robert Riskin (based on the story "Opera Hat" by Clarence Budington Kelland); ph, Joseph Walker; ed, Gene Havlick; art d, Stephen Goosson; fx, Roy Davidson; cos, Samuel Lange

AAN Best Picture; AAN Best Actor: Gary Cooper; *AA Best Director:* Frank Capra; *AAN Best Screenplay:* Robert Riskin; *AAN Best Sound:* John Livadary

Peak inspired lunacy, especially in the courtroom. Here is a shamelessly simple story with a populist point of view, but it is handled with such charm and charisma and acted so well by Cooper and Arthur that it became another Frank Capra classic. Cooper, a rural rube from Vermont, inherits his uncle's vast fortune and becomes national news overnight. The whole town turns out at the train station to see Cooper, tuba player and poet, off to New York, where he will assume the responsibilities of his uncle's business and move into an enormous mansion. But cynical news editor George Bancroft does not fall for Cooper's image of a simple, honest man. Bancroft assigns Arthur to interview Cooper, with explicit instructions not to spare the ridicule, but the aggressive reporter cannot corral Cooper. When she fakes a faint in front of his residence, the gallant Cooper picks her up and takes care of her. She tells him she's unemployed, and then begins wheedling him for information.

Capra directs flawlessly as he captures the prosaic character of Longfellow Deeds; Cooper is tailor-made for the role, natural and authentic. Both he and Arthur remained favorites of Capra, who would use Cooper again in MEET JOHN DOE, Arthur in YOU CAN'T TAKE IT WITH YOU, and MR. SMITH GOES TO WASHINGTON. Capra never had any doubt in casting Cooper for the role of Longfellow Deeds—his first and only choice—but he was in a quandary over the female lead until he spotted Arthur in a minor western. The director was at his high-water mark at Columbia, allowed by Columbia studio chief Harry Cohn to function as he pleased without front office interference. Capra insisted that only Cooper play the lead in the film, causing the production to be delayed for six months while Cooper fulfilled other duties and costing Columbia $100,000. Cohn did not want any more postponements so he okayed Arthur and the production got under way. Arthur literally shook with nerves before each scene, believing she could not pull it off. Yet she was an original in front of the cameras.

The supporting cast is extraordinary, notably Dumbrille, Bancroft, and that venerable character player Warner, who had appeared in many a Capra film and played Christ in DeMille's classic KING OF KINGS. The film achieved immense popularity and gleaned a fortune for Columbia chiefly because of the gangling, rumpled, taciturn Cooper, who was one of the most durable film stars in history and ranked in the top-10 list for 15 years. In 1939 he made almost $500,000, making him the highest paid American actor that year, and would earn more than $10 million throughout his long career.

MR. HOLLAND'S OPUS

1996 142m c Drama		★★
Interscope Communications/The Charlie Mopic Company (U.S.)		PG

Richard Dreyfuss (Glenn Holland), Glenne Headly (Iris Holland), Jay Thomas (Bill Meister), Olympia Dukakis (Principal Jacobs), William H. Macy (Vice Principal Wolters), Alicia Witt (Gertrude Lang), Terrence Howard (Louis Russ), Damon Whitaker (Bobby Tidd), Jean Louisa Kelly (Rowena Morgan), Alexandra Boyd (Sarah Olmstead)

p, Ted Field, Michael Nolin, Robert W. Cort; d, Stephen Herek; w, Patrick Sheane Duncan; ph, Oliver Wood; ed, Trudy Ship; m, Michael Kamen; prod d, David Nichols; art d, Dina Lipton; fx, Bob Riggs; chor, Bruce McDonald; cos, Aggie Guerard Rodgers

AAN Best Actor: Richard Dreyfuss

MR. HOLLAND'S OPUS wants desperately to be the baby boomer IT'S A WONDERFUL LIFE. It's too bad that position is already held by FORREST GUMP.

In 1964, Glenn Holland (Richard Dreyfuss) becomes a high school music teacher. He intends the job to be temporary, just something to pay the bills until his "real" career as a composer takes off. Holland discovers his gift for teaching and the positive impact the act of learning has on a child's self-esteem. Pretty soon, Mr. Holland is organizing a marching band, and his wife Iris (Glenne Headly) is pregnant. In a tragic twist, their son, Cole, is born deaf. Suddenly, it's 1980 and Mr. Holland is deciding whether or not to accompany his star pupil, beautiful ingenue Rowena Morgan (Jean Louisa Kelly), to New York where she wants to pursue a career on Broadway. Mr. Holland considers the notion, but decides not to. In the meantime, his troubled relationship with his son seems to be reaching a head.

MR. HOLLAND'S OPUS is a real tearjerker, but when the tears come, you feel like a jerk. Patrick Sheane Duncan's script is a formula of connect-the-dots cloying moments, and Stephen Herek directs it with all the push-button manipulation and ham-fisted subtlety he brought to THE MIGHTY DUCKS. They should at least be ashamed of the mawkish use of John Lennon's music and memory. Dreyfuss gives a very able performance as the earnest Every-ham, for which he received a Best Actor Oscar nomination.

MR. HULOT'S HOLIDAY
(LES VACANCES DE MONSIEUR HULOT)

1953 85m bw Comedy		★★★★½
Cady/Gaumont (France)		/U

Jacques Tati (Mr. Hulot), Nathalie Pascaud (Martine), Louis Perrault (Fred), Michelle Rolla (The Aunt), Andre Dubois (Commandant), Suzy Willy (Commandant's Wife), Valentine Camax (Englishwoman), Lucien Fregis (Hotel Proprietor), Marguerite Gerard (Strolling Woman), Rene Lacourt (Strolling Man)

p, Jacques Tati, Fred Orain; d, Jacques Tati; w, Jacques Tati, Henri Marquet, Pierre Aubert, Jacques Lagrange; ph, Jacques Mercanton, Jean Mousselle; ed, Suzanne Baron, Charles Bretoneiche, Jacques Grassi; m, Alain Romans; prod d, Henri Schmitt; art d, R. Brian Court, Henri Schmitt

AAN Best Original Screenplay: Jacques Tati, Henri Marquet

Director Jacques Tati turned his attention to those French who wrongly believe that a coastal holiday will be a time of rest and relaxation with this delightful film. Featuring the first appearance of M. Hulot (played by Tati himself, in the tradition of the great silent comedians), MR. HULOT'S HOLIDAY takes place at a coastal resort in Brittany. Chaos seems to follow Hulot wherever he goes, but he somehow makes it

through life without ever really noticing. Like all vacationers, Hulot (and director Tati) spends a great deal of time observing other vacationers. There is the comely Martine (Nathalie Pascaud), whom Hulot would like to get to know better, but is too shy to confront directly; the workaholic businessman (Jean-Pierre Zola, later seen in MY UNCLE) who cannot stop to relax; the burly British old maid (Valentine Camax); the besieged waiter (Raymond Carl); the former military man who still thinks he's leading a battalion (Andre Dubois); the beachcombing couple (Rene Lacourt and Marguerite Gerard), and countless other unidentified persons who are equally important to the scenery. There is no plot (as the prologue warns us), only a seemingly endless stream of events—with and without Hulot—that carry the film through to the end. With very little dialogue and a creative use of sound, Tati (the actor and director) gives us an entirely new way of looking at a very familiar landscape.

MISTER ROBERTS

1955 123m c War/Comedy/Drama		★★½
Orange (U.S.)		/U

Henry Fonda (Lt. Doug Roberts), James Cagney (Captain), Jack Lemmon (Ens. Frank Thurlowe Pulver), William Powell (Doc), Ward Bond (C.P.O. Dowdy), Betsy Palmer (Lt. Ann Girard), Philip Carey (Mannion), Nick Adams (Reber), Harry Carey Jr. (Stefanowski), Ken Curtis (Dolan)

p, Leland Hayward; d, John Ford, Mervyn LeRoy; w, Joshua Logan, Frank S. Nugent (based on the play by Logan and Thomas Heggen and the novel by Heggen); ph, Winton C. Hoch; ed, Jack Murray; m, Franz Waxman; art d, Art Loel; cos, Moss Mabry

AAN Best Picture; AA Best Supporting Actor: Jack Lemmon; AAN Best Sound: William A. Mueller

Mister Nowhere. This stodgy film version of the famous Broadway success was one performance too many. Hank Fonda plays the title role of the cargo officer dying to leave his supply ship for the glories of battle like a wounded spaniel, all sad eyes and monotoned whining. James Cagney, as the megalomaniacal captain with the palm tree, acts like something out of a cartoon. The Tasmanian Devil is much funnier, folks. William Powell is good, but he doesn't have much to do as the sympathetic ship's doctor. That leaves it up to Jack Lemmon, in his film debut as Ensign Pulver, to pump some life—and some humor—into this baby. To his immense credit, he does it. Oscar voters, with their usual inferiority complex about theater, probably felt they had to give this heavy, dull film some kind of honor, and they were so grateful for the Lemmon-fresh pledge that they voted for him lock, stock and barrel. John Ford began the film, came to blows (literally) with Fonda, who had played the role about a million times on stage and didn't want to change a thing, and then suffered a gall-bladder attack. Mervyn LeRoy, way past his peak as a director, took over for a time, and even Josh Logan, who helmed the Broadway production, directed some scenes. The behind-the-scenes tinkering shows.

MR. SMITH GOES TO WASHINGTON

1939 125m bw Political		★★★★★
Columbia (U.S.)		/U

Jean Arthur (Saunders), James Stewart (Jefferson Smith), Claude Rains (Sen. Joseph Paine), Edward Arnold (Jim Taylor), Guy Kibbee (Gov. Hubert Hopper), Thomas Mitchell (Diz Moore), Eugene Pallette (Chick McGann), Beulah Bondi (Ma Smith), H.B. Warner (Sen. Fuller), Harry Carey (President of the Senate)

p, Frank Capra; d, Frank Capra; w, Sidney Buchman (based on the novel The Gentleman from Montana by Lewis R. Foster); ph, Joseph Walker; ed, Gene Havlick, Al Clark; m, Dimitri Tiomkin; art d, Lionel Banks; cos, Robert Kalloch

AAN Best Picture; AAN Best Actor: James Stewart; AAN Best Supporting Actor: Harry Carey; AAN Best Supporting Actor: Claude Rains; AAN Best Director: Frank Capra; AA Best Original Story: Lewis R. Foster; AAN Best Screenplay: Sidney Buchman; AAN Best Editing: Gene Havlick, Al Clark; AAN Best Score: Dimitri Tiomkin; AAN Best Art Direction: Lionel Banks; AAN Best Sound: John Livadary

Stellar Capra-corn Americana. This great film works on the premise that all that is necessary for evil to triumph is the inaction of good men. Against this danger, director Frank Capra shows a naive everyman to be the true guardian of democratic ideals. James Stewart gives the performance that made him a star as Jefferson Smith, an innocent bumpkin selected by cynical politicians to replace a recently deceased senator in the belief that he can be manipulated by the state's esteemed senior senator, Joseph Paine (Claude Rains). Smith sets off for Washington full of ideals and dreams of working with his idol, Paine, little realizing that he is expected to be a rubber stamp for a crooked scheme to finance a new dam that will profit only Paine and his cronies. The Washington press immediately sizes Smith up as a gullible novice, getting him off to a rocky start, but his idealism captivates Saunders (Jean Arthur), his cynical new secretary. Saunders proves to be a valuable mentor as the innocent Smith slowly comes to realize that his altruistic view of the world doesn't necessarily jibe with reality, and he sets out to expose those who make a mockery of the country he loves so dearly.

While MR. SMITH GOES TO WASHINGTON is the most moral of films, it is so artfully filled with real emotion that it never becomes heavy-handed. Capra supervised every element of the production and used a variety of techniques to accelerate the story line without disrupting it, making every move by every player meaningful and illustrating his credo of "one man, one film." This inspiring masterpiece received 11 Oscar nominations but won only for Best Original Story. Stewart is tops and the rest of the much-loved cast, featuring such familiar veterans as Thomas Mitchell, Edward Arnold, William Demarest and especially Harry Carey, provides unforgettable support.

MOBY DICK

1956   116m   c   Adventure   ★★★½
Moulin   (U.K.)   /U

Gregory Peck (Capt. Ahab), Richard Basehart (Ishmael), Leo Genn (Starbuck), Harry Andrews (Stubb), Bernard Miles (Manxman), Orson Welles (Father Mapple), Mervyn Johns (Peleg), Noel Purcell (Carpenter), Frederick Ledebur (Queequeg), James Robertson Justice (Capt. Boomer)

p, John Huston, Vaughan N. Dean; d, John Huston; w, John Huston, Ray Bradbury (based on the novel by Herman Melville); ph, Oswald Morris; ed, Russell Lloyd; m, Philip Stainton; art d, Ralph Brinton, Stephen Grimes; fx, Gus Lohman; cos, Elizabeth Haffenden

Not too sea-worthy. John Huston gives a passionate and faithful rendering of Herman Melville's novel in MOBY DICK, aided by a stellar cast. The film opens as a man (Richard Basehart) enters the whaling town of New Bedford in 1840, and, in voiceover, makes the famous declaration "Call me Ishmael." He signs on board the *Pequod*, commanded by peg-legged Capt. Ahab (Gregory Peck). Once under way, the wild-eyed, stony, horribly scarred Ahab assembles his crew to tell them that this will be no routine whaling expedition but a mission of vengeance against the great white whale Moby Dick, which tore off his leg and scarred him for life. He whips them into a frenzy, and when Moby Dick is finally sighted, the crew is as obsessed with killing it as Ahab is. Filmed at considerable danger to cast and crew, MOBY DICK, under Huston's strong direction, is one of the most historically authentic, visually stunning, and powerful adventures ever made. Inevitably, many critics disagreed with Huston's interpretation of Melville's classic. Two fishbones to pick: Peck and Genn's miscasting. But there's Welles in rare form, fine whaling scenes, the first glimpse of Moby Dick, good use of color (akin to old whaling prints) and a literate adaptation by Ray Bradbury. When MOBY is good, it's a whale of a time. Huston received the New York Film Critics Best Director Award.

MODERN ROMANCE

1981   93m   c   Comedy   ★★★½
Columbia   (U.S.)   R/15

Albert Brooks (Robert Cole), Kathryn Harrold (Mary Harvard), Tyann Means (Waitress), Bruno Kirby (Jay), Jane Hallaren (Ellen), Karen Chandler (Neighbor), Dennis Kort (Health Food Salesman), Bob Einstein (Sporting Goods Salesman), Virginia Feingold (Bank Receptionist), Thelma Leeds (Mother)

p, Andrew Scheinman, Martin Shafer; d, Albert Brooks; w, Albert Brooks, Monica Johnson; ph, Eric Saarinen; ed, David Finfer; m, Lance Rubin; prod d, Edward Richardson

Albert Brooks directed, cowrote, and stars in this brilliantly funny and at times uncomfortably perceptive comedy. Brooks plays Robert, a film editor trapped in an on-again, off-again relationship with Mary (Kathryn Harrold). After breaking up (again) with Mary, Robert is torn between freedom and love. Attempting to forget her, he invests hundreds of dollars in jogging clothes and vitamins, ventures into the LA singles scene (pre-AIDS), mopes, and buries himself in his work (editing a really bad science fiction film for an exploitation studio). None of it works, and soon he's pursuing Mary again in the hope of winning her back—which he does, until anxiety, paranoia, and doubt return to threaten the relationship once again. In addition to being one of the most realistic, insightful romantic comedies ever made, MODERN ROMANCE also offers a detailed and uproarious glimpse into the technical side of the movie business. A progressive, innovative comic filmmaker, Brooks began to find the large audience he deserves with LOST IN AMERICA.

MODERN TIMES

1936   85m   bw   Comedy   ★★★★★
Chaplin   (U.S.)   /U

Charles Chaplin (A Worker), Paulette Goddard (Gamine), Henry Bergman (Cafe Owner), Tiny Sandford (Big Bill/Worker), Chester Conklin (Mechanic), Hank Mann, Louis Natheaux (Burglars), Stanley Blystone (Sheriff Couler), Allan Garcia (Company Boss), Sammy Stein (Foreman)

p, Charles Chaplin; d, Charles Chaplin; w, Charles Chaplin; ph, Roland Totheroh, Ira Morgan; m, Charles Chaplin; art d, Charles D. Hall, J. Russell Spencer

Charlie Chaplin's sentimental but keenly satirical swipe at the mechanization of everyday life is by consensus the last of the great silent features. Talkies were predominant in Hollywood as early as 1929, but this 1936 film reflects (and thematizes) Chaplin's resistance to change—though we do hear his voice for the first time during a nonsense song.

As with most Chaplin, MODERN TIMES proceeds as a loosely linked series of comic and/or melodramatic setpieces. (One critic of the time complained that the film is really a quartet of two-reelers strung together: "The Shop," "The Jailbird," "The Watchman," and "The Singing Waiter.") The film follows Chaplin's familiar tramp persona through a day at the factory (the feeding machine experiment and Charlie's work-induced twitches are highlights), his accidental arrest (and jailhouse encounter with cocaine) when he's labeled a Communist, a stint working at an emporium (where he again displays the remarkable skating prowess he had first revealed in THE RINK twenty years earlier), and a brief engagement as a waiter, during which he's called upon suddenly to perform a song. Along the way he picks up and romances Paulette Goddard's impoverished waif. The narrative culminates in the famous final image of Chaplin and Goddard on the road together, facing an uncertain future with unquenchable optimism.

Despite its loose-knit structure, this remarkable picture—three years in the making—presents a powerful and coherent indictment of the mechanized workplace and the post-Ford "industrialization" of everyday life. At the same time, MODERN TIMES stands as one of Chaplin's most perfectly balanced mixtures of humor and pathos. The gags are impeccably timed and beautifully edited, and Chaplin's scenes with Paulette Goddard, in particular, glow with warmth. (Part of their chemistry doubtless stemmed from their offscreen love; she was Chaplin's third wife.)

The loving care that went into every detail of this film is evident, from Chaplin's own musical score to his makeshift sound effects (e.g., blowing bubbles in a pail of water to simulate a rumbling stomach). Chaplin would continue to delight audiences with his later movies, but all of them featured recorded dialogue—after this one, the master of mime was forced to adapt to modern times.

MOGAMBO

1953   115m   c   Adventure/Romance   ★★★★
MGM   (U.S.)

Clark Gable (*Victor Marswell*), Ava Gardner (*Eloise Y. Kelly*), Grace Kelly (*Linda Nordley*), Donald Sinden (*Donald Nordley*), Philip Stainton (*John Brown Pryce*), Eric Pohlmann (*Leon Boltchak*), Laurence Naismith (*Skipper*), Denis O'Dea (*Father Josef*), Asa Etula (*Young Native Girl*)

p, Sam Zimbalist; d, John Ford; w, John Lee Mahin (based on the play "Red Dust" by Wilson Collison); ph, Robert Surtees, Freddie Young; ed, Frank Clarke; art d, Alfred Junge; cos, Helen Rose

AAN Best Actress: Ava Gardner; *AAN Best Supporting Actress:* Grace Kelly

An action-packed remake of RED DUST (1932), this is an oddity in the Ford canon, lacking his stock company and many of the themes that make up his unmistakable signature. Showgirl Eloise "Honey Bear" Kelly (Gardner), waiting for a steamer in the African jungle, meets safari leader Victor Marswell (Gable, reprising his earlier role). Sex and love follow, but when anthropologist Donald Nordley (Sinden) and his prim but horny wife Linda (Kelly) arrive, Marswell decides to apply his blowtorch to her iceberg. This not only distresses Honey Bear, but may also prove deadly for one third of the love triangle.

MOGAMBO lacks the engaging rauchiness of the superior RED DUST and the wild banter between Gable and his ideal co-star Jean Harlow. Here the verbal sparring goes on between Gardner and Kelly, while Gable wisely replaces his young buck of yore with a more weatherbeaten bwana. Ford provides action all the way, trekking his cameras through Kenya, Tanganyika, and Uganda. Instead of using a traditional score for the film, Ford insisted that the sounds of Africa would be more effective on the soundtrack. The absence of lush music was a rarity for an MGM production; executives thought such devices too experimental for their "family" audience, but they deferred to the great Ford. There are scenes, reminiscent of Ford's westerns, in which he visually exploits the lavish African landscape. In one scene, Gable stoically marches toward the camera through a gauntlet of spear-holding tribesmen while the horizon spreads beyond him, a scene not unlike the finale of MY DARLING CLEMENTINE, in which Henry Fonda (as Wyatt Earp) rides away from the camera, down a road stretching into infinity.

More cultured than RED DUST, MOGAMBO (meaning "to speak") is also slightly less vibrant, but it deserves praise for not really trying to duplicate the earlier film (which Ford never saw). Kelly, teetering on the brink of major stardom, is quite effective as the repressed wife, and Gardner gives one of the most appealing, relaxed performances of her career. Considering that then-hubby Frank Sinatra was at a career low (this was just before FROM HERE TO ETERNITY) and that she had a miscarriage during production makes her achievement all the more impressive.

Gable held up production, too, when he flew back to the US because he only trusted his own dentist. MGM had wanted to get rid of their high-priced star of twenty years for some time, and Gable left the studio, $400K pension in hand, after completing his next film, BETRAYED. MOGAMBO, however, proved such a bonanza (returning almost $5 million on its initial release) that MGM soon regretted its decision. The story provided the blueprint for one of Ann Sothern's "Maisie" series, CONGO MAISIE (1940), and Gable did RED DUST on the radio in 1940 with Sothern as well.

MOMMIE DEAREST

1981   129m   c   Biography   ★★½
Paramount   (U.S.)   PG/

Faye Dunaway (*Joan Crawford*), Diana Scarwid (*Christina Crawford as an Adult*), Steve Forrest (*Greg Savitt*), Howard da Silva (*Louis B. Mayer*), Mara Hobel (*Christina as a Child*), Rutanya Alda (*Carol Ann*), Harry Goz (*Al Steele*), Michael Edwards (*Ted Gelber*), Jocelyn Brando (*Barbara Bennett*), Priscilla Pointer (*Mrs. Chadwick*)

p, Frank Yablans; d, Frank Perry; w, Frank Yablans, Frank Perry, Tracy Hotchner, Robert Getchell (based on the book by Christina Crawford); ph, Paul Lohmann; ed, Peter E. Berger; m, Henry Mancini; prod d, Bill Malley; art d, Harold Michelson; cos, Irene Sharaff

"No wire hangers—ever!" That this apparently banal phrase has now achieved something like immortality is a reflection of the unbridled extravagance of Faye Dunaway's performance in MOMMIE DEAREST—every line, every glance, every Crawford-esque tic and mannerism is greeted by howls of gleeful recognition among camp cognoscenti. Joan Crawford (Dunaway, in a remarkable makeup job) comes off as a cartoon monster in this over-the-top biopic, which blithely mixes fact, legend, and—especially—elements of Crawford's unique screen persona. The film begins in 1939, when Crawford, already a huge star but unhappy and childless, decides to adopt two children. It ends with her death, when the grown-up kids are left out of her will. A neurotic, driven perfectionist, Crawford takes her frustrations out on her children—especially the rebellious Christina (Mara Hobel as a child, Diana Scarwid as an adult)—who are instructed to call her "Mommie Dearest." Largely from Christina's viewpoint, we see Crawford's succession of lovers and husbands, career ups and downs (mainly downs), fantastic egotism, and dependence on and abusiveness toward her children—especially the infamous scene in which she punishes Christina for using wire clothes hangers instead of wooden ones. Based on the best-selling expose by the real Christina Crawford, MOMMIE DEAREST did poorly upon initial release but has since picked up a dedicated cult following. Needless to say, a number of biographical facts (Crawford actually adopted four children) are ignored by the screenplay.

MON ONCLE D'AMERIQUE
(LES SOMNAMBULES)

1980   125m   c   Drama/Romance   ★★★★½
Andrea/TF-1   (France)   PG/A

Gerard Depardieu (*Rene Ragueneau*), Nicole Garcia (*Janine Garnier*), Roger Pierre (*Jean Le Gall*), Nelly Borgeaud (*Arlette Le Gall*), Marie Dubois (*Therese Ragueneau*), Pierre Arditi (*Zambeaux*), Gerard Darrieu (*Leon Veestrate*), Philippe Laudenbach (*Michel Aubert*), Alexandre Rignault (*Jean's Grandfather*), Guillaume Boisseau (*Jean as a Child*)

p, Philippe Dussart; d, Alain Resnais; w, Jean Gruault (based on the works of Prof. Henri Laborit); ph, Sacha Vierny; ed, Albert Jurgenson; m, Arie Dzierlatka

AAN Best Original Screenplay: Jean Gruault

Director Alain Resnais connects three "case histories" in MON ONCLE D'AMERIQUE, on odd, intellectually stimulating film that takes chances with narrative as it also works as a philosophical essay.

MON ONCLE D'AMERIQUE employs the scientific theories of Henri Laborit to explain the actions of three disparate characters, Jean, Janine and Rene, who are first introduced in broad sketches. Jean Le Gall (Roger Pierre), a government official and family man, falls for Janine Garnier (Nicole Garcia) an actress, who later changes her career and links up Rene Ragueneau (Gerard Depardieu) a textile plant manager and family man.

MON ONCLE D'AMERIQUE presents an unusual narrative structure in that the three main characters are only completely linked by the last reel and even then only tenuously. With a nod to Balzac, Resnais and screenwriter Jean Gruault seems to be in sync with nouvelle vague "brother," Jean-Luc Godard, whose concurrent 1980 "comeback" film, EVERY MAN FOR HIMSELF uses a similar device. MON ONCLE D'AMERIQUE punctuates the three characters' stories with Dr. Laborit's narration, which comments on brain functioning, the nervous system, and behavior types, in theories that sound like a blend of Freud, Piaget, and Noam Chomsky.

Beyond the structure, however, MON ONCLE D'AMERIQUE is less artistically adventurous than earlier Resnais work (HIROSHIMA MON AMOUR, LAST YEAR AT MARIENBAD), where even his great cinematographer, Sacha Vierny, shoots in a comparatively conventional manner. Still, MON ONCLE D'AMERIQUE neatly fits into the Resnais ouevre. By establishing a near-Proustian concern for memory and the impact of social conditions on human behavior (ending with images of a war-torn city that go far outside the "story"), Resnais makes a moving and lasting, if downbeat, statement.

MONA LISA

1986 104m c Crime   ★★★½
Palace (U.K.)   R/18

Bob Hoskins (George), Cathy Tyson (Simone), Michael Caine (Mortwell), Clarke Peters (Anderson), Kate Hardie (Cathy), Robbie Coltrane (Thomas), Zoe Nathenson (Jeannie), Sammi Davies (May), Rod Bedall (Terry), Joe Brown (Dudley)

p, Stephen Woolley, Patrick Cassavetti; d, Neil Jordan; w, Neil Jordan, David Leland; ph, Roger Pratt; ed, Lesley Walker; m, Michael Kamen; prod d, Jamie Leonard; art d, Gemma Jackson; cos, Louise Frogley

AAN Best Actor: Bob Hoskins

Irish director Neil Jordan (THE CRYING GAME) showed early promise with this "Hollywood-ready" blend of slick visual style and fairly standard genre narrative. MONA LISA has the quality of an outstanding audition.

George (Bob Hoskins), a recently released convict, has just served a seven-year sentence after taking the fall for his mob boss, Mortwell (Michael Caine). Looking to collect his due, George meets with Mortwell and is informed that he's been assigned a job chauffeuring a high-class black call girl, Simone (Cathy Tyson). George and Simone take an intense dislike to each other at first, but gradually their relationship warms up. Nearly every night, Simone has George drive her through an area where the streetwalkers gather to ply their trade. Here Simone searches for her only friend, Cathy (Kate Hardie), a 15-year-old whore who once worked for the same pimp (Clarke Peters). Eventually George agrees to descend into the underworld to bring back the young woman, a plot device in the grand tradition of TAXI DRIVER and HARDCORE.

Hoskins is tremendous, giving a sensitive, multi-faceted performance that infuses the film with an inner life. Tyson is perfect as Simone, bringing an enigmatic and exotic air to the role that captures the essence of the title. The ever-reliable Caine is good as the sometimes charming villain. The plot's similarity to Martin Scorsese's TAXI DRIVER is not lost on director Jordan, who quotes the earlier film several times. The film often is charming and distinctively offbeat, particularly in scenes featuring the delightful Robby Coltrane as Thomas, George's gentle giant of a roommate. MONA LISA is a detailed, thoughtful film that sensitively explores the emotions within its seedy, exploitative milieu.

MONKEY BUSINESS

1931 77m bw Comedy   ★★★★
Paramount (U.S.)   /U

Groucho Marx (Groucho), Harpo Marx (Harpo), Chico Marx (Chico), Zeppo Marx (Zeppo), Thelma Todd (Lucille), Tom Kennedy (Gibson), Ruth Hall (Mary Helton), Rockliffe Fellowes (Joe Helton), Harry Woods ("Alky" Briggs), Ben Taggart (Capt. Corcoran)

d, Norman Z. McLeod; w, Arthur Sheekman (based on a story by S.J. Perelman, W.B. Johnstone, Roland Pertwee); ph, Arthur Todd

One of the Marx Brothers' funniest films, MONKEY BUSINESS was their first to be written directly for the screen and is noticeably less stagy than earlier efforts. The boys have stowed away on an ocean liner and race from stateroom to stateroom in order to keep from being clapped in the brig. Harpo gets involved with a Punch and Judy show and delights all of the kids on the vessel (as well as all the adults in the audience). The Marxes become embroiled with Fellowes and Woods, a pair of well-dressed and well-heeled gangsters. Hall, the daughter of a hoodlum, is kidnapped and winds up in a barn after being at a masquerade ball. In the finale, Zeppo, the "straight" brother, goes after the tough hoodlum, while Groucho leaps from one bale of hay to another, offering one-liners as punctuation to the punches. Things slow down a bit when Chico tickles the ivories and Harpo plucks the harp. Thelma Todd handles the female ingenue work well enough and dances the tango well with Groucho. All members of the supporting cast are as effective as they can be in the midst of the comedic cyclone.

MONSIEUR HIRE

1989 81m c Thriller   ★★★★
Cinea/Hachette/FR3 (France)   /15

Michel Blanc (M. Hire), Sandrine Bonnaire (Alice), Luc Thuillier (Emile), Andre Wilms (Inspector)

p, Philippe Carcassonne, Rene Cleitman; d, Patrice Leconte; w, Patrice Leconte, Patrick Dewolf (based on the novel Les Fiancailles de Monsieur Hire by Georges Simenon); ph, Denis Lenoir; ed, Joelle Hache; m, Michael Nyman

A superb thriller containing the ugliest portrait of French provincialism since Henri-Georges Clouzot's LE CORBEAU, Patrice Leconte's MONSIEUR HIRE is set in a Parisian suburb in which conformity reigns supreme. Based on the Georges Simenon novel that also inspired Julien Duvivier's PANIQUE, MONSIEUR HIRE is a penetrating psychological portrait of a love-starved outsider who, by the film's end, arouses the audience's protective instincts. When a young girl is murdered, a dogged police investigator (Wilms) immediately suspects Hire (Blanc), a loner distrusted and hated by his neighbors. Tormented by children who play vicious pranks on him, Hire is hounded mercilessly by the detective. Hire resembles his tormenter in that he is an ever-vigilant soul, if in a less acceptable form—for the outcast is a voyeur who spies on Alice (Bonnaire), the woman who has moved in across the way. Eventually, Alice spots her secret admirer and, surprisingly, pays him a visit rather than reporting him to the police. An uninhibited free spirit, she is drawn to Hire and allows him to share the simple pleasures of his life with her. Despite continual harassment from the detective, Hire even makes plans to move to Switzerland with Alice, who, unfortunately, has a ne'er-do-well boyfriend (Thuillier). The denouement provides a heartrending exploration of duplicity and betrayal, with a particularly effective freeze-frame halting the action just before it flows into the twist ending.

Rather than jazz up the suspense through the conventional device of cross-cutting, director Leconte works within the frame to create a sense of inexorable doom. MONSIEUR HIRE doesn't move at a fast clip; instead, it involves the viewer in a downward spiral by making us co-voyeurs with the title character, whose life has been a study in self-protective detachment. The audience is implicated in this point of view, eyeing Bonnaire hungrily through her window as Leconte's camera pulls back to an over-the-shoulder shot of Blanc doing the same. In another dazzling, sexually provocative sequence that puts the same motif to very different purposes, the film cuts from an over-the-shoulder shot of Bonnaire watching Thuillier as he enjoys a brutal boxing match to a shot of Blanc fondling her.

Anchored by a haunting performance from Blanc as the voyeur who throws years of self-control to the winds, MONSIEUR HIRE is a study of blindness on two levels: that of prejudice and that of love. As a result of this blindness, both the deceiver and the deceived become victims of fate in this icily compelling film.

MONSIEUR VERDOUX

1947 102m bw Crime   ★★★★
Chaplin (U.S.)   /PG

Charles Chaplin (Henri Verdoux/Varney/Bonheur/Floray/Narrator), Mady Correll (Mona Verdoux, His Wife), Allison Roddan (Peter Verdoux, Their Son), Robert Lewis (Maurice Bottello), Audrey Betz (Martha Bottello), Martha Raye (Annabella Bonheur), Ada May (Annette, Her Maid), Isobel Elsom (Marie Grosnay), Marjorie Bennett (Marie's Maid), Margaret Hoffman (Lydia Floray)

p, Charles Chaplin; d, Charles Chaplin; w, Charles Chaplin (based on an idea by Orson Welles); ph, Roland Totheroh, Curt Courant, Wallace Chewing; ed, Willard Nico; m, Charles Chaplin; art d, John Beckman

AAN Best Original Screenplay: Charles Chaplin

Chaplin, that master comedian, cannot seem to decide here which way to go, either into straight drama or farcical crime, but his black humor is in force nevertheless and he has produced a compelling film about the notorious Landru, better known as "Bluebeard." Instead of WWI—when Landru was busy wooing and murdering scores of women, mostly rich spinsters bereft of the males who had gone to fight at the front—Chaplin sets his tale during the late 1930s, when France was on the brink of war with Germany. Though happily married, with a young son, Chaplin feels the need to murder after losing his bank-clerk job. To support his family he romances rich widows and women with savings and is quickly supplied with a countless stream of victims. Raye is exceptional as the one woman who proves his nemesis, and Chaplin is mesmerizing as the droll little methodical killer who becomes especially eccentric and scary when being tried for mass murder. Chaplin attempts to lift this depressing little film out of the pitch darkness of nightmare with little touches that sometimes fail to amuse. He falls into a lake and is rescued by his intended drowning victim; his little boy pulls a cat's tail and he wonders where the child learned such cruelty. Little of it is funny, even though the great silent comedian subtitled this effort "A Comedy of Murders." Had Chaplin played the role straight rather than reaching too far for empathy and some bizarre black laughs, it might have been a minor masterpiece. As it is, MONSIEUR VERDOUX is a curiosity with flashes of brilliance, but definitely not one of Chaplin's best. It is not recommended for children, and to say that about any Chaplin film ought to indicate how frightening this sinister little picture really is. Later Chaplin stated that he made this film to protest the A-bomb. The film was utterly rejected by audiences worldwide when released, although it has gained some critical admirers and cult status since.

MONTE CARLO

1930 90m bw Musical/Comedy   ★★★★
Paramount (U.S.)   /PG

Jack Buchanan (Count Rudolph Falliere), Jeanette MacDonald (Countess Vera von Conti), ZaSu Pitts (Maria, Vera's Maid), Claud Allister (Prince Otto von Seibenheim), Lionel Belmore (Duke Gustave von Seibenheim, His Father), Tyler Brooke (Armand, Rudolph's Friend), John Roche (Paul, the "Real" Hairdresser), Albert Conti (Prince Otto's Companion/M.C.), Helen Garden ("Lady Mary" in Stage Opera), Donald Novis ("M. Beaucaire" in Stage Opera)

p, Ernst Lubitsch; d, Ernst Lubitsch; w, Ernest Vajda, Vincent Lawrence (based on the play *The Blue Coast* by Hans Muller and the novelette "Monsieur Beaucaire" by Booth Tarkington and Evelyn Sutherland); ph, Victor Milner; ed, Merrill White; m, Richard Whiting, W. Franke Harling; cos, Travis Banton

MONTE CARLO did much to advance the role of the sound film, still very much in its infancy when this musical comedy was made in 1929. The immensely talented Ernst Lubitsch was able to so integrate the fluid cinematic techniques he'd used in silents with the new-found discovery of sound that the outcome here is delightful. On the verge of marrying a prince (Claude Allister), countess Jeanette MacDonald dumps the Teutonic twit and boards the "Blue Express" train for Monte Carlo. In Monaco, with little money left, MacDonald checks into a posh hotel, and is spotted immediately in the casino by a wealthy count (Buchanan) who believes that touching MacDonald's golden tresses will bring him good luck. But when Buchanan strokes MacDonald's hair, it's the countess who begins winning magically, and, not knowing the count's true station in life, she hires him as her hairdresser-chauffeur-valet. Playing along just to be close to her, Buchanan calls MacDonald nightly, and, without identifying himself, sings his love for her. As her money again begins to run out and she is forced to reconsider marrying Allister, MacDonald grows increasingly frustrated. While attending "Monsieur Beaucaire" (an opera about a gentleman who poses as a commoner to be near the woman he loves), MacDonald spots Buchanan in a box seat and realizes that he is anything but common. When she confronts him, Buchanan admits that he is also the mysterious caller, and the two live happily and wealthily forever. Very sweet but not too much so, MONTE CARLO is a charming musical comedy generously blessed with the famous Lubitsch touch. MacDonald looks ravishing and is in wonderful voice; her comic skills are also on prominent display here, especially when she frizzes her hair in frustration. Costar Buchanan, who wasn't give the chance to transfer his legendary stage charisma to the screen often enough, fares less well. (He wouldn't appear in another American feature until THE BAND WAGON [1953].) Musical selections include: "Day of Days," "Give Me a Moment, Please," "This is Something New to Me," "Women, Just Women," "She'll Love Me and Like It," "Always in All Ways."

MONTY PYTHON AND THE HOLY GRAIL

1975 89m c Historical/Comedy   ★★★★
Python (U.K.)   PG/15

Graham Chapman (King Arthur/Hiccoughing Guard/Three-Headed Knight), John Cleese (Second Soldier with a Keen Interest in Birds/Large Man with Dead Body/Black Knight/Mr. Newt, a Village Blacksmith Interested in Burning Witches/A Quite Extraordinarily Rude Frenchman/Tim the Wizard/Sir Lancelot), Terry Gilliam (Patsy/Arthur's Trusty Steed/The Green Knight/Soothsayer/Bridgekeeper/Sir Gawain, the First to be Killed by the Rabbit), Eric Idle (The Dead Collector/Mr. Blint, a Village Ne'er-Do-Well Very Keen on Burning Witches/Sir Robin/The Guard Who Doesn't Hiccough but Tries to Get Things Straight/Concorde, Sir Lancelot's Trusty Steed/Roger the Shrubber, a shrubber/Broth), Neil Innes (The First Self-Destructive Monk/Robin's Least Favourite Minstrel/The Page Crushed by a Rabbit/The Owner of a Duck), Terry Jones (Dennis's Mother/Sir Bedevere/Three-Headed Knight/Prince Herbert), Michael Palin (1st Soldier with a Keen Interest in Birds/Dennis/Mr. Duck, a Village Carpenter Who Is Almost Keener Than Anyone Else to Burn Witches/Three-Headed Knight/Sir Galahad/King of Swamp Castle/Brother Maynard's Roommate), Connie Booth (The Witch), Carol Cleveland (Zoot and Dingo), Bee Duffell (Old Crone to Whom King Arthur Said "Ni—")

p, Mark Forstater; d, Terry Gilliam, Terry Jones; w, Graham Chapman, John Cleese, Terry Gilliam, Eric Idle, Terry Jones, Michael Palin; ph, Terry Bedford; ed, John Hackney; m, Neil Innes, De Wolfe; prod d, Roy Smith

A zany, hysterically funny, and sometimes brilliant if sometimes sophomoric send-up of every medieval movie ever made, brought to you by the wacky six-member cast of BBC-television's "Monty Python's Flying Circus." Superior to their first film, and AND NOW FOR SOMETHING COMPLETELY DIFFERENT (which was only a series of their televison vignettes released for the theaters), HOLY GRAIL is told in a straight (well all right, fairly straight) narrative structure that follows King Arthur (Chapman) and his knights in their search for the legendary Holy Grail. What transpires in the next 90 minutes is nearly impossible to describe to those unfamiliar with the lunacy of the Python bunch (the six male actors play nearly all the parts, including women's roles), but some of the highlights are well worth mentioning (this film must be seen to be understood). Due to the lack of horses in the kingdom (and a low budget), Chapman and his knights are followed throughout the movie by their servants, who smack two coconuts together to simulate the sound of hoofbeats. One of Chapman's first battles is against the Black Knight (Cleese), who refuses to let the king pass. A reluctant Chapman is then forced to cut the man limb from limb until all that is left of Cleese is a torso that yells at the King to come back and fight like a man. Meanwhile, Sir Lancelot (once again Cleese) rushes into a castle and hacks up several wedding guests in a bloody frenzy in an attempt to rescue an effeminate prince who really doesn't need to be rescued. After Cleese calms down and surveys the carnage, he manages a feeble, "I just get carried away" as an apology. Of course, every fan of this film has his favorite moment (the Trojan Rabbit, the Knights Who Say "Ni", Robin and his Minstrels, the killer rabbit, the Holy Hand Grenade and the crazed bridgekeeper). But, all the insanity finally leads to a climactic battle scene populated with hundreds of costumed extras, which is stopped before it really gets started by a few carloads of policemen who interrupt the shooting and grab the camera. Not only is HOLY GRAIL a strange, occasionally sidesplitting film, but it paints a grubby, muddy, and vile portrait of life in the middle ages. The set design and visual style are detailed and rich, lending such credence to the film that at the end, when modern-day police arrive to break things up, it is a real shock. A must see.

MONTY PYTHON'S LIFE OF BRIAN

1979 93m c Religious/Comedy   ★★★★
Warner Bros./Orion (U.K.)   R/15

Terry Jones (The Virgin Mandy/The Mother of Brian, a Ratbag/Colin/Simon the Holy Man/Saintly Passer-By), Graham Chapman (1st Wise Man/Brian Called Brian/Biggus Dickus), Michael Palin (2nd Wise Man/Mr. Big Nose/Francis a Revolutionary/Mrs. A. Who

Casts the Second Stone/Ex-leper/Ben, an Ancient Prisoner/Pontius Pilate, Roman Governor/A Boring Prophet/Eddie/Nisus Wettus), John Cleese (3rd Wise Man/Reg, Leader of the Judean People's Front/Jewish Official at the Stoning/Centurion of the Yard/Deadly Dirk/Arthur), Kenneth Colley (Jesus the Christ), Gwen Taylor (Mrs. Big Nose/Woman with Sick Donkey/Young Girl), Eric Idle (Mr. Cheeky/Stan Called Loretta, a Confused Revolutionary/Harry the Haggler, Beard and Stone Salesman/Culprit Woman, Who Casts the First Stone/Intensely Dull Youth/Otto, the Nazarene Jailer's Assistant/Mr. Frisbee III), Terence Bayler (Gregory/Revolutionaries and Masked Commandos/Dennis), Carol Cleveland (Mrs. Gregory/Elsie), Charles McKeown (Man Further Forward/Revolutionaries and Masked Commandos/Roman Soldier Stig/Giggling Guard/A False Prophet/Blind Man)

p, John Goldstone; d, Terry Jones; w, Graham Chapman, John Cleese, Terry Gilliam, Eric Idle, Terry Jones, Michael Palin; ph, Peter Biziou; ed, Julian Doyle; m, Geoffrey Burgon, Andre Jacquemin, David Howman, Eric Idle; art d, Roger Christian; cos, Hazel Pethig, Charles Knode; anim, Terry Gilliam

Of all the feature films concocted by the British comedy troupe "Monty Python's Flying Circus," LIFE OF BRIAN is their most sustained effort, with a truly linear plot line. While it may lack the sheer comic anarchy of their other work, it is probably their funniest collective effort.

In Judea, a mother tends her newborn infant. Three wise men come to herald his birth and then find out that they want the manger next door. This is the birthplace of one Brian Cohen, not Jesus Christ.

Forward to the year 33 AD. Brian joins the People's Front of Judea, a small group of would-be terrorists. Brian aids a PFJ plot to kidnap the wife of Pontius Pilate (Michael Palin), the Roman governor of Jerusalem. But inside Pilate's house, the PFJ run into another terrorist group with the same plan, and all are captured by Roman guards while squabbling among themselves. Brian escapes and hides from the soldiers by posing as a streetcorner preacher, extemporizing a sermon that is derided by his audience of jaded Messiah-seekers. As soon as he attempts to leave, however, he attracts followers, and the more he runs, the more they're persuaded that he is the true Messiah.

The Pythons spent rather a lot of time denying that LIFE OF BRIAN was blasphemous, which it clearly is not (though that didn't stop pickets and calls for bans across the US and Great Britain—mostly from people who hadn't seen the film). Aside from such usual Python subjects of mirth as pompous public officials, men dressed as women, and do-gooders who spend too much time arguing parliamentary procedure ever to accomplish anything, the main subject of satire here is not religion but religious fanaticism. And even that is of a fairly inoffensive variety, making fun of those who just want to have a formula for behavior so that they don't have to bother thinking for themselves.

Chapman is as perfect a lead here as he was as King Arthur in HOLY GRAIL—he looks so straight, noble and stalwart, but there's always that crazed glint lurking in the back of his eyes. Everyone in the troupe is at the peak of their form, and BRIAN contains too many hilarious bits to single out the best.

Watch for a quick cameo by George Harrison, who funded LIFE OF BRIAN so the story goes, because he figured it was the only way he would ever get to see another Python movie.

MONTY PYTHON'S THE MEANING OF LIFE

1983 107m c Comedy ★★★
Celandine/Python (U.K.) R/18

Graham Chapman, John Cleese, Terry Gilliam, Eric Idle, Terry Jones, Michael Palin, Carol Cleveland, Judy Loe, Simon Jones, Andrew MacLachlan

p, John Goldstone; d, Terry Jones; w, Graham Chapman, John Cleese, Terry Gilliam, Eric Idle, Terry Jones, Michael Palin; ph, Peter Hannan; ed, Julian Doyle; m, Eric Idle, John Du Prez; prod d, Harry Lange; art d, Richard Dawking; chor, Arlene Phillips; cos, James Acheson; anim, Terry Gilliam

For their fourth film, the "Monty Python" troupe reverted to the vignette structure used in their first (and weakest) feature, AND NOW FOR SOMETHING COMPLETELY DIFFERENT. While the sketches are loosely structured to convey elements of life (e.g., birth, education, sex, food, the military, and death), the film is uneven and disconnected. It gets off to a promising start with a marvelous pre-credit sequence depicting a British financial building being raided by swashbuckling pirates and turned (literally) into a giant ship. Many of the sketches show the Pythons' deranged, offbeat humor at its best, but the film begins to pale long before the end and relies on some revolting bits such as a "live" organ transplant and the spectacular (and graphic) explosion of an obese glutton. This is definitely not for anyone with delicate sensibilities.

MOON AND SIXPENCE, THE

1942 89m c/bw Drama ★★★★
UA (U.S.) /A

George Sanders (Charles Strickland), Herbert Marshall (Geoffrey Wolfe), Steven Geray (Dirk Stroeve), Doris Dudley (Blanche Stroeve), Eric Blore (Capt. Nichols), Albert Basserman (Doctor Coutras), Molly Lamont (Mrs. Strickland), Elena Verdugo (Ata), Florence Bates (Tiara Johnson), Heather Thatcher (Rose Waterford)

p, David L. Loew; d, Albert Lewin; w, Albert Lewin (based on a novel by W. Somerset Maugham); ph, John Seitz; ed, Richard L. Van Enger; m, Dimitri Tiomkin; prod d, Gordon Willis; art d, F. Paul Sylos

AAN Best Score: Dimitri Tiomkin

Though Marshall is the svelte-voiced narrator of this riveting story, it is Sanders as heartless artist Charles Strickland who makes this film a standout. He is a broker who decides to discard his career to take up his passion, painting. To that end he convinces Dirk Stroeve (Geray), a successful but mediocre painter, to aid him in developing his art and, during the process, when Stroeve takes Strickland into his home as a protege, the cad seduces Stroeve's wife. Strickland's friend Geoffrey (Marshall) later finds the rake in Tahiti, where Strickland comes to grips with his own personality and discovers his great talent, producing masterpieces until his tragic death.

The Maugham story on which this film is based unabashedly profiles the profligate career of the great Paul Gauguin, and Sanders plays this introspective, cruel-streaked genius to the hilt. Lewin's direction is terse, swift, and often magnificent as he chronicles Strickland's meteoric career and love life, the best part of the film being that set in the tropics toward the end. Here a sepia tone is employed to capture some of the illustrative flavor of the paintings shown and, near the finale, employs color to potent effect. Seitz's camerawork is terrific and the supporting cast, especially Geray and Blore, as a drunkard, is excellent.

MOON IS BLUE, THE

1953 99m bw Comedy ★★
UA (U.S.) /PG

William Holden (Donald Gresham), David Niven (David Slater), Maggie McNamara (Patty O'Neill), Tom Tully (Michael O'Neill), Dawn Addams (Cynthia Slater), Fortunio Bonanova (Television Announcer), Gregory Ratoff (Taxi Driver), Hardy Kruger (Sightseer), Johanna Matz (His Wife)

p, Otto Preminger, F. Hugh Herbert; d, Otto Preminger; w, F. Hugh Herbert (based on his play); ph, Ernest Laszlo; ed, Ronald Sinclair, Otto Ludwig; m, Herschel Burke Gilbert; prod d, Nicolai Remisoff; cos, Don Loper

AAN Best Actress: Maggie McNamara; AAN Best Editing: Otto Ludwig; AAN Best Song: Herschel Burke Gilbert (Music), Sylvia Fine (Lyrics)

No one today is likely to mistake this smarmy little sex farce for a good film, but it is significant historically as one of the nails in the coffin of Hollywood's self-imposed Production Code. Otto Preminger, an Austrian bull running amuck in the china shop of Hollywood censorship, refused to take the words "virgin", "pregnant", "mistress," and "seduction" out of his script, based on a popular Broadway farce. The film was released without the MPAA seal of approval, and was a solid box office success. The rest, as they say, is history.

The story—which hinges on whether a thirty-something architect (William Holden) or a forty-something roue (David Niven) will get a twenty-something virgin (Maggie McNamara) into bed—follows a painfully predictable line. Holden and Niven are fine, but McNamara, a rather amateurish performer here making her film debut, comes across like a recent drop-out from the Audrey Hepburn Spirited Gamine Academy. (She would act in only three more films before her suicide in 1978.) Luckily, the scene in the taxi where some of the "dirty" words are used comes fairly early on, so you can skip the rest and just read about it in some film history text. Try watching TROUBLE IN PARADISE or THE MAJOR AND THE MINOR instead.

MOONLIGHTING

1982 97m c Drama   ★★★★
Miracle (U.K.)   PG

Jeremy Irons (Nowak), Eugene Lipinski (Banaszak), Jiri Stanislav (Wolski), Eugeniusz Hackiewicz (Kudaj), Dorothy Zienciowska (Lot Airline Girl), Edward Arthur (Immigration Officer), Denis Holmes (Neighbor), Renu Setna (Junk Shop Owner), David Calder (Supermarket Manager), Judy Gridley (Supermarket Supervisor)

p, Mark Shivas, Jerzy Skolimowski; d, Jerzy Skolimowski; w, Jerzy Skolimowski, Boleslaw Sulik, Barry Vince, Danuta Witold Stok; ph, Tony Pierce-Roberts; ed, Barrie Vince; m, Stanley Myers, Hans Zimmer; prod d, Tony Woollard; cos, Jane Robinson

One month after martial law was declared in Poland in the wake of the Solidarity uprising, Jerzy Skolimowski began work on this political allegory about a group of four Polish workers in London. Led by the only English speaker among them, their foreman, Nowak (Jeremy Irons), the group arrives to renovate a flat for their Polish boss. Working illegally at what by English standards are cut rates, they must live on the site under uncomfortable living arrangements. When Soviet troops roll into Warsaw, Nowak learns of the events, but, driven by private anxieties and determined to avoid dissent, schemes to conceal the news from his men. As budgetary and scheduling pressures mount, he must take increasingly drastic and draconian measures to do so. MOONLIGHTING contains no manifestos or crude symbols. Its politics are almost entirely limned in the actions and thoughts of Nowak, who is beautifully portrayed by Irons in the performance that made him one of the most respected actors of the decade. The better-educated and more highly paid Nowak is sympathetically characterized even as he mirrors the actions of the Polish authorities, cutting off his men's access to information and family ties, the workers' hierarchy (including the bosses back home) serving as a microcosm of Polish society. Director-cowriter Skolimowski never fails to truly dramatize his themes, however—creating that rarity, a "political film" that is also deeply personal, true to life, and morally and emotionally complex.

MOONRAKER

1979 126m c Spy/Adventure   ★★★
UA (U.K.)   PG

Roger Moore (James Bond), Lois Chiles (Holly Goodhead), Michel Lonsdale (Drax), Richard Kiel (Jaws), Corinne Clery (Corinne Dufour), Bernard Lee ("M"), Geoffrey Keen (Frederick Gray), Desmond Llewelyn ("Q"), Lois Maxwell (Miss Moneypenny), Emily Bolton (Manuela)

p, Albert R. Broccoli; d, Lewis Gilbert; w, Christopher Wood (based on the novel by Ian Fleming); ph, Jean Tournier; ed, John Glen; m, John Barry; prod d, Ken Adam; art d, Max Douy, Charles Bishop; fx, Derek Meddings, John Evans, John Richardson; cos, Jacques Fonteray

AAN Best Visual Effects: Derek Meddings, Paul Wilson, John Evans

A space-age James Bond (Moore) pursues evil to the final frontier in this big-budget entry that cost as much as the first eight Bond films put together. Bond is assigned to search for a missing space shuttle, and along the way he discovers a plot by Drax (Lonsdale) to take over the world by replacing its population with the super race he has bred in the huge space station to which Bond comes for their final battle. Richard Kiel, a dentist's dream, repeats his role from THE SPY WHO LOVED ME as the indestructible, steel-toothed Jaws. Lois Chiles plays the mandatory Bond love interest, and the film marks the last appearance of Lee as M. The gadgets are up to the usual Bond standards, but fancy effects do not a movie make, and 007 is less satisfying floating around

in space than when his feet are more or less firmly planted on the ground. John Barry and Hal David collaborated on the theme song, which was sung by Shirley Bassey.

MOONSTRUCK

1987 102m c Romance/Comedy   ★★★★
MGM (U.S.)   PG

Cher (Loretta Castorini), Nicolas Cage (Ronny Cammareri), Vincent Gardenia (Cosmo Castorini), Olympia Dukakis (Rose Castorini), Danny Aiello (Johnny Cammareri), Julie Bovasso (Rita Cappomaggi), John Mahoney (Perry), Louis Guss (Raymond Cappomaggi), Feodor Chaliapin Jr. (Loretta's Grandfather), Anita Gillette (Mona)

p, Patrick Palmer, Norman Jewison; d, Norman Jewison; w, John Patrick Shanley; ph, David Watkin; ed, Lou Lombardo; m, Dick Hyman; prod d, Philip Rosenberg; chor, Lofti Travolta

AAN Best Picture; AA Best Actress: Cher; AAN Best Supporting Actor: Vincent Gardenia; AA Best Supporting Actress: Olympia Dukakis; AAN Best Director: Norman Jewison; AA Best Original Screenplay: John Patrick Shanley

Oscar-nominated for Best Picture in 1987, this delightful romantic comedy directed by Norman Jewison and deftly scripted by John Patrick Shanley features excellent ensemble performances and an acting tour de force from Cher. A 38-year-old widow, Loretta Castorini (Cher), works as a bookkeeper and lives in Brooklyn with her very Italian-American family: her father, Cosmo (Vincent Gardenia), a prosperous plumber; her mother, Rose (Olympia Dukakis); and her grandfather (Feodor Chaliapin). Her longtime boyfriend, Johnny Cammareri (Danny Aiello), proposes to her; although not passionately in love with him, she accepts. However, Johnny must travel to his mother's deathbed in Sicily before the wedding. Meanwhile, Loretta meets Ronny (Nicholas Cage), Johnny's brother, to whom Johnny hasn't spoken in five years, and they are instantly attracted to each other. MOONSTRUCK brilliantly captures its Italian-American milieu. Director Jewison and screenwriter Shanley have fashioned a charming, funny tale of infidelity and transcendent love whose cultural setting provides both content and context. A symbol of the undeniable power and unpredictability of passionate love, the moon that glows magically over the Manhattan skyline as the events in the film transpire is there not only for Cher and Cage but also for Gardenia and Dukakis. Cher turns in an outstanding performance that deservedly won her an Academy Award for Best Actress. Although Cage stumbles at points, the supporting performances are all superb and wonderfully nuanced. The moon and the whole of the film are beautifully photographed by Oscar winner David Watkin. Simply stated, it is difficult not to be swept up by this charming picture.

MORGAN!

1966 97m bw Comedy/Drama   ★★★
Quintra (U.K.)   /A

Vanessa Redgrave (Leonie Delt), David Warner (Morgan Delt), Robert Stephens (Charles Napier), Irene Handl (Mrs. Delt), Newton Blick (Mr. Henderson), Nan Munro (Mrs. Henderson), Bernard Bresslaw (Policeman), Arthur Mullard (Wally), Graham Crowden (Counsel), Peter Cellier (2nd Counsel)

p, Leon Clore; d, Karel Reisz; w, David Mercer (based on the television play "A Suitable Case for Treatment" by David Mercer); ph, Larry Pizer, Gerry Turpin; ed, Victor Proctor, Tom Priestley; m, John Dankworth; art d, Philip Harrison

AAN Best Actress: Vanessa Redgrave; AAN Best Costume Design: Jocelyn Rickards

In the late 1950s and early 1960s, British films were densely populated with angry young men. In MORGAN! the young man is not only angry, he's crazier than a bedbug in Bedlam. By altering the nature of the role from the original TV play, the creators of this film seem to be saying that anything is possible if the leading character is deranged. With that premise, all normalcy is tossed out the window and we are asked to accept the lead as he is, crazy or not. By today's standards, this picture is somewhat dated. The technique often overwhelms the story, with innumerable slow-motion shots, freeze frames, and surrealistic scenes.

Warner is Morgan, a London artist married to Leonie (Redgrave), a woman considerably above his working-class standing. He spends his time daydreaming about swinging through the jungle, which understandably alienates his spouse. (Clips of KING KONG and TARZAN movies are used in the dream sequences.) Leonie secures a divorce, and Morgan, who was supposedly in Greece, shows up on the day it is to be granted. He wants her back and is upset at her plans to marry a priggish art dealer (Stephens) closer to her own social status. Morgan's crazed attempts to win Leonie back involve, among other things, bombs, skeletons, kidnapping, and gorilla suits. A Mona Lisa smile from Leonie and a hammer and sickle motif end the film on an enigmatic note.

The director's attempt to blend reality and fantasy is sometimes successful, but the humor is strained as a result and doesn't always work. It's a bizarre film, too heavy in places and not light enough in others. The picture was released in England as MORGAN: A SUITABLE CASE FOR TREATMENT. Czech director Reisz has made some fascinating films, especially SATURDAY NIGHT AND SUNDAY MORNING. Here, however, he tries so hard to be interesting that the effort shows in every frame.

MORNING GLORY

1933   74m   bw   Drama   ★★★
RKO   (U.S.)   /A

Katharine Hepburn (Ada Love/"Eva Lovelace"), Douglas Fairbanks Jr. (Joseph Sheridan), Adolphe Menjou (Louis Easton), Mary Duncan (Rita Vernon), C. Aubrey Smith (Robert Harley Hedges), Don Alvarado (Pepe Velez, the Gigolo), Fred Santley (Will Seymour), Richard Carle (Henry Lawrence), Tyler Brooke (Charles Van Dusen), Geneva Mitchell (Gwendolyn Hall)

p, Pandro S. Berman; d, Lowell Sherman; w, Howard J. Green (based on a play by Zoe Akins); ph, Bert Glennon; ed, William Hamilton; m, Max Steiner; art d, Van Nest Polglase, Charles Kirk; cos, Walter Plunkett

AA Best Actress: Katharine Hepburn

Hepburn received her first Oscar nomination for this, her third film, won the Oscar for her role, and was three times as good as the picture itself. The story paralleled Hepburn's own real-life experience so there was an undeniable streak of reality in her performance. Hepburn leaves a tiny burg in New England. She enters New York City as stagestruck as is humanly possible, but she soon learns that there are a lot of worms in the Big Apple and it's not the most hospitable place to seek fame and fortune. She encounters veteran actor Smith, who has been around since stages were lit by candles, and he takes an interest in her, teaches her a few tricks about acting, and squires her to the right parties. He brings her to a cocktail bash tossed by Duncan, a successful actress and neurotic woman in the Margo Channing (Bette Davis's role in ALL ABOUT EVE) mold. Hepburn hasn't eaten anything so she gets very drunk on champagne and performs two Shakespearean soliloquies for the sake of the startled party-goers. Later, Hepburn takes up with slick Menjou, a manager, then tosses him aside in favor of young playwright Fairbanks, who has written a new show that Duncan is to star in. When the actress goes off the deep end and leaves the show on opening night, guess who steps in, does the role, and is an overnight sensation?

By the story outline, it's easy to see where ALL ABOUT EVE got some of its characters and inspiration. The young actress, the older and temperamental star, the playwright, the manager should be evident. The picture was remade as STAGE STRUCK with Susan Strasberg as the aspiring hopeful and Henry Fonda and Christopher Plummer as the men in her life. That film was not as successful as this one, which was raised in entertainment value by Hepburn's glowing performance. By 1933, the combination of backstage manipulations and overnight success was already a cliche that had been covered many times before. Merian C. Cooper served as the executive producer, and if that seems familiar, it's because he was also responsible for such films as THE FOUR FEATHERS, KING KONG, FORT APACHE, MIGHTY JOE YOUNG, THE QUIET MAN, and many more.

MOROCCO

1930   90m   bw   Romance/War   ★★★★
Paramount   (U.S.)

Gary Cooper (Tom Brown), Marlene Dietrich (Amy Jolly), Adolphe Menjou (Mons. Le Bessiere), Ullrich Haupt (Adjutant Caesar), Juliette Compton (Anna Dolores), Francis McDonald (Cpl. Tatoche), Albert Conti (Col. Quinnevieres), Eve Southern (Mme. Caesar), Michael Visaroff (Barratire), Paul Porcasi (Lo Tinto)

p, Hector Turnbull; d, Josef von Sternberg; w, Jules Furthman (based on the novel Amy Jolly by Benno Vigny); ph, Lee Garmes, Lucien Ballard; ed, S.K. Winston; m, Karl Hajos; art d, Hans Dreier; cos, Travis Banton

AAN Best Actress: Marlene Dietrich; AAN Best Director: Josef Von Sternberg; AAN Best Cinematography: Lee Garmes; AAN Best Art Direction: Hans Dreier (Art Direction)

Marlene Dietrich's first American film is an atmospheric tale of love during wartime, exquisitely directed by Josef von Sternberg. Amy Jolly (Dietrich), a German singer, arrives in North Africa and is hired as the lead act in a cabaret frequented by members of the Foreign Legion. Pursued by Le Bessier (Adolphe Menjou), a worldly gentleman, she finds herself attracted to handsome Legionnaire Tom Brown (Gary Cooper), who ultimately tests the strength of her love.

Like many of Sternberg's most memorable films, MOROCCO is an intelligently observed, passionately realized story of sexual obsession, slim on plot but heavy on atmosphere. Don't look for realism here: it's a sumptuous, overheated Orientalist fantasy peopled with characters (especially Dietrich) who couldn't exist anywhere in the real world, let alone in a Moroccan desert city. MOROCCO would go a long way toward establishing Dietrich's unique star persona (THE BLUE ANGEL was held back from the US market until this Americanized Dietrich could be presented). Camera wizard Lee Garmes was ordered by Sternberg to shoot Dietrich only from one side (an idea borrowed from Garbo films). But Dietrich's comparatively irregular features presented special problems. Garmes compensated with what he called "north light," positioning the key above her and slightly forward. It hollowed her cheeks, shadowed her heavy eyelids, and masked the dimensions of her wide nose. Dietrich was thrilled with the effect; she would insist on similar lighting in movies, public appearances, and photo shoots for the length of her career.

Sternberg and Cooper didn't get along well, and the star resented the director's use of German on the set. Sternberg retaliated by blocking scenes so that Dietrich stands above Cooper, and he's forced to look up to her. Perhaps because of Cooper's mood of angry resignation, he delivers a fey, inadvertently effective performance. His effete mannerisms—tucking a rose behind his ear, smoking with a limp wrist, kissing behind a fan—create a satisfying contrast with Dietrich's androgyny (which is most apparent when she kisses a woman on the mouth in a nightclub scene).

MOSCOW ON THE HUDSON

1984   115m   c   Comedy/Drama   ★★★½
Columbia   (U.S.)   R/15

Robin Williams (Vladimir Ivanoff), Maria Conchita Alonso (Lucia Lombardo), Cleavant Derricks (Lionel Witherspoon), Alejandro Rey (Orlando Ramirez), Savely Kramarov (Boris), Elya Baskin (Anatoly), Oleg Rudnik (Yury), Alexander Beniaminov (Vladimir's Grandfather), Ludmila Kramarevsky (Vladimir's Mother), Ivo Vrzal (Vladimir's Father)

p, Paul Mazursky; d, Paul Mazursky; w, Paul Mazursky, Leon Capetanos; ph, Don McAlpine; ed, Richard Halsey; m, David McHugh; prod d, Pato Guzman; art d, Michael Molly, Peter Rothe; cos, Albert Wolsky

A loving, dramatic comedy that resembles early Frank Capra in its patriotism and sentiment, this movie just misses on several levels but has enough humor to make you smile and enough corn to warm anyone's heart. Vladimir Ivanoff (Robin Williams) is a saxophonist with a Russian circus visiting the US on a tour. Just before leaving New York, Vladimir is in Manhattan's trendiest department store, Bloomingdale's, when he makes the decision to defect. He races around the store, chased by KGB men, and hides under a counter handled by Lucia Lombardo (Maria Conchita Alonso). After the cops come in and Vladimir tells them he's defecting, he is taken to Harlem by security guard Lionel Witherspoon (Cleavant Derricks), whose family welcomes him. It isn't long before Vladimir and Lucia are an item, and she tries to help him get official status in the US through an immigration attorney (Alejandro Rey). There is no great story to speak of, just the adjustments Vladimir must make to become an American.

MOSQUITO COAST, THE

1986 117m c Adventure   ★★★½
Warner Bros.   (U.S.)   R/PG

Harrison Ford *(Allie Fox)*, Helen Mirren *(Mother)*, River Phoenix *(Charlie)*, Jadrien Steele *(Jerry)*, Hilary Gordon *(April)*, Rebecca Gordon *(Clover)*, Jason Alexander *(Clerk)*, Dick O'Neill *(Mr. Polski)*, Alice Sneed *(Mrs. Polski)*, Tiger Haynes *(Mr. Semper)*

p, Jerome Hellman; d, Peter Weir; w, Paul Schrader (based on the novel by Paul Theroux); ph, John Seale; ed, Thom Noble; m, Maurice Jarre; prod d, John Stoddart; art d, John Wingrove; fx, Larry Cavanaugh; cos, Gary Jones

A courageous and serious film that explores the limits of the mythic American virtues of persistence, inventiveness, and rugged individualism. Allie Fox (Harrison Ford) is an eccentric inventor, a wildly optimistic can-do kind of guy. Disgusted with what he perceives to be a dying America, Fox takes his wife (Helen Mirren) and four children, including 15-year-old Charlie (River Phoenix), to an unsettled area near Honduras called the Mosquito Coast. Fox buys the deed to an isolated town that turns out to be nothing but a few shacks and a handful of residents. But he mercilessly pushes his family, the locals, and himself, driven by an obsessive desire to recreate society along Utopian lines. His dream world is shaken when three gun-toting terrorists show up. Unfortunately, as Fox's dreams and sanity begin to fall apart, so does the film, but it's memorable and intense up to that point. Schrader's screenplay, based on an allegorical novel by Paul Theroux, suggests that the very qualities that allow people and nations to achieve greatness may also plant the seeds of future destruction.

MOST DANGEROUS GAME, THE

1932 63m bw Thriller/Adventure   ★★★½
RKO   (U.S.)

Joel McCrea *(Bob Rainsford)*, Fay Wray *(Eve Trowbridge)*, Leslie Banks *(Count Zaroff)*, Robert Armstrong *(Martin Trowbridge)*, Steve Clemente, Noble Johnson *(Tartar Servants)*, Hale Hamilton

p, Merian C. Cooper, Ernest B. Schoedsack; d, Ernest B. Schoedsack, Irving Pichel; w, James Ashmore Creelman (based on a story by Richard Connell); ph, Henry Gerrard; ed, Archie Marshek; m, Max Steiner

This is a grim and morose film with strong undertones of sadism and, toward the end, brutality. It is also a genuinely frightening film involving Banks as a mad Russian count who lords over a mist-enshrouded island and waits like a vicious spider for wayward ships to wreck themselves on the dangerous reefs surrounding his sinister domain. One of the sinking ships delivers up flotsam in the form of McCrea, Wray, and Armstrong, who are, at first, warmly welcomed to Banks's lavish estate. But slowly, as Banks describes his passion for hunting the wild beasts on the island, he begins to finger a scar on his forehead, one caused by a lion. Before they can realize their horrible situation, the shipwrecked survivors are compelled to flee into the thorny wilderness of the island with their host hunting them as he would animals, armed with bow and arrows, to give them a sporting chance. With Banks are his henchmen and a pack of the most vicious dogs ever unleashed in any film. Directors Schoedsack and Pichel dwell on the hunt, showing the victims fleeing madly through the brush and forests, narrowly missing death at the claws of wild animals or plunging into bottomless gorges. The hounds are shown in quick closeups that are terrifyingly abrupt, and telescopic shots cutting from the hunter to the hunted heighten the tension. Banks is relentless in his pursuit, crazily blowing his hunting horn and drawing his bow with an accuracy that proves deadly. He finally meets the grim fate he has designed for the others, plunging to his death while his own bloodthirsty hounds close in on

him. There are wonderful atmospherics to this film—the count's looming, black castle, the primeval forests of the island—the same kind of environment producers Cooper and Schoedsack would create for their horror masterpiece, KING KONG, a year later. The studio thought that showing some decapitated heads, victims of Banks's unnatural hunts, might upset viewers, so these scenes were later cut. Wray, Armstrong, and Steiner, who composed the eerie score, would all be effectively used in KING KONG. The dark theme of this movie would be employed in countless films to come, as well as in radio and television programs. RKO would remake this film as A GAME OF DEATH and United Artists would explore the idea in RUN FOR THE SUN.

MOTHER AND THE WHORE, THE
(LA MAMAN ET LA PUTAIN)

1973 210m bw Drama   ★★★★
Losange/Elite/Cine Qua Non/Simar/V-M   (France)   /X

Bernadette Lafont *(Marie)*, Jean-Pierre Leaud *(Alexandre)*, Francoise Lebrun *(Veronika)*, Isabelle Weingarten *(Gilberte)*, Jacques Renard *(Friend)*, Jean-Noel Picq, Jessa Darrieux, Marinka Matuszewski, Genevieve Mnich, Berthe Grandval

p, Pierre Cottrell; d, Jean Eustache; w, Jean Eustache; ph, Pierre Lhomme, Jacques Renard, Michel Cenet; ed, Jean Eustache, Denise de Casabianca

If any film signified that the French New Wave had come to an end, it was THE MOTHER AND THE WHORE, a grueling three-and-a-half hour study that may be one of the more enlightening works the cinema has ever produced. Set against a background of Paris cafes and tiny one-room apartments, it traces the amorous adventures of Leaud, an irresponsible young man who pretends to be a leftist intellectual. He is really little more than a victim of the postwar existentialist thought that paved the way for the materialistic attitudes of the early 1970s and a generation filled with empty ideals. One morning, Leaud feels an extraordinary need to marry. Leaving the small flat he shares with Lafont, his lover and willing meal ticket, he sets out to pop the question to his old girlfriend. Leaud brings the girl to a cafe where he engages in a long pseudo-intellectual monologue while asking for her hand. She flatly refuses, responding, "What novel are you being a character in?" (Leaud characteristically perceives himself in such terms.) Later that same day, he passes by a cafe where he spots the vampirish-looking Lebrun staring at him. He gets her phone number and agrees to meet her later. After several failed attempts to meet her, the two eventually arrange to meet at a cafe. Lebrun works as a nurse, a job that allows her enough money to pay for her dingy room, to buy pretty clothes, and to keep herself numbed with alcohol. Other than this, the only thing that interests her is sex, and she has no qualms about sleeping with any passing stranger. Leaud and Lebrun start a shaky affair that consists mainly of meeting in cafes and long monologues on Leaud's part. To Lebrun, he has become much more than her usual casual fling. She even calls him while he is spending the evening with Lafont, then sleeps with both of them. Lafont attempts suicide and the tension created by the triangle continually mounts until a gruesome climax in which Lebrun, who has seemed aloof and unaffected to this point, delivers a tear-filled soliloquy revealing her self-perception as a sexual object. Leaud follows her to her room and asks her to marry him. She accepts while vomiting into a bucket which he holds.

Prior to THE MOTHER AND THE WHORE, director Eustache had worked as an assistant for New Wave directors, most notably Jean-Luc Godard. (He even appeared briefly in WEEKEND). His first two solo efforts were medium-length features that were of some interest, but this picture proved he was a perceptive filmmaker. However, Eustache's career was very short. After THE MOTHER AND THE WHORE won both the Grand Prix and the International Critics Award at Cannes, he made only one more feature before his suicide in 1980. THE MOTHER AND THE WHORE captures a sense of realism rare in any type of film, for it brings us deep beneath the surface of the characters's exteriors.

MOTHER INDIA

1957 152m c Drama   ★★★½
Mehboob Productions Ltd.   (India)

Nargis Dutt *(Radha)*, Sunil Dutt *(Birju)*, Raj Kumar *(Shamulu)*

p, Mehboob Khan; d, Mehboob Khan; w, V. Mirza, Ali Raza; m, Naushad; prod d, V.H. Palnitkar

The most popular film in Indian history—it's said to have been playing somewhere in the country every day since its release. This epic melodrama is so widely known and deeply revered that Indira Gandhi used the title on election posters and campaigned with star Nargis Dutt at her side. Radha (Nargis) is a rural matriarch who loses her husband (Raj Kumar) after a farming accident. With her sons, she struggles to survive despite the machinations of a singularly villainous landlord. When wayward son Birju (Sunil Dutt) becomes an outlaw, Radha must act to restore order to the community.

Director Mehboob Khan's very Indian brand of Marxism is neatly represented by his production company's logo, which combines the hammer and sickle with the symbol denoting "Om." The film is unmistakably left-leaning but curiously compromised—after it makes about as strong a case for killing the local *zamindar* (landlord) as could be imagined, it suggests that actually doing so would be a violation of *dharma* (order, propriety). Salvation lies not in violence but in adherence to the traditional values embodied in the archetypal mother figure, unforgettably played by Nargis Dutt. For Nargis, who had earlier specialized in urban sophisticates (AWAARA), the peasant Radha was a marked religion; it nevertheless became the definitive role of her career. Having conducted a notorious affair with Raj Kapoor (India's greatest star and a formidable director), she soon married co-star Sunil Dutt and settled down, redeeming herself in the eyes of the Indian public. Their son, musclebound Sunjay Dutt, became India's leading action star during the 1980s.

MOULIN ROUGE

1952   123m   c   Biography   ★★★★
Romulus   (U.K.)   /PG

Jose Ferrer *(Henri de Toulouse-Lautrec/The Comte de Toulouse-Lautrec)*, Colette Marchand *(Marie Charlet)*, Suzanne Flon *(Myriamme Hayem)*, Zsa Zsa Gabor *(Jane Avril)*, Katherine Kath *(La Goulue)*, Claude Nollier *(Countess de Toulouse-Lautrec)*, Muriel Smith *(Aicha)*, Georges Lannes *(Patou)*, Walter Crisham *(Valentin Dessosse)*, Mary Clare *(Mme. Loubet)*

p, John Huston; d, John Huston; w, Anthony Veiller, John Huston (based on the novel by Pierre La Mure); ph, Oswald Morris; ed, Ralph Kemplen; m, Georges Auric; art d, Paul Sheriff; cos, Marcel Vertes, Juliaes Squire, Schiaparelli

AAN Best Picture; AAN Best Actor: Jose Ferrer; AAN Best Supporting Actress: Colette Marchand; AAN Best Director: John Huston; AAN Best Editing: Ralph Kemplen; AA Best Art Direction: Paul Sheriff, Marcel Vertes; AA Best Costume Design: Marcel Vertes

Jose Ferrer made his mark with portrayals of real, or famous fictional, characters (CYRANO DE BERGERAC, the Dauphin in JOAN OF ARC); his role here can be seen as a combination of the two, since Huston's treatment of the life of artist Toulouse-Lautrec takes took many liberties with the truth. Nonetheless, Ferrer does a fine job of limming the deformed (a childhood illness caused his legs to stop growing) artist, playing most of the film on his knees. MOULIN ROUGE was filmed in France and England and had a few interesting people in small roles. Look hard for horrormeisters Christopher Lee and Peter Cushing, as well as a young Tutte Lemkow (British choreographer/actor who was the Fiddler in FIDDLER ON THE ROOF). The first 25 minutes of the movie are outstanding, with a cancan sequence setting the tone for what is to come. This and other dance sequences completely eclipse similar scenes in Jean Renoir's FRENCH CAN-CAN and Walter Lang's CAN CAN.

MOUSE THAT ROARED, THE

1959   83m   c   Comedy/War   ★★★★
Open Road   (U.K.)   /U

Peter Sellers *(Tully Bascombe/Grand Duchess Gloriana XII/Prime Minister Count Mountjoy)*, Jean Seberg *(Helen)*, David Kossoff *(Prof. Kokintz)*, William Hartnell *(Will)*, Timothy Bateson *(Roger)*, MacDonald Parke *(Snippet)*, Monty Landis *(Cobbley)*, Leo McKern *(Benter)*, Harold Kasket *(Pedro)*, Colin Gordon *(BBC Announcer)*

p, Jon Penington, Walter Shenson; d, Jack Arnold; w, Roger MacDougall, Stanley Mann (based on the novel *The Wrath of the Grapes* by Leonard Wibberley); ph, John Wilcox; ed, Raymond Poulton; m, Edwin Astley; art d, Geoffrey Drake; cos, Anthony Mendleson

THE MOUSE THAT ROARED is the outlandish, sidesplitting tale of the fortunes of the Duchy of Grand Fenwick, a mythical land on the verge of bankruptcy because its one export, a fine wine, has been copied and undercut by a US company. Grand Fenwick's prime minister (Peter Sellers) and female monarch (Sellers again) cook up a scheme to solve the problem: they will declare war on the States, lose immediately, then get back in the black with all the aid that the US usually bestows upon its beaten foes. They send out an "army" of 20, clad in armor and carrying bows and arrows, led by Tully Bascombe (Sellers once more). Of course, the arrival of these ragtag warriors in New York leads to a series of very funny situations, including the group's inadvertent acquisition of the "Q-bomb," a weapon that makes them a genuine threat. In the meantime, Bascombe meets and falls in love with Helen (Jean Seberg), the daughter of a scientist. Besides the wonderful Sellers, there are fine performances from all, especially Leo McKern as the pompous leader of Grand Fenwick's "loyal opposition." An inferior sequel, MOUSE ON THE MOON, was directed by Richard Lester.

MRS. DOUBTFIRE

1993   120m   c   Comedy/Drama   ★★½
Blue Wolf Productions/Fox   (U.S.)   PG-13/PG

Robin Williams *(Daniel Hillard/Mrs. Iphegenia Doubtfire)*, Sally Field *(Miranda Hillard)*, Pierce Brosnan *(Stu)*, Harvey Fierstein *(Frank)*, Polly Holliday *(Gloria)*, Lisa Jakub *(Lydia Hillard)*, Matthew Lawrence *(Chris Hillard)*, Mara Wilson *(Natalie Hillard)*, Robert Prosky *(Mr. Lundy)*, Anne Haney *(Mrs. Sellner)*

p, Marsha Garces Williams, Robin Williams, Mark Radcliffe; d, Chris Columbus; w, Randi Mayem Singer, Leslie Dixon (from the novel *Alias Madame Doubtfire* by Anne Fine); ph, Donald McAlpine; ed, Raja Gosnell, Alexandra Fitzpatrick; m, Howard Shore; prod d, Angelo Graham; art d, W. Steven Graham; fx, John McLeod; cos, Marit Allen

AA Best Makeup: Greg Cannom, Ve Neill, Yolanda Toussieng

The first film, to our knowledge, to propose cross-dressing as a form of marriage therapy, MRS. DOUBTFIRE became one of the biggest hits of 1993, grossing over $220 million at the US box office.

Daniel Hillard (Robin Williams) is a San Francisco voice-over artist whose "principles" (read—New Age posturing) and "love of life" (read—infuriating childishness) prevent him from holding down a job. Daniel's naive exuberance makes him a hit with his kids, but has exhausted the patience of his wife (Sally Field), who sues for divorce and gets custody of the beloved children. In his desperation to spend more time with the extra-cute youngsters, Daniel does what any red-blooded male in his position would do: he impersonates a British nanny and lands a job taking care of his own offspring.

The manifold problems of MRS. DOUBTFIRE are hardly worth listing. Daniel is so hopelessly immature, and played with such puppy-dog overkill by Williams, that it's impossible to root for him—until you meet his wife, whom Sally Field makes even less appealing. But once Williams gets into costume and can hide—as he did in ALADDIN—behind an artfullly constructed facade, he becomes hugely entertaining. He's still one of the funniest performers around, and when he gets on a roll—even if it's a sub-standard TOOTSIE role—you just don't want him to get off.

MRS. MINIVER

1942   134m   bw   Drama/War   ★★★
MGM   (U.S.)   /U

Greer Garson *(Mrs. Kay Miniver)*, Walter Pidgeon *(Clem Miniver)*, Teresa Wright *(Carol Beldon)*, Dame May Whitty *(Lady Beldon)*, Henry Travers *(Mr. Ballard)*, Reginald Owen *(Foley)*, Miles Mander *(German Agent's Voice)*, Henry Wilcoxon *(Vicar)*, Richard Ney *(Vin Miniver)*, Clare Sandars *(Judy Miniver)* p, Sidney Franklin; d, William Wyler; w, Arthur Wimperis, George Froeschel, James Hilton, Claudine West (based on the novel by Jan Struther); ph, Joseph Ruttenberg; ed, Harold F. Kress; m, Herbert Stothart; art d, Cedric Gibbons, Urie McCleary; fx, A. Arnold Gillespie, Warren Newcombe; cos, Robert Kalloch

AA Best Picture; AAN Best Actor: Walter Pidgeon; *AA Best Actress:* Greer Garson; *AAN Best Supporting Actor:* Henry Travers; *AA Best Supporting Actress:* Teresa Wright; *AAN Best Supporting Actress:* May Whitty; *AA Best Director:* William Wyler; *AA Best Screenplay:* George Froeschel, James Hilton, Claudine West, Arthur Wimperis; *AA Best Cinematography:* Joseph Ruttenberg; *AA Best Editing:* Harold F. Kress; *AAN Best Sound:* Douglas Shearer; *AAN Best Visual Effects:* A. Arnold Gillespie, Warren Newcombe, Douglas Shearer

Frightfully nice, it's like war at teatime. MRS. MINIVER tells of the British people's will to survive the German bombing raids and fight to the end for their own human dignity. Director William Wyler achieves his goal by concentrating on the inhabitants of the country village of Belham, especially the middle-class Miniver family—lovely Kay Miniver (Greer Garson), gallant husband Clem (Walter Pidgeon), brave eldest son Vin (Richard Ney) and adorable younger children Toby and Judy (Christopher Severn and Clare Sandars). As the country slips into war, Vin falls in love with noble Carol (Teresa Wright), the teenage daughter of crotchety village matriarch Lady Beldon (Dame May Whitty). As romance grows and the village prepares for its annual flower-growing competition, German bombs begin to decimate the once-peaceful countryside and a downed German aviator seeks refuge with the Minivers. Villagers die, the Miniver home is bombed, and the church is reduced to rubble, but the people's spirit is strengthened when the vicar (Henry Wilcoxon) delivers a powerful speech, and the flower show goes on.

When Winston Churchill saw the film, he maintained that MRS. MINIVER would prove more valuable than the combined efforts of six divisions. At Oscar time, this heavy-handed film was named Best Picture; statuettes were also given to Garson, Wyler, Wright, cinematographer Ruttenberg and the screenwriters. Garson gave the longest (5 1/2 minute) speech in Oscar history; never mind she didn't deserve the award. Ponder her as an actress: totally ordinary, though lovely. Just when you've settled into that opinion, she does something brilliant. Resigned to being wrong, you watch as she settles back into self-satisfied mediocrity. Did that. Quite right. Lovely.

MUCH ADO ABOUT NOTHING

1993 111m c Comedy/Drama   ★★★
Renaissance Films/Samuel Goldwyn Company   PG-13/PG
/American Playhouse/BBC Films (U.K.)

Emma Thompson *(Beatrice)*, Kenneth Branagh *(Benedick)*, Robert Sean Leonard *(Claudio)*, Keanu Reeves *(Don John)*, Denzel Washington *(Don Pedro)*, Michael Keaton *(Dogberry)*, Kate Beckinsale *(Hero)*, Richard Briers *(Leonato)*, Brian Blessed *(Antonio)*, Gerard Horan *(Borachio)*

p, Stephen Evans, David Parfitt, Kenneth Branagh; d, Kenneth Branagh; w, Kenneth Branagh (from the play by William Shakespeare); ph, Roger Lanser; ed, Andrew Marcus; m, Patrick Doyle; prod d, Tim Harvey; art d, Martin Childs; cos, Phyllis Dalton

Kenneth Branagh's second screen adaptation of Shakespeare—the first was HENRY V—is a spritely, sun-drenched production decked out with a high-profile international cast.

In Sicily, Leonato (Richard Briers), Governor of Messina, eagerly greets Don Pedro (Denzel Washington), Prince of Aragon, and his men as they return victorious from war. Claudio (Robert Sean Leonard), Don Pedro's most honored comrade, falls in love with Hero (Kate Beckinsale), Leonato's virtuous and beautiful young daughter. Benedick (Kenneth Branagh), another of Don Pedro's companions, resumes his wittily antagonistic acquaintanceship with Beatrice (Emma Thompson), Leonato's niece. Don Pedro arranges to bring both young couples together, but a dark spell is cast over the proceedings by Don Pedro's jealous half-brother, Don John (Keanu Reeves), whose schemes temporaily disrupt the couples' plans and cause the usual Shakesperean complications before true love prevails.

Lushly photographed and superbly acted, MUCH ADO brought one of Shakespeare's most finely crafted romantic comedies to a popular audience. Though he loaded the production with Hollywood names (alongside a fine ensemble of British players), Branagh's approach to the play itself is quite conventional; very little cutting or updating has been done to the text, and the cast perform in period costume; the interracial casting seems the only nod to modernity. Branagh's use of trendy extended tracking and steadicam shots is sometimes distracting, but overall this is a jouyous romp whose forced jollity is only occasionally wearing.

MUMMY, THE

1932 72m bw Horror   ★★★★★
Universal (U.S.)   /15

Boris Karloff *(Im-Ho-Tep/Ardeth Bey)*, Zita Johann *(Helen Grosvenor/Princess Anck-es-en-Amon)*, David Manners *(Frank Whemple)*, Edward Van Sloan *(Professor Muller)*, A.S. Byron *(Sir Joseph Whemple)*, Bramwell Fletcher *(Norton)*, Noble Johnson *(the Nubian)*, Leonard Mudie *(Professor Pearson)*, Katherine Byron *(Frau Muller)*, Eddie Kane *(Doctor)*

p, Carl Laemmle Jr.; d, Karl Freund; w, John Balderston (based on a story by Nina Wilcox Putnam, Richard Schayer); ph, Charles Stumar; ed, Milton Carruth; art d, Willy Pogany; fx, John P. Fulton

Absolutely marvelous. Following his triumph as the monster in FRANKENSTEIN, Boris Karloff created yet another unforgettable horror character with the help of makeup man Jack Pierce. THE MUMMY opens at an Egyptian archeological dig in 1921 as a group of scientists examine their most recent finding—a sarcophagus in an unmarked grave. The coffin in which the mummy rests has been stripped of all religious markings that would have ensured an afterlife for the deceased, proof that the 3700-year-old corpse was buried in disgrace. Interred with the mummy is a large box upon which is written a warning to those who would dare open it—this, however, is a horror movie, and were no one to open the box we would never be treated to Karloff's magnificent wrappings. THE MUMMY was the directorial debut of the brilliant German cinematographer, Freund, who had photographed such classic German silents as THE LAST LAUGH; VARIETY; and METROPOLIS, as well as DRACULA in the US. Though THE MUMMY is not an overtly terrifying film (with the exception of the mummy's revival at the beginning), Freund creates an uneasy atmosphere of dread and foreboding. His camera is remarkably mobile, with impressive tracking and crane shots that float through the action, creating an eerie mood. Although made during a time when many films suffered from a lack of music, THE MUMMY has a full score, an effectively muted collection of themes perfectly suited to the carefully paced, mystical feel of the film. Though the technical credits are excellent, it is Karloff who carries the day. Makeup genius Pierce once again molded his magic to the actor, and the combination of linen, fuller's earth, and clay used to create the recently discovered mummy took over eight hours a day to apply. The effect is startling, though Karloff only appears as the mummy briefly. Perhaps more impressive is the more subtle makeup Pierce created for Karloff in his reincarnated state. The mass of delicate wrinkles on Karloff's face and hands, combined with the actor's deliberately gentle, flowing movements, creates a being who looks as if he may fall apart at any moment. It is a tribute to Karloff's immense skill that he can lend dignity and conviction to such a role. The supporting roles are also well-handled, with Johann making an appealingly offbeat heroine and Van Sloan crusading against yet another movie monster. The relationship between Karloff's mummy and Johann, whom he believes to be the reincarnation of his lost love, lends the film conviction and a certain pathos amidst the horror. The re-creation of the days of the pharaohs is also quite effective, and the scene wherein Karloff is wrapped alive, eyes going wider as his mouth is covered, is unforgettable. One of the rare horror films to somehow include a touch of the poetic, this stately yet brilliantly absorbing work still works beautifully today. Four inferior, shlocky sequels followed: THE MUMMY'S HAND; THE MUMMY'S TOMB; THE MUMMY'S GHOST; and THE MUMMY'S CURSE. Hammer Films of England revived the series beginning with THE MUMMY in 1959.

MUPPET MOVIE, THE

1979 98m c Musical/Children's ★★★
ITC (U.K.) G/U

GUEST STARS: Charles Durning (Doc Hopper), Austin Pendleton (Max), Scott Walker (Frog Killer), Mel Brooks (Prof. Krassman), Carol Kane (Miss.), MUPPET PERFORMERS: Jim Henson (Kermit the Frog/Rowlf/Dr. Teeth/Waldorf), Frank Oz (Miss Piggy/Fozzie Bear/Animal/Sam the Eagle), Jerry Nelson (Floyd Pepper/Crazy Harry/Robin the Frog/Lew Zealand), Richard Hunt (Scooter/Statler/Janice/Sweetums/Beaker), Dave Goelz (The Great Gonzo/Zoot/Dr. Bunsen Honeydew)

p, Jim Henson; d, James Frawley; w, Jerry Juhl, Jack Burns; ph, Isidore Mankofsky; ed, Christopher Greenbury; m, Paul Williams; prod d, Joel Schiller; art d, Les Gobruegge; cos, Calista Hendrickson, Gwen Capetanos

AAN Best Score: Paul Williams, Kenny Ascher; AAN Best Song: Paul Williams, Kenny Ascher

This charming children's film was the first to star the successful television puppets (two sequels followed). The loose plot follows Kermit the Frog and Fozzie Bear as they travel cross-country on their way to fame and fortune in Hollywood. On the road they pick up a variety of passengers (muppet and human) and sing a dozen songs. The special effects are handled very well; highlights feature Kermit riding a bicycle and rowing a boat. Cute without being insipid, funny without being childish, THE MUPPET MOVIE contains enough magic to please all ages.

MUPPET TREASURE ISLAND

1996 99m c Children's/Comedy/Musical ★★½
Jim Henson Productions/Walt Disney Pictures (U.S.) G/U

Tim Curry (Long John Silver), Kevin Bishop (Jim Hawkins), Billy Connolly (Billy Bones), Jennifer Saunders (Mrs. Bluveridge), Frederick Warder (Calico Jerry), Peter Greeves (Black Eyed Pea), Danny Blackner (Short Stack Stevens), Harry Jones (Easy Pete)

p, Brian Henson, Martin G. Baker; d, Brian Henson; w, Jerry Juhl jim Hart, Kirk Thatcher; ph, John Fenner; ed, Michael Jablow; m, Hans Zimmer; prod d, Val Strazovec; art d, Alan Cassie; fx, Nick Allder, Tom Smith; cos, Polly Smith

This fanciful adaptation of Robert Louis Stevenson's classic adventure novel features plenty of not-too-menacing pirates and exactly the sort of schtick one has come to expect from the Muppets, making for an entertaining diversion for both children and adults.

Orphan Jim Hawkins (Kevin Bishop) and his friends Rizzo the Rat and the Great Gonzo toil in a tavern, fantasizing about adventure on the high seas. When a patron dies and leaves the infamous Captain Flint's treasure map in Jim's hands, the threesome find themselves aboard the Hispainiola, an unusual ship helmed by Captain Smollett (Kermit the Frog). Also aboard is a peg-legged cook named Long John Silver (Tim Curry), who has secretly stocked the crew with pirates. Once the ship reaches Skeleton Island, Silver and his pirates take Jim hostage and set out to find Flint's buried treasure for themselves.

The second Muppet movie produced since the death of creator Jim Henson, MUPPET TREASURE ISLAND suggests that the Muppets (now under the direction of Henson's son, Brian) are charting a new course—literary adaptations. At the movie's outset, Stevenson's sense of adventure and the Muppet mixture of wit, slapstick, and self-reflexive references are blended well. Once the story goes to sea, however, the mix is less successful. Curry, who's usually over the top with relish, seems restrained alongside the Muppet scene-stealers, and young Bishop simply doesn't stand a chance. Adding to their handicap are the songs provided by Barry Mann and Cynthia Weil, none of which are particularly memorable. But while not as good as THE MUPPET CHRISTMAS CAROL, it's hard to harbor too much ill will towards a movie so eager to entertain.

MURDER

1930 92m bw Mystery ★★★★
British Intl. (U.K.) /PG

Herbert Marshall (Sir John Menier), Norah Baring (Diana Baring), Phyllis Konstam (Dulcie Markham), Edward Chapman (Ted Markham), Miles Mander (Gordon Druce), Esme Percy (Handel Fane), Donald Calthrop (Ion Stewart), Amy Brandon Thomas (Defence), Marie Wright (Miss Mitcham), Hannah Jones (Mrs. Didsome)

p, John Maxwell; d, Alfred Hitchcock; w, Alma Reville, Walter C. Mycroft, Alfred Hitchcock (based on the novel and play Enter Sir John by Clemence Dane and Helen Simpson); ph, Jack Cox; ed, Emile De Ruelle, Rene Harrison; m, John Reynders; art d, John Mead

An atypical Hitchcock film which depends on the element of surprise rather than his usual building of suspense. Diana Baring, a young actress, is accused of killing one of her friends, tried, and sentenced to death by a jury. Jury member Sir John Menier (Marshall), an actor-manager and gentleman knight, remains unconvinced of her guilt and makes an attempt to locate the actual murderer. Visually astonishing, MURDER also makes creative use of sound by recording a character's spoken thoughts on the soundtrack. While the innocent person accused became a staple of Hitchcock's later films, the director would expand on this idea of theatricality in his mystery STAGE FRIGHT. Hitchcock also directed a German version of MURDER, entitled MARY, starring Alfred Abel.

MURDER, MY SWEET

1945 95m bw Mystery ★★★★½
RKO (U.S.) /PG

Dick Powell (Philip Marlowe), Claire Trevor (Velma/Mrs. Grayle), Anne Shirley (Ann), Otto Kruger (Amthor), Mike Mazurki (Moose Malloy), Miles Mander (Mr. Grayle), Douglas Walton (Marriott), Don Douglas (Lt. Randall), Ralf Harolde (Dr. Sonderborg), Esther Howard (Mrs. Florian)

p, Adrian Scott; d, Edward Dmytryk; w, John Paxton (based on the novel Farewell, My Lovely by Raymond Chandler); ph, Harry Wild; ed, Joseph Noriega; m, Roy Webb; art d, Albert S. D'Agostino, Carroll Clark; fx, Vernon L. Walker; cos, Edward Stevenson

Near perfect, my sweet. Hard-boiled detective Philip Marlowe (Powell) is hired by ex-con Moose Malloy (Mazurki) to find his missing girl-friend Velma. Shortly thereafter, Marlowe is hired by socialite Mrs. Grayle (Trevor) to find a valuable jade necklace that has been stolen from her. Dividing his time between the seedy underworld and the ritzy digs of the upper class, Marlowe finds blackmail, doublecrosses, corruption, and murder on both sides of the tracks. Much to Marlowe's surprise, both cases dovetail into one. Considered one of the quintessential film noir films, this tough, sardonic, and unusually witty film brought one-time movie crooner Powell back from the brink of career catastrophe and made him a superstar. Not even Humphrey Bogart's portrayal of Marlowe in THE BIG SLEEP could match Powell's portrayal of the down-and-out gumshoe. Director Edward Dmytryk uses every cinematic trick in the book here, creating a truly bleak and disorienting netherworld populated by a variety of sordid characters. Here's Mazurki's best in his catalogue of hoods, our fave Shirley performance, but it's Miss Trevor who rises to the top, like a dangerous cup of posioned cream, viewing after viewing.

MURDER ON THE ORIENT EXPRESS

1974 128m c Mystery ★★★½
Paramount (U.K.) PG

Albert Finney (Hercule Poirot), Lauren Bacall (Mrs. Hubbard), Martin Balsam (Bianchi), Ingrid Bergman (Greta Ohlsson), Jacqueline Bisset (Countess Andrenyi), Jean-Pierre Cassel (Pierre Paul Michel), Sean Connery (Col. Arbuthnot), John Gielgud (Beddoes), Wendy Hiller (Princess Dragomiroff), Anthony Perkins (Hector McQueen)

p, John Brabourne, Richard Goodwin; d, Sidney Lumet; w, Paul Dehn (based on the novel by Agatha Christie); ph, Geoffrey Unsworth; ed, Anne V. Coates; m, Richard Rodney Bennett; prod d, Tony Walton; art d, Jack Stephens; cos, Tony Walton

AAN Best Actor: Albert Finney; *AA Best Supporting Actress:* Ingrid Bergman; *AAN Best Adapted Screenplay:* Paul Dehn; *AAN Best Cinematography:* Geoffrey Unsworth; *AAN Best Score:* Richard Rodney Bennett; *AAN Best Costume Design:* Tony Walton

Elegant and stylish in the best Agatha Christie tradition—a thoroughly entertaining if poky whodunit. Hercule Poirot (a showy Finney) is aboard the luxurious Orient Express in 1934, traveling across Asia and Europe to Paris. When an American financier (Richard Widmark) is found dead—stabbed a dozen times—Poirot is prevailed upon by railway executive Bianchi (Balsam) to solve the case. Through an elaborate re-creation of the crime, he does just that. For years Christie refused to have this story filmed, but MURDER ON THE ORIENT EXPRESS was worth the wait. Even Ingrid knew she didn't deserve her supporting Oscar, but she is fine, and sentimental Academy members slept well that night. Very enjoyable, but frankly, too many stars for its own good.

MURIEL
(MURIEL, OU LE TEMPS D'UN RETOUR)

1963 115m c Drama ★★★★★
Argos/Alpha/Eclair/Pleiade/Dear (France/Italy) /A

Delphine Seyrig *(Helene)*, Jean-Pierre Kerien *(Alphonse)*, Nita Klein *(Francoise)*, Jean-Baptiste Thierree *(Bernard)*, Claude Sainval *(de Smoke)*, Laurence Badie *(Claudie)*, Jean Champion *(Ernest)*, Jean Daste *(The Goat Man)*, Martine Vatel *(Marie-Dominique)*, Philippe Laudenbach *(Robert)*

p, Anatole Dauman; d, Alain Resnais; w, Jean Cayrol (based on the story by Cayrol); ph, Sacha Vierny; ed, Kenout Peltier, Eric Pluet, Claudine Merlin; m, Hans Werner Henze; art d, Jacques Saulnier

Alain Resnais's third feature and first color film once again concerns memory. Helene (Delphine Seyrig) is a widow who sells antiques from her Boulogne-sur-Mer apartment. She shares the place with her eccentric filmmaker stepson, Bernard (Jean-Baptiste Thierree), a 22-month veteran of the Algerian War, during which he took part in the torture and murder of a young woman named Muriel. Bernard is haunted by the memory of Muriel, spending much time watching a grainy 8mm film of her and filming the surroundings in his neighborhood. He talks of Muriel to Helene, who assumes the woman is a girl friend she has yet to meet. Helene, meanwhile, is reunited with a past lover, Alphonse (Jean-Pierre Kerien), another veteran of Algeria, but they cannot recapture what they once had, if they had anything at all. Alphonse arrives at Helene's with his mistress, Francoise (Nita Klein), whom he introduces as his niece. While Helene, her present lover, de Smoke (Claude Sainval), and Alphonse try to sort out their emotions, Francoise shows an attraction to Bernard, who is involved with Marie-Dominique (Martine Vatel). MURIEL marked the second time Resnais worked with screenwriter Jean Cayrol, who previously contributed the commentary for Resnais's short documentary masterpiece NIGHT AND FOG. Their collaboration here produced a technical and thematic masterpiece that makes brilliant and confounding use of montage, sound construction, overlapping dialogue, and color photography. With MURIEL, Resnais' true filmmaking style had finally begun to emerge, employing characters who are real people (not named after cities or designated by letters) with memories that cut deeply into their personalities and relationships. The videotape is in French with English subtitles, though in most of the washed-out prints of the film the reportedly excellent use of color is hardly evident.

MURMUR OF THE HEART
(LE SOUFFLE AU COEUR)

1971 118m c Drama/Comedy ★★★★
Nouvelles Editions/Marianne/Vides/Franz Seitz (France/Italy/West Germany)

Lea Massari *(Clara Chevalier)*, Benoit Ferreux *(Laurent Chevalier)*, Daniel Gelin *(the Father)*, Marc Winocourt *(Marc)*, Fabien Ferreux *(Thomas)*, Michel Lonsdale *(Father Henri)*, Ave Ninchi *(Augusta)*, Gila von Weitershausen *(Freda)*, Micheline Bona *(Aunt Claudine)*, Henri Poirier *(Uncle Leonce)*

p, Vincent Malle, Claude Nedjar; d, Louis Malle; w, Louis Malle; ph, Ricardo Aronovich; ed, Suzanne Baron; m, Charlie Parker, Sidney Bechet, Gaston Freche, Henri Renaud; art d, Jean-Jacques Caziot, Philippe Turlure

AAN Best Adapted Screenplay: Louis Malle

Of all the French New Wave directors, Malle has proved the most versatile and accessible. He isn't afraid to handle delicate issues and he approaches his subjects with sensitivity and wit. Incest, perhaps the most unspeakable of all taboos, was the subject of MURMUR OF THE HEART. Malle's comic take makes for a wonderful, tender film which accurately portrays all the joys and agonies of adolescent sexuality. Ferreux is Laurent, the 14-year-old son of a French gynecologist. His mother Clara (Massari), who had married his father when she was 16, is a kindred spirit and his closest confidante. Laurent's older brothers take him to a prostitute for his first sexual experience, but the drunken boys interrupt the tentative beginnings. Laurent later contracts scarlet fever, which leaves him with a heart murmur, and his mother takes him to a health health spa to recuperate. Mother and son are both rejected by prospective lovers at a Bastille Day celebration and somehow turn to each other, with surprising results.

MURMUR is a film alive with energy. One never forgets those terrible moments of early adolescence, and this film recaptures the feelings with honesty, humor and sensitivity. Backed by a wonderful jazz score, the drama is made believable by its characters. Massari and Ferreux have a marvelous chemistry that makes their relationship honest and understandable. Their lovemaking is treated in a subtle manner; Malle never dwells upon it, nor does he make it seem like a moment of depraved abandon. Instead, this is a special moment for two people who cannot explain their actions to outsiders. Rather than create a paean to incest, Malle has created a song of life.

MUSIC BOX

1989 124m c Drama ★★★★
Carolco (U.S.) PG-13/15

Jessica Lange *(Ann Talbot)*, Armin Mueller-Stahl *(Michael Laszlo)*, Frederic Forrest *(Jack Burke)*, Lukas Haas *(Michael "Mikey" Talbot)*, Donald Moffat *(Harry Talbot)*, Michael Rooker *(Karchy Laszlo)*, Cheryl Lynn Bruce *(Georgine Wheeler)*, Mari Torocsik *(Magda Zoldan)*, J.S. Block *(Judge Erwin Silver)*, Sol Frieder *(Istvan Boday)*

p, Irwin Winkler; d, Constantin Costa-Gavras; w, Joe Eszterhas; ph, Patrick Blossier; ed, Joele Van Effenterre; m, Philippe Sarde; prod d, Jeannine Claudia Oppewall; art d, Bill Arnold; chor, Eva Nemeth, Karoly Nemeth; cos, Rita Salazar

AAN Best Actress: Jessica Lange

As with BETRAYED, critics took director Costa-Gavras to task for not approaching the subject of MUSIC BOX (the prosecution of WWII Nazi war criminals residing in the US) with more passion. Yet, what MUSIC BOX arguably loses by keeping its emotions reined in is more than made up for by a deliberately detailed, deeply disturbing realism. Jessica Lange plays Ann Talbot, the troubled attorney who helps her father, Michael Laszlo, played by Armin Mueller-Stahl, with what she first assumes to be a case of mistaken identity. A Hungarian immigrant after the war, Mueller-Stahl claimed on his application for citizenship to have been a farmer. After decades of raising a family in America on a steelworker's pay, Mueller-Stahl is now faced with deportation on the nominal charge of having lied about his former occupation. In fact, he is being sent back to Hungary to be tried for wartime atrocities he is accused of committing as part of that country's Nazi collaborationist police force. He admits to having been with the police but claims innocence on the atrocity charges, saying he left the force in reaction to the very brutality of which he is accused. Up against badgering prosecutor Forrest, who is fueled by righteous rage, Lange is nevertheless able to puncture the testimony of key government witnesses. Masterfully she then builds her own case, presenting the deportation as a revenge-motivated sham orchestrated by the Hungarian communist government against Mueller-Stahl for his disruption of a cultural exchange with the US several years earlier. While preparing her case, though, she discovers a series of large payments—Mueller-Stahl dismisses them as loans—to a fellow immigrant subsequently killed in a hit-and-run accident. As she investigates these irregularities, she is forced to reevaluate the very foundations of her belief in herself and her family.

Throughout the film, Costa-Gavras chooses not to chastise or harangue. There is nothing shrill about his style here, nor about the performances he elicits from the uniformly excellent cast he has assembled. Rather, MUSIC BOX conveys a feeling of sadness and dread over American innocence, so easily turned to willful ignorance. Costa-Gavras defines Ann Talbot's dilemma as one shared by the nation.

MUSIC MAN, THE

1962   151m   c   Musical   ★★★★
Warner Bros.   (U.S.)   /U

Robert Preston (Harold Hill), Shirley Jones (Marian Paroo), Buddy Hackett (Marcellus Washburn), Hermione Gingold (Eulalie MacKechnie Shinn), Paul Ford (Mayor Shinn), Ewart Dunlop, Oliver Hix, Jacey Squires, Olin Britt (The Buffalo Bills), Pert Kelton (Mrs. Paroo)

p, Morton Da Costa; d, Morton Da Costa; w, Marion Hargrove (based on the musical by Meredith Willson, Franklyn Lacey); ph, Robert Burks; ed, William Ziegler; m, Meredith Willson; art d, Paul Groesse; chor, Onna White, Tom Panko

AAN Best Picture; AAN Best Editing: William Ziegler; AA Best Score: Ray Heindorf; AAN Best Art Direction: Paul Groesse, George James Hopkins; AAN Best Costume Design: Dorothy Jeakins; AAN Best Sound: George R. Groves

A nostalgic mix of corn, laughs, exuberance, and infectious songs. Robert Preston reprises his greatest Broadway role as Prof. Harold Hill, a traveling salesman/con man who arrives in River City, Iowa, in 1912 and persuades its citizens that the town is headed for moral ruin because of its new pool room. The way to keep the town youth from being corrupted is to start a band, says Hill, adding that he will sell the instruments and teach the kids how to play. His real plan is to take the money and run before the instruments arrive. Prim librarian Marian Paroo (Jones) questions Hill's credentials, but he sells her on his revolutionary "Think System," by which all one has to do is think a tune to be able to play it. As he attempts to swindle the townsfolk, Hill alternately charms and exasperates the mayor (Ford), his wife (Gingold), and the members of the town council (played by the barbershop quartet, the Buffalo Bills, who provide some delightful musical interludes).

Preston is a true joy in this film, perhaps as ideally suited for the role as Yul Brynner was for the King of Siam. Though the charming rogue has long been a staple in the entertainment world, few played the role as engagingly as Preston does here. The other performances are notable, particularly the lovely Jones, the delightful Gingold and Ford, and little, lisping Ron Howard. Splendid, but this is, and will always be, Preston's picture. Absurdly, he didn't even get a *nomination* for Best Actor, though the film was cited, losing to LAWRENCE OF ARABIA. Meredith Willson's songs, which are among the best ever to grace a musical production, include "Till There Was You" and the stirring "76 Trombones," which provides the unforgettable climax.

MUSIC ROOM, THE

(JALSAGHAR)

1958   95m   bw   Drama   ★★★★½
Edward Harrison   (India)   /U

Chhabi Biswas (Huzur Biswambhar Roy), Padma Devi (His Wife), Pinaki Sen Gupta (Khoka, His Son), Tulsi Lahari (Manager of Roy's Estate), Kali Sarkar (Roy's Servant), Ganga Pada Basu (Mahim Ganguly), Akhtari Bai, Salamat Khan (Singers), Roshan Kumari (Kathak Dancer), Pratap Mukhopdhya

p, Satyajit Ray; d, Satyajit Ray; w, Satyajit Ray (based on a novel by Tarashankar Banerjee); ph, Subrata Mitra; ed, Dulal Dutta; m, Dakhin Mohan Takhur, Asis Kumar, Robin Majumder; art d, Bansi Chandragupta

One of Satyajit Ray's finest works, THE MUSIC ROOM is also one of the most meditative and lyrical. Its basic concern is the demise of an aristocratic household led by Biswas. Feeling a growing resentment toward his neighbors' elaborate parties, Biswas decides to hold his own

and sells his wife's jewels to finance it. Shortly afterward his wife and son die at sea during a thunderstorm, which sends Biswas into seclusion. Four years later, when his neighbor plans a party in his newly built music room, Biswas decides to have his own party. He scrounges together all the money he has left and throws an elegant party. He loses his sanity, however, and takes off on his son's horse. He is thrown from the animal and dies in the arms of his servants. Beautifully photographed, THE MUSIC ROOM is a fine example of Ray's directorial mastery. Released in India in 1958, shortly before the completion of his Apu trilogy.

MUTE WITNESS

1995   90m   c   Thriller/Mystery/Drama   ★★★
Comet Films/Avrora Media/Cobblestone Pictures/Patmos   R/18
Films   (Germany/U.K./Russia)

Marina Sudina (Billy Hughes), Fay Ripley (Karen Hughes), Evan Richards (Andy Clarke), Oleg Jankowskij (Larsen), Igor Volkov (Arkadi), Sergei Karlenkov (Lyosha), Alexander Buriev (Strohbecker), Alec Guinness (The Reaper), Alexander Piatov (Wartschuk), Nikoai Pastuhov (Janitor)

p, Alexander Buchman, Norbert Soentgen, Anthony Waller; d, Anthony Waller; w, Anthony Waller; ph, Egon Werdin; ed, Peter Adam; m, Wilbert Hirsch; prod d, Matthias Kammermeier; art d, Barbara Becker; fx, Victor Orlov, Pavel Terchov, Christian Burgdorff, Optical Arts; cos, Svetlana Luzanova

After a great start, this offbeat, self-referential genre picture begins to lose steam, but it's still a promising feature debut for writer-director Anthony Waller.

Andy (Evan Richards), a cocky American director, is shooting a film in Russia on antiquated sound stages with a local cast and crew. One night after shooting, Billy (Marina Sudina), a mute special effects artist, goes back to the studio to retrieve a needed prop and stumbles upon two crew members making a porn movie. As Billy watches, the movie abruptly becomes a snuff film when the unsuspecting actress is murdered on camera. A careless move on Billy's part alerts the murderers to her presence, and they chase her through the winding corridors and basement tunnels. Billy is rescued by Andy and his girlfriend and the police are called, but the two crew members insist that they were just testing some special effects. Billy is unable to produce any hard evidence that a murder has occurred. Only enigmatic Inspector Larsen (Oleg Jankowskij) seems to be on Billy's side. Or is he?

An entertaining thriller about innocents abroad, MUTE WITNESS keenly pays homage to the conventions of the thriller genre, but eventually trips over its own cleverness. The nail-biting first half applies frightening twists to a cliched situation—a girl trapped in a scary place filled with dangerous people. The film owes quite a bit to Robert Siodmak's THE SPIRAL STAIRCASE, as well as the many Hitchcock nail-biters in which nightmarish foreigners menace fresh-faced Americans. Sudina's Billy is a spunky and resourceful heroine, but the twists and turns of her predicament ultimately become too implausible.

MUTINY ON THE BOUNTY

1935   132m   bw   Adventure   ★★★★★
MGM   (U.S.)   /A

Charles Laughton (Capt. William Bligh), Clark Gable (1st Mate Fletcher Christian), Franchot Tone (Roger Byam), Herbert Mundin (Smith), Eddie Quillan (Ellison), Dudley Digges (Bacchus), Donald Crisp (Burkitt), Henry Stephenson (Sir Joseph Banks), Francis Lister (Capt. Nelson), Spring Byington (Mrs. Byam)

p, Irving Thalberg; d, Frank Lloyd; w, Talbot Jennings, Jules Furthman, Carey Wilson (based on the novels Mutiny On The Bounty and Men Against the Sea by Charles Nordhoff, James Norman Hall); ph, Arthur Edeson; ed, Margaret Booth; m, Herbert Stothart; art d, Cedric Gibbons, Arnold Gillespie

AA Best Picture; AAN Best Actor: Clark Gable; AAN Best Actor: Charles Laughton; AAN Best Actor: Franchot Tone; AAN Best Director: Frank Lloyd; AAN Best Screenplay: Jules Furthman, Talbot Jennings, Carey Wilson; AAN Best Editing: Margaret Booth; AAN Best Score: Nat W. Finston, Herbert Stothart, Metro-Goldwyn-Mayer Music Department

A bounty for viewers. Few adventures can approach MUTINY ON THE BOUNTY for its action-filled dramatization of good vs. evil. 1935's top grosser, the film confirmed Gable as Hollywood's biggest male star and gave Laughton the most famous role of his career. The film's basis in fact only adds sweep to this bracing saga of a 1788 ship mutiny.

The film opens as the Bounty gracefully sets sail from Portsmouth, England to Tahiti to gather breadfruit trees. Shipboard life, though, soon hits rough seas as conflicts arise between the vicious, bullying Capt. Bligh (Laughton) and his courageous first mate, Fletcher Christian (Gable), with idealistic midshipman Roger Byam (Tone) caught in the middle. The stay in Tahiti proves to be a momentary respite, even though Bligh seethes over Christian's romance with the island chief's daughter (Movita Castaneda). On the homeward voyage, Bligh becomes even more barbaric, and it's only a matter of time before Christian takes action.

Expertly crafted and brilliantly acted, MUTINY ON THE BOUNTY is one of the most durable and engrossing adventure films ever made. For the first and only time in motion-picture history, three actors from the same film—Gable, Laughton, and Tone—were nominated for Oscars in the Best Actor division. Lloyd's rich direction captures the exotic South Sea island of Tahiti and the rigors of the hardscrabble voyage and gives the cast its full head (Digges is especially good). Gable, in splendid form, was originally afraid of wearing breeches and a small ponytail, and he also thought his American accent would stand out too much. (If anything, it works by contributing to a certain xenophobia in his struggles against the unhandsome and genuinely British Laughton.) His Christian is full of integrity and courage, and is even surprisingly tender in the oddly bisexual edge of the film's Tahiti scenes. The superb Laughton, meanwhile, relishing his self-righteous villainy, gave impersonators a lifetime of work uttering "Mr. Christian, come here!". Tone, an underrated actor, is also sturdy, and gets to strut his stuff in the courtroom finale. Although the production of the film was dogged by backstage sniping, scripting problems, expensive location footage ruined by tropical humidity, and the loss of $50K worth of equipment, you'd never know it to look at the result.

The film was remade under the same title in 1962. Trevor Howard was a compelling Bligh, but Marlon Brando's weird attempt to turn Christian into an effeminate fop could have made the film a camp classic if only he weren't so serious about it. As it is, his grand experiment entirely sabotages the film. 1984, meanwhile, brought us THE BOUNTY. Anthony Hopkins aimed for a more complex Bligh, but Mel Gibson was extremely bland and the undertaking entirely lacked the epic scope that made the 1935 version so bracing.

MY BEAUTIFUL LAUNDRETTE

1985 93m c Drama   ★★★★
Working Title/SAF/Channel 4 (U.K.)   R/15

Daniel Day Lewis *(Johnny)*, Saeed Jaffrey *(Nasser)*, Roshan Seth *(Papa)*, Gordon Warnecke *(Omar)*, Shirley Ann Field *(Rachel)*, Rita Wolf *(Tania)*, Richard Graham *(Genghis)*, Winston Graham, Dudley Thomas *(Jamaicans)*, Derrick Branche *(Salim)*

p, Sarah Radclyffe, Tim Bevan; d, Stephen Frears; w, Hanif Kureishi; ph, Oliver Stapleton; ed, Mick Audsley; m, Ludus Tonalis; prod d, Hugo Luczyc-Whyhowski; cos, Lindy Hemming

AAN Best Original Screenplay: Hanif Kureishi

An offbeat winner. Director Stephen Frears and screenwriter Hanif Kureishi have fashioned a wonderfully fresh examination of the political and racial climate of Margaret Thatcher's Britain. Omar (Gordon Warnecke) is a young Pakistani living in London with his father (Roshan Seth), a drunk who was previously one of Pakistan's leading intellectuals. When Papa asks his brother Nasser (Saeed Jaffrey), an underworld crime boss, to find work for Omar, Nasser makes him the manager of a run-down laundrette, and Omar enterprisingly employs Johnny (Daniel Day Lewis), a London street punk and boyhood friend whom he has not seen since Johnny joined a fascist group. In addition to becoming work partners, Omar and Johnny also become lovers. In the meantime, Johnny's friends have turned against him, baffled by his devotion to the "Pakis." Kureishi has come up with at least a half-dozen complex characters whose lives are brilliantly woven together in the film's relatively short 93 minutes. Amidst all the conflicts of racism,

sexuality, bigotry, violence, and politics, MY BEAUTIFUL LAUNDRETTE still manages to be humorous and entertaining, largely because of Frears's skill as a director and marvelous performances all round. Beautifully handled, warmly intelligent and insightful, extremely entertaining.

MY BODYGUARD

1980 96m c Drama   ★★★★
20th Century Fox (U.S.)   PG

Chris Makepeace *(Clifford)*, Adam Baldwin *(Linderman)*, Matt Dillon *(Moody)*, Paul Quandt *(Carson)*, Joan Cusack *(Shelley)*, Dean R. Miller *(Hightower)*, Tim Reyna *(Koontz)*, Richard Bradley *(Dubrow)*, Denise Baske *(Leilani)*, Hank Salas *(Mike)*

p, Don Devlin; d, Tony Bill; w, Alan Ormsby; ph, Michael D. Margulies; ed, Stu Linder; m, Dave Grusin; prod d, Jackson DeGovia

This is essentially a tale of revenge, but not along the lines of some mindless vigilante movie; this is revenge with intelligence and sensitivity. Young Makepeace moves to Chicago with his motel manager father, Mull, and grandmother, Ruth Gordon (doing her wisecracking, randy old lady bit). His new high school is ruled by Dillon, who extorts money from classmates ostensibly so they won't be pummeled by Baldwin, a huge, reclusive hulk whom everyone fears. Makepeace tries to befriend Baldwin and finds him to be a very troubled young man. This is a heartwarming film, superbly directed by ex-actor Tony Bill. Makepeace is excellent as the slight protagonist, and Baldwin is perfect as the brooding, misunderstood mammoth. Dave Grusin's score adds immeasurably to the tone.

MY BRILLIANT CAREER

1979 98m c Drama   ★★★★
New South Wales/GUO/Analysis (Australia)   G/U

Judy Davis *(Sybylla Melvyn)*, Sam Neill *(Harry Beecham)*, Wendy Hughes *(Aunt Helen)*, Robert Grubb *(Frank Hawdon)*, Max Cullen *(Mr. McSwat)*, Patricia Kennedy *(Aunt Gussie)*, Aileen Britton *(Grandma Bossier)*, Peter Whitford *(Uncle Julius)*, Carole Skinner *(Mrs. McSwat)*, Alan Hopgood *(Father)*

p, Margaret Fink; d, Gillian Armstrong; w, Eleanor Witcombe (based on the novel by Miles Franklin); ph, Don McAlpine; ed, Nicholas Beauman; m, Nathan Waks; prod d, Luciana Arrighi; cos, Anna Senior

AAN Best Costume Design: Anna Senior

Late in the 19th century in the Australian outback everyone in a small farming community knows his or her place and what is expected. All except Sybylla Melvyn (Judy Davis), that is, a headstrong young woman who wants a career—an idea that shocks her family and friends. Resisting the rigid codes of society and the marriage proposal of a wealthy man, Harry Beecham (Sam Neill, in a fine portrayal), Sybylla plows ahead with pluck and charm.

Davis gives a lively and humanistic performance, and the direction by Gillian Armstrong (MRS. SOFFEL, HIGH TIDE), in her feature debut, matches her heroine's character: strong, with a good sense of wanting to get something done and then doing it. The *mise-en-scene* is well composed, and the story is well told in this wonderful Australian work. Based on a true story, MY BRILLIANT CAREER was one of the key films in the resurgence of Australian cinema in the late 1970s and early 80s.

MY COUSIN VINNY

1992 119m c Comedy   ★★★
Palo Vista Productions/Peter V. Miller Investment Corporation (U.S.)   R/15

Joe Pesci *(Vincent La Guardia Gambino)*, Ralph Macchio *(Bill Gambini)*, Marisa Tomei *(Mona Lisa Vito)*, Mitchell Whitfield *(Stan Rothenstein)*, Fred Gwynne *(Judge Chamberlain Haller)*, Lane Smith *(Jim Trotter, III)*, Austin Pendleton *(John Gibbons)*, Bruce McGill *(Sheriff Farley)*, Maury Chaykin *(Sam Tipton)*, Pauline Meyers *(Constance Riley)* p, Dale Launer, Paul Schiff; d, Jonathan Lynn; w, Dale Launer; ph, Peter Deming; ed, Tony Lombardo; m, Randy Edelman; prod d, Victoria Paul; art d, Randall Schmook, Michael Rizzo; cos, Carol Wood

AA Best Supporting Actress: Marisa Tomei

Clocking in at just under two hours, MY COUSIN VINNY moves at an extremely leisurely pace for a Hollywood farce. But that's just one indication of what makes this appealingly quirky comedy stand apart from more run-of-the-mill fare. Driving across the country on their way to college, Bill Gambini and Stan Rothenstein (Ralph Macchio and Mitchell Whitfield) are arrested in Alabama. Thinking they've been accused of shoplifting, they sign confessions, only to discover they've been charged with murder. Enter Bill's cousin, Vincent La Guardia Gambino (Joe Pesci), a lawyer who graduated from law school six years earlier but who only passed the bar exam six weeks ago and has never been in a courtroom. Up against a curmudgeonly judge, Chamberlain Haller (Fred Gwynne), and a wily district attorney, Jim Trotter, III (Lane Smith), Vinny rises to the occasion, with the unexpected help of his leggy girlfriend Mona Lisa Vito (Marisa Tomei), a self-taught automotive expert.

Joe Pesci projects a surprising depth here, shrewdly bringing down his usual cartoonish Brooklyn bravado a few notches. The film also benefits from a well-crafted plot, courtesy of screenwriter and co-producer Dale Launer (RUTHLESS PEOPLE, DIRTY ROTTEN SCOUNDRELS), that puts a fresh twist on stock situations and characters.

The film's cast is a comfortable ensemble of reliable veterans like Gwynne and McGill, underrated performers like Macchio and at least one hot newcomer in Tomei, an accomplished comedienne with intelligence and talent to match her knockout looks. British director Jonathan Lynn (NUNS ON THE RUN) keeps planting unexpected grace notes along the way, making this a rare comedy that never quite wears out its welcome.

MY DARLING CLEMENTINE

1946 97m bw Western   ★★★★★
Fox (U.S.)   /A

Henry Fonda *(Wyatt Earp)*, Linda Darnell *(Chihuahua)*, Victor Mature *(Doc Holliday)*, Walter Brennan *(Old Man Clanton)*, Tim Holt *(Virgil Earp)*, Cathy Downs *(Clementine)*, Ward Bond *(Morgan Earp)*, Alan Mowbray *(Granville Thorndyke)*, John Ireland *(Billy Clanton)*, Roy Roberts *(Mayor)*

p, Samuel G. Engel; d, John Ford; w, Samuel G. Engel, Winston Miller (based on a story by Sam Hellman from the novel *Wyatt Earp, Frontier Marshall* by Stuart N. Lake); ph, Joseph MacDonald; ed, Dorothy Spencer; m, Cyril J. Mockridge, David Buttolph; art d, James Basevi, Lyle Wheeler; fx, Fred Sersen; cos, Rene Hubert

Perhaps the best orchestrated western of all time, courtesy of the modest Mr. Ford. No western figure inspired more cinematic lore than the indomitable Wyatt Earp, and Fonda, back from WWII, gives a definitive portrayal of the famous frontier lawman.

Earp and his brothers (Bond, Holt and Don Garner) have driven their cattle to the outskirts of rough-and-tumble Tombstone, Arizona. Coming upon their campsite is Old Man Clanton (Brennan), who offers the Earps a cut-rate price for their herd. Wyatt rejects the offer and heads into town, leaving his youngest brother as watchman. In Tombstone Earp manages to rid the town of a bothersome drunken Indian, and the grateful townsfolk offer him the job of sheriff. He doesn't accept the position until he discovers the Clantons have stolen his cattle and killed his brother. Then it's time for the remaining Earps to strap on their guns, shore up Wyatt's mysterious, alcoholic friend Doc Holliday (Mature), and head for the OK Corral.

Dramatic and brooding, with shadows at night and blinding light at day under a sky that never ends, MY DARLING CLEMENTINE doesn't follow history exactly, but Ford is much more concerned with the myth of the West. The scene where Wyatt brings harmony to Tombstone by eliminating the disruptive element—notably, a Native American—is almost a prototypical expression of the genre's obsession with the formation of community. The most famous scene in this regard, however, is the dance at the church-founding social, where Wyatt and Clementine (Downs) walk down the street like it was a wedding aisle. Fonda was rarely better, his Midwest accent and measured delivery

perfect for the part. His chair-balancing makes wonderful use of his lanky body, and his deliberately stiff but gracefully folksy dance with Clementine is a brilliant bit of acting. The often underrated Mature is also outstanding, acting out the tormented Holliday with amazing passion and restraint. Darnell's luscious noir persona is effective, even if she is too glamorized and seems about as Latina as "My Wild Irish Rose." Downs, meanwhile, cast as a refined parallel to Darnell, isn't much of an actress, but then this isn't much of a part; schoolteacher Clementine is less a character than the embodiment of civilization from the East, and the ingenue fills the bill admirably. Finally, Brennan, downright chilling as Clanton, will make you forget every rerun of THE REAL MCCOYS you ever watched.

As with other Ford films, there is no sustained score; Newman merely provides haunting little variations of the title song on a harmonica, and other western ballads on fiddles or guitars as needed. The script is lean and tight, and MacDonald's startling photography, under the Master's guidance, provides graphics so sweeping that the whole of the West seems bounded by the frame.

Many other films about Wyatt Earp have been made: LAW AND ORDER with Walter Huston; two films named FRONTIER MARSHAL with George O'Brien and Randolph Scott in the role; TOMBSTONE, THE TOWN TOO TOUGH TO DIE with Richard Dix; WICHITA with Joel McCrea; GUNFIGHT AT THE O.K. CORRAL with Burt Lancaster; HOUR OF THE GUN with James Garner; and DOC with Harris Yulin. This, however, is the definitive rendering, if only for the sequence at the church dance. If that scene doesn't either give you chills or make you cry, see your doctor immediately.

MY DINNER WITH ANDRE

1981 110m c Drama   ★★★
Andre (U.S.)   PG/A

Wallace Shawn *(Wally)*, Andre Gregory *(Andre)*, Jean Lenauer *(Waiter)*, Roy Butler *(Bartender)*

p, George W. George, Beverly Karp; d, Louis Malle; w, Wallace Shawn, Andre Gregory; ph, Jeri Sopanen; ed, Suzanne Baron; m, Allen Shawn; prod d, David Mitchell; art d, Stephen McCabe; cos, Jeffrey Ullman

Louis Malle's somewhat overrated MY DINNER WITH ANDRE is a filmed conversation between two friends, and whether you find the movie profound, pretentious, or entertaining will depend on how interesting you find the talk.

The main speaker is real-life theater director and playwright Andre Gregory, a seeker after enlightenment who details his occasionally bizarre quest as he dines with an old, very different friend (real-life actor/playwright Wallace Shawn) whom he hasn't seen in a long time. Wally is more concerned with creature comforts than with quixotic spiritual searches and serves as Andre's philosophical foil as the two men talk and eat (in real time) at a fancy New York restaurant.

Although Malle provided the minimal direction, the film really belongs to Shawn and Gregory, who also cowrote the script.

MY FAIR LADY

1964 170m c Musical/Comedy   ★★
Warner Bros. (U.S.)   /U

Audrey Hepburn *(Eliza Doolittle)*, Rex Harrison *(Prof. Henry Higgins)*, Stanley Holloway *(Alfred P. Doolittle)*, Wilfrid Hyde-White *(Col. Hugh Pickering)*, Gladys Cooper *(Mrs. Higgins)*, Jeremy Brett *(Freddy Eynsford-Hill)*, Theodore Bikel *(Zoltan Karpathy)*, Isobel Elsom *(Mrs. Eynsford-Hill)*, Mona Washbourne *(Mrs. Pearce)*, John Alderson *(Jamie)*

p, Jack L. Warner; d, George Cukor; w, Alan Jay Lerner (based on a musical play by Alan Jay Lerner, Frederick Loewe and the play *Pygmalion* by George Bernard Shaw); ph, Harry Stradling; ed, William Ziegler; m, Frederick Loewe; prod d, Cecil Beaton; art d, Gene Allen; chor, Hermes Pan; cos, Cecil Beaton

AA Best Picture; AA Best Actor: Rex Harrison; *AAN Best Supporting Actor:* Stanley Holloway; *AAN Best Supporting Actress:* Gladys Cooper; *AA Best Director:* George Cukor; *AAN Best Adapted Screenplay:* Alan Jay Lerner; *AA Best Cinematography:* Harry Stradling; *AAN Best Editing:* William Ziegler; *AA Best Score:* Andre Previn; *AA Best*

Art Direction: Gene Allen, Cecil Beaton, George James Hopkins; *AA Best Costume Design:* Cecil Beaton; *AA Best Sound:* George R. Groves

Just fairly fair; call it the revenge of Mary Poppins. Audrey's effortless swan can't redeem the fact that she's a Givenchy mannequin picturesquely dusted with Jack Warner's cigar ashes, when we meet her "playing" an ugly duckling. Hepburn specialized in Cinderella variations (ROMAN HOLIDAY, SABRINA) but was getting too mature, too sophisticated to play the waif bit without outside plot stimuli (danger—CHARADE, broken heart—BREAKFAST AT TIFFANY'S, etc.). Anyway, Shaw's original Eliza is not quite as waifish as she is raffish. Hepburn can't summon up the guts to guttersnipe, and when she opens her mouth wide to presumably sing (dubbed by Marni Nixon, who deserves a special Oscar for all the stars she made look good) like she's never even seen a singer in her entire life, it's a shock and a laugh at the same time.

Otherwise, the Lerner and Loewe musical emerges as an overly long, sometimes enjoyable dinosaur. Perhaps there is truthfully no way to liberate Shaw—his writing is heavy, obtuse. Adding wonderful songs ("On the Street Where You Live," "I Could Have Danced All Night," "Get Me to the Church on Time") only makes it come up heavily trimmed, like a fancy Christmas turkey. The film makes you feel bloated and tired. But it made a fortune at the box office and undeservedly took Oscars in almost every category—with the exception of Best Actress, which ironically went to MARY POPPINS's Julie Andrews, who was Harrison's fair lady on Broadway.

Henry Higgins (Harrison) bets fellow linguist Col. Hugh Pickering (Hyde-White) that he can turn Cockney flower girl Eliza Doolittle (Hepburn) into a lady with elocution so pure no one will suspect her origins. She is, of course, a huge success at a fancy ball, but Higgins has a few lessons in humanity to learn from his "creation."

Yes, Harrison is mechanically expert, like a graduate with honors from the Lord Olivier School of Going through the Motions (we think, belatedly, we'd have preferred orignal choice Cary Grant opposite Andrews). But film always pointed up his hatefulness. It's hard not to think of dead Carole Landis lying on her bathroom floor when he waxes sentimental. Frankly, we hate this damned thing.

MY FAVORITE BLONDE

1942 78m bw Spy/Comedy ★★★½
Paramount (U.S.) /A

Bob Hope *(Larry Haines)*, Madeleine Carroll *(Karen Bentley)*, Gale Sondergaard *(Mme. Stephanie Runick)*, George Zucco *(Dr. Hugo Streger)*, Lionel Royce *(Karl)*, Walter Kingsford *(Dr. Faber)*, Victor Varconi *(Miller)*, Otto Reichow *(Lanz)*, Charles Cane *(Turk O'Flaherty)*, Crane Whitley *(Ulrich)*

p, Paul Jones; d, Sidney Lanfield; w, Don Hartman, Frank Butler (based on a story by Melvin Frank and Norman Panama); ph, William Mellor; ed, William O'Shea; m, David Buttolph; art d, Hans Dreier, Robert Usher

Carroll is a beautiful spy who posesses plans involving the shipment of war planes to England and is being chased by Nazis who want the plans for themselves. While in New York, she escapes from them by ducking into a small dressing room at a theater. Coincidentally this is the dressing room of Hope, a wisecracking ladies' man who's preparing his performing penguin for its debut. Without much pleading, the lovely Carroll convinces Hope to aid her escape. From there it's a comic cross-country chase with lots of disguises and silliness. Hope is wonderful, with something smart to say no matter what the situation. His smug behavior is very funny (far and away superior to anything he ever did in the television work that made him rich) and the pacing is as good as it usually is in these Hope comedies. His old partner from the ROAD films, the wonderfully laid back Bing Crosby, makes a cameo (as he so often did in Hope's solo comedies) as a man giving the two travelers directions. "No, it can't be," mutters Hope after the benefactor leaves. Some good fun, but the poor penguin is treated like a toy rather than an animal. Penguins are inherently funny animals (as television's "Monty Python's Flying Circus" proved time and again), and there was no need for the knockabout treatment of the bird.

MY FAVORITE BRUNETTE

1947 87m bw Mystery/Comedy ★★★★
Paramount (U.S.) /PG

Bob Hope *(Ronnie Jackson)*, Dorothy Lamour *(Carlotta Montay)*, Peter Lorre *(Kismet)*, Lon Chaney Jr. *(Willie)*, Charles Dingle *(Maj. Simon Montague)*, Reginald Denny *(James Collins)*, Frank Puglia *(Baron Montay)*, Ann Doran *(Miss Rogers)*, Willard Robertson *(Prison Warden)*, Jack LaRue *(Tony)*

p, Daniel Dare; d, Elliott Nugent; w, Edmund Beloin, Jack Rose; ph, Lionel Lindon; ed, Ellsworth Hoagland; m, Robert Emmett Dolan; art d, Hans Dreier, Earl Hedrick; fx, Gordon Jennings; cos, Edith Head

In what ranks as one of his best comedies, Hope plays a harried baby photographer who is asked by his private-eye pal to watch his detective business for a few days while he goes on vacation. Hope agrees and finds himself getting involved with a lot more than watching dust settle. Believing Hope to be the real private eye, Lamour hires him to search for her uncle, a wealthy baron who has vanished, and gives the dubious detective a map, warning him to guard it with his life. Hope goes off to the palatial estate of a former associate of the missing man, Dingle, who introduces Hope to a wheelchair-bound man who is supposedly Lamour's uncle. Hoyt, a doctor who is present, insists that Lamour has a few screws loose. Hope is just about convinced of the veracity of Dingle and Hoyt's story until he is about to leave and spots the "disabled" baron walking about. When Hope snaps a quick picture, Dingle gets one of his crazed henchmen (Lorre in a wonderful self-parody) to knock out Hope and recover the film. In an effort to determine the importance of the map, Hope and Lamour pay a visit to the geologist who drew it, but Lorre has killed him, framing Hope for the murder. Minutes before Hope is to be executed, fresh evidence is discovered by Lamour, and the executioner, furious that his day has been ruined, takes off his hood and reveals himself to be none other than Hope's offscreen (and sometimes onscreen) pal Bing Crosby. "Boy," says Hope as he turns to the camera, "he'll take any kind of a part!" This is a classic Hope film, with one gag following another in rapid succession. Particularly good is Lorre, who was known at this stage in his career for doing films that approached this genre seriously. And Chaney's characterization of a dumb sanitarium guard so tough he cracks walnuts with his eyelids is great fun. Alan Ladd is equally amusing in his cameo role of the vacationing detective.

MY FAVORITE WIFE

1940 88m bw Comedy ★★★★
RKO (U.S.) /U

Irene Dunne *(Ellen Arden)*, Cary Grant *(Nick Arden)*, Randolph Scott *(Stephen Burkett)*, Gail Patrick *(Bianca)*, Ann Shoemaker *(Ma)*, Scotty Beckett *(Tim Arden)*, Mary Lou Harrington *(Chinch Arden)*, Donald MacBride *(Hotel Clerk)*, Hugh O'Connell *(Johnson)*, Granville Bates *(Judge)*

p, Leo McCarey; d, Garson Kanin; w, Sam Spewack, Bella Spewack (based on a story by Leo McCarey, Sam Spewack, and Bella Spewack); ph, Rudolph Mate; ed, Robert Wise; m, Roy Webb; art d, Van Nest Polglase, Mark-Lee Kirk; cos, Howard Greer

AAN Best Original Screenplay: Leo McCarey, Bella Spewack, Samuel Spewack; *AAN Best Score:* Roy Webb; *AAN Best Art Direction:* Van Nest Polglase, Mark-Lee Kirk

After Grant and Dunne made such a success of THE AWFUL TRUTH, they were reteamed for this up-to-date version of the "Enoch Arden" story. Producer McCarey was supposed to direct, but he had a terrible auto accident just before shooting, so Kanin was handed the task and came through with a fast-moving, often amusing film.

You all know the story. Ellen (Dunne), shipwrecked for seven years, returns to discover that her husband Nick (Grant) has just had her declared legally dead and has married Bianca (Patrick). Ellen wants her man back and proceeds to make him jealous over Stephen (Scott), the man she was shipwrecked with all those years. Meanwhile, Bianca is getting mentally disturbed. Love will find a way.

Lots of laughs for the first three-quarters of the film but then it peters out for the expected finale. A scene-stealing Bates helps out, though. Remade, not as well, as MOVE OVER, DARLING, which starred Doris Day and James Garner in the Dunne and Grant roles.

MY FAVORITE YEAR

1982 92m c Comedy   ★★★★
Brooksfilms (U.S.)   PG

Peter O'Toole (Alan Swann), Mark Linn-Baker (Benjy Stone), Jessica Harper (K.C. Downing), Joseph Bologna (King Kaiser), Bill Macy (Sy Benson), Lainie Kazan (Belle Carroca), Anne DeSalvo (Alice Miller), Basil Hoffman (Herb Lee), Lou Jacobi (Uncle Morty), Adolph Green (Leo Silver)

p, Michael Gruskoff; d, Richard Benjamin; w, Norman Steinberg, Dennis Palumbo (based on a story by Dennis Palumbo); ph, Gerald Hirschfeld; ed, Richard Chew; m, Ralph Burns; prod d, Charles Rosen; cos, May Routh

AAN Best Actor: Peter O'Toole

A delightful film presenting a poignant portrait of television in the early 1950s. Benjy Stone (Mark Linn-Baker) is a fledgling writer for a live comedy television show hosted by zany, tough, yet soft-hearted King Kaiser (Joseph Bologna). Benjy is assigned to chaperone the unpredictable, boozing, onetime Hollywood swashbuckler Alan Swann (Peter O'Toole), who is to appear on television in a Kaiser skit. Arriving in Manhattan drunk and uncontrollable, Swann begins to lead Stone in a wild night of revelry, and over the next several days, the famous guest is involved in a series of escapades. On the show itself he staggers about with the near-DTs, forgetting his lines and getting into a fight with a bunch of union goons invading the set over Kaiser's past insults. O'Toole is superb as the former matinee idol, and Bologna is outstanding as the brusque and brawling comic. Linn-Baker, who would later go on to his own television series in 1986, is excellent, playing out a real-life incident where novice comedy writer Mel Brooks was assigned to chaperone the colorful Errol Flynn before he appeared on Sid Caesar's "Your Show of Shows." Cameron Mitchell plays a union crime boss with lead-foot accuracy and deadpan deadliness. Richard Benjamin's direction surprisingly provides a dizzy pace and inventive set-ups, aided greatly by cinematographer Gerald Hirschfeld and editor Richard Chew.

MY FRIEND FLICKA

1943 89m c Children's   ★★★★
Fox (U.S.)   /U

Roddy McDowall (Ken McLaughlin), Preston Foster (Rob McLaughlin), Rita Johnson (Nell), James Bell (Gus), Jeff Corey (Tim Murphy), Diana Hale (Hildy), Arthur Loft (Charley Sargent), Jimmy Aubrey

p, Ralph Dietrich; d, Harold Schuster; w, Lillie Hayward, Francis Edwards Faragoh (based on the novel by Mary O'Hara); ph, Dewey Wrigley; ed, Robert Fritch; m, Alfred Newman; art d, Richard Day, Chester Gore; cos, Herschel

A wonderful film, beautifully photographed and sensitively told. McDowall is a young boy who longs for a colt of his own. His rancher father finally gives in and is displeased when the boy chooses the foal from an unruly mare. But through painstaking work by McDowall, the colt is trained and nurtured, eventually growing to become a fine mare and a loyal companion. The performances and direction are as fine as they come. The humanistic qualities within the film come through well, without being the least bit overbearing or overly sentimental. The color photography is wonderful, capturing all the grandeur of the Rocky Mountains. Perfect for the whole family. A sequel was made with almost the same cast: THUNDERHEAD, SON OF FLICKA. Later a series on television.

MY LEFT FOOT

1989 98m c Biography   ★★★★½
Granada (Ireland)   R/PG

Daniel Day-Lewis (Christy Brown), Ray McAnally (Mr. Brown), Brenda Fricker (Mrs. Brown), Ruth McCabe (Mary Carr), Fiona Shaw (Dr. Eileen Cole), Eanna MacLiam (Old Benny), Alison Whelan (Old Sheila), Declan Croghan (Old Tom), Hugh O'Conor (Young Christy), Cyril Cusack (Lord Castlewelland)

p, Noel Pearson; d, Jim Sheridan; w, Shane Connaughton, Jim Sheridan (based on the book by Christy Brown); ph, Jack Conroy; ed, J. Patrick Duffner; m, Elmer Bernstein; prod d, Austin Spriggs; cos, Joan Bergin

AAN Best Picture; AA Best Actor: Daniel Day-Lewis; *AA Best Supporting Actress:* Brenda Fricker; *AAN Best Director:* Jim Sheridan; *AAN Best Adapted Screenplay:* Jim Sheridan, Shane Connaughton

Thank god, an insolent hoof. Stories about people overcoming devastating handicaps have long been grist for the filmmaker's mill. The title of this screen adaptation of Christy Brown's best-selling autobiography refers to the only limb over which Brown, crippled since birth by a severe case of cerebral palsy, ever had any control. Daniel Day-Lewis plays the acclaimed Irish-born artist and author, as the film intercuts flashbacks of his formative years with scenes at a stately Dublin home in 1959. There, the wheelchair-bound Brown, guest of honor at a benefit dinner for a cerebral palsy foundation, first meets Mary (Ruth McCabe), a young nurse assigned to care for him for the evening. Presented with a copy of Brown's book, Mary leafs through its pages, and the author's life is re-created on the screen, beginning with his early years as the ninth of 13 surviving children (out of 22) in a close-knit, working-class Irish Catholic family. That MY LEFT FOOT succeeds as well as it does is in large part due to a superb supporting cast and the virtuoso performances of Hugh O'Conor and Day-Lewis, who play Brown as child and adult, respectively. Undoubtedly, MY LEFT FOOT begs comparison with GABY, A TRUE STORY, the depiction of another cerebral palsy victim. Indeed, the films are like two sides of the same coin. While the less satisfying GABY focuses on the dour aspects of its subject's plight, the better-scripted, more entertaining MY LEFT FOOT is filled with wit and unselfconscious humor. To Brown's credit, his portrayal is unerringly tough, sometimes surprisingly sensual. It keeps FOOT from maudlin static. A rich cinematic experience, this uplifting British production will leave you in awe of the extraordinary Christy Brown.

MY LIFE AS A DOG
(MITT LIV SOM HUND)

1985 101m c Comedy/Drama   ★★★½
AB/Svensk (Sweden)   PG-13/PG

Anton Glanzelius (Ingemar Johansson), Anki Liden (His Mother), Tomas von Bromssen (Uncle Gunnar), Manfred Serner (Erik), Melinda Kinnaman (Saga), Ing-Marie Carlsson (Berit), Kicki Rundgren (Aunt Ulla), Lennart Hjulstrom (Konstnaren), Leif Erickson (Farbor Sandberg), Christina Carlwind (Fru Sandberg)

p, Waldemar Bergendahl; d, Lasse Hallstrom; w, Lasse Hallstrom, Reidar Jonsson, Brasse Brannstrom, Per Berglund (based on the novel by Jonsson); ph, Jorgen Persson, Rolf Lindstrom; ed, Christer Furubrand, Susanne Linnman; m, Bjorn Isfalt; art d, Lasse Westfelt; cos, Inger Pehrsson, Susanne Falck

AAN Best Director: Lasse Hallstrom; *AAN Best Adapted Screenplay:* Lasse Hallstrom, Reidar Jonsson, Brasse Brannstrom, Per Berglund

This critically acclaimed Swedish film, which also won kudos for its talented star, Anton Glanzelius, is a tragicomic, sensitive portrayal of adolescence set in 1959. The film centers on 12-year-old Ingemar Johansson (Glanzelius), who lives with his abusive brother (Manfred Serner) and terminally ill mother (Anki Liden). He is not discouraged, however—sure, he has it bad, but not as bad as Laika, the Soviet spacedog who starved to death while in orbit and whose fate haunts the boy. Ingemar's life has begun to spin out of control, and, like Laika, there's little he can do to stop it. When Ingemar is sent away for the summer to stay with relations, he meets a menage of eccentric—and sexually intimidating—villagers; eventually, these experiences give him a sustaining inner strength. Writer-director Lasse Hallstrom's tale is an episodic rite of passage, a story in which the emotions are touching but never sappy, the main character has the integrity and complexity of a real child with real troubles, and the glimpses of village life are rich and engaging. Not just another charming film about growing up, but an expertly directed tale that takes a small, simple subject and colors it with invention and inspiration.

MY LIFE TO LIVE
(VIVRE SA VIE)
1962 85m bw Drama   ★★★★★
Pleiade   (France)

Anna Karina *(Nana)*, Sady Rebbot *(Raoul)*, Andre Labarthe *(Paul)*, Guylaine Schlumberger *(Yvette)*, Gerard Hoffman *(the Cook)*, Monique Messine *(Elizabeth)*, Paul Pavel *(A Journalist)*, Dimitri Dineff *(A Youth)*, Peter Kassowitz *(A Young Man)*, Eric Schlumberger *(Luigi)*

p, Pierre Braunberger; d, Jean-Luc Godard; w, Jean-Luc Godard; ph, Raoul Coutard; ed, Agnes Guillemot; m, Michel Legrand

An early stunner from Jean-Luc Godard and one of the seminal films of the French New Wave. The filmmaker's fourth feature stars his then-wife, Anna Karina, as Nana, a Parisian sales clerk who, after separating from her husband, Paul (Labarthe), tries to make it as an actress. After seeing Dreyer's silent classic THE PASSION OF JOAN OF ARC, she abandons the idea and turns to prostitution. The film is divided into 12 tableaux, which take place in cafes, in a record store, at a police station, and on the streets of Paris. The scenes and the issues raised range from prostitution (with quoted facts and figures on the subject) to experiments with narration and autobiographical elements (Godard narrating, Karina starring). In Godard's typically dense and provocative style, we also have many allusions to films and literature (Renoir's NANA, Zola's *Nana*, Truffaut's JULES AND JIM, Dreyer and Falconetti, and Edgar Allen Poe's "The Oval Portrait"), as well as an absorbing discussion on linguistic philosophy with Brice Parain).

Through this complex and intriguing network we have an abundance of humor and many uniquely touching vignettes. Karina is considerably more at home in front of the camera than in her earlier films, and Godard has by this point clearly learned how to bring out the very best that's in her. MY LIFE TO LIVE represents an interesting mix of those facets Godard has explored more individually in his earlier films—the genre elements of BREATHLESS, the politics of LE PETIT SOLDAT, and the narrative experimentation of A WOMAN IS A WOMAN. Technically MY LIFE TO LIVE was (and perhaps still is) far ahead of its time, knocking down the traditional walls of sound recording. Godard refused to mix the sound in the studio (except for Michel Legrand's barely used score), instead applying the same rule for sound and image—to capture them directly—and amended his "jump-cut" style of editing by allowing shots to last from six to eight minutes as the camera wandered through the set. MY LIFE TO LIVE also contains one of Godard's greatest and most personal scenes—a reading of Charles Baudelaire's translation of "The Oval Portrait," the story of an artist whose wife dies just as he finishes her portrait. Although Godard does not play Nana's lover in this scene, he does provide the character's voice. As we hear Godard reading Poe's words, we see the face of his wife, Anna Karina as Nana, and realize that, like Poe, Godard is painting a portrait of his wife. The finale is memorable and puts a suitable spin on this early mix of cinematic experimentation and the sociological concerns which would continue to distinguish's this great filmmaker's work as the decade progressed.

MY LITTLE CHICKADEE
1940 83m bw Comedy/Western   ★★½
Universal   (U.S.)   /A

W.C. Fields *(Cuthbert J. Twillie)*, Mae West *(Flower Belle Lee)*, Joseph Calleia *(Jeff Badger)*, Dick Foran *(Wayne Carter)*, Margaret Hamilton *(Mrs. Gideon)*, George Moran *(Clarence)*, Si Jenks *(Deputy)*, Gene Austin *(Himself)*, Russell Hall *(Candy)*, Otto Heimel *(Coco)*

p, Lester Cowan; d, Edward F. Cline; w, Mae West, W.C. Fields; ph, Joseph Valentine; ed, Edward Curtiss; m, Frank Skinner; art d, Jack Otterson; cos, Vera West

Neither the best of the West nor the lillies of the Fields. Teaming Mae and W.C. in a Wild West spoof seemed inspired, and the marquee values brought plenty of people to the box office, but the film plays like two middling star vehicles uneasily spliced together.

Flower Belle (West), a woman whose corsets are tighter than her morals, is thrown out of town by righteous townsfolk after she's romanced by a masked bandit. On board a train, she's courted by snake oil salesman Cuthbert J. Twillie (Fields) and marries him to gain respectability while she continues searching for her lover's identity.

Mutual admirers Fields and West interact fairly well in their occasional scenes together, but her diamond-bright polish and his ambling, martini-fueled improvisations don't entirely mix. We don't have Abbott and Costello or Laurel and Hardy here, but rather two comics used to toplining alone. (It was cute, though, to end the film with his inviting her to "come up and see me sometime" and her responding, "Yeah, I'll do that, my little chickadee.") West parries both saloon owner Jeff Badger (Calleia) and crusading newspaperman Wayne Carter (Foran) with ease, and has a real comic highlight when she takes over a classroom for an indisposed teacher, but Fields comes off rather better. (The quality of his work is rarely affected by the quality of the film as a whole.) His attempts to get into Flower Belle's bed are hilarious, and the poker scene in the bar is a classic if only for the moment when Fuzzy Knight asks, "Is this a game of chance?" and Fields replies, "Not the way I play it."

MY MAN GODFREY
1936 94m bw Comedy   ★★★★½
Universal   (U.S.)   /A

William Powell *(Godfrey Parke)*, Carole Lombard *(Irene Bullock)*, Alice Brady *(Angelica Bullock)*, Eugene Pallette *(Alexander Bullock)*, Gail Patrick *(Cornelia Bullock)*, Alan Mowbray *(Tommy Gray)*, Jean Dixon *(Molly, Maid)*, Mischa Auer *(Carlo)*, Robert Light *(Faithful George)*, Pat Flaherty *(Mike)*

p, Gregory La Cava; d, Gregory La Cava; w, Morrie Ryskind, Eric Hatch, Gregory La Cava (based on the story "1101 Park Avenue" by Eric Hatch); ph, Ted Tetzlaff; ed, Ted J. Kent; m, Charles Previn; art d, Charles D. Hall; cos, Brymer, Travis Banton

AAN Best Actor: William Powell; *AAN Best Actress:* Carole Lombard; *AAN Best Supporting Actor:* Mischa Auer; *AAN Best Supporting Actress:* Alice Brady; *AAN Best Director:* Gregory Lacava; *AAN Best Original Screenplay:* Eric Hatch, Morris Ryskind

A silvery romp. The flaw is that it never delivers on the satire it starts with, dissolving into Cinderella fantasy along the way. But the leads are so impeccable that the seam never shows and the greatly underrated La Cava directs with precision. Of all the great comediennes, Lombard's innocently unflappable center was unique. She's like an eternal playmate—a quality only Harlow shared. It's a pity the two never played sisters.

Anyway, MY MAN GODFREY is comedy with a social conscience, although the message's subtlety has to be unearthed from all the humor. The flaky, endearing Irene Bullock (Lombard) and the dark, calculating Cornelia (Patrick) are two Park Avenue brats in the midst of a scavenger hunt party. Among other items on their list is a "forgotten man" from one of Manhattan's hobo jungles. Irene for once bests her snobbish sister when she convinces down-and-out Godfrey (Powell) to come back to the party with her. Godfrey, however, turns out to be more than the Bullock family ever bargained for when when Irene hires him as butler.

The rich are made to look very foolish and the poor appear very noble in this film, something that Depression audiences must have appreciated. Two years later, a film inspired by this one, MERRILY WE LIVE, was released, but it and the flat 1957 remake of MY MAN GODFREY were inferior attempts at recreating the chemistry of this film. Powell and Lombard, married in 1931 and divorced in 1933, were still friendly enough to make a marvelous onscreen team. One of the better, if not the best, of the famous screwball comedies of the era, GODFREY stands as an excellent example of witty scripting, direction, and editing. With Eugene Palette (growling some of the best lines, and certainly one of the strangest, funniest men ever), Alice Brady (great in these dithery roles), and Mischa Auer (in his famous monkey imitation) among the congress of nitwits. Look fast—there's Janie Wyman in the party scene.

MY NAME IS IVAN
(IVANOVO DETSTVO)

1962 97m bw Drama/War   ★★★★
Mosfilm (U.S.S.R.)   /PG

Kolya Burlyayev (Ivan), Valentin Zubkov (Capt. Kholin), Ye. Zharikov (Lt. Galtsev), S. Krylov (Cpl. Katasonych), Nikolai Grinko (Col. Gryaznov), D. Milyutenko (Old Man), V. Malyavina (Masha), I. Tark-ovskaya (Ivan's Mother), Andrei Konchalovsky, Ivan Savkin

d, Andrei Tarkovsky; w, Vladimir Osipovich Bogomolov, Mikhail Pa-pava (based on the short story "Ivan" by Vladimir Osipovich Bogo-molov); ph, Vadim Yusov; ed, L. Feyginova; m, Vyacheslav Ovchinnikov; art d, Ye. Chernyayaev; fx, V. Sevostyanov, S. Mukhin

This first feature from Soviet director Andrei Tarkovsky, an intense cinematic poem about war and childhood, presents the most horrific account of war's ravaging effect on a child's innocence since Roberto Rossellini's GERMANY, YEAR ZERO. Like Rossellini's Edmund, Tarkovsky's Ivan (Kolya Burlyayev) is a 12-year-old man/boy who has known little else but war—war that has forced him to become an adult and (in the irony of the actual translated title) robbed him of his childhood. When first seen, Ivan might be assumed to be an average youngster until he is shown trekking, neck-deep, through a murky swamp. This swamp is at the enemy's front line, to which Ivan, a member of a WWII Russian military intelligence unit, has been sent to gather information on troop movements. Ivan has only a cause and a country; his town has been overrun by the Germans, his father mur-dered, his mother shot and killed, his sister blown apart by a bomb. Although his superiors are pleased with his efforts, they protectively transfer him to the rear, but Ivan rebels at this and is allowed to go on one more mission. Much more than a war film about a young boy, MY NAME IS IVAN is a pure film experience. Tarkovsky fills the frame with beautiful images composed in extreme high, low, or tilted angles; uses an unpredictable editing style that alternates between rapid, jarring cuts and carefully composed long takes; employs a stark black-and-white contrast, which often turns natural scenery into abstract imagery; and constructs a soundtrack that is as inventive as his visuals. Comple-menting Tarkovsky's vision is the performance of Burlyayev, whose face expresses both determination and tenderness. Highly praised upon its release—it won awards at the Venice Film Festival for Best Film, Director, and Actor—MY NAME IS IVAN has found a new audience with the rising international recognition of Tarkovsky.

MY NIGHT AT MAUD'S
(MA NUIT CHEZ MAUD)

1969 105m bw Drama   ★★★★
F.F.P./Losange/Carrosse/Renn/Deux   GP/12
Mondes/Gueville/Simar/Pleiade (France)

Jean-Louis Trintignant (Jean-Louis), Francoise Fabian (Maud), Marie-Christine Barrault (Francoise), Antoine Vitez (Vidal), Leonide Kogan (Concert Violinist), Anne Dubot (Blonde Friend), Guy Leger (Preacher), Marie Becker (Marie, Maud's Daughter), Marie-Claude Rauzier (Student)

p, Pierre Cottrell, Barbet Schroeder; d, Eric Rohmer; w, Eric Rohmer; ph, Nestor Almendros; ed, Cecile Decugis; art d, Nicole Rachline

AAN Best Foreign Language Film ; AAN Best Adapted Screenplay: Eric Rohmer

Tantalizingly witty, beautifully shot. The fourth of Eric Rohmer's "Six Moral Tales," MY NIGHT AT MAUD'S stars Jean-Louis Trintignant as Jean-Louis, a devout Catholic in love with Francoise (Marie-Christine Barrault), a pretty student he sees in church but is too shy to approach. When Jean-Louis runs into Vidal (Antoine Vitez), an old friend, Vidal invites him to dinner at the home of his bohemian lover, Maud (Francoise Fabian). There, Maud, Vidal (a Marxist professor), and Jean-Louis become involved in a lively conversation about the philosophy of Pascal and freedom of choice. In light of the bad snowstorm outside and the heavy drinking inside, Jean-Louis is per-

suaded to stay overnight at Maud's, but despite his hostess's advances does not make love to her. Later, he finally meets, and then marries, Francoise, only to find years later that she is the former mistress of Maud's husband. As in all of Rohmer's films, there is little "action" in MY NIGHT AT MAUD'S, but there is a great deal of intelligent and fascinating conversation as the characters question, expose, and explain their motivations and feelings (hence the "morality" of the tale). In Jean-Louis's case, his belief in premarital chastity is at issue. Photo-graphed in black-and-white by Nestor Almendros, the film nicely captures the snowbound mood of the Christmas season, and the ensem-ble acting is excellent. The film was nominated for Best Foreign-Lan-guage Film and Best Original Screenplay Oscars, and won the New York Film Critics Best Screenwriting award.

MY OWN PRIVATE IDAHO

1991 102m c Drama   ★★★★
Idaho Productions (U.S.)   R/18

River Phoenix (Mike Waters), Keanu Reeves (Scott Favor), James Russo (Richard Waters), William Richert (Bob Pigeon), Rodney Harvey (Gary), Chiara Caselli (Carmella), Michael Parker (Digger), Jessie Thomas (Denise), Flea (Budd), Grace Zabriskie (Alena)

p, Laurie Parker; d, Gus Van Sant; w, Gus Van Sant; ph, Eric Alan Edwards, John Campbell; ed, Curtiss Clayton; prod d, David Brisbin; art d, Kenneth A. Hardy; cos, Beatrix Aruna Pasztor

A genuinely poetic voice is heard in MY OWN PRIVATE IDAHO. Taking the form of a road movie, blended with elements borrowed from the two parts of Shakespeare's Henry IV, the film chronicles the misadventures of Mike Waters (River Phoenix), a lonesome young hustler who suffers from narcolepsy—he passes out at stressful mo-ments and must literally depend on strangers to protect him. After one such fit at the opening of the film, Mike awakens in a Seattle flophouse, being fellated by a balding, overweight john. Later, he's picked up and taken to the home of a rich matron, where he meets Scott Favor (Keanu Reeves), the rebellious son of the mayor of Portland. After Mike has another fit, Scott carries him to a safe place to sleep it off. The next day Mike meets Hans (Udo Kier), a rich German, falls asleep again, and ends up in Portland with Scott. Led by the Falstaffian Bob Pigeon (William Richert), Mike, Scott and several other hustlers take over a derelict building, only to be cleared out by a police raid. The police are searching for Bob, but they also let Scott know that he must go to see his disapproving father, which he does before setting off with Mike on a motorbike to look for Mike's mother. The search takes them to Idaho, Snake River, and Italy, before the two return to the West Coast to fulfil their very different destinies.

Van Sant (MALA NOCHE, DRUGSTORE COWBOY) combines a realistic grasp of the underside of urban life with a visual sense that is by turns playful and elegiac. In one scene, a group of real-life hustlers exchange stories in a dingy coffee bar, with the director perfectly capturing the aimlessness and pathos which pervade their lives. In a more light-hearted set piece, the covers of a rack of gay porn magazines come to life with pop-art brio (a similar sensibility is evident in the screens of bright, 60s colors which divide up the film's sections.) Perhaps most memorably, Waters's narcoleptic trances are accompa-nied by fleeting images of extraordinary beauty: leaping fish in a silver stream; a lonely road; a bank of quickly moving clouds; a wooden house falling from the heavens.

Van Sant's attempt to impose a Shakesperean conceit on his material is much less successful. Though Richert brings an enjoyable Falstaffian swagger to the Henry IV sequences, most of the other actors seem ill at ease with Van Sant's self-consciously theatrical blend of Shakes-perean dialogue and contemporary street slang. All these sequences pale in comparison to the understated pathos of the quiet scenes. In the most moving of these—a nighttime, roadside confession by Mike of his love for Scott—Van Sant casts a gently hypnotic spell that is not easily forgotten.

MY PAL TRIGGER

1946 79m bw Western ★★★½
Republic (U.S.) /U

Roy Rogers *(Roy Rogers)*, George "Gabby" Hayes *(Gabby Kendrick)*, Dale Evans *(Susan)*, Jack Holt *(Brett Scoville)*, LeRoy Mason *(Carson)*, Roy Barcroft *(Hunter)*, Sam Flint *(Sheriff)*, Kenne Duncan *(Croupier)*, Ralph Sanford *(Auctioneer)*, Francis McDonald *(Storekeeper)*

p, Armand Schaefer; d, Frank McDonald; w, Jack Townley, John K. Butler (based on a story by Paul Gangelin); ph, William Bradford; ed, Harry Keller; art d, Gano Chittenden; fx, Howard Lydecker, Theodore Lydecker

Roy Rogers named this as his favorite of all his films, and one can see why. It's well plotted, with lively direction and much better camera work than most of the Singing Cowboy's films. Rogers plays a horse trader planning to mate a prize mare with a stallion belonging to his pal Gabby Kendrick (Gabby Hayes). A gambler (Jack Holt) with similar plans for his own mare tries to steal the stallion, which escapes and mates with Rogers's mare. When the gambler catches up to the horse, he shoots it. Rogers is blamed, but he and his now-pregnant mare escape capture and leave town, with Roy determined to return to clear his name and unmask the real villain. This is the quintessential Rogers film, with some fine acting (undoubtedly some of the best the genre would produce) and, of course, musical numbers by the Sons of the Pioneers and duets by Rogers and Dale Evans.

MY 20TH CENTURY

1989 104m bw Comedy/Drama ★★★★
Mafilm/Friedlander/ICAIC (Hungary/Canada)

Dorotha Segda *(Dora/Lili/Mother)*, Oleg Jankowski *(Z)*, Peter Andorai *(Thomas Alva Edison)*, Gabor Mathe *(X)*, Paulus Manker *(Weininger)*, Gyula Kery, Andrei Schwartz, Sandor Tery, Sandor Czvetko, Endre Koronszi

d, Ildiko Enyedi; w, Ildiko Enyedi; ph, Tibor Mathe; ed, Maria Rigo; m, Laszlo Vidovszky; prod d, Zoltan Labas; cos, Agnes Gyarmathy

Filmed in shimmering black and white that suggests a fairy tale, this film has such breathtaking visuals it makes one mourn that black-and-white cinematography has fallen into disfavor. This is a dazzling celebration of feminism, mechanical progress, unbreakable familial ties, and early 20th century history. Despite the occasionally slack pace, it is a magical achievement that creates its own universe.

Taking the form of a fable, the film outlines a world of unlimited possibilities. In Hungary in 1880, identical twin girls are separated while selling matches. The different paths of the girls, Lili and Dora (both played by Segda) unwind over many years before they serendipitously cross once more. Aglow with fervor, Lili has become a radical determined to free the masses, while Dora leans toward the pleasures of the flesh. To his total confusion, a man known as Z (Jankowski) meets both women while traveling on the Orient Express, believing them to be one fascinating creature. Intercut with this dual romance are depictions of technological breakthroughs of the time, including the tale of a laboratory dog who outsmarts his scientist keepers, and commentary by Thomas Alva Edison (Andorai). Somehow this fanciful comedy of errors seems to be a logical extension of the progress-driven world in the early 1900s; the characters exist in a shining new world where anything can happen. Since creativity charges the air, the ingenuity of the characters in getting themselves out of scrapes seems only natural. At the film's climax, Lili (en route to eliminate the minister of the interior) encounters her long-lost sister in a hall of mirrors, where the women effect a liberating union.

In his debut film, director Enyedi dexterously unfolds a fanciful tale layered with whimsical and historical segments that touch tangentially on the main storyline. Never tied to a linear structure, it is full of delightful asides, such as the story of the monkey whose naivete about human beings lands him in captivity. The best way to enjoy MY 20TH CENTURY is to approach it as a fantastic cavalcade in which human truths are revealed by accident. Despite the fact that the characters wander through a technological wonderland, the most magical proposition of the film lies not in inventiveness but in the capacity of the spirit to reinvent itself. A liberating experience from a filmmaking visionary.

MY UNCLE
(MON ONCLE)

1958 110m c Comedy ★★★★
Specta/Gray/Alter/Cady (France) /U

Jacques Tati *(M. Hulot)*, Jean-Pierre Zola *(M. Arpel)*, Adrienne Servantie *(Mme. Arpel)*, Alain Becourt *(Gerald Arpel)*, Lucien Fregis *(M. Pichard)*, Betty Schneider *(Betty, Landlord's Daughter)*, Yvonne Arnaud *(Georgette, Arpel's Maid)*, Dominique Marie *(Neighbor)*, J.F. Martial *(Walter)*, Andre Dino *(Sweep)*

p, Jacques Tati; d, Jacques Tati; w, Jacques Tati, Jacques Lagrange, Jean L'Hote; ph, Jean Bourgoin; ed, Suzanne Baron; m, Franck Barcellini, Alain Romans; art d, Henri Schmitt, Pierre Etaix

AA Best Foreign Language Film

Tati followed MR. HULOT'S HOLIDAY with this impressive satire on modern gadgetry and the people who devote their lives to technological convenience. Tati has described his own comedy as "laughter born of a certain fundamental absurdity. Some things are not funny of themselves but become so on being dissected." It is this quality that Tati's films share with such satires as Rene Clair's A NOUS LA LIBERTE, Charles Chaplin's MODERN TIMES, and even Albert Brooks's LOST IN AMERICA. Tati again casts himself as Hulot, a lanky fellow with a raincoat and umbrella who stumbles through life. Content to live in his neglected quarters, Hulot is in direct contrast to the very modern Arpels, comprising his sister (Servantie), brother-in-law (Zola), and nephew, Gerald (Alain Becourt). The Arpels live in a modernized, desensitized suburb, their angular house hidden from the street by a clanging gate, and fronted by a fountain with an obscene metal fish spurting water from its mouth. Inside are gadgets meant to save time but which only waste it—and make noise. Hulot's humble, simple life attracts young Gerald, whose playfulness has no place in the modern world.

Less a condemnation of technology than of its worshippers, MY UNCLE is simultaneously entertaining, intelligent, and technically inventive. It makes vivid use of saturated color schemes and contains some truly great shots which suggest that the house has a life of its own, as when the Arpels walk back and forth before their round bedroom windows, giving the impression from the outside that the house is rolling its eyes.

MYSTERIOUS DR. FU MANCHU, THE

1929 80m bw Mystery ★★★
Paramount (U.S.)

Warner Oland *(Dr. Fu Manchu)*, Jean Arthur *(Lia Eltham)*, Neil Hamilton *(Dr. Jack Petrie)*, O.P. Heggie *(Nayland Smith)*, William Austin *(Sylvester Wadsworth)*, Claude King *(Sir John Petrie)*, Charles Stevenson *(Gen. Petrie)*, Noble Johnson *(Li Po)*, Evelyn Selbie *(Fai Lu)*, Charles Giblyn *(Weymouth)*

d, Rowland V. Lee; w, Florence Ryerson, Lloyd Corrigan (based on the story by Sax Rohmer); ph, Harry Fischbeck; ed, George Nichols Jr.

The first of the popular Sax Rohmer (Arthur Sarsfield Ward) mystery novels to be made into a talking feature is a fairly good job, reaching the same level of chilling suspense as the novels and later radio shows. Benevolent looking, overweight Oland (known for his renditions of Charlie Chan) is the evil green-eyed Chinese doctor bent on revenge against the British officer who commanded forces during the Boxer rebellion. It was during this time that Oland's wife and son were killed, warping the doctor's mind to the extent that all he can think about is vengeance. To assist him, he uses the daughter of an English official killed during the Rebellion. The girl is put into a trance and forced to do Oland's dirty work. After having killed several of the British officers he is after, Oland then attempts to gain vengeance against King and son Hamilton. But before this can happen, Scotland Yard is aware of Oland's pattern, and warns King before he meets with a disastrous end. Oland is quite convincing in the title role that would later be shared by such greats as Boris Karloff and Christopher Lee. The eerie atmosphere and steadily building suspense make this early entry in the series as frightening as those made in the 1960s.

MYSTERY OF THE WAX MUSEUM, THE

1933 73m c Horror   ★★★★
Warner Bros. (U.S.)   /A

Lionel Atwill *(Ivan Igor)*, Fay Wray *(Charlotte Duncan)*, Glenda Farrell *(Florence Dempsey)*, Frank McHugh *(Jim)*, Gavin Gordon *(Harold Winton)*, Edwin Maxwell *(Joe Worth)*, Holmes Herbert *(Dr. Rasmussen)*, Arthur Edmund Carewe *(Sparrow)*, Allen Vincent *(Ralph Burton)*, Monica Bannister *(Joan Gale)*

p, Henry Blanke; d, Michael Curtiz; w, Don Mullaly, Carl Erickson (based on a play by Charles Belden); ph, Ray Rennahan; ed, George Amy; art d, Anton Grot

Lionel Atwill and Fay Wray are teamed here for the second time in a Michael Curtiz-directed, Warner Brothers-produced two-strip Technicolor horror film (their first pairing was in DR. X in 1932). The film opens in London, in 1921, as the brilliant sculptor Ivan Igor (Atwill) is hard at work on his latest creation, surrounded by beautiful wax sculptures of female historical figures. Having eschewed the more sensational—and, therefore, more lucrative—figures of killers like Jack the Ripper in favor of these beautiful creations, Ivan finds his wax museum on the brink of bankruptcy. A fight over finances between Ivan and his partner, Joe Worth (Edwin Maxwell), results in the museum's destruction by fire, the "death" of the wax figures, and Ivan's near death. The scene then shifts to New York City, 1933, where the grey-haired Ivan is confined to a wheelchair, his hands crippled from the fire. When a wealthy socialite dies and her corpse is stolen from the morgue, tough-talking female reporter Florence Dempsey (Glenda Farrell) investigates the case. The strange disappearance of the corpse coincides suspiciously with Ivan's preparation for the opening of his new museum,in which the wax beauties have a remarkably lifelike appearance.

Feared to be lost for many years, MYSTERY OF THE WAX MUSEUM gained a mighty reputation when film historians' memories of the movie were jogged by the 1953 3-D remake, HOUSE OF WAX. When a print of the original film surfaced in the late 1960s, however, many critics were disappointed with it, shrugging it off as a silly mystery picture, though their initial reaction was entirely unfounded. An amazing film filled with stunning sets (by Anton Grot), exceptional moments, and perhaps Atwill's greatest performance, THE MYSTERY OF THE WAX MUSEUM is also a very adult film that deals explicitly with drug addiction, necrophilia, and insanity. Notable for its wonderful use of color, it was also one of the first horror films to be set in the everyday reality of modern-day New York and not in a mystical foreign land.

MYSTERY TRAIN

1989 113m c Comedy   ★★★½
MTI (U.S.)   R/15

Masatoshi Nagase *(Jun)*, Youki Kudoh *(Mitzuko)*, Screamin' Jay Hawkins *(Night Clerk)*, Cinque Lee *(Bellboy)*, Nicoletta Braschi *(Luisa)*, Elizabeth Bracco *(Dee Dee)*, Sy Richardson *(News Vendor)*, Tom Noonan *(Man in Diner)*, Stephen Jones *(The Ghost)*, Rufus Thomas *(Man in Station)*

p, Jim Stark; d, Jim Jarmusch; w, Jim Jarmusch; ph, Robby Muller; ed, Melody London; m, John Lurie; prod d, Dan Bishop; cos, Carol Wood

New York-based filmmaker Jim Jarmusch continues his deadpan Cook's Tour of America with MYSTERY TRAIN, a trio of tangentially related stories set in Memphis, Tennessee.

All three tales center on the run-down Arcade Hotel, where every room is a shrine to Memphis's favorite son, Elvis Aron Presley. A candidate for the wrecking ball, the Arcade is staffed by two dedicated souls (legendary rhythm & blues performer Screamin' Jay Hawkins and Cinque Lee, Spike's younger brother) who seem to have no existence beyond the front desk. As the film's first episode, "Far from Yokohama," opens, Jun (Masatoshi Nagase) and Mitzuko (Youki Kudoh), two teenaged devotees of American culture, check into the Arcade, where they argue over rock 'n' roll favorites, make love, listen to Elvis on the hotel radio, and remain undisturbed by everything that occurs—even the gunshot they hear near checkout time. The Arcade also plays host to Luisa (Nicoletta Braschi), an Italian woman visiting the States to bring her dead husband back to Italy. The focus of the second

episode, "A Ghost," Luisa is harassed by a low-life who promises her she will be visited by visions of Elvis. The third episode, "Lost in Space," involves Dee Dee (Elizabeth Bracco), her alcohol-crazed lover (Joe Strummer), her nervous-wreck brother (Steve Buscemi), and their fast-talking pal (Rick Aviles) as they get involved in a shooting. At checkout time, all the characters go their separate ways.

As with STRANGER THAN PARADISE and DOWN BY LAW, Jarmusch focuses his offbeat sensibility on urban iconoclasts, small-town oddballs, and bewildered strangers. Not surprisingly, MYSTERY TRAIN will work best for those who share Jarmusch's fondness for America's pop culture junkyard; he's a true original, but Jarmusch's originality lies in a quirky viewpoint that may leave some audience members cold. Others who abandon themselves to his deadpan drollery and Robby Muller's witty cinematography, which makes squalor look festive, will be rewarded with a cockeyed valentine to the cradle of rock 'n' roll.

N

NAKED

1993 131m c Drama   ★★★★
Thin Man Films/British Screen/First Independent/Channel   /18
Four (U.K.)

David Thewlis *(Johnny)*, Katrin Cartlidge *(Sophie)*, Greg Cruttwell *(Jeremy)*, Lesley Sharp *(Louise)*, Claire Skinner *(Sandra)*, Peter Wight *(Brian)*, Elizabeth Berrington *(Giselle)*, Ewen Bremner *(Archie)*, Deborah MacLaren *(Woman In Window)*, Carolina Giametto *(Masseuse)*

p, Simon Channing-Williams; d, Mike Leigh; w, Mike Leigh; ph, Dick Pope; ed, John Gregory; m, Andrew Dickinson; prod d, Alison Chitty; art d, Eve Stewart; cos, Lindy Hemming

Blackly funny and corrosively sad, Mike Leigh's NAKED is a rambling portrait of a young man flying apart at a breakneck pace. Like Leigh's earlier films, which include HIGH HOPES (1988) and LIFE IS SWEET (1991), NAKED is an artfully unpolished, ensemble portrait of a group of people who are resolutely undistinguished, if not exactly ordinary.

The film opens on a violent sexual encounter in a Manchester alley. Rape? Consensual rough sex? A casual pickup gone awry? It's impossible to tell, but Johnny (David Thewlis)—who's ferociously clever, cruelly funny, and passably attractive—steals a car and flees to London, where he looks up his old girlfriend, Louise (Lesley Sharp); seduces her drugged-out roommate, Sophie (Katrin Cartlidge); and wreaks havoc on the lives of everyone he meets. Meanwhile, sleek, disdainful, and apparently wealthy Jeremy (Greg Crutwell) rapes and terrorizes various women, including Sophie. Their paths eventually cross, during a very dark night of the soul.

NAKED's greatest accomplishment is that one is forced to empathize with Johnny, however loathsome his behavior. His wit is unfailingly mean, his intelligence without direction or purpose. He feels cheated—by women, by England, by the world, by God—and retaliates by humiliating everyone within range, by any means necessary. He's sexually vicious and practices conversation as a blood sport. His imagination is gridlocked with apocalyptic fantasies drawn from the Bible, the prophecies of Nostradamus, James Gleick's *Chaos*, and the tabloids.

Working from a script developed out of improvisations with the cast, Leigh has created one of the most abrasive—and articulate—characters in recent screen history. His work is triumphantly matched by that of Thewlis, with both director and actor taking awards at the 1993 Cannes festival, and Thewlis picking up a raft of prizes in the US.

NAKED CITY, THE

1948 96m bw Crime   ★★★★
Universal (U.S.)   /A

Barry Fitzgerald *(Lt. Dan Muldoon)*, Howard Duff *(Frank Niles)*, Dorothy Hart *(Ruth Morrison)*, Don Taylor *(Jimmy Halloran)*, Ted de Corsia *(Garzah)*, House Jameson *(Dr. Stoneman)*, Anne Sargent *(Mrs. Halloran)*, Adelaide Klein *(Mrs. Batory)*, Grover Burgess *(Mr. Batory)*, Tom Pedi *(Detective Perelli)*

p, Mark Hellinger; d, Jules Dassin; w, Albert Maltz, Malvin Wald (based on a story by Malvin Wald); ph, William Daniels; ed, Paul Weatherwax; m, Miklos Rozsa, Frank Skinner; art d, John DeCuir; cos, Grace Houston

AAN Best Story: Malvin Wald; *AA Best Cinematography:* William H. Daniels; *AA Best Editing:* Paul Weatherwax

This superlative film set the pattern for myriad documentary-type dramas to come. Its producer, Hellinger, patterned the tale after the tabloid newspaper stories he wrote in his youth, and he narrates the picture with the same kind of terse but poignant vitality that was the hallmark of his sensational prose. Though basically a crime story—with, oddly, only character actor Fitzgerald as its star—the film is also a romance with the city itself, one where Hellinger embraces soiled urchins and immaculate society ladies with equal passion. The story opens with the bathtub murder of a beautiful blonde playgirl. The police are left with no clues. Fitzgerald and his brash young assistant, Taylor, are assigned the case and spend most of their time running down weak leads that reveal nothing. In the process, the routine of their lives is detailed, as the various suspects and would-be witnesses who make up much of the story are presented. Fitzgerald, a cop for 30 years, is relentless in his pursuit of criminals. Taylor, who lives in a modest home and kisses his wife good-bye every morning on his way to headquarters, tries to please his superiors and cover up his lack of experience, but he slowly learns the wily ways of the cop under Fitzgerald's expert tutelage.

Shot completely on location in New York City, THE NAKED CITY chronicles the grim urban landscape and depicts its everyday life and citizens, embracing swank Fifth Avenue, Broadway, kids playing hop-skip-and-jump in the streets, straphangers en route to work and back on the crowded subways. More than 100 locations were employed, with the brilliant cameraman Daniels shooting most of his scenes from inside a van parked along the streets, using a one-way mirror and tinted windows so that passers-by were oblivious to the camera's presence. In the late 1950s and early 60s, a long-running ABC TV series used this film's title to show the "slice-of-life" style of drama the original film typified, and also employed Hellinger's postscript in this, his last feature production, a line which became a household phrase: "There are eight million stories in the naked city. This has been one of them."

NAKED GUN: FROM THE FILES OF POLICE SQUAD!, THE

1988 85m c Comedy   ★★★½
Paramount (U.S.)   PG-13/15

Leslie Nielsen *(Lt. Frank Drebin)*, George Kennedy *(Capt. Ed Hocken)*, Priscilla Presley *(Jane Spencer)*, Ricardo Montalban *(Vincent Ludwig)*, O.J. Simpson *(Nordberg)*, Nancy Marchand *(Mayor)*, John Houseman *(Driving Instructor)*, Reggie Jackson *(Right Fielder)*, Jeannette Charles *(Queen Elizabeth II)*, Curt Gowdy

p, Robert K. Weiss; d, David Zucker; w, Jerry Zucker, Jim Abrahams, David Zucker, Pat Proft; ph, Robert Stevens; ed, Michael Jablow; m, Ira Newborn; prod d, John J. Lloyd; cos, Mary Vogt

The Zucker, Abrahams, and Zucker writing-directing team, who made a huge splash with AIRPLANE!, based THE NAKED GUN on their hilarious but short-lived TV show "Police Squad." Leslie Nielsen reprises his role as bumbling police lieutenant Frank Drebin, who becomes embroiled in a case involving suave heroin smuggler Vincent Ludwig (Ricardo Montalban). Drebin falls for Ludwig's assistant, Jane (Priscilla Presley), who is just as dim and clumsy as he is. Meanwhile, Drebin's boss (George Kennedy) learns that there will be an assassination attempt on Queen Elizabeth (played by look-alike Jeannette Charles) during her visit to Los Angeles.

Merely recounting the plot of any ZAZ comedy utterly fails to convey the lunacy and, believe it or not, charm of the production. From the inspired opening credit sequence, in which a camera mounted behind the flashing light of a police car drives down city streets, through a car wash, into a building, down a corridor, and finally into a women's locker room; to the sight of the villain falling off a tier at a ballpark and being crushed by a bus, a steamroller, and then a marching band, THE NAKED GUN is a continuous stream of verbal and visual gags that come so fast, you don't have time to realize how bad/old/corny they are.

NAKED LUNCH

1991 115m c Science Fiction/Fantasy/Drama   ★★★
Naked Lunch Productions/Recorded Picture Co.   R/18
(U.K./Canada)

Peter Weller *(William Lee)*, Judy Davis *(Joan Frost/Joan Lee)*, Ian Holm *(Tom Frost)*, Julian Sands *(Yves Cloquet)*, Roy Scheider *(Dr. Benway)*, Monique Mercure *(Fadela)*, Nicholas Campbell *(Hank)*, Michael Zelniker *(Martin)*, Robert A. Silverman *(Hans)*, Joseph Scorsiani *(Kiki)*

p, Jeremy Thomas; d, David Cronenberg; w, David Cronenberg (from the novel by William S. Burroughs); ph, Peter Suschitzky; ed, Ronald Sanders; m, Howard Shore; prod d, Carol Spier; art d, James McAteer; fx, Chris Walas Inc; cos, Denise Cronenberg

A grotesquely humorous concoction, cooked up by Canadian director David Cronenberg with a little help from America's favorite underground novelist, William Burroughs. The Burroughs novel from which the movie is adapted is nearly devoid of narrative, but Cronenberg has sidestepped this problem by making a film *about* the writing of *Naked Lunch*. The movie combines elements from Burroughs's life—particularly the accidental shooting of his wife during a drunken game of "William Tell"—with scenes from several of his books to tell the story of his trnasformation into a writer. It opens in New York City in the early 1950s, where Burroughs's alter ego, Bill Lee (Peter Weller), is working as an exterminator. His problems begin when his wife, Joan (Judy Davis), turns him on to the narcotic qualities of the bug powder he uses. Under the influence of the powder, Lee hallucinates his way into an alternative realm where he is a secret agent for a ring of giant, infinitely disgusting beetles. The bugs instruct him to kill his wife and go to Interzone, a fictional city loosely modeled on Tangiers. There, Lee encounters an assortment of literary types and other shady characters, has conversations with typewriters which metamorphose into—you guessed it—giant bugs, and indulges in some exotic, mind-altering substances.

The result is a hallucinatory, often stomach-turning take on the bohemian life that incorporates loosely drawn portraits of Burrough's contemporaries—Jack Kerouac, Allen Ginsberg, Paul and Jane Bowles—as well as conjuring up the nightmares of drug addiction and the excruciatingly painful process of writing itself. The director has come up with some of his most imaginative—and unpalatable—images to date, ranging from two-foot beetles which speak through sphincter-like openings in their backs, to giant, rubbery creatures which secrete a sticky, narcotic fluid from—ahem—organs that sprout from their heads. A treat for Cronenberg fans, though this could hardly be called a gripping, or emotionally involving, story; you're more likely to need a can of bug spray than a hanky.

NAKED PREY, THE

1966 96m c Adventure   ★★★½
Theodora/Sven Persson (U.S./South Africa)   /PG

Cornel Wilde *(Man)*, Gert Van den Bergh *(2nd Man)*, Ken Gampu *(Warrior Leader)*, Patrick Mynhardt *(Safari Overseer)*, Bella Randels *(Little Girl)*, Jose Sithole, Richard Mashiya, Eric Sabela, Joe Diaminl, Frank Mdhluli

p, Cornel Wilde; d, Cornel Wilde; w, Clint Johnston, Donald A. Peters; ph, H.A.R. Thomson; ed, Roger Cherrill; cos, Freda Thompson

AAN Best Original Screenplay: Clint Johnston, Don Peters

An early cinema staple, the chase film, is resurrected, pure and simple, by star-producer-director Cornel Wilde. He plays a tour guide in the South African bush near the end of the 19th century, leading several men on an ivory hunting expedition. Despite his warnings, the party offends local tribesmen. Bad move. Ambushed, the men are taken back to the tribesmen's village for ritual torture and execution. (One especially horrifying, unforgettable image has a victim encased in clay except for a breathing tube, being roasted alive on a spit.) The guide, for whom the natives presumably have some respect, is offered "The Chance of the Lion." Stripped naked, he is given a head start of a few hundred yards. Then six warriors, each of whom has killed ten lions, set out to hunt him down, and the chase is on.

Wilde's fifth directorial outing was easily his best, tautly constructed and rapidly paced. (Fewer than 15 minutes pass between the credits and the start of Wilde's race for life.) His habit of beginning or ending scenes with shots of animal predators snaring their prey is obvious and becomes rather tiresome, but some of the imagery, such as a bird being caught or one frog devouring another, is extraordinary. The film is nothing but an extremely vivid and suspenseful chase, so pared down that there's absolutely no characterization whatsoever—let alone consideration of the environmental or racial issues and attitudes on rampant display here. Thank heavens for those white redcoats, right?

NAKED SPUR, THE

1953 91m c Western ★★★★
MGM (U.S.) /A

James Stewart (Howard Kemp), Janet Leigh (Lina Patch), Robert Ryan (Ben Vandergroat), Ralph Meeker (Roy Anderson), Millard Mitchell (Jesse Tate)

p, William H. Wright; d, Anthony Mann; w, Sam Rolfe, Harold Jack Bloom; ph, William Mellor; ed, George White; m, Bronislau Kaper; art d, Cedric Gibbons, Malcolm Brown

AAN Best Original Screenplay: Sam Rolfe, Harold Jack Bloom

Another superb western from director Anthony Mann who, along with Budd Boetticher, created an outstanding series of engrossing, thoughtful, and challenging films that helped keep the genre fresh and vital during the 1950s. Stewart is excellent as Howard Kemp, the obsessed, disillusioned Civil War veteran who returns home to find he has lost his land. To raise the money needed to regain his land, Kemp decides to become a bounty hunter and enters the Colorado Territory in search of escaped killer Ben Vandergroat (Robert Ryan), who has a $5,000 reward on his head. Vandergroat is accompanied by Lina Patch (Janet Leigh), a lonely young woman who wants to escape to California. While searching for Vandergroat, Kemp picks up a pair of companions; Jesse Tate (Millard Mitchell), a grizzled prospector, and Roy Anderson (Ralph Meeker), a dishonorably discharged Union soldier. The two drifters believe Kemp to be a lawman and agree to help him capture Vandergroat; they corner the fugitive, together with Patch, on a rugged hillside and take them prisoner. When they learn that Kemp is a mere bounty hunter, however, they demand an equal share of the reward. Kemp refuses, and Vandergroat sees a chance to escape, via a clever campaign to pit the men against each other during the seven-day trip through dangerous Indian territory back to Abilene.

NAKED SPUR is a superb, tautly directed western in which Mann's protagonists, once again, allow the desire for vengeance to consume their inherent qualities of honor and decency. The journey becomes a process of near-religious revelation that finally allows one of them to achieve a bitterly earned state of grace.

NAME OF THE ROSE, THE

1986 130m c Mystery ★★★
Bernd Eichinger/Bernd Schaefers/Neue R/18
Constantin/Cristaldifilm/Ariane (U.S.)

Sean Connery (William of Baskerville), F. Murray Abraham (Bernardo Gui), Christian Slater (Adso of Melk), Elya Baskin (Severinus), Feodor Chaliapin Jr. (Jorge de Burgos), William Hickey (Ubertino de Casale), Michel Lonsdale (The Abbot), Ron Perlman (Salvatore), Volker Prechtel (Malachia), Helmut Qualtinger (Remigio de Varagine)

p, Bernd Eichinger; d, Jean-Jacques Annaud; w, Andrew Birkin, Gerard Brach, Howard Franklin, Alain Godard; ph, Tonino Delli Colli; ed, Jane Seitz; m, James Horner; prod d, Dante Ferretti; art d, Giorgio Giovannini, Rainer Schaper; fx, Adriano Pischiutta; cos, Gabriella Pescucci

Based on the witty, flashily erudite first novel by Italian semiotician and journalist Umberto Eco, this medieval murder mystery is a little slow-moving but ultimately rewarding. At an Italian monastery in 1327, the Franciscans, who live in religious poverty, and the Dominicans, who enjoy a life of luxury, meet to debate whether the Catholic church should be in the business of accruing wealth. William of Baskerville (Connery), a brilliant English monk (whose Holmesian manner is reinforced by his name, taken from *The Hound of the Baskervilles*), and his teenage novice, Adso of Melk (Slater), arrive early, and when murders begin occurring, the abbot (Lonsdale) requests that they begin an investigation. But even as William begins looking into the matter, the murders continue, seemingly following the prophecy of the Apocalypse. The more rational clues lead to the monastery's extraordinary library, but before the Englishman can find the truth, the Dominicans and, most important, his old rival Bernardo Gui (Abraham), the Inquisitor, arrive and matters become even more complicated as Gui sees the Devil's hand in the murders. Gifted cinematographer Tonino Delli Colli has given the film an appropriately dark look, and the many odd-looking monks appear as if they have stepped from the set of a Fellini picture. Much of the $18 million production was shot at Kloster Eberbach, a 12th-century monastery near Frankfurt, West Germany.

NARROW MARGIN, THE

1952 71m bw Thriller ★★★
RKO (U.S.) /PG

Charles McGraw (Walter Brown), Marie Windsor (Mrs. Neall), Jacqueline White (Ann Sinclair), Gordon Gebert (Tommy Sinclair), Queenie Leonard (Mrs. Troll), David Clarke (Kemp), Peter Virgo (Densel), Don Beddoe (Gus Forbes), Paul Maxey (Jennings), Harry Harvey (Train Conductor)

p, Stanley Rubin; d, Richard Fleischer; w, Earl Fenton (based on a story by Martin Goldsmith, Jack Leonard); ph, George E. Diskant; ed, Robert Swink; art d, Albert S. D'Agostino, Jack Okey

AAN Best Original Screenplay: Martin Goldsmith, Jack Leonard

A competent B movie from RKO that takes place almost entirely on board a train from Chicago to Los Angeles. Walter Brown (McGraw) is a hard-boiled detective who, with his partner, Gus Forbes (Beddoe), is assigned to escort a racketeer's widow (Windsor) to a West Coast court where she will give testimony before a grand jury. However, three thugs aboard the train are trying to shut her up—permanently. Unfortunately for the gang members, they do not know what the widow looks like, so they bump off anyone they suspect might be their quarry. While far from a masterpiece, THE NARROW MARGIN is a well-executed programmer that turned a fantastic profit for RKO, considering its meager $230,000 budget. Audiences loved the film—thrilling at the plot twists, the characters, and the trick train photography—making it into one of the studio's most profitable B movies.

NASHVILLE

1975 159m c Drama ★★★★★
Paramount (U.S.) R/AA

David Arkin (Norman Chauffeur), Barbara Baxley (Lady Pearl), Ned Beatty (Delbert Reese), Karen Black (Connie White), Ronee Blakley (Barbara Jean), Lily Tomlin (Linnea Reese), Timothy Brown (Tommy Brown), Keith Carradine (Tom Frank), Geraldine Chaplin (Opal), Robert DoQui (Wade)

p, Robert Altman; d, Robert Altman; w, Joan Tewkesbury; ph, Paul Lohmann; ed, Sidney Levin, Dennis M. Hill; m, Richard Baskin

AAN Best Picture; AAN Best Supporting Actress: Ronee Blakely; AAN Best Supporting Actress: Lily Tomlin; AAN Best Director: Robert Altman; AA Best Song: Keith Carradine

Robert Altman's triumph; one of the best American movies of the 70s and one of the most complex, expertly constructed narratives ever. Sprawling over two and one-half hours and never flagging, it successfully introduces and exposes 24 different characters, brilliantly critiquing the country music industry as a microcosm of American society.

NASHVILLE's songs, many of them written by the actors, are more integral to the storyline than is usually the case but, even if you do not cotton to country sounds, the effect is still overwhelming. Altman cuts back and forth between the characters with such aplomb that the audience never loses track of the narrative, which all takes place on one climactic weekend in the Country Music Capital of America. A huge music festival is taking place in Nashville, and at the same time a political rally is slated to promote the candidacy of the never-seen presidential hopeful Hal Phillip Walker, who leads a new entity known as the Replacement Party. Though Walker's politics are not deeply plumbed, he sounds vaguely like George Wallace did when he was running on his third-party ticket. Walker's aides, Michael Murphy and Beatty, know what kind of people the candidate appeals to, and they prevail upon several of the top country music singers to help their cause. Henry Gibson, playing a veteran performer who appears to be patterned after Hank Snow, is the *eminence grise* whom most of the younger performers venerate. Despite his down-home smile as he sings, Gibson is a mean, rotten, self-serving man who would sell his mother for a gold record. Also in the top echelon is Blakley, a country music queen and authentic folk artist (said to be based on Loretta Lynn, who was angry about it) who has just recovered from a mental breakdown and is teetering on the edge of another. The festival has attracted singers from all over the country, each hoping to have a moment in the sun, be discovered, and take a place in the country pantheon. Carradine is one of a trio of folk singers. He's nothing more than skin stretched over lechery and is currently sleeping with partner Allan Nicholl's wife, Cristina Raines. That doesn't stop him from plucking favors from Lily Tomlin, Beatty's neglected wife, and Chaplin, a hilariously irritating BBC correspondent who is covering the festival for the listeners in the British Isles. Blakley's first concert is a flop, as she can't handle appearing in front of a crowd after such a long layoff, and her husband-manager, Allan Garfield, tells the annoyed assemblage that she will give them all a free concert in a couple of days to make up for this one—and to keep her crown from being stolen by Karen Black, doing a poisonous turn as a combo Tammy Wynette-Lynn Anderson. Beatty comes to Blakley and Garfield and asks her to appear for Walker at the rally, and she agrees. Beatty and Murphy stage a small fund-raising stag party and hire waitress Gwen Welles to sing, knowing she's so desperate for fame that they can force her to strip. (The leering men at the stag were actually played by some members of the Nashville Chamber of Commerce, and they turned in a totally convincing performance.) After she finishes, Beatty vainly attempts to bed Welles. On the day of the rally, David Hayward, whom we've seen flit in and out of the film carrying a violin case, comes to the stage and shoots Gibson and Blakley after their singing has stopped the show.

There are other rich characterizations: Barbara Harris, a dearranged white trash runaway out for her big break; Baxley, as Johnson's longtime cynical, bullshit mistress; Keenan Wynn as a Bible Belt family man, with Duvall as an eternal groupie; Tim Brown (magnificently playing a character based on Charlie Pride) is the black singer who has crossed over to become a success in the white world; Scott Glenn is the faithful puppy-dog serviceman who is entranced by Blakley; Jeff Goldblum plays a local freak; Arkin as a chauffeur who witnesses everything; and David Peel is Gibson's son, a boy who does whatever his father asks and hates every minute of it. On top of all that, Elliott Gould and Julie Christie come in to do cameos as themselves, two movie stars tub-thumping a new project.

Amazingly, the movie was shot for about $2 million in less than 45 days, with much of the dialogue improvised by the performers.

NATIONAL LAMPOON'S ANIMAL HOUSE

| 1978 109m c Comedy | ★★★½ |
| Universal (U.S.) | R/15 |

John Belushi *(John "Bluto" Blutarsky)*, Tim Matheson *(Eric "Otter" Stratton)*, Peter Reigert *(Donald "Boon" Schoenstein)*, John Vernon *(Dean Vernon Wormer)*, Tom Hulce *(Larry "Pinto" Kroger)*, Cesare Danova *(Mayor Carmine DePasto)*, Mary Louise Weller *(Mandy Pepperidge)*, Stephen Furst *(Kent "Flounder" Dorfman)*, James Daughton *(Greg Marmalard)*, Bruce McGill *(Daniel "D-Day" Simpson)*

p, Matty Simmons, Ivan Reitman; d, John Landis; w, Harold Ramis, Douglas Kenney, Chris Miller; ph, Charles Correll; ed, George Folsey Jr.; m, Elmer Bernstein; art d, John Lloyd; fx, Henry Millar; cos, Deborah Nadoolman

Rude, rough, tasteless, but often hilarious, this movie was a huge hit with young audiences and grossed more than $80 million. Supposedly based on the actual college experiences of the screenwriters (specifically Miller's year at Dartmouth), it served to introduce to films the anarchistic talents of Belushi as he played off the fine work by Hulce, Matheson, and others. The story takes place in the early 1960s, before the Vietnam War had heated up. Hulce and the rotund Furst attempt to join fraternities on their Faber College campus, but they are turned away and wind up at Delta House, a pigsty where they are welcomed by Matheson. The school's dean, Vernon, is keeping an eye on this particular house because its boozing members all have rotten grades and break nearly every school edict with their raucous "toga parties," in which the revelers dress up in bed sheets. Vernon, who would like to shut down the place, enlists Daughton, the head of the conservative Omega House, in his scheme, but he hasn't bargained on the tenacity, ingenuity, and unbelievably gross taste of his targets. This was the first of those crazy-college-antics films and remains, in most ways, the best.

NATIONAL VELVET

| 1944 125m c Drama | ★★★★ |
| MGM (U.S.) | /U |

Mickey Rooney *(Mi Taylor)*, Donald Crisp *(Mr. Brown)*, Elizabeth Taylor *(Velvet Brown)*, Anne Revere *(Mrs. Brown)*, Angela Lansbury *(Edwina Brown)*, Juanita Quigley *(Malvolia Brown)*, Jackie "Butch" Jenkins *(Donald Brown)*, Reginald Owen *(Farmer Ede)*, Terry Kilburn *(Ted)*, Alec Craig *(Tim)*

p, Pandro S. Berman; d, Clarence Brown; w, Theodore Reeves, Helen Deutsch (based on the novel by Enid Bagnold); ph, Leonard Smith; ed, Robert J. Kern; m, Herbert Stothart; art d, Cedric Gibbons, Urie McCleary; fx, Warren Newcombe; cos, Irene

AA Best Supporting Actress: Anne Revere; *AAN Best Director:* Clarence Brown; *AAN Best Cinematography:* Leonard Smith; *AA Best Editing:* Robert J. Kern; *AAN Best Art Direction:* Cedric Gibbons, Urie McCleary, Edwin B. Willis, Mildred Griffiths

Perhaps the only time Elizabeth Taylor's costar matched her visual scene stealing. He's a horse, albeit a gelding. One of MGM's most beloved films, NATIONAL VELVET was the picture that made a star out of Taylor. The place is Sussex, England, where radiant Velvet Brown (Taylor) wins a horse that she names Pie and plans to enter in the Grand National. With the help of Mi Taylor (Rooney) she begins to rigorously train the animal, though she hasn't the money to enter the National. But Velvet's mother (Anne Revere) has been saving money she won as a young girl by swimming the English Channel, and she parts with it so Velvet can enter the race. Velvet, Mi and the horse then go off on their adventurous quest for the Grand National title. The movie features one of the best horse racing sequences ever filmed, as well as a host of winning performances. Although Taylor had already made her mark in four films, this was the one that really thrust her into the spotlight. Surprisingly she was not the first choice for the role, as Katharine Hepburn, Shirley Temple, and Margaret Sullavan were all candidates to play it. Angela Lansbury finally got one young role that wasn't opportunistic—here she's dreamy and romantic—English peaches and cream. And Jackie "Butch" Jenkins is an outstanding little brother, so ugly his cuteness makes you smile even hours after the movie. The film was remade as INTERNATIONAL VELVET starring Tatum O'Neal, and we grow ashen whenever we think of it.

NATURAL, THE

| 1984 134m c Sports | ★★★ |
| Natural (U.S.) | PG |

Robert Redford *(Roy Hobbs)*, Robert Duvall *(Max Mercy)*, Glenn Close *(Iris)*, Kim Basinger *(Memo Paris)*, Wilford Brimley *(Pop Fisher)*, Barbara Hershey *(Harriet Bird)*, Robert Prosky *(The Judge)*, Richard Farnsworth *(Red Blow)*, Joe Don Baker *(The Whammer)*, John Finnegan *(Sam Simpson)*

p, Mark Johnson; d, Barry Levinson; w, Roger Towne, Phil Dusenberry (based on the novel by Bernard Malamud); ph, Caleb Deschanel; ed, Stu Linder; m, Randy Newman; prod d, Angelo Graham, Mel Bourne; art d, James J. Murakami, Speed Hopkins; fx, Roger Hensen; cos, Bernie Pollack, Gloria Gresham

NATURAL BORN KILLERS

AAN Best Supporting Actress: Glenn Close; AAN Best Cinematography: Caleb Deschanel; AAN Best Score: Randy Newman; AAN Best Art Direction: Angelo Graham, Mel Bourne, James J. Murakami, Speed Hopkins, Bruce Weintraub

Transforming Bernard Malamud's fabulist first novel into a mythical morality play, THE NATURAL follows the fortunes of Roy Hobbs (Robert Redford) as the 19-year-old farm boy makes his way to try out with the Cubs. En route, he wins a bet by striking out the Whammer (Joe Don Baker), a slugger of Ruthian proportions, proving greatness is in his future. But in Chicago, a mysterious women (Barbara Hershey) lures Roy to her hotel room and shoots him with a silver bullet. Fifteen years later, in 1939, Roy joins the hapless New York Knights and literally knocks the cover off the ball, leading the team back into contention. The Knights' owner (Robert Prosky), who is betting against his own team, sends Roy a beautiful temptress (Kim Basinger) so that he falls into a terrible slump, but his virtuous former girlfriend (Glenn Close) appears to revive his hitting. Without using his familiar "Wonderboy" bat for the big game, Roy still blasts an awe-inspiring home run into the lights, setting off a magical shower of fireworks to the strains of Randy Newman's evocative score. Somewhat overly sentimental, lacking the novel's subtlety, and less interesting when the action leaves the ball park, Barry Levinson's beautifully shot film is nonetheless a charming fairy tale. Redford, who played baseball at the University of Colorado, gives an appropriately iconic performance as Roy Hobbs—part Shoeless Joe Jackson (EIGHT MEN OUT), part Joe Hardy (DAMN YANKEES)—and the supporting roles are also well handled, especially Wilford Brimley as the manager. Filmed partly in Buffalo's War Memorial Stadium, a minor league park built in the 1930s, THE NATURAL also offers an appearance by "Super" Joe Charboneau, who had his own miracle season with the Cleveland Indians before disappearing from the big leagues.

NATURAL BORN KILLERS

1994 120m c Action/Thriller   ★★★
New Regency Productions/Ixtlan Productions/Alcor Films/J.D.   R/18
Productions   (U.S.)

Woody Harrelson (Mickey Knox), Juliette Lewis (Mallory Knox), Robert Downey Jr. (Wayne Gale), Tommy Lee Jones (Dwight McClusky), Tom Sizemore (Jack Scagnetti), Rodney Dangerfield (Mallory's Dad), Russell Means (Old Indian), Edie McClurg (Mallory's Mom), Balthazar Getty (Gas Station Attendant), Joe Grifasi (Duncan Homolka)

p, Jane Hamsher, Don Murphy, Clayton Townsend; d, Oliver Stone; w, David Veloz, Richard Rutowski, Oliver Stone (from a story by Quentin Tarantino); ph, Robert Richardson; ed, Hank Corwin, Brian Berdan; m, Trent Reznor; prod d, Victor Kempster; art d, Alan R. Tomkins, Margery Zweizig; fx, Matt Sweeney, Steve Luport, Frank L. Pope, James Schwalm, Lucinda Strub, Rebecca Marie; cos, Richard Hornung; anim, Mike Smith

Wildly unconventional, corrosively satirical, savagely violent and vulgar, NATURAL BORN KILLERS is more self-consciously radical (in form, if not necessarily in content) than any other major studio release in recent memory. If it isn't the masterpiece it aspires to be—director Oliver Stone lacks, and may never attain, the kind of intellectual acuity that most of us still expect from artists—it's unquestionably a watershed.

Woody Harrelson and Juliette Lewis play Mickey and Mallory Knox, a post-utopian Bonnie and Clyde on a cross-country killing spree. If Bonnie and Clyde liked to think of themselves as Depression-era Robin Hoods, Mickey and Mallory have no such illusions—as a TV psychiatrist (Steven Wright) observes: "They know the difference between right and wrong. They just don't give a damn." On their way to racking up 52 victims, the couple become international celebrities, thanks mostly to the attentions of a lurid TV tabloid show hosted by the unapologetically venal Wayne Gale (Robert Downey, Jr.). After a series of increasingly hallucinatory adventures on the road, Mickey and Mallory are apprehended and imprisoned. Nothing, however, can stand in the way of true love (or Nielsen ratings): while deranged Warden McClusky (Tommy Lee Jones) schemes to have the Knoxes murdered, Mickey plots escape, using a live interview with Wayne Gale as a pretext for inciting an apocalyptic prison riot.

This astonishingly violent, technically brilliant satire of televisual culture baffled critics at the time of its release—as did A CLOCKWORK ORANGE 23 years earlier—and its indecorous brand of humor will strike many as insolent, even repellent. Stone, in a smart recovery from the disastrous HEAVEN AND EARTH, has wisely let his obsession with "significance" yield to his instinctive feel for pulp. Paradoxically, the result may be his most significant film. Accessing some of the farthest reaches of previously marginalized culture—direct-to-video splatter, cyberpunk, S&M, anime, serial killer fandom—NBK decisively wrenches mainstream cinema into the anarchic realm of post-modern pop.

NAUGHTY MARIETTA

1935 106m bw Musical   ★★★★
MGM (U.S.)   /A

Jeanette MacDonald (Princess Marie de Namours de la Bonfain, "Marietta Franini"), Nelson Eddy (Capt. Richard Warrington), Frank Morgan (Governor Gaspard d'Annard), Elsa Lanchester (Mme. d'Annard), Douglas Dumbrille (Prince de Namours de la Bonfain), Joseph Cawthorn (Herr Schuman), Cecilia Parker (Julie), Walter Kingsford (Don Carlos de Braganza), Greta Meyer (Frau Schuman), Akim Tamiroff (Rudolpho, Puppet Master)

p, Hunt Stromberg; d, W.S. Van Dyke II; w, John Lee Mahin, Frances Goodrich, Albert Hackett (based on the operetta by Victor Herbert, Rida Johnson Young); ph, William Daniels; ed, Blanche Sewell; art d, Cedric Gibbons; cos, Adrian

AAN Best Picture; AA Best Sound: Douglas Shearer

Nelson Eddy made his full-fledged debut in this, the first of eight films in which he costarred with Jeanette MacDonald. Rita Johnson Young and Victor Herbert's hoary operetta was dusted off, given a new screenplay, new lyrics by Gus Kahn, and the result was a neatly paced (by "One-Take" Woodie Van Dyke) Best Picture nominee that only slightly belies its stage origins. Fleeing an arranged marriage to a Spanish grandee (Walter Kingsford), French princess Marie de Namours de la Bonfain (MacDonald) switches places with her maid and boards a ship bound for Louisana, where its female passengers are to become colonial brides. En route the ship is attacked by pirates, but the women are soon rescued by a group of soldiers led by Capt. Richard Warrington (Eddy), with whom the princess, now calling herself Marietta, falls in love. In New Orleans, she continues to conceal her identity, avoiding marriage by claiming to be a woman of ill repute. Eventually Capt. Warrington comes to the realization that he is in love with Marietta, but several hurdles stand in the way of their happiness, including arrest and the appearance of the princess' father (Douglas Dumbrille), who is determined to take his daughter back to her marital obligations in France. A much underrated if not great film, NAUGHTY MARIETTA features some particulary amusing supporting work by Harold Huber and Edward Brophy. Eddy is actually much better than most would have it, and his singing is quite stirring. MacDonald, though, is really the one in excellent form here, whether blasting the lengthy final high C of the "Italian Street Song" right in Nelson Eddy's face or doing an hilarious impersonation of a gluttonous, bespectacled woman on board the ship. One should admit, though, that the film isn't nearly as good some of her others, most notably THE MERRY WIDOW, where her comedic talents are in full bloom.

NAVIGATOR, THE

1988 92m c/bw Adventure/Fantasy   ★★½
Arenafilm/Film Investment Group (New Zealand)   PG/U

Bruce Lyons (Connor), Chris Haywood (Arno), Hamish McFarlane (Griffin), Marshall Napier (Searle), Noel Appleby (Ulf), Paul Livingston (Martin), Sarah Pierse (Linnet), Mark Wheatley (Tog 1), Tony Herbert (Tog 2), Jessica Cardiff-Smith (Esme)

p, John Maynard, Gary Hannam; d, Vincent Ward; w, Vincent Ward, Kely Lyons, Geoff Chapple; ph, Geoffrey Simpson; ed, John Scott; m, Davood A. Tabrizi; prod d, Sally Campbell; art d, Mike Becroft; cos, Glenys Jackson

THE NAVIGATOR is a singular experience, a time-warp, Chinese-box puzzle of a film that bespeaks the obsessed vision of its writer-director Vincent Ward. It begins in 1348 in Cumbria, England, where a psychic young boy, Griffin (Hamish McFarlane), dreams of a way to save his village from the advancing black plague. He leads his brother (Bruce Lyons) and four other men on a tunnelling expedition that somehow transports them to present-day New Zealand, and presents them with a chance to ward off the plague. But Griffin has also foreseen that, along the way, one of their number will be betrayed and another will die.

Ward has constructed a haunting fable that only occasionally lapses into self-parody, ^a la Monty Python. THE NAVIGATOR is certainly visually stylish, and employs a battery of cinematic effects—the mixed use of black and white with color, time-lapse views of clouds scampering across ominous skies, dizzying tracking shots up spiral staircases, etc. Worth a look.

NEAR DARK

1987 95m c Horror   ★★★½
F/M (U.S.)   R/18

Adrian Pasdar (Caleb), Jenny Wright (Mae), Lance Henriksen (Jesse), Bill Paxton (Severen), Jenette Goldstein (Diamondback), Tim Thomerson (Loy), Joshua Miller (Homer), Marcie Leeds (Sarah), Kenny Call (Deputy Sheriff), Ed Corbett (Ticket Seller)

p, Steven-Charles Jaffe, Eric Red; d, Kathryn Bigelow; w, Eric Red, Kathryn Bigelow; ph, Adam Greenberg; ed, Howard Smith; m, Tangerine Dream; prod d, Stephen Altman; art d, Dian Perryman; fx, Steve Galich, Dale Martin; cos, Joseph Porro

An auspicious solo directing debut from Kathryn Bigelow, NEAR DARK combines such diverse genres as horror, western, crime, and romance into what may be the first vampire road movie.

Set in the contemporary American Southwest, the film begins as Caleb (Adrian Pasdar), a bored farm boy, spots the beguiling Mae (Jenny Wright) at his usual Friday night hangout. By the break of dawn, Caleb has been bitten in the neck by Mae and befriended by a bizarre "family" of vampires—led by Jesse (Lance Henriksen), undead since before the Civil War—who travel across the country in a Winnebago. To his horror, Caleb learns that he has been "nipped" (i.e., he's almost a full-fledged vampire), and to graduate he must kill and drink blood. Sensing that Mae is in love with the boy, Jesse gives Caleb a week to perform his first kill.

Although several movie genres are represented here, NEAR DARK is most obviously based on Nicholas Ray's feature debut, THEY LIVE BY NIGHT (Bigelow's characters literally *must* live by night). Both films focus on a young couple desperately in love but trapped in a lifestyle they detest by their surrogate families (bank robbers and vampires, respectively). Bigelow, who codirected THE LOVELESS with Monty Montgomery in 1982, and coscreenwriter Eric Red (THE HITCHER) demonstrate a keen understanding of the history of American cinema and create a unique film that explores the conventions of the vampire movie while moving it from dank European castles to modern-day Southwestern America. Bigelow sees the vampire (the word is never used in the film) as a nomadic outlaw, much like the fabled gunslingers of the Old West or the bands of bank robbers that roved the landscape during the Depression.

NETWORK

1976 120m c Drama   ★★★★
MGM (U.S.)   R/15

Faye Dunaway (Diana Christensen), William Holden (Max Schumacher), Peter Finch (Howard Beale), Robert Duvall (Frank Hackett), Wesley Addy (Nelson Chaney), Ned Beatty (Arthur Jensen), Arthur Burghardt (Great Ahmed Kahn), Bill Burrows (TV Director), John Carpenter (George Bosch), Jordan Charney (Harry Hunter)

p, Howard Gottfried; d, Sidney Lumet; w, Paddy Chayefsky; ph, Owen Roizman; ed, Alan Heim; m, Elliot Lawrence; prod d, Philip Rosenberg; cos, Theoni V. Aldredge

AAN Best Picture; AA Best Actor: Peter Finch; AAN Best Actor: William Holden; AA Best Actress: Faye Dunaway; AAN Best Supporting Actor: Ned Beatty; AA Best Supporting Actress: Beatrice Straight; AAN Best Director: Sidney Lumet; AA Best Original Screenplay: Paddy Chayefsky; AAN Best Cinematography: Owen Roizman; AAN Best Editing: Alan Heim

Paddy Chayefsky takes on television (his first true love), with somewhat self-congratulatory ardor.

Finch, a veteran newsman for the mythical United Broadcasting System, is sent over the mental edge when he is told that he will be fired after a quarter of a century on the air. He can't handle the situation and tells his audience that he intends to commit suicide on his final broadcast the following week. Ratings go straight through the roof, and his fan mail comes in by the carload. On the night he plans to put a gun to his head, Finch relents, apologizes to the millions watching (it's his largest audience ever), and stands up like an electronic Messiah to shout "go to your nearest window and yell as loud as you can, 'I'm mad as hell and I'm not going to take it anymore!'" His audience does just that. Dunaway, a programming executive at UBS, knows how to exploit this, so she signs Finch to a weekly show in which he can let it all hang out. This idea is opposed by Holden, the man in charge of network news and an old pal of Finch. He can see that Finch is on the edge of insanity and he can't stand the thought of the news being used to further ratings. Dunaway's bosses like the idea and fire Holden for his disagreement. Finch's program, a melange of various items, goes on and is a smash hit. Dunaway, now a star at the network, has other innovations in mind. She intends doing a show about urban guerrillas, but instead of hiring actors, she wants the terrorists to play themselves. Holden and Dunaway meet again and are soon involved; Holden then leaves his wife, Straight, in the most moving (and least gimmicky) scene in the film, as he tells her why he is departing.

NETWORK gives out several superb scenes, including one in which the communist guerrillas' lawyers argue with the network's representatives over the ancillary rights and syndication money that will accrue from their show. There's an amazing display of acting talent, even though director Lumet doesn't quite tie all the strands together. Finch's spouting *is* impressive, but we prefer Holden's sardonic edge, even if his big speeches seem the most predictably written. For Dunaway fans, there are some great moments: Faye zipping up her briefcase in a manic state, and that rattling teacup. With her strangely undersized mouth of yellow baby teeth, she's a believable media carnivore.

NEVER GIVE A SUCKER AN EVEN BREAK

1941 71m bw Comedy   ★★★½
Universal (U.S./France)   /U

W.C. Fields (The Great Man), Gloria Jean (His Niece), Leon Errol (The Rival), Billy Lenhart (Butch), Kenneth Brown (Buddy), Anne Nagel (Mlle. Gorgeous), Franklin Pangborn (The Producer), Mona Barrie (The Producer's Wife), Margaret Dumont (Mrs. Hemogloben), Susan Miller (Ouliotta Delight Hemogloben)

d, Edward F. Cline; w, John T. Neville, Prescott Chaplin (based on a story by W.C.); ph, Charles Van Enger; ed, Arthur Hilton; m, Frank Skinner; art d, Jack Otterson, Richard H. Riedel; cos, Vera West

The great W.C. Fields at his wild antics again, this time spoofing Hollywood, or at least the insanity of producing films as he perceived it. Fields was later accused of biting the hand that fed him, but he gnawed on anything that moved anyway, while providing one belly laugh after another. Many of Fields's comedies mix sentiment, satire and surrealism, and this one is no exception—it simply goes further in almost every direction possible. Thus, while it is not his best film, it *is* pure Fields. Much of the "plot" consists of Fields trying to pitch a story to a Hollywood producer (Pangborn), though this is not made immediately clear to viewers. Memorable moments include Fields's encounter with an obnoxious greasy-spoon waitress (Jody Gilbert); his diving out of an airplane in mid-flight to retrieve (successfully!) a bottle of booze he has accidentally dropped; his encounters with a gorilla and with Ouliotta Delight Hemogloben (Miller) and her man-hungry matron of a mother (the peerless Dumont); and a crazy car chase en route to a maternity ward.

Despite (or perhaps because of) the lack of sense, the great comedian provides so much offbeat humor that the plotlessness makes little difference. Oddly, this spoof of Hollywood realistically capped Fields's own movie career. The great comedian had pretty much run out his options in Hollywood by the time of NEVER GIVE A SUCKER AN EVEN BREAK and knew that Universal was planning to sidetrack his career in favor of the more slapstick Abbott and Costello, the dynamic duo who would dominate comedy at the studio through the 1940s. In this film Fields thumbs his considerable nose at the industry that was ousting him. Fields had insisted that this film be called THE GREAT MAN; unhappy with the title NEVER GIVE A SUCKER AN EVEN BREAK, he later commented: "It doesn't matter anyway. Their title won't fit on a marquee, so they'll cut it down to 'W.C. Fields—Sucker.'"

Fields wrote the script in about four months and it brought a wrathful response from the Hollywood's Breen Office, which labeled the screenplay "vulgar and suggestive" and claimed that Fields made too many references to drinking and liquor. Out came the scissors, but Fields got revenge of sorts. In one scene in the film he turns directly to the camera and whines: "This scene was supposed to be in a saloon but the censor cut it out. It'll play just as well." Later the script was "cleaned up" by a bevy of hack writers assigned by Universal. "They produced the worst script I ever read. I was going to throw it in their faces," Fields stated, "when the director (Cline) told me not to. He said: 'We'll shoot your own script. They won't know the difference.' We did—and they didn't."

NEVER ON SUNDAY
(POTE TIN KYRIAKI)
1960 97m bw Comedy/Drama ★★★
Melina (Greece) /X

Melina Mercouri (*Ilya*), Jules Dassin (*Homer*), George Foundas (*Tonio*), Titos Vandis (*Jorgo*), Mitsos Liguisos (*The Captain*), Despo Diamantidou (*Despo*), Dimos Starenios (*Poubelle*), Dimitris Papamichael (*A Sailor*), Alexis Salomos (*Noface*)

p, Jules Dassin; d, Jules Dassin; w, Jules Dassin; ph, Jacques Natteau; ed, Roger Dwyre; m, Manos Hadjidakis; cos, Denny Vachlioti

AAN Best Actress: Melina Mercouri; *AAN Best Director:* Jules Dassin; *AAN Best Original Story and Screenplay:* Jules Dassin; *AA Best Song:* Manos Hadjidakis; *AAN Best Costume Design:* Denny Vachlioti

Filmed in Greece for a pittance (under $200,000), this colorful arthouse comedy broke through to the mainstream market and made a ton of money. NEVER ON SUNDAY is the brainchild of Jules Dassin, an American writer-director who ran afoul of Red-baiters in the 1950s and had to go to Europe to earn a living. He helmed RIFIFI, then went to Greece, where he met and married Melina Mercouri, NEVER ON SUNDAY's star. Although the film is a standard "hooker with a heart of gold" story, audiences were very much taken with its unfamiliar locale. Dassin not only wrote, produced, and directed, but also costarred as Homer, a tweedy American Grecophile who comes to Piraeus and encounters the local peasantry, who are slightly taken aback by his open ways. Homer loves Greece and everything about it. He soon meets Ilya (Mercouri), a prostitute who takes pride in her work and sees nothing immoral about the way she earns her living. Ilya takes customers six days a week and reserves Sunday for seeing the great Greek plays, none of which she actually comprehends. Homer intends to reform Ilya, but old habits are hard to break. Most of the dialogue is in English with a few speeches in Greek with titles.

NEVER SAY NEVER AGAIN
1983 137m c Spy ★★½
Woodcote/Taliafilm (U.K.) PG

Sean Connery (*James Bond*), Klaus Maria Brandauer (*Largo*), Max von Sydow (*Blofeld*), Barbara Carrera (*Fatima Blush*), Kim Basinger (*Domino*), Bernie Casey (*Felix Leiter*), Alec McCowen (*Q/Algy*), Edward Fox (*M*), Pamela Salem (*Miss Moneypenny*), Valerie Leon (*Lady in Bahamas*)

p, Jack Schwartzman; d, Irvin Kershner; w, Lorenzo Semple Jr. (based on a story by Kevin McClory, Jack Whittingham and Ian Fleming); ph, Douglas Slocombe; ed, Robert Lawrence, Ian Crafford; m, Michel Legrand; prod d, Philip Harrison, Stephen Grimes; art d, Leslie Dilley, Michael White, Roy Stannard; fx, David Dryer, Ian Wingrove; cos, Charles Knode

Sean Connery returns to action after a 12-year absence from his role as 007. The title is based on his comment that he would never do a James Bond film again following DIAMONDS ARE FOREVER. Basically a remake of THUNDERBALL, the film opens with an aging Bond trying to get back in shape at a special clinic. When SPECTRE psycho Largo (Brandauer) hijacks a couple of American cruise missiles, Bond is

assigned the case. Fatima Blush (Carrera), a gorgeous but deadly SPECTRE agent, does her best bring an end to Bond's illustrious career, but, surviving the requisite high-speed chase, he eventually catches up with Largo and his beautiful companion Domino (Basinger) on the villain's yacht. Connery delivers his usual charming performance, and Brandauer (MEPHISTO, OUT OF AFRICA) makes a great Bond villain. Gone is the excessive gadgetry that mars Bond films, and, as a result, the characters are more prominent and colorful. This was director Irvin Kershner's first film following the huge success of THE EMPIRE STRIKES BACK. Lani Hall croons the title song, written by Alan and Marilyn Bergman.

NEVERENDING STORY, THE
(DIE UNENDLICHE GESCHICHTE)
1984 94m c Fantasy/Science Fiction ★★★½
Neve Constantin/WDR (West Germany) PG/U

Barret Oliver (*Bastian*), Gerald McRaney (*Bastian's Father*), Drum Garrett, Darryl Cooksey, Nicholas Gilbert (*Bullies*), Thomas Hill (*Koreander*), Deep Roy (*Teeny Weeny*), Tilo Pruckner (*Night Hob*), Moses Gunn (*Cairon*), Noah Hathaway (*Atreyu*)

p, Bernd Eichinger, Dieter Geissler; d, Wolfgang Petersen; w, Wolfgang Petersen, Herman Weigel (based on the novel by Michael Ende); ph, Jost Vacano; ed, Jane Seitz; m, Klaus Doldinger, Giorgio Moroder; prod d, Rolf Zehetbauer; art d, Gotz Weidner, Herbert Strabel, Johann Iwan Kot; fx, Brian Johnson; cos, Diemut Remy; anim, Steve Archer

Only a certified grump could dislike this engaging fantasy that wends its way into the imagination and is a delight on most levels. Bastian (Barret Oliver) is a troubled lad who has just lost his mother. He lives with his father (Gerald McRaney), who lectures Bastian about the boy's penchant for daydreaming. The lad has to fend off school bullies and is having difficulty adjusting to being motherless. One day, instead of going to school, he wanders into a weird bookstore and borrows a book called *The Neverending Story*. As Bastian turns the pages, the story comes to life. A childlike empress (Tami Stronach), who is not well, lives in a land called "Fantasia" and fears that it will be taken over if she dies. So she sends Atreyu (Noah Hathaway), a young warrior, off to find a cure for her lingering illness. What menaces Fantasia is a plague of "nothing": when the inhabitants of Earth lose hope and forget their aspirations, Fantasia is due to crumble as a direct result. Atreyu's voyage is fraught with peril, and he meets a cast of fantastic characters. Bastian is so enthralled by the story that he is plunged into it as a character. Made on a budget of more than $27 million, the film features state-of-the-art puppetry, animation, opticals, and makeup. THE NEVERENDING STORY owes much to ALICE IN WONDERLAND and THE DAY THE EARTH STOOD STILL in some sequences, but director Wolfgang Petersen combines the elements into a charming film that is excellent for children and won't put any adults to sleep, either.

NEW AGE, THE
1994 110m c Comedy/Drama ★★★★
Ixtlan Productions/Addis-Wechsler/Regency Enterprises/Alcor R/
Films (U.S.)

Peter Weller (*Peter Witner*), Judy Davis (*Katherine Witner*), Patrick Bauchau (*Jean Levy*), Rachel Rosenthal (*Sarah Friedberg*), Adam West (*Jeff Witner*), Paula Marshall (*Alison Gale*), Bruce Ramsay (*Misha*), Tanya Pohlkotte (*Bettina*), Susan Traylor (*Ellen Saltonstall*), Corbin Bernsen (*Kevin Bulasky*)

p, Keith Addis, Nick Wechsler; d, Michael Tolkin; w, Michael Tolkin; ph, John J. Campbell; ed, Suzanne Fenn; m, Mark Mothersbaugh; prod d, Robin Standefer; art d, Kenneth A. Hardy; cos, Richard Shissler

Michael Tolkin's THE NEW AGE is something new, a comedy of horrors that's brittle, hypnotically hip, and so cool it almost freezes the audience out. It's like an update of Preston Sturges's THE PALM BEACH STORY in which the enviable rich people are no longer daffy eccentrics but energy vampires who feed off each other.

In the midst of the 1990-91 recession, LA literary agent Peter (Peter Weller) impulsively decides to find his bliss. He contemptuously walks out on his boss Kevin (Corbin Bernsen), without regard for the needs of his high-strung wife Katherine (Judy Davis), a graphic designer who is facing an exodus of clients. Primed by an assortment of gurus who flit through their social set, Peter and Katherine imprudently decide to invest in their own upscale clothing store, Hip-ocracy. Thereafter, the couple must undergo the kinds of humiliation, large and small, from which people of their class were well insulated in the glory days of American capitalism.

Michael Tolkin sets a difficult task for himself with THE NEW AGE: to satirize the tenets of New Age philosophizing while mustering the requisite sympathy for two fantastically overprivileged lost souls. The film suggests that West Coast swamis-for-hire have twisted legitimate spiritual quests into a religion of success in which the mantra is "Gimme!" As in THE RAPTURE, Tolkin treats a recognizable assortment of fanatics and frauds with a certain sympathy (in an interview about THE RAPTURE's apocalyptic Christians, he asked seriously, "What if they're right?"); as a result, the comedy is overwhelmed with pain and bitterness.

NEW LAND, THE
(NYBYGGARNA)

1972 161m c Drama ★★★
Svensk (Sweden) PG/AA

Max von Sydow *(Karl Oskar)*, Liv Ullmann *(Kristina)*, Eddie Axberg *(Robert)*, Hans Alfredson *(Jonas Petter)*, Halvar Bjork *(Anders Mansson)*, Allan Edwall *(Danjel)*, Peter Lindgren *(Samuel Nojd)*, Pierre Lindstedt *(Arvid)*, Oscar Ljung *(Petrus Olausson)*, Karin Nordstrom *(Judit)*

p, Bengt Forslund; d, Jan Troell; w, Bengt Forslund, Jan Troell (based on the novel *The Emigrants* by Vilhelm Moberg); ph, Jan Troell; ed, Jan Troell; m, Bengt Ernryd, George Oddner; art d, P.A. Lundgren; cos, Ulla-Britt Soderlund

AAN Best Foreign Language Film

This touching sequel to THE EMIGRANTS follows the struggle of von Sydow and Ullmann during their first decade in America. The story includes a futile trek to the Southwest to search for gold. The film is a subtle depiction of the hardships people face as they try to find a niche for themselves. The story moves slowly at times, but this helps to focus on the changes that the characters undergo. Nominated for Best Foreign Film in 1972. Edited for television under the title THE IMMIGRANT SAGA.

NEW YORK, NEW YORK

1977 155m c Musical ★★★½
UA (U.S.) PG

Robert De Niro *(Jimmy Doyle)*, Liza Minnelli *(Francine Evans)*, Lionel Stander *(Tony Harwell)*, Mary Kay Place *(Bernice)*, George Memmoli *(Nicky)*, Murray Moston *(Horace Morris)*, Barry Primus *(Paul Wilson)*, Georgie Auld *(Frankie Harte)*, Dick Miller *(Palm Club Owner)*, Leonard Gaines *(Artie Kirks)*

p, Irwin Winkler, Robert Chartoff; d, Martin Scorsese; w, Earl Mac Rauch, Mardik Martin (based on a story by Rauch); ph, Laszlo Kovacs; ed, Irving Lerner, Marcia Lucas, Tom Rolf, Bert Lovitt, David Ramirez; m, Ralph Burns; prod d, Boris Leven; art d, Harry Kemm; fx, Richard Albain; chor, Ron Field; cos, Theadora Van Runkle

Martin Scorsese's attempt at making an old-fashioned musical, NEW YORK, NEW YORK never found much of an audience, but remains a visually fascinating rumination on the genre.

New York City. 1945. USO singer Francine Evans (Liza Minnelli) and aspiring sax player Jimmy Doyle (Robert De Niro) meet cute during the V-J Day revelry, audition for a job together, and later end up in the employ of big band leader Frankie Harte (Georgie Auld, who dubbed De Niro's sax playing), falling deeply in love and marrying. Jimmy eventually takes over Harte's band, and when Francine returns to New York to have their baby, he becomes involved with her replacement singer (Mary Kay Place). Francine and Jimmy have a son, but in time their marriage disintegrates as Francine becomes a hit recording artist (singing the kind of tunes her husband despises) and film star, while Jimmy turns to jazz and later opens his own club, en route to the film's distinctly downbeat ending.

NEW YORK, NEW YORK cost almost $9 million, and it's uneven in spots—the result of being drastically edited from its original four-hour length (among the slashes was the 12-minute, $300,000 "Happy Endings" production number, later reinserted for the film's 1981 rerelease). Nevertheless, the film is a treat for the ears as well as the eyes. De Niro gives an outstanding performance, masterfully conveying Jimmy's vanity, selfishness, and egotism. Minnelli is nothing less than brilliant, more than deserving of an Oscar nomination that never came her way. Place (THE BIG CHILL, television's "Mary Hartman, Mary Hartman") got her first big break here, and longtime Roger Corman favorite Miller, comic Gaines, and rotund Memmoli all contribute fine work.

NEXT STOP, GREENWICH VILLAGE

1976 111m c Comedy ★★★★
Fox (U.S.) R/X

Lenny Baker *(Larry Lapinsky)*, Shelley Winters *(Mrs. Lapinsky)*, Ellen Greene *(Sarah)*, Lois Smith *(Anita)*, Christopher Walken *(Robert)*, Dori Brenner *(Connie)*, Antonio Fargas *(Bernstein)*, Lou Jacobi *(Herb)*, Mike Kellin *(Mr. Lapinsky)*, Michael Egan *(Herbert)*

p, Paul Mazursky, Tony Ray; d, Paul Mazursky; w, Paul Mazursky; ph, Arthur J. Ornitz; ed, Richard Halsey; m, Bill Conti; prod d, Philip Rosenberg; cos, Albert Wolsky

Anyone who spent time in New York's Greenwich Village in the early 1950s will attest to the accuracy of this wonderful, nostalgic look at that era. It's essentially Mazursky's own story, and he manages to capture the time and the people with a loving touch. Baker is the young man who graduates from Brooklyn College in 1953 and makes the decision to leave his family, Kellin and Winters, and switch boroughs to Manhattan. Winters, the ultimate Jewish mother, is totally against it, but he leaves anyway and takes up residence in the Village, where he takes a job at a health food place, then starts his acting lessons with Egan, a proponent of the "Method." He is soon part of "the scene," and his pals include nutty Brenner (who later married Andre Previn and became an important songwriter); Smith, who is always teetering on the brink of suicide; Walken, the WASPish poet who speaks in epigrams; and Fargas, a black homosexual with a Jewish name. The tight-knit group members are symbiotic and help each other when needed, so when Smith tries suicide, they pour coffee into her. When Baker's sweetheart, Greene, becomes pregnant they arrange an abortion. Baker is out of money and due to be tossed out of his apartment, so the others stage a "rent party" to raise the cash. Baker learns that a major studio wants to cast some juvenile delinquents and he hopes to get one of the parts. (In real life, Mazursky was in THE BLACK-BOARD JUNGLE as "Stoker.") Winters and Kellin come to see how Baker is living, and Winters is shocked when she learns that Baker and Greene are sleeping together. Before she can faint, Kellin takes Winters home to Brooklyn. The group is saddened to learn that Smith's customary suicide attempt worked this time, and they share their grief with each other. Baker gets a chance at the role, then Greene announces that she is going off to Mexico with Walken, Fargas, and Brenner. Baker and Greene make love for the last time and she takes this opportunity to inform him that she is also Walken's lover. An argument erupts as Winters and Kellin enter the apartment surreptitiously. Greene leaves, and Baker understands that this part of his life is now finished. Baker bids his pals farewell, goes to his job, and gets the call about the role. He is to report to Hollywood within the week. At the last supper with Winters and Kellin, she reminds him to never forget where he came from.

Baker was simply marvelous in the leading role. He went on to play in the Broadway hit musical, "I Love My Wife," before dying of cancer. Mazursky's real acting career began in Stanley Kubrick's first feature, FEAR AND DESIRE, which was followed by THE BLACKBOARD JUNGLE. Co-producer Tony Ray, director Nicholas Ray's son, later married his father's ex-wife, Gloria Grahame. In a small role, look for Jeff Goldblum. Conti's music is outstanding and evokes the period without parodying it.

NIAGARA

1953 92m c Thriller ★★★★
Fox (U.S.) /PG

Marilyn Monroe (*Rose Loomis*), Joseph Cotten (*George Loomis*), Jean Peters (*Polly Cutler*), Max Showalter (*Ray Cutler*), Denis O'Dea (*Inspector Sharkey*), Richard Allan (*Patrick*), Don Wilson (*Mr. Kettering*), Lurene Tuttle (*Mrs. Kettering*), Russell Collins (*Mr. Qua*), Will Wright (*Boatman*)

p, Charles Brackett; d, Henry Hathaway; w, Charles Brackett, Walter Reisch, Richard Breen; ph, Joseph MacDonald; ed, Barbara McLean; m, Sol Kaplan; art d, Lyle Wheeler, Maurice Ransford; fx, Ray Kellogg; cos, Dorothy Jeakins

Everyone's honeymoon haven at one time, Niagara Falls, is the deceptive setting for this offbeat, absorbing film with bowstring-tight direction from Hathaway and superb performances from Cotten as a jealous husband and Monroe as his neurotic wife. Newlyweds Peters and Adams arrive at their Niagara honeymoon cottage and meet another couple, Cotten and Monroe. Monroe, from the beginning, confides about her husband being considerably older than she; he is depressed, and has just been released from a mental institution. Peters later sees Monroe kissing a young man, Allan, and learns that the couple plans to murder Cotten.

The film is breathtakingly photographed, in lurid Technicolor that heightens the sensual energy of the Monroe persona. Jean Peters is lovely and effective in a difficult part; the script calls for her to be in Monroe's shadow, yet she's the stronger of the two. Cotten makes a marvelous antihero, and Richard Allan's dark, macho seductiveness makes an exciting contrast to Monroe.

NICHOLAS AND ALEXANDRA

1971 183m c Biography/War ★★★½
Horizon (U.K.) GP/PG

Michael Jayston (*Nicholas II*), Janet Suzman (*Alexandra*), Roderic Noble (*Alexis*), Ania Marson (*Olga*), Lynne Frederick (*Tatiana*), Candace Glendenning (*Marie*), Fiona Fullerton (*Anastasia*), Harry Andrews (*Grand Duke Nicholas*), Irene Worth (*the Queen Mother*), Tom Baker (*Rasputin*)

p, Sam Spiegel; d, Franklin J. Schaffner; w, James Goldman, Edward Bond (based on a book by Robert K. Massie); ph, Freddie Young; ed, Ernest Walter; m, Richard Rodney Bennett; prod d, John Box; art d, Jack Maxsted, Ernest Archer, Gil Parrondo; fx, Eddie Fowlie; cos, Yvonne Blake, Antonio Castillo

AAN Best Picture; AAN Best Actress: Janet Suzman; AAN Best Cinematography: Freddie Young; AAN Best Score: Richard Rodney Bennett; AA Best Art Direction: John Box, Ernest Archer, Jack Maxsted, Gil Parrondo, Vernon Dixon; AA Best Costume Design: Yvonne Blake, Antonio Castillo1

This lavish, overlong production chronicles the downfall of the last Russian czar Nicholas II (Michael Jayston), and his wife Alexandra (Janet Suzman). The film concentrates on their troubled family life, especially the affliction of their only son, Alexis (Roderic Noble), with hemophilia. Nicholas's preoccupation with this tragedy influences state decisions and increases his disengagement from his starving people, while Alexandra falls completely under the influence of the profligate peasant monk Rasputin (Tom Baker), believing that his mystic powers can heal her son. Rasputin's power increases in the Imperial Court despite Nicholas's weak efforts to maintain authority; meanwhile, hundreds are slaughtered at the Winter Palace, fueling Lenin (Michael Bryant) and Trotsky's (Brian Cox) crusade to overthrow "Bloody Nicholas." As the tide of assassination and unrest rises, an ill-prepared Russia suffers terrible losses in WWI, setting the stage for revolution in 1917 and the execution of the deposed czar and family in July 1918. While it remains a treat for the eyes, NICHOLAS AND ALEXANDRA suffers from the filmmakers' attempts to tell too much. Its overview of more than two decades of tumultuous, epochal history develops few of its famous figures beyond caricature (although Baker, of "Dr. Who" fame, plays Rasputin with flamboyance and verve), and the failure to bring Nicholas and Alexandra to life—despite the script's intimate and sympathetic treatment of the pair—is especially critical. Shot on loca-

tion in Spain and Yugoslavia, the film won Oscars for Best Art Direction, Set Decoration, and Costumes. It was also nominated for Best Picture (losing to THE FRENCH CONNECTION), Best Actress (Suzman, who lost to Jane Fonda for KLUTE), Best Score, and Best Cinematography.

NICHOLAS NICKLEBY

1947 108m bw Drama ★★
Ealing (U.K.) /U

Cedric Hardwicke (*Ralph Nickleby*), Stanley Holloway (*Vincent Crummles*), Alfred Drayton (*Wackford Squeers*), Cyril Fletcher (*Alfred Mantalini*), Bernard Miles (*Newman Noggs*), Derek Bond (*Nicholas Nickleby*), Sally Ann Howes (*Kate Nickleby*), Mary Merrall (*Mrs. Nickleby*), Sybil Thorndike (*Mrs. Squeers*), Vera Pearce (*Mrs. Crummles*)

p, Michael Balcon; d, Alberto Cavalcanti; w, John Dighton (based on the novel by Charles Dickens); ph, Gordon Dines; ed, Leslie Norman; m, Lord Berners; art d, Michael Relph; fx, Lionel Banes, Cliff Richardson; cos, Marion Horn

Following within a year of the release of David Lean's popular and highly regarded GREAT EXPECTATIONS, it was inevitable that this adaptation of a Dickens novel would be compared to the earlier effort. It was, and it came up lacking. Bond is the young man who toils in a boys' school in Yorkshire where he has been apprenticed by his thoroughly reprehensible uncle, played by Hardwicke. Conditions at the school are appalling, and Bond befriends one of the students, Aubrey Woods, who has been the victim of much of the brutality at the school. They escape, join a traveling theatrical troupe, and enjoy a series of adventures, with Bond meeting and falling in love with Jill Balcon. Their relationship is complicated by the fact that Hardwicke has provided testimony that sent Balcon's father to debtor's prison as part of an an attempt to force Balcon to marry him. Drayton, Hardwicke's henchman, kidnaps Woods and, though he is rescued by Bond, he dies from the abuse he has been subjected to by Hardwicke. Bond discovers that Woods was Hardwicke's son, and that Hardwicke had abandoned the boy at an early age to acquire a fortune that rightfully belonged to Woods. When Bond reveals his discovery, the shamed Hardwicke kills himself, and Bond and Balcon find happiness together. Casting couldn't be better and Cavalcanti has created an authentic Dickensian mood, but too much story is compressed into the film, making it difficult to follow. The producer's daughter, Jill, made her screen debut here, as did Woods, both coming from the British stage. Neither would make much of a mark in the movie world, however.

NIGHT AND THE CITY

1950 95m bw Crime ★★★★
Fox (U.K.)

Richard Widmark (*Harry Fabian*), Gene Tierney (*Mary Bristol*), Googie Withers (*Helen Nosseross*), Hugh Marlowe (*Adam Dunn*), Francis L. Sullivan (*Phil Nosseross*), Herbert Lom (*Kristo*), Stanislaus Zbyszko (*Gregorius*), Mike Mazurki (*Strangler*), Charles Farrell (*Beer*), Ada Reeve (*Molly*)

p, Samuel G. Engel; d, Jules Dassin; w, Jo Eisinger (based on the novel by Gerald Kersh); ph, Mutz Greenbaum; ed, Nick De Maggio, Sidney Stone; m, Franz Waxman; art d, C.P. Norman; cos, Oleg Cassini, Margaret Furse

A dark, brooding *noir*, with Widmark riveting as a hustling promoter who sinks into the quagmire of his own ambitions. The film is set in London, where Widmark works for the obese Sullivan, owner of a sleazy dive. Widmark steers suckers to the joint on the promise of witnessing some racy shows, but it's all pretty tame stuff—even the very proper Tierney sings there, she being a disapproving girlfriend of wily Widmark. Tierney keeps after Widmark to get a decent job, but the con is in his blood and he is obsessed with developing a big money scheme. He overhears famed wrestler Zbyszko talking to his protege Ken Richmond in a huge sports arena owned by Zbyszko's son, Lom. Before Widmark is thrown out of the arena for hustling customers to Sullivan's club, he learns that Zbyszko is disgusted by the fake wrestling matches his son offers to the public. Zbyszko believes that only his traditional Greco-Roman wrestling is a pure sport. Widmark later goes to Zbyszko and cons him into believing that he will promote the long-neglected Greco-Roman wrestling and bring it back to the popularity it once enjoyed. The legendary wrestler agrees to lend his name to the enterprise, which incenses the powerful Lom, who threatens to kill Widmark if he misuses Lom's father. On the other hand, if he truly promotes Greco-Roman wrestling, Lom tells Widmark, he can go ahead. . . .

NIGHT AND THE CITY is an uncompromising, exciting, anxiety-inducing film that is seen entirely through Widmark's desperate viewpoint. Director Dassin relentlessly displays London without charm and grace, showing only the seamy side where Widmark and his kind live out their unscrupulous lives without thought of love or compassion. Everything is cold and calculating, one character greedily using another for human control. The world Widmark desires to enter is that controlled by the Loms and Sullivans—who belong to a very exclusive club. They are as crooked and immoral as Widmark, but they have the money and the connections, and Widmark only aspires to be a loftier version of his own venal self. Despite the feeling of lonely helplessness that pervades the film, the story proceeds at such a frenetic pace that it's utterly captivating. Widmark's performance is nothing short of remarkable. Greene's camerawork is exceptional, as is Waxman's score. The wrestling scene between Zbyszko, a former heavyweight wrestling champion, and Mazurki is one of the most heart-pounding matches ever filmed. Remade, with mixed results, in 1992.

NIGHT AT THE OPERA, A

1935 90m bw Comedy ★★★★
MGM (U.S.) /U

Groucho Marx *(Otis B. Driftwood)*, Chico Marx *(Fiorello)*, Harpo Marx *(Tomasso)*, Kitty Carlisle *(Rosa Castaldi)*, Allan Jones *(Riccardo Baroni)*, Walter Woolf King *(Rodolfo Lassparri)*, Sig Rumann *(Herman Gottlieb)*, Margaret Dumont *(Mrs. Claypool)*, Edward Keane *(Captain)*, Robert Emmett O'Connor *(Detective Henderson)*

p, Irving Thalberg; d, Sam Wood; w, George S. Kaufman, Morrie Ryskind, Al Boasberg, Bert Kalmar, Harry Ruby (based on a story by James Kevin McGuinness); ph, Merritt Gerstad; ed, William LeVanway; m, Herbert Stothart; art d, Cedric Gibbons, Ben Carre; chor, Chester Hale; cos, Dolly Tree

The Marx Brothers' most popular film and Groucho's favorite, before MGM queered their joyful anarchy. (Groucho must have loved the money which started rolling in; actually, the Marx Bros. were far more at home at Paramount.) Groucho, Chico, and Harpo join forces to disrupt the stuffy world of opera by wreaking havoc on the music, stage, and audience. Otis B. Driftwood (Groucho) tries to con rich Mrs. Claypool (Margaret Dumont, in fabulous form) into investing her money in an opera company, while Tomasso (Harpo) and Fiorello (Chico) join the fray and take it upon themselves to help advance the careers of two struggling young singers, Allan Jones and Kitty Carlisle—both begging for a stagehand to drop twin sandbags and kill the misery they subject an audience to. OPERA is their first at MGM, in case you hadn't guessed, after being dropped by Paramount and the first without Zeppo. Producer Irving Thalberg had faith in them but thought their films for Paramount lacked cohesive stories and enough time to work out the routines, so he prevailed upon them to take a 50-minute precis of the best scenes on the road. They toured four cities with writers George S. Kaufman and Morrie Ryskind in the audience for 24 days and polished the gags until they were ready to film. The result was a huge success and the picture was a hit. Today it is fondly remembered for such classic comedy bits as Groucho and Chico drafting a contract, the stateroom scene, and the hilarious climax where the brothers make a shambles of "Il Trovatore." Sans DUCK SOUP, we'll watch this any day.

NIGHT MOVES

1975 100m c Mystery ★★★½
Hiller/Layton (U.S.) R/

Gene Hackman *(Harry Moseby)*, Susan Clark *(Ellen Moseby)*, Edward Binns *(Ziegler)*, Harris Yulin *(Marty Heller)*, Kenneth Mars *(Nick)*, Janet Ward *(Arlene Iverson)*, James Woods *(Quentin)*, Anthony Costello *(Mary Ellman)*, John Crawford *(Tom Iverson)*, Melanie Griffith *(Delly Grastner)*

p, Robert M. Sherman; d, Arthur Penn; w, Alan Sharp; ph, Bruce Surtees; ed, Dede Allen; m, Michael Small; prod d, George Jenkins; fx, Marcel Vercoutere, Joe Day; cos, Rita Riggs

This excellent contemporary noir features some of the best work of both director Arthur Penn and actor Gene Hackman. Hackman is a small-time private eye working in Los Angeles. Fading movie actress Ward hires him to find Griffith, her wild teenage daughter who has run off to the Florida Keys to be with her stepfather, Crawford, and his mistress, Warren. Hackman finds the girl easily and returns her to her mother, but the next day she is killed in an accident while filming a stunt for a movie. After watching footage of the accident, Hackman becomes convinced Griffith was murdered, and the clues lead him back to the Florida Keys. Although the mystery itself is at times confusing and ultimately pointless, NIGHT MOVES is wholly engrossing and thematically rich, with much material reflecting the disillusionment of post-Watergate America. In particular, Penn and screenwriter Sharp are out to revise the mythos of the private eye; here, no longer a Chandler-esque knight-errant, he's an impotent anachronism—by the time he solves the mystery it's too late to do anything about it. The last shot, with Hackman circling aimlessly in a boat called the "Point of View," says it all. The film marked the feature debut of 17-year-old Melanie Griffith. Especially interesting when viewed as a forerunner to Francis Coppola's THE CONVERSATION, also starring Hackman as a character named Harry.

NIGHT MUST FALL

1937 117m bw Thriller ★★★★
MGM (U.S.) /A

Robert Montgomery *(Danny)*, Rosalind Russell *(Olivia)*, Dame May Whitty *(Mrs. Bransom)*, Alan Marshal *(Justin)*, Merle Tottenham *(Dora)*, Kathleen Harrison *(Mrs. Terence)*, Matthew Boulton *(Belsize)*, Eily Malyon *(Nurse)*, E.E. Clive *(Guide)*, Beryl Mercer *(Saleslady)*

p, Hunt Stromberg; d, Richard Thorpe; w, John Van Druten (based on a play by Emlyn Williams); ph, Ray June; ed, Robert J. Kern; m, Edward Ward; art d, Cedric Gibbons; cos, Dolly Tree

AAN Best Actor: Robert Montgomery; *AAN Best Supporting Actress:* May Whitty

Due primarily to an amazing performance by Robert Montgomery, this superb, nerve-tingling thriller improves on Emlyn Williams's already shocking stage hit. Whitty is a fussy, domineering grande dame living in a cottage in Essex, England, with niece Russell and several cowed servants. Just after Russell and Whitty hear that a "very flashy" woman guest in a nearby inn has vanished, Montgomery appears, claiming that he has been working as a page boy at the inn but is now looking for a new job. Montgomery brings with him a heavy hatbox that he places in a closet after being hired as a handyman by the wheelchair-bound Whitty. He waits hand and foot upon her, flattering Whitty at every opportunity, but exchanges barbs with Russell, who distrusts him. When asked about the missing woman, Montgomery describes her in chilling detail, revealing his psychopathic personality and further arousing Russell's suspicion.

NIGHT MUST FALL is directed with great care by Richard Thorpe, who evokes every bit of suspense intended by playwright Williams (who played the role of the killer on stage, though not nearly as subtly as Montgomery does). Producer Hunt Stromberg saw the play in London and insisted on making it into a film. Although MGM boss Louis B. Mayer thought it was an awful idea, he reluctantly agreed to allow Stromberg, his most successful producer, to undertake the project. Mayer was outraged when Stromberg cast Montgomery, the popular star of frothy MGM comedies, in the role of the killer, but the critical and popular success of the film proved him wrong. The film was remade by the studio nearly 20 years later, starring Albert Finney, Susan Hampshire, and Mona Washbourne, but the remake lacked the tautness and dramatic impact of the original.

NIGHT OF THE HUNTER, THE

1955 93m bw Thriller ★★★★★
UA (U.S.) /PG

Robert Mitchum *(Preacher Harry Powell)*, Shelley Winters *(Willa Harper)*, Lillian Gish *(Rachel)*, Evelyn Varden *(Icey Spoon)*, Peter Graves *(Ben Harper)*, Billy Chapin *(John)*, Sally Jane Bruce *(Pearl)*, James Gleason *(Birdie)*, Don Beddoe *(Walt Spoon)*, Gloria Castillo *(Ruby)*

p, Paul Gregory; d, Charles Laughton; w, James Agee (based on the novel by Davis Grubb); ph, Stanley Cortez; ed, Robert Golden; m, Walter Schumann; art d, Hilyard Brown; fx, Jack Rabin, Louis DeWitt; cos, Jerry Bos

Actor Charles Laughton's only directorial effort is a brilliantly eerie tale of religious madness, greed, innocence, and murder set in the rural South during the Great Depression. Harry Powell (Mitchum), a psychopathic preacher with the word "Love" tattooed on the fingers of his right hand and "Hate" tattooed on the left, is driven by repressed sexual desires to murder women. While in jail for driving a stolen car, Powell meets young Ben Harper (Graves), a bank robber condemned to death for killing a man during a heist. Powell is certain Harper has stashed the loot ($10,000) from the robbery somewhere, but is unable to get Harper to reveal where. Powell is released shortly after Harper is executed, and the mad preacher tracks down his cellmate's widow, Willa (Winters). Powell soon persuades the idiotic Willa to marry him—much to the dismay of her son, John (Chapin), who senses what the preacher is really after and knows that the money is hidden inside one of the dolls of his sister, Pearl (Bruce). Powell soon becomes frustrated with the ignorant Willa and murders her, turning his attention to the children. John and Pearl take the doll and flee into the countryside with the murderous Powell always one step behind them.

Working from a script by James Agee (THE AFRICAN QUEEN), Laughton created what he called "a nightmarish sort of Mother Goose tale," employing an eclectic mix of visual styles (German expressionism, D.W. Griffith) to convey both the horror of Powell's quest and the idyllic flight of the children to the safety of the farm of an old spinster (Gish). In addition to Stanley Cortez's stunning cinematography, the film boasts Robert Mitchum's greatest performance—a chilling essay that would unfortunately typecast him for much of his career. Beautiful, haunting, poetic, and intensely personal, THE NIGHT OF THE HUNTER is a unique, terrifying masterpiece. The adaptation of the Davis Grubb novel was the last film work by James Agee. Audiences didn't know *what* to make of this one; it bombed, and the great Laughton never directed again.

NIGHT OF THE IGUANA, THE

1964 125m bw Drama ★★½
Seven Arts (U.S.) /X

Richard Burton *(Rev. T. Lawrence Shannon)*, Ava Gardner *(Maxine Faulk)*, Deborah Kerr *(Hannah Jelkes)*, Sue Lyon *(Charlotte Goodall)*, James Ward *(Hank Prosner)*, Grayson Hall *(Judith Fellowes)*, Cyril Delevanti *(Nonno)*, Mary Boylan *(Miss Peebles)*, Gladys Hill *(Miss Dexter)*, Billie Matticks *(Miss Throxton)*

p, Ray Stark; d, John Huston; w, Anthony Veiller, John Huston (based on the play by Tennessee Williams); ph, Gabriel Figueroa; ed, Ralph Kemplen; m, Benjamin Frankel; art d, Stephen Grimes; cos, Dorothy Jeakins

AAN Best Supporting Actress: Grayson Hall; *AAN Best Cinematography:* Gabriel Figueroa; *AAN Best Art Direction:* Stephen Grimes; *AA Best Costume Design:* Dorothy Jeakins

Based on the Williams play that won the New York Drama Critics Award for 1961-62, THE NIGHT OF THE IGUANA is alternately fascinating and boring. It served to put the sleepy little village of Puerto Vallarta on the Mexican vacation map, and visitors to the town are still shown the rotting sets for the movie as part of their "official" tour. Burton is a defrocked Episcopalian priest who now earns his living as a tour guide. He's taking a group of schoolteachers around. Lyon, the junior member of the group, finds him attractive, so he squires her to his ratty hotel room, where they are discovered by Hall. The older woman threatens to have him sacked for his dalliance with Lyon unless

he ceases. The group are supposed to be quartered in a plush inn, but Burton takes them to a run-down place owned by friend Gardner, who has just been widowed. The teachers balk, but they are stranded while Burton tinkers with their bus and must now remain at the seedy hotel. Burton falls ill with fever and tells Gardner that Hall means to have him fired, so Gardner won't let Hall use the phone to call Burton's employers. Kerr, a poor artist, and her grandfather, Delevanti, a poorer poet, have been working their way across Mexico by selling her sketches and arranging readings by him, and they arrive at the hotel broke. Ward, the tour's bus driver, soon becomes Lyon's suitor. He repairs the bus and leaves, as tour leader, with the teachers. Kerr, Burton, Delevanti, and Gardner remain at the hotel, and Kerr and Burton become friends. But Burton's mind seems to be on the verge of crumbling. Gardner loves Burton although she sees that his existence might be better served by Kerr and offers her hotel to the two of them. Meanwhile Delavanti, who has been working on the same poem for 20 years, finally finishes it and dies. Kerr leaves, after burying her grandfather, and Burton and Gardner stay on at the shuttered hostelry as the picture ends. We're never certain whether Hall's jealousy of the relationship, if it can be called that, between Lyon and Burton, stems from her attraction to Burton or to Lyon. Gardner is depicted as an aging nymphomaniac, whose two hotel boys, Fidelman Duryan and Roberto Leyva, meet a number of her needs.

The offscreen conduct of cast and crew was almost as weird as the film itself. Burton's wife, Elizabeth Taylor, was on hand throughout the filming, sticking like glue to Burton's side, reportedly to make sure her husband's eyes didn't turn too far in Gardner's direction. Gardner, on the other hand, spent most of her time driving a sports car wildly through the surf along the beach. Director Huston cultivated paranoia by providing guns for the leading players with which to protect themselves from unknown dangers. Lyon, who began her career as the title character in LOLITA, was making her second film appearance chaperoned by her mother. Her movie life was, at best, erratic (TONY ROME, SEVEN WOMEN, etc.), and she later retired to become a teacher in Los Angeles. The iguana mentioned in the title refers to a long lizard that can be seen roaming the streets and hotels of Puerto Vallarta—and looks far more ferocious than it is.

NIGHT OF THE LIVING DEAD

1968 90m bw Horror ★★★★
Image Ten (U.S.) /18

Judith O'Dea *(Barbara)*, Russell Streiner *(Johnny)*, Duane Jones *(Ben)*, Karl Hardman *(Harry Cooper)*, Keith Wayne *(Tom)*, Judith Ridley *(Judy)*, Marilyn Eastman *(Helen Cooper)*, Kyra Schon *(Karen)*, Bill Heinzman, Charles Craig

p, Russell Streiner, Karl Hardman; d, George Romero; w, John A. Russo (based on a story by Romero); ph, George Romero; ed, George Romero; prod d, Vincent Survinski; fx, Regis Survinski, Tony Pantanello

Pittsburgh-based industrial filmmaker George Romero gathered together a loyal cast and youthful crew from the local talent, scrounged up enough money to shoot on weekends, and made motion picture history. The first truly modern horror movie, NIGHT OF THE LIVING DEAD is the most influential work to emerge in the genre since PSYCHO. Despite mostly unprofessional acting, near nonexistent production values, homemade special effects, and cheap grainy black-and-white film stock, the film is a triumph. It's also a sign of its times—the era of the Vietnam War abroad and social upheaval at home—in which good does not triumph over evil, and likable people die just as brutally and unexpectedly as the despicable ones. The violence, which was extreme in its day, reflects the horrors Americans were seeing each night on the evening news, and patriarchal values and institutions are depicted in a critical manner. The horror movie would never be the same again.

Barbara (O'Dea) and her brother, Johnny (Streiner), have driven many miles at the behest of their mother to honor their dead father by placing a wreath on his grave. Neither is enthusiastic about the annual task. Johnny reminisces about how he used to frighten his sister when they were children. "They're coming to get you, Barbara!" he intones ominously in his best Boris Karloff fashion. Though now grown up and ostensibly too mature to be affected by such juvenile scare tactics,

Barbara is still unnerved by her brother's creepy performance. Johnny sees an odd-looking fellow lurching unsteadily in the distance. "Look, there's one of them now!" The fun and games abruptly stop, however, when the weird man savagely grabs Barbara. Johnny leaps to his sister's defence but he's knocked down by the maniac. His head strikes a tombstone, apparently killing him. Barbara races for her life back to the car, leaps in, and discovers that the keys are in Johnny's pocket. The maniac bangs on the windows, desperate to get at her. Barbara releases the emergency brake and the car rolls down a hill away from her clumsy pursuer. She gets out and runs to an old farmhouse where she is soon joined by Ben (Jones), a young black man. Ben informs Barbara that the recently dead have been returning to life to eat the living. He sets about fortifying the house by nailing boards over doors and windows, without much help from Barbara, who has gone into a semi-catatonic state.

Thus the stage is set for one of the most nightmarish films ever made, and one that's still hard to laugh off today. Things get a bit talky once all the characters gather in the farmhouse, but NIGHT OF THE LIVING DEAD grips in the manner of a good "Twilight Zone" episode. Produced for less than $150,000, the film was booked in a haphazard manner—rejected by Columbia because it wasn't in color and by American International Pictures because it had no romance and a downbeat ending—and turned up at kiddie matinees, scaring the daylights out of unprepared youngsters. NIGHT OF THE LIVING DEAD then found its niche on the midnight movie circuit and went on to become one of the most successful independent films of all time. Romero made two (far bloodier) sequels, DAWN OF THE DEAD and DAY OF THE DEAD; all three movies are essential viewing for horror fans.

NIGHT OF THE SHOOTING STARS, THE

1981 106m c Drama/War ★★★
RAI-TV/Ager/Premier (Italy) R/A

Omero Antonutti (Galvano), Margarita Lozano (Concetta), Claudio Bigagli (Corrado), Massimo Bonetti (Nicole), Norma Martelli (Ivana), Enrica Maria Modugno (Mara), Sabina Vannucchi (Rosanna), Dario Cantarelli (Priest), Sergio Dagliana (Olinto), Giuseppe Furia (Requiem)

p, Giuliani G. De Negri; d, Paolo Taviani, Vittorio Taviani; w, Vittorio Taviani, Paolo Taviani, Giuliani G. De Negri, Tonino Guerra; ph, Franco Di Giacomo; ed, Roberto Perpignani; m, Nicola Piovani; art d, Gianni Sbarra

On the night of San Lorenzo (a magical evening during which many Europeans believe wishes may become fulfilled), a shooting star darts across the sky, sending a grown woman into a recollection of her childhood. As the star passes her window, she relates the events that took place in her small town during the last days of WWII: With the advancing Allies pushing the last remnants of the German army out of Italy, the Nazis enact sick and desperate revenge on the Italian civilians, staging vicious attacks on the old men, women, and children left in the villages. The members of the small town of San Miniato are divided in their opinions as to whether to remain in their village and risk dealing with the Germans, or to attempt traveling across the back roads, dodging attacks from sadistic Blackshirts, in an effort to meet the advancing Allies. One group made up of various segments of the town's population sets out on the journey, with all the old prohibitions breaking down as the people pull together in an effort to survive. An elderly peasant man with natural leadership ability is chosen to guide the group to safety. Despite a few voices of dissent, the old man brings ingenuity to his assignment and keeps the group's spirits up by showing a humane concern for all and encouraging them to watch out for one another. During the journey, he develops a romantic relationship with an aristocratic woman who has always admired him but could never let him know because of their difference in class. Once he has guided the group out of danger, however, the townspeople immediately resume the societal roles that previously divided them. The Taviani brothers, who gained international attention with 1977 Cannes Film Festival Golden Palm winner PADRE PADRONE, approached this film in much the same way as they did their earlier effort—using an imaginative combination of events and showing them as remembered by the narrator as she reminisces about the magical moments of her childhood—and came up with a dazzling, immensely popular film that earned them the Special Jury Prize at Cannes.

NIGHT ON EARTH

1992 130m c Drama/Comedy ★★★
Locus Solus/Black Snake Productions (U.S.) R/15

Gena Rowlands (Victoria Snelling), Winona Ryder (Corky), Armin Mueller-Stahl (Helmut Grokenberger), Giancarlo Esposito (YoYo), Rosie Perez (Angela), Isaach De Bankole (Driver), Beatrice Dalle (Blind Woman), Roberto Benigni (Gino), Paolo Bonacelli (Priest), Matti Pellonpaa (Mika)

p, Jim Jarmusch; d, Jim Jarmusch; w, Jim Jarmusch; ph, Frederick Elmes; ed, Jay Rabinowitz; m, Tom Waits; cos, Magda Bava, Claire Fraisse, Alexandra Welker, Gordon Barbara

This global shaggy-dog story is director/writer/producer Jim Jarmusch's most accessible work to date. The film comprises five segments, each of which is set in a taxi, that take place simultaneously at different points around the globe. Starring a very cool collection of international actors, and directed by the king of the American alternative movie scene, these funny yet poignant stories could be described as joined at the hip.

NIGHT ON EARTH begins at sunset on a winter's day in L.A., and then moves through nighttime in New York, Paris, Rome, and finally Helsinki, where the sun is rising as the last section comes to an end. The basic connection is the relationship between driver and passenger that each story explores, though the segments are also linked in other, less obvious, ways. As with the best short stories, the segments are less about plot—very little actually *happens*—than they are about character, dialogue, and mood. Jarmusch is a master of all these elements, and clearly has an intuitive rapport with his cast. The best of the actors—Giancarlo Esposito and Armin Mueller-Stahl in New York, Isaach de Bankole and Beatrice Dalle in Paris, Roberto Benigni in Rome, and Matti Pellonpaa in Helsinki—bring the proceedings to three-dimensional life, mining the script for laughs and even coaxing social and political overtones from Jarmusch's minimalist writing. On a purely visual level, the casting choices are inspired. De Bankole, as a brusque, defensive Ivory Coast native transplanted to Paris, has a face that radiates sullen pride; and Pellonpaa, who subdues a cabful of Helsinki drunks with a story that moves the film from comedy to elegy, has a hang-dog expression that cannot be rivalled. All this is perfectly complemented by the director's moody evocation of the five night-shrouded urban settings. The film's only low points come courtesy of Winona Ryder, who unforgivably mugs her way through the glib first segment; and Rosie Perez, whose high-pitched whining in the New York section reminds you what it's like to be trapped in a cab with a driver who won't shut up.

NIGHT TO REMEMBER, A

1958 123m bw Disaster ★★★★
Rank (U.K.) /PG

Kenneth More (Herbert Lightoller), Ronald Allen (Clarke), Robert Ayres (Peuchen), Honor Blackman (Mrs. Lucas), Anthony Bushell (Capt. Rostron), John Cairney (Murphy), Jill Dixon (Mrs. Clarke), Jane Downs (Mrs. Lightoller), James Dyrenforth (Col. Gracie), Michael Goodliffe (Thomas Andrews)

p, William McQuitty; d, Roy Ward Baker; w, Eric Ambler (based on the book by Walter Lord); ph, Geoffrey Unsworth; ed, Sidney Hayers; m, William Alwyn; art d, Alex Vetchinsky; cos, Yvonne Caffin

A NIGHT TO REMEMBER treats in brilliant, semi-documentary style the night of April 14, 1912, when the luxury liner *Titanic* struck an iceberg and sank, taking 1,513 passengers and crew members (out of a total complement of 2,224 on board) to the bottom of the ocean on on the fifth day of her maiden voyage from Southampton to New York. Although Kenneth More is ostensibly the star, this multi-layered production boasts more than 200 speaking parts. Sticking pretty closely to the facts, Baker and Ambler have constructed a startling drama, uncluttered by fictional sub-plots. Made for a mere $1,680,000, A NIGHT TO REMEMBER looks much more expensive, with superb costumes and sets. Though far superior to Fox's TITANIC of 1953, this critically acclaimed film met with only lukewarm box-office support.

NIGHT TRAIN TO MUNICH

1940 90m bw Spy/War ★★★★
Gaumont (U.K.) /A

Margaret Lockwood (*Anna Bomasch*), Rex Harrison (*Gus Bennett*), Paul Henreid (*Karl Marsen*), Basil Radford (*Charters*), Naunton Wayne (*Caldicott*), James Harcourt (*Axel Bomasch*), Felix Aylmer (*Dr. John Fredericks*), Wyndham Goldie (*Dryton*), Roland Culver (*Roberts*), Eliot Makeham (*Schwab*)

p, Edward Black; d, Carol Reed; w, Sydney Gilliat, Frank Launder (based on a story by Gordon Wellesley); ph, Otto Kanturek; ed, R.E. Dearing; art d, Alex Vetchinsky

AAN Best Original Screenplay: Gordon Wellesley

One of the finest spy films ever, NIGHT TRAIN reflects the immense talents of its brilliant director, Carol Reed, and of scripters Frank Launder and Sydney Gilliat. After Hitler's conquest of Czechoslovakia, Anna Bomasch (Margaret Lockwood) is arrested. Her father, Axel (James Harcourt), who possesses technical information the Nazis want, has fled to England, but Anna is interred in a concentration camp. There, she meets Karl Marsen (Paul Henreid), with whom she manages to escape to England, and in London she contacts music hall performer Gus Bennett (Rex Harrison)—who is actually a British secret agent—to get in touch with her father. In short order the Bomasches, duped by Marsen—who is himself a Gestapo plant—are taken to Germany, where the Nazis threaten Anna to secure Axel's cooperation. Bennett follows, infiltrates the Naval Ministry in Berlin, and discovers that the Bomasches are on the night train to Munich. With the help of two comedic cricketers played by Naunton Wayne and Basil Radford (who performed the same service in Alfred Hitchcock's THE LADY VANISHES), Bennett boards the train and is able to free father and daughter, leading to the trio's final flight to Switzerland, with Marsen and the SS in hot pursuit. Though action-packed with one harrowing scene after another, the film is not broadly played, and Reed employs subtlety over bravado. Its portrayal of the Germans, too, is fairly balanced, without the propagandistic characterizations that would mark films made later in the war. Harrison is perfect as the daring, suave British spy; Lockwood is fine as his love interest; and Henried is appropriately subtle as the deceiving Marsen in this gripping, razor-edged melodrama that mounts to a stunning climax.

NIGHTHAWKS

1981 99m c Crime ★★★½
Universal (U.S.) R/18

Sylvester Stallone (*Deke DaSilva*), Billy Dee Williams (*Matthew Fox*), Lindsay Wagner (*Irene*), Persis Khambatta (*Shakka*), Nigel Davenport (*Peter Hartman*), Rutger Hauer (*Wulfgar*), Hilarie Thompson (*Pam*), Joe Spinell (*Lt. Munafo*), Walter Mathews (*Commissioner*), E. Brian Dean (*Sergeant*)

p, Martin Poll; d, Bruce Malmuth; w, David Shaber (based on a story by David Shaber and Paul Sylbert); ph, James A. Contner; ed, Christopher Holmes; m, Keith Emerson; prod d, Peter Larkin; fx, Ed Drohan, Walter Tatro, Dick Smith, Nick Allder; cos, Robert DeMora, John Falabella

Deke DaSilva (Sylvester Stallone) and Matthew Fox (Billy Dee Williams) are New York cops assigned to track down terrorist Wulfgar (Rutger Hauer). In London, Wulfgar planted a bomb in a London department store, killing several children and incurring the wrath of terrorist leaders. He resumes his career with financing from Shakka (Persis Khambatta). Soon DaSilva and Wulfgar are engaged in a violent battle of wits, while DaSilva struggles to save his marriage to Irene (Lindsay Wagner). This very effective thriller features a chilling performance by Hauer as the emotionless killing machine. Stallone and Williams are also credible, and the film makes good use of its New York locations.

NIGHTMARE ALLEY

1947 111m bw Crime ★★★★
Fox (U.S.) /A

Tyrone Power (*Stanton Carlisle*), Joan Blondell (*Zeena*), Coleen Gray (*Molly*), Helen Walker (*Dr. Lilith Ritter*), Taylor Holmes (*Ezra Grindle*), Mike Mazurki (*Bruno*), Ian Keith (*Pete*), Julia Dean (*Mrs. Peabody*), James Flavin (*Clem Hoatley*), Roy Roberts (*McGraw*)

p, George Jessel; d, Edmund Goulding; w, Jules Furthman (based on the novel by William Lindsay Gresham); ph, Lee Garmes; ed, Barbara McLean; m, Cyril J. Mockridge; art d, Lyle Wheeler, J. Russell Spencer; fx, Fred Sersen; cos, Bonnie Cashin

Power is simply terrific as Stanton Carlisle, a sideshow hustler who makes it to the big time through underhanded methods that ultimately bring about his horrific ruination. Carlisle gets a menial job with a cheap carnival and becomes fascinated with a mind-reading act performed by Pete and Zeena (Keith and Blondell). Becoming the show's barker, Carlisle entices carnival patrons to another attraction as well: an illegal geek show featuring a "half-man, half-beast" who works in a pit and bites the heads off live chickens. Here the geek is a fallen carney performer, a dipsomaniac who conducts his ghastly routines so he can be paid off with a quart of booze each evening. In no time, Carlisle is made a part of the mind-reading act; plying Pete with friendship and liquor, he later replaces the older man in the act after accidentally giving him some poisonous wood alcohol. Carlisle then seduces Zeena into recreating with him a more spectacular version of the act which relies on a secret word code which enables the spiritualist to discern the questions Carlisle has gathered from patrons in the audience. Molly (Gray), a pretty sideshow artist, falls for Carlisle, who, incurring the wrath of the carnival people, marries the girl and moves to Chicago. A successful nightclub artist there, he fascinates Lilith (Walker), a sultry psychologist who agrees to give him confidential information about her wealthy clients in return for a substantial cut of the take. Molly, however, finds it increasingly hard to bilk people, and Lilith discovers some damning information about Carlisle from Zeena.

Although it could not include all the terrifying detail of Gresham's shocking novel, Furthman's script potently reveals the sleazy world of the spiritual con artist. Carefully constructing Power's rise and fall, director Goulding is merciless in his inspection of a character who is rotten through and through. Power, who had Fox buy the rights of the novel for him, gives the performance of his career, proving that he was not merely a matinee idol but a player who could dig deep inside himself and produce a memorable and telling characterization. Goulding was then Power's favorite director; they had worked together in the worthy 1946 adaptation of Somerset Maugham's THE RAZOR'S EDGE. Goulding was noted for eliciting excellent performances from his actors, as he did in GRAND HOTEL, DARK VICTORY, THE GREAT LIE, and CLAUDIA.

Walker is a standout as the cold-blooded psychologist and Blondell excels as the frowzy but calculating sprirualist, the essence of cheapness. Gray is also fine as the stupid but loving wife who can forgive any crime. Mockridge's score is eerie and perfectly suited to the shadowy images captured in Garmes's photography.

NIGHTMARE ON ELM STREET, A

1984 91m c Horror ★★★½
New Line (U.S.) R/18

John Saxon (*Lt. Thompson*), Ronee Blakley (*Marge Thompson*), Heather Langenkamp (*Nancy Thompson*), Amanda Wyss (*Tina Gray*), Nick Corri (*Rod Lane*), Johnny Depp (*Glen Lantz*), Robert Englund (*Fred Krueger*), Charles Fleischer (*Dr. King*), Joseph Whipp (*Sgt. Parker*), Mimi Meyer-Craven (*Nurse*)

p, Robert Shaye, Sara Risher; d, Wes Craven; w, Wes Craven; ph, Jacques Haitkin; ed, Rick Shaine; m, Charles Bernstein; prod d, Gregg Fonseca; fx, Jim Doyle; cos, Dana Lyman

"One, two; Freddy's comin' for you/Three, four; better lock your door/Five, six; grab your crucifix/Seven, eight; gonna stay up late/Nine, ten; never sleep again."

A NIGHTMARE ON ELM STREET, one of the most intelligent and terrifying horror films of the 1980s, begins and ends with this haunting children's song. This was the film that introduced the world to Freddy

Krueger, the horribly scarred man with the ragged slouch hat, dirty red-and-green striped sweater, and metal gloves with knives at the tips. Freddy (Robert Englund), a genius of a monster who exists in his victims' dreams and preys on them in the vulnerability of sleep, has returned to the town where years before he was burnt alive as a child killer by locals who took the law into their own hands. Now he's back to take revenge on their kids. In an era in which the horror film has become little more than a mindless exercise in gratuitous high-tech bloodletting, A NIGHTMARE ON ELM STREET (like most of Wes Craven's films) brought some hope to those concerned about the fate of the genre. This movie intelligently probes into the audience's terror of nightmares and combines it with another horrific element—the very real fear of killers in one's own neighborhood. The teenagers in the film, who are paying for the sins of their parents, are not simply fodder for the special-effects crew but have distinct personalities and are independent and intelligent. The initial success of the movie was based on the audience's insecurity: we are never sure whether the characters are dreaming because the line between nightmare and reality is blurred, and, as a result, the terror is almost nonstop. The success of the sequels, while still based in the dream-versus-reality premise, has become increasingly dependent on the heroic pose of Freddy Krueger, played with energy and humor by Robert Englund.

NIGHTS OF CABIRIA
(LE NOTTI DI CABIRIA)
1957 110m bw Drama   ★★★★½
Marceau (Italy)   /15

Giulietta Masina *(Cabiria)*, Francois Perier *(Oscar D'Onofrio, Accountant)*, Amedeo Nazzari *(Alberto Lazzari, Movie Star)*, Aldo Silvani *(Hypnotist)*, Franca Marzi *(Wanda Cabiria's Friend)*, Dorian Gray *(Jessy Lazzari's Girl Friend)*, Mario Passante *(Cripple in the "Miracle" Sequence)*, Pina Gualandri *(Matilda the Prostitute)*, Polidor *(The Monk)*, Enio Girolami

p, Dino De Laurentiis; d, Federico Fellini; w, Federico Fellini, Ennio Flaiano, Tullio Pinelli, Pier Paolo Pasolini; ph, Aldo Tonti, Otello Martelli; ed, Leo Catozzo; m, Nino Rota; art d, Piero Gherardi; cos, Piero Gherardi

AA Best Foreign Language Film

Masina's finest film performance, perhaps husband Fellini's as well. NIGHTS OF CABIRIA lacks the lyrical simplicity that made LA STRADA such a magical experience, but is an impressive enough display of Fellini's fascinating visual style to have warranted the Academy Award for Best Foreign-Language Film. Set in a district on the outskirts of Rome, the film focuses on Cabiria (Masina), a near-perfect embodiment of the prostitute with a heart of gold. She's the type who understands misfortune to be part and parcel of life, but never loses faith in the value of life itself. When misfortune does come her way, Cabiria shrugs it off and continues walking the streets for money. A handsome movie star picks her up during a brawl with his girlfriend. He takes her to his fabulous home, but quickly discards her when he is through with her services. Eventually someone does fall in love with Cabiria—the shy and withdrawn Oscar D'Onofrio (Francois Perier)—or at least she believes this to be the case. Perhaps the most difficult aspect of NIGHTS OF CABIRIA is accepting Masina as a prostitute: this sweet and naive-looking woman, who stole audiences' hearts with her childlike innocence in LA STRADA, isn't at all typical of women selling themselves on the streets, but does express the dismal point that fate makes no exceptions. Her Cabiria is a sucker for a sob story, and this very flaw gives her a saving grace. As in the majority of Fellini's films, the emphasis here is on visual elements rather than on straight narrative form, relying on small details and eccentricities to breathe life into Cabiria. The film was the basis for the Broadway and film version of *Sweet Charity*.

9 TO 5
1980 110m c Comedy   ★★★
IPC (U.S.)   PG/15

Jane Fonda *(Judy Bernly)*, Lily Tomlin *(Violet Newstead)*, Dolly Parton *(Doralee Rhodes)*, Dabney Coleman *(Franklin Hart, Jr.)*, Sterling Hayden *(Tinsworthy)*, Elizabeth Wilson *(Roz)*, Henry Jones *(Hinkle)*, Lawrence Pressman *(Dick)*, Marian Mercer *(Missy Hart)*, Ren Woods *(Barbara)*

p, Bruce Gilbert; d, Colin Higgins; w, Colin Higgins, Patricia Resnick (based on a story by Patricia Resnick); ph, Reynaldo Villalobos; ed, Pembroke J. Herring; m, Charles Fox; prod d, Dean Edward Mitzner; art d, Jack G. Taylor Jr.; fx, Chuck Gaspar, Matt Sweeney; cos, Ann Roth

AAN Best Song: Dolly Parton (Music & Lyrics)

Recently divorced Jane Fonda takes an office job and soon becomes pals with fellow secretaries Dolly Parton (in a sensational movie debut) and Lily Tomlin. Their boss is male chauvinist Dabney Coleman, who is trying to land Parton in bed. While smoking dope one night the women hatch a plan to take revenge on their cruel boss. Lots of laughs, little sense, and pure fantasy. Produced by Fonda's company, NINE TO FIVE is an amusing way to spend 110 minutes, but hardly memorable. Later made into a short-lived TV series. The title song received an Oscar nomination.

1918
1985 91m c Drama   ★★★½
Guadalupe (U.S.)

William Converse-Roberts *(Horace Robedaux)*, Hallie Foote *(Elizabeth Robedaux)*, Rochelle Oliver *(Mrs. Vaughn)*, Michael Higgens *(Mr. Vaughn)*, Matthew Broderick *(Brother)*, Jeanne McCarthy *(Bessie)*, Bill McGhee *(Sam)*, L.T. Felty *(Mr. Thatcher)*, Horton Foote Jr. *(Jessie)*, Tom Murrel *(Stanley)*

p, Lillian V. Foote, Ross Milloy; d, Ken Harrison; w, Horton Foote (based on his play); ph, George Tirl; ed, Leon Seith; art d, Michael O'Sullivan; cos, Van Broughton Ramsey

This thoughtful and carefully detailed story examines life on the WWI homefront in a rural Texas town that, in its own way, is forever changed by the war's far-reaching effects. Horace (William Converse-Roberts) and Elizabeth Robedaux (Hallie Foote) are a young married couple with an 8-month-old daughter. Their home, where much of the film's action takes place, has been paid for by Elizabeth's wealthy parents (Michael Higgens, Rochelle Oliver), who exert a domineering influence over the two. Horace has claimed he would fight in the war if he could be assured his wife and baby would be properly taken care of. His father-in-law promises to care for the family and leaves Horace no excuse. Elizabeth is furious with her husband and father, but matters take a sudden turn when the flu epidemic sweeps the country. 1918 is a multilayered work that delves deeply into the complexities of its characters and how they cope with the encroaching specter of death both at home and abroad. Foote gives a strong central performance that anchors the film with honest, deeply felt emotions. The screenplay, by her father, Horton Foote, is based on family experiences. The direction by Ken Harrison is thoughtful, allowing the events to unfold naturally in long takes. The small moments of everyday life are as prominent as the war in Europe, an important factor 1918 reflects with care and intelligence, complemented by its exact period detail.

1984
1955 94m bw Drama/Science Fiction   ★★½
Holiday (U.K.)   /15

Michael Redgrave *(Gen. O'Connor)*, Edmond O'Brien *(Winston Smith)*, Jan Sterling *(Julia)*, David Kossoff *(Charrington the Junk Shop Owner)*, Mervyn Johns *(Jones)*, Donald Pleasence *(Parsons)*, Carol Wolveridge *(Selina Parsons)*, Ernest Clark *(Outer Party Announcer)*, Patrick Allen *(Inner Party Official)*, Ronan O'Casey *(Rutherford)*

p, N. Peter Rathvon; d, Michael Anderson; w, William Templeton, Ralph Gilbert Bettinson (based on the novel by George Orwell); ph, C. Pennington-Richards; ed, Bill Lewthwaite; m, Malcolm Arnold; art d, Terence Verity; fx, B. Langley, George Blackwell, N. Warwick; cos, Barbara Gray

Great liberties were taken with the story written by Orwell and published in 1949, a year before Orwell passed away. Those liberties were to the detriment of one of the most powerful and depressing books ever written. The year is, of course, 1984, and London is the capital of one of three world communities of Oceania. It's after the first atomic war, and everyone in London (and everywhere else) is constantly watched by TV cameras (which are also screens) and by "Big Brother" and his faceless aides. The surroundings are drab, and no individuality will be tolerated. The walls are festooned with posters which read "War Is Peace," "Freedom Is Slavery," and "Big Brother Is Watching You." And he is. O'Brien works for the state and finds that he cannot handle the stultifying atmosphere of being ruled by the Minsitry of Love because he is falling for Sterling. They begin to have a clandestine affair which will be life-threatening if ever uncovered by the Anti-Sex League or the Thought Police. Sterling and O'Brien make plans to overthrow Big Brother and they are joined in their cabal by Redgrave, but he is, in reality, a member of the Government who eventually informs on them. Since there are two-way microphones in every residence, the deepest fears of every citizen have been audiotaped and are known to the authorities. When someone is brought in, they are taken to Room 101, where they have to confront their innermost fears. In the case of O'Brien, it's rats, and when he must face the little furry things, he breaks. The end of the movie is varied, depending on which country you see it in. The British version has Sterling and O'Brien killed. The American version has O'Brien betraying Sterling and so successfully brainwashed that he shouts for the love of Big Brother rather than "down with Big Brother," the words he screams as his last epithet in England. The last words of the book are also different. After O'Brien's character is bumped off, the comment is made that "he loved Big Brother." Another version of the film was made in the 1980s which was equally depressing and ultimately unsuccessful with the critics and the public. Perhaps this is one of those novels that defies cinematization and must be savored in one's brain, rather than with the ears and eyes. The same could be said for Huxley's *Brave New World*.

1984

1984 117m c Drama/Science Fiction ★★★
Umbrella/Rosenblum/Virgin (U.K.) R/X

John Hurt *(Winston Smith)*, Richard Burton *(O'Brien)*, Suzanna Hamilton *(Julia)*, Cyril Cusack *(Charrington)*, Gregor Fisher *(Parsons)*, James Walker *(Syme)*, Andrew Wilde *(Tillotson)*, David Trevena *(Tillotson's Friend)*, David Cann *(Martin)*, Anthony Benson *(Jones)*

p, Simon Perry; d, Michael Radford; w, Michael Radford, Jonathan Gems (based on the novel by George Orwell); ph, Roger Deakins; ed, Tom Priestley; m, The Eurythmics, Dominic Muldowney; prod d, Allan Cameron; art d, Martyn Hebert, Grant Hicks; cos, Emma Porteous

In this admirable attempt at bringing George Orwell's classic novel to the screen, director Michael Radford is perhaps too faithful to his source material. This is the well-known story of Winston Smith (John Hurt), a citizen of Oceania whose job it is to rewrite history for Big Brother, the autocratic symbol of a repressive regime that has forbidden such things as freedom of thought and expression—including sex. Winston becomes involved in an illicit love affair with Julia (Suzanna Hamilton), a young woman who works in the Ministry of Truth. Unfortunately for Winston, a high-ranking member of the government, O'Brien (Richard Burton), who has looked upon him as a protege, discovers the rebellion. Orwell wrote his novel in 1948, and his vision of the future is unrelentingly bleak. Radford chooses to present a view of the future as it might have looked to Orwell in 1948. This is not a future made up of colorful blinking lights and high-tech manufacturing; it is a gray, dull, stark, depressing world possessed of little visual stimulation. The performances in the film are excellent, and its look is entirely appropriate and mesmerizing—but only for a while. The basic flaw in 1984 is that it is just too painful, too depressing, and too slow to watch.

1900
(NOVECENTO)

1976 245m c Drama ★★★½
PEA/Artistes Associes (Italy) R/18

Burt Lancaster *(Alfredo Berlinghieri, Grandfather)*, Romolo Valli *(Giovanni)*, Anna-Maria Gherardi *(Eleonora)*, Laura Betti *(Regina)*, Robert De Niro *(Alfredo Berlinghieri, Grandson)*, Paolo Pavesi *(Al-*

fredo as a Child), Dominique Sanda *(Ada)*, Sterling Hayden *(Leo Dalco)*, Gerard Depardieu *(Olmo Dalco)*, Roberto Maccanti *(Olmo as a Child)*

p, Alberto Grimaldi; d, Bernardo Bertolucci; w, Franco Arcalli, Bernardo Bertolucci, Giuseppe Bertolucci; ph, Vittorio Storaro; ed, Franco Arcalli; m, Ennio Morricone; art d, Ezio Frigerio; cos, Gitt Magrini

Like a delicious pasta salad, ruined with intermittent slabs of Velveeta cheese. It's the portable Bernardo Bertolucci film, but it's too heavy to lift. The director wanted to make a collective-memory, "popular" film—there's no denying some brilliant, definitive moments in this left-wing homage to peasant life—if that's your thing. But somewhere Bertolucci got popular culture confused with pulp. Sometimes, this looks like animated Harold Robbins.

1900 captures everything that characterizes the director: his concern with the class dialectic and the battle between Marxism and Fascism, his painterly images of Italy, his historical scope, and his "divided hero" (to borrow a phrase from critic Robin Wood). While it may be a masterpiece at its original length of 320 minutes, 1900's American, British, and videocassette release is a shortened, somewhat erratic 245-minute version. The plot is about as grand and baroque as one can get, entailing the history of the Italian people and politics in the first half of the 1900s, from the organization of the peasant class to the rise of socialism to the fall of Fascism. This political dialectic is personified in Bertolucci's two central characters (the "divided hero"), Alfredo (Robert De Niro), born into a bourgeois clan of landowners, and Olmo (Gerard Depardieu), born into a peasant family, who share the same birthday, January 27, 1901 (the day Verdi died, another point of homage). Although they grow up the best of friends, their friendship turns into a love/hate relationship. As an adult, the weak Alfredo is put in charge of his family's property but is merely a puppet controlled by his evil foreman, Attila (Donald Sutherland), while the Marxist Olmo becomes a leading union organizer. Even in its shortened version, 1900 is an achievement of considerable genius, directed by Bertolucci but made possible by the combined efforts of collaborator-cinematographer Vittorio Storaro, composer Ennio Morricone, art director Enzo Frigerio, costumer Gitt Magrini, and a phenomenal cast that includes an international Who's Who of performers. But if this were an American work would we be so impressed?

NINOTCHKA

1939 110m bw Comedy ★★★★★
MGM (U.S.) /U

Greta Garbo *(Lena Yakushova, "Ninotchka")*, Melvyn Douglas *(Count Leon Dolga)*, Ina Claire *(Grand Duchess Swana)*, Sig Rumann *(Michael Ironoff)*, Felix Bressart *(Buljanoff)*, Alexander Granach *(Kopalski)*, Bela Lugosi *(Commissar Razinin)*, Gregory Gaye *(Count Alexis Rakonin)*, Richard Carle *(Vaston)*, Edwin Maxwell *(Mercier)*

p, Ernst Lubitsch; d, Ernst Lubitsch; w, Charles Brackett, Billy Wilder, Walter Reisch (based on a story by Melchior Lengyel); ph, William Daniels; ed, Gene Ruggiero; m, Werner R. Heymann; art d, Cedric Gibbons, Randall Duell; cos, Adrian

AAN Best Picture; AAN Best Actress: Greta Garbo; *AAN Best Original Screenplay:* Melchior Lengyel; *AAN Best Original Screenplay:* Charles Brackett, Walter Reisch, Billy Wilder

Garbo laughs. So read the advertising for the star's first outright comedy, and it brilliantly sums up the appeal of this remarkable film. Director Ernst Lubitsch has the actress gracefully step down from her pedestal as the stern Communist who warms to the appeal of Paris champagne and playboy Melvyn Douglas. Combining farce, romance and satire, yet still maintaining moments of that soaring Garbo intensity, NINOTCHKA is special indeed.

When three Soviet emissaries (Bressart, Rumann, Granach, whose work could not possibly be bettered) arrive in Paris on a mission, it's not long before Paris arrives on them instead. And so, super efficient Comrade Ninotchka (Garbo) appears to retrieve jewelry in the possession of the former Grand Duchess Swana (Claire). It is the Soviet government's contention that the property of the aristocrats properly belongs to the people. The two women's tussle over the goods becomes complicated, however, when Swana's swain Leon (Douglas) becomes infatuated with the frosty commissar.

Many of Garbo's films rely on her presence alone for their appeal. That's not the case here. Working from a brittle, witty script by no less than Wilder, Brackett, and Reisch, the gifted Lubitsch brings his patented "touch" to scene after scene. From the bumbling emissaries' arithmetic about ringing for hotel maids to Ninotchka's hilarious "execution scene" the film bubbles merrily throughout. Garbo rarely had a paramour as adroit as Douglas, who wears a dinner jacket with the flair of Astaire and the polish of Powell. He plays the gushy romantic dialogue early on with the perfect combination of conviction and playfulness, and one of the film's beauties is watching Garbo shift gears into this mode herself. The lovely scene in a cafe where Douglas cracks Ninotchka up only when he falls off his chair remains a highlight of both film comedy and screen romance.

An adroit satire of both Communism and capitalism, NINOTCHKA still manages a healthy heartiness and a sweet sadness. Its success inspired pallid imitations from COMRADE X with Lamarr and Gable to THE IRON PETTICOAT with Hepburn and Hope. A musical remake, SILK STOCKINGS, featured some good Fred Astaire-Cyd Charisse dancing and a show-stealing turn by Janis Paige, but had little sparkle and even less depth. Garbo would attempt, but fail, to repeat this film's magic with her next, TWO-FACED WOMAN, with George Cukor (at one point slated for NINOTCHKA) directing.

NIXON

1995 190m c/bw Drama/Biography/Political   ★★★
Cinergi Productions/Illusion Entertainment Group   R/15
/Hollywood Pictures (U.S.)

Anthony Hopkins *(Richard M. Nixon)*, Joan Allen *(Pat Nixon)*, Powers Boothe *(Alexander Haig)*, Ed Harris *(E. Howard Hunt)*, Bob Hoskins *(J. Edgar Hoover)*, E.G. Marshall *(John Mitchell)*, David Paymer *(Ron Ziegler)*, David Hyde Pierce *(John Dean)*, Paul Sorvino *(Henry Kissinger)*, Mary Steenburgen *(Hannah Nixon)*

p, Clayton Townsend, Oliver Stone, Andrew G. Vajna; d, Oliver Stone; w, Stephen J. Rivele, Christopher Wilkinson, Oliver Stone; ph, Robert Richardson; ed, Brian Berdan, Hank Corwin; m, John Williams; prod d, Victor Kempster; art d, Donald Woodruff, Richard F. Mays, Margery Zweizig; fx, F. Lee Stone, Peter Kuran, Christer Hokanson, Chris Loudon; cos, Richard Hornung

AAN Best Actor: Anthony Hopkins; *AAN Best Supporting Actress:* Joan Allen; *AAN Best Original Screenplay:* Stephen J. Rivele, Christopher Wilkinson, Oliver Stone; *AAN Best Dramatic Score:* John Williams

A lurching, addlebrained biopic that lacks even the crackpot energy of JFK, Oliver Stone's NIXON struggles to invest its nakedly venal subject with tragic dignity.

Even more than NATURAL BORN KILLERS, it's offered as a Big Statement: We're meant to see Nixon as a flawed but quintessentially *American* figure, to understand (and rationalize) his criminal foibles as a disturbing reflection of our own dark side. What's *really* disturbing — if not precisely surprising — is how closely Stone identifies with his brooding, paranoid antihero. Anthony Hopkins, miscast in the title role, gives the kind of self-consciously hammy performance that automatically qualifies for an Oscar nomination; Joan Allen is a one-dimensional Pat.

One's appreciation of the screenplay (by Stephen J. Rivele, Christopher Wilkinson, and Stone) will probably depend on one's familiarity with real events. Opening and closing on the ill-starred President's "final days", NIXON loops back and forth through well-trodden historical ground (the Checkers speech, the Nixon-Kennedy debates, the Hiss case, etc.), semi-factual elaborations of little-known events (Nixon's strict Quaker upbringing in Whittier, California, his marital woes), and outright fabrications (a sinister meeting with Hoover at the racetrack, a blackmail attempt by an imaginary Texas power broker played by Larry Hagman, TV's J.R. Ewing). All of it is refracted through Stone's peculiar penchant for seeing diabolical connections everywhere. In this case, a link is made between Nixon's supposed involvement in the Bay of Pigs invasion and his ultimate vulnerability

to the "military-industrial complex." Ironically, the film posits a nutty theory of the Kennedy assassination that is completely inconsistent with the equally nutty theory offered in Stone's JFK.

NO GREATER GLORY

1934 117m bw Drama   ★★★★
Columbia (U.S.)   /U

George Breakston *(Nemecsek)*, Jimmy Butler *(Boka)*, Jackie Searl *(Gereb)*, Frankie Darro *(Feri Ats)*, Donald Haines *(Csonakos)*, Rolf Ernest *(Ferdie Pasztor)*, Julius Molnar *(Henry Pasztor)*, Wesley Giraud *(Kolnay)*, Beaudine Anderson *(Csele)*, Bruce Line *(Richter)*

d, Frank Borzage; w, Jo Swerling (based on the novel *The Paul Street Boys* by Ferenc Molnar); ph, Joseph August; ed, Viola Lawrence

This is a fine and honest film with excellent performances by its youthful cast. George Breakston plays a frail youngster who idolizes gang leader Jimmy Butler. The gang is modeled after an army, complete with uniforms and a flag. Breakston's ill health makes him something of an outcast, but he is allowed to join up as a private, the only enlisted soldier in an army otherwise composed of officers. Butler despises him for his weakness, but Breakston cannot see this, so great is his admiration and his need to belong. When their flag is stolen by a rival gang of older boys called "The Red Shirts," Breakston takes it upon himself to retrieve the banner. He invades the enemy camp in a driving rain and confronts their leader Frankie Darro, who repeatedly shoves the younger boy's head under water. Darro cannot break the boy's spirit and gradually comes to respect his pluck. Breakston catches pneumonia and is forced to remain in bed but, when he learns that Butler's gang is taking on the Red Shirts, he sneaks off to join the battle. The excitement is too much for him and he dies fighting for his cause. Butler, realizing the true meaning of strength and courage, tearfully watches as Breakston's mother carries away the limp body of her son.

Breakston is all heart and innocent emotion, the epitome of admiring, loyal youth. Butler, whose career was tragically cut short by his death in World War II, is equally fine. His portrayal of the handsome, serious-minded idol is believable and moving. This film also serves as an allegory of the futility of war and what it does to the best of men. The film is based on an autobiographical novel by noted Hungarian playwright Ferenc Molnar. Sensitive adaptation and direction bring out the honesty and spirit of the book.

NO TIME FOR SERGEANTS

1958 111m bw Comedy   ★★★½
Warner Bros. (U.S.)   /U

Andy Griffith *(Will Stockdale)*, Myron McCormick *(Sgt. King)*, Nick Adams *(Ben Whitledge)*, Murray Hamilton *(Irvin Blanchard)*, Howard Smith *(Gen. Bush)*, Will Hutchins *(Lt. Bridges)*, Sydney Smith *(Gen. Pollard)*, James Millhollin *(Psychiatrist)*, Don Knotts *(Manual Dexterity Corporal)*, Jean Willes *(WAF Captain)*

p, Mervyn LeRoy; d, Mervyn LeRoy; w, John Lee Mahin (based on the play by Ira Levin from the novel by Mac Hyman); ph, Harold Rosson; ed, William Ziegler; m, Ray Heindorf; art d, Malcolm Brown; fx, Louis Lichtenfield

Mac Hyman's hilarious novel, which then became a TV special, which then became a Broadway smash (script by Ira Levin), now comes to the screen with all of the fun intact. Andy Griffith played the role on TV and the stage and gets his chance to show how humorous he is in this, his second film, after a sensational debut in A FACE IN THE CROWD. He's a Georgia backwoods boy who is inducted into the peacetime Air Force when his country sends him "Greetings." His sergeant is McCormick (also repeating his Broadway role), a man who thinks that being in the service is a fine way to spend one's life, as long as nobody creates a ruckus. But that's exactly what Griffith does, as his warm naivete and questioning ways throw a monkey wrench into the sedate peacetime service. It's an episodic farce with one bright scene after another and some terrific acting by everyone. Griffith is sent to psychiatrist Millhollin and totally confounds the doctor. After he and Adams fall out of a plane and are posted as "missing, presumed dead," they turn up at their own funeral in a scene reminiscent of Mark Twain's *Tom Sawyer*.

The film is clearly the inspiration for TV's much cruder "Gomer Pyle." Note Don Knotts and veteran Benny Baker in small roles, as well as a man who went on to star in TV's M*A*S*H after he changed his name from Jameel Farah to Jamie Farr.

NO WAY OUT

1987 114m c Crime/Thriller ★★★
Neufeld, Ziskin, Garland (U.S.) R/15

Kevin Costner (*Lt. Cmdr. Tom Farrell*), Gene Hackman (*David Brice*), Sean Young (*Susan Atwell*), Will Patton (*Scott Pritchard*), Howard Duff (*Sen. Willy Duvall*), George Dzundza (*Dr. Sam Hesselman*), Jason Bernard (*Maj. Donovan*), Iman (*Nina Beka*), Fred Dalton Thompson (*Marshall*), Leon Russom (*Kevin O'Brien*)

p, Laura Ziskin, Robert Garland; d, Roger Donaldson; w, Robert Garland (based on the novel *The Big Clock* by Kenneth Fearing); ph, John Alcott; ed, Neil Travis; m, Maurice Jarre; prod d, J. Dennis Washington, Kai Hawkins; art d, Anthony Brockliss; fx, Jack Monroe, Terry Frazee, Ken Durey

Kevin Costner displays some charisma, for once, in a twisty, stylish espionage thriller. Tom Farrell (Costner) is a Naval officer working in the Pentagon who discovers that his lover, Susan (Young), is also the mistress of his boss, Secretary of Defense Brice (Hackman). When Brice arrives unexpectedly at Susan's lavish duplex, Tom sneaks out a side door, and although Brice sees Tom in the dark street outside, he cannot identify him. Brice then explodes with jealousy, and he and Susan get into a fierce argument that leads to Susan's accidental fall over a railing to her death. A shaken Brice returns to his offices in the Pentagon and there seeks the help of another aide, the ruthlessly ambitious Scott Prichard (Patton), who goes to Susan's duplex, wipes away fingerprints, and removes all traces of his boss. Next, to throw off investigators, he introduces a theory that the killer is a KGB mole long rumored to be operating in the Pentagon. Ironically, Tom, who knows that Brice is the real culprit, is then put in charge of ferreting out the fictitious enemy agent. A worthy remake of the film noir classic THE BIG CLOCK, NO WAY OUT adds, among other things, a delightfully subversive twist ending. Good performances from a strong cast.

NOBODY'S FOOL

1994 112m c Drama ★★★½
Skillet Pictures/Scott Rudin Productions/Cinehaus (U.S.) R/15

Paul Newman (*Donald "Sully" Sullivan*), Jessica Tandy (*Miss Beryl*), Bruce Willis (*Carl Roebuck*), Melanie Griffith (*Toby Roebuck*), Dylan Walsh (*Peter*), Pruitt Taylor Vince (*Rub Squeers*), Gene Saks (*Wirf*), Josef Sommer (*Clive Peoples, Jr.*), Philip Seymour Hoffman (*Officer Raymer*), Philip Bosco (*Judge Flatt*)

p, Scott Rudin, Arlene Donovan; d, Robert Benton; w, Robert Benton (based on the novel by Richard Russo); ph, John Bailey; ed, John Bloom; m, Howard Shore; prod d, David Gropman; art d, Dan Davis; fx, Tom Ryba; cos, Joseph G. Aulisi

AAN Best Actor: Paul Newman; *AAN Best Adapted Screenplay:* Robert Benton

This thoughtful character study of an aging misfit is such a welcome rarity in 1990s Hollywood that it was perhaps overpraised on release; still, Paul Newman's Oscar-nominated performance and Robert Benton's solid, unobtrusive direction combine to create a resonant if unsurprising meditation on growing old in America.

Sixty years old, unemployed, and alone, Donald "Sully" Sullivan (Newman) has spent the better part of his life shirking responsibility in weather-beaten North Bath, New York. Having walked out on his family years before, Sully leads a dead-end existence, drinking, playing cards with his buddy Rub (Pruitt Taylor Vince), and renting a room in the house of his old schoolteacher, Miss Beryl (Jessica Tandy). Sully supports himself by doing periodic construction work for hard-headed Carl Roebuck (Bruce Willis), while pursuing a fruitless lawsuit against his boss for a partially disabling knee injury. Sully seems comfortable with his long, downward spiral, but when his estranged son Peter (Dylan Walsh) and his family come to town for Thanksgiving, he's forced to confront issues that he's long repressed.

Newman's performance is more than the stock collection of curmudgeonly tics that we've come to expect from major stars playing older men; he manages to suggest a great deal more about Sully's past foibles and present-day class resentments than is contained in Robert Benton's episodic script, based on the novel by Richard Russo. Willis and Griffith are both surprisingly good, and John Bailey's camera turns a ramshackle neighborhood of Poughkeepsie (standing in for the fictional town) into something close to a character in itself. NOBODY'S FOOL is to be commended just for acknowledging the existence of old age in the context of youth-obsessed pop culture; more importantly, the film is refreshingly frank about the everyday struggles of many senior citizens in an era of fractured families and a disappearing social safety net.

NONE BUT THE LONELY HEART

1944 113m bw Drama ★★★★
RKO (U.S.) /A

Cary Grant (*Ernie Mott*), Ethel Barrymore (*Ma Mott*), Barry Fitzgerald (*Twite*), June Duprez (*Ada*), Jane Wyatt (*Aggie Hunter*), George Coulouris (*Jim Mordiney*), Dan Duryea (*Lew Tate*), Konstantin Shayne (*Ike Weber*), Eva Leonard Boyne (*Ma Chalmers*), Morton Lowry (*Taz*)

p, David Hempstead; d, Clifford Odets; w, Clifford Odets (based on the novel by Richard Llewellyn); ph, George Barnes; ed, Roland Gross; m, Hanns Eisler; prod d, Mordecai Gorelik; art d, Albert S. D'Agostino, Jack Okey; fx, Vernon L. Walker; cos, Renie

AAN Best Actor: Cary Grant; *AA Best Supporting Actress:* Ethel Barrymore; *AAN Best Editing:* Roland Gross; *AAN Best Score:* C. Bakaleinikoff, Hanns Eisler

This was a daring and inventive film in its day, and Grant, playing the dedicated outsider, and Barrymore, as his cockney mother, are superb. The time is just prior to WWII and the place is Whitechapel in the East End of London. Through these mean streets wanders Grant, a shiftless but lighthearted young man whose mother, Barrymore, runs a dingy second-hand furniture store. Grant and his mother exchange barbs whenever they meet; however, Grant is seldom home to occupy his room above the store. Instead, he vagabonds his way through the area, cadging cigarettes and food from friendly shopkeepers who have known him since boyhood. Particularly concerned about Grant and protective of his mother is the local pawnbroker, Shayne, who dispenses wisdom and wit, as does family friend Fitzgerald, a drifter. Though cellist Wyatt is in love with Grant, he forsakes her for sultry Duprez, the divorced wife of British underworld leader Coulouris. The gangster persuades Grant to join his band of thieves, knowing that Grant will spend his ill-gotten gain on the high-living Duprez.

Odets's powerful script and direction do well by the Llewellyn novel, and the film is uncompromising in its portrayal of slum life. NONE BUT THE LONELY HEART was not a box-office winner, but has remained a critical favorite, boosted by a dedicated cast. To get Barrymore into the film during its hurried production schedule, RKO paid the expenses of closing the long-running play "The Corn Is Green," in which the actress was starring.

NORMA RAE

1979 110m c Drama ★★★★
Fox (U.S.) PG

Sally Field (*Norma Rae*), Beau Bridges (*Sonny*), Ron Leibman (*Reuben*), Pat Hingle (*Vernon*), Barbara Baxley (*Leona*), Gail Strickland (*Bonnie Mae*), Morgan Paull (*Wayne Billings*), Robert Broyles (*Sam Bolen*), John Calvin (*Ellis Harper*), Booth Colman (*Dr. Watson*)

p, Tamara Asseyev, Alexandra Rose; d, Martin Ritt; w, Irving Ravetch, Harriet Frank Jr.; ph, John A. Alonzo; ed, Sidney Levin; m, David Shire; prod d, Walter Scott Herndon; art d, Tracy Bousman

AAN Best Picture; AA Best Actress: Sally Field; *AAN Best Adapted Screenplay:* Irving Ravetch, Harriet Frank, Jr.; *AA Best Song:* David Shire (Music), Norman Gimbel (Lyrics)

Sally Field won her first Oscar for her performance in the title role, a complex portrayal of an working-class southern woman who matures into a complete person when she is faced with labor woes and must grow up or fall by the wayside. Field is one of many overworked and underpaid workers at a cotton mill where management doesn't seem to realize that the days of slavery are over. Her father, Hingle, dies for lack of proper medical attention, while her mother, Baxley, is rapidly going deaf from the incessant din of the factory's equipment. The place is functioning without a union, and when New York labor organizer Leibman arrives to establish one, the workers fear for their jobs. When Field and Leibman first meet, his aggressive personality irritates her, while her lack of ambition does the same to him; but as the film progresses, so does their mutual respect. A divorced woman with two children (one of whom is illegitimate), Field marries Bridges, who becomes jealous of her relationship with Leibman once she decides to to join the union organizer in his efforts to unite the workers. Field begins undermining management from within and eventually manages to rally the workers into a strike. Production at the mill ceases, and management must capitulate in order to keep production rolling.

The simple story is enlivened by an intelligent, compassionate screenplay, whose sole deficiency is that it makes no attempt to represent the management point of view. Field's performance is flawless. Audiences thronged to see NORMA RAE, which made more money than just about any other union movie with the possible exception of ON THE WATERFRONT. (NORMA RAE grossed well over $10 million on initial release.) The film's technical excellence is at least partly due to director Ritt's using the same crew he used on many of his films about the south; Alonzo, Levin, and Herndon have a history of working well with each other and with Ritt.

NORTH BY NORTHWEST

1959   136m   c   Spy   ★★★★
MGM   (U.S.)   /PG

Cary Grant (Roger O. Thornhill), Eva Marie Saint (Eve Kendall), James Mason (Phillip Vandamm), Jessie Royce Landis (Clara Thornhill), Leo G. Carroll (Professor), Philip Ober (Lester Townsend), Josephine Hutchinson (Handsome Woman), Martin Landau (Leonard), Adam Williams (Valerian), Edward Platt (Victor Larrabee)

p, Alfred Hitchcock; d, Alfred Hitchcock; w, Ernest Lehman; ph, Robert Burks; ed, George Tomasini; m, Bernard Herrmann; prod d, Robert Boyle; art d, William A. Horning, Merrill Pye; fx, A. Arnold Gillespie, Lee LeBlanc

AAN Best Original Screenplay: Ernest Lehman; AAN Best Editing: George Tomasini; AAN Best Art Direction: William A. Horning, Robert Boyle, Merrill Pye, Henry Grace, Frank McKelvy

One of Hitchcock's most famous films, NORTH BY NORTHWEST has everything—thrills, suspense, mystery, and black humor, as well as dark undertones of sexual exploitation and covert political machination. Roger Thornhill (Grant, in perennially spectacular form) is a successful advertising executive in New York City who is lunching with mother (Landis, the exact same age as Grant) at Plaza Hotel's Oak Room when he answers the wrong page, one for a George Kaplan, and is mistaken for Kaplan. It becomes an identity which Thornhill cannot shake and one that drags him across the country in the face of death with the pretty Eve Kendall (a rather wooden Saint) at his side. The great suspense director was at his most entertaining, creating a helter skelter action film where the hero is propelled from one breathless situation to the next. It is filled with classic scenes—the two most memorable being the crop-dusting sequence in which Thornhill is terrorized by an aerial menace, and the chase across the face of Mt. Rushmore. The title of the film paraphrases Hamlet: I am but mad north-northwest; when the wind is southerly I know a hawk from a handsaw," an implication that neither Thornhill, Hitchcock, nor Hamlet is mad. Although NORTH BY NORTHWEST is available on videotape, no small screen viewing can match the Technicolor, VistaVision experience of seeing this one in the theater. With James Mason, a study in velvet villany, but looking dowdy for once, next to Grant, and Landau as a chillingly effeminate gunsel.

NORTH DALLAS FORTY

1979   119m   c   Sports   ★★★½
Paramount   (U.S.)   R/18

Nick Nolte (Phillip Elliott), Mac Davis (Maxwell), Charles Durning (Coach Johnson), Dayle Haddon (Charlotte), Bo Svenson (Jo Bob Priddy), Steve Forrest (Conrad Hunter), G.D. Spradlin (B.A. Strothers), Dabney Coleman (Emmett), Savannah Smith (Joanne), Marshall Colt (Art Hartman)

p, Frank Yablans; d, Ted Kotcheff; w, Frank Yablans, Ted Kotcheff, Peter Gent (based on the novel by Gent); ph, Paul Lohmann; ed, Jay Kamen; m, John Scott; prod d, Alfred Sweeney; cos, Dorothy Jeakins

Pro football fans may be disillusioned by this excellent, honest, and often brutal expose of the play-for-pay game. Phillip Elliott (Nick Nolte) is a veteran pass-catcher for the North Dallas Bulls, who bear a strong resemblance to the Dallas Cowboys—not surprising given that the film is based on a novel by former Cowboy wide receiver Pete Gent. The coaches (G.D. Spradlin and Charles Durning) and team owner (Steve Forrest) feel the fiercely independent Elliott has an attitude problem because of his blatant cynicism and his awareness of how he and his teammates are constantly being manipulated by management. Cast aside after being callously used to motivate a fellow player, the receiver comes to realize there is more to life than football, but that he loves the game just the same. Country singer Mac Davis, making his film debut, is quite good as the quarterback who is Elliott's best friend and knows how to play the game both on and off the field and Bo Svenson is effective as a big, dumb defensive lineman. The National Football League refused to help with the production of this film in any way, so the action is kept to a minimum (though what is shown is brutal), but the locker room atmosphere and the off-the-field drama smack of authenticity in NORTH DALLAS FORTY, as telling a depiction of pro football as any to be found. Note the presence of one-time Oakland Raider behemoth John Matuszak, who went on to appear in films such as CAVEMAN and THE GOONIES before his death in 1989.

NORTHWEST PASSAGE

1940   125m   c   Adventure   ★★★★★
MGM   (U.S.)   /A

Spencer Tracy (Maj. Robert Rogers), Robert Young (Langdon Towne), Walter Brennan (Hunk Marriner), Ruth Hussey (Elizabeth Browne), Nat Pendleton (Capt. Huff), Louis Hector (Rev. Browne), Robert Barrat (Humphrey Towne), Lumsden Hare (Gen. Amherst), Donald MacBride (Sgt. McNott), Isabel Jewell (Jennie Coit)

p, Hunt Stromberg; d, King Vidor, Jack Conway; w, Laurence Stallings, Talbot Jennings (based on the novel by Kenneth Roberts); ph, Sidney Wagner, William V. Skall; ed, Conrad A. Nervig; m, Herbert Stothart; art d, Cedric Gibbons, Malcolm Brown

AAN Best Cinematography: Sidney Wagner, William V. Skall

One of the greatest adventure films of all time, this Vidor classic owes much of its success to the rugged Tracy, who plays celebrated Indian fighter Robert Rogers, leader of Rogers' Rangers. Tracy is earthy and eloquent as the frontier leader who knows no fear in a wilderness rife with terror and bloodshed. Set in 1759, the film opens with talented artist Young arriving home in Portsmouth, New Hampshire, to sheepishly explain to his family that he has been expelled from Harvard because of the snide political comments he has inserted into his cartoons. Naturally, his criticism is aimed at the British, which alienates fiancee Hussey's Tory family. Young and his roughneck sidekick, Brennan, get drunk in a pub one night and tell off Hussey's stuffed-shirt father, Hector. As a result, Young's arrest is ordered, but he and Brennan escape into the wilderness, later stopping at a wayside inn, where they meet Tracy. After a night of hard drinking, Young and Brennan wake up outside the military post at Crown Point, headquarters of Tracy's rangers. Tracy entices Young to join the Rangers as a mapmaker, and Brennan tags along. Soon Young and Brennan are boating along with hundreds of other leather-clad veterans of many an Indian war. Their goal is St. Francis, the headquarters of the vicious, French-backed Abenaki tribe, which has conducted bloody raids into colonial territory under British control.

NOSFERATU, THE VAMPIRE

Based on Kenneth Roberts's well-researched novel about Rogers's exploits, NORTHWEST PASSAGE is a rousing adventure all the way, full of thundering action. Its depiction of the colonial era is amazingly convincing, thanks to the perfectionist techniques of director Vidor, who went at the $2 million production with the vigor and relentless energy of Robert Rogers himself. In fact, Vidor, who began working on the film with an incomplete script (new portions of which were flown daily to the production's Idaho location), believed that he was shooting a prologue for a film that would also include Rogers's search for the Northwest Passage. However, producer Hunt Stromberg and MGM decided to confine the film to Rogers's adventures during the Indian Wars, bringing Jack Conway in to shoot an ending to the film while Vidor was in New York. To make his "prologue," Vidor took his almost all-male cast into the wilds of Idaho, around Lake Payette, which resembled the New England terrain of 200 years earlier.

In his first Technicolor film, Vidor made good use of the lush locations; Wagner and Skall's cinematography is absolutely breathtaking, capturing the rich blues of the lakes and the deep greens of the forests (although they had some trouble with the colors of the ranger costumes, until special dyes were ordered to tone down the kelly green hues). The film is marred only by its racism, pretty virulent even by Hollywood standards.

NOSFERATU, THE VAMPIRE
(NOSFERATU, PHANTOM DER NACHT)

1979 107m c Horror   ★★★
Fox   (France/West Germany)   PG/15

Klaus Kinski (Count Dracula), Isabelle Adjani (Lucy Harker), Bruno Ganz (Jonathan Harker), Roland Topor (Renfield), Walter Ladengast (Dr. Van Helsing), Dan Van Husen (Warden), Jan Groth (Harbormaster), Carsten Bodinus (Schrader), Martje Grohmann (Mina), Rijk de Gooyer (Town Official)

p, Werner Herzog; d, Werner Herzog; w, Werner Herzog (based on the novel Dracula by Bram Stoker and the film script NOSFERATU by Henrik Galeen); ph, Jorg Schmidt-Reitwein; ed, Beate Mainka-Jellinghaus; m, Popol Vuh, Florian Fricke, Richard Wagner, Charles Gounod; prod d, Henning von Gierke, Ulrich Bergfelder; art d, Henning von Gierke; fx, Cornelius Siegel; cos, Gloria Storch

After capturing the attention of American critics and public with ambitious, unique, and powerful films, German director Werner Herzog remade what he considers to be the most visionary and important of all German films, F.W. Murnau's 1922 silent masterpiece, NOSFERATU. Held together by the sheer power of Klaus Kinski's performance as the vampire, NOSFERATU, THE VAMPIRE evokes several scenes (practically shot-for-shot) from the Murnau classic while slightly altering some of the original's thematic structures. In Murnau's film, the vampire is pure evil invading a small German community (Herzog feels that the 1922 film adumbrated the rise of Nazism in Germany). Herzog's vampire is much more sympathetic. An outcast from society (as are all of Herzog's protagonists), Kinski's Nosferatu longs for contact, acceptance, and even love from the humans who fear and revile him. Sadly, his curse and death's-head appearance forever prevent this. The vampire's undead state and need for blood seem to be presented as a horrible, irreversible *disease*, rather than an inherently evil harbinger of hell. While this isn't exactly an innovation in the development of the horror film (Tod Browning's DRACULA, 1931, starring Bela Lugosi, had moments of pathos, as does George Romero's MARTIN), Herzog and Kinski succeed here because they convey a sense of pity for a creature so visually repulsive it's hard to look at him.

As with most of Herzog's films, the story behind the production is almost more interesting than the film itself. Unable to shoot in Bremen, as Murnau did in 1922, Herzog prepared to settle for the Dutch town of Delft. Still bitter over their occupation by the Nazis during WWII, the citizens of Delft were less than enthusiastic about this small army of German filmmakers invading their town. When Herzog announced his plan to release 11,000 rats into the streets of Delft for the scene in which Nosferatu arrives (the director wanted grey rats but could only obtain white ones, which his crew painted grey), the Delft *burgermeister* categorically refused and told the apparently insane German that his town had just spent months clearing the canals of their own home-grown rats and had no intention of reinfesting the area with laboratory

rats from Hungary. Nonplussed, Herzog moved his rats to a more accommodating city, Schiedam, where he was allowed to shoot, albeit on a smaller scale.

NOSTALGHIA

1983 120m c/bw Drama   ★★★★
Sovin/RAI-TV/Opera   (U.S.S.R./Italy)   /15

Oleg Yankovsky (Andre Gortchakov), Domiziana Giordano (Eugenia), Erland Josephson (Domenico), Patrizia Terreno (Gortchakov's Wife), Delia Boccardo (Domenico's Wife), Laura De Marchi (Chambermaid), Milena Vukotic (Civil Servant), Alberto Canepa (Farmer)

d, Andrei Tarkovsky; w, Andrei Tarkovsky, Tonino Guerra; ph, Giuseppe Lanci; ed, Amedeo Salfa, Erminia Marani; m, Ludwig van Beethoven, Giuseppe Verdi; prod d, Andrea Grisanti; fx, Paolo Ricci; cos, Lina Nerli Taviani

A meditative film by visionary Soviet filmmaker Tarkovsky that lures viewers into its mysterious, mystical world and completely envelops them for a two-hour stretch. Yankovsky is a Soviet architecture professor who travels to northern Italy's Tuscan Hills to research an exiled 18th-century Russian composer who committed suicide there. Away from his homeland, Yankovsky becomes nostalgic suffering with his unfulfilled desire to return to a home that is out of reach. The melancholy Yankovsky becomes involved with Giordano, his volatile, strong-minded interpreter. Their relationshop, however, is never consummated and gradually deteriorates. Their romance is strained even further by Yankovsky's growing friendship with Josephson, a batty Italian professor who years ago locked his family inside their house and awaited Armageddon—for seven years. Josephson proves too much for Giordano, who makes plans to return to her lover in Rome. Yankovsky finds Josephson living among the rain-soaked ruins of a 16th-century spa. In this ancient crumbling structure is a large, placid mineral bath that Josephson unsuccessfully tries to wade across (its waters are chest-high) while holding a lit candle. His crazy belief is that to save mankind he must cross the bath without letting the candle flame extinguish. Having once again failed, Josephson makes a public proclamation. He climbs atop Michelangelo's statue of Marcus Aurelius in Rome, plays Beethoven's "Ode to Joy" on a portable turntable, and shouts prophetic doomsday messages to those who'll listen. At the same time, Yankovsky has taken up Josephson's plight to cross the bath. His first two attempts fail, each time the candle flame flickering out in the swirling drafts of hot air. Back atop the statue, Josephson soaks himself with kerosene and sets himself ablaze. As he burns to death, Yankovsky completes a successful trip across the waters. The candle burns, but Yankovsky's energy is extinguished. Struggling at the water's edge to stay alive, Yankovsky envisions his homeland as the snow covers its grassy hills.

The final sequence of NOSTALGHIA is one of the most captivating ever put on film. The viewer becomes completely swept away by Tarkovsky's world where the elements reign supreme—fire and water are everywhere. The atmosphere Tarkovsky creates is one of constantly dripping water, unsettling mists, and dew seeping through the eternally damp walls. Coupled with these memorable visuals is a remarkable highlighting of sounds (a job admirably performed by Remo Ugolinelli) such as the echoing drip of water or the swirling of the drafts. NOSTALGHIA is not a film for everyone—if it is fast-paced action you desire, then you will quickly be snoring. Instead of excitement, the feeling one gets after seeing NOSTALGHIA is one of utter relaxation that makes us long for the world we left behind in the theater.

NOTHING BUT A MAN

1964 95m bw Drama   ★★★
Du Art   (U.S.)   /A

Ivan Dixon (Duff Anderson), Abbey Lincoln (Josie Dawson), Gloria Foster (Lee), Julius Harris (Will Anderson), Martin Priest (Driver), Leonard Parker (Frankie), Yaphet Kotto (Jocko), Stanley Greene (Rev. Dawson), Helen Lounck (Effie Simms), Helene Arrindell (Doris)

p, Robert Young, Michael Roemer, Robert Rubin; d, Michael Roemer; w, Michael Roemer, Robert Malcolm Young; ph, Robert Young; ed, Luke Bennett; prod d, William Rhodes; cos, Nancy Ruffing

A well-intentioned, independently made film describing the life of a black man in the 1960s South. Basically, all the title character (Dixon) wants to do is live simply. While working for the railroad in Alabama, he falls in love with Lincoln, the daughter of the minister (Greene). Greene does not like Dixon, so the couple goes to Birmingham to see Dixon's father, a dying alcoholic. Dixon also visits his illegitimate son, who has been abandoned by his mother and left in the care of a woman not related to him. Lincoln wants to marry, but Dixon does not want to assume the responsibility. The couple finally weds, and Dixon gets a job at the town sawmill. When he won't ingratiate himself to his racist white employers, he is fired and labeled a troublemaker. He then finds work at a gas station but is still harassed by the townspeople. After beating and berating his wife, out of frustration, he returns to Birmingham to watch his father die. Facing the situation is a step toward manhood, and he begins to come to terms with his responsibilities. He gets his son and goes back to Lincoln to try to live in peace and dignity. The film garnered a great deal of praise, at the time of its release, for its realistic recounting of the life of a black laborer in the South and for refusing to sentimentalize the subject matter.

NOTHING SACRED

1937   75m   c   Comedy   ★★★★★
Selznick   (U.S.)   /A

Carole Lombard *(Hazel Flagg)*, Fredric March *(Wally Cook)*, Charles Winninger *(Dr. Enoch Downer)*, Walter Connolly *(Oliver Stone)*, Sig Rumann *(Dr. Emile Egglehoffer)*, Frank Fay *(MC)*, Maxie Rosenbloom *(Max Levinsky)*, Margaret Hamilton *(Drug Store Lady)*, Troy Brown *(Ernest Walker)*, Olin Howlin *(Baggage Man)*

p, David O. Selznick; d, William A. Wellman; w, Ben Hecht, Ring Lardner Jr., Budd Schulberg (based on the story "Letter to the Editor" by James H. Street); ph, W. Howard Greene; ed, Hal C. Kern, James E. Newcom; m, Oscar Levant; art d, Lyle Wheeler; fx, Jack Cosgrove; cos, Travis Banton, Walter Plunkett

A marvelous black comedy full of wit and journalistic wisdom in the grand and capricious style of Hecht (who co-authored, with Charles MacArthur, THE FRONT PAGE), this film is all the more stunning thanks to the outrageous and hilarious performance of super comedienne Lombard. This was one of the first of the screwball comedies, a classic of the genre which is just as funny today as when it was first filmed.

March is an ambitious newsman who gets into big trouble when he tries to pass off a black New Yorker as the "Sultan of Marzipan," a potentate who is about to donate $500,000 to establish an art institute (the man is actually penniless and doesn't know Marzipan from Manhattan). When Connolly, the editor of March's sensation-seeking tabloid, finds out about the impersonation, he becomes livid and demotes March to writing obituaries. Meanwhile, Lombard, a working girl in Warsaw, Vermont, who longs to visit New York City, is routinely examined by her less than competent doctor, Winninger; the bumbling doctor sadly tells Lombard that she has radium poisoning and has not much longer to live. News of this tragedy reaches March and he sets out to write a great sob story, but by the time he reaches Lombard, Winninger has changed his diagnosis: Lombard is as healthy as can be. March won't hear of it; he has a great story and refuses to allow the truth to ruin his fabulous tale. He persuades Lombard to go through with the charade, promising that she will not only see New York but will enter the great city in style. She agrees, and by the time March begins grinding out the tragedy in daily installments in his paper, New York is weeping loudly.

Hecht had a great deal of fun writing NOTHING SACRED for the screen, plucking the background from his own newspaper experiences. The fake sultan, for instance, was based upon a prank Hecht himself had concocted, one in which his eccentric poet friend Maxwell Bodenheim, then unknown, pretended to be a foreign potentate visiting Chicago where Hecht was working as a spectacular journalist. Lombard is wonderfully funny here, playing a role that was made for her madcap talent, and March, recognized as a great dramatic player, showed a considerable flair for comedy.

NOTORIOUS

1946   101m   bw   Thriller/Spy   ★★★★★
RKO   (U.S.)   /U

Cary Grant *(Devlin)*, Ingrid Bergman *(Alicia Huberman)*, Claude Rains *(Alexander Sebastian)*, Louis Calhern *(Paul Prescott)*, Mme. Konstantin *(Mme. Sebastian)*, Reinhold Schunzel *(Dr. Anderson)*, Moroni Olsen *(Walter Beardsley)*, Ivan Triesault *(Eric Mathis)*, Alexis Minotis *(Joseph)*, Wally Brown *(Mr. Hopkins)*

p, Alfred Hitchcock; d, Alfred Hitchcock; w, Ben Hecht; ph, Ted Tetzlaff; ed, Theron Warth; m, Roy Webb; art d, Albert S. D'Agostino, Carroll Clark; fx, Vernon L. Walker, Paul Eagler; cos, Edith Head

AAN Best Supporting Actor: Claude Rains; *AAN Best Original Screenplay:* Ben Hecht

This brilliant Hitchcock offering combines romance, suspense, and international intrigue with unforgettable performances from Grant and Bergman. The thriller trappings are merely trim: what's really at hand is a twisted love affair between Grant and Bergman that hints at sadomasochism. He's untrusting, passive, and unsympathetic; she's shady, agressive, and alcoholic. It's a dangerous chocolate box of poisoned candy, Hitchcock's ode to the dementia of passion. Dig in.

Alicia Huberman (Bergman), the daughter of a convicted Nazi spy, has an international jet set reputation as a playgirl, causing American agent Devlin (Grant) to fall in love with her. Devlin, in an effort to uncover a Nazi plot, enlists Alicia's aid in Rio de Janeiro. They contact Nazi agent Alexander Sebastian (Rains), whom Alicia must eventually marry. Meanwhile, Devlin and she must discover how the Sebastian plot is being engineered.

With the blistering onscreen romance between Grant and Bergman—two of the most popular stars in Hollywood—and the creation of one of Hitchcock's greatest "MacGuffins"—the secret uranium shipments—NOTORIOUS emerges as one of Hitchcock's most masterful and sophisticated efforts. The passionate kissing scene in which the lovers devour one another instead of their chicken dinner still retains all of its power. Ingrid Bergman was certainly never sexier: here's the woman who scandalized America with her torrid, extramarital affair. Next to the protagonists, Rains's expert villany is mama's boyism gone awry. And no wonder. With Mme. Leopoldine Konstantin chomping cigars, Hitch really flails away at motherhood. The camera swoons right along with us in a dizzying manner. Best shot: the key. You can't miss it.

NOW, VOYAGER

1942   117m   bw   Drama   ★★★★
Warner Bros.   (U.S.)   /PG

Bette Davis *(Charlotte Vale)*, Paul Henreid *(Jerry D. Durrance)*, Claude Rains *(Dr. Jaquith)*, Gladys Cooper *(Mrs. Henry Windle Vale)*, Bonita Granville *(June Vale)*, John Loder *(Elliott Livingston)*, Ilka Chase *(Lisa Vale)*, Lee Patrick *("Deb" McIntyre)*, James Rennie *(Frank McIntyre)*, Charles Drake *(Leslie Trotter)*

p, Hal B. Wallis; d, Irving Rapper; w, Casey Robinson (based on the novel by Olive Higgins Prouty); ph, Sol Polito; ed, Warren Low; m, Max Steiner; art d, Robert Haas; fx, Willard Van Enger; cos, Orry-Kelly

AAN Best Actress: Bette Davis; *AAN Best Supporting Actress:* Gladys Cooper; *AA Best Score:* Max Steiner

Now, Bette: A glittering, slushy take on the ugly duckling transformation. It's Olive Higgins Prouty, at it again (she also penned *Stella Dallas*, the durable soap opera from which three films, including the Barbara Stanwyck classic, were made), with a title lifted from Walt Whitman's *Leaves of Grass*, a conceit enough to raise a dead poet. Irving Rapper directs as if he wants to stay out of the way of Davis and Cooper—perfectly understandable.

As usual, Davis has to overplay her hand at Jekyll/Hyde transformation. Beforehand, she's got unplucked eyebrows like last spring's dead caterpillars, hair like a mudpuddle with a net over it, and glasses and shoes borrowed from the first continental congress. It sets a satisfyingly camp feeling of self-sacrifice over the entire proceedings. Later she *is* artfully styled; you have the feeling Davis is shedding her own New England repression, which is exactly what she means for you to feel.

Davis plays the dowdy, frustrated daughter of Cooper, with whom she lives in their oppressive Boston mansion. Davis is close to a nervous breakdown because she can't get any love from Cooper, who also forces her to dress "sensibly." Chase, Davis's sister-in-law, worries about Davis's mental condition and enlists the services of famed psychiatrist Rains, who sees that Davis is near collapse and recommends that she leave her lonely home and take refuge at his sanitarium. There, Davis begins a regimen that begins to restore her mental and physical health; she drops pounds and gains confidence daily, transforming into a self-assured swan within three months (a feat none of us can seem to master so quickly). At Rains's suggestion, Davis boards a liner for South America. On the cruise, she meets Henreid, whose wife pretends to be in bad health to keep her unhappy husband from ending their marriage. On a stopover in Rio, Davis and Henreid enjoy a wonderful day and night together, then wake up to discover that their ship has already left the port. They stay in Rio for a few days and Davis experiences passionate love for the first time in her life, although she understands from the start that Henreid will never leave his wife.

Though VOYAGER is best remembered for the scene in which Henreid lights two cigarettes simultaneously and then hands one to Davis, this pleasurable, popular tearjerker is Davis's show all the way. She claimed to have worked extensively on the screenplay, deleting some of Casey Robinson's hard work in favor of Prouty's original words. Cooper is an excellent choice for the matriarchal dowager; Davis always stood in awe (or angry envy) of stage actors, and their scenes have a weight the rest of the picture lacks. Henreid and Rains, both great friends of Davis's (and supposedly Rains was a lover) contribute smooth work. The marvelous Ilka Chase is wasted here, and Bonita Granville is grating. The Polito camerawork finally settles down to Davis-devotion and Steiner's Oscar-winning score clings to her like flypaper. It's Grade-A schlock, but not without depth: critics have detected feminist overtones in this movie, one in which men prove eminently dispensable in the quest for happiness.

NUMBER TWO
(NUMERO DEUX)
1975 88m c Drama ★★★★
Sonimage/Bela (France) /X

Sandrine Battistella *(Wife)*, Pierre Dudry *(Husband)*, Alexandre Rignault *(Grandpa)*, Rachel Stefanopoli *(Grandma)*

d, Jean-Luc Godard; w, Jean-Luc Godard

Announced by Godard as a remake of BREATHLESS (a ploy to get financing), this video project has almost nothing to do with his 1959 masterpiece. Battistella and Dudry are a dissatisfied couple who suffer from physical ailments. Battistella is stricken with chronic constipation, and her husband is unable to perform sexually. They teach their children about sex by showing them, and the grandparents, naked, speak directly to the camera. As Richard Roud writes, "although NUMERO DEUX is a frustrating film about frustration, a constipated film about constipation, it is not entirely without a sense of hope." Shot on videotape (and later transferred to film), the majority of the picture uses only a portion of the screen, usually the upper-left and the lower-right portions. The finish, however, relieves the tension this creates by opening up the entire screen. To further his interests in video, Godard built a studio in Grenoble where his tape experiments for French television continued until 1980 with the release of EVERY MAN FOR HIMSELF, marking his much-awaited return to commercial filmmaking and international distribution. An audacious film.

NUN'S STORY, THE
1959 149m c Religious/Biography ★★★★
Warner Bros. (U.S.) /U

Audrey Hepburn *(Sister Luke/Gabrielle Van Der Mal)*, Peter Finch *(Dr. Fortunati)*, Edith Evans *(Mother Emmanuel Superior General)*, Peggy Ashcroft *(Mother Mathilde)*, Dean Jagger *(Dr. Van Der Mal)*, Mildred Dunnock *(Sister Margharita)*, Beatrice Straight *(Mother Christophe)*, Patricia Collinge *(Sister William)*, Eva Kotthaus *(Sister Marie)*, Ruth White *(Mother Marcella)*

p, Henry Blanke; d, Fred Zinnemann; w, Robert Anderson (based on the book by Kathryn C. Hulme); ph, Franz Planer; ed, Walter Thompson; m, Franz Waxman; art d, Alexander Trauner; cos, Marjorie Best

AAN Best Picture; AAN Best Actress: Audrey Hepburn; *AAN Best Director:* Fred Zinnemann; *AAN Best Adapted Screenplay:* Robert Anderson; *AAN Best Cinematography:* Franz Planer; *AAN Best Editing:* Walter Thompson; *AAN Best Score:* Franz Waxman; *AAN Best Sound:* George R. Groves

A superbly restrained piece of filmmaking, with Zinnemann directing in simple, unadorned style and Hepburn giving a truly radiant performance. Hepburn is the daughter of Belgian surgeon Jagger, and she has the desire to become a nursing nun in the Congo, which was still overseen by Belgium at the time, several years prior to WWII. After experiencing the rigors of a convent, Hepburn goes off to a school where she learns tropical medicine. Her desire to go to the Congo is sidetracked when she is first assigned to a mental hospital in Belgium, where she is almost killed by a maniacal patient whom she thought she could handle. Eventually, she travels to the Congo, where she is disappointed by her assignment. She'd hoped to do her nursing with natives, but is sent, instead, to a hospital for Europeans where she meets crusty Finch, a dedicated surgeon who has no room in his life for women or religion and devotes himself to medicine. Hepburn understands that she must shed her old ways and plunges into her work. Assigned to escort a Belgian official back to the motherland, she arrives there just as the war is beginning. When Jagger is killed by Nazis as he's helping refugees escape, she realizes that she is incapable of keeping her dispassionate attitude and that she must leave the convent in order to fight against the oppressors.

This was perhaps the only movie from this studio (Warners) in which there was no music over the final titles. No one could decide if Waxman should write an upbeat or a downbeat theme because the choice would imply an editorial decision on the part of the filmmakers, something that Zinnemann zealously and successfully avoided all the way through. Jack Warner fought against that viewpoint, but Zinnemann prevailed, and the end credits are accompanied by silence. Assistant director Piero Mussetta used 70 members of Rome's Royal Opera Ballet to stage a sequence in which nuns are involved in various rituals. That sequence should be viewed by every film student as an exercise in how to handle a large group. It's hard to believe that this rare and moving film did not win one single Oscar of the six for which it was nominated; most went to BEN-HUR, with the others going to Simone Signoret and the screenplay for ROOM AT THE TOP.

NUTTY PROFESSOR, THE
1963 107m c Comedy ★★★½
Paramount (U.S.) /PG

Jerry Lewis *(Prof. Julius Ferris Kelp/Buddy Love)*, Stella Stevens *(Stella Purdy)*, Del Moore *(Dr. Hamius R. Warfield)*, Kathleen Freeman *(Millie Lemmon)*, Med Flory, Skip Ward, Norman Alden *(Football Players)*, Howard Morris *(Father Kelp)*, Elvia Allman *(Mother Kelp)*, Milton Frome *(Dr. Leevee)*

p, Jerry Lewis, Ernest D. Glucksman; d, Jerry Lewis; w, Jerry Lewis, Bill Richmond (based on a story by Lewis); ph, W. Wallace Kelley; ed, John Woodcock; m, Walter Scharf; art d, Hal Pereira, Walter Tyler; fx, Paul K. Lerpae; cos, Edith Head

Jerry Lewis's best film stars the often moronic comic as Julius F. Kelp, a bumbling professor of chemistry at a small college who falls hopelessly in love with one of his more popular students, Stella Purdy (Stella Stevens). Seeking to improve his looks, Kelp whips up a chemical potion and is transformed into an overbearing and obnoxious but dashing singer who calls himself Buddy Love. Though totally conceited, Buddy Love (Lewis in a dual role) succeeds in winning over Stella. Unfortunately, his formula has a way of wearing off at the wrong times. Although only tangentially related to horror films, THE NUTTY PROFESSOR can be seen as a strange companion piece to the *Dr. Jekyll and Mr. Hyde* films, in which the dark, menacing side of an otherwise harmless character seeps through to the forefront. Much has been made of Buddy Love's resemblance to Lewis's former partner, Dean Martin, but the person Love really resembles is the pompous, self-important and bitter Jerry Lewis of talk shows and telethons.

NUTTY PROFESSOR, THE

1996 95m c Comedy ★★½
Imagine Entertainment (U.S.) PG-13/12

Eddie Murphy (Sherman Klump/Buddy Love/Lance Perkins/Papa Klump/Mama Klump/Grandma Klump/Ernie Klump), Jada Pinkett (Carla Purty), James Coburn (Harlan Hartley), Larry Miller (Dean Richmond), Dave Chappelle (Reggie Warrington), John Ales (Jason), Patricia Wilson (Dean's Secretary), Jamal Mixon (Ernie Clump, Jr.), Nichole McAuley (Fit Woman), Hamilton Von Watts (Health Instructor)

p, Brian Grazer, Russell Simmons; d, Tom Shadyac; w, David Sheffield, Barry W. Blaustein, Tom Shadyac, Steve Oedekerk (based on the motion picture written by Jerry Lewis and Bill Richmond); ph, Julio Macat; ed, Don Zimmerman; m, David Newman; prod d, William Elliott; art d, Greg Papalia; fx, Jon Farhat, Burt Dalton; cos, Ha Nguyen

AA Best Makeup: Rick Baker, David Leroy Anderson

Eddie Murphy devised this comeback for himself using a remake of Jerry Lewis's classic THE NUTTY PROFESSOR, but it fails to match the original.

Sherman Klump (Eddie Murphy), a kindly overweight science teacher, conducts extra-curricular weight-loss experiments on lab hamsters. Carla (Jada Pinkett), a new grad student, takes a liking to the misunderstood professor, and agrees to a date. Sherman's efforts to lose weight are futile, and his date goes from bad (as his family, all played by Murphy, trade insults over dinner) to worse (a nightclub comic pokes fun at Sherman s size). In desperation, Sherman decides to test his hamster formula on himself, and transforms, temporarily, into the lean, dashing "Buddy Love" (Murphy again). Carla finds Buddy attractive, but is put off by his mean streak. At a ritzy party for Harlan Hartley (James Coburn), a wealthy college donor, Sherman and his alter ego reveal themselves at the same time, astonishing the crowd. Sherman thinks that his days are numbered, but Hartley is so impressed by the experiment, that he insists Sherman continue his work for the school. Sherman (sans Buddy) also finds Carla proudly waiting for him on the dance floor.

This remake strains a little too hard for laughs with excessive, occasionally grotesque special effects. Neither Murphy nor director Tom Shadyac succeed in duplicating the brilliant way the Lewis film played with the two sides of Lewis's public persona—introverted nerd and extroverted lounge lizard. Murphy simply cannot pull off the sensitive scenes convincingly, because his characters have always been based on his jovial, devilish personality. Murphy does shows signs of his old comic skill as Buddy becomes increasingly deranged, but this NUTTY PROFESSOR is generally just mean-spirited and depressing.

O

O LUCKY MAN!

1973 186m c Comedy ★★★★
Memorial/Sam (U.K.) R/15

Malcolm McDowell (Mick Travis), Ralph Richardson (Monty/Sir James Burgess), Rachel Roberts (Gloria Rowe /Mme. Paillard/Mrs. Richards), Arthur Lowe (Mr. Duff /Charlie Johnson /Dr. Munda), Helen Mirren (Patricia Burgess), Dandy Nichols (Tea Lady /Neigh-

bor), Mona Washbourne (Sister Hallett /Usher/Neighbor), Michael Medwin (Army Captain /Power Station Technician /Duke of Belminster), Mary McLeod (Mrs. Ball/Vicar's Wife /Salvation Army Woman), Vivian Pickles (Welfare Lady)

p, Michael Medwin, Lindsay Anderson; d, Lindsay Anderson; w, David Sherwin (based on an idea by Malcolm McDowell); ph, Miroslav Ondricek; ed, David Gladwell, Tom Priestley; m, Alan Price; prod d, Jocelyn Herbert; art d, Alan Withy; fx, John Stears; cos, Elsa Fennell

Bizarre, loosely conceived sequel to IF. . ., in which Malcolm McDowell again plays Mick Travis, now a Candide-like coffee salesman bent on achieving corporate success. Travis's Kafkaesque, state-of-the-nation odyssey takes in a businessmen's sex club; a military camp where he's arrested and tortured; a medical research center where experiments include attaching a human head to a pig's body; an affair with the hippie daughter (Helen Mirren) of a corrupt industrialist (Ralph Richardson); and a scheme involving the sale of Napalm to an African nation that lands Travis in prison.

A variety of framing and distancing devices give a determinedly modernist dimension to Travis's blackly humorous adventures: his travels are punctuated by musical interludes, courtesy of Alan Price, that provide a neo-Brechtian commentary on the action; scenes are divided by blackouts that highlight the episodic nature of the proceedings; members of Anderson's informal repertory company each play several different roles; and Travis's exploits end with him being selected to play the lead role in the film we have just seen. A lucky man, indeed.

OBJECTIVE, BURMA!

1945 142m bw War ★★★★
Warner Bros. (U.S.) /PG

Errol Flynn (Maj. Nelson), James Brown (Sgt. Treacy), William Prince (Lt. Sid Jacobs), George Tobias (Gabby Gordon), Henry Hull (Mark Williams), Warner Anderson (Col. Carter), John Alvin (Hogan), Mark Stevens (Lt. Barker), Richard Erdman (Nebraska Hooper), Anthony Caruso (Miggleori)

p, Jerry Wald; d, Raoul Walsh; w, Ranald MacDougall, Lester Cole (based on a story by Alvah Bessie); ph, James Wong Howe; ed, George Amy; m, Franz Waxman; art d, Ted Smith; fx, Edwin DuPar

AAN Best Original Screenplay: Alvah Bessie; AAN Best Editing: George Amy; AAN Best Score: Franz Waxman

This is one of the finest WWII films made during the war, and Errol Flynn, discarding his usual impudent and pranksterish style, is terrific as the straightforward and very human leader of 50 American paratroops who drop behind enemy lines to destroy a Japanese radar station. The commandos complete their mission successfully, but while waiting to rendezvous with the rescue planes they are attacked by a force of Japanese and have to fight their way out of the Burmese jungle on foot. Flynn gives one of his most convincing and powerful performances, and Raoul Walsh's direction is nothing less than excellent, with the great action director maintaining a harrowing pace, providing a wealth of interesting military detail, and delivering one thrilling scene after another. Alvah Bessie, who would later become one of the "Hollywood Ten" writers indicted by HUAC, provided the engrossing story, marked by its relative lack of patriotic speechifying and some marvelously entertaining banter between the experienced commandos. Exceptional, too, is the dynamic, masterful score by Franz Waxman, which fits the mood and menace of the mysterious jungle and incorporates the sounds of wild animals and exotic birds. James Wong Howe's splendid photography, with its naturalistic lighting, lends a great deal of authenticity to the jungle scenes, especially when one considers that the film was shot almost entirely on the "Lucky" Baldwin Santa Anita ranch outside Pasadena. The film received rave reviews and heavy box-office support in the US, but when OBJECTIVE, BURMA! was released in England, the British press exploded, claiming that the film minimized the efforts of the British in Burma by giving the impression that an American commando team liberated the area by themselves. The film was banned in Britain until 1952, when prints were reissued with a prologue extolling the British contribution to the campaign.

ODD COUPLE, THE

1968 105m c Comedy ★★★½
Paramount (U.S.) G/15

Jack Lemmon *(Felix Ungar)*, Walter Matthau *(Oscar Madison)*, John Fiedler *(Vinnie)*, Herb Edelman *(Murray)*, David Sheiner *(Roy)*, Larry Haines *(Speed)*, Monica Evans *(Cecily)*, Carole Shelley *(Gwendolyn)*, Iris Adrian *(Waitress)*, Heywood Hale Broun *(Sportswriter)*

p, Howard W. Koch; d, Gene Saks; w, Neil Simon (based on the play by Simon); ph, Robert B. Hauser; ed, Frank Bracht; m, Neal Hefti; art d, Hal Pereira, Walter Tyler; fx, Paul K. Lerpae; cos, Jack Bear

AAN Best Adapted Screenplay: Neil Simon; AAN Best Editing: Frank Bracht

A film adaptation of a Neil Simon play, which means that it resembles an old, Manhattan-set syndicated sitcom. Gene Saks directing, which means that it looks like neither he nor the cast ever left the theater. The good news is that, as sitcom-style theater goes, THE ODD COUPLE is often highly amusing, with Lemmon and Matthau ideally cast as prissy neatnik and unmitigated slob. You all know the plot—both men have botched their marriages and try living together without killing each other. With gay domestic partnerships increasingly visible on the American family landscape, this film gingerly dancing around its own queerness does seem either ahead of its time or rather dated, but even if you take your Simon straight, so to speak, he does have a fairly good ear for a wisecrack, and the supporting cast is thankfully expert. The plot, nothing more than a premise based on Simon's real-life brother, Danny, goes nowhere, but then it's not really supposed to. Of course, if you don't feel like renting this video sitcom, you can always watch the actual sitcom with Tony Randall and Jack Klugman, still a big success in syndication. It's the same damn thing.

ODD MAN OUT

1947 116m bw Drama ★★★★★
Two Cities (U.K.) /PG

James Mason *(Johnny McQueen)*, Robert Newton *(Lukey)*, Kathleen Ryan *(Kathleen)*, Robert Beatty *(Dennis)*, William Hartnell *(Barman)*, F.J. McCormick *(Shell)*, Fay Compton *(Rosie)*, Beryl Measor *(Maudie)*, Cyril Cusack *(Pat)*, Dan O'Herlihy *(Nolan)*

p, Carol Reed; d, Carol Reed; w, F.L. Green, R.C. Sherriff (based on the novel by F.L. Green); ph, Robert Krasker; ed, Fergus McDonell; m, William Alwyn; prod d, Roger Furse; art d, Ralph Brinton; fx, Stanley Grant, Bill Warrington

AAN Best Editing: Fergus McDonell

Reed, one of Britain's finest directors, made his name with this haunting, lyrical masterpiece about a doomed fugitive. In perhaps the greatest performance of his illustrious career, Mason plays Johnny, an IRA leader who breaks out of jail and then plans a payroll holdup of a mill in Belfast to fund his underground operations. Though he abhors violence, Johnny accidentally kills a man during the holdup, and is himself critically wounded. Left behind by the panicky driver of the getaway car, Johnny stumbles away, descending into a nightmare as he becomes more and more delirious from his wound. He is harbored by a bunch of strange people who either want to help him or sell him to the British authorities. Sweetheart Kathleen (Ryan) and Johnny's IRA pals are in the meantime searching frantically for him. The man is hidden in deserted buildings and even in a junkyard bathtub for a while. On another occasion, two spinsters take him in, serve him tea, and then discover he is wounded, bandaging him before he departs. He finally falls into the clutches of an eccentric painter (Newton), who wants to catch the look of death in Johnny's eyes before it's too late. Struggling free from this madman, Johnny makes his way toward the docks in a final desperate effort to escape. Kathleen finally finds him there, but so do the police. The finale is very powerful.

Mason's performance as the dying fugitive, enhanced by that unique voice, is nothing less than great. Johnny's escalating pain, his lingering pride and the desperate look he gives an uncomprehending

child searching for a ball are searingly intense. Ryan, who debuted here, never had the chance to impact like this again, and marvelous performances are contributed by Cusack and O'Herlihy as Mason's chief lieutenants. The fascinating McCormick steals most of his scenes as a rag-picking bum who hides Johnny, and Newton positively gorges himself on the scenery in a wild portrait of the artist as a crazed man.

Early on, Reed, aided by Krasker's gritty cinematography, establishes a deeply somber mood in this modern odyssey to doom and death in an uncaring world. Each frame is another lethal step for Johnny as Reed poetically captures his last moments on earth. The plot and character development are touchingly constructed and enhanced by a magnificent score by Alwyn. Though Mason is initially presented as a culprit, his agonizing plight slowly transfigures him into a Christ-like figure. Visually reminiscent of John Ford's THE INFORMER, ODD MAN OUT also shares thematic concerns with Ford's THE FUGITIVE, insofar as both films depict an intolerable fate for a man who is basically decent but is condemned for his own altruistic beliefs. A great work of art, ODD MAN OUT is a painting on celluloid, evoking the best canvases of Goya and Velasquez. (Check out the weird shot of what manifests itself in Johnny's beer bubbles.) Although it was not popular at the box office, the film quickly won worldwide plaudits and established Reed as a great director.

ODDS AGAINST TOMORROW

1959 95m bw Crime ★★★★
Harbel (U.S.) /A

Harry Belafonte *(Johnny Ingram)*, Robert Ryan *(Earl Slater)*, Shelley Winters *(Lorry)*, Ed Begley *(Dave Burke)*, Gloria Grahame *(Helen)*, Will Kuluva *(Bacco)*, Richard Bright *(Coco)*, Lew Gallo *(Moriarity)*, Fred J. Scollay *(Cannoy)*, Carmen de Lavallade *(Kitty)*

p, Robert Wise; d, Robert Wise; w, Abraham Polonsky, Nelson Gidding (based on the novel by William P. McGivern); ph, Joseph Brun; ed, Dede Allen; m, John Lewis; art d, Leo Kerz; cos, Anna Hill Johnstone

A crackling crime caper that includes an overlay of racial tension, ODDS AGAINST TOMORROW was the first film out of Belafonte's own producing entity and proved that he wasn't just another pretty face and froggy voice. Robert Ryan, who was a liberal in real life, plays a psychotic racist similiar to the anti-Semitic character he played in CROSSFIRE. Belafonte is a gambling junkie, a man whose love for the horses has caused his marriage to fall apart. He's a childish nightclub singer and is now in danger from the harassment of Kuluva, a gay gangster in the employ of the people who hold Belafonte's IOUs. Ryan is an ex-con looking for a big score and Begley is a former cop who has been cashiered from the force for illegal dealings. This unlikely trio unite to rob an upstate New York bank of $150,000. Belafonte desperately needs his share of the swag to call off Kuluva, who is now threatening to kill Belafonte's wife and daughter. Ryan is married to Winters, though dallying with Grahame, who gets vicarious thrills before they make love when she pleads with Ryan to tell her how it feels to murder someone. Ryan's anti-black feelings are overcome by Begley and the robbery takes place. But everything goes awry. A gas station jockey spots Ryan. Belafonte witnesses an accident and must give his version of the incident; then he switches places with the food delivery man who brings the bank's night workers their refreshments. The regular guy shows up and so do the cops. Begley is shot, and when he can't get the getaway car's keys to his buddies, he takes his own life, rather than suffer the ignominy of arrest. Ryan and Belafonte escape and flee to an oil storage area not unlike the one in the final scenes of WHITE HEAT.

This is a fine slice of noir that didn't get the box-office attention it deserved. It features a terrific jazz score by John Lewis, pianist for the Modern Jazz Quartet, and, in small roles, Cicely Tyson, Wayne Rogers, and Zohra Lampert. Blacklisted scripter Abraham Polonsky was omitted from the credits in favor of a front, John O. Killens. In 1996, the Writer's Guild of America officially restored Polonsky's credit.

OF HUMAN BONDAGE

1934 83m bw Drama ★★★★
RKO (U.S.) /A

Leslie Howard *(Philip Carey)*, Bette Davis *(Mildred Rogers)*, Frances Dee *(Sally Athelny)*, Reginald Owen *(Thorpe Athelny)*, Reginald Denny *(Harry Griffiths)*, Kay Johnson *(Norah)*, Alan Hale *(Emil Miller)*, Reginald Sheffield *(Dunsford)*, Desmond Roberts *(Dr. Jacobs)*, Tempe Piggott *(Landlady)*

p, Pandro S. Berman; d, John Cromwell; w, Lester Cohen (based on the novel by W. Somerset Maugham); ph, Henry Gerrard; ed, William Morgan; m, Max Steiner; art d, Van Nest Polglase, Carroll Clark; fx, Vernon L. Walker; cos, Walter Plunkett

Cautious adaptation of Somerset Maugham's tragic tale features the electric performance by Bette Davis that made her a star. Today, it looks a trifle much, but given time and circumstance—the stylized acting of the early sound era, and her desire to be noticed—it's a blistering job.

Club-footed Philip Carey (Howard) studies painting in Paris but realizes that his work will never be more than second-rate, so he returns to England and begins to study medicine. Davis is Mildred, a blond tart whom he meets in the restaurant where she works as a waitress. She manipulates his affection cruelly, but even though she later breaks off the relationship to marry Emil Miller (Hale) and he takes solace with sympathetic Norah (Johnson), Philip can only think of Mildred. When a pregnant Mildred returns after Emil has abandoned her, Philip takes her in, but she runs away again, this time with Philip's friend Harry (Denny). And yet she returns one last time. . .

Thanks to wonderful performances by the leads, this version of the Maugham story is certainly the finest. Howard's quiet, studied performance is just right. Davis came by her role the hard way. After RKO acquired the novel for production, studio executives were shocked to learn that none of their leading ladies wanted the part of the sluttish Mildred. Katharine Hepburn, Ann Harding, and Irene Dunne all rejected the role. Davis, however, was languishing in unimportant roles at Warners, and she began to lobby Jack Warner to loan her to RKO for the part. The actress threw herself into the role, adopting a Cockney accent which she refused to discard when off-camera. She even supervised her own makeup so that it would convey Mildred's decline from syphilis. Davis's natural tendency to slouch worked very well for Mildred; within a few years this tendency would be gone for good. She was profoundly disappointed when she failed to receive an Oscar nomination as Best Actress, but this film was her watershed picture.

OF MICE AND MEN

1939 107m bw Drama ★★★★
Hal Roach (U.S.) /A

Burgess Meredith *(George)*, Betty Field *(Mae)*, Lon Chaney Jr. *(Lennie)*, Charles Bickford *(Slim)*, Roman Bohnen *(Candy)*, Bob Steele *(Curley)*, Noah Beery Jr. *(Whit)*, Oscar O'Shea *(Jackson)*, Granville Bates *(Carlson)*, Leigh Whipper *(Crooks)*

p, Lewis Milestone; d, Lewis Milestone; w, Eugene Solow (based on the novel by John Steinbeck); ph, Norbert Brodine; ed, Bert Jordan; m, Aaron Copland; art d, Nicolai Remisoff; fx, Roy Seawright

AAN Best Picture; *AAN Best Score:* Aaron Copland; *AAN Best Sound:* Elmer Raguse

John Steinbeck's moving, poweful story of two ranch hands trying to find a safe haven in a hostile world comes to the screen with penetrating compassion under the deft hand of director Milestone. The huge, childlike, slightly retarded Lennie (Chaney) and the sharp, protective George (Meredith) wander the rural West, looking for work during the Great Depression. Hired as hands at a ranch, they fantasize about owning a farm themselves one day, where George will be in charge and Lennie can tend to the small, furry, barnyard animals. Lennie, unfortunately, can't always control his passions, or the tremendous strength with which he can act on them. When the ranch owner's vicious son Curley (Steele) begins browbeating the men too much, the trouble begins. Things get even worse when Curley's bored, flirtatious wife (Field) begins toying with the baffled Lennie, and George realizes he must do something about his friend.

Though grim and offbeat, OF MICE AND MEN is a noble morality tale that can be appreciated for its simplicity. The acting is faultless and Copland's score is magnificent. Hollywood censorship deserves at least a modest amount of praise for not completely eviscerating a powerfully adult story. This was Chaney's finest performance ever; equally impressive are Meredith, Bickford, Field, Bohnen (in an especially moving turn as the pathetic Candy), and B-film cowboy star Steele. Remade by clumsier hands, and with too much gloss, in 1992.

OFFICER AND A GENTLEMAN, AN

1982 126m c Romance/War ★★★½
Lorimar (U.S.) R/15

Richard Gere *(Zack Mayo)*, Debra Winger *(Paula Pokrifki)*, David Keith *(Sid Worley)*, Robert Loggia *(Byron Mayo)*, Lisa Blount *(Lynette Pomeroy)*, Lisa Eilbacher *(Casey Seeger)*, Louis Gossett Jr. *(Sgt. Emil Foley)*, Tony Plana *(Emiliano Della Serra)*, Harold Sylvester *(Perryman)*, David Caruso *(Topper Daniels)*

p, Martin Elfand; d, Taylor Hackford; w, Douglas Day Stewart; ph, Donald Thorin; ed, Peter Zinner; m, Jack Nitzsche; prod d, Philip Jefferies; art d, John V. Cartwright

AAN Best Actress: Debra Winger; *AA Best Supporting Actor:* Louis Gossett, Jr.; *AAN Best Original Screenplay:* Douglas Day Stewart; *AAN Best Editing:* Peter Zinner; *AAN Best Score:* Jack Nitzsche; *AA Best Song:* Jack Nitzsche (Music), Buffy Sainte-Marie (Music), Will Jennings (Lyrics)

Lou Gossett, Jr., won a much-deserved Best Supporting Actor Oscar for his stellar portrayal of a drill instructor in this story of determination and love set against the backdrop of a Naval Aviation Officer Candidate School. Richard Gere plays Zack Mayo, a would-be flyer with a tough-luck background who, like his classmates, must survive the rigors of training under draconian Marine sergeant Emil Foley (Gossett) before moving on to flight school. Sgt. Foley singles out Zack for special derision, and though he pushes his charge to the limit, the feisty Zack refuses to give up, eventually tangling with the DI in martial-arts battle. Meanwhile, Zack and classmate Sid Worley (David Keith), the film's tragic figure, become involved with a couple of local girls, millworkers Paula Pokrifki (Debra Winger, who received a Best Actress nomination for her fine performance) and Lynette Pomeroy (Lisa Blount). Paula becomes convinced that Zack is like all the other officer candidates who do their training, take advantage of local women, and then disappear forever once they've earned their white uniform. Douglas Day Stewart's Oscar-nominated screenplay is generally involving (if a little overheated), but it is ultimately compromised by its sexism, particularly in the finale, which leaves Paula with only one hope for happiness—to be carried off by a dashing knight. Nonetheless, the performances are uniformly strong, with Gere offering some of his best work—though it pales in comparison with Gossett's *tour de force* as the tough, principled Sgt. Foley, which he patterned after real-life army DI Bill Dower (familiar to some from his appearances in Miller Lite commercials). The film's memorable theme song, "Up Where We Belong" (sung by Joe Cocker and Jennifer Warnes), also won an Academy Award.

OFFICIAL STORY, THE
(LA HISTORIA OFICIAL)

1985 112m c Drama ★★★½
Historias Cine (Argentina) /15

Hector Alterio *(Roberto)*, Norma Aleandro *(Alicia)*, Chela Ruiz *(Sara)*, Chunchuna Villafane *(Ana)*, Hugo Arana *(Enrique)*, Patricio Contreras *(Benitez)*, Guillermo Battaglia *(Jose)*, Maria-Luisa Robledo *(Nata)*, Jorge Petraglia *(Macci)*, Analia Castro *(Gaby)*

p, Marcelo Pineyro; d, Luis Puenzo; w, Luis Puenzo, Aida Bortnik; ph, Felix Monti; ed, Juan Carlos Macias; m, Atilio Stampone; prod d, Abel Facello; art d, Abel Facello; cos, Tiky Garcia Estevez

AA Best Foreign Language Film ; *AAN Best Original Screenplay:* Luis Puenzo, Aida Bortnik

The first important film to emerge from Argentina after the fall of its military regime, THE OFFICIAL STORY is a deeply moving drama examining one of the saddest chapters in that country's history. The tranquil lives of Alicia (Norma Aleandro), a history professor; her husband, Roberto (Hector Alterio), a high-powered businessman; and their five-year-old daughter, Gaby (Analia Castro), are thrown into turmoil when an old friend who was tortured and exiled by the military reveals that, under the junta, babies were taken from political prisoners and sold to well-connected adoptive parents. Realizing that Gaby may be one of these children, Alicia begins to investigate her daughter's background and meets Sara (Chela Ruiz), one of the women who march each day at the Plaza de Mayo to protest the disappearance of loved ones in the junta's "dirty war." Coming to grips with her political naivete, Alicia confronts Alterio, who proves to be deeply involved with the reprehensible junta. An impressive feature debut by Luis Puenzo, who invests his scenes with tremendous emotional impact, THE OFFICIAL STORY won the 1986 Oscar for Best Foreign-Language Film. Poignantly political, its power derives from the depiction of the junta's tragic effect on individual lives. The screenplay was written with Aleandro (a political exile who returned to her native Argentina after the change of government) in mind, and she delivers a *tour de force* performance that won her the Best Actress Award at Cannes. Originally, Puenzo intended to shoot the film in secret, using hidden 16mm cameras, but the junta was voted out of office just after cowriter Aida Bortnik completed the screenplay.

OH! WHAT A LOVELY WAR

1969 144m c War/Musical   ★★★½
Accord (U.K.)   G/PG

Ralph Richardson *(Sir Edward Grey)*, Meriel Forbes *(Lady Grey)*, Wensley Pithey *(Archduke Franz Ferdinand)*, Ruth Kettlewell *(Duchess Sophie)*, Ian Holm *(President Poincare)*, John Gielgud *(Count Berchtold)*, Kenneth More *(Kaiser Wilhelm II)*, John Clements *(Gen. von Moltke)*, Paul Daneman *(Czar Nicholas II)*, Pamela Abbott *(Czarina)*

p, Brian Duffy, Richard Attenborough, Len Deighton; d, Richard Attenborough; w, Len Deighton (based on Joan Littlewood's stage production of Charles Chilton's play *The Long, Long Trail*); ph, Gerry Turpin; ed, Kevin Connor; m, Alfred Ralston; prod d, Don Ashton; art d, Harry White; fx, Ron Ballanger; chor, Eleanor Fazan; cos, Anthony Mendleson

Richard Attenborough's directorial debut is a sprawling, highly stylized musical satire of WWI featuring some of Britain's very finest actors—Ralph Richardson, Laurence Olivier, Michael Redgrave, John Mills, Jack Hawkins, Ian Holm, and Vanessa Redgrave among them. After an opening that finds Europe's heads of state choosing up sides when Archduke Franz Ferdinand is killed during a royal photo session, OH, WHAT A LOVELY WAR traces WWI through a series of surreal set pieces, alternating between the front lines in France and the English homefront, where generals and diplomats conduct a distant war that is actually waged by the young and poor. In particular, the film focuses on the Smith family, whose sons, seduced into the service in the carnival atmosphere of Brighton, all end up dying for their country. Meanwhile, the sacrifices of the British aristocracy, as embodied by Eleanor (Susannah York) and Stephen (Dirk Bogarde), are limited to boycotting German wine. Against a backdrop that includes flashing neon messages and a cricket scoreboard that keeps tally of the war's casualties, a series of musical numbers from 1914-18 are performed and given a distinctly antiwar slant that won considerable support from the British Left for this film and its inspiration, Joan Littlewood's 1963 stage adaptation of Charles Chilton's radio play "The Long, Long Trail." The rights to the play were purchased by producer Brian Duffy and novelist Len Deighton, the latter of whom had his name taken off the film before its release because of differences with Attenborough. OH, WHAT A LOVELY WAR is not a flawless film but is thoughtful and enthralling.

OKLAHOMA!

1955 145m c Western/Musical   ★★★
Magna (U.S.)   G/U

Gordon MacRae *(Curly)*, Gloria Grahame *(Ado Annie)*, Gene Nelson *(Will Parker)*, Charlotte Greenwood *(Aunt Eller)*, Shirley Jones *(Laurey)*, Eddie Albert *(Ali Hakim)*, James Whitmore *(Carnes)*, Rod Steiger *(Jud Fry)*, Barbara Lawrence *(Gertie)*, Jay C. Flippen *(Skidmore)*

p, Arthur Hornblow Jr.; d, Fred Zinnemann; w, Sonya Levien, William Ludwig (based on the musical by Richard Rodgers, Oscar Hammerstein II, from the play *Green Grow the Lilacs* by Lynn Riggs); ph, Robert Surtees; ed, Gene Ruggiero; m, Richard Rodgers; prod d, Oliver Smith; art d, Joseph C. Wright; chor, Agnes De Mille; cos, Orry-Kelly, Motley

AAN Best Cinematography: Robert Surtees; *AAN Best Editing:* Gene Ruggiero, George Boemler; *AA Best Score:* Robert Russell Bennett, Jay Blackton, Adolph Deutsch; *AA Best Sound:* Fred Hynes

Watch it for the songs. A paean to Oklahoma's "Sooner" pioneers, it's a watchable, if hardly terrific, rendering of an innovative Broadway landmark. Boys (MacRae and Nelson) meet girls (Jones and Grahame); boys almost lose girls, all complicated by the villainous Jud Fry (Steiger, in a ridiculously hammy, off-key performance as the farm-hand-from-hell). Although the score is, by now, deeply embedded in the minds of anyone who has ears, it gets spirited renditions here that are worth listening to. MacRae, in the best-remembered role of his career, gets the film off to a wonderful start with "Oh, What a Beautiful Morning." A very young Jones also makes a nice impression and became an instant star (though her film career never did take root), and Grahame, Greenwood, Albert and Lawrence have fun with their parts as well. In the Dream Ballet, choreographer Agnes DeMille followed what she did onstage and replaced non-dancing Jones and MacRae with Bambi Lynn and James Mitchell, respectively, thus unfortunately encouraging filmmakers to cast movie stars without musical comedy talent in adaptations of Broadway shows. OKLAHOMA! was actually shot outside of Nogales, Arizona, where the cast and crew put in nearly eight months of work, delayed by flash floods, one of which washed away a car containing a week's worth of film. Easy come, easy go.

OLD DARK HOUSE, THE

1932 70m bw Horror   ★★★★
Universal (U.S.)   /PG

Boris Karloff *(Morgan)*, Melvyn Douglas *(Roger Penderell)*, Charles Laughton *(Sir William Porterhouse)*, Gloria Stuart *(Margaret Waverton)*, Lilian Bond *(Gladys DuCane)*, Ernest Thesiger *(Horace Femm)*, Eva Moore *(Rebecca Femm)*, Raymond Massey *(Philip Waverton)*, Brember Wills *(Saul Femm)*, Elspeth Dudgeon *(Sir Roderick Femm)*

p, Carl Laemmle Jr.; d, James Whale; w, Benn W. Levy, R.C. Sherriff (based on the novel *Benighted* by J.B. Priestley); ph, Arthur Edeson; ed, Clarence Kolster; art d, Charles D. Hall; fx, John P. Fulton

"No beds! They can't have beds!" A uniquely bizarre, wonderfully funny and exciting haunted house film with an all-star cast directed by the brilliant James Whale. Loosely based on J.B. Priestley's novel *Benighted*, the story has a group of stranded travelers forced to seek refuge at the strange house of the Femm family. Philip Waverton (Massey), his wife Margaret (Stuart) and their friend Roger Penderell (Douglas) arrive first. Inside lurks a "home" presided over by the 102 year-old bedridden patriarch Sir Roderick (Elspeth Dudgeon, an actress billed in the credits as "John Dudgeon" and brilliant in the role). Also featured are his atheist son Horace (Thesiger), his religious fanatic daughter Rebecca (Moore), and their older brother Saul (Wills), a crazed pyromaniac kept locked in his room upstairs. Hovering around the action is the house's hulking, mute, scarred, and slightly psychotic butler Morgan (Karloff, in his first starring role). Two more stranded travelers, Sir William Porterhouse (Laughton) and his "companion" Gladys DuCane (Bond), arrive soon after, and then the fun starts. The horrors here are not supernatural and arise solely from the madnesses of the Femm household, particularly when Morgan gets drunk and lets Saul loose. The suspense builds incredibly in the final showdown between Penderell and the mad Saul.

Handled in the uniquely theatrical manner that makes James Whale's work instantly recognizable, THE OLD DARK HOUSE is nonetheless never "stagy," benefitting as it does from Edeson's wonderful camerawork. The first glimpse of the foreboding house is still among the best of its kind, and the lighting of the stark indoor sets quite stunning. The marvelous screenplay is full of memorable bits, such as the harsh Rebecca's retelling of past family debaucheries or Saul's genuinely creepy conversation with Penderell near the end. The dialogue is often hilarious, but it takes a cast as brilliant as this one to make the most of it. Massey's early speech about the water trickling down his neck or his remarks about seeing the house ("Perhaps it might be wiser to push on") are beautifully handled. With his typically demonstrative aplomb, Whale gives us these moments *as* we see an extreme close-up of Massey's neck or just after the house stands illuminated by flashes of lightning. Douglas can shift from glib wisecracks to a warm and touching romance with Bond in moments, and she and Stuart are appealing leading ladies here. Laughton affects a marvelous Lancashire accent as a hearty, bluff man, and yet he can also touch the heart when speaking about his deceased wife. Karloff may not speak here but his acting is as effective as ever and he and Wills demonstrate a remarkable rapport together. His final embrace of the crazed man is unexpectedly powerful. If we had to reserve top honors, though, they would have to go to Thesiger and Moore, whose work is absolutely flawless. When Eva Moore eats her dinner at warp speed or Ernest Thesiger makes "Have a potato" a classic highlight of a film, you know you're in the presence of rare talents.

As historian William K. Everson has noted, former stage actor and director Whale knows how to emphasize an actor's entrances and exits, or to delay them as needed (as in the case of Saul). His striking flair for composition and editing works an audience over thoroughly, and he adds to the film's impact by deliberately playing with the buildup of suspense. Brilliantly performed, staged and timed, a sly parody on the English household, THE OLD DARK HOUSE stands alongside THE BRIDE OF FRANKENSTEIN and ONE MORE RIVER as one of Whale's most sublime achievements.

OLD MAN AND THE SEA, THE

1958   86m   c   Drama   ★★★
Warner Bros.   (U.S.)   /U

Spencer Tracy *(The Old Man)*, Felipe Pazos *(The Boy)*, Harry Bellaver *(Martin)*, Don Diamond, Don Blackman, Joey Ray, Richard Alameda, Tony Rosa, Carlos Rivera, Robert Alderette

p, Leland Hayward; d, John Sturges; w, Peter Viertel (based on the novella by Ernest Hemingway); ph, James Wong Howe, Floyd Crosby, Tom Tutwiler, Lamar Boren; ed, Arthur Schmidt; m, Dimitri Tiomkin; art d, Art Loel, Edward Carrere; fx, Arthur S. Rhoades

AAN Best Actor: Spencer Tracy; *AAN Best Cinematography:* James Wong Howe; *AA Best Score:* Dimitri Tiomkin

Years before A RIVER RUNS THROUGH IT, the original fish story. This was a near-impossible film to make, but Warner Bros. and Sturges tackled the job sensibly and, with Tracy in bravura form, it came off surprisingly well. Tracy plays a semi-literate Cuban fisherman whose pedantic efforts to practice his trade only cause snickers of derision from his community. Regarded as a fool, he only receives respect from the small boy (Pazos) who brings him coffee every morning. Most of the film is Tracy alone onscreen, as he goes head to head with a gigantic marlin, which, if landed, would be the catch of a lifetime. The struggle and its outcome form a story of irony, achievement and sadness, a battle of man vs. both the elements and his own pride.

THE OLD MAN AND THE SEA is an allegorical tale providing Tracy with a worthy one-man show, and his work has a powerful impact laced with humor and an overwhelming sense of stoic heroism. (Unlike his Portuguese fisherman in CAPTAINS COURAGEOUS, however, Tracy here does not attempt any kind of accent, which does stand out a bit in his scenes with the rest of the cast.) Sturges's direction, given the confining nature of the settings, is masterful, and the cinematography headed by Howe and pieced together by many others is sometimes stunning. (The contribution of much of the footage by many sources, however, has a tendency to present alternating and inconsistent color patterns from scene to scene.)

Attempts to film on location encountered problems; landing an actual marlin proved impossible; and Hayward fired original director Fred Zinneman over, among other things, disagreements about the script. Eventually, much of the film was shot (using a rubber fish) in a huge water tank at Warner Bros! Although Tracy would state that "This is for the birds" during the painfully protracted shoot, his disillusionment doesn't affect his performance, and he received kudos from most of the critics. One exception was Hemingway, who grouched that the film looked like the work of "a rich, fat actor."

OLD YELLER

1957   83m   c   Children's/Drama   ★★★½
Walt Disney Productions   (U.S.)   G/U

Dorothy McGuire *(Katie Coates)*, Fess Parker *(Jim Coates)*, Tommy Kirk *(Travis Coates)*, Kevin Corcoran *(Arliss Coates)*, Jeff York *(Bud Searcy)*, Beverly Washburn *(Lisbeth Searcy)*, Chuck Connors *(Burn Sanderson)*, Spike the Dog *(Old Yeller)*

p, Walt Disney; d, Robert Stevenson; w, Fred Gipson, William Tunberg (based on the novel by Fred Gipson); ph, Charles P. Boyle; ed, Stanley Johnson; m, Oliver Wallace; art d, Carroll Clark; cos, Chuck Keehne, Gertrude Casey

Set in Texas in 1869, Disney Studios' first and best attempt at a boy-and-his-dog film tells the story of a farm family whose head, Jim Coates (Fess Parker), must go on a cattle drive for three months, leaving his 15-year-old son, Travis (Tommy Kirk), in charge. When Travis's younger brother, Arliss (Kevin Corcoran), finds a stray yellow dog and decides to adopt him, Travis is frustrated by this breach of his authority. But his mother (Dorothy McGuire) approves of the dog's presence and reminds Travis that his little brother is lonely. Soon the dog, Old Yeller, has won the hearts of the whole family. Their attachment to the dog will serve as a test for their strength and love in this powerful and moving film. Sequel: SAVAGE SAM.

OLIVER!

1968   153m   c   Musical   ★★★★
Warwick/Romulus   (U.K.)   G/U

Ron Moody *(Fagin)*, Shani Wallis *(Nancy)*, Oliver Reed *(Bill Sikes)*, Harry Secombe *(Mr. Bumble)*, Mark Lester *(Oliver Twist)*, Jack Wild *(The Artful Dodger)*, Hugh Griffith *(The Magistrate)*, Joseph O'Conor *(Mr. Brownlow)*, Peggy Mount *(Widow Corney)*, Leonard Rossiter *(Mr. Sowerberry)*

p, John Woolf; d, Carol Reed; w, Vernon Harris (based on the play by Lionel Bart from the novel *Oliver Twist* by Charles Dickens); ph, Oswald Morris; ed, Ralph Kemplen; m, Lionel Bart; prod d, John Box; art d, Terence Marsh; fx, Allan Bryce; chor, Onna White; cos, Phyllis Dalton

AA Best Picture; *AAN Best Actor:* Ron Moody; *AAN Best Supporting Actor:* Jack Wild; *AA Best Director:* Carol Reed; *AA Best Adapted Screenplay:* Vernon Harris; *AAN Best Cinematography:* Oswald Morris; *AAN Best Editing:* Ralph Kemplen; *AA Best Score:* John Green; *AA Best Art Direction:* John Box, Terence Marsh, Vernon Dixon, Ken Muggleston; *AAN Best Costume Design:* Phyllis Dalton; *AA Best Sound:* Shepperton Studio Sound Department

Sweetened Dickens, a contradiction in kind. If the works of Charles Dickens have their moments of sentiment, they're well-earned, thanks to the savagry and deprivation abundant in the master storyteller's plots. Here, Carol Reed tries to balance the story elements by rendering the story as a fable; the moments of tenderness are intellectualized. Given that *Oliver!* could easily get that perfunctory cuteness that packs the matinees with old ladies, it's a wise move. But being English himself and probably knowing Dickens better than we do, why didn't Carol Reed restore the Dickensian flavor that could give OLIVER! some bite? OLIVER! is the familiar story of young Oliver Twist (strongly played by Mark Lester), an orphan who prefers life on the streets to the hard labor of a foster family or life in a vile orphanage. One day he meets another street urchin, the Artful Dodger (Jack Wild, in an equally strong performance), who tells him of a group of young hooligans that will consider him "part of the family." All Oliver has to do is learn to pickpocket and give his earnings to Fagin (Ron Moody), the crusty criminal gang leader; in return he'll have a "family" and a place to stay.

OLIVER TWIST

OLIVER! is better than most screen musicals of the 1960s, a period when oversized, poorly rendered songfests virtually killed the genre. The score, while hardly immortal, is well served by the actors and Oliver Reed for once found a character he could sink his loathsome self into.

OLIVER TWIST

1948 105m bw Drama ★★★★½
Cineguild (U.K.) /U

Robert Newton (*Bill Sikes*), Alec Guinness (*Fagin*), Kay Walsh (*Nancy*), Francis L. Sullivan (*Mr. Bumble*), Henry Stephenson (*Mr. Brownlow*), Mary Clare (*Mrs. Corney*), John Howard Davies (*Oliver Twist*), Josephine Stuart (*Oliver's Mother*), Henry Edwards (*Police Official*), Ralph Truman (*Monks*)

p, Ronald Neame, Anthony Havelock-Allan; d, David Lean; w, David Lean, Stanley Haynes (based on the novel by Charles Dickens); ph, Guy Green; ed, Jack Harris; m, Arnold Bax; fx, Joan Suttie, Stanley Grant; cos, Margaret Furse

David Lean's version of Charles Dickens's *Oliver Twist* is not as enthralling as his GREAT EXPECTATIONS, but it is a fine film in its own right. This time Alec Guinness (EXPECTATIONS was his first film) plays Fagin, Anthony Newley is the Artful Dodger, and the then-unknown and now-forgotten John Howard Davies is Oliver Twist. (Actually, some may recognize Davies as the British television producer responsible for "Monty Python's Flying Circus" and "Fawlty Towers.") Guinness's performance ran into some trouble from Jewish pressure groups—seven minutes of his performance was excised—and the film finally entered the country in 1951. Many of the novel's characters have been excised or compressed to fit the time frame of the film, but only the most die-hard Dickensians will protest. The sets are as much a part of the story as the dialogue, and set designer John Bryan's work is effectively photographed by Guy Green. All the acting is first-rate, and there is not a false note from the cast.

OMEN, THE

1976 111m c Horror ★★
Fox (U.S.) R/18

Gregory Peck (*Robert Thorn*), Lee Remick (*Katherine Thorn*), David Warner (*Jennings*), Billie Whitelaw (*Mrs. Baylock*), Leo McKern (*Bugenhagen*), Harvey Stevens (*Damien*), Patrick Troughton (*Father Brennan*), Martin Benson (*Father Spiletto*), Anthony Nicholls (*Dr. Becker*), Holly Palance (*Young Nanny*)

p, Harvey Bernhard; d, Richard Donner; w, David Seltzer; ph, Gilbert Taylor; ed, Stuart Baird; m, Jerry Goldsmith; art d, Carmen Dillon; fx, John Richardson

AA Best Score: Jerry Goldsmith; *AAN Best Song*: Jerry Goldsmith

This silly and bloody, but at times very effective, horror film takes THE EXORCIST one step further by concentrating, not on possession by the Devil, but on the Antichrist himself. Robert Thorn (Gregory Peck) is a highly respected American ambassador to England whose wife, Katherine (Lee Remick), gives birth to a stillborn child. Thorn is encouraged by a priest to switch his dead child with the living baby of a mother who died during childbirth. Five years later, strange things begin happening in the Thorn household, all of which can be traced to their boy, Damien (Harvey Stevens), who, unbeknownst to his surrogate parents, is the Antichrist. Regardless of its rather questionable premise, execution (unintentionally funny dialogue abounds), or taste, THE OMEN is a fairly entertaining horror picture that made an obscene amount of money and spawned two sequels, DAMIEN—OMEN II and THE FINAL CONFLICT, neither of which was very good. The films were originally conceived as four parts, tracing Damien's rise to power from his childhood through adulthood and eventually to Armageddon, but patron interest slacked off considerably after the second film, forcing the producers to cut the saga short at three.

ON GOLDEN POND

1981 109m c Comedy/Drama ★★★½
ITC/IPC/AFD/Universal (U.S.) PG

Katharine Hepburn (*Ethel Thayer*), Henry Fonda (*Norman Thayer, Jr.*), Jane Fonda (*Chelsea Thayer Wayne*), Doug McKeon (*Billy Ray*), Dabney Coleman (*Bill Ray*), William Lanteau (*Charlie Martin*), Christopher Rydell (*Sumner Todd*)

p, Bruce Gilbert; d, Mark Rydell; w, Ernest Thompson (based on his play); ph, Billy Williams; ed, Robert Wolfe; m, Dave Grusin; prod d, Stephen Grimes; cos, Dorothy Jeakins

AAN Best Picture; *AA Best Actor*: Henry Fonda; *AA Best Actress*: Katharine Hepburn; *AAN Best Supporting Actress*: Jane Fonda; *AAN Best Director*: Mark Rydell; *AA Best Adapted Screenplay*: Ernest Thompson; *AAN Best Cinematography*: Billy Williams; *AAN Best Editing*: Robert L. Wolfe; *AAN Best Score*: Dave Grusin; *AAN Best Sound*: Richard Portman, David Ronne

Retired professor Norman Thayer, Jr. (Henry Fonda), and his wife Ethel (Katharine Hepburn) are spending the summer at their New England cottage, just as they have done for nearly 50 years. The Thayers' daughter Chelsea (Jane Fonda) arrives at the cottage with her fiance Bill Ray (Dabney Coleman) and Billy (Doug McKeon), his son from a previous marriage. They plan for Billy to stay at the cottage while Jane Fonda and Coleman head for a summer in Europe. The gruff Norman and the irritating Billy are immediately at odds—much as the father and daughter have always been. The two come to a better understanding of one another over the course of the summer, however, while Fonda also tries to come to terms with his mortality. A beautifully photographed movie filled with poignancy, humor, and (of course) some superb acting. Henry Fonda was 75 when this picture was made and must have known he didn't have much time. There could have been no finer final curtain for him than this.

ON HER MAJESTY'S SECRET SERVICE

1969 140m c Spy ★★★½
UA (U.K.) M/PG

George Lazenby (*James Bond*), Diana Rigg (*Tracy Draco*), Telly Savalas (*Ernst Stavro Blofeld*), Ilse Steppat (*Irma Bunt*), Gabriele Ferzetti (*Marc Ange Draco*), Yuri Borienko (*Gruenther*), Bernard Horsfall (*Campbell*), George Baker (*Sir Hilary Bray*), Bernard Lee ("*M*"), Lois Maxwell (*Miss Moneypenny*)

p, Albert R. Broccoli, Harry Saltzman; d, Peter Hunt; w, Richard Maibaum, Simon Raven (based on the novel by Ian Fleming); ph, Michael Reed, Egil Woxholt, Roy Ford, John Jordan, Willy Bogner, Alex Barbey, Ken Higgins; ed, John Glen; m, John Barry; prod d, Syd Cain; art d, Robert Laing; fx, John Stears; cos, Marjorie Cornelius

This might have been the best of the James Bond series if it had starred Sean Connery instead of Australian model George Lazenby, whom the producers grabbed after a frantic talent search when Connery turned down the role. When Bond is ordered to cease his pursuit of old nemesis Blofeld (played by Savalas this time), 007 turns in his license to kill and returns to Portugal to pick up the trail. There he falls for Tracy (Rigg), the ravishing daughter of Draco (Ferzetti), an organized crime kingpin. Draco helps Bond locate the Swiss mountaintop stronghold from which Blofeld plans to engineer universal sterilization unless he is granted a title of nobility and amnesty for his past crimes. After rescuing Tracy from Blofeld's clutches and seemingly doing away with him once and for all, Bond marries her and they *almost* live happily ever after. Based on one of the best of Ian Fleming's Bond novels, ON HER MAJESTY'S SECRET SERVICE benefited from an extremely well-written script that finally revealed a bit more of Bond's character. Lazenby, however, had no previous acting experience, and his lackadaisical performance limits the whole production, yet it still manages to remain one of the more entertaining Bond films.

ON THE BEACH

1959 133m bw Science Fiction/Drama/War ★★½
Kramer (U.S.) /A

Gregory Peck *(Dwight Towers)*, Ava Gardner *(Moira Davidson)*, Fred Astaire *(Julian Osborn)*, Anthony Perkins *(Peter Holmes)*, Donna Anderson *(Mary Holmes)*, John Tate *(Adm. Bridie)*, Lola Brooks *(Lt. Hosgood)*, John Meillon *(Swain)*, Lou Vernon *(Davidson)*, Guy Doleman *(Farrel)*

p, Stanley Kramer; d, Stanley Kramer; w, John Paxton, James Lee Barrett (based on the novel by Nevil Shute); ph, Giuseppe Rotunno, Daniel Fapp; ed, Frederic Knudtson; m, Ernest Gold; prod d, Rudolph Sternad; art d, Fernando Carrere; fx, Lee Zavitz; cos, Joe King, Fontana Sisters

AAN Best Editing: Frederic Knudtson; *AAN Best Score:* Ernest Gold

Based on Nevil Shute's popular novel, this flawed but moving end-of-the-world drama is set in Australia in 1964, after nuclear war has eliminated life in the northern hemisphere. While the folks down under await the nuclear fallout that will eventually kill them, the US *Sawfish*, a submarine commanded by Dwight Towers (Gregory Peck), ventures to California, only to learn that the radio signal still being transmitted from San Diego is being produced by a soda bottle—everyone at home is dead (dramatically reinforced by some extraordinary shots of a deserted San Francisco). Back in Australia, the principal characters deal with their imminent deaths in their own way: scientist Julian Osborn (Fred Astaire) enters and wins an auto race, then asphyxiates himself; Australian naval officer Peter Holmes (Anthony Perkins) and his wife, Mary (Donna Anderson), take their child's and their own lives; good-time girl Moira Davidson (Ava Gardner) tries to drink her fears away, then falls for Towers, who eventually returns with his crew to the US to die at home. Produced and directed by Stanley Kramer, this unremittingly bleak message film was intended to have a big impact and premiered simultaneously in 18 cities on all seven continents. And though it occasionally goes over the top with its melodrama and lacks some technical credibility, ON THE BEACH remains a powerful, well-acted, deftly photographed film in the tradition of THE WORLD, THE FLESH AND THE DEVIL; FAIL SAFE; DR. STRANGELOVE; and TESTAMENT. Its effective use of "Waltzing Matilda" also contributed to making that most Australian of songs a hit in the US.

ON THE TOWN

1949 98m c Musical ★★★★
MGM (U.S.) /U

Gene Kelly *(Gabey)*, Frank Sinatra *(Chip)*, Betty Garrett *(Brunhilde Esterhazy)*, Ann Miller *(Claire Huddesen)*, Jules Munshin *(Ozzie)*, Vera-Ellen *(Ivy Smith)*, Florence Bates *(Mme. Dilyovska)*, Alice Pearce *(Lucy Shmeeler)*, George Meader *(Professor)*, Bern Hoffman *(Worker)*

p, Arthur Freed; d, Gene Kelly, Stanley Donen; w, Adolph Green, Betty Comden (based on the musical play by Comden, Green and Leonard Bernstein, from the ballet *Fancy Free* by Jerome Robbins); ph, Harold Rosson; ed, Ralph E. Winters; m, Leonard Bernstein, Roger Edens, Saul Chaplin, Conrad Salinger; art d, Cedric Gibbons, Jack Martin Smith; fx, Warren Newcombe; chor, Gene Kelly, Stanley Donen; cos, Helen Rose

AA Best Score: Roger Edens, Lennie Hayton

Just a trifle forced, like Gene Kelly. And stolen by a tapping whirlwind named Annie Miller, flying through the Museum of Natural History in a blaze of green gingham. But New York City never looked more beautiful or exciting on screen than in ON THE TOWN, a breakthrough film that, for the first time, took the musical out of the claustrophobic sound stages and onto the streets for on-location shooting. Perfectly fusing story, songs, and dances, with no production number staged merely for its own sake, ON THE TOWN is so energetic and vital that the screen barely contains it; the actors seem ready to leap off and dance up the aisles. The slim story follows sailors Gabey (Gene Kelly), Chip (Frank Sinatra), and Ozzie (Jules Munshin) during their 24-hour pass in New York. In the subway, they note the picture of this month's "Miss Turnstiles," with whom Gabey is especially taken; later they meet Miss Turnstiles—one Ivy Smith (Vera-Ellen)—in the flesh, but she vanishes

into the rush-hour crowd. Chasing after her, they enlist the help of cabbie Brunhilde Esterhazy (Betty Garrett), who takes a fancy to Chip. Continuing their search, they meet anthropologist Claire Huddesen (Ann Miller), who sets her sights on Ozzie. The group splits into three units—Brunhilde and Chip, Claire and Ozzie, and Gabey—to look for Ivy, agreeing to meet on the Empire State Building's observation deck that night. After a day of romantic adventures and misadventures, they rendezvous at the appointed site, Gabey squiring Ivy, whom he mistakenly believes to be a big star in her position as Miss Turnstiles. By the time she gets around to telling him she's really just a no-name dancer from a tiny town (as it happens, the same tiny town *he's* from), it makes no difference to the smitten Gabey, and, after a run-in with the cops that forces the gobs to pretend they're girls, they return to their ship exactly 24 hours from the time they left.

Loius B. Mayer didn't want the film to go on location, while Kelly wanted to shoot the entire picture in New York, leading to a compromise in which Kelly was allowed one frantic week of location shooting, filming the Bronx, the Battery, Coney Island, Brooklyn, the Empire State Building, Times Square, the Statue of Liberty, Fifth Avenue, Radio City, the Bronx Zoo, Central Park, Carnegie Hall, the subway, Wall Street, Grant's Tomb, and the Brooklyn Navy Yard. Perhaps it was the short shooting schedule that contributed to the frantic pace of the film, a jampacked tour without a wasted second. There may have been better songs and even better performances in other musicals, but for effervescent energy nothing has yet come close to the joyous, influential ON THE TOWN. One quibble: Leonard Bernstein's innovative Broadway score is here diminished by Hollywood-style orchestration and much tinkering.

ON THE WATERFRONT

1954 108m bw Drama ★★★★½
Columbia (U.S.) /PG

Marlon Brando *(Terry Malloy)*, Karl Malden *(Father Barry)*, Lee J. Cobb *(Johnny Friendly)*, Rod Steiger *(Charley Malloy)*, Pat Henning *("Kayo" Dugan)*, Eva Marie Saint *(Edie Doyle)*, Leif Erickson *(Glover)*, James Westerfield *(Big Mac)*, Tony Galento *(Truck)*, Tami Mauriello *(Tillio)*

p, Sam Spiegel; d, Elia Kazan; w, Budd Schulberg (based on a story suggested by a series of articles by Malcolm Johnson); ph, Boris Kaufman; ed, Gene Milford; m, Leonard Bernstein; art d, Richard Day; cos, Anna Hill Johnstone

AA Best Picture; *AA Best Actor:* Marlon Brando; *AAN Best Supporting Actor:* Lee J. Cobb; *AAN Best Supporting Actor:* Karl Malden; *AAN Best Supporting Actor:* Rod Steiger; *AA Best Supporting Actress:* Eva Marie Saint; *AA Best Director:* Elia Kazan; *AA Best Story and Screenplay:* Budd Schulberg; *AA Best Cinematography:* Boris Kaufman; *AA Best Editing:* Gene Milford; *AAN Best Score:* Leonard Bernstein; *AA Best Art Direction:* Richard Day

A *tour de force* for director Elia Kazan, star Marlon Brando and, perhaps above all, cinematographer Boris Kaufman. ON THE WATERFRONT is a gritty, no-holds-barred drama about the corruption-glutted New York docks and the dock workers' excruciating struggle to make a living under the control of corrupt unions. Cobb is gangster union boss Johnny Friendly, and Steiger his crooked lawyer, Charley Malloy. Charley's brother, Terry (Brando), a former boxer, hangs around the docks and runs errands for Johnny, who gives handouts to those who do his bidding. Already a has-been as a young man, Terry keeps pigeons on a rooftop and dreams about his days as an promising fighter. Johnny tells Terry to ask a truculent union worker who is holed up in his apartment to meet him on the roof of his tenement. The worker shows up, and two of Johnny's goons push him off to his death as Terry watches in shock. Later, Terry tells some of Johnny's other thugs, "I thought they were only gonna lean on him a little," to which Truck (onetime heavyweight boxer "Two-ton" Tony Galento) replies, "The canary could sing but he couldn't fly!" Terry later meets Edie (Saint), the murdered man's sister, and begins to feel responsible for the death. She introduces him to Father Barry (Malden), who tells Terry that the dead man was killed because he was going to expose Johnny and his henchmen. The priest then exhorts Terry to provide the crime commission with information that will smash the dock racketeers.

Brando is spectacular as the ex-fighter who finds his conscience and risks his life for his newfound principles. The realistic dialogue is poetic in its simplicity, and the seedy tenements and clammy docks are strikingly captured. Kazan sets every scene with menace and suspense, evoking a pitiless world where tough hope is requisite for survival. Cobb is a great villain, exercising his power with a payoff, a sneering smile, and a booming voice, and his goons are really frightening characters, many of them former real-life boxers with faces scarred by years in the ring. Saint is an island of sanity and decency, but the attempt to use Malden as a symbol of good in a troubled world is awfully pat. The film is a draining experience from beginning to end, relentless in its portrayal of inhumanity. And it is all the more grim and hard-hitting because of the steel-gray look of cinematographer Kaufman's startling, neo-documentary approach.

A controversial film of its time because of its violence, raw language (at one point Terry tells the priest to "go to hell"), and its daring in representing labor unions in a negative light, WATERFRONT enjoyed a surprising box office success to match its critical acclaim, taking in $9.5 million on a $900,000 investment.

ONCE UPON A TIME IN AMERICA

1984   227m   c   Crime   ★★★★
Ladd   (U.S.)   R/18

Robert De Niro (Noodles), James Woods (Max), Elizabeth McGovern (Deborah), Treat Williams (Jimmy O'Donnell), Tuesday Weld (Carol), Burt Young (Joe), Joe Pesci (Frankie), Danny Aiello (Police Chief Aiello), Bill Forsythe (Cockeye), James Hayden (Patsy)

p, Arnon Milchan; d, Sergio Leone; w, Leo Benvenuti, Piero De Bernardi, Enrico Medioli, Franco Arcalli, Franco Ferrini, Sergio Leone, Stuart Kaminsky (based on the novel The Hoods by Harry Grey); ph, Tonino Delli Colli; ed, Nino Baragli; m, Ennio Morricone; art d, Carlo Simi, James Singelis; cos, Gabriella Pescucci, Nino Baragli

Italian director Sergio Leone returned to the screen after a 12-year absence, and the result is this ambitious, sprawling, insightful, frustrating, and ultimately challenging gangster film. Its structure is incredibly complex, flashing back and forth from the 20s to the 30s, to the 60s, basically following a group of Jewish boys who meet in the 1920s on Manhattan's Lower East Side. The story concentrates on the mercurial, borderline psychotic Max (James Woods) and Noodles (Robert De Niro), who has loved Deborah (Elizabeth McGovern) since they were children. The gang is virtually destroyed in 1933, but Noodles escapes and goes into hiding for 35 years, returning to New York in 1968 after receiving a mystifying letter. Though it's a confusing movie that has sparked debate and criticism, ONCE UPON A TIME IN AMERICA is visually stunning, rich in detail, and filled with outstanding performances.

ONCE UPON A TIME IN CHINA
(WONG FEI-HUNG)

1991   112m   c   Action/Historical/Martial Arts   ★★★★
Film Workshop   (Hong Kong)

Jet Li (Wong Fei-hung), Yuen Biao (Leung Foon), Jacky Cheung (Buck Teeth Sol), Rosamund Kwan (Aunt Yee), Kent Cheng (Porky Lang)

p, Raymond Chow; d, Tsui Hark; w, Tsui Hark, Yuen Kai-chi, Leung Yiu-ming, Tang Pik-yin; ph, David Chung, Bill Wong, Arthur Wong, Lam Kwok-wah, Chan Tung-chuen, Chan Pui-kai; ed, Mak Chi-sin; m, James Wong; prod d, Lau Man-hung; art d, Yee Chung-man; cos, Yu Ka-on

Tsui Hark's ONCE UPON A TIME IN CHINA is a truly dazzling achievement, even measured against Tsui's own considerable accomplishments and the hyperbolic standards of Hong Kong filmmaking, where riotous visual excess and surreal cross-cultural appropriations are the norm.

The year is 1875. Master Wong Fei-hung (Jet Li), a Confucian bone setter and righteous martial artist, establishes a clinic in Canton province and takes on several apprentices, including the comic Porky Lang (Kent Cheng) and Buck Teeth Sol (Jacky Cheung). Also in the mix is beautiful Aunt Yee (Rosamund Kwan), who has returned to China after many years abroad, bringing with her some strange and modern ideas. When Wong's clinic is burned down, he and his companions set out to

right the many wrongs they see around them. A rival kung-fu master, divorced from the spiritual component of his training, forces Wong to engage in a series of spectacular showdowns, but the real villain is creeping Westernization, embodied in the American soldiers who encourage opium addiction and coerce poor peasants to sail for America, where they'll wind up virtual slaves to the railroad barons.

For fans of Hong Kong films, Tsui Hark is a superstar on the level of a Steven Spielberg or George Lucas. Born in Vietnam and trained at the University of Texas, he has written, directed, and produced dozens of the most striking Hong Kong movies never seen in US theaters. The adventures of Master Wong are a longtime staple of Hong Kong genre cinema, so for Chinese viewers ONCE UPON A TIME IN CHINA is a revisionist exercise in the vein of YOUNG GUNS: the characters, settings, and situations are familiar, but they're all delivered with a distinctly contemporary twist. The title, with its knowing nod to Sergio Leone's remaking of American national fables, ONCE UPON A TIME IN THE WEST, is the tip-off that Tsui's aim is to dust off old genre conventions and present them, refreshed and revitalized, to a new generation of movie buffs.

ONCE UPON A TIME IN CHINA is a virtual non-stop festival of kung-fu display. Battles are staged in spectacular locales: at the opera, where the bad guys hide beneath brilliant traditional costumes and make-up; in a bizarrely out-of-place European-style restaurant; and in an enemy fortress full of ladders, which are deployed to astonishing effect. The action is lightning-fast (though it shows few signs of the overcranking that Hong Kong pictures often use to up the ante) and balletically staged, living up to the choreographic potential often claimed—but seldom truly realized—for martial arts pictures by their highbrow admirers.

ONCE UPON A TIME IN THE WEST

1969   165m   c   Western   ★★★★★
Rafran/San Marco   (U.S./Italy)   M/15

Henry Fonda (Frank), Claudia Cardinale (Jill McBain), Jason Robards Jr. (Cheyenne), Charles Bronson (The Man "Harmonica"), Frank Wolff (Brett McBain), Gabriele Ferzetti (Morton), Keenan Wynn (Sheriff), Paolo Stoppa (Sam), Marco Zuanelli (Wobbles), Lionel Stander (Barman)

p, Fulvio Morsella; d, Sergio Leone; w, Sergio Leone, Sergio Donati (based on a story by Dario Argento, Bernardo Bertolucci, Leone); ph, Tonino Delli Colli; ed, Nino Baragli; m, Ennio Morricone; art d, Carlo Simi; cos, Carlo Simi

Sergio Leone's masterpiece. In ONCE UPON A TIME IN THE WEST, Leone pulls together all the themes, characterizations, visuals, humor, and musical experiments of the three "Dollars" films and comes up with a true epic western. It is a stunning, operatic film of breadth, detail, and stature that deserves to be considered among the greatest westerns ever made. Although the original release in America was a severely edited version (Paramount wanted to cram an extra show in every night to sell more popcorn), the film was rereleased, uncut, in 1984. (The videotape version is also uncut.) ONCE UPON A TIME IN THE WEST's credit sequence is perhaps one of the most famous in cinema history. It unfolds slowly, deliberately, as Leone lingers on the strange behavior of Frank's (Fonda) three hired killers (two of whom are Jack Elam and Woody Strode in unforgettable cameos) who await the arrival of a train carrying "the Man" (Bronson), a stranger who has asked for an audience with Frank. The perfectly realized details—water dripping on Strode's bald head, Elam trying to shoo a pesky fly, and the third gang member cracking his knuckles—brings the scene immediately to life and create an almost unbearable sense of anticipation. It doesn't let up from there.

A series of galvanizing confrontations and shootouts built around a landowning whore-turned-widow (Cardinale), a scheming railroad magnate (Ferzetti), and the Man's mysterious reason for stalking the cold-blooded Frank, ONCE UPON A TIME IN THE WEST is often mesmerizing cinema. Casting baby blue-eyed, open-faced Fonda, with that underlying edge of hardness which Leone loved in Fonda's John Ford films, as a ruthless killer was a stroke of genius. His best bits: Frank's murder of a little boy, and the finale with the harmonica. Another major distinction is Morricone's brilliant score, featuring distinct themes for each of the four main characters (tuneless harmonica for Bronson, biting electric guitar for Fonda, humorous banjo for Robards's charming outlaw, and a lush, romantic score for Cardinale). What is really striking, though, is that Morricone based his composition on the script rather than shot footage, and Leone had his cast adapt their body rhythms to the score. The paths Leone was struggling to develop in his previous three westerns finally merge and take shape here. Called a "dance of death" by some critics who picked up on the strange relationship between the music and the actors, the film is an operatic eulogy for the western hero.

ONCE WERE WARRIORS

1994 99m c Drama ★★★
Communicado/New Zealand Film Commission/Avalon Studios/New Zealand On Air (New Zealand) RV18

Rena Owen (Beth Heke), Temuera Morrison (Jake Heke), Mamaengaroa Kerr-Bell (Grace Heke), Julian Arahanga (Nig Heke), Taungaroa Emile (Boogie Heke), Rachael Morris Jr. (Polly Heke), Joseph Kairau (Huata Heke), Clifford Curtis (Bully), Pete Smith (Dooley), George Henare (Bennett)

p, Robin Scholes; d, Lee Tamahori; w, Riwia Brown (based on the novel by Alan Duff); ph, Stuart Dryburgh; ed, Michael Horton; m, Murray Grindlay, Murray McNabb; prod d, Michael Kane; art d, Shayne Radford; cos, Michael Kane

A huge hit in New Zealand, where it surpassed JURASSIC PARK's box-office take, ONCE WERE WARRIORS is a fairly conventional look at lives blighted by poverty and cultural disenfranchisement. Still, it's hard-hitting stuff, and a welcome antidote to the sentimentalized picture of the Maoris—New Zealand's indigenous people—in 1993's THE PIANO.

The film opens with an image of New Zealand countryside that seems too placid and beautiful to be true. It is: the shot widens, and we're looking at a billboard in the middle of a squalid slum inhabited by urbanized Maoris. Proud, stubborn Beth Heke (Rena Owen) is making the best of a bad marriage to sexy, brutal ne'er-do-well Jake (Temuera Morrison). They have five children, no car, and a rundown house in a shabby neighborhood; what passes for fun is pub crawling and marathon drinking parties that frequently end in violence. When Jake loses his job and goes on the dole, their fragile family disintegrates with terrifying speed. Jake beats Beth, eldest son Nig (Julian Arahanga) joins a brutal gang, and adolescent Boogie (Taungaroa Emile) is placed in a group home for troubled boys. Thirteen-year-old Grace (Mamaengaroa Kerr-Bell), a shy dreamer, tries to shield her younger siblings from the chaos around them, but herself becomes its victim.

There's little new here, but uniformly powerful performances (especially Owen's) give the tale unexpected power and depth, and the exotic details—like the elaborate tribal tattoos worn by Nig's gang, or the Maori chants Boogie learns in reform school—make the Heke family's descent into misery seem fresher than it otherwise might.

ONE-EYED JACKS

1961 141m c Western ★★★½
Pennebaker (U.S.) /PG

Marlon Brando (Rio), Karl Malden (Dad Longworth), Katy Jurado (Maria), Pina Pellicer (Louisa), Slim Pickens (Lon), Ben Johnson (Bob Amory), Sam Gilman (Harvey), Larry Duran (Modesto), Timothy Carey (Howard Tetley), Miriam Colon (Redhead)

p, Frank P. Rosenberg; d, Marlon Brando; w, Guy Trosper, Calder Willingham (based on the novel The Authentic Death of Hendry Jones by Charles Neider); ph, Charles Lang; ed, Archie Marshek; m, Hugo Friedhofer; art d, Hal Pereira, Joseph MacMillan Johnson; fx, John P. Fulton, Farciot Edouart; chor, Josephine Earl; cos, Yvonne Wood

AAN Best Cinematography: Charles Lang, Jr.

Make room for Marlon. This offbeat, indulgent western, the only film directed by La Marlon, is almost as strange as his later THE MISSOURI BREAKS, but it does pack a wallp for patient viewers. Rio (Brando) and Dad (Malden) are bandits who rob a Mexican bank in 1880 but end up having to share a horse during their getaway. Realizing that they cannot outdistance the posse on one horse, Rio sends Dad off to find a second mount while he holds off the posse. Dad, however, gives up trying to find another horse, and rides off with the loot. Rio is of course

caught when his ammo runs out, and goes to prison. Breaking out after five years of brutal treatment, Rio eventually meets Dad again, still a nasty and deceptive man but now sheriff of a small town, with a wife (Jurado) and stepdaughter (Pellicer). It's not Father's Day, folks—Dad knows he's in trouble, so he takes steps to protect himself against the vengeful Rio.

Brando took over the film from Stanley Kubrick after the two disagreed on character development. The story draws heavily upon the legend of Billy the Kid (the father-son relationship between Malden and Brando is almost identical to that between lawman Pat Garrett and the outlaw William Bonney; the escape from jail and the abusive guard are obviously drawn from the Kid's own experiences). It is also fraught with too many pensive moments in which Brando, obviously in love with his own performance, broods and ponders. The painfully exacting star took all the time in the world behind the camera as well, spending six months shooting a film scheduled for two, exposing over a million feet of film. Marshek and others edited the film down to 141 minutes but it was still overlong, with scenes that played up Brando's martyr-like character (the whipping scene is almost a duplication of the Crucifixion). Lang's photography of the spectacular Monterey Peninsula, the windswept, ocean-lapped coast and rocky coastline, is outstanding, and Brando's performance, weird or not, is dynamic and intriguing. Malden is a classic study in guile, but the talented Jurado is unfortunately only a prop, and Pellicer is unconvincing as the naive girl. (This was Pellicer's only US film; after a short-lived career in Mexican pictures, she committed suicide at the age of 24.) Costing over $6 million (with an original budget of only $1.8 million), it only returned $4.3 million. This tale of basic revenge shows man as vile and contemptuous of his fellow man, a view repeatedly seen through the eyes of the often smug but never boring Brando.

ONE FALSE MOVE

1992 105m c Crime/Drama ★★★★
IRS Media (U.S.) R/18

Cynda Williams (Fantasia/Lila), Bill Paxton (Dale "Hurricane" Dixon), Billy Bob Thornton (Ray Malcolm), Jim Metzler (Dud Cole), Michael Beach (Pluto), Earl Billings (McFeely), Natalie Canerday (Cherylann)

p, Jesse Beaton, Ben Myron; d, Carl Franklin; w, Billy Bob Thornton, Tom Epperson; ph, James L. Carter; ed, Carole Kravitz; m, Peter Haycock, Derek Holt; prod d, Gary T. New; art d, Dana Torrey; cos, Ron Leamon

A superbly understated thriller from director Carl Franklin, an AFI graduate whose previous work was limited to Roger Corman outings like NOWHERE TO RUN and FULL FATHOM FIVE. ONE FALSE MOVE opens in suburban Los Angeles with the brutal murder of several family members and friends as part of a cash and cocaine robbery. The culprits are an interracial trio made up of a sadistic redneck sociopath, Ray Malcolm (Billy Bob Thornton, who co-wrote the screenplay); Pluto (Michael Beach), a would-be criminal genius who has a mean way with a knife; and Fantasia (Cynda Williams), the femme fatale who set up the slaughter. Piecing together accounts provided by neighbors with voices recorded on a videocam, LA cops Cole and McFeely (Jim Metzler and Earl Billings) identify Pluto and Ray, both ex-cons, and discover they're on their way to Star City, Arkansas, where Ray has an uncle. (In fact, the trio's plan is to go to Houston, convert the coke into cash, and then pass through Star City so that Fantasia can see her baby boy.) As Ray, Pluto, and Fantasia wend their way through the Southwest on a road trip that becomes increasingly fraught and futile, Cole and McFeely go to Star City, where they team up with local sheriff Dale "Hurricane" Dixon (Bill Paxton) to wait for the killers.

ONE FALSE MOVE is a finely observed character study punctuated by some highly suspenseful, and sometimes grisly, confrontations. Franklin gives a low-key, realistic feel to the criminals' travels, throwing in docudrama-style titles to show which towns they're driving through. The killer trio's road experiences are intercut with the LA cops' almost vacation-like stay in Star City, where Dixon amuses the big-city boys with his puppyish enthusiasm and aspirations to join the LA force. The cast is uniformly first rate, with Paxton an immensely charming small-town hero, Metzler suggesting a youthful Gig Young, and Beach and Thornton a memorably evil duo.

ONE FLEW OVER THE CUCKOO'S NEST

1975 129m c Drama ★★★★
Fantasy (U.S.) R/18

Jack Nicholson *(Randle Patrick McMurphy)*, Louise Fletcher *(Nurse Mildred Ratched)*, William Redfield *(Harding)*, Michael Berryman *(Ellis)*, Brad Dourif *(Billy Bibbit)*, Peter Brocco *(Col. Matterson)*, Dean R. Brooks *(Dr. John Spivey)*, Alonzo Brown *(Miller)*, Scatman Crothers *(Turkle)*, Mwako Cumbuka *(Warren)*

p, Saul Zaentz, Michael Douglas; d, Milos Forman; w, Lawrence Hauben, Bo Goldman (based on the novel by Ken Kesey and the play by Dale Wasserman); ph, Haskell Wexler, William A. Fraser, Bill Butler; ed, Richard Chew, Lynzee Klingman, Sheldon Kahn; m, Jack Nitzsche; prod d, Paul Sylbert; art d, Edwin O'Donovan; cos, Aggie Guerard Rodgers

AA Best Picture; AA Best Actor: Jack Nicholson; *AA Best Actress:* Louise Fletcher; *AAN Best Supporting Actor:* Brad Dourif; *AA Best Director:* Milos Forman; *AA Best Adapted Screenplay:* Lawrence Hauben, Bo Goldman; *AAN Best Cinematography:* Haskell Wexler, Bill Butler; *AAN Best Editing:* Richard Chew, Lynzee Klingman, Sheldon Kahn; *AAN Best Score:* Jack Nitzsche

Ken Kesey's grim satire of institutionalized authority, bracingly filmed by Milos Forman. This romp through a microcosmic lunatic ward with an energetic, wisecracking Nicholson turns unforgettably ugly at the end.

Doing time on a prison farm, Nicholson gets out of work detail and escapes the rigors of prison life by pretending to be crazy. Shipped to a mental asylum, he becomes the prisoner of a much more hateful system, presided over by a quietly sadistic head nurse, Fletcher. To his amazement Nicholson finds his fellow inmates are "no crazier than any other SOB on the street." To bring life to the dead atmosphere, Nicholson introduces card games (with pornographically illustrated cards), organizes basketball games, and even conducts a field trip for his fellow inmates, but at every turn Fletcher is there to administer punishment, attempting to break Nicholson's spirit. After Nicholson smuggles two floozies into the ward for an evening of booze and sex, Fletcher determines to squelch his rebellion—by any means necessary.

Jarring and electrifying drama, ONE FLEW OVER THE CUCKOO'S NEST is consummately acted by a talented ensemble including several future stars. Nicholson is at his peak; Fletcher's characteristic rigidity works well here. Actor Kirk Douglas acquired the rights to Wasserman's play (based on Kesey's novel) and had a great success with it on Broadway in the 1960s; by the time the film was made, he was too old to play the lead and turned the property over to his son Michael, who brought in Forman as director. This picture marked the screen debuts of gigantic Cree Indian painter Will Sampson, Brad Dourif, and Christopher Lloyd, and of Brooks (who was superintendent of the Damasch State Mental Hospital in Salem, Oregon, where the picture was filmed). Danny DeVito had acted on screen, but was almost unknown. Tom McCall, a former Oregon governor, plays a news commentator.

ONE HUNDRED AND ONE DALMATIANS

1961 79m c Children's/Animated ★★★½
Walt Disney Productions (U.S.) G/U

VOICES OF: Rod Taylor *(Pongo)*, Lisa Davis *(Anita)*, Cate Bauer *(Perdita)*, Ben Wright *(Roger Radcliff)*, Frederic Worlock *(Horace)*, J. Pat O'Malley *(Jasper/Miscellaneous Dogs)*, Betty Lou Gerson *(Cruella De Vil/Miss Birdwell)*, Martha Wentworth *(Nani/Goose/Cow)*, Tom Conway *(Collie)*, George Pelling *(Great Dane)*

p, Walt Disney; d, Wolfgang Reitherman, Hamilton Luske, Clyde Geronimi; w, Bill Peet (based on a book by Dodie Smith); ed, Donald Halliday, Roy M. Brewer Jr.; m, George Bruns; prod d, Ken Anderson; art d, Ken Anderson; anim, Milt Kahl, Marc Davis, Oliver M. Johnston Jr., Franklin Thomas, John Lounsbery, Eric Larson, Hal King, Cliff Nordberg, Eric Cleworth, Art Stevens, Hal Ambro, Bill Keil, Dick Lucas, Les Clark, Blaine Gibson, John Sibley, Julius Svendsen

Three hundred artists worked on this project for three years and came up with one of the best feature cartoons ever produced by Disney Studios. The story, a romance with an interesting detective twist, is combined with exquisite caricatures of both humans and dogs. The plot revolves around a dog, Pongo, and his master, Roger, who fall for Anita and her dog, Perdita. Roger and Anita marry, allowing Pongo and Perdita to be together and produce a litter of 15 Dalmatian puppies. Wicked Cruella De Vil is overly persistent in her desire to have all 15 puppies, but Roger refuses her, prompting the wealthy woman to hire a pair of cockney crooks to steal the pups. Roger and Anita try everything to locate them, but to no avail, so Pongo resorts to the "twilight bark," a system of dog signals that locates the puppies in a deserted mansion on the outskirts of London. Pongo, assisted by a dog named the Colonel, a horse, and a cat, then sets out to rescue the puppies, discovering in the process a total of 99 Dalmatians that the evil Cruella has gathered to make herself a rare coat. Throughout the story are subtle visual elements creating an atmosphere that transcends mere cartoon reality. The characters are also evocatively voiced by a cast that includes Rod Taylor as Pongo. For fun, note the physical resemblance between many of the dogs and their masters.

101 DALMATIANS

1996 103m c Children's/Comedy ★★
Great Oaks Entertainment/Walt Disney Pictures (U.S.) G/U

Glenn Close *(Cruella De Vil)*, Jeff Daniels *(Roger)*, Joely Richardson *(Anita)*, Joan Plowright *(Nanny)*, Hugh Laurie *(Jasper)*, Mark Williams *(Horace)*, John Shrapnel *(Skinner)*, Tim McInnerny *(Alonzo)*, Hugh Fraser *(Frederick)*, Zohren Weiss *(Herbert)*

p, John Hughes, Ricardo Mestres; d, Stephen Herek; w, John Hughes (based on the novel *The One Hundred and One Dalmatians* by Dodie Smith); ph, Adrian Biddle; ed, Trudy Ship; m, Michael Kamen; prod d, Assheton Gorton; art d, Alan Tomkins, John Ralph; fx, Michael Owens, Chrissie England, George Gibbs, Industrial Light & Magic, Jim Henson's Creature Shop; cos, Anthony Powell, Rosemary Burrows

This live-action remake of one of Disney's best, most commercially successful animated features is long and loud, but short on any real wit or charm.

Anita (Joely Richardson) is a put-upon fashion designer working for Queen Bitch of London, Cruella DeVil (Glenn Close). She suffers the insults of her boss-from-hell as well as her very un-p.c. fashion ideas involving the use of furs from various endangered species. One day in the park, she meets Roger (Jeff Daniels), a video game designer. Actually, it's their pet dalmatians, Pongo and Perdy, who begin the introductions, by falling instantly in love. The human owners immediately follow suit and are married. It is not long before the patter of little feet is heard, belonging to the amazing litter of 15 puppies which Perdy bestows on them. Cruella unfortunately learns of this blessed event and becomes obsessed with turning them all into the coat of her dreams.

The dogs Pongo and Perdy give by far the best performances in the film. Hack Disney house director Stephen Herek (THE MIGHTY DUCKS, MR. HOLLAND'S OPUS) leaves no antic stone unturned, lavishing them with closeups in which they run the gamut of emotions, from the elation of first love to blissful parenthood to childless sorrow. The humans fare decidedly less well than the dogs. Daniels could have given this performance in his sleep, and Richardson manages to give a slight impression of charm in her seriously undeveloped role. And Close, of course, has a field day: in her chiaroscuro hair and gaudy-baroque Anthony Powell ensembles, she's a visual joke that wears progressively thinner with her every cackling, snorting scene.

ONE HUNDRED MEN AND A GIRL

1937 85m bw Musical ★★★★
Universal (U.S.)

Deanna Durbin *(Patricia Cardwell)*, Leopold Stokowski *(Himself)*, Adolphe Menjou *(John Cardwell)*, Alice Brady *(Mrs. Frost)*, Eugene Pallette *(John R. Frost)*, Mischa Auer *(Michael Borodoff)*, Billy Gilbert *(Garage Owner)*, Alma Kruger *(Mrs. Tyler)*, Jack Smart *(Marshall, the Doorman)*, Jed Prouty *(Tommy Bitters)*

p, Joe Pasternak; d, Henry Koster; w, Bruce Manning, Charles Kenyon, James Mulhauser, Hans Kraly (based on a story by Hans Kraly); ph, Joseph Valentine; ed, Bernard W. Burton

AAN Best Picture; AAN Best Original Story: Hans Kraly; *AAN Best Editing:* Bernard W. Burton; *AA Best Score:* Charles Previn, Universal Studio Music Department; *AAN Best Sound:* Homer Tasker

Charming, still. There are many child stars who have been horrors to work with, but that was not the case with Deanna Durbin, who was surely one of the most agreeable tykes ever to don greasepaint. She began her career with Judy Garland in an MGM short, EVERY SUNDAY, but the studio dropped her and kept Garland. It wasn't that her voice wasn't resonant; it was merely that the studio felt there was only room for one teen singer (BIG mistake) and opted for Judy. Durbin was signed by Universal, cast in THREE SMART GIRLS, and did so well that they top-lined her in this one, which turned out to be a box-office winner that took the studio from the brink of bankruptcy. Menjou is a trombonist without a place to blow. His problem is shared by many of his musician friends, so our perky heroine forms an orchestra and convinces the eminent Leopold Stokowski to conduct it in concert. The orchestra is a hit and all ends well.

Many of Durbin's films (and Durbin herself) have been long underrated as being just too sweet for words, but this is hardly the case, partly because Durbin herself adds such an agreeable touch of spunk and spice to her standard "nice girl" roles. Her first ten films for Universal play delightfully today. ONE HUNDRED MEN AND A GIRL, for instance, is smoothly entertaining from start to finish, with an excellent mix of classical and pop music. The music includes selections from Liszt, Verdi, Wagner, Tschaikovsky and Mozart as well as tunes like "It's Raining Sunbeams" and "A Heart That's Free".

ONE OF OUR AIRCRAFT IS MISSING

1941 90m bw War ★★★½
Archers/British National (U.K.) /U

Godfrey Tearle (*Sir George Corbett*), Eric Portman (*Tom Earnshaw*), Hugh Williams (*Frank Shelley*), Bernard Miles (*Geoff Hickman*), Hugh Burden (*John Glyn Haggard*), Emrys Jones (*Bob Ashley*), Googie Withers (*Jo de Vries*), Pamela Brown (*Else Meertens*), Joyce Redman (*Jet van Dieren*), Hay Petrie (*Burgomeister*)

p, Michael Powell, Emeric Pressburger; d, Michael Powell, Emeric Pressburger; w, Michael Powell, Emeric Pressburger; ph, Ronald Neame; ed, David Lean; art d, David Rawnsley

AAN Best Original Screenplay: Michael Powell, Emeric Pressburger; *AAN Best Visual Effects:* Ronald Neame, C.C. Stevens

During WWII, squadrons of heavy Wellington bombers take off from Britain at dusk and cross the English Channel for a raid on Stuttgart. On the return flight, six crewmen on one plane are forced to bail out over German-occupied Holland. Some Dutch children help them evade a German patrol; then, disguised, they are aided by an underground network that enables them to reach the coast and to return to Britain in a small boat. Almost immediately after being reunited with their squadron they are back in the air, flying even more dangerous missions into Germany. The second Michael Powell-Emeric Pressburger collaboration (the first on which Pressburger was codirector), this film does not reach the heights of their previous, similarly plotted picture, THE INVADERS. The best sequences are the opening ones, precisely detailing the raid as the men concentrate on their duties, adjusting instruments while their planes shake under the anti-aircraft fire all around them. The performances—of the stiff-upper-lip variety—are all good, especially Godfrey Tearle's as the aircraft commander, Googie Withers's as an important link in the chain of rescuers, and Scottish character actor Hay Petrie's as an apoplectic burgomeister. The film's worth as a propaganda piece was considerable, but too many long-winded speeches about people uniting to fight the Germans date the film somewhat now.

ONE, TWO, THREE

1961 115m bw Comedy ★★★½
Mirisch/Pyramid (U.S.) /U

James Cagney (*C.R. MacNamara*), Horst Buchholz (*Otto Ludwig Piffl*), Pamela Tiffin (*Scarlett Hazeltine*), Arlene Francis (*Phyllis MacNamara*), Lilo Pulver (*Ingeborg*), Howard St. John (*Hazeltine*), Hanns Lothar (*Schlemmer*), Lois Bolton (*Mrs. Hazeltine*), Leon Askin (*Peripetchikoff*), Peter Capell (*Mishkin*)

p, Billy Wilder; d, Billy Wilder; w, Billy Wilder, I.A.L. Diamond (based on the play *Egy, Ketto, Harom* by Ferenc Molnar); ph, Daniel Fapp; ed, Daniel Mandell; m, Andre Previn; art d, Alexander Trauner; fx, Milt Rice

AAN Best Cinematography: Daniel L. Fapp

James Cagney left the movie business for more than 20 years after finishing his role in ONE, TWO, THREE and it's no wonder; he needed at least that much time to rest up after the fastest-moving comedy made in the 1960s, and surely one of the funniest. This film begins at mach one and gets somewhere near the speed of light by the time it finishes. As a matter of fact, it's often too furiously quick for its own good as the dialogue comes at the ears with Uzi-like speed. Cagney is the fast-talking, hard-driving, self-made man who heads up Coca-Cola's bottling interests in Germany. His attitude is similar to the man who once ran General Motors and said, "What's good for General Motors is good for America." And since there is nothing in Europe more American than Coca-Cola, Cagney is determined to bring it to everyone with two lips and a gullet. Cagney would like to become chief of all the European operations and is working toward that end when Tiffin, the teenage daughter of St. John—one of the heavyweights at Coca-Cola's Georgia headquarters—arrives, and Cagney has to baby-sit her for two weeks as she makes her way through a tour of the Continent. Cagney does his best to squire the dippy Tiffin, in the hope that her behavior will get him his desired promotion, but things go awry when she falls hard for Buchholz, a dedicated East Berlin Communist hippy. Cagney learns that St. John is coming to Germany at the same time he discovers Tiffin has married Buchholz. He plants a copy of that most capitalistic of papers, *The Wall Street Journal*, on Buchholz, figuring the youth will be clapped in irons and an annulment can be secured. Then he learns that Tiffin is expecting Buchholz's baby, so he has to get the kid out of jail and train him to be a capitalist in order to make him a suitable son-in-law for St. John. Cagney successfully springs Buchholz, spends a few bucks to purchase a royal title for him, and gives him a crash course in American business. Buchholz impresses St. John so much that the pleased father-in-law hands the plum job of running Europe to his new relation, the father of his unborn grandchild. Cagney winds up going back to Atlanta with wife Francis. He did his job too well and lost the promotion he'd hoped for.

Cagney plays this part with such verve and energy that he seems to be a much younger man than he was (62) and even appears to be a new actor eager to impress the studio with his abilities. But that was always the way Cagney played things—to the hilt. Many of the jokes were taken right from the period's headlines and were already dated by the time the film was released. It was based on a one-act play by the master farceur Molnar and expanded beautifully by Wilder and Diamond. Filmed on location in West Berlin and at the studios in Munich (where Wilder had been before the war), it won no awards except the laughter of those who saw it. Fapp got an Oscar nomination for his cinematography. Previn's score was perfect, and the use of several old ditties was excellent, including "Yes, We Have No Bananas" (Frank Silver, Irving Cohn). It would be better to watch this alone as the sound of chuckling in a theater will drown out many of the clever lines.

ONLY ANGELS HAVE WINGS

1939 121m bw Drama ★★★★
Columbia (U.S.) /A

Cary Grant (*Geoff Carter*), Jean Arthur (*Bonnie Lee*), Richard Barthelmess (*Bat McPherson*), Rita Hayworth (*Judith McPherson*), Thomas Mitchell (*Kid Dabb*), Sig Rumann (*Dutchman*), Victor Kilian (*Sparks*), John Carroll (*Gent Shelton*), Allyn Joslyn (*Les Peters*), Don "Red" Barry (*Tex Gordon*)

p, Howard Hawks; d, Howard Hawks; w, William Rankin (uncredited), Eleanore Griffin (uncredited), Jules Furthman (based on a story by Howard Hawks); ph, Joseph Walker, Elmer Dyer; ed, Viola Lawrence; m, Dimitri Tiomkin, Manuel Maciste, M.W. Stoloff; art d, Lionel Banks; fx, Roy Davidson, Edwin C. Hahn; cos, Robert Kalloch

AAN Best Visual Effects: Roy Davidson, Edwin C. Hahn

An amazing adventure film in which the adventure is primarily confined to a shabby saloon, this Grant-Arthur vehicle clearly bears the mark of director Howard Hawks. Grant, the head of a broken-down air freight company, sends courageous pilots over the treacherous Andes Mountains in Peru. Arthur becomes involved with one such pilot, Noah Beery, Jr., then quickly switches her attention to the hardboiled Grant. Several other pilots (Joslyn, Carroll, and Barry) are much taken with Arthur, but she only has eyes for the all-business Grant, who fails to return her affection. Enter Barthelmess, a pilot who tarnished his reputation in an accident years earlier in which another flier was killed. The guilt-ridden Barthelmess is washed up as a pilot, but Grant gives him a job anyway. Hayworth, Barthelmess's sexy, cuckolding wife, tries to seduce Grant and almost succeeds before Grant realizes he really loves the smart-talking Arthur. Although the other pilots have made a pariah of Barthelmess, he proves that he's made of courageous stuff by volunteering to take on the most hazardous missions. Meanwhile, Mitchell—an elderly pilot who acts as surrogate father to Grant and whose brother was killed in the accident that ruined Barthelmess's reputation—is losing his sight but won't admit it. Grant keeps him on the ground to protect him. But when Grant prepares to undertake a dangerous flight himself, Mitchell goes in his place.

ONLY ANGELS HAVE WINGS is a powerful character study, and director Hawks and his fine, predominantly male cast carefully develop the personalities of an interesting collection of characters. Though much of the dialogue is predictable, the story is strong, the acting is outstanding, and Hawks's cameras move with fluid grace through the confining sets.

Rita Hayworth gives a notable performance as a vamp, and supporting players Allyn Joslyn and John Carroll are jaded, sardonic live wires. Richard Barthelmess, as the film's most complex character, plays his role stoically, failing to invest his washed-up flier with the necessary emotional depth. This was an important comeback attempt for Barthelmess, who had experienced lean years since his days as a silent screen star. Regrettably, the meaty part he was given was left on the kitchen table, half-eaten, and Barthelmess never again appeared in a major film as a lead. The special effects, particularly the fine aerial sequences, earned Roy Davidson and Edwin C. Hahn an Oscar nomination in a category recognized for the first time by the Academy. The film was also nominated for Best Black-and-White Cinematography.

OPEN CITY
(ROMA, CITTA APERTA)

1945 105m bw War/Drama ★★★★
Excelsa (Italy) /A

Anna Magnani *(Pina)*, Aldo Fabrizi *(Don Pietro Pellegrini)*, Marcell Pagliero *(Giorgio Manfredi)*, Maria Michi *(Marina)*, Harry Feist *(Maj. Bergmann)*, Francesco Grandjacquet *(Francesco)*, Giovanna Galletti *(Ingrid)*, Vito Annichiarico *(Marcello Pina's Son)*, Carla Revere *(Lauretta)*, Nando Bruno *(Agostino)*

p, Roberto Rossellini; d, Roberto Rossellini; w, Sergio Amidei, Federico Fellini, Roberto Rossellini (based on a story by Amidei and Alberto Consiglio); ph, Ubaldo Arata; m, Renzo Rossellini

AAN Best Original Screenplay: Federico Fellini, Sergio Amidei

In its time, OPEN CITY was an innovative fusion of documentary and melodrama. Filmed on the streets, without the use of sound recorders (dialogue was dubbed in later), during the months just after the Allies liberated Italy from the grip of Fascism, the film has the appearance of a documentary. The actors, except for Anna Magnani (then a sometime dance-hall girl), were all nonprofessionals. The backgrounds were not constructions on a Cinecitta lot, but actual apartments, shops, and streets—a change for those used to sets and costumes. Set in Rome, 1943-44, the story brings together two enemy forces—the Communists and the Catholics—and unites them in the fight for their country's liberation. Manfredi (Marcello Pagliero) is a Resistance leader wanted by the Germans who must deliver some money to his compatriots. Hiding out in the apartment block of Francesco (Francesco Grandjacquet) and his pregnant fiancee, Pina (Magnani), Manfredi plans to let a Catholic priest, Don Pietro (Aldo Fabrizi), make the delivery. When their building is raided, Francesco is arrested and hauled away. Pino chases after him, screaming, and is gunned down in the middle of the street. Manfredi takes refuge in the apartment of his mistress, Marina (Maria Michi). She's a drug addict who, unknown to him, snitches for her dealer, an outrageous lesbian Gestapo agent (Giovanna Galleti). As excellent as OPEN CITY is, it has often been criticized for its simplistic moral scheme and emotional manipulation. Renzo Rossellini's score and various comic contrivances, for instance, don't jibe with the supposedly objective aims of neorealist cinema. Most videotape copies offer prints of mediocre quality and often unreadable subtitles.

OPERATION MAD BALL

1957 105m bw War/Comedy ★★★
Columbia (U.S.) /U

Jack Lemmon *(Pvt. Hogan)*, Kathryn Grant *(Lt. Betty Bixby)*, Ernie Kovacs *(Capt. Paul Locke)*, Arthur O'Connell *(Col. Rousch)*, Mickey Rooney *(M/Sgt. Yancy Skibo)*, Dick York *(Cpl. Bohun)*, James Darren *(Pvt. Widowskas)*, Roger Smith *(Cpl. Berryman)*, William Leslie *(Pvt. Grimes)*, Sheridan Comerate *(Sgt. Wilson)*

p, Jed Harris; d, Richard Quine; w, Jed Harris, Blake Edwards, Arthur Carter (based on the play by Arthur Carter); ph, Charles Lawton Jr.; ed, Charles Nelson; m, George Duning; art d, Robert Boyle

Lemmon received his first starring role in this military comedy which also served as the screen debut of the brilliant television comedian Ernie Kovacs. Based on a play, OPERATION MAD BALL centers on a group of bored WWII GIs stationed at an Army medical unit in France who try to improve morale by throwing a "Mad Ball" for the nurses. Unfortunately, all the nurses are officers and the enlisted men are forbidden to fraternize with them. The mastermind behind this plan is Lemmon, a fast-talking private who sneaks around behind the back of his by-the-book captain, Kovacs. Lemmon arranges for the party to be held at a hotel run by Jeanne Manet, a shifty French local out to make a fast buck off the GIs.

Rooney shines as the clever master sergeant who can dig up anything Lemmon needs at a moment's notice, and Grant (Mrs. Bing Crosby) is likable as Lemmon's disapproving girlfriend. The film is filled with some funny rapid-fire dialogue adapted by playwright Carter and producer Harris with help from a young Blake Edwards. OPERATION MAD BALL was the obsession of actor Richard Quine, who saw the property as his ticket into directing. Quine brought the screenplay to Columbia studio chief Harry Cohn and refused to sell it unless he could direct. Cohn balked at first but gave in with the proviso that Cohn and Jed Harris, who produced the show on Broadway and whom Cohn hated, would never meet. At one point in the shooting, Quine decided to film the climactic party scene at night and served the cast real alcohol so that everyone would be relaxed and in a party mood. When Cohn learned of the costly overtime shoot, he stormed onto the set and demanded an explanation. Quine explained his logic and invited the mogul to stay, have a drink, and watch the shooting. This seemed to appease Cohn, and he sat out of camera range sipping a drink and had a good time.

Kovacs grabbed eagerly at the chance to work his special magic on the big screen. He tackled the role of Capt. Paul Locke with verve and a malevolent zest and garnered good reviews. Unfortunately, Hollywood didn't really know what to do with Kovacs and typecast him in the role for much of his brief movie career. Of the nine movies Kovacs appeared in, he played a captain four times (OPERATION MAD BALL, OUR MAN IN HAVANA, WAKE ME WHEN IT'S OVER, and SAIL A CROOKED SHIP). Frustrated by this short-sighted casting which handcuffed his creativity, Kovacs took out an ad in *Variety* which simply read, "No more [*] [!!] captains."

OPERATION PETTICOAT

1959 124m c Comedy/War ★★★½
Granarte (U.S.) /U

Cary Grant *(Adm. Matt Sherman)*, Tony Curtis *(Lt. Nick Holden)*, Joan O'Brien *(Lt. Dolores Crandall)*, Dina Merrill *(Lt. Barbara Duran)*, Arthur O'Connell *(Sam Tostin)*, Gene Evans *(Molumphrey)*, Dick Sargent *(Stovall)*, Virginia Gregg *(Maj. Edna Hayward)*, Robert F. Simon *(Capt. J.B. Henderson)*, Robert Gist *(Watson)*

p, Robert Arthur; d, Blake Edwards; w, Stanley Shapiro, Maurice Richlin (based on a story by Paul King, Joseph Stone); ph, Russell Harlan, Clifford Stine; ed, Ted J. Kent, Frank Gross; m, David Rose; art d, Alexander Golitzen, Robert E. Smith; cos, Bill Thomas

AAN Best Original Screenplay: Paul King, Joseph Stone, Stanley Shapiro, Maurice Richlin

After the end of WWII, Adm. Matt Sherman (Cary Grant) reads over his log from the USS *Sea Tiger*, the submarine he captains. Sherman is about to turn over the command of the sub to Lt. Nick Holden (Tony Curtis), who is assigned to squire it until it is destroyed and replaced by a nuclear vessel. The movie unwinds in flashback as Sherman recalls some of the events in the sub's life—particularly how that life was renewed when he became determined to raise the *Sea Tiger* in the wake of an attack in Manila Bay. It's December 1941 and, with help from Holden, who secures the supplies and gear to help restore the badly damaged sub, Sherman and his crew take to the waters. Along the way, they are joined by five stranded nurses, a couple of Filipino families, and a goat. The sailors ferry them out of harm's way, especially enjoying the presence of the nurses—a chesty bunch who always seem to be passing the hot young sailors in the sub's very narrow corridors. They also paint the sub pink. There's not much story to speak of, and the jokes are more than a bit sexist, but the gags are bright and Blake Edwards's direction adroit enough to make OPERATION PETTICOAT an enjoyable time. A TV series was later attempted, but never came close to the energy of the movie.

ORDET

1955 126m bw Drama ★★★★★
Palladium (Denmark)

Henrik Malberg *(Morten Borgen)*, Emil Hass Christensen *(Mikkel Borgen)*, Preben Lerdorff-Rye *(Johannes Borgen)*, Cay Kristiansen *(Anders Borgen)*, Birgitte Federspiel *(Inger Mikkel's Wife)*, Ejner Federspiel *(Peter Skraedder)*, Ove Rud *(Pastor)*, Ann Elisabeth Rud *(Maren Borgen Mikkel's Daughter)*, Susanne Rud *(Lilleinger Borgen Mikkel's Daughter)*, Gerda Nielsen *(Anne Skraedder)*

p, Carl-Theodor Dreyer; d, Carl-Theodor Dreyer; w, Carl-Theodor Dreyer (based on the play by Kaj Munk); ph, Henning Bendtsen; ed, Edith Schussel; m, Poul Schierbeck; art d, Erik Aaes

Makes Ingmar Bergman look like Neil Simon. Based on the play by Kaj Munk, this inspirational drama focuses on one of director Dreyer's favorite themes, the conflict between institutional religion and personal faith.

Set in a staunchly God-fearing Danish village, ORDET tells the story of Morten Borgen (Malberg) and his three sons. Mikkel (Christensen) is filled with religious doubt. Anders (Kristiansen), meanwhile, is involved in a romance complicated by differences of faith. The central character, Johannes (Lerdorff-Rye), has the biggest problem of all: He believes he is Christ and his extreme faith is viewed as madness. Things change when he is visited by the Holy Spirit and Mikkel's wife is resurrected at her funeral.

Although any plot summary of ORDET would border on the ludicrous, the film is nothing of the kind. This is an overwhelming emotional and intellectual experience, thanks both to its subject matter and its austere yet potent presentation. Dreyer's rigorously spare visual style (the film contains only 114 shots in 126 minutes) perfectly conveys his metaphysical themes and creates a meditative and genuinely inspirational mood. Not to be missed, certainly by anyone who loved his great THE PASSION OF JOAN OF ARC.

ORDINARY PEOPLE

1980 124m c Drama ★★★½
Wildwood (U.S.) R/15

Donald Sutherland *(Calvin)*, Mary Tyler Moore *(Beth)*, Judd Hirsch *(Berger)*, Timothy Hutton *(Conrad)*, M. Emmet Walsh *(Swim Coach)*, Elizabeth McGovern *(Jeannine)*, Dinah Manoff *(Karen)*, Fredric Lehne *(Lazenby)*, James B. Sikking *(Ray)*, Basil Hoffman *(Sloan)*

p, Ronald L. Schwary; d, Robert Redford; w, Alvin Sargent (based on the novel by Judith Guest); ph, John Bailey; ed, Jeff Kanew; art d, Phillip Bennett, Michael Riva; cos, Bernie Pollack

AA Best Picture; AAN Best Actress: Mary Tyler Moore; *AA Best Supporting Actor:* Timothy Hutton; *AAN Best Supporting Actor:* Judd Hirsch; *AA Best Director:* Robert Redford; *AA Best Adapted Screenplay:* Alvin Sargent

Robert Redford chose to adapt Judith Guest's novel as his first directorial effort, with impressive results. Timothy Hutton (son of actor Jim Hutton) also debuts here, as Conrad, a potentially suicidal teen who is consumed with guilt over the drowning death of his brother (Doebler), compounded by the resentment his mother (Moore, in an astounding performance that made a dramatic departure from her clean-cut image) directs at him for having survived. As tensions mount, Conrad's father

(Sutherland) becomes increasingly distanced from his wife and depressed by his inability to communicate with, let alone restore, his family. When Conrad's new girlfriend (McGovern) kills herself, he is able to achieve a breakthrough with his psychiatrist (Hirsch), deciding he wants to live.

Although the story is admittedly slight, Redford demonstrates a tremendous understanding of his subjects, wealthy white suburbanites who struggle to conceal the rage and fear that eats away at them. His quiet, gentle direction is epitomized in memorably painful moments, such as the famous photo scene, when the squelched feelings threaten to explode. Several times, the film escapes easy resolutions, hanging on difficult moments longer than expected and refusing to slide into artificial closure. The script, which has the difficult task of illustrating the inner lives of essentially inarticulate people, is strongest in its characterization of the mother, whose own misery is withheld until Moore's heart-breaking final sequence (her own son died around the time of this production).

Redford was rewarded, not only with critical praise and a huge box-office hit, but with a surprising slew of Oscars, including Best Picture (beating out the infinitely more deserving RAGING BULL). Nonetheless, it would be eight years before he would direct again (THE MILAGRO BEANFIELD WAR), and he has yet to equal the sure touch and depth of insight shown in this film (with the possible exception of QUIZ SHOW, which is better directed but less emotionally resonant).

ORGANIZER, THE
(LES CAMARADES)

1964 126m bw Drama ★★★
Lux/Vides/Mediterranee/Avala (France/Italy/Yugoslavia) /A

Marcello Mastroianni *(Prof. Sinigaglia)*, Renato Salvaroti *(Raoul)*, Annie Girardot *(Niobe)*, Gabriella Giorgelli *(Adele)*, Bernard Blier *(Martinetti)*, Folco Lulli *(Pautasso)*, Francois Perier *(Maestro Di Meo)*, Vittorio Sanipoli *(Baudet)*, Giuseppe Cadeo *(Cenerone)*, Elvira Tonelli *(Cesarina)*

p, Franco Cristaldi; d, Mario Monicelli; w, Agenore Incrocci, Furio Scarpelli, Mario Monicelli; ph, Giuseppe Rotunno; ed, Ruggero Mastroianni; m, Carlo Rustichelli; art d, Mario Garbuglia; cos, Piero Tosi

AAN Best Original Screenplay: Scarpelli Age, Mario Monicelli

A coproduction of several companies, this powerful labor film won a number of awards, including four at the Argentina Film Festival in 1964, and a nomination by the Academy for Best Screenplay. Workers are toiling an ungodly number of hours at a Turin textile plant in the late 1800s. A worker is hurt because of his weariness, and three of his fellows (Tonelli, Lulli, and Blier) approach the company's bosses for some relief; but Sanipoli, the foreman, spurns them. The workers plan to retaliate by leaving work an hour before quitting time. Lulli gives the order, but Sanipoli won't let the workers go, and Lulli is rewarded for his attempted rebellion by suspension from his job without pay for a fortnight. The workers turn to Mastroianni, a professor who has come to stay in Turin with his pal, Perier, a schoolteacher. Mastroianni has made some political noises and is in semihiding, but he surfaces long enough to help the workers plan a strike. The bosses agree to lift Lulli's suspension and rescind any fine, but that's all they'll do, so the strike takes place. Management calls in the goons, but the angered workers meet the scabs at the train station, and violence follows during which Lulli is killed. Newspapers get the story and make it a cause celebre. Then the commissioner of the Turin police force tells the scabs that they must leave the city before any more deaths occur. Management, realizing that Mastroianni is behind the uprising, uses coercion to get the police to arrest the professor. He escapes the long arm of the law by staying with Girardot, a local lady of the evening. Sanipoli manages to talk Blier into going back to the mill for the good of all. At that, Mastroianni emerges from Girardot's apartment to make an impassioned speech that galvanizes the other mill employees. As one, they descend on the factory, where they are met by waiting soldiers who fire on the workers, killing a young teenager. Mastroianni is taken in by the police, and the workers go back to their labors. In the end the workers' plight seems the same, but they have made their presence felt, and unionism is the next step. Excellent film with good performances, although 20 minutes could have been cut out easily. Directed by the man who did what may be the best Italian comedy ever, BIG DEAL ON MADONNA STREET.

ORLANDO

1993 92m c Drama/Historical   ★★½
Adventure Pictures/Lenfilm/Spectator Entertainment   /PG
International/Sigma Films/Mikado Film/Rio Film
(U.K./Netherlands/Italy/France)

Tilda Swinton (Orlando), Billy Zane (Shelmerdine), Lothaire Bluteau (The Khan), John Wood (Archduke Harry), Charlotte Valandrey (Sasha), Heathcote Williams (Nick Greene/Publisher), Quentin Crisp (Queen Elizabeth I), Peter Eyre (Mr. Pope), Thom Hoffman (William of Orange), Kathryn Hunter (Countess)

p, Christopher Sheppard; d, Sally Potter; w, Sally Potter (from the novel by Virginia Woolf); ph, Alexei Rodionov; ed, Herve Schneid; art d, Michael Buchanan, Michael Howells, Stanislav Romanovsky, Igor Gulyenko; fx, Effects Associates; chor, Jacky Lansley

AAN Best Art Direction: Jan Roeles, Ben Van Os; *AAN Best Costume Design:* Sandy Powell

Suffocatingly beautiful, ORLANDO is a precious trifle whose literary pedigree intimidated audiences into ignoring its sublime silliness. It's visually intoxicating, with its lavish ruffs and furbelows, stately homes and manicured gardens, jewels and silks and elaborately curled hair, but there's less to ORLANDO than meets the eye.

Based on the 1928 novel by Virginia Woolf, ORLANDO opens in 17th century London. Orlando (Tilda Swinton) is an aristocratic youth, androgynous in the fashion of the time and gravely determined to translate life, of which he knows little, into art, of which he knows even less. Orlando captures the fancy of aging Queen Elizabeth I (Quentin Crisp), a crone who orders him not to grow old or wither. Orlando obeys, inexplicably remaining fresh-cheeked as centuries slip past. A romantic to his core, Orlando suffers mightily his unrequited love for the enchanting Russian princess Sasha (Charlotte Valandrey); when she proves false, he seeks out an extended term as England's ambassador to Arabia. One day, Orlando falls into a deep sleep and, when he awakens days later, has undergone a miraculous sex change. Orlando's adventures continue, and she spends the ensuing centuries refusing to behave differently simply because she's now a woman.

ORLANDO is undeniably ravishing, and its politics are almost suspiciously in tune with the times. But beneath the glittering surface is precious little substance: this is a date movie for aspiring intellectuals, a source of smug satisfaction at having chosen to see a thought-provoking movie, unspoiled by the realization that there isn't much to think about.

ORPHANS

1987 115m c Drama   ★★★★
Lorimar (U.S.)   R/15

Albert Finney (Harold), Matthew Modine (Treat), Kevin Anderson (Phillip), John Kellogg (Barney), Anthony Heald (Man in Park), Novella Nelson (Mattie), Elizabeth Parrish (Rich Woman), B. Constance Barry (Lady in Crosswalk), Frank Ferrara (Cab Driver), Clifford Fearl (Doorman)

p, Alan J. Pakula, Susan Solt; d, Alan J. Pakula; w, Lyle Kessler (based on the play by Lyle Kessler); ph, Don McAlpine; ed, Evan Lottman; m, Michael Small; prod d, George Jenkins; art d, John J. Moore; chor, Lynnette Barkley; cos, John Boxer

After the dismal failure of 1986's DREAM LOVER, director Alan J. Pakula returned to top form with the screen version of the popular 1985 Lyle Kessler play *Orphans*. Basically a three-man show, ORPHANS deals with a pair of orphaned brothers, Treat (Matthew Modine) and Phillip (Kevin Anderson), who live in a dilapidated old house in a seedy part of Newark, New Jersey. Treat, a potentially dangerous petty thief, is the dominant sibling. Fearing that he will lose his brother just as he lost his parents, Treat keeps Phillip imprisoned in his own home. Harold (Albert Finney) is brought home by Treat as a potential kidnapping victim, but he quickly begins to take control of the situation. It's not often that a play can survive the transition from stage to screen without

suffering some loss. ORPHANS, however, does. Kessler (who wrote both the stage play and the screenplay) worked his claustrophobic, prisonlike setting to the film's advantage. More important to the success of ORPHANS is the brilliant acting by all three leads. Finney turns in a spectacular performance. Modine displays another facet of his acting ability as the violent, emotionally confused Treat. Anderson, whose image changes as his character becomes readied for the outside world, keeps pace with (and often surpasses) his costars. Part fairy tale and part heightened reality, ORPHANS manages to strike an emotional chord with almost everyone who sees it.

ORPHEUS
(ORPHEE)

1949 112m bw Fantasy   ★★★★½
Andre Paulve (France)   /PG

Jean Marais (Orpheus), Maria Casares (The Princess), Marie Dea (Eurydice), Francois Perier (Heurtebise), Juliette Greco (Aglaonice), Edouard Dermit (Cegeste), Henri Cremieux (Friend in Cafe), Pierre Bertin (Police Commissioner), Roger Blin (Writer), Jacques Varennes

p, Emil Darbon; d, Jean Cocteau; w, Jean Cocteau (based on the play by Jean Cocteau); ph, Nicolas Hayer; ed, Jacqueline Sadoul; m, Georges Auric, Christophe Willibald Gluck; art d, Jean d'Eaubonne

A compelling cinematic allegory from one of the great artists of the twentieth century, ORPHEUS is the perfect example of magical filmmaking. Updating the Greek myth and adding an autobiographical element—the story is now set in contemporary Paris—Cocteau casts his longtime companion Jean Marais as Orpheus, a famous poet married to Eurydice (Marie Dea). When a fellow poet, the handsome young Cegeste (Edouard Dermit), is hit by a passing motorcyclist in front of a popular cafe, Orpheus is invited by an elegant and mysterious Princess (Maria Casares) to accompany her and the dead poet to her chalet. There, the Princess brings Cegeste "back to life" (by ingeniously running the film backwards for that one shot, Cocteau was able to perform such magic) and disappears through a liquescent mirror into the Underworld. Later, after being chauffeured home by the Princess's servant, the angel Heurtebise (Francois Perier), Orpheus devotes himself to his poetry, scribbling down indecipherable messages transmitted to him over a car radio. He ignores everything but the radio and fails to even notice when Eurydice is killed. Heurtebise, who has fallen in love with Eurydice during Orpheus's preoccupation with poetry, comes to suspect that the Princess overstepped her authority as an Angel of Death by killing Eurydice in order to make room for herself in Orpheus's life. Together, Heurtebise and Orpheus pass through the mirror and journey into the Underworld to find the Princess and Eurydice.

Awarded the top prize at the 1950 Venice Film Festival, ORPHEUS was instantly heralded as a masterpiece. It was blessed with perfect casting (though Cocteau had considered both Greta Garbo and Marlene Dietrich for Casares's role), photographic innovation, indelible imagery and an exceptional score by Georges Auric. The film is as much about the creative process as it is about death, but even those who miss its many meanings will still be hypnotized by its style and beauty. As with all Cocteau's films, the written word cannot adequately describe the visual sensations he creates, sensations that do not diminish with the passage of time.

OSSESSIONE

1942 112m bw Drama   ★★★½
ICI Roma (Italy)   /PG

Clara Calamai (Giovanna), Massimo Girotti (Gino), Juan De Landa (The Husband), Elia Marcuzzo (Lo Spagnuolo), Dhia Cristani (Anita), Vittorio Duse (The Lorry Driver), Michele Riccardini, Michele Sakara

p, Libero Solaroli; d, Luchino Visconti; w, Mario Alicata, Antonio Pietrangeli, Gianni Puccini, Giuseppe De Santis, Luchino Visconti (based on the novel *The Postman Always Rings Twice* by James M. Cain); ph, Aldo Tonti, Domenico Scala; ed, Mario Serandrei; m, Giuseppe Rosati; art d, Gino Rosati

The first directorial effort in the brilliant, though sporadic, career of Luchino Visconti was made in 1942 but not shown in the US until 1959 because of copyright problems. Based on the James M. Cain novel *The Postman Always Rings Twice,* the film is a sizzling love story set against a background of murder and adultery along the backroads of the Italian countryside. The nomadic Gino (Massimo Girotti), a man living under the illusion that attachments only act as a hindrance, happens upon the roadside inn run by Giovanna (Clara Calamai) and her older, grotesque-looking husband (Juan de Landa). One look at this couple tells their entire story: she is young, beautiful, and full of passion, married to a man unequal to her in all areas except one—money. Giovanna soon takes a romantic interest in the visitor, discovering the spark that never ignited with her husband. It's a potentially murderous situation.

Despite its exquisitely hardboiled source material and film noir plot, OSSESSIONE is often cited as the first harbinger of neorealism. The film was shot in the Italian countryside (as opposed to the studios—a technique favored by Jean Renoir, with whom Visconti apprenticed) and showed the Italian people living in their natural environs. Because the Fascist government of 1942 had complete control over film production in Italy, Visconti had to have his script okayed before shooting. The government saw nothing wrong with the script he presented, but was quite shocked with the final product, which displayed an Italy in contrast to the stylized depiction common to Italian films of the time. Fearful of political overtones, the government temporarily shelved the film, only to put it back into circulation after Mussolini saw and enjoyed it. As a portrayal of the conflict between moral conscience and uncontrollable passion, between the need to maintain a secure existence and the desire to remain free of any confining forces, OSSESSIONE is a powerful statement, and a remarkable first film from Visconti.

OTHELLO

1952 90m bw Drama ★★★½
Mercury (U.S./France/Italy) /U

Orson Welles (*Othello*), Michael MacLiammoir (*Iago*), Suzanne Cloutier (*Desdemona*), Robert Coote (*Roderigo*), Hilton Edwards (*Brabantio*), Michael Laurence (*Cassio*), Fay Compton (*Emilia*), Nicholas Bruce (*Lodovico*), Jean Davis (*Montano*), Doris Dowling (*Bianca*)

p, Orson Welles; d, Orson Welles; w, Orson Welles (based on the play by William Shakespeare); ph, Anchisi Brizzi, G.R. Aldo, Georges Fanto, Oberdan Trojani, Alverto Fusi; ed, Jean Sacha, John Shepridge, Renzo Lucidi, William Morton; m, Angelo Francesco Lavagnino, Alberto Barberis; art d, Alexander Trauner; cos, Maria De Matteis

Orson Welles's version of the Shakespearean tragedy, with the director also turning in a magnificent performance as the title character. Though he had spent only three weeks shooting his MACBETH, Welles devoted four years to this picture, a production that proceeded by fits and starts as he struggled to scrape together cash from various sources. (As part of his fund-raising efforts, Welles did acting duties in Henry King's PRINCE OF FOXES, Henry Hathaway's THE BLACK ROSE, and Carol Reed's THE THIRD MAN.) Though the final result cannot disguise its on-again, off-again production history—sloppy sound synchronization, cutaways to hide absent actors, lines dubbed by performers other than those onscreen—it nonetheless stands as an important part of the Welles canon, and one of the finest screen adaptations of Shakespeare. The text of the original play has been slashed to its bare bones, with bravura cinematography and editing also helping make this a taut, visceral experience. Michael MacLiammoir, an old Abbey Theatre friend of Welles's, makes a truly devious and convincing Iago, and Suzanne Cloutier is a serenely beautiful Desdemona. OTHELLO co-won the Best Feature Film prize at Cannes in 1952, but enjoyed little commercial success in the US at the time. A partially restored version was released to considerable critical acclaim in 1992.

OUR DAILY BREAD

1934 74m bw Drama ★★★
Viking (U.S.) /A

Karen Morley (*Mary Sims*), Tom Keene (*John Sims*), John Qualen (*Chris*), Barbara Pepper (*Sally*), Addison Richards (*Louie*), Harry Holman, Billy Engle, Frank Minor, Henry Hall, Ray Spiker

p, King Vidor; d, King Vidor; w, King Vidor, Elizabeth Hill, Joseph L. Mankiewicz; ph, Robert Planck; ed, Lloyd Nosler; m, Alfred Newman

This was part of an intended film trilogy by Vidor, and a film that he always considered equal in quality to his majestic silent classic THE CROWD. It is not, but it has a certain poignancy, quaintness, and simplicity that make it a strong document of hard times in the early 1930s. During the depth of the Depression, Morley and Keene, down and out like most Americans, inherit a dilapidated farm and seek to save it and themselves by inviting homeless but hard-working people to join them in a farm collective, or loosely organized commune. While everyone slaves away at tilling the soil and eking out a few meals a day, Keene grows restless and depressed. Then Pepper—a slovenly, slatternly city girl—arrives and quickly seduces Keene, persuading him to run away with her. He deserts Morley and his fellow workers and heads for the city in the middle of a drought, the wheat withering under a blazing sun. As he makes his way with Pepper, Keene suddenly discovers a hidden stream and his thoughts go back to the needy people of his farm. He cannot desert them after all and races back to tell one and all that water is at hand and, if they all work like demons, they might be able to divert the stream and irrigate the crops, saving their future. Men, women, and children pour forth with tools and form a chain of workers who run ahead of the diverted stream, furiously digging a ditch and shoring it up with boulders, chopping down trees and bushes, anything in the water's path, until it flows freely downhill into the valley, where the farm and thirsty crops await. The jubilant farm workers (some so excited that they cartwheel across the screen) are saved and so, too, is Morley's marriage. The ever-faithful wife is reunited with her errant husband and the world is once more bearable, if not overly hopeful. The film was shot on a shoestring after Irving Thalberg, production chief at MGM, told Vidor that he wanted no part of a film dealing with farm communes (or any kind of picture offering a strong socialist message). Vidor nevertheless went ahead and produced a film of sincerity and powerful emotions, even though his actors, except for Morley and a few others, were amateurs. One report stated that Vidor was compelled to use Pepper—a thoroughly inept actress—at the insistence of one of Vidor's financial backers. She nevertheless is surprisingly convincing as the city tramp and has become a minor cult-film figure. Most of the film reflects Vidor's great vitality, especially the spectacular irrigation scenes at the end, some of the most dramatic and dynamic moments ever put on celluloid. Yet much of the film lacks the overall polish and professionalism that a first-rate budget would have given it. It is obvious that Vidor was inspired by the Soviet film THE EARTH THIRSTS (1930) by Yuli Rayzman; it is also true that the scenes showing crowds of Chinese farmers massing to ward off the locusts in THE GOOD EARTH (1936) were inspired by this Vidor production.

OUR HITLER, A FILM FROM GERMANY
(HITLER, EIN FILM AUS DEUTSCHLAND)
1977 450m c Drama ★★★
OMNI Zoetrope (West Germany)

Heinz Schubert, Peter Kern, Helmut Lange, Rainer von Artenfels, Martin Sperr, Peter Moland, Johannes Buzalski, Alfred Edel, Amelie Syberberg, Harry Baer

d, Hans-Jurgen Syberberg; w, Hans-Jurgen Syberberg; ph, Dietrich Lohmann; ed, Jutta Brandstaedter; m, Richard Wagner; art d, Hans Gailling; cos, Barbara Gailling, Brigitte Kuhlenthal

German director Hans-Jurgen Syberberg, who was born in 1935 and grew up under Nazi rule, presents an epic nightmare ruminating on the effect Adolf Hitler had and continues to have on Germany and on humankind. Originally presented on German television in four parts, OUR HITLER's American release (at seven and a half hours) is generally shown in two parts. Syberberg presents a simple theme: Such evil as occurred in Hitler could never have existed without the support, however unwitting, of the rest of humanity. (The word "our" was added to the American title by its distributor, Francis Ford Coppola, driving the point home further.) The presentation is the stuff of nightmares. The music of Hitler's beloved Richard Wagner is included to suggest a sort of decadent, modern Wagnerian opera. Syberberg's vision is not an optimistic one; it is forthright and brutal in its honesty, a vision of humanity's dark, unsettling dreams.

OUR MAN IN HAVANA

1959 111m bw Comedy   ★★★★
Kingsmead (U.K.)   /A

Burl Ives (*Dr. Hasselbacher*), Alec Guinness (*Jim Wormold*), Brul Ives (*Dr. Hasselbacher*), Maureen O'Hara (*Beatrice Severn*), Ernie Kovacs (*Capt. Segura*), Noel Coward (*Hawthorne*), Ralph Richardson ("*C*"), Jo Morrow (*Milly Wormold*), Paul Rogers (*Hubert Carter*), Gregoire Aslan (*Cifuentes*)

p, Carol Reed; d, Carol Reed; w, Graham Greene (based on his novel); ph, Oswald Morris; ed, Bert Bates; m, Hermanos Deniz; art d, John Box; cos, Phyllis Dalton

As hilarious as it is absurd, this droll comedy about spies in Cuba stars the prodigiously talented Guinness. The real world of espionage is ridiculous enough, but director Reed manages to make it seem even sillier by putting an innocuous vacuum cleaner salesman (Guinness) in the the middle of all the clandestine goings-on. Guinness, the owner of a small store in Havana, is approached by Coward, a master spy who enlists him as an agent. Realizing he will be making good money for every tidbit of information he passes along to headquarters in London, and wanting that money to be able to buy the good things in life for his daughter (Morrow), but knowing there is no real information to gather, Guinness begins to invent information. Kovacs, the reportedly brutal chief of police, who has cast a covetous eye on Morrow, gets reports that Guinness has been acting in a furtive manner. Kovacs spies on Guinness, while Guinness spies on Kovacs, and the whole affair begins to expand crazily. However, the intrigue ceases to be phony when Guinness is forced to dispatch a very real enemy. Nevertheless, Guinness eventually has to admit to the fabricated nature of the information he has been providing to British intelligence, and he is ordered back to London, where he meets an unexpected fate. Mixing subtle comedy with sinister consequences, OUR MAN IN HAVANA is probably Guinness' drollest film. Guinness is superb as the greedy but imaginative shop owner, but Kovacs, as the posturing police chief, and Coward, as the British master spy, steal the film, which was shot in Havana shortly after the Cuban Revolution.

OUR RELATIONS

1936 65m bw Comedy   ★★★★
Stan Laurel/Hal Roach (U.S.)   /U

Stan Laurel (*Himself/Alfie Laurel*), Oliver Hardy (*Himself/Bert Hardy*), Sidney Toler (*Captain of the S.S. Periwinkle*), Alan Hale (*Joe Groagan, the Waiter*), Daphne Pollard (*Mrs. Daphne Hardy*), Betty Healy (*Mrs. Betty Laurel*), Iris Adrian (*Alice, the Beer Garden Girl*), Lona Andre (*Lily, the Other Cafe Girl*), James Finlayson (*Finn, the Chief Engineer*), Arthur Housman (*Inebriated Stroller*)

p, Stan Laurel, L.A. French; d, Harry Lachman; w, Richard Connell, Felix Adler, Charles Rogers, Jack Jevne (based on the short story "The Money Box" by William Jacobs); ph, Rudolph Mate; ed, Bert Jordan; m, LeRoy Shield; art d, Arthur I. Royce, William Stevens; fx, Roy Seawright

Perhaps the best Laurel and Hardy feature, OUR RELATIONS marked Stan Laurel's first credit as a producer, and he does an excellent job in this elaborate picture that owes a great deal to Shakespeare's "Comedy Of Errors." Stan and Ollie, sailors on shore leave, have a valuable diamond ring to deliver. Knowing that in the past they've spent all their money while on liberty, they give their cash to Sidney Toler, their captain, telling him to hold it in safekeeping and not to return it until after their ship has sailed. The town they are visiting is the same place where their twin brothers now live in domestic harmony with their henpecking wives, Daphne Pollard and Betty Healy. Stan and Ollie meet two girls, Iris Adrian and Lona Andre, in a local waterfront dive, while nearby, their twins are quaffing beer with their mates in another tavern. Need we say that the duos are soon mixed? The diamond ring turns up missing, and when Stan and Ollie can't locate the jewel, gangsters Ralf Harolde and Noel Madison trap the pair in cement blocks and leave them on a pier where they will soon fall into the water. Naturally, it all comes together in the end with the right husbands re-matched with the correct wives and the twins reunited after a long separation. Several funny scenes include Laurel and Hardy attempting to convince Toler to give them back their money; a set-piece in a hotel

room where they have been placed without clothing; and their difficulty (as the married men) to make beer-hall owner Alan Hale, Sr., understand that they had not been there earlier with Adrian and Andre. Amidst all the fun, there is real danger to the boys when they come up against the villains. This was the first and only time they worked with director Harry Lachman, who was not known for his comedic skills. (His most famous feature was DANTE'S INFERNO, 1935; he also did a couple of CHARLIE CHAN films.) He seems to just turn on Rudolphe Mate's camera and let the boys have their way with the humor. A standout comedy role was played by Arthur Housman as a drunk, and Stanley Sandford, one of the wharf rats, was appearing in his final film of the 23 he made with Laurel and Hardy. In one of her first roles, Iris Adrian was developing the character she would play for the next several decades, the brash blonde with a heart of gold. Despite the excellence of this film, other Laurel and Hardy movies are better remembered.

OUR TOWN

1940 90m bw Drama   ★★★★
Principal Artists (U.S.)   /A

Frank Craven (*Mr. Morgan, the Narrator*), William Holden (*George Gibbs*), Martha Scott (*Emily Webb*), Fay Bainter (*Mrs. Gibbs*), Beulah Bondi (*Mrs. Webb*), Thomas Mitchell (*Dr. Gibbs*), Guy Kibbee (*Editor Webb*), Stuart Erwin (*Howie Newsome*), Philip Wood (*Simon Stinson*), Doro Merande (*Mrs. Soames*)

p, Sol Lesser; d, Sam Wood; w, Thornton Wilder, Frank Craven, Harry Chandlee (based on the play by Thornton Wilder); ph, Bert Glennon; ed, Sherman Todd; m, Aaron Copland; prod d, William Cameron Menzies, Harry Horner

AAN Best Picture; AAN Best Actress: Martha Scott; *AAN Best Score:* Aaron Copland; *AAN Best Art Direction:* Lewis J. Rachmil; *AAN Best Sound:* Thomas Moulton

Sam Wood directed this version of Thorton Wilder's Pulitzer Prize-winning play about the multiple relationships among the folks in a small New England town. The "our town" genre—studies of the relationships that mold a community—became a welcome staple of the movies. Wilder must be given credit for establishing such an important form.

Our Town is brought to the screen with wonderful characterizations by an inspired cast. Small-town America is typified by Craven, the down-home narrator who profiles the lives of citizens of Grover's Corners. Scott is the idealistic but hard-working daughter of the local newspaper editor, and Holden is the son of the local physician who falls in love with Scott, goes through a difficult courtship, and finally wins her hand in marriage. Life in this quaint small town is shown in three periods—1901, 1904, and 1913—with the attention basically focused upon two families, those of Holden and Scott. The result is a moving portrait of small-town America before WWII.

Remaining faithful to Wilder's script, director Wood skillfully conveys the laughter, love, and pain in the lives of Wilder's heartwarming characters. And the techniques Wood employs to tell their stories are marvelous to behold: a dazzling series of dissolves, evocative lighting, and montages that effectively capture the flavor of the periods depicted. Scott, appearing in her first film, is splendid, as is Holden. Mitchell as the physician, Kibbee as the editor, and their wives, played by Bainter and Bondi, all provide sturdy supporting performances. Wood's outstanding direction is enhanced by a stirring score by Copland and lovely sets by Menzies, who is a genius at capturing any locale.

OUR VINES HAVE TENDER GRAPES

1945 105m bw Drama   ★★★★
MGM (U.S.)   /U

Edward G. Robinson (*Martinius Jacobson*), Margaret O'Brien (*Selma Jacobson*), James Craig (*Nels Halverson*), Agnes Moorehead (*Bruna Jacobson*), Jackie "Butch" Jenkins (*Arnold Hanson*), Morris Carnovsky (*Bjorn Bjornson*), Frances Gifford (*Viola Johnson*), Sara Haden (*Mrs. Bjornson*), Louis Jean Heydt (*Mr. Faraassen*), Francis Pierlot (*Minister*) p, Robert Sisk; d, Roy Rowland; w, Dalton Trumbo (based on the novel *For Our Vines Have Tender Grapes* by George Victor Martin); ph, Robert Surtees; ed, Ralph E. Winters; m, Bronislau Kaper; art d, Cedric Gibbons, Edward Carfagno; fx, A. Arnold Gillespie, Danny Hall; cos, Irene, Kay Carter

Few films touch the heart so deeply as this one and fewer still present such moving performances. Robinson is terrific as the Norwegian-born Wisconsin farmer and father of O'Brien; he's a widower who is strict with his precocious offspring but also loving and tender. In O'Brien's world there are daily tragedies, such as the time she accidentally kills a squirrel, but her understanding father is always there to comfort her. Robinson hears that a huge circus is passing through town on a train; since his daughter will not have the opportunity to see the circus in performance, Robinson drives with O'Brien in the middle of the night to the train station and offers one of the foremen of the circus a few dollars if he'll only bring one of the elephants off the train for a few minutes. O'Brien is filled with wonder at the sight of the great, gentle beast. When attractive Gifford arrives in Benson Junction to teach school, a great deal of excitement ensues, especially among the children and gossipy neighbors, who observe how handsome town editor Craig is drawn to her. Craig proposes after a while, but Gifford draws back, fearing that she will be bored to death in the small farming community. Craig is called to serve in WWII and asks Gifford to wait for him, but she cannot make such a commitment. Later, a near tragedy almost consumes the town when O'Brien and her cousin, Jenkins, disappear. The community is in an uproar as a frantic search for the children is conducted during torrential spring rains. They are found alive but soaking wet in a bathtub that has taken them on a perilous journey through the swollen waters of a nearby stream. Robinson doesn't know whether to spank or hug his adventurous child and opts for the latter. But he is severe with O'Brien when she refuses to let Jenkins borrow her skates. Robinson is the personification of a man who knows when to display emotion, such as explaining to his daughter, upset at Craig's induction into the service, that to preserve "peace on earth," one must be willing to fight for peace. All of the lessons taught by Robinson come to fruition when the town gathers to hear that a neighbor's farm has been struck by lightning and that the resultant fire has wiped him out. O'Brien is the first to stand up in church and offer her prize calf to the destitute farmer, which starts a run of charity through the parishioners. Robinson beams in pride at his daughter and then forgoes his own plans for a new barn to help the stricken neighbor. This wonderful outpouring of neighborly generosity and compassion is witnessed by schoolteacher Gifford, who then and there decides that Benson Junction is not a dull place after all but one of the grandest spots on earth in which to live. She resolves to stay there and wait for Craig to return from the war.

Supporting Robinson with marvelous performances are O'Brien, who furthered her juvenile career in films mightily with this entry, as did Jenkins, one of Louis B. Mayer's favorite child actors. Moorehead is excellent and sports a mild Norwegian accent in an underplayed part, and Morris, as the retarded neighbor who dies, displays fine talent. Craig and Gifford made such convincing and gentle lovers that MGM teamed them again in SHE WENT TO THE RACES (1945) and LITTLE MR. JIM (1946). Released just after V-J Day, OUR VINES HAVE TENDER GRAPES was written with great care by the talented Trumbo, whom Robinson had earlier befriended (he was later criticized for this friendship by citizens siding with HUAC during the Sen. Joseph McCarthy era, when Trumbo was part of the "Hollywood Ten").

OUT OF AFRICA

1985 150m c Romance   ★★½
Universal (U.S.)   PG

Meryl Streep *(Karen Blixen-Finecke)*, Robert Redford *(Denys Finch Hatton)*, Klaus Maria Brandauer *(Baron Bror Blixen-Finecke)*, Michael Kitchen *(Berkeley)*, Malick Bowens *(Farah)*, Joseph Thiaka *(Kamante)*, Stephen Kinyanjui *(Kinanjui)*, Michael Gough *(Delamere)*, Suzanna Hamilton *(Felicity)*, Rachel Kempson *(Lady Belfield)*

p, Sydney Pollack; d, Sydney Pollack; w, Kurt Luedtke (based on *Out of Africa* and other writings by Isak Dinesen, *Isak Dinesen: The Life of a Storyteller* by Judith Thurman, and *Silence Will Speak* by Errol Trzebinski); ph, David Watkin; ed, Fredric Steinkamp, William Steinkamp, Pembroke J. Herring, Sheldon Kahn; m, John Barry,

Wolfgang Amadeus Mozart; prod d, Stephen Grimes; art d, Herbert Westbrook, Colin Grimes, Clifford Robinson; fx, David Harris; cos, Milena Canonero

AA Best Picture; AAN Best Actress: Meryl Streep; *AAN Best Supporting Actor:* Klaus Maria Brandauer; *AA Best Director:* Sydney Pollack; *AA Best Adapted Screenplay:* Kurt Luedtke; *AA Best Cinematography:* David Watkin; *AAN Best Editing:* Fredric Steinkamp, William Stienkamp, Pembroke Herring, Sheldon Kahn; *AA Best Score:* John Barry; *AA Best Art Direction:* Stephen Grimes, Josie MacAvin; *AAN Best Costume Design:* Milena Canonero; *AA Best Sound:* Chris Jenkins, Gary Alexander, Larry Stensvold, Peter Handford

There was very little to begin with here—a delicate, lyrical, autobiographical tale written by an austere, refined woman who brought an opera glass instead of a microscope to her life. The author, Isak Dinesen, recounts the tale of lost loves and old imperial Africa. Karen (Meryl Streep) is the well-born woman who marries Baron Bror Blixen-Finecke (Klaus Maria Brandauer), a playboy who bestows a title upon her, promises her eternal bliss on an African plantation in 1914, and then leaves her alone to run things. Bror is nothing more than a drinker, spendthrift, and womanizer. Denys Finch Hatton (Robert Redford) is an enigmatic white hunter who falls in love with the plantation-bound Karen.

Streep, affecting the most inarticulate and cumbersome accent in any film within the last three decades, strives a little too mightily to bring reason and substance to a role that has neither. Streep's performances started becoming strangled by her highly deliberate technique as early as THE FRENCH LIEUTENANT'S WOMAN, and in this one she's so rarefied as to leave one completely cold. Redford, meanwhile, is at once too old, not in the least British (which wouldn't have been so bad if manic Meryl hadn't attempted to be *so* Danish), and obviously quite bored. To make up for the lack of real story here, director Sydney Pollack shoots endless travelogue footage in soft light and pleasing colors. The movie is not drama and far from a compelling romance. Needless to say, the prestige and technical polish on display here were enough to win this flick a passel of Oscars.

OUT OF THE PAST

1947 97m bw Mystery   ★★★★★
RKO (U.S.)   /A

Robert Mitchum *(Jeff Bailey)*, Jane Greer *(Kathie Moffett)*, Kirk Douglas *(Whit Sterling)*, Rhonda Fleming *(Meta Carson)*, Richard Webb *(Jim)*, Steve Brodie *(Fisher)*, Virginia Huston *(Ann)*, Paul Valentine *(Joe)*, Dickie Moore *(The Kid)*, Ken Niles *(Eels)*

p, Warren Duff; d, Jacques Tourneur; w, James M. Cain (uncredited), Frank Fenton (uncredited), Geoffrey Homes (based on the novel *Build My Gallows High* by Geoffrey Homes); ph, Nicholas Musuraca; ed, Samuel E. Beetley; m, Roy Webb; art d, Albert S. D'Agostino, Jack Okey; fx, Russell A. Cully; cos, Edward Stevenson

This quintessential film noir catapulted contract player Robert Mitchum into superstardom and set the standard for the genre for years to come. Boasting a typically confusing and convoluted plot line, the film follows laconic private eye Jeff Bailey (Mitchum) as he is lured into a fateful quagmire when hired by notorious gangster Whit Sterling (Douglas) to find his mistress, Kathie Moffett (Greer), who shot him and ran off with $40,000. Jeff traces Kathie to Mexico, but when he meets the seductive *femme fatale* he falls in love with her and willingly becomes involved in an increasingly complicated web of double-crosses, blackmail, and murder. Directed with supreme skill by Jacques Tourneur (CAT PEOPLE, I WALKED WITH A ZOMBIE) and brilliantly photographed by Nicholas Musuraca, this is an unrelentingly gloomy film set in a dark world of greed and deceit where love is just another device to ensnare the gullible. It was here that Mitchum created what became his iconographic screen persona: the droopy-eyed cynic who accepts fate with a studied nonchalance. Jane Greer is equally superb, perfecting the role of the *femme fatale* with a combination of erotic fire and cool detachment. Her first appearance in the film—cutting a sultry silhouette as she enters a dark cantina from the bright white outdoors—is one of the great entrances in film history. A seminal genre film, certainly among the greatest whose influence is still felt today, OUT OF THE PAST was remade as the distinctly inferior AGAINST ALL ODDS.

OUT-OF-TOWNERS, THE

1970 98m c Comedy
Jalem (U.S.)

★★★½
G/U

Jack Lemmon (George Kellerman), Sandy Dennis (Gwen Kellerman), Milt Kamen (Counterman), Sandy Baron (TV Man), Anne Meara (Woman in Police Station), Robert Nichols (Man in Airplane), Ann Prentiss (Airline Stewardess), Ron Carey (Boston Cab Driver), Philip Bruns (Officer Meyers), Graham Jarvis (Murray)

p, Paul Nathan; d, Arthur Hiller; w, Neil Simon; ph, Andrew Laszlo; ed, Fred Chulack; m, Quincy Jones; art d, Charles Bailey, Walter Tyler; cos, Forrest T. Butler, Grace Harris

If playwriting success were gauged solely on money in the bank, Neil Simon would likely be tops in his field; having brought laughter to so many, he probably deserves that status. In his script for THE OUT-OF-TOWNERS, he mines gold from a field that had been virtually tapped out. Lemmon is an Ohio businessman on his way to New York with his wife, Dennis, to talk about taking a job in the Big Apple. Anticipating dining in one Manhattan's fine restaurants, they refuse an in-flight meal. Their intention is to sup, check into a good hotel, have the appointment the following morning, and return to Dayton. But things don't work out the way they were planned. The plane cannot land in New York because of fog, so it's shunted to Boston. In Beantown, Lemmon and Dennis learn that their luggage is missing; then they have to take a crowded, foodless train to New York. Arriving in a driving rainstorm, they learn that the city has been crippled by a number of strikes, including walkouts by the transit workers and the garbage collectors. They walk a distance to the Waldorf only to learn that the hotel has cancelled their reservation. Jarvis, an apparently sweet man, says he can find them a room; instead, he steals all of their money. With no cash, they decide to try the police, who tell them they can be put up at a local armory for the night. On their way there, the police car is hijacked by crooks, and Lemmon and Dennis are tossed out in Central Park, where they spend the night. The next morning, Lemmon is taken to be a rapist by two joggers, who beat him up. Then he is chased by a police officer on a horse who thinks Lemmon is a child molester. In an attempt to get to his interview, Lemmon hitches a ride in the car of a Cuban official, Carlos Montalban, but the auto is sidetracked by angry anti-Castro demonstrators. When he finally gets to his appointment, Lemmon looks seedy and totally unpresentable, but the company offers him the job anyway. Lemmon decides that New York is no place for him and Dennis, and he turns the job down, preferring to stay in quiet, tranquil Ohio.

While it's implausible that all of these mishaps would befall a couple in 24 hours, none of these occurrences is beyond the realm of belief, and Simon has cleverly strung them together in one of his best screenplays. Director Hiller happily keeps Dennis' quirky mannerisms to a minimum and lets Lemmon do his thing (and a wonderful thing it is), with all secondary roles well cast. The picture did well at the box office and enhanced Lemmon's reputation as one of Hollywood's finest comedic actors. Many of Simon's plays have not transferred well to the screen (with the notable exceptions of THE ODD COUPLE and BAREFOOT IN THE PARK), perhaps because he writes differently for the stage. But when Simon has written directly for the screen, he has done much better, as he did with this film, THE GOODBYE GIRL, and THE HEARTBREAK KID.

OUTLAND

1981 109m c Science Fiction
Ladd/Warner Bros. (U.K.)

★★
R/15

Sean Connery (O'Niel), Peter Boyle (Sheppard), Frances Sternhagen (Lazarus), James B. Sikking (Montone), Kika Markham (Carol), Clarke Peters (Ballard), Steven Berkoff (Sagan), John Ratzenberger (Tarlow), Nicholas Barnes (Paul O'Niel), Manning Redwood (Lowell)

p, Richard A. Roth; d, Peter Hyams; w, Peter Hyams; ph, Stephen Goldblatt; ed, Stuart Baird; m, Jerry Goldsmith; prod d, Philip Harrison; art d, Malcolm Middleton; fx, John Stears; chor, Anthony Van Laast; cos, John Mollo

AAN Best Sound: John K. Wilkinson, Robert W. Glass, Jr., Robert Thirwell, Robin Gregory

HIGH NOON in outer space. Connery is the marshal on Io, Jupiter's third moon, home for a mining colony. His investigation of some strange outbreaks of violence uncovers a plot involving the managing company, led by Boyle, and a drug that increases productivity but has dangerous side effects. Connery wants to bring the culprits to justice, but no one else on Io wants anything to do with the battle, so he is left to face company henchmen alone. Connery and Boyle are fine, but the wholesale lifting of HIGH NOON's plot (there's even an on-screen digital readout periodically displayed, counting down the minutes until the big confrontation) certainly undermines interest. The film has an appealing look to it, although many of the visuals bear a striking resemblance to those seen in ALIEN.

OUTLAW, THE

1943 126m bw Western
Hughes (U.S.)

★

Jack Beutel (Billy the Kid), Jane Russell (Rio), Thomas Mitchell (Pat Garrett), Walter Huston (Doc Holliday), Mimi Aguglia (Guadalupe), Joe Sawyer (Charley), Gene Rizzi (Stranger), Frank Darien (Shorty), Pat West (Bartender), Carl Stockdale (Minister)

p, Howard Hughes; d, Howard Hughes, Howard Hawks; w, Jules Furthman; ph, Gregg Toland; ed, Otho Lovering, Wallace Grissell; art d, Perry Ferguson; fx, Roy Davidson

Shabby, contrived, cornball western, but a marvelous curiosity. The movie as such is forgettable, but Howard Hughes's cynically brilliant commodification of Jane Russell's bosom was a triumph of Hollywood marketing and a harbinger of things to come. THE OUTLAW is a very loose retelling of the legend of Billy The Kid (Jack Beutel), with Walter Huston as Doc Holliday and Thomas Mitchell as lawman Pat Garrett. When the devastating Rio (Russell) enters the picture, old friends Billy and Doc are soon at each other's throats.

Hughes hired Howard Hawks to direct, nagged him to distraction, then took over the reins himself, presiding over the set with a demented attention to detail. Despite the best efforts of cameraman Gregg Toland, the resulting film is static and amateurish; the publicity campaign surrounding its release, however, was a masterpiece. Armed with stills of 19-year-old Russell revealing a remarkable decolletage (while stooping to pick up a pair of milk pails!), Hughes spent tens of thousands of dollars purposely to agitate the censor and arouse public indignation. He released the film in San Francisco in 1943 after United Artists refused to distribute it; it was quickly closed down by civic groups (which is just what he wanted). Meanwhile, legendary publicist Russell Birdwell leased thousands of billboards from coast to coast for three years, plastering a suggestive photo of the scantily clad Russell reclining on a bed of hay, gun in hand. By 1946, when Hughes finally released the film, audiences flocked to theaters, hoping to answer the question splashed across every newspaper ad: "What are the two reasons for Jane Russell's rise to stardom?"

OUTLAW JOSEY WALES, THE

1976 135m c Western
Malpaso (U.S.)

★★★★
R/18

Clint Eastwood (Josey Wales), Chief Dan George (Lone Watie), Sondra Locke (Laura Lee), Bill McKinney (Terrill), John Vernon (Fletcher), Paula Trueman (Grandma Sarah), Sam Bottoms (Jamie), Geraldine Keams (Little Moonlight), Woodrow Parfrey (Carpetbagger), Joyce Jameson (Rose)

p, Robert Daley; d, Clint Eastwood; w, Philip Kaufman, Sonia Chernus (based on the book Gone to Texas by Forrest Carter); ph, Bruce Surtees; ed, Ferris Webster; m, Jerry Fielding; prod d, Tambi Larsen

AAN Best Score: Jerry Fielding

An underrated early directorial effort by Clint Eastwood. The film opens as Union guerillas known as "redlegs" destroy the home and family of Missouri farmer Josey Wales (Eastwood). He joins up with Confederate soldiers to get his revenge, and, after years of battle, refuses to surrender to Terrill (McKinney), the man responsible for his family's death. He even rescues Jamie (Bottoms), a wounded young rebel, from the Union soldiers, who send Terrill and the reluctant Fletcher (Vernon) after them. Josey and Jamie next pick up two Cherokees (George and Keams), a stray dog, and, after rescuing them from Comanches, an elderly woman (Trueman) and her granddaughter (Locke). The old woman is so grateful that she offers to let Josey and his ragtag bunch live at the farmhouse her son built. Josey manages to make peace with the Comanches, but the Union soldiers are another story.

Whereas Eastwood's homage to director Sergio Leone, HIGH PLAINS DRIFTER, was bleak from start to finish, THE OUTLAW JOSEY WALES begins with life (Eastwood and his family) and ends with life (the communal family). In between is a long period of healing and rebuilding wherein Eastwood re-examines the "man with no name" screen persona he developed with Leone. THE OUTLAW JOSEY WALES is a cautiously optimistic epic, deeply rooted in the history of America. Wales, despite his efforts, is not a loner. Instead of surrendering and assimilating into the "rebuilt" post-war society full of carpetbaggers, Klansmen, and dishonor, Wales and his group create their own society, steeped in honor, mutual respect and love. Bolstered by Surtees's magnificent cinematography, Fielding's fine score and an excellent supporting cast highlighted by the scene-stealing dry wit of Chief Dan George, JOSEY WALES affirms life and community with bracing conviction.

OUTSIDER, THE

1980 128m c Drama   ★★★½
Cinematic Arts (U.S.)   R/AA

Craig Wasson (*Michael Flaherty*), Patricia Quinn (*Siobhan*), Sterling Hayden (*Seamus Flaherty*), Niall Toibin (*Farmer*), Elizabeth Begley (*Mrs. Cochran*), T.P. McKenna (*John Russell*), Frank Grimes (*Tony Coyle*), Bosco Hogan (*Finbar Donovan*), Niall O'Brien (*Emmet Donovan*), Joe Dowling (*Pat*)

p, Philippe Modave; d, Tony Luraschi; w, Tony Luraschi (based on the novel *The Heritage of Michael Flaherty* by Colin Leinster); ph, Ricardo Aronovich; ed, Catherine Kelber; m, Ken Thorne; art d, Franco Fumagalli; cos, Judy Dolan

One of the better films concerning the tensions in Northern Ireland, THE OUTSIDER stars Craig Wasson as a young Irish-American inspired by his grandfather's patriotic tales of fighting the British years ago. He arrives in Belfast and discovers he is the target of an IRA plot. The IRA is planning to arrange his death so that it appears to be the work of the British army, thereby turning him into an American martyr and raising funds from sympathetic Irish-Americans. The occupying British are no more flatteringly portrayed than the IRA. The production (which came in at under $3 million) begins and ends in Detroit, but most of it was shot in Dublin, substituting for Belfast.

OUTSIDERS, THE

1983 91m c Drama   ★★★
Zoetrope (U.S.)   PG/15

Matt Dillon (*Dallas Winston*), Ralph Macchio (*Johnny Cade*), C. Thomas Howell (*Ponyboy Curtis*), Patrick Swayze (*Darrel Curtis*), Rob Lowe (*Sodapop Curtis*), Emilio Estevez (*Two-Bit Matthews*), Tom Cruise (*Steve Randle*), Glenn Withrow (*Tim Shephard*), Diane Lane (*Cherry Valance*), Leif Garrett (*Bob Sheldon*)

p, Fred Roos, Gray Frederickson; d, Francis Ford Coppola; w, Kathleen Rowell (based on the novel by S.E. Hinton); ph, Stephen H. Burum; ed, Anne Goursaud; m, Carmine Coppola; prod d, Dean Tavoularis; cos, Marge Bowers

In the early 1980s, after his "Godfather" films (1972, 1974) and APOCALYPSE NOW (1979), works of epic scale, Francis Ford Coppola began choosing small projects and blowing them up to preposterous proportions. Such is the case with THE OUTSIDERS, an awkward, splashy melo based on a popular teenage novel by S.E. Hinton (who makes a cameo appearance here as a nurse). Set in Oklahoma of the 1950s, the story hinges on a conflict between the "greasers"—leather-clad poor kids with Elvis-style pompadours—and their affluent high school classmates, the "Socs." Dallas Winston (Matt Dillon) leads his rebellious buddies on a succession of typical teenage adventures, but when two fellow gang members (Ralph Macchio and C. Thomas

Howell) have a run-in with their rivals, events take a violent turn. Charismatic Dillon, a believable J.D., gets solid support from a cast that went on to populate some of the better youth pictures in years to come. The fault lies in Coppola's unduly reverent approach to a sudsy story. Sometimes laughably, the movie attempts to evoke REBEL WITHOUT A CAUSE, but it lacks the emotional conviction and psychological insight of Nicholas Ray's classic work. Nevertheless, Coppola's grandiose vision pays off in some stunning camerawork, and a barely repressed homoeroticism sometimes strikes sparks.

OVER THE EDGE

1979 95m c Drama   ★★★½
Orion (U.S.)   PG

Michael Kramer (*Carl*), Pamela Ludwig (*Cory*), Matt Dillon (*Richie*), Vincent Spano (*Mark*), Tom Fergus (*Claude*), Harry Northrup (*Doberman*), Andy Romano (*Fred Willat*), Ellen Geer (*Sandra Willat*), Richard Jamison (*Cole*), Julia Pomeroy (*Julia*)

p, George Litto; d, Jonathan Kaplan; w, Charlie Haas, Tim Hunter; ph, Andrew Davis; ed, Robert Bargere; m, Sol Kaplan; prod d, James William Newport; fx, Richard E. Johnson

IF. . . comes to suburbia. In a Californian prefab community, teenagers are bored silly; the developers, in their haste to make a buck, have failed to make any provision for the needs of young people. They turn for entertainment to the Big Three: sex, drugs, and rock 'n' roll. Carl (Michael Kramer) is harassed by the local cop, who likes to shake down kids for drugs. Receiving no support from his boosterish parents, he begins to hang out with Richie (Matt Dillon, in his film debut), a local hood who carries a pistol. Deadly violence, and an invigorating all-out assault on the high school building, ensue. With OVER THE EDGE, director Jonathan Kaplan (THE ACCUSED, HEART LIKE A WHEEL) graduated from exploitation films to shoot a memorably offbeat teen rebellion picture. Perceptive, kinetic, and believable, with a vigorous rock score featuring The Ramones and Cheap Trick.

OX-BOW INCIDENT, THE

1943 75m bw Western   ★★★★★
Fox (U.S.)   /A

Henry Fonda (*Gil Carter*), Dana Andrews (*Donald Martin*), Mary Beth Hughes (*Rose Mapen*), Anthony Quinn (*Juan Martines*), William Eythe (*Gerald Tetley*), Harry Morgan (*Art Croft*), Jane Darwell (*Ma Grier*), Matt Briggs (*Judge Daniel Tyler*), Harry Davenport (*Arthur Davies*), Frank Conroy (*Maj. Tetley*)

p, Lamar Trotti; d, William A. Wellman; w, Lamar Trotti (based on the novel by Walter Van Tilburg Clark); ph, Arthur Miller; ed, Allen McNeil; m, Cyril J. Mockridge; art d, Richard Day, James Basevi; cos, Earl Luick

AAN Best Picture

The finest indictment of lynching ever made, and we're not forgetting LeRoy's THEY WON'T FORGET or Lang's FURY either. THE OX-BOW INCIDENT is a powerful portrait of mob violence that rises to the level of tragedy.

Fonda and Morgan play two travelers who ride into Bridger's Wells, Nevada, a dying town, and head for the local saloon after finishing a cattle drive. Soon thereafter someone races in to announce that a popular local rancher has been shot by rustlers. Although a storekeeper (Davenport) cautions against rash action in the absence of the local sheriff, many locals form a posse anyway. Under the leadership of a pompous ex-Confederate officer (Conroy) who suddenly appears in his old Civil War uniform, the posse rides off. The strangers join the posse largely to keep the townspeople from unfairly suspecting them.

The posse eventually finds three exhausted homesteaders (Andrews, Quinn and Francis Ford) and, although the evidence against them is largely circumstantial, they are convicted of the crime on the spot. The three are given no real trial, just enough time to write farewell letters to loved ones and to "make their peace with God". The men, are of course, innocent, and the memorable finale has Fonda reading aloud the letter Andrews wrote to his family.

Fonda gives a compassionate performance; good work is also done by Darwell, Davenport, Hurst, and Conroy. Quinn only has a small role as one of the victims, but he is terrific as the indignant lynch candidate who is about to be hanged, not for past crimes, but for something he did not do. Wellman's direction of this superb cast is nothing less than awesome; he coaxes subtle performances from some of his players, properly bombastic renderings from others. In keeping with its somber subject matter, the whole film has a gritty, worn-out look, right down to the threadbare costumes on the actors. Much of the credit for the film's tone is due to Miller's outstanding photography, supported by a downbeat score from Mockridge. Although scenes at the beginning and the end of the film offer realistic-looking western exteriors, Wellman insisted that the bulk of the film be shot on a set with painted backdrops, mostly since the bulk of the story occurs at night. On the set he could better control the nuances of lighting he wanted. Some critics complained about the "claustrophobic" look and feel of the picture because of its set-bound image, but it is exactly that atmosphere that helps to create the mood of pervasive doom and maniacal intent of the two dozen "average citizens" to commit a capital crime.

P

PADRE PADRONE

1977 114m c Drama   ★★★½
Radio Italiano (Italy)   /18

Omero Antonutti (Gavino's Father), Saverio Marconi (Gavino), Marcella Michelangeli (Gavino's Mother), Fabrizio Forte (Gavino as a Child), Marino Cenna (Servant/Shepherd), Stanko Molnar (Sebastiano), Nanni Moretti (Cesare)

p, Giuliani G. De Negri; d, Paolo Taviani, Vittorio Taviani; w, Vittorio Taviani, Paolo Taviani (based on a book by Gavino Ledda); ph, Mario Masini; ed, Roberto Perpignani; m, Egisto Macchi; art d, Gianni Sbarra

This is the simple story of a boy's growth into manhood under the despotism of his father. At age six, Gavino (played as a child by Fabrizio Forte) is pulled out of school and taken by his father (Omero Antonutti) into the mountains to become a shepherd. His father tries to control his son's life in every respect, with a comportment bordering on the sadistic. As he grows to manhood, Gavino (played as a young man by Saverio Marconi) begins to discover things for himself and rebel against his father's authority, eventually escaping from the patriarch's rule but encountering his changed father one last time in the film's denouement. Originally filmed by the Taviani brothers for Italian television, PADRE PADRONE is a fine example of a strong ensemble telling a story naturally, without intrusion by the directors. Using both professional actors and untrained locals from the Sardinian countryside, this story of the virtual imprisonment of young Sardinians by the sheep and pastures of their land unfolds simply and yet with great power. The winner of the grand prize at the Cannes Film Festival of 1977, the tale is based in truth: the real-life Gavino underwent similar experiences before escaping at age 20, going on to become a linguistics professor, and writing a book about his experiences.

PAISAN

(PAISA)

1946 120m bw War   ★★★★★
Organizational Films/Foreign Film (Italy)   /A

Carmela Sazio (Carmela), Robert Van Loon (Joe), Alfonsino Pasca (Boy), Maria Michi (Francesca), Renzo Avanzo (Massimo), Harriet White (Harriet), Dotts Johnson (MP), William Tubbs (Capt. Bill Martin), Dale Edmonds (Dale), Carlo Piscane (Peasant in Sicily Story)

p, Roberto Rossellini, Rod E. Geiger, Mario Conti; d, Roberto Rossellini; w, Sergio Amidei, Federico Fellini, Roberto Rossellini, Annalena Limentani (based on stories by Victor Haines, Marcello Pagliero, Amidei, Fellini, Rossellini, Klaus Mann, Vasco Pratolini); ph, Otello Martelli; ed, Eraldo Da Roma; m, Renzo Rossellini

AAN Best Original Screenplay: Alfred Hayes, Federico Fellini, Sergio Amidei, Marcello Pagliero, Roberto Rossellini

PAISAN, perhaps Rossellini's greatest achievement, is one of those rare segmented films that never loses steam as it moves through six chronologically ordered sequences beginning with the Allied invasion of Sicily in 1943 and concluding with liberation in 1945. In addition to moving across time, the film transports the viewer northward throughout Italy, each episode observing a slice of regional life. In the first, a New Jersey soldier (Van Loon) gets the job of guarding a young Sicilian woman (Sazio) who refuses to say anything or betray any emotion. The story details his attempts to win her over with no knowledge of Italian. In Naples, meanwhile, a black MP (Johnson) falls into a drunken sleep and has his shoes stolen by a street urchin. He finds the boy living in a cavern with a horde of homeless Neapolitans and decides that others need his shoes more than he. In the Roman tale, an American soldier (Gar Moore) meets Francesca (Michi), a streetwalker. He drunkenly reminisces about a woman he met as his tank rolled into the city. Francesca recognizes him—she was that woman, but he is too drunk to know it. On to Florence, where an American nurse (White) and an Italian partisan (Gigi Gori) scramble through German lines in a suspensful episode which shows that John Sturges has nothing on Rossellini. In the fifth episode, three army chaplains (Catholic, Protestant, and Jewish) have an amusing yet telling ecumenical encounter with Franciscan monks at a rural monastery. And the final episode brings action: a shootout with the Germans against a group of OSS and British. The shot with the baby is stunning.

A film unlike any other the world had seen, PAISAN is OPEN CITY without the melodrama. Rossellini doesn't have De Sica's ability to coax brilliant dramatic performances out of nonprofessionals, yet there's an amazing honesty about the actors' sometimes awkward presence in this film. Despite the film's slice-of-life approach, it is anything but a flat, uninvolving newsreel. Rossellini in fact uses newsreel techniques precisely to point out the propaganda inherent in their purportedly "objective" style. PAISAN is instead a wartime portrait full of humor, pathos, romance, tension, and warmth. Handled in a seemingly direct manner, free of ornamental flourishes, PAISAN highlights the power of the neorealist style better than almost any other film.

PAJAMA GAME, THE

1957 101m c Musical   ★★★★
Warner Bros. (U.S.)   /U

Doris Day (Kate "Babe" Williams), John Raitt (Sid Sorokin), Carol Haney (Gladys Hotchkiss), Eddie Foy Jr. (Vernon Hines), Reta Shaw (Mabel), Barbara Nichols (Poopsie), Thelma Pelish (Mae), Jack Straw (Prez), Ralph Dunn (Hasler), Owen Martin (Max)

p, George Abbott, Stanley Donen; d, George Abbott, Stanley Donen; w, George Abbott, Richard Bissell (based on the Broadway musical by Bissell, Abbott and the novel Seven and a Half Cents by Bissell); ph, Harry Stradling; ed, William Ziegler; art d, Malcolm Bert; chor, Bob Fosse; cos, William, Jean Eckart

A terrific movie comes out of this simple idea: Katie "Babe" Williams (Doris Day) works in a pajama factory. She and her coworkers want a 7.5-cent raise, but management refuses, so she leads a grievance committee and takes their complaints to shop superintendent Sid Sorokin (John Raitt), spoiling the whole movement when she falls in love. Day is an utter delight in the role, funny and intelligent even in pajamas, and the choreography by Bob Fosse is energetic. The dancing isn't just left to the actors, however; the camera moves are carefully planned to give the hoofing the best look possible, and the inventive pans and tracking shots seem wonderfully natural and add to the fun. The camera even serves as an additional dance partner, doing a unique, comic tango with Carol Haney. This is a movie that knows how to move! Codirectors George Abbott and Stanley Donen lift the film from its Broadway roots to produce a cinematic musical that everyone will enjoy, with a smash-hit score. Excellent second banana work from Haney, Eddie Foy, Jr., Barbara Nichols, and Thelma Pelish.

PAKEEZAH

1971 175m c Drama/Musical ★★★★½
Mahal Pictures (India)

Meena Kumari *(Sahebjan/Nargis)*, Ashok Kumar *(Shahabuddin)*, Raj Kumar *(Salim)*, Veena *(Nawabjan)*, Pratima Devi, Altaf, Parveen Paul, Lotan, Chandabai, Meenakshi

p, Kamal Amrohi; d, Kamal Amrohi; w, Kamal Amrohi; ph, Joseph Wirsching; m, Naushad, Ghulam Mohammed; prod d, Guari Shankar; cos, Meena Kumari

A passionate, opulent Indian melodama, far removed from the rarefied aesthetics of Satyajit Ray. Arguably the greatest achievement of Hindi popular cinema, Kamal Amrohi's tribute to his ill-starred wife, Meena Kumari (who died of drink shortly after the film's release), rivals Sirk and Minnelli in its quasi-feminist subversion of melodramatic norms. Kumari plays the title character, a Muslim courtesan who longs for escape from a Lucknow brothel; Raj Kumar is the wealthy young man who loves her, to the horror of his parents. In keeping with the conventions of Indian commercial films, the narrative proceeds at a leisurely pace and pauses frequently for song and dance sequences (which are uniformly enchanting); it builds powerfully, however, and climaxes in a moment of unforgettable hysteria as a barefoot Kumari dances on broken glass at Kumar's wedding to another woman.

Due to financial and marital problems, as well as Kumari's declining health, PAKEEZAH was filmed intermittently over nearly a decade; fortunately, it was shot roughly in sequence, and the marked deterioration of Kumari's beauty over time only reinforces the tragic quality of her portrayal. The soundtrack songs, performed by Mohammed Rafi and Lata Mangeshkar (who holds a place in the *Guinness Book of World Records* for having recorded more songs than anyone else in history), are considered classics in India and sound lovely even to untrained Western ears. While PAKEEZAH was enthusiastically received by British critics and audiences after its London premiere, it has been neglected in recent years; filmmaker/critic Peter Wollen, however, named it as one of the ten best movies ever made in the 1992 "Sight and Sound" poll.

PAL JOEY

1957 111m c Musical/Comedy ★★★★
Essex/George Sidney (U.S.) /PG

Rita Hayworth *(Vera Simpson)*, Frank Sinatra *(Joey Evans)*, Kim Novak *(Linda English)*, Barbara Nichols *(Gladys)*, Bobby Sherwood *(Ned Galvin)*, Hank Henry *(Mike Miggins)*, Elizabeth Patterson *(Mrs. Casey)*, Robin Morse *(Bartender)*, Frank Wilcox *(Col. Langley)*, Pierre Watkin *(Mr. Forsythe)*

p, Fred Kohlmar; d, George Sidney; w, Dorothy Kingsley (based on the *New Yorker* stories by John O'Hara, the musical play by O'Hara, Richard Rodgers, Lorenz Hart); ph, Harold Lipstein; ed, Viola Lawrence, Jerome Thoms; m, Nelson Riddle; art d, Walter Holscher; chor, Hermes Pan; cos, Jean Louis

AAN Best Editing: Viola Lawrence, Jerome Thoms; *AAN Best Art Direction:* Walter Holscher, William Kiernan, Louis Diage; *AAN Best Costume Design:* Jean Louis; *AAN Best Sound:* John P. Livadary

PAL JOEY's original source was John O'Hara's series of fictional "letters," published in the *New Yorker*, from a mythical dancer who signed all the missives, "Your Pal Joey." O'Hara was approached by producer George Abbott, who talked him into adapting the stories into a book for a musical. Rodgers and Hart came aboard and the play was a success, with sensational, sexy tunes. In this bowdlerized film adaptation, Joey is not a dancer but a singer. Sinatra does a bang-up job as Joey, a saloon singer who arrives in San Francisco with a gleam in his eye, a tuxedo in his suitcase, and not a penny in his pocket. He gets a job at a nightclub, and soon has his way with most of the club chorines, the hold-out being Linda (Kim Novak), a sweet ingenue. When Joey and the band (led by real-life bandleader Bobby Sherwood) are booked for a private soiree at the posh home of wealthy widow Vera (Rita Hayworth), Joey recognizes her as a former stripper. Vera has eyes for Joey, who is himself rapidly falling for Linda, and decides to finance him in his own nightspot, the Chez Joey. Noting, however, that there is more between Joey and Linda than a professional relationship, she holds back the money and tells Joey he cannot open the club if Linda remains with the establishment. Turning over a new leaf, erstwhile heel Joey won't give in, but Linda begs Vera to go ahead with the deal. Vera says she'll do so if Linda will get lost, and offers to end Joey's years of poverty by marrying him, a tempting prospect—but Joey makes the right choice. Some of Rodgers and Hart's best songs ever are in this score, including Sinatra's classic rendition of "The Lady Is a Tramp." (Novak and Hayworth's singing voices are dubbed.) Add gorgeous costumes, excellent choreography by Hermes Pan, and snappy direction by George Sidney to the tunes and what you have is a don't-miss picture.

PALE RIDER

1985 115m c Western ★★★½
Malpaso (U.S.) R/15

Clint Eastwood *(Preacher)*, Michael Moriarty *(Hull Barret)*, Carrie Snodgress *(Sarah Wheeler)*, Christopher Penn *(Josh LaHood)*, Richard Dysart *(Coy LaHood)*, Sydney Penny *(Megan Wheeler)*, Richard Kiel *(Club)*, Doug McGrath *(Spider Conway)*, John Russell *(Stockburn)*, Charles Hallahan *(McGill)*

p, Clint Eastwood; d, Clint Eastwood; w, Michael Butler, Dennis Shryack; ph, Bruce Surtees; ed, Joel Cox; m, Lennie Niehaus; prod d, Edward Carfagno; fx, Chuck Gaspar; cos, Glenn Wright

The quiet calm of a beautiful autumn day is broken by the thundering sound of hooves coming down the hillside. A cadre of men employed by powerful strip-miner Coy LaHood (Richard Dysart) rides into a small mining encampment and begins shooting up the place. One of the terrorists kills the dog of young Megan Wheeler's (Sydney Penny). As Megan buries her pet, she says a prayer, begging the Lord to send someone to defend them. Later Megan sits with her widowed mother (Carrie Snodgress) and reads from the Bible: "And I saw, and behold, a pale horse, and its rider's name was death, and hell followed him." Then a lone horseman (Clint Eastwood), dressed as a preacher, rides into camp. From its breathtaking opening, PALE RIDER heralds the return of the western. Although PALE RIDER is definitely a step down from producer-director Eastwood's masterpiece, THE OUTLAW JOSEY WALES and even from HIGH PLAINS DRIFTER (which it most resembles), it had been so long since a quality western had hit America's screens that it appears as if Eastwood purposely set out to remind audiences of all the elements that make the genre work. Eastwood has a deep love and understanding for the genre, and it shows in every frame of PALE RIDER. The supernatural elements of the story are incidental and handled in a restrained, subtle manner that does not distract from the story but enhances it, bringing another dimension to the oft-told tale. Eastwood the director has delivered a thought-provoking, well-crafted western.

PALM BEACH STORY, THE

1942 90m bw Comedy ★★★★
Paramount (U.S.) /U

Claudette Colbert *(Gerry Jeffers)*, Joel McCrea *(Tom Jeffers)*, Mary Astor *(Princess Centimillia)*, Rudy Vallee *(J.D. Hackensacker III)*, Sig Arno *(Toto)*, Robert Warwick *(Mr. Hinch)*, Arthur Stuart Hull *(Mr. Osmond)*, Torben Meyer *(Dr. Kluck)*, Jimmy Conlin *(Mr. Asweld)*, Victor Potel *(Mr. McKeewie)*

p, Paul Jones; d, Preston Sturges; w, Preston Sturges; ph, Victor Milner; ed, Stuart Gilmore; m, Victor Young; art d, Hans Dreier, Ernst Fegte; cos, Irene

Preston Sturges at full tilt, with Claudette Colbert and Joel McCrea, Rudy Vallee, and Mary Astor. Joel is a crazy young architect who has dreams of building a magnificent airport. Claudette is his adoring wife who, in search of investment money for her beloved's dreams, runs away to Palm Beach with the Ale and Quail Club and meets Rudy, the incredibly normal zillionaire J.D. Hackensacker III, who of course falls in love with her. Rudy's sister, Mary, falls for Joel. In the end all's set right again and each Jack has his Jill. It's hard to describe Sturges' special brand of comedy. Perhaps it's realistic farce. He takes a perfectly natural action and lets it run on just too long to the point of slight but affectionate absurdity.

McCrea and Sturges had just come off the wonderful SULLIVAN'S TRAVELS, which took telling aim at Hollywood. They teamed again to snipe at the idle rich with this hysterically funny fairy tale. Colbert was never lovelier or more energetic than she is here, blithely delivering Sturges's sophisticated dialogue. Vallee is delightful as the somewhat naive and eccentric billionaire, carefully cataloging every cent he spends. As his sister, Astor is wickedly caustic, especially when dealing with her incomprehensible lover, Arno. As in SULLIVAN'S TRAVELS, McCrea is well-cast, adeptly playing off the film's wild collection of characters. All the other roles are carefully cast and virtually anyone who walks on screen delivers a memorable witticism. Though this film may lack the satirical bite of Sturges's great comedies such as SULLIVAN'S TRAVELS or MIRACLE AT MORGAN'S CREEK, it remains a delight.

PAPER CHASE, THE

1973 112m c Comedy/Drama ★★½
Fox (U.S.) PG

Timothy Bottoms (*Hart*), Lindsay Wagner (*Susan Kingsfield*), John Houseman (*Prof. Kingsfield*), Graham Beckel (*Ford*), Edward Herrmann (*Anderson*), Bob Lydiard (*O'Connor*), Craig Richard Nelson (*Bell*), James Naughton (*Kevin*), Regina Baff (*Asheley*), David Clennon (*Toombs*)

p, Robert C. Thompson, Rodrick Paul; d, James Bridges; w, James Bridges (based on the novel by John Jay Osborn Jr.); ph, Gordon Willis; ed, Walter Thompson; m, John Williams; art d, George Jenkins

AA Best Supporting Actor: John Houseman; *AAN Best Adapted Screenplay:* James Bridges; *AAN Best Sound:* Donald O. Mitchell, Lawrence O. Jost

John Houseman had already distinguished himself as a writer (JANE EYRE), a producer (EXECUTIVE SUITE, THE BAD AND THE BEAUTIFUL) and the story editor of CITIZEN KANE before winning the Best Supporting Actor Oscar for this, his second role. Bottoms is a Minnesota-bred law student who comes to Harvard and the lecture hall of Houseman, an instructor who seemingly takes great pleasure in puncturing his students' egos. Bottoms falls in love with Wagner. Essentially, this is a military school plot with a change of venue. Bridges secured an Oscar nomination for his adaptation of the novel, and the film was also nominated for Best Sound.

PAPER MOON

1973 102m c Comedy/Drama ★★★½
Saticoy (U.S.) PG/A

Ryan O'Neal (*Moses Pray*), Tatum O'Neal (*Addie Loggins*), Madeline Kahn (*Trixie Delight*), John Hillerman (*Sheriff Hardin/Jess Hardin*), P.J. Johnson (*Imogene*), Jessie Lee Fulton (*Miss Ollie*), James N. Harrell (*Minister*), Lila Water (*Minister's Wife*), Noble Willingham (*Mr. Robertson*), Bob Young (*Gas Station Attendant*)

p, Peter Bogdanovich; d, Peter Bogdanovich; w, Alvin Sargent (based on the novel *Addie Pray* by Joe David Brown); ph, Laszlo Kovacs; ed, Verna Fields; prod d, Polly Platt; fx, Jack Harmon; cos, Pat Kelly, Sandra Stewart

AA Best Supporting Actress: Tatum O'Neal; *AAN Best Supporting Actress:* Madeline Kahn; *AAN Best Adapted Screenplay:* Alvin Sargent; *AAN Best Sound:* Richard Portman, Les Fresholtz

Bogdanovich's warmest film, featuring charming performances from real-life father and daughter Ryan and Tatum O'Neal. Driving a Model-T roadster in the Depression year of 1936, O'Neal stops to pay his respects at the funeral of one of his former girlfriends. Neighbors explain that the woman's death has left an "adorable" 9-year-old daughter an orphan and beg him to take the child to relatives in St. Joseph, Missouri. O'Neal takes Tatum O'Neal along with him and almost instantly regrets his generosity. The little girl smokes, swears, and exhibits altogether unchildlike behavior. After taking sly vengeance on the brother of the man who caused the death of Tatum's mother in a car accident, defrauding him of $200, O'Neal buys a new car and then takes Tatum to a train station, buying her a ticket for St. Joseph. Rather than get on the train, she creates a scene in the station restaurant, screaming that O'Neal owes her $200. Since he got it from the family

that inadvertently caused her mother's death, she asserts, it is therefore her rightful inheritance—and he's probably her father to boot. O'Neal gives in and takes her along on his roadway adventures through Kansas and Missouri, where he works a variety of con games on the gullible rurals.

PAPER MOON offers brilliant, bittersweet images and an entertaining story. The O'Neals are excellent, but Madeline Kahn almost steals the film in a small turn as a travelling floozy. Bogdanovich's direction is fast, furious, and full of fun. As with THE LAST PICTURE SHOW, the director opted for black-and-white cinematography (beautifully done by Kovacs) in a world swimming in color celluloid, to achieve an historical feel. "I have more affection, more affinity for the past," Bogdanovich later stated. "Since I am more interested in it, it comes easier for me." This was Tatum O'Neal's film debut, and no one would ever forget it, especially Tatum O'Neal, who won a Best Supporting Actress Oscar for her performance (over costar Kahn). For Bogdanovich, the grown-up little girl provided "one of the most miserable experiences of my life." The picture was filmed on location near Hays, Kansas, and St. Joseph, Missouri. The highly effective musical backdrop for the picture is a procession of period tunes from the record collection of Rudi Fehr.

PAPER, THE

1994 112m c Drama ★★★
Imagine (U.S.) R/

Michael Keaton (*Henry Hackett*), Robert Duvall (*Bernie White*), Glenn Close (*Alicia Clark*), Marisa Tomei (*Martha Hackett*), Randy Quaid (*McDougal*), Jason Robards (*Graham Keighley*), Jason Alexander (*Marion Sandusky—Parking Commissioner*), Spalding Gray (*Paul Bladden—Sentinel Editor*), Catherine O'Hara (*Susan*), Lynne Thigpen (*Janet*)

p, Brian Grazer, Frederick Zollo; d, Ron Howard; w, David Koepp, Stephen Koepp; ph, John Seale; ed, Daniel Hanley, Michael Hill; m, Randy Newman; prod d, Todd Hallowell; art d, Maher Ahmad; fx, Hugo Cimmelli; cos, Rita Ryack

AAN Best Original Song: Randy Newman

Director Ron Howard attempts the Great American Newspaper Picture and mostly pulls it off. The film's greatest weakness is that he and screenwriters David and Stephen Koepp (the latter a journalist himself) love those scrappy newshounds too much; THE PAPER doesn't even try for the appropriately acid bite of, say, any version of THE FRONT PAGE.

"In 24 hours your world can change," goes the slogan of *The New York Sun*, a Big Apple tabloid; the maxim applies to reporters as well as readers. City Editor Henry Hackett (Michael Keaton) loves street-level news business, but he's got a tempting job offer from a stuffy, "quality" rival daily; a pregnant wife to consider; and a nemesis in the shape of the *Sun*'s managing editor, Alicia Clark (Glenn Close), who doubts his story sense. Their antagonism boils over with the day's big story, a mob hit on some white businessmen, disguised as a racial murder.

Howard weaves multiple subplots and supporting characters into the main story with finesse, imposing order, good humor, and straight-ahead momentum on a naturally chaotic subject. Some components work better than others; the troubles of a weary editor-in-chief (Robert Duvall) seeking detente with his estranged daughter are standard melodrama, and Randy Quaid deserves more time as a legendary beat reporter who has been "demoted" to a Jimmy Breslin-style columnist. But the ensemble performances are terrific and, thanks to the breezy pace, the flaws hardly matter.

PAPILLON

1973 150m c Prison ★★★★
Corona/General Production (U.S.) PG/18

Steve McQueen (*Henri Charriere Papillon*), Dustin Hoffman (*Louis Dega*), Victor Jory (*Indian Chief*), Don Gordon (*Julot*), Anthony Zerbe (*Toussaint Leper Colony Chief*), Robert Deman (*Maturette*), Woodrow Parfrey (*Clusoit*), Bill Mumy (*Lariot*), George Coulouris (*Dr. Chatal*), Ratna Assan (*Zoraima*) p, Robert Dorfmann, Franklin J. Schaffner; d, Franklin J. Schaffner; w, Dalton Trumbo, Lorenzo Semple Jr. (based on the autobiographical novel by Henri Charriere); ph, Fred Koenekamp; ed, Robert Swink; m, Jerry Goldsmith; prod d, Tony Masters; art d, Jack Maxsted; cos, Anthony Powell

AAN Best Score: Jerry Goldsmith

A grim, authentically brutal film about the escape of notorious French felon Henri "Papillon" Charriere (Steve McQueen) from the supposedly inescapable prison fortress of Devil's Island. The story begins in the streets of Marseilles in the 1930s, with French soldiers escorting a large group of prisoners to the docks. Among them are McQueen, a convicted murderer, and Hoffman, a big-time stock swindler who still has a lot of money hidden. During the ensuing voyage, a couple of brutal murderers attempt to kill Hoffman but McQueen saves him. Once in Cayenne McQueen thinks only about escape. He attacks a guard who abuses Hoffman, and makes a break, only to be later recaptured. McQueen spends most of his time in solitary confinement for repeated escape attempts. Here he staves off starvation, madness, and disease while his body deteriorates. He and William Smithers, the commandant of the solitary confinement compound, engage in a contest of wills and slowly age together, their hair turning white over the years. Finally returned to the main prison, McQueen is received warmly by Hoffman, who is now living a (relatively) cushy life, paying off the guards and the warden for favorable treatment. Hoffman tries to persuade McQueen to serve out his time and wait for parole, but eventually joins him in an escape attempt just as harrowing as life on the inside.

PAPILLON was produced with consummate technical skill and offers brilliant acting by McQueen and Hoffman. Schaffner, who expertly captured the gritty story of PATTON, does not flinch from showing every conceivable horror of the French penal system. Excellent supporting performances are provided by Zerbe, as the compassionate leader of a leper colony, Jory, as a stoic Indian chief, and Coulouris, as a venal prison doctor. Even scriptwriter Trumbo, who had become a cult figure by the time of this film, gets into the act, appearing as the commandant of the penal colony at the beginning of the film. Shot on location in Spain and Jamaica, PAPILLON was costly, but earned $22 million in its US release. PAPILLON was originally rated R by the MPAA for its extreme violence, but Allied Artists appealed and the rating was changed to PG.

PARALLAX VIEW, THE

1974 102m c Thriller   ★★★½
Paramount (U.S.)   R/15

Warren Beatty *(Joseph Frady)*, Hume Cronyn *(Editor Edgar Rintels)*, William Daniels *(Austin Tucker)*, Paula Prentiss *(Lee Carter)*, Kelly Thordsen *(Sheriff L.D.)*, Earl Hindman *(Deputy Red)*, Chuck Waters *(Busboy-Assassin)*, Bill Joyce *(Sen. Carroll)*, Bettie Johnson *(Mrs. Carroll)*, Bill McKinney *(Art, an Assassin)*

p, Alan J. Pakula; d, Alan J. Pakula; w, David Giler, Lorenzo Semple Jr. (based on the novel by Loren Singer); ph, Gordon Willis; ed, John W. Wheeler; m, Michael Small; prod d, George Jenkins; art d, George Jenkins; cos, Frank Thompson

A popular senator is shot by a waiter at the Seattle Space Needle. Three years later Lee (Prentiss), a television reporter who was on the scene, goes to newspaper reporter Joe Frady (Beatty) frightened for her life. Assassination witnesses have been systematically killed, she says, and Lee knows that she's next. Frady discounts her fears as irrational paranoia, but after her supposed suicide, doubt creeps into his mind. He begins investigating the story and uncovers a huge conspiracy involving the mysterious "Parallax Corporation," a secret company that recruits assassins to eliminate troublemakers on their "list." Alan J. Pakula's taut direction maintains a neat balance between the real and the perceived; things are not what they appear to be. He presents disorienting shots and editing patterns with characters often filmed behind glass or curtains, allowing only a partial look at the whole scene. The most compelling aspects are of course the political and historical overtones. The fictional assassination was a deliberate attempt to suggest a possible explanation for the John F. Kennedy assassination. Using historical parallels (the photographs implying a second gunman at Dallas; the fact that many of the assassination witnesses died mysteriously in the years following 1963), Pakula created a possible,

though fictional, explanation in a film steeped in American symbolism. The film was released in June 1974, after the studio had let the controversial work sit for several months. This is one of the best political thrillers of the 1970s.

PARDON MON AFFAIRE
(UN ELEPHANT CA TROMPE ENORMEMENT)

1977 105m c Comedy/Romance   ★★★½
Gaumont/La Gueville (France)   PG/X

Jean Rochefort *(Etienne)*, Claude Brasseur *(Daniel)*, Guy Bedos *(Simon)*, Victor Lanoux *(Bouly)*, Daniele Delorme *(Marthe)*, Anny Duperey *(Charlotte)*, Martine Sarcey *(Esperanza)*, Marthe Villalonga *(Mouchy)*

p, Alain Poire, Yves Robert; d, Yves Robert; w, Jean-Loup Dabadie (based on the story by Robert, Dabadie); ph, Rene Mathelin; ed, Gerard Pollicand; m, Vladimir Cosma

Yves Robert, the director responsible for THE TALL BLONDE MAN WITH ONE BLACK SHOE and its sequel, struck again with this pleasant, enjoyable mixture of comedy and drama about husbands and their affairs. Etienne (Jean Rochefort) is a Parisian civil servant who, while in his company parking lot, gazes at the bright red dress of a pretty young woman (Anny Duperey) as it is blown up above her waist by a rush of air. Although he is happily married to Marthe (Daniele Delorme, wife of director Robert) and has never even thought of having an affair, Etienne becomes enamored of this mystery woman. In the meantime, he and his three best friends witness the result of years of dalliances when one of them, Bouly (Victor Lanoux), comes home one day to find that his wife has left him, taking along his children and every last possession. Robert successfully creates a number of believable characters with honest emotions and places them in lightly humorous situations, and the result falls somewhere between broad comedy (one memorable scene has a character pretending to be blind and causing havoc in an elegant restaurant) and heartfelt drama (Bouly's reaction to his wife's departure), as if Robert was attempting a farcical French version of John Cassavetes's HUSBANDS. Many of the same names reunited for the less successful sequel, PARDON MON AFFAIRE, TOO! Remade in Hollywood as THE WOMAN IN RED.

PARENTHOOD

1989 124m c Comedy   ★★★½
Imagine (U.S.)   PG-13/15

Steve Martin *(Gil Buckman)*, Tom Hulce *(Larry Buckman)*, Rick Moranis *(Nathan)*, Jason Robards Jr. *(Frank Buckman)*, Martha Plimpton *(Julie)*, Mary Steenburgen *(Karen Buckman)*, Dianne Wiest *(Helen)*, Keanu Reeves *(Tod)*, Harley Kozak *(Susan)*, Leaf Phoenix *(Garry)*

p, Brian Grazer; d, Ron Howard; w, Lowell Ganz, Babaloo Mandel (based on a story by Lowell Ganz, Babaloo Mandel, Ron Howard); ph, Don McAlpine; ed, Michael Hill, Daniel Hanley; m, Randy Newman; prod d, Todd Hallowell; art d, Christopher Nowak; cos, Ruth Morley

AAN Best Supporting Actress: Dianne Wiest; *AAN Best Song:* Randy Newman

Occasionally corny, yet thoroughly entertaining, PARENTHOOD is a movie by, for, and about parents. Four generations are portrayed by an all-star cast, delivering a lesson in child-rearing worthy of Dr. Spock. Jason Robards plays Frank, the head of the Buckman clan. Gil (Steve Martin), Helen (Dianne Wiest), Susan (Harley Kozak), and Larry (Tom Hulce) are his children; all of them have kids of their own. Gil tries to balance his career with being the attentive father Frank never was; divorcee Helen has her hands full with son Garry (Leaf Phoenix), who is badly in need of a male role model, rebellious teenage daughter Julie (Martha Plimpton), and burn-out son-in-law Tod (Keanu Reeves). Susan does her best to give her toddler a childhood while husband Nathan (Rick Moranis) has the precocious kid studying karate, long division, and Kafka. With his own illegitimate son in tow, prodigal son Larry has returned home deeply in debt to some very rough customers. All of these situations get worse before they get better, but by film's end the family is closer than ever. PARENTHOOD's coscreenwriters Ron Howard, Lowell Ganz, and Babaloo Mandell—the fathers of 14 children in all—have produced a funny, poignant script with very contemporary humor. It is the acting, though, that shines brightest in the movie. Rarely has such a formidable array of talent been assembled for one film, and theirs is truly an ensemble effort. While PARENTHOOD crosses the border into schmaltz a number of times, the movie runs the gamut of realistic emotions, and one scene or another is bound to hit home with the parents who see the film.

PARIS BELONGS TO US
(PARIS NOUS APPARTIENT)

1960 120m bw Mystery   ★★★
Ajym/Carrosse (France)

Betty Schneider (Anne Goupil), Giani Esposito (Gerard Lenz), Francoise Prevost (Terry Yok), Daniel Crohem (Philip Kaufman), Francois Maistre (Pierre Goupil), Jean-Claude Brialy (Jean Marc), Jean-Marie Robain (De Georges), Brigitte Juslin, Noelle Leiris, Monique Le Poirier

p, Roland Nonin; d, Jacques Rivette; w, Jacques Rivette, Jean Gruault; ph, Charles Bitsch; ed, Denise de Casabianca; m, Philippe Arthuys

Schneider, after overhearing a discussion on the suicide of a young Spaniard, is compelled to learn why the youth's life ended so tragically. She gets involved with Esposito, a theater director, and takes a part in his production of Shakespeare's "Pericles." She becomes worried for Esposito's life when he tells her that the Spaniard was part of a worldwide conspiracy and that he is targeted for murder by the same organization. She also meets Crohem, an American victim of McCarthyism, who is responsible for informing the Spaniard and Esposito of the organization. Eventually it is revealed that Crohem made the whole thing up, but not before Esposito's paranoia gets the better of him and he commits suicide.

Along with Claude Chabrol's LE BEAU SERGE, this first feature by Jacques Rivette kindled the flame that became known as the French New Wave. Production began in the early summer of 1958 with money borrowed from the magazine Rivette (and his New Wave counterparts) worked for, Cahiers du Cinema. Technicians, actors, and lab fees were all on credit, with no money exchanged until the film's release in 1960. Without so much as a car, Rivette and his entourage of film enthusiasts worked whenever they could, spending Sundays trying to raise enough money to begin filming again on Mondays. With the help of Chabrol and Truffaut, whose first films were already receiving acclaim at the Cannes Film Festival, PARIS was finally released—a stepping stone toward French cinema's rebirth.

PARIS, TEXAS

1984 150m c Drama   ★★★★
Road Movies/Argos/Westdeutscher/Channel 4/Pro-Ject   R/15
(France/West Germany)

Harry Dean Stanton (Travis Clay Henderson), Nastassia Kinski (Jane), Dean Stockwell (Walt Henderson), Aurore Clement (Anne), Hunter Carson (Hunter), Bernhard Wicki (Dr. Ulmer), Viva Auder (Woman on TV), Socorro Valdez (Carmelita), Tommy Farrell (Screaming Man), John Lurie (Slater)

p, Don Guest; d, Wim Wenders; w, Sam Shepard (based on a story adapted by L.M. Kit Carson); ph, Robby Muller; ed, Peter Pryzgodda; m, Ry Cooder; art d, Kate Altman; cos, Birgitta Bjerke

Epic but intimate, PARIS, TEXAS combines the European sensibility of director Wim Wenders with the expansive locations of the American West.

Amid the desert and brilliant sky of Big Bend, Texas, Travis Clay Henderson (Harry Dean Stanton) aimlessly wanders under the boiling sun. He stops in a tavern and promptly collapses, awakening in the care of a German doctor (Bernhard Wicki). Assuming the catatonic Travis is mute, the doctor calls a number in his wallet and reaches Travis's brother, Walt (Dean Stockwell), who lives in Los Angeles with his French wife (Aurore Clement) and Hunter (Hunter Carson), Travis's seven-year-old son by his estranged wife, Jane (Nastassia Kinski). It turns out Travis has been missing and assumed dead for four years. Walt brings him back to L.A. for a reunion with Hunter, who subsequently joins his father on a quixotic quest for family, true love, and Jane.

PARIS, TEXAS features neither sweeping themes, grandiose sets, nor a cast of thousands, but from its opening shots one senses its uniquely epic quality. The vast landscapes recall those of John Ford, but instead of John Wayne it's Stanton who wanders across the frame, a modern American father in suit and tie, displaced, aimless, and emotionally dead, on an odyssey to find himself. He knows where he began—in Paris, Texas—but not where he is going. Although based on stories by Sam Shepard, the film's vision of America is wholly that of Wenders, a German director deeply fascinated by Americana. As the title suggests, Wenders' America is a by-product of the European imagination.

Superbly scripted, the film features wonderful performances from all its major players. Equally brilliant, especially in a film that emphasizes script and character, is the cinematography by Robby Muller, perfectly capturing the notion of "America." A final factor in PARIS, TEXAS's success is the remarkably haunting score by blues musician Ry Cooder.

PARTING GLANCES

1986 90m c Drama   ★★★
Rondo (U.S.)   /15

Richard Ganoung (Michael), John Bolger (Robert), Steve Buscemi (Nick), Adam Nathan (Peter), Kathy Kinney (Joan), Patrick Tull (Cecil), Yolande Bavan (Betty), Richard Wall (Douglas), Jim Selfe (Douglas' Sidekick), Kristin Moneagle (Sarah)

p, Yoram Mandel, Arthur Silverman; d, Bill Sherwood; w, Bill Sherwood; ph, Jacek Laskus; ed, Bill Sherwood; prod d, John Loggia; art d, Daniel Haughey, Mark Sweeney; cos, Sylvia Heisel

Unlike several major studio productions, in which homosexuality is used either as an issue or as comic relief, PARTING GLANCES takes an inside look at New York's gay community. The pain and joys of love, unspoken cultural rules, and the specter of AIDS are all dealt with in an energetic manner that balances the story's varying shades of emotion.

Michael (Richard Ganoung) is a pleasant young man about to end a six-year relationship with his live-in lover, Robert (John Bolger). Robert is preparing to leave for Africa, ostensibly to accept an employment opportunity, but also to give himself a little breathing room from Michael's steady companionship. Before going to a dinner to be hosted by Robert's boss, Cecil (Patrick Tull), and his wife, Michael drops by the apartment of Nick (Steve Buscemi), a cynical New Wave musician who is dying of AIDS. Later, as the evening of farewells continues, Michael becomes more despondent.

The plot is fairly simple, but the affection displayed by PARTING GLANCES's marvelous ensemble makes these everyday events something more than commonplace. At the center of it all is Ganoung, who handles his key role well. Buscemi's performance as the dying musician is another standout. Writer-director Bill Sherwood shows marvelous talent in his feature debut. He deals with touchy issues in a forthright manner and doesn't allow these events to unfold without a well-aimed sense of humor. Sadly, Sherwood himself succumbed to AIDS complications in early 1990.

PASSAGE TO INDIA, A

1984 163m c Drama   ★★★½
John Heyman/Edward Sands/HBO (U.K.)   PG

Judy Davis (Adela Quested), Victor Banerjee (Dr. Aziz), Peggy Ashcroft (Mrs. Moore), James Fox (Richard Fielding), Alec Guinness (Godbole), Nigel Havers (Ronny Heaslop), Richard Wilson (Turton), Antonia Pemberton (Mrs. Turton), Michael Culver (McBryde), Art Malik (Mahmoud Ali)

p, John Brabourne, Richard Goodwin; d, David Lean; w, David Lean (based on the play by Santha Rama Rau and the novel by E.M. Forster); ph, Ernest Day; ed, David Lean; m, Maurice Jarre; prod d, John Box; art d, Leslie Tomkins, Clifford Robinson, Ram Yedekar, Herbert Westbrook; cos, Judy Moorcroft

AAN Best Picture; AAN Best Actress: Judy Davis; AA Best Supporting Actress: Peggy Ashcroft; AAN Best Director: David Lean; AAN Best Adapted Screenplay: David Lean; AAN Best Cinematography: Ernest Day; AAN Best Editing: David Lean; AA Best Score: Maurice Jarre;

AAN Best Art Direction: John Box, Leslie Tomkins, Hugh Scaife; AAN Best Costume Design: Judy Moorcroft; AAN Best Sound: Graham V. Hartstone, Nicolas LeMessurier, Michael A. Carter, John Mitchell

At 75, David Lean, whose epics THE BRIDGE ON THE RIVER KWAI, LAWRENCE OF ARABIA, and DOCTOR ZHIVAGO garnered 19 Oscars, returned to work after a 14-year absence with this adaptation of the E.M. Forster novel about sexual repression and racial prejudice in 1924 India. Set in the fictional town of Chandrapore, the story concerns Adela Quested (Judy Davis) who has settled in India and is to marry Ronny Heaslop (Nigel Havers), a town magistrate. She is befriended by the charming Dr. Aziz (Victor Banerjee), but it's a friendship that ultimately leads to tragedy. Lean does an excellent job of conveying the repressive nature of British society captured in the novel. Although the story makes for a movie that is often slow going, it is also a beautiful and evocative film fueled by an excellent performance from Davis and Peggy Ashcroft.

PASSAGE TO MARSEILLE

1944 110m bw Drama/War   ★★★½
Warner Bros. (U.S.)   /PG

Humphrey Bogart (Matrac), Claude Rains (Capt. Freycinet), Michele Morgan (Paula), Philip Dorn (Renault), Sydney Greenstreet (Maj. Duval), Peter Lorre (Marius), George Tobias (Petit), Victor Francen (Capt. Patain Malo), Helmut Dantine (Garou), John Loder (Manning)

p, Hal B. Wallis; d, Michael Curtiz; w, Casey Robinson, John C. Moffitt (based on the novel Men Without a Country by Charles Nordhoff, James Norman Hall); ph, James Wong Howe; ed, Owen Marks; m, Max Steiner; art d, Carl Jules Weyl; fx, Jack Cosgrove, Edwin DuPar, Byron Haskin, Roy Davidson, Rex Wimpy; cos, Leah Rhodes

With adventurer Humphrey Bogart as his lead, director Michael Curtiz here offers a slam-bang action film, one with a tricky plot whose narrative unfolds through a complicated series of flashbacks-within-flashbacks and flash forwards, but that is nevertheless exciting and absorbing all the way. A group of prisoners who have escaped the dreaded prison at Cayenne in French Guiana are picked up by a passing French freighter, commanded by Malo (Victor Francen), who is loyal to Free France but who hides his sympathies from the fascistic Maj. Duval (Sydney Greenstreet), a French officer sympathetic to the Vichy government. The rescued men claim they are survivors of a torpedoed ship, but eventually their true identities are learned. They are Matrac (Bogart), a French journalist who opposed the Nazi takeover of his country from within, and his criminal comrades Marius (Peter Lorre), Garou (Helmut Dantine), Renault (Philip Dorn), and Petit (George Tobias). All are loyal to the Free French, and when Maj. Duval plans to turn the ship over to the Vichy government, Matrac and his comrades fight to keep the ship from the clutches of the collaborators. Although Curtiz draws superb performances from his great cast, many of whom (Bogart, Lorre, Greenstreet, Dantine, Claude Rains, Corinna Mura, and Louis Mercier) appeared in Warner Bros.' recent smash hit CASABLANCA, which was also directed by Curtiz, the story is more than a little confusing because of the unwieldy flashbacks used to tell the tale. Yet the great action director packs the film with marvelous adventure and exciting scenes, not to mention stirring patriotism. Warners attempted to time PASSAGE TO MARSEILLE's release to coincide with what the studio thought would be the invasion of southern France, but when this failed to take place the film was distributed without an international news event to boost the production (as had been the case with CASABLANCA, released just after American troops landed in Africa and Allied leaders met in that African city for top-level conferences). James Wong Howe's gritty photography helps set the mood, and Max Steiner's music dynamically establishes patriotic fervor.

PASSENGER, THE

1975 123m c Drama   ★★★★
CIC/Concordia/C.I.P.I/Champion (Italy)   PG/A

Jack Nicholson (David Locke), Maria Schneider (Girl), Jenny Runacre (Rachel Locke), Ian Hendry (Martin Knight), Steven Berkoff (Stephen), Ambroise Bia (Achebe), Jose Maria Caffarel (Hotel Keeper), James Campbell (Witch Doctor), Manfred Spies (German Stranger), Jean Baptiste Tiemele (Murderer)

p, Carlo Ponti; d, Michelangelo Antonioni; w, Mark Peploe, Peter Wollen, Michelangelo Antonioni (based on a story by Peploe); ph, Luciano Tovoli; ed, Franco Arcalli, Michaelangelo Antonioni; art d, Piero Poletto; cos, Louise Stjernsward

In this visually stunning adventure David Locke (Jack Nicholson) is a reporter sent to northern Africa on a mission to interview a band of guerrillas. After a battle with a Jeep that refuses to travel through sand, Locke winds up in a blisteringly hot, rundown hotel. There he is confused with another hotel guest, Robertson (Chuck Mulvehill), to whom he bears a striking resemblance. When he discovers Robertson dead in his room, Locke is presented with a perfect opportunity to escape his hell of a life. He switches passport photos and personal belongings and places the corpse in his own room. Looking through "his" daily planner, he finds a number of women's names and various appointments. Curious, he decides to keep a rendezvous and discovers that Robertson was a gun runner who supplied foreign governments with plans and documents. In the meantime he meets an enigmatic young woman (Maria Schneider) to whom he is magnetically drawn, causing him to ignore and avoid the efforts of his wife and best friend to locate him. THE PASSENGER could probably be analyzed until the end of time, each viewing uncovering a different path to understanding the film as a whole. What is more interesting than the "whys" and "hows" of the plot however, are the "where" and "when." Locke and the girl are very much a part of their environment, whether it's the sandy wastelands of northern Africa or the exquisitely organic Gaudi architecture of Barcelona. The girl has no history—she just is—a state of being to which Locke also aspires.

PASSION FISH

1992 136m c Drama/Romance   ★★★½
Atchafalaya Films Inc./Esperanza Productions (U.S.)   R/15

Mary McDonnell (Mary-Alice Culhane), Alfre Woodard (Chantelle), David Strathairn (Rennie), Vondie Curtis Hall (Sugar LeDoux), Angela Bassett (Dawn/Rhonda), Lenore Banks (Nurse Quick), William Mahoney (Max), Nelle Stokes (1st Therapist), Brett Ardoin (2nd Therapist), Michael Mantell (Dr. Kline)

p, Sarah Green, Maggie Renzi; d, John Sayles; w, John Sayles; ph, Roger Deakins; ed, John Sayles; m, Mason Daring; prod d, Dan Bishop, Dianna Freas; cos, Cynthia Flynt

AAN Best Actress: Mary McDonnell; AAN Best Original Screenplay: John Sayles

After attempting historical dramas and multi-character urban sagas, John Sayles returns here to the kind of small, intimate film with which he first established his reputation.

PASSION FISH opens on a typically vivid Sayles image: soap opera actress Mary-Alice Culhane (Mary McDonnell) lying immobile in a hospital bed, watching herself walking and talking on TV. The nurse tells her she's been paralyzed from the waist down in a traffic accident (she was on her way to have her legs waxed), but her fear and anger have immobilized her as well: she refuses to participate in her physical therapy, and drowns her sorrows in endless TV watching and drinking. Moving back to her Louisiana Bayou hometown, Mary-Alice goes through a succession of caretakers ranging from Russian authoritarians to biker chicks. The last hope for this self-proclaimed "bitch on wheels" is the quiet Chantelle (Alfre Woodard), who needs the job badly enough that she can't quit, but refuses to indulge Mary-Alice's tantrums. Both women, it turns out, are trying to start over in life, grappling with new identities and responsibilities, and their isolated situation, as well as the subtle magic of the bayou, soon begins to change them.

Never maudlin, and never opting for big dramatic climaxes, PASSION FISH succeeds most of the time, thanks to a typically deft Sayles screenplay and two fine, understated performances from McDonnell and Woodard. For viewers willing to accomodate themselves to its rhythms, which are as unhurried as its bayou setting, Sayles has cooked up an affecting story, one that takes the audience on a slow ride into the swampland with two of its denizens, trying to re-define themselves in the second act of their lives.

PASSION OF ANNA, THE
(EN PASSION)

1969 100m c Drama   ★★★
Cinematograph (Sweden)   R/AA

Liv Ullmann (Anna Fromm), Bibi Andersson (Eva Vergerus), Max von Sydow (Andreas Winkelman), Erland Josephson (Elis Vergerus), Erik Hell (Johan Andersson), Sigge Furst (Verner), Svea Holst (Verner's Wife), Annika Kronberg (Katarina), Hjordis Pettersson (Johan's Sister), Lars-Owe Carlberg

d, Ingmar Bergman; w, Ingmar Bergman; ph, Sven Nykvist; ed, Siv Kanalv; prod d, P.A. Lundgren; fx, Ulf Nordholm; cos, Mago

Max von Sydow, an ex-convict who lives alone in an island farmhouse, is visited one day by the crippled Ullmann, who requests to use the phone. Ullmann soon leaves, but forgets to take her purse with her. Von Sydow looks through it, finds her name, address, and a letter from her husband which discusses their unhappy marriage. He returns the purse and is introduced to Josephson and Andersson, friends of Ullmann's. Eventually Ullmann moves into von Sydow's farmhouse. Tensions between the two begin to rise, partially due to reports of a crazed murderer who is on the loose. In a fit of anger, von Sydow goes after Ullmann with an ax. Later, the *real* maniac strikes at von Sydow's farm, setting his barn on fire. Ullmann rescues von Sydow from the scene of the blaze, and drives frantically down the road. Von Sydow accuses Ullmann of trying to kill him, perhaps as she killed her husband and son years earlier in the auto accident that left her crippled. Hailed by many as a masterpiece, THE PASSION OF ANNA (only Bergman's second film in color) employs some interesting techniques, such as interviews with each of the four main actors and also sheds some light on many of the baroque mannerisms and symbols that have come to be associated with Bergman. It still contains, however, that element of coldness which has turned many viewers against Bergman. Filmed on the island of Faro, a one-time home for Bergman.

PASSPORT TO PIMLICO

1949 84m bw Comedy   ★★★
Ealing/Eagle-Lion (U.K.)   /U

Stanley Holloway (Arthur Pemberton), Hermione Baddeley (Eddie Randall), Margaret Rutherford (Prof. Hatton-Jones), Paul Dupuis (Duke of Burgundy), Basil Radford (Gregg), Naunton Wayne (Straker), Jane Hylton (Molly), Raymond Huntley (Mr. Wix), Betty Warren (Connie Pemberton), Barbara Murray (Shirley Pemberton)

p, Michael Balcon; d, Henry Cornelius; w, T.E.B. Clarke; ph, Lionel Barnes, Cecil Cooney; ed, Michael Truman; m, Georges Auric; art d, Roy Oxley; cos, Anthony Mendleson

AAN Best Original Screenplay: T.E.B. Clarke

A light British comedy about an unexploded bomb that suddenly goes off and unearths documents stating that part of London belongs to Burgundy, France. Halloway becomes the head of the new government; new borders are drawn and new customs barriers are put into effect. A fresh comedy with some well-aimed satirical arrows from producer Balcon's Ealing Studios, famous for their sophisticated, irreverent comedies.

PAT AND MIKE

1952 95m bw Comedy   ★★★★
MGM (U.S.)   /U

Spencer Tracy (Mike Conovan), Katharine Hepburn (Pat Pemberton), Aldo Ray (Davie Hucko), William Ching (Collier Weld), Sammy White (Barney Grau), George Mathews (Spec Cauley), Loring Smith (Mr. Beminger), Phyllis Povah (Mrs. Beminger), Charles Bronson (Hank Tasling), Frank Richards (Sam Garsell)

p, Lawrence Weingarten; d, George Cukor; w, Ruth Gordon, Garson Kanin; ph, William Daniels; ed, George Boemler; m, David Raksin; art d, Cedric Gibbons, Urie McCleary; fx, Warren Newcombe; cos, Orry-Kelly

AAN Best Original Screenplay: Ruth Gordon, Garson Kanin

After playing a sports-hating character 10 years earlier in WOMAN OF THE YEAR, Katharine Hepburn essays the role of an all-around athlete not unlike the great Babe Didrikson Zaharias (who plays herself here) in this marvelous romantic comedy, which paired her again with real-life companion Spencer Tracy. Pat (Hepburn), a perky PE instructor at a southern California college and gifted athlete, falls apart whenever her professor fiance, Collier (William Ching), comes to watch her compete. Mike (Tracy), a somewhat shady sports promoter, recognizes her talent and persuades her to turn pro. Despite his unsuccessful attempt to get her to throw a match, she begins winning golf and tennis tournaments under his guidance, and gradually they fall for each other. What did you expect? Still, the point isn't what happens, but how it happens, and under the direction of George Cukor—working from the script by Garson Kanin and Ruth Gordon—Tracy and Hepburn turn in unforgettable performances. Shot mostly at the Riviera Country Club in Pacific Palisades, PAT AND MIKE gave Hepburn an opportunity to display her authentic athletic ability amidst a cast that included pro golfers Helen Dettweiler and Betty Hicks, as well as tennis professionals Don Budge and Pancho Gonzales. Chuck Connors, on loan from his job as the Triple A Los Angeles Angels's first sacker, makes his film debut as a police captain. Oscar nominated for Best Screenplay.

PAT GARRETT AND BILLY THE KID

1973 106m c Western   ★★★½
Gordon Carroll/Sam Peckinpah (U.S.)   R/18

James Coburn (Pat Garrett), Kris Kristofferson (Billy the Kid), Bob Dylan (Alias), Jason Robards Jr. (Gov. Lew Wallace), Richard Jaeckel (Sheriff Kip McKinney), Katy Jurado (Mrs. Baker), Slim Pickens (Sheriff Baker), Chill Wills (Lemuel), John Beck (Poe), Rita Coolidge (Maria)

p, Gordon Carroll; d, Sam Peckinpah; w, Rudy Wurlitzer; ph, John Coquillon; ed, Roger Spottiswoode, Garth Craven, Robert Wolfe, Richard Halsey, David Berlatsky, Tony De Zarraga; m, Bob Dylan; art d, Ted Haworth; fx, Augie Lohman

After director Sam Peckinpah handed in his final cut of PAT GARRETT AND BILLY THE KID, which he considered his finest film, the hierarchy at MGM saw fit to radically reedit it. The approximately 15 minutes cut from the film so drastically altered Peckinpah's structure and pacing that the incensed director tried to get his name removed from the credits. A restored version of Peckinpah's original film was given a very limited rerelease in 1990, but the initial-release version remains the one that most viewers will be able to see and it is a very choppy affair.

James Coburn is Pat Garrett; Kris Kristofferson is Billy the Kid. Feeling that the time has come for him to settle down, aging desperado Garrett switches sides of the law and puts on a badge; he is assigned to hunt down his old friend Billy. Apprehended and sentenced to hang, Billy shoots his way out of jail and hits the trail, accompanied by a former printer, Alias (Bob Dylan, who contributed the film's score). Back in New Mexico, Billy puts a gang together. Meanwhile, Garrett hires Alamosa Bill (Jack Elam), another former criminal, to help him, and the territorial governor, Lew Wallace (Jason Robards), engages Poe (John Beck) to bring Billy to justice. The manhunt begins.

Among the important scenes cut from the initial release of film was an epilogue that reveals Garrett to have been killed by the same man who ordered the outlaw-turned-lawman to shoot Billy. A prologue was also cut, as were a scene between Garrett and his wife, and the roles of Barry Sullivan, Elisha Cook, Jr., and Dub Taylor. Indeed, at those moments when the film begins to hit its stride, awkward edits undermine its development. Nevertheless the film is visually stunning, and Peckinpah makes great use of his Durango, Mexico, locations. He and screenwriter Rudy Wurlitzer (TWO-LANE BLACKTOP; WALKER) also make cameo appearances.

PATHER PANCHALI

1955 112m bw Drama ★★★★★
West Bengal Government (India) /U

Kanu Banerji *(Harihar the Father)*, Karuna Banerji *(Sarbojaya the Mother)*, Subir Banerji *(Apu)*, Runki Banerji *(Durga as a child)*, Umas Das Gupta *(Durga as a young girl)*, Chunibala Devi *(Indirtharkun the Old Aunt)*, Reva Devi *(Mrs. Mookerji)*, Rama Gangopadhaya *(Ranu Mookerji)*, Tulshi Chakraborty *(Schoolmaster)*, Harimoran Nag *(Doctor)*

p, Satyajit Ray; d, Satyajit Ray; w, Satyajit Ray (based on the novel by Bibhutibhusan Bandopadhaya); ph, Subrata Mitra; ed, Dulal Dutta; m, Ravi Shankar; art d, Banshi Chandra Gupta

Satyajit Ray's debut film, and the first installment in his "Apu Trilogy," quietly and intently studies a family living in the grip of poverty in a Bengal village. This was the first film of a great body of work characterized by visual beauty, humor, and emotional generosity, and announced the arrival of a major new director on the world scene, as well as the debut of Indian cinema in the West.

The father, a struggling writer, sets off to seek his fortune in the city, leaving his wife to take care of the children and an elderly aunt. Mere survival is a struggle for the poor family and the mother worries about how much the old lady eats. What follows is a series of perfectly ordinary events with a cumulative emotional power which may make some western viewers forever question the way Hollywood tells our stories. It's a powerful, unforgettable experience to watch characters whose lives are so different from our own, but whose concerns are ultimately universal. The remaining two films of the trilogy, APARAJITO and THE WORLD OF APU, follow the son, Apu (here played by Subir Banerji), into manhood and fatherhood.

Commissioned in 1945 to illustrate a children's version of the popular novel *Pather Panchali*, Ray became interested in bringing the novel to the screen, even though he had no previous film experience (nor did most of his crew). The production began sporadically on weekends, and was often interrupted by cash shortages before the Bengal government helped finish the picture. Like all Ray's best films, PATHER PANCHALI is influenced by the work of Jean Renoir (Ray visited the set of THE RIVER during its production in India) and of the Italian neorealists.

PATHS OF GLORY

1957 86m bw War ★★★★★
Bryna (U.S.) /PG

Kirk Douglas *(Col. Dax)*, Ralph Meeker *(Cpl. Paris)*, Adolphe Menjou *(Gen. Broulard)*, George Macready *(Gen. Mireau)*, Wayne Morris *(Lt. Roget)*, Richard Anderson *(Maj. Saint-Auban)*, Joseph Turkel *(Pvt. Arnoud)*, Timothy Carey *(Pvt. Ferol)*, Peter Capell *(Col. Judge)*, Susanne Christian *(The German Girl)*

p, James B. Harris; d, Stanley Kubrick; w, Stanley Kubrick, Calder Willingham, Jim Thompson (based on the novel by Humphrey Cobb); ph, Georg Krause; ed, Eva Kroll; m, Gerald Fried; art d, Ludwig Reiber

Stanley Kubrick's first great film established the epic style that has served him so well since. This is a harrowing and still very effective antiwar film that ranks with Lewis Milestone's epic ALL QUIET ON THE WESTERN FRONT in its power. The split between officers and men has never been so sharply delineated. The film was banned in France when it first appeared for eighteen years because of its anti-militarist stance.

Col. Dax (Kirk Douglas) is the commander of the battle-decimated 701st Infantry Regiment of the French Army during WWI, dug in along the Western Front in a brutally stalemated war. It is 1916, and the Allies have been struggling to overcome an equally determined German war machine for two years. Dax's hope that his regiment will be relieved from front-line duty is destroyed when corps commander Gen. Broulard (Adolphe Menjou) orders Gen. Mireau (George Macready), the divisional general in charge, to make an all-out attack against an impregnable German position nicknamed "the Ant Hill." The battle scenes showing the suicidal attack on the Ant Hill are devastating and brutally authentic, the barrage through which Dax leads his men (Kubrick's camera moving inexorably through the carnage) is a hurri-

cane of death. Three soldiers are selected to be court-martialed unjustly to serve as scapegoats for the military humiliation. Dax is the officer charged with their defense but the powers-that-be confound his efforts.

This is a director's film: Kubrick profiles naked power and the effects thereof with a visual excitement seldom seen on the screen; his attitude toward the actions he portrays is always felt. One particularly striking and effective strategy is the tendency to utilize mesmerizing but inhuman tracking shots for the trenches and battlegrounds while using elegant circling camera movements for the comfortable surroundings of the officers' chateau.

Though its condemnation of war is overwhelming, PATHS OF GLORY offers more optimism than is usual for the pessimistic Kubrick. The film may be read as a testament to human courage, compassion, and spirit that battles valiantly for survival despite the efforts of tyrants to vanquish principle and humanity.

PATRIOT GAMES

1992 113m c Thriller/Action ★★½
Neufeld/Rehme Productions/Paramount (U.S.) R/15

Harrison Ford *(Jack Ryan)*, Anne Archer *(Dr. Cathy Ryan)*, Patrick Bergin *(Kevin O'Donnell)*, Sean Bean *(Sean Miller)*, Thora Birch *(Sally Ryan)*, James Fox *(Lord Holmes)*, Samuel L. Jackson *(Robby Jackson)*, Polly Walker *(Annette)*, James Earl Jones *(Admiral James Greer)*, Richard Harris *(Paddy O'Neil)*

p, Mace Neufeld, Robert Rehme; d, Phillip Noyce; w, W. Peter Iliff, Donald Stewart (from the novel by Tom Clancy); ph, Donald McAlpine; ed, Neil Travis, William Hoy; m, James Horner; prod d, Joseph Nemec III; art d, Joseph P. Lucky; cos, Norma Moriceau

PATRIOT GAMES is a stolid, reactionary thriller in which the good old nuclear family becomes the last line of defense against that favorite action-movie staple, a group of international terrorists. In this wooden adaptation of Tom Clancy's best-seller, Harrison Ford plays Jack Ryan, an ex-C.I.A. analyst who single-handedly foils an I.R.A. kidnap attempt while on vacation in London. Ryan kills one of the terrorists, which makes the young man's elder brother, Sean Miller (Sean Bean), *really* mad—so mad, he spends the rest of the movie either scowling moodily into the distance, or trying to do away with Ryan and his family. Just in case there were any doubt about how bad the bad guys are, it's explained to us that Miller and his colleagues are not part of the regular I.R.A., but of an "ultra-violent" fringe group. The good guys, on the other hand, are a picture-perfect WASP family portrayed with all the depth and sincerity of an L.L. Bean catalog. Ryan is a reluctant hero who, when asked why he intervened in the kidnap attempt, looks brave and earnest and says, "I just couldn't stand by and watch those people get killed." His devoted wife Cathy (Anne Archer) is a brilliant eye surgeon who sails blithely into the operating room, performs a minor medical miracle, and then skips out in time to pick up her precocious daughter from school.

The action scenes in PATRIOT GAMES are handled efficiently, if unremarkably, by director Phillip Noyce (DEAD CALM), and a little extra color is provided by some good supporting players, particularly James Fox and Samuel L. Jackson. Our favorite parts, though, were the moments of unintentional humor, mostly courtesy of Ms. Archer. Her insufferably goody-goody performance makes you wish Glenn Close would show up brandishing a kitchen knife.

PATTON

1970 170m c War/Biography ★★★★½
Fox (U.S.) PG

George C. Scott *(Gen. George S. Patton, Jr.)*, Karl Malden *(Gen. Omar N. Bradley)*, Michael Bates *(Field Marshal Sir Bernard Law Montgomery)*, Edward Binns *(Maj. Gen. Walter Bedell Smith)*, Lawrence Dobkin *(Col. Gaston Bell)*, John Doucette *(Maj. Gen. Lucian K. Truscott)*, James Edwards *(Sgt. William George Meeks)*, Frank Latimore *(Lt. Col. Henry Davenport)*, Richard Munch *(Col. Gen. Alfred Jodl)*, Morgan Paull *(Capt. Richard N. Jenson)*

p, Frank McCarthy, Frank Caffey; d, Franklin J. Schaffner; w, Francis Ford Coppola, Edmund H. North (based on the books *Patton: Ordeal and Triumph* by Ladislas Farago and *A Soldier's Story* by Gen. Omar

N. Bradley); ph, Fred Koenekamp; ed, Hugh S. Fowler; m, Jerry Goldsmith; art d, Urie McCleary, Gil Parrondo; fx, L.B. Abbott, Art Cruickshank

AA Best Picture; AA Best Actor: George C. Scott; *AA Best Director:* Franklin J. Schaffner; *AA Best Adapted Screenplay:* Francis Ford Coppola, Edmund H. North; *AAN Best Cinematography:* Fred Koenekamp; *AA Best Editing:* Hugh S. Fowler; *AAN Best Score:* Jerry Goldsmith; *AA Best Art Direction:* Urie McCleary, Gil Parrondo, Antonio Mateos, Pierre-Louis Thevenet; *AA Best Sound:* Douglas Williams, Don Bassman; *AAN Best Visual Effects:* Alex Weldon

What PATHS OF GLORY attempted to show about the relationships between officers and men of the first World War, PATTON in part attempts to do for the second. Patton, of course, is best remembered as the general who slapped a soldier. But George C. Scott, under the direction of Franklin Schaffner, creates a much more colorful and ambiguous portrait. This WWII spectacle is immense but Scott's virtuoso performance looms larger than any of its battles. His characterization can appeal to both hawks and doves; it can appreciated either as a critique or a paean. He's insensitive to his men's plight on some occasions, gentle as a loving father on others. Patton's eccentricity may very well have been an important ingredient of victory. PATTON is a war movie of unusual depth and a landmark in screen biographies.

Beginning with a classic six-minute speech by Patton about the fighting spirit of Americans, the film traces the legendary WWII exploits of "Old Blood and Guts" from his defeat of Rommel's *Afrika Korps* at El Guettar to the invasion of Sicily, during which he disobeys orders and beats rival Field Marshal Montgomery (Michael Bates) to Messina. We also see his loss of command for slapping a battle-fatigued soldier because he has been hospitalized but has no wounds. Then, after sitting out D-Day as a decoy, Patton is given command of the 3rd Army, winning one mighty battle after another with his armored troops and eventually speeding to the rescue of the encircled 101st Airborne Division at Bastogne, ending Hitler's last great counteroffensive in the Battle of the Bulge. Following the war, Patton is sent into involuntary retirement after his highly vocal criticism of the Soviet Union, and the film ends with his farewell to his faithful staff.

Scott won a richly deserved Academy Award (which he refused) for his performance. Sturdy support is provided by Karl Malden as Gen. Omar Bradley, Edward Binns as Maj. Gen. Walter Bedell Smith, John Doucette as Maj. Gen. Lucian K. Truscott, and Bates as Montgomery. Franklin J. Schaffner's direction is majestic particularly in his masterful handling of complex battle scenes; shot in 70-millimeter, Dimension 150, these broad, impersonal spectacles have a macabre beauty that gives the viewer a serene God's-eye-view of modern warfare. Fox hoped to duplicate the success of its black-and-white blockbuster, THE LONGEST DAY, by spending a fortune on this spectacular film, which was shot on location in England, Spain, Morocco, and Greece.

PAULINE AT THE BEACH
(PAULINE A LA PLAGE)

1983 94m c Drama/Comedy   ★★★½
Losange/Ariane (France)   R/15

Amanda Langlet (*Pauline*), Arielle Dombasle (*Marion*), Pascal Greggory (*Pierre*), Feodor Atkine (*Henry*), Simon de la Brosse (*Sylvain*), Rosette (*Louisette*)

p, Margaret Menegoz; d, Eric Rohmer; w, Eric Rohmer; ph, Nestor Almendros; ed, Cecile Decugis; m, Jean-Louis Valero

For the third in Eric Rohmer's series of "Comedies and Proverbs," the director shifts from Paris to the coast of Normandy. Pauline (Amanda Langlet) is a teenager on vacation with her older, recently divorced cousin, Marion (Arielle Dombasle). They become involved with three men during a beachside vacation. Marion carries on with a writer, Henry (Feodor Atkine), and tries to ignore the advances of old friend, Pierre (Pascal Greggory), while Pauline meets a boy her own age, Sylvain (Simon De La Brosse), and has her first sexual experiences. This film is close in spirit to the work of Jean Renoir. Rohmer confines much of it to the beach and a vacation home, turning his directorial attention to the interplay among the five main characters as they move in and out of rooms, spied through windows and doors and forced to become masters of romantic deception. Instead of characteristically

following one determined individual, Rohmer intertwines his characters and lets their paths overlap. Pauline, though singled out in the title, tends to function more as an observer caught in the whirlwind of love and romance. Rohmer was named Best Director at the Berlin Film Festival for PAULINE.

PAWNBROKER, THE

1965 114m bw Drama/War   ★★★★
Landau/Unger/Pawnbroker (U.S.)   /X

Rod Steiger (*Sol Nazerman*), Geraldine Fitzgerald (*Marilyn Birchfield*), Brock Peters (*Rodriguez*), Jaime Sanchez (*Jesus Ortiz*), Thelma Oliver (*Ortiz's Girl*), Marketa Kimbrel (*Tessie*), Baruch Lumet (*Mendel*), Juano Hernandez (*Mr. Smith*), Linda Geiser (*Ruth Nazerman*), Nancy R. Pollock (*Bertha*)

p, Roger Lewis, Philip Langner; d, Sidney Lumet; w, David Friedkin, Morton Fine (based on the novel by Edward Lewis Wallant); ph, Boris Kaufman; ed, Ralph Rosenblum; m, Quincy Jones; art d, Richard Sylbert; cos, Anna Hill Johnstone

AAN Best Actor: Rod Steiger

Although there have been numerous films about the post-Vietnam era and the war's psychological aftereffects on the soldier returning home, very few pictures have dealt with the similar predicament of those who lived through WWII (or WWI, for that matter). THE PAWNBROKER, one of the seminal American films of the 1960s, focuses on Sol Nazerman (Rod Steiger), a middle-aged concentration camp survivor who lost his entire family to the Nazis and now runs a pawnshop in Harlem. That he remained alive is a source of bewilderment and pain. He has lost faith in God and man; he is emotionless and totally removed from the world that surrounds his run-down shop. Shop assistant Jesus Ortiz (Jaime Sanchez) and social worker Marilyn Birchfield (Geraldine Fitzgerald) try to get through Sol's icy exterior, but to no avail. Instead, Sol becomes increasingly cruel and offensive. Meanwhile, he conducts an affair with Tessie (Marketa Kimbrell), a fellow camp survivor whose husband was a victim of Nazi atrocities.

Directed by Sidney Lumet in a gritty, raw style that was fashionable at the time, THE PAWNBROKER is memorable today for its innovative use of flashbacks—in this case quick cuts lasting only a fraction of a second—to represent the disturbing, unrelenting flashes of Sol's memory. Also unforgettable is Steiger's towering performance as the volatile survivor, a powder keg of hateful remembrances. The soundtrack was composed by Quincy Jones.

PAYDAY

1972 102m c Drama   ★★★★
Cinerama (U.S.)   R/X

Rip Torn (*Maury Dann*), Anna Capri (*Mayleen*), Elayne Heilveil (*Rosamond*), Michael C. Gwynne (*Clarence*), Jeff Morris (*Tally*), Cliff Emmich (*Chauffeur*), Henry O. Arnold (*Ted*), Walter Bamberg (*Bridgeway*), Linda Spatz (*Sandy*), Eleanor Fell (*Galen Dann*)

p, Martin Fink, Don Carpenter; d, Daryl Duke; w, Don Carpenter; ph, Richard C. Glouner; ed, Richard Halsey

Torn is a fading country singer in this excellent, overlooked drama. The film chronicles the last 36 hours of Torn's life, as he travels from one honky-tonk to the next. Torn is a cruel, egotistical performer who knows his career is on the skids. Screenwriter Carpenter and director Duke capture in unglamorized fashion the grind of being on the road, the groupies, the payoffs, and the drugs. The film has no heroes or villains, and every character is three-dimensional. Gwynne is Torn's ruthless manager, Capri is the singer's mistress, and Heilveil makes her debut as an innocent groupie. Torn's brilliant performance deserves more recognition, as does the film, which examines the dark side of the music business and the struggle for success and fame.

PEDESTRIAN, THE
(DER FUSSGANGER)

1974 97m c Drama/War ★★★½
Cinerama (West Germany) PG/

Gustav Rudolf Sellner *(Heinz Alfred Giese)*, Ruth Hausmeister *(Inge Maria Giese)*, Maximilian Schell *(Andreas Giese)*, Manuel Sellner *(Hubert Giese)*, Elsa Wagner *(Elsa Giese)*, Dagmar Hirtz *(Elke Giese)*, Michael Weinert *(Michael Giese)*, Peter Hall *(Rudolf Hartmann)*, Alexander May *(Alexander Markowitz)*, Christian Kohlund *(Erwin Gotz)*

p, Maximilian Schell, Zev Braun; d, Maximilian Schell; w, Maximilian Schell; ph, Wolfgang Treu, Klaus Koenig; ed, Dagmar Hirtz; m, Manos Hadjidakis

AAN Best Foreign Language Film

A powerful and revealing film about death, guilt, and Germany's involvement in wartime atrocities, THE PEDESTRIAN focuses on an aging industrialist, Heinz Alfred Giese (Gustav Rudolf Sellner), who prefers not to remember the events of WWII. In fact, he prefers to be involved with life as little as possible. Since the death of his son Andreas (Maximilian Schell) in an auto accident in which Giese was driving (resulting in the loss of his license, hence the title), his whole life has centered around his grandson, Hubert (Manuel Sellner). Although Giese would rather forget his past, Alexander Markowitz (Alexander May), the senior editor of a newspaper, begins a probe into Giese's involvement in the massacre of a Greek village. With the help of two witnesses—a survivor of the attack (Fani Fotinou) and a former German soldier (Walter von Varndal)—Markowitz discovers that Giese was involved in the massacre and could have prevented it. When the story is printed, Giese becomes the target of moral outrage and violence. This strong indictment of his generation's complacency is especially damning because its villain is not a monster but a well-respected businessman and a loving grandfather. Produced, directed, and written by Maximilian Schell, THE PEDESTRIAN received a Golden Globe award for Best Film and an Oscar nomination for Best Foreign Film.

PEE-WEE'S BIG ADVENTURE

1985 90m c Comedy ★★★½
Aspen/Shapiro (U.S.) PG/U

Pee-wee Herman *(Himself)*, Elizabeth Daily *(Dottie)*, Mark Holton *(Francis)*, Diane Salinger *(Simone)*, Judd Omen *(Mickey)*, Irving Hellman *(Neighbor)*, Monte Landis *(Mario)*, Damon Martin *(Chip)*, David Glasser, Gregory Brown

p, Robert Shapiro, Richard Gilbert Abramson; d, Tim Burton; w, Phil Hartman, Paul Reubens, Michael Varhol; ph, Victor J. Kemper; ed, Billy Weber; m, Danny Elfman; prod d, David L. Snyder; fx, Chuck Gaspar; cos, Aggie Guerard Rodgers; anim, Rich Heinrichs

Pee-wee Herman is not like the other boys. "I'm a loner. . . a rebel," he announces to his would-be girlfriend. He's a comic rebel without a pause. Inspired lunacy, PEE-WEE'S BIG ADVENTURE is one of the most inventive films in recent memory. This clever and wholly original work incorporates a wide variety of cinematic tools with a fresh and unique sense of style. Pee-wee Herman, a creation of writer-comedian Paul Reubens, is a great comic creation on a par with Chaplin's Little Tramp. Somewhat reminiscent of the most popular Jerry Lewis screen persona, Pee-wee is a magical, happy-go-lucky, occasionally mischievous little boy living in an adult body. What makes this seemingly moronic character work on an intelligent level is the cartoonlike environment he inhabits. In both structure and content, PEE-WEE'S ADVENTURE often resembles a Warner Brothers cartoon. Like those classic animations, this film thrives on easily identifiable characterizations, simple plot motivations, throwaway gags, and an often surreal sense of logic, all mixed together with talent and ingenuity. The story gets started when the pride and joy of Pee-wee's life, his shiny red bicycle, is stolen. The police are of no help, so a crazed Pee-wee consults a fraudulent fortune-teller who tells him his bike is in the basement of the Alamo in Texas. Naturally, Pee-wee takes to the road.

The episodic plot is a perfect format for Reuben's comedy. For many this character was rather hard to take prior to this marvelous movie. In his nightclub act and numerous appearances on "Late Night with David Letterman," Pee-wee was bit too disturbingly manic, regressive, and grotesquely fey for some genteel sensibilities. He's just as frenetic and sexually ambiguous here but he is so thoroughly contextualized within his own beautifully realized world that he allows even the most traditional among us to get the joke. The smart and wacky script by Rubens and Phil Hartman (of television's "Saturday Night Live" and "The Simpsons) is given added vibrance by director Tim Burton (BEETLEJUICE, BATMAN, EDWARD SCISSORHANDS, and FRANKENWEENIE). Burton's background as a Disney animator is perfect for the film; he gives PEE-WEE'S BIG ADVENTURE a wonderfully cartoonish look through design, lighting, and camera angles. Two stars were born with the release of this film—one in front of the camera and one behind it. One could also make a case for a third star here: Soundtrack composer Danny Elfman from the rock group Oingo Bongo provides a witty and manic score that bolsters every scene.

PEEPING TOM

1960 109m c Thriller ★★★★★
Anglo-Amalgamated (U.K.) /X

Karl Boehm *(Mark Lewis)*, Moira Shearer *(Vivian)*, Anna Massey *(Helen Stephens)*, Maxine Audley *(Mrs. Stephens)*, Esmond Knight *(Arthur Baden)*, Bartlett Mullins *(Mr. Peters)*, Shirley Ann Field *(Diane Ashley)*, Michael Goodliffe *(Don Jarvis)*, Brenda Bruce *(Dora)*, Martin Miller *(Dr. Rosan)*

p, Michael Powell; d, Michael Powell; w, Leo Marks; ph, Otto Heller; ed, Noreen Ackland; m, Brian Easdale; art d, Arthur Lawrence; chor, Wally Stott

With its incredibly complex structure—which implicates the audience in the central character's crimes—PEEPING TOM is a remarkable examination of the psychology of filmmaking and film viewing, and one of the most disturbing films ever made.

Mark Lewis (Boehm), a focus-puller at a film studio, works part-time at a corner cigar store taking pornographic photos of women. One night, he approaches a prostitute on the street, goes to her apartment, and murders her while filming the event.

Mark rents out most of the house he owns, and a young tenant named Helen (Anna Massey) takes a liking to her landlord. When she screens movies of himself as a young boy, Helen is horrified by scenes of Mark's father (Michael Powell), a quack psychologist, tormenting the boy—part of the psychologist's studies in fear, Mark explains.

A dancer working at the film studio (Moira Shearer) is the next victim of Mark's grisly obsession. Increasingly attracted to Helen, he tries to repress his cinematic obsession by leaving his camera at home when they go out, but his perverted impulses begin to get the best of him.

Michael Powell, who, along with partner Emeric Pressburger, was one of the cornerstones of the British film industry during the 1940s, was vilified by the British press following PEEPING TOM's release in 1960. The director of THE LIFE AND DEATH OF COLONEL BLIMP, STAIRWAY TO HEAVEN, BLACK NARCISSUS, and THE RED SHOES had made a rich and provocative psychological horror film, but critics in his homeland found it completely repugnant. The film was quickly butchered by the studio and was shown briefly in US second-run houses. It wasn't until 1979, however, that a restored version was released due to the efforts of director Martin Scorsese, a devout fan of the picture. Sadly, Powell's career never recovered from the critical attacks, and he made only a handful of features and shorts before his death in 1990.

PEGGY SUE GOT MARRIED

1986 104m c Fantasy/Comedy ★★★
Rastar (U.S.) PG-13/15

Kathleen Turner *(Peggy Sue)*, Nicolas Cage *(Charlie Bodell)*, Barry Miller *(Richard Norvik)*, Catherine Hicks *(Carol Heath)*, Joan Allen *(Maddy Nagle)*, Kevin J. O'Connor *(Michael Fitzsimmons)*, Barbara Harris *(Evelyn Kelcher)*, Don Murray *(Jack Kelcher)*, Maureen O'Sullivan *(Elizabeth Alvorg)*, Leon Ames *(Barney Alvorg)* p, Paul R. Gurian; d, Francis Ford Coppola; w, Jerry Leichtling, Arlene Sarner; ph, Jordan Cronenweth; ed, Barry Malkin; m, John Barry; prod d, Dean Tavoularis; art d, Alex Tavoularis; cos, Theadora Van Runkle

AAN Best Actress: Kathleen Turner; *AAN Best Cinematography:* Jordan Cronenweth; *AAN Best Costume Design:* Theadora Van Runkle

A bittersweet cross between OUR TOWN and IT'S A WONDERFUL LIFE, PEGGY SUE GOT MARRIED tells the poignant story of Peggy Sue Bodell (Kathleen Turner). She's a 43-year-old housewife on the verge of a divorce from Charlie (Nicholas Cage), an obnoxious philanderer who is locally famous for his tacky TV commercials for his retail appliance business. Peggy Sue squeezes into her old prom dress and goes to her 25th high school reunion to meet all her old friends from James Buchanan High. Subsequently named queen of the reunion, she ascends the podium to accept her crown, and passes out. Tossed into a time warp, she awakens in 1960, a 43-year-old consciousness in an ostensibly 17-year-old body. This feat requires a suspension of disbelief on the part of the audience but Turner pulls it off admirably. The film asks a powerful question: If we had a chance to go back and do it all again, would we do it the same way? Or would we rewrite our lives to create a new outcome?

Released the year after BACK TO THE FUTURE, there were inevitable comparisons. However, PEGGY SUE GOT MARRIED is a more grown up and fatalistic film (even if it is ultimately inferior) that eschews cartoonish exaggeration for a more realistic approach to its subject matter. The film features good acting from almost everyone, the one notable exception being the annoying Cage who adopts a grating constricted voice for the role. The movie has many lovely moments and just as many dead spots, but its strengths make this atypical film from Francis Coppola a worthwhile viewing experience.

PEKING OPERA BLUES
(DAO MA DAN)

1986   104m   c   Martial Arts/Comedy   ★★★★
Cinema City   (Hong Kong)

Brigitte Lin, Sally Yeh, Cherie Chung, Mark Cheng, Ling Pak Hoi

p, Tsui Hark, Claudie Chung; d, Tsui Hark; w, To Kwok Wai; ph, Poon Hang Sang; ed, David Wu; m, James Wong; art d, Vincent Wai, Ho Kim Sing, Leung Chi Hing; fx, Cinefex Workshop; chor, Ching Sui Tung; cos, Ng Po Ling

A delightfully frenetic comedy-adventure, PEKING OPERA BLUES serves as a terrific introduction to the energetic popular cinema of Hong Kong. Set in China circa 1913, the fast-paced and complicated story centers on three young women from different social classes who become embroiled in a revolutionary plot to overthrow the military government. Surprisingly, one of the key players in the revolution is the beautiful Lin Ching Hsia, the daughter of China's most powerful general. She and a male accomplice are ordered to steal some secret documents from her father's safe. Through a series of slapstick circumstances, a winsome but dim-witted street performer, a disaffected soldier, and the attractive daughter of the local opera house owner become involved in the plot and wind up comrades of the revolutionaries. Together, the five do battle with the army, the generals, and the secret police, with most of the zany action revolving around the colorful opera house. After a series of nonstop seductions, disguises, gunfights, kung-fu skirmishes, gymnastics, chases, double crosses, separations and reunions, the heroes succeed in getting the valued documents to the revolutionary leaders. The film ends with the five on horseback vowing to meet again someday before going their separate ways.

In an era in which most American films are either lifeless bores or cynical exercises in mass marketing (or both), PEKING OPERA BLUES is a welcome burst of manic energy that never fails to please. The skillful combination of breathtaking action and slapstick comedy in this film is nearly indescribable. Martial arts coordinator Ching Sui Tung's innovative choreography of the film's numerous action scenes is superb and the cast boasts three of Hong Kong's most popular actresses—Lin Ching Hsia, Cherie Chung, and Sally Yeh. They make a splendidly vivacious team and their ensemble comedic timing is

flawless. Tsui Hark directs with a verve and style little seen on American screens and, while he always entertains, he also slips in some genuinely touching scenes and social observations.

A massive box-office hit in Hong Kong, the film proved popular with festival audiences in Europe and North America, who discovered that Hong Kong cinema had come a long way since the martial arts cheapies of the early 1970s.

PELICAN BRIEF, THE

1993   140m   c   Thriller   ★★
Warner Bros./Pakula Productions   (U.S.)   PG-13/12

Julia Roberts *(Darby Shaw)*, Denzel Washington *(Gray Grantham)*, Sam Shepard *(Thomas Callahan)*, John Heard *(Gavin Verheek)*, Tony Goldwyn *(Fletcher Coal)*, James B. Sikking *(FBI Director F. Denton Voyles)*, William Atherton *(Bob Gminski)*, Robert Culp *(President of the United States)*, Stanley Tucci *(Khamel)*, Hume Cronyn *(Justice Abraham Rosenberg)*

p, Alan J. Pakula, Pieter Jan Brugge; d, Alan J. Pakula; w, Alan J. Pakula (from the novel by John Grisham); ph, Stephen Goldblatt; ed, Tom Rolf, Trudy Ship; m, James Horner; prod d, Philip Rosenberg; art d, Robert Guerra; fx, Conrad Brink, Lynda Lemon, John Nelson; cos, Albert Wolsky

In this slow, talky adaptation of John Grisham's best-seller, Alan Pakula—director of subtle and suspenseful thrillers like KLUTE and ALL THE PRESIDENT'S MEN—is undone by the stubborn shortcomings of his source material. Grisham's ramshackle plot has no suspense, yields no surprises, and demands almost constant explanations to get to its ending.

The plot is set in motion by the baffling murders of two Supreme Court justices, a curmudgeonly liberal (Hume Cronyn) and a closeted Republican homosexual (Ralph Cosham); all they have in common is a pro-environment inclination. Spirited and beautiful law student Darby Shaw (Julia Roberts) puts together a brief theorizing that the culprit could be a shadowy oil millionaire determined to tap a billion-dollar oil reserve in the fragile Louisiana bayou habitat of the endangered brown pelican. Her lover (Sam Shepard) shows the brief to a friend in the FBI, Verheek (John Heard), and suddenly Darby is the most hunted woman in America. *Washington Herald* reporter Gray Grantham (Denzel Washington) becomes her ally as she seeks to evade her shadowy pursuers and find out the truth behind a scandal that reaches to the highest levels of government.

THE PELICAN BRIEF is a shallow bore. Grisham's characters are rudimentary, and both Roberts and Washington are stiff and over-earnest. Normally, the bad guys could be relied upon to enliven the action, but THE PELICAN BRIEF's creepy oilman has only one scene in the book and none in the screen version, which may be the most realistic aspect of the film—in real life, bad guys almost invariably appear only in the damage they do. In the movies, however, staying true to life makes for a long and trying evening.

PELLE THE CONQUEROR
(PELLE EROVRAREN)

1987   160m   c   Drama   ★★★
Svensk/Danish Film Institute/Swedish Film Institute   PG-13/15
/DR TV/SID   (Denmark/Sweden)

Max von Sydow *(Pappa Lasse)*, Pelle Hvenegaard *(Pelle, His Son)*, Erik Paaske *(Farm Foreman)*, Bjorn Granath *(Farmhand Erik)*, Axel Strobye *(Kongstrup)*, Astrid Villaume *(Mrs. Kongstrup)*, Troels Asmussen *(Rud)*, John Wittig *(Schoolteacher)*, Anne Lise Hirsch Bjerrum *(Karna)*, Sofie Grabol *(Miss Sine)*

p, Per Holst; d, Bille August; w, Bille August (based on volume one of a novel by Martin Andersen Nexo); ph, Jorgen Persson; ed, Janus Billeskov Jansen; m, Stefan Nilsson; prod d, Anna Asp; cos, Kicki Ilander, Gitte Kolvig, Birthe Qualmann

AA Best Foreign Language Film ; *AAN Best Actor:* Max Von Sydow

Bille August, the director of TWIST AND SHOUT (1986), the most commercially successful Danish film ever, followed that teen drama with this Swedish-Danish coproduction set in the 1890s and starring Max von Sydow as an impoverished Swedish widower who moves to Bornholm, a

Danish island in the Baltic, hoping to improve his lot in life. He takes along his seven-year-old son, Hvenegaard, but instead of finding a better life, they are reduced to virtual slavery. A grim story of deprived and depraved humanity unfolds, focusing on both the oppressed and the oppressors. An Oscar winner for Best Foreign Film, this is an often brutal tale which is boosted by a powerful performance from Von Sydow.

PENNIES FROM HEAVEN

1936 80m bw Musical   ★★★
Columbia (U.S.)   /U

Bing Crosby *(Larry)*, Madge Evans *(Susan)*, Edith Fellows *(Patsy)*, Donald Meek *(Gramps)*, John Gallaudet *(Hart)*, Louis Armstrong *(Henry)*, Tom Dugan *(Crowbar)*, Nana Bryant *(Miss Howard)*, Charles Wilson *(Warden)*, Harry Tyler *(Concessionaire)*

p, Emanuel Cohen; d, Norman Z. McLeod; w, Jo Swerling (based on the story "The Peacock's Feather" by Katherine Leslie Moore); ph, Robert Pittack; ed, John Rawlins; m, Arthur Johnston; art d, Stephen Goosson

AAN Best Song: Arthur Johnston (Music), Johnny Burke (Lyrics)

An amusing musical, notable mainly for its fine selection of songs, including the Academy Award-nominated title tune penned by Johnny Burke and Arthur Johnston. The film opens with Crosby serving a jail sentence for smuggling (for which he has been wrongly convicted). Before he is released he is given a note by a murderer who is about to meet his end in the gas chamber. The killer's note contains the name and address of his victim's relatives. As a final request, he asks Crosby to locate the relatives and move them into his abandoned family estate. Crosby finds the relatives—a 10-year-old girl, Fellows, and her grandfather, Meek—living in squalor. At Crosby's urging, Fellows and Meek pack their bags and head for their new home, only to find that it looks haunted. To make the place more inviting, Crosby comes up with the idea of turning it into a restaurant called the Haunted House Cafe. To draw the crowds he croons a number of Johnston and Burke tunes, with the title tune being nominated for an Oscar for Best Song. Other numbers include "One, Two, Button Your Shoe," "So Do I," "Let's Call a Heart a Heart," "Now I've Got Some Dreaming to Do," "What This Country Needs," and "Skeleton in the Closet."

PENNIES FROM HEAVEN

1981 108m c Musical   ★★★★
MGM (U.S.)   R/15

Steve Martin *(Arthur)*, Bernadette Peters *(Eileen)*, Christopher Walken *(Tom)*, Jessica Harper *(Joan)*, Vernel Bagneris *(Accordion Man)*, John McMartin *(Mr. Warner)*, John Karlen *(Detective)*, Jay Garner *(Banker)*, Robert Fitch *(Al)*, Thomas Rall *(Ed)*

p, Herbert Ross, Nora Kaye; d, Herbert Ross; w, Dennis Potter (based on the television series by Dennis Potter); ph, Gordon Willis; ed, Richard Marks; m, Marvin Hamlisch, Billy May; art d, Fred Tuch, Bernie Cutler; chor, Danny Daniels; cos, Bob Mackie

AAN Best Adapted Screenplay: Dennis Potter; *AAN Best Costume Design:* Bob Mackie; *AAN Best Sound:* Michael J. Kohut, Jay M. Harding, Richard Tyler, Al Overton

MGM mistakenly thought Dennis Potter's acclaimed British television miniseries "Pennies from Heaven" could be profitably condensed into a feature, so they cast Martin in the role originated by Bob Hoskins and asked Martin's flame at the time, Peters, to costar. The result is a moving, highly eccentric examination of the relationship between "real life" and popular culture that bombed at the box office.

    PENNIES FROM HEAVEN is a musical in which the actors lip-synch to original recordings from the 1930s. There is no attempt to achieve verisimilitude (Martin at one point is seen singing with a woman's voice); rather, in Potter's conceit, the saccharine songs are meant to reflect the characters' poignantly unrealistic aspirations, or to stand in for emotions they cannot otherwise articulate. Martin plays a Depression-era sheet-music salesman who falls for Peters, even though he's married to Harper. The intervention of a sinister tramp leads to tragedy.

To many, the movie—with its incredible sets, mammoth dance sequences, and intentional air of melodramatic overstatement—seemed too big in comparison to its supposedly mundane characters and concerns, and it was badly received. Most critics didn't get the point, while those who did tended to prefer the more modest TV production. Not for everyone, but those who respond to it will find it unforgettable.

PEOPLE VS. LARRY FLYNT, THE

1996 130m c Biography   ★★★½
Phoenix Pictures/Ixtlan Productions (U.S.)   R/18

Woody Harrelson *(Larry Flynt)*, Courtney Love *(Althea Leasure)*, Edward Norton *(Isaacman)*, Brett Harrelson *(Jimmy Flynt)*, Miles Chapin *(Miles)*, Donna Hanover *(Ruth Carter Stapleton)*, James Cromwell *(Charles Keating)*, Crispin Glover *(Arlo)*, Vincent Schiavelli *(Chester)*, James Carville *(Simon Leis)*

p, Oliver Stone, Janet Yang, Michael Hausman; d, Milos Forman; w, Scott Alexander, Larry Karaszewski; ph, Philippe Rousselot; ed, Christopher Tellefsen; m, Thomas Newman; prod d, Patrizia Von Brandenstein; art d, James Nezda, Shawn Hausman; fx, Rodman Kiser; cos, Theodor Pistek, Arianne Phillips

AAN Best Actor: Woody Harrelson; *AAN Best Director:* Milos Forman

A warm, fuzzy movie for armchair liberals, THE PEOPLE VS. LARRY FLYNT whitewashes the life of the infamous pornographer for the benefit of viewers who are all for the First Amendment—so long as it doesn't protect anything too unpleasant.

    In 1972, Larry Flynt (Woody Harrelson), is running a string of Cincinnati strip clubs when he hits on the idea of publishing a newsletter featuring nude photographs of his strippers. The idea is a big success, largely because the pictures are substantially more explicit than those found in mainstream men's magazines like *Playboy*. Expanded to magazine format, *Hustler* becomes a huge hit. Aided by his wife and business partner Althea (Courtney Love), a former stripper, Flynt becomes a wealthy man by testing the limits of obscenity and good taste. But as the national mood of the late 1970s grows more conservative, the relentlessly provocative Flynt becomes the object of numerous obscenity lawsuits.

    You'd be hard-pressed to find another biopic that whitewashes its subject so thoroughly as THE PEOPLE VS. LARRY FLYNT. Director Milos Forman would like you to believe that Flynt's vulgar catalogue of racism, sexism, and anything else that might be construed as offensive is simply a more honest variation on *Playboy*. Of course, we expect controversial subjects to be watered down in mass-market films, but in a film whose purpose is to salute our Constitutional right to free speech, the contents of *Hustler* properly are an issue: the filmmakers' argument is seriously compromised by their failure to trust their audience with the knowledge of what kind of material that right protects. Despite lacking the courage of its convictions, THE PEOPLE VS. LARRY FLYNT is generally an intelligent and entertaining film. Harrelson's good-ol'-boy raunchiness is amusing, and singer Courtney Love gives an astonishingly good performance in her first substantial film role.

PEOPLE WILL TALK

1951 110m bw Comedy   ★★★★
Fox (U.S.)   /A

Cary Grant *(Dr. Noah Praetorius)*, Jeanne Crain *(Annabel Higgins)*, Finlay Currie *(Shunderson)*, Hume Cronyn *(Prof. Elwell)*, Walter Slezak *(Prof. Barker)*, Sidney Blackmer *(Arthur Higgins)*, Basil Ruysdael *(Dean Lyman Brockwell)*, Katherine Locke *(Miss James)*, Will Wright *(John Higgins)*, Margaret Hamilton *(Miss Pickett)*

p, Darryl F. Zanuck; d, Joseph L. Mankiewicz; w, Joseph L. Mankiewicz (based on the play "Dr. Praetorius" by Curt Goetz); ph, Milton Krasner; ed, Barbara McLean; m, Johannes Brahms, Richard Wagner; art d, Lyle Wheeler, George W. Davis; fx, Fred Sersen; cos, Charles LeMaire

Joseph L. Mankiewicz had just won two Oscars for ALL ABOUT EVE (writing, directing) and the year before that two more for the same tasks on A LETTER TO THREE WIVES. He took on a big challenge here, adapting Curt Goetz's play, "Dr. Praetorius," making it into an odd amalgam of wit, satire, high drama, and glistening dialog. Grant is an early crusader in the medical profession who thinks that the mind can cure just as well, if not better, than massive doses of medicine. He believes in treating the patient rather than the disease, a practice that delights his charges but horrifies his colleagues, who are far more traditional and hidebound in their diagnoses. Grant is teaching at a medical school and living what is thought to be a strange life. His servant and best friend is Currie, a murderer who has been sent to jail twice. His other friend is Slezak, a rotund scientist who loves model trains and knockwurst, not necessarily in that order. Grant's enemy at the school is Cronyn, a sourpuss anatomy instructor who feels more at home dissecting corpses than talking to humans. One day, while Grant is teaching his students, Crain, an aspiring young doctor, faints during the lecture. Grant is soon aware that she's newly pregnant, and when she tries to kill herself, he says that his first diagnosis was wrong, then marries her. Crain's father is Blackmer, a drunk and a loser, but a man with what Tennessee Williams called "the charm of the defeated." In between his classes, Grant conducts the school's orchestra in Wagner and Brahms. Out of spite, Cronyn contacts the dean, Ruysdael, and brings up a few interesting things about Grant's medical background, obliging Grant to defend himself to the school's board of directors. He explains his philosophy of medicine and eventually wins over the listeners. While all this is going on, Grant is spending his time at home convincing Crain that he really does love her and didn't marry her out of pity for her plight. The designation "sophisticated" applies well to PEOPLE WILL TALK, and Grant gives one of his best performances, a carefully controlled job of acting that never becomes farce. The movie is mature and frank, and Mankiewicz uses the opportunity to take a few potshots at academic hypocrisy.

PEPE LE MOKO

1937 90m bw Crime/Romance ★★★★½
Hakim/Paris (France) /PG

Jean Gabin (Pepe le Moko), Mireille Balin (Gaby Gould), Line Noro (Ines), Lucas Gridoux (Inspector Slimane), Gabriel Gabrio (Carlos), Fernand Charpin (Regis), Saturnin Fabre (Grandfather), Gilbert Gil (Pierrot), Roger Legris (Max), Gaston Modot (Jimmy)

p, Robert Hakim, Raymond Hakim; d, Julien Duvivier; w, Julien Duvivier, Henri Jeanson, Henri La Barthe, Jacques Constant (based on the book by Henri La Barthe); ph, Jules Kruger, Marc Fossard; ed, Marguerite Beauge; m, Vincent Scotto, Mohamed Yguerbouchen; prod d, Jacques Krauss

Based on the life of a real criminal who hid in the Casbah under the protection of his pals, PEPE LE MOKO stars Jean Gabin as the title thief, brigand, and charmer, who has surrounded himself with loyal gang members and keeps them in line through the sheer force of his personality, never resorting to violence. Tired of life with his moll, Ines (Line Noro), and of being on the run, Pepe yearns for his old days in Paris. He falls in love with a gorgeous tourist, Gaby Gould (Mireille Balin), but in the process lets his guard down and gives Algerian police inspector Slimane (Lucas Gridoux) the opportunity to finally nab him.

PEPE LE MOKO owes a thematic and stylistic debt to the early Hollywood gangster films, most notably Howard Hawks' SCARFACE, but director Julien Duvivier took the conventional mix of love and bullets and made it into dark poetry.Indeed this film is cited as a prime example of the Poetic Realism movement in France. The camera undulates through dingy realistic sets cloaked in deep shadow. The performances are so naturalistic that the actors don't seem to be acting, and the lack of sentimentality deserves special praise.

The film's success and the universality of its themes can be attested to by the fact that a Hollywood version, ALGIERS, was made immediately after PEPE LE MOKO and released in the States before the original could be imported. Charles Boyer turned the part of Pepe down when it was offered by Duvivier, then starred in the US version when Gabin refused to make the trip to Hollywood, explaining that he, like French wine, "didn't travel well." WhenWW II started, the French government banned the film as too depressing and demoralizing, especially since the news from the front was also bleak. The Germans took over and their puppet government retained the ban, but the moment the war ended, PEPE LE MOKO was again shown and hailed as a classic.

PEPPERMINT SODA
(DIABOLO MENTHE)

1977 97m c Drama/Comedy ★★★½
Alma/Alexandre/Gaumont (France) PG/

Eleonore Klarwein (Anne Weber), Odile Michel (Frederique Weber), Coralie Clement (Perrine Jacquet), Marie Veronique Maurin (Muriel Gazau), Valerie Stano (Martine Dubreuil), Anne Guillard (Sylvie Le Garrec), Corinne Dacla (Pascal Carimil), Veronique Vernon (Evelyne Delacroix), Francoise Berlin (Mlle. Sassy), Arlette Bonnard (Mme. Poliakoff)

d, Diane Kurys; w, Diane Kurys; ph, Philippe Rousselot; ed, Joele Van Effenterre; m, Yves Simon

A thoroughly charming picture which brings to life the loves and fears of two teenaged sisters. Kurys marks her directing debut with a semi-autobiographical story starring Klarwein as the 13-year old Anne (Kurys's age in 1963—the setting of the film) and Michel as her 15-year old sibling. Living with their divorced mother, Ferjac, the girls discover and talk about the things that interest teenage girls—boys, sex, school, and politics (they are French). Lacking a boyfriend, Klarwein steams open her older sister's love letters from her boyfriend. Klarwein's confused reaction to men is further illustrated by her dislike for her mother's boyfriend. It is only from her father that she gets what she wants (a ski trip), but not until she shows her disapproval at his leaving home.

A sensitive portrayal of teens which compares with Truffaut's Antoine Doinel series (THE 400 BLOWS through LOVE ON THE RUN) and George Roy Hill's A LITTLE ROMANCE. Kurys continued exploring her growing years with ENTRE NOUS and C'EST LA VIE. For the curious, the film's title refers to an "adult" drink that Klarwein nearly gets a chance to taste.

PERFECT WORLD, A

1993 130m c Crime/Drama ★★½
Malpaso Productions (U.S.) PG-13/15

Kevin Costner (Butch Haynes), Clint Eastwood (Red Garnett), Laura Dern (Sally Gerber), T.J. Lowther (Phillip Perry), Keith Szarabajka (Terry Pugh), Leo Burmester (Tom Adler), Paul Hewitt (Dick Scuttle), Bradley Whitford (Bobby Lee), Ray McKinnon (Bradley), Bruce McGill (Paul Saunders)

p, Mark Johnson, David Valdes; d, Clint Eastwood; w, John Lee Hancock; ph, Jack N. Green; ed, Joel Cox, Ron Spang; m, Lennie Niehaus; prod d, Henry Bumstead; art d, Jack G. Taylor Jr.; fx, John Frazier, David Amborn, J.W. McCormick; cos, Erica Edell Phillips

In a perfect world, screenwriters would be forbidden from using cute pre-teens to make up for creaky plots; Clint Eastwood would stop churning out his patented over-the-hill-but-still-tough routine; and there would be an injunction against Kevin Costner doing death scenes, especially ones as long and meandering as a cross-Texas road trip.

A PERFECT WORLD starts out quite well, with Butch Haynes (Costner) and a companion breaking out of a Texas prison and, after a tense confrontation with a terrified family, making off with 7-year-old Phillip Perry (T.J. Lowther) as a hostage. Hot on their heels are an initially promising team that includes Eastwood, as grizzled Texas Ranger Red Garnett, and Laura Dern, as inexperienced but independent criminologist Sally Gerber.

You know things have started to go wrong when Butch, after getting rid of his fellow escapee, starts to shape up as the loving father figure that young Phillip has never had. As Butch and the boy's drive turns into one warm, fuzzy episode after another, the team that is pursuing them comes to a physical, and dramatic, halt. With their high-tech trailer stuck in a field, Garnett and his deputies can do nothing either to pursue Butch, or to develop the character relations set up earlier. Throw in a transformation scene in which Costner turns—with a supreme lack of conviction—into a psycho killer, and you have a movie experience that's a long, long way from perfect.

PERFORMANCE

1970 105m c Drama ★★★
Goodtimes Enterprises (U.K.) R/X

James Fox (Chas Devlin), Mick Jagger (Turner), Anita Pallenberg (Pherber), Michele Breton (Lucy), Ann Sidney (Dana), John Bindon (Moody), Stanley Meadows (Rosebloom), Allan Cuthbertson (The Lawyer), Anthony Morton (Dennis), Johnny Shannon (Harry Flowers)

p, Sanford Lieberson; d, Nicolas Roeg, Donald Cammell; w, Donald Cammell; ph, Nicolas Roeg; ed, Antony Gibbs, Brian Smedley-Aston; art d, John Clark

Visually dazzling, finely acted investigation into such diverse matters as identity, sexuality, violence, power, and underground culture in late 1960s London.

James Fox stars as Chas, a sadistic petty gangster who has trouble fitting in, even with his hoodlum cohorts. Chas gets into trouble with the mob after carrying out a murder for personal—as opposed to business—reasons, and hides out in the basement of "retired" rock star Turner while he waits to skip the country. Turner has secluded himself in the house in order to lament the loss of his powers of "incantation," which seems primarily to mean that he indulges in a lot of drug-taking and sex with two female companions. Soon, Turner senses a connection between Chas's brutally violent nature and his own dried-up creative powers, and he draws the young hood into his world. Introduced to hallucinogenic drugs, Chas begins wearing androgynous clothes and even admits he is sexually attracted by Turner, before the mob shows up again and things turn sour.

Uneven, dated, and—at least during the first half-hour—too frantically paced, PERFORMANCE is nevertheless a haunting meditation on human identity from co-directors Donald Cammel and Nicolas Roeg (Roeg had previously worked as a cinematographer on films including FAHRENHEIT 451 and FAR FROM THE MADDING CROWD). Questions of role-playing, imagery and individuality are explored in uniquely visual terms, particularly by the directors' intriguing use of mirror shots. Mick Jagger's performance is a pleasant surprise, and his presence in the film accounted for most of the limited commercial success it enjoyed at the time of its initial release. PERFORMANCE has since become a much-discussed cult classic. Originally released with an "X" rating in the U.S., the film was subsequently re-edited and re-catalogued as an "R."

PERSONA

1966 81m bw Drama ★★★★★
Svensk (Sweden) /X

Bibi Andersson (Nurse Alma), Liv Ullmann (Actress Elisabeth Vogler), Gunnar Bjornstrand (Mr. Vogler), Margareta Krook (Dr. Lakaren), Jorgen Lindstrom (The Boy)

p, Ingmar Bergman; d, Ingmar Bergman; w, Ingmar Bergman; ph, Sven Nykvist; ed, Ulla Ryghe; m, Lars-Johan Werle; prod d, Bibi Lindstrom; art d, Bibi Lindstrom; fx, Evald Andersson; cos, Mago

This is Ingmar Bergman's chaste exploration of psychosis. It's not a horror story but a poem, and remarkable for that. This is one of the director's masterworks. Opening with a sequence that includes a bare bulb projecting onto a screen, the countdown leader of the first reel, and short film clips from slapstick comedies and cartoons, Bergman reminds us that we are in the act of watching a film. Gradually, however, the story gets underway. Ullmann plays an actress who mysteriously stops speaking after a performance of "Electra" and is sent by a psychiatrist to a seaside cottage where she is looked after by nurse Andersson. Using light and shadow masterfully, Bergman and his cinematographer, Sven Nykvist, accentuate the resemblance between the two women, drawing the viewer into a psychodrama that is more the nurse's story than the patient's, as Andersson pours her soul out to the silent Ullmann. She gradually appears to be just as troubled as her patient, whose personality she seems to be assuming. The shot of their two faces merged near the end of the film is one of the great images of cinema.

PERSONA has variously been interpreted as an exploration of the role of the artist, an embodiment of the psychoanalytic process, and as a meditation on Bergman's favorite existential themes. In any case, it is a film of great emotional intensity that benefits from the superlative performances of Ullmann—who reacts only with facial and body gestures—and Andersson, who speaks for both of them as she slips into a kind of subtle madness.

PERSONAL BEST

1982 124m c Sports ★★★
Geffen (U.S.) R/18

Mariel Hemingway (Chris Cahill), Scott Glenn (Terry Tingloff), Patrice Donnelly (Tory Skinner), Kenny Moore (Denny Stites), Jim Moody (Roscoe Travis), Kari Gossviller (Penny Brill), Jodi Anderson (Nadia "Pooch" Anderson), Maren Seidler (Tanya), Martha Watson (Sheila), Emily Dole (Maureen)

p, Robert Towne; d, Robert Towne; w, Robert Towne; ph, Michael Chapman, Allan Gornick Jr.; ed, Ned Humphreys, Jere Huggins, Jacqueline Cambas, Walt Mulconery, Bud Smith; m, Jack Nitzsche, Jill Fraser; prod d, Ron Hobbs; fx, Dale Newkirk; cos, Linda Henrikson, Ron Heilman

Oscar-winning screenwriter Robert Towne (CHINATOWN; SHAMPOO) made his directorial debut with this uneven but affecting study of romantic and athletic commitment set against the background of women's track and field. At the 1976 Olympic trials, pentathlete Tory Skinner (onetime track star Patrice Donnelly in her film debut) and hurdler Chris Cahill (Mariel Hemingway) meet after the former qualifies for the US team, while the latter runs badly. The two become lovers, and Tory persuades her reluctant coach, Terry Tingloff (Scott Glenn), to allow Chris to train with her under his guidance. Eventually, Tingloff convinces Chris to train for the pentathlon, creating a rivalry between Chris and Tory that leads to the breakup of their relationship. Later, Chris falls for Denny (Kenny Moore), a onetime Olympic medalist in swimming; then, against Tingloff's wishes, Chris renews her friendship with Tory during the 1980 Olympic trials.

Although Towne's script is a little talky and heavy-handed, he nonetheless captures the essence of the competitive impulse, exploring both the "killer instinct" and the inner drive to compete only with oneself. The lesbian love story at the film's center is less well developed, but still engaging, its poignancy heightened by the well-cast Hemingway's understated performance. Visually, PERSONAL BEST is frequently interesting, if occasionally studied. Towne's over-reliance on slow motion ultimately undercuts the poetry of motion he seeks to convey, but his camera placement during the track and field action is almost always inventive, as is the film's editing. Moreover, PERSONAL BEST offers a detailed, believable insider's portrait of the world of track and field. This very different sports film isn't for everyone, but patient viewers should find many small pleasures in it. Olympic marathoner Frank Shorter and veteran sportscaster Charlie Jones provide the commentary during the Olympic trials.

PETER PAN

1953 76m c Animated/Children's ★★★★
Walt Disney Productions (U.S.) G/U

VOICES OF: Bobby Driscoll (Peter Pan), Kathryn Beaumont (Wendy), Hans Conried (Capt. Hook/Mr. Darling), Bill Thompson (Mr. Smee), Heather Angel (Mrs. Darling), Paul Collins (Michael Darling), Tommy Luske (John), Candy Candido (Indian Chief), Tom Conway (Narrator)

p, Walt Disney; d, Hamilton Luske, Clyde Geronimi, Wilfred Jackson; w, Ted Sears, Bill Peet, Joe Rinaldi, Erdman Penner, Winston Hibler, Milt Banta, Ralph Wright (based on the play by James M. Barrie); m, Oliver Wallace, Edward Plumb; anim, Milt Kahl, Franklin Thomas, Wolfgang Reitherman, Ward Kimball, Eric Larson, Oliver M. Johnston, Marc Davis, John Lounsbery, Les Clark, Norman Ferguson

PETER PAN is a wonderful movie. Patriarch Mr. Darling (whose voice is provided by Hans Conried) is annoyed that daughter Wendy (voiced by Kathryn Beaumont) insists on telling stories to the other children about a mythical boy known as Peter Pan. When Mr. and Mrs. Darling leave for a night on the town, Peter Pan (voiced by Bobby Driscoll) and fairy sidekick Tinker Bell magically appear in Wendy's room. They all take a magical trip to Never Never Land, where they get involved in a series of adventures that include a confrontation with the evil Captain Hook (Conried, in a dual role). Lots of laughs, fabulous animation, and excellent voicing by the actors. The picture cost more than $4 million to make, a huge amount for a film in 1953. Lest you wonder why it came in so high, you should know that Disney filmed a live-action version of the movie first in order to give his artists something to base their sketches upon.

PETRIFIED FOREST, THE

1936 83m bw Crime ★★★★
Warner Bros. (U.S.) /A

Leslie Howard (*Alan Squier*), Bette Davis (*Gabrielle Maple*), Genevieve Tobin (*Mrs. Chisholm*), Dick Foran (*Boze Hertzlinger*), Humphrey Bogart (*Duke Mantee*), Joe Sawyer (*Jackie*), Porter Hall (*Jason Maple*), Charley Grapewin (*Gramp Maple*), Paul Harvey (*Mr. Chisholm*), Eddie Acuff (*Lineman*)

p, Henry Blanke; d, Archie Mayo; w, Charles Kenyon, Delmer Daves (based on the play by Robert E. Sherwood); ph, Sol Polito; ed, Owen Marks; m, Bernhard Kaun; art d, John Hughes; fx, Warren Lynch, Fred Jackman, Willard Van Enger; cos, Orry-Kelly

One of the variants on the GRAND HOTEL theme halfway between the pleasant comings and goings at that hostelry and the screaming disasters of, say, THE POSEIDON ADVENTURE. This screen version of Robert E. Sherwood's smash play is handled with great care by director Archie Mayo and a sterling cast. This was the film that catapulted Humphrey Bogart to fame, but without Leslie Howard's insistence on Bogart for the part of Duke Mantee, Bogart might never have gotten his big movie break.

This film is really about the confrontation between intellectualism and brute force. Howard, an idealistic writer and world traveler who has grown weary of life's cruelties, finds himself penniless and hitch-hiking through the Arizona desert. As he passes the renowned Petrified Forest, it occurs to him that he is like it, an ossified relic of the past. Stopping at a dilapidated service station restaurant run by grumpy Porter Hall, Howard meets and falls in love with poet Bette Davis, Hall's daughter. She dreams of studying in Paris. Dick Foran, a college halfback who pumps gas for Hall, is in love with Davis, and therefore jealous of Howard; but Howard assures him that he has little to worry about. When a rich couple, Paul Harvey and Genevieve Tobin, arrive at the station, Davis persuades them to take Howard along with them to California. After Howard departs, Hall, Davis, Foran, and Charley Grapewin, Hall's ancient father, hear on the radio that the ruthless gangster Duke Mantee and his henchmen, on the run after committing murders in Oklahoma, are headed into Arizona. On the road, Mantee (Bogart) and his gang are stalled by a broken down car. When Harvey's car comes along, they order the occupants out and drive off with the rich man's auto. Bogart then storms into Hall's service station cafe and holds everyone prisoner, waiting to join up with another carload of henchmen and his gun moll. When Howard, Harvey, Tobin, and their chauffeur, John Alexander, return to the cafe, Bogart holds them hostage as well. Howard challenges Bogart with words Bogart doesn't understand, calling the gangster "the last great apostle of rugged individualism." Howard makes a quiet pact with Bogart, requesting that Bogart shoot him before leaving.

Howard was born for the role of the fatalistic lover and lapsed idealist of THE PETRIFIED FOREST. He had played it to the hilt on Broadway, as did Bogart with the Mantee role in the 1935 stage play. But when it came to casting the film, Jack Warner wanted no part of Bogart, who had appeared in small roles in B films some years earlier. He selected Edward G. Robinson to play Duke Mantee. When Howard heard this, he went to Warner, telling him that if Bogart did not get the role of gangster, he (Howard) would drop out of the picture. Warner needed Howard, so he cast Bogart, who went on to become one of the studio's greatest stars. Bogart's gangster was clearly based on Public Enemy No. 1, John Dillinger (as was Sherwood's original character). Coincidentally, Bogart closely resembled Dillinger, and after studying films of the gangster to perfect his mannerisms, he was a sensation. Yet the Duke Mantee role was also a curse, typecasting Bogart for years to come in the ruthless gangster mold, until 1941 when he appeared as a sympathetic gangster in HIGH SIERRA and, in the same year, as Sam Spade in THE MALTESE FALCON. Davis, too, is outstanding as the culture-hungry girl who yearns to escape the desert and the ominous Petrified Forest. This success of this film would soon land her meatier

roles. The film was remade as ESCAPE IN THE DESERT. In 1955, Bogart, Lauren Bacall, and Henry Fonda would reenact the original play in an excellent television production.

PETULIA

1968 105m c Drama/Comedy ★★★½
Petersham (U.S./U.K.) R/X

Julie Christie (*Petulia Danner*), George C. Scott (*Archie Bollen*), Richard Chamberlain (*David Danner*), Arthur Hill (*Barney*), Shirley Knight (*Polo*), Pippa Scott (*May*), Kathleen Widdoes (*Wilma*), Roger Bowen (*Warren*), Richard Dysart (*Motel Receptionist*), Ruth Kobart

p, Raymond Wagner; d, Richard Lester; w, Larry Marcus, Barbara Turner (based on the novel *Me and the Arch Kook Petulia* by John Haase); ph, Nicolas Roeg; ed, Anthony Gibbs; m, John Barry; prod d, Tony Walton; art d, Dean Tavoularis; cos, Tony Walton, Arlette Nastat

PETULIA was a transitional work for director Richard Lester, a cross between the jump-cutting gimmickry of his earlier films (A HARD DAY'S NIGHT, THE KNACK) and the more conventional storytelling of JUGGERNAUT and ROBIN AND MARIAN. Extravagantly praised by some critics and dismissed by others, it is nevertheless one of the best American films of the sixties (if largely by default). Archie Bollen (George C. Scott) meets Petulia Danner (Julie Christie) at a San Francisco charity function with countercultural pretensions (The Grateful Dead and Big Brother and the Holding Company provide the entertainment). Bollen doesn't know that Petulia recognizes him as the surgeon who operated on a young mexican boy whom she and her husband David (Richard Chamberlain) had befriended on a recent trip to Tijuana. David is an abusive husband who may have caused the boy's injuries. Through flashbacks, which come at a rate of maybe one every ten minutes, we see a large portion of the Tijuana trip, and the subsequent surgery in all its gory detail. Bollen, meanwhile, has his own problems. Divorced, his ex-wife has married a man he despises, and he spends most of his free time either on absurd "divorced Dad" excursions with his two sons (their trip to Alcatraz is a highlight), or trying to figure out exactly what Petulia means to him. PETULIA is both a finely observed comedy of manners set in the San Francisco of the late sixties, and an absorbing drama about abuse and betrayal. Nicholas Roeg did the cinematography.

PEYTON PLACE

1957 162m c Drama ★★
Fox (U.S.) /15

Lana Turner (*Constance MacKenzie*), Hope Lange (*Selena Cross*), Lee Philips (*Michael Rossi*), Lloyd Nolan (*Dr. Matthew Swain*), Diane Varsi (*Allison MacKenzie*), Arthur Kennedy (*Lucas Cross*), Russ Tamblyn (*Norman Page*), Terry Moore (*Betty Anderson*), Barry Coe (*Rodney Harrington*), David Nelson (*Ted Carter*)

p, Jerry Wald; d, Mark Robson; w, John Michael Hayes (based on the novel by Grace Metalious); ph, William Mellor; ed, David Bretherton; m, Franz Waxman; art d, Lyle Wheeler, Jack Martin Smith; fx, L.B. Abbott; cos, Adele Palmer, Charles Le Maire

AAN Best Picture; AAN Best Actress: Lana Turner; *AAN Best Supporting Actor:* Arthur Kennedy; *AAN Best Supporting Actor:* Russ Tamblyn; *AAN Best Supporting Actress:* Hope Lange; *AAN Best Supporting Actress:* Diane Varsi; *AAN Best Director:* Mark Robson; *AAN Best Adapted Screenplay:* John Michael Hayes; *AAN Best Cinematography:* William Mellor

Tawdry potboiler based on one of the best-selling novels of all time. Not to be confused with the suggestive, subversive melodramas of Sirk and Minnelli, this is the kind of hypertensive trash that gives melodrama a bad name, cynically tempering its naughty bits with smug moralizing. The fact that the film won an "A" rating from the Catholic Legion of Decency, meaning it was deemed "acceptable to all," is a dead giveaway.

Into the small New England community of Peyton Place comes a new school principal (Philips), a hotshot Ph.D with "advanced" educational ideas. In no time at all, he meets Turner, a widow with a teenage daughter, Varsi. He's surprised when Turner spurns his amorous advances and he retaliates by sniping at her for the way she treats Varsi when the teen's birthday party turns into a petting fest. Wealthy Coe marries Moore, a sensuous young woman, despite his father's annoyance. Meanwhile, Varsi is having a sincere friendship with Tamblyn, whose mother, Erin O'Brien-Moore, is a domineering woman who resents his friendship with anyone. At the same time, Lange, the stepdaughter of the school's drunken caretaker, Kennedy, is raped by Kennedy, and she later kills him (accidentally, of course). The war begins, and the town's respectable veneer falls to pieces.

PHANTOM LADY

1944 87m bw Mystery
Universal (U.S.)

★★★★
/A

Franchot Tone *(Jack Marlow)*, Ella Raines *(Carol "Kansas" Richman)*, Alan Curtis *(Scott Henderson)*, Aurora Miranda *(Estela Monteiro)*, Thomas Gomez *(Inspector Burgess)*, Fay Helm *(Ann Terry)*, Elisha Cook Jr. *(Cliff March)*, Andrew Tombes *(Bartender)*, Regis Toomey, Joseph Crehan *(Detectives)*

p, Joan Harrison; d, Robert Siodmak; w, Bernard C. Schoenfeld (based on the novel by Cornell Woolrich); ph, Elwood Bredell; ed, Arthur Hilton; m, H.J. Salter; art d, John B. Goodman, Robert Clatworthy; cos, Vera West, Kenneth Hopkins

A superb thriller, and the first American film by German director Siodmak to enjoy any significant success. Alan Curtis plays an innocent man accused of murdering his wife, with Ella Raines, as his secretary, and Thomas Gomez, as an off-duty copy, engaging in a search for the man's female alibi, a mysterious woman (Fay Helm) whose existence is denied by every witness. Adapted from a novel by Cornell Woolrich, with suitably Expressionistic camera angles and moody lighting.

PHANTOM OF LIBERTY, THE
(LE FANTOME DE LA LIBERTE)

1974 104m c Drama
Greenwich (France)

★★★★
R/X

Jean-Claude Brialy *(Mr. Foucauld)*, Monica Vitti *(Mrs. Foucauld)*, Milena Vukotic *(Nurse)*, Michel Lonsdale *(Hatter)*, Michel Piccoli *(2nd Prefect)*, Claude Pieplu *(Commissioner)*, Paul Frankeur *(Innkeeper)*, Julien Bertheau *(1st Prefect)*, Adriana Asti *(Prefect's Sister)*, Adolfo Celi *(Dr. Legendre)*

p, Serge Silberman; d, Luis Bunuel; w, Luis Bunuel, Jean-Claude Carriere; ph, Edmond Richard; ed, Helene Plemiannikov

An uproarious summary of Luis Bunuel's surrealistic concerns in a collection of anecdotes starring Jean-Claude Brialy, Michel Piccoli, and Monica Vitti. THE PHANTOM OF LIBERTY jumps from place to place and time to time in a manner that follows the (il)logic of dreams. The film opens in the Napoleonic era with Spanish patriots urging on the firing squad that's about to execute them with shouts of things like "Down with Liberty!" and "Up with Chains!" Following this is a scene of a maid reading to a child the story we have just witnessed. Again the scene changes to show a man selling supposedly pornographic postcards that are actually shots of entirely non-pornographic French tourist attractions. A nurse then makes the mistake of wandering into a poker game played by a group of monks. A man with a rifle kills passers-by from the top of a Montparnasse building and is hailed as a hero. A missing girl helps the police fill out a report on her disappearance. And, in perhaps the most memorable sequence, a group of elegantly dressed dinner guests sit on toilet seats as they converse around a dining room table. They sheepishly request to be excused when hunger strikes and then creep off to a room containing a private little stall where they may dine.

This is a crazy, subversively funny film about convention-bound characters who have a hard time dealing with sexuality and freedom. It's heartening to see that Bunuel could still ruffle as many feathers at age 75 as he did in 1928 and 1930 with UN CHIEN ANDALOU and L'AGE D'OR.

PHANTOM OF THE OPERA

1943 92m c Horror
Universal (U.S.)

★★★
/A

Nelson Eddy *(Anatole Garron)*, Susanna Foster *(Christine DuBois)*, Claude Rains *(Enrique Claudin)*, Edgar Barrier *(Inspector Raoul de Chagny)*, Leo Carrillo *(Signor Feretti)*, Jane Farrar *(Biancarolli)*, J. Edward Bromberg *(Amiot)*, Fritz Feld *(Lecours)*, Frank Puglia *(Villeneuve)*, Steven Geray *(Vercheres)*

p, George Waggner; d, Arthur Lubin; w, Eric Taylor, Hans Jacoby, Samuel Hoffenstein (based on the novel *Le Fantome de l'Opera* by Gaston Leroux); ph, Hal Mohr, W. Howard Greene; ed, Russell Schoengarth; m, Edward Ward, George Waggner; art d, John B. Goodman, Alexander Golitzen; cos, Vera West

AA Best Cinematography: Hal Mohr, W. Howard Greene; *AAN Best Score:* Edward Ward; *AA Best Art Direction:* Alexander Golitzen, John B. Goodman, Russell A. Gausman, Ira S. Webb; *AAN Best Sound:* Bernard B. Brown

Universal Studios' elaborate and expensive remake of their classic 1925 silent horror film THE PHANTOM OF THE OPERA boasts fabulous sets, gorgeous costumes, and stunning Technicolor photography—but fails in the horror department, because of an excess of music and low comedy. Draining much of the fear, suspense, and mystery out of the original Gaston Leroux material, this remake posits Enrique Claudin (Claude Rains)—the future "Phantom"—as a somewhat frail, middle-aged violinist with the Paris Opera who is in love from afar with Christine DuBois (Susanna Foster), a pretty and talented singer in the chorus. Although Christine doesn't even know the violinist exists, Enrique devotes his entire life to her, sacrificing his musical future just to make her happy. Universal spent $1.5 million on PHANTOM OF THE OPERA and every dollar is on the screen. While the opera house set is the same one used in the original, many additional sets were constructed and dressed up with elaborate and expensive wares. Rains, who had just finished playing what would later become his best-remembered role—that of Capt. Louis Renault in CASABLANCA—managed to bring a sense of pathos and menace to the Phantom. The sparse and briefly seen makeup of the disfigured violinist is merely serviceable; wisely, no attempt was made to duplicate or surpass Lon Chaney's amazing visage in the original. While this version can be quite entertaining at times, it is frustrating that the horror elements are used merely as a plot device to propel the story along to the next elaborate opera scene—a structure that pleased neither horror fans nor opera buffs. PHANTOM OF THE OPERA won Oscars for Best Color Cinematography and Best Color Interior Decoration (John B. Goodman, Alexander Golitzen, R.A. Gausman, Ira S. Webb), receiving nominations for Best Sound Recording and Best Musical Score.

PHANTOM OF THE OPERA, THE

1962 84m c Horror
Hammer (U.K.)

★★★
/A

Herbert Lom *(The Phantom)*, Heather Sears *(Christine Charles)*, Thorley Walters *(Lattimer)*, Edward De Souza *(Harry Hunter)*, Michael Gough *(Lord Ambrose D'Arcy)*, Martin Miller *(Rossi)*, Miles Malleson *(Philosophical Cabby)*, Miriam Karlin *(Charwoman)*, John Harvey *(Vickers)*, Harold Goodwin *(Bill)*

p, Anthony Hinds; d, Terence Fisher; w, Anthony Hinds (based on a story by Gaston Leroux); ph, Arthur Grant; ed, Alfred Cox; m, Edwin Astley; prod d, Bernard Robinson; art d, Don Mingaye

Following successful reinterpretations of such horror film icons as Frankenstein, Dracula, the Mummy, and the Wolfman, Hammer Studios turned its attention to the classic tale of THE PHANTOM OF THE OPERA. Fully aware that its small-budget efforts would be closely compared with the two previous big-budget American versions (in 1925 starring Lon Chaney, Sr., and again in 1943 starring Claude Rains), Hammer bravely forged ahead and managed to produce a film that, while no classic, stands as a well-crafted thriller with some chilling, memorable moments. Shifting the action from Paris to London, the film tells the familiar story of a grotesquely disfigured composer who haunts an opera house and falls hopelessly in love with a beautiful singer.

Hammer's THE PHANTOM OF THE OPERA was originally to have starred the studio's favorite Dracula, Christopher Lee, but a last-minute switch was made in favor of Lom. While he could not hope to equal Chaney's classic tour-de-force or even Rains's memorable portrayal, Lom succeeded admirably in creating an alternately malevolent, sympathetic, and even tragic character. Hammer had hired professional maskmakers to create the phantom's mask, but they failed to come up with a suitable design. Director Fisher tried to shoot around Lom's masked scenes while awaiting the result of the maskmaker's work, but he finally grew impatient and had Hammer's makeup man, Roy Ashton, construct a crude mask out of cloth, tape, and gauze. The effect is perfect because the mask looks like something the Phantom would have made for himself while combing the dank sewers beneath the opera house. Despite the film's low budget, the production has the usual Hammer eye for detail and looks as if it had an expensive treatment. Gough turns in his usual fine performance as the evil opera benefactor, while Sears (whose singing was dubbed by opera singer Pat Clark) and De Souza are serviceable as the standard heroine and hero.

PHANTOM TOLLBOOTH, THE

1970 90m c Animated/Children's/Fantasy ★★★½
MGM (U.S.) G/U

Butch Patrick (Milo), VOICES OF: Mel Blanc, Daws Butler, Candy Candido, Hans Conried, June Foray, Patti Gilbert, Shepard Menken, Cliff Norton, Larry Thor

p, Chuck Jones, Abe Levitow, Les Goldman; d, Chuck Jones, Abe Levitow, David Monahan; w, Chuck Jones, Sam Rosen (based on the book by Norton Juster); ph, Lester Shorr; ed, Jim Faris; m, Dean Elliott; prod d, Maurice Noble; art d, George W. Davis, Charles K. Hagedon; anim, Irv Spence, Bill Littlejohn, Richard Thompson, Tom Ray, Philip Roman, Alan Zaslove, Edwin Aardal, Ed DeMattia, Xenia, Lloyd Vaughan, Carl Bell

This fine adaptation of the children's book by Norton Juster was Chuck Jones's and MGM's first animated feature. Butch Patrick stars (in the live-action sequences) as Milo, a bored youngster who cannot maintain an interest in anything. One day the "phantom tollbooth" appears in his bedroom and Milo drives his toy car into it. He is then transported through the magic of animation into a strange and wonderful world broken up into two camps, letters and numbers. Unfortunately, letters and numbers are at war with each other (each thinking they are more important to society), and Milo soon finds himself caught in the middle. Aided by a dog called Tock, Milo strives mightily to restore the land to peace, in a charming film that combines some fairly sophisticated ideas (demons from the "Mountains of Ignorance" cause much of the trouble, and Milo tries to restore "Rhyme and Reason" to the land) with cute and likable characters that are sure to grab a child's attention.

PHILADELPHIA

1993 119m c Drama ★★★
TriStar (U.S.) PG-13/12

Tom Hanks (Andrew Beckett), Denzel Washington (Joe Miller), Antonio Banderas (Miguel Alvarez), Ron Vawter (Bob Seidman), Joanne Woodward (Sarah Beckett), Jason Robards (Charles Wheeler), Robert Ridgely (Walter Kenton), Paul Lazar (Dr Klenstein), Bradley Whitford (Jamey Collins), Tracey Walter (Librarian)

p, Edward Saxon, Jonathan Demme; d, Jonathan Demme; w, Ron Nyswaner; ph, Tak Fujimoto; ed, Craig McKay; m, Howard Shore; prod d, Kristi Zea; art d, Tim Galvin; cos, Colleen Atwood

AA Best Actor: Tom Hanks; AA Best Original Song: Bruce Springsteen; AAN Best Original Song: Neil Young; AAN Best Original Screenplay: Ron Nyswaner; AAN Best Makeup: Alan D'Angerio, Carl Fullerton

The first mainstream Hollywood film to deal with the subject of AIDS, and one of the few to feature gay characters in a serious dramatic context, PHILADELPHIA is highly competent and equally—if surprisingly—conventional.

Handsome, self-assured young corporate lawyer Andrew Beckett (Tom Hanks) is fired by his white-shoe Philadelphia firm when his sleek, self-satisfied employers—including Charles Wheeler (Jason Robards) and Bob Seidman (Ron Vawter)—discover that he's HIV posi-

tive. With the support of his family—especially his mother, Sarah (Joanne Woodward)—and his lover, Miguel (Antonio Banderas), Beckett sues. But the only lawyer who will take his case is local ambulance chaser Joe Miller (Denzel Washington), who's not sure he wants to be associated with a high profile case about homosexual prejudice.

PHILADELPHIA fails to create complex characters or finely nuanced drama, but it succeeds in its real goal; the education of an audience whose thinking about AIDS and gay life has been shaped by notions of perversion and divine retribution. Screenwriter Ron Nyswaner and director Jonathan Demme assemble a drama filled with familiar elements: the importance of family (and, especially, a mother's love for her children); the decent little man pitted against a smugly uncaring system; the mismatched legal team of affluent white suburbanite Beckett and struggling, black, city-bred Miller. Strong performances from Hanks and Washington are among the film's greatest assets. Doomsayers foretold that the movie would fail to find a mainstream audience and that this would insure the subject's relegation, once again, to the independent arena, but the dire predictions proved false.

PHILADELPHIA STORY, THE

1940 112m bw Comedy ★★★★
MGM (U.S.) /PG

Cary Grant (C.K. Dexter Haven), Katharine Hepburn (Tracy Lord), James Stewart (Macauley Connor), Ruth Hussey (Elizabeth Imbrie), John Howard (George Kittredge), Roland Young (Uncle Willie), John Halliday (Seth Lord), Mary Nash (Margaret Lord), Virginia Weidler (Dinah Lord), Henry Daniell (Sidney Kidd)

p, Joseph L. Mankiewicz; d, George Cukor; w, Donald Ogden Stewart, Waldo Salt (based on the play by Philip Barry, uncredited); ph, Joseph Ruttenberg; ed, Frank Sullivan; m, Franz Waxman; art d, Cedric Gibbons, Wade B. Rubottom; cos, Adrian

AAN Best Picture; AA Best Actor: James Stewart; AAN Best Actress: Katharine Hepburn; AAN Best Supporting Actress: Ruth Hussey; AAN Best Director: George Cukor; AA Best Screenplay: Donald Ogden Stewart

George Cukor directed this classic comedy talkfest that offers special pleasures for fans of Katharine Hepburn, James Stewart, and Cary Grant. Tracy Lord (Hepburn), the daughter of a super-wealthy family living in a ritzy suburb of Philadelphia, is slated to marry George Kittredge (Howard), a stuffed-shirt coal company executive. Previously she had been married to C.K. Dexter Haven (Grant) in a stormy short-lived relationship that ended largely because Tracy couldn't deal with Dexter's drinking and irresponsible ways. As her wedding nears, Dexter shows up at the estate, ostensibly to attend the nuptials, but really to protect the reputation of his ex-in-laws. Dexter has learned that publisher Sidney Kidd (Daniell) plans to run an expose about Tracy's stagedoor Johnny father (Halliday), revealing in Spy magazine details of his chronic womanizing. To mollify the publisher, Dexter, who works for Kidd, arranges for the magazine's chief scandal reporter, Mike Conner (Stewart), and photographer Liz Imbrie (Hussey) to report on the wedding for the magazine. Mike has a healthy skepticism about the ways of the rich until he gets smitten by Tracy, who grows more unsure of her desires as her wedding nears. Indeed most of the major characters must decide whom they really love before the film is over. Of course, all must end happily even if unexpectedly.

With such a stellar cast, a fine director working in the type of picture he did best, and some genuinely witty dialogue, this film has all the ingredients for a great comedy. And it is great, though there have been many funnier comedies. The film has an unfortunate tendency to take itself too seriously for long stretches. Mike's shameless adoration of Tracy and the cloying speeches he's forced to deliver in her praise try our credulity and patience. A very strong case is being made here for the sheer irresistibility of the film's female star. The film also strenuously drives home the point that people born poor aren't necessarily noble while men born rich aren't necessarily cads. No need to stop the presses for this little news bulletin!

This was a project especially dear to Hepburn. Two years prior to the release of THE PHILADELPHIA STORY, Hepburn had been branded "box-office poison" by a leading exhibitor, thus prompting her to look for a Broadway show suitable for her talents. Playwright Barry wrote the role of Tracy expressly for Hepburn, who covered 25 percent of the play's cost and took no salary, shrewdly opting to take 45 percent of the considerable profits. Joseph Cotten played the Cary Grant role while Van Heflin originated Stewart's part. The cagy actress also purchased the film adaptation rights and eventually succeeded in getting Louis B. Mayer not only to pay her $250,000 for them but also won the right to select her own director, screenwriter, and costars. Grant accepted his role only on the proviso that he receive top billing, which he did. He then demanded a then-whopping salary of $137,000 and got it. (Grant later donated his entire salary from the film to the British War Relief Fun.)

The film became a box-office smash. It broke all records at Radio City Music Hall with a return of almost $600,000 in six weeks. Hepburn, who won the coveted New York Film Critics Award, lost the Oscar to Ginger Rogers for her role in KITTY FOYLE. The film was poorly remade as a musical, HIGH SOCIETY, in 1956, starring Bing Crosby, Frank Sinatra, and Grace Kelly.

PIANO, THE

1993 120m c Drama/Historical ★★★★
Jan Chapman Productions/CiBy 2000 (New Zealand) R/15

Holly Hunter *(Ada McGrath)*, Sam Neill *(Stewart)*, Harvey Keitel *(George Baines)*, Anna Paquin *(Fiona McGrath)*, Kerry Walker *(Aunt Morag)*, Genevieve Lemon *(Nessie)*, Tungia Baker *(Hira)*, Ian Mune *(Reverend)*, Peter Dennett *(Head Seaman)*

p, Jan Chapman; d, Jane Campion; w, Jane Campion; ph, Stuart Dryburgh; ed, Veronika Jenet; m, Michael Nyman; prod d, Andrew McAlpine; cos, Janet Patterson

AA Best Actress: Holly Hunter; *AA Best Supporting Actress:* Anna Paquin; *AA Best Original Screenplay:* Jane Campion; *AAN Best Picture*Jan Chapman; *AAN Best Director:* Jane Campion; *AAN Best Cinematography:* Stuart Dryburgh; *AAN Best Costume Design:* Janet Patterson; *AAN Best Editing:* Veronika Jenet

A period love story with strange metaphysical inclinations, Jane Campion's THE PIANO garnered lavish—though not unanimous—critical acclaim and a raft of awards. This is a film of mysterious beauty and subtle passion, set in a past so alien it might as well be another galaxy and peopled with characters so odd it's hard to believe they're not real.

Ada (Holly Hunter), a 19th-century Scottish woman of formidable and eccentric intelligence who hasn't spoken since childhood, is sent with her gravely beautiful daughter Flora (Anna Paquin)—conceived out of wedlock and her mother's intermediary with the speaking world—to the wilds of New Zealand to marry Stewart (Sam Neill), a farmer whose spirit has been deformed by hardship and displaced decorum. Though speechless, Ada is a gifted pianist who plays with an intensity that simultaneously enthralls and frightens the average listener. Stewart refuses to have her piano hauled to his isolated farm, but Baines (Harvey Keitel), an uneducated Englishman gone native, buys the instrument and arranges for Ada to give him piano lessons in his hut. Their increasingly erotic liaison eventually transforms the lives of all concerned.

Though without explicit sex scenes, THE PIANO is intensely sensual—when Ada massages Stewart's bare flesh or plays for the naked Baines, the sexual charge is almost palpable—and Campion's eye is extraordinary. She searches out the detail that makes the image, and the image that tells the story more eloquently than words ever could. Her film is a compelling examination of the wondrously strange ways in which people treat one another, the poetically eccentric accommodations they make to life's incomprehensible cruelty and flashes of brilliant wonder.

PICKPOCKET

1959 75m bw Crime ★★★★
Lux (France) /A

Martin Lassalle *(Michel)*, Marika Green *(Jeanne)*, Pierre Leymarie *(Jacques)*, Pierre Pelegri *(Police Inspector)*, Kassagi *(Master Pickpocket)*, Pierre Etaix *(Accomplice)*, Dolly Scal *(Michel's Mother)*, Cesar Gattegno *(Detective)*

p, Agnes Delahaie; d, Robert Bresson; w, Robert Bresson (based on the novel *Crime and Punishment* by Feodor Dostoyevsky); ph, L.H. Burel; ed, Raymond Lamy; m, Jean-Baptiste Lully; art d, Pierre Charbonnier

Using Dostoyevsky's *Crime and Punishment* as a point of departure, director Bresson has created a wonderful study of a criminal on the road to redemption in PICKPOCKET (released in Paris in 1959). Lassalle stars as a lonely young man who resigns himself to the fate of becoming a pickpocket. An initial attempt is unsuccessful, and he is easily caught. It is during his arrest that Lassalle's consciousness is raised on the rights and wrongs of theft. When his sickly mother dies, Green and Leymarie, his two closest friends, offer advice and solace. Lassalle, however, chooses to return to crime, taking lessons from master pickpocket Kassagi. The police inspector observes Lassalle's criminal life but fails to arrest him, partly because of flimsy evidence and partly because he is intrigued with Lassalle's ideas. When Lassalle's partners in crime are arrested, the pickpocket flees France, leaving behind Green, who has by now fallen in love with him. When he returns years later he finds Green unmarried and with a child. Again he resorts to stealing and again he is caught. Green visits him in his cell, and for the first time he realizes that he loves her. In the memorable final moments, Green and Lassalle embrace through the bars of the cell as he tells her, "What a strange way I have traveled to find you at last." As Bresson has so often done in his films, PICKPOCKET details a man's struggle between his inner feelings and his attempt to survive in society. What separates PICKPOCKET from so many other films is Bresson's use of Lassalle's inner voice (which corresponds to the written words in his diary) as a narrative element. Those familiar with the work of screenwriter-director Paul Schrader will note a few similarities in style and thought, which comes as no surprise since Schrader wrote a book entitled *Transcendental Style on Film: Ozu, Bresson, and Dreyer*. Elements of TAXI DRIVER's narrative (voiceover and diary passages corresponding) are lifted from PICKPOCKET, as in the final line of AMERICAN GIGOLO. While Schrader's transcendental style has failed to achieve the status of Bresson or Ozu or Dreyer (TAXI DRIVER, his finest achievement, comes closest), he has, at least, brought an interesting philosophical element into American film.

PICKUP ON SOUTH STREET

1953 80m bw Crime/Spy ★★★★
Fox (U.S.) /A

Richard Widmark *(Skip McCoy)*, Jean Peters *(Candy)*, Thelma Ritter *(Moe)*, Murvyn Vye *(Capt. Dan Tiger)*, Richard Kiley *(Joey)*, Willis Bouchey *(Zara)*, Milburn Stone *(Winoki)*, Henry Slate *(MacGregor)*, Jerry O'Sullivan *(Enyart)*, Harry Carter *(Dietrich)*

p, Jules Schermer; d, Samuel Fuller; w, Samuel Fuller (based on the story "Blaze of Glory" by Dwight Taylor); ph, Joseph MacDonald; ed, Nick De Maggio; m, Leigh Harline; art d, Lyle Wheeler, George Patrick; fx, Ray Kellogg; cos, Travilla

AAN Best Supporting Actress: Thelma Ritter

A brutal melodrama set against a backdrop of New York's seedy underworld, PICKUP ON SOUTH STREET delves into the shadowy world of federal agents and communist spies. Widmark is a petty crook, a three-time loser whose actions are motivated solely by greed. When he steals a wallet from the purse of Peters, he finds himself in deeper trouble than he ever imagined. Inside the wallet is top-secret microfilm that Peters is unwittingly transporting for her lover, Kiley, a communist spy she believes to be a patent lawyer. When Kiley discovers that the microfilm has been stolen, he demands that Peters find Widmark and get the film back. Also on Widmark's track are two federal agents who have been shadowing Peters. Both the agents and Peters get information on Widmark's whereabouts from Ritter, an aging ex-pickpocket who supplements her scant income from tie peddling by selling information on underworld criminals. Peters tries to use sex to get the microfilm from Widmark but fails. The agents appeal to Widmark's sense of patriotism, but this, too, fails since Widmark doesn't care about the effect of communism on the American way of life. With all the interest that has been shown in the microfilm, Widmark knows that it is worth a great deal of money, so he holds out for an offer from Kiley. By now Peters has fallen for Widmark, and has turned against Kiley, whom she sees as un-American. Kiley attempts to buy Widmark's address from

Ritter, but she proudly refuses to sell to a communist—at any price. Enraged, Kiley kills Ritter. Widmark now has a reason to keep the microfilm out of Kiley's hands—not because Kiley is a communist but because the spy killed a friend of Widmark's. Kiley then returns to Peters (who by now has obtained the film) and mercilessly beats her when he learns of her part in the scheme. After discovering that some of the microfilm is missing and obtaining Widmark's waterfront address, Kiley pays the thief a visit. Widmark eludes Kiley and follows him to a subway station, where Widmark manages to steal back the microfilm. In retaliation for the death of Ritter and the attack on Peters, Widmark pounds Kiley into the pavement and turns him over to the federal agents. Only after Kiley is killed is it revealed that his contact is none other than the federal agent who has been heading up the search for the spy. Having assisted the feds, Widmark is left to finish his romance with Peters and to return to his gutter life.

This provocative film from Sam Fuller is based on "Blaze of Glory," a straightforward story about drug pushers written by Dwight Taylor. Although this original story line was retained in the dubbed version of the film released in France under the title LA PORTE DE LA DROGUE, Fuller decided to politicize the American version of the film. Unfortunately, PICKUP ON SOUTH STREET has been viewed by some as rabidly anticommunist, an assessment that ignores the depth and complexity that Fuller brings to the film. Like so many of Fuller's heroes, Widmark's Skip McCoy fights to retain his individuality in the face of societal pressures. Yet McCoy doesn't foil the communist scheme because of his devotion to the American ideal but because Kiley, who just happens to be a communist spy, has done McCoy wrong. Both Widmark and Peters are superb, but it is Ritter, as the seedy but much-loved Moe, who gives the film its emotional punch, and her performance earned an Oscar nomination for Best Supporting Actress—something of an oddity for a Fuller-directed B movie.

PICNIC

1955 115m c Drama ★★★★
Columbia (U.S.) /A

William Holden (Hal Carter), Rosalind Russell (Rosemary Sydney), Kim Novak (Madge Owens), Betty Field (Flo Owens), Susan Strasberg (Millie Owens), Cliff Robertson (Alan), Arthur O'Connell (Howard Bevans), Verna Felton (Mrs. Helen Potts), Reta Shaw (Linda Sue Breckenridge), Nick Adams (Bomber)

p, Fred Kohlmar; d, Joshua Logan; w, Daniel Taradash (based on the play by William Inge); ph, James Wong Howe; ed, Charles Nelson, William Lyon; m, George Duning; prod d, Jo Mielziner; art d, William Flannery; chor, Miriam Nelson; cos, Jean Louis

AAN Best Picture; AAN Best Supporting Actor: Arthur O'Connell; AAN Best Director: Joshua Logan; AA Best Editing: William A. Lyon, Charles Nelson; AAN Best Score: George Duning; AA Best Art Direction: William Flannery, Jo Mielziner, Robert Priestley

Joshua Logan's faithful screen adaptation of William Inge's Pulitzer Prize-winning play about small-town America. PICNIC features a bravura performance by Holden as a drifter come to a small Kansas town just as the community is preparing to celebrate Labor Day. Seeking out old college friend Robertson in the hope of landing a job with Robertson's father, the richest man in the county, Holden is invited to join in the festivities. What's more, Robertson insists that Holden meet his fiancee, the beautiful Novak, and she and the drifter fall in love at first sight. Holden struts about the town flexing his muscles, and most of the local ladies, including Novak's naive younger sister, Strasberg, and schoolmarm Russell, fall for the handsome stranger. Holden brags about his adventures, and Russell gets drunk while admiring him, thrusting aside her reliable date, O'Connell, and losing control, ripping Holden's shirt right off his back in her seizure of lust. Along with this humiliation, Holden is forced into a fight with Robertson so that he beats up his old friend and then must run from the law, dragging Novak with him. He finally persuades her to return home, confessing that he's nothing but a bum and a liar. Novak does go home, and Holden exits the way he arrived, by hopping a freight train. Novak, however, realizes that her love for Holden is stronger than the security of home and she takes a bus heading in the same direction as the train, intending to catch up with the love of her life.

Holden is brilliant; Novak, in her first major role, was terrified of botching the job but performs admirably. The love scenes between the two have real fire, and the sequence showing their dance together is as sensual as any recorded on film. Hollywood lore has it that Holden didn't believe he was up to the famous slow dance with Novak. Logan, who rubbed every scene in the film to high gloss, took Holden to roadhouses and compelled him to dance with choreographer Nelson to jukebox songs until the actor was confident he could perform on the dance floor. Cinematographer Howe circled the two dancers with his camera, showing them mostly from the waist up, their eyes riveted to each other, capturing the love scene in one take. That scene became one of the most famous of the 1950s and it made "Moonglow" a sensational hit. The film was shot in Hutchinson, Kansas, and in Columbia's Burbank Studio.

PICNIC AT HANGING ROCK

1975 110m c Drama ★★★
Atlantic (Australia) PG/A

Rachel Roberts (Mrs. Appleyard), Dominic Guard (Michael Fitzhubert), Helen Morse (Dianne De Poiters), Jacki Weaver (Minnie), Vivean Gray (Miss Greta McGraw), Kirsty Child (Dora Lumley), Anne Lambert (Miranda), Karen Robson (Irma), Jane Vallis (Marion), Christine Schuler (Edith Horton)

p, Jim McElroy, Hal McElroy; d, Peter Weir; w, Cliff Green (based on the novel by Joan Lindsay); ph, Russell Boyd; ed, Max Lemon; m, Bruce Smeaton; art d, David Copping; cos, Judy Dorsman

The critical recognition of Australia's film industry in the late 1970s can, to a large degree, be credited to the works of Peter Weir. After his first feature, THE CARS THAT ATE PARIS, films such as PICNIC AT HANGING ROCK and THE LAST WAVE exhibited a peculiar and fascinating mystical quality that revealed a distinctive sensibility. Unfortunately Weir's decidedly personal vision is often rather murky.

PICNIC AT HANGING ROCK recounts the strange story of four girls and their teacher from a boarding school in Victoria who go for a picnic at nearby Hanging Rock on a beautiful St. Valentine's Day in 1900. One of the girls, Edith (Christine Schuler), takes a nap and wakes to find that the other three have removed their shoes and stockings to climb higher. They vanish. The police are called in but they are unsuccessful in their search. A young Englishman conducts a search of his own with odd and inconclusive results.

An exceedingly beautiful film, PICNIC AT HANGING ROCK seems to aspire to be an existential thriller of some sort. At times the film seems to thread in BLACK NARCISSUS territory with its depiction of barely controlled sexual hysteria and its eccentric lyrical quality. It's all pretty overheated and underexplained but this arty vague and possibly supernatural movie lingers on in the memory.

PICTURE OF DORIAN GRAY, THE

1945 110m c/bw Horror ★★★½
MGM (U.S.) /A

George Sanders (Lord Henry Wotton), Hurd Hatfield (Dorian Gray), Donna Reed (Gladys Hallward), Angela Lansbury (Sybil Vane), Lowell Gilmore (Basil Hallward), Peter Lawford (David Stone), Richard Fraser (James Vane), Reginald Owen (Lord George Farmoor), Lydia Bilbrook (Mrs. Vane), Morton Lowry (Adrian Singleton)

p, Pandro S. Berman; d, Albert Lewin; w, Albert Lewin (based on the novel by Oscar Wilde); ph, Harry Stradling; ed, Ferris Webster; m, Herbert Stothart; art d, Cedric Gibbons, Hans Peters

AAN Best Supporting Actress: Angela Lansbury; AA Best Cinematography: Harry Stradling; AAN Best Art Direction: Cedric Gibbons, Hans Peters, Edwin B. Willis, John Bonar, Hugh Hunt

This subtle and frightening adaptation of the classic Oscar Wilde novel allows the audience's imagination to do most of the scaring. Hurd Hatfield stars as the title character—a young aristocrat in 19th-century London whose gentle, angelic appearance is dangerously deceptive. Coaxed by the manipulative and hedonistic Lord Henry Wotton (George Sanders), Dorian grows as evil and scandalous as his mentor, becoming a philandering louse who entertains sadistic and perverse thoughts, alluding to (unseen) orgies and unspeakable evils. At the height of his vanity, Dorian has his portrait painted, and, in a Faustian pact, trades his soul for eternal youth. As a result, the portrait ages hideously, while Dorian's appearance never changes. In much the same manner as Val Lewton's horror films, THE PICTURE OF DORIAN GRAY frightens the audience by mere suggestion, without ever resorting to distracting visual representations of the horrible. All the infamy of Hatfield's character is implied, resulting in a building up of evil so horrible that it becomes unspeakable. The only visual shock the audience is subjected to is the portrait itself (which one never expects to see when it pops onto the screen in Technicolor with a violent musical crash), painted in a brilliantly grotesque style by Ivan Albright. THE PICTURE OF DORIAN GRAY not only frightened many viewers, it also earned the respect of the Motion Picture Academy, which bestowed upon the film two Oscar nominations—one to Angela Lansbury (as Dorian's jilted fiancee) for Best Supporting Actress and another to Cedric Gibbons and Hans Peters for Best Black-and-White Art Direction—and one statuette for the deep-focus camerawork of Harry Stradling.

PIERROT LE FOU

1965 110m c Crime/Romance ★★★★
Rome/Paris/SNC/DEG (France/Italy) /A

Jean-Paul Belmondo *(Ferdinand Griffon, "Pierrot")*, Anna Karina *(Marianne Renoir)*, Dirk Sanders *(Fred, Marianne's Brother)*, Raymond Devos *(Man on the Pier)*, Graziella Galvani *(Ferdinand's Wife)*, Roger Dutoit, Hans Meyer *(Gangsters)*, Jimmy Karoubi *(Dwarf)*, Krista Nell *(Mme. Staquet)*, Pascal Aubier *(2nd Brother)*

p, Georges de Beauregard; d, Jean-Luc Godard; w, Jean-Luc Godard (based on the novel *Obsession* by Lionel White); ph, Raoul Coutard; ed, Francoise Collin; m, Antoine Duhamel, Antonio Vivaldi; art d, Pierre Guffroy

Like BAND OF OUTSIDERS before it and the incomprehensible MADE IN USA afterward, Jean-Luc Godard's PIERROT LE FOU is based on a pulp detective novel, providing the filmmaker with a simple story on which to hang his personal, artistic and philosophical beliefs.

Ferdinand Griffon (Jean-Paul Belmondo) leaves behind his Parisian wife and child during a party and takes off on an adventure with Marianne Renoir (Anna Karina), the family baby-sitter with whom he had an affair five years earlier. The following morning a man is found in Marianne's apartment with scissors sticking out of his throat. They set out for the Riviera (heading south, as the characters in Godard's previous film, ALPHAVILLE, hoped to do) in the hope of locating Marianne's gunrunner brother. Ferdinand spends his time writing a journal, but Marianne grows increasingly impatient and gets herself involved once more in gangster activities. Again the result is a mobster—a dwarf—being found with scissors in his throat.

The pair is separated when Ferdinand is kidnapped and tortured by gangsters who are interested in finding Marianne. Ferdinand eventually meets up with her and learns that her brother is really her lover. A double cross follows, and Ferdinand ends up shooting them both. Having had enough of the adventure, Ferdinand phones his wife in Paris but cannot get through to her. He goes to the top of a hill, paints his face blue, ties red and yellow sticks of dynamite to his head, and lights the fuse.

PIERROT LE FOU was Godard's tenth film in six years (not including four sketches that he contributed to compilation films) and perhaps the first to contain all the elements that have been called "Godardian." He combined everything that came before—the romanticism of BREATHLESS, the inner monologue externalized in LE PETIT SOLDAT, the structural divison of MY LIFE TO LIVE, and the epic odyssey of CONTEMPT—with the linguistic diary format that would overpower some of his later films.

Working from the outline provided by Lionel White's novel *Obsession*, Godard was able to proceed without a script and create what he called "a completely spontaneous film." Spontaneous or not, PIERROT LE FOU is arguably one of the few Godard pictures to have the desired balance of romance, adventure, violence, and humor on one side, and philosophy, literary and cinematic allusion, and Brechtian distancing on the other.

The film was lensed quickly in May, June, and July 1965 and then edited even more rapidly for a showing at the Venice Film Festival at the end of August. Despite the mixed reaction that inevitably accompanies a new Godard film, it was soon elevated to the position of runner-up in the prestigious *Sight and Sound* poll of 1972.

PILLOW BOOK, THE

1996 126m c Erotic/Romance/Drama ★★½
Kasander/Wigman Productions/Woodline Films/Alpha /18
Film/Channel Four Films/Studio Canal Plus/Delux Productions
(U.K./Netherlands/France)

Vivian Wu *(Nagiko Kiohara)*, Yoshi Oida *(The Publisher)*, Ken Ogata *(The Father)*, Ewan McGregor *(Jerome)*, Hideko Yoshida *(Sei Shonagon/The Aunt/The Maid)*, Judy Ongg *(The Mother)*, Yutaka Honda *(Hoki)*, Ken Mitsuishi *(The Husband)*, Barbara Lott *(Jerome's Mother)*, Miwako Kawai

p, Kees Kasander; d, Peter Greenaway; w, Peter Greenaway; ph, Sacha Vierny; ed, Chris Wyatt, Peter Greenaway; prod d, Wilbert van Dorp, Andree Putman, Emi Wada; art d, Koichi Hamamura, Vincent De Pater; cos, Dien van Straalen, Koji Tatsuno, Martin Margiela, Emi Wada

An excellent introduction to the films of Peter Greenaway, this seductive eye-candy masquerading as thought-provoking art cinema wears its brain on its sleeve, or—more accurately—its bare skin.

Nagiko (Vivian Wu)—namesake of Sei Shonagon, the author of a 10th-century collection of sensual writings called *The Pillow Book*—cherishes the memory of the birthday ritual devised by her father (Ken Ogata), a writer and skilled calligrapher who writes birthday greetings on her upturned face. As an adult, Nagiko finds the act of writing on the body suffused with erotic potential, and the scent of paper reminds her of human skin, an apparently quixotic detail that experienced viewers of Greenaway films will know can only have ominous significance. A series of unsatisfactory affairs with calligraphers behind her, she falls in love with bisexual translator Jerome (Ewan McGregor). He becomes her link to a publisher (Yoshi Oida) who once humiliated her father and against whom she plots an elaborate revenge.

With its attractive cast, beguiling score, and relatively straightforward narrative, this dark fable of letters and lust is one of Greenaway's most accessible works, although it retains the hallmarks of his earlier films: obsessions with ritual, with counting, with densely layered and embedded images, sex in conjunction with grotesque violence, and the transformation of life into literature. While undeniably exquisite, the entire enterprise carries a faint whiff of orientalism—naked Asian flesh (to be fair, McGregor, the only European with a significant role, bares all as well) and an obsession with mysterious Eastern arts—that's a bit troubling in so conspicuously learned an enterprise.

PILLOW TALK

1959 105m c Comedy ★★★½
Arwin (U.S.) /A

Rock Hudson *(Brad Allen)*, Doris Day *(Jan Morrow)*, Tony Randall *(Jonathan Forbes)*, Thelma Ritter *(Alma)*, Nick Adams *(Tony Walters)*, Julia Meade *(Marie)*, Allen Jenkins *(Harry)*, Marcel Dalio *(Pierot)*, Lee Patrick *(Mrs. Walters)*, Mary McCarty *(Nurse Resnick)*

p, Ross Hunter, Martin Melcher; d, Michael Gordon; w, Stanley Shapiro, Maurice Richlin (based on a story by Russell Rouse, Clarence Greene); ph, Arthur E. Arling; ed, Milton Carruth; m, Frank DeVol; art d, Alexander Golitzen, Richard H. Riedel; cos, Bill Thomas, Jean Louis

AAN Best Actress: Doris Day; *AAN Best Supporting Actress:* Thelma Ritter; *AA Best Story and Screenplay:* Russell Rouse, Clarence Greene, Stanley Shapiro, Maurice Richlin; *AAN Best Score:* Frank DeVol; *AAN Best Art Direction:* Richard H. Riedel, Russell A. Gausman, Ruby R. Levitt

PILLOW TALK was the first of the witty, well-produced sex comedies featuring Day and Hudson. Hudson, a playboy songwriter, and Day, a successful, independent interior designer, learn to loathe each other when they are forced to share a party line during a Manhattan phone-line shortage. Day gets increasingly angry every time she tries to make a call and hears Hudson coming on to yet another unsuspecting woman he's trying to bed. After listening to enough of his suave baloney, Day begins causing trouble. Naturally, Hudson thinks she's an uptight old hag, and eventually they agree to take turns using the phone every half-hour. Coincidentally, Hudson's buddy, Randall, is in love with Day and the phone-sharers finally meet when Randall brings her to see the progress of a Broadway show he's funding and for which Hudson is writing the tunes. Surprised by Day's good looks, Hudson pretends to be a dopey Texan and begins to work his charms on her. Day quickly realizes who Hudson is and puts an end to the romance. Now hooked, Hudson seeks advice from Day's maid, Ritter (who nearly steals the movie), and she suggests that Hudson let Day decorate his apartment. This ploy back-fires, however, when the not-to-be-fooled Day gets her licks in by doing over Hudson's pad in a hideous manner. Frustrated because he can get her no other way, Hudson does some quick thinking and states that he hopes his apartment will be to her liking when they get married.

Though PILLOW TALK is silly and at times overly "cute," it was the first time Day was allowed to show a more sexually frank side to her character, and Hudson was able to prove he was more than just a good-looking hunk. The combination clicked, leaving the two among the most popular stars of the next five years. It was also among the bigger box-office successes of its day, taking in $7.5 million in domestic distribution.

PIMPERNEL SMITH

1941 100m bw Spy/War   ★★★½
British National (U.K.)   /U

Leslie Howard (Prof. Horatio Smith), Francis L. Sullivan (Gen. von Graum), Mary Morris (Ludmilla Koslowski), Hugh McDermott (David Maxwell), Raymond Huntley (Marx), Manning Whiley (Bertie Gregson), Peter Gawthorne (Sidimir Koslowski), Allan Jeayes (Dr. Beckendorf), Dennis Arundell (Hoffman), Joan Kemp-Welch (Teacher)

p, Leslie Howard; d, Leslie Howard; w, Anatole de Grunwald, Roland Pertwee, Ian Dalrymple (based on a story by A.G. MacDonnell, Wolfgang Wilhelm); ph, Mutz Greenbaum; ed, Douglas Myers; m, John Greenwood

Leslie Howard more or less reprises his most famous swashbuckling role, that of THE SCARLET PIMPERNEL, as that tale of disguise and rescue is transplanted from Paris during the Reign of Terror to Germany under the Nazis. Prof. Horatio Smith (Howard), an absent-minded professor of archaeology, is supposedly involved in the search for Aryan artifacts near Switzerland, but secretly he runs refugees over the border to safety while disguising himself in a bewildering variety of get-ups. Meanwhile, Gen. von Graum (Francis L. Sullivan), a corpulent Gestapo officer, sets out to stop the elusive "Pimpernel." Eventually Smith's students figure out what their professor is up to and help him smuggle a large group of persecuted scientists across the border. Smith then goes back one more time, all the way to Berlin, to free Ludmilla Koslowski (Mary Morris), a young woman being held by the Gestapo. This was Howard's first solo directorial effort (he codirected PYGMA-LION earlier) and he does a creditable job, keeping the film moving with the right mixture of action and suave, stiff-upper-lip heroism; however, his relaxed acting and immensely likable screen presence are what carry the film.

PINK FLAMINGOS

1972 95m c Comedy   ★★★½
Saliva Films (U.S.)   NC-17/

Divine (Divine/Babs Johnson), David Lochary (Raymond Marble), Mink Stole (Connie Marble), Mary Vivian Pearce (Cotton), Edith Massey (Miss Edie), Danny Mills (Crackers), Channing Wilroy (Channing), Cookie Mueller (Cookie), Paul Swift (Egg Man), Susan Walsh (Suzie—Blonde in Basement)

p, John Waters; d, John Waters; w, John Waters; ph, John Waters; ed, John Waters; prod d, Vincent Peranio; art d, Vincent Peranio; cos, Van Smith

Billed as "the most disgusting picture of all time," this absolutely uninhibited exercise in scatology and low camp was the breakthrough film for Baltimore-based independent filmmaker John Waters, who later entered the commercial mainstream with such films as HAIR-SPRAY and SERIAL MOM. The improbable star of this ultra-low

budget cinematic gross-out is 300-pound transvestite Divine, whose willingness to do virtually anything in front of the camera, along with an undeniable screen presence, made PINK FLAMINGOS a favorite on the campus and midnight-movie circuits. Gleefully grotesque Babs Johnson (Divine) lives in a trailer park with her simpleminded son, Crackers (Danny Mills), and revolting Mama Edie (Edith Massey), who is obsessed with eggs. Everyone agrees that Babs is the "filthiest person in the world"; her status draws the envy of black-market baby farmers Raymond and Connie Marble (David Lochary and Mink Stole), who vow to "out-filthy" their rival. The resulting competition encompasses acts of arson, bestiality, cannibalism, castration and coprophagy. Waters's early films sought to explode the conventions of bourgeois taste, which he saw as fraudulent and oppressive; ironically, bourgeois taste now cheerfully embraces the sensibility (if not, perhaps, the explicit grossness) of PINK FLAMINGOS. To commemorate the film's 25th-anniversary, Waters prepared a special edition of his trash epic, which included an addendum of never-before-seen footage and a commentary from the director himself.

PINK FLOYD—THE WALL

1982 99m c Musical   ★★
Tin Blue/Goldcrest (U.K.)   R/15

Bob Geldof (Pink), Christine Hargreaves (Pink's Mother), James Laurenson (Pink's Father), Eleanor David (Pink's Wife), Kevin McKeon (Young Pink), Bob Hoskins (Rock 'n' Roll Manager), David Bingham (Little Pink), Jenny Wright (American Groupie), Alex McAvoy (Teacher), Ellis Dale (English Doctor)

p, Alan Marshall; d, Alan Parker; w, Roger Waters (based on the album "The Wall" by Pink Floyd); ph, Peter Biziou; ed, Gerry Hambling; prod d, Brian Morris; art d, Chris Burke, Clinton Cavers; fx, Martin Gutheridge, Graham Longhurst; anim, Gerald Scarfe

This overlong, tedious film based on the multimillion-selling record album by Pink Floyd stars Boomtown Rats singer and "Live Aid" organizer Bob Geldof as Pink, a successful, narcissistic, and wholly unsympathetic rock star on the verge of burnout. Driven to the edge by the news that his wife has left him for another man, Pink spirals into a neurotic conglomeration of flashbacks and fantasies detailing his life. A child of WWII, he grows up amidst the horrors and ruins of wartime Britain. Eventually he becomes a star singer, in the process discovering his power to manipulate a crowd for his own satisfaction (much as his own schoolteachers manipulated and dehumanized him when he was a boy). Cut off from human feeling, Pink slowly builds a wall around himself to deflect suffering. While the music may be interesting and effective on vinyl, on film it becomes repetitious and pretentious, despite director Alan Parker's flair for flashy visuals. Thematically the film is banal, and even its simple themes of alienation, loneliness, and paranoia are muddled and sapped of relevancy by the overblown treatment. Geldof is effective in the lead, and the animation sequences by political cartoonist Gerald Scarfe are interesting and well executed, though too long. Rabid Pink Floyd fans have supported this film enthusiastically since its inception and look upon it as one of the greatest rock 'n' roll films of all times (it isn't).

PINK PANTHER, THE

1964 113m c Comedy   ★★★½
Mirisch/G&E (U.S.)   /PG

David Niven (Sir Charles Lytton), Peter Sellers (Inspector Jacques Clouseau), Robert Wagner (George Lytton), Capucine (Simone Clouseau), Claudia Cardinale (Princess Dala), Brenda de Banzie (Angela Dunning), Fran Jeffries (Greek "Cousin"), Colin Gordon (Tucker), John Le Mesurier (Defense Attorney), James Lanphier (Saloud)

p, Martin Jurow; d, Blake Edwards; w, Blake Edwards, Maurice Richlin; ph, Philip Lathrop; ed, Ralph E. Winters, Marshall M. Borden, David Zinnemann; m, Henry Mancini; art d, Fernando Carrere; fx, Lee Zavitz; chor, Hermes Pan; cos, Yves Saint-Laurent

AAN Best Score: Henry Mancini

Writer-director Blake Edwards hit paydirt with the character of Inspector Clouseau, a Tati-like police inspector in an over-large trenchcoat who is sublimely indifferent to the physical realities that surround him.

Peter Sellers brought magnificent life to the character and it lasted through a number of movies until Sellers' death. (Clouseau has occasionally been played by others, most recently by Italian comic Roberto Benigni.)

Niven, in a role not unlike his RAFFLES character (or the part played by Cary Grant in TO CATCH A THIEF almost a decade before), is a famous jewel thief who is suave beyond belief, fairly dripping with sophistication. He is vacationing at the Alpine resort of Cortina D'Ampezzo, where all the skiers are swathed in clothes by famous French designers. One of the guests is Cardinale, an Indian princess who owns the famous "Pink Panther" gem, a bauble of immeasurable value. Niven wants the jewel and will stop at nothing to get it. He has been the scourge of Interpol for the previous 15 years, as he's pulled off one daring robbery after another. All that time, Niven has been tailed by Sellers, a French inspector, who also wants to nail Niven's female accomplice. The fact that Sellers can never seem to catch up with Niven must have something to do with the fact that his wife, Capucine, is Niven's lover and is therefore able to alert Niven before Sellers can nab him. Meanwhile, Niven's American-born nephew, Wagner, is being supported by his uncle under the pretext that he is a college student. Wagner seems, however, to have inherited a predisposition for his uncle's "occupation." Niven is moving in on Cardinale and the gem when Wagner arrives, also intent on purloining the "Panther."

Though he has less time on screen than the other principals, Sellers steals the film. The ensuing follow-up pictures proved his staying power. Gorgeous photography and sets, huge guffaws, and lots of fun. Mancini took an Oscar nomination and stuck around to do the music for several sequels.

PINKY

1949　102m　bw　Drama　★★★★
Fox　(U.S.)　/A

Jeanne Crain *(Pinky, Patricia Johnson)*, Ethel Barrymore *(Miss Em)*, Ethel Waters *(Granny Dysey Johnson)*, William Lundigan *(Dr. Thomas Adams)*, Basil Ruysdael *(Judge Walker)*, Kenny Washington *(Dr. Canady)*, Nina Mae McKinney *(Rozelia)*, Griff Barnett *(Dr. Joe McGill)*, Frederick O'Neal *(Jake Walters)*, Evelyn Varden *(Melba Wooley)*

p, Darryl F. Zanuck; d, Elia Kazan; w, Philip Dunne, Dudley Nichols (based on the novel *Quality* by Cid Ricketts Sumner); ph, Joseph MacDonald; ed, Harmon Jones; m, Alfred Newman; art d, Lyle Wheeler, J. Russell Spencer; cos, Charles LeMaire

AAN Best Actress: Jeanne Crain; *AAN Best Supporting Actress:* Ethel Barrymore; *AAN Best Supporting Actress:* Ethel Waters

Producer Darryl F. Zanuck, who had attacked anti-Semitism in GENTLEMAN'S AGREEMENT in 1947, tackled the subject of prejudice against African Americans in this film. Crain plays the eponymous Pinky (a term used in the black community to described those whose complexions are light enough that they can pass for white), a bright young woman who has been studying nursing at a school in New England. Lundigan, a white physician, would like to marry her, but Crain believes the interracial union could never work, suspects Lundigan of being more "tolerant" than committed, and is unwilling to be absorbed into the white world. Sadly, she leaves and returns to the southern town of her birth. Crain's grandmother, Waters, works for feisty dowager Barrymore, and when the old woman becomes ill, Crain becomes her nurse and stays on until her death. Barrymore leaves her estate to Crain, but her family contests the legacy because Crain is black, claiming that Crain exerted undue influence on the dying Barrymore. The dispute is taken to court, where Crain wins the estate. Afterwards, she turns it into a nursing home and school for blacks. Zanuck initially asked John Ford to direct PINKY, but he was reportedly relieved, nevertheless, when Ford (who didn't get along with actress Waters and felt little enthusiasm for the story) asked to be taken off the picture two weeks into shooting, since Zanuck had misgivings about Ford's ability to create credible black characters. After Ford's exit, Zanuck immediately called in Elia Kazan; eight weeks later the film was completed, Ford's footage totally scrapped. Today, PINKY is still remarkable for its sincerity and directness, especially when one considers its date of origin. This is a mature film, with great respect for the

humanity of people who are able to transcend social barriers and care for one another. Crain, Waters, and Barrymore all received Oscar nominations for their performances.

PINOCCHIO

1940　88m　c　Children's/Fantasy/Animated　★★★★★
Walt Disney Productions　(U.S.)　/U

VOICES OF: Dick Jones *(Pinocchio)*, Christian Rub *(Geppetto)*, Cliff Edwards *(Jiminy Cricket)*, Evelyn Venable *(The Blue Fairy)*, Walter Catlett *(J. Worthington Foulfellow)*, Frankie Darro *(Lampwick)*, Charles Judels *(Stromboli the Coachman)*, Don Brodie *(Barker)*

p, Walt Disney; d, Ben Sharpsteen, Hamilton Luske; w, Ted Sears, Otto Englander, Webb Smith, William Cottrell, Joseph Sabo, Erdman Penner, Aurelius Battaglia (based on the story by Carlo Collodi); m, Paul J. Smith; art d, Charles Philippi, Hugh Hennesy, Dick Kelsey, Terrell Stapp, John Hubley, Ken Anderson, Kendall O'Connor, Thor Putnam, McLaren Stewart, Al Zinnen; anim, John Lounsbery, Charles A. Nichols, Art Palmer, Fred Moore, Eric Larson, Milt Kahl, Ward Kimball, Franklin Thomas, Vladimir Tytla, Arthur Babbitt, Wolfgang Reitherman

AA Best Score: Leigh Harline, Paul J. Smith, Ned Washington; *AA Best Song:* Leigh Harline (Music), Ned Washington (Lyrics)

This was Disney's second full-length animated feature and it may well be the greatest of the studio's cartoon classics.

A technical tour de force, PINOCCHIO was brilliantly crafted with an awesome attention to detail and verisimilitude. This film showcased all of Disney's innovative techniques when they were still fresh. The episodic story of the wooden puppet who earns real life by learning to be a good person was an unusual but inspired choice for adaptation. Emotionally rich, humorous, and periodically terrifying, the film offers images so startling and memorable that generations of children have been enthralled by it.

This timeless story focuses on a wooden puppet that wants nothing more than to be a real boy, a wish echoed by its creator, Geppetto. One night, the Blue Fairy descends from the skies and promises to turn Pinocchio into a flesh-and-blood little boy if he swears to be brave and unselfish and to learn right from wrong. The Blue Fairy even assigns Pinocchio a conscience, in the form of Jiminy Cricket. This is, of course, the film that features what would become the Disney theme song, "When You Wish upon a Star," sung by the inimitable Cliff Edwards, the voice of Jiminy Cricket. Pinocchio must undergo many harrowing life lessons before his dream comes true.

PINOCCHIO boasts the first extensive use of the Disney-developed multiplane camera. This allows for a convincing illusion that the animation camera is actually moving in three dimensions through different planes of action in the way a dolly or tracking shot functions in a live action film. The animators have further refined their animation of human figures which had still been a bit shaky in their first feature, SNOW WHITE. With both FANTASIA and PINOCCHIO in release in 1940, the future must have seemed bright and interesting at the Disney studios. Then came DUMBO, BAMBI, the studio strike, WWII, and a long stretch of declining success with animated features from which Disney was not able to recover artistically. Some would argue did this recovery finally occured with the release of THE LITTLE MERMAID but this film and BEAUTY AND THE BEAST were, at best, a return to form rather than new plateaus for the animated feature. See PINOCCHIO again and again. A marvel and a joy to behold, it's the real thing. It's the stuff that dreams—and nightmares—are made of.

PIRATE, THE

1948　102m　c　Musical　★★★½
MGM　(U.S.)　/U

Judy Garland *(Manuela)*, Gene Kelly *(Serafin)*, Walter Slezak *(Don Pedro Vargas)*, Gladys Cooper *(Aunt Inez)*, Reginald Owen *(The Advocate)*, George Zucco *(The Viceroy)*, The Nicholas Brothers *(Specialty Dancers)*, Lester Allen *(Uncle Capucho)*, Lola Deem *(Isabella)*, Ellen Ross *(Mercedes)*

p, Arthur Freed; d, Vincente Minnelli; w, Albert Hackett, Frances Goodrich, Joseph L. Mankiewicz (uncredited), Joseph Than, Lillian Braun, Anita Loos, Wilkie Mahoney (based on a play by S.N.

Behrman); ph, Harry Stradling; ed, Blanche Sewell; m, Cole Porter; art d, Cedric Gibbons, Jack Martin Smith; chor, Robert Alton, Gene Kelly; cos, Tom Keogh, Barbara Karinska

AAN Best Score: Lennie Hayton

The story is wearisome and the acting fever-pitched, but the music and dancing in this colorful film are spectacular. The setting is the Caribbean Island of San Sebastian in the 1820s, where young Manuela (Judy Garland) fantasizes about the notorious pirate Macoco, better known as "Mack the Black." Serafin (Gene Kelly), a strolling minstrel, falls in love with Manuela, and tries to win her heart by impersonating Macoco. Meanwhile, Don Pedro (Walter Slezak), the mayor of the town and Manuela's fiance by arrangement, schemes against Serafin, who nonetheless persists in his charade, boldly demanding that the town hand Manuela over to him lest he unloose his fierce pirates. Manuela discovers his fraud, however, and a knock-down, drag-out fight between the fiery lovers takes place while they sing/shout Cole Porter's "Love of My Life." To his peril, Serafin learns that Don Pedro is *really* Macoco incognito; Manuela, however, has never known this and is by now hopelessly in love with the street performer. Eventually, she joins his troupe of players, ending the film with a reprise of "Be a Clown" in which Garland and Kelly sing and dance with several of their teeth blackened and big red noses gleaming. THE PIRATE is an old-fashioned lavish MGM musical, dripping with lush color and peppered with wonderful numbers. Little care is given to the script and the dramatics, but the film is a scenic treat, offering magnificent sets and a frenetic pace typical of director Vincente Minnelli (then Garland's husband). Filming was slowed down considerably by Garland's emotional illness; she was on the verge of a breakdown and delayed the proceedings with paranoiac attacks directed at Minnelli, Kelly, and Porter. A financial failure that cost MGM $3,768,000 and earned back only $2,290,000 in its initial release, THE PIRATE has earned a cult following, chiefly for its extravagant choreography, especially in the sweeping "Nina" and "Mack the Black" numbers, danced energetically by Kelly. A special treat is the appearance of the Nicholas Brothers, who dance with Kelly in the first "Be a Clown" number; they were edited out of this scene in southern theaters at the time of release.

PIT AND THE PENDULUM, THE

1961 85m c Horror ★★★½
Alta Vista (U.S.) /15

Vincent Price *(Nicholas Medina)*, John Kerr *(Francis Barnard)*, Barbara Steele *(Elisabeth Barnard Medina)*, Luana Anders *(Catherine Medina)*, Anthony Carbone *(Dr. Charles Leon)*, Patrick Westwood *(Maximillian the Butler)*, Lynn Bernay *(Maria)*, Larry Turner *(Nicholas as a Child)*, Mary Menzies *(Isabella)*, Charles Victor *(Bartolome)*

p, Roger Corman; d, Roger Corman; w, Richard Matheson (based on a story by Edgar Allan Poe); ph, Floyd Crosby; ed, Anthony Carras; m, Les Baxter; prod d, Daniel Haller; art d, Daniel Haller; fx, Pat Dinga; cos, Marjorie Corso

The second and one of the best films in Roger Corman's Edgar Allan Poe series stars Vincent Price as Nicholas Medina, owner of a large and spooky castle with an elaborate torture chamber built by his father during the Spanish Inquisition. Stricken with grief after the death of his wife, Elisabeth (Barbara Steele, in her American film debut), Nicholas becomes obsessed with the notion that he accidentally buried her alive. Elisabeth's brother, Francis Barnard (John Kerr), suspects foul play and travels to the castle looking for answers. He finds Nicholas slowly going mad and claiming to hear Elisabeth's voice calling to him. Eventually it is revealed that Elisabeth is not dead at all, but has conspired with her lover, family doctor Charles Leon (Anthony Carbone), to drive her husband insane. Corman brought in THE PIT AND THE PENDULUM on a 15-day shooting schedule, and the result is a very entertaining horror film with chills, humor, and a bravura performance by Price, who was just beginning to finely hone his wickedly delightful, villainous characters. Shot in lush and almost garish color by cinematographer Floyd Crosby (who also shot Corman's previous Poe film, THE HOUSE OF USHER), the picture includes some impressive techniques and camera movement. Screenwriter Richard Matheson did a fine job of adapting Poe's rather limited (for films) short story by saving the dungeon sequences for the climax and then creating a rather interesting plot line to lead up to it. One of Corman's and AIP's best.

PIXOTE

1981 127m c Drama ★★★★½
Embrafilm (Brazil) /18

Fernando Ramos da Silva *(Pixote)*, Marilia Pera *(Sueli)*, Jorge Juliao *(Lilica)*, Gilberto Moura *(Dito)*, Jose Nilson dos Santos *(Diego)*, Edilson Lino *(Chico)*, Zenildo Oliveira Santos *(Fumaca)*, Claudio Bernardo *(Garatao)*, Tony Tornado *(Cristal)*, Jardel Filho *(Sapatos Brancos)*

p, Paulo Francini; d, Hector Babenco; w, Hector Babenco, Jorge Duran (based on the novel *Infancia Dos Martos* by Jose Louzeiro); ph, Rodolfo Sanchez; ed, Luiz Elias; m, John Neschling; art d, Clovis Bueno

A grim, disturbing and engrossing portrait of children living in poverty on the streets of Sao Paulo, PIXOTE is one of the most powerful films ever made on the subject of urban degradation.

The story focuses on Pixote (da Silva), a boy abandoned by his parents, who becomes a streetwise pimp and eventually a murderer by the age of 10. The film depicts a life of unrelenting squalor and hopelessness, and director Babenco does not flinch from confronting his audience with the most grisly details of his subjects' lives: violence in the reformatory; an aborted baby in a bucket in a bathroom; the young hero suddenly reverting to infancy, suckling at the breast of a momentarily sympathetic prostitute.

PIXOTE draws on a tradition of films in which innocence is stripped from the young, from Rossellini's GERMANY YEAR ZERO to Truffaut's THE 400 BLOWS. In its combination of a documentary-like approach influenced by neorealism with a sometimes surreal visual sense, it clearly owes most to Bunuel's LOS OLVIDADOS. In fact, the director had originally intended to make a documentary and had completed 200 hours of interviews with reformatory children for this purpose. When he was denied further access to the reformatories, he turned to the streets and hired slum children to portray themselves, building scenes around improvisation workshops that allowed the youths to contribute their own experiences to the picture. In 1986, in a tragic and ironic coda to the making of the film, da Silva was killed in a shootout with police after allegedly resisting arrest for an assault.

PLACE IN THE SUN, A

1951 122m bw Drama ★★★★
Paramount (U.S.) /A

Montgomery Clift *(George Eastman)*, Elizabeth Taylor *(Angela Vickers)*, Shelley Winters *(Alice Tripp)*, Anne Revere *(Hannah Eastman)*, Keefe Brasselle *(Earl Eastman)*, Fred Clark *(Bellows)*, Raymond Burr *(Marlowe)*, Herbert Heyes *(Charles Eastman)*, Shepperd Strudwick *(Anthony Vickers)*, Frieda Inescort *(Mrs. Vickers)*

p, George Stevens; d, George Stevens; w, Michael Wilson, Harry Brown (based on the novel *An American Tragedy* by Theodore Dreiser and the play by Patrick Kearney); ph, William Mellor; ed, William Hornbeck; m, Franz Waxman; art d, Hans Dreier, Walter Tyler; fx, Gordon Jennings; cos, Edith Head

AAN Best Picture; AAN Best Actor: Montgomery Clift; AAN Best Actress: Shelley Winters; AA Best Director: George Stevens; AA Best Original Screenplay: Michael Wilson, Harry Brown; AA Best Cinematography: William C. Mellor; AA Best Editing: William Hornbeck; AA Best Score: Franz Waxman; AA Best Costume Design: Edith Head

A ponderous version of Dreiser's *An American Tragedy*, based on the real-life murder of Grace Brown by her social-climbing boyfriend Chester Gillette at Big Moose Lake, New York, in 1906. The film opens with Clift on a highway trying to hitch a ride. Taylor drives past him in a shiny sports car, beeps her horn in a flirtatious manner, and keeps going. Clift gapes after her, awed by her stunning beauty. When Clift arrives in the city looking for a job in his uncle's bathing-suit factory, he is amazed to discover that Taylor is his cousin. The uncle, Heyes, puts Clift to work in the factory, giving him a menial job, but providing the young man with the security Clift's doting mother, Revere, has prayed for. Clift looks from afar at the grand life style, the foreign cars, clothes, and the estate of Heyes and Taylor and, goaded by unbridled ambition, decides to reach upward. Meanwhile, he combats his loneliness by getting involved with Winters, who works in the factory. As his affair with Winters deepens, so does

Clift's association with Heyes and his upper-crust family. Clift is invited to a party at Heyes's mansion where he meets and instantly falls in love with the ravishing Taylor, and she with him. In a whirlwind of torrid trysts, Clift and Taylor fall so deeply in love that they plan to wed. Clift is on the verge of elevating himself from the lower class into the ranks of the super rich, but Winters dashes his plans by telling Clift that she is pregnant and insisting that he marry her.

Dreiser's story was first filmed in 1931 by Josef von Sternberg in a much starker, more realistic manner. This version is almost cartoony by comparison, with Elizabeth Taylor, at the peak of her MGM-sorority loveliness, balanced against an unbelievably plain Shelley Winters. It's as if there were no middle ground in this small town, just extremes of wealth and poverty, beauty and drabness. Taylor was only 17 when Stevens cast her in her rich-girl role, but the studio tried to promote a romance between the young actress and Clift. The liaison didn't require much prompting; Clift fell in love with his leading lady and helped her through her most difficult scenes, with spellbinding results. Meanwhile, A PLACE IN THE SUN marked the beginning of Winters' journey from B-bombshell to character actress. Though Stevens at first refused to consider her for the role (he couldn't see beyond the brassy blondes she had played for years), she became indelibly linked to this part and was asked to play many similar types in the future. A PLACE IN THE SUN also marked the last screen appearance for Revere, who was branded a communist by the House Un-American Activities Committee and blacklisted.

PLACES IN THE HEART

1984 112m c Drama   ★★★½
Tri-Star (U.S.)   PG

Sally Field *(Edna Spalding)*, Lindsay Crouse *(Margaret Lomax)*, Ed Harris *(Wayne Lomax)*, Amy Madigan *(Viola Kelsey)*, John Malkovich *(Mr. Will)*, Danny Glover *(Moze)*, Yankton Hatten *(Frank)*, Gennie James *(Possum)*, Lane Smith *(Albert Denby)*, Terry O'Quinn *(Buddy Kelsey)*

p, Arlene Donovan; d, Robert Benton; w, Robert Benton; ph, Nestor Almendros; ed, Carol Littleton; m, John Kander, Howard Shore; prod d, Gene Callahan; art d, Sydney Z. Litwack; fx, Bran Ferren; cos, Ann Roth

AAN Best Picture; AA Best Actress: Sally Field; *AAN Best Supporting Actor:* John Malkovich; *AAN Best Supporting Actress:* Lindsay Crouse; *AAN Best Director:* Robert Benton; *AA Best Original Screenplay:* Robert Benton; *AAN Best Costume Design:* Ann Roth

Set in Texas in 1930, this film stars Sally Field as Edna Spalding, a mother of two whose lawman-husband has just been killed by a drunk. Near penniless, she is stunned to learn that the bank is about to foreclose on her property, which includes a 40-acre cotton field. Determined to keep her home, she decides to plant and harvest the cotton, though she's ill equipped to do so. She hires wandering laborer Moze (Danny Glover) to help and takes in blind boarder Mr. Will (John Malkovich) to generate some cash, and the little group struggles to make a go of it. Director Robert Benton (KRAMER VS. KRAMER) effectively re-creates depression-era Texas in this moving tale that landed the second Oscar for Field (her first came for NORMA RAE). Malkovich's terrific performance generated an Oscar nomination, while Benton was nominated for Best Director and Best Screenplay, winning the latter. The film was also nominated as Best Picture but lost to AMADEUS.

PLAN 9 FROM OUTER SPACE

1959 79m bw Science Fiction   ★★½
J. Edward Reynolds (U.S.)

Gregory Walcott *(Jeff Trent)*, Mona McKinnon *(Paula Trent)*, Duke Moore *(Lt. Harper)*, Tom Keene *(Col. Tom Edwards)*, Vampira *(The Ghoul Woman)*, Bela Lugosi *(The Ghoul Man)*, Tor Johnson *(Police Inspector Clay)*, Lyle Talbot *(Gen. Roberts)*, Dudley Manlove *(Eros)*, John Breckinridge *(The Ruler)*

p, Edward D. Wood Jr.; d, Edward D. Wood Jr.; w, Edward D. Wood Jr.; ph, William C. Thompson; ed, Edward D. Wood; m, Gordon Zahler

The cult reputation earned by Edward D. Wood Jr.'s bizarre sci-fi epic has been one of the film industry's strangest "success" stories. Using two minutes of footage Wood had shot featuring his friend Bela Lugosi

that was to be used for a never-realized project (Lugosi died days later), the bargain-basement director, responsible for such other noteworthy oddities as GLEN OR GLENDA? (AKA: I CHANGED MY SEX), BRIDE OF THE MONSTER, and JAIL BAIT, put before the cameras "the sworn testimony of miserable souls who survived the ordeal of graverobbers from outer space!" This claim was intoned with all seriousness by the film's host and narrator, famed TV psychic (and close personal friend of the director) Criswell, whose impassioned prologue and epilogue to PLAN 9 FROM OUTER SPACE frame the fantastic tale of aliens using resurrected human zombies to conquer the earth. Alongside—or rather, as well as—Lugosi, the cast includes Vampira, a popular LA TV horror-show hostess; ex-wrestler Tor Johnson, a friend of Wood's; and Joanna Lee, who went on to become a highly successful TV scriptwriter.

PLAN 9 could be the movie for which the critical cliche "it's so bad, it's good" was coined. Voted "The Worst Film of All Time" in a readers' poll for the 1980 book *The Golden Turkey Awards*, Wood's *piece de resistance* so shamelessly ignores all the rules of filmmaking that it's impossible not to be impressed by the director's implacable indifference to "production values." For most of the film, Wood's wife's chiropractor stands in for Lugosi and, even though his face is always hidden by his Dracula cape, it's still obvious he's not the legendary horror star—the two men have entirely different builds. (Meanwhile, the real Lugosi footage, shot two years previously, is repeated over and over throughout the movie.) Some flying saucers seen attacking LA are, in fact, paper plates. In the cemetery scenes, a concrete floor is clearly visible under the "grass," as are some ratty-looking mattresses, there to cushion the fall of a woman who is dropped to the ground; it's obvious, too, that the tombstones are made out of cardboard. There are inexplicable shifts from day to night in the course of several scenes, and the same set of furniture appears in different rooms in Trent's house. Hardly THE REMAINS OF THE DAY, but some would claim it's more fun.

PLANES, TRAINS, AND AUTOMOBILES

1987 93m c Comedy   ★★★
Paramount (U.S.)   R/15

Steve Martin *(Neal Page)*, John Candy *(Del Griffith)*, Laila Robins *(Susan Page)*, Michael McKean *(State Trooper)*, Kevin Bacon *(Taxi Racer)*, Dylan Baker *(Owen)*, Carol Bruce *(Joy Page)*, Olivia Burnette *(Marti)*, Diana Douglas *(Peg)*, William Windom *(Boss)*

p, John Hughes; d, John Hughes; w, John Hughes; ph, Don Peterman; ed, Paul Hirsch; m, Ira Newborn; prod d, John W. Corso; art d, Harold Michelson; cos, April Ferry

The guru of teenager movies, John Hughes, enters the world of adults with this seasonal comedy about the horrors of transportation in America. Two days before Thanksgiving, yuppie marketing consultant Neal Page (Steve Martin) races from Manhattan to catch a plane home to Chicago, only to find that his flight has been delayed. Hours later, he boards the plane and ends up next to Del Griffith (John Candy), a huge slob wearing a polyester suit. When the flight is detoured to Wichita, it's just the beginning of Page's trip and his association with Griffith. With a concept as thin as this, PLANES, TRAINS AND AUTOMOBILES could have easily become a repetitious bore. Instead, producer-director-writer Hughes infuses his film with an appealing sense of sentiment and humanity—not to mention many hilarious scenes. Candy finally has a bravura role and proves himself to be not only a superb comedian but also a fine actor. Martin, in the less flamboyant of the two roles, is excellent as well. Hughes's insistence on cramming the film with a glut of pop songs (which in most cases do nothing to complement the action) is unfortunate.

PLANET OF THE APES

1968 112m c Science Fiction   ★★★★
Apjac (U.S.)   G/PG

Charlton Heston *(George Taylor)*, Roddy McDowall *(Cornelius)*, Kim Hunter *(Dr. Zira)*, Maurice Evans *(Dr. Zaius)*, James Whitmore *(President of the Assembly)*, James Daly *(Honorius)*, Linda Harrison *(Nova)*, Robert Gunner *(Landon)*, Lou Wagner *(Lucius)*, Woodrow Parfrey *(Maximus)*

PLATOON

p, Arthur P. Jacobs; d, Franklin J. Schaffner; w, Michael Wilson, Rod Serling (based on the novel *Monkey Planet* by Pierre Boulle); ph, Leon Shamroy; ed, Hugh S. Fowler; m, Jerry Goldsmith; art d, Jack Martin Smith, William Creber; fx, John Chambers, L.B. Abbott, Art Cruickshank, Emil Kosa Jr.; cos, Morton Haack

AAN Best Score: Jerry Goldsmith; *AAN Best Costume Design:* Morton Haack

"Get your stinking paws off me, you damn dirty ape!" An outstanding science-fiction film that spawned four sequels, an animated cartoon series, a live-action TV series, bubble-gum cards, Halloween masks, and a rash of plastic models. Massive marketing notwithstanding, the original film is still quite an achievement. Heston plays the commander of a lengthy outer-space mission that is interrupted when the spaceship crashes on an unknown planet. He and two other survivors make their way through an arid wasteland into a lush forest where they observe what appears to be a tribe of Stone Age humans. A bizarre horn cries, and the sounds of hoofbeats and gunfire are heard, sending the savages running into the woods. The confused astronauts are shocked to see that the armed horsemen are actually gorillas wearing leather uniforms. Welcome to the planet of the apes, where they wear the clothes and do the talking, and we have reverted to our (natural?) savage state.

PLANET OF THE APES is a success on many levels, with a witty, intelligent script by Rod Serling and a suitably hot-tempered, athletic performance from Charlton Heston. Roddy McDowall and Kim Hunter are highly effective as a sympathetic ape scientist and doctor, respectively, with John Chambers's superb latex makeup allowing them a full range of expressive facial gestures. (Chambers won a special Oscar for his work.) None of the sequels (BENEATH THE PLANET OF THE APES, ESCAPE FROM THE PLANET OF THE APES, CONQUEST OF THE PLANET OF THE APES, BATTLE FOR THE PLANET OF THE APES) lived up to the original and, partly in reaction to all the marketing push, the "Apes" series eventually spiraled into self-parody.

PLATOON

1986 111m c War   ★★★★
Hemdale (U.S.)   R/15

Tom Berenger *(Sgt. Barnes)*, Willem Dafoe *(Sgt. Elias)*, Charlie Sheen *(Chris)*, Forest Whitaker *(Big Harold)*, Francesco Quinn *(Rhah)*, John C. McGinley *(Sgt. O'Neill)*, Richard Edson *(Sal)*, Kevin Dillon *(Bunny)*, Reggie Johnson *(Junior)*, Keith David *(King)*

p, Arnold Kopelson; d, Oliver Stone; w, Oliver Stone; ph, Robert Richardson; ed, Claire Simpson; m, Samuel Barber; prod d, Bruno Rubeo; art d, Rodel Cruz, Doris Sherman Williams; fx, Yves De Bono

AA Best Picture; AAN Best Supporting Actor: Tom Berenger; *AAN Best Supporting Actor:* Willem Dafoe; *AA Best Director:* Oliver Stone; *AAN Best Original Screenplay:* Oliver Stone; *AAN Best Cinematography:* Robert Richardson; *AA Best Editing:* Claire Simpson; *AA Best Sound:* John "Doc" Wilkinson, Richard Rogers, Charles "Bud" Grenzback, Simon Kaye

Chris (Charlie Sheen), a green recruit and child of privilege who dropped out of college and enlisted, finds himself in Vietnam as a member of a platoon divided against itself. On one side is Sgt. Barnes (Tom Berenger), a horribly scarred veteran of several tours of duty—a morally corrupt, remorseless killing machine. The men who follow him seek clear-cut solutions to the complicated realities they face. On the other side is veteran sergeant Elias (Willem Dafoe), who, though equally skilled in the ways of death, still retains some semblance of humanity and attempts to impose a sense of compassion and responsibility on his men. Chris is caught between these two in what he describes as a "battle for possession of my soul."

PLATOON is a shattering experience. Writer-director Stone, a Vietnam veteran, used his first-hand knowledge to create one of the most realistic war films ever made, one whose success lies in the mass of detail Stone brings to the screen, bombarding the senses with vivid sights and sounds that have the feel of actual experience. Stone captures the heat, the dampness, the bugs, the jungle rot, and, most important, the confusion and fear experienced by the average soldier. The men in PLATOON do perform heroic acts on occasion, but the heroism isn't motivated by love of country or idealism—it is motivated by pure terror, by desperation, by a desire to end the madness one way or another. Never before in a war film has stark terror among soldiers been such a tangible, motivating force. There is nothing appealing in Stone's war; it doesn't have a "recruitment flavor." However, while PLATOON has no equal when it comes to capturing the reality of the combat experience, it falters when Stone attempts to apply greater meaning to his vision. The film's battle between the forces of good and evil as represented by the two sergeants is heavy-handed, as is Sheen's totally unnecessary voice-over narration, which dilutes the power of Stone's visuals. On an incredibly low budget of $6.5 million, Stone brought his cast and crew to the Philippines and shot PLATOON in a swift 54 days. To everyone's surprise, the film was a massive hit with the critics and the public.

PLAY IT AGAIN, SAM

1972 85m c Comedy   ★★★½
Apjac/Rollins-Joffe (U.S.)   PG/15

Woody Allen *(Allan Felix)*, Diane Keaton *(Linda Christie)*, Tony Roberts *(Dick Christie)*, Jerry Lacy *(Humphrey Bogart)*, Susan Anspach *(Nancy Felix)*, Jennifer Salt *(Sharon)*, Joy Bang *(Julie)*, Viva *(Jennifer)*, Mari Fletcher *(Fantasy Sharon)*, Diana Davila *(Girl in Museum)*

p, Arthur P. Jacobs; d, Herbert Ross; w, Woody Allen (based on the play by Allen); ph, Owen Roizman; ed, Marion Rothman; m, Billy Goldenberg, Max Steiner; prod d, Ed Wittstein; cos, Anna Hill Johnstone

A true film buff's film about a film buff, Allan Felix (Allen), who is obsessed with CASABLANCA. The impish, neurotic Allan patterns his personality after Humphrey Bogart but has nothing of the actor's tough guy image. When Allan's wife (Anspach), leaves him she explains, "You're one of life's great watchers. I'm not like that, I'm a doer." While the distressed Allan laments over his lack of "cool," he is visited by Bogart (Lacy), who sits in a dark corner of the room, wearing his usual trenchcoat and smoking a cigarette. Bogart gives him advice: "Dames are simple. I never met one that didn't understand a slap in the mouth or a slug from a forty-five." To boost his spirits Allan's married friends, Linda (Diane Keaton) and Dick (Woody Allen good-luck charm Tony Roberts), try to fix him up with another woman. Their meddling and Allan's attempts to emulate his hero lead him into many failures and one undesired success in the game of love, but at least our hero gets to play a scene from CASABLANCA at the finale.

Based on Allen's Broadway play (Allen, Roberts, Keaton, and Lacy all appeared in the stage version, which opened on February 12th, 1969, and ran for 453 performances), PLAY IT AGAIN, SAM differs somewhat from Allen's earlier pictures. Allen handed over the directorial reins here to Herbert Ross, a craftsman, but a director who has no recognizable style of his own. What Ross brings to Allen's play is a sense of control and drama as opposed to the slapstick vignettes of TAKE THE MONEY AND RUN and BANANAS. Still, PLAY IT AGAIN, SAM is clearly Allen's film. (Atypical, however, for an Allen film is the location. A strike in New York caused filming to move to San Francisco.) Though his character is the typical neurotic Allen hero, he strikes a common chord with film audiences. What Allen hits on in PLAY IT AGAIN, SAM is a cultural phenomenon unique to the movie era—audiences living their lives as a movie. While not every audience can relate to the New York intellectual idiosyncracies of ANNIE HALL, they can relate on a gut emotional level to an average man idolizing a movie star. For film buffs, Allen has included countless film references (Erich von Stroheim, Francois Truffaut, Ida Lupino), film posters, and, of course, clips and music from CASABLANCA. Composer Goldenberg borrows heavily from the themes of Max Steiner, which are heard throughout, as is the unforgettable "As Time Goes By" and an Oscar Peterson composition titled "Blues for Allan Felix." Also deserving special mention is Lacy's flawless portrayal of Bogart, which consistently makes one feel as if Allen somehow got the real Bogart for this film.

PLAY MISTY FOR ME

1971 102m c Thriller   ★★★½

Malpaso (U.S.)   R/18

Clint Eastwood *(Dave Garland)*, Jessica Walter *(Evelyn Draper)*, Donna Mills *(Tobie Williams)*, John Larch *(Sgt. McCallum)*, Jack Ging *(Dr. Frank Dewan)*, Irene Hervey *(Madge Brenner)*, James McEachin *(Al Monte)*, Clarice Taylor *(Birdie)*, Don Siegel *(Murphy the Bartender)*, Duke Everts *(Jay Jay)*

p, Robert Daley; d, Clint Eastwood; w, Jo Heims, Dean Riesner (based on a story by Jo Heims); ph, Bruce Surtees; ed, Carl Pingitore; m, Dee Barton; art d, Alexander Golitzen; cos, Helen Colvig, Brad Whitney

This was Clint Eastwood's directorial debut and it far surpasses other attempts in the genre, such as the popular FATAL ATTRACTION, for thrills, suspense, and insight into sexual obsession. Dave Garland (Eastwood) is a Carmel, California, disc jockey who gets a call every night from a mysterious woman listener who requests that he play the Erroll Garner classic "Misty." After breaking up with his girlfriend Tobie (Mills), Dave looks for action in the local bars and meets Evelyn (Walter), a rather high-strung but seductive woman who, he learns, is the mysterious voice that requests "Misty." The lustful pair adjourn to Evelyn's apartment and they sleep together with the understanding that it will be a one-night stand. Unfortunately for Dave, Evelyn is quite mad and absolutely refuses to leave him alone despite the fact that he has patched up his relationship with Tobie. Evelyn's jealous rage is at first suicidal, then quite murderous. A superior thriller, PLAY MISTY FOR ME proved that popular actor Eastwood could direct himself in a film, concentrate on every aspect of the production from the visuals to the performances, and complete the shooting ahead of schedule and under budget. What he delivered was an engrossing study of how loneliness and longing can be transformed into irrational rage after a thoughtless act of selfish indulgence. Much of the credit must go to Jessica Walter for her outstanding performance which somehow manages to be chilling while at the same time sympathetic.

PLAYER, THE

1992 123m c Comedy/Mystery   ★★★★

Avenue Entertainment/Spelling Entertainment (U.S.)   R/15

Tim Robbins *(Griffin Mill)*, Greta Scacchi *(June Gudmundsdottir)*, Fred Ward *(Walter Stuckel)*, Whoopi Goldberg *(Detective Avery)*, Peter Gallagher *(Larry Levy)*, Brion James *(Joel Levison)*, Cynthia Stevenson *(Bonnie Sherow)*, Vincent D'Onofrio *(David Kahane)*, Dean Stockwell *(Andy Civella)*, Richard E. Grant *(Tom Oakley)*

p, David Brown, Michael Tolkin, Nick Wechsler; d, Robert Altman; w, Michael Tolkin (from his novel); ph, Jean Lepine; ed, Geraldine Peroni, Maysie Hoy; m, Thomas Newman; prod d, Stephen Altman; art d, Jerry Fleming; cos, Alexander Julian

AAN Best Director: Robert Altman; *AAN Best Adapted Screenplay:* Michael Tolkin; *AAN Best Editing:* Geraldine Peroni

A hilarious and deftly convincing satire of contemporary Hollywood, courtesy of industry "bad boy" Robert Altman. Lighter in tone than classic exposes like THE BAD AND THE BEAUTIFUL, THE PLAYER sees Tinseltown as run by power brokers who are not so much ruthless as they are inept and insecure. The film's lackadaisical plot, about a production executive (Tim Robbins) who murders a writer (Vincent D'Onofrio), is really just an excuse for an Altmanesque tour of make-believe-land. Along the way, we encounter the dead man's girlfriend, a radiantly composed artist who never completes a painting (Greta Scacchi); an industry whiz-kid who gives great car-phone (Peter Gallagher); a veteran producer who drops Julia Roberts's name into every other sentence (Dean Stockwell); and a preening studio security chief who doesn't think twice about checking his reflection in the back of a coffee-spoon (Fred Ward). The daily rituals of a studio executive's life—speaker-phone conferences, power lunches, private screenings—are portrayed with an authenticity reinforced by the presence of scores of real celebrities, playing themselves in cameo roles.

Among the film's choicer moments: Buck Henry (who wrote THE GRADUATE) pitching an idea for "The Graduate 2," in which a bed-ridden Mrs. Robinson would move in with Benjamin and Elaine;

Whoopi Goldberg, playing a police detective, picking up an Oscar in a studio office and mimicking the speech which the *real* Goldberg gave after winning the award for GHOST; and the murdered writer's funeral, where the best tribute the dead man's friends can muster is to read aloud from the screenplay he was working on before he died ("Long, slow pan across room," etc.) Though it's a canny piece of work, THE PLAYER doesn't compare with Altman's multi-layered masterpiece, NASHVILLE. The earlier film made the world of country music a mirror for American society at large, using its immediate setting to address wider, more universal issues. THE PLAYER looks no further than Hollywood, perhaps because Hollywood is incapable of looking beyond itself.

PLAYTIME

1967 120m c Comedy   ★★★★½

Specta-Films (France)

Jacques Tati *(M. Hulot)*, Barbara Dennek *(Young Tourist)*, Jacqueline Lecomte *(Her Friend)*, Leon Doyen *(Porter)*, Georges Montant *(M. Giffard)*, John Abbey *(Mr. Lacs)*, Valerie Camille *(Mr. Lacs's Secretary)*, Henri Piccoli *(Important Gentleman)*, France Rumilly *(Eyeglass Saleswoman)*, France Delahalle *(Client at the Strand)*

p, Rene Silvera; d, Jacques Tati; w, Jacques Tati, Jacques Lagrange, Art Buchwald; ph, Jean Badal, Andreas Winding; ed, Gerard Pollicand; m, Francis Lemarque, David Stein, James Campbell; prod d, Eugene Roman

Jacques Tati's familiar comic character, Monsieur Hulot, weaves his way through Tati's most ambitious and costly film, the award-winning PLAYTIME.

A group of American tourists arrive at Orly Airport, among them a pretty young woman named Barbara (Barbara Dennek). As a bus transports them to their hotel in Paris, M. Hulot (Jacques Tati) attempts to keep an appointment with M. Giffard (Georges Montant), who works in a large, ultramodern office building. That evening, Hulot runs into an old army buddy (Yves Barsacq) who invites him to his apartment, the residential equivalent of a display window in a department store. An elegant, new (but unfinished) supper club opens its doors for business. One of its customers is Barbara; another is Hulot. Havoc ensues as the management tries to accommodate a capacity turnout and, at the same time, complete construction of the club. Most of the clientele manage to have a splendid time nonetheless and at dawn, they move on to a local snack bar. Among them are Hulot and Barbara, who have paired off.

PLAYTIME was the most elaborate and ambitious film of Tati's career. It took 100 workers more than five months to build the movie's huge setting, an ultramodern mini-city which was nicknamed "Tativille" and became an actual tourist attraction until it was razed to make room for a highway. Initially released in 70mm and stereophonic sound, the three-hour-plus picture was gradually whittled down to less than half of its original length, but nothing could save it from commercial disaster. Nonetheless, Tati was enormously proud of PLAYTIME and, although it was not his final film, regarded it as the climactic work and crowning glory of his career.

The notion of technology developing beyond people's capacity to cope with it is a familiar one that has frequently been treated in films of science, horror, and strident satire. Tati alone chose to take the theme into the perennially unfashionable realm of benign comedy. His mechanical monsters are more annoying than harmful and the beings who control and are controlled by them are not villains and victims but, invariably, innocents as guileless as they are hapless.

PLAZA SUITE

1971 114m c Comedy   ★★★★

Paramount (U.S.)   GP/PG

Walter Matthau *(Sam Nash/Jesse Kiplinger/Roy Hubley)*, Maureen Stapleton *(Karen Nash)*, Jose Ocasio *(Waiter)*, Dan Ferrone *(Bellhop)*, Louise Sorel *(Miss McCormack)*, Barbara Harris *(Muriel Tate)*, Lee Grant *(Norma Hubley)*, Jenny Sullivan *(Mimsey Hubley)*, Tom Carey *(Borden Eisler)*

p, Howard W. Koch; d, Arthur Hiller; w, Neil Simon (based on the play by Neil Simon); ph, Jack Marta; ed, Frank Bracht; m, Maurice Jarre; art d, Arthur Lonergan; cos, Jack Bear

To his credit, Neil Simon never stops trying to expand. With several solid successes in the comedy genre behind him, he attempted something here that wasn't merely a pack of one-liners but had an underlying pathos and humanity. George C. Scott and Maureen Stapleton opened on Broadway in the show, which ran more than 1,000 performances with Mike Nichols directing. Stapleton returns to do one of the three vignettes, as does Lee Grant, who did the Road Show version playing another of the parts, and Barbara Harris in the middle segment. Simon's plays are almost always one-set jobs, and the task of adapting them for the screen is not an enviable one, since movie fans will often carp that they are photographed stage plays of people talking with no cinematic value. Since this picture takes place in one suite at New York's Plaza Hotel, its staginess was all the more evident. The only unifying force in the trio of stories is Matthau in a tour-de-force job as three very different men. There were to be four stories in the original, and the one that was dropped was used as the basis for Simon's original screenplay of THE OUT-OF-TOWNERS. Director Hiller had just come off LOVE STORY, and there was some doubt as to whether he could direct a comedy.

The first segment has Matthau and Stapleton as a middle-aged couple trying to revive their failing marriage in what they believe is the same suite they occupied on their wedding night. In the second segment, Matthau is a Hollywood producer who attempts to seduce Harris with his endless store of motion picture anecdotes. The final, funniest sketch has Matthau driven to distraction when his daughter locks herself in the bathroom and refuses to come out for her wedding ceremony.

Of the female roles, Harris steals the picture. Critics were divided in their assessment of PLAZA SUITE, but we have to stand in the "pro" corner, although Simon has had some terrible adaptations (STAR SPANGLED GIRL) and even some bummer screenplays of his own, as in THE SLUGGER'S WIFE.

PLENTY

1985 125m c Drama/War   ★★★
Fox (U.S.)   R/15

Meryl Streep (*Susan Traherne*), Charles Dance (*Raymond Brock*), Tracey Ullman (*Alice Park*), John Gielgud (*Sir Leonard Darwin*), Sting (*Mick*), Ian McKellen (*Sir Andrew Charleson*), Sam Neill (*Lazar*), Burt Kwouk (*Mr. Aung*), Pik Sen Lim (*Mme. Aung*), Andre Maranne (*Villon*)
p, Edward R. Pressman, Joseph Papp; d, Fred Schepisi; w, David Hare (based on his play); ph, Ian Baker; ed, Peter Honess; m, Bruce Smeaton; prod d, Richard MacDonald; art d, Tony Reading, Adrian Smith; cos, Ruth Myers

Adapted by playwright-director David Hare ("A Map of the World", WETHERBY) from his own play, PLENTY follows the fortunes of Englishwoman Susan Traherne (Meryl Streep) from her thrilling days as a courier behind the lines in occupied France through the boredom she experiences in her postwar life. During the war, in France, she has a brief but passionate affair with a dashing young British agent called Lazar (Sam Neill). When she returns to England after the war, she is unable to forget him. Taking a stab at bohemian life, she becomes involved in a calculated relationship with Mick (Sting), a working-class gent she's decided will make a suitable father for her child. When they fail to produce a baby, however, Susan drops Mick and eventually marries Raymond Brock (Charles Dance), a patient, polished foreign service officer she follows around the globe. But the life of a diplomat's wife is hardly satisfying for the increasingly frustrated and neurotic Susan, and her cruelty to her husband worsens as the years pass. On its face, director Fred Schepisi's film concerns a woman whose warped personality becomes less rational and more malicious as she realizes she will never recapture the excitement of her life during wartime; however, Hare's well-crafted screenplay also uses Susan as a symbol of the squandered hopes for a better postwar Britain. Middle-class Susan and working-class Mick's inability to produce a child is symbolic of postwar Labor governments' failure to eliminate class division and inequity from British society, even in a time of economic "plenty." Intriguing and generally overlooked, PLENTY works on both levels.

Employing yet another flawless accent, Streep delivers an excellent, restrained but edgy performance, well supported by Dance, Sting, and Ullman, who plays her best friend.

PLOUGHMAN'S LUNCH, THE

1983 107m c Drama   ★★★★
Greenpoint (U.K.)   R/15

Jonathan Pryce (*James Penfield*), Tim Curry (*Jeremy Hancock*), Rosemary Harris (*Ann Barrington*), Frank Finlay (*Matthew Fox*), Charlie Dore (*Susan Barrington*), David De Keyser (*Gold*), Nat Jackley (*Mr. Penfield*), Bill Paterson (*Lecturer*), William Maxwell, Paul Jesson
p, Simon Relph, Ann Scott; d, Richard Eyre; w, Ian McEwan; ph, Clive Tickner; ed, David Martin; m, Dominic Muldowney; prod d, Luciana Arrighi; art d, Michael Pickwoad; cos, Luciana Arrighi

BBC radio journalist and would-be historian James Penfield (Jonathan Pryce) is an unbridled opportunist and self-promoter. He is at work on a book about the 1956 Suez Canal crisis in which his aim is to interpret events in a politically popular manner that will enhance his career. He pursues television-documentary researcher Susan Barrington (Charlie Dore), mainly because her mother (Rosemary Harris) is an expert on Suez. As he gets more involved with these characters and his work, it becomes more difficult to determine just who is using whom. First-time director Richard Eyre has created a gripping film that honestly explores political morality in the 1980s. Pryce is superb as the self-interested corporate-social climber, and the entire film plays like THE GRADUATE stood on its head.

POCAHONTAS

1995 87m c Animated/Musical/Romance   ★★★
Walt Disney (U.S.)   G/

VOICES OF: Irene Bedard (*Pocahontas—Speaking Voice*), Judy Kuhn (*Pocahontas—Singing Voice*), Mel Gibson (*Captain John Smith*), Russell Means (*Chief Powhatan*), David Ogden Stiers (*John Ratcliffe*), Linda Hunt (*Grandmother Willow*), Joe Baker (*Lon*), Billy Connolly (*Ben*), Christian Bale (*Thomas*), John Kassir (*Meeko*)
p, James Pentecost; d, Mike Gabriel, Eric Goldberg; w, Carl Binder, Susannah Grant, Philip LaZebnik (from a story by Glen Keane, Joe Grant, Ralph Zondag, Burny Mattinson, Ed Gombert, Kaan Kaylon, Francis Glebas, Robert Gibbs, Bruce Morris, Todd Kurosawa, Duncan Majoribanks, and Chris Buck); ed, H. Lee Peterson; m, Alan Menken, Stephen Schwartz; art d, Michael Giaimo; anim, Glen Keane, John Pomeroy, Duncan Majoribanks, Ruben Aquino, Nik Ranieri, Dave Prulksma, Chris Buck, Ken Duncan

AA Best Musical or Comedy Score: Alan Menken, Stephen Schwartz; *AA Best Original Song:* Alan Menken, Stephen Schwartz "Colors of the Wind"

Balancing historical revisionism on the one hand and a cherished story of early America on the other, POCAHONTAS is a candy-coated lesson in tolerance and the ennobling power of love. English adventurer John Smith (voiced by Mel Gibson) and his crew arrive in the New World in 1607, under the command of rapacious Governor Ratcliffe (David Ogden Stiers), who lusts for gold. Smith and Algonquian maiden Pocahontas (newcomer Irene Bedard) fall in love. Relations between the Native Americans and the settlers quickly deteriorate and war seems inevitable, but Pocahontas saves Smith's life and her selflessness shames everyone into doing the right thing.

POCAHONTAS breaks the Disney mold in several small but significant ways. Unlike generations of animated princesses, the capable Pocahontas doesn't waste much time waiting for her prince. She's too busy canoeing over waterfalls, harvesting corn, and chatting with a wise old tree spirit (Linda Hunt). It's also the first Disney film based on the life of a real person, though it's been widely criticized for the many liberties taken with historical fact. And it doesn't have a doggedly happy ending—the chaste lovers part at the end, returning to their own people rather than running off together to seek improbable bliss. Still, in many respects, POCAHONTAS embodies the Disney style flawlessly. It's technically polished, gently preachy, and a beautifully realized piece of feature-length animation. But it's visually subdued, all cool greens and blues, and the score is unusually bland: there's nothing here to match THE LION KING's toe-tapping "Hakuna Matata" number.

POCKETFUL OF MIRACLES

1961 136m c Crime/Comedy ★★★½
Franton (U.S.) /U

Glenn Ford *(Dave, the Dude, Conway)*, Bette Davis *(Apple Annie, "Mrs. E. Worthington Manville")*, Hope Lange *(Elizabeth "Queenie" Martin)*, Arthur O'Connell *(Count Alfonso Romero)*, Peter Falk *(Joy Boy)*, Thomas Mitchell *(Judge Henry G. Blake)*, Edward Everett Horton *(Hutchins, the Butler)*, Mickey Shaughnessy *(Junior)*, David Brian *(Governor)*, Sheldon Leonard *(Steve Darcey)*

p, Frank Capra; d, Frank Capra; w, Hal Kanter, Harry Tugend, Jimmy Cannon (based on the story "Madame La Gimp" by Damon Runyon and the screenplay LADY FOR A DAY by Robert Riskin); ph, Robert Bronner; ed, Frank P. Keller; m, Walter Scharf, Peter Ilich Tchaikovsky; art d, Hal Pereira, Roland Anderson; fx, Farciot Edouart; chor, Nick Castle; cos, Edith Head, Walter Plunkett

AAN Best Supporting Actor: Peter Falk; *AAN Best Song:* James Van Heusen (Music), Sammy Cahn (Lyrics); *AAN Best Costume Design:* Edith Head, Walter Plunkett

This was Frank Capra's swan song as a producer-director, and although it was not well received upon initial release, it's still a good movie with some outstanding performances. New York gangster Dave "the Dude" Conway (Glenn Ford) is a superstitious type who believes he can't come to any harm as long as he continues to buy his daily apple from Apple Annie (Bette Davis), a drunken fruit vendor. In essence, Dave's belief is that "an apple a day keeps the Mafia away," and although his bodyguard, Joy Boy (Peter Falk), and chauffeur, Junior (Mickey Shaughnessy), think it's a lot of hooey, his girlfriend (Hope Lange) goes along with whatever Dave wants. When Apple Annie isn't at her usual street corner one morning, Dave goes looking for her. He finds her in deep depression because her daughter, Louise (Ann-Margret, in her first role), who thinks her mother is a wealthy matron, is coming to pay a visit. With Dave's help, Apple Annie is able to pull off her charade as "Mrs. E. Worthington Manville," even receiving help from the mayor, the governor, and a horde of real socialites. A remake of Capra's picture LADY FOR A DAY.

POINT BLANK

1967 92m c Crime ★★★★½
Bernard/Winkler (U.S.)

Lee Marvin *(Walker)*, Angie Dickinson *(Chris)*, Keenan Wynn *(Fairfax, "Yost")*, Carroll O'Connor *(Brewster)*, Lloyd Bochner *(Frederick Carter)*, Michael Strong *(Stegman)*, John Vernon *(Mal Reese)*, Sharon Acker *(Lynne)*, James B. Sikking *(Hired Gun)*, Sandra Warner *(Waitress)*

p, Judd Bernard, Robert Chartoff; d, John Boorman; w, Alexander Jacobs, David Newhouse, Rafe Newhouse (based on the novel *The Hunter* by Richard Stark (*aka* Donald E. Westlake)); ph, Philip Lathrop; ed, Henry Berman; m, Johnny Mandel; art d, George W. Davis, Albert Brenner; fx, Virgil Beck, J. McMillan Johnson; cos, Margo Weintz

The ultimate arty 60s thriller, and we mean that as a compliment. John Boorman's second film (after HAVING A WILD WEEKEND) and his first US production, POINT BLANK layers some of the stylistic traits of the French New Wave onto a quintessentially American thriller. The result is a breathtakingly composed genre classic, and a surprisingly complex allegory of modern urban life.

After pulling off a successful heist from the mob, Walker (Lee Marvin) is double-crossed by his wife (Sharon Acker) and his partner-in-crime (John Vernon), who shoots him and leaves him for dead in a cell of the now-deserted Alcatraz prison. Walker survives, escapes, and moves to L.A. There, he begins a search for revenge (and for his share of the loot) that takes him through successively elevated ranks of an organized crime syndicate that is increasingly hard to distinguish from a legitimate business organization. After he tracks down his wife, she commmits suicide; he is then aided in his quest by her sister, Chris (Angie Dickinson), and by a shadowy figure (Keenan Wynn) who steers Walker toward each fresh target with unerring accuracy.

A deceptively simple action film, POINT BLANK actually succeeds on many levels. As a thriller, it is fast, suspenseful, and peppered with the kind of brilliantly stylized violence now associated with Quentin Tarantino. On a purely visual level, it is an absolute treasure; Philip Lathrop's widescreen compositions continually make you want to stop the film to take in particular images, or re-run particularly impressive scenes: Walker fighting two hoods in a nightclub, against a swirling psychedelic backdrop, to the strains of the house R&B band; Chris futilely pounding Walker with her fists, until she sinks into a useless heap at his feet (he never flinches); Walker trashing a sports car just to intimidate his passenger.

Based on the novel by Richard Stark (*aka* Donald Westlake), POINT BLANK reaches beyond genre conventions to make pertinent social and existential observations. Its artsy effects (time lapses, echoing dialogue-flashbacks, etc.) suggest an alternative storyline, in which our hero dies in that opening scene, and the entire revenge plot is a dream/wish-fulfilment experienced in his last moments of consciousness. And Walker, anachronistically seeking retribution according to a code that seems outmoded in contemporary, corporate LA, is a figure both brutal and poignant—a fully realized tragic hero.

POLICE

1984 113m c Crime ★★★
TF1/Gaumont (France)

Gerard Depardieu *(Mangin)*, Sophie Marceau *(Noria)*, Richard Anconina *(Lambert)*, Pascale Rocard *(Marie Vedret)*, Sandrine Bonnaire *(Lydie)*, Franck Karoui *(Rene)*, Jonathan Leina *(Simon Slimane)*, Meaachou Bentahar *(Claude)*

p, Emmanuel Schlumberger; d, Maurice Pialat; w, Catherine Breillat, Sylvie Danton, Jacques Fieschi, Maurice Pialat (based on a story by Catherine Breillat); ph, Luciano Tovoli; ed, Yann Dedet; m, Henryk Mikolaj Gorecki; art d, Constantine Mejinsky; cos, Malika Brahim

A hard-bitten expose of the volatile Parisian criminal underworld, starring Gerard Depardieu as a brawny, animalistic cop who crosses over to the other side of the law when it suits him.

The film opens with a long, purposely tedious interrogation scene as Mangin (Depardieu) plays a game of cat-and-mouse with a nervous North African drug dealer. Mangin follows his leads to drug dealer Simon (Jonathan Leina), a Tunisian who has come to Paris with his many brothers and his streetwise, sensual teenage sister Noria (Sophie Marceau). Mangin nabs them both and throws them into jail. Upon her release, Noria contrives a clever plan to steal a cache of drug money, gradually luring Mangin into the scam.

If not wholly successful as a narrative, POLICE displays a welcome stylistic restraint. Director Pialat not only allows his actors the freedom of improvisation, but also avoids censoring their characters, passing no judgment on their moral qualities. Certain scenes drag, others are perhaps too diffuse and improvisatory. Depardieu is excellent, though his abrupt change from brute to sensitive lover is perhaps too conspicuous. Marceau proves her range by turning in a performance poles apart from her charming, dewy teenager in LA BOUM.

POLTERGEIST

1982 114m c Horror ★★
MGM-UA (U.S.) PG/15

Craig T. Nelson *(Steve)*, JoBeth Williams *(Diane)*, Beatrice Straight *(Dr. Lesh)*, Dominique Dunne *(Dana)*, Oliver Robins *(Robbie)*, Heather O'Rourke *(Carol Anne)*, Zelda Rubinstein *(Tangina)*, Martin Casella *(Marty)*, Richard Lawson *(Ryan)*, Michael McManus *(Tuthill)*

p, Steven Spielberg, Frank Marshall; d, Tobe Hooper; w, Steven Spielberg, Michael Grais, Mark Victor; ph, Matthew F. Leonetti; ed, Michael Kahn; m, Jerry Goldsmith; prod d, James H. Spencer; cos, L.J. Mower

AAN Best Score: Jerry Goldsmith; *AAN Best Visual Effects:* Richard Edlund, Michael Wood, Bruce Nicholson; *AAN Best Sound Effects Editing:* Stephen Hunter Flick, Richard L Anderson

A vapid, silly horror movie with occasional moments of promise that ultimately fails due to an overdose of cuteness.

Steve and Diane (Craig T. Nelson and JoBeth Williams) are a happy suburban couple who suddenly find that their perfect house in the perfect neighborhood has begun acting funny, scaring their perfect children. They really sit up and take notice, however, when wide-eyed young daughter Carol Anne (Heather O'Rourke) becomes possessed by late-night television and gets sucked into limbo by God knows what. Enter clairvoyant Tangina (Zelda Rubinstein), who surmises that the subdivision was built on a sacred Indian burial ground and that the gods aren't happy. POLTERGEIST is frustrating because one gets a hint of what director Tobe Hooper *really* wanted to do, but it's obvious that he was restrained by producer Steven Spielberg. The problem is, some of the truly horrifying moments slip through the censorship cracks, scaring little kids (and their parents), leaving POLTERGEIST a very disjointed, uneven movie.

POOR COW

1967 101m c Drama   ★★½
Vic/Fenchurch (U.K.)   /15

Carol White *(Joy)*, Terence Stamp *(Dave)*, John Bindon *(Tom)*, Kate Williams *(Beryl)*, Queenie Watts *(Aunt Emm)*, Geraldine Sherman *(Trixie)*, James Beckett, Billy Murray *(Tom's Friends)*, Simon King *(Johnny, Age 1 1/2)*, Stevie King *(Johnny, Age 3)*

p, Joseph Janni; d, Kenneth Loach; w, Kenneth Loach, Nell Dunn (based on her novel); ph, Brian Probyn; ed, Roy Watts; m, Donovan; art d, Bernard Sarron

By-the-book British realism from often interesting director Ken Loach (RIFF-RAFF). Joy (Carol White), a lumpen Cockney housewife, suffers in a dingy London flat with her swinish husband (John Bindon), a petty thief; when he's sent to jail, she moves in with Dave (Terence Stamp), who's a criminal associate of her husband. Surprisingly, Dave turns out to be a gentle and caring man who treats Joy's son with affection; but their fleeting happiness ends when Dave is also arrested. On her own, Joy ekes out a living as a barmaid and sometime nude model, treating herself to an occasional affair. She begins divorce proceedings, but when her husband is released she resolves to patch things up for the benefit of their son. While the film deserves praise for its unusual sensitivity to a woman's point of view, it's earnest to a fault and sometimes painfully dreary.

PORGY AND BESS

1959 138m c Musical   ★★★½
Goldwyn (U.S.)   /A

Sidney Poitier *(Porgy)*, Dorothy Dandridge *(Bess)*, Sammy Davis Jr. *(Sportin' Life)*, Pearl Bailey *(Maria)*, Brock Peters *(Crown)*, Leslie Scott *(Jake)*, Diahann Carroll *(Clara)*, Ruth Attaway *(Serena)*, Clarence Muse *(Peter)*, Everdinne Wilson *(Annie)*

p, Samuel Goldwyn; d, Otto Preminger; w, N. Richard Nash (based on the operetta by George Gershwin, Ira Gershwin, DuBose Heyward, the play by DuBose Heyward, Dorothy Heyward, and the novel by DuBose Heyward); ph, Leon Shamroy; ed, Daniel Mandell; m, George Gershwin; prod d, Oliver Smith; art d, Serge Krizman, Joseph C. Wright; chor, Hermes Pan; cos, Irene Sharaff

AAN Best Cinematography: Leon Shamroy; *AA Best Score:* Andre Previn, Ken Darby; *AAN Best Costume Design:* Irene Sharaff; *AAN Best Sound:* Gordon E. Sawyer, Fred Hynes

With a budget of over $6 million, why wasn't this classic American operetta a classic American movie? Perhaps the fault lies in Samuel Goldwyn's decision to fire director Rouben Mamoulian in favor of Otto Preminger—if anyone could muddle a great saga, it was Preminger. The crippled Porgy (Sidney Poitier) loves Bess (Dorothy Dandridge), a floozy adored by many men, including Crown (Brock Peters), a tough stevedore, and Sportin' Life (Sammy Davis, Jr.), who supplies her with heroin and who is always trying to lure her away from life in Catfish Row. After Crown kills a man in an argument over a game of craps and must flee the police, Bess settles in with Porgy. When Crown returns, wanting Bess back, Porgy kills him in turn, then hides out, while Bess agrees to follow Sportin' Life to New York. Porgy comes back to Catfish Row, learns that she's left, and is determined to follow her as the film ends—a simple story carried into the stratosphere by the glorious music. Poitier, not yet a star, initially accepted the role of Porgy, then

declined, reportedly because of feeling within the black community that the story was racist, until producer Goldwyn and Mamoulian again convinced him to do the project. His singing voice and Dandridge's are dubbed; Davis, Pearl Bailey (as Maria), and Peters all do their own singing. (As Clara, Diahann Carroll, a wonderful nightclub singer lacking operatic range, also has her voice looped.) Shooting was delayed when fire decimated the Goldwyn lot, and in the month it took to rebuild everything, Goldwyn and Mamoulian began to have "creative differences." Thus Preminger was called in to replace Mamoulian, with rather heavy-handed results. The brilliant score by the Gershwins and DuBose Heyward, however, will last forever, while Preminger's veteran cameraman, Leon Shamroy, did a wonderful job and the art direction by Serge Krizman and Joseph Wright is sensational.

PORK CHOP HILL

1959 97m bw War   ★★★★
Melville (U.S.)   /PG

Gregory Peck *(Lt. Clemons)*, Harry Guardino *(Forstman)*, Rip Torn *(Lt. Russell)*, George Peppard *(Fedderson)*, James Edwards *(Cpl. Jurgens)*, Bob Steele *(Kern)*, Woody Strode *(Franklin)*, George Shibata *(Lt. O'Hashi)*, Norman Fell *(Sgt. Coleman)*, Robert Blake *(Velie)*

p, Sy Bartlett; d, Lewis Milestone; w, James R. Webb (based on a story by S.L.A. Marshall); ph, Sam Leavitt; ed, George Boemler; m, Leonard Rosenman; prod d, Nicolai Remisoff; cos, Edward Armand

A grim, harrowing film detailing a single brutal Korean War battle, PORK CHOP HILL was directed by veteran helmsman Lewis Milestone and is the third entry in his informal trilogy devoted to 20th-century military conflict (ALL QUIET ON THE WESTERN FRONT was set during WWI, and A WALK IN THE SUN during WWII). Gregory Peck plays the commander of an Army company that is ordered to take Pork Chop Ridge, an inconsequential tactical objective. Compounding the seeming pointlessness of the assignment are the Panmunjom peace talks, which the troops believe may end the war at any minute, so that they are reluctant to participate in what may be its final battle. PORK CHOP HILL is an ode to the common American infantryman, soldiers who manage to retain their honor and dignity despite being ordered into an insane action by a top brass unwilling to lose face to the enemy, even though the conflict's end appears imminent. Peck is outstanding as the resolute but compassionate commander, and Rip Torn, Harry Guardino, Woody Strode, James Edwards (veteran of Sam Fuller's excellent Korean War film THE STEEL HELMET), and Robert Blake provide solid support. Moreover, Milestone employs his considerable technical skills to create an authentic and memorable cinematic experience, projecting a grim realistic air that captures the forlorn atmosphere of the meaningless mission. Sam Leavitt's photography is topnotch and depicts this heroic battle in such stark detail that the viewer can almost smell the acrid fumes of cordite and taste the dust blown from the dead ridge. This powerful movie and HAMBURGER HILL, which deals similarly with an assault during the Vietnam War, would make a very interesting double bill.

PORT OF SHADOWS
(QUAI DES BRUMES)

1938 91m bw Drama   ★★★★
Gregor Rabinovitch (France)

Jean Gabin *(Jean)*, Michele Morgan *(Nelly)*, Michel Simon *(Zabel)*, Pierre Brasseur *(Lucien Laugardier)*, Robert Le Vigan *(Michel Krauss)*, Jenny Burnay *(Lucien's Friend)*, Marcel Peres *(Chauffeur)*, Rene Genin *(Doctor)*, Edouard Delmont *(Panama)*, Raymond Aimos *(Quart-Vittel)*

p, Gregor Rabinovitch; d, Marcel Carne; w, Jacques Prevert (based on the novel *Le Quai Des Brumes* by Pierre Mac Orlan); ph, Eugene Schuftan, Louis Page; ed, Rene Le Henaff; m, Maurice Jaubert; prod d, Alexander Trauner

This marvelous distillation of the prevailing mood in prewar France was the first feature to win critical acclaim for the directing-writing team of Marcel Carne and Jacques Prevert (who had collaborated on JENNY and BIZARRE, BIZARRE, and who would later create the beloved CHILDREN OF PARADISE). Gabin plays a deserter who comes to the port of Le Havre looking for passage to a distant country. In a local dive he becomes attracted to Morgan, ward of the owner of a shop that is a front for illicit dealing. When Gabin comes to Simon's shop to buy a gift for Morgan, the evil Simon promises Gabin a passport and money if he will kill one of Simon's enemies. Gabin refuses. But hope for Gabin's escape comes when visionary artist Le Vigan gives the deserter his own passport before walking out on the quay and drowning himself.

A classic of French poetic realism, PORT OF SHADOWS conveys a deeply fatalistic belief that humankind is at the mercy of malevolent fate, a message that is communicated both through the simple story line and through the superb fog-shrouded sets (the work of Alexander Trauner) and forbidding locations. Ironically, PORT OF SHADOWS was originally to have been a German production. Carne was introduced to the Mac Orlan novel on which the picture is loosely based by Raoul Ploquin, then head of French productions at UFA in Berlin. Nazi propaganda minister Josef Goebbels turned thumbs down on the project, however; he considered this story of a deserter to be decadent. The rights were sold to French producer Gregor Rabinovitch, who envisioned a lighter, happier film, and so quarreled constantly with Carne. Carne also had political problems within his own country, primarily with the French minister of war, who would not permit the word "deserter" to be used and insisted that Gabin's soldier's uniform be treated respectfully. As a result, writer Prevert was forced to deviate from the novel in almost every respect. Notably, in the book, Morgan's heroine is no tempest-tossed innocent; she is a prostitute who murders her pimp and ends up wealthy. Banned from being shown during the Nazi occupation of France.

PORTRAIT OF A LADY, THE

1996 144m c Drama ★★★½
Propaganda Films (New Zealand/U.K./U.S.) PG-13/12

Nicole Kidman (Isabel Archer), John Malkovich (Gilbert Osmond), Barbara Hershey (Madame Serena Merle), Martin Donovan (Ralph Touchett), Shelley Winters (Mrs. Touchett), John Gielgud (Mr. Touchett), Richard E. Grant (Lord Warburton), Shelley Duvall (Countess Gemini), Christian Bale (Edward Rosier), Viggo Mortensen (Caspar Goodwood)

p, Monty Montgomery, Steve Golin; d, Jane Campion; w, Laura Jones (based on the novel by Henry James); ph, Stuart Dryburgh; ed, Veronika Jenet; m, Wojiech Kilar; prod d, Janet Patterson; art d, Martin Childs; cos, Janet Patterson

AAN Best Supporting Actress: Barbara Hershey; *AAN Best Costume Design:* Janet Patterson

Director Jane Campion's feminist intentions are clear in this adaptation of Henry James's classic novel. While it lacks the power and originality of her previous films, PORTRAIT offers much to be admired.

Isabel Archer (Nicole Kidman), a young American orphan, has come to live at the English estate of her wealthy aunt and uncle (John Gielgud and Shelley Winters) and their consumptive son, Ralph (Martin Donovan). An independently minded young woman, Isabel declines two attractive marriage proposals. She instead finds inspiration in the worldly independence of a mysterious widow, Madame Merle (Barbara Hershey), and the two become fast friends. After her uncle dies, Isabel is bequeathed a surprisingly large fortune and she travels to Italy, where Madame Merle introduces her to Gilbert Osmond (John Malkovich). An American expatriate with exquisite taste but little money, Osmond seduces Isabel into marriage. Soon, however, Osmond lets his true nature be known, and Isabel's dream of independence becomes a nightmare of imprisonment.

Campion takes the title of James's novel fully to heart, offering up an enticing visual portrait of a woman constrained by the limits of a patriarchal society. Despite a few too many obvious visual metaphors, Campion takes some commendable risks, such as fantasy sequences and changes in film speed. Kidman's thoughtful portrayal has depth, but she's unable to measure up to the character's strength and intelligence. At this point in his career, Malkovich's villain feels cliched, but Hershey is a revelation: her complex portrayal of a ruthless woman torn between the need to provide for herself and a genuine horror at her own manipulations is both chilling and heartbreaking. Drawing parallels

between the 19th century and the present, Campion creates her own portrait of modern femininity, while exposing the persistent social structures with which it is necessarily framed.

PORTRAIT OF JENNIE

1948 86m c/bw Romance ★★★★
Vanguard (U.S.)

Jennifer Jones (Jennie Appleton), Joseph Cotten (Eben Adams), Ethel Barrymore (Miss Spinney), Cecil Kellaway (Mr. Matthews), David Wayne (Gus O'Toole), Albert Sharpe (Mr. Moore), Florence Bates (Mrs. Jekes the Landlady), Lillian Gish (Mother Mary of Mercy), Henry Hull (Eke), Esther Somers (Mrs. Bunce)

p, David O. Selznick; d, William Dieterle; w, Paul Osborn, Peter Berneis, Leonardo Bercovici (based on the novel by Robert Nathan); ph, Joseph August; ed, William Morgan; m, Dimitri Tiomkin; prod d, J. McMillan Johnson; art d, Joseph B. Platt; fx, Clarence Slifer, Paul Eagler, J. McMillan Johnson; cos, Lucinda Ballard, Anna Hill Johnstone

AAN Best Cinematography: Joseph August; *AA Best Visual Effects:* Paul Eagler, Joseph McMillan Johnson, Russell Shearman, Clarence Slifer, Charles Freeman, James G. Stewart

An eerie love story, PORTRAIT OF JENNIE offers superb performances from Cotten, as a struggling painter, and Jones, as a girl from the past with whom he falls in love. It is 1932, the nadir of the Depression, and Cotten, a young painter who feels that his work lacks depth, sits glumly in New York City's Central Park, contemplating his not-so-bright future. A beautiful young girl, Jones, approaches him and begins to speak with him, using strange words that belong to a previous era, mentioning that she attends a convent school and that her parents are trapeze artists at Hammerstein's Opera House. She sings Cotten a haunting song, then disappears as abruptly as she appeared. Afterwards, Cotten struggles on with his art, encouraged by wealthy art dealer Barrymore, who takes a motherly interest in him, buying his water colors even though she knows they are poor, and suggesting that he try a new medium. Jones turns up periodically throughout that winter, while Cotten finds work painting a mural on the wall of an Irish saloon, a commission arranged by Cotten's good friend Wayne, a cab driver. Each time Jones reappears through the following spring and summer, she seems older by years, growing up from adolescence to young womanhood. Cotten asks her to sit for a portrait and finishes it just as she tells him she's about to graduate from college. When Barrymore and her associate, Kellaway, see the portrait of Jones, they hail it as a startling, innovative work by the hitherto unpromising Cotten that will surely establish his artistic reputation. Yet Cotten is haunted by Jones and begins to look into her background, discovering that her parents were killed in a highwire accident. Moreover, he finds out from Gish, the mother superior at an all-girl college, that Jones was in fact killed during a hurricane in New England in the 1920s. Cotten refuses to believe that the girl he painted is a ghost, but on the eve of the hurricane's anniversary, he rushes to New England. There, Jones comes to him during a raging storm and tells him that their love will live across the barriers of time, then vanishes for good. Eventually, Cotten begins to doubt he ever really met the beautiful girl, but when he finds her scarf, he begins to believe that he will meet his true love again in the afterlife after all.

Dieterle's direction is sensitive and the sequences are wonderfully constructed, with no scene bruising the next. He draws forth stellar performances, especially from Cotten; Jones is seen too briefly, but projects a genuinely ethereal quality during her moments on the screen. August's photography is stunning, and Tiomkin's lyrical score, drawn from Claude Debussy's themes (principally "The Afternoon of a Faun") is highly memorable. The foreword of the film, written by Ben Hecht, sums up the story's effect: "Out of the shadows of knowledge, and out of a painting that hung on a museum wall, comes our story, the truth of which lies not on our screen but in your heart." (A similar story of love that crosses mortal boundaries is at the core of a Hecht romance of considerable note, MIRACLE IN THE RAIN.)

POSTCARDS FROM THE EDGE

1990 101m c Comedy/Drama   ★★★
Columbia (U.S.)   R/15

Meryl Streep (Suzanne Vale), Shirley MacLaine (Doris Mann), Dennis Quaid (Jack Falkner), Gene Hackman (Lowell), Richard Dreyfuss (Dr. Frankenthal), Rob Reiner (Joe Pierce), Mary Wickes (Grandma), Conrad Bain (Grandpa), Annette Bening (Evelyn Ames), Simon Callow (Simon Asquith)

p, Mike Nichols, John Calley; d, Mike Nichols; w, Carrie Fisher (based on her novel); ph, Michael Ballhaus; ed, Sam O'Steen; m, Carly Simon; prod d, Patrizia Von Brandenstein; art d, Kandy Stern; cos, Ann Roth

AAN Best Actress: Meryl Streep; AAN Best Song: Shel Silverstein

Adapted by Fisher from her first novel, POSTCARDS FROM THE EDGE is yet further proof that Hollywood makes its best films about what it knows best—making films in Hollywood. But while POSTCARDS is entertainingly observant of the filmmaking scene, too much time is taken up with the cliched mother-daughter drama at the film's core. Continuing in the dark comedy vein she began in SHE DEVIL, Streep, as actress Suzanne Vale, starts at rock bottom. Working on a film, Suzanne is so addled by a cocaine habit that her director, Lowell (Hackman), must threaten her life just to get her focused. When she overdoses on sedatives while in bed with Jack Falkner (Quaid), the womanizing producer anonymously wheels her into a hospital emergency room. There her stomach is pumped by a doctor (Dreyfuss) who later asks her out on a date. During her rehabilitation, Suzanne must contend with a therapist (CCH Pounder from BAGDAD CAFE) whose grab-bag of self-help slogans is enough to drive a patient back to drugs. Upon completing her clinical rehab, Suzanne finds she is only able to find work on a low-budget cop movie. She's also required to live with her domineering, alcoholic, entertainer-mom, Doris (MacLaine playing Debbie Reynolds), the too-obvious cause of Suzanne's problems.

Director Nichols and Fisher manage to slip a few provocative ideas in here. Notably, Suzanne's return to sobriety is hardly rewarding; instead it provides her with a new sensitivity to the apathy and treachery of agents, producers, directors, lovers, and, most importantly, her mother. Suzanne's personal struggle is also contrasted throughout with Doris's nonstop, unrepentant boozing. The film suggests that sedation is an almost reasonable response to such a crazy life. In the final analysis, POSTCARDS is a mixed bag. There are a number of entertaining moments; however, potentially rich characters and situations wither from lack of development for the sake of the central relationship, which is never wholly convincing.

POSTMAN ALWAYS RINGS TWICE, THE

1946 113m bw Crime   ★★★★
MGM (U.S.)   /PG

Lana Turner (Cora Smith), John Garfield (Frank Chambers), Cecil Kellaway (Nick Smith), Hume Cronyn (Arthur Keats), Leon Ames (Kyle Sackett), Audrey Totter (Madge Gorland), Alan Reed (Ezra Liam Kennedy), Jeff York (Blair), Charles Williams (Jimmie White), A. Cameron Grant (Willie)

p, Carey Wilson; d, Tay Garnett; w, Harry Ruskin, Niven Busch (based on the novel by James M. Cain); ph, Sidney Wagner; ed, George White; m, George Bassman; art d, Cedric Gibbons, Randall Duell; cos, Irene, Marion Herwood Keyes

The best version of James M. Cain's torrid, hard-hitting romance comes to startling life under Garnett's shrewd direction, surprisingly at MGM. The studio threw in the towel on Turner's sweet parts and let her turn on the blowtorch and expose the seething passions. Although 1946 censors assured some downplaying of the heat between the leads, from the moment surly Garfield sees the "Man Wanted" sign, and Turner's lipstick rolls tauntingly across the floor, we know we're in for dangerous pulp romance. By the time the camera tilts from Turner's foot to the top of her white-hot visage, we know what the goods are and that Garfield's horny drifter is sold. If Turner is more girlish than Stanwyck in DOUBLE INDEMNITY, we also know it's a ruse she knows works with men.

Drifter Frank Chambers (Garfield) stops at a California roadside cafe owned by the amiable Nick Smith (Kellaway), who offers him a job as a handyman. Frank is disinclined toward such menial work until he catches a glimpse of Nick's siren wife, Cora (La Lana). He immediately takes the job and then begins making advances to a most receptive lady. The two become lovers ("Give me a kiss or I'll sock ya!") but what are they going to do about Nick?

Except for two scenes in which Turner wears black (one when she contemplates suicide and the other when she goes to her mother's funeral), the alluring platinum blond actress wears nothing but white in the film, further propelling her haughty phosphorescent steaminess: this angelically venal little trollop begged to be dirtied up. Though she is a femme fatale here, Turner is a softer, more emotionally vulnerable Lucrezia Borgia than her sisterly counterparts in other Cain stories. Even at the end she is seeking love, not revenge, telling Garfield after the murder that she wants "kisses that come from life, not death." So impressed was Cain with Turner's performance that he presented her with a leather-bound first edition of the novel, inscribing it, "For my dear Lana, thank you for giving a performance that was even finer than I expected."

The critical and public response to THE POSTMAN ALWAYS RINGS TWICE was enormous. Turner and Garfield won kudos from the critics, and the supporting players, especially Ames and Cronyn, received plaudits. The studio announced in 1972 that it would remake this film noir classic, but delays in casting and directing stalled the production until 1980 when Bob Rafelson took over the chore of directing Jack Nicholson and Jessica Lange. The remake was much less satisfying and much more crudely sexual, with Nicholson ravishing Lange on the kitchen table. For all the 80s heaving and pawing, the 1946 version is far more suggestive.

POSTMAN, THE
(IL POSTINO)

1994 113m c Comedy/Drama   ★★★½
Cecchi Gori Group/Tiger Cinematographica/Pentafilm   PG/15
/Esterno Mediterraneo Film/Blue Dahlia Productions/Le Studio
Canal Plus/K2T (Italy/France/Belgium)

Massimo Troisi (Mario Ruoppolo), Philippe Noiret (Pablo Neruda), Maria Grazia Cucinotta (Beatrice Russo), Linda Moretti (Donna Rosa), Renato Scarpa (Telegraph Operator), Anna Bonaiuto (Matilde), Mariana Rigillo (Di Cosimo), Bruno Alessandro (Pablo Neruda's Voice), Sergio Solli, Carlo di Maio

p, Mario Cecchi Gori, Vittorio Cecchi Gori, Gaetano Daniele; d, Michael Radford; w, Anna Pavignano, Michael Radford, Furio Scarpelli, Giacomo Scarpelli, Massimo Troisi (from a story by Furio Scarpelli and Giacomo Scarpelli based on the novel Burning Patience by Antonio Skarmeta); ph, Franco Di Giacomo; ed, Roberto Perpignani; m, Luis Enrique Bacalov; prod d, Lorenzo Baraldi; cos, Gianni Gissi

AAN Best Picture; AAN Best Actor: Massimo Troisi; AAN Best Director: Michael Radford; AAN Best Adapted Screenplay: Anna Pavignano, Michael Radford, Furio Scarpelli, Giacomo Scarpelli, Massimo Troisi; AA Best Dramatic Score: Luis Enrique Bacalov

In 1952, exiled Chilean dissident and poet Pablo Neruda traveled to Europe, where a nervous, deeply anti-Marxist Italian government tried to kick him out, eventually depositing him on the isle of Capri. That a famous Communist should have found himself living in a rich man's villa, learning about life from the "simplest people in the world," is the arch conceit underlying this finely wrought film.

Massimo Troisi plays Mario Ruoppolo, a listless fellow who lives with his father in a tiny fishing village. Mario has never liked fishing, and at his father's urging he finally finds a job as a postman, working for the district's Postmaster (Renato Scarpa), a Marxist. His village has never before needed a postman, but the arrival of Neruda (Philippe Noiret) has changed everything. To the shy Mario, Neruda is a charismatic but baffling figure. Only when Mario sets out to win the heart of his own Beatrice (Maria Grazia Cucinotta) does he begin to understand the real power of poetry.

Based on Burning Patience by Antonio Skarmeta, this film was a labor of love for Troisi, who sought Radford (1984, WHITE MISCHIEF) to direct and who shares a screenplay credit. The film has a gentle political edge, knocking Marxists and Christian Democrats with equal cheerfulness, and Troisi's self-deprecating humor, sly delivery, and melancholic charm are inimitable. Troisi, who suffered from a congenital heart defect, postponed surgery to complete the film, and died the day after shooting wrapped. The actor's fate hangs over every minute of THE POSTMAN (which he shot in small bursts, often an hour or less in a day), and necessarily frames the audience's response. When, toward the end, Mario discovers that Neruda has forgotten all about him, he shrugs it off, saying he was a fool to expect more. It is impossible to be unmoved by a dying man's despairing assumption that nobody will remember him.

PRAISE MARX AND PASS THE AMMUNITION

1970 90m c Political/Comedy   ★★
Mithras   (U.K.)   /X

John Thaw *(Dom)*, Edina Ronay *(Lucy)*, Luis Mahoney *(Julius)*, Anthony Villaroel *(Arthur)*, Helen Fleming *(Clara)*, David David *(Lal)*, Tanya *(Paraguayan Girl)*, Eva Enger *(Swedish Girl)*, Tandy Cronyn *(American Girl)*, Tina Packer *(Air Hostess)*

p, Maurice Hatton; d, Maurice Hatton; w, Maurice Hatton (based on an idea by Maurice Hatton, Michael Wood); ph, Charles Stewart; ed, Eduardo Guedes, Tim Lewis; m, Carl Davis; art d, Nick Pollock

Thaw stars as a Marxist who travels around Britain trying to start a revolution but who spends most of his time in bed with the women willing to listen to his political rambling. Suspected by party leaders of not being a "true" revolutionary, Thaw is captured and brought before a tribunal located in a warehouse. College-level theoretical political discourse is thrown back and forth until the cops come and break things up. Pretty tedious unless one enjoys pretentious counterculture nostalgia.

PRANCER

1989 103m c Drama   ★★★½
Raffaella/Nelson/Cineplex Odeon   (U.S.)   G/U

Sam Elliott *(John Riggs)*, Rebecca Harrell *(Jessica Riggs)*, Cloris Leachman *(Mrs. McFarland)*, Rutanya Alda *(Aunt Sarah)*, John Joseph Duda *(Steve Riggs)*, Abe Vigoda *(Dr. Orel Benton)*, Michael Constantine *(Mr. Stewart/Santa)*, Ariana Richards *(Carol Wetherby)*, Mark Rolston *(Herb Drier)*, Johnny Galecki *(Billy Quinn)*

p, Raffaella De Laurentiis, Greg Taylor, Mike Petzold; d, John Hancock; w, Greg Taylor (based on his story); ph, Misha Suslov; ed, Dennis M. O'Connor; m, Maurice Jarre; prod d, Chester Kaczenski; art d, Marc Dabe; cos, Denny Burt

Plucky nine-year-old Jessica Riggs (Rebecca Harrell) resolutely believes in Santa Claus even though her schoolmates think she's a baby. When she finds Prancer, one of Saint Nick's famous reindeer, injured in nearby forest, Jessica secretly nurses the reindeer back to health, aided by an elderly veterinarian (Abe Vigoda). However, her attempts to help Prancer are complicated when she confides in a shopping-mall Santa (Michael Constantine), who spills the beans to the press, and by her father (Sam Elliott), who sells the reindeer to a merchant for use as part of a promotional stunt. When children's films are released for the holidays, one's heart sinks at the memory of such saccharine seasonal "gems" as SANTA CLAUS: THE MOVIE, and television's "It Came upon a Midnight Clear"; however, PRANCER marches to the beat of a different little drummer boy. Sensitively directed by John Hancock and filmed in the Indiana area where he grew up, the movie benefits from an authentic atmosphere, fleshed-out characters who behave as if they live in the real world, and an especially charming performance by Harrell. Good family films are as rare as flying reindeer, but PRANCER deserves to join the select ranks of those Christmas movies we return to again and again.

PREDATOR

1987 107m c Thriller/Science Fiction   ★★★½
Gordon/Silver/Davis/American Entertainment   R/18
Partners   (U.S.)

Arnold Schwarzenegger *(Maj. Alan "Dutch" Schaefer)*, Carl Weathers *(Dillon)*, Elpidia Carrillo *(Anna)*, Bill Duke *(Mac)*, Jesse Ventura *(Sgt. Blain)*, Sonny Landham *(Billy)*, Richard Chaves *(Pancho)*, R.G. Armstrong *(Gen. Phillips)*, Shane Black *(Hawkins)*, Kevin Peter Hall *(Predator)*

p, Lawrence Gordon, Joel Silver, John Davis; d, John McTiernan; w, Jim Thomas, John Thomas; ph, Don McAlpine; ed, John F. Link II, Mark Helfrich; m, Alan Silvestri; prod d, John Vallone; art d, Frank Richwood, Jorge Saenz, John K. Reinhart Jr.; fx, R/Greenberg, Joel Hynek, Stuart Robertson, Dream Quest Images, Al Di Sarro, Laurencio Cordero, Stan Winston

AAN Best Visual Effects: Joel Hynek, Robert M. Greenberg, Richard Greenberg, Stan Winston

Crisply stylish and suspenseful, making brilliant use of optical special effects, PREDATOR is one of Schwarzenegger's best. Director McTiernan (DIE HARD) nimbly sustains suspense throughout this tale of a special forces platoon assigned to locate an unnamed menace lurking in the jungles of Central America. The film is one of the cleverest of the many action pictures that allegorize Vietnam—its hardbitten soldiers, ill used by a government that lies to them about the real nature of their mission, face an invisible enemy that picks them off using guerilla tactics. In the end, however, the creature proves curiously sympathetic, and its final confrontation with Major Dutch Schaefer (Schwarzenegger) has tragic overtones.

PRESIDENT'S ANALYST, THE

1967 103m c Spy/Comedy   ★★★½
Panpiper   (U.S.)   /A

James Coburn *(Dr. Sidney Schaefer)*, Godfrey Cambridge *(Don Masters)*, Severn Darden *(Kropotkin)*, Joan Delaney *(Nan Butler)*, Pat Harrington Jr. *(Arlington Hewes)*, Barry Maguire *(Old Wrangler)*, Jill Banner *(Snow White)*, Eduard Franz *(Ethan Allan Cocket)*, Walter Burke *(Henry Lux)*, Will Geer *(Dr. Lee Evans)*

p, Stanley Rubin; d, Theodore J. Flicker; w, Theodore J. Flicker; ph, William A. Fraker; ed, Stuart Pappe; m, Lalo Schifrin; prod d, Pato Guzman; art d, Hal Pereira, Al Roelofs; cos, Jack Bear

Though it's now somewhat dated, at the time of its release this picture was a mostly-on-the-mark satire of American culture and international politics in the 1960s. Coburn plays a psychiatrist who serves his country as the analyst for the president of the United States. It isn't long before some in the government become concerned about what Coburn has learned in this position, and he's marked for assassination. However, other nations figure Coburn might be able to supply them with valuable information, and soon agents from around the globe are tracking the hapless psychiatrist. Among those in pursuit are American agent Cambridge, his longtime friend and adversary Russian agent Darden, and Arte Johnson and Martin Horsey as a couple of humorless "FBR" agents. Mindless bureaucracy, Cold War mentality, blind liberalism, and psychoanalysis are spoofed in this fast-paced comedy.

PRESUMED INNOCENT

1990 127m c Crime/Mystery   ★★★½
Mirage   (U.S.)   R/15

Harrison Ford *(Rusty Sabich)*, Brian Dennehy *(Raymond Horgan)*, Raul Julia *(Sandy Stern)*, Bonnie Bedelia *(Barbara Sabich)*, Paul Winfield *(Judge Larren Lyttle)*, Greta Scacchi *(Carolyn Polhemus)*, John Spencer *(Detective Lipranzer)*, Joe Grifasi *(Tommy Molto)*, Tom Mardirosian *(Nico Della Guardia)*, Anna Maria Horsford *(Eugenia)*

p, Sydney Pollack, Mark Rosenberg; d, Alan J. Pakula; w, Frank Pierson, Alan J. Pakula (based on the novel by Scott Turow); ph, Gordon Willis; ed, Evan Lottman; m, John Williams; prod d, George Jenkins; art d, Bob Guerra; fx, C5, Inc.; cos, John Boxer

If they gave an Oscar for the year's most claustrophobic film, PRE-SUMED INNOCENT could have won it in a walk. Everything about this film is as cramped, clenched, and constricted as Harrison Ford's face, which looks like a tightly balled-up fist here. However, Ford's perpetually coiled-up state also makes him a natural murder suspect in this adaptation of attorney Scott Turow's best-selling novel. Ford plays prosecuting attorney Rusty Sabich, the quintessential good soldier right down to his Roman Centurion haircut. But Sabich serves a degraded master, District Attorney Raymond Horgan (Brian Dennehy), a soured idealist whose principles have been compromised by years of deals made to keep the wheels of justice from grinding to a halt. As the film begins, Horgan is making a halfhearted run at re-election, but his campaign is fatally rocked by the sordid rape-murder of his star prosecutor in the sex-crimes division, the brilliant, beautiful, and ambitious Carolyn Polhemus (Scacchi). The list of suspects narrows to a single name when Sabich's fingerprints are found on a beer glass five feet from Polhemus' body and when tests reveal that the killer's blood type also matches that of Sabich, who had an affair with Polhemus that ended messily.

The solution to this whodunit will hardly surprise any of the millions who have read Turow's novel. However, neither the book nor the movie hinges on the killer's disclosure. Despite cinematographer Gordon Willis's penchant for underlit scenes of Sabich implausibly poring over legal documents in near-darkness, and Pakula's overemphasis on Sabich's weariness and dessication, PRESUMED INNOCENT is never less than engrossing.

PRETTY BABY

1978 109m c Drama   ★★★½
Paramount (U.S.)   R/18

Keith Carradine (*E.J. Bellocq*), Susan Sarandon (*Hattie*), Brooke Shields (*Violet*), Frances Faye (*Mme. Nell Livingston*), Antonio Fargas (*Professor, Piano Player*), Gerrit Graham (*Highpockets*), Mae Mercer (*Mama Mosebery*), Diana Scarwid (*Frieda*), Barbara Steele (*Josephine*), Matthew Anton (*Red Top*)

p, Louis Malle; d, Louis Malle; w, Polly Platt (based on a story by Platt and Malle, from the book *Storyville, New Orleans: Being an Authentic Account of the Notorious Redlight District* by Al Rose); ph, Sven Nykvist; ed, Suzanne Baron, Suzanne Fenn; prod d, Trevor Williams; fx, Maureen Lambray; cos, Mina Mittleman

AAN Best Score: Jerry Wexler

Beautifully shot and subtly rendered, but too slowly told for its ambiguities to really be effective. Violet (Brooke Shields) lives with her mother, Hattie (Susan Sarandon), a prostitute in 1917 New Orleans. Her touching innocence seems unaffected even when, at the age of twelve, her virginity is auctioned off for the princely sum of $400. After leaving the brothel to live for a while with photographer E.J. Bellocq (a real-life figure), Violet is eventually reunited with her mother, who has escaped the brothel for a more "respectable" life on the outside.

The strength of Malle's film lies in its simultaneous presentation of two viewpoints: that of Violet, whose sweetly innocent appreciation of her life is so convincing that we feel her entry into "civilized" society will be her downfall; and that of Bellocq, who sees the girl and her surroundings as both erotically compelling and artistically challenging. Cinematographer Nykvist does a superlative job of capturing this luxuriant world-unto-itself, but the pace is so slow that, by the end, we've given up caring about Malle's characters, let alone his critique of bourgeois morality.

PRETTY IN PINK

1986 96m c Comedy/Drama   ★★★
Paramount (U.S.)   PG-13/15

Molly Ringwald (*Andie Walsh*), Harry Dean Stanton (*Jack Walsh*), Jon Cryer (*Phil "Duckie" Dale*), Andrew McCarthy (*Blane McDonough*), Annie Potts (*Iona*), James Spader (*Steff McKee*), Jim Haynie (*Donnelly*), Alexa Kenin (*Jena*), Kate Vernon (*Benny*), Andrew Dice Clay (*Bouncer*)

p, Lauren Shuler; d, Howard Deutch; w, John Hughes; ph, Tak Fujimoto; ed, Richard Marks; m, Michael Gore; prod d, John W. Corso; chor, Kenny Ortega

Andie Walsh (Molly Ringwald) is a kid from the wrong side of the tracks. She's a self-confident high-school senior who dresses in handmade clothes, works in a record store, and lives in a modest home with her unemployed father (Harry Dean Stanton). Times are tough for Andie in school, where she and her friends are tormented by the wealthy students who make up the majority of the student body, and where her worst fear is that she won't get invited to the senior prom. Her best friend, "Duckie" (Jon Cryer), talks matter-of-factly with her father about marrying Andie, but he never thinks of taking her to the prom—a social event that most of the poor kids avoid. To her surprise, she is asked to go to the dance by the charming Blaine (Andrew McCarthy), who's not as snobbish as the rest of his elitist friends. As in all of John Hughes's films, PRETTY IN PINK touches a chord with today's teens (as well as anyone who has been that age), but at the same time seems to pander somewhat to the audience's expectations. Interestingly, however, the finest moments in PRETTY IN PINK come not from the script by Hughes, but from Howard Deutch's careful direction. While the script contains trite and unbelievable dialogue, the superbly convincing performances make up for these faults.

PRETTY POISON

1968 89m c Thriller   ★★★½
Lawrence Turman/Molino (U.S.)   /15

Anthony Perkins (*Dennis Pitt*), Tuesday Weld (*Sue Ann Stepanek*), Beverly Garland (*Mrs. Stepanek*), John Randolph (*Azenauer*), Dick O'Neill (*Bud Munsch*), Clarice Blackburn (*Mrs. Bronson*), Joe Bova (*Pete*), Ken Kercheval (*Harry Jackson*), Don Fellows (*Detective*), Parker Fennelly (*Night Watchman*)

p, Marshal Backlar, Noel Black; d, Noel Black; w, Lorenzo Semple Jr. (based on the novel *She Let Him Continue* by Stephen Geller); ph, David Quaid; ed, William Ziegler; m, Johnny Mandel; art d, Jack Martin Smith, Harold Michelson; fx, Ralph Winigar, Billy King; cos, Ann Roth

A fascinating thriller that was mostly ignored at the time of its release, this is a fine film with a terrific performance by Tuesday Weld. Perkins is again a mentally unstable young man. As a youth, after a fight with his aunt, he kills the woman by burning down her house, though he claims he didn't know she was inside. As the film opens, he's recently been released from prison and is being watched carefully by parole officer Randolph. He gets a job with a lumber company and meets Weld, a pert high-school student. To impress her, he tells her he's with the CIA and in town to investigate nasty business at the lumber company. The two soon begin a relationship, though Weld's domineering mother, Garland, thinks Perkins is a nut and tells her daughter to stay away from him. It isn't long before Perkins finds that Weld's sweet face hides a killer's psyche, and he finds himself caught in a murder wrap as he is cleverly manipulated by the calculating Weld. It's up to the wily Randolph to figure out what really happened. This was Noel Black's directorial debut, and he maintains a brisk pace and a necessary level of tension throughout. Perkins, of course, is fine in the kind of role he excels at, but it's Weld's performance that really makes the film something special. She is superb as the pretty young thing whose exterior cloaks an ice-cold killer. With this film and her fine performances in such movies as SOLDIER IN THE RAIN; THE CINCINNATI KID; and WHO'LL STOP THE RAIN?, she consistently proved herself to be an actress of depth who is much more than a pretty face and a silly name. The picture was made in Great Barrington, Massachusetts.

PRETTY WOMAN

1990 119m c Comedy/Romance   ★★½
Silver Screen Partners/Touchstone (U.S.)   R/15

Richard Gere (*Edward Lewis*), Julia Roberts (*Vivian Ward*), Ralph Bellamy (*James Morse*), Jason Alexander (*Phillip Stuckey*), Laura San Giacomo (*Kit De Luca*), Alex Hyde-White (*David Morse*), Amy Yasbeck (*Elizabeth Stuckey*), Elinor Donahue (*Bridget*), Hector Elizondo (*Hotel Manager*), Judith Baldwin (*Susan*)

p, Arnon Milchan, Steven Reuther; d, Garry Marshall; w, J.F. Lawton; ph, Charles Minsky; ed, Priscilla Nedd; m, James Newton Howard; prod d, Albert Brenner; art d, David M. Haber; fx, Gary Zink; cos, Marilyn Vance-Straker

AAN Best Actress: Julia Roberts

None too pretty. Director Garry Marshall, the sophisticated talent who gave the world "Laverne and Shirley," comes a cropper with this Happy Hooker harangue. Yes, Julia Roberts's goofy good looks and giggly charm have a certain glimmer about them, rather like expensively wrapped Christmas candy, but she's an actress of considerable shallowness. If anyone gets unwrapped in this film, it's Richard Gere, whose body is, interestingly enough, more on display than Roberts's or Laura San Giacomo's (who, by the way, gives the film's funniest performance). Maybe that's why some feminists liked the film—though most of them knew better. Otherwise, Gere's performance as a corporate takeover specialist who picks up a pneumatic fantasy whore is strictly paint-by-numbers. The silly script lurches from one jarring, implausible moment to another, and Marshall directs like he was wearing earplugs and boxing gloves on the set. OK, PRETTY WOMAN is supposed to be a fairy tale, but whose? Bound to offend prostitutes and millionaires everywhere, this flick is not the street-smart "Pgymalion" it desperately wants to be.

PRICK UP YOUR EARS

1987 111m c Biography	★★★½
Civilhand Zenith (U.K.)	R/18

Gary Oldman (*Joe Orton*), Alfred Molina (*Kenneth Halliwell*), Vanessa Redgrave (*Peggy Ramsay*), Wallace Shawn (*John Lahr*), Lindsay Duncan (*Anthea Lahr*), Julie Walters (*Elsie Orton*), James Grant (*William Orton*), Janet Dale (*Mrs. Sugden*), Dave Atkins (*Mr. Sugden*), Margaret Tyzack (*Mme. Lambert*)

p, Andrew Brown; d, Stephen Frears; w, Alan Bennett (based on the biography by John Lahr); ph, Oliver Stapleton; ed, Mick Audsley; m, Stanley Myers; prod d, Hugo Luczyc-Wyhowski; art d, Philip Elton; cos, Bob Ringwood

Stephen Frears's PRICK UP YOUR EARS chronicles the rise and tragic demise of Joe Orton, the gay playwright whose brief but dazzling career spawned the brilliant farces *Loot*, *Entertaining Mr. Sloan* and *What the Butler Saw* and made a lasting contribution to the English-language theater.

Born John Orton in Leicester, England, Orton died at age 34 in 1967 when his longtime lover, Kenneth Halliwell, crushed his skull with a hammer before downing two handfuls of Nembutal to take his own life. PRICK UP YOUR EARS opens with this grisly event, then unfolds in flashbacks as biographer John Lahr (Wallace Shawn) researches Orton's brief life.

This is director Frears's second film with an openly homosexual theme, the first being 1986's acclaimed MY BEAUTIFUL LAUNDRETTE, and he attempts to delve deeply into the relationship between the two protagonists. In real life, however, Halliwell was not the bearish brute that Molina's physical presence indicates; those who knew him say that he had a certain charm of his own as well as a Svengali influence over Orton. Other than the unfortunate miscasting of Molina, an otherwise superb actor, and Wallace Shawn's grating performance, everyone else is right on the money. Oldman, fresh from his triumph as Sex Pistol Sid Vicious in SID AND NANCY, is the key and holds it all together.

PRIDE AND PREJUDICE

1940 117m bw Drama	★★★★½
MGM (U.S.)	/U

Greer Garson (*Elizabeth Bennet*), Laurence Olivier (*Mr. Darcy*), Mary Boland (*Mrs. Bennet*), Edna May Oliver (*Lady Catherine de Bourgh*), Maureen O'Sullivan (*Jane Bennet*), Ann Rutherford (*Lydia Bennet*), Frieda Inescort (*Miss Caroline Bingley*), Edmund Gwenn (*Mr. Bennet*), Karen Morley (*Charlotte Lucas*), Heather Angel (*Kitty Bennet*)

p, Hunt Stromberg; d, Robert Z. Leonard; w, Aldous Huxley, Jane Murfin (based on the play by Helen Jerome and the novel by Jane Austen); ph, Karl Freund; ed, Robert J. Kern; m, Herbert Stothart; art d, Cedric Gibbons, Paul Groesse; chor, Ernst Matray; cos, Adrian, Gile Steele

AA Best Art Direction: Cedric Gibbons, Paul Groesse

We may be prejudiced, but MGM can be proud. A remarkable example of Hollywood's not choking on the prestige adorning the filming of a classic, PRIDE AND PREJUDICE is an unusually successful adaptation of Jane Austen's most famous novel. Although the satire is slightly reduced and coarsened and the period advanced in order to use more flamboyant costumes, the spirit is entirely in keeping with Austen's sharp, witty portrait of rural 19th century social mores. The film tells the familiar story of Mr. and Mrs. Bennet (Gwenn and Boland) and their five marriageable daughters. Jane (O'Sullivan) falls for the wealthy Mr. Bingley (Bruce Lester), but, unsure of her love and discouraged by his snooty sister (Inescourt) and his haughty friend Mr. Darcy (Olivier), he leaves town without any promises. The middle daughter, Mary (Marsha Hunt) is goofy and bookish, the fourth child Kitty (Angel) insecure and suggestible and the youngest, Lydia (Rutherford), overly flirtatious. Troubles really brew when Lydia runs off with a caddish officer (Edward Ashley) and when Darcy, who feels himself too "proud" to fall for just any woman, flips for the second Bennet daughter, the independent Elizabeth (Garson). She, however, "prejudiced" against him because of his arrogance, will have none of him. Meanwhile, her mother plans for her to wed their foppish cousin, Mr. Collins (Melville Cooper).

The screenplay, by Aldous Huxley and old hand Jane Murfin, retains much of the novel's famous dialogue (e.g., the opening conversation between Mr. and Mrs. Bennet). They have also added a few scenes to "open up" the action a bit; our favorites are the hilarious carriage race and the enchanting archery lesson. The sets and costumes are lovingly rendered and the cinematography by Karl Freund evokes a glorious sense of period. PRIDE AND PREJUDICE represents the finest directorial work by MGM perennial Robert Z. Leonard. Liked by actors whom he indulged, Leonard generally crafts his work smoothly but it often lacks personality or imagination. Here, however, the pacing is perfect and the details just right. For personality, all one has to do is turn to that amazing cast. Garson never did anything better than her Elizabeth Bennet. Genteel but not precious, witty yet not forced, spirited but never vulgar, Garson's Elizabeth is an Austen heroine incarnate. Olivier, too, has rarely been better in a part requiring the passion of his Heathcliff from WUTHERING HEIGHTS but strapping it into the straitjacket of snobbery. As Mr. Bennet, Gwenn makes a wonderfully wry and composed foil for his wife's antics, and Cooper rarely had the chance to huff and fluff quite so amusingly again.

PRIDE OF THE MARINES

1945 119m bw War	★★★★
Warner Bros. (U.S.)	/A

John Garfield (*Al Schmid*), Eleanor Parker (*Ruth Hartley*), Dane Clark (*Lee Diamond*), John Ridgely (*Jim Merchant*), Rosemary DeCamp (*Virginia Pfeiffer*), Ann Doran (*Ella Merchant*), Warren Douglas (*Kebabian*), Don McGuire (*Irish*), Tom D'Andrea (*Tom*), Rory Mallinson (*Doctor*)

p, Jerry Wald; d, Delmer Daves; w, Albert Maltz, Marvin Borowsky (based on a story by Roger Butterfield); ph, Peverell Marley; ed, Owen Marks; m, Franz Waxman; art d, Leo K. Kuter; fx, L. Robert Burgs

AAN Best Original Screenplay: Albert Maltz

A grand and emotional study in heroism, PRIDE OF THE MARINES is a tour de force for rugged Garfield and a film that allowed director Daves to introduce some startling psychological techniques which made this film exceptional. Based on the true story of Al Schmid, the film shows us Garfield as a workingman in Philadelphia who courts and marries Parker on the eve of WW II. Garfield enlists in the Marines and is sent to Guadalcanal, where he and his small machine gun crew receive orders to be on the alert for a massive Japanese attack. With extraordinary heroism, they fend off the assault, but not before Garfield is blinded. Now, in readjusting to life and marriage without his sight, Garfield must display heroism of a different kind.

Garfield is brilliant in his portrayal of Schmid, and Daves's direction is superb, utilizing remarkable techniques such as double printings, negative images, and telescopic shots which all add to the eerie and unnerving experience Garfield is undergoing in his rehabilitation. The battle scenes in this film are some of the most harrowing ever shot. The idea for the film was largely Garfield's. He read an article about Schmid in *Life* magazine and contacted writer Maltz, suggesting a script be written about the man. Maltz had worked on the film DESTINATION TOKYO, also directed by Daves, and Garfield felt he would be the ideal writer to handle the project. Daves was brought into the project a short time later. This film, along with AIR FORCE and DESTINATION TOKYO, was one of Garfield's favorite films made at Warner Bros. PRIDE OF THE MARINES was a box office smash, released just as WWII came to a close, timed perfectly with the public's curiosity about rehabilitating a generation of wounded American servicemen. Co-author Maltz later became one of the "Hollywood Ten," and some of the dialogue in PRIDE OF THE MARINES was later recalled by the House Un-American Activities Committee, particularly those lines dealing with social consciousness and working class arguments (mostly expressed by Clark), as an example of communistic philosophy insidiously inserted into movies. The film nevertheless remains a deeply moving, sensitive production, and one of the finest war films ever made.

PRIDE OF THE YANKEES, THE

1942 127m bw Biography/Sports ★★★★½
RKO (U.S.) /U

Gary Cooper (*Lou Gehrig*), Teresa Wright (*Eleanor Gehrig*), Walter Brennan (*Sam Blake*), Dan Duryea (*Hank Hanneman*), Babe Ruth (*Himself*), Elsa Janssen (*Mom Gehrig*), Ludwig Stossel (*Pop Gehrig*), Virginia Gilmore (*Myra*), Bill Dickey (*Himself*), Ernie Adams (*Miller Huggins*)

p, Samuel Goldwyn; d, Sam Wood; w, Jo Swerling, Herman J. Mankiewicz (based on a story by Paul Gallico); ph, Rudolph Mate; ed, Daniel Mandell; m, Leigh Harline; prod d, William Cameron Menzies; art d, Perry Ferguson, McClure Capps; fx, Jack Cosgrove; cos, Rene Hubert

AAN Best Picture; AAN Best Actor: Gary Cooper; AAN Best Actress: Teresa Wright; AAN Best Original Story: Paul Gallico; AAN Best Screenplay: Herman J. Mankiewicz, Jo Swerling; AAN Best Cinematography: Rudolph Mate; AA Best Editing: Daniel Mandell; AAN Best Score: Leigh Harline; AAN Best Art Direction: Perry Ferguson, Howard Bristol; AAN Best Sound: Thomas Moulton; AAN Best Visual Effects: Jack Cosgrove, Ray Binger, Thomas T. Moulton

Eloquently written (by Herman Mankiewicz and Jo Swerling from a story by Paul Gallico), stunningly photographed, and directed with great sensitivity, THE PRIDE OF THE YANKEES is the sweet, sentimental, and utterly American story of Lou Gehrig, the "Iron Man" first baseman of the indefatigable New York Yankees of the 1920s and 30s. Gary Cooper is exceptional as Gehrig and Teresa Wright marvelous as his sweetheart (and later wife), Eleanor.

Gehrig leads the Yankees to the World Series, becoming one of the best ever to play the game, until, in 1939, he learns that he has a lethal neurological disease (amyotrophic lateral sclerosis, since known as Lou Gehrig's disease) and has only a short time to live. He retires from baseball and makes a dramatic farewell at Yankee Stadium (perhaps the most famous scene in any sports film), standing at home plate and stating, "Some people say I've had a bad break, but I consider myself to be the luckiest man on the face of the earth."

THE PRIDE OF THE YANKEES is the story of a simple man with extraordinary talent and a soaring spirit that made him the idol of every American schoolboy. Although the film keeps the on-field action to a minimum, Cooper, a righthander, spent many weeks under the tutelage of Lefty O'Doul learning to bunt and throw lefthanded like Gehrig. To complete the illusion, Cooper wore a uniform with the numbers reversed and ran to third base instead of first so that when the film was processed, in reverse, he would appear to be swinging from the left side of the plate. Among the real-life Bronx Bomber teammates who appear in the film are Babe Ruth, Bill Dickey, Mark Koenig, and Bob Meusel.

PRIME CUT

1972 88m c Crime ★★★
Cinema Center (U.S.) R/18

Lee Marvin (*Nick Devlin*), Gene Hackman (*"Mary Ann"*), Angel Tompkins (*Clarabelle*), Gregory Walcott (*Weenie*), Sissy Spacek (*Poppy*), Janit Baldwin (*Violet*), William Morey (*Shay*), Clint Ellison (*Delaney*), Howard Platt (*Shaughnessy*), Les Lannom (*O'Brien*)

p, Joe Wizan; d, Michael Ritchie; w, Robert Dillon; ph, Gene Polito; ed, Carl Pingitore; m, Lalo Schifrin; art d, Bill Malley; fx, Logan Frazee; cos, Patricia Norris

Hackman is a degenerate Kansas City cattleman who sells as many girls as he does cows. Chicago gangster Marvin is sent to teach him a lesson on behalf of factory owners who are fed up with Hackman's insolence. Some of the more interesting aspects of this violent film from director Michael Ritchie are an unlikely setting for a gangster film (a country fair), a wheatfield chase scene (a la NORTH BY NORTHWEST), and a switch in casting (Hackman playing the louse and Marvin playing the relatively good guy). Ritchie breaks tradition by portraying the rural population as far more despicable than the city folk, referring to Chicago as being "as peaceful as anyplace anywhere." Sissy Spacek makes her film debut as one of Hackman's commodities.

PRIME OF MISS JEAN BRODIE, THE

1969 116m c Drama/Comedy ★★★★
Fox (U.K.) M/15

Maggie Smith (*Jean Brodie*), Robert Stephens (*Teddy Lloyd*), Pamela Franklin (*Sandy*), Gordon Jackson (*Gordon Lowther*), Celia Johnson (*Miss MacKay*), Diane Grayson (*Jenny*), Jane Carr (*Mary McGregor*), Shirley Steedman (*Monica*), Lavinia Lang (*Emily Carstairs*), Antoinette Biggerstaff (*Helen McPhee*)

p, Robert Fryer; d, Ronald Neame; w, Jay Presson Allen (based on the play by Allen from the novel by Muriel Spark); ph, Ted Moore; ed, Norman Savage; m, Rod McKuen; prod d, John Howell; art d, Brian Herbert; cos, Elizabeth Haffenden, Joan Bridge

AA Best Actress: Maggie Smith; AAN Best Song: Rod McKuen

Prime, indeed. In the Edinburgh of 1932, Smith teaches in an upscale private girls' school. She inspires her students with her ideas on art, music, and politics—the latter based on romantic notions that lead her to express admiration for the *fascisti* in Italy. Smith has assembled a small coterie of adoring students—including Carr, Grayson and Franklin—who follow her around. She even arranges to take them with her on one of her occasional visits to the country home of Jackson, a fellow teacher who is more interested in her than she is in him. Actually, she is romantically involved with Stephens, another teacher and a sometime painter, whose jealousy she hopes Jackson's attentions will arouse. Stephens, however, a married Catholic with children, balks at breaking up his marriage to make a commitment to Smith. Dour headmistress Johnson, meanwhile, takes a dim view of Smith's influence and has her suspicions about the impropriety of the teacher's actions. Young follower Franklin, annoyed by Smith's evaluation of her as scholarly and practical—and of Grayson as a romantic beauty—determines to seduce Stephens away from Smith.

Celia Johnson makes a formidable adversary for Smith, and Smith's then-husband Stephens is dead-on right as the art professor. Pamela Franklin, accomplished and lovely, does the best she can with the film's most difficult plot-fulcrum role. The movie loses some steam when it turns to romantic melodrama, but Smith keeps you watching to see how she works with it. Work she does, managing at the same time to make her unique brand of magic look easy as breathing. The film is slightly marred by Rod McKuen's insufferable title song.

PRINCE AND THE PAUPER, THE

1937 120m bw Adventure ★★★½
Warner Bros./First National (U.S.) /U

Errol Flynn (*Miles Hendon*), Claude Rains (*Earl of Hertford*), Henry Stephenson (*Duke of Norfolk*), Barton MacLane (*John Canty*), Billy Mauch (*Tom Canty*), Bobby Mauch (*Prince Edward*), Alan Hale (*Captain of the Guard*), Eric Portman (*1st Lord*), Montagu Love (*Henry VIII*), Robert Warwick (*Lord Warwick*)

p, Robert Lord; d, William Keighley; w, Laird Doyle (based on the novel by Mark Twain and the play by Catherine Chishold Cushing); ph, Sol Polito; ed, Ralph Dawson; m, Erich Wolfgang Korngold; art d, Robert Haas; fx, Willard Van Enger, James Gibbons; cos, Milo Anderson

This Mark Twain doppelganger tale of rags and royalty in 16th-century England is sumptuously produced and full of high drama and adventure, with Errol Flynn swashbuckling between the precocious Mauch twins—Bill and Bobby. The look-alikes decide that they will switch roles as a lark, one being Prince Edward (later King Edward VI), the other a beggar boy. Despite the beggar boy's outlandish behavior in his new station, the royal court and advisors accept him as the heir to the throne. The true Edward, however, is submerged in low-life London and, when he decides he's had enough of the game, asserts that he is the real prince. Miles Hendon (Flynn), a soldier of fortune, meets the real Edward and is amused by his claims to the throne, thinking him mad until he begins to believe the emphatic urchin just as the impostor is about to be crowned king. Enemies at court send an assassin (Alan Hale) after the boy, but he is prevented from carrying out his evil task by Miles, who saves the real king-to-be at the last moment.

PRINCE AND THE SHOWGIRL, THE

1957   117m   c   Comedy   ★★★½
Marilyn Monroe/L.O.P.   (U.K.)   /PG

Marilyn Monroe *(Elsie Marina)*, Laurence Olivier *(Charles)*, Sybil Thorndike *(Queen Dowager)*, Richard Wattis *(Northbrooke)*, Jeremy Spenser *(King Nicholas)*, Esmond Knight *(Hoffman)*, Paul Hardwick *(Major Domo)*, Rosamund Greenwood *(Maud)*, Aubrey Dexter *(The Ambassador)*, Maxine Audley *(Lady Sunningdale)*

p, Laurence Olivier; d, Laurence Olivier; w, Terence Rattigan (based on the play *The Sleeping Prince* by Rattigan); ph, Jack Cardiff; ed, Jack Harris; m, Richard Addinsell; chor, William Chappell; cos, Beatrice Dawson

By combining the light comic skills of Monroe and the grand acting ability of Olivier, THE PRINCE AND THE SHOWGIRL manages to succeed not only as pleasant entertainment but also as a wonderful mixture of two very different screen personalities. It's 1911 in London, and Monroe plays a flighty American showgirl who catches the eye of the prince regent of Carpathia, Olivier, who is in town for the coronation of George V.

Produced and directed by Olivier and financed by Monroe's newly formed production company (she reportedly was to receive a phenomenal 75 percent of the profits), THE PRINCE AND THE SHOWGIRL shows both actors in fine form. Monroe—in this, her 25th picture—had turned 30 and was as beautiful as ever, delivering a comic performance which is among her very finest. Olivier had already familiarized himself with the role on the British stage in the Rattigan play "The Sleeping Prince," which costarred his miscast wife, Vivien Leigh. Initially Rattigan had expressed reservations about having an actor of Olivier's stature playing a character the author had envisioned as a mundane bureaucrat. But Rattigan needn't have worried; after much ballyhoo in the press, the play opened to rave reviews. What's more, the casting of Monroe in place of Leigh brought the film a remarkable balance between two of film's most arresting screen personalities.

PRINCE OF FOXES

1949   107m   bw   Adventure/Historical   ★★★★
Fox   (U.S.)   /A

Tyrone Power *(Andrea Corsini)*, Orson Welles *(Cesare Borgia)*, Wanda Hendrix *(Camilla Verano)*, Everett Sloane *(Mario Belli)*, Marina Berti *(Angela Borgia)*, Katina Paxinou *(Mona Zeppo Constanza)*, Felix Aylmer *(Count Marc Antonio Verano)*, Leslie Bradley *(Don Esteban)*, Joop van Hulzen *(D'Este)*, James Carney *(Alphonso D'Este)*

p, Sol C. Siegel; d, Henry King; w, Milton Krims (based on the novel by Samuel Shellabarger); ph, Leon Shamroy; ed, Barbara McLean; m, Alfred Newman; art d, Lyle Wheeler, Mark-Lee Kirk; fx, Fred Sersen; cos, Vittorio Nino Novarese

AAN Best Cinematography: Leon Shamroy; *AAN Best Costume Design:* Vittorio Nino Novarese

Great adventure, a literate script, and fine performances combine in PRINCE OF FOXES to produce splendid entertainment, directed with marvelous briskness by Henry King. Set during the Italian Renaissance, the film opens with Welles, as the notorious Cesare Borgia, outlining his plans for the domination of Italy to his trusted aide, Power. Welles tells Power that the city-state cannot be taken of Ferrara by force, its fortress being too well-manned and well-defended by the Duke Alfonso D'Este (van Hulzen), cannon-maker extraordinaire. He assigns Power

to persuade van Hulzen to marry Welles's sister, the scheming Lucrezia Borgia. This Power does, with considerable guile and brass, after which he is instructed by Welles to seduce the young Hendrix—wife of the elderly Aylmer, who presides over a neighboring duchy—and then to turn over Aylmer's mountain fortress to Welles. En route to Aylmer's duchy, Power, an aspiring painter, stops to visit his mentor, art dealer Eduardo Ciannelli, and arranges to have one of his own works on display when Hendrix inspects Ciannelli's collection. She spots Power's work and admires it, after which the artist makes a gift of it to her. Hendrix, in turn, invites Power to visit her and Aylmer. However, having thus inveigled his way into Aylmer's court, Power soon realizes that the old duke is an honorable, decent man whose deep love for Hendrix is more paternal than sexual, and he cannot bring himself to betray Hendrix and Aylmer's trust. Deciding he can no longer wait for Power to deliver the duchy, Welles orders his men to march against the mountain fortress. Power offers his sword to Aylmer and Hendrix, betraying his master to join in the heroic defense of the stronghold. Welles's troops eventually overcome the defenders, however, and Aylmer is dead by the time Hendrix and Power surrender the duchy. After Sloane, Power's erstwhile friend and advisor, reports to Welles that he has discovered that Power's mother (Paxinou) is a peasant, Welles realizes that his former aide, now his prisoner, has not only betrayed him but is not of noble birth, and allows Sloane to gouge out Power's eyes before a dinner party at which Hendrix begs for Power's life. However, Sloane has really clutched two grapes over Power's eyes and offered this gore up as the real thing, whispering to Power to scream in feigned pain. Power is led away, but soon organizes a plot to retake Citta del Monte and free Hendrix.

Beautifully photographed on location in Italy by cinematographer Leon Shamroy, this Fox production is both tasteful and lavish, with Power exceptional in his portrait of an ambitious but honorable Renaissance man. Unfortunately, the exquisite costuming suffers somewhat as a result of Fox's decision to shoot in black and white, even though King had begged for color. Welles, who makes a wholly sinister Cesare Borgia, took the role because he was desperately in need of cash to fuel his own projects. But he couldn't resist the urge to direct, and reportedly infuriated King when, during his scenes, he would upbraid his fellow actors for not reacting correctly to his evil, powerful character.

PRINCE OF THE CITY

1981   167m   c   Crime   ★★★½
Orion   (U.S.)   R/15

Treat Williams *(Daniel Ciello)*, Jerry Orbach *(Gus Levy)*, Richard Foronjy *(Joe Marinaro)*, Don Billett *(Bill Mayo)*, Kenny Marino *(Dom Bando)*, Carmine Caridi *(Gino Mascone)*, Tony Page *(Raf Alvarez)*, Norman Parker *(Rick Cappalino)*, Paul Roebling *(Brooks Paige)*, Bob Balaban *(Santimassino)*

p, Burtt Harris; d, Sidney Lumet; w, Jay Presson Allen, Sidney Lumet (based on the book by Robert Daley); ph, Andrzej Bartkowiak; ed, John J. Fitzstephens; m, Paul Chihara; prod d, Tony Walton; art d, Edward Pisoni; cos, Anna Hill Johnstone

AAN Best Adapted Screenplay: Jay Presson Allen, Sidney Lumet

PRINCE OF THE CITY is an excellent, if overlong, fictional treatment of a true story, set in the 1960s. New York cop Daniel Ciello (Treat Williams) reluctantly turns informer on his pals and colleagues after being recruited by the US Justice Department to expose police corruption, especially the involvement of the cops in the drug trade. Williams gives a fine performance, the rest of the cast is also excellent, and director Sidney Lumet's eye for detail is sure throughout this authentic look at the dirtier side of police work.

PRINCE OF TIDES, THE

1991   132m   c   Drama/Romance   ★★½
Barwood Films/Longfellow Productions/Columbia   (U.S.)   R/15

Nick Nolte *(Tom Wingo)*, Barbra Streisand *(Dr. Susan Lowenstein)*, Blythe Danner *(Sallie Wingo)*, Kate Nelligan *(Lila Wingo Newbury)*, Jeroen Krabbe *(Herbert Woodruff)*, Melinda Dillon *(Savannah Wingo)*, George Carlin *(Eddie Detreville)*, Jason Gould *(Bernard Woodruff)*, Brad Sullivan *(Henry Wingo)*, Maggie Collier *(Lucy Wingo)* p, Barbra Streisand, Andrew Karsch; d, Barbra Streisand; w, Becky Johnston, Pat Conroy (from the novel by Conroy); ph, Stephen Goldblatt; ed, Don Zimmerman; m, James Newton Howard; prod d, Paul Sylbert; art d, W. Steven Graham; cos, Ruth Morley

AAN Best Picture; *AAN Best Actor*: Nick Nolte; *AAN Best Supporting Actress*: Kate Nelligan; *AAN Best Adapted Screenplay*: Pat Conroy, Becky Johnston; *AAN Best Cinematography*: Stephen Goldblatt; *AAN Best Score*: James Newton Howard; *AAN Best Art Direction*: Paul Sylbert, Caryl Heller

Directed with loving care by Barbra Streisand, this adaptation of the best-seller also boasts a serious flaw: Streisand herself. Narrated by Tom Wingo (Nolte) in flashbacks intercut with present-day sequences, THE PRINCE OF TIDES tells the story of his family, a poor white clan from the South Carolina tidewater emotionally crippled by a never-talked-about event which took place during Tom's childhood. Only years later, following yet another suicide attempt by Tom's twin sister Savannah (Dillon), a Greenwich Village poet, is the family demon exorcised.

Savannah, who has lost her will to live, does not respond to therapy. At the request of Dr. Susan Lowenstein (Streisand), Tom flies north to shed light on his sister's troubled psyche. Tom, too, has been left emotionally scarred by the mysterious childhood event. An unemployed high-school teacher and football coach, the father of three, he spends depressing days as house-husband to wife Sallie (Danner), a doctor who's thinking of leaving him for her lover. Over a six-week period with Dr. Susie, Tom explores the fragments of the Wingo past. His own confidence slowly returns—partly thanks to a soft-focus love affair with Dr. Sue, partly thanks to his successful coaching in football of her withdrawn, preppy son Bernard (Gould, Streisand's son by Elliott). What pigskin won't do for a guy.

Therapists will be scornful of Lowenstein's quick cure of the Wingo family trauma (i.e. remember the past, and all will be well), especially since she dispenses her expertise *gratis*—not to mention the fact that she tumbles into bed with her "client." Most moviegoers, though, are probably willing to let this slip by. What *doesn't* wash is La Strident's glamorous characterization of the sophisticated New York shrink. As star, director and co-producer, Streisand shifts the book's focus from the Wingo past to the Tom-Susan love affair. This could have worked had Streisand directed herself better—if, indeed, she had directed herself at all. Instead of a performance, we get smirks, poses, campy shots that linger on her outrageously long manicured fingernails, and radiant, cloying smiles. Streisand's inadequacies, though, are more than compensated for by Nolte's compelling Tom. He brings conviction and depth to the role, treading a fine line between self-pity and self-respect and exposing his frailties with a rare sensitivity. He also manages to keep a straight face during a scene where La Babs orders dinner in French—now *that's* acting.

PRINCESS BRIDE, THE

1987 98m c Adventure/Children's/Comedy ★★★★
Act III (U.S.) PG

Cary Elwes *(Westley)*, Mandy Patinkin *(Inigo Montoya)*, Chris Sarandon *(Prince Humperdinck)*, Christopher Guest *(Count Rugen)*, Wallace Shawn *(Vizzini)*, Andre the Giant *(Fezzik)*, Fred Savage *(The Grandson)*, Robin Wright *(Buttercup, the Princess Bride)*, Peter Falk *(The Grandfather)*, Peter Cook *(The Impressive Clergyman)*

p, Arnold Scheinman, Rob Reiner; d, Rob Reiner; w, William Goldman (based on his novel); ph, Adrian Biddle; ed, Robert Leighton; m, Mark Knopfler; prod d, Norman Garwood; art d, Keith Pain, Richard Holland; fx, Nick Allder; cos, Phyllis Dalton

AAN Best Song: Willy DeVille

A hilarious mixture of Errol Flynn swashbuckler and Monty Python send-up, THE PRINCESS BRIDE works as love story, as adventure, and as satire. In the framing story, a sick 10-year-old (Fred Savage) is visited by his grandfather (Peter Falk), who reads him *The Princess Bride*, a "kissing" story set in a medieval make-believe land. In it, the beautiful Buttercup (Robin Wright) reluctantly becomes engaged to a prince (Chris Sarandon) when her true love, Westley (Cary Elwes), disappears. Soon, however, she is kidnapped by a crafty Sicilian (Wallace Shawn) and his hirelings, Spanish swordsman Inigo Montoya

(Mandy Patinkin) and gargantuan Fezzik (Andre the Giant). Buttercup is rescued by a mysterious man in black, who turns out to be Westley; but after surviving the Dreaded Fireswamp, they are apprehended by the prince. Buttercup agrees to marry the prince when he promises to free Westley, but the dashing lad is actually tortured to death—or is he? With the help of a wizened miracle maker (Billy Crystal), Inigo and Fezzik join forces with Westley to fight the forces of evil. With tongues in cheeks and hearts on sleeves, director Rob Reiner and scripter William Goldman create a dazzling adventure for younger viewers, while at the same time hilariously satirizing the same genre. Goldman's screenplay, adapted from his own novel, made the rounds for 14 years before finally making it to the screen. The wait was worth it. When it comes to pleasing both kids and adults, you can't do much better than THE PRINCESS BRIDE.

PRISONER OF SHARK ISLAND, THE

1936 95m bw Prison/Biography ★★★★
Fox (U.S.) /A

Warner Baxter *(Dr. Samuel A. Mudd)*, Gloria Stuart *(Mrs. Peggy Mudd)*, Joyce Kay *(Marth Mudd)*, Claude Gillingwater *(Col. Jeremiah Dyer)*, Douglas Wood *(Gen. Ewing)*, Fred Kohler Jr. *(Sgt. Cooper)*, Harry Carey *(Commandant of Fort Jefferson "Shark Island")*, Paul Fix *(David Herold)*, John Carradine *(Sgt. Rankin)*, Francis McDonald *(John Wilkes Booth)*

p, Darryl F. Zanuck; d, John Ford; w, Nunnally Johnson (based on the life of Dr. Samuel A. Mudd); ph, Bert Glennon; ed, Jack Murray; art d, William Darling; cos, Gwen Wakeling

Warner Baxter is smashing as a doctor who treats the ankle of fugitive assassin John Wilkes Booth, played by Francis McDonald. Arrested shortly thereafter, Baxter is charged with being part of the conspiracy to murder President Abraham Lincoln. Dragged away from his wife, Gloria Stuart, and their small child, Baxter is convicted on scant evidence and sent to prison for life at Fort Jefferson on Shark Island in the Dry Tortugas. There he is considered, even by the black guards, to be a worthy "southern gentleman" doctor determined to care for prisoners and their captors alike when they fall sick. When a yellow fever epidemic breaks out, Baxter, risking his own life, saves the lives of many. For this heroic act, Baxter's case is reopened; exonerated of being part of the Lincoln conspiracy, he returns to his family. This based-on-fact story about the injustice meted out to one man is handled beautifully by director John Ford, whose cameras, under Bert Glennon's expert guidance, starkly depict the horrors of prison life. Baxter underplays his role superbly, eliciting viewer sympathy early on. Ford leaves no doubt as to the man's innocence by stating the facts of the case right at the beginning of the film. The good doctor's sympathies are revealed when Baxter, while treating Booth, refers to Abraham Lincoln as the only salvation Southerners can look to. There are some slight similarities between this film and I AM A FUGITIVE FROM A CHAIN GANG and LES MISERABLES, but THE PRISONER OF SHARK ISLAND is a distinctive Ford film with his imprint on every frame, offering a taut, believable script by Nunnally Johnson. Typical of the reverential Ford is the scene depicting the assassination. Frank McGlynn, who played Lincoln many times, is shown seated in his box; when the shot that ends his life rings out, only McGlynn's hand is shown slumping, then a quick full shot of the lifeless body dissolves into a magnificent portrait of the President.

PRISONER OF ZENDA, THE

1937 101m bw Romance/Adventure ★★★★★
Selznick (U.S.) /U

Ronald Colman *(Rudolph Rassendyl/King Rudolf V)*, Madeleine Carroll *(Princess Flavia)*, Douglas Fairbanks Jr. *(Rupert of Hentzau)*, Mary Astor *(Antoinette De Mauban)*, C. Aubrey Smith *(Col. Zapt)*, Raymond Massey *(Black Michael)*, David Niven *(Capt. Fritz von Tarlenheim)*, Eleanor Wesselhoeft *(Cook)*, Byron Foulger *(Johann)*, Montagu Love *(Detchard)* p, David O. Selznick; d, John Cromwell, George Cukor, W.S. Van Dyke II; w, John Balderston, Wells Root, Donald Ogden Stewart (based on the novel by Anthony Hope and the play by Edward Rose); ph, James Wong Howe; ed, Hal C. Kern, James E. Newcom; m, Alfred Newman; art d, Lyle Wheeler; fx, Jack Cosgrove; cos, Ernest Dryden.

AAN Best Score: Alfred Newman, Selznick International Pictures Music Department; *AAN Best Art Direction:* Lyle Wheeler

Hollywood movies don't get much classier. The great Anthony Hope adventure is adapted for the screen with loving loyalty to the story, and Cromwell's helmsmanship is decisive and full of affection for the tale. Colman plays the doppelganger roles of Rudolph Rassendyl and Prince Rudolf of the mythical European kingdom of Ruritania. The film opens by showing Rassendyl arriving in the city of Strelsau, startling citizens who believe that the prince is traveling in disguise by sporting a goatee instead of his usual mustache. He is also spotted by Col. Zapt (Smith) and Capt. von Tarlenheim (Niven), aides to the Prince, and he ends up dining with his royal double who is, as it turns out, a distant cousin. The next morning, however, the Prince lies in a coma, having been drugged by a servant in the employ of the Prince's brother "Black" Michael (Massey) and his villainous cohort Rupert of Hentzau (Fairbanks). Zapt vows that Michael will never sit on the throne and presses Rudolph to substitute for the Prince, through the coronation if need be, until the real Prince recovers. Of course this not only entails weathering additional attempts on the future King Rudolf V's life, but also standing in for His Majesty in the business of love, convincing Princess Flavia (Carroll) that he is indeed her fiance.

Director Cromwell does a marvelous job in extracting great performances from his leading players, as well as carefully developing the Colman-Carroll romance, which is touched with gentility and poetic grace. Cromwell was brought in by Selznick because the producer knew that this director would bring out the best from the cast and that he would stay within his budget. Selznick nevertheless hedged his bets and had George Cukor, famed as a "woman's director," helm the final scene between Colman and Carroll. This shows in Carroll's departure from her pose as the soft and gentle Flavia, as she becomes abruptly assertive, her voice rising to tell Colman that she must do her duty. Action director W.S. Van Dyke was also used to help with the exciting duel between Colman and Fairbanks. Selznick was repeatedly warned not to revive this Ruritanian adventure, his advisors telling him that the production was doomed. Selznick, however, rightly reasoned that he could capture the public's interest by highlighting the coronation scenes, since the public was already keyed to the upcoming crowning of Britain's Edward VIII. He was right. The film was a smash, enhancing the careers of everyone involved.

Colman was not really a swashbuckling type, although he retained some of that image after appearing in the silent version of BEAU GESTE and 1935's CLIVE OF INDIA. Voted Hollywood's handsomest actor (at age 46) the same year that ZENDA appeared, Colman is the essence of gentlmanly dash. He is matched by a true Hollywood princess, Madeleine Carroll, in what she would later call her favorite role. The great climactic duel staged between Colman and Fairbanks (in a scene-stealing, roguish performance that would have done his father proud) with Colman parrying words as well as blades, suggests more than it really shows. And the carefully masked split screen effects enabling the two Colmans to chat and shake hands are handled with skill.

Beyond the flawless visual elegance provided by Cromwell and ace cameraman Howe, the script by Balderston, Root, and Stewart is witty, literate, and lyrical, and Newman's sweeping, memorable score one of that composer's finest. The design of the picture is often stunning and earned an Oscar nomination for Lyle Wheeler. The dark, saturnine Raymond Massey is the perfect scheming Prince Michael, while Mary Astor does beautifully as the ill-fated mistress who proves a surprise ally for the good guys. That unofficial dean of Hollywood's British community, Sir C. Aubrey Smith, is charming, quaint, and heroically stalwart as the king's aide, and David Niven shows great promise as his brave protege.

PRIVATE BENJAMIN

1980 109m c Comedy/War ★★½
Warner Bros. (U.S.) R/15

Goldie Hawn *(Judy Benjamin)*, Eileen Brennan *(Capt. Doreen Lewis)*, Armand Assante *(Henri Tremont)*, Robert Webber *(Col. Clay Thornbush)*, Sam Wanamaker *(Teddy Benjamin)*, Barbara Barrie *(Harriet Benjamin)*, Mary Kay Place *(Pvt. Mary Lou Glass)*, Harry Dean Stanton *(Sgt. Jim Ballard)*, Albert Brooks *(Yale Goodman)*, Alan Oppenheimer *(Rabbi)*

p, Nancy Meyers, Charles Shyer, Harvey Miller; d, Howard Zieff; w, Nancy Meyers, Charles Shyer, Harvey Miller; ph, David M. Walsh; ed, Sheldon Kahn; m, Bill Conti; prod d, Robert Boyle; art d, Jeff Howard; fx, Robert Peterson; cos, Betsy Cox

AAN Best Actress: Goldie Hawn; *AAN Best Supporting Actress:* Eileen Brennan; *AAN Best Original Screenplay:* Nancy Meyers, Charles Shyer, Harvey Miller

Goldie Hawn brings that old standby, the service comedy, into the 1980s in this funny tale of a Jewish girl who decides to be all that she can be in the all-new Army. After her second husband (wonderfully played by Albert Brooks) dies while they are making love, Hawn enlists in the Army, much to the chagrin of her well-to-do parents, Sam Wanamaker and Barbara Barrie. The reality of Army life under demanding commanding officer Eileen Brennan turns out to be a far cry from Hawn's notion that she'll have her own room to decorate and the opportunity to visit exciting locales. The pampered Hawn's reactions to rigorous training exercises, her interactions with her superiors, and a not-quite-successful love affair with French physician Armand Assante while on duty in Europe inspire plenty of laughs. Hawn makes the most of the script, written by Nancy Meyers, Charles Shyer, and Harvey Miller, providing many funny moments in her performance. Brennan, as her lesbian-leaning CO, Robert Webber (as the unit commander) and Mary Kay Place (as Judy's sidekick) also provide strong support.

PRIVATE FUNCTION, A

1985 93m c Comedy ★★★
Hand Made (U.K.) R/15

Michael Palin *(Gilbert Chilvers)*, Maggie Smith *(Joyce Chilvers)*, Denholm Elliott *(Dr. Swaby)*, Richard Griffiths *(Allardyce)*, Tony Haygarth *(Sutcliff)*, John Normington *(Lockwood)*, Bill Paterson *(Wormold)*, Liz Smith *(Mother)*, Alison Steadman *(Mrs. Allardyce)*, Jim Carter *(Inspector Noble)*

p, Mark Shivas; d, Malcolm Mowbray; w, Alan Bennett (based on a story by Bennett, Mowbray); ph, Tony Pierce-Roberts; ed, Barrie Vince; m, John Du Prez; prod d, Stuart Walker; art d, Judith Lang, Michael Porter; cos, Phyllis Dalton

To sum up this movie in two words, one would have to flip a coin to decide whether it is "hysterically tasteless" or "tastelessly hysterical." It is surely one or the other, and perhaps both. The time is 1947. England is just recovering from the war, and there are still many restrictions on the inhabitants of the Yorkshire town where the action takes place. There could be a brisk trade in black market items, but Wormold (Bill Paterson), the local inspector from the Food Ministry, keeps tabs on everyone, making certain that nobody is growing food or breeding livestock illegally. Gilbert (Michael Palin) and Joyce Chilvers (Maggie Smith) are a married couple with little in common. He's a quiet podiatrist, and she is a lower-class hoyden who wants to move up to the middle class. When Joyce learns that some village big shots have bribed a local farmer to keep an unlicensed pig for them and fatten it up, she convinces Gilbert that they should abduct the animal. Once they have a supply of sausages and chops, there is no question they will be welcomed into the town's fanciest homes. Now the trouble begins. This movie is a vicious satire of class distinctions mixed with some of the grossest humor ever seen on-screen. But the British love their scatology and their sociology, so the two seem to blend. The result is a film that you don't have to be British to enjoy, just brutish.

PRIVATE LIFE OF HENRY VIII, THE

1933 97m bw Biography   ★★★★
London Films (U.K.)   /U

Charles Laughton (Henry VIII), Robert Donat (Thomas Culpepper), Lady Tree (Henry's Old Nurse), Binnie Barnes (Katherine Howard), Elsa Lanchester (Anne of Cleves), Merle Oberon (Anne Boleyn), Wendy Barrie (Jane Seymour), Everley Gregg (Catherine Parr), Franklin Dyall (Thomas Cromwell), Miles Mander (Wriothesley)

p, Alexander Korda, Ludovico Toeplitz; d, Alexander Korda; w, Lajos Biro, Arthur Wimperis; ph, Georges Perinal; ed, Harold Young, Stephen Harrison; m, Kurt Schroeder; art d, Vincent Korda; chor, Espinosa; cos, John Armstrong

AAN Best Picture; AA Best Actor: Charles Laughton

An admirable glutton. And a resurrection for England's film industry, with palms going to Korda, and French cinematograper Georges Perinal. Many costume epics were made in the silent years and some even touched upon the life of the monarch, but this is the one that will be remembered. Laughton's performance was outstanding and won the first Oscar ever for a British-made movie. Korda called upon his brother Vincent to be set designer and the nepotism was worthwhile, as Vincent managed to make this picture look far more expensive than the 60,000 pounds it cost to produce it in just five weeks. The attitude taken was to dispense with the public utterances and show the intimate side of the monarch, a technique Korda was to use again in the less fulfilling THE PRIVATE LIFE OF DON JUAN.

There is a great deal of humor in this picture, which details the life of Henry VIII and five of his six wives. The first wife, Catherine of Aragon, is dispensed with in a prologue that explains that she was far "too respectable to be included." Merle Oberon is Anne Boleyn, his first spouse pictured, who is soon beheaded after failing to give Henry a male heir. Wendy Barrie plays Jane Seymour and dies giving birth. Henry next marries Lanchester (Anne of Cleves), wearing an odd wig and doing her best to look terrible in order to justify the film's most famous line, uttered by Laughton with a regal sigh as he enters the bedroom, "The things I've done for England." Lanchester, using a German accent, is the only performer to come close to Laughton in scene-stealing, nearly swiping their sequences entirely. That marriage leads to divorce, and Henry next marries Binnie Barnes, who loses her head after losing her heart to Laughton's pal, Robert Donat. At the finale, after raving and roaring and ranting, eating like an animal, ruling his roost like a cock of the walk, Laughton is shown to be a tranquil, almost whipped man at the hands of his last mate, Everley Gregg, a sharp-faced shrew.

Laughton was only 33 at the time this film was made but already a veteran of nine movies and many stage productions. There are several standout scenes, not the least of which are the "eating" sequences with Laughton chewing on a chop, then tossing the remains over his shoulder. Actually, the eating bits are sexier than the bedroom scenes, and one wonders if Tony Richardson didn't study them for his directing of TOM JONES. Until this movie was released, there had been a mild recession in costume epics, but they came back with a flurry when the totals were in on the profits, about 10 times the cost. Korda's sets, which were poverty-stricken at best, were photographed so well by Perinal that no one realized how frail they were.

PRIVATE LIFE OF SHERLOCK HOLMES, THE

1970 125m c Comedy/Mystery   ★★★½
Phalanx/Mirisch (U.S./U.K.)   GP/PG

Robert Stephens (Sherlock Holmes), Colin Blakely (Dr. John H. Watson), Irene Handl (Mrs. Hudson), Stanley Holloway (1st Gravedigger), Christopher Lee (Mycroft Holmes), Genevieve Page (Gabrielle Valladon), Clive Revill (Rogozhin), Tamara Toumanova (Petrova), George Benson (Inspector Lestrade), Catherine Lacey (Old Lady)

p, Billy Wilder; d, Billy Wilder; w, Billy Wilder, I.A.L. Diamond (based on the characters created by Sir Arthur Conan Doyle); ph, Christopher Challis; ed, Ernest Walter; m, Miklos Rozsa; prod d, Alexander Trauner; art d, Tony Inglis; fx, Wally Veevers, Cliff Richardson; chor, David Blair; cos, Julie Harris

This unjustly forgotten Billy Wilder film takes on the much-loved character of Sherlock Holmes and attempts to humanize him by examining his vulnerabilities: his ambiguous sexuality and his cocaine addiction. Told via an unpublished manuscript by Dr. Watson (Blakely), the story begins with a bored, frustrated Sherlock Holmes (Stephens), who turns to cocaine between cases. One evening a beautiful Belgian woman, Gabrielle Valladon (Page), turns up at 221B Baker Street asking Holmes to find her missing husband. Although warned by his mysterious brother, Mycroft (Lee), to abandon the case, Holmes persists and the trail leads to Scotland's Loch Ness, where Holmes and Watson come face to face with the legendary monster. Although the film was cut by more than 30 minutes by United Artists, what is left of this satirical, intimate look at the revered character is intriguing and wholly entertaining. Nevertheless it it bombed at the box office. The sets were designed under the direction of Alexander Trauner, who re-created, in detail, the Victorian atmosphere of Holmes's London residence, including a massive back-lot reproduction of Baker Street. The score by Miklos Rozsa is one of his most impressive, and he can be seen conducting it during the ballet sequence. Robert Stephens is an excellent, never-before-seen Holmes, one with wild mood swings which veil his insecurities. Colin Blakely's Dr. Watson is loyal, humorous, and energetic, while Christopher Lee as Mycroft is excellent, making him the only actor in Holmes screen history to play both the detective (in the German-made SHERLOCK HOLMES AND THE NECKLACE OF DEATH) and his brother.

PRIVATE LIVES

1931 92m bw Comedy   ★★★★½
MGM (U.S.)   /A

Norma Shearer (Amanda Chase Paynne), Robert Montgomery (Elyot Chase), Reginald Denny (Victor Paynne), Una Merkel (Sibyl Chase), Jean Hersholt (Oscar), George Davis (Bellboy)

d, Sidney Franklin; w, Hans Kraly, Richard Schayer, Claudine West (based on the play by Noel Coward); ph, Ray Binger; ed, Conrad A. Nervig; art d, Cedric Gibbons; cos, Adrian

PRIVATE LIVES is one of those enduring scripts that can't be hurt, even by ordinary actors; in the case of this film, the acting is excellent, and the result is charming. Norma Shearer and Robert Montgomery play Amanda and Elyot, a once-married couple who have divorced and wed other mates. He's now married to Sibyl (Merkel) and she to Victor (Denny). Both Sibyl and Victor are conservative sorts, devoid of the joy and madness that once attracted Amanda and Elyot to one another. By a coincidence, both couples are honeymooning at the French hotel where Amanda and Elyot had spent their first two weeks of marriage years before. For a time we see the divorced pair struggling to show affection to their new spouses, a tall order when considering the surpassingly bland Sibyl and the stuffed-shirt Victor. Since their suites are next to each other, it isn't long before our fireball lovers meet on their balconies, at once delighted and stunned to see one another. In no time, the newlyweds are quarreling; the formerly-weds, convinced that they are still in love, leave their fresh spouses behind and go to a mountain chalet to have another honeymoon. Of course, their passion is as volatile as it ever was, and they are soon arguing viciously between romantic interludes. The words become blows, and when Sibyl and Victor finally catch up with the elopers they are in the midst of a battle royale. Amanda and Elyot reconcile with Victor and Sibyl, but when the latter two get into an argument over breakfast, the true lovers realize that even the most placid types get into scrapes. What the impish pair do and how the word "Sollochs" helps them make for an amusingly sweet finale.

Noel Coward wrote and starred in PRIVATE LIVES onstage with Gertrude Lawrence in a 1930 London production, then brought it to New York with Laurence Olivier and Jill Esmond in the secondary roles. Producer Irving Thalberg, Shearer's husband, made a film record of this production to aid cast and crew in bringing its unique flavor to the cinema. One of the film's joys is that it achieves a faithful reproduction of the original without seeming a mere copy. The actors don't convince as British (only Denny was), but that really doesn't matter. Shearer and Montgomery attack their roles with such zest and comic elan that we don't miss the spirits of Noel and Gertie hanging around. Opening up the play for a spot of mountain climbing (and a *very* pre-Code sleeping scene), director Franklin does a fine job in preventing his film from becoming stagy.

PRIZZI'S HONOR

1985 129m c Romance/Comedy/Crime ★★★★
ABC (U.S.) R/15

Jack Nicholson (*Charley Partanna*), Kathleen Turner (*Irene Walker*), Robert Loggia (*Eduardo Prizzi*), John Randolph (*Angelo "Pop" Partanna*), William Hickey (*Don Corrado Prizzi*), Lee Richardson (*Dominic Prizzi*), Michael Lombard (*Filargi "Finlay"*), Anjelica Huston (*Maerose Prizzi*), George Santopietro (*Plumber*), Lawrence Tierney (*Lt. Hanley*)

p, John Foreman; d, John Huston; w, Richard Condon, Janet Roach (based on the novel by Condon); ph, Andrzej Bartkowiak; ed, Rudi Fehr, Kaja Fehr; m, Alex North; prod d, J. Dennis Washington; art d, Michael Helmy, Tracy Bousman; fx, Connie Brink; cos, Donfeld

AAN Best Picture; AAN Best Actor: Jack Nicholson; AAN Best Supporting Actor: William Hickey; AA Best Supporting Actress: Anjelica Huston; AAN Best Director: John Huston; AAN Best Adapted Screenplay: Richard Condon, Janet Roach; AAN Best Editing: Rudi Fehr, Kaja Fehr; AAN Best Costume Design: Donfeld

Director John Huston, one-time master of film noir, returns to the form with a black comedy about the Mafia. The film benefits from some stellar performances from Jack Nicholson, Kathleen Turner, and William Hickey. This was the penultimate film from the ailing great director. It is also one of his best.

Charley Partanna (Nicholson) is an aging dopey hit man who works for a powerful New York Mafia family. He spots luscious Irene Walker (Turner) at a gangster wedding and loses his heart. She's ostensibly a tax consultant living in Los Angeles, and soon Charley finds himself flying westward to court her. Then he discovers that she is really a hit woman for the mob. With this, at least, Charley can identify, but when he learns that Irene has cheated his own Mafia family—the Prizzis—out of a great sum of money, his loyalties are painfully divided. The finale is a shocker finish few viewers will ever forget. It's all good and funny in a cynical, bleak sort of way, reflecting the then 78-year-old Huston's perspective of the world. A lesser-known director might have been pilloried for bad taste. Huston was not only tolerated but cheered.

The film received a host of Oscar nominations, including Best Picture, Best Actor (Nicholson), Best Supporting Actor (Hickey), Best Costume Design, Best Direction, Best Editing, and Best Screenplay from Another Medium (Richard Condon, Janet Roach). Anjelica Huston (the director's daughter) won an Oscar as Best Supporting Actress.

PRODUCERS, THE

1967 88m c Comedy ★★★★
Springtime/Crossbow (U.S.) /PG

Zero Mostel (*Max Bialystock*), Gene Wilder (*Leo Bloom*), Dick Shawn (*Lorenzo St. Du Bois*), Kenneth Mars (*Franz Liebkind*), Estelle Winwood (*Old Lady*), Christopher Hewett (*Roger De Bris*), Andreas Voutsinas (*Carmen Giya*), Lee Meredith (*Ulla*), Renee Taylor (*Eva Braun*), Michael Davis (*Production Tenor*)

p, Sidney Glazier; d, Mel Brooks; w, Mel Brooks; ph, Joseph Coffey; ed, Ralph Rosenblum; m, John Morris; art d, Charles Rosen; chor, Alan Johnson; cos, Gene Coffin

AAN Best Supporting Actor: Gene Wilder; AA Best Original Screenplay: Mel Brooks

Mel Brooks's first and funniest, a spoof of Broadway theater that has earned a deservedly devoted cult following. Forewarned, though, is forearmed: Mostel, genius that he is, doesn't scale his performances down at all for film. The first half hour you feel you're in the presence of comedy's king. After that, you gradually begin to feel bludgeoned by shrill overkill.

Mostel is a down-and-out but still pompous theater producer who desperately wants to regain his former glory. Wilder is his new, meek accountant who finds his books an utter disaster. He tells Mostel that the only way he will ever recover is to produce an enormous hit or, he whimsically suggests, to collect a lot of money from investors for a play

guaranteed to fail. That way Mostel could keep most of the investors' money. Mostel persuades Wilder not only to doctor the books but to become his partner in the production. They exhaust themselves soliciting and reading the worst scripts ever penned until they hit upon a play that is a surefire flop, "Springtime for Hitler," written by Mars, a Nazi fanatic living in Yorkville. Next, Mostel woos and wins the backing of every spinster in New York, taking in hundreds of thousands of dollars to back his doomed play. Although everything possible is done to make the play an unbearably tasteless flop, disaster strikes when it proves a smash hit.

THE PRODUCERS raised Mostel to new heights of zany appeal and made a star of Wilder, who proceeded to beat this kind of role into the ground in a series of subsequent films. Our favorite among the investors: Estelle Winwood, as "Touch Me, Feel Me"—she takes the material and runs with it. Highlights: the opening number, opening night; "I'm hysterical! I'm wet and I'm hysterical! I'm in *pain* and I'm wet and I'm hysterical!"

PROJECTIONIST, THE

1970 88m c Drama/Comedy ★★★½
Maglan (U.S.) PG/A

Chuck McCann (*Projectionist/Captain Flash*), Ina Balin (*The Girl*), Rodney Dangerfield (*Renaldi/The Bat*), Jara Kohout (*Candy Man/Scientist*), Harry Hurwitz (*Friendly Usher*), Robert Staats (*TV Pitchman*), Robert King (*Premiere Announcer*), Stephen Phillips (*Minister*), Clara Rosenthal (*Crazy Lady*), Jacquelyn Glenn (*Nude on Bearskin*)

p, Harry Hurwitz; d, Harry Hurwitz; w, Harry Hurwitz; ph, Victor Petrashevic; ed, Harry Hurwitz; m, Igo Kantor, Erma E. Levin

Long before ZELIG, THE PURPLE ROSE OF CAIRO, and DEAD MEN DON'T WEAR PLAID, there was THE PROJECTIONIST, an innovative low-budget oddity with a cult following. McCann plays the title character, a lovable nebbish who sees himself as part of every movie he's ever seen, including newsreels. In the imaginary role of Captain Flash, fearless defender of the downtrodden, McCann does battle with the Bat, who is played in McCann's dreamworld by Dangerfield (in his film debut). When he meets Balin, she immediately becomes part of his cinematic fantasy, cast as an imperiled Pauline whom McCann must save with regularity from the clutches of Dangerfield. McCann's mind movies feature archival footage from CASABLANCA, GUNGA DIN, DAMES, FORT APACHE, THE BIRTH OF A NATION, and many other Hollywood classics.

PROOF

1992 86m c Drama ★★★½
House & Moorhouse Films (Australia) R/15

Hugo Weaving (*Martin*), Genevieve Picot (*Celia*), Russell Crowe (*Andy*), Heather Mitchell (*Martin's Mother*), Jeffrey Walker (*Young Martin*), Daniel Pollock (*Gary—the Punk*), Frank Gallacher (*Vet*), Frankie J. Holden (*Brian—Policeman*), Saskia Post (*Waitress*), Belinda Davey (*Doctor*)

p, Lynda House; d, Jocelyn Moorhouse; w, Jocelyn Moorhouse; ph, Martin McGrath; ed, Ken Sallows; m, Not Drowning Waving; prod d, Patrick Reardon; cos, Cerri Barnett

Australian filmmaker Jocelyn Moorhouse made an auspicious debut with PROOF, a dry, dark comedy about a blind photographer and his efforts to find someone to trust. The disabled individual in question, Martin (Hugo Weaving), does little but walk his dog in the park and take pictures, using a modern auto-focus camera and aiming at sounds, or objects he feels with his hands. Since he can never see what he shoots, he needs someone to describe what he has photographed. Martin's housekeeper, Celia (Genevieve Picot), is an attractive but dour figure who has become obsessed with her employer, and is constantly trying to seduce him. The two are locked in battle, Martin despising Celia and she tormenting him in infinite, petty ways. A new factor enters the equation when Martin befriends Andy (Russell Crowe), a likable restaurant dishwasher.

PROOF unfolds with the clarity and purity of a fable. The metaphor of the blind photographer is an intriguing premise, and Moorhouse sustains it brilliantly as a way of commenting on the extent to which we all depend on those around us for confirmation of our own perceptions. For all its cerebral thematics, however, what is most remarkable about PROOF is how firmly and easily it stays on a human level. Moorhouse has written three full, rich characters who come vividly alive as acted by the excellent cast. Though the film is unabashedly unrealistic from the outset, it never for a moment feels contrived.

PROVIDENCE

1977 104m c Drama ★★★★
Action/SFP (France/Switzerland) R/X

John Gielgud (*Clive Langham*), Dirk Bogarde (*Claude Langham*), Ellen Burstyn (*Sonia Langham*), David Warner (*Kevin Woodford*), Elaine Stritch (*Helen Weiner/Molly Langham*), Denis Lawson (*Dave Woodford*), Cyril Luckham (*Dr. Mark Eddington*), Kathryn Leigh-Scott (*Miss Boon*), Milo Sperber (*Mr. Jenner*), Anna Wing (*Karen*)

p, Yves Gasser, Yves Peyrot, Klaus Hellwig; d, Alain Resnais; w, David Mercer; ph, Ricardo Aronovich; ed, Albert Jurgenson; m, Miklos Rozsa; art d, Jacques Saulnier; cos, Catherine Leterrier, Yves Saint-Laurent, John Bates

Alain Resnais's PROVIDENCE is truly a breakthrough film, a provocative attempt to synthesize past and future, literature and cinema, into a disarming but totally compelling present tense.

The film takes place on the eve of the 78th birthday of Clive Langham (John Gielgud), a dying novelist. He lives alone in his country estate in Providence, Rhode Island, battling alcoholism, the memory of his dead wife, and a chronic rectal disorder. At night, he struggles to write what appears to be his last novel, basing the characters on his own children. In this malevolent fiction, his son, Claude (Dirk Bogarde), and daughter-in-law, Sonia (Ellen Burstyn), are unhappily married and constantly—if wittily—sparring. Another, illegitimate son, Kevin Woodford (David Warner) a former soldier on trial, prosecuted by Claude, for killing an old man who turned into a werewolf. Claude is the prosecuting attorney, but the defendant is acquitted, and soon falls in love with Sonia. This, however, does not upset Claude as much as it disgusts him.

The increasingly inebriated Clive decides to give Claude a mistress, but the character he creates, Helen (Elaine Stritch), is the image of his dead wife—an older woman with a terminal disease, whom Clive continually mistakes for her prototype. As he labors to complete his retributive narrative, characters disintegrate further and further, delivering each other's dialogue and hopelessly confusing the story. Settings, too, change inexplicably. The next morning, Clive's children pay a birthday visit and prove a far cry from the ailing novelist's representations of them.

Director Alain Resnais—who collaborated with novelists Marguerite Duras in HIROSHIMA MON AMOUR, Alain Robbe-Grillet in LAST YEAR AT MARIENBAD, and Jorge Semprun in LA GUERRE EST FINIE—joined forces here with playwright David Mercer, best known for his *A Suitable Case for Treatment* (filmed by Karel Reisz as MORGAN!). PROVIDENCE should put those who attack Resnais for being pretentious and cold at ease, especially in light of Gielgud's virtuoso performance. Filled with brilliant wit, PROVIDENCE is a superb instance of inventive filmmaking with a comic touch and an intellectual theme.

PSYCHO

1960 109m bw Horror ★★★★★
Paramount (U.S.) /15

Anthony Perkins (*Norman Bates*), Janet Leigh (*Marion Crane*), Vera Miles (*Lila Crane*), John Gavin (*Sam Loomis*), Martin Balsam (*Milton Arbogast*), John McIntire (*Sheriff Chambers*), Lurene Tuttle (*Mrs. Chambers*), Simon Oakland (*Dr. Richmond*), Frank Albertson (*Tom Cassidy*), Patricia Hitchcock (*Caroline*)

p, Alfred Hitchcock; d, Alfred Hitchcock; w, Joseph Stefano (based on the novel by Robert Bloch); ph, John L. Russell Jr.; ed, George Tomasini; m, Bernard Herrmann; prod d, Joseph Hurley, Robert Clatworthy; fx, Clarence Champagne; cos, Helen Colvig

AAN Best Supporting Actress: Janet Leigh; *AAN Best Director:* Alfred Hitchcock; *AAN Best Cinematography:* John L Russell; *AAN Best Art Direction:* Joseph Hurley (Art Direction), Robert Clatworthy (Art Direction), George Milo (Set Decoration)

Perhaps no other film changed Hollywood's perception of the horror film so drastically as did PSYCHO. Nowadays, when any psychological thriller featuring a loony with a knife is designated "Hitchcockian" in some quarters, it's easy to forget just what a dramatic change of pace this was for Hitchcock. Though renowned for stories of murder, intrigue, and high adventure, Hitchcock's Hollywood films of the 1950s generally boasted top drawer production values, big stars, picturesque surroundings, and, more often than not, Technicolor. In comparison to the likes of, say, NORTH BY NORTHWEST, PSYCHO was intentionally sleazy and cheap both in look and subject matter.

The now familiar plot concerns Norman Bates (Anthony Perkins), a nervous, bird-like motel proprietor who lives under the domineering influence of his aged invalid mother. Norman takes care of Mother and, in return, she protects the disturbingly boyish man from temptation and corruption, particularly in the form of attractive single women who come to stay at the motel. Marion Crane (Janet Leigh) stops at the Bates Motel after impulsively fleeing from her workplace with a large sum of stolen money. She had hoped this cash would allow her married lover, Sam Loomis (John Gavin), to divorce his wife and marry her. After chatting with Norman, Marion appears to resolve to return the money. However Mother intervenes, leaving a bloody mess for Norman to clean up. After he's scrubbed down the bathroom, the dutiful son places the corpse in the trunk of Crane's rented car and sinks all the evidence in a nearby swamp. The situation gets tense for Norman when Marion's sister, Lila (Vera Miles), Marion's lover, Sam, and private investigator Milton Arbogast (Martin Balsam) arrive to ask some questions.

PSYCHO is not at all like the many movies that tried to imitate it. It's got a jet black sense of humor that becomes increasingly apparent upon repeated viewings and there's no doubt that it is masterful filmmaking. Hitchcock himself approached it almost as a technical joke: he wanted to see what would happen to audiences if you killed off the star in the first reel. The film is a textbook example of audience manipulation, as Hitchcock shifts our identification from character to character with the alacrity of a magician.

Inspired by the life of the demented, cannibalistic Wisconsin killer Ed Gein (whose gruesome acts would also inspire THE TEXAS CHAIN SAW MASSACRE and DERANGED), PSYCHO's importance to the horror genre cannot be overestimated. The influence comes not only from the Norman Bates character (who has since been reincarnated in a staggering variety of forms), but also from Hitchcock's use of pop psychological themes (the probable cause of the mayhem stems from the character's perverse familial and sexual history rather than an outside supernatural agency); Bernard Herrmann's famed all-string instruments score (his innovative nerveracking violin "screams" have been oft-mimicked); and new levels of screen violence. One intriguing difference between PSYCHO and the horror films of today is in the age of the characters. There isn't a teenager in sight in the Hitchcock classic—a revealing sign of the subsequent evolution of the genre *and* the downward shift in the age of moviegoing audiences.

PUBLIC ENEMY, THE

1931 83m bw Crime ★★★★½
Warner Bros. (U.S.) /A

James Cagney (*Tom Powers*), Jean Harlow (*Gwen Allen*), Edward Woods (*Matt Doyle*), Joan Blondell (*Mamie*), Beryl Mercer (*Ma Powers*), Donald Cook (*Mike Powers*), Mae Clarke (*Kitty*), Leslie Fenton (*Nails Nathan*), Robert Emmett O'Connor (*Paddy Ryan*), Murray Kinnell (*Putty Nose*)

p, Darryl F. Zanuck; d, William A. Wellman; w, Kubec Glasmon, John Bright, Harvey Thew (based on the original story *Beer and Blood* by John Bright); ph, Dev Jennings; ed, Ed McCormick; art d, Max Parker; cos, Earl Luick, Edward Stevenson

AAN Best Original Screenplay: John Bright, Kubec Glasmon

Fascinating and brutally realistic, THE PUBLIC ENEMY, along with LITTLE CAESAR, BAD COMPANY, and SCARFACE, set the pattern for the gangster films of the 1930s. It also made a star of its volatile leading man, James Cagney, and confirmed director William Wellman as a major force in talkies.

The film opens with two young Irish boys, Tom (Frank Coghlan) and Matt (Frankie Darro), growing up in the shantytown South Side of Chicago, circa 1909, and learning a life of crime from Putty Nose (Kinnell), a fence. As adults, Tom (now played by Cagney) and Matt (Woods) move into robbery but, on a warehouse heist, a panicky Tom fires his gun needlessly and the police descend. Tom and Matt escape, but not before killing a cop. Putty Nose skips town, and the two young crooks move into bootlegging on the advice of Paddy Ryan (O'Connor). (In a scene which memorably uses the offscreen sound of a discordant piano, Matt and Tom square their accounts with Putty Nose.) Working for Nails Nathan (Fenton), the two are successful in their new racket, and move into an apartment with Mamie (Blondell) and Kitty (Clarke), two blondes they have picked up. Tom, the more nasty and aggressive of the two, continues to rise up in the gangster hierarchy, especially after Nails is killed in a freak accident by a horse. (So used to killing are Tom and Matt that they even execute the unfortunate animal.) The price of success, though, is great, as Tom's crusading brother Mike (Cook) prevents their mother (Mercer) from accepting the largesse of Tom's misdeeds. Even though Tom takes up with the seductive Gwen (Harlow), gang warfare takes its toll. The film's famous final shot, with "I'm Forever Blowing Bubbles" playing on a victrola, is still, even after exposure to today's graphic filmic violence, horrifying.

THE PUBLIC ENEMY is one of the most realistic gangster films ever produced. Wellman's direction is a frontal attack on the subject; other than handling a number of violent deaths offscreen, he spares no brutality of emotion, action, or thought in his grim portrayal of a lethal criminal. Cagney is *the* gangster of his day, cocky, tough as nails, and utterly without conscience, a character molded into evil by his environment. We see only the criminal world; the one cop shown in detail is Tom's father, a brute who walks around the house in half his uniform, communicating with his unruly child via a razor strop. Photographer Dev Jennings shot the film emphasizing sharp contrasts: glaring sunlit exteriors and grainy gray interiors that fade to black alleyways and gutters.

Tom's casual brutality scars the memory in shot after shot. The moment best remembered, of course, is the one in which Cagney smashes half a grapefruit in Clarke's face when she taunts him with the suggestion that maybe he's found a new lover. Everyone connected with this famous scene recalls it differently—whose idea it was, was Cagney really supposed to hit her, was Clarke prepared, etc. Whatever the case, Clarke is unfortunately remembered more for this small role than any other she played, and Cagney was for years to come offered a grapefruit whenever he entered a restaurant.

PULP FICTION

1994   149m   c   Crime/Thriller   ★★★★
Jersey Films   (U.S.)   R/18

John Travolta *(Vincent Vega)*, Samuel L. Jackson *(Jules Winfield)*, Uma Thurman *(Mia Wallace)*, Harvey Keitel *(The Wolf)*, Tim Roth *(Pumpkin)*, Amanda Plummer *(Honey Bunny)*, Maria de Medeiros *(Fabienne)*, Ving Rhames *(Marsellus Wallace)*, Eric Stoltz *(Lance)*, Rosanna Arquette *(Jody)*

p, Lawrence Bender; d, Quentin Tarantino; w, Quentin Tarantino, Roger Avary (based on stories by Quentin Tarantino and Roger Avary); ph, Andrzej Sekula; ed, Sally Menke; prod d, David Wasco; art d, Charles Collum; fx, Larry Fioritto; cos, Betsy Heimann

AA Best Original Screenplay: Quentin Tarantino, Roger Avary; *AAN Best Picture*; *AAN Best Actor:* John Travolta; *AAN Best Supporting Actor:* Samuel L. Jackson; *AAN Best Supporting Actress:* Uma Thurman; *AAN Best Director:* Quentin Tarantino; *AAN Best Editing:* Sally Menke

Witty, stylish, and romantic to its dark heart, PULP FICTION is a compulsively funny and strangely dreamy look at the criminals, hangers-on, and low-life scum who populate a glamorously sleazy Los Angeles of the mind.

After an introductory sequence featuring a pair of small-time holdup artists (Amanda Plummer and Tim Roth), we meet talkative hit men Jules Winfield (Samuel Jackson) and Vincent Vega (John Travolta), who are on their way to deal with some drug-dealing college kids who've made the mistake of trying to double-cross crime kingpin Marsellus (Ving Rhames). Their visit with the college boys takes a nasty turn after they find a briefcase—which emits a strange, radiant light—that Marsellus has sent them to retrieve. In the next episode, Vincent beards the boss's wife, Mia (Uma Thurman), through an evening on the town; their date turns ugly after she accidentally snorts an overdose of heroin. Lastly, we meet Butch (Bruce Willis), a nearly-washed up boxer who is being paid by Marsellus to take a dive in an upcoming fight. But Butch has other plans: he fights to win and then flees. By the end, all these seemingly disparate plot elements have been pulled together through a daring series of narrative somersaults.

Movie-mad writer-director Quentin Tarantino's second feature is a witty, violent, and unexpectedly redemptive tour-de-force. The movie skims along on a sea of lurid cliches, but these are twisted, transfigured, and given astonishingly fresh life: from the washed-up boxer and his French sex-kitten girlfriend, to the platform shoes enshrined on a hippie drug dealer's wall, to the mysterious suitcase whose glowing contents strike viewers dumb, PULP FICTION pays homage to its B-movie past while existing comfortably in its own perfectly realized world.

For all the violent action—and there's plenty—talk is paramount: the all-star cast is awash in words, endlessly debating such issues as whether a foot massage is tantamount to adultery or the relative filthiness of pigs and dogs, while beset by serial sex maniacs, contract gunmen, and bottom feeders of every stripe. No one and nothing is quite what it seems, from the billing and cooing couple of the opening sequence to the coolly professional killer who sees the light during a routine hit, to the raven-haired seductress whose evening out takes a sudden turn for the nightmarish. Yet PULP FICTION isn't all flash and chronological sleight-of-hand. It's driven by an astonishingly pure romantic impulse: it's filled with people who want to be saved, though most of them have no more idea about how to go about saving themselves than fish flopping around on the bottom of a boat. Without its commitment to an idea of salvation, PULP FICTION would be little more than a terrific parlor trick; with it, it's something far richer and more haunting.

PUMPKIN EATER, THE

1964   118m   bw   Drama   ★★★★
Romulus   (U.K.)   /X

Anne Bancroft *(Jo Armitage)*, Peter Finch *(Jake Armitage)*, James Mason *(Bob Conway)*, Janine Gray *(Beth Conway)*, Cedric Hardwicke *(Mr. James, Jo's Father)*, Rosalind Atkinson *(Mrs. James, Jo's Mother)*, Alan Webb *(Mr. Armitage, Jake's Father)*, Richard Johnson *(Giles)*, Maggie Smith *(Philpot)*, Eric Porter *(Psychiatrist)*

p, James Woolf; d, Jack Clayton; w, Harold Pinter (based on the novel *The Pumpkin Eater* by Penelope Mortimer); ph, Oswald Morris; ed, James B. Clark; m, Georges Delerue; art d, Edward Marshall; cos, Motley

AAN Best Actress: Anne Bancroft

Bancroft, in an Oscar-nominated performance, plays a twice-married mother of six. She divorces her second husband (Johnson) and takes up with Finch, a highly successful screenwriter. The two marry; it seems like a perfect marriage until Bancroft realizes her philandering husband will never buckle down to her notions of marital fidelity. She gives birth to her seventh child and suffers a nervous breakdown. This, along with an encounter with an unbalanced woman at her hairdresser's, sends Bancroft to a psychiatrist (Porter). He is not much help. Bancroft's father dies, and she discovers that she is once more expecting a baby. She refuses to accompany Finch to a film location in Morocco but agrees to his arguments for sterilization. Later she runs into Mason, a man who once made a pass at her. Mason reveals that Finch has been having an affair with his wife (Gray), who is now expecting a child. In an ugly scene Bancroft confronts Finch and returns to Johnson. After she spends the night with her former husband, Johnson gets a phone call from old-friend Finch, whose father has just died. Bancroft goes to the funeral, but Finch pretends not to notice her. As she chases him, she slips and falls in the mud. Demoralized once more, she goes to their unfinished country house and spends the night alone. In the morning she wakes to the sound of her children as Finch leads them up a hill. Bancroft resigns herself to life, for good or ill, with the man. This is a fine film, encompassing the joys and tragedies of life: birth and death, marriage and divorce, love and hate. The leads give their characters life. They seem to be real people on the screen, not actors in a drama. Bancroft lends her role real depth, switching moods with eerie and wonderful believability. Mason, in a small supporting role, is nothing short of excellent. The script, by noted playwright Pinter, is complex and painful but often exhibits a good sense of the comic as well. The direction, slow and even-handed, allows the story to develop at its own pace, gradually building in speed as the story's intensity grows. This is a fine and sensitive work, a truthful portrait of human foibles and complexities. The film was charismatic character-actor Hardwicke's final one; he died the year of its release.

PURPLE ROSE OF CAIRO, THE

1985 84m c/bw Comedy/Fantasy ★★★½
Jack Rollins/Charles H. Joffe (U.S.) PG

Mia Farrow (Cecilia), Jeff Daniels (Tom Baxter/Gil Shepherd), Danny Aiello (Monk), Dianne Wiest (Emma), Van Johnson (Larry), Zoe Caldwell (The Countess), John Wood (Jason), Milo O'Shea (Fr. Donnelly), Deborah Rush (Rita), Irving Metzman (Theater Manager)

p, Robert Greenhut; d, Woody Allen; w, Woody Allen; ph, Gordon Willis; ed, Susan E. Morse; m, Dick Hyman; prod d, Stuart Wurtzel; art d, Edward Pisoni; cos, Jeffrey Kurland

AAN Best Original Screenplay: Woody Allen

The premise here is unique, but it wears thin after the first reel, even though director-writer Woody Allen strives mightily to keep things humming. Cecilia (Mia Farrow) is married to loutish, womanizing Monk (Danny Aiello) and lives a miserable life as a diner waitress. Her only escape from the woes of the depression is in the local movie house. Cecilia is particularly absorbed by a film (fictional) entitled "The Purple Rose of Cairo" starring a simon-pure hero (Jeff Daniels). She watches the same movie over and over, and then the miracle occurs. The hero suddenly faces the camera on-screen and begins to talk to Cecilia in the audience, then he startles the rest of the on-film actors by stepping out of the screen and into the theater, asking Cecilia to show him what real life is all about. He falls in love with her and she with him, but Monk and the Hollywood moguls are concerned. It's all a clever gimmick, of course, and Allen pulls it off well technically, but the story is as one-dimensional as the fictional Daniels. Where Allen succeeds is in his re-creation of the old studio programmers of the 1930s, something he had done briefly before in ZELIG. Allen has done better than this, but THE PURPLE ROSE OF CAIRO is a sweet little film and an interesting diversion for his legion of followers.

PURSUED

1947 101m bw Mystery/Western ★★★½
United States (U.S.) /PG

Teresa Wright (Thorley Callum), Robert Mitchum (Jeb Rand), Judith Anderson (Medora Callum), Dean Jagger (Grant Callum), Alan Hale (Jake Dingle), Harry Carey Jr. (Prentice McComber), John Rodney (Adam Callum), Clifton Young (The Sergeant), Ernest Severn (Jeb, Age 8), Charles Bates (Adam, Age 10)

p, Milton Sperling; d, Raoul Walsh; w, Niven Busch; ph, James Wong Howe; ed, Christian Nyby; m, Max Steiner; art d, Ted Smith; fx, William McGann, Willard Van Enger; cos, Leah Rhodes

An offbeat, film noir western/murder mystery which stars Robert Mitchum as Jeb Rand, a man pursued for his entire life by unseen (by him) assailants. Told in flashback, the film tells Jeb's story beginning when, as a young boy, his entire family was slaughtered—a vision that haunts him into adulthood. When the killers discover that Jeb was the only family member to survive, they vow to kill him too. He spends his life trying to find out who is responsible and why his adopted mother agreed to raise him. While not a mystery in the truest sense, PURSUED is one of the darkest films ever made—one in which the main character spends his entire life (and the duration of the film) being victimized by everyone around him. Although some of the motives are made clear in an early scene, Mitchum's character knows nothing of the mysterious

events which envelop him. It's not completely a western (it's merely a western location) and it's not completely a mystery, but it is a film which stretches the parameters of both genres.

PYGMALION

1938 96m bw Comedy ★★★★★
MGM (U.K.) /U

Leslie Howard (Prof. Henry Higgins), Wendy Hiller (Eliza Doolittle), Wilfrid Lawson (Alfred Doolittle), Marie Lohr (Mrs. Higgins), Scott Sunderland (Col. Pickering), Jean Cadell (Mrs. Pearce), David Tree (Freddy Eynsford-Hill), Everley Gregg (Mrs. Eynsford-Hill), Leueen MacGrath (Clara Eynsford-Hill), Esme Percy (Count Aristid Karpathy)

p, Gabriel Pascal; d, Anthony Asquith, Leslie Howard; w, George Bernard Shaw, W.P. Lipscomb, Cecil Lewis, Ian Dalrymple, Anthony Asquith (based on the play by George Bernard Shaw); ph, Harry Stradling; ed, David Lean; m, Arthur Honegger; art d, Laurence Irving; cos, Prof. Czettell, Worth, Schiaparelli

AAN Best Picture; AAN Best Actor: Leslie Howard; AAN Best Actress: Wendy Hiller; AA Best Screenplay: George Bernard Shaw; AA Best Adapted Screenplay: Ian Dalrymple, Cecil Lewis, W.P. Lipscomb

Shaw's magnificent comedy, a 1913 stage smash, was never better served than here, with Howard and Hiller perfectly matched as thoroughly mismatched lovers. Howard is Henry Higgins, a wealthy phonetics professor who encounters Cockney flower girl Eliza Doolittle (Hiller) and bets his friend Col. Pickering (Sunderland) that he can transform the uncouth and thick-accented woman ("a squashed cabbage leaf," he calls her) into a grand lady within three months. Eliza's hilarious lessons include speaking with marbles in her mouth to perfect her elocution. (When she swallows one, Higgins calmly notes, "That's all right. We have plenty more.") Eliza turns out to be a huge success at the ball, but what to do with her now?

The film, which Howard codirected with Asquith, is a delight from beginning to end. Hiller is splendid, making an amazing transformation from illiterate to lady. Eliza's first public test, when she takes tea with Henry's mother (Lohr, marvelous) is sidesplittingly funny. You may have tears in your eyes when Eliza goes on about her father's drinking and the fate of her deceased aunt's lovely straw hat. The curmudgeonly Shaw originally wanted Charles Laughton for Higgins, but Howard went way beyond the playwright's dour expectations, becoming the epitome of the intellectual tyrant. Sunderland is excellent as Pickering, and Lawson, as Doolittle the dustman, is stupendous. Lawson's speeches, along with other philosophical diatribes, were cut, despite producer Pascal's promises to Shaw; the playwright despised the interpolated "happy" ending, which was also used in the stage and screen versions of MY FAIR LADY.

Q

Q

1982 100m c Horror ★★★½
United Film Distribution (U.S.) R/15

Michael Moriarty (Jimmy Quinn), Candy Clark (Joan), David Carradine (Detective Shepard), Richard Roundtree (Sgt. Powell), James Dixon (Lt. Murray), Malachy McCourt (Police Commissioner), Fred J. Scollay (Capt. Fletcher), Peter Hock (Detective Clifford), Ron Cey (Detective Hoberman), Mary Louise Weller (Mrs. Pauley)

p, Larry Cohen; d, Larry Cohen; w, Larry Cohen; ph, Fred Murphy; ed, Armond Lebowitz; m, Robert O. Ragland; fx, Steve Neill, David Allen, Randall William Cook, Peter Kuran

Larry Cohen once again proves himself to be among the most creative, original, and intelligent American horror film directors in this bizarre masterwork, which successfully combines a *film noir* crime story with a good old-fashioned "giant monster" movie. Michael Moriarty turns in a brilliant performance as Jimmy Quinn, an ex-con, former junkie, and small-time hood looking to make one big score. After robbing a Manhattan diamond center, he hides out in the tower of the Chrysler Building and discovers a large hole in the dome of the structure, containing a huge nest with an equally large egg and several partially devoured human corpses. Meanwhile, the New York City police have been plagued by a bizarre string of deaths, and Detective Shepard (David Carradine) and Sgt. Powell (Richard Roundtree) have been investigating reports of people being snatched off rooftops. What all soon find out is that the Aztec god Quetzalcoatl, the winged serpent, is flying over Manhattan. Though Q's premise seems fairly silly (so does KING KONG's), Cohen's handling of the material is superior; he really convinces us that the idea of a giant bird living in a nest at the top of the Chrysler building isn't as implausible as it sounds. Cohen packs the film with stunning visuals and makes the most of New York City's architecture, capitalizing on its dozens of facades with birds and birdlike carvings. Q bombed at the box office because it was nearly impossible to package into a nice, simple ad campaign, but the film is a skillful combination of genres, sporting some fine acting and a literate, fascinating script with dashes of biting humor, that is well worth seeing.

Q&A

1990   134m   c   Crime/Drama   ★★½
Regency International Pictures-Odyssey Distributors   R/18
Ltd.   (U.S.)

Nick Nolte *(Lt. Mike Brennan)*, Timothy Hutton *(Al Reilly)*, Armand Assante *(Bobby Texador)*, Patrick O'Neal *(Kevin Quinn)*, Lee Richardson *(Leo Bloomenfeld)*, Luis Guzman *(Detective Luis Valentin)*, Charles Dutton *(Detective Sam Chapman)*, Jenny Lumet *(Nancy Bosch)*, Paul Calderon *(Roger Montalvo)*, International Chrysis *(Jose Malpica)*

p, Arnon Milchan, Burtt Harris; d, Sidney Lumet; w, Sidney Lumet (based on the book by Edwin Torres); ph, Andrzej Bartkowiak; ed, Richard Cirincione; m, Ruben Blades; prod d, Philip Rosenberg; art d, Beth Kuhn; cos, Ann Roth, Neil Spisak

An attempt to return to the police corruption territory which had provided Lumet with two of his best films (SERPICO and PRINCE OF THE CITY), Q&A is a pungent, graphic drama sabotaged by a stupid romantic sub-plot, misjudged casting and a truly abysmal soundtrack. Hailed by his peers as one of the finest cops in New York, Lt. Mike Brennan (Nick Nolte) is, in fact, one of the dirtiest men on the force. In the film's opening scene, he kills an unarmed Latino drug dealer in cold blood, then plants a gun on him. When more officers arrive on the scene, Brennan claims he shot the dealer in self-defense. Still, this incident requires an investigation by the DA's office, and cop turned assistant DA Al Reilly (Timothy Hutton) is assigned to the case. This being Reilly's first investigation, chief of homicide Kevin Quinn (Patrick O'Neal) briefs him on how to go about it: Reilly will ask questions regarding the incident, a stenographer will record Brennan's answers (the Q&A of the title) and, after a few interviews with some witnesses, the whole matter will be neatly cleared up. In their initial meeting, Brennan explains his side of the story in suspiciously thorough detail; then Reilly learns his own former girlfriend, Nancy (Jenny Lumet, the director's daughter), is now romantically involved with Bobby Texador (Armand Assante), a drug dealer who is also a witness. The young assistant DA decides to launch a full investigation of this seemingly simple matter and events take a dangerous turn. The trail of corruption leads from drug dealers to Brennan and, ultimately, Quinn.

Q&A is authentic and uncompromising in its depiction of racism within the police force, probably coming closer to capturing the casually offensive repartee of New York cops than any other film. It also does a fine job of evoking Lumet's much-loved city, from smoky bars to cluttered station houses to opulent criminal hideaways. But while creating this dark, seedy world, Lumet overstuffs Q&A with plot. Providing little or no character motivation, he trivializes the film's central concerns (racism and corruption) with his banal, cliched treatment of the relationship between Riley and Nancy. Matters aren't

helped by the fact that Hutton is miscast, while Jenny Lumet seems simply incapable of acting. Nolte, meanwhile, turns in a riveting performance, superbly aided and abetted by Luis Guzman and Charles Dutton as his initially loyal colleagues. The work of these three alone makes Q&A worth seeing, though you'll cringe every time the film's embarassing theme song comes thudding over the soundtrack.

QUADROPHENIA

1979   120m   c   Drama   ★★★★
Who Films   (U.K.)   R/X

Phil Daniels *(Jimmy Michael Cooper)*, Mark Wingett *(Dave)*, Philip Davis *(Chalky)*, Leslie Ash *(Steph)*, Garry Cooper *(Pete)*, Toyah Wilcox *(Monkey)*, Sting *(The Ace Face)*, Trevor Laird *(Ferdy)*, Gary Shail *(Spider)*, Kate Williams *(Mrs. Cooper)*

p, Roy Baird, Bill Curbishley; d, Franc Roddam; w, Dave Humphries, Martin Stellman, Franc Roddam, Pete Townshend; ph, Brian Tufano; ed, Mike Taylor; m, The Who; prod d, Simon Holland; chor, Gillian Gregory

In 1964 London, Jimmy (Phil Daniels) and his pals are Mods, dividing their time between dancing and brawling with Rockers. QUADROPHENIA episodically depicts Jimmy's struggles with his seemingly empty existence, alleviated only by his relationships with his pals, most of whom are in the same grim boat. Adapted from a double album written by Pete Townshend and performed by the Who (who also acted as executive producers for the film), QUADROPHENIA is one of the best films about youth ever made, beautifully illustrating the frustrations of being young and bright but still having no future. First-time director Franc Roddam does a fine job with his young cast and his re-creation of period detail is nearly perfect. Daniels gives an amazing performance as the confused Jimmy, looking for an identity and coming literally to the brink of self-destruction—so intense and full of divergent emotions, he seems ready to explode at any moment.

QUEEN CHRISTINA

1933   97m   bw   Historical/Romance   ★★★★★
MGM   (U.S.)   /U

Greta Garbo *(Queen Christina)*, John Gilbert *(Don Antonio De la Prada)*, Ian Keith *(Magnus)*, Lewis Stone *(Chancellor Oxenstierna)*, Elizabeth Young *(Ebba Sparre)*, C. Aubrey Smith *(Aage)*, Reginald Owen *(Prince Charles)*, Georges Renavent *(French Ambassador)*, Gustav von Seyffertitz *(General)*, David Torrence *(Archbishop)*

p, Walter Wanger; d, Rouben Mamoulian; w, H.M. Harwood, Salka Viertel, S.N. Behrman (based on a story by Salka Viertel, Margaret R. Levino); ph, William Daniels; ed, Blanche Sewell; m, Herbert Stothart; art d, Alexander Toluboff, Edwin B. Willis; cos, Adrian

A revelation, wrung from the usual MGM Bio identikit, but given shape by Mamoulian's painterly eye, and immortality by Garbo's ability to transcend. Even when the script serves up great clumps of unleavened bread, Garbo imbues it with living emotion. Although the same cannot be said of still-handsome Gilbert's Spanish Ambassador, their love scenes capture the depth of overwhelming emotion in an unparalleled, perfectly beautiful way. If some of Garbo's other performances have dated, this one documents her magical strangeness in a way that has stood the test of time.

Garbo's CHRISTINA is a decisive queen, ruling Sweden with wisdom and compassion. Her former lover, Magnus (Keith), attempts to arrange a marriage between Christina and a dashing prince, but she will have nothing to do with political unions. Then, while out riding, she encounters Don Antonio (Gilbert), the newly appointed ambassador from Spain. Intrigued by the gallant Spaniard, Christina decides to discover his real nature by disguising herself as a man. She goes to an inn where she knows Don Antonio is staying. He befriends her, and, unaware that she is a woman, invites Christina to spend the night in his room. She eventually reveals her identity and the two fall in love, spending two glorious days and nights together. Their idyll over, Christina returns to her court and receives Don Antonio officially, pretending she knows him only as an official representative of a foreign power. He is there, he informs her, to ask for her hand in marriage—for the king of Spain. She does not respond, but instead continues to meet him secretly. When the manipulative Magnus discovers their meetings, he rouses the public against Don Antonio, labeling him a trifling interloper.

In QUEEN CHRISTINA, Garbo had her way, making use of an iron-clad contract that paid her $250,000 a film, gave her the choice of director, cameraman, leading man, and, in fact, the entire cast, if she cared to select the extras. She had seen a young British actor, Laurence Olivier, in an Ann Harding vehicle, WESTWARD PASSAGE, and liked him. Olivier was signed to play the Spanish ambassador and came to the studio to rehearse with Garbo, at Mamoulian's suggestion. The rehearsal was a disaster, as Garbo froze up. Olivier was told to forget about appearing in a Garbo film, and Mamoulian immediately called Gilbert, asking him to help warm up the woman he had starred with in the heyday of the silent era. The effect he had on her was amazing. Still, the studio proposed other leading players, *anyone* but Gilbert, but Garbo refused anyone else. Much has been said about Garbo's magnanimous insistence that Gilbert, the fallen star, join her in a major film to rescue his almost lost career. She was reportedly no longer in love with him but was returning the favor he had extended to her at the beginning of *her* career, when he demanded she costar with him in the silent classic FLESH AND THE DEVIL. But not until Gilbert signed his contract to do QUEEN CHRISTINA did Mayer give up trying to replace him. Chief of production Irving Thalberg and Garbo hoped for a comeback for Gilbert, but even though he was touching in his role, the public was no longer interested, having bought the myth, sponsored by Mayer, about the actor's inadequacy in talkies.

QUEEN MARGOT
(LA REINE MARGOT)

1994   143m   c   Drama/Historical/Romance   ★★★
Renn Productions/France 2 Cinema/Films Nef   R/18
Filmproduktion/Wing RCS Films & TV
(France/Germany/Italy)

Isabelle Adjani *(Marguerite de Valois—the Queen Margot)*, Vincent Perez *(Joseph de la Mole)*, Virna Lisi *(Catherine de Medici)*, Jean-Hugues Anglade *(Charles IX)*, Daniel Auteuil *(Henri of Navarre)*, Otto Tausig *(Mendes)*, Thomas Kretschmann *(Nancay)*, Pascal Greggory *(Duc d'Anjou)*, Julien Rassam *(Alencon)*, Jean-Claude Brialy *(Coligny)*

p, Claude Berri; d, Patrice Chereau; w, Patrice Chereau, Daniele Thompson (based on the novel by Alexander Dumas); ph, Philippe Rousselot; ed, Francois Gedigier, Helene Viard; m, Goran Bregovic; prod d, Richard Peduzzi, Olivier Radot; fx, Georges Demetrau; cos, Moidele Bickel

AAN Best Costume Design: Moidele Bikel

A lavish historical spectacle, QUEEN MARGOT is the sort of film Hollywood never made, teeming with violence, sex, and colorful period accessories, all legitimized with a veneer of historical importance. It's sumptuous and entertaining, but keeping up with the huge cast and complicated plot is no easy task.

In 1572, during the reign of Catholic King Charles IX (Jean-Hugues Anglade), France is torn by religious strife: Protestants and Catholics vie for political control, and power-behind-the-throne Catherine de Medici (Virna Lisi) decides to placate the Protestants by wedding her daughter Marguerite de Valois (Isabelle Adjani), better known as Margot, to the Protestant Henri of Navarre (Daniel Auteuil). Their arranged marriage is the catalyst of a series of intrigues, massacres, and murders.

QUEEN MARGOT manages—though only barely—to survive the film's relentless focus on the basest aspects of life among the "silk-and-vultures" who were France's 16th-century elite. Most of the film veers between scenes of ghastly violence and scenes of steamy sex (in a curious nod to American conventions, the violence is extremely graphic, while the bedroom scenes involve no frontal nudity). Margot's relationship with her older brothers is unmistakably incestuous and, generally speaking, her carnal desires take precedence over all other concerns; when Protestant zealots refer to her as the Catholic whore, it's hard to take issue with their assessment.

Based on the historical novel by Alexandre Dumas, QUEEN MARGOT was directed with tremendous attention to visual detail by Patrice Chereau, whose background lies in theater and opera. In con-

trast to most Hollywood epics of this size and scope, the film wallows in the period's nasty details as lovingly as its sumptuous ones: it's filled with rich silks and lavishly embroidered fabrics, and they're all grimy.

QUEEN OF HEARTS

1989   112m   c   Comedy/Romance   ★★★★
Enterprise/TVS/Nelson   (U.K.)   PG

Vittorio Duse *(Nonno)*, Joseph Long *(Danilo)*, Anita Zagaria *(Rosa)*, Eileen Way *(Mama Sibilla)*, Vittorio Amandola *(Barbariccia)*, Roberto Scateni *(Falco)*, Stefano Spagnoli *(Young Eddie)*, Alec Bregonzi *(Headwaiter)*, Ronan Vivert *(Man in Pig Scene)*, Matilda Thorpe *(Woman in Pig Scene)*

p, John Hardy; d, Jon Amiel; w, Tony Grisoni; ph, Mike Southon; ed, Peter Boyle; m, Michael Convertino; prod d, Jim Clay; art d, Philip Elton; cos, Lindy Hemming

A jewel of a film from director Jon Amiel, who directed Dennis Potter's award-winning "The Singing Detective." QUEEN OF HEARTS is a mystical fable of love and revenge, seen through the imaginative eyes of a child. Now grown, Eddie (Ian Hawkes) narrates the flashback story of his close-knit Italian family, who emigrate to England after WWII, when his father, Danilo (Joseph Long), and mother, Rosa (Anita Zagaria), elope, escaping her arranged marriage to the wealthy Barbariccia (Vittorio Amandola). On the advice of a talking pig, Danilo makes enough money gambling to become the proprietor of a London restaurant, the Lucky Cafe, supporting his family until Barbariccia, who has also emigrated and become the owner of several gambling houses, wins everything Danilo owns in a card game. The stage is then set for the STING-like scam the family works to get even with Barbariccia. There may be a few Italian immigrant family cliches along the way, but the characters in QUEEN OF HEARTS are treated sensitively, with much humor and warmth—never patronized. Much credit has to go to the film's wonderful cast, handpicked by director Amiel from what he called "a treasure trove" of relative unknowns.

QUEST FOR FIRE

1981   97m   c   Adventure/Historical   ★★★
ICC/Cine-Trail/Belstar   (France/Canada)   R/15

Everett McGill *(Naoh Ulam Tribe Member)*, Ron Perlman *(Amoukar Ulam Tribe Member)*, Nameer El-Kadi *(Gaw Ulam Tribe Member)*, Rae Dawn Chong *(Ika Ivaka Tribe Member)*, Gary Schwartz, Frank Olivier Bonnet, Jean-Michel Kindt, Kurt Schiegl, Brian Gill, Terry Fitt

p, John Kemeny, Denis Heroux, Jacques Dorfmann, Vera Belmont; d, Jean-Jacques Annaud; w, Gerard Brach (based on the novel *La Guerre de Feu* by J.H. Rosny, Sr.); ph, Claude Agostini; ed, Yves Langlois; m, Philippe Sarde; prod d, Brian Morris, Guy Comtois; art d, Clinton Cavers; fx, Martin Malivoire; cos, John Hay, Penny Rose

AA Best Makeup: Sarah Monzani, Michele Burke

A fascinating look at what the life of early man may have been like, QUEST FOR FIRE stars Everett McGill, Ron Perlman, and Nameer El-Kadi as members of a prehistoric tribe, the Ulams, who are sent out to find fire after their only source is accidentally extinguished. They find another, barbarous tribe, the Ivakas, who to the amazement of the Ulams can create fire using flint and sticks. The three rescue Ika (Rae Dawn Chong) from the cruel Ivakas and take her along, with the secret of firestarting. The characters register humor, grief, happiness, anxiety, and other everyday emotions, creating realistic personalities that the audience can identify with. Desmond Morris, author of "The Naked Ape," created a body language for the film based on actual simian gestures, while famed novelist Anthony Burgess created a primitive language. Although occasionally bleak, the film affords many pleasurable moments, showing early man learning to laugh and expressing delight and amazement at the sight of fire. The film received an Academy Award for Best Make-Up.

QUESTION OF SILENCE, A
(DE STILTE ROND CHRISTINE M.)

1983 92m c Crime   ★★★½
Sigma (Netherlands)   R/15

Cox Habbema *(Dr. Janine Van Den Bos)*, Edda Barends *(Christine M.)*, Nelly Frijda *(Waitress)*, Henriette Tol *(Secretary)*, Eddy Brugman *(Rudd)*, Dolf DeVries *(Boutique Manager)*, Kees Coolen *(Police Inspector)*, Onno Molenkamp *(Pathologist)*, Hans Croiset *(Judge)*, Eric Plooyer

p, Matthijs van Heijningen; d, Marleen Gorris; w, Marleen Gorris; ph, Frans Bromet; ed, Hans Van Dongen; m, Lodewijk De Boer, Martijn Hasebos; prod d, Harry Ammerlaan

This controversial film focuses on three women—housewife Christine M. (Edda Barends), waitress Annie (Nelly Frijda), and secretary Andrea (Henriette Tol)—who, though unacquainted, spontaneously kill a male boutique owner when he catches one of them shoplifting. They are arrested and assigned a female psychiatrist, Dr. Janine Van Den Bos (Cox Habbema), who prepares a plea of insanity. Christine appears to be the most deeply affected of the threesome, slipping into a state of shock and refusing to utter a word. As Dr. Van Den Bos talks with Annie and Andrea, she begins to have her doubts about the insanity plea, and the murder makes increasingly more sense to her. Each of the three women was dealing with her own frustrations with men: the housewife was a slave to housekeeping duties and a victim of a thoughtless husband; the waitress subjected to rude comments by male customers; and the secretary constantly treated as a subordinate at the executive office where she worked. Instead of confirming the expected insanity pleas, Dr. Van Den Bos tells the courtroom that the women are fully responsible for the crime against the patronizing shopkeeper. But to the surprise of the males in the courtroom, all the women present unite in a grand show of female solidarity. QUESTION OF SILENCE is the first feature from writer-director Marleen Gorris, who hit upon the idea after reading an article about a working-class woman's arrest for shoplifting. Instead of putting three murderesses on trial, this superb, disturbing feminist film turns the tables and puts male society on the stand—which will undoubtedly anger as many viewers as it thrills.

QUIET MAN, THE

1952 129m c Romance/Comedy   ★★★★★
Argosy (U.S.)   /U

John Wayne *(Sean Thornton)*, Maureen O'Hara *(Mary Kate Danaher)*, Barry Fitzgerald *(Michaeleen Flynn)*, Ward Bond *(Fr. Peter Lonergan)*, Victor McLaglen *(Red Will Danaher)*, Mildred Natwick *(Mrs. Sarah Tillane)*, Francis Ford *(Dan Tobin)*, Eileen Crowe *(Mrs. Elizabeth Playfair)*, May Craig *(Woman at Railway Station)*, Arthur Shields *(Rev. Cyril Playfair)*

p, Merian C. Cooper, John Ford, Michael Killanin; d, John Ford; w, Frank S. Nugent, Richard Llewellyn (based on the story by Maurice Walsh); ph, Winton C. Hoch, Archie Stout; ed, Jack Murray; m, Victor Young; art d, Frank Hotaling; cos, Adele Palmer

AAN Best Picture; AAN Best Supporting Actor: Victor McLaglen; AA Best Director: John Ford; AAN Best Screenplay: Frank S. Nugent; AA Best Cinematography: Winton Hoch, Archie Stout; AAN Best Art Direction: Frank Hotaling, John McCarthy, Jr., Charles Thompson; AAN Best Sound: Daniel J. Bloomberg

Epic romantic comedy, but so thick on the blarney, that it helps to be Irish, at least to a degree. Otherwise, it may be hard to get a grasp on the turbulent traditions, fiesty sentimentality and burning coldness that exists in the Irish soul. That understood, cook a corned beef and invite the neighbors over.

THE QUIET MAN is Ford's sentimental journey into the past of his ancestral Ireland, a journey enacted by Ford's onscreen alter ego, John Wayne. The story begins in the 1920s, when American Sean Thornton (Wayne), a quiet fellow but a former boxer with a brutal past, arrives in Innisfree. He is met by the elfin, capricious Michaeleen Flynn (Fitzgerald), the village cabman. Sean is off to a little cottage—his birthplace, White O'Mornin'—which he has bought from a local widow (Natwick). En route, he sees in the distance a beautiful, red-haired woman framed by trees, a soft wind rippling her skirts and hair.

She seems a vision of a lost world, and Wayne asks Flynn, "Is that real?" (Quips the cabbie, "Only a mirage brought on by your terrible thirst!") Wayne is really asking about the scene itself, rather than than the lovely woman gracing it, and recalls his dead mother as she described Innisfree to him as a child. Arriving at his cottage, he tells Flynn, "I'm Sean Thornton and I was born in that little cottage. I'm home and home I'm going to stay." It's almost a declaration of war against the perils of the present in favor of the safety of the past.

In buying his land, Sean has alienated the richest, toughest man in the area, Red Will Danaher (McLaglen), who is doubly peeved over his being a "dirty Yank". Though his land looks fertile, Sean turns up nothing but rocks when he tries to plow it for planting. He battles the present for the illusion of the past at every turn, and is even upbraided for his romanticism when he proudly shows off his cottage to a neighbor, who inspects its thatched roof and immaculately painted walls, remarking that "It looks the way all Irish cottages should, and seldom do. And only an American would think of painting it emerald green." One day, Sean enters his cottage to find his neighbor Mary Kate (O'Hara) cleaning up for him, a gesture suggesting more than communal fellowship. Just as she is about to flee, Sean attempts to kiss her. She gives him a stiff-armed slap, but, before running off, encourages him with a kiss of her own. Later, Sean meets Red Will, Mary Kate's brutish brother, in the local pub. When Sean extends his hand, the powerful Irishman squeezes it with all his might and the ex-boxer responds with his own pressure, until both are wincing in pain.

Witnessing this first confrontation between the two giants is a group of locals—most of whom hate Red Will and side with Sean. Sean has already befriended Father Lonergan (Bond), though he goes out of his way to say nothing of his past. But the local Protestant clergyman (Shields) knows Sean's dark secret and tells him so privately. The minister, a onetime amateur boxer, has kept a scrapbook about boxers the world over and knows that "Trooper Thorn" retired after accidentally killing a man in the ring. Discredited, Sean moved with his prize money to Ireland to find the peace, happiness, and beauty of his boyhood. A memorable fight with Red Will, though, awaits the "quiet man."

A love story that packs a fearsome punch, THE QUIET MAN is a passionate, full-blooded film. Ford constructs the picture carefully, and lavishes the tale with some of the most visually extraordinary scenes ever filmed. Some of these, such as the idealistic vision of O'Hara in the glen herding her sheep, are presented in muted, diffused tones that suggest an ethereal world—into which Wayne has barged. THE QUIET MAN is Ford's symbolic homecoming, in which he shapes his own longing and memories in the form of living, full-blooded characters, who are at the same time representative types. Wayne is Ford's youth; O'Hara his great love, as well as all the women of Ireland; McLaglen, the sentimental bully; Bond, the priest who would rather fish than pray, though fishing is also a form of prayer; Shields, the patient outsider; Natwick, the typical Irish widow; Fitzgerald, the local conscience and historian (he also delivers the film's best line after seeing the broken wedding bed: "Impetuous! Homeric!"). The wonderful performances by Ford's stock company in these roles help make THE QUIET MAN an utterly moving and fascinating portrait of rural life in Ireland.

QUILOMBO

1984 114m c Historical   ★★★★
CDK (Brazil)

Antonio Pompeo *(Zumbi)*, Zeze Motta *(Dandara)*, Tony Tornado *(Ganga Zumba)*, Vera Fischer *(Ana de Ferro)*, Antonio Pitanga *(Acaiuba)*, Mauricio do Valle *(Domingos Jorge Velho)*, Daniel Filho *(Carrilho)*, Joao Nogueira *(Rufino)*, Jorge Coutinho *(Sale)*, Grande Otelo *(Baba)*

p, Augusto Arraes; d, Carlos Diegues; w, Carlos Diegues; ph, Lauro Escorel Filho; ed, Mair Tavares

This is a spectacular, brilliantly colored historical epic that explores the beginnings of Quilombo de Palmares, the Brazilian slave nation in the mid-1600s. Director Diegues described the nation as "the first democratic society that we know of in the Western hemisphere." The picture begins as the slaves revolt and violently murder their Portuguese owners. Taking to the forests of northeastern Brazil, the slaves form a nation, free from the oppression of slave owners. They are soon joined by other oppressed peoples such as Jews and poor white farmers. A government is created and a leader elected—Ganga Zumba, played by Tornado. The Portuguese, however, retaliate and attempt to conquer the nation. Diegues previously scored on American art-house screens with BYE BYE BRAZIL and XICA. Here, he successfully manages to mix history with folklore. Exquisitely photographed and lavishly produced, the film has a great deal of action, culminating with some intense battle sequences, but it often loses sight of its story. More than examining a historic period, QUILOMBO, like Diegues's other films, comments on the present state of Brazil as well as the nation's possible future.

QUIZ SHOW

1994   120m   c   Drama/Historical   ★★★½
Baltimore Pictures/Dreyfuss-James Productions/Hollywood PG-13/15
Pictures   (U.S.)

John Turturro *(Herb Stempel)*, Rob Morrow *(Richard Goodwin)*, Ralph Fiennes *(Charles Van Doren)*, Paul Scofield *(Mark Van Doren)*, David Paymer *(Dan Enright)*, Hank Azaria *(Albert Freedman)*, Christopher McDonald *(Jack Barry)*, Johann Carlo *(Toby Stempel)*, Elizabeth Wilson *(Dorothy Van Doren)*, Allan Rich *(Robert Kintner)*

p, Robert Redford, Michael Jacobs, Julian Krainin, Michael Nozik; d, Robert Redford; w, Paul Attanasio (based on the book "Remembering America: A Voice From the Sixties" by Richard N. Goodwin); ph, Michael Ballhaus; ed, Stu Linder; m, Mark Isham; prod d, Jon Hutman; art d, Tim Galvin; cos, Kathy O'Rear

AAN Best Picture; AAN Best Supporting Actor: Paul Scofield; *AAN Best Director:* Robert Redford; *AAN Best Adapted Screenplay:* Paul Attanasio

A meditation on the loss of moral character in America, director Robert Redford's recounting of the 1950's quiz show scandals has much to recommend it, but fails to answer the $64,000 question—"so what?"

New York, 1957. Herb Stempel (John Turturro) is the reigning champion on "Twenty-One," one of the big-money quiz shows drawing huge new audiences to the fledgling medium of television. Stempel is seemingly unbeatable, but network and sponsor think he's a "schmuck with a face for radio," and they want him off the show. Enter Columbia professor Charles Van Doren (Ralph Fiennes), a handsome WASP with an impeccable intellectual pedigree. "Twenty-One" producer Dan Enright (David Paymer) convinces Van Doren to participate in a fraudulent scheme: in order to guarantee his continuing appearance on the show, he's supplied with the answers in advance.

Ironically, the scandal that threatened to bring down television served as the impetus for the three networks to take monopolistic control over the entire industry, from production to broadcast, ending TV's "Golden Age" and ushering in the so-called "Vast Wasteland" era of the 60s. QUIZ SHOW's success is likewise defined by its unintended consequences. It purports to reveal the genesis of a morally ambiguous culture that accepts, and even expects, deception. Assuming that's true, however, the contemporary mass audience, raised on televisual values and inured to fraudulence, will presumably shrug off Redford's charges with bemused apathy.

Formally, QUIZ SHOW deserves a great deal of praise. It's a blessedly old-fashioned, well-made and well-acted narrative; the scenes involving the Van Doren and Stempel families, and the show's producers, stand out, while Rob Morrow (as crusading attorney Richard Goodwin) makes an unnecessary meal out of his character's Boston accent.

QUO VADIS

1951   171m   c   Historical   ★★★½
MGM   (U.S.)   /PG

Robert Taylor *(Marcus Vinicius)*, Deborah Kerr *(Lygia)*, Leo Genn *(Petronius)*, Peter Ustinov *(Nero)*, Patricia Laffan *(Poppaea)*, Finlay Currie *(Peter)*, Abraham Sofaer *(Paul)*, Marina Berti *(Eunice)*, Buddy Baer *(Ursus)*, Felix Aylmer *(Plautius)*

p, Sam Zimbalist; d, Mervyn LeRoy; w, John Lee Mahin, S.N. Behrman, Sonya Levien (based on the novel by Henryk Sienkiewicz); ph, Robert Surtees, William V. Skall; ed, Ralph E. Winters; m, Miklos Rozsa; art d, William McCoy, Cedric Gibbons, Edward Carfagno; fx, Thomas Hayward, A. Arnold Gillespie, Donald Jarnhaus; chor, Madi Obolensky, Auriel Millos; cos, Herschel McCoy

AAN Best Picture; AAN Best Supporting Actor: Leo Genn; *AAN Best Supporting Actor:* Peter Ustinov; *AAN Best Cinematography:* Robert Surtees, William V. Skall; *AAN Best Editing:* Ralph E. Winters; *AAN Best Score:* Miklos Rozsa; *AAN Best Art Direction:* William A. Horning, Cedric Gibbons, Edward C. Carfagno, Hugh Hunt; *AAN Best Costume Design:* Herschel McCoy

One of MGM's biggest box-office hits, the epic QUO VADIS offers a spectacular cast to match its overwhelming production; there's plenty to enjoy, but don't look for greatness. Over it all looms a loony Ustinov as Emperor Nero, despite director LeRoy's best efforts to keep him from chewing the scenery as he enjoyably steals the show. Taylor is the nominal star, playing Marcus Vinicius, a Roman army commander who returns victorious to the Eternal City in the 1st Century AD. After receiving a hero's welcome from the empress (Laffan), Marcus meets Lygia (Kerr), a hostage who is the Christian daughter of a defeated king. He lusts after her, but is put off by her oversized pal Ursus (the aptly named Baer), and further rejected by Lygia because he is a pagan. Angered, Marcus makes Lygia his slave, but is still unable to make her his mistress. How he manages forms the core of the story.

The acting is good, especially that of Kerr, Taylor, and Genn (as the gentle advisor to the emperor), but it's the wild Ustinov who scoops up every scene he's in, giving one of the most outlandish performances ever filmed. Ustinov tested for the role of the lyre-playing little arsonist in 1949, but the film was slow to develop. A year later, MGM wired Ustinov that they were still interested in him for the part but they were worried that he might be too young for the role. Ustinov wired back, "If you wait much longer I shall be too old. Nero died at thirty-one." (Tony Thomas, *Ustinov in Focus.*)

Shot in six months at a cost of almost $7 million, QUO VADIS gleaned $25 million in world rentals and became the second all-time grosser after GONE WITH THE WIND. It led the way for all those crazy religious epics which dominated popular postwar production: SALOME, IVANHOE, THE ROBE, DAVID AND BATHSHEBA, THE SILVER CHALICE, and BEN HUR, which would surpass its boxoffice take. Enhancing this epic's success was the fine score by Miklos Rozsa, who, along with MGM librarian George Schneider, located all the known instruments of the period and then, although no clear record of the era's music remained, pieced his score together through slave songs, Christian hymns, marches, and fanfares played on modern instruments (using the Scottish clarsach to approximate the sound of the ancient lyre, for example). QUO VADIS was nominated for eight Oscars, but the lions were passed over. Imagine that.

R

RABID

1977   91m   c   Science Fiction/Horror   ★★
Cinepix/Dibar   (Canada)   R/

Marilyn Chambers *(Rose)*, Frank Moore *(Hart Read)*, Joe Silver *(Murray Cypher)*, Howard Ryshpan *(Dr. Dan Keloid)*, Patricia Gage *(Dr. Roxanne Keloid)*, Susan Roman *(Mindy Kent)*, Roger Periard *(Lloyd Walsh)*, Lynne Deragon *(Nurse Louise)*, Terry Schonblum *(Judy Glasberg)*, Victor Desy *(Claude LaPointe)*

p, John Dunning; d, David Cronenberg; w, David Cronenberg; ph, Rene Verzier; ed, Jean LaFleur; art d, Claude Marchand; fx, Joe Blasco, Al Griswold; cos, Erla Gliserman

A virtual remake of THEY CAME FROM WITHIN, RABID finds director David Cronenberg more in control of his narrative and his visual style than in his previous films, but the results are still somewhat uneven. Once again Cronenberg explores sexually transmitted horror, but this time through none other than hardcore porno starlet Marilyn Chambers, who makes her legitimate debut here as Rose, a woman seriously injured in a motorcycle accident. A local plastic surgeon uses the opportunity to experiment with some new skin grafts he's been developing, but somehow the surgery goes awry and soon Rose sports a grotesque, phallus-like organ in her armpit that sucks blood out of her unsuspecting lovers (the original treatment of the film was entitled "Mosquito"). This soon leads to an epidemic that turns the citizens of Montreal into rabid, blood-seeking, sex-crazed monsters that drool green slime.

Once again, Cronenberg has made a rather frustrating film. Although RABID is full of interesting ideas, they are not particularly well developed or presented by Cronenberg's unfocused script. And while the film has an uneasy sense of humor, Cronenberg again overplays his most visceral sequences, including the well-shot but pointless car crash. As with THEY CAME FROM WITHIN, the performances are weak, and while Chambers does add some resonance to the film as a sexual icon, her acting ability is decidedly limited.

RACHEL, RACHEL

1968 101m c Drama   ★★★½
Kayos (U.S.)   R/X

Joanne Woodward (*Rachel Cameron*), James Olson (*Nick Kazlik*), Kate Harrington (*Mrs. Cameron*), Estelle Parsons (*Calla Mackie*), Donald Moffat (*Niall Cameron*), Terry Kiser (*Preacher*), Franco Corsaro (*Hector Jonas*), Bernard Barrow (*Leighton Siddley*), Geraldine Fitzgerald (*Rev. Wood*), Nell Potts (*Rachel as a Child*)

p, Paul Newman; d, Paul Newman; w, Stewart Stern (based on the novel *A Jest of God* by Margaret Laurence); ph, Gayne Rescher; ed, Dede Allen; m, Jerome Moross, Erik Satie, Robert Schumann; art d, Robert Gundlach; cos, Domingo Rodriguez

AAN Best Picture; AAN Best Actress: Joanne Woodward; *AAN Best Supporting Actress:* Estelle Parsons; *AAN Best Adapted Screenplay:* Stewart Stern

Woodward, Parsons, Stern (screenwriter), and the picture itself were all nominated for Oscars, and Newman and Woodward both won awards from the New York Film Critics. While other directors were impressing with their flash and technique in the 1960s, Newman chose to make a small, understated, and very sensitive film as his directorial debut. It was sometimes halting and quite spare, but the overall effect was excellent and business was meritorious, something no one expected. Newman had trouble securing the financing and was saved by then-production chief Ken Hyman, a man with some foresight who recognized the need for this kind of story. Shot on location at various Connecticut sites, the film was a departure for Woodward, who had been made into a glamour girl in her early years and resented it.

Woodward is a lonely, bored spinster who lives with her widowed mother, Harrington. Her best friend, Parsons, makes what has to be termed a "pass" at Woodward, who decides she had better find out what men are like before she falls into a homosexual pattern. Woodward is sexually naive, frustrated, and willing to learn, so when Olson, a childhood friend, comes back to the small town to visit his parents, she is easy for him to seduce.

The film's double-word title is made more intriguing because Newman uses his and Woodward's daughter, Nell Potts, as the young Rachel; and Woodward is occasionally replaced by Potts to indicate that the child in her still remains. In the final scene, for example, as Woodward climbs on the bus to Oregon, she waves farewell to Potts, finally bidding good-bye to the child she's been. In later years, a horde of "women's pictures" would appear, but this one was the first in the cycle and one of the best. It could have been a drab, weepy story, but Stern and Newman collaborated to make it an inspiring one that proves one is never too old to change one's life.

RACKET, THE

1951 88m bw Crime   ★★★★
RKO (U.S.)   /A

Robert Mitchum (*Capt. McQuigg*), Lizabeth Scott (*Irene*), Robert Ryan (*Scanlon*), William Talman (*Johnson*), Ray Collins (*Welch*), Joyce MacKenzie (*Mary McQuigg*), Robert Hutton (*Ames*), Virginia Huston (*Lucy Johnson*), William Conrad (*Turck*), Walter Sande (*Delaney*)

p, Edmund Grainger; d, John Cromwell, Nicholas Ray; w, William Wister Haines, W.R. Burnett (based on the play by Bartlett Cormack); ph, George E. Diskant; ed, Sherman Todd; m, Paul Sawtell, Roy Webb; art d, Albert S. D'Agostino, Jack Okey; cos, Michael Woulfe

This hard-hitting melodrama was the second film adaptation of Bartlett Cormack's popular 1920s play from Howard Hughes, who released a version in 1928 and updated the story here to tie it in with the then-controversial Kefauver crime hearings, which had captured the TV viewing audience of the day. Mitchum (in a switch from his usual casting) plays a tough, honest police captain in a midwestern city who, on the eve of an important election, battles to wrest control of the city's government from crime boss Ryan.

Director Cromwell does a fine job of keeping up a lightning pace here, and elicits a great performance from Ryan, who is truly sinister in his profile of the gang boss striving to change his unalterably violent character. Mitchum is solid if not enthusiastic in his role as an honest cop, and the rest of the cast (particularly Collins and Conrad) is excellent, though Scott, while appropriately sultry and attractive, is little more than window dressing in her role. After taking over RKO in 1948, Hughes immediately scheduled THE RACKET for production, banking on the success of the 1928 film version, though the remake is more faithful to Cormack's play (in which Cromwell had appeared as an actor). The city profiled, of course, is Chicago and its corrupt politics of the 1920s. Cromwell had been directing films on and off at RKO since 1932; this picture marked his last such assignment for the studio.

RADIO DAYS

1987 85m c Comedy   ★★★½
Orion (U.S.)   PG

Woody Allen (*Narrator*), Seth Green (*Little Joe*), Julie Kavner (*Mother*), Michael Tucker (*Father*), Dianne Wiest (*Aunt Bea*), Josh Mostel (*Uncle Abe*), Renee Lippin (*Aunt Ceil*), William Magerman (*Grandpa*), Leah Carrey (*Grandma*), Joy Newman (*Ruthie*)

p, Robert Greenhut; d, Woody Allen; w, Woody Allen; ph, Carlo Di Palma; ed, Susan E. Morse; prod d, Santo Loquasto; art d, Speed Hopkins; cos, Jeffrey Kurland

AAN Best Original Screenplay: Woody Allen; *AAN Best Art Direction:* Santo Loquasto, Carol Joffe, Les Bloom, George DeTitta, Jr.

Writer-director Woody Allen draws on his own past in this nostalgic piece, cross-cutting between the Brooklyn of his youth, in this case the Rockaway area, and the uptown life being led by radio personalities. Allen gives us a typical yet intriguing family in Rockaway. Joe (Seth Green) is the youthful protagonist who lives with his parents (Julie Kavner and Michael Tucker), grandparents (Willian Magerman and Leah Carrey), maiden aunt Bea (Dianne Wiest), uncle Abe (Josh Mostel, son of Zero), Abe's wife Ceil (Renee Lippin), and their daughter Ruthie (Joy Newman). In voice-over, Allen (who doesn't appear in the film) relates stories about members of this household. While life goes on in Brooklyn, Allen intercuts stories about radio and its personalities, many of the tales focusing on Sally White (Mia Farrow), a cigarette girl with a dreadful "Noo Yawk" accent who dreams of radio stardom. If this summary sounds disjointed, so is the film. There is no real story, just a succession of funny and nostalgic interludes. Allen presents a host of anecdotes and remembrances of things past, but one wishes it could have been slightly more cohesive. One of the joys in this picture is the soundtrack of songs of the period that will delight anyone who lived in those radio days.

RAFFLES

1930 70m bw Crime/Romance   ★★★½
UA (U.S.)   /U

Ronald Colman (*A.J. Raffles*), Kay Francis (*Lady Gwen Manders*), Bramwell Fletcher (*Bunny Manders*), Frances Dade (*Ethel Crowley*), David Torrence (*McKenzie*), Alison Skipworth (*Lady Kitty Melrose*), Frederick Kerr (*Lord Harry Melrose*), John Rogers (*Crawshaw*), Wilson Benge (*Barraclough*), Virginia Bruce (*Blonde*)

p, Samuel Goldwyn; d, Harry d'Abbadie D'Arrast, George Fitzmaurice; w, Sidney Howard (based on the novel *the Amateur Cracksman* by Ernest William Hornung and the play "Raffles, The

Amateur Cracksman" by E.W. Hornung, Eugene Wiley Presbrey); ph, George Barnes, Gregg Toland; ed, Stuart Heisler; art d, William Cameron Menzies, Park French

AAN Best Sound: Oscar Lagerstrom

After being adapted for the stage, Ernest William Hornung's novel *The Amateur Cracksman* came to the screen twice in the silent era, with John Barrymore and House Peters cast as the roguish A.J. Raffles in the 1914 and 1925 versions, respectively. In this first sound version of the story, Ronald Colman is the famed British cricket player who spends his evenings as "The Amateur Cracksman," an equally famous criminal who consistently eludes Scotland Yard. Colman falls in love with beautiful socialite Kay Francis and manages to wangle an invitation to a weekend bash thrown by blue-blood Alison Skipworth, who owns an extremely valuable—and very tempting—necklace.

Having established himself with moviegoers as Bulldog Drummond, Colman found himself in another crowd-pleasing role as the lovable Raffles. Opening to almost unanimously favorable reviews, RAFFLES marked a farewell to silent films for Sam Goldwyn's production company. A firm believer in the future of sound films, Goldwyn quickly made the transition, and this picture was the last that his company produced in both silent and sound versions. Goldwyn's faith in sound recording resulted in an Oscar nomination for sound recordist Oscar Lagerstrom. The picture was begun under the direction of Harry d'Abbadie D'Arrast (LAUGHTER), but he was fired and his name struck from the credits by Goldwyn after endless disagreements between the two. His replacement, George Fitzmaurice, an able craftsman, had been responsible for bringing D'Arrast to Hollywood from France eight years earlier. RAFFLES was remade, practically scene for scene, in 1939 with David Niven and Olivia de Havilland in the leads, and again in 1960 as EL RAFFLES MEXICANO, a Spanish-language picture with Rafael Bertrand as The Amateur Cracksman.

RAGGEDY MAN
1981 94m c Drama   ★★★
Universal (U.S.)   PG/15

Sissy Spacek *(Nita)*, Eric Roberts *(Teddy)*, Sam Shepard *(Bailey)*, William Sanderson *(Calvin)*, Tracey Walker *(Arnold)*, R.G. Armstrong *(Rigby)*, Henry Thomas *(Harry)*, Carey Hollis Jr. *(Henry)*, Ed Geldart *(Mr. Calloway)*, Bill Thurman *(Sheriff)*

p, Burt Weissbourd, William D. Wittliff; d, Jack Fisk; w, William D. Wittliff; ph, Ralf D. Bode; ed, Edward Warschilka; m, Jerry Goldsmith; art d, John Lloyd; cos, Joe I. Tompkins

A compelling but oddly empty film, RAGGEDY MAN stars Spacek as a young divorcee who struggles to raise her two sons in Texas during WWII. Since her divorce, she has been harassed by local low-lifes who believe that all divorced women are looking for stand-in husbands. Two men in particular (Sanderson and Walker) have refused to leave her alone. Another local character, Shepard, a mysterious down-and-outer, also haunts Spacek's existence. Her life changes dramatically when Roberts, a young sailor, arrives on the scene and captivates both Spacek and her sons. His eventual departure, however, sends the story rushing toward a disturbing climax that isn't completely in keeping with everything that has preceded it. Fine performances by Spacek and Roberts, combined with able direction from Spacek's husband, Fisk (directing his first feature), make this one well worth a look.

RAGING BULL
1980 129m c/bw Biography/Sports   ★★★★★
UA (U.S.)   R/18

Robert De Niro *(Jake LaMotta)*, Cathy Moriarty *(Vickie LaMotta)*, Joe Pesci *(Joey)*, Frank Vincent *(Salvy)*, Nicholas Colasanto *(Tommy Como)*, Theresa Saldana *(Lenore)*, Frank Adonis *(Patsy)*, Mario Gallo *(Mario)*, Frank Topham *(Toppy/Handler)*, Lori Anne Flax *(Irma)*

p, Irwin Winkler, Robert Chartoff; d, Martin Scorsese; w, Paul Schrader, Mardik Martin (based on the book by Jake LaMotta with Joseph Carter, Peter Savage); ph, Michael Chapman; ed, Thelma Schoonmaker; prod d, Gene Rudolf; art d, Alan Manser, Kirk Axtell, Sheldon Haber

AAN Best Picture; AA Best Actor: Robert DeNiro; *AAN Best Supporting Actor:* Joe Pesci; *AAN Best Supporting Actress:* Cathy Moriarty; *AAN Best Director:* Martin Scorsese; *AAN Best Cinematography:* Michael Chapman; *AA Best Editing:* Thelma Schoonmaker; *AAN Best Sound:* Donald O. Mitchell, Bill Nicholson, David J. Kimball, Les Lazarowitz

RAGING BULL is an uncompromisingly brutal and emotionally devastating movie based on the life of middleweight boxing champion Jake LaMotta. The film chronicles the life of the fighter from 1941 until the mid-1960s and is chiefly concerned with the irrational and violent LaMotta's struggle to find peace within himself. Loosely based on LaMotta's autobiography and filmed in gorgeous black and white, the story begins in 1941 and follows LaMotta (Robert De Niro), who is managed by his brother, Joey (Joe Pesci), as he pursues the middleweight championship. During his rise to the crown the hostile LaMotta is distracted by both the local mafia's efforts to control his career and his romance with 15-year-old Vickie (Cathy Moriarty). Eventually LaMotta divorces his first wife to marry Vickie, but the extremely paranoid and insanely jealous boxer abuses both his wife and his brother when he unjustly suspects them of wrongdoing. LaMotta eventually wins the championship (in a bout with Frenchman Marcel Cerdan), but quickly relinquishes it to his nemesis, Sugar Ray Robinson (Johnny Barnes), who defeated LaMotta five out of the six times they met. The collapse of his boxing career coincides with the destruction of his personal life, and, estranged from both his brother and his wife, the now-bloated boxer begins the long road back to personal salvation.

Fueled by Martin Scorsese's brilliant direction and a magnificent Oscar-winning performance by De Niro—who gained nearly 50 pounds to play the older, fatter LaMotta—RAGING BULL is one of the most powerful boxing films ever made. Often unpleasant and painful to watch, the film is a no-holds-barred look at a violent man in a brutal sport, in which, amazingly, the wholly unsympathetic LaMotta attains a state of grace at the end that is inspiring. As usual, the director is examining maleness in this film, and RAGING BULL has a way of zeroing in on masculine values and codes, and how they weigh men down. The film's senseless feel for violence forces you to consider its place in the male idenity—it's easier for most men to retreat into than honest emotion. Many people feel BULL was the best movie of the 80s; like the decade, it leaves a sour taste that lingers long after.

RAGTIME
1981 155m c Historical   ★★★
Sunley (U.S./U.K.)   PG/15

James Cagney *(Police Commissioner Waldo)*, Brad Dourif *(Younger Brother)*, Moses Gunn *(Booker T. Washington)*, Elizabeth McGovern *(Evelyn Nesbit)*, Kenneth McMillan *(Willie Conklin)*, Pat O'Brien *(Delmas)*, Donald O'Connor *(Evelyn's Dance Teacher)*, James Olson *(Father)*, Mandy Patinkin *(Tateh)*, Howard E. Rollins Jr. *(Coalhouse Walker, Jr.)*

p, Dino De Laurentiis; d, Milos Forman; w, Michael Weller (based on the novel by E.L. Doctorow); ph, Miroslav Ondricek; ed, Anne V. Coates, Anthony Gibbs, Stanley Warnow; m, Randy Newman; prod d, John Graysmark; art d, Patrizia von Brandenstein, Tony Reading; chor, Twyla Tharp; cos, Anna Hill Johnstone

AAN Best Supporting Actor: Howard E. Rollins, Jr.; *AAN Best Supporting Actress:* Elizabeth McGovern; *AAN Best Adapted Screenplay:* Michael Weller; *AAN Best Cinematography:* Miroslav Ondricek; *AAN Best Score:* Randy Newman; *AAN Best Song:* Randy Newman; *AAN Best Art Direction:* John Graysmark, Patrizia Von Brandenstein, Anthony Reading, George DeTitta, Sr., George DeTitta, Jr., Peter Howitt; *AAN Best Costume Design:* Anna Hill Johnstone

Although more than $32 million was pumped into this kaleidoscopic portrait of American life in 1906, RAGTIME is too long, too splintered in its characterizations, and too much of a good thing squeezed dry. The most impressive aspect of the film is the return, after a 20-year hiatus, of top-billed Cagney, at age 81, to play a feisty NYC police commissioner.

Based on Doctorow's novel, the film balances several themes and four families—one factual, three fictional. The most compelling story is that of the infamous Thaw-White murder case, in which mad millionaire Harry K. Thaw (Robert Joy) kills famed architect Stanford

White (Norman Mailer) over the affections of Thaw's showgirl wife Evelyn Nesbit (Elizabeth McGovern). This story was better told in THE GIRL IN THE RED VELVET SWING. A second plot line follows the disintegration of an upper-class American family led by Mary Steenburgen and James Olson; their complacency is disturbed by black ragtime artist Coalhouse Walker (Howard E. Rollins Jr.), who arrives to woo a pregnant young woman living in their home. Walker's sense of dignity turns to rage when he is abused by local racists; he gathers a band of revolutionaries who are joined by Steenburgen's younger brother (Dourif), a munitions expert. Another plotline follows starving immigrant artist Patinkin, who encounters Nesbit by chance and later sets off to make his fortune in Hollywood. An exploration of the down side of the American Dream, RAGTIME is not always convincing, and under Forman's occasionally heavy-handed direction, its performances are uneven. Ambitious, but only sporadically engaging.

RAIDERS OF THE LOST ARK

1981   115m   c   Adventure   ★★★★½
Lucasfilm   (U.S.)   /PG

Harrison Ford (Indiana Jones), Karen Allen (Marion Ravenwood), Paul Freeman (Belloq), Ronald Lacey (Toht), John Rhys-Davies (Sallah), Denholm Elliott (Brody), Wolf Kahler (Dietrich), Anthony Higgins (Gobler), Alfred Molina (Satipo), Vic Tablian (Barranca)

p, Frank Marshall; d, Steven Spielberg; w, Lawrence Kasdan (based on a story by George Lucas, Philip Kaufman); ph, Douglas Slocombe, Paul Beeson; ed, Michael Kahn; m, John Williams; prod d, Norman Reynolds; art d, Leslie Dilley; fx, Richard Edlund, Kit West; cos, Deborah Nadoolman; anim, John Van Vliet, Kim Knowton, Garry Waller, Lording Doyle, Scott Caple, Judy Elkins, Sylvia Keuler, Scott Marshal

AAN Best Picture; AAN Best Director: Steven Spielberg; AAN Best Cinematography: Douglas Slocombe; AA Best Editing: Michael Kahn; AAN Best Score: John Williams; AA Best Art Direction: Norman Reynolds, Leslie Dilley, Michael Ford,; AA Best Sound: Bill Varney, Steve Maslow, Gregg Landaker, Roy Charman; AA Best Visual Effects: Richard Edlund, Kit West, Bruce Nicholson, Joe Johnston

The 1930s-style adventure serial was never better served than in this spectacular cliffhanger to end all cliffhangers. Indeed RAIDERS OF THE LOST ARK totally transcends its modest source material. Packed with astounding action setpieces, this movie was crafted with such polish, humor, and elan that it became an instant classic. This was the film that Spielberg made while still smarting from the massive flop of 1941, his large-scale period slapstick comedy about invasion paranoia in southern California on the eve of WWII. Spielberg described it as "work for hire" for his old pal executive producer George Lucas, but it comes off as a labor of love.

Harrison Ford went stellar with this perfect portrayal of archaeologist Dr. Indiana Jones, a distinguished scholar who sheds his spectacles to live a life of high adventure outside of the classroom. Ford's performance is an underrated but remarkable achievement; he succeeds in fully embodying a comic-book style hero without ever descending into camp. It's a brilliantly stylized portrayal that is now burned into our pop-cultural memory.

Set in 1936, the film follows Jones on his US intelligence mission to find the Ark of the Covenant, which reputedly still contains the Ten Commandments. The catch is that the Ark is also being sought by agents of Adolf Hitler, who resort to all manner of treachery to stop our hero. Aided by Marion Ravenwood (Karen Allen), his tough, beautiful, hard-drinking ex-flame, Indy escapes one outrageous life-threatening situation after another in the quest that takes him from Nepal to Cairo.

Most viewers are powerless to resist the kinetic pleasures of this endlessly inventive action adventure. Some naysayers have correctly pointed out that the film gave new life to late and unlamented racial stereotypes—cowering natives of color and all that—and that initially proto-feminist Marion is all-too-soon reduced to screeching for Indy to rescue her. It is difficult to resuscitate dead genres without bringing back their offensive aspects and assumptions, but RAIDERS OF THE LOST ARK could have been far worse on these counts. This is great filmmaking, warts and all.

The action, though fairly intense, is extremely witty and playful. The violent setpieces have the imaginatively stylized quality of the progressively escalating gags in a vintage 1940s Tex Avery cartoon. Spielberg demonstrates a delightfully oblique approach to action. He also has a sharp eye for simultaneous movement on several planes of action. The supporting performances are outstanding, as are the stuntwork and special effects. Shot in Hawaii, France, Tunisia, and at Elstree Studios in England—in just 73 days for $22.8 million—this perpetual motion machine has made more than $200 million and inspired two sequels (INDIANA JONES AND THE TEMPLE OF DOOM and INDIANA JONES AND THE LAST CRUSADE).

RAILWAY CHILDREN, THE

1970   108m   c   Historical/Children's   ★★★
EMI   (U.K.)   G/U

Dinah Sheridan (Mother), Bernard Cribbins (Perks Railway Porter), William Mervyn (Old Gentleman), Iain Cuthbertson (Father), Jenny Agutter (Bobbie), Sally Thomsett (Phyllis), Peter Bromilow (Doctor), Ann Lancaster (Ruth), Gary Warren (Peter), Gordon Whiting (Russian)

p, Robert Lynn; d, Lionel Jeffries; w, Lionel Jeffries (based on a novel by E. Nesbit); ph, Arthur Ibbetson; ed, Teddy Darvas; m, Johnny Douglas; art d, John Clark; fx, Pat Moore, John Richardson; cos, Elsa Fennell

An effective children's film set in Britain during the Edwardian period and starring Sheridan as the wife of a British Foreign Office employee who is falsely accused of treason and imprisoned. Forced by disgrace and lack of income to move from their lush surroundings to the Yorkshire moors, Sheridan sells the idea to her children as sort of a game (they "pretend" to be poor). The kids take to their new surroundings quickly, and it is only a matter of time until they have made new friends and sunk roots in the area. The village they now live in is located near a railway, and much of their play time is spent among the trains. Among their new friends is a wealthy resident of the area who volunteers to help them clear their father's name. Well acted, nicely scripted, and produced with the right amount of heart and sentiment.

RAIN MAN

1988   128m   c   Drama   ★★★½
Guber-Peters   (U.S.)   R/15

Dustin Hoffman (Raymond Babbitt), Tom Cruise (Charlie Babbitt), Valeria Golino (Susanna), Jerry Molen (Dr. Bruner), Jack Murdock (John Mooney), Michael Roberts (Vern), Ralph Seymour (Lenny), Lucinda Jenney (Iris), Bonnie Hunt (Sally Dibbs), Kim Robillard

p, Mark Johnson; d, Barry Levinson; w, Ronald Bass, Barry Morrow (based on a story by Morrow); ph, John Seale; ed, Stu Linder; m, Hans Zimmer; prod d, Ida Random; cos, Bernie Pollack

AA Best Picture; AA Best Actor: Dustin Hoffman; AA Best Director: Barry Levinson; AA Best Original Screenplay: Ronald Bass, Barry Morrow; AAN Best Cinematography: John Seale; AAN Best Editing: Stu Linder; AAN Best Score: Hans Zimmer; AAN Best Art Direction: Ida Random, Linda DeScenna

Well written, smartly directed, and sensitively performed, RAIN MAN depicts the one-sided relationship between two brothers, self-centered Los Angeles hustler Charlie Babbitt (Tom Cruise) and the older Raymond (Dustin Hoffman), an autistic resident of a home for the mentally disabled. Their father's estate, worth $3 million, has been left in trust to Raymond, and figuring he can force the trustee to turn over half of the inheritance, Charlie abducts Raymond and attempts to fly him back to Los Angeles. Raymond—an idiot savant who can cite airline crash statistics and other bizarre facts and figures in astounding detail—refuses to fly, however, forcing the pair to drive from Cincinnati to LA in their father's car. As they make their way across the country, the emotionally unreachable Raymond becomes the catalyst for Charlie's transformation from a self-absorbed character incapable of intimacy into a caring and sympathetic adult. RAIN MAN rises above the banality of its concept—another buddy movie crossbred with a road picture—to become a genuinely moving and intelligent look at what it means to be human. Hoffman delivers a magnificent stunt of a performance; Cruise brings depth and conviction to the emotional development of his character; and Valeria Golino (as Charlie's girlfriend) gives the film an extra spark.

RAIN PEOPLE, THE

1969 101m c Drama ★★★
Warner Bros. (U.S.) R/AA

James Caan (Jimmie "Killer" Kilgannon), Shirley Knight (Natalie Ravenna), Robert Duvall (Gordon), Marya Zimmet (Rosalie), Tom Aldredge (Mr. Alfred), Laurie Crewes (Ellen), Andrew Duncan (Artie), Margaret Fairchild (Marion), Sally Gracie (Beth), Robert Modica (Vinny Ravenna)

p, Bart Patton, Ronald Colby; d, Francis Ford Coppola; w, Francis Ford Coppola (based on his story "Echoes"); ph, Wilmer C. Butler; ed, Blackie Malkin; m, Ronald Stein; art d, Leon Ericksen

This is one of those "better luck next time" pictures—and, of course, next time meant THE GODFATHER for Coppola. He'd already directed five films without much success: the vile little TONIGHT FOR SURE!, the disastrous FINIAN'S RAINBOW, and the unjustly overlooked THE TERROR, DEMENTIA 13, and YOU'RE A BIG BOY NOW. Although studios had some confidence in his writing ability, his directorial work was seriously in question. This odd odyssey was not a hit, even though over the years it has been regarded as one of Coppola's more personal pictures and has attained a limited following. Knight plays Natalie, a childless Long Island housewife married to a decent man, Vinny (Modica). She learns she's pregnant and can't decide what to do, so she bolts, calling her husband from time to time to apologize, and to tell him of the baby and her thoughts on aborting it. Eager for sexual experience, Natalie picks up Jimmie (Caan), a brain-damaged former football player whose prospective job in West Virginia falls through when his former girlfriend's father (Duncan) sees Jimmie's current state. Traveling around with Jimmie through the South and Midwest, she eventually meets Gordon (Duvall), a widowed cop, when he pulls her over for speeding in Nebraska. Natalie begins a dalliance with Gordon, but her sexual and emotional odyssey ultimately results in a tragic conflict between the two men.

Too many flashbacks spoil the narrative, and Knight's character is confused, not very sympathetic, and not clearly motivated. Caan, who had played athletes in several films, is convincingly wooden here. Shot in Colorado, Tennessee, Nebraska, New York, and West Virginia, THE RAIN PEOPLE was was somewhat ahead of its time as a "feminist" movie (even if it does punish its heroine for her desires), predating STAND UP AND BE COUNTED and AN UNMARRIED WOMAN in the 1970s. The title is from a line by Caan that is hardly right for the retarded youth—"The rain people are made of rain, and when they cry, they disappear altogether"—whatever that means. The movie races all over the place in a hurry to illuminate the "little people" who live in quiet desperation. It's a bit too noisy for that, and yet there is enough about it to warrant attention.

RAINING STONES

1993 90m c Comedy/Drama ★★★½
Parallax Pictures (United Kingdom) /15

Bruce Jones (Bob), Julie Brown (Anne), Gemma Phoenix (Coleen), Ricky Tomlinson (Tommy), Tom Hickey (Father Barry), Mike Fallon (Jimmy), Jonathan James (Tansey), Ronnie Ravey (Butcher), Lee Brennan (Irishman), Karen Henthorn (Young Mother)

p, Sally Hibbin; d, Kenneth Loach; w, Jim Allen; ph, Barry Ackroyd; ed, Jonathan Morris; m, Stewart Copeland; prod d, Martin Johnson; art d, Fergus Clegg

A bittersweet working-class comedy that resonates far beyond its immediate milieu, RAINING STONES may be Ken Loach's most approachable film and, ironically, his most slyly political.

Bob (Bruce Jones), wife Anne (Julie Brown), and daughter Coleen (Gemma Phoenix) live in Manchester, where jobs are scarce and Bob is reduced to sheep-rustling with best friend Tommy (Ricky Tomlinson) to make ends meet. Coleen's first Holy Communion is approaching and Bob can't afford to buy her a dress, so he embarks on some quick-money misadventures, often with Tommy in tow, which include drain-cleaning and robbing lawn turf from an absent homeowner. Bob's van

is stolen and he borrows heavily from a loan shark, but money gets squandered in the pub almost as fast as it comes in. Soon, the loan shark turns violent, with Coleen's first Communion only days away. What's a father to do? "We start off with all these big ideas," observes Anne. "I'll live and die in this flat and nobody will even know."

RAINING STONES has a cumulative power that draws you into its bleak, but never humorless, world and produces some beautiful moments of recognition. Loach avoids pat answers and stereotypes, his apparent lack of style belying a sophisticated grasp of character development and episodic narrative drive. The naturalistic acting is uniformly excellent, in tune with Loach's uncompromising vision of a world in which an uncaring political/economic system turns decent, hard-working people into scavengers who will steal from one another. RAINING STONES ends on an upbeat note, but not until Loach has illuminated one family's struggle and despair.

RAINMAKER, THE

1956 121m c Comedy ★★★
Paramount (U.S.) /A

Burt Lancaster (Starbuck), Katharine Hepburn (Lizzie Curry), Wendell Corey (File), Lloyd Bridges (Noah Curry), Earl Holliman (Jim Curry), Cameron Prud'Homme (H.C. Curry), Wallace Ford (Sheriff Thomas), Yvonne Lime (Snookie), Dottie Bee Baker (Belinda), Dan White (Deputy)

p, Hal B. Wallis; d, Joseph Anthony; w, N. Richard Nash (based on the play by N. Richard Nash); ph, Charles Lang; ed, Warren Low; m, Alex North; art d, Hal Pereira, Walter Tyler; fx, John P. Fulton; cos, Edith Head

AAN Best Actress: Katharine Hepburn; *AAN Best Score:* Alex North

THE MUSIC MAN may have owed something to this story, since both concern confidence men who come to small towns to peddle their scams, then fall for spinsters. Nash wrote the film as a television play then expanded it to work on the Broadway stage, where it ran 124 performances with Geraldine Page in the Hepburn role and Prud'Homme as her father, under the direction of Anthony, who also did this film and, later, the musical version, "110 in the Shade." Composer North garnered an Oscar nomination, as did Hepburn, her seventh. The main problem is that the film is far too talky, and the leads are somewhat grizzled for the situation. Hepburn is a hick-town spinster in an arid area of the Southwest. (She never really convinces anyone that she's a country girl because that New England accent and her flighty mannerisms constantly intrude.) Lancaster is a brash, lively con artist who comes to the burg claiming that he can bring rain to the drought-ravaged locale for the sum of $100. He is taken into Prud'Homme's house and allowed to live in one of the outbuildings. Hepburn's brothers are Bridges, who never quite buys Lancaster's spiel, and Holliman, an oafish young man who is wooing town beauty Lime. Once Lancaster is ensconced, he begins to change things around. Hepburn is being courted, albeit reluctantly, by the town's lawman, Corey, but he doesn't seem to be able to pop the question, and time is a-wasting in her old maid life. Lancaster convinces the plain Hepburn that she is gorgeous, and once she feels that's true, her attitude about herself begins to alter. She's been told for years by everyone, mostly her brother Bridges, that she is, at best, plain, but the intrusion of Lancaster works a minor miracle on her self-confidence. She now has a duo of suitors in Lancaster and Corey, who suddenly awakens to the fact that she is a terrific woman. At the end, there is a coincidental downpour, and Lancaster, it should go without saying, takes all the credit before departing for his next conquest. Behind him, he has left a changed woman, and his visit has been the most exciting thing to happen to the tiny village in its history. Lancaster does one of his ELMER GANTRY bravura performances and was a perfect selection, although a little timeworn at 43. Hepburn was pushing 50 and Corey was 7 years younger. The difference in all their ages was revealed by the close-ups and worked against the believability of the story. Still, it's a pleasant movie with more than many laughs.

RAISE THE RED LANTERN
(DAHONG DENGLONG GAOGAO GUA)

1991   125m   c   Drama   ★★★★★
Era International/Salon Productions/China Film   PG
Co-Production Corporation   (China/Hong Kong)

Gong Li (Songlian), Ma Jingwu (Master Chen Zuoqian), He Caifei (Meishan), Cao Cuifeng (Zhuoyun), Jin Shuyuan (Yuru), Kong Lin (Yan'er), Ding Weimin (Mother Song), Cui Zhigang (Doctor Gao), Chu Xiao (Feipu), Cao Zhengyin (Old Servant)

p, Chiu Fu-sheng; d, Zhang Yimou; w, Ni Zhen (from the novel Wives and Concubines by Su Tong); ph, Zhao Fei; ed, Du Yuan; m, Zhao Jiping; art d, Cao Jiuping, Dong Huamiao; cos, Huang Lihua

AAN Best Foreign Language Film

A masterpiece. The historical dramas of Zhang Yimou, a master "Fifth Generation" filmmaker who emerged from the reopened Beijing Film Academy during the liberal climate of the early 1980s, resonate with subtexts of repression, resistance and retribution. Though Zhang's screenplay for RAISE THE RED LANTERN (based on the 1989 novel *Wives and Concubines* by Su Tong) got a stamp of approval from the Chinese censors, the finished production was banned at home while playing to great praise abroad.

Set in a wealthy 1920s Chinese household, the tale has the timeless quality of a fable, as a lovely nineteen-year-old named Songlian (Gong Li), forced to set aside her academic ambitions, resignedly sells herself to a rich man who already has three wives. "Let me be a concubine," she declares. "Isn't that a woman's fate?" Songlian arrives at the ancient, sprawling palace of Master Chen (Ma Jingwu), where she is welcomed as "Fourth Sister" in the aristocrat's harem. But beneath the polite surface boils a cauldron of intrigue and hatred, as rival wives scheme to win the Master's favor from day to day. As the freshest arrival, Songlian gets the most of Chen's sexual attentions, until he's dragged away by the complaints of wife number three, Meishan (He Caifei), a onetime opera star who now craves the spotlight at home. Songlian is comforted by Second Sister, Zhuoyun (Cao Cuifeng), a kind-looking matron who is later accurately described by Meishan as having the face of the Buddah and the heart of a scorpion.

Almost all of this superbly rendered tragedy takes place within the confines of the Master's vast estate, and Zhang Yimou uses a mostly stationary camera to frame the characters within careful compositions of doorways, portals, canopies and courtyards; the severe, rigid style effectively turns the sumptuous residence into a metaphorical prison compound. As bleak as the material sounds, there is a certain sardonic humor, mostly from the spirited Meishan and even the Master himself, who's absolutely baffled as to why his spouses seem so discontented.

This sumptuously shot $1 million production was financed by Taiwanese interests through a Hong Kong intermediary, and it was Hong Kong that submitted RAISE THE RED LANTERN as its official candidate for the 1992 Academy Award for best foreign language film, a move disapproved by Beijing.

RAISIN IN THE SUN, A

1961   127m   bw   Drama   ★★★★
Paman/Doris   (U.S.)   /A

Sidney Poitier (Walter Lee Younger), Claudia McNeil (Lena Younger), Ruby Dee (Ruth Younger), Diana Sands (Beneatha Younger), Ivan Dixon (Asagai), John Fiedler (Mark Lindner), Louis Gossett Jr. (George Murchison), Stephen Perry (Travis), Joel Fluellen (Bobo), Roy E. Glenn Sr. (Willie Harris)

p, David Susskind, Philip Rose; d, Daniel Petrie; w, Lorraine Hansberry (based on the play by Lorraine Hansberry); ph, Charles Lawton Jr.; ed, William Lyon, Paul Weatherwax; m, Laurence Rosenthal; art d, Carl Anderson

Hansberry's lovely adaptation of her 1959 Broadway hit about a black family in financial straits reunites seven of the original cast in the film version.

McNeil is the matriarch of a family living in cramped quarters on Chicago's south side (where all the location shots were done). Her husband has just died and she receives a check for $10,000 from the insurance company, quite a sizeable sum at the time. McNeil wants to get out of the ghetto and buy a decent house, then use the rest of the windfall to put her daughter through med school. But Poitier, her angry, ambitious son, has other ideas.

The performances are uniformly excellent, with Poitier illuminating the limitations placed on black men in American society and McNeil handling the role of the matriarch with unflinching emotional honesty. Look for Gossett in a small part as a black youth fixated by WASP values. Since much of the action takes place in the tiny apartment, director Petrie had to pull out all the stops to keep it from being stage-bound, and, with the help of cinematographer Lawton, he succeeded.

RAISING ARIZONA

1987   94m   c   Comedy   ★★★
Circle   (U.S.)   PG-13/15

Nicolas Cage (H.I. McDonnough), Holly Hunter (Edwina), Trey Wilson (Nathan Arizona, Sr.), John Goodman (Gale), William Forsythe (Evelle), Sam McMurray (Glen), Frances McDormand (Dot), Randall "Tex" Cobb (Leonard Smalls), T.J. Kuhn (Nathan Arizona, Jr.), Lynne Dumin Kitei (Florence Arizona)

p, Ethan Coen, Mark Silverman; d, Joel Coen; w, Ethan Coen, Joel Coen; ph, Barry Sonnenfeld; ed, Michael R. Miller; m, Carter Burwell; prod d, Jane Musky; art d, Harold Thrasher; cos, Richard Hornung

The promise that was evident in BLOOD SIMPLE, the Coen brothers' remarkably assured debut, is fulfilled in RAISING ARIZONA, an entertaining, energetic, and stylish comedy about a simple but loving couple who long to be parents.

H.I. "Hi" McDonnough (Nicholas Cage) is a hopelessly inept petty crook who attempts to go straight after he marries prison officer Edwina (Holly Hunter), and they settle down in a trailer in the middle of the Arizona desert. They long for a normal family life, but are childless and unable to adopt due to Hi's criminal past. When Hi and Edwina read that the wife of wealthy furniture dealer Nathan Arizona (Trey Wilson) has given birth to quintuplets, they decide to steal one for themselves.

RAISING ARIZONA is populated with excellent performances, especially from its two leads. Cage creates a homey and thoroughly likable character who earns the respect of the audience, but Hunter is the real surprise. Appearing in her first starring role, the stage veteran displays so much energy that she forces the audience to pay attention. The supporting cast is equally impressive, particularly John Goodman and William Forsythe as a couple of escaped convicts who pay a visit to their old friend Cage. Former professional boxer Randall "Tex" Cobb is also memorable as a thoroughly bizarre and very menacing bounty hunter.

RAMBLING ROSE

1991   112m   c   Drama/Romance/Comedy   ★★★★
Carolco   (U.S.)   R/15

Laura Dern (Rose), Robert Duvall (Daddy Hillyer), Diane Ladd (Mother Hillyer), Lukas Haas (Buddy Hillyer), John Heard (Willcox "Buddy" Hillyer), Kevin Conway (Doctor Martinson), Robert Burke (Police Chief Dave Wilkie), Lisa Jakub (Doll Hillyer), Evan Lockwood (Waski Hillyer), Matt Sutherland (Billy)

p, Renny Harlin; d, Martha Coolidge; w, Calder Willingham (from his novel); ph, Johnny Jensen; ed, Steveny Cohen; m, Elmer Bernstein; prod d, John Vallone; art d, Christiaan Wagener; cos, Jane Robinson

AAN Best Actress: Laura Dern; AAN Best Supporting Actress: Diane Ladd

Directed by Martha Coolidge from a screenplay by Calder Willingham based on his autobiographical novel, RAMBLING ROSE is a humorous coming of age story with a barbed central message.

When Rose (Laura Dern) becomes part of the eccentric Hillyer household in 1935, she proves more of a disruptive element than anyone could have anticipated. A tall country girl with flowing golden hair, she quickly captivates the Hillyer children, especially 13-year-old Buddy (Lukas Haas). Rose, in turn, is awed by the genteel, learned Mother (Diane Ladd) and courtly Daddy (Robert Duvall). Rose's failing is that she . . . rambles. Beautiful, naive, and sexually uninhibited, she has an overriding need for emotional—and physical—affection. As the narrator (an adult Buddy, played by John Heard) observes, the result is "one damnable commotion."

Coolidge does a supremely assured job of bringing the period to life, handling her story with a charm that does not blunt the edge of its message. Dern is impeccable as a heroine whose unbridled sexuality is matched by a complete lack of guile, and Robert Duvall is superb as a Southern gentleman completely nonplussed by the combination. Lukas Haas is winning, and Diane Ladd paints a finely observed portrait of a compassionate, intellectual Southern matron.

RAMBLING ROSE deals with cultural misogyny and sexual oppression in a human, comic way accessible to all. An intelligent screenplay, deft direction, and excellent production values make this a quietly compelling gem.

RAN
1985 160m c Historical/War   ★★★★★
Herald Ace/Nippon Herald/Greenwich   (France/Japan)   R/15

Tatsuya Nakadai (*Lord Hidetora Ichimonji*), Akira Terao (*Tarotakatora Ichimonji*), Jinpachi Nezu (*Jiromasatora Ichimonji*), Daisuke Ryu (*Saburonaotora Ichimonji*), Mieko Harada (*Lady Kaede*), Yoshiko Miyazaki (*Lady Sue*), Kazuo Kato (*Ikoma*), Masayuki Yui (*Tango*), Peter (*Kyoami*), Hitoshi Ueki (*Fujimaki*)

p, Masato Hara, Serge Silberman; d, Akira Kurosawa; w, Akira Kurosawa, Hideo Oguni, Masato Ide (based on "King Lear" by William Shakespeare); ph, Takao Saito, Masaharu Ueda, Asakazu Nakai; ed, Akira Kurosawa; m, Toru Takemitsu; prod d, Yoshiro Muraki, Shinobu Muraki; art d, Yoshiro Muraki; cos, Emi Wada

AAN Best Director: Akira Kurosawa; *AAN Best Cinematography:* Takao Saito, Masaharu Ueda, Asakazu Nakai; *AAN Best Art Direction:* Yoshiro Muraki, Shinobu Muraki; *AA Best Costume Design:* Emi Wada

At age 75, Akira Kurosawa, Japan's greatest living director, created one more magnificent work that will surely stand the test of time. In RAN, Kurosawa turned to Shakespeare for inspiration—as he had in THRONE OF BLOOD nearly 30 years before—and chose to film a Japanese adaptation of "King Lear." Set in 16th-century Japan, RAN (the Japanese character for fury, revolt, and madness—chaos) begins as Hidetora Ichimonji (Tatsuya Nakadai), an aging warlord who has acquired power through 50 years of ruthless bloodshed, announces his intention to divide his kingdom among his three sons, each of whom will live at one of three outlying castles. While the elder sons thank him for the honor, the youngest calls his father senile and mad, noting—prophetically—that it will only be a matter of time until the ambitious brothers begin battling for possession of the whole domain. In the process, Hidetora and his kingdom are consigned to a tragic and spectacular end. For more than 10 years, Kurosawa wanted desperately to make RAN, and, on the strength of KAGEMUSHA's success, he was finally able to obtain funding for this, the most expensive film ever made in Japan (though the $11 million budget is small by Hollywood standards). Partly shot at two of that country's most revered landmarks (the ancient castles at Himeji and Kumamoto; the third castle was constructed of plastic and wood on the slopes of Mount Fuji), RAN is a visually stunning epic, containing some of the most beautiful, colorful, breathtaking imagery ever committed to celluloid. As he grew older, Kurosawa began to shoot his films in a more traditionally Japanese style (static takes, little camera movement, no flamboyant editing). Here, especially in the battle scenes, he adopts a detached, impassive camera, heightening the tragedy by giving the audience a godlike but powerless perspective on all the madness and folly unfolding onscreen. At the same time, Kurosawa infuses the film with deep human emotion, aided by uniformly superb performances. The work of a mature artist in complete control of his medium, RAN is a true cinematic masterwork of sight, sound, intelligence, and—most important—passion.

RANCHO DELUXE
1975 93m c Western/Comedy   ★★★½
UA   (U.S.)   R/

Jeff Bridges (*Jack McKee*), Sam Waterston (*Cecil Colson*), Elizabeth Ashley (*Cora Brown*), Charlene Dallas (*Laura Beige*), Clifton James (*John Brown*), Slim Pickens (*Henry Beige*), Harry Dean Stanton (*Curt*), Richard Bright (*Burt*), Patti D'Arbanville (*Betty Fargo*), Maggie Wellman (*Mary Fargo*)

p, Elliott Kastner; d, Frank Perry; w, Thomas McGuane; ph, William A. Fraker; ed, Sidney Katz; m, Jummy Buffett; art d, Michael Haller

Frank Perry's second comedy (after DIARY OF A MAD HOUSE-WIFE) is an underrated anti-western about modern-day cattle rustlers. Jack McKee (Jeff Bridges) and Cecil Colson (Sam Waterston) ply their trade with chainsaws, high-powered rifles and a pick-up truck. When they steal a steer from the ranch of John Brown (Clifton James), a newcomer who sold a profitable restaurant business in Schenectady to make it as a cattle rancher in Montana, the adventure begins. Brown is so bored with his new life that the sleuthing associated with catching the two becomes an obsession. His ranch hands, (Harry Dean Stanton and Richard Bright), no dyed-in-the-wool cowpokes themselves, make a deal with McKee and Colson to relieve Brown of a large portion of his cattle, completely oblivious to the fact that the elderly 'detective' Henry Biege (Slim Pickens) that Brown has brought to the case and his 'niece', Laura (Charlene Dallas), are not nearly as incompetent as they seem. Scripted by novelist Thomas McGuane, RANCHO DELUXE is an often hilarious look at how the vast societal upheaval of the sixties and the creeping industrialization which began at the turn of the century were changing the face of the 'old west.'

RANCHO NOTORIOUS
1952 89m c Western   ★★★★
Fidelity   (U.S.)   /PG

Marlene Dietrich (*Altar Keane*), Arthur Kennedy (*Vern Haskell*), Mel Ferrer (*Frenchy Fairmont*), Lloyd Gough (*Kinch*), Gloria Henry (*Beth*), William Frawley (*Baldy Gunder*), Lisa Ferraday (*Maxine*), John Raven (*Chuck-a-Luck Dealer*), Jack Elam (*Geary*), George Reeves (*Wilson*)

p, Howard Welsch; d, Fritz Lang; w, Daniel Taradash (based on the story "Gunsight Whitman" by Sylvia Richards); ph, Hal Mohr; ed, Otto Ludwig; m, Emil Newman; prod d, Wiard Ihnen; cos, Joe King, Don Loper

The last of Fritz Lang's three westerns, following THE RETURN OF JESSE JAMES and WESTERN UNION, RANCHO NOTORIOUS is a bizarre, strangely poetic, and highly personal ballad of a man transformed by revenge. Kennedy plays cowhand Vern Haskell who, at the film's opening, is flirting with his fiancee (Henry), who works at the general store. Soon afterwards, two outlaws hold up the store, and when Vern returns, he learns that the woman "wasn't spared anything." Vern begins a quest for revenge and eventually finds one of the killers, shot in the back by the other. The man's last words point him toward a criminal hideout, a ranch run by former barroom singer Altar Keane (Dietrich). Insinuating himself into the gang holed up at Altar's place, Vern attempts to find out which man killed his fiancee.

RANCHO NOTORIOUS combines the quintessential Lang theme of a man ruled by fate with the generic elements of the western. Although set in the West, it is not a classic western in the style of John Ford. Whereas Ford, along with other western-movie pioneers, has a sense of American mythmaking, Lang is still absorbed in his German heritage, with its external, physical representation of inner turmoil. Like Lang's hero in THE BIG HEAT, Vern is a basically good man turned inside out by thoughts of revenge. In both movies, fate leads a man to express his dark side, bringing tragedy to a *femme fatale* (Gloria Grahame in THE BIG HEAT, Dietrich here) in the process.

Lang's experience with RKO and notorious studio head Howard Hughes was far from happy. Even though Lang was to have been consulted before any reediting was undertaken, the film was recut under producer Welsch's orders. Lang also had troubles with Dietrich, here playing an aging woman for the first time. Like her Altar Keane character, Dietrich could not accept the effects of mortality, begging cameraman Mohr to make her look as lovely as he had for 1939's DESTRY RIDES AGAIN. Lang was no angel on the set, either; by the film's end he and Dietrich were not even speaking to each other.

None of those problems, however, appear to have affected the film. Dietrich's songs and performance are superb (especially fun is her first scene, in which she rides a man, as if on horseback, in a drunken barroom contest). Her portrayal of a woman torn between two men, and between youth and old age, is a revelation, and the rest of the cast, especially Kennedy, is similarly excellent. The garish color is oddly effective in conveying the sense of gloom which hangs over so many of Lang's films. Missing from the credits was actor Lloyd Gough who, because he refused to testify before the House Un-American Activities Committee, was blacklisted and had his name removed by Hughes.

RANDOM HARVEST

1942 125m bw Drama ★★★½
MGM (U.S.) /U

Ronald Colman *(Charles Rainier)*, Greer Garson *(Paula)*, Philip Dorn *(Dr. Jonathan Benet)*, Susan Peters *(Kitty)*, Reginald Owen *("Biffer")*, Edmund Gwenn *(Prime Minister)*, Henry Travers *(Dr. Sims)*, Margaret Wycherly *(Mrs. Deventer)*, Bramwell Fletcher *(Harrison)*, Arthur Margetson *(Chetwynd)*

p, Sidney Franklin; d, Mervyn LeRoy; w, Claudine West, George Froeschel, Arthur Wimperis (based on the novel by James Hilton); ph, Joseph Ruttenberg; ed, Harold F. Kress; m, Herbert Stothart; art d, Cedric Gibbons, Randall Duell; chor, Ernst Matray; cos, Robert Kalloch

AAN Best Picture; *AAN Best Actor:* Ronald Colman; *AAN Best Supporting Actress:* Susan Peters; *AAN Best Director:* Mervyn LeRoy; *AAN Best Original Screenplay:* George Froeschel, Claudine West, Arthur Wimperis; *AAN Best Score:* Herbert Stothart; *AAN Best Art Direction:* Cedric Gibbons, Randall Duell, Edwin B. Willis, Jack D. Moore

Amnesia, that standard movie plot device, was never used better than in this filmed adaptation of James Hilton's popular 1940 novel. The setting is England, where WWI veteran Colman is hospitalized for shell shock, having lost his memory in battle. When the armistice is declared, Colman wanders out of the hospital during a joyous celebration and meets Garson, who takes him to a country village to help him put his life back together. Although Colman is unable to regain his memory, he builds a new identity and discovers he has a talent for writing. In time, he and Garson fall in love, marry, and have a child.

The idyll ends when Colman is hit by a car: the accident restores his old memories, but wipes out his last three years with Garson. He returns to his relatives and works in the family business. After much struggle, Garson locates her husband and gets a job as his secretary (on a psychiatrist's advice, she doesn't let on who she is). Colman has a new fiancee and is embarking on a political career. But since he still fails to recognize his ex-wife. . .

RANDOM HARVEST is a deeply moving film, marked by superb direction of its intricate story from Mervyn LeRoy, and by the strong performances of Colman and Garson (who's better here than she was in her Oscar-winning turn the same year in MRS. MINIVER). Their scenes together are sensitive and heartfelt, giving a depth to the implausible plot that allows the proceedings to transcend soap opera. Made at a cost of $2 million, RANDOM HARVEST brought in $4.5 million at the box office, made record receipts for Radio City Music Hall, and became one of the top 25 money-making films of its year. On the strength of its success, Colman won renewed respect in Hollywood and Garson's future at MGM was assured.

RANSOM

1996 121m c Thriller/Action ★★★
Ransom Productions/Segue Productions/Imagine R/15
Entertainment/Touchstone Pictures/Scott Rudin
Productions (U.S.)

Mel Gibson *(Tom Mullen)*, Gary Sinise *(Jimmy Shaker)*, Rene Russo *(Kate Mullen)*, Delroy Lindo *(Agent Lonnie Hawkins)*, Lili Taylor *(Maris Connor)*, Brawley Nolte *(Sean Mullen)*, Liev Schreiber *(Clark Barnes)*, Donnie Wahlberg *(Cubby Barnes)*, Evan Handler *(Miles Roberts)*, Nancy Ticotin *(Agent Kimba Welch)*

p, Scott Rudin, Brian Grazer, B. Kipling Hagopian; d, Ron Howard; w, Richard Price, Alexander Ignon (from a story by Cyril Hume and Richard Maibaum); ph, Piotr Sobocinski; ed, Dan Hanley, Mike Hill; m, James Horner; prod d, Michael Corenblith; art d, John Kasarda; cos, Rita Ryack

The men behind two of 1995's most successful movies, BRAVE-HEART star Mel Gibson and APOLLO 13 director Ron Howard, teamed up the following year for this kidnapping thriller.

Self-made airline magnate Tom Mullen (Gibson) and his beautiful wife Kate (Rene Russo) seem to have it all, until their young son Sean (Brawley Nolte) is kidnapped. The abductors, led by lovers Maris Connor (Lili Taylor) and Jimmy Shaker (Gary Sinise), demand a $2 million ransom, and FBI agent Lonnie Hawkins (Delroy Lindo) recommends paying up. After a disastrous first drop attempt, Tom refuses to make a second, and instead goes on TV and offers the $2 million as a bounty on the kidnappers heads. Shaker, determined to get the money at any cost, eliminates his cohorts and steps forward as the boy's savior, but when he shows up later to collect the reward, Sean's terrified reaction to his voice tips Tom off to the truth. They all take to the streets for the final shoot-out.

At its core, RANSOM wants to be a game of psychological "chicken" between the father and the kidnapper. The "big twist" of Mullen's refusal to pay the ransom was used as the film's selling point: basically, assuring audiences that Gibson would take matters into his own hands in his familiar car-leaping, window-busting fashion. That said, RANSOM remains a surprisingly effective suspense yarn, with many compelling scenes—the byzantine course of the first drop is terrific—due in part to the multiple script rewrites by Richard Price (CLOCKERS). Across the board, the cast gives excellent performances

RASHOMON

1950 90m bw Drama ★★★★★
Daiei (Japan) /X

Toshiro Mifune *(Tajomaru)*, Machiko Kyo *(Masago)*, Masayuki Mori *(Takehiro)*, Takashi Shimura *(Firewood Dealer)*, Minoru Chiaki *(Priest)*, Kichijiro Ueda *(Commoner)*, Fumiko Homma *(Medium)*, Daisuke Kato *(Policeman)*

p, Jingo Minoura; d, Akira Kurosawa; w, Shinobu Hashimoto, Akira Kurosawa (based on the short story "Yabu no Naka" and the novel *Rasho-Mon* by Ryunosuke Akutagawa); ph, Kazuo Miyagawa; m, Fumio Hayasaka; art d, So Matsuyama

AAN Best Art Direction: Matsuyama, H. Motsumoto

One of the most brilliantly constructed films of all time, RASHOMON is a monument to Akira Kurosawa's greatness, combining his well-known humanism with an experimental narrative style that has become a hallmark of film history. The central portion of the film revolves around four varying points of view of the rape of a woman and the death of her husband in a forest. Set in the 11th century, the film opens with a framing device, the conversation between three men—a woodcutter (Takashi Shimura), a priest (Minoru Chiaki), and a commoner (Kichijiro Ueda)—who have taken refuge from a rainstorm under the ruins of the stone Rashomon Gate. The priest relates the details of a trial he witnessed in a prison courtyard involving the rape of Masago (Machiko Kyo) and the murder of her samurai husband Takehiro (Masayuki Mori). As he explains, the audience is shown the four main defendants: Masago; the bandit Tajomaru (Toshiro Mifune); the spirit of Takehiro, which has been conjured by a medium; and the woodcutter, who admits that he witnessed the murder. Each of their viewpoints is depicted, the "truth" changing with each new defendant's explanation. Based on two short stories by Japanese author Ryunosuke Akutagawa ("In the Grove," the inspiration for the central crime story, and "Rashomon," the basis for the framing scenes), RASHOMON is a reflection of Kurosawa at his most Eisensteinian. Here he uses a juxtaposition of shots and a varying sequence of events to tell an essentially visual story. Although the film has been described by some as being about the search for truth, it is much more than that, as the framing story hints. Like the ruins of the Rashomon Gate (the film is after all named RASHOMON and not IN THE GROVE), the humanity Kurosawa depicts is crumbling and in danger of completely collapsing. While philosophers contend there are many truths, logic asserts there is only one, and, therefore, three of the four testifying characters in this film must be lying. Since Kurosawa's interests lie chiefly in human nature (and not philosophy or narrative structure), it follows that RASHOMON is not about truth but human fallibility, dishonesty, and selfishness. Like so many Kurosawa films, RASHOMON also contains some of the most amazing performances you are likely to find anywhere, especially that of the wildly fascinating Toshiro Mifune as the bandit. The videocassette is available in both dubbed and subtitled versions.

RAW DEAL

1948 79m bw Crime ★★★
Reliance/Eagle-Lion (U.S.) /18

Dennis O'Keefe (*Joe Sullivan*), Claire Trevor (*Pat*), Marsha Hunt (*Ann Martin*), John Ireland (*Fantail*), Raymond Burr (*Rick Coyle*), Curt Conway (*Spider*), Chili Williams (*Marcy*), Richard Fraser, Whit Bissell, Cliff Clark (*Men*)

p, Edward Small; d, Anthony Mann; w, Leopold Atlas, John C. Higgins (based on a story by Arnold B. Armstrong, Audrey Ashley); ph, John Alton; ed, Al DeGaetano; m, Paul Sawtell; art d, Edward L. Ilou; fx, George J. Teague

A hard-hitting gangster film with lots of action, good dialog, and fine performances by all, especially Trevor as a gun moll. O'Keefe is serving time for a crime of which he was innocent. His one-time associates arranged a frame, and O'Keefe is determined to get even with them when he breaks out of jail. With the aid of Trevor, his lover and pal, O'Keefe flees prison and is on his way to wreak revenge. While inside he was visited by Hunt, a social worker; he decides that she would be a good hostage in case the cops close in, so he kidnaps her. The three begin a trip to get Burr and his gang, the men responsible for O'Keefe's stint in prison. It isn't long before O'Keefe begins to fall for Hunt, much to the jealous consternation of Trevor, who has risked her life and her freedom for O'Keefe. Hunt, a heretofore legal and solid citizen, finds this all very exciting, and when O'Keefe has a battle with Ireland, one of the thugs, and loses, O'Keefe pleads with Hunt to save him, which she does by shooting Ireland in the back. Now she's a full part of the underworld. Hunt thinks she is in love with O'Keefe, but he wants her out of this hard life, so he temporarily sends her off while he goes to execute Burr—playing a pyromaniacal part in the best Laird Cregar style. O'Keefe bursts into the hideout as Burr is experimenting with some flames, and Burr shoots O'Keefe. Then the place goes up in a conflagration, and Burr leaps out the window to escape the heat and smoke and falls to his death. As O'Keefe is dying from the gunshot wound, Hunt holds him in her arms, and Trevor watches. A *film noir* picture in the best tradition, with fast-paced direction by Mann and superior photography by Alton. Whit Bissell (still known at the time as "Whitner") does a small role as a hood.

RAZOR'S EDGE, THE

1946 146m bw Drama/War ★★★★
Fox (U.S.) /15

Tyrone Power (*Larry Darrell*), Gene Tierney (*Isabel Bradley*), John Payne (*Gray Maturin*), Anne Baxter (*Sophie Nelson*), Clifton Webb (*Elliott Templeton*), Herbert Marshall (*Somerset Maugham*), Lucile Watson (*Mrs. Louise Bradley*), Frank Latimore (*Bob MacDonald*), Elsa Lanchester (*Miss Keith*), Fritz Kortner (*Kosti*)

p, Darryl F. Zanuck; d, Edmund Goulding; w, Lamar Trotti (based on the novel by W. Somerset Maugham); ph, Arthur Miller; ed, J. Watson Webb; m, Alfred Newman; art d, Richard Day, Nathan Juran; fx, Fred Sersen; chor, Harry Pilcer; cos, Charles LeMaire, Oleg Cassini

AAN Best Picture; AAN Best Supporting Actor: Clifton Webb; *AA Best Supporting Actress:* Anne Baxter; *AAN Best Art Direction:* Richard Day, Nathan Juran, Thomas Little, Paul S. Fox

Larry Darrell (Tyrone Power) is an idealistic youth, a former WW I pilot whose experiences in battle have caused him to question the moral values and the very fiber of his society. Returning to Chicago, Larry disturbs his high-society fiancee, Isabel (Gene Tierney), with his inexplicable urge to seek out the real meaning of life. He balks at the thought of joining the social *creme de la creme*, and instead embarks on a quest to find intellectual and spiritual freedom, journeying to Paris and Nepal, where he finds an elderly Hindu mystic who brings peace to his troubled mind and spirit. Ten years later, Larry is reunited with Isabel and his former friends, all of whom have undergone various degrees of suffering—physically, emotionally, and financially. More melodrama than romance than war film, THE RAZOR'S EDGE—based on the classic novel by Somerset Maugham—depicts a generation of people affected by war, by the senselessness of battlefield deaths and war's constant reminders of mortality. The film examines the possible futility of life, including the certain futility of war, and provides an intelligent and thoughtful counterpoint to the many films that celebrate glory in battle.

RE-ANIMATOR

1985 86m c Horror ★★★
Re-Animated (U.S.) /18

Jeffrey Combs (*Herbert West*), Bruce Abbott (*Dan Cain*), Barbara Crampton (*Megan Halsey*), David Gale (*Dr. Carl Hill*), Robert Sampson (*Dean Halsey*), Gerry Black (*Mace*), Carolyn Purdy-Gordon (*Dr. Harrod*), Peter Kent (*Melvin the Re-Animated*), Barbara Pieters (*Nurse*), Ian Patrick Williams (*Swiss Professor*)

p, Brian Yuzna; d, Stuart Gordon; w, Dennis Paoli, William J. Norris, Stuart Gordon (based on the story "Herbert West, The Re-Animator" by H.P. Lovecraft); ph, Mac Ahlberg; ed, Lee Percy; m, Richard Band; art d, Robert Burns; fx, Anthony Doublin, John Naulin; cos, Robin Burton

H.P. Lovecraft, a Rhode Island native and recluse, wrote a large number of short stories, most of which were published only in lurid pulp magazines like *Weird Tales*. He has since been acclaimed as the most important and influential writer of horror and fantasy to appear post-Poe and pre-King. Several attempts to film Lovecraft's eerie tales of monsters and madness have been made, ranging from DIE, MONSTER, DIE to THE DUNWICH HORROR. While RE-ANIMATOR fails as a faithful adaptation of Lovecraft, it is an incredibly demented movie in its own right that combines a plethora of downright disgusting grand guignol with disturbing black humor. Herbert West (Jeffrey Combs) is an intense young med student determined to make a scientific breakthrough and bring the dead back to life. He works at home on mysterious experiments and finally, using the glowing green fluid he has developed, revivifies a dead cat. The next stop is the med school morgue, where Herbert reanimates a human corpse. Of course, this and every other cadaver he brings to life becomes a bit difficult to subdue. A major-league splatterfest, RE-ANIMATOR has a number of horrifying moments, made even more macabre by the grisly humor evident in almost every unforgettable scene (the most memorable and bizarre being the sex scene with a cadaver's detached head). Perhaps the film's only drawback is the somewhat arch self-consciousness of the performers, who are constantly winking at the viewer as the horrible is defused into the safely ludicrous. Director-coscreenwriter Stuart Gordon again turned his attention to Lovecraft in FROM BEYOND.

REAL LIFE

1979 99m c Comedy ★★★½
Paramount (U.S.) PG

Dick Haynes (*Harris*), Albert Brooks (*Himself*), Charles Grodin (*Warren Yeager*), Frances Lee McCain (*Jeanette Yeager*), Matthew Tobin (*Dr. Howard Hill*), J.A. Preston (*Dr. Ted Cleary*), Mort Lindsey (*Himself*), Joseph Schaffler (*Paul*), Phyllis Quinn (*Donna*), James Ritz (*Jack*)

p, Penelope Spheeris; d, Albert Brooks; w, Albert Brooks, Monica Johnson, Harry Shearer; ph, Eric Saarinen; ed, David Finfer; m, Mort Lindsey; art d, Linda Spheeris, Linda Marder

Comedian-filmmaker Albert Brooks established himself as a major force in film comedy with this devastating satire on the interplay between the media and "real life." Brooks plays someone not unlike himself, an obnoxious documentary filmmaker who sets out to find a "typical American family" and then film their lives for a year. He chooses an Arizona clan headed by Charles Grodin and Frances Lee McCain, who are at first enchanted with their sudden fame. But things turn sour. Normal family problems are blown up by filmmaker Brooks into crises of disastrous proportions—McCain's trip to the gynecologist, for example, becomes an expose on her doctor. Eventually the family comes apart at the seams and members stop talking to each other. Brooks desperately tries to manipulate the family members so that they will do *something* in front of the cameras. Before long, he begins to lose his grip.

REAL LIFE was inspired by the PBS television documentary "An American Family," which followed the lives of the Loud family and serendipitously documented the couple's breakup and divorce. At the time of that program's airing, critics and psychologists debated whether the presence of cameras in the household contributed to the collapse of the family—whether the documentary merely *recorded* the events or helped to shape them. REAL LIFE delivers a pointed critique of the influence of media on our lives; it is also one of the funniest looks at filmmaking ever put on screen. With REAL LIFE, Brooks pushed his way into the forefront of American comedy. Subsequent films, including LOST IN AMERICA and DEFENDING YOUR LIFE, are as insightful and funny as his first.

REAR WINDOW

1954   112m   c   Thriller   ★★★★★
Paramount   (U.S.)   /PG

James Stewart *(L.B. "Jeff" Jeffries)*, Grace Kelly *(Lisa Carol Fremont)*, Wendell Corey *(Detective Thomas J. Doyle)*, Thelma Ritter *(Stella)*, Raymond Burr *(Lars Thorwald)*, Judith Evelyn *(Miss Lonely Hearts)*, Ross Bagdasarian *(Songwriter)*, Georgine Darcy *(Miss Torso)*, Sara Berner *(Woman on Fire Escape)*, Frank Cady *(Fire Escape Man)*

p, Alfred Hitchcock; d, Alfred Hitchcock; w, John Michael Hayes (based on the story "It Had to Be Murder" by Cornell Woolrich); ph, Robert Burks; ed, George Tomasini; m, Franz Waxman; art d, Hal Pereira, Joseph MacMillan Johnson; fx, John P. Fulton; cos, Edith Head

AAN Best Director: Alfred Hitchcock; *AAN Best Original Screenplay:* John Michael Hayes; *AAN Best Cinematography:* Robert Burks; *AAN Best Sound:* Loren L. Ryder

This much-loved Hitchcock picture, based on the Cornell Woolrich story "It Had to Be Murder," is a superb example of suspense filmmaking, especially when one considers the technical limitations of its single set. Magazine photographer Stewart has a broken leg and is confined to a wheelchair in his Greenwich Village apartment, where he has nothing to do but passively sit back and watch the mundane day-to-day activities that take place in the courtyard outside his rear apartment window. His neighbors are conspicuously unconscious of their own vulnerability to Stewart's constant gaze. He watches housewives, newlyweds (the only persons who actually draw the shades on *their* rear windows), a composer in a posh apartment, a lonely woman he dubs Miss Lonely Hearts, a Broadway ballerina, and, of particular interest, Lars Thorwald (Burr). After playing the voyeur for some time, Stewart begins to suspect that Thorwald has murdered his wife. Since Stewart is immobile, he enlists the aid of Kelly, a cool, blonde fashion model (here at her loveliest and most beguiling) who, because she is desperately in love with him, agrees to do his dangerous "legwork".

This, of all Hitchcock films, is an exercise in voyeurism, in which the audience has no choice but to assume the role of voyeur. It's like being Hitchcock for 112 minutes. "Look out the window, see things you shouldn't see," says Stewart's nurse Ritter, and look out the window the viewer does, having the same single and mounting terrifying perspective as does Stewart. One of the film's early ad campaigns read, "If you do not experience delicious terror when you see REAR WINDOW, then pinch yourself—you are most probably dead."

REBECCA

1940   130m   bw   Thriller   ★★★★
Selznick   (U.S.)   /PG

Laurence Olivier *(Maxim de Winter)*, Joan Fontaine *(Mrs. de Winter)*, George Sanders *(Jack Favell)*, Judith Anderson *(Mrs. Danvers)*, Nigel Bruce *(Maj. Giles Lacy)*, C. Aubrey Smith *(Col. Julyan)*, Reginald Denny *(Frank Crawley)*, Gladys Cooper *(Beatrice Lacy)*, Philip Winter *(Robert)*, Edward Fielding *(Frith)*

p, David O. Selznick; d, Alfred Hitchcock; w, Robert E. Sherwood, Joan Harrison (based on the novel by Daphne du Maurier, adapted by Philip MacDonald, Michael Hogan); ph, George Barnes; ed, James Newcom, Hal C. Kern; m, Franz Waxman; art d, Lyle Wheeler

AA Best Picture; AAN Best Actor: Laurence Olivier; *AAN Best Actress:* Joan Fontaine; *AAN Best Supporting Actress:* Judith Anderson; *AAN Best Director:* Alfred Hitchcock; *AAN Best Screenplay:* Robert E. Sherwood, Joan Harrison; *AA Best Cinematography:* George

Barnes; *AAN Best Editing:* Hal C. Kern; *AAN Best Score:* Franz Waxman; *AAN Best Art Direction:* Lyle Wheeler; *AAN Best Visual Effects:* Jack Cosgrove, Arthur Johns

A landmark: Hitchcock's Oscar, his first Hollywood film and his second Daphne du Maurier adaptation in a row (JAMAICA INN preceded). REBECCA is women's gothic melo-romance, but Hitchcock makes it a film about his distrust and dislike for women. He must have enjoyed a private chuckle over the women he knew would flood theaters to see it.

Fontaine stars as the unnamed narrator and shy, young, second wife of the urbane and handsome Maxim de Winter (Olivier). They meet and fall in love while vacationing on the Riviera. Following their quick marriage, they return to Maxim's vast English estate, Manderley. His wife is introduced to an army of servants who immediately, though subtly, display hostility toward her, as they all adored Rebecca, Maxim's first wife, whose death is shrouded in secrecy. As the servants become more hostile, the second wife grows more fearful, until she finally learns what happened to Rebecca. REBECCA was a prestige project for producer David O. Selznick, who was still coming down off the high of GONE WITH THE WIND. As with that 1939 classic, Selznick surrounded REBECCA with publicity including a massive talent hunt for this film's leads. Loretta Young, Margaret Sullavan, Olivia de Havilland, Vivien Leigh (Olivier's intended bride and GONE WITH THE WIND star), and Anne Baxter were all mentioned, but it was the 22-year-old Fontaine who was ultimately selected for the part.

Depending on your own feelings, you will find Fontaine either endearing or totally maddening. Whichever, she's right in the part; and Hitchcock's relentless camera seems to luxuriate in her emotional masochism. Olivier seems oddly out of command here—perhaps he and Welles should have switched off acting chores on REBECCA and JANE EYRE. The supporting roles are rendered quite well indeed. Anderson, Sanders, and Florence Bates all reveled in nasty roles; they look delighted sharpening their talons on Fontaine's little brown wren.

REBEL WITHOUT A CAUSE

1955   111m   c   Drama   ★★★★
Warner Bros.   (U.S.)   /PG

James Dean *(Jim)*, Natalie Wood *(Judy)*, Sal Mineo *(Plato)*, Jim Backus *(Jim's Father)*, Ann Doran *(Jim's Mother)*, Corey Allen *(Buzz)*, William Hopper *(Judy's Father)*, Rochelle Hudson *(Judy's Mother)*, Virginia Brissac *(Jim's Grandma)*, Nick Adams *(Moose)*

p, David Weisbart; d, Nicholas Ray; w, Stewart Stern (based on Irving Shulman's adaptation of "The Blind Run", a story by Dr. Robert M. Lindner); ph, Ernest Haller; ed, William Ziegler; m, Leonard Rosenman; prod d, William Wallace; art d, Malcolm Bert; cos, Moss Mabry

AAN Best Supporting Actor: Sal Mineo; *AAN Best Supporting Actress:* Natalie Wood; *AAN Best Original Screenplay:* Nicholas Ray

In this powerful study of juvenile violence, Dean is riveting as a teenager groping for love from a society he finds alien and oppressive. This film forever linked Dean to the restless 1950s generation; even though the indicted parents are caricatures, it's the best of its kind. Dean is Jim, a troublemaker who has caused his parents to move from one town to another before settling in L.A. Much of Jim's problem stems from the smothering but superficial love he receives from his domineering mother (Doran) and weak-willed father (Backus). Waiting at the police station after being picked up for being drunk and disorderly, he notices Judy (Wood), a girl taken in for walking the streets after curfew, and Plato (Mineo), a disturbed rich kid brought in for killing a litter of puppies. Entering his new high school the next day, Jim spots Judy and asks her for a date. She rejects him and drives off with her hot-rodding, black leather-jacketed boyfriend Buzz (Allen). Jim and Buzz later get into a knife fight, and Jim finally accepts Buzz's challenge in which both boys drive cars at breakneck speed to the edge of a cliff, diving out before they go over the edge. Whoever jumps out first is, of course, considered a coward. The game has surprising results.

The mundane plot is somehow made forceful in this directorial gem. Perfectionist director Ray spent hours researching hundreds of teenage police cases before filming. Transcending what might have been merely a teen exploitation film, REBEL draws heavily upon the presence of the intense and fascinating Dean. The young actor's appearance here electrified audiences, especially teenagers, who identified with this powerful symbol of their alienated generation. There is much of Marlon Brando's character from THE WILD ONE (1953), and critics accused Dean of mimicking Brando's brooding, mumbling delivery, but Dean was later recognized as an actor of singular stature. Wood and Mineo, although fine in their roles, serve mainly as dramatic foils for Dean's brooding. Many adults saw the film as promoting violence; with this picture the clean-cut juvenile ideal of yore moved into the adult world of film noir. Warners executives initially proposed, of all people, Tab Hunter and Jayne Mansfield (it would have been a classic, but of another kind). Ray, however, insisted upon Dean and Wood. He had been impressed by Dean's work in EAST OF EDEN, and drove the actor mercilessly on the set.

The tragedy of the film was relived offscreen, as all three principals died prematurely. Mineo was murdered in West Hollywood. He became one of the stars of a chic gay set and spent money crazily on clothes, fast cars, and even a $250,000 estate for his parents in Long Island. On the eve of the Academy Awards, he was so convinced that he would win for REBEL that he gave a party at which a huge banner was strung across the facade of his home reading: "Congratulations, Sal!" He didn't win, and the banner was yanked down and burned before dawn the next day. When Mineo was murdered in 1976, little was left of his fortune. On the wall, however, in an expensive frame, was a prized possession: a poster for REBEL WITHOUT A CAUSE ironically captioned: "Teenage terror torn from today's headlines."

Wood drowned in a still-mysterious accident while boating off Catalina Island with her husband, Robert Wagner, and Christopher Walken. Dean himself was killed in a perverse replay of the "chickie run" in REBEL, speeding at more than 100 mph in a racing car on a public highway in California. Besides killing himself, he seriously injured two other people. Only two hours before his death, Dean was given a ticket for driving 75 mph in a 45 mph zone. "So what?" he responded, before gunning his car down the road toward doom.

RED
(TROIS COULEURS: ROUGE)
1994 100m c Drama   ★★★★
Marin Karmitz Productions/Tor Film Studios/CAB   R/15
Productions (France/Poland/Switzerland)

Irene Jacob (Valentine), Jean-Louis Trintignant (Judge Joseph Kern), Frederique Feder (Karin), Jean-Pierre Lorit (Auguste), Samuel Lebihan (The Photographer), Marion Stalens (Veterinary Surgeon), Teco Celio (Barman), Bernard Escalon (Record Dealer), Jean Schlegel (Neighbor), Elzbieta Jasinska (Woman)

p, Marin Karmitz, Gerard Ruey; d, Krzysztof Kieslowski; w, Krzysztof Kieslowski, Krzysztof Piesiewicz; ph, Piotr Sobocinski; ed, Jacques Witta; m, Zbigniew Preisner; prod d, Claude Lenoir; cos, Corinne Jorry

AAN Best Director: Krzysztof Kieslowski; AAN Best Original Screenplay: Krzysztof Piesiewicz, Krzysztof Kieslowski; AAN Best Cinematography: Piotr Sobocinski

RED, the final film in Krzysztof Kieslowski's THREE COLORS trilogy, shrewdly weaves together the disparate lead characters from all three films, while telling its own moving and clever tale.

RED takes place in contemporary Carouge, a suburb of Geneva, where several residents are united by fate. One night, a young model, Valentine (Irene Jacob), accidentally hits a dog while driving home from a fashion show. She takes the wounded animal to the home of its owner (Jean-Louis Trintignant), a reclusive retired judge who likes to spy on his neighbors by using an elaborate phone-tapping system. Meanwhile, one of the judge's neighbors and spying victims, weather forecaster Karin (Frederique Feder), cheats on her boyfriend, Auguste (Jean-Pierre Lorit), a Swiss law student.

Many film critics were shocked (and a few were skeptical) when the 53-year old Krzysztof Kieslowski announced at Cannes in 1993 that RED would be his final film. While RED lands tonally somewhere between the serious, enigmatic BLUE and the lighter but more eccentric WHITE, the three films together constitute a humanistic statement about the need for connection. In RED, Kieslowski underscores his theme with bold, often humorous cinematic brushstrokes that challenge the inherent sentimentality of the project.

RED is a superb European co-production, from the touching performances by Jacob and Trintignant, to the restless, roving camerawork by Piotr Sobocinski, to the stunning production design by Claude Lenoir. Academy rules disqualified it from competing for the Oscar for Best Foreign Language Film, since its multi-national participants did not meet country-of-origin guidelines (perhaps in reaction, Academy members awarded Kieslowski with a Best Director nomination).

RED BADGE OF COURAGE, THE
1951 69m bw War/Western   ★★★★★
MGM (U.S.)   /U

Audie Murphy (Henry Fleming the Youth), Bill Mauldin (Tom Wilson the Loud Soldier), Douglas Dick (Lieutenant), Royal Dano (Tattered Man), John Dierkes (Jim Conlin the Tall Soldier), Arthur Hunnicutt (Bill Porter), Andy Devine (Fat Soldier), Robert Easton (Thompson), Smith Ballew (Captain), Glenn Strange (Colonel)

p, Gottfried Reinhardt; d, John Huston; w, John Huston, Albert Band (based on the novel by Stephen Crane, adapted by Band); ph, Harold Rosson; ed, Ben Lewis; m, Bronislau Kaper; art d, Cedric Gibbons, Hans Peters

John Huston always insisted that this Civil War battle picture examining the fine line between cowardice and bravery, "could have been" his greatest film, and certainly it is among the director's best, despite the tampering of studio executives. Audie Murphy, the most decorated hero of WWII, is Henry Fleming, a youth who joins the Union army and grows restless waiting for the orders that will take him into battle. When news finally comes that his unit is to join others for an impending battle, he turns braggart. But faced with the enemy, Murphy runs in terror, only to confront his fear later and return to his unit for another battle. Huston's direction is vivid in every scene; the film's battle sequences, however, are its most impressive element. In more pensive moments, THE RED BADGE OF COURAGE is a moving study of Americans fighting Americans, and the reluctance many of them bring to this awful task. Much of the credit for the overall visual effect of the film goes to cameraman Harold Rosson, who lends it a gritty, hardscrabble feel, marvelously capturing the period. Huston left the production immediately after its completion to fly across the world to make THE AFRICAN QUEEN, leaving his film in the hands of studio chiefs who cut it as they saw fit. They removed much of the director's questioning of the necessity for warfare (unacceptable during the Cold War), adding narration by James Whitmore and reducing the running time to a scant 69 minutes. Because the film didn't play well with premiere audiences, MGM sent it out without fanfare, offering it as a second feature on double bills— hardly a way to recoup production costs. Audiences failed to identify with the film's grim realism and its mostly unknown cast, and the classic Crane story wasn't enough of a draw to insure box-office success. Huston maintained that the movie as he filmed it was one of his favorites, and in the 1970s an attempt was made to revive the uncut version. To Huston's knowledge, however, a print of his original cut no longer existed, so the idea was dropped.

RED DESERT
(IL DESERTO ROSSO)
1964 116m c Drama   ★★★★★
Film Duemila/Federiz/Francoriz (France/Italy)   /X

Monica Vitti (Giuliana), Richard Harris (Corrado Zeller), Carlo Chionetti (Ugo), Xenia Valderi (Linda), Rita Renoir (Emilia), Aldo Grotti (Max), Valerio Baroleschi (Valerio), Giuliano Missirini (Workman), Lili Rheims (Workman's Wife), Emanuela Paola Carboni (Girl in Fable)

p, Antonio Cervi; d, Michelangelo Antonioni; w, Michelangelo Antonioni, Tonino Guerra; ph, Carlo Di Palma; ed, Eraldo Da Roma; m, Giovanni Fusco, Vittorio Gelmetti; art d, Piero Poletto; fx, Franco Freda; cos, Gitt Magrini

A masterpiece of color cinematography, RED DESERT uses its carefully rendered color scheme to heighten the emotional impact of Michelangelo Antonioni's portrayal of the alienating effect of the modern world on one woman. Giuliana (an atypically brunette Monica Vitti in a marvelous performance) lives in the northern Italian town of Ravenna with her husband, Ugo (Carlo Chionetti), a factory engineer who fails to appreciate the depth of her despair, and with her young son, Valerio (Valerio Bartoleschi), upon whom she dotes. The city's grim industrial landscape weighs heavily on Giuliana. Corrado (Richard Harris), who has come to recruit workers for a South American project, is attracted to her and understands her depression, realizing that the auto accident ostensibly responsible for her malaise was really a suicide attempt. Giuliana's struggle to come to terms with her environment is not easily resolved. As the film ends and her son asks her why birds don't fly through the poisonous yellow smoke of factory, she is able to tell him it's "because they have learned to fly around it," illustrating the separate peace she must make with technology.

An extremely disturbing film, RED DESERT captures a rare beauty that extends the boundaries of film art in its use of color and setting. In attempting to depict Giuliana's perception of the destructive influence of technology on the natural environment, Antonioni went so far as to enhance the bleakness of his industrial wasteland by literally painting the marshlands gray, and Giuliana's sense of isolation is further reenforced by a frightening electronic soundtrack. Not an easy film to watch because of its very deliberate pacing, but well worth the effort.

RED RIVER

1948 125m bw Western   ★★★★★
UA (U.S.)   /U

John Wayne *(Tom Dunson)*, Montgomery Clift *(Matthew Garth)*, Joanne Dru *(Tess Millay)*, Walter Brennan *(Groot Nadine)*, Coleen Gray *(Fen)*, John Ireland *(Cherry Valance)*, Noah Beery Jr. *(Buster McGee)*, Harry Carey *(Mr. Millville)*, Harry Carey Jr. *(Dan Latimer)*, Paul Fix *(Teeler Yacy)*

p, Howard Hawks; d, Howard Hawks; w, Borden Chase, Charles Schnee (based on the novel *The Chisholm Trail* by Borden Chase); ph, Russell Harlan; ed, Christian Nyby; m, Dimitri Tiomkin; art d, John Datu Arensma; fx, Don Steward

AAN Best Original Screenplay: Borden Chase; *AAN Best Editing:* Christian Nyby

There have been many classic westerns but this Hawks masterpiece certainly ranks among the best of the genre. Along with Ford's MY DARLING CLEMENTINE, it's probably the best of all the 1940s westerns—an unforgettable sweeping spectacle with the kind of grandeur few westerns achieved.

Wayne, as Tom Dunson, is shown as a young, determined man at the opening of RED RIVER. He and his companion Groot (Brennan) intend to head south, toward Texas and the Red River, leaving behind Tom's sweetheart Fen (Gray). When Tom and Groot see black smoke trailing behind them in the distance, they know that Indians have attacked the wagon train, but the two men must soon deal with an attack on their own wagon. The next day they find young Matthew Garth (Micky Kuhn), a survivor from the wagon train massacre, and take him along on their journey to Texas. Dunson eventually lays claim to a substantial expanse of land, successfully defeating a wealthy Mexican who also claims the territory. Years pass, and Tom Dunson owns a sprawling cattle empire. Matthew (now played by Clift) has fought in the Civil War and has returned to become Tom's right-hand man. Needing cash, Tom In need of cash, Wayne decides to drive a herd of cattle north and sell them. But he doesn't take the advice of Matt's friend, hired gun Cherry Valance (Ireland), and pushes his herds through a painfully difficult route. Men start deserting him, but Tom mercilessly drives both his crew and his cattle on. Matthew is unable to confront his father figure for a long time, but an eventual showdown is inevitable.

Hawks fills every frame of this movie with action and drama. Borden Chase, author of the original novel, always resented the changes Hawks made to his story (especially the ending), but the plot and characterization are steady and strong nonetheless. Wayne gives a terrific performance, certainly one of the best of his career, and Clift matches him all the way, Matthew's sensitive but determined manner a perfect counterpoint to Dunson's ruthlessness. It was Hawks who insisted that the marvelous Brennan remove his false teeth for the running gag with Chief Yowlachie; at first the 42-year-old balked at the idea, but he quickly remembered that it was Hawks who had expanded his Oscarwinning role in COME AND GET IT. All of the supporting players, especially Ireland, Beery, the Careys, and Fix, are memorable, and Dru firmly joins the ranks of the strong women who invade a man's world

in Hawks's films. Harlan's photography is stunning, sweeping through the horizonless plains and covering the vast territory the cowboys must travel in their odyssey: storms, rivers, canyons, distant buttes all encompassed beautifully. Matching the elegance of the cinematography is Tiomkin's stirring score.

At this point in his career, Hawks was already an established master of the directorial craft. His work had included comedies (HIS GIRL FRIDAY), war films (AIR FORCE), and mysteries (THE BIG SLEEP), all classics. This was his first western, and he quickly exhibited his mastery of that genre as well as he once again considered the status of the male hero and the bonding he makes with others in the name of professionalism. RED RIVER, which would gross almost $5 million in its initial release, was seen by the public and critics alike as a classic, and it remains so today.

RED ROCK WEST

1993 98m c Crime/Drama   ★★★½
Black Crow Productions/Propaganda Films (U.S.)   R/15

Nicolas Cage *(Michael Williams)*, Dennis Hopper *(Lyle)*, Lara Flynn Boyle *(Suzanne Brown)*, J.T. Walsh *(Wayne Brown)*, Craig Reay *(Jim)*, Vance Johnson *(Mr. Johnson)*, Robert Apel *(Howard)*, Bobby Joe McFadden *(Old Man)*, Dale Gibson *(Kurt)*, Ted Parks *(Cashier)*

p, Sigurjon Sighvatsson, Steve Golin; d, John Dahl; w, John Dahl, Rick Dahl; ph, Marc Reshovsky; ed, Scott Chestnut; m, William Olvis; prod d, Robert Pearson; art d, Don Diers; fx, Frank Ceglia; cos, Terry Dresbach

One of the more successful entries in the crowded ranks of early 90s neo-noir thrillers, RED ROCK WEST is the tale of a hapless drifter caught in a web of corruption in a remote western town. It offers suspense, wit, genuine surprises, and a trio of top-notch performances.

Hard-luck case Michael (Nicolas Cage) finds himself broke in the town of Red Rock, where bar owner Wayne Brown (J.T. Walsh) mistakes him for "Lyle from Dallas," whom he's hired for a job. Eager for work, Michael plays along with the misunderstanding, only to find out he's being offered $10,000 to murder Wayne's wife, Suzanne (Lara Flynn Boyle). Michael informs Suzanne of Wayne's intentions, whereupon she doubles the money offered if Michael will turn around and kill Wayne. Michael takes the money and tries to run, but finds himself trapped in the inevitable web of violence, corruption, and double-dealing, which only gets worse when the real Lyle from Dallas (Dennis Hopper) arrives on the scene.

Released directly to video in 1993, RED ROCK WEST surfaced theatrically in 1994, thanks to the enthusiasm of one San Francisco exhibitor and a handful of critics. A cleverly plotted drama of infidelity, greed, and bad luck, it's truer to the spirit of classic film noir than many of the rival offerings released at about the same time (DREAM LOVER, CHINA MOON, etc.). Cage is the near-perfect embodiment of a modern-day noir hero and the rest of the cast is equally fine. There's hardly a false note in a script that stands out for its structure and consistency, and the story never stops twisting and turning. The result is stylish, suspenseful and satisfying.

RED SHOES, THE

1948 133m c Dance   ★★★★★
Archers (U.K.)   /U

Anton Walbrook *(Boris Lermontov)*, Moira Shearer *(Victoria Page)*, Marius Goring *(Julian Craster)*, Leonide Massine *(Grischa Ljubov)*, Robert Helpmann *(Ivan Boleslawsky)*, Albert Basserman *(Sergei Ratov)*, Esmond Knight *(Livy)*, Ludmilla Tcherina *(Irina Boronskaja)*, Jean Short *(Terry)*, Gordon Littman *(Ike)*

p, Michael Powell, Emeric Pressburger; d, Michael Powell, Emeric Pressburger; w, Michael Powell, Emeric Pressburger, Keith Winter; ph, Jack Cardiff; ed, Reginald Mills; m, Brian Easdale; art d, Hein Heckroth, Arthur Lawson; chor, Robert Helpmann; cos, Hein Heckroth

AAN Best Picture; AAN Best Story: Emeric Pressburger; *AAN Best Editing:* Reginald Mills; *AA Best Score:* Brian Easdale; *AA Best Art Direction:* Hein Heckroth, Arthur Lawson

Magical. Although THE RED SHOES is the ultimate ballet film, you don't have to be a balletomane to enjoy this backstage love story distinguished by glorious dancing, superb acting, and masterful direction. After the successful staging of a new ballet, impresario Boris Lermontov (Walbrook, obviously modeled on Serge Diaghilev) admits two new members to his company: Victoria Page (Shearer), a gifted young ballerina, and Julian Craster (Goring) an equally talented composer. After Julian acquits himself well as an arranger, Boris gives him a chance to collaborate on a new ballet, "The Red Shoes," with Victoria. A breathtaking 20-minute ballet based on Hans Christian Anderson's story about a pair of magical shoes that permit their wearer to dance gloriously but tragically prevent her from stopping, it brings great acclaim to both Julian and Victoria, who have fallen in love. When Julian leaves the company, Victoria follows, marrying him over the objections of the jealous Boris, who avers that she is ruining her brilliant future. Owning the rights to "The Red Shoes," Boris prevents her from dancing her greatest role until, much later, he gives her one more opportunity to perform in Monaco. Doing so, however, means she will miss the premiere of Julian's new work. The three principals confront one another just before the performance as the film builds to its memorable climax.

THE RED SHOES began as a Pressburger script commissioned by producer Alexander Korda for wife Merle Oberon, whose dancing was to have been done by a double. Pressburger and collaborator Powell then bought the script back from Korda and co-helmed this extraordinary tale of romance and artistic obsession. According to Lermontov, there is hardly the time to be both a ballerina and a loving wife. While some may quibble with this, the film's tension becomes such that you totally understand why dancing or composing becomes the most important thing in the world to those gifted and dedicated enough to do them. The parallels between Victoria's story and that of the ballet are obvious without being too heavy-handed. The ballet, meanwhile, is so engrossing that it flies breathlessly by. Full of audacious lighting, dance modernisms and swirling plastic, it is gloriously unafraid of its own pretensions. The always impassioned but usually more subdued Walbrook does a magnificent job essaying the driven impresario, and the unusual-looking Goring is convincing and compelling as well. Shearer, whose gorgeous red hair is beautifully rendered by Cardiff's opulent Technicolor photography, was a Sadler's Wells ballerina who proved to be a much better actress than anyone had dreamed. This bewitching performer covers the emotional gamut quite skillfully and would ever after be identified with this role. Praise should also go to the other dancers in the cast—Massine, Tcherina, and Helpmann (who also did the choreography). They all perform with great assurance and grace, onstage or off. The film's backstage detail remains intoxicating and when it comes to the more melodramatic aspects of the film, Powell and Pressburger let the naysayers be damned.

RED SORGHUM
(HONG GAOLIANG)
1987 91m c Drama   ★★★★
Xi'an (China)   /15

Gong Li (Nine, the Grandmother), Jiang Weng (Yu, the Grandfather), Jiu Ji (Their Son), Ji Cun Hua (Sanpao, the Bandit Chief), Teng Rujun (Luohan), Cui Cun-hua

d, Zhang Yimou; w, Chen Jianyu, Zhu Wei, Mu Yan; ph, Gu Changwei; ed, Du Yuan; m, Zhao Jiping; prod d, Yang Gang

A devastating first feature from Zhang Yimou, one of the "Fifth Generation" of Chinese filmmakers, previously known as the photographer of Chen Kaige's THE BIG PARADE and YELLOW EARTH and as the lead actor in Wu Tianming's OLD WELL. RED SORGHUM won the Golden Bear at the Berlin Film Festival and was acclaimed at the New York Film Festival, marking a new level of Western interest in Chinese cinema. The film opens in the 1930s, an unseen narrator informing us that this story is about his grandparents. The grandmother (Gong Li) is a pretty 18-year-old whose name means "Nine," called thus because she was the ninth child, born on the ninth day of the ninth month. Sold in exchange for a donkey, Nine is prepared for a wedding to a leprosy-infected winemaker. When her wedding party is attacked by a masked bandit, the bandit tries to rape the young woman, but the chair-bearers, led by the strong Yu (Jiang Weng), attack and kill him. Later, before the wedding, Nine and Yu make love in the sorghum fields, and the leprous winemaker is found murdered. Nine takes charge of the distillery, marries Yu and eventually has a son. China is in the midst of

war, and invading Japanese soldiers have recruited the winemakers to trample the fields to make way for a new road. The Chinese are treated savagely by the Japanese; at the close, a solar eclipse turns the sky and the sorghum field a deep red.

Although the visual style of RED SORGHUM is one of resounding natural beauty—wide-screen horizon shots, flowing sorghum fields, heavenly sunsets—and the directorial style invokes myth and legend, the film does incorporate a certain level of realism. Shown in great detail are the distilling of the sorghum, the preparation of an ox-head meal at the butcher's, the trampling of the fields, and the bloody butchering of an ox during the Japanese attack—all of which contrast with the sense of fable Zhang Yimou creates. While the film essentially seems a sentimental ballad to the director's grandparents (and to their generation), RED SORGHUM is also a documentary on the color red—the red of sorghum, wine, a bridal robe, blood, the Communist victory, solar eclipses, and camera filters.

Some of RED SORGHUM's best moments come from the violent yoking together of moments of humor and pathos. The male bearers transporting the young bride-to-be, for example, sing a raucous, vulgar song and make her trip as bumpy as possible, while the poor Nine looks alternately sick and suicidal. When the men hear her terrible sobbing from inside and realize their mistake, though, they carry on ceremoniously. Much of the film's humor comes from Jiang Weng, a large man, bare-chested and bald, who recalls some of Toshiro Mifune's clownish antics. Gong Li's character is equally compelling—a powerful, independent woman who drinks and works like a man but who has a coy, girlish sexuality.

REDS
1981 200m c Historical/Biography/War   ★★★½
Paramount (U.S.)   PG/15

Warren Beatty (John Reed), Diane Keaton (Louise Bryant), Edward Herrmann (Max Eastman), Jerzy Kosinski (Grigory Zinoviev), Jack Nicholson (Eugene O'Neill), Paul Sorvino (Louis Fraina), Maureen Stapleton (Emma Goldman), Nicolas Coster (Paul Trullinger), M. Emmet Walsh (Speaker at the Liberal Club), Ian Wolfe (Mr. Partlow)

p, Warren Beatty; d, Warren Beatty; w, Warren Beatty, Trevor Griffiths; ph, Vittorio Storaro; ed, Dede Allen, Craig McKay; m, Stephen Sondheim, Dave Grusin; prod d, Richard Sylbert; art d, Simon Holland; cos, Shirley Russell

AAN Best Picture; AAN Best Actor: Warren Beatty; AAN Best Actress: Diane Keaton; AAN Best Supporting Actor: Jack Nicholson; AA Best Supporting Actress: Maureen Stapleton; AA Best Director: Warren Beatty; AAN Best Original Screenplay: Warren Beatty, Trevor Griffiths; AA Best Cinematography: Vittorio Storaro; AAN Best Editing: Dede Allen, Craig McKay; AAN Best Art Direction: Richard Sylbert, Michael Seirton; AAN Best Costume Design: Shirley Russell; AAN Best Sound: Dick Vorisek, Tom Fleischman, Simon Kaye

Produced, directed, and cowritten by Warren Beatty, who also stars as radical journalist John Reed, REDS is a sprawling yet highly personal epic. Focusing on Reed's tempestuous relationship with feminist Louise Bryant (Diane Keaton), the $45-million production also encompasses a capsule history of the American Left in the early 20th century and depicts the Russian Revolution, which Reed chronicled in Ten Days That Shook the World. Punctuated by the reminiscences of a number of Reed's real-life contemporaries (shot in stark black and white and unidentified, although they include Rebecca West, Henry Miller, and Hamilton Fish) the three-hour-plus marathon shifts the action among a variety of American locales and from the States to the Soviet Union. Among the larger-than-life figures given the personal treatment are Louise's one-time lover Eugene O'Neill (Jack Nicholson), Emma Goldman (magnificently portrayed by Maureen Stapleton, who won a Best Supporting Actress Oscar for her work), Communist party chief Grigory Zinoviev (novelist Jerzy Kosinski), and Max Eastman (Edward Herrmann). Beatty, has created a film of DOCTOR ZHIVAGO-like scope and majesty, yet REDS succeeds best in its smallest moments, focusing on the interaction among its carefully drawn characters. Keaton fails to bring the necessary depth to her portrayal and relies too much on her familiar, quirky film persona; but Beatty gives a highly nuanced, appropriately energized performance, and the supporting players are uniformly excellent. The film's chief attribute, however, is also one of its major flaws. In presenting an up-close, personal look at the lives of its famous figures—particularly Reed and Bryant in their love affair and marriage—the film sometimes gives short shrift to the world-shaking events that are its unique subject. Nonetheless, the brilliantly designed and photographed REDS is a beautiful, passionate film, both in its stunningly recreated action scenes and its quietest moments.

REMAINS OF THE DAY, THE

1993 134m c Drama/Historical/Romance ★★★½
Merchant Ivory/Columbia (U.S.) PG/U

Anthony Hopkins (Stevens), Emma Thompson (Miss Kenton), James Fox (Lord Darlington), Christopher Reeve (Lewis), Peter Vaughan (Father), Hugh Grant (Cardinal), Michael Lonsdale (Dupont D'Ivry), Tim Pigot-Smith (Benn), John Haycraft (Auctioneer), Caroline Hunt (Landlady)

p, Mike Nichols, John Calley, Ismail Merchant; d, James Ivory; w, Ruth Prawer Jhabvala (from the novel by Kazuo Ishiguro); ph, Tony Pierce-Roberts; ed, Andrew Marcus; m, Richard Robbins; prod d, Luciana Arrighi; art d, John Ralph; chor, Elizabeth Aldrich; cos, Jenny Beavan, John Bright, Cosprop

AAN Best Picture Ismail Merchant, Mike Nichols, John Calley; AAN Best Actor: Anthony Hopkins; AAN Best Actress: Emma Thompson; AAN Best Director: James Ivory; AAN Best Original Score: Richard Robbins; AAN Best Adapted Screenplay: Ruth Prawer Jhabvala; AAN Best Art Direction: Luciana Arrighi, Ian Whittaker; AAN Best Costume Design: Jenny Beaven, John Bright

THE REMAINS OF THE DAY is yet another quietly intense, dignified period drama from the producing-directing-writing team of Ismail Merchant, James Ivory, and Ruth Prawer Jhabvala. Though it offers a host of fine performances in a smoothly crafted, adult drama of unfulfilled love, it lacks the cumulative dramatic impact of the team's best work.

During the 1930s, Miss Kenton (Emma Thompson) is hired by Lord Darlington (James Fox), as is the elderly Stevens (Peter Vaughan), who has spent his life in service. Darlington's perfect butler, the younger Stevens (Anthony Hopkins), attempts to cover for his father's failing abilities, but Miss Kenton points out the dangers of the older man's continuing on. Stevens reacts with scorn, yet the repressed butler also begins to develop deeper feelings for Miss Kenton, as does she for him. Their painfully repressed relationship is played out against the backdrop of world affairs, as Darlington becomes involved with Nazism while trying to keep England out of WWII.

As with many of this team's other films, THE REMAINS OF THE DAY is intelligently and respectfully faithful to its prestigious source, in this case Kazuo Ishiguro's Booker Prize-winning novel. Though the film teeters dangerously close to what lurks just beyond the edge of many Merchant-Ivory productions—camp—its telling vignettes are adroitly sketched, Tony Pierce-Roberts' luscious cinematography is quietly expressive, and the acting lends freshness and urgency to a drama which could have been just so much highbrow soap.

REMBRANDT

1936 84m bw Biography ★★★★
London Films (U.K.) /A

Charles Laughton (Rembrandt van Rijn), Gertrude Lawrence (Geertje Dirx), Elsa Lanchester (Hendrickje Stoffels), Edward Chapman (Fabrizius), Walter Hudd (Banning Cocq), Roger Livesey (Beggar Saul), John Bryning (Titus van Rijn), Allan Jeayes (Dr. Tulp), John Clements (Gavaert Flink), Raymond Huntley (Ludvig)

p, Alexander Korda; d, Alexander Korda; w, Carl Zuckmayer, Lajos Biro, June Head, Arthur Wimperis; ph, Georges Perinal, Richard Angst; ed, William Hornbeck, Francis D. Lyon; m, Geoffrey Toye; prod d, Vincent Korda; fx, Ned Mann; cos, John Armstrong

This box-office failure wonderfully exposes the creative process of the artist and presents an unromanticized look at one of art's geniuses. The film confines itself to the final 27 years of the Dutchman's life, beginning shortly after the death of Rembrant's first wife, with Rembrandt, played by Charles Laughton, busily at work on "The Night Watch." The men who appear in the famous painting, all of whom have paid a fee for the privilege of sitting for the master, are unhappy with the way they have been painted, but Rembrandt, true to his vision, will not allow them to criticize his work. With his first wife buried, he turns to the female closest to him, Geertje (Gertrude Lawrence), his housekeeper and sometime model, a vulgar woman he might never have noticed were he still happily married. The moment he begins his alliance with Geertje, things go rotten. First, he must sell his regal house and most of his assets in order to satisfy his outstanding bills. Then, when he turns his attentions on the maid, Hendrickje (Elsa Lanchester), Geertje leaves him. Hendrickje is soon pregnant, and they are married after she gives birth. When Hendrickje dies, Rembrandt becomes almost instantly old, a doddering old fool on the brink of total senility. Producer-director Alexander Korda, an art collector, teamed up with his brother in designing a marvelous "look" to the movie, each scene looking as though it were taken from one of Rembrandt's own paintings. Laughton did his research by traveling to Holland, studying the art and whatever biographical material he could lay hands on, then steeped himself in the information and entered into the persona of the painter, offering a superb, complex characterization that must rank among his best, and, perhaps, one of the best biographical roles in film history. Laughton dominated the film in the title role, as he'd done before in the roles of Henry, Nero, Javert, and Bligh. He was in every scene but one, giving such a restrained performance that audiences expecting his thespian fireworks were disappointed. That the movie was not a hit does not detract from the achievements of the Kordas, Laughton, and everyone associated with this tasteful, mostly accurate, and satisfying motion picture.

REMEMBER THE NIGHT

1940 86m bw Comedy/Romance ★★★½
Paramount (U.S.) /A

Barbara Stanwyck (Lee Leander), Fred MacMurray (John Sargent), Beulah Bondi (Mrs. Sargent), Elizabeth Patterson (Aunt Emma), Willard Robertson (Francis X. O'Leary), Sterling Holloway (Willie), Charles Waldron (Judge, New York), Paul Guilfoyle (District Attorney), Charles Arnt (Tom), John Wray (Hank)

p, Mitchell Leisen; d, Mitchell Leisen; w, Preston Sturges; ph, Ted Tetzlaff; ed, Doane Harrison; m, Frederick Hollander; art d, Hans Dreier, Roland Anderson; cos, Edith Head

You'd have to be a grump not to like this funny, sentimental blend of pathos, drama and zaniness. It may have been former art director Leisen's best directorial effort, mainly due to the superior Sturges script. Sturges had a way with designing a picture so it could get right to the brink of syrup, then pull back with an hysterical comedy sequence. Conversely, just as the humor was about to disintegrate into chaotic slapstick, Sturges would throw a curve that put the story back onto a firm, dramatic footing. Stanwyck is a tough cookie with a shoplifting habit. Christmas is approaching and she decides to give herself a present, a bracelet of diamonds. She's caught by the security people and sent to jail to await trial. She's been in twice before for the same sort of crime and the judge decides to deal with her after the Christmas holidays. MacMurray is to prosecute her in his job as assistant district attorney. He's going home to Indiana for the holiday and when he learns that Stanwyck is also from the same state, he gets her out of jail in his custody. He takes her to her home, but her mother, Georgia Caine, wants nothing to do with her. MacMurray takes her to his home to meet his mother, Bondi, his aunt, Patterson, and their handyman, Holloway. Stanwyck has never been part of such a loving family and is struck by the closeness. She and MacMurray are soon in love but she holds back, fearing that it could never be permanent. She considers fleeing, then changes her mind and returns to New York for the trial. Her defense attorney, Robertson (who usually played the stern judge or vicious no-nonsense prosecutor) makes an impassioned and funny plea on Stanwyck's behalf, but that all goes out the window when she pleads guilty and accepts the brief jail term. It goes without saying that MacMurray will be waiting for her when she is released. It could have been maudlin and dreary in many other hands but Leisen and Sturges have made this a wonderful Yuletide movie that's good watching any time of year. Three songs: "Easy Living" (Ralph Rainger, Leo Robin, sung by Martha Mears in a nightclub sequence), "Back Home in Indiana" (James F. Hanely, Ballard MacDonald, performed by Mears and the King's Men), and "End of a Perfect Day" (Carrie Jacobs Band, sung by Holloway as Stanwyck plays the piano).

REPO MAN

1984 92m c Science Fiction/Comedy ★★★½
Edge City (U.S.) R/18

Harry Dean Stanton *(Bud)*, Emilio Estevez *(Otto)*, Tracey Walter *(Miller)*, Olivia Barash *(Leila)*, Sy Richardson *(Lite)*, Susan Barnes *(Agent Rogers)*, Fox Harris *(J. Frank Parnell)*, Tom Finnegan *(Oly)*, Del Zamora *(Lagarto)*, Eddie Velez *(Napo)*

p, Jonathan Wacks, Peter McCarthy; d, Alex Cox; w, Alex Cox; ph, Robby Muller; ed, Dennis Dolan; m, Tito Larriva, Steven Hufsteter; art d, J. Rae Fox, Lynda Burbank; fx, Robby Knott, Roger George; cos, Theda Deramus

The youth cult film of 1984, REPO MAN marked the auspicious debut of writer-director Alex Cox, born in Britain and educated as a lawyer at Oxford before relocating to Los Angeles to study at UCLA Film School on a Fulbright scholarship.

Otto (Emilio Estevez) is a disaffected youth in Los Angeles who loses his supermarket stock boy job as the film opens. He spends the night wandering through the punk underground before he encounters Bud (Harry Dean Stanton), who tells him that his wife left her car in a bad neighborhood and offers Otto $25 to drive it out for him. Otto accepts but is indignant when he learns that Bud lied to him and that he has just helped repossess a car. Later, however, he listens to offers of big money and sets off to learn the trade under Bud's tutelage. Meanwhile, a nuclear physicist (Fox Harris), who has had himself lobotomized to stop guilt feelings about his work on the neutron bomb, has stolen something dangerous and glowing and put it in the trunk of his 1964 Chevy Malibu. A nuclear device of some sort? The decomposing body of an alien with spectacular powers? Several government agencies are after the car and offer a $20,000 reward for whoever finds it, a prize that makes it the most sought-after car in the city.

REPO MAN looks at the neon-lit, horizontal sprawl of Los Angeles in a way that no one had before, and a great deal of credit for the film's distinctive look goes to German cinematographer Robby Muller, who'd already distinguished himself via numerous collaborations with Wim Wenders. Cox's familiarity with the punk milieu is impressive, and he would continue in this vein for his follow-up, SID AND NANCY. The performances vary wildly in their quality, with Stanton and Estevez taking top honors and most of the other characters little more than cartoons. Still, REPO MAN is one of the most original films of recent memory, with an edge of black humor and punk sensibility—wickedly funny, ceaselessly inventive, and never boring.

REPULSION

1965 104m bw Horror ★★★★★
Compton/Tekli (U.K.) /18

Catherine Deneuve *(Carol Ledoux)*, Ian Hendry *(Michael)*, John Fraser *(Colin)*, Patrick Wymark *(Landlord)*, Yvonne Furneaux *(Helen Ledoux)*, Renee Houston *(Miss Balch)*, Helen Fraser *(Bridget)*, Valerie Taylor *(Mme. Denise)*, James Villiers *(John)*, Hugh Futcher *(Reggie)*

p, Gene Gutowski; d, Roman Polanski; w, Roman Polanski, Gerard Brach, David Stone; ph, Gilbert Taylor; ed, Alastair McIntyre; m, Chico Hamilton; art d, Seamus Flannery

One of the most frightening and disturbing pictures ever made, REPULSION contains a scene in which a man's face is slashed with a razor until he dies, captured by Polanski's camera with a clinical expertise that pushes the viewer's nervous system to the edge. REPULSION has often been compared to PSYCHO, but Polanski's film, rather than presenting a portrait of a psychotic killer from outside, pulls the audience into the crazed individual's mind.

Deneuve plays a Belgian manicurist working in London and living in an apartment with her sister, Furneaux. She becomes increasingly unhinged, apparently due to her feelings about sex, which simultaneously repulses and attracts her, and about which she is constantly reminded by the presence of Furneaux's lover. When her sister goes on holiday, Deneuve is left to fend for herself and becomes the victim of

terrifying, destructive hallucinations within the confines of the apartment. REPULSION tells a simple story, but Polanski turns it into something undeniably brilliant. The director-writer took great pains in creating the proper composition and details for his nightmarish black-and-white visuals, extracting maximum hallucinatory effect from the apartment set. A powerfully engrossing film that owes much to the realistic, nearly silent performance of Deneuve, REPULSION was Polanski's first English-language feature. The director makes a cameo appearance as a spoons player.

REQUIEM FOR A HEAVYWEIGHT

1962 85m bw Sports ★★★½
Columbia (U.S.) /A

Anthony Quinn *(Mountain Rivera)*, Jackie Gleason *(Maish Rennick)*, Mickey Rooney *(Army)*, Julie Harris *(Grace Miller)*, Stanley Adams *(Perelli)*, Madame Spivy *(Ma Greeny)*, Herbie Faye *(Bartender)*, Jack Dempsey *(Himself)*, Muhammad Ali *(Ring Opponent)*, Steve Belloise *(Hotel Desk Clerk)*

p, David Susskind; d, Ralph Nelson; w, Rod Serling (based on his TV play); ph, Arthur J. Ornitz; ed, Carl Lerner; m, Laurence Rosenthal; art d, Burr Smidt; cos, John Boxer

Six years after Jack Palance brilliantly essayed the character of Mountain Rivera on television's "Playhouse 90," Anthony Quinn took on the role of the battered boxer for this big-screen adaptation of Rod Serling's Emmy-winning teleplay. As the film begins, Rivera, a veteran of 17 years in the ring, is beaten senseless by a younger, faster opponent (played by Cassius Clay, soon to be Muhammad Ali), going down for the count in the seventh round. His longtime manager, Gleason, who assured mobster Spivy that his fighter wouldn't last past the first few rounds, is given three weeks to compensate her for her betting losses—or else. Rivera has been told that he may go blind if he fights again, so he tries to get a job to come up with the money with the help of Harris, a caring employment counselor. Gleason, however, sabotages his interview for a position at a summer camp. Disappointed with Gleason but ever loyal, Rivera compromises his dignity by donning an Indian war bonnet and entering the professional wrestling ring to save his manager's life. Quinn, Gleason, and Rooney, as Rivera's erstwhile trainer, turn in magnificent performances in this unforgettable drama of abiding friendship and the abuse of trust. However, director Ralph Nelson, who also helmed the original 1956 television production, asked that his name be removed from the credits when nonessential scenes that had been cut from the original release print were reinstated to make the feature longer. Although those scenes, which slow down the narrative, certainly work against the film, REQUIEM FOR A HEAVYWEIGHT remains a thoroughly engaging movie.

RESERVOIR DOGS

1992 99m c Crime/Drama ★★★★
Dog Eat Dog Productions (U.S.) R/18

Harvey Keitel *(Mr. White/Larry)*, Tim Roth *(Mr. Orange/Freddy)*, Michael Madsen *(Mr. Blonde/Vic)*, Christopher Penn *(Nice Guy/Eddie)*, Steve Buscemi *(Mr. Pink)*, Lawrence Tierney *(Joe Cabot)*, Randy Brooks *(Holdaway)*, Kirk Baltz *(Marvin Nash)*, Eddie Bunker *(Mr. Blue)*, Quentin Tarantino *(Mr. Brown)*

p, Lawrence Bender; d, Quentin Tarantino; w, Quentin Tarantino; ph, Andrzej Sekula; ed, Sally Menke; m, Karyn Rachtman; prod d, David Wasco; cos, Betsy Heimann

RESERVOIR DOGS heralded the arrival of an extraordinary new talent leading a first-rate cast in one of 1992's most original releases. Most of the film deals with the aftermath of a jewelry heist gone awry. The protagonists are strangers who address each other using false names assigned by the heist's organizer, Joe Cabot (Lawrence Tierney). Wounded Mr. Orange (Tim Roth) is screaming and flailing in the back seat of a car driven by Mr. White (Harvey Keitel). They return to the gang rendezvous, an abandoned warehouse somewhere in Los Angeles, where they meet Mr. Pink (Steve Buscemi), who has escaped with the stolen diamonds. Convinced there is a traitor in their gang, Pink proposes to White that they simply leave Orange (who is, unbeknownst to them, an undercover cop) to die and split the jewels. Their deliberations are interrupted by Mr. Blonde (Michael Madsen), who has brought along a cop (Kirk Baltz) he took as a hostage. Later, "Nice Guy" Eddie (Christopher Penn) arrives, sent by his father, Cabot, to try and straighten out the mess. Things only get more complicated, however, leading to a climax that is both blood-soaked and, in its formal symmetry, darkly funny.

As in GLENGARRY GLEN ROSS, the actual heist in RESERVOIR DOGS is never seen. Instead, we get flashbacks that etch in the backgrounds of key players White, Orange, Blonde, Eddie and Joe. We also see bits and pieces of the post-heist chase that both punctuate the warehouse scenes with some tautly handled action and reveal further complications underpinning what's going on. RESERVOIR DOGS betrays the influence of Godard in the fragmentation of its narrative, which deconstructs the criminal subculture as a parody of "legitimate" capitalism. The film's look and themes also recall those of Howard Hawks. Avoiding artful, fussy compositions, Tarantino constructs much of RESERVOIR DOGS from simple medium-shot long takes. Tarantino also puts a postmodernist spin on the classic Hawksian theme of professionalism. The gangsters keep debating and defining the meaning of the term, while their actions undercut their words by proving these addled psychopaths to be anything but "professional." For Tarantino, the age of heroic competence is as dead as his characters are at the fadeout.

RETURN OF MARTIN GUERRE, THE
(RETOUR DE MARTIN GUERRE, LE)

1982　111m　c　Historical　★★★½
La Societe Francaise/France Region 3/Marcel　/15
Dassault/Roissi/Palace　(France)

Gerard Depardieu (Martin Guerre), Bernard-Pierre Donnadieu (Martin Guerre), Nathalie Baye (Bertrande de Rols), Roger Planchon (Jean de Coras), Maurice Jacquemont (Judge Rieux), Isabelle Sadoyan (Catherine Boere), Rose Thiery (Raimonde de Rols), Maurice Barrier (Pierre Guerre), Stephane Peau (Young Martin), Sylvie Meda (Young Bertrande)

p, Daniel Vigne; d, Daniel Vigne; w, Daniel Vigne, Jean-Claude Carriere; ph, Andre Neau; ed, Denise de Casabianca; m, Michel Portal; art d, Alain Negre; cos, Anne-Marie Marchand

AAN Best Costume Design: Anne-Marie Marchand

Set in 16th-century France, this engrossing period piece is based on existing records of an actual court case tried in a small village. Two youngsters, Martin Guerre and Bertrande de Rols, enter into a marriage of convenience at the behest of their peasant families. After a number of years, the strangely distant Martin disappears from the village, leaving behind his chaste, love-starved wife (Nathalie Baye). When Martin (Gerard Depardieu) returns, nine years later, he receives a warm welcome from the townsfolk and Bertrande, who has remained faithful to him. However, when Martin experiences occasional lapses of memory and fails to recognize faces, accusations fly—some of the villagers accusing him of being an impostor in the belief that the real Martin lost a leg in combat. Bertrande grows increasingly confused, at times defending her husband who has discovered a newfound affection for her, but on other occasions condemning him with her silence. The matter becomes even more confused when another man claiming to be Martin Guerre (Bernard Pierre Donnadieu) arrives in the village. One of the most successful art-house films of the 1980s, THE RETURN OF MARTIN GUERRE relies on two powerful performers—Depardieu, who is perfectly cast as the mysterious peasant, and Baye, whose demanding role calls for carefully measured silence and reserve. In his second cinematic outing, television director Daniel Vigne realized that he need only stick to the original facts to create a captivating film. Anne-Marie Marchand's costumes received an Oscar nomination. The year 1993 saw the release of SOMMERSBY, a bloodless American remake of MARTIN GUERRE starring Richard Gere and Jodie Foster.

RETURN OF THE JEDI

1983　133m　c　Science Fiction　★★½
Lucasfilm　(U.S.)　PG/U

Mark Hamill (Luke Skywalker), Harrison Ford (Han Solo), Carrie Fisher (Princess Leia), Billy Dee Williams (Lando Calrissian), Anthony Daniels (See Threepio (C-3PO)), Peter Mayhew (Chewbacca), James Earl Jones (Voice of Darth Vader), Alec Guinness (Ben Obi-Wan Kenobi), Frank Oz (Yoda), Ian McDiarmid (Emperor Palpatine)

p, Howard Kazanjian, Robert Watts, Jim Bloom; d, Richard Marquand; w, Lawrence Kasdan, George Lucas (based on a story by Lucas); ph, Alan Hume, Jack Lowin, James Glennon; ed, Sean Barton, Marcia Lucas, Duwayne Dunham, Arthur Repola; m, John Williams; prod d, Norman Reynolds; art d, Fred Hole, James Schoppe, Joe Johnston; fx, Roy Arbogast, Kit West, Richard Edlund, Dennis Muren, Ken Ralston; chor, Gillian Gregory; cos, Aggie Guerard Rodgers, Nilo Rodis-Jamero; anim, James Keefer

AAN Best Score: John Williams; AAN Best Art Direction: Norman Reynolds, Fred Hole, James Schoppe, Michael Ford; AAN Best Sound: Ben Burtt, Gary Summers, Randy Thom, Tony Dawe; AAN Best Sound Effects Editing: Ben Burtt

The first STAR WARS trilogy comes to an end with RETURN OF THE JEDI, technically the most sophisticated of the bunch, and a favorite among fans.

R2-D2 (Kenny Baker) and C-3PO (Anthony Daniels) are sent to the palace of loathsome space gangster Jabba the Hutt to deliver a message from Luke (Mark Hamill), who asks that Jabba negotiate for the freedom of the imprisoned Han Solo (Harrison Ford). But the droids are also imprisoned, and soon Princess Leia (Carrie Fisher), Chewbacca (Peter Mayhew), Lando Calrissian (Billy Dee Williams), and Luke are all gathered in Jabba's lair. After a daring escape, Luke goes to consult with Yoda about his destiny. The dying Yoda (Frank Oz) confirms that Darth Vader (voiced by James Earl Jones) is indeed Luke's father, and reveals that Leia is his twin sister.

RETURN OF THE JEDI does not hold up particularly well independent of the preceding two films. Characterization here is a given: If you don't know who Luke, Leia, Solo, et al are and what they mean to one another, you won't find out by watching this film. The dialogue is repetitive ("I won't give in to the dark side of the Force!" "You will!") and significant characters from earlier films—notably bounty hunter Boba Fett and Yoda—are dispatched without fanfare, and the whole business has a slightly rushed, perfunctory feel at the same time that it feels oddly attenuated. The chattering, spear-rattling, calculatedly adorable Ewoks, the furry inhabitants of the planet Endor, are unbearable—it's no wonder that cynical viewers cheer when one finally bites the dust. Still, the space battles are well-staged (the debt owed to JEDI by the far slicker INDEPENDENCE DAY is conspicuous) and various loose narrative threads are neatly pulled together.

RETURN OF THE PINK PANTHER, THE

1975　115m　c　Mystery/Comedy　★★★½
UA　(U.K.)　PG

Peter Sellers (Inspector Jacques Clouseau), Christopher Plummer (Sir Charles Litton), Catherine Schell (Claudine Litton), Herbert Lom (Chief Inspector Dreyfus), Peter Arne (Col. Sharki), Burt Kwouk (Cato), Andre Maranne (Francois), Gregoire Aslan (Chief of Police), Peter Jeffrey (Gen. Wadafi), David Lodge (Jean Duval)

p, Blake Edwards; d, Blake Edwards; w, Frank Waldman, Blake Edwards; ph, Geoffrey Unsworth; ed, Tom Priestley; m, Henry Mancini; prod d, Peter Mullins; art d, Peter Mullins; fx, John Gant; cos, Bridget Sellers

This was the third in the "Pink Panther" series, which starred Sellers. Alan Arkin and director Bud Yorkin had attempted their version with INSPECTOR CLOUSEAU, but it couldn't compare to the comedy engendered by Sellers under Edwards's direction. This sequel took in more than $30 million and earned every cent. The famous diamond named in the title has been stolen from the museum where it had been residing for the past several years. Blame is laid at the feet of retired jewel thief Plummer (doing the David Niven role established in THE PINK PANTHER), though he is innocent. Plummer is married to Schell and is in danger of being arrested for a crime he didn't commit, so he must find out who the real crook is. Lom, again Sellers's boss, reluctantly gives Sellers the task of solving the crime. A series of sight gags and misplaced-word jokes follows, with Sellers playing off Aslan and Arne, two Middle Eastern cops; Victor Spinetti and Mike Grady, employees at a Gstaad resort; and all of the villains, led by Eric Pohlmann in an imitation of Sydney Greenstreet. The picture comes to life only when Sellers is onscreen, and the rest of the time it's just vamping. The locations were visually satisfying with scenes being shot at Gstaad, Switzerland, the French Riviera, Marrakesh, and Casablanca. The picture races along like a "Road Runner" cartoon with occasional stops to catch its breath. Try to see it on television in a room alone because the laughter in a full-theater audience might cause you to miss some good lines. Julie Andrews, who is Edwards's wife, did a small cameo as a chambermaid, but the scene was cut out in the final print. Edwards comes from directorial genes, as his grandfather, J. Gordon Edwards, was in charge of the lensing of many films.

RETURN OF THE SECAUCUS SEVEN

1980 110m c Drama   ★★★½
Salsipuedes (U.S.)   R/AA

Mark Arnott *(Jeff)*, Gordon Clapp *(Chip)*, Maggie Cousineau *(Frances)*, Brian Johnston *(Norman Gaddis)*, Adam LeFevre *(J.T.)*, Bruce MacDonald *(Mike)*, Jean Passanante *(Irene)*, Maggie Renzi *(Kate)*, John Sayles *(Howie)*, David Strathairn *(Ron)*

p, William Aydelott, Jeffrey Nelson; d, John Sayles; w, John Sayles; ph, Austin de Besche; ed, John Sayles; m, Mason Daring

After scripting low-budget horror films such as PIRANHA and BATTLE BEYOND THE STARS for Roger Corman, acclaimed novelist and short story writer John Sayles made an auspicious directorial debut with THE RETURN OF THE SECAUCUS SEVEN, a more authentic and charming portrait of the same territory explored in the glossier THE BIG CHILL.

In the late 1960s seven friends were arrested in Secaucus, New Jersey, on their way to a march on the Pentagon. Ten years after graduating from college, the forgotten "Secaucus Seven" and a few companions come together at the New Hampshire home of Mike (Bruce MacDonald) and Kate (Maggie Renzi, coproducer of LIANNA, THE BROTHER FROM ANOTHER PLANT, MATEWAN). Over the course of the few days they spend together, much is revealed about their past and present lives and romances.

Shot in 1978 on a miniscule budget (reportedly $40,000) and using inexperienced actors, Sayles succeeds in creating an intelligent and often compelling study of former 1960s political activists coming to grips with their lives. Though that's about all THE RETURN OF THE SECAUCUS SEVEN offers, it is nevertheless an honest examination of the characters and their relationships. Fans of Sayles's work will note the presence of Gordon Clapp and David Strathairn, both of whom appear in the director's MATEWAN and EIGHT MEN OUT.

REVENGE OF THE NERDS

1984 90m c Comedy   ★★★½
Interscope (U.S.)   R/18

Robert Carradine *(Lewis)*, Anthony Edwards *(Gilbert)*, Timothy Busfield *(Poindexter)*, Andrew Cassese *(Wormser)*, Curtis Armstrong *(Booger)*, Larry B. Scott *(Lamar)*, Brian Tochi *(Takashi)*, Julie Montgomery *(Betty)*, Michelle Meyrink *(Judy)*, Ted McGinley *(Stan)*

p, Ted Field, Peter Samuelson; d, Jeff Kanew; w, Steve Zacharias, Jeff Buhai (based on a story by Tim Metcalfe, Miguel Tejada-Flores, Zacharias, Buhai); ph, King Baggot; ed, Alan Balsam; m, Thomas Newman; prod d, James Schoppe; fx, Joe Unsinn; chor, Dorain Grusman; cos, Radford Polinsky, Deborah Hopper

This funny movie is about 10 rungs above the usual teenage-college films. Lewis (Robert Carradine) and Gilbert (Anthony Edwards) are the essential nerds, in that Gilbert is a shy computer genius and Lewis is a boy with an annoying laugh and a huge overbite. When they arrive at Adams College and try to join fraternities, they are turned aside as they are so nerdy. In desperation, they join with other nerds to start their own branch of Lambda Lambda Lambda, an all-black fraternity that is functioning on other campuses. All the while, they are being closely watched by the jock contingent led by Stan (Ted McGinley), who is also the chairman of the Greek council. The jocks begin to make life miserable for the nerds, but revenge is on its way. This picture is hipper than NATIONAL LAMPOON'S ANIMAL HOUSE; PORKY'S; and all of the other teenage films lumped together. It's engaging, hysterically funny at times, wildly satiric, and has fewer lapses of good taste than most.

REVERSAL OF FORTUNE

1990 120m c Drama   ★★★★
Edward R. Pressman/Shochiku Fuji/Sovereign (U.S.)   R/15

Jeremy Irons *(Claus von Bulow)*, Glenn Close *(Sunny von Bulow)*, Ron Silver *(Alan M. Dershowitz)*, Annabella Sciorra *(Carol)*, Uta Hagen *(Maria)*, Fisher Stevens *(David Marriott)*, Christine Baranski *(Andrea Reynolds)*, Mano Singh, Felicity Huffman, Alan Pottinger

p, Edward R. Pressman, Oliver Stone; d, Barbet Schroeder; w, Nicholas Kazan (based on the book by Alan Dershowitz); ph, Luciano Tovoli; ed, Lee Percy; m, Mark Isham; prod d, Mel Bourne; cos, Judianna Makovsky, Milena Canonero

AA Best Actor: Jeremy Irons; *AAN Best Director:* Barbet Schroeder; *AAN Best Adapted Screenplay:* Nicholas Kazan

A cool, quirky adaptation of lawyer Alan Dershowitz's book about his successful appeal of Claus von Bulow's conviction for the attempted murder of his wife, Martha "Sunny" von Bulow. Neither docudrama nor out-and-out fiction, REVERSAL OF FORTUNE is somewhere in between, a darkly humorous, determinedly ambiguous delight. Schroeder begins with Sunny (Glenn Close), who narrates the film from the vantage point of her "persistent vegetative state"—recalling William Holden's ghostly narration of SUNSET BOULEVARD. She summarizes the first murder trial, which ended with Claus (Jeremy Irons) convicted and released on bail pending appeal. The drama really begins when Claus approaches Harvard Law professor Dershowitz (Ron Silver) to handle the case. Dershowitz is initially reluctant to accept Claus—an arrogant, elitist, decadent multi-millionaire—as a client. Ultimately, though, he is caught up in the challenge of defending the indefensible. Working with a small army recruited from his classes, Dershowitz demolishes the prosecution case, which had Claus injecting Sunny with enough insulin to bring about her coma. After a second trial, Claus is acquitted. Did he do it? Schroeder isn't saying.

Irons's canny performance dominates the film. He plays the role with apparent frankness and dignity rather than melodramatic villainy, and Schroeder's camera frames him in isolation to convey his bleakness and solitude. Claus remains, above all, enigmatic. The movie finally "guesses" that Claus didn't mean to kill Sunny, and Sunny didn't necessarily mean to kill herself. In fact, the point of Schroeder's film is not "whodunit?", but the suggestion that, in the end, legal guilt and moral culpability are not the same thing at all. REVERSAL OF FORTUNE is one of those rare films that deals with class difference in supposedly classless America, which makes for an unusually provocative tragicomedy of (bad) manners.

RHAPSODY IN BLUE

1945 139m bw Musical/Biography   ★★★½
Warner Bros. (U.S.)   /U

Robert Alda *(George Gershwin)*, Joan Leslie *(Julie Adams)*, Alexis Smith *(Christine Gilbert)*, Charles Coburn *(Max Dreyfus)*, Julie Bishop *(Lee Gershwin)*, Albert Basserman *(Prof. Frank)*, Morris Carnovsky *(Poppa Gershwin)*, Rosemary DeCamp *(Momma Gershwin)*, Anne Brown *(Bess)*, Herbert Rudley *(Ira Gershwin)*

p, Jesse L. Lasky; d, Irving Rapper; w, Howard Koch, Elliot Paul (based on a story by Sonya Levien); ph, Sol Polito; ed, Folmar Blangsted; m, George Gershwin; art d, John Hughes, Anton Grot; fx, Ray Davidson, Willard Vanenger; chor, LeRoy Prinz

AAN Best Score: Ray Heindorf, Max Steiner; *AAN Best Sound:* Nathan Levinson

George Gershwin died before he was 40, but his music continues to be a source of delight and inspiration. Like NIGHT AND DAY and WORDS AND MUSIC—film biographies about Cole Porter and Rogers and Hart, respectively—RHAPSODY IN BLUE has little to do with the *real* life of its subject, but, as is the case with those films, its subject's wonderful songs are the main attraction. In telling its story of the Gershwin Brothers' rise to fame from Manhattan's Lower East Side, RHAPSODY IN BLUE offers the usual scenes of song-plugging, struggle, failure, rehearsals, and backstage life; episodes in New York, London, and Paris; goes so far as to invent a character who never existed (played by Joan Leslie); and alters others to the point of laughability. In his second film, Robert Alda won't be confused for Laurence Olivier, but he does contribute a relatively convincing portrayal of George Gerswhin, while Herbert Rudley, as Ira, looks very much like the master wordsmith at the same age and carries off his part well. There are many celebrity impersonations, as well as appearances by several stars playing themselves, but the film's best lines belong to Gershwin's good friend Oscar Levant (as himself), who contributes piano solos along with Ray Turner. Max Steiner did the musical adaptation with orchestrations by Ray Heindorf and Ferde Grofe, composer of the "Grand Canyon Suite." Given this lineup and Gershwins' timeless tunes, it would be possible to remove all the talk, leave the music, and still have a good movie; and, of course, in the age of remote-control "mute" buttons, that's an option.

RICHARD III

1955   158m   c   Historical/War   ★★★½
Big Ben/London Films   (U.K.)   /U

Laurence Olivier *(King Richard III)*, Ralph Richardson *(Buckingham)*, Claire Bloom *(Lady Anne)*, John Gielgud *(Clarence)*, Cedric Hardwicke *(King Edward IV)*, Mary Kerridge *(Queen Elizabeth)*, Pamela Brown *(Jane Shore)*, Alec Clunes *(Hastings)*, Stanley Baker *(Henry Tudor)*, Michael Gough *(Dighton)*

p, Laurence Olivier; d, Laurence Olivier, Anthony Bushell; w, Alan Dent, Laurence Olivier, Colley Cibber, David Garrick (based on the play by William Shakespeare); ph, Otto Heller; ed, Helga Cranston; m, William Walton; prod d, Roger Furse; art d, Carmen Dillon; fx, Wally Veevers; cos, H. Nathan, L. Nathan

AAN Best Actor: Laurence Olivier

Laurence Olivier's third Shakespeare film, after HENRY V and HAMLET, and in some ways the most suitable of the three for his rather cold talents. For once, Olivier finds a part in which he can fully exploit his chilly magnetism, and the viewer can only root for his vicious but charismatic cripple.

The picture begins with Richard, Duke of York (Olivier) enviously observing the coronation of Edward IV (Cedric Hardwicke)—the sun (son) of York that illuminates Richard's metaphorical winter of discontent. Richard sets about scheming for the throne, arranging the deaths of Clarence (John Gielgud) and Edward's young heirs, and incidentally seducing Lady Anne (Claire Bloom). After Edward's death, he becomes protector and then king, but must face the House of Tudor in a bloody battle at Bosworth Field.

The battle scene was the first shot (in Spain); during shooting Olivier was accidentally pierced by a bolt from the film's stunt archer that was supposed to hit the protected horse (an animal that had been trained to fall and play dead on command). Olivier continued the scene until a natural break in the action was called for, then asked for medical aid. (The limp he sports as Richard is real, a result of the accident.) It took three hours each day to put on Olivier's complex makeup—the same prosthetics he wore on stage, including a false nose, hunched back, false hand, and black pageboy wig.

RICHARD III was not a hit when it was released in England, so the producers made a unique deal with the NBC television network in the US in which the networks acquired the rights to broadcast the film for the sum of $500,000 (in later years it was re-released to resounding success, and has been the most financially rewarding of Olivier's Shakespeare films).

This film lacks the cinematic boldness of Olivier's earlier screen Shakespeare; there's nothing here to match the gloomy *mise-en-scene* of HAMLET or the cocky theatrical conceits of HENRY V. But his riveting performance transcends his conventional directing and utterly dominates the movie. Indeed, this filmed record of Olivier's Richard has intimidated generations of actors—how can they hope to compete with an interpretation both so brilliant and so familiar to audiences?

Olivier and Alexander Korda had hoped to film a version of "Macbeth," with Vivien Leigh as Lady Macbeth, but Korda died a year after RICHARD III was made, and lack of interest in the project caused it to be tabled. The British Film Academy gave RICHARD III Best British Film, Best Film, and Best Actor awards.

RICHARD III

1995   104m   c   Drama/Historical/War   ★★★½
Bayly/Pare Productions/United Artists/First Look   R/15
Pictures   (U.K./U.S.)

Ian McKellen *(Richard III)*, Annette Bening *(Queen Elizabeth)*, Maggie Smith *(The Duchess of York)*, Nigel Hawthorne *(Clarence)*, John Wood *(King Edward IV)*, Robert Downey Jr. *(Earl Rivers)*, Kristin Scott Thomas *(Lady Anne)*, Jim Broadbent *(Buckingham)*, Jim Carter *(Lord Hastings)*, Bill Paterson *(Richard Ratcliffe)*

p, Lisa Katselas Pare, Stephen Bayly; d, Richard Loncraine; w, Ian McKellen, Richard Loncraine (adapted from the stage production by Richard Eyre, based on the play by William Shakespeare); ph, Peter Biziou; ed, Paul Green; m, Trevor Jones; prod d, Tony Burrough; art d, Choi Ho Man, Richard Bridgland; fx, John Evans; cos, Shuna Harwood

AAN Best Art Direction: Tony Burrough; *AAN Best Costume Design:* Shuna Harwood

Ian McKellen's delightfully sinister portrait of a power-hungry sociopath highlights this oddly breezy adaptation of Shakespeare's play. This is a flawed and far from definitive rendering, but it is nonetheless dynamic and enjoyably revisionist.

McKellen and director-co-writer Richard Loncraine have completely re-envisioned the setting of the 1592 historical drama. The hunchbacked Duke of Gloucester still malevolently murders his family members one by one, climbing his way to the top to become King Richard III, but now his coup takes place among the aristocratic, pro-fascist Clivenden Set of the 1930s.

By reinventing the material in a timely and imaginative way, RICHARD III succeeds where other recent Shakespeare-on-film adaptations fail. This version brazenly moves around chunks of text, shifts the story to a more recent and comprehensible era, and irreverently spoofs the sacrosanct material. However, the film does not take its revisionist point quite far enough. The look is appropriately elegant, but only a few scenes stand out as truly eye-catching (e.g., a fascist rally shot like TRIUMPH OF THE WILL in 3-strip Technicolor, Richard's fiery death scene). Moreover, the parallels between Richard's ascent and the rise of European fascism make for interesting allegory, but McKellen and Loncraine stop far short of driving the point home with reference to the present day.

McKellen's forceful and frighteningly funny performance is matched by Kristin Scott Thomas's mournful, masochistic Lady Anne. They are both well supported by Nigel Hawthorne, Maggie Smith, and Jim Broadbent in parts that amount to showy cameos. Far less successful are the performances by two American actors clearly added to the film for marquee value, Annette Bening and Robert Downey Jr.

RIDE THE HIGH COUNTRY

1962   94m   c   Western   ★★★★★
MGM   (U.S.)

Randolph Scott *(Gil Westrum)*, Joel McCrea *(Steve Judd)*, Mariette Hartley *(Elsa Knudsen)*, Ronald Starr *(Heck Longtree)*, R.G. Armstrong *(Joshua Knudsen)*, Edgar Buchanan *(Judge Tolliver)*, John Anderson *(Elder Hammond)*, L.Q. Jones *(Sylvus Hammond)*, Warren Oates *(Henry Hammond)*, James Drury *(Billy Hammond)*

p, Richard E. Lyons; d, Sam Peckinpah; w, N.B. Stone Jr.; ph, Lucien Ballard; ed, Frank Santillo; m, George Bassman; art d, George W. Davis, Leroy Coleman

A much-loved revisionist Western, director Peckinpah's second feature film proved to be a bittersweet swan song for the Old West and a classy farewell to the screen for actors Scott and—for some years—McCrea. Set at the turn of the century, the film opens in the town of Hornitos, which is in the midst of a celebration. Down the crowded main street rides Steve Judd (McCrea), an aging former lawman who has seen better days. He mistakenly thinks the cheers of the crowd are for him, but is abruptly reminded of the changing times when a car nearly runs him over. Steve has been hired to escort a gold shipment from the mining town of Coarse Gold back to a bank in Hornitos, but the banker is taken aback by his age. (An especially good scene has Steve reading over his contract in the bathroom so the banker can't see that he needs spectacles.) The old lawman is finally given the job, and he sets out to hire help for the trip. He runs into Gil Westrum (Scott), a fellow former lawman who has survived by dressing up as the dandified "Oregon Kid," selling out his former heroic image. Steve hires Gil and his young sidekick Heck Longtree (Starr), but Gil plans to steal the gold at the first opportunity.

In RIDE THE HIGH COUNTRY, director Peckinpah began what was to be an obsession with men who have lived past their era in history and find it difficult to adapt to changing times (THE WILD BUNCH; THE BALLAD OF CABLE HOGUE; and PAT GARRETT AND BILLY THE KID all share this theme). His two protagonists, in some ways mirror images of each other, are wracked with guilt for sometimes failing to live up to the standards they have set for themselves. What separates them, though, from the scoundrels they invariably encounter is a personal code of honor they both try to uphold. Eventually, these tortured souls attain a sort of grace because they do what it takes to regain their self-respect. Soon after producer Lyons talked McCrea and Scott into doing the film, McCrea—who had originally agreed to play the part of Gil Westrum, the lawman gone bad—felt uncomfortable with the role (he had never played a villain before, albeit, here, a sympathetic one) and asked Lyons if he could see how Scott felt about switching parts. Later that same afternoon, Lyons received a call from Scott who confessed that he was feeling insecure about his role and wondered if McCrea would mind a swap. Much to the actors' relief, the roles were switched. The only problem left was to decide who would receive top billing, but a public coin toss at the Brown Derby restaurant solved that one.

Shooting was planned on location at Mammoth Lake in the High Sierras, but after four days it began to snow, and cost-conscious MGM insisted the production be moved to a more workable area, using soap suds to simulate snow. Shooting was completed in an astounding 26 days, but a shake-up at MGM saw Peckinpah supporter Sol Siegel ousted and replaced by Joseph R. Vogel, who barred the director from the studio, forcing him to consult with editors and sound mixers by phone. The film was dumped onto the bottom half of double bills, but proved an astounding popular and critical success in Europe, winning First Prize at the Cannes Film Festival, the Grand Prize at the Brussels Film Festival (beating out Federico Fellini's 8 1/2), and the Silver Goddess from the Mexican Film Festival for Best Foreign Film. Peckinpah's attention to detail and character makes this film a multifaceted jewel to be studied and enjoyed again and again. The honest, subtle, and consummately skillful performances by Scott and McCrea and promising newcomer Mariette Hartley continue to draw viewers in.

RIDER ON THE RAIN
(LE PASSAGER DE LA PLUIE)

1970 119m c Thriller   ★★★½
Greenwich/Medusa (France/Italy)   GP/18

Marlene Jobert (Melancolie "Mellie" Mau), Charles Bronson (Col. Harry Dobbs), Annie Cordy (Juliette), Jill Ireland (Nicole), Gabriele Tinti (Tony), Jean Gaven (Toussaint), Marc Mazza (The Stranger), Corinne Marchand (Tania), Jean Piat (M. Armand), Marika Green (Hostess at Tania's)

p, Serge Silberman; d, Rene Clement; w, Sebastien Japrisot, Lorenzo Ventavoli; ph, Andreas Winding; ed, Francoise Javet; m, Francis Lai; art d, Pierre Guffroy; cos, Rosine Delamare

A young woman (Jobert) who lives in a small seaside resort in France happens to see a stranger exit from a bus; later, he seems to be following her. That evening the stranger breaks into Jobert's home after her husband has left. The stranger rapes Jobert; she kills him with a shotgun and disposes of the body in the ocean. After a few days the stranger's body washes up on the beach, making newspaper headlines. Jobert goes to a wedding reception and meets Bronson, an American who accuses her of murder. The victim, it seems, was a sex fiend who escaped from prison and stole $60,000 from the US Army. Bronson demands that Jobert return an airline bag that held the money, but Jobert ignores his threats. The pursuit begins.

RIDER ON THE RAIN is a tightly plotted, well-executed thriller in which Bronson's three stock expressions are put to superb use by director Rene Clement. The locations, on the French coast and in Paris, are used effectively; combined with careful cinematography, the scen-

ery adds greatly to the story's inherent tension. This stylish, Hitchcockian suspenser was filmed in French and dubbed into English for American distribution, but the dubbing was unusually well done. RIDER ON THE RAIN helped make Bronson a star in France, giving him the clout that eventually led to international fame.

RIDERS OF THE PURPLE SAGE

1931 58m bw Western   ★★★
Fox (U.S.)   /U

George O'Brien (Jim Lassiter), Marguerite Churchill (Jane Withersteen), Noah Beery Sr. (Judge Dyer), Yvonne Pelletier (Bess), James Todd (Venters), Stanley Fields (Oldring), Shirley Nails (Fay Larkin), Lester Dorr (Judkins), Frank McGlynn Sr. (Jeff Tull)

d, Hamilton MacFadden; w, John Goodrich, Philip Klein, Barry Connors (based on the novel by Zane Grey); ph, George Schneiderman; ed, Al DeGaetano

O'Brien plays a cowboy out to rescue his kidnapped sister (Nails) in this adaptation of the noted Grey novel. Though a bit creaky as far as dialogue goes, there are several sequences that feature topnotch action. A wide-angle lens was used in the photography with great effect. O'Brien is fine as the hero and fits the characterization of the strong, silent type. This first sound version was followed by a sequel, THE RAINBOW TRAIL, in 1932. Two silent versions were also filmed, the first in 1918 with William Farnum and the second in 1925 with silent legend Tom Mix. Mix also made a sequel to his version. A second sound version, starring George Montgomery, was produced by Fox in 1941. *Riders of the Purple Sage* was the first really successful novel by noted western writer Grey, who formerly caught fish for a living.

RIDICULE
(LE RIDICULE)

1996 102m c Historical/Drama   ★★★½
Epithete/Cinea/France 3 Cinema/Investimage 4/Procirep/Gras   R/15
Savoye (France)

Charles Berling (Ponceludon de Malavoy), Jean Rochefort (Marquis de Bellegarde), Fanny Ardant (Madame de Blayac), Judith Godreche (Mathilde de Bellegarde), Bernard Giraudeau (Abbot de Vilecourt), Bernard Dheran (Monsieur de Montalieri), Carlo Brandt (Knight de Milletail), Jacques Mathou (Abbot de l'Epee), Urbain Cancelier (Louis XVI), Albert Delpy (Baron de Gueret)

p, Gilles Legrand, Frederic Brillion, Philippe Carcassonne; d, Patrice Leconte; w, Remi Waterhouse, Michel Fessler, Eric Vicaut; ph, Thierry Arbogast; ed, Joelle Hache; m, Antoine Duhamel; prod d, Ivan Maussion; cos, Christian Gasc

AAN Best Foreign Language Film

Thanks largely to a wonderfully literate script, RIDICULE is a flavorful divertissement which recalls the great French period films of yore. Somewhere, Guitry and Duvivier are smiling.

In the Versailles of Louis XVI, country aristocrat Ponceludon de Malavoy (Charles Berling) comes to court with the hope of pleading the cause of his disease-ridden people. He is taken under the wing of the Marquis de Bellegarde (Jean Rochefort), who agrees to coach Malavoy in the Byzantine ways of court etiquette and, above all, language. In a palace that worships a well-turned phrase, having a reputation for a sharp tongue is the only way of gaining access to the King. Fortunately, Malavoy (a natural wit) is a sensation. He allows himself to be seduced by the formidable Madame de Blayac (Fanny Ardant), but really loves the Marquis's independent daughter, Mathilde (Judith Godreche). While those around him rise and fall, Malavoy inches closer to an audience with the King, until a venom of a deadlier sort—jealousy—leads to his undoing.

Remi Waterhouse's lovingly crafted script is a highly inventive, wonderfully wicked bauble. The barbed repartee flows like wine, and the battles of wits are as absorbing as any sports match. The bright, brainy cast revels in the rococo garb and effervescent dialogue. Berling is at once fresh, intelligent, and dashing, while Ardant is perfect as the brilliant Comtesse cum courtesan. Shot on the dream location of the gardens of Versailles, the production is handsome and, best of all, looks lived in. Anyone expecting a lavish spectacle on the order of MARIE ANTOINETTE or DANGEROUS LIAISONS will be disappointed by the relatively low-key but historically evocative decor.

RIFF-RAFF

1991 94m c Comedy/Drama/Political ★★★
Parallax Productions/Channel Four (U.K.)

Robert Carlyle *(Stevie)*, Emer McCourt *(Susan)*, Jimmy Coleman *(Shem)*, George Moss *(Mo)*, Ricky Tomlinson *(Larry)*, David Finch *(Kevin)*, Richard Belgrave *(Kojo)*, Ade Sapara *(Fiaman)*, Derek Young *(Desmonde)*, Bill Moores *(Smurph)*

p, Sally Hibbin; d, Kenneth Loach; w, Bill Jesse; ph, Barry Ackroyd; ed, Jonathan Morris; m, Stewart Copeland; prod d, Martin Johnson

Following a foray into commercial cinema with the political thriller HIDDEN AGENDA, British director Ken Loach returned to his roots in social realism with a bittersweet comedy-drama about London construction workers.

The film's slight plot focuses on Stevie (Robert Carlyle), who moves to London from his home in Glasgow, where he has served a prison term for theft. Stevie finds work with an unscrupulous building contractor whose disregard for safe working conditions is balanced by his willingness to hire laborers without checking their backgrounds or identities. This suits Stevie's colorful, polyglot co-workers, most of whom use false names in order to continue drawing welfare benefits.

Loach has made an insightful, quietly affecting study of people who, amidst the economic wreckage of post-Thatcherite Britain, have been reduced to outcasts in their own country—converting rundown buildings into condos for the rich, while having to break into abandoned buildings for homes of their own. Using a neo-documentary style and improvisational acting techniques, the director has brought emotional resonance and humor to a script by the late Bill Jesse, a struggling comedy writer and playwright who had been supporting himself as a construction laborer; he died shortly after the film's completion. The result is an aptly moving epitaph, mining both poignancy and humor from its ostensibly grim subject matter. This English-language film was released in a subtitled version in the US, which is a big help for American viewers attempting to unravel the crazy quilt of accents—Scottish, Liverpudlian, Cockney, African—that weave the story together.

RIFIFI

1954 117m bw Crime ★★★★★
Indus/Pathe/Prima (France) /X

Jean Servais *(Tony le Stephanois)*, Carl Mohner *(Jo Le Suedois)*, Robert Manuel *(Mario)*, Jules Dassin *(Cesar)*, Magali Noel *(Viviane)*, Marie Sabouret *(Mado)*, Janine Darcey *(Louise)*, Pierre Grasset *(Louis Grutter)*, Robert Hossein *(Remi Grutter)*, Marcel Lupovici *(Pierre Grutter)*

p, Rene G. Vuattoux; d, Jules Dassin; w, Jules Dassin, Rene Wheeler, Auguste Le Breton (based on the novel by Le Breton); ph, Philippe Agostini; ed, Roger Dwyre; m, Georges Auric; art d, Auguste Capelier

This landmark caper film shows the robbery of a Parisian jewelry store and the complications that follow for the thieves—mastermind Tony (Jean Servais), a recently released ex-con who may or may not have a terminal respiratory problem; Jo (Carl Mohner), whom Tony served time to protect; safecracker Cesar (the film's director, Jules Dassin, acting under the pseudonym Perlo Vita); and Mario (Robert Manuel)—all of them surprisingly decent men. The film's centerpiece is a 28-minute sequence that captures the robbery itself in fascinating detail, employing neither dialogue nor music, allowing only the actual sounds of the thieves at work to be heard. Once the heist is accomplished, life doesn't get any easier for the crooks, as Tony's gangster rival (Marcel Lupovici) and cohorts get violently greedy after learning about the robbery through Cesar's indiscretion. The kidnapping of Jo's son and plenty of shooting follow before RIFIFI (French slang for "trouble") is over.

This was the second European-made film for writer-director-actor Dassin, an American who plied his trade abroad after the House Un-American Activities Committee made life difficult at home. Dassin, whose wonderful you-are-there direction won him a share of the Best

Director award at Cannes, also manages to inject more than a little humor into this tension-filled genre classic, preceded by the likes of THE ASPHALT JUNGLE and followed by films like BIG DEAL ON MADONNA STREET and Dassin's own TOPKAPI.

RIGHT STUFF, THE

1983 192m c Biography ★★★★
Ladd Co. (U.S.) PG/15

Sam Shepard *(Chuck Yeager)*, Scott Glenn *(Alan Shepard)*, Ed Harris *(John Glenn)*, Dennis Quaid *(Gordon Cooper)*, Fred Ward *(Gus Grissom)*, Barbara Hershey *(Glennis Yeager)*, Kim Stanley *(Bancho Barnes)*, Veronica Cartwright *(Betty Grissom)*, Pamela Reed *(Trudy Cooper)*, Scott Paulin *(Deke Slayton)*

p, Irwin Winkler, Robert Chartoff; d, Philip Kaufman; w, Philip Kaufman (based on the book by Tom Wolfe); ph, Caleb Deschanel; ed, Glenn Farr, Lisa Fruchtman, Stephen A. Rotter, Tom Rolf, Douglas Stewart; m, Bill Conti; prod d, Geoffrey Kirkland; art d, Richard Lawrence, Stewart Campbell, Peter Romero; fx, Gary Gutierrez, Jordan Belson

AAN Best Picture; AAN Best Supporting Actor: Sam Shepard; *AAN Best Cinematography:* Caleb Deschanel; *AA Best Editing:* Glenn Farr, Lisa Fruchtman, Stephen A. Rotter, Douglas Stewart, Tom Rolf; *AA Best Score:* Bill Conti; *AAN Best Art Direction:* Geoffrey Kirkland, Richard J. Lawrence, W. Stewart Campbell, Peter Romero, Pat Pending, George R. Nelson; *AA Best Sound:* Mark Berger, Tom Scott, Randy Thom, David MacMillan; *AA Best Sound Effects Editing:* Jay Boekelheide

Funny, trenchant account, based on Tom Wolfe's book, of the dawn of the space age, seen as both a shameless piece of media mythmaking, and as an act of genuine courage on the part of the first astronauts. The movie spans about 15 years, beginning with Chuck Yeager (Sam Shepard) breaking Mach 1, and concluding with a huge barbecue at the Astrodome at which President Johnson (Donald Moffat) hosts the astronauts. In between, it depicts their arduous training and complex personal lives, and the absurd lengths to which they have to go to satisfy the public's demand for real-life heroes. Director-writer Philip Kaufman's script brings a wealth of humor to a faithful retelling of the astronauts' fascinating stories, the actors fit smoothly into their roles and even physically resemble their characters, and the direction is well-paced and visually exciting.

RING-A-DING RHYTHM

1962 73m bw Musical/Comedy ★★½
Amicus (U.K.)

Helen Shapiro *(Helen)*, Craig Douglas *(Craig)*, Felix Felton *(Mayor)*, Arthur Mullard *(Police Chief)*, Timothy Bateson *(Coffeeshop Owner)*, Hugh Lloyd *(Usher)*, Ronnie Stevens, Frank Thornton *(TV Directors)*, Derek Nimmo *(Head Waiter)*, Mario Fabrizi *(Spaghetti Eater)*

p, Richard Lester; d, Richard Lester; w, Milton Subotsky; ph, Gilbert Taylor; ed, Bill Lenny; m, Ken Thorne; prod d, Al Marcus; art d, Maurice Carter; cos, Gamp Ferris, Maude Churchill

Richard Lester's first feature proved to be an effective springboard for his highly stylized direction, employing techniques (unusual camera angles, quick cuts) that he polished further in the Beatles' A HARD DAY'S NIGHT. The plot here is not unlike a number of 50s films in which a town's upstanding citizens react vehemently to the corrupting spread of demon rock 'n' roll, forcing the kids to stand up for their rights. In this case, the mayor of an English town, Felton, goes so far as to take away one coffeeshop's license for having a jukebox. A pair of crafty local teens, Shapiro and Douglas, counterattack by trying to put together a festival that will demonstrate the merits of traditional jazz (then an important part of British counterculture) and rock 'n' roll, traveling to a London TV studio to try to persuade some big-name performers to appear. This plot gives Lester an opportunity to creatively showcase a number of pop, rock, and trad jazz stars, including Del Shannon, Chubby Checker, Gary "U.S." Bonds, Gene Vincent, Chris Barber's Jazz Band and the Temperance Seven.

RIO BRAVO

1959 141m c Western   ★★★★
Armada (U.S.)   /PG

John Wayne (John T. Chance), Dean Martin (Dude), Ricky Nelson (Colorado Ryan), Angie Dickinson (Feathers), Walter Brennan (Stumpy), Ward Bond (Pat Wheeler), John Russell (Nathan Burdette), Pedro Gonzalez-Gonzalez (Carlos), Estelita Rodriguez (Consuelo), Claude Akins (Joe Burdette)

p, Howard Hawks; d, Howard Hawks; w, Jules Furthman, Leigh Brackett (based on a story by Barbara Hawks McCampbell); ph, Russell Harlan; ed, Folmar Blangsted; m, Dimitri Tiomkin; art d, Leo K. Kuter; cos, Marjorie Best

Annoyed that the acclaimed and popular HIGH NOON portrayed a sheriff so afraid of his adversaries that he spends most of the movie asking the townsfolk for help, director Howard Hawks decided to make a filmed response, namely RIO BRAVO. A lengthy, leisurely paced film, RIO BRAVO is set in a small Texas border town, Rio Bravo, that is under the control of evil cattle baron Russell and his dim-witted brother, Akins. When Akins commits a murder, the sheriff (Wayne), throws him in jail to await the arrival of a US Marshall. Russell lays seige to the jailhouse, and Wayne is forced to rely on the town drunk (Martin), a cranky old cripple (Brennan), and an untested young gunslinger (Nelson) for help.

With its simple plotline, familiar characters, songs, and frequent humor, RIO BRAVO is outstanding entertainment. However, the film has been overrated by some zealous critics, who either ignore its weak points or defend them as praiseworthy oddities. As enjoyable as the film is, it has flaws that prevent it from reaching the classic status of RED RIVER—particularly the casting. Pop star Ricky Nelson was cast on the basis of his great popularity with teenagers rather than because of any acting talent, a decision that ensured additional box office from young girls who wouldn't normally think of going to see a western. Despite his moneymaking potential, however, Nelson simply couldn't act, and Hawks must have known it. The singer is given the fewest lines possible for a third-billed actor, and he is physically restricted to the background or alongside the other leads. He is never given center stage alone—this is no Montgomery Clift (Wayne's costar in RED RIVER). Also somewhat weak is Angie Dickinson. While she is given all the right Hawksian dialog and her character is the quintessential Hawks woman, tough enough to stand up to any man who comes her way, she doesn't possess the spunkiness of a Jean Arthur or the sultriness of a Lauren Bacall. Wayne, however, turns in a fine performance (though not as good his work in RED RIVER), and Walter Brennan is superb as the grouchy, nasty old man who is undyingly loyal to his friends. The real revelation, however, is Dean Martin, in a part he obviously understood well. His role as the drunken deputy who redeems himself is crucial to the film, and the singer-actor handles his part with skill. Hawks enjoyed working with Martin, whom he found eager and willing to take direction.

RIO BRAVO was very successful commercially, and Hawks later used two variations of the story (with the same character types, similar situations, sometimes even the same sets) in his last two westerns, EL DORADO and RIO LOBO. All cowritten by Leigh Brackett, the films form a sort of informal trilogy, although they become successively weaker. Though Hawks was inspired to make RIO BRAVO as a rebuttal to HIGH NOON, his daughter, Barbara Hawks McCampbell, an aspiring writer, came up with the basic plotline that later became the film's climax—outlaws holed up in a house, while the heroes explode sticks of dynamite by shooting them like clay targets—and was paid and given screen credit for the story. Overall, RIO BRAVO is an excellent film featuring strong, proud, but very human characters who fight against their various handicaps and pull together to do a job and do it right. The people in RIO BRAVO have the same kind of deep affection and understanding for one another as do close family members who are not afraid to speak truthfully for fear of hurting each other's feelings, and it is that aspect of the film that is so appealing. Director John Carpenter's second feature, ASSAULT ON PRECINCT 13, is an updated remake of RIO BRAVO.

RIO GRANDE

1950 105m bw Western/War   ★★★★
Argosy (U.S.)   /U

John Wayne (Lt. Col. Kirby Yorke), Maureen O'Hara (Mrs. Kathleen Yorke), Ben Johnson (Trooper Tyree), Claude Jarman Jr. (Trooper Jeff Yorke), Harry Carey Jr. (Trooper Daniel "Sandy" Boone), Chill Wills (Dr. Wilkins), J. Carrol Naish (Gen. Philip Sheridan), Victor McLaglen (Sgt. Maj. Quincannon), Grant Withers (Deputy Marshal), Peter Ortiz (Capt. St. Jacques)

p, John Ford, Merian C. Cooper; d, John Ford; w, James Kevin McGuinness (based on the story "Mission with No Record" by James Warner Bellah); ph, Bert Glennon; ed, Jack Murray; m, Victor Young; art d, Frank Hotaling; fx, Howard Lydecker, Theodore Lydecker; cos, Adele Palmer

This fine portrait of the US Cavalry was the third in John Ford's magnificent trilogy about the troopers of the Old West, following FORT APACHE and SHE WORE A YELLOW RIBBON. Lt. Col. Kirby Yorke (John Wayne) is a tough commanding officer at a remote cavalry post whose hard edge is softened when his only son, Jeff (Claude Jarman, Jr.), reports for duty. After dropping out of West Point, the shamed Jeff has enlisted in the Cavalry and now wants to prove himself to his father. Kirby is cool toward the boy, promising no favoritism, and explains what Army life is really about: "Put out of your mind any romantic ideas that it's a way of glory. It's a life of suffering and hardship, an uncompromising devotion to your oath and your duty." Jeff is taken under the wings of fun-loving troopers Tyree (Ben Johnson) and Boone (Harry Carey, Jr.), who keep an eye on the young man, and the arrival of Kathleen Yorke (Maureen O'Hara), Kirby's estranged wife and Jeff's mother, adds some tension to the scene. She is determined to buy back Jeff's enlistment, and in the process rekindles Kirby's love for her. An excellent post-Civil War tale with romance (Wayne and O'Hara), humor (Johnson, Carey, and Victor McLaglen), and music (a few tunes by the Sons of the Pioneers), RIO GRANDE is one of Ford's great achievements. As in FORT APACHE and SHE WORE A YELLOW RIBBON, Ford creates a powerful portrait of the wild, remote Southwest during the Indian wars, presenting the traditions and exploits of the old cavalry in very realistic terms, showing them in action as tired, dirty, wounded men performing their assignments in pain and discomfort and emphasizing the real glory of these soldiers as typified by their leader Kirby. The director's camera angles, broadly encompassing whole lines of riding cavalrymen, accentuate their prosaic nobility and dedication to taming the frontier. Much of the score nicely supports the story, indicating the cavalrymen's Irish background and sentimentality, especially in the inclusion of the fine Sons of the Pioneers song "I'll Take You Home Again, Kathleen."

RIO LOBO

1970 114m c Western   ★½
Malabar/Cinema Center (U.S.)   G/PG

John Wayne (Col. Cord McNally), Jorge Rivero (Capt. Pierre Cordona), Jennifer O'Neill (Shasta Delaney), Jack Elam (Phillips), Victor French (Ketcham), Susana Dosamantes (Maria Carmen), Christopher Mitchum (Tuscarora), Mike Henry (Sheriff Tom Hendricks), David Huddleston (Dr. Jones), Bill Williams (Sheriff Pat Cronin)

p, Howard Hawks; d, Howard Hawks; w, Leigh Brackett, Burton Wohl (based on a story by Burton Wohl); ph, William Clothier; ed, John Woodcock; m, Jerry Goldsmith; prod d, Robert Smith; fx, A.D. Flowers, Cliff Wenger; cos, Luster Bayless, Ted Parvin

This is probably the hardest film to watch that either Howard Hawks or John Wayne ever took part in, surpassing even Wayne's early days in Republic's "Three Mesquiteer" series for forced acting and situations. The 1930s pictures are more forgivable because the budgets were limiting and the outings were approached routinely. But for such a refined director as Hawks to end his career on a note like this, having made some of the finest films in the history of American cinema, is an atrocity not worth the silver used in the negative. The story isn't so bad, taking place soon after the Civil War. Union captain Wayne teams up with two Confederate soldiers to track down the man responsible for stealing a shipment of gold. Their efforts land them in the middle of a town being terrorized by a crooked sheriff. Wayne and company put an end to the sheriff's tyranny by rallying the townspeople to stand up for their rights. Witty lines are injected that would normally provide a chuckle but are so poorly delivered here that veiwers are left sighing. The common Hawksian theme of male comradeship can be found in the relationship between Wayne and his Confederate cohorts, but the way Wayne and his supporting cast walk through their roles is ridiculous. Rivero and O'Neill face the Duke like beginning stars in the shadow of a great master, something Wayne is aware of and can't seem to shake. Only the performance of Elam remains lively, but it is the type of characterization he has done dozens of times. A sad finale to Hawks's magnificent career.

RISE OF LOUIS XIV, THE
(LA PRISE DE POUVOIR PAR LOUIS XIV)
1966 100m c Biography   ★★★
O.R.T.F. (France)   G/U

Jean-Marie Patte *(King Louis XIV)*, Raymond Jourdan *(Jean Baptiste Colbert)*, Silvagni *(Cardinal Mazarin)*, Katherina Renn *(Queen Anne of Austria)*, Dominique Vincent *(Mme. du Plessis)*, Pierre Barrat *(Nicolas Fouquet)*, Fernand Fabre *(Michel Le Tellier)*, Francoise Ponty *(Louise de la Valliere)*, Joelle Langeois *(Marie Therese)*, Jacqueline Corot *(Mme. Henrietta)*

d, Roberto Rossellini; w, Philippe Erlanger, Jean Gruault; ph, Georges Leclerc; ed, Armand Ridel; art d, Maurice Valay; cos, Christiane Coste

This is Roberto Rossellini's sparse, near-documentary look at the young Sun King (Jean-Marie Patte) and at how he codified and choreographed an empire, framing fashions to ensure absolute obedience. No detail of the artful young king's designs and graces—which culminated in the structured elegance of the court at Versailles—is too small to be captured by the camera, while the big events, the executions and rebellions, are, quite properly, trivialized. What won obeisance for playboy Louis was fashion, carefully crafted for conquest. Rossellini's pans and zooms follow these strategies of manners and mores intimately: Louis's dying mentor Mazarin (Silvagni) rouges his pallid cheeks prior to his audience with the young king; Louis demands more height to his wigs to enhance his stature and more lace to his jacket to gain attention; the king choreographs the rituals attendant on funerals, cabinet meetings, banquets. The complexities of Louis's life-structurings consolidate his previously shaky power—all eyes are on the young king, hoping to spot each new nuance, each fad-to-be—and intrigues and plots are forgotten in this atmosphere of utter attendance: the Sun King is all-powerful. A revival of sorts for Rossellini, this picture would set the standard for its genre, playing as important a part in film history as did his earliest Neo-Realist films. Like PAISAN, its predecessor of 20 years, the film is constructed of episodes, each giving the observer a chance to bear witness to a reality, a view of history not of battles and bravado, but of guile, manipulation, and role-playing charisma.

RISING SUN
1993 129m c Thriller   ★★★
Fox (U.S.)   R/18

Sean Connery *(John Connor)*, Wesley Snipes *(Web Smith)*, Harvey Keitel *(Tom Graham)*, Cary-Hiroyuki Tagawa *(Eddie Sakamura)*, Kevin Anderson *(Bob Richmond)*, Mako *(Yoshida-San)*, Ray Wise *(Senator John Morton)*, Stan Egi *(Ishihara)*, Stan Shaw *(Phillips)*, Tia Carrere *(Jingo Asakuma)*

p, Peter Kaufman; d, Philip Kaufman; w, Philip Kaufman (from the original screenplay based on the novel by Michael Crichton); ph, Michael Chapman; ed, Stephen A. Rotter, William S. Scharf; m, Toru Takemitsu; prod d, Dean Tavoularis; art d, Angelo Graham; fx, Larry L. Fuentes, Industrial Light & Magic, Mark A.Z. Dippe; cos, Jacqueline West

Directed by Philip Kaufman from the best-selling novel by Michael Crichton, RISING SUN is a triumph of style over content. Like BLADE RUNNER, the film grafts a fiercely modernist feel onto characters and themes right out of a 1940s film noir—an impressive achievement that more than makes up for a ponderous storyline.

Most of the factors deemed anti-Japanese in Crichton's novel have been removed or softened for the film, which revolves around the murder of a young woman at the LA office of a huge Asian corporation.

The key players are John Connor (Sean Connery), a police detective whose love of all things Japanese has many colleagues doubting his motives, and Web Smith (Wesley Snipes), Connor's younger, slow-on-the-uptake partner. The murder, it seems, has been recorded on a video disk that has then been electronically adjusted to twist the facts. As Connor and Smith uncover successive layers of digital cover-up, the disk becomes both the fulcrum on which the investigation turns, and a metaphor for the detective process itself.

Kaufman gives RISING SUN a brilliant, high-tech-meets-urban-grunge sheen, conjuring extremes of opulence and sleaze and suggesting a moral shadowland where every character is compromised. Connery is in his element as the almost mystically gifted Connor, though Snipes can't make us believe in Smith's stupidity—15 minutes into the film, he's the only one in the theater who still hasn't figured out what's going on.

RISKY BUSINESS
1983 98m c Comedy   ★★★½
Geffen (U.S.)   R/18

Tom Cruise *(Joel)*, Rebecca De Mornay *(Lana)*, Joe Pantoliano *(Guido)*, Richard Masur *(Rutherford)*, Bronson Pinchot *(Barry)*, Curtis Armstrong *(Miles)*, Nicholas Pryor *(Joel's Father)*, Janet Carroll *(Joel's Mother)*, Shera Danese *(Vicki)*, Raphael Sbarge *(Glenn)*

p, Jon Avnet, Steve Tisch; d, Paul Brickman; w, Paul Brickman; ph, Reynaldo Villalobos; ed, Richard Chew; m, Tangerine Dream; prod d, William J. Cassidy; cos, Robert de Mora

One of the key films of the 1980s, and proof that a teen sex comedy could merit serious consideration. Smart, stylish, and cynical about the values of its time, this movie aspires to be THE GRADUATE for its generation and it comes pretty close. The affluent teenaged hero is poised on the brink of manhood, eager for the promised pleasures of maturity and fearful of the responsibilities. One wrong step could destroy a potentially bright future. The title refers to both sex and capitalist endeavor; RISKY BUSINESS documents a time in which everything has become a commodity.

Like Fellini's 8 1/2, RISKY BUSINESS begins with a revealing dream of its stymied protagonist. A steamy sexual encounter is nightmarishly transformed into a crucial college entrance examination to which Joel (Tom Cruise) has arrived too late: there will no future for our young protagonist. Joel, we learn, lives in a fashionable Chicago suburb with his alarmingly straight parents (Nicholas Pryor and Janet Carroll). They go off on a trip leaving their outwardly model son in charge. His thoughts soon turn to sex and the "adult" ads in a local newspaper. After an unsettling initial encounter with a black transvestite, Joel is referred to the services of the spectacular Lana (Rebecca De Mornay), who visits his home and rocks his world. The morning after, the kittenish hooker surveys her upscale surroundings and proposes to Joel a plan that could net them a lot of money. She and her associates have something that the neighborhood boys want and Joel has an empty house where they can all gather. What sounds like a risky but potentially profitable plan is complicated by the intervention of Guido the Killer Pimp (Joe Pantoliano) and the equally frightening interviewer from Princeton University, Mr. Rutherford (Richard Masur).

Cruise is likable and credible in the lead. His youthful nervousness and exuberance in the early part of the film—particularly his starmaking solo dance around the empty house—are joyous to behold. De Mornay is sexy and touching, and Bronson Pinchot and Curtis Armstrong are memorable in supporting roles. Paul Brickman does a slickly professional job directing his own darkly satirical screenplay and Tangerine Dream provide the dreamy electronic score.

RITA, SUE AND BOB TOO!
1986 95m c Comedy   ★★★
Film Four/Umbrella/British Screen (U.K.)   R/18

Michelle Holmes *(Sue)*, Siobhan Finneran *(Rita)*, George Costigan *(Bob)*, Lesley Sharp *(Michelle, Bob's Wife)*, Willie Ross *(Sue's Father)*, Patti Nicholls *(Sue's Mother)*, Kulvinder Ghir *(Aslam)*, Paul Oldham *(Lee)*, Bryan Heeley *(Michael)*

p, Sandy Lieberson, Patsy Pollock; d, Alan Clarke; w, Andrea Dunbar (based on her plays "The Arbor," "Rita, Sue and Bob Too"); ph, Ivan Strasburg; ed, Stephen Singleton; m, Michael Kamen; art d, Len Huntingford; cos, Cathy Cook

Sue (Michelle Holmes) and Rita (Siobhan Finneran) are hefty teenage girls who live in a deteriorating housing project in economically depressed north England. As the film opens, they trek across town to baby-sit for Bob (George Costigan) and Michelle (Lesley Sharp), a middle-class suburban couple. Instead of driving the baby-sitters home at the end of the evening, George takes them out on the darkened moors, where he produces a condom for their inspection and then proposes they put it to use. After a bit of glib demurring, the girls accept. All three are more or less delighted by the experience and repeat it frequently. But their cozy arrangement runs into problems. Based on two plays by Andrea Dunbar, this is a sex comedy in which the on-screen sex (which is limited) is far less important than the idea of that sex. With their *menage a trois*, the girls are capable of bringing some excitement to their lives even if the surrounding world wallows in hopeless inertia. Although there are some slow sections, RITA, SUE AND BOB TOO! provides a number of good laughs and also more than a few empathetic winces.

RIVER, THE

1951 99m c Drama   ★★★★★
Oriental-International Films/Theatre Guild   (India)   /U

Nora Swinburne *(The Mother)*, Esmond Knight *(The Father)*, Arthur Shields *(Mr. John)*, Thomas E. Breen *(Captain John)*, Radha Shri Ram *(Melanie)*, Suprova Mukerjee *(Nan)*, Patricia Walters *(Harriet)*, Adrienne Corri *(Valery)*, Richard Foster *(Bogey)*, Penelope Wilkinson *(Elizabeth)*

p, Kenneth McEldowney; d, Jean Renoir; w, Jean Renoir, Rumer Godden (based on the novel by Rumer Godden); ph, Claude Renoir, Ramananda Sen Gupta; ed, George Gale; m, M.A. Partha Sarathy; prod d, Eugene Lourie; art d, Bansi Chandragupta

Jean Renoir's first film in color, THE RIVER is an extraordinarily rich and almost therapeutically heartening movie about an English family living in Bengal. Part coming-of-age story, part empathetic travelogue, part philosophic poem, THE RIVER was cited by Renoir as "one film that corresponds almost exactly to my initial concept of it."

Harriet (Patricia Walters), a bright and sensitive adolescent, lives with her large family in a big house overlooking the Ganges River. One day, a handsome young American named Captain John (Thomas E. Breen) arrives at the home of his cousin, Mr. John (Arthur Shields), a widower who lives next door to Harriet's family. A somewhat mysterious and romantic figure who has lost a leg in the war, Captain John becomes the immediate object of new and unfamiliar longings in Harriet, in her only slightly older but considerably riper friend, Valery (Adrienne Corri), and, perhaps, in Mr. John's half-Indian daughter, Melanie (Radha Shri Ram), the least flighty of the three girls.

Before contracting to film THE RIVER, Renoir required producer Kenneth McEldowney, a Beverly Hills florist, to agree to four stipulations: (1) Renoir would be allowed to make a reconnaissance trip to India, all expenses paid; (2) he would write the script in collaboration with Rumer Godden, author of the source novel; (3) he would have final cut; and (4) the film would include no elephant hunt, a staple ingredient of English-language movies set in India. Rumer Godden's semiautobiographical script (co-written with Renoir) for THE RIVER is superb. The visuals of Renoir and crew fully live up to the words of Godden. Dense with documentary and aesthetic asides but, amazingly, never sidetracked by them, Renoir's "mural" movie blesses its viewers with a multitude of riches and bonuses, including a series of mini-travelogues spotted throughout. THE RIVER is further graced by the presence of its three young leading ladies: Radha Shri Ram, a precociously, hauntingly grave beauty recruited from the world of Hindu dance; Adrienne Corri, a robust, red-headed nymph; and Patricia Walters as Harriet, a homely girl who yearns to be "outstandingly beautiful" and becomes so in her last onscreen moments with Captain John.

Anyone who still believes in family sentiment, but is disheartened by Hollywood's characteristically mawkish and insincere treatment of it, is urged to immediately take a voyage on Renoir's river.

RIVER RUNS THROUGH IT, A

1992 123m c Drama   ★★½
The Big Sky Motion Picture Co./North Fork Motion Picture   PG
Company   (U.S.)

Craig Sheffer *(Norman MacLean)*, Brad Pitt *(Paul MacLean)*, Tom Skerritt *(Reverend MacLean)*, Brenda Blethyn *(Mrs. MacLean)*, Emily Lloyd *(Jesse Burns)*, Edie McClurg *(Mrs. Burns)*, Stephen Shellen *(Neal Burns)*, Joseph Gordon-Levitt *(Young Norman)*, Vann Gravage *(Young Paul)*, Robert Redford *(Narration)*

p, Patrick Markey, Robert Redford; d, Robert Redford; w, Richard Friedenberg (from the novella by Norman MacLean); ph, Philippe Rousselot; ed, Lynzee Klingman, Robert Estrin; m, Mark Isham; prod d, Jon Hutman; art d, Walter Martishius; cos, Bernie Pollack

AAN Best Adapted Screenplay: Richard Friedenberg; *AA Best Cinematography:* Philippe Rousselot; *AAN Best Score:* Mark Isham

Directed by Robert Redford, A RIVER RUNS THROUGH IT employs picture-postcard scenery as a backdrop for a mildly engaging family melodrama. Norman (Craig Sheffer) and Paul MacLean (Brad Pitt) grow up in a Montana town under the stern but loving guidance of their Presbyterian minister father, Reverend MacLean (Tom Skerritt), and soft-spoken mother (Brenda Blethyn). After school lessons, the Reverend lets the boys share his greatest passion—fly fishing. To the elder MacLean, the sport is almost a religion. Young Paul is continually rebelling against the Reverend, while Norman is the responsible one. When they grow up, Norman goes away to college and Paul stays in Montana, becoming a newspaper reporter. When Norman returns from college, he is disturbed by Paul's gambling, drinking and skirt-chasing, but can do little to stop his brother's downward spiral, which eventually leads to a tragic end. Meanwhile, Norman falls in love with Jesse Burns (Emily Lloyd), a flapper from an eccentric Methodist family.

Some 12 years after making his directorial debut with ORDINARY PEOPLE, Robert Redford once again turns his attention to the story of a family. His directorial style, however, involves little more than a tendency to use huge close-ups of every performer—particularly Sheffer and Pitt, who are continually shown looking at each other, even when they have nothing to say. While Redford centers on the actors, the screenplay wallows in cliches. Richard Friedenberg, who adapted Norman MacLean's autobiographical novella, does little to make this depiction of 1920s Montana fresh, and Norman's narration is chock-full of neo-philosophical platitudes: "Life is not a work of art," etc. Compounding the situation is the fact that fly fishing isn't the most visually dynamic of sports. Even set against the Sierra Club beauty of Redford's Montana, it's hard to get excited by fisherman casting their lines into the water.

RIVER'S EDGE

1987 99m c Drama   ★★★½
Hemdale   (U.S.)   R/18

Crispin Glover *(Layne)*, Keanu Reeves *(Matt)*, Ione Skye *(Clarissa)*, Daniel Roebuck *(Samson "John" Tollette)*, Dennis Hopper *(Feck)*, Joshua Miller *(Tim)*, Roxana Zal *(Maggie)*, Josh Richman *(Tony)*, Phil Brock *(Mike)*, Tom Bower *(Bennett)*

p, Sarah Pillsbury, Midge Sanford, David Streit; d, Tim Hunter; w, Neal Jimenez; ph, Frederick Elmes; ed, Howard Smith, Sonya Sones; m, Jurgen Knieper; prod d, John Muto; art d, Mick Muhlfriedel; cos, Claudia Brown

One of the most haunting films of the 1980s, RIVER'S EDGE looks at a suburban, postpunk generation which has no causes, no morals, no feelings, and, worst of all, no future.

This controversial drama, based on a notorious 1981 murder case profiled in *Rolling Stone*, opens with John Tollette (Daniel Roebuck), a hulking teenager who strangles his girlfriend Jamie (Danyi Deats, in the ultimate thankless role) and then matter-of-factly tells his friends about it. Matt (Keanu Reeves) and Clarissa (Ione Skye), the murdered girl's best friend, are disturbed, but Layne (Crispin Glover), a speed freak, views the situation differently. In his eyes, Jamie was a friend, but now she's dead; John is also their friend, but he's still alive and needs their help. As tensions within the group escalate, John and Layne take refuge with Feck (Dennis Hopper), a burned-out biker from the 1960s who had killed his own beloved girlfriend and has now given his heart to a blow-up sex doll named Ellie.

RIVER'S EDGE owes its success, in large part, to Neal Jimenez's superb screenplay, which digs beneath the facades that contemporary teenagers hide behind and yields honest and complex portraits. This generation's postpunk worldview is rooted in nihilism, detachment, and fear of nuclear annihilation—nothing matters to them except friends, rock 'n' roll, and getting stoned.

RIVER'S EDGE also boasts the best cast of unknowns since Francis Ford Coppola's THE OUTSIDERS. Reeves and Skye are superb as the moral centers of the film, Roebuck is great as the killer, and the supporting performaces are also impressive. Glover and Hopper go over the top and get away with it.

ROAD HOUSE

1948   95m   bw   Thriller   ★★★
Fox   (U.S.)   /A

Ida Lupino (Lily Stevens), Cornel Wilde (Pete Morgan), Celeste Holm (Susie Smith), Richard Widmark (Jefty Robbins), O.Z. Whitehead (Arthur), Robert Karnes (Mike), George Andre Beranger (Lefty), Ian MacDonald (Police Captain), Grandon Rhodes (Judge), Jack G. Lee (Sam)

p, Edward Chodorov; d, Jean Negulesco; w, Edward Chodorov (based on a story by Margaret Gruen, Oscar Saul); ph, Joseph La Shelle; ed, James B. Clark; m, Cyril J. Mockridge; art d, Lyle Wheeler, Maurice Ransford; fx, Fred Sersen; cos, Kay Nelson

A stylish and perverse film noir which stars Widmark as the owner of a roadhouse near the Canadian border and Wilde as his best friend and manager. When they hire Lupino as the joint's singer and piano player, the friendship takes a strange turn. Widmark becomes obsessed with Lupino, who in turn finds herself attracted to Wilde. Wilde, however, also the object of cashier Holm's desires, remains aloof. When Widmark goes away on a hunting trip, Wilde finally gives in to Lupino and the two become lovers. When Widmark returns and is told by Wilde of the new situation, Widmark's dark side comes to light. He stages a robbery which points to Wilde as the guilty party. Rather than watch the framed Wilde go to jail, however, he persuades the judge to release the "criminal" into his custody. Widmark's form of imprisonment is a psychological one—forcing Wilde to stay on at the roadhouse but keeping him from Lupino and, ultimately, his freedom. To further torment him, Widmark arranges for a trip to a lodge nestled in the woods, placing Wilde even closer to the border than before. Widmark hopes that his "prisoner" will make an attempt to escape across the border, thereby giving Widmark the chance to shoot him. Meantime, Holm, who has come along to the lodge, is still silently in love with Wilde. A chance finally comes to escape, and Wilde and Lupino run off into the woods. Holm tries to warn them that Widmark is on their trail, hunting them with a psychotic vengeance, but in the process she is wounded by the crazed hunter. A battle follows between Widmark and Wilde. Lupino, determined to fight for her man, intervenes and guns down Widmark for the animal he is. A strong movie scattered with land mines of psychotic characters, ROAD HOUSE has a disturbing quality of psychological torture to it—a quality magnified by the claustrophobic atmosphere of the stylized diner and the false outdoors of the studio's sound stage. Wilde does fine as the victimized lover, Widmark plays his archetypal villain with his usual intensity, and Lupino is remarkable in her raw toughness. Holm, however, is the one who keeps ROAD HOUSE from going over the edge by playing a normal girl with a foothold on reality. Adding to the film's atmosphere is Lupino's delivery of a few bluesy numbers including "Again," (Dorcas Cochran, Lionel Newman), "One for My Baby" (Johnny Mercer, Harold Arlen), and "The Right Time."

ROAD TO MOROCCO

1942   83m   bw   Comedy/Musical   ★★★★
Paramount   (U.S.)   /U

Bing Crosby (Jeff Peters), Bob Hope (Turkey Jackson), Dorothy Lamour (Princess Shalmar), Anthony Quinn (Mullay Kasim), Dona Drake (Mihirmah), Mikhail Rasumny (Ahmed Fey), Vladimir Sokoloff (Hyder Khan), George Givot (Neb Jolla), Andrew Tombes (Oso Bucco), Leon Belasco (Yusef)

p, Paul Jones; d, David Butler; w, Frank Butler, Don Hartman; ph, William Mellor; ed, Irene Morra; art d, Hans Dreier, Robert Usher; chor, Paul Oscard; cos, Edith Head

AAN Best Original Screenplay: Frank Butler, Don Hartman; *AAN Best Sound:* Loren Ryder

The third, and best, in the "Road" series, ROAD TO MOROCCO has everything going for it. Bob Hope and Bing Crosby were not yet tired of the formula, and their breezy acting wafts the picture along in a melange of gags, songs, thrills, and calculated absurdities. The duo had already sent up adventure movies in ROAD TO SINGAPORE and jungle films in ROAD TO ZANZIBAR—the next target was the Arabian Nights. Jeff Peters (Crosby) and Turkey Jackson (Hope) are the lone survivors of a Mediterranean shipwreck. They land on a beach, mount a passing camel, and go off toward Morocco, where they learn that things aren't swell. The area is parched, the people poor, and foreigners looked upon with scorn. The two are penniless and hungry when a local merchant offers Jeff money to sell Turkey into slavery as the personal plaything of Princess Shalmar (Dorothy Lamour). Jeff makes the deal, Turkey is forcibly removed to the palace, and life in Morocco gets increasingly difficult for everyone thereafter. The picture is filled with great gags and one-liners, including Hope's lament for the Oscar he might have won; the camel's complaint that "this is the screwiest picture I've ever been in!"; Hope's appearance in drag; and the backfire of the "patty cake" routine, after which it's remarked, "Hmmm. That gag sure got around." And there are countless more, delivered at a pace that never lets up.

ROAD WARRIOR, THE

1981   94m   c   Science Fiction/Action   ★★★★
Warner Bros.   (Australia)   R/X

Mel Gibson (Max), Bruce Spence (Gyro Captain), Vernon Wells (Wez), Emil Minty (Feral Kid), Mike Preston (Pappagallo), Kjell Nilsson (Humungus), Virginia Hey (Warrior Woman), Syd Heylen (Curmudgeon), Moira Claux (Big Rebecca), David Slingsby (Quiet Man)

p, Byron Kennedy; d, George Miller; w, Terry Hayes, George Miller, Brian Hannat; ph, Dean Semler; ed, David Stiven, Tim Wellburn, Michael Chirgwin; m, Brian May; art d, Graham Walker; fx, Jeffrey Clifford, Kim Priest; cos, Norma Moriceau

Director George Miller, whose MAD MAX set new standards of kinetic, visceral excitement, surpasses himself with the sequel. The film is set in a savage, post-apocalyptic world devoted solely to the pursuit of gasoline with which to fuel surviving vehicles. Max (Mel Gibson), whose wife and child were killed in the previous movie, has become an alienated drifter. He is led by the Gyro Captain (Bruce Spence) to a small oil refinery populated by the "good" people under the leadership of Pappagallo (Mike Preston). Their precious encampment is continuously besieged by an army of grotesque, nomadic desert rats led by a massive bodybuilder known as the Humungus (Kjell Nilsson), who wants their gasoline. In one of the most spectacular chase scenes ever put on film, Max and his comrades fight off a series of vicious high-speed attacks from a convoy of bizarre vehicles.

Miller brings every visual trick in the book into play, creating a stunningly detailed, vibrant new world that never ceases to amaze. He pulls all the fresh and original elements of MAD MAX together, and straightens out his earlier muddled narrative style into a strict linear plot that rips along at a breathtaking pace. In addition, THE ROAD WARRIOR has a connotative richness unusual for an action film, drawing equally on cinematic history (Max's relationship with The Feral Kid echoes SHANE), classical literature (the film is replete with references to the *Iliad*), and myth (Miller was a devotee of scholar-guru Joseph Campbell long before his work on myth and the heroic tradition became inescapably trendy during the late 1980s). Perhaps needless to say, this is the film that made Mel Gibson an international star.

ROARING TWENTIES, THE

1939 104m bw Crime ★★★★
Warner Bros. (U.S.) /PG

James Cagney *(Eddie Bartlett)*, Priscilla Lane *(Jean Sherman)*, Humphrey Bogart *(George Hally)*, Jeffrey Lynn *(Lloyd Hart)*, Gladys George *(Panama Smith)*, Frank McHugh *(Danny Green)*, Paul Kelly *(Nick Brown)*, Elisabeth Risdon *(Mrs. Sherman)*, Edward Keane *(Pete Henderson)*, Joe Sawyer *(Sgt. Pete Jones)*

p, Samuel Bischoff; d, Raoul Walsh, Anatole Litvak; w, Jerry Wald, Richard Macaulay, Robert Rossen (based on a story by Mark Hellinger); ph, Ernest Haller; ed, Jack Killifer; m, Heinz Roemheld, Ray Heindorf; art d, Max Parker; fx, Byron Haskin, Edwin DuPar; cos, Milo Anderson

A fitting finale to a decade of memorable gangster films. This slick, whirlwind-paced crime melodrama is another tour de force for James Cagney, making it a companion piece to ANGELS WITH DIRTY FACES. It was the brainchild of journalist-turned-producer Mark Hellinger, who assures audiences in voice-over during the opening credits that what they are about to see is based upon real people and events he covered as a newsman during the 1920s, when the gangster was king and Prohibition was nothing more than a bad law that elevated the gangster to his deadly throne.

The picture opens with three WWI doughboys, Eddie Bartlett (Cagney), George Hally (Bogart) and Lloyd Hart (Lynn) discussing their future plans in a bomb crater during a battle in France. Hart intends to become a lawyer, and Eddie plans on going back to repairing cabs, but Hally explains that he is determined to put his Army weapons training to good use. Back home, Eddie becomes a successful bootlegger, hires Hally away from a rival gin peddler, and employs Hart to handle legal affairs for the legit end of his business. When war breaks out between the rival gangs, Hally, tired of playing second fiddle, helps set Eddie up in a trap that backfires. Later, Hally decides to go after Hart, who is now a crusading attorney. Chorus girl Jean (Lane) begs Eddie for help, and the stage is set for a climactic confrontation between Cagney and Bogart. Viewers aren't likely to forget Cagney's walk down the street at the end of the film.

Walsh's direction of this third and last film in which Cagney and Bogart appeared together is awesomely swift, encompassing a decade in slick episodes, interspersed with newsreel footage of gangsters, rumrunning, and booze being made on an assembly line. Eddie is shown to be a good man ruined by the excesses of the times. Though he has gone bad, strains of decency are apparent in his relationship with Hart and Jean, and in his self-sacrificing attempt to save them from the violence of Hally.

Cagney gives a supercharged performance, particularly when he is down-and-out and acting the role of a drunk in a stupor. Bogart is icily sinister as a man devoid of human kindness or affection, while George is terrific as the loyal saloon gal who will go to the Devil for her man.

Cagney's role is based upon the spectacular rise and fall of New York gangster Larry Fay, a colorful and enigmatic underworld character who promoted the career of brassy nightclub singer Texas Guinan (the role model for Panama). Fay also reputedly provided the inspiration for F. Scott Fitzgerald's *The Great Gatsby*. This would be Cagney's last gangster film for a decade, until he took on the psychotic lead role in WHITE HEAT, working again with his good friend Walsh.

ROBE, THE

1953 135m c Religious ★★½
Fox (U.S.) /U

Richard Burton *(Marcellus Gallio)*, Jean Simmons *(Diana)*, Victor Mature *(Demetrius)*, Michael Rennie *(Peter)*, Jay Robinson *(Caligula)*, Dean Jagger *(Justus)*, Torin Thatcher *(Sen. Gallio)*, Richard Boone *(Pilate)*, Betta St. John *(Miriam)*, Jeff Morrow *(Paulus)*

p, Frank Ross; d, Henry Koster; w, Albert Maltz (originally uncredited), Philip Dunne (based on the novel by Lloyd C. Douglas), Gina Kaus; ph, Leon Shamroy; ed, Barbara McLean; m, Alfred Newman; art d, Lyle Wheeler, George W. Davis; fx, Ray Kellogg

AAN Best Picture; AAN Best Actor: Richard Burton; AAN Best Cinematography: Leon Shamroy; AA Best Art Direction: Lyle Wheeler, George W. Davis, Walter M. Scott, Paul S. Fox; AA Best Costume Design: Charles LeMaire, Emile Santiago

Fighting for fashion, in widescreen no less. A heavy Biblical dirge, bulging with blandfilmitis bigbudgetitis, THE ROBE was the first film in CinemaScope, Hollywood's answer to the threat of TV. Audiences (primarily Catholic schoolchildren dragged kicking and screaming by their teachers) dutifully poured into theaters to watch orgy-weary Roman officer turned luminous Christian Richard Burton (very stiff in a part he considered prissy and silly) and his equally shiny and suffering co-star Jean Simmons (who deserves better) fight for a bolt of cloth that J.C. (and we don't mean Joan Crawford) wore before his death. Their opponent is evil emperor Caligula (Jay Robinson, in a flamboyant camp classic performance that must be seen to be believed). Luckily, Dick and Jean, who have an unfortunate date with death, have Demetrius (the Mature Vic, giving the film's best performance) on their side. He rescues the rumpled but revered wrap just in time to tote it with him to the sequel, DEMETRIUS AND THE GLADIATORS, where he must face a more dangerous lioness than any Caligula ever kept penned up: Susie Hayward. Stick with THE TEN COMMANDMENTS, or try watching FELLINI SATYRICON instead.

ROBERTA

1935 105m bw Musical/Comedy ★★★★
RKO (U.S.) /U

Irene Dunne *(Stephanie)*, Fred Astaire *(Huck Haines)*, Ginger Rogers *(Countess Scharwenka/Lizzie Gatz)*, Randolph Scott *(John Kent)*, Helen Westley *(Roberta/Aunt Minnie)*, Victor Varconi *(Ladislaw)*, Claire Dodd *(Sophie)*, Luis Alberni *(Voyda)*, Ferdinand Munier *(Lord Delves)*, Torben Meyer *(Albert)*

p, Pandro S. Berman; d, William A. Seiter; w, Jane Murfin, Sam Mintz, Allan Scott, Glenn Tryon (from the musical play *Roberta* by Jerome Kern and Otto Harbach based on the novel *Gowns By Roberta* by Alice Duer Miller); ph, Edward Cronjager; ed, William Hamilton; m, Jerome Kern; art d, Van Nest Polglase, Carroll Clark; chor, Fred Astaire, Hermes Pan; cos, Bernard Newman

AAN Best Song: Jerome Kern, Dorothy Fields, Jimmy McHugh

The least-seen and appreciated of the magical Astaire-Rogers series at RKO, this now seems, along with TOP HAT and SWING TIME, one of the three wonder films of the series. Astaire and Rogers persistently upstage the romantic leads, Irene Dunne and Randolph Scott, and they simply fly, largely unburdened by the plot.

John Kent (Scott) is a former football star touring Europe with a swing band led by his pal Huck Haines (Astaire, in a role that combined those performed by Bob Hope and George Murphy in the Broadway original). In Paris they visit the salon of noted designer Mme. Roberta, actually John's Aunt Minnie (a marvelous Westley), where they encounter Stephanie (Dunne), a Russian princess employed there since the Revolution. They also meet Countess Scharwenka (Rogers), who, as with the other women, is not what she seems—she's an old girlfriend of Huck's using an aristocratic Polish stage name. John becomes involved with Stephanie, Huck and his old flame rekindle their passion, and together the four set to it that the fashion show goes on at the finale.

What's hung on this frivolous plot are some of Jerome Kern's most beautiful tunes and a set of dances that leave audiences waiting impatiently for the return of Astaire and Rogers. Thankfully they return frequently. "I'll Be Hard to Handle" remains one of their greatest ever, partly because it firmly establishes the personas of "Fred and Ginger" in the popular imagination. Astaire, a great light comedian, makes the most of his many savage wisecracks, and a hilarious Rogers steals practically every scene in which she appears. Astaire does one of his all-time greatest solos to "I Won't Dance," a brilliantly choreographed and performed routine. Two other brief duets, a touchingly simple yet dramatic romantic turn to "Smoke Gets in Your Eyes", and a blistering final recap of "I Won't Dance" make this film dancer-happy to the max.

ROBIN AND MARIAN

1976 106m c Romance/Adventure ★★★
Columbia (U.K.) PG

Sean Connery (*Robin Hood*), Audrey Hepburn (*Maid Marian*), Robert Shaw (*Sheriff of Nottingham*), Richard Harris (*King Richard*), Nicol Williamson (*Little John*), Denholm Elliott (*Will Scarlett*), Kenneth Haigh (*Sir Ranulf de Pudsey*), Ronnie Barker (*Friar Tuck*), Ian Holm (*King John*), Bill Maynard (*Mercadier*)

p, Denis O'Dell; d, Richard Lester; w, James Goldman; ph, David Watkin; ed, John Victor Smith; m, John Barry; prod d, Michael Stringer; art d, Gil Parrondo; fx, Eddie Fowlie; cos, Yvonne Blake

ROMEO AND JULIET for senior citizens. What might have been a wonderful movie is only so-so due to Lester's typically (but here unnecessarily) busy direction and a ponderous script by James Goldman, who had so much success with THE LION IN WINTER that some of his lines for this seem like bon mots he may have cut from that screenplay. Twenty years have passed since the bandit who robbed from the rich to give to the poor ran off to fight in the Crusades with his beloved king. He's now back, in the form of wizened Connery, and in the two decades since he left much has transpired. His love, Marian, is still a maid; she's become a nun, in fact. The king (Harris), meanwhile, has become a madman dedicated to amassing a fortune. The one thing remaining constant in Robin's life is that the sheriff of Nottingham (Shaw) is still eager to see him hang. Robin hooks up with some of the old gang (including Nicol Williamson, all wrong as Little John), kidnaps Marian and gets involved in some spirited adventures, climaxing with a long, cruel duel with the nasty sheriff.

The film's greatest asset is the teaming of Connery and Hepburn. Their more quiet and amusing moments together are as luminous as one would expect, and the coda is very touching indeed. Taken as a whole, ROBIN AND MARIAN is a spotty picture that's sometimes satirical, a trifle pretentious, occasionally exciting. If the powers that be had decided to shoot an all-out comedy that showed Connery creakily trying to recapture his old derring-do, it might have made more sense. Hepburn came back to movies after a nine-year absence to accept this role and had nothing but praise for Lester's quick direction. The trouble is that it's either too quick or too slow, and neither he nor the screenwriter achieve a supple balance between the rueful laughter of maturity and the depressing horrors of medieval bloodshed and old age. You just don't know where you stand with this one.

ROBIN HOOD: PRINCE OF THIEVES

1991 143m c Action/Adventure/Historical ★★½
Morgan Creek/Trilogy Entertainment Group (U.S.) PG-13/PG

Kevin Costner (*Robin of Locksley/Robin Hood*), Morgan Freeman (*Azeem*), Mary Elizabeth Mastrantonio (*Maid Marian*), Christian Slater (*Will Scarlett*), Alan Rickman (*Sheriff of Nottingham*), Geraldine McEwan (*Mortianna*), Michael McShane (*Friar Tuck*), Brian Blessed (*Lord Locksley*), Michael Wincott (*Guy of Gisborne*), Nick Brimble (*Little John*)

p, Richard B. Lewis, Pen Densham, John Watson; d, Kevin Reynolds; w, Pen Densham, John Watson (from the story by Densham); ph, Doug Milsome; ed, Peter Boyle; m, Michael Kamen; prod d, John Graysmark; art d, Alan Tomkins, Fred Carter, John F. Ralph; cos, John Bloomfield

AAN Best Song: Michael Kamen (Music), Bryan Adams (Lyrics), Robert John Lange (Lyrics)

One of 1991's biggest hits, for reasons increasingly obscure. Costner and company struggle desperately to make the Robin Hood legend relevant to contemporary audiences.

With the help of Azeem (Morgan Freeman), young nobleman Robin of Locksley (Kevin Costner) escapes from a Middle Eastern prison and makes his way home to England, where a rude surprise awaits him. His father has been murdered, King Richard is in exile, and Prince John has usurped the throne. Locally, the wicked Sheriff of Nottingham (Alan Rickman), has laid siege to the countryside. Robin gathers his merry men and fights back, pausing only for romance with the lovely, strongwilled Maid Marian (Mary Elizabeth Mastrantonio).

If nothing else, ROBIN HOOD: THE PRINCE OF THIEVES is resolutely politically correct, positing a feminist Marian, adding women to the band of merry men, and inventing the incongruous Azeem, a black Muslim. Costner's surprisingly portly Robin is less a dashing force of justice than a decent kind of guy forced by circumstance to do the right thing because the wrong thing—embodied in the flamboyantly wicked Sheriff of Nottingham—is so obviously unacceptable. He's a Robin Hood for an age when no one believes in heroes.

Director Kevin Reynolds (FANDANGO) has no flair for action: the climactic battle is so ineptly shot and edited that it is difficult to tell who is smiting whom. While Costner is lifeless and speaks strangely (he was said to have attempted a British accent, then abandoned it during shooting), Mastrantonio is an acceptably vivacious Marian. As the Sheriff of Nottingham, Alan Rickman, swaggering through his scenes in sinister black, hissing one-liners and basically acting up a storm, is so theatrically vile that he seems to be in another movie altogether; one can't help but think it's a more entertaining movie than ROBIN HOOD: PRINCE OF THIEVES.

ROBOCOP

1987 103m c Crime/Science Fiction ★★★½
Orion (U.S.) R/18

Peter Weller (*Alex J. Murphy/Robocop*), Nancy Allen (*Anne Lewis*), Ronny Cox (*Richard "Dick" Jones*), Kurtwood Smith (*Clarence J. Boddicker*), Miguel Ferrer (*Robert Morton*), Robert DoQui (*Sgt. Reed*), Dan O'Herlihy (*The Old Man*), Ray Wise (*Leon Nash*), Felton Perry (*Johnson*), Mario Machado

p, Arne L. Schmidt; d, Paul Verhoeven; w, Edward Neumeier, Michael Miner; ph, Jost Vacano; ed, Frank J. Urioste; m, Basil Poledouris; prod d, William Sandell; art d, Gayle Simon; fx, Dale Martin, Rob Bottin, Craig Davies, Peter Ronzani; cos, Erica Edell Phillips

AAN Best Editing: Frank J. Urioste; *AAN Best Sound:* Michael J. Kohut, Carlos DeLarios, Aaron Rochin, Robert Wald

A first-rate production full of nonstop action and inventive special effects but what truly makes ROBOCOP spellbinding is a superior script. Intelligent and satirical, it has the quality of cutting-edge British comic books such as the "Judge Dred" series. Kudos to the screenwriting team of Michael Miner and Edward Neumeier.

It's the not-too-distant future in crime-ridden Old Detroit. A corporate conglomerate is running the city and, under the direction of Richard Jones (Ronny Cox), has developed a huge metal android to combat rampant street crime. When this creation demonstrates a murderous "glitch," Robert Morton (Miguel Ferrer) sees an opportunity to advance his company position by building a better cop machine. He gets his chance when cop Alex Murphy (Peter Weller) is brutally killed by a gang of sadistic hoodlums. Murphy's body is reconstructed by technicians and dubbed RoboCop. It proves to be more than effective against street criminals thereby elevating Morton to top corporate management. This motivates the scheming Jones to make a pact with supervillain Boddicker (Kurtwood Smith) to destroy RoboCop.

Though extremely violent, ROBOCOP showcases an invigorating style even in its goriest scenes. Paul Verhoeven makes every scene sparkle with tilted angles, oddball twists, and special-effects wonders. ROBOCOP effectively conveys a combination of reality and fantasy in a hard-boiled world of humane robots and unfeeling humans.

ROCCO AND HIS BROTHERS
(ROCCO ET SES FRERES)

1960 175m bw Drama ★★★★
Titanus/Marceau (France/Italy) /15

Alain Delon (*Rocco Parondi*), Renato Salvatori (*Simone Parondi*), Annie Girardot (*Nadia*), Katina Paxinou (*Rosaria Parondi*), Roger Hanin (*Morini*), Paolo Stoppa (*Boxing Impresario*), Suzy Delair (*Luisa*), Claudia Cardinale (*Ginetta*), Spiros Focas (*Vincenzo Parondi*), Max Cartier (*Ciro Parondi*)

p, Giuseppe Bordogni; d, Luchino Visconti; w, Luchino Visconti, Suso Cecchi D'Amico, Pasquale Festa Campanile, Massimo Franciosa, Enrico Medioli (based on the novel *The Bridge of Ghisolfa* by Giovanni Testori); ph, Giuseppe Rotunno; ed, Mario Serandrei; m, Nino Rota; art d, Mario Garbuglia; cos, Piero Tosi

Luchino Visconti's episodic prize-winning study of five brothers and their widowed mother transplanted from rural Sicily to industrial Milan in northern Italy is violent, deliberately operatic, and makes ambiguous social statements. The characters' relationships are explored over a period of 12 years, with concentration chiefly on Delon and Salvatori as they alternately enjoy and abuse the affections of Girardot, a prostitute who yearns to be free. She loves Delon, but he sacrifices her to the brutal Salvatori because the latter seems to have greater need of her love. Unable to return Salvatori's affection or to put up with his possessiveness, she returns to her former profession. Enraged, he stabs her to death (the 13 on-screen stabbings in European versions are cut to three for American audiences). ROCCO exists in a variety of running times. The American premiere audience found the 175-minute version overlong and began walking out before the film's final scene ended; but the raped 95-minute version should be avoided.

ROCK AROUND THE CLOCK

1956   77m   bw   Musical   ★★★
Columbia   (U.S.)   /U

Bill Haley and the Comets, The Platters, Tony Martinez and His Band, Frankie Bell and His Bellboys (Themselves), Alan Freed (Himself), Johnnie Johnston (Steve Hollis), Alix Talton (Corinne Talbot), Lisa Gaye (Lisa Johns), John Archer (Mike Dennis), Henry Slate (Corny LaSalle)

p, Sam Katzman; d, Fred F. Sears; w, Robert E. Kent, James B. Gordon; ph, Benjamin Kline; ed, Saul A. Goodkind, Jack Ogilvie; art d, Paul Palmentola; chor, Earl Barton

The rock 'n' roll movie. Producer Sam Katzman and director Fred Sears again pooled their exploitative talents to deliver a film not so much *about* rock 'n' roll, but a film that *was* rock 'n' roll. The story is barely evident—legendary rock deejay Alan Freed discovers Bill Haley and the Comets in a mountain village and brings them back to New York, where they quickly become a musical phenomenon. Katzman was correct in assuming that if rock concerts could cause youth riots, so could a movie. In England, soon after a couple of screenings, young rockers were tearing up the seats and dancing up a storm. Of course all their moms and dads were bowled over with shock and banned the film from the theaters. Even now it can still make the feet move to the beat. Haley's tunes include "Razzle Dazzle," "Happy Baby," "See You Later, Alligator," "Rudy's Rock," and the greatest rocker of them all "Rock around the Clock." And then there's "The Great Pretender," "Only You" (The Platters), "Codfish and Potatoes," "Sad and Lonely," "Cuero," "Mambo Capri" (Tony Martinez), and "Giddy Up, Ding Dong," "We're Gonna Teach You to Rock" (Freddie Bell).

ROCK 'N' ROLL HIGH SCHOOL

1979   93m   c   Musical/Comedy   ★★★★
New World   (U.S.)   PG/15

P.J. Soles (Riff Randell), Vincent Van Patten (Tom Roberts), Clint Howard (Eaglebauer), Dey Young (Kate Rambeau), Mary Woronov (Evelyn Togar), Dick Miller (Police Chief Klein), Paul Bartel (Mr. McGree), Alix Elias (Coach Steroid), Don Steele (Screamin' Steve Stevens), Loren Lester (Fritz Hansel)

p, Michael Finnell; d, Allan Arkush; w, Richard Whitley, Russ Dvonch, Joseph McBride (based on a story by Arkush, Joe Dante); ph, Dean Cundey; ed, Larry Bock, Gail Werbin; m, The Ramones; art d, Marie Kordus; chor, Siana Lee Hall; cos, Jack Buehler

When tickets for an upcoming concert by her favorite rock band, the Ramones, go on sale, aspiring teenage songwriter Riff Randell (P.J. Soles) skips school to be the first in line, enraging Evelyn Togar (Mary Woronov), the no-nonsense principal of Vince Lombardi High School, who has dedicated herself to putting an end to her charges' obsession with rock 'n' roll. Aided by a couple of aggressive henchmen (Loren Lester and Daniel Davies), Togar does everything in her power to see that no backbeat bopping deters her students from their studies, including confiscating all of the Ramones' concert tickets Riff has purchased. Meanwhile, under the guidance of the school's resident operator, Eaglebauer (Clint Howard), Tom Roberts (Vince Van Patten), a handsome but hopelessly unhip football player, pursues Riff, while smart but not particularly sexy Kate Rambeau (Dey Young) tries to win Tom's

affections. The action heats up—both in Tom's van and between Togar and the students—and after an attempted record burning, Riff, the kids, *and* the Ramones prove once again that winning isn't everything, it's the only thing, turning Lombardi High into Rock 'n' Roll High School. Written by Joe Dante and directed by Allan Arkush, this refreshingly wacky teenage film is filled with warped humor (including mice exploding to Ramones music), and makes wonderful use of the "so dumb they're smart" Ramones, who stepped to the fore when Cheap Trick backed out of the project. Nothing is taken seriously and nothing should be—it's only rock 'n' roll.

ROCK, THE

1996   136m   c   Action/Prison/Adventure   ★★
Simpson-Bruckheimer Productions/Hollywood   R/15
Pictures   (U.S.)

Sean Connery (John Patrick Mason), Nicolas Cage (Stanley Goodspeed), Ed Harris (General Francis X. Hummel), John Spencer (FBI Director Womack), David Morse (Major Tom Baxter), William Forsythe (Ernest Paxton), Michael Biehn (Commander Anderson), Vanessa Marcil (Carla Pestalozzi), John C. McGinley (Marine Captain Hendrix), Gregory Sporleder (Captain Frye)

p, Don Simpson, Jerry Bruckheimer; d, Michael Bay; w, David Weisberg, Mark Rosner, Douglas S. Cook (from a story by David Weisberg and Douglas S. Cook); ph, John Schwartzman; ed, Richard Francis-Bruce; m, Nick Glennie-Smith, Hans Zimmer; prod d, Michael White; art d, Mark Mansbridge, Ed McAvoy; fx, Hoyt Yeatman, Michael Meinardus, Dream Quest Images; cos, Bobbie Read

AAN Best Sound: Kevin O'Connell, Greg P. Russell, Keith A. Wester

Sean Connery's crafty character may quote Oscar Wilde, but don't expect too much intelligence from THE ROCK. In this last film from the team of Jerry Bruckheimer and Don Simpson (Simpson died in early 1996), the TOP GUN producers go out with a bang—and then some.

Deranged General Francis X. Hummel (Ed Harris) leads a group of renegade Marines in a takeover of San Francisco's notorious, now-derelict prison, Alcatraz. Hummel threatens to launch a several missiles containing a deadly biological chemical unless the US government makes reparations to the families of the 80-odd soldiers who died in covert military operations. FBI biochemist Stanley Goodspeed (Nicolas Cage) must defuse the chemical explosives, but in order to get to Alcatraz, he is forced to work with John Patrick Mason (Connery), a wily, bitter convict who once served time at Alcatraz. With Goodspeed's scientific expertise and Mason's keen knowledge of Alcatraz's layout, the mission should be a success—if they can only learn to trust one another.

Distinctive only in its relentless, pummeling style of editing, THE ROCK borrows so heavily from recent action-adventure pictures (DIE HARD, etc.) that it becomes a virtual index of genre devices. But they are assembled into a very clunky story, fraught with shifts in tone and weighed down by laborious subplots and atrocious dialogue. Typically, the film's best performer, Harris, has the worst lines. Along with an overbearing patriotism and a smattering of homophobia, there are also a few disturbing plot developments, such as when nerd-turned-hero Goodspeed becomes a vengeful, remorseless killer. One of the few things that can be said in the film's favor, however, is that the filmmakers did refrain from making the bad guy Middle Eastern.

ROCKY

1976   119m   c   Sports   ★★★★
UA   (U.S.)   PG

Sylvester Stallone (Rocky Balboa), Talia Shire (Adrian), Burt Young (Paulie), Carl Weathers (Apollo Creed), Burgess Meredith (Mickey), Thayer David (Miles Jergens), Joe Spinell (Tom Gazzo), Jimmy Gambina (Mike), Bill Baldwin (Fight Announcer), Aldo Silvani (Cut Man)

p, Irwin Winkler, Robert Chartoff; d, John G. Avildsen; w, Sylvester Stallone; ph, James Crabe; ed, Richard Halsey, Scott Conrad; m, Bill Conti; prod d, William J. Cassidy; art d, James H. Spencer; fx, Garrett Brown; chor, Sylvester Stallone; cos, Robert Cambel, Joanne Hutchinson

AA Best Picture; AAN Best Actor: Sylvester Stallone; AAN Best Actress: Talia Shire; AAN Best Supporting Actor: Burgess Meredith; AAN Best Supporting Actor: Burt Young; AA Best Director: John G. Avildsen; AAN Best Original Screenplay: Sylvester Stallone; AA Best Editing: Richard Halsey, Scott Conrad; AAN Best Song: Bill Conti (Music), Carol Connors (Lyrics), Ayn Robbins (Lyrics); AAN Best Sound: Harry Warren Tetrick, William McCaughey, Lyle Burbridge, Bud Alper

Better films have been made about the world of sports, but for many ROCKY is *the* sports movie. As drenched in sentiment as it is in sweat, as much love story as fight film, this classic tale of a tireless "bum" who makes good is one of the most uplifting films ever made. Set primarily in working-class Philadelphia, it follows the fortunes of Rocky Balboa (Sylvester Stallone), a 30-year-old club fighter who earns his living as a collections man for a loan shark. His boxing career has hit bottom, but Rocky's love life is looking up. He clumsily but endearingly woos Adrian (Talia Shire), the shy, repressed sister of Paulie (Burt Young), Rocky's friend who engineers their strange first date, and in no time, Rocky and Adrian are deeply in love. When a challenger's injury leaves the Ali-like world heavyweight champion Apollo Creed (ex-Oakland Raider linebacker Carl Weathers) without an opponent for his upcoming title defense, the boisterous champ decides to give a nobody a chance and chooses Rocky, "the Italian Stallion." Urged on by Mickey (Burgess Meredith), his crotchety old manager, and to the accompaniment of Bill Conti's rousing theme "Gonna Fly Now," Rocky undergoes grueling training for his title long shot: doing one-armed push-ups, pounding slabs of meat in a slaughterhouse freezer, making his now-famous run through the Philadelphia streets and up the steps of its art museum. Come fight time, Rocky wants only to go the distance with Creed, to prove he isn't "just another bum from the neighborhood." Surprising everyone, he gives the fight of his life, narrowly losing a split decision. Amid the post-fight hubbub, Rocky and Adrian meet in a loving mid-ring clinch. Establishing a formula that would be duplicated over and over (especially in its own sequels—see ROCKY series), the film slowly draws the audience into Rocky's struggle, until his triumph becomes that of every "little guy" who's dreamed of making it big. Reminiscent of Marlon Brando's Terry Malloy (ON THE WATERFRONT) and Paul Newman's Rocky Graziano (SOMEBODY UP THERE LIKES ME), Stallone's Rocky is magnificent, mirroring the actor's own battle for Hollywood success. As a struggling actor and screenwriter known mainly for THE LORDS OF FLATBUSH, Stallone, inspired by New Jersey club boxer Chuck Wepner's courageous loss to Muhammad Ali (a 15th-round TKO), wrote ROCKY's screenplay in three days. Determined to star in it himself, he turned down a quarter-million-dollar offer for his script, won the part, and, under John Avildsen's Oscar-winning direction, gave the screen one of its most memorable characters. The fairy-tale championship match is generally well choreographed (by Stallone), and the training montage, in its originality, remains more gripping than the many glossier imitations it inspired. Expertly paced, benefiting from well-drawn characters and an evocative, often funny script, ROCKY simply pushes all the right buttons. Former heavyweight champ and Philly native Joe Frazier appears as himself.

ROCKY II

1979 119m c Sports ★★★½
UA (U.S.) PG

Sylvester Stallone (Rocky Balboa), Talia Shire (Adrian), Burt Young (Paulie), Carl Weathers (Apollo Creed), Burgess Meredith (Mickey), Tony Burton (Apollo's Trainer), Joe Spinell (Gazzo), Leonard Gaines (Agent), Sylvia Meals (Mary Anne Creed), Frank McRae (Meat Foreman)

p, Irwin Winkler, Robert Chartoff; d, Sylvester Stallone; w, Sylvester Stallone; ph, Bill Butler; ed, Danford B. Greene, Stanford C. Allen, Janice Hampton, James Symons; m, Bill Conti; art d, Richard Berger; chor, Sylvester Stallone; cos, Tom Bronson, Sandra Berke

Considerably less satisfying than the original ROCKY, but head and shoulders above the later installments, ROCKY II picks up the saga of "the Italian Stallion" during the last two rounds of his gutsy loss to world champ Apollo Creed (Carl Weathers). After the bout, Rocky (Sylvester Stallone) and Adrian (Talia Shire), his no-longer-mousy

sweetheart, marry and use his fight purse to buy a car and condo. Soon Rocky learns that if he enters the ring again he runs the risk of being blinded in the eye he injured fighting Apollo. He does his best to provide for Adrian but is laid off by the slaughterhouse where he works with his brother-in-law, Paulie (Burt Young). Worried about the future—which is about to include a new baby—Rocky accepts a rematch with Apollo, who is anxious to prove Rocky's showing in their first bout was a fluke.

All the endearing characters from Part One are back, as is Bill Conti's familiar music—indeed, the sequel is a virtual remake of the original film. This time Stallone both wrote and directed the film, and though his handling of the actors and camera is less assured than John Avildsen's in ROCKY, he keeps things moving at a good pace and delivers another charming performance himself.

ROCKY HORROR PICTURE SHOW, THE

1975 100m c Comedy/Horror/Musical ★★
Adler/White (U.K.) R/15

Tim Curry (Dr. Frank N. Furter), Susan Sarandon (Janet Weiss), Barry Bostwick (Brad Majors), Richard O'Brien (Riff Raff), Jonathan Adams (Dr. Everett Scott), Nell Campbell (Columbia), Peter Hinwood (Rocky Horror), Patricia Quinn (Magenta), Meat Loaf (Eddie), Charles Gray (Criminologist)

p, Michael White, John Goldstone; d, Jim Sharman; w, Jim Sharman, Richard O'Brien (based on the stage musical by O'Brien); ph, Peter Suschitzky; ed, Graeme Clifford; m, Richard O'Brien; prod d, Brian Thomson; art d, Terry Ackland Snow; fx, Wally Veevers; chor, David Toguri; cos, Sue Blane, Richard Pointing, Gillian Dods

This film has become the official definition of a cult movie—so much so that the audience watching (or more accurately, participating in) the picture is the most interesting element. What happens on the screen is secondary.

Based on a British musical stage play by O'Brien (who also appears in the film and wrote all the music), RHPS eventually made it to the screen with the help of Lou Adler and Michael White. After a short run in New York it closed, but soon was revived on the midnight circuit. It is the story of Brad and Janet (Bostwick and Sarandon) whose car breaks down during a rainstorm in Ohio. They look for shelter in a mansion, which turns out to be the residence of Dr. Frank N. Furter, wildly played by Curry. They soon find themselves in the middle of a convention of alien transsexuals from the planet Transsexual in the galaxy Transylvania. Curry is ready to reveal his Frankenstein-esque creation—a monster named Rocky who is to be the ultimate sexual male. What follows, in a nutshell, is sex, cannibalism (Meat Loaf is appropriately eaten), murder, seduction, more sex, people being turned into statues, RKO Radio Pictures being spoofed, and Brad and Janet (dammit!) escaping before everything is blown up. The film itself is trash—its script and direction poor, its music mediocre—but audience participation has given it a kind of immortality. SHOCK TREATMENT was a sequel of sorts.

ROLLERBALL

1975 129m c Sports/Science Fiction ★★★
UA (U.S.) R/15

James Caan (Jonathan E.), John Houseman (Bartholomew), Maud Adams (Ella), John Beck (Moonpie), Moses Gunn (Cletus), Pamela Hensley (Mackie), Barbara Trentham (Daphne), Ralph Richardson (Librarian), Shane Rimmer (Team Executive), Alfred Thomas (Team Trainer)

p, Norman Jewison; d, Norman Jewison; w, William Harrison (based on his story "Rollerball Murders"); ph, Douglas Slocombe; ed, Anthony Gibbs; m, Andre Previn, Johann Sebastian Bach, Peter Ilich Tchaikovsky, Dmitri Shostakovich, Tomaso Albinoni; prod d, John Box; art d, Robert Laing; fx, Sass Bedig, John Richardson, Joe Fitt; cos, Julie Harris

It is the year 2018 and society is rid of war and poverty, and the only violence left is supplied by the corporation-controlled rollerball teams, who fight to the bloody finish with spikes and motorcycles in a sport combining roller derby, football, and hockey. When champion roller-ball player Caan is asked to retire because the corporate executives who rule the world are fearful that he has become too popular with the masses, he fights the move. To get rid of him, the corporate executives decide to change the rollerball rules and make it a fight to the death. Produced and directed by Norman Jewison, this science-fiction film envisions a time when major corporations will control the populace by offering them a brutal and compelling entertainment to distract from the real social issues at hand and act as a funnel for their frustrations, hatred, and resentment. While the questions raised about the relationship between corporate power and sporting events are valid and intriguing, ROLLERBALL is, unfortunately, hopelessly heavy-handed and ponderous. From its gloomy and solemn air to the overbearing use of baroque music, the film is far too self-important for its own good. Luckily, the performances of Caan and Richardson are excellent, and the rollerball sequences are fast-paced and interesting.

ROLLING THUNDER

1977 99m c Drama/War　　　　　　　　　　　　★★★
TBC Film　(U.S.)　　　　　　　　　　　　　　　R/

William Devane (*Maj. Charles Rane*), Tommy Lee Jones (*Johnny Vohden*), Linda Haynes (*Linda Forchet*), Lisa Richards (*Janet*), Dabney Coleman (*Maxwell*), Cassie Yates (*Candy*), Lawrason Driscoll (*Cliff*), Luke Askew (*Automatic Slim*), James Victor (*Lopez*), Cassie Yates (*Candy*)

p, Norman T. Herman; d, John Flynn; w, Paul Schrader, Heywood Gould (from a story by Paul Schrader); ph, Jordan Cronenweth; ed, Frank P. Keller; m, Barry De Vorzon; art d, Steve Berger; fx, Richard Helmer

Hot on the heels of TAXI DRIVER came a new film penned by its prolific screenwriter (soon to be director), Paul Schrader, and shot on a shoestring by in Texas by director John Flynn. ROLLING THUNDER stars Devane (in a superb performance) as a Vietnam POW who, after years in captivity, is returned home along with cellmate Jones. Devane is given a hero's welcome by his little Texas town and presented with a small fortune in silver dollars—one for each day he was a prisoner. While all this attention is heartwarming, he has also come home to a wife who no longer loves him, a son who doesn't remember him, and a society that doesn't understand him. Emotionally deadened by his wartime experiences ("You learn to love the pain," the vet ominously tells his wife's lover), Devane only comes alive after his wife and son are killed by thieves who invade their home to steal the silver coins. The thugs try to torture information out of Devane by shoving his hand down a garbage disposal, but he refuses to break—a macho display that brings about his family's deaths. Fitted with a hook to replace his mangled hand, Devane, with the help of his former comrade Jones, goes to Mexico in search of vengeance. While ROLLING THUNDER suffers from Schrader's predictable obsessions with masculine ritual and gunplay, Devane and Jones enhance the material with their nuanced, sensitive portrayals of men who have lost their souls in another land. The scenes of their attempted readjustment are unforgettable, especially those in which the obviously tormented Jones rots away in the bosom of his stiflingly polite family, who refuse to discuss the war with him. Aside from TAXI DRIVER, this is probably the best of the shortlived Vietnam vet-as-vigilante subgenre, which also included GOOD GUYS WEAR BLACK (1979) and THE EXTERMINATOR (1980).

ROMAN HOLIDAY

1953 119m bw Romance/Comedy　　　　　　　　★★★★
Paramount　(U.S.)　　　　　　　　　　　　　　/U

Gregory Peck (*Joe Bradley*), Audrey Hepburn (*Princess Anne*), Eddie Albert (*Irving Radovich*), Hartley Power (*Mr. Hennessy*), Laura Solari (*Hennessy's Secretary*), Harcourt Williams (*Ambassador*), Margaret Rawlings (*Countess Vereberg*), Tullio Carminati (*Gen. Provno*), Paolo Carlini (*Mario Delani*), Claudio Ermelli (*Giovanni*)

p, William Wyler; d, William Wyler; w, Ian McLellan Hunter, John Dighton (based on a story by Dalton Trumbo); ph, Franz Planer, Henri Alekan; ed, Robert Swink; m, Georges Auric; art d, Hal Pereira, Walter Tyler; cos, Edith Head

AAN Best Picture; AA Best Actress: Audrey Hepburn; *AAN Best Supporting Actor:* Eddie Albert; *AAN Best Director:* William Wyler; *AA Best Story:* Ian McLellan Hunter; *AAN Best Screenplay:* Ian McLellan Hunter, John Dighton; *AAN Best Cinematography:* Frank Planer, Henry Alekan; *AAN Best Editing:* Robert Swink; *AAN Best Art Direction:* Hal Pereira, Walter Tyler; *AA Best Costume Design:* Edith Head

Delicious, and delectable Audrey's Oscar-winning American debut. But not such a difficult feat with William Wyler backing you up. The secret is in the way Wyler, who had been away from comedy for about 18 years, builds an atmosphere of charm that leads us to her. And it didn't hurt Hepburn at all that she came along during a time when Monroe's sex doll influence had Hollywood brimming over with sex bombs from all over; or that Wyler cast her opposite dependable, protective Gregory Peck. The film gained 10 Academy Award nominations—amazing for a comedy—with Oscars awarded (beside Hepburn) to costumer Edith Head, and Ian McClellan Hunter for the film's story. Charming, wistful, and frothy, it earned strong receipts at the box office. Hepburn, who had previously appeared in six European movies and in "Gigi" on Broadway (selected for her role in that play by author Colette herself, who met the actress in the south of France and was immediately struck by her gamine beauty.), ROMAN HOLIDAY auspiciously presents her. She *is* infectious as Anne, a princess on holiday in Rome, where her ever-present coterie includes Rawlings, her chaperon, and Carminati, an aide. Overprotected all her life, she hasn't the vaguest idea of what the world outside her castle and her small country is like. Now in her teenage years, she is beginning to rebel against the formality and constrictions of her royal position and, seeing her chance to see how the other half lives, escapes her claustrophobic entourage. While they conduct a frantic search for her, she falls asleep on a park bench and meets Peck, one of the many reporters who have been trying to interview the princess, who has hitherto been shielded from the world's press corps by her aides. Peck knows he has a major scoop in meeting Hepburn, but initially pretends not to know who she is, taking her on a sightseeing tour of Rome while Albert, a news photographer, secretly snaps pictures of her as she plays hookey. For 24 hours, Peck shows Hepburn the famous sights, as well as some that are less familiar, since it is necessary to evade the police who are looking everywhere for the missing princess. Peck takes her on a motorcycle, they go dancing, and the pair land in some minor scrapes; all the while, the hard-boiled reporter falls harder for the guileless, beautiful Hepburn.

The film also has enough adventure and excitement to satisfy, and the faintly bittersweet note of the ending is made deliciously palatable by its artistic rightness. ROMAN HOLIDAY inspired several imitations, but none came close to the charming insouciance of the original. Hunter, picking up his Oscar, was fronting for blacklisted Dalton Trumbo, who was awarded a posthumous statuette in 1993.

ROMAN SCANDALS

1933 85m bw Musical/Comedy　　　　　　　　★★★½
UA　(U.S.)　　　　　　　　　　　　　　　　/PG

Eddie Cantor (*Eddie*), Ruth Etting (*Olga*), Gloria Stuart (*Princess Sylvia*), David Manners (*Josephus*), Verree Teasdale (*Empress Agrippa*), Edward Arnold (*Emperor Valerius*), Alan Mowbray (*Majordomo*), Jack Rutherford (*Manius*), Grace Poggi (*Slave Dancer*), Willard Robertson (*Warren F. Cooper*)

p, Samuel Goldwyn; d, Frank Tuttle; w, William Anthony McGuire, George Oppenheimer, Arthur Sheekman, Nat Perrin (based on a story by George S. Kaufman, Robert E. Sherwood); ph, Gregg Toland; ed, Stuart Heisler; art d, Richard Day; chor, Busby Berkeley; cos, John Harkrider

This was Eddie Cantor's fourth of six films for Samuel Goldwyn and second only to THE KID FROM SPAIN in popularity. Goldwyn had originally hoped to star Cantor in a musical version George Bernard Shaw's "Androcles and the Lion," but that failing, he hired Robert Sherwood and George S. Kaufman to fashion a story that would take Cantor to ancient Rome. Disappointed with their effort (so much so that Sherwood and Kaufman had to sue to collect their promised fee), Goldwyn hired Nat Perrin, George Oppenheimer, Arthur Sheekman, and William Anthony to punch up the screenplay. This time too many cooks didn't spoil this broth, and ROMAN SCANDALS is one of the best, funniest Cantor-Goldwyn associations. It opens with Cantor as a delivery boy in West Rome, Oklahoma, then shifts to the long dream sequence that makes up most of the film and finds him as the official food taster for the evil Emperor Valerius (Edward Arnold) in ancient Rome. The slim plot includes a love story between Princess Sylvia (Gloria Stuart) and Josephus (David Manners), Eddie proving the emperor to be a fraud, and a satire of BEN HUR's chariot race, shot by Ralph Cedar. Busby Berkeley, in his last choreographic job before going on to Warner Bros. and into film history, provides one scene wherein The Goldwyn Girls (Lucille Ball among them) are totally nude except for long blonde wigs. Ruth Etting, who contributes but one song here, later had a film made of her life, LOVE ME OR LEAVE ME, starring Doris Day and James Cagney.

ROMAN SPRING OF MRS. STONE, THE

1961   103m   c   Drama   ★★★½
Seven Arts/Anglo-Amalgamated   (U.S./U.K.)   /X

Vivien Leigh *(Karen Stone)*, Warren Beatty *(Pablo di Leo)*, Coral Browne *(Meg)*, Jill St. John *(Bingham)*, Lotte Lenya *(Contessa Magda Terribili-Gonzales)*, Jeremy Spenser *(Young Man)*, Stella Bonheur *(Mrs. Jamison-Walker)*, Josephine Brown *(Lucia)*, Peter Dyneley *(L. Greener)*, Carl Jaffe *(Baron)*

p, Louis de Rochemont; d, Jose Quintero; w, Gavin Lambert, Jan Read (based on the novel by Tennessee Williams); ph, Harry Waxman; ed, Ralph Kamplen; m, Richard Addinsell; prod d, Roger Furse; art d, Herbert Smith; cos, Pierre Balmain, Bumble Dawson

AAN Best Supporting Actress: Lotte Lenya

This picture grows better with age. Leigh was 48, and her husband, Olivier, had just left her for a younger woman. Beatty was 23, eager, ambitious, and sincerely wanting to change his image after SPLENDOR IN THE GRASS. Based on Tennessee Williams's only novel, the screenplay by Lambert became far more explicit in many ways than the subtle, short book. The film preserves many of Williams's bon mots, some of which went right over the heads of the movie's detractors.

Leigh is a fading actress who has just failed in a role more appropriate for a younger woman. She decides that it's time for a vacation in Europe. Her wealthy husband sickens and dies on the way to Italy, but she continues to Rome. When the widow admits to a friend (Browne) that she could use some male companionship, Browne sets her up with high-society pimp Lenya, who provides the widow with a handsome Italian boy (Beatty). Needless to say, Leigh falls in love, and heartbreak results.

The lines are pure Williams. When Lenya has a complaint, Leigh retorts: "The beautiful make their own laws." Beatty mentions a middle-aged woman he knows of who died in bed with her throat cut. Leigh, who has been concentrating on her card hand, looks up and says, "After three more years of this, assassination would be a convenience." Lenya is superb; the great German actress never had much success in US movies, although she will always be remembered as the villainess in FROM RUSSIA WITH LOVE. The assistant director, who went on to great success, was Peter Yates.

ROMANCING THE STONE

1984   105m   c   Adventure/Romance   ★★★½
Fox   (U.S.)   PG

Michael Douglas *(Jack Colton)*, Kathleen Turner *(Joan Wilder)*, Danny DeVito *(Ralph)*, Zack Norman *(Ira)*, Alfonso Arau *(Juan)*, Manuel Ojeda *(Zolo)*, Holland Taylor *(Gloria)*, Mary Ellen Trainor *(Elaine)*, Eve Smith *(Mrs. Irwin)*, Joe Nesnow *(Super)*

p, Michael Douglas; d, Robert Zemeckis; w, Diane Thomas; ph, Dean Cundey; ed, Donn Cambern, Frank Morriss; m, Alan Silvestri; prod d, Lawrence G. Paull; art d, Augustin Ituarte; chor, Jeffrey Hornaday; cos, Marilyn Vance

AAN Best Editing: Donn Cambern, Frank Morriss

A rousing, old-fashioned romantic adventure about Joan Wilder (Kathleen Turner), an author of lusty, best-selling bodice-rippers whose own life is a colorless bore. The picture opens as a tearful Joan is completing her latest literary fantasy. She's snapped out of her reverie by the arrival of a strange package that contains some sort of treasure map pointing the way to a fabulous gemstone. Then follows a frantic phone call from

her sister, who is being held captive by an evil art dealer, Ira (Zack Norman), and his snarling cousin, Ralph (Danny DeVito). Her sister's husband has disappeared in Colombia, and it was he who sent Joan the map. Ira and Ralph threaten to kill Joan's sister unless the treasure map is turned over to Ralph in Colombia. So timid Joan takes off for the jungles of South America only to discover that Zolo (Manuel Ojeda), a corrupt military official, is also after the map. Luckily, she is rescued by a handsome, American soldier-of-fortune, Jack Colton (Michael Douglas), and together they go after the treasure. ROMANCING THE STONE moves like lightning through its 105-minute running time, barely giving viewers a chance to catch their breath. Although comparisons with Steven Spielberg's RAIDERS OF THE LOST ARK are inevitable, it is the interplay between Turner and Douglas that gives the film its real charm. Norman and DeVito score strongly in roles that would have been played by Sydney Greenstreet and Peter Lorre 30 years ago, and the whole film has the feel of an old Warner Bros. thriller with broadly comic overtones. An inferior sequel, THE JEWEL OF THE NILE, was released the following year.

ROMANTIC ENGLISHWOMAN, THE

1975   115m   c   Comedy/Romance   ★★★½
Dial/Meric/Matalon   (U.K./France)   R/15

Glenda Jackson *(Elizabeth Fielding)*, Michael Caine *(Lewis Fielding)*, Helmut Berger *(Thomas)*, Marcus Richardson *(David Fielding)*, Kate Nelligan *(Isabel)*, Rene Kolldehoff *(Herman)*, Michel Lonsdale *(Swan)*, Beatrice Romand *(Catherine)*, Anna Steele *(Annie)*, Nathalie Delon *(Miranda)*

p, Daniel M. Angel; d, Joseph Losey; w, Tom Stoppard, Thomas Wiseman (based on the novel by Wiseman); ph, Gerry Fisher; ed, Reginald Beck; m, Richard Hartley; art d, Richard MacDonald; cos, Ruth Myers

Caine is a successful writer whose imagination becomes increasingly vivid when his wife, Jackson, travels to Europe. Separated by hundreds of miles and angry emotions, Jackson forgets about her husband and becomes attracted to German drug-smuggler Berger. She returns home to Caine in Britain, and the pair invite Berger to stay with them. Caine is intent on having the fellow help do some writing, but instead finds him fondling his wife. Jackson runs away with Berger, but Caine pursues and retrieves his wife. This intelligent film (a comedy, of sorts) from Joseph Losey explores Luigi Pirandello's concept of characters being under control of the author.

ROMEO AND JULIET

1936   127m   bw   Romance/Historical   ★★★★
MGM   (U.S.)   /U

Norma Shearer *(Juliet)*, Leslie Howard *(Romeo)*, Edna May Oliver *(Nurse to Juliet)*, John Barrymore *(Mercutio)*, C. Aubrey Smith *(Lord Capulet)*, Basil Rathbone *(Tybalt)*, Andy Devine *(Peter)*, Henry Kolker *(Friar Lawrence)*, Violet Kemble-Cooper *(Lady Capulet)*, Ralph Forbes *(Paris)*

p, Irving Thalberg; d, George Cukor; w, Talbot Jennings (based on the play by William Shakespeare); ph, William Daniels; ed, Margaret Booth; m, Herbert Stothart; art d, Cedric Gibbons; chor, Agnes De Mille; cos, Oliver Messel, Adrian

AAN Best Picture; AAN Best Actress: Norma Shearer; *AAN Best Supporting Actor:* Basil Rathbone; *AAN Best Art Direction:* Cedric Gibbons, Frederic Hope, Edwin B. Willis

MGM production chief and lover of the classics Irving Thalberg spared no expense in this excellent filming of Shakespeare's famous tragedy/romance, starring the queen of the MGM lot, Norma Shearer (Thalberg's wife) and the sensitive Leslie Howard. The eternal Romeo and Juliet story is here brought alive with verve and lavish, gorgeous production values. George Cukor was a good choice to direct this romance, able to communicate to his cast his own passion for the characters. Although Howard and Shearer are technically too old for their roles (the characters were teenagers), they perform splendidly, rendering their parts with great sensitivity. She flutters girlishly a bit too much early on and is not quite right in the balcony scene; her reading of the famous potion speech is, however, superb. Howard, more reticent than one would like, nonetheless performs with considerable grace.

Shearer was 34 when she did the film; Howard was 46 and refused the part at first, saying that he was too old. Barrymore gives a spritely, compelling, if somewhat strange performance in the role of Mercutio, delivered with a slight Irish brogue. On the set, Barrymore vexed the gentle Cukor no end by inserting foul words into the beautiful Shakespearean lines. The rest of the cast is fine, and the film as a whole is rather better than some would have it.

ROMEO AND JULIET

1968 138m c Historical/Romance ★★★★
British Home Entertainment/Verona/DEG (U.K./Italy) PG

Olivia Hussey *(Juliet)*, Leonard Whiting *(Romeo)*, Milo O'Shea *(Friar Laurence)*, Murray Head *(The Chorus)*, Michael York *(Tybalt)*, John McEnery *(Mercutio)*, Pat Heywood *(The Nurse)*, Natasha Parry *(Lady Capulet)*, Robert Stephens *(Prince of Verona)*, Keith Skinner *(Balthazar)*

p, Anthony Havelock-Allan, John Brabourne; d, Franco Zeffirelli; w, Franco Zeffirelli, Masolino D'Amico, Franco Brusati (based on the play by William Shakespeare); ph, Pasqualino De Santis; ed, Reginald Mills; m, Nino Rota; prod d, Lorenzo Mongiardino; art d, Luciano Puccini, Emilio Carcano; cos, Danilo Donati

AAN Best Picture; AAN Best Director: Franco Zeffirelli; AA Best Cinematography: Pasqualino DeSantis; AA Best Costume Design: Danilo Donati

This beautiful version of the Veronese love story was by far the most successful at the box office, although Zeffirelli took a huge chance casting two unknowns in the leads. Whiting was 17 and Hussey was 15, the closest any screen actors have actually come to the ages of the characters. It's a visually stunning adaptation with much action, broad humor, and eroticism. The Italian director had made THE TAMING OF THE SHREW the year before with Elizabeth Taylor and Richard Burton. Although that film was not a big hit, his backers felt that his assured direction merited another attempt at Shakespeare, and the project was filmed in Tuscany at Pienza, Gubbio, Artena, and in the palace once owned by the Borgias. In order to take the onus off the relatively inexperienced leads, Zeffirelli trimmed some of the longer speeches, used reaction shots to break matters up, and gave the actors bits of business to do so they wouldn't seem like talking heads. That technique was successful, although both leads did betray their youth on several occasions. Major excisions in the text include, unforgivably, Juliet's potion speech. Laurence Olivier was around to lend his mellifluous voice as a narrator, a definite plus, but the director is the true star here as he gives us rousing crowd scenes, vicious fights, and a brief nude scene. The sets are magnificent, the supporting actors excellent, and the costumes attractive enough to warrant an Oscar for Donati, beating out another period piece that year, OLIVER!

ROOM AT THE TOP

1959 115m bw Drama ★★★★½
Romulus (U.K.) /15

Laurence Harvey *(Joe Lampton)*, Simone Signoret *(Alice Aisgill)*, Heather Sears *(Susan Brown)*, Donald Wolfit *(Mr. Brown)*, Ambrosine Phillpotts *(Mrs. Brown)*, Donald Houston *(Charles Soames)*, Raymond Huntley *(Mr. Hoylake)*, John Westbrook *(Jack Wales)*, Allan Cuthbertson *(George Aisgill)*, Mary Peach *(June Samson)*

p, John Woolf, James Woolf; d, Jack Clayton; w, Neil Paterson (based on the novel by John Braine); ph, Freddie Francis; ed, Ralph Kemplen; m, Mario Nascimbene; art d, Ralph Brinton

AAN Best Picture; AAN Best Actor: Laurence Harvey; AA Best Actress: Simone Signoret; AAN Best Supporting Actress: Hermione Baddeley; AAN Best Director: Jack Clayton; AA Best Adapted Screenplay: Neil Paterson

A ruthless indictment of the British class system, ROOM AT THE TOP is a hallmark, seminal film in the social realist British "kitchen sink" movement, which produced such movies as SATURDAY NIGHT AND SUNDAY MORNING, A TASTE OF HONEY, and THIS SPORTING LIFE. But ROOM set the trend and lured adults back into theaters in droves, thanks to its frank treatment of sexuality and the blaze of energy brought to it by the magnificence and suffering of the incomparable Signoret. You may not agree, but we think (because of *her*) it stands the test of time. Laurence Harvey, the film's ruthless anti-hero, hopes to gatecrash past his working-class origins. Arriving in a bleak Yorkshire industrial town, he secures a low-paying job as a government accountant, but soon realizes that professional skill won't bring social status. He sets his cap for Sears, the naive young daughter of millionaire industrialist Wolfit, who tries to break up the romance by shipping Sears off to the Continent. Harvey then begins an affair with Signoret, a married woman 10 years his senior. When Sears returns, love clashes with ambition.

Based on the "angry young man" novel by John Braine, ROOM AT THE TOP broke new ground in its realistic dialogue, sexual frankness (it received an X certificate in Britain), and bitter condemnation of provincialism and class-consciousness. Jack Clayton, who had previously directed only the mid-length THE BESPOKE OVERCOAT, was hailed as an important new voice in British cinema on its strength, while screenwriter Neil Paterson and Simone Signoret both won Oscars for their work. It also took Best Picture and Best Foreign Actress (Signoret) British Film Academy awards, as well as another Best Actress for Signoret at Cannes. Among the supporting performers Wolfit and Phillpotts (as Harvey's wealthy future in-laws) are especially good. ROOM AT THE TOP memorably conveys the snobbery, poverty, desperation, and politics of class in provincial England. A sequel, LIFE AT THE TOP, also starred Harvey, but otherwise failed to live up to the standard of the original.

ROOM SERVICE

1938 78m bw Comedy ★★
RKO (U.S.) /U

Groucho Marx *(Gordon Miller)*, Chico Marx *(Harry Binelli)*, Harpo Marx *(Faker Englund)*, Lucille Ball *(Christine)*, Ann Miller *(Hilda Manney)*, Frank Albertson *(Leo Davis)*, Donald MacBride *(Gregory Wagner)*, Clifford Dunstan *(Joseph Gribble)*, Philip Loeb *(Timothy Hogarth)*, Philip Wood *(Simon Jenkins)*

p, Pandro S. Berman; d, William A. Seiter; w, Morrie Ryskind (based on the play by John Murray and Allen Boretz); ph, J. Roy Hunt; ed, George Crone; art d, Van Nest Polglase, Al Herman; cos, Renie

The hit Broadway comedy by Boretz and Murray was not given a great treatment by RKO and the Marx Brothers. Harpo didn't play the harp, Chico didn't play the piano, and Groucho didn't have Margaret Dumont to play with. It cost more than a quarter of a million dollars for the stage rights, and despite the fact that the budget was low, the movie still lost almost $400,000 the first time around. Scenarist Ryskind did what he could to adapt the farce for the unique talents of the Marxes, but the result was just another comedy. Gordon Miller (Groucho; his character's ordinary name immediately spells trouble) and Harry Binelli (Chico) are living at a Broadway hotel, planning a new stage show and waiting for financing to come through. How they bamboozle a young playwright (Albertson) and keep a hotel executive (MacBride) at bay make for some frantic but not especially inspired situations.

Besides wasting the talents of the brothers Marx in an insufficiently absurd film, ROOM SERVICE also soft-pedals up-and-coming comic ingenues Lucille Ball and Ann Miller. MacBride, though his standard blowhard role is spread a bit thick sometimes, is the only cast member given a role worthy of his talents. In 1944, RKO remade the film as a musical, STEP LIVELY. Who would *ever* guess that Adolphe Menjou, George Murphy, Frank Sinatra and Gloria DeHaven could be funnier than the Marx Brothers and Lucille Ball? Truth is stranger than fiction, folks.

ROOM WITH A VIEW, A

1985 115m c Comedy/Drama ★★★★
Cinecom (U.K.) PG-13/PG

Maggie Smith *(Charlotte Bartlett)*, Helena Bonham Carter *(Lucy Honeychurch)*, Denholm Elliott *(Mr. Emerson)*, Julian Sands *(George Emerson)*, Daniel Day Lewis *(Cecil Vyse)*, Simon Callow *(Rev. Beebe)*, Judi Dench *(Miss Lavish)*, Rosemary Leach *(Mrs. Honeychurch)*, Rupert Graves *(Freddy Honeychurch)*, Patrick Godfrey *(Mr. Eager)* p, Ismail Merchant; d, James Ivory; w, Ruth Prawer Jhabvala (based on the novel by E.M. Forster); ph, Tony Pierce-Roberts; ed, Humphrey Dixon; m, Richard Robbins; prod d, Gianni Quaranta, Brian Ackland-Snow; cos, Jenny Beavan, John Bright

AAN Best Picture; AAN Best Supporting Actor: Denholm Elliott; *AAN Best Supporting Actress:* Maggie Smith; *AAN Best Director:* James Ivory; *AA Best Adapted Screenplay:* Ruth Prawer Jhabvala; *AAN Best Cinematography:* Tony Pierce-Roberts; *AA Best Art Direction:* Gianni Quaranta, Brian Ackland-Snow, Brian Savegar, Elio Altramura; *AA Best Costume Design:* Jenny Beavan, John Bright

Made for only $3 million, this Merchant-Ivory production was nominated for eight Oscars and won three. The droll comedy of manners and morals begins in 1907, when Lucy Honeychurch (Helena Bonham Carter) goes off to Italy in the company of Charlotte Bartlett (Maggie Smith), her maiden cousin and spinster chaperone. They arrive in Florence and take up residence at the Pensione Bertolini, where they meet the charming Mr. Emerson (Denholm Elliott) and his son, George (Julian Sands). It's evident from the start that George finds Lucy pleasing to gaze upon, and on a visit to Fiesole, the town high above Florence, he takes the opportunity to kiss the young girl. Charlotte witnesses the kiss and insists they leave for England at once. Back in Surrey, where Lucy lives with her mother (Rosemary Leach) and ne'er-do-well brother, Freddy (Rupert Graves), Lucy settles into her relationship with Cecil (Daniel Day Lewis), the twit to whom she is engaged. But the Emersons move into a vacant villa in the area, and uninhibited passion again enters Lucy's safe world. It's hard to believe A ROOM WITH A VIEW cost so little; the costumes and sets are dazzling and the acting is superb—from two-time Oscar-winner Smith to the smallest role, there's not a false note.

ROPE

1948   80m   c   Thriller   ★★★
Transatlantic   (U.S.)   /PG

James Stewart *(Rupert Cadell)*, John Dall *(Shaw Brandon)*, Farley Granger *(Philip)*, Joan Chandler *(Janet Walker)*, Cedric Hardwicke *(Mr. David Kentley's Father)*, Constance Collier *(Mrs. Atwater)*, Edith Evanson *(Mrs. Wilson the Governess)*, Douglas Dick *(Kenneth Lawrence)*, Dick Hogan *(David Kentley)*

p, Sidney Bernstein, Alfred Hitchcock; d, Alfred Hitchcock; w, Arthur Laurents, Hume Cronyn, Ben Hecht (based on the play "Rope's End" by Patrick Hamilton); ph, Joseph Valentine, William V. Skall; ed, William Ziegler; m, David Buttolph; art d, Perry Ferguson; cos, Adrian

Hitchcock's first film in color is famous for appearing to be one continuous take. It tells of two cocky young collegiates, Shaw and Philip (Dall and Granger), who murder a weak-willed friend, David (Hogan), simply for the thrill of it. Strangling their friend with rope, they stuff his corpse into an antique chest and then ready the apartment for a cocktail party. Among the guests are David's father (Hardwicke), his fiancee (Chandler), and Rupert Cadell (Stewart), a philosophy professor whose discussions of Nietzsche's "superman" theory have inspired the murderers. Shaw, the more arrogant of the two, insists that dinner be served from the chest and makes veiled references to the crime such as "I could kill you." Philip, on the other hand, reacts nervously to such purposely ironic comments. As times passes, the guests become concerned by David's absence and the increasingly morbid conversation.

Although the story of this verbose film is intriguing, it's not top-drawer Hitchcock. Like LIFEBOAT before it, ROPE is an experiment in overcoming technical restrictions—a task which always thrilled Hitchcock. Here, all of his energies go into technique, but, paradoxically, ROPE seems favorable to the actors because it plays like so much theater. The construction of ROPE is simple—eight 10-minute takes cut together (except for the opening and a few reverse-angle shots) to appear as one continuous shot. (Feature films generally have about 600 shots.) Since the maximum length of a reel of 35mm film is around 10 minutes, the reels were joined by stopping the camera behind a character with his back filling the entire frame. Not surprisingly, there were many other hurdles for Hitchcock and his crew to overcome. Ziegler's job was to choreograph the actors' movements with a small scale model of the set. Valentine's camera

needed the freedom to travel through the set without crashing into things, so breakaway walls on rollers were built. A special camera dolly was invented (by head grip Morris Rosen) to allow for greater freedom of movement.

Valentine was only experienced with black-and-white photography, so he was unable to capture the color Hitchcock needed during sundown. Technicolor advisor Skall was brought in and, after Valentine left the production due to illness, reshot the final five reels. Special care was also taken on the New York City skyline; since the film took place in real time, night had to fall over the city. A set was built which encompassed 35 square miles of skyline, including such landmarks as the Empire State Building and the Chrysler Building. (The skyline included an ad for Reduco, featuring a before and after silhouette of Hitchcock—a gag also used in a newspaper in LIFEBOAT.) Correct cloud formations were even constructed from spun glass and chickenwire under the advice of a meteorologist.

Hitchcock later said, "I undertook ROPE as a stunt," and that's how it plays. Stewart seems uncomfortable playing an intellectual; his dull performance never displays the disturbance or authority that it needs. Dall and Granger, by contrast, are superb. Their characters and their thinly shrouded homosexuality were based on the murderous exploits of Richard Leopold and Nathan Loeb, wealthy Chicago teenagers who, in 1924, killed 14 year-old Bobbie Franks just to see if they could pull it off. Because of the homosexuality in ROPE, however discreet, the film was initially banned in Chicago (perhaps because it evoked memories of the real case), Spokane, Memphis, and Seattle, and was morally condemned in many other towns. Only after an "adults only" policy was enacted in Chicago, and the opening murder scene deleted in Sioux City, Iowa, could the film be shown in those cities. The Leopold/Loeb case also was the basis for SWOON, a stylish, if self-indulgent, 1992 feature by independent New York filmmaker Tom Kalin.

ROSE, THE

1979   134m   c   Musical   ★★★
Fox   (U.S.)   R/15

Bette Midler *(Rose)*, Alan Bates *(Rudge)*, Frederic Forrest *(Dyer)*, Harry Dean Stanton *(Billy Ray)*, Barry Primus *(Dennis)*, David Keith *(Mal)*, Sandra McCabe *(Sarah)*, Will Hare *(Mr. Leonard)*, Rudy Bond *(Monty)*, Don Calfa *(Don Frank)*

p, Marvin Worth, Aaron Russo; d, Mark Rydell; w, Bo Goldman, Bill Kerby, Michael Cimino (based on the story by Kerby); ph, Vilmos Zsigmond; ed, Robert Wolfe; m, Paul A. Rothchild; prod d, Richard MacDonald; art d, James Schoppe; chor, Toni Basil; cos, Theoni V. Aldredge

AAN Best Actress: Bette Midler; *AAN Best Supporting Actor:* Frederic Forrest; *AAN Best Editing:* Robert L. Wolfe, C. Timothy O'Meara; *AAN Best Sound:* Theodore Soderberg, Douglas Williams, Paul Wells, Jim Webb

Bette Midler turns in a magnificent performance as a dissipated, Janis Joplin-like rock singer. Exhausted from touring, Rose (Midler) tells her manager (Alan Bates) that she wants a year off to rest, and when he resists, the singer goes into a tailspin. One night she picks up Dyer (Frederic Forrest), a chauffeur, and embarks on the most fulfilling romance of her life. Dyer cannot deal with the penalties of fame that come with Rose's success, however, and eventually he leaves her to her music. A triumphant performance before a hometown audience turns out to be her last as the troubled singer resorts to a fatal combination of booze and drugs. Midler successfully brings her charged stage persona to the screen, presenting a convincing portrait of the backstage life of a rock 'n' roll performer. Forrest, as the chauffeur, and Harry Dean Stanton, in a cameo as a country singer, add an earthy contrast to the glamorous aspects of rock stardom. Only Bates is wasted in a relatively minor role as the manager whose hunger for success is greater than Rose can handle.

ROSE MARIE

1936 110m bw Musical/Comedy ★★★★½
MGM (U.S.) /U

Jeanette MacDonald (Marie de Flor), Nelson Eddy (Sgt. Bruce), James Stewart (John Flower), Reginald Owen (Myerson), George Regas (Boniface), Robert Greig (Cafe Manager), Una O'Connor (Anna), Jimmy Conlin (Joe the Piano Player), Lucien Littlefield (Storekeeper), Dorothy Gray (Edith)

p, Hunt Stromberg; d, W.S. Van Dyke II; w, Frances Goodrich, Albert Hackett, Alice Duer Miller (based on the operetta by Otto Harbach, Oscar Hammerstein II, Rudolf Friml, Herbert Stothart); ph, William Daniels; ed, Blanche Sewell; m, Rudolf Friml, Herbert Stothart; art d, Cedric Gibbons, Joseph C. Wright, Edwin B. Willis; chor, Chester Hale, William von Wymetal; cos, Adrian

Of all the Jeanette MacDonald-Nelson Eddy films, ROSE MARIE made the most money and is the best remembered. Grace Moore was to star but due to a schedule conflict, MacDonald, coming off her smash hit collaboration with Eddy, NAUGHTY MARIETTA, replaced her. As opera star Marie de Flor, she pleads with the Canadian priemer (Alan Mowbray) to release convicted bank robber John Flower (James Stewart, in his second film), but when he kills a man during a breakout, Marie leaves the opera (five acts of Charles Gounod's "Romeo et Juliette" amazingly compressed into roughly six minutes) and hires Boniface (George Regas), a half-breed guide, to take her into the wilderness in search of Flower. After Boniface double-crosses Marie, stealing all her money, she survives by becoming a saloon singer. Enter handsome Sgt. Bruce (Eddy) of the Mounties, whose mission it is to bring in Flower and who falls for the lovely Marie, then learns of her connection to the escapee. However, a Mountie always gets his man, and so does Sgt. Bruce, though by film's end he's also gotten his woman. A few laughs, excellent singing, and gorgeous photography all contribute to making this a must-see for Eddy-MacDonald fans. Her opening impersonation of a pampered prima donna is hilarious, an ample reminder of MacDonald's formidable if not always utilized comic talents. Although composer Rudolf Friml is always remembered for ROSE MARIE, it was actually MGM musical director Herbert Stothart who wrote many of the tunes. Under no circumstances confuse this offering, retitled INDIAN LOVE CALL for television showings, with the remake, which is inferior, despite its wide-screen, color treatment.

ROSE TATTOO, THE

1955 117m bw Drama ★★★★
Paramount (U.S.) /A

Anna Magnani (Serafina Delle Rose), Burt Lancaster (Alvaro Mangiacavallo), Marisa Pavan (Rosa Delle Rose), Ben Cooper (Jack Hunter), Virginia Grey (Estelle Hohengarten), Jo Van Fleet (Bessie), Sandro Giglio (Father De Leo), Mimi Aguglia (Assunta), Florence Sundstrom (Flora), Dorrit Kelton (Schoolteacher)

p, Hal B. Wallis; d, Daniel Mann; w, Tennessee Williams, Hal Kanter (based on the play by Williams); ph, James Wong Howe; ed, Warren Low; m, Alex North; art d, Hal Pereira, Tambi Larsen; cos, Edith Head

AAN Best Picture; AA Best Actress: Anna Magnani; AAN Best Supporting Actress: Marisa Pavan; AA Best Cinematography: James Wong Howe; AAN Best Editing: Warren Low; AAN Best Score: Alex North; AA Best Art Direction: Hal Pereira, Tambi Larsen, Sam Comer, Arthur Krams; AAN Best Costume Design: Edith Head

Tennessee Williams wrote "The Rose Tattoo" as a stage vehicle for Anna Magnani several years before this film appeared, but at that time she was still struggling with English and declined the role. Five years later, after a fairly successful run, Williams did the screenplay and Mann, the director of the stage production, handled the directing. Magnani, by this time, had more confidence in her command of the language (plus the safety afforded by retakes) and took the role, her first US job. The result was a hit.

Magnani, a Sicilian-born widow with a 15-year-old daughter (Pavan) enounters Lancaster, a banana hauler like her late husband who (also like her husband) sports a rose tattoo on his chest, symbolizing

virility. She's drawn to Lancaster but reveres her husband's memory so much that she holds her emotions in check—until she discovers the truth about her late spouse.

Magnani later appeared opposite Marlon Brando in THE FUGITIVE KIND, another Williams piece, but never came close in any of her other US pictures to her dynamic performance here. North's excellent music helps the mood enormously. Pavan, the sister of the tragic Pier Angeli, later married Jean-Pierre Aumont.

ROSEMARY'S BABY

1968 136m c Horror ★★★★
Paramount (U.S.) R/18

Mia Farrow (Rosemary Woodhouse), John Cassavetes (Guy Woodhouse), Ruth Gordon (Minnie Castevet), Sidney Blackmer (Roman Castevet), Maurice Evans (Hutch), Ralph Bellamy (Dr. Sapirstein), Victoria Vetri (Terry Fionoffrio), Patsy Kelly (Laura-Louise), Elisha Cook Jr. (Mr. Nicklas), Charles Grodin (Dr. Hill)

p, William Castle; d, Roman Polanski; w, Roman Polanski (based on the novel by Ira Levin); ph, William A. Fraker; ed, Sam O'Steen, Bob Wyman; m, Krzysztof Komeda; prod d, Richard Sylbert; art d, Joel Schiller; fx, Farciot Edouart; cos, Anthea Sylbert

AA Best Supporting Actress: Ruth Gordon; AAN Best Adapted Screenplay: Roman Polanski

Roman Polanski's first American movie and his second masterpiece of horror (REPULSION was released in 1965) is set under the sunny skies of modern-day New York City. There are no creepy characters and no eerie locations, just a happy young couple expecting their first child. Newlyweds Rosemary (Mia Farrow) and unemployed actor Gus (John Cassavetes) have just moved into their new apartment in a gothic Central Park building (shot in the famous Dakota, home of the late John Lennon). Their neighbors, the elderly Minnie (Ruth Gordon) and Roman Castevet (Sidney Blackmer), are friendly but a bit intrusive. Rosemary learns that she is pregnant but feels a strange sense of anxiety. She seems to remember a vague dream in which she was raped by a savage beast. She has mysterious scratches on her stomach. Her doctor prescribes a curious elixir. It's perhaps not surprising that Rosemary becomes fixated by the idea that she has been impregnated by Satan and is now carrying his unholy child in her womb while living among a coven of witches.

Truly frightening because so much of it is so plausible, ROSEMARY'S BABY is one of the finest examples of modern horror, a milestone in the evolution of the genre. Although the subject matter is ultimately supernatural, the treatment is very realistic. Perhaps the film's most disturbing aspect is that the fears and anxiety that Rosemary experiences initially seem like an understandable response for a neurasthenic young woman to have when an "alien" being is growing within her. The brilliance of the film is that it takes this realistic basis and builds upon it with supernatural metaphors that make pregnancy a rich and strange condition.

ROUND MIDNIGHT

1986 133m c Drama ★★★★
PECF/Little Bear (France/U.S.) R/PG

Dexter Gordon (Dale Turner), Francois Cluzet (Francis Borier), Gabrielle Haker (Berangere), Sandra Reaves-Phillips (Buttercup), Lonette McKee (Darcey Leigh), Christine Pascal (Sylvie), Herbie Hancock (Eddie Wayne), Bobby Hutcherson (Ace), Pierre Trabaud (Francis's Father), Frederique Meininger (Francis's Mother)

p, Irwin Winkler; d, Bertrand Tavernier; w, Bertrand Tavernier, David Rayfiel (based on incidents in the lives of Francis Paudras and Bud Powell); ph, Bruno de Keyzer; ed, Armand Psenny; m, Herbie Hancock; prod d, Alexander Trauner; art d, Pierre Duquesne; cos, Jacqueline Moreau

ROUND MIDNIGHT might easily be called the best jazz film ever made, and not only because, aside from 1988's BIRD, the competition is so weak. The film's quality lies not just in its vivid portrayal of the bebop milieu, but also in its sensitive examination of the turbulent forces within an artist compelled to create on a nightly basis, despite personal consequences. Dedicated to jazz greats Lester Young and Bud Powell, the film begins in 1959 as black bebop jazzman Dale Turner

(Dexter Gordon), "the greatest tenor saxophone player in the world," leaves New York City for Paris. Alcoholic, ill, and apparently a former heroin addict, Turner plays nightly at Paris' famous Blue Note club to adoring fans, who appreciate him and his fellow expatriates' music. One of his most fervent admirers, Francis (Francois Cluzet), forms a close friendship with Turner, who moves in with him. Together the two try to bring Turner's self-destructive impulses under control, until Turner decides to risk a return to the US. The irony of ROUND MID-NIGHT—a sadly familiar one recognized in the plot—is that it took a Frenchman, director-cowriter and jazz lover Betrand Tavernier, to make this most accurate and intelligent film about the distinctly American art of jazz. Casting musicians (including Wayne Shorter, Tony Williams, Ron Carter, and Herbie Hancock, who did the Oscar-winning score) as his actors and insisting that the music be recorded live on the set with cameras rolling, Tavernier captures the complex relations among the players at work; the process has never been shown so well in a narrative film. Turner (an amalgam of various figures, including Young, Powell, and Gordon himself) is brilliantly played by the great Gordon, who contributed much of the dialogue, suggested changes in the script, and eventually received a Best Actor Oscar nomination. The aging Gordon's playing is well below the standards of his prime, but the soundtrack became a best seller anyway.

ROXANNE

1987 107m c Comedy/Romance	★★★½
Columbia (U.S.)	PG

Steve Martin (Charlie "C.D." Bales), Daryl Hannah (Roxanne Kowalski), Rick Rossovich (Chris McDonell), Shelley Duvall (Dixie), John Kapelos (Chuck), Fred Willard (Mayor Deebs), Max Alexander (Dean), Michael J. Pollard (Andy), Shandra Beri (Sandy), Brian George (Dr. David Schepisi)

p, Michael Rachmil, Daniel Melnick; d, Fred Schepisi; w, Steve Martin (based on the play "Cyrano de Bergerac" by Edmond Rostand); ph, Ian Baker; ed, John Scott; m, Bruce Smeaton; prod d, Jackson DeGovia; art d, David Fischer; fx, Bill Orr; cos, Richard Bruno, Tish Monaghan

Unlike many of his comedic contemporaries, Steve Martin likes to take risks. Martin served as executive producer and wrote the screenplay for this modernization of Edmond Rostand's "Cyrano de Bergerac," which stars Martin as C.D. Bales, the fire chief in a small northwestern town, a much beloved and witty man who happens to have a huge nose. C.D. has hired Chris McDonell (Rick Rossovich), a handsome dimwit who knows his way around hoses but not around women. Roxanne Kowalski (Daryl Hannah) is an astronomer who has rented a local house for the summer, and in scant moments we see that C.D. is mad about Roxanne. But Roxanne gets a look at Chris and falls for him, whereupon Chris asks C.D. for help in wooing her. C.D. agrees, albeit reluctantly. Many wonderful jokes dot the picture, but it is, in essence, a love story and most satisfying in that respect. The bright, literate screenplay sometimes descends into slapstick but stays close enough to its source that it pays homage without sacrificing originality. Martin makes his character amiable and downright lovable; Hannah shows a fire she hadn't demonstrated in previous efforts. In an era when romance seems to have taken second place to sex, it's heartwarming to see a film like ROXANNE bring back the loveliness of love.

ROYAL FAMILY OF BROADWAY, THE

1930 68m bw Drama/Comedy	★★★★
Paramount (U.S.)	/U

Ina Claire (Julia Cavendish), Fredric March (Tony Cavendish), Mary Brian (Gwen Cavendish), Henrietta Crosman (Fanny Cavendish), Charles Starrett (Perry Stewart), Arnold Korff (Oscar Wolff), Frank Conroy (Gilbert Marshall), Royal C. Stout (Joe), Elsie Edmond (Della), Murray Alper (McDermott)

d, George Cukor, Cyril Gardner; w, Herman J. Mankiewicz, Gertrude Purcell (based on the play The Royal Family by George S. Kaufman and Edna Ferber); ph, George Folsey; ed, Edward Dmytryk

AAN Best Actor: Fredric March

When George S. Kaufman and Edna Ferber's thinly veiled parody of the acting Barrymores, "The Royal Family," opened in Los Angeles, Fredric March took on the role Otto Kruger had played on Broadway. Paramount studio bosses were so impressed by March's performance that they cast him in the lead in their film version of the play, THE ROYAL FAMILY OF BROADWAY (the name was changed to prevent confusion), and he responded by gaining an Oscar nomination and a huge following. Adapters Herman Mankiewicz and Gertrude Purcell wisely jettisoned some extraneous subplots and hammered out a tight script that George Cukor snappily directed, with assistance from Cyril Gardner.

Henrietta Crosman, matriarch of the famous acting Cavendishes, lives in a fabulous apartment and talks of her ancient theatrical triumphs. When son March arrives, he is not welcomed: by leaving the stage for the movies, he has incurred the wrath of the purists in the family. With March in the movies, daughter Ina Claire semi-retired, and a second daughter (Brian) unwilling to carry on the family tradition, Crosman accepts an offer to go on tour with a repertory company. The tour proves too much for her and she suffers a heart attack while performing. Her children must now decide whether to pick up the torch.

Even though March is on screen less than the other leads, his presence is extraordinarily powerful in the film's flashiest role. His impression of John Barrymore is nearly flawless, capturing every gesture, every raised eyebrow, every sneer perfectly. Although the film's humor is tempered by the drama of Crosman's demise, the screenwriters crafted her death so skillfully that even this heart-tugging scene has funny moments. A must-see for anyone who loves the theater, THE ROYAL FAMILY OF BROADWAY was edited by Edward Dmytryk, later the director of such films as THE JUGGLER, RAIN-TREE COUNTY, and WALK ON THE WILD SIDE.

ROYAL FLASH

1975 98m c Historical/Comedy/Adventure	★★★
Fox (U.K.)	PG/15

Malcolm McDowell (Harry Flashman), Alan Bates (Rudi von Sternberg), Florinda Bolkan (Lola Montez), Oliver Reed (Otto von Bismarck), Britt Ekland (Duchess Irma), Lionel Jeffries (Kraftstein), Tom Bell (de Gautet), Joss Ackland (Sapten), Christopher Cazenove (Hansen), Roy Kinnear (Old Roue)

p, David V. Picker, Denis O'Dell; d, Richard Lester; w, George Mac-Donald Fraser (based on the novel by Fraser); ph, Geoffrey Unsworth; ed, John Victor Smith; m, Ken Thorne; prod d, Terence Marsh; art d, Alan Tomkins

Spirited adaptation of one of George MacDonald Fraser's Flashman novels, which follow cowardly, lascivious, lovable Harry Flashman—the bully from Tom Brown's Schooldays—through a military career that lands him in the center of seemingly every major historical event of the 19th Century. Here, Flashman (Malcolm McDowell) is found toadying in Continental high society, where he encounters a young Otto von Bismarck (Oliver Reed) and sinister nobleman Rudi von Sternberg (Alan Bates). They use Flashman to advance their political schemes, hatching a plan by which he must pose as a Prussian nobleman and wed a duchess (Britt Eckland). Inevitably, Flashman is exposed; kinetic swordplay and hairsbreadth escapes ensue as our antihero quakes with abject terror. Lester's energetic direction enlivens the baroque plot; movie buffs will recognize frequent echoes of THE PRISONER OF ZENDA (1937).

ROYAL WEDDING

1951 93m c Musical/Comedy	★★★★
MGM (U.S.)	/U

Fred Astaire (Tom Bowen), Jane Powell (Ellen Bowen), Peter Lawford (Lord John Brindale), Sarah Churchill (Anne Ashmond), Keenan Wynn (Irving Klinger/Edgar Klinger), Albert Sharpe (James Ashmond), Viola Roache (Sarah Ashmond), Henri Letondal (Purser), James Finlayson (Cabby), Alex Frazer (Chester)

p, Arthur Freed; d, Stanley Donen; w, Alan Jay Lerner; ph, Robert Planck; ed, Albert Akst; art d, Cedric Gibbons, Jack Martin Smith; fx, Warren Newcombe; chor, Nick Castle

AAN Best Song: Burton Lane (Music), Alan Jay Lerner (Lyrics)

On the eve of the royal wedding of then-Princess Elizabeth and Philip Mountbatten, an American brother and sister vaudeville act, Ellen (Jane Powell) and Tom Bowen (Fred Astaire), ventures to London to perform. There Tom falls in love with Anne Ashmond (Sarah Churchill, daughter of Sir Winston Churchill, making her only US film appearance) a music hall dancer, while Ellen becomes involved with an English lord (Peter Lawford). The picture ends with couples married, after the usual misunderstandings and rocky romantic plot twists. That's about it for the story, but what shines here are the great songs by Alan Jay Lerner and Burton Lane (among them the Oscar-nominated "Too Late Now"), the singing, and the dancing, including two of the most spectacular Astaire routines ever devised. In the first, he dances with a hat rack that nearly comes alive as his partner; in the second and most celebrated, the legendary hoofer seems to be dancing on the walls and ceiling of a room—accomplished by building the room so it could be rotated at the same speed as the camera, with the camera operator strapped in and shooting upside down. Although Nick Castle is listed as choreographer, it seems likely that it was Astaire's genius that inspired these dazzling routines. When all is said and done, Stanley Donen's first solo directorial assignment, after his work with Gene Kelly, is a lovely bit of frou-frou.

RUGGLES OF RED GAP

1935 76m bw Comedy ★★★★
Paramount (U.S.) /U

Charles Laughton (*Marmaduke Ruggles*), Mary Boland (*Effie Floud*), Charlie Ruggles (*Egbert Floud*), ZaSu Pitts (*Mrs. Judson*), Roland Young (*George Van Bassingwell*), Leila Hyams (*Nell Kenner*), Maude Eburne (*Ma Pettingill*), Lucien Littlefield (*Charles Belknap-Jackson*), Leota Lorraine (*Mrs. Belknap-Jackson*), James Burke (*Jeff Tuttle*)

p, Arthur Hornblow Jr.; d, Leo McCarey; w, Walter DeLeon, Harlan Thompson, Humphrey Pearson (based on the play and novel by Harry Leon Wilson); ph, Alfred Gilks; ed, Edward Dmytryk; m, Ralph Rainger, Sam Coslow; art d, Hans Dreier, Robert Odell; cos, Travis Banton

AAN Best Picture

RUGGLES OF RED GAP is one of the great comedies of all time, a wonderful source of pleasure. Charles Laughton is brilliantly cast as Marmaduke Ruggles, the ultimate valet. His aristocratic, impoverished English master (Roland Young) loses him in a poker game in Paris to a rough-and-ready visiting American rancher, played by actor Charlie Ruggles. Laughton, Ruggles, and one of Ruggles's buddies have a hysterically funny night on the town before Laughton packs up everything and goes to Red Gap, a brawling frontier town in the West. The locals there take Laughton for a British aristocrat, and he decides that since he is here in the land of the free, he no longer has to be an indentured servant. He falls for and marries ZaSu Pitts, and leaves Ruggles and his wife (Mary Boland) to open a restaurant with Pitts. Eventually, Young comes to visit the small town, meets Maude Eburne, falls in love with her, and decides to stay in Red Gap. Seventy-six fast-moving minutes directed with an eye toward huge laughs, RUGGLES OF RED GAP ends with a startling scene where the slightly tipsy Laughton recites Lincoln's "Gettysburg Address," his masterful reading and palpable sincerity overcoming the incongruity of the scene to win over on-screen listeners and generations of audiences.

Laughton had already shown himself to be a superb dramatic actor in MUTINY ON THE BOUNTY and HENRY VIII, but few knew that he could be funny as well as pompous, underplay as well as emote, and show a subtle comedic side, which he did masterfully in this film. The versatile Leo McCarey deftly directs the picture, making it one his best films. Harry Leon Wilson's 1915 novel was first done by Essanay as a silent starring Taylor Holmes in 1918, and again by Paramount in 1923, with a youthful Edward Everett Horton in the lead. The picture was remade as FANCY PANTS, starring Bob Hope, but the remake was a tepid imitation of McCarey's hilarious version.

RULES OF THE GAME
(LA REGLE DU JEU)

1939 110m bw Drama ★★★★★
Nouvelle Edition Francaise (France) /PG

Marcel Dalio (*Robert de la Chesnaye*), Nora Gregor (*Christine de la Chesnaye*), Roland Toutain (*Andre Jurieu*), Jean Renoir (*Octave*), Mila Parely (*Genevieve de Marrast*), Paulette Dubost (*Lisette*), Gaston Modot (*Schumacher*), Julien Carette (*Marceau*), Odette Talazac (*Charlotte de la Plante*), Pierre Magnier (*The General*)

d, Jean Renoir; w, Jean Renoir (in collaboration with Carl Koch, Camille Francois, and the cast); ph, Jean Bachelet, Jacques Lemare, Jean-Paul Alphen, Alan Renoir; ed, Marguerite Renoir, Marthe Huguet; m, Roger Desormieres, Camille Saint-Saens, Salabert, E. Rose, Vincent Scotto, Wolfgang Amadeus Mozart, Johann Strauss, Frederic Chopin, Monsigny, G. Claret, Camille Francois, Delonnel Garnier; art d, Eugene Lourie, Max Douy; cos, Coco Chanel

One of cinema's most monumental achievements, Renoir's RULES OF THE GAME passionately tackles the pre-WWII French class system, and succeeds in bringing forth the complexities and frailties underlying bourgeois civility. When aviator Andre Jurieu (Toutain) is met by his friend Octave (director Renoir) and ecstatic reporters after a record-setting flight, he tells the radio audience that he undertook the adventure for the love of a woman—who failed to greet him at the airport. This woman, Christine (Gregor), is in the meantime preparing for an evening out with her husband, Robert de la Chesnaye (Dalio), who knows of his wife's affair and doesn't want to lose her. Toward this end, he tries to end his relationship with his adoring mistress (Parely). Octave, the character with the clearest understanding of his environment, admits to Andre that he too cares for Christine (although, like the others, he has difficulty distinguishing love from "friendship"), and maintains that Andre will never win her because he doesn't heed "the rules" of society. Later the two are among the guests at a weekend shooting party at de la Chesnaye's country estate (a remarkably beautiful location evoking the works of the director's father, Auguste Renoir, and that is greatly enhanced by the gorgeous deep-focus photography). Everyone, servants included, brings along their own little drama, to be played out during and after the hunt—a brutal game complete with its own rigid rules threatening to spill over into the domestic, "civilized" sphere.

RULES OF THE GAME has a flavor like no other film, its tone covering farce, satire, and tragedy alike. Renoir extracts great power from sequences such as the slaughter of the rabbits, an act done with the utmost cool by the aristocrats partying in the country. Later Robert displays his latest mechanical toy for his guests, and a stunning dolly shot carries us into several planes of action, as seductions and murderous chases occur among both servants and masters. So many things here unfold with the beauty of inevitability (e.g. what Christine sees through a set of binoculars during the hunt) and yet the film breathes surprise, improvisation, reversal. No stone is left unturned as Renoir explores the follies of love, the contradictory class relations and the casual anti-Semitism inhabiting these barren people.

The acting is great, with Dalio and Carette giving perhaps the performances of their careers as the self-indulgent host and the hilarious and sneaky poacher of rabbits and wives alike. Toutain, Parely, and Modot, meanwhile, as would-be lover, mistress, and cuckold respectively, superbly cover a range of types frustrated by love. Dubost manages to be both very appealing and appropriately vague as the blithe and careless maid, and the actors embodying the guests and servants are perfectly cast. (Could Magnier's marvelously fading military man have inspired, if only by osmosis, Richard Bennett's character in THE MAGNIFICENT AMBERSONS?) Renoir, as the hapless, compassionate yet insightful friend to all, proves himself a terrific actor, leaving one to regret that he didn't act more often. His Octave, the most likable character in the film, is appropriately its emotional center. And finally Gregor (a real-life aristocrat and sometime actress who would commit suicide in the late 1940s), carefully coached by Renoir, gives perhaps her most impressive performance. Interested in her at the time, Renoir realizes her limitations and turns them into strengths. The Austrian actress's flawed French and slightly remote quality are well-nigh perfect for the role of an outsider tossed amidst a rampaging sea of desire.

The ending is one of incredible poignancy, and if anything brilliantly highlights the film's already intense reflexivity. A labor of love and passion, RULES OF THE GAME was borne of Renoir's discontent with the complacency of his French contemporaries as the country faced occupation. Relentlessly booed at its 1939 Paris premiere and banned by both the French and Vichy governments, the film is a classic example of audience revulsion to a perceptive critique of their world. Renoir aimed to create "an exact description of the bourgeoisie of our time" and he evidently struck a very raw nerve. It wasn't until 1959 that the film was restored to its nearly original form at 110 minutes. The Venice Film Festival premiere of the restored version quickly put the film onto nearly every list of greatest films ever made, a position it has justly retained. Alain Resnais considered this film the most overwhelming experience he had ever had at the cinema, and while those knowledgeable in French history may pick up on more, several viewings of this unique film (what it takes) will get you hooked too.

RULING CLASS, THE

| 1972 | 148m | c | Comedy | ★★★½ |
| Keep | (U.K.) | | | R/X |

Peter O'Toole *(Jack, 14th Earl of Gurney)*, Alastair Sim *(Bishop Lampton)*, Arthur Lowe *(Tucker)*, Harry Andrews *(13th Earl of Gurney)*, Coral Browne *(Lady Claire Gurney)*, Michael Bryant *(Dr. Herder)*, Nigel Green *(McKyle)*, William Mervyn *(Sir Charles Gurney)*, Carolyn Seymour *(Grace Shelley)*, James Villiers *(Dinsdale Gurney)*

p, Jules Buck, Jack Hawkins; d, Peter Medak; w, Peter Barnes (based on the play by Barnes); ph, Ken Hodges; ed, Ray Lovejoy; m, John Cameron; prod d, Peter Murton; fx, Roy Whybrow; chor, Eleanor Fazan; cos, Ruth Myers

AAN Best Actor: Peter O'Toole

Overly long, controversial comedy with plenty of tragedy mixed in, this was adapted by the playwright, Peter Barnes, for the screen and might have benefitted from some disinterested pruning. It is nevertheless a vigorous, and sometimes wildly funny, assault on classbound British mores.

Andrews, a peer, accidentally loses his life while performing what seems to be a nightly ritual: he dons long underwear, a tutu, and a Napoleonic hat, puts a silken noose around his neck, and dangles contentedly. Peter O'Toole, the family lunatic, gets the peerage and estate; manservant Lowe gets 30,000 pounds; the rest of the family gets stiffed. The formerly servile Lowe begins spouting communist slogans, swilling booze, and telling the family exactly what he thinks of them. O'Toole returns from a mental institution dressed as Jesus Christ; he spends many hours on a huge cross in the living room and distributes wealth to the meek and downtrodden, infuriating the rest of the family. They decide they have only one means by which to rectify matters: have O'Toole sire a child, then toss him back into the looney bin so the family can assume control of the money by becoming the unborn child's guardians.

Hardly a segment of British society comes out of this film unscathed: the public school system, Parliament, snobbery, religion, homosexuals, servants, the upper classes, and just about everything else that can be decried. It's caustic and funny, but often goes too far and stays too long in making its points. O'Toole was nominated for an Oscar as the mad earl and bites off Barnes's speeches with Shavian diction. Lowe steals every scene he's in, while Sim's role as a doddering bishop is one of his best in a long career. A lot of money was spent on this movie, making it one of the best-produced British films of the year. Interiors were done at Twickenham with locations shot in Buckinghamshire, Lincolnshire, Surrey, Hampshire, and London.

RUMBLE FISH

| 1983 | 105m | c/bw | Drama | ★★★★½ |
| Zoetrope | (U.S.) | | | R/18 |

Matt Dillon *(Rusty James)*, Mickey Rourke *(Motorcycle Boy)*, Diane Lane *(Patty)*, Dennis Hopper *(Father)*, Diana Scarwid *(Cassandra)*, Vincent Spano *(Steve)*, Nicolas Cage *(Smokey)*, Christopher Penn *(B.J.)*, Laurence Fishburne *(Midget)*, William Smith *(Patterson)*

p, Fred Roos, Doug Claybourne; d, Francis Ford Coppola; w, S.E. Hinton, Francis Ford Coppola (based on a novel by S.E. Hinton); ph, Stephen H. Burum; ed, Barry Malkin; m, Stewart Copeland; prod d, Dean Tavoularis; chor, Michael Smuin; cos, Marge Bowers

If THE OUTSIDERS was a GODFATHER for teens, RUMBLE FISH was APOCALYPSE NOW. Filmed in dreamy black-and-white with an occasional dab of color, RUMBLE FISH is an unabashed art film. Deliriously expressionistic visually and aurally, it owes at least as much to the work of Jean Cocteau, Kenneth Anger, and F.W. Murnau as to the juvenile delinquent sagas of the 1950s. Set in Tulsa, Oklahoma, RUMBLE FISH tells of a somewhat slow-witted but charismatic teenager, Rusty James (Dillon), who idolizes his elder brother, the Motorcycle Boy (Rourke). The Motorcycle Boy has repudiated his gang-leader past and disapproves of Rusty's fighting but really has no practical advice to offer his sibling. He's intelligent enough to know that he has done nothing admirable to earn his local notoriety; he's just a very cool dude in a way that his hot-headed and increasingly dopey younger brother can never hope to match. Rusty, though, is too blinded by hero-worship and addled by injury-induced deliriums and booze to see things clearly. The person most annoyed by the former gang leader's lofty reputation is Officer Patterson (Smith) who ominously watches the Motorcycle Boy from behind his jet black shades.

Coppola has never made a more beautiful film. The rumble sequence alone is a rousingly choreographed frenzy that deserves to be studied by generations of film students. Hinton collaborated with the director in adapting her eccentric but profoundly moving novel for the screen. The resulting film is an amazingly sensitive recreation of the sensibility of the literary work. Burum's black-and-white cinematography utilizes deep focus and time-lapse effects to reflect the peculiar point-of-view of the protagonists. The fighting fish to which the title refers are in color though they float in a black-and-white pet shop window. The innovative score from Copeland (formerly drummer for The Police) plays a major part in creating mood, blending perfectly with Coppola's striking images. Often it sounds like ticking clocks, thereby heightening the sense that time is running out for these characters. Clocks are also a recurring visual motif.

RUMBLE FISH also contains some truly outstanding performances. Rourke gives what may be his most satisfying performance as the impossibly cool Motorcycle Boy. One never knows whether he is truly insane, as several characters assert, or just suffers from what his father calls "acuteness of the senses." Dillon shines through with a heartbreaking portrayal of a vulnerable teen increasingly lost in a mental fog. Lane is quite touching and believable as Rusty's long-suffering girlfriend, and Spano shows great range in an atypical role as Rusty's nerdy pal. Hopper is likewise superb, his ravaged but still beautiful face suggesting a fallen angel.

This is not a film for all audiences; indeed it is difficult to imagine to what audience it is targeted. Some wags even had the temerity to christen this minor masterpiece as "Mumble Fish." Give it a try. It might change your life.

RUN SILENT, RUN DEEP

| 1958 | 93m | bw | War | ★★★ |
| Hecht/Hill/Lancaster | (U.S.) | | | /U |

Clark Gable *(Cmdr. Richardson)*, Burt Lancaster *(Lt. Jim Bledsoe)*, Jack Warden *(Mueller)*, Brad Dexter *(Cartwright)*, Don Rickles *(Ruby)*, Nick Cravat *(Russo)*, Joe Maross *(Kohler)*, Mary LaRoche *(Laura)*, Eddie Foy III *(Larto)*, Rudy Bond *(Cullen)*

p, Harold Hecht; d, Robert Wise; w, John Gay (based on a novel by Cmdr. Edward L. Beach); ed, George Boemler; m, Franz Waxman; art d, Edward Carrere; fx, A. Arnold Gillespie

After his lucrative teaming with Gary Cooper in VERA CRUZ, Burt Lancaster and his partners, Harold Hecht and James Hill, decided to pair Lancaster with the fading but still popular Clark Gable. Gable plays Commander Richardson, the only survivor when the submarine he commands is sunk by a Japanese destroyer dubbed "Bongo Pete." Back at Pearl Harbor, he is given command of another submarine, the *Nerka*, but on it he encounters much dissension. Lt. Bledsoe (Lancaster), the sub's executive officer, is upset because he expected to get the command, and the crew refuses to trust a commander who is the sole survivor of a sunken vessel. Richardson battles frequently with Bledsoe, who is just short of mutinous, and drills the crew repeatedly in a tricky maneuver designed to torpedo "Bongo Pete" head on, an operation he calls the "down the throat shot." Ordered to stay well clear of Japan's dangerous Bongo Straits, the obsessed commander disobeys and pursues the destroyer. Gable, two years and three films away from death, is plainly too old for his role, but he makes the most of it with a very good performance. The entire film, in fact, is one of the better submarine dramas ever made, tense and claustrophobic, with a minimum of dalliances back at the base (in defiance of the Hollywood dictum that no movie without a love interest can succeed). On the set, things were rather tense, with Lancaster and his two partners arguing over the script, while Gable worried about what was going to happen to his character when the dust settled. Although reasonably successful at the box office, RUN SILENT, RUN DEEP was ultimately overshadowed by another film that put an old star and a new star in a submarine, OPERATION PETTICOAT, with Cary Grant and Tony Curtis.

RUNAWAY TRAIN

1985 111m c Prison/Thriller   ★★★½
Northbrook (U.S.)   R/18

Jon Voight (Manny), Eric Roberts (Buck), Rebecca De Mornay (Sara), Kyle T. Heffner (Frank Barstow), John P. Ryan (Ranken), T.K. Carter (Dave Prince), Kenneth McMillan (Eddie MacDonald), Stacey Pickren (Ruby), Walter Wyatt (Conlan), Edward Bunker (Jonah)

p, Menahem Golan, Yoram Globus; d, Andrei Konchalovsky; w, Djordje Milicevic, Paul Zindel, Edward Bunker (based on the screenplay by Akira Kurosawa, Ryuzo Kikushima, Hideo Oguni); ph, Alan Hume; ed, Henry Richardson; m, Trevor Jones; prod d, Stephen Marsh; art d, Joseph T. Garrity; fx, Keith Richins, Rick H. Josephsen, Bob Riggs, Tassilo Baur, Ray Brown; cos, Katherine Dover

AAN Best Actor: Jon Voight; AAN Best Supporting Actor: Eric Roberts; AAN Best Editing: Henry Richardson

The action in this superlative film is relentless and gripping from beginning to end. Manny (Jon Voight) is a hard-as-nails prison inmate who, with vicious punk Buck (Eric Roberts), escapes from a brutal Alaskan prison. They emerge into a blizzard and grope their way toward the train tracks, clambering aboard a passing train. They are unaware that the engineer has just suffered a fatal heart attack. Frantic passenger Sara (Rebecca De Mornay), a railroad employee, encounters the hiding convicts and begs them to save the train and her. The tough cons make it to the engineer's cab, and then their brutal ordeal to stop this train begins—an exercise in raw courage and chilling perils that drives both convicts to the brink of madness. What's more, Ranken (John P. Ryan), the prison warden who has a long-standing vendetta with Manny, is after the train as well. Voight is powerful and absorbing, and Roberts gives a fascinating performance as his cretinous sidekick. This is the second American-made film by Russian director Andrei Konchalovsky, and he does an outstanding job with his material and actors. Based on an original screenplay by Japanese master Akira Kurosawa.

RUTHLESS PEOPLE

1986 93m c Comedy   ★★★½
Touchstone/Silver Screen Partners II (U.S.)   R/18

Danny DeVito (Sam Stone), Bette Midler (Barbara Stone), Judge Reinhold (Ken Kessler), Helen Slater (Sandy Kessler), Anita Morris (Carol), Bill Pullman (Earl), William Schilling (Police Commissioner), Art Evans (Lt. Bender), Clarence Felder (Lt. Walters), J.E. Freeman (Bedroom Killer)

p, Michael Peyser; d, Jim Abrahams, David Zucker, Jerry Zucker; w, Dale Launer; ph, Jan De Bont; ed, Arthur Schmidt; m, Michel Colombier; art d, Don Woodruff; cos, Rosanna Norton; anim, Sally Cruikshank

This is a wacky, tasteless, hilarious reworking of O. Henry's classic short story "The Ransom of Red Chief." The movie begins as millionaire garment manufacturer Sam Stone (Danny DeVito) is having dinner with Carol (Anita Morris), his sultry mistress. He is

planning to murder Barbara (Bette Midler), his overweight and shrewish wife, unaware that Carol is cheating on him with her hunky, clunky beau, Earl (Bill Pullman). Before Sam can kill Barbara, however, she is kidnapped by a sweet young couple, Ken (Judge Reinhold) and Sandy (Helen Slater), who are seeking revenge against Sam for using an idea of Sandy's to make a fortune without paying her one cent in royalties. They tell Sam that Barbara will be tortured and killed if he breathes one word of the kidnapping to the police or the press. Naturally, Sam thinks his troubles are over, but he's wrong. Everyone in the movie seems to have a comic moment, because the laughs are piled on top of each other. Call it rude, crude, and lewd, but you also have to call it very funny.

RYAN'S DAUGHTER

1970 192m c Romance/War   ★★½
Faraway (U.K.)   R/15

Robert Mitchum (Charles Shaughnessy), Sarah Miles (Rosy Ryan), Trevor Howard (Father Collins), Christopher Jones (Randolph Doryan), John Mills (Michael), Leo McKern (Tom Ryan), Barry Foster (Tim O'Leary), Archie O'Sullivan (McCardle), Marie Kean (Mrs. McCardle), Evin Crowley (Moureen)

p, Anthony Havelock-Allan; d, David Lean; w, Robert Bolt; ph, Freddie Young; ed, Norman Savage; m, Maurice Jarre; prod d, Stephen Grimes; art d, Roy Walker; fx, Robert MacDonald; cos, Jocelyn Rickards

AAN Best Actress: Sarah Miles; AA Best Supporting Actor: John Mills; AA Best Cinematography: Freddie Young; AAN Best Sound: Gordon K. McCallum, John Bramall

The best thing about this much-vaunted, overlong Irish epic love triangle is its gorgeous photography by Young. The rest is an expensive potboiler (costing more than $12 million) in which Mitchum saunters through his role as a schoolteacher, cuckolded by trampy wife Miles. The marriage between Miles, the daughter of saloonkeeper McKern, and Mitchum is passionless, the result of Mitchum's lack of interest in sex. Troubled by this absence of lovemaking, Miles consults the parish priest, Howard, who tells her that she should be thankful she's married to such a saint of a man. Then shell-shocked British officer Jones arrives, assigned to suppress associations between the IRA and German spies (it's 1916 and WWI is raging). Miles and Jones are much taken with each other and make wild love in empty buildings and open meadows. Halfwit Mills finds a button ripped off Jones' uniform during one of the love scenes between Miles and Jones and parades around the village square with it, offering it up as evidence against the sinful Miles. Mitchum does not respond to the resulting gossip, preferring to let the romance dissipate. IRA leader Foster then arrives with a boatload of guns sent by the Germans, but, believing the British will make fierce reprisals against the town, Mitchum informs on the gun-runners and the British swoop in. Believing that it was Miles who told her British lover about the weapons, the townspeople swarm into Mitchum's house, strip Miles, and shave her head. Knowing now that he has lost Miles, Jones blows himself up with a hand grenade. Miles and Mitchum pack their things and head for a new life in Dublin.

Directed by fine craftsman Lean, RYAN'S DAUGHTER is self-indulgent and dull, a long-winded period piece that is so introspective that its love scenes, presented in a frenetic style, appear out of place. Miles is only vaguely interesting, Jones boring, and Mitchum so detached that he appears to be thinking about anything but this film. Only Mills, essaying the village idiot, provides a spark to an otherwise aimless and lifeless film. The whole thing is a great disappointment from a great director. Lean and Bolt—actress Miles' husband, and the director's frequent collaborator—spent five years making the picture, which was photographed on location on the Dingle Peninsula, Ireland's rainiest area. Cast and crew spent a full year there, once shooting only a minute of screen time in a 10-day period because of the awful weather.

S

SABOTAGE

1936 76m bw Thriller/Spy   ★★★½
Gaumont (U.K.)   /PG

Sylvia Sidney *(Sylvia Verloc)*, Oscar Homolka *(Karl Verloc)*, John Loder *(Sgt. Ted Spencer)*, Desmond Tester *(Steve)*, Joyce Barbour *(Renee)*, Matthew Boulton *(Supt. Talbot)*, S.J. Warmington *(Hollingshead)*, William Dewhurst *(A.S. Chatman)*, Austin Trevor *(Vladimir)*, Torin Thatcher *(Yunct)*

p, Michael Balcon, Ivor Montagu; d, Alfred Hitchcock; w, Charles Bennett, Ian Hay, Alma Reville, Helen Simpson, E.V.H. Emmett (based on the novel *The Secret Agent* by Joseph Conrad); ph, Bernard Knowles; ed, Charles Frend; m, Louis Levy

Terrorist Karl Verloc (Homolka) is engaged in a bombing spree in London using a trusting young boy Stevie (Tester), the little brother of his wife Sylvia (Sidney), to deliver the packages of destruction without knowing their contents. Meanwhile, neighborhood grocer Ted Spencer (Loder), actually an undercover Scotland Yard detective, is investigating Verloc's activities. A tense and chilling espionage picture, SABOTAGE contains one sequence that many consider among the director's most excruciatingly suspenseful; Hitchcock, however, later called it a mistake. While delivering a package containing a time bomb, the unknowing Stevie is delayed several times along the way, and ends up on a public bus which stops and starts in traffic as the bomb ticks away. In an interview with Truffaut years later, Hitchcock observed that "the boy was involved in a situation that got him too much sympathy from the audience, so that when the bomb exploded and he was killed, the public was resentful." Truffaut called the sequence a near abuse of cinematic power, and Hitchcock agreed, although his posture of repentance is difficult to reconcile with comparable cruelties in, for instance, PSYCHO and FRENZY. SABOTAGE was banned in several countries where censors viewed it as a handbook for terrorism. Based on a Joseph Conrad novel entitled *The Secret Agent*, the film's title was changed to SABOTAGE to avoid confusion with Hitchcock's previous picture SECRET AGENT. The confusion came later, however, in 1942, when Hitchcock directed SABOTEUR. If you're not confused yet, SABOTAGE was originally released in the US as A WOMAN ALONE.

SABOTEUR

1942 108m bw Spy/War   ★★★★
Universal (U.S.)   /A

Priscilla Lane *(Patricia Martin)*, Robert Cummings *(Barry Kane)*, Otto Kruger *(Charles Tobin)*, Alan Baxter *(Freeman)*, Clem Bevans *(Neilson)*, Norman Lloyd *(Frank Fry)*, Alma Kruger *(Mrs. Henrietta Sutton)*, Vaughan Glaser *(Phillip Martin)*, Dorothy Peterson *(Mrs. Mason)*, Ian Wolfe *(Robert, the Butler)*

p, Frank Lloyd, Jack H. Skirball; d, Alfred Hitchcock; w, Peter Viertel, Joan Harrison, Dorothy Parker (based on an original story by Hitchcock); ph, Joseph Valentine; ed, Otto Ludwig; m, Charles Previn, Frank Skinner; art d, Jack Otterson

This film, Hitchcock's first contribution to wartime American propaganda, is as polished and suspenseful as any the great director would make. A forerunner to NORTH BY NORTHWEST, SABOTEUR tells a similar story of an innocent man accused of murder and chasing a bunch of insidious spies across the country. Barry Kane (Robert Cummings) is a simple factory worker in an airplane plant whose best friend is killed in a fire. It turns out the extinguisher Kane handed him was filled with gasoline, engulfing his friend in flames before burning the whole factory down. An investigation points to Kane as the saboteur, forcing him to flee across the country to find the real fifth columnist. Along the way he meets Pat Martin (Priscilla Lane), the only one who believes

his story. SABOTEUR is no doubt best remembered for its harrowing Statue of Liberty (actually a Universal backlot) finale, in which Cummings chases his man to the Lady's torch. Hitchcock had originally hoped to cast Gary Cooper and Barbara Stanwyck in the leads, with Harry Carey, Sr., in the role of master spy Charles Tobin.

SABRINA

1954 112m bw Romance/Comedy   ★★★½
Paramount (U.S.)   /U

Humphrey Bogart *(Linus Larrabee)*, Audrey Hepburn *(Sabrina Fairchild)*, William Holden *(David Larrabee)*, Walter Hampden *(Oliver Larrabee)*, John Williams *(Thomas Fairchild)*, Martha Hyer *(Elizabeth Tyson)*, Joan Vohs *(Gretchen Van Horn)*, Marcel Dalio *(Baron)*, Marcel Hillaire *(The Professor)*, Nella Walker *(Maude Larrabee)*

p, Billy Wilder; d, Billy Wilder; w, Billy Wilder, Samuel Taylor, Ernest Lehman (based on the play *Sabrina Fair* by Taylor); ph, Charles Lang; ed, Arthur Schmidt; m, Frederick Hollander; art d, Hal Pereira, Walter Tyler; fx, John P. Fulton, Farciot Edouart; cos, Edith Head

AAN Best Actress: Audrey Hepburn; *AAN Best Director:* Billy Wilder; *AAN Best Screenplay:* Billy Wilder, Samuel Taylor, Ernest Lehman; *AAN Best Cinematography:* Charles Lang, Jr.; *AAN Best Art Direction:* Hal Pereira Walter Tyler, Sam Comer, Ray Moyer; *AA Best Costume Design:* Edith Head

Three recent Oscar winners and the sure guidance of Wilder helped make this familiar Cinderella story into something more than it might have been under other auspices. Holden was 36 at the time, a bit old for a dissolute playboy. Further, he is eclipsed by Bogart's performance as his older brother, an unaccustomed comedy role that showed Bogie could play for laughs as well as sneers. Wilder had already won an Oscar, and co-author Lehman was to be the recipient of the coveted statuette later, so this was a formidable team. The story isn't much, but it's the treatment and the witty dialogue that set it apart from the ordinary.

Holden and Bogart are the wealthy sons of Hampden and Walker. Holden lives for fast cars and faster women; Bogart is a hard-headed businessman. Also living on the estate are Williams, the chauffeur, and his impressionable daughter, Hepburn. She's mad about Holden, and attempts suicide when she realizes he's only toying with her. Williams sends her to France, where she is transformed into a sophisticated lady of fashion. In the US, Bogart seeks to enhance the family's wealth by marrying Holden off to heiress Hyer. Hepburn returns to Long Island, and once Holden gets a look at this new version, he falls for her. Hepburn is determined to win Holden, but Bogart and Hampden are determined to prevent the match. To take her mind off Holden, bachelor Bogart pretends to be courting her. The expected romantic complications follow.

A charming, if often-seen, tale, paced with alacrity by Wilder from the adaptation of Taylor's hit play which had starred Margaret Sullavan, SABRINA was a resounding hit at the box office and with the critics and proved that silk purses were still possible from less than perfect sources. Bogart had been making movies for more than two decades, but this was his first effort for Paramount. He and Wilder did not get along and had differing views of what was funny. Whoever won those battles will never be known, but the results were satisfying, as Bogart played drawing-room comedy with aplomb.

SACCO AND VANZETTI
(SACCO E VANZETTI)

1971 120m c Historical   ★★★
Jolly/Unidis/Theatre Le Rex (Italy/France)   GP/AA

Gian Maria Volonte *(Bartolomeo Vanzetti)*, Riccardo Cucciolla *(Nicola Sacco)*, Cyril Cusack *(Frederick Katzmann)*, Milo O'Shea *(Fred Moore)*, Geoffrey Keen *(Judge Webster Thayer)*, William Prince *(William Thompson)*, Rosanna Fratello *(Rosa Sacco)*, Claude Mann *(Journalist)*, Edward Jewesbury, Armenia Balducci

p, Arrigo Colombo, Giorgio Papi; d, Giuliano Montaldo; w, Giuliano Montaldo, Fabrizio Onofri, Ottavio Jemma; ph, Silvano Ippoliti; ed, Nino Baragli; m, Ennio Morricone; art d, Aurelio Crugnola; cos, Enrico Sabbatini

The American judicial system has a long and spotted history of convicting and executing those whose political views defy the status quo. One most notorious such trial was that of Sacco and Vanzetti, two Italian immigrants and admitted anarchists who were convicted and sent to the electric chair as a result of the 1920s red scare. This English-dubbed version of the tale accurately portrays the facts, with clear sympathy shown towards the two defendants. Cucciolla and Volonte (the latter from A FISTFUL OF DOLLARS and FOR A FEW DOLLARS MORE) portray the duo, who are brought up on charges of murder when two employees of a shoe store are killed in a robbery. After a sham trial in which Cucciolla and Volonte are tried more for their politics than for the actual crime, they are found guilty and sentenced to death. The case causes worldwide commotion as literally thousands of people rally behind them over the course of the next six years. However, despite some evidence of their innocence, Cucciolla and Volonte are executed on August 23, 1927. Though overall an impressive and accurate retelling of this miscarriage of justice, the film is not without its faults. The major problem is length. Considering the scope of actual time and the myriad events that took place over those seven years, two hours is simply insufficient for the story. Worst of all is an annoying theme song by Joan Baez which is packed with such insincere (and ultimately condescending) lyrics as, "Here's to you, Sacco and Bart/Something, something forever in my heart." The film is at its strongest when allowed to simply speak for itself. This is a story fraught with natural emotion, portrayed with sincerity and genuine sympathy for its doomed protagonists. In the end, SACCO AND VANZETTI becomes an eloquent portrait of two simple men swept up in the fury of political self-righteousness, a portrait which is not flattering to the American way of justice, to say the least.

SACRIFICE, THE
(OFFRET-SA CRIFICATIO)
1986 145m c Drama   ★★★★
Swedish Film Institute/Argos/Film Four/Josephson &   PG/15
Nykvist/Swedish Television/SVT 2/Sandrew/French Ministry of
Culture   (France/Sweden)

Erland Josephson (Alexander), Susan Fleetwood (Adelaide), Valerie Mairesse (Julia), Allan Edwall (Otto), Gudrun Gisladottir (Maria), Sven Wollter (Victor), Filippa Franzen (Marta), Tommy Kjellqvist (Little Man)

d, Andrei Tarkovsky; w, Andrei Tarkovsky; ph, Sven Nykvist; ed, Andrei Tarkovsky, Michal Leszczylowski; m, Johann Sebastian Bach, Watazumido Shuoo; art d, Anna Asp; fx, Svenska Stuntgruppen, Lars Hoglund, Lars Palmqvist, Richard Roberts, Johan Toren; cos, Inger Pehrsson

The final film from one of Russia's greatest filmmakers, Andrei Tarkovsky, was also his first to receive any widespread recognition in the US. Like all of Tarkovsky's work, it tackles complex themes and concerns that most directors would never approach. THE SACRIFICE is about a number of things, none obvious and none remaining wholly consistent from one viewing to the next; it is a poetic vision, filled with the symbolism peculiar to Tarkovsky's imagination. It is also a visually stunning, hauntingly beautiful, brilliant piece of art. THE SACRIFICE opens as Alexander (Erland Josephson) and his six-year-old son are busily planting a tree along the sandy, barren shore of the small island where the family is vacationing. During this vacation, it is announced on the radio that WWIII has begun—and the complete destruction of Europe by nuclear arms is certain. Later, when Alexander is alone, he gets down on his hands and knees to ask forgiveness from his creator, begging for the terrible events that are transpiring to be undone. He promises to do anything—give up all his possessions, even part with his son—if only things will be returned to normal. More than a beautiful film, THE SACRIFICE is a hopeful message to future generations to live in harmony with nature and with one another (which only gains in power by virtue of its dedication to the filmmaker's son). By December 29, 1986, less than a year after this movie was completed, Tarkovsky would fall victim to the cancer that he already knew would kill him. Aware that this would probably be his last film, Tarkovsky makes a conscious plea that we consider the damage done to the planet before it's too late, and seems to be saying that for all the modern world's astounding scientific progress, there is nothing to compensate for the loss of our spiritual essence—creating a dangerous gap between human

consciousness and the natural world. While perhaps not the most typical of Tarkovsky's works (the Swedish cast, Sven Nykvist's photography, and the Faro location occasionally lend it a Bergmanesque quality), THE SACRIFICE is a brilliant picture that should not be missed.

[SAFE]
1995 123m c Drama   ★★★★
American Playhouse Theatrical Films/Chemical Films/Good   R/15
Machine/Kardana/Channel Four Films   (U.S.)

Julianne Moore (Carol White), Peter Friedman (Peter Dunning), Xander Berkeley (Greg White), Susan Norman (Linda), Kate McGregory Stewart (Claire), Mary Carver (Nell), Steven Gilborn (Dr. Hubbard), April Grace (Susan), Peter Crombie (Dr. Reynolds), Ronnie Farer (Barbara)

p, Christine Vachon, Lauren Zalaznick; d, Todd Haynes; w, Todd Haynes; ph, Alex Nepomniaschy; ed, James Lyons; m, Ed Tomney; prod d, David Bomba; art d, Anthony Stabley; cos, Nancy Steiner

Controversial, undeniably brilliant alternative filmmaker Todd Haynes (POISON, SUPERSTAR: THE KAREN CARPENTER STORY) reached the mainstream with this dreamy but tough-minded satire. It's about a fragile housewife (Julianne Moore) who develops a mysterious syndrome called Multiple Chemical Sensitivity — as one character puts it, she's "allergic to the 20th Century."

In the sterile landscape of California's San Fernando Valley, suburban homemaker Carol White (Moore, in a stunning performance) slowly discovers that she's allergic to her new sofa. Next, she has a terrifying choking attack caused by exhaust fumes on the freeway. Both Carol's husband Greg (Xander Berkeley) and her physician, Dr. Hubbard (Stephen Gilborn), dismiss the malady as emotional. But Carol continues to experience adverse reactions to everything from her hairspray to the food she eats. Desperate, Carol tries everything, winding up in a "wellness center" near Albuquerque, New Mexico. There, doctors, gurus, and assorted lost souls fail to halt Carol's inexorable retreat from reality.

[SAFE] sounds like a disease-of-the-week TV movie, but it transforms the formulaic material into something original and spellbinding. Much as Douglas Sirk and Rainer Werner Fassbinder reimagined the conventions of melodrama, director Todd Haynes—who was indeed inspired by a TV movie, THE BOY IN THE PLASTIC BUBBLE—turns the form on its head. Haynes keeps viewers at arm's-length through the cool detachment of his technique. Viewers unused to his elliptical style may have difficulty discerning his point of view (many experienced similar difficulties the previous year with Michael Tolkin's masterly THE NEW AGE), but few will fail to register his disdain for the overweening gurus who advise their clients that sick people are responsible for their own diseases.

SAINT JACK
1979 112m c Crime   ★★½
Playboy/Shoals Creek/Copa de Oro   (U.S.)   R/X

Ben Gazzara (Jack Flowers), Denholm Elliott (William Leigh), James Villiers (Frogget), Joss Ackland (Yardley), Rodney Bewes (Smale), Mark Kingston (Yates), Lisa Lu (Mrs. Yates), Monika Subramaniam (Monika), Judy Lim (Judy), George Lazenby (Senator)

p, Roger Corman; d, Peter Bogdanovich; w, Peter Bogdanovich, Howard Sackler, Paul Theroux (based on the novel by Theroux); ph, Robby Muller; ed, William Carruth; art d, David Ng

In Singapore circa 1971, Gazzara is an American pimp who tries to become an independent operator. This arouses the anger of the local mobsters who want to put him out of business. He finally knuckles under after heavy pressure and goes to work for an American mobster (played by director Bogdanovich in a good quirky performance). He's forced to photograph an important senator in the arms of a young male prostitute, but eventually Gazzara's conscience catches up with him. The film uses the locations well and Gazzara's performance is an actor's dream. But SAINT JACK never quite becomes the "important" film it seems to aspire to be. The story is told in too meandering a style and the many well-acted characterizations never mesh together. This was Bogdanovich's first film in three years. After a promising early career, he got sidetracked creating films for his various mistresses and trying to recapture dead genres (DAISY MILLER and AT LONG LAST LOVE are massive disappointments considering they were made by the director of THE LAST PICTURE SHOW). SAINT JACK helped Bogdanovich regain his critical strength, but it wasn't until 1985's MASK that he was accepted by the public again. SAINT JACK was produced by Roger Corman, who had given the director his start in 1964 with THE WILD ANGELS. Serving as executive producer was Playboy's Hugh Hefner, which may explain some of the film's unnecessary steamier moments.

SAINT STRIKES BACK, THE

1939 67m bw Mystery ★★★½
RKO (U.S.) /A

George Sanders (*Simon Templar*), Wendy Barrie (*Val Travers*), Jonathan Hale (*Inspector Henry Fernack*), Jerome Cowan (*Cullis*), Neil Hamilton (*Allan Breck*), Barry Fitzgerald (*Zipper Dyson*), Robert Elliott (*Chief Inspector Webster*), Russell Hopton (*Harry Donnell*), Edward Gargan (*Pinky Budd*), Robert Strange (*Police Commissioner*)

p, Robert Sisk; d, John Farrow; w, John Twist (based on the novel *Angels of Doom* by Leslie Charteris); ph, Frank Redman; ed, Jack Hively; art d, Van Nest Polglase, Albert S. D'Agostino; cos, Renie

George Sanders plays the Robin Hood-like sleuth in this second installment in "The Saint" series, having taken over the role from Louis Hayward. In this one, the Saint and Inspector Henry Fernack (Hale, reprising his role from THE SAINT IN NEW YORK) are bound for San Francisco to prove that the murdered father of Val Travers (Barrie) was not the brains behind a series of clever murders. Sanders, on loan from 20th Century-Fox, takes the role and makes it his own. Until this film he had been slowly working his way into the Hollywood system after coming from England. Wendy Barrie does a nice job as the female lead, good support is provided in the secondary roles, and spine-tingling direction makes the most of a clever script. After this film The Saint was a guaranteed winner in the public eye and RKO had a monster hit on its hands.

SAINT, THE

1997 114m c Thriller/Crime ★★½
Rysher Entertainment/Robert Evans Company PG-13/12
/Paramount (U.S.)

Val Kilmer (*Simon Templar*), Elisabeth Shue (*Dr. Emma Russell*), Rade Serbedzija (*Ivan Tretiak*), Valery Nikolaev (*Ilya Tretiak*), Henry Goodman (*Dr. Lev Botvin*), Alun Armstrong (*Chief Inspector Teal*), Michael Byrne (*Tretiak's Aide — Vereshagin*), Evgeny Lazarev (*President Karpov*), Irina Apeximova (*Frankie*), Lev Prigunov (*General Sklarov*)

p, David Brown, Robert Evans, William J. MacDonald, Mace Neufeld; d, Phillip Noyce; w, Jonathan Hensleigh, Wesley Strick (from a story by Jonathan Hensleigh, based on the character created by Leslie Charteris); ph, Phil Meheux; ed, Terry Rawlings; m, Graeme Revell; prod d, Joseph Nemec III; art d, Alan Cassie, Leslie W. Tomkins; fx, Robert Grasmere, George Gibbs, Andrew Eio, Bob Bridges; cos, Marlene Stewart

A huge, expensively produced action machine designed to ensnare the MISSION: IMPOSSIBLE crowd.

Evil Russian oil billionaire Ivan Tretiak (Rade Serbedzija) hires international man of mystery Simon Templar (Val Kilmer) to purloin an energy formula from idealistic scientist Emma Russell (Elisabeth Shue), intending to use it to take over Russia or some such megalomaniacal thing. But Templar—a wounded loner who's spent a lifetime displacing his passions into in high-tech skullduggery—falls for the meek and virtuous Russell, who wants to give cold fusion to the shivering world. *Quelle* calamity!

Forget the title: this monolith is so far removed from the sophisticated pulp adventurer (played on TV by a pre-*Bond* Roger Moore, and in old movies by George Sanders) dreamed up by novelist Leslie Charteris that his name doesn't even merit a "based on the character created by" credit. In keeping with modern tastes, Templar has been darkened and dirtied up, metamorphosed into Batman (minus the rubber fetish gear) by way of a traumatic childhood, a damaged psyche, and a meaningful quirk: he takes the names of Catholic saints as his

aliases. Kilmer slips in and out of a series of ludicrously elaborate disguises, some more convincing than others, while poor Shue shuffles through the role of a sexy, book-reading babe pretending to be a dowdy lady scientist in knee socks. Tretiak's psycho son (Valery Nikolaev) and his droogies provide the villainous rush that keeps our heroes constantly on the run, and the whole business is beautifully photographed.

SALAAM BOMBAY!

1988 113m c Drama ★★★★
Mirabai (India) /15

Shafiq Syed (*Krishna/Chaipau*), Sarfuddin Qurrassi (*Koyla*), Raju Barnad (*Keera*), Raghubir Yadav (*Chillum*), Nana Patekar (*Baba*), Aneeta Kanwar (*Rekha*), Hansa Vithal (*Manju*), Mohanraj Babu (*Salim*), Chandrashekhar Naidu (*Chungal*), Ramesh Deshavani

p, Mira Nair; d, Mira Nair; w, Sooni Taraporevala (based on a story by Nair, Sooni Taraporevala); ph, Sandi Sissel; ed, Barry Alexander Brown; m, L. Subramaniam; prod d, Mitch Epstein

AAN Best Foreign Language Film

The breakthrough film for onetime documentarist Mira Nair (INDIA CABARET), who later entered the English-language mainstream with MISSISSIPPI MASALA. Nair leavens her story of a desperately impoverished 11-year-old (Shafiq Syed) with enough sentimentality to insure broad audience appeal.

Abandoned by his family, unable to read or write, unsure even of the name of his native village, the boy arrives in the Bombay slums where he hopes to raise enough money to return to his family. He makes a few rupees a day delivering tea, and in the process comes into contact with a variety of seedy characters: a pimp (Nana Patekar), his prostitute wife (Aneeta Kanwar), a drug-addicted pusher (Raghubir Yadav) who works for the pimp, the pimp's daughter (Hansa Vithal), and a naive peasant girl called "Sweet Sixteen" (Chanda Sharma), a prostitute-to-be whose virginity is being auctioned off to the highest bidder. As time wears on, however, the youngster's surrogate family collapses around him.

Shot in the slums of Bombay with child actors recruited by Nair from the street, SALAAM BOMBAY! is moving and well-crafted, but far from original. Like Satyajit Ray's early work, it is heavily indebted to the Italian neo-realist tradition and implicitly contemptuous of mainstream Indian cinema. Nair uses her characters' devotion to Bombay musicals to make a rather tired point about the contrast between their squalid lives and the fantasies purveyed by commercial cinema. In one place, this strategy notably backfires: when the protagonist and his friends visit the cinema, the clip we see them viewing—a comic dance number from MR. INDIA performed by Indian megastar Sridevi—is far more arresting than anything in SALAAM BOMBAY! Nair's film received the prestigious Camera d'Or for best first feature at the 1988 Cannes Film Festival.

SALO, OR THE 120 DAYS OF SODOM
(SALO, O LE 120 GIORNATE DI SODOMA)

1975 117m c Drama ★★½
PEA/Les Productions Artistes Associes (Italy/France)

Paolo Bonacelli (*The Duke*), Giorgio Cataldi (*The Monsignore*), Uberto Paolo Quintavalle (*His Excellency*), Aldo Valletti (*The President*), Caterina Boratto (*Signora Castelli*), Elso di Giorgi (*Signora Maggi*), Helene Surgere (*Signora Vaccari*), Sonia Saviange (*The Pianist*), Ines Pellegrini (*Maid*)

p, Alberto Grimaldi; d, Pier Paolo Pasolini; w, Pier Paolo Pasolini (based on the novel *Le 120 Journees de Sodome* by the Marquis de Sade; Sergio Citti; ph, Tonino delli Colli; ed, Nino Baragli; m, Ennio Morricone; prod d, Dante Ferretti; art d, Dante Ferretti; cos, Danilo Donati

Uncompromisingly violent, apocalyptic, and repulsive, SALO is the last film directed by Pier Paolo Pasolini, who was beaten to death by a male prostitute shortly before its release. Very loosely based on Sade's notorious fantasy of consensual sexual cruelty, *Les 120 Journees de Sodome*, this brutally explicit film is set in 1944 during the waning days of Italian fascism. A cabal of four authority figures—a magistrate, a banker, a duke, and a monsignor—lures a group of young men and women to an isolated villa, where they are subjected to unrelenting, ritualistic torture. The director, a Marxist with anarchistic leanings, presumably means to allegorize the institutionalization of violence under late capitalism—"It is the first time I am making a film about the modern world," he said—while transgressing every conceivable convention of bourgeois taste. The result, despite moments of undeniably brilliant insight, is nearly unwatchable, extremely disturbing, and often literally nauseous.

SALT OF THE EARTH

1954   94m   bw   Docudrama   ★★★★
Intl. Union of Mine, Mill and Smelter Workers   (U.S.)   /A

Rosaura Revueltas (*Esperanza Quintero*), Will Geer (*Sheriff*), David Wolfe (*Barton*), Melvin Williams (*Hartwell*), David Sarvis (*Alexander*), Juan Chacon (*Ramon Quintero*), Henrietta Williams (*Teresa Vidal*), Ernest Velasquez (*Charley Vidal*), Angela Sanchez (*Consuelo Ruiz*), Joe T. Morales (*Sal Ruiz*)

p, Paul Jarrico, Sonja Dahl Biberman, Adolfo Barela; d, Herbert Biberman; w, Michael Wilson, Michael Biberman; ph, Leonard Stark, Stanley Meredith; ed, Ed Spiegel, Joan Laird; m, Sol Kaplan; prod d, Sonja Dahl Biberman, Adolfo Barela

Landmark semi-documentary account of a strike by Mexican-American mineworkers in the American Southwest which was released at the height of McCarthyism and led to the imprisonment and/or blacklisting of several of the key figures involved. This was one of the first films to deal with the rights of Chicanos and to depict women as playing a central role in the labor movement.

SALT OF THE EARTH was filmed using actual participants of the real-life struggle on which it is based (Chacon, a non-professional actor, does an amazing job in his real-life role). The film rises above the level of agitprop by avoiding sloganeering and using the real words of real people to tell its story. Its feminism, too, is real and unforced, with women simply being shown struggling alongside—and when necessary defying—their male counterparts.

Naturally a film with such liberal leanings became a source of controversy in the 1950s; SALT OF THE EARTH was doubly cursed, for its content and its background. Producer Paul Jarrico had been banned from Hollywood, but this could not stop him. He joined with director Herbert Biberman, a member of the "Hollywood Ten," who had served a 5-month prison sentence for being an uncooperative House Un-American Activities Committee (HUAC) witness. They wanted to create a film company which would give work to blacklisted members of the film industry. Their intent was to create stories, as the two wrote 20 years later, "drawn from the living experiences of people long ignored in Hollywood—the working men and women of America." As it turns out, this was their only production, made in association with the International Mine, Mill, and Smelter Workers. They were lucky to make the film at all; shortly after production began in early 1953 the pro-McCarthy establishment press sought to discredit the film and filmmakers. Hollywood actor Walter Pidgeon, then president of the Screen Actors Guild, upon receiving a letter from a New Mexico schoolteacher warning of "Hollywood Reds... shooting a feature-length anti-American racial-issue propaganda movie" alerted his contacts in government, ranging from members of HUAC to officials of the FBI and CIA. Donald Jackson, a member of HUAC, claimed he would do everything he could to prevent the screening of "this communist-made film," citing non-existent scenes as examples of the film's Red leanings. Even billionaire Howard Hughes, head of RKO, got on the bandwagon and came up with a plan to stop the film's processing and distribution. The local population near the shooting site also got into the act. Vigilante groups took action, picking fights with crew members and setting fire to real union headquarters. Local merchants refused to do business with anyone in the production. One group threatened to take out the company "in pine boxes," and finally the New Mexico State Police had to come in to protect the filmmakers.

Problems were compounded when Revueltas, a Mexican actress, was arrested by immigration officials for a minor passport violation. She returned to Mexico, and the film had to be completed with a double. Some of her scenes were also shot in her native country on the pretext of being test shots for a future production. (Sadly, the Red fever of this country spilled over into Mexico, and Revueltas was blacklisted there for her work in this film. The talented actress would never work again.)

SALT OF THE EARTH enjoyed critical acclaim in Europe but, due to continued blacklisting, did not enjoy wide US release until 1965, when it became a rallying point for the political activism of that decade.

SALVADOR

1986   123m   c   Drama/War   ★★★★
Hemdale   (U.K.)   R/18

James Woods (*Richard Boyle*), James Belushi (*Dr. Rock*), Michael Murphy (*Ambassador Thomas Kelly*), John Savage (*John Cassady*), Elpidia Carrillo (*Maria*), Tony Plana (*Maj. Max*), Colby Chester (*Jack Morgan*), Cynthia Gibb (*Cathy Moore*), Will MacMillian (*Col. Hyde*), Valerie Wildman (*Pauline Axelrod*)

p, Gerald Green, Oliver Stone; d, Oliver Stone; w, Oliver Stone, Richard Boyle; ph, Robert Richardson; ed, Claire Simpson; m, Georges Delerue; prod d, Bruno Rubeo; art d, Melo Hinojosa; fx, Yves De Bono; cos, Kathryn Morrison

AAN Best Actor: James Woods; *AAN Best Original Screenplay:* Oliver Stone, Richard Boyle

Caustic, vivid, and without question the best major film about recent conflicts in Latin America. This often-overlooked Oliver Stone effort is in some ways better than his Oscar-winning Vietnam film PLATOON. Although there have been other major films dealing with conflict in Latin America (Chile in MISSING; Nicaragua in UNDER FIRE), none has conveyed the chaos, tension, and fear within the region as convincingly as SALVADOR.

Based on the experiences of real-life journalist Richard Boyle, the film begins in 1980, as the unemployed veteran reporter (played brilliantly by James Woods) heads down to El Salvador with his buddy, Dr. Rock (James Belushi), an out-of-work disc jockey. Promising drink, drugs, and an endless supply of cheap whores, Boyle cons his friend into coming along to a place where he can make some quick money covering a "little guerrilla war." Once they cross the border, however, things begin to get dangerous as Boyle becomes embroiled in the devastating civil war.

Director Stone persuasively conveys the turmoil and horror of life in El Salvador; at the same time, he shows the rebirth of conscience in a cynical, self-absorbed journalist whose problems pale in comparison with the atrocities suffered by the Salvadoran people. Woods is superb, and it is a tribute to his considerable dramatic skill that he manages to elicit sympathy for a uniquely obnoxious character. But if Woods' performance is one of the most challenging and fascinating to hit the screen in some time, it is Stone's stinging portrayal of El Salvador that gives the film its disturbing tone. Limning the chaotic events of 1980-81, Stone recreates the confusion, terror, senselessness, and despair felt by Salvadorans, while jaded Americans—government, military, and press—blithely ignore the realities of the country's predicament. Stone's camera suggests photojournalism, always on the move, running, swirling, probing, trying to get as close as possible to the truth of the tragedy in El Salvador.

SALVATORE GIULIANO

1961   125m   bw   Biography/Crime   ★★★
Lux/Vides/Galatea   (Italy)   /X

Frank Wolff (*Gaspare Pisciotta*), Salvo Randone (*President of Viterbo Assize Court*), Federico Zardi (*Pisciotta's Defense Counsel*), Pietro Cammarata (*Salvatore Giuliano*), Fernando Cicero (*Bandit*), Sennuccio Benelli (*Reporter*), Bruno Ekmar (*Spy*), Max Cartier (*Francesco*), Giuseppe Calandra (*Minor Official*), Cosimo Torino (*Frank Mannino*)

p, Franco Cristaldi; d, Francesco Rosi; w, Francesco Rosi, Suso Cecchi D'Amico, Enzo Provenzale, Franco Solinas; ph, Gianni Di Venanzo; ed, Mario Serandrei; m, Piero Piccioni; art d, Sergio Canevari, Carlo Egidi; cos, Marilu Carteny

This film is based on the true story of Salvatore Giuliano, an important Sicilian Mafia chieftain who was found shot full of holes on July 5, 1950. The film opens with the bullet-ridden remains found in a sunny courtyard. After his wake and funeral begin, the mobster's career is portrayed in flashbacks. Cammarata is the gangster who becomes involved with some guerrilla activities in postwar Sicily. When the group breaks up, a number of his men continue to follow Cammarata as he stages a minor war against legal authorities. He has a group of peasants slaughtered at a Communist rally, which triggers violent confrontations between gangsters and the law. Slowly, his men grow disillusioned with him and they abandon the man. Wolff, Cammarata's second-in-command, also abandons his boss but, like many of the outlaws, is tried and thrown in jail. There, Wolff is poisoned by members of the Mafia, a group he joined after leaving Cammarata. This is an interesting gangster picture, made in the heart of the Mafia's birthplace. The use of camera technique is excellent, coupled with a strong sense of direction. The acting is equally good, making full use of the cast's respective talents. Non-professional actors, as well as professionals, were used with fine results. However, the film is severely hampered for American audiences by the confusing plot line that was clearly designed with more local audiences in mind. The political, historical, and social references are not always clear, which can be distracting, yet this still works and works well.

SAMMY AND ROSIE GET LAID

1987 100m c Drama ★★★½
Cinecom/Film Four   (U.K.) R/18

Shashi Kapoor *(Rafi Rahman)*, Claire Bloom *(Alice)*, Ayub Khan Din *(Sammy)*, Frances Barber *(Rosie Hobbs)*, Roland Gift *(Danny/Victoria)*, Wendy Gazelle *(Anna)*, Suzette Llewellyn *(Vivia)*, Meera Syal *(Rani)*, Badi Uzzaman *(Ghost)*

p, Tim Bevan, Sarah Radclyffe; d, Stephen Frears; w, Hanif Kureishi; ph, Oliver Stapleton; ed, Mick Audsley; m, Stanley Myers; prod d, Hugo Luczyc-Whyowski; cos, Barbara Kidd

Director Stephen Frears and screenwriter Hanif Kureishi, the team that produced the splendid MY BEAUTIFUL LAUNDRETTE, join forces again to provide a cynically humorous and apocalyptic portrait of life in Prime Minister Margaret Thatcher's England. Sammy (Ayub Khan Din) and Rosie (Frances Barber), a young interracial married couple, lead a bohemian existence in a marginal London neighborhood. Theirs is a relationship based on "freedom plus commitment," meaning that they sleep with whomever they want but still love each other. Into this genially amoral world comes Sammy's father, Rafi Rahman (Shashi Kapoor, a huge star in India), a charming rogue who has not seen his son in years. Having made a fortune in his murderous political dealings in Pakistan, Rafi has returned to transfer his wealth into his son's account on the condition that Sammy and Rosie buy a house in a respectable part of England and that they supply him with a grandson. Though he has blood on his own hands, Rafi is appalled by the violence, squalor, and social unrest. The beloved London of his youth has become a living hell in his eyes. Sammy and Rosie's friends disapprove of Rafi's political sins while he is revolted by their "perverted" sexuality and left wing views. Only the strikingly handsome mulatto street person named Danny (Roland Gift, lead singer for the Fine Young Cannibals)—but who prefers to be called "Victoria"—looks up to Rafi and follows him around town. However, before long, the charismatic scoundrel's old crimes come back to haunt him.

SAMMY AND ROSIE GET LAID is a biting satire that does its best to achieve screenwriter Kureishi's stated aim to "get as much filth and anarchy into the cinema as possible." In addition to literate hard-hitting scripting and smooth direction, the movie is features excellent performances. However, this is a case where a film is simply too ambitious. Kureishi does an admirable job of juggling numerous balls in the air for the first half of the film—dealing with issues of politics, class, drugs, and interracial strife and attraction—but he becomes less graceful in the film's second half after a bravura triple split screen sex scene. Matters become increasingly contrived as the film collapses in exhaustion from thematic overload. Still it's a fairly impressive achievement as a whole.

SAMSON AND DELILAH

1949 131m c Religious ★★★½
Paramount (U.S.) /U

Hedy Lamarr *(Delilah)*, Victor Mature *(Samson)*, George Sanders *(Saran of Gaza)*, Angela Lansbury *(Semadar)*, Henry Wilcoxon *(Ahtur)*, Olive Deering *(Miriam)*, Fay Holden *(Hazel)*, Julia Faye *(Hisham)*, Russ Tamblyn *(Saul)*, William Farnum *(Tubal)*

p, Cecil B. DeMille; d, Cecil B. DeMille; w, Vladimir Jabotinsky, Harold Lamb, Jesse Lasky Jr., Fredric M. Frank (based on the story in the Bible and the book *Judge and Fool* by Vladimir Jabotinsky); ph, Dewey Wrigley, George Barnes; ed, Anne Bauchens; m, Victor Young; art d, Hans Dreier, Walter Tyler; fx, Gordon Jennings, Paul K. Lerpae, Devereaux Jennings; chor, Theodore Kosloff; cos, Edith Head, Gus Peters, Dorothy Jeakins, Gwen Wakeling, Elois Jenssen

AAN Best Cinematography: George Barnes; *AAN Best Score:* Victor Young; *AA Best Art Direction:* Hans Dreier, Walter Tyler, Sam Comer, Ray Moyer; *AA Best Costume Design:* Edith Head, Dorothy Jeakins, Elois Jenssen, Gile Steele, Gwen Wakeling; *AAN Best Visual Effects:*

Late but classic Cecil B. DeMille blockbuster, and one of the director's top money-makers, about biblical strong man Samson (Victor Mature), vanquished by the soft curves of the vixen Delilah (Hedy Lamarr).

SAMSON AND DELILAH was tried and true ground for the great DeMille, best remembered for his spectacular interpretations of the Bible (KING OF KINGS, SIGN OF THE CROSS, THE TEN COMMANDMENTS) and other extravagant historical recreations (CLEOPATRA, THE CRUSADES). Here DeMille, the master of the crowd scene, is in top form managing thousands of extras, particularly in the savage battle scenes in which Samson destroys the Philistine army with the jawbone of an ass. DeMille spent $3 million to film the Old Testament story, but the movie gained enormous and immediate returns, filling Paramount's coffers with more than $12 million from its initial release, the largest box-office take the studio had enjoyed to date.

SAN FRANCISCO

1936 115m bw Romance/Disaster ★★★★
MGM (U.S.) /A

Clark Gable *(Blackie Norton)*, Jeanette MacDonald *(Mary Blake)*, Spencer Tracy *(Father Tim Mullin)*, Jack Holt *(Jack Burley)*, Ted Healy *(Matt)*, Margaret Irving *(Della Bailey)*, Jessie Ralph *(Maisie Burley)*, Harold Huber *(Babe)*, Al Shean *(Professor)*, William Ricciardi *(Baldini)*

p, John Emerson, Bernard H. Hyman; d, W.S. Van Dyke II, D.W. Griffith; w, Anita Loos, Erich von Stroheim (based on a story by Robert E. Hopkins); ph, Oliver T. Marsh; ed, Tom Held; m, Edward Ward; art d, Cedric Gibbons, Arnold Gillespie, Harry McAfee; fx, A. Arnold Gillespie, James Basevi; chor, Val Raset; cos, Adrian

AAN Best Picture; AAN Best Actor: Spencer Tracy; *AAN Best Director:* W.S. Van Dyke; *AAN Best Original Story:* Robert Hopkins; *AA Best Sound:* Douglas Shearer

This film left no doubt that MGM was the most formidable studio in Hollywood. Star power, a great, rowdy story, and one of the most awesome special effects sequences in the history of film made SAN FRANCISCO a blockbuster. The pairing of Gable and Tracy here is historic: Tracy envied Gable's roguish charm and romantic image; Gable thought Tracy the finest actor on screen.

Gable stars as the brassy, colorful boss of the infamous Paradise beer garden, who ensnares starving MacDonald into a contract singing for him, although she also gains fame with Nob Hill patrons of the San Francisco Opera and amazingly finds time to inspire churchgoers, trilling in priest Tracy's choir. Yes, Jeanette overdoes it a bit, and why not? She's The Belle of San Francisco. Until the special effects, this is a Lifetime Achievement period piece for McDonald, with the rough 'n' ready leads battling over her soul and other extremities. It almost holds the picture together while we're waiting for the Big Rumble.

And rumble it does: the great old historic sites of San Francisco are shown breaking to pieces under the strain of the tremendous earthquake. City Hall collapses, fountains disintegrate, and office and residential buildings sway and tumble as the quake grips the entire city. Everywhere people are looking for lost loved ones. A long view of the city shows widespread fires breaking out, and a series of quick shots show firemen helpless to combat them because the water mains are broken. A second tremor begins, and this time the very streets split. But when The King finds Jeanette, she's still in concert.

SAN FRANCISCO is the biggest film Van Dyke ever directed, a work he maintains at a fantastic pace, hustling along his actors to keep time with the gaudy, bawdy era he presented in the background. Although Van Dyke certainly earned the credit for his astounding, technically flawless film, his mentor and the father of American silent film (and creator of almost all the techniques used thereafter in the sound era), D.W. Griffith, appeared at MGM one day and Van Dyke asked "the master" if he cared to direct any of the scenes in the film. He did, but just which scene the great Griffith directed is still in debate. One report had it that he directed one of MacDonald's operatic scenes, another one of the mob scenes at the Paradise club. But it was also rumored that the he directed the gem of this golden film, the incredible 20-minute earthquake and fire sequence, or at least that portion which was not achieved by the special effects of Gillespie and the uncredited James Basevi.

Van Dyke did not forget others of the silent era and tried to put to work many of the silent stars who were then unemployed and suffering during that year of the Great Depression, including Flora Finch; one-time Vitagraph star Naomi Childers; Jean Acker, who had been Rudolph Valentino's first wife and a leading lady in her own right during the silent days; King Baggot and Rhea Mitchell, whom Van Dyke had directed in the 1918 silent film THE HAWK'S LAIR. Even silent film director Erich von Stroheim got into the act, writing some additional dialogue for Loos's script.

SANDS OF IWO JIMA

1949   110m   bw   War   ★★★★
Republic   (U.S.)   /PG

John Wayne *(Sgt. John M. Stryker)*, John Agar *(Pfc. Peter Conway)*, Adele Mara *(Allison Bromley)*, Forrest Tucker *(Pfc. Al Thomas)*, Wally Cassell *(Pfc. Benny Regazzi)*, James Brown *(Pfc. Charlie Bass)*, Richard Webb *(Pfc. Shipley)*, Arthur Franz *(Cpl. Robert Dunne/Narrator)*, Julie Bishop *(Mary)*, James Holden *(Pfc. Soames)*

p, Edmund Grainger; d, Allan Dwan; w, Harry Brown, James Edward Grant (based on a story by Brown); ph, Reggie Lanning; ed, Richard L. Van Enger; m, Victor Young; art d, James Sullivan

AAN Best Actor: John Wayne; *AAN Best Original Screenplay:* Harry Brown; *AAN Best Editing:* Richard L. Van Enger; *AAN Best Sound:* Republic Sound Department

Unlike John Wayne's many WWII films in which he single-handedly destroys whole Japanese battalions, SANDS OF IWO JIMA presents him as a believable, vulnerable human being. Sgt. John M. Stryker (Wayne), a battle-toughened Marine, prepares a group of recruits for combat, driving them hard without worrying about making friends, although he is hurt when Pfc. Peter Conway (John Agar) hopes aloud that his newborn son won't be anything like Stryker. Later, in combat on Tarawa, Stryker's men grow furious with him when he refuses to rescue a Marine who has been separated from the squad, because to do so would give away their position. After Tarawa, they go to Hawaii for some R & R, where Stryker shows his heart of gold to a young mother forced into prostitution. The Marines' biggest test comes on Iwo Jima, and Stryker's men perform magnificently as they inch their way up Mt. Suribachi, but their leader is killed and Conway, now his disciple, must try to fill Stryker's big shoes. This is one of Wayne's finest performances, earning him an Oscar nomination. Directed with marvelous restraint by old hand Allan Dwan, SANDS OF IWO JIMA features appearances by three of the Marines who actually participated in the famous flag-raising on Mt. Suribachi—Ira Hayes, Rene Gagnon, and John Bradley.

SANSHO THE BAILIFF
(SANSHO DAYU)

1954   125m   bw   Drama   ★★★★★
Daiei/Kyoto   (Japan)

Yoshiaki Hanayagi *(Zushio)*, Kyoko Kagawa *(Anju)*, Kinuyo Tanaka *(Tamaki)*, Eitaro Shindo *(Sansho)*, Akitake Kono *(Taro)*, Masao Shimizu *(Masauji Taira)*, Ken Mitsuda *(Prime Minister Morozane Fujiwara)*, Chieko Naniwa *(Ubatake)*, Kikue Mori *(Priestess)*, Kazukimi Okuni *(Norimura)*

p, Masaichi Nagata; d, Kenji Mizoguchi; w, Yahiro Fuji, Yoshikata Yoda (based on the story "Sansho Dayu" by Ogai Mori); ph, Kazuo Miyagawa; ed, Mitsuji Miyata; m, Fumio Hayasaka, Kanahichi Odera, Tamekichi Mochizuki; art d, Kisaku Ito

A classic of Japanese and world cinema, SANSHO THE BAILIFF, set in the 11th century, tells the story of Zushio (Yoshiaki Hanayagi) and his struggle within the limits of feudal society. The film begins as family members—mother Tamaki (Kinuyo Tanaka), sister Anju (Kyoko Kagawa), and Zushio—travel through the woods in search of their exiled patriarch. They are soon assaulted by kidnappers, and Tamaki is sold into prostitution and exiled to Sado Island, while the children are sold as slaves to a powerful and cruel bailiff, Sansho (Eitaro Shindo). Ten years pass, and Zushio has become as evil as Sansho, for whom he now works as an overseer at a labor compound. Haunted by thoughts of his dead father and his exiled mother, Zushio prepares his escape, planning to leave with Anju. She, however, in order to keep from burdening her brother or from revealing his whereabouts, drowns herself. When Zushio reaches his destination, Kyoto, he discovers that his father has become a folk hero immortalized in song. In recognition of his father's stature, Zushio is granted the post of governor, and he takes it upon himself to abolish slavery and to banish the bailiff from his land. Having performed his service to humanity, he resigns, resumes his search for his mother, and finds her, now blind, facing the sea. Perhaps Kenji Mizoguchi's greatest achievement, SANSHO THE BAILIFF is a visually mesmerizing picture that pays great and careful attention to the smallest details of nature and environment, highlighted by Mizoguchi's use of the long take and deep-focus shots. In an attempt to film life as he sees it, Mizoguchi and his cinematographer, Kazuo Miyagawa, capture images much as a painter might—using the entire palette of contrasts and colors to create a richly textured atmosphere. The film was not released in the US until 1969.

SANTA CLAUSE, THE

1994   95m   c   Children's/Comedy/Fantasy   ★★★½
Outlaw Productions/Walt Disney Productions   (U.S.)   PG/

Tim Allen *(Scott Calvin)*, Judge Reinhold *(Neal)*, Wendy Crewson *(Laura)*, Eric Lloyd *(Charlie)*, David Krumholtz *(Bernard)*, Larry Brandenburg *(Detective Nunzio)*, Mary Gross *(Ms. Daniels)*, Paige Tamada *(Elf—Judy)*, Peter Boyle *(Mr. Whittle)*, Judith Scott *(Susan)*

p, Brian Reilly, Jeffrey Silver, Robert Newmyer; d, John Pasquin; w, Steve Rudnick, Leo Benvenuti; ph, Walt Lloyd; ed, Larry Bock; m, Michael Convertino; prod d, Carol Spier; art d, James McAteer; fx, John Sullivan, Buena Vista Visual Effects, Denise Davis; cos, Carol Ramsey

A tale of a suburban single father thrust into the role of St. Nick, THE SANTA CLAUSE offers a holiday-themed fantasy with appeal to both children and parents. It's an ideal debut vehicle for the talents of TV sitcom star Tim Allen ("Home Improvement").

When Santa Claus falls from a roof on the night before Christmas and sustains a fatal injury, the homeowner, divorced single father and toy company exec Scott Calvin (Tim Allen), has no choice but to don Santa's suit, hop into the sleigh, and continue Santa's rounds, accompanied by his young son Charlie (Eric Lloyd). When the job is done, Scott finds himself at the North Pole being lectured by head elf Bernard (David Krumholtz), who informs him that he has exactly eleven months to get his affairs in order and prepare for next Christmas. By putting on the red suit, Bernard explains, Scott activated the "Santa Clause," which makes him contractually bound to perform Santa's duties. To make matters worse, Scott's growing, Santa-esque eccentricities prompt his ex-wife to file for sole custody of Charlie.

With stronger emotional highs and lows, THE SANTA CLAUSE could have become a Christmas perennial on the order of IT'S A WONDERFUL LIFE or the original MIRACLE ON 34TH STREET. Unlike those earlier movies, the screenplay soft-pedals inherent domestic conflicts—e.g., the rivalry between Scott and his former wife's new husband over Charlie's affections—that might have made the narrative more involving and resonant. Nevertheless, THE SANTA CLAUSE is a charming, if mild, fantasy, distinguished by a gentle directorial touch that strikes a deft balance between dramatic and fantastic elements. At the heart of the film are engaging performances by the two male leads—Allen, as the bewildered single father, and young Lloyd, who responds plausibly as a son whose father becomes a new man in his eyes overnight. While the film breaks no new ground, it offers the kind of simple, well-crafted, family entertainment that used to be a staple of the Disney studio. THE SANTA CLAUSE was the surprise hit of 1994, earning domestic grosses of more than $100 million.

SANTA FE TRAIL

1940 110m bw Historical/Adventure   ★★★½
First National   (U.S.)   /U

Errol Flynn *(Jeb Stuart)*, Olivia de Havilland *(Kit Carson Holliday)*, Raymond Massey *(John Brown)*, Ronald Reagan *(George Armstrong Custer)*, Alan Hale *(Barefoot Brody)*, Guinn "Big Boy" Williams *(Tex Bell)*, Van Heflin *(Rader)*, Henry O'Neill *(Cyrus Holliday)*, William Lundigan *(Bob Holliday)*, John Litel *(Harlan)*

p, Robert Fellows; d, Michael Curtiz; w, Robert Buckner; ph, Sol Polito; ed, George Amy; m, Max Steiner; art d, John Hughes; fx, Byron Haskin, H.F. Koenekamp; cos, Milo Anderson

Despite its misleading title, this roaring, action-packed film, directed with great vigor by Curtiz, is not a western and has little to do with the Santa Fe Trail. And though it purports to deal with a serious segment of American history, even that is inaccurate.

Flynn is his ever-dashing self as he appears at West Point, playing the southern-born J.E.B. Stuart, who later became the South's greatest cavalryman during the Civil War. He arrives, along with mule and dog, wearing an outlandish uniform of his own design which so confuses the sentinels at the post that they mistakenly call out an honor guard to salute what appears to be a high-ranking officer of a foreign power. This auspicious arrival is soon ended when it is learned that Flynn is nothing more than a new cadet reporting to the Point for training. Other than his academic studies, Flynn's real enemy at the Point is Heflin, a wild-eyed radical abolitionist who is out to change the class and caste system of America. He is a secret follower of the fanatic John Brown, and his political activities finally get Heflin cashiered from the Point. Flynn and his friends (Reagan, playing George Armstrong Custer; David Bruce, essaying Phil Sheridan; Wilcox, playing Longstreet; William Marshall, enacting the role of George Pickett; and George Haywood, playing John Hood) all graduate from the Point in 1854 and are assigned to a western post in Kansas where they must combat the illegal activities of the dreaded Brown, played by Massey. A travesty of history, SANTA FE TRAIL is nonetheless a rousing adventure yarn, offering a great romp for Flynn and providing a bevy of colorful characterizations. De Havilland is at her feisty, attractive best, while Reagan has the "best friend" role, losing her to the handsome Flynn. Massey, who overacts frantically as Brown, would play him again in SEVEN ANGRY MEN in 1955. The film's gratuitous patriotism is countered by the tentative sympathies Reagan and a few others utter on behalf of Massey, stating that he may be misdirected but that his ambition to free the slaves is a worthy one.

SAPPHIRE

1959 92m c Mystery   ★★★
Artna   (U.K.)   /A

Nigel Patrick *(Supt.)*, Yvonne Mitchell *(Mildred)*, Michael Craig *(Inspector Learoyd)*, Paul Massie *(David Harris)*, Bernard Miles *(Ted Harris)*, Olga Lindo *(Mrs. Harris)*, Earl Cameron *(Dr. Robbins)*, Gordon Heath *(Paul Slade)*, Jocelyn Britton *(Patsy)*, Harry Baird *(Johnny Fiddle)*

p, Michael Relph; d, Basil Dearden; w, Janet Green, Lukas Heller (based on the screenplay by Green); ph, Harry Waxman; ed, John D. Guthridge; m, Philip Green; art d, Carmen Dillon

Good detective yarn starring Patrick and Craig as detectives of Scotland Yard who are investigating the murder of a young black woman whose light-colored skin allowed her to pass as white. Suspects range from Massie, as the girl's white boyfriend, and his parents, who feared for their son's career, to the black youths the girl tosses aside when she is accepted by whites. Craig's prejudice, as well as just about everyone else's, adds a good deal of tension to the sleuthing, which Patrick pursues in a highly dignified, professional manner despite the additional obstacles. Material stays on safe ground about shedding light on the problem of racial prejudice which was rampant in England in the late 1950s. The picture was made shortly after race riots occurred in London and Nottingham.

SARATOGA

1937 94m bw Comedy   ★★★½
MGM   (U.S.)   /A

Jean Harlow *(Carol Clayton)*, Clark Gable *(Duke Bradley)*, Lionel Barrymore *(Grandpa Clayton)*, Walter Pidgeon *(Hartley Madison)*, Frank Morgan *(Jesse Kiffmeyer)*, Una Merkel *(Fritzi O'Malley)*, Cliff Edwards *(Tip O'Brien)*, George Zucco *(Dr. Beard)*, Jonathan Hale *(Frank Clayton)*, Hattie McDaniel *(Rosetta)*

p, Bernard H. Hyman; d, Jack Conway; w, Anita Loos, Robert E. Hopkins; ph, Ray June; ed, Elmo Veron; m, Edward Ward; art d, Cedric Gibbons, John S. Detlie; cos, Dolly Tree

Jean Harlow gave her last screen performance—one of her best—in this sharp-witted and charming trackside comedy that pairs the actress with Clark Gable. Harlow, who died before the film's completion, stars as Carol Clayton, the daughter of a horse breeder (Jonathan Hale) who through gambling loses his Saratoga farm to his bookmaker friend Duke Bradley (Clark Gable). After her father dies of a heart attack, Carol forbids her stockbroker fiance, Hartley Madison (Walter Pidgeon), to make any more trackside wagers—much to the chagrin of Duke, who had planned to win back the money he lost to Hartley at Belmont. While Carol and Duke carry on a love-hate flirtation, the bookmaker schemes with his old friend Fritzi (Una Merkel) to recoup his losses, persuading top jockey Dixie Gordon (Frankie Darro) to ride Fritzi's horse in an upcoming race against Hartley's steed. By now Carol has fallen for Duke and broken off her engagement, but Duke nobly ends their budding romance, respecting her late father's wishes that she be sheltered from the wicked ways of the track. Heartbroken, Carol purchases Frankie's contract from Fritzi, and the stage is set for Duke's ruin until kind-hearted Fritzi saves the day. After Harlow died in June 1937, it was decided to use a stand-in for her remaining scenes, in which Mary Dees and Geraldine Dvorak are photographed from behind while wearing a large floppy hat, with Paula Winslow speaking for the character (whom screenwriters Anita Loos and Robert Hopkins gave a cold and cough).

SATURDAY NIGHT AND SUNDAY MORNING

1960 90m bw Drama   ★★★★
Woodfall   (U.K.)   /PG

Albert Finney *(Arthur Seaton)*, Shirley Ann Field *(Doreen Gretton)*, Rachel Roberts *(Brenda)*, Hylda Baker *(Aunt Ada)*, Norman Rossington *(Bert)*, Bryan Pringle *(Jack)*, Robert Cawdron *(Robboe)*, Edna Morris *(Mrs. Bull)*, Elsie Wagstaffe *(Mrs. Seaton)*, Frank Pettitt *(Mr. Seaton)*

p, Tony Richardson; d, Karel Reisz; w, Alan Sillitoe (based on his novel); ph, Freddie Francis; ed, Seth Holt; m, John Dankworth; art d, Ted Marshall

In a scant 89 minutes, Sillitoe and Reisz create a world and immerse the viewer in it. This was 23-year-old Finney's first major film (he'd done a bit in THE ENTERTAINER earlier that year) and the resulting performance remains a fresh revelation. It's another of the "angry young men" pictures (e.g., ROOM AT THE TOP) and this is one that lingers. Sillitoe, who also wrote THE LONELINESS OF THE LONG DISTANCE RUNNER, adapted his own novel here with major results.

Finney is a lathe operator in a small town near Nottingham. He is a lively young man devoted to pleasure and thumbing his nose at authority. As he says, "All I want is a good time. The rest is propaganda." To that end, he spends his weekends boozing and brawling and bedding down any woman he can. He makes a good wage; he has plenty of discretionary money to spend. He hates his job but is willing to put in his week at the lathe in return for the fun he can have with his pay envelope. He's having an affair with Roberts, who is married to his fellow worker, Pringle. Finney enjoys the sexual liaisons with Roberts, but that's as far as he will go with her; she wants more. At the same time, Finney meets Field, a beautiful, old-fashioned young woman with strict morals. Finney finds himself falling in love with Field, but she won't sleep with him unless there is a commitment, something Finney cannot bear to make. Then Roberts announces that she's pregnant.

The story seems slim at best, but Reisz's sharp direction and the superb editing combine with Sillitoe's grasp of the argot to make this a compelling, if somewhat difficult to understand, movie. The accents in that area of England are almost impossible for US ears (and even many London auricles) to fathom, so it had to be looped in places where the words blurred. Sillitoe, who used to work in a Midlands factory, captures the nuances perfectly in his script, and Reisz, who was in his early thirties at the time, does a smashing job in his first feature after having worked in the documentary field. Despite Finney's youth, he was already a veteran Shakespearean actor and had once taken over for Olivier when Sir Larry was felled by injury on the eve of a performance of *Coriolanus* at Stratford. It was a sensational outing for Finney, and great things were in store. Roberts was excellent and her performance (not unlike that of Simone Signoret in ROOM AT THE TOP), like Finney's, was also honored with a BFA award. One of the best of the "kitchen sink" pictures of the era, SATURDAY NIGHT AND SUNDAY MORNING has more than its share of humor to temper the highly charged drama, and it stands out in every department—the sex is steamy, the language is raw, the emotions are strong. Still a must-watch.

SATURDAY NIGHT FEVER

1977 119m c Drama ★★★★
Paramount (U.S.) R/PG

John Travolta *(Tony Manero)*, Karen Lynn Gorney *(Stephanie)*, Barry Miller *(Bobby C.)*, Joseph Call *(Joey)*, Paul Pape *(Double J)*, Donna Pescow *(Annette)*, Bruce Ornstein *(Gus)*, Julie Bovasso *(Flo)*, Martin Shakar *(Frank)*, Sam Coppola *(Fusco)*

p, Robert Stigwood; d, John Badham; w, Norman Wexler (based on the *New York* magazine article "Tribal Rites of the New Saturday Night" by Nik Cohn); ph, Ralf D. Bode; ed, David Rawlins; m, Barry Gibb, Robin Gibb, Maurice Gibb, David Shire; prod d, Charles Bailey; chor, Lester Wilson; cos, Patrizia Von Brandenstein, Jennifer Nichols

AAN Best Actor: John Travolta

Reminiscent of both MARTY and SATURDAY NIGHT AND SUNDAY MORNING, this hugely popular picture and its even more popular soundtrack album (more than 27 million copies of which have been sold) raked in nearly $200 million. Moreover, John Travolta's heartfelt portrayal of Tony Manero, a directionless young clerk in a Brooklyn paint store, catapulted him to stardom. Refusing to compete with his seminarian brother (Martin Shakar) for his father's approval, Tony lives for the weekend, strutting his stuff on the disco dance floor with his girlfriend, Annette (Donna Pescow), whom he shuns after meeting Stephanie (Karen Lynn Gorney), an upwardly mobile, smart-stepping miss who becomes his partner for a big dance contest. Tony's tempestuous relationship with Stephanie, his desertion of Annette, and the pleasures and problems of his neighborhood buddies make up the rest of the film, which reaches its tragic climax in a scene at the Verrazano Bridge, where Bobby C. (Barry Miller), overcome with worries about the baby he has fathered out of wedlock, precariously scales the bridge.

The story here is really secondary to character and milieu, as director John Badham and his actors create a convincing portrait of frustrated 1970s working-class youth and the escape offered by the swirling lights and pulsing rhythms of the disco. Although technically not a musical—no one in the cast sings—this highly energized film has more songs than many musicals proper, most courtesy of the Bee Gees, who reached their creative and popular apex here. It also features some great dancing by Travolta, who made a triumphant critical comeback in 1994's PULP FICTION, during the same period that a 70s nostalgia boom turned SNF into a college cult favorite and the Bee Gees' "Tragedy" briefly re-appeared on the *Billboard* charts. The sequel, STAYING ALIVE, is nowhere near as involving.

SAVAGE NIGHTS
(LES NUITS FAUVES)

1993 126m c Erotic/Drama/Romance ★★★
Banfilm Ter/La Sept/Erre Produzioni/SNC (France/Italy) /18

Cyril Collard *(Jean)*, Romane Bohringer *(Laura)*, Carlos Lopez *(Samy)*, Corine Blue *(Laura's Mother)*, Claude Winter *(Jean's Mother)*, Rene-Marc Bini *(Marc)*, Maria Schneider *(Noria)*, Clementine Celarie *(Marianne)*, Laura Favali *(Karin)*, Denis D'Archangelo *(Cabaret Singer)*

p, Nella Banfi; d, Cyril Collard; w, Cyril Collard (based on his novel *Les Nuits Fauves*); ph, Manuel Teran; ed, Lise Beaulieu; prod d, Jacky Macchi, Katja Kosenina; cos, Regine Arniaud

Coming on the heels of the sentimental PHILADELPHIA, it was predictable that SAVAGE NIGHTS would be heralded as a tough-minded AIDS movie—one that dares to address the complicity of some victims in the transmission of the disease. The film has a fascinating, trenchant first hour, collapses of its own weight before the end, and lingers like a bad dream—to its credit.

Jean (director Cyril Collard) is an HIV-positive, bisexual filmmaker who drowns his anxiety in passion. He auditions 17-year-old boutique clerk Laura (Romane Bohringer), who fails the screen test but becomes Jean's lover. Almost concurrently, Jean auditions and seduces Samy (Carlos Lopez), who hustles tricks at Mr. Andre's, a louche, anything-goes bordello. Despite developing KS lesions, Jean pursues Laura; at first she doesn't quibble over his admission of bisexuality. After he and Samy have a failed menage with a Swiss streetwalker, he confesses his health status to Laura, but she refuses to allow a condom to interfere with their passion.

This ambitious, passionate movie means to shock its audience. Collard, who was himself struggling with AIDS as he shot the film, may have regarded it as a final statement, and accordingly tried to make it as bold as possible—perhaps to a fault. Often his actors (including himself) project grand Parisian posturing rather than suffering, and Collard's screenplay lets Bohringer's character rant on to the point of irritation about what she will soon be missing (namely Collard—it's as though a Greek chorus were lamenting his charms). Nor does the film's golden, overly pretty cinematography do much to strengthen its story line.

NIGHTS swept France's Cesar Awards: Best Debut Film, Best Editing, Best Female Newcomer (Romane Bohringer), and Best Picture of the Year. Collard's death of AIDS complications at age 35, three days before the awards, added a mythic, poignant touch to NIGHTS' day in the sun.

SAVE THE TIGER

1973 100m c Drama ★★★
Filmways/Jalem/Cirandinha (U.S.) R/AA

Jack Lemmon *(Harry Stoner)*, Jack Gilford *(Phil Greene)*, Laurie Heineman *(Myra the Hitchhiker)*, Norman Burton *(Fred Mirrell)*, Patricia Smith *(Janet Stoner)*, Thayer David *(Charlie Robbins)*, William Hansen *(Meyer)*, Harvey Jason *(Rico)*, Liv von Linden *(Ula)*, Lara Parker *(Margo the Prostitute)*

p, Steve Shagan; d, John G. Avildsen; w, Steve Shagan; ph, James Crabe; ed, David Bretherton; m, Marvin Hamlisch; art d, Jack Collis

AA Best Actor: Jack Lemmon; *AAN Best Supporting Actor:* Jack Gilford; *AAN Best Adapted Screenplay:* Steve Shagan

Director John Avildsen has a knack for using small budgets to make "big" movies. First it was JOE, then this film, then his triumph with ROCKY.

The action of SAVE THE TIGER takes place in about a day and a half in the life of a man who is trapped by his own indulgences. Businesss is rotten, and Lemmon, the managing partner of Capri Casuals, a Los Angeles garment manufacturing company, finds himself daydreaming about his youth. After a nightmare-filled night, he rises in his sumptuous Beverly Hills home; says goodbye to his wife, Smith, who is on her way to a relative's funeral; and gets into his Lincoln for the long drive downtown. On the street, he picks up Heineman, a liberated young woman who proposes that they go to bed together. Lemmon balks. At the office, he and partner Gilford try to figure a way out of their dire financial straits (they owe a bundle and there isn't a bank in town willing to give them a loan). Lemmon suggests torching the company's Long Beach warehouse to collect insurance money, but Gilford won't hear of it. When Burton, a conservative out-of-town client who lets his hair down in LA, arrives to see the new line from Capri, Lemmon arranges for him to be entertained by call girl Parker. Later, in a porno movie house, Lemmon meets with David, who is willing to burn down the warehouse for a price. Outside the theater, Bif Elliott is raising funds to protect wildlife, particularly lions and tigers—hence the film's title. Things continue in this vein, with the increasingly pressured Lemmon eventually breaking down in front of the audience at a fashion show, convinced that the assembled clients are his dead comrades-in-arms from WWII.

SAVE THE TIGER is an uneven but engaging look at a man whose lust for success has bankrupted not only his company but his conscience. Yet despite his illegal and immoral practices, we are drawn to Lemmon's Harry Stoner.

SAY ANYTHING

1989   100m   c   Comedy/Drama ★★★★
Gracie/Cameron Crowe   (U.S.) PG-13/15

John Cusack *(Lloyd Dobler)*, Ione Skye *(Diane Court)*, John Mahoney *(James Court)*, Lili Taylor *(Corey Flood)*, Amy Brooks *(D.C.)*, Pamela Segall *(Rebecca)*, Jason Gould *(Mike Cameron)*, Loren Dean *(Joe)*, Joan Cusack *(Constance)*, Glenn Walker Harris Jr. *(Jason)*

p, Polly Platt; d, Cameron Crowe; w, Cameron Crowe; ph, Laszlo Kovacs; ed, Richard Marks; m, Richard Gibbs, Anne Dudley, Nancy Wilson; prod d, Mark Mansbridge; cos, Jane Ruhm

A far cry from the standard Hollywood teen romance, SAY ANYTHING is the extraordinary directorial debut of Cameron Crowe (who adapted his own novel for the hilariously inventive FAST TIMES AT RIDGEMONT HIGH). Set in Seattle, Crowe's wonderfully nuanced screenplay develops a complex triangular relationship involving a gifted and ambitious high-school graduate, Diane Court (Ione Skye), her doting father, James (John Mahoney), and Lloyd Dobler (John Cusack), the likable, underachieving classmate who falls for her. The relationship of father and daughter is tested when Diane is wooed by Lloyd, an Army brat who lives with his unmarried sister (real-life sibling Joan Cusack) and her young son (Daniel Will-Harris). His best friends, Corey and D.C. (Lili Taylor and Amy Brooks) know just how sensitive, creative, and loving Lloyd is. Diane, too, is won over by Lloyd's generosity of spirit, but her father wants nothing to stand in the way of her success, and pressures her to break up with Lloyd. Seldom have such complexity, emotional depth, honesty, and realism been invested in what is ostensibly a teen love story. Crowe's script is full of careful observations, and his camera unobtrusively serves the spot-on production design, the witty but believable dialog, and especially the outstanding performances by Skye (RIVER'S EDGE; A NIGHT IN THE LIFE OF JIMMY REARDON), Mahoney (MOONSTRUCK; SUSPECT; BETRAYAL), and Cusack, whose Lloyd Dobler is an exceedingly winning portrayal.

SAYONARA

1957   147m   c   War/Drama ★★★★
Goetz/Pennebaker   (U.S.) /PG

Marlon Brando *(Maj. Lloyd Gruver)*, Ricardo Montalban *(Nakamura)*, Red Buttons *(Joe Kelly)*, Patricia Owens *(Eileen Webster)*, Martha Scott *(Mrs. Webster)*, James Garner *(Capt. Mike Bailey)*, Miiko Taka *(Hana-ogi)*, Miyoshi Umeki *(Katsumi)*, Kent Smith *(Gen. Webster)*, Douglas Watson *(Col. Craford)*

p, William Goetz; d, Joshua Logan; w, Paul Osborn (based on the novel by James A. Michener); ph, Ellsworth Fredricks; ed, Arthur Schmidt, Philip W. Anderson; m, Franz Waxman; art d, Ted Haworth; chor, LeRoy Prinz; cos, Norma Koch

AAN Best Picture; AAN Best Actor: Marlon Brando; AA Best Supporting Actor: Red Buttons; AA Best Supporting Actress: Miyoshi Umeki; AAN Best Director: Joshua Logan; AAN Best Adapted Screenplay: Paul Osborn; AAN Best Cinematography: Ellsworth Fredericks; AAN Best Editing: Arthur P. Schmidt, Philip W. Anderson; AA Best Art Direction: Ted Haworth, Robert Priestley; AA Best Sound: George Groves

This beautifully photographed and often moving story of racial prejudice features Marlon Brando as Lloyd Gruver, an Army major reassigned to a Japanese air base in the midst of the Korean conflict. In Japan, Gruver sees the US military's racism against the Japanese, which goes so far as to forbid servicemen from marrying Japanese women. Although at first indifferent to the situation, Gruver is forced to take a stand when his buddy Joe Kelly (Red Buttons) falls in love with a local woman, Katsumi (Miyoshi Umeki), and becomes determined to marry her, going over the heads of the military high command and petitioning

Congress for permission. Sticking by his comrade, Gruver risks the wrath of his superiors when he agrees to be Kelly's best man at the ceremony. What's more, Gruver himself falls in love with a beautiful Japanese dancer, Hana-ogi (Miiko Taka), and finds himself in the same predicament as Kelly. SAYONARA is a sensitive work, sparing neither Americans nor Japanese in condemning prejudice. This updating of the "Madame Butterfly" theme is a powerful, well-told story, with a statement on racism that remains timeless. It was certainly topical: when filming began, in 1956, more than 10,000 American servicemen had defied extant regulations and married Japanese women (as the novel's author, James A. Michener, had done earlier). The film received 10 Academy Award nominations, including Best Picture (it lost to THE BRIDGE ON THE RIVER KWAI), Best Director, Best Actor (Brando lost to Alec Guinness for RIVER KWAI), Best Cinematography, Best Screenplay, and Best Editing. Oscars went to the film for Sound, Art Direction, and Set Decoration, as well as to Buttons and Umeki for their supporting performances.

SCANDAL

1989   114m   c   Biography/Political ★★★
Palace/British Screen   (U.K.) R/18

John Hurt *(Stephen Ward)*, Joanne Whalley-Kilmer *(Christine Keeler)*, Bridget Fonda *(Mandy Rice-Davies)*, Ian McKellen *(John Profumo)*, Leslie Phillips *(Lord Astor)*, Britt Ekland *(Mariella Novotny)*, Roland Gift *(Johnnie Edgecombe)*, Jeroen Krabbe *(Eugene Ivanov)*, Daniel Massey *(Mervyn Griffith-Jones)*, Jean Alexander *(Mrs. Keeler)*

p, Stephen Woolley; d, Michael Caton-Jones; w, Michael Thomas; ph, Mike Molloy; ed, Angus Newton; m, Carl Davis; prod d, Simon Holland; art d, Chris Townsend; cos, Jane Robinson

Michael Caton-Jones's SCANDAL peeks under the bedsheets of Britain's ruling class with a rehashing of the Profumo Affair, the early 60s sex scandal that eventually toppled the Conservative Party from power. Minister of War John Profumo (Ian McKellan) is romantically linked to accused prostitute Christine Keeler (Joanne Whalley-Kilmer), who, as it happened, was also involved with Soviet attache Eugene Ivanov (Jeroen Krabbe), an alleged spy. Keeler met both men through Dr. Stephen Ward (John Hurt), a high-society osteopath. Meanwhile, teenage beauty Mandy Rice-Davies (Bridget Fonda), another Ward protegee, was bedhopping with the high and mighty of two continents, and the whole crew were reported to be frequent participants at extravagant orgies. Instead of sleaze, director Caton-Jones and screenwriter Michael Thomas deliver a vindication of the affair's chief scapegoats—Ward and Keeler—in the form of a two-hour nostalgia trip (complete with imitation Beatles), with some complex and powerful performances. The screen is filled with memorabilia of 1960s London: miniskirts, smoke-filled dens of West Indians, rows of tenements, opportunistic newsmen from tabloids. Overall, however, the direction is uninspired. One problem with SCANDAL is that, compared to scandals of the 80s, the Profumo affair is rather tame. If it's a poke at England's Conservatives you're looking for, the honest fiction of Mike Leigh's HIGH HOPES did more to make them bleed than the pointless fact of SCANDAL.

SCANNERS

1981   102m   c   Horror ★★★
Filmplan   (Canada) R/18

Stephen Lack *(Cameron Vale)*, Jennifer O'Neill *(Kim)*, Patrick McGoohan *(Dr. Paul Ruth)*, Lawrence Dane *(Keller)*, Charles Shamata *(Gaudi)*, Adam Ludwig *(Crostic)*, Michael Ironside *(Darryl Revok)*, Victor Desy *(Dr. Gatineau)*, Mavor Moore *(Trevellyan)*, Robert Silverman *(Pierce)*

p, Claude Heroux; d, David Cronenberg; w, David Cronenberg; ph, Mark Irwin; ed, Ronald Sanders; m, Howard Shore; art d, Carol Spier; fx, Dick Smith, Gary Zeller, Henry Pierrig, Dick Smith, Chris Walas

SCANNERS is a nifty science fiction comic-book of a movie that makes excellent use of its low budget and hastily-written script. The film boasts a few extraordinary set pieces and some inspiredly gory special effects, as well as some resonant visual metaphors for the telepathic condition.

Ephemerol, an experimental tranquilizer, was tested on pregnant women during the 1940s and produced some severe long range side effects. Before the drug was taken off the market, 236 babies were born to the women tested. They were found to possess the ability to read minds. Dubbed "scanners," these powerful telepaths spread out through North America for decades until many were sought and rounded up by two mysterious and competing corporations: Consec, headed by Dr. Paul Ruth (McGoohan), and Biocarbon Amalgamated, headed by the deadly Darryl Revok (Ironside), a scanner assassin. Cameron Vale (Lack) is a homeless drifter with the gift. He is abducted from the street and ends up in the healing hands of Dr. Ruth, who gives him medication that allows him to control his power. Vale is informed that Revok plans to take over the world with an army of evil scanners. He must link up with his farflung "brethren" so they can determine their own futures.

Notorious for the scene in which Ironside uses his awesome scanning power to literally explode the head of another man, SCANNERS is relatively conventional by Cronenberg standards—though wildly imaginative by normal ones. Despite the loose ends and inconsistencies, SCANNERS is a memorable and absorbing genre entertainment that has spawned several direct-to-video sequels. Cronenberg displays more confidence as a visual stylist here than in his previous films, but his storytelling abilities are not much in evidence. Matters aren't helped by Lack's weak lead performance, though his large, emotive eyes add poignance to his predicament. Fortunately McGoohan (of television's "Secret Agent" and "The Prisoner") is on hand to provide an eccentrically entertaining performance as the fatherly Dr. Ruth. Ironside is fantastic as the lethal Revok, helping make this a popular cult favorite.

SCARECROW

1973 112m c Drama   ★★★
Warner Bros. (U.S.)   R/18

Gene Hackman *(Max)*, Al Pacino *(Lion)*, Dorothy Tristan *(Coley)*, Ann Wedgeworth *(Frenchy)*, Richard Lynch *(Riley)*, Eileen Brennan *(Darlene)*, Penny Allen *(Annie)*, Richard Hackman *(Mickey)*, Al Cingolani *(Skipper)*, Rutanya Alda *(Woman in Camper)*

p, Robert M. Sherman; d, Jerry Schatzberg; w, Garry Michael White; ph, Vilmos Zsigmond; ed, Evan Lottman; m, Fred Myrow; prod d, Albert Brenner; cos, Jo Ynocencio

This is a good look at a pair of losers that is a bit too episodic. Hackman has recently been released from San Quentin where he did some hard time for assault. He's on his way to Pittsburgh where he hopes to open a car wash on the modest savings he's accumulated. Pacino is a seaman who has just completed a voyage. The two men hit it off and decide to go east together. On the trip, they have adventures in bars, diners, and various residences belonging to former loves and old pals. As they near their destinations, Pacino becomes nervous about seeing his wife, Allen, whom he left while she was pregnant. Hackman does his best to encourage him, but Pacino is beginning to crumble. He's never seen his child, and, when he phones ahead to Detroit and talks to Allen (in a very sensitive portrayal), she lies, telling him that the child he'd thought she had was never born. She says she miscarried early and all of his trepidation about meeting his child was for naught. Pacino goes into a violent form of nervous breakdown. The final scenes show Hackman using his savings to pay for Pacino's hospital care, his hopes of opening his own business tossed aside in favor of helping his only friend. Hackman gives another splendid, compelling performance. Pacino's characterization is rather weak, however. His roles in DOG DAY AFTERNOON and THE GODFATHER are better indications of his talents. There are points where writer White has created unrealistic lines for Pacino instead of allowing the character to emerge subtly and become part of the story. Brennan does well as a barroom floozie, and Tristan scores as one of Hackman's ex-girlfriends. The picture looks wonderful and captures the grittiness of the road. Schatzberg had been a photographer and his collaboration with Zsigmond is fruitful in that respect for much of the film, though they are both occasionally guilty of gratuitous Hollywood gloss. The ending is not consistent with Hackman's behavior all the way through. Given the box office potency of the two stars, the receipts were disappointing, although the movie eventually did make a small profit. No four-letter word seems to have been omitted.

SCARFACE

1932 99m bw Biography/Crime   ★★★★★
Caddo (U.S.)   /15

Paul Muni *(Tony Camonte)*, Ann Dvorak *(Cesca Camonte)*, Karen Morley *(Poppy)*, Osgood Perkins *(Johnny Lovo)*, Boris Karloff *(Gaffney)*, George Raft *(Guino Rinaldo)*, Vince Barnett *(Angelo)*, C. Henry Gordon *(Inspector Guarino)*, Inez Palange *(Tony's Mother)*, Edwin Maxwell *(Commissioner)*

p, Howard Hughes; d, Howard Hawks; w, Ben Hecht, Seton I. Miller, John Lee Mahin, W.R. Burnett, Fred Pasley (based on the novel by Armitage Trail); ph, Lee Garmes, L.W. O'Connell; ed, Edward Curtiss; m, Adolph Tandler, Gus Arnheim; prod d, Harry Olivier

One of Hawks's undisputed masterpieces, and a landmark in the screen depiction of gangsters. Though the gangster genre had recently exploded with LITTLE CAESAR and PUBLIC ENEMY, it was SCARFACE (a.k.a. "Scarface, the Shame of a Nation") that depicted the professional hood as a murderous beast. In earlier films of the genre, a great deal of attention was paid to developing the background of the criminal and placing the blame for his antisocial activities on his environment. But with SCARFACE, all of that was dispensed with to give audiences for the first time an adult, fully developed monster who thrived on murder and power.

The first scene of SCARFACE shows Tony Camonte (Muni) only in shadow, whistling a few bars of an Italian aria before shooting a victim and then walking calmly away. It's obvious that the career shown on screen is that of the notorious Al Capone. Tony is honestly portrayed as the typical gangster of the era; he is brutal, arrogant, and stupid (Truffaut said Hawks directed Muni to make him look and move like an ape; it's likely), a homicidal maniac who revels in gaudy clothes, fast cars, and machine guns, because their rapid fire allows him to kill more people at a single outing. (The number of deaths recorded in this ultra-violent film is 28, with many more reported as occurring off-camera.) But Tony is also insanely jealous of his slinky sister (Ann Dvorak), to the point where his feelings toward her are obliquely incestuous. Tony works for Johnny Lovo (Osgood Perkins), a more sophisticated and clever hoodlum who, in turn, is the chief lieutenant of Big Louis (Harry Vejar), the city's nominal crime boss. (Perkins's role is based on Johnny Torrio, the creator of organized crime in America, and Vejar is a duplicate of Chicago's old-time crime czar, Big Jim Colosimo.) Tony is arrested for the murder shown in the opening scene, but the mob lawyer soon has him freed on a special writ. Tony encourages Johnny to kill Louis since he won't take advantage of the new Prohibition law and go into bootlegging liquor. But when Johnny tells Tony to leave the North Side boss (Boris Karloff) alone, and especially after Tony meets Johnny's sexy mistress (Karen Morley), it's clear that Tony's tactics are only going to intensify.

SCARFACE was the most violent, bloody film the genre had seen. Hawks outdid himself, running his cameras with the action in vivid truck and dolly shots often missing from the static early talkies of the period. Note in particular how Hawks uses the symbol of an "X" to indicate death (the rafters of a ceiling, Karloff's bowling score, Raft's apartment number, etc.) Aiding the director was cameraman Lee Garmes, whose sharp contrasts created some of the starkest images ever captured on screen. Producer Howard Hughes spared no expense, but he also interfered with Hawks (as he did with other directors), insisting that Hawks present all decisions for his approval. In fact, the production was almost cancelled because of the incessant squabbling between the producer and director.

Little of the original novel was kept except for the title. Profiling the gangster and his tempestuous sister as modern-day Borgias was Hawks's idea, with the incest relationship brilliantly suggested as the emotional weakness that destroys the unthinking gangster. Hecht had been offered $20,000 by Hawks to write the script, but wanted instead $1,000 a day in cash—not a particularly advantageous deal since he finished the script in 11 days.

Muni is superb in his role of the maniac killer, and Morley is perfect as his ice-cool moll. Raft, meanwhile, with his tuxedo and pomaded hair parted in the middle, is also excellent as Muni's right-hand man, a killer who does Muni's bidding without question. Muni and Raft became stars overnight because of SCARFACE, and both received lucrative long-term Hollywood contracts.

SCARFACE

1983   170m   c   Crime   ★★★★
Universal   (U.S.)   R/18

Al Pacino (*Tony Montana*), Steven Bauer (*Manny Ray*), Michelle
Pfeiffer (*Elvira*), Mary Elizabeth Mastrantonio (*Gina*), Robert Loggia
(*Frank Lopez*), Miriam Colon (*Mama Montana*), F. Murray Abraham
(*Omar*), Paul Shenar (*Alejandro Sosa*), Harris Yulin (*Bernstein*),
Angel Salazar (*Chi Chi*)

p, Martin Bregman, Peter Saphier; d, Brian De Palma; w, Oliver Stone
(based on the 1932 film script by Ben Hecht); ph, John A. Alonzo; ed,
Jerry Greenberg, David Ray; m, Giorgio Moroder; art d, Ed Richardson; fx, Ken Pepiot, Stan Parks; cos, Patricia Norris

A beautiful, at times poetic exercise in excess from Brian DePalma.
Based on the classic 1932 gangster film of the same name, the screenplay (written by Oliver Stone) follows the plot of its source almost to
the letter. A Cuban refugee with a violent streak is unstoppable in his
quest for the American dream. Fresh off the boat from Cuba, two-bit
hood Tony Montana (Pacino) lies his way into the country and into a
spot in Freedom Town (a camp in Florida for refugees to live in while
they wait for their green cards). It's not long before he and his right-
hand man Manny (Stephen Bauer) enter the world of crime. They
murder a political figure for drug dealer Frank Lopez (Robert Loggia)
to get their green cards and are soon on his payroll. They make a drug
buy at a Miami Beach motel, but the deal goes sour, and one of
Montana's cohorts is chopped up with a chainsaw by a group of
fanatical Colombians. After nearly being killed himself, Tony kills the
Colombians and brings both the money and the cocaine to Lopez. This
gives Tony a more prominent role in the organization. His duties include
serving as chauffeur to Lopez's beautiful but cocaine-addicted wife,
Elvira (Michelle Pfeiffer). Tony tries to make peace with his long-suffering mother and sister, whom he has not visited for sometime. One
night he shows up at their doorstep flashing money, but his mother
(Miriam Colon) wants nothing to do with him. His sister Gina (Mary
Elizabeth Mastrantonio) is seduced by the money, however. Tony's
feelings for his sister are a bit on the incestuous side, and he dominates
the girl, refusing to let her date. After a bad business deal and an
argument over Elvira, Lopez attempts to have Tony killed. In a brilliant
sequence, Tony and two assassins shoot it out in a crowded club. After
killing the assassins, Tony murders Lopez, marries Elvira and becomes
the most powerful drug lord in Florida. He makes deals with Bolivian
drug kingpin Sosa (Paul Shenar) and lives in a mansion with body-
guards and surveillance equipment. However, Manny is secretly dating
Gina (though warned not to), Elvira has become increasingly zombie-
like, and his money is not earning the interest it should. Moreover, he
also has become a selfish, paranoid drug addict. He is set up by the cops
and arrested. To avoid prison, Tony agrees to assassinate an anti-drug
politician who is exposing Sosa's business practices. Tony travels to
New York to execute the hit, but the target shows up with his wife and
kids. Tony refuses to go through with the hit. When he returns home,
Sosa threatens to kill him for backing out of the deal, and Tony
challenges him to "go to war."

Jammed with action sequences and unbearably tense moments, the
film depicts the seediest aspects of the American underworld. Stone's
screenplay twists gangster movie conventions, and DePalma demonstrates an unusual understanding of the genre. The latter's skill with the
camera is certainly his strongest talent. Although not as flashy as some of
his work (such as DRESSED TO KILL or CARRIE), it is a showboat of
cinematic style (the most memorable composition is an overhead shot of
Pacino soaking in an obscenely large bath tub). In addition to the high-octane action sequences, SCARFACE offers some excellent acting (especially from Loggia). An undeniably effective, visceral experience.

SCARLET EMPRESS, THE

1934   110m   bw   Biography/Historical   ★★★★★
Paramount   (U.S.)   /A

Marlene Dietrich (*Sophia Frederica*), John Lodge (*Count Alexei*),
Sam Jaffe (*Grand Duke Peter*), Louise Dresser (*Empress Elizabeth*), Maria Sieber (*Sophia as a Child*), C. Aubrey Smith (*Prince

August*), Ruthelma Stevens (*Countess Elizabeth*), Olive Tell (*Princess Johanna*), Gavin Gordon (*Gregory Orloff*), Jameson Thomas
(*Lt. Ostvyn*)

d, Josef von Sternberg; w, Manuel Komroff (based on the diary of
Catherine the Great); ph, Bert Glennon; ed, Josef von Sternberg; m,
Felix Mendelssohn, Peter Ilich Tchaikovsky, Richard Wagner, Josef
von Sternberg; art d, Hans Dreier, Peter Ballbusch, Richard Kollorsz;
fx, Gordon Jennings; cos, Travis Banton

For lovers of cinema, this film is practically a religious experience.
Like Griffith's INTOLERANCE, Von Stroheim's GREED or
Ophuls's LOLA MONTES, this is one of those masterpieces which
contemporaries just couldn't grip. Josef von Sternberg's name was
scarlet in Hollywood after he made this costly, indulgent box-office
failure, but his work has been entirely vindicated by the passing of
time. A highly romanticized rendering of the life of Catherine the
Great, from her childhood through her arranged married to the
half-witted Peter (Jaffe) and her later usurping of the throne of
Russia, THE SCARLET EMPRESS represents Sternberg's ultimate
recreation of a world from his own eccentric mind. Marlene Dietrich
exists in this never-never-land like some incredible goddess who
manifests various aspects of human personality and desire, from
wide-eyed, open-mouthed innocence through cynical worldliness to
political ambition. It's a real credit to Dietrich that she's both credible
throughout these changes and ironically distanced in a way that she
alone could pull off. The crazed intensity of the film pits her aggressive seduction of the entire Russian army versus Peter's rights as heir
and his manic desires. Jaffe matches Dietrich in brilliance with his
remarkable facial expressions, whispered lunacies and childishly
temperamental displays. Stealing much of the film is Louise Dresser
as the queen who regrets passing her throne onto Peter and who
attempts to prime Catherine to be a baby machine. She plays the role
like a pushy, middle-aged matchmaking mother from the windy
Midwest, and it works beautifully. Also worthy of mention is the
stunningly handsome John Lodge (who later gave up acting for
politics) as the emissary who brings the young princess to the
Russian court and later becomes her lover. Delivering his suggestive
lines through clenched teeth, he makes an ideal object of desire in
the lavish Russian court. As his large dark uniform covers the frame
during one seduction of Catherine, we get a striking visual rendering
of her initiation into court politics.

In terms of visuals, THE SCARLET EMPRESS is a symphony
verging on insanity. From the cuckoo clock of the woman who exposes
herself to the long roving shots surveying a grotesque wedding dinner,
Sternberg paints a rich tapestry of decadence. Most memorable of all is
the statuary of deformed gargoyles and slaughtered people decorating
most of the palace. But it's not just the sets which tell the story here. The
staging, frame composition and camera movement produce moments of
great beauty as well. Consider the shot showing a locket Catherine
discards as it bounces down from one tree branch to another, or the scene
where Catherine is being hairdressed and garbed for her wedding. Or, for
a saucier moment, notice how Sternberg tilts his camera slightly after Peter
strips one of Catherine's soldier lovers of his rank. As critic Charles Silver
has noted, with the men's groins now in frame as well, we realize that the
soldier wears other medals which distinguish him in the Russian court.
Sternberg loves to clutter his frame, using veils, smoke and shadows to
distance us from his characters. A portrait of Catherine lounging on her
bed as she fingers a screen drawn around her focuses so intently on the
netting that Catherine becomes an inscrutable blur enmeshed in her own
reverie. Greatest of all, though, in their combination of photography, lights
and editing, are three moments whose emotional impact comes from the
filming and not the writing. As a child Catherine is told of the powers and
horrors of ruling, and she envisions an incredible montage of torture
scenes, climaxing with the unforgettable shot of a man being used as a
clapper inside a giant bell. (The dissolve which links this scene to the next
is unforgettable.) The finale, meanwhile, done largely without dialogue to
the strains of the "The Ride of the Valkyries", builds great momentum as
Catherine rides her horse up the palace steps to declare her ultimate
triumph. But the scene of scenes is Catherine's wedding to Peter. A frame
jammed with crosses; powerful cuts between the pleased Queen, the
helpless emissary, the eccentric Peter and the desperate Catherine; the
lingering, increasingly tight closeups of Dietrich behind yet another

veil—what can one say? See this film on a large screen and in 35 mm if at all possible. The film does justice to the visual possibilities of cinema as few others have done, so do justice to the film when watching it.

SCARLET PIMPERNEL, THE

1935 85m bw Adventure ★★★★
London Films   (U.K.) /U

Leslie Howard (*Sir Percy Blakeney*), Merle Oberon (*Lady Marguerite Blakeney*), Raymond Massey (*Chauvelin*), Nigel Bruce (*The Prince of Wales*), Bramwell Fletcher (*The Priest*), Anthony Bushell (*Sir Andrew Ffoulkes*), Joan Gardner (*Suzanne de Tournay*), Walter Rilla (*Armand St. Just*), Mabel Terry-Lewis (*Countess de Tournay*), O.B. Clarence (*Count de Tournay*)

p, Alexander Korda; d, Harold Young, Rowland V. Brown, Alexander Korda; w, S.N. Behrman, Robert E. Sherwood, Arthur Wimperis, Lajos Biro (based on the novel by Baroness Orczy); ph, Harold Rosson; ed, William Hornbeck; m, Arthur Benjamin; prod d, Vincent Korda; fx, Ned Mann; cos, John Armstrong, Oliver Messel

Classic Korda adventure. THE SCARLET PIMPERNEL is based on a romantic novel about deposed French aristocrats, written by the daughter of deposed Hungarian aristocrats; this powerful film secured lasting fame for Leslie Howard.

Sir Percy Blakeney (Howard) is a mild-mannered aristocrat in the court of the Prince of Wales. While large numbers of aristocrats in France are guillotined in the Reign of Terror, Blakeney loses the respect of his wife, Lady Marguerite (Merle Oberon), for being so ineffectual, and he in turn believes that she has been responsible for the arrest of some old friends of hers. Meanwhile, Robespierre (Ernest Milton) and the rest of the French revolutionary government are troubled by a series of daring rescues of condemned nobles, pulled off by the mysterious agency of a man who leaves behind him a small red flower—a pimpernel—for which he comes to be named. The Scarlet Pimpernel adopts a variety of disguises as he saves the gentry from the guillotine. Suspecting English involvement, the French send one of their most capable individuals, Chauvelin (Raymond Massey), to London, ostensibly to serve as ambassador, but really to discover the identity of the Pimpernel. Chauvelin persuades Lady Marguerite to help bait a trap for the Pimpernel, in return for the lives of her arrested friends.

Although directed by Harold Young, the film is much more the work of its producer, Alexander Korda, another transplanted Hungarian (Howard too, for that matter, was the son of Hungarian immigrants). The first director hired was Rowland Brown, director of QUICK MILLIONS, BLOOD MONEY, and author of several respected screenplays. He also had a reputation for getting fired, however, and on the first day of shooting he butted heads with Korda and lost. The producer took over directing for that day, hired Young the next day, and kept a tight rein on him throughout the production. Much of the film was shot outdoors, contrary to the general practice in England at the time. The impressive production resources of Korda's studio are very much in evidence. Korda imported Hal Rosson from Hollywood to shoot the film, and the cinematographer was ecstatic at the varied English skies. Howard gives a wonderful performance, languid and almost effeminate as Sir Percy, and richly deserving of his wife's contempt, but dashing and daring as the Pimpernel. He is supported by Massey in fine form as the villain, and Merle Oberon, as empty as ever.

The novel served as the basis of several silent films, and was remade in 1950 as THE ELUSIVE PIMPERNEL, with David Niven in the title role. The sequel suffers from having been originally shot as a musical; the way it's edited, you can see where the numbers were cut.

The best remembered thing about the original classic adventure is the little bit of doggerel that Howard makes up to throw off suspicion: "They seek him here, they seek him there / The Frenchies seek him everywhere / Is he in Heaven? Is he in Hell? / That damned elusive Pimpernel."

SCARLET STREET

1945 103m bw Crime ★★★★★
Diana   (U.S.) /A

Edward G. Robinson (*Christopher Cross*), Joan Bennett (*Kitty March*), Dan Duryea (*Johnny Prince*), Margaret Lindsay (*Millie*), Rosalind Ivan (*Adele Cross*), Jess Barker (*Janeway*), Arthur Loft (*Dellarowe*), Samuel S. Hinds (*Charles Pringle*), Vladimir Sokoloff (*Opo Lejon*), Charles Kemper (*Patcheye*)

p, Fritz Lang; d, Fritz Lang; w, Dudley Nichols (based on the novel and play *La Chienne* by Georges de la Fouchardiere, Mouezy-Eon); ph, Milton Krasner; ed, Arthur Hilton; m, H.J. Salter; art d, Alexander Golitzen, John B. Goodman; fx, John P. Fulton; cos, Travis Banton

Fritz Lang brings his eye for the bleak to this grim but brilliant noir (done before in a 1931 French film, LA CHIENNE, which featured Michel Simon and director Jean Renoir). Robinson, a cashier for a large New York city clothing retailer, spends his spare time painting. At a company banquet held in his honor for two decades of employment, he is characterized as one of those faceless people who make things tick but never receive their due, except at dinners like this. When Robinson leaves the party, he finds Bennett being attacked in the street. He fends off the mugger by using his umbrella as a saber and takes Bennett to have a quiet drink at a bar. Robinson finds this young woman fascinating and can't bear to tell her what he really does for a living, so he lies about it and lets her think he is a renowned artist. Robinson is married to Ivan, a shrewish woman who heckles him unmercifully for his lack of ambition. It isn't long before he thinks he is in love with Bennett, who continues to lead him on and doesn't make him aware of her relationship with Duryea, a hoodlum living on the edge of legality. Since they reckon that Robinson is a good mark, Bennett and Duryea conspire to have him rent a studio where he can meet Bennett for their trysts. Robinson does that and hauls several of his art works to the studio. Duryea brings in a professional critic, Barker, to look at the work; he is impressed. The cost of maintaining the separate residence is cutting into Robinson's savings, and he is at a loss to figure how to pay for his passion. Duryea removes Robinson's name from the art and puts Bennett's signature on the work. Robinson is annoyed at this, but when the pictures are acknowledged to be the work of a talented person, Robinson takes solace in the fact that someone appreciates him. Robinson begins to embezzle cash from his company, then learns that Ivan's first husband, long thought dead, is actually still alive. That means he can divorce Ivan and marry Bennett. When he races to the studio to tell Bennett the good news, he finds her and Duryea in each other's arms. He watches surreptitiously until Duryea exits, then walks in and has a confrontation with Bennett. When she taunts him with the news that he's been a patsy all along, he does something he (even more, perhaps, than Duryea) will regret the rest of his days.

One of the quintesstial expressions of the noir sensibility, SCARLET STREET does not flinch from the harsher aspects of its sordid story. Robinson, Bennett and Duryea are all in splendid form, and the incredible visuals entrap the feckless Robinson long before plot circumstances do. The paintings for the film were done by John Decker, the artist who palled around with such luminaries as Errol Flynn, John Barrymore, and W.C. Fields.

SCENES FROM A MARRIAGE

1973 168m c Drama ★★★
Cinematograph   (Sweden) PG/15

Liv Ullmann (*Marianne*), Erland Josephson (*Johan*), Bibi Andersson (*Katarina*), Jan Malmsjo (*Peter*), Anita Wall (*Mrs. Palm*), Gunnel Lindblom (*Eva*), Barbro Hiort af Ornas (*Mrs. Jacobi*)

p, Ingmar Bergman; d, Ingmar Bergman; w, Ingmar Bergman; ph, Sven Nykvist; ed, Siv Lundgren; cos, Inger Pehrsson

One of the finest of Ingmar Bergman's late-period films, SCENES FROM A MARRIAGE was in its original form a six-episode, 300-minute Swedish television series; Bergman cut it for US release. Here the director-writer again proves that he is one of film's best, and most theatrical, directors of actresses, giving the inimitable Ullmann a superb script that casts her in the role of an abandoned wife forced to deal with her weak husband Josephson's involvement with a younger woman. Filmed almost entirely in extreme close-ups by the masterful Sven

Nykvist, Ullmann's face conveys a variety of expressions reminiscent of Renee Falconetti in Carl Dreyer's silent THE PASSION OF JOAN OF ARC. The film is not without its faults, especially a certain choppiness resulting from the paring of the television version. (Its made-for-television visual content, however, should be admirably suited to videocassette.) There is little plot to speak of—the film's chief force lying in its dramatization of marital trauma—but viewers will be deeply moved by the marvelous acting and the honesty of Bergman's screenplay.

SCENT OF A WOMAN

1992 157m c Drama   ★★★
City Light Films/Universal (U.S.)   R/15

Al Pacino (Lt. Col. Frank Slade), Chris O'Donnell (Charlie Simms), James Rebhorn (Mr. Trask), Gabrielle Anwar (Donna), Philip S. Hoffman (George Willis Jr.), Richard Venture (W.R. Slade), Bradley Whitford (Randy), Rochelle Oliver (Gretchen), Margaret Eginton (Gail), Tom Riis Farrell (Garry)

p, Martin Brest; d, Martin Brest; w, Bo Goldman (from the characters created by Ruggero Maccari and Dino Risi, from the novel Il Buio e il Miele by Giovanni Arpino); ph, Donald E. Thorin; ed, William Steinkamp, Michael Tronick, Harvey Rosenstock; m, Thomas Newman; prod d, Angelo Graham; art d, W. Steven Graham; chor, Jerry Mitchell, Paul Pellicoro; cos, Aude Bronson-Howard

AAN Best Picture; AA Best Actor: Al Pacino; AAN Best Director: Martin Brest; AAN Best Adapted Screenplay: Bo Goldman

Thanks to a landmark performance by Al Pacino, SCENT OF A WOMAN is an agreeably watchable film. If they'd made it half an hour shorter and re-written the ending, it could have been a great one.

Pacino plays Frank Slade, a brilliant ex-Lieutenant Colonel whose career was cut short by a stupid accident. Now blind and embittered and living in New Hampshire with relatives, Slade has planned to exit this life in glorious style: after one last, hedonistic New York City weekend—the Waldorf, the Oak Room, etc.—he plans to don his dress blues for the last time and casually blow out his brains.

The unwitting accomplice to Slade's plan is Charlie Simms, (Chris O'Donnell), an earnest, hard-up scholarship student at nearby cradle of WASP manhood, Baird College. Charlie, who has problems of his own—he witnessed a student prank and is faced with expulsion unless he sneaks on the culprits—thinks he's going to earn $300 baby-sitting the abrasive Slade over Thanksgiving weekend. Instead, he finds himself on a whirlwind, induction-into-manhood tour of Manhattan.

Most of the adventures that befall Frank and Charlie are entirely unbelievable. Pacino inhabits the role with such passion and conviction, however, that we suspend our skepticism and delight in watching him dance a tango, test-drive a Ferrari or simply rail at his lot.

The dialogue ranges from the insightful to the crassly sentimental, and there's no dramatic structure to speak of. Nevertheless, Pacino, with commendable support from O'Donnell, makes us overlook these shortcomings—until the end, that is, when a hammy show-down at Baird College finally pushes the credibility meter off the scale.

SCHINDLER'S LIST

1993 185m c/bw Drama/Historical/War   ★★★★★
Amblin/Universal (U.S.)   R/15

Liam Neeson (Oskar Schindler), Ben Kingsley (Itzhak Stern), Ralph Fiennes (Amon Goeth), Caroline Goodall (Emilie Schindler), Jonathan Sagalle (Poldek Pfefferberg), Embeth Davidtz (Helen Hirsch), Andrzej Seweryn (Julian Scherner), Norbert Weisser (Albert Hujar), Elina Lowensohn (Diana Reiter), Malgoscha Gebel (Victoria Klonowska)

p, Steven Spielberg, Gerald R. Molen, Branko Lustig; d, Steven Spielberg; w, Steve Zaillian (from the novel Schindler's Ark by Thomas Keneally); ph, Janusz Kaminski; ed, Michael Kahn, Bill Kimberlin; m, John Williams; prod d, Allan Starski; art d, Maciej Walczak, Ewa Tarnowska, Ryszard Melliwa, Grzegorz Piatkowski; fx, Bruce Minkus, Industrial Light & Magic, Steve Price; cos, Anna Biedrzycka-Sheppard

AA Best Picture: Steven Spielberg, Branko Lustig, Gerald R. Molen; AA Best Director: Steven Spielberg; AA Best Cinematography: Janusz Kaminski; AA Best Adapted Screenplay: Steve Zaillian; AA Best Original Score: John Williams; AA Best Editing: Michael Kahn;

AA Best Art Direction: Ewa Braun, Allan Starski; AAN Best Actor: Liam Neeson; AAN Best Supporting Actor: Ralph Fiennes; AAN Best Costume Design: Anna Biedrzycka-Sheppard; AAN Best Sound: Andy Nelson, Steve Pederson, Scott Millan, Ron Judkins; AAN Best Makeup: Christina Smith, Matthew Mungle, Judith A. Cory

The seven Academy Awards and virtually unanimous acclaim accorded to SCHINDLER'S LIST were entirely merited. Director Steven Spielberg has achieved something close to the impossible—a morally serious, aesthetically stunning historical epic that is nonetheless readily accessible to a mass audience.

In 1941, the Jews of Nazi-occupied Kracow are dispossessed of their businesses and herded into a tiny, squalid ghetto. Small-time entrepreneur Oskar Schindler (Liam Neeson), a gentile, conceives of a get-rich-quick scheme that involves Itzhak Stern (Ben Kingsley), an accountant and member of the local judenrat (Jewish council), and an enamelware plant where cheap labor is supplied by ghetto Jews.

Stern sees a way to save Jewish lives: factory employees, classified as essential workers, are exempt from "resettlement" in concentration camps. Against his better judgment, Schindler looks the other way as Stern adds musicians, academics, rabbis, and cripples to the factory rolls. Within a year, the Final Solution is well underway, and a monstrous Nazi commandant, Amon Goeth (Ralph Fiennes), brutally liquidates the ghetto and ships surviving Jews to a forced labor camp. Schindler bribes the cynical Goeth to permit re-establishment of the factory within camp walls, and business continues more or less as before. But Schindler is changing, and at great risk to himself, he begins to take an active role in protecting his workers.

Though based on fact, SCHINDLER'S LIST is neither history, nor the "definitive" film version of the Holocaust some reviewers wanted it to be. It's an intensely personal meditation on the nature of heroism and moral choice, rendered on the kind of rich, dreamlike cinematic canvas that only Hollywood can realize. Far from a departure for Spielberg, SCHINDLER'S LIST is the fulfillment of his singular talent for achieving high seriousness—as with EMPIRE OF THE SUN—within and despite the constraints of corporate filmmaking.

SCOUNDREL, THE

1935 76m bw Drama/Comedy   ★★★★
Paramount (U.S.)   /A

Noel Coward (Anthony Mallare), Julie Haydon (Cora Moore), Stanley Ridges (Paul Decker), Rosita Moreno (Carlotta), Martha Sleeper (Julia Vivian), Hope Williams (Margie), Ernest Cossart (Jimmy Clay), Everley Gregg (Mildred Langwiter), Eduardo Ciannelli (Maurice Stern), Helen Strickland (Mrs. Rollinson)

p, Ben Hecht, Charles MacArthur; d, Ben Hecht, Charles MacArthur; w, Ben Hecht, Charles MacArthur; ph, Lee Garmes; ed, Arthur Ellis; art d, Walter E. Keller

AA Best Original Story: Ben Hecht, Charles MacArthur

This is a smart-set literati piece starring Noel Coward as a New York publisher who is a marionette master, pulling the strings of everyone around him while scattering bons mots like rose petals. He is a charming heel who loves 'em, leaves 'em, and remains the main topic of conversation at swank hotels, various watering spots, and brittle cocktail parties. Julie Haydon, a young author, is in love with Stanley Ridges, and Coward means to break them up and make her his own. Meanwhile, he meets his female counterpart in Hope Williams, who is just as world-weary, cynical, and cunning as he is. Coward gets aboard a Bermuda-bound flight which crashes, killing everyone aboard. But he gets a new lease on life and is allowed to return to this world, never to rest until he finds someone, anyone, who mourns his passing. In the end, Coward makes peace with his Maker and is allowed to have eternal salvation. The metaphysical conclusion left many in the audience wondering what it all meant, and some of the actors were mystified as well. The picture is mostly talk with very little action. Coming off their sensational debut as co-authors-directors-producers of CRIME WITHOUT PASSION, Ben Hecht and Charles MacArthur made the virtually unreleasable ONCE IN A BLUE MOON. (It was held for a year before it was let slip out.) They followed up with this movie, which must be one of the earliest existential films produced. Hecht and MacArthur were not true directors who knew how to make the screen dance with images, and their lack of expertise is evident throughout. Yet the wonderful words spoken by almost everyone in the cast keep the movie afloat. To star in their original work, which owes a bit to the Hecht novel *Fantazius Mallare* and to his well-known *A Jew In Love*, they chose Noel Coward, who was making his talking picture debut after having done a silent juvenile bit in Griffith's HEARTS OF THE WORLD in 1918. This movie was made at the Astoria, Long Island, lot and was a favorite of sophisticates, pseudo-sophisticates, and anyone who could recognize the real-life people upon whom the screenplay was based.

SCREAM

1996 100m c Horror ★★★½
Wes Craven Films/Woods Entertainment/Dimension Films R/18
(U.S.)

Neve Campbell *(Sidney)*, Drew Barrymore *(Casey)*, Skeet Ulrich *(Billy)*, Courteney Cox *(Gale Weathers)*, David Arquette *(Dewey)*, Rose McGowan *(Tatum)*, Matthew Lillard *(Stuart)*, Henry Winkler *(Principal Himbry)*, Lawrence Hecht *(Mr. Prescott)*, Jamie Kennedy *(Randy)*

p, Cary Woods, Cathy Konrad; d, Wes Craven; w, Kevin Williamson; ph, Mark Irwin; ed, Patrick Lussier; m, Marco Beltrami; prod d, Bruce Alan Miller; art d, David Lubin; fx, Frank Ceglia, Kamar Bitar; cos, Mathew Clayton Hooey, Gary J. Saldutti

Director Wes Craven continues his reign as one of horror's kingpins with this self-reflexive twist on "dead-teen" movies. The film mixes sly humor and grisly deaths into a tale that both updates and satirizes the slasher genre.

Small-town virgin Sidney Prescott (Neve Campbell) is being stalked by a masked psycho-killer who's already slaughtered two of her class-mates and may have also murdered her mom—exactly one year earlier. Is it the video store geek (Jamie Kennedy)? Sidney's hunky and too-good-to-be-true boyfriend Billy (Skeet Ulrich)? Her dad (Lawrence Hecht), who's supposedly away on business but can't be located? Class weirdo Stuart (Matthew Lillard), who's dating Sidney's perky best friend (Rose McGowan)? The high-strung, teen-hating school principal (Henry Winkler)? Or could it be the janitor in the Freddy Krueger sweater?

Unlike most modern horror movies, which are little more than exploitation cash cows, director Craven and scriptwriter Kevin Williamson have created a surprisingly clever thriller, which embraces the genre even as it subverts it. It's fast-paced and complex enough to keep viewers guessing, and while never aiming for outright comedy, the in-jokes will get laughs from knowing viewers. Better still, in a change from the teen horror films of the 80s, the cast actually has an opportunity to act! Campbell is sympathetic as the emotionally abused (but strong-willed) heroine; McGowan is full of attitude and sex appeal, and Drew Barrymore's small but pivotal role sets the edgy tone for the entire film. But above all, this is Craven's show. He knows how to ladle on the thrills, get an audience to jump, or pull back for a laugh.

SEA HAWK, THE

1940 126m bw Romance/Adventure/War ★★★★★
Warner Bros. (U.S.) /U

Errol Flynn *(Capt. Geoffrey Thorpe)*, Brenda Marshall *(Donna Maria Alvarez de Cordoba)*, Claude Rains *(Don Jose Alvarez de Cordoba)*, Flora Robson *(Queen Elizabeth)*, Donald Crisp *(Sir John Burleson)*, Henry Daniell *(Lord Wolfingham)*, Alan Hale *(Carl Pitt)*, Una O'Con-nor *(Martha)*, William Lundigan *(Danny Logan)*, James Stephenson *(Abbott)*

p, Henry Blanke; d, Michael Curtiz; w, Howard Koch, Seton I. Miller; ph, Sol Polito; ed, George Amy; m, Erich Wolfgang Korngold; art d, Anton Grot; fx, Byron Haskin, H.F. Koenekamp; cos, Orry-Kelly

AAN Best Score: Erich Wolfgang Korngold; *AAN Best Art Direction:* Anton Grot; *AAN Best Sound:* Nathan Levinsony; *AAN Best Visual Effects:* Byron Haskin, Nathan Levinson

First class, rousing adventure with the inimitable Flynn swashing away, aided by top Curtiz direction and bracing Korngold score. Everything else clicks, too: the cinematography of Sol Polito, terrific Warners production values and a cast of character actors hard to match in any era.

As the film opens, Spain's King Philip II (Montagu Love) instructs his advisors to devise a plan to conquer England and continental Europe. To placate England's Queen Elizabeth (Flora Robson), he sends Don Jose Alvarez de Cordoba (Claude Rains), his crafty ambas-sador, to soothe the Virgin Queen's fears and disguise Spain's inten-tions. En route, the Spanish galleon carrying Don Jose and his niece, Donna Maria (Brenda Marshall), is sunk by a British ship commanded by Geoffrey Thorpe (Flynn). The dashing captain takes the indignant ambassador and Maria on board, bringing them safely to England. Despite his fine manners, Thorpe is a dedicated "Sea Hawk," one of a half-dozen British sea captains who foresee war and have been raiding Spanish coastal forts and seizing Philip's treasures to fund a British fleet, all with Elizabeth's unofficial approval. Although Thorpe's gal-lantry soon wins over Maria, Don Jose intrigues to capture him in Panama, where Spanish forces waylay the Englishman.

Warners lavished a then-staggering $1.7 million on THE SEA HAWK, with gorgeous results. The 31-year-old Flynn, at the peak of his spectacular career, is magnificent in his swashbuckling role; Mar-shall was never more radiant; Rains is deliciously evil; and Robson makes a wonderfully witty and intelligent Elizabeth. Eschew shortened versions; you want all 127 minutes.

SEA OF LOVE

1989 113m c Mystery/Thriller ★★★½
Martin Bregman (U.S.) R/18

Al Pacino *(Frank Keller)*, Ellen Barkin *(Helen)*, John Goodman *(Sher-man)*, Michael Rooker *(Terry)*, William Hickey *(Frank Keller, Sr.)*, Richard Jenkins *(Gruber)*, Paul Calderon *(Serafino)*, Gene Canfield *(Struk)*, Larry Joshua *(Dargan)*, John Spencer *(Lieutenant)*

p, Martin Bregman, Louis A. Stroller; d, Harold Becker; w, Richard Price; ph, Ronnie Taylor; ed, David Bretherton; m, Trevor Jones; prod d, John Jay Moore; cos, Betsy Cox

A thriller featuring a mysterious femme fatale, an involving plot, and some nice offbeat twists, SEA OF LOVE owes a good deal to Hitch-cock, and to such recent efforts as FATAL ATTRACTION and JAG-GED EDGE, though it can claim plenty of originality as well. Several men who have responded to the personals in a popular New York magazine have been found murdered in their beds. Twenty-year veteran cop Frank Keller (Al Pacino), a stressed-out borderline alcoholic, and Sherman (John Goodman), a jolly family man, team up to track the killer, planting an ad and "dating" the respondents. Breaking the first rule of investigation, Keller gets deeply involved with one respondent, a tough and savvy single mother (Ellen Barkin). He becomes caught in a web of infatuation and rough, steamy sex, despite signs that she might be the killer. Beyond its slight (though satisfying) plot, SEA OF LOVE's strength lies in the realism of its characterizations. Writer Richard Price is a master at contriving sympathetic, believable charac-ters. His dialogue here, the skewed, elliptical jargon of urban social maneuvering, is dead on. Director Harold Becker (THE ONION FIELD; TAPS) skillfully and unobtrusively supports the drama with just the right lighting, details, and mood. Pacino gives perhaps his best film performance since DOG DAY AFTERNOON; Barkin matches him well as the hard-bitten, voraciously carnal suspect. SEA OF LOVE captures the emotional risk and false hope of the urban singles scene so accurately it's almost painful to watch.

SEA WOLF, THE

1941 100m bw Drama ★★★★
Warner Bros. (U.S.) /PG

Edward G. Robinson *(Wolf Larsen)*, John Garfield *(George Leach)*, Ida Lupino *(Ruth Webster)*, Alexander Knox *(Humphrey Van Wey-den)*, Gene Lockhart *(Dr. Louie Prescott)*, Barry Fitzgerald *(Cooky)*, Stanley Ridges *(Johnson)*, Francis McDonald *(Svenson)*, David Bruce *(Young Sailor)*, Howard da Silva *(Harrison)*

p, Henry Blanke; d, Michael Curtiz; w, Robert Rossen (based on the novel by Jack London); ph, Sol Polito; ed, George Amy; m, Erich Wolfgang Korngold; art d, Anton Grot; fx, Byron Haskin, H.F. Koenekamp

AAN Best Visual Effects: Byron Haskin, Nathan Levinson

After a ferryboat capsizes in a fog-shrouded sea, the scavenger ship the *Ghost* picks up two survivors: Knox, an author and scholar, and the sad, sick Lupino. Captained by the brutal, callous Robinson—who rules his seagoing fiefdom both by physical might and strategic cunning—the *Ghost* is manned by shanghaied sailors who have been pressed into service with belaying pins and Mickey Finns in the old British way, except for Garfield, a surly young sailor who has signed on to escape the clutches of the law. Robinson refuses to take Knox and Lupino to shore. Instead, he presses them both into service, telling the reluctant but somewhat fascinated Knox, "You're soft, like a woman. This voyage ought to do you a lot of good." To humiliate the scholar, but also to gain his company—for the cruel captain is a secret intellectual who, when closeted in his cabin, reads poetry and philosophy—Robinson makes Knox the cabin boy for the duration of the voyage. In this servitude, Knox functions as a captive intellectual audience of one for Robinson as the captain elucidates his Nietzschean superman theories. During one of these discourses, Robinson is suddenly seized with a headache that is literally blinding. He attempts to hide this fact, both because he despises weakness and because his condition threatens his absolute control over his crew. Robinson exerts authority over his men more in the manner of a chess master than a ship's master, manipulating them mentally, divining their weaknesses, and dividing them in order to conquer them. As his condition worsens, however, he becomes locked into a relationship of mutual dependence and fascination with Knox which becomes the ultimate test of each man's character.

THE SEA WOLF contains little of the prolixity of Jack London's philosophically oriented novel, yet it is true to the spirit of the book. The megalomania of the ship's master is wonderfully expressed in Edward G. Robinson's fine portrayal of the contemptuous captain. Alexander Knox's reserve makes a perfect foil for Robinson's sneering bombast; in his screen debut, this fine stage actor is beautifully restrained. Ida Lupino, in her role as a loser, gives one of her best screen performances; John Garfield is also fine as her masculine counterpart; and a laudable assemblage of Warner Bros. stock-company character actors ably supports the leads. Required to work a romance into London's all-male work to satisfy studio formula, screenwriter Robert Rossen did very well with the unenviable task. He added the characters played by Garfield and Lupino, which help flesh out the story, substituting for the novel's uncinematic dialogue. Warner's all-purpose director, Michael Curtiz, performed up to par, shooting all the seafaring scenes in studio tanks. THE SEA WOLF earned an Oscar nomination for Best Special Effects. Erich Wolfgang Korngold's score melds well with the excellent sound effects—the constant creaking of timbers under stress, the whipping of ratlines—that create the ambience of a ship at sea.

SEANCE ON A WET AFTERNOON

1964   115m   bw   Crime   ★★★★
Beaver/Allied   (U.K.)   /A

Kim Stanley *(Myra Savage)*, Richard Attenborough *(Billy Savage)*, Mark Eden *(Charles Clayton)*, Nanette Newman *(Mrs. Clayton)*, Judith Donner *(Amanda Clayton)*, Patrick Magee *(Supt. Walsh)*, Gerald Sim *(Sgt. Beedle)*, Margaret Lacey *(Woman at 1st Seance)*, Maria Kazan *(Other Woman at Seance)*, Lionel Gamlin *(Man at Seances)*

p, Richard Attenborough, Bryan Forbes; d, Bryan Forbes; w, Bryan Forbes (based on the novel by Mark McShane); ph, Gerry Turpin; ed, Derek York; m, John Barry; art d, Ray Simm

AAN Best Actress: Kim Stanley

In this eerie tale, Myra Savage (Kim Stanley), a medium, claims contact with "the other side" through her late son Arthur, a stillborn child whose death Myra cannot come to accept. Myra's husband, Billy (Richard Attenborough, the British actor who would later direct MAGIC, CRY FREEDOM, and GANDHI), does his best to keep her happy, knowing well that she is walking a tightrope between insanity and rationality. He is a weak man and adores Myra, so he can deny her nothing. Myra would like some publicity for her flagging business, so she concocts a plan to have Billy kidnap a wealthy child and collect his ransom. Myra will then offer the services of her psychic powers to the bereaved family and, of course, "find" the child. An atmospheric film, SEANCE ON A WET AFTERNOON succeeds because of Bryan Forbes' excellent

direction and the superb performances of both Kim Stanley (in a rare film appearance) and Attenborough (who also produced). While the film can be slow going in spots, Stanley's portrayal of the emotionally unfit Myra Savage is riveting as she gradually loses her grip on reality and slips into a dark psychological abyss.

SEARCH, THE

1948   105m   bw   Drama   ★★★★
Prasens   (U.S.)   /U

Montgomery Clift *(Ralph Stevenson)*, Aline MacMahon *(Mrs. Murray)*, Jarmila Novotna *(Mrs. Malik)*, Wendell Corey *(Jerry Fisher)*, Ivan Jandl *(Karel Malik)*, Mary Patton *(Mrs. Fisher)*, Ewart G. Morrison *(Mr. Crookes)*, William Rogers *(Tom Fisher)*, Leopold Borkowski *(Joel Makowsky)*, Claude Gambier *(Raoul Dubois)*

p, Lazar Wechsler; d, Fred Zinnemann; w, Richard Schweizer, David Wechsler, Paul Jarrico; ph, Emil Berna; ed, Hermann Haller; m, Robert Blum

AAN Best Actor: Montgomery Clift; *AAN Best Director:* Fred Zinnemann; *AA Best Story:* Richard Schweizer, David Wechsler; *AAN Best Screenplay:* Richard Schweizer, David Wechsler

Clift was making his first movie, RED RIVER, when he was approached by Zinnemann to read the first draft of the script by Peter Viertel, and he liked it enough to commit to making THE SEARCH (which, as it turned out, was released before RED RIVER). When Swiss producer Wechsler hired his son to help rewrite the screenplay, Clift became angered and began to substitute his own words for those in the script. Attorneys were called in to mediate, and, in the end, the younger Wechsler and co-author Schweizer won an Oscar for a screenplay that contained many of Clift's words.

THE SEARCH begins in a camp for children who have been orphaned or displaced by WWII. Among them is Jandl, a traumatized 9-year-old Czech who hasn't seen his mother since he was torn from her arms at the age of five. Frightened, Jandl escapes from a Red Cross ambulance; soon, he's living like a frightened animal in the burnt-out houses of the city, foraging for food in trash cans. He is nearly starved when Clift, an American soldier, finds him and takes him home. Jandl is hostile, fearful, and makes attempts to leave, but Clift begins to convince the boy of his good intentions. Clift attempts to trace Jandl's history with the help of his pal Corey, but it's a brick wall. Meanwhile, Jandl's mother, Novotna, continues her search for the boy.

A rather saccharine ending mars the believablity of the plot, and audiences might have liked it better if Novotna's character were not so wonderful and Jandl had gotten a new lease on life by going to the US with Clift. Zinnemann and Clift received Oscar nominations and Jandl won a special juvenile Oscar for his haunting portrayal of the tragic child. Jandl was discovered singing with a youth choir in Prague, and, after this picture, it was just assumed that he would stay in films, but his parents refused, and he disappeared from sight. Zinnemann had been with MGM, but they dropped his contract while he was shooting this film, so he signed with RKO. However, after the picture was released, Zinnemann's star again rose, so they re-signed him for a great deal more money. THE SEARCH was shot entirely in the American Occupied Zone of Germany, the first movie to be made there after the war. With THE SEARCH and RED RIVER released the same year, Clift became a huge star and was given a *Life* magazine cover. Only 27, he received $75,000 for this film. He brought along his friend and mentor, Mira Rostova, who stood behind the camera and gave her approval on each scene. Zinnemann objected to this, so she stayed away but spent almost every night before shooting going over each nuance of the next day's pages. Only four professional actors appeared in the movie: Clift, who was under contract to Howard Hawks; Corey, on loan from Hal Wallis; Novotna, an opera star at the Met; and MacMahon. The others were locals, and their unfamiliar presence lent an air of credibility to the project. This superior movie made the world aware of the plight of these children and money poured in to the UNRRA to help their plight.

SEARCHERS, THE

1956 119m c Western ★★★★★
Warner Bros. (U.S.) /PG

John Wayne (*Ethan Edwards*), Jeffrey Hunter (*Martin Pawley*), Vera Miles (*Laurie Jorgensen*), Ward Bond (*Capt. Rev. Samuel Clayton*), Natalie Wood (*Debbie Edwards*), John Qualen (*Lars Jorgensen*), Olive Carey (*Mrs. Jorgensen*), Henry Brandon (*Chief Scar*), Ken Curtis (*Charlie McCorry*), Harry Carey Jr. (*Brad Jorgensen*)

p, Merian C. Cooper, C.V. Whitney; d, John Ford; w, Frank S. Nugent (based on the novel by Alan LeMay); ph, Winton C. Hoch; ed, Jack Murray; m, Max Steiner; art d, Frank Hotaling, James Basevi; fx, George Brown; cos, Frank Beetson, Ann Peck

"What makes a man to wander?/What makes a man to roam?/What makes a man leave bed and board and turn his back on home?/Ride away, ride away, ride away."

This sad and beautiful song accompanies the opening credits of what may be the finest and most ambitious film from director John Ford, America's premier poet of the Western. Part of what makes this classic film so remarkable is that these questions are never answered directly—an oddity for a product of Hollywood where loose ends are rarely allowed. This is the ultimate cult film for the new Hollywood. It is quoted and alluded to in numerous films such as HARDCORE, TAXI DRIVER, CLOSE ENCOUNTERS OF THE THIRD KIND, and STAR WARS.

As THE SEARCHERS begins, we hear the extraordinarily beautiful strains of Max Steiner's score over darkness. A cabin door opens to reveal the harsh beauty of the arid Monument Valley in the distance. The silhouette of a frontier woman moves into the doorway. Far beyond we see a tiny figure on horseback approaching. "Ethan?" queries the woman uncertainly. The figure dismounts and walks toward the house. The woman is Martha Edwards (Dorothy Jordan), the wife of Ethan's brother. She is joined on the porch by her husband, Aaron (Walter Coy), their teenaged daughter, Lucy (Pippa Scott), 10-year-old Debbie (Lana Wood), and teenaged Ben (Robert Lyden). Ethan's clothes are filthy and he wears a faded Confederate coat. The children chant "Uncle Ethan! Uncle Ethan!" Ethan Edwards has finally come home—three years after the end of the Civil War.

John Wayne gives the performance of his career as Ethan Edwards, one of the most intriguing characters the American cinema has given us. Ethan is a mysterious obsessive man who rides in from the waste-lands of Monument Valley into a small frontier farm settled by his brother years earlier. He has been missing since the end of the Civil War in which he fought for the Confederacy. He never turned up at the surrender to give up his sword and saber. He is also inexplicably carrying a large quantity of gold and, in the words of the local captain of the Texas Rangers, Reverend Samuel Clayton (Ward Bond), Ethan "fits a lot of descriptions."

The last family member to arrive is Martin Pawley (Jeffrey Hunter). Now nearly grown, Martin was saved years ago by Ethan when his parents were slaughtered by Indians. Ethan left him in the care of Aaron, who has raised him as his own son, but because Martin is one-eighth Cherokee, Ethan now treats him as a boarder rather than as one of the family.

The tranquility of the Edwards' lives is shattered when the local Commanche tribe goes on the warpath. Most of the men are lured away from the farm and the Edwards' farm is attacked. Most of the family is brutally murdered and the two daughters are abducted. The men form a search party and go off in hot pursuit. The ravaged body of the older girl is found and buried while the search for Debbie continues. When the winter snows come, most of the men turn back. Ethan is undaunted by this temporary setback. He and Martin resolve to continue the search and they do—for seven years. As the months drag on, Martin is amazed by Ethan's knowledge of the Indians' ways and his ability to read their signs and speak their language, but comes to realize that his guide is also a fanatical racist who intends to kill Debbie when they find her because she has become a "squaw."

THE SEARCHERS is an extremely rich film that continues to reveal new nuances with each viewing. The genre's traditional opposition between "Civilization" and "Wilderness" has rarely been as powerfully represented dramatically or visually. Ethan sees himself as an agent of civilization but his skills ally him with the forces of wilderness. He can find nowhere where he can be at peace and accepted. His difficulty in accepting a Native American as part of his family mirrors America's tensions regarding civil rights and integration in the 1950s. In a genre that has often be justly condemned for its racism, THE SEARCHERS—while hardly politically correct by modern standards—was a major breakthrough for Ford, Wayne, and the genre. The traditional Western hero and the Cavalry is shown in an unusually critical light. Furthermore the Native American point of view is considered for a change. By balancing points of view, Ford deepens and informs our understanding of the story. Equally well managed is the film's balance of drama and humor. THE SEARCHERS is essentially a tragedy, and without its humorous passages the film would have been almost too grim to bear (as was Alan LeMay's novel). The humor grows out of and illuminates character; even the hard-driven Ethan reveals a sense of irony and wit.

Ford's poetic visual sensibility has never been more richly demonstrated. The film provides an opportunity for numerous striking portraits of John Wayne set against the western vistas in color and widescreen. If you had to pick an ultimate Western still, it would probably come from this film. THE SEARCHERS is also that rare sound film in which more is revealed through facial expression, physical stance, and subtle gesture than through dialogue. Deep and complex insights into characters are all beautifully conveyed by body language. All in all, this is about as good as Hollywood filmmaking gets. A deeply emotional experience that is also a grand entertainment, THE SEARCHERS is a true American masterpiece.

SEARCHING FOR BOBBY FISCHER

1993 110m c Drama ★★★½
Paramount/Mirage Productions (U.S.) PG

Max Pomeranc (*Josh Waitzkin*), Joe Mantegna (*Fred Waitzkin*), Joan Allen (*Bonnie Waitzkin*), Ben Kingsley (*Bruce Pandolfini*), Laurence Fishburne (*Vinnie*), Michael Nirenberg (*Jonathan Poe*), Robert Stephens (*Poe's Teacher*), David Paymer (*Kalev*), William H. Macy (*Tunafish Father*), Dan Hedaya (*Tournament Director*)

p, Scott Rudin, William Horberg; d, Steve Zaillian; w, Steve Zaillian (from the book by Fred Waitzkin); ph, Conrad L. Hall; ed, Wayne Wahrman; m, James Horner; prod d, David Gropman; art d, Gregory Keen; cos, Julie Weiss

AAN Best Cinematography: Conrad L. Hall

A rare family film that's not afraid to inject conflict and complexity into its images of domestic happiness.

Based on the real-life story of chess prodigy Josh Waitzkin, SEARCHING begins with the seven-year-old boy (Max Pomeranc) becoming enthralled by the matches he sees being played in New York's Washington Square Park. Josh, it turns out, harbors a rare talent for the game and, encouraged by his sportswriter father (Joe Mantegna), begins to learn more about it from two markedly different teachers: Vinnie (Laurence Fishburne), a kind of chess bum who apparently lives in the park and plays with a fast, streetwise style; and Bruce Pandolfini (Ben Kingsley), a reclusive scholar with a purist intellectual approach. Josh soon becomes a chess star, moving some to compare him to the young Bobby Fischer. (Excerpts from Fischer's life are narrated in voice-over by Josh, providing a poignant parallel to his own story.) Success, however, brings the inevitable pitfalls. His father's support starts to look like obsession, causing friction within the family; and Josh's confidence and innocence are fractured by the appearance of a brilliant young rival.

Though SEARCHING finally ties up its loose ends a little too neatly, what comes before that is a joy; an engrossing, witty story about far more than chess, directed with a flawless eye for detail and superbly performed by some of the best actors around—including young Mr. Pomeranc.

SECONDS

1966 106m bw Mystery/Thriller ★★★★
Paramount (U.S.) /X

Rock Hudson (*Antiochus "Tony" Wilson*), Salome Jens (*Nora Marcus*), John Randolph (*Arthur Hamilton*), Will Geer (*Old Man*), Jeff Corey (*Mr. Ruby*), Richard Anderson (*Dr. Innes*), Murray Hamilton (*Charlie Evans*), Karl Swenson (*Dr. Morris*), Khigh Dhiegh (*Davalo*), Frances Reid (*Emily Hamilton*) p, Edward Lewis; d, John Frankenheimer; w, Lewis John Carlino (based on the novel *Seconds* by David Ely); ph, James Wong Howe; ed, Ferris Webster, David Webster; m, Jerry Goldsmith; art d, Ted Haworth

AAN Best Cinematography: James Wong Howe

Middle-aged New York businessman Arthur Hamilton (John Randolph) is blackmailed into accepting the services of a clandestine organization which provides paunchy middle-aged businessmen with new lives through plastic surgery, physical reconditioning and reckless career placement. The end result is that Arthur Hamilton is transformed into Tony Wilson (Rock Hudson), a swinging bachelor and abstract painter with a groovy pad by the California seashore, a girlfriend (Salome Jens), and a butler (Wesley Addy) who is unusually anxious for his boss to indulge in heavy partying activities. Unfortunately, Tony Wilson still acts a lot like Arthur Hamilton: he can't hold his liquor and he's afraid of girls. After hosting a disastrous cocktail party for some of his neighbors, Wilson is shipped back to corporate headquarters for some fine tuning. He's willing to give it another try and has some thoughtful suggestions for his next "placement" and for the future of the program. The Old Man (Will Geer), the founder of the organization that got him into this mess in the first place, is appreciative, but nonetheless has other ideas for the body of Tony Wilson and the soul of Arthur Hamilton.

SECONDS received mixed reviews, and was critically savaged at the Cannes Film Festival, but repeated showings on late night television have improved its reputation to the point where it is now considered a cult classic. The film features a surprisingly good performance by Rock Hudson, an impeccable supporting cast and stunning cinematography by screen veteran James Wong Howe.

SECRET AGENT

1936   83m   bw   Spy   ★★★½
Gaumont   (U.K.)   /U

Madeleine Carroll *(Elsa Carrington)*, John Gielgud *(Edgar Brodie/Richard Ashenden)*, Peter Lorre *(The General)*, Robert Young *(Robert Marvin)*, Percy Marmont *(Caypor)*, Florence Kahn *(Mrs. Caypor)*, Lilli Palmer *(Lilli)*, Charles Carson *("R")*, Michel Saint-Denis *(Coachman)*, Andreas Malandrinos *(Manager)*

p, Michael Balcon, Ivor Montagu; d, Alfred Hitchcock; w, Charles Bennett, Ian Hay, Jesse Lasky Jr., Alma Reville (based on the play by Campbell Dixon, from the stories "Triton" and "The Hairless Mexican" in the book *Ashenden* by W. Somerset Maugham); ph, Bernard Knowles; ed, Charles Frend; cos, Joe Strassner

One of a string of British espionage thrillers Hitchcock directed in the mid-1930s (THE 39 STEPS preceded it in 1935 and SABOTAGE followed in 1936), this one begins in England, 1916, with the funeral of war hero and famed novelist Edgar Brodie (Gielgud). The funeral is a ruse, however, with Brodie still very much alive and in the service of British Intelligence. He is given a new identity, Richard Ashenden, and sent to Switzerland to terminate an enemy agent—although no one knows the identity or description of the agent. Also assigned to the mission are agents Elsa Carrington (Carroll), who is undercover as Ashenden's wife, and The General (Lorre), a demented, sexually charged, professional killer, and together they chase through the Swiss Alps to carry out their operation. SECRET AGENT bursts with not-so-hidden sexual innuendos and a heavy dose of comic dialogue, as well as Lorre's unrestrained lunatic comic performance. Based on two Somerset Maugham stories (for the espionage angle) and a Campbell Dixon play (for the romance), SECRET AGENT did not perform at the box office as well as Hitchcock had hoped. Although the director has cited this film among his favorites, he felt that its fault was in having a main character with whom the audience could not identify. London-based animator Len Lye (who had, in 1934, invented a technique for painting directly on film) had created, for the climactic train crash scene, a piece of brightly colored film which was to make it appear as if the film itself had burst into flames. Proving too much of a distraction, the effect was eliminated in the film's preview screenings.

SECRET GARDEN, THE

1993   101m   c   Children's/Drama   ★★★
American Zoetrope/Warner Bros.   (U.S.)   G/U

Kate Maberly *(Mary Lennox)*, Heydon Prowse *(Colin Craven)*, Andrew Knott *(Dickon)*, Maggie Smith *(Mrs. Medlock)*, Laura Crossley *(Martha)*, John Lynch *(Lord Craven)*, Walter Sparrow *(Ben Weatherstaff)*, Irene Jacob *(Mary's Mother/Lilias Craven)*, Frank Baker *(Government Official)*, Valerie Hill *(Cook)*

p, Fred Fuchs, Fred Roos, Tom Luddy; d, Agnieszka Holland; w, Caroline Thompson (from the novel by Frances Hodgson Burnett); ph, Roger Deakins; ed, Isabelle Lorente; prod d, Stuart Craig; art d, Peter Russell; fx, John Evans, Digby Milner, Peter Dawson, Peter Pickering, Simon Hewitt; cos, Marit Allen

Polish director Agnieszka Holland, who scored an art-house hit in the US with EUROPA, EUROPA, deserved to find her way into the hearts of a larger audience with this reworking of Frances Hodgson Burnett's classic childrens' tale. Though it can get laborious, and produces the odd unintended chuckle, THE SECRET GARDEN is charming and sometimes chillingly authentic.

At the center of the film is young Mary Lennox, winningly played by English actress Kate Maberly in her feature debut. Orphaned by an earthquake in India, Mary is sent to a forbidding Gothic house in the north of England to be looked after by her widower uncle, Lord Craven (John Lynch). Since he wants nothing to do with her, she is effectively left in the charge of the dour, mean-spirited housekeeper, Mrs. Medlock (Maggie Smith). Things look rather grim until Mary discovers a garden that her aunt had tended and that Craven declared off-limits after her death, as well as a companion on each side of the great English class divide: Colin (Heydon Prowse), Craven's invalid son; and Dickon (Andrew Knott), a young, Yorkshire Dr. Dolittle who walks and talks with the animals.

While there's nothing subtle about the story's metaphors of growth and rebirth, Holland avoids cliches as deftly as she does the hero/villain syndrome. The dark, oppressive characters have reasons for being that way, and Mary and Colin can be just as obnoxious as they are sympathetic.

SECRET LIFE OF WALTER MITTY, THE

1947   105m   c   Fantasy/Comedy   ★★★★
Goldwyn   (U.S.)   /U

Danny Kaye *(Walter Mitty)*, Virginia Mayo *(Rosalind van Hoorn)*, Boris Karloff *(Dr. Hugo Hollingshead)*, Fay Bainter *(Mrs. Mitty)*, Ann Rutherford *(Gertrude Griswold)*, Thurston Hall *(Bruce Pierce)*, Konstantin Shayne *(Peter van Hoorn)*, Florence Bates *(Mrs. Griswold)*, Gordon Jones *(Tubby Wadsworth)*, Reginald Denny *(RAF Colonel)*

p, Samuel Goldwyn; d, Norman Z. McLeod; w, Ken Englund, Everett Freeman (based on the story by James Thurber); ph, Lee Garmes; ed, Monica Collingwood; m, David Raksin; art d, George Jenkins, Perry Ferguson; fx, John P. Fulton; cos, Irene Sharaff

Though James Thurber offered to give producer Sam Goldwyn $10,000 *not to* film his classic short story, the rights to which Goldwyn had purchased, THE SECRET LIFE OF WALTER MITTY is still an outstanding production and possibly Kaye's best film. Thurber's tale about a middle-aged man who escapes reality by imagining himself in all sorts of heroic situations doesn't lose much in the film adaptation.

Though it slips into slapstick toward the end, THE SECRET LIFE OF WALTER MITTY is enjoyable and presents more genuinely funny scenes than most comedies. Goldwyn sank more than $3 million into this sumptuous showcase for Kaye, parading his statuesque Goldwyn Girls through some of the star's big musical numbers. Mayo is alluring, Bainter is terrific as the overbearing mom, and Hall stands out as the ghoulish publisher. Without the aid of makeup, Karloff also does a great burlesque of himself as the monster from FRANKENSTEIN. And throughout the film there is that memorable sound of Kaye's imaginary life-saving machine—"pucketa, pucketa, pucketa."

SECRET OF NIMH, THE

1982 82m c Animated/Children's ★★★
MGM-UA (U.S.) G/U

VOICES OF: Derek Jacobi (*Nicodemus*), Elizabeth Hartman (*Mrs. Brisby*), Arthur Malet (*Ages*), Dom DeLuise (*Jeremy*), Hermione Baddeley (*Auntie Shrew*), John Carradine (*Great Owl*), Peter Strauss (*Justin*), Paul Shenar (*Jennar*), Tom Hattan (*Farmer Fitzgibbons*), Shannen Doherty (*Teresa*)

p, Don Bluth, Gary Goldman, John Pomeroy; d, Don Bluth; w, Don Bluth, Gary Goldman, John Pomeroy, Will Finn (based on the novel *Mrs. Frisby and the Rats of N.I.M.H.* by Robert C. O'Brien); ph, Joe Jiuliano, Charles Warren, Jeff Mellquist; ed, Jeffrey Patch; m, Jerry Goldsmith; fx, D.A. Lanpher, Tom Hush

This superbly animated (but weakly scripted) tale was produced by Don Bluth, who left Disney Studios when he became dissatisfied with the quality of their animated films in the 1970s, taking a dozen of Disney's best animators with him. The result is a return to the lush, finely detailed animation seen in the best Disney features. This is the story of a mother mouse's desperate attempt to move her family to a new location before they are killed by the farmer who is soon to plow his field. Although hindered by her son's illness, the mother mouse gets help from some escaped laboratory rats with superior intelligence. Among the actors who lend their vocal talents to the proceedings are Dom DeLuise and the fine British stage actor Derek Jacobi.

SECRET OF ROAN INISH, THE

1995 102m c Fantasy/Romance/Children's ★★★½
Skerry Movies Corporation/Peter Newman Productions (U.S.) PG/

Jeni Courtney (*Fiona Coneelly*), Mick Lally (*Hugh Coneelly*), Eileen Colgan (*Tess Coneelly*), Richard Sheridan (*Eamon*), John Lynch (*Tadhg*), Cillian Byrne (*Jamie*), Susan Lynch (*Selkie Woman*), Frankie McCafferty, Fergal McElheron, Brendan Conroy

p, Maggie Renzi, Sarah Green; d, John Sayles; w, John Sayles (based on the book *The Secret of Ron Mor Skerry* by Rosalie K. Fry); ph, Haskell Wexler; ed, John Sayles; m, Mason Daring; prod d, Adrian Smith; art d, Henry Harris; fx, Trevor Neighbour; cos, Consolata Boyle

A change of pace from filmmaker John Sayles, better known for realistic dramas, this is a lush, allegorical fairy tale filmed in Ireland. Darkly lyrical and imbued with a genuine sense of magic, ROAN INISH has the haunted quality of Irish folk music.

In late 1940s Ireland, an unemployed widower sends his young daughter, Fiona (Jeni Courtney), to live with her grandparents, Tess (Eileen Colgan) and Hugh Coneelly (Mick Lally), in a northwest coast fishing village. Hugh tells Fiona the story of how, years earlier, her baby brother, Jamie, was swept out to sea in his cradle, and Fiona becomes obsessed with finding the boy. Fiona's search begins on the nearby island of Roan Inish ("seal island"), where she soon finds herself on the trail of a mysterious half-human sea creature called the Selkie.

During the 1980s, John Sayles earned a reputation as a maker of serious, topical independent films about worthy subjects. Ironically, this seemingly innocuous children's fantasy is his most satisfying film to date. Thanks to his earnest, straightforward approach to unlikely material (the source is a 1957 novella, *Secret of the Ron Mor Skerry*, by Rosalie K. Fry), Sayles ends up tempering the excesses of what might have been sentimental blarney. Here, he creates a fresh, captivating mise-en-scene, simultaneously realistic and magical (Haskell Wexler's cinematography of the Irish locales is crucial here). A highlight is the Selkie myth, which is depicted with a refreshing minimum of camera tricks and special effects. Another great sequence is the Old Hollywood-style montage illustrating the children's rebuilding of the cottage on Roan Inish. In all, this is family entertainment in the best sense of the term.

SECRETS & LIES

1995 142m c Drama ★★★★½
CiBy 2000/Thin Man Films (U.K.) R/15

Timothy Spall (*Maurice*), Phyllis Logan (*Monica*), Brenda Blethyn (*Cynthia*), Claire Rushbrook (*Roxanne*), Marianne Jean-Baptiste (*Hortense*), Elizabeth Berrington (*Jane*), Michele Austin (*Dionne*), Lee Ross (*Paul*), Lesley Manville (*Social Worker*), Ron Cook (*Stuart*)

p, Simon Channing-Williams; d, Mike Leigh; w, Mike Leigh; ph, Dick Pope; ed, John Gregory; m, Andrew Dickson; prod d, Alison Chitty, Georgina Lowe; cos, Maria Price

AAN Best Picture; *AAN Best Actress:* Brenda Blethyn; *AAN Best Supporting Actress:* Marianne Jean-Baptiste; *AAN Best Director:* Mike Leigh; *AAN Best Original Screenplay:* Mike Leigh

Winner of the Palme d'Or at Cannes, Mike Leigh's SECRETS & LIES is a fascinating, brilliantly acted slice-of-life drama.

After the death of her adoptive mother, Hortense (Marianne Jean-Baptiste), a young black woman living in London, learns that Cynthia (Brenda Blethyn), a white, middle-aged single parent, is her birth mother. When Hortense telephones her, Cynthia is initially shocked, but agrees to meet her at a coffeeshop. When they see each other, Cynthia assumes there has been a mistake, until she remembers having had a one-night stand with a black man. The two develop an understanding, and Cynthia decides to present Hortense to her family at the 21st birthday party of Roxanne (Claire Rushbrook), Cynthia's other daughter.

On paper, the plot of a Mike Leigh film often sounds like the stuff of TV soap opera, and that's especially true in the case of SECRETS & LIES. But where soaps breed familiarity over time, Leigh and his actors hone characters so sharply that viewers become as familiar with them over the running time of a film as they would with people they have known for years. Leigh's films are staged simply, not because of laziness or indifference, but because he has in every case found the single best point from which to view the proceedings. SECRETS & LIES contains several long scenes shot in single takes that would be impossible for actors working under standard filming conditions: the long take of Cynthia and Hortense at their first meeting is particularly astonishing. This scene alone is enough to merit the Best Actress Award Blethyn received at Cannes, as well as the Oscar nominations for both her and Jean-Baptiste. SECRETS & LIES may be a trifle long, but there isn't a moment that needs to be cut.

SEDUCTION OF MIMI, THE
(MIMI METALLURGICO FERITO NELL'ONORE)

1972 92m c Drama ★★★½
Vera/Euro-International (Italy) R/

Giancarlo Giannini (*Carmelo "Mimi" Mardocheco*), Mariangela Melato (*Fiore*), Agostina Belli (*Rosalia*), Elena Fiore (*Signora Finocchiaro*), Turi Ferro (*Tricarico*), Agostina Belli, Luigi Diberti, Tuccio Musumeci, Ignazio Pappalardo, Rosaria Rapisarda

p, Daniele Senatore, Romano Cardarelli; d, Lina Wertmuller; w, Lina Wertmuller; ph, Dario Di Palma; ed, Franco Fraticelli; m, Piero Piccioni

This early film by Lina Wertmuller earned her the Best Director prize at the Cannes Film Festival and stars Giancarlo Giannini as a Sicilian metallurgist named Mimi. After refusing to vote for the Mafia candidate in a local election, Mimi loses his factory job and decides to head north for work. Although professing to be communist, he is eager to get rich, enjoy a life of luxury, and step on his fellow workers. Leaving behind his wife, Rosalia (Agostina Belli), whom he cruelly dominates and castigates for her infertility, Mimi finds work in Turin. There, he falls in love with Fiore (Mariangela Melato), a virgin anarchist who bears him a child. Mimi's idyllic life in the north is sabotaged, however, by the menacing Mafia-controlled authorities who transfer him back to Sicily. A clever examination of the bonds between sexual and political power, and the differences between the "civilized" northern Italians and the "barbaric" southerners, Wertmuller's film comes to life through Giannini's bravura performance; a macho brute and philistine, his Mimi is still a sympathetic character, more victim than victimizer. The videocassette is dubbed in English though, as in LOVE AND ANARCHY, the image appears to have been squeezed into the television format.

SEMI-TOUGH

1977 108m c Comedy/Sports ★★★
UA (U.S.) R/15

Burt Reynolds (*Billy Clyde Puckett*), Kris Kristofferson (*Shake Tiller*), Jill Clayburgh (*Barbara Jane Bookman*), Robert Preston (*Big Ed Bookman*), Bert Convy (*Friedrich Bismark*), Roger E. Mosley (*Puddin*), Lotte Lenya (*Clara Pelf*), Richard Masur (*Phillip Hooper*), Carl Weathers (*Dreamer Tatum*), Brian Dennehy (*T.J. Lambert*) p, David Merrick; d, Michael Ritchie; w, Walter Bernstein (based on the novel by Dan Jenkins); ph, Charles Rosher Jr.; ed, Richard A. Harris; m, Jerry Fielding; prod d, Walter Scott Herndon; cos, Theoni V. Aldredge

Set against the backdrop of professional football, SEMI-TOUGH is both a three-cornered romantic comedy and a scathing satire of self-help movements. Reynolds and Kristofferson are teammates on a fictitious Super Bowl-bound Miami football team owned by Preston, a recent convert to BEAT, the est-like way to a better life "gurued" by Convy. Recently returned from Africa, Preston's twice-divorced daughter, Clayburgh, reappraises her longtime friends, Reynolds and Kristofferson, and finds the latter, whom Convy has led to BEAT, not only a changed man but a suitable fiance. The trouble is Reynolds is in love with Clayburgh; however, being a resourceful guy, he manages to poke a hole in Convy's BEAT bubble, pull off some Super Bowl magic, and make sure that the right guy ends up with Preston's daughter. Based on a book by Dan Jenkins, SEMI-TOUGH is periodically funny and frequently on target in its satire, and it boasts a strong performance from Reynolds (who also starred in the football-themed THE LONGEST YARD). Jenkins's novel did not include the self-help lampooning, which was introduced into the story by screenwriter Bernstein at the insistence of director Ritchie (THE BAD NEWS BEARS; DOWN-HILL RACER). Several sportscasters and former football players appear in the film in character or as themselves, including Joe Kapp, Carl Weathers (ROCKY), Paul Hornung, and Lindsay Nelson.

SENSE AND SENSIBILITY
1995 135m c Drama/Romance ★★★½
Mirage Enterprises (U.S.) PG/U

Emma Thompson *(Elinor Dashwood)*, Kate Winslet *(Marianne Dashwood)*, Alan Rickman *(Colonel Brandon)*, Hugh Grant *(Edward Ferrars)*, Greg Wise *(John Willoughby)*, Emilie Francois *(Margaret Dashwood)*, Elizabeth Spriggs *(Mrs. Jennings)*, Gemma Jones *(Mrs. Dashwood)*, Harriet Walter *(Fanny Dashwood)*, James Fleet *(John Dashwood)*

p, Lindsay Doran; d, Ang Lee; w, Emma Thompson (based on the novel by Jane Austen); ph, Michael Coulter; ed, Tim Squyres; m, Patrick Doyle; prod d, Luciana Arrighi; art d, Philip Elton; fx, Ricky Farns, Randall Balsmeyer; cos, Jenny Beavan, John Bright

AAN Best Picture; AAN Best Supporting Actress: Kate Winslet; *AAN Best Actress:* Emma Thompson; *AA Best Adapted Screenplay:* Emma Thompson; *AAN Best Cinematography:* Michael Coulter; *AAN Best Costume Design:* Jenny Beavan, John Bright; *AAN Best Dramatic Score:* Patrick Doyle

To Hollywood's astonishment, SENSE AND SENSIBILITY was something very close to a blockbuster hit. First-time screenwriter Emma Thompson and director Ang Lee combined their talents for a graceful adaptation of Jane Austen's well-loved novel. If the result is not as sharp as Austen's prose, it is nonetheless as handsome and intelligent an adaptation as one could reasonably expect.

John Dashwood (James Fleet) inherits the entirety of his father's estate, Norland, since law does not permit his father to leave property to John's half-sisters. Prodded by his haughty wife Fanny (Harriet Walter), he minimizes his settlement on his stepmother and her daughters, and the couple moves into Norland. Mrs. Dashwood and her daughters—sensible Elinor (Emma Thompson), passionate Marianne (Kate Winslet), and young tomboy Margaret (Emilie Francois) prepare to vacate their home. Compelled by economics and convention, the three must begin a search for socially suitable husbands — happiness, of course, is only a secondary consideration.

Beautifully helmed by Lee, SENSE AND SENSIBILITY surprised many who saw the Taiwanese director as an odd choice for this comedy of 19th-century British manners. However, Lee's earlier works—e.g., THE WEDDING BANQUET and EAT DRINK MAN WOMAN—are not as far from Austen's worldview as it might seem. These are delicately wrought studies of social mores; especially where marriage is concerned, a highly structured society forces propriety and money to take precedence over love. Lee's frequently distanced framing works as a cinematic rendering of Austen's coolly ironic prose, and his camera angles and moving shots are splendid. Lee also elicits uniformly

excellent performances from his cast, with Thompson and Winslet particularly fine. Thompson also deserves credit for a faithful, intelligent screenplay which never rushes through Austen's plot.

SEPARATE TABLES
1958 98m bw Drama ★★★★½
Clifton/Joanna (U.S.) /PG

Deborah Kerr *(Sibyl Railton-Bell)*, Rita Hayworth *(Ann Shankland)*, David Niven *(Maj. Pollack)*, Wendy Hiller *(Miss Pat Cooper)*, Burt Lancaster *(John Malcolm)*, Gladys Cooper *(Mrs. Railton-Bell)*, Cathleen Nesbitt *(Lady Matheson)*, Felix Aylmer *(Mr. Fowler)*, Rod Taylor *(Charles)*, Audrey Dalton *(Jean)*

p, Harold Hecht; d, Delbert Mann; w, Terence Rattigan, John Gay (based on the play by Rattigan); ph, Charles Lang; ed, Marjorie Fowler, Charles Ennis; m, David Raksin; prod d, Harry Horner; art d, Edward Carrere; cos, Edith Head, Mary Grant

AAN Best Picture; AA Best Actor: David Niven; *AAN Best Actress:* Deborah Kerr; *AA Best Supporting Actress:* Wendy Hiller; *AAN Best Adapted Screenplay:* Terence Rattigan, John Gay; *AAN Best Cinematography:* Charles Lang, Jr.; *AAN Best Score:* David Raksin

Superb drama, marred by an unexpected failure among the brilliant cast. It's Deborah Kerr, overacting a repressed spinster almost to the point of retardation. That Delbert Mann could pull such fine work from the rest of the ensemble makes the usually strong Kerr's performance all the more curious, for hers is a career built on underacting.

Terence Rattigan's original play consisted of two one-acts set in the same Bournemouth, England locale. It was a tour de force for Eric Portman and Margaret Leighton, who played it successfully in London, then in New York during the fall of 1956. Rattigan collaborated with John Gay to blend the two stories into one that used four leads instead of two. The title refers to the practice of seating solo guests at their own dining tables. The small hotel is at the seashore, and the dining room is filled with a host of lonely people. Niven is a very British retired major who waxes on about his experiences in the war's North African campaign, but his stories have the ring of prevarication about them. Cooper is a stern and forceful matriarch (a Cooper specialty; was anyone ever better at these roles?) with daughter, Kerr, a mousey spinster fascinated by Niven but far too shy to let him know. Hiller, who runs the hotel, devotes herself to the comfort of others. It distracts her from troubles with her lover, Lancaster, a reclusive American writer who drinks more than he creates and spends much of his time in his room (with his macho bluster, Lancaster brings a Hemingway feeling to the role). Aging socialite Hayworth, Lancaster's former wife, arrives unexpectedly at the hotel, and everyone's lives begin to unravel simultaneously.

This is adult, intelligent stuff, marvelously shaded by the amalgamation of talents. That Niven and Hiller are sublime is almost to be expected. But one watches Hayworth with genuine surprise, as the poignant divorcee watching her beauty slip away. This kind of part is usually the province of Englishwomen—Vivien Leigh, for example. It's the only mature role she ever got to play. Lancaster, cast against two women whose talents have an air of gentility, is able to tone down his trademark bravura. Besides Miss Kerr, wouldn't it have been lovely to have been spared Vic Damone's insistent croon over the opening credits?

SERGEANT YORK
1941 134m bw War/Biography ★★★★
Warner Bros. (U.S.) /U

Gary Cooper *(Alvin C. York)*, Walter Brennan *(Pastor Rosier Pile)*, Joan Leslie *(Gracie Williams)*, George Tobias *(Michael T. "Pusher" Ross)*, Stanley Ridges *(Maj. Buxton)*, Margaret Wycherly *(Mother York)*, Ward Bond *(Ike Botkin)*, Noah Beery Jr. *(Buck Lipscomb)*, June Lockhart *(Rose York)*, Dickie Moore *(George York)*

p, Jesse L. Lasky, Hal B. Wallis; d, Howard Hawks; w, Abem Finkel, Harry Chandlee, Howard Koch, John Huston (based on *War Diary of Sergeant York* by Sam K. Cowan, *Sergeant York and His People* by Cowan, and *Sergeant York—Last of the Long Hunters* by Tom Skeyhill); ph, Sol Polito, Arthur Edeson; ed, William Holmes; m, Max Steiner; art d, John Hughes

AAN Best Picture; AA Best Actor: Gary Cooper; *AAN Best Supporting Actor:* Walter Brennan; *AAN Best Supporting Actress:* Margaret Wycherly; *AAN Best Director:* Howard Hawks; *AAN Best Original Screenplay:* Harry Chandlee, Abem Finkel, John Huston, Howard Koch; *AAN Best Cinematography:* Sol Polito; *AA Best Editing:* William Holmes; *AAN Best Score:* Max Steiner; *AAN Best Art Direction:* John Hughes, Fred MacLean; *AAN Best Sound:* Nathan Levinson

Predictable, a trifle slow, but ultimately winning. Gary Cooper won his first Oscar for his strong portrayal here of WWI hero Alvin C. York, who single-handedly captured 132 German soldiers during the Meuse-Argonne offensive and became one of America's most decorated and beloved heroes. Beginning in 1916, Howard Hawks' masterfully directed film follows the man from the hills of East Tennessee as he falls in love with Gracie Williams (Joan Leslie) and struggles to hold onto his land. When lightning strikes his rifle, York views it a sign from God and, becoming a pacifist, tries to avoid service in WWI. Eventually he does fight in France, however, and the rest is spectacular military history. Hawks brings the life of this incredible hero to the screen with forceful integrity, and Cooper is wonderful as the country fellow who gets religion and holds onto it, even through the nightmare of war. Technically, the film is faultless, with Hawks keeping his cameras fluid and employing Sol Polito's magnificent photographic skills at every turn.

Jesse Lasky, who saw York in the 1919 Armistice Day Parade, spent years trying to convince the modest Tennessean to allow his story to be filmed, finally winning York's approval provided that the proceeds go to charity and that Gary Cooper play him. At first Cooper refused, but he changed his mind after visiting York. Warner Bros. had hoped to have Michael Curtiz direct SERGEANT YORK, but Cooper wouldn't work with him, and when several others couldn't take the job, Hawks was hired, to the lasting pleasure of all who see this magnificent film. That's Robert Porterfield as Zeb Andrews; he established Barter Theater, Virginia's state theater, the oldest repertory still running in the United States.

SERPICO

1973 129m c Biography/Crime   ★★★★
Artists Entertainment/DEG (U.S.)   R/18

Al Pacino *(Frank Serpico)*, Tony Roberts *(Bob Blair)*, John Randolph *(Chief Sidney Green)*, Jack Kehoe *(Tom Keough)*, Biff McGuire *(Capt. McClain)*, Barbara Eda-Young *(Laurie)*, Cornelia Sharpe *(Leslie)*, John Medici *(Pasquale Serpico)*, Allan Rich *(D.A. Tauber)*, Norman Ornellas *(Rubello)*

p, Martin Bregman; d, Sidney Lumet; w, Waldo Salt, Norman Wexler (based on the book by Peter Maas); ph, Arthur J. Ornitz; ed, Dede Allen, Richard Marks; m, Mikis Theodorakis; prod d, Charles Bailey; art d, Douglas Higgins; cos, Anna Hill Johnstone

AAN Best Actor: Al Pacino; *AAN Best Adapted Screenplay:* Waldo Salt, Wexler Norman

In 1970, police officer Frank Serpico electrified the Knapp Commission investigating the New York City Police Department by testifying that there were as many cops taking payoffs as there were crooks. Peter Maas's biography of Serpico formed the basis of the script by Waldo Salt (MIDNIGHT COWBOY) and Norman Wexler (SATURDAY NIGHT FEVER), and Al Pacino is the title character, an honest cop who refuses to go on the take.

Surrounded by corruption, Frank Serpico is distrusted and harrassed by fellow officers, who suspect him both for his honesty and for his countercultural lifestyle. When the double-dealing and persecution become too much, he tries to inform police commissioner White of the corruption within the department, but the response is discouraging. Frustrated, Serpico takes his story to the *New York Times* editors; the resultant scandal prompts the mayor to initiate a high-profile investigation. Serpico is called to testify, and now both cops and criminals are gunning for him.

All of the actors contribute excellent performances under the assured direction of Sidney Lumet, who replaced John Avildsen on the project. It's a particular pleasure to see Tony Roberts working in a film that *wasn't* directed by Woody Allen, and he is outstanding as Pacino's trusted pal. Oscar-winner F. Murray Abraham (AMADEUS), Mary Louise Weller (ANIMAL HOUSE), M. Emmet Walsh (STRAIGHT TIME), and Hank Garrett (THREE DAYS OF THE CONDOR) also

appear in small but telling roles. But when all is said and done, Pacino is the riveting presence that makes the movie work and it is difficult to imagine any other actor in the part.

SERVANT, THE

1963 115m bw Drama   ★★★½
Springbok (U.K.)   /15

Dirk Bogarde *(Hugo Barrett)*, Sarah Miles *(Vera)*, Wendy Craig *(Susan)*, James Fox *(Tony)*, Catherine Lacey *(Lady Mounset)*, Richard Vernon *(Lord Mounset)*, Ann Firbank *(Society Woman)*, Doris Knox *(Older Woman)*, Patrick Magee *(Bishop)*, Jill Melford *(Younger Woman)*

p, Joseph Losey, Norman Priggen; d, Joseph Losey; w, Harold Pinter (based on the novel by Robin Maugham); ph, Douglas Slocombe; ed, Reginald Mills; m, John Dankworth; prod d, Richard MacDonald; art d, Ted Clements; cos, Beatrice Dawson

Opaque but hypnotically absorbing allegory of power, exploitation, and sublimated sexuality in a class-based society. British screenwriter Harold Pinter and expatriate American director Joseph Losey (he'd run afoul of anti-Communist witch-hunters in the US) married disparate sensibilities to tell the story of a dissipated Cockney servant (Dirk Bogarde) who trades roles with his master (James Fox), a classically effete aristocrat.

Although THE SERVANT's critical reputation has declined in recent years, it was initially received as an important, groundbreaking film, and won British Academy Awards for Best Actor (Bogarde), Most Promising Newcomer (Fox), and Best Cinematography (Douglas Slocombe, whose astonishing credit list encompasses over 70 films, including major works by Alexander Mackendrick, Roman Polanski, Steven Spielberg, John Huston, and Ken Russell). Pinter's adaptation of Robin Maugham's novel employs his customary strategies (e.g., fractured dialogue, cryptic silences, pregnant discussions of ostensible trivialities) but lacks the cockeyed humor of his best work for the stage. (Pinter appears in a cameo as a society man.) After working in major films throughout the 60s, Fox experienced a religious conversion in 1973 and retired from movies for several years. He is the younger brother of Edward Fox (DAY OF THE JACKAL, A BRIDGE TOO FAR), with whom he is often confused.

SET-UP, THE

1949 72m bw Sports   ★★★★
RKO (U.S.)   /PG

Robert Ryan *(Bill "Stoker" Thompson)*, Audrey Totter *(Julie)*, George Tobias *(Tiny)*, Alan Baxter *(Little Boy)*, Wallace Ford *(Gus)*, Percy Helton *(Red)*, Hal Baylor *(Tiger Nelson)*, Darryl Hickman *(Shanley)*, Kenny O'Morrison *(Moore)*, James Edwards *(Luther Hawkins)*

p, Richard Goldstone; d, Robert Wise; w, Art Cohn (based on the poem by Joseph Moncure March); ph, Milton Krasner; ed, Roland Gross; art d, Albert S. D'Agostino, Jack Okey

One of the most realistic and gripping boxing films ever made, THE SET-UP is a tautly constructed, emotionally charged examination of one night in the life of an aging boxer, Stoker Thompson (Robert Ryan). Played out in real time as 72 uninterrupted minutes of Stoker's life, the movie begins as a crowd gathers in front of the arena in anticipation of the evening's bouts. Although almost washed up, Stoker is convinced that if he can win that night's bout he'll be back on the road to the top, "just one punch away" from being able to collect a big purse, open his own tavern, and retire. Meanwhile, his seedy manager (George Tobias) has taken $50 from a hood in return for Stoker's throwing the fight. Since, as of late, Stoker has been getting knocked out regularly after the second round, the manager simply doesn't tell the fighter about the setup. Back in the locker room, Stoker watches as the fighters—ranging from fresh-out-of-high-school talent to punchy veterans—prepare for their bouts, while he awaits the fight of his life. THE SET-UP is an amazingly powerful film. Within a very simple format (the screenplay was based on a poem), director Robert Wise and his performers present a myriad of criticisms and emotions, making for one of the most brutal condemnations of boxing ever filmed. The fighting is shown as dehumanizing and cruel, the audience as a mass of animalistic maniacs who live vicariously through the boxers. Everyone, from trainers to promoters to gangsters, is a seedy, uneducated opportunist; only the fighters themselves are shown to have any self-respect. Ryan gives the best performance of his career as the quiet, inarticulate fighter who is determined to stick with the game because he feels that he's "just one punch away" from success. Ryan, who actually boxed for four years undefeated while at Dartmouth College, handles his role with great subtlety: always soft-spoken and sincere, Stoker clings to his simple beliefs and will take whatever punishment is necessary to retain his self-respect and dignity. The fight scenes in THE SET-UP are among the best ever filmed, surpassed only by those in Martin Scorsese's incredible RAGING BULL.

SEVEN

1995 107m c Thriller/Crime/Action   ★★★½
New Line (U.S.)   R/18

Brad Pitt (Detective David Mills), Morgan Freeman (Lieutenant William Somerset), Gwyneth Paltrow (Tracy), Richard Roundtree (Talbot), John C. McGinley (California), Kevin Spacey (John Doe), John Cassini (Officer Davis), Peter Crombie (Dr. O'Neill), Reg E. Cathey (Dr. Santiago), Richard Portnow (Dr. Beardsley)

p, Arnold Kopelson, Phyllis Carlyle; d, David Fincher; w, Andrew Kevin Walker; ph, Darius Khondji; ed, Richard Francis-Bruce; m, Howard Shore; prod d, Arthur Max; art d, Gary Wissner; fx, Peter Albiez, Danny Cangemi, Greg Kimble, Tim Thompson; cos, Michael Kaplan

Bleak and deeply serious, SEVEN forges the formulaic elements of dozens of lousy movies—mismatched cops, a serial killer, noir trappings—into a compelling one. As dark as an anvil and as subtle as a hammer, SEVEN gets the job done—it entertains, if you accept it on its own implacable terms.

The hard rain that pours down daily on the streets of the unnamed metropolis in which SEVEN is set isn't enough to wash the human filth off the streets. Having spent 34 years in the futile task of street cleaning, detective William Somerset (Morgan Freeman) is set to retire. He wants his last week to pass quietly, but he's charged with training his replacement, David Mills (Brad Pitt), an eager hotshot, new to the city. First thing Monday, they're faced with an unusual murder: an obese man has been force-fed spaghetti until he literally burst, and the word "GLUTTONY" was written in grease on the wall. As Somerset instantly realizes, they're on the trail of a serial killer with a biblical bent: he's staging brilliantly sadistic murders that illustrate each of the Seven Deadly Sins. Greed follows, and the mismatched cops try desperately to identify the madman as he works his way through Sloth, Lust, Pride, and—in a startling conclusion—Envy and Wrath.

SEVEN is unnerving from the opening credits, jarring graphics set to the electronic pulse of Nine Inch Nails' industrial rock. The stench and filth of the gluttony scene is tangible and nauseating. The sloth episode is horrific, and contains a sickening shock, while the rape-murder of lust is almost unimaginably gruesome. Director David Fincher assaults the audience relentlessly; his "Noir York" is a claustrophobic world, colored from a palette of stark grays and the occasional, dingy yellow. Fincher wants to immerse viewers in the rot of this world, and indict its (and our) malaise for the on-screen sins: the murderous John Doe is only a festering symptom.

SEVEN BEAUTIES
(PASQUALINO SETTEBELLEZZE)

1976 115m c Comedy/Drama   ★★★★
Medusa (Italy)   R/18

Giancarlo Giannini (Pasqualino Frafuso), Fernando Rey (Pedro), Shirley Stoler (Commandant), Elena Fiore (Concettina), Enzo Vitale (Don Raffaele), Mario Conti (Totonno), Piero Di Orio (Francesco), Ermelinda De Felice (Mother), Francesca Marciano (Carolina), Lucio Amelio (Lawyer)

p, Lina Wertmuller, Giancarlo Giannini, Arrigo Colombo; d, Lina Wertmuller; w, Lina Wertmuller; ph, Tonino Delli Colli; ed, Franco Fraticelli; m, Enzo Iannacci; art d, Enrico Job

AAN Best Actor: Giancarlo Giannini; AAN Best Director: Linda Wertmuller; AAN Best Original Screenplay: Linda Wertmuller; AAN Best Foreign Language Film:

Memorable, but nasty. The grotesque casting, the surrealistic shooting, and the entire production make one think that Federico Fellini was in charge. But it was Wertmuller who handled the writing and directing Giannini is a small-time crook in Naples during the dark days of WW II. He has seven ugly sisters, none of whom is ever likely to get married, and he is busily supporting them doing whatever he can do to keep their fat bodies and souls together. Giannini is subjected to the terrors of a German prison camp, where gross matron Shirley Stoler forces him to do unspeakable things to her body. In an all-out attempt to survive, Giannini does whatever it is that's necessary to keep from being killed and, finally, manages to live through the war. Wertmuller seems to be saying that Italians are a race willing to do anything to hang on; she strips them of pride and their natural dignity. Giannini's character is a facistic Little Tramp who swallows whatever bull is thrown at him. The picture made a lot of money, proving desensitized audiences were looking for goofball black comedy pratfalls, mixed in with a soupcon of peversion and cruelty. Things haven't changed much since then.

SEVEN BRIDES FOR SEVEN BROTHERS

1954 102m c Musical   ★★★★½
MGM (U.S.)   G/U

Jane Powell (Milly), Howard Keel (Adam Pontabee), Jeff Richards (Benjamin Pontabee), Russ Tamblyn (Gideon Pontabee), Tommy Rall (Frank Pontabee), Howard Petrie (Pete Perkins), Virginia Gibson (Liza), Ian Wolfe (Rev. Elcott), Marc Platt (Daniel Pontabee), Matt Mattox (Caleb Pontabee)

p, Jack Cummings; d, Stanley Donen; w, Albert Hackett, Frances Goodrich, Dorothy Kingsley (based on the story "The Sobbin' Women" by Stephen Vincent Benet); ph, George Folsey; ed, Ralph E. Winters; art d, Cedric Gibbons, Urie McCleary; chor, Michael Kidd; cos, Walter Plunkett

AAN Best Picture; AAN Best Screenplay: Albert Hackett, Frances Goodrich, Dorothy Kingsley; AAN Best Cinematography: George Folsey; AAN Best Editing: Ralph E. Winters; AA Best Score: Adolph Deutsch, Saul Chaplin

Close to perfect. A magical blend of the right story, a great score, and the astonishing choreography of Michael Kidd, SEVEN BRIDES FOR SEVEN BROTHERS is one the big screen's most entertaining musicals. The action takes place in Oregon, where Adam (Howard Keel), the oldest of the Pontabee brothers, who live on a ranch high in the mountains, decides to find a bride. In town, he meets Milly (Jane Powell), a waitress, and woos, marries, and takes her back to the homestead, which is considerably less civilized than she'd expected. Soon Adam's brothers decide they, too, would like some female company, and, taking their inspiration from the story of the "Sobbin' Women" (Sabine women), they kidnap some local beauties, who have to winter at the ranch when an avalanche prevents the townspeople from rescuing them. Come spring, wedding bells ring for all. Based on Stephen Vincent Benet's "The Sobbin' Women," SEVEN BRIDES FOR SEVEN BROTHERS is a rollicking film with a breathless pace, well-defined characters, and incredible vitality under Stanley Donen's direction, marred marginally by an overlying patina of corny Americana. Adolph Deutsch and Saul Chaplin's scoring won an Oscar. The dynamo dancing is mostly due to the terrific male dancers, whose standouts include the barn-raising and the "Lonesome Polecat Lament" ballet. Keel and Powell have an adorable chemistry; neither would ever be this well-matched again, which reminds us we would have preferred Powell in for Kathryn Grayson in KISS ME, KATE. Look for ripe Julie Newmar (then Newmeyer) among the other brides, whom we always found sexier as a wild-maned brunette. The score is by Gene dePaul and Johnny Mercer.

SEVEN DAYS IN MAY

1964 120m bw Thriller/Political/War   ★★★★
Seven Arts/Joel (U.S.)   /U

Burt Lancaster (Gen. James M. Scott), Kirk Douglas (Col. Martin "Jiggs" Casey), Fredric March (President Jordan Lyman), Ava Gardner (Eleanor Holbrook), Edmond O'Brien (Sen. Raymond Clark),

Martin Balsam *(Paul Girard)*, George Macready *(Christopher Todd)*, Whit Bissell *(Sen. Prentice)*, Hugh Marlowe *(Harold McPherson)*, Bart Burns *(Arthur Corwin)*

p, Edward Lewis; d, John Frankenheimer; w, Rod Serling (based on the novel by Fletcher Knebel, Charles Waldo Bailey II); ph, Ellsworth Fredricks; ed, Ferris Webster; m, Jerry Goldsmith; art d, Cary Odell

AAN Best Supporting Actor: Edmond O'Brien; *AAN Best Art Direction:* Cary Odell, Edward G. Boyle

The surprising revelations of the Iran-Contra scandal have given new meaning to this gripping, well-acted political thriller based on Charles Waldo Bailey II's and Fletcher Knebel's 1962 best-seller. SEVEN DAYS IN MAY begins as the President of the United States, Jordan Lyman (Fredric March), signs a nuclear disarmament treaty with the Soviets, outraging the military establishment, particularly Gen. James M. Scott (Burt Lancaster), head of the Joint Chiefs of Staff, who conspires with other Joint Chiefs to stage a coup d'etat. His aide, Marine Col. "Jiggs" Casey (Kirk Douglas), stumbles onto evidence of the plot, including a secret Air Force base, and approaches the president. With only days left before the coup is to take place, Lyman swings into action, but trusted friends Sen. Raymond Clark (Edmond O'Brien) and Paul Girard (Martin Balsam), whom the president has sent to secure the proof needed to expose Scott and his cohorts, are captured and killed in a plane crash, respectively. Armed with incriminating letters from Scott's former mistress (Ava Gardner), Lyman confronts the general, and though the president cannot bring himself to use blackmail he eventually triumphs over Scott. Filmed in stark black and white, unraveling its complicated plot at a rapid clip, this exciting film from John Frankenheimer, the director of the similarly taut THE MANCHURIAN CANDIDATE, packs a grim warning about the military's potential abuse of power. Douglas, who, like Lancaster and March, contributes an outstanding performance, initiated the project after reading galleys of the novel. Given the enthusiastic cooperation of the Kennedy administration (though not of the Pentagon, whom the filmmakers understandably never approached), SEVEN DAYS IN MAY smacks of realism, from its skillfully realized sets to its wholly believable supporting performances by O'Brien, Balsam, and John Houseman. Sure to keep you on the edge of your seat.

7 FACES OF DR. LAO

1964 100m c Science Fiction/Fantasy ★★★½
Galaxy/Scarus (U.S.)

Tony Randall *(Dr. Lao/Merlin the Magician/Pan/The Abominable Snowman/Medusa/The Giant Serpent/Apollonius of Tyana)*, Barbara Eden *(Angela Benedict)*, Arthur O'Connell *(Clint Stark)*, John Ericson *(Ed Cunningham)*, Noah Beery Jr. *(Tim Mitchell)*, Lee Patrick *(Mrs. Howard T. Cassan)*, Minerva Urecal *(Kate Lindquist)*, John Qualen *(Luther Lindquist)*, Frank Kreig *(Peter Ramsey)*, Peggy Rea *(Mrs. Peter Ramsey)*

p, George Pal; d, George Pal; w, Charles Beaumont (based on the novel *The Circus of Dr. Lao* by Charles G. Finney); ph, Robert Bronner; ed, George Tomasini; m, Leigh Harline; art d, George W. Davis, Gabriel Scognamillo; fx, Paul Byrd, Wah Chang, Jim Danforth, Ralph Rodine, Robert R. Hoag

AAN Best Visual Effects: Jim Danforth

Set in the Old West, this is a wonderful fantasy from puppeteer George Pal, whose futurist fancies have delighted many. When Dr. Lao (Tony Randall), an Oriental magician, rides into Abalone with his strange circus, he finds the good citizens threatened by the land-grabbing activities of villainous Clint Stark (Arthur O'Connell). Calling upon his mysterious powers and the services of the bizarre characters who populate the strange circus (all played by Randall), Lao comes to the aid of the crusading young newspaper editor (John Ericson) who tries to prevent Stark's takeover of the town. In the film's most fantastic sequence, Lao's pet fish becomes a seven-headed monster to chase down one of Stark's henchmen. Randall gives a virtuoso multiple-character performance, and the special effects are dazzling, including a few scenes from Pal's ATLANTIS, THE LOST CONTINENT. Makeup man William Tuttle won the first of only two special Academy Awards for his work on this film—before the category was permanently established in 1981.

SEVEN LITTLE FOYS, THE

1955 95m c Musical/Biography ★★★½
Paramount (U.S.) /U

Bob Hope *(Eddie Foy)*, Milly Vitale *(Madeleine Morando)*, George Tobias *(Barney Green)*, Angela Clarke *(Clara)*, Herbert Heyes *(Judge)*, Richard Shannon *(Stage Manager)*, Billy Gray *(Brynie)*, Lee Erickson *(Charley)*, Paul De Rolf *(Richard Foy)*, Lydia Reed *(Mary Foy)*

p, Jack Rose; d, Melville Shavelson; w, Melville Shavelson, Jack Rose; ph, John F. Warren; ed, Ellsworth Hoagland; art d, Hal Pereira, John B. Goodman; chor, Nick Castle; cos, Edith Head

AAN Best Original Screenplay: Melville Shavelson, Jack Rose

Funny and heartwarming, though a little on the cute side, this engaging musical biography of vaudevillian Eddie Foy, Sr. features a socko cameo by multitalented James Cagney, reprising his Oscar-winning role as George M. Cohan. Bob Hope plays Foy, who declares that he'll always do a "single," both onstage and in life, but who, in short order, is married and has seven kids. When his wife (Milly Vitale) dies, Foy has problems adjusting to single parenthood, but before long the kids are not only in the act, but stealing the show. With Eddie, Jr., Foy's real-life son, doing the narrating, we are taken through the various episodes of the family's life. The highlight of the film comes at a Friars Club dinner for Foy, when he and his great pal Cohan get on stage, throw some fast and furious jokes back and forth, and wind up in a splendid dance routine. Cagney reportedly did the role for no pay, even though he and Hope rehearsed their dancing for 10 days. A must see for Hope and Cagney fans.

SEVEN-PER-CENT SOLUTION, THE

1976 113m c Mystery ★★★
Universal (U.K.) PG/15

Alan Arkin *(Sigmund Freud)*, Vanessa Redgrave *(Lola Deveraux)*, Robert Duvall *(Dr. Watson)*, Nicol Williamson *(Sherlock Holmes)*, Laurence Olivier *(Prof. Moriarty)*, Joel Grey *(Lowenstein)*, Samantha Eggar *(Mary Watson)*, Jeremy Kemp *(Baron von Leinsdorf)*, Charles Gray *(Mycroft Holmes)*, Georgia Brown *(Mrs. Freud)*

p, Herbert Ross; d, Herbert Ross; w, Nicholas Meyer (based on his novel); ph, Oswald Morris; ed, Chris Barnes; m, John Addison; prod d, Ken Adam; art d, Peter Lamont; cos, Alan Barrett

AAN Best Adapted Screenplay: Nicholas Meyer (Screenplay); *AAN Best Costume Design:* Alan Barrett

A hit at the box office, this revisionist Sherlock Holmes film is based on the best seller by Nicholas Meyer and places a historical figure (Sigmund Freud) and a fictitious one (Sherlock Holmes) from the late 19th century together in a hypothetical situation. The result is a fascinating film that sees the loyal Dr. Watson (Duvall) scheme to trick his friend Holmes (Williamson) into seeking a cure for his cocaine addiction from the soon-to-be-famous Freud (Arkin). The criminologist and the psychologist come to respect each other's considerable deductive talents, and they team up to rescue one of Arkin's patients (Redgrave) who has been kidnapped. Williamson is a Holmes unlike any other, a man of genius but also a man tormented by things he cannot recall. His obsession with the completely innocent Professor Moriarty (Olivier) is actually a reaction to a long-buried secret in the sleuth's subconscious. Williamson's Holmes actually cries at one point, something Basil Rathbone would never have done. Duvall is a breath of fresh air as well; far from the Nigel Bruce bumbler, he is a capable man and a devoted friend. Production design is nothing short of marvelous, conveying the gentility of the late Victorian era in splendid detail. The music was originally to be composed by Bernard Herrmann, but he died before completing it and was replaced by John Addison. Stephen Sondheim, a mystery buff, contributed a witty saloon song.

SEVEN SAMURAI, THE
(SHICHININ NO SAMURAI)

1954   200m   bw   Drama   ★★★★★
Toho   (Japan)   /15

Takashi Shimura (Kambei), Toshiro Mifune (Kikuchiyo), Yoshio Inaba (Gorobei), Seiji Miyaguchi (Kyuzo), Minoru Chiaki (Heihachi), Daisuke Kato (Shichiroji), Ko Kimura (Katsushiro), Kuninori Kodo (Gisaku), Kamatari Fujiwara (Manzo), Yoshio Tsuchiya (Rikichi)

p, Shojiro Motoki; d, Akira Kurosawa; w, Shinobu Hashimoto, Hideo Oguni, Akira Kurosawa; ph, Asakazu Nakai; ed, Akira Kurosawa; m, Fumio Hayasaka; art d, So Matsuyama

AAN Best Art Direction: Takashi Matsuyama (Art Direction); *AAN Best Costume Design:* Kohei Ezaki

Much imitated, still unsurpassed. By critical consensus one of the best movies ever made, THE SEVEN SAMURAI covers so much emotional, historical, and cinematic ground that that it demands to be viewed over and over again. Director Akira Kurosawa re-imagines the epic westerns of John Ford in a Japanese context, yielding an art-house action picture with cross-cultural appeal.

The film is set in the 1600s during the Sengoku era, when the once-powerful samurai were coming to the end of their rule. A small, unprotected village, which is regularly pillaged by murderous thieves, comes under the protection of a band of these samurai. Kambei (Takashi Shimura) is a veteran warrior who has fallen on hard times and who answers the villagers' appeal for help by gathering six comrades to help defend the town. (Each of the samurai is quickly limned to show us who they are, what they do, and whatever personal quirks they may have.) In return for three small meals daily, the men drill the town on how to fight, but the parties are battling for different reasons. The townspeople are desperate to keep their lives and property intact; the warriors are in it for honor alone. The last of the samurai to join is Kikuchiyo (Toshiro Mifune), a loudmouth who pretends that he is qualified but who is, in reality, a farmer's son who hopes to be accepted by the others. The 40 bandits arrive, and a huge battle takes place. In the end, only three of the warriors survive. Akira Kurosawa's classic tells a simple tale, but one so rich with underlying meaning and cinematic technique that no synopsis can do justice to the film's power. Those viewers under the misconception that foreign films are boring should be thrilled by the staging of this film's brutal action sequences, such as the raid on the town, the violent hand-to-hand combat in the pouring rain, and the epic horseback battles. The action is never shown strictly for its own sake, however. All the characters are so carefully etched that we sincerely grieve when they are killed. One of the most successful of all Japanese films, and one of the most immediately accessible to English-speaking audiences.

SEVEN YEAR ITCH, THE

1955   105m   c   Comedy   ★★★
Fox   (U.S.)   /PG

Marilyn Monroe (The Girl), Tom Ewell (Richard Sherman), Evelyn Keyes (Helen Sherman), Sonny Tufts (Tom McKenzie), Robert Strauss (Kruhulik), Oscar Homolka (Dr. Brubaker), Marguerite Chapman (Miss Morris), Victor Moore (Plumber), Roxanne (Elaine), Donald MacBride (Mr. Brady)

p, Charles K. Feldman, Billy Wilder; d, Billy Wilder; w, Billy Wilder, George Axelrod (based on the play by Axelrod); ph, Milton Krasner; ed, Hugh S. Fowler; m, Alfred Newman; art d, Lyle Wheeler, George W. Davis; fx, Ray Kellogg; cos, Travilla, Charles LeMaire

Entertaining Billy Wilder outing, adapted—and toned down—by George Axelrod from his hit Broadway play. This is probably Monroe's best known film, largely thanks to the scene in which a rush of air from a subway grating sends her skirt flying up around her shoulders.

Tom Ewell plays a book publisher who has been married for seven years, and who stays behind in Manhattan for the summer when his wife (Keyes) and son (Bernard) leave on vacation. Ewell's small building has an upstairs apartment which has been sublet to Monroe, a flighty commercial actress/model who becomes the object of his (mostly imaginary) amorous advances. Ewell's lively imagination sends him into flights of fancy involving both his conquest of Monroe,

and the humiliation which would result from the exposure of his infidelity (Monroe appearing on a local TV show to openly discuss his proclivities, etc.). The picture ends with no adultery having been committed, except in Ewell's mind.

This was Monroe's 23rd movie and Ewell's eighth, since he broke in opposite Judy Holliday in ADAM'S RIB. Monroe was falling in and out of depression during filming, as her marriage to Yankee slugger Joe DiMaggio was ending. Oscar Homolka has a bit part as a psychiatrist.

SEVENTH SEAL, THE
(DET SJUNDE INSEGLET)

1957   105m   bw   Drama   ★★★★★
Svensk   (Sweden)   /15

Max von Sydow (Antonius Block), Gunnar Bjornstrand (Jons), Nils Poppe (Jof), Bibi Andersson (Mia), Bengt Ekerot (Death), Ake Fridell (Blacksmith Plog), Inga Gill (Lisa), Maud Hansson (Tyan), Gunnel Lindblom (Girl), Inga Landgre (Block's Wife)

p, Allan Ekelund; d, Ingmar Bergman; w, Ingmar Bergman (based on his play "Tramalning"); ph, Gunnar Fischer; ed, Lennart Wallen; m, Erik Nordgren; fx, Evald Andersson; chor, Else Fischer; cos, Manne Lindholm

The film that gained Ingmar Bergman an international reputation, THE SEVENTH SEAL is an all-out religious allegory addressing that most-contemplated question, "Does God exist?" Set during a single day in the Middle Ages, the film concerns the philosophical quandary of a knight, Antonius Block (von Sydow), who returns from the Crusades to find his country at the mercy of plague and witchhunts. In the midst of his moral and religious confusion, Antonius is visited by Death (Ekerot), a black-cloaked figure who is ready to call the knight from this earth. Antonius strikes a deal with Death, winning a brief reprieve by inviting him to play a game of chess. Since Death apparently has a soft spot for chess, he agrees. Over the next several hours, Antonius is confronted by some who are unconvinced of God's existence (the Knight's agnostic squire, played by Bjornstrand) and some who are a wandering band of performers). Who survives the plague and who doesn't propels the narrative; the issues, however, are what really matter here.

Long hailed as a masterpiece of cinema, the status of THE SEVENTH SEAL (and, more generally, Bergman's place in the pantheon of great filmmakers) has steadily declined over the years. Still, we must admit to really liking this one. It is most powerful on its first viewing, when the opening burst of light through the sky, the incredible parade of flagellants through the town, and the memorable finale with Death and his conquests have their greatest impact for a viewer. On later viewings the craft of the film remains bracing and its greater concerns stay provocative without becoming heavy-handed. Whatever one thinks of Bergman's philosophical debates on good and evil or God and the Devil, the film nevertheless deserves one's respect. As with so much of this filmmaker's cinema, the acting is of a very high order. Von Sydow's long face makes a perfect portrait of stoicism, and the incredibly versatile Bjornstrand scores again in a change of pace role. Poppe would never again achieve a performance quite as good as this one, his Jof a combination of artlessness and winning grace. Andersson and Lindblom are equally fine, and the details and dignity of the acting throughout render an incredibly effective sense of period. What's most important here is that THE SEVENTH SEAL, for all its downbeat aspects, is so gripping as to be entertaining in an enlightening way. Less austere and more visually striking than some of Bergman's later films.

SEVENTH VEIL, THE

1945   95m   bw   Drama   ★★★★
Theatrecraft/Ortus   (U.K.)   /PG

James Mason (Nicholas), Ann Todd (Francesca Cunningham), Herbert Lom (Dr. Larson), Hugh McDermott (Peter Gay), Albert Lieven (Maxwell Leyden), Yvonne Owen (Susan Brook), David Horne (Dr. Kendal), Manning Whiley (Dr. Irving), Grace Allardyce (Nurse), Ernest Davies (Parker)

p, Sydney Box; d, Compton Bennett; w, Muriel Box, Sydney Box; ph, Reginald Wyer; ed, Gordon Hales; m, Benjamin Frankel; art d, James Carter; cos, Dorothy Sinclair

AA Best Original Screenplay: Muriel Box, Sydney Box

An intelligent and absorbing psychological drama that took the Oscar for Best Screenplay, THE SEVENTH VEIL was shot in under three months on a modest budget of less than 100,000 pounds and proved that a polished movie could be made for a reasonable price. Todd, in her best performance of an up-and-down career in which she never got the acclaim she deserved, is a concert pianist who suffers from fits of depression and attempts suicide. Her hands were once hurt in an accident and she fears that she will lose their use. The picture unreels in flashback as Todd checks into a mental hospital and puts herself in the care of psychiatrist Lom, who guides her through her past and lifts the veils of her memory. With the aid of drugs and hypnosis, Todd goes back to the time when she was brutally caned by a cruel headmistress the night before she was to take her final exams in music. The result was that she failed the test. Todd is an orphan put in the care of crippled and charismatic Mason, a bachelor who dedicates himself to cultivating her talents. When Todd attempts romance with bandleader McDermott, Mason takes her to Paris where she plays brilliantly and delights crowds and critics. Then she falls for Lieven, an artist; in an attempt to put an end to that attachment, Mason steals a car and crashes it with Todd inside; her hands are burned. Now that Todd has discovered why she feels the way she does, she becomes aware that her talent remains, and the recognition of her personal history causes her to race to the arms of the man she truly loves, Mason.

It's a complex picture that only skims the surface of mental illnes, but the attempt was admirable, if a bit simplistic. Still, for the time, praise must be given to the Boxes for their story and to former film editor Bennett for his direction. The producers showed it to audiences on a sneak-preview basis and let them decide the ending. At first, no one was quite sure how to conclude it. But when the cards came in, it was indicated that the audiences felt Todd should wind up with Mason, and so that is implied at the conclusion. Pianist Eileen Joyce did the solos for Todd. Two years before this, Todd electrified London with her stage work in "Lottie Dundass," in which she played opposite Sybil Thorndike. She began her professional career in 1931 in KEEPERS OF YOUTH and eventually became a producer and director of travel films. Czech-born Lom, who later was seen as Peter Sellers's boss in the "Pink Panther" films, was making his fifth film.

SEVENTH VICTIM, THE

1943 71m bw Horror   ★★★★
RKO (U.S.)   /A

Tom Conway (*Dr. Louis Judd*), Kim Hunter (*Mary Gibson*), Jean Brooks (*Jacqueline Gibson*), Hugh Beaumont (*Gregory Ward*), Erford Gage (*Jason Hoag*), Isabel Jewell (*Frances Fallon*), Chef Milani (*Mr. Romari*), Marguerita Sylva (*Mrs. Romari*), Evelyn Brent (*Natalie Cortez*), Mary Newton (*Mrs. Redi*)

p, Val Lewton; d, Mark Robson; w, DeWitt Bodeen, Charles O'Neal; ph, Nicholas Musuraca; ed, John Lockert; m, Roy Webb; art d, Albert S. D'Agostino, Walter E. Keller; cos, Renie

"I runne to death and death meets me as fast/And all my pleasures are like yesterday." This epigraph from the first "Holy Sonnet" by John Donne sets the tone for what is perhaps producer Val Lewton's most personal film, and certainly one of his greatest. While very little in the way of horrific action takes place in THE SEVENTH VICTIM, the film has a haunting, lyrical, overwhelming sense of melancholy and despair to it—death is looked upon as a sweet release from the oppression of a cold, meaningless existence. Kim Hunter makes her film debut as Mary Gibson, an orphan attending a gloomy Catholic boarding school. Informed by the nuns that her older sister, Jacqueline (Jean Brooks), has disappeared and stopped sending tuition money, Mary is forced to go to New York City and find her. With the help of Jacqueline's husband, Gregory (Hugh Beaumont), Mary discovers that her sister has fallen in with a group of satanists who meet in secret and virtually control the lives of their members. No plot description can fully convey the uneasy sense of dread that pervades every frame of this film. Although Mark Robson, who made his directorial debut here, is no Jacques Tourneur, his direction is restrained and effective. Lewton ensured this by seeing to it that all the delicate nuances of mood and character were written into the screenplay. The film includes a number of unforgettable moments: the scene in which Mary persuades Jacqueline's landlord to open up her room—only to find a noose hanging from the ceiling and a chair placed beneath it, Mary watching in horror as the body of a murder victim is transported by its killers on the subway, a precursor to the shower scene in PSYCHO that must have been seen by Hitchcock, and the film's final moment—without a doubt the bleakest ending to any film ever made in Hollywood.

7TH VOYAGE OF SINBAD, THE

1958 87m c Science Fiction/Fantasy   ★★★½
Morningside (U.S.)   /U

Kerwin Mathews (*Capt. Sinbad*), Kathryn Grant (*Princess Parisa*), Richard Eyer (*Baronni the Genie*), Torin Thatcher (*Sokurah the Magician*), Alec Mango (*Caliph*), Danny Green (*Karim*), Harold Kasket (*Sultan*), Alfred Brown (*Harufa*), Nana de Herrera (*Sadi*), Nino Falanga (*Gaunt Sailor*)

p, Charles H. Schneer; d, Nathan Juran; w, Ken Kolb; ph, Wilkie Cooper; ed, Edwin Bryant, Jerome Thoms; m, Bernard Herrmann; art d, Gil Parrendo; fx, Ray Harryhausen

Stop-motion animation master Ray Harryhausen's first color film is also one of the greatest achievements in fantasy filmmaking since KING KONG. For the first time Harryhausen ventures into the realm of myth and legend (his previous films were the modern-day giant monster variety), resuscitating the Sinbad adventure, long thought to be box-office poison. The film opens as Sinbad (Kerwin Mathews) sails to Baghdad, accompanied by Princess Parisa (Kathryn Grant), his future bride. A violent storm blows the ship off course, and the travelers land on the island of Colossa, where they find the sorcerer Sokurah (Torin Thatcher) being chased by a monstrous cyclops from whom he has stolen a magic lamp. Sinbad fends off the cyclops, but only with help from the lamp's genie are they able to escape. During their retreat, the lamp falls into the sea and is recovered by the angry cyclops. Despite the sorcerer's pleas to return for the lamp, Sinbad sails for Baghdad. Sokurah, however, shrinks the princess to miniature size to force Sinbad to see things his way. The rest of the film is an assault of the visually fantastic: Sinbad and his crew battle a baby roc and its giant mother, another cyclops, a fire-breathing dragon, and in the most memorable scene of all, Sinbad has a thrilling sword fight with a living skeleton. Harryhausen would make more magic in such outstanding fantasy features as MYSTERIOUS ISLAND, JASON AND THE ARGONAUTS, and CLASH OF THE TITANS.

SEX, LIES, AND VIDEOTAPE

1989 101m c Drama   ★★★½
Outlaw (U.S.)   R/18

James Spader (*Graham Dalton*), Andie MacDowell (*Ann Millaney*), Peter Gallagher (*John Millaney*), Laura San Giacomo (*Cynthia Bishop*), Ron Vawter (*Therapist*), Steven Brill (*Barfly*), David Foil (*John's Colleague*), Earl Taylor (*Landlord*), Alexandra Root (*Girl on Tape*)

p, Robert Newmyer, John Hardy; d, Steven Soderbergh; w, Steven Soderbergh; ph, Walt Lloyd; m, Cliff Martinez; art d, Joanne Schmidt; cos, James Ryder

AAN Best Original Screenplay: Steven Soderbergh

Like its title, SEX, LIES AND VIDEOTAPE sneaks by quietly, in subtle increments, gradually accumulating force. Graham Dalton (James Spader) arrives at the upscale home of his old college friend John Millaney (Peter Gallagher) and the friend's wife, Ann (Andie MacDowell). The two men have little in common any more: Graham is jobless and alienated; John is an aggressive yuppie attorney. He is also having an affair with his wife's sister, Cynthia (Laura San Giacomo), who's a trouble-maker. Graham and Ann become friendly, and he reveals that he is impotent. They have a falling out over his collection of videotapes, which contain conversations with women who've consented to speak intimately about sex before his camera. Then Cynthia pays him a visit and makes a tape, precipitating a series of emotional revelations. An unusually mature and self-assured fiction-feature debut for director Steven Soderbergh, SEX, LIES AND VIDEOTAPE was the winner of the Cannes Film Festival's top prize, the Palme d'Or, scoring a rare double win when Spader was named Best Actor as well. Notwithstanding the fervency of its reception, this is a quiet film, relying on talk rather than scenes of sex or nudity to make its points, and in the process establishing a far more intimate tone than many more explicit pictures. Soderbergh coaxes remarkably well-nuanced performances from the four principals. Beautifully edited by Soderbergh, the film is evenly paced, its subtleties accreting slowly, and by the end it gathers powerful emotional momentum.

SHADOW OF A DOUBT

1943 108m bw Thriller ★★★★½
Universal (U.S.) /A

Teresa Wright *(Young Charlie)*, Joseph Cotten *(Uncle Charlie)*, Macdonald Carey *(Jack Graham)*, Henry Travers *(Joseph Newton)*, Patricia Collinge *(Emma Newton)*, Hume Cronyn *(Herbie Hawkins)*, Edna May Wonacott *(Ann Newton)*, Wallace Ford *(Fred Saunders)*, Irving Bacon *(Station Master)*, Charles Bates *(Roger Newton)*

p, Jack H. Skirball; d, Alfred Hitchcock; w, Thornton Wilder, Sally Benson, Alma Reville (based on a story by Gordon McDonnell); ph, Joseph Valentine; ed, Milton Carruth; m, Dimitri Tiomkin; art d, John B. Goodman, Robert Boyle

AAN Best Original Screenplay: Gordon McDonell

Deathly Americana; not as fun or spine-tingling as other Hitchcocks, but who's complaining? Hitch's favorite among his own films was based on the case of the real-life "Merry Widow Murderer," Earle Leonard Nelson, a mass strangler of the 1920s. The sly Hitchcock made this chiller all the more frightening by having his crafty homicidal maniac intrude into the tranquility of a warm, middle-class family living in a small town, deeply developing his characters and drawing from the soft-spoken Joseph Cotten one of the actor's most remarkable and fascinating performances.

At the beginning of the film, Charlie (Cotten) is shown wooing and then murdering a woman for her riches. He barely escapes the police and then boards a train, having wired his sister Emma (Collinge) in Santa Rosa, California, that he is coming for an extended stay with the only family he has. (On board the train, as a passenger in his cameo appearance, is director Hitchcock.) In Santa Rosa his niece, also named Charlie (Wright), is delighted to hear that her urbane, witty, and adventurous uncle will be visiting the family. She, her father (Travers), and her young brother and sister (Wonacott and Bates) greet Uncle Charlie at the train station, but are shocked to see him limping on a cane, being helped by porters. He claims to be ill, and the family quickly takes him home, where Emma pampers him. Charlie stops at a bank and makes a scene while depositing $40,000, but his strange behavior is explained as an idiosyncracy by his adoring niece. Gradually, though, Charlie's past comes to town to haunt him, especially when a detective (Carey) shows up. Battling the thought that her beloved uncle could be the mass killer the detective has suggested he is, Charlie tries to get closer to her uncle, hoping to learn about his past and allay her fears.

This is Hitchcock's most penetrating analysis of a murderer—a masterful profile, aided by Cotten's superb performance, of a subtle killer who cannot escape his dark passions, despite a superior intellect. The film's construction is adroit and perfectly calculated, letting the viewer know early on just what kind of man Cotten really is, but providing tension through Cotten's devious charade as a gentle, kind man deserving of his family's love—a tension which fuels the chilling cat-and-mouse game between Cotten and Wright that provides the film's suspenseful center.

Hitchcock took his time in making SHADOW OF A DOUBT, and the care shows. The director got Thornton Wilder to write the screenplay, assuming that the playwright who created "Our Town" would be the perfect scenarist to bring the right kind of ambience and characterization to the film's small, close-knit Santa Rosa. After consulting briefly with Hitchcock, Wilder wandered about Hollywood with a notebook, writing bits and pieces of the screenplay when he could. He and the director took their time developing the intricate story, and Wilder had not finished the screenplay when he enlisted to serve in the Psychological Warfare Division of the Army. To finish the script, Hitchcock boarded a cross-country train to Florida (where Wilder was to begin his training) with the writer, and patiently sat in the next compartment as Wilder periodically emerged to give him another few pages of copy. The great playwright finished the last page of SHADOW

OF A DOUBT just as the train was coming to his stop, and he used the train upon which he and Hitchcock traveled as his model in creating the setting for the gripping finale.

SHADOWLANDS

1993 130m c Biography/Drama/Romance ★★★
Shadowlands Productions/Price Entertainment (U.K.) PG/U

Anthony Hopkins *(Jack Lewis)*, Debra Winger *(Joy Gresham)*, John Wood *(Christopher Riley)*, Edward Hardwicke *(Warnie Lewis)*, Robert Flemyng *(Claude Bird)*, Joseph Mazzello *(Douglas Gresham)*, Gerald Sim *(Superintendent Registrar)*, Peter Firth *(Dr. Craig)*, Julian Firth *(Father John Fisher)*, Julian Fellowes *(Desmond Arding)*

p, Richard Attenborough, Brian Eastman; d, Richard Attenborough; w, William Nicholson (from his play); ph, Roger Pratt; ed, Lesley Walker; m, George Fenton; prod d, Stuart Craig; art d, Michael Lamont; fx, Chris Corbould; cos, Penny Rose

AAN Best Actress: Debra Winger; *AAN Best Adapted Screenplay:* William Nicholson

Nominally a biography of C. S. Lewis, the Oxford lecturer and author of the popular children's books *The Chronicles of Narnia*, Richard Attenborough's SHADOWLANDS is a philosophical three-hankie picture.

Bachelor C.S. "Jack" Lewis (Anthony Hopkins) lives a quiet life of the mind, writing and teaching, and living with his brother Warnie (Edward Hardwicke). Jack's staid existence is shaken when he meets Joy Gresham (Debra Winger), an American poet with whom he has been corresponding, and who embarrasses him with her honesty and forthrightness. After a tense and awkward first encounter they become friends and, despite a romantic distance, soulmates. Joy brings her young son Douglas (Joseph Mazzello) to visit the Lewis brothers and reveals that she has fled her abusive husband. Jack agrees to a mock marriage to Joy so she can gain British citizenship; they live apart until Joy develops cancer and Jack realizes how deeply he feels about her.

The fact that SHADOWLANDS is based on a real-life love affair seems barely relevant; rather than dealing with historical events or social settings, Attenborough focuses almost entirely on the spiritual and personal aspects of this late-blooming romance. The term "tearjerker" is often used in a derogatory sense, but SHADOWLANDS earns the label honestly and may well help rehabilitate the genre by demonstrating its possibilities. Rather than brazenly manipulating its audience to force simple sobs, the film mixes introspection and a richly philosophical narration with its weeping for love lost and life cut short.

SHADOWS

1960 81m bw Drama ★★★★
Lion (U.S.) /X

Hugh Hurd *(Hugh)*, Lelia Goldoni *(Lelia)*, Ben Carruthers *(Ben)*, Anthony Ray *(Tony)*, Dennis Sallas *(Dennis)*, Tom Allen *(Tom)*, David Pokitillow *(David)*, Rupert Crosse *(Rupert)*, David Jones *(David)*, Pir Marini *(Pir)*

p, Maurice McEndree; d, John Cassavetes; ph, Erich Kollmar; ed, Maurice McEndree, Len Appelson; m, Charlie Mingus, Shifi Hadi

While on a radio talk show during the late 1950s, actor John Cassavetes casually mentioned his desire to film an improvisatory project and was soon surprised to receive public donations totaling nearly $20,000. Inspired, Cassavetes scraped together additional funds and, armed with a 16mm camera, he shot the powerful and moving SHADOWS, heralding a vital new era in independent American filmmaking.

Based on a series of improvisations created by members of the Variety Arts Studio, of which Cassavetes was the director, the film depicts the struggle of three black siblings to survive in the mean streets of Manhattan. Hugh (Hugh Hurd), the oldest and a would-be jazz musician, watches over Ben (Ben Carruthers) and Lelia (Lelia Goldoni), both of whom can, and do, pass for white. Darker-skinned than his younger siblings, Hugh has grown increasingly embittered due to the limited opportunities open to him; his artistic potential is being wasted in the dives and strip joints he's forced to play trumpet in just to survive.

Meanwhile, Lelia hooks up with the pretentious New York art crowd and moves among them, teasing and flirting. She has an affair with Tony (Anthony Ray), a young white man, and loses her virginity to him. However, when Tony learns that Lelia is a mulatto, he leaves her. Ben leads a carefree life, hanging out with his friends Tom (Tom Allen) and Dennis (Dennis Sallas), drinking, carousing and getting into trouble. One night the three young men become involved in a vicious street fight. By the film's end, Hugh grows more determined to win over one of the catatonic strip joint audiences, Lelia has taken refuge with friends, and Ben is abandoned by his buddies and left alone to lick his wounds.

Failing to interest American distributors—who, in addition to the obvious issue of content, were put off by the fact that the film was technically spotty and directed by a man heretofore known only as an actor—Cassavetes took SHADOWS to the 1960 Venice Film Festival, where it won the prestigious Critics Award. Shortly thereafter, the film was picked up for British distribution by Lion International. Finally, it made its way to the States and, to Hollywood's surprise, created a minor sensation.

Cassavetes was promptly hailed as a genius by critics and in no time began receiving offers to direct from major studios. The new director accepted Hollywood's embrace, but after making only two films (TOO LATE BLUES and A CHILD IS WAITING) he became frustrated by the limitations imposed on him by producers and returned to independent filmmaking, which allowed him complete control over his art.

While SHADOWS has become somewhat dated over the years and Cassavetes went on to greater heights as a filmmaker, its importance in the development of the American independent movement cannot be overstated, nor can the unique power it still retains. The film perfectly captured a specific time and place, illuminating simple truths regarding the human condition, while unveiling an important, powerful, and visionary new force in the American cinema.

SHAFT

1971 98m c Crime   ★★★
Stirling Silliphant/Roger Lewis (U.S.)   R/15

Richard Roundtree (John Shaft), Moses Gunn (Bumpy Jonas), Charles Cioffi (Lt. Vic Androzzi), Christopher St. John (Ben Buford), Gwenn Mitchell (Ellie Moore), Lawrence Pressman (Sgt. Tom Hannon), Victor Arnold (Charlie), Sherri Brewer (Marcy), Rex Robbins (Rollie), Camille Yarbrough (Dina Greene)

p, Joel Freeman; d, Gordon Parks Sr.; w, John D.F. Black, Ernest Tidyman (based on the novel by Tidyman); ph, Urs Furrer; ed, Hugh A. Robertson; m, Isaac Hayes; art d, Emanuel Gerard; cos, Joseph Aulisi

AAN Best Score: Isaac Hayes; *AA Best Song:* Isaac Hayes

This was the second feature of the longtime still photographer Parks, in which he brought together talent for capturing an image and personal knowledge of life on the streets to create a hard-hitting action thriller. Roundtree plays a private detective hired by Harlem mobster Gunn to find his kidnapped daughter. This requires infiltrating the mob before finding the girl. St. John plays the black militant who assists Roundtree, and Cioffi is the cop who helps keep a gangland war from escalating. Although obvious racial tensions are created, these are kept under check by Parks, who concentrated on the humanistic elements in his character.

SHAKESPEARE WALLAH

1965 115m bw Drama   ★★★
Continental Distributing (India)   /A

Shashi Kapoor (Sanju), Felicity Kendal (Lizzie Buckingham), Madhur Jaffrey (Manjula), Geoffrey Kendal (Mr. Tony Buckingham), Laura Liddell (Mrs. Carla Buckingham), Utpal Dutt (Maharaja), Praveen Paul (Didi), Jim D. Tytler (Bobby), Prayag Raaj (Sharmaji), Pincho Kapoor (Guptaji)

p, Ismail Merchant; d, James Ivory; w, Ruth Prawer Jhabvala, James Ivory (based on a story by Jhabvala); ph, Subrata Mitra; ed, Amit Bose; m, Satyajit Ray

Diverting piece about a bedraggled theatrical troupe engaged in a valiant effort to keep the spirit of Shakespeare alive in post-Independence India. English actress Felicity Kendal stars, and much of the material is based on the experiences of her real-life theatrical family.

Kendal gets involved in an interracial romance with a rich playboy (Shashi Kapoor); Madhur Jaffrey, an Indian actress also known for her books on Indian cuisine, turns in a colorful performance as a movie star. A wryly humorous film from the directing/producing/writing team of James Ivory, Ismail Merchant and Ruth Prawer Jhabvala.

SHALL WE DANCE

1937 101m bw Romance/Musical/Comedy   ★★★★
RKO (U.S.)   /U

Fred Astaire ("Petrov"/Peter P. Peters), Ginger Rogers (Linda Keene), Edward Everett Horton (Jeffrey Baird), Eric Blore (Cecil Flintridge), Jerome Cowan (Arthur Mille—Linda's Manager), Ketti Gallian (Lady Denise Tarrington), William Brisbane (Jim Montgomery), Harriet Hoctor (Harriet Hoctor), Ann Shoemaker (Mrs. Fitzgerald), Ben Alexander (Rooftop Bandleader)

p, Pandro S. Berman; d, Mark Sandrich; w, Allan Scott, Ernest Pagano, P.J. Wolfson (based on the story "Watch Your Step" by Lee Loeb, Harold Buchman); ph, David Abel; ed, William Hamilton; m, George Gershwin; art d, Van Nest Polglase, Carroll Clark; fx, Vernon L. Walker; chor, Hermes Pan, Harry Losee; cos, Irene

AAN Best Song: George Gershwin (Music), Ira Gershwin (Lyrics)

Shall we dance some more, please? For the seventh time in four years, Fred Astaire and Ginger Rogers team up for another frolicsome romp, though this effort doesn't amount to much more than a rehash of their previous films, replete with the usual romantic screw-ups, people pretending to be what they aren't, and too few stylized dances. Thank goodness for Astaire and Rogers and especially for a sensational Gershwin brothers score. Astaire is Petrov, a Russian ballet dancer; Rogers is Linda Keene, a high-powered musical-comedy star. To keep Linda from retiring to marry, Linda's agent (Cowan) suggests that she's already married to Petrov, to the surprise of the breathless press. Petrov and Linda ultimately decide to get married so they can get a very public divorce and clear the air, but true love does blossom amid the many plot complications.

SHALL WE DANCE might have made more of an impact on moviegoers, who, judging from the still huge but slowly declining boxoffice appeal of the Astaire-Rogers efforts, were growing tired of the formula. The film itself still has plenty of shine, but deficiencies exist. The peerless pair enjoy one of their best-ever tap duets with "They All Laughed", one which includes jokes, challenges, hard and soft tap, changes in tempo, a lovely merging of his ballet and her tap and a snappy close. But it's the only duet that measures up. Astaire and Rogers croon "Let's Call the Whole Thing Off" ("you say ee-ther, and I say eye-ther") quite agreeably, but neither quite pulls off the rollerskating routine which follows. Astaire's solo to "Slap That Bass" has some great moments and a blistering finale, but the fuel it provides really doesn't last. The finale, meanwhile, although it offers a clever resolution to the plot, seems more than a bit forced, with Rogers falling back in love with Astaire at the sight of duplicates of herself dancing onstage. The ballet surrounding this climax is a mess, with chorines and ballerinas ambling about in clumps, Astaire looking uncomfortable, and sideshow freak Harriet Hoctor bollixing any impact the number may have. A ballerina-cum-contortionist, Hoctor stops the show dead (and we mean *dead*) when she performs her signature move: kicking herself in the head while bent backwards like a human croquet wicket. Please be sure to share this moment with someone you love, for things like this don't appear in films everyday. The supporting cast (except for the awkward Ketti Gallian) is as expert as it was in earlier RKO musicals, even if the hilarious and gifted duo of Horton and Blore really have to work overtime to put over some of the thin material. Although it didn't initially appear to be hit-laden, George and Ira Gershwin's unfailingly marvelous score ultimately produced a number of standards, including the haunting, Oscar-nominated "They Can't Take That Away From Me." (What a glorious romantic duet that song would have made for Fred and Ginger!) Maybe we've been harsh, because there's still plenty to enjoy in this typically exhilarating Astaire-Rogers effort, but the lack of invention and the slight dearth of dancing do make this a lesser entry in the duo's joint canon.

SHALLOW GRAVE

1994 94m c Thriller/Crime ★★½
Figment Film/Film Four/Channel Four Films/Glasgow R/18
Film Fund (U.K.)

Kerry Fox *(Juliet Miller)*, Christopher Eccleston *(David Stephens)*, Ewan McGregor *(Alex Law)*, Ken Stott *(Detective McCall)*, Keith Allen *(Hugo)*, John Bett *(Brian McKinley)*, Kenneth Bryans *(Senior Police Officer)*, Elspeth Cameron *(Elderly Woman)*, Jean Marie Coffey *(Goth)*, Tony Curren *(Salesman)*

p, Andrew Macdonald; d, Danny Boyle; w, John Hodge; ph, Brian Tufano; ed, Masahiro Hirakubo; m, Simon Boswell; prod d, Kave Quinn; art d, Zoe MacLeod; fx, Tony Steers; cos, Kate Carin

Wildly overpraised by critics in search of a new master of suspense, SHALLOW GRAVE has plenty of visual style but no soul. Three Edinburgh yuppies—Alex (Ewan McGregor), a journalist, David (Christopher Eccleston), an accountant, and Juliet (Kerry Fox), a doctor—are looking for a fourth tenant for their shared apartment. They agree on mysterious Hugo (Keith Allen), who dies of a drug overdose soon after, leaving behind a suitcase full of money. After some debate, the trio decide to slice up the corpse, bury it in the woods, and keep the cash. The scheme begins to unravel when two of Hugo's associates break into the apartment and viciously attack Juliet and Alex. Although David manages to kill the pair, it's only the beginning of the trio's troubles.

Even before its UK release, SHALLOW GRAVE was enthusiastically flacked by the British press, who hailed director Danny Boyle as a "British Quentin Tarantino." While Boyle's visual skill is evident, he lacks the vision and sense of structure that distinguish RESERVOIR DOGS and PULP FICTION; John Hodges's brittle dialogue, furthermore, doesn't come close to the loopy poetry of QT's best writing. Alex, David and Juliet are self-centered, obnoxious louts, the British equivalent of American yuppie scum: there's no possible way to empathize with them. As a result, the plentiful violence is more unpleasant than frightening, several potentially compelling scenes lose their resonance, and the gory, histrionic finale—evidently intended to play as black comedy—just feels excessive.

SHAME
(SKAMMEN)

1968 103m bw Drama ★★★★½
Svensk (Sweden) R/15

Liv Ullmann *(Eva Rosenberg)*, Max von Sydow *(Jan Rosenberg)*, Gunnar Bjornstrand *(Col. Jacobi)*, Sigge Furst *(Filip)*, Birgitta Valberg *(Mrs. Jacobi)*, Hans Alfredson *(Lobelius)*, Ingvar Kjellson *(Oswald)*, Raymond Lundberg *(Jacobi's Son)*, Frank Sundstrom *(Chief Interrogator)*, Willy Peters *(Elder Officer)*

d, Ingmar Bergman; w, Ingmar Bergman; ph, Sven Nykvist; ed, Ulla Ryghe; art d, P.A. Lundgren, Lennart Blomkvist; fx, Evald Andersson; cos, Mago

Ingmar Bergman's SHAME is a tremendously profound and unsettling film about the indignities of war. In remarkably subtle performances, Liv Ullmann and Max von Sydow play a middle-class couple whose quietly honed existence is forever shattered by a mysterious civil war tearing across their homeland.

Former concert violinists Eva and Jan Rosenberg (Liv Ullmann, Max von Sydow) work and live on a small island, where they've escaped the war on the mainland. The apolitical Rosenbergs concern themselves only with selling the produce that they grow in their greenhouse. Despite ominous warnings of an impending invasion, the couple cling to their routine and ponder their future. Without warning, military warplanes fill the sky with explosions and gunfire while an officer warns Jan and Eva to evacuate immediately. Before they have a chance to start their car, Jan and Eva are ambushed by a film crew, who demand to know their political beliefs. Eva says that they have no interest in the war and the two are set free. Later, the Rosenbergs are arrested because of Eva's interview—which has been completely redubbed by a voice spouting revolutionary propaganda.

Considered by many critics to be one of Bergman's masterpieces, SHAME is certainly one of his most accessible. In the 1960s, Bergman moved to Faro, a small Swedish island in the Baltic where he also shot a series of daring and introspective films. In two of those "island" films—PERSONA (1966) and THE PASSION OF ANNA (1969)—he experimented with self-reflexive form and fragmented narratives using the bleak landscape as an existential purgatory where his characters were exiled. But with SHAME, Bergman felt compelled to make a non-political statement about the dehumanization of war as the conflict in Vietnam intensified.

SHAME's power is its simplicity. Cinematographer Sven Nykvist bathes the scenery in harsh sunlight, which gives the film an otherworldly and dreamlike glow. Longtime regulars Ullmann, von Sydow, and Gunnar Bjornstrand embody their characters with a raw emotionalism that's upsetting and not always easy to watch. Bergman hardly shows any violence, yet his spare stylistic touches—phones and automobiles that fail to work, the sound of water lapping against a boat full of doomed passengers—brilliantly convey the horror of destruction and how the greater ideologies of politics don't matter when one is faced with survival and death.

SHAMPOO

1975 109m c Drama/Comedy ★★★½
Columbia (U.S.) R/18

Warren Beatty *(George Roundy)*, Julie Christie *(Jackie Shawn)*, Goldie Hawn *(Jill)*, Lee Grant *(Felicia Carr)*, Jack Warden *(Lester Carr)*, Tony Bill *(Johnny Pope)*, Carrie Fisher *(Lorna Carr)*, Jay Robinson *(Norman)*, George Furth *(Mr. Pettis)*, Ann Weldon *(Mary)*

p, Warren Beatty; d, Hal Ashby; w, Robert Towne, Warren Beatty; ph, Laszlo Kovacs; ed, Robert C. Jones; m, Paul Simon; prod d, Richard Sylbert; art d, Stewart Campbell; cos, Anthea Sylbert

AAN Best Supporting Actor: Jack Warden; *AA Best Supporting Actress:* Lee Grant; *AAN Best Original Screenplay:* Robert Towne, Warren Beatty; *AAN Best Art Direction:* Richard Sylbert, W. Stewart Campbell, George Gaines

Satire of a satyr. Playing a Jay Sebring-like hairdresser/boy toy to the Beverly Hills elite, Beatty mercilessly lampoons his own offscreen image in a bumptious comedy of manners that turns persuasively sombre at the end. The events take place on Election Day, 1968, a date clearly chosen to signify the end of an era. Beatty is fooling around with Grant, an attractive married woman. Their coupling is interrupted by a phone call from Hawn, who represents the closest thing to a serious relationship Beatty can manage; he rushes over to her home and ends up spending the rest of the night with her. Later Beatty talks to a bank loan officer, hoping to get money to open his own hair salon. The loan officer thinks Beatty is a poor risk, and the angered hairdresser retaliates by screaming, "I've got the heads!"

Grant suggests Beatty approach her husband, Warden, for the money. Warden is sleeping with Christie, an old client/lover of Beatty's; he assumes Beatty is gay and doesn't catch on even when he finds his mistress and her lover virtually *in flagrante*. He agrees to consider Beatty's request, and asks Beatty to beard Christie at an election night party. Beatty reluctantly agrees, and the party proves to be a fiasco of drink, boorishness, and sexual betrayal.

Beatty, who produced SHAMPOO and cowrote the script (reportedly working for six years on it), was born to play the aimless, none-too-bright Don Juan. Hawn sums up his character nicely when she shouts at him: "You never stop moving! You never go anywhere!" The film's use of television election returns during the election night party is effective. History is in flux—with Nixon's election, the Swinging Sixties are definitively over—but the overprivileged party guests remain oblivious, caught up in the drama of their own sexual politics. The Beach Boys' popular song "Wouldn't It Be Nice" plays as the credits roll, a black-humored punch line to the film. Fisher made her film debut here as Grant's feisty daughter who seduces Beatty in record time. Reportedly Fisher's mother, Debbie Reynolds, was furious with her daughter for taking the part. SHAMPOO was an enormous success at the box office, taking in some $60 million during its initial release.

SHANE

1953 118m c Western ★★★★
Paramount (U.S.) /PG

Alan Ladd (Shane), Jean Arthur (Marion Starrett), Van Heflin (Joe Starrett), Brandon de Wilde (Joey), Jack Palance (Wilson), Ben Johnson (Chris), Edgar Buchanan (Lewis), Emile Meyer (Ryker), Elisha Cook Jr. (Torrey), Douglas Spencer (Shipstead)

p, George Stevens; d, George Stevens; w, A.B. Guthrie Jr., Jack Sher (based on the novel by Jack Schaefer); ph, Loyal Griggs; ed, William Hornbeck, Tom McAdoo; m, Victor Young; art d, Hal Pereira, Walter Tyler; fx, Gordon Jennings; cos, Edith Head

AAN Best Picture; AAN Best Supporting Actor: Brandon DeWilde; AAN Best Supporting Actor: Jack Palance; AAN Best Director: George Stevens; AAN Best Screenplay: A.B. Guthrie, Jr.; AA Best Cinematography: Loyal Griggs

Self-important, overly solemn, middlingly paced—all harbingers of what would become Stevens's later style. It's the western styled as Arthurian legend, flawlessly cast, undeniably splendid. The thematic attempt really takes off when the Black Knight himself, Jack Palance, arrives, or when a dog mourns the passing of his master. And Brandon de Wilde had a very special line in children's roles—an ability to bring complexity and individual humor to the realm of childhood's longing. We love him very much.

SHANE stars Alan Ladd in the title role of the gunslinger who becomes a young boy's idol. Joe and Marion Starrett (Van Heflin and Jean Arthur) and their adventurous young son Joey (Brandon de Wilde) are struggling to survive on their Wyoming frontier homestead. One day, Shane (Alan Ladd) approaches on horseback and asks for water for himself and his mount. Joe obliges, and before long Shane is helping the family protect its land from villainous cattle baron Ryker (Emile Meyer). Shane stays on as a ranch hand and, in the process, becomes a friend and hero to young Joey. Shane's presence, however, proves to be too much of an obstacle for Ryker, and the inevitable showdown occurs. SHANE is a powerful drama in which the old West of gunslingers and cattle barons bows to the new era of the homesteader and the family. Ladd, who was never better as the doomed hero, and who gives one of the best performances ever seen in any western, knows he is a creature of the past and that he cannot escape his reputation as a hired gun. Although the film is often brutal, there is such a positive sense of morality displayed here that SHANE should be seen by the whole family. How many Academy members knew Paramount had sliced the top and bottom off Griggs's compositions, to accomodate the then-new, wide screen, and therefore had lost some of the color? Ladd learned a bitter lesson from SHANE. Then in the process of leaving Paramount for Warners, the former did no lobbying to earn him a Best Actor nomination. Yet the legacy of character he left behind gave this lonely, taciturn man immortality among children who see this movie.

SHANGHAI EXPRESS

1932 80m bw Drama ★★★★
Paramount (U.S.) /A

Marlene Dietrich (Shanghai Lily), Clive Brook (Capt. Donald "Doc" Harvey), Anna May Wong (Hui Fei), Warner Oland (Henry Chang), Eugene Pallette (Sam Salt), Lawrence Grant (Rev. Carmichael), Louise Closser Hale (Mrs. Haggerty), Gustav von Seyffertitz (Eric Baum), Emile Chautard (Maj. Lenard), Claude King (Albright)

d, Josef von Sternberg; w, Jules Furthman (based on a story by Harry Hervey); ph, Lee Garmes; m, W. Franke Harling; art d, Hans Dreier; cos, Travis Banton

AAN Best Picture; AAN Best Director: Josef Von Sternberg; AA Best Cinematography: Lee Garmes

The fourth of the Josef von Sternberg-Marlene Dietrich collaborations (following THE BLUE ANGEL, MOROCCO, and DISHONORED), SHANGHAI EXPRESS is a mystical and exotic story of love and destruction, a film for which both star and director became legends. The film begins at the Peking Railroad as China's great train, the Shanghai Express, is being boarded and loaded with baggage. En route to Shanghai is a mixed assortment of characters, including Dietrich, a lady of questionable reputation known as "the White Flower of the Chinese coast;" Clive Brook, a British Medical Corps officer; Warner Oland, a shady half-caste merchant with a penchant for carrying a cane; and Anna Mae Wong, an American-bred Chinese prostitute with plans for starting anew in marriage. The time of the journey is one of great political unrest, with the possibility of bands of rebels attacking the train looming large. Before the train even leaves the station, arrests are made. Brook is surprised to find that he is traveling with Dietrich, a past love of his whom he deserted. Because of his constant work and busy schedule, he has never heard of her reputation as a glamorous prostitute and seductress. But he soon begins to understand Dietrich and the power she holds over men. In the meantime, it becomes clear to everyone on board that Oland is a rebel leader, desperate over the arrest of his aides. Along the way, Oland orders the train stopped at an old station that has been taken over for use as rebel headquarters, while he makes plans to take hostages from among his fellow first-class passengers. Oland, like Brook, is strongly attracted to the elusive Dietrich, but when the rebel leader asks Dietrich to be his mistress, she turns him down flat. But Oland pressures Dietrich by threatening to torture Brook. Only then—in order to save Brook—does Dietrich give in. Brook, however, is unaware of what she has done. Oland's fate is sealed, however, not by Dietrich or Brook, but by Wong, the prostitute in search of redemption, who has earlier been raped by the insatiable rebel leader. As Oland returns to his room, Wong stabs him to death, thereby freeing herself, the Shanghai Express, and the love between Dietrich and Brook.

Though von Sternberg insisted the film was based on a one-page treatment handed him by Harry Hervey, the story of THE SHANGHAI EXPRESS is clearly drawn from Guy de Maupassant's classic short story of a French prostitute during the Franco-Prussian war, "Boule de Suif." The final film, however, is all von Sternberg, his enigmatic creation, Dietrich, filling the screen with her stunning persona. Dietrich, as always, gave von Sternberg the exact performance he had envisioned, but feuds and hard feelings ran rampant between the director and the remainder of the cast. Von Sternberg was something of a tyrant on the set, and actors received the brunt of his wrath. Lending further credence to his tyrannical image on the set, von Sternberg, who had nearly lost his voice from shouting, dismissed a suggestion from Sam Jaffe to use a megaphone, instead hooking up a public address system. This enthusiasm and complete control over the production paid off for the director and for SHANGHAI EXPRESS come Oscar time. The film was nominated for Best Picture (losing to GRAND HOTEL), von Sternberg received a nomination for Best Director (his second in a row), and Lee Garmes walked away with a statuette for his cinematography.

SHANGHAI TRIAD
(YAO A YAO YAO DAO WAIPO QIAO)

1995 108m c Drama/Crime ★★★½
Shanghai Film Studios/Alpha Films/UGC Images/La Sept R/15
Cinema (China/France)

Gong Li (Bijou—Xiao Jinbao), Li Baotian (Tang, the Triad Boss), Wang Xiaoxiao (Shuisheng, the Boy), Li Xuejian (6th Uncle), Sun Chun (Song, Tang's No. 2), Fu Biao (Tang's No. 3), Chen Shu (Shi Ye), Liu Jiang (Fat Yu), Jiang Baoying (Cuihua, the Widow), Yang Qianquan (Ah Jiao)

p, Jean-Louis Piel; d, Zhang Yimou; w, Bi Feiyu (freely adapted from the novel Men Gui (Gang Law) by Li Xiao); ph, Lu Yue; ed, Du Yuan; m, Zhang Guangtian; prod d, Cao Jiuping; art d, Huang Xinming, Ma Yongming; chor, Wang Qing; cos, Tong Huamiao

AAN Best Cinematography: Lu Yue

This gorgeously appointed gangster picture, a departure for acclaimed Chinese art-house director Zhang Yimou, looks like a Hollywood genre movie—in fact, it looks a lot like BILLY BATHGATE. Here, however, the volatile gangster's moll (Gong Li) is moved—often literally—to center stage.

Zhang was criticized in the US for making an apparently apolitical film, but political controversy nevertheless attended the 1995 New York Film Festival showing of SHANGHAI TRIAD. At the request of the Chinese Government—angered by another festival entry, Tiananmen Square massacre documentary THE GATE OF HEAVENLY PEACE—Zhang had to abandon his plans to attend the Festival. In addition, SHANGHAI TRIAD marked the apparent end of the longtime collaboration of Zhang and star Gong Li, which has often been compared to the intense professional and personal relationship between Josef von Sternberg and Marlene Dietrich. Gong had appeared in all seven of Zhang's features.

Simultaneously over- and underdressed in extravagant shades of red and gold, Gong Li is a star in the old-fashioned Hollywood sense: she's China's first screen diva, easily outshining the bravura gunplay and macho posturing of an essentially generic story line, about warring gangsters and their women in the Shanghai underworld of 1930. The film represents a retreat from the explicitly political concerns of TO LIVE (which landed the director in serious trouble with P.R.C. authorities), but there's a distinct satirical subtext underlying Zhang's Chinese Gangland, a place of limitless greed, self-destructive ritual and fatal hubris. Arguably, Zhang was up to something that in 1995 was far more dangerous than criticizing China's Maoist past — with necessary subtlety, he was contemplating its bleak capitalist future.

SHAWSHANK REDEMPTION, THE

1994   142m   c   Prison/Drama ★★★½
Columbia/Castle Rock   (U.S.) R/15

Tim Robbins (Andy Dufresne), Morgan Freeman (Ellis Boyd "Red" Redding), Bob Gunton (Warden Norton), William Sadler (Heywood), Clancy Brown (Captain Hadley), Gil Bellows (Tommy), Mark Rolston (Bogs Diamond), James Whitmore (Brooks Hatlen), Jeffrey DeMunn (1946 DA), Larry Brandenburg (Skeet)

p, Niki Marvin; d, Frank Darabont; w, Frank Darabont (based on the short story "Rita Hayworth and Shawshank Redemption" by Stephen King); ph, Roger Deakins; ed, Richard Francis-Bruce, David Johnson; m, Thomas Newman; prod d, Terence Marsh; art d, Peter Smith; cos, Elizabeth McBride

AAN Best Picture; AAN Best Actor: Morgan Freeman; AAN Best Adapted Screenplay: Frank Darabont; AAN Best Cinematography: Roger Deakins; AAN Best Editing: Richard Francis-Bruce; AAN Best Original Score: Thomas Newman; AAN Best Sound: Robert J. Litt, Elliot Tyson, Michael Herbick, Willie Burton

A "life-affirming" tale about life imprisonment, THE SHAWSHANK REDEMPTION is the kind of old-fashioned entertainment that easily overvalued in an era of diminishing expectations. This reverent adaptation of an unremarkable 1982 Stephen King novella was received tepidly at the box office—due in part to advertising that offered no clue as to what the movie was about—but gained a remarkably enthusiastic following and surprised many by netting seven Oscar nominations.

In mid-1940s Maine, banker Andy Dufresne (Tim Robbins) is tried and convicted for the murder of his wife and her lover. He is sentenced to life at Shawshank prison, where he meets affable lifer Ellis Boyd "Red" Redding (Morgan Freeman), whose applications for parole are turned down on an annual basis. Known as one who can get things—for a price—Red secures for Andy a pinup of Rita Hayworth and a rock hammer to pursue his geological hobbies. Both items turn out to be crucial parts of a scheme that the mild-mannered banker nurses through years of painstaking preparation.

Whereas some Stephen King adapters have seemed intent on transcending or trashing their source material, writer-director Frank Darabont succeeds through fidelity to the text; the few deviations make this subdued male love story even more audience-friendly. The film benefits greatly from elegant cinematography by Roger Deakins and a poignant score by Thomas Newman. Freeman creates an endearing portrait of a decent man with a dark deed in his past, and Tim Robbins gives what may be his most accomplished portrayal. The excellent supporting cast includes James Whitmore, cute as the dickens as old-timer Brooks Hatlen, and William Sadler as a con who starts out scary and ends up lovable.

Which brings us to the film's greatest limitation: prison hasn't looked this inviting since 1940s Hollywood. Nothing seems to build character like a long stint at Shawshank, which on the whole seems not much worse than a downmarket summer camp. This makes for a crowd-pleasing story that has little to do with the messy complexities of reality.

SHE DONE HIM WRONG

1933   66m   bw   Comedy ★★★★½
Paramount   (U.S.) /A

Mae West (Lady Lou), Cary Grant (Capt. Cummings), Owen Moore (Chick Clark), Gilbert Roland (Serge Stanieff), Noah Beery Sr. (Gus Jordan), David Landau (Dan Flynn), Rafaela Ottiano (Russian Rita), Dewey Robinson (Spider Kane), Rochelle Hudson (Sally Glynn), Tammany Young (Chuck Connors)

p, William Le Baron; d, Lowell Sherman; w, Mae West, Harvey Thew, John Bright (based on the play "Diamond Lil" by Mae West); ph, Charles Lang; ed, Al Hall; art d, Robert Usher; chor, Harold Hecht; cos, Edith Head

AAN Best Picture

Marvelously crude melodrama dished up with generous portions of undiluted West in her first starring vehicle. Re-creating her bediamonded demimonde, Diamond Lil, for the screen, she wriggles her way through some lowdown dirty blues ditties, seduces young Cary Grant's righteous Salvation Army crusader, kicks asses and takes names. Little-known director Lowell Sherman ably evokes the gaudy squalor of the Bowery at the turn of the century, and West establishes herself as a persona happiest squabbling among the chiselers and moneylenders.

West already reigned supreme on Broadway when Hollywood beckoned her at around age 40 (West was hazy about age) to support George Raft in NIGHT AFTER NIGHT. With SHE DONE HIM WRONG, West became an enormous star. She made 12 movies altogether, 10 of which she wrote either alone or with collaborators. Amazingly, SHE DONE HIM WRONG was shot in 18 days, plus one week of rehearsal, as West fiddled with the lines to mislead the censors.

West's Lou must rank as one of the first truly liberated women ever seen onscreen as she runs a Bowery saloon, fronting for owner Noah Beery, Sr. Cary Grant, a captain at the local mission, spends more than the usual amount of time in the bar in what seems to be an attempt to save her immortal soul; before long the buxom West is in love with the youthful Grant. Having been the mistress of Beery, who plies her with diamonds, West knows she's in trouble when her heart begins to obscure the glow of the gems. But Beery is discovered to be running a counterfeiting ring and, as a sideline, sending young women to San Francisco to be pickpockets. Gilbert Roland and Rafaela Ottiano have been passing the bogus money that Beery needs to pay for West's diamonds. Then, in a jealous battle with West, Ottiano gets herself killed.

Remember what we said about crude melodrama? Scenes like the latter obviously recall the touring shows West herself must have seen growing up as a tyke in turn of the century Brooklyn. West's original character of Lil was derived from her mother, a former French corset model whose husband (West's Irish prizefighter father) referred to her affectionately as "Champagne Til". And some of Lil was undoubtedly West herself: as a child, West's mother spoiled her outrageously, always dressing her in minature versions of her own elaborate gowns. West never lost her taste for long skirts, fancy fabrics, wasp waists and cornucopic picture hats.

She had spotted Grant on the Paramount lot and asked to have him in the picture, a request that pleased director Lowell Sherman, who liked Grant's work with Marlene Dietrich in BLONDE VENUS. But West, who never saw other women's movies, didn't know that. Eyeing Grant up and down, West said to Sherman, "If he can talk, I'll take 'im." In the years to come, West always played variations on this "Diamond Lil" role in everything she did, tacking on other character names. "Why should I go good, when I'm packin' 'em in 'cause I'm bad?", West once asked.

SHE WORE A YELLOW RIBBON

1949   103m   c   Western/War ★★★★
Argosy   (U.S.) /U

John Wayne (Capt. Nathan Brittles), Joanne Dru (Olivia Dandridge), John Agar (Lt. Flint Cohill), Ben Johnson (Sgt. Tyree), Harry Carey Jr. (Lt. Ross Pennell), Victor McLaglen (Sgt. Quincannon), Mildred Natwick (Mrs. Abby Allshard), George O'Brien (Maj. Mack Allshard), Arthur Shields (Dr. O'Laughlin), Francis Ford (Barman) p, John Ford, Merian C. Cooper; d, John Ford; w, Frank S. Nugent, Laurence Stallings (based on the stories "War Party" and "The Big Hunt" by James Warner Bellah); ph, Winton C. Hoch, Charles P. Boyle; ed, Jack Murray; m, Richard Hageman; art d, James Basevi; fx, Jack Cosgrove, Jack Caffee; cos, Michael Meyers, Ann Peck

AA Best Cinematography: Winton Hoch

The second film in John Ford's "Cavalry Trilogy" features John Wayne at his best and boasts some incredible, Oscar-winning Technicolor photography of Monument Valley. Capt. Nathan Brittles (Wayne) is a career officer in the US Cavalry marking the final days before his forced retirement from the service. In the wake of the massacre of Custer and the Seventh Cavalry, the local Indians are becoming agitated, and, worse, confident. Brittles is assigned to escort two women (Joanne Dru and Mildred Natwick) from the fort to the stagecoach stop at Sudrow's Wells, but the Indians are on the warpath and there is little chance now to evacuate the women from the area. Wayne gives one of the finest performances of his career here, in the first serious role Ford gave him. (Wayne himself later said that Ford never respected him as an actor until he made RED RIVER.) As Capt. Brittles—the character a full generation older than the actor—Wayne is at his most human, a man who has made the Army his whole life, even sacrificing the lives of his family to its service, and now having to watch his Army career end on a note of failure. The passing of time is the film's recurring theme, suggested as Brittles arrives late with his troops, is forced to retire because of his age, leaves a dance to speak to his dead wife; even the inscription on the watch the troopers give him, "Lest we forget," plays on this theme of time lost and recalled. Ford's main inspiration for the film's scenic look was the western paintings of Frederic Remington. On the set, the director clashed with cinematographer Winton Hoch, a technical perfectionist who would endlessly fiddle with his camera while the cast baked in the sun. One day in the desert, when a line of threatening clouds darkened the horizon, indicating a thunderstorm, Hoch started to pack up his equipment. Ford ordered him to continue shooting, and Hoch did so, but filed an official protest with his union. The shot that emerged, of a fantastic purple sky with jagged streaks of lightning reaching toward earth in the distance, was breathtaking and helped Hoch win an Oscar for his work on the film. After decades of terribly washed-out color prints of SHE WORE A YELLOW RIBBON, the film has recently been restored to its original glory and may soon be available on home video in pristine condition.

SHENANDOAH

1965 105m c War
Universal (U.S.)

★★★½
/PG

James Stewart *(Charlie Anderson)*, Doug McClure *(Sam)*, Glenn Corbett *(Jacob Anderson)*, Patrick Wayne *(James Anderson)*, Rosemary Forsyth *(Jannie Anderson)*, Phillip Alford *(Boy Anderson)*, Katharine Ross *(Ann Anderson)*, Charles Robinson *(Nathan Anderson)*, James McMullan *(John Anderson)*, Tim McIntire *(Henry Anderson)*

p, Robert Arthur; d, Andrew V. McLaglen; w, James Lee Barrett; ph, William Clothier; ed, Otho Lovering; m, Frank Skinner; art d, Alexander Golitzen, Alfred Sweeney; cos, Rosemary Odell

AAN Best Sound: Waldon O. Watson

An offbeat performance from James Stewart as Virginia farmer Charlie Anderson makes SHENANDOAH an involving and entertaining look at one family's attempt to deal with the Civil War. A prosperous farmer with six sons and one daughter, Charlie is a widower whose wife died during the birth of Boy (Phillip Alford). Charlie, who is opposed to slavery, tries to maintain a neutral stance in the conflict between North and South. However, a number of events threaten to change his pacifist leanings: 16-year-old Boy is captured by Union soldiers; Confederate son-in-law Sam (Doug McClure) is called to duty; son James (Patrick Wayne) and his wife, Ann (Katharine Ross), are murdered by Confederate looters; and another son, Jacob (Glenn Corbett), is killed by a Confederate guardsman. Andrew V. McLaglen's excellent direction and carefully crafted battle scenes successfully combine with one of the best supporting casts you're likely to find outside of a John Ford film, including Harry Carey, Jr., Warren Oates, Strother Martin, Denver Pyle, George Kennedy, Paul Fix, and Bob Steele.

SHE'S GOTTA HAVE IT

1986 84m c/bw Comedy/Drama
Spike Lee Joint/Forty Acres and a Mule (U.S.)

★★★
R/18

Tracy Camila Johns *(Nola Darling)*, Tommy Redmond Hicks *(Jamie Overstreet)*, John Canada Terrell *(Greer Childs)*, Spike Lee *(Mars Blackmon)*, Raye Dowell *(Opal Gilstrap)*, Joie Lee *(Clorinda Bradford)*, Epatha Merkinson *(Dr. Jamison)*, Bill Lee *(Sonny Darling)*, Cheryl Burr *(Ava)*, Aaron Dugger *(Noble)*

p, Shelton J. Lee; d, Spike Lee; w, Spike Lee; ph, Ernest Dickerson; ed, Spike Lee; m, Bill Lee; prod d, Wynn Thomas; art d, Ron Paley; cos, John Michael Reefer

Combining a lively, topical theme with stylish filmmaking techniques, NYU Film School alum Spike Lee won instant recognition for SHE'S GOTTA HAVE IT, his promising but flawed feature debut.

Nola Darling (Tracy Camila Johns) is a young, black Brooklyn woman whose bed is a shrine visited with great frequency by three very different boyfriends. She can't, however, pick the one she likes best. First there's Jamie Overstreet (Tommy Redmond Hicks), a sensitive, well-mannered sort who smothers Nola with his overpossessiveness. Then there's Greer Childs (John Canada Terrell), a self-absorbed fashion model. The most likable character is the third beau, Mars Blackmon (director Lee), an unemployed bicycle messenger who always manages to make Nola—and audiences—laugh.

Combining humor, drama, and documentary techniques, Lee has created an energetic film that takes an unflinching look at modern sexuality—specifically black sexuality. The film is filled with scenes of the main characters speaking to the camera, commenting on the story and their rival characters—adding a sense of authenticity it might otherwise lack. Although the film's small budget and tight shooting schedule (lensed in 15 days on Super 16mm) is betrayed by sloppy editing, unpolished sound and an occasional flat performance, particularly Johns in the lead role, SHE'S GOTTA HAVE IT still bursts with the energy and technical command that have quickly established Lee as a major force in American cinema. The Mars Blackmon character lived on in a series of commercials for Nike sneakers shot by Lee.

SHINE

1996 105m c Drama
Momentum Films (Australia/U.K.)

★★★½
PG-13/12

Geoffrey Rush *(David as an Adult)*, Armin Mueller-Stahl *(Peter)*, Lynn Redgrave *(Gillian)*, Noah Taylor *(David as a Young Man)*, John Gielgud *(Cecil Parkes)*, Alex Rafalowicz *(David as a Child)*, Googie Withers *(Katharine Susannah Prichard)*, Sonia Todd *(Sylvia)*, Nicholas Bell *(Ben Rosen)*

p, Jane Scott; d, Scott Hicks; w, Jan Sardi (from a story by Scott Hicks); ph, Geoffrey Simpson; ed, Pip Karmel; m, David Hirschfelder; prod d, Vicki Niehus; cos, Louise Wakefield

AA Best Actor: Geoffrey Rush; *AAN Best Picture; AAN Best Supporting Actor:* Armin Mueller-Stahl; *AAN Best Director:* Scott Hicks; *AAN Best Film Editing:* Pip Karmel; *AAN Best Original Dramatic Score:* David Hirschfelder; *AAN Best Original Screenplay:* Jan Sardi, Scott Hicks (story)

Based on the true story of David Helfgott, a gifted pianist whose troubled private life cut short a brilliant career, Scott Hicks's film is neither exploitative nor excessively sentimental, managing the difficult task of relating familiar screen material in a fresh way.

As a little boy, David (Alex Rafalowicz) is forced to learn piano by his domineering father, Peter (Armin Mueller-Stahl), a Holocaust survivor who was denied the opportunity to play music during his own upbringing. David shows great promise as a teenager and wins a scholarship to study in America, but a resentful Peter forbids him to leave home. Later, through the encouragement of an elderly writer, Katharine Susannah Prichard (Googie Withers), David defies his father and leaves to study at London's Royal College of Music. But his success there is matched by mounting pressures, and after Katharine dies, David suffers a nervous breakdown. After receiving electro-shock therapy, David is committed to an institution where he is forbidden to ever play the piano.

SHINE succeeds better than many other stories about artists overcoming adversity because it does not condescend to either the characters or the audience. David's jabbering adult self may be a bit annoying at first, but in the hands of Geoffrey Rush (whose performance as the adult David won him an Academy Award for Best Actor) he becomes a fully rounded character. Likewise, the father-son melodrama at the heart of the film resists becoming a simplistic power struggle. Rush is well-supported by the entire cast, particularly Mueller-Stahl, who turns in one of his best performances as the psychotic stage-father. SHINE's classical production will particularly thrill music lovers (most of the music is played by Helfgott himself), but the film's emotional force can be appreciated by all audiences.

SHINING, THE

1980 146m c Horror   ★★★★
Warner Bros. (U.K.)   R/18

Jack Nicholson (Jack Torrance), Shelley Duvall (Wendy Torrance), Danny Lloyd (Danny), Scatman Crothers (Halloran), Barry Nelson (Ullman), Philip Stone (Grady), Joseph Turkel (Lloyd), Anne Jackson (Doctor), Tony Burton (Durkin), Lia Beldam (Young Woman in Bathtub)
p, Stanley Kubrick; d, Stanley Kubrick; w, Stanley Kubrick, Diane Johnson (based on the novel by Stephen King); ph, John Alcott; ed, Ray Lovejoy; m, Bela Bartok, Wendy Carlos, Rachel Elkind, Gyorgi Ligeti, Krzysztof Penderecki; prod d, Roy Walker; art d, Leslie Tomkins; cos, Milena Canonero

With remarkable visual panache and a keen sense of irony, Stanley Kubrick rehabilitates Stephen King's trashy, terrifying novel. Not a horror film in any traditional sense, but a perversely comic, occasionally frightening melodrama of intrafamilial rage, THE SHINING retains the Oedipal structure of King's narrative while running rings around its pulpy sensibility.

Jack Torrance (Nicholson) is a former schoolteacher hoping to find the solitude necessary to write a novel, so he accepts a position as the off-season caretaker of a Colorado resort, the Overlook Hotel. Because the winter storms are so fierce in this isolated mountain region, the hotel is often cut off from the rest of civilization. When he accepts the job, Jack is warned that the isolation can be devastating (some years earlier the caretaker axed his wife and two daughters to death). Jack and his wife, Wendy (Duvall), and their son, Danny (Lloyd), journey by car to the Overlook. Danny possesses the psychic gift that the hotel's chef (Crothers) calls "the shining"—he can "see" events from the future and the past. He can also project his thoughts into the minds of others. Danny senses something evil about the hotel and, while riding his bike through its labyrinthine halls, has visions of the carnage of past murders. His only playmate in this lonely environment is his "imaginary" friend, Tony. The emotionally vulnerable Jack—he's a recovering alcoholic with a history of violent episodes—is bedeviled by visions as well. Before long he begins to succumb to the hotel's supernatural forces and becomes possessed by thoughts of chopping up his family.

The film begins with astounding aerial footage of the Torrances' car driving through breathtaking mountain landscapes, accompanied by Wendy Carlos' mournful electronic score. There's also some impressive Steadicam work as the camera follows directly behind Danny, riding his Big Wheel bike through the winding corridors of the hotel. Cinematographer John Alcott (A CLOCKWORK ORANGE, BARRY LYNDON) does his usual outstanding job in each of these sequences. The film is rich thematically as well as visually—it's interesting to see how well the themes of the novel coincide with Kubrick's ongoing obsessions—but dramatically somewhat unsatisfying; it seems to have been conceived as a horror film for people who have lost patience with the genre. Duvall and Lloyd are excellent, while Nicholson's performance is over the top, complete with rolling eyes and hyperactive eyebrows. By the time of the climactic chase, he's lurching around like a cut-rate Quasimodo.

SHIP OF FOOLS

1965 148m bw Drama   ★★★★
Columbia (U.S.)   /A

Vivien Leigh (Mary Treadwell), Simone Signoret (La Condesa), Jose Ferrer (Rieber), Lee Marvin (Tenny), Oskar Werner (Dr. Schumann), Elizabeth Ashley (Jenny), George Segal (David), Jose Greco (Pepe), Michael Dunn (Glocken), Charles Korvin (Capt. Thiele)
p, Stanley Kramer; d, Stanley Kramer; w, Abby Mann (based on the novel by Katherine Anne Porter); ph, Ernest Laszlo; ed, Robert C. Jones; m, Ernest Gold; prod d, Robert Clatworthy; fx, Albert Whitlock, Farciot Edouart, John Burke; cos, Bill Thomas, Jean Louis

AAN Best Picture; AAN Best Actor: Oskar Werner; AAN Best Actress: Simone Signoret; AAN Best Supporting Actor: Michael Dunn; AAN Best Adapted Screenplay: Abby Mann; AA Best Cinematography: Ernest Laszlo; AA Best Art Direction: Robert Clatworthy, Joseph Kish; AAN Best Costume Design: Bill Thomas, Jean Louis

GRAND HOTEL at sea. It's the early 1930s, and an oceanliner peopled with a cross-section of society is leaving Vera Cruz for Bremerhaven. In the high class section are several well-to-do people, while steerage holds sugar workers returning to Spain after a season of work in Cuba. There are several wealthy Germans on the ship, and all are asked to sit at the captain's table save two—Heinz Ruhmann, a Jew, and Dunn, a dwarf. Werner, the ship's doctor and a man with a bad heart, makes time with Signoret, a Spaniard being deported for her political activities. Drunken satyr Marvin is a failed baseball player whose career went awry because he couldn't hit the outside curve ball. Also on the ship are unmarried lovers Segal and Ashley, flirtatious divorcee Leigh (in her last screen role), evangelist Wengraf, and dancer Greco. All of the above stories are interwoven, soap opera style, so we never follow any single story for any lengthy period of time. It's an adult picture with graphic language and important themes, the main one being Nazism. Superb acting in an Abby Mann script that seldom descends into bathos.

SHOCK CORRIDOR

1963 101m c/bw Drama   ★★★½
Allied Artists (U.S.)   /15

Peter Breck (Johnny Barrett), Constance Towers (Cathy), Gene Evans (Boden), James Best (Stuart), Hari Rhodes (Trent), Larry Tucker (Pagliacci), William Zuckert (Swanee), Philip Ahn (Dr. Fong), Neyle Morrow (Psycho), John Matthews (Dr. Cristo)
p, Samuel Fuller; d, Samuel Fuller; w, Samuel Fuller (based on his scenario); ph, Stanley Cortez, Samuel Fuller; ed, Jerome Thoms; m, Paul Dunlap; art d, Eugene Lourie; fx, Charles Duncan, Lynn Dunn; chor, Jon Gregory; cos, Einar Bourman

Good example of Fuller's "tabloid" filmmaking style, displaying the contradictory politics and pugnacious visual style that earned him the label "American primitive."

A self-serving reporter (Breck) has himself confined to an asylum so he can uncover a murder and win a Pulitzer Prize. He is sucked into the maelstrom of the asylum, which is presented as a microcosm of contemporary society, and eventually loses his mind. Fuller plays cinematic bully here, forcefully confronting us with unpleasant characters and situations in a way that makes us rethink our preconceptions about insanity and civilization. The bravura camerawork, by Stanley Cortez, is a marvel. Original release prints included some color sequences the director had shot in Japan and Africa as early as 1955. Fuller followed this piece with what was probably one of his best works, THE NAKED KISS.

SHOESHINE
(SCIUSCIA)

1946 93m bw Prison   ★★★½
Lopert (Italy)   /A

Rinaldo Smordoni (Giuseppe), Franco Interlenghi (Pasquale), Aniello Mele (Raffaele), Bruno Ortensi (Arcangeli), Pacifico Astrologo (Vittorio), Francesco de Nicola (Ciriola), Antonio Carlino (L'Abruzzese), Enrico de Silva (Giorgio), Antonio Lo Nigro (Righetoo), Angelo D'Amico (Siciliano)
p, Paolo W. Tamburella; d, Vittorio De Sica; w, Cesare Zavattini, Sergio Amidei, Adolfo Franci, Cesare Viola, Vittorio De Sica (based on a story by Zavattini); ph, Anchise Brizzi; m, Alessandro Cicognini

AAN Best Original Screenplay: Sergio Amidei, Adolfo Franci, C G Viola, Cesare Zavattini

Along with THE BICYCLE THIEF and UMBERTO D, this film is one of the three neorealist masterpieces produced through the collaborative efforts of director Vittorio De Sica and screenwriter Cesare Zavattini.

Like so many of the films of the neorealist movement, SHOESHINE is simply real life projected on a screen. After spying on a pair of shoeshine boys for a year in war-torn Rome, De Sica and Zavattini decided to bring their story to the screen with two nonprofessionals in the lead roles. Giuseppe (Rinaldo Smordoni) and Pasquale (Franco Interlenghi) are waifs who survive by harassing American soldiers—the only ones in postwar Italy with spare change—into spending a few lire to have their boots cleaned. Despite their bleak surroundings, these shoeshine boys still have innocent dreams and hopes, and, in fact, are saving their earnings to buy a handsome white horse. When Giuseppe's brother approaches them with a black market opportunity to make some quick money, they jump at the chance, buy their dream horse, and refuse to let it out of their sight, even going so far as to sleep in the stable with it. This brief moment in paradise is short-lived, however, and they are arrested, taken to a reformatory, and locked away. The longer they stay in their damp, vermin-infested cells, the more hardened the youngsters become. A powerful indictment of the Italian penal system and, on a larger scale, the brutal inevitability of the loss of innocence.

SHOOT THE PIANO PLAYER
(TIREZ SUR LE PIANISTE)
1960 80m bw Crime   ★★★★★
Pleiade (France)   /X

Charles Aznavour (Charlie Kohler/Edouard Saroyan), Marie Dubois (Lena), Nicole Berger (Theresa), Michele Mercier (Clarisse), Albert Remy (Chico Saroyan), Jacques Aslanian (Richard Saroyan), Richard Kanayan (Fido Saroyan), Claude Mansard (Momo), Daniel Boulanger (Ernest), Serge Davri (Plyne)

p, Pierre Braunberger; d, Francois Truffaut; w, Francois Truffaut, Marcel Moussy (based on the novel Down There by David Goodis); ph, Raoul Coutard; ed, Cecile Decugis, Claudine Bouche; m, Georges Delerue; art d, Jacques Mely

A marvelously funny movie about sadness. For his follow-up to THE 400 BLOWS (1959), Francois Truffaut chose not to deliver another episode of his autobiography, nor to study childhood, but to pay homage to Hollywood gangster films. Deciding to adapt David Goodis's pulp novel Down There, Truffaut chose Charles Aznavour, one of France's most popular singers and songwriters, to play the role of Charlie Kohler, a honky-tonk cafe piano player who has given up his life as the famed concert pianist Edouard Saroyan. He becomes mixed up in the underworld affairs of his brother, Remy, and fears not only for his own safety, but for that of his adolescent brother, Kanayan. In the process he falls in love with Dubois but has trouble mustering the courage to court her. As he gets entangled deeper and deeper in the underworld and in romance, Aznavour reveals who he really is, how he got "down there," and why he doesn't ever want to go back.

SHOOT THE PIANO PLAYER is a magnificent picture, not because of its debt to the gangster genre, but because of Truffaut's personal approach to that genre. Truffaut doesn't concern himself with plot mechanisms—since these have been provided for him countless times by Hollywood—but instead uses the conventions as a frame upon which to hang his own ideas (in much the same way the science-fiction genre served him in FAHRENHEIT 451), which burst out into all kinds of witty explorations. Said Truffaut, "The idea behind SHOOT THE PIANO PLAYER was to make a film without a subject, to express all I wanted to say about glory, success, downfall, failure, women, and love by means of a detective story. It's a grab bag." More than anything, it is a collection of beautifully scripted and photographed moments, many of which do nothing to further the narrative, but give the film a soul. One such moment lasts only a split second: A heartless club owner swears that he is telling the truth and proclaims, "If I am lying, may my mother drop dead." At that instant, Truffaut cuts to a shot of a decrepit old woman dropping to the floor. The casting of Aznavour is brilliant, the actor combining the proper blend of cafe piano man and classical pianist—a figure who loses everything he has ever loved, except his music.

SHOOTING, THE
1971 82m c Western   ★★★★
Proteus/Favorite (U.S.)   R/A

Jack Nicholson (Billy Spear), Millie Perkins (Woman), Warren Oates (Willett Gashade), Will Hutchins (Coley), B.J. Merholz (Leland Drum), Guy El Tsosie (Indian), Charles Eastman (Bearded Man)

p, Monte Hellman, Jack Nicholson; d, Monte Hellman; w, Adrien Joyce; ph, Gregory Sandor; ed, Monte Hellman; m, Richard Markowitz

Moody, absurdist anti-Western from cult director Monte Hellman (TWO-LANE BLACKTOP), anchored by the charismatic presence of young Jack Nicholson. Warren Oates plays a bounty hunter on an existential quest for a man who may be his twin brother; he's joined by flirtatious Perkins, fatally naive Hutchins, and mysterious gunman Nicholson. A clash of wills in the vast desert leads to a violent, surrealistic confrontation.

Minimal dialogue, spatial disorientation, and a tone of cynical revisionism characterize this little-known, strikingly unconventional film. Nicholson's minimalist performance is arresting, and Perkins (a minor starlet in the 50s) is good in her unusual role. THE SHOOTING was filmed simultaneously with the equally fascinating RIDE IN THE WHIRLWIND during a six-week period in 1965. Both films were produced on minuscule budgets by Nicholson and director Hellman, with an uncredited Roger Corman serving as executive producer. WHIRLWIND, whose sparse dialogue and bleak thematic material is strikingly similar, was scripted by Nicholson (THE SHOOTING was penned by Adrien Joyce, who later wrote FIVE EASY PIECES for Nicholson). Despite excellent reviews after screenings at the Montreal Film Festival and Cannes, no distributor would touch the film, and Nicholson was forced to sell the rights to a French producer who later went bankrupt. After sitting on the shelf for a few years, both films began to turn up on late-night TV, developing a word-of-mouth reputation that won them limited screenings after the success of EASY RIDER.

SHOOTIST, THE
1976 100m C Western   ★★★★
DEG (U.S.)   PG

John Wayne (John Bernard Books), Lauren Bacall (Bond Rogers), Ron Howard (Gillom Rogers), James Stewart (Dr. Hostetler), Richard Boone (Sweeney), Hugh O'Brian (Pulford), Bill McKinney (Cobb), Harry Morgan (Marshall Thibido), John Carradine (Beckum), Sheree North (Serepta)

p, M.J. Frankovich, William Self; d, Don Siegel; w, Miles Hood Swarthout, Scott Hale (based on the novel by Glendon Swarthout); ph, Bruce Surtees; ed, Douglas Stewart; m, Elmer Bernstein; prod d, Robert Boyle; fx, Augie Lohman; cos, Moss Mabry, Luster Bayless, Edna Taylor

AAN Best Art Direction: Robert F. Boyle, Arthur Jeph Parker

Eloquent last hurrah for a man who superseded mere movie-star status to become an icon of American culture, with Wayne playing aging, legendary gunfighter J.B. Brooks. Opening with a black-and-white montage of scenes from Wayne's earlier westerns, the film traces Brooks's career from 1871 to 1901, when THE SHOOTIST is set. As we move through scenes from RED RIVER, HONDO, RIO BRAVO and EL DORADO, Wayne ages before our eyes until he rides up before the camera and the film turns to color. During this sequence a voice-over spoken by Howard tells us that Wayne has killed 30 men in 30 years but was never an outlaw—he even spent time as a lawman. Wayne's credo: "I won't be wronged, I won't be insulted, and I won't be laid a hand on. I don't do these things to other people and I expect the same from them." Wayne rides into Carson City, Nevada, where he is informed by the doctor (James Stewart) that his cancer. The drama of his life's end is complicated by the presence of a beautiful widow, played by Lauren Bacall, and a host of young gunfighters looking to prove their worth by going up against him.

THE SHOOTIST is an uneven, elegiac tribute to a great career. The script leaves a lot to be desired, but is compensated for by some fine performances (especially Wayne's), Bruce Surtees' poignant cinematography, and Don Siegel's carefully paced direction.

SHOP AROUND THE CORNER, THE

1940 97m bw Comedy/Romance ★★★★★
MGM (U.S.) /U

James Stewart (Alfred Kralik), Margaret Sullavan (Klara Novak), Frank Morgan (Hugo Matuschek), Joseph Schildkraut (Ferencz Vadas), Sara Haden (Flora), Felix Bressart (Pirovitch), William Tracy (Pepi Katona), Inez Courtney (Ilona), Charles Halton (Detective), Charles Smith (Rudy)

p, Ernst Lubitsch; d, Ernst Lubitsch; w, Samson Raphaelson (based on the play "Parfumerie" by Nikolaus Laszlo); ph, William Daniels; ed, Gene Ruggiero; m, Werner R. Heymann; art d, Cedric Gibbons, Wade B. Rubottom

Delectable Hungarian pastry, served up by masters all around. This may be the best romantic comedy ever made. The great Ernst Lubitsch handles his "small" theme brilliantly, bringing the lives of everyday people to the screen as he had never done before.

In contrast to the glamorous heroes of other Lubitsch films, James Stewart's everyman sales clerk is as prosaic as they come. Working in a leather goods shop in Budapest, Stewart is the top clerk and a trusted friend of the owner, Morgan. Together, Morgan and Stewart head a tightly knit force of workers, all eager to please. Among them are Stewart's closest ally, Bressart, an aging clerk who leads a simple life and avoids confrontation; Schildkraut, a braggart who flashes his newly acquired wealth; and Tracy, an aspiring clerk who is constantly being bossed around. Trouble brews when the unemployed Sullavan enters the shop and begs Morgan to hire her as Christmas help. He rudely refuses; before she leaves, however, she impresses Morgan by selling a musical cigar box to a fat woman for use as a candy box. Morgan gives her a job, much to Stewart's consternation.

But Stewart has another distraction, as he confides to Bressart: through a lonely-hearts ad, Stewart has met a wonderful girl, though he knows her only by her box number. After exchanging a number of increasingly romantic letters with the charming lady of Box 237, Stewart makes a date to meet her in the flesh. Sullavan is herself carrying on an epistolary romance with a man she's never met and whose name she doesn't know—Stewart, of course. While Sullavan and Stewart may love each other in their anonymous letters, however, they feel only an increasing mutual dislike at the shop.

While THE SHOP AROUND THE CORNER lacks the immediate impact of the more spectacular TO BE OR NOT TO BE or HEAVEN CAN WAIT, this late entry from Lubitsch touches viewers deeply. The director renders a broad array of characters and emotions with a delicacy unusual even for him. Lubitsch said of the film: "As for human comedy, I think I never was as good as in THE SHOP AROUND THE CORNER. Never did I make a picture in which the atmosphere and the characters were truer than in this picture."

The film features a James Stewart many of us have forgotten once existed—his touch is delicate and precise. He's perfectly matched by Sullavan, a forgotten genius who never gave a bad performance. And this is perhaps Morgan's finest portrayal. These three had also completed Borzage's THE MORTAL STORM the same year. SHOP was later turned into a musical for Judy Garland and Van Johnson, IN THE GOOD OLD SUMMERTIME—one of Garland's most formulaic efforts.

SHOP ON MAIN STREET, THE

(OBCHOD NA KORZE)

1965 128m bw War/Drama ★★★★★
Barrandov (Czechoslovakia) /A

Jozef Kroner (Tono Brtko), Ida Kaminska (Rozalie Lautmann), Hana Slivkova (Evelina Brtko), Frantisek Zvarik (Marcus Kolkotsky), Helena Zvarikov (Rose Kolkotsky), Martin Holly (Imro Kuchar), Martin Gregory (Katz), Adam Matejka (Piti Baci), Mikulas Ladizinsky (Marian Peter), Eugen Senaj (Blau)

p, Jaromir Lukas, Jordan Balurov; d, Jan Kadar, Elmar Klos; w, Jan Kadar, Elmar Klos, Ladislav Grosman (based on the story "Obchod Na Korze" by Grosman); ph, Vladimir Novotny; ed, Jaromir Janacek, Diana Heringova; m, Zdenek Liska; art d, Karel Skvor

AA Best Foreign Language Film ; AAN Best Actress: Ida Kaminska

Among the most highly praised Eastern European films of the 1960s, THE SHOP ON MAIN STREET is a profoundly moving tragicomedy set against a WWII backdrop of racial hatred and fascism. Tono Brtko (Kroner) seemingly walks through life without any guiding morals or principles. He is content just to get by—though his domineering wife, Evelina (Slivkova), who longs for a more comfortable existence, tries to force him into working for her fascist brother-in-law, Marcus (Zvarik). One night Marcus brings news that Tono has been appointed Aryan comptroller of a Jewish button shop, a job that will bring money and status. Tono visits the shop the next day, informing the aged, frail, and rheumatic proprietress, Rozalie (Kaminska), that he is now in charge. She, however, too deaf to understand and too blind to read his authorization, begins bossing him around. Only later does Tono learn that the shop is completely bankrupt, and that the old woman is supported by her fellow Jewish merchants. He eventually agrees to the charade of working as Rozalie's assistant and forms a strong friendship with her that transcends racial, religious, and political divisions. But the Nazis soon appear, setting off a series of ironic—and highly dramatic—developments.

Codirected by the team of Kadar and Klos, THE SHOP ON MAIN STREET is a relatively straightforward narrative, without the stylistic virtuosity of so many other films by young Eastern European filmmakers. What the film lacks in flash, however, it makes up for in craftsmanship and intelligence. The acting is excellent throughout, and Kroner and Kaminska are both spellbinding. When Tono must decide between turning Rozalie over to the Nazis or trying to hide her, the film's careful buildup begins to pay off. When the elderly woman finally realizes what is happening around her and Tono desperately tries to shut her up, you may feel your guts wrenching in awe, terror and pity. Mixing a comic tone with a tragic subject, the film paints a uniquely vivid portrait of wartime persecution and enforces the view that the greatest, most inhumane of tragedies can strike anyone at any time.

SHORT CUTS

1993 189m c Drama ★★★½
Sandcastle 5/Avenue Pictures/Fine Line Features (U.S.) R/18

Tim Robbins (Gene Shepard), Tom Waits (Earl Piggot), Lily Tomlin (Doreen Piggot), Madeleine Stowe (Sherri Shepard), Peter Gallagher (Stormy Weathers), Anne Archer (Claire Kane), Fred Ward (Stuart Kane), Buck Henry (Gordon Johnson), Andie MacDowell (Ann Finnigan), Jack Lemmon (Paul Finnegan)

p, Robert Altman, Scott Bushnell; d, Robert Altman; w, Robert Altman, Frank Barhydt (from short stories and a poem by Raymond Carver); ph, Walt Lloyd; ed, Geraldine Peroni; m, Mark Isham; prod d, Stephen Altman; art d, Jerry Fleming; cos, John Hay

AAN Best Director: Robert Altman

With SHORT CUTS, director/co-screenwriter Robert Altman revisits the format of his 1975 masterpiece NASHVILLE, presenting a panorama of intertwined Southern California lives adapted from works by Raymond Carver. The result is quirky, sometimes brilliant, and mostly ice-cold.

Waitress Doreen (Lily Tomlin) is married to Earl (Tom Waits), a drunken lout who may have importuned to her daughter Honey (Lili Taylor). Honey's husband Bill (Robert Downey Jr.) is an aspiring makeup artist who pals around with Jerry (Chris Penn), who runs a pool maintenance service and is frustrated and disturbed by his wife Lois' (Jennifer Jason Leigh) career in phone sex. Claire (Anne Archer) and Stuart (Fred Ward) meet surgeon Ralph (Matthew Modine) and his painter wife Marian (Julianne Moore) at a concert featuring cellist Zoe Trainer (Lori Singer); the couples plan a barbecue, after Stuart takes a fishing trip during which he and his buddies discover a dead, naked woman in a stream. Marian's sister Sherri (Madeleine Stowe) decides to let her motorcycle cop husband Gene's (Tim Robbins) affair with Betty (Frances McDormand) play itself out. Betty's jealous, estranged husband, Stormy Weathers (Peter Gallagher), watches. Doreen runs over Casey Finnigan (Zane Cassidy), son of Ann (Andie MacDowell) and news anchor Howard (Bruce Davison). Their lives—and those of many others—overlap and intertwine, until an earthquake shakes up everyone and everything involved.

Altman's "Carver soup" didn't please all the author's admirers, many of whom felt that, by changing the locale and tone of Carver's stories and linking them to form an integrated web, the director had dispensed with exactly what was Carveresque about his source. It's hard not to be impressed, though, by Altman's narrative legerdemain—he sustains at least ten major stories, each of which has depth, definition, and dramatic interest—or the first-rate contributions of the players. The film is fascinating and complex, and benefits from a densely textured soundtrack that makes it as interesting to listen to as to watch.

SHORT FILM ABOUT KILLING, A
(KROTKI FILM O ZABIJANIU)

1988 84m c Drama/Political ★★★★
Polish Corporation for Film Production/Tor Film Unit/Zespoly /18
Filmowe/Telewizja Polska/Sender Freies Berlin (Poland)

Miroslaw Baka (Jacek Lazar—The Murderer), Krzysztof Globisz (Piotr Balicki—The Lawyer), Peter Jan Tesarz (Waldemar Rekowski—The Taxi Driver), Zbigniew Zapasiewicz (Bar Examiner), Barbara Dziekan-Vajda (Girl in Cinema Box Office), Aleksander Bednarz (Executioner), Jerzy Zass (Court Official), Zdzislaw Tobiasz (Judge), Artur Barcis (Young Man), Krystyna Janda

p, Ryszard Chutkowski; d, Krzysztof Kieslowski; w, Krzysztof Kieslowski, Krzysztof Piesiewicz; ph, Slawomir Idziak; ed, Ewa Smal; m, Zbigniew Preisner; prod d, Halina Dobrowolska; art d, Grazyna Tkaczyk; cos, Malgorzata Obloza, Hanna Cwiklo

A SHORT FILM ABOUT KILLING is an expanded version of Episode Five of late director Krzysztof Kieslowski's DECALOGUE (1988), a ten-part series made for Polish television interpreting the themes of the biblical Ten Commandments in modern stories. This episode, focusing on the Fifth Commandment, brilliantly portrays the dynamics between killer, victim, and legal system.

Jacek (Miroslaw Baka) is a young thug from the countryside, unhappy and restless, who wanders the city aimlessly. Piotr (Krzysztof Globisz) is an idealistic law student who takes and passes his bar exams. Waldemar (Peter Jan Tesarz) is a simple taxi driver and a thoroughly unpleasant character. The film intercuts the lives of these three apparently unrelated figures throughout the course of the day in which their fates will intersect irretrievably. It is with apparent arbitrariness that Jacek finally hails one cab and not another, instructs the driver to take a desolate alternative route, and then brutally murders him. Jacek will be defended unsuccessfully by the young lawyer Piotr, given the death penalty, and hanged by the state.

The relative speed with which the film moves from the murder to capital punishment serves to highlight their moral equivalence. The long buildup that precedes the murders engenders no sympathy but rather adopts the cold perspective of a stranger. In this sense, Kieslowski relies entirely on the crimes themselves to reveal the meanings of the moral commandment. Released in Poland in 1988, this film preceded the success of Kieslowski's later French films, including THE DOUBLE LIFE OF VERONIQUE and the much acclaimed trilogy RED, WHITE and BLUE, which take up similar themes of contingency, fate, and coincidence surrounding and defining human action and responsibility.

SHOT IN THE DARK, A

1964 103m c Mystery/Comedy ★★★★
Mirisch/Geoffrey (U.S./U.K.) /PG

Peter Sellers (Inspector Jacques Clouseau), Elke Sommer (Maria Gambrelli), George Sanders (Benjamin Ballon), Herbert Lom (Chief Inspector Charles Dreyfus), Tracy Reed (Dominique Ballon), Graham Stark (Hercule Lajoy), Andre Maranne (Francois), Douglas Wilmer (Henri Lafarge), Vanda Godsell (Mme. Lafarge), Maurice Kaufmann (Pierre)

p, Blake Edwards; d, Blake Edwards; w, Blake Edwards, William Peter Blatty (based on plays by Harry Kurnitz, Marcel Achard); ph, Christopher Challis; ed, Bert Bates; m, Henry Mancini; prod d, Michael Stringer; cos, Margaret Furse

This picture, the second in the Inspector Clouseau series starring Sellers, was drawn from a French play, "L'idiote," by Marcel Achard, which opened in Paris in the fall of 1960. About a year later Kurnitz presented his adaptation, "A Shot in the Dark," on Broadway, and it is from both these plays that the screenplay was fashioned. Sommer is a chambermaid, in the Parisian residence of Sanders and Reed, who has been accused of murdering her boyfriend. Sellers is mistakenly assigned to the case. His superior, Lom, would like to get him off it because he knows the havoc the man can wreak. ("Give me 10 men like Clouseau and I could destroy the world.") All the clues point to Sommer's guilt, but Sellers believes she is innocent.

The picture is filled with one sight gag after another, many familiar to anyone old enough to remember the glory days of silent comedy. The funniest sustained sequence occurs when Sellers attempts to bed down Sommer, and his aide (Burt Kwouk) leaps into the room ready to conduct the violent judo lesson that was to punctuate many of the later comedies. The original Achard-Kurnitz plays had the lead character a nutty judge, but that was altered in this screenplay to fit the character Sellers played in the first PINK PANTHER film. In the movies that followed, Lom continued as the boss, despite having murdered all of the victims in this one.

SHOUT, THE

1978 87m c Horror ★★★
Recorded Picture (U.K.) R/15

Alan Bates (Crossley), Susannah York (Rachel), John Hurt (Anthony), Robert Stephens (Medical Man), Tim Curry (Robert), Julian Hough (Vicar), Carol Drinkwater (Wife), Nick Stringer (Cobbler), John Rees (Inspector), Susan Wooldridge (Harriet)

p, Jeremy Thomas; d, Jerzy Skolimowski; w, Michael Austin, Jerzy Skolimowski (based on a story by Robert Graves); ph, Mike Molloy; ed, Barrie Vince; m, Rupert Hine, Tony Banks, Michael Rutherford; art d, Simon Holland

THE SHOUT is a strange, disturbing, and elusive tale of a mental patient, Bates, who, having once lived with a tribe of Aborigines, has learned the secret of "the shout," which has the power to kill. Told in flashback during a cricket match that takes place on the grounds of a mental asylum, the film follows Bates's relationship with experimental composer Hurt and his wife, York. Bates moves in with the couple, and gradually his disturbing presence takes its toll. He tells the couple that he killed his own children, demonstrates his ability to kill with his shout, seduces York, and tries to destroy Hurt. Directed by Polish director Jerzy Skolimowski (MOONLIGHTING), THE SHOUT has a certain compelling element that both mystifies and involves the viewer, its unusual story told with equal amounts of obscurity and skill. It has no tidy conclusions or explanations, leaving the audience as baffled at the end as they were at the start, but the film is definitely worth experiencing. Tony Banks and Mike Rutherford of the rock group Genesis contributed to the electronic score, and ROCKY HORROR star Tim Curry has a supporting role.

SHOW BOAT

1936 110m bw Musical ★★★★½
Universal (U.S.) /U

Irene Dunne (Magnolia Hawks), Allan Jones (Gaylord Ravenal), Charles Winninger (Capt. Andy Hawks), Helen Westley (Parthy Hawks), Paul Robeson (Joe), Helen Morgan (Julie), Donald Cook (Steve), Sammy White (Frank Schultz), J. Farrell MacDonald (Windy), Arthur Hohl (Pete)

p, Carl Laemmle Jr.; d, James Whale; w, Oscar Hammerstein II (based on the novel by Edna Ferber and the play by Hammerstein, Jerome Kern); ph, John Mescall; ed, Ted J. Kent, Bernard W. Burton; m, Jerome Kern, Oscar Hammerstein II; art d, Charles D. Hall; fx, John P. Fulton; chor, LeRoy Prinz; cos, Vera West, Doris Zinkeisen

This time around, Universal got it right. Carl Laemmle, Jr., whose father produced the 1929 version of SHOW BOAT that owed more to Edna Ferber's novel than to the 1927 Hammerstein and Kern musical, took over the reins here and the result is splendid. It's still the same romance between gambler Gaylord Ravenal (Jones) and Magnolia Hawks (Dunne), daughter of showboat captain Andy Hawks (Winninger). The stars of this mobile 19th century theatre, Julie (Morgan) and Steve (Cook), must leave the showboat when it is found out that Julie is half-black. Gaylord and Magnolia step in and play their romance onstage and off, but an unlucky gambling streak spells trouble for the young couple.

SHOWBOAT's many-tiered plot is secondary to its extraordinary score, but it does make for some beguiling romance, delightful comedy and potent dramatics. Master director Whale, here essaying his first musical, does some typically marvelous things with the camera and *mise-en-scene* and gets wonderful performances from his cast. Many of them had essayed their roles previously onstage, so their dazzling assurance should come as no surprise. Dunne's lilting soprano does full justice to such favorites as "Make Believe" and "You Are Love" and she is sidesplittingly funny acting the role of a schoolteacher in a barnstorming melodrama aboard the showboat. It is fortunate that Winninger's legendary performance has been captured on film. His greatest moment comes when, with incredible dexterity and panache, he enacts the entire finale of a play before an audience. Jones, too, a likable actor-singer underused by Hollywood, does excellent work as a roguish but loving gambler. The rest of the supporting cast, including the ever-marvelous Westley and the one-and-only Hattie McDaniel, are in grand form, but Robeson and Morgan must be singled out for special praise. Robeson's immortal rendition of "Ol' Man River" is stunningly staged by Whale, as a 270 degree pan sweeps around him and the lyrics are enacted with Expressionistic vignettes. The film really suffers when Robeson is no longer around, but his presence haunts even the last reels. The same goes for Helen Morgan, whose decline at this point in her brief life and career is clearly apparent. She makes Julie almost unbearably poignant. Her tremulous voice and slight gestures convey volumes, and one is grateful when she briefly turns up again in Magnolia's life at just the right moment. When Morgan sings "Bill" (with that amazing close-up near the end), one feels privileged to witness one of the greatest filmed performances of a song in the history of cinema. If you doubt that two minutes of a woman singing can break your heart, guess again.

Universal really poured its money into this film, and it shows in Hall's lovely set designs, Mescall's sumptuous cinematography, and the actual riverboat built for the film. Whale's trademark theatricality lends itself perfectly to this film, and he plays the famous miscegenation scene for all it's worth. The film is only really flawed in the last third, as we are rushed into the 1930s while Magnolia's daughter becomes a stage star herself. It's quite improbable that Capt. Andy and Parthy would still be alive, and other contrivances mar the impact of what has come before.

SHOW BOAT

1951 107m c Musical ★★★½

MGM (U.S.) /U

Kathryn Grayson (*Magnolia Hawks*), Ava Gardner (*Julie LaVerne*), Howard Keel (*Gaylord Ravenal*), Joe E. Brown (*Capt. Andy Hawks*), Marge Champion (*Ellie May Shipley*), Gower Champion (*Frank Schultz*), Robert Sterling (*Stephen Baker*), Agnes Moorehead (*Parthy Hawks*), Adele Jergens (*Cameo McQueen*), William Warfield (*Joe*)

p, Arthur Freed; d, George Sidney; w, John Lee Mahin (uncredited), George Wells, Jack McGowan (based on the musical by Jerome Kern and Oscar Hammerstein II from the novel by Edna Ferber); ph, Charles Rosher; ed, John Dunning; m, Jerome Kern; art d, Cedric Gibbons, Jack Martin Smith; fx, Warren Newcombe, Peter Ballbusch; chor, Robert Alton; cos, Walter Plunkett

AAN Best Cinematography: Charles Rosher; *AAN Best Score:* Adolph Deutsch, Conrad Salinger

Greatly enhanced by its deft use of color, this third film version of Hammerstein and Kern's classic musical is nearly as good as the superlative second and much better than the lackluster first (1936 and 1929, respectively). Yet, as was the case with the 1936 version, the Motion Picture Academy barely acknowledged the film's excellence, nominating only Charles Rosher's cinematography and Adolph Deutsch and Conrad Salinger's musical direction. This time out the story is considerably altered and compressed, with Kathryn Grayson in the role of Magnolia and Ava Gardner as Julie, the much-wronged mulatto who helps save Magnolia's marriage to gambler-turned-entertainer Gaylord Ravenal (Howard Keel). The action is again played out

on a Mississippi riverboat, *The Cotton Blossom*, piloted by Magnolia's father, Capt. Andy Hawks (Joe E. Brown, whom Edna Ferber reputedly had in mind when she created the character of Capt. Andy for the novel whence the musical sprang). Agnes Moorehead plays Capt. Andy's tough cookie spouse and Leif Erickson is the deckhand who reveals Julie's miscegenation to the authorities when she rebuffs his advances. After planning to shoot the film on location in Mississippi, MGM decided it would be more cost effective to keep the cast at home and, like the 1936 production, went to great lengths to create a realistic riverboat, constructing one from scratch that was over 170 feet long, nearly 60 feet high, and cost more than $125,000. Among the film's fine performances are those of Grayson, who had already played Magnolia in a segment of the fanciful biopic of Kern, TILL THE CLOUDS ROLL BY, and Gardner, who did her own singing but had her voice dubbed by Annette Warren after preview audiences reacted coolly to the beautiful leading lady's vocalizing. Although the film's musical numbers are almost entirely the Kern-Hammerstein originals, the finale, "After the Ball," was penned by Charles K. Harris, while P.G. Wodehouse and Guy Bolton wrote new lyrics for "Bill."

SHOWGIRLS

1995 131m c Erotic/Drama ★½

Chargeurs/Carolco/Vegas Productions/United NC-17/18
Artists (U.S.)

Elizabeth Berkley (*Nomi Malone*), Kyle MacLachlan (*Zack Carey*), Gina Gershon (*Cristal Connors*), Glenn Plummer (*James Smith*), Robert Davi (*Al Torres*), Alan Rachins (*Tony Moss*), Gina Ravera (*Molly Abrams*), Lin Tucci (*Henrietta Bazoom*), Greg Travis (*Phil Newkirk*), Al Ruscio (*Mr. Karlman*)

p, Alan Marshall, Charles Evans; d, Paul Verhoeven; w, Joe Eszterhas; ph, Jost Vacano; ed, Mark Goldblatt, Mark Helfrich; m, David A. Stewart; prod d, Allan Cameron; art d, William F. O'Brien; fx, Burt Dalton, Special Effects Unlimited, Inc.; chor, Marguerite Pomerhn-Derricks; cos, Ellen Mirojnick

Perhaps *the* most hyped movie of 1995, SHOWGIRLS was Hollywood's first attempt to mass-market a film with an NC-17 rating. Excoriating reviews, however, scared off everyone but the most intrepid curiosity seekers and the raincoat crowd. Its non-stop display of flesh and sleaze aside, SHOWGIRLS is a cliched and coarsely acted backstage drama whose only possible value lies in its camp posturing.

Brassy young Nomi Malone (Elizabeth Berkley)—a homophone for "know me, alone"—hitchhikes into Las Vegas determined to become a star showgirl. She is befriended by Molly (Gina Ravera), a young costumer, who invites Nomi to share her trailer. Nomi quickly begins clawing her way up the greased pole of the Vegas entertainment industry, first landing a job dancing in a sleazy topless club and later graduating to higher-paying, semi-private lap dances. After performing for hotel entertainment director Zack Carey (Kyle MacLachlan) and Stardust Hotel revue star Cristal Connors (Gina Gershon), Nomi wins an audition in front of a powerful producer and gets a shot at the topless big-time.

This colossal misfire from the writer-director team of Joe Eszterhas and Paul Verhoeven—the creators of BASIC INSTINCT—received the critical censure it so richly merited. Verhoeven claimed he intended to make a provocative movie revealing the harsh, corrupt side of the showgirl business and the glitzmeisters who run it. Instead, he produced an unpleasant gawk at the seamy facade and sleazy back rooms of topless Las Vegas. Eszterhas's story and characters are as superficial as the subject matter, turning the viewer into a voyeur. Berkley's wooden performance only accentuates the script's weaknesses. Her Nomi is witlessly unsympathetic—even in comparison with the despicable snakes who surround her.

SHY PEOPLE

1988 119m c Drama ★★★½

Golan-Globus (U.S.) R/15

Jill Clayburgh (*Diana Sullivan*), Barbara Hershey (*Ruth Sullivan*), Martha Plimpton (*Grace Sullivan*), Merritt Butrick (*Mike Sullivan*), John Philbin (*Tommy Sullivan*), Don Swayze (*Mark Sullivan*), Pruitt Taylor Vince (*Paul Sullivan*), Mare Winningham (*Candy*), Michael Audley (*Louie*), Brad Leland (*Larry*) p, Menahem Golan, Yoram Globus; d, Andrei Konchalovsky; w, Gerard Brach, Andrei Konchalovsky, Marjorie David (based on a story by Konchalovsky); ph, Chris Menges; ed, Alain Jakubowicz; fx, Cal Acord

The fourth American film from Soviet emigre Andrei Konchalovsky (MARIA'S LOVERS; RUNAWAY TRAIN; and DUET FOR ONE preceded), SHY PEOPLE is about a meeting of two people, and two worlds, who initially appear to be diametrically opposed but who, we learn by the film's end, have more in common than we imagined. The film opens in Manhattan, where *Cosmopolitan* reporter Diana Sullivan (Jill Clayburgh) lives with her teenaged coke-sniffing daughter, Grace (Martha Plimpton). At her editor's suggestion, Diana has traced her own roots back to the Louisiana Bayou and talks her bored daughter into accompanying her on a visit to the relatives. As Diana and Grace reveal their urban dependencies, the Cajun cousins reveal their backwoods, superstitious ways. Ruth Sullivan (Barbara Hershey) informs her guests that the family is watched over by her former husband, the outlaw Joe, though he hasn't been seen for over 15 years. The film is full of strange and wonderful events, and in the course of the action the two women grow and change as a result of their exposure to one another. As in his 1985 RUNAWAY TRAIN, Konchalovsky here presents powerful characterizations, beautiful imagery, and philosophical content as entertainment that can appeal to the average filmgoer but that also still has enough depth to stand up to critical analysis.

SID AND NANCY

1986 111m c Biography   ★★★★
Zenith/Initial (U.K.)   R/18

Gary Oldman (*Sid Vicious*), Chloe Webb (*Nancy Spungen*), Drew Schofield (*Johnny Rotten*), David Hayman (*Malcolm McLaren*), Debbie Bishop (*Phoebe*), Tony London (*Steve*), Perry Benson (*Paul*), Anne Lambton (*Linda*), Kathy Burke (*Brenda*), Mark Monero (*Clive*)

p, Eric Fellner; d, Alex Cox; w, Alex Cox, Abbe Wool; ph, Roger Deakins; ed, David Martin; m, Pray for Rain, The Pogues, Joe Strummer; prod d, Andrew McAlpine; art d, J. Rae Fox, Lynda Burbank; cos, Cathy Cook, Theda De Ramus

The sordid, pathetic lives of Sex Pistols bassist Sid Vicious and his groupie girlfriend Nancy Spungen might strike some as unsuitable material for a movie romance, but British filmmaker Alex Cox brings their embattled relationship and tragic end to powerful cinematic life.

SID AND NANCY opens in 1978, as police arrive at New York's Chelsea Hotel to find the body of Nancy (Chloe Webb) in the couple's bathroom and zombie-like Sid (Gary Oldman) staring at the wall and holding a knife. The film then flashes back to 1977 when the couple first meet at the home of Linda (Anne Lambton), a friend of Sid's and Johnny Rotten's (Drew Schofield). Nancy is a loud, whining, American rock 'n' roll groupie who's wound up in London at the height of the punk rock movement. She's impressed when she learns that Linda's guests are members of the infamous Sex Pistols, the brainchild of young entrepreneur Malcolm McLaren (David Hayman). (Sid, born John Ritchie, abandoned his role as drummer for the nascent Siouxsie and the Banshees to replace original Sex Pistol bassist Glen Matlock.) That night, she goes to hear the band, riding high on the British charts with "God Save the Queen," their second single, and later tries to seduce Rotten, but he declares sex "boring" and leaves her to Vicious.

A few days later Sid spots Nancy in a pub and follows her when she runs out yelling and crying; another rocker has absconded with her heroin money. Angry and frustrated, Spungen scrapes her knuckles on a brick wall. "That looks like it hurts," Sid tells her sympathetically. "So does this," he continues, and brutally slams his head into the brick wall, a gesture which Nancy seems to understand and appreciate. Sid then gives Nancy money to buy heroin for both of them; although she's already a full-blown junkie, Sid has never done hard drugs.

SID AND NANCY does not canonize Sid Vicious and Nancy Spungen, the Sex Pistols or the punk movement itself, nor does it glamorize the couple's horrible self-destruction. (Sid died of a heroin overdose on February 2, 1979, before his case could be tried.) Although Cox, abetted by co-screenwriter Abbe Wool, often displays a black, quirky sense of humor, the horror of drug addiction is always at the forefront and never made light of.

The performances of Oldman and Webb, both stage-trained veterans, are simply astonishing. SID AND NANCY will certainly be tough going for viewers unfamiliar with the punk movement and unprepared for the extraordinary amount of cynicism, ignorance, anger, and self-abuse that went hand-in-hand with it, but the film's value lies in its honest, unflinching gaze at a social phenomenon.

SILENCE OF THE LAMBS, THE

1991 118m c Thriller/Mystery/Horror   ★★★★½
Strong Heart Productions/Orion (U.S.)   R/18

Jodie Foster (*Clarice Starling*), Anthony Hopkins (*Dr. Hannibal Lecter*), Scott Glenn (*Jack Crawford*), Ted Levine (*Jame Gumb*), Anthony Heald (*Dr. Frederick Chilton*), Brooke Smith (*Catherine Martin*), Charles Napier (*Sergeant Boyle*), Diane Baker (*Senator Ruth Martin*), Kasi Lemmons (*Ardelia Mapp*), Roger Corman (*FBI Director Hayden Burke*)

p, Edward Saxon, Kenneth Utt, Ron Bozman; d, Jonathan Demme; w, Ted Tally (from the novel by Thomas Harris); ph, Tak Fujimoto; ed, Craig McKay; m, Howard Shore; prod d, Kristi Zea; art d, Tim Galvin; cos, Colleen Atwood

AA Best Picture; *AA Best Actor:* Anthony Hopkins; *AA Best Actress:* Jodie Foster; *AA Best Director:* Jonathan Demme; *AA Best Adapted Screenplay:* Ted Tally; *AAN Best Editing:* Craig McKay; *AAN Best Sound:* Tom Fleischman, Christopher Newman

One of the most talked-about movies of 1991, multiple Academy Award-winner THE SILENCE OF THE LAMBS was actually the second "Hannibal Lecter" film, Michael Mann having previously adapted the character from Thomas Harris's novel *Red Dragon* in 1986's MANHUNTER. But Jonathan Demme's taut thriller proved to have a much greater impact on the public imagination.

FBI trainee Clarice Starling (Jodie Foster) is recruited by the Bureau's behavioral sciences unit to help track down one serial killer by getting inside the head of another who's already behind bars—the notorious Hannibal "the Cannibal" Lecter (Anthony Hopkins), a brilliant but psychopathic psychiatrist. In a series of riveting interviews, Starling reveals personal details about her past to Lecter, in exchange for information that may snare "Buffalo Bill," the murderer who flays his female victims. Tensions escalate when Bill kidnaps the daughter of a U.S. senator and Lecter plots an escape.

While the suspenseful pursuit of the killer is handled well by Demme, the film's principle attraction stems not from the thrill of the hunt, but from the spellbinding skull sessions between Jodie Foster's heroine and Anthony Hopkins's brilliant, menacing villain. Hopkins plays the cannibalistic doctor with a quiet, controlled erudition, lacing his performance with moments of black humor. His Lecter is a sort of satanic Sherlock Holmes whose spasms of violence are all the more terrifying because they erupt from beneath such an intelligent and refined mask.

Although not as overwhelming, Foster's performance is equally impressive. Her strong-yet-vulnerable interpretation of the rookie FBI agent projects a quietly convincing feminism. Although she remains the pupil of the benign patriarch Crawford, Starling rises above the pettiness of her male colleagues. Despite the cinematic and dramatic triumphs of SILENCE OF THE LAMBS, the film's accomplishments cannot be endorsed without reservation. While behavioral scientists within the film offer much psychoanalytical reading of character, the movie itself fails to separate Buffalo Bill's sexual confusion from his homicidal psychopathy. While not central to the story, such a depiction threatens to demonize sexual ambiguity as criminal. Finally, while the amount of violence in this thriller is not unusual, the disturbingly bizarre nature of Lecter's face-eating cannibalism and the misogyny of Buffalo Bill's *modus operandi* may be sufficient reason for many would-be viewers to forego the film's gripping drama.

SILENT RUNNING

1972 89m c Science Fiction   ★★★½
Universal (U.S.)   PG/U

Bruce Dern (*Freeman Lowell*), Cliff Potts (*Wolf*), Ron Rifkin (*Barker*), Jesse Vint (*Keenan*), Steven Brown, Mark Persons, Cheryl Sparks, Larry Whisenhunt (*Drones*)

p, Michael Gruskoff; d, Douglas Trumbull; w, Deric Washburn, Steven Bochco, Michael Cimino; ph, Charles F. Wheeler; ed, Aaron Stell; m, Peter Schickele; fx, Douglas Trumbull, John Dykstra, Richard Yuricich, Richard O. Helmer, James Rugg, Marlin Jones, Richard Helmer, Vernon Archer

In the year 2008, all of Earth's natural plant and animal life has been destroyed by nuclear forces. A group of space stations orbiting Saturn function as outer-space greenhouses, waiting for a time when the planet *may* again be able to support life. When the project is terminated and orders given for the greenhouses to be destroyed, Freeman Lowell (Bruce Dern) kills his three colleagues and takes off in one of the stations, to preserve the potential for life in some other place or time. Lowell is aided in his efforts by three cute robots, known as Huey, Louie and Dewey.

This was a directorial debut for Trumbull, who had previously worked with Stanley Kubrick on the special effects for 2001: A SPACE ODDYSSEY. Like that film, SILENT RUNNING concentrates heavily on special effects, resulting in some stunning imagery. Dern gives an engaging, against-type performance, though the script is stretched out very thin to support a feature-length film. The unusual score is by Peter Schickele, best known for his classical music parodies written under the pseudonym P.D.Q. Bach. Despite the presence of some very dated Joan Baez songs on the soundtrack, SILENT RUNNING has built up a deserved cult status over the years. The writing team of Washburn, Bochco, and Cimino would go on to make the Vietnam drama THE DEER HUNTER.

SILK STOCKINGS

1957 117m c Musical/Comedy   ★★★★
MGM   (U.S.)   /U

Fred Astaire (Steve Canfield), Cyd Charisse (Ninotchka), Janis Paige (Peggy Dainton), Peter Lorre (Brankov), Jules Munshin (Bibinski), Joseph Buloff (Ivanov), George Tobias (Commissar Vassili Markovich), Wim Sonneveld (Peter Ilyitch Boroff), Belita (Dancer Vera), Ivan Triesault (Russian Embassy Official)

p, Arthur Freed; d, Rouben Mamoulian; w, Leonard Gershe, Harry Kurnitz (uncredited), Leonard Spigelgass (based on the musical play by George S. Kaufman, Leueen McGrath, Abe Burrows and the screenplay by Billy Wilder, Charles Brackett, Walter Reisch from *Ninotchka* by Melchior Lengyel); ph, Robert Bronner; ed, Harold F. Kress; m, Cole Porter; art d, William A. Horning, Randall Duell; chor, Hermes Pan, Eugene Loring; cos, Helen Rose

Great light entertainment that paid heavy dividends at the box office, SILK STOCKINGS is the delightful film version of the George S. Kaufman-Leueen McGrath-Abe Burrows-Cole Porter Broadway musical based on Ernst Lubitsch's classic screen comedy NINOTCHKA (1939). Fred Astaire is Hollywood film producer Steve Canfield, who comes to Paris to make a movie, meets touring Soviet composer Peter Ilyitch Boroff (Wim Sonneveld), and persuades him to remain in France to score his film, prompting Commissar Vassili Markovitch (George Tobias, who appeared in both the stage version and in NINOTCHKA) to dispatch of trio of underlings to retrieve the revered composer. In short order, Brankov (Peter Lorre, who is very funny but struggles vainly as a dancer), Bibinski (Jules Munshin), and Ivanov (Joseph Buloff) are contentedly indulging in the pleasures of life in the West. Ninotchka (Cyd Charisse, in the role Greta Garbo essayed so brilliantly), the exemplary Communist sent by Commissar Markovitch to retrieve the retrievers, is not so easily seduced by Western ways or by Steve, who falls in love with her. Despite Steve's marriage proposal, Ninotchka and the others return to the USSR; however, when Brankov, Bibinski, and Ivanov, sent again to Paris as representatives of the Soviet film industry, become partners in a nightclub with Steve, Ninotchka returns to collect her errant comrades, but this time love wins out. Hermes Pan oversaw Astaire's dancing, some of the last really dazzling terping he would do, while Eugene Loring handled the rest of the choreography. Charisse, a great dancer in her own right, gives a terrific performance (vocally looped by Carol Richards). Rouben Mamoulian's direction is brisk but not brilliant; Cole Porter's songs are witty, airy, and tuneful, though not as memorable as many of the renowned tunesmith's other works; and because the chemistry between Charisse and Astaire isn't the equal of that of Garbo and Melvyn Douglas, SILK

STOCKINGS lacks NINOTCHKA's warmth. It does, however, have some wonderful musical moments and is the kind of picture that anyone of any age will enjoy.

SILKWOOD

1983 131m c Biography   ★★★★
20th Century Fox   (U.S.)   R/15

Meryl Streep (Karen Silkwood), Kurt Russell (Drew Stephens), Cher (Dolly Pelliker), Craig T. Nelson (Winston), Diana Scarwid (Angela), Fred Ward (Morgan), Ron Silver (Paul Stone), Charles Hallahan (Earl Lapin), Josef Sommer (Max Richter), Sudie Bond (Thelma Rice)

p, Mike Nichols, Michael Hausman; d, Mike Nichols; w, Nora Ephron, Alice Arlen; ph, Miroslav Ondricek; ed, Sam O'Steen; m, Georges Delerue; prod d, Patrizia von Brandenstein; art d, Richard James; cos, Ann Roth

AAN Best Actress: Meryl Streep; AAN Best Supporting Actress: Cher; AAN Best Director: Mike Nichols; AAN Best Original Screenplay: Nora Ephron, Alice Arlen; AAN Best Editing: Sam O'Steen

Karen Silkwood, a worker at the Kerr-McGee nuclear materials plant in Cimarron, Oklahoma, died in 1974 in a suspect auto accident on her way to meet a *New York Times* reporter to present evidence she had gathered concerning safety violations at her workplace. Based on that story, SILKWOOD is a sensational expose of big business seen through the eyes of average working people. Meryl Streep, in another brilliant portrayal, is the title character, a tough, hard-drinking woman who lives with her boyfriend (Kurt Russell), and a lesbian friend (an engagingly low-key Cher). In the course of her dull, dangerous job at Kerr-McGee, Silkwood is repeatedly contaminated. She begins to suspect a management cover-up of safety measures violations at the plant, and undertakes to get proof of her suspicions for the union brass in Washington. Though her relationship with her boyfriend deteriorates as she plugs more and more of her energy into her spying, she gathers evidence that she intends to give to the reporter, and heads out for the meeting that never took place. The clear implication is that Silkwood was silenced to prevent her from making trouble for the plant. Mike Nichols, in his first venture into movies since THE FORTUNE (1975), elicited superlative performances from the actors, particularly Streep and stage veteran Sudi Bond.

SILVERADO

1985 132m c Western   ★★½
Columbia   (U.S.)   PG-13/PG

Kevin Kline (Paden), Scott Glenn (Emmett), Rosanna Arquette (Hannah), John Cleese (Sheriff Langston), Kevin Costner (Jake), Brian Dennehy (Cobb), Danny Glover (Mal), Jeff Goldblum (Slick), Linda Hunt (Stella), Raymond Baker (McKendrick)

p, Lawrence Kasdan; d, Lawrence Kasdan; w, Lawrence Kasdan, Mark Kasdan; ph, John Bailey; ed, Carol Littleton, Mia Goldman; m, Bruce Broughton; prod d, Ida Random; fx, Roy Arbogast; cos, Kristi Zea

AAN Best Score: Bruce Boughton; AAN Best Sound: Donald O. Mitchell, Rick Kline, Kevin O'Connell, David Ronne

Jammed with enough characters and plot elements to fill at least 10 films, SILVERADO is a big stampede of a movie with ideas and scenes thundering off in dozens of directions. Without things getting out of hand, the plot here sees four unlikely heros—Paden (Kevin Kline), Emmett (Scott Glenn), Jake (Kevin Costner), and Mal (Danny Glover)—team up to rescue the town of Silverado from nasty sheriff Cobb (Brian Dennehy) and his army of goons. The basics are simple enough and definitely the stuff of 1940s westerns, but then writer-director Lawrence Kasdan bloats the plot with dozens of side stories that, in painfully predictable detail, show how each of our heroes has a reason for being in Silverado and why they decide to stick their necks out. Though much of the running time is devoted to these expository passages, it's all very basic and shallow. Between the gratuitous climaxes that seem to occur every 10 minutes, Kasdan parades a myriad of stereotypes before us and never develops them (Rosanna Arquette as the pretty young widow; Jeff Goldblum as the slimy, dandified gambler; Linda Hunt as the tough saloon owner). In fact, he never really explores any of his characters but only provides them with enough motivation to justify the slaughter of dozens of people.

SIN OF MADELON CLAUDET, THE

1931 74m bw Drama ★★★★
MGM (U.S.)

Helen Hayes (Madelon Claudet), Lewis Stone (Carlo Boretti), Neil Hamilton (Larry), Robert Young (Dr. Claudet), Cliff Edwards (Victor), Jean Hersholt (Dr. Dulac), Marie Prevost (Rosalie), Karen Morley (Alice), Charles Winninger (Photographer), Alan Hale (Hubert)

d, Edgar Selwyn; w, Charles MacArthur (based on the play The Lullaby by Edward Knoblock); ph, Oliver T. Marsh; ed, Tom Held; art d, Cedric Gibbons

AA Best Actress: Helen Hayes

Helen Hayes made her sound-film debut in this well-acted soaper scripted by her husband, Charles MacArthur. Jean Hersholt narrates in flashback the story of Hayes, a French girl who falls in love with Neil Hamilton, an American artist. The two move in together without marrying, but their idyllic life is ruined when Hamilton leaves and marries another woman. Hayes then becomes involved with Lewis Stone, but, arrested on jewel theft charges, he kills himself rather than face the law; Hayes, charged as his accomplice, is sentenced to 10 years in prison. On her release, she becomes a streetwalker to support her illegitimate son, Robert Young, sending the money to Hersholt, a doctor tutoring Young in medicine. Young is suspicious about the money because of the irregular sums and sporadic deliveries; however, Hayes lies, telling Young the money is from the estate of his late mother. Eventually Young becomes a successful doctor, setting Hayes up in a Parisian apartment. The film ends as Hersholt finishes his narration. He has been telling the story to Young's wife, a woman upset by Young's devotion to his career. She had been considering leaving him, but after hearing Hayes' story, the woman reconsiders.

Hayes won a well-deserved Oscar for this performance, taking her character from young girl to old woman with astonishing believability. The story piles twist upon emotional twist, coming close to self-parody, but audiences of the day loved the picture. The story had been made numerous times under the title MADAME X. Two silent versions were made in 1915 and 1920, while sound versions were made in 1929, 1937, 1948, 1960 (as THE TRIAL OF MADAME X), 1966, and 1981 as a television film.

SINCE YOU WENT AWAY

1944 172m bw War/Drama ★★★★
UA (U.S.) /U

Claudette Colbert (Anne Hilton), Jennifer Jones (Jane), Shirley Temple (Bridget "Brig" Hilton), Joseph Cotten (Lt. Anthony Willett), Monty Woolley (Col. Smollett), Robert Walker (Cpl. William G. Smollett II), Lionel Barrymore (Clergyman), Hattie McDaniel, Agnes Moorehead (Emily Hawkins), Guy Madison (Harold Smith)

p, David O. Selznick; d, John Cromwell; w, David O. Selznick (based on the book Together by Margaret Buell Wilder, adaptation by Wilder); ph, Stanley Cortez, Lee Garmes, Jack Cosgrove; ed, Hal C. Kern, James E. Newcom, Don DiFaure, Arthur Fellows, Wayland M. Hendrys; m, Max Steiner, Louis Forbes; prod d, William L. Oereira; fx, Jack Cosgrove, Clarence Slifer; chor, Charles Walters

AAN Best Picture; AAN Best Actress: Claudette Colbert; AAN Best Supporting Actor: Monty Woolley; AAN Best Supporting Actress: Jennifer Jones; AAN Best Cinematography: Stanley Cortez, Lee Garmes; AAN Best Editing: James E. Newcom, Hal C. Kern; AA Best Score: Max Steiner; AAN Best Art Direction: Mark-Lee Kirk, Victor A. Gangelin; AAN Best Visual Effects: John R. Cosgrove, Arthur Johns

Focusing on the plight of those left behind when the soldiers went off to fight in WWII, SINCE YOU WENT AWAY was a smash hit with audiences on the home front, grossing well over $4 million at a time when movie ticket prices were as low as 25 cents. Based on a collection of letters written by Ohio newspaper columnist Margaret Buell Wilder to her husband fighting overseas, which Wilder first published in her column, then collected in a book, and finally rewrote as a screen story,

SINCE YOU WENT AWAY is a long, episodic, but always interesting film scripted by producer David O. Selznick from Wilder's adaptation. The film focuses on the wartime life of Colbert and her two daughters (Jones and a teenaged Temple, the latter making her first screen appearance after a layoff of a couple of years) after Colbert's husband leaves his family and his job in the advertising business to go off to fight in the war. Jones is in love with a soldier—Walker, a corporal, who returns from the service to romance her. (Jones and Walker were married in real life at the time, and, though they divorced a year later, their off-screen love is still evident here). Also figuring in the proceedings are Cotten, a family friend and Navy lieutenant who lends his moral support to Colbert and never takes advantage of her loneliness; Wooley, Colbert's acerbic boarder, whose sarcasm provides the film's lighter moments; and Soda, the family's scene-stealing English bulldog.

SINCE YOU WENT AWAY unfolds its loosely structured story realistically—even the battle scenes lack the phony heroics common in WWII films—and the film's three hours pass quickly, sped by its interesting assortment of characters, touchingly portrayed by the cast, its well-written script by Selznick, and its high level of technical accomplishment.

SINGIN' IN THE RAIN

1952 103m c Musical ★★★★★
MGM (U.S.) /U

Gene Kelly (Don Lockwood), Donald O'Connor (Cosmo Brown), Debbie Reynolds (Kathy Selden), Jean Hagen (Lina Lamont), Millard Mitchell (R.F. Simpson), Rita Moreno (Zelda Zanders), Douglas Fowley (Roscoe Dexter), Cyd Charisse (Dancer), Madge Blake (Dora Bailey), King Donovan (Rod)

p, Arthur Freed; d, Gene Kelly, Stanley Donen; w, Adolph Green, Betty Comden (suggested by the song "Singin' in the Rain"); ph, Harold Rosson; ed, Adrienne Fazan; m, Nacio Herb Brown; art d, Cedric Gibbons, Randall Duell; fx, Warren Newcombe, Irving G. Ries; cos, Walter Plunkett

AAN Best Supporting Actress: Jean Hagen; AAN Best Score: Lennie Hayton

Very likely the greatest musical MGM or anyone else ever produced, SINGIN' IN THE RAIN has everything—great songs, great dances, a wonderful, nostalgic story, and a dependable cast, although we're beginning to find Kelly and O'Connor a trifle overanimated in scenes they needn't be (but then whenever we see the talented yet obsequious Mr. Kelly play modest, we get a strange olfactory sensation—that of ham baking). It's admittedly directed (by Gene Kelly and Stanley Donen) with a dazzling pace equal to the speed-crazy era the film profiles, the Roaring Twenties. Asked to create a story that would tie together numbers from the best of MGM's musical output, many of which were penned by Nacio Herb Brown and Arthur Freed, screenwriters Adolph Green and Betty Comden found that some of the finest of those tunes appeared in films made during the transition from silents to talkies, and so they decided to focus their tale on that dynamic period when new stars replaced old; bright, shiny faces took the places of heavily rouged vamps and mascared lotharios.

As the film opens in 1927, dashing Don Lockwood (Kelly) and blonde bombshell Lina Lamont (Jean Hagen) are one of Hollywood's favorite romantic teams, though Lina mistakenly believes their on-screen love is for real. Don and his less famous former partner, song-and-dance man Cosmo Brown (Donald O'Connor), have worked their way to the top the hard way (vaudeville, stuntwork, etc.), and when THE JAZZ SINGER changes the cinematic rules, making a pleasant voice a necessity, Don is ready. Not so Lina, whose shrill voice makes a mockery of the musical their most recent film has been transformed into, despite the best efforts of a stuffy diction coach which are wonderfully lampooned by Don and Cosmo in "Moses Supposes" (written by Comden and Green and Roger Edens). Kathy Selden (Debbie Reynolds, who makes a great flapper—like UNSINKABLE MOLLY BROWN, here's a character with Reynolds's energy level), an aspiring "serious" actress whose life Don enters quite unexpectedly and with whom he falls in love, saves the film when her voice is dubbed for Lina's (ironically, Reynolds's own singing was looped by Betty

Royce—her own voice hadn't much training yet). Although it seems at first that Kathy is destined to remain behind the scenes indefinitely, the film's ending sees to it that fair is fair as true love triumphs.

Contributing some of the most captivating choreography ever filmed, Kelly, more than anyone, is responsible for the delightful ambience of this spectacular musical. His *tour de force* dance to the classic title song (which first appeared in HOLLYWOOD REVUE OF 1929) alone makes the film a must-see; bounding through a rain-clogged street, swinging around a lamppost, splashing and jumping in joy over having fallen in love with Kathy, he creates one of the cinema's most unforgettable moments. Nearly as engaging are the hilarious, highly energized comic dance O'Connor performs with props and sets on a soundstage to "Make 'Em Laugh" and the marvelous "Broadway Ballet" sequence with a wonderful guest appearance by surly Cyd Charisse and her "crazy veil," a 25-foot long piece of white China silk that streamed about her, kept afloat by three airplane motors whirring off-camera. This sequence took a month to rehearse, two weeks to shoot, and cost $600,000, almost a fifth of the overall budget of this superlative musical, one of the most popular films ever. Look for Madge Blake as a saccharine sob sister columnist and Rita Moreno as a flapper actress.

SINGLE WHITE FEMALE

1992   107m   c   Thriller   ★★½
SWF Productions/Guber-Peters Entertainment   R/18
Company   (U.S.)

Bridget Fonda *(Allison Jones)*, Jennifer Jason Leigh *(Hedra Carlson)*, Steven Weber *(Sam Rawson)*, Peter Friedman *(Graham Knox)*, Stephen Tobolowsky *(Mitchell Meyerson)*, Frances Bay *(Elderly Neighbor)*, Michele Farr *(Myerson's Assistant)*, Tara Karsian *(Mannish Applicant)*, Christiana Capetillo *(Exotic Applicant)*, Jessica Lundy *(Talkative Applicant)*

p, Barbet Schroeder; d, Barbet Schroeder; w, Don Roos (from the novel "SWF Seeks Same" by Jon Lutz); ph, Luciano Tovoli; ed, Lee Percy; m, Howard Shore; prod d, Milena Canonero; art d, P. Michael Johnston; cos, Milena Canonero

SINGLE WHITE FEMALE is a stylishly shot thriller with several hair-raising moments. Considering that it's directed by Barbet Schroeder and stars Bridget Fonda and Jennifer Jason Leigh, it's also a major disappointment. Fonda plays Alison Jones, a chic New Yorker who finds herself in need of a roommate after she kicks out her unfaithful boyfriend Sam (Steven Weber). Enter Hedra Carlson (Leigh), who seems like the perfect candidate. Waif-like and dowdy, Hedra helps Alison through her crisis, and obviously derives satisfaction from the fact that her new friend comes to depend on her for support.

When Sam works his way back into Alison's life, Hedra's jealousy is so blatant and intense it prompts Alison into some amateur investigation. Surprise, surprise! Turns out Hedra is no bookish introvert, but a psycho intent on taking over her roommate's life. That's what you get for not checking references.

Like too many contemporary thrillers, SWF starts out with an intriguing psychological premise which it fails to develop. Hedra, we find out, is an identical twin who lost her sister at an early age and is compulsively seeking a replacement. Thus she begins to dress in clothes identical to Alison's and even gets her hair styled in the exact same fashion. When we cut to the chase, though, she behaves just like any other generic movie psycho, killing anyone who gets in her way and covering her tracks with professional efficiency. Despite the formidable talents of the two leads, SWF is resoundingly inauthentic—a particular disappointment given that Schroeder's earlier films, REVERSAL OF FORTUNE and BARFLY, were such keenly observed studies of different social milieux. What we see of Alison and Hedra's lives outside the apartment rings patently untrue, as does Alison's tolerance of her patently manipulative, unhinged roommate. Any single white female that gullible should seek professional help.

SINGLES

1992   99m   c   Romance/Comedy   ★★★½
Warner Bros.   (U.S.)   PG-13/12

Bridget Fonda *(Janet Livermore)*, Campbell Scott *(Steve Dunne)*, Kyra Sedgwick *(Linda Powell)*, Sheila Kelley *(Debbie Hunt)*, Jim True *(David Bailey)*, Matt Dillon *(Cliff Poncier)*, Bill Pullman *(Dr. Jamison)*, James LeGros *(Andy)*, Devon Raymond *(Ruth)*, Camilo Gallardo *(Luiz)*

p, Richard Hashimoto, Cameron Crowe; d, Cameron Crowe; w, Cameron Crowe; ph, Ueli Steiger; ed, Richard Chew; m, Paul Westerberg; prod d, Stephen J. Lineweaver; art d, Mark Haack

Rolling Stone contributor turned writer-director Cameron Crowe pulled off a near-impossible feat with his first film, SAY ANYTHING: he made an intelligent, endearing, non-sappy teen romance. With his follow-up, SINGLES, Crowe ambitiously tackles the romantic lives of a group of twentysomething characters, as played out against an appealing Seattle backdrop. SINGLES is more a series of interlocking vignettes than a straightforward narrative; the film is divided into "chapters" and characters occasionally talk directly to the screen, to introduce themselves or comment on the action. The principals are Linda (Kyra Sedgwick), who works for an environmental agency, and Steve (Campbell Scott), an urban planner, who enjoy an idyllic love affair that gets complicated when Linda discovers she's pregnant. Steve's U-shaped singles apartment complex also houses Janet (Bridget Fonda) and Cliff (Matt Dillon), the clownish lead singer of grunge-metal band Citizen Dick (played by members of Seattle sensation Pearl Jam). Janet, Steve's trusted advisor on matters of the heart, is hung up on Cliff, but Cliff is more devoted to the band than to his quasi-girl-friend, and Janet makes several attempts to win him over before she finally breaks off the relationship.

SINGLES works because it gets so many details right: the discussions about how long to wait after a date before calling someone back, or the strategies people use to convince themselves someone is attracted to them, are skewered with amusing accuracy. Mercifully, Crowe hasn't added a syrupy orchestral score to cue the audience during emotional scenes. Instead, there's music from former Replacements front man Paul Westerberg and some of the Seattle bands who rose to national prominence in 1992: Alice in Chains, Soundgarden and many others. These angry, fiercely contemporary sounds act as an effective counterpoint to the characters' seemingly cool, collected psyches. SINGLES is funny and well-observed and, most notably, plays to its audience's intelligence rather than its libido.

SINK THE BISMARCK!

1960   97m   bw   War/Historical   ★★★★
Fox   (U.K.)   /U

Kenneth More *(Capt. Jonathan Shepard)*, Dana Wynter *(Anne Davis)*, Carl Mohner *(Capt. Lindemann)*, Laurence Naismith *(First Sea Lord)*, Geoffrey Keen *(A.C.N.S.)*, Karel Stepanek *(Adm. Lutjens)*, Michael Hordern *(Commander on King George)*, Maurice Denham *(Cmdr. Richards)*, Michael Goodliffe *(Capt. Banister)*, Esmond Knight *(Captain, Prince of Wales)*

p, John Brabourne; d, Lewis Gilbert; w, Edmund H. North (based on the book by C.S. Forester); ph, Christopher Challis; ed, Peter Hunt; m, Clifton Parker; art d, Arthur Lawson; fx, Howard Lydecker, Bill Warrington

Screenwriter Edmund North knows how to write about war, as he proved with his Oscar-winning screenplay for PATTON. Here, he has fashioned a taut, tense wartime drama out of the real story of how the Germans' most powerful naval fighting machine was destroyed. The film starts with actual newsreel footage as the *Bismarck* is launched in Hamburg to the cheers of the Nazi chiefs in 1938. Flash ahead to 1941 and the War Room of the British Admiralty, where More, still stunned by the death of his wife in an air raid, begins to conduct the campaign to blow the German battleship out of the water. Wynter, a WREN (the British equivalent of a WAVE), is at More's side in the War Room. No sooner does More take over the job when word comes in that the *Bismarck* has left its hiding place and is now steaming toward the battle zone. More has to figure some way to make th most of his sparse fleet, and the news is bad when the *Bismarck* sinks the *Hood*, one of Britain's best, then cripples the cruiser *Prince of Wales*. More's son is a gunner on the *Ark Royal*, a carrier More sends to fight the *Bismarck*. Rushing from Gibraltar, *Ark Royal* damages the behemoth enough to cause it to seek shelter on the French coast. Once the *Bismarck* is slowed down, the British ships *King George V* and *Rodney* are able to catch up with it and finally destroy it in a huge sea battle. The film is a marvel of intercutting, shifting repeatedly from More and Wynter in the War Room, to action aboard the German battleship, to all the other British ships as they begin to tighten the noose. More spends countless hours plotting the destruction of the *Bismark*, grabbing a nap here and there, sharing his personal woes with Wynter, who is always at his side. Although there's a bit of caricature in the portrayal of the Germans, the film is still evenhanded enough in its portrayal of the enemy that the villains remain interesting characters. Actual battle footage is combined with flawless miniature work by Howard Lydecker and Bill Harrington and the effect is stunningly convincing. SINK THE BISMARK is a first-class war drama that ranks with IN WHICH WE SERVE and COCKLESHELL HEROES as examples of how to create excitement with a great script. The most impressive part of North's screenplay is that we are almost able to look inside More's head to see why he does what he does.

SISTER ACT

1992 96m c Comedy/Musical ★★½
Touchstone (U.S.) PG

Whoopi Goldberg *(Deloris)*, Maggie Smith *(Mother Superior)*, Kathy Najimy *(Mary Patrick)*, Wendy Makkena *(Mary Robert)*, Mary Wickes *(Mary Lazarus)*, Harvey Keitel *(Vince LaRocca)*, Bill Nunn *(Eddie Souther)*, Robert Miranda *(Joey)*, Richard Portnow *(Willy)*, Ellen Albertini Dow

p, Teri Schwartz; d, Emile Ardolino; w, Paul Rudnick, Eleanor Bergstein, Jim Cash, Jack Epps Jr., Carrie Fisher, Robert Harling, Nancy Meyers; ph, Adam Greenberg; ed, Richard Halsey; m, Marc Shaiman; prod d, Jackson DeGovia; cos, Molly Maginnis

A tremendous commercial success, Touchstone's SISTER ACT is yet another Disney comedy that keeps threatening to get genuinely interesting, only to veer back into by-the-numbers banality. The main plot is triggered when Reno lounge singer Deloris (Whoopi Goldberg) walks in on her lover, thug Vince LaRocca (Harvey Keitel), killing an informer. Deciding her life expectancy would be severely limited otherwise, Deloris takes an offer from a cop, Eddie Souther (Bill Nunn), to go temporarily undercover until she can testify against LaRocca. Her new identity? A nun in a San Francisco convent presided over by a stern Mother Superior (Maggie Smith), the only person in the place who knows Deloris's true identity. Since Deloris makes an unconvincing holy sister, the Mother Superior strikes a bargain with her: she will confine herself to her room and come out only to coach the convent choir, an ensemble of jaw-dropping ineptness. Deloris soon turns the choir into a hymn-singing girl group whose repertoire includes pop classics like "My Guy" and "I Will Follow Him," reworked into religious anthems.

Though it was SISTER ACT's major selling point, the idea of hip, singing nuns bringing down the house wears thin quickly. Nonetheless, director Emile Ardolino (THREE MEN AND A LITTLE LADY, DIRTY DANCING) largely saves the day by coaxing winning performances from an excellent cast. Goldberg's work here never loses its edge or originality, allowing her to shine opposite Smith, who is so good that she barely seems to be acting. The supporting cast is consistently funny, from veteran performer Wickes to Kathy Najimy, whose maniacally sunny-spirited Sister Mary Patrick keeps threatening to steal the picture.

SISTERS OF THE GION
(GION NO SHIMAI)

1936 70m bw Drama ★★★★
Daiichi Eiga (Japan)

Isuzu Yamada *(Umekichi)*, Yoko Umemura *(O-Mocha)*, Eitaro Shindo, Benkei Shiganoya, Namiko Kawahima, Fumio Okura, Taizo Fukami, Reido Aoi

p, Masaichi Nagata; d, Kenji Mizoguchi; w, Yoshikata Toda (based on a story by Mizoguchi); ph, Minoru Miki

This is one of two excellent films (the other being THE OSAKA ELEGY) that director Kenji Mizoguchi made in 1936. Both were made possible by Daiichi Eiga, the failing studio for whom the director was employed, which gave him complete control before it was shuttered. Like so many of Mizoguchi's works, SISTERS OF THE GION focuses on female characters, in this case two sisters, both of whom are geishas. Umekichi (Isuzu Yamada) is the elder, an experienced prostitute who has become romantically involved with one of her former clients, a bankrupt merchant. Omocha (Yoko Umemura), the younger sister, has different ideas about men and relationships. Having seen the way men treat women, especially her sister, she decides to take the upper hand, manipulating, and ultimately to destroying, a young kimono clerk. In a twist of fate that seems to suggest that gender roles are irreversible, both sisters are victimized by the film's end. This elegant, carefully directed tale shows Mizoguchi's early talents. He manages to elicit beautiful performances from his actresses, establishing himself as one of the great directors of women, and embarking on his career as the greatest cinematic interpreter of the lives of Japanese women. From SISTERS OF THE GION's very beginning, with its rollicking jazz score, Mizoguchi demonstrates his unique mastery of the film frame, moving through the expansive space of a merchant's home in which every last piece of furniture is auctioned off—a masculine material defeat that neatly contrasts with the female romantic defeat at the film's end. (In Japanese; English subtitles.)

SITTING PRETTY

1948 84m bw Comedy ★★★★
Fox (U.S.) /U

Robert Young *(Harry)*, Maureen O'Hara *(Tacey)*, Clifton Webb *(Lynn Belvedere)*, Richard Haydn *(Mr. Appleton)*, Louise Allbritton *(Edna Philby)*, Randy Stuart *(Peggy)*, Ed Begley *(Hammond)*, Larry Olsen *(Larry)*, John Russell *(Bill Philby)*, Betty Lynn *(Ginger)*

p, Samuel G. Engel; d, Walter Lang; w, F. Hugh Herbert (based on the novel *Belvedere* by Gwen Davenport); ph, Norbert Brodine; ed, Harmon Jones; m, Alfred Newman; art d, Lyle Wheeler, Leland Fuller; fx, Fred Sersen; cos, Kay Nelson

AAN Best Actor: Clifton Webb

If ever an actor was born to play a part, it was Clifton Webb in his Oscar-nominated role as Lynn Belvedere, a prissy genius who takes a job as a babysitter. The scene is Hummingbird Hill, a typical suburban community where the three sons of Harry and Tacey (Robert Young and Maureen O'Hara) are so bratty that the family has lost a trio of maids, with little hope of finding another replacement. Tacey advertises in the local paper and in walks Mr. Belvedere, a self-proclaimed genius with definite ideas about raising children. He is stern but fair and it's not long before the boys knuckle under to his discipline. When the baby tosses oatmeal at Belvedere, his response is to toss the goop right back at the baby, thereby establishing his superiority. The neighborhood is filled with gossips and busybodies, and they are all shocked when the real reason for Belvedere's presence is unveiled: he's a writer (besides being a doctor, lawyer, philosopher, and everything else) who has been researching the community. The town is then exposed when Belvedere's book is published and becomes a best-seller. The two sequels to this successful film, MR. BELVEDERE GOES TO COLLEGE and MR. BELVEDERE RINGS THE BELL, were not nearly as witty or biting as the original. In 1985, a TV series was also attempted based on the Webb character.

SIX DEGREES OF SEPARATION

1993 102m c Comedy/Drama ★★★
MGM/New Regency Productions (U.S.) R/

Stockard Channing *(Ouisa Kittredge)*, Will Smith *(Paul)*, Donald Sutherland *(Flan Kittredge)*, Ian McKellen *(Geoffrey)*, Mary Beth Hurt *(Kitty)*, Bruce Davison *(Larkin)*, Richard Masur *(Dr. Fine)*, Anthony Michael Hall *(Trent Conway)*, Heather Graham *(Elizabeth)*, Eric Thal *(Rick)*

p, Fred Schepisi, Arnon Milchan; d, Fred Schepisi; w, John Guare (from his play); ph, Ian Baker; ed, Peter Honess; m, Jerry Goldsmith; prod d, Patrizia Von Brandenstein; art d, Dennis Bradford; cos, Judianna Makovsky

AAN Best Actress: Stockard Channing

Witty, wordy, well-acted satire of contemporary class and race relations, based on John Guare's acclaimed stage play.

Art dealers Ouisa and Flan Kittredge (Stockard Channing, Donald Sutherland) are entertaining a rich South African business partner (Ian McKellen) in their posh Fifth Avenue apartment when a suave and personable young black man bursts in. Paul (Will Smith), who claims to be the son of Sidney Poitier and a college friend of the Kittredges' children, says he's been wounded by muggers. By the end of the evening he has charmed the initially suspicious Kittredges with his culinary and elocutionary talents—so much so that they invite him to stay the night. The next morning, however, they discover Paul in bed with a man he has picked up on the street and throw him out. But that's only the beginning of their involvement with this offbeat confidence man.

Channing holds this sometimes stagy movie together in the pivotal role of Ouisa, the Park Avenue matron who ultimately snaps when Paul makes her realize the ways in which her privileged status has isolated her from the rest of humanity. It is she who invokes the film's title, referring to an old conversational gambit to the effect that any two people in the world can be linked together by a chain of no more than six relationships. For a mainstream Hollywood production, the film is refreshingly frank about race and class in the US; for a darker, more acerbic variation on the same theme, see Wendell B. Harris's brilliant CHAMELEON STREET (1991).

SIX IN PARIS
(PARIS VU PAR. . .)

1965 96m c Comedy/Drama   ★★★
Losange/Barbet Schroeder   (France)

SAINT-GERMAIN-DES-PRES: Barbara Wilkin *(Katherine)*, Jean-Francois Chappey *(Jean)*, Jean-Pierre Andreani *(Raymond)*, GARE DU NORD: Nadine Ballot *(Odile)*, Barbet Schroeder *(Jean-Pierre)*, Gilles Queant *(Stranger)*, RUE SAINT-DENIS: Micheline Dax *(Prostitute)*, Claude Melki *(Leon)*, PLACE DE L'ETOILE: Jean-Michel Rouziere *(Jean-Marc)*, Marcel Gallon *(Victim)*

p, Barbet Schroeder; d, Jean Douchet, Jean Rouch, Jean-Daniel Pollet, Eric Rohmer, Jean-Luc Godard, Claude Chabrol; w, Jean Douchet, Jean Rouch, Georges Keller, Jean-Daniel Pollet, Eric Rohmer, Jean-Luc Godard, Claude Chabrol; ph, Nestor Almendros, Etienne Becker, Alain Levent, Albert Maysles, Jean Rabier; ed, Jackie Reynal; art d, Eliane Bonneau

This six-part compilation film, which opened in Paris in October 1965, is notable for the talent that worked on some of the segments; many of these directors, actors and cinematographers would go on to become central figures of the French New Wave.

In "Saint-Germain-des-Pres," Chappey brings American student Wilkin to his flat for the night. He gets rid of her the next day, announcing that he's flying to Mexico to join his father. Wilkin is later disillusioned when Chappey turns up as a model in her art class. She then allows Andreani to pick her up, only to discover that this boy had loaned his apartment to Chappey for the original affair. The photographer was Almendros, who became a celebrated cinematographer during the 1970s.

In "Gare du Nord," Ballot runs out on her husband (Schroeder) after a fight. She's almost run down by Queant, a handsome stranger in a fancy car. He says he's going to kill himself but will change his mind if Ballot goes away with him. She refuses, and he takes a plunge off a railway bridge.

"Rue Saint-Denis" depicts shy, young Melki bringing prostitute Dax back to his place for a night of fun. His incessant conversation leads to Dax's staying for dinner before they can get to bed.

"Place de l'Etoile," directed by Rohmer, has salesman Rouziere bumping into Gallon, a street person, on his way to work. He hits the poor man with his umbrella during the confrontation, and Gallon falls down. Rouziere is convinced he's killed the derelict and looks for news of his death in the papers. A few weeks later, he sees Gallon engaged in a similar argument with another person at the same place.

"Montparnasse-Levallois" was directed by the bad boy of the *Nouvelle Vague*, Godard, and photographed by noted American documentary filmmaker Maysles. This story has Joanna Shimkus serving as a

lover for two men. She sends each a note telling the site of their respective rendezvous but panics when she thinks she mistakenly switched the notes. She goes to each lover to explain away her mistake and is surprised when each man throws her out, then realizes the mistake was all in her mind.

The last segment, "La Muette," was written and directed by Chabrol. He also plays a man who constantly fights with his wife (Stephane Audran) about money and who flirts with the housemaid. His son, tired of the noise, buys some earplugs for himself. The earplugs end up doing more harm than good when his mother falls down the stairs, and the boy doesn't hear her cry out for help.

SIXTEEN CANDLES

1984 93m c Comedy   ★★★
Channel (U.S.)   PG/15

Molly Ringwald *(Samantha)*, Justin Henry *(Mike Baker)*, Michael Schoeffling *(Jake)*, Haviland Morris *(Caroline)*, Gedde Watanabe *(Long Duk Dong)*, Anthony Michael Hall *(Ted, the Geek)*, Paul Dooley *(Jim Baker)*, Carlin Glynn *(Brenda Baker)*, Blanche Baker *(Ginny)*, Edward Andrews *(Howard)*

p, Hilton A. Green; d, John Hughes; w, John Hughes; ph, Bobby Byrne; ed, Edward Warschilka; m, Ira Newborn; prod d, John W. Corso; cos, Mark Peterson, Marla Denise Schlom

This funny, unpretentious film marked writer John Hughes's first time out as a director. The premise is ordinary, but the film is distinguished by funny gags and excellent performances by Molly Ringwald and Anthony Michael Hall. Samantha (Ringwald) is a high-school sophomore about to turn 16, and her life is dominated by her love for Jake (Michael Schoeffling), a senior and the school heartthrob. In turn, she is followed around by Ted (Hall), a younger boy who is acknowledged to be a nerd. Nothing seems to be going right for Samantha. Her older sister is about to be married, and her parents are overlooking Samantha's birthday, a major moment in her young life. Her grandparents move into her room, and her relationship with her smart-alecky brother (Justin Henry) gets tense. Simultaneously, Samantha has to be kind and caring for Long Duk Dong (Gedde Watanabe), a loony but sweet Japanese exchange student staying at her home. The situations are predictable, but Hughes saves them from being cliches with his attention to detail. Hall and Ringwald became part of the Hollywood "Brat Pack" with this film, and Hughes emerged as a hot director.

SKIPPY

1931 85m bw Children's   ★★★½
Paramount (U.S.)   /U

Jackie Cooper *(Skippy Skinner)*, Robert Coogan *(Sooky Wayne)*, Mitzi Green *(Eloise)*, Jackie Searl *(Sidney)*, Willard Robertson *(Dr. Herbert Skinner)*, Enid Bennett *(Mrs. Ellen Skinner)*, David Haines *(Harley Nubbins)*, Helen Jerome Eddy *(Mrs. Wayne)*, Jack Clifford *(Dogcatcher Nubbins)*, Guy Oliver *(Dad Burkey)*

p, Louis D. Lighton; d, Norman Taurog; w, Joseph L. Mankiewicz, Norman Z. McLeod, Don Marquis, Percy Crosby, Sam Mintz (based on the comic strip by Crosby); ph, Karl Struss

AAN Best Picture; AAN Best Actor: Jackie Cooper; *AA Best Director:* Norman Taurog; *AAN Best Adapted Screenplay:* Joseph Mankiewicz, Sam Mintz

A charming children's picture that doesn't neglect adults, SKIPPY was good enough to merit Oscar nominations for Best Picture, Best Director, Best Story, and for Jackie Cooper as Best Actor. Based on a comic strip by Percy Crosby, it's a simple, adorable tale of boys and girls and their dogs. When a dog belonging to Sooky Wayne (Robert Coogan, younger brother of Jackie Coogan) is captured by the local dogcatcher, Sooky and his friend Skippy Skinner (Jackie Cooper) try to raise money to buy a license for the pooch. In order to get the necessary $3, they try everything. One of their plans is to stage a show, for which they sell tickets, lemonade, etc. They also try smashing Skippy's unbreakable bank by putting it under the wheels of a truck. There are many wonderful moments in the picture, and watching Cooper cry is worth the price of admission. There have been few child actors who have been as convincing as he could be. The sequel was SOOKY.

SLACKER

1991 97m c Comedy   ★★★½
Detour Filmproduction (U.S.)   R/18

Richard Linklater, Rudy Basquez, Jean Caggeine, Jan Hockey, Stephan Hockey, Mark James, Samuel Dietert, Bob Boyd, Terrence Kirk, Keith McCormack

p, Richard Linklater; d, Richard Linklater; w, Richard Linklater; ph, Lee Daniel; ed, Scott Rhodes

An original, narratively innovative, low-budget film from the fringe, SLACKER is a perfectly plotless work that tracks incidental moments in the lives of some one hundred characters who have made the bohemian side of Austin, Texas, their hangout of choice.

Because it lacks any conventional storyline, or even a central character, SLACKER is impossible to synopsize or categorize. The film's organizing sensibility is perhaps best explained by director Richard Linklater himself, who appears onscreen in his film's opening scene. On his way into town, he free-associates to his cab driver: "You know in THE WIZARD OF OZ where Dorothy meets the Scarecrow . . . and they think about going in all those directions and they end up going in that *one* direction? All those other directions, just because they thought about them, became separate realities . . . entirely different movies." SLACKER consists of all those other different movies. Its camera follows one character, splinters off to follow another, then another, never spending more than a few minutes with any one and never returning to a place or person from preceding scenes.

The two forces that hold the film together are its clear sense of place (specifically Austin, more generally college towns) and its intimate knowledge of a certain character type: the "slacker." The term is slang that refers loosely to any number of young underemployed residents of college communities who either lack direction in life or choose an alternative direction. In an hour and a half we meet dozens of these street musicians, espresso czars, co-op kids, sidewalk psychics, paranoid hitchhikers, disgruntled grad students, cafe philosophers, anti-artists, petty thieves, anarchists, post-modernists, dropouts and freaks—slackers all.

While many appear to be lazy and indulgent drags on society, what emerges is a portrait of a collective of creative malcontents. In the clubs, coffeehouses, streets and unfurnished apartments near campus they each spin their idiosyncratic conspiracy theories about modern life, UFOs, Elvis, Madonna, George Bush, popular culture, JFK, Oswald, Marx and various forms of cosmic consciousness. Although there is little action as they practice the fine art of hanging out, their constant talk is full of energy, humor, eccentricity and a warped but discernable intelligence.

Produced on a budget of only $23,000, SLACKER became a surprise hit on the festival circuit. At age 29, director Richard Linklater obtained a major distribution deal from Orion Classics, which blew the original 16mm print up to 35mm and remixed its soundtrack. Such treatment was exceptional for a self-taught, first-time filmmaker who used mostly unpaid amateur talent to create an experiment in cinematic form. But the film's improvisatory, meandering style is actually carefully constructed.

SLAP SHOT

1977 123m c Sports   ★★★
Universal (U.S.)   R/18

Paul Newman (*Reggie Dunlop*), Strother Martin (*Joe McGrath*), Michael Ontkean (*Ned Braden*), Jennifer Warren (*Francine Dunlop*), Lindsay Crouse (*Lily Braden*), Jerry Houser (*"Killer" Carlson*), Andrew Duncan (*Jimm Carr*), Jeff Carlson (*Jeff Hanson*), Steve Carlson (*Steve Hanson*), David Hanson (*Jack Hanson*)

p, Robert J. Wunsch, Stephen Friedman; d, George Roy Hill; w, Nancy Dowd; ph, Victor J. Kemper; ed, Dede Allen; m, Elmer Bernstein; art d, Henry Bumstead; cos, Tom Bronson

Funny, frank, and violent, George Roy Hill's absorbing film about minor league hockey offers a wonderful comic performance from Newman as the aging player-coach of the Charleston Chiefs. Mired in a long losing streak and deserted by their fans, the Chiefs learn that the franchise is to fold at the end of the season because the steel mill that employs most of their Pennsylvania town's populace is closing. Refus-

ing to give up, Newman encourages his team in no-holds-barred play. Surprisingly, three recently acquired, bespectacled brothers (Carlson, Carlson, and Hanson) prove to be the ultimate monsters of high-sticking mayhem, leading the Chiefs to victory after violent victory and filling the stands. This doesn't sit well with leading scorer Ontkean, a Princeton grad committed to "old-fashioned" hockey. Meanwhile, Newman plants stories that the Chiefs' unknown owner is negotiating to sell the club and tries to reconcile with his beautician-wife, Warren. The team is destined to become a tax write-off, but with pride on the line, they take on a club composed of the league's roughest players for the championship—a game with a bizarre finish unlike that of any other sports film. Upon its release, SLAP SHOT gained instant notoriety for its locker-room language, which may offend some but is perfect for its milieu. In fact, screenwriter Dowd based the diction on tape recordings her brother, a minor league hockey player, made in the locker room and on the team bus. In addition to Newman's masterful work, the film includes excellent supporting performances by Martin as the Chiefs' general manager, Duncan as a sportscaster, and Crouse as Ontkean's most unhappy wife. The on-ice violence is hyperreal, the emotions believable, and the laughs plentiful in this slightly off-the-wall comedy.

SLEEPER

1973 88m c Science Fiction/Comedy   ★★★½
Rollins-Joffe (U.S.)   PG

Woody Allen (*Miles Monroe*), Diane Keaton (*Luna Schlosser*), John Beck (*Erno Windt*), Marya Small (*Dr. Nero*), Bartlett Robinson (*Dr. Orva*), Mary Gregory (*Dr. Melik*), Chris Forbes (*Rainer Krebs*), Peter Hobbs (*Dr. Dean*), Spencer Milligan (*Jeb Hrmthmg*), Stanley Ralph Ross (*Sears Wiggles*)

p, Jack Grossberg; d, Woody Allen; w, Woody Allen, Marshall Brickman; ph, David M. Walsh; ed, Ralph Rosenblum; m, Woody Allen; prod d, Dale Hennesy; art d, Dianne Wager; fx, A.D. Flowers, Jerry Endler; cos, Joel Schumacher

Like most of Allen's movies, this one is better than the box-office receipts would indicate; it still looks good many years after it was shot. Allen never lets his actors see a full script while they are shooting, so no one, except Allen, knows what's happening in the film. Consequently, many of the performers were confused by their roles.

A Greenwich Village health food store owner who dabbles in Dixieland jazz, Allen reluctantly goes to the hospital for an ulcer operation in 1973. The operation fails, and the doctors quickly put him into the deep freeze. Two hundred years later, he awakens in a dysutopian future presided over by a Big Brother-style leader. With Keaton, a writer of Rod McKuenesque verse, he sets out to overthrow the government.

There is one sight gag after another, in a physical, Buster Keaton-like fashion, and many barbs puncture contemporary targets. When someone asks what happened to Norman Mailer, Allen says that he donated his ego to science. The McDonald's signs show trillions of hamburgers sold, etc. SLEEPER is a highly inventive science fiction parody that is typical of Allen's tight, well-edited movies, which usually come in under 90 minutes. Costumes by Joel Schumacher are excellent; he later gave up sewing for writing (CAR WASH) and then directing.

SLEEPING CAR MURDER, THE
(COMPARTIMENT TUEURS)

1965 92m bw Mystery/Thriller   ★★★½
PECF/Seven Arts (France)   /X

Yves Montand (*Inspector Grazzi*), Simone Signoret (*Eliane Darres*), Pierre Mondy (*Commissioner*), Catherine Allegret (*Bambi*), Pascale Roberts (*Georgette Thomas*), Jacques Perrin (*Daniel*), Michel Piccoli (*Cabourg*), Jean-Louis Trintignant (*Eric*), Charles Denner (*Bob*), Claude Mann (*Jean-Lou*)

p, Julien Derode; d, Constantin Costa-Gavras; w, Constantin Costa-Gavras, Sebastien Japrisot (based on the novel *Compartiment Tueurs* by Japrisot); ph, Jean Tournier; ed, Christian Gaudin; m, Michel Magne; art d, Rino Mondellini

Costa-Gavras (Z, STATE OF SIEGE, MISSING) made his directorial debut with this tightly constructed suspense thriller. Montand portrays a French police inspector investigating the murder of a woman who was sleeping in a lower berth on a moving train. Aided by his assistant Mann, Montand begins to track down all the passengers who were in the train compartment where the murder took place. Piccoli, an office worker who was on the train, volunteers information but afterward is found murdered. At the same time, two other passengers, Allegret and Perrin, attempt to avoid the police because the latter is a runaway who will be taken back to his parents if found. Perrin was hiding from the conductor in a berth and was aided by Allegret, a young woman traveling to a new job in Paris. After the murder, the pair stumble across the wallet of Signoret, an aging actress who also was a passenger on the train that night. They then go to her home to return it. Before knocking at her door, they notice she is being interrogated by Montand. Perrin and Allegret hide nearby and watch as a young man, Trintignant, slips out the back door of Signoret's house. During the interrogation, Signoret reveals that Perrin was hiding in an upper berth of the compartment. Soon after Montand leaves, Signoret is murdered. Eventually, the police determine that Trintignant was Signoret's lover, and when interrogated, the young man provides an airtight alibi. Meanwhile, Perrin overhears a plot by two men to kill Allegret and he tells the girl to hide out in a hotel. The young runaway then goes to Montand and spills everything he knows. When the police arrive, they thwart the murder attempt on Allegret and capture Trintignant. The suspect reveals that he was only an accomplice; the real killer is Montand's assistant Mann, who masterminded the whole scheme in order to pilfer Signoret's large bank account. Trintignant then goes on to state that Mann is out in the streets of Paris now, seeking to kill Perrin. Montand immediately sets out after Mann and following a thrilling chase, he saves Perrin and captures the killer. THE SLEEPING CAR MURDERS was sort of a family affair for Montand and Signoret, who were married, and for the beautiful Allegret, who is Signoret's daughter by writer director Yves Allegret. While the subject matter of this film is less political than those he would go on to make, Costa-Gavras' taut direction, coupled with a superb cast of foreign actors, propels this somewhat impenetrable mystery along at breakneck speed. It is an intriguing, highly entertaining thriller.

SLEEPING WITH THE ENEMY

1991   99m   c   Thriller/Romance   ★★★
Fox   (U.S.)   R/15

Julia Roberts *(Laura Burney/Sara Waters)*, Patrick Bergin *(Martin Burney)*, Kevin Anderson *(Ben Woodward)*, Elizabeth Lawrence *(Chloe)*, Kyle Secor *(Fleishman)*, Claudette Nevins *(Dr. Rissner)*, Tony Abatemarco *(Locke)*, Marita Geraghty *(Julie)*, Harley Venton *(Garber)*, Nancy Fish *(Woman on Bus)*

p, Leonard Goldberg; d, Joseph Ruben; w, Ronald Bass (from the novel by Nancy Price); ph, John W Lindley; ed, George Bowers; m, Jerry Goldsmith; prod d, Doug Kraner; art d, Joseph P. Lucky; cos, Richard Hornung

With its timely theme of domestic violence, SLEEPING WITH THE ENEMY is both contemporary fairy tale and Hollywood hokum of the highest grade, its sturdy prototype the "woman's picture" of the 40s and 50s. A perfect young beauty named Laura (Julia Roberts) lives with her perfect businessman husband Martin Burney (Patrick Bergin) in their perfect high-tech home by the sea. Laura dutifully conforms to her husband's lifestyle, which is excruciatingly controlled and formal. He also beats her up periodically—a tasteful sadist. The high-tech home begins to resemble a prison tower and the handsome businessman an evil wizard. Laura, with her trailing red tresses, devises a way to escape her tormentor.

Laura seizes her opportunity during a stormy yacht excursion where she jumps into the ocean and fakes her own death. She settles in a baseball and apple pie North Carolina town and begins a new life as Sara Waters. She acquires a suitor (Kevin Anderson), a bearded natural-man drama instructor at the local college. They fall blandly in love. Meanwhile Martin has put two and two together and begins to track his wife down with a bitter vengeance.

SLEEPING WITH THE ENEMY teeters constantly on the verge of silliness but director Joseph Ruben keeps the cornball melodrama scaled down to a pleasant lull. Nothing is overplayed and there's an admirable restraint in the story telling. The scenes speed along at a confident pace. Everything is designed to show off the movie's best asset: Julia Roberts.

SLEEPLESS IN SEATTLE

1993   100m   c   Comedy/Drama/Romance   ★★★
Big Onion Productions/Gary Foster Productions   PG
/TriStar   (U.S.)

Tom Hanks *(Sam Baldwin)*, Meg Ryan *(Annie Reed)*, Bill Pullman *(Walter)*, Rosie O'Donnell *(Becky)*, Rob Reiner *(Jay)*, Rita Wilson *(Suzy)*, Gaby Hoffmann *(Jessica)*, Carey Lowell *(Maggie Baldwin)*, Ross Malinger *(Jonah Baldwin)*, Victor Garber *(Greg)*

p, Gary Foster; d, Nora Ephron; w, Nora Ephron, David S. Ward, Jeffrey Arch (from his story); ph, Sven Nykvist; ed, Robert Reitano; m, Marc Shaiman; prod d, Jeffrey Townsend; art d, Gershon Ginsburg, Charley Beal; fx, Robert M. Riggs, Rick Fichter; cos, Judy Ruskin

AAN Best Original Screenplay: Jeff Arch, Nora Ephron, David S. Ward; AAN Best Original Song: Marc Shaiman, Ramsey McLean

JOE VS. THE VOLCANO co-stars Tom Hanks and Meg Ryan are reunited by director/co-writer Nora Ephron in this equally whimsical, but far more successful, romantic comedy. Superbly acted, beautifully photographed, and resolutely warm and fuzzy, SLEEPLESS IN SEATTLE is a romantic treat.

Recent widower Sam Baldwin (Hanks), a Chicago architect, moves with his eight-year-old son Jonah (Ross Malinger) to Seattle, where he hopes to start fresh, though he's haunted by the memory of his wife, Maggie (Carey Lowell, seen in home movies, dreams, and flashbacks). One night, a desperate Jonah calls a nationwide radio psychologist to see if she can help Sam (whose depression has made him insomniac) find a new wife; Sam, whom the woman dubs "Sleepless in Seattle," is eventually drawn into the conversation.

Sam's call captures the fancy of women across the country; one of them, Annie Reed (Ryan), is a reporter for The Baltimore Sun who is about to be married to the likable-but-dull Walter (Bill Pullman). Annie becomes obsessed with "Sleepless" and, though the course of true love doesn't run smooth, SLEEPLESS IN SEATTLE will not disappoint the romantic at heart.

Despite the inherently downbeat nature of the story, Ephron keeps the movie light, a series of witty riffs on grief, loss, and desperation, loosely held together by a plot that delights in referencing a slew of older movies, particularly AN AFFAIR TO REMEMBER. For a film crafted from so seemingly delicate a conceit, SLEEPLESS has the sturdy feeling of something that will continue to find receptive—if lovesick—audiences for years to come.

SLEUTH

1972   138m   c   Mystery   ★★★★
Palomar   (U.K.)   PG/15

Laurence Olivier *(Andrew Wyke)*, Michael Caine *(Milo Tindle)*, Alec Cawthorne *(Inspector Doppler)*, Margo Channing *(Marguerite)*, John Matthews *(Detective Sgt. Tarrant)*, Teddy Martin *(Police Constable Higgs)*

p, Morton Gottlieb; d, Joseph L. Mankiewicz; w, Anthony Shaffer (based on his play); ph, Oswald Morris; ed, Richard Marden; m, John Addison; prod d, Ken Adam; art d, Peter Lamont; cos, John Furniss

AAN Best Actor: Michael Caine; AAN Best Actor: Laurence Olivier; AAN Best Director: Joseph L. Mankiewicz; AAN Best Score: John Addison

This stylish, intelligent mystery is full of delightfully unexpected twists, and boasts extraordinary performances from Michael Caine and Laurence Olivier. Caine, the owner of a chain of hair salons, is invited to the 16th-century country home of Olivier, a well-known detective novelist with a passion for elaborate games. Olivier reveals that he knows Caine is having an affair with his estranged wife, but instead of being angry, he is delighted and proposes a scheme that will profit both men. Olivier's idea is for Caine to put on a clown disguise and steal his wife's jewels, thereby allowing Olivier to collect the insurance money and Caine to fence the gems and support his lover in the style to which

631

she is accustomed. The film goes through a number of shocking reversals on its way to the surprising but satisfying end. The script, written by Anthony Shaffer from his own stage play, is an actor's dream, and the two stars whip up their roles with relish, pulling the mystery back and forth in this deadly cat-and-mouse game. Director Joseph L. Mankiewicz was determined to keep the unusual nature of his mystery a secret to the audience throughout. Listed in the closing credits as playing Olivier's wife (who appears in the film only as a portrait on Olivier's wall for which actress Joan Woodward posed) is Margo Channing, which film buffs will recognize as the name of Bette Davis's famed character in Mankiewicz's classic film ALL ABOUT EVE.

SLING BLADE

1996 135m c Drama   ★★★½
Shooting Gallery (U.S.)   R/

Billy Bob Thornton (Karl Childers), Dwight Yoakam (Doyle Hargraves), J.T. Walsh (Charles Bushman), John Ritter (Vaughan Cunningham), Lucas Black (Frank Wheatley), Natalie Canerday (Linda Wheatley), James Hampton (Jerry Woolridge), Robert Duvall (Karl's Father), Rick Dial (Bill Cox), Brent Briscoe (Scooter Hodges)

p, Brandon Rosser, David L. Bushell; d, Billy Bob Thornton; w, Billy Bob Thornton (from his screenplay "Some Folks Call It a Sling Blade"); ph, Barry Markowitz; ed, Hughes Winborne; m, Daniel Lanois; prod d, Clark Hunter; cos, Douglas Hall

AA Best Adapted Screenplay: Billy Bob Thornton; AAN Best Actor: Billy Bob Thornton

A long, unusual, and compelling film. Written and directed by its star, Billy Bob Thornton, SLING BLADE concerns a mentally retarded man who experiences love and moral awakening despite his handicaps and memories of a horrifying childhood. Thornton's script garnered him a Best Adapted Screenplay Oscar.

In an Alabama mental institution, Karl Childers (Thornton) tells the story of how he killed both his mother and her young lover while they were having sex. Upon his release at the age of 37, Karl returns to his hometown, where he gets a job as a mechanic. He befriends a young boy, Frank (Lucas Black), whose widowed mother Linda (Natalie Canerday) allows Karl to stay with them. He is treated kindly by both Linda and her longtime friend Vaughan (John Ritter), but is ridiculed by Linda's abusive boyfriend, Doyle (Dwight Yoakam). Though Karl feels at home in his new surroundings, he is haunted by his violent past.

Thornton first introduced Karl Childers in a performance piece, then brought him to the screen the 1993 short film SOME FOLKS CALL IT A SLING BLADE. Thornton's inspired and humane performance earns his character great sympathy and respect, beginning with the movie's most powerful set piece: a long monologue in which Karl relates the key events of his traumatic childhood, his recitation underscored and enhanced by the slow, sad, portentous music of Daniel Lanois. Superbly photographed by Barry Markowitz in small-town Arkansas, SLING BLADE affords respect to both its characters and its viewers by telling its story in long, straightforward, and subtly absorbing takes. Despite a very minor slackening and softening of the plot in the last act, SLING BLADE is a moving, thought-provoking, and accomplished piece of filmmaking.

SLITHER

1973 97m c Crime/Comedy   ★★★
MGM (U.S.)   PG/15

James Caan (Dick Kanipsia), Peter Boyle (Barry Fenaka), Sally Kellerman (Kitty Kopetzky), Louise Lasser (Mary Fenaka), Allen Garfield (Vincent J. Palmer), Richard B. Shull (Harry Moss), Alex Rocco (Man With Ice Cream), Alex Henteloff (Man at Phone Booth), Garry Goodrow (Man with Camera), Len Lesser (Jogger)

p, Jack Sher; d, Howard Zieff; w, W.D. Richter; ph, Laszlo Kovacs; ed, David Bretherton; m, Tom McIntosh; art d, Dale Hennesy; fx, John Coles; cos, Lambert Marks, Janet Strong

A hip, eccentrically amusing road movie, SLITHER marked the debuts of director Zieff, a respected veteran of TV commercials who'd won every major advertising award, and screenwriter/associate producer Richter, who went on to become one of the most expensive, though not necessarily commercial, writers in the movie world.

Caan, just released from jail after serving time for grand theft auto, is hanging out with fellow parolee Shull when the latter is gunned down by snipers. With his final words, Shull tells Caan that he can have lots of money if he finds Boyle and mentions the name Garfield. Caan locates Boyle, who admits that he and the late Shull had stolen over $300,000 and given the money to investment counselor Garfield. Neither man trusted the other, so each had half of the information needed to get the cash. Caan, with Boyle and his wife (Lasser) and a kooky speed freak (Kellerman), hits the road in search of the cash. But a mysterious black van gives chase.

SLITHER features some very funny moments and benefits from fine editing by Bretherton and assured camera work by Kovacs. Zieff later made THE MAIN EVENT, HOUSE CALLS and HEARTS OF THE WEST.

SMALL CHANGE
(L'ARGENT DE POCHE)

1976 105m c Drama/Comedy   ★★★★
Carrosse/Artistes (France)   PG/A

Geory Desmouceaux (Patrick), Philippe Goldman (Julien), Claudio Deluca (Mathieu Deluca), Franck Deluca (Franck), Richard Golfier (Richard), Laurent Devlaeminck (Laurent Riffle), Bruno Staab (Bruno Rouillard), Sebastien Marc (Oscar), Sylvie Grezel (Sylvie), Pascale Bruchon (Martine)

d, Francois Truffaut; w, Francois Truffaut, Suzanne Schiffman; ph, Pierre-William Glenn; ed, Yann Dedet; m, Maurice Jaubert; art d, Jean-Pierre Kohut-Svelko; cos, Monique Dury

Chiefly a collection of vignettes, this sentimental homage to children and their innocent ways focuses on two young boys, Patrick (Geory Desmouceaux) and Julien (Philippe Goldman). Patrick is a shy, slightly plump boy who looks after his paralyzed father and who is infatuated with a schoolmate's mother. His desire for romance is finally satisfied by the film's end, when he gets his first kiss from schoolgirl Martine (Pascale Bruchon). Julien's life is the polar opposite of Patrick's. Long-haired and neglected, he is a present-day "wild child" (see Truffaut's 1972 film, THE WILD CHILD) living in a hovel with his hateful mother and grandmother, who are not beyond physically abusing him. At the center of the children's lives is a schoolteacher (Jean-Francois Stevenin), a thoughtful, fatherly man who eventually becomes a parent himself. The film is filled with adorable youngsters: Sylvie, a seven-year-old with two pet fish and a fuzzy elephant purse that her parents won't let her bring to a restaurant; the Deluca brothers, who offer to play barber to save a classmate some money; and little Gregory, a mischievous tyke too charming to incur ire. Director Francois Truffaut worked his screenplay around the children, using them as his inspiration rather than forcing a script on them. The result is a collection of some of the most natural sequences ever filmed. Although the cast is made up of children, parents will appreciate SMALL CHANGE far more than kids will.

SMART MONEY

1931 90m bw Crime   ★★★½
Warner Bros. (U.S.)   /A

Edward G. Robinson (Nick "The Barber" Venizelos), James Cagney (Jack), Evalyn Knapp (Irene Graham), Ralf Harolde (Sleepy Sam), Noel Francis (Marie), Margaret Livingston (District Attorney's Girl), Maurice Black (The Greek Barber), Boris Karloff (Sport Williams), Morgan Wallace (District Attorney Black), Billy House (Salesman-Gambler)

d, Alfred E. Green; w, Kubec Glasmon, John Bright, Lucien Hubbard, Joseph Jackson (based on the story "The Idol" by Hubbard, Jackson); ph, Robert Kurrle; ed, Jack Killifer

AAN Best Original Screenplay: Lucien Hubbard, Joseph Jackson

After the smashing success of LITTLE CAESAR, Warner Bros. decided to team its two hottest stars, Edward G. Robinson and James Cagney, in a crime picture guaranteed to do big business—it was the only time the two "tough guys" would ever appear on film together. Robinson plays a barber-shop owner in a small town. He has a penchant for gambling, booze, and women, and he exercises his vices by running a gambling den in the back room. Cagney, a barber in Robinson's shop, also serves as his enthusiastic right-hand man. One day, Boris Karloff, a seedy gambler, shows up to try his luck at Robinson's poker table. Despite Karloff's cheating, Robinson wins and then kicks the bum out. The barber's friends marvel at his luck and skill in games of chance and, with Cagney's encouragement, they raise $10,000 to stake Robinson in a big-time syndicate poker game in the city. Robinson decides to try his hand against the big boys, and on his way to the train station he is met by Karloff, who gives him an additonal $1,000 to gamble with. In the city, Robinson is wooed by a pretty girl, Noel Francis, who steers him to a game run by Ben Taggart—a disaster in which Robinson loses everything. Realizing the whole thing was a setup engineered by Francis, Taggart, and one of the gamblers, Ralf Harolde, Robinson vows revenge. He sends for Cagney, and they both get barbering jobs in the city and work out their scheme.

The SMART MONEY script provided Robinson and Cagney with a fast-paced story a bit different from the ones they had previously starred in (more humor and much less violence—the original story was nominated for an Oscar). The film shows the studio's commitment in its top-notch production values. The supporting cast is solid, with an appearance by Karloff, who would soon go on to do FRANKENSTEIN for Universal and reach superstardom of his own. Robinson was a proven star by the time SMART MONEY went before the cameras, and Warner Bros. knew just by watching the rushes from THE PUBLIC ENEMY that Cagney would score big with moviegoers. (Cagney worked on both films at the same time, running from one soundstage to the other.) This isn't to say that Warner Bros. wasn't hedging its bet on the young actor. His role in SMART MONEY is relatively small when compared with Robinson's, and he is totally absent from the middle of the film. THE PUBLIC ENEMY proved to be a smash when released—it's too bad that Cagney's part isn't bigger in SMART MONEY. Meanwhile, Robinson, who still hadn't fully comprehended his popularity in the wake of LITTLE CAESAR, was sent by the studio to New York to attend the premiere of SMART MONEY at the Winter Garden Theater. There his star status became abundantly clear to him when, in order to get into the theater, he had to hide on the floor of the car from throngs of his overzealous fans.

SMASH PALACE

1981 108m c Drama ★★★½
Aardvark Films/New Zealand Film R/18
Commission (New Zealand)

Bruno Lawrence (Al Shaw), Anna Jemison (Jacqui Shaw), Greer Robson (Georgie Shaw), Keith Aberdein (Ray Foley), Desmond Kelly (Tiny), Lynn Robson (Linda), Margaret Umbers (Rose), Sean Duffy (Frank), Bryan Johnson (2nd Police Officer), Terence Donovan (Traffic Officer)

p, Roger Donaldson; d, Roger Donaldson; w, Roger Donaldson, Peter Hansard, Bruno Lawrence; ph, Graeme Cowley; ed, Michael Horton; m, Sharon O'Neill; art d, Reston Griffiths; cos, Annabel Blackett

Former racing champ Al Shaw (Bruno Lawrence) returns to his native New Zealand to take over his father's old auto junk shop. Accompanying him is his pregnant European wife, Jacqui (Anna Jemison), who through the years grows tired of her husband and goes to live with her best friend, police officer Ray Foley (Keith Aberdein). The crazed Shaw attempts reconciliation by kidnapping his daughter and running off into the bush, forcing a widespread hunt for the missing child. Although the plot is fairly thin, the concentration is on the characters and on the growing tension between the married couple. The result is a pointed look into the formation and dissolution of a relationship where neither person is to blame. Lawrence is outstanding as the self-absorbed man whose personality undergoes massive changes in the course of the film.

SMILE

1975 113m c Comedy ★★★★
UA (U.S.) PG/A

Bruce Dern ("Big Bob" Freelander), Barbara Feldon (Brenda Di-Carlo), Michael Kidd (Tommy French), Geoffrey Lewis (Wilson Shears), Nicholas Pryor (Andy DiCarlo), Colleen Camp (Connie Thompson/"Miss Imperial County"), Joan Prather (Robin Gib-son/"Miss Antelope Valley"), Denise Nickerson (Shirley Tolstoy/"Miss San Diego"), Annette O'Toole (Doria Houston/"Miss Anaheim"), Maria O'Brien (Maria Gonzales/"Miss Salinas")

p, Michael Ritchie; d, Michael Ritchie; w, Jerry Belson; ph, Conrad Hall; ed, Richard A. Harris; m, Daniel Osborn, Leroy Holmes, Charles Chaplin; chor, Jim Bates; cos, Patricia Norris

Director Ritchie does a fine job handling a huge cast, with many first-timers, in this satirical glimpse of a real beauty pageant staged in Santa Rosa, California. The original script, written by TV veteran Belson, supplies plenty of laughs, but the picture has so many characters we never get to truly know any of them, and the result, while often hilarious, is ultimately skin-deep, just as the beauty contestants are. Dern is a mobile-home dealer in the town and the chief judge of the contest. His son, Eric Shea, is a pre-teener with an eye toward female flesh and money so he takes some surreptitious shots of the nude beauties and means to sell them to his pals. When that's discovered, father and son have to see a court-ordered psychiatrist, George Skaff, to allow the boy to go back to school. Kidd is a tired choreographer who has received this second-rate assignment and hopes it might lead to a rekindling of his flagging career. The president of the beauty pageant is Lewis, and the prudish female chief of the proceedings is Feldon, who is married to Pryor and is as cold as an Arctic night to him. Cutting between all of these people and the many contestants, Ritchie tries to give us a picture like NASHVILLE with multiple stories going at the same time. The final scenes were staged at the actual pageant, and no one, except Belson and Ritchie, knew the winner, so the conclusion seems realistic. The best of the beauty contestants is Prather, who has to alter her character from naive waif to win-at-any-cost contestant. Pryor eventually shoots her out of frustration, thus reducing the film's level to something near "Tom and Jerry." Before that, however, the picture is superior in many ways. In 1986 a stage musical based on the movie was being financed, with music by Marvin Hamlisch. The music for SMILE was based on Charles Chaplin's original song "Smile," which became a hit for Nat "King" Cole. Osborn's incidental music was appropriate, and some pop tunes by Neil Sedaka, Shirley and Lee, and the Beach Boys were also used. Like many of Ritchie's films, it was sharp but not good-natured, and people stayed away from it in droves. Most of the beauty contest participants were exactly that, and it's a tribute to Ritchie's ability with actors that he gets them to come off as nonactors, which is one of the most difficult things an actor can do.

SMILES OF A SUMMER NIGHT
(SOMMARNATTENS LEENDE)

1955 108m bw Comedy ★★★★★
Svensk (Sweden) /X

Ulla Jacobsson (Anne Egerman), Eva Dahlbeck (Desiree Armfeldt), Margit Carlqvist (Charlotte Malcolm), Harriet Andersson (Petra the Maid), Gunnar Bjornstrand (Fredrik Egerman), Jarl Kulle (Count Malcolm), Ake Fridell (Frid the Groom), Bjorn Bjelvenstam (Henrik Egerman), Naima Wifstrand (Mrs. Armfeldt), Gull Natrop (Malla)

p, Allan Ekelund; d, Ingmar Bergman; w, Ingmar Bergman; ph, Gunnar Fischer; ed, Oscar Rosander; m, Erik Nordgren; art d, P.A. Lundgren; cos, Mago

A heavenly boudoir farce, alternately sardonic to it's inhabitants, then surprisingly tender, this is easily Bergman's finest comedy.

SMILES OF A SUMMER NIGHT is set in turn-of-the-century Sweden and takes place primarily at an old country estate, where love permeates the summer air. As a result of the scheming of actress Desiree Armfeldt (Eva Dahlbeck), a group of former, present, and would-be lovers gathers at her mother's country home, including Desiree's one-time lover Fredrik Egerman (Gunnar Bjornstrand); Anne (Ulla Jacobsson), his 20-year-old, still-virgin wife of two years; Fredrik's son, Henrik (Bjorn Bjelvenstam), a theology student a little younger than his stepmother; Desiree's current lover, Count Malcolm (Jarl Kulle); and his wife, Charlotte (Margit Carlqvist). In the course of this midsummer's eve, Anne runs off with her stepson, Fredrik rekindles his romance with Desiree, and Count Malcolm and Charlotte reconcile their marriage—while the maid, Petra (Harriet Andersson), literally rolls in the hay with a coachman.

SMILES OF A SUMMER NIGHT is erotic and lyrical, full of blithe spirits brilliantly evoked. Though Bergman's staging of the affair occasionally suggests a proscenium is just beyond the frame, the ensemble brings joyful veracity to the romantic complications and well-drawn characters. Influenced by Shakespeare's *A Midsummer Night's Dream*, Bergman's film provided the inspiration for the Broadway musical *A Little Night Music* and Woody Allen's A MIDSUMMER NIGHT'S SEX COMEDY.

SMILIN' THROUGH

1932 96m bw Drama   ★★★★
MGM (U.S.)

Norma Shearer *(Moonyean Clare/Kathleen)*, Fredric March *(Kenneth Wayne/Jeremy Wayne)*, Leslie Howard *(John Carteret)*, O.P. Heggie *(Dr. Owen)*, Ralph Forbes *(Willie Ainley)*, Beryl Mercer *(Mrs. Crouch)*, Margaret Seddon *(Ellen)*, Cora Sue Collins *(Kathleen as a Child)*, Forrester Harvey *(Orderly)*, David Torrence *(Gardener)*

d, Sidney Franklin; w, Ernest Vajda, Claudine West, Donald Ogden Stewart, James Bernard Fagan (based on the play by Jane Cowl, Jane Murfin, Langdon McCormick); ph, Lee Garmes; ed, Margaret Booth; art d, Cedric Gibbons; cos, Adrian

AAN Best Picture

Lovely, simply lovely. SMILIN' THROUGH was first a stage play, then a 1922 silent film starring Norma Talmadge. The story begins in England in 1868, on the day of Norma Shearer's wedding to Leslie Howard. Tragedy strikes during the ceremony, when Shearer's jealous suitor, Fredric March, shows up drunk and crazed. He pulls a pistol and fires at his rival, but the bullet hits Shearer. As she lies dying in Howard's arms, she promises him that she will always be near and that someday they will be reunited. March manages to escape and disappears. Howard spends the rest of his days as a lonely recluse grieving over his loss. Years pass, and Howard's loneliness is interrupted by the arrival of his young niece, who comes to live with the old man after her parents are drowned. One day the niece (played as an adult by Shearer) and a friend are caught in a rainstorm and seek shelter in an empty old house—the same house March had fled long ago. While exploring the place, Shearer meets March's son (also played by March), and there is an instant romantic attraction between the two. Shearer excitedly tells Howard of her discovery, but the old man angrily forbids her to see the son of the man who robbed him of his true love. Soon after, March goes to fight in WWI, and the ghost of the dead woman keeps returning to Howard to beg him to let the young lovers be united.

SMILIN' THROUGH is an example of romantic melodrama at its best. A hit at the box office, the film boasts a superb production and a strong cast who handle their roles with aplomb. La Norma was perhaps never better (and she never looked lovelier), and March, Howard, O.P. Heggie, and Ralph Forbes lend sterling support. One of those rare films whose gorgeous soft-focus look and dreamy, unashamed, sentimental romantic conviction suggests the best of Frank Borzage, SMILIN' THROUGH was remade by Borzage with less success in 1941, with Jeanette MacDonald, Gene Raymond and Brian Aherne.

SMILING LIEUTENANT, THE

1931 102m bw Musical/Comedy   ★★★★½
Paramount (U.S.)   /A

Maurice Chevalier *(Niki)*, Claudette Colbert *(Franzi)*, Miriam Hopkins *(Princess Anna)*, George Barbier *(King Adolf)*, Charlie Ruggles *(Max)*, Hugh O'Connell *(Orderly)*, Robert Strange *(Adjutant von Rockoff)*, Janet Reade *(Lily)*, Lon MacSunday *(Emperor)*, Elizabeth Patterson *(Baroness von Schwedel)*

p, Ernst Lubitsch; d, Ernst Lubitsch; w, Ernest Vajda, Samson Raphaelson, Ernst Lubitsch (based on the operetta *A Waltz Dream* by Leopold Jacobson and Felix Doermann, and the novel *Nux der Prinzgemahl* by Hans Muller); ph, George Folsey; ed, Merrill White; m, Oscar Straus; art d, Hans Dreier

AAN Best Picture

Only six years after the release of EIN WALZERTRAUM, the 1925 German silent based on the operetta inspired by Hans Muller's novel *Nux, der Prinzgemahl*, Ernst Lubitsch gathered Maurice Chevalier,

Claudette Colbert and Miriam Hopkins, moved them into Paramount's Astoria, Long Island, studios, and made this musical as well as a French-language version, LE LIEUTENANT SOURIANT, with the same cast working from a new French script by Jacques Bataille-Henri. The delightful story is set in Vienna, where Niki (Chevalier), an officer of the Royal Guards, shares romance and an apartment with Franzi (Claudette Colbert), a violinist. During a state visit to the Austrian capital by King Adolf (George Barbier), his desperately plain daughter, Princess Anna (Miriam Hopkins), mistakenly believes that the smile Niki has intended for Franzi was actually directed in her royal direction, but is convinced the handsome soldier is only being kind. When Niki protests that he finds the princess attractive, she falls in love with him, and in no time, bound by his duty to his country, he finds himself married to her. Niki refuses to consummate their marriage, however—that is, until Franzi does a makeover job on Anna that sends the guardsman's head reeling.

The operetta plot bears little resemblance to reality, but the players are so good, the dialogue (by Lubitsch, Ernest Vajda and Samson Raphaelson) so witty, and the direction so skillful that no one minds the logic lapses. The music is delightful, and the songs include such bon-bons as "Spruce Up Your Lingerie." Made and released during the Depression, THE SMILING LIEUTENANT offered welcome escapism for a public reeling under too real economic woes. Colbert—warm, sweet, with touches of sadness—is in wonderful form, and proves to be a fine singer to boot. Hopkins, meanwhile, enjoyed her first major opportunity to display her considerable comic prowess as the princess in need of a makeover, and Chevalier is in his best and most typical form. This was the noted French entertainer's first work together with master director Lubitsch after their successful collaboration on THE LOVE PARADE two years earlier, and the result is an utterly charming film that was box-office hit.

SMOKE

1995 112m c Comedy/Drama   ★★★½
Miramax/Nippon Film Development/Smoke   R/15
Productions/Euro Space Productions/Interal (U.S.)

Harvey Keitel *(Auggie Wren)*, William Hurt *(Paul Benjamin)*, Harold Perrineau Jr. *(Thomas "Rashid" Cole)*, Forest Whitaker *(Cyrus Cole)*, Stockard Channing *(Ruby McNutt)*, Victor Argo *(Vinnie)*, Erica Gimpel *(Doreen Cole)*, Clarice Taylor *(Ethel)*, Ashley Judd *(Felicity)*, Malik Yoba *(The Creeper)*

p, Greg Johnson, Peter Newman, Hisami Kuriowa, Kenzo Horikoshi; d, Wayne Wang; w, Paul Auster (based on his story "Auggie Wren's Christmas Story"); ph, Adam Holender; ed, Maisie Hoy; m, Rachel Portman; prod d, Kalina Ivanov; art d, Jeff McDonald; cos, Claudia Brown

Author Paul Auster (THE MUSIC OF CHANCE) teamed up with filmmaker Wayne Wang (CHAN IS MISSING) to create this novel excursion into storytelling.

Auggie Wren (Harvey Keitel) runs a cigar store in the Park Slope neighborhood of Brooklyn, where a colorful assortment of regular customers, including blocked novelist Paul Benjamin (William Hurt), hang out and spin philosophy while puffing on Panatelas. Paul still grieves for his wife, who was killed in a holdup, and dwells obsessively on the contingency of life. When Paul is saved from a hit-and-run collision by a young man who calls himself Rashid (Harold Perrineau, Jr.), some elaborate—if not exactly earth-shattering—events ensue.

Forget the convolutions of the plot. In SMOKE, narrative is about fiction: invented selves and imagined histories, the lies we tell ourselves to make our lives bearable. Auster's script, which appropriately receives top billing, is unabashedly literary: instead of delivering conventional cross-talk, characters spin yarns or regale each other with elaborate fabrications and opinions. Most of these are refreshing and original enough to carry the film through narrative contrivances and unsubtle performances. Wang yields to both the writer and the actors throughout the film, noticeably asserting himself only in the doubled story at the film's conclusion. But his attention to detail is quietly omnipresent and extremely effective: the look, sound, and feel of the locations provide a palpable backdrop against which Auster paints his slightly surreal word pictures.

Wang and Auster enjoyed their collaboration so much that they made a second, improvised film on the same set, with many of the same actors, during the few days left after their main shoot wrapped. That film, BLUE IN THE FACE, was released shortly after SMOKE.

SMOKEY AND THE BANDIT

1977 96m c Comedy   ★½
Rastar (U.S.)   PG

Burt Reynolds (Bandit), Jackie Gleason (Sheriff Buford T. Justice), Sally Field (Carrie), Jerry Reed (Cledus Snow), Mike Henry (Junior Justice), Pat Williams (Little Enos Burdette), Pat McCormick (Big Enos Burdette), Alfie Wise (Traffic Jam Patrolman), George Reynolds (Sheriff Branford), Macon McCalman (Mr. B)

p, Mort Engelberg; d, Hal Needham; w, James Lee Barrett, Charles Shyer, Alan Mandel (based on a story by Needham and Robert L. Levy); ph, Bobby Byrne; ed, Walter Hannemann, Angelo Ross; m, Bill Justis, Jerry Reed; art d, Mark Mansbridge; fx, Art Brewer

AAN Best Editing: Walter Hannemann, Angelo Ross

The first in the series and the best of a lousy lot. Depending on whom you believe, the movie grossed anywhere between $40 million and $70 million; that must be some sort of new record for fooling the public. It was the first picture directed by Needham, one of the highest-paid stuntmen in movies, and is one long, stupid car chase punctuated by four-letter words in a live-action version of the "Roadrunner" cartoons.

The plot is premised on the fact that it once was illegal for Coors to sell their Colorado beer east of Texas unless a special permit was secured. McCormick and Williams play a father-son team of filthy-rich Texans who have a car entered in an Atlanta stock race, which they fully expect to win. In order to celebrate, they'd like to have enough Coors around for themselves and their guests, but the race is the following day and there doesn't seem to be any means to get the beer there in time. Reynolds makes an $80,000 wager that he can drive to Texas and back in the needed 28 hours, and the obligatory chases and stunts ensue.

The stunts in SMOKEY are excellent but the comedy is numbing, and the acting is on a par with a junior high school production of Our Town. Even Gleason comes across badly, and that's a major feat. Adolph Coors and Sons must have been very happy to have a 97-minute commercial for their brew.

SNAKE PIT, THE

1948 108m bw Drama   ★★★½
Fox (U.S.)   /A

Olivia de Havilland (Virginia Stuart Cunningham), Mark Stevens (Robert Cunningham), Leo Genn (Dr. Mark Kirk), Celeste Holm (Grace), Glenn Langan (Dr. Terry), Helen Craig (Miss Davis), Leif Erickson (Gordon), Beulah Bondi (Mrs. Greer), Lee Patrick, Isabel Jewell

p, Anatole Litvak, Robert Bassler; d, Anatole Litvak; w, Frank Partos, Millen Brand (based on the novel by Mary Jane Ward); ph, Leo Tover; ed, Dorothy Spencer; m, Alfred Newman; art d, Lyle Wheeler, Joseph C. Wright; cos, Bonnie Cashin

AAN Best Picture; AAN Best Actress: Olivia DeHavilland; AAN Best Director: Anatole Litvak; AAN Best Original Screenplay: Frank Partos, Millen Brand; AAN Best Score: Alfred Newman; AA Best Sound: 20th Century-Fox Sound Department

Produced under the aegis of 20th Century-Fox studio head Darryl F. Zanuck, this remains one of the best screen explorations of mental illness and its treatment.

In a bravura performance, de Havilland is a disturbed young woman who is put into a mental institution by her husband, Stevens. While he loves his wife, he realizes that she needs more help than he can give her. Luckily, de Havilland's case comes to the attention of Genn, a patient, thoughtful, and caring doctor who devotes much of his time to her. Though the hospital is overcrowded and understaffed, Genn manages to concentrate on her case while desperately trying to keep his hospital from becoming the "snake pit" which most people believe mental institutions to be.

Though the portrayal of the causes and cures of mental illness remains Hollywood-simplistic here, THE SNAKE PIT was one of the first films to seriously examine the subject and treat it with—sometimes harrowing—realism. Producer-director Litvak saw the galley pages to Mary Jane Ward's fictionalized autobiography and immediately paid $75,000 for the film rights. After trying to sell the idea to every other studio in town, Litvak went to his friend Zanuck as a last resort. (Fox rarely took on independent productions.) The studio head was a bit leery about the subject matter, but he felt that films should deal with important subjects, so he agreed to finance the project. Litvak worked closely with Litvak to tighten the script so that its "suspense and urgency" would cause viewers to accept the more unpleasant passages. Litvak spent three months in preproduction researching mental facilities and procedures, and he required his cast and crew to accompany him. De Havilland gave a subtle, passionate performance and was deservedly nominated for a Best Actress Oscar (though she lost to Jane Wyman for JOHNNY BELINDA). THE SNAKE PIT turned out to be a critical and financial success for Zanuck, and the film called such attention to the treatment of mental illness that 26 states passed new legislation pertaining to procedures in state institutions.

SNAPPER, THE

1993 94m c Comedy/Drama   ★★★½
BBC Films (U.K.)   R/15

Tina Kellegher (Sharon), Colm Meaney (Dessie), Ruth McCabe (Kay), Colm O'Byrne (Darren), Eanna Macliam (Craig), Ciara Duffy (Kimberley), Joanne Gerrard (Lisa), Peter Rowen (Sonny), Fionnula Murphy (Jackie), Pat Laffan (George Burgess)

p, Lynda Myles; d, Stephen Frears; w, Roddy Doyle (from his novel); ph, Oliver Stapleton; ed, Mick Audsley; prod d, Mark Geraghty; fx, Gerry Johnston; cos, Consolata Boyle

The amiable SNAPPER is a domestic comedy that never degenerates into sitcom platitudes, even though it was made for TV. Though the film has its share of brisk one-liners and contrived situations played for their obvious comic potential, its appealing mix of sweetness and grit, and ultimate reliance on character to carry the material, make it a pleasant surprise.

Young Sharon Curley (Tina Kellegher) is pregnant, unmarried, and determined to have her baby, the (whipper)snapper of the title. Her parents, Dessie (Colm Meaney) and Kay (Ruth McCabe), are less than thrilled but make the best of things. This becomes increasingly difficult when the rumor begins going about that the baby's father, whom Sharon steadfastly refuses to name, is middle-aged neighbor George Burgess (Pat Laffan). Sharon's situation becomes a local scandal and, as her pregnancy progresses, Sharon learns who her real friends are, forging a new relationship with her parents, particularly her father.

The transformation of gruff "man's man" Dessie into a working model of a sharing, caring new man provides THE SNAPPER with its narrative spine, and what could be an entirely contrived exercise becomes instead an engaging character study. Roddy Doyle, who adapted the screenplay from his own novel, also wrote Alan Parker's THE COMMITMENTS; THE SNAPPER is the second of three books dealing with the same neighborhood and overlapping characters. Well written and directed, THE SNAPPER celebrates common sense and human decency, qualities which triumph over prudishness and restrictive social mores.

SNOW WHITE AND THE SEVEN DWARFS

1937 83m c Children's/Animated   ★★★★★
Walt Disney Productions (U.S.)   G/U

VOICES OF: Adriana Caselotti (Snow White), Harry Stockwell (Prince Charming), Lucille La Verne (The Queen), Moroni Olsen (Magic Mirror), Billy Gilbert (Sneezy), Pinto Colvig (Sleepy/Grumpy), Otis Harlan (Happy), Scotty Mattraw (Bashful), Roy Atwell (Doc), Stuart Buchanan (Humbert)

p, Walt Disney; d, David Hand, Perce Pearce, Larry Morey, William Cottrell, Wilfred Jackson, Ben Sharpsteen; w, Ted Sears, Otto Englander, Earl Hurd, Dorothy Ann Blank, Richard Creedon, Dick Richard, Merrill De Maris, Webb Smith (based on the fairy tale by the Brothers Grimm); m, Frank Churchill, Leigh Harline, Paul J. Smith,

Larry Morey; art d, Charles Philippi, Hugh Hennesy, Terrell Stapp, McLaren Stewart, Harold Miles, Tom Codrick, Gustaf Tenggren, Ken Anderson, Kendall O'Connor, Hazel Sewell; anim, Hamilton Luske, Vladimir Tytla, Fred Moore, Norman Ferguson

AAN Best Score: Leigh Harline, Walt Disney Studio Music Department, Frank Churchill, Leigh Harline, Paul J. Smith

"The only film that made money in 1937 was SNOW WHITE AND THE SEVEN DWARFS," said Mae West. "And that would have made more money if they woulda let *me* play Snow White."

West wasn't far from wrong. Consider Snow White, living with seven devoted, worshipful little men. Obviously, Disney was as naive in ways as the children in his audiences. Maybe that's the secret to his animated successes, or one of them. SNOW WHITE softens the Grimms' fairytale, but then there are the sequences of terror. Timeless they are, and here Expressionistic. Indeed, Disney always seemed to pull the stops out for the moments evoking evil in his animated features. And for all the bird trills of Snow White (never again would Walt's heroine have such a fantasy singing voice, and for that reason, she's the favorite heroine of many animation *auteurs*; certainly, we could all agree she's the most surreal of the sisterhood), and the cuteness of the comic relief inspired by the little men, our nod goes to Eleanor Audley (who would supply the voice for all Disney's memorable villainesses through SLEEPING BEAUTY) and the animated rendering of the Wicked Queen. Did Mr. Disney and Mr. Hitchcock have more than love of terror in common?

Dubbed "Disney's Folly" by its detractors, this masterpiece was a personal success for Walt Disney—the fulfillment of his dream to pioneer animation of unimagined scope. The film opens on a storybook, and as "Some Day My Prince Will Come" plays in the background, the turning pages explain how the orphaned Snow White has been brought up as a servant of a wicked queen. The queen, an icily beautiful woman with piercing eyes, stands before her Magic Mirror and poses her vain, oft-asked question: "Mirror, mirror, on the wall, who is the fairest of them all?" She is shocked when the mirror gives an unexpected answer: "Snow White." The nasty queen then orders that the innocent young woman be killed. Snow White, however, has eight things going for her—Prince Charming and seven dwarfs named Doc, Happy, Sleepy, Sneezy, Bashful, Grumpy, and Dopey.

This is animation as it had never before been experienced. Disney wisely realized the film could only work if it was full of believable characters, and each personality is distinct, from the purity of Snow White to the absolute evil of the queen. This film classic also features some unforgettable songs, including "Whistle While You Work," "Heigh Ho" and "Some Day My Prince Will Come."

SNOWS OF KILIMANJARO, THE

1952 117m c Adventure   ★★★½
Fox (U.S.)   /PG

Gregory Peck *(Harry)*, Susan Hayward *(Helen)*, Ava Gardner *(Cynthia)*, Hildegarde Neff *(Countess Liz)*, Leo G. Carroll *(Uncle Bill)*, Torin Thatcher *(Johnson)*, Ava Norring *(Beatrice)*, Helene Stanley *(Connie)*, Marcel Dalio *(Emile)*, Vincente Gomez *(Guitarist)*

p, Darryl F. Zanuck; d, Henry King; w, Casey Robinson (based on the short story by Ernest Hemingway); ph, Leon Shamroy; ed, Barbara McLean; m, Bernard Herrmann; art d, Lyle Wheeler, John De Cuir; fx, Ray Kellogg; chor, Antonio Triana; cos, Charles LeMaire

AAN Best Cinematography: Leon Shamroy; *AAN Best Art Direction:* Lyle Wheeler, John DeCuir, Thomas Little, Paul F. Fox

One of the more successful attempts to bring Hemingway material to the screen, this story of a writer who has lost his intellectual and emotional bearings after enjoying early commercial success works splendidly under King's sure directorial hand, and is enacted with power and conviction by Peck. Scriptwriter Robinson expanded the origina Hemingway story to incorporate several elements from the writer's own life and, despite some carping from Hemingway purists, the film was an immense box-office success.

As the story begins, Peck is shown half delirious with fever, lying on a cot in an African campsite, his leg infected with gangrene. A rich and popular author, he finds himself with little left to live for as he drifts in and out of consciousness, with his wealthy wife Hayward at his side.

The writer thinks back on his colorful life, seeing himself at age 17 in the Midwest; as a young writer living in Paris and falling in love with Gardner, on whom he bases the heroine of his first novel; traveling around Africa oblivious to Gardner's pregnancy, which is terminated when she falls down a flight of stairs; finally being abandoned by Gardner in Spain, when she realizes he will never settle down with her; re-encountering her during the Spanish Civil War but then being separated from her again; and finally marrying Hayward, whom he initially mistakes for Gardner when he is drunk one night in Paris. The movie ends with him coming to realize the depth of his love for Hayward, and vowing to return to serious work.

This beautifully photographed film, King's favorite, combines many Hemingway tales to make its point, and it features a magnificent score by Herrmann that captures all the exotic locales profiled. Gardner is excellent as the star-crossed lover, but Hayward has a part that is mostly lost inside the flashbacks featuring Gardner. Peck had played a Hemingway hero in THE MACOMBER AFFAIR five years earlier, portraying a white hunter in Africa, and that film had also been written by Robinson. Although the script for SNOWS OF KILIMANJARO is a seamless blend of Robinson's and Hemingway's style, Hemingway didn't like the film, calling Fox mogul Zanuck personally to say that it was a compilation of his stories and that it should have been called "the Snows of Zanuck."

SO PROUDLY WE HAIL

1943 126m bw War/Drama   ★★★★
Paramount (U.S.)   /A

Claudette Colbert *(Lt. Janet Davidson)*, Paulette Goddard *(Lt. Joan O'Doul)*, Veronica Lake *(Lt. Olivia D'Arcy)*, George Reeves *(Lt. John Summers)*, Barbara Britton *(Lt. Rosemary Larson)*, Walter Abel *(Chaplain)*, Sonny Tufts *(Kansas)*, Mary Servoss *(Capt. "Ma" McGregor)*, Ted Hecht *(Dr. Jose Bardia)*, John Litel *(Dr. Harrison)*

p, Mark Sandrich; d, Mark Sandrich; w, Allan Scott; ph, Charles Lang; ed, Ellsworth Hoagland; m, Miklos Rozsa; art d, Hans Dreier, Earl Hedrick; fx, Gordon Jennings, Farciot Edouart, George Dutton

AAN Best Supporting Actress: Paulette Goddard; *AAN Best Original Screenplay:* Allan Scott; *AAN Best Cinematography:* Charles Lang; *AAN Best Visual Effects:* Farciot Edouart, Gordon Jennings, George Dutton

SO PROUDLY WE HAIL is a surprisingly unglamorous Hollywood depiction of the lives of three Army nurses (Goddard, Lake, and Colbert) who survive the battles at Bataan and Corregidor in WWII. The film begins as they arrive back home in the US, then relates their story in flashback, beginning in December 1941. After the attack on Pearl Harbor, the trio's Hawaii-bound ship is diverted to Bataan and finally to Corregidor. Along the way, the women witness the fighting at its most brutal, but also find time for relaxation and romance. Never, however, does SO PROUDLY WE HAIL succumb to pinup star glamour; rather, Mark Sandrich's direction and Allan Scott's screenplay concentrate on the ugly realities of war, the painful scenes including a sequence in which a mother stands by while her son's legs are amputated. All three leads are superbly cast in their nicely balanced characters. Colbert is the mother-hen nurse who avoids romance but eventually winds up married to Reeves; Lake fights a private battle against the Japanese, who killed her boyfriend at Pearl Harbor; and the showy Goddard evenly divides her time between the war and her romance with happy-go-lucky Kansas lad Tufts.

Because of the popularity of its stars, the patriotic spirit of the film, and the novelty of female combat nurses, SO PROUDLY WE HAIL made a sizable dent in the box office. The critics praised its authenticity, which Sandrich went to great lengths to achieve. Having read a news item about 10 nurses who escaped the fall of Corregidor in May 1942, Sandrich, together with Scott, tracked them down. He hired one of them, Lt. Eunice Hatchitt, as a technical advisor and, after receiving permission from the government to tell the nurses' story, began filming. However, although certain to hit box-office gold with Paramount's Claudette Colbert, Veronica Lake, and Paulette Goddard as the stars, Sandrich was also destined to have a battle of egos on his hands. The feuding began when Goddard told a reporter that she preferred working with Lake because "after all, we are closer in age." Colbert was naturally upset at the implication that she was over the hill (and, in fact,

Goddard was wrong—her own birth date is usually cited as 1911, making her seven years younger than Colbert and eight years older than Lake). There were also arguments over how they were photographed and rivalry over their respective technical skills. (Goddard and Lake were considered screen *personalities*, while only Colbert was viewed as an actress.) Often Sandrich would have to retake scenes many times to accommodate Lake's and Goddard's deficiencies, while Colbert needed no more than a couple of takes. Fans of Lake and her famous peek-a-boo hairstyle should be forewarned that she wears her hair short in this picture. Reportedly, the government asked that she not appear as a servicewoman with that hairstyle because there were a number of women factory workers whose long, Lake-inspired hair was getting tangled in the machinery.

SOFT SKIN, THE
(LA PEAU DOUCE)
1964 120m bw Drama   ★★½
Carrosse/SEDIF   (France)

Jean Desailly *(Pierre Lachenay)*, Francoise Dorleac *(Nicole Chomette)*, Nelly Benedetti *(Franca Lachenay)*, Daniel Ceccaldi *(Clement)*, Laurence Badie *(Ingrid)*, Jean Lanier *(Michel)*, Paule Emanuele *(Odile)*, Philippe Dumat *(Reims Cinema Manager)*, Pierre Risch *(Canon)*, Dominique Lacarriere *(Pierre's Secretary)*

d, Francois Truffaut; w, Francois Truffaut, Jean-Louis Richard; ph, Raoul Coutard; ed, Claudine Bouche; m, Georges Delerue; cos, Renee Rouzot

One of Truffaut's least successful, most derivative films, THE SOFT SKIN was a response to the resounding impact of JULES AND JIM. While the latter concentrates on love in the country, Truffaut's aim in THE SOFT SKIN was, as he put it, to create "a violent answer to JULES AND JIM. It's as though someone else had made JULES AND JIM . . . [THE SOFT SKIN shows] a truly modern love; it takes place in planes, in elevators; it has all the harassments of modern life." From its opening, THE SOFT SKIN surely does not seem like a Truffaut film. It is distant, restrained—as the title implies, a "surface" film in which emotions run only skin deep. The story concerns Desailly as Lachenay (named after Truffaut's friend), a literary critic with a wife (Benedetti) and a child, who falls in love with a stewardess (Dorleac) after a trip to Lisbon. Although THE SOFT SKIN is perhaps Truffaut's weakest film, it can also be considered his most daring. Rather than present a conventionally melodramatic love triangle, Truffaut chooses for his leading man a common, albeit somewhat bookish, individual (not nearly so romantic as the characters in the Balzac novels on which the critic is an authority). When fate intervenes and Pierre gets his beautiful dream girl, he begins his downward Hitchcockian spiral, an innocent caught up in a situation he cannot control. In THE SOFT SKIN Balzac (a personal favorite of Truffaut) meets Hitchcock, and the film frame becomes an arena in which Truffaut's two greatest influences do battle.

SOLARIS
1972 165m c Science Fiction   ★★★★
Mosfilm/Magna   (U.S.S.R.)   PG

Nathalie Bondarchuk *(Harey)*, Yuri Yarvet *(Snaut)*, Donatas Banionis *(Kris)*, Anatoli Sonlonitsin *(Sartorius)*, Vladislav Dvorjetzki *(Burton)*, Nikolai Grinko *(Father)*, Sos Sarkissian *(Gibarian)*

d, Andrei Tarkovsky; w, Andrei Tarkovsky, Friedrich Gorenstein (based on the novel by Stanislaw Lem); ph, Vadim Jusov; m, Eduard Artemyer; art d, Mikhail Romadin

Perhaps the most accessible of Tarkovsky's films, certainly free of the overbearing portentousness that would mark later work like THE SACRIFICE. The story concerns a cosmonaut who travels to a distant space station on Solaris. No ordinary planet, Solaris is in fact a superintelligent being capable of giving material form to human desires. Slow, but ravishingly beautiful and charged with a real poignancy.

SOLDIER OF ORANGE
1977 165m c War/Drama   ★★★½
Rank (Netherlands)   R/

Rutger Hauer *(Erik)*, Jeroen Krabbe *(Gus)*, Peter Faber *(Will)*, Derek De Lint *(Alex)*, Eddy Habbema *(Robby)*, Lex Van Delden *(Nico)*, Edward Fox *(Col. Rafelli)*, Belinda Meuldijk *(Esther)*, Susan Penhaligon *(Susan)*, Andrea Domburh *(Queen Wilhelmina)*

p, Rob Houwer; d, Paul Verhoeven; w, Paul Verhoeven, Gerard Soeteman, Kees Holierhoek (based on the autobiography of Erik Hazelhoff Roelfzema); ph, Jan De Bont, Jost Vacano; ed, Jane Speer; m, Rogier Van Otterloo; art d, Roland De Groot; cos, Elly Claus

Carefully crafted by veteran Dutch director Paul Verhoeven (ROBOCOP, THE FOURTH MAN), this WWII drama details the effects of Nazi occupation on a group of Dutch students. Erik (Rutger Hauer) is at first hesitant to join the resistance effort, but after escaping to England he becomes deeply involved, courageously transporting supplies to his comrades in Holland. After the war, he returns home to find that most of his fellow students and resistance fighters have been killed, including onetime student leader Gus (Jeroen Krabbe), while others have come through the war barely affected. An exceptional character study, SOLDIER OF ORANGE is also beautifully photographed by Peter De Bont—the shots of Hauer on the supply boat's windy prow as he travels between Britain and Holland linger long after the film is over. Verhoeven would again work with Krabbe and screenwriter Gerard Soeteman in his haunting THE FOURTH MAN.

SOLDIER'S STORY, A
1984 101m c Mystery   ★★★½
Columbia (U.S.)   PG/15

Howard E. Rollins Jr. *(Capt. Davenport)*, Adolph Caesar *(Sgt. Waters)*, Art Evans *(Pvt. Wilkie)*, David Alan Grier *(Cpl. Cobb)*, David Harris *(Pvt. Smalls)*, Dennis Lipscomb *(Capt. Taylor)*, Larry Riley *(C.J. Memphis)*, Robert Townsend *(Cpl. Ellis)*, Denzel Washington *(Pfc. Peterson)*, William Allen Young *(Pvt. Henson)*

p, Norman Jewison, Ronald L. Schwary, Patrick Palmer; d, Norman Jewison; w, Charles Fuller (based on his stage play "A Soldier's Play"); ph, Russell Boyd; ed, Mark Warner, Caroline Biggerstaff; m, Herbie Hancock; prod d, Walter Scott Herndon; cos, Chuck Velasco, Robert Stewart

AAN Best Picture; AAN Best Supporting Actor: Adolph Caesar; AAN Best Adapted Screenplay: Charles Fuller

Gripping, thanks to spotless direction and Rollins's inspired work, but nothing new to relay. Charles Fuller's powerful play (a Pulitzer Prize-winner, based on Melville's *Billy Budd*) was adapted by Fuller himself for the screen, and the power of the stage presentation is not diminished (which means it's not particularly cinematic, either).

The action takes place at Fort Neal, Louisiana, a base for black soldiers during WWII. Sgt. Waters (Adolph Caesar), a tough African-American topkick and manager of the baseball team, is coming back to the base drunk one night when he is shot to death by a .45-caliber weapon. That's the only clue to his death. Capt. Davenport (Howard E. Rollins, Jr.) is the black Army attorney who is sent to investigate the murder. The white officers on the base, as well as the black soldiers, are astounded at the choice, and Davenport finds that he's not getting any help in his search for the truth. Some of the black troops blame the Klan, while others suggest it might have been one of the white soldiers who ranked at Waters's attitude. A series of flashbacks establishes Waters and the relationship he had with all those around him as Davenport begins his interrogations. What makes this such a good film is the multilayered complexity of the script. Fuller has taken a basic Agatha Christie-type plot and bathed it in social issues; A SOLDIER'S STORY is an insightful period drama as well as a totally engaging character study. The picture does become a trifle talky at times, thus betraying its stage origin, but Fuller's words are almost always interesting and powerful and make worthwhile listening. Caesar's performance stands out. With the addition of two musical treats: "The St. Louis Blues March," one of our favorites, over the credits, and Patti Labelle in a cameo as Big Mary, wailing away and tearing down the house as usual.

SOLID GOLD CADILLAC, THE

1956 99m bw Comedy ★★★★
Columbia (U.S.) /U

Judy Holliday *(Laura Partridge)*, Paul Douglas *(Edward L. McKeever)*, Fred Clark *(Clifford Snell)*, John Williams *(John T. Blessington)*, Hiram Sherman *(Harry Harkness)*, Neva Patterson *(Amelia Shotgraven)*, Ralph Dumke *(Warren Gillie)*, Ray Collins *(Alfred Metcalfe)*, Arthur O'Connell *(Jenkins)*, Richard Deacon *(Williams)*

p, Fred Kohlmar; d, Richard Quine; w, Abe Burrows (based on the play by George S. Kaufman and Howard Teichmann); ph, Charles Lang; ed, Charles Nelson; m, Cyril J. Mockridge; art d, Ross Bellah; cos, Jean Louis

AAN Best Art Direction: Ross Bellah, William R. Kiernan, Louis Diage; *AA Best Costume Design:* Jean Louis

A charming, often hysterically funny poke at big business, government, and the plight of the underdog. The script was by Abe Burrows, based on the hit Broadway play starring a much older Josephine Hull, written by Kaufman and Teichmann. Burrows would later be involved with another successful comedy on the same general subject entitled HOW TO SUCCEED IN BUSINESS WITHOUT REALLY TRYING. The original play was to have had a younger woman, but when Hull, who was so delicious in ARSENIC AND OLD LACE, became available, she was paged for the part. In the film Holliday has the role, and a love story was added to fill the romantic gaps. She plays her patented daffy blonde with a heart of gold who owns 10 shares in a massive company. The board of directors of the organization are a panel of stern-visaged prigs including Clark, Williams, Sherman, Collins, and Dumke. Holliday shows up at a stockholders meeting and protests some of the shenanigans of the board. At first, she is a mere fly in their gargantuan ointment, but her presence is duly noted by the press, and things begin to happen. The former head of the company is Douglas, a hard-driving tycoon who has given up his role as top man on that totem pole in order to donate his services to the government, for which he is functioning as a "dollar-a-year" man. Holliday meets the bombastic Douglas and enlists him in her quest to secure representation for the small stockholders. When Douglas learns that his former aides have stabbed him in the back in their running of the company he started and nurtured, he joins with Holliday to get proxy votes from all the little people and to regain his position with the firm. O'Connell is the "don't rock the boat" office manager who is Holliday's boss, and Patterson is the secretary who aids and abets Holliday's mischief. George Burns handles the narrating chores in the same way Fred Allen did it (pre-recorded) on Broadway. The narration provides a few funny lines and bridges some of the gaps. The title stems from Holliday's fervent wish to own a solid gold cadillac. At the film's conclusion, with Douglas and Holliday united and running the company, she gets her desire.

The humor in the screenplay seldom derives from one-liners. Rather, it is in the situations, the caricatures that are the targets for its darts, and the unflagging energy of Holliday and Douglas as two utterly different people who find love with each other and blend to defeat the pompous executives. Kaufman, who was known as the "Great Collaborator," wrote with more people than the average sit-com scribe. His partners included Moss Hart (YOU CAN'T TAKE IT WITH YOU, among others), Edna Ferber (THE ROYAL FAMILY OF BROADWAY), Marc Connelly (MERTON OF THE MOVIES), Morrie Ryskind (A NIGHT AT THE OPERA), and Ring Lardner, Sr.

SOME CAME RUNNING

1959 137m c Drama ★★★★
MGM (U.S.) /A

Frank Sinatra *(Dave Hirsh)*, Dean Martin *(Bama Dillert)*, Shirley MacLaine *(Ginny Moorhead)*, Martha Hyer *(Gwen French)*, Arthur Kennedy *(Frank Hirsh)*, Nancy Gates *(Edith Barclay)*, Leora Dana *(Agnes Hirsh)*, Betty Lou Keim *(Dawn Hirsh)*, Larry Gates *(Prof Robert Haven French)*, Steven Peck *(Raymond Lanchak)*

p, Sol C. Siegel; d, Vincente Minnelli; w, John Patrick, Arthur Sheekman (based on the novel by James Jones); ph, William Daniels; ed, Adrienne Fazan; m, Elmer Bernstein; art d, William A. Horning, Urie McCleary; cos, Walter Plunkett

AAN Best Actress: Shirley MacLaine; *AAN Best Supporting Actor:* Arthur Kennedy; *AAN Best Supporting Actress:* Martha Hyer; *AAN Best Song:* James Van Heusen, Sammy Cahn; *AAN Best Costume Design:* Walter Plunkett

The protagonist of Jean-Luc Godard's CONTEMPT won't remove his hat, even in the bathtub, because he wants to look like Dean Martin in SOME CAME RUNNING—a nice index of the reverence with which Vincente Minnelli's eloquent, passionate melodramas were regarded by French New Wave critics, who saw in them an ironic encapsulization of American culture. Expertly condensed by studio hacks Sheekman and Patrick from a massive, windy best-seller by James Jones (*From Here To Eternity*), this film captures the disillusionment of returning WWII vets, and brilliantly addresses itself to many of the director's characteristic concerns—masculine fear of domestication and attendant resentment of women; the tensions of masculine friendship; women's complicity in their own oppression; the compromises demanded of artists functioning under capitalism.

As the film opens, unsuccessful novelist and WWII vet Sinatra returns to his home town of Parkman, Illinois, with a new manuscript under one arm and a charming floozy, MacLaine, draped over the other. Their appearance creates a minor sensation in the small town, in which, of course, superficial respectability masks a hotbed of corruption and sexual intrigue. Sinatra's brother is Kennedy, a rigid businessman married to Dana but having an affair with his assistant, Nancy Gates. Hyer teaches at the local college and finds Sinatra intriguing, but the jaded Sinatra is impatient with her refusal to sleep with him. He befriends Martin, an easygoing, superstitious gambler with whom he enjoys endless card games and drinking bouts. The two are casually contemptuous of MacLaine, who is sexually available and thus, to their minds, less desirable than the icy Hyer; MacLaine endures many cruelties out of love for Sinatra. Eventually, Sinatra's frustration with the town's ubiquitous hypocrisy boils over; his subsequent recklessness leads to tragedy.

SOME LIKE IT HOT

1959 120m bw Crime/Comedy ★★★★★
Ashton/Mirisch (U.S.) /PG

Marilyn Monroe *(Sugar Kane)*, Tony Curtis *(Joe/Josephine)*, Jack Lemmon *(Jerry/Daphne)*, George Raft *(Spats Columbo)*, Pat O'Brien *(Mulligan)*, Joe E. Brown *(Osgood E. Fielding III)*, Nehemiah Persoff *(Little Bonaparte)*, Joan Shawlee *(Sweet Sue)*, Billy Gray *(Sig Poliakoff)*, George E. Stone *(Toothpick Charlie)*

p, Billy Wilder; d, Billy Wilder; w, Billy Wilder, I.A.L. Diamond (based on Robert Thoeren and M. Logan's screenplay for the film FANFARES OF LOVE); ph, Charles Lang; ed, Arthur Schmidt; m, Adolph Deutsch; art d, Ted Haworth; cos, Orry-Kelly, Milt Rice

AAN Best Actor: Jack Lemmon; *AAN Best Director:* Billy Wilder; *AAN Best Adapted Screenplay:* Billy Wilder, I.A.L. Diamond; *AAN Best Cinematography:* Charles Lang, Jr.; *AAN Best Art Direction:* Ted Haworth Edward G. Goyle; *AA Best Costume Design:* Orry-Kelly

Nobody's perfect—except Billy Wilder in top form. One of the most well-loved of Hollywood comedies, Wilder's masterly spoof of gangster films and gender roles revels in invention and effervescent high camp. It's February, 1929, and Joe (Tony Curtis) and Jerry (Jack Lemmon) are two unemployed musicians desperate for work. The pair accidentally witness the St. Valentine's Day Massacre, watching mobster Spats Columbo (George Raft) and his henchmen wipe out Toothpick Charlie (George E. Stone) and his gang. Forced to leave town in a hurry, Joe and Jerry take the first job they can get: playing in Sweet Sue's all-girl band. Dressing up as women, the two join the rest of the band on their train ride to Florida. Both Joe, who adopts Josephine as his *nom de* drag, and Jerry, who becomes Daphne, are thrown for a loop when they meet Sweet Sue's lead singer, the pneumatic Sugar Kane (Marilyn Monroe)—"jello on springs," says Jerry.

SOME LIKE IT HOT expands a one-joke premise with hysterical results, due in no small part to the contributions of the near-perfect ensemble, with each of the major characters shining like a perfect jewel. Lemmon and Curtis are marvelous as the men-turned-women, creating believable characters and generally eschewing the lower forms of camp. Monroe is at her best, delightfully spoofing her dizzy blonde image. Billy Wilder and I.A.L. Diamond's witty script is full of clever twists, throwing in unexpected turns at a frantic pace. The script was written with Lemmon in mind, but at one point Frank Sinatra was considered as a possible replacement. Fortunately, this alternative casting fell through when Monroe expressed interest in doing the film. Although Monroe's presence was welcomed, both cast and crew learned to regret it as she lived up to her reputation as a "difficult" performer, consistently showing up late, forgetting her lines, and spending endless time in her dressing room. Wilder took to writing her lines on furniture in the hope that it would help the legendary actress to get through her scenes, but even this drastic effort failed. What's more, the other actors resented Monroe's antics, and Curtis compared kissing her to kissing Hitler. Nevertheless, Monroe still demonstrates her marvelous comic touch and sings three songs: "I Wanna Be Loved By You," "Running Wild," and "I'm Through with Love."

Ironically, Monroe's constant absences led to the creation of the film's classic exit line. Knowing Monroe's unreliability, Wilder took to shooting around her. It was decided that the film would end on a closeup of Lemmon and Joe E. Brown, as Daphne/Jerry explains to the lovesick Osgood E. Fielding III why s/he can't marry him. "We wrote it the night before we had to shoot it," Diamond explained in an interview, "and I mentioned a line I'd considered using at some earlier point. . . . Billy said, 'Do you think it's strong enough for the tag of the picture?' And I said, 'I don't know.' But it was getting to be eleven o'clock at night, so we wrote it that way, and he said, 'Well, maybe we'll think of something better on the set.' Fortunately, we didn't think of anything better on the set."

Monroe, unpopular on the set, wasn't invited to the wrap party. But she may have had the last laugh since she received 10 percent of the film's gross; the film made over $8 million in its initial release and would make several million more over the next few years. Said Wilder after the difficult shoot: "You have to be orderly to shoot disorder; this was the best disorder we ever had."

SOMEBODY UP THERE LIKES ME

1956   113m   bw   Sports/Biography   ★★★½
MGM   (U.S.)   /A

Paul Newman (Rocky Graziano), Pier Angeli (Norma), Everett Sloane (Irving Cohen), Eileen Heckart (Ma Barbella), Sal Mineo (Romolo), Harold J. Stone (Nick Barbella), Joseph Buloff (Benny), Sammy White (Whitey Bimstein), Arch Johnson (Heldon), Robert Lieb (Questioner)

p, Charles Schnee; d, Robert Wise; w, Ernest Lehman (based on the autobiography of Rocky Graziano written with Rowland Barber); ph, Joseph Ruttenberg; ed, Albert Akst; m, Bronislau Kaper; art d, Cedric Gibbons, Malcolm Brown

AA Best Cinematography: Joseph Ruttenberg; AAN Best Editing: Albert Akst; AA Best Art Direction: Cedric Gibbons, Malcolm Brown, Edwin B. Willis, Keogh Gleason

After pulling no punches in his brilliant study of the downside of professional boxing, THE SET-UP, director Robert Wise presents a much more upbeat picture of the fight game in this entertaining biography of one-time middleweight champion Rocky Graziano. Paul Newman plays the New York slum-bred fighter, the son of a boxer whose career was stifled by the bottle. In and out of trouble for most of his young life, Rocky drifts from petty crime to reform school, from a dishonorable discharge from the Army to Leavenworth Prison. In the joint, however, Rocky is encouraged to develop his boxing talents, and when he is released he is taken under the wing of small-time manager Irving Cohen (Everett Sloane). Under Cohen's guidance, Rocky begins winning fights, but it isn't until he meets and marries Norma (Pier Angeli) that Rocky becomes a big winner. In time, he battles Tony Zale (brilliantly boxed by Courtland Shepard) for the championship, losing their first fight, but taking the title in the second. Newman, who spent time with Graziano and observed his speech patterns, mannerisms, movements, and boxing style, worked himself into peak condition for the role, lifting weights and sparring with top professionals, and his portrayal of the scrappy, often tongue-tied, but wholly likable boxer is superb. Although the role was originally intended for James Dean, Newman makes it his own, delivering such memorable lines as "I'll drink from the bottle like the rest of the boys" when asked if he needs a cup to complete his boxing garb.

SOMEONE TO WATCH OVER ME

1987   106m   c   Thriller/Romance   ★★★
Columbia   (U.S.)   R/15

Tom Berenger (Mike Keegan), Mimi Rogers (Claire Gregory), Lorraine Bracco (Ellie Keegan), Jerry Orbach (Lt. Garber), John Rubinstein (Neil Steinhart), Andreas Katsulas (Joey Venza), Tony DiBenedetto (T.J.), James Moriarty (Koontz), Mark Moses (Win Hockings), Daniel Hugh Kelly (Scotty)

p, Thierry de Ganay, Harold Schneider; d, Ridley Scott; w, Howard Franklin; ph, Steven Poster; ed, Claire Simpson; m, Michael Kamen; prod d, Jim Bissell; art d, Christopher Burian-Mohr, John J. Moore; cos, Colleen Atwood

Hot on the heels of FATAL ATTRACTION came SOMEONE TO WATCH OVER ME, another film about a happily married man who strays from the marital bed. Mike Keegan (Tom Berenger) is a New York police detective who lives in Queens with his ex-cop wife, Ellie (Lorraine Bracco), and their young son. When wealthy socialite Claire Gregory (Mimi Rogers) witnesses a murder, Keegan is assigned to protect her from the killer. Cold and aloof at first, Claire begins to warm to the handsome, shy, and somewhat dim-witted detective. Although SOMEONE TO WATCH OVER ME has some major problems with plot plausibility, its emphasis is properly on the people involved in the romantic triangle and not the machinations of a contrived story line. Much of the credit for what works in the film should go to the excellent cast. Berenger is superb, and Rogers proves here that she can handle a lead role with class and aplomb. Bracco, however, steals the picture with a refreshing energy and wit.

SOMETHING WILD

1986   113m   c   Drama/Comedy   ★★★½
Religioso Primitiva   (U.S.)   R/18

Jeff Daniels (Charles Driggs), Melanie Griffith (Audrey Hankel), Ray Liotta (Ray Sinclair), Tracey Walter (The Country Squire), Margaret Colin (Irene), Dana Preu ("Peaches"), Jack Gilpin (Larry Dillman), Su Tissue (Peggy Dillman), Kristin Olsen (Tracy), John Sayles (Motorcycle Cop)

p, Jonathan Demme, Kenneth Utt; d, Jonathan Demme; w, E. Max Frye; ph, Tak Fujimoto; ed, Craig McKay; m, John Cale, Laurie Anderson; prod d, Norma Moriceau; art d, Stephen J. Lineweaver

One bright Friday afternoon in lower Manhattan, Charles Driggs (Jeff Daniels), a successful young tax consultant, capriciously skips out of a tiny diner without paying his lunch check. Just outside, he is stopped by Audrey Hankel (Melanie Griffith), a Louise Brooks-clone in black wig and vaguely African attire. She calls herself "Lulu," presumably a reference to Brooks' character in PANDORA'S BOX. She tells Charles that she saw him walk out on the check and threatens to turn him in. Declaring that Charles is actually a "closet rebel," she decides instead that he'd be game for a road trip. Before he knows what is happening, Charles finds himself in Audrey's convertible being driven to New Jersey. Through Audrey he is temporarily freed from his normal bourgeois restraints. They have a wild adventure on the road as they engage in some petty theft, mildly kinky sex, and finally attend Audrey's high school reunion. This modern screwball comedy takes a frightening dark turn when they encounter Audrey's psychotic ex-husband, Ray (Ray Liotta), who has just gotten out of jail.

Since his early films, director Jonathan Demme has demonstrated a sharp eye for the American landscape and its people. With a keen wit and an optimistic compassion, Demme has creates vividly human characters whose quirks have the ring of truth about them. With a screenplay from first-time screenwriter E. Max Frye and superior performances from his principal cast, Demme has created a unique and likable film in SOMETHING WILD. John Cale and Laurie Anderson compiled the film's rousing rock soundtrack which features nearly 50 songs.

Some viewers were alarmed at the dark violent turn the story takes more than halfway through but close viewing reveals that the audience is subtly being prepared for this tonal shift from early on. This is a film that benefits greatly from a second screening. Demme keeps his quirky narrative twisting and turning so that the viewer can never predict what will happen next. He draws us in with humor and then grabs us by the throat, bringing us face-to-face with the failures of the American dream. A filmmaker with a small but devoted following, he would not have a major popular hit until the 1991 blockbuster, THE SILENCE OF THE LAMBS.

SOMMERSBY

1993 112m c Drama/Historical/Romance   ★★★
New Regency Films/Warner Bros. (U.S.)   PG-13/12

Richard Gere *(Jack)*, Jodie Foster *(Laurel)*, Lanny Flaherty *(Buck)*, Wendell Wellman *(Travis)*, Bill Pullman *(Orin)*, Brett Kelley *(Little Rob)*, William Windom *(Reverend Powell)*, Clarice Taylor *(Esther)*, James Earl Jones *(Judge Issacs)*, Frankie Faison *(Joseph)*

p, Arnon Milchan, Steve Reuther; d, Jon Amiel; w, Nicholas Meyer, Sarah Kernochan (from story by Meyer and Anthony Shaffer based on the screenplay *Le Retour de Martin Guerre* by Daniel Vigne and Jean-Claude Carriere); ph, Philippe Rousselot; ed, Peter Boyle; m, Danny Elfman; prod d, Bruno Rubeo; art d, P. Michael Johnston; fx, Gregory S. Hull; chor, Colleen Kelly; cos, Marilyn Vance-Straker

Like BREATHLESS, THREE MEN AND A BABY and COUSINS, SOMMERSBY is a Hollywood remake of a successful French film, this time THE RETURN OF MARTIN GUERRE. With the setting switched from 16th-century France to post-civil war Tennessee, the story remains largely the same: a man returns home after an absence of several years to reclaim his wife and property, but is so changed as to arouse suspicions about his real identity.

As played by Richard Gere, Jack Sommersby seems transformed from a spoilt, mean-spirited landowner into a paragon of heroism and virtue. By day, he leads his wife (Jodie Foster) and tenants in an enlightened, profit-sharing scheme to bring prosperity back to his war-ravaged estate by growing tobacco; by night, he takes time out from reading Homer to his young son to single-handedly rout KKK gangs who beat up his emancipated black workers.

"Sommersby" is made with enough intelligence to overcome its credulity-straining premise, and handles its outdoor scenes with epic charm. It's fun to watch the farmers nurture their precious tobacco seed into full-grown plants, at one point fighting off an invasion of swollen, wormlike bugs. The worms are only slightly less appealing, however, than Richard Gere, whose facial expressions run the gamut from smug to smarmy. Gere's pairing opposite Jodie Foster is a fatal flaw here, with her self-contained performance reflecting his glib narcissism. Though it's billed as a romantic drama, SOMMERSBY is better at recreating a time and place than at sparking even the faintest glimmer of passion. On this particular tobacco farm, there's plenty to smoke, but no fire.

SON OF FRANKENSTEIN

1939 95m bw Horror   ★★★★
Universal (U.S.)   /H

Basil Rathbone *(Baron Wolf von Frankenstein)*, Boris Karloff *(The Monster)*, Bela Lugosi *(Ygor)*, Lionel Atwill *(Inspector Krogh)*, Josephine Hutchinson *(Elsa von Frankenstein)*, Donnie Dunagan *(Peter von Frankenstein)*, Emma Dunn *(Amelia)*, Edgar Norton *(Thomas Benson)*, Perry Ivins *(Fritz)*, Lawrence Grant *(Burgomaster)*

p, Rowland V. Lee; d, Rowland V. Lee; w, Willis Cooper (based on characters created by Mary Shelley); ph, George Robinson; ed, Ted J. Kent; m, Frank Skinner; art d, Jack Otterson; fx, John P. Fulton; cos, Vera West

The third film in the Universal "Frankenstein" series and the last feature film appearance by Boris Karloff as the monster, SON OF FRANKEN-STEIN boasts some stunning set design by Russell Gausman, a good script, and a magnificent cast. Set 25 years after the end of THE BRIDE OF FRANKENSTEIN, the film begins as the late Baron von Franken-stein's son, Wolf (Basil Rathbone), returns to his homeland and receives a weak welcome from the burgomaster, who presents him with a box containing his father's papers. Once safe in his castle, Wolf is visited by Inspector Krogh (Lionel Atwill), who warns him that he is not welcomed by the villagers, who fear that he will continue his father's experiments. Wolf laughs off their suspicions, but the next day, while wandering the ruins of his father's laboratory, he meets Ygor (Bela Lugosi). The deceased Baron's assistant now hides among the ruins,

guarding his "friend"—the comatose Frankenstein monster (Karloff) laid out on a slab, immobile, but very much alive. Wolf becomes obsessed with the idea of bringing the monster back to full power, then vindicating his father by teaching the creature to behave. SON OF FRANKENSTEIN is a rousing, memorable addition to the series, and features a collection of superb portrayals from Lugosi (who delivers the performance of his career and nearly steals the film), Rathbone (in a part originally planned for Peter Lorre), and Lionel Atwill (who milks his false arm for all it's worth), though Karloff is a bit of a disappoint-ment—his beloved monster turned into little more than a mute robot. Dwight Frye, who had been Frankenstein's assistant in the first two films, unfortunately had his entire role as one of the villagers cut out. While the offbeat vision and humor of James Whale (the director of the first two FRANKENSTEIN films) are missing, Rowland Lee manages to create a memorable world all his own. The series would go downhill from here and end with a rousing parody of the whole genre in ABBOTT AND COSTELLO MEET FRANKENSTEIN.

SON OF PALEFACE

1952 95m c Western/Comedy   ★★★½
Paramount (U.S.)   /U

Bob Hope *(Junior)*, Jane Russell *(Mike)*, Roy Rogers *(Himself)*, Bill Williams *(Kirk)*, Lloyd Corrigan *(Doc Lovejoy)*, Paul E. Burns *(Ebenezer Hawkins)*, Douglas Dumbrille *(Sheriff McIntyre)*, Harry von Zell *(Stoner)*, Iron Eyes Cody *(Indian Chief)*, Wee Willie Davis *(Blacksmith)*

p, Robert L. Welch; d, Frank Tashlin; w, Frank Tashlin, Robert Welch, Joseph Quillan; ph, Harry Wild; ed, Eda Warren; m, Lyn Murray; art d, Hal Pereira, Roland Anderson; fx, Gordon Jennings, Paul K. Lerpae, Farciot Edouart; chor, Josephine Earl

AAN Best Song: Jack Brooks

A very funny sequel to THE PALEFACE that took four years to put on the screen while Hope made a few other pictures. This time, Hope plays his own son. The original character of the pioneer dentist was played by Hope, and now he comes back, again with Russell, as the Harvard graduate who goes west to claim the inheritance left by his father. Russell is a bandit who sings in a saloon known as "The Dirty Shame." Hope teams with Rogers and Trigger (playing themselves) to nab a crook who has been robbing various gold shipments. They suspect that the criminal may be Russell. She thinks Rogers is a handsome guy and has the warms for him, but he would rather kiss his horse, so, rarity of rarities, Hope gets the girl.

SON OF PALEFACE is a satire of every cowboy cliche, with Hope getting the chance to rattle off one-liners while the action takes in Indian uprisings, lynch mobs, posses, ghost towns, mirages, deserts, quick-draws, saloon brawls—in other words, everything that John Wayne ever did for real. Tashlin was receiving his first directorial credit; he had co-directed THE LEMON DROP KID with Sid Lanfield but was not credited. He'd written THE PALEFACE with Ed Hartmann and was rewarded with this assignment, a job he didn't muff. It's fast and witty, and all the rootin' tootin' shootin' cannot be taken seriously for a moment. Tashlin was a one-time cartoonist, and it shows as he sets up the scenes like animated sequences, much to the picture's benefit. In the original, Ray Evans and Jay Livingston wrote the Oscar tune "Buttons and Bows" and they wisely bring it back for another go-around with new lyrics, as sung by Hope, Rogers, and Russell.

Rogers had been the king of the small western movies for over a decade, but after this movie, began to limit his appearances. He did a small guest bit in ALIAS JESSE JAMES, then a role in MACKIN-TOSH AND T.J. Other than those, he spent most of his time tending his huge real estate investments which are worth over $100 million.

SONG OF BERNADETTE, THE

1943 156m bw Religious/Biography   ★★★★
Fox (U.S.)   /U

Jennifer Jones *(Bernadette Soubirous)*, William Eythe *(Antoine)*, Charles Bickford *(Peyremaie)*, Vincent Price *(Dutour)*, Lee J. Cobb *(Dr. Dozous)*, Gladys Cooper *(Sister Vauzous)*, Anne Revere *(Louise Soubirous)*, Roman Bohnen *(Francois Soubirous)*, Mary Anderson *(Jeanne Abadie)*, Patricia Morison *(Empress Eugenie)* p, William Perlberg; d, Henry King; w, George Seaton (based on the novel by Franz Werfel); ph, Arthur Miller; ed, Barbara McLean; m, Alfred Newman; art d, James Basevi, William Darling; fx, Fred Sersen; cos, Rene Hubert

AAN Best Picture; AA Best Actress: Jennifer Jones; *AAN Best Supporting Actor:* Charles Bickford; *AAN Best Supporting Actress:* Gladys Cooper; *AAN Best Supporting Actress:* Anne Revere; *AAN Best Director:* Henry King; *AAN Best Screenplay:* George Seaton; *AA Best Cinematography:* Arthur Miller; *AAN Best Editing:* Barbara McLean; *AA Best Score:* Alfred Newman; *AA Best Art Direction:* James Basevi, William Darling, Thomas Little; *AAN Best Sound:* E.H. Hansen

This film depicts the stirring true story of the woman who had a vision of the Virgin Mary in a grotto at Lourdes in 1858. Jennifer Jones is Bernadette Soubirous, a peasant girl whose family lives in the town jail because they have no place of their own. One morning, Bernadette is gathering sticks of wood near the grotto when she is visited by the Virgin (Linda Darnell). Bernadette is directed to dig at the grotto for a healing water with curative power for the lame and the halt. Everyone scoffs at her except her devout mother and, eventually, Peyremaie (Charles Bickford), a local priest. He helps her get into a convent, and, after many years of defending her vision, Bernadette is canonized by the Catholic Church. Since that time, millions have flocked to Lourdes to bathe in the Holy Water. Jones is touching in an Oscar-winning performance.

SONG OF THE SOUTH

1946   94m   c   Animated/Children's ★★★★
Walt Disney Productions   (U.S.) /U

Ruth Warrick *(Sally)*, Bobby Driscoll *(Johnny)*, Luana Patten *(Ginny)*, Lucile Watson *(Grandmother)*, Hattie McDaniel *(Aunt Tempy)*, Glenn Leedy *(Toby)*, James Baskett *(Uncle Remus)*, Nicodemus Stewart *(Voice of Brer Bear)*, Johnny Lee *(Voice of Brer Rabbit)*, George Nokes

p, Walt Disney; d, Harve Foster, Wilfred Jackson; w, Dalton Raymond, Morton Grant, Bill Peet, George Stallings, Ralph Wright, Maurice Rapf (based on *Tales of Uncle Remus* by Joel Chandler Harris); ph, Gregg Toland; ed, William Morgan; m, Daniele Amfitheatrof, Paul J. Smith; art d, Perry Ferguson; fx, Ub Iwerks; cos, Mary Wills; anim, Milt Kahl, Erick Larson, Oliver M. Johnston Jr., Les Clark, Marc Davis, John Lounsbery, Don Lusk, Tom Massey, Murray McClellan, Jack Campbell, Hal King, Harvey Toombs, Ken O'Brien, Al Coe, Hal Ambro, Cliff Nordberg, Rudy Larriva

AAN Best Score: Daniele Amfitheatrof, Paul J. Smith, Charles Wolcott; *AA Best Song:* Allie Wrubel (Music), Ray Gilbert (Lyrics)

This Disney charmer is also the studio's most controversial production. Set in the Reconstruction South, it stars Bobby Driscoll as Johnny, a white little boy who goes to live on his grandmother's plantation after his parents separate. Upset by things he can't understand, Johnny runs away and meets former slave Uncle Remus (James Baskett). Uncle Remus decides to trick Johnny into going home, telling the boy he would also like to run away, but must stop home for a few things. As Uncle Remus packs, he tells Johnny a story, and the film moves into a marvelous combination of live action and animation in a bright cartoon setting in which Brer Rabbit, too, has an adventure while running away from home. SONG OF THE SOUTH's cartoon sequences are as fine as anything produced by the Disney animators. The live action projected into a cartoon setting transcends gimmickry, with the actors and caricatures carefully matched within the frame. Baskett's excellent performance (for which he received an honorary Academy Award) makes the technique work that much better. The film's idyllic portrayal of the Reconstruction setting was controversial, however, particularly among black Americans. The NAACP and the National Urban League, among others, protested the stereotypes in the film, though Disney officials of course maintained the film was "a sincere effort to depict American folklore, to put the Uncle Remus stories into pictures." Included is the well-known song "Zip A Dee Doo Dah."

SONG TO REMEMBER, A

1945   113m   c   Musical/Biography ★★★½
Columbia   (U.S.) /U

Paul Muni *(Professor Joseph Elsner)*, Merle Oberon *(George Sand)*, Cornel Wilde *(Frederic Chopin)*, Stephen Bekassy *(Franz Liszt)*, Nina Foch *(Constantia)*, George Coulouris *(Louis Pleyel)*, Sig Arno *(Henri Dupont)*, Howard Freeman *(Kalbrenner)*, George Macready *(Alfred DeMusset)*, Claire DuBrey *(Mme. Mercier)*

p, Louis F. Edelman; d, Charles Vidor; w, Sidney Buchman (based on the story by Ernst Marischka); ph, Tony Gaudio, Allen Davey; ed, Charles Nelson; m, Miklos Rozsa; art d, Lionel Banks, Van Nest Polglase; cos, Walter Plunkett, Travis Banton

AAN Best Actor: Cornel Wilde; *AAN Best Original Screenplay:* Ernst Marischka; *AAN Best Cinematography:* Tony Gaudio, Allen M. Davey; *AAN Best Editing:* Charles Nelson; *AAN Best Score:* Miklos Rozsa, Morris Stoloff; *AAN Best Sound:* John Livadary

As a fictional tale of a composer who gives his all for his music, this is a fine picture; as a biography, it bears as much resemblance to the truth as NIGHT AND DAY did to the life of Cole Porter. Nonetheless, Cornell Wilde earned an Oscar nomination for his convincing performance as Frederic Chopin, whom screenwriter Sidney Buchman presents as a revolutionary Polish patriot (though, in fact, his support of Polish nationalism was never so zealous). Top-billed Paul Muni, in his only Technicolor film, portrays Chopin's mentor Prof. Joseph Elsner, while Merle Oberon essays the role of novelist George Sand, whom the infatuated Chopin meets in Paris and follows to Majorca, where he becomes consumptive (the real-life relationship between Sand and Chopin was considerably less whirlwind, lasting some 10 years), resulting in his death when he refuses to cancel a concert tour whose proceeds are earmarked for the cause.

SONS AND LOVERS

1960   99m   bw   Drama ★★★½
Fox   (U.K.) /A

Trevor Howard *(Walter Morel)*, Dean Stockwell *(Paul Morel)*, Wendy Hiller *(Mrs. Morel)*, Mary Ure *(Clara Dawes)*, Heather Sears *(Miriam Lievers)*, William Lucas *(William)*, Conrad Phillips *(Baxter Dawes)*, Donald Pleasence *(Pappleworth)*, Ernest Thesiger *(Henry Hadlock)*, Rosalie Crutchley *(Miriam's Mother)*

p, Jerry Wald; d, Jack Cardiff; w, Gavin Lambert, T.E.B. Clarke (based on the novel by D.H. Lawrence); ph, Freddie Francis; m, Mario Nascimbene; art d, Lionel Couch; cos, Margaret Furse

AAN Best Picture; AAN Best Actor: Trevor Howard; *AAN Best Supporting Actress:* Mary Ure; *AAN Best Director:* Jack Cardiff; *AAN Best Adapted Screenplay:* Gavin Lambert, T.E.B. Clarke; *AA Best Cinematography:* Francis Freddie; *AAN Best Art Direction:* Tom Morahan, Lionel Couch

They might well have titled this SON AND MOTHER, for the famous relationship between a mother and son is at the center of this respectful adaptation of Lawrence's autobiographical novel. A few characters have been altered and a sister has been dropped in the transition from print to the screen, but these changes hardly call attention to themselves.

The story is set in Nottingham, where Hiller and Howard have raised three sons on Howard's miner's wages. Hiller is a forceful woman who manages men like puppets. Stockwell is the sensitive son who longs to pursue a career as an artist in London. After romancing naive local lass Sears for a while, Stockwell takes up with an older woman, Ure, who is married to Phillips. Hiller puts an end to her son's relationship with Sears, and when Ure leaves her husband for Stockwell, Hiller is livid. Stockwell listens to his mother but knows he should follow his heart; however, he appears powerless to free himself of her grasp. No matter what he does or where he goes, Stockwell feels Hiller's presence. The love that Hiller should be giving her husband is, instead, showered upon Stockwell. When one of his brothers dies in a mining accident and the other goes off to London, Stockwell is forced to abandon his dreams in order to be near his bereaved mother. Hiller eventually dies, and Stockwell leaves for London, looking forward to a life away from the claustrophobic town, but we know that the specter of his dear mother will always be with him.

Many works have been written about the domination of sons by mothers, but few have come close to the insights of Lawrence's classic, and it is much to the film's credit that a great deal of its dialogue comes straight from the novel. The film's period details are excellent, and the direction by cinematographer-turned-director Cardiff (who photographed such films as THE RED SHOES, LEAVE HER TO HEAVEN and THE AFRICAN QUEEN) is first rate. All of the actors acquit themselves well, even in the most menial roles. Crutchley is exquisite as Sears' mother and veteran Thesiger (who, at 81, was making his penultimate film in a career that begain in 1918) is equally memorable. Cardiff's assistant on the film was Peter Yates, who later directed such films as BULLITT and BREAKING AWAY.

SONS OF THE DESERT

1933 68m bw Comedy   ★★★★
MGM   (U.S.)   /U

Stan Laurel (Himself), Oliver Hardy (Himself), Charley Chase (Himself), Mae Busch (Mrs. Lottie Chase Hardy), Dorothy Christy (Mrs. Betty Laurel), Lucien Littlefield (Dr. Horace Meddick), John Elliott (Exalted Exhausted Ruler), Charley Young, John Merton, William Gillespie

p, Hal Roach; d, William A. Seiter; w, Frank Craven, Byron Morgan; ph, Kenneth Peach; ed, Bert Jordan; chor, David Bennett

One of Stan Laurel and Oliver Hardy's best feature-length films, SONS OF THE DESERT is a comedic send-up of masonic lodge conventions. Based on the team's silent two-reeler WE FAW DOWN, the story involves Laurel and Hardy's trip to a convention of the Sons of the Desert. Because their wives don't want them to attend the convention, the pair pretend to take an ocean cruise to Honolulu for the sake of Hardy's health. Instead, they attend their convention in grand style and are even filmed by a newsreel crew covering the festivities. Upon their return home they discover that, not only did the ship that they supposedly sailed on sink, but their wives saw the newsreel they were featured in. Thus, their ruse is exposed. Songs include "Honolulu Baby" and "Sons of the Desert." SONS is faster by far than most L&H vehicles, though their childish innocence is left mercifully intact. Chase is a riot as an irritatingly madcap conventioneer. And as Johnny Carson's Matinee Host used to say, "featuring the ever popular Mae Busch" (as Mrs. Hardy; that's Dorothy Christy as Mrs. Laurel.)

SOPHIE'S CHOICE

1982 157m c Drama   ★★★
ITC   (U.S.)   R/15

Meryl Streep (Sophie Zawistowska), Kevin Kline (Nathan Landau), Peter MacNicol (Stingo), Josef Sommer (Narrator), Rita Karin (Yetta Zimmerman), Stephen D. Newman (Larry), Greta Turken (Leslie Lapidus), Josh Mostel (Morris Fink), Marcell Rosenblatt (Astrid Weinstein), Moishe Rosenfeld (Moishe Rosenblum)

p, Alan J. Pakula, Keith Barish; d, Alan J. Pakula; w, Alan J. Pakula (based on the novel by William Styron); ph, Nestor Almendros; ed, Evan Lottman; m, Marvin Hamlisch; prod d, George Jenkins; art d, John J. Moore; cos, Albert Wolsky

AA Best Actress: Meryl Streep; *AAN Best Adapted Screenplay:* Alan J. Pakula; *AAN Best Cinematography:* Nestor Almendros; *AAN Best Score:* Marvin Hamlisch; *AAN Best Costume Design:* Albert Wolsky

Meryl Streep essays another foreign accent in this overwrought melodrama. Adapted from William Styron's wildly ambitious semiautobiographical novel (its first line is "Call me Stingo"—get it?), the film follows Stingo (Peter MacNicol), a cornpone author who moves into a Brooklyn boarding house in 1947 and meets driven Nathan Landau (Kevin Kline) and mysterious Sophie Zawistowska (Meryl Streep), a Polish woman with a past. For most of the film one wonders what Sophie's "choice" is: is she to choose between Nathan and Stingo? But then the film flashes back to monochrome sepia to depict war, concentration camps, and the moment of revelation.

Competently directed by Pakula and featuring gorgeous cinematography by Almendros, SOPHIE'S CHOICE is an overlong, fairly schlocky film that takes itself too seriously. Streep emotes in customary fashion; Kline overacts wildly; MacNicol is charming in an unforgiving role.

SORRY, WRONG NUMBER

1948 89m bw Thriller   ★★★★
Paramount   (U.S.)   /15

Barbara Stanwyck (Leona Stevenson), Burt Lancaster (Henry Stevenson), Ann Richards (Sally Lord Dodge), Wendell Corey (Dr. Alexander), Harold Vermilyea (Waldo Evans), Ed Begley (James Cotterell), Leif Erickson (Fred Lord), William Conrad (Morano), John Bromfield (Joe), Jimmy Hunt (Jimmy Lord)

p, Hal B. Wallis, Anatole Litvak; d, Anatole Litvak; w, Lucille Fletcher (based on her radio play); ph, Sol Polito; ed, Warren Low; m, Franz Waxman; art d, Hans Dreier, Earl Hedrick; fx, Gordon Jennings; cos, Edith Head

AAN Best Actress: Barbara Stanwyck

A gripping film version of the classic 22-minute radio play which was made famous by Agnes Moorehead in a tour-de-force performance in 1943. Because Moorehead was not a "star" in Hollywood, Barbara Stanwyck was given the role in the movie version and she made it her own. Leona Stevenson (Stanwyck) is a whining, domineering, paranoid, hypochondriac New York heiress who has developed a psychosomatic illness that has made her a bed-ridden invalid. She lives in a fancy apartment with her milquetoast husband Henry (Lancaster), her only contact with the outside world being the telephone. One evening, while trying to reach Henry at the office, she overhears two men confirming plans for a murder. She tries to contact the outside world—the police, the phone company, Henry—to warn them of the impending violence, but time is quickly running out and the hour of the murder is approaching. The film's title is also its last line of dialogue.

SORRY, WRONG NUMBER is a wonderful premise which made for a taut, fast-paced 22-minute radio play, but at 89 minutes, much of them told in flashback, the suspense ebbs somewhat. Both Lancaster and Stanwyck are excellent.

SOUND OF MUSIC, THE

1965 174m c Musical/Biography   ★★½
Fox   (U.S.)   G/U

Julie Andrews (Maria), Christopher Plummer (Capt. Von Trapp), Eleanor Parker (The Baroness), Richard Haydn (Max Detweiler), Peggy Wood (Mother Abbess), Charmian Carr (Liesl), Heather Menzies (Louisa), Nicholas Hammond (Friedrich), Duane Chase (Kurt), Angela Cartwright (Brigitta)

p, Robert Wise; d, Robert Wise; w, Ernest Lehman (based on the musical play by Richard Rodgers, Oscar Hammerstein II, Howard Lindsay, Russel Crouse); ph, Ted McCord; ed, William Reynolds; m, Richard Rodgers; prod d, Boris Leven; fx, L.B. Abbott, Emil Kosa Jr.; chor, Marc Breaux, Dee Dee Wood; cos, Dorothy Jeakins

AA Best Picture; AAN Best Actress: Julie Andrews; *AAN Best Supporting Actress:* Peggy Wood; *AA Best Director:* Robert Wise; *AAN Best Cinematography:* Ted McCord; *AA Best Editing:* William Reynolds; *AAN Best Score:* Irwin Kostal; *AAN Best Art Direction:* Boris Leven, Walter M. Scott, Ruby Levitt; *AAN Best Costume Design:* Dorothy Jeakins; *AA Best Sound:* James P. Corcoran, Fred Hynes

We'd give anything to be little Von Trapp children, living our lives in the confines of this film. We'd refuse to wear clothes made from curtains. We'd sing loudly (like off-key Ethel Mermans) when we were hiding from Nazis, and never compromise our talent to sing before Papa's guests. We'd snatch Eleanor Parker's Eva Gabor wig, moon nuns, and wet Julie's bed during "My Favorite Things." What fun we'd have. And make this travesty real. For despite the political danger, we know it's leading to music swells and Andrews's million-dollar wedding gown—enough to make Grace Kelly and Princess Di and Elizabeth Taylor slap their mothers. It's so perfectly contrived and mechanical and fresh as a daisy, it's infuriating. And only the sly, insistently subversive Christopher Plummer is on our side.

Maria (Julie Andrews) is a young postulant at a nunnery who quickly realizes that the cloister is not for her. Yet she still believes in the values espoused by the church, so she goes out into the world and radiantly attempts to bring what she's learned to the lay world. Soon Maria is hired by Austrian widower Capt. Von Trapp (Christopher Plummer) as a governess for his seven singing children. Noting that the children seem cowed by their disciplinarian father, she strives to open their lives to joy. They live in one of the most beautiful sections of the Alps, but only learn to appreciate the surrounding vistas when Maria, with her fresh outlook, shows them what they have. All that is soon threatened by Nazi rule in Austria, forcing the Von Trapps to flee while en route to Salzburg for a musical festival in which they are to perform. A staple of 1960s Hollywood films, THE SOUND OF MUSIC delivered an unforgettable Julie Andrews performance (simultaneously damning her career; we'd have preferred the more authentic Mary Martin), and presented a most postcard view of Austria. The songs are hard to forget—"The Sound of Music," "Do Re Mi," "My Favorite Things," "Edelweiss", "Climb Every Mountain", and our pick of the litter, "The Lonely Goatherd"—but we're trying. So you expected a *serious* review?

In a nutshell: lovely to look at, scripted competently, with a few chilling moments about the lurking Nazis. But Wise can't direct Plummer to play along. And who does Eleanor Parker think she is—Anne Baxter standing in for Joan Crawford?

SOUNDER

1972   105m   c   Drama   ★★★½
Radnitz/Mattel   (U.S.)   G/U

Cicely Tyson *(Rebecca Morgan)*, Paul Winfield *(Nathan Lee Morgan)*, Kevin Hooks *(David Lee Morgan)*, Carmen Mathews *(Mrs. Boatwright)*, Taj Mahal *(Ike)*, James Best *(Sheriff Young)*, Yvonne Jarrell *(Josie Mae Morgan)*, Eric Hooks *(Earl Morgan)*, Sylvia Kuumba Williams *(Harriet)*, Janet MacLachlan *(Camille Johnson)*

p, Robert B. Radnitz; d, Martin Ritt; w, Lonne Elder III (based on a novel by William H. Armstrong); ph, John A. Alonzo; ed, Sidney Levin; m, Taj Mahal; prod, Walter Scott Herndon; cos, Nedra Watt

AAN Best Picture; AAN Best Actor: Paul Winfield; *AAN Best Actress:* Cicely Tyson; *AAN Best Adapted Screenplay:* Lonne Elder, III

Heartbreaking and intelligent, SOUNDER celebrates a family's dedication to each other through whatever travails befall them. In 1930s Louisiana, Nathan and Rebecca Morgan (Winfield and Tyson) are sharecroppers raising their three children and their dog, Sounder, as best they can in the poverty of the Depression. Nathan does the farming and hunts for game to feed his family. Rebecca takes in washing, and the trio of children take an equal part in doing the other tasks. Not much game is to be had, however, and when Nathan is arrested for stealing a ham, the family is torn apart. Rebecca and the children now begin a backbreaking schedule as they strive to work the land, make their quota, and keep body and soul together.

Adapted from a slim book that won the 1970 Newberry Award for children's literature, SOUNDER is one of the truest examples of a "family film" ever made and a triumph for all concerned. A sequel, SOUNDER, PART 2, followed in 1976, with Harold Sylvester and Ebony Wright taking over the roles played here by Winfield and Tyson.

SOUTH PACIFIC

1958   171m   c   Musical   ★★★½
South Pacific/Magna   (U.S.)   /U

Rossano Brazzi *(Emile De Becque)*, Mitzi Gaynor *(Nellie Forbush)*, John Kerr *(Lt. Cable)*, Ray Walston *(Luther Billis)*, Juanita Hall *(Bloody Mary)*, France Nuyen *(Liat)*, Russ Brown *(Capt. Brackett)*, Jack Mullaney *(Professor)*, Ken Clark *(Stewpot)*, Floyd Simmons *(Harbison)*

p, Buddy Adler; d, Joshua Logan; w, Paul Osborn (based on the play by Oscar Hammerstein II, Richard Rodgers, Logan, from the book *Tales of the South Pacific* by James A. Michener); ph, Leon Shamroy; ed, Robert Simpson; art d, Lyle Wheeler, John DeCuir, Walter M. Scott, Paul S. Fox; fx, L.B. Abbott; chor, LeRoy Prinz; cos, Dorothy Jeakins

AAN Best Cinematography: Leon Shamroy; *AAN Best Score:* Alfred Newman, Ken Darby; *AA Best Sound:* Fred Hynes

SOUTH PACIFIC isn't the screen classic it should have been, but despite the fact that it pales in comparison with the long-running Rodgers and Hammerstein Broadway musical on which it is based, the film still stands up as terrific entertainment. Inspired by James Mich-

ener's book *Tales of the South Pacific*, both the stage musical and the movie were directed by Joshua Logan—not entirely a good thing, since he allows his actors to resort to stage techniques that aren't always suited to the close-up medium of film. Set on an island in (you guessed it) the South Pacific, the story concerns Nellie Forbush (Mitzi Gaynor), a midwestern nurse who falls in love with Emile De Becque (Rossano Brazzi), a widowed planter who is much older, has children, and is set in his ways (shades of THE KING AND I). At the same time, Lt. Cable (John Kerr), a young Marine, falls for Liat (France Nuyen), a local native girl.

Ray Walston steals every scene in which he appears as a SeaBee conniver not unlike Sergeant Bilko, and Juanita Hall is wonderful as she repeats her stage role as Bloody Mary, though her singing is dubbed by Muriel Smith. Brazzi's voice work was provided by Giorgio Tozzi, and Bill Lee sang for Kerr, but Gaynor handled vocal chores herself. Made for $5 million, SOUTH PACIFIC was shot on location in Hawaii with a large cast that includes such names as Tom Laughlin (BILLY JACK), Ron Ely (TV's "Tarzan"), Doug McClure, and a non-speaking cameo by Joan Fontaine. Ultimately, though, it is the glorious Rodgers and Hammerstein songs that really distinguish the film.

SOUTHERN COMFORT

1981   100m   c   Drama/War   ★★★½
Phoenix/Cinema Group   (U.S.)   R/

Keith Carradine *(Spencer)*, Powers Boothe *(Hardin)*, Fred Ward *(Reece)*, Franklyn Seales *(Simms)*, T.K. Carter *(Cribbs)*, Lewis Smith *(Stuckey)*, Les Lannom *(Casper)*, Peter Coyote *(Poole)*, Carlos Brown *(Bowden)*, Brion James *(Trapper)*

p, David Giler; d, Walter Hill; w, Michael Kane, Walter Hill, David Giler; ph, Andrew Laszlo; ed, Freeman Davies; m, Ry Cooder; prod d, John Vallone

Arguably writer-director Walter Hill's best film to date, SOUTHERN COMFORT works both as a pure action film and as an extremely effective allegory of America's involvement in Vietnam. Vaguely reminiscent of John Boorman's DELIVERANCE, the film follows a group of National Guardsmen on maneuvers in the swamps of Louisiana. These weekend warriors, ill-equipped for their task, are given to horseplay and bickering. While out in the country, they "borrow" some canoes from local Cajuns, and soon find themselves pursued by the angry backwoodsmen. When one Guardsman (Lewis Smith) makes the mistake of shooting at the Cajuns, albeit with blanks, the enraged locals return the fire with real bullets, killing the detachment's commander (Peter Coyote), the only real soldier in the bunch. A deadly battle ensues as the Guardsmen attempt to escape from the swamp before more blood is shed. Unfamiliar with the terrain and extremely disorganized, the soldiers are no match for their pursuers. Tautly directed by Hill, superbly shot by Andrew Lazlo, and boasting an excellent score by Ry Cooder that incorporates authentic Cajun music, SOUTHERN COMFORT is a gripping, atmospheric, and disturbing film. Without straining to make his points, Hill evokes the American struggle in Southeast Asia by pitting a group of directionless recruits in unfamiliar terrain against enigmatic guerrillas. The director also considers the tensions that result when a diverse group of men is thrown together an extreme situation.

SOUTHERNER, THE

1945   91m   bw   Drama   ★★★★½
UA   (U.S.)   /A

Zachary Scott *(Sam Tucker)*, Betty Field *(Nona Tucker)*, Beulah Bondi *(Granny Tucker)*, Bunny Sunshine *(Daisy Tucker)*, Jay Gilpin *(Jot Tucker)*, Percy Kilbride *(Harmie Jenkins)*, Blanche Yurka *(Ma Tucker)*, Charles Kemper *(Tim, the Narrator)*, J. Carrol Naish *(Henry Devers)*, Norman Lloyd *(Finlay Hewitt)*

p, David L. Loew, Robert Hakim; d, Jean Renoir; w, Jean Renoir, Hugo Butler, William Faulkner (uncredited), Nunnally Johnson (based on the novel *Hold Autumn in Your Hand* by George Sessions Perry); ph, Lucien Andriot; ed, Gregg Tallas; m, Werner Janssen

AAN Best Director: Jean Renoir; *AAN Best Score:* Werner Janssen; *AAN Best Sound:* Jack Whitney

A remarkably naturalistic portrayal of one family's struggle to start a farm in the South. With the coming of autumn, Scott, a man hardened by his years of working fields for other people, decides to work his own land on the advice of his dying uncle. He is given a plot of unused, out-of-the-way land and packs his wife Field, children Sunshine and Gilpin, grandmother Bondi, a dog, and all of their possessions onto a beat-up truck. What they find is a plot of unkempt, though workable, land and a dilapidated shanty that isn't fit for animals. The family gets settled in, fix the front porch, put a fire in the stove, and do their best to make the space livable. When Scott realizes the well doesn't work, he pays a visit to a neighboring farm which, after years of toiling, has become what Scott hopes his will be. The farm belongs to Naish, an embittered man who cannot appreciate the success of his hard work without thinking about how it caused the deaths of his wife and child. Naish is less than hospitable and only reluctantly agrees to let Scott use his well on the condition that Scott supply a new rope when the old one wears thin. As time passes and winter arrives, Scott and his family plow the land and ready it for a cotton crop. For days the family goes without any decent food, surviving on mash, until Scott successfully smokes a possum out of a hollow tree. Mealtime brings the family together and gives Scott reason to thank the Lord with a simple prayer. Come spring, Gilpin is stricken with pellagra, or "spring sickness," forcing Scott to plant vegetables and find milk for the boy's nourishment. The vegetables begin to grow, but Scott has no money left for milk. Out of desperation he appeals again to Naish, who, in front of Scott, proceeds to use an entire bucket of fresh milk for pig slop while refusing to spare even a drop for a sick child. Kemper, a friend of Scott's from the city who has offered the farmer a factory job, does all he can to help by buying the family a cow, thereby saving the boy's life.

In the meantime, Scott's rivalry with Naish grows stronger when Naish's livestock are found in Scott's vegetable garden. Scott goes angrily to Naish's farm and a brawl begins between them, with Naish finally being thrown into the pig pen. In retaliation, Naish grabs his rifle and heads for the river where Scott is washing up. Before Naish can fire off a shot, he sees Scott's fishing line pull taut. Both he and Scott know that the fish that has been hooked is "Lead Pencil," a legendary giant catfish with whiskers as thick as lead pencils. It's been Naish's dream to catch the fish, so rather than shoot Scott, he helps him pull in the catch. The pair strike a deal: Naish will let Scott farm his vegetable garden and use his well, and in exchange Scott will let Naish have the glory of catching "Lead Pencil." Summer comes, the cotton crop shows promise, and Scott has hopes of life improving for him and the family. While they are in town for a wedding, a terrible rainstorm rages for hours. When the family arrives back at the farm, they find their crop completely destroyed, their house battered by the storm's high winds, and the river rising high onto Scott's property. Near his wit's end, Scott must consider how his family is going to survive and what the fate of his farm will be.

THE SOUTHERNER, Renoir's most critically respected American film, is a superb depiction, in spirit if not in historical authenticity, of the plight of the farmer. The southerner of the title is not only the heroic Scott, but also the angry Naish (who, like all Renoir's "evil" characters, has his reasons for being so), the obstinate grandmother, and the unbreakable Field. As with such great pictures as OUR DAILY BREAD, THE GRAPES OF WRATH and the brilliant government documentaries of Pare Lorentz to which THE SOUTHERNER is most similar (PLOW THAT BROKE THE PLAINS and THE RIVER), this picture makes characters of the land, the cotton, the plow, and the water, granting them the same importance as the actors. In THE SOUTHERNER, man is just another element which makes up the whole of the natural world; he is not in control of the divine elements but subject to them. With the original Hugo Butler script (he later dropped out of the production, in reverence to Renoir who, Butler felt, could rewrite the script however he pleased) of the Perry novel *Hold Autumn in Your Hand*, Renoir and his producers, Loew and Hakim, were able to convince Hollywood to make their film.

Not surprisingly, Renoir, a native of France who had only been in the US since 1940, found it difficult to fully capture the dialogue and dialect of the southern people. Nunnally Johnson, who had scripted THE GRAPES OF WRATH, was first brought in, followed by William Faulkner (both received no screen credit), who that year also had a hand in THE MALTESE FALCON and TO HAVE AND HAVE NOT.

Faulkner, who had known Renoir since the director's first American film, SWAMP WATER, and felt he was the greatest contemporary director, would later remark that working on THE SOUTHERNER had given him more pleasure than any other Hollywood production.

SPARTACUS

1960 196m c Historical/War ★★★★½
Bryna (U.S.) /PG

Kirk Douglas (*Spartacus*), Laurence Olivier (*Marcus Licinius Crassus*), Tony Curtis (*Antoninus*), Jean Simmons (*Varinia*), Charles Laughton (*Gracchus*), Peter Ustinov (*Lentulus Batiatus*), John Gavin (*Julius Caesar*), Nina Foch (*Helena Glabrus*), Herbert Lom (*Tigranes*), John Ireland (*Crixus*)

p, Edward Lewis; d, Stanley Kubrick, Anthony Mann; w, Dalton Trumbo (based on the novel by Howard Fast); ph, Russell Metty, Clifford Stine; ed, Robert Lawrence, Robert Schulte, Fred Chulack; m, Alex North; prod d, Alexander Golitzen; art d, Eric Orbom; cos, Bill Thomas, Valles

AA Best Supporting Actor: Peter Ustinov; *AA Best Cinematography:* Russell Metty; *AAN Best Editing:* Robert Lawrence; *AAN Best Score:* Alex North; *AA Best Art Direction:* Alexander Golitzen, Eric Orbom, Russell A. Gausman, Julia Heron; *AA Best Costume Design:* Bill Thomas, Valles

Although this is the only one of Stanley Kubrick's pictures over which he did not have complete control (he was brought in by Kirk Douglas to direct when Anthony Mann was fired after the first week of shooting), SPARTACUS is still a remarkable epic—one of the greatest tales of the ancient world ever to hit the screen. It's especially strong, and more typical of Kubrick, in the first half—before satire gives way to sentiment.

It tells the true story of a slave rebellion that panicked Rome for more than two years circa 73 BC, though some historical facts have been Hollywoodized (including Spartacus's demise—he was hacked to death in battle, not crucified). Spartacus (Douglas) is a rebellious Libyan slave purchased by Lentulus Batiatus (Peter Ustinov), the proprietor of a school for gladiators. Like his fellow trainees, he is rigorously trained in fighting skills in order to be profitably peddled to Roman coliseum owners. Discovering in himself and his fellow gladiators a spark of human dignity, Spartacus helps to lead a revolt and organize an army of slaves that will descend on Rome and liberate all oppressed men from the tyrannical rule of the patricians, specifically Marcus Crassus (Laurence Olivier). Also playing parts in this battle between free will and oppression are Gracchus (Charles Laughton), a senator engaged in a political power struggle with Crassus; Varinia (Jean Simmons), the beautiful slave and wife of Spartacus whom Crassus previously arranged to purchase; and young Julius Caesar (John Gavin), a student of Gracchus who later allies himself with Crassus.

More visually restrained than usual for Kubrick (the Technirama equipment made camera movement difficult), SPARTACUS instead concentrates on the *mise-en-scene*, most notably in the preparation of the massive final battle scene, as the various Roman military units position themselves like pieces on some gigantic chessboard. SPARTACUS today remains a stirring, intelligent comment on the spirit of revolt, largely due to Dalton Trumbo's literate and impassioned screenwriting (this was the blacklisted Trumbo's first screen credit in over a decade). Severely cut for its 1967 re-release, the film was largely restored in 1991. The restorers took advantage of this opportunity to insert some footage that was considered too suggestive for the film's initial release, a thinly-veiled attempted seduction of Curtis by Olivier. The soundtrack of this sequence had been lost and, since Olivier had recently died, his dialogue was indetectably redubbed by Anthony Hopkins.

SPEED

1994 115m c Action/Thriller ★★★½
Fox (U.S.) R/

Keanu Reeves (*Jack Traven*), Dennis Hopper (*Howard Payne*), Sandra Bullock (*Annie*), Joe Morton (*Captain McMahon*), Jeff Daniels (*Harry*), Alan Ruck (*Stephens*), Glenn Plummer (*Jaguar Owner*), Richard Lineback (*Norwood*), Beth Grant (*Helen*), Hawthorne James (*Sam*)

p, Mark Gordon; d, Jan De Bont; w, Graham Yost; ph, Andrzej Bartkowiak; ed, John Wright; m, Mark Mancina; prod d, Jack DeGovia; art d, John R. Jensen; fx, John Frazier, Boyd Shermis, Sony Pictures Imageworks; cos, Ellen Mirojnick

AA Best Sound: Gregg Landaker, Steve Maslow, Bob Beemer, David R.B. MacMillan; *AA Best Sound Effects:* Stephen Hunter Flick; *AAN Best Editing:* John Wright

Acclaimed cinematographer Jan De Bont's directing debut is a mindless, implausible, and thoroughly gripping adventure movie. SPEED parlays its crackerjack premise into a satisfying but instantly forgettable rollercoaster ride of explosions, car crashes, and awesome hardware.

Jack Traven (Keanu Reeves) is an irreverent LA cop who insists on doing things his way; he and his partner Harry Temple (Jeff Daniels) specialize in defusing bombs. They rescue an elevator full of people from mad bomber-extortionist Howard Payne (Dennis Hopper), but their triumph turns sour when he returns with an even more audacious plan. There's a bomb on a city bus. Once the bus goes over 50mph, the bomb is armed. If it then drops below 50mph, it blows up. If any passengers are taken off, it blows up. If Payne doesn't get his $3.7 million ransom, it blows up. Jack must figure out how to rescue the commuters—including spunky Annie (Sandra Bullock), who takes over driving duty when the bus driver is shot—and get Payne, all before 11 a.m.

SPEED lives up to its title, delivering carefully crafted action/adventure thrills without ever breaking out of the genre rut. Though the film runs out of steam near the end, as long as the action stays on the bus, it's thrilling. De Bont deploys helicopters, motorcycles, police cars, and SWAT teams with aplomb; Reeves, except for the rare occasions when he's called upon to do more than flex his muscles or utter terse one-liners, makes an appealing action hero.

SPELLBOUND

1945   111m   bw   Thriller   ★★★★
Selznick/Vanguard   (U.S.)   /PG

Ingrid Bergman *(Dr. Constance Peterson)*, Gregory Peck *(John "J.B." Ballantine)*, Jean Acker *(Matron)*, Donald Curtis *(Harry)*, Rhonda Fleming *(Mary Carmichael)*, John Emery *(Dr. Fleurot)*, Leo G. Carroll *(Dr. Murchison)*, Norman Lloyd *(Garmes)*, Steven Geray *(Dr. Graff)*, Paul Harvey *(Dr. Hanish)*

p, David O. Selznick; d, Alfred Hitchcock; w, Ben Hecht, Angus Macphail (based on the novel *The House of Dr. Edwardes* by Francis Beeding [Hilary St. George Saunders, John Palmer]); ph, George Barnes, Rex Wimpy; ed, William Ziegler, Hal C. Kern; m, Miklos Rozsa; prod d, James Basevi; art d, John Ewing; fx, Jack Cosgrove; cos, Howard Greer

AAN Best Picture; AAN Best Supporting Actor: Michael Chekhov; *AAN Best Director:* Alfred Hitchcock; *AAN Best Cinematography:* George Barnes; *AA Best Score:* Miklos Rozsa; *AAN Best Visual Effects:* Jack Cosgrove

An intriguing Hitchcock thriller which probes the dark recesses of a man's mind through psychoanalytic treatment and the love of a woman. Dr. Edwardes (Peck), a young psychiatrist, begins a new assignment as the director of a modern mental asylum. His behavior, however, is rather strange and eccentric, causing Dr. Peterson (Bergman), a brilliant but emotionally icy doctor, to grow suspicious. When she discovers that the doctor's real initials are J.B., she doubts that he is really Dr. Edwardes. She wonders not only what happened to Dr. Edwardes, but who J.B. really is, thereby involving herself professionally and emotionally as she falls in love with J.B. while digging into his past.

Generated by David O. Selznick, who purchased the rights because of his keen interest in psychoanalysis, the film often gets bogged down in psychiatric and psychoanalytic jargon, but it is counterbalanced by the love story that develops between J.B. and Dr. Peterson. Depending on the viewer's preference, the breakthrough to J.B.'s mystery can be credited to one of two things: the success of modern psychiatry or the power of love. As Hitchcock describes it, the film is "a manhunt story wrapped up in pseudo-psychoanalysis." Although heavy on dialogue, it is not without some brilliant visual touches, most obviously the heralded dream sequence created by avant-garde artist Salvador Dali. In its original conception it was far longer and more complex than the

two-minute sequence that finally appeared. It was to have run 22 minutes (much of which was actually shot but edited out) and included a disturbing sequence described by Hitchcock: "He [Dali] wanted a statue to crack like a shell falling apart, with ants crawling all over it, and underneath, there would be Ingrid Bergman, covered by ants! It just wasn't possible." As it happened, Hitchcock did not even shoot the dream sequence, returning instead to London. The brilliant visual stylist Josef von Sternberg was first considered as the director of the sequence, but William Cameron Menzies (THINGS TO COME) was finally chosen, though he later expressed dissatisfaction and asked that his name be removed from the credits.

SPETTERS

1980   109m   c   Drama   ★★★
VSE   (Netherlands)   R/18

Toon Agterberg *(Eve)*, Maarten Spanjer *(Hans)*, Hans Van Tongeren *(Reen)*, Marianne Boyer *(Maya)*, Renee Soutendijk *(Fientje)*, Jeroen Krabbe *(Henkhof)*, Rutger Hauer *(Witkamp)*, Peter Tuinman, Yvonne Valkenberg, Rudi Falkenhagen

p, Joop Van Den Ende; d, Paul Verhoeven; w, Gerard Soeteman; ph, Jost Vacano; ed, Ine Schenkkan; m, Ton Scherpenzeel; art d, Dick Schillemans, Peter Jasuai; cos, Yan Tax

A flashy, fast-paced drama, SPETTERS is the story of Dutch teenage motorcycle enthusiasts Eve (Toon Agterberg), Hans (Maarten Spanjer), and Reen (Hans Van Tongeren), all of whom dream of being as tough and successful as motorcycle champ Witkamp (Rutger Hauer). Their youthful rebellion ends tragically for both Reen, who is crippled in an accident, and Eve, who is raped, beaten, and killed by a gang of violent homosexuals. Providing a sexual outlet for the teenagers, and just about every other biker on the wharf, is Fientje (Renee Soutendijk), a conniving creature who runs a greasy spoon with her gay brother. SPETTERS is a violent, action-packed assault on the sensibilities of all but the most hardened filmgoers, not surprising given that it was directed by Paul Verhoeven, who would go on to score a major success in the US with his ultraviolent ROBOCOP (1987). Here he demonstrates his penchant for startling visuals, explicit sex, and graphic violence, though his intelligent direction is anything but careless or irresponsible. The beautiful blonde Soutendijk and Jeroen Krabbe would later costar again in another Verhoeven film, THE FOURTH MAN.

SPIRAL STAIRCASE, THE

1946   83m   bw   Thriller   ★★★★★
RKO/Vanguard   (U.S.)   /PG

Dorothy McGuire *(Helen Capel)*, George Brent *(Prof. Warren)*, Ethel Barrymore *(Mrs. Warren)*, Kent Smith *(Dr. Parry)*, Rhonda Fleming *(Blanche)*, Gordon Oliver *(Steve Warren)*, Elsa Lanchester *(Mrs. Oates)*, James Bell *(Constable)*, Charles Wagenheim *(Desk Clerk)*, Ellen Corby *(Neighbor)*

p, Dore Schary; d, Robert Siodmak; w, Mel Dinelli (based on the novel *Some Must Watch* by Ethel Lina White); ph, Nicholas Musuraca; ed, Harry Marker, Harry Gerstad; m, Roy Webb; art d, Albert S. D'Agostino, Jack Okey; fx, Vernon L. Walker

AAN Best Supporting Actress: Ethel Barrymore

The setting in this suspense-filled film is an old, dark Gothic mansion located in New England at the turn of the century. Young innocent Helen Capel (McGuire), long ago made mute due to a childhood trauma, is a servant for Mrs. Warren (Barrymore), a cantankerous, widowed invalid. The wealthy widow has two sons: one (Oliver), a hell-raiser, and the other (Brent), a gentle professor for whom Helen carries a secret torch. When three local girls—all physically handicapped—are murdered, everyone worries that Helen will be next. The tension builds as her suspicion of the killer's identity proves wrong and she is forced to confront the real madman.

Dorothy McGuire, one of the finest actresses of her day, gives a touching and totally convincing pantomime performance as the victimized mute in this prototype old-dark-house thriller. Not one thriller convention has been neglected in a picture that is virtually guaranteed to suffuse audiences with gooseflesh: creaking doors, wind-gusted curtains, flickering candles, cutaways to the menacing eyes of the unseen, unknown murdering maniac, every element of terror is in place.

Director Robert Siodmak, a gifted craftsman noted for his expressionistic style, had made a number of atmospheric suspense films for Universal before joining with producer Dory Schary and RKO for this one. Ethel Barrymore, Elsa Lanchester, and George Brent all turn in brilliant performances. Author White's novel was substantially modified for the film; in the book, the menaced serving girl had been a cripple rather than a mute, and the setting was contemporary England. Dismally remade in Britain in 1975 under the direction of Peter Collinson.

SPIRIT OF ST. LOUIS, THE

1957 135m c Biography ★★★½
Warner Bros. (U.S.) /U

James Stewart (Charles A. Lindbergh), Murray Hamilton (Bud Gurney), Patricia Smith (Mirror Girl), Bartlett Robinson (B.F. Mahoney), Robert Cornthwaite (Knight), Sheila Bond (Model/Dancer), Marc Connelly (Father Hussman), Arthur Space (Donald Hall), Harlan Warde (Boedecker), Dabbs Greer (Goldsborough)

p, Leland Hayward; d, Billy Wilder; w, Billy Wilder, Wendell Mayes, Charles Lederer (based on the book by Charles A. Lindbergh); ph, Robert Burks, Peverell Marley; ed, Arthur Schmidt; m, Franz Waxman; art d, Art Loel; fx, H.F. Koenekamp, Louis Lichtenfield

AAN Best Visual Effects: Louis Lichtenfield

Billy Wilder's re-creation of Charles A. Lindbergh's 1927 solo flight from New York to Paris is an intelligent piece, marked by James Stewart's strong performance as the brave pilot. The story, based on Lindbergh's autobiography, opens as Lindbergh is working as an airmail pilot. His flying goals go well beyond his mail route, however, and he begins to think about a solo voyage across the Atlantic, something no single pilot has ever accomplished. Lindbergh tries to find financial backers for his dream and, after much struggle, finds a willing group in St. Louis, Missouri. He has a special plane built for the trip, dubbing it *The Spirit of St. Louis* in honor of his backers. On the day he is to take off from New York, Lindbergh is forced to spend some time on the ground while waiting for the rain to stop and, in flashback, reflects on his career.

This is a well-told story, capturing the thoughts and feelings of a man alone under the most extraordinary conditions. Stewart is sincere and thoughtful in his depiction of the 1920s' greatest hero, and Wilder's direction shows the monotony of the flight while largely sidestepping the tedium which ever threatens to emerge. Perhaps the real star, though, is Waxman's marvelous score. The film gives a complete picture of Lindbergh, one that shows this dangerous journey to be the fulfillment of a devotion to and pure love of flying. The film was nominated for a Best Special Effects Oscar.

SPIRIT OF THE BEEHIVE, THE
(EL ESPIRITU DE LA COLMENA)

1973 98m c Drama ★★★★
Ellas Querejeta (Spain) /AA

Ana Torrent (Ana), Isabel Telleria (Isabel), Fernando Fernan Gomez (Fernando), Teresa Gimpera (Teresa), Jose Villasante (the Monster), Lally Soldavilla (Milagros), Juan Margallo (the Fugitive), Miguel Picazo (the Doctor)

p, Elias Querejeta; d, Victor Erice; w, Francisco J. Querejeta (based on an idea by Erice, Angel Fernandez Santos); ph, Luis Cuadrado; ed, Pablo del Amo; m, Luis de Pablo; art d, Adolfo Cofino

A haunting, atmospheric film that focuses on a young girl's obsession with the Frankenstein monster. Ana (the stunning Ana Torrent), a charming eight-year-old, lives in a Castillian village in 1940, just after the end of the Spanish Civil War. Although the village has been spared the destruction of battle, the after-effects of war are still felt, and the villagers buckle under Francoist repression. Ana's mother (Teresa Gimpera) shares a dream world with an imaginary lover; her father (Fernando Fernan Gomez) tends a beehive and ponders existence in an ongoing work he calls "The Spirit of the Beehive." After watching the 1931 James Whale-Boris Karloff version of FRANKENSTEIN, Ana begins to worry about the monster, and returns daily to the old house where her 10-year-old sister (Isabel Telleria) says he can be found. Eventually, an escaped convict becomes a surrogate for the monster, but though he is killed, Ana continues to cling to the idea that the

monster's spirit exists, holding on to the power of imagination. Slow-moving but lyrical, Victor Erice's stunning feature-film directorial debut carefully re-creates the post-Civil War period, but much more is at work here than appears at first glance. SPIRIT OF THE BEEHIVE is a thought-provoking, highly symbolic work about the isolation engendered by Franco's stultifying reign, made by one of a generation of Spanish filmmakers forced to cloak their political messages in allegory.

SPITFIRE

1942 90m bw War/Biography ★★★½
Misbourne/British Aviation (U.K.) /A

Leslie Howard (R.J. Mitchell), David Niven (Geoffrey Crisp), Rosamund John (Diana Mitchell), Roland Culver (Cmdr. Bride), Anne Firth (Miss Harper), David Horne (Higgins), J.H. Roberts (Sir Robert MacLean), Derrick de Marney (S.L. Jefferson), Rosalyn Boulter (Mabel Livesey), Tonie Edgar Bruce (Lady Houston)

p, Leslie Howard, George King, John Stafford, Adrian Brunel; d, Leslie Howard; w, Anatole de Grunwald, Miles Malleson (based on a story by Henry C. James, Katherine Strueby); ph, Georges Perinal; ed, Douglas Myers; m, William Walton; art d, Paul Sheriff

Leslie Howard, who also produced and directed here, made his last screen appearance in this above-average biography with a strong propaganda message. Howard plays R.J. Mitchell, who designed the Spitfire fighter plane, the weapon that would foil Hitler's plans to invade England by air. The film opens as a squadron of fighter pilots sits at a base, awaiting the next wave of German planes. Squadron leader Geoffrey Crisp (David Niven) begins to tell the men about his close friend Mitchell, the designer of their craft, and the details of the origin of the Spitfire are related in a lengthy flashback that makes up most of the film's running time. This was Howard's last film before he was shot out of the sky by the Luftwaffe while returning from a semi-secret diplomatic mission in Lisbon. (There are rumors that the Germans knew Churchill was to be attending a meeting in Casablanca and that Howard's plane was used as a decoy.) Niven was actually detached from the service to appear in SPITFIRE, and his smooth performance is probably the best in the film. Howard's direction is assured and keeps the story from getting bogged down in its message. The score, by "serious" composer William Walton, is superb.

SPLASH

1984 111m c Fantasy/Comedy/Romance ★★★½
Touchstone (U.S.) PG

Tom Hanks (Allen Bauer), Daryl Hannah (Madison), Eugene Levy (Walter Kornbluth), John Candy (Freddie Bauer), Dody Goodman (Mrs. Stimler), Shecky Greene (Mr. Buyrite), Richard B. Shull (Dr. Ross), Bobby Di Cicco (Jerry), Howard Morris (Dr. Zidell), Tony DiBenedetto (Tim the Doorman)

p, Brian Grazer; d, Ron Howard; w, Lowell Ganz, Babaloo Mandel, Bruce Jay Friedman (based on the story by Grazer, Friedman); ph, Don Peterman; ed, Daniel Hanley, Michael Hill; m, Lee Holdridge; prod d, Jack T. Collis; art d, John B. Mansbridge; fx, Mitch Suskin; cos, May Routh, Charles De Muth, Jody Berke

AAN Best Original Screenplay: Lowell Ganz, Babaloo Mandel, Bruce Jay Friedman, Brian Grazer

An "alien" picture from an alien source (Disney with a new moniker), SPLASH, for all its nudity and hip humor, is a throwback to pictures of days past such as NEPTUNE'S DAUGHTER (1914) and MR. PEABODY AND THE MERMAID (1948). Nevertheless, young viewers who never heard of the aforementioned thought that this film was wildly creative and flocked to the theaters. The premise is simple: boy meets girl, boy falls for girl, but girl is not girl at all—she's a mermaid. Mermaid Madison (Daryl Hannah) meets Allen Bauer (Tom Hanks), a bright, young man who is a wholesale fruit and vegetable dealer in New York. Allen works with his brother, Freddie (John Candy), a smarmy playboy pudge. Madison is human when on dry land but the moment she is touched by saltwater, she reverts to her half-woman, half-fish form. Walter Kornbluth (Eugene Levy), a scientist who suspects that Madison is a mermaid, tracks her and Allen until he finally pours water on Madison, transforming her in front of hundreds on a New York street.

Naturally, some mean government types get interested at this point. Director Ron Howard has a good sense of the whimsical, and his film is sweet and unpretentious, though somewhat ribald when one realizes the studio from whence it sprang.

SPLENDOR IN THE GRASS

1961 124m c Drama ★★★
NBI/Newton (U.S.) /X

Natalie Wood (Wilma Dean Loomis), Warren Beatty (Bud Stamper), Pat Hingle (Ace Stamper), Audrey Christie (Mrs. Loomis), Barbara Loden (Ginny Stamper), Zohra Lampert (Angelina), Fred Stewart (Del Loomis), Joanna Roos (Mrs. Stamper), Jan Norris (Juanita Howard), Gary Lockwood (Toots)

p, Elia Kazan; d, Elia Kazan; w, William Inge; ph, Boris Kaufman; ed, Gene Milford; m, David Amram; art d, Richard Sylbert; chor, George Tapps; cos, Anna Hill Johnstone

AAN Best Actress: Natalie Wood; AA Best Original Story and Screenplay: William Inge

SPLENDOR IN THE GRASS has a few firsts attached to it. It was Beatty's debut in the movies; it was Inge's first work done specifically for the screen; and it was Kazan's first picture that failed to satisfy. A self-consciously Freudian melodrama of repressed sexuality and its consequences, the film takes place in 1925 in Kansas, where Inge grew up. Beatty and Wood are high schoolers who can't consummate their love due to social constraints. Their frustration is exacerbated by Wood's shrewish mom (Christie) and Beatty's rigid, unloving dad (Hingle); madness and heartbreak result.

The title comes from Wordsworth: "There's nothing can bring back the hour / Of splendor in the grass, of glory in the flower / We will grieve not, but rather find / Strength in what remains behind." What remains of interest after more than three decades is Zohra Lampert's excellent work in a small but crucial part, and a key role in the evolution of Beatty's star image. Beatty was in his early twenties and had just appeared in Inge's play "A Loss of Roses" in 1959, after having been discovered by Josh Logan and Inge while working in a small playhouse in New Jersey. Despite that play's failure, Inge was mesmerized by Beatty and wrote this screenplay for him. Later, he would adapt James Leo Herlihy's novel All Fall Down into a screenplay for Beatty after Beatty himself had impressed another epicene playwright, Tennessee Williams, sufficiently to get the plum role in THE ROMAN SPRING OF MRS. STONE. While making this film, Beatty began the off-screen amours that have since become legendary. Wood was married to Robert Wagner (the first time around) and she was the first of many who would fall for Beatty.

In small bits, note Phyllis Diller as Texas Guinan, Sandy Dennis in her first film, and Gary Lockwood in his third. Youth exploitation pictures were all the rage at the time, and while this is better than some in execution and intent, it's still exactly that.

SPRINGTIME IN THE ROCKIES

1942 91m c Musical ★★★½
Fox (U.S.) /U

Betty Grable (Vicky), John Payne (Dan), Carmen Miranda (Rosita), Cesar Romero (Victor), Charlotte Greenwood (Phoebe Gray), Edward Everett Horton (McTavish), Frank Orth (Bickle), Harry Hayden (Brown), Jackie Gleason (Dan's Agent), Chick Chandler (Stage Manager)

p, William LeBaron; d, Irving Cummings; w, Walter Bullock, Ken Englund, Jacques Thery (based on a story by Philip Wylie); ph, Ernest Palmer; ed, Robert Simpson; art d, Richard Day, Joseph C. Wright; chor, Hermes Pan

Grable and Payne are a pair of Broadway performers and lovers who prove the truth of the old saying that those who love together also fight together. The biggest problem seems to be that Payne can't keep his mind off other women, which piques Grable to no end. To get even, she hooks up with Romero as though she intends to marry him. Payne retaliates by romancing his Brazilian secretary, Miranda. Though the premise is slight, music, dance, comedy, and even some drama are combined in a very astute manner. Much of the action is played out against the backdrop of Lake Louise, Alberta, and Palmer's Technicolor cinematography fills the screen with the beauty of the Canadian Rockies. The story sets up Grable and Romero as dancing partners, and they do a little hoofing to the accompaniment of Harry James and His Music Makers. This was the first film to give Grable top billing, and it's still easy to see why she became a wartime favorite, even if the irrepressible Miranda does steal the film.

SPY WHO CAME IN FROM THE COLD, THE

1965 112m bw Spy ★★★★
Salem (U.K.) /A

Richard Burton (Alec Leamas), Claire Bloom (Nan Perry), Oskar Werner (Fiedler), Peter Van Eyck (Hans-Dieter Mundt), Sam Wanamaker (Peters), George Voskovec (East German Defense Attorney), Rupert Davies (Smiley), Cyril Cusack (Control), Michael Hordern (Ashe), Robert Hardy (Carlton)

p, Martin Ritt; d, Martin Ritt; w, Paul Dehn, Guy Trosper (based on the novel by John Le Carre); ph, Oswald Morris; ed, Anthony Harvey; m, Sol Kaplan; prod d, Hal Pereira, Tambi Larsen; art d, Edward Marshall; cos, Motley

AAN Best Actor: Richard Burton; AAN Best Art Direction: Hal Pereira, Tambi Larsen, Edward Marshall, Josie MacAvin

Gripping grit, with a perfect performance from Burton, before Liz and alcohol robbed him of his center.

Spying is a grim, desperate business that is at once boring and exciting, with dirty work behind the scenes and hardly any derring-do. This superb adaptation of John Le Carre's novel artfully conveys that sense. Audiences must have preferred the more glamorous spies like James Bond because this film, which was one of the best ever made on the subject, failed to gather much interest at the box office. Produced and directed by Martin Ritt in Ireland and England, with some second-unit lensing in Europe, the film stars Richard Burton as a burnt-out case, a man who is looking forward to getting out of the spy game and retiring from British Intelligence. Just before he is to leave, Burton is called back to London and put on the carpet. It seems that several of his sub-agents have been caught by Van Eyck, who is Burton's counterpart on the East Berlin side. Van Eyck is a former Nazi who has taken over as chief of operations for the Communists, and his handiwork is putting a crimp in the British operations. Since it is well known that Burton is tired of what he's doing, Burton's boss, Cusack, gives him his final assignment. He is to masquerade as a drunk who wants to defect to the East Germans. If it works and Burton gets inside the Communist operations, he can find out if there is a "mole" in their own organization as well as get the goods on what's happening inside the East German operation. As part of his cover, Burton takes a job at a library and there meets Bloom, a member of the Communist party. He has a fling with her, then later, acting the drunken bully, he beats a shopkeeper and ends up in jail. When he is released, he is contacted by East German agents who believe he is ready to defect. He is taken to East Berlin, where he is grilled by Werner, Van Eyck's top assistant. Werner is convinced that Van Eyck is a double agent and believes Burton can provide information proving his theory. Burton genuinely believes the idea is absurd and continually insists that to Werner. Nevertheless, Werner has gathered enough evidence to have Van Eyck arrested, and a trial is begun to determine Van Eyck's fate. Burton is stunned when Bloom is brought in to testify at the trial, and he suddenly realizes his bosses have set him up—Van Eyck is indeed a double agent, and the whole plot has been constructed to discredit Werner, who is getting too close to the truth.

Burton's performance garnered him one of his five Oscar nominations (he lost that year to Lee Marvin in CAT BALLOU—an amazing example of middle-class taste). It's sad Burton never won, sad because one suspects a low self-belief at work in him. He probably drank to quell the early demons of deprivation, but could not obliterate them enough to still the pain. He had been touted as the next Olivier (we think he's far more interesting—and conveys heart behind the technique), before settling for celebrity as Taylor's consort. An affirmation of worth from Hollywood might have told Burton his talent not only was always apparent, but superceded his celebrity status.

There are no gimmicks, no fast cars that turn into airplanes, no weapons that fire lasers, just a tense battle of wits shot in stark black and white. The title refers to the time when an outside spy has to "come in from the cold" and take a sedentary job as another spy's control or even some menial desk assignment until the mandatory age limit forces retirement. Only Graham Greene has come close to Le Carre in detailing the emotional drudgery of the espionage world.

SPY WHO LOVED ME, THE

1977 125m c Spy   ★★
Eon   (U.K.)   PG

Roger Moore (James Bond), Barbara Bach (Maj. Anya Amasova), Curt Jurgens (Karl Stromberg), Richard Kiel (Jaws), Caroline Munro (Naomi), Walter Gotell (Gen. Gogol), Geoffrey Keen (Minister of Defense), Bernard Lee ("M"), Shane Rimmer (Capt. Carter), Bryan Marshall (Commander Talbot)

p, Albert R. Broccoli; d, Lewis Gilbert; w, Christopher Wood, Richard Maibaum (based on the novel by Ian Fleming); ph, Lamar Boren, Claude Renoir; ed, John Glen; m, Marvin Hamlisch; prod d, Ken Adam; art d, Peter Lamont; fx, Derek Meddings, Alan Maley, John Evans; cos, Ronald Paterson

AAN Best Score: Marvin Hamlisch; AAN Best Song: Marvin Hamlisch (Music), Carole Bayer Sager (Lyrics); AAN Best Art Direction: Ken Adam, Peter Lamont, Hugh Scaife

James Bond (Moore) teams with a beautiful Russian secret agent, Maj. Anya Amasova (Bach), to stop the Captain Nemo-esque Karl Stromberg (Jurgens) from using two stolen nuclear-armed submarines to destroy life on the Earth's surface so he can create an undersea kingdom. Stromberg dispatches 7-foot-2-inch, steel-toothed Jaws (Kiel) to take Bond out of the picture, and 007 leads the indestructible behemoth on a globe-trotting chase.

As the Bond series moved deeper into the 1970s, the emphasis moved away from the inventive scripts that made the best Sean Connery films fine examples of the spy genre and toward the kind of feats of daring and visual spectacle that abound in THE SPY WHO LOVED ME. Take for example Bond's daring jump off a 90-foot cliff, a feat that ski jumper Rick Sylvester was paid $30,000 to accomplish and which took 10 days to shoot. The largest studio set to date was also built to house the submarines and for Stromberg's menacing headquarters, and shooting was done in Egypt, Sardinia, Malta, Scotland, Okinawa, Switzerland, and Nassau.

STAGE DOOR

1937 83m bw Comedy/Drama   ★★★★★
RKO   (U.S.)   /U

Katharine Hepburn (Terry Randall), Ginger Rogers (Jean Maitland), Adolphe Menjou (Anthony Powell), Gail Patrick (Linda Shaw), Constance Collier (Catherine Luther), Andrea Leeds (Kaye Hamilton), Samuel S. Hinds (Henry Sims), Lucille Ball (Judy Canfield), Pierre Watkin (Richard Carmichael), Franklin Pangborn (Harcourt)

p, Pandro S. Berman; d, Gregory La Cava; w, Morrie Ryskind, Anthony Veiller, Gregory La Cava (based on the play by Edna Ferber, George S. Kaufman); ph, Robert de Grasse; ed, William Hamilton; art d, Van Nest Polglase, Carroll Clark; cos, Muriel King

AAN Best Picture; AAN Best Supporting Actress: Andrea Leeds; AAN Best Director: Gregory Lacava; AAN Best Original Screenplay: Morris Ryskind, Anthony Veiller

A stellar cast, superb direction, and a screenplay even better than the stage play on which it was based, all add up to one of the best movies about show business—or about women living together—ever made. Hepburn is a wealthy debutante from an important family. She has come to New York to seek a career on the stage and, rather than take a Park Avenue apartment far removed from the mainstream, she checks into a theatrical boarding house for young, aspiring actresses. The luck of the draw puts her in a room with Rogers (in one of her finest performances), a sarcastic tough cookie who heckles everyone. The two of them are like flint and steel and are close to hair-pulling on a few occasions. All the actresses in the boarding house spend most of their time discussing work, food, and potential husbands. But the ins and outs of their professional lives are central. Ball (who was appearing in her twenty-seventh movie at the age of 27) has been invited to dinner by some lumber barons from the Northwest and she asks Rogers to double date with her. Rogers has a short fuse, and there is no mistaking her

likes and dislikes. Among the latter is Patrick, who is more of a mistress to Broadway producer Menjou than she is an actual working actress. Leeds hasn't worked for more than 12 months and she's trying to save some money, so she often foregoes meals. She thinks she may have a chance for the ingenue lead in a new play Menjou is planning, "Enchanted April." (The actual play shown was a rewrite of The Lake, a failed Hepburn vehicle that she starred in after making SPITFIRE.)

Rogers and Miller audition for Menjou with the Hal Borne-Mort Greene song "Put Your Heart Into Your Feet and Dance," and he is taken by them, especially by Rogers. He gets them a job at a nightspot in which he has a financial stake. Menjou asks Rogers for a date and she accepts—not that she finds the old lecher attractive, she just wants to make sure she and Miller get the dance job and she also wants to give the needle to Patrick. Soon Patrick is replaced by Rogers, and fumes about the turn of events. Leeds and Hepburn go together to audition for Menjou's play, but the reading is cancelled. Leeds faints from hunger in the reception area and Hepburn promptly tells Menjou off for the cavalier fashion in which he treats actors. Although he's in his office and apparently not busy, he is sending the actors away as a power play. Now attorney Watkin enters the picture, telling Menjou that a wealthy client, Hinds (who is Hepburn's father), will back Menjou's show if Hepburn is hired for the lead.

Directing his first film since MY MAN GODFREY, La Cava showed that he could handle a large group of actors as well as he could do a straight two-lead comedy. So much work was done on the script that co-author of the play George S. Kaufman suggested waggishly that it should have been called "Screen Door." Legend has it that La Cava ordered the actresses to the studio for two weeks of rehearsal and familiarization with the boarding house set. Then he had a stenographer take their dialogue down as they sat around between rehearsals, and their words were incorporated into the script. The large cast includes Eve Arden (in her fourth film and already taking out a patent on her no-nonsense spinsters), Franklin Pangborn, Grady Sutton, and Jean Rouverol, who later became a well-known screenwriter with her husband, Hugo Butler. For years, impressions of Hepburn have used the line she speaks in while acting onstage: "The calla lillies are in bloom again." The best line in the film, though, is Rogers' marvelous barb to a friend over the phone when Gail Patrick enters the scene: "Hold on, gangrene just set in." The best prop, meanwhile, is the cat forever draped over Eve Arden's shoulders. A brilliant script and strong, realistic acting make this film a treat to the eyes and ears, and it affords the additional pleasure of seeing all those future stars like Ball, Miller, Arden, and Jack Carson in their early days.

STAGE DOOR CANTEEN

1943 132m bw Musical/War   ★★★★
UA   (U.S.)   /U

Cheryl Walker (Eileen), William Terry (Ed "Dakota"Smith), Marjorie Riordan (Jean Rule), Lon McCallister ("California"), Margaret Early (Ella Sue), Sunset Carson ("Texas"), Dorothea Kent (Mamie), Fred Brady ("Jersey" Wallace), Marion Shockley (Lillian), Patrick O'Moore (Australian)

p, Sol Lesser; d, Frank Borzage; w, Delmer Daves; ph, Harry Wild; ed, Hal C. Kern; m, Freddie Rich; prod d, Harry Horner, Clem Beauchamp; art d, Hans Peters; cos, Albert Dano

AAN Best Score: Frederic E. Rich; AAN Best Song: James Monaco (Music), Al Dubin (Lyrics)

In this boy-meets-canteen-girl story set in a Stage Door Canteen in Manhattan, three enlisted men on a one-day pass in New York fall in love with three young hostesses at the canteen. The story is nothing special, but the cast is: everybody who was anybody at the time, from Katharine Hepburn to Johnny Weissmuller to Gypsy Rose Lee to violinist Yehudi Menuhin, makes an appearance. The story is a trifle, but you'll want to see this movie in its full 132 minutes to revel in the sight of its 65 guest stars, playing themselves and seeming to have more fun than they had playing characters. The American Theatre Wing operated several Stage Door Canteens, with the flagship location on West 44th Street in Manhattan, and 90 percent of the movie's profits went back to the Theatre Wing to help defray expenses for the venues. In WWII, officers went to the officer's clubs, but at the Stage Door Canteen, you had to be ranked below officer status to be admitted. Jammed from start to finish with stars, music, laughs, tears, and pure entertainment, STAGE DOOR CANTEEN casts Cheryl Walker as Eileen, a young hostess at the Canteen who falls for soldier Dakota Smith (William Terry), while Jean Rule (Marjorie Riordan) hits it off with California (Lon McCallister) and Mamie (Dorothea Kent) goes ga-ga for Texas (Michael Harrison, aka Sunset Carson). The three soldiers meet the three women at the Canteen while on a one-day pass in New York; when their ship is delayed, they spend another day, and another, until love is in full bloom, despite the prohibition against hostesses seeing servicemen outside of the Canteen. When the boys finally do go off to war, they know the girls will be waiting for them upon their return. That's about it for plot, but writer Delmer Daves and director Frank Borzage insert into the story a cavalcade of musical and comedy numbers and many cameo appearances. In the cameos, Katherine Cornell makes her only film appearance doing a snippet of "Romeo and Juliet," George Jessel reprises his famous phone call to "Mama," Harpo Marx runs around like a nut, George Raft is seen as a dishwasher, Lunt and Fontanne have an argument, and Paul Muni rehearses his new play. Fred Rich's score gained an Oscar nomination, as did Al Dubin and Jimmy Monaco for "We Mustn't Say Goodbye," sung by Lanny Ross.

STAGE FRIGHT

1950 111m bw Thriller   ★★★★
Warner Bros./First National   (U.K.)   /A

Jane Wyman *(Eve Gill/Doris Tinsdale)*, Marlene Dietrich *(Charlotte Inwood)*, Michael Wilding *(Wilfrid O. "Ordinary" Smith)*, Richard Todd *(Jonathan Cooper)*, Alastair Sim *(Commodore Gill)*, Kay Walsh *(Nellie Goode)*, Sybil Thorndike *(Mrs. Gill)*, Miles Malleson *(Mr. Fortesque)*, Hector MacGregor *(Freddie Williams)*, Joyce Grenfell *("Lovely Ducks")*
p, Alfred Hitchcock; d, Alfred Hitchcock; w, Whitfield Cook, Alma Reville, James Bridie, Ranald MacDougall (based on the stories "Man Running" and "Outrun the Constable" by Selwyn Jepson, uncredited); ph, Wilkie Cooper; ed, E.B. Jarvis; m, Leighton Lucas; cos, Christian Dior, Milo Anderson

The standard British murder mystery is raised to a higher plateau by Hitchcock in STAGE FRIGHT, but still falters in comparison to the best of the master's works. Over the opening credits a theatrical safety curtain rises, revealing not a stage but London street life—the actual stage for Hitchcock's mystery. Eve Gill (Wyman) is an acting student at the Royal Academy of Dramatic Art (RADA) when she runs into a former boyfriend, Jonathan Cooper (Todd), who explains how his mistress, stage and singing star Charlotte Inwood (Dietrich, in marvelous form), came to him wearing a dress bloodied when she killed her husband. Because of his involvement with the singer, Jonathan is suspected and must turn to Eve for help. The plot twists are many. STAGE FRIGHT was far from being one of Hitchcock's most memorable or successful films, drawing criticism for both his provocative use of false flashbacks and the relative absence of any real threat of danger. Hitchcock's main interest in the film, and its most fascinating aspect today, is the concentration on acting and deception. Like MURDER in 1930 (and the same year's ALL ABOUT EVE), STAGE FRIGHT has an actress as the heroine. Here Eve gets her finest training not from RADA (where Hitchcock's daughter Patricia was enrolled, and where some of the film was photographed) but from real life. Her character's performance is not a simple one, forcing her to appear as something different to everyone—an actress, a maid, a Nancy Drew-type, and a newspaper reporter—with London serving as her stage, and death being her greatest fright. Shot at England's Elstree Studios, it was the last film Hitchcock shot in his home country until 1971 when he returned to film FRENZY. A special treat is Dietrich singing two of her standards: Cole Porter's "The Laziest Gal in Town" and Edith Piaf's "La Vie en Rose."

STAGECOACH

1939 97m bw Western   ★★★★★
UA   (U.S.)   /U

Claire Trevor *(Dallas)*, John Wayne *(The Ringo Kid)*, John Carradine *(Hatfield)*, Thomas Mitchell *(Dr. Josiah Boone)*, Andy Devine *(Buck Rickabaugh)*, Donald Meek *(Mr. Samuel Peacock)*, Louise Platt *(Lucy Mallory)*, George Bancroft *(Sheriff Curly Wilcox)*, Berton Churchill *(Henry Gatewood)*, Tim Holt *(Lt. Blanchard)*

p, Walter Wanger; d, John Ford; w, Dudley Nichols (based on the short story "Stage to Lordsburg" by Ernest Haycox); ph, Bert Glennon; ed, Dorothy Spencer, Walter Reynolds; m, Richard Hageman, W. Franke Harling, Louis Gruenberg, Leo Shuken, John Leipold; art d, Alexander Toluboff; fx, Ray Binger; cos, Walter Plunkett

AAN Best Picture; AA Best Supporting Actor: Thomas Mitchell; AAN Best Director: John Ford; AAN Best Cinematography: Bert Glennon; AAN Best Editing: Otho Lovering, Dorothy Spencer; AA Best Score: Richard Hageman, Frank Harling, John Leipold, Leo Shuken; AAN Best Art Direction: Alexander Toluboff

The classic western, STAGECOACH is one of John Ford's greatest frontier epics. This western eclipsed all films in the genre that had gone before it, and so vastly influenced those that followed that its stamp can be found in most superior westerns made since Ford stepped into Monument Valley for the first time. Set in a landscape of endless horizons, STAGECOACH is a wonderful, broad portrait of pioneer life in the untamed Great Southwest, as well as an in-depth character study of eight people, all diverse in their pursuits and all traveling to separate fates on a journey packed with danger.

High peril is present from the first scenes, which depict Geronimo on the warpath and telegraph wires cut by raiding Apaches. Leaving the town of Tonto, New Mexico, by stagecoach are a motley bunch of Western types. Doc Boone (Mitchell) is a conniving drunkard, long ago kicked out of the medical profession for malpractice. Dallas (Trevor) is a prostitute whose sexual exploits have so unnerved the local women that they have banded together to oust her from their scandal-mongering society. Hatfield (Carradine), meanwhile, is a shady gambler with the manners of a southern gentleman, with his own mysterious reasons for leaving Tonto. He pretends, however, that his real motivation is to offer the withdrawn Lucy (Platt), who is pregnant and married to a cavalry officer, his "protection" as she travels to be with her husband. Henry Gatewood (Churchill), a pompous and demanding banker, gets aboard the coach carrying a small valise which is locked and which he will not let go of, while Samuel Peacock (Meek), a whiskey salesman, carries a sample case. These six strangers make up the passenger list, and riding on top on the driver's seat is Buck (Devine), a garrulous type with an aversion to Indians, and tough, gruff, but fair-minded Curly (Bancroft), a lawman riding "shotgun." Before they've been on the trail very long they pick up the Ringo Kid (Wayne, in a star-making performance), whose horse has gone lame. The stagecoach is set, so to speak, so bring on the adventure!

Ford had not directed a western in 13 years before making STAGECOACH, his previous film in the genre being THREE BAD MEN. This film came as a shock to the movie community, in that Ford was no longer thought of as a western director; now he had, almost out of the blue, produced the greatest western ever seen. He would later state that "STAGECOACH blazed the trail for the 'adult' western," but this discounted too many great silent films of the genre, including his own and those of William S. Hart, who made many "adult" westerns, such as HELL'S HINGES and TUMBLEWEEDS. But STAGECOACH was nonetheless an important, sterling prototype, with in-depth characters and allegorical themes running just beneath the surface of the plot. Moveover, Ford employs a dazzling array of technical skills in presenting this film, as well as framing each breathtaking scene as if it were a painting. The landscape of the awesome Monument Valley serves both as a backdrop and a constant reminder of the freedom of the frontier and the dangers inherent in enjoying that freedom. With its arid plains, 4,000 feet above sea level, and jutting buttes, some reaching 1,500 feet, Monument Valley still startles audiences of this film today. During the 1880s, stagecoaches had actually crossed this enormous valley, and Ford made excellent use of the old coach trails which are seen running through the broad expanses like old scars. Marvelously cast and acted, stunningly shot and featuring a beautifully effective musical score, the exciting STAGECOACH was poorly remade in 1966 with Alex Cord, Ann-Margret and Bing Crosby.

STAIRWAY TO HEAVEN

1946 104m c/bw Fantasy/Romance ★★★★½
Archers/Independent Producers (U.K.) /A

David Niven (*Squadron Leader Peter D. Carter*), Kim Hunter (*June*), Roger Livesey (*Dr. Reeves*), Robert Coote (*Bob Trubshawe*), Marius Goring (*Conductor 71*), Raymond Massey (*Abraham Farlan*), Kathleen Byron (*An Angel*), Richard Attenborough (*English Pilot*), Bonar Colleano (*American Pilot*), Joan Maude (*Chief Recorder*)

p, Michael Powell, Emeric Pressburger; d, Michael Powell, Emeric Pressburger; w, Michael Powell, Emeric Pressburger; ph, Jack Cardiff; ed, Reginald Mills; m, Allan Gray; prod d, Alfred Junge; art d, Arthur Lawson; fx, Douglas Woolsey, Henry Harris; cos, Hein Heckroth

Made by Powell and Pressburger at the instigation of the Ministry of Information to promote goodwill between Britain and the US, STAIRWAY TO HEAVEN achieves an almost impossible task—blending fantasy and reality with deftness and impeccable taste.

The plot concerns an RAF pilot, Niven, who is forced to bail out of his flaming plane as it is dropping out of the sky. With all his fellow crew members either dead or having parachuted to safety and his own chute riddled with bullet holes, Niven gets on the radio and shares what he believes to be his last words with an American WAC, Hunter. Niven, a poet, has a romantic conversation with Hunter and falls hopelessly in love with her voice. When he finally jumps for his life, he lands in the ocean and is washed safely ashore. By some fateful coincidence he meets Hunter and the pair fall in love. Although Niven appears to be healthy, he actually is suffering from brain damage and must undergo an operation. Meanwhile, in heaven it is realized that a terrible mistake has been made, that Niven, who was scheduled to die, has somehow lived. This discovery is made by Heavenly Conductor Number 71, Goring, a Frenchman who was beheaded in his country's revolution. While Goring and his superiors debate Niven's fate, Niven argues that because of their mistake and because he has fallen in love with Hunter, he should be allowed to remain on Earth.

Shining with surrealistic cinematic bravura (the fantasy sequences were shot in black and white, the earthly ones in color), STAIRWAY TO HEAVEN is a marvel, with a notable contribution from production designer Junge. Most remarkable is his monumental stairway which reaches majestically into the heavens, peopled with a cast of history's dead. Niven and Livesey enjoy two of their finest roles, Hunter is warm and appealing, Goring a quirky delight, and such actors as Coote, Massey and Abraham Sofaer (as God, no less) are clearly having a blast. Chosen as the first of the Royal Command Film Performances, STAIRWAY TO HEAVEN garnered some critical acclaim in Britain but was generally attacked by stuffy detractors who felt it was anti-British. It received a far warmer welcome in the US.

STAKEOUT

1987 115m c Crime ★★★½
Touchstone/Silver Screen Partners III (U.S.) R/15

Richard Dreyfuss (*Chris Leece*), Emilio Estevez (*Bill Reimers*), Madeleine Stowe (*Maria McGuire*), Aidan Quinn (*Richard "Stick" Montgomery*), Dan Lauria (*Phil Coldshank*), Forest Whitaker (*Jack Pismo*), Ian Tracey (*Caylor Reese*), Earl Billings (*Capt. Giles*), Jackson Davies (*FBI Agent Lusk*), J.J. Makaro

p, Jim Kouf, Cathleen Summers; d, John Badham; w, Jim Kouf; ph, John Seale; ed, Tom Rolf, Michael Ripps; m, Arthur B. Rubinstein; prod d, Philip Harrison; art d, Richard Hudolin, Michael Ritter

It doesn't matter that this film is a traditional cop vs. killer picture, since it is presented in very human terms and sparkles with top-flight performances from Richard Dreyfuss, Emilio Estevez, and Madeleine Stowe. Chris Leece (Dreyfuss) is a plainclothes detective on the Seattle police force, a man with a thankless job and an empty life until he and his partner, Bill Reimers (Estevez), are assigned to stake out the home of Maria McGuire (Stowe), the former girlfriend of escaped killer Stick Montgomery (Aidan Quinn). Chris meets Maria when he pretends to be a phone repairman and bugs her phones, and they are quickly attracted to each other. But fugitive Montgomery plans to retrieve not only the loot from his last job (hidden in Maria's apartment) but also his girl. STAKEOUT is a well-handled, quick-paced, and often funny film that accurately details the humdrum routine of police work.

Director John Badham expertly mixes just the right amount of action with a very delightful romance. This movie is a virtuoso return for Dreyfuss, who is captivating in his role.

STALAG 17

1953 120m bw Comedy/War ★★★★½
Paramount (U.S.) /PG

William Holden (*Sefton*), Don Taylor (*Lt. Dunbar*), Otto Preminger (*Oberst Von Scherbach*), Robert Strauss (*"Animal" Stosh*), Harvey Lembeck (*Harry*), Richard Erdman (*Hoffy*), Peter Graves (*Price*), Neville Brand (*Duke*), Sig Rumann (*Schultz*), Michael Moore (*Manfredi*)

p, Billy Wilder; d, Billy Wilder; w, Billy Wilder, Edwin Blum (based on the play by Donald Bevan, Edmund Trzcinski); ph, Ernest Laszlo; ed, Doane Harrison, George Tomasini; m, Franz Waxman; art d, Hal Pereira, Franz Bachelin; fx, Gordon Jennings

AA Best Actor: William Holden; *AAN Best Supporting Actor:* Robert Strauss; *AAN Best Director:* Billy Wilder

The trenchant trenches of a German POW camp, uneven but not without its gallows humor fascination. Made just eight years after the end of WWII, writer-director Wilder's classic black comedy is too cross-pollinated by slapstick Germans, who interfere with the abrasive edge of satirical statements on free enterprise and oppressed peoples banding together to become a variation on witch-hunting fascists. But the film did amazing things for Holden. Even in SUNSET BOULEVARD he was transforming from the handsome juvenille lead of yore. His performance made him Bogie's successor to American Cynicism; without a doubt, Holden was one of the finest actors of his generation, thanks to his scrunched-face concentration which surprised you with its quick-change range. Holden plays Sefton, the glib loner whose scams and scheming make life in Stalag 17 bearable for him but incurs the wrath of his fellow POWs. Still, they willingly participate in the games and attractions (like observing female Russian prisoners through a telescope) he operates for fun and profit. When two prisoners are killed while trying to escape, the Americans come to believe an informer is in their midst, and suspicion falls on Sefton. Later, after the camp's sadistic commandant, Von Scherbach (brilliantly played by director Preminger, in a take on Stroheim in LA GRANDE ILLUSION), learns how newcomer Dunbar (Don Taylor) managed to blow up a train, the POWs are certain Sefton is the rat and make life miserable for him.

Unlike previous POW films, Wilder and co-writer Edwin Blum's script, based on the play by Donald Bevan and Edmund Trzcinski, presents the prisoners not as paragons of patriotic virtue but as real, self-interested, bored soldiers trying to survive. Holden is magnificent as the heel-turned-hero, but STALAG 17 is full of wonderful, well-directed performances, including Sig Rumann as the barracks guard (the prototype for John Banner's Sgt. Schultz on "Hogan's Heroes," the long-running TV series inspired by the film); Gil Stratton, Jr., as Sefton's gopher; Harvey Lembeck and Robert Strauss as the barracks clowns; and real-life war hero Neville Brand. Peppered with Wilder's distinctive biting wit, STALAG 17 was justly a hit with the critics and at the box office.

STALKER

1979 161m c/bw Science Fiction ★★★½
Mosfilm Unit 2 (U.S.S.R.) /PG

Aleksandr Kaidanovsky (*Stalker*), Nikolai Grinko (*Professor*), Anatoly Solonitsin (*Writer*), Alisa Freindlikh (*Stalker's Wife*), Natasha Abramova ("*Monkey*"—*Stalker's Daughter*), F. Yurna, E. Kostin, R. Rendi

p, Alexandra Demidova; d, Andrei Tarkovsky; w, Boris Strugatsky, Arkady Strugatsky (based on their novel *Roadside Picnic*); ph, Aleksandr Knyazhinsky; ed, L. Feiginovoi; m, Eduard Artemyev; prod d, Andrei Tarkovsky; art d, A. Merkulov; cos, N. Fominoi

Andrei Tarkovsky's STALKER is a metaphysical allegory in the guise of a sci-fi adventure, that like most of this visionary director's films, alternates between mesmerizing brilliance and intense boredom.

In a futuristic and desolate industrial wasteland, there exists a supernatural "Zone" which contains a miraculous "Room," where all of one's wishes will be granted. The Zone has been declared off limits, but unauthorized guides known as Stalkers still lead travellers inside.

One such Stalker (Aleksandr Kaidanovsky) meets a Writer (Anatoly Solonitsin), and a Professor (Nikolai Grinko) who hire him to take them into the Zone, and the Stalker agrees to do so, despite his wife's (Alisa Freindlikh) fears that he'll be imprisoned again. The Writer says he's going there because he's lost his inspiration and the Professor claims to be going for scientific reasons. The three men sneak past a police guard, then travel down railroad tracks until they reach the Zone. The men work their way through a complex tunnel system, and after emerging from the final tunnel, known as the "meat grinder," they reach the threshold of the mysterious Room.

STALKER is an impenetrable film about the inexplicable mysteries of the universe, that's open to myriad interpretations. Anyone looking for a typical sci-fi film will be sorely disappointed, for Tarkovsky merely uses the basic plot as a metaphor, with the trip to the Zone being a spiritual journey into the heart of one's soul. The Stalker, Writer, and Professor, represent Blind Faith, Jaded Art, and Amoral Science, respectively, and the characters spend most of the trip philosophizing. The methodical tracking shots and lumbering movements of the actors are so painfully slow that one feels the weight and gravity of each and every shot, but just when one is lulled into a narcotized state, Tarkovsky comes up with some stunning cinematic moments, such as the mystical framing scenes, where the earsplitting roar of a train shaking the Stalker's house is undercut by the soothing sound of Beethoven's "Ode to Joy." Tarkovsky was undoubtedly a serious artist, but his films operate on their own private wavelength of sometimes maddening deliberateness which can create a hypnotic and soporific effect simultaneously and STALKER certainly has its share of both, but it also has enough hauntingly beautiful images and profound ideas to linger in one's mind.

STAND AND DELIVER

1988   105m   c   Biography   ★★★
American Playhouse   (U.S.)   PG/15

Edward James Olmos (Jaime Escalante), Lou Diamond Phillips (Angel), Rosana DeSoto (Fabiola Escalante), Andy Garcia (Ramirez), Ingrid Oliu (Lupe), Karla Montana (Claudia), Vanessa Marquez (Ana), Mark Eliot (Tito), Patrick Baca (Javier), Will Gotay (Pancho)

p, Tom Musca; d, Ramon Menendez; w, Ramon Menendez, Tom Musca; ph, Tom Richmond; ed, Nancy Richardson; m, Craig Safan; cos, Kathryn Morrison

AAN Best Actor: Edward James Olmos

Another one of those teachers who uses entertainment to save young souls, this time in East Los Angeles. Based on a true story, the movie stars Edward James Olmos as Jaime Escalante, a math teacher at East LA's Garfield High. Escalante's class is filled with kids who have no desire to learn—they come late to class, can't do multiplication, talk and eat in class, and live in fear of gang violence. Escalante, however, is no ordinary high school teacher—he's a Movie Teacher (cf. DEAD POET'S SOCIETY), so he wear costumes, engages in amateur theatrics (he dresses as a chef and violently slices up apples to illustrate the concept of fractions), and refers to his class as a "show." Gradually the students respond to his style. With his school facing a loss of accreditation, Escalante makes a radical request—to prepare his students for the Advanced Placement exams in Calculus. Carefully scripted and well acted, STAND AND DELIVER is sentimental and utterly predictable but better than many films of this kind. First-time director Ramon Menendez, a Cuban UCLA graduate, gives the charismatic Olmos a showcase.

STAND BY ME

1986   87m   c   Comedy   ★★★½
Columbia   (U.S.)   R/15

Wil Wheaton (Gordie Lachance), River Phoenix (Chris Chambers), Corey Feldman (Teddy Duchamp), Jerry O'Connell (Vern Tessio), Richard Dreyfuss (The Writer), Kiefer Sutherland (Ace Merrill), Casey Siemaszko (Billy Tessio), Gary Riley (Charlie Hogan), Bradley Gregg (Eyeball Chambers), Jason Oliver (Vince Desjardins)

p, Andrew Scheinman, Bruce A. Evans, Raynold Gideon; d, Rob Reiner; w, Raynold Gideon, Bruce A. Evans (based on the novella *The Body* by Stephen King); ph, Thomas Del Ruth; ed, Robert Leighton; m, Jack Nitzsche; prod d, J. Dennis Washington; fx, Richard L. Thompson, Henry Millar; cos, Sue Moore

AAN Best Adapted Screenplay: Raynold Gideon, Bruce A. Evans

From the moment we hear the Ben E. King-Mike Stoller-Jerry Lieber hit "Stand By Me," we know we're in for a nostalgia trip, but STAND BY ME is a lot more than that. The picture is framed by the reminiscences of a writer (Richard Dreyfuss). Hearing about a friend's death, he recalls the summer of 1959, when he and his 12-year-old friends spent their time hanging around doing what boys do. Gordie (Wil Wheaton) is the writer as a youth, and he's joined by Chris (River Phoenix), a somewhat older kid who's considered bad because of his family, Teddy (Corey Feldman), an erratic boy whose father is in a mental hospital, and pudgy Vern (Jerry O'Connell). Vern hears his older brother (Casey Siemaszko) tell a pal that his gang found the body of a missing boy while they were out for a spin in a stolen car, and when he repeats the story to his own pals, they set out to find the body.

Directed by Rob Reiner from a semi-autobiographical Stephen King story, STAND BY ME is a sentimental film that works because of its unsentimental moments—in particular, its sometimes embarrassingly honest portrayal of what interests boys and how they talk about it. Reiner elicits some excellent performances from his young cast (River Phoenix is a standout) and Kiefer Sutherland is memorable as a menacing teen hood.

STAR!

1968   175m   c   Musical/Biography   ★★★½
Fox   (U.S.)   G/U

Julie Andrews (Gertrude Lawrence), Richard Crenna (Richard Aldrich), Michael Craig (Sir Anthony Spencer), Daniel Massey (Noel Coward), Robert Reed (Charles Fraser), Bruce Forsyth (Arthur Lawrence), Beryl Reid (Rose), John Collin (Jack Roper), Alan Oppenheimer (Andre Charlot), Richard Karlan (David Holtzman)

p, Saul Chaplin; d, Robert Wise; w, William Fairchild; ph, Ernest Laszlo; ed, William Reynolds; prod d, Boris Leven; fx, L.B. Abbott, Art Cruickshank, Emil Kosa Jr.; chor, Michael Kidd; cos, Donald Brooks

AAN Best Supporting Actor: Daniel Massey; *AAN Best Cinematography:* Ernest Laszlo; *AAN Best Score:* Lennie Hayton; *AAN Best Song:* James Van Heusen (Music), Sammy Cahn (Lyrics); *AAN Best Art Direction:* Boris Leven, Walter M. Scott, Howard Bristol; *AAN Best Costume Design:* Donald Brooks; *AAN Best Sound:* 20th Century-Fox Studio Sound Department

Gertrude Lawrence was a huge star in England and on Broadway, but not in movies, and this cinematic biography left audiences wondering why Fox spent about $14 million to tell her story. Julie Andrews, on the other hand, was a huge marquee star after MARY POPPINS and THE SOUND OF MUSIC, and director Robert Wise and producer Saul Chaplin thought she would make a smashing Lawrence. Viewers disagreed, and the picture plummeted from its opening day. (It was re-released in a cut version, titled THOSE WERE THE HAPPY TIMES, a year later, but with no success either.) The film begins during WWII, as Lawrence, starring in the musical play *Lady in the Dark*, watches a newsreel about her own life. The film flashes back to 1915 in Clapham, England, when she leaves home to join her vaudevillian father (Bruce Forsyth), who is working in a run-down Brixton music hall. Gertrude decides to follow in her dad's footsteps and gets a job as a chorine in one of Andre Charlot's famous revues. Though Charlot (Alan Oppenheimer) is annoyed when she steals scenes and throws carefully rehearsed sketches out of whack, stage manager Jack Roper (John Collin) steps in and keeps her from getting fired. Jack and Gertrude marry but cannot agree on her role as a wife (he wants her to stay home; she wants to perform). After their daughter is born, Gertrude leaves. She becomes great friends with Noel Coward (Daniel Massey, who actually was Coward's godson), who uses his influence to get her a spot in Charlot's latest show, and she is instantly acclaimed as a new find after the opening in New York. Her career and romantic prospects soar, but her relationship with her neglected daughter (Jenny Agutter) is poor; moreover, she spends all her considerable earnings and overtaxes herself to pay her debts. After her success in Coward's *Tonight at 8:30*, she appears in *Susan and God*, showing she can play drama, then meets banker and theatrical dabbler Richard Aldrich (Richard Crenna) and appears in his staging of *Skylark*. Afterward, she moves on to *Lady in the Dark*, marries Aldrich, and is happy and fulfilled at last. There the picture ends, though in real life Lawrence lived another eight years and died at age 54. The movie lost millions, but it deserved a better fate for its enormous score, top-flight production, excellent choreography, and fine acting.

STAR 80

1983 102m c Biography   ★★★★
Ladd/Warner Bros. (U.S.)   R/18

Mariel Hemingway *(Dorothy Stratten)*, Eric Roberts *(Paul Snider)*, Cliff Robertson *(Hugh Hefner)*, Carroll Baker *(Dorothy's Mother)*, Roger Rees *(Aram Nicholas)*, David Clennon *(Geb)*, Josh Mostel *(Private Detective)*, Lisa Gordon *(Eileen)*, Sidney Miller *(Nightclub Owner)*, Keith Hefner *(Photographer)*

p, Wolfgang Glattes, Kenneth Utt; d, Bob Fosse; w, Bob Fosse (based on "Death of a Playmate" by Teresa Carpenter); ph, Sven Nykvist; ed, Alan Heim; m, Ralph Burns; art d, Jack G. Taylor Jr., Michael Bolton; cos, Albert Wolsky

Brilliant and sickening. Bob Fosse's version of the short life and gory death of *Playboy* "Playmate of the Year" Dorothy Stratten focuses on the machinations and tacky ambitions of her boyfriend/murderer Paul Snider, hypnotically played by Eric Roberts. Stratten (Mariel Hemingway, who underwent breast augmentation for the role) is shown as sweet small-town girl, easy prey for sleazy mediocrity Snider, who promises to make her a star. He marries her and brings her to Los Angeles, where she *does* become a star (a starlet, anyway—Stratten did an acceptable job in one film, Peter Bogdanovich's THEY ALL LAUGHED), she dumps Snider for the glitzy, cocaine-snorting Playboy mansion crowd, hangs out with Hef (Cliff Robertson) and has an affair with Aram Nicholas (a fictionalized Bogdanovich, played by Roger Rees). Snider reacts with murderous rage. Fosse's last film is a disturbing essay on sex, violence and showbiz in a world where attractive women function as tokens of exchange between men. A must-see that is guaranteed to ruin your day.

STAR IS BORN, A

1937 111m c Drama   ★★★★½
Selznick (U.S.)

Janet Gaynor *(Esther Blodgett/Vicki Lester)*, Fredric March *(Norman Maine)*, Adolphe Menjou *(Oliver Niles)*, Andy Devine *(Danny McGuire)*, May Robson *(Lettie)*, Lionel Stander *(Libby)*, Owen Moore *(Casey Burke)*, Elizabeth Jenns *(Anita Regis)*, J.C. Nugent *(Theodore Smythe)*, Clara Blandick *(Aunt Mattie)*

p, David O. Selznick; d, William A. Wellman; w, Dorothy Parker, Alan Campbell, Robert Carson, David O. Selznick, William A. Wellman, Ring Lardner Jr., Budd Schulberg, John Lee Mahin (based on the story by Wellman, Carson); ph, W. Howard Greene; ed, James E. Newcom; m, Max Steiner; art d, Lyle Wheeler; fx, Jack Cosgrove; cos, Omar Kiam

AAN Best Picture; AAN Best Actor: Fredric March; *AAN Best Actress:* Janet Gaynor; *AAN Best Director:* William Wellman; *AA Best Original Story:* William A. Wellman, Robert Carson; *AAN Best Screenplay:* Alan Campbell, Robert Carson, Dorothy Parker

March is a movie superstar whose heyday has slipped by, although he is still held in high esteem by his producer and studio head, Menjou. Everyone, except March, seems to know that he is losing popularity with the public and his films are seeing less and less box-office success. At a Hollywood party where he drinks too much, as usual, March meets and is attracted to Gaynor, who is serving sandwiches and, in his cups, he proposes to make her a star. She has been longing to become an actress and has been starving while waiting for Central Casting to call her for her big break. This call never comes, which annoys her boarding house owner, Kennedy, no end. March winds up breaking the dishes Gaynor is responsible for and charming her into leaving the party with him, later painting for her a life of splendor and happiness as a movie star, encouraging her to follow his lead. March persuades a reluctant

Menjou to give Gaynor a screen test Impressed, Menjou decides to make her a star. March and Gaynor marry and, while her career accelerates, his takes a complete nosedive. Soon he's the most unemployable actor in Hollywood, shamelessly getting drunk in public and embarrassing a wife who loves him in spite of himself.

A STAR IS BORN captures wonderfully the hustle of Hollywood, especially in scenes which show Gaynor being physically (and painfully) prepared for stardom by having her perfectly acceptable face redone by cosmetic experts, facial experts, eyebrow experts, hair stylists, and makeup magicians—these scenes lack the forced "let's kid Judy" energy of the 1954 version—they're colder. It profiles the behind-the-scenes machinations of stars and producers, and it shows that, however accidentally, a person of talent, sincerity, and good-heartedness sometimes slips through the corrosive Hollywood system to become a star. The film is marvelously constructed by Wellman, who elicited superb performances from his stars.

The dialogue created for this film is tough, and most of the words Stander is given to growl portray him and the many Hollywood types similar to his character as vindictive and ruthless, people without pity, charisma, or compassion. Even after March dies of drowning, Stander can only spit out vicious quips: "First drink of water he's had in 20 years, and then he had to get it by accident. How do you wire congratulations to the Pacific Ocean?" Producer Menjou is no less cynical when evaluating the movie-going public: "Fans will write to anyone for a picture. It only takes a three-cent stamp, and that makes pictures cheaper than wallpaper." Of course, much of this acid-dripping dialogue stemmed from the black humor for which "Algonquin Round Table" member Dorothy Parker was famous.

STAR IS BORN, A

1954 176m c Musical   ★★★★★
Transcona (U.S.)   PG/A

Judy Garland *(Esther Blodgett/Vicki Lester)*, James Mason *(Norman Maine)*, Jack Carson *(Matt Libby)*, Charles Bickford *(Oliver Niles)*, Tommy Noonan *(Danny McGuire)*, Lucy Marlow *(Lola Lavery)*, Amanda Blake *(Susan Ettinger)*, Irving Bacon *(Graves)*, Hazel Shermet *(Libby's Secretary)*, James Brown *(Glenn Williams)*

p, Sidney Luft; d, George Cukor; w, Moss Hart (based on the Dorothy Parker, Alan Campbell, Robert Carson screenplay from a story by William A. Wellman, Carson, based on the film WHAT PRICE HOLLYWOOD); ph, Sam Leavitt; ed, Folmar Blangsted, Craig Holt; m, Harold Arlen; prod d, Gene Allen; art d, Malcolm Bert; fx, H.F. Koenekamp; chor, Lize Bechtold Blyth, Eric Durst; cos, Jean Louis, Mary Ann Nyberg, Irene Sharaff

AAN Best Actor: James Mason; *AAN Best Actress:* Judy Garland; *AAN Best Score:* Ray Heindorf; *AAN Best Song:* Harold Arlen (Music), Ira Gershwin (Lyrics); *AAN Best Art Direction:* Malcolm Bert, Gene Allen, Irene Sharaff, George James Hopkins; *AAN Best Costume Design:* Jean Louis, Mary Ann Nyberg, Irene Sharaff

Judy Garland is at her peak, pulling out all the stops, daring the gods in this dark, weighty fable of the price one pays to be at the top. This version, directed by Cukor, is lent all manner of mythic significance by Garland, teetering on the abyss before the slide. There would be other triumphs in concert, but this is the peak of her film career. Here she finally exposed her powerful dramatic range, coupled with the magnificent singing voice that she pushed further than anyone could imagine. Her genius is attached to an uncomfortable, intense plot that allows reason for the tremulous mannerisms and bottomless, dark eyes.

The plot essentially follows that of the original 1936 film (directed by William Wellman and starring Janet Gaynor and Fredric March). A young singer (Garland) saves Norman Maine (James Mason), a star actor, from making a drunken fool of himself on stage. Later, a sober Norman hears her sing and decides to help this incredible talent get started in pictures. Eventually (after she changes her name from Esther Blodgett to Vicki Lester), he manages to get her the lead in a big musical. As Vicki's star rises, however, Norman's begins to fall. The two elope, but their happiness is short-lived, and Norman's drinking increases when he is cut by his studio. Frustrated by the fickleness of his public and "friends," he drunkenly interrupts the Oscar ceremonies where Vicki has won the award for Best Actress, humbly pleading for a job and accidentally slapping his wife during the presentation ceremony. Despite all Vicki's attempts to find Norman work in Hollywood, his slide cannot be stopped by his wife's love.

Director George Cukor previously filmed the story as WHAT PRICE HOLLYWOOD? in 1932. Here he delivers a much more savage film, allowing moments and characters to speak for themselves in a way that give A STAR IS BORN that much more power. Garland is well matched by Mason, who imbues Norman's hellish descent with a deep sense of self-understanding, a dignified awareness of what is transpiring and ultimate acceptance of fate. And in the scenes of drunkenness, a threatening aura of danger that seems to give him an unhuman kind of vigor and strength. If Mason looks healthier than Garland sometimes, it works. Policing and caretaking an addict takes enormous energy; sometimes the toll is greater on the spouse than the addict themselves. Mason's work on STAR is the equal of any good performance you can name.

Harold Arlen and Ira Gershwin provided Garland with songs that would become standards in her concert repertoire, including the ten-ton torch song, "The Man That Got Away" (which earned an Oscar nomination for Best Song), rendered by Garland with incredible emotional power. Leonard Gershe's classic "Born in a Trunk" sequence is also one of Garland's finest moments, a near-autobiographical musical sequence that shows the star's rise, incorporating the songs "I'll Get By," "You Took Advantage of Me," "Black Bottom," "Peanut Vendor," "My Melancholy Baby," and "Swanee." After Garland's Oscar-nominated performance lost to Grace Kelly's amateur thesping in THE COUNTRY GIRL, many in Hollywood felt that she was being punished by her peers for her past troubles, and Groucho Marx sent a telegram to Garland saying that the loss "was the biggest robbery since Brink's."

Warners stupidly cut A STAR IS BORN considerably after its premiere, but Cukor's version was eventually partially restored through the reinsertion of recovered soundtrack with production stills and some alternate takes that had somehow survived, giving the film a continuity that unfeeling hands had removed. Seemingly vindicated, Cukor passed away the night before he was to see his restored film, which reopened in 1983 to enthusiastic crowds. George Hoyningen-Huene consulted on the color, which gives the film either somber depth or hysterical, raw splashes of color—it's exactly right. If this version is more closely aligned with showbiz tradition than the 1937 version, it works, largely because it underlines the Garland legend. With Jack Carson in a definitive role as a bastard press agent, and Lucy Marlow and Joan Shawlee as putrid starlet and columnist and Tommy Noonan, surprisingly effective as Garland's jazz musician pal, in the best role of his career.

STAR IS BORN, A
1976 140m c Musical ★★★
Warner Bros. (U.S.) R/15

Barbra Streisand *(Esther Hoffman)*, Kris Kristofferson *(John Norman Howard)*, Gary Busey *(Bobby Ritchie)*, Oliver Clark *(Gary Danziger)*, Vanetta Fields, Clydie King *(The Oreos)*, Marta Heflin *(Quentin)*, M.G. Kelly *(Bebe Jesus)*, Sally Kirkland *(Photographer)*, Joanne Linville *(Freddie)*

p, Jon Peters; d, Frank Pierson; w, John Gregory Dunne, Joan Didion, Frank Pierson (based on a story by William A. Wellman, Robert Carson); ed, Peter Zinner; m, Roger Kellaway; prod d, Polly Platt; art d, William M. Hiney; fx, Chuck Gaspar; chor, David Winters; cos, Shirley Strahm, Seth Banks

AAN Best Cinematography: Robert Surtees; *AAN Best Score:* Roger Kellaway; *AA Best Song:* Barbra Streisand (Music), Paul Williams (Lyrics); *AAN Best Sound:* Robert Knudson, Dan Wallin, Robert Glass, Tom Overton

The fourth remake of this story, this is a fairly good, though overlong, film, executive-produced by Barbra Streisand and produced by her companion of the time, Jon Peters. Rock star John Norman Howard (Kris Kristofferson) takes solace in booze while his career slides. After a particularly embarrassing concert performance, the sullen star visits a nightclub where the interracial female singing trio "The Oreos" is performing. Impressed by the talents of Oreo Esther Hoffman (Streisand), John gets her an audition that leads to a recording contract.

An album is released, Esther becomes a star, and she and John marry. But, as everyone watching expects, trouble looms in paradise as her career soars and his plummets. John ruins Esther's Grammy acceptance speech, staggering onstage to interrupt her triumph. Eventually he leaves her and dies in a car crash. The picture should have ended there; unfortunately, a lengthy coda follows, with Esther performing a concert dedicated to her late husband. Streisand fans will love this extra footage, but others will yawn. The songs, from several sources but mostly by Paul Williams and Kenny Ascher, range in quality from "Watch Closely Now" (a dreadful, interminable tune sung too often by Kristofferson) to "Evergreen," cowritten by Streisand and Williams. Director Frank Pierson clashed repeatedly with Streisand and later made some much-publicized charges blasting the star for megalomania.

STAR TREK II: THE WRATH OF KHAN
1982 113m c Science Fiction ★★★½
Paramount (U.S.) PG

William Shatner *(Adm. James T. Kirk)*, Leonard Nimoy *(Mr. Spock)*, DeForest Kelley *(Dr. Leonard "Bones" McCoy)*, Ricardo Montalban *(Khan Noonian Singh)*, James Doohan *(Chief Engineer Montgomery "Scotty" Scott)*, Walter Koenig *(Chekov)*, George Takei *(Sulu)*, Nichelle Nichols *(Cmdr. Uhura)*, Bibi Besch *(Dr. Carol Marcus)*, Merritt Butrick *(David Marcus)*

p, Robert Sallin; d, Nicholas Meyer; w, Jack B. Sowards (based on a story by Sowards and Harve Bennett and on the TV series "Star Trek"); ph, Gayne Rescher; ed, William Dornisch; m, James Horner; prod d, Joseph R. Jennings; art d, Michael Minor, Ken Ralston, Jim Veillieux, Alan Howarth

Of the first three Trek films, #2 comes closest to the spirit of the TV series. It's conceived as a sequel to the "Space Seed" episode from the 1967 show, in which Kirk had banished the evil Khan (Ricardo Montalban) to the edge of the universe. Now Khan is back and looking for revenge, via a device capable of reversing creation. This is one of the most popular in the series, thanks to a high action quotient (including a tensely staged space battle), a suitably campy turn by Montalban, and the shock value of Spock's "death." There is some novelty value, too, in the focus on Kirk's family life back on Earth.

STAR TREK IV: THE VOYAGE HOME
1986 119m c Fantasy/Science Fiction ★★★
Paramount (U.S.) PG

William Shatner *(James T. Kirk)*, Leonard Nimoy *(Mr. Spock)*, DeForest Kelley *(Dr. Leonard "Bones" McCoy)*, James Doohan *(Chief Engineer Montgomery "Scotty" Scott)*, George Takei *(Sulu)*, Walter Koenig *(Chekov)*, Nichelle Nichols *(Comdr. Uhura)*, Majel Barrett *(Dr. Christine Chapel)*, Jane Wyatt *(Amanda, Spock's Mother)*, Catherine Hicks *(Dr. Gillian Taylor)*

p, Harve Bennett; d, Leonard Nimoy; w, Harve Bennett, Steve Meerson, Peter Krikes, Nicholas Meyer (based on a story by Leonard Nimoy, Harve Bennett, and the TV series created by Gene Roddenberry); ph, Don Peterman; ed, Peter E. Berger; m, Leonard Rosenman; prod d, Jack T. Collis; art d, Joe Aubel, Pete Smith; fx, Michael Lantieri; cos, Robert Fletcher

AAN Best Cinematography: Don Peterman; *AAN Best Score:* Leonard Rosenman; *AAN Best Sound:* Terry Porter, Dave Hudson, Mel Metcalfe, Gene S. Cantamessa; *AAN Best Sound Effects Editing:* Mark Mangini

With directorial tongue firmly in cheek, Leonard Nimoy again takes the helm (he had begun his career with the lumbering third episode), in this environmentally-minded installment which sends our heroes back in time to 1986 San Francisco. Spock gives a Vulcan pinch to a punk, Kirk gets lost on a bus, and we learn the importance of saving the whales. (A huge space probe is threatening to destroy 23rd-century Earth unless a whale—by then extinct—can be found for it to "chat" with.) By far the silliest and most self-mocking of the series, with the interplay between Spock and Kirk veering somewhere between Hope and Crosby and Cheech and Chong, but also one of the most successful, grossing around $110 million.

STAR TREK: FIRST CONTACT

1996 105m c Science Fiction/Adventure ★★★
Rick Berman (U.S.) PG-13/12

Patrick Stewart (*Captain Jean-Luc Picard*), Jonathan Frakes (*Commander William Riker*), Brent Spiner (*Lieutenant Commander Data*), LeVar Burton (*Lieutenant Commander Geordi La Forge*), Michael Dorn (*Lieutenant Commander Worf*), Gates McFadden (*Dr. Beverly Crusher*), Marina Sirtis (*Counselor Deanna Troi*), Alfre Woodard (*Lily Sloane*), James Cromwell (*Zefram Cochrane*), Alice Krige (*Borg Queen*)

p, Rick Berman; d, Jonathan Frakes; w, Rick Berman, Brannon Braga, Ronald D. Moore (from a story by Rick Berman, Brannon Braga and Ronald D. Moore, based on characters created by Gene Rodenberry); ph, Matthew F. Leonetti; ed, John W. Wheeler; m, Jerry Goldsmith; prod d, Herman Zimmerman; art d, Ron Wilkinson; fx, Terry D. Frazee, Jeff Olson, Scott Rader, Adam Howard, Industrial Light & Magic; cos, Deborah Everton

AAN Best Makeup: Michael Westmore, Scott Wheeler, Jake Garber

The eighth film in the STAR TREK movie series, FIRST CONTACT continues the tradition of the even-numbered entries' superiority. It's the second STAR TREK movie to feature the cast of TV's "The Next Generation," and the first with no members of the original show's cast.

In the 24th century, Captain Jean-Luc Picard (Patrick Stewart) is breaking in a new Starship Enterprise when the Borg, a notoriously fearsome race of cyborgs, attack. Rather than fight fair, the Borg travel back to the 21st century to alter the course of human events to their advantage, and it's up to Picard and crew to stop them.

Saving the universe is small potatoes compared to the real mission assigned to Jonathan Frakes (who plays Commander William Riker and also directed), Stewart, and company. This installment's prime directive: Save the STAR TREK franchise! Without the popular cast of the original series or the guidance of the late Gene Roddenberry, the future looked uncertain. However, now free of the demands of "classic TREK" mythology, FIRST CONTACT demonstrates that Trek flicks can actually be decent films. The story line follows up on a popular "Next Generation" episode, in which Picard is captured and assimilated by the Borg. All the show's favorites—including Picard, Data (Brent Spiner), Deanna (Marina Sirtis), and Worf the Klingon (Michael Dorn)—reprise their roles. The film may be action-heavy, but it features a smartly-written script and, in a big departure from TREK tradition, camp-free acting. Stewart and Alice Krige, who stars as the dangerously seductive Borg Queen, both give performances of surprising depth.

STAR WARS

1977 121m c Science Fiction ★★★★½
20th Century Fox (U.S.) PG/U

Mark Hamill (*Luke Skywalker*), Harrison Ford (*Han Solo*), Carrie Fisher (*Princess Leia Organa*), Peter Cushing (*Grand Moff Tarkin*), Alec Guinness (*Ben (Obi-Wan) Kenobi*), Anthony Daniels (*See Threepio (C3PO)*), Kenny Baker (*Artoo-Detoo (R2D2)*), Peter Mayhew (*Chewbacca*), David Prowse (*Lord Darth Vader*), James Earl Jones (*Voice of Lord Darth Vader*)

p, Gary Kurtz; d, George Lucas; w, George Lucas; ph, Gilbert Taylor; ed, Paul Hirsch, Marcia Lucas, Richard Chew; m, John Williams; prod d, Jonathan Barry; art d, Norman Reynolds, Leslie Dilley; fx, John Dykstra, John Stears, Grant McCune, Robert Blalack, Richard Edlund, Les Bowie, Industrial Light & Magic; cos, John Mollo, Ron Beck; anim, Adam Beckett

AAN Best Picture; AAN Best Supporting Actor: Alec Guinness; *AAN Best Director:* George Lucas; *AAN Best Original Screenplay:* George Lucas; *AA Best Editing:* Marcia Lucas, Paul Hirsch, Richard Chew; *AA Best Score:* John Williams; *AA Best Art Direction:* Jonathan Barry, Norman Reynolds, Leslie Dilley, Roger Christian; *AA Best Costume Design:* John Mollo; *AA Best Sound:* Don MacDougall, Ray West, Bob Minkler, Derek Ball; *AA Best Visual Effects:* John Stears, John Dykstra, Richard Edlund, Grant McCune, Robert Blalack

"A long time ago, in a galaxy far far away," reads the opening title of STAR WARS, introducing not only this one film but, in effect, a whole new wave in Hollywood filmmaking. From this point on, American films changed—for better or worse—as did audience expectations. STAR WARS left viewers craving more; "bigger and better" spectacles became the rage for years afterwards, although much that followed paled in comparison. It soon became common to hear casual fans conversing about previously arcane special effects in a critical and knowledgeable manner.

There's no denying the appeal of this historic blockbuster. What's fascinating from a cinematic point of view is the magnificently derivative nature of the film. It's an enormous summary of characters, styles, and plot points that surveys 40 years of film history. There's probably not a frame in it that doesn't have some cinematic antecedent—Lucas quotes with such enthusiastic abandon that he doesn't balk at referencing even THE TRIUMPH OF THE WILL. This is not necessarily a criticism. STAR WARS brought back for a new generation many of the most attractive elements of studio-era moviemaking, and it did so in breathless anthology form. For some young filmgoers this film acted as a doorway to the glory of the movies.

STAR WARS presents a cast of characters who have become part of our collective consciousness: Mark Hamill is the callow youth Luke Skywalker; Harrison Ford is the rugged, roguish adventurer Han Solo; and Carrie Fisher is the lovely, spunky Princess Leia. Also along for the ride are a pair of adorable 'droids, R2D2 (Kenny Baker) and C3PO (Anthony Daniels); Chewbacca (Peter Mayhew), the fierce, towering bearlike Wookie navigator who's really a softie at heart; and Obi-Wan Kenobi (Alec Guinness), the wise old hermit who is actually a great Jedi Master.

Luke is an "orphan" (see THE EMPIRE STRIKES BACK) living with his aunt and uncle on their farm on a dusty remote planet called Tatooine. He yearns for a life of high adventure. He wants to go offworld to join the academy like his friends, but his uncle needs help with the coming harvest. Meanwhile, the Imperial Senate has been disbanded and the galaxy has been taken over by the evil Emperor. The Empire's greatest weapon, the dreaded Death Star, is a huge globular craft able to disintegrate entire planets. This fearsome device is commanded by the sinister Grand Moff Tarkin (Peter Cushing) and his feared masked aide, Darth Vader (David Prowse, voiced by the uncredited James Earl Jones). Princess Leia acquires the plans for the craft and hides them in R2D2, who is jettisoned in an escape pod with the fussy translator 'droid C3PO. R2D2 has been programmed to find Obi-Wan Kenobi, but first he ends up on the Skywalker farm. The little 'droid wanders off one night to fulfill his mission; Luke follows and meets old Ben Kenobi who offers to teach him the mysterious ways of the Force. The rest is movie history.

STARDUST MEMORIES

1980 90m bw Comedy ★★½
UA (U.S.) PG/15

Woody Allen (*Sandy Bates*), Charlotte Rampling (*Dorrie*), Jessica Harper (*Daisy*), Marie-Christine Barrault (*Isobel*), Tony Roberts (*Tony*), Daniel Stern (*Actor*), Amy Wright (*Shelley*), Helen Hanft (*Vivian Orkin*), John Rothman (*Jack Abel*), Anne DeSalvo (*Sandy's Sister*)

p, Robert Greenhut; d, Woody Allen; w, Woody Allen; ph, Gordon Willis; ed, Susan E. Morse; prod d, Santo Loquasto; art d, Michael Molly

After flirting with autobiography in a few films, Woody Allen dug directly into personal experience to fashion this tale. Allen plays a prominent comedian-turned-film-director who attends a weekend film seminar where he is surrounded by hordes of adoring critics and fans who mine his every word looking for profundity and hidden meanings. The usual Allen neuroses and problems with women are given an episodic treatment, with a number of jokes along the way, but the film has an underlying angry tone that Allen fails to blend successfully with the comedy. Allen is to be commended for broadening the psychology and themes of his films, but STARDUST MEMORIES remains a disappointing outing, despite its many laughs and inside jokes. (The head of United Artists, Andy Albeck, plays a film chief who is worried that his new movie has no laughs.)

STARGATE

1994   119m   c   Science Fiction/Adventure   ★★★
Le Studio Canal Plus/Centropolis Film/Carolco   PG-13/PG
(U.S./France)

Kurt Russell *(Colonel Jonathan "Jack" O'Neil)*, James Spader *(Dr. Daniel Jackson)*, Jaye Davidson *(Ra)*, Viveca Lindfors *(Catherine)*, Alexis Cruz *(Skaara)*, Mili Avital *(Sha'uri)*, Leon Rippy *(General W.O. West)*, John Diehl *(Lieutenant Kawalsky)*, Carlos Lauchu *(Anubis)*, Djimon *(Horus)*

p, Joel B. Michaels, Oliver Eberle, Dean Devlin; d, Roland Emmerich; w, Roland Emmerich, Dean Devlin; ph, Karl Walter Lindenlaub; ed, Michael J. Duthie, Derek Brechin; m, David Arnold; prod d, Holger Gross; art d, Peter Murton, Frank Bollinger, Mark Zuelzke; fx, Kit West; cos, Joseph Porro

Lavishly produced and designed, this science fiction epic became one of the biggest commercial hits of 1994, despite a second-hand storyline and ponderous tone that were pounced upon by most critics.

Nerdy Egyptologist Daniel Jackson (James Spader) is called upon to assist in a classified Air Force project near the great pyramid of Giza. The Feds suspect that a huge circular structure discovered near the pyramid is a "StarGate"—a teleportation device that links the earth with another site far off in the universe. Jackson deciphers the hieroglyphic code on the structure and, accompanied by a military team led by Colonel Jack O'Neil (Kurt Russell), embarks on a perilous journey to the unknown. They emerge into a bizarre desert civilization ruled by a Machiavellian tyrant (Jaye Davidson) who claims to be the sun god Ra.

This was an expensive film to make, and every penny spent is visible onscreen. It incorporates excellent special effects, burnished cinematography that gives the distant planet a convincing other-worldly aura, highly effective action sequences populated by legions of meticulously costumed extras, and towering sets of which Cecil B. DeMille would surely have been proud. Given these assets, STARGATE rides out the bumps in its fanciful story. The film handles its all-important human elements capably, and leavens its high-tech bravado with just the right amount of comic relief. Though overblown and overlong, it rewards viewers with meticulously designed thrills and conveys a genuine sense of wonder—no small feat in these times of post-modern cinematic ennui.

STARMAN

1984   115m   c   Science Fiction/Romance   ★★★
Columbia   (U.S.)   PG

Jeff Bridges *(Starman)*, Karen Allen *(Jenny Hayden)*, Charles Martin Smith *(Mark Shermin)*, Richard Jaeckel *(George Fox)*, Robert Phalen *(Maj. Bell)*, Tony Edwards *(Sgt. Lemon)*, John Walter Davis *(Brad Heinmuller)*, Ted White *(Deer Hunter)*, Dirk Blocker, M.C. Gainey *(Cops)*

p, Larry Franco; d, John Carpenter; w, Bruce A. Evans, Raynold Gideon; ph, Donald Morgan; ed, Marion Rothman; m, Jack Nitzsche; prod d, Daniel Lomino; fx, Roy Arbogast, Bruce Nicholson, Michael McAlister; cos, Andy Hylton, Robin Bush

AAN Best Actor: Jeff Bridges

In this pleasant surprise from director John Carpenter, Jenny Hayden (Karen Allen) is a young Wisconsin widow still grieving over the loss of her husband. She spends her evenings looking through photo albums and watching home movies of their brief time together. One night, a bright blue light zooms from outer space and flies into Jenny's home. It hovers over the photo album and runs the home movies until it has assimilated enough characteristics of Earthlings to take on the shape of one—Jenny's dead husband. She is shocked and confused when confronted with this man who looks just like her late husband (Jeff Bridges). The alien manages to explain that he has come with greetings in return for the message Earth sent into space on *Voyager II*. His people have arranged for him to be picked up in the Arizona desert in a few days, and he forces Jenny to drive him there. Meanwhile, the government, represented by a National Security Council agent (Richard Jaeckel), is out to capture the alien in order to study him. Jenny's fear is eventually overcome by her compassion for the vulnerable being who is almost childlike in his sense of wonder about Earth and its inhabi-

tants. Slowly, hesitantly, they fall in love, knowing that he must return to his planet or die. STARMAN is a wonderful film that combines science fiction, road movies, and romance into an engaging, very entertaining whole. While the plot may have some holes and the story may be a bit hard to swallow, the film works due to the performances by Bridges and Allen. Carpenter directs the film in a straightforward manner, and the brief forays into special effects and pyrotechnics are handled deftly without distracting from the basic story line. STARMAN is an enjoyable film filled with the kind of sensitivity, love, and humor seldom seen on today's screens.

STARS LOOK DOWN, THE

1939   104m   bw   Drama   ★★★★
Grand National   (U.K.)   /A

Michael Redgrave *(David Fenwick)*, Margaret Lockwood *(Jenny Sunley)*, Emlyn Williams *(Joe Gowan)*, Nancy Price *(Martha Fenwick)*, Allan Jeayes *(Richard Barras)*, Edward Rigby *(Robert Fenwick)*, Cecil Parker *(Stanley Millington)*, Linden Travers *(Laura Millington)*, Milton Rosmer *(Harry Nugent)*, George Carney *(Slogger Gowan)*

p, Isadore Goldsmith; d, Carol Reed; w, J.B. Williams (based on the novel by A.J. Cronin); ph, Ernest Palmer, Henry Harris, Mutz Greenbaum; ed, Reginald Beck; m, Hans May; art d, James Carter

Made in 1939, but released in the US at around the same time as HOW GREEN WAS MY VALLEY, this superb view of the plight of British miners was unfortunately overlooked at the box office. Though related in subject, THE STARS LOOK DOWN is much grimmer than John Ford's classic.

Based on a novel by A.J. Cronin, Carol Reed's first major film is set in a bleak coal mining town in northern England, where Rigby and Price have struggled to give their son (Redgrave) an opportunity for a better life and a university education. Rigby works in the mine with his younger son (Desmond Tester) and attempts to organize his fellow miners, who are working under dangerous conditions. While away at school, Redgrave meets Lockwood. A vain young woman, Lockwood has been rejected by Williams, and now traps Redgrave into marriage. When Williams, an unctuous type, renews his affair with Lockwood, Redgrave leaves her and turns his attention to helping the miners back home, who have been forced to return to work after an aborted strike. Redgrave, who has ambitions of becoming an MP, tries to rally support for the union, but to no avail. After a cave-in at the mine in which many—including Rigby and Tester—are killed, he decides to stay in the small town and devote his life to improving the lot of the miners.

At once topical and enduring, this powerful drama influenced by the social realism of the British documentary greatly enhanced the growing reputation of Reed, then a young director. Shot partially at a colliery in Cumberland, THE STARS LOOK DOWN was also an important film for the young Michael Redgrave, who was still fresh from the British stage (and from THE LADY VANISHES). He gives a strong performance, as do Lockwood and Williams, with Rigby and Price lending fine support.

STARTING OVER

1979   106m   c   Romance/Comedy   ★★★½
Paramount   (U.S.)   R/15

Burt Reynolds *(Phil Potter)*, Jill Clayburgh *(Marilyn Homberg)*, Candice Bergen *(Jessica Potter)*, Charles Durning *(Michael "Mickey" Potter)*, Frances Sternhagen *(Marva Potter)*, Austin Pendleton *(Paul)*, Mary Kay Place *(Marie)*, MacIntyre Dixon *(Dan Ryan)*, Jay O. Sanders *(Larry)*, Charles Kimbrough *(Salesman)*

p, Alan J. Pakula, James L. Brooks; d, Alan J. Pakula; w, James L. Brooks (based on the novel by Dan Wakefield); ph, Sven Nykvist; ed, Marion Rothman; m, Marvin Hamlisch; prod d, George Jenkins; cos, John Boxer

AAN Best Actress: Jill Clayburgh; *AAN Best Supporting Actress:* Candice Bergen

In perhaps his best performance, Burt Reynolds, cast here against type, stars as a lonely man whose wife leaves him to spread her wings and try to build a career as a singer-songwriter (although she exhibits a striking lack of talent). Stunned when she announces her desire for freedom, he goes to Boston where he is consoled by Durning and

Sternhagen, a duo of relatives who also happen to be psychiatrists. At first Reynolds has no idea that in addition to yearning for freedom Bergen is having an affair with her boss. Struck by this new situation, Reynolds soon meets Clayburgh, a schoolteacher who shies away from any commitment. He also joins a divorced men's group, which provides some touching and funny moments. Reynolds shaved off his moustache for the film and with it went his hirsute, macho image; he presents instead a feeling and vulnerable man. Bergen's character is gently made fun of. In a very funny sequence, she sings her dreadful autobiographical songs in a caterwauling screech. While all of the acting is top-notch, Reynolds steals the show with his underplaying and understanding of the role. He has been quoted as saying, "It was very close to the story of my life," and his grasp of the character's emotions is evident from the start. Audiences like to see their heroes in familiar roles, however, and the film was not the great success its producers hoped for, although it grossed over $20 million on initial release. Brooks, the producer-screenwriter who came from the "Mary Tyler Moore Show," later went on to make a name for himself as a director-writer-producer with TERMS OF ENDEARMENT.

STATE FAIR

1945 100m c Musical   ★★★★
Fox (U.S.)   /U

Jeanne Crain (*Margy Frake*), Dana Andrews (*Pat Gilbert*), Dick Haymes (*Wayne Frake*), Vivian Blaine (*Emily Joyce*), Charles Winninger (*Abel Frake*), Fay Bainter (*Melissa Frake*), Donald Meek (*Hippenstahl*), Frank McHugh (*McGee*), Percy Kilbride (*Miller*), Harry Morgan (*Barker*)

p, William Perlberg; d, Walter Lang; w, Oscar Hammerstein II, Sonya Levien, Paul Green (based on the novel by Phil Stong); ph, Leon Shamroy; ed, J. Watson Webb; art d, Lyle Wheeler, Lewis Creber; fx, Fred Sersen

AAN Best Score: Charles Henderson, Alfred Newman; *AA Best Song:* Richard Rodgers (Music), Oscar Hammerstein, II (Lyrics)

This second version of STATE FAIR improves on its predecessor of 1933. Oscar Hammerstein based his screenplay on the 1933 adaptation of Phil Stong's bucolic novel, and, with Richard Rodgers, contributed the score. The story is virtually the same, but the addition of the marvelous songs made the musical remake a smash. It's still pleasant mid-summer in Iowa, where Abel and Melissa Frake (Charles Winninger and Fay Bainter) are the parents of the teenage Margy (Jeanne Crain) and Wayne (Dick Haymes). Abel wants to enter his pig at the state fair and treats the porker like a king, lavishing more attention on the beast that his wife. Melissa is preparing her locally famous pickles and mincemeat, hoping to win a blue ribbon herself. At the fair, Wayne falls for Emily (Vivian Blaine), a dance-band singer, and Margy meets Pat (Dana Andrews), a newspaper reporter. After the obligatory romantic complications, Abel's pig hogs the show, Melissa's mincemeat is spiked with brandy and gets the judges tipsy enough to award her the prize, and the couples wind up happy. The story is as light as cotton candy, but everyone has such a good time and rural life seems so sweetly appealing that urbanites flocked to real state fairs after this movie was released.

STATE OF SIEGE
(ETAT DE SIEGE)

1972 120m c Political/Thriller   ★★★½
Reggana/Cinema 10/Unidis/Euro Intl./Dieter Geissler   PG/X
(France/U.S./Italy/West Germany)

Yves Montand (*Philip Michael Santore*), Renato Salvatori (*Capt. Lopez*), O.E. Hasse (*Carlos Ducas*), Jacques Weber (*Hugo*), Jean-Luc Bideau (*Este*), Evangeline Peterson (*Mrs. Santore*), Maurice Teynac (*Minister of Internal Security*), Yvette Etievant (*Woman Senator*), Harald Wolff (*Minister of Foreign Affairs*), Nemesio Antunes (*President of the Republic*)

p, Jacques Perrin; d, Constantin Costa-Gavras; w, Franco Solinas, Constantin Costa-Gavras; ph, Pierre-William Glenn; ed, Francoise Bonnot; m, Mikis Theodorakis; prod d, Jacques D'Ovidio; art d, Jacques d'Ovidio

Taking aim at the repressive right-wing government of a Latin American country (a thinly veiled Uruguay) and the support it received from at least one employee of the US Agency for International Development (AID), Costa-Gavras offers here another tightly knit political thriller along the lines of his Z, MISSING and THE CONFESSION. Set in the 1970s, STATE OF SEIGE chronicles the kidnaping of AID "traffic expert" Philip Santore (Yves Montand) by Tupamaro-like left-wing guerrillas who are determined to prove he is behind the introduction of sophisticated torture methods in their country and in others as well—an international criminal. As the guerrillas try to extract a confession from the wounded but cool Santore, the government's search begins to zero in on their location, with tension mounting as the demand for a prisoner exchange is rejected by the government. When Santore confesses, his captors are left with the difficult decision of whether or not to execute him. Told mostly in flashback and allegedly based on the case of real-life AID officer Daniel Mitrione, STATE OF SIEGE was banned from the American Film Institute theater in Washington upon its release, its opponents arguing that it glorified assassination and was violently anti-American. Never one to pull political punches, Costa-Gavras delivers yet another impassioned, intensely dramatic indictment of the abuse of power.

STATE OF THE UNION

1948 124m bw Political   ★★★★
Liberty (U.S.)

Spencer Tracy (*Grant Matthews*), Katharine Hepburn (*Mary Matthews*), Van Johnson (*Spike McManus*), Angela Lansbury (*Kay Thorndyke*), Adolphe Menjou (*Jim Conover*), Lewis Stone (*Sam Thorndyke*), Howard Smith (*Sam Parrish*), Maidel Turner (*Lulubelle Alexander*), Raymond Walburn (*Judge Alexander*), Charles Dingle (*Bill Hardy*)

p, Frank Capra; d, Frank Capra; w, Anthony Veiller, Myles Connolly (based on the play by Howard Lindsay, Russel Crouse); ph, George Folsey; ed, William Hornbeck; m, Victor Young; art d, Cedric Gibbons, Urie McCleary; fx, A. Arnold Gillespie; cos, Irene

Spencer Tracy stars in this political drama as a millionaire aircraft manufacturer who is seeking the Republican presidential nomination. A party outsider, Tracy isn't given much of a chance to capture the nomination. Further, his personal life is not the kind most voters would find endearing. He has been separated from his wife, Hepburn, for some years, and is having an affair with Lansbury, a wealthy newspaper publisher. With Lansbury's newspapers supporting Tracy's candidacy, he could become a much more legitimate contender for the nomination. Still, his personal life needs to be set straight, so he asks Hepburn to return to him and pose as his loving wife during the campaign. Hepburn agrees but makes it clear that it will be on a temporary basis and that she won't stay beyond his election, if he ever gets the nomination. Tracy's campaign picks up steam and Menjou, a powerful political boss, gives Tracy his substantial support. Also joining the campaign is Johnson, a successful newspaperman who takes a leave from his job to serve as Tracy's publicist. Tracy had begun the campaign with strong convictions, but as the campaign grind continues and as the nomination becomes a very real possibility, he is soon making accommodations and compromises, most suggested to him by Lansbury and Menjou. Hepburn watches her husband alter his values to suit others, and she becomes upset by these developments. Her love for Tracy has started to return and she can't bear to see him sell out. At a dinner party, she tells him that she thinks his advisers are morally bankrupt and urges him to distance himself from them and to retain his own sense of values. Tracy is moved by Hepburn's words and then on a radio broadcast, announces to the listening audience that he is taking his name off the nominating slate because he feels he is not worthy of consideration on the voters' part. He then returns to Hepburn's open arms.

One of the joys of the Broadway hit upon which this film is based was that the authors changed the dialogue almost weekly to reflect what was happening in the news. In making the movie, the dialogue obviously was frozen, but many of the jokes and barbs were clearly aimed at events surrounding the 1948 presidential election pitting President Harry S. Truman against Republican challenger Thomas E. Dewey. The film was originally set to star Gary Cooper and Claudette Colbert, and when that casting fell through, Tracy was immediately picked for the male lead. Despite the fact that Hepburn had turned down the same role in the play, she was anxious to do it opposite Tracy in the film and a deal was struck. There was much tension on the set between Hepburn and Menjou. During this time the government had begun to investigate the Hollywood community, searching for communists, a practice Hepburn deplored and Menjou supported. This may have helped the picture, since the characters played by Hepburn and Menjou are adversaries throughout the film. The acting is first-rate as are the script, direction, and technical credits. Though it may seem somewhat dated to younger audiences, it remains an entertaining and uplifting movie experience.

STATE OF THINGS, THE

1982 121m bw Drama ★★★½
Gray City (U.S.) /AA

Isabelle Weingarten *(Anna)*, Rebecca Pauly *(Joan)*, Jeffrey Kime *(Mark)*, Geoffrey Carey *(Robert)*, Camilla Mora *(Julia)*, Alexandra Auder *(Jane)*, Patrick Bauchau *(Friedrich)*, Paul Getty III *(Dennis)*, Viva Auder *(Kate)*, Samuel Fuller *(Joe)*

p, Chris Sievernich; d, Wim Wenders; w, Wim Wenders, Robert Kramer; ph, Henri Alekan, Fred Murphy; ed, Barbara von Weitershausen; m, Jurgen Knieper; art d, Ze Branco; cos, Maria Gonzaga

Wim Wenders's THE STATE OF THINGS is a comically bleak look at the clash between the auteurist European filmmaking sensibility and the commercial Hollywood style, that mirrors its subject by being more of a private diary than a traditional narrative film.

German director Friedrich "Fritz" Munro (Patrick Bauchau) is in Portugal shooting his first American film, a low-budget science-fiction movie, when he learns that the company has run out of film. Fritz assures everyone that Gordon (Allen Garfield, billed here as Allen Goorwitz), the film's producer, will come through with more money, but in the meantime the production shuts down. Fritz soon travels to L.A. to look for Gordon. He eventually finds him hiding out in a huge mobile home, and goes inside to talk to him. As they drive through the night, Gordon explains that he's on the run from the loan sharks, who demanded their money back after they screened the film's rushes and saw that they were in black-and-white and that the film had no story.

THE STATE OF THINGS is a deeply personal work that came about as a result of the numerous interruptions of Wenders's trouble-plagued American debut HAMMETT (1982). While visiting friends in Lisbon who were working on Raul Ruiz's THE TERRITORY (1983), Wenders borrowed most of that film's cast and crew and decided to quickly improvise and shoot a film that would be a comment on his difficulties in Hollywood. The film's poetic black-and-white photography is starkly beautiful, and Wenders's use of sound and music is as impressive as ever, but the conditions under which the film was made accounts for its often self-indulgent, desultory quality, and the improvisations of the cast quickly become tiresome, apart from Samuel Fuller's robust performance as Fritz s grizzled Hollywood cameraman, and the mobile-home finale where Fritz rambles on about "life, death, images, and art," while Gordon completely ignores him and sings a morose little ditty about Hollywood (written by Goorwitz/Garfield himself). The film is an existential study of the nature of creativity (Fritz echoes Wenders's preference for atmosphere and mood over plot and structure), and what it feels like to be a stranger in a strange land (the L.A. scenes are shot like a sci-fi film, with alienated overhead shots of traffic, parking lots, fast-food restaurants and monolithic office buildings).

STAVISKY

1974 115m c Political/Biography ★★★½
Ariane/Cerita/Euro Intl. (France) PG/A

Jean-Paul Belmondo *(Serge Alexandre Stavisky)*, Charles Boyer *(Raoul)*, Francois Perier *(Borelli)*, Anny Duperey *(Arlette)*, Michel Lonsdale *(Mezy)*, Claude Rich *(Bonny)*, Marcel Cuvilier *(Bosseaud)*, Jacques Spiesser *(Granville)*, Gigi Balista *(Henriet)*, Roberto Bisacco *(Montalvo)*

d, Alain Resnais; w, Jorge Semprun; ph, Sacha Vierny; ed, Albert Jurgenson; m, Stephen Sondheim

A fascinating true story of the man who almost brought down the French government. Serge Stavisky committed suicide on January 3, 1934. The Russian-born promoter had been involved with the issuance

of phony bonds and several other crimes, but he had evidently been protected by officials in high places (he supposedly distributed millions of francs in bribes). When one of the officials was murdered, there were accusations that this man in the public prosecutor's office was silenced to keep from spilling the beans. Factions from all of the parties began stirring up trouble and claiming that it was due to the basic corruption in the elected government. Riots began on February 6-8, and a general strike was called. The government teetered and fell, then a new coalition was formed by people who had been outside of the Stavisky influence, and France went on. That's how it ended. How it all happened is the subject of the movie by Resnais, a different kind of film from the director who helmed LAST YEAR AT MARIENBAD and HIROSHIMA, MON AMOUR. The screenplay is by the man who wrote Z, so it is literate and has more than a bit of politics attached. Belmondo plays the title role, a small-time hustler who migrates to France, becomes an embezzler, and uses his personal charm and diabolical tactics to rise quickly to a place of economic importance with a rash of bold moves. Belmondo's wife is Duperey, who goes along with his machinations, and Boyer is a poor Spanish nobleman who dreams of stirring up a civil war in Spain and taking over after the current regime has been destroyed. The picture belongs to Belmondo, who oozes confidence as he makes his way up through the whirlpools of politics and emerges as the most powerful man in the country. Then, when it seems as though he's gone too far, all of his associates desert him and he is left with only one recourse, the taking of his own life. With that, he duplicates what his father did upon hearing that his son had been clapped in jail. The picture is technically brilliant, visually stunning, and ceaselessly interesting. But the hero is a villain without much to like, and audiences want someone to root for; thus, this movie did not make a great deal at the box office. Sondheim's music is a bit too intellectual for the emotions seen on-screen.

STEALING BEAUTY
(LO BALLO DA SOLA)

1996 119m c Romance/Drama ★★½
Fiction Cinematografica/Recorded Picture Company R/15
/UGC Images (Italy/U.K./France)

Liv Tyler *(Lucy Harmon)*, Jeremy Irons *(Alex Parrish)*, Sinead Cusack *(Diana Grayson)*, Carlo Cecchi *(Carlo Lisca)*, Jean Marais *(M. Guillaume)*, Donal McCann *(Ian Grayson)*, D.W. Moffett *(Richard Reed)*, Stefania Sandrelli *(Noemi)*, Rachel Weisz *(Miranda Fox)*, Joseph Fiennes *(Christopher Fox)*

p, Jeremy Thomas; d, Bernardo Bertolucci; w, Susan Minot (from a story by Bernardo Bertolucci); ph, Darius Khondji; ed, Pietro Scalia; m, Richard Hartley; prod d, Gianni Silvestri; art d, Domenico Sica; cos, Louise Stjernsward, Giorgio Armani

It's refreshing to see director Bernardo Bertolucci return to smaller-scale film making, but STEALING BEAUTY, the tale of a young girl's sexual awakening, lacks the artistic and political passion of his early work.

Following her mother's suicide, young American Lucy Harmon (Liv Tyler) travels to Tuscany for the summer, staying with her mother's friends Ian and Diana Grayson (Donal McCann and Sinead Cusack). She reads her mother's diaries, trying to figure out the identity of her biological father. Lucy spends her time posing for Ian and getting to know the other houseguests: Alex (Jeremy Irons), a terminally-ill playwright; Guillaume (Jean Marais), an elderly French art dealer; Miranda (Rachel Weisz), Diana's daughter from a previous marriage; Richard (D.W. Moffett), Diana's boyfriend; and Noemi (Stefania Sandrelli), an advice columnist. The assorted expatriates take an interest in Lucy's many dilemmas, particularly the teenager's desire to lose her virginity. By the end of the summer, Lucy has succeeded in both her aims.

STEALING BEAUTY's main problem is its screenplay, written by Bertolucci and novelist Susan Minot. The setting and structure of the drama invoke Chekhov, but the dialogue sounds pretentious, forcing the talented cast to struggle with poorly-written roles. Bertolucci keeps the images looking sumptuous throughout, although the endless parade of life, love, food, and beauty dulls the palate. The best-known actors, Irons and Marais, tend to overplay the two potentially most moving parts. Tyler makes her Henry James-style heroine more appealing than she might have been; Cusack is given little to work with as Diana but hints at a great untold story behind her character; and McCann lends solidity to the role of Ian.

STEEL HELMET, THE

1951 84m bw War ★★★★
Deputy (U.S.) /A

Gene Evans *(Sgt. Zack)*, Robert Hutton *(Pvt. "Conchie" Bronte)*, Richard Loo *(Sgt. "Buddhahead" Tanaka)*, Steve Brodie *(Lt. Driscoll)*, James Edwards *(Cpl. "Medic" Thompson)*, Sid Melton *(Joe, 2nd GI)*, Richard Monahan *(Pvt. Baldy)*, William Chun *("Short Round")*, Harold Fong *(The Red)*, Neyle Morrow *(1st GI)*

p, Samuel Fuller; d, Samuel Fuller; w, Samuel Fuller; ph, Ernest Miller; ed, Philip Cahn; m, Paul Dunlap; art d, Theobold Holsopple; fx, Ben Southland, Ray Mercer; cos, Alfred Berke

Scripted in a week, shot in 10 days, and released only six months after the start of the Korean War, Sam Fuller's THE STEEL HELMET stands as one of the best films about that war or any war. Dark, violent, and disturbing, this film doesn't celebrate duty, honor, and heroism; it shows men simply trying to survive the madness. Evans, a wounded sergeant whose platoon has been wiped out, is saved from sniper fire by Chun, a South Korean orphan nicknamed "Short Round" (a name adopted by Steven Spielberg for his cute Asian kid in INDIANA JONES AND THE TEMPLE OF DOOM). With the kid tagging along, Evans meets up with a group of raw recruits, and agrees to lead them in exchange for a box of cigars. The tiny group then proceeds to an ancient Buddhist temple which is to be used as an army observation post. Before long, the Americans find themselves furiously besieged by the enemy.

THE STEEL HELMET is a film made for an audience tired of war. The world had welcomed home its battle-weary soldiers from WWII only five years before, and many were less than enthusiastic when another war—one neither so popular nor so ideologically clear-cut—dragged men away again. This time the public wondered whether the bloodshed was necessary. THE STEEL HELMET reflects these doubts. Those soldiers who are not confused and scared are cold and cynical. The rules of this war are different from the last. The enemy looks exactly like the people the soldiers are supposed to be defending. A confused soldier asks Evans, "How do you tell a North Korean from a South Korean?" Evans replies, "If he's running with you he's a South Korean. If he's running after you he's a North Korean." Director Fuller emphasizes this confusion visually. The film is very claustrophobic (most of the action takes place on a single set) and the characters nearly always seem to be immersed in smoke and fog. Things are never what they seem. GI Monahan's snoring is mistaken for the whistle of incoming shells, Buddhist priests turn out to be North Korean soldiers in disguise, and Loo, the intelligent and brave South Korean soldier, isn't trusted by the American lieutenant. By the end of the film, the American soldiers who have survived are on the brink of madness. Fuller's final comment on the situation comes with the closing credit, which reads, "There is no end to this story." He spoke the truth: his movie became the model for nearly every Vietnam war film.

STEEL MAGNOLIAS

1989 118m c Comedy/Drama ★★★
Rastar (U.S.) PG/15

Sally Field *(M'Lynn Eatenton)*, Dolly Parton *(Truvy Jones)*, Shirley MacLaine *(Ouiser Boudreaux)*, Daryl Hannah *(Annelle Dupuy Desoto)*, Olympia Dukakis *(Clairee Belcher)*, Julia Roberts *(Shelby Eatenton Latcherie)*, Tom Skerritt *(Drum Eatenton)*, Dylan McDermott *(Jackson Latcherie)*, Kevin J. O'Connor *(Sammy Desoto)*, Sam Shepard *(Spud Jones)*

p, Ray Stark; d, Herbert Ross; w, Robert Harling (based on his play); ph, John A. Alonzo; ed, Paul Hirsch; m, Georges Delerue; prod d, Gene Callahan, Edward Pisoni; art d, Hub Braden, Michael Okowita; chor, Spencer Henderson; cos, Julie Weiss

AAN Best Supporting Actress: Julia Roberts

Based on screenwriter Robert Harling's award-winning off-Broadway play, STEEL MAGNOLIAS tells the story of six southern women whose lives interconnect in a beauty parlor in their small Louisiana town. M'Lynn Eatenton (Sally Field), mother of headstrong Shelby (Julia Roberts), is worried about her daughter's upcoming marriage, fearing for the children that the diabetic, seizure-prone Shelby wants to have. Their friends at the beauty parlor—Truvy (Dolly Parton), who runs the parlor; Annelle (Daryl Hannah), her assistant; Clairee (Olympia Dukakis), an aristocratic widow; and Ouiser (Shirley MacLaine), the town scold—gossip and cope with a variety of problems, among them a failing marriage for Truvy, and some chameleonlike changes for Annelle. Shelby marries and has her baby, but just when things look rosy, tragedy rears its head. STEEL MAGNOLIAS is an old-fashioned "klatsch" film, a prefeminist relic in which a group of women eschew the public world of men in favor of the community of the coffee table. Their world is shown as inferior to men's in terms of power but superior to it in emotion and insight into the things that "really matter." Not surprisingly, the "klatscher" myth has been concocted largely by men (most notably by George Cukor). Here director Herbert Ross (TURNING POINT) gets generally strong performances from his ensemble, and an especially good one from Field in a role that really doesn't suit her. The film was shot on location in Natchitoches, Louisiana, hometown of actor-turned-writer Harling, who based his play on the experiences of his own mother and sister.

STELLA DALLAS

1937 104m bw Drama ★★★★
UA (U.S.) /U

Barbara Stanwyck *(Stella Martin Dallas)*, John Boles *(Stephen Dallas)*, Anne Shirley *(Laurel Dallas)*, Barbara O'Neil *(Helen Morrison)*, Alan Hale *(Ed Munn)*, Marjorie Main *(Mrs. Martin)*, Edmund Elton *(Mr. Martin)*, George Walcott *(Charlie Martin)*, Gertrude Short *(Carrie Jenkins)*, Tim Holt *(Richard)*

p, Samuel Goldwyn; d, King Vidor; w, Sarah Y. Mason, Victor Heerman (based on the novel by Olive Higgins Prouty and the play by Harry Wagstaff Gribble, Gertrude Purcell); ph, Rudolph Mate; ed, Sherman Todd; art d, Richard Day; cos, Omar Kiam

AAN Best Actress: Barbara Stanwyck; *AAN Best Supporting Actress:* Anne Shirley

Grand Vidor soap opera, boasting a brilliant Stanwyck performance. She's a tough cookie, a bit of a shrew and a grasping woman who snares Boles, a well-born young man whose family lost its old money when his father committed suicide. Boles has moved to a tiny New England town where he meets Stanwyck. He had been engaged to O'Neil, a woman of the same social level as himself, but when his fortune was lost he left, and she took up with another. Stanwyck is aware of his background from reading the tabloids. They have a daughter, but the difference in their classes continues to keep them distanced from one another. When Boles is offered a job in New York and asks Stanwyck to come with him, she fears being laughed at by his society friends, so he goes south and she stays in the mill town.

Stanwyck begins running around with the rough-hewn, hard-drinking friends of her youth but she remains a good mother, almost too good, as she lavishes love and affection on the child (played as an adult by Shirley). Hale would like to marry Stanwyck, but her life is devoted to her daughter. One day, while riding a train, Hale gets abusive and offends many of the townspeople, who associate him with Stanwyck and Shirley. When Shirley invites her friends to a birthday party, she and Stanwyck are snubbed in a particularly touching scene. Boles would like a divorce so he can wed O'Neil, a widow with two sons, but Stanwyck will not give her consent. Shirley and Stanwyck visit a posh resort on the strength of Boles's cash, and on this trip Stanwyck learns that her coarse behavior and garish clothing stand in the way of Shirley's happiness.

Despite unforgettable work in a slew of other films, Stanwyck was quoted as saying that this was the best acting she'd ever done and it remained her favorite role. Only 30 years old at the time of STELLA, she had to be aged considerably to look right as the mother of an adult daughter. The role demanded a vast range of emotion, and Stanwyck wrung every last smile and tear out of every speech. Even when she was simply reacting, Stanwyck emanated frustration channeled into maternal martyrdom, but without an ounce of self-pity. She is well-supported by Shirley and Hale, with John Boles his typical handsome if rather stolid self and Barbara O'Neill fine as the noble rich woman. The film was remade in 1990 as STELLA, with Bette Midler having some effective moments, with no help from anyone else.

STEPFATHER, THE

1987 90m c Horror/Thriller ★★★½
ITC (U.S.) R/18

Terry O'Quinn *(Jerry Blake, the Stepfather/Henry Morrison/Bill Hodgkins)*, Jill Schoelen *(Stephanie Maine)*, Shelley Hack *(Susan Blake)*, Charles Lanyer *(Dr. Bondurant)*, Stephen Shellen *(Jim Ogilvie)*, Stephen Miller *(Al Brennan)*, Robyn Stevan *(Karen)*, Jeff Schultz *(Paul Baker)*, Lindsay Bourne *(Art Teacher)*, Anna Hagan *(Mrs. Leitner)*

p, Jay Benson; d, Joseph Ruben; w, Donald E. Westlake (based on a story by Carolyn Lefcourt, Brian Garfield, Westlake); ph, John Lindley; ed, George Bowers; m, Patrick Moraz; prod d, James William Newport; art d, David Willson; cos, Mina Mittleman

Just when it looked like slasher movies were wholly irredeemable, director Joseph Ruben came along to prove there is some intelligent life in this otherwise bereft subgenre. Featuring a fascinating script by novelist Donald Westlake, some taut direction, and an absolutely absorbing performance by Terry O'Quinn, THE STEPFATHER is not just another slice-and-dice thriller. Loosely based on a real-life case, the film begins in a picturesque suburb, where a rugged-looking, bearded man (O'Quinn) washes blood from his hands, cuts his hair, shaves, and changes clothes to emerge a completely different person. As he walks downstairs, we see that the man's entire family has been massacred. One year later, the man resurfaces as Jerry Blake—in a new suburb, with a new job, a new wife (Shelley Hack), and a teenage stepdaughter (Jill Schoelen). Gradually the secret madness and alternate lives of Jerry Blake begin to surface. THE STEPFATHER fits in nicely among such examinations of the seedy underbelly of "perfect" family life as Alfred Hitchcock's SHADOW OF A DOUBT and David Lynch's BLUE VELVET. Although the last part of the picture disintegrates into some typical slasher-movie conventions and a plethora of clumsy Hitchcock homages, the majority of the film is *definitely* not typical. Fueled by an intense and intricate performance by O'Quinn, the movie is a fascinating examination of America's predilection for appearances over substance. Jerry Blake is the consummate actor, masking his crazed state with an air of friendliness and easy charm, whose false veneer of bliss has been spoon-fed to his diseased mind via television. He wants the perfect TV family; but when reality rears its ugly head and day-to-day problems cannot be dealt with in a matter of minutes, his repressed rage erupts.

STEPFORD WIVES, THE

1975 114m c Science Fiction/Comedy ★★½
Palomar/Fadsin (U.S.) PG/15

Katharine Ross *(Joanna)*, Paula Prentiss *(Bobby)*, Peter Masterson *(Walter)*, Nanette Newman *(Carol)*, Patrick O'Neal *(Dale Coba)*, Tina Louise *(Charmaine)*, Carol Rossen *(Dr. Fancher)*, William Prince *(Artist)*, Paula Trueman *(Welcome Wagon Lady)*, Remak Ramsay *(Atkinson)*

p, Edgar J. Scherick; d, Bryan Forbes; w, William Goldman (based on the novel by Ira Levin); ph, Owen Roizman; ed, Timothy Gee; m, Michael Small; prod d, Gene Callahan; fx, Dick Smith

Ira Levin is an eclectic writer who has done comedy-drama *(Sleuth)*, adventure *(The Boys from Brazil)*, thrillers *(Rosemary's Baby)*, and science fiction such as *The Stepford Wives*. But Goldman's screenplay and Forbes's ponderous direction slow his exciting novel to a laborious pace. Goldman, an often excellent writer, scripted BUTCH CASSIDY AND THE SUNDANCE KID, and Forbes proved himself with SEANCE ON A WET AFTERNOON, as well as many other films. So what happened here? The first hour takes what feels like two, and the last 44 minutes goes like an Indy car, so the pace is alternately snail's and Lamborghini's. Ross and her husband, Masterson, leave the hectic world of Manhattan and settle in the small, tranquil town of Stepford, Connecticut (actually shot in Westport). She meets the local wives, who seem weird to her, talking about dumb things and sounding like Procter & Gamble commercials. The two women who perplex her most are

Louise and Newman (Forbes's wife in real life). They are perfect—they're devoted to their husbands, to keeping their homes squeaky clean, to having every hair in place, etc. This odd contentment gnaws at Ross. Her only normal friend is also a newcomer, Prentiss. O'Neal is the important man in the town and runs a men's club that Ross and Prentiss would like to know more about. After much palaver, the truth comes out. These women are not women at all, just flawlessly executed robot replicas of the real wives who came to Stepford, and who knows what's happened to the originals? The only difference is that these women never argue with their husbands, do everything that's asked of them, and fulfill every male chauvinist fantasy ever imagined. Ross would like to expose the truth once she learns it, but by that time it's too late. She and Prentiss are seen at the conclusion as two of a gaggle of Stepford Wives, happily exchanging recipes in the supermarket as they shop for their hubbies' favorite dishes. The film has more than a passing similarity to THE INVASION OF THE BODY SNATCHERS, although that was played totally serious and this has more than a few laughs, particularly when the wives are acting in their "whatever you want, darling" mode. With 15 minutes cut out of the opening 60, this would have been a whizzer.

STERILE CUCKOO, THE

1969 108m c Romance/Comedy ★★★½
Boardwalk (U.S.) PG/X

Liza Minnelli *(Pookie)*, Wendell Burton *(Jerry)*, Tim McIntire *(Charlie Schumacher)*, Elizabeth Harrower *(Landlady)*, Austin Green *(Pookie's Father)*, Sandra Faison *(Nancy Putnam)*, Chris Bugbee *(Roe)*, Jawn McKinley *(Helen Upshaw)*, Fred Lerner, A. Frederick Gooseen

p, Alan J. Pakula; d, Alan J. Pakula; w, Alvin Sargent; ph, Milton Krasner; ed, Sam O'Steen, John W. Wheeler; m, Fred Karlin; art d, Roland Anderson; fx, Charles Spurgeon; cos, Jennifer Parsons, John A. Anderson

AAN Best Actress: Liza Minnelli; *AAN Best Song:* Fred Karlin (Music), Dory Previn (Lyrics)

Pakula's directorial debut, after he had produced pictures directed by his partner, Robert Mulligan, is thoroughly crafted. Unlike many firsttimers (especially during the indulgent late 60s), Pakula uses understatement, avoids cinematic tricks, and carefully guides young stars Minnelli (who was nominated for an Oscar) and Burton, who was making his screen debut after starring on Broadway for three years in the title role of "You're a Good Man, Charlie Brown." Shot primarily at the Hamilton College campus in upstate New York, the film is a youth-oriented tearjerker that is just perceptive enough to transcend the genre.

Minnelli and Burton meet on a bus going up to school; her quirky behavior during the ride embarrasses him and he's relieved to discover that they're attending different colleges. He's a quiet young man studying etymology; she's a motherless waif with a neglectful father. Burton settles into his dorm room with slob McIntire, a beer-drinking boor and bore who talks endlessly of his sexual conquests, and is stunned when Minnelli arrives and announces that she intends to spend the weekend. The strained relationship develops into romance, but the two have different expectations for the future.

Minelli's boilerplate "lovable kook" is a matter of taste—Liza worshippers should swoon; others may wince. Burton, who seemed to disappear after his next picture, FORTUNE AND MEN'S EYES, is excellent. The syrupy theme song, "Come Saturday Morning" (Fred Karlin, Dory Previn), was a big hit for The Sandpipers.

STING, THE

1973 129m c Crime/Comedy ★★½
Richard D. Zanuck/David Brown (U.S.) PG

Paul Newman *(Henry Gondorff/Mr. Shaw)*, Robert Redford *(Johnny Hooker/Kelly)*, Robert Shaw *(Doyle Lonnegan)*, Charles Durning *(Lt. William Snyder)*, Ray Walston *(J.J. Singleton)*, Eileen Brennan *(Billie)*, Harold Gould *(Kid Twist)*, John Heffernan *(Eddie Niles)*, Dana Elcar *(FBI Agent Polk)*, Jack Kehoe *("Erie Kid")* p, Tony Bill, Julia Phillips, Michael Phillips; d, George Roy Hill; w, David S. Ward; ph, Robert Surtees; ed, William Reynolds; m, Scott Joplin, John Philip Sousa; art d, Henry Bumstead; fx, Bob Warner, Albert Whitlock; cos, Edith Head

AA Best Picture; AAN Best Actor: Robert Redford; AA Best Director: George Roy Hill; AA Best Adapted Screenplay: David S. Ward; AAN Best Cinematography: Robert Surtees; AA Best Editing: William Reynolds; AA Best Score: Marvin Hamlisch; AA Best Art Direction: Henry Bumstead, James Payne; AA Best Costume Design: Edith Head; AAN Best Sound: Ronald K. Pierce, Robert Bertrand

Vastly overrated Crooks-R-Us—this time *you* wear the moustache, enhanced by fine period trappings and flavor. Ultimately empty stuff, but preferable to BUTCH CASSIDY.

By reuniting director George Roy Hill and actors Robert Redford and Paul Newman (BUTCH CASSIDY AND THE SUNDANCE KID), THE STING emerged an equally successful entertainment, outgrossing every other picture of the year. Frightening. The story begins in September, 1936, in Joliet, Illinois. The city is run by corrupt officials, and the numbers racket runs rampant. When two-bit drifter Redford and his partner, Robert Earl Jones, the veteran bunco artist of the area, con one of the racketeers out of a $5,000 delivery, they find themselves mixed up with the big boys in Chicago and their head man, Shaw, a sleazy gangster who would gladly kill a drifter like Redford to retain control of his operation. Police lieutenant Durning shakes down Redford, who has already gambled away most of the money, threatening to kill him if he doesn't pay it back. Jones, who has decided to retire from the con game and get into a legitimate business is killed by two of Shaw's thugs. On the run from Joliet police and Shaw's goons, Redford heads for Chicago to meet a friend of Jones, a man described as "the greatest con artist of them all," Newman. Determined to avenge the murder of Jones, Redford makes plans to "sting" Shaw out of a fortune. Newman, a drunk who lives in backroom squalor in a joint run by Brennan, is wary of hooking up with the still inexperienced Redford. Newman is, however, finally convinced, and they set the gears into motion.

Much of the film's success is a result of its visual brilliance: the aged look of Surtees' photography evokes a feeling of nostalgia, and the art direction, set decoration, and costuming are equally effective. Marvin Hamlisch did a fine job of adapting Scott Joplin's classic rags, especially "The Entertainer," which was soon a radio commonplace and sparked a renewed interest in the composer.

STIR CRAZY

1980 111m c Prison/Comedy ★★★
Columbia (U.S.) R/15

Gene Wilder *(Skip Donahue)*, Richard Pryor *(Harry Monroe)*, Georg Stanford Brown *(Rory Schultebrand)*, JoBeth Williams *(Meredith)*, Miguel Suarez *(Jesus Ramirez)*, Craig T. Nelson *(Deputy Ward Wilson)*, Barry Corbin *(Warden Walter Beatty)*, Charles Weldon *(Blade)*, Nicolas Coster *(Warden Henry Sampson)*, Joel Brooks *(Len Garber)*

p, Hannah Weinstein; d, Sidney Poitier; w, Bruce Jay Friedman; ph, Fred Schuler; ed, Harry Keller; m, Tom Scott; prod d, Alfred Sweeney; chor, Scott Salmon; cos, Patricia Edwards

An essentially empty script is made palatable by Richard Pryor's ability to be funnier than his material. Pryor and Gene Wilder are two losers from New York who decide to drive to California to change their luck. Along the way they stop in a small town and take a job requiring them to wear woodpecker costumes. When two crooks don identical outfits and rob the local bank, Pryor and Wilder are arrested for the crime, convicted, and given 120-year prison terms. Wilder is his usual hyperactive self, but director Sidney Poitier gets as much as he can out of the uninspired script.

STOLEN CHILDREN, THE
(IL LADRO DI BAMBINI)

1992 108m c Drama ★★★★
Erre Produzioni/Alia Film/Arena Films/Vega Film /15
(Italy/France/Switzerland)

Enrico Lo Verso *(Antonio)*, Valentina Scalici *(Rosetta)*, Giuseppe Ieracitano *(Luciano)*, Florence Darel *(Martine)*, Marina Golovine *(Nathalie)*, Fabio Alessandrini *(Grignani)*, Agnostino Zumbo *(Priest At Children's Home)*, Vincenzo Peluso *(Neopolitan Carabiniere)*, Maria Pia Di Giovanni *(Mother)*, Vitalba Andrea *(Antonio's Sister)*

p, Angelo Rizzoli, Stefano Munafo; d, Gianni Amelio; w, Gianni Amelio, Sandro Petraglia, Stefano Rulli (from a story by Rulli, Petraglia and Amelio); ph, Tonino Nardi, Renato Tafuri; ed, Simona Paggi; m, Franco Piersanti; art d, Andrea Crisanti, Giuseppe M. Gaudino

Inspired by a newspaper article about a woman who prostituted her eight-year-old daughter, this rigorous, immensely affecting portrait of a pair of emotionally damaged children marks an entirely successful revival of Italian neo-realist filmmaking.

In a Milan slum, a woman (Maria Pia Di Giovanni) is arrested for prostituting her eleven-year-old daughter Rosetta (Valentina Scalici). Emotionally stunted Antonio (Enrico Lo Verso), a shy, 25-year-old *carabiniere*, and his partner Grigani (Fabio Alessandrini) are ordered to deliver the sullen, rebellious Rosetta and her brother Luciano (Giuseppe Ieracitano) to a Catholic orphanage in northern Italy. Grigani abandons the group to visit his girlfriend in Bologna and Antonio and the children are turned away from the orphanage. The trio head south on a three-day trip, mostly by train, to a home for troubled children in Sicily. En route, the children begin to shed their defenses and Antonio becomes increasingly attached to them, even though he knows he must soon turn them over to the authorities.

With a background in socially conscious Italian TV movies, director Gianni Amelio made STOLEN CHILDREN in what he terms a "naked" style, improvising on the script, shooting in unadorned, unpicturesque locations and casting several non-professional performers, including the two extraordinary children. The straightforward, linear narrative takes its time in getting beneath the skin of the characters, in a manner that recalls the documentary-like 1940s classics of Roberto Rossellini and, perhaps most closely, de Sica's 1949 THE BICYCLE THIEF. Though the film has a deep, cumulative emotional pull, it offers no solutions to the problems encountered: the power of STOLEN CHILDREN lies in its unsettled, unfinished quality.

STOLEN KISSES
(BAISERS VOLES)

1968 90m c Romance/Comedy ★★★★
Carrosse/Artistes (France) R/X

Jean-Pierre Leaud *(Antoine Doinel)*, Delphine Seyrig *(Fabienne Tabard)*, Michel Lonsdale *(M. Tabard)*, Claude Jade *(Christine Darbon)*, Harry-Max *(M. Henri Tabard)*, Daniel Ceccaldi *(M. Darbon)*, Claire Duhamel *(Mme. Darbon)*, Catherine Lutz *(Mme. Catherine)*, Andre Falcon *(M. Blady)*, Paul Pavel *(Julien)*

p, Marcel Berbert; d, Francois Truffaut; w, Francois Truffaut, Bernard Revon, Claude de Givray; ph, Denys Clerval; ed, Agnes Guillemot; m, Antoine Duhamel; art d, Claude Pignot

AAN Best Foreign Language Film

Sadly complacent comedy of French charm, and Paris was never so beguiling. STOLEN KISSES covers the installment in the life of Antoine Doinel (Jean-Pierre Leaud), which began in THE 400 BLOWS and continued through the LOVE AT TWENTY episode entitled "Antoine and Colette." The film picks up as Doinel is discharged from the army at age 20. Unable to make Christine (Claude Jade) love him, he continues his search for the perfect woman. In the process Doinel lands a job with a detective agency, where the rookie Sherlock Holmes bungles every case he investigates. He finally gets a simple assignment in a shoe store after demonstrating his "technical proficiency" by wrapping a shoe box. Doinel is supposed to discover why the store's owner, M. Tabard (Michel Lonsdale), feels hated and whether there is a conspiracy against him; but while working late one night, he begins an affair with Tabard's wife, Fabienne (Delphine Seyrig). Dismissed, as Truffaut's work often is, as overly charming and simplistic, STOLEN KISSES was oddly enough made during a time of extremely intense political crisis in Paris, with a sidebar of artistic controversy. Dedicated to Henri Langlois and his Cinematheque Francaise, STOLEN KISSES was made while Truffaut worked with a defense committee that fought for the reinstatement of the Cinematheque director. Langlois, who in his lifetime was probably responsible for the film education of every aspiring director in France, was ordered removed by Minister of Culture Andre Malraux—a move met with opposition by the entire international film community. Truffaut stated, "If STOLEN KISSES is good, it will be thanks to Langlois." As violence erupted in the streets of Paris, Truffaut continued his filming, but, instead of making the political film one might expect to emerge from a period of revolt, the director chose to reaffirm his belief in cinema.

STONE BOY, THE

1984 93m c Drama   ★★★½
Fox   (U.S.)   PG/

Robert Duvall (Joe Hillerman), Frederic Forrest (Andy Jansen), Glenn Close (Ruth Hillerman), Wilford Brimley (George Jansen), Jason Presson (Arnold Hillerman), Gail Youngs (Lu Jansen), Cindy Fisher (Amalie), Susan Blackstone (Nora Hillerman), Dean Cain (Eugene Hillerman), Kenneth Anderson

p, Joe Roth, Ivan Bloch; d, Christopher Cain; w, Gina Berriault (based on her short story); ph, Juan Ruiz-Anchia; ed, Paul Rubell; m, James Horner; prod d, Joseph G. Pacelli; art d, Stephanie Wooley; cos, Gail Viola

At first glance, the story for this quiet, sensitive film would seem to bear a resemblance to ORDINARY PEOPLE. But this is *really* about ordinary people—Montana farmers who have to cope with tragedy using strength from within and without help from a professional shrink. Director Chris Cain shows enormous talent as he leads the actors through tricky territory. Arnold (Jason Presson) and Eugene Hillerman (Dean Cain, the director's son) are brothers living on a farm in Montana. They rise early to go duck hunting, but their happy plans soon turn tragic as Eugene is accidentally shot by Arnold's gun. Arnold becomes quiet, doesn't know what to do. His brother is dead and he realizes he'll have to tell everyone what happened, but he can't face the fact right away. When he finally returns home to break the terrible news to his parents (Robert Duvall and Glenn Close), he is immediately left outside of their sorrow. Since Arnold is not in tears or hysterical, his father misreads that as his not caring. His mother also can't fathom Arnold's tranquil behavior, but she is less stern. As the whirlpool swims around him, Arnold gets quieter and quieter, becoming a "stone boy" in that he cannot be part of the swirling madness of a family in chaos. A langorous movie with little of the tear jerking and often obvious sequences one might have expected, THE STONE BOY pulls no punches and makes very few statements. All it seems to do is present the story very simply and let the audience decide what's right and what's wrong.

STORMY MONDAY

1988 93m c Crime/Romance   ★★★½
British Screen/Film Four/Moving Picture (U.K.)   R/15

Melanie Griffith (Kate), Tommy Lee Jones (Cosmo), Sting (Finney), Sean Bean (Brendan), James Cosmo, Mark Long, Brian Lewis, Derek Hoxby, Heathcote Williams, Prunella Gee

p, Nigel Stafford-Clark; d, Mike Figgis; w, Mike Figgis; ph, Roger Deakins; ed, David Martin; m, Mike Figgis; prod d, Andrew McAlpine; cos, Sandy Powell

This feature debut from British writer-director-composer Mike Figgis is a tautly constructed, deftly executed crime thriller. The action is set in Newcastle, England, an economically depressed city desperate for jobs. American business magnate-gangster, Cosmo (Tommy Lee Jones), is launching an ambitious money-laundering scheme by buying up lots of real estate. One man refuses all of Jones's lucrative offers: Finney (Sting), the owner of a successful jazz club. Caught up in the conflict are Kate (Melanie Griffith), an American who has worked for Cosmo as a call girl, and Brendan (Sean Bean), a young jazz enthusiast. When two thugs from London are hired to "persuade" Finney to sell his club, he turns the tables and sends the head assassin back to London

with a broken arm. But Cosmo escalates the violence. STORMY MONDAY draws its strength from subtle shadings of character and a vivid evocation of its setting, Newcastle. The little violent action there is takes place either very quickly or offscreen. Figgis's moody realization of the screenplay is quietly effective and brimming with visual nuance and irony—particularly in its perceptive take on the contradictions of the global economy.

STORMY WEATHER

1943 77m bw Musical   ★★★½
Fox   (U.S.)   /U

Lena Horne (Selina Rogers), Bill Robinson (Corky), Cab Calloway and His Band, Fats Waller, The Nicholas Brothers (Themselves), Ada Brown (Ada), Dooley Wilson (Gabe), Ned Stanfield, Johnny Horace (The Shadracks), Emmett "Babe" Wallace (Chick Bailey)

p, William LeBaron; d, Andrew L. Stone; w, Frederick Jackson, Ted Koehler, H.S. Kraft (based on a story by Jerry Horwin, Seymour B. Robinson); ph, Leon Shamroy; ed, James B. Clark; art d, James Basevi, Joseph C. Wright; fx, Fred Sersen; chor, Clarence Robinson; cos, Helen Rose

Because it contains performances by many of the great black musical stars of its day, STORMY WEATHER will be studied for years to come. The slim story into which the acts are incorporated concerns veteran entertainer Corky (Bill Robinson), who, as he reflects on his career, flashes back to a number of scenes that are all neat musical bits in themselves. (A few were later released as short subjects in black theaters.) Corky's struggles and rise in show business, as well as his split and eventual reconciliation with his wife (Lena Horne), are thinly sketched, with a cavalcade of musical numbers in between. Cab Calloway, Fats Waller, Robinson, Horne, Mae Johnson, The Nicholas Brothers, Babe Wallace, Ada Brown, and many others are featured; about the only cast member who doesn't perform is Dooley Wilson, whose singing was so important in CASABLANCA. Horne, who had just completed CABIN IN THE SKY, was 26, making the 65-year-old Robinson old enough to be her grandfather, not her husband, but the discrepancy is overlooked. Jazz fans will recognize Zutty Singleton at the drums, Coleman Hawkins playing sax, and Taps Miller on trumpet, among several others.

STORY OF A CHEAT, THE
(LE ROMAN D'UN TRICHEUR)

1936 83m bw Drama   ★★★★½
Cineas   (France)

Sacha Guitry (The Cheat), Jacqueline Delubac (Young Woman), Rosine Derean (The Jewel Thief), Marguerite Moreno (The Countess), Pauline Carton (Mme. Morlot), Gaston Dupray (Waiter), Serge Grave (The Cheat), Pierre Assy (The Cheat), Frehel (Singer), Henri Pfeifer (M. Charbonnier)

d, Sacha Guitry; w, Sacha Guitry (based on his novel Memoires D'un Tricheur); ph, Marcel Lucien; ed, Myriam; m, Adolphe Borchard

An exciting, funny, innovative, and brilliant effort from one of France's most prolific playwrights and filmmakers, Sacha Guitry. Considered to be Guitry's masterpiece, THE STORY OF A CHEAT is told to the audience by the cheat (Guitry, as usual, playing the role) himself, as he writes his memoirs in a Parisian cafe, while on the screen we see the events he is speaking of, acted out without dialogue. All we get to hear is Guitry's witty commentary. His life story begins with the first time he is caught being a cheat, an act which gets him sent to his room without supper. In a stroke of luck, however, his entire family eat poison mushrooms that evening and die. Thus begins a long string of events in which Guitry benefits from his cheating instead of paying for it. Not only is the film itself unique, with its cutting back and forth between past and present and its use of reverse motion and wipes, but its title sequence is also exceptional. Like Francois Truffaut's FAHRENHEIT 451, the credits are spoken by the director, but here we see the characters and filmmakers involved. Not surprisingly, his experimentation and humor have gone on to influence greatly those who've seen the picture, especially the filmmakers of the New Wave. It was chiefly the favorable criticism of filmmakers such as Truffaut, Jean-Luc Godard, and Alain Resnais (who cited THE STORY OF A CHEAT as one of the primary influences of HIROSHIMA MON AMOUR) that have brought about the reassessment of Guitry. An outstanding contribution to cinematic and narrative technique which Guitry never quite equaled again.

STORY OF A THREE DAY PASS, THE
(LA PERMISSION)
1967 87m bw Drama ★★★½
OPERA (France)

Harry Baird (Turner), Nicole Berger (Miriam), Christian Marin (Hotelman), Pierre Doris (Peasant), Hal Brav, Tria French

p, Guy Belfond; d, Melvin Van Peebles; w, Melvin Van Peebles; ph, Michel Kelber; ed, Liliane Korb; m, Mickey Baker, Melvin Van Peebles

An impressive first feature from Melvin Van Peebles has a black American soldier, Baird, stationed in France and visiting Paris on a three-day pass. He meets and falls for a French girl, Berger, and together they spend his last two days living a poetically romantic existence. Upon his return, he is demoted by his captain for having dated a white girl. The film is a moving and brutally honest achievement from Van Peebles, who moved to Paris after living in San Francisco, Mexico, and Holland. He started in Paris (without knowing the language) as an author, eventually writing in French and becoming eligible for admission to the French Cinema Center as a director. He then applied for a grant and received $70,000 after expecting no more than $10,000. With a completed film, Van Peebles went back to the US as a French filmmaker, confusing and surprising everyone when they learned he was actually a black American. Actress Berger, who also appeared in Francois Truffaut's SHOOT THE PIANO PLAYER, was killed just a short time after completing this picture.

STORY OF ADELE H., THE
(L'HISTOIRE D'ADELE H.)
1975 97m c Biography ★★★★
Carrosse/Artistes (France) PG/A

Isabelle Adjani (Adele Hugo), Bruce Robinson (Lt. Albert Pinson), Sylvia Marriott (Mrs. Saunders), Reubin Dorey (Mr. Saunders), Joseph Blatchley (Mr. Whistler), M. White (Col. White), Carl Hathwell (Lt. Pinson's Batman), Ivry Gitlis (Hypnotist), Cecil De Sausmarez (Mr. Lenoir), Raymond Falla (Judge Johnstone)

p, Marcel Berbert; d, Francois Truffaut; w, Francois Truffaut, Jean Gruault, Suzanne Schiffman, Jan Dawson (based on the book Le Journal d'Adele Hugo by Frances V. Guille); ph, Nestor Almendros; ed, Yann Dedet; m, Maurice Jaubert; art d, Jean-Pierre Kohut-Svelko; cos, Jacqueline Guyot

AAN Best Actress: Isabelle Adjani

Truffaut's hauntingly poetic tale of obsession stars the beautiful Isabelle Adjani as Adele Hugo, daughter of France's most beloved author, Victor Hugo. The picture opens in Halifax, Nova Scotia, in 1863, after Adele has left her father's Guernsey home to seek out Albert Pinson (Bruce Robinson), a young English lieutenant who wants nothing to do with the determined young woman. Although her obsession with Pinson grows to the point that she announces to her father a pending engagement, Adele's only real contact with him is from a distance—spying on him while he makes love to another woman, or following him (or those she believes to be him) in the streets. Adele is obsessed not only with the lieutenant, but also with her own writing, paying frequent visits to a local bookstore to buy reams of paper and then retreating to her room to scrawl indecipherable coded messages in her journal.

One of Truffaut's most complex films, a love story that shows only one half of an affair, THE STORY OF ADELE H. combines the fascination with obsessive women that fills his films (Catherine from JULES AND JIM, Julie Kohler from THE BRIDE WORE BLACK, Camille Bliss from SUCH A GORGEOUS KID LIKE ME) with his love of books, diaries and the process of writing (FAHRENHEIT 451 and THE WILD CHILD). The true story of Adele Hugo is already engrossing; unable to live up to her father's expectations, she thought she could not fill the void in his heart after his favorite daughter, Leopoldine, drowned. Truffaut's disturbing film on the subject is as difficult to walk away from as it is to watch.

STORY OF ALEXANDER GRAHAM BELL, THE
1939 97m bw Biography ★★★½
Fox (U.S.) /U

Don Ameche (Alexander Graham Bell), Loretta Young (Mrs. Bell), Henry Fonda (Tom Watson), Charles Coburn (Gardner Hubbard), Spring Byington (Mrs. Hubbard), Gene Lockhart (Thomas Sanders), Sally Blane (Gertrude Hubbard), Polly Ann Young (Grace Hubbard), Georgiana Young (Berta Hubbard), Bobs Watson (George Sanders)

p, Kenneth MacGowan; d, Irving Cummings; w, Lamar Trotti (based on a story by Ray Harris); ph, Leon Shamroy; ed, Walter Thompson; cos, Royer

THE STORY OF ALEXANDER GRAHAM BELL is the film for which Don Ameche will be best remembered, despite his Oscar-winning performance in COCOON more than 40 years later. The film opens in 1873 with Alexander Graham Bell (Ameche) trying to earn his living by working with deaf-mutes while spending his off-hours inventing. Bell is soon enamored of a pretty young Scot (Loretta Young) whom he has been asked to teach. They fall in love, and she asks her father to unbuckle his copious money belt to back one of Bell's inventions. Bell hopes to perfect a process whereby he can use the same kind of wires Western Union uses for sending dots and dashes to transmit the sound of a human voice. After much trial and error, he succeeds and, in doing so, becomes one of the most famous inventors in history. Not even remotely factual, this Hollywood-invented story is an enjoyable feature nonetheless, especially when the boyish and earnest Ameche is onscreen.

STORY OF ESTHER COSTELLO, THE
1957 103m bw Drama ★★★★
Romulus/Valiant (U.K.) /A

Joan Crawford (Margaret Landi), Rossano Brazzi (Carlo Landi), Heather Sears (Esther Costello), Lee Patterson (Harry Grant), Ron Randell (Frank Wenzel), Fay Compton (Mother Superior), John Loder (Paul Marchant), Denis O'Dea (Father Devlin), Sidney James (Ryan), Bessie Love (Matron in Art Gallery)

p, Jack Clayton, David Miller; d, David Miller; w, Charles Kaufman (based on the novel by Nicholas Monsarrat); ph, Robert Krasker; ed, Ralph Kemplen; m, Georges Auric; art d, George Provis, Tony Masters; cos, Jean Louis

A powerful if sometimes seamy look at a problem more famously dealt with in THE MIRACLE WORKER. Crawford is a wealthy American, estranged from her husband, who is visiting her birthplace in Ireland when she meets Sears, a young girl who is deaf, blind, and mute as a result of psychological trauma. Since there is no specialized medical service in her small town, Sears' condition has remained untreated. At the urging of a local priest, the childless Crawford decides to take Sears into her life as a surrogate daughter. After much struggle and many years, the girl begins to respond to treatment. Then Brazzi, Crawford's ex, reappears. From Crawford, he wants money; from Sears—now grown to young womanhood—he wants something else.

It's more melodramatic than THE MIRACLE WORKER, and the focus is as much on the people around the girl as the girl herself. Crawford showed off her acting range in familiar melo territory, and the result was a Best Actress Award from the British Film Academy. A strong story, good acting, and a most literate script from Charles Kaufman, who also wrote the screenplay for FREUD.

STORY OF G.I. JOE, THE
1945 109m bw Biography/War ★★★★
UA (U.S.)

Burgess Meredith (Ernie Pyle), Robert Mitchum (Lt. Walker), Freddie Steele (Sgt. Warnicki), Wally Cassell (Pvt. Dondaro), Jimmy Lloyd (Pvt. Spencer), Jack Reilly (Pvt. Murphy), William Murphy (Pvt. Mew), William Self (Cookie Henderson), Dick Rich (Sergeant at Showers), Billy Benedict (Whitey)

p, Lester Cowan; d, William A. Wellman; w, Leopold Atlas, Guy Endore, Philip Stevenson (based on the book by Ernie Pyle); ph, Russell Metty; ed, Otho Lovering, Al Joseph; m, Ann Ronell, Louis Applebaum; art d, James Sullivan, David Hall

AAN Best Supporting Actor: Robert Mitchum; *AAN Best Original Screenplay:* Leopold Atlas, Guy Endore, Philip Stevenson

This story of the greatest of America's WWII combat correspondents, Ernie Pyle, immortalizes the man who celebrated the common soldier in his dispatches and books (*Brave Men* and *Here Is Your War*). As the film begins, Pyle (Burgess Meredith) catches up with a tired platoon of infantrymen in Italy, observing and comforting them as they fight through town after town, enduring death, misery, boredom, and fear. Leading the platoon is Lt. Walker (Robert Mitchum), a tough but likable officer who is respected and admired by his men. The film has no real story, only the consistent wearing down of the men through combat and fatigue. Meredith is superb, conveying the humanity and caring of Pyle, but it is Mitchum, in a star-making performance, who steals the show. This great picture had the full cooperation of Pyle, who was killed in the South Pacific before seeing THE STORY OF G.I. JOE.

STORY OF LOUIS PASTEUR, THE

1936 85m bw Biography   ★★★★
Warner Bros. (U.S.)   /A

Paul Muni (*Louis Pasteur*), Josephine Hutchinson (*Mme. Pasteur*), Anita Louise (*Annette Pasteur*), Donald Woods (*Jean Martel*), Fritz Leiber (*Dr. Charbonnet*), Henry O'Neill (*Roux*), Porter Hall (*Dr. Rosignol*), Raymond Brown (*Dr. Radisse*), Akim Tamiroff (*Dr. Zaranoff*), Walter Kingsford (*Napoleon III*)

p, Henry Blanke; d, William Dieterle; w, Sheridan Gibney, Pierre Collings (based on the story by Gibney, Collings); ph, Tony Gaudio; ed, Ralph Dawson; art d, Robert Haas; cos, Milo Anderson

AAN Best Picture; AA Best Actor: Paul Muni; *AA Best Screenplay:* Pierre Collings, Sheridan Gibney

This film biography stars Paul Muni as Louis Pasteur, the French scientist who worked to find a cure for anthrax and hydrophobia. His colleagues at the Medical Academy are convinced his experiments are a waste of time and ridicule his research, so he and his family move to the French countryside, where he can conduct his experiments in peace. Authorities soon learn that the sheep in Pasteur's area are disease-free as a result of his efforts, a finding which causes some stir in the Medical Academy, as Pasteur is now praised for his ground-breaking work by his former critics. THE STORY OF LOUIS PASTEUR is well told, with an intelligent script, excellent performances, and careful attention to scientific accuracy. Muni offers a fine characterization that shows the famed scientist as a man faced with extraordinary obstacles.

STORY OF QIU JU, THE
(QIU JU DA GUANSI)

1992 114m c Comedy/Drama/Political   ★★★★
Sil-Metropole Organization/Beijing Film   PG/12
Academy-Youth Film Studio (China/Hong Kong)

Gong Li (*Wan Qiu Ju*), Lei Laosheng (*Wan Shantung—Village Head*), Liu Peiqi (*Wan Qing Lai—Husband*), Yang Liuchun (*Meizi*), Ge Zhijun (*Officer Li*), Zhu Qanqing, Cui Luowen, Yang Huiqin, Wang Jianfa, Lin Zi

p, Ma Fung-kwok; d, Zhang Yimou; w, Liu Heng (from the novel *The Wan Family's Lawsuit* by Chen Yuanbin); ph, Chi Xiaoling, Yu Xiaoqun; ed, Du Yuan; m, Zhao Jiping; art d, Cao Jiuping

Preeminent Chinese director Zhang Yimou ventures onto contemporary terrain for the first time with this lovingly detailed, gently satirical tale of a country woman's campaign to seek redress for a minor grievance. Star Gong Li delivers a meticulously scaled performance in a daringly unglamorous role.

Qiu Ju (Gong Li) is a pregnant farm laborer driven to seek justice when the village elder, Shantung (Lei Laosheng), kicks her husband (Liu Peiqi) in the groin after the husband has mocked the elder over his inability to sire a son. After being assured by the village apothecary that her husband is not permanently damaged, Qiu Ju demands an apology from the culprit. Shantung dismisses her semi-articulate request, mov-

ing Qiu Ju to visit the local magistrate, Officer Li (Ge Zhijun). Li acts as a mediator between the two parties, suggesting that Shantung pay 200 yuan for lost labor and medical expenses. Shantung agrees, but refuses to apologize; he further insults Qiu Ju by throwing the money on the ground so she will have to bow to him to pick it up. Qiu Ju's crusade then leads her far from her village, through increasingly labyrinthine bureaucracies, developing a momentum of its own that eventually proves disastrous for one of the characters.

Using real settings and, in some cases, real people interacting spontaneously with Gong Li as a hidden camera records the action, Zhang gives his film a distinctly documentary feel. Yet much of QIU JU plays almost like a Preston Sturges farce in which an ordinary person's quest for justice is taken to comical extremes. Along the way, Zhang provides a rich, lively tapestry of modern Chinese daily life and a powerful warning about what can happen when the traditional process of saving face is neglected.

STORY OF VERNON AND IRENE CASTLE, THE

1939 90m bw Musical/Biography   ★★★½
RKO (U.S.)   /U

Fred Astaire (*Vernon Castle*), Ginger Rogers (*Irene Castle*), Edna May Oliver (*Maggie Sutton*), Walter Brennan (*Walter Ash*), Lew Fields (*Himself*), Etienne Girardot (*Papa Aubel*), Janet Beecher (*Mrs. Foote*), Rolfe Sedan (*Emile Aubel*), Leonid Kinskey (*Artist*), Robert Strange (*Dr. Foote*)

p, George Haight, Pandro S. Berman; d, H.C. Potter; w, Richard Sherman, Oscar Hammerstein II, Dorothy Yost (based on the books *My Husband* and *My Memories of Vernon Castle* by Irene Castle); ph, Robert de Grasse; ed, William Hamilton; art d, Van Nest Polglase, Perry Ferguson; fx, Vernon L. Walker, Douglas Travers; chor, Hermes Pan; cos, Walter Plunkett, Edward Stevenson, Irene Castle

This fine film biography of the title beloved dance team was Ginger Rogers and Fred Astaire's final film together for RKO. (Astaire and Rogers teamed once again a decade later, in MGM's THE BARKLEYS OF BROADWAY, but the magic of their pairing had largely fled.) After Irene Foote (Rogers), the daughter of a well-known New Rochelle physician, meets vaudeville performer Vernon Castle (Astaire), they fall in love, marry, go to Paris, and become a famous ballroom dancing duo. Soon all the world wants to be like the Castles: not only do they invent several dance steps, but their hair is duplicated in wigs, cigars are named after him, and they have their own line of cosmetics. During WWI, Vernon becomes a pilot with the Canadian Royal Flying Corps, while Irene works on the silent film PATRIA by herself. He sends for her to join him in Texas, where he has a huge romantic reunion planned, including an orchestra to play for them alone. All does not go as planned, however, and sudden tragedy strikes the Castles.

The fact that the real Vernon Castle was British didn't enter into matters; Astaire was not required to mimic an English accent because hardly anyone had ever heard the famed dancer speak. The details of the team's meteoric rise to stardom are sketchily intertwined among the many songs in the score, with Edna May Oliver providing supporting highlights as the agent who had faith in the happy couple and pushed hard to make them stars. The real Irene Castle (upon whose books the film is based) served as technical advisor, and the dancing re-creates the Castles' original steps with little in the way of alteration by Astaire and choreographer Hermes Pan. The score contains a tremendous number of songs, and it's a tribute to the talents of musical director Victor Baravalle, who died before the film was released, that they feel right and never seem crammed in for their own sake. Astaire and Rogers are both in very fine form, and if the final image of their ghosts dancing down a path comes across as exceptionally moving, it's because this film is as much a farewell to this amazing duo as it is to the characters they play onscreen.

STORY OF WOMEN

1988 110m c Drama   ★★★
MK2/Camelia/La Sept/La Sofica Sofinergie/A2 (France)

Isabelle Huppert (*Marie*), Francois Cluzet (*Paul*), Niels Tavernier (*Lucien*), Marie Trintignant (*Lulu/Lucie*), Louis Ducreux, Michel Beaune, Dominique Blanc, Marie Bunel p, Marin Karmitz; d, Claude Chabrol; w, Colo Tavernier O'Hagan, Claude Chabrol (based on *Une Affaire de Femmes* by Francis Szpiner); ph, Jean Rabier; ed, Monique Fardoulis; m, Matthieu Chabrol

In a German-occupied French village in 1941, Marie (Isabelle Huppert) struggles to eke out an existence for herself and two children, then begins supporting her family in style by performing amateur abortions. Her husband, Paul (Fracois Cluzet), whom Marie grows to despise, returns from the war a broken man, but when her affair with a young collaborator (Nils Tavernier) becomes increasingly overt, Paul turns informer, and Marie finds herself standing trial in Paris for her "crime against the state."

Loosely based on the life of Marie-Louise Giraud, an actual abortionist who was executed by the Vichy government, this absorbing account of a dark period in French history is technically impressive on every level. Chabrol's economical control of cinematic narrative, as usual, stands him in good stead, lending his depiction of the nightmare of the Occupation the kind of melodramatic tension that is his specialty. STORY OF WOMEN unfolds with inexorable logic, though it is too schematic in conception to achieve real tragic power. Huppert (who took the best actress award at the 1988 Venice Film Festival for her performance here) remains stoically in character throughout, daring viewers to sympathize with her cool demeanor, but even her fine work is not enough to overcome the problems in the script.

STRAIGHT TIME

1978   114m   c   Crime   ★★★★
First Artists/Sweetwall   (U.S.)   R/18

Dustin Hoffman *(Max Dembo)*, Theresa Russell *(Jenny Mercer)*, Harry Dean Stanton *(Jerry Schue)*, Gary Busey *(Willy Darin)*, M. Emmet Walsh *(Earl Frank)*, Sandy Baron *(Manny)*, Kathy Bates *(Selma Darin)*, Edward Bunker *(Mickey)*, Fran Ryan *(Cafe Owner)*, Rita Taggart *(Carol Schue)*

p, Stanley Beck, Tim Zinnemann; d, Ulu Grosbard; w, Alvin Sargent, Edward Bunker, Jeffrey Boam (based on the novel *No Beast So Fierce* by Bunker); ph, Owen Roizman; ed, Sam O'Steen, Randy Roberts; m, David Shire; prod d, Stephen Grimes; art d, Richard Lawrence; cos, Bernie Pollack

A gripping, disturbing, and unglamorized portrait of a professional thief who thrives on the thrill and danger of his actions. Hoffman, in one of the best performances of his career, plays a thief who is released from prison after a six-year sentence for armed robbery. Hoffman tries to go straight but is continually thwarted by slimy parole officer Walsh, as well as his old friends, a motley assortment of junkies and small-time hoods.

Based on ex-convict Edward Bunker's novel *No Beast So Fierce*, STRAIGHT TIME was an obsessive labor of love for its star, who had purchased the rights to the novel in 1972. Hoffman struck a deal with First Artists that would give him the right to direct the film and supervise the final cut. To research his role Hoffman had himself booked at Los Angeles County Jail and went through the procedure all inmates go through (this was later re-created for the film in documentarylike fashion). Hoffman also sneaked into San Quentin prison and mingled with the prisoners for several hours incognito to get the feel of prison life. The actor also interviewed ex-cons and visited their homes. During production, however, Hoffman found that acting and directing were too much for him, so he hired his old friend Grosbard to take over the helm. When the filming was completed, First Artists president Phil Feldman took control of the film and refused Hoffman his right to final cut (Feldman was the same man who tampered with Sam Peckinpah's THE WILD BUNCH, cutting over 20 minutes of character development behind the director's back). Hoffman sued for damages. The studio, which thought the film was a disaster, dumped the movie into release, where it received bad reviews and little box office attention. Hoffman's case was thrown out, and to this day the actor speaks little of it. But Hoffman has nothing to be ashamed of. STRAIGHT TIME is a powerful film that shows a criminal as he is. The film has no tired explanations for Hoffman's behavior, no fingers are pointed, no apologies or excuses are offered. Hoffman is a habitual criminal and that is the way he is. Though the parole system is taken to task for the "Catch 22"-type restrictions given to ex-cons, this is not presented as an excuse

for Hoffman's return to crime—only a match that ignites the fuse already inside the man. The performances in STRAIGHT TIME are nothing less than superb. Walsh is perfect as the slimy parole officer who couldn't care less about his charges. Busey once again proves his versatility and is unforgettable as the pathetic addict. Russell is fine as the naive girl willing to let Hoffman drift through her life, and Stanton practically steals the film as the ex-thief yearning to escape from the boredom of his suburban lifestyle. Grosbard's direction is straightforward and professional. A highlight is the electrifying scene of a jewelry store robbery.

STRANGE DAYS

1995   145m   c   Science Fiction/Thriller/Drama   ★★½
First Light/Lightstorm Entertainment   (U.S.)   R/18

Ralph Fiennes *(Lenny Nero)*, Angela Bassett *(Lornette "Mace" Mason)*, Juliette Lewis *(Faith Justin)*, Tom Sizemore *(Max Peltier)*, Michael Wincott *(Philo Gant)*, Vincent D'Onofrio *(Burton Steckler)*, Glenn Plummer *(Jeriko One)*, Brigitte Bako *(Iris)*, Richard Edson *(Tick)*, William Fichtner *(Dwayne Engelman)*

p, James Cameron, Steven-Charles Jaffe; d, Kathryn Bigelow; w, James Cameron, Jay Cocks (from a story by James Cameron); ph, Matthew F. Leonetti; ed, Howard Smith; m, Graeme Revell; prod d, Lilly Kilvert; fx, John Warnke; art d, Terry Frazee, James Lima, Digital Domain, Michael "Tony" Meagher; cos, Ellen Mirojnick

Despite its high-tech trappings, slick surfaces and relentless self-reflexivity, Kathryn Bigelow's STRANGE DAYS is shopworn pulp. Though executed with superior style and showy performances, it fails to realize the potential of its premise.

In the last days of 1999, former vice cop Lenny Nero (Ralph Fiennes) prowls a chaotic Los Angeles dealing illegal "clips." These are contraband recordings of sensory experiences made directly from the brains of individuals equipped with the Superconducting Quantum Interference Device (SQUID), a device easily secreted under a hat or hairpiece. A principled pusher, Lenny refuses to deal in "snuff" clips. He uses the forbidden technology himself to relive his own happier days with Faith Justin (Juliette Lewis) who has since become a rising pop star under the control of menacing promoter Philo Gant (Michael Wincott). Lenny keeps tabs on Faith through his friend Max Peltier (Tom Sizemore), a former cop turned bodyguard. In turn, Lenny's friend Lornette "Mace" Mason (Angela Bassett), a formidable security specialist, keeps a protective eye on him. He'll need it: before long, Lenny and Mace are swept up in a murder conspiracy that threatens to bring about a racial apocalypse.

A cultural by-product of the videotaped beating of black motorist Rodney King by LA police, the film seems a calculated attempt to restore the audience's faith in (white) police authority. Bigelow's decision to let authority off the hook eliminated any possibility that STRANGE DAYS could make a meaningful statement about the racial, social, and economic meaning of the Rodney King beating and the subsequent LA riots. There's nothing here about how American society actually *works* as the end of the 20th Century approaches. What's left is pure sensation and visually stylish pyrotechnics. There's very little at stake; the generic elements function as a template for empty virtuosity.

STRANGE LOVE OF MARTHA IVERS, THE

1946   116m   bw   Crime   ★★★★
Paramount   (U.S.)   /A

Barbara Stanwyck *(Martha Ivers)*, Van Heflin *(Sam Masterson)*, Lizabeth Scott *(Toni Marachek)*, Kirk Douglas *(Walter O'Neil)*, Judith Anderson *(Mrs. Ivers)*, Roman Bohnen *(Mr. O'Neil)*, Darryl Hickman *(Sam Masterson as a Boy)*, Janis Wilson *(Martha Ivers as a Girl)*, Ann Doran *(Secretary)*, Frank Orth *(Hotel Clerk)*

p, Hal B. Wallis; d, Lewis Milestone; w, Robert Rossen (based on the story "Love Lies Bleeding" by Jack Patrick); ph, Victor Milner; ed, Archie Marshek; m, Miklos Rozsa; art d, Hans Dreier, John Meehan; fx, Farciot Edouart; cos, Edith Head

AAN Best Original Screenplay: Jack Patrick

A dark and perverse melodrama which stars Stanwyck as the wicked Martha Ivers, a wealthy and powerful woman who has gained control of the small town of Iverstown, Pennsylvania, after inheriting a large family fortune. She lives with her weakling husband Walter (Douglas, in his first film), a district attorney who is preparing to make a bid for mayor. What no one in the town knows, however, is that Martha and Walter share a deep secret—as a young girl, Martha murdered her aunt while planning to elope with then-sweetheart Sam Masterson. In order to protect the family name, an innocent man was executed for the crime. After a long absence, Sam (Heflin) returns to Iverstown. The couple fear that he is preparing to blackmail them, but their paranoia only makes him more curious about Martha's childhood secret. A cruel *film noir* which, although it starts somewhat slowly, builds to a frenzied state of suspense in which the characters, all of them vile, have a perverse hold over one another. The result is an often gripping film which shows the collaborative efforts of such talents as Wallis, Milestone, Rossen, Rozsa, art director Hans Dreier, and costumer Edith Head. This film also includes among its credits four future directors: screenwriter Rossen, Kirk Douglas, assistant director Robert Aldrich, and, as a bit player, Blake Edwards.

STRANGER, THE

1946 95m bw Thriller/War   ★★★★
International Pictures (U.S.)   /A

Edward G. Robinson *(Wilson)*, Loretta Young *(Mary Longstreet)*, Orson Welles *(Prof. Charles Rankin/Franz Kindler)*, Philip Merivale *(Judge Longstreet)*, Richard Long *(Noah Longstreet)*, Byron Keith *(Dr. Jeff Lawrence)*, Billy House *(Potter)*, Konstantin Shayne *(Konrad Meinike)*, Martha Wentworth *(Sara)*, Isabel O'Madigan *(Mrs. Lawrence)*

p, Sam Spiegel; d, Orson Welles; w, Anthony Veiller, John Huston (uncredited), Orson Welles (based on the story by Victor Trivas, Decla Dunning); ph, Russell Metty; ed, Ernest Nims; m, Bronislau Kaper; art d, Perry Ferguson; cos, Michael Woulfe

AAN Best Original Screenplay: Victor Trivas

After having made three commercial disasters in a row (THE MAGNIFICENT AMBERSONS; JOURNEY INTO FEAR; and IT'S ALL TRUE), Orson Welles was badly in need of a hit that would right him in the eyes of Hollywood. The result was THE STRANGER, the most restrained and conventional of Welles's films, but still a thrilling entertainment. Set shortly after WWII, the film casts Edward G. Robinson as Wilson, a Nazi hunter assigned the task of finding the infamous Franz Kindler, one of the architects of the genocide of the Jews. Wilson traces Kindler to the sleepy college town of Hartford, Connecticut, where he comes to suspect that Prof. Charles Rankin (Welles) is actually Kindler hiding behind a new identity. Although Rankin does a fine job of casting doubt on Wilson's suspicions, the latter's dogged pursuit of the truth wins out and Kindler is exposed. In THE STRANGER, Welles gives us one of the cinema's most realistic and chilling portrayals of a Nazi. His Franz Kindler is not a cartoon character in uniform spouting propaganda and clicking his heels, but an arrogant, cynical, amoral, and wholly self-confident creature who believes that he is superior to anyone he meets—evil incarnate. Robinson is also quite good as the hunter determined to catch his prey. Technically, as one expects with Welles, the film is superb. THE STRANGER is not as wildly creative as his other films, but all the Welles trademarks are present, including superior lighting, inventive camera angles, strong transitions, and characters silhouetted in darkness.

STRANGER, THE
(L'ETRANGER)

1967 104m c Drama   ★★
Master Marianne Casbah/DEG (Algeria/France/Italy)   /AA

Marcello Mastroianni *(Arthur Meursault)*, Anna Karina *(Marie Cardona)*, Bernard Blier *(Defense Counsel)*, Georges Wilson *(Examining Magistrate)*, Bruno Cremer *(Priest)*, Pierre Bertin *(Judge)*, Jacques Herlin *(Director of Home)*, Marc Laurent *(Emmanuel)*, Georges Geret *(Raymond)*, Alfred Adam *(Prosecutor)*

p, Dino De Laurentiis; d, Luchino Visconti; w, Suso Cecchi D'Amico, Georges Conchon, Emmanuel Robles, Luchino Visconti (based on the novel by Albert Camus); ph, Giuseppe Rotunno; ed, Ruggero Mastroianni; m, Piero Piccioni; art d, Mario Garbuglia; cos, Piero Tosi

Mastroianni plays the existential Meursault, a French clerk living in Algiers who one day, for no other reason than the bright sunshine, shoots and kills a young Algerian. He is brought to trial, where he is forced to answer questions about an affair he had shortly after the death of his mother and his failure to cry at his mother's funeral. While awaiting the guillotine, Mastroianni refuses to be swayed by the prison priest's beliefs and chooses instead to think about life and existence. As is often the case when a great filmmaker brings the work of a great novelist to the screen, THE STRANGER is an utter failure, in terms of Camus. Director-writer Visconti fails to come close to Camus' style and seems unsure of his own, as if he chose to make the film in the hopes of producing a failure. All that can be said in the movie's favor lies in its stupendous technical achievements and the fine performances of Mastroianni (who somehow seems perfect as Meursault) and Karina.

STRANGER ON THE THIRD FLOOR

1940 64m bw Crime   ★★★★
RKO (U.S.)   /A

Peter Lorre *(Stranger)*, John McGuire *(Michael Ward)*, Margaret Tallichet *(Jane)*, Charles Waldron *(District Attorney)*, Elisha Cook Jr. *(Joe Briggs)*, Charles Halton *(Meng)*, Ethel Griffies *(Mrs. Kane)*, Cliff Clark *(Martin)*, Oscar O'Shea *(Judge)*, Alec Craig *(Defense Attorney)*

p, Lee Marcus; d, Boris Ingster; w, Frank Partos; ph, Nicholas Musuraca; ed, Harry Marker; m, Roy Webb; art d, Van Nest Polglase; fx, Vernon L. Walker

This extremely weird B movie has been hailed as the first true *film noir*, and it certainly has all the *noir* elements, both visual and thematic. Feeling guilty because his eyewitness testimony has sent a man who could be innocent to the electric chair, reporter Michael Ward (McGuire) returns to his apartment in a state of depression. On the stairs he notices an odd-looking little man wearing a white scarf (Lorre) loitering in the building and chases him off. In his room, the reporter realizes that his nosy next door neighbor, Mr. Meng (Halton), isn't doing his usual loud snoring. Tired and upset, Michael wonders if Meng is dead and recalls the several nasty, and public, run-ins he has had with the man. Falling asleep, Michael has a nightmare where he is wrongly accused of his neighbor's murder and is sentenced to die in the electric chair. Upon awakening, Michael checks on Meng and to his horror, finds the man murdered. Arrested for the crime, Michael must rely on his fiance, Jane (Tallichet), to track down the mysterious man in the white scarf.

First-time director Boris Ingster, cinematographer Nicholas Musuraca, and art director Van Nest Polglase created a frightening, claustrophobic, and nightmarish urban environment ruled by indifference, injustice, and moral corruption. The forces of order (the police, district attorney, juries, judges, and institutions) are the true villains here as they quickly and carelessly dispense judgement on citizens. Lorre's killer is obviously mad (an escaped mental patient), but in his brief screen time he is seen to be a sympathetic victim of harsh and thoughtless treatment (he describes being held in a straight-jacket and doused with ice-water). Ingster's direction shows the heavy influence of the Germanic expressionist films of the 1920s and the film is a visual delight. He never again directed anything nearly as interesting or influential as this nearly forgotten B picture.

STRANGER THAN PARADISE

1984 95m bw Drama   ★★★★
Grokenberger/ZDF/Cinesthesia (U.S./West Germany)   R/15

John Lurie *(Willie)*, Eszter Balint *(Eva)*, Richard Edson *(Eddie)*, Cecillia Stark *(Aunt Lottie)*, Danny Rosen *(Billy)*, Rammellzee *(Man with Money)*, Tom Docillo *(Airline Agent)*, Richard Boes *(Factory Worker)*, Rockets Redglare, Harvey Perr

p, Sara Driver; d, Jim Jarmusch; w, Jim Jarmusch; ph, Tom DiCillo; ed, Jim Jarmusch, Melody London; m, John Lurie, Aaron Picht

A bleak but mordantly funny portrait of three aimless characters who discover that "paradise" isn't such an easy place to find. Displaying a hip formalism, Jim Jarmusch's second feature (his first, 1980's PERMANENT VACATION, received scant exposure) is divided into three distinct sections; individual sequences within each section are presented in one sustained take, and are separated by blackouts. The first finds Willie (John Lurie, of Lounge Lizard renown), a Hungarian emigre and self-styled hipster, living in a stark, dreary section of New York City. Willie's day-to-day existence is interrupted when his relatives ask him to house his young female cousin, Eva (Eszter Balint), upon her arrival from the old country. Willie dutifully, but reluctantly, obliges. Eva, however, is anything but a helpless foreigner and promptly goes about her own business. Still, when she departs 10 days later, a strange affection has developed between them.

In the second section, Willie and his buddy Eddie (Richard Edson) decide to head for Cleveland in the dead of winter to visit Eva, who now lives there with her irritable Aunt Lotte (Cecilia Stark). Once again, the characters do little of import together, spending their time staring at TV and visiting Lake Erie. In the third and final section, the trio abandons the frozen north for Florida, where they check into an empty seaside motel and the boys squander most of their money at the dog races. Then Eva suddenly comes into a huge stash of loot.

Although STRANGER THAN PARADISE's premise is inarguably slight, Jarmusch compensates for it with the sheer stylishness of the film. Fortunately, he also transcends the obvious theme of alienation, fashioning instead an ironic comedy about communication and the lack thereof. The film received the Camera d'Or at the 1984 Cannes Film Festival and was cited as best picture of the year by the National Society of Film Critics. Jarmusch went on direct such films as MYSTERY TRAIN and NIGHT ON EARTH.

STRANGERS KISS

1984 93m c/bw Romance   ★★★★
Kill   (U.S.)   R/15

Peter Coyote *(Stanley, the Director)*, Victoria Tennant *(Carol Redding/Betty)*, Blaine Novak *(Stevie Blake/Billy)*, Dan Shor *(Farris, the Producer)*, Richard Romanus *(Frank Silva)*, Linda Kerridge *(Shirley)*, Carlos Palomino *(Estoban)*, Vincent Palmieri *(Scandelli)*, Jay Rasumny *(Jimmy)*, Jon Sloan *(Mikey)*

p, Douglas Dilge; d, Matthew Chapman; w, Blaine Novak, Matthew Chapman (based on a story by Novak); ph, Mikhail Suslov; ed, William Carruth; m, Gato Barbieri; art d, Virginia Randolph; cos, Tracy Tynan

A stylish, charming, honest, romantic, and obsessive look at filmmaking during the B-movie days of the 1950s that transcends its period setting and speaks to filmmakers and viewers of all times. Stanley (Peter Coyote) is a crazed, manipulative director who is driven to make his picture "Strange and Dangerous" at all costs. With his sheepish, boy-wonder producer, Farris (Dan Shor), at his side, Stanley meets with gangster Frank Silva (Richard Romanus) about funding the film. The likable but dangerous Silva agrees, with one condition—that his girl friend Carol (Victoria Tennant) get the lead role. Distressed at the lack of chemistry between Carol and her dopey, insecure costar, Stevie Blake (Blaine Novak), Stanley plots to have his stars fall in love, a scheme that will permanently sever his financial tie with Silva. Photographed in cool, vibrant color reminiscent of the 1950s and scored with a jazzy saxophone melody, STRANGERS KISS stuns with one fresh scene after another. The film shines on all levels, from technique to acting performances, from the direction to the script. What is most apparent in STRANGERS KISS is the director's and screenwriter's love for filmmaking. For anyone who is enthralled by that strange species known as "filmmakers" or for those who just love well-made entertainment reminiscent of a bygone era, STRANGERS KISS is highly recommended.

STRANGERS ON A TRAIN

1951 101m bw Thriller   ★★★★★
Warner Bros.   (U.S.)   /PG

Farley Granger *(Guy Haines)*, Ruth Roman *(Anne Morton)*, Robert Walker *(Bruno Antony)*, Leo G. Carroll *(Sen. Morton)*, Patricia Hitchcock *(Barbara Morton)*, Laura Elliot *(Miriam)*, Marion Lorne *(Mrs. Antony)*, Jonathan Hale *(Mr. Antony)*, Howard St. John *(Capt. Turley)*, John Brown *(Prof. Collins)*

p, Alfred Hitchcock; d, Alfred Hitchcock; w, Raymond Chandler, Czenzi Ormonde, Whitfield Cook (based on the novel by Patricia Highsmith); ph, Robert Burks; ed, William Ziegler; m, Dimitri Tiomkin; art d, Ted Haworth; fx, H.F. Koenekamp; cos, Leah Rhodes

AAN Best Cinematography: Robert Burks

Gripping all the way, this is a Hitchcock thriller in which, through happenstance, two men, completely different, are drawn inexorably together and toward an uncommon goal—murder. Hitchcock opens this electrifying film by showing two sets of male feet, those of Guy Haines (Granger) and Bruno Antony (Walker), hurrying towards a train. Guy wears conservative-looking shoes, Bruno black and white spectator shoes, and from their very movements, the sure gait of Guy, the anxious steps of Bruno, the viewer can easily tell, once the two are shown fully on camera, their distinctive personalities. After some club car chit-chat in which both men discuss some personal problems, Bruno proposes, *in theory*, of course, that they each murder the person vexing the other person's life—Bruno would murder Guy's wife in exchange for Guy murdering Bruno's father. Guy is appalled at the idea, but is even more appalled when Bruno carries out his half of the deal and then expects Guy to do the same.

STRANGERS ON A TRAIN ranks at the top of Hitchcock's most accomplished works, a masterpiece that is so carefully constructed and its characters so well developed that the viewer is quickly intimate and comfortable with the story long before Bruno turns killer. After reading Patricia Highsmith's novel, Hitchcock paid $7,500 for the rights to adapt the book and then went about having a rough draft written for the screen, later bringing in Raymond Chandler to do the finished script—a collaboration which was thoroughly frustrating for both parties. At first Hitchcock insisted that he work at Chandler's side, working out every detail of the film as he, Hitchcock, envisioned it, a routine that soon had the brilliant, booze-sipping Chandler nervous and often upset. Chandler's script nevertheless was the basic one employed by Hitchcock, although the director later asked his favorite writer, Ben Hecht, to come in and "spruce it up." Since Hecht was engaged on several other projects, he assigned Czenzi Ormonde, who worked for him, to clean up some of the dialogue and tighten some scenes before Hecht himself gave final approval. Granger is excellent as the innocent victim of the evil plot, and Walker (who would make only one more film before his death) is, like Joseph Cotten's "Uncle Charlie" in SHADOW OF A DOUBT, one of Hitchcock's most diabolical and charismatic villains—a frightening alter ego to the film's hero. Remade in 1969 as ONCE YOU KISS A STRANGER, and the basis for the 1987 comedy THROW MOMMA FROM THE TRAIN.

STRAPLESS

1989 97m c Drama   ★★★½
Granada/Film Four   (U.K.)   R/15

Blair Brown *(Dr. Lillian Hempel)*, Bruno Ganz *(Raymond Forbes)*, Bridget Fonda *(Amy Hempel)*, Alan Howard *(Mr. Cooper)*, Michael Gough *(Douglas Brodie)*, Hugh Laurie *(Colin)*, Suzanne Burden *(Romaine Salmon)*, Camille Coduri *(Mrs. Clark)*, Gary O'Brien *(Mr. Clark)*, Julian Bunster *(Carlos)*

p, Rick McCallum; d, David Hare; w, David Hare; ph, Andrew Dunn; ed, Edward Marnier; m, Nick Bicat; prod d, Roger Hall

From the writer of PLENTY and writer-director of WETHERBY, British playwright David Hare, comes yet another decidedly odd but utterly irresistible study of isolation, loneliness, and strength. Blair Brown stars as a cancer specialist and expatriate American, Dr. Lillian Hempel, who meets shady, romantic Raymond Forbes (Bruno Ganz) while touring the continent. Enchanted but cautious, Lillian lunches with him but balks at a later rendezvous at his hotel and returns to England without giving him her address. Soon Raymond abruptly shows up on Lillian's doorstep, having obtained her home address from a hotel where she stayed, and resumes his courtship. When he proposes marriage, Lillian again balks, though she agrees to move in with him. Raymond's idea of playing house turns out to be an extended stay at a casino-hotel that ends on an ominous note when he bounces a check in attempting to cover his betting losses. Lillian makes good on Raymond's bad check and returns home. In the face of the mounting chaos in her life, Lillian suffers a minor breakdown but impulsively agrees to marry Raymond, who carries over his romantic excesses into their domestic life.

STRAPLESS is an ode to both independence and interdependence. While Lillian's repression and forced isolation lead her to be seduced by Raymond's romanticism, her independent strength allows her to take the experience on its own terms and use it to enrich her own life. That strength leads her to break out of her shell and become a participant in the lives of those around her. At the same time, her sister learns from Lillian the need to pull back and tend to her inner needs to make a proper environment for her new baby.

In spite of its dreamy allegorical tone and terse political overtones, STRAPLESS is anything but dour and preachy. Instead it is alive with feeling for its characters and their world. Though beautifully controlled under Hare's direction, STRAPLESS is full of poignant, human moments of precise observation, gentle comedy, and penetrating drama. It's also full of exquisite performances, especially from Brown, Ganz, and Fonda, who make the most of the rich roles Hare has written for them.

STRATEGIC AIR COMMAND

1955 114m c Drama ★★★
Paramount (U.S.) /U

James Stewart *(Lt. Col. Robert "Dutch" Holland)*, June Allyson *(Sally Holland)*, Frank Lovejoy *(Gen. Ennis C. Hawkes)*, Barry Sullivan *(Lt. Col. Rocky Samford)*, Alex Nicol *(Ike Knowland)*, Bruce Bennett *(Gen. Espy)*, Jay C. Flippen *(Doyle)*, James Millican *(Gen. Castle)*, James Bell *(Rev. Thorne)*, Richard Shannon *(Aircraft Commander)*

p, Samuel J. Briskin; d, Anthony Mann; w, Valentine Davies, Beirne Lay Jr. (based on his story); ph, William Daniels, Tom Tutwiler; ed, Eda Warren; m, Victor Young; art d, Hal Pereira, Earl Hedrick; fx, John P. Fulton; cos, Edith Head

AAN Best Original Screenplay: Beirne Lay, Jr.

A smash hit movie, mainly due to the sensational airplane footage. Not a war movie, not even an action picture, it's a made-up tale about a St. Louis Cardinals third baseman who is ordered back to service and put into the SAC. Stewart is the veteran hot-corner man who must leave the game of baseball when he's called into the Air Force (this actually did happen to superstar Ted Williams who was drafted to serve as a pilot during the Korean War after already having served in WWII). Like Williams, Stewart already put in his time during the battles of WWII and thinks that the authorities have singled him out because he's a star. He'd much prefer hot grounders to hot jets and makes known his feelings loud and clear. Nevertheless, he must do his country's bidding and acquiesces. He is an experienced pilot and they need men like him to handle the new B-36 and B-47 jets that have the capability of delivering the atomic bomb wherever the President orders it to be dropped. Stewart's wife is Allyson (as in THE GLENN MILLER STORY and THE STRATTON STORY) and she is expecting a child. Once in the service, Stewart settles into his job and grows to respect Lovejoy, a tough but fair commanding officer who combines a gruff manner with a soft side. There is no question that the SAC is important to the nation's security and Stewart soon comes to appreciate that, despite Allyson's whining that her husband's job is keeping him from her.

A fairly sappy story, totally contrived, with dialogue they wouldn't dare use on TV soap operas. What makes it so much fun to watch is the spectacular aerial scenes as shot by Thomas Tutwiler with Paul Mantz at the plane's controls. Mantz, who was one of the best movie pilots ever, died in a crash while making FLIGHT OF THE PHOENIX. His long-time partner was Frank Tallman (their company was TallMantz Aviation) who also died in a light-plane accident. Due to the nature of the movie, the SAC lent support and planes to the production so if there was anything at all that might have had a negative aspect, it was never seen. This was more of a staged documentary than anything else and served to quash the complaints of the taxpayers who were carping about the billions spent on defense.

STRAW DOGS

1971 118m c Crime ★★★★
ABC/Amerbroco/Talent Associates (U.K.) R/X

Dustin Hoffman *(David Sumner)*, Susan George *(Amy Sumner)*, Peter Vaughan *(Tom Hedden)*, T.P. McKenna *(Maj. Scott)*, Del Henney *(Charlie Venner)*, Ken Hutchison *(Scutt)*, Colin Welland *(Rev. Hood)*, Jim Norton *(Cawsey)*, Sally Thomsett *(Janice)*, Donald Webster *(Riddaway)*

p, Daniel Melnick; d, Sam Peckinpah; w, David Zelag Goodman, Sam Peckinpah (based on the novel *The Siege of Trencher's Farm* by Gordon M. Williams); ph, John Coquillon; ed, Paul Davies, Roger Spottiswoode, Tony Lawson; m, Jerry Fielding; prod d, Ray Simm; art d, Ken Bridgeman; cos, Tiny Nicholls

AAN Best Score: Jerry Fielding

STRAW DOGS is one of Sam Peckinpah's finest films, a relentless study in violence and machismo that is shocking, not only for its explicit gore, but for the degree to which it manipulates "civilized" audiences. Even the most passive viewer may find himself silently cheering on the carnage at the film's climax—an act that, in retrospect, gives much cause for discomfort.

David Sumner (Dustin Hoffman), a quiet mathematician, and his wife Amy (Susan George) seek to escape urban violence by moving to her birthplace, a small Cornish village. They hire four locals to build a garage and it isn't long before they start making life unpleasant for David. Led by Charlie (Del Henney), an ex-boyfriend of Amy's, the four workers ridicule David and ogle Amy, who seems to encourage their attentions. David, trying to win their acceptance, accepts an invitation to accompany them on a hunting trip; they desert him, and two of the men return to the cottage and rape Amy, who is ambivalent about the experience and doesn't tell her husband.

Some time later, the couple attend a local church function where Amy, haunted by memories of the rape, has a breakdown. Driving home in a dense fog, they knock down Henry (David Warner), the town simpleton. Unbeknownst to the couple, Henry has just strangled a young girl who taunted him. They take the injured man back to their home and, when an angry mob (including David's tormentors) learn of Henry's whereabouts and lay siege to the house, David resolves to fight them. What follows is a brilliantly edited, spectacularly violent climax.

STRAW DOGS generated tremendous controversy upon its release in 1971. Many found the violence too graphic and gratuitous, as well as taking offence at the film's neolithic sexual politics: by resorting to brutal, deadly violence, the man proves himself true master of his "property"—his house and his wife. The film is played as a power struggle between husband and wife (David and Amy play several symbolic games of chess during the proceedings), with Amy pushing her partner's tolerance to breaking point. Her strategies include teasing the workers and disrupting David's work, while he counters by abusing her cat and accepting the hunting invitation. But David's checkmate comes when—after he's killed a few men and become shockingly abusive—he compels Amy to shoot one of the assailants. David has thus "won" the game, losing everything that he stood for in the process. This cynical premise, combined with the fact that David has actually enjoyed the violence, is difficult to swallow.

STRAW DOGS contains one of Hoffman's most layered performances, with the final explosion of violence all the more believable thanks to his initial, mild-mannered quietude. George combines suggestive sexuality with spitefulness to create an equally unforgettable character. Peckinpah handles everything with consummate skill, exerting complete control over his audience's responses. STRAW DOGS is full of arresting images (the mesmerizing opening dissolve was borrowed by David Cronenberg for the beginning of THE FLY), perfectly complemented by Jerry Fielding's eerie, Oscar-nominated score. Whatever your reservations about its content and philosophy, STRAW DOGS remains one of the strongest and most memorable statements about violence ever put on screen.

STRAY DOG
(NORA INU)

1949 122m bw Crime ★★★½
Shin Toho (Japan)

Toshiro Mifune *(Murakami)*, Takashi Shimura *(Sato)*, Ko Kimura *(Yuro)*, Keiko Awaji *(Harumi)*, Reisaburo Yamamoto *(Hondo)*, Noriko Sengoku *(Girl)*

p, Sojiro Motoki; d, Akira Kurosawa; w, Ryuzo Kikushima, Akira Kurosawa (based on a novel by Kurosawa); ph, Asakazu Nakai; ed, Yoshi Sugihara; m, Fumio Hayasaka; art d, So Matsuyama

This gripping, but somewhat flawed, Akira Kurosawa film details the efforts of young police detective Murakami (Toshiro Mifune) to recover his pistol after it is stolen from him on a crowded bus. Murakami becomes obsessed with finding the gun, taking personal responsibility for all the crimes committed with it—including murder—chasing his own criminal impulses by vicariously experiencing the killer's deeds.

Kurosawa has indicated that he considers STRAY DOG a failure in its concern with technique over character. While the analysis is debatable, technical lapses do mar the film more than the script or performances. A sloppy pace; indifferent narration; and an unbearably long montage sequence comprising nearly 10 minutes of dissolves and double-exposures, distract from the fascinating character study and threaten to cause the whole film to collapse under a ponderous weight. Despite this, STRAY DOG is a powerful film and well worth seeing.

STREAMERS

1983 118m c Drama/War   ★★★½
UA Classics (U.S.)   R/18

Matthew Modine (Billy), Michael Wright (Carlyle), Mitchell Lichtenstein (Richie), David Alan Grier (Roger), Guy Boyd (Rooney), George Dzundza (Cokes), Albert Macklin (Martin), B.J. Cleveland (Pfc. Bush), Bill Allen (Lt. Townsend), Paul Lazar (MP Lieutenant)

p, Robert Altman, Nick J. Mileti; d, Robert Altman; w, David Rabe (based on the play by Rabe); ph, Pierre Mignot; ed, Norman Smith; prod d, Wolf Kroeger; art d, Steve Altman; cos, Scott Bushnell

In the 1980s, Robert Altman (NASHVILLE, THE PLAYER) seemed more interested in the stage than the screen, directing movie versions of critically acclaimed plays such as *Secret Honor*, *Come Back to the 5 and Dime, Jimmy Dean, Jimmy Dean*, and *Fool for Love*. STREAMERS, based on a play by David Rabe, is set in an Army barracks circa 1965, where a group of young soldiers awaits assignment to Vietnam. The draftees come from a variety of backgrounds and include two blacks, a country boy, and a Yale-educated homosexual. They are confronted by two brutal sergeants, veterans of the Korean War. Sexual and racial tensions build as the men await their transfer orders in the claustrophobic barracks, and eventually shocking violence erupts. Rabe uses the microcosmic barracks as a site for exploring the explosive emotions and issues that preoccupied Americans during the Vietnam War, and on stage, the play was an excruciatingly intense experience. Altman, working in a cooler medium, wisely opts for a somewhat distanced approach. This very low-budget film feels more stagebound than the director's other stage-to-screen projects, but Altman elicits marvelous performances from his cast—especially Matthew Modine, Michael Wright and George Dzundza. The title is Army slang for paratroopers whose chutes have failed to open.

STREET SCENE

1931 80m bw Drama   ★★★★
UA (U.S.)   /A

Sylvia Sidney (Rose Maurrant), William Collier Jr. (Sam Kaplan), Estelle Taylor (Anna Maurrant), Beulah Bondi (Emma Jones), Max Montor (Abe Kaplan), David Landau (Frank Maurrant), Matt McHugh (Vincent Jones), Russell Hopton (Steve Sankey), Greta Granstedt (Mae Jones), Tom Manning (George Jones)

p, Samuel Goldwyn; d, King Vidor; w, Elmer Rice (based on his play); ph, George Barnes; ed, Hugh Bennett; m, Alfred Newman; art d, Richard Day

Elmer Rice's Pulitzer Prize-winning play about the lives and loves of the people who live on a West Side Manhattan street proved to have national appeal under the sure hand of director King Vidor. To insure quality, eight of the original Broadway cast were hired to reprise their roles, including Beulah Bondi, who made her screen debut here and went on to have a long film career. Practically all of the shooting was done on a huge street set. It's summer and the windows are open. The neighborhood people can't bear to stay in their stifling apartments, so the action takes place outside. As the film opens, the big topic of conversation is the love affair between mature woman Estelle Taylor and Russell Hopton, a man who collects for the milk company. Taylor's husband, David Landau, suspicious of Hopton and his wife, is just waiting to catch them. As the sun rises, Taylor's daughter, Sylvia

Sidney, goes off to work, while Landau mentions that he has to travel to Connecticut for the day. After Landau leaves, Sidney's beau, Max Montor, sees Hopton surreptitiously make his way to Taylor's flat. The shades come down—every other shade on the block is up to let in fresh air—and within a few seconds Landau is back in the apartment. Screams are heard, noises of a fight, then a single shot rings out. The people on the street turn their eyes to the sound, the shade comes up, and Hopton stands at the window. Then there's another shot, and Hopton disappears. An instant later, Landau, looking crazed, comes running out of the brownstone with the gun in his hand; the people on the street shrink back when he tells them to scatter. Landau turns the corner and disappears down an alley as police cars and ambulances rush into the street. A crowd gathers, eager to watch but not to help, waiting to see what will happen next.

Featuring excellent acting all around, STREET SCENE moves very quickly, with hardly a wasted word. Although somewhat dated by today's standards, it must be judged by those of the 1930s, when it was a stunning achievement. The play ran for more than two years and is still revived often. An added dimension was composer Alfred Newman's main theme (since used in many films), which ranks, to this day, among the most evocative pieces of music ever written, immediately conjuring up the crowded streets, the hustle, and the oppressive claustrophobia of the Big Apple.

STREET SMART

1987 95m c Crime   ★★★
Golan-Globus (U.S.)   R/18

Christopher Reeve (Jonathan Fisher), Morgan Freeman (Fast Black), Kathy Baker (Punchy), Mimi Rogers (Alison Parker), Jay Patterson (Leonard Pike), Andre Gregory (Ted Avery), Anna Maria Horsford (Harriet), Frederick Rolf (Joel Davis), Erik King (Reggie), Michael J. Reynolds (Art Sheffield)

p, Menahem Golan, Yoram Globus; d, Jerry Schatzberg; w, David Freeman; ph, Adam Holender; ed, Priscilla Nedd; m, Robert Irving III, Miles Davis; prod d, Dan Leigh; art d, Serge Jacques; cos, Jo Ynocencio

AAN Best Supporting Actor: Morgan Freeman

Jonathan Fisher (Reeve) is a magazine journalist who gets an assignment to write about the lifestyle of a pimp. When he can't get any real pimps to talk to him, Fisher creates a fictional portrait that is chosen as a cover story and turns him into a celebrity with his own TV news show. Fisher then gets to know "Fast Black" (Freeman), a vicious, high-powered pimp who is being charged with murder. Meanwhile, an assistant D.A. comes to believe that Fast Black is the real-life subject of Fisher's article, and subpoenas the writer's (non-existent) notes as evidence in the trial. Fast Black exerts pressure on Fisher to create false notes that will provide him with an alibi; Fisher resists, until he realizes how far the pimp will go to get what he wants.

Thanks to a terrific performance by Freeman and slick direction by Jerry Schatzberg, this is a fast-moving, intermittently riveting crime drama. Reeve is good as the naive writer who gets in over his head, and Kathy Baker is outstanding as one of Fast Black's "girls."

STREETCAR NAMED DESIRE, A

1951 125m bw Drama   ★★★★
Warner Bros. (U.S.)   /15

Vivien Leigh (Blanche DuBois), Marlon Brando (Stanley Kowalski), Kim Hunter (Stella Kowalski), Karl Malden (Mitch), Rudy Bond (Steve Hubbell), Nick Dennis (Pablo Gonzales), Peg Hillias (Eunice Hubbell), Wright King (Young Collector), Richard Garrick (Doctor), Ann Dere (The Matron)

p, Charles K. Feldman; d, Elia Kazan; w, Tennessee Williams, Oscar Saul (adapted from the play by Williams); ph, Harry Stradling; ed, David Weisbart; m, Alex North; art d, Richard Day; cos, Lucinda Ballard

AAN Best Picture; AAN Best Actor: Marlon Brando; AA Best Actress: Vivien Leigh; AA Best Supporting Actor: Karl Malden; AA Best Supporting Actress: Kim Hunter; AAN Best Director: Elia Kazan; AAN Best Screenplay: Tennessee Williams; AAN Best Cinematography:

Harry Stradling; *AAN Best Score:* Alex North; *AA Best Art Direction:* Richard Day, George James Hopkins; *AAN Best Costume Design:* Lucinda Ballard; *AAN Best Sound:* Colonel Nathan Levinson

In this consensual screen classic, Marlon Brando is electrifying as working-class hunk Stanley Kowalski, reprising his Broadway role in Tennessee Williams's most famous play. Elia Kazan, who directed the play in New York, made the trek west for the film, joined by Brando, Kim Hunter, Karl Malden, Rudy Bond, Nick Dennis, Peg Hillias, and Edna Thomas from the stage version. Only Jessica Tandy, who had been a smash as Blanche DuBois on Broadway, was replaced—studio chiefs felt that she wasn't well-known enough for the movie. The role went to Vivien Leigh, who had been starring in a London presentation of the play directed by her husband, Laurence Olivier. The resulting film is an actors' showcase and a flamboyant, sometimes uneasy admixture of Manhattan and Hollywood sensibilitites.

The film opens with Blanche (Leigh) arriving in New Orleans, where she intends to stay with her pregnant sister Stella Kowalski (Hunter) and her brutish husband Stanley (Brando). (To get to their seedy apartment, Blanche has to take a streetcar named Desire—named for a New Orleans street.) Stella, an earthy, pragmatic woman, seems happy in her marriage to the trashy but overtly sexual Stanley, but Blanche is delicate, morose, and deeply neurotic. Stanley immediately sees through Blanche's southern-belle facade and the two are quickly at odds. As sexual and financial tensions escalate, Stanley sets out to reveal the truth about Blanche.

A STREETCAR NAMED DESIRE features some of the finest ensemble acting ever offered on the screen, speaking some Williams's most vivid dialogue. Kazan's direction, however, sometimes verges on the pedestrian, as though he's struggling to recreate his Broadway staging in a much more visually demanding medium. Leigh, in the final great triumph of her screen career, is the very picture of tattered magnificence. She's like a cracked figurine from *The Glass Menagerie* come to life; her emotional choices are tragic and horrifying at the same time. Brando's character is strictly scratch, mumble, flex, and roar, but it's telegraphed a through force-of-nature persona. As countless subsequent productions have shown, Brando has no peer when it comes to conveying the physical threat and sexual potency that make the character work. Kim Hunter is more than adequate in the most sketchily written role. Three minutes of footage censored from the original were restored in a 1994 video re-release.

STRICTLY BALLROOM

1992 92m c Comedy/Dance/Romance ★★½
M&A Film Corporation (Australia) PG

Paul Mercurio (*Scott Hastings*), Tara Morice (*Fran*), Bill Hunter (*Barry Fife*), Barry Otto (*Doug Hastings*), Pat Thompson (*Shirley Hastings*), Gia Carides (*Liz Holt*), Peter Whitford (*Les Kendall*), John Hannan (*Ken Railings*), Sonia Kruger-Taylor (*Tina Sparkle*), Pip Mushin (*Wayne Burns*)

p, Tristam Miall, Ted Albert; d, Baz Luhrmann; w, Baz Luhrmann, Craig Pearce; ph, Steve Mason; ed, Jill Bilcock; m, David Hirshfelder; prod d, Catherine Martin; cos, Trathie Angus

Australian director Baz Luhrman's first film takes satirical potshots at an easy target, the world of competitive ballroom dancing, adding a dash of John Waters-style camp into the mix for extra effect. Welcome to STRICTLY BALLROOM, a world of deeply regimented dancing competition (hence the title, implying no deviations from set form) that mirrors the rigid social order of the Waratah (southern Australia) districts.

Competition is keen, especially between Kim Rallings (John Hannan), a drunken, platinumed lothario, and Scott Hastings (Paul Mercurio), the earnest, handsome, self-absorbed, rising-star son of dance school owners. When Scott departs from the time-honored formula during a samba competition, he causes a furor among the powers-that-be of the Dance Federation: Scott's coach, Les Kendall (Peter Whitford); corrupt Federation president, Barry Fife (Bill Hunter); and Scott's own parents, Shirley and Doug Hastings (Pat Thomson, Barry Otto). Scott's ambitious partner Liz (Gia Carrides) deserts him, and Scott joins forces with ugly duckling newcomer Fran (Tara Morice). Is

it a surprise that she blossoms into a impassioned and seductive dancer, or that Scott ignores every obstacle and succeeds in doing things his own way?

One would have to be heartless not to be engaged by STRICTLY BALLROOM's romantic, dewy sentiment, but the predictable plot is difficult to bear, as are the broad characterizations. Some spirited performances breathe life into the limp central idea, and BALLROOM's cast demonstrates genuine dance talent; costume designer Angus Strathie and choreographer John "Cha Cha" O'Connell appear to have enjoyed their work, and Luhrman has given the entire enterprise his loving, detailed attention—it looks terrific.

STRICTLY DISHONORABLE

1931 94m bw Comedy ★★★½
Universal (U.S.) /A

Paul Lukas (*Count Di Ruva*), Sidney Fox (*Isabelle Parry*), Lewis Stone (*Judge Dempsey*), George Meeker (*Henry Greene*), William Ricciardi (*Tomasso*), Sidney Toler (*Mulligan*), Samuel Bonello, Carlo Schipa (*Waiters*), Natalie Moorhead (*Lilli*), Joe Torilla (*Cook*)

p, Carl Laemmle Jr.; d, John M. Stahl; w, Gladys Lehman (based on the play by Preston Sturges); ph, Karl Freund, Jackson Rose; ed, Arthur Tavares, Maurice Pivar

Preston Sturges's second stage play (written when he was still in his twenties) became a Broadway hit and was filmed twice: this version and the remake in 1951 that starred Janet Leigh and Ezio Pinza. Screenwriter Gladys Lehman wisely stuck close to the original, and the laughs are many. Paul Lukas portrays a rakehell opera-singer. In an illegal speakeasy one night, he meets naive southerner Sidney Fox, who is engaged to boorish George Meeker. Lukas lets her know that his intentions are strictly dishonorable but it matters not to petite Fox, who is, by this time, disgusted with her aggravating suitor. The speak is owned by William Ricciardi (reprising his role in the play, as did Meeker) and frequented by Sidney Toler, a cop who turns the other way when he sees the illegal alcohol being poured in his own glass. Lewis Stone almost steals the movie as a one-time judge who has given up the law in favor of tippling. When Fox leaves Meeker and has no place to stay, Lukas offers her the use of his apartment, making certain she knows that he is a bounder, a cad, and a ne'er-do-well. Despite her admitted degeneracy, Fox still wants to be with him, and he almost seduces her when Stone points out that she is little more than a child, and that he (Lukas) would be remiss if he allowed himself to fall prey to passion. Lukas leaves Fox in his apartment and goes up to Stone's apartment to spend the night, but the realization of love suddenly intrudes.

The writing is sharp, the characters are well drawn, and the comedy timing is on a par with the best movies of the era. And watching the patrician Stone as a drunk is great entertainment.

STRIKE UP THE BAND

1940 120m bw Musical/Comedy ★★★½
MGM (U.S.) /U

Mickey Rooney (*Jimmy Connors*), Judy Garland (*Mary Holden*), Paul Whiteman and His Orchestra (*Themselves*), June Preisser (*Barbara Frances Morgan*), William Tracy (*Phillip Turner*), Ann Shoemaker (*Mrs. Connors*), Larry Nunn (*Willie Brewster*), George Lessey (*Mr. Morgan*), Francis Pierlot (*Mr. Judd*), Harry McCrillis (*Booper Barton*)

p, Arthur Freed; d, Busby Berkeley; w, Herbert Fields (uncredited), Kay Van Riper (uncredited), John Monks Jr., Fred Finklehoffe; ph, Ray June; ed, Ben Lewis; art d, Cedric Gibbons, John S. Detlie; cos, Dolly Tree, Gile Steele

AAN Best Score: Georgie Stoll, Roger Edens; *AAN Best Song:* Roger Edens, Arthur Freed; *AA Best Sound:* Douglas Shearer

Mickey Rooney and Judy Garland, two of the great young stars of their day, team up in this musical comedy as a pair of high school students. Mary (Garland) works in the library after school, and Jimmy (Rooney) spends his free time practicing the drums. He wants to smack the skins in a dance band, but his widowed mother yearns for him to become a doctor. Jimmy and a bunch of his pals form an orchestra with the intention of entering a contest sponsored by big band "King of Jazz" Paul Whiteman. The kids manage to scrape together the money for their trip to the coast, but when one of them needs an emergency operation, Jimmy decides to pay for it and sacrifice his big chance. Luckily, Paul Whiteman is in town and Jimmy and his boys get a chance to play for him anyway. Rooney and Garland deliver their usual energy-packed performances, but one unexpected scene is a standout: as Jimmy uses a bowl of fruit to illustrate an idea he has for a musical number, the fruit turns into little animated puppet models (masterminded by George Pal) that perform "Do the Conga." Also included is the big band classic "Sing, Sing, Sing."

STRIPES

1981 106m c Comedy	★★★
Columbia (U.S.)	R/15

Bill Murray (John Winger), Harold Ramis (Russell Zitsky), Warren Oates (Sgt. Hulka), P.J. Soles (Stella), Sean Young (Louise), John Candy (Ox), John Larroquette (Capt. Stillman), Judge Reinhold (Elmo), John Voldstad (Aide), John Diehl (Cruiser)

p, Ivan Reitman, Dan Goldberg; d, Ivan Reitman; w, Len Blum, Dan Goldberg, Harold Ramis; ph, Bill Butler; ed, Eva Ruggiero, Michael Luciano, Harry Keller; m, Elmer Bernstein; prod d, James H. Spencer; chor, Ronn Forella; cos, Richard Bruno

Though it's occasionally tasteless and eventually crumbles, STRIPES is an often hilarious film that provided Bill Murray with a perfect opportunity in which to display his comedic skills. Murray stars as John Winger, an irresponsible goof-off who, as the film opens, has just lost his job, his girl, his apartment and his car. As he ponders his fate with his equally unsuccessful best friend, Russell Zitsky (Harold Ramis), a man who teaches English to recent immigrants, it occurs to him that enlisting in the Army seems to be a sensible career move. He persuades Zitsky to go along on the adventure and soon they find themselves in boot camp surrounded by a group of misfits that includes the overweight Ox (John Candy), the temperamental Psycho (Conrad Dunn), the dopey Cruiser (John Diehl), and druggie Elmo (Judge Reinhold in his film debut). Given the unenviable task of presiding over this collection of dolts is tough Army veteran Sgt. Hulka (Warren Oates), and it isn't long before Winger finds his way to the sergeant's bad side. While STRIPES was ideally suited to Murray's wise-ass, rebel-who-has-no-use-for-a-cause character, what really makes the film work is his relationship with Ramis. The two make a delightful comedy team, with the somewhat more sensible Ramis serving as the perfect foil to Murray. His expressive face and low-key manner provide a comic perspective that serves to enhance Murray's clowning. The rest of the cast is also first-rate, especially Oates who imbues his weary sergeant with an unexpected wit and intelligence. While basic training has been the subject of countless screen comedies, the subject is one which offers great comic potential, and this film exploits that potential. Unfortunately, it flags considerably once basic ends and the characters set off on their inane adventure behind enemy lines.

STUDENT PRINCE, THE

1954 107m c Musical	★★½
MGM (U.S.)	/U

Ann Blyth (Kathie), Edmund Purdom (Prince Karl), John Ericson (Count Von Asterburg), Louis Calhern (King of Karlsburg), Edmund Gwenn (Prof. Juttner), S.Z. Sakall (Joseph Ruder), Betta St. John (Princess Johanna), John Williams (Lutz), Evelyn Varden (Queen), John Hoyt (Prime Minister)

p, Joe Pasternak; d, Richard Thorpe; w, William Ludwig, Sonya Levien (based on the operetta by Dorothy Donnelly, Sigmund Romberg, and the novel and play by Wilhelm Meyer-Foerster); ph, Paul C. Vogel; ed, Gene Ruggiero; m, Sigmund Romberg; art d, Cedric Gibbons, Randall Duell; fx, Warren Newcombe; chor, Hermes Pan; cos, Helen Rose, Walter Plunkett

A remake of the 1927 picture based on the musical by Romberg and Donnelly and the straight play by Meyer-Foerster, this film is a pleasant trifle with some good musical numbers that were sung by Mario Lanza, but came out of the mouth of Purdom. Lanza had been scheduled to play the German prince, but his weight was always fluctuating, and when his temper began to rise and fall with the speed of his avoirdupois, the decision was made to toss him out and use Purdom. Since Lanza

had already pre-recorded the tunes, that wasn't too tough, although the sound of the round tenor tones coming out of Purdom's slim chest does seem ludicrous, for a while. After the shock of it is over, the picture has its moments. Purdom is Karl, a prince with all the accoutrements of the royal purple. His father is the king (Calhern), who feels that the prince needs to go out and see what the real world is like before he comes back to the princess (St. John) with whom a marriage has been arranged. He goes to Heidelberg, where he meets Kathie (Blyth), the daughter of a local innkeeper (Sakall). They fall in love, but when the king falls ill and dies, Karl must assume his position as king.

Unrequited love is the theme and 1954 audiences liked their love requited, so the picture didn't fare as well as the studio had hoped. The stalwart and handsome if unexciting Purdom got lots of build-up and later starred in THE EGYPTIAN, yet his career never did take off. The Romberg-Donnelly songs (with some revised lyrics by Paul Francis Webster) include "Golden Days," "Serenade," "Deep in My Heart," "To the Inn We're Marching," "Drink, Drink, Drink," and "Come Boys, Let's All Be Gay, Boys," a song that causes gales of laughter these days because the meaning of its title has changed over the years. Webster and Nicholas Brodszky added three new tunes to the score ("I'll Walk with God", "Beloved," and "Summertime in Heidelberg"), none of which was up to the original. The editing by Ruggiero was a standout and Pan's choreography properly rousing, but the time had passed for such corn by 1954.

STUNT MAN, THE

1980 129m c Comedy/Drama	★★★★
Fox (U.S.)	R/X

Peter O'Toole (Eli Cross), Steve Railsback (Cameron), Barbara Hershey (Nina Franklin), Allen Garfield (Sam), Alex Rocco (Jake), Sharon Farrell (Denise), Adam Roarke (Raymond Bailey), Philip Bruns (Ace), Chuck Bail (Chuck Barton), John Garwood (Gabe)

p, Richard Rush; d, Richard Rush; w, Larry Marcus, Richard Rush (based on the novel by Paul Brodeur); ph, Mario Tosi; ed, Jack Hofstra, Caroline Ferriol; m, Dominic Frontiere; art d, James Schoppe; cos, Rosanna Norton

AAN Best Actor: Peter O'Toole; AAN Best Director: Richard Rush; AAN Best Adapted Screenplay: Lawrence B. Marcus Richard Rush

Peter O'Toole, a megalomaniacal film director, tyrannizes his writer and plays games with his actors, manipulating their actions in reality, just as he does in the story he is filming. Steve Railsback is on the run from the law, and he stumbles upon the movie company as they shoot a scene on the beach. After his top stuntman is killed, O'Toole, who has shielded Railsback from the law, persuades the young man to take the dead man's place. Railsback is then thrust into the not-so-glamorous world of moviemaking and gets involved with Barbara Hershey, O'Toole's beautiful star and lover. Lawrence B. Marcus's script, which pits real life against reel life, offers plenty of wit, with most of the bons mots handed to O'Toole.

SUBJECT WAS ROSES, THE

1968 107m c Drama	★★★★
MGM (U.S.)	/A

Patricia Neal (Nettie Cleary), Jack Albertson (John Cleary), Martin Sheen (Timmy Cleary), Don Saxon (Nightclub Master of Ceremonies), Elaine Williams (Woman), Grant Gordon (Man in Restaurant)

p, Edgar Lansbury; d, Ulu Grosbard; w, Frank D. Gilroy (based on his play); ph, Jack Priestley; ed, Jerry Greenberg; m, Lee Pockriss; art d, George Jenkins; cos, Anna Hill Johnstone

AAN Best Actress: Patricia Neal; AA Best Supporting Actor: Jack Albertson

Frank Gilroy's Pulitzer Prize-winning drama was beautifully realized in this film adaptation WWII has just ended, and Sheen returns home from the battle to live with parents Neal and Albertson. In the years since he's been away, his parents' marriage has disintegrated into rancor, disagreements and highly charged hostility. Before he left, Sheen was the apple of Neal's eye and only had a passing relationship with Albertson. Now that he's matured, however, he has a closer tie to

Albertson, finding that they are two of a kind. Sheen can't bear to see his parents at such loggerheads and attempts to mediate their differences without standing in either's corner.

Neal begins a subtle campaign of sabotage against Albertson but Sheen sees through this and confronts his mother by saying that he will not side with her or Albertson in any dispute, preferring to remain completely neutral. Neal can't handle Sheen's attitude but she later discovers Sheen drunk and arguing with Albertson in much the same way he had argued with her. Sheen, despite the booze he's ingested, makes some sense. This situation will never get better as long as things remain the same. He thinks that his parents must work out their marital differences without using him as a referee, so he tells them that he is going to leave and strike out on his own.

The movie was not a hit, despite the terrific acting, sharp writing, and outstanding direction from Grosbard, who also staged the play. Never does the emotion explode into oratory, so almost every scene has an underlying tension that continues to bubble.

SUCH A GORGEOUS KID LIKE ME
(UNE BELLE FILLE COMME MOI)

1973 100m c Comedy/Drama   ★★★
Carrosse   (France)   R/

Bernadette Lafont (Camille Bliss), Claude Brasseur (Monsieur Murene), Charles Denner (Arthur), Guy Marchand (Sam Golden), Andre Dussollier (Stanislas Previne), Philippe Leotard (Clovis Bliss), Anne Kreis (Helene), Gilberte Geniat (Isobel Bliss), Daniele Girard (Florence Golden), Martine Ferriere (Prison Secretary)

p, Marcel Berbert; d, Francois Truffaut; w, Francois Truffaut, Jean-Loup Dabadie (based on the novel by Henry Farrell); ph, Pierre-William Glenn; ed, Yann Dedet; m, Georges Delerue; art d, Jean-Pierre Kohut-Svelko; cos, Monique Dury

An often ignored film by Truffaut, this black comedy is about women and their seemingly magical hold over men. Lafont, who first appeared in his 1957 short, LES MISTONS, takes up where she left off some 15 years earlier. In LES MISTONS she was tormented by a quintet of young boys who were very much in love with her. Here Lafont is able to take revenge on her tormentors.

The picture starts with a sociologist, Dussollier, preparing to write a book called *Criminal Women* (which he never gets to publish). He visits a women's prison and decides to interview convicted murderess Lafont, passing up offers to interview a woman who dismembered her victims and another who strangles them using only one hand. Dussollier discovers that Lafont is indirectly responsible for the deaths of her father and her mother-in-law, and was unsuccessful in her attempts to kill attorney Brasseur and husband Leotard with rat poison. She is eventually acquitted of her crime and rises to become a famed singer, not because of her voice (which is wretched) but because of the publicity that surrounds her case. Backstage at one of her performances, she is confronted by Leotard and Dussollier kills Leotard. But Lafont still has her own unique resources at hand.

SUCH A GORGEOUS KID LIKE ME, though it may not initially seem Truffautesque, has roots in a number of his previous films. He compares this film to THE WILD CHILD. Lafont's murderous female character is also seen in JULES AND JIM and THE BRIDE WORE BLACK (and to a lesser, non-violent extent in THE STORY OF ADELE H.). While it may not be an audience pleaser, SUCH A GORGEOUS KID LIKE ME is a definite must for those who are interested in learning about the "total" Truffaut.

SUGAR CANE ALLEY
(RUE CASES NEGRES)

1983 103m c Drama   ★★★½
Su Ma Fa/Orca/NEF Diffusion   (France)   PG/

Garry Cadenat (Jose), Darling Legitimus (M'Man Tine), Douta Seck (Medouze), Joby Bernabe (M. Saint-Louis), Francisco Charles (Le Gereur), Marie-Jo Descas (La Mere de Leopold), Marie-Ange Farot (Mme. Saint-Louis), Henri Melon (M. Roc), Eugene Mona (Douze Orteils), Joel Palcy (Carmen)

p, Michel Loulergue, Alix Regis; d, Euzhan Palcy; w, Euzhan Palcy (based on the novel La Rue Cases Negres by Joseph Zobel); ph, Dominique Chapius; ed, Marie-Josephe Yoyotte; m, Groupe Malavoi; art d, Hoang Thanh At; cos, Isabelle Filleul

Set in the French colony of Martinique in the 1930s, this stark, charming film takes a look at life in "Rue Cases Negres," a wooden-shack community isolated in the middle of a sugar plantation. While the adults toil in the fields, the children romp the "alley," but for many of the youngsters this will be their last summer on the plantation. The brightest among them will find better jobs or go on to school, while the less fortunate will remain to assist their parents in the fields. Most prominently featured is Jose (Garry Cadenat), a frolicsome 11-year-old who earns a prestigious scholarship to a school in Fort-de-France. This well-acted film is an unexpected delight, showing that a ray of hope can materialize amid the despondency of a shantytown. SUGAR CANE ALLEY was a double prizewinner at the Venice Film Festival, taking a Silver Lion and Darling Legitimus garnering a Best Actress award.

SUGARBABY
(ZUCKERBABY)

1985 86m c Drama/Comedy   ★★★½
Pelemele   (West Germany)   /15

Marianne Sagebrecht (Marianne), Eisi Gulp (Huber 133), Toni Berger (Old Subway Driver), Manuela Denz (Huber's Wife), Will Spindler (Funeral Director), The Paul Wurges Combo (Dance Hall Band), Hans Stadlbauer

d, Percy Adlon; w, Percy Adlon; ph, Johanna Heer; ed, Jean-Claude Piroue; m, Dreieier; cos, Regina Batz, Silvia Risa

The first installment of Percy Adlon's delightful "Marianne" trilogy, SUGARBABY stars the utterly winning Marianne Sagebrecht in a sweetly romantic story which also bears the rare distinction of being a Teutonic comedy.

Marianne (Sagebrecht) is a hugely overweight mortuary attendant who, while commuting to work one morning on the subway, becomes infatuated with the conductor (Eisi Gulp), a handsome, blond hunk in a tight-fitting uniform. She quickly determines to win him over and, failing to locate him the following day, goes to great lengths to procure his name and route number: Huber 133. Next, under the guise of finding work for her nephew, she gets her hands on the complex work schedule for subway drivers. After an obsessive search, she finally figures out Huber's schedule. In the meantime, Marianne has been preparing herself for her future lover, buying sexy lingerie (which must be specially ordered in her size), flashy high heels and pink satin sheets. Although it seems likely that all this preparation will backfire, Huber, nicknamed "Sugarbaby" by Marianne, accepts her invitation to dinner and romance quickly blossoms.

Adlon combines the free-spirited energy of his characters with technique to match, fashioning a magnificent lighting scheme that relies heavily on color effects, a minimalist set reduced to the barest essentials and a frantic camera style that allows the camera to wander, sway, and zig-zag through the set. Rather than creating a feeling of pretension or intrusive stylization, however, Adlon's film is lighthearted and energetic. He lets no barriers stand in his way and, as a result, the entire picture is an engaging, intelligent entertainment. And in Marianne, marvelously incarnated by Sagebrecht, viewers will find a lovable heroine with whom most would gladly spend time in the real world.

SUGARLAND EXPRESS, THE

1974 109m c Adventure   ★★★★
Universal   (U.S.)   PG

Goldie Hawn (Lou Jean Poplin), Ben Johnson (Capt. Tanner), Michael Sacks (Officer Slide), William Atherton (Clovis Poplin), Gregory Walcott (Officer Mashburn), Steve Kanaly (Jessup), Louise Latham (Mrs. Looby), Harrison Zanuck (Baby Langston), A.L. Camp (Mr. Nocker), Jessie Lee Fulton (Mrs. Nocker)

p, Richard D. Zanuck, David Brown; d, Steven Spielberg; w, Hal Barwood, Matthew Robbins (based on a story by Spielberg, Barwood, Robbins); ph, Vilmos Zsigmond; ed, Edward Abroms, Verna Fields; m, John Williams; art d, Joe Alves; fx, Frank Brendel

This is Steven Spielberg's first effort at the helm in feature filmmaking (the earlier DUEL being a made-for-TV movie), and it contains much of the raw sense of adventure (though without the technical gadgetry) that would make his later films so popular and such good clean fun. After his success with THE SUGARLAND EXPRESS, he went on to direct the highly profitable, beloved, and much-imitated JAWS in 1975. Based on a true story, this film features Hawn playing a woman who helps her husband, Atherton, escape from prison. She needs him to join her in the fight against forces who want to put her child up for adoption. What ensues is one long chase across America's highways. Throughout the film, more and more police, and the media, want in on the action. Spielberg exhibits that he still had a bit to learn in the world of filmmaking, but the lighthearted tone of the beginning takes a dive into an abyss that shocks many viewers. With this role, Hawn further proves she was an actress of some talent and not just an attractive woman to be taken lightly.

SULLIVAN'S TRAVELS

1941 91m bw Comedy/Drama ★★★★★
Paramount (U.S.) /A

Joel McCrea *(John L. Sullivan)*, Veronica Lake *(The Girl)*, Robert Warwick *(Mr. Lebrand)*, William Demarest *(Mr. Jones)*, Franklin Pangborn *(Mr. Casalais)*, Porter Hall *(Mr. Hadrian)*, Byron Foulger *(Mr. Valdelle)*, Margaret Hayes *(Secretary)*, Robert Greig *(Sullivan's Butler)*, Eric Blore *(Sullivan's Valet)*

p, Paul Jones; d, Preston Sturges; w, Preston Sturges; ph, John Seitz; ed, Stuart Gilmore; m, Leo Shuken, Charles Bradshaw; art d, Hans Dreier, Earl Hedrick; fx, Farciot Edouart; cos, Edith Head

A Hollywood variation on *Gulliver's Travels* and just as successful as satire. This brilliant, often devastating look at Hollywood and the real world behind its tinsel is arguably Preston Sturges's greatest film. McCrea, in one of his best roles, plays a successful Hollywood film director who has made nothing but lightweight films with titles like "So Long, Sarong." When he is suddenly struck with the desire to make a searing drama about human suffering, his studio bosses (Warwick and Hall) laugh and tell him that the proposal is ridiculous, since McCrea has no personal experience of such difficulty. Accordingly, McCrea sets out to suffer. He will don hobo clothes and, with only 10 cents in his pocket, go forth into poverty and experience adversity for himself. Knowing they can't change his mind, Warwick and Hall humor the eccentric director's whim, but decide to turn McCrea's nomadic adventure into a publicity stunt that will benefit the studio. To this end they provide him with a publicity entourage and a luxury van that follows McCrea as he travels on foot, and that carries McCrea's butler, Greig, and valet, Blore, who both urge their employer to give up this mad idea, telling him that the poor insist upon their privacy and don't want him intruding upon it.

Though the plot may sound a bit contrived, everything in this wonderful film works. And it presents a spectacular array of emotions and situations that allow for Sturges's magical direction and script to quickly turn all the film's sharp corners with his characters. SULLIVAN'S TRAVELS is a wonderful comedy-drama, the type of a one-of-a-kind film for which Sturges—basically a writer with a good sense of camera use and visuals, who as a director was always trying out new techniques—was noted. Unlike many of his other films, which were made for sheer entertainment value, SULLIVAN'S TRAVELS contains a message, which Sturges himself later explained: "SULLIVAN'S TRAVELS is the result of an urge, an urge to tell some of my fellow filmwrights that they were getting a little too deep-dish and to leave the preaching to the preachers."

SUMMER HOLIDAY

1948 92m c Musical/Comedy ★★★★
MGM (U.S.) /U

Mickey Rooney *(Richard Miller)*, Gloria DeHaven *(Muriel McComber)*, Walter Huston *(Nat Miller)*, Frank Morgan *(Uncle Sid)*, Jackie "Butch" Jenkins *(Tommy Miller)*, Marilyn Maxwell *(Belle)*, Agnes Moorehead *(Cousin Lily)*, Selena Royle *(Mrs. Miller)*, Michael Kirby *(Arthur Miller)*, Shirley Johns *(Mildred Miller)*

p, Arthur Freed; d, Rouben Mamoulian; w, Frances Goodrich, Albert Hackett, Irving Brecher, Jean Holloway (based on the play "Ah, Wilderness!" by Eugene O'Neill); ph, Charles Schoenbaum; ed, Albert Akst; m, Harry Warren; art d, Cedric Gibbons, Jack Martin Smith; chor, Charles Walters; cos, Irene, Walter Plunkett

This fine musical version of Eugene O'Neill's "Ah, Wilderness!" stars Mickey Rooney as a boy struggling with the pitfalls of adolescence. In early 1900s New England we meet the Miller clan: Nat (Walter Huston), a newspaper editor and staunch upholder of Yankee tradition; his wife (Selena Royle), ever the doting mother; Richard (Rooney), their oldest son; and Tommy ("Butch" Jenkins), their youngest. Also living in their comfortable household are an old maid cousin (Agnes Moorehead) and a bachelor uncle (Frank Morgan). Richard is extraordinarily bright and has big ideas about changing the world. He adores neighbor Muriel McComber (Gloria DeHaven), but has been forbidden to see her by her conservative father. Peeved at his inability to see the girl he loves, Richard goes off on a drunk, meets a dance-hall girl, spends every cent he has, and gets kicked out of the bar. Naturally, he catches hell from his dad, but by the end he and Muriel are finally allowed to be together.

A sweet movie with good work by all the actors, SUMMER HOLIDAY benefits immeasurably from director Mamoulian's inventiveness and the handsome cinematography and production values. Even if "The Stanley Steamer" is an obvious attempt to cash in on the appeal of "The Trolley Song" from the very similar MEET ME IN ST. LOUIS, the songs are quite appealing and eminently suitable. An earlier version of the O'Neill play appeared in 1935 as AH, WILDERNESS, with Rooney playing the role of the younger brother.

SUMMER OF '42

1971 102m c Drama ★★★
Warner Bros. (U.S.) PG/X

Jennifer O'Neill *(Dorothy)*, Gary Grimes *(Hermie)*, Jerry Houser *(Oscy)*, Oliver Conant *(Benjie)*, Katherine Allentuck *(Aggie)*, Christopher Norris *(Miriam)*, Lou Frizzell *(Druggist)*, Walter Scott *(Dorothy's Husband)*, Robert Mulligan *(Narrator)*, Maureen Stapleton *(Voice of Hermie's Mother)*

p, Richard A. Roth; d, Robert Mulligan; w, Herman Raucher; ph, Robert Surtees; ed, Folmar Blangsted; m, Michel Legrand; prod d, Albert Brenner

AAN Best Adapted Screenplay: Herman Raucher; *AAN Best Cinematography:* Robert Surtees; *AAN Best Editing:* Folmar Blangstad; *AA Best Score:* Michel Legrand

People who actually recall 1942 will more greatly appreciate the waves of nostalgia that bathe this affectionate coming-of-age drama, set on a tiny island off New England. Director Mulligan (as the adult Hermie) narrates his recollections, and all of the names used in the story were the real names of the people involved (or so claimed screenwriter Raucher, who wrote the screenplay in less than two weeks). Grimes is the 15-year-old whose life we observe on the tranquil island, where the horrors of war seem a million miles away. Grimes and his friends, Houser and Conant, pal around together, get into minor scrapes, go see movies like NOW, VOYAGER, and spend a great deal of time poring over an educational sex manual. Houser reads the manual as though it were the Bible and he a seminary student; Grimes is more interested in the practical aspects of sex and yearns for O'Neill, an "older woman" in her twenties who is married to absent soldier Scott.

SUMMERTIME

1955 100m c Romance ★★★★
Lopert/London Films (U.S.) /PG

Katharine Hepburn *(Jane Hudson)*, Rossano Brazzi *(Renato Di Rossi)*, Isa Miranda *(Signora Fiorina)*, Darren McGavin *(Eddie Jaeger)*, Mari Aldon *(Phyl Jaeger)*, Jane Rose *(Mrs. McIlhenny)*, MacDonald Parke *(Mr. McIlhenny)*, Gaitano Audiero *(Mauro)*, Andre Morell *(Englishman)*, Jeremy Spenser *(Vito)* p, Ilya Lopert; d, David Lean; w, David Lean, H.E. Bates (based on the play *The Time of the Cuckoo* by Arthur Laurents); ph, Jack Hildyard; ed, Peter Taylor; m, Alessandro Cicognini; art d, Vincent Korda

AAN Best Actress: Katharine Hepburn; *AAN Best Director:* David Lean

Based loosely on Arthur Laurents's play *The Time Of The Cuckoo*, SUMMERTIME is a romance set in Venice. Hepburn is an Ohio old maid who works as a secretary and has saved her money for a trip to Venice. She's traveling alone, and, on her first night there, she wanders around the city and sees lovers walking hand in hand. She meets Audiero, a charming child who hustles tourists, and he becomes her guide to the wonders of the city.

The next day, they go sightseeing and meet Brazzi who owns an antique shop. They fall in love, and there's a whirlwind montage as they walk, hand in hand, through the twisting streets of the main island. While waiting for Brazzi in the Piazza San Marco, she's approached by Spenser, a young man who tells her that Brazzi will be late. She soon learns that he is Brazzi's son and that her lover has a wife and family he's never mentioned. Although hurt by this revelation, Hepburn realizes that this is the most romantic interlude of her spinsterish existence; she's not about to end it now.

Touching, warm, often funny and lushly photographed. SUMMERTIME comes as close to capturing the essence of Venice as you will ever see. Lean had earlier directed BRIEF ENCOUNTER, so the story was familiar to him, although the terrain was vastly altered. There are places where the picture could have used some pruning, especially in the travelogue portions, but Hepburn and Brazzi emerge as the best middle-aged couple (short of Hepburn and Tracy) of the 1950s.

SUN ALSO RISES, THE

1957 129m c Drama ★★★★
Fox (U.S.) /A

Tyrone Power *(Jake Barnes)*, Ava Gardner *(Lady Brett Ashley)*, Mel Ferrer *(Robert Cohn)*, Errol Flynn *(Mike Campbell)*, Eddie Albert *(Bill Gorton)*, Gregory Ratoff *(Count Mippipopolous)*, Juliette Greco *(Georgette)*, Marcel Dalio *(Zizi)*, Henry Daniell *(Doctor)*, Bob Cunningham *(Harris)*

p, Darryl F. Zanuck; d, Henry King; w, Peter Viertel (based on the novel by Ernest Hemingway); ph, Leo Tover; ed, William Mace; m, Hugo Friedhofer, Alexander Courage; art d, Lyle Wheeler, Mark-Lee Kirk; cos, Charles LeMaire, Fontana Sisters

Author Hemingway's paean to the Lost Generation in the wake of WWI has been adapted to the screen more faithfully than have any of his other works. Power is the aimless postwar expatriate drifting around Europe, seeking thrills to compensate for his impotence, the result of a war wound. In the company of sultry prostitute Greco, he threads his way through the bistros of Paris. He's still in love with beautiful aristocrat Gardner, who helped him recover from his wounds during the war. She is being pursued by amorous Greek tycoon Ratoff, and also by young would-be writer Ferrer. Power sets off for Pamplona with his trusted friend, fellow expatriate Albert, arriving only to find that Gardner, Ferrer, and Ratoff have preceded him there to witness the annual running of the bulls. The group is joined by carefree Scottish playboy Flynn, Gardner's former fiance. Behind the hilarity and fun, tensions mount, as all the men lust after Gardner while she wants only Power.

Producer Zanuck greatly admired Hemingway, whom he had met in Paris, introduced by screenwriter Viertel, years before. Zanuck and Hemingway both wintered in Sun Valley for a number of years and were great friends, but their friendship had been flawed by Hemingway's reaction to Zanuck's production of THE SNOWS OF KILIMANJARO. At 43, Power was old for the role. This was to be the actor's second-to-last film, and his last for Fox; he died of a heart attack the following year. This was one of Flynn's last pictures, and his self-parody is a joy, the best thing in the film. The fourth-billed Flynn had, for the first time in years and over his weak protests, accepted less than the top spot in the credits, an honor he had been accorded ever since his success in CAPTAIN BLOOD. Power's habitually petulant facial expression is wrong for this film; a contrapuntal masculinity would have served the story better. Ferrer is fine in his part as the resentful introvert. His wife Audrey Hepburn, who joined him on location in both Pamplona and in

Morelia, Mexico (which doubled for the Spain location), was the one who suggested Greco to Zanuck for the role of the sympathetic prostitute. Greco was then singing at the Waldorf-Astoria in New York City, but she had a substantial cult following in Europe, where she had appeared in movies. This was her US film debut. She and producer Zanuck had an on-location romance which was to continue long past the picture's release. Touted as a Zanuck "find," Evans had been a clothing manufacturer. He had actually been "found" by Norma Shearer, whose late husband, Irving Thalberg, he had portrayed in THE MAN WITH A THOUSAND FACES (not yet released at the time). Evans later became production chief at Paramount. Zanuck, goaded by the mischievous Flynn, actually ran with the bulls himself at Pamplona, but only after carefully timing himself to make certain he could stay ahead of them. The picture was reported to have cost $5 million, but it made money for the studio.

SUNDAY IN THE COUNTRY, A
(UN DIMANCHE A LA CAMPAGNE)

1984 94m c Drama ★★★★½
Sara/A2 (France) G/18

Louis Ducreux *(M. Ladmiral)*, Sabine Azema *(Irene)*, Michel Aumont *(Gonzague/(Edouard))*, Genevieve Mnich *(Marie-Therese)*, Monique Chaumette *(Mercedes)*, Claude Winter *(Mme. Ladmiral)*, Thomas Duval *(Emile)*, Quentin Ogier *(Lucien)*, Katia Wostrikoff *(Mireille)*, Valentine Suard

p, Alain Sarde; d, Bertrand Tavernier; w, Bertrand Tavernier, Colo Tavernier (based on the novella *Monsieur Ladmiral Va Bientot Mourir* by Pierre Bost); ph, Bruno de Keyzer; ed, Armand Psenny; m, Gabriel Faure, Louis Ducreux, Marc Perrone; prod d, Patrice Mercier; cos, Yvonne Sassinot de Nesle

This beautiful film details a day in the life of an elderly painter, Ladmiral (Louis Ducreux), a holdover from the days of the French Impressionists. On one average Sunday in 1912, Ladmiral entertains his son (Michel Aumont) and the latter's family. They walk through the picturesque grounds of Ladmiral's country estate, prepare dinner, and tell wonderful stories about life and art. Unexpectedly, Ladmiral's daughter, Irene (Sabine Azema), pays a rare visit. Although Irene is the troubled outcast of the family, she is still her father's favorite, making this otherwise average Sunday exciting and worthwhile.

The story line may appear simple and undramatic, but the movie's beauty lies in this simplicity. The old painter's Sunday is serene. He is an old man who has lived a quiet life and enjoys reminiscing, his surroundings are bathed in a peaceful light, his canvas quietly awaits his artistic touch. The sum of these simple parts is a rich view of life. Betrand Tavernier, named Best Director at the Cannes Film Festival for this film, successfully evokes the essence of French life in the early 20th century. Tavernier and cinematographer Bruno de Keyzer have made a conscious effort to attain the appearance of French Impressionist painting. In fact, A SUNDAY IN THE COUNTRY is nothing short of a painting come to life.

SUNDAY, BLOODY SUNDAY

1971 110m c Drama ★★★½
Vectia (U.K.) R/X

Glenda Jackson *(Alex Greville)*, Peter Finch *(Dr. Daniel Hirsh)*, Murray Head *(Bob Elkin)*, Peggy Ashcroft *(Mrs. Greville)*, Tony Britton *(George Harding)*, Maurice Denham *(Mr. Greville)*, Bessie Love *(Answering Service Lady)*, Vivian Pickles *(Alva Hodson)*, Frank Windsor *(Bill Hodson)*, Thomas Baptiste *(Prof. Johns)*

p, Joseph Janni; d, John Schlesinger; w, Penelope Gilliatt; ph, Billy Williams; ed, Richard Marden; m, Ron Geesin, Wolfgang Amadeus Mozart; prod d, Luciana Arrighi; art d, Norman Dorme; cos, Jocelyn Richards

AAN Best Actor: Peter Finch; *AAN Best Actress:* Glenda Jackson; *AAN Best Director:* John Schlesinger; *AAN Best Adapted Screenplay:* Penelope Gilliatt

Too deliberate, but among Schlesinger's best; a strong drama about a *menage a trois* among homosexual Finch, heterosexual Jackson, and bisexual Head, who alternates between the other two. Time may decree the film a classic.

Written by *New Yorker* magazine movie critic Gilliatt, the plot presents Finch as a middle-aged bachelor doctor in London who shares his answering service with Jackson, a divorced woman who works at an employment agency. Both of them know Windsor and Pickles, a happy couple in the area, and both of them sleep with Head, a younger designer of modern sculpture. Both Jackson and Finch are aware of each other because Head is an honest sort, almost to the point of naivete. Windsor and Pickles have five children and need some time away from home, so Jackson and Head offer to stay at their home and tend the quintet while the parents go off to attend an educational seminar. On Saturday morning Head excuses himself from Jackson and only says he's "going out." She knows that he's on his way to see Finch, and the thought of it knocks her off her strict diet and into an orgy of fudge consumption. At Finch's the two men discuss an upcoming vacation to Italy, then Head returns to an annoyed Jackson, who resents having to share her lover with a man.

The characters are terribly civilized about the whole thing—too civilized, in fact, with only Jackson betraying any real emotion. The major problem with this film is that it is not easy to see what an intelligent man like Finch and an equally intelligent woman like Jackson see in each other—his character is not realized nearly so well as those of the other two. Schlesinger said that he conceived the idea of the film on the basis of some people he knew, then hired Gilliatt. She, on the other hand, claims total responsibility for the idea because she'd written a novel with a similar plot. Perhaps their differences explain the movie's unresolved undercurrent.

SUNDOWNERS, THE

1960 133m c Drama   ★★★★½
Warner Bros. (U.S.)   /U

Deborah Kerr *(Ida Carmody)*, Robert Mitchum *(Paddy Carmody)*, Peter Ustinov *(Venneker)*, Glynis Johns *(Mrs. Firth)*, Dina Merrill *(Jean Halstead)*, Chips Rafferty *(Quinlan)*, Michael Anderson Jr. *(Sean)*, Lola Brooks *(Liz)*, Wylie Watson *(Herb Johnson)*, John Meillon *(Bluey)*

p, Fred Zinnemann, Gerry Blattner; d, Fred Zinnemann; w, Isobel Lennart (based on the novel by Jon Cleary); ph, Jack Hildyard; ed, Jack Harris; m, Dimitri Tiomkin; art d, Michael Stringer; cos, Elizabeth Haffenden

AAN Best Picture; *AAN Best Actress:* Deborah Kerr; *AAN Best Supporting Actress:* Glynis Johns; *AAN Best Director:* Fred Zinnemann; *AAN Best Adapted Screenplay:* Isobel Lennart

A splendid, sprawling saga of Australia. Set in the 1920s, it's the story of a single family, how they interact with the pioneers around them, how they extract a living from the land, how they live and love and cope. Lennart's adaptation of the Cleary novel is full of wit, sly philosophy and solid, motivated action. The title refers to those people who roam the land and live wherever they stop when the sun sets.

Mitchum is married to Kerr, and the two travel the land with their son, Anderson. They have no money, just a great love and a continuing hope that things will get better. Still, tiring of this nomadic existence, Kerr and Anderson yearn for a place where they can hang their hats. But instead of settling down, Mitchum takes a job leading more than a thousand sheep on a long trek to Cawndilla in western Australia. Since there are so many sheep to look after, Mitchum has to ask Ustinov, a onetime ship's captain, to help.

The journey is arduous and filled with excitement. Along the way, the four stop and visit with another group of Sundowners who have given up the road for a sedentary existence. Kerr and Anderson envy the life led by this family, but Mitchum pays it no mind. Mitchum and company continue on, finally delivering their sheep and collecting their fee. Then the four take jobs on a large station, with Kerr hoping they will be able to save enough money to buy their own spread.

Mitchum is splendid and Kerr was nominated for an Academy Award, as were Johns, Zinnemann, Lennart, and the picture itself. Kerr plays with little makeup and her natural beauty shines through all the dust. Johns is also a delight in her small but telling role, and Ustinov does his usual excellent job. Indeed, every aspect of the movie is first-rate, and even the smallest roles are wonderfully cast, including Australia's favorite actor, Chips Rafferty, as the sheep-shearing foreman. (Rafferty was in just about every Australian movie made in the 1940s, 1950s and 1960s, with his most famous appearance being in THE OVERLANDERS.) Big, funny, tender and humane all at the same time, THE SUNDOWNERS is a true "family" film, without any of the cloying connotations of that term.

SUNSET BOULEVARD

1950 110m bw Drama   ★★★★★
Paramount (U.S.)   /PG

William Holden *(Joe Gillis)*, Gloria Swanson *(Norma Desmond)*, Erich von Stroheim *(Max von Mayerling)*, Nancy Olson *(Betty Schaefer)*, Fred Clark *(Sheldrake)*, Lloyd Gough *(Morino)*, Jack Webb *(Artie Green)*, Cecil B. DeMille, Hedda Hopper, Buster Keaton

p, Charles Brackett; d, Billy Wilder; w, Billy Wilder, Charles Brackett, D.M. Marshman Jr. (based on the story "A Can of Beans" by Brackett, Wilder); ph, John Seitz; ed, Doane Harrison, Arthur Schmidt; m, Franz Waxman, Richard Strauss; art d, Hans Dreier, John Meehan; fx, Gordon Jennings, Farciot Edouart; cos, Edith Head

AAN Best Picture; *AAN Best Actor:* William Holden; *AAN Best Actress:* Gloria Swanson; *AAN Best Supporting Actor:* Erich Von Stroheim; *AAN Best Supporting Actress:* Nancy Olson; *AAN Best Director:* Billy Wilder; *AA Best Story and Screenplay:* Charles Brackett, Billy Wilder, D.M. Marshman, Jr.; *AAN Best Cinematography:* John F. Seitz; *AAN Best Editing:* Arthur Schmidt, Doane Harrison; *AA Best Score:* Franz Waxman; *AA Best Art Direction:* Hans Dreier, John Meehan, Sam Comer, Ray Moyer

No other motion picture about Hollywood comes near Billy Wilder's searing, uncompromising and utterly fascinating portrait of the film community. Beneath it all is vanity, madness, murder, and a twisted obsession with filmdom's past. Wilder's work is a sardonic portrait of an aging silent film star and a cynical young man who is engulfed by the demented siren's delusions.

The movie opens with a jolt: the bullet-riddled body of a young man is seen floating face down in the pool next to a mansion. The ghostly voice of Joe Gillis (William Holden) recounts the events leading up to his death, which are shown in flashback. A hack screenwriter, Joe is hounded by creditors and desperate for cash. After failing to sell a script—his last hope—he's driving aimlessly when he spots a couple of repo men who are after his car. He speeds off, gets a flat, and pulls into the driveway of a dilapidated mansion, where he hears an arresting female voice calling down to him, ordering him into the house. Max (Erich von Stroheim), a severe-looking, bald-headed butler, waves Joe inside, where he is shown into the august presence of silent screen star Norma Desmond (Gloria Swanson). After lamenting the current state of the film industry, she offers Joe a job writing a reworking of *Salome*, which she plans to use as a comeback vehicle. Joe knows it's a pipe dream, but he needs the work. The creepily seductive Norma insists that he stay with her while working on the script. Observed by Norma and the somber, silent Max, Joe becomes a virtual prisoner of the actress and her strange past.

SUNSET BOULEVARD is Billy Wilder's sour, insightful critique of showbiz nostalgia—the myths by which a tawdry, profit-driven industry has managed to define itself as a dream machine of unfailing glamour. Essentially satirical, the film works equally well for those fans who read it as straightforward melodrama, largely because of Swanson's remarkable performance. This was a comeback for Swanson, who achieved what her tragic character in SUNSET BOULEVARD could not. Yet the attention she received upon her return to Hollywood still couldn't match the adulation lavished on Swanson in the 1920s, when tens of thousands turned out to cheer her in mammoth parades. Swanson was thus in a singular position to empathize with her character's longing for Hollywood's past glories. As Norma says: "We didn't need dialogue. We had faces then." There is much of Norma Desmond that *is* Swanson. Not only did she allow Wilder to exploit her hard-earned image, but she let him incorporate her silent career, including footage of her work in von Stroheim's QUEEN KELLY, into the film. Swanson, however, was never the neurotic, mentally disturbed creature that Norma is off-screen. Before Swanson was chosen, Wilder and producer-coscenarist Charles Brackett talked about the possibility of using Mary Pickford, Mae Murray, Pola Negri, or even Mae West as Norma. It is unlikely that any of them could have come close to the magnificent performance given by Swanson, whose penetrating, courageous grasp of the character astounded critics, public, and peers. In 1989, SUNSET BOULEVARD was selected by the National Film Registry of the Library of Congress as one of 25 landmark films, leading examples of American cinematic art.

SUNSHINE BOYS, THE

1975 111m c Comedy ★★★½
UA (U.S.) PG

Walter Matthau *(Willy Clark)*, George Burns *(Al Lewis)*, Richard Benjamin *(Ben Clark)*, Lee Meredith *(Nurse in Sketch)*, Carol Arthur *(Doris)*, Rosetta LeNoire *(Nurse)*, F. Murray Abraham *(Mechanic)*, Howard Hesseman *(Commercial Director)*, James Cranna *(TV Director)*, Ron Rifkin *(TV Floor Manager)*

p, Ray Stark; d, Herbert Ross; w, Neil Simon

AAN Best Actor: Walter Matthau; *AA Best Supporting Actor:* George Burns; *AAN Best Adapted Screenplay:* Neil Simon; *AAN Best Art Direction:* Albert Brenner, Marvin March

One of the best films ever made from a Neil Simon play, an engaging homage to the tradition of vaudeville in which the two halves of a once-famous double act (they now hate each other) re-team for a TV special.

The film opens in the 1970s with Matthau as a semi-retired comic scraping by doing commercials that his agent/nephew Benjamin has secured for him. He's auditioning for a silly potato chip TV spot for advertising director Hesseman when he blows his lines and decides that this isn't show business and he no longer wants to be a part of it. A nostalgic TV special is coming up, and Benjamin books Matthau on it, hoping that he will put aside his rancor toward his former partner, Burns, and unite this last time for the benefit of all those people who never saw them together in the flesh. Burns and Matthau haven't spoken in decades, and the mere mention of Burns is enough to send Matthau's blood pressure soaring. But he buries his enmity and agrees to see his erstwhile friend. The two men meet and began rehearsing the sketch that made them household names way back when they were known as the Sunshine Boys, but battles begin immediately as they argue over the first words of the sketch.

THE SUNSHINE BOYS is a solid movie with stellar performances from all—seldom have Simon's lines been delivered with as much bite and wit as they are here. This was Burns' first film in 35 years and he was perfect, earning a Best Supporting Actor Oscar at the age of 79. Matthau earned a nomination for Best Actor (he lost to Jack Nicholson for ONE FLEW OVER THE CUCKOO'S NEST, which collected most of the statuettes in 1975), and nominations also went to the screenplay and the art direction. Simon's inspiration for the story came from real-life vaudevillians Smith and Dale. In their very advanced years, the comics teamed to do their "Dr. Kronkheit" sketch on the Ed Sullivan show, reviving a classic piece of comedy for a whole new generation of viewers.

SUPERCOP

1992 96m c Action/Crime/Martial Arts ★★★½
Golden Way (Hong Kong)

Jackie Chan *(Detective Kevin Chan aka Fu Sheng)*, Michelle Yeoh *(Director Yang aka Hana)*, Maggie Cheung *(May)*, Bill Tung *(Uncle Bill)*, Tsang Kong *(Chaibat aka Big Brother Wei)*, Yuen Wah *(Panther)*, Josephine Koo *(Madame Chaibat)*, Philip Chan *(Inspector Chan)*, Lo Lieh *(Thai General)*, Shum Wai *(Drug Dealer)*

p, Willie Chan, Edward Tang; d, Stanley Tong; w, Edward Tang, Fibe Ma, Lee Wei-yee; ph, Ardy Lam; ed, Cheung Yiu-chung, Cheung Kar-fei; m, Joel McNeely; prod d, Wong Yue Man; art d, But Yiu Kwong; cos, Hung Wei-chuk

With this second sequel to his enormously popular POLICE STORY, Jackie Chan edges ever closer to matching American action films in scope, even if his budgets are lower. This one cost $10 million, paltry by U.S. standards but huge for a Hong Kong film; one can only wish that the care lavished on the stunt sequences had been applied to the screenplay as well.

Chan is Kevin Chan, who is drafted by his Hong Kong superiors to be the "supercop" requested by the police force in mainland China. They need someone to help them bring down an international drug ring

run by Big Brother Wei (Ken Tsang), and Chan seems to fit the bill. But first, he must prove himself to Chinese police director Yang (Michelle Khan), and does so in a martial arts duel with the best fighter on her squad. He then goes undercover in a prison camp, where he helps Wei's younger brother, known as "The Panther" (Yuen Wah) "escape" from the place. After some initial doubt, Wei's gang accepts Chan into their midst, but soon it looks like his cover might be blown.

SUPERCOP: POLICE STORY III shares many of the strengths and weaknesses of Chan's latter-day films. After he moved away from the pure martial arts films that made his name (including the amazing PROJECT A, which remains one of the best kung-fu films ever made), his movies became more dependent on plot and large-scale stunts than his incredible hand-to-hand combat choreography. Like ARMOR OF GOD (another Chan title to get U.S. exposure recently), POLICE STORY III is overly dependent on plot for the first two-thirds, and the action doesn't come as enjoyably thick and fast as in his all-martial-arts fests. But, as in most Asian genre films, the final half-hour makes it all worthwhile, and what makes Chan's work continually astonishing is that the actor does all his own stunts.

The movie also benefits from Chan's considerable comic skills — he's always incorporated humor into his films, and isn't afraid to be the butt of the jokes — and from costar Khan (also known as Michelle Yeoh), who proves to be every bit the martial artist he is. In fact, she may be the best of all the female sidekicks that have populated recent action films, treated with neither overt sensitivity nor sentimentality; she gets knocked down and jumps up again as much as Chan, and rarely gets into situations where she's dependent on him to save her. The scene in which Chan takes on Yang's best fighter, surprisingly and disappointingly, is done with sped-up visuals, but the action gets better as it goes along, culminating in the astonishing, extended final sequence that ends atop a speeding train. As usual, the film ends with outtakes of Chan and Khan getting into alternately funny- and painful-looking accidents in the course of shooting the action scenes.

SUPERFLY

1972 96m c Action/Crime ★★★★
Warner Bros. (U.S.) R/18

Ron O'Neal *(Youngblood Priest)*, Carl Lee *(Eddie)*, Sheila Frazier *(Georgia)*, Julius Harris *(Scatter)*, Charles McGregor *(Fat Freddie)*, Nate Adams *(Dealer)*, Polly Niles *(Cynthia)*, Yvonne Delaine *(Mrs. Freddie)*, Henry Shapiro *(Robbery Victim)*, K.C. *(Pimp)*

p, Sig Shore; d, Gordon Parks Jr.; w, Phillip Fenty; ph, James Signorelli; ed, Bob Brady; m, Curtis Mayfield; cos, Nate Adams

This interesting feature is one of the few Hollywood films that takes an honest look at the lives of African-Americans in the ghetto. O'Neal plays a Harlem cocaine pusher whose success (via connections with corrupt police officials) has gained him the respect and envy of the neighborhood. He wants to retire from the business and enjoy the comforts this life has brought him, but first he must make one last million-dollar dope deal.

The moral ambiguity of the film may disturb some viewers, but the film smacks of realistic grit throughout. Parks, one of the few blacks to direct in Hollywood, had a real feeling for the Harlem locations and the language of its residents. The action sequences are good, and a fine score by Mayfield helps out as well. SUPERFLY was financially backed by a group of Harlem businessmen, marking one of the first times a Black-oriented film was actually financed by Blacks. It was also one of the first to use a nonwhite cast and crew. Director Parks was the son of Gordon Parks, Sr., the director of the "Shaft" movies. A sequel, SUPERFLY T.N.T., followed.

SUPERMAN

1978 143m c Science Fiction ★★★
Warner Bros. (U.S.) PG

Marlon Brando *(Jor-El)*, Gene Hackman *(Lex Luthor)*, Christopher Reeve *(Superman/Clark Kent)*, Ned Beatty *(Otis)*, Jackie Cooper *(Perry White)*, Glenn Ford *(Pa Kent)*, Trevor Howard *(1st Elder)*, Margot Kidder *(Lois Lane)*, Jack O'Halloran *(Non)*, Valerie Perrine *(Eve Teschmacher)*

p, Pierre Spengler; d, Richard Donner; w, Mario Puzo, David Newman, Leslie Newman, Robert Benton (based on the story by Puzo, from the comic strip created by Jerry Siegel, Joe Shuster); ph, Geoffrey Unsworth; ed, Stuart Baird; m, John Williams; prod d, John Barry; fx, Colin Chilvers, Roy Field, Derek Meddings, Zoran Perisic, Denys Coop, Les Bowie; cos, Yvonne Blake

AAN Best Editing: Stuart Baird; AAN Best Score: John Williams; AAN Best Sound: Gordon K. McCallum, Graham Hartshone, Nicolas Le-Messurier, Roy Charman

"You'll believe a man can fly," the ads said, and by SUPERMAN's end that's just about true. Christopher Reeve essays the title role and makes it his own, combining correctly chiseled features with a likable comic humanity, while the film itself nicely balances special effects with the romance of Superman and Lois Lane (Margot Kidder). The story opens on the planet Krypton, where Superman's father (Marlon Brando) sends his son off to Earth, where he grows up to be "mild-mannered reporter" Clark Kent. Flying around in tights and cape, Superman-alias-Clark saves the day—and Lois—a number of times. Eventually he rescues all mankind from the evil Lex Luthor (Gene Hackman) and his assistants (Ned Beatty and Valerie Perrine, in an excellent bit of comic caricature) as they plot to take over the world. Lois is killed in the course of events, but Superman circles the globe at such terrific speed that its rotation is reversed, bringing his beloved back to life. The film burdens itself with too many story lines and an overlong (though beautifully photographed) prologue, but things really get moving when Reeve takes the screen. A worldwide hunt was conducted to find the right man for the role, with Robert Redford, Burt Reynolds, Nick Nolte, Kris Kristofferson, Sylvester Stallone, Ryan O'Neal, Clint Eastwood, and Charles Bronson among the candidates. So excellent is Reeve, however, that it is nearly impossible to think of anyone else as the Man of Steel.

SUPERMAN II

1980   127m   c   Science Fiction   ★★★½
Warner Bros.   (U.S./U.K.)   PG

Gene Hackman (Lex Luthor), Christopher Reeve (Clark Kent/Superman), Ned Beatty (Otis), Jackie Cooper (Perry White), Sarah Douglas (Ursa), Margot Kidder (Lois Lane), Jack O'Halloran (Non), Valerie Perrine (Eve Teschmacher), Susannah York (Lara), Clifton James (Sheriff)

p, Pierre Spengler; d, Richard Lester; w, Mario Puzo, David Newman, Leslie Newman (based on a story by Puzo, from characters created by Jerry Siegel, Joe Shuster); ph, Geoffrey Unsworth, Robert Paynter; ed, John Victor-Smith; m, Ken Thorne; prod d, John Barry, Peter Murton; art d, Maurice Fowler; fx, Colin Chilvers, Roy Field, Zoran Perisic; cos, Yvonne Blake, Sue Yelland

Poking fun at its American mythos, but never descending into camp comedy, this sequel makes for a wonderful time. Christopher Reeve reprises his role as the bumbling reporter/Man of Steel with marvelous success. The film opens with a fury as terrorists who have taken over the Eiffel Tower threaten to blow it up with a nuclear bomb. Lois Lane (Margot Kidder), ever the inquisitive reporter, tries to interview the terrorists and finds herself in more trouble than she bargained for. Fortunately, Superman comes to save the day, rescuing Lois and flinging the bomb into outer space. But this sets off a nuclear explosion that frees some bad guys (Terence Stamp, Sarah Douglas, and Jack O'Halloran) from the cosmic prison they were sentenced to in SUPERMAN. The movie hits full stride as the villains come to take over Earth, not knowing their fellow Kryptonian is that planet's hero. The result is an especially fun movie and a rare instance of a sequel that not only equals, but even betters, its original. The same cannot be said for SUPERMAN III or SUPERMAN IV: THE QUEST FOR PEACE, despite Reeve's continued command of the role.

SUPPORT YOUR LOCAL SHERIFF

1969   96m   c   Western/Comedy   ★★★
Cherokee   (U.S.)   G/PG

James Garner (Jason McCullough), Joan Hackett (Prudy Perkins), Walter Brennan (Pa Danby), Harry Morgan (Mayor Olly Perkins), Jack Elam (Jake), Bruce Dern (Joe Danby), Henry Jones (Preacher Henry Jackson), Walter Burke (Fred Johnson), Dick Peabody (Luke Danby), Gene Evans (Tom Danby)

p, William Bowers; d, Burt Kennedy; w, William Bowers; ph, Harry Stradling Jr.; ed, George W. Brooks; m, Jeff Alexander; art d, Leroy Coleman; fx, Marcel Vercoutere; cos, Norman Burza, Florence Hackett

This entertaining spoof of western movie cliches features Garner as a stranger who stops off at a small town en route to Australia, a running joke that works well through the rest of the film. He's engaged as the new sheriff, taking the job because he can't afford the boomtown's inflated prices. He hires Elam, the town drunk, as a deputy. After Garner arrests Dern and has the outlaw help build the new jail, Dern's father, Brennan, gets angry and summons the rest of his family to rescue the wayward son. A climactic street shootout results in a win by Garner as he holds a gang off with an apparently empty cannon. Unlike the later BLAZING SADDLES (1974), SUPPORT YOUR LOCAL SHERIFF has a good time with the western cliches but still shows respect for the formula western. Garner underplays winningly; Brennan is hilarious in a virtual parody of his role in MY DARLING CLEMENTINE (1946).

SURE THING, THE

1985   94m   c   Comedy   ★★★
Monument   (U.S.)   PG-13/15

John Cusack (Walter "Gib" Gibson), Daphne Zuniga (Alison Bradbury), Anthony Edwards (Lance), Boyd Gaines (Jason), Lisa Jane Persky (Mary Ann Webster), Viveca Lindfors (Prof. Taub), Nicollette Sheridan (The Sure Thing), Tim Robbins (Gary Cooper), Fran Ryan (Louise), George Memmoli (Al)

p, Roger Birnbaum, Andrew Scheinman; d, Rob Reiner; w, Steven L. Bloom, Jonathan Roberts; ph, Robert Elswit; ed, Robert Leighton; m, Tom Scott; prod d, Lilly Kilvert; fx, John Frazier, Jeff Wischnack; cos, Durinda Wood

A charming surprise, THE SURE THING is IT HAPPENED ONE NIGHT with acne. It's life in the Ivy League. Walter "Gib" Gibson (John Cusack) is a junk food junkie, a beer-swilling freshman who lives for women but strikes out more often than a pitcher. Alison Bradbury (Daphne Zuniga) is an all-American lass who has planned her life down to where she'll retire. They meet in a writing class and sparks fly, but the wrong kind of sparks. They hate each other on sight, or so it seems. Gib's pal, Lance (Anthony Edwards), invites him to spend Christmas in the West and says that he can arrange a date in California with a girl who is "a sure thing." Gib plans to drive out with a California-bound couple. At the same time, Alison arranges to go with the same couple to visit her own boy friend in California. Lots of good music, good humor, affection, and more than some passing philosophy as writers Steven L. Bloom and Jonathan Roberts poke fun at the effete East and the laidback West.

SUSPICION

1941   99m   bw   Thriller   ★★★★
RKO   (U.S.)   /PG

Cary Grant (Johnnie Aysgarth), Joan Fontaine (Lina McLaidlaw), Cedric Hardwicke (Gen. McLaidlaw), Nigel Bruce (Beaky Thwaite), Dame May Whitty (Mrs. McLaidlaw), Isabel Jeans (Mrs. Newsham), Heather Angel (Ethel, Maid), Auriol Lee (Isobel Sedbusk), Reginald Sheffield (Reggie Wetherby), Leo G. Carroll (Capt. Melbeck)

d, Alfred Hitchcock; w, Samson Raphaelson, Joan Harrison, Alma Reville (based on the novel Before the Fact by Frances Iles); ph, Harry Stradling; ed, William Hamilton; m, Franz Waxman; art d, Van Nest Polglase, Carroll Clark; fx, Vernon L. Walker; cos, Edward Stevenson

AAN Best Picture; AA Best Actress: Joan Fontaine; AAN Best Score: Franz Waxman

SUSPICION is so grimly powerful that its Hollywood-style happy ending has infuriated audiences for years. Cary Grant plays penniless society wastrel Johnnie Aysgarth, who cynically romances Lina McLaidlaw (Joan Fontaine), the sheltered daughter of wealthy parents. Rapidly approaching old maidenhood, Lina escapes her oppressive home by marrying Johnnie, even though she's been warned that he's a fortune hunter and an incorrigible playboy. Apparently true to form, Johnnie becomes involved in an embezzlement scheme, which is complicated when his friend Beaky (Nigel Bruce, playing his usual lovable bumbler) dies in Paris under curious circumstances; Lina begins to suspect that Johnnie murdered him. Now Lina imagines that she's to be Johnnie's next victim and seems to find her suspicions confirmed in his every action. The tension mounts (and the humor of the film's first half subsides) as Lina becomes increasingly fearful, especially since she can find no convincing evidence that her charming husband is a killer. Soon, she's afraid to drink her nightly glass of milk, brought to her in bed by Johnnie in one of the director's most famous sequences (the milk glows ominously—Hitchcock had a light bulb placed in the glass). But the milk isn't poisoned, and the climax occurs later, when the couple are driving along a rocky cliff high above the ocean.

Based on Frances Iles's novel *Before the Fact*, in which the husband really is a murderer, SUSPICION's ending disappointed many, especially considering the slow, delicious building of Hitchcockian suspense that preceded it. With REAR WINDOW and VERTIGO, the film is one of Hitchcock's most trenchant critiques of spectatorship, as the frustrating passivity displayed by bookish fantasist Lina seems driven by a perverse desire to watch the narrative unfold. Joan Fontaine's Oscar was widely considered a compensation for the Oscar she *didn't* receive for the previous year's REBECCA.

SWEET BIRD OF YOUTH

1962 120m c Drama ★★½
Roxbury/MGM (U.S.) /X

Paul Newman *(Chance Wayne)*, Geraldine Page *(Alexandra Del Lago)*, Shirley Knight *(Heavenly Finley)*, Ed Begley *("Boss" Finley)*, Rip Torn *(Thomas J. Finley)*, Mildred Dunnock *(Aunt Nonnie)*, Madeleine Sherwood *(Miss Lucy)*, Philip Abbott *(Dr. George Scudder)*, Corey Allen *(Scotty)*, Barry Cahill *(Bud)*

p, Pandro S. Berman; d, Richard Brooks; w, Richard Brooks (based on the play by Tennessee Williams); ph, Milton Krasner; ed, Henry Berman; art d, George W. Davis, Urie McCleary; fx, Lee LeBlanc; cos, Orry-Kelly

AAN Best Actress: Geraldine Page; *AA Best Supporting Actor:* Ed Begley; *AAN Best Supporting Actress:* Shirley Knight

Williams's steamy play gets the Richard Brooks whitewash—as with CAT ON A HOT TIN ROOF. Instead of Newman's hustler getting castrated, it's the original stage piece that gets emasculated here. Newman, Page, Sherwood, and Torn repeat their Broadway roles, and Hollywood replaced Sidney Blackmer, Diana Hyland, and Martine Bartlett with Begley, Knight, and Dunnock—all in good form. Admittedly, Brooks was under orders to make changes to the play in order to secure approval from the Production Code. But he doesn't allow the expert cast to go to the mat like they need to.

Newman is a gigolo who thinks he can make it in film; all he needs is a break. In Florida, he meets Page, a fading movie star who is at the end of her tether. Her last movie is, she is certain, a dismal flop. When she meets Newman and she gives her a ride to his home town, she begs him for more gin. Later, when they stay in a motel together, she demands an oxygen inhalator. Then she asks Newman if he can find her some hashish to smoke. In order to keep the virile Newman at her side, she tells him that she can help him get his start in Hollywood by introducing him to the right people. They travel to Newman's hometown before going back to California. Newman wants to see his one-time girlfriend, Knight, who is the apple of her father's (Begley's) eye. Begley, a corrupt politician who runs the area, hates Newman with a passion because the last time Newman came through town he left Knight pregnant and she had to get an abortion. (In the play, she was liberally infected with syphilis by her lover and had to have her ovaries removed.) Begley wants to get even with Newman for what he did to Knight, so he plots revenge with his lackey son, Torn.

All of Williams's Southern Gothic themes are intermingled here: violence, familial conflict, sexual neurosis, the mentality of the mob. Most of it comes across as overheated nonsense, but Page's egomaniacal telephone soliloquy at the film's climax is reason enough to tune in. (For devotees of camp, BIRD was filmed for TV in 1989 in an almost total misfire directed by Nicholas Roeg, with Mark Harmon more flaccid than Newman, Rip Torn moving up a generation to Begley's role, the underrated Valerie Perrine in for Sherwood, and Elizabeth Taylor playing Alexandra Del Lago like a pretty Marie Dressler.)

SWEET CHARITY

1969 157m c Musical/Comedy ★★★½
Universal (U.S.) G/A

Shirley MacLaine *(Charity Hope Valentine)*, Sammy Davis Jr. *(Big Daddy)*, Ricardo Montalban *(Vittorio Vitale)*, John McMartin *(Oscar Lindquist)*, Chita Rivera *(Nickie)*, Paula Kelly *(Helene)*, Stubby Kaye *(Herman)*, Barbara Bouchet *(Ursula)*, Alan Hewitt *(Nicholsby)*, Dante D'Paulo *(Charlie)*

p, Robert Arthur; d, Bob Fosse; w, Peter Stone (based on the play by Neil Simon, Cy Coleman, Dorothy Fields, adapted from the screenplay "Notti Di Cabiria" by Federico Fellini, Tullio Ponelli, Ennio Flaiano); ph, Robert Surtees; ed, Stuart Gilmore; m, Cy Coleman; art d, Alexander Golitzen, George Webb; chor, Bob Fosse; cos, Edith Head

AAN Best Score: Cy Coleman; *AAN Best Art Direction:* Alexander Golitzen, George C. Webb, Jack D. Moore; *AAN Best Costume Design:* Edith Head

SWEET CHARITY is a very good musical that should have been a great musical. Bob Fosse, making his film directorial debut, couldn't convey the verve he injected into the play to the movie version, which starred Shirley MacLaine as Charity, a dime-a-dance hostess in a tacky New York ballroom whose boyfriend takes all of her hard-earned savings, pushes her off a low bridge in Central Park, and absconds with the cash. Charity, however, is a die-hard optimist, down but not out. Walking along the street one evening, she comes across Italian movie star Vittorio (Ricardo Montalban) in a furious argument with his lover, Ursula (Barbara Bouchet). Vittorio takes the gamine Charity out for a night on the town in Ursula's stead—but just when sparks seem about to strike, a contrite Ursula shows up at his apartment, leaving Charity stuck hiding in a closet while Vittorio and Ursula make up. Later, Charity is trapped in a stalled elevator with Oscar (John McMartin), a mild-mannered and terribly claustrophobic insurance clerk. The two hit it off, but the romance is complicated because Oscar doesn't know Charity works in a dance hall. Eventually he does find out what she does for a living but still wants to marry her. After meeting her friends (Paula Kelly and Chita Rivera), seeing her place of employment, and discovering she wears a tattoo, however, he backs out. The film ends, as a depressed Charity is handed a flower by a band of hippies in Central Park, after which she takes new heart. Cy Coleman and Dorothy Fields wrote the fine score for the play and two new numbers for the movie, and their songs, along with Fosse's choreography and some fine supporting performances, provide the film's high points. MacLaine works very hard at not seeming to work hard but gives a somewhat studied portrayal nonetheless.

SWEET SMELL OF SUCCESS

1957 96m bw Drama ★★★★★
Hecht-Hill-Lancaster (U.S.) /A

Burt Lancaster *(J.J. Hunsecker)*, Tony Curtis *(Sidney Falco)*, Susan Harrison *(Susan Hunsecker)*, Martin Milner *(Steve Dallas)*, Sam Levene *(Frank D'Angelo)*, Barbara Nichols *(Rita)*, Jeff Donnell *(Sally)*, Joseph Leon *(Robard)*, Edith Atwater *(Mary)*, Emile Meyer *(Harry Kello)*

p, James Hill; d, Alexander Mackendrick; w, Clifford Odets, Ernest Lehman (based on the short story "Tell Me About It Tomorrow" by Lehman); ph, James Wong Howe; ed, Alan Crosland Jr.; m, Elmer Bernstein; art d, Edward Carrere

Emerging from a posh nightclub into the rain-slicked streets of midtown Manhattan, where a couple of hoodlums can be seen rolling a drunk, ruthless showbiz journalist J.J. Hunsecker experiences a pre-dawn epiphany. "I love this dirty town," he exclaims.

The moment is typical of SWEET SMELL OF SUCCESS, Alexander Mackendrick's perverse, masterly romance of urban menace and moral decay. Best known as the director of lovably quirky Ealing comedies (e.g., THE MAN IN THE WHITE SUIT), Mackendrick turns to film noir with a vengeance, evincing a very British fascination with (and simultaneous distaste for) naked American ambition. With the assistance of legendary cinematographer James Wong Howe, he fashions a stark, neon-lit urban landscape that seems to comprehend and surpass all of its predecessors in the genre.

Sidney Falco (Tony Curtis) is a Broadway flack whose income depends on getting media exposure for his showbiz clients. The most coveted form of publicity is a mention in the syndicated newspaper column written by Hunsecker (Burt Lancaster), a Walter Winchell type with a nationwide audience and sufficient clout to intimidate the President. Desperate to plant items for his clients, Falco panders shamelessly to the columnist. Hunsecker, who spends his evenings sipping coffee in a trendy nightspot, is a sternly forbidding, collosally repressed bachelor with no apparent interest in women apart from his younger sister Susan (Susan Harrison). Neurotically overprotective of Susan, who lives with him in an implicitly incestuous arrangement, Hunsecker feels threatened by her blossoming romance with jazz musician Steve Dallas (Martin Milner). Hunsecker pressures Falco to break up the relationship; should he fail, he'll lose all access to the column.

After fabricating a blind item implying that the young musician is a pot-smoking Communist, Falco inveigles a cigarette girl (Barbara Nichols) into sleeping with an entertainment reporter; in exchange for her favors, the reporter runs the item. Dallas loses his gig and is forced to appeal to Hunsecker, who offers to get him his job back if he agrees to stay away from Susan. Dallas furiously refuses. Hunsecker then extracts a promise from his sister that she will not see Dallas again. She soon breaks her word, however, meeting the musician at a secluded spot by the river, where he persuades her that she is being manipulated by her older brother. When Hunsecker discovers the couple's surreptitious reunion, he again turns to Falco to scotch the romance. This time Falco is guaranteed a period of carte blanche access to the column should his machinations succeed. Unable to resist the lucrative offer, Falco plants a reefer in Dallas's topcoat pocket and tips police detective Harry Kello (Emile Meyer). Kello finds the marijuana and viciously beats Dallas with pair of shot-loaded gloves.

As Falco celebrates, he receives a call from Susan, who sounds suicidal. He races to the Hunseckers' apartment and tries to comfort the half-dressed girl while sitting on her bed. Hunsecker arrives and, assuming the worst, tosses Falco out and interrogates Susan. Knowing that Falco is mixed up in her boyfriend's persecution, she refuses to defend him. In a jealous rage, Hunsecker calls Kello and informs the sadistic detective that he's been hoodwinked by Falco. Kello tracks Falco down near a highway overpass and, as the younger man shouts his defiance, again pulls on his sinister gloves. Meanwhile, Susan packs a suitcase and walks out of her brother's apartment forever.

SWEET SMELL OF SUCCESS captures the sleazy allure of Manhattan like no other film; Howe's atmospheric night-for-night location shooting turns a Broadway juice bar into a cross between a Weegee photo and an Edward Hopper canvas. The charmingly venal Sidney Falco was a breakthrough role for Tony Curtis, whose frequent miscasting, particularly in costume adventures, had become something of a Hollywood joke. Here, comfortable for once in an urban milieu, Curtis does a remarkable job, managing to elicit sympathy without compromising his character's essential tawdriness. His brash 50s hepcat—a kid who's risen a little above his station and masks his insecurities with manufactured bravado—is a reminder that Cool wasn't invented by James Dean (who never even played a city boy). Lancaster, vividly sinister, seems ready to implode from surplus repression. Co-screenwriter Clifford Odets ("Golden Boy") contributes passages of lyrical slang to a Freudian scenario based on a novella by Ernest Lehman (NORTH BY NORTHWEST). The brisk jazzy score was contributed by Elmer Bernstein, who makes canny use of the Chico Hamilton Quintet.

SWEET SWEETBACK'S BAADASSSSS SONG

1971 97m c Action/Drama   ★★★★
Cinemation Industries   (U.S.)   X/

Melvin Van Peebles *(Sweetback)*, Simon Chuckster *(Beetle)*, Hubert Scales *(Mu-Mu)*, John Dullaghan *(Commissioner)*, Rhetta Hughes *(Old Girl Friend)*, West Gale, Niva Rochelle, Nick Ferrari, Ed Rue, Mario Van Peebles

d, Melvin Van Peebles; w, Melvin Van Peebles; ph, Bob Maxwell; ed, Melvin Van Peebles; m, Melvin Van Peebles

A landmark in Black filmmaking in the U.S., this angry, extravagant, loud, belligerent movie reaches a high pitch early on and stays there. It's written, directed, photographed, scored by, and stars Melvin Van Peebles, who'd always wanted to be a filmmaker, went to France to do a conventional film (STORY OF A THREE DAY PASS), came back to try his hand in Hollywood (WATERMELON MAN), and finally wound up here, an independent in full control of his product.

The narrative is linear and relatively unimaginative. Sweetback (Van Peebles), who's working in a brothel when the film begins, is finally moved to action, stomps a couple of cops unconscious, then begins running. He runs for the rest of the film, finally escaping to Mexico.

SWEET SWEETBACK is not an easy film to admire: it's violent, even sadistic, obscene, frenzied, painful. Some critics condemned it for trading on a classic Black stereotype, the "buck." On the surface, the film has all the extreme elements of the most cynical "Blaxploitation" movies, but Van Peebles actually uses these elements in order to comment upon them. The pain with which he washes the screen is meant to be transmuted into anger by audiences, and then into political action. Obviously, this didn't happen, and probably never could. But the film succeeds as a *cri de coeur*, an announcement that Black militancy has reached your neighborhood theater and that things will never be the same.

SWEET SWEETBACK caused considerable controversy among Black commentators and critics, but it remains one of very few Black films from the 1970s to spring entirely from a Black artistic sensibility. Although this independent release didn't appear on *Variety* charts, it grossed more than $10 million, thus becoming one of the most financially rewarding independent productions of all time.

SWEETIE

1989 97m c Comedy   ★★★★
Arenafilm   (Australia)   /15

Genevieve Lemon *(Dawn)*, Karen Colston *(Kay)*, Tom Lycos *(Louis)*, Jon Darling *(Gordon)*, Dorothy Barry *(Flo)*, Michael Lake *(Bob)*, Andre Pataczek *(Clayton)*, Jean Hadgraft *(Mrs. Schneller)*, Paul Livingston *(Teddy Schneller)*, Louise Fox *(Cheryl)*

p, John Maynard; d, Jane Campion; w, Jane Campion, Gerard Lee (based on an idea by Jane Campion); ph, Sally Bongers; ed, Veronika Heussler; m, Martin Armiger; prod d, Peter Harris; cos, Amanda Lovejoy

To appreciate the complexity and uniqueness of SWEETIE, Jane Campion's remarkably assured first feature, try to imagine Roman Polanski's REPULSION reworked as a romantic comedy or Brian De Palma's SISTERS refashioned as a farce.

Kay (Karen Colston) is a gaunt, withdrawn young woman whose life is ruled by superstition. A control freak, she fervidly accepts a fortune teller's prediction that she'll meet a man with a question mark on his forehead and promptly steals a coworker's fiance (Tom Lycos) who fits the bill: he sports a wayward curl of hair over a beauty mark. For a while, the uptight woman relaxes, but her phobic behavior is never completely overcome. When her obese sister Dawn (Genevieve Lemon) appears on the scene, unannounced and uninvited, we begin to understand just why Kay's a paranoid bundle of repression. Manipulative and alternately petulant or hysterical, the eponymous "Sweetie" gobbles life voraciously, sampling food and men with the same relish; she's a female Peter Pan straitjacketed in a little girl's frilly party dress. Not surprisingly, her wildly inappropriate behavior has brought her family to the end of its rope.

In this darkly stylish debut, New Zealander Campion has fashioned a slapstick domestic tragedy. In addition to being a remarkable visual stylist (brilliantly aided by cinematographer and former classmate Sally Bongers), Campion elicits miracles of acting from her cast. In this comically heightened version of reality, the actors might all too easily have overplayed the laughs and forced the tears; instead they are effectively disquieting and colorful. Cruelly honest and pitilessly funny, SWEETIE is one of the nakedest explorations of familial love and desperation ever filmed.

SWEPT AWAY...BY AN UNUSUAL DESTINY IN THE BLUE SEA OF AUGUST

1974 116m c Drama/Comedy ★★★½
Medusa (Italy) R/X

Giancarlo Giannini (Gennarino), Mariangela Melato (Raffaella)

p, Romano Cardarelli; d, Lina Wertmuller; w, Lina Wertmuller; ph, Giulio Battiferri, Giuseppe Fornari, Stefano Ricciotti; m, Piero Piccioni; cos, Enrico Job

Aboard a chartered yacht a group of wealthy northern Italians discuss a variety of topics while basking in the sun. The snobbish Melato takes particular delight in taunting Giannini, a Sicilian deckhand, ridiculing his smelly shirt and communist ideology. Surely, Giannini is the last man on earth Melato would ever want to be shipwrecked with on a desert isle. SWEPT AWAY is a wild romp and certainly lives up to its elongated title. When destiny does indeed shipwreck the two, none of Melato's arrogance can keep this two-person war between the sexes and classes from taking some passionately amorous turns. Director-screenwriter Lina Wertmuller's 11th film (the fourth to gain a US release) provoked much controversy for what many perceived as a reactionary, sexist treatment of Melato's role by Wertmuller, a self-described feminist. (One beating scene goes on for a *long* time.) The argument has merit, although it ignores the broadness of Wertmuller's treatment here of some of her favorite themes. Gender and class politics are ever-present throughout the story, but laced with a delightfully satiric bite that provokes laughter as well as thought. Giannini and Melato are perfectly matched as the combatants/lovers, providing a chemistry that lends Wertmuller's parable some degree of naturalism and honesty. With lesser actors the story might never have worked, and it certainly wouldn't have made such a splash at the box office.

SWIMMER, THE

1968 94m c Drama ★★½
Horizon/Dover (U.S.) PG/

Burt Lancaster (Ned Merrill), Janet Landgard (Julie Hooper), Janice Rule (Shirley Abbott), Tony Bickley (Donald Westerhazy), Marge Champion (Peggy Forsburgh), Nancy Cushman (Mrs. Halloran), Bill Fiore (Howie Hunsacker), John Garfield Jr. (Ticket Seller), Kim Hunter (Betty Graham), Rose Gregorio (Sylvia Finney)

p, Frank Perry, Roger Lewis; d, Frank Perry, Sydney Pollack; w, Eleanor Perry (based on the short story by John Cheever); ph, David Quaid, Michael Nebbia; ed, Sidney Katz, Carl Lerner, Pat Somerset; m, Marvin Hamlisch; art d, Peter Dohanos; cos, Anna Hill Johnstone, Elizabeth Stewart

Frequently silly but oddly memorable and unsettling, THE SWIMMER is an underrated blend of existential fable and social satire. Based on a *New Yorker* short story by John Cheever, it's buoyed by the music of a 22-year-old Marvin Hamlisch making his film scoring debut.

It's a summer day in suburban Connecticut, and successful advertising executive Ned Merrill (Burt Lancaster), clad only in swim trunks, finds himself several miles from home. Rather than walk straight back to his house, he decides to "swim" home, touring the pools of all his friends and neighbors. These include Betty Graham (Kim Hunter), on whom he once harbored a crush; Julie Hooper (Janet Landgard, in her film debut), who used to baby-sit his daughters and lust after him, but meets his latterday advances with bewilderment; and his former mistress, Shirley Abbott (Janice Rule), who shatters Ned with her assertion that she never loved him. Many of those Ned encounters are openly critical, commenting on his failed marriage or the children who have turned their backs on him. Each of these revelations seems to come as a shock, as though he's been unaware of them until now. As the journey continues, Ned's life is seen to be progressively disintegrating, until he reaches his own home, a dilapidated place which has clearly been empty for years, and breaks down in tears.

A collaboration between director Frank Perry (DAVID AND LISA) and his then-wife and screenwriter, Eleanor Perry, THE SWIMMER was deemed too confusing by its producers, who brought in Sydney Pollack to turn the Lancaster/Rule scene into a neater ending. Much of the film is still confusing, not to mention portentous and credibility-straining, but it remains genuinely affecting. Shot on location in Westport, Connecticut.

SWIMMING TO CAMBODIA

1987 87m c Drama/Comedy ★★★½
Screenliner Productions/Cinecom International Films /18
/Swimming Company (U.S.)

Spalding Gray, Sam Waterston, Ira Wheeler

p, Renne A. Shafransky; d, Jonathan Demme; w, Spalding Gray (from his performance piece); ph, John Bailey; ed, Carol Littleton; m, Laurie Anderson; prod d, Sandy McLeod

A surprisingly compelling film adaptation of Spalding Gray's one-man, two-evening stage performance about his experiences in Cambodia while filming a small role in Roland Joffe's THE KILLING FIELDS. Director Jonathan Demme has boiled the original monologue down to 87 minutes that still manage to encompass everything from Gray's search for his "perfect" moment, to his adventures in Hollywood (where, among other things, he auditions for a TV show opposite Farrah Fawcett), to his grisly evocation of the reign of the Khmer Rouge, whom he at one point compares to upstate New York hicks. Gray is a spellbinding monologist, and Demme constructs a perfect, uncluttered showcase for his subject's powers. All we get is Gray, a table, a glass of water, a couple of maps, and some "sound images" courtesy of Laurie Anderson; but that's enough to create a mesmerizing odyssey through the mind of a uniquely talented performer, as well as through one of the gorier chapters of modern history.

SWINDLE, THE
(IL BIDONE)

1955 92m bw Drama ★★★½
Titanus/SGC (France/Italy) /A

Broderick Crawford (Augusto), Richard Basehart (Picasso), Franco Fabrizi (Roberto), Giulietta Masina (Iris), Lorella De Luca (Patrizia), Giacomo Gabrielli (Vargas), Sue Ellen Blake (Anna), Alberto De Amicis (Rinaldo), Irene Cefaro (Marisa), Xenia Valderi (Luciana)

p, Mario Derecchi; d, Federico Fellini; w, Federico Fellini, Ennio Flaiano, Tullio Pinelli (based on a story by Fellini, Flaiano); ph, Otello Martelli; ed, Mario Serandrei, Giuseppe Vari; m, Nino Rota

To many people the films of Fellini are an obnoxious blend of tiresome episodes filled with ugly characters and extreme symbolism. Others find these same elements to be a magical universe filled with the forces influencing an individual's fate. They appreciate the revealing caricatures, lively costumes and sets, and extenuating sounds that create a poetic vision. The latter camp will find much to entertain themselves with in THE SWINDLE, a film similar to its predecessor, LA STRADA, in its depiction of a man who goes through life almost blind to its wonders and with little pity for other humans. Crawford plays a petty thief who teams up with Basehart and Fabrizi to swindle poor people. Fabrizi is the first to back out of these schemes—not to redeem himself but to go on to "better" things. Of the three, his character is the least sympathetic because his acts of thievery are done so casually. In a moment of enlightenment, Basehart forsakes this lifestyle to return to his wife Masina who, as in LA STRADA, looks on the events with her large round eyes. She is the direct opposite of the soulless Fabrizi. This leads Crawford to assemble another bunch to assist in his operations. In the touching final scenes, Crawford is dressed in a bishop's robes in order to execute a scheme when he is approached by an invalid, Blake, who takes him for the real thing, bending down to kiss his hand. Crawford finally feels remorse for his deeds, realizing that he has been taking advantage of people who are driven by pure faith. But by this time it's too late for him to repent. A very dark vision that isn't always pleasant to look at but is nonetheless fascinating. The film did not get a US release until 1962.

SWING SHIFT

1984 113m c Drama/War ★★★½
Warner Bros. (U.S.) PG

Goldie Hawn *(Kay Walsh)*, Kurt Russell *(Lucky Lockhart)*, Christine Lahti *(Hazel Zanussi)*, Fred Ward *(Biscuits Toohey)*, Ed Harris *(Jack Walsh)*, Sudie Bond *(Annie)*, Holly Hunter *(Jeannie Sherman)*, Patty Maloney *(Laverne)*, Lisa Pelikan *(Violet Mulligan)*, Susan Peretz *(Edith Castle)*

p, Jerry Bick; d, Jonathan Demme; w, Nancy Dowd, Bo Goldman, Ron Nyswaner; ph, Tak Fujimoto; ed, Craig McKay; m, Patrick Williams; prod d, Peter Jamison; art d, Bo Welch; cos, Joe I. Tompkins

AAN Best Supporting Actress: Christine Lahti

This latter-day look at "Rosie the Riveter" stars Goldie Hawn as Kay Walsh, whose husband, Jack (Ed Harris), is sent off to fight in WWII. Kay goes to work at an aircraft factory where she meets Lucky (Kurt Russell), whose heart problem has kept him out of uniform. They begin an affair, and Kay also develops a close friendship with her "loose" (i.e., emancipated) neighbor, Hazel (Christine Lahti). When Jack comes home on furlough, he discovers Kay's infidelity and goes back to war with a broken heart. In turn, Lucky, feeling rejected, sleeps with the lonely Hazel, upsetting relations among the three civilians. SWING SHIFT's view of adultery isn't very palatable—since Jack is at least as likable, if not more, than Lucky and seems to have a "good" marriage with Kay. Many castigated the film for using wartime hardships to justify Kay's affair and tarnish the patriotic image of the homefront Rosies. A fairer assessment suggests that director Jonathan Demme's characteristic generosity toward his characters and refusal to make absolute moral judgments are strong points, while the feminist subtext adds freshness to the story. The dullness of Kay and Lucky's romance, however, does damage the film, and may be the result of friction between Demme and Hawn, who reportedly had another director brought in to shoot new scenes that conventionalized the love triangle and downplayed Lahti's Hazel. Supporting Actress Oscar. Released at 113, 100, and 99 minutes, the movie is on videocassette at 100 minutes.

SWING TIME

1936 105m bw Musical/Romance ★★★★★
RKO (U.S.) /U

Fred Astaire *(John "Lucky" Garnett)*, Ginger Rogers *(Penelope "Penny" Carrol)*, Victor Moore *(Dr. Cardetti)*, Helen Broderick *(Mabel Anderson)*, Eric Blore *(Mr. Gordon)*, Betty Furness *(Margaret Watson)*, George Metaxa *(Ricardo Romero)*, Landers Stevens *(Judge Watson)*, John Harrington *(Dice Raymond)*, Pierre Watkin *(Al Simpson)*

p, Pandro S. Berman; d, George Stevens; w, Howard Lindsay, Allan Scott (based on a story by Erwin Gelsey); ph, David Abel; ed, Henry Berman; m, Jerome Kern; art d, Van Nest Polglase, Carroll Clark; fx, Vernon L. Walker; chor, Hermes Pan; cos, Bernard Newman, John Harkrider

AA Best Song: Jerome Kern (Music), Dorothy Fields (Music)

TOP HAT may be more energetic and glossy, but SWING TIME is arguably the most magical of the ten films Fred Astaire and Ginger Rogers made together. Their dancing and acting rapport are at a peak and director George Stevens shows more finesse than Mark Sandrich in lending the couple's rocky romance a genuinely heartfelt quality. This film seems to be more *about* the Astaire-Rogers mystique than any of the others, so it's especially poignant when Fred sings that he's "Never Gonna Dance" if he can't have Ginger.

The story tells of "Lucky" Garnett (Astaire), a gambler and and dancer engaged to Margaret Watson (Furness, in her pre-consumer advocacy days). When Lucky shows up late for his wedding, Margaret's father (Landers Stevens, the director's real-life father) tells him not to return until he earns $25,000 to prove that he's not just a layabout. Once Lucky meets dance teacher Penny Carrol (Rogers), however, his main problem is to *keep* from earning the 25 grand, since, of course, he falls in love with Penny. Highlights include a complex and delightful routine to "Pick Yourself Up," one of the greatest of the Astaire-Rogers light courtship duets, just as their luminous turn to "Waltz in Swing Time" stands today as one of their finest romantic turns. Their last duet, to the

aforementioned "Never Gonna Dance," really signals the end of the Astaire-Rogers golden years; this number, with the scene preceding it, constitutes the team's most touching five minutes together on film.

SWING TIME also features Astaire's incredible solo dance to "Bojangles of Harlem," perhaps the only blackface number on film which doesn't make one squirm today. His skin made up *as* an African-American rather than a minstrel-show caricature of one, Astaire dances an obvious tribute to the great Bill Robinson, even if the black dancer he more closely approximates is John Bubbles of PORGY AND BESS fame. The marvelous score, with music by Jerome Kern and lyrics by Dorothy Fields, consists of one classic song after another, and they are all stunningly staged. Astaire's rendition of "The Way You Look Tonight" comes while Rogers washes her hair. Her final appearance gently mocks the tender lyric, but her rubbing of Astaire's shoulder confirms the sentiment of the moment. "A Fine Romance," meanwhile, that famous sardonic love duet, appears while the couple walks around a gorgeous set of a snowy inn, the final swishing of the car's wiper blades perfectly rounding out the tune. The supporting cast, led by the acerbic Broderick, the sweetly bumbling Moore and the unctuous Blore, adds plenty of laughs, and, at the center of it all, Hollywood's ideal couple shines at their brightest. A film to cherish.

SWISS FAMILY ROBINSON

1960 126m c Children's ★★★½
Walt Disney Productions (U.K.) G/U

John Mills *(Father)*, Dorothy McGuire *(Mother)*, James MacArthur *(Fritz)*, Janet Munro *(Roberta)*, Sessue Hayakawa *(Pirate Chief)*, Tommy Kirk *(Ernst)*, Kevin Corcoran *(Francis)*, Cecil Parker *(Capt. Moreland)*, Andy Ho *(Auban)*, Milton Reid *(Big Pirate)*

p, Bill Anderson; d, Ken Annakin; w, Lowell S. Hawley (based on the novel by Johann Wyss); ph, Harry Waxman; ed, Peter Boita; m, William Alwyn; prod d, John Howell; art d, John Howell; fx, Danny Lee, Walter Stones; cos, Julie Harris

Disney's version of the famous novel is a superior adventure following the exploits of the title family. Father and Mother Robinson (John Mills and Dorothy McGuire) and their three sons, Fritz, Francis, and Ernst (James MacArthur, Kevin Corcoran, and Tommy Kirk), flee Napoleon and look for someplace to live in the South Seas, but in the course of the search they are chased by pirates and their ship is pounded by an angry sea. After the ship's crew deserts the sinking vessel with only the family on board, the Robinsons crash along a rocky shore and emerge to find a tropical island Eden. Since the ship, which is only half-submerged, is filled with food and gear, they prepare to settle in. Numerous adventures follow in this exciting and humorous picture filled with classic Disney touches. It's a tongue-in-cheek movie that avoids the sappy sentiment of so many "family" films and concentrates on sheer entertainment instead. The scenery is lush and colorful; the film's success made Tobago a tourist haven for many years afterward.

T

T-MEN

1947 91m bw Crime ★★★★
Eagle-Lion (U.S.) /A

Dennis O'Keefe *(Dennis O'Brien)*, Alfred Ryder *(Tony Genaro)*, Mary Meade *(Evangeline)*, Wallace Ford *(Schemer)*, June Lockhart *(Tony's Wife)*, Charles McGraw *(Moxie)*, Jane Randolph *(Diana)*, Art Smith *(Gregg)*, Herbert Heyes *(Chief Carson)*, Jack Overman *(Brownie)*

p, Aubrey Schenck; d, Anthony Mann; w, John C. Higgins (based on a story by Virginia Kellogg); ph, John Alton; ed, Fred Allen; m, Paul Sawtell; art d, Edward C. Jewell; fx, George J. Teague; cos, Frances Ehren

AAN Best Sound: Sound Services Inc.

One of Anthony Mann's finest forays into film noir, T-MEN was also one of the director's first financial triumphs. O'Keefe and Ryder are two treasury agents determined to crack a successful counterfeiting ring after a fellow agent is killed during the investigation. In order to obtain first-class information, the agents pose as underworld hoods and infiltrate a powerful Detroit mob family headed by Kosta. They discover that Ford, a sleazy LA-based hood with a penchant for steam baths, may hold the key to the counterfeiting ring, so the agents ingratiate themselves with him. Ford is afraid he'll soon be knocked off by the boys in Detroit, and his fears are justified; they have sent McGraw to kill him. Suspecting that Ryder is a T-Man, Ford informs McGraw of his suspicions, hoping that he'll be allowed to live. McGraw accepts the news and then locks Ford in a steam bath and turns the steam on full blast. The sadistic killer stands and watches as the hysterical Ford tries to smash the glass in the tiny window, to no avail. Meanwhile, Ryder finally cracks the secret of the counterfeiting operation, just as McGraw and the gang, O'Keefe among them, arrive intending to kill him.

When PRC studios and Britain's J. Arthur Rank organization merged to form Eagle-Lion, the new owners encouraged better scripts and more artistic creativity while providing bigger budgets to achieve their goals. Director Mann rose to the occasion and began a series of fascinating film noir crime dramas (T-MEN, RAW DEAL, and THE BLACK BOOK) with superb cinematographer John Alton. Presented in a documentary-like style with narration by Reed Hadley, T-MEN shifts from the bureaucratic staunchness of a voiceover to the shadowy, out-of-control world of film noir. In what would become a major theme in Mann's later work (especially in his westerns with Jimmy Stewart), the film examines the thin line between the law and the lawless, the hunters and the hunted. Though lawmen O'Keefe and Ryder plunge themselves into the criminal element with fervor, they are party to acts only sanctioned by society if one wears a badge. These themes are illustrated beautifully by Alton's visuals, which put the agents in the same shadowy light as the criminals. The film is at its most shocking during the steam bath murder and the scene is intense and horrifying enough to disturb most sensitive viewers. Mann and Alton's work for Eagle-Lion was so distinguished that MGM took note and signed both of them.

TAKE ME OUT TO THE BALL GAME

1949 93m c Sports/Musical   ★★★★
MGM (U.S.)   /U

Frank Sinatra *(Dennis Ryan)*, Esther Williams *(K.C. Higgins)*, Gene Kelly *(Eddie O'Brien)*, Betty Garrett *(Shirley Delwyn)*, Edward Arnold *(Joe Lorgan)*, Jules Munshin *(Nat Goldberg)*, Richard Lane *(Michael Gilhuly)*, Tom Dugan *(Slappy Burke)*, Murray Alper *(Zalinka)*, Wilton Graff *(Nick Donford)*

p, Arthur Freed; d, Busby Berkeley; w, Harry Tugend, Harry Crane (uncredited), George Wells (based on a story by Gene Kelly and Stanley Donen); ph, George Folsey; ed, Blanche Sewell; m, Roger Edens; art d, Cedric Gibbons, Daniel B. Cathcart; fx, Warren Newcombe, Peter Ballbusch; chor, Gene Kelly, Stanley Donen; cos, Helen Rose, Valles

Dennis Ryan (Frank Sinatra) and Eddie O'Brien (Gene Kelly) are a popular song-and-dance team on the vaudeville circuit who spend their summers playing baseball in a semiprofessional league. Ready to begin a new season, the pair are surprised and delighted to find that a woman, K.C. Higgins (Esther Williams), is the new team owner as well as their manager. Both men find her attractive, but K.C. is only interested in fielding a good team. When Eddie is benched for moonlighting as a dance director for a nightclub chorus line, he falls under the spell of Joe Lorgan (Edward Arnold), a seemingly benevolent man who in reality is a big-time gambler, and trouble brews for Eddie and his team.

While there's not much baseball played here, this is an amiable film, marked by the enjoyable cast and some lively, if not memorable, music. TAKE ME OUT TO THE BALL GAME was Sinatra and Kelly's follow-up to ANCHORS AWEIGH, and the two are again well-matched partners. The film was based on an original idea of Kelly and Stanley Donen's that closely resembled a minor 1930 film, THEY LEARNED ABOUT WOMEN. After concocting the story, Kelly and Donen asked for the chance to direct, but it was decided to bring in the legendary Busby Berkeley—who had fallen on hard times—and the film turned out to be his last directorial effort. Kelly and Donen, however, were allowed to direct TAKE ME OUT TO THE BALL GAME's musical sequences and producer Arthur Freed was impressed enough to allow them to direct the next Kelly-Sinatra film, the classic ON THE TOWN, later that year.

TAKE THE MONEY AND RUN

1969 85m c Crime/Prison/Comedy   ★★★½
Heywood/Hillary/Palomar (U.S.)   M/PG

Woody Allen *(Virgil Starkwell)*, Janet Margolin *(Louise)*, Marcel Hillaire *(Fritz)*, Jacquelyn Hyde *(Miss Blaire)*, Lonny Chapman *(Jake)*, Jan Merlin *(Al)*, James Anderson *(Chain Gang Warden)*, Howard Storm *(Fred)*, Mark Gordon *(Vince)*, Micil Murphy *(Frank)*

p, Charles H. Joffe; d, Woody Allen; w, Woody Allen, Mickey Rose; ph, Lester Shorr, Fouad Said; ed, Ralph Rosenblum, James T. Heckert, Ron Kalish, Paul Jordan; m, Marvin Hamlisch; art d, Fred Harpman; fx, A.D. Flowers

Woody Allen's first directorial achievement is a frequently hilarious, sometimes misfiring satire of crime movies. Allen plays the typical shlemiel, a put-upon wimp who becomes a compulsive criminal. Told in semidocumentary fashion, with a rambling narration by Jackson Beck (who was heard as the narrator on radio's "Superman" for years), it prefigures Allen's work years later in ZELIG.

One-liners galore, lots of episodic scenes and some good satire, with the intercutting of actual news footage to establish the era (President Richard Nixon and Dwight Eisenhower figure prominently). A bit of homage to Claude Lelouch in the love scenes between Allen and Margolin, then into the jail sequences that can best be appreciated by those familiar with I AM A FUGITIVE FROM A CHAIN GANG, THE LAST MILE, or any of several jail movies. A spotty picture with many delicious moments, including a sequence where Allen hires an over-the-hill movie director (Hillaire) to pretend he is shooting a film about a bank robbery so that Allen and his men can use that as a cover for their actual robbery of the institution. Everything is going well until a rival gang arrives with the same intention. Several inside jokes are unfathomable to viewers from the hinterlands.

TAKING OF PELHAM ONE TWO THREE, THE

1974 104m c Crime   ★★★½
Palomar/Palladium (U.S.)   R/15

Walter Matthau *(Lt. Garber)*, Robert Shaw *(Blue)*, Martin Balsam *(Green)*, Hector Elizondo *(Grey)*, Earl Hindman *(Brown)*, James Broderick *(Denny Doyle)*, Dick O'Neill *(Correll)*, Lee Wallace *(The Mayor)*, Tom Pedi *(Caz Dolowicz)*, Beatrice Winde *(Mrs. Jenkins)*

p, Gabriel Katzka, Edgar J. Scherick; d, Joseph Sargent; w, Peter Stone (based on the novel by John Godey); ph, Owen Roizman; ed, Jerry Greenberg, Robert Q. Lovett; m, David Shire; art d, Gene Rudolf; cos, Anna Hill Johnstone

This exciting, suspenseful drama of a subway car held for ransom begins with Matthau, a New York transit cop, giving some visiting Japanese a guided tour of the subway control center. Matthau mocks and insults the party, not realizing that his guests speak English. Meanwhile, in the subway tunnels of New York, a train pulls out of the Pelham station at 1:23 p.m. Aboard are four men wearing identical hats, glasses, mustaches, and raincoats. The group, led by Shaw, separates one car from the train, taking the conductor (Broderick) and the passengers on board hostage. Their demands are chillingly simple: the city must pay $1 million ransom in exactly one hour or else they will begin killing hostages. A dialogue begins over the radio between Matthau and Shaw as the detective tries to negotiate a safe release for the hostages. One of the kidnappers, Balsam, is suffering from a bad cold, and Matthau blesses him with each sneeze. Shaw eventually has Broderick killed when the demands have not been met. The ransom money is finally delivered, and the gang make their plan to escape.

Though Matthau and Shaw spend most of the film communicating through a microphone, the tension between the two is well developed. The editing back and forth is sharp, accentuating the two strong performances and adding to the suspense. Shaw is excellent as the cold-blooded killer, with a steely performance that fascinates as well as frightens. The one low point is the slice-of-life group of passengers aboard the subway. Each hostage is a stereotype, ranging from a mother with two bratty children to a streetwise pimp, to Gorrin's know-it-all old man. The direction is sharp, using the small, darkened world of the subway to its fullest, and backed by Shire's exciting jazz score that complements the suspense. The film was advertised in many large cities with posters displayed in subway stations, but this ad campaign emphasizing every commuter's nightmare was dumped when subway riders across the country complained.

TAKING OFF

1971 92m c Comedy/Drama	★★★½
Forman/Crown/Hausman (U.S.)	R/18

Lynn Carlin (Lynn Tyne), Buck Henry (Larry Tyne), Linnea Heacock (Jeannie Tyne), Georgia Engel (Margot), Tony Harvey (Tony), Audra Lindley (Ann Lockston), Paul Benedict (Ben Lockston), Vincent Schiavelli (Schiavelli), David Gittler (Jamie), Ike Turner

p, Alfred W. Crown; d, Milos Forman; w, Milos Forman, John Guare, Jean-Claude Carriere, John Klein; ph, Miroslav Ondricek; ed, John Carter; art d, Robert Wightman; cos, Peggy Farrell

Milos Forman's first US movie is a rather dated look at the mores of the country he had just adopted. At the time of its release, critics welcomed the Czech-born Forman's skewed perspective on a transitional period of American culture, but today the film, like so much else from the late 60s and early 70s, can best be appreciated as a historical curio.

Heacock is a a teenager who has run away from her affluent Long Island home and settled in New York's East Village, where she hopes to make a career as a singer. Parents Carlin and Henry team up with Lindley, who also has a runaway child, to search for their daughter amidst the countercultural milieu that they fear and despise. At first, they're repelled, but it isn't long before they begin to respond to the allure of marijuana and sexual freedom.

The movie is more satire than farce, and satire "is what closes on Saturday nights," said George S. Kaufman. Kaufman was right, and this movie did nowhere near the business it deserved, although it did serve to introduce Forman to the US audience after his European successes with LOVES OF A BLONDE and THE FIREMAN'S BALL. Henry had done cameo appearances in THE GRADUATE and CATCH-22 and here has a full-fledged leading role. His work is exemplary, and he more than holds his own with the other, more experienced actors. Carlin first came to prominence in FACES, although her career never went as far as her talent could have taken her. Heacock was an amateur whom Forman spotted in Central Park. Forman enjoys using nonprofessionals and always seems to evoke excellent results from them. The promise of this first US movie was realized when Forman distinguished himself with ONE FLEW OVER THE CUCKOO'S NEST and AMADEUS. The script was written by a formidable quartet composed of Forman, playwright Guare (whose "The House of Blue Leaves" won several Tony Awards in June, 1986), French author Carriere (who co-wrote BELLE DU JOUR and THE MILKY WAY), and Klein.

TALE OF TWO CITIES, A

1935 120m bw Historical	★★★★★
MGM (U.S.)	/U

Ronald Colman (Sydney Carton), Elizabeth Allan (Lucie Manette), Edna May Oliver (Miss Pross), Blanche Yurka (Mme. DeFarge), Reginald Owen (Stryver), Basil Rathbone (Marquis St. Evremonde), Henry B. Walthall (Dr. Manette), Donald Woods (Charles Darnay), Walter Catlett (Barsad), Fritz Leiber (Gaspard)

p, David O. Selznick; d, Jack Conway; w, W.P. Lipscomb, S.N. Behrman (based on the novel by Charles Dickens); ph, Oliver T. Marsh; ed, Conrad A. Nervig; m, Herbert Stothart; art d, Cedric Gibbons, Frederic Hope; cos, Dolly Tree

AAN Best Picture; AAN Best Editing: Conrad A. Nervig

Easily the best film version of Charles Dickens's classic novel (out of at least seven), A TALE OF TWO CITIES follows the turmoil and aftermath of the French Revolution. Sydney Carton (Colman) is a world-weary London barrister in love with Lucie Manette (Allan). She thinks of him only as a friend, however, and marries Charles Darnay (Woods), a descendant of a noble Frenchman who is also Carton's look-alike. Darnay's uncle, the Marquis St. Evremonde (Rathbone), is a heartless tyrant who is killed at the Revolution's onset. As the nephew of the hated Marquis, Darnay is arrested in Paris and sentenced to death. Lucie is frantic with worry over her husband, and Carton, devoted to Lucie but seeing no hope of happiness, goes to Paris, where he frees Darnay and takes his place in prison. His last words as he ascends the scaffold have become so identified with Colman that they are almost impossible to say without slipping into his distinctive accent: "It is a far, far better thing that I do than I have ever done; it is a far, far better rest that I go to than I have ever known."

This superb, lavish production features an MGM stock company playing very small role to perfection, and Colman gives one of the best performances of his life in a role he had long wanted to play. He captures Carton's intellectualism, cynicism, self-pity and nobility in equal measure, achieving a richness of characterization that would have pleased Dickens himself. Equally memorable is Blanche Yurka as the sinister Mme. DeFarge. This is nastiness to rival Mercedes McCambridge's ripe, blistering work in JOHNNY GUITAR. And, as in that Nicholas Ray film, Yurka has her own Joan Crawford to confront: the inimitable Edna May Oliver, representing the forces of virtue. Their final struggle is one of the highlights of the film. The film, has, in fact, many great moments, among the most beautiful of which is Carton's walk through the snow as the holiday carolers go by. The finale, as Carton awaits death, is equally powerful and touching. In a small role as a seamstress also being executed, Isabel Jewell gets to pull off yet another marvelous dramatic vignette.

One of director Jack Conway's finest efforts, the film never suffers from a sense that the novel has been compressed or rushed. Moving, fresh and aware of its effects, this film stands as one of Hollywood's finest adaptations of a novel. Its huge and deserved success gave producer David O. Selznick the freedom to walk away from MGM (and his father-in-law, Louis B. Mayer) and set up Selznick International Pictures. "Tis a far, far better thing" indeed.

TALES OF MANHATTAN

1942 118m bw Comedy	★★★½
Fox (U.S.)	/A

Charles Boyer (Paul Orman), Henry Fonda (George), Ginger Rogers (Diane), Rita Hayworth (Ethel Halloway), Charles Laughton (Charles Smith), Paul Robeson (Luke), Ethel Waters (Esther), Edward G. Robinson (Larry Browne), Cesar Romero (Harry Wilson), J. Carrol Naish (Costello)

p, Boris Morros, Sam Spiegel; d, Julien Duvivier; w, Ben Hecht, Ferenc Molnar, Donald Ogden Stewart, Samuel Hoffenstein, Alan Campbell, Ladislas Fodor, Laslo Vadnay, Laszlo Gorog, Lamar Trotti, Henry Blankfort, Buster Keaton (uncredited), Edmund Beloin, William Morrow; ph, Joseph Walker; ed, Robert Bischoff; m, Sol Kaplan; art d, Richard Day, Boris Leven; cos, Irene, Dolly Tree, Bernard Newman, Gwen Wakeling, Oleg Cassini

TALES OF MANHATTAN follows the adventures of a fancy tail coat as it goes from riches to rags. A famous actor (Charles Boyer) initially buys the coat, only to be told the garment carries a curse. Later, it winds up with a man (Cesar Romero) whose fiancee (Ginger Rogers) finds a love letter in one of the pockets. He insists the coat belongs to his pal (Henry Fonda), but his strategy backfires when, impressed by the letter's passion, she runs off with the friend. The cursed jacket then passes from a composer (Charles Laughton) to an impoverished lawyer (Edward G. Robinson), who wears it to a college reunion, where three former classmates decide to help him get back on his feet. Next to own the garment is a crook (J. Carrol Naish) who wears it while he pulls off a job. Pocketing the loot, he boards a plane, but during the flight he throws the coat out the window, forgetting it's stuffed with $40,000. The money flutters to the ground and is picked up by two sharecroppers (Paul Robeson and Ethel Waters) who take it to the local preacher, while the coat ends up on a scarecrow. TALES OF MANHATTAN unfolds with charm. Under the fine direction of Julien Duvivier (who directed the similarly episodic UN CARNET DU BAL, 1938), the episodes flow smoothly. It has, however, been criticized for its simplistic presentation of blacks in the final episode, and Robeson later denounced the film. Also unfortunate is that what might have been the best sequence, featuring W.C. Fields, didn't make the final cut.

TALES OF TERROR

1962 90m c Horror   ★★★½
Alta Vista   (U.S.)   /X

Vincent Price (Locke/Fortunato/Valdemar), MORELLA: Maggie Pierce (Lenora), Leona Gage (Morella), Edmund Cobb (Driver), THE BLACK CAT: Peter Lorre (Montresor), Joyce Jameson (Annabel), Lennie Weinrib, John Hackett (Policemen), THE CASE OF MR. VALDEMAR: Basil Rathbone (Carmichael), Debra Paget (Helene)

p, Roger Corman; d, Roger Corman; w, Richard Matheson; ph, Floyd Crosby; ed, Anthony Carras; m, Les Baxter; art d, Daniel Haller; fx, Pat Dinga

The fourth entry in Roger Corman's Edgar Allan Poe series, this film is an anthology of three short pieces based on tales by Poe, and all three—"Morella," "The Black Cat," and "The Case of Mr. Valdemar"—feature Vincent Price in the starring role. In "Morella," Price is an embittered widower who has lived alone in his gloomy mansion since the death of his wife, Gage, after giving birth some 26 years ago. His daughter, Pierce, arrives and finds that her father loathes her because he blames her for his wife's death. Prowling around the house, Pierce finds Gage's mummified body lying on a bed. Price explains he couldn't bear to have her beauty buried beneath the ground, so he had her corpse moved into the house. Pierce reveals to her father that she is dying and only has a few months left. Father and daughter are reconciled, but that night Pierce dies and her body becomes possessed by Gage, who has been waiting all these years to return and wreak her vengeance on Price—the father of the baby that killed her. In "The Black Cat," Lorre is superb as a drunken loser whose behavior forces his wife to seek comfort in the arms of wine-taster Price. To get even, Lorre captures his wife and her lover and walls them up in the cellar. Unbeknownst to him, however, the family cat is also entombed, and its wails give the scheme away. The final story, "The Case of Mr. Valdemar," features Price as a dying man who has fallen under the spell of an evil mesmerist, Rathbone. Price agrees to be the subject of an experiment wherein Rathbone will put him in a state of hypnosis at the moment of death, which will, perhaps, prevent him from dying. The trick works, but when the evil Rathbone attempts to steal Price's wife and estate, Price snaps out of the spell and attacks the mesmerist, his dead flesh melting around him. "Morella," the scariest of the tales, is an interesting precursor to THE TOMB OF LIGEIA (1965). "The Black Cat" combines the title Poe tale with Poe's "The Cask of Amontillado." It is a wonderfully funny prototype of THE RAVEN (1963), with both Lorre and Price having a grand time poking fun at the material and themselves. The final story has several memorable moments—especially when Price's disembodied voice can be heard pleading for release from his undead state—but the ending is marred by some unnecessary optical effects that obscure his melted visage (indeed, the production stills from this tale are more frightening than what appears in the movie).

TALK OF THE TOWN, THE

1942 118m bw Comedy   ★★★★
Columbia   (U.S.)   /U

Cary Grant (Leopold Dilg), Jean Arthur (Nora Shelley), Ronald Colman (Michael Lightcap), Edgar Buchanan (Sam Yates), Glenda Farrell (Regina Bush), Charles Dingle (Andrew Holmes), Emma Dunn (Mrs. Shelley), Rex Ingram (Tilney), Leonid Kinskey (Jan Pulaski), Tom Tyler (Clyde Bracken)

p, George Stevens; d, George Stevens; w, Irwin Shaw, Sidney Buchman (based on a story by Sidney Harmon, adapted by Dale Van Every); ph, Ted Tetzlaff; ed, Otto Meyer; m, Frederick Hollander; art d, Lionel Banks, Rudolph Sternad; fx, Donald Starling; cos, Irene

AAN Best Picture; AAN Best Original Screenplay: Sidney Harmon; AAN Best Original Screenplay: Sidney Buchman, Irwin Shaw; AAN Best Cinematography: Ted Tetzlaff; AAN Best Editing: Otto Meyer; AAN Best Score: Frederick Hollander, Morris Stoloff; AAN Best Art Direction: Lionel Banks, Rudolph Sternad, Fay Babcock

The contrivance of plot is compensated by one of the most genial casts in history. Full of wonderful bon mots, TOWN is acted with comic fervor by Grant, Arthur, and Colman.

Colman plays a renowned law professor who wants to spend a quiet summer writing while he awaits an appointment to the Supreme Court. He takes lodgings in the home of Arthur, a schoolteacher, but Colman's summer proves to be anything but quiet. Grant, who has escaped from jail after being labeled as the man behind a deadly factory fire, has taken refuge in the house as well. Arthur tells the bearded professor that Grant is the gardener, taking great care to protect Grant's secret. Colman is set in his ways when it comes to legalities, but what's more, he soon learns the real reason for Grant's stay at the house. It turns out that Grant was framed by a corrupt local government. The foreman who supposedly died in the blaze is very much alive, and both Colman and Grant develop an active interest in Arthur.

Grant, Arthur, and Colman are a terrific threesome, playing well off one another in a finely constructed love triangle. Both men want Arthur, yet Colman never lets his desire for her take precedence over the justice that must be done. Stevens directs his cast well, handling the double-edged story with grace and style. He originally shot two endings, one with Colman getting Arthur, and the other having Arthur pair with Grant. Both endings were shown in preview screenings, and audience polls decided how the film would end. This was Colman's first film at Columbia since 1937's LOST HORIZON. Much to his delight, he learned that Stevens had arranged it so the actor would not have to deal with studio chief Harry Cohn during TALK OF THE TOWN's production. At the time Colman had been experiencing some popularity problems at the box office, and this hit film gave his career the desired boost.

TALL BLOND MAN WITH ONE BLACK SHOE, THE
(LE GRAND BLOND AVEC UNE CHAUSSURE NOIRE)

1972 90m c Mystery/Comedy   ★★½
Gueville/Madeline/Gaumont   (France)   PG/AA

Pierre Richard (Francois), Bernard Blier (Milan), Jean Rochefort (Toulouse), Mireille Darc (Christine), Jean Carmet (Maurice), Colette Castel (Paulette), Paul Le Person (Perrache), Jean Obe (Botrel), Robert Castel (Georghiu), Roger Caccia (M. Boudart)

p, Alain Poire, Yves Robert; d, Yves Robert; w, Yves Robert, Francis Veber; ph, Rene Mathelin; ed, Ghislaine Desjonqueres; m, Vladimir Kosma

Filled with dry humor and featuring an understated comic performance by the expressionless Pierre Richard, this French farce concentrates on the silly aspects of the espionage world. Because of infighting in the French Secret Service, chief Louis Toulouse (Jean Rochefort) sets a trap for an ambitious underling, Bernard Milan (Bernard Blier), who is after his job. As a result, the innocent Francois Perrin (Richard), a tall blond with one black shoe, is randomly chosen as a decoy to trap Milan, who immediately puts his men to work on Francois's past, his contacts, his mission, and his real identity, convinced that he is a "superagent." In the tradition of the silent comics, Francois walks through this danger zone of espionage completely oblivious to the gangs of assassins out to kill him.

What is especially funny about the film is its send-up of the genre. Milan and his top agents assume that every one of Francois' actions has a double meaning: if he goes to the dentist, they think it is to meet a contact; when he plays the violin, they think it is a secret signal. They even try to decode an innocent message inscribed on a photo from his mistress. A sequel followed in 1974 titled, appropriately enough, RETURN OF THE TALL BLOND MAN WITH ONE BLACK SHOE. The original was remade in 1985 as THE MAN WITH ONE RED SHOE, starring Tom Hanks.

TALL MEN, THE

1955 122m c Western   ★★★½
Fox (U.S.)   /U

Clark Gable *(Ben Allison)*, Jane Russell *(Nella Turner)*, Robert Ryan *(Nathan Stark)*, Cameron Mitchell *(Clint Allison)*, Juan Garcia *(Luis)*, Harry Shannon *(Sam)*, Emile Meyer *(Chickasaw)*, Steve Darrell *(Colonel)*, Will Wright *(Gus, the Bartender)*, Robert Adler *(Wrangler)*

p, William A. Bacher, William B. Hawks; d, Raoul Walsh; w, Sydney Boehm, Frank S. Nugent (based on the novel by Clay Fisher); ph, Leo Tover; ed, Louis Loeffler; m, Victor Young; art d, Lyle Wheeler, Mark-Lee Kirk; fx, Ray Kellogg; cos, Travilla

Texas brothers Gable and Mitchell, who had ridden with Quantrill's Raiders during the Civil War, head North to Montana in search of gold. Desperate for cash, the men waylay Ryan, a wealthy businessman transporting $20,000. The fast-thinking Ryan turns the robbery to his advantage, however, by offering Gable and Mitchell a chance to be his partners in what is to be an arduous and fateful cattle drive from Texas to Montana.

Shot in CinemaScope and color by cinematographer Leo Tover, THE TALL MEN is a beautiful film to look at and also boasts a good script, solid performances, and typically fine direction from veteran director Walsh. Though the action is supposed to take place in Texas and Montana, Walsh learned that there were not enough longhorn cattle in the area to make a decent herd for the film. The cast and crew were sent to Durango, Mexico, where large herds of longhorn roamed the countryside. Walsh was assisted by a man named Carlos, the governor's son-in-law. Carlos spoke English, was a fan of American movies, and had good connections with the local cattle ranchers. According to Walsh's autobiography, after one week of shooting, a pistol-packing representative of the beef-growers' association, Diaz, showed up on the set and demanded more money for the cattle. The governor's son-in-law reminded the man that they had signed a contract which stated a specific price for the cattle. According to Walsh, when this did not faze the cattleman, "my self-appointed protector jumped in his car and raised more dust between us and the town. When he came back, he was driving a truck with 10 soldiers in it. That was the end of the holdup. The soldiers prodded Diaz into the truck after taking his gun away. 'You can roll your cameras now,' Carlos grinned, 'but I would advise you to get out of town the day you finish the picture.'"

The rest of the shooting proceeded smoothly, though director Walsh and his cast enjoyed playing tricks and teasing each other. Walsh roomed with Gable, Ryan roomed with Mitchell, and Russell had a house to herself. One night the director borrowed a tame skunk that had been "deodorized" by two young Mexican boys and tossed it into Gable's bedroom. When Gable spotted the creature, he yelled for help, and Walsh calmly advised the actor to slowly get out of bed and whistle to the skunk because skunks are afraid of whistling. So Gable stood in the corner whistling "Ol' Man River" and "If I Loved You," while Walsh came over and picked up the little beast. The next day Gable told the entire company how brave Walsh was for removing the animal. Somehow, Walsh managed to keep a straight face through the entire affair.

TALL T, THE

1957 78m c Western   ★★★★
Columbia (U.S.)   /U

Randolph Scott *(Pat Brennan)*, Richard Boone *(Usher)*, Maureen O'Sullivan *(Doretta Mims)*, Arthur Hunnicutt *(Ed Rintoon)*, Skip Homeier *(Billy Jack)*, Henry Silva *(Chink)*, John Hubbard *(Willard Mims)*, Robert Burton *(Tenvoorde)*, Robert Anderson *(Jace)*, Fred Sherman *(Hank Parker)*

p, Harry Joe Brown; d, Budd Boetticher; w, Burt Kennedy (based on the story "The Captive" by Elmore Leonard); ph, Charles Lawton Jr.; ed, Al Clark; m, Heinz Roemheld; art d, George Brooks

Veteran cowboy actor Scott is on the trail again, but this is not the standard shoot-'em-up. The story has more suspense than most. Scott is captured by Boone and his thugs, who have also kidnaped newlyweds O'Sullivan and Hubbard. The film moves along at a brisk pace and includes elements of both comedy and drama. Boone and his boys want to rob a stagecoach, but the slimy Hubbard, in an attempt to save

himself, tells them that O'Sullivan comes from a wealthy family, and it would be easier to get money by holding her for ransom. From there, the tension builds as Scott plans to outwit their captors.

This film has received a fair amount of critical analysis in recent years, particularly in light of the interest paid to genre films. Burt Kennedy's script and Budd Boetticher's direction have been applauded as solid in this psychological western which makes use of modern adult themes and depicts the struggle between good and evil as a complicated one—too complicated, in fact, for a black-and-white presentation. Rather, the viewer is shown how elements outside humans' control can influence the struggle and make clear-cut conclusions impossible. Scott is the strong-willed, laconic representation of the (pre-Eastwood) Western man pitted against an equally strong-minded, laconic villain. The struggle between Scott and Boone is depicted as a delicate balance of power in which Scott, the force of good, is not necessarily stronger—or even better in all aspects of his life, he is merely more wily in the end. THE TALL T, like the Leone westerns to follow, used the American West as the perfect setting for an eternal struggle, the outcome of which is always a crap shoot.

TAMING OF THE SHREW, THE
(LA BISBETICA DOMATA)

1967 122m c Comedy   ★★★½
Royal/FAI (U.S./Italy)

Elizabeth Taylor *(Katharina)*, Richard Burton *(Petruchio)*, Cyril Cusack *(Grumio)*, Michael Hordern *(Baptista)*, Alfred Lynch *(Tranio)*, Alan Webb *(Gremio)*, Victor Spinetti *(Hortensio)*, Roy Holder *(Biondello)*, Mark Dignam *(Vincentio)*, Bice Valori *(The Widow)*

p, Richard Burton, Elizabeth Taylor, Franco Zeffirelli; d, Franco Zeffirelli; w, Paul Dehn, Suso Cecchi D'Amico, Franco Zeffirelli (based on the play by William Shakespeare); ph, Oswald Morris, Luciano Trasatti; ed, Peter Taylor, Carlo Fabianelli; m, Nino Rota; prod d, John De Cuir; art d, Giuseppe Mariani, Elven Webb; fx, Augie Lohman; cos, Irene Sharaff, Danilo Donati

AAN Best Art Direction: Renzo Mongiardino (Art Direction), John DeCuir (Art Direction), Elven Webb (Art Direction), Giuseppe Mariani (Art Direction), Dario Simoni (Set Decoration), Luigi Gervasi (Set Decoration); *AAN Best Costume Design:* Irene Sharaff, Danilo Donati

The Liz and Dick Show, Part II. The Battling Burtons go at it again onscreen in this follow-up to their joint triumph in WHO'S AFRAID OF VIRGINIA WOOLF? And, although it may initially be hard to picture La Liz reciting blank verse, both she and the film are fine. Zeffirelli is famous (or infamous) for his sometimes unsubtle editing of Shakespeare's plays when he turns them into films that "ordinary folk" can understand (a piece of advice, Franco: we're not that stupid). Purists will doubtless be upset by this flick, but the bawdy humor is engaging, the photography and musical score work just fine, and the most famous married couple in the world at that time are really having a ball here. Not really an actress noted for playing feminists, La Liz manages the transition from spoiled filly—typecasting here, folks—to submissive wife—which is all the eight-times-around Mrs. Hilton Fisher Burton Warner Fortensky whoever really wants after all, right?

TAMPOPO

1986 114m c Comedy   ★★★½
Itami (Japan)   /18

Ken Watanabe, Tsutomu Yamazaki, Nobuko Miyamoto, Koji Yakusho, Rikiya Yasuoka, Kinzo Sakura, Shuji Otaki

p, Yasushi Tamaoki, Seigo Hosogoe; d, Juzo Itami; w, Juzo Itami; ph, Masaki Tamura; ed, Akira Suzuki; m, Kunihiko Murai; art d, Takeo Kimura

A hilarious comedy from Japan concerned exclusively with food, TAMPOPO begins in a movie theater as we (the viewing audience) sit watching the audience in the film. In walks a suave yakuza attended by his girlfriend and an entourage of goons. Gangster and moll sit down in the front row, while the henchmen set up a table filled with delectable food. As the gangster eats, he suddenly notices us watching him, leans forward into the camera, and asks, "What are you eating?" He then informs us that he hates noise in movie theaters—especially people who crinkle wrappers and eat loudly. Of course, a man behind him is eating too noisily, and the gangster angrily threatens to kill the confused moviegoer if he continues. He then sits down to enjoy the show, urging us to do the same. Now TAMPOPO proper begins, a string of rollicking comic vignettes concerning food that—more or less—tell the story of a heroic truck driver and his sidekick's attempts to help a young widow improve her noodle-shop business.

The second feature by director Juzo Itami (preceded by THE FUNERAL, 1984), TAMPOPO is a wonderfully funny and creative film with a cornucopia of comical characters in absurd situations. These loony elements combine to offer some perceptive observations about human joy, fear, and passion for food. TAMPOPO also satirizes filmmaking (with references to THE SEVEN SAMURAI, American westerns, Steven Spielberg, and Japanese yakuza films), though Itami's film is itself heavily indebted to Luis Bunuel. With his first two films (his "Taxing Woman" entries, unfortunately, have less bite), Itami moved to the forefront of the irreverent young Japanese directors who have recently put a comedic spotlight on Japanese society, finding some very funny and disturbing truths about life there.

TARGETS

1968 90m c Horror/Crime ★★★★½
Saticoy (U.S.) /X

Boris Karloff (Byron Orlok), Tim O'Kelly (Bobby Thompson), Nancy Hsueh (Jenny), James Brown (Robert Thompson), Sandy Baron (Kip Larkin), Arthur Peterson (Ed Loughlin), Mary Jackson (Charlotte Thompson), Tanya Morgan (Ilene Thompson), Monty Landis (Marshall Smith), Peter Bogdanovich (Sammy Michaels)

p, Peter Bogdanovich; d, Peter Bogdanovich; w, Peter Bogdanovich (based on a story by Polly Platt and Peter Bogdanovich); ph, Laszlo Kovacs; ed, Peter Bogdanovich; m, Charles Greene, Brian Stone; prod d, Polly Platt

On target. An unconventional horror picture that draws a comparison between the real-life horror of the 1966 Charles Whitman murder spree and the fictional horrors of movie legend Boris Karloff, TARGETS opens with a film clip (the flood scene) from Roger Corman's 1963 film, THE TERROR. The clip then ends, revealing a screening room occupied by aging horror star Byron Orlok (Karloff, extremely moving here), filmmaker Sammy Michaels (played by director Bogdanovich), and some film executives. Orlok informs them that he's had enough of horror films and plans to return to his home in England. He is aware that his films no longer frighten people and that the public is only affected by the horrors in the headlines, stating, "The world belongs to the young. Make way for them. Let them have it. I am an anachronism." Meanwhile, in a gun shop across the street, a clean-cut young man, Bobby Thompson (Tim O'Kelly), adds a high-powered rifle to the already huge arsenal of weapons stashed in his car trunk. Thompson begins a bloody rampage, first murdering his wife, then sniping at innocent drivers from a tower near a highway. TARGETS' brilliant finale, set at a drive-in premiere of the latest Orlok opus, puts both of these horrors—the movieland fiction of Orlok and the real-life danger of Thompson—up on the screen together. Down below, the audience screams in fright, not at Orlok but at Thompson, whose rifle shots are picking them off one by one. TARGETS is an insightful comment on the changing state of the horror film: Whereas Karloff's films concerned gruesome monsters with frightening physical attributes, TARGETS is about—to use Bogdanovich's phrase—"the ghouls next door," the all-American killers who are all the more frightening because the deformities exist *inside* their heads.

TARNISHED ANGELS, THE

1957 91m bw Drama ★★★★
Universal (U.S.) /A

Rock Hudson (Burke Devlin), Robert Stack (Roger Shumann), Dorothy Malone (LaVerne Shumann), Jack Carson (Jiggs), Robert Middleton (Matt Ord), Alan Reed (Col. Fineman), Alexander Lockwood (Sam Hagood), Christopher Olsen (Jack Shumann), Bob Wilke (Hank), Troy Donahue (Frank Burnham)

p, Albert Zugsmith; d, Douglas Sirk; w, George Zuckerman (based on the novel Pylon by William Faulkner); ph, Irving Glassberg; ed, Russell Schoengarth; m, Frank Skinner; art d, Alexander Golitzen, Alfred Sweeney; fx, Clifford Stine; cos, Bill Thomas

The best-ever adaptation of a Faulkner novel for the screen, directed with passion and perception by Sirk. The once underrated director, now recognized as a master of implicitly subversive melodrama, draws excellent portrayals from Hudson (who had come a long way as an actor by this point), Stack, Malone, and Carson in an authentic and stimulating Depression-era drama of racing pilots and daredevil exploits.

Stack arrives in New Orleans in 1932 with his barnstorming troupe, his wife Malone, his son, Olsen, and his loyal-unto-death mechanic, Carson. They have arrived to participate in an air show and race, with Stack hoping to win the big prize money with a dilapidated plane. Hudson, an idealistic reporter for one of the local newspapers, is assigned to write some features about the air show, so he interviews Stack and his family, intrigued by their gypsyish lifestyle. As he comes to know these people, his initial sarcastic attitude toward them changes to one of respect. Middleton, a wealthy old man who lusts after Malone, gives Stack a plane to fly in the air show, but wants Malone in return. Stack, meanwhile, proves himself master of the air until his plane develops a problem while turning the last pylon to win the race.

The acting is first-rate here, and the script is outstanding, full of wit, black humor, and occasional fine poetic monologues, especially the lines delivered by Stack when he wistfully looks back upon WWI and those of Hudson when he returns drunk to his newspaper and describes the lives of the nomads of the air. Sirk does a marvelous job with his action scenes, all of which appear realistic. Faulkner saw this film and considered it the best picture ever made of his work. The author based much of his story on the exploits of his own brother, Dean Faulkner, who was a barnstorming pilot in the early 1930s.

TARZAN AND HIS MATE

1934 105m bw Adventure/Romance ★★★½
MGM (U.S.)

Johnny Weissmuller (Tarzan), Maureen O'Sullivan (Jane Parker), Neil Hamilton (Harry Holt), Paul Cavanagh (Martin Arlington), Forrester Harvey (Beamish), William Stack (Pierce), Desmond Roberts (Van Ness), Nathan Curry (Saidi), Paul Porcasi (Mons. Gironde)

p, Bernard H. Hyman; d, Jack Conway, Cedric Gibbons; w, Howard Emmett Rogers, Leon Gordon (based on the story by James Kevin McGuinnes and the characters created by Edgar Rice Burroughs); ph, Charles Clarke, Clyde De Vinna; ed, Tom Held

The second MGM "Tarzan" film, a sequel to TARZAN THE APE MAN, features Johnny Weissmuller and Maureen O'Sullivan as its eponymous pair. The story is as scant as O'Sullivan's costume: the jungle couple are living together atop the trees when O'Sullivan's civilized beau, Neil Hamilton, arrives on the scene with greedy ivory hunter Paul Cavanagh. The outsiders are still searching for Mutia Escarpment, the elephant burial grounds, and Cavanagh wounds one pachyderm in the hope that it will lead them to the grounds. When he objects to the merciless treatment of his animal friends, Weissmuller is shot and left to die. His ape companions rescue him and he regains his health, but Hamilton and Cavanagh are not so fortunate; after making it to the burial grounds, they and their bearers are devoured by lions. Stampeding elephants rescue O'Sullivan before she too becomes lunch, and the jungle lovers are reunited.

The most interesting aspect of this "Tarzan" installment is its adult appeal: Weissmuller and O'Sullivan's Tarzan and Jane are obviously living in sexual freedom as they swing through the trees. O'Sullivan's character, a formerly civilized Londoner, has thrown away all inhibitions here; she wears her revealing animal-skin outfit only so others "won't think [her] immodest," but sleeps in the nude, and one scene—clipped from the film after Legion of Decency protests—reveals her bare breasts as Weissmuller and a stand-in for O'Sullivan go skinny-dipping. Not surprisingly, the Hays Code brought about changes in later "Tarzan" films. To appease those who wanted double beds for the pair (a rather unfeasible arrangement in the treetops), a jungle house was built for them, complete with four walls and ceiling. So began the downfall of the series. Although the first talkie TARZAN was directed by W.S. Van Dyke, with Cedric Gibbons as art director,

MGM finally gave in to Gibbons' wishes and let him direct here. The move proved less than successful, however, and Gibbons was relieved of his duties after a few weeks (MGM made its "Tarzan" films slowly and carefully, with large budgets and generous shooting schedules). Gibbons was replaced by the more experienced Jack Conway, who directed most of the film, but did not receive screen credit.

TARZAN, THE APE MAN

1932 99m bw Adventure/Romance ★★★★
MGM (U.S.)

Johnny Weissmuller (Tarzan), Neil Hamilton (Harry Holt), Maureen O'Sullivan (Jane Parker), C. Aubrey Smith (James Parker), Doris Lloyd (Mrs. Cutten), Forrester Harvey (Beamish), Ivory Williams (Riano), Cheta the Chimp

p, Irving Thalberg; d, W.S. Van Dyke II; w, Cyril Hume, Ivor Novello (based on the characters created by Edgar Rice Burroughs); ph, Harold Rosson, Clyde De Vinna; ed, Ben Lewis, Tom Held; art d, Cedric Gibbons

The original swinger, with the original call of the wild. A legend was born when MGM cast Johnny Weissmuller, a 28-year-old Olympic swimming champion, as Tarzan in this film. The Edgar Rice Burroughs character had been popular in silent films, but this was the first sound version. Jane Parker (Maureen O'Sullivan), her father (C. Aubrey Smith), and her boyfriend (Neil Hamilton) venture into the African wilds in search of the ivory-laden Elephant's Graveyard and experience great danger in the process. Fears are heightened when Tarzan's jungle yell is heard, and before long, Jane is screaming and kicking as Tarzan carries her into the treetops. Her father and suitor threaten to shoot Tarzan, but after she is released, Jane defends the ape-man with whom she is falling in love. She is soon swinging through the trees under his arm, clowning around with the captivating chimp Cheta, and taking swims with Tarzan. Their happiness is threatened, however, when they are captured by pygmies and lowered into a pit with a giant ape.

The first of six MGM Weissmuller-O'Sullivan "Tarzan" adventures, TARZAN, THE APE MAN suffers in technological comparison with today's Steven Spielbergian jungle adventures, but still has enough thrills to put most modern films to shame. The near-nonstop excitement holds up wonderfully, making this one of Hollywood's most memorable adventure films. And the two leads, through countless casting calls, have never been beaten. Okay, Bo Derek, you can clean the cage now.

TASTE OF HONEY, A

1961 100m bw Drama ★★★★½
Woodfall (U.K.) /18

Dora Bryan (Helen), Rita Tushingham (Jo), Robert Stephens (Peter), Murray Melvin (Geoffrey), Paul Danquah (Jimmy), David Boliver (Bert), Moira Kaye (Doris), Herbert Smith (Shoe Shop Proprietor), Valerie Scarden (Woman in Shoe Shop), Rosalie Scase (Nurse)

p, Tony Richardson; d, Tony Richardson; w, Shelagh Delaney, Tony Richardson (based on the play by Delaney); ph, Walter Lassally; ed, Anthony Gibbs; m, John Addison; art d, Ralph Brinton; cos, Sophie Harris

A taste of the British "Kitchen Sink" school at its best. Honest depiction of life in the British working class with an offbeat treatment, superb acting, realistic direction, and a complex script.

Tushingham plays a 17-year-old who lives with her promiscuous, alcoholic mother, Bryan, in various furnished rooms Tushingham is gawky, not terribly attractive, and desperate to be held. On holiday in Blackpool, she wanders around the docks and meets Danquah, a black sailor on a brief shore leave. She sleeps with him. On returning home, she discovers that her mother has impulsively married current boyfriend Stephens; the girl is to be left on her own. She secures employment in a shoe store and meets Melvin, a gentle and kind homosexual who needs a place to stay. They move in together. Then Tushingham realizes that she's carrying Danquah's child.

The movie was shot for a pittance on location in Blackpool and on the Salford docks. Delaney was only 19 when she wrote the play, which had a long run in the West End as well as on Broadway after first trying out at Stratford-upon-Avon in May 1958. Tushingham had been a backstage worker and did a bit in Arnold Wesker's play "The Kitchen"

at Liverpool Rep before she answered an ad, walked in, auditioned, and won this plum role. Bryan had spent most of her career as a comedienne in movies since she began in ODD MAN OUT. Casting her here was an inspired choice as she showed her scope. If you have a sharp ear, you may be able to recognize Johnny Dankworth's theme from SATURDAY NIGHT AND SUNDAY MORNING, which was uncredited. Richardson coproduced that film with Harry Saltzman, so it can be assumed he had permission for the tune's use. The hit song "A Taste of Honey" had nothing to do with this film. It was written by Ric Marlow and Bobby Scott and traded on the success of the movie, which won Cannes Film Festival awards for Melvin and Tushingham as well as British Film Academy Awards for Best Picture, Best Actress (Bryan), Best Screenplay (Delaney and Richardson), and Most Promising Actress (Tushingham).

TAXI BLUES

1990 110m c Drama ★★★½
Marin Karmitz Productions/Lenfilm Studios
/Ask Eurofilm/La Sept (France/U.S.S.R.)

Pyotr Nikolajevitch Mamonov (Liocha), Piotr Zaitchenko (Schlikov), Vladimir Kachpour (Old Netchiporenko), Natalia Koliakanova (Christina), Hal Singer (Himself), Elena Saphonva (Nina—Liocha's Wife), Serguei Gazarov (Administrator), Evgueni Gortchakov (Bald Musician in the Taxi), Dimitri Prigov (Writer Typing in the Train), Igor Zolotovitsky (Petiountchik)

p, Marin Karmitz; d, Pavel Lounguine; w, Pavel Lounguine; ph, Denis Evstigneef; ed, Elizabeth Guido; m, Vladimir Chekassine; art d, Valery Yourkevitch; cos, Natalia Dianova

The precedent-shattering TAXI BLUES, helmed by screenwriter-turned-director Pavel Lounguine, is a wrenching, prolonged study in impotence and frustration.

Schlikov (Pyotr Zaitchenko) is a solidly working-class Russian taxi driver, racist and largely friendless, with the burly build of a bully. Liocha (Piotr Nikolajevitch Mamonov) is a flamboyant, self-destructive Jewish jazz musician. When Liocha stiffs Schlikov for a 70-ruble fare one drunken evening, Schlikov tracks him down, beats him up and takes his saxophone. However, Schlikov is sufficiently intrigued by Liocha to offer him vodka and a bed in his flat—much to the anger of Schlikov's neighbor, the rabidly anti-Semitic Netchiporenko (Vladimir Kachpour).

Shot in Moscow over a four-month period in 1989, with the flowering of perestroika already showing signs of blight and the crumbling of the Soviet Union soon to come, TAXI BLUES proved a rude shock to the struggling Russian film establishment.

Lounguine, who also wrote the screenplay, has described his style here as "extremist" and the story as autobiographical. The film has some of the narrative looseness of the French New Wave, as well as plenty of that movement's characteristic handheld camerawork. Although Lounguine has termed it a comedy, Westerners will find it only occasionally amusing. To its credit, the film, styled mostly as a two-character study, never falters into an "Odd Couple"-style formula. Both characters, as superbly played by Zaitchenko and Mamonov (whom Lounguine calls "the oldest Russian rock star, mythical in Moscow for his excesses") are equally disagreeable, making audience identification nearly impossible. The excesses of both are delineated in long, boisterous, often ugly scenes (including a rape) that seem to verge on escaping directorial control.

TAXI DRIVER

1976 112m c Drama ★★★★★
Bill-Phillips (U.S.) R/18

Robert De Niro (Travis Bickle), Cybill Shepherd (Betsy), Jodie Foster (Iris Steensman), Peter Boyle (Wizard), Harvey Keitel (Sport), Albert Brooks (Tom), Leonard Harris (Charles Palantine), Martin Scorsese (Passenger), Diahnne Abbott (Concession Girl), Frank Adu (Angry Black Man)

p, Michael Phillips, Julia Phillips; d, Martin Scorsese; w, Paul Schrader; ph, Michael Chapman; ed, Marcia Lucas, Tom Rolf, Melvin Shapiro; m, Bernard Herrmann; art d, Charles Rosen; fx, Tony Parmelee; cos, Ruth Morley

AAN Best Picture; AAN Best Actor: Robert De Niro; *AAN Best Supporting Actress:* Jodie Foster; *AAN Best Score:* Bernard Herrmann

A landmark of 70s American cinema that announced to the world the arrival of director Martin Scorsese, screenwriter Paul Schrader and star Robert De Niro. Though critics remain divided over the ultimate merits of TAXI DRIVER, it is an undeniably brilliant, nightmarish portrait of one man's personal hell.

TAXI DRIVER is an alarmingly plausible character study of Vietnam vet Travis Bickle (De Niro), an alienated insomniac who spends his nights driving a New York cab. Much of what we see of the city is viewed through his windshield. After long night shifts, he still can't sleep and spends hours in porno theatres or alone in his squalid room. He has nothing but contempt for the "scum" he sees all around him and prophesies that someday a big rain will come and clean all the filth from the streets. Travis' world brightens a little when he sees a beautiful blonde woman, Betsy (Cybill Shepherd), in the campaign offices of presidential candidate Charles Palantine (Leonard Harris). He quickly develops a crush on her, and she finds him intriguing enough to agree to go out with him. When he takes her, though, to a porn film (the only type of movie he knows) she walks out in disgust. An even more frustrated Travis then meets Iris (Jodie Foster), a 12-year-old runaway turned prostitute who is managed by a long-haired pimp known as Sport (Harvey Keitel). Travis becomes obsessed with "rescuing" Iris from her situation, turning himself into a one-man killing machine as he prepares for a bloody crusade which he believes will put the world to rights.

TAXI DRIVER is a fevered, paranoid take on the perils of contemporary urban life. Scorsese paints a picture of New York City with stark, unforgettable images—steaming sewers, rainslicked streets, glaring neon lights—that together constitute a vision of hell on earth. All this is helped immensely by Bernard Herrmann's visceral score (his last; he passed away a day after its completion), and Michael Chapman's grainy cinematography. The climactic killing sequence is a sustained, hallucinatory triumph of shot composition and editing—as stomach-churning as it is technically astonishing. (Much of the negative critical reaction to the film focused on Scorsese's moral stance toward this bloodbath, claiming—short-sightedly—that it is portrayed as a positive, cleansing ritual that redeems Travis' character. TAXI DRIVER is far more ironic and multi-layered than such an interpretation suggests.)

De Niro's mesmerizing performance is central to the film's success. He appears in nearly every scene and we see nearly everything through his skewed vision. He commands the screen and evokes such power and authority—even during Travis's meekest moments—that we are inexorably drawn into his life. Shepherd is highly effective as the Hitchcockian icy blonde, and the young Jodie Foster effortlessly conveys both youthful innocence and a street-smart, wise-beyond-her-years quality. Her breakfast scene with De Niro is riveting. In smaller roles, Boyle is great fun as an eccentric cabbie; comedian/filmmaker Albert Brooks plays Shepherd's somewhat nerdy co-worker; and Harvey Keitel makes a memorably sleazy Sport.

TAXI DRIVER won the Golden Palm at the Cannes Film Festival, and Scorsese and De Niro were honored as Best Director and Best Actor by the New York Film Critics.

TAXING WOMAN, A
(MARUSA NO ONNA)

1987 127m c Comedy   ★★★½
Itami/New Century (Japan)   /18

Nobuko Miyamoto *(Ryoko Itakura, Tax Inspector),* Tsutomu Yamazaki *(Hideki Gondo),* Masahiko Tsugawa *(Assistant Chief Inspector Hanamura),* Hideo Murota *(Ishii, Motel President),* Shuji Otaki *(Tsuyuguchi, Tax Office Manager),* Daisuke Yamashita *(Taro Gondo),* Shinsuke Ashida, Keiju Kobayashi, Mariko Okada, Kiriko Shimizu
p, Yasushi Tamaoki, Seigo Hosogoe; d, Juzo Itami; w, Juzo Itami; ph, Yonezo Maeda; ed, Akira Suzuki; m, Toshiyuki Honda

Continuing his series of hilariously incisive examinations of modern Japanese culture (burial rites in THE FUNERAL, food in TAMPOPO), director Juzo Itami here turns his gaze on that most sacred of contemporary obsessions—money. Part social satire, part procedural drama, A TAXING WOMAN takes its title from spunky, dedicated tax agent

Ryoko Itakura (wonderfully acted by Nobuko Miyamoto, Itami's wife), who uses her demure looks to lull tax cheats into false confidence before she lowers the boom. Most of the film details her determined attempt to get the goods on suave "adult motel" tycoon Hideki Gondo (Tsutomu Yamazaki), who launders his money through the *yakuza* (gangsters), phony corporations, real estate, and his mistress. He's sharp, but Ryoko's sharper; and by the end, not only are the interests of the Japanese Tax Office served, but love (though unrequited) makes an appearance. Although not as out-and-out loopy as TAMPOPO, Itami's portrait of money-mad Japanese society has a biting satiric edge. The boundless energy of the Japanese seems to be what really fascinates the director, who is well on his way to becoming the leading chronicler of life in modern-day Japan. His 1988 sequel to this film, A TAXING WOMAN'S RETURN, is less satisfying than the original.

TEA AND SYMPATHY

1956 122m c Drama   ★★★½
MGM (U.S.)   /X

Deborah Kerr *(Laura Reynolds),* John Kerr *(Tom Robinson Lee),* Leif Erickson *(Bill Reynolds),* Edward Andrews *(Herb Lee),* Darryl Hickman *(Al),* Norma Crane *(Ellie Martin),* Dean Jones *(Ollie),* Jacqueline de Wit *(Lilly Sears),* Tom Laughlin *(Ralph),* Ralph Votrian *(Steve)*
p, Pandro S. Berman; d, Vincente Minnelli; w, Robert Anderson (based on the play by Anderson); ph, John Alton; ed, Ferris Webster; m, Adolph Deutsch; art d, William A. Horning, Edward Carfagno; cos, Helen Rose

Watered-down version of a landmark Broadway play that dealt with alleged homosexuality and an older woman's desire to prove the machismo of the suspect young man.

John Kerr is a married woman with three children who returns to his exclusive prep school in New England for a reunion. In a flashback to his troubled years at the school, we see that he is inept at every sport except tennis (which is regarded as a sissy pastime), which sets him apart from the other boys. He wears his hair long and spends his off-hours in romantic pastimes which the other students scorn. His roommate is Hickman, who is slightly embarrassed by Kerr's behavior but defends him to the others. Kerr's housemaster is big, hearty Erickson, a smiling boor who emphasizes masculine games for his charges. Erickson is in league with Andrews, Kerr's father, who shares the housemaster's belief that the boy should have his hair cut and make an attempt to get into the mainstream of the school's activities. Kerr is shunned by almost everyone at the school except Hickman and Erickson's wife, played by Deborah Kerr. She is a sensitive woman who realizes that this lad is in trouble. (He reminds her of her late first husband, a boy who volunteered for the Army during WWII in order to show everyone that he was fearless and left her widowed.) Gradually, her feelings for the boy deepen into something more than maternal concern.

The two Kerrs and Erickson all effectively reprised the roles they had played in the stage version, which opened in September, 1953, and ran for more than 700 performances. Since Anderson himself wrote the screenplay (with the censors looking over his shoulder), any bowdlerization must be attributed to him. Minnelli's direction is true to the material.

TEAHOUSE OF THE AUGUST MOON, THE

1956 123m c Comedy   ★★★★
MGM (U.S.)   /U

Marlon Brando *(Sakini),* Glenn Ford *(Capt. Fisby),* Machiko Kyo *(Lotus Blossom),* Eddie Albert *(Capt. McLean),* Paul Ford *(Col. Purdy),* Jun Negami *(Mr. Seiko),* Nijiko Kiyokawa *(Miss Higa Jiga),* Mitsuko Sawamura *(Little Girl),* Harry Morgan *(Sgt. Gregovich),* Shichizo Takeda *(Ancient Man)*
p, Jack Cummings; d, Daniel Mann; w, John Patrick (based on the novel by Vern J. Sneider and the play by Patrick); ph, John Alton; ed, Harold F. Kress; m, Saul Chaplin; art d, William A. Horning, Eddie Imazu; chor, Masaya Fujima

This charming adaptation of the novel and play shows that Brando has a flair for comedy. In a prologue, Okinawan Brando introduces himself and the other players and asserts with pride that Okinawa has the honor of being the most subjugated place in history. It has been overrun by the Chinese and the Japanese and, now, the US. Glenn Ford, an American officer, is charged with bringing "civilization" to a small village. With Brando as his official interpreter, Glenn Ford is supposed to start a women's club, build a schoolhouse, and establish democracy according to the plan sent out from Washington. The villagers, however, have other plans: what they desire most is a teahouse with plenty of geisha girls.

Paul Ford, a befuddled colonel, had played the same role on Broadway more than 1,000 times and yet managed to bring a freshness to it for the screen. He was later to do the same kind of role on TV's "You'll Never Get Rich" when he played Sgt. Bilko's (Phil Silvers) commanding officer. Kyo spoke no English when she accepted the role. She had previously been seen in GATE OF HELL and RASHOMON. The music was mostly Okinawan and Japanese, and that lent authenticity to the affair. Although David Wayne was a marvel in the play (which won the Tony as Best Play that year), he was not a movie star, so when Brando indicated he wanted the part, he got it. Brando does one of his best roles here, submerging his own powerful personality. He spent months learning the proper way to move like an Asian. Some of the humor is labored, and Glenn Ford overplays a bit, but the ultimate result is a charming, though somewhat talky, movie that elevates whimsy to a new high.

10

1979 122m c Comedy ★★★
Orion (U.S.) R/18

Dudley Moore *(George)*, Julie Andrews *(Sam)*, Bo Derek *(Jenny)*, Robert Webber *(Hugh)*, Dee Wallace Stone *(Mary Lewis)*, Sam Jones *(David)*, Brian Dennehy *(Bartender)*, Max Showalter *(Reverend)*, Rad Daly *(Josh)*, Nedra Volz *(Mrs. Kissel)*

p, Blake Edwards, Tony Adams; d, Blake Edwards; w, Blake Edwards; ph, Frank Stanley; ed, Ralph E. Winters; m, Henry Mancini; prod d, Rodger Maus; fx, Fred Cramer; cos, Patricia Edwards

AAN Best Score: Henry Mancini; *AAN Best Song:* Henry Mancini (Music), Robert Wells (Lyrics)

A funny if somewhat retrograde film that sent Dudley Moore's career soaring briefly, while making some telling points about the problems of middle age. Moore is a successful songwriter with four Oscars to his name. Suffering from a combination of ennui and self-doubt, Moore sees a limousine go past in his ritzy neighborhood. In it is Derek, on her way to get married to Jones at a Beverly Hills church. This is the woman of Moore's dreams, whom he rates "11" on a scale of one to 10. Moore learns Derek's identity, and impulsively follows the newly-wed couple to Mexico, where he commences a blundering pursuit of Derek.

Derek enjoyed brief stardom on the basis of her part in this film but has failed to achieve any further success. Several standout comedy bits include Moore getting drunk, being stung on the nose by a bee, and burning his feet on the hot beach sand. Moore also played the piano (which he does well) in the band that provided the background music. Mancini and Robert Wells's song "It's Easy to Say" was nominated for an Oscar. The movie made about $40 million, thus qualifying it as the "sleeper" of 1979.

TEN COMMANDMENTS, THE

1956 219m c Religious ★★★½
Paramount (U.S.) /U

Charlton Heston *(Moses)*, Yul Brynner *(Rameses)*, Anne Baxter *(Nefretiri)*, Edward G. Robinson *(Dathan)*, Yvonne De Carlo *(Sephora)*, Debra Paget *(Lilia)*, John Derek *(Joshua)*, Cedric Hardwicke *(Sethi)*, Nina Foch *(Bithiah)*, Martha Scott *(Yochabel)*

p, Cecil B. DeMille; d, Cecil B. DeMille; w, Aeneas MacKenzie, Jesse Lasky Jr., Jack Gariss, Fredric M. Frank (based on the novels *The Prince of Egypt* by Dorothy Clarke Wilson, *Pillar of Fire* by the Rev. J.H. Ingraham, and *On Eagle's Wings* by the Rev. G.E. Southon, and in accordance with the Bible, the ancient texts of Josephus, Eusebius, Philo, and The Midrash); ph, Loyal Griggs, John F. Warren, W. Wallace Kelley, Peverell Marley; ed, Anne Bauchens; m, Elmer Bernstein; art

d, Hal Pereira, Walter Tyler, Albert Nozala; fx, John P. Fulton; chor, LeRoy Prinz, Ruth Godfrey; cos, Edith Head, Ralph Jester, John Jensen, Dorothy Jeakins, Arnold Friberg

AAN Best Picture; *AAN Best Cinematography:* Loyal Griggs; *AAN Best Editing:* Anne Bauchens; *AAN Best Art Direction:* Hal Pereira, Walter H. Tyler, Albert Nozaki, Sam M. Comer, Ray Moyer; *AAN Best Costume Design:* Edith Head, Ralph Jester, John Jensen, Dorothy Jeakins, Arnold Friberg; *AAN Best Sound:* Loren L. Ryder; *AA Best Visual Effects:* John Fulton

A great big wallow, sublime hootchy-kootchy hokum, peppered with lightning that does automatic writing and an unsurpassed homage to the joys of jello. Director-producer Cecil B. DeMille ended his great career with this gigantic production, packed with enormous crowd scenes, lavish spectacles, and wide-screen special effects orchestrated with dazzling brilliance.

DeMille's Exodus (a tale he had also filmed in 1923) opens as the Egyptian pharaoh is told that the deliverer of the enslaved Hebrews will soon be born. He orders the slaughter of all newborn Jewish males, but one is placed on a basket in the Nile, found by the pharaoh's sister, and brought up as her own. Years pass and the now-adult Moses (Charlton Heston) has become a beloved prince, much to the chagrin of Rameses (Yul Brynner), the pharaoh's son. When Moses's lineage is revealed, he is banished into the desert, but after several peaceful years, he learns of his destiny in his encounter with the burning bush. The film then depicts his return and his confrontation with Rameses II, the mass exodus of the Hebrews, Moses's parting of the Red Sea, his receipt of the Ten Commandments, the Jews' worship of the idolatrous Golden Calf, and their 40 years of wandering as punishment. Finally, the aged Moses watches Joshua lead his people into the Promised Land.

DeMille tells the biblical story on a scale no other filmmaker ever attempted, yet the star cast cannot be overwhelmed by the epic production, even if the orgy did take three weeks to film. The exodus itself is truly moving, and Hardwicke lends a convincing old Pharaoh. Heston's stalwart prophet really does look like Michelangelo's Moses—how can he miss? Brynner and Baxter supply velvet and villainy, Robinson and Vincent Price are accomplished camps, and Paget and DeCarlo contribute beautous support. THE TEN COMMANDMENTS eventually grossed over $80 million, enjoying several re-releases, and DeMille's vision remains a powerful one, a testament to his inestimable talent as the master of epic vulgarity and self-justified righteousness.

10 RILLINGTON PLACE

1970 111m c Crime ★★★½
Genesis/Filmways/Columbia (U.K.) GP/15

Richard Attenborough *(John Reginald Christie)*, Judy Geeson *(Beryl Evans)*, John Hurt *(Timothy John Evans)*, Pat Heywood *(Mrs. Ethel Christie)*, Isobel Black *(Alice)*, Miss Riley *(Baby Geraldine)*, Phyllis McMahon *(Muriel Eady)*, Ray Barron *(Workman Willis)*, Douglas Blackwell *(Workman Jones)*, Gabrielle Daye *(Mrs. Lynch)*

p, Martin Ransohoff, Leslie Linder; d, Richard Fleischer; w, Clive Exton (based on the book by Ludovic Kennedy); ph, Denys Coop; ed, Ernest Walter; m, John Dankworth; art d, Maurice Carter

Richard Attenborough portrays murderer John Reginald Christie, whose actions led to the hanging of an innocent man and the eventual abolition of capital punishment in Britain. The film picks up in 1944 as Christie coaxes a young lady into his flat, then rapes and strangles her, burying the body in his back yard. Several years later, Timothy John Evans (Hurt) and wife Beryl (Geeson), along with their baby daughter, move into the building and are charmed by Christie, who claims all sorts of medical and legal knowledge. When Beryl learns she is pregnant, the young couple allows Christie to perform an abortion. Instead of performing an abortion Christie rapes and murders Beryl, then tells Timothy his wife died during the operation and suggests he go away and leave their daughter in his care. The none-too-bright Timothy does as he is told, and that same night Christie kills his daughter. Eventually Timothy goes to the police and confesses to murdering Beryl. At his trial he relates the facts but is condemned by perjured testimony from Christie and hanged. Christie goes on to take the lives of several other victims, including his own wife, before justice is served.

Based on the historical Christie-Evans case, this painstakingly accurate film was shot in the building next door to the one where the actual killings took place. After filming was completed, the entire block, now renamed Ruston Close, was razed and council houses were built on the location. Attenborough is excellent as the banal, middle-class killer, and John Hurt is effective as usual as the man too dim to keep himself from being executed for a crime he didn't commit. 10 RILLINGTON STREET is somber and frightening and omits the stylistic flourishes that marred director Richard Fleischer's previous excursion into the world of true crime, THE BOSTON STRANGLER. Fleischer directed two other suspense-filled films that same year, THE LAST RUN and SEE NO EVIL.

TENANT, THE
(LE LOCATAIRE)

1976 124m c Horror	★★★½
Paramount (France)	R/18

Roman Polanski (*Trelkovsky*), Isabelle Adjani (*Stella*), Shelley Winters (*Concierge*), Melvyn Douglas (*Mr. Zy*), Jo Van Fleet (*Mme. Dioz*), Bernard Fresson (*Scope*), Lila Kedrova (*Mme. Gaderian*), Claude Dauphin (*Husband*), Claude Pieplu (*Neighbor*), Rufus (*Badar*)

p, Andrew Braunsberg; d, Roman Polanski; w, Roman Polanski, Gerard Brach (based on the novel *Le Locataire Chimerique* by Roland Topor); ph, Sven Nykvist; ed, Francoise Bonnot; m, Philippe Sarde; prod d, Pierre Guffroy; art d, Claude Moesching, Albert Rajau; cos, Jacques Schmidt

Roman Polanski's psychological horror film stars Polanski himself as Trelkovsky, a Polish office clerk in Paris. He rents an apartment in a quiet building whose elderly residents seem to feel malevolence toward the new tenant from the start. After he learns that the previous occupant jumped from the apartment window, he visits the dying woman—who is covered head to toe in wrappings—in the hospital, and meets her friend Stella (Isabelle Adjani). The woman suddenly lets out a blood-curdling scream and dies, an event that forms a bond between Trelkovsky and Stella, who nearly become lovers but drift apart. Meanwhile, Trelkovsky, while experiencing increasing difficulty with his fellow tenants—they complain that he makes noise (though we don't see or hear anything) and threaten to "take steps"—grows steadily more obsessed with uncovering the mystery of the deceased woman and her fate and becomes positive his neighbors are trying to kill him. As the film progresses, however, his paranoia seems less and less justified, and his actions more and more insane.

In many ways, THE TENANT is Polanski's REPULSION (1965) with the director in the Catherine Deneuve role. In both films, a character's vision of the world clashes with "reality" to the point that no sense can be made of either, and in both the conflict leads to violence. We are never really sure that there isn't a plot against Polanski, even though logic suggests he is imagining everything, and this uneasy sense that maybe Polanski's character is right makes the film extremely, scarily effective (it is also surprisingly funny). Technically, THE TENANT is superb, with stunning camerawork by Sven Nykvist, an eerie score by Philippe Sarde, and thoroughly convincing performances from the entire cast.

TENDER MERCIES

1983 89m c Drama	★★★½
EMI (U.S.)	PG

Robert Duvall (*Mac Sledge*), Tess Harper (*Rosa Lee*), Betty Buckley (*Dixie*), Wilford Brimley (*Harry*), Ellen Barkin (*Sue Anne*), Allan Hubbard (*Sonny*), Lenny Von Dohlen (*Robert*), Paul Gleason (*Reporter*), Michael Crabtree (*Lewis Menefee*), Norman Bennett (*Rev. Hotchkiss*)

p, Philip S. Hobel, Mary-Ann Hobel, Horton Foote, Robert Duvall; d, Bruce Beresford; w, Horton Foote; ph, Russell Boyd; ed, William Anderson; m, George Dreyfus; art d, Jeannine Oppewall; chor, Nick Felix; cos, Elizabeth McBride

AAN Best Picture; *AA Best Actor*: Robert Duvall; *AAN Best Director*: Bruce Beresford; *AA Best Original Screenplay*: Horton Foote; *AAN Best Song*: Austin Roberts, Bobby Hart

This low-key drama set in Texas is one of the continuing stories of screenwriter Horton Foote's life in the hinterlands. Robert Duvall, who won an Oscar for his performance, is Mac Sledge, a down-and-out singer who has recently broken up with his wife, Dixie (Betty Buckley), also a country singer. Mac gets rip-roaring drunk and wakes up in a motel-gas-station owned by a religious widow, Rosa Lee (Tess Harper), with a young son (Allan Hubbard). Rosa offers Mac a job, so he stays on, and the two fall in love. Meanwhile, Dixie and her manager (Wilford Brimley) are lurking in the background, and Mac attempts to patch matters up with her and their daughter (Ellen Barkin). He also tries to make a comeback.

TENDER MERCIES is an episodic gem that offers little in the way of action or melodrama but gets by on fine performances (particularly from Barkin and from Duvall, who does his own singing), atmospheric cinematography, and spare, unglamorous writing. Australian director Bruce Beresford's first American assignment, the film bears interesting comparison with Englishman Michael Apted's COAL MINER'S DAUGHTER (another outsider's vision of the world of country), and with Foote's later, probably superior, THE TRIP TO BOUNTIFUL.

TENTH VICTIM, THE
(LA DECIMA VITTIMA)

1965 92m c Science Fiction	★★★
Champion/Concordia/Les Films (France/Italy)	/A

Marcello Mastroianni (*Marcello Polletti*), Ursula Andress (*Caroline Meredith*), Elsa Martinelli (*Olga*), Salvo Randone (*Professor*), Massimo Serato (*Lawyer*), Evi Rigano (*Victim*), Milo Quesada (*Rudi*), Luce Bonifassy (*Lidia*), Anita Sanders (*Relaxatorium Girl*), Mickey Knox (*Chet*)

p, Carlo Ponti; d, Elio Petri; w, Elio Petri, Ennio Flaiano, Tonino Guerra, Giorgio Salvioni (based the on short story "The Seventh Victim" by Robert Sheckley); ph, Gianni Di Venanzo; ed, Ruggero Mastroianni; m, Piero Piccioni; art d, Piero Poletto; chor, Gino Landi; cos, Giulio Coltellacci

A bizarre, pop look at life in the future which stars Mastroianni and Andress as participants in a game of legalized murder known as "Man Hunt," a replacement for violence and war. Andress must kill her tenth victim to achieve the pinnacle of success, and Mastroianni happens to be the chosen one. He also is plotting to kill her, which confuses the situation, especially when they fall in love. Petri creates an eccentric and flamboyant world, with some of his wackier invention including Andress's deadly, double-barreled bra and a trendy nightery called Club Masoch.

TEOREMA

1968 93m c Drama	★★★★
Aetos (Italy)	/X

Terence Stamp (*Visitor*), Silvana Mangano (*Mother*), Massimo Girotti (*Father*), Anne Wiazemsky (*Daughter*), Laura Betti (*Maid*), Andres Jose Cruz Soublette (*Son*), Alfonso Gatto (*Doctor*), Ninetto Davoli (*Messenger*), Susanna Pasolini (*Old Peasant*), Adele Cambria

p, Franco Rossellini, Manolo Bolognini; d, Pier Paolo Pasolini; w, Pier Paolo Pasolini (based on his novel); ph, Giuseppe Ruzzolini; ed, Nino, m, Ennio Morricone, Wolfgang Amadeus Mozart; art d, Luciano Puccini; fx, Goffredo Rocchetti; cos, Marcella De Marchis, Roberto Capucci

A heavily symbolic and highly intellectual look at the bourgeois milieu and the effect that a mysterious visitor, Stamp, has on one specific family. Into the life of a prominent Milanese family walks Stamp, an angelic-looking stranger (although Pasolini acknowledges that he may also represent the devil), whose spiritual sexuality touches each member of the household in a different way, elevating each to a certain level of grace. He becomes involved with Mangano, the wife; Girotti, the husband; Wiazemsky, their daughter; Cruz, their son; and Betti, the housemaid. Then one day Stamp leaves as mysteriously as he arrived. The family feels the void, can no longer attain the level of spirituality that Stamp provided, and falls back into the worldliness of the bourgeoisie. Mangano tries to recapture that state by wandering the streets and picking up lovers at random; Wiazemsky enters a catatonic trance and completely withdraws from her society; Cruz becomes an artist whose dissatisfaction with his paintings prompts him to urinate on them; and Girotti relinquishes control of his factory to the workers and wanders naked through a vast wasteland. Only Betti, the maid, can survive without Stamp. This is because she, unlike the family that employs her, is from the peasant class and has a naive faith to sustain her—not only in Stamp's divinity but in what he has taught her faith can do. Instead of deteriorating, Betti returns to her village, performs miracles for the peasants, and even levitates. For her brilliant performance (the rest of the cast is equally admirable), Betti was awarded the Best Actress prize at the 1968 Venice Film Festival. The film's release, like so many of Pasolini's films, was shrouded in controversy. The left wing of the Italian Catholics gave the film an award for its "mysticism" while the Catholic right unleashed a scathing attack on the picture. According to Pasolini (whose self-analysis is usually more confusing than clarifying): "The point of the film is roughly this: a member of the bourgeoisie, whatever he does, is always wrong . . . anything done by the bourgoisie, however sincere, profound, and noble it is, is always on the wrong side of the track." Pasolini had hoped to include Orson Welles in the cast, although he didn't make clear whether he would have had Stamp's or Girotti's role. In either case, the mind boggles.

TERMINATOR, THE

1984   108m   c   Science Fiction/Thriller   ★★★★
Hemdale/Pacific Western   (U.S.)   R/18

Arnold Schwarzenegger (Terminator), Michael Biehn (Kyle Reese), Linda Hamilton (Sarah Connor), Paul Winfield (Traxler), Lance Henriksen (Vukovich), Rick Rossovich (Matt), Bess Motta (Ginger), Earl Boen (Silberman), Dick Miller (Pawn Shop Clerk), Shawn Schepps (Nancy)

p, Gale Anne Hurd; d, James Cameron; w, James Cameron, Gale Anne Hurd, William Wisher Jr.; ph, Adam Greenberg; ed, Mark Goldblatt; m, Brad Fiedel; art d, George Costello; fx, Stan Winston, Gene Warren Jr., Peter Kleinow; cos, Hillary Wright

Back before Arnold Schwarzenegger's ascendence to his current status as Hollywood's designated Action Hero of choice, husband to Kennedys, and buddy of presidents, he was still willing to play villains. As such he made an indelible impression as the titular character of THE TERMINATOR. This was the film that demonstrated to the dubious everyone that the musclebound fellow with that outrageous accent might be more than just another passing blip on our pop culture radar screens. The sleeper hit of fall 1984, THE TERMINATOR is an intelligent, smoothly crafted, and stylish low-budget science fiction action movie that astounded fans of the genre. This was an enormous career booster for writer-director James Cameron (ALIENS, THE ABYSS, TERMINATOR 2) as well as stars Schwarzenegger and Linda Hamilton (TV's cult favorite "Beauty and the Beast" and TERMINATOR 2).

The movie opens in the hellish Los Angeles of the year 2029. We see a world destroyed by nuclear war and run by sophisticated machines that have decided to obliterate the weak humans who created them. The action then shifts back to Los Angeles in 1984. In two separate locations, two men—the Terminator (Arnold Schwarzenegger) and Kyle Reese (Michael Biehn)—materialize out of what appear to be small electrical storms and wander off into the night. The next day, after having stolen several deadly weapons and a car, the Terminator looks up the name "Sarah Connor" in the phone book. There are three Sarah Connors listed. The stoical mystery man sets off to kill each of them. Two of the women are killed, but the third (Linda Hamilton) has gone out for the evening. Noticing she is being followed by Reese, the nervous Sarah ducks into a nightclub aptly named Tech Noir and tries to disappear into the crowd. But the Terminator has traced her to the nightclub. Fortunately for her so has Reese. From him Sarah will learn about her destiny and that of the human race.

THE TERMINATOR is an amazingly effective picture that becomes doubly impressive when one considers its small budget. Looking better than most big-budget efforts, it contains dozens of impressive visual effects, including some very good stop-motion animation. For our money, this film is far superior to its mega-grossing mega-budgeted sequel. This is fresh, exciting, and surprisingly witty viewing. Like most genre films made post-STAR WARS, it alludes to many other works. However, this film went a bit further than most. The producers

were successfully sued by cult fantasy author Harlan Ellison who claimed that significant chunks of plot and imagery were lifted from two of his celebrated teleplays for "The Outer Limits," a beloved science fiction series from the early 1960s. The two episodes in question are "Soldier" and "Demon with a Glass Hand." Anyone who has seen those episodes will readily agree that THE TERMINATOR took its homage a bit too far.

TERMINATOR 2: JUDGMENT DAY

1991   135m   c   Science Fiction/Action   ★★★½
Pacific Western/Le Studio Canal Plus/Lightstorm   R/15
Entertainment/Carolco   (U.S.)

Arnold Schwarzenegger (The Terminator), Linda Hamilton (Sarah Connor), Robert Patrick (T-1000), Edward Furlong (John Connor), Earl Boen (Dr. Silberman), Joe Morton (Miles Dyson), S. Epatha Merkerson (Tarissa Dyson), Castulo Guerra (Enrique Salceda), Danny Cooksey (Tim), Jenette Goldstein (Janelle Voight)

p, James Cameron; d, James Cameron; w, James Cameron, William Wisher; ph, Adam Greenberg; ed, Conrad Buff, Mark Goldblatt, Richard A. Harris; m, Brad Fiedel; prod d, Joseph Nemec III; art d, Joseph P. Lucky; fx, Stan Winston, Dennis Muren; cos, Marlene Stewart

AAN Best Cinematography: Adam Greenberg; AAN Best Editing: Conrad Buff, Mark Goldblatt, Richard A. Harris; AA Best Sound: Tom Johnson, Gary Rydstrom, Gary Summers, Lee Orloff; AA Best Visual Effects: Dennis Muren, Stan Winston, Gene Warren, Jr., Robert Skotak; AA Best Makeup: Stan Winston, Jeff Dawn; AA Best Sound Effects Editing: Gary Rydstrom, Gloria S. Borders

The single bona fide blockbuster hit of 1991, TERMINATOR 2: JUDGMENT DAY dazzled its global audience with astonishing special effects and re-confirmed Arnold Schwarzenegger's mega-star status. Trend-setting visuals compensate for a plot that lacks the imagination and edge of the 1984 original.

The film opens with a vision of a future, war-ravaged L.A., where human rebels led by an adult John Connor (Michael Edwards) do battle with silvery, skeletal robots. A voiceover informs us that two "intelligent machines" have been dispatched to the past, one to protect the young Connor, the other to kill him. On late 20th-century Earth, young John Connor (Edward Furlong) finds himself pursued by two androids. The one who would be his guardian (Arnold Schwarzenegger) is a replica of the Terminator model T-800 which dominated the original film; the other is a newer model, the T-1000 (Robert Patrick), which takes on the appearance of a young policeman—the first human it dispatches after arriving on Earth. During their first encounter, the "good" Terminator gets the drop on his rival, but a barrage of shotgun shells leaves puncture wounds that heal as we watch—the T-1000 is made of liquid metal that seems impossible to permanently damage. It is also, as we soon discover, able to assume the exact shape and appearance of anything with which it comes into contact. Now convinced that androids from the future really do exist, John realizes that his mother, Sarah Connor (Linda Hamilton), is far from crazy. (Because of her ravings about killer robots, Sarah has been diagnosed as a paranoid schizophrenic and detained in Pescadero State Hospital.) Now the boy and his Terminator must somehow free Sarah, destroy the T-1000, and prevent an impending nuclear apocalypse.

Though Arnold Schwarzenegger is the nominal star of TERMINATOR 2: JUDGMENT DAY, the show is stolen by extraordinary special effects, particularly the "morphing" in which the liquid metal T-1000 transforms itself into a multitude of organic and inorganic forms. The process was seen earlier, in a less fully developed form, in director James Cameron's 1989 release THE ABYSS. (It's interesting, however, how quickly such high-tech effects now become commonplace, and audiences jaded—within months after T2's release, morphing was ubiquitous on TV commercials.)

On a dramatic level, the film is less satisfactory. Like an increasing number of big-budget extravaganzas, it bears all the hallmarks of having been created by a demography-minded committee. Thus the violence is offset by a more user-friendly Schwarzenegger, who says things like "Hasta la vista, baby" and is forbidden to kill anyone. Meanwhile, Linda Hamilton is given a lot of New Age, motherly things to say, especially during her sojourn in the desert ("If a machine can learn the value of human life, then maybe we can, too."). Nevertheless, her muscle-bound, gun-toting persona is refreshing. Flaws aside, TERMINATOR 2 is an enjoyable, often exhilarating piece of filmmaking, with a wry sense of humor to boot.

TERMS OF ENDEARMENT

1983   130m   c   Comedy/Drama   ★★★½
Paramount   (U.S.)   PG/15

Debra Winger *(Emma Horton)*, Shirley MacLaine *(Aurora Greenway)*, Jack Nicholson *(Garrett Breedlove)*, Danny DeVito *(Vernon Dahlart)*, Jeff Daniels *(Flap Horton)*, John Lithgow *(Sam Burns)*, Betty King *(Rosie)*, Lisa Hart Carroll *(Patsy Clark)*, Huckleberry Fox *(Toddy)*, Megan Morris *(Melanie)*

p, James L. Brooks, Penney Finkelman, Martin Jurow; d, James L. Brooks; w, James L. Brooks (based on the novel by Larry McMurtry); ph, Andrzej Bartkowiak; ed, Richard Marks, Sidney Wolinsky; m, Michael Gore; prod d, Polly Platt; art d, Harold Michelson; cos, Kristi Zea, Anthony J. Faso

AA Best Picture; *AA Best Actress:* Shirley MacLaine; *AAN Best Actress:* Debra Winger; *AA Best Supporting Actor:* Jack Nicholson; *AAN Best Supporting Actor:* John Lithgow; *AA Best Director:* James L. Brooks; *AA Best Adapted Screenplay:* James L. Brooks; *AAN Best Editing:* Richard Marks; *AAN Best Score:* Michael Gore; *AAN Best Art Direction:* Polly Platt, Harold Michelson, Tom Pedigo, Anthony Mondello; *AAN Best Sound:* Donald O. Mitchell, Rick Kline, Kevin O'Connell, Jim Alexander

Lopsided comedy turned tearjerker, saved by excellent performances. TV veteran James Brooks ("Mary Tyler Moore Show") wrote, directed, and co-produced the film which examines a 30-year period in the lives of Aurora Greenway (Shirley MacLaine) and her daughter, Emma (as a child, Jennifer Josey; as an adult, Debra Winger). Aurora is guilty of "smother" love, and, as Emma grows up, she can't wait to escape her mother's suffocating hold. In the face of her mother's anger, Emma marries Flap (Jeff Daniels), has three children, and moves away. All the while, Aurora is wooed by ex-astronaut Garrett Breedlove (Jack Nicholson), an uncouth bachelor whose persistence and unfailing good humor begin to wear her down.

Winger is absolutely winning all the way, with a deathbed scene that may not have been equalled since Bette Davis lay down in DARK VICTORY. MacLaine works like a slow-cooker. The early scenes are her usual stabs at caricature (almost every choice in a dining room scene is wrong), but she is freed by Nicholson; their scenes have a great element of play to them. About the time she demands better hospital treatment for her daughter, she begins to take chances and ventures into virtuoso territory. Nicholson, while certainly not worth the $1 million pricetag for his services, delivers an amusing variation on himself. Brooks writes some of the best dialogue around, but the film is directed in a perfunctory fashion, and many scenes go on far too long. Needless to say, it was a huge commercial success; it's one of those movies that manipulates you into thinking it touched you while it's balancing its bank account. And the box-office profited by gossip that the leading ladies despised each other—making it one of those detective watches for more hardened viewers. Something for everyone, indeed.

TERROR IN A TEXAS TOWN

1958   80m   bw   Western   ★★★½
UA   (U.S.)

Sterling Hayden *(George Hansen)*, Sebastian Cabot *(Ed McNeil)*, Carol Kelly *(Molly)*, Eugene Martin *(Pepe Mirada)*, Ned Young *(Johnny Crale)*, Victor Millan *(Jose Mirada)*, Ann Varela *(Rosa Mirada)*, Sheb Wooley *(Baxter)*, Fred Kohler Jr. *(Weed)*, Steve Mitchell *(Keeno)*

p, Frank N. Seltzer; d, Joseph H. Lewis; w, Ben L. Perry; ph, Ray Rennahan; ed, Frank Sullivan, Stefan Arnsten; m, Gerald Fried; art d, William Ferrari

A minor cult classic, the last film directed by a major cult talent, Joseph H. Lewis (GUN CRAZY, MY NAME IS JULIA ROSS). This offbeat, low-budget western casts Sterling Hayden as George Hansen, a Swede who returns home from the sea to find that his father, a farmer, has

gunned down by the greedy Johnny Crale (Young), who wants to buy up everyone's land in order to drill for oil. At the final showdown, it's six-shooter vs. harpoon.

A leisurely paced, almost hypnotic western, TERROR IN A TEXAS TOWN relies more on characterization and form than on plot. Although the film's title and the final confrontation sound campy, this flick is lean, mean, and grippingly serious. Sharp-eyed viewers will recognize Sheb Wooley, who made the charts in 1958 with his immortal hit, "Purple People Eater."

TESS

1979   170m   c   Drama   ★★★
Renn/Burrill   (France/U.K.)   PG

Nastassia Kinski *(Tess Durbeyfield)*, Leigh Lawson *(Alec d'Urberville)*, Peter Firth *(Angel Clare)*, John Collin *(John Durbeyfield)*, David Markham *(Rev. Mr. Clare)*, Rosemary Martin *(Mrs. Durbeyfield)*, Richard Pearson *(Vicar of Marlott)*, Carolyn Pickles *(Marian)*, Pascale de Boysson *(Mrs. Clare)*, Tony Church *(Parson Tringham)*

p, Claude Berri; d, Roman Polanski; w, Roman Polanski, Gerard Brach, John Brownjohn (based on the novel *Tess of the d'Urbervilles* by Thomas Hardy); ph, Geoffrey Unsworth, Ghislain Cloquet; ed, Alastair McIntyre, Tom Priestley; m, Philippe Sarde; prod d, Pierre Guffroy; art d, Jack Stephens; chor, Sue Lefton; cos, Anthony Powell

AAN Best Picture; *AAN Best Director:* Roman Polanski; *AA Best Cinematography:* Geoffrey Unsworth, Ghislain Cloquet; *AAN Best Score:* Philippe Sarde; *AA Best Art Direction:* Pierre Guffroy Jack Stephens; *AA Best Costume Design:* Anthony Powell

Roman Polanski's delicate, visually rich adaptation of Thomas Hardy's classic novel places the supremely photogenic Nastassja Kinski in the title role. Peasant girl Tess Durbeyfield is sent to the estate of the wealthy d'Urbervilles by her desperate father after he learns that the two families are distantly related. It turns out, however, that the d'Urbervilles are not the d'Urbervilles after all, but a family that bought the noble line's name. Alec d'Urberville (Leigh Lawson), the cocky young master of the household, takes Tess as his lover, but later she returns home, disillusioned and pregnant. After the death of her baby, Tess is left to work on a dairy farm, where she falls in love with Angel Clare (Peter Firth). Their romance leads to a marriage that ends abruptly on their wedding night when her outraged husband refuses to accept her past. With nowhere else to go, Tess returns to Alec, a decision that leads to a violent end.

Visually, TESS is a masterpiece, capturing in amazing detail the scenery and atmosphere of the England of yore. The film's chief drawback, however, is its lack of vitality. Instead of Hardy's passionate tale of ruin and disenchantment, TESS is cautious and reserved.

TEST PILOT

1938   118m   bw   Drama   ★★★★
MGM   (U.S.)   /A

Clark Gable *(Jim Lane)*, Myrna Loy *(Ann Barton)*, Spencer Tracy *(Gunner Sloane)*, Lionel Barrymore *(Howard B. Drake)*, Samuel S. Hinds *(Gen. Ross)*, Arthur Aylesworth *(Frank Barton)*, Claudia Coleman *(Mrs. Barton)*, Gloria Holden *(Mrs. Benson)*, Louis Jean Heydt *(Benson)*, Ted Pearson *(Joe)*

p, Louis D. Lighton; d, Victor Fleming; w, Vincent Lawrence, Waldemar Young, Howard Hawks (based on a story by Frank Wead); ph, Ray June; ed, Tom Held; m, Franz Waxman; cos, Dolly Tree

AAN Best Picture; *AAN Best Original Screenplay:* Frank Wead; *AAN Best Editing:* Tom Held

One of the best Hollywood aviation dramas, TEST PILOT sparkles with a great cast and sprightly direction by Fleming, a "man's director" who had the good sense to feature a great female performer, Loy, in this action film. Gable plays a world-renowned test pilot who meets and marries farm girl Loy. She wants him to settle down, but Gable—who calls the sky "that lady all dressed in blue"—deeply enjoys putting his life on the line. When Army general Hinds requests that Gable test the Army's new B-17 bomber, Gable accepts the challenge. Loy is on the verge of a crackup by the time Gable and his copilot-buddy Tracy climb into the bomber. Gable pushes the plane beyond its presumed limit and keeps going, trying to reach 30,000 feet. The bomber cannot take the pressure and gives out, plummeting earthward in a screaming nosedive. . .

According to some sources (though not Lynn Tornabee, author of the Gable biography *Long Live the King*), it was actually Tracy who, during the production of this film, gave Gable the sobriquet for which he would be forever known. Reportedly, as Tracy attempted to drive into the MGM lot one morning, his car was blocked by scores of screaming female fans who were besieging Gable, demanding that the star sign their pictures of him. Tracy beeped his horn, but the fans ignored him. Finally, the frustrated Tracy stood up in his convertible and shouted at Gable, "Long live the king! And now, for Christ's sake, let's get inside and go to work!" The prop department subsequently made Gable a cardboard crown lined with rabbit's fur, after which Ed Sullivan heard about the incident and conducted a nationwide poll to find out who the king and queen of Hollywood really were. Fans overwhelmingly elected Gable and Loy. Tracy was frequently frustrated at having to perform in support of screen idol Gable and is said to have stretched out some of his own scenes to insure that he would make a good impression. Regardless, the rapport of the three leads is the film's greatest strength. Buoyed as well by its stunning aerial photography, TEST PILOT was a box-office smash.

TESTAMENT

1983 90m c Science Fiction/Drama/War   ★★★
Entertainment Events/American Playhouse (U.S.)   PG/

Jane Alexander (*Carol Wetherly*), William Devane (*Tom Wetherly*), Ross Harris (*Brad Wetherly*), Roxana Zal (*Mary Liz Wetherly*), Lukas Haas (*Scottie Wetherly*), Philip Anglim (*Hollis*), Lilia Skala (*Fania*), Leon Ames (*Henry Abhart*), Lurene Tuttle (*Rosemary Abhart*), Rebecca De Mornay (*Cathy Pitkin*)

p, Jonathan Bernstein, Lynne Littman; d, Lynne Littman; w, John Sacret Young (based on the story "The Last Testament" by Carol Amen); ph, Steven Poster; ed, Suzanne Pettit; m, James Horner; prod d, David Nichols; art d, Linda Pearl; cos, Julie Weiss

AAN Best Actress: Jane Alexander

Set in a small town in northern California, this flawed but moving film begins by establishing the pattern of everyday life for an average American family, then rips it apart by introducing the nightmare of nuclear apocalypse. Tom and Carol Wetherly (William Devane and Jane Alexander), the loving parents of three children (Lukas Haas, Ross Harris, and Roxana Zal), joke, bicker, and make love until one day Tom doesn't come home from work because war has broken out. Thereafter, the film shows the effects of fallout, both physical and psychological, on the little town and particularly the Wetherlys. As living conditions deteriorate, looting begins, and people start dying, including two of the Wetherly children; Carol and her surviving son search for solace in the past, stirring their memories with home movies of happier times. Ultimately, they find the will to go on into the bleak future.

While TESTAMENT is less sensational than the similar TV movie, "The Day After," first-time director Lynne Littman lays on the sentiment and symbolism a little thickly, and some may find the pre-disaster sequences slow going. The acting is undeniably strong, particulary Alexander's heartfelt performance.

TESTAMENT OF DR. MABUSE, THE
(DAS TESTAMENT DES DR. MABUSE)

1933 122m bw Science Fiction/Crime   ★★★★★
Nero/Constantine/Deutsche Universal (Germany)   /A

Rudolf Klein-Rogge (*Dr. Mabuse*), Oscar Beregi Sr. (*Prof. Dr. Baum*), Karl Meixner (*Hofmeister*), Theodor Loos (*Dr. Kramm*), Otto Wernicke (*Commissioner Karl Lohmann*), Klaus Pohl (*Muller*), Wera Liessem (*Lilli*), Gustav Diesel (*Kent*), Camilla Spira (*Juwelen-Anna*), Rudolph Schundler (*Hardy*)

p, Fritz Lang; d, Fritz Lang; w, Fritz Lang (based on the characters from the novel by Norbert Jacques); ph, Fritz Arno Wagner, Karl Vash; m, Hans Erdmann; prod d, Karl Vollbrecht, Emile Hasler; art d, Karl Vollbrecht, Emil Hasler

A haunting, suspenseful sequel to the great Fritz Lang's 1922 silent DR. MABUSE, THE GAMBLER picks up where the original left off—with Rudolf Klein-Rogge, reprising his role as the mad Dr. Mabuse, in a cell in an insane asylum. When Mabuse dies, Prof. Baum (Oskar Beregi), the director of the asylum, becomes possessed by the dead doctor's spirit and is compelled to carry out the madman's master plan to destroy the state through theft, violence, murder, and destruction. Although Baum engineers these chaotic acts, he manages to lead a double life, retaining his position at the asylum. Interwoven into this story is the tale of two lovers—Lilli (Wera Liessem) and Kent (Gustav Diesel), a member of Baum's gang who wants out and manages to prove the connection between Mabuse's plans and the chaos that is rocking Berlin.

Filmed in 1932 and coscripted by Lang's wife, Thea von Harbou, THE TESTAMENT OF DR. MABUSE was made during the Nazi party's rise to power, and completed just before Lang fled, without von Harbou (who would become a top Nazi screenwriter), to the US. Whether or not it was Lang's intention, there are distinct parallels between THE TESTAMENT OF DR. MABUSE and the real-life events of the day—Prof. Baum symbolizing all those whose minds had become controlled by the thought of carrying out the "master plan." It should come as no surprise, then, that this remarkable testament to Lang's artistry was banned, and nearly destroyed, by the Nazis.

TESTAMENT OF ORPHEUS, THE
(LE TESTAMENT D'ORPHEE)

1959 79m c/bw Drama   ★★★★★
Editions Cinegraphiques (France)   /A

Jean Cocteau (*Himself, the Poet*), Edouard Dermit (*Cegeste*), Jean-Pierre Leaud (*The Schoolboy*), Henri Cremieux (*The Professor*), Francoise Christophe (*The Nurse*), Maria Casares (*The Princess*), Francois Perier (*Heurtebise*), Yul Brynner (*The Court Usher*), Daniel Gelin (*The Intern*), Nicole Courcel (*The Young Mother*)

p, Jean Thuillier; d, Jean Cocteau; w, Jean Cocteau; ph, Roland Pontoiseau; ed, Marie-Josephe Yoyotte; m, Georges Auric, Martial Solal, Johann Sebastian Bach, George Frederick Handel, Christophe Gluck; art d, Pierre Guffroy

Poet-filmmaker-sculptor-painter Jean Cocteau bade a fond farewell to cinema with this free-flowing, spirited collection of images and scenes that includes characters from his past films and personal friends. What there is of a story retreads the ground of Cocteau's THE BLOOD OF A POET (1930) and ORPHEUS (1949), bringing his cinematic career (which is difficult to separate from his other pursuits) full circle. For fans of Cocteau, everything in this picture will strike a familiar chord—a poet lives, must die, is resurrected, and must die again to qualify for immortality. Cocteau again employs some of the most inventive and beautiful photographic manipulations ever done in films, including the reverse motion techniques that never fail to bring a smile to his devotees. The cast reads like a cultural who's who—Pablo Picasso, Charles Aznavour, Francoise Sagan, Brigitte Bardot, Roger Vadim, Jean-Pierre Leaud, and, yes, Yul Brynner. Also making appearances are familiar faces from ORPHEUS, including Jean Marais, Maria Casares, Edouard Dermit, Francois Perier, and Henri Cremieux. Francois Truffaut, in honor of one of his masters, assisted with the production and financing of the picture. A pure, personal poem from one of the greats, THE TESTAMENT OF ORPHEUS allows Cocteau to live on forever.

TEX

1982 103m c Drama   ★★★
Walt Disney Productions (U.S.)   PG

Matt Dillon (*Tex McCormick*), Jim Metzler (*Mason McCormick*), Meg Tilly (*Jamie Collins*), Bill McKinney (*Pop McCormick*), Frances Lee McCain (*Mrs. Johnson*), Ben Johnson (*Cole Collins*), Emilio Estevez (*Johnny Collins*), Phil Brock (*Lem Peters*), Jack Thibeau (*Coach Jackson*), Zeljko Ivanek (*Hitchhiker*)

p, Tim Zinnemann; d, Tim Hunter; w, Tim Hunter, Charlie Haas (based on the novel by S.E. Hinton); ph, Ric Waite; ed, Howard Smith; m, Pino Donaggio; prod d, Jack T. Collis; art d, John B. Mansbridge

Matt Dillon takes his urban toughness to Oklahoma as Tex, a young farmboy raised by his elder brother when their mother dies and their father wanders away. The film probes the pitfalls of growing up, tackling such subjects as sex, boozing, and fighting—three areas the Disney folks have stayed clear of in the past. Dillon, though occasionally annoying, turns in a decent performance, as do Jim Metzler as his brother and Meg Tilly (THE BIG CHILL, PSYCHO II, AGNES OF GOD) as his girlfriend. The screenplay is based on a teen novel by S.E. Hinton (who also appears in the film).

TEXAS CHAINSAW MASSACRE, THE

1974 83m c Horror	★★★★
Vortex/Henkel/Hooper (U.S.)	R/X

Marilyn Burns *(Sally)*, Allen Danziger *(Jerry)*, Paul A. Partain *(Franklin)*, William Vail *(Kirk)*, Teri McMinn *(Pam)*, Edwin Neal *(Hitchhiker)*, Jim Siedow *(Old Man)*, Gunnar Hansen *(Leatherface)*, John Dugan *(Grandfather)*, Jerry Lorenz *(Pickup Driver)*

p, Tobe Hooper; d, Tobe Hooper; w, Kim Henkel, Tobe Hooper; ph, Daniel Pearl; ed, Sallye Richardson, Larry Carroll; m, Tobe Hooper, Wayne Bell; art d, Robert Burns

Though its exploitation title would suggest that THE TEXAS CHAIN SAW MASSACRE is just another mindless gore-fest, it is in fact an intelligent, absorbing, and deeply disturbing horror film that is nearly bloodless in its depiction of violence. Using the age-old technique of suggestion, combined with a gritty, well-executed (no pun intended) visual style, the film seems much bloodier than it actually is. Disturbed by news reports that vandals have been desecrating the remote Texas cemetery where her grandfather is buried, Burns and her wheelchair-bound brother, Partain, gather some of their friends and take the family van to see if their grandfather's grave is still intact. While in the area they decide to visit the old farmhouse where Grandpa lived. Nearby is another farmhouse—one decorated with grisly items made from human and animal skin and bones—in which resides a family of unemployed slaughterhouse workers, the most frightening of whom is "Leatherface" (Hansen), who wears a mask of human flesh and has a way with a chainsaw.

Obviously based on real-life Wisconsin farmer Ed Gein (whose grotesque exploits also inspired Hitchcock's PSYCHO), THE TEXAS CHAIN SAW MASSACRE is one of the best examples of the "horror of the family" subgenre, which takes as its subject the American family—traditionally a wholesome, positive force—and examines its dark side, the side that is claustrophobic, stifling, and incestuous. Tobe Hooper's film is deeply disturbing and is meant to be. The best films in the horror genre don't exist just to "scare" people but to examine the darker impulses, fears, taboos, and repressed desires found in human beings and to purge them from our collective subconscious.

THAT HAMILTON WOMAN

1941 128m bw Biography/War	★★½
UA (U.S.)	/A

Vivien Leigh *(Emma Hart Hamilton)*, Laurence Olivier *(Lord Horatio Nelson)*, Alan Mowbray *(Sir William Hamilton)*, Sara Allgood *(Mrs. Cadogan-Lyon)*, Gladys Cooper *(Lady Nelson)*, Henry Wilcoxon *(Capt. Hardy)*, Heather Angel *(Street Girl)*, Halliwell Hobbes *(Rev. Nelson)*, Gilbert Emery *(Lord Spencer)*, Miles Mander *(Lord Keith)*

p, Alexander Korda; d, Alexander Korda; w, Walter Reisch, R.C. Sherriff; ph, Rudolph Mate; ed, William Hornbeck; m, Miklos Rozsa; prod d, Vincent Korda; fx, Lawrence Butler; cos, Rene Hubert

AAN Best Cinematography: Rudolph Mate; *AAN Best Art Direction:* Vincent Korda, Julia Heron; *AA Best Sound:* Jack Whitney; *AAN Best Visual Effects:* Lawrence Butler, William H. Wilmarth

A drunken crone (played by Vivien Leigh), jailed on charges of theft and assault, begins to tell the story of her life to a cellmate, and the tale of THAT HAMILTON WOMAN unfolds in flashback. In 1786, young Emma Hart (Leigh) arrives at the court of Naples, expecting to wed the British ambassador's nephew. He proves a rascal, but Emma's *joie de vivre* soon attracts the ambassador himself, Sir William Hamilton (Alan Mowbray), and she eventually becomes his bride. Seven years later, British naval hero Lord Nelson (Laurence Olivier) arrives in Naples, seeking the king's aid in the war against Napoleon, and the rest, as they

say, is history—or at least producer-director Alexander Korda's version of such. The film traces the growth in Naples of Emma and Nelson's love (to which her husband turns a blind eye, though tongues wag back home) and their return to England, where the lovers set up house, although Nelson's wife refuses to divorce him. The war goes badly, and Emma persuades Nelson to return to his command, leading to his mortal wounding in the victory at Trafalgar, which in turn begins her slide into despair. Despite the marquee pull of newlyweds Olivier and Leigh (she fresh from GONE WITH THE WIND), THAT HAMILTON WOMAN was not the hit its makers hoped it would be—though it reportedly *was* Winston Churchill's favorite movie. Korda, shooting in the US with little money, was forced to film quickly, without the lavish sets that were his specialty, and the script's "tastefulness"—which downplays Nelson's sensuality and alters facts in making Emma pay for her sins later in the classic Hollywood style—while pleasing to 1941 censors and strengthening its propaganda value for then-embattled Britain, also lowers the level of excitement. For a more accurate account, see Glenda Jackson and Peter Finch in THE NELSON AFFAIR (1973).

THAT MAN FROM RIO
(L'HOMME DE RIO)

1964 114m c Comedy/Adventure	★★★
Ariane/Artistes/Dear (France/Italy)	/U

Jean-Paul Belmondo *(Adrien Dufourquet)*, Francoise Dorleac *(Agnes)*, Jean Servais *(Prof. Catalan)*, Simone Renant *(Lola)*, Milton Ribeiro *(Tupac)*, Ubiracy de Oliveira *(Sir Winston)*, Adolfo Celi *(Senor De Castro)*, Daniel Ceccaldi, Roger Dumas, Sabu do Brasil

p, Alexandre Mnouchkine, Georges Dancigers; d, Philippe de Broca; w, Jean-Paul Rappeneau, Ariane Mnouchkine, Daniel Boulanger, Philippe de Broca; ph, Edmond Sechan; ed, Laurence Mery-Clark, Francoise Javet; m, Georges Delerue; fx, Gil Delamare

AAN Best Original Screenplay: Jean-Paul Rappeneau, Ariane Mnouchkine, Daniel Boulanger, Philippe DeBroca

A wacky adventure yarn that begins with French air force pilot Belmondo on an eight-day pass to visit girlfriend Dorleac in Paris. Unfortunately Belmondo arrives just in time to see Dorleac kidnaped by South American Indians who are trying to get a hold of a set of valuable statues that, when assembled, will point the way to an Amazon treasure. Dorleac is taken because her late father led an expedition in the area, so the Indians suspect she knows where the statues are. After a lengthy series of misadventures in the jungle, Belmondo and Dorleac eventually escape and return to Paris just in time for Belmondo to return to his unit. Belmondo, as always, is a delight. The film received an Oscar nomination for Best Screenplay.

THAT OBSCURE OBJECT OF DESIRE
(CET OBSCUR OBJECT DU DESIR)

1977 100m c Drama	★★★★½
Greenwich/Galaxie/Inine (France/Spain)	R/X

Fernando Rey *(Mathieu)*, Carole Bouquet, Angela Molina *(Conchita)*, Julien Bertheau *(Judge)*, Milena Vukotic *(Traveler)*, Andre Weber *(Valet)*, Pierre Pieral *(Psychologist)*, Maria Asquerino, Ellen Bahl, Valerie Blanco

p, Serge Silberman; d, Luis Bunuel; w, Luis Bunuel, Jean-Claude Carriere (based on the novel *La Femme et la Pantin* by Pierre Louys); ph, Edmond Richard; ed, Helene Plemiannikov; art d, Pierre Guffroy

AAN Best Foreign Language Film ; AAN Best Adapted Screenplay: Luis Bunuel, Jean-Claude Carriere

The final film from the 77-year-old Luis Bunuel shows the playful director in as outrageous form as ever, casting two women—the graceful Carole Bouquet and the saucy Angela Molina—in the role of Conchita, a beautiful but elusive Spanish girl who becomes the object of obsession for Mathieu (Fernando Rey, his voice dubbed into French by Michel Piccoli), an upstanding French businessman. Widowed seven years ago, Mathieu regards love and sex moralistically, priding himself on his ability to count on one hand the number of times he had sex with a woman he didn't love. When he sees Conchita, however, his mind overflows with thoughts of her. Although Conchita professes her love to Mathieu, she leaves him and flees to Switzerland, only to return later as his maid. When Mathieu finally manages to bed her, she is dressed in such an impenetrable outfit (a chastity belt of sorts) that he is unable to satisfy his uncontrollable sexual urge.

This straightforward tale of obsessive love is colored with the always amazing Bunuelian touches. Mathieu's story is framed by a train trip in which he speaks of Conchita to his fellow passengers: a French official, a woman and her teenage daughter, and a dwarf psychologist. Also prevalent throughout the picture is a rash of bombings by a terrorist group that calls itself the Revolutionary Army of the Infant Jesus. The most fascinating aspect of THAT OBSCURE OBJECT OF DESIRE, however, is the character of Conchita, who is exactly what the title promises—so obscure that Bunuel chose to cast two actresses in her role. LAST TANGO IN PARIS star Maria Schneider was originally cast to play Conchita by herself, but she was replaced early in the shooting. In a stroke of genius, Bunuel then cast two women in the same role—a completely logical dualism, since Conchita seems to vary greatly in her feelings for Mathieu, loving him one day and leaving him the next.

THAT TOUCH OF MINK

1962 99m c Romance/Comedy   ★★★
Granley/Arwin/Nob Hill (U.S.)   /U

Cary Grant *(Philip Shayne)*, Doris Day *(Cathy Timberlake)*, Gig Young *(Roger)*, Audrey Meadows *(Connie)*, Alan Hewitt *(Dr. Gruber)*, John Astin *(Beasley)*, Richard Sargent *(Young Man)*, Joey Faye *(Short Man)*, John Fiedler *(Mr. Smith)*, Willard Sage *(Hodges)*

p, Martin Melcher, Stanley Shapiro; d, Delbert Mann; w, Stanley Shapiro, Nate Monaster; ph, Russell Metty; ed, Ted J. Kent; m, George Duning; art d, Alexander Golitzen, Robert Clatworthy; cos, Norman Norell, Rosemary Odell

AAN Best Original Screenplay: Stanley Shapiro, Nate Monaster; *AAN Best Art Direction:* Alexander Golitzen, Robert Clatworthy, George Milo; *AAN Best Sound:* Walden O. Watson

A bouncy if rather smarmy comedy from the mind of Stanley Shapiro, who also contributed to PILLOW TALK and LOVER COME BACK. Shapiro and coauthor Monaster have come up with a thin plot but scads of funny dialogue enhanced by Grant, Day, and Young in enjoyable performances. Day is out of work in New York and about to cash her unemployment check when Grant's passing limousine splashes her with mud. Grant is a corporate raider who has spent his life gobbling up companies and neglecting his personal life. (Humphrey Bogart did the same role in SABRINA.) Day walks into the local automat. Grant sends Young, his tippling financial advisor, into the restaurant to offer Day money for her muddied dress. Meadows, Day's roommate (in a wisecracking, Eve Arden-like role), and Young tell Day to give Grant what-for if she is so indignant at him. Day marches into Grant's fabulous office, where her wrath is soon assuaged by Grant's incomparable suavity. When Grant has to make a business trip to Maryland, he invites her to join him and she agrees. Thus begins a whirlwind journey as he takes her to Philadelphia for drinks, to the UN where he gives a speech, then down to Baltimore for dinner and a game between the Yankees and the Orioles. (Seen briefly are Mickey Mantle, Roger Maris, and Yogi Berra as themselves.) This cat-and-mouse game has to end eventually, and it does when Grant asks Day if she'd like to go to Bermuda with him. The lady doth protest at first, but when Grant plies her with lavish clothing (designed by Rosemary Odell) and a full-length mink coat, Day changes her mind. As nighttime approaches in their vacation spot, Day realizes that this is nothing out of Plato; Grant wants to take Richmond here, and there is no getting away from it. Day conveniently breaks out in a rash, leaving Grant to spend the night playing cards. The romantic trip becomes a disaster. Day feels awful about what's happened and wants another chance. Prior to their next date, Day begins to drink to relax herself and falls off a terrace. Grant feels that the whole affair has been a waste of time and won't call her anymore. Day is frustrated and wants to make Grant jealous, so she asks Young for his help. Young arranges a motel tryst with Astin, an unemployment clerk with a lecherous gleam in his eye. Then Young notifies Grant so he can rescue Day from this fate. Once Day is out of Astin's clutches, Grant realizes that she is the woman for him. Skin problems, though, once again enter the picture.

Most of the jokes are verbal rather than slapstick in this script, which, rather surprisingly, copped an Oscar nomination. The film whips along like a Formula One car under Mann's capable direction. The main problem is that 58-year-old Grant and 38-year-old Day were getting slightly long in the tooth for this kind of "will she or won't she?" story. Astin is excellent, appearing in his second movie after WEST SIDE STORY. Right after this, he teamed with Marty Ingels in his first TV series, "I'm Dickens, He's Fenster."

THAT'LL BE THE DAY

1974 90m c Drama   ★★★
Goodtimes (U.K.)   PG/15

David Essex *(Jim MacLaine)*, Ringo Starr *(Mike)*, Rosemary Leach *(Mrs. MacLaine)*, James Booth *(Mr. MacLaine)*, Billy Fury *(Stormy Tempest)*, Keith Moon *(J.D. Clover)*, Rosalind Ayres *(Jeanette)*, Robert Lindsay *(Terry)*, Beth Morris *(Jean)*, James Ottaway *(Grand-dad)*

p, Sandy Lieberson, David Puttnam; d, Claude Whatham; w, Ray Connolly (based on his story); ph, Peter Suschitzky; ed, Michael Bradsell; art d, Brian Morris

A surprisingly adept rock 'n' roll youth film set in the late 1950s starring real-life rocker David Essex (his big hit was "Rock On") as an alienated, working-class youth who goes through his rights of passage. Ex-Beatle Starr is fine as Essex's buddy. Insightful, well written and acted, THAT'LL BE THE DAY is an honest, realistic youth anthem that soon spawned a sequel, STARDUST, which is just as good.

THEATRE OF BLOOD

1973 104m c Horror   ★★★★
UA (U.K.)   R/18

Vincent Price *(Edward Lionheart)*, Diana Rigg *(Edwina Lionheart)*, Ian Hendry *(Peregrine Devlin)*, Harry Andrews *(Trevor Dickman)*, Coral Browne *(Miss Chloe Moon)*, Robert Coote *(Oliver Larding)*, Jack Hawkins *(Solomon Psaltery)*, Michael Hordern *(George Maxwell)*, Arthur Lowe *(Horace Sprout)*, Robert Morley *(Meredith Merridew)*

p, John Kohn, Stanley Mann; d, Douglas Hickox; w, Anthony Greville-Bell; ph, Wolfgang Suschitzky; ed, Malcolm Cooke; m, Michael J. Lewis; prod d, Michael Seymour; fx, John Stears; chor, Tutte Lemkow; cos, Michael Baldwin

After the horrible deaths of three of his colleagues in the prestigious London Theatre Critics Circle, Peregrine Devlin (Ian Hendry) approaches the baffled police with a bizarre theory: perhaps the murders are being committed by Edward Lionheart (Vincent Price), an aging Shakespearean actor who was outraged when the Critic's Circle award went to another actor. So incensed was Lionheart, that he pushed his way onto the stage, stole the award, and jumped into the Thames, supposedly killing himself. Since the three murders closely parallel deaths detailed in the plays of Shakespeare, the cops think that Devlin may be right. The now-insane Lionheart, aided by his lovely though equally mad daughter, Edwina (Diana Rigg), and a group of derelicts who rescued him from the Thames, is indeed killing the critics.

Clearly inspired by the success of the "Dr. Phibes" series, THEATRE OF BLOOD goes one better by allowing Price to glory in his peculiarly Gothic acting style. He is wonderful here, delighting in every grotesque killing and relishing the excerpts from Shakespeare while outfitted in a variety of outlandish costumes. While Price dominates the film with his superb performance, he is ably supported by a top-notch cast—all of whom agreed to do the film in homage to Price. Director Douglas Hickox wisely chooses a very fluid cinematic style to provide a contrast to the distinctly theatrical script. He skillfully intertwines hilarious black humor with some surprisingly intense Grand Guignol effects. Wholly entertaining and memorable, THEATRE OF BLOOD is ripe camp, an excellent film, and a lasting tribute to the career of one of the most important actors in the genre.

THELMA & LOUISE

1991 128m c Drama/Adventure/Comedy ★★★★
Percy Main Productions (U.S.) R/15

Geena Davis *(Thelma)*, Susan Sarandon *(Louise)*, Harvey Keitel *(Hal)*, Michael Madsen *(Jimmy)*, Christopher McDonald *(Darryl)*, Stephen Tobolowsky *(Max)*, Brad Pitt *(J.D.)*, Timothy Carhart *(Harlan)*, Lucinda Jenney *(Lena the Waitress)*, Jason Beghe *(State Trooper)*

p, Ridley Scott, Mimi Polk; d, Ridley Scott; w, Callie Khouri; ph, Adrian Biddle; ed, Thom Noble; m, Hans Zimmer; prod d, Norris Spencer; art d, Lisa Dean; cos, Elizabeth McBride

AAN Best Actress: Geena Davis; *AAN Best Actress:* Susan Sarandon; *AAN Best Director:* Ridley Scott; *AA Best Original Screenplay:* Callie Khouri; *AAN Best Cinematography:* Adrian Biddle; *AAN Best Editing:* Thom Noble

THELMA & LOUISE is a rowdy, feminist road movie in which a pair of gutsy, independent women discover the strength of sisterhood during a hell-raising, joy-riding escape from the laws of men. One of the most hotly debated films of 1991, it features outstanding performances from stars Geena Davis and Susan Sarandon.

Louise (Sarandon) is a strong-willed waitress who convinces her friend Thelma (Davis), a timid housewife, to join her on a weekend camping trip. Against the wishes of Darryl (Christopher McDonald), her possessive, sexist husband, Thelma sneaks away for the outing. Along the way the pair let loose at a country bar, drinking and dancing; Thelma flirts mildly with a handsome but abusive man, Harlan (Timothy Carhart). Harlan attempts to rape Thelma in the parking lot and is discovered by Louise, who shoots and kills him. The women decide that the police are not likely to believe their version of events, so they flee in a panic.

From Arkansas they head through Oklahoma, where they pick up J.D. (Brad Pitt), a young cowboy stud who has a one-night stand with Thelma. He also steals the money Louise had convinced Jimmy (Michael Madsen), her sometime boyfriend, to withdraw from her savings account. Again victimized by men, they turn desperado, robbing stores to finance their attempted escape to Mexico. Because Louise refuses to take the direct route through Texas (where, it turns out, she herself was once raped), their getaway turns into an extended driving tour of the Southwest. Along the way they feel oddly empowered by their ability to assert themselves against authority, and develop a penchant for improvised holdups. But all the while, the FBI is closing in.

Critical reaction to THELMA & LOUISE indicated that many male viewers felt threatened by these pistol-packing female outlaws, but complaints about the movie's chauvinist treatment of men are largely unjustified. Gender warfare aside, THELMA & LOUISE is a fun, breezy roadtrip across the Western landscape. In the natural grandeur of this setting, director Scott abandons his trademark high-tech atmospherics in favor of a bright, glossy, photographic style that makes picture postcards of the Route 66 backdrop. Yet actresses Davis and Sarandon manage to upstage even Monument Valley. Together they forge a believable and appealing bond that carries the film through some of its improbable plot twists. Even the daring finish—a freeze-frame apotheosis of the duo's leap into the Grand Canyon—works, thanks to the vividness of Davis's and Sarandon's portrayals. It all adds up to a highly enjoyable ride.

THEM!

1954 93m bw Science Fiction ★★★½
Warner Bros. (U.S.) /PG

James Whitmore *(Sgt. Ben Peterson)*, Edmund Gwenn *(Dr. Harold Medford)*, Joan Weldon *(Dr. Patricia Medford)*, James Arness *(Robert Graham)*, Onslow Stevens *(Brig. Gen. O'Brien)*, Sean McClory *(Maj. Kibbee)*, Chris Drake *(Officer Ed Blackburn)*, Sandy Descher *(Little Girl)*, Mary Alan Hokanson *(Mrs. Lodge)*, Don Shelton *(Captain of Troopers)*

p, David Weisbart; d, Gordon Douglas; w, Ted Sherdeman, Russell Hughes (based on a story by George Worthing Yates); ph, Sid Hickox; ed, Thomas Reilly; m, Bronislau Kaper; art d, Stanley Fleischer; fx, Ralph Ayres, William Mueller, Francis J. Scheid; cos, Edith Head

AAN Best Visual Effects:

THEM! is one of the best of a 1950s spate of monster movies rooted in nuclear paranoia. Whitmore and Drake, two New Mexico state troopers patrolling the desert, happen across a trailer home that has been peeled open like a sardine can and gutted. Hiding nearby is a little girl who is nearly catatonic from fear. All she can utter is the word "Them." As the mystery deepens, FBI man Arness, scientist Gwenn, and his daughter Weldon (a scientist in her own right), are called in to help in the investigation. Eventually they learn that secret atomic testing in the area has spawned a colony of 20-foot-long ants. Realizing that if the queen is able to mate, the world may be overrun by the giant creatures, Whitmore and company hurriedly work to locate the nest and destroy it. They trace the creatures to the Los Angeles drainage system (in perhaps the best use of that overly photographed location). Armed with large flame throwers, they confront the monstrous critters.

THEM! pulls all this off quite convincingly. The giant ants do look a bit phony, but they are never on screen long enough to become bothersome. In fact, the image of dozens of giant ants in their underground nest is unforgettable. There was no stop-motion animation used in the film. Instead, two actual-sized models were constructed by prop man Dick Smith (one entire ant, and another front section for closeups). Special effects supervisor Ayres was nominated for an Academy Award for his work on the film. The film is produced and performed with such seriousness that one becomes engrossed in the logistics of dealing with such creatures and forgets about plausibility. THEM! was Warner Brothers' highest grossing film of 1954 and inspired countless imitations, all of which were inferior to the original.

THEODORA GOES WILD

1936 94m bw Comedy ★★★½
Columbia (U.S.) /A

Irene Dunne *(Theodora Lynn)*, Melvyn Douglas *(Michael Grant)*, Thomas Mitchell *(Jed Waterbury)*, Thurston Hall *(Arthur Stevenson)*, Rosalind Keith *(Adelaide Perry)*, Spring Byington *(Rebecca Perry)*, Elisabeth Risdon *(Aunt Mary)*, Margaret McWade *(Aunt Elsie)*, Nana Bryant *(Ethel Stevenson)*, Henry Kolker *(Jonathan Grant)*

p, Everett Riskin; d, Richard Boleslawski; w, Sidney Buchman (based on a story by Mary E. McCarthy); ph, Joseph Walker; ed, Otto Meyer; m, M.W. Stoloff; art d, Stephen Goosson; cos, Bernard Newman

AAN Best Actress: Irene Dunne; *AAN Best Editing:* Otto Meyer

Dunne's first starring comedy role after several weepers was good enough to secure her an Oscar nomination, her second after the 1931 CIMARRON. Dunne plays the title role, a New England woman who writes a steamy best-seller about the morals of a sleepy little town located north of New York City. The book takes off and she decides to see the big city for herself. Once she arrives in Manhattan she meets the ultrasophisticated artist (Douglas) who did the illustrations for her book, and her escapades begin, arising from her situation as a fish out of water in New York. The quaint and hard-bitten Yankees from her village are examined vis-a-vis the sharp Big Apple types and the film draws the conclusion that there are nuts in both places.

The idea was to produce a screwball comedy on the style of some of Capra's Columbia pictures, but this movie had the wrong Riskin (producer Everett, rather than Capra's longtime associate and screenwriter, Robert) and it just wasn't wacky enough, despite a valiant try by Dunne to breathe life into Buchman's modest if clever script. Her efforts did earn her a Best Actress Oscar nomination, but she lost to Luise Rainer for THE GREAT ZIEGFELD.

Director Boleslawski, the Polish stage director who cut his teeth with the Moscow Arts Theatre, made a number of fine films, most notably CLIVE OF INDIA, THE PAINTED VEIL, and LES MISERABLES, which he directed in succession in 1934-35.

THERE'S NO BUSINESS LIKE SHOW BUSINESS

1954 117m c Musical ★★★½
Fox (U.S.) /U

Ethel Merman *(Molly Donahue)*, Donald O'Connor *(Tim Donahue)*, Marilyn Monroe *(Vicky)*, Dan Dailey *(Terrance Donahue)*, Johnny Ray *(Steve Donahue)*, Mitzi Gaynor *(Katy Donahue)*, Richard Eastham *(Lew Harris)*, Hugh O'Brian *(Charles Gibbs)*, Frank McHugh *(Eddie Duggan)*, Rhys Williams *(Father Dineen)*

p, Sol C. Siegel; d, Walter Lang; w, Phoebe Ephron, Henry Ephron (based on a story by Lamar Trotti); ph, Leon Shamroy; ed, Robert Simpson; m, Irving Berlin; art d, Lyle Wheeler, John De Cuir; fx, Ray Kellogg; chor, Robert Alton

AAN Best Original Screenplay: Lamar Trotti; *AAN Best Score:* Alfred Newman, Lionel Newman; *AAN Best Costume Design:* Charles LeMaire, Travilla, Miles White

Packed with tunes by the incomparable Irving Berlin, this entertaining musical concerns the plight of the Five Donahues, a vaudeville act comprised of Molly and Terrence Donahue (Ethel Merman and Dan Dailey) and their children. Steve (Johnny Ray), the oldest child, who goes off to become a priest, is the first of the brood to leave. Next brother Tim (Donald O'Connor) and sister Katy (Mitzi Gaynor) get antsy and decide to carry on the family tradition in New York. Katy's romance with songwriter Charles Gibbs (Hugh O'Brian) is no problem, but Tim's involvement with nightclub hatcheck girl and aspiring singer Vicky (Marilyn Monroe) is another story. When he believes that Vicky is cheating on him, Tim gets drunk and ends up in an automobile accident. Ultimately, though, things work out for the best, as they have a way of doing in musicals, and all of the Donahues come together for one more big number, the rousing title tune.

THERE'S NO BUSINESS LIKE SHOW BUSINESS is packed with every vaudeville cliche the movies have ever conjured up, yet it is presented in a fresh, colorful, heartwarming manner. Merman is a standout, but the lively cast never allows the singer to dominate, and Monroe, in particular, adds much-needed buoyancy to the somewhat flat story, turning up the temperature with her sexy rendition of "Heat Wave."

THESE THREE

1936 93m bw Drama ★★★★½
UA (U.S.) /U

Miriam Hopkins *(Martha Dobie)*, Merle Oberon *(Karen Wright)*, Joel McCrea *(Dr. Joseph Cardin)*, Catharine Doucet *(Mrs. Lily Mortar)*, Alma Kruger *(Mrs. Tilford)*, Bonita Granville *(Mary Tilford)*, Marcia Mae Jones *(Rosalie Wells)*, Carmencita Johnson *(Evelyn)*, Mary Anne Durkin *(Joyce Walton)*, Margaret Hamilton *(Agatha)*

p, Samuel Goldwyn; d, William Wyler; w, Lillian Hellman (based on her play "The Children's Hour"); ph, Gregg Toland; ed, Daniel Mandell; m, Alfred Newman; art d, Richard Day; cos, Omar Kiam

AAN Best Supporting Actress: Bonita Granville

One of Wyler's finest films, and the occasion for one of the finest Goldwynisms. When warned that the play he'd just bought, Lillian Hellman's *The Children's Hour*, was about lesbians, Goldwyn supposedly replied, "That's okay: we'll turn them into Americans." Although Hellman's screenplay jettisons explicit lesbianism in conformance with the Hays Code, the resulting movie abounds with repressed eroticism and is far superior to Wyler's post-Code remake THE CHILDREN'S HOUR. Bonita Granville, in an Oscar-nominated role, plays Mary Tilford, a mean, vicious girl who is censured by her teachers at a posh private school run by college friends Martha and Karen (Miriam Hopkins and Merle Oberon). Martha is an austere Yankee type, while Karen is a warm woman who is in love with local doctor Joseph Cardin (Joel McCrea). He reciprocates her passion but maintains a close friendship with Martha. Mary retaliates by telling her grandmother (Alma Kruger) that Martha and Joe had been "carrying on" in a bedroom near the student's quarters. The grandmother knows that Mary is a compulsive liar but believes her when the lie is corroborated by nine-year-old Rosalie (Marcia Mae Jones, every bit as good as Granville). Mary, it seems, is blackmailing the other girl with the knowledge

that Rosalie has stolen a watch. Charges and countercharges are hurled, and though the truth eventually comes out, important changes have occurred in everyone's lives.

Lillian Hellman's *The Children's Hour* appeared on Broadway for over 600 performances. Samuel Goldwyn took advantage of the notoriety of Hellman's first stage effort by releasing the movie while the play was still running. He'd purchased the rights for $50,000, but the Production Code people insisted he remove much of what made the play such a sensation. Goldwyn hired Hellman to make the alterations. Despite the script changes, though, there are many moments when it seems that Hopkins is more interested in Oberon than McCrea. However one reads it, THESE THREE is gripping, adult cinema. Oberon gives one of her best dramatic performances and McCrea is also quite fine. The two child actresses have the showiest parts, but the real performances to watch are those of Alma Kruger and Miriam Hopkins. Hopkins, in particular, has rarely been better, her intense, high-strung quality perfectly suited to the role of a woman unable to stop her world from falling apart around her. In both cases, the major problem was making the audience believe in the character portrayed by Granville (Karen Balkin in the remake). This was the first of eight collaborations for Goldwyn and Wyler and the first for Wyler and the masterful Gregg Toland, who died at 44 after having photographed almost half of Goldwyn's output. Despite Granville's superb acting, she lost the Oscar for Best Supporting Actress to Gale Sondergaard for her work in ANTHONY ADVERSE. Other than MAID OF SALEM (1937) and some Nancy Drew movies, Granville never really did get another chance at bat, eventually marrying millionaire Jack Wrather and becoming a producer. Her work in THESE THREE was a revelation for audiences accustomed to seeing sweet little girls like Shirley Temple onscreen.

THEY DIED WITH THEIR BOOTS ON

1942 140m bw Western/Biography/War ★★★★
Warner Bros. (U.S.) /U

Errol Flynn *(George Armstrong Custer)*, Olivia de Havilland *(Elizabeth Bacon Custer)*, Arthur Kennedy *(Ned Sharp)*, Charley Grapewin *(California Joe)*, Gene Lockhart *(Samuel Bacon)*, Anthony Quinn *(Crazy Horse)*, Stanley Ridges *(Maj. Romolus Taipe)*, John Litel *(Gen. Phil Sheridan)*, Walter Hampden *(Sen. Sharp)*, Sydney Greenstreet *(Gen. Winfield Scott)*

d, Raoul Walsh; w, Wally Klein, Aeneas MacKenzie; ph, Bert Glennon; ed, William Holmes; m, Max Steiner; art d, John Hughes; cos, Milo Anderson

If one can ignore the blatantly fictitious nature of this Hollywood "biography" of the still-controversial George Armstrong Custer, THEY DIED WITH THEIR BOOTS ON is a wholly entertaining movie, fueled by Raoul Walsh's direction and Errol Flynn's energetic performance. The film follows Custer (Flynn) from his youth as a West Point cadet to his service in the Civil War and finally to his days with the Seventh Cavalry, which ended with the massacre at Little Big Horn on June 25, 1876. Walsh creates a rousing film, its pace as fast as the many cavalry charges the dashing Custer leads. Unfortunately, the picture does not adhere to the facts and, in many instances, strays far afield to keep Custer's legend intact, going so far as to invest the cavalry commander with impassioned sympathy for the plight of the Indians! Though historically inaccurate, THEY DIED WITH THEIR BOOTS ON still provides sprawling, exciting epic action, with huge masses of men moved in the Civil War scenes, and particularly in the final battle against the Indians, with great skill by Walsh. Walsh used more than 1,000 extras, with mostly Filipinos doubling for the Sioux because, not surprisingly, only 16 real Sioux from the reservation at South Dakota's Fort Yates answered the casting call (the rest, presumably, refusing to insult the memories of their ancestors). Dozens of stuntmen were injured in horse falls, so many that the studio had to set up a field hospital at the location site to handle the daily injuries, with doctors and nurses—and veterinarians—attending the scores of riders and horses hobbling in for treatment after battle scenes. Indeed, three stuntmen died during the filming of this wild actioner: one from a broken neck, another from a heart attack, and, in the most bizarre and gruesome death, one impaled on his own sword—which was real at his own insistence. Despite the film's wanton distortion of history, THEY DIED

WITH THEIR BOOTS ON did paint a fairly sympathetic portrait of the Indians. Director Walsh later stated: "Most westerns had depicted the Indian as a painted, vicious savage. In THEY DIED WITH THEIR BOOTS ON I tried to show him as an individual who only turned violent when his rights as defined by treaty were violated by white men."

THEY DRIVE BY NIGHT

1940 93m bw Drama   ★★★★½
Warner Bros. (U.S.)

George Raft (*Joe Fabrini*), Ann Sheridan (*Cassie Hartley*), Ida Lupino (*Lana Carlsen*), Humphrey Bogart (*Paul Fabrini*), Gale Page (*Pearl Fabrini*), Alan Hale (*Ed J. Carlsen*), Roscoe Karns (*Irish McGurn*), John Litel (*Harry McNamara*), Henry O'Neill (*District Attorney*), George Tobias (*George Rondolos*)

p, Mark Hellinger; d, Raoul Walsh; w, Jerry Wald, Richard Macaulay (based on the novel *The Long Haul* by A.I. Bezzerides); ph, Arthur Edeson; ed, Oliver S. Garretson, Thomas Richards; m, Adolph Deutsch; art d, John Hughes; fx, Byron Haskin, H.F. Koenekamp, James Gibbons, John Holden, Edwin DuPar; cos, Milo Anderson

Amid tough competition, Ida Lupino steals it. This cult classic is one of the best road movies to emerge from a major studio in the 1940s. Raft and Bogart are truck-driving brothers who have left the large company run by Hale and bought their own truck to work as independents. The first half of the film details their rise as they drive all night, skimp on needed repairs, and struggle to keep their fledgling business afloat. Bogart is married to Page, who resents his neglect of her in favor of the business. One night, when Bogart and Raft are pulled over at a roadside diner, they meet waitress Sheridan. She has a sharp tongue and a mane of red hair, and Raft is almost instantly attracted to her. Later, the hitchhiker the two men pick up turns out to be Sheridan, who has quit her job in the face of her boss's continued advances. Raft sets her up with a room in a boardinghouse. Shyly, he makes some romantic comments, which Sheridan turns away without being discouraging. Bogart falls asleep at the wheel one night and loses his arm in the subsequent accident, forcing Raft to take a job with Hale as traffic manager. Lupino, Hale's venomous wife, sets her sights on Raft, but he refuses to fool around with the boss's wife. Lupino then decides to get rid of her husband, leaving him drunk and unconscious in the car while she closes the door and leaves the engine running. She offers to share with Raft the company she has inherited, but when he refuses, Lupino goes to the police and tells them that Raft forced her to kill her husband. In no time Raft is arrested and charged. Sheridan comes to jail and pleads with Lupino to tell the truth, but Lupino tells her that she will take Raft with her wherever she goes. Things go badly for Raft in court, with circumstantial evidence implicating him and the testimony of his friends doing nothing to clear him. But several people have yet to be heard from, and help comes from the strangest of places.

A loose remake of BORDERTOWN (in which Bette Davis asphyxiates husband Eugene Pallette in order to win Paul Muni), THEY DRIVE BY NIGHT could have been another routine film but for Lupino's incredibly forceful performance and Raft's smooth depiction of the tough trucker. Bogart—still wallowing in the lull in his career between the time THE PETRIFIED FOREST established him as a serious actor and the time HIGH SIERRA finally made him a star—is very good, especially when he is embittered by the loss of his arm. Walsh's direction is as forceful and vigorous as always and this film is among his very best.

THEY LIVE

1988 93m c Science Fiction   ★★★½
Alive (U.S.)   R/18

Roddy Piper (*John Nada*), Keith David (*Frank*), Meg Foster (*Holly*), George "Buck" Flower (*Drifter*), Peter Jason (*Gilbert*), Raymond St. Jacques (*Street Preacher*), Jason Robards III (*Family Man*), John Lawrence (*Bearded Man*), Susan Barnes (*Brown-haired Woman*), Sy Richardson (*Black Revolutionary*)

p, Larry Franco; d, John Carpenter; w, John Carpenter (based on the short story "Eight O'Clock in the Morning" by Ray Nelson); ph, Gary B. Kibbe; ed, Frank Jimenez, Gib Jaffe; m, John Carpenter, Alan Howarth; fx, Frank Carrisosa, Roy Arbogast; cos, Robin Bush

A rare left-leaning Hollywood film from the Reagan era, John Carpenter's THEY LIVE is an erratically amusing throwback to the science-fiction paranoia films of the 1950s. Set in Los Angeles in the near future, the movie shows a society in which the rich have gotten richer while the middle class has eroded and the ranks of the poor and homeless have swelled (sound familiar?). A construction worker called John Nada (professional wrestler Roddy Piper) stumbles on some unusual sunglasses. When he looks through their lenses, he can see what advertising, television shows, and even paper currency are *really* saying; even scarier, the glasses expose the legions of briefcase-toting yuppies as alarming-looking aliens. Nada and his friend Frank (Keith David) track down a band of rebels and enlist in their effort to destroy Cable 54, the television station that keeps the populace from seeing things clearly. Carpenter is trying for a satire of advertising and consumerism under late capitalism, and although the film is great fun at first—especially when depicting the world through Nada's glasses—it rarely rises above the intellectual level of a comic book.

THEY LIVE BY NIGHT

1949 95m bw Crime   ★★★★★
RKO (U.S.)   /A

Cathy O'Donnell (*Keechie*), Farley Granger (*Bowie*), Howard da Silva (*Chickamaw*), Jay C. Flippen (*T-Dub*), Helen Craig (*Mattie*), Will Wright (*Mobley*), Marie Bryant (*Singer*), Ian Wolfe (*Hawkins*), William Phipps (*Young Farmer*), Harry Harvey (*Hagenheimer*)

p, John Houseman; d, Nicholas Ray; w, Charles Schnee, Nicholas Ray (based on the novel *Thieves Like Us* by Edward Anderson); ph, George E. Diskant; ed, Sherman Todd; m, Woody Guthrie, Leigh Harline; art d, Albert S. D'Agostino, Al Herman; fx, Russell A. Cully

Nicholas Ray's energetic first feature, THEY LIVE BY NIGHT tells the tragic story of two doomed lovers and of their short, fast life together before they are torn apart by the criminal world.

As the film opens, Granger and O'Donnell are shown kissing. A title is superimposed: "This boy and this girl were never properly introduced to the world we live in." In this manner, the young lovers' saga hits the screen. Granger, a decent enough fellow whose greatest fault is his naivete, joins a prison break engineered by da Silva and Flippen, two callous criminals who spare no sentimental thought for Granger's innocence, but simply take him along because they need a third hand for a bank job. An auto accident caused by da Silva injures Granger, who recovers in a dark hideout. He is nursed to health by O'Donnell, a young woman who quickly falls in love with Granger, sensing that he is not like his two partners. Granger returns O'Donnell's affections and the two are soon involved in passionate romance. Soon they make it legal, marrying in the dilapidated office of a justice of the peace. When da Silva asks him to join another bank job, Granger is not strong enough to say no, but it's not long before Flippen is killed and da Silva has angrily gone off on his own. Soon da Silva, too, is killed, leaving Granger the last of the gang and still sought by the police. The young fugitive wants nothing more than a quiet home for himself and his wife, but his fate has been sealed.

More than a standard cops-and-robbers tale, THEY LIVE BY NIGHT is a Depression-era saga about lovers on the run. Entangled in a fate they cannot escape, and over which they have absolutely no control, they love to the fullest before they are inevitably, tragically separated. Though based on the novel *Thieves Like Us* by Edward Anderson (later filmed by Robert Altman under Anderson's title), THEY LIVE BY NIGHT owes an equal debt to the Bonnie and Clyde myth, which, while it bears no resemblance to this film in plot, has permeated the cinema's image of lovers on the run. (It's an image that can also be seen in 1949's GUN CRAZY and the 1937 Fritz Lang picture YOU ONLY LIVE ONCE.) Ray undertook the project enthusiastically, bringing to his film a personal style and vision evident from its beginning. After Granger and O'Donnell's kiss at the opening, a getaway car carrying the three criminals is seen traveling down a dusty road, pursued by police. Rather than shoot with a standard camera set-up, Ray demanded that the scene be photographed from a helicopter, a highly unorthodox idea that has now become a standard element of the cinematic lexicon. Not only did this sequence open the film with a burst of unharnessed energy, it also conveyed a sense of godlike fate, looking down on Granger and relentlessly pursuing him. Beautifully acted, THEY LIVE BY NIGHT stands today as one of the most poignant and unforgettable noirs ever made.

THEY MADE ME A FUGITIVE

1947 78m bw Crime ★★★★
Shipman/Gloria/Alliance (U.K.)

Sally Gray (*Sally*), Trevor Howard (*Clem Morgan*), Griffith Jones (*Narcey*), Rene Ray (*Cora*), Mary Merrall (*Aggie*), Vida Hope (*Mrs. Fenshawe*), Ballard Berkeley (*Inspector Rockliffe*), Phyllis Robins (*Olga*), Eve Ashley (*Ellen*), Charles Farrell (*Curley*)

p, Nat A. Bronsten, James Carter; d, Alberto Cavalcanti; w, Noel Langley (based on the novel *Convict Has Escaped* by Jackson Budd); ph, Otto Heller; ed, Marjorie Saunders; m, Marius-Francois Gaillard; art d, Andrew Mazzei

Although film noir in the United States has received the attention it deserves, the same cannot be said for British noir, a movement equally downbeat and striking but more indebted to French poetic realism than to German Expressionism. THEY MADE ME A FUGITIVE, though more Teutonic than some other British noirs, is nonetheless one of the finest representations of the postwar malaise which also infected Great Britain. Trevor Howard is Clem, an RAF officer who falls from grace, winds up a crook, gets framed by Narcey (Jones), and is thrown in the pen. Getting out, Clem heads for London's Soho district, seeking revenge on Narcey and his dope-dealing gang. It's up to Sally (Gray) to try to save him from sinking too low.

Artfully sculpted and suspenseful, THEY MADE ME A FUGITIVE makes for gripping, adult cinema. Few stars began their film careers with more outstanding films made back to back than did Howard, who plumbs the depths of Clem's decline without ever sinking into bathos. He is well supported by Gray as a sympathetic noir blonde, and by a seasoned cast of British veterans, with Jones especially good as the chilling Narcey. With its striking compositions and starkly dramatic lighting, the film shows the mastery of director Alberto Cavalcanti, an eclectic talent who began making short avant-garde silent films in France, made several outstanding features (DEAD OF NIGHT, WENT THE DAY WELL?) in Great Britain and later attempted to imitate Hollywood's industrial success when he headed up the short-lived Vera Cruz studios in Brazil.

THEY SHOOT HORSES, DON'T THEY?

1969 129m c Drama ★★★★
Palomar (U.S.) M/15

Jane Fonda (*Gloria Beatty*), Michael Sarrazin (*Robert Syverton*), Susannah York (*Alice*), Gig Young (*Rocky*), Red Buttons (*Sailor*), Bonnie Bedelia (*Ruby*), Bruce Dern (*James*), Michael Conrad (*Rollo*), Al Lewis (*Turkey*), Robert Fields (*Joel*)

p, Irwin Winkler, Robert Chartoff, Sydney Pollack; d, Sydney Pollack; w, James Poe, Robert E. Thompson (based on the novel by Horace McCoy); ph, Philip Lathrop; ed, Fredric Steinkamp; m, Johnny Green; prod d, Harry Horner; fx, Blondie Anderson; chor, Tom Panko; cos, Donfeld

AAN Best Actress: Jane Fonda; *AA Best Supporting Actor:* Gig Young; *AAN Best Supporting Actress:* Susannah York; *AAN Best Director:* Sydney Pollack; *AAN Best Adapted Screenplay:* James Poe, Robert E. Thompson; *AAN Best Editing:* Fredric Steinkamp; *AAN Best Score:* John Green, Albert Woodbury; *AAN Best Art Direction:* Harry Horner, Frank McKelvy; *AAN Best Costume Design:* Donfeld

An allegorical, socially conscious response to the injustices of the Depression era, THEY SHOOT HORSES, DON'T THEY? has managed to survive the late 1960s, unlike so many other films of that period, without appearing the least bit dated. Preparing the audience for the inevitable, the film begins with Robert Syverton (Sarrazin) standing trial for murder, the details of which are purposely vague. The scene then switches to Chicago's famous Aragon Ballroom, where a dance marathon is about to get underway. Among the contestants is Gloria Beatty (Fonda), an independent, disagreeable loner who seems to enjoy lashing out at those around her. She replaces her original partner with Robert, a drifter with no real desire to participate. Also wearing

numbers on their backs are a pregnant farm woman (Bedelia), her husband (Dern), a sailor and veteran marathoner with heart trouble (Buttons), and a Jean Harlow clone (York) who hopes to be discovered while dancing in the spotlight. As the master of ceremonies, whose job it is to keep the audience content and the dancers dancing, is the sleazy, unshaven Rocky (Young). Everyone's reason for participating is simple—three meals a day and a chance at winning the $1,500 prize, a bonanza in the days of record unemployment and bread lines. The tension builds as the emcee goads the dancers to self-destruction and the driven contestants fight among themselves. Several deaths result, and when Robert is asked why he has committed murder, responds, "They shoot horses, don't they?"

Although it is at times heavy-handed, THEY SHOOT HORSES, DON'T THEY? is a *tour de force* of acting. Fonda, best known at the time as Roger Vadim's wife and the sex toy of BARBARELLA, here got her first chance to prove herself as a serious, dramatic actress. For bringing such gritty, sweaty, hopeless self-degradation to the screen, Fonda received universal praise, as well as an Oscar nomination for Best Actress. Young is superb in his role, a sharp switch from his usual *bon vivant* parts. The rest of the acting is similarly fine, even though Sarrazin, in what is admittedly one of the film's less interesting parts, doesn't really bring enough presence or imagination to his performance. Pollack does one of his best jobs of directing, even if his primary strength lies in his rapport with actors. The look of the film is just right and Pollack skillfully evokes the ratty atmosphere amid which explosive emotions come to a boil. At one point camerawork was even done on roller skates to achieve just the right effect for the bedraggled characters on the dance floor. The film uses much Depression-era music for period flavor and contains many references to the Hollywood of that era. This kind of reflexivity helps highlight the dance floor as an arena of action, a microcosm of America, and the parallels with the situation in Vietnam are pretty obvious. Based on a 1935 novel feted by French existentialists and first purchased by Charlie Chaplin, THEY SHOOT HORSES, DON'T THEY? remains a suitably glum yet cathartic film experience.

THEY WERE EXPENDABLE

1945 135m bw War ★★★★★
MGM (U.S.) /A

Robert Montgomery (*Lt. John Brickley*), John Wayne (*Lt. J.G. "Rusty" Ryan*), Donna Reed (*2nd Lt. Sandy Davyss*), Jack Holt (*Gen. Martin*), Ward Bond (*"Boots" Mulcahey*), Marshall Thompson (*Ens. Snake Gardner*), Paul Langton (*Ens. Andy Andrews*), Leon Ames (*Maj. James Morton*), Arthur Walsh (*Seaman Jones*), Donald Curtis (*Lt. J.G. "Shorty" Long*)

p, John Ford; d, John Ford, Robert Montgomery; w, Frank Wead (based on the book by William L. White); ph, Joseph August; ed, Frank E. Hull, Douglas Biggs; m, Herbert Stothart; art d, Cedric Gibbons, Malcolm Brown; fx, A. Arnold Gillespie

AAN Best Sound: Douglas Shearer (Sound); *AAN Best Visual Effects:* A. Arnold Gillespie, Donald Jahraus, R. A. MacDonald, Michael Steinore

In direct contrast to the flag-waving, jingoistic propaganda films typical of Hollywood during WWII, John Ford's THEY WERE EXPENDABLE is a somber and moving account of America's defeat in the Philippines early in the war. Filming this grim failure, Ford beautifully and poetically captures the heroism and bravery of the men and women who fought there—and does so without impassioned speechifying or gushing patriotism. Instead, Ford commemorates the quiet and uncomplaining devotion to duty, the will to serve, and the nobility of sacrifice of those left in an untenable situation. Based on the exploits of Lt. John Bulkeley, commander of Motor Torpedo Boat Squadron No. 3 (the predecessor of the Navy PT boat force), the film follows the coolly professional lieutenant (Robert Montgomery, in one of his best performances), renamed "Brickley" for the film, and his hot-headed executive officer, Lt. J.G. "Rusty" Ryan (John Wayne), as they struggle to get the Navy to accept the PT boats as a valuable new tool in the war effort. The top commanders, however, see no use for the unit and relegate Brickley and crew to running messages and ferrying supplies. As Bataan and Corregidor fall to the Japanese, however, the PT unit proves itself valuable by sinking many enemy ships, although the effort proves too little too late. Japan emerges triumphant and the American brass is forced to leave their troops stranded before the enemy and to flee to Australia, where they will regroup and plan their return.

From the time Ford shot THEY WERE EXPENDABLE to the day he died, the director was ambivalent about the film, his opinion of the work alternating between disapproval and satisfaction. This may have been largely due to the fact that he was pressured into making THEY WERE EXPENDABLE soon after having seen action himself in the South Pacific as a documentary filmmaker for the Navy. Capt. Ford had lost 13 men in his unit and the making of this film no doubt stirred painful memories for the director, memories he may have preferred to ignore when asked to discuss his films later in life. Despite Ford's ambivalence, THEY WERE EXPENDABLE is one of the greatest films to come out of WWII, a lasting and poignant tribute to those who go in harm's way.

THEY WON'T FORGET

1937 95m bw Drama ★★★★
Warner Bros. (U.S.) /A

Claude Rains (Andrew J. Griffin), Gloria Dickson (Sybil Hale), Edward Norris (Robert Paerry Hale), Otto Kruger (Michael Gleason), Allyn Joslyn (William P. Brock), Lana Turner (Mary Clay), Linda Perry (Imogene Mayfield), Elisha Cook Jr. (Joe Turner), Cy Kendall (Detective Laneart), Clinton Rosemond (Tump Redwine)

p, Mervyn LeRoy; d, Mervyn LeRoy; w, Robert Rossen, Aben Kandel (based on the novel Death in the Deep South by Ward Greene); ph, Arthur Edeson; ed, Thomas Richards; m, Adolph Deutsch; art d, Robert Haas

Aspiring secretary Turner takes a class in her southern hometown, learning dictation and touch-typing from young Norris, a recent arrival from the North. After class, Turner repairs to a local soda fountain (a scene that brings to mind the apocryphal tale of Turner's "discovery" in Schwab's drugstore), then heads back out into the street, where a Confederate Day parade is in progress. The camera tracks the sweatered Turner's progress, catching her figure from every angle, while a marching band plays the rebel anthem "Dixie" in the background. Returning to the deserted classroom to retrieve her misplaced vanity case—having earlier told Norris that she doesn't "feel dressed without [her] lipstick"—Turner hears the ominous sound of footsteps in the hallway. As her face, in closeup, contorts with fear, the film dissolves to a symbolic musket blast at the Confederate Day commemoration. Back at school, Rosmond, the black janitor, finds Turner's body and alerts authorities to the murder. District attorney Rains, who has long nursed political ambitions, decides to try to convict northern teacher Norris, rather than the most obvious suspect in the crime, Rosmond. "Anyone can convict a Negro in the South," says the ambitious Rains, who wants a better challenge than Rosmond might afford him.

Chiefly known now for introducing Turner to cinema audiences—she'd done bits before, but had never gotten billing—THEY WON'T FORGET (which followed close on the heels of Fritz Lang's famed lynch-mob film FURY) was touted by some critics as a true classic and cited by the National Board of Review as one of the ten best of 1937. The screenplay closely follows its source, Ward Greene's novel Death in the Deep South, which was in turn based on a true incident that occurred in Atlanta in 1915. Turner, though sixth-billed and featured only in the first few minutes of the film, nonetheless makes a vivid impression as the fresh-faced, blossoming adolescent victim. Director LeRoy's 75-foot tracking shot of Turner's sensual strut established in every viewer's mind the sex-related nature of her character's murder without in any way risking the wrath of the censors; if the character was violated, the Production Code was not.

THIEF

1981 122m c Crime ★★★½
UA (U.S.) R/X

James Caan (Frank), Tuesday Weld (Jessie), Willie Nelson (Okla), James Belushi (Barry), Robert Prosky (Leo), Tom Signorelli (Attaglia), Dennis Farina (Carl), Nick Nickeas (Nick), W.R. Brown (Mitch), Norm Tobin (Guido)

p, Jerry Bruckheimer, Ronnie Caan; d, Michael Mann; w, Michael Mann (based on the book The Home Invaders by Frank Hohimer); ph, Donald Thorin; ed, Dov Hoenig; m, Tangerine Dream; prod d, Mel Bourne; art d, Mary Dodson

Frank (James Caan) is a professional thief, one of the best in the business, who wants to make one last big score so he can settle down with his girlfriend Jessie (Tuesday Weld). That desire gets him involved with vicious big-time mobster Leo (Robert Prosky) and the robbery of a high-security vault in Los Angeles, aided by his friend Barry (Jim Belushi). This was the first feature film for director Michael Mann (MANHUNTER, TV's "Miami Vice"), and it was a stunner. Mann demonstrates an understanding of the casting, location, costumes, music (a superior score by Tangerine Dream), and visuals. The performances by Caan, Prosky, Belushi, and Weld are nothing less than terrific. Caan has his best role since THE GODFATHER, but Prosky (TV's "Hill Street Blues") nearly steals the film by underplaying the role of the powerful mob chieftain. This film is brutally realistic in its street language and violence, so sensitive viewers should be warned.

THIEF OF BAGHDAD, THE

1940 106m c Fantasy ★★★★★
London Films (U.K.) /U

Conrad Veidt (Jaffar), Sabu (Abu), June Duprez (Princess), John Justin (Ahmad), Rex Ingram (Djinni), Miles Malleson (Sultan), Morton Selten (King), Mary Morris (Halima), Bruce Winston (Merchant), Hay Petrie (Astrologer)

p, Alexander Korda; d, Ludwig Berger, Michael Powell, Tim Whelan, Zoltan Korda, William Cameron Menzies, Alexander Korda; w, Lajos Biro, Miles Malleson; ph, Georges Perinal, Osmond Borradaile; ed, William Hornbeck, Charles Crichton; m, Miklos Rozsa; prod d, Vincent Korda; fx, Lawrence Butler, Tom Howard, John Mills; cos, Oliver Messel, John Armstrong, Marcel Vertes

AA Best Cinematography: George Perinal; AAN Best Score: Miklos Rozsa; AA Best Art Direction: Vincent Korda; AA Best Visual Effects: Lawrence Butler, Jack Whitney

Perhaps the most splendid fantasy film ever made. Alexander Korda produced, Michael Powell and five others directed this breathtaking attempt to capture The Arabian Nights on film. An early example of outstanding Technicolor work, this became a cult favorite among young Hollywood directors of the 1970s such as Francis Coppola and George Lucas. The special effects, though quaint by today's standards, still deliver the goods. This lively collection of incidents from the Arabian Nights fables makes most modern fantasy blockbusters look anemic in comparison.

Abu (Sabu), a charming street urchin, is thrown into a Baghdad dungeon for thievery. Before long, Prince Ahmad (John Justin), the deposed ruler of the realm, joins him there. Ahmad has been overthrown by his righthand man, the evil grand vizier, Jaffar (Conrad Veidt). The unlikely duo manage to escape and flee to exotic Basra, where Ahmad is smitten by Basra's princess (June Duprez). Learning that Jaffar is about to abduct the beauty, Ahmad and Abu try to thwart the plan, but the wicked magician turns them into a blind beggar and a dog respectively. When the princess promises to wed Jaffar, he revokes his curse, and sails back to Baghdad with her. All seems lost until Abu—after a series of adventures involving a genie, an "All-Seeing Eye," and a magic carpet—finds a way to save the day.

Although six directors worked on the film, it remains surprisingly seamless as it maintains such a consistent grandeur and even pace. The marvelous set designs by Vincent Korda seem truly out of this world, and Miklos Rozsa has created a dynamic and memorable score. Conrad Veidt, looking cool and cruel in his dashing black outfits, is one of the screen's great villains. Sabu is simply adorable as the little thief of Baghdad. Duprez's unusual but stunning beauty is only enhanced by the rich Technicolor and the handsome Justin looks just right as the wan prince. African-American actor Rex Ingram is outstanding in the small but unforgettable role of the genie.

THIEVES LIKE US

1974 123m c Crime ★★★½
UA (U.S.) R/AA

Keith Carradine (Bowie), Shelley Duvall (Keechie), John Schuck (Chicamaw), Bert Remsen (T-Dub), Louise Fletcher (Mattie), Ann Latham (Lula), Tom Skerritt (Dee Mobley), Al Scott (Capt. Stammers), John Roper (Jasbo), Mary Waits (Noel)

p, Jerry Bick; d, Robert Altman; w, Calder Willingham, Joan Tewkesbury, Robert Altman (based on the novel by Edward Anderson); ph, Jean Boffety; ed, Lou Lombardo

A well-done remake of THEY LIVE BY NIGHT that's slightly long but unusually free of Altman's customary indulgences. A 1930s crime story with humor and humanity, THIEVES LIKE US owes more than a passing nod to BONNIE AND CLYDE and BADLANDS in theme and treatment. Young killer-crook Carradine escapes from a Mississippi jail with older, hard-bitten criminals Remsen and Schuck. After a brief respite, they return to the only way they know how to make a living: robbing banks.

Unlike BONNIE AND CLYDE, there is a real love story between Carradine and Duvall that comes across. The music and background sounds were supplied by John Dunning, who is credited for "radio research." He provided radio shows like "Gangbusters," "The Heart of Gold," remote band broadcasts, and an actual "Romeo and Juliet" dramatization that is heard while Duvall and Carradine are making love. Most of the killings are referred to rather than seen, so this is a character study more than a violence film. The executive producer was George Litto, who used to be Altman's agent and was making his bow in production. Litto was later responsible for a few of De Palma's debacles. Fletcher, wife of producer Bick, makes her film debut in this picture. Remsen, who is one of Altman's stock company, has another career as one of the most respected casting directors in Hollywood. Coscreenwriter Tewksbury makes a cameo.

THIN ICE

1937 78m bw Musical/Comedy/Romance ★★★
Fox (U.S.)

Sonja Henie (Lili Heiser), Tyrone Power (Prince Rudolph), Arthur Treacher (Nottingham), Raymond Walburn (Uncle Dornic), Joan Davis (Orchestra Leader), Alan Hale (Baron), Sig Rumann (Prime Minister), Melville Cooper (Krantz), Maurice Cass (Count), George Givot (Alex)

p, Raymond Griffith; d, Sidney Lanfield; w, Boris Ingster, Milton Sperling (based on the play "Der Komet" by Attila Obok); ph, Robert Planck, Edward Cronjager; ed, Robert Simpson; art d, Mark-Lee Kirk; chor, Harry Losee; cos, Royer

Smile, Sonja. Skate, Sonja. Just don't try to act. One of the most popular and best-remembered of the dozen ice musicals the three-time Olympic skater made in Hollywood in the late 1930s and early 40s, THIN ICE casts her as a skating instructor (surprise, surprise) who is romanced by a prince (Power) masquerading as a reporter. Having won the gold medal in ice skating in 1928, 1932 and 1936, the Norwegian Henie drove a hard bargain with 20th Century-Fox, who carefully built a series of bland but genial light entertainments around her. She does have a certain placid charm, her dimples are adorable (if you like that sort of thing) and, though her skating may seem less dazzling to an age used to triple toe loops and double axis, she's still pretty impressive on those blades. Her numbers are lavishly mounted and showcase her admirably, though she's got more competition on dry land opposite the impossibly gorgeous looks of a very young Power. Henie is also surrounded with plenty of contract second bananas, especially rubber-limbed, rubbed-faced Joan Davis. Thin ice, maybe, but reasonably sturdy entertainment, if you keep your expectations modest.

THIN MAN, THE

1934 93m bw Mystery/Comedy ★★★★½
MGM (U.S.) /A

William Powell (Nick Charles), Myrna Loy (Nora Charles), Maureen O'Sullivan (Dorothy Wynant), Nat Pendleton (Lt. John Guild), Minna Gombell (Mimi Wynant), Porter Hall (MacCauley), Henry Wadsworth (Tommy), William Henry (Gilbert Wynant), Harold Huber (Nunheim), Cesar Romero (Chris Jorgenson)

p, Hunt Stromberg; d, W.S. Van Dyke II; w, Albert Hackett, Frances Goodrich (based on the novel by Dashiell Hammett); ph, James Wong Howe; ed, Robert J. Kern; m, William Axt; art d, Cedric Gibbons, David Townsend, Edwin B. Willis; cos, Dolly Tree

AAN Best Picture; AAN Best Actor: William Powell; AAN Best Director: W.S. Van Dyke; AAN Best Adapted Screenplay: Frances Goodrich, Albert Heckett

Nick Charles (Powell) is a retired detective who has married the wealthy Nora (Loy) and now intends to devote himself to looking after her money and doing some serious drinking. (You can tell this film was made just after the repeal of Prohibition.) They travel to New York for the holidays, and there meet Dorothy (O'Sullivan), who asks Nick to help her find her missing father (Ellis). He's an inventor who months before went into seclusion to work on a project but hasn't been heard from since. Nick, whose reputation precedes him, isn't anxious to end his happy retirement, but Nora, eager for thrills, prods him into it. Together with their wire-haired terrier Asta, the newlyweds solve the case.

Praise should go to the writers of the film's delightful dialogue and to the underrated Van Dyke, a director of craft who knows how to make a film move. The story, meanwhile, faithfully taken from Hammett's novel, proves eminently serviceable if not quite the stuff of genius. What really makes THE THIN MAN an enduring classic, though, is the interplay between Powell and Loy, one of the greatest happily married couples ever to flicker on a screen. The repartee they shoot back and forth is priceless, as in one scene the morning after a gunman has broken into their suite and superficially wounded Nick before being subdued and hauled away. As they read the morning papers about the event, Powell says, "I'm a hero, I was shot twice in the Tribune." Loy: "I read you were shot five times in the tabloids." "It's not true. He didn't come anywhere near my tabloids," Powell parries. Loy has a terrific comic bit entering a scene loaded down with packages and dragged by their feisty pooch, and Powell has great fun shooting the balls off a Christmas tree with his favorite present, a gun. Loy and Powell proved so popular that they were teamed twelve more times during their careers (thirteen if you count her cameo in THE SENATOR WAS INDISCREET), six of the pairings coming in the THIN MAN series. These sleuthfests would continue with lessening success for 13 years, but at their peak (the first three films), Nick and Nora were one of the best movie buys around. Loy and Powell set a style for connubial comic banter which many performers still attempt in vain to duplicate today.

THING, THE

1951 87m bw Science Fiction ★★★★
Winchester (U.S.)

Kenneth Tobey (Capt. Pat Hendry), James Arness (The Thing), Margaret Sheridan (Nikki Nicholson), Robert Cornthwaite (Dr. Arthur Carrington), Douglas Spencer (Ned "Scotty" Scott), James Young (Lt. Ed Dykes), Dewey Martin (Bob), Robert Nichols (Lt. Ken Erickson), William Self (Sgt. Barnes), Eduard Franz (Dr. Stern)

p, Howard Hawks; d, Christian Nyby, Howard Hawks; w, Charles Lederer (based on the story "Who Goes There" by Don A. Stuart); ph, Russell Harlan; ed, Roland Gross; m, Dimitri Tiomkin; art d, Albert S. D'Agostino, John Hughes; fx, Don Steward, Linwood Dunn

Classic sci-fi chiller about a slimy alien presence (James Arness, who would later be Marshall Dillon on TV's "Gunsmoke") that invades an arctic station. THE THING is very much a film of its producer, Howard Hawks, although Christian Nyby, Hawks's editor on RED RIVER, was credited as director. Hawks's style, themes, and handling of actors arguably dominate the film.

Set in the subzero environment of the North Pole, the film follows an Air Force captain, Tobey, as he and his crew fly to Polar Expedition Six—a group of scientists led by Cornthwaite who are studying arctic conditions—to investigate reports that a flying craft of some sort has crashed into the ice. At the base camp Tobey finds an old flame, Sheridan, who is working as Cornthwaite's secretary. Sheridan is a tough woman in the Hawksian mold, and the romantic banter between her and Tobey is a joy to watch. When Tobey meets with Cornthwaite, he is shown pictures of the strange object as it streaked across the sky. A party is organized to investigate the crash site, and when they arrive they discover that the object has sunk into the ice and has been frozen.

The soldiers, scientists, and Spencer, a journalist, fan out to determine the shape of the object. When they all take their places at the edge of the object, they have formed a perfect circle.

The men decide to melt the ship out of the ice by detonating thermite bombs around it, but the plan goes awry and the ship is destroyed. Gravely disappointed, the men head back for their plane only to discover something else frozen in the ice—an alien. Using axes, they cut out a block of ice encasing the extraterrestrial corpse and bring it back to the base camp. While the soldiers and scientists debate over what to do with the creature, the ice melts and the eight-foot tall thing breaks free of its prison, very much alive—and not at all friendly.

THE THING was based rather loosely on a science-fiction story by John W. Campbell, Jr. (it was first published under his pseudonym, Don A. Stuart), in which the alien had the ability to change its shape at will, causing havoc among the soldiers who begin to suspect *each other* of harboring the monster. Lederer's screenplay (rumor has it that frequent Lederer-Hawks collaborator Ben Hecht had a hand in it as well) streamlines the narrative and allows Hawks to concentrate on the human interaction in the face of crisis. Whereas the original story (and Carpenter's remake) is a study of paranoia among comrades, Hawks's film revels in the interworkings of a tough group of professionals capable of handling any crisis if they stick together. The characters operate as an ensemble with no one being given much solo screen time. Their unity is what the film is about, a familiar Hawksian theme.

In a genre often dependent upon elaborate special effects, THE THING is relatively stark and restrained. The monster is only glimpsed in shadows and darkness, thus allowing the imagination of the audience fill in the terrifying details. Harlan's cinematography and Tiomkin's eerie early electronic score (he used a theremin) provide enough chills to satisfy any horror fan. No ray-guns, strange costumes, or futuristic inventions are needed here; even the spaceship is only suggested, never seen. The fact that the alien closely resembles a man heightens the sense of personal, human struggle that is the cornerstone of all good drama.

THING, THE

1982   108m   c   Science Fiction   ★★
Universal (U.S.)   R/18

Kurt Russell (MacReady), Wilford Brimley (Blair), T.K. Carter (Nauls), David Clennon (Palmer), Keith David (Childs), Richard Dysart (Dr. Copper), Charles Hallahan (Norris), Peter Maloney (Bennings), Richard Masur (Clark), Donald Moffat (Garry)

p, David Foster, Lawrence Turman; d, John Carpenter; w, Bill Lancaster (based on the story "Who Goes There?" by John W. Campbell, Jr.); ph, Dean Cundey; ed, Todd Ramsay; m, Ennio Morricone; prod d, John J. Lloyd; art d, Henry Larrecq; fx, Roy Arbogast, Albert Whitlock, Leroy Routly, Rob Bottin, Michael Clifford

A major disappointment. Horror director John Carpenter let the special effects run amok in this remake of the 1951 science-fiction classic THE THING, and they ooze over everything in the film. The plot is pared down to the essentials: a group of American scientists in the Antarctic find the frozen remains of an alien, which they soon thaw out. The only problem is that the alien is not dead, and it springs back to life, taking on whatever form suits its purpose (dogs, men, etc.). The cast is superb, but unfortunately the actors are not allowed to show their stuff because their characters are nothing more than fodder for the effects, and their performances are limited to standing around grimacing at the gore. Kurt Russell once again sleepwalks through his role (as he did in ESCAPE FROM NEW YORK), and the ending of the film is unsatisfying and ambiguous. The effects are absolutely fantastic, complicated, and grotesque, but this remake ultimately fails because it is more an exercise in technique than an essay in human terror.

THINGS CHANGE

1988   105m   c   Comedy/Crime   ★★★½
Filmhaus (U.S.)   PG

Don Ameche (Gino), Joe Mantegna (Jerry), Robert Prosky (Joseph Vincent), J.J. Johnston (Frankie), Ricky Jay (Mr. Silver), Mike Nussbaum (Mr. Greene), Jack Wallace (Repair Shop Owner), Dan Conway (Butler), Willo Hausman (Miss Bates), Gail Silver (Housemaid)

p, Michael Hausman; d, David Mamet; w, David Mamet, Shel Silverstein; ph, Juan Ruiz-Anchia; ed, Trudy Ship; m, Alaric Jans; prod d, Michael Merritt; cos, Nan Cibula

THINGS CHANGE is a surprisingly light, upbeat follow-up to David Mamet's dark directorial debut, HOUSE OF GAMES. One of the most powerful Mafia dons in the country, Mr. Greene (Mike Nussbaum), has murdered someone. An elderly Sicilian bootblack, Gino (Don Ameche), who bears more than a passing resemblance to the don, agrees to take the fall and is turned over to the custody of Jerry (Joe Mantegna), a mob goon who is "on probation." Jerry feels sorry for the old guy and impulsively decides to take him to Lake Tahoe before a final fling before jail. Because of Jerry's reticence, the staff of the mob-owned hotel treats the mysterious old man as if he were an important Mafia don. After some suspenseful moments, Jerry takes Gino back to Chicago to find things have changed in an unexpected way.

In an era in which most American comedies rely on big gags, blunt jokes, or elaborate slapstick for laughs, Mamet has taken audience expectations and played upon them brilliantly, without ever delivering the anticipated payoff. Much of the charm of THINGS CHANGE lies in the characters. Mamet's dialogue is crisp, the wit dry, and there are plenty of great lines in the film, most of which are delivered flawlessly.

THINGS TO COME

1936   113m   bw   Science Fiction   ★★★★
London Films (U.K.)   /PG

Raymond Massey (John Cabal/Oswald Cabal), Edward Chapman (Pippa Passworthy/Raymond Passworthy), Ralph Richardson (The Boss), Margaretta Scott (Roxana/Rowena), Cedric Hardwicke (Theotocopulos), Maurice Braddell (Dr. Harding), Sophie Stewart (Mrs. Cabal), Derrick de Marney (Richard Gordon), Ann Todd (Mary Gordon), Pearl Argyle (Catherine Cabal)

p, Alexander Korda; d, William Cameron Menzies; w, H.G. Wells, Lajos Biro (based on the book The Shape of Things to Come by H.G. Wells); ph, Georges Perinal; ed, Charles Crichton, Francis D. Lyon; m, Arthur Bliss; prod d, Vincent Korda; fx, Ned Mann, Lawrence Butler, Edward Cohen, Harry Zech, Wally Vaevers, Ross Jacklin; cos, John Armstrong, Rene Hubert, Marchioness of Queensbury

Not since Fritz Lang's METROPOLIS had there been a science fiction film of such epic scope and vision as Alexander Korda's production of H.G. Wells's 1933 treatise on the future, The Shape of Things to Come. Set in an urban metropolis known as Everytown, the film charts the course of a chilling future in which war, disease, and totalitarianism nearly destroy mankind.

THINGS TO COME is best remembered for its prescient depiction of massive aerial bombing, which was to change the face of war (and urban England) within three years of its release. Eager to have Wells's participation in the project, producer Korda approached the great author and offered him the chance to write the screenplay. Two years and four drafts later, with considerable help from Korda, writer Lajos Biro, and director William Menzies, the script was completed. Wells was allowed to wander around the set during production influencing every detail of the film from the costumes and set design to the blocking of the actors. Everything about THINGS TO COME, its strengths and its considerable weaknesses, may be directly attributed to Wells. While the epic scope of the film and its vision of the future are impressive, the human element is sorely lacking. The dialogue is very stilted and uninteresting: there is little interaction among characters and everyone makes speeches. It is a tribute to Massey's skill as an actor that the speeches play as well as they do.

Though the film fails as a human drama, it succeeds impressively in the scenes of devastation and reconstruction—a purely visual experience. Korda's brother Vincent was in charge of the production design and he plundered every new concept in architecture, industry, and design for the Everytown of 2036. Famed Hungarian futurist Laszlo Moholy-Nagy was hired to contribute his vision, but his designs were scrapped as too impractical. Wells, of course, had final approval on everything, but eventually he grew frustrated with the filmmaking process and admitted he knew little about making movies. Menzies, one of the most influential art directors in the history of motion pictures, was the perfect choice to direct the film (though Lewis Milestone was signed on at one time). Though his skill in directing actors was negligible, Menzies possessed a true feel for design and knew how to photograph it. At Wells' insistence, Arthur Bliss was brought in before production started to compose the score based on the script and Wells' suggestions. (The author felt that the music should be incorporated into the filmmaking process from the beginning, instead of after the filming was completed.) The resulting music was thus wholly integrated with the visuals. Bliss's work on the film proved so popular with the critics and the public that his music for THINGS TO COME was the first movie score to be recorded commercially and sold in record stores. When it was all over, Korda had spent over $1.5 million on THINGS TO COME, an incredible sum for the time. The film failed to ignite the box office, but it eventually made money. The original release in Britain ran 130 minutes, but the running time was cut for the US. (There are several different versions of the film now in distribution, running the gamut from 96 min. to 130 min.) Despite its flaws, THINGS TO COME is a truly epic work which continues to fascinate.

THIRD MAN, THE

1949 104m bw Thriller ★★★★★
London Films (U.K.) /PG

Joseph Cotten *(Holly Martins)*, Orson Welles *(Harry Lime)*, Alida Valli *(Anna Schmidt)*, Trevor Howard *(Maj. Calloway)*, Paul Hoerbiger *(Porter)*, Ernst Deutsch *(Baron Kurtz)*, Erich Ponto *(Dr. Winkel)*, Siegfried Breuer *(Popescu)*, Bernard Lee *(Sgt. Paine)*, Geoffrey Keen *(British Policeman)*

p, David O. Selznick, Alexander Korda, Carol Reed; d, Carol Reed; w, Graham Greene; ph, Robert Krasker; ed, Oswald Hafenrichter; m, Anton Karas; prod d, Vincent Korda, Joseph Bato, John Hawkesworth

AAN Best Director: Carol Reed; AA Best Cinematography: Robert Krasker; AAN Best Editing: Oswald Hafenrichter

A gripping, beautifully structured picture and a *tour de force* from British director Carol Reed. American pulp novelist Holly Martins (Cotten) arrives in bleak postwar Vienna, having been promised a job by old friend Harry Lime (Welles). Holly soon is informed that his dear friend Harry is dead, killed in an accident and, in fact, his body is about to be lowered into a grave. He attends the funeral, where he meets the beautiful Anna (Valli), Lime's one-time love. Inquiring of British officer Calloway (Howard) about Lime, Holly learns that his friend was a racketeer. Holly vows to carry out his own investigation into Lime's background and clear him of the crimes Calloway insists he committed. What results makes for a powerful examination of friendship and loyalty in the face of social obligations.

There's so much to recommend THE THIRD MAN that one can only scratch the surface in mentioning its strengths. It gives the incredibly intoxicating feel of being a happy accident, and yet the ingredients are all there. Anton Karas's amazing zither music will haunt you for the rest of your life, and yet you will never mind. The camerawork of genius Krasker (Britain's greatest at that time) makes marvelous use of realistic city locales, darkly menacing alleys and inventively canted framings. The dozens of references to Harry Lime really prime us for his delayed appearance, and Orson Welles's enigmatic performance is so electric that one is not disappointed. (That entrance, in fact, remains one of cinema's greatest.) Cotten, meanwhile, gives a tangy yet subtle spin to the concept of the Ugly American abroad, and Howard lends both sympathy and edge to the determined police inspector. Valli, an intense and gifted Italian star, gives a poignant performance as well. Reed's direction has perhaps never been better, from the thrilling chase through the sewers to the accusations of the little boy to the quieter romantic moments, and Graham Greene's script is both adult and suspenseful. It's hard to choose just one scene to sum up this poetic thriller, but the legendary scene on the ferris wheel may best represent its perfect blend of great writing, acting, and directing. The fadeout, too, is unforgettable.

—30—
1959 96m bw Drama ★★★
Mark VII (U.S.)

Jack Webb *(Sam Gatlin)*, William Conrad *(Jim Bathgate)*, David Nelson *(Earl Collins)*, Whitney Blake *(Peggy Gatlin)*, Louise Lorimer *(Bernice Valentine)*, James Bell *(Ben Quinn)*, Nancy Valentine *(Jan Price)*, Joe Flynn *(Hy Shapiro)*, Richard Bakalyan *(Carl Thompson)*, Dick Whittinghill *(Fred Kendall)*

p, Jack Webb; d, Jack Webb; w, William Bowers; ph, Edward Colman; ed, Robert M. Leeds; m, Ray Heindorf; art d, Feild M. Gray, Gibson Holley

Interesting feature directed by and starring Webb as the managing editor of a newspaper working the late shift on a more or less typical Thursday night. Conrad is the crusty city editor, Lorimer, the dowager rewrite-woman who has seen it all and remained above it, and Nelson, the much put-upon copy boy. The film starts as Webb arrives in the city room late after his regular visit to the graves of his first wife and child. He is having trouble with his new wife, who wants to adopt a child, something Webb just can't bring himself to do. As the night goes on, two news items come into prominence: the first concerns a little girl who wanders into the city's storm drains and becomes lost as a storm begins to fill the sewers; the second is the story of an attempt by Air Force pilots, Lorimer's grandson among them, to set a new record flying from Hawaii to Washington, DC. The whole office holds its breath as the search for the girl continues while the waters rise, and as the planes disappear. Eventually the girl is found and the story is the headline, but the plane story is less happy, for the planes are discovered to have crashed with no survivors. Lorimer is visibly distressed and Webb tells her to go home, but she insists on writing up the story of her grandson's death before going. Webb comes to some conclusions about life and death during the evening's events and tells his wife that he no longer opposes adopting a child. Well-done newspaper story has the usual faults of Webb's films—dialogue staccato to the point of silliness and a directorial style serviceable at best, but it works here, especially in the later scenes as the staff gets down to the real work of getting the paper out. Conrad is very good as the city editor and Lorimer gives a convincing performance as a woman whose job is more important than her emotions. An accurate and memorable newspaper film.

39 STEPS, THE

1935 85m bw Spy ★★★★★
Gaumont (U.K.) /U

Madeleine Carroll *(Pamela)*, Robert Donat *(Richard Hannay)*, Lucie Mannheim *(Miss Smith/Annabella)*, Godfrey Tearle *(Prof. Jordan)*, Peggy Ashcroft *(Margaret)*, John Laurie *(John)*, Helen Haye *(Mrs. Jordan)*, Wylie Watson *(Mr. Memory)*, Frank Cellier *(Sheriff Watson)*, Peggy Simpson *(Young Maid)*

p, Michael Balcon, Ivor Montagu; d, Alfred Hitchcock; w, Charles Bennett, Alma Reville, Ian Hay (based on the novel by John Buchan); ph, Bernard Knowles; ed, Derek Twist; m, Louis Levy; prod d, Otto Wendorff, Albert Jullion; fx, Jack Whitehead; cos, Joe Strassner

Along with THE LADY VANISHES, one of Hitchcock's best British films, and a prototype for so much of what would follow in his American career. For those who love a grand spy mystery, a wild chase, and a harrowing portrait of an innocent man struggling to prove his innocence while the world turns inexplicably against him, THE 39 STEPS is ideal. Richard Hannay (Donat) is on vacation in London when he meets a mysterious woman (Mannheim) who tells him of a spy ring which she is trying to crack. She doesn't know the identity of the masterspy, but does know that he is missing a portion of the little finger on his right hand. She also cryptically mentions something about "The 39 Steps." Later she is murdered—before Hannay can learn anything more. His own life now in danger, Hannay flees to a town in Scotland which she has circled on a map, and sets out to find the man with the disfigured finger. Along the way he meets Pamela (Carroll), who decides to assist him after the crooks handcuff her to him. An encounter with a memory expert proves to be the key to uncracking this corker.

This is one of the best films of its genre and it richly displays Hitchcock's complete and playful mastery of the language of filmmaking. The handcuffing sequence (which still influences films today, e.g., the remake of D.O.A.) is one of the cinema's greatest. Hitch also has great fun with the sound bridge linking a screaming woman with a train whistle, and the final assassination attempt recalls THE BIRTH OF A NATION. Carroll makes for an appealing heroine and Donat brings his oddly wispy quality to the man on the run. He looks curiously androgynous in this film; the oh-so-trim mustache and his lilting voice add a vulnerability to his character which distinguishes it from the run-of-the-mill hero. Tearle is splendid, as is Watson in his most famous role, but who we really like are Peggy Ashcroft and John Laurie. This gifted stage actress and this striking, reliable actor of many films lend something intense to the married couple Hannay encounters while on the run. Ashcroft is extremely moving as a woman strangled in her marriage and home life, desperately grateful for whatever the strange Hannay may bring into it. Scenes such as this linger in the memory as long as the more typically Hitchcockian setpieces, and it does credit to the master director's versatility. (It somehow seems more his style that he actually handcuffed Carroll and Donat on the set one day to get them used to their scenes together. . . he of course then vanished from the set!)

THIRTY SECONDS OVER TOKYO

1944 138m bw War ★★★★
MGM (U.S.) /A

Spencer Tracy (Lt. Col. James H. Doolittle), Van Johnson (Capt. Ted W. Lawson), Robert Walker (David Thatcher), Phyllis Thaxter (Ellen Jones Lawson), Tim Murdock (Dean Davenport), Scott McKay (Davey Jones), Gordon McDonald (Bob Clever), Don DeFore (Charles McClure), Robert Mitchum (Bob Gray), John R. Reilly (Shorty Manch)

p, Sam Zimbalist; d, Mervyn LeRoy; w, Dalton Trumbo (based on the book by Capt. Ted W. Lawson, Robert Considine); ph, Harold Rosson, Robert Surtees; ed, Frank Sullivan; m, Herbert Stothart; art d, Cedric Gibbons, Paul Groesse; fx, A. Arnold Gillespie, Warren Newcombe, Donald Jahraus

AAN Best Cinematography: Robert Surtees, Harold Rosson; AA Best Visual Effects: A. Arnold Gillespie, Donald Jahraus, Warren Newcombe, Douglas Shearer

In 1942, 131 days after the Japanese bombing of Pearl Harbor, an American force retaliated, bombing the major Japanese cities of Tokyo and Yokohama. This picture, a quasi-documentary re-creation of that event, was authored by one of the survivors of the raid, Ted Lawson (played here by Van Johnson). Since land bases near the target are unavailable—and in-flight refueling techniques undeveloped—a dangerous, untried tactic must be employed for the top-secret mission: for the first time in history, twin-engine bombers are to take off from the deck of an aircraft carrier. Because the planes are too large to land on a carrier deck, after the attack they must continue on to mainland China—occupied by the Japanese—and then make their way to Allied-held territory as best they can. Weeks of preparation and training take place before the aircraft and their crews are finally loaded aboard the USS Hornet. Following a final shipboard briefing by mission leader Lt. Col. Jimmmy Doolittle (Spencer Tracy), the fliers man their twin-engine Mitchell bombers and are catapulted from the flight deck. The remainder of the film follows the adventures of Lawson's crew only. A well-made war film, THIRTY SECONDS OVER TOKYO was sufficiently accurate to prompt all the real-life principals to approve the use of their names in the picture. Screenwriter Dalton Trumbo wisely elected not to attempt to alter the limited perspective of Lawson's memoir by including more of the details of the famous raid. In the actual event, all 16 participating bombers made it to China, although three men died in crashes and eleven others were captured by the Japanese, who executed three of them. Although top-billed, Tracy's appearance here is basically a cameo, with Johnson the real star of the film.

THIRTY-TWO SHORT FILMS ABOUT GLENN GOULD

1993 94m c Biography ★★★
Max Film (Canada) /U

Colm Feore (Glenn Gould), Derek Keurvorst (Gould's Father), Katya Lada (Gould's Mother), Devon Anderson (Glenn Age—3), Joshua Greenblatt (Glenn Age—8), Sean Ryan (Glenn Age—13), Kate Hennig (Chambermaid), Sean Doyle (Porter), Sharon Bernbaum (Female Guide), Don McKellar (Concert Promoter)

p, Niv Fichman; d, Francois Girard; w, Francois Girard, Don McKellar; ph, Alain Dostie; ed, Gaetan Huot; m, Johann Sebastian Bach, Richard Wagner, Ludwig Von Beethoven, Glenn Gould, Richard Strauss, Tony Hatch, Jean Sibelius, Sergei Prokofiev, Alexander Scriabin, Paul Hindemith, Arnold Schoenberg; art d, John Rubino; cos, Linda Muir

The title of this offbeat Canadian feature, which echoes Beethoven's "Thirty Two Variations in C Minor" (one of which is heard in the film), reflects the style and structure employed by director Francois Girard in his treatment of the reclusive concert pianist and recording artist Glenn Gould (Colm Feore). Between intertitles borrowed from the lexicon of classical music (the Prelude, the Fugue, the Theme and Variations), Girard weaves together a series of impressions, interviews, and dramatizations in an attempt to find cinematic correlatives for musical forms. The result is less a biopic than a meditation on creativity, isolation, and the nature of communication in a technological age.

After his retirement from the concert stage, Gould became a cult figure in classical music, with all that that implies; his work is still subjected to probing critical analysis, revisionist interpretations, and not a few vitriolic attacks. It is probably impossible to separate Gould's personal history from the continuing reassessment of his performing career, and Girard and co-writer Don McKellar nimbly sidestep the pitfalls of critical debate by narrowing their focus to specific moments and impressions. Without attempting a sweeping, comprehensive summation of Gould-the-man or Gould-the-performer, Girard and McKellar still manage to suggest greater depths of artistry and personality than the conventions of traditional film biography might allow.

THIS BOY'S LIFE

1993 115m c Drama ★★★½
Knickerbocker Films (U.S.) R/15

Robert De Niro (Dwight), Ellen Barkin (Caroline), Leonardo DiCaprio (Toby), Jonah Blechman (Arthur Gayle), Eliza Dushku (Pearl), Chris Cooper (Roy), Carla Gugino (Norma), Zack Ansley (Skipper), Tracey Ellis (Kathy), Kathy Kinney (Marian)

p, Art Linson; d, Michael Caton-Jones; w, Robert Getchell (from the autobiography by Tobias Wolff); ph, David Watkin; ed, Jim Clark; m, Carter Burwell; prod d, Stephen J. Lineweaver; art d, Sandy Cochrane; fx, Nick Lawson, Mike Vezina; cos, Richard Hornung

Based on Tobias Wolff's brilliant memoir of the same title, THIS BOY'S LIFE is a well-acted film about an extremely painful adolescence. In capturing the compelling battle between a boy and his abusive stepfather, director Michael Caton-Jones cannily avoids obvious sentimentality, opting to let a rather brutal story tell itself.

1957. Angel-faced but troubled Toby "Jack" Wolff (Leonardo DiCaprio) and his brassy blonde mom, Caroline (Ellen Barkin), hit the road in search of a better life. Caroline is wooed by Dwight (Robert De Niro), an auto mechanic who lives far away in Concrete, Washington with his three kids, and marries him to give Toby a stable family life. Neither is happy: Dwight is a sadistic disciplinarian whose abuse Toby suffers for the sake of his mother, while Caroline endures a loveless marriage for the sake of her son. The conflict between Dwight and Toby escalates frighteningly, and the two are soon locked in a brutal battle of wills.

Screenwriter Robert Getchell's adaptation often simplifies its source, but for the most part he and Caton-Jones remain faithful to Wolff's remarkable story. Young DiCaprio makes a very strong impression in his first leading role, delineating the many moods of adolescence with ease. Robert De Niro often seems forced in comparison; in fact, his savage portrayal stands as the movie's main blemish. Still, this is powerful and moving stuff.

THIS GUN FOR HIRE

1942 80m bw Crime/Spy ★★★★½
Paramount (U.S.) /15

Veronica Lake (Ellen Graham), Robert Preston (Michael Crane), Laird Cregar (Willard Gates), Alan Ladd (Philip Raven), Tully Marshall (Alvin Brewster), Mikhail Rasumny (Slukey), Marc Lawrence (Tommy), Pamela Blake (Annie), Harry Shannon (Steve Finnerty), Frank Ferguson (Albert Baker)

p, Richard Blumenthal; d, Frank Tuttle; w, Albert Maltz, W.R. Burnett (based on the novel *A Gun for Sale* by Graham Greene); ph, John Seitz; ed, Archie Marshek; m, David Buttolph; art d, Hans Dreier

Outstanding *film noir*, based on Graham Greene's novel *A Gun For Sale*, which presents one of the most disturbed (and disturbing) killers ever to cross the screen. Ladd is scary because he doesn't care; he is simply a killing machine hired out by whoever will pay. Only when Lake takes the time to break through the emotional fortress that he has built around himself does Ladd show any signs of humanity.

This is the film that made Alan Ladd a star. Although director Tuttle had originally intended to cast Preston in the lead role, he later decided to hunt for an unknown. When Tuttle was introduced to Ladd, the director was convinced that the 28-year-old blonde could make the cold-blooded killer Phillip Raven a sympathetic character. Contracted at $300 per week, Ladd underwent screen tests, and even had his hair dyed black in keeping with his character's name. Though the film was conceived as a Lake-Preston vehicle, it soon became quite apparent that the studio had something in Ladd, and the script was reworked during production to favor the actor. The film became, in more ways than one, the Alan Ladd story—with all the attention being paid to him and his role. As a result, the film's romantic angle was soon tossed away and Preston reduced to a plot device. But even though Ladd and Lake did not so much as exchange a kiss, they still became one of Hollywood's hottest and most bankable love teams, with three more pictures following—THE GLASS KEY; THE BLUE DAHLIA; and SAIGON.

THIS GUN FOR HIRE was originally to have begun with a dream in which a young Raven (played by Dickie Jones) is seen murdering his aunt and guardian (Hermine Sterler) after she attacks him and injures his wrist. This rather morbid beginning was omitted, however, and the film begins, instead, with Ladd awaking from the dream. THIS GUN FOR HIRE was remade in 1957 as the James Cagney-directed SHORT CUT TO HELL.

THIS HAPPY BREED

1944 110m c Drama   ★★★★
Two Cities (U.K.)   /A

Robert Newton *(Frank Gibbons)*, Celia Johnson *(Ethel Gibbons)*, John Mills *(Billy Mitchell)*, Kay Walsh *(Queenie Gibbons)*, Stanley Holloway *(Bob Mitchell)*, Amy Veness *(Mrs. Flint)*, Alison Leggatt *(Aunt Sylvia)*, Eileen Erskine *(Vi)*, John Blythe *(Reg)*, Guy Verney *(Sam Ledbetter)*

p, Noel Coward, Anthony Havelock-Allan; d, David Lean; w, David Lean, Ronald Neame, Anthony Havelock-Allan (based on the play by Noel Coward); ph, Ronald Neame; ed, Jack Harris; m, Noel Coward, Muir Mathieson; art d, C.P. Norman

Based on Noel Coward's hit play (in which he also starred), this cavalcade of British life between wars was one of the top moneymakers in the UK in 1944, but it took three more years to reach US screens. Laurence Olivier narrates the episodic story of a family that lives in a small row house, totally indistinguishable from all the other houses surrounding it. This average working-class family includes father Newton, mother Johnson, and their two children, Walsh (who just happened to be married to director Lean at the time) and Blythe. WWI is ending and Newton, who has served four years in the army, is coming home to take Johnson and the children away from the home they've occupied with Johnson's mother, Veness, and her sister, Leggart. The whole group moves into a larger residence in Clapham and looks forward to a happy life. But life isn't always pleasant for Leggart and Veness, who battle constantly. To get out of the house and away from Veness' sharp tongue, Leggart, a spinster, volunteers for just about every committee and charity group around. Meanwhile, the children continue to grow and become increasingly independent, watched over by Newton (in an understated performance that is a departure from his usual scene-stealing tactics). When a general strike occurs, Blythe is right in the middle of it, coming home one evening with bruises and cuts sustained in a riot. Hoping to better her lot, Walsh takes a job in a fashionable beauty salon in London's posh West End. She's been dating Mills, the sailor son of Holloway, who lives next door, and it is just assumed that they will eventually wed. At the same time, Blythe is engaged to Betty Fleetwood. The applecart is overturned when Walsh runs off with a married man, and the family is crushed. Blythe and Fleetwood are

married, but tragedy strikes when both are killed in an auto crash and the news is given to the family in one of the most memorable scenes in British cinema.

Coward and Lean codirected IN WHICH WE SERVE, and the great actor-playwright was impressed enough by Lean's work to hand the director the film rights for this film as well as for "Brief Encounter" and "Blithe Spirit." Here Lean is partnered with cinematographer Neame (who later became a producer and director) and writer Havelock-Allan. In 1944, there were almost no color cameras in England, but somehow they managed to find one of them for this film, although the color is muted and not nearly as stark as the process used in the US at the time. Still, this is an immensely charming movie, with many tears and many moments of warmth. Newton is excellent, and Johnson, who could look glamorous when the part called for it, is deliberately dressed dowdily and de-glamorized for her role here, she which performs with great aplomb.

THIS IS SPINAL TAP

1984 82m c Comedy   ★★★½
Spinal Tap (U.S.)   R/15

Rob Reiner *(Marty DiBergi)*, Michael McKean *(David St. Hubbins)*, Christopher Guest *(Nigel Tufnel)*, Harry Shearer *(Derek Smalls)*, R.J. Parnell *(Mick Shrimpton)*, David Kaff *(Viv Savage)*, Tony Hendra *(Ian Faith)*, Bruno Kirby *(Tommy Pischedda)*, Kimberly Stringer, Chazz Dominguez

p, Karen Murphy; d, Rob Reiner; w, Christopher Guest, Michael McKean, Harry Shearer, Rob Reiner; ph, Peter Smokler; ed, Kent Beyda, Kim Secrist, Robert Leighton; m, Christopher Guest, Michael McKean, Harry Shearer, Rob Reiner; prod d, Bryan Jones; cos, Renee Johnston

Hilarious pseudo-documentary spoof of a British rock group that was so on-target in its satire, many viewers took it for the real thing.

Spinal Tap is an aging British heavy metal band who are limping their way across the US while Marty DiBergi (Reiner) makes a "rockumentary" film about them. (Reiner is a Yank who has been following the group since they burst onto the scene 17 years before. Now that they're fading, he decides to tell their story rather than make some commercials for Wheat Thins.) Every disaster that can befall a rock group happens to Nigel Tufnel (Guest), David St. Hubbins (McKean), and Derek Smalls (Shearer). Management woes, promotional difficulties, nonexistent hotel accommodations, phony business people, props that don't work, and an album that hasn't yet been distributed in the stores, all add up to major problems.

The American cast make pretty convincing English rockers, and the album-of-the-film, "The Best of Spinal Tap," became a hit in Japan. In 1992, the group became the stuff of pop-culture legend, releasing a follow-up album, "Break Like the Wind," completing a national tour of the US, and even appearing in animated form on hit Fox TV show "The Simpsons."

THIS IS THE ARMY

1943 120m c Musical/War   ★★★
Warner Bros. (U.S.)   /U

Irving Berlin *(Himself)*, George Murphy *(Jerry Jones)*, Joan Leslie *(Eileen Dibble)*, George Tobias *(Maxie Stoloff)*, Alan Hale *(Sgt. McGee)*, Charles Butterworth *(Eddie Dibble)*, Rosemary DeCamp *(Ethel)*, Dolores Costello *(Mrs. Davidson)*, Una Merkel *(Rose Dibble)*, Stanley Ridges *(Maj. Davidson)*

p, Jack L. Warner, Hal B. Wallis; d, Michael Curtiz; w, Casey Robinson, Claude Binyon (based on the play by Irving Berlin); ph, Bert Glennon, Sol Polito; ed, George Amy; art d, John Keonig, John Hughes; fx, Jack Cosgrove; chor, LeRoy Prinz, Robert Sidney; cos, Orry-Kelly

AA Best Score: Ray Heindorf; AAN Best Art Direction: John Hughes, Lieutenant John Koenig, George James Hopkins; AAN Best Sound: Nathan Levinson

This star-studded musical salute to the American soldier is filled with Irving Berlin's songs and morale-boosting patriotism. Taken from Berlin's stage play, which opened July 4, 1942, THIS IS THE ARMY also adapts portions of Berlin's earlier musical "Yip Yip Yaphank." Jerry Jones (George Murphy) is a big-time Broadway star who, at the beginning of WWI, is drafted into the service and given the job of putting on a big show. He does his bit and, when the show ends, cast and crew go off to fight in Europe. Years pass and Jerry is now a producer with a son, Johnny (Ronald Reagan, who joined Murphy in rising through California politics), who is drafted in WWII and given the same job as his father. Johnny writes a terrific show *and* marries sweetheart Eileen Dibble (Joan Leslie). The show tours the country and at the final performance, before the boys go to war, Irving Berlin (as himself) comes onstage in Washington to sing. The plot is just barely enough to hang the musical numbers on, but it's the tunes that count. Berlin used his clout to get the Army to lend him more than 300 soldiers for the stage show, promising to donate more than a million dollars from the show's receipts to a relief fund for the families the boys left behind.

THIS LAND IS MINE

| 1943 | 103m | bw | War | ★★★½ |
| RKO | (U.S.) | | | /A |

Charles Laughton (*Arthur Lory*), Maureen O'Hara (*Louise Martin*), George Sanders (*George Lambert*), Walter Slezak (*Maj. Erich von Keller*), Kent Smith (*Paul Martin*), Una O'Connor (*Mrs. Emma Lory*), Philip Merivale (*Prof. Sorel*), Thurston Hall (*Mayor Henry Manville*), George Coulouris (*Prosecuting Attorney*), Nancy Gates (*Julie Grant*)

p, Jean Renoir, Dudley Nichols; d, Jean Renoir; w, Dudley Nichols; ph, Frank Redman; ed, Frederic Knudtson; m, Lothar Perl; prod d, Eugene Lourie; art d, Albert S. D'Agostino, Walter E. Keller; fx, Vernon L. Walker; cos, Renie

AA Best Sound: Stephen Dunn

Set "somewhere in Europe" (clearly Jean Renoir's French homeland), THIS LAND IS MINE stars Charles Laughton as a cowardly schoolteacher, Arthur Lory, who whimpers during air raids and can only be comforted by his overly possessive mother (Una O'Connor). Arthur chooses to keep a low profile and go about his business unnoticed until his mentor, Prof. Sorel (Philip Merivale), lights a patriotic spark in him. Aware of his cowardice, he turns to fellow schoolteacher Louise Martin (Maureen O'Hara), who is sympathetic both to his fears and to the cause of the Resistance, of which her brother Paul (Kent Smith) is an active member who throws bombs at German officers. As much as he tries to remain neutral, Arthur finds himself increasingly sympathetic to the Resistance movement.

Although some consider THIS LAND IS MINE preachy and overly talky, it must be praised for its understanding of humanity. Instead of painting the Germans as mighty evildoers and the French as innocent victims, Renoir took a more daring and honest approach, implicating the French as being partly responsible for the Occupation, when many citizens collaborated with the Nazis to ensure that they would remain immune from punishment and that their orderly lives would not be shattered by the invaders. Renoir avoided propagandistic cliches and took into consideration human nature; human nature, however, is not what people look for in war heroes and patriotic messages. Although long considered a propaganda film, THIS LAND IS MINE is more correctly seen as anti-propagandistic. There is no black and white, no good or evil. There is only grey, and, in that grey area, an understanding of the frailty of human nature.

THIS MAN MUST DIE
(QUE LA BETE MEURE)

| 1970 | 115m | c | Thriller | ★★★★ |
| Boetie/Rizzoli | (France/Italy) | | | GP/A |

Michel Duchaussoy (*Charles Thenier*), Caroline Cellier (*Helene Lanson*), Jean Yanne (*Paul Decourt*), Anouk Ferjac (*Jeanne*), Marc Di Napoli (*Philippe Decourt*), Maurice Pialat (*Police Inspector*), Guy Marly (*Jacques Ferrand*), Lorraine Rainer (*Anna Ferrand*), Stephane Di Napoli (*Michel Thenier*), Louise Chevalier (*Mme. Levenes*)

p, Andre Genoves; d, Claude Chabrol; w, Claude Chabrol, Paul Gegauff (based on the novel *The Beast Must Die* by Nicholas Blake); ph, Jean Rabier; ed, Jacques Gaillard; m, Pierre Jansen; art d, Guy Littaye

One of Chabrol's best films. When Duchaussoy's son is killed by a hit-and-run driver, the quiet author of children's books can think only of revenge. He begins a search for the killer, recording each step he

takes in a diary. First, he meets a farmer who tells him that on the day of the accident he saw a damaged sports car in which TV personality Cellier was a passenger. Duchaussoy travels to Paris and meets Cellier. Soon the two are having an affair, and the writer learns that Cellier's brother-in-law (Yanne) runs an auto repair shop. Immediately, Yanne becomes Duchaussoy's prime suspect. Eventually Duchaussoy grows close to Yanne's son (Marc Di Napoli), who tells the writer that he plans to kill his father. Duchaussoy then takes Yanne out on a sailboat to drown him. However, Yanne pulls a pistol on the vengeful writer, saying that he's read Duchaussoy's diary. Duchaussoy leaves Paris with Cellier, but the plot twists don't end there. Another of the quietly handled but solidly engrossing melodramas Chabrol was making at the time, and well worth the effort.

THIS SPORTING LIFE

| 1963 | 129m | bw | Sports | ★★★★ |
| Independent Artists | (U.K.) | | | /15 |

Richard Harris (*Frank Machin*), Rachel Roberts (*Mrs. Hammond*), Alan Badel (*Weaver*), William Hartnell (*Johnson*), Colin Blakely (*Maurice Braithwaite*), Vanda Godsell (*Mrs. Weaver*), Arthur Lowe (*Slomer*), Anne Cunningham (*Judith*), Jack Watson (*Len Miller*), Harry Markham (*Wade*)

p, Karel Reisz; d, Lindsay Anderson; w, David Storey (based on the novel by Storey); ph, Denys Coop; ed, Peter Taylor; m, Roberto Gerhard; art d, Alan Withy; cos, Sophie Devine

AAN Best Actor: Richard Harris; *AAN Best Actress:* Rachel Roberts

From its virtuoso opening shot of a rugby scrum—from the bottom, looking up—to its final emotionally draining moments, THIS SPORTING LIFE is a captivating, visceral film experience. Not only is Lindsay Anderson's (IF; O LUCKY MAN!) first feature film one of the most poignant sports-centered movies ever made, it is also a landmark in the history of British cinema, an "Angry Young Man" classic. Adapted by David Storey (who played professional rugby at one time) from his own novel, the film follows the fortunes of Frank Machin (Richard Harris), a loutish former Yorkshire coal miner who bashes his way to local celebrity as a professional rugby player. Although pursued by a number of women, Frank starves for the love of his landlady, Mrs. Hammond (Rachel Roberts), a bitter, passionless widow, who eventually has a physical relationship with Frank but refuses to give herself to him emotionally. Meanwhile, Frank remains the darling of the rugby club's management and supporters, and as long as he performs on the field, his sullen rebelliousness is tolerated. In time, Mrs. Hammond grows tired of Frank's callousness, they fight terribly, and he moves out. Realizing how much he needs her love, Frank tries to patch things up, but tragedy awaits his attempt at reconciliation. Finally, Frank is left only with the violent world of rugby, in which he is only as good as his last game. THIS SPORTING LIFE is both a biting indictment of class-based exploitation (the club owners treat the players as mindless beasts) and a tragic story of love that founders on suppressed feelings and unconscious macho insensitivity. Harris gives an extraordinary, gut-wrenching performance reminiscent of young Marlon Brando, and Roberts brings considerable complexity to her exceptional portrayal of a woman whose emotional life is as dormant as Frank's is frustrated. The game action is hard-hitting and well captured, and cinematographer Denys Coop's gritty, detailed black and white is in the best tradition of British kitchen-sink realism.

THOMAS CROWN AFFAIR, THE

| 1968 | 102m | c | Crime | ★★★ |
| Mirisch/Simkoe/Solar | (U.S.) | | | R/PG |

Steve McQueen (*Thomas Crown*), Faye Dunaway (*Vicky Anderson*), Paul Burke (*Eddy Malone*), Jack Weston (*Erwin Weaver*), Biff McGuire (*Sandy*), Yaphet Kotto (*Carl*), Todd Martin (*Benjy*), Sam Melville (*Dave*), Addison Powell (*Abe*), Sidney Armus (*Arnie*)

p, Norman Jewison; d, Norman Jewison; w, Alan R. Trustman; ph, Haskell Wexler; ed, Hal Ashby, Ralph E. Winters, Byron Brandt; m, Michel Legrand; art d, Robert Boyle; fx, Pablo Ferro Films; cos, Ron Postal, Theadora Van Runkle, Alan Levine

AAN Best Score: Michel Legrand; *AA Best Song:* Michel Legrand, Alan Bergman, Marilyn Bergman

A very expensive caper picture that drowns in its own artiness, using multi-images, cinematic tricks, and other pretentious film gimmicks—all of which detract from the story. Set and partially filmed in Boston, it's the tale of a self-made millionaire, McQueen, who decides that he has been a member of the Establishment long enough. With the help of aides who never actually meet him, McQueen arranges a brilliant bank robbery that nets millions. McQueen pays off his assistants (most notable is Weston) and banks the remainder, almost $3 million, in Switzerland. The bank's insurance company pays off the loss, then assigns its number one investigator, Dunaway, to the case. She is working in league with police officer Burke, and, through a totally unbelievable gut instinct, she picks McQueen as the most likely suspect (audiences groaned at this jump of logic). Dunaway moves in on McQueen, and the two recognize each other as the enemy. In an artsy sequence, Jewison sends his camera around the two (the way it was done in A MAN AND A WOMAN) as they fall in love after a chess game that parodies the eating sequence in TOM JONES. Dunaway is completely ga-ga over McQueen and thinks she can get him off without a prison sentence if he gives back the money. The chances of that are slim to none, and McQueen wants to see if she really loves him or is using her body as part of her investigation. McQueen says he's about to pull off another caper and wants her to meet him in a local cemetery after the job's done. She shows up there with Burke, and the money is in a garbage can. McQueen's Rolls-Royce arrives, and she thinks it's him. But no—further double-cross ensues.

Split-screen techniques, which were all the rage after having been seen to great advantage at the 1964 World's Fair, are used time and again. The Bergman song "The Windmills of Your Mind," written with Legrand, won an Oscar, and Legrand was nominated for his music. The supervising film editor was Hal Ashby, who also was associate producer. Walter Hill (who later became a writer-director) was one of the assistant directors and, thankfully, picked up none of Jewison's bad ideas. Trustman was a practicing attorney when he wrote the script; he has since written several more films. McQueen is charming, reads his lines well, and shows that he isn't just another short actor with an interesting face. Watching the film today, one can sense the era in which it was filmed, as many other movies of that period made the mistake of placing technique over characterization.

THOSE MAGNIFICENT MEN IN THEIR FLYING MACHINES; OR HOW I FLEW FROM LONDON TO PARIS IN 25 HOURS AND 11 MINUTES

1965 133m c Comedy ★★★½
Fox (U.K.) G/U

Stuart Whitman (Orvil Newton), Sarah Miles (Patricia Rawnsley), James Fox (Richard Mays), Alberto Sordi (Count Emilio Ponticelli), Robert Morley (Lord Rawnsley), Gert Frobe (Col. Manfred von Holstein), Jean-Pierre Cassel (Pierre Dubois), Eric Sykes (Courtney), Terry-Thomas (Sir Percival Ware-Armitage), Irina Demick (Brigitte/Ingrid/Marlene/Francoise/Yvette/Betty)

p, Stan Margulies; d, Ken Annakin; w, Jack Davies, Ken Annakin; ph, Christopher Challis; ed, Gordon Stone, Anne V. Coates; m, Ron Goodwin; prod d, Tom Morahan; art d, Jim Morahan; fx, Richard Parker, Ron Ballanger; cos, Osbert Lancaster, Dinah Greet; anim, Ralph Ayres

AAN Best Original Screenplay: Jack Davies, Ken Annakin

This rip-roaring comedy takes place in 1910, when English press bigwig Lord Rawnsley (Robert Morley) sets out to prove that Great Britain is No. 1 in the air. Putting up 10,000 pounds as a prize, he invites the world's best pilots to compete in an air race from London to Paris. All sorts of dandy planes arrive, but Rawnsley roots for his daughter's (Sarah Miles's) fiance, Richard Mays (James Fox), a Royal Navy lieutenant. Other contenders include an Italian count (Alberto Sordi); a fanatical Prussian who will die before he lets anyone else win (Gert Frobe); a Frenchman (Jean-Pierre Cassel) followed by a sextet of women (all played by Irina Demick); a villainous Brit (Terry-Thomas); an inscrutable Japanese (Yujiro Ishihara); and American barnstormer Orvil Newton (Stuart Whitman), who decides that Rawnsley's daughter is the woman for him. After a series of slapstick mishaps, the competitors are winnowed until only the Italian and the two romantic rivals remain. Heroism and fair play are the order of the day in the big finish,

but it's up to Rawnsley's daughter to decide which of the competitors has won her heart. Good, clean fun, with fast and furious action, good cinematography, crisp dialogue, wonderful planes, and a host of some of the funniest people in movies in the cast.

THOUSAND CLOWNS, A

1965 117m bw Comedy/Drama ★★★★
UA (U.S.)

Jason Robards Jr. (Murray Burns), Barbara Harris (Sandra), Martin Balsam (Arnold Burns), Barry Gordon (Nick), Gene Saks (Leo), William Daniels (Albert)

p, Fred Coe; d, Fred Coe; w, Herb Gardner (based on his play); ph, Arthur J. Ornitz; ed, Ralph Rosenblum; m, Don Walker; cos, Ruth Morley

AAN Best Picture; AA Best Supporting Actor: Martin Balsam; AAN Best Adapted Screenplay: Herb Gardner; AAN Best Score: Don Walker

This warm and wonderful comedy-drama is a paean to non-conformity. Robards is an out-of-work writer who quit his last job writing a kiddie TV show called "Chuckles the Chipmunk" when he could no longer stand the stupidity. Unemployed for five months, he needs cash to help support his nephew, Gordon, a bright 12-year-old whom his sister dropped off one afternoon seven years ago, then vanished. Gordon is illegitimate and, after living with Robards this long, more like a son than a nephew. The relationship between them is warm, loving, and respectful. Robards has never legally adopted Gordon, so a social worker, Harris, comes by to see if she can straighten out the situation. With her is Daniels, a prissy man who is a by-the-book social worker. Unless Robards can prove that he has a real job, they are going to have to take Gordon out of the ratty apartment and give him a foster home. Of course, Harris and Robards become romantically involved. Harris now has a personal stake in keeping the family together but can she and Gordon persuade Robards to return to the daily grind of a regular job? Will he willingly become one of the "thousand clowns" one sees running for the morning bus?

Touching and often funny, A THOUSAND CLOWNS offers superb performances by everyone, especially the young Gordon who read lines like a seasoned pro. Saks, who is also a well-known stage and film director, is sensational as the grotesque "Chuckles", a portrayal that is actually more memorable than Balsam's as Robard's brother, the agent, who won the Best Supporting Actor Oscar for his role.

THOUSAND EYES OF DR. MABUSE, THE
(DIE TAUSEND AUGEN DES DR. MABUSE)

1960 103m bw Crime/Science Fiction ★★★½
CCC/CEI Incom Criterion (France/Italy/West Germany) /A

Dawn Addams (Marion Menil), Peter Van Eyck (Henry B. Travers), Gert Frobe (Comm. Krauss), Wolfgang Preiss (Jordan/Cornelius), Werner Peters (Hieronymous P. Mistelzweig), Andrea Checchi (Insp. Berg), Rene Kolldehoff (The Clubfoot), Howard Vernon ("No. 12"), Jean-Jacques Delbo (Deiner the Servant), Christiane Maybach (Pretty Blonde)

p, Fritz Lang; d, Fritz Lang; w, Fritz Lang, Heinz Oskar Wuttig (based on an idea by Jan Fethke, from a character created by Norbert Jacques); ph, Karl Lob; ed, Walter Wischniewsky, Walter Wischniewsky; m, Bert Grund, Gerhard Becker; art d, Erich Kettelhut, Johannes Ott; cos, Ina Stein

Noted German director Lang returned to his native land to make his last film, a fine, low-budget sequel to his prewar films dealing with the notorious Dr. Mabuse, DR. MABUSE DER SPIELER (1922) and THE TESTAMENT OF DR. MABUSE (made in 1932, but not released in the US until 1943). Lang had fled Germany after Hitler, impressed with Lang's METROPOLIS, offered him a position as the official Nazi filmmaker. (Lang expected the offer to be a trap and feared the Nazis would learn of his mother's Jewish background.) Lang went to France, where he directed one film. In 1934, in London, he was signed by producer David O. Selznick to a one-picture deal with MGM. He sailed to the US and became a citizen in 1935. Taking his inspiration from an actual Nazi blueprint on how to bug a hotel, Lang fashioned this story about a series of strange murders in Berlin's fictional Hotel Luxor.

Authorities come to believe the man behind the crimes may be someone who believes he is a reincarnation of the evil Dr. Mabuse. Van Eyck is an American millionaire who saves Addams from killing herself at the Luxor, and the two become involved in the investigation. Frobe (later of GOLDFINGER) is the police commissioner who thinks that either Preiss or Peters is the killer. Preiss is a supposedly blind clairvoyant, and Peters is an insurance salesman. Lang fills his eerie tale with a tightly controlled *mise-en-scene*, a world of hidden cameras, two-way mirrors, and mistaken impressions. This film, which was dubbed into English for American release, is pure cinema, using camera angle, shot composition, and lighting to achieve an overwhelming power that stays long after the final reel goes through the projector. Five sequels followed in the wake of this film's enormous popularity: THE RETURN OF DR. MABUSE (1961); SCOTLAND YARD HUNTS DR. MABUSE (1963); DR. MABUSE'S RAYS OF DEATH (1964); THE INVISIBLE DR. MABUSE (1965) and THE TERROR OF DR. MABUSE (1965).

THOUSANDS CHEER

1943 126m c Musical   ★★★½
MGM (U.S.)   /U

Kathryn Grayson *(Kathryn Jones)*, Gene Kelly *(Eddie Marsh)*, Mary Astor *(Hyllary Jones)*, Jose Iturbi *(Himself)*, John Boles *(Col. Jones)*, Richard Simmons *(Capt. Avery)*, Ben Blue *(Chuck)*, Frank Jenks *(Sgt. Koslack)*, Frank Sully *(Alan)*, Wally Cassell *(Jack)*

p, Joe Pasternak; d, George Sidney; w, Paul Jarrico, Richard Collins (based on the story "Private Miss Jones"by Jarrico, Collins); ph, George Folsey; ed, George Boemler; m, Herbert Stothart; art d, Cedric Gibbons, Daniel B. Cathcart; cos, Irene

AAN Best Cinematography: George Folsey; *AAN Best Score:* Herbert Stothart; *AAN Best Art Direction:* Cedric Gibbons, Daniel B. Cathcart, Edwin B. Willis, Jacques Mersereau

The Louis B. Mayer axiom that MGM had "more stars than there are in heaven" was proven true by this flag-waving wartime extravaganza. Promising opera singer Kathryn Jones (Kathryn Grayson) puts her career on hold to keep house for her Army colonel father (John Boles) after he and his wife (Mary Astor) separate. Kathryn's life becomes further complicated by the arrival of Pvt. Eddie Marsh (Gene Kelly), a former circus trapeze artist who doesn't much like the Army way of life but who wants to transfer to the Air Corps and realizes that by winning over Kathryn he may be able to wangle the transfer he's after from her father. Along the way, of course, he discovers that he really loves Kathryn, her parents go to great lengths to keep the two apart, and Eddie puts himself on the line to demonstrate his love for her.

Despite the rather perfunctory storyline, much of the film is taken up with the star-studded show that Kathryn organizes, featuring not only Eddie's trapeze act but a raft of MGM stars, including Eleanor Powell, Frank Morgan, Lucille Ball, Marsha Hunt, Red Skelton, Anne Sothern, and John Conte. The whole affair is emceed by Mickey Rooney, who does a very funny impression of Clark Gable (who was unable to appear in the film because he was in the service) and Lionel Barrymore from TEST PILOT. Filled with great comedy bits, boasting loud but nostalgically fun color and first-rate production values, THOUSANDS CHEER is two hours plus of solid entertainment.

THREE BROTHERS

1980 113m c Drama   ★★★½
Iter Film/Artificial Eye/Gaumont (Italy)   PG/A

Philippe Noiret *(Raffaele Giuranna)*, Charles Vanel *(Donato Giuranna)*, Michele Placido *(Nicola Giuranna)*, Vittorio Mezzogiorno *(Rocco Giuranna/Young Donato)*, Andrea Ferreol *(Raffaele's Wife)*, Maddalena Crippa *(Giovanna)*, Sara Tafuri *(Rosaria)*, Marta Zoffoli *(Marta)*, Tino Schipinzi *(Raffaele's Friend)*, Simonetta Stefanelli *(Young Donato's Wife)*

p, Giorgio Nocella, Antonio Macri; d, Francesco Rosi; w, Francesco Rosi (based on the story, "The Third Son," by A. Platonov); ph, Pasqualino De Santis; ed, Ruggero Mastroianni; m, Piero Piccioni; art d, Andrea Crisanti

AAN Best Foreign Language Film

Directed by Francesco Rosi, whose films have long explored Italy's complex sociopolitical milieu, THREE BROTHERS delivers a symbolic state-of-the-society message. Three brothers, each representing a significant segment of the Italian body politic, return to the village of their youth to attend their mother's funeral. Raffaele (Philippe Noiret) is a Roman judge presiding over the trial of a terrorist whose life is consequently in constant danger; Rocco (Vittorio Mezzogiorno) is a self-sacrificing teacher; and Nicola (Michele Placido) is a factory worker and organizer. None of the brothers is as happy or at peace with the world as is their father (Charles Vanel), who has lived his life simply and close to the land. Though the talk periodically becomes a little ponderous, Rosi's *mise-en-scene* speaks volumes about the fragmented lives of his characters and an Italy on the brink of social disintegration.

THREE CABALLEROS, THE

1944 70m c Animated/Musical   ★★★★
Walt Disney Productions (U.S.)   G/U

VOICES OF: Jose Olivera *(Joe Carioca)*, Joaquin Garay *(Panchito)*, Fred Shields, Sterling Holloway, Frank Graham, Aurora Miranda, Carmen Molina, Dora Luz, Nestor Amarale, Almirante

p, Norman Ferguson; d, Norman Ferguson, Clyde Geronimi, Jack Kinney, Bill Roberts, Harold Young; w, Homer Brightman, Ernest Terrazzas, Ted Sears, Bill Peet, Ralph Wright, Elmer Plummer, Roy Williams, William Cottrell, Del Connell, James Bodrero; ph, Ray Rennahan; ed, John Haliday; art d, Richard Irvine; chor, Billy Daniels, Aloysio Oliveira, Carmelita Maracci; anim, Ward Kimball, Eric Larson, Fred Moore, John Lounsbery, Les Clark, Milt Kahl, Hal King, Franklin Thomas, Harvey Toombs, Bob Carlson, John Sibley, Bill Justice, Oliver M. Johnston Jr., Milt Neil, Marvin Woodward, John Patterson

AAN Best Score: Edward Plumb, Paul J. Smith, Charles Wolcott; *AAN Best Sound:* C.O. Slyfield

A smashing follow-up to SALUDOS AMIGOS, this is one of the most dazzling achievements of the cartoon genre. Donald Duck opens presents on his birthday, the first of which is a movie projector. He puts film on the projector and we are plunged into the tale of Pablo the Penguin, who is sick and tired of the Antarctic cold and wants to live in the tropics, and a story about a little Mexican boy who finds a donkey with wings. Donald's next present is a large book. The moment he opens it, up pops Joe Carioca (from SALUDOS AMIGOS), then we're off on one of the fastest-moving cartoon sequences ever devised, as the two travel to Brazil, where Donald meets and falls in love with Aurora Miranda (in a huge production number that's as elaborate as anything Busby Berkeley ever choreographed). A breakneck trip around Mexico follows, during which Donald, Joe, and Panchito the rooster cavort with beautiful women and dance with animated plants (as well as with Carmen Molina, who does her trademark "Jesusita" number). THREE CABALLEROS also includes the famous sequence in which Donald gets into the soundtrack, represented by a moving line. So much more happens on-screen that no synopsis of this fast and funny picture will begin to do it justice. A must for all ages.

THREE CAME HOME

1950 106m bw War   ★★★★
Fox (U.S.)   /A

Claudette Colbert *(Agnes Keith)*, Patric Knowles *(Harry Keith)*, Florence Desmond *(Betty Sommers)*, Sessue Hayakawa *(Col. Suga)*, Sylvia Andrew *(Henrietta)*, Mark Keuning *(George)*, Phyllis Morris *(Sister Rose)*, Howard Chuman *(Lt. Nekata)*, Drue Mallory, Virginia Keiley

p, Nunnally Johnson; d, Jean Negulesco; w, Nunnally Johnson (based on a book by Agnes Newton Keith); ph, Milton Krasner; ed, Dorothy Spencer; m, Hugo Friedhofer; art d, Lyle Wheeler, Leland Fuller

A powerful and moving picture that examines life in a Japanese POW camp from a woman's point of view. Colbert plays American writer Agnes Newton Keith, who is married to British administrator Knowles. They live in the East Indian islands and, shortly after the outbreak of WWII, are arrested along with other noncombatants, then imprisoned in a concentration camp. They are given paltry food rations, as well as beatings and other humiliations. Colbert refuses to lose her spirit and, at one point, risks punishment to spend a few minutes with her husband. Hayakawa is the US-educated Japanese colonel who runs the camp, a man torn between obedience to orders and the dictates of his conscience. The prisoners, including children, fight to maintain a semblance of dignity, hoping to survive until the GIs arrive. Based on Keith's autobiography, this film ably develops the intricate relationships among its characters. Colbert is stunning in the lead; Hayakawa, a former silent-film actor, creates a character of high intensity and internal struggle. A fine film in all departments.

THREE COINS IN THE FOUNTAIN

1954 101m c Romance   ★★★
Fox (U.S.)   /U

Clifton Webb (*Shadwell*), Dorothy McGuire (*Miss Francis*), Jean Peters (*Anita*), Louis Jourdan (*Prince Dino Di Cessi*), Maggie McNamara (*Maria*), Rossano Brazzi (*Georgio*), Howard St. John (*Burgoyne*), Kathryn Givney (*Mrs. Burgoyne*), Cathleen Nesbitt (*Principessa*), Vincent Padula (*Dr. Martinelli*)

p, Sol C. Siegel; d, Jean Negulesco; w, John Patrick (based on the novel by John H. Secondari); ph, Milton Krasner; ed, William Reynolds; m, Victor Young; art d, Lyle Wheeler, John De Cuir; cos, Dorothy Jeakins

AAN Best Picture; AA Best Cinematography: Milton Krasner; *AA Best Song:* Jule Styne (Music), Sammy Cahn (Lyrics)

This pleasant boy-meets-girl story (times three) is more distinguished for its photography and title song than for its predictable plot. This was the first CinemaScope picture ever made on location, and Rome and Venice never looked better. Peters, McGuire, and McNamara are a trio of American women living in Rome in a posh apartment. A legend states that if you throw a coin into the Fountain of Trevi and you want to come back to the Eternal City, your wish will be granted. McNamara had come to work as a secretary and meets Italian prince Jourdan, whose mother, Nesbitt, is watching out that some gold digger doesn't snap him up. McNamara is naive but also sharp in some ways and eventually captures Jourdan as her own. McGuire is a quiet older woman who works as the secretary to Webb, an American writer who prefers living in Rome. She finally convinces Webb that she should be his life's companion and the final scene between the two, as she goes wading in the Trevi Fountain, is a lovely moment. Peters is a high-powered executive who has had it with the board rooms and now wants to find a simpler existence. She falls for Brazzi—a wolf who haunts the Via Veneto—and by the time the movie is over, he's donned sheep's clothing, for real. That's about it for the story. There are the customary romantic complications, but the conclusion is as easy to spot as an elephant at a mouse picnic. There are a few sexy (for the time) lines of dialogue but a general feeling of traditional romance sweetens the tales. The same director, Negulesco, handled another movie about a trio of women on the make, HOW TO MARRY A MILLIONAIRE. It was later remade, sort of, as THE PLEASURE SEEKERS with Negulesco again directing.

THREE COMRADES

1938 100m bw Drama   ★★★★
MGM (U.S.)   /A

Robert Taylor (*Erich Lohkamp*), Margaret Sullavan (*Pat Hollmann*), Franchot Tone (*Otto Koster*), Robert Young (*Gottfried Lenz*), Guy Kibbee (*Alfons*), Lionel Atwill (*Franz Breuer*), Henry Hull (*Dr. Heinrich Becker*), George Zucco (*Dr. Plauten*), Charley Grapewin (*Local Doctor*), Monty Woolley (*Dr. Jaffe*)

p, Joseph L. Mankiewicz; d, Frank Borzage; w, F. Scott Fitzgerald, Edward E. Paramore (based on the novel by Erich Maria Remarque); ph, Joseph Ruttenberg; ed, Frank Sullivan; m, Franz Waxman; art d, Cedric Gibbons, Paul Groesse

AAN Best Actress: Margaret Sullavan

Erich Maria Remarque's international best-seller was brought to the screen here with a stellar cast and a script cowritten by F. Scott Fitzgerald. The scene is post-WWI Germany, a time and place of want and astronomical inflation, where Deutschmarks are borne to the marketplace in wheelbarrows to be exchanged for a beefsteak. Three

returning German soldiers—Taylor, Tone, and Young—are among the many war-weary, now homeless, hopeless young men who travel from the trenches of France to their war-ravaged homeland. Prewar friends, the three reunite and decide to try their luck in the republic-to-be's emerging automobile market, pooling their meager resources to set up a repair shop. Working with bits and pieces of salvaged wrecks, they put together a car of their own—which they affectionately dub "Heinrich"—and scramble for business in the intensely competitive field. Motoring on a highway, the three engage in an informal race with the owner of a shiny new automobile, Atwill. Victorious, they stop to eat at an inn and are joined by the vanquished Atwill. Saying, "You wiped me off the map!" Atwill admires their scrap-heap amalgam and introduces them to his driving companion, the lovely Sullavan. The travelers dine together, and Taylor persuades Sullavan to give him her telephone number. He renews the acquaintance the following day, visiting her in the elegant apartment in which Atwill has established the beauty, a child of wealth now reduced to poverty. Sullavan ultimately joins the trio of comrades, but is reluctant to marry Taylor because she suffers from tuberculosis. Eventually, she is persuaded by Taylor's two friends to live what remains of her life to the fullest, and she and Taylor wed amidst the ominous setting of an unstable, pre-Hitler Germany. Young is killed in a street riot; Sullavan, refusing further treatment for her malady, hastens her own demise. As the film ends, Tone and Taylor—joined by the spirits of their late companions (in double exposure)—face a most uncertain future.

Sullavan is superb in this bleak drama, her throaty voice and striking looks at their very best. (She was to gain an Oscar nomination for her role and was named the year's best actress by the New York Film Critics Association.) The actress was a bit difficult during filming, however. According to a long-standing superstition, she refused to work until a rainfall occurred, and she also protested that some of coscripter Fitzgerald's dialogue was unspeakable. Producer Mankiewicz agreed with his star and, with the help of other studio writers, rewrote and excised much of the script, to Fitzgerald's great disgruntlement and later vilification of Mankiewicz. In fact, Mankiewicz was himself a talented screenwriter and understood far better than the proud novelist the basic elements of a good visual presentation. (Other scenes were edited out for less obvious reasons, among them several that concerned the rise of Naziism. Objections were raised by the Breen Office—the industry's self-censorship group—and the film was also cut as a result of studio chief Louis B. Mayer's reluctance to offend the Germans and lose the export market.) Although he continued to write screenplays, and was even signed by the studio at the enormously high salary (for the time) of $1,250 weekly, this was to be Fitzgerald's only *credited* sceenwriting assignment. Sullavan's leading man, Taylor, is unconvincing in his role, which he had not wanted to play. Cinemogul Mayer had to persuade the actor that the part would lend him prestige and help to erase the pretty-boy image he had developed over the course of his career. The picture is well directed by romance-drama specialist Borzage, but overlong, and only partly redeemed by Sullavan's splendid performance.

THREE CROWNS OF THE SAILOR
(LES TROIS COURONNES DU MATELOT)

1983 117m c/bw Fantasy   ★★★
L'Institut de l'Audiovisuel/Antenne 2 (France)   /15

Jean-Bernard Guillard (*The Sailor*), Philippe Deplanche (*The Student*), Jean Badin (*The Officer*), Nadege Clair (*Maria*), Lisa Lyon (*Mathilde*), Claude Derepp (*The Captain*), Frank Oger (*The Blindman*), Raoul Guillet, Hugo Santiago (*Voices*), Jose De Carvalho

p, Jean Lefaux, Maya Feuiette, Jose-Luis Vasconselos; d, Raul Ruiz; w, Raul Ruiz, Emilio de Solar, Francois Ede; ph, Sacha Vierny; ed, Janine Verneau, Valeria Sarmiento, Jacqueline Simoni-Adamus, Pascale Sueur; m, Jorge Arriagada

A strongly praised work of surrealism from expatriate Chilean director Ruiz—living and working in France since 1973—about a story-telling sailor, Guillard, who catches a student murdering his tutor. He proceeds to regale the lad with tales of his bizarre adventures in South American ports visiting the seedy opium dens and frequenting the brothels. It's not what happens in THREE CROWNS OF THE SAILOR but how it happens. Following the tradition of surrealism set in the 1920s, Ruiz directs this film with no basis in logic or reality—dreamy locations are filled with macabre individuals speaking mystical nonsense. As difficult as it is to pin down, THREE CROWNS OF THE SAILOR is thoroughly enjoyable just as long as you don't try to understand it.

THREE DAYS OF THE CONDOR

1975 117m c Thriller   ★★★½
Wildwood/Paramount (U.S.)   R/AA

Robert Redford *(Joe Turner)*, Faye Dunaway *(Kathy Hale)*, Cliff Robertson *(Higgins)*, Max von Sydow *(Joubert)*, John Houseman *(Mr. Wabash)*, Addison Powell *(Atwood)*, Walter McGinn *(Sam Barber)*, Tina Chen *(Janice)*, Michael Kane *(Wicks)*, Don McHenry *(Dr. Lappe)*
p, Stanley Schneider; d, Sydney Pollack; w, Lorenzo Semple Jr., David Rayfiel (based on the novel *Six Days of the Condor* by James Grady); ph, Owen Roizman; ed, Fredric Steinkamp, Don Guidice; m, Dave Grusin; prod d, Stephen Grimes; art d, Gene Rudolf; fx, Augie Lohman; cos, Joseph G. Aulisi

AAN Best Editing: Fredric Steinkamp, Don Guidice

Redford is the bookish and bespectacled reader for the Literary Historical Society, but the organization actually serves as a CIA front located in a brownstone in Manhattan. One day he goes out to get lunch for the others (it's his turn), and while he's picking up the food, killers armed with automatic weapons enter the building and massacre everyone there. Redford returns with lunch and finds all his coworkers murdered. Fearing that he may be next, he goes to a phone booth and calls headquarters, identifying himself by his code name, "Condor." He is told to meet an agent at a nearby hotel, but when the fellow CIA man tries to kill him, Redford realizes its own organization is responsible for the slaughter. Determined to survive and to blow the whistle on the CIA, Redford kidnaps woman photographer Dunaway and forces her to help him. Based on James Grady's novel *Six Days of the Condor* (the film compresses the time frame of the novel), this taut espionage thriller gained greater plausibility during its shooting when a sudden raft of sensational post-Watergate news items began coming out of Washington regarding illegal wiretaps, surveillance, and killings motivated by political expediency. What was once merely a fanciful exploitation on the corrupt inner workings of covert organizations. The public ate it up and the film was a hit at the box office.

THREE FACES OF EVE, THE

1957 91m bw Drama   ★★★
Fox (U.S.)

Joanne Woodward *(Eve)*, David Wayne *(Ralph White)*, Lee J. Cobb *(Dr. Luther)*, Edwin Jerome *(Dr. Day)*, Alena Murray *(Secretary)*, Nancy Kulp *(Mrs. Black)*, Douglas Spencer *(Mr. Black)*, Terry Ann Ross *(Bonnie)*, Ken Scott *(Earl)*, Mimi Gibson *(Eve)*
p, Nunnally Johnson; d, Nunnally Johnson; w, Nunnally Johnson (based on a book by Corbett H. Thigpen, M.D., and Hervey M. Cleckley, M.D.); ph, Stanley Cortez; ed, Marjorie Fowler; m, Robert Emmett Dolan; art d, Lyle Wheeler, Herman A. Blumenthal; cos, Renie

AA Best Actress: Joanne Woodward

Joanne Woodward's showy but nonetheless highly impressive performance in the tile role required her to play three roles with enough separation in the characterizations to make the audience believe she was a woman with a trio of personalities bubbling inside her. Woodward is married to Wayne, an insensitive clod. She is emotionally disturbed, has headaches, and forgets things, so she decides she needs the professional help of a psychiatrist, although Wayne thinks she's faking it. At first, Cobb, the doctor, gives her the usual advice: get more rest, try to calm down, etc. Woodward goes home to Wayne and her daughter, Ross, but her mental woes continue. She returns to Cobb's office later, but instead of being an unsure housewife, she is suddenly a loose woman with an attitude of total irresponsibility. She denies being the mother of Ross and lives for hedonistic pleasure. Wayne is rapidly getting disgusted with Woodward, but Cobb is intrigued when one of Woodward's personality switches occurs while she's in his presence. Eventually, a third person emerges. This one is a well-balanced woman who speaks in a different pattern. Whereas the first two talk in southern

dialect, this one sounds as though she went to Cornell and graduated *summa cum laude*. Cobb uses hypnotic techniques on Woodward and is able to conjure up each "face" by merely suggesting that she step forward. The next step is to try to merge the three faces of Eve.

It's an interesting psychological tale that is not without humor, much of which is supplied by the witty narration of Alistair Cooke. The movie is based on a true story, documented by the psychiatrists who treated the woman in real life, but the ultimate solution as represented is both too simplistic and underexplained. The film is basically a two-character piece featuring Woodward and Cobb and probably would have made a very good play. Cinematically, it's lacking on several levels. Wayne, a marvelous actor, was apparently directed to play his role for laughs in order to take the edge off Woodward's dramatics. The mixture of styles works against the ultimate outcome.

THREE GODFATHERS, THE

1948 106m c Western   ★★★★
Argosy (U.S.)   /A

John Wayne *(Robert Marmaduke Hightower)*, Pedro Armendariz *(Pedro "Pete" Roca Fuerte)*, Harry Carey Jr. *(William Kearney, "The Abilene Kid")*, Ward Bond *(Perley "Buck" Sweet)*, Mildred Natwick *(The Mother)*, Charles Halton *(Mr. Latham)*, Jane Darwell *(Miss Florie)*, Mae Marsh *(Mrs. Perley Sweet)*, Guy Kibbee *(Judge)*, Dorothy Ford *(Ruby Latham)*
p, John Ford, Merian C. Cooper; d, John Ford; w, Laurence Stallings, Frank S. Nugent (based on the story by Peter B. Kyne); ph, Winton C. Hoch; ed, Jack Murray; m, Richard Hageman; art d, James Basevi

John Ford's THE THREE GODFATHERS is a wonderful, sentimental western about a bad man who redeems himself. It is also a tribute to Ford's mentor and friend, actor Harry Carey, who died in 1947. The film follows a trio of outlaws—Robert Marmaduke Hightower (John Wayne), "Pete" Roca Fuerte (Pedro Armendariz), and "The Abilene Kid" (Harry Carey, Jr.)—who flee a posse after robbing the bank at Welcome. After losing their horses in a desert sandstorm, they arrive at Terrapin Tanks, where they find an abandoned woman in labor. After giving birth, the dying woman (Mildred Natwick) begs the men to save her baby, and they agree, deciding to bring it to the nearby town of New Jerusalem—a hazardous journey with a biblical analogy not lost on the outlaws. Only Hightower makes it, however, stumbling into New Jerusalem with the baby on Christmas Eve. Later, the sheriff of Welcome (Ward Bond) offers to drop the charges if the outlaw will give up custody of the baby, but Hightower's response shouldn't surprise anyone. Ford first filmed this story in 1919 as MARKED MEN with Harry Carey, who also appeared in the first version of the story, THREE GODFATHERS, in 1916. This version, Ford's first color film, begins as a silhouetted cowboy astride Carey's favorite horse rides to the top of a hill, pushing his hat back on his head as the words "Dedicated to Harry Carey, a bright star in the early western sky" appear.

THREE LITTLE WORDS

1950 102m c Biography/Musical   ★★★★
MGM (U.S.)   /U

Fred Astaire *(Bert Kalmar)*, Red Skelton *(Harry Ruby)*, Vera-Ellen *(Jessie Brown Kalmar)*, Arlene Dahl *(Eileen Percy)*, Keenan Wynn *(Charlie Kope)*, Gale Robbins *(Terry Lordel)*, Gloria DeHaven *(Mrs. Carter DeHaven)*, Phil Regan *(Himself)*, Harry Shannon *(Clanahan)*, Debbie Reynolds *(Helen Kane)*
p, Jack Cummings; d, Richard Thorpe; w, George Wells (based on the lives and songs of Bert Kalmar and Harry Ruby); ph, Harry Jackson; ed, Ben Lewis; art d, Cedric Gibbons, Urie McCleary; chor, Hermes Pan

AAN Best Score: Andre Previn

An utter delight, this musical biography portrays the lives of composers Bert Kalmar (Fred Astaire) and Harry Ruby (Red Skelton). Kalmar is a vaudeville song-and-dance man and would-be magician who turns to writing lyrics after a knee injury puts an end to his dancing. Ruby plays the piano at a Coney Island honky-tonk and also writes lyrics, though he dreams of playing baseball. Eventually, the two meet, and a great songwriting team is born; they go on to write numerous hits for Broadway and the movies. A misunderstanding ends the partnership, but Kalmar's wife, Jessie (Vera-Ellen), and Ruby's wife, Eileen (Arlene Dahl), finally bring the two men back together for a happy, if somewhat fictionalized, conclusion. For the most part, though, this movie sticks to the facts, and it never fails to entertain. Astaire is as suave as usual and dances a couple numbers with Vera-Ellen, while Skelton gives one of the best performances of his career. The film is sparked by wonderful supporting work by Vera-Ellen and Dahl. Appearing as themselves in cameo roles are Phil Regan and Harry Mendoza. Ruby himself served as technical advisor.

3 MEN AND A BABY

1987 99m c Comedy   ★★½
Touchstone/Silver Screen Partners III/Jean Francois   PG/
Lepetit/Interscope   (U.S.)

Tom Selleck (*Peter Mitchell*), Steve Guttenberg (*Michael Kellam*), Ted Danson (*Jack Holden*), Nancy Travis (*Sylvia*), Margaret Colin (*Rebecca*), Lisa Blair, Michelle Blair (*Mary, the Baby*), Celeste Holm (*Mrs. Holden*), Philip Bosco (*Detective Melkowitz*), Derek De Lint (*Jan Clopatz*)

p, Ted Field, Robert W. Cort, Edward Teets; d, Leonard Nimoy; w, James Orr, Jim Cruickshank (based on the French film TROIS HOMMES ET UN COUFFIN by Coline Serreau); ph, Adam Greenberg; ed, Michael A. Stevenson; m, Marvin Hamlisch; prod d, Peter Larkin; art d, Dan Yarhi; fx, Michael Kavanagh; cos, Larry Wells

Peter Mitchell (Tom Selleck), Jack Holden (Ted Danson), and Michael Kellam (Steve Guttenberg) are three swinging bachelors who share an opulent penthouse apartment in Manhattan. Their unfettered existence is quickly thrown into turmoil, however, when they're forced to care for a baby girl who unexpectedly turns up on their doorstep. Relentless in its pursuit of "cute," this comedy (a remake of the French film TRES HOMMES ET UN COUFFIN) proved enormously popular at the box office. The leads acquit themselves fairly well, but the biggest winner is Selleck, whose low-key charm and gift for light comedy are put to good use here.

THREE MEN AND A CRADLE
(TROIS HOMMES ET UN COUFFIN)

1985 100m c Comedy   ★★★
Flach/TF1/Soprofilm   (France)   PG-13/

Roland Giraud (*Pierre*), Michel Boujenah (*Michel*), Andre Dussollier (*Jacques*), Philippine Leroy Beaulieu (*Sylvia*), Dominique Lavanant (*Madame Rapons*), Marthe Villalonga (*Antoinette*), Annick Alane (*Pharmacist*)

p, Jean-Francois Lepetit; d, Coline Serreau; w, Coline Serreau; ph, Jean-Yves Escoffier; ed, Catherine Renault; m, Franz Schubert; art d, Ivan Maussion

AAN Best Foreign Language Film

An engaging French comedy about three bachelors who find an abandoned baby at their door (a plot line direct from John Ford's THREE GODFATHERS). Though many of jokes are familiar and the outcome easily predictable, the picture scored an Oscar nomination as Best Foreign-Language Film (it lost to THE OFFICIAL STORY) and French Cesars for Best Picture, Best Screenplay, and Best Supporting Actor (Michel Boujenah). The film begins with the arrival of a baby in a basket before the closed door of goofy roommates Jacques (Andre Dussollier), Pierre (Roland Giraud), and Michel (Boujenah), one of whom, it turns out, is the unwitting father. The men become increasingly attached to the cute little bundle and soon become jealous of one another's paternalism. Things take a more complex turn when Jacques hides a smuggled cache of heroin in the baby's diapers, and the trio gets drawn into a drug-dealing subplot. The most popular picture in France during the 1985-86 film year (handily beating out such contenders as RAMBO II; OUT OF AFRICA; ROCKY IV; and BACK TO THE FUTURE), THREE MEN AND A CRADLE was also, of course, the movie that inspired the 1987 Hollywood remake THREE MEN AND A BABY, which performed similar magic at the box office.

THREE MUSKETEERS, THE

1948 126m c Adventure/Comedy   ★★★★
MGM (U.S.)   /U

Lana Turner (*Countess Charlotte de Winter*), Gene Kelly (*D'Artagnan*), June Allyson (*Constance Bonacieux*), Van Heflin (*Robert Athos*), Angela Lansbury (*Queen Anne*), Frank Morgan (*King Louis XIII*), Vincent Price (*Richelieu the Prime Minister*), Keenan Wynn (*Planchet*), John Sutton (*George*), Gig Young (*Porthos*)

p, Pandro S. Berman; d, George Sidney; w, Robert Ardrey (based on the novel by Alexandre Dumas); ph, Robert Planck; ed, Robert J. Kern, George Boemler; m, Herbert Stothart; art d, Cedric Gibbons, Malcolm Brown; fx, Warren Newcombe; cos, Walter Plunkett

AAN Best Cinematography: Robert Planck

THE THREE MUSKETEERS is a rollicking version of the oft-filmed Dumas classic, with Gene Kelly playing the role of D'Artagnan with great panache. The film opens as D'Artagnan leaves his country home for Paris, to join the famed Musketeers. He proves his ability in a duel with Athos (Van Heflin) and adopts the "one for all and all for one" motto, joining the Musketeers in serving King Louis XIII (Frank Morgan). Prime Minister Richelieu (Vincent Price) plots to end the king's reign, enlisting Louis's mistress, Lady de Winter (Lana Turner), in his evil scheme. The Musketeers, however, are not about to let that happen.

Kelly is a sheer delight, attacking the swashbuckling story with enormous zest. His acrobatics are a sight to behold, a marvelous extension of his much loved dancing skills. This was Kelly's favorite role in his nonmusical films, and he had hoped his performance here would convince MGM to let him do a musical version of "Cyrano de Bergerac." Alas, it didn't. The supporting cast is marvelous, especially Morgan in a wonderful portrayal of King Louis XIII.

THREE MUSKETEERS, THE

1974 105m c Adventure/Comedy   ★★★★
Fox (U.K.)   PG/U

Oliver Reed (*Athos*), Raquel Welch (*Constance*), Richard Chamberlain (*Aramis*), Michael York (*D'Artagnan*), Frank Finlay (*Porthos*), Christopher Lee (*Rochefort*), Jean-Pierre Cassel (*Louis XIII*), Geraldine Chaplin (*Anne of Austria*), Simon Ward (*Duke of Buckingham*), Faye Dunaway (*Milady*)

p, Michael Alexander, Ilya Salkind; d, Richard Lester; w, George MacDonald Fraser (based on the novel by Alexander Dumas); ph, David Watkin; ed, John Victor Smith; m, Michel Legrand; cos, Yvonne Blake, Ron Talsky

The oft-told tale by Dumas gets a terrific rendering here. York is a happy rustic youth, a bit of a bumbler, but with such high spirits that he is instantly lovable. He would like to become part of the Musketeers, the leaders of whom are Reed, Chamberlain, and Finlay, a trio more intrigued by cleavage and cash than by any sort of loyalty to their king, Cassel, who is, at best, an idiot. Cassel's wife is Chaplin, a duplicitous queen who is having a royal fling with Ward, a peer of England. Evil cardinal Charlton Heston learns of the affair and plans to use it to destroy the queen, opening the door for him to assume a more influential role with the king. He enlists the aid of the adventurous and ambitious Dunaway in his scheme. Meanwhile, the Musketeers have taken a liking to York, and he has fallen in love with Welch, Chaplin's best friend and lady-in-waiting. She is on to Heston's plot and tells York about it, and the four swordsmen set out to foil Heston's scheme. In the past, the story had been so trifled with by filmmakers that it seldom resembled what Dumas had written. Here, writer Fraser and director Lester went back to the original and hewed closely to the source material, but adding a lot of fun. Some good slapstick combines with moments of real drama and menace to make this movie a winner. The producer, Salkind, paid the cast for one picture but shot two at the same time without telling them. In 1975, Salkind brought out a sequel, THE FOUR MUSKETEERS, and the cast banded together to sue the producer for more wages. They were awarded a considerable sum, though not nearly as much as if they'd been hired to make two movies. Despite glowing reviews, the movie did not knock audiences over at the box office, although it turned a tidy profit after all the receipts were counted.

THREE SMART GIRLS

1937 86m bw Musical/Comedy ★★★★
Universal (U.S.) /A

Deanna Durbin *(Penny Craig)*, Binnie Barnes *(Donna Lyons)*, Alice Brady *(Mrs. Lyons)*, Ray Milland *(Lord Michael Stuart)*, Charles Winninger *(Judson Craig)*, Mischa Auer *(Count Arisztid)*, Nan Grey *(Joan Craig)*, Barbara Read *(Kay Craig)*, Ernest Cossart *(Binns the Butler)*, Hobart Cavanaugh *(Wilbur Lamb)*

p, Joe Pasternak; d, Henry Koster; w, Adele Comandini, Austin Parker (based on the story by Adele Comandini); ph, Joseph Valentine; ed, Ted J. Kent; art d, John Harkrider; cos, John Harkrider

AAN Best Picture; AAN Best Original Story: Adele Commandini; *AAN Best Sound:* Homer G. Tasker

In her film debut, 14-year-old singing sensation Deanna Durbin is cast as Penny Craig, one of three sisters who try to keep their father from marrying a gold digger. Penny is the devoted matchmaker who tries everything to bring about her parents' reconciliation before her father exchanges vows with his new love. By the picture's finale, Penny's efforts have been all too successful—her sisters have found prospective husbands, and her mother and father have rekindled their romance. Penny is still single, however, though thoroughly content with everyone's newfound happiness.

A highly pleasing first cousin to the screwball comedies of the day, THREE SMART GIRLS wisely centers on Durbin, a wonderful singer and a genuinely charming screen personality. The film earned Academy Award nominations for Best Picture (losing to THE GREAT ZIEGFELD), Best Original Story, and Best Sound. It spawned two sequels, THREE SMART GIRLS GROW UP, and HERS TO HOLD, both starring Durbin. There was also a remake, THREE DARING DAUGHTERS, which put Jane Powell in the Durbin role.

3:10 TO YUMA

1957 92m bw Western ★★★½
Columbia (U.S.) /A

Van Heflin *(Dan Evans)*, Glenn Ford *(Ben Wade)*, Felicia Farr *(Emmy)*, Leora Dana *(Alice Evans)*, Henry Jones *(Alex Potter)*, Richard Jaeckel *(Charlie Prince)*, Robert Emhardt *(Mr. Butterfield)*, Sheridan Comerate *(Bob Moons)*, George Mitchell *(Bartender)*, Robert Ellenstein *(Ernie Collins)*

p, David Heilweil; d, Delmer Daves; w, Halsted Welles (based on the story by Elmore Leonard); ph, Charles Lawton Jr.; ed, Al Clark; m, George Duning; art d, Frank Hotaling; cos, Jean Louis

This fine western opens with Heflin as a rancher whose family is suffering from the devastating effects of a long drought. Heflin needs $200 to build a well, then learns he can obtain the money as a reward for delivering Ford, a notorious outlaw now in the hands of the law, to the state prison in Yuma, Arizona. Though this will put Heflin in great personal danger, the peaceful man accepts the assignment, knowing what the money will mean to his family. Heflin and Ford hole up in a small hotel in another town while waiting for the train to Yuma. The outlaw begins toying with Heflin's mind, talking in a friendly manner about Heflin's job and financial situation. Playing psychological games, Ford tries to convince Heflin to take $10,000 to look the other way while he escapes. Heflin finds himself in a quandary, desperately needing the money yet being bound by his word to carry out the job. Ford's gang, led by Jaeckel, discovers where their leader is hidden and sets out to rescue him. The town officials abandon Heflin rather than put themselves in danger, leaving him to face off with the outlaws. Ford ends up assisting Heflin, helping his captor on to the 3:10 to Yuma, explaining: "I owed you that." Heflin has come through the ordeal, body and integrity intact, and, as if in answer to this baptism by fire, the skies burst forth with rain, putting an end to the drought.

Much like HIGH NOON, this film deals with a man alone after town officials have passed on their duties, leaving him to face both his adversaries and his conscience. Daves's direction is gritty, confining much of the story to the small hotel room, with a hard-hitting use of close-ups. His outdoor sequences are equally good, particularly the portrait of a land desperate for water. Heflin is superior in the role with

his intense portrait of a man caught between personal needs and social duties. Ford is equally good, mixing amiable feelings with monstrous qualities. This is a landmark western, redefining what the genre was capable of doing, and is one of Daves's best works.

3 WOMEN

1977 122m c Drama ★★★
Lion's Gate (U.S.) PG/AA

Shelley Duvall *(Millie Lammoreaux)*, Sissy Spacek *(Pinky Rose)*, Janice Rule *(Willie Hart)*, Robert Fortier *(Edgar Hart)*, Ruth Nelson *(Mrs. Rose)*, John Cromwell *(Mr. Rose)*, Sierra Pecheur *(Mr. Bunweill)*, Craig Richard Nelson *(Dr. Maas)*, Maysie Hoy *(Doris)*, Belita Moreno *(Alcira)*

p, Robert Altman; d, Robert Altman; w, Robert Altman; ph, Charles Rosher Jr.; ed, Dennis M. Hill; m, Gerald Busby; art d, James Vance; fx, Modern Film Effects

3 WOMEN is one of Robert Altman's better pictures, although it still suggests that he believes an enigma is more important than a beginning, middle and end. Pinky Rose (Sissy Spacek), a naive young woman, arrives at a California desert community and hits it off immediately with Millie Lammoreaux (Shelly Duvall), a fellow Texan and her coworker at a nursing home that specializes in the treatment of arthritis. The fashion-conscious Millie lives in a singles apartment complex and spends her nights drinking beer at a nearby motorcycle bar. Pinky moves in with Millie and befriends Willie (Janice Rule), the silent, pregnant wife of the complex's alcoholic owner, Edgar (Robert Fortier), a former movie stuntman.

Pinky, who worships her indifferent roommate, begins borrowing Millie's clothes, using the same expressions, and generally aping Millie. Millie plans a party for some prospective suitors, but the men don't arrive and she storms out, only to return later that night with Edgar, who's roaring drunk. A distraught Pinky leaps into the swimming pool in an apparent suicide attempt. She's rescued by Willie and taken to the hospital, where Millie remains at her side until she recovers. After recuperating, Pinky returns to the apartment, but the roles have changed.

Altman supposedly based his screenplay on a dream he had while his wife was in surgery. While the maverick director's fans will praise 3 WOMEN's narrative richness, his detractors will find it incomprehensible and tedious. Typically, however, the acting, particularly from Duvall and Spacek, is first-rate.

THREEPENNY OPERA, THE
(DIE DREIGROSCHENOPER)

1931 113m bw Opera ★★★
Nero/Tobis Klangfilm/Warner Bros. (U.S./Germany)

Rudolf Forster *(Mackie Messer)*, Carola Neher *(Polly)*, Reinhold Schunzel *(Tiger Brown)*, Fritz Rasp *(Peachum)*, Valeska Gert *(Mrs. Peachum)*, Lotte Lenya *(Jenny)*, Herman Thimig *(Vicar)*, Ernst Busch *(Street-Singer)*, Vladimir Sokoloff *(Smith)*, Paul Kemp

p, Seymour Nebenzal; d, G.W. Pabst; w, Leo Lania, Bela Balasz, Ladislas Vajda, Solange Bussi, Andre Mauprey, Ninon Steinhoff (based on the play by Bertolt Brecht, adapted from *The Beggar's Opera* by John Gay); ph, Fritz Arno Wagner; ed, Hans Oser, Henri Rust; m, Kurt Weill; prod d, Andre Andrejew

Less revered today than the Bertolt Brecht play or the Kurt Weill songs, G.W. Pabst's film version of "The Threepenny Opera" is still a fine example of pre-Hitler German filmmaking. In the German version available on videocassette (a French version exists with a different cast, while the planned English version was never completed), Rudolf Forster plays the infamous Mackie Messer, or Mack the Knife, an underworld gangster of the 1890s whose territory is London. A dashing and respected criminal, Mackie is best of friends with the corrupt police chief, Tiger Brown (Reinhold Schunzel). After meeting Polly (Carola Neher), Mackie decides to marry her. In a dusty underground warehouse—the room lavishly prepared with goods stolen from London's top shops—the wedding is attended by a crowd of beggars and thieves, as well as Tiger Brown. Polly, however, is the daughter of Peachum (Fritz Rasp), the king of the beggars, who strongly opposes the marriage. He puts pressure on Tiger Brown to send Mackie to the gallows, threatening to organize a beggars' revolt to disrupt the queen's upcoming coronation if the police chief does not accede to his wishes.

Based on the John Gay satire of 1728, "The Beggar's Opera," Pabst's film lacks the punch that made the Brecht-Weill collaboration so potent when it hit the stage in 1928. The sting of social criticism is lessened here, with greater emphasis placed on dramatics; in fact, Brecht was so disappointed with the director's interpretation that he ended his own work on the screenplay. What the film lacks in Brechtian qualities, however, it makes up for in the aesthetics of Pabst. Having previously exposed the seedier side of London in the silent PANDORA'S BOX, Pabst once again brings it to the screen here in a unique mixture of realism and expressionism, taking great care to evoke the textures of London's underworld—populated by the lowest of lowlifes—in both his visuals and his soundtrack. Although there is a noticeable absence of some of Weill's tunes—"Ballad of Sexual Dependency," "The Ballad for the Hangman," and "The Tango Ballad"—the film does open and close with the Ernst Busch rendition of "Moritat," a song which became the 1957 pop music hit "Mack the Knife." Also prominently featured is "Pirate Jenny" (Brecht-Weill), delivered by the inimitable Lenya.

THRONE OF BLOOD
(KUMONOSUJO)
1957 110m bw Drama/War   ★★★★½
Brandon (Japan)   /PG

Toshiro Mifune *(Taketoki Washizu)*, Isuzu Yamada *(Asaji)*, Takashi Shimura *(Noriyasu Odagura)*, Minoru Chiaki *(Yoshaki Miki)*, Akira Kubo *(Yoshiteru)*, Takamaru Sasaki *(Kuniharu Tsuzuki)*, Yoichi Tachikawa *(Kunimaru)*, Chieko Naniwa *(Witch)*

p, Akira Kurosawa, Sojiro Motoki; d, Akira Kurosawa; w, Hideo Oguni, Shinobu Hashimoto, Ryuzo Kikushima, Akira Kurosawa (based on the play "Macbeth" by William Shakespeare); ph, Asaichi Nakai; ed, Akira Kurosawa; m, Masaru Sato; art d, Yoshiro Muraki, Kohei Ezaki

Kabuki *Macbeth*, and like nothing you've ever seen. A truly remarkable film combining beauty and terror to produce a mood of haunting power, THRONE OF BLOOD was the brilliant fulfillment of Japanese master Akira Kurosawa's longtime ambition to bring Shakespeare to Japanese audiences. Kurosawa set the story in feudal Japan, and the transposition of cultures is surprisingly successful, with all the plot elements intact. After putting down a mutinous rebellion for their lord, warriors Taketoki Washizu (Toshiro Mifune) and Yoshaki Miki (Minoru Chiaki) are called to the main castle for an audience. Riding through the dense and foggy forest that protects the warlord's castle, they encounter a mysterious old woman bathed in white light and mist. When questioned, the woman prophesies that Washizu will be given command of a castle and soon become warlord, but his reign will be brief and his throne will be occupied by his friend's son thereafter. When it appears her predictions are coming true, Washizu grows increasingly corrupted by his own ambitions. THRONE OF BLOOD is filled with unforgettable, haunting imagery. Departing from his usual (very Western) fluid camera style and fast-paced editing, Kurosawa borrowed here from the conventions of Noh theater. While the visuals are gorgeous, the compositions are static and stagy, concentrating on the emotional moment as it seems to hang in the air, unaltered by editing or camera movement. The visual and acting styles work marvelously with the material, although the film is somewhat cold and detached, containing little of the exhilarating passion found in Kurosawa's other work. Kurosawa has a lot of fun with the advance of Birnam Wood, Yamanda's Lady Macbeth is a virtuoso fright and Mifune's demise is in the most grand, outrageous Kabuki fashion. This is filmmaking with risk and greatness in its blood.

THROW MOMMA FROM THE TRAIN
1987 88m c Comedy   ★★½
Orion (U.S.)   PG-13/15

Danny DeVito *(Owen Lift)*, Billy Crystal *(Larry Donner)*, Anne Ramsey *(Momma)*, Kim Greist *(Beth)*, Kate Mulgrew *(Margaret)*, Branford Marsalis *(Lester)*, Rob Reiner *(Joel)*, Bruce Kirby, Oprah Winfrey, Joey DePinto

p, Larry Brezner; d, Danny DeVito; w, Stu Silver; ph, Barry Sonnenfeld; ed, Michael Jablow; m, David Newman; prod d, Ida Random; art d, William Elliott; cos, Marilyn Vance

AAN Best Supporting Actress: Anne Ramsey

Making a surprisingly assured directorial debut that is hampered only by a weak script, Danny DeVito stars as Owen Lift, a childlike 40-year-old bachelor whose life is totally dominated by his mean-spirited mother (Anne Ramsey). Owen meets Larry Donner (Billy Crystal), a hapless would-be writer whose ex-wife (Kate Mulgrew) ran off with his only completed manuscript, sold it as her own, and is now a millionaire. Owen gets it into his head that Larry wants to "swap" murders with him, with each committing an unmotivated crime that cannot be traced—Owen's momma for Larry's ex-wife. After beginning as a promising black comedy, THROW MOMMA FROM THE TRAIN deteriorates into a repetitive affair that betrays the brazen nastiness with which it began. DeVito does a nice job modulating his own performance, managing to evoke sympathy for his loony character. Crystal, sadly, is hampered by a script that limits him to spells of griping, whining, and full-blown hysteria.

THUNDERBALL
1965 130m c Spy   ★★★
Eon (U.K.)   GP/PG

Sean Connery *(James Bond)*, Claudine Auger *(Domino Derval)*, Adolfo Celi *(Emilio Largo)*, Luciana Paluzzi *(Fiona Volpe)*, Rik Van Nutter *(Felix Leiter)*, Bernard Lee *("M")*, Martine Beswicke *(Paula Caplan)*, Guy Doleman *(Count Lippe)*, Molly Peters *(Patricia Fearing)*, Desmond Llewelyn *("Q")*

p, Kevin McClory; d, Terence Young; w, Richard Maibaum, John Hopkins (based on the characters created by Ian Fleming and the story by McClory, Jack Whittingham, Fleming); ph, Ted Moore, Lamar Boren; ed, Peter Hunt; m, John Barry; prod d, Ken Adam; art d, Peter Murton; fx, John Stears; cos, Anthony Mendleson

AA Best Visual Effects: John Stears

This relatively disappointing fourth entry in the James Bond series centers on the hijacking of a NATO bomber carrying a nuclear payload. After sweating out the effects of his louche lifestyle at a health spa, James Bond (Sean Connery) is dispatched to the sunny Bahamas, where the aircraft is hidden underwater. SPECTRE's No. 2 man, Emilio Largo (Adolfo Celi), is behind the scheme, and Bond, well-equipped with state-of-the art spy gadgetry, catches up with the villain and his equally well-equipped mistress, Domino (Auger), who eventually embraces both Bond and his cause. Bond locates the downed plane and calls in American aqua-paratroops, who do underwater battle with SPECTRE scuba divers while 007 chases Largo, who flees in his yacht-turned-hydrofoil.

With THUNDERBALL, the wildly popular Bond series started to slip, substituting gadgets and gimmicks for story and character development. The action is reasonably well-staged, but the film is overlong and occasionally draggy. THUNDERBALL was meant to be the first in the series, but Bond creator Ian Fleming engaged in a long legal battle over the rights to his novel, eventually losing in court to Kevin McClory. However, McClory was unable to put together a workable package to turn the novel into a movie, largely because Sean Connery was by now under contract to regular Bond producers Cubby Broccoli and Harry Saltzman. Eventually, Saltzman, Broccoli, and McClory struck a deal that gave McClory the producer credit and a percentage of the profits (McClory also retained the right to produce a remake after a 10 years had elapsed; the result was 1983's NEVER SAY NEVER AGAIN). Despite its shortcomings, the film was the top moneymaker of 1966, grossing more than any other picture in the series. Julie Christie, Raquel Welch, and Faye Dunaway—then relatively unknown players—were all considered for the role of Domino before Claudine Auger was chosen. Welch was actually signed to play the part, but Broccoli reluctantly released her as a favor to 20th Century-Fox production head Richard Zanuck, who wanted her for FANTASTIC VOYAGE. Tom Jones sings the title song, written by John Barry and Don Black.

THUNDERBOLT AND LIGHTFOOT

1974   114m   c   Crime   ★★★½
Malpaso   (U.S.)   R/18

Clint Eastwood *(John "Thunderbolt" Doherty)*, Jeff Bridges *(Lightfoot)*, Geoffrey Lewis *(Goody)*, Catherine Bach *(Melody)*, Gary Busey *(Curly)*, George Kennedy *(Red Leary)*, Jack Dodson *(Vault Manager)*, Gene Elman, Lila Teigh *(Tourists)*, Burton Gilliam *(Welder)*

p, Robert Daley; d, Michael Cimino; w, Michael Cimino; ph, Frank Stanley; ed, Ferris Webster; m, Dee Barton; art d, Tambi Larsen; fx, Sass Bedig

AAN Best Supporting Actor: Jeff Bridges

Before the disastrous HEAVEN'S GATE and YEAR OF THE DRAGON, and before the success of THE DEER HUNTER, intermittently brilliant director Michael Cimino directed his marvelous first film, THUNDERBOLT AND LIGHTFOOT. Eastwood, whose production company produced the film, had become impressed with Cimino after Cimino coauthored the screenplay for another Eastwood vehicle, MAGNUM FORCE (1973). The film is a crisp, well-written cast caper movie sporting some stunning landscapes and a fine core of performances (Bridges earned an Academy Award nomination as Best Supporting Actor). Young drifter Bridges hooks up with ex-thief Eastwood, who has been on the lam from his former partners for several years because they believe he set them up and took off with the loot from a government vault they robbed in Montana. The two remaining members of his gang, Kennedy, a sadistic war buddy of Eastwood, and Lewis, a likable dimwit, are in pursuit of revenge and hot on Eastwood's tail. The thief, therefore, reluctantly strikes up a friendship with Bridges to escape. Bridges admires Eastwood and wants to prove himself worthy of his friendship, so the crazy kid takes part in the dangerous maneuvering. Eventually Kennedy and Lewis corner the pair and prepare to kill them. Eastwood convinces Kennedy he has no idea where the money is (it was hidden behind the blackboard of an old schoolhouse that no longer exists) and their lives are spared. With nothing better to do, Bridges convinces the group it should rob the same vault, the same way, all these years later because no one would suspect another attempt (they shot their way into the vault with a Howitzer cannon). After some elaborate planning, the four men successfully execute the robbery, but their getaway goes awry. . .

THUNDERBOLT AND LIGHTFOOT is a multifaceted caper film told in fine detail with richly developed characters. Eastwood is nearly overshadowed by Bridges, Kennedy, and Lewis, who brings great depth to his weak-willed, somewhat stupid, character without resorting to cliches. Here, as well as in THE DEER HUNTER, Cimino's main characters—Eastwood and De Niro—seem detached from their peers and unmoved by their environment, until events beyond their control force them to realize what it was they had. It is only then that they experience a melancholy sense of loss. Cimino's first two films succeed because he allows well-drawn characters to affect the audience, not the epic scale of the production. The power of THUNDERBOLT AND LIGHTFOOT and THE DEER HUNTER stems from their eloquent, complex, honest characters.

THUNDERHEAD—SON OF FLICKA

1945   78m   bw   Drama   ★★★★
Fox   (U.S.)   /U

Roddy McDowall *(Ken McLaughlin)*, Preston Foster *(Rob McLaughlin)*, Rita Johnson *(Nelle)*, James Bell *(Gus)*, Diana Hale *(Hildy)*, Carleton Young *(Maj. Harris)*, Ralph Sanford *(Mr. Sargent)*, Robert Filmer *(Tim)*, Alan Bridge *(Dr. Hicks)*

p, Robert Bassler; d, Louis King; w, Dwight Cummins, Dorothy Yost (based on a novel by Mary O'Hara); ph, Charles Clarke; ed, Nick De Maggio; m, Cyril J. Mockridge; art d, Lyle Little, Fred J. Rode

An enjoyable and engaging tale, this follow-up to MY FRIEND FLICKA is every bit as entertaining as the original. Ken McLaughlin (Roddy McDowall, returning from the original film) is trying to break in Thunderhead, the title horse. The all-white colt is trained for racing, and Ken enters him in competition. At a county race it appears Thunderhead is going to win when the horse suddenly pulls a tendon. Ken is content to restrict his use of Thunderhead to his father's ranch, but

trouble brews when the albino horse who sired Thunderhead goes wild. That horse causes trouble for all the ranchers in the valley by stealing mares, but eventually it is challenged by Thunderhead. The brave colt saves Ken, then takes on the albino. The two horses engage in a terrific fight, with Thunderhead defeating his renegade father. Ken's horse returns to his master, but shows a desire to live free on the range. Though heartbroken, Ken understands what is best for his friend and allows the horse to go free. The film is well acted, though the players are really secondary to the real stars of the film: the horses and the beautiful Utah locations. Perfect family viewing.

THUNDERHEART

1992   118m   c   Thriller   ★★★
TriBeCa Productions/Waterhorse Productions/TriStar   (U.S.)   R/15

Val Kilmer *(Ray Levoi)*, Sam Shepard *(Frank Coutelle)*, Graham Greene *(Walter Crow Horse)*, Fred Dalton Thompson *(William Dawes)*, Fred Ward *(Jack Milton)*, Sheila Tousey *(Maggie Eagle Bear)*, Chief Ted Thin Elk *(Grandpa Sam Reaches)*, John Trudell *(Jimmy Looks Twice)*, Julius Drum *(Richard Yellow Hawk)*, Sarah Brave *(Maisy Blue Legs)*

p, Robert De Niro, Jane Rosenthal, John Fusco; d, Michael Apted; w, John Fusco; ph, Roger Deakins; ed, Ian Crafford; m, James Horner; prod d, Dan Bishop; art d, Bill Ballou; cos, Susan Lyall

THUNDERHEART is a thoughtful, atmospheric thriller set on a North Dakota Native American reservation in the 1970s. Loosely based on a real-life incident, the film involves a series of murders, a deadly, government-backed uranium mining operation, and the attempts of a group of American Indian activists to protect their land and culture.

Val Kilmer stars as Ray Levoi, a one-quarter Sioux F.B.I. agent who is assigned to the murder investigation as a token Indian (the natives mockingly refer to him as the "Washington Redskin"). His partner, tough old-timer Frank "Cooch" Coutelle (Sam Shepard), is more interested in making a quick arrest than in getting to the root of the situation. Levoi, though, suspects the case is more complex than it seems. Influenced and impressed by some of the Indians (particularly savvy native cop Walter Crow Horse, winningly played by Graham Greene), he overcomes his initial embarrassment about his Indian blood and discovers the meaning of his heritage. As he uncovers a trail of conspiracy and corruption, Levoi is forced to decide where his true sympathies lie.

THX 1138

1971   88m   c   Science Fiction   ★★½
American Zoetrope   (U.S.)   PG/15

Robert Duvall *(THX 1138)*, Donald Pleasence *(SEN 5241)*, Don Pedro Colley *(SRT)*, Maggie McOmie *(LUH 3417)*, Ian Wolfe *(PTO)*, Sid Haig *(NCH)*, Marshall Efron *(TWA)*, John Pearce *(DWY)*, Johnny Weissmuller Jr., Robert Feero *(Chrome Robots)*

p, Lawrence Sturhahn; d, George Lucas; w, George Lucas, Walter Murch (based on a story by Lucas); ph, David Myers, Albert Kihn; ed, George Lucas; m, Lalo Schifrin; art d, Michael Haller; cos, Donald Longhurst

George Lucas's feature debut is muted, brooding sci-fi, expanded (under the auspices of Francis Ford Coppola) from the short film with which Lucas won the 1967 National Student Film Festival. A young Robert Duvall plays THX (pronounced "Thix"), who attempts to escape from a futuristic society located beneath the Earth's surface. Reminiscent of the repressive societies described in George Orwell's *1984*, Aldous Huxley's *Brave New World*, and especially E.M. Forster's "The Machine Stops," Duvall's society has outlawed love and sex, with drugs as mandatory dietary supplements. McOmie plays Duvall's love interest, who awakens him to the pleasures of love after she and Duvall stop taking the libido-stifling drugs. They're arrested, and in prison she discovers she's pregnant. They hook up with Pleasence, who persuades the two to escape with him. Ponderous and largely static, this film shows little of the movie-making flair Lucas would later exhibit—except for a tense, stylishly edited car chase, in which the director makes impressive use of a relatively low budget, and a few flashes of wit, like the computerized confession boxes. Sharp-eyed Lucas fans may have noticed that in AMERICAN GRAFFITI, Paul Le Mat's Deuce Coupe sports license plates that read "THX 138."

TICKET TO HEAVEN

1981 107m c Drama ★★★
UA (U.S.) PG/

Nick Mancuso (David), Saul Rubinek (Larry), Meg Foster (Ingrid), Kim Cattrall (Ruthie), R.H. Thompson (Linc Strunk), Jennifer Dale (Lisa), Guy Bond (Eric), Dixie Seatle (Sarah), Paul Soles (Morley), Harvey Atkin (Mr. Stone)

p, Vivienne Leebosh; d, Ralph L. Thomas; w, Ralph L. Thomas, Anne Cameron (based on the book Moonwebs by Josh Freed); ph, Richard Leiterman; ed, Ron Wisman; m, Micky Erbe, Maribeth Solomon; prod d, Susan Longmire; art d, Jill Scott; cos, Lynda Kemp

Fascinating if one-sided examination of the power of religious cults and the methods they employ to attract new members. Mancuso is good as the vulnerable youth who seeks solace and comfort in a cult after enduring a messy breakup with his girlfriend. The film details Mancuso's conversion, his parents' efforts to locate him, and his "deprogramming"—which seems as much of a brainwashing as anything he gets from the cult. Rubinek (UNFORGIVEN, TRUE ROMANCE) steals the film with ease.

TIE ME UP! TIE ME DOWN!
(ATAME)

1990 101m c Comedy/Romance/Erotic ★★½
El Deseo (Spain)

Victoria Abril (Marina), Antonio Banderas (Ricky), Francisco Rabal (Maximo Espejo), Loles Leon (Lola), Julieta Serrano (Alma), Maria Barranco, Rossy de Palma

p, Agustin Almodovar; d, Pedro Almodovar; w, Pedro Almodovar; ph, Jose Luis Alcaine; ed, Jose Salcedo; m, Ennio Morricone; prod d, Esther Garcia

This outrageous title is a little deceiving, especially for a film from Spain's most controversial export, Pedro Almodovar. The director's usual campy, boisterous hilarity has been replaced in TIE ME UP! TIE ME DOWN! by anguished—albeit offbeat—romantic heterosexual yearning.

Ricky (Antonio Banderas) is released from a mental institution with one burning ambition. On a previous escape from the hospital, he met and made love to Marina (Victoria Abril), a junkie and former porn star. Obsessed by the memory of her, he determines to seek her out again and win her love. He finds her on the set of a legitimate film, working under the direction of the aged Maximo Espejo (Francisco Rabal), who is also obsessed with her. Marina has no recollection of Ricky when she sees him, but he trails her home and kidnaps her. Tying her up in her own apartment, he makes her a captive audience for his desperate romantic overtures. She is at first fiercely resistant to him, but gradually succumbs, especially when he returns to her bruised and bloodied after an attempt to score drugs for her. Eventually, Marina's sister, Lola (Loles Leon), comes to the rescue, but by that time, Marina's fate is (happily) sealed.

The shock effects of Almodovar's earlier work were considerably diluted in his Lubitschian crazy-love roundelay, WOMEN ON THE VERGE OF A NERVOUS BREAKDOWN, and TIE ME UP!, despite its bondage theme and lightly sadomasochistic overtones, makes a similar attempt to enter the mainstream. The film recalls Hitchcock's THE 39 STEPS, with its bickering handcuffed lovers, as well as the sweeping romantic intensity of Douglas Sirk's 1950s trash-fests. Ennio Morricone's ubiquitous music contributes to this attempt to explore the traditions of classic cinema, but it lacks the savvy, finger-popping verve of the more street-smart scores of other Almodovar films. The screenplay lacks the frantic multitude of characters that have typified Almodovar's work, and the non-sequiturs and comic asides we have come to expect are also kept to a minimum. Staying with TIE ME UP! demands some patience, but the director's timing never fails him, and he brings things to a close on an upbeat note.

TIGER BAY

1959 105m bw Crime ★★★½
Independent Artists (U.K.) /PG

John Mills (Supt. Graham), Horst Buchholz (Korchinsky), Hayley Mills (Gillie), Yvonne Mitchell (Anya), Megs Jenkins (Mrs. Phillips), Anthony Dawson (Barclay), George Selway (Detective Sgt. Harvey), Shari (Christine), George Pastell (Poloma Captain), Marne Maitland (Dr. Das)

p, John Hawkesworth; d, J. Lee Thompson; w, John Hawkesworth, Shelley Smith (based on the novel Rodolphe et le Revolver by Noel Calef); ph, Eric Cross; ed, Sidney Hayers; m, Laurie Johnson; art d, Edward Carrick

A Polish sailor on leave, Korchinsky (Horst Buchholz), heads into Tiger Bay to visit his girlfriend, Anya (Yvonne Mitchell). He finds that she is now living with another man and guns her down in a fit of anger. Their noisy argument attracts the attention of 12-year-old Gillie (Hayley Mills), a lonely tomboy who witnesses the murder through a mail slot. She gets hold of the murder weapon, convinced that having a gun will make her popular with her peers when they play cowboys and Indians. In time, the precocious youngster is confronted by a police detective (her real-life father, John Mills), but she frustrates him by reciting a convincing string of lies that get him deeper into the situation than she ever imagined. TIGER BAY operates on several levels, creating a thriller of varying intensity with the warm relationship that develops between Gillie and Korchinsky at its center. Korchinsky's interest in the girl grows from a desperate need to keep his crime a secret into genuine affection. Likewise, Gillie sees this as an adventure which will make her popular with playmates, until she develops strong feelings for the sailor. This was Hayley Mills's film debut, and she gives quite a performance for an actress of any age.

TIM BURTON'S THE NIGHTMARE BEFORE CHRISTMAS

1993 75m c Fantasy/Musical/Animated ★★★½
Skellington Productions/Touchstone (U.S.) PG

VOICES OF: Danny Elfman (Jack Skellington (songs)/ Barrel/Clown with the Tear Away Face), Chris Sarandon (Jack Skellington), Catherine O'Hara (Sally/Shock), William Hickey (Evil Scientist), Glenn Shadix (Mayor), Paul Reubens (Lock), Ken Page (Oogie Boogie), Ed Ivory (Santa), Susan McBride (Big Witch W W D), Debi Durst (Corpse Kid/Corpse Mom/Small Witch)

p, Denise DiNovi, Tim Burton; d, Henry Selick; w, Caroline Thompson (from the story and characters by Tim Burton); ph, Pete Kozachik; ed, Stan Webb; m, Danny Elfman; art d, Deane Taylor; fx, Ariel Velasco Shaw, Pete Kozachik; anim, Eric Leighton

AAN Best Visual Effects: Gordon Baker, Pete Kozachik, Eric Leighton, Ariel Velasco Shaw

There's a new Santa Claus in town, and if you're lucky your Christmas gifts could include a hungry snake or a severed, shrunken head.

Welcome to THE NIGHTMARE BEFORE CHRISTMAS, producer Tim Burton's animated, musical vision of a world where skeletons are considered handsome and spiders tasty. Working within the relatively obscure techniques of stop-motion animation (by which puppets are manipulated, one frame at a time, to create the illusion of movement), Burton and director Henry Selick have pulled off a spectacular visual coup, revolving around a character known as Jack the Pumpkin King. Frustrated with the limitations of his native Halloween-town, which is peopled by assorted macabre types and presided over by a (literally) two-faced mayor, Jack tries to conquer neighboring Christmastown, where the nice people live.

NIGHTMARE betrays almost demonic powers of invention, every frame crammed with eye-catching (and frequently eyebrow-raising) detail. It's also appealing to the ears, courtesy of Danny Elfman's infectious, amusing songs. Yet the richness of the canvas only draws our attention to the weakness of the narrative. Burton seems to waver between rooting for the scary guys and the cuddly ones, and his indecision makes it hard for us to respond on an emotional level. The result, though refreshingly different from mainstream animated fare, is ultimately more trick than treat.

TIME AFTER TIME

1979 112m c Science Fiction/Thriller ★★★
Orion/Warner Bros. (U.K.) PG/15

Malcolm McDowell *(Herbert G. Wells)*, David Warner *(Dr. John Lesley Stevenson)*, Mary Steenburgen *(Amy Robbins)*, Charles Cioffi *(Lt. Mitchell)*, Laurie Main *(Inspector Gregson)*, Andonia Katsaros *(Mrs. Turner)*, Patti D'Arbanville *(Shirley)*, Keith McConnell *(Harding)*, Geraldine Baron *(Carol)*, James Garrett *(Edwards)*

p, Herb Jaffe; d, Nicholas Meyer; w, Nicholas Meyer (based on a story by Karl Alexander and Steven Hayes); ph, Paul Lohmann; ed, Donn Cambern; m, Miklos Rozsa; prod d, Edward Carfagno; fx, Larry Fuentes, Jim Blount; cos, Sal Anthony, Yvonne Kubis

What if Jack the Ripper (David Warner) were really an old friend of H.G. Wells (Malcolm McDowell) and what if H.G. Wells actually invented a time machine and what if Jack the Ripper used it to escape to San Francisco circa 1979 and what if H.G. Wells figured out a way to follow him? What if H.G. fell in love with a kooky bank officer (Mary Steenburgen) and what if Jack tried to kill her? It's convoluted and the plot device that allows Wells to follow Jack is laughable, but this is such a conscientious undertaking you might as well take a look.

Meyer had tried this historical twist before with his screenplay for THE SEVEN-PERCENT SOLUTION, in which Sherlock Holmes meets Sigmund Freud, but TIME AFTER TIME actually works better. It's a well-crafted blend of fiction and history boosted by some excellent special effects. McDowell is marvelous as the free-thinking Victorian who is suddenly confronted with the future—a spectacle he finds both wonderful and horrifying. Steenburgen, in her first major role, does an engaging turn as the daffy bank worker, and the chemistry between the two is good. (They fell in love while making TIME AFTER TIME and were later married.) Meyer makes a fine directorial debut, pacing the film for optimal suspense despite some obvious holes in the script. For some more sophisticated treatments of time travel, see Alain Resnais' JE T'AIME, JE T'AIME, or Chris Marker's LA JETEE, a haunting parable composed almost entirely of still images.

TIME BANDITS

1981 110m c Science Fiction/Fantasy/Comedy ★★★★
HandMade (U.K.) PG

John Cleese *(Robin Hood)*, Sean Connery *(King Agamemnon)*, Shelley Duvall *(Pansy)*, Katherine Helmond *(Mrs. Ogre)*, Ian Holm *(Napoleon)*, Michael Palin *(Vincent)*, Ralph Richardson *(Supreme Being)*, Peter Vaughan *(Ogre)*, David Warner *(Evil Genius)*, David Rappaport *(Randall)*

p, Terry Gilliam; d, Terry Gilliam; w, Michael Palin, Terry Gilliam; ph, Peter Biziou; ed, Julian Doyle; m, Mike Moran; prod d, Millie Burns; art d, Norman Garwood

Gilliam and Palin, from Monty Python's Flying Circus, masterminded this madcap journey through history. A curious boy, Kevin (David Warnock) is whisked out of his dreary English home by six mischievous dwarfs who possess a map stolen from the Supreme Being (Sir Ralph Richardson) that reveals gaps in the universe. Utilizing these "time holes," they travel through history encountering the likes of Robin Hood (Cleese), Greek warrior King Agamemnon (Connery), and Napoleon (Holm)—and robbing them of their treasures. God wants his map back and he keeps popping up at the most inopportune times for Kevin and the time bandits. The Evil Genius (David Warner) also wants to get his hands on this great treasure. Who will win?

This wild and sometimes woolly fantasy is delivered in the customary chaotic Python style, resulting in an onslaught of witticisms and slapstick. We can also see definite signs of the major filmmaker Gilliam (director of BRAZIL, THE ADVENTURES OF BARON MUNCHHAUSEN, THE FISHER KING) would later become. In many ways, this remains his most satisfying film. However, be warned: this film is unusually dark for a modern children's film. At times a grimly comic fairy tale, TIME BANDITS offers little reassurance. It's a tough world out there—even in our imaginative life. Perhaps that is why we need heroes so badly.

Connery, in particular, stands out in a sterling cast. His portrayal of Agamemnon emerges as an idealized surrogate father that any boy would love to have. Cleese is priceless as a primly officious Robin

Hood. The band of little people is also splendid, especially the late David Rappaport as their leader, Randall. Chances are good that this eccentric film will gain in stature in the years to come.

TIME MACHINE, THE

1960 103m c Science Fiction ★★★★
Galaxy (U.K./U.S.) G/PG

Rod Taylor *(George)*, Alan Young *(David Filby/James Filby)*, Yvette Mimieux *(Weena)*, Sebastian Cabot *(Dr. Philip Hillyer)*, Tom Helmore *(Anthony Bridewell)*, Whit Bissell *(Walter Kemp)*, Doris Lloyd *(Mrs. Watchell)*, Bob Barran *(Eloi Man)*, Paul Frees *(Voice of the History Machine)*

p, George Pal; d, George Pal; w, David Duncan (based on the novel by H.G. Wells); ph, Paul C. Vogel; ed, George Tomasini; m, Russell Garcia; art d, George W. Davis, William Ferrari; fx, Gene Warren, Tim Baer, Wah Chang

AA Best Visual Effects: Gene Warren, Tim Baar

This smashing science-fiction adaptation of H.G. Wells's famous novel has more creativity in every frame than most latter-day rip-offs have in their entirety. Rod Taylor plays George, an inventor who confounds his contemporaries in Victorian England by unveiling his new time machine. His friends think he's lost his mind, but after they leave, George takes off in his machine, whizzing through time but not through space. Therefore, all of his adventures take place in the same general area of England but at various points in history. He makes brief stops at both World Wars, the atomic confrontations of the future (1966 according to this film), and even as far ahead as the year 802,701. In this futuristic era, he finds humanity divided into two groups—the Eloi, normal-looking humans who live above ground, and the Morlocks, horrifying mutants who live beneath the ground. The Eloi are a vapid, incredibly passive lot, and George is stunned to learn that they are nothing more than cattle for the cannibalistic Morlocks. He falls in love with Weena (Yvette Mimieux), one of the Eloi, and sets out to help her people overcome their oppressors. Producer-director George Pal had already made quite a name for himself with his "Puppetoon" stop-motion animation techniques, and here he again delivers some amazing special effects.

TIME OF THE GYPSIES

1989 142m c Drama ★★★★
Forum Film/Sarajevo (Yugoslavia) R/15

Davor Dujmovic *(Perhan)*, Bora Todorovic *(Ahmed)*, Ljubica Adzovic *(Grandmother)*, Elvira Sali *(Danira)*, Sinolicka Trpkova *(Azra)*, Husnija Hasimovic *(Merdzan)*

p, Mirza Pasic; d, Emir Kusturica; w, Emir Kusturica, Gordan Mihic; ph, Vilko Filac; m, Goran Bregovic

The third film from the Yugoslavian director of the acclaimed WHEN FATHER WAS AWAY ON BUSINESS was inspired by a newspaper article on the inter-European trade in young Gypsy children. The result is an extraordinary epic that employs an elliptical, fantastic style influenced by Latin American magic realism and features nonprofessional, gypsy actors delivering most of their dialogue in Romanian (a language the director barely understands). It's a remarkable achievement.

A kindhearted Gypsy teenager, Perhan (Dujmovic, who costarred in WHEN FATHER WAS AWAY), is forced to leave his ramshackle home in the Skopje ghetto to accompany his young sister Danira (Sali) on a journey to a hospital where she is to undergo an operation on her bad leg, courtesy of Ahmed (Todorovic), the richest man in the ghetto. Danira and Perhan become separated, and he spends the rest of the film trying to find her so that he can return home and marry Azra (Trpkova), the girl of his dreams. During his odyssey Perhan loses his innocence and learns the brutal ways of the world.

Kusturica has said that his style in this film is a mixture of Ford and Bunuel, and GYPSIES has telling echoes of both, bringing its characters vividly and vitally to life. But there are also echoes of Coppola's GODFATHER films here—in GYPSIES' operatic tone and tragic vision, as well as the parallels between both films' treatment of a criminal ethnic subculture. Kusturica also conveys a genuine sense of wonder at the Gypsies' ability to live, love, and dream amid the squalor by which they are surrounded. This is a major work that augurs well for the director's future.

TIME OF YOUR LIFE, THE

1948 109m bw Comedy/Drama ★★★½
UA (U.S.) /A

James Cagney (Joe), William Bendix (Nick), Wayne Morris (Tom), Jeanne Cagney (Kitty Duval), Broderick Crawford (Policeman), Ward Bond (McCarthy), James Barton (Kit Carson), Paul Draper (Harry), Gale Page (Mary L), James Lydon (Dudley)

p, William Cagney; d, H.C. Potter; w, Nathaniel Curtis (based on the play by William Saroyan); ph, James Wong Howe; ed, Walter Hannemann, Truman K. Wood; m, Carmen Dragon, Reginald Beane; art d, Wiard Ihnen; cos, Courtney Haslam

This warm and engaging adaptation of Saroyan's superlative comedy represents a labor of love by James Cagney and his brother, producer William Cagney.

The film, set in a San Francisco waterfront saloon, is told in a helter skelter fashion, as Cagney (who remains seated through almost the entire picture) functions as the calm, controlling eye of the human hurricane that whirls on the screen. Cagney is a barroom philosopher, endlessly drinking expensive champagne as he indulges in his own peculiarities. He enjoys listening to old records as he sits, sending Morris, an earnest, mildly retarded young man, on various errands, placing bets on horses, picking up children's toys, and buying gum that this good friend loves to chew in big wads. Bendix, a member of the original Broadway cast, is the bartender. Cagney's real-life sister Jeanne is a down-on-her-luck streetwalker with a self-mocking sense of humor. Barton plays "Kit Carson," a quintessential old-timer, whom Cagney constantly prods into telling stories about the Wild West. In the end, the world inside the saloon is threatened, but Cagney at last rises from his chair to defend his terrain and friends.

The story's message—encouraging people to live out their dreams—is simple, and Cagney's performance is a delight. The supporting cast is marvelous, an eclectic and enjoyable bunch that keeps the film moving along at a bouncy pace. Potter's direction allows the material to flow freely, giving his cast every opportunity to excel without letting the camera call attention to itself. This was the third film Cagney did in conjunction with his brother William. The first two (JOHNNY COME LATELY and BLOOD ON THE SUN) had not done well at the box office, so the Cagney brothers were determined to find a script of quality that would also be popular with filmgoers. It wasn't: THE TIME OF YOUR LIFE lost $500,000 at the box office. It was the only Cagney picture ever to lose money, and, though the actor was proud of his artistic achievement, he remained disappointed that this never caught on with the public.

TIN DRUM, THE
(DIE BLECHTROMMEL)

1979 142m c Drama/War ★★★½
Artemis/Hallelujah Argos (France/Yugoslavia/Poland/West R/X
Germany)

David Bennent (Oskar Matzerath), Mario Adorf (Alfred Matzerath), Angela Winkler (Agnes Matzerath), Daniel Olbrychski (Jan Bronski), Katharina Thalbach (Maria), Charles Aznavour (Sigismund Markus), Heinz Bennent (Greff), Andrea Ferreol (Lina Greff), Fritz Hakl (Bebra), Mariella Oliveri (Raswitha Raguna)

p, Franz Seitz, Anatole Dauman; d, Volker Schlondorff; w, Franz Seitz, Volker Schlondorff, Jean-Claude Carriere, Gunter Grass (based on the novel The Tin Drum by Grass); ph, Igor Luther; ed, Suzanne Baron; m, Friedrich Meyer, Maurice Jarre; prod d, Nicos Perakis; art d, Nicos Perakis; fx, Georges Jaconelli

AA Best Foreign Language Film

Winner of the Academy Award for Best Foreign-Language Film and cowinner (along with APOCALYPSE NOW) of the top prize at the Cannes Film Festival, THE TIN DRUM is a startlingly successful realization of an "unfilmable" novel by Gunter Grass, the leading German practitioner of magical realism.

Oskar (David Bennent), born to a German rural family in the 1920s, becomes disgusted with the behavior of adults and decides, on his third birthday, not to grow any more, preferring instead to beat his tin drum (a birthday present) and shatter glass with his shrill scream. As he "ages," little Oskar continues to observe the hypocritical behavior of adults, beating out a constant tattoo on his tin drum to control the world around him. His small stature also makes for a very peculiar relationship with a teenage girl, Maria (Katharina Thalbach), who is also mistress to a much older, and bigger, man. THE TIN DRUM is a disturbing film, rich with black humor, that takes a decidedly bitter and horrific look at the German people. Director Volker Schlondorff brilliantly translates Grass' allegorical treatment of the rise of Nazism and manages to suggest much of the novelist's complex critique of German notions of history. Only Oskar, in his singularly demented way, is the voice of reason, proclaiming, "Once there was a credulous people who believed in Santa Claus, but Santa Claus turned out to be the gas man." The film is often difficult to watch and downright frightening, especially due to the haunting face of 12-year-old actor Bennent.

TIN MEN

1987 112m c Comedy ★★★
Touchstone/Silver Screen Partners II (U.S.) R/15

Richard Dreyfuss (Bill "BB" Babowsky), Danny DeVito (Ernest Tilley), Barbara Hershey (Nora Tilley), John Mahoney (Moe, Partner to "BB"), Jackie Gayle (Sam, Tilley's Partner), Stanley Brock (Gil), Seymour Cassel (Cheese), Bruno Kirby (Mouse), J.T. Walsh (Wing), Richard Portnow (Carly)

p, Mark Johnson; d, Barry Levinson; w, Barry Levinson; ph, Peter Sova; ed, Stu Linder; m, David Steele, Andy Cox; prod d, Peter Jamison; cos, Gloria Gresham

Director Barry Levinson (RAINMAN; GOOD MORNING, VIETNAM) returns to his hometown of Baltimore for this story of a battle between two aluminum siding salesmen in 1963. The trouble begins when Bill "BB" Babowsky (Richard Dreyfuss) backs his new Cadillac into the car owned by Ernest Tilley (Danny DeVito), who is busy arguing with his wife Nora (Barbara Hershey) at the time. Soon the two men are locked in a comical struggle for revenge. Though much of the plot action is downright silly, Dreyfuss, DeVito, and Hershey offer wonderful performances, and director Levinson keeps things moving with some nice comic touches. As he did in his first film, DINER, Levinson again effectively uses a diner setting in which the characters are allowed to engage in some rambling but very funny dialogue. Comedian Jackie Gayle provides some hilarious observations.

TIN PAN ALLEY

1940 92m bw Musical ★★½
Fox (U.S.) /U

Alice Faye (Katie Blane), Betty Grable (Lily Blane), Jack Oakie (Harry Calhoun), John Payne (Skeets Harrigan), Allen Jenkins (Sgt. Casey), Esther Ralston (Nora Bayes), Harold Nicholas, Fayard Nicholas (Dance Specialty), Ben Carter (Boy), John Loder (Reggie Carstair)

p, Kenneth MacGowan; d, Walter Lang; w, Robert Ellis, Helen Logan (based on a story by Pamela Harris); ph, Leon Shamroy; ed, Walter Thompson; art d, Richard Day, Joseph C. Wright; chor, Seymour Felix; cos, Travis Banton

AA Best Score: Alfred Newman

Harry Calhoun (Jack Oakie) and Skeets Harrigan (John Payne), a pair of struggling songsmiths, persuade the singing-and-dancing Blane sisters—Katie (Alice Faye) and Lily (Betty Grable, written into the film after her success with DOWN ARGENTINE WAY)—to perform one of their compositions. Later, Harry and Skeets have their first hit with a song they stumble on and buy from another songwriter (Elisha Cook, Jr.). When Lily lands a part in a big show, Katie decides to become part of Harry and Skeets's music publishing business; however, after they allow another, big-name singer (Esther Ralston) to perform a song that seems destined to be a hit, Katie calls it quits and joins Lily in London, where the sisters become big stars. Back in Tin Pan Alley, Skeets passes over a war song that has been submitted to the publishers, and not only does WWI break out and the song become a hit, but the brothers lose their shirts and end up in the Army. In England, on their way to the trenches, Harry and Skeets go AWOL and see the sisters, setting the stage for a happy postwar reunion. Directed at a breezy pace by Walter Lang and full of familiar old tunes, this entertaining musical (remade in 1950 as I'LL GET BY) bubbles with energy. Payne and Faye play well off each other, Oakie and Grable provide strong support, and Ralston, once known as the "American Venus," makes her last major appearance here. Significantly, "The Sheik of Araby," the movie's big production number, was edited after the Hays Office complained that an excess of female flesh was displayed in the sequence.

TITANIC

1953 98m bw Historical ★★★½
Fox (U.S.) /A

Clifton Webb (Richard Sturges), Barbara Stanwyck (Julia Sturges), Robert Wagner (Giff Rogers), Audrey Dalton (Annette Sturges), Thelma Ritter (Mrs. Maude Young), Brian Aherne (Capt. E.J. Smith), Richard Basehart (George Healey), Allyn Joslyn (Earl Meeker), James Todd (Sandy Comstock), William Johnstone (John Jacob Astor)

p, Charles Brackett; d, Jean Negulesco; w, Charles Brackett, Walter Reisch, Richard Breen; ph, Joseph MacDonald; ed, Louis Loeffler; m, Sol Kaplan; art d, Lyle Wheeler, Maurice Ransford; fx, Ray Kellogg; chor, Robert Alton; cos, Dorothy Jeakins

AA Best Story and Screenplay: Charles Brackett, Walter Reisch, Richard Breen; AAN Best Art Direction: Lyle Wheeler, Maurice Ransford, Stuart Reiss

The Titanic disaster of April 15, 1912 has been filmed several times, and this time the tragedy gets the full Hollywood melodrama treatment. Stanwyck is the mother of two children and the wife of Webb, whom she is leaving, because he is a snobbish socialite. She is taking her children back to America with her to keep them from their father's corrupting influence. Webb manages to get passage on the ship by buying the third-class tickets of a Basque family whom he has persuaded to catch another ship. He and Stanwyck have a number of confrontations on board before she drives him away once and for all by telling him that her son, Harper Carter, is not his child. Wagner is a young college student who falls in love with Dalton, Stanwyck's daughter. Basehart is a priest defrocked for alcoholism. The ship's captain, Aherne, is pushing for a record crossing-time, and is ignoring warnings of icebergs in the area. Finally the inevitable disaster strikes the "unsinkable" ship, and an underwater spur on a berg tears a long hole in the side of the ship. Before long, the ship begins to list, and the passengers start for the lifeboats, only to discover that there are entirely too few to hold all of them.

Despite an overly melodramatic main story line, the film is quite effective in conveying the panic and the calm of the sinking. A 20-foot-long model of the ship is featured in scenes of the sinking which are a tour de force of special effects. Even the actors were affected by the magnitude of the tragedy they were re-creating. Stanwyck later said: "The night we were filming the scene of the dying ship in the outdoor tank at Twentieth Century-Fox, it was bitter cold. I was 47 feet up in a lifeboat swinging on the davits. The water below was agitated into a heaving, rolling mass and it was thick with other lifeboats full of women and children. I looked down and thought: if one of these ropes snaps now, it's good-bye for you. Then I looked up at the faces lining the rail, those left behind to die with the ship. I thought of the men and women who had been through this thing. We were re-creating an actual tragedy and I burst into tears. I shook with great racking sobs and couldn't stop."

TO BE OR NOT TO BE

1942 99m bw War/Drama/Comedy ★★★★★
UA (U.S.) /U

Carole Lombard (Maria Tura), Jack Benny (Joseph Tura), Robert Stack (Lt. Stanislav Sobinski), Felix Bressart (Greenberg), Lionel Atwill (Rawitch), Stanley Ridges (Prof. Alexander Siletsky), Sig Rumann (Col. Ehrhardt), Tom Dugan (Bronski), Charles Halton (Dobosh), Peter Caldwell (Wilhelm Kunze)

p, Ernst Lubitsch; d, Ernst Lubitsch; w, Edwin Justus Mayer (based on a story by Lubitsch, Melchior Lengyel); ph, Rudolph Mate; ed, Dorothy Spencer; m, Miklos Rozsa; prod d, Vincent Korda; fx, Lawrence Butler; cos, Irene

AAN Best Score: Werner Heymann

A masterpiece of satire and one of the more controversial films of its day, TO BE OR NOT TO BE is a brilliant example of how comedy can be as effective in raising social and political awareness as a serious propaganda film, while still providing hilarious entertainment.

The film begins in Poland, 1939, where Joseph Tura (Jack Benny), a tremendously vain Polish actor, and his wife, Maria (Carole Lombard), a conceited national institution in Warsaw, are starring in an anti-Nazi stage play that subsequently is censored and replaced with a production of "Hamlet." Maria has taken a fancy to a young Polish fighter pilot, Sobinski (Robert Stack), who is called to duty when Germany invades Poland. In England, he and his fellow pilots in the Polish squadron of the RAF bid farewell to their much-loved mentor, Prof. Siletsky (Stanley Ridges), who confides to them that he is on a secret mission to Warsaw. Sobinski, however, begins to suspect that Siletsky is a spy and flies to Warsaw to stop him from keeping an appointment with Nazi colonel Ehrhardt (Sig Rumann)—an appointment that will destroy the Warsaw underground. There, Sobinski enlists the aid and special talents of the Tura's theater group to save and protect the Resistance.

A satire built around a rather complex spy plot and directed with genius by Ernst Lubitsch, TO BE OR NOT TO BE lampoons the Nazis and paints the Poles as brave patriots fighting for their land, for whom Hamlet's question "To be or not to be" takes on national implications. Released in 1942, in the midst of America's involvement in WWII, the film drew a great deal of criticism from people who felt that Lubitsch, a German (though he left long before Hitler's rise), was somehow making fun of the Poles. TO BE OR NOT TO BE is also remembered as the last screen appearance for the dazzling Lombard, who, just after the film's completion, was killed in a plane crash while on her way to Hollywood for a war bonds spot on Benny's radio show. TO BE was a perfect and brash finale to Lombard's great comic genius, especially because of it's examination of play-acting. Was there ever as playful a spirit on a movie set as Lombard? The film came from an idea by Melchior Lengyel—as did NINOTCHKA. Mel Brooks's remake of the story was released in 1983, with Brooks and Anne Bancroft playing the leads. While not as good, it's a perfectly watchable, if unecessary, tribute to the original, with Bancroft faring better than Brooks.

TO CATCH A THIEF

1955 103m c Crime/Romance/Comedy ★★½
Paramount (U.S.) /PG

Cary Grant (John Robie), Grace Kelly (Frances Stevens), Jessie Royce Landis (Mrs. Jessie Stevens), John Williams (H.H. Hughson), Charles Vanel (Bertani), Brigitte Auber (Danielle Foussard), Jean Martinelli (Foussard), Georgette Anys (Germaine), Roland Lessaffre (Jean Hebey), Rene Blancard (Commissioner Lepic)

p, Alfred Hitchcock; d, Alfred Hitchcock; w, John Michael Hayes (based on the novel by David Dodge); ph, Robert Burks; ed, George Tomasini; m, Lyn Murray; art d, Hal Pereira, Joseph MacMillan Johnson; fx, John P. Fulton; cos, Edith Head

AA Best Cinematography: Robert Burks; AAN Best Art Direction: Hal Pereira, Joseph McMillan Johnson, Sam Comer, Arthur Krams; AAN Best Costume Design: Edith Head

Catch a thief? Throw it back. Notable as perhaps Hitchcock's worst film during perhaps his greatest decade, TO CATCH A THIEF is schoolboy naughtiness and schoolgirl slush, all decked out in chic French finery and looking mighty expensive. This doughy, stale piece of puff pastry casts Grant as a former thief whose modus operandi is being appropriated by some new crook along the French Riviera. Understandably miffed at all the suspicion blowing his way, he sets out to find out the real villain. His "girl Friday" in this one is elegant Grace Kelly, sniffing that Monaco air like she's got the crown on already. She's at her sexiest and most playful here, but the tired Grant doesn't look like he wants to tussle much. The dialogue is sexy, too, but Hitch's "wink, wink, nudge, nudge" has all the delicacy of oatmeal. If you can't figure out the real thief's identity in about twenty minutes, your Captain Crunch spy decoder ring should be taken away forever. Topping off this non-caloric sundae is a fashion extravaganza without even the camp appeal of those in THE WOMEN or the same year's LUCY GALLANT. Palms to Jesse Royce Landis, though, for giving the film's best performance. Lightweight to the point of zero gravity, this mildly enjoyable but overlong piece of K-Mart sophistication today seems a mere footnote to the career of the man in the director's chair.

TO DIE FOR

1995 100m c Crime/Comedy/Drama   ★★★
LH Productions/Laura Ziskin Productions/Columbia (U.S.)   R/15

Nicole Kidman (Suzanne Stone), Matt Dillon (Larry Maretto), Joaquin Phoenix (Jimmy Emmett), Casey Affleck (Russell Hines), Illeana Douglas (Jancie Maretto), Alison Folland (Lydia Mertz), Dan Hedaya (Joe Maretto), Wayne Knight (Ed Grant), Kurtwood Smith (Earl Stone), Holland Taylor (Carol Stone)

p, Laura Ziskin; d, Gus Van Sant; w, Buck Henry (based on the novel by Joyce Maynard); ph, Eric Alan Edwards; ed, Curtiss Clayton; m, Danny Elfman; prod d, Missy Stewart; art d, Vlasta Svoboda; fx, Laird McMurray Film Services; cos, Beatrix Aruna Pasztor

Not *just* another facile attempt to blame societal ills on TV, TO DIE FOR leavens its heavy-handed satire of mainstream American values with genuine empathy for its marginal characters. Adapted from Joyce Maynard's fact-based novel about a New Hampshire teacher who bullied her teenaged lover into murdering her husband, TO DIE FOR was a comeback of sorts for both director Gus Van Sant—whose EVEN COWGIRLS GET THE BLUES (1994) was a genuine debacle—and screenwriter Buck Henry, who hadn't written a critical or commercial hit since 1978's HEAVEN CAN WAIT.

Little Hope, New Hampshire, is the center of a media whirlwind involving lovely local weathergirl Suzanne Stone (Nicole Kidman) and murder most foul. Suzanne is the brightly chatty narrator of her own bizarre story. Hell-bent on conquering the world of television — "You're nobody in America unless you're on TV," Suzanne coos, "because what's the point of doing something worthwhile if nobody's watching?" — she's prepared to bump off anyone who stands in her way. Which is too bad for hubby Larry (Matt Dillon), a small-town tavern-keeper who saw his best days in high school.

A solid narrative with a disappointing and obvious subtext, TO DIE FOR opts to finger the usual suspects: TV, unseemly ambition, and some generalized flaw in the American character. Kidman's wildly overrated performance shows some comic flair, but the part is woefully underwritten. Dillon fares better in a role that could easily have descended into caricature: his death scene has a tragic humanity that the film rarely achieves with the other "straight" characters. Van Sant and Henry's contempt for Middle America rivals Robert Altman's; they can't even be bothered to get the details right. None of the film's TV recreations have the ring of truth, a substantial liability in this media-mad context.

TO EACH HIS OWN

1946 122m bw Drama   ★★★★
Paramount (U.S.)   /A

Olivia de Havilland (Miss Josephine Norris), John Lund (Capt. Bart Cosgrove/Gregory Piersen), Mary Anderson (Corinna Piersen), Roland Culver (Lord Desham), Phillip Terry (Alex Piersen), Bill Goodwin (Mac Tilton), Virginia Welles (Liz Lorimer), Victoria Horne (Daisy Gingras), Griff Barnett (Mr. Norris), Alma Macrorie (Belle Ingham)

p, Charles Brackett; d, Mitchell Leisen; w, Charles Brackett, Jacques Thery (based on a story by Brackett); ph, Daniel Fapp; ed, Alma Macrorie; m, Victor Young; art d, Hans Dreier, Roland Anderson; fx, Gordon Jennings, Farciot Edouart; cos, Edith Head

AA Best Actress: Olivia de Havilland; *AAN Best Original Story:* Charles Brackett

What might have been a trite soap opera is elevated to the status of superior emotional drama by a wise script, sensitive direction, and an Oscar-winning performance by de Havilland, her first and the first for an actress at Paramount. Covering 27 years in the life and times of a woman who loved neither wisely nor well, it begins during the blitz on

London. Middle-aged de Havilland is an air raid warden and marches her beat with confidante Culver, a peer of the realm and another warden. When she learns that a handsome US pilot, Lund, is in town, her thoughts flash back to an earlier time in her life, when her love affair with a dashing pilot (also played by Lund) resulted in a disastrous pregnancy.

Lund, who had already established himself on Broadway, made his film debut here. An interesting sidelight is that de Havilland hadn't worked for two years. She'd been on suspension from Warner Bros. and was trying to break a contract which they claimed included all of her suspension time. She sued the studio successfully and the result was a law that limited studios to a seven-year agreement with an actor, with no clause regarding suspensions. That became known as the "de Havilland Decision," and actors have thanked her ever since. Leisen and de Havilland had worked together in HOLD BACK THE DAWN, and when she asked for him to direct, he passed on it at first, then was convinced when the studio gave him script approval as well as several other concessions. It was sentimental but never bathetic. Leisen knew that de Havilland had given a star performance and on the wrap day gifted her with a bracelet that featured a mini-Oscar. His prophecy was on the money, and she took the Oscar home at the next awards ceremony. Brackett's story was nominated for a statuette, but that was it from the Academy. Audiences loved it, and credit must be given to the studio for attempting a "soft" picture at the time. No one expected it to do as well as it did. Good editing by Macrorie and Victor Young's music kept the mood swings right on target. Miss de Havilland's winning of the Oscar was a surprise to many who had placed their bets on the formidable quartet of losers in 1946. They were Celia Johnson for BRIEF ENCOUNTER, Jane Wyman in THE YEARLING, Jennifer Jones for DUEL IN THE SUN, and Rosalind Russell as SISTER KENNY.

TO HAVE AND HAVE NOT

1944 100m bw Drama   ★★★★
Warner Bros. (U.S.)   /PG

Humphrey Bogart (Harry Morgan), Walter Brennan (Eddie), Lauren Bacall (Marie Browning), Dolores Moran (Helene De Bursac), Hoagy Carmichael (Cricket), Walter Molnar (Paul De Bursac), Sheldon Leonard (Lt. Coyo), Marcel Dalio (Gerard), Walter Sande (Johnson), Dan Seymour (Capt. M. Renard)

p, Howard Hawks; d, Howard Hawks; w, Jules Furthman, William Faulkner (based on the novel by Ernest Hemingway); ph, Sid Hickox; ed, Christian Nyby; m, Franz Waxman; art d, Charles Novi; fx, Roy Davidson; cos, Milo Anderson

The dialogue is sharp, the direction first-rate, and the acting superb, but TO HAVE AND HAVE NOT is undoubtedly best remembered for the on- and offscreen romance between Bogart and Bacall. Warner Bros. wanted another CASABLANCA, and in many ways Bogart's character here resembles his classic portrait of Rick Blaine.

It is WWII and France has just fallen to the Nazi occupation. Bogart, living on the island of Martinique, is the owner of a cabin cruiser, the *Queen Conch*, on which he takes wealthy customers on fishing trips. Working with him is Brennan, a not-too-bright alcoholic with an amiable demeanor. Bogart is approached by Dalio, a member of the French resistance, who asks Bogart to help smuggle one of the underground movement's top leaders (Molnar) into Martinique. Bogart, who cares little for politics, turns him down. Bacall appears, asking Bogart for help in getting off the island. Now Bogart agrees to make the dangerous run for Dalio.

Stylish and loaded with humor, this immensely entertaining film was the result of a argument between director Hawks and novelist Ernest Hemingway. On a fishing trip in Florida with the author, Hawks tried to convince Hemingway that he should come to Hollywood to work on a screenplay. When Hemingway indicated no interest in Hawks's proposal, the filmmaker reportedly responded by boasting that he could make a film out of Hemingway's worst book, which Hawks felt was *To Have and Have Not*. Hemingway's novel is set in Cuba and the Florida Keys in the 1930s. In it, the character Bogart plays is less heroic, a married man with children, who is forced to run booze and men on his boat when his financial situation becomes desperate. Hawks kept the title and the character, then threw out the Hemingway story.

The next task for Hawks was casting. Bogart seemed perfect for the part of Harry Morgan, but who was fiery enough to play opposite him? Hawks took a chance on an unknown talent named Betty Bacall, a beautiful 18-year-old New York model who was virtually unknown in Hollywood. Hawks had become interested in Bacall after his wife spotted her on the cover of *Vogue*. The electricity between the two stars was always intended to be the heart of the film, but Bogart and Bacall's onscreen romance had a steamy verisimilitude that went way beyond anybody's expectations. As it became obvious the two were becoming involved, Hawks reportedly warned Bacall that the 45-year-old Bogart was just using his young costar to escape from a bad marriage and that when the filming was over, Bogart would forget about her. Worried that Bacall's infatuation with Bogart would cause the young actress to blow her big chance, Hawks is said to have threatened to sell her contract to Monogram. Of course, this was an empty threat, and some have even suggested that Hawks used the offscreen affair to heighten the on-screen romance. (Tellingly, in the film Bogart and Bacall refer to each other as "Steve" and "Slim," the pet names Hawks and his wife had for each another.)

TO KILL A MOCKINGBIRD

1962   129m   bw   Drama   ★★★★
Universal   (U.S.)   /PG

Gregory Peck *(Atticus Finch)*, Mary Badham *(Jean Louise "Scout" Finch)*, Phillip Alford *(Jem Finch)*, John Megna *(Dill Harris)*, Frank Overton *(Sheriff Heck Tate)*, Robert Duvall *(Arthur "Boo" Radley)*, Rosemary Murphy *(Miss Maudie Atkinson)*, Ruth White *(Mrs. Dubose)*, Brock Peters *(Tom Robinson)*, Estelle Evans *(Calpurnia)*

p, Alan J. Pakula; d, Robert Mulligan; w, Horton Foote (based on the novel by Harper Lee); ph, Russell Harlan; ed, Aaron Stell; m, Elmer Bernstein; art d, Alexander Golitzen, Henry Bumstead; cos, Rosemary Odell, Viola Thompson

AAN Best Picture; AA Best Actor: Gregory Peck; *AAN Best Supporting Actress:* Mary Badham; *AAN Best Director:* Robert Mulligan; *AA Best Adapted Screenplay:* Horton Foote; *AAN Best Cinematography:* Russell Harlan; *AAN Best Score:* Elmer Bernstein; *AA Best Art Direction:* Alexander Golitzen, Henry Bumstead, Oliver Emert

Peck's peak. Based on Harper Lee's semiautobiographical, Pulitzer Prize-winning novel of 1960, TO KILL A MOCKINGBIRD is a hauntingly nostalgic portrayal of childhood mischief set in a racially divided Alabama town in the 1930s. If the film's tone sometimes seems overly righteous, it's offset by a poetic lyricism that is difficult to resist embracing.

Gregory Peck plays incorruptible lawyer Atticus Finch, a widower with two children, 10-year-old Alford and tomboyish 6-year-old Badham. During the summer, Alford and Badham amuse themselves by rolling each other down the street in a tire or playing in a treehouse. What occupies them most, however, is the creaky wooden house where Robert Duvall lives. According to neighborhood legend, Duvall is crazy and chained to his bed by his father, though he has never been seen, at least by the children. While the kids play, Peck agrees to represent a black man who is accused of raping a young white woman. A number of people try to pressure him into stepping down from the case, but his pursuit of justice is unwavering. As the trial proceeds, Peck, Alford, and especially Badham learn as much about each other as they do about their own fears and prejudices.

Since its release, this intelligent, atmospheric film has been warmly received by audiences responding not only to their own childhood, but also to the heroic image portrayed by Peck, a shining example of citizenship and affectionate fatherhood.

There is also a superb score by Elmer Bernstein. The language, emotions, and general subject matter of the trial scenes may be a bit rough for some children, but in Peck's solid, idealistic hands, all good things triumph. This was Robert Duvall's film debut.

TO LIVE
(HUOZHE)

1994   125m   c   Historical/Political/Drama   ★★★★
ERA International Ltd./Shanghai Film Studios   (China/Taiwan)   /12

Ge You *(Fugui)*, Gong Li *(Jiazhen)*, Niu Ben *(Town Chief Niu)*, Guo Tao *(Chunsheng)*, Jiang Wu *(Wan Erxi)*, Ni Dahong *(Long'er)*, Liu Tianchi *(Adult Fengxia)*, Zhang Lu *(Teenage Fengxia)*, Xiao Cong *(Fengxia—as a child)*, Dong Fei *(Youqing)*

p, Chiu Fu-Sheng; d, Zhang Yimou; w, Yu Hua, Lu Wei (based on the novel by Yu Hua); ph, Lu Yue; ed, Du Yuan; m, Zhao Jiping; prod d, Cao Jiuping; cos, Dong Huamiao

Boasting superb central performances from Ge You and the astonishing Gong Li, Zhang Yimou's TO LIVE is truly epic in its historical scope while retaining the emotional intimacy of such earlier masterworks as RED SORGHUM, JU DOU, and RAISE THE RED LANTERN.

The eldest son of a prominent local family, Fugui (Ge You) is indolent by nature but passionate about gambling. Although his wife, Jiazhen (Gong Li), threatens to leave him, Fugui soon loses his family's fortune and is reduced to selling thread on the street. With the long-suffering Jiazhen, Fugui struggles to hold his family together through years of social turmoil, coping with a harrowing stint in the Nationalist Army and the brutal upheavals of Mao's Great Leap Forward and the Cultural Revolution.

Visually, TO LIVE is surprisingly straightforward, even static, lacking the cinematic sweep of Chen Kaige's FAREWELL, MY CONCUBINE. Instead, Zhang has created a domestic drama on an epic scale, choosing to view historic events through the lens of a nuclear family. He's also chosen to focus on performances, and his two stars don't disappoint. Known for her breathtaking beauty and spitfire intensity, Gong Li once again confirms her status as one of the screen's most affecting actresses. Ge You is a revelation: he delivers a subtle, beautifully nuanced, and deeply humane performance for which he was honored as Best Actor at the 1994 Cannes Film Festival.

Although TO LIVE raised the hackles of the Chinese government during its production (Zhang was subsequently banned from participating in any foreign co-productions), it is not by any means an attack on the PRC; still, it doesn't flinch from depicting the fearful consequences of Mao's utopianism. The film's greatest achievement transcends partisan politics: TO LIVE breathes new and persuasive life into what has a become a humanist cliche, depicting the triumph of the human spirit as the ability to persevere, if not exactly flourish, under the most difficult conditions.

TO LIVE AND DIE IN L.A.

1985   116m   c   Crime   ★★★½
New Century/SLM   (U.S.)   R/

William L. Peterson *(Richard Chance)*, Willem Dafoe *(Rick Masters)*, John Pankow *(John Vukovich)*, Debra Feuer *(Bianca Torres)*, John Turturro *(Carl Cody)*, Darlanne Fluegel *(Ruth Lanier)*, Dean Stockwell *(Bob Grimes)*, Steve James *(Jeff Rice)*, Robert Downey Jr. *(Thomas Bateman)*, Michael Greene *(Jim Hart)*

p, Irving H. Levin; d, William Friedkin; w, William Friedkin, Gerald Petievich (based on the novel by Petievich); ph, Robby Muller; ed, Scott Smith, Bud Smith; m, Wang Chung; prod d, Lilly Kilvert; art d, Buddy Cone; fx, Phil Corey; cos, Linda Bass

An astonishing, brilliantly edited car chase—with pursuer and pursued speeding the wrong way along the LA Freeway—is one of many pleasures in this darkly stylish crime film, director William Friedkin's best effort since THE EXORCIST. Richard Chance (William L. Petersen) is a Secret Service agent whose partner (Michael Greene) is brutally slain by a counterfeiting gang led by Rick Masters (Willem Dafoe). Chance is now teamed with tyro John Vukovich (John Pankow) and is determined to bring his partner's killer to justice. His quest leads him into the world of Masters, a talented artist who has given up painting and turned to making superb reproductions of $20 bills. Extremely violent, subversively homoerotic, and visually remarkable, with an electric soundtrack by Wang Chung.

TO SIR, WITH LOVE

1967 105m c Drama   ★★★
James Clavell (U.K.)   /PG

Sidney Poitier *(Mark Thackeray)*, Christian Roberts *(Denham)*, Judy Geeson *(Pamela Dare)*, Suzy Kendall *(Gillian Blanchard)*, Lulu *(Barbara Pegg)*, Faith Brook *(Mrs. Evans)*, Geoffrey Bayldon *(Weston)*, Edward Burnham *(Florian)*, Gareth Robinson *(Tich)*, Grahame Charles *(Fernman)*

p, James Clavell; d, James Clavell; w, James Clavell (based on the novel by E.R. Braithwaite); ph, Paul Beeson; ed, Peter Thornton; m, Ron Grainer; art d, Tony Woollard

A sentimental picture starring Poitier as an engineer from British Guiana who, because he is black, cannot find work in his field. He accepts a teaching position in a slummy high school in London's East End. He quickly learns that he signed on for more than he bargained for—the students are poorly educated, viciously rebellious, and downright crude to authority figures. Rather than end up like the previous string of instructors—who gave up on the students—Poitier tries an unorthodox method. Instead of relying on textbooks, Poitier teaches from experience. His belief is that the students must be treated like adults in order for them to behave as such. Gradually Poitier gains the students' trust and respect. What makes TO SIR, WITH LOVE such an enjoyable film is the mythic nature of Poitier's character. He manages to come across as a real person, while simultaneously embodying everything there is to know about morality, respect, and integrity. The film's success baffled Columbia executives who just didn't know how to market it. In an attempt to learn why people liked the film so much, they even handed out questionnaires—a method that proved fruitless. One factor in the picture's popularity and its sustaining charm is the tuneful title song, which was a top hit for Lulu and is heard throughout the film. TO SIR, WITH LOVE went on to become the eighth largest grosser of the year, raking in $7.2 million.

TO SLEEP WITH ANGER

1990 95m c Drama   ★★★½
Edward R. Pressman/SVS (U.S.)   PG/15

Danny Glover *(Harry Mention)*, Richard Brooks *(Babe Brother)*, Paul Butler *(Gideon)*, Mary Alice *(Suzie)*, Carl Lumbly *(Junior)*, Sheryl Lee Ralph *(Linda)*, Vonetta McGee *(Pat)*, Wonderful Smith *(Preacher)*, Ethel Ayler *(Hattie)*

p, Caldecot Chubb, Thomas S. Byrnes, Darin Scott; d, Charles Burnett; w, Charles Burnett; ph, Walt Lloyd; ed, Nancy Richardson; m, Stephen James Taylor; prod d, Penny Barrett; art d, Troy Myers; cos, Gaye Shannon-Burnett

Although with this movie writer-director Charles Burnett received considerable attention as one of a "new wave" of black filmmakers, he had already been making films for more than a decade. An atypical look at suburban middle-class black life, TO SLEEP WITH ANGER boasts a rich and resonant screenplay, strong performances, and expressive direction.

Danny Glover, who used some of his post-LETHAL WEAPON clout to finance the film, won for himself a rare opportunity to show his dramatic range. Harry Mention (Glover), a hard-bitten drifter, shows up one day at the suburban Los Angeles home of Gideon (Paul Butler) and his wife Suzie (Mary Alice). He is an old friend who grew up with the couple in the South. The household is filled with tension, much of it created by son Samuel (Richard Brooks), who resents hard-working, successful older brother Junior (Carl Lumbly). Junior, meanwhile, resents the way his parents dote on Samuel, despite the fact that Junior does all the heavy work around the house while supporting his pregnant wife, Pat (Vonetta McGee). Harry's arrival initially adds some excitement to the family life, but his behavior develops an insidious edge. He starts bringing his old friends into the house: blues singers, gamblers, and other shady characters who drink heavily and have vaguely violent pasts. We learn that Harry himself may have been involved with a couple of murders. When Gideon is disabled by a stroke, Harry assumes control of the household with bleak results, exploiting the family's weaknesses and tensions.

What really sticks out in TO SLEEP WITH ANGER is its richness of imagery. The opening credits play over an image of Gideon sitting placidly in a chair as flames burn first on his feet and eventually over his entire body as the hymn "Precious Memories" plays on the soundtrack. Other memorable scenes include shots of the kid next door struggling to play a trumpet, undercutting the stereotypes about blacks and music; Harry cutting his toenails in Gideon's favorite chair as Gideon lies stricken upstairs; and the poignant montage showing the deterioration of Gideon's beloved garden in the wake of his illness.

TOBACCO ROAD

1941 84m bw Comedy/Drama   ★★★★
Fox (U.S.)   /A

Charley Grapewin *(Jeeter Lester)*, Marjorie Rambeau *(Sister Bessie)*, Gene Tierney *(Ellie May Lester)*, William Tracy *(Duke Lester)*, Elizabeth Patterson *(Ada Lester)*, Dana Andrews *(Dr. Tim)*, Slim Summerville *(Henry Peabody)*, Ward Bond *(Lov Bensey)*, Grant Mitchell *(George Payne)*, Zeffie Tilbury *(Grandma Lester)*

p, Darryl F. Zanuck; d, John Ford; w, Nunnally Johnson (based on the play by Jack Kirkland and the novel by Erskine Caldwell); ph, Arthur Miller; ed, Barbara McLean; m, David Buttolph; art d, Richard Day, James Basevi

A twisty, humorous antithesis to the usual Fordian style of family bonding, TOBACCO ROAD is a beautifully photographed examination of life among the "poor white trash" of Georgia's Tobacco Road area during the Depression. One of three Nunnally Johnson-scripted Ford films—following the PRISONER OF SHARK ISLAND and THE GRAPES OF WRATH—TOBACCO ROAD takes the long-running Kirkland play, which opened in 1933 and was based on the popular Caldwell novel, and turns it into a strangely distorted story of individualism and integrity. The film opens with the apocalyptic statement, "All that they were, and all that they had, is gone with the wind and the dust," establishing a somber tone for this character study of man battered by the elements. But Ford, not to be easily pigeon-holed, plays much of the film for laughs. Cast as husband and wife, Grapewin and Patterson do their best to hold their family together while struggling to pay the bills. Grandmother Tilbury just gets up and leaves one day, walking into the forest, presumably to die, and is never seen again. Tracy, the rambunctious son, is more concerned with buying a car, blowing its horn, and making a wreck of it after one day than he is with helping his father in daily affairs. It is this car, however, that brings the family together in admiration of its design. The unity, however, is short-lived.

A masterful combination of Ford's pictorial skills and Johnson's character sketches (which also can be seen in the classic Jean Renoir portrait of the South, THE SOUTHERNER, to which Johnson and William Faulkner contributed), TOBACCO ROAD is an oddity in Ford's filmography, which is full of movies that celebrate family values, the love of the land, the work ethic, and honesty. In this film, however, these qualities are parodied, and the result, while unorthodox, is highly enjoyable, making TOBACCO ROAD perhaps Ford's most underrated achievement. Photographed by Arthur C. Miller, the man responsible for the breathtaking visuals of HOW GREEN WAS MY VALLEY (for which he won an Oscar), TOBACCO ROAD is, if nothing else, a marvel to look at.

TOKYO STORY
(TOKYO MONOGATARI)

1953 136m bw Drama   ★★★★★
Shochiku/Ofuna (Japan)   /U

Chishu Ryu *(Shukishi Hirayama)*, Chieko Higashiyama *(Tomi Hirayama)*, So Yamamura *(Koichi)*, Kuniko Miyake *(Fumiko)*, Haruko Sugimura *(Shige Kaneko)*, Nobuo Nakamura *(Kurazo Kaneko)*, Kyoko Kagawa *(Kyoko)*, Setsuko Hara *(Noriko)*, Shiro Osaka *(Keiso)*, Eijiro Tono *(Sanpei Numata)*

p, Takeshi Yamamoto; d, Yasujiro Ozu; w, Yasujiro Ozu, Kogo Noda; ph, Yushun Atsuta; ed, Yoshiyasu Hamamura; m, Takanobu Saito; prod d, Tatsuo Hamada, Itsuo Takahashi; art d, Tatsuo Hamada, Itsuo Takahashi; cos, Taizo Saito

TOKYO STORY, Ozu's masterpiece and a landmark in Japanese cinema, didn't make it to the US until 19 years after its initial release, but American critics were immediately taken with this stately, powerful critique of the family and its discontents. An elderly couple (Ryu and Higashiyama) journey with their youngest daughter (Kagawa) to Tokyo to visit their doctor son (Yamamura) and a daughter (Sugimura) who runs a beauty salon. The children are too busy to meet with their parents, so they send them to a resort. After a sleepless night in the noisy resort the parents return to Tokyo. Before leaving, however, the mother spends a night with the widow (Hara) of another son, and the father visits some old drinking buddies. As it turns out, only this daughter-in-law gives the elderly couple the attention and love they need. The couple's own children soon have cause to regret their neglect, but their emotional ties to their parents have been all but severed by then. It comes as no surprise that they can so easily return to their own self-absorbed lives.

The film may not sound like much in a bald summary, but Ozu's cinema is remarkably powerful for those willing to give it a chance. Ryu is a familiar face in the films of many fine directors, and his marvelous low-key performance is but one of many in the film. Delicately constructed and deliberately leisurely, TOKYO STORY allows its dramatic content and thematic concerns to envelop an audience the way social mores envelop the films' characters. Ozu seems at once critical of certain aspects of Japanese tradition and reconciled to their status and use value. His trademark stylistics are equally intriguing, from his casually non-mainstream editing patterns to his limited camera movement. Most famous of all, though, are Ozu's trademark *tatami*-level shots. Using a special camera dolly to simulate the three-foot height of the average person kneeling or sitting on a *tatami* pad, Ozu creates a way of seeing the world that is specifically Japanese. Although one should resist seeing this great filmmaker simply as the most traditional of Japanese directors, his films do mirror the basics of contemporary Japan in a manner fascinating for those interested in this complex culture.

Of Yasujiro Ozu's 53 films only a few have been released in the US, and 34 were silents directed before 1936, many of which have been destroyed.

TOM BROWN'S SCHOOLDAYS

1951   93m   bw   Drama   ★★
Talisman   (U.K.)   /U

John Howard Davies (*Tom Brown*), Robert Newton (*Dr. Arnold*), Diana Wynyard (*Mrs. Arnold*), Hermione Baddeley (*Sally Harrowell*), Kathleen Byron (*Mrs. Brown*), James Hayter (*Old Thomas*), John Charlesworth (*East*), John Forrest (*Flashman*), Michael Hordern (*Wilkes*), Max Bygraves (*Coach Guard*)

p, Brian Desmond Hurst; d, Gordon Parry; w, Noel Langley (based on the novel by Thomas Hughes); ph, C. Pennington-Richards, Ray Sturgess; ed, Kenneth Heeley-Ray; m, Richard Addinsell; art d, Fred Pusey

This is a saccharine screen version of the Thomas Hughes classic, emphasizing the battles between new boy at school Davies and the brute he must contend with, Forrest. A new headmaster is also introduced, portrayed by Newton. He deals with problems in a manner the boys are not very accustomed to; that is, he treats his students as human beings instead of untrained animals. Davies is almost too likable in the lead role, while his counterpart is likewise almost too nasty, but this helps to play up the heavy dramatics. This film is a remake of TOM BROWN'S SCHOOL DAYS.

TOM JONES

1963   131m   c   Comedy   ★★★★★
Woodfall   (U.K.)   /PG

Albert Finney (*Tom Jones*), Susannah York (*Sophie Western*), Hugh Griffith (*Squire Western*), Edith Evans (*Miss Western*), Joan Greenwood (*Lady Bellaston*), Diane Cilento (*Molly Seagrim*), George Devine (*Squire Allworthy*), David Tomlinson (*Lord Fellamar*), Joyce Redman (*Mrs. Waters/Jenny Jones*), George A. Cooper (*Fitzpatrick*)

p, Tony Richardson; d, Tony Richardson; w, John Osborne (based on the novel by Henry Fielding); ph, Walter Lassally; ed, Anthony Gibbs; m, John Addison; prod d, Ralph Brinton; art d, Ted Marshall; cos, John McCorry

AA Best Picture; AAN Best Actor: Albert Finney; *AAN Best Supporting Actor:* Hugh Griffith; *AAN Best Supporting Actress:* Diane Cilento; *AAN Best Supporting Actress:* Edith Evans; *AAN Best Supporting Actress:* Joyce Redman; *AA Best Director:* Tony Richardson; *AA Best Adapted Screenplay:* John Osborne; *AA Best Score:* John Addison; *AAN Best Art Direction:* Ralph Brinton, Ted Marshall, Jocelyn Herbert, Josie MacAvin

A rollicking comedic condensation of Fielding's sprawling novel about a lusty young man's adventures in 18th-Century England, TOM JONES was an enormous box office success that won four Oscars for Best Picture, Best Screenplay, Best Direction, and Best Score.

Featuring superb performances from Albert Finney and Susannah York and marking the film debut of Lynn Redgrave, TOM JONES is a brilliant melding of naturalistic 18th-Century backgrounds with frantic, Keystone Kops-style slapstick and silent film devices like undercranking, titles, wipes, stop-motion photography, etc. Cutting down and molding Fielding's huge 1749 episodic novel was a gargantuan task. Screenwriter Osborne, best known for social realist works like LOOK BACK IN ANGER, may have seemed an odd choice (Richardson and Osborne were both from the "Angry Young Man" school), but he succeeded beyond all expectations.

Several set pieces stand out in memory: the huge stag hunt at the estate of Griffith; the Georges Feydeau-style bedroom farce at the inn; but, most of all, the famous Redman-Finney scene which, while it shows nothing sexual—just two people staring into each others' eyes as they rip food apart and stuff it in their faces—remains among the most cheekily erotic few minutes in cinema. The other achievement of TOM JONES was that it put Fielding's novel back onto the best-seller lists, more than two centuries after it was published.

TOMMY

1975   111m   c   Musical   ★½
Columbia   (U.K.)   PG/15

Ann-Margret (*Nora Walker Hobbs*), Oliver Reed (*Frank Hobbs*), Roger Daltrey (*Tommy Walker*), Elton John (*Pinball Wizard*), Eric Clapton (*Preacher*), Jack Nicholson (*Specialist*), Robert Powell (*Capt. Walker*), Paul Nicholas (*Cousin Kevin*), Tina Turner (*Acid Queen*), Barry Winch (*Young Tommy*)

p, Robert Stigwood, Ken Russell; d, Ken Russell; w, Ken Russell (based on the musical drama by Pete Townshend, John Entwistle, and Keith Moon); ph, Dick Bush, Ronnie Taylor, Robin Lehman; ed, Stuart Baird; m, Pete Townshend, Roger Daltrey, John Entwistle, Keith Moon; art d, John Clark; chor, Gillian Gregory; cos, Shirley Russell

AAN Best Actress: Ann-Margret; *AAN Best Score:* Peter Townshend

Fans of the Who beware. Ken Russell applies his rococo outpourings to Pete Townshend's rock opera and botches not only the visuals but the fine score. With its beginnings as a 1969 album by the Who, one of rock music's most beloved and respected bands, TOMMY went on to become a stage smash in England. Then Russell, with his taste for the flamboyant and meaningless, added Ann-Margret and Oliver Reed, cast lead singer Roger Daltrey in the title role, and wasted a number of talents in useless cameos. The story, told entirely in song, centers on Tommy, a "deaf, dumb, and blind kid" who shuns the rest of the world after the death of his father. His mother, Ann-Margret, and stepfather, Reed, bring him to a doctor, Jack Nicholson, for treatment, but nothing seems to help—that is, until Tommy discovers pinball. "Playing by sense of smell," he beats even the Pinball Wizard (Elton John) and eventually breaks free and starts life anew. Drummer Keith Moon is a highlight as perverted Holiday Camp counsellor Uncle Ernie, Eric Clapton transfers his real-life role as rock guitar god to the screen, and Tina Turner is explosive as the Acid Queen but comes and goes with little explanation. Regrettably, Townshend's extraordinary songs are mauled by Ann-Margret, Reed, and Nicholson. Daltrey, however, proves himself an engaging screen presence and would continue to find work as an actor.

TONI
(LES AMOURS DE TONI)
1935 90m bw Drama   ★★★½
d'Aujourd'hui (France)

Charles Blavette (Antonio "Toni" Canova), Celia Montalvan (Josepha), Jenny Helia (Marie), Edouard Delmont (Fernand), Andrex (Gaby), Andre Kovachevitch (Sebastian), Max Dalban (Albert), Paul Bozzi (Jacques Bozzi the Guitarist), Jacques Mortier

p, Pierre Gault; d, Jean Renoir; w, Jean Renoir, Carl Einstein (based on material gathered by Jacques Levert); ph, Claude Renoir; ed, Marguerite Renoir, Suzanne de Troeye; m, Paul Bozzi

TONI has often been called the first "neorealist" film, preceding Luchino Visconti's OSSESSIONE by seven years; since the Italian director was one of Jean Renoir's assistants on the project, its influence on his work seems clear. Basing his film on police files dealing with an incident that occurred in the small town of Les Martigues, Renoir, seeking authenticity, brought his crew to that town and used its citizens as characters. The story centers on Toni (Charles Blavette), an Italian laborer who falls in love with his landlady (Jenny Helia) and then with a Spanish woman, Josepha (Celia Montalvan). After receiving permission from Josepha's father to marry her, Toni discovers that she has been raped by a sleazy foreman, whom Josepha ends up marrying, eventually deserts, and accidentally kills. Not surprisingly, Toni takes the blame. An insightful portrayal of male-female relationships and a skillful rendering of its near-pulp novel plot (again predating Visconti's adaptation of James M. Cain), TONI is nonetheless far from perfect, riddled with numerous technical weaknesses and some seemingly improvised direction. Still, it is clearly one of Renoir's important technical experiments.

TOOTSIE
1982 116m c Comedy/Romance   ★★½
Columbia (U.S.)   PG/15

Dustin Hoffman (Michael Dorsey/Dorothy Michaels), Jessica Lange (Julie), Teri Garr (Sandy), Dabney Coleman (Ron), Charles Durning (Les), Bill Murray (Jeff), Sydney Pollack (George Fields), George Gaynes (John Van Horn), Geena Davis (April), Doris Belack (Rita)

p, Sydney Pollack, Dick Richards; d, Sydney Pollack; w, Larry Gelbart, Elaine May (uncredited), Murray Schisgal (based on a story by Don McGuire, Gelbart); ph, Owen Roizman; ed, Fredric Steinkamp, William Steinkamp; m, Dave Grusin; prod d, Peter Larkin; cos, Ruth Morley

AAN Best Picture; AAN Best Actor: Dustin Hoffman; AA Best Supporting Actress: Jessica Lange; AAN Best Supporting Actress: Teri Garr; AAN Best Director: Sydney Pollack; AAN Best Original Screenplay: Larry Gelbart, Murray Schisgal, Don McGuire; AAN Best Cinematography: Owen Roizman; AAN Best Editing: Fredric Steinkamp, William Steinkamp; AAN Best Song: Dave Grusin (Music), Alan Bergman (Lyrics), Marilyn Bergman (Lyrics); AAN Best Sound: Arthur Piantadosi, Les Fresholtz, Dick Alexander, Les Lazarowitz

A sitcom ode to the Hoffman ego. Like Hoffman in drag, it doesn't look at itself very closely; it might crack the mirror. Rather than confront what it sets up, it takes the one joke and runs—till it runs out of steam. Paging Billy Wilder.

TOOTSIE is about a man who pretends to be a woman in order to secure employment as an actor-actress. Michael Dorsey (Dustin Hoffman), a stage actor trying to make ends meet, dresses in drag and auditions for a part as a mature woman at a New York soap opera. Everyone is fooled, and he gets the part. His rise to fame as "Dorothy Michaels" is almost instant, but his personal relationships become a minefield.

The film's problem is its sitcom style, which doesn't really allow for the suspension of disbelief Wilder achieved in SOME LIKE IT HOT. It leaves one no choice but to try and accept Hoffman at, well, face value. As Dorothy, Hoffman's Dorsey is hardly believable as a woman, much less an actress or someone playing an actress. Except for Lange (at the peak of her beauty, playing a sterotype with such

effortless ease that she almost steals the film) and Murray (who *does* steal the film), the rest of the cast lacks comic energy—they're not sprightly enough.

The screenplay is credited to Larry Gelbart and Murray Schisgal, but many writers contributed to it, including Elaine May; meanwhile, Hoffman's tantrums escalated set conditions to a hellish state, with Pollack, playing Hoffman's agent, and Bill Murray, Geena Davis, and Dabney Coleman around to take sides. The make-up artists worked as best they could to transform the raw material at hand—hiding Hoffman's burro ears and temporarily capping his large teeth.

TOP GUN
1986 110m c Drama/War   ★★
Paramount (U.S.)   PG/15

Tom Cruise (Lt. Pete Mitchell), Anthony Edwards (Lt. Nick Bradshaw), Kelly McGillis (Charlotte Blackwood), Tom Skerritt (Cmdr. Mike Metcalf), Val Kilmer (Tom Kasanzky), Michael Ironside (Dick Wetherly), Rick Rossovich (Ron Kerner), Barry Tubb (Henry Ruth), Whip Hubley (Rick Neven), Clarence Gilyard Jr. (Evan Gough)

p, Don Simpson, Jerry Bruckheimer; d, Tony Scott; w, Jim Cash, Jack Epps Jr.; ph, Jeffrey L. Kimball; ed, Billy Weber, Chris Lebenzon; m, Harold Faltermeyer; prod d, John De Cuir; fx, Gary Gutierrez

AAN Best Editing: Billy Weber, Chris Lebenzon; AA Best Song: Giorgio Moroder (Music), Tom Whitlock (Lyrics); AAN Best Sound: Donald O. Mitchell, Kevin O'Connell, Rick Kline, William B. Kaplan; AAN Best Sound Effects Editing: Cecelia Hall, George Watters, II

This paean to hotshot Navy fighter pilots and high technology attracted mass audiences despite its familiar plot and characters so vapid they vanish from memory as soon as the house lights come up. Brash young pilot Lt. Pete Mitchell (Tom Cruise), nicknamed "Maverick" for his individualistic flying style, is sent to Miramar Naval Air Station, where he trains with the country's best fighter pilots. The best student from each class wins the prized "Top Gun" award, and the privilege of remaining at Miramar as an instructor. Maverick's chief competition is Tom Kasanzky (Val Kilmer), nicknamed "Ice Man," and eventually an international incident arises that allows the pilots to prove themselves. In an unlikely subplot, Maverick has an affair with Charlotte Blackwood (Kelly McGillis), a civilian expert on the physics of high-speed jet performance.

What TOP GUN contributes to the genre is an increased emphasis on military hardware and an almost homoerotic attraction for male bodies, mostly sweaty ones. In the final analysis, though, everything that happens on the ground is irrelevant to the real heart of the film, the flying sequences. Much praised, the airborne footage seamlessly intercuts live action shots of planes with special effects models. But for all the skill of their execution, the flying scenes are often confusing, rarely giving any idea of where the planes are in relation to one another. Jets streak by and pilots spin their heads around yelling, "Where'd he go? Where'd he go?" until the beepers aboard their planes tell them they've been shot down. Ultimately, TOP GUN is a facile movie in which Americans kill Russians with aplomb—proving their inherent superiority—and Tom Cruise gets the girl.

TOP HAT
1935 101m bw Comedy/Musical/Romance   ★★★★★
RKO (U.S.)   /U

Fred Astaire (Jerry Travers), Ginger Rogers (Dale Tremont), Edward Everett Horton (Horace Hardwick), Helen Broderick (Madge Hardwick), Erik Rhodes (Alberto Beddini), Eric Blore (Bates), Lucille Ball (Flower Clerk), Leonard Mudie (Flower Salesman), Edgar Norton (Hotel Manager), Gino Corrado (Hotel Manager)

p, Pandro S. Berman; d, Mark Sandrich; w, Dwight Taylor, Allan Scott (based on the musical The Gay Divorcee by Dwight Taylor, Cole Porter and the play The Girl Who Dared by Alexander Farago, Aladar Laszlo); ph, David Abel; ed, William Hamilton; art d, Van Nest Polglase, Carroll Clark; fx, Vernon L. Walker; chor, Fred Astaire, Hermes Pan; cos, Bernard Newman

AAN Best Picture; AAN Art Direction: Carroll Clark, Van Nest Polglase; AAN Best Song: Irving Berlin

The fourth pairing of Fred Astaire and Ginger Rogers and the first with a screenplay written specifically for them, TOP HAT is the quintessential Astaire-Rogers musical, complete with a silly plot, romance, dapper outfits, art deco sets, and plenty of wonderful songs and dance numbers. Set in London (though the story really unfolds in Hollywood's mythical Fred-and-Ginger-Land), TOP HAT's tale of mistaken identity concerns American song-and-dance man Jerry Travers (Astaire), who becomes as enamored of lovely Dale Tremont (Rogers) as she is of him. Problems arise, however, when Dale comes to believe that Jerry is the husband (whom she's never met) of her good friend Madge (Broderick) and rebuffs his advances, finally fleeing to Venice with Madge. Jerry and Horace Hardwick (Horton), Madge's real husband and the producer of the show in which Jerry stars, follow them to Venice, and the confusion grows as Dale tells Madge that Horace has been unfaithful. Dale then marries her dress designer, Albert (Rhodes), before Jerry gets a chance to straighten things out. Not to worry: Horace's faithful butler (Eric Blore) to the rescue.

An effervescent musical that was the perfect panacea for Depression-era audiences, this wonderfully whimsical reworking of 1934's THE GAY DIVORCEE (whose leading players are reunited here) offers perhaps the most famous Astaire-Rogers duet, "Cheek to Cheek", wherein the dancers shift from effortless gliding to moves of dazzling exuberance. Despite the problems it caused in filming, La Ginger was absolutely right about not changing the famous feathered dress—it does move beautifully, and she looks as light as a feather dancing in it. Built around Irving Berlin's hit-laden score, TOP HAT also boasts Astaire's brilliant, signature solo number, "Top Hat, White Tie and Tails." Fred and Ginger once again display their incredible rapport as actors as well as dancers, and the supporting cast is uniformly perfect, even though Rhodes's Italian caricature so offended Italian officials (and even the top guy, Mussolini himself), that TOP HAT, like THE GAY DIVORCEE (in which Rhodes played a similar character), was banned in Italy. With over $3 million in receipts, TOP HAT was RKO's biggest moneymaker of the decade. Tip top.

TOP SECRET!

1984 90m c Comedy/Spy/Musical   ★★★
Paramount (U.S.)   PG/15

Omar Sharif *(Cedric)*, Jeremy Kemp *(Gen. Streck)*, Warren Clarke *(Col. Von Horst)*, Tristram Jellinek *(Maj. Crumpler)*, Val Kilmer *(Nick Rivers)*, Billy J. Mitchell *(Martin)*, Major Wiley *(Porter)*, Gertan Klauber *(Mayor)*, Richard Mayes *(Biletnikov)*, Peter Cushing *(Bookstore Proprietor)*

p, Jon Davison, Hunt Lowry; d, Jim Abrahams, David Zucker, Jerry Zucker; w, Jim Abrahams, David Zucker, Jerry Zucker, Martyn Burke; ph, Christopher Challis; ed, Bernard Gribble; m, Maurice Jarre; prod d, Peter Lamont; art d, John Fenner, Michael Lamont; fx, Nick Allder; chor, Gillian Gregory; cos, Emma Porteous

A strange mix that might have been titled "Beach Blanket Espionage," this overlooked comedy by Zucker, Abrahams, and Zucker doesn't always work, nor does it measure up to their hilarious AIRPLANE!. It is, nevertheless, very funny as it lampoons two genres: the spy movie and the teenage musical. While in East Germany to perform at big cultural festival, rock star Nick Rivers (Val Kilmer) finds himself embroiled in international intrigue involving an East German plot to take over West Germany, an imprisoned scientist (Michael Gough), and his beautiful daughter, Hillary (Lucy Gutteridge), who, naturally, becomes Nick's love interest. While helping Hillary thwart the takeover scheme, Nick, in the tradition of countless Elvis films, bursts into song on the slightest provocation. Equally without rhyme or reason is the movie's plot. In parodying pictures like THE SPY WHO CAME IN FROM THE COLD, Zucker, Abrahams, and Zucker present a narrative that is hopelessly convoluted, but that, of course, is exactly their intention as they pile joke upon joke, filling their film with inventive sight gags. Omar Sharif appears as a spy and is uproarious in what amounts to a cameo appearance, even though he gets top billing. This film hits more than it misses.

TOPAZ

1969 126m c Spy   ★★★
Universal (U.S.)   PG/A

John Forsythe *(Michael Nordstrom)*, Frederick Stafford *(Andre Devereaux)*, Dany Robin *(Nicole Devereaux)*, John Vernon *(Rico Parra)*, Karin Dor *(Juanita de Cordoba)*, Michel Piccoli *(Jacques Granville)*, Philippe Noiret *(Henri Jarre)*, Claude Jade *(Michele Picard)*, Michel Subor *(Francois Picard)*, Roscoe Lee Browne *(Philippe Dubois)*

p, Alfred Hitchcock; d, Alfred Hitchcock; w, Samuel Taylor (based on the novel by Leon Uris); ph, Jack Hildyard; ed, William Ziegler; m, Maurice Jarre; prod d, Henry Bumstead; fx, Albert Whitlock; cos, Edith Head

An espionage story that takes the cameras to Copenhagen, Paris, New York City, Harlem, Virginia, and a California hacienda that doubles as Cuba. Loosely based on the true-life exploits of French spy Philippe de Vosjoli and the 1962 "Sapphire" scandals in which top French officials were uncovered as Soviet agents, the film has a sense of authenticity but fails to fire up as much suspense as most of Hitchcock's intrigues. With an international cast of semirecognizable names (Michel Piccoli, Philippe Noiret, and just one American, John Forsythe), TOPAZ gleaned most of its attention from the star status of its director. Hitchcock considered the film a disaster because it went into production without a finished script (in complete antithesis to his normal working methods of full preparedness), without full casting, and without an ending.

TOPKAPI

1964 120m c Comedy/Crime   ★★★★
Filmways (U.S.)   /U

Melina Mercouri *(Elizabeth Lipp)*, Peter Ustinov *(Arthur Simpson)*, Maximilian Schell *(William Walter)*, Robert Morley *(Cedric Page)*, Akim Tamiroff *(Geven)*, Gilles Segal *(Giulio)*, Jess Hahn *(Fischer)*, Titos Vandis *(Harback)*, Ege Ernart *(Maj. Tufan)*, Senih Orkan

p, Jules Dassin; d, Jules Dassin; w, Monja Danischewsky (based on the novel *The Light of Day* by Eric Ambler); ph, Henri Alekan; ed, Roger Dwyre; m, Manos Hadjidakis; art d, Max Douy; cos, Denny Vachlioti

AA Best Supporting Actor: Peter Ustinov

Dassin went back to his hit RIFIFI and spoofed it with this enjoyable, fast-moving tale of a caper pulled by some of the most delightful characters ever assembled on one screen. Filmed on location in Istanbul and Greece, TOPKAPI cleverly employs every cinematic trick in the book—to an accompaniment of clever dialogue. As long as you realize TOPKAPI failed to accomplish what it set out to do—top RIFIFI—and if you don't care—this is glamorous, hambone stew.

Sexpot Mercouri (Dassin's real-life wife) and her lover want to steal a priceless dagger from the heavily secured museum in Istanbul known as Topkapi. To pull off the job, they enlist aid: Morley is an addled but brilliant British inventor and expert in electronics and burglar alarms, Segal is a mute acrobat who could climb a sheer wall with his fingernails and Hahn is a muscular, remarkably strong lout. While in Kavala, Greece, the gang hires Ustinov, a low-life con artist, to drive an expensive car across the border into Turkey. Ustinov doesn't know that the car carries weapons and gear for the robbery; when he is stopped at the border, one of the Turkish police (Ernart) thinks that some terrorists are using him as a dupe. Rather than arrest Ustinov, Ernart asks him to infiltrate the group that his hired him to report back. Ustinov delivers the goods (some bombs, a high-powered rifle) to the gang's villa in Turkey. The daring robbery is carefully calculated. The floor of the museum is wired so that a single step will set off the alarm, so Hahn will hold a rope and lower Segal through a window. Then Segal will hang from the rope, reach down, and take the dagger without ever touching the floor. Meanwhile, at the gang's sumptuous mansion, the alcoholic cook, Tamiroff, is convinced that Mercouri and the others are Soviet agents. He passes this intelligence on to Ustinov, who still doesn't know about the robbery, and Ustinov informs Ernart. The robbery is about to take place when Tamiroff accidentally crushes

Hahn's powerful hand with a door. With the strong man immobilized, Ustinov is pressed into service as the one to hold the rope, a job for which the paunchy Brit is obviously ill-equipped.

The film was based on a little-known book by Ambler and was adapted beautifully by screenwriter Danischewsky. Mercouri is the only woman of consequence in the movie, and she has a field day surrounded by the men—indeed, her touch is lighter than usual. A Supporting Oscar went to Ustinov (who keeps his numerous awards in a glass case in his bathroom. When a producer was scandalized by his placing kudos in such a room, Ustinov explained that it was the only location in his residence where he could ponder his achievements without seeming egotistical.). A great movie—with lots of laughs, a bit of the aforementioned RIFIFI, a smidgeon of BEAT THE DEVIL, and some of its own originality.

TOPPER

1937 98m bw Science Fiction/Comedy   ★★★★
MGM   (U.S.)   /A

Constance Bennett (Marion Kerby), Cary Grant (George Kerby), Roland Young (Cosmo Topper), Billie Burke (Henrietta Topper), Alan Mowbray (Wilkins), Eugene Pallette (Casey), Arthur Lake (Elevator Boy), Hedda Hopper (Mrs. Stuyvesant), Virginia Sale (Miss Johnson), Theodore von Eltz (Hotel Manager)

p, Hal Roach; d, Norman Z. McLeod; w, Jack Jevne, Eric Hatch, Eddie Moran (based on the novel The Jovial Ghosts by Thorne Smith); ph, Norbert Brodine; ed, William Terhune; m, Edward T. Powell, Hugo Friedhofer; art d, Arthur Rouce; fx, Roy Seawright; cos, Samuel Lange, Irene, Howard Schraps

AAN Best Supporting Actor: Roland Young; AAN Best Sound: Elmer Raguse

Sophisticated, but a touch too mild, saved by an ebullient cast. Low-budget comedy producer Hal Roach, who had made a fortune on his Laurel and Hardy shorts, finally decided to risk a big-budget, feature-length comedy, and he came up with a winner that spawned two sequels, a television series, and a made-for-television remake.

George and Marion Kerby (Cary Grant and Constance Bennett) are a young, wealthy, happy-go-lucky married couple whose main pursuit in life is having a good time. Though they are the chief stockholders in a bank, their minds are on anything but business. One night, while driving recklessly in their big car, they hit a tree and are killed. Their spirits walk out of the wreck, but are dismayed to learn that they have not ascended to the heavens but are still on Earth, albeit in a rather astral form (they can turn invisible at will). George and Marion then decide that they will probably be trapped on Earth forever unless they make amends for their frivolous lifestyle by doing something of value.

The orignal casting for the film—Harlow for Bennett, W.C. Fields for Young—might have made for a screwier, more frenetic mix. Harlow's comedic touch had a more childlike sense of mischief. When she died a month before filming, Bennett, whose box-office was languishing due to too many formulaic weepies, landed the risk of TOPPER. She's a teasing minx, rather than a playful kitten. But audiences responded enthusiastically to her portrayal. Additional laughs result from TOPPER's special effects—the invisible duo makes objects appear to move by themselves. Avoid the the computer-colored version, which recently appeared on the market.

TORCH SONG TRILOGY

1988 120m c Drama   ★★★
Howard Gottfried-Ronald K. Fierstein (U.S.)   R/15

Anne Bancroft (Ma), Matthew Broderick (Alan), Harvey Fierstein (Arnold Beckoff), Brian Kerwin (Ed), Karen Young (Laurel), Eddie Castrodad (David), Ken Page (Murray), Charles Pierce (Bertha Venation), Axel Vera (Marina Del Rey), Benji Schulman (Young Arnold)

p, Howard Gottfried; d, Paul Bogart; w, Harvey Fierstein (based on his play); ph, Mikael Salomon; ed, Nicholas C. Smith; m, Peter Matz; prod d, Richard Hoover; chor, Scott Salmon; cos, Colleen Atwood

When Harvey Fierstein's "Torch Song Trilogy" premiered Off-Broadway in the early 1980s, it became a word-of-mouth sensation for its caustically humorous homosexual script and performances. The film stays close to the stage production, with a story set in New York City

between 1971 and 1980 that follows the roller-coaster love life of a gravel-voiced female impersonator (Fierstein). Fierstein falls for both a handsome and tender young hunk (Brian Kerwin) and a 21-year-old fashion model (Matthew Broderick), tries to act as a father to a teenage boy (Eddie Castrodad), and all the way battles his domineering mother (Anne Bancroft). Fierstein gives a strong and winning performance, and much of his story is funny and heartfelt. Kerwin and Broderick are merely perfunctory in their roles, but Bancroft nearly single-handedly destroys the picture with her scenery chewing. She's Harvey's mother because she's a star and because the script says so, not because the audience believes her.

TORN CURTAIN

1966 126m c Spy   ★★½
Universal (U.S.)

Paul Newman (Prof. Michael Armstrong), Julie Andrews (Sarah Sherman), Lila Kedrova (Countess Kuchinska), Hansjorg Felmy (Heinrich Gerhard), Tamara Toumanova (Ballerina), Ludwig Donath (Prof. Gustav Lindt), Wolfgang Kieling (Hermann Gromek), Gunter Strack (Prof. Karl Manfred), David Opatoshu (Mr. Jacobi), Gisela Fischer (Dr. Koska)

p, Alfred Hitchcock; d, Alfred Hitchcock; w, Brian Moore (based on a story by Moore); ph, John F. Warren; ed, Bud Hoffman; m, John Addison; prod d, Hein Heckroth; art d, Frank Arrigo; cos, Edith Head

This was Alfred Hitchcock's fiftieth film and one of his least successful, despite the box-office names of Paul Newman and Julie Andrews. Michael Armstrong (Newman) is a top US nuclear physicist who defects to East Germany in order to get a secret formula in the possession of enemy scientist Gustav Lindt (Donath). Having Newman play a physicist at the peak of his sly but only semi-articulate animal sexiness (HUD, COOL HAND LUKE) is like having Elizabeth Taylor play Golda Meir. Putting Julie Andrews in a Hitchcock film at all, meanwhile, proves that a spoonful of sugar doesn't help the medicine go down. . . in the most de-light-ful way. Dull and way too long, TORN CURTAIN is only memorable for one very shocking and brutal scene in which Armstrong and a farmer's wife (played by Carolyn Conwell) have to murder a Soviet soldier. They stab the man, choke him, and finally gas him in the kitchen stove, graphically showing just how difficult can be to kill a human being.

TORTILLA FLAT

1942 105m bw Drama   ★★★★
MGM   (U.S.)   /U

Spencer Tracy (Pilon), Hedy Lamarr (Dolores "Sweets" Ramirez), John Garfield (Danny), Frank Morgan (The Pirate), Akim Tamiroff (Pablo), Sheldon Leonard (Tito Ralph), John Qualen (Jose Maria Corcoran), Donald Meek (Paul D. Cummings), Connie Gilchrist (Mrs. Torrelli), Allen Jenkins (Portagee Joe)

p, Sam Zimbalist; d, Victor Fleming; w, John Lee Mahin, Benjamin Glazer (based on the novel by John Steinbeck); ph, Karl Freund; ed, James E. Newcom; m, Franz Waxman; art d, Cedric Gibbons, Paul Groesse; fx, Warren Newcombe; cos, Robert Kalloch, Gile Steele

AAN Best Supporting Actor: Frank Morgan

This excellent adaptation of Steinbeck's novel features Tracy and Tamiroff as two ne'er-do-wells constantly in search of a free meal in their home of Monterey, California. Garfield is an eager young man who considers himself to be wealthy after inheriting two houses located on Tortilla Flat. Proud of his new status, Garfield allows Tracy and his friends to move into one of the homes, keeping the other for himself. But Garfield's newfound wealth—not to mention his attraction to local cannery worker Lamarr—soon threatens come between the pals.

TORTILLA FLAT is an affectionate tale, told with sensitivity and a wonderfully offbeat sense of humor. Steinbeck's engaging characters are well treated by the talents of this ensemble and by Fleming's caring direction. Lamarr is excellent (she considered this the best of all her roles) as the level-headed, spunky woman who refuses to settle for anything she doesn't want. Her relationship with Garfield, a mixture of attraction and suspicion, is realistic and honest, a rarity for a screen romance. Garfield puts his heart into his portrayal of the earnest Danny, contributing a memorable characterization that complements Lamarr's wonderful work. Tracy's lovable rogue and Morgan's holy roller add to the film's cast of colorful characters. Indeed, Morgan received a well-deserved Oscar nomination as Best Supporting Actor, though he lost that year to Van Heflin in JOHNNY EAGER.

Fleming captures the nuances and ambience of life in this small town, a sincere effort that guides the performers with care through the material. MGM built an entire village over three acres of land for the film that Garfield dearly wanted to do, though he had to wait some time before Warner Bros. agreed to loan him to MGM. Louis B. Mayer, MGM's head, also liked the idea of Garfield in the role, and, reportedly, the powerful mogul was not above some unorthodox pressuring to get his man. Mayer is said to have threatened to expose Warner Bros. for not making good on their pledges to certain charitable groups unless Garfield was allowed to make the film.

TOTAL RECALL

1990 109m c Action/Science Fiction ★★
Mario Kassar-Andrew Vajna-Carolco-Ronald Shusett (U.S.) R/18

Arnold Schwarzenegger *(Doug Quaid)*, Rachel Ticotin *(Melina)*, Sharon Stone *(Lori Quaid)*, Ronny Cox *(Cohaagen)*, Michael Ironside *(Richter)*, Marshall Bell *(George/Kuato)*, Mel Johnson Jr. *(Benny)*, Michael Champion *(Helm)*, Roy Brocksmith *(Dr. Edgemar)*, Ray Baker *(McClane)*

p, Buzz Feitshans; d, Paul Verhoeven; w, Ronald Shusett, Dan O'Bannon, Gary Goldman (based on a story by Ronald Shusett, Dan O'Bannon, Jon Povill, from the short story "We Can Remember It for You Wholesale" by Phillip K. Dick); ph, Jost Vacano; ed, Frank J. Urioste; m, Jerry Goldsmith; prod d, William Sandell; art d, James Tocci, Jose Rodriguez Granada; fx, Rob Bottin, Thomas L. Fisher, Eric Brevig; cos, Erica Edell Phillips; anim, Jeff Burks

AAN Best Sound: Nelson Stoll, Michael J. Kohut, Carlos DeLarios, Aaron Rochin; *AA Best Visual Effects:* Eric Brevig, Rob Bottin, Tim McGovern, Alex Funke; *AAN Best Sound Effects Editing:* Stephen H. Flick

Ugly, stupid, loud, offensive, and pointlessly violent—let's not mince words—this film should be called TOTAL REJECT. This is prime example of an unfortunate tendency in modern blockbuster moviemaking. Runningly mindlessly amok drunk on money and contempt, TOTAL RECALL is overloaded with inelegant special effects, bone-crunching "action," hideously cheesy make up effects, and gaping plot holes. That's entertainment? Any intelligent science fiction fan would be well advised to steer clear of this turkey and read a book instead. The late great Philip K. Dick must be retching in his grave at this "adaptation" of his short story, "We Can Remember It for You Wholesale." One would never know from watching this headache-inducing movie that Dick was one of the most cerebral writers in science fiction. Part of what makes this film so infuriating is that the premise is pure gold but the execution is insulting to the audience. Still it does have its passionate admirers. It takes all kinds. . . .

Set in the year 2084, TOTAL RECALL tells the story of Doug Quaid (Schwarzenegger), a construction worker with a beautiful wife (Sharon Stone) and a nice home. This society of the future has provided a fairly good life for Quaid. Mars has become a colony of Earth but Quaid has never had time to vacation there though he dreams of it every night (and of a mysterious woman he has never met). Quaid decides to pay a visit to Rekall Inc., a "travel" service that specializes in implanting artificial memories of vacations into its customers' brains. One can recline in a high-tech chair and enjoy all the pleasures of a vacation at an accelerated rate with none of the fuss. Quaid purchases a memory of a trip to Mars. Included in the package is Rekall's special "Ego Trip" which allows the customer to take his "trip" as another person. Quaid chooses to travel as a fictional secret agent. When the doctors begin the implant, something goes terribly wrong. Even before the memory is implanted, Quaid becomes crazed, claiming that he *is* a secret agent from Mars. Is this a previous implant or is it a real memory that had been obscured? The doctors subdue and tranquilize Quaid and release him. Later, Quaid is attacked by coworkers and nearly killed by his wife. She confirms that he really is an agent posing as a construction worker. She also explains that she is not really his wife but actually another agent

assigned to watch him. After fighting off would-be killers and learning more about his past (with the help of a pre-recorded message from himself), Quaid escapes to Mars to unlock the rest of the mystery.

Up to this point TOTAL RECALL is fascinating as it deals with some recurring themes from Dick's fiction such as the search for identity, the slippery nature of reality, and the effect of drugs on perception. Rumor has it that Matthew Broderick was originally slated to star. If he had been the protagonist, this would have been a radically different film, probably a much better one. Broderick would have been credible as a regular Walter Mitty-type who discovers that he may have had, unbeknownst to himself, a secret life of high adventure. In contrast, who could be less convincing as a regular guy than Schwarzenegger? The Arnold can be just fine in the right vehicle (e.g. THE TERMINATOR and PREDATOR) but here his presence, and the obligatory tone that goes with it, turns an interesting science fiction premise into just another noisy dumb shoot-em-up. Pity.

TOTO LE HEROS

1991 90m c Drama/Comedy/Fantasy ★★★★
Iblis Films/Les Productions Philippe Dussart/Metropolis PG-13/15
Filmprodukion/RTBF Telefilms/FR3 Films Production/Zweites
Deutsches Fernsehen/Jacqueline Pierreux
(Belgium/France/Germany)

Michel Bouquet *(Thomas—As an Old Man/Voice of Adult Thomas)*, Mireille Perrier *(Voice of Evelyne As an Old Woman/ Adult Evelyne)*, Jo De Backer *(Thomas—As an Adult)*, Thomas Godet *(Thomas—As a Child)*, Sandrine Blancke *(Alice)*, Fabienne Loriaux *(Thomas's Mother)*, Klaus Schindler *(Thomas's Father)*, Patrick Waleffe *(Voice of Thomas's Father)*, Didier DeNeck *(Mr. Kant)*, Peter Bohlke *(Alfred—As an Old Man)*

p, Pierre Drouot, Dany Geys; d, Jaco Van Dormael; w, Jaco Van Dormael; ph, Walther Vanden Ende; ed, Susana Rossberg; m, Pierre Van Dormael; art d, Hubert Pouille; cos, Suzanne Van Well

A remarkable, visually enchanting first feature from former professional clown Jaco Van Dormael. TOTO skips back and forth through time, unraveling the obsessed thoughts of the bitter, retired Thomas Van Hosebroeck (Michel Bouquet). Thomas is convinced that, as a baby, he was accidentally switched with neighbor Alfred Kant, who grew up in the lap of luxury while Thomas had to endure the hardships and indignities of a tough working-class upbringing. Thomas's troubled childhood includes falling in love with his sister Alice (in his eyes they aren't really related), who is killed when, at Thomas's urging, she sets a retaliatory fire on Alfred's property. As an adult, Thomas begins an affair with Alfred's wife, Evelyne, who agrees to run away with Thomas but is late for their train-station rendezvous. (Certain he's been abandoned again, Thomas leaves the station, failing to see Evelyne arrive an instant later.) At sixty, Thomas at last perceives an opportunity to get even with his lifelong secret nemesis, now a prominent industrialist, via a plot involving political terrorists. Recurring throughout Thomas's daydreams is Toto, an archetypal fantasy figure who looks like a stockier version of Inspector Clouseau and is perpetually doing battle with the forces of evil (gangster stand-ins for Alfred).

One can hardly imagine any other way for the intricate, metaphysical premise of TOTO to unfold, other than through this controlled explosion of impressions. The multi-flashback structure uses recurrent motifs and coincident images, notably of family, fire and flight, to vividly evoke the wonders and horrors of childhood.

TOUCH OF CLASS, A

1973 105m c Comedy/Romance ★★★★
Brut (U.K.) PG/AA

George Segal *(Steve Blackburn)*, Glenda Jackson *(Vicki Allessio)*, Paul Sorvino *(Walter Menkes)*, Hildegard Neil *(Gloria Blackburn)*, Cec Linder *(Wendell Thompson)*, K. Callan *(Patty Menkes)*, Mary Barclay *(Martha Thompson)*, Michael Elwyn *(Cecil)*, Nadim Sawalha *(Night Hotel Manager)*, Ian Thompson *(Derek)*

p, Melvin Frank; d, Melvin Frank; w, Melvin Frank, Jack Rose; ph, Austin Dempster; ed, Bill Butler; m, John Cameron; prod d, Terrence Marsh; art d, Alan Tomkins; cos, Ruth Myers

AAN Best Picture; *AA Best Actress:* Glenda Jackson; *AAN Best Adapted Screenplay:* Melvin Frank, Jack Rose; *AAN Best Score:* John Cameron; *AAN Best Song:* Georgie Barrie (Music), Sammy Cahn (Lyrics)

Joseph E. Levine (THE GRADUATE, THE LION IN WINTER, CARNAL KNOWLEDGE) picked a winner when he elected to present this very funny film about infidelity in London. Segal is an American insurance executive living in London with wife (Neil) and children. He's playing softball in the regular Sunday game near the Albert Memorial in Hyde Park one Sunday when he meets Jackson, a divorcee with two children of her own. Segal suggests that they have a tryst in Spain and is very surprised when she agrees. Making excuses to his wife, Segal takes Jackson to Malaga for what he hopes will be a sexual idyll. But Segal's friend Sorvino is on the same plane. Farcical complications, and romance, ensue.

The company behind the film was Brut Productions, part of the Brut cosmetics firm headed by George Barrie. Barrie always fancied himself a composer and cowrote the film's Oscar-nominated song (lyrics by Sammy Cahn), "All That Love Went to Waste," as well as two other tunes. Shot on location in Spain and London, and interiors were done at Lee Studios in London. The picture did quite well at the box office. Segal is charming, but everyone knew he could play comedy. The big surprise was Jackson's impeccable comic timing, which some likened to that of Katharine Hepburn. The softball scene at the start of the film features many of the expatriate Americans who lived in London at the time and played regularly. Frank was not nominated for his direction, but he should have been. The film is in excellent taste and is a tribute to Frank and his cowriter, Jack Rose. Later, George Barrie would team up with Frank's former partner, Norman Panama, and produce I WILL, I WILL. . . FOR NOW with less than spectacular results.

TOUCH OF EVIL

1958 95m c Crime   ★★★★★
Universal (U.S.)   /PG

Charlton Heston *(Ramon Miguel "Mike" Vargas)*, Janet Leigh *(Susan Vargas)*, Orson Welles *(Hank Quinlan)*, Joseph Calleia *(Pete Menzies)*, Akim Tamiroff *("Uncle Joe" Grandi)*, Val DeVargas *(Pancho)*, Ray Collins *(District Attorney Adair)*, Dennis Weaver *(Motel Clerk)*, Joanna Moore *(Marcia Linnekar)*, Mort Mills *(Schwartz)*

p, Albert Zugsmith; d, Orson Welles, Harry Keller; w, Orson Welles (based on the novel *Badge of Evil* by Whit Masterson); ph, Russell Metty; ed, Virgil Vogel, Aaron Stell; m, Henry Mancini; art d, Alexander Golitzen, Robert Clatworthy; cos, Bill Thomas

Wild Welles rides again—adapting a shelved script written by Paul Manash for Albert Zugsmith, King of the Bs, from Whit Masterson's novel *Badge of Evil* (which Welles never bothered to read). The result? A film about love of film even more than the stinking, perverse little thriller it presents itself as. Already famous for directing perhaps the greatest film ever made, CITIZEN KANE, Welles opens TOUCH OF EVIL with what may be the greatest single shot ever put on film. It is a spectacular tracking crane shot which crosses the Mexican/US border, thereby visually foreshadowing the thematic elements to come—the differences that exist between two peoples, the Mexican and the Americans; the line Charlton Heston's character crosses from being a law-abiding husband to a vengeful madman; and the line Orson Welles's character crosses from good cop to evil cop. When a car explodes after crossing the border, both US cop Hank Quinlan (Welles) and Mexican narcotics agent Mike Vargas (Heston) begin their investigations. Almost immediately Quinlan has a suspect, Sanchez (Victor Millan), a young Mexican who is involved with the dead man's daughter Marcia (Moore). In order to secure a conviction, Quinlan plants some dynamite in Sanchez's flat, but Vargas is wise to Quinlan's game. With help from Pete Menzies (Calleia), a long-time friend of Quinlan's, Vargas investigates Quinlan's past, all the while trying to solve the murder and protect his wife (Leigh) from a number of dangerous locals. Directing his first film in America since 1948's MACBETH, Welles was originally just supposed to act in TOUCH OF EVIL. The misunderstanding that led to this bizarre and twisted masterpiece began when Heston read a script based on the novel *Badge of Evil*. Hearing that Welles was involved, and assuming that his involvement meant as actor *and* director, Heston told producer Zugsmith that he would love to do the project.

Rather than lose Heston, Zugsmith managed to get Universal to agree to let Welles direct, on the condition that he could also rewrite. Although much of the mystery element is revealed to the audience, it is Vargas who cannot unravel all the threads and make his clues add up to anything.

This nightmarish descent into dark entertainment has so much weirdness going on it's amazing. Marlene Dietrich, reprising her GOLDEN EARRINGS drag, smoking cigars and scraping pots, almost steals it. Complete with German accent and huge, light eyes at half mast, she's the most surreal excuse for a Mexican gypsy you've ever seen. When she sees Welles, big as a house with a false nose, it's the film's best line and a prophecy of Wellesian doom: "You're a mess, honey. You've been eating too much candy." Like Dietrich, Heston skips the Mexican accent as well. He looks like a muscular, surly version of an El Greco. Janet Leigh is at her most perversely innocent, and besides lots of grisly scenes (a murder by Welles the worst), there are a slew of outrageous cameos by Welles crony Joseph Cotten, Zsa Zsa Gabor (totally unaware what kind of film she's making), Dennis Weaver (unbelievably loopy), Ray Collins and the wildest, Mercedes McCambridge as a butch bitch biker. The blonde in the exploding car is Joi Lansing, the poor man's Mamie Van Doren. EVIL was filmed at Universal, with some locations at Venice Beach. It's greatly enhanced by Mancini's dangerous, Latin Rock score. Go for the rediscovered (1976) 108 minute version. Baroque, maddening, and totally inspired.

TOUS LES MATINS DU MONDE

1991 114m c Drama/Biography/Musical   ★★★½
Film par film/Divali Films/DD Productions/Sedif/FR3 Films   /12
Production/Paravision International   (France)

Jean-Pierre Marielle *(Monsieur de Saint Colombe)*, Gerard Depardieu *(Marin Marias)*, Anne Brochet *(Madeleine)*, Guillaume Depardieu *(Young Marin Marais)*, Caroline Sihol *(Madame de Sainte Colombe)*, Carole Richert *(Toinette)*, Violaine Lacroix *(Young Madeleine)*, Nadege Teron *(Young Toinette)*, Myriam Boyer *(Guignotte)*, Jean-Claude Dreyfus *(Abbe Mathieu)*

p, Jean-Louis Livi, French Ministry of Culture, Canal Plus; d, Alain Corneau; w, Alain Corneau, Pascal Quignard (from his novel); ph, Yves Angelo; ed, Marie-Josephe Berroyer; m, Jordi Savall; prod d, Yves Angelo; cos, Corrine Jorry

TOUS LES MATINS DU MONDE recounts the real-life story of master 17th-century French musician M. de Saint Colombe (Jean-Pierre Marielle) and his brilliant protege, Marin Marais. A grandly sentimental, eccentric romance, the film also tackles some hefty philosophical and aesthetic questions. It's a heady, intoxicating mix. The film's framing narrative introduces us to the mature Marais (a periwigged Gerard Depardieu at his bloated, foppish best), surrounded by his adoring students in the royal musical chambers. Despite having found fame and fortune as musical director at the court of Louis XIV, Marais is unfulfilled. Compared to his former mentor, the legendary Saint Colombe, Marais feels like an impostor. In flashback, he ruefully recalls his salad days as a student of Saint Colombe and lover of his mentor's elder daughter, Madeleine (Anne Brochet).

Though he's not on screen for very long, Gerard Depardieu gives a marvelously fussy performance as the older Marais. In an impressive film debut, his 21-year-old son Guillaume portrays the aspiring artist as a young man with real charm and conviction. Anne Brochet exudes a winning blend of naivete and sophistication and Jean-Pierre Marielle's deadpan portrayal of Saint Colombe is wonderfully offbeat, filled with either long silences or aphorisms. ("Urinating is a chromatic descent; music exists to say things words cannot say.") The driving force of TOUS LES MATINS, though, is the music—original compositions of Saint Colombe and Marais, with additional works by Lully, Couperin and Savall, conducted and performed by Jordi Savall and the Concert of Nations.

TOUT VA BIEN

1972 95m c Drama   ★★★½
Lido/Empire (France)   /X

Jane Fonda *(She)*, Yves Montand *(He)*, Vittorio Caprioli *(Factory Manager)*, Jean Pignol *(Delegate)*, Pierre Ondry *(Frederic)*, Ilizabeth Chauvin *(Genevieve)*, Eric Chartier *(Lucien)*, Yves Gabrielli *(Leon)*

p, Jean-Pierre Rassam; d, Jean-Luc Godard, Jean-Pierre Gorin; w, Jean-Luc Godard, Jean-Pierre Gorin; ph, Armand Marco; ed, Kernout Peitier

Jean-Luc Godard's most commercial film since WEEKEND and his strongest attempt to bring political thought into popular film. In order to deliver his message of class struggle Godard signed two famous actors—Jane Fonda and Yves Montand. The plot of TOUT VA BIEN exists only, as Godard says in the film, to provide "a story for those who shouldn't still need one." Fonda is an American news reporter living in Paris with her husband, Montand, a former "New Wave" film director, who has turned to directing commercials. They pay a visit to a sausage factory and find themselves in the middle of a work stoppage. The workers spout Maoist slogans and read political speeches into the cameras while taking over the factory's corporate offices. The plant manager is locked in his office and not even allowed to go to the bathroom. TOUT VA BIEN ends without neatly tying up the narrative, letting "each individual create his own history."

It is different from Godard's other political films (WIND FROM THE EAST, SEE YOU AT MAO, and VLADIMIR ET ROSA to name a few). It received a commercial release (many of his other political films were shown only to workers and students), had two "movie stars" and even received financial backing from Paramount (which opted not to distribute). The most impressive visuals are a multileveled cutaway of an office building which allows a view of all the offices at the same time, and a bravura tracking shot through an ultra-modern supermarket. TOUT VA BIEN was a noble effort to bring anti-bourgeois cinema to the masses; needless to say, the masses stayed home.

TOWERING INFERNO, THE

| 1974 165m c Disaster | ★★ |
| Fox/Warner Bros. (U.S.) | PG/ |

Steve McQueen *(Fire Chief Michael O'Hallorhan)*, Paul Newman *(Doug Roberts)*, William Holden *(Jim Duncan)*, Faye Dunaway *(Susan Franklin)*, Fred Astaire *(Harlee Claiborne)*, Susan Blakely *(Patty Simmons)*, Richard Chamberlain *(Roger Simmons)*, Jennifer Jones *(Lisolette Mueller)*, O.J. Simpson *(Security Chief Jernigan)*, Robert Vaughn *(Sen. Gary Parker)*

p, Irwin Allen; d, John Guillermin, Irwin Allen; w, Stirling Silliphant (based on the novels *The Tower* by Richard Martin Stern and *The Glass Inferno* by Thomas M. Scortia, Frank M. Robinson); ph, Fred Koenekamp, Joseph Biroc, Jim Freeman; ed, Harold F. Kress, Carl Kress; m, John Williams; prod d, William J. Creber; art d, Ward Preston; fx, A.D. Flowers, Logan Frazee, L.B. Abbott; cos, Paul Zastupnevich

AAN Best Picture; AAN Best Supporting Actor: Fred Astaire; *AA Best Cinematography:* Fred J. Koenekamp, Joseph Biroc; *AA Best Editing:* Harold F. Kress, Carl Kress; *AAN Best Score:* John Williams; *AA Best Song:* Al Kasha, Joel Hirschhorn; *AAN Best Art Direction:* William Creber, Ward Preston, Raphael Bretton; *AAN Best Sound:* Theodore Soderberg, Herman Lewis

Burn, baby, burn—and it's not a disco inferno, either. The disaster film which mercifully signaled the end of a cycle, THE TOWERING INFERNO places an all-star cast consisting mostly of has-beens and never-weres in a spangly glass tower, only to torch the sucker. Faye Dunaway looks stoned, Paul Newman and Steve ("When are you architects going to learn?") McQueen look bored, William Holden looks sick, O.J. Simpson gets to rescue a cat, Richard Chamberlain is unpleasant, and Fred Astaire and Jennifer Jones act as if the film were entitled THE COWERING INFERNO. No wonder everybody's so afraid of burning to death here—their characters are cardboard!

TOY STORY

| 1995 80m c Animated/Fantasy/Children's | ★★★½ |
| Walt Disney Pictures/PIXAR Productions (U.S.) | G/PG |

VOICES OF: Tom Hanks *(Woody)*, Tim Allen *(Buzz Lightyear)*, Don Rickles *(Mr. Potato Head)*, Jim Varney *(Slinky Dog)*, Wallace Shawn *(Rex)*, John Ratzenberger *(Hamm)*, Annie Potts *(Bo Peep)*, John Morris *(Andy)*, Erik Von Detten *(Sid)*, Laurie Metcalf *(Mrs. Davis)*

p, Ralph Guggenheim, Bonnie Arnold; d, John Lasseter; w, Joss Whedon, Andrew Stanton, Joel Cohen, Alec Sokolow (from an original story by John Lasseter, Pete Docter, Andrew Stanton, and Joe Ranft); ed, Robert Gordon, Lee Unkrich; m, Randy Newman; art d, Ralph Eggleston; anim, Pete Docter, Rich Quade, Ash Brannon, Pixar Animation Studios

AAN Best Original Screenplay: Joss Whedon, Andrew Stanton, Joel Cohen, Alec Sokolow; story by John Lasseter, Pete Docter, Andrew Stanton, Joe Ranft; *AAN Best Musical or Comedy Score:* Randy Newman; *AAN Best Original Song:* Randy Newman "You've Got a Friend"

Kids are mad about it; it's far from painful for parents; the voice of Mr. Potato Head is Don Rickles. What more could you ask?

Clever, fast-moving, and unobtrusively self-conscious, Disney's marketing triumph describes a struggle for status between two toys—old favorite Woody, a low-tech talking cowboy voiced by Tom Hanks, and newcomer Buzz Lightyear (voice of Tim Allen), an arrogant space ranger who threatens to upset the toy box. The mismatched heroes must team up against a vicious brat who's fond of mutilating his playthings and turning them into scary mutants. Needless to say, Woody and Buzz learn to set aside their differences and respect each other along the way, imparting a valuable lesson to viewers too young to have seen the LETHAL WEAPON films.

Billed as the first feature film constructed entirely of computer animation, TOY STORY is a visual masterpiece that must truly be seen to be believed. The brainchild of director John Lasseter and his team of computer animators at Pixar, TOY STORY genuinely makes viewers forget they're watching an animated film. For its considerable techincal achievements—which took four years and an army of computer animators to complete—TOY STORY was given a special Academy Award. Its bravura set pieces—notably the astonishing toy's-eye-view flying sequence—mark new milestones in animation. That such astonishing amounts of money, technology, and highly-skilled labor were put to use in constructing a kiddie matinee presumably says something disturbing about American capitalism and culture, but we'd rather not think about it.

TRADING PLACES

| 1983 106m c Comedy | ★★★ |
| Paramount (U.S.) | R/15 |

Dan Aykroyd *(Louis Winthorpe III)*, Eddie Murphy *(Billy Ray Valentine)*, Ralph Bellamy *(Randolph Duke)*, Don Ameche *(Mortimer Duke)*, Denholm Elliott *(Coleman)*, Kristin Holby *(Penelope Witherspoon)*, Paul Gleason *(Clarence Beeks)*, Jamie Lee Curtis *(Ophelia)*, James Belushi *(Harvey)*, Al Franken

p, Aaron Russo; d, John Landis; w, Timothy Harris, Herschel Weingrod; ph, Robert Paynter; ed, Malcolm Campbell; m, Elmer Bernstein; prod d, Gene Rudolf; cos, Deborah Nadoolman

AAN Best Score: Elmer Bernstein

The plot of this fine comedy owes more than a passing nod to Mark Twain's *The Prince and the Pauper*: street hustler Billy Ray Valentine (Eddie Murphy) and upscale yuppie Louis Winthorpe III (Dan Aykroyd) are forced to switch positions in life to resolve a bet between two rich brothers, Mortimer and Randolph Duke (Don Ameche and Ralph Bellamy), who frame Winthorpe and welcome Valentine into their business in his place. The rise of Valentine and the fall of Winthorpe are a source of great fun. The street hustler proves that his years in back alleys have stood him in good stead, providing him with all sorts of fresh business ideas. In Winthorpe's case, however, it is only when he meets and falls for hooker Ophelia (Jamie Lee Curtis) that he begins to appear in a sympathetic light. Although it tends to rely heavily on slapstick in the second half, the movie provides plenty of laughs and is one of director Landis's best efforts—despite overtones of racism that were perhaps intended ironically but have no business in the story.

TRAFFIC
(TRAFIC)

1972 89m c Comedy ★★★★
Corona (France) G/

Jacques Tati (*Mons. Hulot*), Maria Kimberly (*Maria, the Public Relations Girl*), Marcel Fravel (*Truck Driver*), Honore Bostel (*Managing Director of ALTRA*), Tony Kneppers (*Dutch Garage Proprietor*), Francois Maisongrosse (*Francois*), Franco Ressel, Mario Zanuelli

p, Robert Dorfmann; d, Jacques Tati; w, Jacques Tati, Jacques Lagrange; ph, Marcel Weiss, Edward Van Der Enden; ed, Maurice Laumain, Sophie Tatischeff, Jacques Tati; m, Charles Dumont; art d, Adrien de Rooy

Jacques Tati's fifth picture in 25 years (his fourth, PLAYTIME, was not released until 1973), TRAFFIC is a collection of sight gags concerning the modern problem of automobile overpopulation. Tati again plays himself in this English-dubbed outing—the rain-coated, pipe-smoking eccentric—though now he has invented an ultramodern camping vehicle. With Kimberly, the public relations girl of his firm, he plans to take his new car from Paris to an Amsterdam auto show. A long series of misadventures befalls them.

Any plot synopsis of a Tati picture proves to be fruitless since what is most important are the visual gags. So vital are the visuals that Tati rarely uses dialogue, thereby negating the need for subtitles. One of the picture's funniest moments is Tati's attempt to climb the vines that cling to a house, pulling them down in the process. Instead of stopping there, however, he yanks them back up and winds up hanging upside down by his foot, refusing to give in and yell for help. Many of the film's brightest moments do not even include Tati (it was his wish that he would eventually be only a minor character in his films). One gag has Kimberly thinking that her dog has been crushed by the back wheel of her sports car. She is unaware that a group of mischievous passersby simply put one of their coats (which are made from the same fur as the dog) under the wheel. Other brilliant bits are created through montage. Various people are seen picking their noses while waiting for traffic to advance; or a connection is made between the car a person drives and that person's physical appearance; or a connection between the person and the movement of their windshield wipers. Tati, who's brilliant at commenting on modernization, here again provides insights into modern life that make for one of the freshest and funniest pictures to hit the screen in years.

TRAIL OF THE LONESOME PINE, THE

1936 102m c Drama ★★★½
Paramount (U.S.) /A

Sylvia Sidney (*June Tolliver*), Fred MacMurray (*Jack Hale*), Henry Fonda (*Dave Tolliver*), Fred Stone (*Judd Tolliver*), Nigel Bruce (*Mr. Thurber*), Beulah Bondi (*Melissa*), Robert Barrat (*Buck Falin*), Spanky McFarland (*Buddy*), Fuzzy Knight (*Tater*), Otto Fries (*Corsey*)

p, Walter Wanger; d, Henry Hathaway; w, Grover Jones, Harvey Thew, Horace McCoy (based on the novel by John Fox Jr.); ph, W. Howard Greene, Robert C. Bruce; ed, Robert Bischoff; art d, Hans Dreier

AAN Best Song: Louis Alter (Music), Sideny Mitchell (Lyrics)

This was the first outdoor Technicolor three-strip film and Henry Fonda's first movie in color. Set in the backwoods of Kentucky in the early years of the 20th century, it's the story of feudin' and fussin' mountain people. Two clans have been battling for years, and, as the movie begins, Robert Barrat's family is firing at the cabin of Fred Stone's family, just as Beulah Bondi is giving birth to a daughter. Time passes and Sylvia Sidney grows up under the watchful eye of her brother, Fonda. He is almost killed in a fight with the rival clan, but Fred MacMurray, an engineer who has come to the locale with the railroad, saves his life. Fonda wants to keep his sister away from city slickers like MacMurray, believing she would be better off in love with a local boy. The advent of the railroad has brought new prosperity. MacMurray arranges for Sidney to be accepted by a school in Louisville, but Fonda is angered and lets MacMurray know it. The two men get into a fist fight, but then stop to fend off the Barrat clan, who have launched an onslaught on the railroad camp. The workers are frightened for their lives and leave the area in a shambles. Younger brother Spanky

McFarland is killed in the battle, so, when Sidney returns from school in Louisville, she calls for a blood bath. MacMurray angers her when he attempts to inject a modicum of sanity into the proceedings. Fonda realizes that the feud must cease and offers to meet the rival clan leader. Barrat accepts and the time is set for the ritual handshake. In the meantime, however, Fonda is shot by one of Barrat's clan. Barrat can't believe what's happened and pays a visit to the Stone house to express his sorrow as Fonda lies moments from death. Fonda bids Stone and Barrat to shake hands, then watches as Sidney and MacMurray move close to each other.

Often poignant, filled with action, well-photographed, and even scored with four songs, this is a slice of Americana that proved successful at the box office. Cecil B. DeMille's version (1916) starred Charlotte Walker in the Sidney role, while Mary Miles Minter played the part in the 1923 version, directed by Charles Maigne. McFarland, who was only eight years old and already a veteran of several "Our Gang" shorts, shows his versatility in this film. Years later, Al Capp admitted that he'd based his famed "Li'l Abner" character on Fonda's role, and collectors of comic book lore will recognize some of Capp's early drawings as looking quite a bit like Fonda. Fuzzy Knight does a fine job acting and warbling the tunes. The song "Melody from the Sky" earned an Oscar nomination for Best Song. Other songs were: "Stack O' Lee Blues" (which may have been "Stagger Lee"), and "When It's Twilight on the Trail" (all by Sidney Mitchell and Lou Alter), plus Harry Carroll's "Trail of the Lonesome Pine."

TRAIN, THE
(LE TRAIN)

1965 140m bw Thriller/War ★★★★
Artistes/Ariane/Dear (France/Italy/U.S.) /PG

Burt Lancaster (*Labiche*), Paul Scofield (*Col. von Waldheim*), Jeanne Moreau (*Christine*), Michel Simon (*Papa Boule*), Suzanne Flon (*Miss Villard*), Wolfgang Preiss (*Herren*), Richard Munch (*Von Lubitz*), Albert Remy (*Didont*), Charles Millot (*Pesquet*), Jacques Marin (*Jacques*)

p, Jules Bricken; d, John Frankenheimer; w, Franklin Coen, Frank Davis, Walter Bernstein, Albert Husson (based on the novel *Le Front de l'Art* by Rose Valland); ph, Jean Tournier, Walter Wottitz; ed, David Bretherton, Gabriel Rongier; m, Maurice Jarre; prod d, Willy Holt; fx, Lee Zavitz; cos, Jean Zay

AAN Best Original Screenplay: Franklin Coen, Frank Davis

A superior WWII film that provides plenty of edge-of-the-seat thrills, THE TRAIN also poses a rather serious philosophical question: Is the preservation of art worth a human life? Set in France in the summer of 1944, with the Germans in retreat, the film begins as a German colonel, von Waldheim (Paul Scofield), is ordered to transport the collection of the Jeu de Paume Museum—including numerous masterpieces—by train to the Fatherland. The curator of the museum gets word of the plan to the Resistance, and they persuade Labiche (Burt Lancaster), a railway inspector, to try to save the priceless works of art. THE TRAIN was originally to have been helmed by Arthur Penn, but during the first two weeks of shooting the director had some severe disagreements with Lancaster and producer Jules Bricken and left the production. Lancaster then called in John Frankenheimer, whom he had just worked with on SEVEN DAYS IN MAY (they had also collaborated on THE YOUNG SAVAGES and THE BIRDMAN OF ALCATRAZ). The film was shot entirely on location in France, and Frankenheimer employed a number of cameras shooting simultaneously so that the action with the trains would be captured from several different angles with as few takes as possible. His camera placement perfectly captures the massive trains (no models or miniatures were used) from every conceivable perspective, and their movement is directly contrasted with the chess game played by Labiche and von Waldheim. The acting in the film is superb, with Scofield taking top honors as the obsessed German colonel, though veteran French character actor Michel Simon nearly steals the film as a determined old engineer.

TRAINSPOTTING

1995   93m   c   Drama   ★★★½
Figment Films/Noel Gay Motion Picture Company   R/18
/Channel Four Films   (U.K.)

Ewan McGregor *(Mark Renton)*, Ewen Bremner *(Spud)*, Jonny Lee Miller *(Sick Boy)*, Kevin McKidd *(Tommy)*, Robert Carlyle *(Begbie)*, Kelly Macdonald *(Diane)*, Peter Mullan *(Swanney)*, James Cosmo *(Mr. Renton)*, Eileen Nicholas *(Mrs. Renton)*, Susan Vidler *(Allison)*

p, Andrew Macdonald; d, Danny Boyle; w, John Hodge (based on the novel by Irvine Welsh); ph, Brian Tufano; ed, Masahiro Hirakubo; prod d, Kave Quinn; art d, Tracey Gallacher; fx, Grant Mason, Tony Steers; cos, Rachael Fleming

AAN Best Adapted Screenplay: John Hodge

Perhaps the most influential, certainly the most hotly debated, UK film of the 90s. Brought to you by the writer-producer-director team that made their debut with SHALLOW GRAVE, TRAINSPOTTING is a rambling chronicle of high times in low company—DRUGSTORE COWBOY goes to Edinburgh. By turns cheeky, surreal, exhilarating, and stomach-churning, it follows assorted days in the lives of mangy Mark Renton (Ewan McGregor) and the scabby crew of junkies, deadbeats, thieves, liars, and nut jobs he calls friends.

TRAINSPOTTING proves that no novel—not even one as loosely structured and reliant on interior monologue as Welsh's—is unfilmable. Renton may be a degenerate boil on society's backside, but he also makes a clever, witty screen hero. Though the film softens the edges of Welsh's book, it doesn't back off from its most controversial theme; these characters are not duped by evil drug pushers, but consciously choose drugs over the banality of. . . well, pretty much everything else. While getting the squalor and degradation of the junkie lifestyle down to the last grotesque detail, TRAINSPOTTING also captures the way drug addiction gives structure and purpose to aimless lives, and evokes the breathtaking rapture of a fix. All this and a happy ending, too.

TRAPEZE

1956   105m   c   Drama   ★★★½
Susan   (U.S.)   /U

Burt Lancaster *(Mike Ribble)*, Tony Curtis *(Tino Orsini)*, Gina Lollobrigida *(Lola)*, Katy Jurado *(Rosa)*, Thomas Gomez *(Bouglione)*, Johnny Puleo *(Max the Dwarf)*, Minor Watson *(John Ringling North)*, Gerard Landry *(Chikki)*, Jean-Pierre Kerien *(Otto)*, Sidney James *(Snake Charmer)*

p, James Hill; d, Carol Reed; w, James R. Webb, Liam O'Brien (based on the novel *The Killing Frost* by Max Catto); ph, Robert Krasker; ed, Bert Bates; m, Malcolm Arnold; art d, Rino Mondellini; fx, Jack Lannan

Despite some stiff acting and a ponderous script, this was a smash at the box office, if only because audiences got to see Lancaster, himself a former circus performer, playing against the attractive Lollobrigida and the handsome Curtis. Lancaster is a lame acrobat who is famed for having done the impossible, a "triple" off the trapeze before having the accident that caused his limp. Two somersaults in mid-air are a commonplace, but a triple is the stuff of which high flyer's dreams are made. He's working as a rigger for a Parisian circus when Curtis arrives, eager to meet Lancaster and learn from him. Curtis is the son of a former circus friend of Lancaster and wants to learn to do a triple. Lancaster does everything he can to discourage Curtis, but circus-owner Gomez would love to have some enormous starring act to help business. After a while, Curtis wears Lancaster down and the older man decides that he might recapture his own glory by helping Curtis achieve the feat. The two men become very close. Lollobrigida is a scheming member of a tumbling act who would like to have the fame and fortune that trapeze artists merit. She begins using her wiles on Lancaster, but he has no interest, so she turns to the more naive Curtis. The high-wire work is very exciting and Reed's direction of the triple is breathtaking. These assets more than compensate for the shortcomings of the remainder of the movie. Seen briefly is Johnny Puleo, the little person who served for so many years as one of the Harmonica Rascals with Borah Minevitch. The ambience of circus life is quite well conveyed.

TREASURE ISLAND

1934   109m   bw   Adventure   ★★★½
MGM   (U.S.)   /U

Wallace Beery *(Long John Silver)*, Jackie Cooper *(Jim Hawkins)*, Lionel Barrymore *(Billy Bones)*, Otto Kruger *(Dr. Livesey)*, Lewis Stone *(Capt. Alexander Smollett)*, Nigel Bruce *(Squire Trelawney)*, Charles "Chic" Sale *(Ben Gunn)*, William V. Mong *(Pew)*, Charles McNaughton *(Black Dog)*, Dorothy Peterson *(Mrs. Hawkins)*

p, Hunt Stromberg; d, Victor Fleming; w, John Lee Mahin, Leonard Praskins, John Howard Lawson (based on the novel by Robert Louis Stevenson); ph, Ray June, Harold Rosson, Clyde De Vinna; ed, Blanche Sewell; m, Herbert Stothart; art d, Cedric Gibbons, Merrill Pye, Edwin B. Willis; cos, Dwight Franklin

Robert Louis Stevenson's *Treasure Island* transfers easily from the page to the screen in this first sound version of the classic adventure tale. Wallace Beery plays the famous Long John Silver and Jackie Cooper takes the role of the doughty Jim Hawkins. The film opens at a rough-and-tumble coastal pub where young Jim meets the drunken Billy Bones (Lionel Barrymore) and learns that the old rummy has a secret map of an island in the Caribbean where a trove was left by a well-known pirate. When Billy Bones dies, Jim and two friends book passage on a ship run by Capt. Smollett (Lewis Stone). What they don't know, at first, is that practically all of the ship's men are one-time associates of the late pirate and one step from being cutthroats. What's more, all of them want their share of the booty. A beautiful production, a fine score, and a strong script all contribute to making this a respectable version of Stevenson's work.

TREASURE ISLAND

1950   96m   c   Adventure   ★★★★
Walt Disney Productions   (U.K.)   G/U

Bobby Driscoll *(Jim Hawkins)*, Robert Newton *(Long John Silver)*, Basil Sydney *(Capt. Smollett)*, Walter Fitzgerald *(Squire Trelawney)*, Denis O'Dea *(Dr. Livesey)*, Ralph Truman *(George Merry)*, Finlay Currie *(Capt. Bones)*, John Laurie *(Pew)*, Francis de Wolff *(Black Dog)*, Geoffrey Wilkinson *(Ben Gunn)*

p, Perce Pearce; d, Byron Haskin; w, Lawrence E. Watkin (based on the novel by Robert Louis Stevenson); ph, Freddie Young; ed, Alan Jaggs; m, Clifton Parker; prod d, Tom Morahan

This was Disney's first totally live-action movie, and it is, by far, the best film version of the familiar Stevenson story. Disney regular Bobby Driscoll takes on the coveted role of Jim Hawkins, and a number of reliable British actors round out the cast. This version has a marvelous full-bodied visual style that never appears to be studio-bound. When Disney wanted to rerelease the film in the 1970s, the MPAA rating system had arrived, and because of some rather graphic violence, the movie was given the dreaded (by Disney) "PG" rating. The offending scenes had to be snipped to acquire the desired "G" rating, depriving audiences of some excitement, but this remains an extremely satisfying film.

TREASURE OF THE SIERRA MADRE, THE

1948   126m   bw   Adventure   ★★★★★
Warner Bros.   (U.S.)   /PG

Humphrey Bogart *(Fred C. Dobbs)*, Walter Huston *(Howard)*, Tim Holt *(Curtin)*, Bruce Bennett *(Cody)*, Barton MacLane *(McCormick)*, Alfonso Bedoya *(Gold Hat)*, Arturo Soto Rangel *(Presidente)*, Manuel Donde *(El Jefe)*, Jose Torvay *(Pablo)*, Margarito Luna *(Pancho)*

p, Henry Blanke; d, John Huston; w, John Huston (based on the novel by Berwick Traven Torsvan); ph, Ted McCord; ed, Owen Marks; m, Max Steiner; art d, John Hughes; fx, William McGann, H.F. Koenekamp

AAN Best Picture; *AA Best Supporting Actor:* Walter Huston; *AA Best Director:* John Huston; *AA Best Screenplay:* John Huston

Arguably John Huston's greatest film, this powerful study of masculinity under pressure retains its power. There's gold in them thar hills and Humphrey Bogart, Walter Huston, and Tim Holt are hell-bent to find it. The rather preachy B. Traven novel about greed and its tragic consequences is made more lively and much more human by the father-and-son team of actor Walter Huston and director/writer John, with the invaluable assistance of Bogart. What a nice present to give your father at the end of his career. Bogart gives one of his most memorable performances as Fred C. Dobbs, an ordinary guy who gets transformed and finally consumed by greed.

On the bum in Tampico, Mexico, Bogart is reduced to panhandling. He meets and befriends another struggling American, Holt, and the two of them go to work for a shady contractor, MacLane, who takes them to a remote site where they slave away, their pay withheld until the job is done. When the work is finished and they return to Tampico, MacLane says he must go and pick up the payroll. Bogart and Holt complain that they don't have a cent, even to buy a beer, and he gives them a few dollars. They go to a cantina and drink, then check in at a flophouse where they take bunks next to a colorful, garrulous old man (Huston). Huston is regaling the other tramps about prospecting for gold, explaining that he has been at it since the Klondike days, having dug up fortunes and spent them. As Huston spins his tales, he adds that greed is usually the undoing of all prospectors. Bogart goes to sleep and the next day he and Holt look for MacLane and learn that he has a reputation for not paying his workers. They run into him on the street and have to beat him nearly senseless to get him to come up with their pay. Now that they have a little money, they decide prospecting might be a good idea, so they find Huston and ask if he wants to join them. He agrees, and says he's got a little money he can put into the venture. Just then, a young Mexican boy (Robert "Bobby" Blake, veteran of OUR GANG comedies and later famous as TV's "Baretta") who had earlier sold Bogart a lottery ticket, shows up and tells Bogart that his ticket is a winner. Bogart then adds his winnings to the stake and the three men set out to get the gear and equipment they'll need. The three start out as good buddies but wind up in a murderous tangle.

Both director John Huston and his distinguished father, Walter, won Oscars for this film, the only time father and son won the coveted gold statuettes. (In 1985, a third generation of the family won an Oscar when Anjelica Huston, John's daughter and Walter's granddaughter, was named Best Supporting Actress for her role in PRIZZI'S HONOR—also directed by John Huston.)

TREE GROWS IN BROOKLYN, A

1945 128m bw Drama   ★★★★
Fox   (U.S.)   /A

Dorothy McGuire (Katie), Joan Blondell (Aunt Sissy), James Dunn (Johnny Nolan), Lloyd Nolan (McShane), Peggy Ann Garner (Francie Nolan), Ted Donaldson (Neeley Nolan), James Gleason (McGarrity), Ruth Nelson (Miss McDonough), John Alexander (Steve Edwards), B.S. Pully (Christmas Tree Vendor)

p, Louis D. Lighton; d, Elia Kazan; w, Tess Slesinger, Frank Davis (based on the novel by Betty Smith); ph, Leon Shamroy; ed, Dorothy Spencer; m, Alfred Newman; art d, Lyle Wheeler; fx, Fred Sersen; cos, Bonnie Cashin

AA Best Supporting Actor: James Dunn; AAN Best Screenplay: Frank Davis, Tess Slesinger

Elia Kazan's first directorial assignment in films proved to be one of the most endearing, honest family dramas of the era and is still timeless enough to be watched and savored decades later. Set in the Williamsburg area of Brooklyn in the first years of the 20th century, this film memorably captures the local ambiance, and the struggle of the urban poor, as it focuses on the drama of one Irish family. Matriarch McGuire worries about every penny because her husband, amiable loser Dunn, can't ever seem to earn enough to support her and their children (Donaldson and Garner). Protagonist Garner wants to write and dreams of a better life elsewhere. In the tenement there is a small tree that heroically withstands the harsh winter and the humid summer; for Garner, it becomes a symbol of survival, particularly when death strikes the family.

This episodic, charmingly sentimental movie is a trifle lengthy but never tedious. McGuire had only made one movie before, the charming CLAUDIA, and was only about 13 years older than Garner and 13 years younger than Dunn at the time of shooting. Kazan did not fall into the trap to which so many first-time directors are prey, i.e., impressing the eye with cinematic tricks. Instead, he wisely concentrated on evoking

memorable performances from all concerned, and none was more rewarding than that of Dunn, who had starred in many B movies for years before getting the opportunity to show his stuff here. Dunn, for many years, had been a notorious heavy drinker, and when he was first proposed for the role of the Irish singing waiter, Fox executives said no, that he was unreliable and a drunk. But studio boss Zanuck was persuaded that that was exactly what Dunn would be playing and, against all advice, cast the easygoing tippler in the role.

TREE OF WOODEN CLOGS, THE
(L'ALBERO DEGLI ZOCCOLI)

1978 185m c Drama   ★★★★½
G.P.C. Gruppo/Gaumont   (Italy)   /A

Luigi Ornaghi (Batisti), Francesca Moriggi (Batistina), Omar Brignoli (Minek), Antonio Ferrari (Tuni), Teresa Brescianini (Widow Runk), Giuseppe Brignoli (Grandpa Anselmo), Carlo Rota (Peppino), Pasqualina Brolis (Teresina), Massimo Fratus (Pierino), Francesca Villa (Annetta)

d, Ermanno Olmi; w, Ermanno Olmi; ph, Ermanno Olmi; ed, Ermanno Olmi; m, Johann Sebastian Bach

Approaching verite in style, and heavily influenced by American documentarist Robert Flaherty's ethnological classics, this naturalistic portrayal of Italian peasants neither glorifies their lives nor looks down on them. Olmi, who directed, scripted, photographed, and edited the film, concentrates on three peasant families (all finely acted by nonprofessionals) and their daily existence for the period of about one year. They live on an estate governed by a practically nonexistent landlord and work his land with the greatest of care and devotion. Interestingly, however, the least important facet of THE TREE OF WOODEN CLOGS is its plot. Instead, the focus is on the bond between people, as well as their relationship to the land. Olmi resists the urge to overly moralize the lives of these people as he considers what is beautiful as well as what is stagnant about their lives. At times he seems to suggest that here may reside a model for human existence, but he is generally content to present the film as an extended vignette. (It is interesting, though, how Olmi largely fails to consider the class relations structuring certain aspects of these people's lives.) A memorable picture which takes a sensitive, poetic look at a remarkable group of human beings without getting too romanticized about it, THE TREE OF WOODEN CLOGS was winner of the Golden Palm at the 1978 Cannes Film Festival, making it the second Italian film in a row to take top honors (the 1977 winner was the Taviani Brother's PADRE PADRONE).

TREES LOUNGE

1996 94m c Comedy/Drama   ★★★
LIVE Entertainment/Addis/Wechsler/Hanley-Wyman   R/15
/Seneca Falls Productions   (U.S.)

Steve Buscemi (Tommy Basilio), Mark Boone Jr. (Mike), Chloe Sevigny (Debbie), Michael Buscemi (Raymond), Anthony LaPaglia (Rob), Elizabeth Bracco (Theresa), Daniel Baldwin (Jerry), Carol Kane (Connie), Debi Mazar (Crystal), Seymour Cassel (Uncle Al)

p, Brad Wyman, Chris Hanley; d, Steve Buscemi; w, Steve Buscemi; ph, Lisa Rinzler; ed, Kate Williams; m, Evan Lurie; prod d, Steve Rosenzweig; art d, Jennifer Alex; cos, Mari-An Ceo

Steve Buscemi—leading character actor of countless independent American films and a particular favorite of the Coen brothers and Quentin Tarantino—takes his turn behind the camera, and it's a winner.

Thirty-one-year-old Tommy Basilio (Buscemi) is what is commonly known as a loser. He's been fired from his job at the garage, has lost his girlfriend (Elizabeth Bracco) to his ex-best friend/ex-boss (Anthony LaPaglia), has been getting a little to comfy with his ex-girlfriend's underage niece (Chloe Sevigny), and he can't even cut it driving his late uncle's (Seymour Cassel) ice cream truck, because he gives kids the creeps. Tommy is also an alcoholic, and the greater part of his day is spent in a stupor on a bar stool at the Trees Lounge, chumming it up the with other not so beautiful losers.

It's clear from the outset that writer-director Buscemi has seen his share of John Cassavetes films. With his own fine ensemble cast, he's quite capable of capturing a similar sense of improvisatory spontaneity—Carol Kane's worn-out bartender and Debi Mazar's lacquered cookie in stiletto heels are superb creations. But where Cassavetes often uncovered the grotesquerie underlying such desperate lives (usually after one round too many), Buscemi's vison is rooted in compassion and a quirky humor that's entirely his own. Set in the Long Island, NY town of Valley Stream (Buscemi's home town), the film perfectly captures the suburban malaise that can waylay those New Yorkers who left the big city with dreams of a better life amid the green grass, picket fences, and corner bars.

TREMORS

1990 96m c Comedy/Horror ★★★
No Frills/Wilson-Maddock (U.S.) PG-13/15

Kevin Bacon (Valentine McKee), Fred Ward (Earl Basset), Finn Carter (Rhonda LeBeck), Michael Gross (Burt Gummer), Reba McEntire (Heather Gummer), Bobby Jacoby (Melvin Plug), Charlotte Stewart (Nancy), Tony Genaro (Miguel), Ariana Richards (Minday), Richard Marcus (Nestor)

p, Brent Maddock, S.S. Wilson; d, Ron Underwood; w, S.S. Wilson, Brent Maddock (based on a story by S.S. Wilson, Brent Maddock, and Ron Underwood); ph, Alexander Gruszynski; ed, O. Nicholas Brown; m, Ernest Troost; prod d, Ivo Cristante; art d, Donald Maskovich; fx, Gene Warren Jr.

TREMORS fondly recalls monster movies of the 50s, and wisely treads a middle path between knowing sendup and cannily crafted chiller.

Trying to escape their dead-end life in the desert town of Perfection (population 14), handymen Val (Kevin Bacon) and Earl (Fred Ward) find themselves sidetracked when corpses mysteriously begin piling up around them, the causes of death ranging from the strange (an old drunk is found halfway up an electrical tower dead from dehydration) to the unknown. When the handymen have a run-in with some creepy tentacled creatures that have apparently made lunch out of a road crew, they realize they are in deep trouble and retreat to the town to spread some hysteria and prepare for Mankind's last stand against a really disgusting menace: giant, foul-smelling, flesh-eating, mutant maggots.

TREMORS bends its movie cliches just enough to keep the action interesting and entertaining. One of the most fondly held conventions of 50s horror films was to withhold a straight-on view of the monsters until late in the picture; in TREMORS the beasts emerge early in the action, which, in another departure from convention, takes place almost entirely in broad daylight. The special effects are first-rate, with the maggots easily withstanding extended camera scrutiny. Another up-ended convention places a female scientist (Finn Carter) in the thick of the action, although she contributes little to our knowledge of the beasts and, before long, becomes irritated by the questions of the excited townsfolk. It turns out that the dumbest guys in the movie, Val and Earl, contribute the most towards eradicating the big bugs, with their prime motivation being to get the job done so they can continue their rudely interrupted journey out of Perfection.

You don't have to be a perennial late-night movie vidiot to get a kick out of TREMORS. It's fast-moving fun for kids of all ages who harbor a secret delight in movies starring gooey, smelly monsters. It's also very well cast, with Ward and Bacon proving affable and enjoyable comedy leads. Carter also has an offbeat appeal as the irritable woman of science, while Michael Gross and country star Reba McEntire, in a most unlikely film debut (she also wrote and sings the end-credit song, "Why Not Tonight?"), provide solid support as a survivalist couple who dispatch one of the creatures in a hail of bullets. It may not top anyone's 10-best list, but TREMORS is nevertheless solid entertainment.

TRIAL, THE
(LE PROCES)

1963 118m bw Drama ★★★½
Paris Europa/Hisa (France/Italy/West Germany) /X

Anthony Perkins (Josef K), Orson Welles (Hastler), Jeanne Moreau (Miss Burstner), Romy Schneider (Leni), Elsa Martinelli (Hilda), Akim Tamiroff (Bloch), Arnoldo Foa (Inspector A), William Kearns (1st Assistant Inspector), Jess Hahn (2nd Assistant Inspector), Suzanne Flon (Miss Pittl)

p, Yves Laplanche, Miguel Salkind, Alexander Salkind; d, Orson Welles; w, Orson Welles (based on the novel by Franz Kafka); ph, Edmond Richard; ed, Yvonne Martin; m, Jean Ledrut, Tomaso Albinoni; art d, Jean Mandaroux; cos, Helen Thibault

Welles applied his bravura directorial style to Kafka's landmark 1925 novel about Joseph K (Perkins), an office clerk who gets arrested without being told why.

The film opens over a series of pin-screen pictures (a technique using pins, cloth, light, and shadows created by A. Alexeieff) of a guard in front of a huge door, preventing a man from entering. For years the man awaits entrance through the door which leads to the Law, but he never gains admittance. The narrator (Welles) then explains, "It has been said that the logic of this story is the logic of a dream. Do you feel lost in a labyrinth? Do not look for a way out. You will not be able to find one . . . There is no way out."

Kafka's novel doesn't translate well into film, being too dependent on the internal thoughts and frustrations of Joseph K during his quest. Aware of this problem, Welles has chosen to concentrate on the atmosphere of K's world, accompanied by the dreamy musical leitmotif of Albinoni's "Adagio." The sets are typical Welles baroque—massive structures which engulf K in the same way Xanadu swallowed Charles Foster Kane in CITIZEN KANE. These sets alone—with their haunting shadows and claustrophobic walls and ceilings—make THE TRIAL essential viewing. Welles's enthusiasm for the film is remarkable: "Say what you like, but THE TRIAL is the best film I ever made."

The film's genesis goes back to Miguel and Alexander Salkind, the father-and-son producing team, who offered Welles a list of 15 classic novels which were in public domain. Welles was to choose one that he wanted to film and, without much enthusiasm (Welles admits he had a "lack of profound sympathy for Kafka"), he agreed to The Trial. Production began in Zagreb, Yugoslavia, but was soon shut down for lack of funds. Skipping out on bills owed them, Welles and his entourage returned to Paris to complete the film at the abandoned Gare d'Orsay train station, an overwhelming structure which seems to have been built with Welles in mind. Although the film has its admirers, its opening was less than favorable. Originally scheduled to play the 1962 Venice Film Fest, it did not open until December 21 of that year in Paris. Not only did Welles have to overcome financial and scheduling restrictions, but he had problems with the casting. He had first cast himself as a priest, but when no suitable actor could be found for the advocate, Welles took over the role, scrapping the footage he had already shot. Shot in English, THE TRIAL was dubbed for its foreign-language releases, which had a variety of running times. Two players were cut from the US release: Katina Paxinou, as a scientist, and Van Doude, who played an archivist.

The chief difference between Welles's Joseph K and Kafka's is in the extent of their guilt. While Kafka stresses ambiguity, Welles is clear in his feelings: "He is a little bureaucrat. I consider him guilty . . . He belongs to a guilty society; he collaborates with it." Welles further points to his differences with Kafka: "I do not share Kafka's point of view in The Trial. I believe that he is a good writer, but Kafka is not the extraordinary genius that people today see in him." Nonetheless, Kafka's story is far more successful as a novel than a film.

TRIAL OF JOAN OF ARC
(PROCES DE JEANNE D'ARC)

1962 65m bw Historical ★★★
Pathe (France)

Florence Carrez (Jeanne D'Arc), Jean-Claude Fourneau (Bishop Cauchon), Marc Jacquier (Jean Lemaitre), Roger Honorat (Jean Beaupere), Jean Gillibert (Jean de Chatillon), Andre Regnier (D'Estivet), Michel Herubel (Frere Isambart de la Pierre), Philippe Dreux (Frere Martin Ladvenu), Jean Darbaud (Nicolas de Houppeville), E.R. Pratt (Warwick)

p, Agnes Delahaie; d, Robert Bresson; w, Robert Bresson (based on "Proces de Condamnation et de Rehabilitation de Jeanne D'Arc"); ph, L.H. Burel; ed, Germaine Artus; m, Francis Seyrig; art d, Pierre Charbonnier; cos, Lucilla Mussini

The most commonly known film rendition of the famous French legend of Joan of Arc is the 1920s version by Dreyer in which Falconetti gave a stunning performance of the girl burned as a witch. From the outset of this newer project, Bresson chose an entirely different angle from that of Dreyer, for he was concerned with creating a more objective rendition, unprejudiced by the filmmaker's camera technique and personal manipulations. His efforts were fairly successful. He based the script solely on the notes from the trial, with Carrez playing Joan in a manner that makes her appear brighter and more scheming than she has usually been represented. Joan was a French peasant girl brought to trial as an enemy of the government, and after enduring a long court case and torture she was burned as a witch. Unlike the earlier version, Bresson concentrates quite heavily on the psychological and physical torture, showing how Joan broke down during the trial and recanted her faith. The purpose of Bresson was not to destroy the myth of Joan of Arc; what he did was reveal the processes that helped to create a legend.

TRIP TO BOUNTIFUL, THE

1985 105m c Drama ★★★★
Bountiful/Film Dallas (U.S.) PG/U

Geraldine Page (*Mrs. Watts*), John Heard (*Ludie Watts*), Carlin Glynn (*Jessie Mae*), Richard Bradford (*Sheriff*), Rebecca De Mornay (*Thelma*), Kevin Cooney (*Roy*), Norman Bennett, Harvey Lewis (*Bus Ticket Men*), Kirk Sisco (*Ticket Agent*), David Tanner (*Billy Davis*)

p, Sterling Van Wagenen, Horton Foote; d, Peter Masterson; w, Horton Foote (based on his play); ph, Fred Murphy; ed, Jay Freund; m, J.A.C. Redford; prod d, Neil Spisak; art d, Philip Lamb; cos, Gary Jones

AA Best Actress: Geraldine Page; AAN Best Adapted Screenplay: Horton Foote

A luminous performance by Geraldine Page and one of the most touching pictures of the decade. The year is 1947; the place, Houston, Texas. Mrs. Watts (Page) is an elderly woman given to humming hymns and living the remaining years of her life with her wimp son, Ludie (John Heard), and his shrewish wife, Jessie Mae (Carlin Glynn), in a cramped apartment. Mrs. Watts's heart is weak, she has spells, and she can't get along with Jessie Mae at all. She has but one fervent desire left in her life: she wants to return to Bountiful, the small Texas town where she was born and grew up. The memories of the tranquility of Bountiful haunt her constantly as a reminder of a better time and life. When the stress gets too much for her, Mrs. Watts hides her pension check from Ludie and Jessie Mae and plans her escape. The movie is wonderfully made, and the first-time direction by stage director Peter Masterson is extraordinary. No guns, no violence, no nudity—just a caring story that will wet the driest eye and warm the coldest heart. Every single role is perfectly cast and perfectly played, and Horton Foote's script is a marvel of economy.

TRISTANA

1970 95m c Drama ★★★★
Epoca/Talia/Selenia/Corona (Spain/Italy/France) GP/A

Catherine Deneuve (*Tristana*), Fernando Rey (*Don Lope*), Franco Nero (*Horacio*), Lola Gaos (*Saturna*), Antonio Casas (*Don Cosme*), Jesus Fernandez (*Saturno*), Vicente Soler (*Don Ambrosio*), Jose Calvo (*Bellringer*), Fernando Cebrian (*Dr. Miquis*), Candida Losada (*Senora Burguesa*)

d, Luis Bunuel; w, Luis Bunuel, Julio Alejandro (based on the novel *Tristana* by Benito Perez Galdos); ph, Jose F. Aguayo; ed, Pedro del Rey; art d, Enrique Alarcon; cos, Rosa Garcia

AAN Best Foreign Language Film

A tauting black comedy with Surrealist touches. Bunuel's reworking of Benito Perez Galdos' novel, like all the works of this prolific filmmaker, has much beneath its surface. In a role that capitalizes on her placid beauty, Deneuve is a young woman who becomes the ward of hypocritical aristocrat Rey, who makes much of the fact that he hasn't taken advantage of her beauty. The truth is—he has. Prior to receiving an inheritance from his sister, the more-or-less-impoverished Rey refuses to take a job because he believes a man of his social standing is above menial labor. Instead, he sells all his belongings. At the same time he sees himself as a leader of the common man and makes great speeches to his cronies about improving the lot of the masses. Deneuve leaves the protection of Rey's home when she falls in love with artist

Nero, but she is unwilling to make a commitment to him, so she returns to Rey, who asks for her hand. After losing a leg because of a tumor, she accepts Rey's proposal and begins a passionless marriage despite her continued love for Nero.

Perhaps what makes this work so powerful is Bunuel's subtle use of key situations to represent much larger ideas. In comparison with such Bunuel masterpieces as VIRIDIANA and LOS OLVIDADOS, TRISTANA's assault on religion and politics is tame. Nevertheless, Bunuel's subtle presentation here (he uses, very little camera movement and little music), effectively conveys a world in desperate need of change.

TROUBLE IN MIND

1985 111m c Crime/Romance ★★
Raincity (U.S.) R/15

Kris Kristofferson (*Hawk*), Keith Carradine (*Coop*), Lori Singer (*Georgia*), Genevieve Bujold (*Wanda*), Joe Morton (*Solo*), Divine (*Hilly Blue*), George Kirby (*Lt. Gunther*), John Considine (*Nate Nathanson*), Dirk Blocker (*Rambo*), Albert Hall (*Leo*)

p, Carolyn Pfeiffer, David Blocker; d, Alan Rudolph; w, Alan Rudolph; ph, Toyomichi Kurita; ed, Sally Allen, Tom Walls; m, Mark Isham; prod d, Steven Legler; fx, Bob Burns; cos, Tracy Tynan

An ambitious but ultimately pretentious film that attempts to mix film noir, Theater of the Absurd, romance, and science fiction but falls flat on almost all counts. It's set in the near future in the mythical town of Rain City. The place is ruled by martial law but populated with 1940s gangsters and 1950s diners. Hawk (Kris Kristofferson) is an ex-cop who has just come back from jail for having killed a man in self-defense. He looks up his old flame, Wanda (Genevieve Bujold), who is now running a cafe. He would like to put his life together, mind his own business, and have a pleasant few years. Coop (Keith Carradine) and Georgia (Lori Singer) are a newlywed couple who have come to Rain City to try to find jobs. When work doesn't materialize, Coop gets involved with crook Solo (Joe Morton), soon dealing in stolen goods. When Hawk learns what's transpiring, he takes it upon himself to save Coop and protect Georgia. TROUBLE IN MIND is offbeat, unique, and interesting, and for that alone it should be noted. It is a shame that none of the elements ever come together, so this film winds up being a beautiful, atmospheric mess.

TROUBLE IN PARADISE

1932 83m bw Comedy ★★★★★
Paramount (U.S.) /15

Miriam Hopkins (*Lily Vautier*), Kay Francis (*Mariette Colet*), Herbert Marshall (*Gaston Monescu/La Valle*), Charlie Ruggles (*the Major*), Edward Everett Horton (*Francois Filiba*), C. Aubrey Smith (*Adolph Giron*), Robert Greig (*Jacques the Butler*), George Humbert (*Waiter*), Rolfe Sedan (*Purse Salesman*), Luis Alberni (*Annoyed Opera Fan*)

p, Ernst Lubitsch; d, Ernst Lubitsch; w, Grover Jones, Samson Raphaelson (based on the play "The Honest Finder" by Laszlo Aladar); ph, Victor Milner; m, W. Franke Harling; art d, Hans Dreier; cos, Travis Banton

For six decades this film has been unmatched in the realm of sophisticated farce. Films from THE AWFUL TRUTH to THE LADY EVE to SOME LIKE IT HOT are sublime on their more modest social scale and in their basic Americanness. By contrast, TROUBLE IN PARADISE has all the class and Continental elegance one associates with the Paramout of the 1930s. Made before the Production Code clampdown of 1934, this Lubitsch masterpiece shows his talent for sly sexual innuendo at its most witty and polished. The result is pure caviar, only tastier.

The story tells of two jewel thieves, Gaston (Marshall) and Lily (Hopkins), who together work at bilking a merry widow, Mariette Colet (Francis), out of a small fortune. They secure jobs as her secretary and maid, but trouble begins in paradise when Gaston starts falling for his lovely prey and when one of her many suitors (Horton), a former victim of Gaston's, begins to recognize Mme. Colet's new secretary.

The many laughs in this consistently delightful souffle come not only from Raphaelson's marvelous screenplay but also from Lubitsch's supple visual wit. On one hand there's delightful repartee about a former secretary who enjoyed an antique bed a bit too much, and on the other we have the sexy silhouette of Gaston and Mariette cast over a chaise lounge. From the opening shot of an operatic gondolier who turns out to be a garbageman to a police report about theft and tonsils translated for Italian officials, this film is full of unforgettable moments of merriment.

The cast, too, is peerless. In one of his earliest Hollywood efforts, Herbert Marshall does the greatest work of his career. Too often maligned for playing stodgy consorts to dynamic star actresses such as Garbo, Davis, and Shearer, Marshall here gets to display his impeccable timing and supple grace. Frequently hilarious, his quiet approach and crushed velvet voice still let him remain suave throughout. Even Cary Grant would be hard pressed to match this portrayal. (He'd be too frantic.) Kay Francis, too, that popular sufferer of countless "women's films" with her "twoublesome" r's, gives of her very best. With her sleek, glamorous style and elegantly wry line readings, she is light, sexy, and totally captivating. Her doorway caresses and her finger-snapping seduction of Gaston are priceless. Miriam Hopkins was luckier in that she had many more chances to display her comic flair in film. Today one of the most underrated and unfairly maligned stars of the 1930s, the brittle, feisty Hopkins can rattle off witty banter at a breakneck pace or she can be deliciously languorous and coy. Her enjoyment of her own sexuality is heady even today and the thieving competition between Gaston and Lily, in which escalating crimes turn into escalating passion, remains one of the greatest scenes of foreplay ever caught on film. Ruggles and Horton prove yet again that they are two of the greatest farceurs in Hollywood, and the rest of the cast is equally choice. (One standout is Leonid Kinskey, whose bit as a leftist radical only foregrounds the satiric anarchy of the entire film.) Beautifully handled from start to finish, gleamingly shot and full of Dreier's incredible Art Deco designs, TROUBLE IN PARADISE is Lubitsch's greatest film and one of the indisputable highlights of comic cinema.

TROUBLE WITH HARRY, THE

1955 99m c Comedy ★★★½
Paramount (U.S.) /PG

Edmund Gwenn *(Capt. Albert Wiles)*, John Forsythe *(Sam Marlowe, the Painter)*, Shirley MacLaine *(Jennifer Rogers, Harry's Wife)*, Mildred Natwick *(Miss Graveley)*, Mildred Dunnock *(Mrs. Wiggs)*, Jerry Mathers *(Arnie Rogers, Harry's Son)*, Royal Dano *(Calvin Wiggs)*, Parker Fennelly *(Millionaire)*, Barry Macollum *(Tramp)*, Dwight Marfield *(Dr. Greenbow)*

p, Alfred Hitchcock; d, Alfred Hitchcock; w, John Michael Hayes (based on the novel by Jack Trevor Story); ph, Robert Burks; ed, Alma Macrorie; m, Bernard Herrmann; art d, Hal Pereira, John B. Goodman; fx, John P. Fulton; cos, Edith Head

A quiet, picturesque Vermont autumn, its leaves in full color, provides the setting for this splendid Hitchcock black comedy in which Harry Worp just won't stay dead. Shirley MacLaine, in her film debut, is Jennifer Rogers, a young mother who recognizes Harry's corpse as that of her dead husband. She is certain that she accidentally killed him. Retired sea captain Albert Wiles (Gwenn), and the dotty old Miss Graveley (Natwick) also believe they are the murderers. Enter eccentric painter Sam Marlowe (Forsythe), a tongue-in-cheek nod to gumshoes Sam Spade and Philip Marlowe, who tries to get to the bottom of Harry's death. Two love stories are interspersed as Jennifer and Sam fall for each other, and the captain and Miss Graveley do the same. Jerry Mathers, of "Leave It to Beaver" fame, is MacLaine's often-hysterical young son.

TRUE BELIEVER

1989 103m c Crime/Mystery ★★★
Lasker-Parkes (U.S.) R/

James Woods *(Eddie Dodd)*, Robert Downey Jr. *(Roger Baron)*, Margaret Colin *(Kitty Greer)*, Yuji Okumoto *(Shu Kai Kim)*, Kurtwood Smith *(Robert Reynard)*, Tom Bower *(Cecil Skell)*, Miguel Fernandes *(Art Esparza)*, Charles Hallahan *(Vincent Dennehy)*, Sully Diaz *(Maraquilla Esparza)*, Misan Kim *(Mrs. Kim)*

p, Walter F. Parkes, Lawrence Lasker; d, Joseph Ruben; w, Wesley Strick; ph, John Lindley; ed, George Bowers; m, Brad Fiedel; prod d, Lawrence Miller; art d, Jim Pohl; cos, Erica Edell Phillips

Idealistic recent law school graduate Roger Baron (Robert Downey, Jr.) journeys to New York to work as a clerk for his idol, Edward Dodd (James Woods), whose inventive tactics in civil rights cases in 1960s and 70s made him one of the country's most respected attorneys. Sadly, Dodd is now a dope-smoking shyster who plies his trade in the service of sleazy drug dealers, but when Roger manages to get him to take the case of an unjustly imprisoned Korean (Yuji Okumoto), Dodd uncovers a conspiracy and redeems himself as a committed "true believer." Though its plot is thoroughly implausible, TRUE BELIEVER is still an intriguing and entertaining mystery, thanks to the performance of Woods and the direction of Joseph Ruben, who revitalizes the tired premise (crusading lawyer frees innocent man) by providing exhilarating pace and inventive action. Woods clearly relishes his chance to display a wide range of emotions within his patented maverick persona, and Downey also acquits himself well in a much less challenging role.

TRUE CONFESSIONS

1981 108m c Crime ★★★★
UA (U.S.) R/15

Robert De Niro *(Des Spellacy)*, Robert Duvall *(Tom Spellacy)*, Charles Durning *(Jack Amsterdam)*, Ed Flanders *(Dan T. Champion)*, Burgess Meredith *(Seamus Fargo)*, Rose Gregorio *(Brenda Samuels)*, Cyril Cusack *(Cardinal Danaher)*, Kenneth McMillan *(Frank Crotty)*, Dan Hedaya *(Howard Terkel)*, Gwen Van Dam *(Mrs. Fazenda)*

p, Irwin Winkler, Robert Chartoff; d, Ulu Grosbard; w, John Gregory Dunne, Joan Didion (based on the novel by Dunne); ph, Owen Roizman; ed, Lynzee Klingman; m, Georges Delerue; prod d, Stephen Grimes; art d, Stewart Campbell; chor, Alfonse L. Palermo; cos, Joe I. Tompkins

Underrated at the time of release, TRUE CONFESSIONS is a fascinating film that exposes the dark underside of the Catholic Church and fixes it firmly in the seedy, corrupt world of film noir. The first on-screen teaming of De Niro and Duvall (they appeared in GODFATHER II but never in the same scene), the film is largely set in Los Angeles in the 1940s. Tom Spellacy (Duvall) is a hard-boiled homicide detective whose investigation of the grisly murder of a porno starlet leads him to believe that his brother Des (De Niro), an ambitious Catholic monsignor, is involved with corrupt local businessman Jack Amsterdam (Durning)—Spellacy's chief suspect. Adapted by the husband-and-wife team of Dunne and Didion from Dunne's fine novel, all of the characters in TRUE CONFESSIONS are corrupt to the core. The period detail is letter-perfect, the cast is uniformly excellent, and Delerue's score is haunting and evocative. TRUE CONFESSIONS is a thoughtful but deeply disturbing film, and its frank portrayal of corruption and murder makes it for adults only.

TRUE GRIT

1969 128m c Western ★★★★
Paramount (U.S.) G/PG

John Wayne *(Reuben J. "Rooster" Cogburn)*, Glen Campbell *(La Boeuf)*, Kim Darby *(Mattie Ross)*, Jeremy Slate *(Emmett Quincy)*, Robert Duvall *(Ned Pepper)*, Dennis Hopper *(Moon)*, Alfred Ryder *(Goudy)*, Strother Martin *(Col. G. Stonehill)*, Jeff Corey *(Tom Chaney)*, Ron Soble *(Capt. Boots Finch)*

p, Hal B. Wallis; d, Henry Hathaway; w, Marguerite Roberts (based on the novel by Charles Portis); ph, Lucien Ballard; ed, Warren Low; m, Elmer Bernstein; prod d, Walter Tyler; fx, Dick Johnson; cos, Dorothy Jeakins

AA Best Actor: John Wayne; *AAN Best Song:* Elmer Bernstein (Music), Don Black (Lyrics)

An enormously entertaining adventure that is as much about John Wayne's image as it is about a girl seeking revenge for her father's murder. Mattie Ross (Kim Darby) is a level-headed 14-year-old who goes to Rooster Cogburn (Wayne) after her father is killed. The murderer, Tom Chaney (Jeff Corey), has since fled into Indian territory, and Mattie wants a man of "true grit" to help bring him to justice. Cogburn, a paunchy US marshal with a patch over one eye, admires Mattie's spunk and agrees to take on the job. Joining them is La Boeuf (Glen Campbell), a Texas Ranger whom Mattie despises. He, too, is searching for Chaney, hoping to collect a reward offered by the family of a murdered Texas politician. Much of the film's entertainment comes from the obvious contrasts and subtle similarities between Cogburn and Mattie. Cogburn is fat, drunken, and not entirely honest, but he has an underlying sense of honor, that "true grit" that Mattie demands. Although Wayne's characterizations in STAGECOACH and THE SEARCHERS are more complex, TRUE GRIT provides him with some of his most memorable screen moments. He reprised the role in ROOSTER COGBURN, costarring with Katharine Hepburn. TRUE GRIT was redone for television in 1978, with Warren Oates in the lead role, but neither project approached this film in either quality or spirit.

TRUE LIES

1994 141m c Action/Adventure ★★★½
Lightstorm Entertainment (U.S.) R/15

Arnold Schwarzenegger (Harry Tasker), Jamie Lee Curtis (Helen Tasker), Tom Arnold (Gib), Bill Paxton (Simon), Tia Carrere (Juno Skinner), Charlton Heston (Spencer Trilby), Art Malik (Aziz), Eliza Dushku (Dana Tasker), Grant Heslov (Faisil), Marshall Manesh (Khaled)

p, James Cameron, Stephanie Austin; d, James Cameron; w, James Cameron; ph, Russell Carpenter; ed, Conrad Buff, Mark Goldblatt, Richard A. Harris, Shawn Broes, Scott Michael Keppler; m, Brad Fiedel; prod d, Peter Lamont; art d, Robert Laing, Michael Novotny; fx, Thomas L. Fisher, John Bruno, Jacques Stroweis, Patrick McClung; chor, Lynn Hockney; cos, Marlene Stewart

AAN Best Visual Effects: John Bruno, Thomas L. Fisher, Jacques Stroweis, Patrick McClung

A James Bond pastiche for the 1990s, TRUE LIES is hugely elaborate and ultimately disturbing, a big empty gloss on action formulas with an ugly edge that belies its all-in-good-fun surface.

Special agent Harry Tasker (Arnold Schwarzenegger) emerges from the water outside a heavily guarded mansion, peels off his wetsuit to reveal the dinner jacket underneath, and strolls into a swanky party. He tangos with a treacherous woman (Tia Carrere), steals some computer files, and escapes in a spectacular flurry of gunfire and masked pursuers on skis. Now for the joke: Harry goes home to mousy wife Helen (Jamie Lee Curtis) and the sham of his domestic life, in which he pretends to be a computer salesman. Helen is so bored by household routine that she's on the verge of giving in to smarmy used-car salesman Simon (Bill Paxton), who woos her by claiming to be a spy. For the rest of the film, Harry must serve two masters: while pursuing Arab terrorists led by charismatic Aziz (Art Malik), he attempts to save his marriage, which involves using the Agency's considerable resources to terrorize Simon and Helen.

It's hard to separate TRUE LIES the movie from TRUE LIES the $120 million phenomenon. Above all, this is a smirking monument to self-referential excess: everything is big, bigger, biggest, from the action sequences to the star, and when something doesn't work on the level of spectacle, it's played as a joke. On the surface, TRUE LIES is an affectionate homage to James Bond movies, ratcheted up to meet the action/adventure expectations of today's audiences.

But TRUE LIES also picks up a lot of nasty subtext from the Bond films and expands upon it (deliberately or not), and the larky atmosphere is ultimately poisoned by racism, homophobia, and misogyny. In the wake of the film's release, many noted that no other racial stereotype is so widely tolerated as that of Arabs as wild-eyed terrorists in kaffiyehs, and TRUE LIES panders to that image shamelessly. It also puts forth, without a trace of irony, the idea that exotic women are two-faced temptresses, as well as the notion that all women are whores at heart, and stupid ones at that. True lies, indeed.

TRUE LOVE

1989 104m c Comedy ★★★
Forward Films (U.S.) R/15

Annabella Sciorra (Donna), Ron Eldard (Michael), Star Jasper (J.C.), Aida Turturro (Grace), Roger Rignack (Dom), Michael J. Wolfe (Brian), Kelly Cinnante (Yvonne), Rick Shapiro (Kevin), Suzanne Costallos (Fran), Vinny Pastore (Angelo)

p, Richard Guay, Shelley Houis; d, Nancy Savoca; w, Nancy Savoca, Richard Guay; ph, Lisa Rinzler; ed, John Tintori; prod d, Lester Cohen; art d, Pamela Woodbridge; cos, Deborah Anderko

The top prize-winner at the 1989 US Film festival, TRUE LOVE is a low-budget feature debut which, while no landmark, is an entertaining comedy filled with likable characters. Like fellow NYU alum Martin Scorsese, first-time director Nancy Savoca turned for inspiration to her own working-class Italian-American roots to create this story. The film centers on the strong but somewhat empty-headed Donna (Annabella Sciorra) who is determined to get her man Michael (Ron Eldard) to the altar. Michael doesn't mind getting engaged and exchanging an occasional "I love you," but who would rather pal around with his neighborhood buddies than actually exchange marriage vows. The story is as old as the movies themselves, but the uncanny resemblance its people and situations bear to real life makes TRUE LOVE enjoyable. The characters are created with care and a feeling for individuality, and each scene comes to life with humor and poignancy. Among the cast, the most pleasant surprise is Sciorra, in her first feature.

TRUE ROMANCE

1993 119m c Action/Thriller ★★★½
True Romance Productions/Morgan Creek/Davis Films (U.S.) R/18

Christian Slater (Clarence Worley), Patricia Arquette (Alabama Whitman), Dennis Hopper (Clifford Worley), Val Kilmer (Elvis (uncredited)), Gary Oldman (Drexl Spivey), Brad Pitt (Floyd - Dick's Roomate), Christopher Walken (Vincenzo Coccotti), Bronson Pinchot (Elliot Blitzer), Samuel L. Jackson (Big Don), Michael Rapaport (Dick Ritchie)

p, Samuel Hadida, Steve Perry, Bill Unger; d, Tony Scott; w, Quentin Tarantino; ph, Jeffrey L. Kimball; ed, Michael Tronick, Christian Wagner; m, Hans Zimmer; prod d, Benjamin Fernandez; art d, James J. Murakami; fx, Robert Henderson, Mike Meinardus, Larry Shorts; cos, Susan Becker

TRUE ROMANCE is about as good as contemporary Hollywood movies get. It boasts an engaging pair of leads (Christian Slater and Patricia Arquette); a snappy plot; dialogue that bristles with great one-liners; a gallery of accurately, hilariously observed minor characters; and a happy ending complete with a slew of corpses. What more could you ask?

The story begins in Detroit, where Alabama Whitman (Arquette), a call-girl with three days' experience, bumps into—or, more exactly, tips a carton of popcorn over—lowly store clerk Clarence Worley (Slater) during a kung fu triple bill at Clarence's local theater. Within a matter of hours, Alabama has renounced her nascent career and found true love; Clarence, meanwhile, has got himself into a bloody shootout with Alabama's former "manager" and found himself in possession of a suitcase full of cocaine—not to mention a really cheesy pair of sunglasses. The couple head off to LA in an attempt to sell their loot that involves them with a supremely bad actor (Dick Ritchie), whom we first see auditioning for "T.J. Hooker"; an unctuous movie producer (Saul Rubinek); his fawning, preppy assistant (Bronson Pinchot); a band of pursuing mafia hit men; and a bunch of wisecracking LA cops.

TRUE ROMANCE blends and recycles elements of scores of crime and road movies, from BONNIE AND CLYDE to BADLANDS, but it does so with enough energy and verve to create something entirely fresh and infectiously entertaining. The filmmakers demonstrate a passion for pop culture that gives everything an air of comic-book unreality, while also making for some genuinely haunting moments. Highlights: the gloriously un-PC scene in which Clarence's dad (Dennis Hopper) faces off against a mob lieutenant (Christopher Walken); and the bloody, protracted motel-room battle (trimmed for theatrical release, restored for video) between Alabama and a goon who—like the audience—gets more than he bargained for.

TRUE STORIES

1986 89m c Comedy ★★★½
True Stories Ventures (U.S.) PG

David Byrne *(Narrator)*, John Goodman *(Louis Fyne)*, Swoosie Kurtz *(Miss Rollings)*, Spalding Gray *(Earl Culver)*, Alix Elias *(The Cute Woman)*, Annie McEnroe *(Kay Culver)*, Roebuck "Pops" Staples *(Mr. Tucker)*, Humberto Larriva *(Ramon)*, John Ingle *(The Preacher)*, Matthew Posey *(The Computer Guy)*

p, Gary Kurfirst; d, David Byrne; w, David Byrne, Beth Henley, Stephen Tobolowsky; ph, Ed Lachman; ed, Caroline Biggerstaff; m, David Byrne, The Talking Heads; prod d, Barbara Ling; chor, Meredith Monk, Dee McCandless, Gene Menger; cos, Elizabeth McBride

David Byrne, then the front man for the Talking Heads, makes his feature film directorial debut with a deliciously offbeat and affectionate look at American madness. Byrne himself plays the narrator, a friendly outsider every bit as strange as the oddball characters he observes. Wearing a large cowboy hat, he talks to the camera as he drives along in a big red convertible. Virtually plotless, the film follows Byrne as he takes us on a tour of Virgil, Texas, and its inhabitants. We meet the "Laziest Woman in the World" (Swoozie Kurtz); the "Lying Woman" (Jo Harvey Allen), who spices up her mundane workday with incredible stories; a civic leader (Spalding Gray) and his wife (Annie McEnroe), who haven't spoken directly to each other in 15 years; a paranoid preacher (John Ingle) who sees conspiracy around every corner; and the man who comes closest to being the film's main character, Louis Fyne (John Goodman), a lovable panda-bear of a man who is looking for matrimony with a capital "M." Supposedly inspired by bizarre clippings found in the slezoid tabloids that adorn grocery checkout line, TRUE STORIES attempts to provide a fond, kindly glimpse of the heartland of America. Some were offended by what they perceived to be the film's smug hipness and sense of superiority. We could not disagree more. It's a lovely loving film that also has some terrific Talking Heads tunes. The actors all do amazingly well with their rather sketchy characterizations. All in all, this is a commendable first effort from neophyte director Byrne. We hope to hear—and see—more from him.

TRULY, MADLY, DEEPLY

1991 105m c Romance/Fantasy ★★★½
BBC Films (U.K.) PG

Juliet Stevenson *(Nina)*, Alan Rickman *(Jamie)*, Bill Paterson *(Sandy)*, Michael Maloney *(Mark)*, Carolyn Choa *(Translator)*, Christopher Rozycki *(Titus)*, Keith Bartlett *(Plumber)*, David Ryall *(George)*, Stella Maris *(Maura)*

p, Robert Cooper; d, Anthony Minghella; w, Anthony Minghella; ph, Remi Adefarasin; ed, John Stothart; m, Barrington Pheloung; prod d, Barbara Gasnold; cos, James Keast

The first feature film from writer-director Anthony Minghella, TRULY, MADLY, DEEPLY is a funny, touching story about dealing with bereavement and learning to love again.

Nina (Juliet Stevenson) is having a hard time getting over the sudden death of her lover Jamie (Alan Rickman). London is a lonely place, she finds, as she returns home from work every day to an empty flat—empty, that is, save for a recent infestation of rats. The memory of her relationship with Jamie is always on her mind, the music he played on his cello echoing her thoughts at every turn. Sandy (Bill Paterson), who runs the translation agency where she works, tries to shake Nina out of the doldrums, but without success. Titus (Christopher Rozycki), another colleague who wants to fix up her rundown flat, is smitten with her, but she good-humoredly ignores his advances. Nina admits to her bereavement therapist that she feels as though Jamie is somehow still around. Lost in her memories, Nina begins to slip away from reality and, in the process, literally wills her dead lover back in the form of a ghost.

Labelled by many critics as a "thinking person's GHOST," TRULY, MADLY, DEEPLY is sensitively written and charmingly acted. Juliet Stevenson brings tremendous depth to a role that was created specifically for her, and Alan Rickman proves himself capable of something quite different from the bad-guy roles (DIE HARD, ROBIN HOOD: PRINCE OF THIEVES) for which he's best known. Minghella's background in TV, though (he worked with the late Jim Henson on a

series of European folk tales for NBC and created the BBC drama series, "What If It's Raining") is evident in the limited scope of the piece, particularly its rather uninspired visuals. Special mention should go to Barrington Pheloung for his lilting, poignant musical score.

TRUST

1991 90m c Romance/Comedy/Drama ★★★
Zenith Productions/Last Moment Films/True Fiction R/15
Pictures (U.S.)

Adrienne Shelly *(Maria Coughlin)*, Martin Donovan *(Matthew Slaughter)*, Merritt Nelson *(Jean Coughlin)*, John McKay *(Jim Slaughter)*, Edie Falco *(Peg Coughlin)*, Marko Hunt *(John Coughlin)*

p, Bruce Weiss; d, Hal Hartley; w, Hal Hartley; ph, Michael Spiller; ed, Nick Gomez; m, Phil Reed; prod d, Daniel Ouellette; art d, Julie Fabian; cos, Claudia Brown

The second full-length film from director-screenwriter Hal Hartley, TRUST displays all the characteristics which made his first feature, THE UNBELIEVABLE TRUTH, a cult hit—suburban Long Island settings, deadpan dialogue mixing metaphysical ponderings with *non sequiturs*, understated black humor. TRUST, though, fails to break any new ground, and lacks some of the spontaneous charm of the previous work.

The film begins with seventeen-year-old Maria Coughlin (Adrienne Shelly) confronting her father John (Marko Hunt) with the news that she's pregnant and plans to drop out of high school. He insults her; she slaps him and leaves home; he falls down dead of a heart attack. Maria wanders the town and meets Rachel, a despondent housewife who confides all her woes in Maria and gives her money for food. Maria fights off a would-be-rapist shopkeeper while trying to buy beer, and emerges from the store to find that a baby has been kidnapped; she suspects Rachel of the crime. Maria hides out in an old abandoned house where she meets Matthew Slaughter (Martin Donovan), a troubled young man who carries around a hand grenade his father brought back from Korea just in case he decides to kill himself. With Matthew, Maria faces—*inter alia*—angry parents, a search for the missing baby, an abortion, and some twisted sexual intrigue.

TRUST is stylishly photographed and crammed with quirky, offbeat incidents and dialogue. As in THE UNBELIEVABLE TRUTH, Adrienne Shelley gives an engaging performance as a confused, alienated suburban girl who meets up with an enigmatic, potentially violent stranger. Hartley has an appealing and distinctive world-view; those who enjoyed THE UNBELIEVABLE TRUTH, however, may feel as though they've seen it all before, and that it was better structured and more convincingly performed the first time around.

TRUTH OR DARE

1991 118m c/bw Documentary/Musical ★★★
Propaganda Films (U.S.) R/18

Madonna, Donna Delory, Niki Harris, Luis Camacho, Oliver Crumes, Salim Gauwloos, Jose Guitierez, Kevin Stea, Gabriel Trupin, Carlton Wilborn *(Dancers)*

p, Tim Clawson, Jay Roewe, Steve Golin, Sigurjon Sighvatsson; d, Alek Keshishian; ph, Robert Leacock, Doug Nichol, Christophe Lanzenberg, Marc Reshovsky, Daniel Pearl, Toby Phillips; ed, Barry Alexander Brown, John Murray; chor, Vincent Paterson

Shot during 1989's "Blonde Ambition" world tour, TRUTH OR DARE is a documentary look at Madonna Louise Ciccone, arguably the most famous woman in the world today.

Director Alek Keshishian, who cut his teeth on music video, follows the pop diva from stage to hotel room to parties, press conferences, rehearsals and shopping expeditions. He photographs her talking to her family, eating, getting her hair done and horsing around with her dancers, back-up singers and other tour personnel, then intercuts the footage—shot in self-conscious B&W—with color footage of her elaborate stage show. The result is a surprisingly engaging portrait of a media phenomenon for whom the distinction between "onstage" and "offstage" is almost irrelevant.

Keshishian is ruthless, showing Madonna as she bitches at the tech crew, strips in her dressing room, prays at her mother's grave (there's a wireless mike concealed in the dirt) and fellates a bottle during a parlor game—the "Truth or Dare" of the title. About the only thing Keshishian doesn't show is Madonna at home cleaning the toilet, but that's because she's on the road, wrapped in the cocoon of touring ritual and intense, superficial camaraderie. But you get the sense that this is her real life; when then-boyfriend Warren Beatty passes through and suggests she isn't interested in living off-camera, the remark sounds unexpectedly profound.

Madonna is a star for the voyeuristic age, an age when wars start on television and confession is only good for the soul if it's picked up by the wires. When the camera captures Madonna observing two of her male dancers kiss, she's absorbed by the same contradictory spectacle audiences experience when they look at TRUTH OR DARE: intimacy designed to be watched.

TUCKER: THE MAN AND HIS DREAM

1988 111m c Biography   ★★★★
Lucasfilm (U.S.)   PG

Jeff Bridges (Preston Tucker), Joan Allen (Vera Tucker), Martin Landau (Abe Karatz), Frederic Forrest (Eddie Dean), Mako (Jimmy Sakuyama), Lloyd Bridges (Sen. Homer Ferguson), Elias Koteas (Alex Tremulis), Christian Slater (Junior), Nina Siemaszko (Marilyn Lee Tucker), Anders Johnson (Johnny Tucker)

p, Fred Roos, Fred Fuchs; d, Francis Ford Coppola; w, Arnold Schulman, David Seidler; ph, Vittorio Storaro; ed, Priscilla Nedd; m, Joe Jackson, Carmine Coppola; prod d, Dean Tavoularis; fx, David Pier; chor, Paula Smuin; cos, Milena Canonero

AAN Best Supporting Actor: Martin Landau; AAN Best Art Direction: Dean Tavoularis, Armin Ganz; AAN Best Costume Design: Milena Canonero

A long-delayed dream project for director Francis Ford Coppola, TUCKER: THE MAN AND HIS DREAM was one of the most visually sumptuous American films of the 1980s. In a style that hearkens back to the boundless optimism of 1940s American advertising art, the film tells the story of Preston Tucker—part inventor, part con man—who in the late 1940s attempted to produce his own car, which he dubbed the Tucker Torpedo, "The Car of Tomorrow—Today!" Tucker (Jeff Bridges) has worked his way up in the auto industry and starts up a company to build his dream car. Meanwhile, the big three auto manufacturers in Detroit get wind of Tucker's scheme and set out to squash the tiny interloper.

A glorious celebration of the creative process, TUCKER is Coppola's most overtly autobiographical film, even though it is about someone else's life. Coppola's treatment of the material is remarkably upbeat and joyous. Even when things get extremely dark for our hero, the film's style remains peversely buoyant. Tucker's increasingly frenzied upbeat renditions of "Hold That Tiger" begin to take on the quality of madness. As with Frank Capra heroes, there is a strong suggestion of dark undercurrents beneath the surface optimism. While a darker film would have been more honest, TUCKER: THE MAN AND HIS DREAM is a gorgeous, fluid, wonderfully exhilarating movie. Continuing and expanding upon the visual experiments he began in the notorious commercial flop ONE FROM THE HEART, Coppola fills TUCKER with some flawlessly executed scene transitions that will startle even the most jaded audience.

TUNE IN TOMORROW

1990 108m c Comedy/Romance   ★★★
Polar (U.S.)   PG-13/12

Barbara Hershey (Aunt Julia), Keanu Reeves (Martin Loader), Peter Falk (Pedro Carmichael), Bill McCutcheon (Puddler), Patricia Clarkson (Aunt Olga), Jerome Dempsey (Sam/Sid), Peter Gallagher (Richard Quince), Dan Hedaya (Robert Quince), Buck Henry (Fr. Serafim), Hope Lange (Margaret Quince)

p, John Fiedler, Mark Tarlov; d, Jon Amiel; w, William Boyd (based on the novel Aunt Julia and the Scriptwriter by Mario Vargas Llosa); ph, Robert Stevens; ed, Peter Boyle; m, Wynton Marsalis; prod d, Jim Clay; chor, Quinny Sacks; cos, Betsy Heiman

TUNE IN TOMORROW, the screen adaptation of Mario Vargas Llosa's acclaimed novel Aunt Julia and the Scriptwriter, is an amiable comedy that overcomes its faults with the sheer charm of its performers and the talent of its director, Jon Amiel.

The film, which takes place in 1951, stars Barbara Hershey as Aunt Julia, a 36-year-old divorcee who comes to New Orleans in search of a new husband but instead begins a secret romance with her 21-year-old nephew—by marriage—Martin (Keanu Reeves), who is a newswriter at a local radio station. Another new arrival to town is eccentric scriptwriter Pedro Carmichael (Peter Falk), who is hired by Martin's bosses at WXBU to raise their sagging ratings. Dedicated to turning Martin into a "true artist," Pedro begins manipulating Aunt Julia and Martin's relationship, as well as using their actual exchanges as dialogue for his radio show.

Amiel would seem to be the perfect choice to direct TUNE IN TOMORROW. The story-within-the-story construction of the film echoes the style of "The Singing Detective," the brilliant mini-series that Amiel directed for British television, and the overall sentimental tone of the script matches the feel of Amiel's 1989 release QUEEN OF HEARTS. But these two styles fail to mesh. Although extremely funny, the outrageous melodrama of the soap opera feels like an intrusion on the relationships of the real characters. The drama that unfolds between Reeves and Hershey (which remains the most interesting thing in the film) always seems to get shortchanged in favor of a cheap laugh or kooky sight-gag. The film does work, despite the wildly uneven screenplay, mainly due to the performances. Falk is hilarious (especially funny is the inspiring speech he gives his radio actors before they go on the air), Hershey, as usual, is wonderful; only Reeves seems to be struggling, and his forced southern accent is a bit distracting. Robert Stevens's photography is terrific, Jim Clay's production design is strikingly authentic, and Wynton Marsalis's score is a standout.

TUNES OF GLORY

1960 106m c Drama/War   ★★★½
Hi Mark (U.K.)   /PG

Alec Guinness (Lt. Col. Jock Sinclair), John Mills (Lt. Col. Basil Barrow), Dennis Price (Maj. Charlie Scott), Susannah York (Morag Sinclair), John Fraser (Cpl. Piper Fraser), Allan Cuthbertson (Capt. Eric Simpson), Kay Walsh (Mary), John MacKenzie (Pony Major), Gordon Jackson (Capt. Jimmy Cairns), Duncan Macrae (Pipe Maj. MacLean)

p, Colin Lesslie; d, Ronald Neame; w, James Kennaway (based on his novel); ph, Arthur Ibbetson; ed, Anne V. Coates; m, Malcolm Arnold

AAN Best Adapted Screenplay: James Kennaway

A powerful and highly effective tale of military life during peacetime, TUNES OF GLORY follows two very different officers in a Scottish Highland regiment. Director Ronald Neame and the producers cast against type in giving the suave Alec Guinness the role of crude, up-from-the-ranks Lt. Col. Jock Sinclair, who had bravely led his troops to victory at El Alamein, while John Mills must convince the audience that he is Lt. Col. Basil Barrow, an Oxbridge type who is all spit, polish, and protocol. Sinclair is the interim commander of the 200-year-old unit, a man of war with little interest in commanding a peacetime unit, which suffers from a lack of discipline in the ranks. Rules are easily bent; dress rehearsals are not taken seriously. Enter military man Barrow, sent to replace Sinclair. Devoted to restoring the faded glory of the regiment, he demands respect from everyone and ruffles many feathers. However, some who served under Sinclair, appreciating his personal bravery and abilities but hating his boorish ways, flock to Barrow in the hope that he will bring back their former days of glory.

Mills and Guinness are the center of the movie and it's a tossup as to which is better, though Mills won the Best Actor Award at the 1960 Venice Film Festival. The film is all acting and character, nicely accented by the Scottish bagpipe music of Malcolm Arnold.

TURNING POINT, THE

1977 119m c Dance   ★★★
Hera (U.S.)   PG

Anne Bancroft *(Emma Jacklin)*, Shirley MacLaine *(Deedee Rodgers)*, Mikhail Baryshnikov *(Kopeikine)*, Leslie Browne *(Emilia Rodgers)*, Tom Skerritt *(Wayne Rodgers)*, Martha Scott *(Adelaide)*, Antoinette Sibley *(Sevilla)*, Alexandra Danilova *(Dahkarova)*, Starr Danias *(Carolyn)*, Marshall Thompson *(Carter)*

p, Herbert Ross, Arthur Laurents; d, Herbert Ross; w, Arthur Laurents; ph, Robert Surtees; ed, William Reynolds; prod d, Albert Brenner; chor, John Cranko, Alvin Ailey, Marius Petipa, George Balanchine, Dennis Nahat, Alexander Minz, Jean Coralli, Jules Perrot, Harald Lander, Kenneth MacMillan, Frederick Ashton, Michel Fokine, Lev Ivanov; cos, Albert Wolsky

AAN Best Picture; AAN Best Actress: Anne Bancroft; *AAN Best Actress:* Shirley MacLaine; *AAN Best Supporting Actor:* Mikhail Baryshnikov; *AAN Best Supporting Actress:* Leslie Browne; *AAN Best Director:* Herbert Ross; *AAN Best Original Screenplay:* Arthur Laurents; *AAN Best Cinematography:* Robert Surtees; *AAN Best Editing:* William Reynolds; *AAN Best Art Direction:* Albert Brenner, Marvin March; *AAN Best Sound:* Theodore Soderberg, Paul Wells, Douglas O. Williams, Jerry Jost

Only the second ballet-based picture (the first was THE RED SHOES) to ever make a dent with popular audiences, THE TURNING POINT is a well-made soap opera with a story that right out of a 1930s backstage musical.

The American Ballet Theatre is touring the US and makes a stop in Oklahoma City. The company's star is Bancroft, painfully thin, dedicated to dance, and having very little life away from her work. Living in DC is her former associate, MacLaine, who opted for love and marriage 20 years before when they were rivals for the prima ballerina role in the company. MacLaine is married to Skerritt; they have three children and a successful ballet school. MacLaine goes to the performance and is bothered by her choice in life. Had she stayed with the ABT and continued, would that prima ballerina on the stage be her and not Bancroft? MacLaine introduces 19-year-old daughter Browne to Bancroft, who recognizes herself and MacLaine in the ambitious girl. Bancroft arranges an audition for Browne, and she is accepted. As the new season approaches, Browne bids farewell to her parents and goes to New York to prepare for her work in the ABT. Bancroft has been a star for many years, and the time has come for her to hang up her tutu. The leading roles are being given to younger ballerinas, and Bancroft realizes that the moment is near when she will begin to teach more than dance. This is depressing for Bancroft, and she wonders if MacLaine didn't make the right decision by marrying Skerritt way back then. Browne is comfortably ensconced in New York by now and has been joined by MacLaine, apparently as a chaperone. But the truth is that MacLaine wants to see if she did right by leaving the ballet. Browne is the lever between the women as they both coach her in various regimens while keeping an eye on each other.

THE TURNING POINT features a few laughs, lots of maudlin moments, superior dancing from a host of real ballerinas, and an occasionally perceptive script. Executive producer Nora Kaye (wife of the director) is herself a former famed ballerina, and producer-director Ross is a one-time choreographer. Ross does his best to convince us that Bancroft can dance, but his fiddling with fast cuts and closeups won't fool anyone who knows anything about ballet.

TURTLE DIARY

1985 97m c Comedy/Drama   ★★★½
United British Artists Britannic (U.K.)   PG

Glenda Jackson *(Neaera Duncan)*, Ben Kingsley *(William Snow)*, Richard Johnson *(Mr. Johnson)*, Michael Gambon *(George Fairbairn)*, Rosemary Leach *(Mrs. Inchcliff)*, Eleanor Bron *(Miss Neap)*, Harriet Walter *(Harriet)*, Jeroen Krabbe *(Sandor)*, Nigel Hawthorne *(Publisher)*, Michael Aldridge *(Mr. Meager)*

p, Richard Johnson; d, John Irvin; w, Harold Pinter (based on the novel by Russell Hoban); ph, Peter Hannan; ed, Peter Tanner; m, Geoffrey Burgon; prod d, Leo Austin; art d, Diane Danklefsen, Judith Lang; cos, Elizabeth Waller

An intelligent, witty, offbeat, and somewhat eccentric comedy based on the novel by Russell Hoban. Neaera Duncan (Glenda Jackson) is a writer-artist who specializes in children's books. But she has come to a creative crossroads and is wondering if she has what it takes to go on. Shy Neaera lives comfortably by herself in a roomy London flat, and her only pal in the building is her enigmatic next-door neighbor Johnson (Richard Johnson). William Snow (Ben Kingsley) is a clerk in a bookshop who lives in a teeming boardinghouse populated by odd characters. William isn't happy at the job or at the rooming house, but he is doing his best to cope. Neaera and William come together at the local aquarium where both are fond of the huge turtles that swim endlessly from one end of the tank to the other. And both speculate about what would happen if these giant turtles were released into the sea. A simple tale well told. No murders, no rapes, no teenage dancing, no hardware—just good talk and lovely characters. This is a totally engaging movie, even if you don't care a whit about turtles.

12 ANGRY MEN

1957 95m bw Drama   ★★★★
Orion/Nova (U.S.)   /U

Henry Fonda *(Juror No. 8)*, Lee J. Cobb *(Juror No. 3)*, Ed Begley *(Juror No. 10)*, E.G. Marshall *(Juror No. 4)*, Jack Warden *(Juror No. 7)*, Martin Balsam *(Juror No. 1)*, John Fiedler *(Juror No. 2)*, Jack Klugman *(Juror No. 5)*, Edward Binns *(Juror No. 6)*, Joseph Sweeney *(Juror No. 9)*

p, Henry Fonda, Reginald Rose; d, Sidney Lumet; w, Reginald Rose (based on his television play); ph, Boris Kaufman; ed, Carl Lerner; m, Kenyon Hopkins; art d, Robert Markell

AAN Best Picture; AAN Best Director: Sidney Lumet; *AAN Best Adapted Screenplay:* Reginald Rose

Lumet's debut, Rose's adaptation of his television play: verbose, stage-bound, predictable and acted to within an inch of its life. This classic courtroom drama begins in the final hours of a trial for murder in a hot, muggy New York City courtroom. The tired trial judge gives 12 weary jurors their instructions, exhorting them to adhere to the basic rule that weights the scales of justice: the defendant must be seen to be innocent unless proven guilty beyond a reasonable doubt. The jurors shuffle slowly to their chamber and consider the case of a teenage Puerto Rican boy accused of knifing his father to death. Expecting a rapid verdict in what appears a conclusive case, the jury foreman invites an immediate vote. When the ballots are tallied, 11 prove to be for conviction. Fonda is the lone holdout. They deliberate, and the character of each emerges.

Though the film now appears anachronistic, MEN was a landmark film in its day, one which brought a new style to cinema. The teleplay-turned-movie made use of a single static set—an actual New York City jury room—and had a total of 365 separate takes, nearly all of them from different angles. The result was cinema heresy that *worked*. Director Lumet, making his film debut (though he was accomplished in stage and television productions), was teaching lessons to the old-timers. With cameraman Kaufman (the brother of famed Soviet director Dziga Vertov), Lumet carefully plotted and sketched every visual nuance. As had been his habit with theatrical productions, he also rehearsed his cast for a full two weeks before the actual 20-day shoot. The resulting real-time drama made film history.

This was Fonda's one experience as a movie producer. He had admired the television play authored by co-producer Rose and had attempted to get Hollywood's established studios interested in it, with little success. Released as a conventional booking in large theaters, the film failed to make a profit, and Fonda never received his deferred salary. Despite his financial loss, Fonda remembered it fondly as one of his three best efforts (along with THE GRAPES OF WRATH and THE OX-BOW INCIDENT). Fonda is fine in the picture, and the others in the cast (whom he hand-picked) were the leading stage and TV actors of Gotham, whose wonderful work was rewarded in many cases by eventual cinematic stardom. The film is an unsettling one in many ways, as much an indictment as an affirmation of America's jury system. One wonders what might have happened had Fonda's voice-of-reason character not been present. The technique of the film has been repeated since, but this is the one that set the precedent.

TWELVE CHAIRS, THE

1970   94m   c   Comedy   ★★★½
Crossbow/UMC   (U.S.)   GP/U

Ron Moody (*Ippolit Vorobyaninov*), Frank Langella (*Ostap Bender*), Dom DeLuise (*Father Fyodor*), Mel Brooks (*Tikon*), Bridget Brice (*Young Woman*), Robert Bernal (*Curator*), David Lander (*Engineer Bruns*), Andreas Voutsinas (*Nikolai Sestrin*), Vlada Petric (*Sevitsky*), Diana Coupland (*Mme. Bruns*)

p, Michael Hertzberg; d, Mel Brooks; w, Mel Brooks (based on a novel by Ilya Arnoldovich Ilf, Yevgeniy Petrov, translated by Elizabeth Hill, Doris Mudie as *Diamonds to Sit On*); ph, Djordje Nikolic; ed, Alan Heim; m, John Morris; art d, Mile Nokolic; cos, Ruth Myers

One of Mel Brooks's best films, THE TWELVE CHAIRS was made before he discovered that nothing succeeds like excess. Based on a Russian novel from the 1920s that was translated into English by Doris Mudie and Elizabeth Hill and retitled *Diamonds to Sit On*, this fast-paced period piece is well-made, funny, and a pleasure to watch from start to finish. Shot on location in Yugoslavia, it begins as Moody, a onetime nobleman's son now reduced to working as a clerk for the government, is told by his dying mother that the family fortune was hidden in one of a set of a dozen chairs 10 years previously. In an attempt to claim the money, Moody returns to the family's former home and makes the mistake of telling his story to Langella, a beggar with big ideas. Now that Langella knows the secret, he is cut in as a partner when he promises to help Moody. DeLuise, a Russian Orthodox priest who heard the old woman's final confession, is now also searching for the jewels. DeLuise visits the Department of Housing, where Langella masquerades as a clerk, sending the priest on a wild goose chase to Siberia to see Lander, who supposedly has the chairs. Meanwhile, Moody and Langella find a few of the chairs reposited in a museum. They wait until the museum closes, then rip up the chairs but find nothing for their efforts. Learning that some of the remaining chairs are being used as props by a small theatrical company, Langella and Moody insinuate themselves into the acting company, slash the chairs, and are again stymied when they find zilch. As the search continues, they discover that a Russian circus performer is using one of the chairs in a highwire act. The two destroy that chair, too, but again they come up with nothing. Eleven chairs have been found and there is but one left. In a railway employees' clubroom, Moody and Langella learn that the final chair was already dismantled by the workers and that the jewels were used to provide all of the accouterments and chess games for the retired workers. The search has ended sadly, and Langella is preparing to part company with Moody, but he changes his mind when Moody goes into his "epilepsy" act and several people stop on the street to toss him some money. It becomes clear that Langella and Moody will continue their relationship as long as Moody can quiver and Langella can shout at the passers-by and gather the loose coins they toss.

Brooks plays a small role as the onetime valet of Moody's father who is now acting as the janitor in the family's old house. He does a drunk routine that is a marvel of timing and understatement (which is rare for Brooks). Unfortunately, DeLuise is out of his class opposite Moody and Langella. Moody's work proves that his brilliance in OLIVER was anything but a fluke. Langella plays it straight, which is perfect in the script by Brooks. All in all, THE TWELVE CHAIRS is a charming movie about larceny in Communist Russia, with a few moments of questionable taste that make it less than apporopriate for the kids.

TWELVE MONKEYS

1995   130m   c   Science Fiction/Fantasy/Drama   ★★★½
Atlas Entertainment/BBC/Polygram/Classico   R/15
/Shochiku/Telemunchen/UGC/Universal
(U.S./U .K./Germany/Japan/France)

Bruce Willis (*James Cole*), Madeleine Stowe (*Kathryn Railly*), Brad Pitt (*Jeffrey Goines*), Christopher Plummer (*Dr. Goines*), Jon Seda (*Jose*), David Morse (*Dr. Peters*), Frank Gorshin (*Dr. Fletcher*), Irma St. Paule (*Poet*), Joey Perillo (*Detective Franki*), Harry O'Toole (*Louie/Raspy Voice*)

p, Charles Roven; d, Terry Gilliam; w, David Peoples, Janet Peoples (inspired by the film LA JETTE written by Chris Marker); ph, Roger Pratt; ed, Mick Audsley; m, Paul Buckmaster; prod d, Jeffrey Beecroft; art d, William Ladd Skinner; fx, Anthony Simonaitis, Vincent Montefusco, Kent Houston, Susi Roper, Peerless Camera Co.; cos, Julie Weiss

AAN Best Supporting Actor: Brad Pitt; *AAN Best Costume Design:* Julie Weiss

A glorious dystopian downer, ready-made for years of fan-boy dissection. For once, the packagers didn't outsmart themselves: a creative match made in movie heaven—director Terry Gilliam (BRAZIL) plus screenwriter David Peoples (BLADE RUNNER)—yielded an instant cult classic that's everything you wanted it to be.

Perhaps more important, TWELVE MONKEYS is none of the things you hoped it *wouldn't* be: it's a time-travel movie that doesn't get bogged down in time-travel technicalities, a killer-virus movie without Dustin Hoffman or that adorable monkey (title notwithstanding, there are no monkeys at all), a Brad Pitt movie in which Hollywood's leading pretty boy looks even worse than he did in SEVEN, a Bruce Willis movie without a single smart-ass one-liner. It's BRAZIL crossed with THE TERMINATOR, and just when you think the production design is in danger of overwhelming the story, Gilliam goes for a note of pure, inevitable tragedy and hits it solidly.

In the near future, the planet's surface has been devastated by a deadly virus; the few human survivors have fled underground. James Cole (Willis), a prisoner, is ordered to participate in a bizarre experiment: he's to travel back in time and gather information about the fatal outbreak before it occurs. But nothing works out quite the way it's supposed to, and what Cole finds in the past is his own inexorable fate. It may not mean anything to anyone except die-hard movie buffs, but we're compelled to mention that the screenplay is loosely based on Chris Marker's 1962 experimental classic, LA JETEE. It was an act of sheer hubris to remake Marker's futuristic meditation on *temps perdu*—told almost entirely in still images—as a big-budget, mainstream picture starring Bruce Willis. That Terry Gilliam managed to make TWELVE MONKEYS into a clever, complex, and poignant success is as astonishing as it is satisfying.

TWELVE O'CLOCK HIGH

1949   132m   bw   War   ★★★★½
Fox   (U.S.)   /U

Gregory Peck (*Gen. Frank Savage*), Hugh Marlowe (*Lt. Col. Ben Gately*), Gary Merrill (*Col. Keith Davenport*), Dean Jagger (*Maj. Harvey Stovall*), Millard Mitchell (*Gen. Pritchard*), Robert Arthur (*Sgt. McIllhenny*), Paul Stewart (*Capt. "Doc" Kaiser*), John Kellogg (*Maj. Cobb*), Robert Patten (*Lt. Bishop*), Lee MacGregor (*Lt. Zimmerman*)

p, Darryl F. Zanuck; d, Henry King; w, Sy Bartlett, Beirne Lay Jr. (based on their novel); ph, Leon Shamroy; ed, Barbara McLean; m, Alfred Newman; art d, Lyle Wheeler, Maurice Ransford

AAN Best Picture; AAN Best Actor: Gregory Peck; *AA Best Supporting Actor:* Dean Jagger; *AA Best Sound:* 20th Century-Fox Sound Department

Firm film, peak Peck in this Henry King-directed drama about the physical and emotional stress that results from giving the "maximum effort" day after day. The film opens obscurely and hauntingly as a bald, bespectacled man, Harvey Stovall (Dean Jagger), wanders through postwar England, arriving at the edge of a former American air base, now overgrown with weeds. As the onetime major looks into the sky, his memory takes over: bomber squadrons return from the daylight missions in Germany. The 918th Bomber Group is under the command of Col. Keith Davenport (Gary Merrill), a likable leader who operates as a friend to his men. However, it is Col. Davenport's identification with his men—boys really—that leads to his downfall. Overly concerned with their health and well-being (after a seemingly endless succession of dangerous bombing missions, the squadron is a jumble of wounds and jangled nerves), the colonel is unable to meet the demands of his superiors, Gen. Pritchard (Millard Mitchell) and Gen. Frank Savage (Peck). Davenport is relieved of his duties and replaced by Gen. Savage, a callous martinet who tries to whip the men back into shape, immediately cutting back on three-day passes, closing the local bar, demanding that he be saluted and that everyone be properly uniformed. Most of the pilots put in for a transfer; however, one confused but heroic young pilot, Lt. Bishop (Bob Patten), rallies them. Moved by his men's show of unity, Savage becomes increasingly friendly, identifying with them even more than his predecessors had.

One of the first films to take a complex look at WWII heroism, TWELVE O'CLOCK HIGH is not afraid to show its fighting men as vulnerable. Four years after the war's end, audiences no longer needed the blatant propaganda that filled wartime screens. Instead, Savage's character (based on the real life and nervous breakdown of Air Corps Maj. Gen. Frank A. Armstrong) is entirely human—a man with real emotions, fears, and inadequacies. Peck gives a flawless portrayal of Gen. Savage, but the film's pivotal performance is Jagger's Maj. Stovall. Stovall is an introspective, older military man; friend and assistant to both Davenport and Savage, he has lived through one world war and now holds together the frayed ends of the 918th Bomber Group. In addition to the fine acting, TWELVE O'CLOCK HIGH features some gorgeous camerawork by Leon Shamroy and one of the most horrifying aerial attack sequences ever put on film. Judging from this picture alone, the subsequent devaluation of King's work is a gross injustice.

TWENTIETH CENTURY

1934   91m   bw   Comedy   ★★★½
Columbia   (U.S.)   /A

John Barrymore *(Oscar Jaffe)*, Carole Lombard *(Mildred Plotka/Lily Garland)*, Roscoe Karns *(Owen O'Malley)*, Walter Connolly *(Oliver Webb)*, Ralph Forbes *(George Smith)*, Dale Fuller *(Sadie)*, Etienne Girardot *(Matthew J. Clark)*, Herman Bing, Lee Kohlmar *(Bearded Men)*, James Burtis *(Train Conductor)*

p, Howard Hawks; d, Howard Hawks; w, Charles MacArthur, Ben Hecht (based on their play, adapted from the play "Napoleon on Broadway" by Charles Bruce Milholland); ph, Joseph August; ed, Gene Havlick

Though the film has a large cast, TWENTIETH CENTURY remains essentially a one-man show for John Barrymore, who plays one of the most preposterous and memorable characters to spring from the minds of Ben Hecht and Charles MacArthur. Directed with breakneck pace by Howard Hawks (as in his later Hecht-MacArthur adaptation, HIS GIRL FRIDAY [1940]), it's the story of a maniacal Broadway director (Barrymore) who transforms shopgirl Carole Lombard from a talented amateur to a smashing Great White Way success adored by public and press. For three years, Barrymore has been both Lombard's lover and her Svengali, shepherding her career, controlling her behavior, and directing her plays. They battle regularly, but make up passionately. Now a huge star of the New York stage, Lombard yearns for some peace and respite from the manic Barrymore. One final disagreement does the trick, and Lombard heads for the palm trees of Hollywood and a screen career. Barrymore's fortunes subsequently plummet, causing creditors to dog his heels in Chicago. To escape, he boards the Twentieth Century Limited train in the Windy City, accompanied by his manager, Walter Connolly, and press representative Roscoe Karns, heading for what they hope will be newfound success in New York. As luck would have it, Lombard and her new fiance, football player Ralph Forbes, are also on the train. Barrymore despises the ruggedly handsome Forbes and doesn't bother to hide his disdain as he moves in on Lombard (who has become as big a star on the screen as she was on the stage), trying to convince her to appear in his latest production. The remainder of the picture is a farcical series of biting verbal exchanges, opening and closing doors, hurled insults, thrown kisses, a madcap procession of

several weird characters on board the train, and some of the biggest laughs Barrymore ever received. In the end, as expected, Barrymore has convinced Lombard that Broadway is the place for her, and by the time the Twentieth Century pulls into Grand Central Station, she is safely under his influence once more. Barrymore is a wonder as he does imitations of camels, tramples over his fellow actors' lines, sprinkles his dialog with foreign phrases, and generally leaves the rest of the cast looking like his stooges. The picture was not a hit when it first came out, perhaps because its satire of flamboyant theater people failed to capture the imagination of moviegoing audiences; later it became the basis for the Broadway musical "On the Twentieth Century."

20,000 LEAGUES UNDER THE SEA

1954   120m   c   Science Fiction   ★★★★
Walt Disney Productions   (U.S.)   /U

Kirk Douglas *(Ned Land)*, James Mason *(Capt. Nemo)*, Paul Lukas *(Prof. Pierre Aronnax)*, Peter Lorre *(Conseil, His Assistant)*, Bob Wilke *(1st Mate of "Nautilus")*, Carleton Young *(John Howard)*, Ted de Corsia *(Capt. Farragut)*, Percy Helton *(Diver)*, Ted Cooper *(Mate of "Abraham Lincoln")*, Eddie Marr *(Shipping Agent)*

p, Walt Disney; d, Richard Fleischer; w, Earl Felton (based on the novel *Twenty Thousand Leagues under the Sea* by Jules Verne); ph, Franz Planer, Ralph Hammeras, Till Gabbani; ed, Elmo Williams; m, Paul J. Smith, Johann Sebastian Bach; art d, John Meehan; fx, John Hench, Joshua Meador; cos, Norman Martien

AAN Best Editing: Elmo Williams; *AA Best Art Direction:* John Meehan, Emile Kuri; *AA Best Visual Effects:*

One of the best Disney live action films and a classic fantasy-adventure, 20,000 LEAGUES UNDER THE SEA is a fairly respectful adaptation of Jules Verne's prophetic tale (published in 1870) of submarines and atomic power. It's 1868 and San Francisco is agog over reports of a sea-roving "monster" that devours any ship that ventures near it. Many voyages are canceled and the government is forced to send a warship to investigate and clear the sea lanes. That ship is sunk by the heinous "creature" and only three people survive the ordeal: a professional harpoonist (Kirk Douglas), a professor from the Nautical Museum in Paris (Paul Lukas), and his aide (Peter Lorre). They are plucked from the sea by the dreaded "monster" which is actually the *Nautilus*, a fabulous submarine. The sub is commanded by Capt. Nemo (James Mason), scientist, inventor, crazed visionary, and radical peace activist. He's taken to sinking ships in a well-meaning effort to end warfare at sea. In an awesome adventure brimming over with fantastic elements, one sequence rises above the fray to become indelible: the fight with the giant squid. The marvelous sets—with their quaint blend of Victorian and futuristic elements—are worth the price of admission alone. The direction is sharp as are the special effects. All the major performances are fun but James Mason is a standout. Dare we say it? It's fun for the entire family!

20,000 YEARS IN SING SING

1933   81m   bw   Prison   ★★★★
Warner Bros./First National   (U.S.)

Spencer Tracy *(Tom Connors)*, Bette Davis *(Fay)*, Lyle Talbot *(Bud)*, A.S. Byron *(Warden Long)*, Grant Mitchell *(Dr. Ames)*, Warren Hymer *(Hype)*, Louis Calhern *(Joe Finn)*, Sheila Terry *(Billie)*, Edward McNamara *(Chief of Guards)*, Spencer Charters *(Daniels)*

p, Robert Lord; d, Michael Curtiz; w, Courtney Terrett, Robert Lord, Wilson Mizner, Brown Holmes (based on the book by Lewis E. Lawes); ph, Barney McGill; ed, George Amy; m, Bernhard Kaun; art d, Anton Grot; cos, Orry-Kelly

The praises of a prison, the famous Sing Sing, are sung in this picture authored by Sing Sing's long-term reform warden, Lewis E. Lawes. Cocksure criminal Spencer Tracy is sent to the slammer on a felony rap. There he is greeted by the kindly warden, A.S. Byron, who explains that good behavior brings certain privileges. Tough-guy Tracy starts a near-riot and gets 90 days in solitary, where he resolves to escape. He joins some prisoners who are planning an escape attempt until he discovers that their plan is set for Tuesday (he has an odd superstition relating to the days of the week). Beaten at last, he determines to win parole through good behavior. Meanwhile, Tracy's girlfriend

Davis—attempting to win his parole by other means—seeks the assistance of powerful mob chief Harold Huber. In return for his help, Huber wants Davis's favors. While speeding down a street in a car, Davis repels the gangster's groping and is seriously injured in the resulting automobile crash. When warden Byron hears of her condition, he offers Tracy—now a trusty—compassionate leave to visit Davis. On the outside, however, Tracy runs into some detectives who mistake him for an escapee. A disastrous shootout follows.

Tracy's role in the film seems tailored more to James Cagney's cinematic persona than to his own—indeed, Cagney, who made the mold in a number of gangster films, was Jack Warner's first choice for the part. But Tracy handled the characterization beautifully. Davis' performance is excessively histrionic; not even domineering director Michael Curtiz could hold the actress back. This was to be the only time that two-time Oscar winners Davis and Tracy worked together. At the time the picture was made, author Lawes was the warden of Sing Sing and cooperated in every possible way for the production, allowing the film crew to enter the prison to shoot and permitting real prisoners to play in the mob scenes. The film was the first of many to be based on Lawes's accounts of prison life; others include OVER THE WALL, YOU CAN'T GET AWAY WITH MURDER, INVISIBLE STRIPES, and CASTLE ON THE HUDSON, the latter a remake of 20,000 YEARS IN SING SING, starring John Garfield, Ann Sheridan, and Pat O'Brien. Despite the grimness of its subject matter, 20,000 YEARS IN SING SING is laced with humor.

TWENTY-FOUR EYES
(NIJUSHI NO HITOMI)
1954   158m   c   Drama   ★★★★
Shochiku   (Japan)

Hideko Takamine *(Miss Oishi)*, Chishu Ryu, Toshiko Kobayashi, Shizue Natsukawa, Nijiko Kiyokawa, Yumeji Tsukioka, Ushio Akashi, Chieko Naniwa

p, Ryotaro Kuwata; d, Keisuke Kinoshita; w, Keisuke Kinoshita (based on the novel by Sakae Tsuboi); ph, Hiroshi Kusuda; ed, Yoshi Sugiwara; m, Chuji Kinoshita

The only film available on videotape from the masterful Keisuke Kinoshita, whose brilliance is practically unknown in the US, TWENTY-FOUR EYES chronicles 20 years in the lives of a loving teacher (Hideo Takemine, the star of 11 Kinoshita films) and 12 of her pupils in a small Inland Sea village. Concerned in many of his films with youth, purity, and innocence, the prolific Kinoshita directed some of the most visually inventive and audacious movies to come out of Japan—from his early WOMAN (a 1948 romantic thriller that has the urgency of a Hollywood B-movie) to CARMEN COMES HOME (a wild 1951 musical satire about a bubbly stripper) to THE BALLAD OF NARAYAMA (his 1958 adaptation of the popular ballad about old age that contains some of the most remarkable lighting schemes and set designs ever put on film). Yet this is his most popular film. It centers on the teacher as she watches helplessly as her pupils are called to join the war effort, leading to much sorrow and the inevitable loss of innocence. An interesting complement to this film is Masahiro Shinoda's 1985 film MACARTHUR'S CHILDREN, a less impressive effort about the effect of the American presence on a group of schoolchildren at the close of WWII. The videocassette is in Japanese with English subtitles.

TWILIGHT'S LAST GLEAMING
1977   146m   c   Historical/Thriller/War   ★★★½
Geria/Lorimar/Bavaria   (U.S./West Germany)   R/AA

Burt Lancaster *(Lawrence Dell)*, Richard Widmark *(Martin MacKenzie)*, Charles Durning *(President Stevens)*, Melvyn Douglas *(Zachariah Guthrie)*, Paul Winfield *(Willis Powell)*, Burt Young *(Augie Garvas)*, Joseph Cotten *(Arthur Renfrew)*, Roscoe Lee Browne *(James Forrest)*, Gerald S. O'Loughlin *(Brig. Gen. Michael O'Rourke)*, Richard Jaeckel *(Capt. Stanford Towne)*

p, Merv Adelson; d, Robert Aldrich; w, Ronald M. Cohen, Edward Huebsch (based on the novel *Viper Three* by Walter Wager); ph, Robert B. Hauser; ed, Michael Luciano, Maury Weintrobe; m, Jerry Goldsmith; prod d, Rolf Zehetbauer; art d, Werner Achmann; fx, Henry Millar, Willy Neuner; cos, Tom Dawson

A flawed but nonetheless highly exciting political thriller, TWILIGHT'S LAST GLEAMING has some deeply disturbing things to say about the powers that be in America. The action begins in 1981 (the near future for this 1977 release) and centers on former US Air Force general Lawrence Dell (Burt Lancaster), a Vietnam veteran who served five years as a POW. Upon his return, Dell became a vocal advocate of disclosing the truth behind US involvement in Southeast Asia in the hope that a post-Watergate America would forgive its government and have renewed faith in its leaders. Because of his radical stance, however, Dell is eventually sent to prison on trumped-up manslaughter charges. Still determined, he recruits three inmates (Paul Winfield, Burt Young, and William Smith) to help him escape and take over a nearby SAC base that he helped design. Once in control of the base, Dell demands that the president (Charles Durning) reveal the truth about the Vietnam War to the American people by reading National Security Council document 9759 on national television. If these demands are not met, Dell promises to send the nine Titan missiles to their targets in the Soviet Union. TWILIGHT'S LAST GLEAMING is a stunning indictment of the arrogance of America's decision makers and the lengths to which they will go to maintain "business as usual." At the same time it also dramatizes the danger of our unthinking faith in technology. Tellingly, it comes as a deep shock to the military that their usually reliable machines and detailed procedures seem to have gone haywire on the day of the siege, leaving them powerless to stop Dell. Though a bit slow at the outset and suffering from some occasional lapses of logic, Robert Aldrich's film—shot in Germany with no cooperation from the US military—is a fascinating, tension-filled effort. Lancaster contributes a fine performance as the righteous, populist general, and Durning is superb as the president who comes to share Lancaster's high hopes. Further, Aldrich uses some remarkable split-screen techniques that add to the film's tension and speed up the complicated expository passages. Despite some flaws, TWILIGHT'S LAST GLEAMING is a gripping drama that will have you on the edge of your seat until the bitter end.

TWISTER
1996   117m   c   Thriller   ★★★
Amblin Entertainment/Universal/Warner Bros.   (U.S.)   PG-13/

Bill Paxton *(Bill Harding)*, Helen Hunt *(Jo Harding)*, Cary Elwes *(Dr. Jonas Miller)*, Jami Gertz *(Melissa)*, Lois Smith *(Aunt Meg)*, Alan Ruck *(Dusty)*, Philip Seymour Hoffman *(Rabbit)*, Abraham Benrubi *(Bubba)*, Nicholas Sadler *(Kubrick)*, Sean Whalen *(Sanders)*

p, Kathleen Kennedy, Ian Bryce, Michael Crichton; d, Jan De Bont; w, Michael Crichton, Anne-Marie Martin; ph, Jack N. Green; ed, Michael Khan; m, Mark Mancina; prod d, Joseph Nemec III; art d, Dan Olexiewicz; fx, Stefen Fangmeier, John Frazier, Habib Zargarpour, Henry La Bounta, Industrial Light & Magic; cos, Ellen Mirojnick

AAN Best Visual Effects: Stefen Fangmeier, John Frazier, Habib Zargarpour, Henry La Bounta; *AAN Best Sound:* Steve Maslow, Gregg Landaker, Kevin O'Connell, Geoffrey Patterson

A by-the-numbers blockbuster with even less in the way of plot than JURASSIC PARK, TWISTER stormed the US box office in the summer of 1996 and became one of the top 10 all-time grossers within six weeks of its release.

Bill (Bill Paxton) has abandoned the wild life of chasing tornadoes for a sedate berth as a weatherman and imminent marriage to therapist Melissa (Jami Gertz); he just needs wife Jo (Helen Hunt) to sign the divorce papers. Meanwhile, spunky Jo and her group of scrappy, pure-hearted tornado chasers are trying to beat the big, bad corporate-financed tornado chasers—you can tell them by their glossy black vans—to some Very Important Discovery about the structure of killer twisters.

That's about all. But the barebones plotting is beside the point: TWISTER stands or falls on the tornado effects, and they're stupendous, even if the lion's roar incorporated into the sound mix errs a tad on the side of overstatement (the twister is a monster—we get it). Those who recall that Bill Paxton once had an edgy, feral appeal should be forewarned that TWISTER batters him into two-dimensional blandness; anyone fooled by the synopsis into hoping for an entertaining hybrid of disaster movie brouhaha and comedy-of-remarriage high jinks will be sorely disappointed. Extreme-weather buffs, thrill-ride junkies, and anyone else in search of utterly mindless entertainment need look no further.

2 DAYS IN THE VALLEY

1996   105m   c   Crime/Thriller/Comedy   ★★★
Rysher Entertainment/Redemption/MGM   (U.S.)   R/18

Danny Aiello (Dosmo Pizzo), James Spader (Lee Woods), Greg Cruttwell (Allan Hopper), Jeff Daniels (Alvin Strayer), Teri Hatcher (Becky Foxx), Charlize Theron (Helga Svelgen), Glenne Headly (Susan Parish), Peter Horton (Roy Foxx), Marsha Mason (Audrey Hopper), Paul Mazursky (Teddy Peppers)

p, Jeff Wald, Herb Nanas; d, John Herzfeld; w, John Herzfeld; ph, Oliver Wood; ed, Jim Miller, Wayne Wahrman; m, Anthony Marinelli; prod d, Catherine Hardwicke; art d, Kevin Constant; fx, Larry Fioritto; cos, Betsy Heimann

Promoted at the time of its release as a Quentin Tarantino-style thriller, 2 DAYS IN THE VALLEY is actually more reminiscent of the complex, multi-character films of Alan Rudolph.

Has-been hitman Dosmo Pizzo (Danny Aiello) is hired by sociopath Lee Woods (James Spader) to assist in a contract killing, but Dosmo soon discovers he's meant to be the fall guy. After he murders his target and shoots Dosmo, Lee and his sexy partner Helga (Charlize Theron) try to collect their fee from the victim's widow, Becky (Teri Hatcher). The money, however, is locked in a safe back at the crime scene—Becky's house. Meanwhile, saved by his bulletproof vest, Dosmo hides out in the home of art dealer Allan Hopper (Greg Cruttwell), whom Dosmo takes hostage along with Allan's abused assistant, Susan (Glenne Headly), his half-sister, Audrey (Marsha Mason), and Teddy Peppers (Paul Mazursky), a down-and-out director. Lee's attempt to recover his money and Dosmo's thirst for revenge lead the two men back to the scene of the crime for a bloody showdown.

Despite the busy plot, writer-director John Herzfeld is really more interested in characters than story, and 2 DAYS works best as a showcase for its ensemble cast. But while the film's focus may be on sympathetic losers Dosmo and Teddy, Herzfeld's most engaging characters are the unrepentant bad guys. Spader steals the film as an ice-cool killer with a macabre sense of humor; Cruttwell is only slightly less odious here than the monstrous yuppie he played in Mike Leigh's NAKED (1993); and Theron, as Spader's dangerous, spandex-sheathed consort, makes a memorable debut. While this admirably ambitious film may ultimately fail in achieving all it hopes for, it still has enough small virtues to make for entertaining viewing.

TWO ENGLISH GIRLS
(LES DEUX ANGLAISES ET LE CONTINENT)

1971   108m   c   Drama   ★★★½
Carosse/Simar/Cinetel   (France)   R/

Jean-Pierre Leaud (Claude Roc), Kika Markham (Anne Brown), Stacey Tendeter (Muriel Brown), Sylvia Marriott (Mrs. Brown), Marie Mansart (Madame Roc), Philippe Leotard (Diurka), Irene Tunc (Ruta), Mark Peterson (Mr. Flint), David Markham (Palmist), Georges Delerue (Claude's Business Agent)

p, Claude Miler; d, Francois Truffaut; w, Francois Truffaut, Jean Gruault (based on the novel by Henri-Pierre Roche); ph, Nestor Almendros; ed, Yann Dedet; m, Georges Delerue; art d, Michel de Broin; cos, Gitt Magrini

Francois Truffaut's TWO ENGLISH GIRLS is a love story examining the complications of one man's romance with two women, in a reversal of JULES AND JIM (both films are based on novels by Henri-Pierre Roche). Set at the beginning of the 20th century, the film focuses on Claude (Jean-Pierre Leaud), a young art critic and aspiring author who charms his way through life. In Paris he meets Anne (Kika Markham), a liberated young woman who invites him to spend the summer at the seaside cottage she shares with her sister, Muriel (Stacey Tendeter). Though Anne shows some initial interest in Claude, she secretly intends that he fall in love with the puritanical Muriel. Her plot works, but when she herself has a tryst with Claude, the situation becomes increasingly intense. One of Truffaut's darker films, TWO ENGLISH GIRLS is compared much too often to its companion piece, JULES AND JIM.

Both films shine light on the personality of Roche (Truffaut had access to his unpublished diaries), mainly through the characters of Catherine (Jeanne Moreau in JULES AND JIM) and Claude. However, TWO ENGLISH GIRLS is more interestingly viewed as a precursor to Truffaut's later film THE STORY OF ADELE H., with Muriel bearing remarkable similarities to Adele Hugo.

TWO FOR THE ROAD

1967   112m   c   Comedy/Drama   ★★★½
Fox   (U.K.)   /PG

Audrey Hepburn (Joanna Wallace), Albert Finney (Mark Wallace), Eleanor Bron (Cathy Manchester), William Daniels (Howard Manchester), Claude Dauphin (Maurice Dalbret), Nadia Gray (Francoise Dalbret), Georges Descrieres (David), Gabrielle Middleton (Ruth Manchester), Jacqueline Bisset (Jackie), Judy Cornwell (Pat)

p, Stanley Donen; d, Stanley Donen; w, Frederic Raphael; ph, Christopher Challis; ed, Richard Marden, Madeleine Gug; m, Henry Mancini; art d, Willy Holt, Marc Frederix; fx, Gilbert Manzon; cos, Hardy Amies, Ken Scott, Michele Posier, Paco Rabanne, Mary Quant, Foale and Tuffin

AAN Best Original Screenplay: Frederic Raphael

Like a cheap wine, TWO FOR THE ROAD has not stood up well to the passing of time. What seemed so chic in 1967 looks like a soap opera with jumpcuts today. Still, one must measure it by the temper of the times; in 1967, it was on the money. A small cult of aficionados feels that the film remains one of the best of the genre.

Audrey Hepburn and architect Albert Finney are a married couple taking a car trip from England to the French Riviera. They are about to visit the home of Dauphin, the Frenchman who helped the successful Finney get his first break. From the nature of the biting dialogue between the two, it's obvious that this is a marriage in jeopardy. Flash back to a dozen years before when Finney and Hepburn first met. He's a backpacking student looking at European buildings, and she's one of several female music students going to a festival. Finney is attracted to Jacqueline Bisset but winds up with Hepburn as the other women all come down with chicken pox. They travel together to the edge of the sea and decide they are in love and will get married. Flash forward to their next trip on the Continent. They are newlyweds traveling with William Daniels, Eleanor Bron, and their incorrigible daughter, Gabrielle Middleton. This little girl is enough to sour any woman from having a child, but Hepburn manages to overcome her hatred for the little brat. She and Finney make a pact never again to travel with anyone else. On yet another trip along the same road, Hepburn tells Finney that she is pregnant, and they meet Dauphin, who gives Finney his chance to go from minor jobs to major homes in the south of France. The film cuts between past, present, and future, presenting Finney having a one-night stand with Karyn Balm and Hepburn submitting to the amorous advances of Georges Descrieres, a sober intellectual who turns out to be far too dour for Hepburn's lighthearted personality. The two are reunited and realize that, through it all, they love each other and no amount of petty quarreling or even major spats will ever divide them.

Finney's character remains essentially the same throughout, a slightly boorish lout. Hepburn changes visibly from a naive waif to a mature wife and mother to a bored matron. There were some complaints that Hepburn was too old for Finney, but she is actually just about seven years his senior. Her career had been twice the length of Finney's, and people were just used to seeing her more often. The usually fastidious Hepburn was dressed by Mary Quant, Paco Rabanne, Ken Scott, and others, and, wonder of wonders, she even wore blue jeans. Location scenes were done in Paris, Nice, St. Tropez, La Colle sur le Loup, and Beauallon. Good aerial photography by Guy Tabary and an excellent score by Henry Mancini also enhance the film. Although Bron plays an American, she is actually a British actress who scored in HELP, ALFIE, WOMEN IN LOVE, and the Dudley Moore-Peter Cook production, BEDAZZLED, also directed by Stanley Donen. Donen's direction here is a trifle trendy and frantic, with sometimes jarring results.

TWO HUNDRED MOTELS

1971 98m c Musical/Experimental/Fantasy ★★★
UA (U.K.) R/X

The Mothers of Invention *(Themselves)*, Theodore Bikel *(Rance Muhammitz)*, Ringo Starr *(Larry the Dwarf/Frank Zappa)*, Keith Moon *(Hot Nun)*, Jimmy Carl Black *(Lonesome Cowboy Burt)*, Martin Lickert *(Jeff)*, Janet Ferguson, Lucy Offerall *(Groupies)*, Pamela Miller *(Interviewer)*, Don Preston *(Bif Debris)*

p, Jerry Good, Herb Cohen; d, Frank Zappa, Tony Palmer; w, Frank Zappa, Tony Palmer (based on a story by Zappa); ph, Tony Palmer; ed, Richard Harrison, Barry Stephens; m, Frank Zappa; prod d, Calvin Schenkel; art d, Leo Austin; fx, Bert Luxford; chor, Gillian Lynne; cos, Sue Yelland; anim, Mara Kam

Always ahead of his time, avant-garde musician Zappa anticipates the rock video in what can best be described as the visual equivalent to any of his recordings in the late 1960s and early 1970s. TWO HUNDRED MOTELS is a hodgepodge of color and sound linked by ex-Beatle Starr playing Zappa, complete with curly-locked wig and the signature goatee. The film is a marvelous whirl of color and visual effects, with some fine animation and Zappa's delicious wit present throughout the entire production. This was the first color production to be transferred from videotape to film, and the technique works well. The special visual effects available at the time were used to create some amazing surreal images and optical illusions. This is certainly not for everyone, and sometimes the picture causes eyestrain, but, for the adventurous, TWO HUNDRED MOTELS is definitely a film to experience. Zappa codirected with Palmer, taking credit for "characterizations." Palmer was said to have directed the visuals and was also responsible for the shooting script from the "story" and screenplay by Zappa. Watch for Moon, the drummer of The Who, in a cameo as a nun!

TWO-LANE BLACKTOP

1971 102m c Drama ★★★★
Universal (U.S.) R/X

James Taylor *(The Driver)*, Warren Oates *(G.T.O.)*, Laurie Bird *(Girl)*, Dennis Wilson *(The Mechanic)*, David Brake *(Needles Station Attendant)*, Richard Ruth *(Needles Station Mechanic)*, Rudolph Wurlitzer *(Hot Rod Driver)*, Jaclyn Hellman *(Driver's Girl)*, Bill Keller *(Texas Hitchhiker)*, Harry Dean Stanton *(Oklahoma Hitchhiker)*

p, Michael S. Laughlin; d, Monte Hellman; w, Rudy Wurlitzer, Will Corry (based on a story by Corry); ph, Jackson Deerson; ed, Monte Hellman; cos, Richard Bruno

Real-life rock stars Taylor and Wilson (the latter a member of the Beach Boys) are a pair of car freaks driving down the endless roads of the American Southwest in search of a race. They drive an old 1955 Chevy, using race winnings to keep the souped-up auto in shape. The pair have little to say to each other beyond car talk. At a small Arizona diner they meet Bird, who gets in the car with them, no questions asked. After winning another race, Taylor and Bird make love; the next evening it's Wilson's turn with her. Later the three meet up with Oates, an older drifter who travels across the US in his brand new GTO. He challenges them to a cross-country race to Washington, DC, with the winner taking ownership of the loser's car. Along the way the participants' interest in the race begins to wane. Wilson suggests to Bird that they ride off together. Taylor enters a race in Memphis, and Bird, bored with the younger men, heads off to North Carolina with Oates. Later she takes off with a motorcyclist, and Oates continues his aimless driving. Eventually, Wilson and Taylor find another race to run, and the movie ends ominously as they drive away from the camera down a two-lane road and the film burns and melts in the gate, leaving only a bright white light. Certainly not an average car chase movie, TWO-LANE BLACK-TOP is perhaps director Monte Hellman's finest film. Known for his small, brooding existential westerns (THE SHOOTING, RIDE IN THE WHIRLWIND), Hellman once again brings to life characters desperately searching for meaning. Oates, a close personal friend of Hellman's and lead player in nearly all his films, is magnificent in TWO-LANE BLACKTOP, bringing a perfect blend of comedy, mystery, and pathos to his role. It is a powerful and memorable screen appearance that is somewhat weakened by the amateur support from nonactors Taylor, Wilson, and Bird, whose limited abilities required

delicate handling by Hellman. Expectations were high for this somber film, with the studio convinced they had another EASY RIDER on their hands. *Esquire* magazine ran a cover story on the film, reprinted screenwriter Wurlitzer's screenplay in its entirety, and proclaimed it "the movie of the year." The predictions fell far short; the majority of the movie-going public failed to understand the picture and found its portrayal of youthful boredom to be just that: boring. TWO-LANE BLACKTOP is very similar to the work of popular European existential filmmakers, but the fickle American "art house" crowd stayed away in droves, obviously preferring that their serious psychological dramas be imported from abroad.

TWO OF US, THE
(LE VIEIL HOMME ET L'ENFANT)

1967 86m bw Drama/Comedy ★★★★
Valoria/PAC/Renn (France) /U

Michel Simon *("Gramps")*, Alain Cohen *(Claude)*, Luce Fabiole *("Granny")*, Roger Carel *(Victor)*, Paul Preboist *(Maxime)*, Charles Denner *(Claude's Father)*, Zorica Lozic *(Claude's Mother)*, Jacqueline Rouillard *(Teacher)*, Aline Bertrand *(Raymonde)*, Sylvine Delannoy *(Suzanne)*

p, Paul Cadeac; d, Claude Berri; w, Claude Berri, Michel Rivelin, Gerard Brach; ph, Jean Penzer; ed, Sophie Coussein, Denise Charvein; m, Georges Delerue; art d, Georges Levy, Maurice Petri

Life's joys and sorrows are given a fine, sensitive treatment in this autobiographical first feature from Claude Berri, who was one of many Jewish children sent by Parisian parents to live in the French countryside during the Occupation. This film, an honest portrait of one such boy, was considered by Francois Truffaut to be one of the best films ever made about the Occupation. Ten-year-old Claude (Alain Cohen, in a touching, natural performance) is sent to live with the parents of his father's Catholic friends. "Gramps" (Michel Simon), the cranky old man who looks after Claude, takes an immediate liking to the boy and begins teaching him about anti-Semitism, not realizing that his young friend is a Jew. A warm friendship grows between the two, despite their differences in age and religion. Some genuinely comic moments also arise, including Claude's accusation that the old man is a Jew (he cites Gramps's big nose as evidence). Through everything, the two remain the best of friends, bound together by the trials of everyday living, the problems incurred by the war, and the old man's aging dog. Georges Delerue delivers a moving score, and, in his comeback performance, Simon delivers one of the most memorable portrayals of his brilliant career.

TWO OR THREE THINGS I KNOW ABOUT HER
(DEUX OU TROIS CHOSES QUE JE SAIS D'ELLE)

1966 90m c Drama ★★★★★
Anouchka/Argos/Carrosse/Parc (France) /X

Marina Vlady *(Juliette Janson)*, Anny Duperey *(Marianne)*, Roger Montsoret *(Robert Janson)*, Jean Narboni *(Roger)*, Christophe Bourseiller *(Christophe)*, Marie Bourseiller *(Solange)*, Raoul Levy *(The American)*, Joseph Gehrard *(M. Gerard)*, Helena Bielicic *(Girl in Bath)*, Robert Chevassu *(Meter-Reader)*

p, Raoul Levy; d, Jean-Luc Godard; w, Jean-Luc Godard (based on a letter from Catherine Vimenet that appeared in *Le Nouvel Observateur*); ph, Raoul Coutard; ed, Francoise Collin, Chantal Delattre; m, Ludwig van Beethoven; cos, Gitt Marrini

Arguably the greatest film made by arguably the most important world director to emerge since WWII. Not recognized as one of Godard's foremost achievements at the time, TWO OR THREE THINGS now seems the richest of his films, made at the perfect halfway moment between his playful iconoclasm and his later political anger. What little "plot" there is concerns a housewife (Vlady) who works part-time on the sly as a prostitute. What Godard and crew milk from this topic is extraordinary: a sociologically oriented dissection of modern middle-class life as an act of prostitution.

The film's title alone suggests the richness of what unfolds—"her" is at once our heroine Juliette, actress Vlady, Paris, consumerism, politics, structuralism and about a dozen other things. The use of disjunctive editing, saturated color schemes, endless quotation (from

Marx to Wittgenstein) and deadpan performance style make this film deliberately "difficult" to engage. Godard is challenging us, asking us to consider how we watch films and how we live our lives. Unforgettable moments are numerous: the opening introductions of Vlady as Vlady, then Vlady as Juliette; the little boy recounting his dream of Vietnam while his mother lies covered in the red, white and blue of her nightgown and bedding; the babysitter, paid with canned goods, attempting to comfort a squalling child while lovers tryst in adjoining rooms; two naked women wearing airline tote bags on their heads. Perhaps greatest of all is the satiric final shot of a Paris neighborhood constructed from grocery goods, and the amazing close-up wherein a cup of coffee becomes the cosmos. (As we stare in awe, the whispering voice-over of Godard himself considers the philosophical terrain underpinning contemporary French intellectual thought.) Shot at the same time as MADE IN U.S.A. (Godard filmed one in the mornings, the other in the afternoons), TWO OR THREE THINGS I KNOW ABOUT HER is a uniquely rewarding film that requires *many* viewings—a brilliant, powerful and overtly political film that's still relevant today.

TWO RODE TOGETHER

1961   108m   c   Western   ★★½
Columbia   (U.S.)   /PG

James Stewart *(Guthrie McCabe)*, Richard Widmark *(Lt. Jim Gary)*, Shirley Jones *(Marty Purcell)*, Linda Cristal *(Elena de la Madriaga)*, Andy Devine *(Sgt. Darius P. Posey)*, John McIntire *(Maj. Frazer)*, Paul Birch *(Edward Purcell)*, Willis Bouchey *(Mr. Harry J. Wringle)*, Henry Brandon *(Chief Quanah Parker)*, Harry Carey Jr. *(Ortho Clegg)*

p, Stan Shpetner; d, John Ford; w, Frank S. Nugent (based on the novel *Comanche Captives* by Will Cook); ph, Charles Lawton Jr.; ed, Jack Murray; m, George Duning; art d, Robert Peterson; cos, Frank Beetson

John Ford attempts to make an adult western with this film, which seems to fall between the cracks; it's too grown-up for the children's audience and much too simplistic to be deemed a psychological film. There are attempts at comedy that barely induce a smile, and the picture winds up yawnable, one of Ford's very few bores. Gorgeous scenery and a fine acting job by Stewart in an unaccustomed semivillain role don't overcome the lackluster production overseen by TV veteran Shpetner. Stewart, a corrupt sheriff in a small town, spends most of his time seated on the verandah of the saloon run by Annelle Hayes collecting a 10 percent tithe on illicit goings-on in the village. Widmark approaches Stewart for some help. Some years before Comanche Indians kidnapped a group of whites, and Widmark wants to rescue them to bring them back to their anxious families. Stewart reckons he might help but only if Widmark arranges a bounty of $500 to be paid for each hostage recovered. The promise of the fee plus the chance to flee from the matrimonially minded Hayes is enough to get Stewart off his duff and into the plains. They ride into the camp of Indian Brandon and secure the release of David Kent, a white boy who has been raised as an Indian, plus Cristal, a Mexican woman who had been the forced squaw of Indian warrior Woody Strode. Strode is not thrilled that they want to take away his woman and he gets into a battle with Stewart, who kills him. Widmark and Stewart bring the duo of Cristal and Kent back to the Army fort and none of the waiting families recognizes Kent. He is finally claimed by Nolan, a woman who is mentally incompetent. She thinks that the wild youth is her son and wants him. She unties Kent and he promptly kills her. The settlers capture Kent and string him up before Jones, a settler in love with Widmark, can let them know that the boy is her brother. None of the prissy women at the Army fort will have a thing to do with the tainted Cristal since, in their eyes, any woman who has lived with Indians must be a harlot. Cristal is brokenhearted and thinks that the ways of civilization are far too uncivilized. Stewart shrugs and prepares to go back to his old job as sheriff of the small town but learns that he's lost his position to his deputy, who now occupies the same spot on Hayes's verandah. Stewart takes Cristal's hand, understands that they are both outcasts, and rides off with her to find something better over the next hill as the picture goes to black. Filmed in southwest Texas, it more than resembles Ford's THE SEARCHERS in several ways but comes nowhere close to the power of the former. The picture is almost totally devoid of anything to break the despair of a mission unaccomplished. Good supporting work from a host of actors but there is a vague feeling that we've seen it before, and better.

2001: A SPACE ODYSSEY

1968   160m   c   Science Fiction   ★★★★½
Hawk/MGM   (U.S./U.K.)   /U

Keir Dullea *(David Bowman)*, Gary Lockwood *(Frank Poole)*, William Sylvester *(Dr. Heywood Floyd)*, Daniel Richter *(Moonwatcher)*, Leonard Rossiter *(Smyslov)*, Margaret Tyzack *(Elena)*, Robert Beatty *(Halvorsen)*, Sean Sullivan *(Michaels)*, Frank Miller *(Mission Controller)*, Alan Gifford *(Poole's Father)*

p, Stanley Kubrick; d, Stanley Kubrick; w, Stanley Kubrick, Arthur C. Clarke (based on the short story "The Sentinel" by Clarke); ph, Geoffrey Unsworth, John Alcott; ed, Ray Lovejoy; prod d, Tony Masters, Harry Lange, Ernest Archer; art d, John Hoesli; fx, Stanley Kubrick, Wally Veevers, Douglas Trumbull, Con Pederson, Tom Howard, Colin J. Cantwell, Bryan Loftus, Frederick Martin, Bruce Logan, David Osborne, John Jack Malick; cos, Hardy Amies

AAN Best Director: Stanley Kubrick; *AAN Best Original Story and Screenplay:* Stanley Kubrick, Arthur C. Clarke; *AAN Best Art Direction:* Tony Masters, Harry Lange, Ernie Archer; *AA Best Visual Effects:* Stanley Kubrick

A beautiful, confounding picture that had half the audience cheering and the other half snoring. Kubrick clearly means to say something about the dehumanizing effects of technology, but exactly *what* is hard to say. One of those works presumed to be profound by virtue of its incomprehensibility, 2001 is nevertheless an astounding visual experience—one to be enjoyed, if possible, only on the big screen.

The film opens with (as a title modestly announces) The Dawn of Man. Man dawns when a tribe of apelike hominids is visited by a huge black monolith, which instructs them in the use of tools and weapons. Cut to the year 2001, when a scientist (Sylvester) is investigating a baffling archaeological discovery on the moon—it is, of course, a huge black monolith, which later sends a signal in the direction of the planet Jupiter. Dissolve to a year later, as a spaceship makes its way to Jupiter. Dullea and Lockwood run the ship with the help of HAL 9000, the most sophisticated computer ever devised. HAL turns on its human masters, killing Lockwood, and Dullea ventures further into space, eventually confronting a huge black monolith. Later, after witnessing a truly spectacular light show, he enounters a relatively small black monolith.

The screenplay—which is often quite witty, especially in the largely satirical Sylvester sequences—probably was meant sincerely, but has the feel of something that was never thought through. Kubrick seems to have understood that, with the emergence of drug culture and middle-class spiritual yearnings during the late 60s, anything really huge and really vague stood a good chance of being received as something really deep. If so, Kubrick's strategy worked: made at a cost of $10.5 million, the film began to build slowly but eventually took in almost $15 million in North America, then about half that upon rerelease in the slightly shorter version (141 minutes) in 1972. Many hailed it as a religious experience, and underground newspapers counseled readers to time their ingestion of hash brownies so as to be optimally stoned during the psychedelic final scenes. Clarke's short story was first made into a novel, then into the screenplay that MGM financed for $6 million. The budget kept rising, and the studio execs feared a disaster. The casting of Lockwood, Dullea, and Sylvester, three undynamic actors (in these roles), must have been deliberate, as Kubrick didn't want anything in the way of his vision (whatever that was). 2001 continues to annoy and delight audiences; for sheer spectacle, it may be unsurpassed. Its relatively low-tech special effects, masterfully engineered by Douglas Trumbull, remain more astonishing and persuasive than much of today's computer-generated gimmickry.

TWO WOMEN
(LA CIOCIARA)

1960   105m   bw   Drama/War   ★★★★
C.C. Champion/Marceau/Cocinor/S.G.C.   (Italy/France)   /X

Sophia Loren *(Cesira)*, Jean-Paul Belmondo *(Michele)*, Eleanora Brown *(Rosetta)*, Raf Vallone *(Giovanni)*, Renato Salvatori *(Florindo)*, Carlo Ninchi *(Michele's Father)*, Andrea Checchi *(Fascist)*, Pupella Maggio, Emma Baron, Bruna Cealti p, Carlo Ponti; d, Vittorio De Sica; w, Cesare Zavattini, Vittorio De Sica (based on the novel by Alberto Moravia); ph, Gabor Pogany, Mario Capriotti; ed, Adriana Novelli; m, Armando Trovajoli; art d, Gastone Medin; cos, Elio Costanzi

AA Best Actress: Sophia Loren

Mama Mia! Loren deservedly won a Best Actress Oscar—the first to a non-American actress in a foreign-language film—for this Vittorio De Sica film, adapted by screenwriter Cesare Zavattini from an Alberto Moravia novel. It's not a great De Sica-Zavattini collaboration; much of the movie suffers from poor pacing and listlessness, but Loren is a marvel to behold.

She plays Cesira, a young widow in 1943 Italy who leaves her grocery store in San Lorenzo in the hands of her sometime lover (Raf Vallone), fleeing Allied bombing with her teenage daughter, Rosetta (Eleanora Brown), to return to her native village. There, after an arduous journey, she meets Michele (Jean-Paul Belmondo), the intellectual son of a local farmer with whom Rosetta falls in love, though he falls for her lovely mother. As the town grows increasingly besieged by bombing and shortages, Michele is forced to guide some fleeing Germans on an escape route, while Cesira and Rosetta go back to Rome for safety. Along the way, mother and daughter suffer a tragedy that changes both their lives forever, despite Cesira's best efforts to protect her child from the ravages of war. Loren also won the Best Actress Award at Cannes and the same honor from the British Film Academy; more important, she demonstrated in this film that she was a mature actress with talent to match her looks. And that deglamourized, she was still magnificent. But Eleanora Brown's role (originally meant for Loren, with Magnani to play the mother; the latter refused) is underwritten, Belmondo's character is a rehashed cliche, and Loren's affair with Vallone has had all the sex sucked out of it. It's almost as though everyone pinned their hopes on a big, international success for Loren, so they side-stepped her earth mother getting too carnal. But if the plot turns feel predictable, Loren rises to their occasions with the primal maternal force almost as old as time itself.

De Sica (who also won an Oscar for the film) and Zavattini's previous collaborations included SHOESHINE, THE BICYCLE THIEF, and UMBERTO D., while TWO WOMEN doesn't match the greatness or simplicity of those neo-realist masterworks, it remains a remarkably moving, humane vision of individual struggle in an inhumane world.

U

UGETSU MONOGATARI

1953 96m bw Drama ★★★★★
Daiei (Japan) /X

Machiko Kyo *(Lady Wukasa)*, Masayuki Mori *(Genjuro)*, Kinuyo Tanaka *(Miyagi)*, Sakae Ozawa *(Tobei)*, Mitsuko Mito *(Ohama)*, Sugisaku Aoyama *(Old Priest)*, Ryosuke Kagawa *(Village Chief)*, Kichijiro Tsuchida *(Silk Merchant)*, Mitsusaburo Ramon *(Captain of Tamba Soldiers)*, Ichisaburo Sawamura *(Genichi)*

p, Masaichi Nagata; d, Kenji Mizoguchi; w, Matsutaro Kawaguchi, Yoshikata Yoda (based on two classic tales by Akinari Ueda); ph, Kazuo Miyagawa; ed, Mitsuji Miyata; m, Fumio Hayasaka, Ichiro Saito; art d, Kisaku Ito; chor, Kinshichi Kodera; cos, Kusune Kainosho

AAN Best Costume Design: Tadaoto Kainoscho

Set in 16th-century Japan, this lyrical, enchanting film by Mizoguchi is one of Japanese cinema's greatest masterpieces. As civil warfare ravages the land, Genjuro and Tobei (Mori and Ozawa), peasant potters, dream of finding glory. They risk their own and their families' lives making pottery to sell at market and then head for the big city. Genjuro leaves his wife behind when he is taken in by a noblewoman (Kyo) who

is not what she seems. Tobei, meanwhile, pursues his longstanding desire to become a samurai, something he achieves when, with extreme luck, he manages to kill an established warrior. What happens to the two men's wives (Tanaka and Mito), however, is another story.

Mizoguchi's background as a painter shows in the lovely and artful compositions he sets before the viewer. The image of Lady Wukasa, her servant, and Genjuro trekking through the high reeds is, among many others, unforgettable. Mizoguchi, however, does not neglect the soundtrack, and the use of offscreen sound during such moments as the opening approach of the raiders skillfully suggests the threat to village life. The aesthetic appeal of UGETSU, however, is not merely indulged for its own sake; rather, the film uses the resources of film to explore a recurrent theme in this filmmaker's work. Like a painter determined to catch one vista in canvas after canvas, Mizoguchi considers how the price of indulging men's desires is often the suffering of women. This is done in individual shots (e.g. the highway robbers in the background gorging themselves on food the victimized Miyagi was carrying) as well as in the film as a whole. On another level the film can be read as paralleling the plight of post-WWII Japan. Either way, the film's subtle mix of realism and fantasy (consider a tracking shot with a near-invisible dissolve which "impossibly" links a sensual bath with a picnic) makes for challenging viewing. Working within Japanese genre conventions which seek to validate traditional values, Mizoguchi also considers their inherent contradictions. Look carefully at the pan and tracking shot as the errant Genjuro thinks he's returning to home and hearth near the end and you will witness a great moment in the history of cinema as both art and social commentary.

ULZANA'S RAID

1972 103m c Western/War ★★★★
Universal (U.S.) R/18

Burt Lancaster *(McIntosh)*, Bruce Davison *(Lt. Garnett DeBuin)*, Jorge Luke *(Ke-Ni-Tay)*, Richard Jaeckel *(Sergeant)*, Joaquin Martinez *(Ulzana)*, Lloyd Bochner *(Capt. Gates)*, Karl Swenson *(Rukeyser)*, Douglas Watson *(Maj. Cartwright)*, Dran Hamilton *(Mrs. Riordan)*, John Pearce *(Corporal)*

p, Carter DeHaven; d, Robert Aldrich; w, Alan Sharp; ph, Joseph Biroc; ed, Michael Luciano; m, Frank DeVol; art d, James Vance

One of the greatest films made by often overlooked director Robert Aldrich, ULZANA'S RAID isn't a true war film, but within its traditional western format, Aldrich and screenwriter Alan Sharp transform the material into an effective and damning allegory of America's involvement in Vietnam. Set in Arizona during the late 1880s, the film centers on Lancaster, a hard-riding scout who accompanies idealistic, young lieutenant Davison in his pursuit of a group of rapacious renegade Apaches led by Martinez (playing Ulzana). On the trail it becomes apparent that Lancaster and Davison hold radically different views of Martinez's actions—the scout is cold and cynical, while Davison's Christian morality is incensed by the Apache atrocities. As the film progresses it poses a complex series of questions about the nature of heroism, racism, and American imperialism. However, as an allegorical indictment of the Vietnam War, ULZANA'S RAID avoids the preachy stance of similarly themed westerns such as SOLDIER BLUE, benefiting from Aldrich's stark, violent treatment of Sharp's well-developed script. Regrettably, this challenging film was much abused by its studio, and several different versions were circulated, including a European cut containing alternative takes and slightly altered scene construction (most noticeable in the film's opening section). This was the third time Lancaster and Aldrich had worked together, after a lapse of 18 years (their previous collaborations, APACHE and VERA CRUZ), and they would soon team again on TWILIGHT'S LAST GLEAMING.

UMBERTO D.

1952 89m bw Drama ★★★★★
Amato/Rizzoli (Italy)

Carlo Battisti *(Umberto Domenico Ferrari)*, Maria Pia Casilio *(Maria)*, Lina Gennari *(Landlady)*, Alberto Albani Barbieri *(Fiance)*, Elena Rea *(Sister)*, Ileana Simova *(Surprised Woman)*, Memmo Carotenuto *(Voice of Light)*

p, Vittorio De Sica; d, Vittorio De Sica; w, Cesare Zavattini, Vittorio De Sica (based on a story by Zavattini); ph, Aldo Graziati; ed, Eraldo di Roma; m, Alessandro Cicognini; prod d, Virgilio Marchi

AAN Best Original Screenplay: Cesare Zavattini

Simple on its surface but actually multi-layered and complex, this shattering portrait of an old man is an indictment of postwar Italy and its treatment of the aged. Umberto Domenico Ferrari (non-pro Carlo Battisti, a university professor) is a retired civil servant with no friends, family, or prospects, and only his dog, Flike, to keep him company. His meager pension does not provide enough for him to both eat and afford shelter, so Umberto is far behind on his rent for the room he has lived in for three decades. When he used to work during the day, his landlady (Lina Gennari) rented his room to lovers, but since his continual presence isn't adding to her income, she is planning to evict him. Umberto is one of many elderly people who voice their opposition to the way the government is treating pensionsers. Depressed by the lack of response, he determines there is no way out but suicide. He puts those thoughts aside, however, when he realizes that his dog would be at the mercy of the streets. One of the greatest films of all time and one of the handful of masterpieces to emerge from the Italian neo-realist period, UMBERTO D. is as cerebral as it is emotional, as bleak as it is warm. There is no sentimentality or pandering for sympathy in De Sica's direction. The emotions one feels watching Umberto and Flike are cathartic. This is a remarkable collaboration by De Sica, Battista, and screenwriter Cesare Zavattini.

UMBRELLAS OF CHERBOURG, THE
(LES PARAPLUIES DE CHERBOURG)

1964 90m c Musical   ★★★½
Madeleine/Parc/Beta   (France/West Germany)

Catherine Deneuve *(Genevieve Emery)*, Nino Castelnuovo *(Guy)*, Anne Vernon *(Mme. Emery)*, Ellen Farner *(Madeleine)*, Marc Michel *(Roland Cassard)*, Mireille Perrey *(Aunt Elise)*, Jean Champion *(Aubin)*, Harald Wolff *(Dubourg)*, Dorothee Blank *(Girl in Cafe)*

p, Mag Bodard; d, Jacques Demy; w, Jacques Demy; ph, Jean Rabier; ed, Anne-Marie Cotret; m, Michel Legrand; art d, Bernard Evein; cos, Real, Jacqueline Moreau

AAN Best Foreign Language Film ; *AAN Best Original Screenplay:* Jacques Demy; *AAN Best Score:* Michel Legrand, Jacques Demy; *AAN Best Score:* Michel Legrand; *AAN Best Song:* Michel Legrand (Music), Jacques Demy (Lyrics), Norman Gimbel (Lyrics)

Although inspired by the Hollywood musical, Jacques Demy's vibrant, inventive film forgoes the familiar backdrop of a Broadway show or movie premiere to revel instead in the myth and magic of everyday romance, in all its sentimental and banal glory. Not quite a musical or an operetta, THE UMBRELLAS OF CHERBOURG is, as Demy has described it, "a film in color and song." What separates it from the Hollywood musical is Demy and composer Michel Legrand's decision to deliver all the dialogue—every last meaningless word—in song form. Divided into three acts—Departure, Absence, Return—and set in Cherbourg on the coast of Normandy, the film begins with the blossoming romance of two young lovers: Genevieve (the beautiful 19-year-old Catherine Deneuve), who works in her mother's umbrella store, and Guy (Nino Castelnuovo), a service station attendant. They fall in love, have an evening of romantic bliss, and are then separated when Guy receives his draft notice. In the second act, Genevieve learns that she is pregnant and, after failing to hear from Guy, agrees to marry the accommodating Roland (Marc Michel) and move to Paris. Voila, Guy returns to Cherbourg. A feast of movement, color, and song, THE UMBRELLAS OF CHERBOURG transforms the quotidian into a celebration. By inflating the life of a common shop girl into a musical spectacle, Demy succeeds in turning a tedious existence into a fantasy, yet he and cinematographer Jean Rabier and art director Bernard Evein do so without creating a false world. Instead they discover the "poetic realism" in Genevieve's world of umbrellas, hat, chairs, and shop windows.

UN COEUR EN HIVER

1992 105m c Drama/Romance   ★★★★
Film Par Film/Cinea/FR3 Film Productions/DA Film   /12
/Sedis/Roissy Films   (France)

Daniel Auteuil *(Stephane)*, Emmanuelle Beart *(Camille)*, Andre Dussollier *(Maxime)*, Elisabeth Bourgine *(Helene)*, Brigitte Catillon *(Regine)*, Maurice Garrel *(Lachaume)*, Myriam Boyer *(Madame Amet)*, Stanislas Carre DeMalberg *(Brice)*, Jean-Luc Bideau *(Ostende)*

p, Philippe Carcassonne, Jean-Louis Livi; d, Claude Sautet; w, Yves Ulmann, Claude Sautet; ph, Yves Angelo; ed, Jacqueline Thiedot; m, Maurice Ravel; cos, Corrine Jorry

Passion without eroticism, melancholia without mawkishness, a love triangle with only two active participants—UN COEUR EN HIVER breaks the rules so tenderly and assuredly that the viewer, like its main character, sees no danger until it's too late.

Passive Stephane (Daniel Auteuil) is a master repairer/restorer of violins. His partner in business and society is Maxime (Andre Dussollier), an outgoing older man. Their relationship is so intimate and comfortable that one almost suspects the men might be the screen's most contented lovers, until Maxime drops the bombshell that he's just left his unseen wife and children for their new client Camille (Emmanuelle Beart), a beautiful young violin virtuoso whom he plans to marry. Stephane responds to Camille's intrusion like a perfect gentleman, with only the faintest trace of reserve, but she falls madly, perversely in love with him, even as she moves in with Maxime. How will this repressed triangle work itself out?

UN COEUR EN HIVER unfolds in the rarefied world of concert violinists, where director Claude Sautet (once a music critic) finds apt metaphors for Stephane's soulless civility: he can tune an instrument to perfect pitch, but gave up playing because there was no personality to his technique. A cool and intelligent story of jealousy and obsession, Sautet's film leaves viewers puzzling to the last: does Stephane subtly, deliberately seduce Camille, or is he a bewildered victim of inescapable fate? Auteuil and Beart deliver fine, nuanced performances, and UN COEUR EN HIVER won Cesars (France's Oscar) for Best Director and Best Supporting Actor (Andre Dussollier).

UNBEARABLE LIGHTNESS OF BEING, THE

1988 171m c Romance/Erotic/War   ★★½
Orion   (U.S.)   R/18

Daniel Day-Lewis *(Tomas)*, Juliette Binoche *(Tereza)*, Lena Olin *(Sabina)*, Derek De Lint *(Franz)*, Erland Josephson *(The Ambassador)*, Pavel Landovsky *(Pavel)*, Donald Moffat *(Chief Surgeon)*, Daniel Olbrychski *(Interior Ministry Official)*, Stellan Skarsgard *(The Engineer)*, Tomek Bork *(Jiri)*

p, Saul Zaentz; d, Philip Kaufman; w, Jean-Claude Carriere, Philip Kaufman (based on the novel by Milan Kundera); ph, Sven Nykvist; ed, Walter Murch; m, Mark Adler, Keith Richards, Leos Janacek; prod d, Pierre Guffroy; fx, Trielli Brothers; cos, Ann Roth

AAN Best Adapted Screenplay: Jean-Claude Carriere, Philip Kaufman; *AAN Best Cinematography:* Sven Nykvist

Phil Kaufman's film version of Milan Kundera's acclaimed novel opens in Prague shortly before the Soviet invasion of 1968, where Tomas (Daniel Day-Lewis), a brilliant playboy surgeon, lives a "light" existence free of commitment. Tomas falls in love with the shy, provincial Tereza (Juliette Binoche), eventually marrying her. He continues to womanize, though, especially with the similarly free and easy Sabina (Lena Olin), defending his adultery by insisting that sex and love are not the same thing. When the Soviet tanks roll into Prague, Sabina flees to Geneva, but Tomas and Tereza stay behind—she snapping pictures of the clampdown, riots, demonstrations, and violence. Eventually they, too, head for Geneva, and Tomas resumes his liaison with Sabina. When Tereza decides to return to Czechoslovakia, Tomas follows her home. There they sustain the weight of Soviet influence fairly easily, until authorities discover that Tomas once wrote an anti-Communist article. Though Tomas, typically, wrote the piece on a whim, he refuses to renounce it and suffers professionally. In the meantime, he continues to philander and Tereza continues to try to understand his philosophy of sex versus love. With its distinguished international cast and crew, volatile historical backdrop, and numerous erotic scenes, all filtered through the eye of American director Kaufman (THE RIGHT STUFF), THE UNBEARABLE LIGHTNESS OF BEING is the perfect European art film for American audiences who thirst for movies that are "intellectual" but not so much so that they can't understand them. Unfortunately, for all its credentials and the virtuoso performances of its three leads, this lengthy movie doesn't add up to much. It fails to explore its themes—love and hedonism, freedom and commitment (political and sexual)—in depth, floating haphazardly from scene to scene without emotional or intellectual development. Shot in Geneva and Lyon, France (the latter town standing in for Prague, where Kundera's work is banned), the film places greater stress on the actual events of the 1968 Soviet invasion than does its source, incorporating real black-and-white footage of the time with simulated shots featuring Binoche and Day-Lewis.

UNBELIEVABLE TRUTH, THE

1990 90m c Comedy/Drama   ★★★½
Action Features   (U.S.)   R/15

Adrienne Shelly *(Audry Hugo)*, Robert Burke *(Josh Hutton)*, Christopher Cooke *(Vic Hugo)*, Julia Mueller *(Pearl)*, Mark Bailey *(Mike)*, Gary Sauer *(Emmet)*, Katherine Mayfield *(Liz Hugo)*, David Healy *(Todd Whitbread)*, Matt Malloy *(Otis)*, Edie Falco *(Jane, the Waitress)*

p, Bruce Weiss; d, Hal Hartley; w, Hal Hartley; ph, Michael Spiller; ed, Hal Hartley; m, Jim Coleman, Wild Blue Yonder, The Brothers Kendall; prod d, Carla Gerona; cos, Kelly Reichardt

THE UNBELIEVABLE TRUTH proved a promising feature-film debut for writer-director Hal Hartley, who was dubbed "the Godard of Long Island" by critics with more sense of humor than of substance. In the vein of Jim Jarmusch's STRANGER THAN PARADISE and the work of David Lynch, THE UNBELIEVABLE TRUTH searches for the unexpected, bizarre, and magical essence of prosaic American locales. For director Hartley, that locale is Lindenhurst, Long Island, hometown of Josh Hutton (Robert Burke), a paroled convict who, as the film opens, returns to the area (where everyone remembers the details of his crime differently) because he has nowhere else to go. Haunted by a past that includes the manslaughter of his sweetheart and a prison stretch for killing her grieving father in an argument about her death, Hutton is too shell-shocked to begin his life anew until he meets Audry Hugo (Adrienne Shelly), a high-school student with an obsessive fear of nuclear attack. When Audry's father, garage owner Vic (Christopher Cooke), agrees to hire Josh for his exceptional mechanical skills, Audry and Josh can no longer suppress their growing mutual attraction.

Hartley exhibits a born filmmaker's eye for composition and camera placement in this offbeat, dryly humorous film. His screenwriting skills are less solid, however, and the film is further damaged by the uneven quality of its cast, which weakens the already delicate balance in this black comedy. Although Burke makes the ideal loner hero, Shelly is saddled with a role that's more a collection of nonconformist attitudes than a true character. More damaging is the casting of Cooke, whose delineation of the harried middle-class father is amateurish.

Despite these flaws, THE UNBELIEVABLE TRUTH captivates with its committedly off-center vision of suburban angst. Long Island becomes a world of identity crises, serendipitous occurrences, and amusing non-sequiturs. It's an impressive, if not always cogent, attempt to mine humor out of tragic circumstances, and it manages to send up small-town life without being condescending—no mean feat. Unfortunately, Hartley's subsequent features, from TRUST to SIMPLE MEN to AMATEUR, seem to have mined the exact same territory, to increasingly meager dramatic and emotional effect.

UNCLE BUCK

1989 100m c Comedy   ★★½
Universal   (U.S.)   PG/12

John Candy *(Uncle Buck Russell)*, Jean Kelly *(Tia Russell)*, Gaby Hoffman *(Maizy Russell)*, Macaulay Culkin *(Miles Russell)*, Amy Madigan *(Chanice Kobolowski)*, Elaine Bromka *(Cindy Russell)*, Garrett M. Brown *(Bob Russell)*, Laurie Metcalf *(Marcie Dahlgren-Frost)*, Jay Underwood *(Bug)*, Brian Tarantina *(Rog)*

p, John Hughes, Tom Jacobson; d, John Hughes; w, John Hughes; ph, Ralf D. Bode; ed, Lou Lombardo, Tony Lombardo, Peck Prior; m, Ira Newborn; prod d, John W. Corso; chor, Miranda Garrison; cos, Marilyn Vance

The late John Candy, in what may be his most celebrated role, stars as the eponymous Buck. He's a painfully inept, irredeemable slob who becomes a most unlikely baby-sitter for eight-year-old Miles (Macaulay Culkin), six-year-old Maizy (Gaby Hoffman), and teenaged Tia (Jean Kelly) when Buck's brother and sister-in-law have to leave town to visit a sick relative. Supposedly ill-equipped to take care of children, Uncle Buck keeps Maizy and Miles amused and eventually wins the reluctant respect of Tia by protecting her from her creepy boyfriend. In the process, however, he nearly ruins his own eight-year relationship with Chanice (Amy Madigan). Mostly thanks to Candy's sympathetic performance, the film has become a video perennial; like many John Hughes films, however, it has a distinctly reactionary subtext—Buck proves his worth not so much by winning the hearts of the kiddies as by exerting patriarchal authority over Tia.

UNCONQUERED

1947 146m c Adventure   ★★★½
Paramount   (U.S.)

Gary Cooper *(Capt. Christopher Holden)*, Paulette Goddard *(Abigail Martha "Abby" Hale)*, Howard da Silva *(Martin Garth)*, Boris Karloff *(Guyasuta)*, Cecil Kellaway *(Jeremy Love)*, Ward Bond *(John Fraser)*, Katherine DeMille *(Hannah)*, Henry Wilcoxon *(Capt. Steele)*, C. Aubrey Smith *(Lord Chief Justice)*, Victor Varconi *(Capt. Simson Ecuyer)*

p, Cecil B. DeMille; d, Cecil B. DeMille; w, Charles Bennett, Fredric M. Frank, Jesse Lasky Jr. (based on the novel *The Judas Tree* by Neil H. Swanson); ph, Ray Rennahan; ed, Anne Bauchens; m, Victor Young; art d, Hans Dreier, Walter Tyler; fx, Gordon Jennings, Farciot Edouart, Wallace Kelley, Paul K. Lerpae, Devereaux Jennings; chor, Jack Crosby; cos, Gwen Wakeling, Barbara Karinska

AAN Best Visual Effects: Farciot Edouart, Devereux Jennings, Gordon Jennings, Paul Lerpae, George Dutton

Another of Cecil B. DeMille's bloated epics about the shaping of America, UNCONQUERED stars Goddard as an indentured servant sentenced to 14 years of servitude in the American colonies. On the voyage across from England, she meets Cooper, a Virginia militia captain who takes an immediate liking to her, despite the fact that he is already engaged. Goddard also attracts the eye of da Silva, a scurrilous trader. When his attentions grow too lewd, she slaps him, prompting da Silva to try to buy her contract. He is foiled on the docks, though, when Cooper bids higher and immediately gives Goddard her freedom. However, da Silva has too many other nefarious schemes in the works to be bothered by a little setback like this. Most notably, he marries the daughter of Seneca chief Karloff and agitates the Indians to unite to drive the white men back into the sea, using muskets da Silva sells them. At Fort Pitt, Cooper's fiancee tells him that she has fallen in love with another man, a development that doesn't seem to bother Cooper much. Goddard, however, falls into da Silva's hands again when he manages to get hold of her contract and convince her that Cooper's purchase was fraudulent. He puts her to work in a saloon he owns, managed by the crude Mazurki. She scrubs the floor while the men make rude comments, but Cooper isn't long in rescuing her. Jealous of her husband's attentions toward Goddard, da Silva's Indian wife arranges with the tribe to have Goddard kidnapped. Goddard is tied to a stake and is about to be tortured when Cooper comes on the scene to rescue her yet again. They arrive back at the fort just as the Indians attack with flaming arrows. Cooper helps the settlers fight off the Indians, then manages to kill da Silva and Mazurki in a shootout in a stable. As the film ends, Cooper and Goddard are about to be married.

This huge and expensive production never really comes together. Over $5 million and 102 days were spent on the film, but it was savaged by the critics and ignored by the public. Fearing the flaming arrows that had already sent 30 extras to the hospital with burns, Goddard created problems for the director when she refused to climb the ramparts of the fort during the attack sequence. To teach her a lesson DeMille picked one lowly extra for an important part in the scene, succoring the wounded on the ramparts. Goddard was vindicated, though, when the extra joined the others at the hospital.

Karloff wasn't very good as the Indian chief, though his dedication to the part was impressive. He had originally intended to speak the role in gibberish, but DeMille insisted that he learn Seneca, which he did. In addition, the actor had recently undergone back surgery and under his bonnet, furs, and loincloth was a massive brace. Cooper is good but looks a little old to be gallivanting about the frontier, and Goddard tries too hard to be glamorous, destroying her character. Da Silva is a worthy villain and the rest of the cast is more than adequate, but the whole thing sinks under its own grand weight. DeMille simply tries too hard to get in everything, even one of his patented bathtub scenes, played here in a barrel by Goddard. The film lost a fortune at the box office.

UNDER FIRE

1983 127m c Drama/War	★★★
Lion's Gate (U.S.)	R/15

Nick Nolte *(Russell Price)*, Ed Harris *(Oates)*, Gene Hackman *(Alex Grazier)*, Joanna Cassidy *(Claire)*, Alma Martinez *(Isela)*, Holly Palance *(Journalist)*, Ella Laboriel *(Nightclub Singer)*, Oswaldo Doria *(Boy Photographer)*, Fernando Elizondo *(Businessman)*, Hamilton Camp *(Regis Seydor)*

p, Jonathan T. Taplin; d, Roger Spottiswoode; w, Ron Shelton, Clayton Frohman (based on a story by Frohman); ph, John Alcott; ed, John Bloom; m, Jerry Goldsmith; art d, Agustin Ytuarte, Toby Rafelson; fx, Laurencio Cordero, Jesus Duran; cos, Cynthia Bales

AAN Best Score: Jerry Goldsmith

Flawed but still fascinating, UNDER FIRE looks at the Nicaraguan revolution through the eyes of Russell Price (Nick Nolte), an American photojournalist who uses his camera to distance himself from reality. In Managua, Price's noncommittal attitude is put to the test by the startling contrast between the high life enjoyed by the supporters of President Anastasio Somoza (Rene Enriquez) and the reality experienced by most Nicaraguans. The American begins to realize that the plush Hotel Continental, home of the press corps, is an obscene imperialist outpost that distances the reporters from the people they are supposed to be covering. None of this, however, is news to Claire (Joanna Cassidy), a National Public Radio reporter, and under her influence Price eventually becomes actively involved with the revolutionaries, faking a picture of a slain leader so that it will appear that he is still alive. The sensational photo brings network news anchor Alex Grazier (Gene Hackman) to Managua where he is shot and killed by one of Somoza's National Guardsmen (mirroring the horrifying true-life murder of ABC correspondent Bill Stewart by Somoza's troops in 1979—an event that was captured on videotape and shown to a shocked American audience). Price records the whole incident on film, and his pictures create worldwide outrage that helps sound the death knell for Somoza's government. Nolte gives one of his best performances as the photographer who suddenly finds himself looking past what he sees in the viewfinder in this insightful look at revolution and the world of journalism. Director Roger Spottiswoode, who edited a number of Sam Peckinpah movies, succeeds brilliantly in creating the chaotic last days of Somoza's government while at the same time incisively evaluating the moral dilemma faced by war correspondents. Where the film falters, however, is screenwriter Ron Shelton's (BULL DURHAM) overly simplistic view of both Somoza and the Sandinistas. Shown to be the white knights riding to the rescue of the oppressed masses, the Sandinistas are given almost embarrassingly reverent treatment with no hint of the ideological divisions, confusion, and suffering that would follow their takeover (problems at least hinted at in Oliver Stone's remarkable SALVADOR).

UNDER SIEGE

1992 100m c Action/Thriller	★★½
Le Studio Canal Plus/Alcor Films/Regency Enterprises (U.S.)	R/15

Steven Seagal *(Casey Ryback)*, Gary Busey *(Commander Krill)*, Tommy Lee Jones *(William Strannix)*, Erika Eleniak *(Jordan Tate)*, Colm Meaney *(Daumer)*, Patrick O'Neal *(Captain Adams)*, Michael Des Barres *(Damiani)*, Nick Mancuso *(Tom Breaker)*, Bernie Casey *(Commander Harris)*, Damian Chapa *(Tackman)*

p, Steven Reuther, Arnon Milchan, Steven Seagal; d, Andrew Davis; w, J.F. Lawton, John Mason, Michael Rae; ph, Frank Tidy; ed, Robert A. Ferretti, Dennis Virkler, Don Brochu, Dov Hoenig; m, Gary Chang; prod d, Bill Kenney; art d, Bill Hiney; cos, Richard Bruno

AAN Best Sound: Don Mitchell, Frank A. Montano, Rick Hart, Scott Smith; *AAN Best Sound Effects Editing:* John Leveque, Bruce Stambler

Despite some occasional flashes of inspiration, this is yet another B movie with bloated production values. Instantly tagged as "DIE HARD on a battleship," UNDER SIEGE gives us Steven Seagal as Casey Ryback, a former Navy SEAL who, because of his resistance to the US invasion of Panama, has been demoted to the post of cook on the USS Missouri. He's called on to do more than sling hash when the ship's second-in-command, Commander Krill (Gary Busey), arranges a "surprise" party for the Captain's birthday featuring rock singer Strannix (Tommy Lee Jones), outside caterers and a topless dancer (Erika Eleniak). Strannix turns out to be a renegade CIA agent who, with his "caterers," takes over the ship with an eye to removing and selling its weaponry. But he hasn't reckoned on Ryback, who teams up with the topless dancer and a few of the ship's officers to put matters to rights.

During its opening scenes, UNDER SIEGE threatens to achieve something like DIE HARD's blend of wit, ingenuity and action, with Jones and Busey making highly entertaining, creepy-funny villains. Once the stolid Seagal takes over, however, we settle into a predictable high-tech groove of explosions, gunplay and gore. Though as capable at staging explosions as anybody, director Davis still betrays no more feeling for character or suspense than he did in his earlier films, THE PACKAGE and ABOVE THE LAW.

UNDER THE ROOFS OF PARIS
(SOUS LES TOITS DE PARIS)

1930 96m bw Drama	★★★
Tobis (France)	/A

Albert Prejean *(Albert)*, Pola Illery *(Pola)*, Edmond T. Greville *(Louis)*, Gaston Modot *(Fred)*, Paul Olivier *(Drunkard)*, Bill Bocket *(Bill)*, Jane Pierson *(Neighborhood Woman)*, Raymond Aimos *(Thief)*, Thomy Bourdelle *(Francois)*

d, Rene Clair; w, Rene Clair; ph, Georges Perinal, Georges Raulet; ed, Rene Le Henaff; art d, Lazare Meerson

Billed upon its release as "the most beautiful film in the world," UNDER THE ROOFS OF PARIS may well have fit that description—at least at the time. In this first "100 percent French talking and singing film," Rene Clair was determined to make sound and visuals equal partners. Instead of simply employing synchronous sound techniques, he chose to use sound only when needed, refusing to toss in dialogue just for the sake of doing so.

The story itself is a simple one. Street singer Albert (Prejean) and Pola (Illery) are lovers, though she enjoys flirting with his best friend, Louis (Greville). When Albert finds himself in prison for a crime he didn't commit, the door is open for Pola and Edmond to act upon their mutual attraction. Upon his release from prison, Albert is enraged by Pola and Edmond's romance, but the final arrangement the three arrive at is unexpected indeed. In 1931, using practically the same set of technicians, Clair went on to make his two of his greatest films—LE MILLION and A NOUS LA LIBERTE, improvements which continued his experiments with sound. Much of this film's visual style, however, can be attributed to the great art director Lazare Meerson, who collaborated with Clair on the director's greatest works.

UNDER THE VOLCANO

1984 112m c Drama	★★★½
Ithaca/Conacine (U.S.)	R/15

Albert Finney *(Geoffrey Firmin)*, Jacqueline Bisset *(Yvonne Firmin)*, Anthony Andrews *(Hugh Firmin)*, Ignacio Lopez Tarso *(Dr. Vigil)*, Katy Jurado *(Senora Gregoria)*, James Villiers *(Brit)*, Dawson Bray *(Quincey)*, Carlos Riquelme *(Bustamante)*, Jim McCarthy *(Gringo)*, Rene Ruiz *(Dwarf)*

p, Moritz Borman, Wieland Schulz-Keil; d, John Huston; w, Guy Gallo (based on the novel by Malcolm Lowry); ph, Gabriel Figueroa; ed, Roberto Silvi; m, Alex North; prod d, Gunther Gerzso; art d, Jose Rodriguez Granada; cos, Angela Dodson

AAN Best Actor: Albert Finney; *AAN Best Score:* Alex North

A bizarre journey into the mystical Mexican underworld in 1939, UNDER THE VOLCANO is set during the morbid holiday known as the Day of the Dead—a day on which the souls of the dead spew forth from hell amid the colorful and lively festivities of the village of Cuernavaca. Geoffrey Firmin (Albert Finney), a former British consul, is there for the celebration, drinking himself to death. The spirit of celebration is alive, but Geoffrey appears lifeless, almost zombielike as he wanders the streets. His former wife, Yvonne (Jacqueline Bisset), arrives, and with the help of Geoffrey's brother, Hugh (Anthony Andrews), tries to get him away from Mexico to a farm in the US, hoping it will curb his drinking. After wandering about the village pathetically for hours on end, Geoffrey slips away and winds up in a sleazy bar-whorehouse, drinking himself into oblivion. Based on the 1947 novel by Malcom Lowry, who began the work in 1936 at the age of 27, UNDER THE VOLCANO has been a project kicked around Hollywood since the book's publication. Lowry, a suicidal alcoholic, wrote the novel without any clear narrative line, relying instead on marvelously visual images, thereby causing many people to label the novel "unfilmable"—until it ended up in the lap of John Huston. The result is very much worth the wait, bringing to life the mysticism of Mexico with a superb script by Guy Gallo, exquisite photography, and the unparalleled performance by Finney.

UNFAITHFULLY YOURS

1948   105m   bw   Comedy   ★★★★★
Fox   (U.S.)   /15

Rex Harrison *(Sir Alfred de Carter)*, Linda Darnell *(Daphne de Carter)*, Barbara Lawrence *(Barbara Henshler)*, Rudy Vallee *(August Henshler)*, Kurt Kreuger *(Anthony)*, Lionel Stander *(Hugo Standoff)*, Edgar Kennedy *(Detective Sweeney)*, Alan Bridge *(House Detective)*, Julius Tannen *(Tailor)*, Torben Meyer *(Dr. Schultz)*

p, Preston Sturges; d, Preston Sturges; w, Preston Sturges; ph, Victor Milner; ed, Robert Fritch; m, Gioacchino Rossini, Richard Wagner, Peter Ilich Tchaikovsky; art d, Lyle Wheeler, Joseph C. Wright; fx, Fred Sersen; cos, Bonnie Cashin

The last of Sturges's Hollywood films, and one of his finest. This farce of misconceptions, infidelities, and murder is a brilliantly stylish work that imaginatively squeezes everything it can from the film medium.

Harrison, in a marvelous performance, is a famous British conductor married to Darnell. The two are much in love, but, when Harrison returns from Europe, a seed of jealously is planted in his mind by his brother-in-law, Vallee. It seems that Vallee had a private detective, Kennedy, follow Darnell through her daily activities, and his report, which Harrison refuses to look at, suggests that Darnell indulged in some extracurricular activities with Harrison's private secretary, Kreuger, when the conductor was abroad. Harrison tears up the report and throws it out of his hotel room, but eventually the pages are put back together and wind up back in Harrison's hands. This time Harrison burns the document, nearly setting his dressing room ablaze. However, Harrison slowly begins to think there just might be something to the report, so he goes to Kennedy's office. Kennedy, it turns out, is a big fan of Harrison (who loves how the conductor "handles Handel") and dredges up the original report from his files. Now Harrison's jealous imagination goes wild. That night, as he begins conducting Rossini's "Semiramide" overture at a concert, the camera zeros in on Harrison's eye. The scene flashes to Harrison and Darnell as they return to their hotel room. As part of an elaborate plan, Harrison has arranged for Darnell to spend a night on the town with Kreuger. Using his straight razor, Harrison murders his wife, then sets up the room so Kreuger will appear to be the culprit. Harrison's plan works to perfection, and the conductor laughs maniacally when Kreuger is found guilty of the crime. The music comes to a conclusion, and the camera pulls away from Harrison's eye, back to the concert. The entire scenario has taken place in his mind, as do the next two sequences. To the accompaniment of Wagner's "Tannhauser" overture, Harrison imagines writing a fat check for Darnell, enabling her to run off with her young lover. Finally, with

Tchaikovsky's "Francesca da Rimini" wafting in the background, Harrison challenges Darnell and Kreuger to a game of Russian roulette. He ends up with a bullet in his temple as the concert comes to an end. Harrison, now convinced that Darnell and Kreuger are dallying behind his back, returns to his hotel room and tries to set up the murderous plan he imagined during the concert. His real-life plans are a disaster, and Harrison finally realizes that Kennedy's report was the result of many misconceptions.

UNFAITHFULLY YOURS is a near perfect combination of sound and image. Sturges orchestrates the fantasy sequences with care and precision, using editing and performance rhythms that are in perfect synch with the underscoring music. Harrison is a sheer delight, turning in a devilish performance brimming with wit and style. Darnell, Kreuger, Vallee, and Lawrence fill out the lead roles with elegance and wit, while consummate character player Kennedy adds a nice touch of buffoonery. Sturges had gotten the idea of music affecting the conductor's thoughts while writing the screenplay for THE POWER AND THE GLORY. "I had a scene all written and had only to put it down on paper. To my surprise, it came out quite unlike what I had planned," Sturges said later. "I sat back wondering what the hell had happened, then noticed that someone had left the radio on in the next room and realized that I had been listening to a symphony broadcast from New York and that this, added to my thoughts, had changed the total." (Quoted in James Curtis, *Between Flops*.)

Despite many critical plaudits, UNFAITHFULLY YOURS never caught on with the public—an undeserved fate for a film of such brilliance. It was remade in 1984 by Howard Zieff with Dudley Moore and Nastassja Kinski as leads.

UNFORGIVEN

1992   130m   c   Western   ★★★★½
Malpaso Productions/Warner Bros.   (U.S.)   R/15

Clint Eastwood *(William Munny)*, Gene Hackman *(Sheriff "Little Bill" Daggett)*, Morgan Freeman *(Ned Logan)*, Richard Harris *(English Bob)*, Jaimz Woolvett *(The "Schofield Kid")*, Saul Rubinek *(W.W. Beauchamp)*, Frances Fisher *(Strawberry Alice)*, Anna Thomson *(Delilah Fitzgerald)*, David Mucci *(Quick Mike)*, Rob Campbell *(Davey Bunting)*

p, Clint Eastwood; d, Clint Eastwood; w, David Peoples; ph, Jack N. Green; ed, Joel Cox; m, Lennie Niehaus; prod d, Henry Bumstead; art d, Rick Roberts, Adrian Gorton

AA Best Picture; AAN Best Actor: Clint Eastwood; *AA Best Supporting Actor:* Gene Hackman; *AA Best Director:* Clint Eastwood; *AAN Best Original Screenplay:* David Webb Peoples; *AAN Best Cinematography:* Jack N. Green; *AA Best Editing:* Joel Cox; *AAN Best Art Direction:* Henry Bumstead, Janice Blackie-Goodine; *AAN Best Sound:* Les Fresholtz, Vern Poore, Dick Alexander, Rob Young

One of Eastwood's finest outings to date, an elegiac western that ironically undermines the conventions of the genre, only to deliver a finale as legendary as the shootout at the O.K. Corral.

Wyoming, the 1880s. William Munny (Clint Eastwood) is a former murderer who, transformed by the love of a good woman, gave up a life of indiscriminate killing to raise a family and try his hand at pig farming. With his wife now dead and his farm a failure, Munny is lured back into his old ways by the "Schofield Kid" (Jaimz Woolvett), an aspiring young gunfighter who brings the older man word of a bounty being offered in the frontier town of Big Whiskey. (After a cowboy slashed the face of a prostitute there, the woman's co-workers have offered a reward for the death of the attacker and his accomplice.) Munny refuses the young man's offer of partnership but later reconsiders, teaming up with his old sidekick Ned Logan (Morgan Freeman) and setting off to join Schofield. The journey will bring him up against "Little Bill" Daggett (Gene Hackman), the autocratic sheriff of Big Whiskey, as well as forcing him to acknowledge that killing is, in fact, what he does best.

It's easy to see why Eastwood was drawn by this script, written by David Webb Peoples (BLADE RUNNER) in the 1970s. Munny is descended in a direct line from Eastwood's two most famous characters: the Man with No Name, from his 60s Westerns with Sergio Leone; and Dirty Harry, the anti-hero of Don Siegel's cop thrillers. Leone's presence is most strongly felt in the revisionist content of UNFOR-

GIVEN, while Siegel's influence is manifest in the film's lean, moody, no-nonsense style. Both of Eastwood's directorial mentors are acknowledged in the film's on-screen dedication, "to Sergio and Don."

The West of UNFORGIVEN is a place of few illusions, despite a mythology of heroism symbolized by Beauchamp (Saul Rubinek), a pulp biographer who has written heavily embellished accounts of the life of notorious gunslinger "English Bob" (marvelously played by Richard Harris). At one point, Little Bill ruptures this mythology by telling Beauchamp the inglorious real story behind one of the scenes described in his books—a pattern that is reprised throughout the film, as awe-struck tales of earlier heroes and exploits are undercut by cynical, down-to-earth dismissals. Eastwood as director finally turns this strategy on its head at the film's climax, when Munny pulls off a gunslinging feat of genuinely mythic proportions.

As with Leone's masterworks, UNFORGIVEN depicts a West driven solely by forces of commerce, not ideals of freedom or manifest destiny, with killing being Munny's sole marketable skill. Yet, just as Eastwood's occasional efforts to abandon his nihilist screen persona have been inconclusive, so is Munny haunted by his inability to escape the role society has decreed for him. Though he's the only protagonist left standing when the smoke clears, his story is the only one with the status of tragedy, his flaw being his very invincibility.

The cast is universally strong. Hackman, Freeman and Harris don't do anything they haven't done before, but the roles suit their personae to a degree where they approach archetypal status. The same applies to Eastwood, who casts himself as part of an ensemble rather than as the conscious star. And that's as it should be. With UNFORGIVEN, Eastwood achieves a new level of authority as a filmmaker and actor who has nothing to prove.

UNINVITED, THE

1944 98m bw Horror   ★★★★
Paramount (U.S.)   /A

Ray Milland (Roderick Fitzgerald), Ruth Hussey (Pamela Fitzgerald), Donald Crisp (Cmdr. Bench), Cornelia Otis Skinner (Miss Holloway), Dorothy Stickney (Miss Hird), Barbara Everest (Lizzie Flynn), Alan Napier (Dr. Scott), Gail Russell (Stella Meredith), Jessica Newcombe (Miss Ellis), John Kieran (Foreword Narrator)

p, Charles Brackett; d, Lewis Allen; w, Dodie Smith, Frank Partos (based on the novel by Dorothy Macardle); ph, Charles Lang; ed, Doane Harrison; m, Victor Young; art d, Hans Dreier, Ernst Fegte; fx, Farciot Edouart

AAN Best Cinematography: Charles Lang

An unusual and fascinating item, a ghost story that takes itself seriously. Milland and his sister, Hussey, buy a house on the Cornish cliffs and are soon bedeviled by phenomena such as cold spots in rooms, the smell of mimosas permeating the air, and the dog refusing to go upstairs. They are often visited by a local girl, Russell, whose grandfather, Crisp, forbids her to go into the house. It's suspected that the place is haunted by the spirit of Russell's mother, who fell from the cliffs to her death. More strange things happen, such as flowers wilting immediately in a room, and eventually the phantom itself is seen at the top of the stairs (one of the most convincing and scary ghosts to appear on the screen). Russell is confined by her grandfather to an asylum, but Milland and Hussey figure out that it is not one but two ghosts that haunt their home, carrying their rivalry from life beyond the grave. They eventually solve the mystery surrounding the death of Russell's mother, and when they do the spirits depart.

This film was greatly influenced by Val Lewton's productions for RKO in which the horror is only suggested, and almost never shown—for the monster in one's mind is much more frightening than the one on the screen. Some of the film doesn't work so well; it drags in spots and much of it seems a direct cop from REBECCA (house on the cliffs, scary folks coming in and out talking about the dead woman who lived there before, etc., and the advertising for the film went out of its way to compare itself to the Hitchcock film). Milland is as good as ever, and the rest of the cast does an admirable job, particularly Crisp and Skinner. Although the film garnered favorable reviews and decent returns at the box office, it would be many years before Hollywood would get serious about the spirit world again (THE HAUNTING).

UNION PACIFIC

1939 135m bw Western   ★★★★
Paramount (U.S.)   /U

Barbara Stanwyck (Mollie Monahan), Joel McCrea (Jeff Butler), Akim Tamiroff (Fiesta), Robert Preston (Dick Allen), Lynne Overman (Leach Overmile), Brian Donlevy (Sid Campeau), Robert Barrat (Duke Ring), Anthony Quinn (Jack Cordray), Stanley Ridges (Gen. Casement), Henry Kolker (Asa M. Barrows)

p, Cecil B. DeMille; d, Cecil B. DeMille; w, Walter DeLeon, C. Gardner Sullivan, Jesse Lasky Jr., Jack Cunningham (based on the novel Trouble Shooters by Ernest Haycox); ph, Victor Milner, Dewey Wrigley; ed, Anne Bauchens; m, George Antheil, Sigmund Krumgold, John Leipold; art d, Hans Dreier, Roland Anderson; fx, Gordon Jennings, Loren L. Ryder, Farciot Edouart; cos, Natalie Visart

AAN Best Visual Effects: Farciot Edouart, Gordon Jennings, Loren Ryder

After finishing his pirate epic THE BUCCANEER, Cecil B. DeMille was caught in a quandary regarding his next picture. Should it concern planes, ships, or trains? Deciding on trains, he faced another choice: the Union Pacific or the Sante Fe? The producer-director of spectacles reportedly flipped a coin, and UNION PACIFIC landed face up.

McCrea stars in this lavishly produced western, playing the supervisor of the construction of the Union Pacific Railroad. While on the job, he meets Stanwyck, a tough but feminine postmistress for the railroad. McCrea falls for her; meanwhile, Kolker, a seedy politician with a financial interest in the rival Central Pacific line, hires crooked gambler Donlevy to delay construction of the line. Aided by Preston, a comrade of McCrea's from the Civil War, Donlevy sets up a gambling den and begins distracting the Union Pacific workers with the prospect of gambling, liquor, and fast women. The lure of a good time causes havoc at the railroad—as does the robbery of the payroll, performed by Preston. Stanwyck, who has been seeing Preston as well as McCrea, learns that Preston is responsible for the theft and talks him into returning the money. Soon after, the train is attacked by Indians. Stanwyck holds her ground to fight alongside McCrea and Preston, and it looks as though they will all be slaughtered. Will the cavalry arrive in time?

UNION PACIFIC is a big, sprawling western epic produced with the usual DeMille extravagance and eye for detail. DeMille gained the cooperation of the Union Pacific Railroad, which made available heaps of old records and papers pertaining to the line's construction. In addition to the research material, the Union Pacific supplied DeMille with vintage trains and experienced crews to run them. The film was shot on locations in Utah and Oklahoma, and at the Canoga Park lot in Hollywood, where the reenactment of the golden spike ceremony was staged. Moreover, the actual golden spike (driven on May 10, 1869) that was used at that ceremony was loaned to the production by Stanford University and brought to Hollywood in great secrecy. DeMille, who assembled his usual cast of thousands for the production, was delighted by Stanwyck's professional enthusiasm as she toughed it through the action scenes with the men. The director had to undergo an operation during the production, and much of the location shooting was directed by Arthur Rosson and James Hogan during his absence. When DeMille returned to the production, he directed from a stretcher and was carried from set to set by crew members.

Even the premiere of UNION PACIFIC was a spectacle. DeMille arranged for a special Union Pacific train to carry the cast on a five-day trip from Los Angeles to Omaha, where the film was to open (and where the railway line started). There were stops along the way, of course, and special events were planned at each. In Omaha a three-day celebration with the citizenry in period costume was held, and the UNION PACIFIC cast—also in costumes—joined in. The film was a big hit at the box office, prompting Paramount Studios finally to give DeMille *carte blanche* on future productions.

UNMARRIED WOMAN, AN

1978 124m c Drama/Comedy   ★★★
Fox (U.S.)   R/18

Jill Clayburgh *(Erica)*, Alan Bates *(Saul)*, Michael Murphy *(Martin)*, Cliff Gorman *(Charlie)*, Pat Quinn *(Sue)*, Kelly Bishop *(Elaine)*, Lisa Lucas *(Patti)*, Linda G. Miller *(Jeannette)*, Andrew Duncan *(Bob)*, Daniel Seltzer *(Dr. Jacobs)*

p, Paul Mazursky, Tony Ray; d, Paul Mazursky; w, Paul Mazursky; ph, Arthur J. Ornitz; ed, Stuart Pappe; m, Bill Conti; prod d, Pato Guzman; cos, Albert Wolsky

AAN Best Picture; AAN Best Actress: Jill Clayburgh; *AAN Best Original Screenplay:* Paul Mazursky

AN UNMARRIED WOMAN became a beacon of the women's movement in the 1970s, though its tentative feminism seems tame by today's standards. Jill Clayburgh, in the title role, learns to take control of her own life after her schlump of a husband (beautifully played by Michael Murphy) leaves her for a girl he met in Bloomingdale's.

Set in the New York milieus Mazursky knows so well, AN UNMARRIED WOMAN has some great insights and is superbly acted by all involved. The director populates the film with his usual, very real and attractive modern characters, but you may think it cops out in the end, when Clayburgh falls into the arms of romantic SoHo painter Alan Bates. Nonetheless, Mazursky spares nobody and nothing with his comic darts. Some of the most hysterically funny scenes occur when Clayburgh and her three pals (Quinn, Bishop, and Miller) have regular luncheons in which they let down their hair and frankly talk about their sex lives.

UNTIL THE END OF THE WORLD

1991 178m c Science Fiction   ★★½
Trans Pacific Films/Road Movies Film/Argos Films/Village   R/15
Roadshow   (France/Germany/Australia)

William Hurt *(Trevor McPhee/Sam Farber)*, Solveig Dommartin *(Claire Tourneur)*, Sam Neill *(Eugene Fitzpatrick)*, Max Von Sydow *(Henry Farber)*, Rudiger Vogler *(Philip Winter)*, Ernie Dingo *(Burt)*, Jeanne Moreau *(Edith Farber)*, Lois Chiles *(Elsa)*, Chick Ortega *(Chico)*, Elena Smirnowa *(Krasikova)*

p, Jonathan Taplin; d, Wim Wenders; w, Wim Wenders, Peter Carey (from the story by Wenders and Solveig Dommartin); ph, Robby Muller; ed, Peter Przygodda; m, Graeme Revell; prod d, Thierry Flamand, Sally Campbell; art d, Ian Gracie; cos, Montserrat Casanova

Wim Wenders'S UNTIL THE END OF THE WORLD is really two movies, joined rather awkwardly at the hip. The first half of this three-hour marathon is an enjoyable, off-the-cuff road movie with a post-modernist, technological spin; the second is a half-baked, indulgent meditation on the nature of the recorded image.

The year is 1999, and the world is on the brink of a nuclear confrontation. Claire Tourneur (Solveig Dommartin), a disenchanted young bohemian, is involved in a lackluster relationship with novelist Eugene Fitzpatrick (Sam Neill). Driving across Europe on her way home from a decadent party, she has a car accident that involves her with two bank robbers, Chico and Raymond (Chick Ortega and Eddy Mitchell). Claire ends up agreeing to transport their heist to Paris in exchange for a cut of the proceeds. Then she meets Sam Farber (William Hurt), an enigmatic traveler who steals some of the loot from her car before going on his mysterious way. Enraged and intrigued, Claire sets off to track him down. Her quest takes her around the world in a cosmopolitan blur of languages, cultures and high-tech computer images, ending in the Australian outback, where Sam's father (Max von Sydow) has a laboratory.

Sam, it develops, has been using a special camera to collect images from his global trek. His father is working on a process that will enable Sam's mother (Jeanne Moreau) to "see" these images, even though she is blind. Convinced by an absence of radio signals that a nuclear holocaust has taken place, everyone devotes themselves to helping with Mr. Farber's experiments. Their work bears fruit; the machine not only gives sight to the blind but also allows users to view their dreams on screen. These beautiful images, however, prove dangerously addictive.

One of the most highly respected directors of the New German Cinema, Wim Wenders completed a remarkable trilogy of road movies—ALICE IN THE CITIES, WRONG MOVE and KINGS OF THE ROAD—early in his career, and made a partial return to the genre with PARIS, TEXAS. (His production company is even called Road Movies.) The themes which illuminated those earlier movies, though—the difficulty of communication, the nature of wanderlust, urban alienation—get skimpy treatment here. The first half of the film is a flip, engaging romp which offers us some stylish visuals and a knowing, *fin de siecle* attitude. Once the film gets bogged down in the outback, however, it comes to a virtual stop. Wenders seems to be saying something pretty banal about the emotional emptiness of the recorded image as opposed to the "real thing." If that's the point, why make a film at all? Worth seeing nevertheless, if only for the outstanding soundtrack and the nicely realized dream images.

UNTOUCHABLES, THE

1987 119m c Crime   ★★
Paramount   (U.S.)   R/15

Kevin Costner *(Eliot Ness)*, Sean Connery *(James Malone)*, Charles Martin Smith *(Oscar Wallace)*, Andy Garcia *(George Stone)*, Robert De Niro *(Al Capone)*, Richard Bradford *(Mike)*, Jack Kehoe *(Walter Payne)*, Brad Sullivan *(George)*, Billy Drago *(Frank Nitti)*, Patricia Clarkson *(Catherine Ness)*

p, Art Linson; d, Brian De Palma; w, David Mamet; ph, Stephen H. Burum; ed, Jerry Greenberg, Bill Pankow; m, Ennio Morricone; art d, William Elliott; cos, Marilyn Vance

AA Best Supporting Actor: Sean Connery; *AAN Best Score:* Ennio Morricone; *AAN Best Art Direction:* Patrizia Von Brandenstein, Hal Gausman; *AAN Best Costume Design:* Marilyn Vance-Straker

THE UNTOUCHABLES pits Chicago crime kingpin Al Capone (Robert De Niro) against mild-mannered Eliot Ness (Kevin Costner), a Treasury agent assigned to smash Capone's bootleg empire. Ness recruits wily street cop James Malone (Sean Connery), who knows the ins and outs of the Chicago underworld, after which more recruits are added to form the nucleus of what will later be known as "the untouchables"—lawmen who cannot be bought or corrupted. The whole thing is sloppy, a stew brewed by writer David Mamet and served steaming hot by director Brian De Palma as true crime history, which it is not. In real life, Ness and Capone never met, and Ness had nothing to do with getting the evidence that sent Capone to prison for income tax evasion. There is something cartoonish about THE UNTOUCHABLES, with De Niro doing an impersonation of Rod Steiger's excellent portrayal in CAPONE. Costner's interpretation is one of dreary indifference, without the forcefulness the role demands. Connery, however, is terrific as the wizened veteran cop.

UNZIPPED

1995 80m c Documentary   ★★★½
Hachette Filipacchi Productions/Elle Magazine   (U.S.)   R/15

Isaac Mizrahi, Nina Santisi, Eartha Kitt, Sandra Bernhard, Naomi Campbell, Mark Morris, Madonna, Roseanne

p, Michael Alden; d, Douglas Keeve; ph, Ellen Kuras; ed, Paula Heredia

Burned by Robert Altman's READY TO WEAR? Don't let that scare you away from UNZIPPED, a flossy, crowd-pleasing documentary about *haute couture*. The subject is designer Isaac Mizrahi, who's about to start a new collection and is desperately casting about for inspiration. It comes in the form of Loretta Young, radiant in a snowdrift, in 1935's CALL OF THE WILD. "Think Eskimos!" squeals the irrepressible Mizrahi, and the race against time is on. Supermodels, celebrity friends, opinionated magazine editors: Mizrahi eclipses them all with his bitchy wit and camp-inflected dedication to the ephemeral world of fashion. The only person who steals his spotlight is his kvelling mom, who knew her son was a genius when at age five he noticed the daisies on her shoes. And oh, that climactic fashion show: it's a genuine thrill.

UP IN ARMS

1944 106m c Musical/Comedy/War ★★★★
Goldwyn (U.S.) /U

Danny Kaye *(Danny Weems)*, Constance Dowling *(Mary Morgan)*, Dinah Shore *(Virginia Merrill)*, Dana Andrews *(Joe Nelson)*, Louis Calhern *(Col. Ashley)*, George Mathews *(Blackie)*, Benny Baker *(Butterball)*, Elisha Cook Jr. *(Info Jones)*, Lyle Talbot *(Sgt. Gelsey)*, Walter Catlett *(Maj. Brock)*

p, Don Hartman; d, Elliott Nugent; w, Don Hartman, Allen Boretz, Robert Pirosh (based on the play *The Nervous Wreck* by Owen Davis, Sr.); ph, Ray Rennahan; ed, Daniel Mandell, James E. Newcom; m, Ray Heindorf; art d, Perry Ferguson, Stewart Chaney, McClure Capps; fx, Clarence Slifer, Ray Binger; chor, Danny Dare

AAN Best Score: Louis Forbes, Ray Heindorf; *AAN Best Song:* Harold Arlen (Music), Ted Koehler (Lyrics)

This is the lavish musical comedy that introduced 31-year-old vaudeville and stage star Danny Kaye to the movie audience. He plays confirmed hypochondriac Danny Weems, who is so fearful of illness that he works as a medical building's elevator operator—if disease strikes, help is no more than a scream away. When Danny and his best pal, Joe (Dana Andrews), are drafted into the Army, he must tell the woman he loves, Mary (Constance Dowling), that they are going off to war. Accordingly, Mary—who really likes Joe—joins the WACs with her friend Virginia (Dinah Shore), who signs on as a nurse because, of course, she's in love with Danny. The boys are shipped out to the Far East, but fate and the screenwriters intervene when Mary and Virginia, who came to bid them goodbye, are trapped on the ship. Not being a nurse like Virginia, Mary must stow away to avoid court-martial, and is shunted around the ship to escape the eagle eye of the martinet captain (Louis Calhern). Soon enough, Mary is discovered, Danny takes the blame, and things look bleak as Danny is placed in an Army jail after the ship docks. Then the Japanese attack and take Danny prisoner, but in a series of wonderfully funny escapades our neurotic hero escapes and even manages to nab some of the enemy. Kaye's superb comic timing is already in full evidence, allowing him to dominate every scene. Excellent choreography, superb sets, fine costumes, and a host of songs (several by Harold Arlen and Ted Koehler) round out the enjoyment.

UP IN SMOKE

1978 86m c Comedy ★★★
Paramount (U.S.) R/

Richard "Cheech" Marin *(Pedro De Pacas)*, Tommy Chong *(Man Stoner)*, Stacy Keach *(Sgt. Stedenko)*, Tom Skerritt *(Strawberry)*, Edie Adams *(Tempest Stoner)*, Strother Martin *(Mr. Stoner)*, Louisa Moritz *(Officer Gloria)*, Zane Buzby *(Jade East)*, Anne Wharton *(Debbie)*, Mills Watson *(Harry)*

p, Lou Adler, Lou Lombardo; d, Lou Adler; w, Thomas Chong, Richard "Cheech" Marin; ph, Gene Polito, Jack Willoughby; ed, Lou Lombardo; art d, Leon Ericksen; fx, Knott Limited

"Up in smoke, that's where my money's gone." So goes the opening song of this weedfest/comedy, despised by most critics, parents and lovers of cinema but cherished by anyone who's ever had a bad case of the munchies. The story opens with Man Stoner (Tommy Chong) being tossed out of his parents' plush Hollywood Hills house only to stumble upon Pedro de Pacos ("Cheech" Marin), leader of a rock band and lover of "canabus." What ensues is an 86-minute ride from LA to Mexico and back, with our smoking heroes driving a van made entirely of "Fibreweed" (pure marijuana) across the border, outwitting the cops and the van's owners, and still managing to win a climactic "Battle of the Bands" contest.

The funniest of all the Cheech and Chong movies, UP IN SMOKE provides a feast of gags for the sympathetically minded. Best exchange, on the subject of Pedros's cousin: "He went to Vietnam and came back weirded out." "Nam grass can do weird things to you."

UPTOWN SATURDAY NIGHT

1974 104m c Comedy ★★★
First Artists (U.S.) PG

Sidney Poitier *(Steve Jackson)*, Bill Cosby *(Wardell Franklin)*, Flip Wilson *(The Reverend)*, Richard Pryor *(Sharp Eye Washington)*, Rosalind Cash *(Sarah Jackson)*, Roscoe Lee Browne *(Congressman Lincoln)*, Paula Kelly *(Leggy Peggy)*, Lee Chamberlin *(Mme. Zenobia)*, Johnny Sekka *(Geechie's Henchman)*

p, Melville Tucker; d, Sidney Poitier; w, Richard Wesley; ph, Fred Koenekamp; ed, Pembroke J. Herring; m, Tom Scott; prod d, Alfred Sweeney; fx, Charles Spurgeon

A fine comedy starring and directed by Sidney Poitier, who plays a bored factory worker. He, along with his taxi-driving friend, Cosby, decides to live it up one night, and they venture into a seedy, illegal, underground gambling den for some fun. While they are at the club, gangsters hold up the guests, making off with jewelry, cash, and wallets. When Poitier and Cosby learn that the lottery ticket in Poitier's stolen wallet happens to be worth $50,000, the desperate friends plunge headfirst into the criminal underworld to retrieve it. Pryor turns up as an incompetent private eye, Wilson is a preacher, Browne plays a shady black congressman, and Belafonte steals the movie with a hilarious parody of Marlon Brando's "Godfather" as the mobster who owns the town. The film spawned two sequels: LET'S DO IT AGAIN and A PIECE OF THE ACTION.

URBAN COWBOY

1980 135m c Drama ★★
Paramount (U.S.) PG/15

John Travolta *(Bud)*, Debra Winger *(Sissy)*, Scott Glenn *(Wes)*, Madolyn Smith *(Pam)*, Barry Corbin *(Uncle Bob)*, Brooke Alderson *(Aunt Corene)*, Cooper Huckabee *(Marshall)*, James Gammon *(Steve Strange)*, Betty Murphy *(Bud's Mom)*, Ed Geldart *(Bud's Dad)*

p, Robert Evans, Irving Azoff; d, James Bridges; w, James Bridges, Aaron Latham (based on a story by Latham); ph, Reynaldo Villalobos; ed, David Rawlins; m, Ralph Burns; prod d, Stephen Grimes; art d, Stewart Campbell; chor, Patsy Swayze

If you can accept John Travolta as a Texan, half the problems of URBAN COWBOY have been surmounted. Here he plays a country boy who ventures to the big city to work at an oil refinery. Soon he's immersed in the nightlife that revolves around Gilley's, a cavernous honky-tonk with a famous mechanical bull. He meets sexy Debra Winger and, after a brief, intense courtship, the two are married. Problems, however, soon plague the relationship. Aside from Winger's winning performance, not much else here is interesting, save for Scott Glenn's solid portrayal of a heavy. Director James Bridges fails to instill much life into a narrative peopled with vapid characters.

USED CARS

1980 113m c Comedy ★★★½
Columbia (U.S.) R/15

Kurt Russell *(Rudy Russo)*, Jack Warden *(Roy L. Fuchs/Luke Fuchs)*, Gerrit Graham *(Jeff)*, Frank McRae *(Jim, the Mechanic)*, Deborah Harmon *(Barbara Fuchs)*, Joe Flaherty *(Sam Slaton)*, David L. Lander *(Freddie Paris)*, Michael McKean *(Eddie Winslow)*, Michael Talbott *(Mickey)*, Harry Northrup *(Carmine)*

p, Bob Gale; d, Robert Zemeckis; w, Robert Zemeckis, Bob Gale; ph, Donald Morgan; ed, Michael Kahn; m, Patrick Williams; prod d, Peter Jamison

Before director-writer Bob Zemeckis found success with blockbuster hits ROMANCING THE STONE and BACK TO THE FUTURE, he directed this raunchy, hysterically funny comedy. Kurt Russell turns in a brilliant performance as Rudy Russo, the unscrupulous but likable head salesman of a dying used car lot owned by Roy L. Fuchs (Jack Warden). Roy's brother, Luke (also played by Warden), owns a successful car lot across the street and is conspiring to get Roy's property. When Roy dies Rudy and his colleague Jeff (Gerrit Graham) try to conceal the death from Roy's daughter (Deborah Harmon) and Luke.

Filled with riotous plot twists and effective black humor, this is a truly inventive and memorable comedy, which was virtually ignored at the box office. Fans of television's "Hill Street Blues" may want to look for Betty Thomas as a topless dancer (a role she would no doubt like to forget) bumping and grinding in one of the R-rated commercials with which Rudy jams a Presidential address.

USUAL SUSPECTS, THE

1995   96m   c   Crime/Thriller   ★★★
Rosco Film GmbH/Blue Parrott Productions/Bad Hat Harry   R/18
Productions/PolyGram/Spellings Films International   (U.S.)

Kevin Spacey *(Roger "Verbal" Kint)*, Chazz Palminteri *(Kujan)*, Stephen Baldwin *(McManus)*, Gabriel Byrne *(Dean Keaton)*, Benicio Del Toro *(Fenster)*, Kevin Pollak *(Hockney)*, Pete Postlethwaite *(Kobayashi)*, Suzy Amis *(Edie)*, Giancarlo Esposito *(Jack Baer)*, Dan Hedaya *(Sgt. Rabin)*

p, Bryan Singer, Michael McDonnell; d, Bryan Singer; w, Christopher McQuarrie; ph, Newton Thomas Sigel; ed, John Ottman; m, John Ottman; prod d, Howard Cummings; art d, David Lazan; fx, Roy Downey; cos, Louise Mingenbach

AA Best Supporting Actor: Kevin Spacey; *AA Best Original Screenplay:* Christopher McQuarrie

This twisty and twisted yarn, one of the more successful entries in the post-Tarantino cycle of hip, violent crime flicks, marks a promising major-league debut for director Bryan Singer.

Special investigator Kujan (Chazz Palminteri) grills "Verbal" Kint (Kevin Spacey), a crippled con-man who is the lone survivor of an LA boat explosion that claimed more than 20 victims. Kujan wants to confirm that his nemesis, the rogue cop Keaton (Gabriel Byrne), is actually dead. Kint relates the majority of the film in flashback, beginning with the fateful day when five shifty guys meet in a police-station lineup in New York City. Along with dour Keaton, Kint encounters cheerfully sociopathic McManus (Stephen Baldwin), mordantly sarcastic Hockney (Kevin Pollak), and Fenster (Benicio Del Toro), whose speech is virtually incomprehensible. Together they plot to steal a small fortune in gems from "New York's Finest Taxi Service"—crooked cops who provide escort service for visiting drug kingpins. What follows is a shell-game of violence and betrayal, all hinging on the identity of a mysterious villain called Keyser Soze.

THE USUAL SUSPECTS is an intricately plotted, densely layered story, and although the resolution of Soze's identity is dramatically fulfilling—and not all that surprising—it has the effect of undermining the entire narrative. But fans of taut, self-consciously clever puzzles will find this film a delightful excursion, full of talented actors having great fun with their quirky, nasty characters. Pollak shines early, though his good lines diminish as the film progresses, and Baldwin is surprisingly chilling. Byrne holds the center with his patented brooding intensity, and Del Toro is simply hysterical as a jumble of visual and verbal tics. But it's Spacey who carries the weight of the film, and he rises admirably to the challenge of epitomizing pure evil with a blandly human face.

UTU

1983   104m   c   Drama   ★★★½
Utu/NZ Film Commission   (New Zealand)   R/15

Anzac Wallace *(Te Wheke)*, Bruno Lawrence *(Williamson)*, Kelly Johnson *(Lt. Scott)*, Wi Kuki Kaa *(Wiremu)*, Tim Elliot *(Col. Elliot)*, Ilona Rodgers *(Emily)*, Tania Bristowe *(Kura)*, Martyn Sanderson *(Vicar)*, Faenza Reuben *(Henare)*, John Bach *(Belcher)*

p, Geoff Murphy, Don Blakeney; d, Geoff Murphy; w, Geoff Murphy, Keith Aberdein; ph, Graeme Cowley; ed, Michael Horton, Ian John; m, John Charles; prod d, Ron Highfield; art d, Rick Kofoed; cos, Michael Kane

One of the best films yet to emerge from the budding New Zealand cinema, UTU (Maori for "retribution") deals with the British colonial presence on the islands in the 1870s. Te Wheke (Anzac Wallace) is a Maori in the service of the British army as a scout and guide. One day, while going about his scouting duties, he comes across a village that the British have wiped out in a massacre. It is Wheke's own village, and he then deserts the British to seek revenge against them. With a

small group of similarly angry renegades, he launches a campaign of terror and murder against the British. When they attack an isolated farm, murdering the woman of the house and burning it to the ground, Williamson (Bruno Lawrence) also takes up the search for revenge. Wallace, his face covered with ritual tattoos, is a superb actor, and his conversion from loyal British subject to killer is quite believable. Lawrence, the star of most of the successful films to come from New Zealand, is similarly excellent as he is driven to revenge for the same reasons. The most expensive film in New Zealand's history, UTU was a major success at home and abroad.

VAGABOND
(SANS TOIT NI LOI)

1985   105m   c   Drama   ★★★½
Cine Tamaris/Ministere de la Culture/A2   (France)   /18

Sandrine Bonnaire *(Mona)*, Macha Meril *(Madame Landier)*, Stephane Freiss *(Jean-Pierre)*, Laurence Cortadellas *(Elaine)*, Marthe Jarnias *(Tante Lydie)*, Yolande Moreau *(Yolande)*, Joel Fosse *(Paulo)*, Patrick Lepcynski, Yahiaoui Assouna, Setti Ramdane

p, Oury Milshtein; d, Agnes Varda; w, Agnes Varda; ph, Patrick Blossier; ed, Agnes Varda, Patricia Mazuy; m, Joanna Bruzdowicz

Atmospheric, cold, and distancing, yet somehow engaging, VAGABOND combines a stylized documentary technique with the fictional vision of writer-director Agnes Varda. The picture opens in the dead of winter, as a farmhand discovers a woman's frozen corpse in a ditch—her long hair a tangle of knots, her skin hidden beneath a well-worn leather jacket and filthy blue jeans. This was Mona (Bonnaire), a fiercely independent "vagabond" whose last weeks are reconstructed in flashback and in "interviews" (both with actors and nonprofessionals Varda found during shooting) with people who met Mona. It soon becomes clear, however, that no one really knew her. Mona is not a character many will entirely like or identify with, nor is one expected to. Varda presents her story without any sentiment, and in the process she tells the stories of a number of different people whose lives were altered, perhaps permanently, by their contact with the vagabond.

After working in the shadow of the more popular French New Wave directors for years, the then 57-year-old Varda broke new ground in narrative film with her methods in VAGABOND. Her visual prowess is on ample display as well, potently rendering a rich portrait of Mona and her world. Equal credit for the movie's success, however, must go to Bonnaire, who perfectly transforms herself into the filthy, aimless, and enigmatic wanderer that the role calls for. Bonnaire justly won a French Cesar for her remarkable performance, and the film itself took the Golden Lion for Best Picture at the Venice Film Festival.

VALLEY GIRL

1983   95m   c   Romance   ★★★½
Atlantic   (U.S.)   R/15

Nicolas Cage *(Randy)*, Deborah Foreman *(Julie Richman)*, Elizabeth Daily *(Loryn)*, Michael Bowen *(Tommy)*, Cameron Dye *(Fred)*, Heidi Holicker *(Stacey)*, Michelle Meyrink *(Suzie)*, Tina Theberge *(Samantha)*, Lee Purcell *(Beth Brent)*, Colleen Camp *(Sarah Richman)*

p, Wayne Crawford, Andrew Lane; d, Martha Coolidge; w, Wayne Crawford, Andrew Lane; ph, Frederick Elmes; ed, Eva Gordos; m, Scott Wilk, Marc Levinthal; prod d, Mary Delia Javier

Insightful and genuine, VALLEY GIRL tells the unlikely tale of Julie (Deborah Foreman), a deb from the Valley, and Randy (Nicholas Cage), a punk rocker from Hollywood, falling in love. As prom time approaches, Julie bows to pressure from her friends to stop dating the "creep" from "Hollyweird." She dumps Randy for her old boyfriend, Tommy (Michael Bowen), a mindless jock. Randy tries a number of unsuccessful stunts to win her back, then reluctantly decides to go to the prom and force a confrontation. This simplified Romeo and Juliet tale was written and performed with such heart and care that it is impossible to dislike. The cast is wonderful, headed by the engaging couple of Cage and Foreman and wittily directed by Coolidge. VALLEY GIRL also boasts an eclectic pop score that features songs by Modern English, Josie Cotton, Men at Work, The Plimsouls, Sparks, Psychedelic Furs, and Eddie Grant, among others.

VALLEY OF THE DOLLS

1967 123m c Drama   ★★
Red Lion (U.S.)   GP/

Barbara Parkins (*Anne Welles*), Patty Duke (*Neely O'Hara*), Paul Burke (*Lyon Burke*), Sharon Tate (*Jennifer North*), Tony Scotti (*Tony Polar*), Martin Milner (*Mel Anderson*), Charles Drake (*Kevin Gilmore*), Alexander Davion (*Ted Casablanca*), Lee Grant (*Miriam*), Naomi Stevens (*Miss Steinberg*)

p, David Weisbart; d, Mark Robson; w, Helen Deutsch, Dorothy Kingsley (based on the novel by Jacqueline Susann); ph, William Daniels; ed, Dorothy Spencer; m, John Williams; art d, Jack Martin Smith, Richard Day; fx, L.B. Abbott, Art Cruickshank, Emil Kosa Jr.; chor, Robert Sidney; cos, Travilla

AAN Best Score: John Williams

Pure trash, based on a trashy book, filled to the brim with trashy performances, now becoming a trashy cult film. Based on Jacqueline Susann's novel detailing the horrors of stardom (the author has a bit part as a journalist, which she has trouble pulling off), the film stars Tate, Parkins, and Duke as three aspiring actresses who each attain a degree of success followed by a dependence on pills (nicknamed "dolls"). Tate, who is told by everyone she meets that she has no talent but a great body, meets and marries a young singer, Scotti, who soon is stricken with a fatal illness requiring expensive hospitalization. To pay the bills, Tate appears in European porno films and becomes quite a sensation. Unfortunately, she soon discovers she has breast cancer and needs to have her "talent" removed. Realizing there is no future in porno after such surgery, Tate kills herself by taking an overdose of sleeping pills.

Duke, meanwhile, (who turns in the worst performance of the three, only because she is capable of so much more) lands a minor part in a new Broadway show opposite aging superstar Hayward (who replaced the originally cast Judy Garland, a dropout despite the perquisites proffered by the studio, including the dressing-room pool table she had demanded). The ambitious newcomer makes herself such a nuisance that she soon finds herself out of a job. As luck would have it, Duke winds up doing a quick singing spot on a national television fundraiser and becomes a superstar overnight (oh, sure). Of course, her sudden success leads to a horrible drug addiction that eventually turns her into a pathetic, whining has-been who *should* commit suicide to end the audience's suffering. Unfortunately, she doesn't.

Not all success stories are grim, however, as we follow the likable Parkins from her small East Coast town to New York where she hits it big as a model. This, once again, leads to a bout with the ever-present pills and an unstable love life, but Parkins eventually finds the inner strength to abandon her success and hightail it back to her hometown before she winds up as just another tragic statistic. Banal, ignorant, crass and just plain lousy, this film went on to gross over $20 million, becoming one of 20th Century-Fox's biggest hits ever and reaffirming the belief that the public deserves what it gets.

VAMPYR

(VAMPYR, OU L'ETRANG E AVENTURE DE DAVID GRAY)

1932 83m bw Horror   ★★★★★
Dreyer/Tobis/Klangfilm (France/Germany)

Julian West (*David Gray*), Henriette Gerard (*Marguerite Chopin*), Jan Hieronimko (*Doctor*), Maurice Schutz (*Lord of the Manor*), Rena Mandel (*His Daughter Gisele*), Sybille Schmitz (*His Daughter Leone*), Albert Bras (*Servant*), N. Babanini (*The Girl*), Jane Mora (*The Religious Woman*)

p, Baron Nicolas de Gunzberg, Carl-Theodor Dreyer; d, Carl-Theodor Dreyer; w, Carl-Theodor Dreyer, Christen Jul (based on stories from *In a Glass Darkly* by Joseph Sheridan Le Fanu); ph, Rudolph Mate, Louis Nee; m, Wolfgang Zeller; art d, Hermann Warm, Hans Bittmann, Cesare Silvagni

Much to the dismay of his admirers, Danish filmmaker Dreyer followed his silent masterpiece THE PASSION OF JOAN OF ARC with a horror film. The result, his first foray into sound, was the greatest vampire film ever made and one of the few undisputed masterpieces of the horror genre. Thrillseekers, beware, though, because it's not that kind of film. VAMPYR, rather, is subtly unsettling rather than gory or shocking; it is such stuff as nightmares are made of.

Loosely based on the Le Fanu collection of stories, *In a Glass Darkly*, the film begins as young David Gray (West) arrives in a dark, mysterious European village and takes a room at the inn. That night a strange old man (Schutz) gives gives him a package to be opened in the event of his death. David later witnesses many strange events, among which is the murder of the old man. David meets the dead man's daughters (Schmitz and Mandel) and opens the package, which contains a copy of *Strange Tales of Vampires*. Realizing that the town is at the mercy of one of the undead (Gerard), David struggles to save himself and the two young women.

Such are the bare bones of the plot, but its unfolding, leisurely and fragmented, is not of tantamount importance. What really matters are features like the muffled offscreen sounds and the lack of dialogue explaining them; the misty shooting style (achieved via filters and by working at dawn); and Zeller's spare but sinister music (a highlight is his "Shadow Polka"). The sequence using this music subtly suggests the vampire's power. Angry at the villagers's revels she cannot join, she stands alone, framed in silhouette by a doorway and with large wheels around her. She shrieks for quiet and, without a cutaway, Dreyer lets us her command has been obeyed. Another sequence, in which the one-legged gamekeeper's shadow leaves his body behind to do the vampire's bidding, is also left unexplained. Throughout VAMPYR, a deep, muffling sense of terror slowly envelops both village and viewer, reinforced by Dreyer's brilliantly disjunctive construction of space. Mate's cinematography creates many memorable images, from the scythe-bearer by the water to the tainted elder sister awakening to the call of bloodlust as she eyes her innocent sibling. The marvelous Schmidt (remembered in the title role of Frank Wysbar's classic FERRYMAN MARIA), in the difficult role of the semi-vampire daughter, makes this moment one of the most horrific in the entire film. Best of all, though, are two more famous sequences. The doctor, one of the vampire's accomplices, meets his doom in a flour mill, smothered by the cascading (and purifying) white dust as the agonizingly slow workings of fate and the machinery take their toll. Earlier, David, after donating blood to help a victim, dreams of his own burial. Handled largely from David's view, with the sealing of the coffin lid, the ride to the cemetery and the icy glimpse of the elderly vampiress through the coffin window, this imitated but never duplicated sequence must rank among the greatest uses of point-of-view camera ever filmed. Sensual but remote and vague, gripping and yet somehow unsatisfying, VAMPYR is yet another of Dreyer's brilliant meditations on faith, love and salvation. For him, the vampire's curse haunts the soul foremost, and this unique film experience is likely to haunt your memory long after the film runs out.

VANISHING, THE

(SPOORLOOS)

1986 120m c Mystery/Drama   ★★★★
Golden Egg Films/MGS Film/Ingrid Productions (Netherlands) /12

Gene Bervoets (*Rex Hofman*), Johanna Ter Steege (*Saskia Wagter*), Bernard-Pierre Donnadieu (*Raymond Lemorne*), Gwen Eckhaus (*Lienexe*), Bernadette LeSache (*Simone Lemorne*), Tania Latarjet (*Denise*), Lucille Glenn (*Gabrielle*), Roger Souza (*Manager*), Caroline Apperre (*Cashier*), Pierre Forget (*Farmer Laurent*)

p, Anne Lordon, George Sluizer; d, George Sluizer; w, George Sluizer, Tim Krabbe (adapted from his novel *The Golden Egg*); ph, Toni Kuhn; ed, George Sluizer, Lin Friedman; m, Henry Vrienten; art d, Santiago Isidro Pin, Cor Spijk; cos, Sophie Dussaud

Through some fiendish alchemy, THE VANISHING manages to scare people out of their wits more effectively than a legion of better-known horror films. This Dutch production has a pleasantly efficient veneer to it that hides a truly awesome undercurrent.

Two young Dutch lovers are motoring through France. They are flushed with optimism and affection for each other. While arguing playfully, Saskia Wagter (Johanna Ter Steege), the young woman, tells Rex Hofman (Gene Bervoets), the young man, her recurring dream. She is trapped in a golden egg in the midst of darkness with no hope of escaping. Recently, she tells Rex, she has dreamt of another egg traveling beside her. When their car stalls in the middle of a dark tunnel, Saskia has an emotional explosion of claustrophobia and abandonment. Her lover cruelly neglects her, going off to get some gas. Returning, the two make up quickly. They stop at a nearby gas station. Saskia goes to make a purchase in the store. Rex waits for her outside. She never comes back. Three years later Rex is still searching for Saskia. As Rex searches, the audience is introduced to Raymond Lemorne (Bernard-Pierre Donnadieu) who, through different time frames, slowly reveals Saskia's fate. It is only in the last few moments of the film that the mystery is fully revealed to us. And those moments are deeply horrific.

The choice of actors in this film is uncanny. Johanna Ter Steege's vanished Saskia is luminous in her opening scenes. Her presence continues to haunt the film after her disappearance. And Bernard-Pierre Donnadieu as Raymond Lemorne does a remarkable job. Lemorne is a sociopath and, unlike the scores of other movie villains, Donnadieu's Lemorne's humanity is not a conceit. His beneficence makes his monstrousness even more hard to take. The director, George Sluizer, lets the whole film play out in a contemporary world of freeways, efficiency lighting and sports commentary spilling over from the radio. Into this banal universe he plays out themes that haven't been so effectively conjured up since the early 60s. Sluizer himself directed a predictably inferior American remake released in 1993.

VANYA ON 42ND STREET

1994 119m c Drama ★★★
The Vanya Company/Laura Pels Productions/New Media
Finance (U.S.) PG/U

Wallace Shawn *(Vanya Voynitsky)*, Julianne Moore *(Yelena)*, Brooke Smith *(Sonya)*, Larry Pine *(Dr. Michael Astrov)*, George Gaynes *(Alexander Serybryakov)*, Lynn Cohen *(Maman)*, Phoebe Brand *(Marina)*, Jerry Mayer *(Waffles)*, Madhur Jaffrey *(Mrs. Chao)*, Andre Gregory *(Himself)*

p, Fred Berner; d, Louis Malle; w, David Mamet (based on the play *Uncle Vanya* by Anton Chekhov); ph, Declan Quinn; ed, Nancy Baker; m, Joshua Redman; prod d, Eugene Lee; cos, Gary Jones

Wallace Shawn, Andre Gregory, and director Louis Malle, the brain trust behind MY DINNER WITH ANDRE, concoct a staged reading of *Uncle Vanya* in Broadway's condemned New Amsterdam Theater, amid the incongruous dilapidation of Times Square.

As the camera roves the abandoned grandeur of the opera-house interior, and the actors prattle and nosh, Andre Gregory, as the play's director, bids us take our seats and we slip effortlessly into a walk-through of the play. Vanya Voynitsky—Uncle Vanya (Wallace Shawn)—is a dreamer in his late 40s, living with his mother (Lynn Cohen) on the estate of Alexander Serybryakov (George Gaynes), a great man and revered thinker in the autumn of his life, whose first wife was Vanya's sister. The marriage produced a daughter, the plain and pure Sonya (Brooke Smith), whose hopes rest on Michael Astrov, the local doctor (Larry Pine). Meanwhile, everyone else's attentions reside with Yelena (vivid Julianne Moore), the 27-year-old beauty who is the professor's second wife.

Louis Malle's direction is elegant and unobtrusive, but this movie (based on an invitation-only workshop production that was celebrated as much for its trendy exclusivity as for its quality) is essentially a filmed record of a work by Gregory and Shawn. Briefly the thinking person's Abbott and Costello after the surprise success of MY DINNER WITH ANDRE, Shawn and Gregory never appear together here, but their mildly arty, anachronistic sensibility—closer to the WWI-era bohemianism of the Provincetown Players than any contemporary avant-garde—pervades the piece. While they want us to admire their boldness in staging *Vanya* as an ironically distanced, modern-dress

sitcom, in fact they chose the safest possible approach to the material. While there are moments of considerable power here—due in particular to standout performances by Moore and Smith—this stripped-down rendering gives us something more like a latterday dysfunctional family than Chekhov's doomed bourgeosie.

VERA CRUZ

1954 94m c Western ★★★
Hecht/Hill/Lancaster (U.S.) /A

Gary Cooper *(Benjamin Trane)*, Burt Lancaster *(Joe Erin)*, Denise Darcel *(Countess Marie Duvarre)*, Cesar Romero *(Marquis de Labordere)*, Sarita Montiel *(Nina)*, George Macready *(Emperor Maximilian)*, Ernest Borgnine *(Donnegan)*, Morris Ankrum *(Gen. Aguilar)*, Henry Brandon *(Danette)*, Charles Bronson *(Pittsburgh)*

p, James Hill; d, Robert Aldrich; w, Roland Kibbee, James R. Webb (based on the story by Borden Chase); ph, Ernest Laszlo; ed, Alan Crosland Jr.; m, Hugo Friedhofer

This broadly played, action-packed western teams Cooper and Lancaster as two American soldiers of fortune on a foray into Mexico during the revolution of 1866. Cooper, a former Confederate major, and Lancaster, a constantly grinning outlaw, leave the US in search of mercenary work. It doesn't matter to them which side they fight for, as long as it pays better than the other. In Mexico they meet a beautiful young girl, Montiel, who falls for Cooper and begs him and his partner to fight for Juarez and the revolutionaries. The American gunslingers are tugged in the opposite direction by Romero, a supporter of Maximilian, who offers them huge sums of cash. While mulling the offers over, Cooper and Lancaster encounter Darcel, a seductive and extremely rich countess who asks them to escort her while she transports a gold shipment from Mexico City to Maximilian's forces in Vera Cruz. The men agree and quickly assemble a motley crew of gunfighters and government regulars to accompany them through the rough territory. On the trail, the wily Darcel suggests that they steal the gold and split it three ways. The Americans agree to the plan, with each suspecting the other of planning double crosses. Maximilian loyalist Romero discovers the plot and takes off with the gold to make sure it gets delivered. The Americans chase Romero to the fort in Vera Cruz, and after a bloody battle, Lancaster manages to get his hands on the gold. Cooper, however, has had a change of heart due to Montiel's revolutionary fervor, and demands Lancaster hand over the gold to Juarez's forces. Lancaster doesn't buy Cooper's commitment to the revolution and refuses to release the gold. Cooper is forced to kill Lancaster in a showdown and then gives the gold to Montiel.

The film is directed with an emphasis on action by Aldrich (who had just guided Lancaster through APACHE the year before), and most of the actors in VERA CRUZ are allowed to ham it up quite a bit. For contrast there is Cooper, forever the tight-lipped, serious professional wary of those around him, especially Lancaster's grinning gunman. The film was produced by Lancaster's own company on a budget of $1.7 million and became quite a hit, grossing more than $11 million worldwide, though critical opinion at the time was extremely negative. Lancaster gladly gave top billing to Cooper, well aware of the older actor's box-office pull. As is typical with director Aldrich's work, the violence is well staged and frequent, going a bit overboard at times specifically with regard to Darcel, who is shown being slapped and knocked about by Lancaster more than once. Aldrich and Lancaster would collaborate again in the 1970s with ULZANA'S RAID and TWILIGHT'S LAST GLEAMING.

VERDICT, THE

1982 129m c Drama ★★★★
Fox (U.S.) R/15

Paul Newman *(Frank Galvin)*, Charlotte Rampling *(Laura Fischer)*, Jack Warden *(Mickey Morrissey)*, James Mason *(Ed Concannon)*, Milo O'Shea *(Judge Hoyle)*, Lindsay Crouse *(Kaitlin Costello Price)*, Edward Binns *(Bishop Brophy)*, Julie Bovasso *(Maureen Rooney)*, Roxanne Hart *(Sally Doneghy)*, James Handy *(Kevin Doneghy)* p, Richard D. Zanuck, David Brown; d, Sidney Lumet; w, David Mamet (based on the novel by Barry Reed); ph, Andrzej Bartkowiak; ed, Peter C. Frank; m, Johnny Mandel; prod d, Edward Pisoni; art d, John Kasarda; cos, Anna Hill Johnstone

AAN Best Picture; AAN Best Actor: Paul Newman; *AAN Best Supporting Actor:* James Mason; *AAN Best Director:* Sidney Lumet; *AAN Best Adapted Screenplay:* David Mamet

This powerful study of a man's fight to regain his dignity features a fine performance from Paul Newman as failed attorney Frank Galvin. He takes on a seemingly open-and-shut case of malpractice, in which a woman lapsed into a coma while having a baby, the apparent victim of a mistake by an anesthesiologist at a prominent Catholic hospital in Boston. At first willing to take a settlement for the victim's family, Galvin realizes after visiting the comatose woman that he should put up a fight on her behalf. Up against the powerful Catholic establishment of Boston, he works to build a case, and, with it, renewed self-respect. He is also battling his dependence on alcohol, another reason behind his downfall. Newman's portrayal of his character is a sympathetic and totally candid performance. Every wart shows, from his alcoholism to the ill-prepared opening statement he delivers in a nervous stammer to the packed courtroom. Small moments come across as something special, and the actor received a well-deserved Oscar nomination for his performance. Sidney Lumet directs effectively, keeping the tension strong, and unfolding David Mamet's intelligent screenplay slowly but with maximum impact.

VERONIKA VOSS
(DIE SEHNS UCHT DER VERONIKA VOSS)

1982 105m bw Drama   ★★★★
Rialto/Maran/Larua/Tango   (West Germany)   R/AA

Rosel Zech *(Veronika Voss)*, Hilmar Thate *(Robert Krohn)*, Cornelia Froboess *(Henriette)*, Annemarie Duringer *(Dr. Katz)*, Doris Schade *(Josefa)*, Erik Schumann *(Dr. Edel)*, Peter Berling *(Fat Film Producer)*, Gunther Kaufmann *(G.I. Dealer)*, Sonja Neudorfer *(Saleswoman)*, Lilo Pempeit *(Her Boss)*

p, Thomas Schuhly; d, Rainer Werner Fassbinder; w, Peter Marthesheimer, Pia Frohlich, Rainer Werner Fassbinder; ph, Xaver Schwarzenberger; ed, Juliane Lorenz; m, Peer Raben; prod d, Rolf Zehetbauer

At the very end of his amazing yet tragically short career, Fassbinder still gives us his Douglas Sirk-influenced view of the world, except this time colored with Billy Wilder's SUNSET BOULEVARD and Robert Aldrich's THE LEGEND OF LYLAH CLARE for good measure. The result, in typical Fassbinder fashion, is a visually incredible portrait of German corruption as well as the UFA star system and the loneliness of once-famous screen star Veronika Voss (Zech). The fading star is drawn into an affair with sportswriter Robert Krohn (Thate), who soon discovers the actress's dependency on drugs. Her doctor (Duringer) fuels her addiction, forcing Voss to turn over all of her personal property in exchange for more morphine. Krohn and his girlfriend bring the doctor to the attention of the authorities, unaware that they, too, are involved in the doctor's scheme. On Easter Sunday, Voss is locked in her room by the doctor. Suffering from withdrawal symptoms after being refused morphine, she is given enough sleeping pills to kill herself. Zech is quite remarkable at the film's close.

One of the most stylish of Fassbinder's many films, VERONIKA VOSS features dizzying camerawork and stark black-and-white photography. Not among Fassbinder's greatest achievements, this striking film is nonetheless a worthy companion piece to his earlier two films about postwar Germany, THE MARRIAGE OF MARIA BRAUN and LOLA. The actual story is loosely based on the life of Sybille Schmitz (VAMPYR, FERRYMAN MARIA) a gifted German film star who committed suicide in the mid-1950s, unable to cope with the loss of her celebrity.

VERTIGO

1958 127m c Thriller   ★★★★★
Paramount   (U.S.)   /PG

James Stewart *(John "Scottie" Ferguson)*, Kim Novak *(Madeleine Elster/Judy Barton)*, Barbara Bel Geddes *(Midge)*, Tom Helmore *(Gavin Elster)*, Henry Jones *(Coroner)*, Raymond Bailey *(Doctor)*, Ellen Corby *(Manageress)*, Konstantin Shayne *(Pop Leibel)*, Lee Patrick *(Older Mistaken Identity)*, Paul Bryar *(Capt. Hansen)*

p, Alfred Hitchcock; d, Alfred Hitchcock; w, Alec Coppel, Samuel Taylor (based on the novel *D'Entre les Morts* by Pierre Boileau and Thomas Narcejac); ph, Robert Burks; ed, George Tomasini; m, Bernard Herrmann; art d, Hal Pereira, Henry Bumstead; fx, John P. Fulton, Farciot Edouart, Wallace Kelly; cos, Edith Head

AAN Best Art Direction: Hal Pereira, Henry Bumstead, Sam Comer, Frank McKelvy; *AAN Best Sound:* George Dutton

The most-discussed work of the master; despairingly sardonic and demanding of multiple viewings. Hitchcock's intensely personal and frighteningly self-revealing picture, VERTIGO is the story of a man (Stewart as Hitch) who is possessed by the image of a former love (Novak as Vera Miles) and becomes increasingly compulsive in his attempts to make another woman (Novak as Novak) over in that image. We'll explain.

Stewart is a former San Francisco policeman who suffers from vertigo—a dizzying sensation brought on by his acrophobia. When he gets a call from a former classmate, shipping magnate Gavin Elster (Helmore), he agrees to play detective and shadow the millionaire's wife Madeleine (Novak) whom Elster fears is going to wind up dead. Elster ominously asks him "Do you believe that someone dead, someone out of the past, can take possession of a living being?" After following Madeleine for a short while Stewart becomes obsessed with her—lost deep in a labyrinthine plot from which he cannot escape.

Based on a novel by Pierre Boileau and Thomas Narcejac (who previously supplied the source material for DIABOLIQUE), VERTIGO appealed to Hitchcock for reasons which become clearer the more one knows about the director's personality. VERTIGO is, in fact, nothing less than Hitchcock revealing himself to his audience—his obsessions and desire to make over women are embodied in Stewart's character and the perfect Hitchcock woman is embodied in Madeleine. VERTIGO is also a masterpiece of filmmaking which includes one of the most important technical discoveries since the dawn of cinema—the dolly-out, zoom-in shot, which visually represents the dizzying sensation of vertigo. The result is a shot unique to Hitchcock, unlike any other before it in film, one which will always bear his stamp.

But more than that, the behind-the-scenes preparation of VERTIGO resembles the story itself. Hitchcock had directed Vera Miles in THE WRONG MAN, and stood poised to make her a star in VERTIGO. This would be, of course, according to Hitchcock tradition: the cool blonde, whose whorish carnality is hidden beneath sleekly understated clothes and simple hair. But his plan went awry when Miles married after filming was over and soon became pregnant ("I lost interest. I couldn't get the rhythm going with her again," said Hitchcock in an interview, but later he threw her a bone in PSYCHO). He convinced Novak to take the role; her somnambulistic quality made her very effective in the role, but he and Edith Head had hell convincing her to tone down.

Yet perhaps Novak is the unsung quintessential Hitch-heroine. Hitchcock himself described Stewart's character's obsession with Novak's as a "form of necrophilia"; it's chilling when you think of the director re-creating his dreamgirl again and again. Novak's heroine is degraded by suffusing her own idenity to become what men want her to be. Did she feel degraded when Hitchcock and Head tried to bury the established Novak? Did it make her feel like a cheap pawn, forced to impersonate a lady, that is in itself an impersonation, within the confines of an acting job (an impersonation anyway)? And how much of her real self—Marilyn Novik—had fused with the manufactured Kim Novak? The latter was a star persona placed in an impossible-to-please situation in the first place. Groomed as a successor to Hayworth and a threat to Monroe, it's small wonder Novak fled the film industry to hide in Big Sur. To examine her within the context of VERTIGO is another dizzying vortex—a virtual vertigo in itself.

VICTIM

1961 100m bw Crime ★★★★
Parkway/Allied (U.K.) /15

Dirk Bogarde *(Melville Farr)*, Sylvia Syms *(Laura Farr)*, Dennis Price *(Calloway)*, Anthony Nicholls *(Lord Fullbrook)*, Peter Copley *(Paul Mandrake)*, Norman Bird *(Harold Doe)*, Peter McEnery *(Jack Barrett)*, Donald Churchill *(Eddy Stone)*, Derren Nesbitt *(Sandy Youth)*, John Barrie *(Detective Inspector Harris)*

p, Michael Relph; d, Basil Dearden; w, Janet Green, John McCormick; ph, Otto Heller; ed, John D. Guthridge; m, Philip Green; art d, Alex Vetchinsky

A powerful film that deals with homosexuality in England and the fact that most of the blackmail cases in that country were aimed against men trying to stay in the closet. In 1961, any homosexual acts were illegal and, while this film was hardly an overt plea to change the laws, it did have some impact; a few years later homosexuality was no longer punishable by time in jail. Bogarde, in one of the best roles of his career to date, plays Melville Farr, a closeted lawyer aware of his own homosexual desires. He is married now to Laura (Syms), who knows about his past affairs but accepts him nonetheless. Some years before, Farr had an affair with construction worker Jack Barrett (McEnery) but denies it. Barrett is now a wanted man, having stolen money from his building company. When he's caught by the police, the truth emerges that Barrett doesn't have a brass farthing to his name. Since a great deal of money had been purloined, this sets the law to wondering where it all went. Barrett needs a lawyer and tries to contact Farr, but the eminent queen's counsel avoids him. When Barrett hangs himself rather than answer any police questions, Farr realizes that his former lover was being blackmailed and that Barrett was trying to protect Farr's good name. The blackmailers are extracting money from several people, including a barber, an actor, a used car salesman and a photographer. (The film earnestly tries to avoid stereotyping, though to some extent these "victims" do represent a variety of "types".) Although it may damage both his career and his marriage, Farr decides to go after the blackmailers and prosecute them himself.

Immensely significant in its plea for tolerance for gay men (interestingly, lesbianism is not discussed here), VICTIM works hard arguing that gays are part of the typical, healthy fabric of society. For that alone, it was highly controversial and was refused the Seal of the Motion Picture Association of America. On its own terms, the film works quite well. The drama is exciting, the writing cogent, the acting often superb and the production and direction by the team of Dearden and Relph quite fine. Every role, no matter how small, is very intelligently cast and even the blackmailers were given some depth and character contradictions. In acting terms, the film quite properly belongs to the dynamic yet sensitive Bogarde, but McEnery, as his former lover, and Price, as a blackmail partner, also stand out. The film does, of course, shy away from certain aspects of its provocative subject matter, and a great deal of emphasis is laid on Farr's heterosexual relations with his wife. (It probably takes up more footage than is actually necessary, but this subplot broadens the role of Farr and is fairly well handled.) A liberal film on the subject of homosexuality rather than the radical film some considered it at the time, VICTIM still stands as an intelligent film attempting to address an important social issue.

VICTORIA THE GREAT

1937 110m c/bw Biography/Historical ★★★★
Imperator (U.K.) /U

Anna Neagle *(Queen Victoria)*, Anton Walbrook *(Prince Albert)*, Walter Rilla *(Prince Ernest)*, Mary Morris *(Duchess of Kent)*, H.B. Warner *(Lord Melbourne)*, Grete Wegener *(Baroness Lehzen)*, C.V. France *(Archbishop of Canterbury)*, James Dale *(Duke of Wellington)*, Charles Carson *(Sir Robert Peel)*, Hubert Harben *(Lord Conyngham)*

p, Herbert Wilcox; d, Herbert Wilcox; w, Miles Malleson, Charles de Grandcourt (based on the play "Victoria Regina" by Laurence Housman); ph, Freddie Young; m, Anthony Collins

This beautiful and elaborate film gives an intimate portrait of England's long-reigning monarch, following her from the first years of her reign to the celebration of her Diamond Jubilee. Neagle is excellent as

Victoria, who assumes the throne at the age of 18. The film details her courtship and marriage to Prince Albert (Walbrook), and a foiled attempt on the queen's life, thwarted when Albert risks death himself to shield Victoria from the would-be assassin. The story then concentrates on the royal couple's domestic life, with such figures as Disraeli, Wellington, and Lincoln introduced peripherally. Closing with the Jubilee, the film switches from black and white to a brilliant Technicolor.

Fictionalizing the lives of the royal family has long been a touchy issue in England, but producer-director Wilcox treats his subject respectfully, avoiding treacly sentiment. Neagle (who would later marry Wilcox) is completely believable as she takes her character from young girl to octogenarian, and is a marvel to watch as she transcends her craft and becomes the character. Released 100 years after Victoria began her reign, the film was enormously popular in England, prompting Wilcox, Neagle, and Walbrook to make a sequel, SIXTY GLORIOUS YEARS (1938), an all-color production that concentrated more on the political events of Victoria's rule. In 1942, Wilcox cut the first portion of VICTORIA THE GREAT into the latter half of SIXTY GLORIOUS YEARS to create a single feature, simply titled QUEEN VICTORIA.

Wilcox began production on VICTORIA THE GREAT after Edward VIII (who later abdicated to marry American divorcee Wallis Warfield Simpson) personally requested that the filmmaker produce a feature about the queen. It took an amazingly short five weeks to film. Attention to period detail was immaculate; Neagle's costumes were copied from Victoria's actual dresses, which were kept at the British Museum. Released in America through RKO, VICTORIA THE GREAT was popular in its initial run at Radio City Music Hall, where it turned a handsome profit, but it did not fare as well in smaller cities. Both Neagle and Wilcox toured the US to promote the film, though this too was not as successful as its backers hoped. However, Wilcox's association with RKO did result in a lucrative agreement with the studio, under which the independent producer was to turn out a number of features under the American company's banner, an arrangement that helped reduce the burden of the United Kingdom's restrictive quotas on domestic screenings of imported films. VICTORIA THE GREAT also features Paul Henreid in his first British film, appearing in a small role under his real name.

VICTOR/VICTORIA

1982 133m c Musical/Comedy ★★★
MGM (U.K.) PG/15

Julie Andrews *(Victor/Victoria)*, James Garner *(King)*, Robert Preston *(Toddy)*, Lesley Ann Warren *(Norma)*, Alex Karras *(Squash)*, John Rhys-Davies *(Cassell)*, Graham Stark *(Waiter)*, Peter Arne *(Labisse)*, Sherloque Tanney *(Bovin)*, Michael Robbins *(Hotel Manager)*

p, Blake Edwards, Tony Adams; d, Blake Edwards; w, Blake Edwards (based on the film VICTOR UND VIKTORIA by Rheinhold Schuenzel, Hans Hoemburg); ph, Dick Bush; ed, Ralph E. Winters; m, Henry Mancini; prod d, Rodger Maus; art d, Tim Hutchinson, William Craig Smith; chor, Paddy Stone; cos, Patricia Norris

AAN Best Actress: Julie Andrews; *AAN Best Supporting Actor:* Robert Preston; *AAN Best Supporting Actress:* Lesley Ann Warren; *AAN Best Adapted Screenplay:* Blake Edwards; *AA Best Score:* Henry Mancini, Leslie Bricusse; *AAN Best Art Direction:* Rodger Maus, Tim Hutchinson, William Craig Smith, Harry Cordwell; *AAN Best Costume Design:* Patricia Norris

A musical boudoir farce, captivating at times, infuriating at others. A British singer (Julie Andrews) and an aging homosexual (Robert Preston) are down-and-out nightclub performers in Paris. Hungry and broke, they're desperate for employment until Toddy (Preston) recasts his friend as the female impersonator singer-dancer Victor/Victoria—putting the chanteuse in the unusual position of being a woman who pretends to be a man who performs as a woman onstage. She is an immediate hit at a local nightclub, where King (James Garner), a gangster from Chicago traveling with his blowsy girlfriend (a Jean Harlowesque Lesley Ann Warren) and his bodyguard, Squash (Alex Karras), sees her perform. King is attracted to Victor/Victoria, but thinks, like everyone else, that she is a transvestite. The burly Squash, meanwhile, watches in amazement as his macho boss apparently loses his yen for beautiful women and becomes attracted to his own kind.

Edwards' film forces audiences to examine their own ideas about gender and sexuality, and that's great. But Andrews, despite looking very Berlin Bowie in her tux, is so safe and sane, she brings no madness of her own to the farce. Everything therefore swirls around a still center—in the film's one good number, "Le Jazz Hot", she climbs a staircase like she has weights on her feet. Nor can she summon any of the impersonator's hauteur or joy to her masquerade. Robert Preston is wonderful—he plays a cliche with such malice and relish, he revitalizes it, and Garner is successful kidding his own past macho image. A platinumed Warren is also quite good, but Edwards makes her dopey sweetness go sour—he humiliates her, especially in a chorus line number that could make a feminist a raging virago. Will someone please give Warren a role worthy of her undeniable talent? The film's best moments are early on: Andrews warbling for disinterested cabaret owners, or the preparation of Victoria to become Victor. After that, this becomes increasingly coarse and overstated. Edwards directs like a grizzly bear whipping up a souffle. The screenplay was based on VIKTOR UND VIKTORIA, a 1933 German film, first refashioned in 1935 into a star vehicle for the ever-delightful Jessie Mathews, FIRST A GIRL.

VIDEODROME

1983 88m c Horror   ★★★½
Filmplan (Canada)   R/18

James Woods (Max Renn), Sonja Smits (Bianca O'Blivion), Deborah Harry (Nicki Brand), Peter Dvorsky (Harlan), Les Carlson (Barry Convex), Jack Creley (Prof. Brian O'Blivion), Lynne Gorman (Masha), Julie Khaner (Briley), Reiner Schwarz (Moses), David Bolt (Rafe)

p, Claude Heroux; d, David Cronenberg; w, David Cronenberg; ph, Mark Irwin; ed, Ronald Sanders; m, Howard Shore; prod d, Carol Spier; art d, Nick Kosonic; fx, Frank Carere, Rick Baker, Michael Lennick; chor, Kirsteen Etherington; cos, Delphine White

Director David Cronenberg's most visionary and audacious film up to the time of its making, VIDEODROME is a fascinating rumination on humanity, technology, entertainment, sex, and politics that is virtually incomprehensible on first viewing and needs to be seen several times before one can even begin to unlock its mysteries. James Woods, in one of the best performances of his career, stars as Max Renn, an ambitious cable television programmer who, in his off hours, is a closet voyeur of sex and violence. Looking for something new, something "sensational" for his cable station, Renn stumbles across a show called "Videodrome" while pirating signals from satellite dishes. The show seems to depict the actual torture and murder of a different victim every night. Fascinated and excited by the program, Renn tries to find out where the show originates. During the investigation, he becomes deeply embroiled in a bizarre, intriguing, and sometimes incomprehensible fusion of television, politics, and mind-control that seems to herald some sort of "New Order" for society.

VIDEODROME very well may be the most incomprehensible mainstream film ever made. As Cronenberg's narrative veers from hallucination to reality and back again—the line between them more blurred each time—he unleashes his bizarre visual imagination, bombarding viewers with such sights as an open stomach cavity that becomes a repository for videocassettes and guns, throbbing television sets, a literal hand-gun, and humans who crack open and spew forth all manner of flesh, blood, and multicolored goo. While these images are undeniably powerful (the throbbing, living television set is amazing) and the film is compulsively watchable, it does tend to become wholly impenetrable toward the end and may leave the uninitiated frustrated or even angry. Nevertheless, this is a remarkable film that will continue to be debated and analyzed for decades to come.

VIKINGS, THE

1958 114m c Adventure/Historical   ★★★
Bryna (U.S.)   /A

Kirk Douglas (Einar), Tony Curtis (Eric), Ernest Borgnine (King Ragnar), Janet Leigh (Princess Morgana), James Donald (Lord Egbert), Alexander Knox (Father Godwin), Frank Thring (King Aella), Maxine Audley (Enid), Eileen Way (Kitala), Edric Connor (Sandpiper)

p, Jerry Bresler; d, Richard Fleischer; w, Dale Wasserman, Calder Willingham (based on the novel The Viking by Edison Marshall); ph, Jack Cardiff; ed, Elmo Williams; m, Mario Nascimbene; prod d, Harper Goff

Viking warriors led by Borgnine raid the English coast, raping and plundering. In one small kingdom, he kills the king and rapes the queen. The child who is born as a result of that assault grows up to be Curtis, a Viking slave who knows nothing of his parentage. He and Douglas, Borgnine's legitimate son, take a dislike to each other and fight a duel, during which Curtis' falcon claws out one of Douglas' eyes. Enraged, Douglas orders the slave tossed into a pit of giant crabs. Curtis is saved when Donald, who was banished from England and is planning his return with Viking help, recognizes an amulet Curtis wears which proclaims his true identity. On another raid, the Norsemen carry off princess Leigh, and Douglas decides he wants her, although she has fallen in love with Curtis. Leigh and Curtis escape one night, and when Douglas and Borgnine chase them, the pursuing boat crashes on the rocks in the fjord and sinks. Borgnine is pulled aboard by Curtis and taken to England as a gift for evil king Thring. Thring orders the old Viking chieftain thrown to their more civilized variation of the giant crab pit—the ravenous wolf pit. Thring laughs when Borgnine asks to die like a Viking, with a sword in his hand, but Curtis takes pity and cuts his hands free and gives him his own sword. Borgnine almost gleefully jumps into the pit with a shout and manages to take a few wolves to Valhalla with him. Thring is outraged, mostly at the loss of his precious wolves, and orders that Curtis' hand be chopped off and he be set adrift in the North Sea. The boat, of course, drifts straight back to Norway where Curtis tells Douglas the fate of his father, and the two decide to put aside their mutual hatred to seek vengeance on Thring. They sail to England and attack the castle, and Douglas then frees Leigh and proposes marriage. She tells him she loves Curtis and, when Douglas vows to kill him, she reveals that they are half-brothers. Curtis shows up and the two fight a duel on the battlements of the castle. Douglas gets the upper hand and is about to kill Curtis, but he hesitates, apparently reluctant to kill his own kin. Curtis knows nothing about any blood ties and uses Douglas' moment of indecision to drive his own blade into his foe. The film concludes as Douglas is given a Viking funeral, set adrift on a burning longship.

A rousing adventure, despite a great deal of out-and-out silliness, this film was a major ordeal to make. The projected $2.5 million budget doubled as the studio leased the rights to an entire fjord, constructed a Viking village on a rock in the middle of it, and built a fleet of longships copied from reproductions in museums. The cast and crew were housed on two ships moored in the fjord and were shuttled back and forth by a fleet of 17 old PT boats. Weather proved a problem: of the 60 shooting days in Norway, 49 were rainy and dark. Finally the camera crew improvised a way to protect the camera from the elements, and some haunting shots of Viking longships gliding through the rain and fog were captured. Douglas and Borgnine give memorably bombastic performances—Douglas leering with his milked-over eye and Borgnine shouting war cries through his bushy beard as he happily meets his death in the wolf pit. Curtis is less memorable and seems as out of place as he always does in these swashbucklers. The production values are all top drawer and, thanks to a publicity campaign that included sending Viking dagger letter openers to reviewers, having seven Norwegians sail a longship from Oslo to New York, and lifting another longship onto the marquee of the New York theater where it debuted, the film was a big moneymaker.

VILLAGE OF THE DAMNED

1960 77m bw Horror/Science Fiction   ★★★
MGM (U.K.)   /A

George Sanders (Gordon Zellaby), Barbara Shelley (Anthea Zellaby), Michael Gwynn (Maj. Alan Bernard), Laurence Naismith (Dr. Willers), John Phillips (Gen. Leighton), Richard Vernon (Sir Edgar Hargraves), Jenny Laird (Mrs. Harrington), Richard Warner (Mr. Harrington), Thomas Heathcote (James Pawle), Alexander Archdale (Coroner) p, Ronald Kinnoch; d, Wolf Rilla; w, Wolf Rilla, Stirling Silliphant, George Barclay (based on the novel *The Midwich Cuckoos* by John Wyndham); ph, Geoffrey Faithfull; ed, Gordon Hales; m, Ron Goodwin; art d, Ivan King; fx, Tom Howard

A very frightening adaptation of the John Wyndham novel about a small English village that becomes the victim of unfriendly aliens. During a 24-hour period all the inhabitants of Midwich are put to sleep, waking to find a dozen of the women pregnant. When these babies are born, their mothers love them as if they were conceived under normal circumstances. However, all of these children look the same, with bright blond hair. The are also possessed of superior intelligence and telekinetic powers. Sanders, a physicist and the husband of Shelley, who has given birth to the leader of the children, undertakes the job of educating these youngsters and soon discovers that their mission is not a friendly one: they plan to take control of the entire planet. Sanders then sees that the children are destroyed, killing himself in the process. Sanders' role required more outward emotion than he had in his repertoire, but this casting mistake is more than compensated for by the weird atmosphere provided by the children. Made in England for less than $300,000, the picture grossed more than $1.5 million in initial release in the US and Canada alone. It spawned a host of possessed-children-as-villains films, including THE OMEN and THE BOYS FROM BRAZIL. This intriguing story also gave rise to a sequel, CHILDREN OF THE DAMNED, which proved every bit as good as the original.

VINCENT AND THEO

1990 138m c Biography ★★★★
Belbo/Central/La Sept/Telepool/RAI Uno/Vara R/15
/Sofica Valor (U.K./France/U.S.)

Tim Roth (*Vincent van Gogh*), Paul Rhys (*Theodore van Gogh*), Jip Wijngaarden (*Sien Hoornik*), Johanna Ter Steege (*Jo Bonger*), Wladimir Yordanoff (*Paul Gauguin*), Jean-Pierre Cassel (*Dr. Paul Gachet*), Bernadette Giraud (*Marguerite Gachet*), Adrian Brine (*Uncle Cent*), Jean-Francois Perrier (*Leon Bouscod*), Vincent Vallier (*Rene Valadon*)

p, Ludi Boeken; d, Robert Altman; w, Julian Mitchell; ph, Jean Lepine; ed, Francois Coispeau, Geraldine Peroni; m, Gabriel Yared; prod d, Stephen Altman; art d, Dominique Douret, Ben Van, Jan Roelfs; cos, Scott Bushnell

Altman tackles the monumental story of Vincent van Gogh and his brother Theo and, for the most part, comes up a winner. Working from a minimalist script by Julian Mitchell, the director offers us a stripped-to-the-bones drama that leaves most screen takes on the artistic life—from the Hollywood bombast of LUST FOR LIFE to the self-conscious quirkiness of Derek Jarman's CARAVAGGIO—way behind.

The film's beginning is the director's most audacious conceit. We see actual footage of the painting "Sunflowers" as it is being auctioned off at Christie's, and Altman, one of the keenest users of sound in all cinema, sustains the soundtrack of the bidding during his opening scene between Vincent and Theo. As the brothers argue over the money their rich uncle sends each month to Vincent to sustain his creative, if uncommercial, journey, the point is clearly made about the often arbitrary elusiveness of artistic success. Familiar ground is subsequently covered, including Vincent's fascination with prostitutes and Theo's syphilitic torment. The story continues through Vincent's uneasy friendship with Gauguin, his encroaching mental instability, Theo's personal financial struggles as a gallery owner, and his troubled courtship and marriage to Jo Bonger (Ter Steege). The fate of the two troubled brothers resolves the action.

As photographed by Jean Lepine, the film is visually stunning. VINCENT AND THEO is brimful of the pictorial splendors of nature and the human form, but they are captured fleetingly, in an off-the-cuff kind of way that suggests the finely attuned peripheral vision, the febrile antennae, of an artist. The early scene of Vincent observing and rapidly sketching the whore as she takes a break from posing, stretches, looks through the window at the moon, and even relieves herself, comes as close to depicting the actual creative process of painting as anything ever filmed. The creation of the sunflower paintings is aptly expressed in the silent, sketchy takes of him out in the fields, experiencing quick frustration more than anything else, with the end result a terse, panning shot of his room in Arles, filled with his finished efforts glowing from the walls.

VIRGIN SPRING, THE
(JUNGFRUKALLAN)

1959 88m bw Drama ★★★
Svensk (Sweden) /X

Max von Sydow (*Herr Tore*), Brigitta Pettersson (*Karin Tore*), Birgitta Valberg (*Mareta Tore*), Gunnel Lindblom (*Ingeri*), Axel Duberg (*Thin Herdsman*), Tor Isedal (*Mute Herdsman*), Ove Porath (*Boy*), Allan Edwall (*Beggar*), Gudrun Brost (*Frida*), Oscar Ljung (*Simon*)

p, Ingmar Bergman, Allan Ekelund; d, Ingmar Bergman; w, Ulla Isaksson (based on the 14th-century ballad "Tores Dotter I Vange"); ph, Sven Nykvist, Rolf Halmquist; ed, Oscar Rosander; m, Erik Nordgren; art d, P.A. Lundgren; cos, Marik Vos

AA Best Foreign Language Film ; AAN Best Costume Design: Marik Vos

The Best Foreign-Language Film Oscar awarded to THE VIRGIN SPRING was director Ingmar Bergman's first Academy Award, and the film still numbers among the director's classics. The story takes place in 13th-century Sweden, as Christianity and folklore vie for dominance in the popular belief. Karin (Birgitta Pettersson), the spoiled young virgin daughter of wealthy landowner Tore (Max von Sydow), is to go to church to light candles for the Virgin, and is allowed to wear a special gown, handmade by 15 virgins, on the occasion. Riding in the woods, Karin is raped, and then killed, by shepherds. The men take her gown, hoping to sell it, and move on, arriving at Tore's house, where they receive food and shelter. Their crime is discovered, however, moving Tore to enact bloody revenge and testing the bereaved father's faith. THE VIRGIN SPRING is based on a medieval ballad, and is full of the folk-tale oppositions (a good sister and a bad one) and motifs (the tell-tale gown, the trio of shepherds) so beloved by Bergman (the film is also true to its origins in its extreme violence). As always, those with little affinity for Bergman's preoccupations will find the film overlong and overdone. Most, however, will be rewarded by the depth of the director's moral and religious questioning, the emotional power of the story and acting, the haunting and symbolic imagery, and the excellent black-and-white photography of Sven Nykvist. Nominated by the Academy for Best Costume Design.

VIRGINIAN, THE

1929 92m bw Western ★★★½
Famous Players/Paramount (U.S.)

Gary Cooper (*The Virginian*), Walter Huston (*Trampas*), Mary Brian (*Molly Stark Wood*), Richard Arlen (*Steve*), Helen Ware ("*Ma*" *Taylor*), Chester Conklin (*Uncle Hughey*), Eugene Pallette ("*Honey*" *Wiggin*), Victor Potel (*Nebraskey*), E.H. Calvert (*Judge Henry*), Tex Young (*Shorty*)

p, Louis D. Lighton; d, Victor Fleming; w, Howard Estabrook, Edward E. Paramore, Grover Jones, Keene Thompson (based on the play by Owen Wister, Kirk La Shelle, and the novel by Owen Wister); ph, J. Roy Hunt, Edward Cronjager; ed, William Shea

Gary Cooper's first all-talkie, this film adaptation of Owen Wister's popular novel established Cooper's heroic image in the public eye. As the title character, Cooper is foreman of a Wyoming ranch. He gives a job to an old friend, Richard Arlen, with whom he is vying for the affections of schoolmarm Mary Brian. Cooper wins out and Arlen goes bad, taking up with local villain Walter Huston to rustle cattle from Cooper's herd. Cooper catches his friend changing brands and warns him, but when Arlen is later caught stealing cattle again, along with two other rustlers, Cooper oversees the lynching of all three. Plagued by guilt, Cooper swears to get Huston, whom he knows to be the leader of the gang. When Brian finds out what Cooper has done, she rejects him. Later, though, in a skirmish with Huston, Cooper is wounded and Brian takes care of him, eventually agreeing to marry him. On their wedding day, Huston brings matters to a head, and the two men square off in the street for a showdown. Cooper is faster on the draw and Huston dies in the dust. The bit for which this film is most remembered occurs during a card game, when Huston calls Cooper an insulting name. Cooper pulls his gun out, lays it on the table and says, "If you want to call me that, smile." The phrase caught on immediately and was used extensively in advertising for the film. Cooper played his role well, and his performance helped him escape the typecasting he had been saddled with. Now he could play rugged male leads instead of juvenile lovers. Huston is even better, his Trampas the essence of western villainy and the standard to be imitated for years to come. This was the third film of the novel, which had previously been done in 1921 starring Dustin Farnum, and in 1923 starring Kenneth Harlan. A major box-office success, it was remade in 1946 with Joel McCrea, and became a television series in 1962 starring James Drury in the title role.

VIRIDIANA

1961 90m bw Drama ★★★★★
Uninci/Films 59/Gustavo Alatriste (Mexico/Spain) /X

Silvia Pinal (Viridiana), Francisco Rabal (Jorge), Fernando Rey (Don Jaime), Margarita Lozano (Ramona), Victoria Zinny (Lucia), Teresa Rabal (Rita), Jose Calvo, Joaquin Roa, Luis Heredia, Jose Manuel Martin

p, Ricardo Munoz Suay; d, Luis Bunuel; w, Luis Bunuel, Julio Alejandro (based on a story by Bunuel); ed, Pedro del Rey; m, Wolfgang Amadeus Mozart, George Frederick Handel; art d, Francisco Canet

Luis Bunuel had been absent from his native land for 25 years when he was invited by the Franco government to produce a film in Spain. The result was VIRIDIANA. Ironically, it was never shown in Spanish theaters, having been banned by the Franco government immediately after its debut at the Cannes Film Festival, where it won the Golden Palm. Pinal plays the title role, a religious novitiate who visits her last remaining relative, the wealthy Don Jaime (Rey), before she takes her vows. Viridiana, firmly intent on resisting the corruption of her uncle's estate, is surprised to find him most gracious, kind, and gentle. He, however, is secretly obsessed with her resemblance to his wife, who died 30 years earlier on their wedding night. After Don Jaime attempts to ravish the nun-to-be, who has obliged the lonely man by putting on his wife's wedding gown, he feels such remorse that he commits suicide. Viridiana inherits the estate, along with Don Jaime's son Jorge (Rabal) and she intends to use her new position to benefit the local poor. Once again her virtuous intentions backfire. Oh, that final card game!

VIRIDIANA is filled with allegories concerning the general state of the world and Spain in particular, conveyed with the master surrealist's usual mix of black humor and stunning images. Foremost among them is the famous "Last Supper," in which a group of thoroughly degenerate beggars carouse drunkenly, in a visual parody of Da Vinci's painting, to the strains of Handel's "Messiah." You will *never* forget this moment. Viridiana, who wishes to redeem these miscreants through her idealism, is mocked in the process—as is the Catholicism that Bunuel believed had to be overthrown if Spain was to avoid becoming a decaying mess like Don Jaime's estate. Viridiana's ineffectual faith is contrasted with Jorge's more beneficial pragmatism. The changes he attempts to realize can perhaps do but minimal good, as indicated in one of Bunuel's most famous jokes: just after Jorge has rescued a dog that was being dragged mercilessly from a cart by buying it from its owner, the director shows another cur in the same predicament, attached to another cart coming from the opposite direction. Still, Jorge does represent a practical approach to achieving modest changes for the better. Immediately after the film was shot, it was shipped to Paris, where it was quickly edited in time for Cannes. Spanish authorities, who had not seen the final print before the festival screening, were shocked when it won the Golden Palm. Further scandal followed the film to Italy, where Bunuel was threatened with a prison sentence if he entered the country. Despite all this controversy, VIRIDIANA has a deceptively artless quality, stemming from the poetic formality with which Bunuel allows the picture to unfold. He steered away from complex and confusing images or camera movement, and created, along with THE EXTERMINATING ANGEL, one of the most magnificent films of his incredible career.

VITELLONI
(I VITELLONI)

1953 103m bw Drama ★★★★
PEG/Cite (Italy/France)

Franco Interlenghi (Moraldo), Franco Fabrizi (Fausto), Alberto Sordi (Alberto), Leopoldo Trieste (Leopoldo), Riccardo Fellini (Riccardo), Leonora Ruffo (Sandra), Lida Baarova (Giulia), Arlette Sauvage (Woman in the Cinema), Maja Nipora (Actress), Jean Brochard (Father of Fausto)

p, Mario de Vecchi; d, Federico Fellini; w, Federico Fellini, Ennio Flaiano (based on the story by Fellini, Flaiano and Tullio Pinelli); ph, Otello Martelli, Luciano Trasatti, Carlo Carlini; ed, Rolando Benedetti; m, Nino Rota; art d, Mario Chiari

AAN Best Original Screenplay: Federico Fellini, Ennio Flaiano, Tullio Pinelli

This semiautobiographical work by Federico Fellini was the first film to bring him a measure of world attention. As in AMARCORD (his film of nearly two decades later), the setting is the seaside town of Rimini, Fellini's birthplace. The plot follows the adventures of five youths who refuse to grow up and accept responsibility. Only one of the gang, Moraldo (Franco Interlenghi, the young boy from SHOESHINE) comes to understand that life in the small town is a relatively empty existence, while his friends are content to play meaningless games that lend momentary security but ultimately make them puppets to forces beyond their control. VITELLONI is filled with the cinematic excesses that were to clutter Fellini's later films, though here they seem much more insightful in describing the tribulations of adolescent rites of passage.

VIVA LAS VEGAS

1964 85m c Musical ★★★½
MGM (U.S.)

Elvis Presley (Lucky Jackson), Ann-Margret (Rusty Martin), Cesare Danova (Count Elmo Mancini), William Demarest (Mr. Martin), Nicky Blair (Shorty Farnsworth), Jack Carter (Himself), Robert B. Williams (Swanson), Bob Nash (Big Gus Olson), Roy Engel (Baker), Barnaby Hale (Mechanic)

p, Jack Cummings, George Sidney; d, George Sidney; w, Sally Benson; ph, Joseph Biroc; ed, John McSweeney Jr.; m, George Stoll; art d, George W. Davis, Edward Carfagno; chor, David Winters; cos, Don Feld

Presley's one really good musical, mainly because it features a female costar, Ann-Margret, who can match the coiffed one in the charisma stakes. Elvis plays Lucky Jackson, a race-car driver who comes to Las Vegas to compete in the upcoming Grand Prix against his arch-rival, Count Elmo Cancini (Cesare Danova). To earn money for a new engine, Presley takes a job as a waiter at a casino, romancing swimming teacher Rusty Martin (Ann-Margret) and singing songs in his spare time before the race. They include: "The Lady Loves Me" (Sid Tepper, Roy C. Bennett); "Viva Las Vegas," "I Need Somebody to Lean On," (Doc Pomus); "What'd I Say" (Ray Charles); "Come On, Everybody" (Stanley Chianese); "Today, Tomorrow and Forever" (Bill Giant, Bernie Baum, Florence Kaye); "If You Think I Don't Need You" (Bob "Red" West); "Appreciation," "My Rival" (Marvin More, Bernie Wayne); "The Climb," "The Yellow Rose of Texas" (Don George); and "The Eyes of Texas Are upon You."

VIVA VILLA!

1934 115m bw Biography ★★★★
MGM (U.S.) /A

Wallace Beery (Pancho Villa), Fay Wray (Teresa), Stuart Erwin (Johnny Sykes), Leo Carrillo (Sierra), Donald Cook (Don Felipe), George E. Stone (Chavito), Joseph Schildkraut (Gen. Pascal), Henry B. Walthall (Madero), Katherine DeMille (Rosita), David Durand (Bugle Boy)

p, David O. Selznick; d, Howard Hawks, Jack Conway; w, Ben Hecht (based on the book by Edgecumb Pinchon, O.B. Stade); ph, James Wong Howe; ed, Robert J. Kern; m, Herbert Stothart; art d, Harry Oliver; cos, Dolly Tree

AAN Best Picture; *AAN Best Adapted Screenplay:* Ben Hecht; *AAN Best Sound:* Douglas Shearer

The life of the famous Mexican bandit and revolutionary is told in this exciting action drama. The film opens as young Pancho Villa (Phillip Cooper) watches his father whipped to death by a soldier for some minor offense. Soon afterward, the boy murders the soldier and takes to the hills where he grows into adulthood and gathers a band of followers who join him in pillaging the homes of the rich and giving part of the proceeds to the poor. On one of these raids, Villa (played as an adult by Wallace Beery) meets an American reporter (Stuart Erwin), and the two become close friends. Later he meets a wealthy landowner (Donald Cook) and his sister (Fay Wray), who are sympathetic to Beery and his goals. They introduce the bandit to the intellectual head (Henry Walthall) of the peasant revolt which is starting to gather strength. Walthall persuades Beery to add his forces to the peasant army as its fighting core. Soon a renegade general (Joseph Schildkraut) joins the rebels with his men, and the resulting body soon sweeps through Mexico to victory. The president resigns and Walthall is named in his place. Beery's army is disbanded and he is sent home to his ranch. When Beery takes up bank robbery and kills a teller in the process, Schildkraut seizes the opportunity to eliminate his closest rival and orders him executed for murder. Walthall pardons Beery on the condition that he leave the country. Schildkraut then murders Walthall and seizes power for himself. Beery returns and reactivates his army, but without the guiding intelligence of Walthall, Beery and his men run wild, robbing and killing almost at random. Cook and Wray refuse to support Beery. He attacks Wray, and when she shoots him in the arm, he orders her flogged. Later a stray bullet fired by one of Beery's men kills her. Beery's forces triumph over Schildkraut's, and, when the general is captured, Beery has him covered in honey and left out for the ants to eat. Beery takes over as president, but with his limited education the job is too much for him. He retires to his ranch once again. Some time later, he visits Mexico City and runs into his old friend Erwin. As they talk, they are spotted by Cook, who shoots the bandit to avenge his sister's death. The mortally wounded Beery feels that momentous last words are in order, so Erwin composes them for him.

Beery's performance as Villa is one of the highlights of his long and diverse career, and his portrayal of the man as equal parts child, crusader, peasant, and murderous bandito is near perfect. When finally completed, the film proved a huge success, earning stacks of money for MGM.

VIVA ZAPATA!

1952 113m bw Biography   ★★★★
Fox   (U.S.)   /PG

Marlon Brando (*Emiliano Zapata*), Jean Peters (*Josefa Espejo*), Anthony Quinn (*Eufemio Zapata*), Joseph Wiseman (*Fernando Aguirre*), Arnold Moss (*Don Nacio*), Alan Reed (*Pancho Villa*), Margo (*La Soldadera*), Harold Gordon (*Don Francisco Madero*), Lou Gilbert (*Pablo*), Mildred Dunnock (*Senora Espejo*)

p, Darryl F. Zanuck; d, Elia Kazan; w, John Steinbeck (based on the novel *Zapata the Unconquered* by Edgcumb Pichon); ph, Joseph MacDonald; ed, Barbara McLean; m, Alex North; art d, Lyle Wheeler, Leland Fuller

AAN Best Actor: Marlon Brando; *AA Best Supporting Actor:* Anthony Quinn; *AAN Best Story and Screenplay:* John Steinbeck; *AAN Best Score:* Alex North; *AAN Best Art Direction:* Lyle Wheeler Leland Fuller, Thomas Little, Claude Carpenter

Great acting exercise, Tabascoed with Brando, peppered with Quinn, but otherwise Kazan/Steinbeck refried beans.

Kazan directs this exciting biography of the peasant who rose to be a revolutionary leader and President of his country with great relish, graphically capturing a bloody era of Mexican history, and Brando gives an electrifying performance. But the adventure lags, marred by pretentious brooding as the script strains to moralize about the corruptive influence of power.

Nor can Brando's acting justify the liberties taken. The real Emiliano Zapata was a small man with large, dark eyes and delicate hands—a tenant-farmer who finally rose up against the tyrannical rule of Porfirio Diaz, as did Pancho Villa in the north, and led an army to victory over Diaz. He waged his civil wars, 1911-19, not to conquer Mexico but to free the land for the peasants of Morelos and other southern provinces. Kazan presents a whitewashed version of the great leader; the historical Zapata was in reality barbaric and did not hesitate to execute his enemies en masse. Quinn is marvelous as the hard-riding, hard-drinking brother willing to die for passion. Frank Silvera as Huerta, Roope as Diaz, and Wiseman as the intense war-mongering journalist are startling villains, not far from their real-life counterparts in posture and character. Gilbert, who acts as Brando's intellectual conscience, is a bit too dramatic and unbelievable in some scenes. Gordon as Madero gives a realistic profile, but Peters and Margo are given little to do. Though he is on camera for only a few scenes, Reed, playing Pancho Villa, captures the brooding charisma of the revolutionary leader.

VOLCANO

1997 105m c Disaster   ★★★
Donner-Shuler/Donner Productions/Fox 2000   PG-13/
/Original Film   (U.S.)

Tommy Lee Jones (*Mike Roark*), Anne Heche (*Dr. Amy Barnes*), Don Cheadle (*Emmit Reese*), Gaby Hoffman (*Kelly Roark*), Keith David (*Lt. Fox*), Jaqueline Kim (*Dr. Jaye Calder*), John Corbett (*Norman Calder*), John Carroll Lynch (*Stan Olber*), Michael Rispoli (*Gator Harris*), Marcello Thedford (*Kevin*)

p, Neal H. Moritz, Andrew Z. Davis; d, Mick Jackson; w, Jerome Armstrong, Billy Ray (based on a story by Jerome Armstrong); ph, Theo Van de Sande; ed, Michael Tronick, Don Brochu; m, Alan Silvestri; prod d, Jackson DeGovia; art d, Scott Rittenour, Tom Reta, William Cruse, Donald Woodruff; fx, Dale Ettema, Mat Beck; cos, Kirsten Everberg

An utterly formulaic throwback to the disaster movies of yesteryear in which a big ol' volcano pokes its snout out from the La Brea tar pits and vomits lava all over some pricy downtown Los Angeles real estate. It's up to Mike Roark (Tommy Lee Jones) from the Office of Emergency Management to sort out this mess of biblical proportions ("It is a foolish man who builds his house upon the sand," Roark intones in his best Old Testament growl), with a little help from a spunky lady seismologist (Anne Heche). Together, they must prevent a rogue lava stream from incinerating the hospital where Roark's sent a slew of sick and injured indivduals, including his own teenage daughter Kelly (Gaby Hoffman).

You always knew it was a bad idea to build a subway in LA, but now you know exactly why. This is a silly movie, but the mayhem is hugely entertaining. So what makes this smoldering inferno a better no-brainer than the feeble DANTE'S PEAK? Three things: 1.) A lava geyser in front of LA's posh Beverly Center is a bigger kick than ash raining down on some dinky town in the Pacific Northwest. 2.) The effects are bigger. 3.) No one says anything as quite as stupid as "Her name was Marion and she loved volcanoes. . ." Even the ridiculous, obligatory, imperiled dog scene is better: VOLCANO's pooch is so cute you're actually happy when it escapes being burned to a cinder, a fate that befalls several less-photogenic supporting characters, who might as well have "volcano fodder" branded on their foreheads.

VON RYAN'S EXPRESS

1965 117m c War   ★★★½
P-R   (U.S.)   /PG

Frank Sinatra (*Col. Joseph L. Ryan*), Trevor Howard (*Maj. Eric Fincham*), Raffaella Carra (*Gabriella*), Brad Dexter (*Sgt. Bostick*), Sergio Fantoni (*Capt. Oriani*), John Leyton (*Orde*), Edward Mulhare (*Constanzo*), Wolfgang Preiss (*Maj. von Klemment*), James Brolin (*Pvt. Ames*), John Van Dreelen (*Col. Gortz*)

p, Saul David; d, Mark Robson; w, Wendell Mayes, Joseph Landon (based on the novel by David Westheimer); ph, William Daniels; ed, Dorothy Spencer; m, Jerry Goldsmith; art d, Jack Martin Smith

AAN Best Sound Effects Editing: Walter A. Rossi

Frank Sinatra stars in this implausible but relatively engaging WWII POW escape film, playing Col. Joseph Ryan, a downed US Army Air Corps pilot who leads 600 British and American prisoners in a dramatic escape through Italy aboard a commandeered train. Aided by some of their Italian jailers, who are anxious to jump sides as the 1943 Allied invasion gets under way, the POWs take over a train and, with some of their number masquerading as Germans guards, set off for neutral Switzerland. Initially called "von Ryan" by the other prisoners, who thought him too accommodating to the enemy, the American colonel proves his courage over and over again as the train makes its way to freedom, fending off attacking Messerschmitts and narrowly escaping a pursuing German troop train. Sinatra is convincing as the gutsy American officer who engineers the escape, and Trevor Howard gives a strong performance as the British major Sinatra replaces as ranking prisoner, but there isn't much else that's believable in VON RYAN'S EXPRESS. Nonetheless, Mark Robson's film is packed with action and occasionally technically impressive, especially in the duel between the train and the German planes that attack it in the mountains of northern Italy. If it's realism you're after, look elsewhere; but if you enjoy straightforward wartime thrills (or films with particularly stupid German soldiers), VON RYAN'S EXPRESS is just the ticket.

WAGES OF FEAR, THE
(LE SALAIRE DE LA PEUR)
1952 140m bw Adventure ★★★★½
Filmsonor/CICC/Vera/Fono Roma (France/Italy) /A

Yves Montand *(Mario)*, Charles Vanel *(Jo)*, Vera Clouzot *(Linda)*, Folco Lulli *(Luigi)*, Peter Van Eyck *(Bimba)*, William Tubbs *(Bill O'Brien)*, Dario Moreno *(Hernandez)*, Jo Dest *(Smerloff)*, Antonio Centa *(Camp Chief)*, Luis de Lima *(Bernardo)*

p, Henri-Georges Clouzot; d, Henri-Georges Clouzot; w, Henri-Georges Clouzot, Jerome Geronimi (based on the novel by Georges Arnaud); ph, Armand Thirard; ed, Henri Rust, Madeleine Gug, Etiennette Muse; m, Georges Auric; prod d, Rene Renoux

Excellent, but nasty stuff. When the powerful oil company that controls the poverty-stricken Central American village of Las Piedras is faced with a well-fire disaster 300 miles away, they call for drivers to haul a load of highly volatile nitroglycerine across the dangerous terrain to the disaster site. After the driving skills of the applicants are tested, four men are chosen—Mario (Yves Montand), a French-raised Corsican; Luigi (Folco Lulli), his husky Italian roommate; Bimba (Peter Van Eyck), a cold and egotistical German; and Jo (Charles Vanel), a fifth choice who has gotten rid of the man before him. Driving two trucks at a snail's pace, they must overcome numerous obstacles to reach their destination, including a rickety wooden platform suspended over a deep ravine, a giant boulder that blocks the road and must be destroyed with a nitro charge, a swamp of oil and their greatest natural danger—fear. A superb suspense film that eats at one's nerves for its entire last half, THE WAGES OF FEAR can almost be thought of as two movies. While director Henri-Georges Clouzot, relying on visuals, devotes the latter portion of the film to the passage of the trucks, he spends the first half building characters and atmosphere—the sweaty, dusty, hellish existence in Las Piedras, which is little better than death. From the opening shot—of four frantic beetles that have been strung together by a mischievous child—it is clear that the four characters are prisoners of the place. Remade in 1977 by William Friedkin as the crummy SORCERER.

WAGONMASTER
1950 86m bw Western ★★★★
Argosy (U.S.) /U

Ward Bond *(Elder Wiggs)*, Ben Johnson *(Travis Blue)*, Harry Carey Jr. *(Sandy Owens)*, Joanne Dru *(Denver)*, Charles Kemper *(Uncle Shiloh Clegg)*, Jane Darwell *(Sister Ledeyard)*, Alan Mowbray *(Dr. A. Locksley Hall)*, Ruth Clifford *(Fleuretty Phyffe)*, Russell Simpson *(Adam Perkins)*, Kathleen O'Malley *(Prudence Perkins)*

p, John Ford, Merian C. Cooper; d, John Ford; w, Frank S. Nugent, Patrick Ford (based on a story by John Ford); ph, Bert Glennon; ed, Jack Murray; m, Richard Hageman; art d, James Basevi; fx, Jack Caffee; cos, Wesley V. Jefferies, Adele Parmenter

When asked by Peter Bogdanovich to comment on WAGONMASTER during their famous interview in 1966, director Ford replied that he thought the film, "along with THE FUGITIVE and THE SUN SHINES BRIGHT . . . came closest to being what I had wanted to achieve." Written by the director's son Patrick together with Frank Nugent, and based on a story by Ford himself, WAGONMASTER is a deceptively simple tale about a Mormon wagon train headed for the promised land. Along the way the group, led by Bond, forges alliances with two young horse traders (Johnson and Carey), four members of a traveling medicine show (Mowbray, Clifford, Francis Ford, and Dru), and a tribe of nomadic Navajo Indians. Bad guys materialize in the form of a sleazy band of varmints known as the Clegg family (Kemper, Arness, Libby, Worden, and Mickey Simpson), who we have seen rob an express office and murder a clerk during the pre-credit sequence.

WAGONMASTER is a first-rate film about solidarity, sacrifice, and tolerance, with Ford displaying consummate skill in everything from the brilliant visual compositions to the casting of the bit players. The relaxed, natural feel of the film is helped by the absence of stars; by putting his supporting players in lead roles, Ford was able to develop their characters in fresh and unexpected ways. Bond, Johnson, and Dru are nothing short of brilliant, turning in performances which, together with breathtaking scenery and an engaging sense of humor, make this well worth repeated watching.

WAIT UNTIL DARK
1967 107m c Thriller ★★★½
Warner Bros. (U.S.) /X

Audrey Hepburn *(Susy Hendrix)*, Alan Arkin *(Roat)*, Richard Crenna *(Mike Talman)*, Efrem Zimbalist Jr. *(Sam Hendrix)*, Jack Weston *(Carlino)*, Samantha Jones *(Lisa)*, Julie Herrod *(Gloria)*, Frank O'Brien *(Shatner)*, Gary Morgan *(Boy)*, Jean Del Val *(The Old Man)*

p, Mel Ferrer; d, Terence Young; w, Robert Carrington, Jane Howard Carrington (based on the play by Frederick Knott); ph, Charles Lang; ed, Gene Milford; m, Henry Mancini; art d, George Jenkins

AAN Best Actress: Audrey Hepburn

A real edge-of-your-seat thriller adapted from a Broadway stage hit written by Frederick Knott, author of DIAL M FOR MURDER. Hepburn, a blind Manhattan housewife, is terrorized by a trio of vicious killers (Crenna, Arkin, and Weston) who are after a fortune in heroin that has been hidden in a toy doll her husband, Zimbalist, gave to her. What follows is an excruciatingly suspenseful battle of wits between the blind Hepburn and her sadistic tormentors. Expertly directed by veteran British helmsman Young (Arthur Penn had directed the stage version), WAIT UNTIL DARK is an exciting, original chiller. Hepburn turns in a strong, realistic performance as the terrorized blind woman—a role she researched diligently with the help of two young blind women from the Lighthouse for the Blind school. For weeks the actress (and director Young) wore a special shade over her eyes and learned how to use a cane properly, feel the texture of different objects, and listen carefully to distinguish the quality and distance of sounds. The film was a tremendous success at the box office, and for added effect, some theater owners turned the house lights off completely during the final 15 minutes.

WAITING TO EXHALE

1995 121m c Drama   ★★½
Schindler-Swerdlow Productions (U.S.)   R/15

Whitney Houston (Savannah), Angela Bassett (Bernadine), Loretta
Devine (Gloria), Lela Rochon (Robin), Gregory Hines (Marvin), Dennis Haysbert (Kenneth), Mykelti Williamson (Troy), Michael Beach
(John, Sr.), Leon Robinson (Russell), Wendell Pierce (Michael)

p, Ezra Swerdlow, Deborah Schindler; d, Forest Whitaker; w, Terry
McMillan, Ronald Bass (based upon the novel by Terry McMillan); ph,
Toyomichi Kurita; ed, Richard Chew; m, Kenneth "Babyface" Edmonds; prod d, David Gropman; art d, Marc Fisichella; fx, Thomas C.
Ford; cos, Judy Ruskin

Had there been no Million Man March, this movie alone might have
prompted one. If there's an African-American male here who isn't a
sneaky, two-timing, narcissistic, wallet-stealing, white-woman-dating,
dope-taking, bad-in-bed, sorry son of a bitch, we missed him: he must
have been hiding in some closet, behind all those fabulous clothes.
Forest Whitaker's adaptation of Terry McMillan's best-selling novel is
more about gender than race, and it comes uncomfortably close to
pinning the blame for all the troubles of black women on black men.
Four genuinely charismatic actresses (Whitney Houston, Angela Bassett, Lela Rochon, and Loretta Devine) play close friends whose
relationship appears to be entirely founded on complaining about their
boyfriends. With its diva-heavy cast, this feels like THE WOMEN for
the '90s — which may mean that its superficial feminism is just an
excuse for a wallow in self-hatred.

WAKE ISLAND

1942 78m bw War   ★★★★
Paramount (U.S.)   /A

Brian Donlevy (Maj. Caton), Macdonald Carey (Lt. Cameron), Robert
Preston (Joe Doyle), William Bendix (Smacksie Randall), Albert
Dekker (Shad McClosky), Walter Abel (Cmdr. Roberts), Mikhail
Rasumny (Probenzky), Don Castle (Pvt. Cunkel), Rod Cameron
(Capt. Lewis), Bill Goodwin (Sergeant)

p, Joseph Sistrom; d, John Farrow; w, W.R. Burnett, Frank Butler; ph,
Theodor Sparkuhl; ed, LeRoy Stone; m, David Buttolph; art d, Hans
Dreier, Earl Hedrick

AAN Best Picture; AAN Best Supporting Actor: William Bendix; AAN
Best Director: John Farrow; AAN Best Original Screenplay: W.R.
Burnett, Frank Butler

The heroic but doomed defense of Wake Island against the Japanese in
the opening days of WWII provided the basis for this slightly fictionalized, immensely popular flag-waver that garnered several Academy
Award nominations. A perfect example of Hollywood's contribution to
the war effort, the film demonstrated that even in defeat there was
victory, and provided needed inspiration for a nation reeling from loss
after loss at the hands of the Japanese. Hunkered down in foxholes and
machine gun nests, the courageous Marine defenders of the island,
under the command of the determined Maj. Caton (Brian Donlevy),
refuse to bend to the assault of countless Japanese troops. For two
weeks they hold on, but with no help coming and ammunition running
low, they are doomed and know it. Still, they refuse to give up, and in
the end, Maj. Caton, Joe Doyle (Robert Preston), Lt. Cameron (Macdonald Carey), Smacksie Randall (William Bendix), and the other
brave Marines prove their mettle.

All the performers are good, particularly Donlevy, brilliantly evoking calm in the face of overwhelming odds, and Bendix. The film was
widely shown to soldiers at training camps all over the country, and
reportedly never failed to rouse cheers. Shot on location on the shores
of the Salton Sea in the California desert.

WALK IN THE SUN, A

1945 117m bw War   ★★★★½
Fox (U.S.)

Dana Andrews (Sgt. Tyne), Richard Conte (Rivera), John Ireland
(Windy), George Tyne (Friedman), Lloyd Bridges (Sgt. Ward), Sterling
Holloway (McWilliams), Herbert Rudley (Sgt. Porter), Norman Lloyd
(Archimbeau), Steve Brodie (Judson), Huntz Hall (Carraway)

p, Lewis Milestone; d, Lewis Milestone; w, Robert Rossen (based on
a story by Harry Brown); ph, Russell Harlan; ed, Duncan Mansfield;
m, Freddie Rich; art d, Max Bertisch

One of the better films to emerge from the final days of WWII, A WALK
IN THE SUN is the story of one infantry platoon, covering one
morning, from the time they hit the beach at Salerno until they reach
and capture their objective, a farmhouse six miles inland. Before they
even get ashore things begin to go badly, and the green lieutenant in
command is killed. A sergeant takes over for a time, but the stress proves
too great and he cracks. The men encounter a German armored car for
which they set up an ambush, raining it with grenades, then continue
on their mission with natural leader Sgt. Tyne (Dana Andrews) now in
command. Eventually, the soldiers reach their objective, but the situation appears suicidal and Sgt. Tyne must devise some way to complete
the mission with a minimum loss of life. Throughout the film, as it
follows the men in battle, the soundtrack picks up their chatty conversations and private thoughts. They think about their place in the great
scheme of the war, about their fear of being killed, and about the hard,
dirty, tedious, and dangerous job of being a front-line foot soldier. A
languorous sense of resignation holds sway over all: weary, hard-bitten,
and somewhat cynical, they are there to do a job, and although they
don't even understand what part they play in the big picture, they do it
anyway, even at the cost of their lives.

Although director Lewis Milestone seemed to have put the pacifism
of his earlier ALL QUIET ON THE WESTERN FRONT on hold for
the duration of WWII, A WALK IN THE SUN mostly avoids the
patriotic posing and outright racism (indeed, the enemy is never given
a face here) of his THE PURPLE HEART from the year before and
instead concentrates on the rugged day-to-day existence of the common
foot soldier. While the film is consistently engaging, some of the
narrative devices Milestone employs, such as the voice-over narration
and the occasional off-screen singing of a somewhat sappy folk song
dedicated to foot soldiers, now seem more of an intrusion on the visuals
than a complement.

WALKABOUT

1971 95m c Adventure/Drama   ★★★★½
20th Century Fox (Australia/U.S.)   PG/AA

Jenny Agutter (Girl), Lucien John (Brother), David Gulpilil (Aborigine),
John Meillon (Father), Peter Carver (No Hoper), John Illingsworth
(Husband), Barry Donnelly (Australian Scientist), Noelene Brown
(German Scientist), Carlo Manchini (Italian Scientist)

p, Si Litvinoff; d, Nicolas Roeg; w, Edward Bond (based on the novel
by James Vance Marshall); ph, Nicolas Roeg; ed, Anthony Gibbs,
Alan Pattillo; m, John Barry; prod d, Brian Eatwell; art d, Terry Gough

One of the most original, visually stunning, and provocative films of
the 1970s, WALKABOUT is timeless in its beauty and unique approach
to a classic coming-of-age story. The film is arguably director Nicolas
Roeg's finest achievement.

While on a picnic with his two children in the Australian outback, a
man goes insane and kills himself. His 14-year-old daughter (Jenny
Agutter), who had witnessed the suicide, tries to prevent her 6-year-old
brother (Lucien John) from discovering their father's dead body by
taking him away into the desert. Lost and hungry, they meet up with a
teenage aborigine (David Gulpilil) who is on a "walkabout," a ritual
during which adolescent aborigine boys must survive several weeks
alone in the desert. He is able to kill animals for food and find water
underneath the ground, thereby providing sustenance for himself, the
boy, and girl. He speaks no English, and the girl has little patience for
his native language. The young boy, however, learns to communicate
with him via signals and gestures. As the trio continue their journey,
the girl slowly becomes comfortable around the aborigine, although she
refuses to acknowledge the mating dance he does in her honor.

WALKABOUT is set in terrain stranger and more awe-inspiring
than that of any science-fiction film. It is filled with hissing lizards,
ominous bugs, blinding red sand, and short, misshapen trees. The film
has a straightforward story, little dialogue, and few characters. Nevertheless, it is a remarkably rich and complex narrative. On a basic level,
the film is about the way traditional roles and "civilized" upbringings
affect people so deeply that the roles cannot be overcome. By placing
the children in a setting that's as scary as it is awe-inspiring,

WALKABOUT presents one of cinema's deepest and most convincing studies of the mysteries and wonders of growing up. A restored version of the film was released in the United States in 1997, containing a scene that had been lost from American prints for years. The aborigine, momentarily separated from the boy and girl, is approached by a white woman. He rebuffs her advances, and she returns to her nearby home, where she lies in bed alone as her husband teaches aborigine children to paint. The scene adds a new dimension to the aborigine, proof that he knew all along that civilization was near, but chose not to bring the boy and girl there.

WALKING TALL

1973 125m c Biography/Crime	★★½
BCP (U.S.)	R/18

Joe Don Baker (Buford Pusser), Elizabeth Hartman (Pauline Pusser), Gene Evans (Sheriff Al Thurman), Noah Beery Jr. (Grandpa Carl Pusser), Brenda Benet (Luan Paxton), John Brascia (Prentiss Parley), Bruce Glover (Grady Coker), Arch Johnson (Buel Jaggers), Felton Perry (Obra Eaker), Richard X. Slattery (Arno Purdy)

p, Mort Briskin; d, Phil Karlson; w, Mort Briskin; ph, Jack Marta; ed, Harry Gerstad; m, Walter Scharf; prod d, Stan Jolley; fx, Sass Bedig; cos, Oscar Rodriguez, Phyllis Garr

Baker stars as real-life Tennessee sheriff Buford Pusser, whose one-man battle against gambling, moonshine whiskey, and prostitution in his county elevated him to folk-hero stature in three movies (WALKING TALL, PART 2 and FINAL CHAPTER—WALKING TALL followed this one) and a shortlived TV series. In this story of an angry redneck with a big stick, Baker smashes all illegal activities in his jurisdiction, much to the dismay of the criminal kingpins in Tennessee. The crooks band together in an effort to eliminate the troublesome sheriff. After several life-threatening beatings and the murder of his wife, Hartman, Baker finally gets *really mad*, grabs his stick, and cleans out the whole town, killing several people. Incredibly, the film grossed over $17 million at the box office, and the sequels were already in the works.

WALL, THE
(LE MUR)

1983 117m c Prison	★★★½
MK2/Guney/TF1/Ministere de la Culture (France)	/18

Tuncel Kurtiz, Ayse Emel Mesci, Nicolas Hossein, Isabelle Tissandier, Malik Berrichi, Ahmet Ziyrek, Ali Berktay, Selahattin Kuzuoglu, Jean-Pierre Colin, Jacques Dimanche

p, Marin Karmitz; d, Yilmaz Guney; w, Yilmaz Guney; ph, Izzet Akay; ed, Sabine Mamou; m, Ozan Garip Sahin, Setrak Bakrirel, Ali Dede Altuntas, Robert Kempler

THE WALL is an unceasingly brutal film about life in a Turkish prison. Director Yilmaz Guney, who died in 1984, served three separate jail sentences (one for murder) before finally escaping in 1981. Working from this firsthand experience in France (in an abbey converted to a jail for the production), Guney brings to the screen a film that stands up defiantly and violently for the rights of the imprisoned. The prison depicted here is a re-creation of the one in Ankara, Turkey, that was the sight of an inmate rebellion in 1976. It segregates men, women, and children but has no policy of separating violent offenders from political dissidents. In an indictment of the barbaric Turkish penal system, Guney presents an overcrowded prison with no windows, heat, hot water, or decent food, and with inhumane visiting conditions. The inmates (mostly children in the film) are treated savagely: one is kicked in the eye, another is forced to swallow a louse found on his body, and yet another is savagely battered on the soles of his feet while his blood-chilling screams are transmitted through the prison's public address system. These children pray to God not to be released but simply to be sent to another prison. Although the subject has been brought to the screen before and certain elements of THE WALL have become cliches, the power of the film's message is not lessened. THE WALL is perhaps not the most artful or poetic picture (although it does contain one of the most amazingly photographed birth scenes in cinema); it is nonetheless one of the most necessary.

WALL STREET

1987 124m c Drama	★★★
American Entertainment (U.S.)	R/15

Charlie Sheen (Bud Fox), Michael Douglas (Gordon Gekko), Martin Sheen (Carl Fox), Terence Stamp (Sir Larry Wildman), Sean Young (Kate Gekko), Daryl Hannah (Darien Taylor), Sylvia Miles (Realtor), James Spader (Roger Barnes), Hal Holbrook (Lou Mannheim), Saul Rubinek (Harold Salt)

p, Edward R. Pressman, A. Kitman Ho; d, Oliver Stone; w, Oliver Stone, Stanley Weiser; ph, Robert Richardson; ed, Claire Simpson; m, Stewart Copeland; prod d, Stephen Hendrickson; art d, John J. Moore, Hilda Stark; cos, Ellen Mirojnick

AA Best Actor: Michael Douglas

Writer-director Oliver Stone, who shows an uncanny knack for anticipating public interest in the subjects he chooses, explores the much-publicized inside trading scandals of the mid-1980s. Set in 1985, the film follows the career of young Wall Street broker Bud Fox (Charlie Sheen) as he scrambles to make his first million. His idol is ruthless big-time corporate raider Gordon Gekko (Michael Douglas). Fox insinuates himself into Gekko's good graces by giving Gekko inside information about an airline, information he has learned from his father (Martin Sheen), an airline mechanic and local representative of his union. With the promise of big financial rewards negating his momentary apprehension about breaking the law, Fox willingly goes to work for Gekko. With WALL STREET, Stone intentionally set out to make a good old-fashioned liberal drama about the evils of unchecked capitalism. This approach results in a film with few shades of gray and lots of moralizing speeches, but Stone nearly pulls it off through his usual visual verve and keen casting instincts. Charlie Sheen is fine as the young, inexperienced kid whose soul is battled for by the forces of good and evil. Better yet is Douglas, whose Gordon Gekko is a predatory animal seducing the weak into his lair.

WALTZ OF THE TOREADORS

1962 104m c Comedy	★★★½
Independent Artists (U.K.)	/15

Peter Sellers (Gen. Leo Fitzjohn), Dany Robin (Ghislaine), Margaret Leighton (Emily Fitzjohn), John Fraser (Robert), Cyril Cusack (Dr. Grogan), Prunella Scales (Estella), Denise Coffey (Sidonia), Jean Anderson (Agnes), Raymond Huntley (President of the Court Martial), Cardew Robinson (Midgeley)

p, Peter de Sarigny; d, John Guillermin; w, Wolf Mankowitz (based on the play by Jean Anouilh); ph, John Wilcox; ed, Peter Taylor; m, Richard Addinsell; prod d, Wilfred Shingleton; art d, Harry Pottle; cos, Beatrice Dawson

Sellers is outstanding as a Leo Fitzjohn, a retired general looking to escape a bleak existence in this fine adaptation of Jean Anouilh's bittersweet stage comedy. The film opens just before the outbreak of WWI. Fitzjohn has retired from the army and now lives on his manor with his shrewish wife, Emily (Leighton), whom he can't stand. Tortured by loneliness, Fitzjohn pines for the days when he had a platonic affair 17 years before with Ghislaine (Robin), a beautiful young Frenchwoman. Surprisingly, Ghislaine arrives at the manor claiming fidelity to the general and demanding that they consummate the relationship. Fitzjohn jumps at the chance, but circumstances force a postponement of their rendezvous and he leaves his former love under the care of his aide, Robert (Fraser). In two days, the aide succeeds where Fitzjohn has failed, and the angry general puts the young soldier in for a court-martial. Fitzjohn learns during the trial that Robert is actually his illegitimate son, so he stops the proceedings and allows the young couple to marry. Unhinged by the reality that he is stuck with Emily for the rest of his life, Fitzjohn considers doing something desperate, but a new arrival on the scene changes his mind.

WANDERERS, THE

1979 113m c Drama   ★★★★
Orion (U.S.)   R/18

Ken Wahl (Richie), John Friedrich (Joey), Karen Allen (Nina), Toni Kalem (Despie Galasso), Alan Rosenberg (Turkey), Jim Youngs (Buddy), Tony Ganios (Perry), Linda Manz (Peewee), William Andrews (Emilio), Erland Van Lidth (Terror)

p, Martin Ransohoff; d, Philip Kaufman; w, Rose Kaufman, Philip Kaufman (based on the novel by Richard Price); ph, Michael Chapman; ed, Ronald Roose, Stuart Pappe; art d, John J. Moore; cos, Robert de Mora

The best of the gang films to be released in 1979 (the list includes THE WARRIORS, WALK PROUD, and BOULEVARD NIGHTS), THE WANDERERS is a strangely compelling film directed with flair by Philip Kaufman (INVASION OF THE BODY SNATCHERS, THE RIGHT STUFF). While basically just a string of vignettes about a gang of Italian-American teenagers living in the Bronx circa 1963, the film has an air of authenticity, as if it episodes were based on adolescent recollections. The performances in the film are uniformly strong, with Wahl, the protagonist, showing a great screen promise he has never fulfilled (FORT APACHE, THE BRONX; and THE SOLDIER being dismal wastes of his talent). Little Linda Manz (DAYS OF HEAVEN and OUT OF THE BLUE) nearly steals the film as a pint-sized tough gal who is the girlfriend of Van Lidth, the giant leader of a rival street gang known as "The Fordham Baldies." Kaufman infuses the film with a wistful sadness for an era about to end with the assassination of JFK. Many incidents will stick with the viewer, including the very funny sequence where all the members of the Fordham Baldies get drunk and join the Marines, and the haunting, almost surrealistic battle with the mysterious and violent rival gang known as "The Ducky Boys." All in all a fascinating film with an outstanding musical score consisting of jukebox hits from the period.

WAR AND PEACE

1956 208m c Drama/War   ★★★★
Ponti/DEG (Italy/U.S.)   /U

Audrey Hepburn (Natasha Rostov), Henry Fonda (Pierre Bezukhov), Mel Ferrer (Prince Andrei Bolkonsky), Vittorio Gassman (Anatole Kuragin), John Mills (Platon Karatayev), Herbert Lom (Napoleon), Oscar Homolka (Gen. Mikhail Kutuzov), Anita Ekberg (Helene Kuragin), Helmut Dantine (Dolokhov), Barry Jones (Count Ilya Rostov)

p, Dino De Laurentiis; d, King Vidor; w, Bridget Boland, Robert Westerby, King Vidor, Mario Camerini, Ennio De Concini, Ivo Perilli, Irwin Shaw (based on the novel by Leo Tolstoy); ph, Jack Cardiff, Aldo Tonti; ed, Stuart Gilmore, Leo Catozzo; m, Nino Rota; art d, Mario Chiari, Franz Bachelin, Gianni Polidori; cos, Maria De Matteis

AAN Best Director: King Vidor; AAN Best Cinematography: Jack Cardiff; AAN Best Costume Design: Marie DeMattesi

King Vidor's version of Tolstoy's great novel seems insufficient at more than three hours and fared ill both with the critics and at the box office, but it does deliver the spectacular visuals expected of historical epics. As Napoleon (Herbert Lom) prepares to invade Russia, the gentle, awkward, intellectual Pierre Bezukhov (Henry Fonda) falls in undeclared love with young Natasha Rostov (Audrey Hepburn). Soon afterward, his father dies—making Pierre the wealthy new Count Bezukhov and a desirable marriage prospect—and Bezukhov marries the luscious, adulterous Helene (Anita Ekberg). Meanwhile, his dear friend Prince Andrei (Mel Ferrer), a haughty, gloomy aide to General Kutuzov (Oscar Homolka), returns home from battle after being wounded. Depressed after his wife's death in childbirth, Andrei rediscovers the joy of life when he, too, falls in love with Natasha, and she with him—the two having been introduced by Pierre, who battles his own spiritual malaise after the failure of his loveless marriage. Andrei returns to the front and is wounded critically in the disastrous Russian defeat at Borodino. Pierre observes the carnage in horror and vows to assassinate Napoleon, but he is captured and held prisoner when the French occupy Moscow. When all looks darkest, however, the Russian

winter sets in, the French are routed, Pierre is reunited with Natasha, and the love that was hinted at in the opening scenes finally comes to fruition.

Lovers of Tolstoy's work are likely to be frustrated by this somewhat static film, which, inevitably, omits a great deal of Tolstoy's characterization, plots, philosophy, and historical analysis, while on the other hand plays up the Pierre-Natasha romance. The performances are similarly limited, though Hepburn charmingly captures the gamine radiance of the young Natasha and Fonda (who felt he was miscast) effectively communicates Pierre's integrity. Cinematographers Jack Cardiff and Aldo Tonti contribute the film's most stunning work, as does Mario Soldati, who directed the battle scenes.

WAR OF THE ROSES, THE

1989 116m c Comedy   ★★★★
Gracie (U.S.)   R/15

Michael Douglas (Oliver Rose), Kathleen Turner (Barbara Rose), Danny DeVito (Gavin D'Amato), Marianne Sagebrecht (Susan), Sean Astin (Josh, Age 17), Heather Fairfield (Carolyn, Age 17), G.D. Spradlin (Harry Thurmont), Trenton Teigen (Josh, Age 10), Bethany McKinney (Carolyn, Age 10), Peter Donat (Larrabee)

p, James L. Brooks, Arnon Milchan; d, Danny DeVito; w, Michael Leeson (based on the novel by Warren Adler); ph, Stephen H. Burum; ed, Lynzee Klingman, Nicholas C. Smith; m, David Newman; prod d, Ida Random; art d, Mark Mansbridge; cos, Gloria Gresham

Few things are sadder, sillier, or scarier than the break-up of a long-married pair, and in THE WAR OF THE ROSES, director Danny DeVito captures this fiasco in its full, blackly comic ingloriousness. After 17 years of wedlock, Barbara Rose (Kathleen Turner) can't stand her husband, Oliver (Michael Douglas). He still loves her—but he loves their big, beautiful, antique-filled house more, and therein lies the cautionary tale, told by Gavin D'Amato (director DeVito), a divorce lawyer who recounts the progressively crazier story to a prospective client. Stuck (for legal reasons) in the house together as they begin divorce proceedings, the Roses escalate tensions until the hostilities erupt into full-scale, no-prisoners war.

DeVito films this tale with a fiendish gusto, yet with psychological realism and meticulous attention to an inexorable logic in the plotting, even as the Roses' war moves from the outlandish to the surreal. At once horrific and hilarious, THE WAR OF THE ROSES is made with a high level of cinematic craft: Turner and Douglas (ROMANCING THE STONE, JEWEL OF THE NILE) again prove to be the quintessential antiromantic screen couple for the antiromantic 1980s, and DeVito exerts a control behind the camera that is otherwise almost nonexistent in contemporary American film comedy.

WAR OF THE WORLDS, THE

1953 85m c Science Fiction   ★★★½
Paramount (U.S.)   /PG

Gene Barry (Dr. Clayton Forrester), Ann Robinson (Sylvia Van Buren), Les Tremayne (Gen. Mann), Lewis Martin (Pastor Matthew Collins), Robert Cornthwaite (Dr. Pryor), Sandro Giglio (Dr. Bilderbeck), William Phipps (Wash Perry), Paul Birch (Alonzo Hogue), Jack Kruschen (Salvatore), Vernon Rich (Col. Heffner)

p, George Pal; d, Byron Haskin; w, Barre Lyndon (based on the novel by H.G. Wells); ph, George Barnes; ed, Everett Douglas; m, Leith Stevens; art d, Hal Pereira, Albert Nozaki; fx, Gordon Jennings, Paul K. Lerpae, Wallace Kelly, Ivyl Burks, Jan Domela, Irmin Roberts, Walter Hoffman, Chesley Bonestell; cos, Edith Head

AAN Best Editing: Everett Douglas; AAN Best Sound: Loren L. Ryder; AA Best Visual Effects:

A key sci-fi film of the 1950s, George Pal's THE WAR OF THE WORLDS is a vividly realized adaptation of the classic H.G. Wells novel, updated from 19th century London to 20th century California. Though it's bogged down by a stiff cast, a yawn-inspiring conventional romance, and a sappy religiosity, it remains a landmark in the history of special effects. The lumbersome triopods of the Wells novel are jettisoned in favor of cool, green, slickly contoured flying saucers that fire death rays accompanied by one of the most fondly remembered sound effects in screen history. Filmed on a relatively modest budget of $2 million ($1.3 million went to special effects), THE WAR OF THE WORLDS was a solid box office hit.

WAR REQUIEM

1989 93m c Experimental ★★★★
Anglo International Films/Liberty Films /PG
/BBC Enterprises (U.K.)

Nathaniel Parker (Wilfrid Owen), Tilda Swinton (Nurse), Laurence Olivier (Old Soldier), Patricia Hayes (Mother), Rohan McCullough, Nigel Terry (Abraham), Owen Teale (Unknown Soldier), Sean Bean (German Soldier)

p, Don Boyd; d, Derek Jarman; w, Derek Jarman (from the poetry of Wilfred Owen); ph, Richard Greatrex; ed, Rick Elgood; m, Benjamin Britten; prod d, Lucy Morahan; cos, Linda Alderson

Marshalling an astonishing parade of images—brutal, exquisite, erotic, and painterly by turns—avant-garde director Derek Jarman supplies visual counterpoint to Benjamin Britten's masterwork, the 1961 oratorio *War Requiem*. Jarman's hallucinatory vision of war draws on the life and verse of WWI poet Wilfred Owen, who was killed on a French battlefield two weeks before the Armistice. Owen's preoccupations—e.g., the Christ-like martyrdom of soldiers, the interplay of sexuality and death, the pity and horror evoked by the mutilation of young bodies—mesh perfectly with those of the director. An anti-war film of surpassing power, WAR REQUIEM can also be read as a metaphorical treatment of the devastation of youth by AIDS. The soundtrack recording of Britten's music, by the London Symphony Orchestra with soloists including Peter Pears and Dietrich Fischer-Dieskau, is first-class. Laurence Olivier's cameo is his last screen appearance.

WARLOCK

1959 121m c Western ★★★★
Fox (U.S.) /U

Richard Widmark (Johnny Gannon), Henry Fonda (Clay Blaisdell), Anthony Quinn (Tom Morgan), Dorothy Malone (Lilly Dollar), Dolores Michaels (Jessie Marlow), Wallace Ford (Judge Holloway), Tom Drake (Abe McQuown), Richard Arlen (Bacon), DeForest Kelley (Curley Burne), Regis Toomey (Skinner)

p, Edward Dmytryk; d, Edward Dmytryk; w, Robert Alan Aurthur (based on the novel by Oakley Hall); ph, Joseph MacDonald; ed, Jack W. Holmes; m, Leigh Harline; art d, Lyle Wheeler, Herman A. Blumenthal; fx, L.B. Abbott; cos, Charles LeMaire

A unique and often overlooked adult western that goes much deeper than most movies in this genre, WARLOCK would seem on the surface to be a fairly standard story. The citizens of the small town of Warlock are a kind, God-fearing lot who live in dread because a group of brawling cowboys, led by Drake, likes to come into town from time to time and shoot up the place. They hire Fonda, a well-known gunslinger, to be local marshal. It's 1881, and men of Fonda's type are either dying of old age or being shot down by younger, faster cowboys, so he's something of an anachronism. He accepts the job on the provision that he also can run the local gambling and dance parlor. Fonda soon meets Michaels, and an attraction between the two grows. Drake and his cohorts mosey back into Warlock accompanied by Widmark, who becomes disenchanted with Drake and his group so he quits the gang and decides to remain in Warlock as Fonda's deputy. Fonda manages to get Drake and the other troublemakers out of town, and for a while law and order reign. The townsfolk decide that they don't need a professional gunslinger anymore, now that Drake and the others have been cowed. Inevitably, however, the bad guys return.

WARLOCK was shot partly in Utah, although not much of the glorious scenery there was utilized. The filmmakers preferred instead to concentrate on the scene within the confines of the small town and the multilayered stories going on among the principals. There's a sense of brooding and Greek tragedy here not usually presented in a cowboy movie. Yet under Dmytryk's strong direction of the Aurthur adaptation, the tone and story lines all work to great advantage. Fonda had bombed in two previous films and had to get back into mainstream movies. While this was hardly a typical western, it did reestablish him in the eyes of the movie-going public as more than the effete Easterner he had portrayed in STAGE STRUCK and 12 ANGRY MEN. Lots of action punctuates the excellent dialogue, enhanced by a strong supporting cast.

WARRIORS, THE

1979 90m c Action ★★★½
Paramount (U.S.) R/18

Michael Beck (Swan), James Remar (Ajax), Thomas Waites (Fox), Dorsey Wrights (Cleon), Brian Taylor (Snow), David Harris (Cochise), Tom McKitterick (Cowboy), Marcelino Sanchez (Rembrandt), Terry Michos (Vermin), Deborah Van Valkenburgh (Mercy)

p, Lawrence Gordon; d, Walter Hill; w, David Shaber, Walter Hill (based on the novel by Sol Yurick); ph, Andrew Laszlo; ed, David Holden; m, Barry DeVorzon; art d, Don Swanagan, Robert Wightman; cos, Bobbie Mannix, Mary Ellen Winston

Kinetic is the word for the films of director Walter Hill. While some of them may lack complex characterizations (particularly true of THE DRIVER and THE WARRIORS), Hill makes up for these deficiencies with stunning visual panache. THE WARRIORS advertised its subject matter in somewhat belligerent terms: "These are the Armies of the Night. They are 100,000 strong. They outnumber the cops five to one. They could run New York City," and as a result the film was widely criticized as an incitement to gang violence. While the film depicts gangs, however, it does so in a highly stylized manner, and the criticism seems therefore to reflect a naive confusion of art with life. Indeed, without moralizing, the film achieves insight into the blighted lives and emotions of the young gang members. Loosely based on Sol Yurick's 1965 novel about a reprehensible New York street gang, THE WARRIORS opens (after a marvelous credits sequence that sets the mood for the movie) at a rally held by Roger Hill, playing the ambitious leader of a gang known as the Riffs, who seeks to unite all the street gangs into one army. Each gang has sent a handful of representatives to the meeting, all of whom have agreed to come unarmed. The leader of a gang called the Rogues, however, pulls a gun, kills Hill, and frames the Warriors for the crime. The film then turns into a battle in which the Warriors try to make it home through enemy territory with every rival gang in the city out to get them. The Warriors finally straggle back to Coney Island, where the truth is revealed, leaving Kelly and his gang in the hands of a very angry group of Riffs.

THE WARRIORS is a visual feast. Director Hill fills the frame with vibrant colors, bright lights, and nonstop motion. The uniforms of the various gangs are unique, funny, fearsome, and more than a bit theatrical. The exciting fight scenes are brilliantly choreographed, and instead of focusing on the violence, Hill concentrates on pure movement (most of the cast were actually dancers). Alongside all the glitz are a few moments of insight into the characters. In a simple but effective scene, the Warriors are sprawled exhausted in a subway car. Two teenage couples fresh from a prom enter and sit opposite gang-leader Beck and his girl, Valkenburgh. The street kids stare at the tuxedos, prom dresses, and flowers of the "wholesome" kids. The visual contrast is enough to suggest the ways in which the street kids have missed out and been denied a normal adolescence.

WATCH ON THE RHINE

1943 114m bw Drama/War ★★½
Warner Bros. (U.S.) /U

Bette Davis (Sara Muller), Paul Lukas (Kurt Muller), Geraldine Fitzgerald (Marthe de Brancovis), Lucile Watson (Fanny Farrelly), Beulah Bondi (Anise), George Coulouris (Teck de Brancovis), Donald Woods (David Farrelly), Henry Daniell (Phili von Ramme), Donald Buka (Joshua Muller), Eric Roberts (Bodo Muller)

p, Hal B. Wallis; d, Herman Shumlin; w, Dashiell Hammett, Lillian Hellman (based on the play by Hellman); ph, Merritt Gerstad, Hal Mohr; ed, Rudi Fehr; m, Max Steiner; art d, Carl Jules Weyl; fx, Jack Holden, Edwin DuPar; cos, Orry-Kelly

AAN Best Picture; AA Best Actor: Paul Lukas; AAN Best Supporting Actress: Lucile Watson; AAN Best Screenplay: Dashiell Hammett

Yawn. Lillian Hellman's respected play was adapted for film by Hellman and Dashiell Hammett, her longtime companion, and helmed by Herman Shumlin, who directed the stage original and cast some of its players here. The resulting drama, intermittently powerful stuff, was nominated for Best Picture, Script, and Supporting Actress (Lucile Watson) Oscars, while Paul Lukas, repeating his stage role, won as Best Actor. Kurt and Sara Muller (Lukas and Bette Davis), refugees from Nazi Germany, arrive with their children after a long absence to visit Sara's mother (Watson) in her Washington, DC, home. Already there are Teck de Brancovis (George Coulouris), a Rumanian count, and his American wife (Geraldine Fitzgerald). The Mullers plan to stay in the US only until Kurt's health improves; then he will return to his "business" abroad, the exact nature of which is unclear. When the count, who socializes at the German embassy, hears of the Gestapo's unsuccessful attempts to crack an underground resistance group, he suspects that Kurt may be one of them and offers to spy on him, then in turn tries to blackmail Kurt, who must take desperate measures to protect himself and his family.

One of the first American films to present the philosophy—rather than just the warmongering—of fascism as a danger, WATCH ON THE RHINE is rather dully helmed by stage director Shumlin, who too often fails to avoid the static pitfalls of so many play adaptations. Lukas and most of the cast (especially Coulouris) are in fine form, though, partially redeeming a film that has not worn particularly well. Davis, too, (in a fairly small role, though top-billed) tones down her usual fireworks here to fairly good effect. She's better in spitfire mode, though.

WATERDANCE, THE

1992   106m   c   Comedy/Drama   ★★★½
No Frills Films/JBW   (U.S.)   R/15

Eric Stoltz (*Joel Garcia*), Wesley Snipes (*Raymond Hill*), William Forsythe (*Bloss*), Helen Hunt (*Anna*), Elizabeth Pena (*Rosa*), William Allen Young (*Les*), James Roach (*Guy in the Electronic Wheelchair*), Henry Harris (*Mr. Gibson*), Tony Genaro (*Victor*), Eva Rodriguez (*Victor's Wife*)

p, Gale Anne Hurd, Marie Cantin; d, Neal Jimenez, Michael Steinberg; w, Neal Jimenez; ph, Mark Plummer; ed, Jeff Freeman; m, Michael Convertino; prod d, Bob Ziembicki; cos, Isis Mussenden

Screenwriter and first-time director Neal Jimenez drew on personal experience for THE WATERDANCE, a tough-minded comedy-drama about three paraplegics adapting to life in a wheelchair. Joel Garcia (Eric Stolz) is a promising young novelist who has broken his neck in a hiking accident. Garcia was having an affair with his married editor, Anna (Helen Hunt), who was about to leave her husband for him when Garcia's accident occurred. With his world turned upside down, Garcia begins having second thoughts about their relationship and questions whether Anna will stay with him in his new, physically dependent condition. He has little regard or use for his wardmates at first, but gradually he gets to know them. A member of a biker gang, Bloss (William Forsythe) was broadsided by a car while riding drunk. Though an unapologetic redneck bigot, Bloss strikes up a bickering friendship with Black wardmate Raymond Hill (Wesley Snipes). Hill continually brags about his sexual conquests, but his only visible partner is his wife, who is divorcing him and taking their daughter with her.

Co-directed with Michael Steinberg, Jimenez populates his episodic tale with characters who are believable rather than heroic, sympathetic if not always likable, and avoids the sentimental or the moralistic by undercutting the tragedy with some barbed humor. The cast is generally good, with Hunt (MR. SATURDAY NIGHT, PEGGY SUE GOT MARRIED) taking top honors for giving substance to a relatively sketchy part. Stolz and Forsythe are solid and Snipes is extraordinary. He disappears so thoroughly into Raymond that it's hard to imagine the same actor as the slick, successful architect in Spike Lee's JUNGLE FEVER. Elizabeth Pena (JACOB'S LADDER) contributes an effective turn as the ward's head nurse. The real star here, though, is Jimenez, a talented filmmaker who clearly has a lot more still to offer.

WATERLOO BRIDGE

1940   103m   bw   Romance   ★★★★
MGM   (U.S.)   /A

Vivien Leigh (*Myra Lester*), Robert Taylor (*Capt. Roy Cronin*), Lucile Watson (*Lady Margaret Cronin*), C. Aubrey Smith (*Duke*), Maria Ouspenskaya (*Mme. Olga*), Virginia Field (*Kitty*), Leo G. Carroll (*Policeman*), Clara Reid (*Mrs. Bassett*), Steffi Duna (*Lydia*), Leonard Mudie (*Parker*)

p, Sidney Franklin; d, Mervyn LeRoy; w, S.N. Behrman, Hans Rameau, George Froeschel (based on the play by Robert E. Sherwood); ph, Joseph Ruttenberg; ed, George Boemler; m, Herbert Stothart; art d, Cedric Gibbons, Urie McCleary; chor, Ernst Matray; cos, Adrian, Gile Steele

AAN Best Cinematography: Joseph Ruttenberg; *AAN Best Score:* Herbert Stothart

In London during WWII, a British colonel, Taylor, is caught in a blackout in his chauffeured army sedan. He steps from the vehicle to tread the pavement of the famed Waterloo Bridge and begins to reminisce. In flashback, Taylor is a handsome young captain on the eve of WWI. He meets and falls in love with ballerina Leigh; they make plans to wed, but before they can do so Taylor's regiment is called into battle. Leigh abandons her performance to bid her lover farewell at Waterloo Station and is fired from the ballet company. Impoverished, she resorts to prostitution. She plies her trade on the Waterloo Bridge where, months later, she meets the returning Taylor—who has spent the intervening time as a POW—and, thinking fast, conceals her profession during the shocking reunion. Their romance continues; it appears that her degradation was no more than a nightmare, best forgotten. But inevitably, her indiscretions come to light.

Leigh is stunning in this second cinematic version of author Sherwood's hit play. (A fine first version was made in 1931 by James Whale and starred Mae Clarke and Douglass Montgomery.) WATERLOO BRIDGE was Leigh's first movie following the record-breaking David Selznick production of GONE WITH THE WIND, which had made her the most visible, most desirable actress in the world. Selznick had loaned Leigh to MGM for the picture in repayment for help that studio's head had given him for the previous picture. Leigh was in the midst of a divorce from her husband Leigh Holman at the time, her romance with Laurence Olivier—also wed at the time—a continuing scandal. She and Olivier had both invested every farthing they had in their planned theatrical production of William Shakespeare's "Romeo and Juliet," and both were desperately in need of money. Olivier accepted the male lead in PRIDE AND PREJUDICE, and the lovers were forced to separate temporarily. Leigh was irate about the parting, believing that Olivier should have gotten the role assigned to Taylor. Taylor drew kudos for his mature, restrained performance, which revitalized his then-fading career by demonstrating that he was more than just another pretty face, although critics were none too tolerant of his "Nebraska accent." Of all his seventy-plus screen performances, this was Taylor's personal favorite. The story was filmed again in 1956 as GABY, a disappointing version starring Leslie Caron and John Kerr.

WATERSHIP DOWN

1978   92m   c   Animated   ★★★
Nepenthe   (U.K.)   PG/U

VOICES OF: John Hurt (*Hazel*), Richard Briers (*Fiver*), Michael Graham-Cox (*Bigwig*), John Bennett (*Capt. Holly*), Simon Cadell (*Blackberry*), Roy Kinnear (*Pipkin*), Richard O'Callaghan (*Dandelion*), Terence Rigby (*Silver*), Ralph Richardson (*Chief Rabbit*), Denholm Elliott (*Cowslip*)

p, Martin Rosen; d, Martin Rosen; w, Martin Rosen (based on the novel by Richard Adams); ed, Terry Rawlings; m, Angela Morley, Malcolm Williamson

Expertly and realistically animated, this version of the popular novel didn't seem to have an audience. It was much too violent for kids, and wasn't the type of picture that an adult would go out and see, in part because it is animated. The spirit of the book is captured here as the rabbits, faced with problems of ecology, are forced to find a new home.

Their trek is filled with surprises and adventures, as well as bloodshed. The job of personifying the rabbits is nicely achieved due to expert readings by the cast.

WATERWORLD

1995 134m c Adventure/Action/Science Fiction ★★¹/₂
King Kona Productions/The Gordon Company/TIG PG-13/12
Productions/Davis Entertainment/Licht/Mueller Film
Corp./Universal (U.S.)

Kevin Costner (Mariner), Dennis Hopper (Deacon), Jeanne Tripple-horn (Helen), Tina Majorino (Enola), Michael Jeter (Gregor), Gerard Murphy (Nord), R.D. Call (Enforcer), Chaim Jeraffi (Drifter #1), Kim Coates (Drifter #2), John Fleck (Doctor)

p, Charles Gordon, John A. Davis, Kevin Costner; d, Kevin Reynolds; w, David Twohy, Peter Rader, Joss Whedon (uncredited); ph, Dean Semler; ed, Peter Boyle; m, James Newton Howard; prod d, Dennis Gassner; art d, David Klassen; fx, Marty Bresin, Michael McAlister, Sean Phillips, Boss Film Studios, Brad Kuehn, Jamie Price, Cinesite; cos, John Bloomfield

AAN Best Sound: Steve Maslow, Gregg Landaker, Keith A. Wester

This is the way the WATERWORLD fiasco ends: not with a bang but a whimper. After all the thud and blunder of its production, the most expensive movie ever made emerged as a marginally better-than-average, entirely forgettable summer action picture. Those who were hoping for a debacle of HEAVEN'S GATE proportions were disappointed: this huge, rather awkward ROAD WARRIOR ripoff managed to turn a slight profit worldwide, partly because star Kevin Costner surrendered his upfront fee.

In a postapocalyptic future world where all land is submerged beneath the surface of the ocean, an amphibious loner called the Mariner (Costner) roams the sea in search of fresh water and dry land, tangling with a gang of punked-out losers led by one-eyed evildoer Deacon (Dennis Hopper, in a nod to his biker-pic background). Tepid love interest is supplied by Jeanne Tripplehorn, but the film's really all about Costner — his image, his ego, and his revamped build — who throws himself around the floating sets with commendable energy.

Of course, any Hollywood spectacle that opens with its superstar protagonist drinking his own urine—distilled, granted, but pee nonetheless—has something going for it. WATERWORLD aspires to laud ecological values—the villains burn oil, smoke cigarettes and eat a processed meat product called "Smeat," while the hero lives at peace with the sea—but in the end, its sheer profligacy undermines the message.

WAY AHEAD, THE

1944 115m bw War ★★★¹/₂
Two Cities (U.K.)

David Niven (Lt. Jim Perry), Raymond Huntley (Davenport), William Hartnell (Sgt. Fletcher), Stanley Holloway (Brewer), James Donald (Lloyd), John Laurie (Luke), Leslie Dwyer (Beck), Hugh Burden (Parsons), Jimmy Hanley (Stainer), Renee Asherson (Marjorie Gillingham)

p, John Sutro, Norman Walker; d, Carol Reed; w, Eric Ambler, Peter Ustinov (based on a story by Eric Ambler); ph, Guy Green; ed, Fergus McDonell; m, William Alwyn; art d, David Rawnsley

Bracing, spirited and lovely. Carol Reed had already developed a reputation in Britain as an accomplished director by the time WWII broke out, so when he joined the Army it was no surprise that he was assigned to the film unit. His 1942 short instructional documentary THE NEW LOT and an idea by Lt. Col. David Niven provided the inspiration for THE WAY AHEAD (a.k.a. THE IMMORTAL BATTALION). Set in the aftermath of the Dunkirk evacuation, the story focuses on Lt. Jim Perry (Niven) as he whips a group of ordinary conscripts into soldiers and then leads them against Rommel's Afrika Korps at El Alamein. This pseudo-documentary was a big success in Britain, earning Reed even greater respect and leading to ODD MAN OUT, THE FALLEN IDOL and THE THIRD MAN, and serving as a patriotic contribution to the war effort.

WAY OUT WEST

1937 65m bw Comedy/Western ★★★★¹/₂
Hal Roach (U.S.) /U

Stan Laurel, Oliver Hardy (Themselves), James Finlayson (Mickey Finn), Sharon Lynne (Lola Marcel), Stanley Fields (Sheriff), Rosina Lawrence (Mary Roberts), James Mason (Anxious Patron), James C. Morton, Frank Mills, David Pepper (Bartenders)

p, Stan Laurel; d, James W. Horne; w, Charles Rogers, Felix Adler, James Parrott (based on a story by Jack Jevne, Charles Rogers); ph, Art Lloyd, Walter Lundin; ed, Bert Jordan; m, Marvin Hatley, LeRoy Shield, Egbert Van Alstyne, J.L. Hill, Nathaniel Shilkret, Irving Berlin, Franz von Suppe; art d, Arthur I. Royce; fx, Roy Seawright

AAN Best Score: Marvin Hatley, Hal Roach Studio Music Department

Laurel and Hardy's only western spoof, WAY OUT WEST, ranks among the best of their films, with more exuberant laughs crammed into its scant 65 minutes than can be found in a dozen modern comedies. With their faithful mule, the boys head into Brushwood Gulch to deliver a gold mine deed to their departed partner's daughter. But they get hopelessly lost, and make the mistake of asking bartender Mickey Finn (James Finlayson) for advice. Finn's scullery maid, Mary Roberts (Rosina Lawrence), is actually the woman they seek, but he deliberately steers them toward his wife, Lola Marcel (Sharon Lynn)—a brassy blonde who is so obviously not the right person that everyone can see she cries crocodile tears upon learning of her "father's" death. Everyone, that is, except Laurel and Hardy. Included is the song "Trail of the Lonesome Pine."

WAY WE WERE, THE

1973 118m c Romance ★★★
Rastar (U.S.) PG

Barbra Streisand (Katie Morosky), Robert Redford (Hubbell Gardiner), Bradford Dillman (J.J.), Lois Chiles (Carol Ann), Patrick O'Neal (George Bissinger), Viveca Lindfors (Paula Reisner), Allyn Ann McLerie (Rhea Edwards), Murray Hamilton (Brooks Carpenter), Herb Edelman (Bill Verso), Diana Ewing (Vicki Bissinger)

p, Ray Stark; d, Sydney Pollack; w, Arthur Laurents, Alvin Sargent (uncredited), David Rayfiel (based on the novel by Laurents); ph, Harry Stradling Jr.; ed, Margaret Booth; m, Marvin Hamlisch; prod d, Stephen Grimes; chor, Grover Dale; cos, Dorothy Jeakins, Moss Mabry

AAN Best Actress: Barbra Streisand; AAN Best Cinematography: Harry Stradling, Jr.; AA Best Score: Marvin Hamlisch; AA Best Song: Marvin Hamlisch (Music), Alan Bergman (Lyrics), Marilyn Bergman (Lyrics); AAN Best Art Direction: Stephen Grimes, William Kiernan; AAN Best Costume Design: Dorothy Jeakins, Moss Mabry

La Babs with a blondish Afro spouting leftist rhetoric? Just call her Harpo Marxist. Here we have an engrossing, if occasionally ludicrous, hit tearjerker with Pollack, Streisand, and Redford doing a good job of bringing Arthur Laurents' script to the screen. It's a great campy romance and it does tell us something about the way we were from the 30s through the 50s, but a lot of the politics of the Blacklist period are missing from the film, apparently cut just before release.

Redford is a handsome WASP college student in the late 1930s. He yearns to be a writer, spends his spare time in mindless social activities, and is politically neutral. Streisand, in her big bid for old-fashioned romantic movie star status, is a radical Jewish student who joins every political organization. She is the butt of many jokes at the college (what a surprise!), and the sharpest barbs come from Redford's pals, though he doesn't feel the same way. They meet briefly at a dance and there is an attraction, but that's put on the back burner. Years pass, and WWII begins. Streisand is on the radio talking politics, and Redford is now a member of the armed forces. They meet again, but he is drunk, so she takes him back to her apartment where he passes out in her bed. Still later, he's a published author, and, while discussing his book, it's evident to both that the attraction they felt in college is still there. Redford's snobbish friends again try to wreck the relationship. She won't put up with their attitude, and Redford decides this might be the time to end their romance. They are reconciled, however, marry and move to California where Redford has received a screenplay assignment. She goes off to Washington to fight against the House Un-American Activities Committee. Streisand fears that Redford is selling out his talent. He begins to agree with her and is soon in trouble with the studio executives. Dillman, an old buddy of Redford, is the wishy-washy producer assigned to the project, and he wants certain changes in the script that Redford is loath to make. While Streisand is away, Redford seeks solace in the arms of an ex-girlfriend. Pregnant, Streisand is distraught and wants to end their marriage. They will wait until after their child is born, then part amicably. Years later, though, they meet again in New York. Redford has now sold out totally and makes his living writing for TV. Streisand has remarried. They meet in Central Park, and in a rather predictable ending, bid each other farewell. She walks away handing out "Ban the Bomb" leaflets as he shakes his head and calls out after her, "You never give up, do you?" Whether the screenwriter was referring to the character or the actress is *anybody's* guess. Give it up, girl.

WAYNE'S WORLD

1992 95m c Comedy   ★★★½
Paramount (U.S.)   PG-13/PG

Mike Myers *(Wayne Campbell)*, Dana Carvey *(Garth Algar)*, Rob Lowe *(Benjamin Oliver)*, Tia Carrere *(Cassandra)*, Brian Doyle-Murray *(Noah Vanderhoff)*, Lara Flynn Boyle *(Stacy)*, Colleen Camp *(Mrs. Vanderhoff)*, Donna Dixon *(Dreamwoman)*, Meat Loaf *(Tiny)*, Ione Skye *(Elyse)*

p, Lorne Michaels; d, Penelope Spheeris; w, Mike Myers, Bonnie Turner, Terry Turner (from the characters created by Mike Myers); ph, Theo Van De Sande; ed, Malcolm Campbell; m, J. Peter Robinson; prod d, Gregg Fonseca; art d, Bruce Miller

Given the huge cultural significance of this film, based on the "Saturday Night Live" sketch starring Mike Myers and Dana Carvey, we felt the situation called for more than just a review. So we asked Dr. Stephen Stratocaster, Professor of Popular Culture at the University of Illinois-Aurora, to interview Wayne and Garth in an attempt to pin down the reason for the film's massive appeal.

S.S.: "I'd like to begin by talking about the plot of your film, which involves an ultra-smooth video producer, played by Rob Lowe. He tries to turn your public-access cable show, which you've been producing from a basement in suburban Illinois, into a mainstream network success. But he also dupes you into giving the show's new sponsor—a video arcade owner—his own spot on the program. Then he tries to iron out the show's rough edges, turning it into a cheesy, plastic version of the real thing. Did you intend this as a satire on the crass, commercial nature of network TV?"

WAYNE: "No way, Professor; we just needed a story so we could string a lot of gags together without it getting too boring."

GARTH: "Yeah, like NAKED GUN!"

S.S.: "I see. Well, let's talk about the other storyline, which involves Wayne falling in love with Cassandra (Tia Carrere), a beautiful Asian woman who sings in a rock band. I was deeply moved, Wayne, by one scene in which you're sitting on the roof of a nightclub with Cassandra, and you launch into fluent Cantonese, a language you've learned specifically so you can get to know her better. I feel the scene says a lot about our current need for a global understanding—an understanding that can best be achieved by studying the languages and customs of other cultures. Is that what you were trying to express?"

WAYNE: "Oui, exactement."

S.S.: "My next question concerns the satirical references to modern pop culture, from TV shows like "Mission Impossible" to sports personalities like Stan Mikita, which saturate your movie. I'm particularly interested in the way you got pop-culture icons to turn in cameo performances. Ed O'Neill, for instance, from TV's "Married With Children," plays a donut-shop manager with a psychopathic conversational style; and rock performer Alice Cooper delivers a speech on the socio-political history of Milwaukee. In addition, you both address the camera directly, as though you *know* you're in a movie. All this makes for a very post-modern, self-referential tone which seems to reflect the media-saturated nature of contemporary society. Was this an effect you were actively seeking?"

WAYNE: "Absolutely, Professor. Our film confronts the cultural emptiness of late 20th-century life head-on, revealing a profound hollowness in the heart of modern man (and babe). But we manage to find humor in the midst of this despair."

S.S.: "Well, thank you, gentlemen, that was most enlightening."

WAYNE: "No, thank *you*, Professor. You've helped us understand our work in a new light . . . NOT!"

WE LIVE AGAIN

1934 85m bw Historical   ★★★★
UA (U.S.)   /15

Anna Sten *(Katusha Maslova)*, Fredric March *(Prince Dmitri Nekhlyudov)*, Jane Baxter *(Missy Kortchagin)*, C. Aubrey Smith *(Prince Kortchagin)*, Sam Jaffe *(Gregory Simonson)*, Ethel Griffies *(Aunt Maria)*, Gwendolyn Logan *(Aunt Sophia)*, Mary Forbes *(Mrs. Kortchagin)*, Jessie Ralph *(Matrona Pavlovna)*, Leonid Kinskey *(Simon Kartinkin)*

p, Samuel Goldwyn; d, Rouben Mamoulian; w, Maxwell Anderson, Leonard Praskins, Preston Sturges, Thornton Wilder (based on the novel *Resurrection* by Leo Tolstoy, uncredited); ph, Gregg Toland; ed, Otho Lovering; m, Alfred Newman; prod d, Sergei Sudeikin; art d, Richard Day; cos, Omar Kiam

This fine adaptation of Tolstoy's oft-filmed novel *Resurrection* begins in the countryside of Czarist Russia. Fredric March is a young prince in love with Anna Sten, a servant girl with whom he has grown up. The dashing March goes into the service and returns after two years to find Sten's affections unchanged. They attend Easter mass at a Russian Orthodox church, and afterwards he seduces her, only to slip away the next morning. He then forgets all about the girl, who, it turns out, is pregnant with his child. Sten tries to recapture his heart and at one point runs through a storm after his train as an oblivious March continues playing cards with fellow army officers. The child dies and Sten, accompanied only by another servant, buries its tiny coffin in unconsecrated ground. Seven years pass and March is engaged to Jane Baxter, the daughter of another prince, C. Aubrey Smith, who invites March to sit as a juror on a case he is trying involving a prostitute charged with murder. The accused is Sten, who is innocent of the crime. March presses for acquittal, but she is found guilty and sentenced to exile in Siberia. March tries to get her released, but she only mocks her former lover's efforts. March decides he must pay for the suffering he has caused Sten, so he gives up his land to his retainers, sells all of his possessions and joins Sten on her long journey to Siberia.

This classic story of redemption is beautifully told under Rouben Mamoulian's strong direction. March and Sten are excellent as the tragic lovers, giving their roles depth and intensity. The photography by master lensman Gregg Toland gives the film a moody, atmospheric look which further enhances the strong emotions of the story. Samuel Goldwyn was furiously trying to promote Sten, an actress he considered to be "the Russian Garbo." This was her follow-up to NANA, and, though she again gave an admirable performance, Sten never caught on as Goldwyn had hoped. Maxwell Anderson and Leonard Praskins both received credit for the screenplay, though neither writer made contributions to the final script. Both had written drafts which were unacceptable by Goldwyn's standards, and Preston Sturges was finally given the assignment at Mamoulian's urging.

According to some reports, Goldwyn was highly impressed with the Russian Orthodox Easter service portrayed in the film, though the music was accidentally recorded backwards. Because of Goldwyn's enthusiasm for the scene, no one dared to tell him of the error and the sequence stayed as it was.

WE THE LIVING

1942 174m bw Drama   ★★★★
Scalera/Duncan Scott (Italy)

Alida Valli *(Kira Argounova)*, Rossano Brazzi *(Leo Kovalensky)*, Fosco Giachetti *(Andrei Taganov)*, Giovanni Grasso *(Tishenko)*, Emilio Cigoli *(Pavel Syerov)*, Cesarina Gherardi *(Comrade Sonia)*, Mario Pisu *(Victor Dunaev)*, Guglielmo Sinaz *(Morozov)*, Gero Zambuto *(Alexei Argounov)*, Annibale Betrone *(Vassili Dunaev)* p, Duncan Scott, Henry Mark Holzer, Erika Holzer; d, Goffredo Alessandrini; w, Anton Giulio Majano (based on the novel by Ayn Rand); ph, Giuseppe Caracciolo; ed, Eraldo Da Roma; m, Renzo Rossellini; art d, Andrea Beloborodoff, Giorgio Abkhasi, Amleto Bonetti; cos, Rosi Gori

They don't make films like this anymore. First shown in Italy in 1942, but banned by Mussolini's government and lost until it was rediscovered and re-edited (after an intensive search by the producers), WE THE LIVING has a syrupy score, misty photography, melodramatic confrontations, heroic renunciations, and suicides in the name of lost ideals. And it works. An adaptation of Ayn Rand's novel, the film mixes lots of anti-Communist politics with its passion, but there's still much passion in this tale set in Russia in the early 1920s. Opposed to the new Bolshevik regime are the lovers Kira Argounova (Alida Valli) and Leo Kovalensky (Rossano Brazzi). When Leo is arrested and subsequently contracts tuberculosis, Kira becomes the mistress of idealistic Party man and secret police member Andrei Taganov (Fosco Giachetti) as a means of paying for Leo's stay at a sanitarium. Unfortunately, Leo repays her sacrifice by becoming as corrupt as his erstwhile oppressors, while Andrei becomes disillusioned with the government and shoots himself after finding out that Kira doesn't care for him. The film ends as Kira, still incorruptibly anti-Red, prepares to leave Russia and Leo forever. Though filled with Rand's predictable dogma, WE THE LIVING is unforgettably romantic, and still stands up as a moving love story and as a declaration of female independence that was way ahead of its time. The lush sets, exquisite cinematography, impeccable black-and-white values, and exceptional casting lend the proceedings much splendor, even if the splendor is preposterous.

WEDDING, A

1978 125m c Comedy/Drama ★★½
Lion's Gate (U.S.) PG/15

Lillian Gish *(Nettie Sloan)*, Ruth Nelson *(Beatrice Sloan Cory)*, Ann Ryerson *(Victoria Cory)*, Desi Arnaz Jr. *(Dino Corelli)*, Belita Moreno *(Daphene Corelli)*, Vittorio Gassman *(Luigi Corelli)*, Nina Van Pallandt *(Regina Corelli)*, Virginia Vestoff *(Clarice Sloan)*, Dina Merrill *(Antoinette Sloan Goddard)*, Pat McCormick *(Mackenzie Goddard)*

p, Robert Altman; d, Robert Altman; w, John Considine, Patricia Resnick, Allan Nicholls, Robert Altman (based on a story by Considine and Altman); ph, Charles Rosher Jr.; ed, Tony Lombardo; m, John Hotchkis

Altman's ambitious film is sadly one of his less successful. A WEDDING is extraordinarily self-indulgent, which is really saying something in light of this great filmmaker's astonishingly uneven career.

The setting is a wedding between the daughter of a southern parvenu family and the scion of a clan that is a combination of old money and Mafia. Altman trots more than 50 characters across the screen in what must have been an attempt to prove that he could top the feat he achieved with the 24 stars he used in NASHVILLE. In this case, though, more is less. So many people appear onscreen in so many snippets of stories that not only is it difficult to care about anyone, it's hard to remember who they are. The movie has no narrative thrust, coming across as a ragged collection of occasionally amusing scenes. This is social satire delivered with a shotgun blast.

That great gray goddess of Hollwood films, Lillian Gish, makes her 100th film appearance, but gets killed off far too early. Arnaz, the groom, is set to marry Amy Stryker, the bride with conspicuous braces. Stryker's sister Mia Farrow has already had an affair with Arnaz and is pregnant by him. Stryker's mother is Carol Burnett. She is bored with husband Paul Dooley (an Altman favorite who played Wimpy in POPEYE) and has a sexual liaison with Arnaz's uncle, McCormick. Arnaz's mother is Van Pallandt, a confirmed heroin addict. The wedding coordinator is Geraldine Chaplin, a lesbian (how amusing!), and John Cromwell is the senile priest who forgets his lines and is so myopic that he speaks to a corpse and wonders why his remarks go unanswered. Perhaps the movie's best moment goes to Howard Duff, a lech and a lush of a doctor. At one point late in the film, during a major dramatic scene, we hear him far off-screen, two floors below, very quietly reply when asked if he wants his glass refilled: "Just to the brim, please!" It's the most thrown-away of all great throwaway lines in the movies.

WEDDING BANQUET, THE
(XIYAN)

1993 107m c Comedy ★★★
Central Motion Picture Corporation /15
/Good Machine Inc. (Taiwan)

Winston Chao *(Wai Tung)*, May Chin *(Wei-Wei)*, Ah-Leh Gua *(Mrs. Gao)*, Sihung Lung *(Mr. Gao)*, Mitchell Lichtenstein *(Simon)*, Neal Huff *(Steve)*, Jeffrey Howard *(Street Musician)*, Anthony "Iggy" Ingoglia *(Restaurant Manager)*, Dion Birney *(Andrew)*, Jeanne Kuo Chang

p, James Schamus, Ted Hope, Ang Lee; d, Ang Lee; w, Ang Lee, Neil Peng, James Schamus; ph, Jong Lin; ed, Tim Squyres; m, Mader; prod d, Steve Rosenzweig; art d, Rachel Weinzimer; cos, Michael Clancy

AAN Best Foreign Language Film

THE WEDDING BANQUET is a farcical, freewheeling account of what happens when one half of an interracial gay couple gets married to a woman in order to satisfy his parents' dearest wish. The film has a universal appeal that crosses all racial and sexual divisions, and will be of particular delight to anyone who has ever experienced an elaborate wedding ceremony.

Manhattanites Gao Wai Tung (Winston Chao) and Simon (Mitchell Lichtenstein) are an ideal same-sex couple: young, attractive, successful. Pressured by his parents in Taiwan to marry, Wai Tung takes up Simon's suggestion that he make a marriage of convenience with Wei-Wei (May Chin), a rebellious, decidedly untraditional artist who needs a green card. Wai Tung's parents (Sihung Lung, Ah-Leh Gua) put a major kink in the proceedings when they come to Manhattan for the wedding. With all five characters in nervously close cohabitation, Wai Tung and Simon's townhouse becomes a setting for Feydeau-esque confusion: the lovers must sleep apart; undomestic Wei-Wei pretends to whip up the flawless Chinese dinners that are, in fact, secretly prepared by Simon; and so on. The wedding ceremony, ensuing banquet, and closely supervised honeymoon bring further complications.

Taiwanese director Ang Lee has pulled off one of the most congenial, richly affectionate extended party sequences ever put on film: the banquet is a creamily photographed, cartoonish modern variant of those elaborate, over-populated Chinese scrolls depicting the human comedy in all its infinite sentiment and absurdity. Lee sustains the bubbling hilarity, but also provides quieter, deeper observation of the characters' motives and moods.

WEDDING IN GALILEE
(NOCE EN GALILEE)

1987 116m c Drama ★★★★
Marisa/LPA/French Ministry of Culture/French Community Ministry/ZDF (Belgium/France)

Ali Mohammed El Akili *(Abu Adel, the Mukhtar)*, Bushra Karaman *(The Mother)*, Nazih Akleh *(Adel, the Groom)*, Makhram Khouri *(Military General)*, Anna Achdian *(Samia, the Bride)*, Sonia Amar *(Sumaya, the Daughter)*, Youssef Abou Warda *(Baccum)*, Eyad Anis *(Hassan)*, Wael Barckouti *(Ziad)*, Juliano Mer Khamis

d, Michel Khleifi; w, Michel Khleifi; ph, Eddy van der Enden; ed, Marie Castro Vasquez; m, Jean-Marie Senia

WEDDING IN GALILEE is a moving and remarkable Belgian-French coproduction about Palestinian wedding customs, military and patriarchal dominance, and the quest for peace in the Middle East. Directed by the 36-year-old, Nazareth-born Michel Khleifi, who resides in Belgium, this film has not come to American shores without its share of accolades. It was awarded the 1987 Cannes Critic's Prize, named Best Film of the Year in Belgium, and took the Grand Prize at the San Sebastian Film Festival—where jury member Alain Tanner said to Khleifi, "Your film is greater than any prize we could give it."

Filmed before the escalation in Palestinian-Israeli tensions of late 1987, WEDDING IN GALILEE is set (and was photographed) in the occupied West Bank, where the village *mukhtar* (elder), played by Akili, has vowed to give his son a great wedding. The obstacle to this planned festivity is the imposed curfew that takes effect every evening at sundown. Akili appeals to the military governor, Khouri, to make an exception in this case, but to no avail. Khouri does propose that the wedding can take place on the condition that he and his Israeli aides are invited as guests of honor. Without pondering the consequences, Akili agrees and parts with the military governor on friendly terms. When he explains to his villagers that the Israelis will be in attendance, there is an immediate split, with hostilities and insults hurled about at once. Even Akili's son, groom-to-be Akleh, disagrees with his father's decision. The wedding, however, *will* take place as Akili has promised.

A rich, lyrical film of many textures, WEDDING IN GALILEE presents Western audiences with a world rarely seen onscreen, familiar only from violent television news reports. As an anthropological film, it is educational and enlightening, presenting foreign locations and nonprofessional actors. But WEDDING IN GALILEE is much more than a film of cultural curiosity. It is a human drama, ranging in tone from comic to poignant, from tense to sensual. Director Michel Khleifi is not afraid to let his camera linger on his locations, allowing it to move through the space and stare out an open window long after the characters have left and the action has ceased. Often the haunting musical score overpowers all other sounds until it is the only thing heard.

WEE WILLIE WINKIE
1937 103m bw Drama/Comedy   ★★★
Fox (U.S.)

Shirley Temple *(Priscilla Williams)*, Victor McLaglen *(Sgt. MacDuff)*, C. Aubrey Smith *(Col. Williams)*, June Lang *(Joyce Williams)*, Michael Whalen *(Lt. "Coppy" Brandes)*, Cesar Romero *(Khoda Khan)*, Constance Collier *(Mrs. Allardyce)*, Douglas Scott *(Mott)*, Gavin Muir *(Capt. Bibberbeigh)*, Willie Fung *(Mohammet Dihn)*

p, Gene Markey; d, John Ford; w, Ernest Pascal, Julien Josephson (based on a story by Rudyard Kipling); ph, Arthur Miller; ed, Walter Thompson; m, Louis Silvers; art d, William Darling; cos, Gwen Wakeling

AAN Best Art Direction: William S. Darling, David Hall

Little Shirley Temple works her charms on India in this starring vehicle, which is very loosely based on a Rudyard Kipling story and directed by, of all people, John Ford, best known for his classic westerns. At the turn of the century, Priscilla (Shirley Temple) and her widowed mother (June Lang) go to live with her grandfather, Col. Williams (C. Aubrey Smith), on a British army base in India. Priscilla goes through maneuvers with the troops, donning a darling pint-sized uniform and managing to win over everyone she comes in contact with, including rebel leader Khoda Khan (Cesar Romero). The entire political situation is solved when Priscilla asks why the two factions are mad at each other, thus bringing about a peaceful resolution.

WEEKEND
1967 103m c Drama   ★★★★½
Comacico/Copernic/Lira/Ascot (France/Italy)   /18

Mireille Darc *(Corinne)*, Jean Yanne *(Roland)*, Jean-Pierre Kalfon *(Leader of FLSO)*, Valerie Lagrange *(His Moll)*, Jean-Pierre Leaud *(Saint-Just/Man in Phone Booth)*, Yves Beneyton *(Member of FLSO)*, Paul Gegauff *(Pianist)*, Daniel Pommereulle *(Joseph Balsamo)*, Yves Alfonso *(Gros Poncet)*, Blandine Jeanson *(Emily Bronte/Girl in Farmyard)*

d, Jean-Luc Godard; w, Jean-Luc Godard; ph, Raoul Coutard; ed, Agnes Guillemot; m, Antoine Duhamel, Wolfgang Amadeus Mozart

A brutally satirical film somewhat reminiscent of the works of Luis Bunuel, this was Jean-Luc Godard's most ambitious and vociferous "revolutionary" movie before he retired to the shelter of the Dziga-Vertov group. It's full of funny anti-bourgeois set pieces including one of the great sequences in all cinema: a full reel, ten-minute tracking shot that proceeds with a stately pace past a very, very long line of stalled automobiles on a French country highway lined with poplars.

This mind boggling film stacks analogy upon analogy and allegory upon allegory with hallucinatory fervor in an episodic odyssey of an unpleasant upper-class Parisian pair out for a weekend trip to visit the wife's mother. Opening with a psychiatric-session monologue by the delicate Darc, clad only in panties and perched first on a desk, then on a refrigerator as she hesitantly describes a sexual encounter involving an egg and an orifice, the movie quickly moves to the carnage of the roadways during a sunny weekend. A bumper-to-bumper carnival of

cars ensues, honking, careening, crashing, overturning, and burning along with their grotesque occupants as Darc and Yanne proceed on their trip. Along the way social values regarding sex, consumerism, and family are explored in myriad surreal ways. The final result can be viewed as a darkly funny vision of Hell that culminates in one possible brave new world. One of the essential films of the 1960s.

WELCOME IN VIENNA
1987 126m bw War   ★★★★
Thalia/ORF/ZDF/SSR/Austrian Ministry
(Austria/West Germany)

Gabriel Barylli *(Freddy Wolff)*, Nicolas Brieger *(Sgt. Adler)*, Claudia Messner *(Claudia Schutte)*, Hubert Mann *(Capt. Karpeles)*, Karlheinz Hackl *(Treschensky)*, Liliana Nelska *(Russian Woman)*, Kurt Sowinetz *(Stodola)*, Joachim Kemmer *(Lt. Binder)*, Heinz Trixner *(Oberst Schutte)*

d, Axel Corti; w, Axel Corti, Georg Stefan Troller; ph, Gernot Roll; ed, Ulrike Pahl, Claudia Rieneck; m, Hans Georg Koch, Franz Schubert; prod d, Matija Barl; cos, Uli Fessler

WELCOME IN VIENNA is the first and only film made on the subject of Austrian and German emigres to the US who joined the US Army and then returned to their homeland in 1944 with the American liberating forces.

Beautifully photographed in grainy black-and-white (which gives a documentary visual quality), the movie opens on Christmas Eve 1944 as the American forces are holed up in a barn in the middle of a snowy field. The two main characters are Barylli, an Austrian Jew who has longed for this return home, and Brieger, a German intellectual who fled to the States in fear of the Nazis and has now become sympathetic to the Communists. Heading their command is a tough-talking, hard-drinking German-American, Kemmer, who firmly believes in Teutonic anti-Semitism. In the battle that follows, a German deserter, Hackl, is captured who turns out to be an opportunistic Viennese and Nazi former friend of Barylli's. Time jumps ahead to May 1945 in Salzburg on the final day of the war as the liberating forces descend on the city. The first girl that Barylli lays eyes on is Messner, a pretty Austrian whose father is a colonel in the *Abwehr* (the Nazi counterintelligence). She informs US authorities that her father is willing to surrender his information, but only if the US receives him with full honors. Barylli has returned to Austria—his home—though he soon finds that things have changed. Thousands of Jews have disappeared, and as many buildings have been reduced to rubble. When he tries to locate his family's apartment, he finds it almost completely destroyed and learns that his family's possessions were sold on the street. The "home" that he hoped to find no longer exists. He works his way up in the ranks of the new government, taking a cultural job because of his smattering knowledge of theater and literature. He falls in love with Messner, who is yet another representation of that Austrian "home" that he cannot recapture. Although she loves him dearly, she uses him as a means to further her career on the stage. Brieger, in the meantime, has become disillusioned in his admiration of Stalin's Communist rule, while Hackl, still the opportunist, has moved into a position of power in the black market. As the film ends, Barylli has lost Messner to the stage and must now decide whether or not to return to America.

Funded by Austrian dollars, directed by Austrian Corti, and cowritten by Austrian expatriate Troller (now living in Paris), WELCOME IN VIENNA is the first film, according to its makers, that deals accurately with Austria's unflattering role during World War II. Echoing Jean Renoir's line of dialogue from RULES OF THE GAME that "Everybody has their reasons," Corti has presented an exceptional look at the human condition. Every element of the picture rings of a desire to tell the truth—from the newsreel quality of the film stock, to the locations and unfaltering performances.

WELCOME TO L.A.

1976 106m c Drama ★★½
UA (U.S.) R/15

Keith Carradine *(Carroll Barber)*, Sally Kellerman *(Ann Goode)*, Geraldine Chaplin *(Karen Hood)*, Harvey Keitel *(Ken Hood)*, Lauren Hutton *(Nona Bruce)*, Viveca Lindfors *(Susan Moore)*, Sissy Spacek *(Linda Murray)*, Denver Pyle *(Carl Barber)*, John Considine *(Jack Goode)*, Richard Baskin *(Eric Wood)*

p, Robert Altman; d, Alan Rudolph; w, Alan Rudolph (based on the music suite "City of the One Night Stands" by Richard Baskin); ph, David Myers; ed, William A. Sawyer, Tom Walls; m, Richard Baskin; cos, Jules Melillo

Although heralded by some as one of the most original and innovative directorial debuts of the 1970s, Alan Rudolph's WELCOME TO L.A., like his REMEMBER MY NAME, seems specifically designed for cult status. It takes an off-beat look at a self-important group of Los Angeles bohemians and their essentially worthless lives, which revolve mainly around sex, drinking, and driving (though not necessarily at the same time). Carradine and his fellow Altman veterans just seem to wander around a lot, and the film's success or failure depends almost entirely on how much you like them.

WELCOME TO THE DOLLHOUSE

1996 87m c Comedy/Drama ★★★½
Suburban Pictures (U.S.) R/

Heather Matarazzo *(Dawn Wiener)*, Brendan Sexton Jr. *(Brandon McCarthy)*, Daria Kalinina *(Missy Wiener)*, Matthew Faber *(Mark Wiener)*, Angela Pietropinto *(Mrs. Wiener)*, Eric Mabius *(Steve Rodgers)*, Bill Buell *(Mr. Wiener)*, Victoria Davis *(Lolita)*, Christina Brucato *(Cookie)*, Christina Vidal *(Cynthia)*

p, Todd Solondz; d, Todd Solondz; w, Todd Solondz; ph, Randy Drummond; ed, Alan Oxman; m, Jill Wisoff; prod d, Susan Block; art d, Lori Solondz; cos, Melissa Toth

Nightmarishly hilarious and stunningly frank, writer-director Todd Solondz's evocation of awkward adolescence is a bracing antidote to the counterfeit nostalgia so egregiously exploited by heartwarming TV sitcoms and saccharine coming-of-age movies.

Eleven-year-old misfit Dawn Wiener (Heather Matarazzo) is the patron saint of cootie girls, complete with nerd glasses and clueless wardrobe. At home, she's a put-upon middle child—her younger sister is an adorable little ballerina; her older brother, a brainy computer geek. At school, the cool girls torment her mercilessly, calling her "wiener dog" and "lesbo" (she's too dorky even to register on the radar of cool boys). Her parents offer little in the way of sympathy or support, and even her teachers treat her with spiteful indifference.

WELCOME TO THE DOLLHOUSE adroitly renders the relentless pecking order of abuse, but it doesn't make the sentimental error of suggesting that people become noble, kind, or empathetic simply by virtue of being persecuted. Dawn (portrayed with spirited honesty by 11-year-old Matarazzo) isn't one of those sensitive, misunderstood outsiders familiar from REBEL WITHOUT A CAUSE or *The Catcher in the Rye*. She's an victim, to be sure, but Solondz refuses to romanticize her predicament: she's abrasive, unsightly, socially maladroit, and exasperatingly complicit in her own ostracism.

WEST SIDE STORY

1961 153m c Musical ★★★★
Mirisch/Seven Arts/Beta (U.S.) /PG

Natalie Wood *(Maria)*, Richard Beymer *(Tony)*, Russ Tamblyn *(Riff)*, Rita Moreno *(Anita)*, George Chakiris *(Bernardo)*, Simon Oakland *(Lt. Schrank)*, Bill Bramley *(Officer Krupke)*, Tucker Smith *(Ice)*, Tony Mordente *(Action)*, Eliot Feld *(Baby John)*

p, Robert Wise; d, Robert Wise, Jerome Robbins; w, Ernest Lehman (based on the stage play by Arthur Laurents, based on a conception by Robbins, inspired by a play by William Shakespeare); ph, Daniel Fapp; ed, Thomas Stanford; m, Leonard Bernstein; prod d, Boris Leven; chor, Jerome Robbins; cos, Irene Sharaff

AA Best Picture; *AA Best Supporting Actor:* George Chakiris; *AA Best Supporting Actress:* Rita Moreno; *AA Best Director:* Jerome Robbins, Robert Wise; *AAN Best Adapted Screenplay:* Ernest Lehman; *AA Best Cinematography:* Daniel L. Fapp; *AA Best Editing:* Thomas Stanford; *AA Best Score:* Saul Chaplin, Johnny Green, Sid Ramin, Irwin Kostal; *AA Best Art Direction:* Boris Leven, Victor A. Gangelin; *AA Best Costume Design:* Irene Sharaff; *AA Best Sound:* Fred Hynes, Gordon E. Sawyer

When it's good, very good; when it's bad, a stinker. WEST SIDE STORY is the filmed version of the hit Broadway musical inspired by "Romeo and Juliet." Jerome Robbins, who conceived the stage version, gets co-director credit here. He was originally slated to direct the entire film, but his perfectionism meant twice the budget. United Artists brought in Robert Wise after less than a month of rehearsals, assigning him direction of the non-musical sequences. Before long, Robbins was booted all together. The numbers he choreographed remain the most inventive, energetic sequences in the film: the lengthy opening sequence (including "The Jet Song"), "America," "I Feel Pretty" and "Cool". If Robbins had done the whole of it, we might be left with a more dynamic and explosive film. But there's no discounting that whenever WEST SIDE STORY proclaims the leads' love it goes predictable on us—musically, first and foremost, so no director could entirely change that. Wise saddled these moments with all the usual—soft-focus camera work, stars in the sky, Rodgers and Hammerstein ballet. Nor is this helped by Natalie Wood and Richard Beymer (dubbed by Marni Nixon and Jim Bryant). When they're not mouthing like fish in tanks, they're wrestling the awkward dialogue of these sequences. Lucky for us, everything—and everyone—else is first-rate; especially the three meaty supporting parts played by Moreno (alas, dubbed also, by Betty Wand—but Moreno acts with fire and can dance), gorgeous, pantherine Chakiris and winning Tamblyn.

Sticking closely to Arthur Laurents's original book, the film follows the escalating tensions between rival teenage gangs the Jets (who are white) and the Sharks (who are Puerto Rican) as they battle for turf in Manhattan's Upper West Side. The Sharks are led by Bernardo, boyfriend of the tempestuous Anita; the Jets follow Riff (Tamblyn). Caught in the middle are Bernardo's sister, Maria (Wood), who has just arrived from Puerto Rico, and Tony (Beymer), a member of the Jets who is Riff's best friend. Tony and Maria fall in love, despite the hatred between their friends and relatives, but the romance is destined to end tragically.

WEST SIDE STORY became one of the most popular film musicals in history, largely on the strength of its youth appeal and the aforementioned Robbins's choreography—a spectacular combination of ballet, acrobatics, and jazz excitingly adapted for the camera. The score by Leonard Bernstein (with lyrics by Stephen Sondheim) has become an acknowledged and much-beloved classic.

WESTERN UNION

1941 93m c Western ★★★★
Fox (U.S.) /U

Randolph Scott *(Vance Shaw)*, Robert Young *(Richard Blake)*, Dean Jagger *(Edward Creighton)*, Virginia Gilmore *(Sue Creighton)*, John Carradine *(Doc Murdoch)*, Slim Summerville *(Herman)*, Chill Wills *(Homer)*, Barton MacLane *(Jack Slade)*, Russell Hicks *(Governor)*, Victor Kilian *(Charlie)*

p, Harry Joe Brown; d, Fritz Lang; w, Robert Carson (based on a story by Zane Grey); ph, Edward Cronjager, Allen Davey; ed, Robert Bischoff, Gene Flowler Jr.; m, David Buttolph; art d, Richard Day, Albert Hogsett; cos, Travis Banton

After the success of his first western, THE RETURN OF FRANK JAMES, German director Lang was assigned to do another, this one based on the construction of the Western Union telegraph line from Omaha, Nebraska, to Salt Lake City, Utah. Randolph Scott stars as an outlaw looking to reform his wicked ways.

The most epic and beautiful of Lang's westerns (it was the director's personal favorite), WESTERN UNION is an outstanding entry in the genre. Lang, who loved the American West and spent much time traveling there, researched the period thoroughly and paid painstaking attention to detail. Having studied American Indians for some time, he was delighted with the opportunity to present them in their full glory, with accurate warpaint and battle gear photographed in beautiful Technicolor. The photography by Cronjager is some of the most beautiful work of the 1940s, and the cast is filled with outstanding character actors such as Carradine, Wills, Summerville, and Kilian. There is much humor in WESTERN UNION, most of it centering around Summerville, the timid cook scared witless of the "Wild West." Lang would make only one more western, RANCHO NOTORIOUS, yet another superior entry from a German director working in a distinctly American genre.

WESTERNER, THE

1940 100m bw Western ★★★★★
UA (U.S.) /U

Gary Cooper *(Cole Hardin)*, Walter Brennan *(Judge Roy Bean)*, Doris Davenport *(Jane-Ellen Mathews)*, Fred Stone *(Caliphet Mathews)*, Paul Hurst *(Chickenfoot)*, Chill Wills *(Southeast)*, Charles Halton *(Mort Borrow)*, Forrest Tucker *(Wade Harper)*, Tom Tyler *(King Evans)*, Arthur Aylesworth *(Mr. Dixon)*

p, Samuel Goldwyn; d, William Wyler; w, Jo Swerling, Niven Busch (based on a story by Stuart N. Lake); ph, Gregg Toland; ed, Daniel Mandell; m, Alfred Newman, Dimitri Tiomkin; art d, James Basevi; fx, Archie Stout, Paul Eagler; cos, Irene Saltern

AA Best Supporting Actor: Walter Brennan; *AAN Best Original Story:* Stuart N. Lake; *AAN Best Art Direction:* James Basevi

A superior western that mixes fine cinematography, terrific performances, and a script of higher caliber than most to produce a film still fondly remembered today. Cooper is a drifter who runs afoul of the law when he is falsely accused of stealing a horse. He is taken in front of Brennan, who serves as a justice of the peace and *is* the "Law west of the Pecos," as a cemetery full of his victims will attest. He tries Cooper in a hasty mockery of justice and sentences him to hang, but Cooper, knowing Brennan's admiration and even love for stage star Lily Langtry (after whom Brennan has named his town), convinces the judge that he is a personal friend of Langtry and will obtain a lock of her hair for the judge if the judge lets him go. Brennan is so love-struck that he doesn't see through this obvious lie, and the two men soon become friends of a sort. That night, Cooper steals Brennan's gun and escapes, stopping at the farm of Stone and his daughter, Davenport. Brennan is conducting a campaign, through his deputies, aimed at driving the homesteaders off the range. Cooper, who has become smitten with Davenport, decides to stay in the area and be the advocate for the homesteaders with Brennan. For a time things go smoothly, and Cooper gives Brennan a lock of Davenport's hair, telling him it is from Langtry; but then Brennan's terrorizing of the farmers takes on new fervor, and Stone is murdered. Cooper sets out for a reckoning with Brennan, but learns that the judge has left Langtry to travel to Fort Davis, where he has bought every seat in the theater to see Langtry in person for the first time. The curtain rises, and it is Cooper who is standing there, guns at the ready. The two men shoot it out in the gaslit hall, and Cooper finally manages to wound Brennan mortally. Dying, Brennan is taken backstage by Cooper to meet his dream, played here by Lilian Bond, whose hand he kisses before he dies.

Cooper was initially reluctant to take the part of the drifter, thinking it too minor for an actor of his stature. Director Wyler shamed him out of that attitude, though, with a variation of the "no small parts, only small actors" bit, and he gave Cooper enough good scenes to make the actor happy. It is Brennan, however, who steals the picture, making Judge Roy Bean one of the most unforgettable characters ever seen in a western film, researching his character and adopting a neck dislocation to represent an injury the historical judge incurred when he was hanged and cut down. Cinematographer Toland's work is superb, filling his western skies with gnarled trees and amazing clouds, and underscoring the story with a strangely somber tone. The score by Tiomkin was completely scrapped at the last minute and a new one written by Alfred Newman, though he did not receive screen credit. Dana Andrews and Forrest Tucker made their debuts here.

WESTWORLD

1973 91m c Science Fiction/Western ★★★½
MGM (U.S.) PG/15

Yul Brynner *(Gunslinger)*, Richard Benjamin *(Peter Martin)*, James Brolin *(John Blane)*, Norman Bartold *(Medieval Queen)*, Dick Van Patten *(Banker)*, Linda Scott *(Arlette)*, Steve Franken *(Technician)*, Michael T. Mikler *(Black Knight)*, Terry Wilson *(Sheriff)*, Majel Barrett *(Miss Carrie)*

p, Paul N. Lazarus III; d, Michael Crichton; w, Michael Crichton; ph, Gene Polito; ed, David Bretherton; m, Fred Karlin; art d, Herman A. Blumenthal; fx, Charles Schulthies

The title refers to a futuristic Disney-type fantasy land which features android Western figures. Benjamin and Brolin are two businessman who come to WESTWORLD to live out their fantasies, and Brynner is the robot Benjamin kills in a saloon fight. Suddenly everything goes haywire, and the machines stalk the visitors. Brynner guns down Brolin, and chases Benjamin. Brynner is very good, his austere presence and unflinching intent making him seem indestructible. The film grossed a healthy $3.4 million in the US and Canada and was the last film from MGM before it dissolved its releasing company. Ten minutes have been deleted from the original footage to allow WESTWORLD's present PG rating. The gardens of movie comedian Harold Lloyd's estate were used for some of the amusement park sequences. The film was followed by a sequel, FUTUREWORLD.

WETHERBY

1985 102m c Drama ★★★½
Greenpoint/Film Four/Zenith (U.K.) R/15

Vanessa Redgrave *(Jean Travers)*, Ian Holm *(Stanley Pilborough)*, Judi Dench *(Marcia Pilborough)*, Marjorie Yates *(Verity Braithwaite)*, Tom Wilkinson *(Roger Braithwaite)*, Tim McInnerny *(John Morgan)*, Suzanna Hamilton *(Karen Creasy)*, Stuart Wilson *(Mike Langdon)*, Mike Kelly *(CID Policeman)*, Diane Whitley

p, Simon Relph; d, David Hare; w, David Hare; ph, Stuart Harris; ed, Christopher Wimble; m, Nick Bicat; prod d, Hayden Griffin; art d, Jamie Leonard; cos, Jane Greenwood, Lindy Hemming

A very intelligent picture that needs to be looked at closely in order to fathom some of its subtleties. David Hare, the playwright of PLENTY, wrote and directed this film, and it's a corker. Wetherby is a small, cold town in Yorkshire. Jean Travers (Vanessa Redgrave) is a local teacher who never married. Her teenage crush was killed in Malaya in the 1950s, and she has never gotten over it. Jean is having a small dinner party in her home for two couples, Stanley (Ian Holm) and Marcia Piborough (Judi Dench), and Roger (Tom Wilkinson) and Verity Braithwaite (Marjorie Yates). When John Morgan (Tim McInnerny) shows up, Jean assumes that he is with one of the couples and they assume that he is a friend of hers. He is neither. The following day, Morgan comes by Jean's home, has a pleasant chat, then, without a bit of warning and apparently no motivation, puts a gun in his mouth and blows his brains out. It is an incredibly shocking moment. The movie flits in the present, the recent past, and sometime in the early 1950s. Hare uses an intriguing technique as he keeps going back to the seemingly ordinary dinner party in memory, and we realize that what we saw before was only the tip of the iceberg. To give away the answer to this enigma might be a disservice to anyone who likes to use his noodle. There are more questions asked than answered in this movie, but the mental gymnastics are well worth the effort. The performances are all first-rate as well, including that of Joely Richardson, Redgrave's daughter with director Tony Richardson, as the young Jean.

WHALES OF AUGUST, THE

1987 90m c Drama ★★★
Alive/Circle/Nelson (U.S.) /U

Bette Davis *(Libby Strong)*, Lillian Gish *(Sarah Webber)*, Vincent Price *(Mr. Nikolai Maranov)*, Ann Sothern *(Tisha Doughty)*, Harry Carey Jr. *(Joshua Brackett)*, Frank Grimes *(Mr. Beckwith)*, Frank Pitkin *(Old Randall)*, Mike Bush *(Young Randall)*, Margaret Ladd *(Young Libby)*, Tisha Sterling *(Young Tisha)* p, Carolyn Pfeiffer, Mike Kaplan; d, Lindsay Anderson; w, David Berry (based on the play by David Berry); ph, Mike Fash; ed, Nicolas Gaster; m, Alan Price; prod d, Jocelyn Herbert; art d, K.C. Fox, Bob Fox; cos, Rudy Dillon, Julie Weiss

AAN Best Supporting Actress: Ann Sothern

It is 1954, and Libby Strong (Bette Davis) and her younger sister Sarah Webber (Lillian Gish) have returned to the small Maine island for the summer, as they have done for the past 60 years. Libby is now blind and Sarah has cheerfully looked after her for 15 years. As girls they had stood on the cliffs and watched for whales. Now the whales come no more. Sarah still anticipates their appearance and wants to put in a new picture window, but Libby, who has grown bitter and cynical, thinks it would be frivolous and vetoes the idea. Tisha Doughty (Ann Sothern), their lifelong friend and the island's resident busybody, pays them a visit and tries to persuade Sarah to put Libby in her daughter's care and to move in with her.

With its extraordinary cast, THE WHALES OF AUGUST would have made cinema history even if its script had been taken from a cereal box. In fact, the screenplay, adapted by David Berry from his own largely autobiographical stage play, isn't one of the film's stronger elements. Suffering from heavy-handed symbolism and offering few real insights, it nonetheless provides the blueprint from which these exceptional actors are able to build their performances. THE WHALES OF AUGUST has more than a few problems, but anyone interested in the art of acting, the history of the cinema, or in seeing an unpatronizing portrait of elderly characters will find the film rewarding.

WHAT A WAY TO GO!

1964	111m	c	Comedy	★★½
Fox	(U.S.)			/15

Shirley MacLaine *(Louisa)*, Paul Newman *(Larry Flint)*, Robert Mitchum *(Rod Anderson)*, Dean Martin *(Leonard Crawley)*, Gene Kelly *(Jerry Benson)*, Robert Cummings *(Dr. Stephanson)*, Dick Van Dyke *(Edgar Hopper)*, Reginald Gardiner *(Painter)*, Margaret Dumont *(Mrs. Foster)*, Roy Gordon *(Minister)*

p, Arthur P. Jacobs; d, J. Lee Thompson; w, Betty Comden, Adolph Green (based on a story by Gwen Davis); ph, Leon Shamroy; ed, Marjorie Fowler; m, Nelson Riddle; art d, Jack Martin Smith, Ted Haworth; fx, L.B. Abbott, Dick Smith, Emil Kosa Jr.; chor, Gene Kelly, Richard Humphrey; cos, Edith Head, Moss Mabry

AAN Best Art Direction: Jack Martin Smith, Ted Haworth, Walter M. Scott, Stuart A. Reiss; *AAN Best Costume Design:* Edith Head, Moss Mabry

Former press agent Jacobs always felt that "bigger was better," so for this, his first venture into film producing, he decided to do a huge comedy, filled with stars, huge sets, and colorful costumes. It all went to prove that bigger isn't better. As the film opens, MacLaine is sharing her tale of woe with psychiatrist Cummings. Seems she's worth $200 million, but she wants to give the money to the IRS because she believes it's cursed. In flashback, the story unfolds, beginning with her refusal to marry the very wealthy Martin. Instead, she weds Van Dyke, a poor shopkeeper. Upset because Martin has told her she's made a big mistake, Van Dyke works tirelessly to amass a fortune and dies from the exertion. MacLaine, now a wealthy widow, meets and marries a series of hapless men—including bohemian painter Newman, high-powered businessman Mitchum, and smalltime entertainer Kelly—each of whom is done in by the effort of keeping her happy.

The size of this production was awesome. Costumer Edith Head had half a million dollars to play with for the more than 70 MacLaine costumes, and jeweler Harry Winston lent a bauble collection of almost $4 million to the production. A musical-extravaganza number featured Kelly and MacLaine in a satire of every nautical musical ever made. Comden, Green, and Jule Styne collaborated on "Musical Extravaganza" and "I Think You and I Should Get Acquainted." Thompson employed several shooting styles. The Van Dyke episode is reminiscent of a silent movie. The Newman section is shot as a French film, right down to the English subtitles. The Mitchum section is a Doris Day-Rock Hudson Universal look-alike. And the Gene Kelly piece resembles a Busby Berkeley production. On paper this picture seemed to have everything going for it. Unfortunately, movies are made on film, and the

sank. The fact was that it simply wasn't very funny. Some interesting cameos include veteran players like Dumont (in her last film after having served so long as the Marx Brothers' foil), former boxer Lou Nova, Tom Conway (in his last role; he is the former "Falcon" of the movies and brother of George Sanders), and comics Lenny Kent, Sid Gould, and Wally Vernon. A real flopperoo—which proves that excess for its own sake means little or nothing to movie audiences.

WHAT EVER HAPPENED TO BABY JANE?

1962	132m	bw	Thriller	★★★★
Aldrich	(U.S.)			/18

Bette Davis *(Jane Hudson)*, Joan Crawford *(Blanche Hudson)*, Victor Buono *(Edwin Flagg)*, Anna Lee *(Mrs. Bates)*, Maidie Norman *(Elvira Stitt)*, Marjorie Bennett *(Mrs. Della Flagg)*, Dave Willock *(Ray Hudson)*, Anne Barton *(Cora Hudson)*, Barbara D. Merrill *(Liza Bates)*, Julie Allred *(Young Jane)*

p, Robert Aldrich; d, Robert Aldrich; w, Lukas Heller (based on the novel by Henry Farrell); ph, Ernest Haller; ed, Michael Luciano; m, Frank DeVol; art d, William Glasgow; fx, Don Steward; chor, Alex Romero; cos, Norma Koch

AAN Best Actress: Bette Davis; *AAN Best Supporting Actor:* Victor Buono; *AAN Best Cinematography:* Ernest Haller; *AA Best Costume Design:* Norma Koch; *AAN Best Sound:* Joseph Kelly

Star wars, trenchantly served, with Davis as wharf rat and Crawford a frantic parakeet. If it sometimes looks like a poisonous senior citizen show with over-the-top spoiled ham, just try to look away. Bringing the screen's queens of sadism and masochism together for this slice of Camp Hollywood gothic horror revitalized the careers of both.

The Hudson sisters—Davis and Crawford—are aging actresses who live in a rotting Los Angeles mansion. Davis had been a spoiled brat vaudeville headliner known as "Baby Jane," but as she grew older her career faded. Crawford lived in her shadow as a girl but had an enormously successful adult career as a screen glamour girl. But she was unable to help Davis gain a career in film, due to the latter's drinking and eccentric behavior. At the peak of her stardom, Crawford suffered a career-ending accident for which Davis was seemingly responsible. Ever since then the two have lived together in mutual enmity, tended to by their maid, Norman. When Davis learns that her wheelchair-bound sister is planning to sell the mansion and put her in a sanitarium, she begins terrorizing Crawford; at the same time, she enlists the service of Buono, a young pianist who she hopes will help her make a comeback. The film then suspensefully builds its way to a conclusion that puts a new spin on the relationship between the two sisters.

As in the best Hitchcock movies, suspense, rather than actual mayhem, drives the film. The screenplay, by Lukas Heller, was based on the novel by Henry Farrell (who also authored the novel HUSH, HUSH SWEET CHARLOTTE and scripted WHAT'S THE MATTER WITH HELEN?).

Aldrich had his hands full balancing the overblown but sensitive egos of the rival actresses. If full-scale battle never erupted, it is still correct to say that battle lines were constantly being drawn. The original choice to star with Davis was Tallulah Bankhead (a far more lethal combination than the eventual one) when the property began floating around Hollywood, but Crawford acquired rights to the property, and offered it to Davis while the latter was unhappily appearing on Broadway in *Night of the Iguana*. Davis commanded a larger salary, Crawford a larger percentage of the gross (Joan's years at Pepsi-Cola paid off). Davis's foot allegedly made contact with Crawford's head during a scene where Baby Jane punts her sister around the living room. Crawford supposedly retaliated by use of the old Veronica Lake trick (see I MARRIED A WITCH) by rigging weights under her robe for a scene where Davis had to drag her, and Davis hurt her back. Crawford shared a private joke on Davis by sending hairdresser Peggy Shannon to MGM to secure her old blonde wig from ICE FOLLIES OF 1939 for Davis to wear. Davis bitched to Aldrich about Crawford's drinking (both were alcoholics) and padded brassieres; Crawford insulted Davis's daughter (who appeared in the film—to put it kindly, she was not burdened by her mother's talent), and the incidents go on and on.

In a bucket of gooey make-up, Davis cried when she saw herself in rushes (the limited budget precluded re-shooting) but her excessive performance is riveting—capturing the malevolence Lynn Redgrave lacked in the 1991 TV remake. Crawford wisely underacts—if her performance isn't as showy as Davis's, it's not any less accomplished.

WHAT'S LOVE GOT TO DO WITH IT

1993 120m c Biography/Musical/Drama ★★★
Touchstone (U.S.) R/18

Angela Bassett *(Tina Turner)*, Laurence Fishburne *(Ike Turner)*, Jenifer Lewis *(Zelma Bullock)*, Phyllis Yvonne Stickney *(Alline Bullock)*, Rae'ven Kelly *(Young Anna Mae)*, Virginia Capers *(Choir Mistress)*, Emery Shaw *(Organ Player)*, Cora Lee Day *(Grandma Georgiana)*, Sherman Augustus *(Reggie)*, Chi *(Fross)*

p, Doug Chapin, Barry Krost; d, Brian Gibson; w, Kate Lanier (from the autobiography *I, Tina* by Tina Turner and Kurt Loder); ph, Jamie Anderson; ed, Lisa Day, Stuart Pappe, Dave Rawlins, Michael J. Hill, Thomas G. Finnan; m, Stanley Clarke; prod d, Stephen Altman; art d, Richard Johnson; chor, Michael Peters; cos, Ruth Carter

AAN Best Actor: Laurence Fishburne; *AAN Best Actress:* Angela Bassett

This enjoyable biopic of rock singer Tina Turner was made at more or less the height of her success, and very much under her control. Adapted from Turner's autobiography, *I, Tina*, it plays something like A STAR IS BORN, plus rhythm and blues soundtrack, minus a third-act death scene.

Shy, gawky, country-raised teenager Anna Mae Bullock (Angela Bassett) joins her mother in the big city and spends her nights at the club where her sister, Alline, works. It's here that she first spies sexy Ike Turner (Laurence Fishburne) and his Kings of Rhythm onstage. When the microphone is passed around for audience participation, it's the little girl with the great big voice who wins the biggest ovation. Recognizing Anna Mae's talent, Ike retools the band around her, christens her Tina, and takes the show on the road. Ike and Tina marry and, while they achieve fame and fortune, their home life descends into a hell of abuse and humiliation. Finally, Tina must find the strength to leave her husband and forge a new career without him.

Two things lift WHAT'S LOVE out of the realm of showbiz boilerplate. One is the music, with knockout production numbers crystallizing major turns in the emotional life of the protagonists: a rousing "Make Me Over" at their first studio session; "Think It's Gonna Work Out Fine" over their bordertown nuptials; "A Fool in Love" at the couple's starmaking first Apollo show, where the beleaguered Tina can barely go on. The other is the two stars: Fishburne and Bassett are both extraordinary, and though the story is inevitably slanted to Tina's perspective, Fishburne makes Ike a complex and compelling presence.

WHAT'S EATING GILBERT GRAPE?

1993 117m c Comedy/Drama ★★★
Gilbert Grape Partners/Meir Teper Productions/DM PG-13/12
Productions (U.S.)

Johnny Depp *(Gilbert Grape)*, Juliette Lewis *(Becky)*, Leonardo DiCaprio *(Arnie Grape)*, Mary Steenburgen *(Betty Carver)*, Crispin Glover *(Bobby McBurney)*, John C. Reilly *(Tucker Van Dyke)*, Darlene Cates *(Momma)*, Laura Harrington *(Amy Grape)*, Mary Kate Schellhardt *(Ellen Grape)*, Kevin Tighe *(Mr. Carver)*

p, Meir Teper, Bertil Ohlsson, David Matalon; d, Lasse Hallstrom; w, Peter Hedges (from his novel); ph, Sven Nykvist; ed, Andrew Mondshein; m, Alan Parker, Bjorn Isfalt; prod d, Bernt Capra; cos, Renee Ehrlich Kalfus

AAN Best Supporting Actor: Leonardo DiCaprio

Whimsical to a fault, WHAT'S EATING GILBERT GRAPE? hangs together in large part because of fine performances by Johnny Depp, as the preciously named Gilbert Grape, and Leonardo DiCaprio, who received an Academy Award nomination for his performance as Gilbert's retarded teenage brother.

Gilbert is encumbered by more burdens than any young man ought to have. He lives in isolated Endora, a dying small town, and stocks shelves at a grocery whose business has decamped to the new mall supermarket. Gilbert's 500-pound mother (Darlene Cates) hasn't left the house since his father hanged himself in the basement, his sisters (Laura Harrington and Mary Kate Schellhardt) quarrel relentlessly, and his retarded brother Arnie (DiCaprio) requires constant supervision. Gilbert's best buddies are a novice undertaker (Crispin Glover) and a gung-ho loser (John C. Reilly) who sees his future in a Burger Barn franchise. And Gilbert is having a desultory affair with frustrated housewife Betty Carver (Mary Steenburgen), whose reckless sexual demands have begun to alarm him. Everyone needs the preternaturally patient Gilbert, whose future seems grimly assured until worldly Becky (Juliette Lewis) and her grandmother (Penelope Branning) coast into town in an ailing camper, opening Gilbert's eyes to the wider world outside Endora.

Based on the first novel by Peter Hedges (who also wrote the screenplay), which has a small but intense cult following, WHAT'S EATING GILBERT GRAPE? is meandering, quirky, and resolutely small in scale. The film is heavy on character and atmosphere and light on action, though what does happen is so bizarre as to verge on the ridiculous. As directed by Swedish filmmaker Lasse Hallstrom (MY LIFE AS A DOG), it's endearingly loopy without degenerating into a carnival tent show.

WHAT'S NEW, PUSSYCAT?
(QUOI DE NEUF, PUSSYCAT?)

1965 108m c Comedy ★★★½
Famous Artists/Famartists (U.S./France) /15

Peter Sellers *(Dr. Fritz Fassbender)*, Peter O'Toole *(Michael James)*, Romy Schneider *(Carole Werner)*, Capucine *(Renee Lefebvre)*, Paula Prentiss *(Liz)*, Woody Allen *(Victor Shakapopulis)*, Ursula Andress *(Rita)*, Eddra Gale *(Anna Fassbender)*, Katrin Schaake *(Jacqueline)*, Richard Burton *(Man in Bar)*

p, Charles K. Feldman; d, Clive Donner; w, Woody Allen; ph, Jean Badal; ed, Fergus McDonell; m, Burt Bacharach; art d, Jacques Saulnier; fx, M. MacDonald; chor, Jean Guelis; cos, Gladys de Segonzac, Mia Fonssagrives, Vicky Tiel

AAN Best Song: Burt Bacharach (Music), Hal David (Lyrics)

A most significant film to buffs in that it marks the first time Woody Allen appeared on screen in a script drawn from his own typewriter. Until this time he'd been a successful nightclub and TV variety show comic, and WHAT'S NEW PUSSYCAT? gave a wider audience to his patented neuroses. It's a good example of the "swinging sixties" style under the broad direction of Clive Donner, who had begun his career in films as an assistant director. O'Toole, fresh from his triumphs in LAWRENCE OF ARABIA and BECKET, shows that he can deliver the goods comedically as well as dramatically; here he takes the role of a lover of gorgeous women who fears nothing in this world save marriage. Sellers is a freaked-out, Beatle-wigged analyst attempting to help O'Toole deal with his problems but is so lecherous himself that he is of little value to the disturbed O'Toole. Allen is an intellectual nebbish whose life is a perpetual attempt to learn why he can't attract women.

WHAT'S NEW, PUSSYCAT? is a classic comedy of its time and captures the period in sight and sound. It doesn't wear as well as a true classic, though, and many of the gags would feel dated 20 years later. Sets and costumes are superb, as are the scenes at the "Crazy Horse." Burt Bacharach's music and Hal David's lyrics helped immensely, with the title tune being reaching No. 3 in pop music polls that year. The movie was a box-office success, appealing, no doubt, to those who doubted the sexual "double standard" as well as the Teutonic psychiatrist so aptly portrayed by Sellers. Richard Burton does a cameo, as does Allen's wife at the time, Louise Lasser. By making O'Toole the editor on a Paris fashion magazine, the tale was able to move with lighting speed and also justify his coming into contact with so many gorgeous women—every man's dream, but most particularly Woody Allen's.

WHAT'S UP, DOC?

1972   94m   c   Comedy   ★★★
Saticoy   (U.S.)   G/U

Barbra Streisand *(Judy Maxwell)*, Ryan O'Neal *(Prof. Howard Bannister)*, Madeline Kahn *(Eunice Burns)*, Kenneth Mars *(Hugh Simon)*, Austin Pendleton *(Frederick Larrabe)*, Sorrell Booke *(Harry)*, Stefan Gierasch *(Fritz)*, Mabel Albertson *(Mrs. Van Hoskins)*, Michael Murphy *(Mr. Smith)*, Graham Jarvis *(Bailiff)*

p, Peter Bogdanovich; d, Peter Bogdanovich; w, Buck Henry, David Newman, Robert Benton (based on a story by Bogdanovich); ph, Laszlo Kovacs; ed, Verna Fields; m, Artie Butler; prod d, Polly Platt; art d, Herman A. Blumenthal; fx, Robert MacDonald; cos, Nancy McArdle, Ray Phelps

Peter Bogdanovich's attempt to revive the screwball comedy genre is more imitation than homage, especially if you've seen the Howard Hawks classic BRINGING UP BABY. Still, the film has plenty of good 1930s slapstick and cartoon humor to hold your attention and to justify Bugs Bunny's famed opening line (which serves as the title) and Porky Pig's equally famed closing: "Th-th-that's all, folks!" Ryan O'Neal, a clumsy, shy professor from Iowa, hopes to win a $20,000 fellowship in musicology. He carries some ancient rocks in a plaid suitcase; the rocks demonstrate his theory on music's prehistoric origins. O'Neal arrives at a San Francisco hotel with his fiancee, Kahn (in her film debut), while other guests with identical suitcases, including the breezy Streisand, are also checking in. Naturally, the suitcases get hopelessly mixed up—a daffy coincidence leading to countless comic scenes. While WHAT'S UP, DOC? may not be as great as the classic screwball comedies of the 1930s and 40s, director Bogdanovich has delivered a film with energy, wit, and a madcap pace that is well worth watching.

WHAT'S UP, TIGER LILY?

1966   80m   c   Comedy   ★★★½
Toho/Benedict   (U.S.)   PG

Tatsuya Mihashi *(Phil Moscowitz)*, Mie Hama *(Terri Yaki)*, Akiko Wakabayashi *(Suki Yaki)*, Tadao Nakamaru *(Shepherd Wong)*, Susumu Kurobe *(Wing Fat)*, Woody Allen *(Narrator/Host/Voice)*, Frank Buxton, Len Maxwell, Louise Lasser, Mickey Rose

p, Woody Allen; d, Senkichi Taniguchi; w, Kazuo Yamada, Woody Allen, Frank Buxton, Len Maxwell, Louise Lasser, Mickey Rose, Bryna Wilson, Julie Bennett; ph, Kazuo Yamada; ed, Richard Krown; m, Jack Lewis, The Lovin' Spoonful

Woody Allen took a low-grade Japanese spy film called KAGI NO KAGI (Key of Keys) and dubbed in new dialogue (improvised with Buxton, Maxwell, Lasser, Rose, Wilson, and Bennett) to create this wonderfully cockeyed movie. The story describes the adventures of Phil Moscowitz, a Japanese James Bond who is searching for the world's greatest egg salad recipe. The balance of world power hangs on whether or not Moscowitz can keep this recipe—"so delicious you could *plotz*"—from falling into the wrong hands. After many plucky escapades, Moscowitz confronts Shepherd Wong, the evil mastermind trying to get the recipe for his own nefarious doings. Moscowitz defeats Wong's henchmen and then returns to his loves, Suki and Terri Yaki. They are eager for him to arrive, "bringing with him the constant promise of joy and fulfillment in its most primitive form." But alas, Moscowitz is now under the delusion that he is a Pan Am jet!

WHAT'S UP, TIGER LILY? is cleverly devised, hinging on a well-developed sense of the absurd. Allen and his cohorts make good use of the source movie's situations, turning its obvious cliches into some wonderful parodic gems. The one-liners spew out like popcorn, an effect that wears a little thin towards the end. Footage of the pop group the Lovin' Spoonful edited into the story also detracts from the pell-mell pacing. Though Allen had limited control over the visual content, many of the themes and ideas he would later develop in such films as LOVE AND DEATH and HANNAH AND HER SISTERS are evident in the dialogue—themes of sexual frustration, psychiatry and neurosis, Judaism, and the influence of movies. Executive producer Saperstein paid only $66,000 for the rights to KEY OF KEYS and certainly got more than his money's worth when he turned it over to the rising comedian. Heard on the soundtrack are Lasser, Allen's second wife, and Rose, cowriter with Allen of TAKE THE MONEY AND RUN and BANANAS.

WHEN A MAN LOVES A WOMAN

1994   125m   c   Drama   ★★½
Touchstone   (U.S.)   R/

Andy Garcia *(Michael Green)*, Meg Ryan *(Alice Green)*, Ellen Burstyn *(Emily)*, Tina Majorino *(Jess Green)*, Mae Whitman *(Casey Green)*, Lauren Tom *(Amy)*, Philip Seymour Hoffman *(Gary)*, Eugene Roche *(Walter)*, Gail Strickland *(Pam)*, Steven Brill *(Madras Tie Guy)*

p, Jordan Kerner, Jon Avnet; d, Luis Mandoki; w, Ronald Bass, Al Franken; ph, Lajos Koltai; ed, Garth Craven; m, Zbigniew Preisner; prod d, Stuart Wurtzel; art d, Steven A. Saklad; fx, Tom Ward; chor, Miranda Garrison; cos, Linda Bass

When a man loves a woman who's an alcoholic, he's going to get a crash course in the modern American culture of addiction and recovery. So will viewers of this would-be old-fashioned tearjerker, in which much of the drama and romance is drained to make room for plenty of instructional preaching.

Alice Green (Meg Ryan) drinks a lot, and her husband, Michael (Andy Garcia), accepts it, even though she alternates between being fun and being an irresponsible and worrisome drunk. Only when she gets so drunk that she falls though the glass shower door is Alice ready to admit she's an alcoholic. While Alice struggles through detox and the beginnings of recovery, Michael struggles at home with their two daughters, eight-year-old Jess (Tina Majorino) and five-year-old Casey (Mae Whitman). After Alice returns home, she and Michael must rebuild their relationship, which isn't as easy as they'd like.

THE DAYS OF WINE AND ROSES is a terrific story about an upper middle-class, San Francisco couple caught in the downward slide of alcoholism. Is there equal drama in the portrait of an upper middle-class, San Francisco couple facing the upward climb of recovery? WHEN A MAN LOVES A WOMAN dodges the question in favor of a glossy, emotional theme park ride—"Recoveryland." Ryan and Garcia give the movie what authenticity it has, but too much time is given to speeches and therapeutic jargon. It's entertaining in a manipulative, TV movie way, but a film that addresses a serious social ill begs to be held to a higher standard.

WHEN FATHER WAS AWAY ON BUSINESS
(OTAC NA SLUZBENOH PUTU)

1985   144m   c   Drama/Comedy   ★★★★
Centar/Forum   (Yugoslavia)   R/15

Moreno D'E Bartolli *(Malik)*, Miki Manojlovic *(Mesha)*, Mirjana Karanovic *(Senija)*, Mustafa Nadarevic *(Zijo)*, Mira Furlan *(Ankica)*, Davor Dujmovic *(Mirza)*, Predrag Lakovic *(Franjo)*, Pavle Vujisic *(Muzamer)*, Eva Ras *(Zivka)*, Aleksandar Dorcev *(Dr. Ljahaov)*

d, Emir Kusturica; w, Abdulah Sidran; ph, Vilko Filac; ed, Andrija Zafranovic; m, Zoran Simjanovic; cos, Divna Jovanovic

AAN Best Foreign Language Film

Director Emir Kusturica deservedly won the prestigious Golden Palm at Cannes with this complex, moving drama, his second feature.

It is the early 1950s in Yugoslavia, which, under the leadership of Marshal Tito, has broken with the USSR. No-one can be sure if their next-door neighbor is just shooting off his mouth, or deliberately trying to bait someone else into making an anti-government statement. If that happens, police arrive in the middle of the night and the individual is soon "away on business." Malik (Moreno D'E Bartolli) is the 6-year-old child who narrates the story of his father, Mesha (Miki Manojlovic), a privileged Labor Ministry official who is sent off to a work camp. The family likes everyone to think that Mesha is in jail for unspecified political actions, but just about everyone knows the truth—that he was set up by his former lover, Ankica (Mira Furlan). Malik and his older brother (Davor Dujmovic) do their best to keep up their mother's (Mirjana Karanovic) spirits while her husband is gone, but that's a tall order when she knows that the man who arrested her husband is her own brother, the local police commissioner, who is also sexually involved with Ankica and wanted to get his competition out of the way.

WHEN FATHER WAS AWAY has its fair share of humor and whimsy; Malik's sleepwalking assumes an almost fairy-tale dimension, and the state propaganda machine is the source of some well-observed laughs. But Kusturica never allows us to entirely forget the harsh underpinnings of his tale, and doesn't flinch from depicting the charming Mesha's less savory qualities. The banished father's chauvinism threatens, on occasion, to strain our sympathy beyond breaking point, and the last scene, in which he exacts a viciously nasty revenge on his former lover, is a masterpiece of emotional manipulation; even though we abhor Micha's behavior, we clutch our seats in the hope that he will *not* be caught red-handed. Not in front of the children, anyway.

WHEN HARRY MET SALLY...

1989 96m c Comedy/Romance   ★★★
Castle Rock/Nelson (U.S.)   R/15

Billy Crystal *(Harry Burns)*, Meg Ryan *(Sally Albright)*, Carrie Fisher *(Marie)*, Bruno Kirby *(Jess)*, Steven Ford *(Joe)*, Lisa Jane Persky *(Alice)*, Michelle Nicastro *(Amanda)*, Gretchen Palmer *(Stewardess)*, Robert Alan Beuth *(Man on Aisle)*, David Burdick *(9-year-old Boy)*

p, Rob Reiner, Andrew Scheinman, Jeffrey Stott, Steve Nicolaides; d, Rob Reiner; w, Nora Ephron; ph, Barry Sonnenfeld; ed, Robert Leighton; m, Marc Shaiman, Harry Connick Jr.; prod d, Jane Musky; cos, Gloria Gresham

AAN Best Original Screenplay: Nora Ephron

Harry (Billy Crystal) meets Sally (Meg Ryan) on a post-graduation drive from the University of Chicago to New York, but when she rebuffs his flip advances, instant antipathy is born. Nonetheless, over the next 10 years in Manhattan, the two bump into each other at various emotionally crucial points in their lives and eventually manage to effect a friendship. Then sex rears its insistent head once more, and, following a period of readjustment, commitment-shy Harry learns that staying an entire night—and possibly an entire life—with one's object of lust is actually possible. The plot may seem anything but fresh (and the borrowings from Woody Allen certainly are stale), but director Rob Reiner has a killer instinct for setting up jokes and punchlines, and is vastly aided by the performances and chemistry of Crystal and Ryan, as well as crisp supporting work from Carrie Fisher and Bruno Kirby.

WHEN THE WIND BLOWS

1986 85m c Animated   ★★★★
Meltdown/British Screen/Film Four/TVC London/Penguin   /PG
Books (U.K.)

VOICES OF: Peggy Ashcroft *(Hilda Bloggs)*, John Mills *(Jim Bloggs)*, Robin Houston *(Announcer)*, James Russell, Matt Irving, David Dundas

p, John Coates; d, Jimmy T. Murakami; w, Raymond Briggs (based on his book); ed, John Cary; m, Roger Waters; fx, Stephen Weston

With its striking simplicity, WHEN THE WIND BLOWS is a moving parable of nuclear holocaust. Told through animation, the story follows a retired English couple, James Bloggs (voiced by John Mills) and his wife, Hilda (voiced by Peggy Ashcroft), as they face the postnuclear winter in a small cottage in the British countryside. World tensions have been building, according to radio reports, and war is imminent. When the bomb goes off, destroying the England James and Hilda love so dearly, they are convinced the situation is merely a temporary crisis and, like WWII, one they can stick out until things get back to normal. Gradually, radiation begin taking its toll on the couple, and small but important details of their lives start to slip out of their control. These developments are handled with a gentle, sympathetic humor that subtly brings out the hopelessness of their plight. Mills and Ashcroft are perfectly cast in their cartoon roles. The variety of animation styles frequently produces captivating visual effects. WHEN THE WIND BLOWS is an eloquent vision of the ultimate tragedy.

WHERE EAGLES DARE

1969 155m c War   ★★★½
Winkast (U.K.)   M/PG

Richard Burton *(John Smith)*, Clint Eastwood *(Lt. Morris Schaffer)*, Mary Ure *(Mary Ellison)*, Patrick Wymark *(Col. Turner)*, Michael Hordern *(Vice Adm. Rolland)*, Donald Houston *(Christiansen)*, Peter Barkworth *(Berkeley)*, Robert Beatty *(Cartwright Jones)*, William Squire *(Thomas)*, Derren Nesbitt *(Maj. von Hapen)*

p, Elliott Kastner; d, Brian G. Hutton; w, Alistair MacLean; ph, Arthur Ibbetson; ed, John Jympson; m, Ron Goodwin; art d, Peter Mullins; fx, Richard Parker, Fred Hellenburgh

A high-powered, big-budget WWII espionage thriller, WHERE EAGLES DARE follows an elite group of Allied commandos, led by John Smith (Richard Burton) and assigned to rescue an American general being held captive by the Nazis in a castle high in the Bavarian Alps. Ably assisted by a young American lieutenant, Morris Schaffer (Clint Eastwood), Smith and his crew of six don German uniforms and parachute into enemy territory. One of their number is found dead after landing, and Smith begins to suspect that one of his men is a double agent. He meets up with a pair of Allied agents, Mary Ellison (Mary Ure) and Heidi (Ingrid Pitt), and they manage to infiltrate the castle, which is accessible only by a tramway. An exciting picture with much derring-do and adventure, WHERE EAGLES DARE is also a lengthy film, though there is more than enough action to keep it moving along. Of course, it's all a bit hard to credit (especially since the Germans can't seem to hit anything with their machine guns), but that's part of the fun. Burton, in a switch from the heavy dramatic roles that made him famous, is excellent as an action hero, but Eastwood is the one who makes it all worthwhile. If it's explosions, gunplay, and wartime treachery that you like, WHERE EAGLES DARE delivers.

WHERE THE BOYS ARE

1960 99m c Comedy   ★★½
Euterpe (U.S.)   /PG

Dolores Hart *(Merritt Andrews)*, George Hamilton *(Ryder Smith)*, Yvette Mimieux *(Melanie)*, Jim Hutton *(TV Thompson)*, Barbara Nichols *(Lola)*, Paula Prentiss *(Tuggle Carpenter)*, Connie Francis *(Angie)*, Chill Wills *(Police Captain)*, Frank Gorshin *(Basil)*, Rory Harrity *(Franklin)*

p, Joe Pasternak; d, Henry Levin; w, George Wells (based on the novel by Glendon Swarthout); ph, Robert Bronner; ed, Fredric Steinkamp; m, George Stoll, Pete Rugolo; art d, George W. Davis, Preston Ames; chor, Robert Sidney; cos, Kitty Mager

It's spring break, and college kids from around the country descend en masse to Fort Lauderdale, Florida. Hart, Mimieux, Prentiss, and Francis are four friends in search of sun, parties, and boys, though not necessarily in that order. The episodic plot line follows each girl in her respective success or failure with members of the opposite gender. Prentiss (in her film debut) is a scatterbrained lass who falls for Hutton, though their relationship takes a jealous turn when Hutton is briefly infatuated with Nichols, a nightclub entertainer who performs an underwater act in a glass tank. Recording star Francis also makes her first film appearance, capitalizing more on her vocal talents than acting ability. Hart meets Ivy Leaguer Hamilton, and romance blooms. Mimieux is determined to get herself an Ivy Leaguer any way she can, mistaking sexual passion for true love.

WHERE THE BOYS ARE is plenty moralistic, yet the film is not without a naive sense of charm. Hart, who doesn't give in so easily to Hamilton, is the pinnacle of everything good and proper, while poor Mimieux gets exactly what she deserves for responding so swiftly to Harrity's importunities—or so the film would have us believe. This sexual moralizing is a bit much, portraying women as either good or bad while the boys who chase them have just one thing in mind. Fortunately, the black-and-white ethics are balanced with the lighter involvements of the other couples. Prentiss and Hutton give their story a silly sweetness, going through predictable situations with fine comic flair. Considering the radical movements that would sweep college campuses in the 1960s, this film holds some interest as a relic of sexual attitudes in the 1950s. A 1984 remake showed just how much Hollywood had changed in portraying sexual antics on screen, though the later film has none of the original's appeal.

WHERE'S POPPA?

1970 83m c Comedy ★★★½
UA (U.S.) R/X

George Segal (*Gordan Hocheiser*), Ruth Gordon (*Mrs. Hocheiser*), Trish Van Devere (*Louise Callan*), Ron Leibman (*Sidney Hocheiser*), Rae Allen (*Gladys Hocheiser*), Vincent Gardenia (*Coach Williams*), Joe Keyes (*Gang Leader*), Alice Drummond (*Woman in Elevator*), Tom Atkins (*Policeman in Apartment*), Florence Tarlow (*Miss Morgiani*)

p, Jerry Tokofsky, Marvin Worth; d, Carl Reiner; w, Robert Klane (based on the novel by Robert Klane); ph, Jack Priestley; ed, Bud Molin, Chic Ciccolini; m, Jack Elliott; art d, Warren Clymer; cos, Albert Wolsky

Once again, George Segal is saddled with a difficult Jewish mother, as he was in NO WAY TO TREAT A LADY and LOST AND FOUND. This time, though, she's little short of a senile psychopath. Robert Klane wrote the screenplay from his hysterical novel, and Reiner directed it, but missed many of the jokes that worked so well in the book.

A New York attorney, Segal, lives with Gordon, his aged and quite senile mother. He has never married because she has fouled up all of his relationships. She deserves to be in a home, but Segal promised his late father that he would look after her. At the beginning of the film, Segal awakens to a local radio show, showers, shaves, puts on a gorilla suit, and races into Gordon's room. We're not sure if he wants to cheer her up or cause her to have a heart attack. She responds by punching him hard in the groin and saying, "You almost scared me to death," as she laughs. Segal, doubled over in pain, mumbles, "Almost is not good enough." Gordon prepares orange slices for Segal's breakfast, then eats them herself, along with breakfast cereal smothered in Coca-Cola. Segal's brother, Leibman, is married to Allen and refuses to help in the care of Gordon, so Segal hires a succession of nurses, but none stay past noon because Gordon is impossible to deal with. Eventually Segal meets and hires Van Devere, a sweet nurse with a strange background. She's been married once, for 32 hours. After her first sexual experience with her husband, she was appalled to find that he'd defecated in bed. Van Devere is thrilled to find a man like Segal, and the two are soon in love, though Gordon does her best to scare the young woman off.

The ultimate black comedy about difficult Jewish mothers, WHERE'S POPPA? can be very funny, but suffers from the non-stop barrage of jokes. A few quieter moments would have allowed the humor more room to breathe. Reiner's son, Rob, a onetime cast member of television's "All in the Family" who would go on to be an acclaimed director in his own right (STAND BY ME, MISERY), makes a cameo appearance. Filmed on location in New York City, WHERE'S POPPA? has become a cult favorite, though it has been radically edited for television showings and must be seen in its entirety to be fully appreciated.

WHILE THE CITY SLEEPS

1956 100m bw Crime ★★★★
Thor (U.S.) /PG

Dana Andrews (*Edward Mobley*), Rhonda Fleming (*Dorothy Kyne*), Sally Forrest (*Nancy Liggett*), Thomas Mitchell (*John Day Griffith*), Vincent Price (*Walter Kyne*), Howard Duff (*Lt. Burt Kaufman*), Ida Lupino (*Mildred Donner*), George Sanders (*Mark Loving*), James Craig (*Harry Kritzer*), John Drew Barrymore (*Robert Manners*)

p, Bert E. Friedlob; d, Fritz Lang; w, Casey Robinson (based on the novel *The Bloody Spur* by Charles Einstein); ph, Ernest Laszlo; ed, Gene Fowler Jr.; m, Herschel Burke Gilbert; art d, Carroll Clark; cos, Norma

Lang's finest film since THE BIG HEAT and his last great success, WHILE THE CITY SLEEPS is a crime drama sending its lead actors on a twisted, dog-eat-dog journey into the underworld in their quest for success. The plot revolves around the aspirations of three newsmen—Mitchell, Sanders, and Craig—each in line for the job of editor-in-chief of a New York tabloid called *The Sentinel*. Upon the death of

newspaper owner Robert Warwick, his manipulative, dilettante son Price takes charge. The city is being terrorized by a sex murderer known as "The Lipstick Killer" (played with conventional dementia by Barrymore), a mama's boy who preys on beautiful woman at night. In a perverse power game, Price offers the newspaper's top position to the man who can crack the case. Naturally, Mitchell, Sanders, and Craig become rivals. Mitchell, a leathery, hard-drinking Irishman, is clear about his motive—he needs the money that the position pays. Sanders, the head of the wire service, is a ruthless cad interested in the societal implications of being the boss. Photo-editor Craig tries to use his romantic link with Price's wife, Fleming, as his inroad to the top job, spending more time wooing her than investigating the crime. To help achieve his goal, Mitchell bribes streetwise reporter Andrews for assistance. Each character's lack of moral values is soon made evident when they all employ the services of women to find the killer—risking the ladies' lives instead of their own. Mitchell agrees to Andrews's plan to use Andrews's fiancee, Forrest, as a decoy for Barrymore. Sanders cons gutsy columnist Lupino into helping him secure information by seducing Andrews, while Craig continues working through Fleming and her influence over Price. Forrest is nearly killed when Barrymore tries to enter her apartment. A climactic chase leads Andrews, hot on the trail of the pathetic killer, to the New York subway system. A battle ensues between him and Barrymore, eventually ending up on the subway tracks. The roar of a northbound train thunders closer, while the lights of a southbound loom larger by the second. At the very last moment, Andrews is tossed past the oncoming train and lands safely, while Barrymore escapes up the stairs only to be apprehended by the police.

Although viewed rather narrow-mindedly by some as an unsuccessful thriller because Lang reveals the killer's identity too early, WHILE THE CITY SLEEPS is clearly more than a thriller. Lang's interest is not in the killer's motivation and methods, but in the journalists' ruthless, morally guilty minds. These are men who are entrusted to uphold society's morals and protect a community, yet they readily put other people in danger for their own benefit. This superbly constructed and multilayered film was Lang's second favorite film, following his 1936 US masterpiece, FURY. Produced independently, WHILE THE CITY SLEEPS was set for release by United Artists, though in the end it was distributed by RKO.

WHILE YOU WERE SLEEPING

1995 100m c Comedy/Romance ★★★
SST Productions/Caravan Pictures/Hollywood Pictures (U.S.) PG

Sandra Bullock (*Lucy Moderatz*), Bill Pullman (*Jack*), Peter Gallagher (*Peter*), Peter Boyle (*Ox*), Jack Warden (*Saul*), Glynis Johns (*Elsie*), Michael Rispoli (*Joe Jr.*), Jason Bernard (*Jerry*), Micole Mercurio (*Midge*), Ally Walker (*Ashley Bacon*)

p, Joe Roth, Roger Birnbaum; d, Jon Turteltaub; w, Daniel G. Sullivan, Fredric Lebow; ph, Phedon Papamichael; ed, Bruce Green; m, Randy Edelman; prod d, Garreth Stover; art d, Chris Cornwell; fx, Guy Clayton Jr.; cos, Betsy Cox

Warm and sentimental, with suitably engaging stars, this romantic comedy remains winning even when it takes the occasional misstep.

Sandra Bullock plays Lucy, a Chicago subway token clerk who has a crush on one of her daily fares, handsome lawyer Peter (Peter Gallagher). When he's mugged and thrown off the platform, Lucy jumps onto the tracks and somehow manages to move his unconscious body out of the way of an oncoming train. At the emergency room, she's mistaken for Peter's fiancee by an overzealous nurse. Thus begins a series of confusions that finds Lucy progressively enmeshed with Peter's loving, if slightly kooky, family—especially his amiable brother Jack (Bill Pullman).

Shot against a wintry Chicago backdrop, WHILE YOU WERE SLEEPING has the warm, cuddly feel of a plush toy. Bullock is appropriately charming, but Pullman, previously typecast as a perennial loser, steals the show. His slightly fuzzy good looks and wry smile have a relaxed appeal that is especially welcome in a time when Hollywood seems dominated by chiseled action heroes and troubled boy-men. Director Jon Turteltaub enhances the clear narrative flow and leisurely pacing of a workmanlike screenplay, exploiting moments of comic relief in situations that could easily collapse into mawkishness or over-the-top sentimentality.

WHISTLE BLOWER, THE

1986 104m c Spy   ★★★
Portreeve (U.K.)   PG

Michael Caine (*Frank Jones*), James Fox (*Lord*), Nigel Havers (*Robert Jones*), Felicity Dean (*Cynthia Goodburn*), John Gielgud (*Sir Adrian Chapple*), Gordon Jackson (*Bruce*), Barry Foster (*Charles Greig*), Kenneth Colley (*Bill Pickett*), Dinah Stabb (*Rose*), Andrew Hawkins (*Allen Goodburn*)

p, Geoffrey Reeve; d, Simon Langton; w, Julian Bond (based on the novel by John Hale); ph, Fred Tammes; ed, Robert Morgan; m, John Scott; prod d, Morley Smith; art d, Chris Burke; cos, Raymond Hughes

Despite a superb performance from the incredibly prolific Michael Caine, THE WHISTLE BLOWER is a ponderous affair that, while intellectually interesting, fails miserably on a cinematic level. The slow, confusing, and convoluted opening introduces widower Caine, a Korean War veteran, patriot, and struggling business machine salesman who launches a one-man investigation into the mysterious death of his son (Havers), an idealistic young man who worked as a Russian translator at GCHQ (Government Communications Headquarters), British intelligence's listening center. The further he digs, the more it becomes apparent that the British government sanctioned the murder of his son because he was about to blow the whistle on the sordid operations of the agency. Because Americans are more used to cinematic portrayals of government involvement in corruption, deceit, and conspiracy, THE WHISTLE BLOWER seems strangely uninvolving. Bond's script and Langton's direction are so very proper, restrained, and subdued that the viewer has trouble maintaining much interest in revelations that should really be news to no one. Not that every spy movie needs James Bond-type action to be successful, but THE WHISTLE BLOWER is mainly dialogue with little visual nuance. As is typical of British productions, the film is brimming with fine acting.

WHISTLE DOWN THE WIND

1961 98m bw Drama   ★★★½
Beaver/Allied Film Makers (U.K.)   /U

Hayley Mills (*Kathy Bostock*), Bernard Lee (*Mr. Bostock*), Alan Bates (*Arthur Blakey*), Diane Holgate (*Nan Bostock*), Alan Barnes (*Charles Bostock*), Norman Bird (*Eddie*), Diane Clare (*Miss Lodge*), Patricia Heneghan (*Salvation Army Girl*), Elsie Wagstaffe (*Auntie Dorothy*), John Arnatt (*Teesdale*)

p, Richard Attenborough; d, Bryan Forbes; w, Keith Waterhouse, Willis Hall (based on the novel by Mary Hayley Bell); ph, Arthur Ibbetson; ed, Max Benedict; m, Malcolm Arnold; art d, Ray Simm

Bryan Forbes's directorial debut was a beauty. Not satisfied to cut his teeth on a proven commercial vehicle, he used the unique novel by Mary Hayley Bell as the basis for this unique film. In today's world, anyone proclaiming himself to be Jesus Christ would be whisked away by the authorities before many moments passed. And children today are a lot keener on life's realities than they were a quarter of a century ago, perhaps due to the influence of television. But on a grim Lancashire farm, a man claiming to be Christ wins the trust of three motherless children who have been strongly influenced by their strict religious training. Mills is the eldest of Lee's children; the others are Barnes and Holgate. The trio finds a bearded man hiding in the family barn. Beards are not common in that area, and when Mills asks the wild-eyed fellow who he is, he mutters, "Jesus Christ." They take him at his word, and do their best to shield and care for him. Only later is it revealed that Bates is a fugitive criminal.

This could have been a mawkish movie if it had gone over the edge, but Forbes kept matters realistic and still managed to enfold several bits of New Testament symbolism into the picture without hammering anyone on the head. The novel's author was Mills' mother (and wife of actor John Mills), and although there is no proof that she wrote the book with her daughter in mind, the youngster was surely the right choice for the role. It was her fourth movie; she had already completed TIGER BAY, POLLYANNA, and THE PARENT TRAP before this. Bates was

wonderful in his difficult role. Prior to this, he had established himself as a stage actor and had appeared in THE ENTERTAINER the year before in his debut. Holgate and Barnes are so delicious in their naivete that they almost steal the film from Mills. It's an allegory, the second film produced by actor Richard Attenborough, who later became the Oscar-winning director of GANDHI.

WHITE
(TROIS COULEURS: BLANC)

1994 92m c Drama/Comedy/Romance   ★★★½
Marin Karmitz Productions (France/Poland/Switzerland)   R/15

Zbigniew Zamachowski (*Karol Karol*), Julie Delpy (*Dominique*), Janusz Gajos (*Mikolaj*), Jerzy Stuhr (*Jurek*), Grzegorz Warchol (*Elegant Man*), Jerzy Nowak (*Old Farmer*), Aleksander Bardini (*Lawyer*), Cezary Harasimowicz (*Inspector*), Jerzy Trela (*Monsieur Bronek*), Cezary Pazura (*Bureau de Change Proprietor*)

p, Marin Karmitz; d, Krzysztof Kieslowski; w, Krzysztof Kieslowski, Krzysztof Piesiewicz, Agnieszka Holland, Edward Zebrowski; ph, Edward Klosinski; ed, Ursula Lesiak; m, Zbigniew Preisner; art d, Halina Dobrowolska, Claude Lenoir

The second film in Krzysztof Kieslowski's THREE COLORS trilogy lacks the power of the first and third installments, BLUE and RED, but produces its own distinct pleasures. WHITE's story of obsessive love is originally told and surprisingly funny.

In a Paris courtroom, Dominique (Julie Delpy), a French woman, divorces her Polish husband, Karol (Zbigniew Zamachowski), a hairdresser, because he has been unable to consummate their marriage. After the hearing, Dominique, who is still angry at Karol, burns their hair salon and frames her ex-husband for the arson. Karol is forced to flee to the Paris subways, where he meets Mikolaj (Janusz Gajos), a businessman who convinces him to return to Poland. In Warsaw, Karol manages to strike it rich and plots a fantastic revenge against his former wife.

Compared to the previous BLUE and subsequent RED, WHITE is a curiosity. The film is distinguished by quirky humor and farcical plot developments, and it is directed in a straightforward, less stylized fashion than the other two films. Still, WHITE effectively continues Kieslowski's search for meaning amidst unusual relationships. Karol's incredible fall-and-rise produces moments ranging from pathos to hilarity, and Zbigniew Zamachowski's performance as Karol ("Charles") deliberately evokes the bittersweet charm of Charlie Chaplin's Little Tramp.

WHITE represents the "equality" section of the French tricolor in an eccentric and rather disturbing way. The national, economic, and sexual "equality" achieved here leaves the bitter aftertaste of revenge, which is at odds with the more optimistic conclusions of the other tricolor films. Indeed, Kieslowski seems to view equality as a chimerical goal—sexual relationships are innately antagonistic, the market (black or white) rewards the ruthless at the expense of the powerless. A more satisfying ending of WHITE occurs at the end of RED, the last story in the trilogy, during which Karol and Dominique reappear together in an unexpected way.

WHITE CHRISTMAS

1954 120m c Musical/Comedy   ★★★
Paramount (U.S.)   /U

Bing Crosby (*Bob Wallace*), Danny Kaye (*Phil Davis*), Rosemary Clooney (*Betty*), Vera-Ellen (*Judy*), Dean Jagger (*Gen. Waverly*), Mary Wickes (*Emma*), John Brascia (*Joe*), Anne Whitfield (*Susan*), Richard Shannon (*Adjutant*), Grady Sutton (*General's Guest*)

p, Robert Emmett Dolan; d, Michael Curtiz; w, Norman Krasna, Norman Panama, Melvin Frank; ph, Loyal Griggs; ed, Frank Bracht; art d, Hal Pereira, Roland Anderson; chor, Robert Alton; cos, Edith Head

AAN Best Song: Irving Berlin

This eagerly awaited musical comedy had all the ingredients for success: two of its day's biggest-box office draws, a solid director, and a score by America's treasure, Irving Berlin. And though it's not as satisfying as it might have been, it still boasts great stars and catchy songs in addition to a love story, and is a perennial holiday favorite.

Bob Wallace (Bing Crosby) and Phil Davis (Danny Kaye) meet during the war and team up afterward to become the hottest song-and-dance duo around. After five years of heady success, they think it's about time to take a vacation, so they travel to a New England ski resort in the company of lovely sister entertainers Betty (Rosemary Clooney) and Judy (Vera-Ellen) for some rest and recuperation. They arrive to find the place in terrible financial condition and in desperate need of an infusion of money, because there hasn't been any snow for almost a year. The man who runs the inn is their old Army topkick, Gen. Waverly (Dean Jagger). Bob and Phil decide to aid Waverly by staging a benefit show that is, of course, a smash. Included is the title song, which Irving Berlin had written for HOLIDAY INN 12 years before. With that tune as the core, the script was fashioned, and several more Berlin tunes were added.

WHITE CLIFFS OF DOVER, THE

1944   126m   bw   War   ★★★½
MGM   (U.S.)   /U

Irene Dunne *(Susan Dunn Ashwood)*, Alan Marshal *(Sir John Ashwood)*, Frank Morgan *(Hiram Porter Dunn)*, Roddy McDowall *(John Ashwood II as a Boy)*, Peter Lawford *(John Ashwood II at age 24)*, Dame May Whitty *(Nanny)*, C. Aubrey Smith *(Colonel)*, Gladys Cooper *(Lady Jean Ashwood)*, Van Johnson *(Sam Bennett)*, John Warburton *(Reggie)*

p, Sidney Franklin; d, Clarence Brown; w, Claudine West, Jan Lustig, George Froeschel (based on the poem "The White Cliffs of Dover" by Alice Duer Miller, with additional material by Robert Nathan); ph, George Folsey; ed, Robert J. Kern, Al Jennings; m, Herbert Stothart; art d, Cedric Gibbons, Randall Duell; fx, A. Arnold Gillespie, Warren Newcombe; cos, Irene

AAN Best Cinematography: George Folsey

Alice Duer Miller's poem was the inspiration for this sentimental look at the ravages of war and at the courage of one woman who lost both her husband and son in the two world wars that dominated this century. Dunne is a Red Cross supervisor in England, awaiting casualties of WWII. At her desk, she ruminates about her past and flashes back to 1914, when she comes to England with Morgan, her father, a newspaper publisher in a medium-sized town in the US. In no time at all, Dunne meets, falls in love with, and marries wealthy and titled Marshal. They are ecstatic, but their happiness is brief; WWI breaks out, and Marshal must serve his country in France, where he is killed on the battlefield. By the time of his death, Dunne has given birth to a son, and though the war is over, she stays in England to raise the boy. Played first by McDowall, then by Lawford, the boy grows to be a credit to his father. WWII breaks out and Dunne becomes a worker for the Red Cross assigned to a hospital in London. The wounded servicemen are brought in for surgery and she is shocked to see that one of them is her son, Lawford, now 24. He is dying of his injuries and she is powerless to help. At the conclusion, Dunne looks out a window and observes a battalion of American soldiers as they march past, the first such warriors to reach the British shores.

At the advent of the war, MGM made several pro-English features, the most successful being MRS. MINIVER. The studio wanted the same type of success again, but couldn't find the right material until producer Franklin happened on Miller's poem (which was given some additional words by Robert Nathan). Dunne was busy on A GUY NAMED JOE, but that production had to go on hiatus while Van Johnson recovered from an auto accident. In the meantime, this one began, and when Johnson was able to get back before the cameras more quickly than anyone had anticipated, Dunne found herself working on two major features at the same time. Beside MRS. MINIVER, MGM had already made GOODBYE, MR. CHIPS and RANDOM HARVEST and was in danger of being classified as a strictly Anglophile studio. This movie didn't achieve the success of the aforementioned films, but still managed a respectable gross of more than $4 million. Good acting, superior production values, sensitive direction, and one of Dunne's finest performances enhance the film. In order to make the settings authentic, MGM hired Major Cyril Seys Ramsey-Hill as technical advisor; he must have done his job because Britons living in the US sobbed at the showings.

WHITE DOG

1982   90m   c   Drama   ★★★½
Edgar J. Scherick   (U.S.)   PG/15

Kristy McNichol *(Julie Sawyer)*, Paul Winfield *(Keys)*, Burl Ives *(Carruthers)*, Jameson Parker *(Roland Gray)*, Lynne Moody *(Molly)*, Marshall Thompson *(Director)*, Bob Minor *(Joe)*, Vernon Weddle *(Vet)*, Christa Lang *(Nurse)*, Tony Brubaker *(Sweeper Driver)*

p, Jon Davison; d, Samuel Fuller; w, Samuel Fuller, Curtis Hanson (based on the novella by Romain Gary); ph, Bruce Surtees; ed, Bernard Gribble; m, Ennio Morricone; prod d, Brian Eatwell

One of the most famous "unseen" films, WHITE DOG never got a theatrical run in the US even though it had a well-known cast, a legendary director, and a powerful subject—racism. Kristy McNichol plays Julie Sawyer, a young actress who adopts a beautiful white stray dog. When a rapist breaks into Julie's home, the dog, which has been playful and gentle up to this, attacks and nearly tears the man limb from limb before the police arrive. The beautiful dog, she learns, has been trained to kill Blacks. A Black animal-trainer, Keys (Paul Winfield), begins an attempt to recondition the dog, although Carruthers (Burl Ives), who runs the training center, maintains that it can never be completely broken of its desire to kill. In the meantime, Julie meets the person who trained the dog in the first place. The rights the award-winning novella by Romain Gary on which the film is based were bought by Paramount 10 years before production began. Once the movie was made, the studio got cold feet, fearing that the volatile subject would incite racial controversy, although Sam Fuller's film is anything but racist. When WHITE DOG finally opened in Paris and London it was hailed as a masterpiece by some critics. The film finally did show up on cable television in January of 1984, in a re-edited version from Paramount that foolishly turned the dog from a killer to one that merely bites.

WHITE HEAT

1949   114m   bw   Crime   ★★★★★
Warner Bros.   (U.S.)   /15

James Cagney *(Arthur Cody Jarrett)*, Virginia Mayo *(Verna Jarrett)*, Edmond O'Brien *(Hank Fallon/Vic Pardo)*, Margaret Wycherly *(Ma Jarrett)*, Steve Cochran *(Big Ed Somers)*, John Archer *(Phillip Evans)*, Wally Cassell *(Giovanni Cotton Valetti)*, Fred Clark *(Daniel Winston, the Trader)*, Ford Rainey *(Zuckie Hommell)*, Fred Coby *(Happy Taylor)*

p, Louis F. Edelman; d, Raoul Walsh; w, Ivan Goff, Ben Roberts (based on a story by Virginia Kellogg); ph, Sid Hickox; ed, Owen Marks; m, Max Steiner; art d, Edward Carrere; fx, Roy Davidson, H.F. Koenekamp; cos, Leah Rhodes

AAN Best Original Screenplay: Virginia Kellogg

Ten years later, a flaming farewell to the 30s gangster picture, scripted like a Greek tragedy on speed. Raoul Walsh supplies the Freudian direction, Cagney the daring acting and sizzling star power. WHITE HEAT is primal, flamboyant stuff—close your eyes and you could be watching a 30s picture. But don't close them more than momentarily; the film's visuals make it linger in the mind's eye.

Cagney plays psychopathic gangster Cody Jarrett, Margaret Wycherly the mother who drives him to crime and whose death makes him go literally berserk. Virginia Mayo is Jarrett's wife, who has a hankering for gang member Big Ed (Steve Cochran), Edmond O'Brien plays a police informant who shares a cell with Jarrett, and John Archer is the FBI agent on the madman's tail.

One of the toughest and most brilliant crime films ever made, WHITE HEAT marked a breakthrough in the explicitly psychological depiction of screen bad guys. Cagney's character was based on notorious real-life gangster Arthur "Doc" Barker, Wycherly's on the equally infamous "Ma" Barker, the alleged catalyst for his criminal exploits. Cagney graphically demonstrates Jarrett's mother fixation when the actor, following one of his epileptic-style seizures, allows her to sit him in her lap and soothe him. This startling scene, like many in this classic film noir, was Cagney's own idea. The prison mess hall sequence, where Jarrett hears of his mother's murder, is the most charged moment in Cagney's outstanding career. The final image, shot atop an actual oil refinery in Torrance, CA, in which Jarrett calls out his warped triumph to his dead mother before blowing himself skyward, is one of the best-known scenes in film history.

WHITE HUNTER, BLACK HEART

1990 112m c Adventure/Drama ★★½
Malpaso/Rastar (U.S.) PG

Clint Eastwood (John Wilson), Jeff Fahey (Pete Verrill), Charlotte Cornwell (Miss Wilding), Norman Lumsden (Butler George), George Dzundza (Paul Landers), Edward Tudor Pole (Reissar), Roddy Maude-Roxby (Thompson), Richard Warwick (Basil Fields), John Rapley (Gun Shop Salesman), Catherine Neilson (Irene Saunders)

p, Clint Eastwood; d, Clint Eastwood; w, Peter Viertel, James Bridges, Burt Kennedy (based on the novel Roman a Clef by Peter Viertel); ph, Jack N. Green; ed, Joel Cox; m, Lennie Niehaus; prod d, John Graysmark; art d, Tony Reading; fx, John Evans, Roy Field; chor, Arlene Phillips; cos, John Mollo

Based on Peter Viertel's roman a clef, WHITE HUNTER, BLACK HEART uses the making of a classic film, THE AFRICAN QUEEN, as the setting for an investigation into the creative process. It's also the story of one enigmatic film director as told by another. Star-director Clint Eastwood plays a thinly disguised John Huston, here called John Wilson.

Set in 1951, the film begins as Wilson has summoned an old friend, writer Pete Verrill (Jeff Fahey), to his Irish estate to recruit him for his latest project—the title of which he never can remember—about a salty, hard-drinking boat captain and a prissy schoolmarm who take on the German navy in Africa during WWII. All Wilson really cares about is that the film will give him a fast infusion of cash to put a dent in personal debts totalling a quarter of a million dollars. Even more important, it will provide him with an all-expenses-paid opportunity to fulfill his longtime dream of going big-game hunting. Meetings with producer Paul Landers (George Dzundza, playing a role modeled on real-life producer Sam Spiegel) and potential backers put the production on track, and Wilson and Verrill begin work on the script. But a major dispute arises over the fate of the leading characters, who, in Wilson's version, are killed, while Verrill insists they should live as the fair reward for their extraordinary heroism. Even after Wilson and Verrill's arrival in Africa, the film continues to take a back seat to the director's planned safari to kill an elephant.

WHITE HUNTER is an ambitious and intriguing project that never amounts to anything more than the sum of its parts—a trait shared by many of Eastwood's other major projects as an independent filmmaker, BIRD. The personification of the post-Hemingway action hero, Eastwood looks and sounds uncomfortable filling Huston's decidedly Hemingwayesque shoes. As the action shifts to Africa, he seems inordinately laid-back as his character's obsession grows. He can't quite get a hold on the first predominantly unsympathetic character he's played since TIGHTROPE. And as a director, Eastwood has yet to pose much of a threat to Huston. WHITE HUNTER, like other Eastwood-directed films, lacks precisely the clear, lean narrative approach that characterizes Huston's best work (including THE AFRICAN QUEEN) or even that of Eastwood's mentor, director Don Siegel (DIRTY HARRY, ESCAPE FROM ALCATRAZ).

WHITE MEN CAN'T JUMP

1992 115m c Sports/Comedy ★★½
Finger Roll Inc/Fox (U.S.) R/15

Wesley Snipes (Sidney Deane), Woody Harrelson (Billy Hoyle), Rosie Perez (Gloria Clemente), Tyra Ferrell (Rhonda Deane), Cylk Cozart (Robert), Kadeem Hardison (Junior), Ernest Harden Jr. (George), John Marshall Jones (Walter), Marques Johnson (Raymond), David Roberson (T.J.)

p, Don Miller, David Lester; d, Ron Shelton; w, Ron Shelton; ph, Russell Boyd; ed, Paul Seydor, Kimberly Ray; m, Bennie Wallace; prod d, Dennis Washington; art d, Roger Fortune

Ron Shelton's second outing since his breakout success with BULL DURHAM aims to be a high-energy remake of THE HUSTLER in a street-basketball setting, but succeeds only intermittently. Playground hoops phenomenon Billy Hoyle (Woody Harrelson) walks onto a tough

Venice court and smokes the competition, including reigning champ Sidney Deane (Wesley Snipes), who is duly impressed. Or so it seems, until Deane conspires with some friends to con Hoyle out of the nest egg he's saved while living with his sexy, volatile girlfriend Gloria Clemente (Rosie Perez). Gloria knocks heads with Sidney's wife Rhonda (Tyra Ferrell), and together they come up with a plan for Sidney and Billy to compete in a sponsored two-on-two playground competition for a $5000 first prize. Sidney and Billy win easily, but Billy loses his half to Sidney on a foolish slam-dunking bet on the way home (thus the film's title). A disgusted Gloria walks out on Billy, but he wins her back by helping her achieve her lifetime ambition to compete on the game show "Jeopardy," which she wins easily. With her winnings, Gloria wants Billy to buy some decent clothes and get a straight job. Instead, Billy wants to take the money and bet it on one last playground match.

WHITE MEN CAN'T JUMP is engaging if inconsistent, with its manifest plot loopholes compensated for by the colorful court scenes, rapid-fire dialogue and enthusiastic performances from all concerned.

WHITE SHEIK, THE
(LO SCEICCO BIANCO)

1952 86m bw Comedy ★★½
Producers Distributors/OFI (France/Italy) /PG

Alberto Sordi (Fernando Rivoli), Brunella Bovo (Wanda Cavalli), Leopoldo Trieste (Ivan Cavalli), Giulietta Masina (Cabiria), Lilia Landi (Felga), Ernesto Almirante (Director of "White Sheik" Strip), Fanny Marchio (Marilena Vellardi), Gina Mascetti (White Sheik's Wife), Enzo Maggio (Hotel Concierge), Ettore Margadonna (Ivan's Uncle)

p, Luigi Rovere; d, Federico Fellini; w, Federico Fellini, Tullio Pinelli, Ennio Flaiano (based on a story by Federico Fellini and Tullio Pinelli from an idea by Michelangelo Antonioni); ph, Arturo Galea; ed, Rolando Bebedetti; m, Nino Rota; art d, Raffaello Tolfo

Federico Fellini's first solo directorial effort (he codirected VARIETY LIGHTS with Alberto Lattuada in 1951) is an enjoyable romp that shows the director's early promise. Newlyweds Wanda (Brunella Bovo) and Ivan Cavalli (Leopoldo Trieste) are honeymooning in Rome. The couple is mismatched: Ivan is conservative in nature, while his bride is full of spontaneity and eager to pursue her dreams. When Wanda learns that the popular photographic comic book "The White Sheik" is being shot nearby, she heads off to ogle the sheik (Alberto Sordi), sending Ivan on a frantic search for her all over Rome and jeopardizing their planned papal audience. When Wanda actually meets her idol, however, the sheik proves to be less than dashing. Already displaying his fascination with the romantic dreams of everyday people, Fellini orchestrates fantasy and reality deftly here as the newlyweds' perceptions of life and of each other change under the pressure of their unusual circumstances. The film falters in its pacing, however, which is somewhat too slow. Originally proposed as a project for Michelangelo Antonioni, THE WHITE SHEIK is not one of Fellini's masterworks (and uncharacteristically farcical), but it is a must-see for those interested in the director's oeuvre and an entertaining piece on its own.

WHO FRAMED ROGER RABBIT

1988 103m c Animated/Comedy/Mystery ★★★
Touchstone/Amblin/Silver Screen Partners III (U.S.) PG

Bob Hoskins (Eddie Valiant), Christopher Lloyd (Judge Doom), Joanna Cassidy (Dolores), Stubby Kaye (Marvin Acme), Alan Tilvern (R.K. Maroon), Richard Le Parmentier (Lt. Santino), Joel Silver (Raoul Raoul, Director), Paul Springer (Augie), Richard Ridings (Angelo), Edwin Craig (Arthritic Cowboy)

p, Robert Watts, Frank Marshall; d, Robert Zemeckis; w, Jeffrey Price, Peter Seaman (based on the book Who Censored Roger Rabbit? by Gary K. Wolf); ph, Dean Cundey; ed, Arthur Schmidt; m, Alan Silvestri; prod d, Elliot Scott, Roger Cain; fx, Peter Biggs, Brian Morrison, Roger Nichols, David Watkins, Brian Lince, Tony Dunsterville, Brian Warner; chor, Quinny Sacks, David Toguri; cos, Joanna Johnston; anim, Richard Williams

AAN Best Cinematography: Dean Cundey; AA Best Editing: Arthur Schmidt; AAN Best Art Direction: Elliot Scott, Peter Howitt; AAN Best Sound: Robert Knudson, John Boyd, Don Digirolamo, Tony Dawe;

AA Best Visual Effects: Ken Ralston, Richard Williams, Edward Jones, George Gibbs; *AA Best Sound Effects Editing:* Charles L. Campbell, Louis L. Edemann

A startling combination of live action and animation, WHO FRAMED ROGER RABBIT? was instantly catapulted into the ranks of cinema classics. While flawlessly delivered, it's overkill—so loud and excessive, it makes our head swim. And its peak comes early on, when Jessica Rabbit sings, "Why Don't You Do Right?". Adult viewers are generally used to only Disney—104 minutes of the racous rukus of Warners style cartoons is well, too much of a dumb thing. This film could only have been made during the decade when Miss Piggy became a star.

Set in Los Angeles circa 1947, the film takes place in a universe where cartoon characters really exist and work alongside human beings. Disdainfully referred to as "Toons" by humans, the cartoon characters are underpaid by human standards and are forced to live in a segregated ghetto known as Toontown. When Maroon Cartoons studio chief R.K. Maroon (Alan Tilvern) is found murdered, it appears that the studio's biggest star, Roger Rabbit, is the culprit. Desperate to clear his name, Roger hires down-on-his-luck private detective Eddie Valiant (Bob Hoskins) to crack the case. A human, Eddie is reluctant to take the case, for he hates Toons because his brother was killed by one. As the plot thickens, however, Roger begins to grow on Eddie and the pair team up to solve the mystery of Toontown, battling the sinister Judge Doom (Christopher Lloyd) in the process.

We salute the technical brilliance of this movie. A small army of animators led by Richard Williams and assisted by Industrial Light and Magic performed the meticulous task of matching animation with camera movement and film noir lighting to give the cartoon characters a 3-D effect. And admittedly Hoskins had a tough job—interacting with thin air and floating props (the Toons handle real objects) because the animation was added to the frame months after principal photography had been completed. Director Bob Zemeckis deserves a Purple Heart for taking on the monumental technical headaches involved in the production and somehow managing to deliver a film that works. A must-see for all ages, but not a work that lingers in the imagination. It's like a sumptous banquet composed entirely of fast food; fills you up but entirely forgettable.

WHOLE TOWN'S TALKING, THE

1935 95m bw Comedy/Crime   ★★★★★
Columbia (U.S.)

Edward G. Robinson *(Arthur Ferguson Jones/Killer Mannion)*, Jean Arthur *(Wilhelmina "Bill" Clark)*, Arthur Hohl *(Detective Sgt. Mike Boyle)*, Wallace Ford *(Healy)*, A.S. Byron *(District Atty. Spencer)*, Donald Meek *(Hoyt)*, Paul Harvey *(J.G. Carpenter)*, Edward Brophy *(Bugs Martin)*, Etienne Girardot *(Seaver)*, James Donlan *(Detective Sgt. Pat Howe)*

p, Lester Cowan; d, John Ford; w, Jo Swerling, Robert Riskin (based on the novel by W.R. Burnett); ph, Joseph August; ed, Viola Lawrence

One of the most underrated of John Ford's early films, THE WHOLE TOWN'S TALKING is a marvelous gangster film told in a comic vein and sporting a superb performance from Edward G. Robinson, playing a timid clerk working for a hardware company. He has a superlative work record and has been on time every morning for eight years. He is in love with one of his coworkers (Jean Arthur) from afar. While he is having lunch with her one day, the police arrive and arrest him, having mistaken him for Public Enemy No. 1, Killer Mannion, recently escaped from prison and the hardware clerk's exact double. After much confusion over his identity, the district attorney is satisfied that Robinson isn't the gangster they are looking for and issues the clerk an identity card he can show police to avoid being arrested by mistake again. Unfortunately, the news about Robinson's misadventure hits all the newspapers—partly because Robinson's boss urges his employee to write about Mannion for the papers—and the real Killer Mannion (also played by Robinson) reads the story. The gangster shows up at the clerk's house and demands that the identity card be turned over to him every evening so that he can move about more freely. The gangster also begins dictating the details of his sordid life to the clerk, to be included in the newspaper column. To ensure the clerk's cooperation, the gangster kidnaps Arthur and the clerk's aunt (Effie Ellsler). Posing as the clerk, the gangster and his thugs commit several robberies in the area and the police put the innocent Robinson in jail for his own protection. To kill two birds with one stone, the gangster decides to pose as the clerk, get into jail, kill a stoolie that once double-crossed him, and then send the clerk out on a bank job where he is sure to be killed—thus "Killer Mannion" would be dead and "Arthur Ferguson" could be released. The clerk heads for the bank, but when he realizes that he's forgotten his gun, he goes back to the gang's hideout. Before entering, he overhears the gangsters joking about the setup. The clerk then decides to act like the gangster, and when the real gangster enters the room, the clerk orders the men to kill him, which they do, thinking the clerk is their boss.

Adapted by screenwriters Jo Swerling and Robert Riskin from a story by W.R. Burnett (who wrote the novel *Little Caesar*), THE WHOLE TOWN'S TALKING is a masterful balance of comedy and drama with a very dark subtext. Robinson the clerk and Robinson the gangster are two sides of the same coin. The clerk is a milquetoast who can't bring himself to tell the woman he loves how he feels about her, but once he dons the identity of the gangster and orders a man to be killed, he is suddenly infused with self-confidence and power which finally enable him to speak his mind and take action. Though the film is essentially a comedy and Robinson the clerk's actions are well enough motivated for his character to remain sympathetic, it is an undeniably chilling and ambiguous moment. Robinson handles the role beautifully, bringing several shadings and subtleties to a double role that could easily have disintegrated into gimmicky silliness. Because of the ambiguity and subtle handling of the darker aspects of the story, director Ford and actor Robinson turned what could have been dismissed as just another light, frivolous entertainment into an evocative work of art.

WHO'LL STOP THE RAIN?

1978 125m c Crime/War   ★★★½
UA (U.S.)   R/18

Nick Nolte *(Ray Hicks)*, Tuesday Weld *(Marge Converse)*, Michael Moriarty *(John Converse)*, Anthony Zerbe *(Antheil)*, Richard Masur *(Danskin)*, Ray Sharkey *(Smitty)*, Gail Strickland *(Chairman)*, Charles Haid *(Eddy)*, David Opatoshu *(Bender)*

p, Herb Jaffe, Gabriel Katzka; d, Karel Reisz; w, Judith Rascoe, Robert Stone (based on the novel *Dog Soldiers* by Stone); ph, Richard H. Kline; ed, John Bloom; m, Laurence Rosenthal

An effective film adaptation of Robert Stone's excellent novel *Dog Soldiers*, WHO'LL STOP THE RAIN? begins in Vietnam and follows jaded, cynical, and bitter photojournalist John Converse (Michael Moriarty) as he arranges to smuggle a large shipment of Asian heroin into the US. To assist him, Converse enlists Vietnam vet Ray Hicks (Nick Nolte). Once a Marine, now working for the Merchant Marine, Hicks can easily smuggle the heroin out of Vietnam and into the docks at Oakland, California, where he is to hook up with Converse's wife, Marge (Tuesday Weld), and await Converse's return to the US. Unfortunately, Antheil (Anthony Zerbe), a corrupt federal drug enforcement agent, has gotten wind of the shipment and has sent two of his men (Richard Masur and Ray Sharkey) to kill Marge and Hicks and confiscate the heroin for his own purposes. Fueled by excellent performances from the entire cast—with Nolte a definite standout—WHO'LL STOP THE RAIN? is a gripping action film that also illustrates the bitter disillusionment of Americans who witnessed the corruption, confusion, and moral chaos of the country's leadership during the Vietnam era. Smartly directed by Karel Reisz (a Czech-born Englishman), whose previous feature was the memorable THE GAMBLER with James Caan, the film boasts fine photography by Richard H. Kline and an unforgettable climax in the surreal ruins of an abandoned hippie commune.

WHOOPEE

1930 94m c Musical/Comedy   ★★★½
UA (U.S.)

Eddie Cantor *(Henry Williams)*, Eleanor Hunt *(Sally Morgan)*, Paul Gregory *(Wanenis)*, Jack Rutherford *(Sheriff Bob Wells)*, Ethel Shutta *(Mary Custer)*, Spencer Charters *(Jerome Underwood)*, Chief Caupolican *(Black Eagle)*, Albert Hackett *(Chester Underwood)*, William H. Philbrick *(Andy McNabb)*, Walter Law *(Judd Morgan)* p, Samuel Goldwyn, Florenz Ziegfeld; d, Thornton Freeland; w, William Conselman (based on the Ziegfeld musical "Whoopee" by William Anthony McGuire, Walter Donaldson, Gus Kahn, the comedy "The Nervous Wreck" by Owen Davis, Sr., and the story "The Wreck" by E.J. Rath); ph, Lee Garmes, Ray Rennahan, Gregg Toland; ed, Stuart Heisler; art d, Richard Day; chor, Busby Berkeley; cos, John Harkrider

AAN Best Art Direction: Richard Day

After the smash hit Broadway show in 1928-29 finished its long run, Sam Goldwyn joined forces with Flo Ziegfeld to re-create "Whoopee" for one of the first Technicolor films, making Eddie Cantor a Goldwyn star and the song "Making Whoopee" a standard. Cantor plays Henry Williams, a hypochondriac whose supposedly poor health causes him to travel West with his nurse-companion Mary Custer (Ethel Shutt). They wind up in Arizona, where busybody Henry pokes his nose into the affairs of Sally Morgan (Eleanor Hunt). Sally is engaged to local sheriff Bob Wells (John Rutherford), but really loves Indian brave Wanenis (Paul Gregory). Henry manages to extricate Sally from Bob's arms into those of Wanenis, who, it later turns out, is really a paleface who had been abandoned and raised by local Native Americans. Several splendid Busby Berkeley production numbers, a bevy of "Goldwyn Girls" (among them a very young Betty Grable), and Oscar-nominated art direction by Capt. Richard Day enliven the silly plot—but the real drawing card is Cantor (just as it was Danny Kaye, when Goldwyn remade this movie as 1944's UP IN ARMS). Neither Goldwyn nor Ziegfeld enjoyed working with a partner, and the two split when Ziegfeld wanted his name first in the billing of the company. Goldwyn released the film in the nadir of the Depression and charged $5 per ticket, the equivalent of a day's pay back then.

WHO'S AFRAID OF VIRGINIA WOOLF?

| 1966 131m bw Drama | ★★★★ |
| Warner Bros. (U.S.) | /15 |

Elizabeth Taylor *(Martha)*, Richard Burton *(George)*, George Segal *(Nick)*, Sandy Dennis *(Honey)*

p, Ernest Lehman; d, Mike Nichols; w, Ernest Lehman (based on the play by Edward Albee); ph, Haskell Wexler; ed, Sam O'Steen; m, Alex North; prod d, Richard Sylbert; cos, Irene Sharaff

AAN Best Picture; AAN Best Actor: Richard Burton; *AA Best Actress:* Elizabeth Taylor; *AAN Best Supporting Actor:* George Segal; *AA Best Supporting Actress:* Sandy Dennis; *AAN Best Director:* Mike Nichols; *AAN Best Adapted Screenplay:* Ernest Lehman; *AA Best Cinematography:* Haskell Wexler; *AAN Best Editing:* Sam O'Steen; *AAN Best Score:* Alex North; *AA Best Art Direction:* Richard Sylbert, George James Hopkins; *AA Best Costume Design:* Irene Sharaff; *AAN Best Sound:* George R. Groves

The Liz and Dick Show. A vitriol Valentine to that most public of famous marriages, The Battling Burtons, in their finest work (together). Our tabloid awareness of their union informs us they were living out their real-life roles, so a side of the viewer champions the authenticity, even when it sometimes looks actorly. Albee's play opened in October, 1962, and shocked even blase New Yorkers with its language and dark subject matter (Uta Hagen and Arthur Hiller created the Broadway roles). The attendent publicity when the film was cast guaranteed an audience no matter what. And many big names had wanted the roles. (Bette Davis wanted to play it opposite Jimmy Stewart, supposedly. Can you imagine Davis doing a parody of herself saying, "What a dump!"? We ideally would have cast Susan Hayward and Henry Fonda.) If Taylor's early scenes sometimes seem more like showing off, she ultimately ropes you in—it's a pity so few films have taken advantage of her bawdy penchant for black comedy. Burton's only disadvantage is his accent; his portrayal seems a trifle more fully realized than hers.

It's two in the morning in New England. Burton is a defeated history professor married to Taylor, a harridan whose father is the president of the college where Burton lectures. After two decades their union is alternately loving and vicious. Taylor likes to compare her weakling husband with her strong father (who is never seen) because she knows it rankles Burton. They have invented a son and talk about him as though he actually exists. Earlier that night, they attended a faculty party where they met Segal and Dennis, a self-proclaimed ladies' man and a sniveling mouse of a woman. The older couple have invited the younger to their comfortable home for a nightcap. Enter Segal and Dennis. She is already tipsy but has more to drink, which makes her worse. Taylor, behaving boorishly, makes advances at Segal which Burton does nothing to stop. Dennis begins to feel sick and Segal gets increasingly drunk. Segal confides to Burton that Dennis trapped him into marriage by pretending to be pregnant. As the late evening drags into early morning, Taylor takes Segal up to her bedroom. Burton stands in the yard below and watches their shadows in the window. Later, Segal mentions Burton's and Taylor's "son," and Burton explodes, vowing to destroy Taylor, who matches his threat.

Producer Lehman's screenplay left most of Albee's play intact, which shocked movie audiences not accustomed to hearing four-letter words cannonading off the screen. At first, the Production Code seal was denied to the movie, but Jack Warner used his personal clout and secured the seal. The play was bought by Warners for half a million dollars; an additional million each went to the Burtons—out of a total budget of $5 million. The movie grossed large numbers at the box office, nearly $15 million the first time around, due, in part, to the draw of the stars.

Dennis in her second role after a small part in SPLENDOR IN THE GRASS was absolutely right in a part that became the definitive Dennis role. The same cannot be said for Segal, who lacks the bulk and WASP look for Nick—where was Robert Redford when Nichols needed him?. Burton and Taylor both took British Oscars for their work. Hiring Nichols (comedy partner of Elaine May) in his directorial debut was a risk because the former nightclub comic had done only lighter work. But the script is fueled by acid, sarcastic dialogue which his direction paces flawlessly, his sense of comic timing serving him well. The film was rehearsed like a play for three weeks before a camera ever turned. This also marked Lehman's debut as a producer. Strong stuff, intensely watchable, but definitely not for children.

WICKER MAN, THE

| 1973 102m c Horror/Mystery | ★★★½ |
| British Lion (U.K.) | R/18 |

Edward Woodward *(Sgt. Neil Howie)*, Christopher Lee *(Lord Summerisle)*, Diane Cilento *(Miss Rose)*, Britt Ekland *(Willow MacGregor)*, Ingrid Pitt *(Librarian-Clerk)*, Lindsay Kemp *(Alder MacGregor)*, Russell Waters *(Harbormaster)*, Aubrey Morris *(Old Gardener-Gravedigger)*, Irene Sunters *(May Morrison)*, Walter Carr *(Schoolmaster)*

p, Peter Snell; d, Robin Hardy; w, Anthony Shaffer; ph, Harry Waxman; ed, Eric Boyd-Perkins; m, Paul Giovanni; art d, Seamus Flannery; chor, Stewart Hopps; cos, Sue Yelland

Sgt. Neil Howie (Woodward) is a devoutly Christian policeman and lay minister, still an unmarried virgin though middle-aged. After receiving an anonymous lead pertaining to the whereabouts of a missing girl, Neil heads out to Summerisle, a Scottish island community within his jurisdiction, in search of clues. What he finds on the island is a pagan cult led by Lord Summerisle (Lee), which offers a human sacrifice every year. Here we have the unusual case of a film about a pagan cult that has developed a cult of its very own. Drastically cut by its original distributors (from 102 minutes to 87 minutes), poorly marketed, and subsequently little seen, THE WICKER MAN developed a reputation as a lost masterpiece of mystery and the macabre. Fueled by actor Christopher Lee's comments that the film contained his best performance, a rabid group of fans went about extolling the movie's virtues. When director Robin Hardy's reconstructed original cut of the film was finally released on videocassette (seven minutes are still missing), opinion over the much-anticipated film was split: people either loved it or hated it. While no masterpiece, the film is a fascinating examination of the conflict between fundamental Christianity and paganism. The performances are uniformly excellent, and Hardy's direction is quite evocative, bizarre, witty, erotic, and downright chilling.

WILD ANGELS, THE

| 1966 83m c Action | ★★★ |
| AIP (U.S.) | |

Peter Fonda *(Heavenly Blues)*, Nancy Sinatra *(Mike)*, Bruce Dern *(Loser/Joey Kerns)*, Lou Procopio *(Joint)*, Coby Denton *(Bull Puckey)*, Marc Cavell *(Frankenstein)*, Buck Taylor *(Dear John)*, Norman Alden *(Medic)*, Michael J. Pollard *(Pigmy)*, Diane Ladd *(Gaysh)* p, Roger Corman; d, Roger Corman; w, Charles B. Griffith; ph, Richard Moore; ed, Monte Hellman; m, Mike Curb; prod d, Rick Beck-Myer; art d, Leon Ericksen

The first of a wave of biker movies that hit American screens in the late 60s, this seminal exploitation film stars soon-to-be cult hero Peter Fonda as the leader of a leather-clad biker gang. When one of the cyclists, Loser (Bruce Dern), is injured, Heavenly Blues (Fonda) and company snatch him from his hospital bed, taking time to trash the place and gang-rape a nurse. Loser dies en route to a hideout, and his comrades requisition a church and hold a funeral service that soon degenerates into a festive, drugged-out orgy. Soon after, the bikers find themselves in a pitched battle with furious local townspeople and police.

Unusually violent for its time, THE WILD ANGELS became one of AIP's most successful films, grossing some $25 million on a production budget of $350,000. Most critics hated the film, but some defenders called it an allegory of America's descent toward nihilism; today, it's of interest as a vivid piece of pop culture history and as a watershed in several careers. Peter Bogdanovich was called in to rewrite the screenplay (he also acted as Corman's assistant and played a small role); Michael J. Pollard went on to a major role in BONNIE AND CLYDE the following year; Monte Hellman, the editor, later directed TWO-LANE BLACKTOP and THE SHOOTING. WILD ANGELS was better received in Europe than in the US, and Corman was invited to bring the picture to the Venice Film Festival—the only US picture that year to be so honored.

WILD AT HEART

1990   126m   c   Comedy/Drama/Romance   ★★½
Polygram-Propaganda   (U.S.)   R/18

Nicolas Cage (Sailor Ripley), Laura Dern (Lula Pace Fortune), Diane Ladd (Marietta Pace), Willem Dafoe (Bobby Peru), Isabella Rossellini (Perdita Durango), Crispin Glover (Dell), Grace Zabriskie (Juana), J.E. Freeman (Marcello Santos), W. Morgan Sheppard (Mr. Reindeer)

p, Monty Montgomery, Steve Golin, Sigurjon Sighvatsson; d, David Lynch; w, David Lynch (based on the novel by Barry Gifford); ph, Frederick Elmes; ed, Duwayne Dunham; m, Angelo Badalamenti; prod d, Patricia Norris; fx, David B. Miller, Louis Lazara, David Domeyer; cos, Patricia Norris

AAN Best Supporting Actress: Diane Ladd

Based on the novel by Barry Gifford, this winner of the Cannes Film Festival's Palme d'Or is a wacky, occasionally inventive road movie that fails to display the vision or the dark intensity of director Lynch's earlier work.

Sailor Ripley (Nicolas Cage), a rebellious, 23-year-old Elvis acolyte, has just been released from prison. Waiting for him on the outside is Lula Fortune (Laura Dern), a 20-year-old, gum-popping, sex-loving cyclone of a gal. Embarking on a journey that takes them from the Carolinas to Texas, they encounter nightmarish accidents and outrageously evil characters, all the while trying to keep one step ahead of Lula's murderous, witchlike mother, Marietta (Diane Ladd, Dern's real-life mother). Interwoven into their cross-country odyssey are numerous references to THE WIZARD OF OZ.

Besides Crispin Glover as a cousin of Lula's who likes to put cockroaches in his underwear, and Willem Dafoe as a psychotic, rotten-toothed ex-marine called Bobby Peru, Lynch's Rogues Gallery includes W. Morgan Sheppard as Mr. Reindeer, a mysterious crime lord who is constantly surrounded by topless hookers; Freddie Jones as a bar patron with a mangled voice; Isabella Rossellini as Perdita, Peru's bleached-blonde girlfriend; Jack Nance, John Lurie, and Scott Coffey as three of the many eccentrics that populate Big Tuna, Texas; and David Patrick Kelly, Calvin Lockhart, and Grace Zabriskie as a trio of psycho killers. At the center of this wild hodge-podge, Cage and Dern turn in undeniably effective performances.

There are many powerful moments in WILD AT HEART—particularly one sequence in which Sailor and Lula come upon the scene of a nighttime accident, and find Sherilyn Fenn (best known for Lynch's TV show "Twin Peaks") wandering in a bloody daze by the side of the road.

But these moments never add up to very much; the film plays as a series of vignettes, each with its own visual or aural or psychological *raison d'etre*, but never really tying into anything else that's going on.

WILD BOYS OF THE ROAD

1933   77m   bw   Drama   ★★★★★
Warner Bros./First National   (U.S.)

Frankie Darro (Eddie Smith), Dorothy Coonan (Sally), Edwin Phillips (Tommy), Rochelle Hudson (Grace), Ann Hovey (Lola), Arthur Hohl (Dr. Heckel), Grant Mitchell (Mr. Smith), Claire McDowell (Mrs. Smith), Sterling Holloway (Ollie), Charley Grapewin (Mr. Cadmust)

p, Robert Presnell; d, William A. Wellman; w, Earl Baldwin (based on the story "Desperate Youth" by Daniel Ahearn); ph, Arthur Todd; ed, Thomas Pratt; art d, Esdras Hartley

WILD BOYS OF THE ROAD is a marvelous piece of Americana, a look at the social confusion of the Depression era. The film's two chief characters, Frankie Darro and Edwin Phillips, are California youths enjoying a comfortable lifestyle with their parents. When the Depression hits and their fathers lose their jobs, the boys hop an eastbound freight train to find work. They soon learn that there are thousands just like themselves, all looking for work, all trying to fight the economic depression that is destroying the country. Darro and Phillips find not only a number of other "wild boys" but also Dorothy Coonan and Rochelle Hudson, tough girls who take to the rails with them. Along the way, this mobile group of naive vagrants become a pack of outlaws when they kill a brakeman who has raped Hudson. The kids are finally forced off the tracks in Ohio, where they assemble their own "sewer city" from sewer pipes and supplies—a city founded on new ideals and a commitment to equality. Their city, however, breeds theft in the nearby community, prompting the police and fire department to wash away the vagrants with fire hoses. The gang moves on, suffering from lack of food and money. After getting involved in a theft ring, they're arrested and hauled off to court, where they get a lesson in New Deal ideology.

Blasted by countless critics for its political stance, WILD BOYS OF THE ROAD, if sometimes naive politically, is still superb entertainment. Director William A. Wellman tackled a straightforward "road movie" structure and applied the simplest of New Deal ideas to it. WILD BOYS OF THE ROAD shows with amazing accuracy the feeling of emptiness and apparent hopelessness that ran rampant in the country. The chief problem with the film is its refusal to lay the blame for the Depression at anyone's feet. The film's finish, though technically a happy ending, is rather mindless, leaving the audience with a "don't worry, everything will be fine" promise. Despite these faults, WILD BOYS OF THE ROAD is one of the finest films about youthful idealism to hit the screen. Costing $203,000 to produce, the film had only minimal success at the box office. Besides the superb Coonan (Wellman's fourth wife), the film is peopled with numerous teens, most of whom were, before and after the film, unknowns, adding to the authenticity of the film's atmosphere. The standout among the cast, however, is the appealing, pint-sized Darro, who became one of the foremost Depression era tough kids of the screen.

WILD BUNCH, THE

1969   143m   c   Western   ★★★★★
Warner Bros.   (U.S.)   R/18

William Holden (Pike Bishop), Ernest Borgnine (Dutch Engstrom), Robert Ryan (Deke Thornton), Edmond O'Brien (Sykes), Warren Oates (Lyle Gorch), Jaime Sanchez (Angel), Ben Johnson (Tector Gorch), Emilio Fernandez (Mapache), Strother Martin (Coffer), L.Q. Jones (T.C.)

p, Phil Feldman; d, Sam Peckinpah; w, Walon Green, Sam Peckinpah (based on a story by Green, Roy N. Sickner); ph, Lucien Ballard; ed, Lou Lombardo; m, Jerry Fielding; art d, Edward Carrere; fx, Bud Hulburd

AAN Best Adapted Screenplay: Walon Green, Roy N. Sickner, Sam Peckinpah; AAN Best Score: Jerry Fielding

An extraordinarily well-made film about anachronistic outlaws in the early 20th century, Sam Peckinpah's THE WILD BUNCH feels like it should have been the final western. This harsh yet elegiac story proved controversial upon its release not only because, like BONNIE AND CLYDE two years before, it upped the ante on American screen violence but also, in industry circles, because of the war it started between the producer, Feldman, and the director.

As with the majority of Peckinpah's work, the studios and producers mutilated the film to suit their needs (to cut its length, to eliminate controversy, to prove their power over the ever-difficult Peckinpah) and distributed a movie vastly different from the one the director had originally envisioned. The cutting occurred while Peckinpah was vacationing in Hawaii, *after* his film had been shown uncut to reviewers on the East Coast. (*New York Times* critic Vincent Canby expressed dismay when he went to see the film again and discovered scenes missing.) Certainly it was not adverse preview reaction that spurred Feldman to make the cuts (the trimmed scenes contained important motivational information vital to the portrayals of the main characters—none of the deletions was a particularly violent scene). These revisions were simply made to bring the film's running time down to two hours, to enable theater owners to turn more of a profit from the feature. With the director's uncut version now readily available on video and laserdisc, there is no reason for anyone to subject themselves to the butchered version.

WILD CHILD, THE
(L'ENFANT SAUVAGE)

1969 90m bw Drama	★★★★½
Carrosse/Artistes (France)	G/

Jean-Pierre Cargol *(Victor the Boy)*, Francois Truffaut *(Dr. Jean Itard)*, Jean Daste *(Prof. Philippe Pinel)*, Francoise Seigner *(Mme. Guerin)*, Paul Ville *(Remy)*, Claude Miler *(M. Lemeri)*, Annie Miler *(Mme. Lemeri)*, Pierre Fabre *(Orderly at Institute)*, Rene Levert *(Police Offical)*, Jean Mandaroux *(Itard's Doctor)*

p, Marcel Berbert; d, Francois Truffaut; w, Francois Truffaut, Jean Gruault (based on *Memoire et Rapport sur Victor de L'Aveyron* by Jean-Marc Gaspard Itard); ph, Nestor Almendros; ed, Agnes Guillemot; m, Antonio Vivaldi; art d, Jean Mandaroux; cos, Gitt Magrini

As in Francois Truffaut's THE 400 BLOWS and SMALL CHANGE, THE WILD CHILD is devoted to the perceptual honesty and education of children. In this case, director and star Truffaut has made a deceptively clear and simple picture on the classic subject (Romulus and Remus, Tarzan) of the socialization of a boy discovered in the forest. Based on an actual case study published in 1806, THE WILD CHILD stars Jean-Pierre Cargol as Victor, a long-haired nature boy who, apparently abandoned in the woods by his parents years earlier, is found and placed in the Institute for the Deaf and Dumb in Paris. The boy is treated as a perverse outcast and freak, but Jean Itard (Truffaut), a patient and enlightened doctor, intervenes and cares for the child in his country home rather than allow him to be sent to an asylum. Raised in an orphanage himself, Truffaut had an affinity for children that was expressed in nearly all his pictures. Probably the director's most ambitious film, THE WILD CHILD spins a modern myth with resonances for parents and children, teachers and students, and even filmmakers, actors and audiences. Its concern with language and images mirrors the longstanding French philosophical interest in linguistics, and through it all Truffaut examines the many issues at hand with warmth, concern and wisdom.

WILD ONE, THE

1953 79m bw Drama	★★★½
Columbia (U.S.)	/PG

Marlon Brando *(Johnny)*, Mary Murphy *(Kathie)*, Robert Keith *(Harry Bleeker)*, Lee Marvin *(Chino)*, Jay C. Flippen *(Sheriff Singer)*, Peggy Maley *(Mildred)*, Hugh Sanders *(Charlie Thomas)*, Ray Teal *(Frank Bleeker)*, John Brown *(Bill Hannegan)*, Will Wright *(Art Kleiner)*

p, Stanley Kramer; d, Laslo Benedek; w, John Paxton (based on a story by Frank Rooney); ph, Hal Mohr; ed, Al Clark; m, Leith Stevens; prod d, Rudolph Sternad; art d, Walter Holscher

The first and best biker movie begins as a group of 40 leather-jacketed motorcyclists roar down a lonely country road straight at the camera. The bikers, who call themselves the Black Rebels, invade a legitimate motorcycle race and try to join the competition, but they are soon thrown out by the mass of motorcycle enthusiasts. Before leaving, a gang member manages to snatch the first-prize trophy and presents it to their leader, Brando. With the trophy strapped to his handlebars, Brando leads his pack of rowdies into the small town of Wrightsville where they drag up and down the street, forcing an old man to drive his car into a light pole. Many of the bikers pile into the local bar, Bleeker's Cafe, which is owned and operated by the sheriff, Keith. Keith is overwhelmed by the disturbance and does little to calm things down as the bikers drink themselves into oblivion. Brando's minions amuse themselves by terrorizing the town, while Brando spots a good-looking girl, Murphy, and follows her into the bar. To his surprise he learns that she is Keith's daughter, and he tries to impress her by giving her the stolen trophy. Though she is intrigued by this strange, somewhat withdrawn, brutish young man, she refuses the gift. More trouble soon thunders into town in the guise of Marvin, a former member of Brando's gang who has left and formed his own pack.

THE WILD ONE was inspired by an incident in 1947 in which a gang of 4,000 motorcyclists took over the small town of Hollister, California, for the Fourth of July weekend and destroyed it. Producer Kramer put together a film that he hoped would illustrate the frustration and alienation felt by a younger generation, and the result became an anthem for disaffected American youth. Brando's performance enthralled audiences, who became fascinated with his contradictory character. He seemed powerful and brutal, but also demonstrated a caring, vulnerable side that he tried hard to repress—laying the groundwork for a whole school of moody antiheroes that would include James Dean in REBEL WITHOUT A CAUSE. Even without these virtues, the film would be immortal merely for the legendary exchange in which Murphy asks Brando, "What are you rebelling against?" and he replies, "What have you got?"

WILD PARTY, THE

1929 77m bw Comedy/Romance	★★★
Paramount (U.S.)	

Clara Bow *(Stella Ames)*, Fredric March *(Gil Gilmore)*, Shirley O'Hara *(Helen Owens)*, Marceline Day *(Faith Morgan)*, Joyce Compton *(Eva Tutt)*, Adrienne Dore *(Babs)*, Virginia Thomas *(Tess)*, Kay Bryant *(Thelma)*, Alice Adair *(Mazie)*, Jean Lorraine *(Ann)*

p, E. Lloyd Sheldon; d, Dorothy Arzner; w, E. Lloyd Sheldon, John V.A. Weaver, George Marion Jr. (based on a story by Warner Fabian); ph, Victor Milner; ed, Otho Lovering; cos, Travis Banton

Though the plot practically grows mold before the viewer's eyes, and some of the production qualities are laughable, THE WILD PARTY remains fascinating to watch from first reel to last. One of the popular happy-go-lucky college-based films of the era, this has an added benefit in featuring Bow in her talkie debut. She is, naturally, a wild party girl who's enrolled in college for the good times rather than to advance her education. Bow and her girlfriends decide to take a class taught by March, not for his stunning classroom abilities, but because he's cute! March is a no-nonsense type and the course proves to be much more difficult than Bow and company had anticipated. To relieve this academic pressure, the coeds pull a few classroom pranks. Bow attends a ball but is kicked out for wearing a low-cut dress. She later goes to a roadhouse, where an inebriated Ben Hendricks tries to have his way with her. March, who inexplicably is also at the roadhouse, puts a stop to this, then gives Bow a lift. Compton, a fellow classmate of Bow's, sees the campus flirt leaving March's car, and her nimble mind immediately assumes there's funny business involved. Gossip spreads thick, so March chews out Bow in front of other students to prove they aren't an item. Bow angrily walks out of the classroom. She and roommate O'Hara go to a party (no one ever studies at this school), where O'Hara falls for Jack Luden. Hendricks, still angry with March for the earlier altercation, finds the professor and shoots him. Bow tells the wounded March of her love for him, giving Compton more fuel for her gossip mill. A letter from O'Hara to Luden turns up, and its spicy contents create a scandal.

It's silly, but so what? Arzner's direction is good and Bow gives an energetic performance, her Brooklyn accent serving the "It" girl's well-known personality with absolute perfection. The advertising campaign played up on this with glee, claiming: "You've had an eyeful of *IT*. . . now get an earful!" March, in only his second film, takes his part seriously, which adds to the picture's inherent campiness. Bow was terrified of making a talkie, but she handled herself well in the funfest. Reportedly, her voice was so loud it blew meters on the sound equipment when she spoke her first line. At times her voice is muddled on the soundtrack, partly the fault of the new technology and partly due to her accent. In England, THE WILD PARTY was released as a silent film. Within a few years Bow would be gone from the screen forever, while March would become one of filmdom's most respected thespians.

WILD REEDS

1994 110m c Drama ★★★★
IMA Films/Les Films Alain Sarde/Canal Plus/La Sept /15
/Arte/IMA Productions/SFP Productions (France)

Frederic Gorny (Henri), Gael Morel (Francois), Elodie Bouchez (Maite), Stephane Rideau (Serge), Michele Moretti (Madame Alvarez), Nathalie Vigne (Young Bride), Laurent Groulout (The Photographer), Jacques Nolot (Monsieur Morelli), Eric Kreikenmayer (Young Bridegroom), Michel Ruhl (Monsieur Cassagne)

p, Alain Sarde, Georges Benayoun; d, Andre Techine; w, Andre Techine, Gilles Taurand, Olivier Massart; ph, Jeanne Lapoirie; ed, Martine Giordano; cos, Elisabeth Tavernier

Andre Techine's lovely coming-of-age film—set in 1962, near the end of the Algerian war for independence—evokes the vulnerability and desperation of adolescence through the stories of a group of teenagers whose lives intersect at a boarding school in southwestern France. The title derives from La Fontaine's fable "The Oak and the Reeds" and serves to place the characters within the broader context of nature: Techine often frames them within a landscape of rolling hills and pans gently across the frame, giving the film the wistful flow of reeds in the wind.

There are four youngsters: Maite (Elodie Bouchez), the feminist, Communist daughter of the school's literature instructor; timid, intelligent Francois (Gael Morel), who's discovering his homosexuality; Serge (Stephane Rideau), the passionate and physical son of emigre Italian farmers; and Henri (Frederic Gorny), older than the rest and an Algerian refugee who supports the reactionary OAS. Moments of passion, beauty, and self-discovery result from this complicated friendship, but the turmoil surrounding the Algerian War soon spills over into the adolescent idyll.

Informed but not constrained by the conventions of 1950s melodramas, WILD REEDS does a remarkable job of exploring the volatile space in which personal affairs and international events intersect. It was produced as part of a series called Tous les garcons et les filles de leur age (All the Boys and Girls of their Time), for which nine directors were invited to make films about teenagers, set in the periods of their own youth. It won four 1994 Cesar awards (the French equivalent of the Oscar), including Best Picture, Director, and Screenplay, and was France's official entry that year for the Academy Award for Best Foreign Language Film.

WILD RIVER

1960 115m c Drama ★★★★
Fox (U.S.) /A

Montgomery Clift (Chuck Glover), Lee Remick (Carol Baldwin), Jo Van Fleet (Ella Garth), Albert Salmi (F.J. Bailey), Jay C. Flippen (Hamilton Garth), James Westerfield (Cal Garth), Big Jeff Bess (Joe John Garth), Robert Earl Jones (Ben), Frank Overton (Walter Clark), Barbara Loden (Betty Jackson)

p, Elia Kazan; d, Elia Kazan; w, Paul Osborn (based on the novels Mud on the Stars by William Bradford Huie and Dunbar's Cove by Borden Deal); ph, Ellsworth Fredricks; ed, William Reynolds; m, Kenyon Hopkins; art d, Lyle Wheeler, Herman A. Blumenthal; cos, Anna Hill Johnstone

Although it was not a great success at the box office (issue-oriented films were not what the public seemed to want in 1960), this dramatic tug-of-war between progress and tradition remains a memorable example of director Kazan at his best. Set in the 1930s, the story focuses on Clift, an agent for the Tennessee Valley Authority (TVA), which is in the process of clearing land to build much-needed dams. This project cannot be accomplished without the demolition of many homes and the relocation of their inhabitants. One of Clift's most unpleasant tasks is the removal of Van Fleet, an 80-year-old widow, from her home. Van Fleet, who has lived on her land for more than 50 years, refuses to leave. As if Clift's plight isn't bad enough, the locals look upon him as an interloper and make his life miserable. Local whites grow particularly hostile when Clift treats the area's blacks fairly, and it isn't long before some of the more racist townsfolk try to beat some sense into the TVA man. Nevertheless, Van Fleet's young widowed granddaughter, Remick, falls in love with Clift and they eventually marry. In time, Van Fleet finally gives up her battle, the land is flooded, and the proud old woman dies shortly after moving into her new home.

An emotionally charged movie that offers little respite for the viewer, WILD RIVER was skillfully scripted by Osborn, masterfully directed by Kazan, and features excellent acting and strong production values. Shot on location in Tennessee at Lake Chickamauga, the Hiwassee River, and in the towns of Cleveland and Charleston, this film was the end of a 25-year dream for Kazan. He had been to the area in the mid-1930s and always wanted to do a movie about the TVA, but it took more than two decades to find a studio and the right script to fulfill his desire. Many nonprofessional Tennesseans appear in the film, lending it a realism seldom seen when Hollywood extras are employed. Kazan's wife, Barbara Loden, plays a small role, and if you keep an eye out you'll see a very young Bruce Dern appearing in his first movie. However, Van Fleet's performance is the film's standout; though she was only 41 at the time the film was made, the actress is completely convincing as an 80-year-old, thanks in no small part to Ben Nye's wonderful makeup work. Clift also gives a fine performance. He was never easy to work with, as he had several personal problems, not the least of which was his drinking and his difficulty in coming to grips with his homosexuality. Reportedly, he'd promised to stay off the sauce for the picture and kept his word until the final week when he went on a bender that almost submarined the movie.

WILD STRAWBERRIES
(SMULTRONSTALLET)

1957 90m bw Drama ★★★★½
Svensk (Sweden) /15

Victor Sjostrom (Prof. Isak Borg), Bibi Andersson (Sara), Ingrid Thulin (Marianne Borg), Gunnar Bjornstrand (Evald Borg), Jullan Kindahl (Agda), Folke Sundquist (Anders), Bjorn Bjelvenstam (Viktor), Naima Wifstrand (Isak's Mother), Gunnel Brostrom (Mrs. Berit Almann), Gertrud Fridh (Isak's Wife)

p, Allan Ekelund; d, Ingmar Bergman; w, Ingmar Bergman; ph, Gunnar Fischer, Bjorn Thermenius; ed, Oscar Rosander; m, Erik Nordgren; art d, Gittan Gustafsson; cos, Millie Strom

AAN Best Original Screenplay: Ingmar Bergman

Possibly Ingmar Bergman's finest film and a landmark in film history. Victor Sjostrom stars as Isak Borg, a medical professor on his way to accept an honorary degree on the 50th anniversary of his graduation from the University at Lund. He rides with his daughter-in-law, Marianne (Ingrid Thulin), who has decided to leave her husband. They don't get along, mainly because the old man reminds her so much of her husband. En route, they stop at Isak's childhood house, where he recalls his family in the days of his youth (although he is unseen by the characters and not present in the flashback). He sees his sweetheart, Sara (Bibi Andersson), picking wild strawberries and carrying on seductively with his brother. Later he is awakened (in the present) by a teenage girl named Sara (again played by Andersson). She asks the old man for a ride, bringing along two male friends. This foray proves less than idyllic, hampered by a car crash and Isak's disturbing nightmares.

WILD STRAWBERRIES is viewed by many as Bergman's greatest achievement. Its most striking segment, which perhaps best illustrates Bergman's technique, is a dream sequence in which Isak walks through a desolate city, is approached by a faceless man, sees a clock without hands, and watches a funeral wagon crash and leave a coffin in the middle of the street. As he nears the coffin, it opens, and the corpse—again Isak—emerges and attempts to pull him into the afterlife. The visual and aural symbolism is chilling, and the entire scene is perfectly integrated into the "reality" of the rest of the picture. Sjostrom, in his final film, delivers one of the finest performances in any Bergman film—a major accomplishment considering the virtuosity that Bergman's actors consistently display.

WILL SUCCESS SPOIL ROCK HUNTER?

1957   94m   c   Comedy   ★★★★
Fox   (U.S.)

Jayne Mansfield (*Rita Marlowe*), Tony Randall (*Rock Hunter*), Betsy Drake (*Jenny*), Joan Blondell (*Violet*), John Williams (*Le Salle*), Henry Jones (*Rufus*), Lili Gentle (*April*), Mickey Hargitay (*Bobo*), Georgia Carr (*Calypso Number*), Groucho Marx (*Surprise Guest*)

p, Frank Tashlin; d, Frank Tashlin; w, Frank Tashlin (based on the play by George Axelrod); ph, Joseph MacDonald; ed, Hugh S. Fowler; m, Cyril J. Mockridge; art d, Lyle Wheeler, Leland Fuller; fx, L.B. Abbott; cos, Charles LeMaire

A panic. Jayne's twin peaks triumph, for which she received a Tony, gets transferred from Hollywood lampoon to advertising satire. Tashlin produced, directed and wrote the screenplay, and in true Tashlin form, it feels like a like an outrageous, gaudy cartoon. The frantic Randall performance, Blondell's usual canny job and Hargitay, Mansfield's real life muscleman husband doing a turn as a TV Tarzan, all score. But it's Jayne's last word on Hollywood Blondes that will have you howling. Her best takes: Seclusion and Catherine the Great. And wait until you see who she really carries a torch for. Jayne's broad comedic talent was only properly utilized twice by Fox. Instead of basing her persona on Marilyn Monroe, her studio should have built her along the lines of a combo of Mae West and Jane Russell, and taken advantage of her unique brand of sexual anarchy. French critics enjoyed this picture immensely, and Jean-Luc Godard had it on his 10-best list. In a small role as one of the scrubwomen appears Minta Durfee, former silent-screen comedienne who worked with Charlie Chaplin, among others, and married Roscoe "Fatty" Arbuckle.

WILLIAM SHAKESPEARE'S ROMEO + JULIET

1996   113m   c   Romance/Drama   ★★
Bazmark Productions   (U.S./Australia/Canada)   PG-13/12

Leonardo DiCaprio (*Romeo*), Claire Danes (*Juliet*), John Leguizamo (*Tybalt*), Harold Perrineau (*Mercutio*), Diane Venora (*Gloria Capulet*), Paul Sorvino (*Fulgencio Capulet*), Brian Dennehey (*Ted Montague*), Pete Postlethwaite (*Father Laurence*), Miriam Margolyes (*The Nurse*), Christina Pickles (*Mrs. Montague*)

p, Gabriella Martinelli, Baz Luhrmann; d, Baz Luhrmann; w, Baz Luhrmann, Craig Pearce (based on the play by William Shakespeare); ph, Don McAlpine; ed, Jill Bilcock; prod d, Catherine Martin; art d, Doug Hardwick; fx, Laurnecio "Chov" Cordero; cos, Kym Barett

AAN Best Art Direction: Catherine Martin, Brigitte Broch

Recklessly energetic, Baz Luhrmann's bold adaptation of *Romeo and Juliet* doesn't so much pump up a classic for easily bored teens as use the play as a pretext for directorial handsprings and back flips.

In the smoggy, crime-filled metropolis of Verona, two corporate dynasties, the Montagues, headed by Mr. Montague (Brian Dennehey), and the Capulets, presided over by Mr. Capulet (Paul Sorvino), compete so viciously that succeeding generations are poisoned by their rivalry. On the eve of her betrothal, Juliet Capulet (Claire Danes) becomes smitten by Romeo Montague (Leonardo DiCaprio), and the lovers prevail upon Juliet's maid (Miriam Margolyes) and Romeo's priest, Father Laurence (Pete Postlethwaite), to facilitate their secret wedding, but happiness proves short-lived for the star-crossed pair.

To their credit, director Baz Luhrmann and co-screenwriter Craig Pearce foster a sense of urgency in their retelling of this centuries-old play by investing the characters with a state of adrenaline overdrive; everyone seems to be hurtling toward premature death. However, Luhrmann doesn't bother to support or dramatize Shakespeare's tragedy-laden text; his startling imagery pushes all the pesky dialogue into the wings where it's left to fend for itself. Unlike the magically revamped RICHARD III (1995), which positioned that upstart's treachery in a 20th century fascist environment, this febrile adaptation is pointlessly updated with pop-culture references and a hip sensibility. Moreover, his abuse of Shakespeare runs a close second to his thrashing of a talented cast. Gloriously photogenic Leonardo DiCaprio gives a

moving performance only when he isn't required to speak; Claire Danes summons up the mournfulness of a cheerleader who's been stood up on prom night. Only Margolyes and Postlethwaite acquit themselves with any dignity.

WILSON

1944   154m   c   Biography   ★★★
Fox   (U.S.)   /U

Alexander Knox (*Woodrow Wilson*), Charles Coburn (*Prof. Henry Holmes*), Geraldine Fitzgerald (*Edith Wilson*), Thomas Mitchell (*Joseph Tumulty*), Ruth Nelson (*Ellen Wilson*), Cedric Hardwicke (*Henry Cabot Lodge*), Vincent Price (*William G. McAdoo*), William Eythe (*George Felton*), Mary Anderson (*Eleanor Wilson*), Sidney Blackmer (*Josephus Daniels*)

p, Darryl F. Zanuck; d, Henry King; w, Lamar Trotti; ph, Leon Shamroy; ed, Barbara McLean; m, Alfred Newman; art d, Wiard Ihnen, James Basevi; fx, Fred Sersen; cos, Rene Hubert

AAN Best Picture; AAN Best Actor: Alexander Knox; *AAN Best Director:* Henry King; *AA Best Original Screenplay:* Lamar Trotti; *AA Best Cinematography:* Leon Shamroy; *AA Best Editing:* Barbara McLean; *AAN Best Score:* Alfred Newman; *AA Best Art Direction:* Wiard Ihnen, Thomas Little; *AA Best Sound:* E.H. Hansen; *AAN Best Visual Effects:* Fred Sersen, Roger Heman

A lavish biography of Woodrow Wilson, this film was Darryl F. Zanuck's first production after he returned from WWII service in North Africa. Knox plays the president, first as the head of Princeton University and the author of books on political theory. He is chosen to run for governor of New Jersey and is such a success that he is soon running for president. He wins and during his first term WWI erupts in Europe. He is steadfast in his determination to keep the US out of the war, keeping with the largely isolationist sentiment of the country. Eventually, though, German attacks on US merchant ships lead Wilson to declare war. After the war is won, thanks to the massive infusion of fresh American boys into the exhausted and depleted Allied armies, Wilson goes to Versailles to help form the peace treaty. He conceives the idea of the League of Nations and convinces most of the former combatants to join, but back in the US he is unable to drum up support; isolationism is still running strong. He goes on a cross-country campaign to bring his idea to the masses, but the trip only ruins his own health and the US votes to stay out of the League.

More than $3 million was spent on the production, and the lavish sets included a nearly perfect re-creation of the White House. Henry Fonda and Gary Cooper were considered for the lead, but eventually a supporting contract player, Knox, was tagged for the role. Zanuck and Lamar Trotti wrote most of the script. Zanuck also oversaw the cutting, seeing that the film moved quickly depite its length. When the film was finally ready, Zanuck reportedly predicted that it would win an Oscar. (It didn't, but when Zanuck did recieve one for GENTLEMAN'S AGREEMENT in 1947 he told the Academy in his acceptance speech, "I should have got this for WILSON.")

WINCHESTER '73

1950   92m   bw   Western   ★★★★
Universal   (U.S.)   /U

James Stewart (*Lin McAdam*), Shelley Winters (*Lola Manners*), Dan Duryea (*Waco Johnny Dean, the Kansas Kid*), Stephen McNally (*Dutch Henry Brown*), Millard Mitchell (*Johnny "High Spade" Williams*), Charles Drake (*Steve Miller*), John McIntire (*Joe Lamont*), Will Geer (*Wyatt Earp*), Jay C. Flippen (*Sgt. Wilkes*), Rock Hudson (*Young Bull*)

p, Aaron Rosenberg; d, Anthony Mann; w, Robert L. Richards, Borden Chase (based on the story by Stuart N. Lake); ph, William Daniels; ed, Edward Curtiss; m, Joseph Gershenson; art d, Bernard Herzbrun, Nathan Juran, Russell A. Gausman, A. Roland Fields; cos, Yvonne Wood

The first collaboration between director Mann and actor Stewart, a team that would create a series of superior westerns that added a new, psychological dimension to the genre.

WINCHESTER '73 begins as Stewart, who is pursuing his father's killer, rides into Dodge City with his friend, Mitchell. The whole town is celebrating the Fourth of July under the watchful eye of the fatherly Wyatt Earp (Geer), who collects pistols from gun-toting strangers and keeps them in his office until they leave. Stewart enters the local saloon and orders a drink. Out of the corner of his eye he sees McNally, and both men spastically grope for their sidearms, only to find empty holsters. Stewart's nerves are frazzled by the event, and he leaves the saloon shaking. The two men square off again, this time in a shooting contest with a brand new "one-of-1,000" Winchester '73 rifle as the first prize. The contestants are evenly matched in an intense fight, but Stewart manages to best McNally and wins the coveted rifle. Before Stewart can leave town with his prize, however, McNally attacks him and steals the rifle. Stewart then sets off on a maniacal pursuit of McNally and his rifle which culminates in a memorable shoot-out with decidedly Oedipal overtones.

WINCHESTER '73 was the first of the so-called "psychological" westerns that became the benchmark of the genre in the 1950s. Mann and Stewart present a basically decent hero driven to the brink of madness by dark forces from his past. Played out against breathtaking landscapes that reflect the emotional turmoil of the main characters, Mann's film gives us one of Stewart's greatest performances, his manic intensity evoking both terror and pathos. The supporting cast is fine, with both Tony Curtis and Rock Hudson appearing in small roles.

WINCHESTER '73 was once a project for Fritz Lang, who worked on the script with Silvia Richards in 1948. Lang eventually walked away from the film, and Mann took over at Stewart's suggestion. Beginning a collaboration that would last through two more westerns (BEND OF THE RIVER, 1952, and THE FAR COUNTRY, 1955), Mann rewrote the script with Borden Chase. WINCHESTER '73 was a great success at the box office and reestablished Stewart (who was suffering a decline in popularity) as one of Hollywood's top actors. In addition to providing both star and director with a career boost, the film launched a whole new series of adult westerns directed by such notables as Mann, Budd Boetticher, Don Siegel, Sam Fuller, and Nicholas Ray.

WIND AND THE LION, THE

1975   119m   c   Adventure/Historical/War   ★★★½
MGM   (U.S.)   PG/A

Sean Connery (Mulay el Raisuli), Candice Bergen (Eden Pedecaris), Brian Keith (Theodore Roosevelt), John Huston (John Hay), Geoffrey Lewis (Gummere), Steve Kanaly (Capt. Jerome), Vladek Sheybal (The Bashaw), Nadim Sawalha (Sherif of Wazan), Roy Jenson (Adm. Chadwick), Deborah Baxter (Alice Roosevelt)

p, Herb Jaffe; d, John Milius; w, John Milius; ph, Billy Williams; ed, Robert Wolfe; m, Jerry Goldsmith; prod d, Gil Parando; art d, Antonio Paton; cos, Richard LaMotte

AAN Best Score: Jerry Goldsmith; AAN Best Sound: Harry W. Tetrick, Aaron Rochin, William McCaughey, Roy Charman

A stirring, if grossly inaccurate, look at the dawn of US interventionism, THE WIND AND THE LION features Brian Keith as a Teddy Roosevelt determined to establish his Presidential identity, having come to office after the death of William McKinley. When a rebellious Arab chieftain, Mulay el Raisuli (Sean Connery), seizes American woman Eden Pedecaris (Candice Bergen) and her children, Roosevelt prepares to send in the Marines. At the same time the Germans land in North Africa in force, looking for a way to turn the situation to their advantage. The chieftain and Eden talk a great deal of philosophy, and the Arab ruler begins to take on heroic stature in the eyes of her son. Eventually, under pressure from Roosevelt, Raisuli releases his hostages to the Marines and is immediately arrested and imprisoned by the Germans. The Marines are none too happy about this development—since Roosevelt had promised Raisuli his freedom if he released his prisoners—so they march into the town (in a scene almost directly stolen from THE WILD BUNCH) and shoot it out with the Germans.

THE WIND AND THE LION is certainly jingoistic to a fault, and its portrayal of the various factions is little above the cartoon level, but thanks to marvelous performances by Keith and Connery, the film works as a maker of myths. The real facts of the incident were not so grand: Raisuli, a brigand chief, kidnapped a balding, overweight businessman who bore no resemblance to the lovely Bergen, to embarrass

the Sultan of Morocco, who was already having troubles with the US. The man was freed after only a couple of days, but before his release was made public, the Republican Party, looking for a rallying issue, announced that a telegram had been sent to the kidnapper demanding the man be freed or Raisuli would be pay with his life. No troops landed. No one was killed. But historical truth isn't what's important here; heroes and myth are the currency of this film, and it delivers two heroes in admirable fashion.

WINDOW, THE

1949   73m   bw   Thriller   ★★★★
RKO   (U.S.)   /A

Barbara Hale (Mrs. Woodry), Bobby Driscoll (Tommy Woodry), Arthur Kennedy (Mr. Woodry), Paul Stewart (Mr. Kellerton), Ruth Roman (Mrs. Kellerton), Anthony Ross (Ross), Richard Benedict (Drunken Seaman), Jim Nolan (Stranger on Street), Ken Terrell (Man), Lee Phelps

p, Frederic Ullman Jr.; d, Ted Tetzlaff; w, Mel Dinelli (based on the novelette The Boy Cried Murder by Cornell Woolrich); ph, William Steiner; ed, Frederic Knudtson; m, Roy Webb; art d, Walter E. Keller, Sam Corso; fx, Russell A. Cully

AAN Best Editing: Frederic Knudtson

Set in the tenement section of New York's Lower East Side, this incredibly tense nail-biter stars Driscoll as a young boy who has a habit of crying wolf. One night, while trying to beat the heat by making his bed on the fire escape, he climbs up to the next floor and sees Stewart and Roman murder a drunken seaman, Benedict. Of course, no one, not even the boy's parents (Kennedy and Hale), believes Driscoll when he tells what he has seen, since they all assume that this is just another of the boy's tales. Danger lurks.

Based on a story by Cornell Woolrich (whose writing was also the basis for Hitchcock's similar REAR WINDOW), THE WINDOW presents a frightening vision of helplessness, vividly conveying childish frustration at being dismissed or ignored by one's parents. Director and onetime cameraman Tetzlaff adroitly injects a maximum of suspense into the film, enabling the audience to identify with Driscoll's predicament and, interestingly, to view his parents as evil, almost as evil as the murderers themselves. Having photographed Hitchcock's NOTORIOUS just three years before, Tetzlaff had, without a shadow of a doubt, learned something of his suspense-building craft from the master of that art (as did just about every working director). By casting the 12-year-old Driscoll, star of such heart-warming Disney pictures as SONG OF THE SOUTH and SO DEAR TO MY HEART, Tetzlaff was able to twist the idyllic Disney image of childhood into a nightmare world of death and violence, in which parents and neighbors are the child's worst fears come true. Adding to the film's effect is the on-location photography and the dark ambience of the tenements, where evil and death seem to lurk in every shadow, where the seaman's corpse is found, and where the pursued boy is nearly killed. (In a perverse twist of fate, it was in an abandoned, crumbling New York City tenement that actor Driscoll was found dead some 20 years later, the victim of an apparent drug overdose.) THE WINDOW, which cost only $210,000 to produce and made many times that at the box office, was voted the best mystery film of the year by the Mystery Writers of America. Editor Knudtson was nominated for an Academy Award, while Driscoll was named Outstanding Juvenile Actor and given a miniature statuette. An exceptional film.

WINGS OF DESIRE
(DER HIMMEL UBER BERLIN)

1987   130m   c/bw   Fantasy   ★★★★½
Road Movies/Argos/WDR   (France/West Germany)   PG-13/15

Bruno Ganz (Damiel), Solveig Dommartin (Marion), Otto Sander (Cassiel), Curt Bois (Homer), Peter Falk (Himself)

p, Wim Wenders, Anatole Dauman; d, Wim Wenders; w, Wim Wenders, Peter Handke; ph, Henri Alekan; ed, Peter Przygodda; m, Jurgen Knieper; prod d, Heidi Ludi; cos, Monika Jacobs

A rich, mystical near-masterpiece. With WINGS OF DESIRE, Wim Wenders creates a visual poem about the walls that exist in our world—those that separate fiction from reality, Heaven from Earth, history from the present, those who observe from those who feel. Bruno Ganz and Otto Sander play two angels who circulate in a black-and-white Berlin, where they "observe, collect, testify to, and preserve" the world around them, unseen by all but innocent children. The angels focus their attentions on three individuals—an octogenarian poet (Curt Bois); an American film and TV star (Peter Falk, playing himself); and a French trapeze artist (Solveig Dommartin). But, while helping these mortals, Ganz also struggles with his own desires to be able to feel, not just emotionally but physically as well. Although WINGS OF DESIRE draws on many sources, from Cocteau's filmic depiction of angels to the writings of Rainer Maria Rilke, the film's roots are perhaps closest to Walter Ruttmann's classic 1927 silent documentary, BERLIN: SYMPHONY OF A CITY. WINGS OF DESIRE, too, is a symphony on Berlin, though under Wenders's direction the city limits (which were then bisected by the Wall) become fantastic, extending far above to include those angels who keep a watchful eye on the world below. WINGS OF DESIRE enjoyed an overwhelmingly positive reception both at the box office—where it exceeded the success normally enjoyed by art-house offerings—and at the hands of the critics. The jury of the 1987 Cannes Film Festival named Wenders Best Director.

WINSLOW BOY, THE

1948 97m bw Drama ★★★½
Anatole de Grunwald/London Films/Eagle-Lion (U.K.) /U

Robert Donat (*Sir Robert Morton*), Margaret Leighton (*Catherine Winslow*), Cedric Hardwicke (*Arthur Winslow*), Basil Radford (*Esmond Curry*), Kathleen Harrison (*Violet*), Francis L. Sullivan (*Attorney General*), Marie Lohr (*Grace Winslow*), Jack Watling (*Dickie Winslow*), Frank Lawton (*John Watherstone*), Neil North (*Ronnie Winslow*)

p, Anatole de Grunwald; d, Anthony Asquith; w, Terence Rattigan, Anthony Asquith, Anatole de Grunwald (based on the play by Rattigan); ph, Freddie Young, Osmond Borradaile; ed, Gerald Turney-Smith; m, William Alwyn; prod d, Andre Andrejew; cos, William Chappell

In 1912 in London, Hardwicke is a retired bank official whose 14-year-old son, North, is expelled from naval college when he is accused of stealing a five-shilling postal order from another cadet. Hardwicke is convinced of his son's innocence but he is prevented by British law and unconcerned bureaucrats from fighting for his son's honor. Stymied at every turn, he hires the most famous attorney in Britain, Donat. Donat makes an impassioned speech in the House of Commons that results in a Petition of Right that allows Hardwicke to sue the Admiralty and make them prove in the courts that his son stole the postal order. The case is making headlines now and Hardwicke's family is facing the consequences: Hardwicke's daughter, suffragette Leighton, is left by her fiance; son Watling is forced to leave Oxford; and various legal fees are bringing Hardwicke almost to bankruptcy. In a courtroom trial, Donat finally gets North to admit the truth about what he was doing when the postal order was stolen: sneaking a cigarette in the locker room. The court finds in favor of North and Donat makes clear that he intends to see a great deal more of Leighton.

The story may seem rather dry, but the performances of Hardwicke, as the father prepared to face ruin to restore his son's honor, and of Donat, as the brilliant lawyer who finally breaks through the boy's own personal code of honor to exonerate him, keep the movie an engrossing experience. Based on the true Archer-Shee case of 1912.

WINTER KILLS

1979 97m c Comedy/Mystery/Political ★★★★
Avco Embassy (U.S.) R/18

Jeff Bridges (*Nick Kegan*), John Huston (*Pa Kegan*), Anthony Perkins (*John Ceruti*), Sterling Hayden (*Z.K. Dawson*), Eli Wallach (*Joe Diamond*), Dorothy Malone (*Emma Kegan*), Tomas Milian (*Frank Mayo*), Belinda Bauer (*Yvette Malone*), Ralph Meeker (*Gameboy Baker*), Toshiro Mifune (*Keith*)

p, Fred Caruso; d, William Richert; w, William Richert (based on the novel by Richard Condon); ph, Vilmos Zsigmond; ed, David Bretherton; m, Maurice Jarre; prod d, Robert Boyle; art d, Norman Newberry

Bridges stars as Nick Kegan, the youngest son of a Kennedyesque family presided over by an eccentric tycoon (Huston). Not wanting to follow in the footsteps of his older brother, who became president and was then assassinated, Nick has drifted through life trying to avoid the influence of his father. But when a dying man claims to have been the "second rifle" at the president's assassination 19 years before, the revelation sets into motion a bizarre series of events which sees Nick dig deeper and deeper into the past to find out who is truly responsible for his brother's assassination. Director William Richert has turned Richard Condon's novel about the insanity of the American power structure into a wickedly funny black comedy spiced up by some deliciously off-the-wall performances. The fact that Richert got the project off the ground at all is a miracle. To be taken seriously by the studio, this first-time director went out and got written commitments from such acting notables as Huston, Bridges, Perkins, and Elizabeth Taylor. Filling out his cast with Mifune, Malone, Hayden, Wallach, and Richard Boone, he began production and acquired Alfred Hitchcock's favorite production designer, Robert Boyle (who also makes a humorous cameo as a hotel desk clerk) to execute the lush, detailed look of the film. About a week before the $6.5 million production was completed, the studio inexplicably pulled the financial plug. Richert finished the project on his own and struck complicated financial deals with Avco Embassy in an effort to complete and distribute it. Though it garnered little attention in theaters, it has become a cult favorite on video.

WISE BLOOD

1979 106m c Drama/Comedy ★★★½
Ithaca/Anthea (U.S./West Germany) PG/15

Brad Dourif (*Hazel Motes*), Ned Beatty (*Hoover Shoates*), Harry Dean Stanton (*Asa Hawks*), Dan Shor (*Enoch Emery*), Amy Wright (*Sabbath Lily*), Mary Nell Santacroce (*Landlady*), John Huston (*Grandfather*)

p, Michael Fitzgerald, Kathy Fitzgerald; d, John Huston; w, Benedict Fitzgerald, Michael Fitzgerald (based on the novel by Flannery O'Connor); ph, Gerry Fisher; ed, Roberto Silvi; m, Alex North; cos, Sally Fitzgerald

At the age of 73, John Huston allowed his affinity for losers to attract him to the least marketable project of his career. The story of an obsessive, young, southern evangelist and several equally eccentric characters affected by him, WISE BLOOD, an unusual mixture of comedy, tragedy, satire, and horror, is an uningratiating but haunting work.

After his army discharge, young Hazel Motes (Brad Dourif) returns to his Southern hometown to find the family house boarded up. After taking a train to the city, he rents a room in a seedy boardinghouse, occupied by Asa Hawks (Harry Dean Stanton), an evangelist who claims to have blinded himself for God, and his daughter, Sabbath Lily (Amy Wright), a teenager who becomes infatuated with Hazel. Hazel becomes a street preacher for the "Church of Truth Without Christ," a secular religion of his own invention. One night, he is approached by Hoover Shoates (Ned Beatty), an opportunist who wants to become Hazel's promoter. The young man rebuffs him. Hazel discovers that Hawks is not blind, and winds up moving in with Sabbath Lily. When Shoates hires a preacher (William Hickey) to compete with Hazel, Hazel tracks down his rival and runs him over.

In the late 1970s, after being being approached about adapting *Wise Blood* by the son of Flannery O'Connor's literary executor, Huston went down to Macon, GA with a crew of only 25 and shot the film in 48 days. Although the movie earned its director a standing ovation at the Cannes Film Festival and his best reviews in years, no major Hollywood studio would distribute it. Nonetheless, Huston declared himself "intensely proud of it, as proud of it as anything I've ever done."

Perfectly cast as Hazel, Dourif parlays all the eccentricity, frustration, righteousness, humorlessness, and rage of youth into one darkly comic package. Wright is splendid as trashy seductress Sabbath Lily. In addition to Huston's keenly focused direction, the film is blessed with bracing, wintry pictures by cinematographer Gerry Fisher, and a melancholy Alex North arrangement of the "Tennessee Waltz" that is so affecting and haunting that it goes a long way toward persuading the viewer that WISE BLOOD's appalling personae are indeed worth caring about and grieving for.

WITCHES, THE

1990 91m c Fantasy ★★★½
Jim Henson/Lorimar (U.K./U.S.) PG

Anjelica Huston (*Mrs. Ernst/Grand High Witch*), Mai Zetterling (*Helga*), Jasen Fisher (*Luke*), Rowan Atkinson (*Mr. Stringer*), Bill Paterson (*Mr. Jenkins*), Brenda Blethyn (*Mrs. Jenkins*), Charlie Potter (*Bruno Jenkins*), Anna Lambton (*Woman in Black*), Jane Horrocks (*Miss Irvine*), Sukie Smith (*Marlene*)

p, Mark Shivas; d, Nicolas Roeg; w, Allan Scott (based on the book by Roald Dahl); ph, Harvey Harrison; ed, Tony Lawson; m, Stanley Myers; prod d, Andrew Sanders; art d, Norman Dorme; fx, Jim Henson's Creature Shop, Steve Norrington, Nigel Booth, John Stephenson; cos, Marit Allen

Never known for the accessibility of his films, director Nicolas Roeg (DON'T LOOK NOW, THE MAN WHO FELL TO EARTH, INSIGNIFICANCE) here has created a wildly entertaining fairy tale.

The film begins in Germany, where a little boy named Luke (Jasen Fisher) listens to bedtime stories read by his grandmother Helga (Mai Zetterling). Helga warns Luke about witches and their insidious ways. Some time after the story-telling session, Luke's parents are killed in a car accident, leaving the boy and his grandmother alone. They travel to England and, when Helga is stricken with a mild attack of diabetes, they head for a seaside resort. Coincidentally, all the witches in England arrive at the resort, summoned there by Mrs. Ernst (Anjelica Huston) for seminars on how to capture British children. While exploring the hotel, Luke stumbles upon a meeting of the witches, who are posing as conventioneers. He is stunned to see Mrs. Ernst transform herself into the frightening Grand High Witch, who announces that she's developed a magic potion that turns children into mice. When the witches discover Luke, he is forced to drink some of the potion and becomes a mouse. It's now up to Luke the mouse, together with his grandmother, to thwart the witches' heinous plans.

Based on a story by Roald Dahl (source author of WILLY WONKA AND THE CHOCOLATE FACTORY, and screenwriter for CHITTY CHITTY BANG BANG), THE WITCHES weaves many classic childhood fears into its entertaining—and genuinely eerie—action. Roeg directs with his usual visual flair, notably excelling during the wondrous mouse point-of-view scenes. (These sequences feature mouse puppets designed by the late Jim Henson, who served as the film's executive producer, the last film in which he was involved before his death in 1990.) In addition to the lively visuals, THE WITCHES features sharp art direction and beautiful locations. The actors seem to be having a good time, particularly Huston, who gives a wonderfully over-the-top performance as the Grand High Witch. Zetterling, making her first appearance in a US release since THE MAN WHO FINALLY DIED in 1967, is impressive, turning in a performance that is both rich and comic, and giving the film its emotional center.

WITCHES OF EASTWICK, THE

1987 118m c Horror/Comedy ★★
Warner Bros. (U.S.) R/18

Jack Nicholson (*Daryl Van Horne*), Cher (*Alexandra Medford*), Susan Sarandon (*Jane Spofford*), Michelle Pfeiffer (*Sukie Ridgemont*), Veronica Cartwright (*Felicia Alden*), Richard Jenkins (*Clyde Alden*), Keith Jochim (*Walter Neff*), Carel Struycken (*Fidel*), Helen Lloyd Breed (*Mrs. Biddle*), Caroline Struzik (*Carol Medford*)

p, Neil Canton, Peter Guber, Jon Peters; d, George Miller; w, Michael Cristofer (based on the novel by John Updike); ph, Vilmos Zsigmond; ed, Richard Francis-Bruce, Hubert C. de La Bouillerie; m, John Williams; prod d, Polly Platt; art d, Mark Mansbridge, Dave Howard Stein; fx, Mike Lanteri, Rob Bottin; cos, Aggie Guerard Rodgers; anim, Ellen Lichtwardt, John Armstrong, Chris Green

AAN Best Score: John Williams; *AAN Best Sound:* Wayne Artman, Tom Beckert, Tom Dahl, Art Rochester

A haphazard and slickly dumb adaptation of John Updike's best-selling novel, THE WITCHES OF EASTWICK is a star-studded special-effects extravaganza about the battle of the sexes. A trio of bored, sexually repressed New England women—Alex (Cher), Jane (Susan Sarandon), and Sukie (Michelle Pfeiffer), each of them left to live without their respective husbands—innocently conjures up a mysterious stranger who, they are convinced, will relieve their frustrations. This mystery man is Daryl Van Horne (Jack Nicholson), the filthy rich, wild-eyed Devil incarnate, who buys a local mansion. Within days, Alex, Jane, and Sukie have all been to bed with the Devil and discovered in themselves the almighty power of the female form. By the finale, the female trinity is pitted against the Devil, a mildly sympathetic misogynist who only wants to be loved *and* have someone to iron his shirts. While the underlying message of THE WITCHES OF EASTWICK may be of interest, the execution by George (MAD MAX) Miller is downright pathetic. The film plays like a TV sitcom, with an overdose of raunch added to the proceedings; when the Devil spews forth his profanities, one almost expects to hear a diabolical laugh track.

WITH A SONG IN MY HEART

1952 116m c Musical/Biography ★★★½
Fox (U.S.) /U

Susan Hayward (*Jane Froman*), Rory Calhoun (*John Burns*), David Wayne (*Don Ross*), Thelma Ritter (*Clancy*), Robert Wagner (*GI Paratrooper*), Helen Westcott (*Jennifer March*), Una Merkel (*Sister Marie*), Richard Allan (*Dancer*), Max Showalter (*Guild*), Lyle Talbot (*Radio Director*)

p, Lamar Trotti; d, Walter Lang; w, Lamar Trotti; ph, Leon Shamroy; ed, J. Watson Webb; art d, Lyle Wheeler, Joseph C. Wright, Earle Hagen; fx, Fred Sersen, Ray Kellogg; chor, Billy Daniel; cos, Charles LeMaire

AAN Best Actress: Susan Hayward; *AAN Best Supporting Actress:* Thelma Ritter; *AA Best Score:* Alfred Newman; *AAN Best Costume Design:* Charles LeMaire; *AAN Best Sound:* Thomas T. Moulton

This fairly accurate film biography stars Susan Hayward as singer Jane Froman, whose story is told in flashback. In 1936 she gets her first break on a Cincinnati radio station, and from there it's on to personal appearances at Radio City Music Hall and across the country. Although she's somewhat ambivalent about the match, Jane eventually marries her mentor, Don Ross (David Wayne). Problems arise, however, as Don becomes jealous of his wife's success. When Jane goes off to entertain the troops during WWII, her plane crashes off the Portuguese coast. Rescued by pilot John Burn (Rory Calhoun), the badly injured singer undergoes a difficult recuperation in a Lisbon hospital, becoming fast friends with her nurse, Clancy (Thelma Ritter, whose character is fictional). John, meanwhile, falls in love with Jane, who stifles her own feelings because she is married. She returns to the US, undergoes a series of painful operations (with faithful Clancy by her side), and works with Don's help to get her career back on track. There are setbacks along the way, including a serious argument with Don, but eventually Jane makes a triumphant comeback and Don frees her to marry John.

Froman provides Hayward's singing voice, to glorious effect, in a host of standards from various writers (with uncredited background vocals provided by the Skylarks, Modernaires, Melody Men, King's Men, Starlighters, and Four Girlfriends). Five-time Oscar nominee Hayward, as always, gives her best, making WITH A SONG IN MY HEART a satisfying film on all levels.

WITHNAIL & I

1987 108m c Drama ★★★½
HandMade (U.K.) R/15

Richard E. Grant (*Withnail*), Paul McGann (*Marwood*), Richard Griffiths (*Monty*), Ralph Brown (*Danny*), Michael Elphick (*Jake*), Daragh O'Malley (*Irishman*), Michael Wardle (*Issac Parkin*), Una Brandon-Jones (*Mrs. Parkin*), Noel Johnson (*General*), Irene Sutcliffe (*Waitress*)

p, Paul M. Heller; d, Bruce Robinson; w, Bruce Robinson (based on his novel); ph, Peter Hannan; ed, Alan Strachan; m, David Dundas; prod d, Michael Pickwoad; art d, Henry Harris; cos, Andrea Galer

A hilarious black comedy and already something of a cult favorite, WITHNAIL & I opens in a cluttered, refuse-ridden flat in North London. This confused mess is home for two out-of-work actors: gaunt, sarcastic, vaguely aristocratic, and dissipated Withnail (Richard E. Grant); and handsome, bespectacled Marwood (Paul McGann), whose journal notations, heard in voice-over, serve as the film's narration. It is 1969, and the pair visit Withnail's wealthy eccentric uncle Monty (Richard Griffiths) in hopes of getting the use of his country cottage for a weekend away to "rejuvenate." Uncle is agreeable, and the two drive off to the cottage only to find it a rustic version of their own flat—ice cold, damp, totally without provisions. As usual, Withnail leaves the practical matters to Marwood to solve. WITHNAIL & I is a wry portrait of 60s low-life bohemia which gets plenty of comic mileage from the rapid-fire repartee, colorfully drawn characters, and occasionally Monty Pythonesque moments of director-writer Bruce Robinson's script.

WITHOUT APPARENT MOTIVE
(SANS MOBILE APPARENT)

1972 102m c Mystery		★★★
President/Cineteleuro (France)		PG/

Jean-Louis Trintignant (Stephane Carella), Dominique Sanda (Sandra Forest), Sacha Distel (Julien Sabirnou), Carla Gravina (Jocelyne Rocca), Paul Crauchet (Francis Palombo), Laura Antonelli (Juliette Vaudreuil), Jean-Pierre Marielle (Perry Rupert-Foote), Stephane Audran (Helene Vallee), Pierre Dominique (Di Bozzo), Erich Segal (Hans Kleinberg)

p, Jacques Strauss; d, Philippe Labro; w, Philippe Labro, Jacques Lanzmann (based on the novel Ten Plus One by Ed McBain); ph, Jean Penzer; ed, Claude Barrois, Nicole Saunier; m, Ennio Morricone; prod d, Andre Hoss

A deft thriller in the hardboiled tradition of Raymond Chandler and Dashiell Hammett, this story of murderous revenge opens with Michel Bardinet, playing a wealthy Frenchman, being gunned down in broad daylight. Trintignant, the detective assigned to the case, can find no motive behind the slaying. Soon two others are killed in the same mysterious way. Trintignant is convinced a link exists between the three deaths, yet he has nothing to go on. A slim thread of hope comes when Sanda, Bardinet's stepdaughter, gives the detective a pocket diary that had belonged to the dead man. The diary contains, among other things, a list of Bardinet's lovers. One woman on this roll call is Gravina, a former passion of Trintignant's as well. Gravina meets the detective at his flat, hoping to rekindle their affair. After it's revealed that she had known all three of the murdered men, Gravina leaves, disappointed this liaison was for business reasons rather than sex. Before Trintignant can catch up with her, a shot rings out, adding Gravina to the list of mysterious sniper killings.

Though the plot, adapted from a pulp novel by Ed McBain, clearly takes its cue from film noir, director Labro takes some interesting chances with his adaptation. Rather than use the classic darkened settings of a 1940s crime film, Labro shoots in the sun-drenched streets of the French Riviera city of Nice. Despite the antithetical settings, the mood is just as dark here as in a good Humphrey Bogart crime story. Labro slowly builds up a feeling of impending doom, holding the mystery's solution until the very end and maintaining a consistent mood. The background music, a pulsating rhythm, enhances the atmosphere. Labro also understands the essentials of creating a thriller, building suspense before letting out the short bursts of violence. As the lone detective, Trintignant also owes a great deal to Bogart. His performance, filled with suppressed emotion, shows the influence of his cinematic forerunner but wisely avoids parodying him. A real surprise in the cast is Erich Segal, better known for his novel Love Story. In his cameo role the author shows a genuine flair for acting and handles his French dialogue with ease.

WITNESS

1985 112m c Crime		★★★★
Paramount (U.S.)		R/15

Harrison Ford (John Book), Kelly McGillis (Rachel), Josef Sommer (Schaeffer), Lukas Haas (Samuel), Jan Rubes (Eli Lapp), Alexander Godunov (Daniel Hochleitner), Patti LuPone (Elaine), Danny Glover (McFee), Brent Jennings (Carter), Angus MacInnes (Fergie)

p, Edward S. Feldman; d, Peter Weir; w, Earl W. Wallace, William Kelley (based on a story by Kelley, Wallace, Pamela Wallace); ph, John Seale; ed, Thom Noble; m, Maurice Jarre; prod d, Stan Jolley; fx, John R. Elliott; cos, Shari Feldman, Dallas Dornan

AAN Best Picture; AAN Best Actor: Harrison Ford; AAN Best Director: Peter Weir; AA Best Original Screenplay: Earl W. Wallace, William Kelley, Pamela Wallace; AAN Best Cinematography: John Seale; AA Best Editing: Thom Noble; AAN Best Score: Maurice Jarre; AAN Best Art Direction: Stan Jolley, John Anderson

Sure-footed thriller, beautifully photographed, with Ford's best performance thus far. Australian director Peter Weir's first Hollywood film examines the tenuous survival of innocence in pockets of post-war America. The story begins as Rachel (Kelly McGillis), a young Amish widow, is traveling into the city with her young son, Samuel (Lukas Haas). While they're waiting for their train in the crowded Philadelphia station, Samuel wanders into the men's room where, undetected, he witnesses a murder. Questioned by tough, cynical cop John Book (Harrison Ford), the boy identifies a narcotics officer (Danny Glover) as the killer. Suspecting a conspiracy and fearing for the safety of his young witness, Book tries to get Samuel and Rachel back to the safe obscurity of Lancaster County, home to a peaceful, idyllic community of Amish farmers. But trouble follows, even as Rachel and Book become attracted to each other. The cast is uniformly excellent, while John Seale's cinematography and Maurice Jarre's score are memorably atmospheric.

WITNESS FOR THE PROSECUTION

1957 114m bw Mystery		★★★★½
Theme (U.S.)		/U

Tyrone Power (Leonard Stephen Vole), Marlene Dietrich (Christine Helm/Vole), Charles Laughton (Sir Wilfrid Robarts), Elsa Lanchester (Miss Plimsoll), John Williams (Brogan Moore), Henry Daniell (Mayhew), Ian Wolfe (Carter), Una O'Connor (Janet MacKenzie), Torin Thatcher (Mr. Meyers), Francis Compton (Judge)

p, Arthur Hornblow Jr.; d, Billy Wilder; w, Billy Wilder, Harry Kurnitz, Larry Marcus (based on the novel and the play by Agatha Christie); ph, Russell Harlan; ed, Daniel Mandell; m, Matty Malneck; art d, Alexander Trauner; cos, Edith Head, Joe King

AAN Best Picture; AAN Best Actor: Charles Laughton; AAN Best Supporting Actress: Elsa Lanchester; AAN Best Director: Billy Wilder; AAN Best Editing: Daniel Mandell; AAN Best Sound: Gordon Sawyer

Dietrich steals it. WITNESS FOR THE PROSECUTION is a witty, terse adaptation of the Agatha Christie hit play brought to the screen with ingenuity and vitality by Billy Wilder. Sir Wilfrid Robarts (Laughton) is a sickly barrister who is told by his doctors and forced by his pesty nurse Miss Plimsoll (Lanchester, Laughton's real-life wife), to retire from criminal cases. When his solicitor Mayhew (Daniell) arrives at his home with murder suspect Leonard Vole (Power), Robarts cannot resist. Hearing Vole's story, Robarts becomes convinced of the man's innocence, but because his only alibi is his wife Christine (Dietrich), prospects for an acquittal look dim. Before their meeting ends, word is received that Vole has inherited a fortune from the deceased's estate. Because of the apparent clarity of Vole's motive, Scotland Yard places him under arrest. Robarts, however, is not completely convinced and continues examining the clues, uncovering more than even he imagined.

Improving on Christie's play, Wilder has rid WITNESS FOR THE PROSECUTION of much of the usual static courtroom scenes and filled the film with an active, visual excitement. Whether it be the fluidity of the camera, the use of an occasional flashback, or the diversion of Robarts's constant medical attention, Wilder succeeds in finding a way to relieve the boredom that typically accompanies the courtroom. Wilder even introduces the Miss Plimsoll character into Christie's scenario to add some life and a comic angle. At the film's halfway point Wilder flashes back to wartime Germany for the standard Dietrich-as-cabaret-singer scene, giving her a chance to show off one of her attractive legs, play the accordion, and deliver "I Never Go There Anymore" (Ralph Arthur Roberts, Jack Brooks). The part, one of her finest, was pure Dietrich, casting her as a woman who throws away everything—her homeland, her reputation, and her life—for the man she loves.

WIZARD OF OZ, THE

1939 101m c/bw Fantasy/Musical	★★★★★
MGM (U.S.)	/U

Judy Garland (Dorothy), Ray Bolger (Hunk/The Scarecrow), Bert Lahr (Zeke/The Cowardly Lion), Jack Haley (Hickory/The Tin Woodsman), Billie Burke (Glinda), Margaret Hamilton (Miss Gulch/The Wicked Witch), Charley Grapewin (Uncle Henry), Clara Blandick (Auntie Em), Pat Walsh (Nikko), Frank Morgan (Prof. Marvel/The Wizard/Guard/Coachman)

p, Mervyn LeRoy; d, Victor Fleming, King Vidor; w, Noel Langley, Florence Ryerson, Edgar Allan Woolf (based on the novel by L. Frank Baum); ph, Harold Rosson; ed, Blanche Sewell; m, Herbert Stothart; art d, Cedric Gibbons; fx, A. Arnold Gillespie; chor, Bobby Connolly; cos, Adrian

AAN Best Picture; AA Best Score: Herbert Stothart; AA Best Song: Harold Arlen (Music), E.Y. Harburg (Lyrics); AAN Best Art Direction: Cedric Gibbons, William A. Horning; AAN Best Visual Effects: A. Arnold Gillespie, Douglas Shearer

There's no place like home, and there will never be another movie like THE WIZARD OF OZ. Forget that it's over 50 years old, that here and there it creaks a tiny bit: it stirs in all of us the feeling of wanting to belong, of having security, but wanting enchantment at the same time. OZ gives us enchantment unparalleled for a hundred different reasons, foremost among which is the ageless appeal of young Judy Garland, perhaps the most beloved of all film actresses. Watching her now, we're aware of all the sadness Garland's life would encompasses (the consummate showbiz pro, she was quick to milk her suffering), but Dorothy captures her poised on the brink of legend, before the ravages of unhappiness set in. And chances are, for most of us, we first saw her in OZ before life took any serious tolls upon us, before broken hearts, or deaths, or money troubles or career disappointments. Sometimes you watch Garland longingly sing "Over the Rainbow" and it sweeps you away to somewhere you can't even explain. THE WIZARD OF OZ is a dazzling fantasy musical, so beautifully directed and acted that it deserves its classic status.

Dorothy (Garland) is a schoolgirl living in Kansas with family and her little dog, Toto. One afternoon, a twister sucks up Dorothy's house and she and Toto are dropped beyond the rainbow into Munchkinland. With a pair of magical red slippers and some advice from Glinda the Good Witch (Billie Burke), Dorothy, Toto and three new friends—the Scarecrow (Ray Bolger), Tin Man (Jack Haley), and Cowardly Lion (Bert Lahr)—follow the yellow brick road to the Emerald City, where they must ask the all-powerful Wizard of Oz (Frank Morgan) to get Dorothy and Toto back home. The Wicked Witch (Margaret Hamilton), however, is determined to get her hands on the slippers, and sends out her flying monkeys to capture the group—as if you needed to know any of this.

Curiously, Garland, forever to be identified with the wide-eyed Dorothy, was not the first choice for the part; both Shirley Temple and Deanna Durbin were considered for the role. Had Jean Harlow not died, ending the loan-out deal to exchange her for IN OLD CHICAGO with Temple for OZ, we'd be watching Temple's forthright moppet, instead of Garland's tender waif. The mind boggles. We could regale you for hours on end with behind the scenes trivia on OZ. Books have been written on nothing but, and they're not hard to find. But we'll toss you a few: Frank Morgan spent half his time on set drunk. Clara Blandick (Auntie Em) was just as unhappy as she appears; she ended up a recluse who eventually took her own life. Harlow's third and last husband, Harold Rosson, did OZ's cinematography and King Vidor did some uncredited directorial work. L.B. Mayer's nickname for Garland was his "little humpback." The original Wizard was to have been W.C.

Fields, the original Tin Man Buddy Ebsen (who fell ill from all the makeup preparation) and the original Wicked Witch was to have been played as an evil siren by Gale Sondergaard. Bolger, Haley, Lahr, and Morgan were not the kindly uncles you might think. All were grizzled showbiz vets not about to give Garland an inch of scene-stealing capacity onscreen; when she takes a scene, it's not because anyone let her. See if you can hear the female Munchkin who runs forward to Garland and shouts "Judy" instead of "Dorothy" after Hamilton's first exit. And watch for inconsistencies in Garland's hairstyles during the time she is beautified in OZ.

WOLF MAN, THE

1941 71m bw Horror	★★★★
Universal (U.S.)	/PG

Claude Rains (Sir John Talbot), Lon Chaney Jr. (Larry Talbot), Evelyn Ankers (Gwen Conliffe), Ralph Bellamy (Capt. Paul Montford), Warren William (Dr. Lloyd), Patric Knowles (Frank Andrews), Maria Ouspenskaya (Maleva), Bela Lugosi (Bela), Fay Helm (Jenny Williams), Leyland Hodgson (Kendall)

p, George Waggner; d, George Waggner; w, Curt Siodmak; ph, Joseph Valentine; ed, Ted J. Kent; art d, Jack Otterson

A feast of horror, for animals of all kinds. Bearing no resemblance to Universal's 1935 film THE WEREWOLF OF LONDON, THE WOLF MAN was given a whole new look and treatment by the studio. Lon Chaney Jr., stars as Larry Talbot, a young British heir who returns to the mansion of his father (Claude Rains) after getting a college education in America. Learning about the legend of the werewolf from antique store employee Gwen (Evelyn Ankers), gypsy fortune teller Maleva (Maria Ouspenskaya), and Maleva's son, Bela (Bela Lugosi), Larry laughs it off as superstition. When the young man hears a bone-chilling wolf's howl and a blood-curdling scream emanating from the foggy moors, however, he rushes to the source of the hideous noises and is attacked and bitten by a vicious, hairy beast. Later, Maleva tells Larry that he will transform into a savage, murderous wolf when the moon is full and that he can only be killed by silver—be it a silver bullet, knife, or cane. Larry tries to deny her superstitious forecast, but when the next full moon arises, his nose becomes a wet snout, his hands and feet turn to paws, and his body is covered with thick fur. An animal trapped in a bedroom, the wolf man crashes through the window and runs off into the night in search of his prey.

Fearing comparison with his famous father, Lon Jr. avoided appearing in horror films, but as he gained confidence in his abilities he agreed to try the genre and created the character with whom he would always be identified—the wolf man. Through the genius of Universal makeup artist Jack Pierce, Chaney underwent a complete transformation nearly as complete as his character's—gaining a rubber snout, fangs, claws, and lots of yak hair. Screenwriter Curt Siodmak patched together the legend of the werewolf by combining elements from lycanthropic folklore, witchcraft, and Bram Stoker's Dracula, creating a new monster for the screen. All elements combined to make a thrilling, scary, and ultimately tragic horror classic. Chaney essayed the role of the werewolf five more times, in FRANKENSTEIN MEETS THE WOLF-MAN, HOUSE OF FRANKENSTEIN, HOUSE OF DRACULA, and ABBOTT AND COSTELLO MEET FRANKENSTEIN, as well as a guest appearance on the television show "Route 66."

WOLFEN

1981 115m c Horror	★★★½
Orion (U.S.)	R/18

Albert Finney (Dewey Wilson), Diane Venora (Rebecca Neff), Edward James Olmos (Eddie Holt), Gregory Hines (Whittington), Tom Noonan (Ferguson), Dick O'Neill (Warren), Dehl Berti (Old Indian), Peter Michael Goetz (Ross), Sam Gray (Mayor), Ralph Bell (Commissioner)

p, Rupert Hitzig; d, Michael Wadleigh; w, David Eyre, Michael Wadleigh (based on the novel by Whitley Strieber); ph, Gerry Fisher; ed, Chris Lebenzon, Dennis Dolan, Martin Bram, Marshall M. Borden; m, James Horner; prod d, Paul Sylbert; art d, David Chapman; fx, Carl Fullerton, Robert Blalack, Betz Bromberg; cos, John Boxer

This straightforward, intelligent film puts a new spin on the werewolf legend, presenting the creatures as a superior species living in the slums of New York City. Police detective Dewey Wilson (Albert Finney) is assigned to investigate the savage murder of a rich industrialist. When the city coroner (Gregory Hines, in his film debut) suggests that the dead man was mutilated by a wild animal, Wilson and criminal psychologist Rebecca Neff (Diane Venora) connect the killing with several murders that have occurred in which the bodies of winos, drug addicts, and bums have been found with their throats ripped out. Further investigation by Wilson and Neff leads to a group of Native American construction workers and to a strange tale of the "Wolfen" that once roamed the land that is now New York City. Directed by Michael Wadleigh, whose only other feature is the 1970 rock documentary WOODSTOCK, WOLFEN is an intelligent, insightful, and visually creative twist on the werewolf legend. Although occasionally preachy, it is a fascinating horror tale that is as engrossing as it is horrifying. The visual effects are sensational, introducing to the screen a previously unseen "Wolfen vision" that, through a variety of optical printing techniques, conveys the wolves' heightened awareness of heat, smell, movement, and texture. The gore effects by Carl Fullerton are effective, if somewhat gratuitous.

WOMAN IN THE DUNES
(SUNA NO ONNA)
1964 123m bw Drama ★★★★
Teshigahara (Japan) /18

Eiji Okada *(Niki Jumpei)*, Kyoko Kishida *(Woman)*, Koji Mitsui, Hiroko Ito, Sen Yano, Ginzo Sekigushi, Kiyohiko Ichiha, Tamutsu Tamura, Hiroyuki Nishimo

p, Kiichi Ichikawa, Tadashi Ohono; d, Hiroshi Teshigahara; w, Kobo Abe (based on the novel *Suna no Onna* by Abe); ph, Hiroshi Segawa; ed, F. Susui; m, Toru Takemitsu

AAN Best Foreign Language Film ; *AAN Best Director:* Hiroshi Teshigahara

A profoundly moving parable told with beautiful simplicity, WOMAN IN THE DUNES begins as Niki Jumpei (Eiji Okada) a reserved entomologist, collects specimens along a Japanese beach. He is met by some villagers, who offer him both a place to sleep and a woman, and is led to a shack located at the bottom of a sand pit, where he climbs down a rope ladder to the woman, Kyoko (Kyoko Kishida). The next morning, he notices that the ladder has been removed. A panicky urge to climb out of the pit is followed by a futile attempt to scale the sand walls, which cascade beneath his feet. Helpless, he watches as Kyoko endlessly shovels the sand into buckets, which are then hoisted by the villagers above. In return, food and water are sent down—no shoveling, no food. Niki soon realizes the necessity of the woman's work. He becomes accustomed to his new lifestyle and takes the woman as his lover. She becomes pregnant, and he must wrestle with his urge to escape and his growing devotion to Kyoko and his new life.

Beautifully photographed and confined almost exclusively to a single set, WOMAN IN THE DUNES is a poetic affirmation of life. As frustrating and claustrophobic as the man's situation may first appear, the film becomes increasingly seductive as it lulls the audience into the woman's sandpit existence. Based on a novel by Kobo Abe.

WOMAN IN THE WINDOW, THE
1945 99m bw Thriller ★★★★
Christie/International Pictures (U.S.) /A

Edward G. Robinson *(Prof. Richard Wanley)*, Joan Bennett *(Alice Reed)*, Raymond Massey *(Frank Lalor)*, Edmund Breon *(Dr. Michael Barkstone)*, Dan Duryea *(Heidt/Doorman)*, Thomas Jackson *(Inspector Jackson)*, Arthur Loft *(Claude Mazard/Frank Howard)*, Dorothy Peterson *(Mrs. Wanley)*, Frank Dawson *(Collins, the Steward)*, Carol Cameron *(Elsie Wanley)*

p, Nunnally Johnson; d, Fritz Lang; w, Nunnally Johnson (based on the novel *Once Off Guard* by J.H. Wallis); ph, Milton Krasner; ed, Marjorie Johnson, Gene Fowler Jr.; m, Arthur Lange; art d, Duncan Cramer; fx, Vernon L. Walker; cos, Muriel King

AAN Best Score: Hugo Friedhofer, Arthur Lange

A gripping psychological thriller which stars Robinson as a fortyish, intellectual college professor who, with his friends, discusses the dangers of becoming too adventurous at their age. Robinson has a wife and children (who are away on vacation) and sees no reason to wander from his staid, secure path. However, while admiring a portrait of a beautiful model in a gallery window, he notices the model, Bennett, standing beside him. Bennett asks if Robinson would like to come up to her apartment under honest pretenses: "I'm not married. I have no designs on you," she assures him. Once in her apartment, this fantasy girl of Robinson's brings about his downfall, though unintentionally. Her boyfriend, wealthy financier Loft, arrives unexpectedly and, thinking that the two are having an affair, begins to slap his mistress around. He then lunges at Robinson, who grabs a nearby scissors and, in self-defense, stabs his attacker in the back. Frightened both of the police and of the disgrace he will cause his family, Robinson plots, with Bennett, to dispose of the body. Battling countless obstacles and nearly getting caught a number of times, they take the corpse, sitting up in the back seat of a car with open, glazed eyes, to a secluded woody area. They manage to carry out their plan without getting caught. Robinson, however, is still subject to mental torture, especially by his friend, Massey, a district attorney who continually talks about the case, unaware that Robinson is the man he's after. Through Massey, Robinson learns all the most intricate details of the investigation and is able to follow the progress of the police. He also learns his mistakes, which mount by the day. Making matters worse is a blackmail scheme engineered by Loft's bodyguard, Duryea, who has discovered Robinson's guilt.

With its terse pacing and elegant camerawork, THE WOMAN IN THE WINDOW was a great box-office success and one of the most praised *films noir* of its time. Robinson, in a role different from his standard gangster part, shines and holds the film's credibility together by turning in a convincing portrayal of a good man who is caught off guard just once (to paraphrase the title of the novel, *Once Off Guard*, on which the film is based). Bennett, in her second Lang film after 1941's MAN HUNT, is dazzlingly alluring as the fantasy girl who comes to life for Robinson. The collaboration between Bennett and Lang was so amiable that they would work together two more times, in SCARLET STREET with Robinson again as costar, and SECRET BEYOND THE DOOR, both produced by her and husband Walter Wanger's own Diana Productions. Although many people feel cheated by the film's ending, Lang always felt (in later interviews) that his decision was justified. Either way, it's still a fine film.

WOMAN IS A WOMAN, A
(UNE FEMME EST UNE FEMME)
1960 80m c Drama ★★★★
Rome/Paris Pathe (France/Italy) /X

Anna Karina *(Angela)*, Jean-Claude Brialy *(Emile Recamier)*, Jean-Paul Belmondo *(Alfred Lubitsch)*, Nicole Paquin *(Suzanne)*, Marie Dubois *(1st Prostitute)*, Marion Sarraut *(2nd Prostitute)*, Jeanne Moreau *(Woman in Bar)*, Catherine Demongeot

p, Carlo Ponti, Georges de Beauregard; d, Jean-Luc Godard; w, Jean-Luc Godard (based on an idea by Genevieve Cluny); ph, Raoul Coutard; ed, Agnes Guillemot, Lila Herman; m, Michel Legrand; art d, Bernard Evein; cos, Bernard Evein

Godard's third feature film and his first in color, A WOMAN IS A WOMAN is one of the most enjoyable of all the master's works. Taking an extremely lighthearted approach, it bursts with a passion for the medium of film expressed in every shot. The plot is very simple and could almost be taken for homage to Hollywood musical comedy, but homage seems much too tacky a term to express the fascination Godard had and the playful manner in which he approached this film. Karina (Godard's wife at the time) plays a stripper living with her boyfriend (Brialy), who refuses to marry her in spite of her expressed desire to have a child. Using an old feminine ploy, she starts to turn her attentions toward another man (Belmondo), easily making him fall in love with her. Sure enough, it works, with the boyfriend breaking down when faced with the prospect of losing the girl he loves.

Every moment of this picture is filled with charm, from Brialy riding a bicycle around their apartment in a strange mating dance to the buffoonish manner in which Belmondo tries to declare his love for

Karina. The loose style almost seems to suggest that Godard just placed the camera down and then told his three stars to play; they look like children who have not yet outgrown the play lot and are unwilling to accept responsibility. The way Karina announces that she wants to have a baby is totally whimsical, a thing to do because that is what couples do when they are in love. Next to Godard's nonstylish stylishness, the most outstanding feature is the mere presence of Karina; her subtle glance and loftiness coincide with little mistakes in technical performance that most directors would not tolerate, but which actually serve to make her that much more human and irresistible. In fact, the picture appears almost to be a private photograph album showcasing the charming Karina in many moods. This is the first of Godard's films to be shot largely in a studio under tightly controlled conditions. The director insisted on using sets with ceilings in the interest of naturalism. This was also Godard's first experience with direct synchronous sound; his previous films had been dubbed. Elements of some of the director's earlier short subjects—most notably the 10-minute UNE FEMME COQUETTE—can be seen in the plot and the characterizations. Raoul Coutard's superlative wide-screen camera work will be diminished on the TV screen.

WOMAN NEXT DOOR, THE
(LA FEMME D'A COTE)

1981 106m c Drama	★★★
Carrosse/TF-1 (France)	R/AA

Gerard Depardieu *(Bernard Coudray)*, Fanny Ardant *(Mathilde Bauchard)*, Henri Garcin *(Philippe Bauchard)*, Michele Baumgartner *(Arlette Coudray)*, Veronique Silver *(Mme. Jouve)*, Philippe Morier-Genoud *(Doctor)*, Roger Van Hool *(Roland Duguet)*, Olivier Becquaert, Nicole Vauthier, Muriel Combe

d, Francois Truffaut; w, Francois Truffaut, Suzanne Schiffman, Jean Aurel; ph, William Lubtchansky; ed, Martine Barraque; m, Georges Delerue; art d, Jean-Pierre Kohut-Svelko; cos, Michele Cerf

This dark entry from Truffaut pairs French superstar Depardieu with newcomer Ardant as former flames who have married other people and now live next door to each other. Depardieu, who has been living a comfortable though joyless bourgeois existence with his wife and young son, tries to avoid Ardant at every turn. A chance meeting at the supermarket, however, opens a floodgate of buried emotions, and the romance is resumed. Gradually, Depardieu and Ardant's mutual obsession builds to a dangerous level that neither can control. As he did in JULES AND JIM and THE STORY OF ADELE H., Truffaut once again displays his interest in obsessive love and the pain and destruction it can cause. Here as in THE SOFT SKIN and THE BRIDE WORE BLACK, the shadow of Hitchcock looms large, resulting in a taut, psychological narrative that stifles the director's poetic impulse. Stage actress Ardant, who makes a stunning starring debut here as the woman obsessed, also appears in Truffaut's final film, CONFIDENTIALLY YOURS.

WOMAN OF THE YEAR

1942 112m bw Comedy/Drama	★★★★
MGM (U.S.)	/A

Spencer Tracy *(Sam Craig)*, Katharine Hepburn *(Tess Harding)*, Fay Bainter *(Ellen Whitcomb)*, Reginald Owen *(Clayton)*, Minor Watson *(William Harding)*, William Bendix *(Pinkie Peters)*, Gladys Blake *(Flo Peters)*, Dan Tobin *(Gerald)*, Roscoe Karns *(Phil Whittaker)*, William Tannen *(Ellis)*

p, Joseph L. Mankiewicz; d, George Stevens; w, Ring Lardner Jr., Michael Kanin; ph, Joseph Ruttenberg; ed, Frank Sullivan; m, Franz Waxman; art d, Cedric Gibbons, Randall Duell; cos, Adrian

AAN Best Actress: Katharine Hepburn; *AA Best Original Screenplay:* Michael Kanin, Ring Lardner, Jr.

The first onscreen pairing of Tracy and Hepburn, a team that would last 25 years until Tracy's death in 1967. He plays a sportswriter for a New York newpaper who becomes angry after hearing Hepburn on a radio broadcast boldly state that baseball should be eliminated until WWII comes to an end. Hepburn, the daughter of diplomat Watson and an international affairs writer, works on the same paper as Tracy, and her remarks begin a battle waged in their respective columns. Once they

meet in person, they are attracted to each other, much to the surprise of their friends and colleagues. Eventually Tracy and Hepburn wed, but their marriage rests on shaky ground. Hepburn's attempts at homemaking are an outright disaster, as she feels her job must come before anything else. Tracy is angered by her lack of commitment to the marriage and ends up getting too drunk to write his column. Hepburn, whose knowledge of sports isn't much better than her abilities as a housewife, pens Tracy's column and the results are catastrophic. Hepburn is voted "Woman of the Year," ironically hearing the news while she is contemplating whether to remain with Tracy. When her father remarries, Hepburn listens closely as marriage vows are read. The words move her and she decides to go back to Tracy with renewed zeal for married life.

WOMAN OF THE YEAR is a marvelous comedy-drama, brimming with wit, style, and sophistication. Hepburn is strong and assured, a woman fueled by intense pride along with a good-sized ego. (Maybe that's why the final breakfast scene, amusing as it is, leaves a bad taste in the mouth, as it milks rather obvious laughs from Hepburn's lack of traditonally "feminine" skills.) Tracy is her male opposite, just as opinionated and just as stubborn. Their chemistry is engaging, a solid teaming that enhances the accomplished script.

Garson Kanin's idea for the film was inspired by renowned columnist Dorothy Thompson. Because of Kanin's other commitments, he was unable to develop the story further, instead giving the project to his brother Michael and Ring Lardner, Jr. The writers concocted a 30,000-word treatment, and Hepburn immediately fell in love with the property. It was decided that Hepburn would talk MGM into buying the script. Hepburn, at 5 feet 7 inches, was already considered to be tall among the actresses on the MGM lot. For her meeting with studio head Louis B. Mayer, Hepburn donned four-inch heels, thus increasing her height to an even more imposing stature. Mayer, who was not a tall man, listened to her every demand. Though Hepburn was convinced she had not succeeded, the strong-minded actress was shocked when she learned Mayer had given her everything she wanted on WOMAN OF THE YEAR. In addition to her own salary of $100,000, Hepburn received a $11,000 commission as a script agent, plus her choice of director and costar. Kanin and Lardner each received $50,000 for their efforts, far beyond the $200 to $300 a week they normally got.

For her leading man, Hepburn had only one choice. She wanted Tracy, but at the time he was on location in Florida, working on MGM's production of THE YEARLING. However, various problems on the set caused that project to be halted (Gregory Peck would eventually play Tracy's role), leaving Tracy free for WOMAN OF THE YEAR. The two were introduced in the studio commissary by producer Mankiewicz. Hepburn, decked out in her four-inch heels, said to her costar, "I'm afraid I'm a little tall for you, Mr. Tracy." "Don't worry, Miss Hepburn," Tracy shot back, "I'll cut you down to my size." (In years to follow, Mankiewicz took credit for the clever retort whenever he told the story.)

WOMAN TIMES SEVEN
(SEPT FOIS FEMME)

1967 99m c Comedy/Drama	★★★
Fox/Cormoran (U.S./France/Italy)	/15

Shirley MacLaine *(Paulette/Maria Terese/Linda/Edith/Eve Minou/Marie/Jeanne)*, FUNERAL PROCESSION: Elspeth March *(Annette)*, AMATEUR NIGHT: Rossano Brazzi *(Giorgio)*, Catherine Samie *(Jeannine)*, Judith Magre *(2nd Prostitute)*, TWO AGAINST ONE: Vittorio Gassman *(Cenci)*, Clinton Greyn *(MacCormick)*, Lex Barker *(Rik)*, THE SUPER-SIMONE: Elsa Martinelli *(Woman in Market)*, Robert Morley *(Dr. Xavier)*

p, Arthur Cohn; d, Vittorio De Sica; w, Cesare Zavattini; ph, Christian Matras; ed, Teddy Darvas, Victoria Mercanton; m, Riz Ortolani; art d, Bernard Evein; cos, Marcel Escoffier

It's difficult enough doing one role well, but playing several parts in the same movie is a nearly impossible feat requiring the talents of an Alec Guinness or a Peter Sellers. MacLaine had not yet achieved the maturity or the acting ability to bring this off, and the result is just ol' Shirl' in a host of different costumes, hairstyles, and makeup. Shot on location in Paris with interiors at the Boulogne Studios, this set out to be a *tour de force* but ends up only a *tour de France*.

In the first segment, she's a widow accompanying the coffin of her late husband to the cemetery; on the way, she finds romance with old friend Sellers. The second piece has MacLaine returning to her home to find her husband, Brazzi, cavorting in the sack with another woman. She storms out and learns some lessons about men from the local streetwalkers. Next, MacLaine is seen as a hippie who attracts the competing sexual attentions of Gassman and Grey, resulting in some lubricious games. In the fourth segment, MacLaine is a grumpy housewife married to Barker, a successful author of trashy novels that feature a wild, passionate heroine. In order to compete with this fantasy figure, she tries to be equally impulsive, but only succeeds in convincing everyone she's gone mad. The fifth episode has MacLaine as a rich Parisian matron plotting to foil a social rival, Adrienne Corri, in a dispute over a designer gown. In No. 6, MacLaine and Alan Arkin are lovers married to other people who make an ill-fated suicide pact. The final section of the film has MacLaine, married to Noiret, out shopping with her best pal, Anita Ekberg. When MacLaine spots Caine watching her, she's flattered that such a handsome man would find her attractive—never dreaming that Caine has been hired to keep an eye on her by her jealous husband.

All of the segments, save the first, run between 14 and 16 minutes. The funeral episode goes about eight minutes, which is all it's worth. Ortolani's music is second-rate, but the rest of the technical credits are all excellent. Special note should be taken of Alex Archambault's hairstyles and the makeup work done by Alberto De Rossi and Georges Bouban. Although Marcel Escoffier gets credit for the well-planned costumes, it was Pierre Cardin who designed MacLaine's gowns.

WOMAN UNDER THE INFLUENCE, A

1974 155m c Drama ★★★★
Faces International Films (U.S.) R/15

Peter Falk *(Nick Longhetti)*, Gena Rowlands *(Mabel Longhetti)*, Matthew Cassel *(Tony Longhetti)*, Matthew Laborteaux *(Angelo Longhetti)*, Christina Grisanti *(Maria Longhetti)*, Katherine Cassavetes *(Mama Longhetti)*, Lady Rowlands *(Martha Mortensen)*, Fred Draper *(George Mortensen)*, O.G. Dunn *(Garson Cross)*, Mario Gallo *(Harold Jensen)*

p, Sam Shaw; d, John Cassavetes; w, John Cassavetes; ph, Caleb Deschanel; ed, Tom Cornwell, David Armstrong, Elizabeth Bergeron, Sheila Viseltear; m, Bo Harwood; art d, Phedon Papamichael; cos, Carole Smith

AAN Best Actress: Gena Rowlands; *AAN Best Director:* John Cassavetes

Tough-minded, moving study of a working-class housewife's mental breakdown, enhanced by superb performances from Rowlands, in the title role, and Falk as her husband. Laborteaux, Grisanti, and Cassel play the children. A kind of tragic duet between the two leads, A WOMAN remains an insightful essay on sexual politics. As Rowlands delicately crosses the line of sanity, it becomes apparent that imposed social roles are the cause.

Both Rowlands (who lost to Ellen Burstyn for ALICE DOESN'T LIVE HERE ANYMORE) and Cassavetes (for direction) were nominated for Oscars for this unexpected minor hit, which grossed well over $6 million the first time around. It began as a theatrical piece for Rowlands, but she balked at having to play such a demanding role nightly and the suggestion was made to transform it into a movie. Cassavetes took out a mortgage on his home, contacted friends and relatives for financing, and then began a two-year shooting schedule dictated by his own personal finances. Cassavetes's work is often mistaken as improvisational, or even as *cinema verite*. In fact, his films are thoughtful celebrations of the art of acting and, in most cases, are shot from precise scripts (even if those scripts are themselves based on extensive improvisational exercises).

WOMEN, THE

1939 132m c/bw Comedy ★★★★½
MGM (U.S.) /A

Norma Shearer *(Mary Haines)*, Joan Crawford *(Chrystal Allen)*, Rosalind Russell *(Sylvia Fowler)*, Mary Boland *(Countess DeLave)*, Paulette Goddard *(Miriam Aarons)*, Joan Fontaine *(Peggy Day)*, Lucile Watson *(Mrs. Moorehead)*, Phyllis Povah *(Edith Potter)*, Florence Nash *(Nancy Blake)*, Virginia Weidler *(Little Mary)*

p, Hunt Stromberg; d, George Cukor; w, Anita Loos, Jane Murfin (based on the play by Clare Boothe Luce); ph, Oliver T. Marsh, Joseph Ruttenberg; ed, Robert J. Kern; m, Edward Ward, David Snell; art d, Cedric Gibbons, Wade B. Rubottom; cos, Adrian

Every feminist's nightmare? In some ways, yes; in others no. Adapted from the hit Broadway play by Clare Boothe (who was later Mrs. Luce, by dint of marriage to the founder of *Time* magazine), THE WOMEN does portray its subjects as inordinately fond of catty gossip, but also has some interesting points to make about female bonding and societal pressures.

Norma Shearer plays Mary Haines, a wealthy and loving woman married to an adoring husband and the mother of sweet Little Mary (Weidler, admirably pulling off a difficult part). Contented Mary, though, has no idea that her mate is having an affair with predatory perfume seller Crystal Allen (Joan Crawford). Mary's girlfriends know, and the bitchiest of the lot, Sylvia Fowler (Rosalind Russell), arranges for Mary to get the news herself from the gossip manicurist (Dennie Moore) who first started circulating the story. Mary's mother, Mrs. Morehead (Lucile Watson), though, advises her to say nothing and simply let the affair play itself out. Unfortunately, Mary encounters Crystal at a fancy clothing salon and, in a blistering scene, the two women exchange words. Mary leaves New York to race to Reno for a six-week divorce and meets the Countess de Lave (Mary Boland), an aging former showgirl who has been married several times. She also encounters younger chorine Miriam Aarons (Paulette Goddard), who is having an affair with Sylvia's husband. Mary and the others check in to a ranch owned by Lucy (Marjorie Main, along with the marvelous Phyllis Povah, the only holdover from the original Broadway cast), a funny and voluble woman. Sylvia arrives, and when she realizes that it was Miriam who stole her husband, a battle ensues between the two women. Mary's surprise, though, is soon tempered as she learns that her former mate, rather than calling her to stop the divorce at the 11th hour, has married Crystal.

Later, when she gets home to New York, Mary discovers that her ex is unhappy in his new marriage, and that Crystal has taken to both spending money with a passion and having an affair with a radio singing cowboy married to the former Countess. Finally showing her mother that she, too, has had her nails done in "Jungle Red", Mary embraces the predatory principles of her friends and artfully tries to win her husband back.

Filled with witty repartee and vicious gossip, THE WOMEN portrays a world where women seem to do nothing but obsess over men. Playwright Clare Boothe always defended her work, claiming that only empty-headed, spoilt rich women were being satirized here. Close examination of the film script, though, reveals considerable insight into female bonding. The several mother-daughter relationships are interestingly portrayed, and even the fights over men, as dramatized in this vast improvement on Boothe's original, are not without their lessons about the roles imposed on women by society.

All the performances are joys. Shearer has never been more restrained, and but for two moments (dropping to her knees to cry at her mother's feet, and the final reconciliation), her performance never falters. Her crying jag in Reno is one of the most convincing of its kind; even technically better actresses like Davis and Hepburn couldn't always pull tears off this well. Another great moment to look for is the way Shearer hits the flowers her errant husband sends her. Crawford, meanwhile, brilliantly revitalized her career with one of her finest acting achievements, a funny, spot-on portrait of the scheming, sexy Crystal. Hard as nails throughout, she uses her velvet voice to great effect, and her parting salvo at the end is a killer ("There's a word for you ladies, but it is seldom used in high society, outside of a kennel"). Russell (in a showcase part that made her a top star) and Goddard (rarely better) are equally good, though perhaps the funniest performance is contributed by the marvelous Boland. Cukor's direction is rich and confident, and the whole production fairly shimmers.

WOMEN IN LOVE

1969 130m c Drama ★★★½
Brandywine (U.K.) R/18

Alan Bates *(Rupert Birkin)*, Oliver Reed *(Gerald Crich)*, Glenda Jackson *(Gudrun Brangwen)*, Jennie Linden *(Ursula Brangwen)*, Eleanor Bron *(Hermione Roddice)*, Alan Webb *(Thomas Crich)*, Vladek Sheybal *(Loerke)*, Catherine Willmer *(Mrs. Crich)*, Sarah Nicholls *(Winifred Crich)*, Sharon Gurney *(Laura Crich)*

p, Larry Kramer; d, Ken Russell; w, Larry Kramer (based on the novel by D.H. Lawrence); ph, Billy Williams; ed, Michael Bradsell; m, Georges Delerue, Peter Ilich Tchaikovsky; art d, Ken Jones; chor, Terry Gilbert; cos, Shirley Russell

AA Best Actress: Glenda Jackson; *AAN Best Director:* Ken Russell; *AAN Best Adapted Screenplay:* Larry Kramer; *AAN Best Cinematography:* Billy Williams

Fine adaptation of D.H. Lawrence's classic novel with some interesting visual sequences typical of director Russell's style.

It is 1920s England. Jackson is a free-thinking artist who, along with her schoolteacher sister, Linden, watches from a graveyard as Gurney and Christopher Gable are married. Later, at an outdoor luncheon given for the couple, the two women meet Reed and Bates. Bates, a school inspector, constantly ruminates on the topic of love and begins a fledgling relationship with Linden. At a picnic at the plush home of Gurney's wealthy family, the newlyweds are lost beneath the dark waters of the estate's lake. When the water is drained from the lake, the two drowned bodies are discovered entwined together in the muddy lake bed. That night Bates and Reed, in a discussion on friendship, strip before a fireplace and engage in a nude wrestling match. After Bates and Linden marry, they go with Reed and Jackson for a honeymoon in Switzerland. Jackson meets Sheybal, a sculptor like herself, and engages in an affair with the bisexual man, when her sister and brother-in-law leave Switzerland. Reed, enraged at Sheybal's intrusion, attacks the man and tries to choke Jackson. Then Reed flees into the snow and wanders until he dies. Bates, stunned by the death, still questions the mystery of relations between men and women.

There are moments of great beauty here, such as the view of Bates and Linden running naked into each other's arms in a wheatfield. The camera is turned horizontally, and the bodies seem to defy gravity, moving up and down within the frame through the golden vegetation. In another, much-heralded piece of editing, Russell cuts from the intertwined bodies of Bates and Linden after a lovemaking session to the cold, stiff corpses of Gurney and Gable on the bottom of the emptied lake. Russell did some of his own camerawork (although Williams received credit as cinematographer) and showed an excellent eye for shot composition and editing rhythms. His ability as a storyteller is less in evidence, however. Despite the passion of the topic and the beauty of the images, the narrative tends toward the static, particularly in the later stages. Russell incorporated many dance images into WOMEN IN LOVE, expanding on what he considered to be a central theme of the novel. He later stated that he "should have turned the whole thing into a musical; it wasn't far off in some ways."

WOMEN ON THE VERGE OF A NERVOUS BREAKDOWN

1988 98m c Drama ★★★★
Lauren Films/El Desea (Spain) /15

Carmen Maura *(Pepa)*, Antonio Banderas *(Carlos)*, Fernando Guillen *(Ivan)*, Julieta Serrano *(Lucia)*, Maria Barranco *(Candela)*, Rossy de Palma *(Marisa)*, Kiti Manver *(Paulina)*, Chus Lampreave, Yayo Calvo, Loles Leon

d, Pedro Almodovar; w, Pedro Almodovar; ph, Jose Luis Alcaine; ed, Jose Salcedo; m, Bernardo Bonezzi; cos, Jose Maria de Cossio

AAN Best Foreign Language Film

In WOMEN ON THE VERGE OF A NERVOUS BREAKDOWN, Pedro Almodovar has written and directed an incisive, fast-paced romp with the serious theme of obsessive love. The film's cascade of missed connections and riotous coincidences is triggered when Ivan (Fernando Guillen) abruptly abandons his longtime lover, Pepa (Carmen Maura). Finding herself pregnant, Pepa frantically tries to track down the elusive Ivan. In the course of her search she discovers some of his secrets, including Lucia (Julieta Serrano), by whom he has fathered a now-grown son. Pepa, distraught and contemplating suicide, prepares a batch of gazpacho laced with enough barbiturates to put a small town into coma and puts her apartment up for rent—after which people start showing up in waves. The pitcher of gazpacho becomes the key to some strange and unexpected events, culminating in a loopy car chase. Almodovar, who was an obscure telephone company employee just six years earlier, consolidates his reputation as a cult moviemaker with this one. He is great at inventing simple but stunning visual jokes and staging running gags. Further, he brings the best out of his uniformly skillful cast, in particular Carmen Maura. An Almodovar regular and consummate farceur, Maura can also play the pathos of the role with moving veracity. The film is flushed with bright light and cartoon hues, nicely accenting the fast-paced stew of incidents.

WONDER MAN

1945 98m c Comedy/Musical ★★★★
Goldwyn (U.S.) /U

Danny Kaye *(Buzzy Bellew/Edwin Dingle)*, Virginia Mayo *(Ellen Shanley)*, Vera-Ellen *(Midge Mallon)*, Donald Woods *(Monte Rossen)*, S.Z. Sakall *(Schmidt)*, Allen Jenkins *(Chimp)*, Edward Brophy *(Torso)*, Steve Cochran *(Ten-Grand Jackson)*, Otto Kruger *(District Attorney R.J. O'Brien)*, Richard Land *(Assistant District Attorney Grosset)*

p, Samuel Goldwyn; d, H. Bruce Humberstone; w, Don Hartman, Melville Shavelson, Philip Rapp, Jack Jevne, Eddie Moran (based on a story by Arthur Sheekman); ph, Victor Milner, William Snyder; ed, Daniel Mandell; m, Ray Heindorf; art d, Ernst Fegte, McClure Capps; fx, John P. Fulton; chor, John Wray

AAN Best Score: Lou Forbes, Ray Heindorf; *AAN Best Song:* David Rose (Music), Leo Robin (Lyrics); *AAN Best Sound:* Gordon Sawyer; *AA Best Visual Effects:* John Fulton, A.W. Johns

In one of his most likable films, Danny Kaye takes on a dual role, playing two brothers—one an entertainer about to marry who is killed when he witnesses a mob hit, and the other an intellectual in love with a librarian. The dead brother's spirit approaches the living brother and asks that he help bring the murderous mobsters to justice. Since the egghead is afraid to get involved, the spirit of the dead brother enters the body of the living one. Not surprisingly, this causes a great deal of confusion, especially for the two women who are now in love with him, the librarian and the dead brother's fiancee. Filled with lots of laughs, WONDER MAN features a splendid performance by Kaye that is spiced with verve and zeal.

WORKING GIRL

1988 113m c Romance ★★★½
Fox (U.S.) R/15

Harrison Ford *(Jack Trainer)*, Melanie Griffith *(Tess McGill)*, Sigourney Weaver *(Katharine Parker)*, Alec Baldwin *(Mick Dugan)*, Joan Cusack *(Cyn)*, Philip Bosco *(Oren Trask)*, Nora Dunn *(Ginny)*, Oliver Platt *(Lutz)*, James Lally *(Turkel)*, Kevin Spacey *(Bob Speck)*

p, Douglas Wick; d, Mike Nichols; w, Kevin Wade; ph, Michael Ballhaus; ed, Sam O'Steen; m, Carly Simon; prod d, Patrizia von Brandenstein; cos, Ann Roth

AAN Best Picture; AAN Best Actress: Melanie Griffith; *AAN Best Supporting Actress:* Sigourney Weaver; *AAN Best Supporting Actress:* Joan Cusack; *AAN Best Director:* Mike Nichols; *AA Best Song:* Carly Simon

Melanie Griffith, excellent in another strong 1988 film, STORMY MONDAY, gives an even more dazzling performance here as Tess McGill, an industrious secretary at a brokerage firm who longs to break out of the secretarial mold. After a run-in with her boss, she finds herself in a last-chance opportunity as the secretary to Katharine Parker (Sigourney Weaver). The astute secretary has an idea for putting together a deal for a client (Philip Bosco). Later, while Katharine recovers from a skiing accident, Tess learns that her boss has been moving ahead on the idea with no apparent intention of giving Tess any credit. Tess decides to engineer the big deal herself, with the help of Jack Trainer (Harrison Ford), an outside deal-maker who also happens to be Katharine's lover. Director Mike Nichols (THE GRADUATE, CATCH-22, BILOXI BLUES) demonstrates again his assured command of the film medium—coaxing outstanding performances from lead and supporting players alike, using the camera to brilliant effect, and infusing the story with tension, romance, and humor. Funny, touching, and ultimately tremendously buoyant—reflecting the optimism engendered by the shortlived 1980s economic boom—WORKING GIRL is a "feel good" movie with some intelligence. However, its Horatio Alger premise—that hard work, pluck, and intelligence are inevitably rewarded in the world of business—may be hard to swallow, particularly in an era of diminishing expectations.

WORKING GIRLS

1986 90m c Drama   ★★★★
Lizzie Borden/Alternate Current (U.S.)   /18

Louise Smith (Molly), Ellen McElduff (Lucy), Amanda Goodwin (Dawn), Marusia Zach (Gina), Janne Peters (April), Helen Nicholas (Mary)

p, Lizzie Borden, Andi Gladstone; d, Lizzie Borden; w, Lizzie Borden, Sandra Kay; ph, Judy Irola; ed, Lizzie Borden; m, David van Tieghem; prod d, Kurt Ossenfort

WORKING GIRLS concentrates on the daily routine of a modern-day Manhattan prostitute in a detached, clinical manner, breaking away from old myths to create an insightful and, in many ways, disturbing interpretation of what has been called the "world's oldest profession." Molly (Louise Smith) is a Yale graduate, nearing 30, who temporarily works in a Manhattan brothel to help make ends meet. The Manhattan brothel she works in appears as a normal office. The girls dress like secretaries, and harmlessly chat about their personal lives, the job, and their general disdain for their boss, as they patiently wait for the day to end so they can go home.

 Director Lizzie Borden's usually sharp eye for detail pervades WORKING GIRLS, and here maintains a high level of interest throughout. The down-to-earth portrayals possess none of the stereotypes popular in media representations of prostitutes, and, as a result, are frighteningly realistic. A film with an interesting and provocative feminist edge.

WORLD ACCORDING TO GARP, THE

1982 136m c Comedy/Drama   ★★½
Pan Arts (U.S.)   R/15

Robin Williams (T.S. Garp), Mary Beth Hurt (Helen Holm), Glenn Close (Jenny Fields), John Lithgow (Roberta Muldoon), Hume Cronyn (Mr. Fields), Jessica Tandy (Mrs. Fields), Swoosie Kurtz (Hooker), James McCall (Young Garp), Peter Michael Goetz (John Wolfe), George Ede (Dean Bodger)

p, George Roy Hill, Robert L. Crawford; d, George Roy Hill; w, Steve Tesich (based on the novel by John Irving); ph, Miroslav Ondricek; ed, Ronald Roose, Stephen A. Rotter; prod d, Henry Bumstead; art d, Woods Mackintosh; cos, Ann Roth; anim, John Canemaker

AAN Best Supporting Actor: John Lithgow; AAN Best Supporting Actress: Glenn Close

Empty shortening of Irving's book reaches for profundity, and comes up courageous but brainless. It's actually a bittersweet string of sketches, attempting to explain a man's growth from birth to adulthood and how he deals with the vices of lust and fanaticism that whirl around him.

 Garp is born to a formidable unmarried mother, Jenny Fields, played by Glenn Close. (The various stages of Garp's childhood are played by Thomas Peter Daikos, Brendon Roth, and James McCall before Robin Williams takes over as Garp reaches young adulthood.) The story follows him through childhood at a boys' prep school, where Jenny is the school nurse, through his high school passions—wrestling, writing,

and sex—to marriage with his high school sweetheart, children, marital disaffection, and a career as a writer. Jenny meanwhile has become a famous feminist, espousing an eccentric cause. The plot details an abundance of comic and tragicomic episodes, outlandish physical, emotional, and sexual adventures. Williams gives another puppy-dog performance—he has yet to land a script that takes advantage of his wildness and anarchy. Although these qualities are undoubtedly couched in the cuteness of Williams's persona, they come from anywhere but. He's like a wild bird with clipped wings. GARP is stolen by Lithgow, who imparts dignity and depth to his role of a king-sized transsexual, and Close's feminist mom. The movie was not a success—even at 136 minutes, GARP still feels like its dialogue and its action are going in opposite directions. Audiences were confused; we're not—we can't work up that much of a lather.

WORLD APART, A

1988 113m c Biography   ★★★★
Working Title/British Screen (U.K.)   PG

Barbara Hershey (Diana Roth), Jodhi May (Molly Roth), Jeroen Krabbe (Gus Roth), Carolyn Clayton-Cragg (Miriam Roth), Merav Gruer (Jude Roth), Yvonne Bryceland (Bertha), Albee Lesotho (Solomon), Linda Mvusi (Elsie), Rosalie Crutchley (Mrs. Harris), Mackay Tickey (Milius)

p, Sarah Radclyffe; d, Chris Menges; w, Shawn Slovo; ph, Peter Biziou; ed, Nicolas Gaster; m, Hans Zimmer; prod d, Brian Morris; cos, Nic Ede

Set in Johannesburg in 1963, A WORLD APART is an utterly convincing, impeccably constructed indictment of apartheid, based on a semi-autobiographical screenplay by Shawn Slovo. (Slovo is the daughter of Joe Slovo, head of the South African Communist Party and one of two white members of the ANC executive council, and Ruth First, who was assassinated by a parcel bomb in Mozambique in 1982.) Jodhi May plays the younger Slovo as a 13-year-old whose world revolves around Spanish dancing lessons, hula-hooping, and swimming in the pool of her equally privileged best friend (Nadine Chalmers). Her world is turned upside down when her father (Jeroen Krabbe), an ANC official, departs in the middle of the night not to return, leaving her journalist mother (Barbara Hershey) both to take care of May and her two younger sisters and to continue the political struggle. Much to May's confusion, Hershey's involvement with the movement makes her, not a bad mother, but a distracted, inattentive one—distant because she fears she cannot trust her daughter with life-and-death secrets. The film is driven by the tension between May's resentment at what she perceives as her mother's neglect of the family, and her gradual acknowledgment of the importance of the political imperatives by which her mother is compelled.

 The feature-film directorial debut of Academy Award-winning cinematographer Chris Menges (THE KILLING FIELDS; THE MISSION), A WORLD APART was the second major film in two years to deal with South African issues, coming soon after Richard Attenborough's 1987 effort, CRY FREEDOM. In A WORLD APART, Menges has chosen to explore apartheid primarily through the eyes of whites, though his black characters—particularly Elsie (Linda Mvusi), the family's live-in maid, and her brother Solomon (Albee Lesotho), a political activist—are considerably more developed than those in Attenborough's film. The performances in A WORLD APART are uniformly excellent, and the extraordinarily moving work of Barbara Hershey, Jodhi May, and Linda Mvusi garnered a shared Best Actress award at the Cannes Film Festival.

WORLD IN HIS ARMS, THE

1952 104m c Adventure   ★★★
Universal (U.S.)   /U

Gregory Peck (Jonathan Clark), Ann Blyth (Countess Marina Selanova), Anthony Quinn (Portugee), John McIntire (Deacon Greathouse), Andrea King (Mamie), Carl Esmond (Prince Semyon), Eugenie Leontovich (Anna Selanova), Sig Rumann (Gen. Ivan Vorashilov), Hans Conried (Eustace), Bryan Forbes (William Cleggett) p, Aaron Rosenberg; d, Raoul Walsh; w, Borden Chase, Horace McCoy (based on the novel by Rex Beach); ph, Russell Metty; ed, Frank Gross; m, Frank Skinner; art d, Bernard Herzbrun, Alexander Golitzen; chor, Hal Belfaer; cos, Bill Thomas

Strong period adventure film set in Alaska that marked the first of three joint projects for Peck and Quinn.

Peck is captain of a vessel that illegally hunts seals. He returns to San Francisco's Barbary Coast after a good voyage and checks into a hotel with his crew. Blyth, a Russian countess, is also a guest there with her coterie of servants. She is fleeing an arranged marriage with Esmond, a Czarist peer, and thinks she can find safety in Sitka, Alaska, under the aegis of her uncle, Rumann, who is the governor general of the area. She approaches Quinn, a Portuguese seal hunter and Peck's rival, and says she'll pay well to be taken north, but Quinn can't raise a crew to make the voyage. When Blyth discovers that Peck has a ship and a crew, she asks him to take her to Alaska. Peck finds her most attractive and doesn't know that royal blood pumps in her veins when he takes her around the city for a nighttime tour of Baghdad by the Bay. By dawn the two become close and decide to get married. They are about to be wed when Esmond, at the helm of a Russian boat, comes into San Francisco harbor, steals Blyth and her entourage, and sets sail for Alaska, promising to kill Rumann if Blyth doesn't fulfill her previous marriage obligation. Peck finds that Blyth is gone, drinks himself into a stupor, has a huge fist fight with Quinn, and winds up broke. To raise money, Peck proposes a bet with Quinn. The two will race to Sitka, and the winner will get the other captain's seal catch as well as his boat. Quinn agrees and the race begins.

Superb sea footage, lots of action, and a robust relationship between Peck and Quinn combine to make this highly enjoyable, despite occasional overtones of anticommunism (this was the time of the Hollywood "witch hunts"). It would be hard to present a seal-hunter as a modern-day hero, but producer Rosenberg and director Walsh admittedly keep the hunting scenes to a minimum. Appearing in his first US film (he'd done two in the UK) is Bryan Forbes, who later abandoned acting for writing, producing, and directing.

WORLD OF APU, THE
(APUR SANSAR)
1959   103m   bw   Drama   ★★★★
Satyajit Ray   (India)   /U

Soumitra Chatterjee (Apurba Kumar Roy), Sharmila Tagore (Aparna), Shapan Mukerji (Pulu), S. Alke Chakravarty (Kajal)

p, Satyajit Ray; d, Satyajit Ray; w, Satyajit Ray (based on the novel Aparajito by Bibhutibhusan Bandopadhaya); ph, Subrata Mitra; ed, Dulal Dutta; m, Ravi Shankar; art d, Banshi Chandra Gupta

THE WORLD OF APU is the third and final installment of Satyajit Ray's "Apu Trilogy," the most famous group of films to come out of India. After following the young character of Apu from his early years (PATHER PANCHALI) to his schooldays (APARAJITO), the trilogy picks up with Soumitra Chatterjee in the role of Apu as a young man. His desire is to become a writer, but a lack of finances has forced him to abandon his university studies. His life changes, however, when he again meets his old friend Pulu (Shapan Mukerji). Together, the two travel to the wedding of Pulu's cousin, Aparna (Sharmila Tagore). When the bridegroom turns out to be insane and the wedding is canceled, Apu agrees to marry Aparna to save her from ridicule. They return to his Calcutta apartment to start a new life, but destiny does not look kindly upon the newlyweds. In this final entry, Ray rounds out the life of Apu, charting his loss of innocence and painting a detailed and textured portrait of Indian life in the process. In Apu, Ray has brought to the screen a character who lives out his story, though he is never able to finally put it on paper. A rich and insightful picture, THE WORLD OF APU, despite being rooted deep in Indian culture, strikes a universal humanistic chord. Exquisitely photographed and scored.

WORLD OF HENRY ORIENT, THE
1964   115m   c   Comedy   ★★★
UA   (U.S.)   /U

Peter Sellers (Henry Orient), Paula Prentiss (Stella), Tippy Walker (Valerie Boyd), Merrie Spaeth (Marian "Gil" Gilbert), Angela Lansbury (Isabel Boyd), Tom Bosley (Frank Boyd), Phyllis Thaxter (Mrs. Gilbert), Bibi Osterwald (Boothy), Peter Duchin (Joe Byrd), John Fiedler (Sidney)

p, Jerome Hellman; d, George Roy Hill; w, Nora Johnson, Nunnally Johnson (based on the novel by Nora Johnson); ph, Boris Kaufman, Arthur J. Ornitz; ed, Stuart Gilmore; m, Elmer Bernstein, Ken Lauber; prod d, James Sullivan; art d, Jan Scott; fx, Dick Smith; cos, Ann Roth

THE WORLD OF HENRY ORIENT is a charming comedy about the agony of adolescent infatuation. Walker and Spaeth are boarding school chums who keep busy pursuing egotistical concert pianist Sellers. The girls, just 14 or so, believe that they are in love with Sellers, a Casanova whose latest conquest is the married Prentiss. Prentiss is convinced that the girls have been hired by her husband to trail her, and after that the groupies' idolatry creates a number of ridiculous situations. This is one of the rare films in which someone steals scenes from Sellers. Walker and Spaeth are a joy—with none of the professional, cloying sweetness so often seen in younger performers—and the best part of the movie is the depiction of the girls, which never strays from truth, even when the teens are on wild flights of fancy. Director George Roy Hill made another, equally charming, tale of young love 15 years later: A LITTLE ROMANCE.

WRITTEN ON THE WIND
1956   99m   c   Drama   ★★★★½
Universal   (U.S.)   /A

Rock Hudson (Mitch Wayne), Lauren Bacall (Lucy Moore Hadley), Robert Stack (Kyle Hadley), Dorothy Malone (Marylee Hadley), Robert Keith (Jasper Hadley), Grant Williams (Biff Miley), Bob Wilke (Dan Willis), Edward Platt (Dr. Paul Cochrane), Harry Shannon (Hoak Wayne), John Larch (Roy Carter)

p, Albert Zugsmith; d, Douglas Sirk; w, George Zuckerman (based on the novel by Robert Wilder); ph, Russell Metty; ed, Russell Schoengarth; m, Frank Skinner; art d, Alexander Golitzen, Robert Clatworthy; fx, Clifford Stine; cos, Bill Thomas, Jay A. Morley Jr.

AAN Best Supporting Actor: Robert Stack; AA Best Supporting Actress: Dorothy Malone; AAN Best Song: Victor Young (Music), Sammy Cahn (Lyrics)

The ultimate in lush melodrama, WRITTEN ON THE WIND is, along with IMITATION OF LIFE, Douglas Sirk's finest directorial effort, and one of the most notable critiques of the American family ever made.

A Texas oil baron (Stack) has a whirlwind romance with a secretary (Bacall) and then marries her, but later has doubts as to whether the child she is expecting is really his. Stacks's nymphomaniac sister (Malone) stokes up his suspicions that his best friend, geologist Rock Hudson, is really the father, and sets off a series of larger-than-life confrontations and crises from which no-one escapes lightly.

WRITTEN ON THE WIND successfully combines all the elements of the genre that has has become synonymous with Sirk's name. Sirk's melodrama, though, diverges from what is usually understood by that term to encompass a highly developed sense of ironic social critique. Some critics have seen his sumptuous visual style, full of parody and cliche, as a kind of Brechtian distancing that draws attention to the artificiality of the film medium, in turn commenting on the hollowness of middle-class American life. The lake in WRITTEN ON THE WIND, for example, is presented as a patently artificial studio interior, ironically pointing up the romantic self-delusion with which Malone sees her world.

WRONG BOX, THE

1966 107m c Comedy   ★★★
Salamander (U.K.)   /U

John Mills (*Masterman Finsbury*), Ralph Richardson (*Joseph Finsbury*), Michael Caine (*Michael Finsbury*), Peter Cook (*Morris Finsbury*), Dudley Moore (*John Finsbury*), Nanette Newman (*Julia Finsbury*), Tony Hancock (*Detective*), Peter Sellers (*Dr. Pratt*), Cicely Courtneidge (*Maj. Martha*), Wilfrid Lawson (*Peacock*)

p, Bryan Forbes; d, Bryan Forbes; w, Larry Gelbart, Burt Shevelove (based on the novel by Robert Louis Stevenson, Lloyd Osbourne); ph, Gerry Turpin; ed, Alan Osbiston; m, John Barry; art d, Ray Simm; cos, Julie Harris

This funny period comedy is based on a story coauthored by Robert Louis Stevenson and Lloyd Osbourne in the last century. Americans Gelbart and Shevelove expanded on the tale, adding a great deal of comedy and writing the script for this gag-filled farce.

Mills and Richardson are brothers in Victorian London. They haven't seen each other for four decades, and for good reason. When they were young lads, they were part of a multi-youth "tontine" and they are the last survivors of the odd pact. Years before, several parents had tossed about $2,800 each into a pool. As the calendar pages were ripped off, the money began to mount through good investments, until it is now quite a bundle. In an extended series of gags, we see how the other members of the strange lottery have gone to their final destinies. Meanwhile, the brothers are each awaiting the news that the other has died, so the remaining one can have all the money.

Sellers is on screen only a few minutes but registers quite well, as does Lawson as the butler. The picture is shot like a British version of a Mack Sennett film, replete with subtitles. All of the smaller roles are deliciously cast, with several of the best comic actors England had to offer in that decade, a heyday of British humor. The picture gets flabby from time to time but comes alive when the old masters, Mills and Richardson, are on screen. The plot works, but there are so many sight gags that fall flat, it begins to pall occasionally. The score is by John Barry and The Temperance Seven perform funeral and military airs.

WRONG MAN, THE

1956 105m bw Crime   ★★★★★
Warner Bros. (U.S.)   /PG

Henry Fonda (*Christopher Emmanuel "Manny" Balestrero*), Vera Miles (*Rose Balestrero*), Anthony Quayle (*Frank O'Connor*), Harold J. Stone (*Lt. Bowers*), Esther Minciotti (*Mrs. Balestrero*), Charles Cooper (*Detective Matthews*), Nehemiah Persoff (*Gene Conforti*), Laurinda Barrett (*Constance Willis*), Norma Connolly (*Betty Todd*), Doreen Lang (*Ann James*)

p, Alfred Hitchcock; d, Alfred Hitchcock; w, Maxwell Anderson, Angus Macphail (based on "The True Story of Christopher Emmanuel Balestrero" by Anderson); ph, Robert Burks; ed, George Tomasini; m, Bernard Herrmann; art d, Paul Sylbert, William L. Kuehl

The bleakest of Hitchcock's films, this stark, deliberate probing of a man wrongfully accused is almost wholly based on fact, creating its drama from a celebrated New York City case. Fonda plays Manny Balestrero, a family man who plays stand-up bass at a Queens nightspot called the Stork Club. Although he doesn't have much money, he manages to keep his life together with the help of his devoted wife, Rose (Miles). When she complains of dental pains, Manny decides to borrow on her life insurance policy (the last place they can borrow money since their debts have already piled too high) to pay for medical attention. Although he makes a practice of picking horses in the race section of the newspaper, he never dares to actually bet on them even though a win could get him out of debt. The following morning, Manny goes to the insurance office where he is identified by the office girls as the man who had robbed them previously. Later that night, he is arrested at the Stork Club. After being identified by a number of witnesses, Manny is interrogated at the police station. When he makes a nervous mistake in a handwriting test (misspelling the word "drawer" as "draw"—the same mistake made on the robber's ransom note), he is fingerprinted, photographed, and imprisoned. Finally released on bail, Manny is joyfully reunited with Rose and hires defense attorney (Quayle). When Manny cannot find any witnesses to provide his alibi,

the prospect of an acquittal looks dim. Meanwhile, Rose begins to crack under the pressure and is no longer able to deal with her husband's trial and defense. Although legal justice is ultimately served, Manny's family must nonetheless pay a considerable price for his freedom.

Having become accustomed to the lighter, more commercial tone of such films as TO CATCH A THIEF; THE TROUBLE WITH HARRY; and THE MAN WHO KNEW TOO MUCH, the public was taken aback when they viewed the unexpectedly bleak, hopeless, Kafka-esque style (more frightening than Orson Welles's THE TRIAL) of THE WRONG MAN. Basing the film on incidents occurring to a real-life Queens bass player that began with his arrest on January 13, 1953 (Hitchcock learned of the case through a *Life* magazine article), Hitchcock takes us to the actual locations—the Stork Club, a Long Island Prudential insurance office, Balestrero's 74th Street Queens home, the asylum where his wife was committed, the actual police station, and Balestrero's prison cell—with the intent of representing the case in all its authenticity. Hitchcock spares us nothing in procedural terms. The questioning of the suspect, for example, is done in necessary tedium, wearing down the audience as much as Fonda's character. We see him fingerprinted—the ink being applied to his fingertips, the printing, the paper he is given to clean his hands. We are forced to sit through the entirety of his handwriting analysis as well. In THE WRONG MAN Hitchcock has succeeded in filming a true story that is indeed Hitchcockian—the idea of the wrong man accused—as if to present evidence to any critics or viewers who thought the director's films were not credible. To add legitimacy to the story's events, Hitchcock even tacked on a prologue in which he introduced himself and then verified that the story about to be shown was based on fact. While the film centers chiefly on Manny's trauma, Hitchcock doesn't ignore the mental torture Rose is put through, temporarily departing from the story of Fonda's conviction to delve further into her problems. It was Miles's first of two appearances in a Hitchcock film (PSYCHO was the second), although she did act in the first episode of the director's television series "Alfred Hitchcock Presents. . . " (one of the handful to be directed by Hitchcock himself). Hitchcock planned to cast her in VERTIGO but had to cast Kim Novak instead when the newly wed actress became pregnant. Don't look for Hitchcock's trademark cameo in this picture; he had originally intended to be seen as a customer walking into the Stork Club but edited himself out of the final print. There are a few other interesting appearances, however—Harry Dean Stanton in one of his countless minor roles, and two giggling girls who later found fame, Bonnie Franklin and Tuesday Weld.

WUTHERING HEIGHTS

1939 103m bw Romance   ★★★★½
Goldwyn (U.S.)   /U

Merle Oberon (*Cathy Linton*), Laurence Olivier (*Heathcliff*), David Niven (*Edgar Linton*), Donald Crisp (*Dr. Kenneth*), Flora Robson (*Ellen Dean*), Hugh Williams (*Hindley Earnshaw*), Geraldine Fitzgerald (*Isabella Linton*), Leo G. Carroll (*Joseph*), Cecil Humphreys (*Judge Linton*), Miles Mander (*Lockwood*)

p, Samuel Goldwyn; d, William Wyler; w, Ben Hecht, Charles MacArthur (based on the novel by Emily Bronte); ph, Gregg Toland; ed, Daniel Mandell; art d, James Vasevi; cos, Omar Kiam

AAN Best Picture; *AAN Best Actor:* Laurence Olivier; *AAN Best Supporting Actress:* Geraldine Fitzgerald; *AAN Best Director:* William Wyler; *AAN Best Screenplay:* Ben Hecht, Charles MacArthur; *AA Best Cinematography:* Gregg Toland; *AAN Best Score:* Alfred Newman; *AAN Best Art Direction:* James Basevi

Haunting, beautiful film version of Emily Bronte's tragic novel, with Olivier at his romance period peak, but marred slightly by Oberon's relative lack of passion.

WUTHERING HEIGHTS is a beautifully told story, displaying impeccable talent both in front of and behind the camera. Wyler had been interested in Bronte's story as a vehicle for Charles Boyer and Sylvia Sidney, who had starred in his 1937 film DEAD END. Hecht and MacArthur were assigned to write the film, and they headed for the island home of drama critic Alexander Woolcott. Here they labored to create a script faithful to the novel, though Woolcott was convinced the two writers would destroy Bronte's passionate and poetic story. Wyler eventually got Goldwyn to back the script, though Boyer was no longer being considered for the lead. The next choice was Olivier, a relative unknown to American audiences at the time. Hecht, who was an uncredited writer on QUEEN CHRISTINA, remembered Olivier from that film. The Briton had originally been hired to play opposite Garbo in that film, but was removed from the production in favor of John Gilbert. Olivier was furious, and had harbored ill feelings towards Hollywood ever since. He was interested in the part of Heathcliff however, and agreed to portray the doomed lover only if his wife, Vivien Leigh, could be his Cathy. But Oberon had already been signed for the role, and Goldwyn would not consider firing her. Leigh was offered the role of Olivier's unloved wife instead, but she turned this down, saying she felt more akin to the tragic lead character. Besides, Leigh had already been featured as the lead in several British films and was simply unwilling to step down for Hollywood. Eventually Olivier agreed to take the role, and Leigh ended up playing Scarlett O'Hara in GONE WITH THE WIND that year. Olivier and Oberon had previously appeared together in THE DIVORCE OF LADY X, a 1938 British film; many believe they made an unforgettable romantic duo.

Though the film understandably condenses Bronte's lengthy novel, Goldwyn spared no expense in creating the right atmosphere for the picture. A tract of 450 acres of land in California's Conejo Hills was transformed into authentic-looking English moors. One thousand heather plants were transplanted, and Goldwyn completed his re-creation by building a period manor on the site. However, he switched the novel's period from the original Regency to the Georgian era. His reasoning was simple: the Georgian period was marked by fancier dresses for women, and he was eager to show off Oberon in beautiful costumes. Gregg Toland won an Academy Award for his brilliant photography, a moody black-and-white perfectly suited to the material.

WUTHERING HEIGHTS
(ABISMOS DE PASION)
1953 90m bw Romance ★★★★
Tepeyac (Mexico)

Irasema Dilian (*Catalina*), Jorge Mistral (*Alejandro*), Lilia Prado, Ernesto Alonso, Luis Aceves Castaneda, Francisco Reiguera, Hortensia Santovena, Jaime Gonzalez

p, Oscar Dancigers; d, Luis Bunuel; w, Luis Bunuel, Julio Alejandro, Dino Maiuri (based on the novel by Emily Bronte); ph, Agustin Jiminez; ed, Carlos Savage; m, Raul Lavista, Richard Wagner

Luis Bunuel's long-planned version of Emily Bronte's novel (the screenplay was written some 20 years before the film was made, but no backer could be found), a favorite work of the Surrealists, shifts the setting from the English moors to a small Mexican estate and turns Heathcliff into Alejandro (Jorge Mistral) and Cathy into Catalina (Irasema Dilian). As the Spanish title implies, the lovers fall into an "abyss of passion"—a place where love exists above and beyond all else. Unlike Hollywood's sanitized backlot version of Bronte, Bunuel's reworking is rooted in the darker aspects of love. The film opens with a slow-motion image of crows as they scatter from a twisted, leafless tree, frightened by an off-screen gunshot. This image of death and decay hangs over the film. The film is flawed (the acting is flatter than usual, the emphasis is overly literary), but it is one of the most passionate and expressionistic works of Bunuel's Mexican period, featuring an ending as brilliant as anything ever accomplished by a surrealist artist.

"X"—THE MAN WITH THE X-RAY EYES
1963 80m c Science Fiction ★★★½
Alta Vista (U.S.)

Ray Milland (*Dr. James Xavier*), Diana Van Der Vlis (*Dr. Diane Fairfax*), Harold J. Stone (*Dr. Sam Brant*), John Hoyt (*Dr. Willard Benson*), Don Rickles (*Crane*), John Dierkes (*Preacher*), Lorie Summers (*Party Dancer*), Vicki Lee (*Young Girl Patient*), Kathryn Hart (*Mrs. Mart*), Carol Irey (*Woman Patient*)

p, Roger Corman; d, Roger Corman; w, Robert Dillon, Ray Russell (based on his story); ph, Floyd Crosby; ed, Anthony Carras; m, Les Baxter; art d, Daniel Haller; fx, Butler-Glouner, Inc.; cos, Marjorie Corso

Memorable, viscerally disturbing sci-fi/horror picture with Ray Milland as Dr. Xavier, a medical scientist who develops a serum that gives him X-ray vision. He's able to see through paper, clothes, and skin (a valuable asset to have around the operating room). As his powers grow stronger, he becomes increasingly demented and loses his job, signing up with a sideshow tout (Don Rickles) as a mind reader. His condition now causes him pain so severe that he needs to wear lead glasses. In agony and desperation, Xavier flees, eventually smashing his car and wandering into a revival meeting. There he hears a preacher quoting the Bible: "If thine eye offend thee, pluck it out." At wit's end, Dr. Xavier chooses to interpret the admonition literally. One of Roger Corman's finest directorial efforts, the movie took top honors at the Trieste Science Fiction Film Festival. In his book of casual horror criticism, *Danse Macabre*, Stephen King claims to have heard of an alternative ending that Corman deemed too horrifying: after tearing out his eyes, Dr. Xavier is supposed to have screamed, "I can still see!"

YAABA
1989 90m c Drama ★★★★
Arcadia/L'Avenir/Thelma/Suisse Romande TV/ZDF /PG
/La Sept/Centre de la Cinemagraphic/Department des
Affaires Etrangeres/Coe (Burkina Faso)

Fatimata Sanga (*Yaaba*), Noufou Ouedraogo (*Bila*), Roukietou Barry (*Nopoko*), Adama Ouedraogo (*Kougri*), Amade Toure (*Tibo*), Sibidou Ouedraogo (*Poko*), Adama Sidibe (*Razougou*), Rasmane Ouedraogo (*Noaga*), Kinda Moumouni (*Finse*), Assita Ouedraogo (*Koudi*)

p, Freddy Denaes, Michel David, Pierre-Alain Meier, Idressa Ouedraogo; d, Idressa Ouedraogo; w, Idressa Ouedraogo; ph, Matthias Kalin; ed, Loredana Cristelli; m, Francis Bebey

Set in a village in Burkina Faso, YAABA concerns two young cousins, Bila (Noufou Ouedraogo) and Nopoko (Roukietou Barry), whose lives are forever changed by their association with the mysterious Sana (Fatimata Sanga), an old woman who has been branded a witch and ostracized by the adults in their village. While carefully depicting the social codes of the village's quarrelsome extended family, director Idrissa Ouedraogo pits the innocence of Bila and Nopoko against the intrigue and superstition among the elders. The curious and sensitive Bila becomes something of a "problem child" when he develops a relationship with the outcast Sana—who, far from being a witch, is a contemplative sort given to dispensing small nuggets of wisdom. Bila savors these nuggets and respectfully calls her "Yaaba" (Grandmother). When Nopoko suffers an injury that leads to an infection that is misdiagnosed as malaria, Sana journeys to get a healer to help her. However, the villagers continue to persecute Sana right up to the film's touching closing.

The winner of the International Critics Prize at the 1989 Cannes Film Festival, YAABA is a visually striking, poignant film that communicates much through refreshingly economical means. Director Ouedraogo (YAM DAABO) filmed this elegant work in his own village, using a nonprofessional cast that renders uniformly convincing and natural performances. Relying on deft *mise-en-scene*, Ouedraogo captures the village's unique rhythms with precision and wrests great emotional power from the simple story.

YAKUZA, THE

1975 112m c Crime ★★★½
Warner Bros./Toei (U.S./Japan) R/AA

Robert Mitchum (*Harry Kilmer*), Ken Takakura (*Tanaka Ken*), Brian Keith (*George Tanner*), Herb Edelman (*Oliver Wheat*), Richard Jordan (*Dusty*), Kishi Keiko (*Tanaka Eiko*), Okada Eiji (*Tono Toshiro*), James Shigeta (*Goro*), Kyosuke Mashida (*Kato Jiro*), Christina Kokubo (*Hanako*)

p, Sydney Pollack; d, Sydney Pollack; w, Paul Schrader, Robert Towne (based on a story by Leonard Schrader); ph, Okazaki Kozo, Duke Callaghan; ed, Fredric Steinkamp, Thomas Stanford, Don Guidice; m, Dave Grusin; prod d, Stephen Grimes; art d, Ishida Yoshiyuki; fx, Richard Parker, Kasai Tomoo; cos, Dorothy Jeakins

Interesting and well-acted, if clumsy, American take on the Japanese gangster genre. Robert Mitchum stars as a private detective who goes to Japan to rescue an American girl who has been kidnapped by a yakuza, with Japanese screen idol Ken Takakura as a former gangster who helps him in his quest. Kishi Keiko plays a woman with whom Mitchum had had a love affair while stationed in Japan at the end of WWII, and whom he now re-encounters.

Written by Paul Schrader from a story by his brother Leonard (the screenplay was then rewritten by famed script doctor Robert Towne), THE YAKUZA was a commendable attempt to expose American audiences to some of the conventions of Japanese genre films. By making the Ken character an anachronistic yakuza who still lives by the codes of the past (he's described as a "lone wolf" by his brother) while trying to exist in present-day capitalist Japan, the filmmakers were able to interestingly compare ancient rituals and values with more contemporary practices. Director Pollack does a workmanlike job, neither giving added resonance to the material, nor ruining a good idea with overbearing direction. His camera is just there to record the performances and really does little else. This film belongs to the actors, and they succeed in making it fascinating viewing. Co-screenwriter Paul Schrader is a student of Japanese culture and cinema, and his obsession with their notion of honor and sacrifice climaxed in 1985 with MISHIMA.

YANKEE DOODLE DANDY

1942 126m bw Musical ★★★★★
Warner Bros. (U.S.) /U

James Cagney (*George M. Cohan*), Joan Leslie (*Mary*), Walter Huston (*Jerry Cohan*), Richard Whorf (*Sam Harris*), George Tobias (*Dietz*), Irene Manning (*Fay Templeton*), Rosemary DeCamp (*Nellie Cohan*), Jeanne Cagney (*Josie Cohan*), S.Z. Sakall (*Schwab*), George Barbier (*Erlanger*)

p, William Cagney; d, Michael Curtiz; w, Robert Buckner, Edmund Joseph (based on a story by Robert Buckner); ph, James Wong Howe; ed, George Amy; art d, Carl Jules Weyl; chor, LeRoy Prinz, Seymour Felix, John Boyle; cos, Milo Anderson

AAN Best Picture; AA Best Actor: James Cagney; *AAN Best Supporting Actor:* Walter Huston; *AAN Best Director:* Michael Curtiz; *AAN Best Original Story:* Robert Buckner; *AAN Best Editing:* George Amy; *AA Best Score:* Ray Heindorf, Heinz Roemheld; *AA Best Sound:* Nathan Levinson

The real George M. Cohan had just had a serious operation and was recuperating at his upstate New York home when he was shown, in a private screening, this film of his life starring the indefatigable James Cagney. The great showman watched the movie without a word. When it was finished he was asked how he liked it. Cohan grinned, shook his head, and paid the great Cagney his highest compliment: "My God, what an act to follow!" This beguiling film, which deservedly won Cagney a Best Actor Oscar, presents an irresistible portrait of song-and-dance man Cohan and of early 20th-century America. It's heartfelt entertainment and anyone who ever whistled a tune, tapped a toe or hummed a bar of music will love it. This was Cagney's favorite film and his favorite number was, in his own words, "when I did the 'wings' coming down the stairs at the White House. Didn't think of it until five minutes before I went on. I didn't consult with the director or anything, I just did it."

YEAR OF LIVING DANGEROUSLY, THE

1983 115m c Adventure/Romance ★★★½
MGM (Australia) PG

Mel Gibson (*Guy Hamilton*), Sigourney Weaver (*Jill Bryant*), Linda Hunt (*Billy Kwan*), Michael Murphy (*Pete Curtis*), Bembol Roco (*Kumar*), Domingo Landicho (*Hortono*), Hermono De Guzman (*Immigration Officer*), Noel Ferrier (*Wally O'Sullivan*), Paul Sonkkila (*Kevin Condon*), Ali Nur (*Ali*)

p, James McElroy; d, Peter Weir; w, David Williamson, Peter Weir, C.J. Koch (based on the novel by Koch); ph, Russell Boyd; ed, Bill Anderson; m, Maurice Jarre; art d, Herbert Pinter; cos, Terry Ryan

AA Best Supporting Actress: Linda Hunt

Ambitious, stylish, and ideologically confused, THE YEAR OF LIVING DANGEROUSLY falters in its attempts to succeed simultaneously as thriller, romance, and political tract, while also encompassing director Peter Weir's penchant for half-baked mysticism. Still, it's a gripping film, set in 1965 as Australian reporter Guy Hamilton (Gibson) arrives in Jakarta, Indonesia. His photographer, Billy Kwan (Hunt), a Chinese-Australian, shows him the ropes, introducing him to the city's poverty and corruption and to various contacts, including Jill Bryant (Weaver), an embassy attache with whom Guy begins a romance. When Jill secures information on a planned Communist coup against President Sukarno and urges Guy to leave, he betrays her confidence and files a major story—for which she is the obvious source. Billy, previously a fence-sitter, now comes out against Sukarno, feeling that he has betrayed Indonesia in much the same way as Guy betrayed Jill (whom Billy also loves). Revolt and reaction explode on all sides.

Weir is only partly successful in attempting to link his various themes symbolically with reflexive images of Indonesian shadow puppetry and Billy's advice to "look at the shadows, not at the puppets," but the director indisputably made the right move in his risky casting of the tiny, gravel-voiced Hunt to play Billy Kwan. Physically convincing in the role, Hunt's achievement is not merely cosmetic; her Billy negotiates among a compelling range of motivations and emotions. Gibson and Weaver, too, enjoy two of their few interesting roles to date, and respond to the challenges put them with intensity and intelligence. The film's hot, humid, seedy ambience is nearly palpable, enhancing this fascinating story of Sukarno's downfall.

Unfortunately, the film's politics are puerile—Weir appears to endorse Kwan's smug rejection of social reform in favor of individual charity—and its historical material is sketchy and misleading. Viewers not already familiar with the events of 1965 in Indonesia will come away no wiser; in particular, they will not learn that the "Communist coup" was an invented cover story for a CIA-engineered military coup against Sukarno that led to one of the bloodiest massacres of the post-war era (according to most estimates, some 500,000 alleged Communists and Sukarno supporters were slaughtered in the space of a few weeks). Considered purely as a romantic adventure, the film mightn't need come to grips with such unpleasant realities, but it desperately wants to be taken seriously. Taken seriously, it largely fails.

YEARLING, THE

1946 134m c Drama ★★★★
MGM (U.S.) /U

Gregory Peck (*Pa Baxter*), Jane Wyman (*Ma Baxter*), Claude Jarman Jr. (*Jody Baxter*), Chill Wills (*Buck Forrester*), Clem Bevans (*Pa Forrester*), Margaret Wycherly (*Ma Forrester*), Henry Travers (*Mr. Boyles*), Forrest Tucker (*Lem Forrester*), Donn Gift (*Fodderwing*), Dan White (*Millwheel*)

p, Sidney Franklin; d, Clarence Brown; w, Paul Osborn (based on the novel by Marjorie Kinnan Rawlings); ph, Charles Rosher, Leonard Smith, Arthur E. Arling; ed, Harold F. Kress; m, Herbert Stothart; art d, Cedric Gibbons, Paul Groesse; fx, Warren Newcombe, Chester M. Franklin

AAN Best Picture; AAN Best Actor: Gregory Peck; *AAN Best Actress:* Jane Wyman; *AAN Best Director:* Clarence Brown; *AA Best Cinematography:* Charles Rosher, Leonard Smith, Arthur Arling; *AAN Best Editing:* Harold Kress; *AA Best Art Direction:* Cedric Gibbons, Paul Groesse, Edwin B. Willis

THE YEARLING is a splendid family film set just after the Civil War in the wilds of southern Florida, where the Baxters—Ma, Pa, and their one surviving child, Jody (Gregory Peck, Jane Wyman, and Claude Jarman)—are having a tough time eking out a living on their small farm. Pa's ambition is to earn enough from his next crop to be able to sink a well nearer the house, so that Ma won't have to tote water. As an only child in the wilderness, Jody needs some company and asks his parents if he might have a pet. When Pa is bitten by a rattlesnake and in danger of dying, Ma and Jody must kill a deer and make an elixir out of its innards. The doe has a fawn, and when Jody begs his parents to allow him to raise the baby, they do. Time passes and the bond between boy and animal deepens, but as the deer grows it begins eating some of the crops so vital to the family's existence. Pa is left with no choice but to tell Jody that the youth must kill his beloved companion. Similar to OLD YELLER in its lessons, THE YEARLING was a huge success and one of MGM's top moneymakers. A remarkable film that is truly for the entire family.

YELLOW EARTH

1984   89m   c   Drama   ★★★½
World Entertainment Release   (China)   /U

Xue Bai *(Ciu Qiao)*, Wang Xueqi *(Gu Qing)*, Tan Tuo *(The Father)*, Liu Qiang *(Hanhan)*

d, Chen Kaige; w, Zhang Ziliang (based on the essay "Sanwen" by Ke Lan); ph, Zhang Yimou

One of a handful of films by the group of young Chinese directors labeled "the Fifth Generation," YELLOW EARTH is set during the skirmishes between China and Japan prior to WWII. Xueqi plays a communist soldier studying the local folk songs of the Shaanxi province. He settles in the house of Tuo, a farmer who continues to plough his barren land in the hope the gods will reward him with a good crop. Along with Tuo is his 10-year-old son, and 14-year-old daughter, Bai, rumored to have the most beautiful voice in the province. The taciturn family slowly begins to open up to Xueqi as he helps them with their daily work, but the tension between his "progressive" ideals and the time-honored protocols of village life leads to tragedy.

   YELLOW EARTH was one of the first "Fifth Generation" films to reach Western eyes and was justifiably celebrated for its daring, colorful visuals and innovative, eye-opening rhythms.

YELLOW SUBMARINE

1968   85m   c   Animated/Musical   ★★★½
King Features/Subafilms   (U.K.)   G/U

Paul McCartney, John Lennon, Ringo Starr, George Harrison *(The Beatles)*, VOICES OF: John Clive *(John)*, Geoffrey Hughes *(Paul)*, Peter Batten *(George)*, Paul Angelis *(Ringo/Chief Blue Meanie)*, Dick Emery *(Lord Mayor/Nowhere Man/Max)*, Lance Percival *(Old Fred)*

p, Al Brodax; d, George Dunning; w, Lee Minoff, Al Brodax, Erich Segal, Jack Mendelsohn (based on a story by Minoff, from the song by John Lennon and Paul McCartney); ph, John Williams; ed, Brian J. Bishop; art d, Heinz Edelmann; fx, Charles Jenkins; anim, Jack Stokes, Robert Balser

A zesty, satisfying celebration of animation, fantasy, love, and the Beatles that pleases the eyes as much as the ears. YELLOW SUBMARINE tells the glorious tale of a make-believe world inhabited by Blue Meanies, a wicked little bunch who suck the color out of people and bop them on the heads with apples. The Beatles and Old Fred are called in to stop the Blue Meanies' rage. The singing heroes hop in their yellow submarine and sail the seas—of green, of science, of time, of monsters, and, best of all, of holes—until they finally reach Pepperland and straighten out the villains by overpowering them with love, love, love. The animation is superb, filled with exciting and unexpected transformations that are thoughtfully complemented by the music. The Fab Four themselves appear in the live-action coda. This was the first animated feature made in Britain in 14 years; no wonder everyone got a hand in it. Director Dunning contributed the memorable "Lucy" section himself. Erich Segal, who wrote the fast-food romance *Love Story*, had a hand in the script.

YENTL

1983   134m   c   Musical   ★★★
Ladbroke/Barwood   (U.S.)   PG

Barbra Streisand *(Yentl)*, Mandy Patinkin *(Avigdor)*, Amy Irving *(Hadass)*, Nehemiah Persoff *(Papa)*, Steven Hill *(Reb Alter Vishkower)*, Allan Corduner *(Shimmele)*, Ruth Goring *(Esther Rachel)*, David De Keyser *(Rabbi Zalman)*, Bernard Spear *(Tailor)*, Doreen Mantle *(Mrs. Shaemen)*

p, Barbra Streisand, Rusty Lemorande; d, Barbra Streisand; w, Barbra Streisand, Jack Rosenthal (based on the short story "Yentl, the Yeshiva Boy" by Isaac Bashevis Singer); ph, David Watkin; ed, Terry Rawlings; m, Michel Legrand; prod d, Roy Walker; art d, Leslie Tomkins; fx, Alan Whibley; chor, Gillian Lynne; cos, Judy Moorcroft

AAN Best Supporting Actress: Amy Irving; *AA Best Score:* Michel Legrand, Alan Bergman, Marilyn Bergman; *AAN Best Song:* Michel Legrand (Music), Alan Bergman (Lyrics), Marilyn Bergman (Lyrics); *AAN Best Song:* Michel Legrand; *AAN Best Art Direction:* Roy Walker, Leslie Tomkins, Tessa Davies

Isaac Bashevis Singer's beautiful short story "Yentl, the Yeshiva Boy" is turned into a musical ego trip in Barbra Streisand's directorial debut. Set in Eastern Europe in 1904, the story concerns the fortunes of Yentl (Streisand), a girl who wants to study the Torah. Strict Jewish law prohibits such knowledge for women, but Yentl won't give in to community pressure, so, after the death of her father, she disguises herself as a young man and leaves home, hoping to be accepted into a yeshiva. In this guise, she falls in love with fellow student Avigdor (Mandy Patinkin), who takes a liking to young Yentl, but never realizes that his friend is really a woman. When Avigdor's engagement to Hadass (Amy Irving) breaks off because her parents disapprove of him, Avigdor asks Yentl to marry Hadass in his stead. Can the deception continue?

   Streisand has undertaken an extremely ambitious project to mark her directorial debut and, while far from perfect, the superstar performer shows undeniable promise. The production values are topflight but Streisand lacks visual skill and relies on the musical numbers to link episodes and detail character motivation. In the opening sequences these songs, all sung by Streisand and structured as musical soliloquies, work quite well but they later become repetitious and intrusive—important characters are tossed aside to make room for her to belt out another tune. In all fairness, however, Streisand is actually quite credible in her role and she elicits beautifully shaded performances from a large cast, particularly Patinkin and Irving. Streisand owned the movie rights to Singer's story for 14 years and finally acquired the clout to bring the project to life after many years of trying. Singer, however, was appalled by the film.

YESTERDAY, TODAY, AND TOMORROW
(IERI, OGGI E DOMANI)

1963   119m   c   Comedy/Drama   ★★★
C.C. Champion/Concordia   (Italy/France)   /X

Sophia Loren *(Adelina/Anna/Mara)*, Marcello Mastroianni *(Carmine/Renzo/Augusto Rusconi)*, Aldo Giuffre *(Pasquale Nardella)*, Agostino Salvietti *(Lawyer Verace)*, Lino Mattera *(Amadeo Scapece)*, Tecla Scarano *(Bianchina Verace)*, Silvia Monelli *(Elvira Nardella)*, Carlo Croccolo *(Auctioneer)*, Pasquale Cennamo *(Police Captian)*, Armando Trovajoli *(Other Man)*

p, Carlo Ponti; d, Vittorio De Sica; w, Eduardo De Filippo, Isabella Quarantini, Cesare Zavattini, Billa Billa Zanuso (based on the story "Troppo Ricca" by Alberto Moravia); ph, Giuseppe Rotunno; ed, Adriana Novelli; m, Armando Trovajoli; art d, Ezio Frigerio; chor, Jacques Ruet; cos, Piero Tosi, Christian Dior, Annamode, Jean Barthet

AA Best Foreign Language Film

This Italian sex trilogy teams up two of that country's biggest stars, Sophia Loren and Marcello Mastroianni, with director Vittorio De Sica. The first and most interesting episode, "Adelina," features Loren as the title Neopolitan who is in trouble with the law and Mastroianni as her husband who discovers a legal loophole: pregnant women cannot be jailed until six months after the child's birth. Adelina duly gets pregnant, and pregnant again, and so on until her mate can no longer take it. "Anna" casts Loren as the Milanese wife of an industrialist who drops her lover (Mastroianni) after he nearly wrecks her beloved sports car. Lastly, in "Mara," the eponymous Roman prostitute (Loren) resists the temptation to seduce a young seminarian (Giovanni Ridolfi) who has fallen in love with her and even takes a one-week vow of chastity herself, much to the frustration of her most devoted client (Mastroianni). Although YESTERDAY, TODAY AND TOMORROW won a Best Foreign-Language Film Academy Award, it's hardly representative of the best work of its stars, director (UMBERTO D, THE BICYCLE THIEF, SHOESHINE), or screenwriters (Cesare Zavattini, De Sica's frequent collaborator, contributes "Anna" and "Mara"). It is, however, an enjoyable romp, buoyed by the professionalism of all concerned.

YESTERDAY'S ENEMY

1959 95m bw War   ★★★★
Hammer (U.K.)   /A

Stanley Baker (Capt. Langford), Guy Rolfe (Padre), Leo McKern (Max), Gordon Jackson (Sgt. MacKenzie), David Oxley (Doctor), Richard Pasco (2nd Lt. Hastings), Russell Waters (Brigadier), Philip Ahn (Yamazaki), Bryan Forbes (Dawson), Wolfe Morris (Informer)

p, Michael Carreras; d, Val Guest; w, Peter R. Newman (based on his television play); ph, Arthur Grant; ed, James Needs, Alfred Cox; art d, Bernard Robinson, Don Mingaye

This disturbing WWII film focuses on the survivors of a battle-decimated brigade as they try to make their way through the Burmese jungle to rejoin the main British force. Led by Baker, the survivors come upon a village where they surprise a small Japanese detachment. Found on a dead Japanese colonel is a coded map that details future Japanese battle strategy. Baker interrogates a captured Burmese agent, demanding an explanation of the code. The prisoner refuses to talk, so Baker carries through a threat to shoot two innocent villagers. In the wake of these executions, the prisoner confesses all. Rolfe and McKern, a priest and reporter, respectively, are appalled by Baker's sadistic actions. Baker tries to get the information to divisional headquarters, but he and his men are captured by Japanese troops. Now Baker is on the receiving end of similar torture. When Baker refuses to talk, the Japanese kill him and his men.

YESTERDAY'S ENEMY takes an unflinching look at the effects of war on the human psyche. Applying their own standards to a situation unlike any either of them has experienced, Rolfe and McKern are unable to fathom Baker's actions. Yet there is no right and wrong in Baker's act. Instead, his brutality is depicted as an evil that has become necessary at a specific moment. The perverse irony of war then reverses the entire situation. Guest's direction is excellent—particularly his skillful building of tension—and the ensemble performances are riveting. Though shot in the studio, the film is highly realistic, putting the viewer in the midst of the Burmese jungle.

YOJIMBO

1961 110m bw Action   ★★★★½
Toho/Kurosawa (Japan)   /A

Toshiro Mifune (Sanjuro Kuwabatake), Eijiro Tono (Gonji the Sake Seller), Seizaburo Kawazu (Seibei), Isuzu Yamada (Orin), Hiroshi Tachikawa (Yoichiro), Kyu Sazanka (Ushitora), Daisuke Kato (Inokichi), Tatsuya Nakadai (Unosuke), Kamatari Fujiwara (Tazaemon), Takashi Shimura (Tokuemon)

d, Akira Kurosawa; w, Akira Kurosawa, Ryuzo Kikushima, Hideo Oguni; ph, Kazuo Miyagawa; m, Masaru Sato; art d, Yoshiro Muraki; cos, Yoshiro Muraki

AAN Best Costume Design: Yoshiro Muraki

Directed by Japanese master Akira Kurosawa, YOJIMBO is the spirited, strangely moralistic tale of Sanjuro Kuwabatake (Toshiro Mifune), a samurai who wanders into a town divided by a civil war. On one side stands silk merchant Tazaemon (Kamatari Fujiwara), on the other sake merchant Tokuemon (Takashi Shimura)—both equally evil. Sanjuro views their conflict as an opportunity to make some money and secure food and lodging. Hired by Tazaemon as a yojimbo (bodyguard), Sanjro puts a devious plan of his own into effect, pretending to enter the

employ of Tokuemon, then secretly killing some of his men. Sanjuro is caught, however, brutally beaten, and tossed in prison. He escapes, in time to witness the momentous battle between the two factions that ultimately brings peace to the war-ravaged village. Kurosawa's entertaining direction, Kazuo Miyagawa's beautiful widescreen photography, and Mifune's eccentric acting combined to make YOJIMBO such a box-office success that Toho Studios asked the director to make another film along similar lines. The result was SANJURO, which again starred Mifune as an unorthodox samurai. Loosely remade in 1964 as A FISTFUL OF DOLLARS.

YOL

1982 111m c Drama   ★★★½
Guney/Cactus (Turkey)   PG/15

Tarik Akan (Seyit Ali), Halil Ergun (Mehmet Salih), Necmettin Cobanoglu (Omer), Serif Sezer (Zine), Meral Orhousoy (Emine), Semra Ucar (Gulbahar), Hikmet Celik (Mevlut)

p, Edi Hubschmid, K.L. Puldi; d, Serif Goren; w, Yilmaz Guney; ph, Erdogan Engin; ed, Yilmaz Guney, Elisabeth Waelchli; m, Sebastian Argol, Kendal

Five Turkish convicts are given a week's leave from prison to visit their loved ones in this extraordinarily painful drama. What has promised to be an emotionally uplifting period of freedom takes a disastrous and tragic turn for each of the prisoners, one of whom comes home to find that his brother has been murdered by police, while another learns of his wife's infidelity. A visually intense examination of Turkish mores and customs (the scene of the prisoner dragging his unfaithful wife into a snowy wasteland is both powerful and alienating for Western audiences), YOL was written by actor-turned-director Yilmaz Guney while he was behind bars and directed, under Guney's supervision, by one of his former assistants. Guney escaped from prison in 1981 and died three years later, after completing his final picture, THE WALL. YOL shared the top prize at Cannes with Costa-Gavras's MISSING.

YOU CAN'T CHEAT AN HONEST MAN

1939 76m bw Comedy   ★★★½
Universal (U.S.)   /U

W.C. Fields (Larson E. Whipsnade), Edgar Bergen, Charlie McCarthy, Mortimer Snerd, Pietro Blacaman, Princess Baba (Themselves), Constance Moore (Vicky Whipsnade), Mary Forbes (Mrs. Bel-Goodie), Thurston Hall (Archibald Bel-Goodie), John Arledge (Phineas Whipsnade)

p, Lester Cowan; d, George Marshall, Edward F. Cline; w, George Marion Jr., Richard Mack, Everett Freeman (based on a story by W.C. Fields); ph, Milton Krasner; ed, Otto Ludwig; art d, Jack Otterson; cos, Vera West

Universal Studios waved big money under comedian Fields's legendary proboscis and wooed him away from Paramount. In his first film for his new studio, Fields returned to the kind of character he loved best—a terminally broke and nomadic huckster who must live by his wits to stay one step ahead of the law. Owner of "Larson E. Whipsnade's Circus Giganticus," Fields is first seen hustling his caravan of wagons over the county line to escape the police he had angered at his previous stop. While setting up tents in a new town, Fields is confronted by ventriloquist Bergen and his smart-aleck dummy Charlie McCarthy. The two are the bane of Fields's existence, but he cannot fire them because of a strange clause in their contract. Luckily for Fields, Bergen has decided to quit because he hasn't been paid in months. The ventriloquist quickly changes his mind, however, when he meets Fields's beautiful daughter, Moore.

Like most Fields vehicles, YOU CAN'T CHEAT AN HONEST MAN is a virtually plotless array of hilarious verbal and visual gags designed to make the most of the comedian's prodigious talents. The script was actually a reworking of two previous projects, a rejected screenplay titled "Grease Paint," written by H.M. Walker in 1933, with added plot lines from Fields' silent movie TWO FLAMING YOUTHS. Once again Fields wrote the story under the pseudonym of "Charles Bogle," but Universal and director Marshall removed several important scenes that Fields felt were essential to his character development. In the film, Fields seems to be an entirely unlikable character with little or no compassion for his workers or family. In the script, Fields began the film with a tender scene where his wife, a trapeze artist who has suffered a fall, dies in his arms. Despite—or perhaps because of—trimmings of this nature, YOU CAN'T CHEAT is one of Fields's most sustained comic triumphs, containing several classic moments.

YOU CAN'T TAKE IT WITH YOU

1938   126m   bw   Comedy   ★★★½
Columbia (U.S.)   /U

Jean Arthur *(Alice Sycamore)*, Lionel Barrymore *(Martin Vanderhof)*, James Stewart *(Tony Kirby)*, Edward Arnold *(Anthony P. Kirby)*, Mischa Auer *(Kolenkhov)*, Ann Miller *(Essie Carmichael)*, Spring Byington *(Penny Sycamore)*, Samuel S. Hinds *(Paul Sycamore)*, Donald Meek *(Poppins)*, H.B. Warner *(Ramsey)*

p, Frank Capra; d, Frank Capra; w, Robert Riskin (based on the play by George S. Kaufman and Moss Hart); ph, Joseph Walker; ed, Gene Havlick; m, Dimitri Tiomkin; art d, Stephen Goosson; cos, Bernard Newman, Irene

AA Best Picture; *AAN Best Supporting Actress:* Spring Byington; *AA Best Director:* Frank Capra; *AAN Best Screenplay:* Robert Riskin; *AAN Best Cinematography:* Joseph Walker; *AAN Best Editing:* Gene Havlick; *AAN Best Sound:* John Livadary

Frank Capra took the phenomenally successful (if somewhat overrated) Kaufman-Hart stage play "You Can't Take It with You" and turned it into this well-received (if somewhat overrated) film. Amazingly, it garnered Capra his third Oscar for Best Director, as well as winning the Best Picture Oscar (it was also nominated for Best Supporting Actress [Byington], screenplay, cinematography, editing, and sound recording).

Barrymore is the eccentric patriarch of a clan of frustrated artists who decided 30 years earlier to retire from the rat-race and use his fortune to encourage friends and family to pursue vocations that really interest them. He has taken up painting, which he does badly, but at least he enjoys himself. His daughter, Byington, has taken up writing mystery novels; her husband, Hinds, tinkers with explosives in the basement. Their daughter Miller desires to be a ballet dancer, and her cynical Russian teacher, Auer, follows her around barking instructions. Miller's husband, Dub Taylor, practices playing the xylophone, while Barrymore's friend Meek invents new toys and party masks. The huge house is a frenzy of bizarre activities and in the center of it all is Barrymore's other granddaughter, Arthur, who is pursuing a relatively normal life by working as a receptionist in the offices of Arnold, a powerful businessman who wants to have Barrymore's mansion torn down so he can build on the property. Arthur is in love with Arnold's son Stewart, who fears that his father will never approve of a girl from such a family. The couple decides to arrange a dinner for the families to be held at Arthur's house, and Barrymore commands the clan to tone down their normal antics in order to make a good impression on Arnold and his stuffy wife, Mary Forbes. Unfortunately, there is confusion over the date of the dinner, and Stewart shows up with his parents a day early. The ensuing madness is unrestrained and hilarious.

YOU CAN'T TAKE IT WITH YOU is an entertaining, if saccharine film, packed with enough loony activity to keep the laughs coming from start to finish. Capra assembled a superb cast of players, and all score solidly in their roles, even if their behavior doesn't today seem as anarchic as it must have then. Capra himself, however, doesn't do as well, turning out a stagey product that represents one of his lesser directorial efforts. Perhaps the most amusing character in the film is Meek, a milquetoast of a man who enjoys sneaking up on family members and scaring them with his latest Halloween mask. YOU CAN'T TAKE IT WITH YOU was the first film for veteran actor Barrymore in which the crippling arthritis which would soon put him in a wheelchair became evident. To remedy the situation, Capra had a fake leg cast put on the actor and explained it by having him state that he broke his leg while sliding down a bannister—just the kind of reckless, carefree act one would expect from his character. Character actor Dub Taylor, who has appeared in hundreds of films and television shows, made his acting debut in this film.

YOU ONLY LIVE ONCE

1937   86m   bw   Crime   ★★★★
UA (U.S.)   /A

Sylvia Sidney *(Joan Graham)*, Henry Fonda *(Eddie Taylor)*, Barton MacLane *(Stephen Whitney)*, Jean Dixon *(Bonnie Graham)*, William Gargan *(Father Dolan)*, Warren Hymer *(Muggsy)*, Charles "Chic" Sale *(Ethan)*, Margaret Hamilton *(Hester)*, Guinn "Big Boy" Williams *(Rogers)*, Jerome Cowan *(Dr. Hill)*

p, Walter Wanger; d, Fritz Lang; w, Gene Towne, Graham Baker (based on a story by Towne); ph, Leon Shamroy; ed, Daniel Mandell; m, Alfred Newman; art d, Alexander Toluboff

This brooding and powerful tale, which suggests the story of Bonnie and Clyde, is one of Lang's best efforts in Hollywood. Fonda and Sidney are excellent as the average Depression-era couple made into criminals through circumstances and just plain bad luck. Fonda is not the average law-abiding citizen, however; he has committed many robberies in the past and has served three prison terms. He vows, however, that he is going straight. He gets a job and marries his patient, long-time sweetheart, Sidney. But his past catches up with him when his landlord turns him and his wife out of their room after finding out he has a record. Soon after, his employer at the trucking firm fires him. Then Fonda's hat is found at the scene of a bank holdup where a guard has been killed. He is quickly tried and sentenced to death. Once in prison, Fonda resolves to fight back against a system that offers him no way of surviving. He pretends to be ill and is sent to the prison hospital. There he obtains a gun and uses the prison doctor as a shield to get to the prison yard. The prison chaplain runs to him to say that he has been pardoned but by then Fonda will believe nothing any authority figure tells him. He thinks the chaplain is trying to hoodwink him into surrendering and, when the priest makes the wrong move, Fonda fires, killing the chaplain. He manages to escape the prison and rejoin wife Sidney. Together they drive toward the Canadian border, trying to get out of a country that has persecuted and hounded them. They do manage to reach the border but their joy is only momentary. A sharpshooting member of the New York State Police raises his rifle and spots the fugitives through his telescopic sights. He fires several rounds which mortally wound both Fonda and Sidney. Sidney is first hit and Fonda takes her in his arms, carrying her the last few steps into Canada, freedom, and death for both of them. This tragedy is distinguished by Lang's meticulous direction and carefully constructed scenes. Fonda gives a terrific performance as the social pariah fighting for his very existence. Sidney's performance is poignant and beautiful. It was once stated that this superb actress had the face of the Great Depression, and this film is undoubtedly the reason for the sobriquet. There is little mirth in this film loaded with permanent steel-gray skies, and the director's murky, diffused shots suggest a kind of unbearable futility to life. His figures, especially in the prison escape scenes, are hazy, almost transparent, as mist covers the yard and searchlights reach out for Fonda who moves like a ghost before them. Fonda held Lang in high regard as a director but felt that Lang pushed his actors too hard in his quest to attain perfection, causing, in the 46-day shooting schedule of this film, his cast and crew to go without sleep and to physically exhaust themselves to achieve the effect he desired. There is a grimness to this film that is often overwhelming, and though it is technically flawless, it offers little hope to the viewer for satisfaction. Justice is not served here, only irony.

YOU ONLY LIVE TWICE

1967   117m   c   Adventure/Spy   ★★★
Eon (U.K.)

Sean Connery *(James Bond)*, Akiko Wakabayashi *(Aki)*, Donald Pleasence *(Ernst Stavro Blofeld)*, Tetsuro Tamba *(Tiger Tanaka)*, Mie Hama *(Kissy Suzuki)*, Teru Shimada *(Osato)*, Karin Dor *(Helga Brandt)*, Lois Maxwell *(Miss Moneypenny)*, Desmond Llewelyn *("Q")*, Charles Gray *(Henderson)*

p, Albert R. Broccoli, Harry Saltzman; d, Lewis Gilbert; w, Roald Dahl, Harold Jack Bloom (based on the novel by Ian Fleming); ph, Freddie Young; ed, Peter Hunt; m, John Barry; prod d, Ken Adam; art d, Harry Pottle; fx, John Stears; cos, Eileen Sullivan

Sean Connery's disenchantment with his starring role is unmistakable in this, the fifth Bond spectacular. After turning in an enervated performance here, Connery refused to renew his contract with the profitable 007 franchise, although he was lured back for 1971's DIAMONDS ARE FOREVER and 1983's NEVER SAY NEVER AGAIN.

When both Russian and American spaceships start disappearing, each country suspects the other is responsible, bringing the planet to the brink of WWIII—exactly what SPECTRE agent Ernst Blofeld (Donald Pleasence), the architect of this international crisis, had in mind. Connery is sent to Japan to investigate. Hoping to give himself a little breathing room, he fakes his own death before exploring the volcano that houses Blofeld's own extraordinary spacecraft.

Limited by a Bond formula that demanded, among other things, that 007 be involved with at least three women, screenwriter Roald Dahl produced a contrived scenario that prevents YOU ONLY LIVE TWICE from ever really taking off. The film was also hampered by the last-minute casting of Pleasence to replace Jan Werich. Pleasence experimented with a variety of disfigurements and disabilities—finally settling on a facial scar—but nothing made him look quite sinister enough. Despite its obvious shortcomings and $10 million budget (staggering by mid-1960s standards), YOU ONLY LIVE TWICE was a tremendous commercial success. Nancy Sinatra sings the wistful title song, and the action scenes are enhanced by some of composer John Barry's best work for the Bond series.

YOU WERE NEVER LOVELIER

1942 97m bw Musical	★★★½
Columbia (U.S.)	/U

Fred Astaire (Robert Davis), Rita Hayworth (Maria Acuna), Adolphe Menjou (Edwardo Acuna), Leslie Brooks (Cecy Acuna), Adele Mara (Lita Acuna), Isobel Elsom (Mrs. Maria Castro), Gus Schilling (Fernando), Barbara Brown (Mrs. Delfina Acuna), Douglas Leavitt (Juan Castro), Catherine Craig (Julia Acuna)

p, Louis F. Edelman; d, William A. Seiter; w, Michael Fessier, Ernest Pagano, Delmer Daves (based on the story and screenplay "The Gay Senorita" by Carlos Olivari, Sixto Pondal Rios); ph, Ted Tetzlaff; ed, William Lyon; m, Jerome Kern; art d, Lionel Banks, Rudolph Sternad; chor, Val Raset; cos, Irene

AAN Best Score: Leigh Harline; AAN Best Song: Jerome Kern (Music), Johnny Mercer (Lyrics); AAN Best Sound: John Livadary

The second and last screen pairing of Fred Astaire and Rita Hayworth features the former as Robert Davis, an American dancer stranded in Buenos Aires. Desperate for funds (he lost his money gambling), he seeks work at the hotel owned by Edwardo Acuna (Adolphe Menjou), where Xavier Cugat and His Orchestra are currently playing. Edwardo, however, has more pressing matters to deal with: his eldest daughter is about to wed and his two youngest want to, but his second child, Maria (Hayworth), is ruining everyone's plans. Edwardo has a strict rule for his children: they must marry in order of their age, and Maria's romantic ideals are so lofty no man can measure up to them. Edwardo has been secretly sending her flowers and love notes, hoping to put a dent in her fantasies. Robert is mistaken for a messenger and sent to deliver the latest bouquet, and Maria thinks he's her mystery man. Edwardo now hires Robert to play Maria's secret admirer, but idealistic Maria has a counter to every argument for marriage. More complications arise when Mrs. Acuna starts wondering who her spouse has been sending billets-doux, but all works out happily in the end, of course. Hayworth is a wonderful complement to Astaire in the dance numbers, gliding about the floor with natural ease and looking ravishing. Her singing is dubbed for the film by Nan Wynn.

YOUNG AND INNOCENT

1937 84m bw Crime	★★★½
G.B./Gaumont (U.K.)	/U

Nova Pilbeam (Erica Burgoyne), Derrick de Marney (Robert Tisdall), Percy Marmont (Col. Burgoyne), Edward Rigby (Old Will), Mary Clare (Aunt Margaret), John Longden (Inspector Kent), George Curzon (Guy), Basil Radford (Uncle Basil), Pamela Carme (Christine Clay), George Merritt (Sgt. Miller)

p, Edward Black; d, Alfred Hitchcock; w, Charles Bennett, Alma Reville, Anthony Armstrong, Edwin Greenwood, Gerald Savory (based on the novel A Schilling for Candles by Josephine Tey); ph, Bernard Knowles; ed, Charles Frend; m, Louis Levy; art d, Alfred Junge

One of Hitchcock's more charming efforts, this thriller stars the endearing 18-year-old Pilbeam as Erica Burgoyne, the daughter of police constable Col. Burgoyne (Marmount), who is heading an investigation into the strangulation death of an actress whose body has washed ashore, along with the murder weapon—the belt of a raincoat. The prime, and in fact only, suspect is Robert Tisdall (de Marney) who maintains his innocence, despite the fact that everything is against him—he was friendly with the dead woman, he was included in her will, and his raincoat is missing. After giving the suspect a ride to a desolate farmhouse, Erica is faced with the choice of helping Tisdall prove his innocence, despite her fear of the repercussions of her father and his office. Naturally she finds herself falling in love with him, and he with her, and together the young and innocent fugitives must steer clear of the authorities and find the real murderer. While not generally considered one of Hitchcock's finer films, YOUNG AND INNOCENT, because of its simplicity (or innocence, in keeping with the title), is often overlooked, especially in light of the director's other British successes, THE MAN WHO KNEW TOO MUCH, THE 39 STEPS, and THE LADY VANISHES. Although its plot is simply a reworking of THE 39 STEPS without the spy angle, YOUNG AND INNOCENT has a certain delightful charm to it, due entirely to the young Pilbeam, with her glowing Sylvia Sidney-type face. The film also boasts some of Hitchcock's most memorable visual effects, namely a remarkable crane and dolly shot which travels across a grand ballroom and into the face of the murderer with his twitching eye.

YOUNG AT HEART

1955 117m c Musical	★★★
Arwin (U.S.)	/U

Doris Day (Laurie Tuttle), Frank Sinatra (Barney Sloan), Gig Young (Alex Burke), Ethel Barrymore (Aunt Jessie), Dorothy Malone (Fran Tuttle), Robert Keith (Gregory Tuttle), Elisabeth Fraser (Amy Tuttle), Alan Hale Jr. (Robert Neary), Lonny Chapman (Ernest Nichols), Frank Ferguson (Bartell)

p, Henry Blanke; d, Gordon Douglas; w, Liam O'Brien (based on the screenplay for the film FOUR DAUGHTERS by Julius J. Epstein, Lenore Coffee, from the story "Sister Act" by Fanny Hurst); ph, Ted McCord; ed, William Ziegler; art d, John Beckman; fx, H.F. Koenekamp; cos, Howard Shoup

This is a smooth but empty musical remake of 1938's FOUR DAUGHTERS, sans one daughter. Laurie Tuttle (Doris Day) and sisters Fran and Amy (Dorothy Malone and Elizabeth Fraser) live with their father (Robert Keith) and Aunt Jessie (Ethel Barrymore). When Alex Burke (Gig Young), a composer working on a musical comedy, arrives on the scene, both Laurie and Fran fall in love with him. Alex calls in a friend, the embittered pianist and composer Barney Sloan (Frank Sinatra), to help him arrange the musical's score, and Barney promptly falls for Laurie, who has gotten engaged to Alex. On the eve of her wedding to Alex, however, Laurie finds out about Fran's feelings for Alex; Laurie then nobly backs out of the wedding and heads for the city with Barney. They get married, and in time she comes to love him truly, though he is unconvinced of the sincerity of her emotion. Bad luck strikes again and again, until Barney finally comes to have faith in Laurie's love and they embark on married life anew. Despite all the talent involved, this soap opera fails to generate much interest, especially since Day and Sinatra generate few sparks.

YOUNG DR. KILDARE

1938 81m bw Drama	★★★½
MGM (U.S.)	/A

Lew Ayres (Dr. James Kildare), Lionel Barrymore (Dr. Leonard Gillespie), Lynne Carver (Alice Raymond), Nat Pendleton (Joe Wayman), Jo Ann Sayers (Barbara Chanler), Samuel S. Hinds (Dr.

Stephen Kildare), Emma Dunn *(Mrs. Martha Kildare),* Walter Kingsford *(Dr. Walter Carew),* Nella Walker *(Mrs. Chanler),* Pierre Watkin *(Mr. Chanler)*

p, Lou Ostrow; d, Harold S. Bucquet; w, Harry Ruskin, Willis Goldbeck (based on characters created by Max Brand); ph, John Seitz; ed, Elmo Veron; m, David Snell; art d, Cedric Gibbons, Malcolm Brown

Newly graduated from medical school, Ayres returns to his home town and the prospect of joining his father's medical practice. To the disappointment of his parents and his sweetheart, Carver, Ayres elects to accept a proffered internship in a large New York City hospital. There he incurs adverse publicity in the newspapers when a powerful politician dies while under his care. He is exonerated of blame when it is discovered that an ambulance attendant failed to follow Ayres's orders to administer oxygen to the alcoholic politician. Crusty old wheelchair-bound diagnostician Barrymore takes the young man under his abrasive wing, to Ayres's discomfort. (Ayres has yet to learn that Barrymore's bark is directed mostly at those in whom he sees some potential.) One of Ayres's patients is Sayers, daughter of wealthy Watkin and Walker. Sayers has attempted suicide, and eminent psychiatrist Monty Woolley has adjudged her mentally unbalanced, decreeing that she be institutionalized. Ayres disagrees with the opinion and countermands the decision on his own authority. As the youthful physician is about to be discharged for insubordination, the ever-irascible Barrymore—who agrees with his diagnosis—appoints Ayres as his new assistant.

The first of MGM's "Dr. Kildare" series, this was not the first filmed adaptation of author Brand's characters. That honor belongs to INTERNES CAN'T TAKE MONEY, starring Joel McCrea and Barbara Stanwyck. MGM had recently started its "Hardy Family" series to considerable acclaim, and Louis B. Mayer wanted another profitable series vehicle. He assigned the HARDY staff to search for something suitable and settled on a hospital theme partly because of the nearly infinite plot variations it appeared to afford and partly because it offered a continuing role for his favorite actor, Barrymore (who had only recently suffered the crippling hip injury that required him to use a wheelchair). Ayres, with his gentle manner, was a fortuitous selection as Kildare, though he was none too pleased with the series at the outset (he's been quoted as saying of this initial entry, "Frankly, I thought it was terrible"). Ayres and Barrymore were to work together in eight more films in the series (Barrymore continued beyond these eight, with other actors assuming the young doctor characterization). Players Pendleton, Hinds, Dunn, and Kingsford were to become regulars on the series. Actress Laraine Day joined the group in the next picture in the series, CALLING DR. KILDARE. The studio's feature-release series ended in 1947 with DARK DELUSION, but the young doctor and his mentor were to be rejuvenated on television.

YOUNG FRANKENSTEIN

1974	108m	bw	Comedy/Horror	★★★★½
Fox	(U.S.)			PG/15

Gene Wilder *(Dr. Frederick Frankenstein),* Peter Boyle *(Monster),* Marty Feldman *(Igor),* Madeline Kahn *(Elizabeth),* Cloris Leachman *(Frau Blucher),* Teri Garr *(Inga),* Kenneth Mars *(Inspector Kemp),* Gene Hackman *(Blind Hermit),* Richard Haydn *(Herr Falkstein),* Liam Dunn *(Mr. Hilltop)*

p, Michael Gruskoff; d, Mel Brooks; w, Gene Wilder, Mel Brooks (based on the characters from the novel *Frankenstein* by Mary Wollstonecraft Shelley); ph, Gerald Hirschfeld; ed, John C. Howard; m, John Morris; art d, Dale Hennesy; fx, Hal Millar, Henry Miller Jr.; cos, Dorothy Jeakins

AAN Best Adapted Screenplay: Gene Wilder, Mel Brooks; *AAN Best Sound:* Richard Portman, Gene Cantamessa

Mel Brooks's follow-up to his enormously successful western spoof, BLAZING SADDLES, tackles the horror genre—specifically, FRANKENSTEIN and THE BRIDE OF FRANKENSTEIN. This time Brooks tones down his broad humor a bit to create a work that is both an affectionate parody and a knowledgeable homage to its cinematic forebears. Gene Wilder plays Dr. Frederick Frankenstein (now defiantly pronounced "FRONK-en-steen"), a med school lecturer who

thinks his infamous grandfather's work is "doo-doo." The younger Frankenstein must finally face his destiny when he inherits his grandfather's Transylvanian estate. Once there, he meets Igor (pronounced "eye-gore" and played by the eye-popping Marty Feldman), whose hunchback inexplicably changes from the left side to the right throughout the movie; Inga (Teri Garr), a young woman who will assist the doctor; and Frau Blucher (Cloris Leachman), a hideous old woman who causes horses to whinny in fright at the mere mention of her name. Eventually, Frederick finds his grandfather's private library and a copy of his book, *How I Did It.* Of course, Frederick cannot keep himself from righting his grandfather's wrongs and creating a new monster (Peter Boyle), a big, dumb corpse with a zipper round his neck and an abnormal brain in his head. The laughs come along at a fast and furious rate. One of the film's highlights is the "Puttin' on the Ritz" duet performed by Frederick and the Monster.

YOUNG FRANKENSTEIN is Brooks's most accomplished work, combining his well-known brand of comedy with stylish direction and a uniformly excellent cast. The handsome black-and-white cinematography really captures the look of an early 1930s film. The direction achieves a seemingly impossible task, balancing Brooks's off-the-wall humor within the framework of the style of a classic Universal Frankenstein film. The Frankenstein castle, with its cobwebs, dust, skulls, original lab equipment, and strange goings-on, could easily have been inhabited by Boris Karloff or Bela Lugosi. Wilder, wildly funny here, later attempted his own genre spoof, HAUNTED HONEYMOON, which came nowhere near YOUNG FRANKENSTEIN.

YOUNG LIONS, THE

1958	167m	bw	War	★★★★
Fox	(U.S.)			/PG

Marlon Brando *(Christian Diestl),* Montgomery Clift *(Noah Ackerman),* Dean Martin *(Michael Whiteacre),* Hope Lange *(Hope Plowman),* Barbara Rush *(Margaret Freemantle),* May Britt *(Gretchen Hardenberg),* Maximilian Schell *(Capt. Hardenberg),* Dora Doll *(Simone),* Lee Van Cleef *(Sgt. Rickett),* Liliane Montevecchi *(Francoise)*

p, Al Lichtman; d, Edward Dmytryk; w, Edward Anhalt (based on the novel by Irwin Shaw); ph, Joseph MacDonald; ed, Dorothy Spencer; m, Hugo Friedhofer; art d, Lyle Wheeler, Addison Hehr; fx, L.B. Abbott; cos, Adele Balkan, Charles LeMaire

AAN Best Cinematography: Joe MacDonald; *AAN Best Score:* Hugo Friedhofer; *AAN Best Sound:* Carl Faulkner

A somewhat bloated adaptation of Irwin Shaw's sprawling WWII novel, THE YOUNG LIONS follows three soldiers—one German, two American—from the time of their enlistment until the end of the war. Christian Diestl (Marlon Brando) is an idealistic young German who believes in Hitler and becomes a lieutenant in the Wehrmacht. As he makes his way from the occupation of Paris to duty in Rommel's Afrika Korps and then back into Europe, Diestl becomes disillusioned and embittered over Nazi brutality and comes to hate his uniform and everything it represents. Meanwhile, in the US, a young Jew, Noah Ackerman (Montgomery Clift), and a popular singer, Michael Whiteacre (Dean Martin), meet as draftees and become fast friends. Although patriotic and dedicated, Ackerman becomes the victim of the Army's anti-Semitism, and is forced to fight his fellow Americans before ever facing the Germans. As the years go by, the fates of Ackerman, Whiteacre, and Diestl grow closer, until they eventually intersect outside a concentration camp. Great departures were made in the script from Shaw's original story, mostly in the character of the German, Diestl. In the book, he is an unredeemed Nazi to the last, and in the final confrontation kills the Jewish soldier, then is killed by the other American. It was largely Brando who made the German a sympathetic character, arguing that Shaw had written his book in the immediate, angry aftermath of the war, although Shaw later told the actor that he wouldn't have changed his opinions even if he had written the book 10 years later. Although Edward Dmytryk's direction was never more than workmanlike and the film is bit overlong and draggy at times, it does contain a pair of worthwhile performances from Brando and Clift.

YOUNG MAN WITH A HORN

1950 111m bw Musical   ★★★★
Warner Bros. (U.S.)   /PG

Kirk Douglas (*Rick Martin*), Lauren Bacall (*Amy North*), Doris Day (*Jo Jordan*), Hoagy Carmichael (*Smoke Willoughby*), Juano Hernandez (*Art Hazzard*), Jerome Cowan (*Phil Morrison*), Mary Beth Hughes (*Margo Martin*), Nestor Paiva (*Louis Galba*), Orley Lindgren (*Rick as a Boy*), Walter Reed (*Jack Chandler*)

p, Jerry Wald; d, Michael Curtiz; w, Carl Foreman, Edmund H. North (based on the novel by Dorothy Baker); ph, Ted McCord; ed, Alan Crosland Jr.; art d, Edward Carrere; cos, Milo Anderson

Inspired by the tragic life of jazz cornet player Bix Beiderbecke, who died at age 28 in 1931 after a long battle with alcoholism, YOUNG MAN WITH A HORN stars Kirk Douglas as the great musician's fictional counterpart, Rick Martin. While pianist Smoke Willoughby (Hoagy Carmichael) reminisces about the talented trumpeter, Rick's life is shown in flashback, beginning with his youthful fascination with music and Art Hazzard (Juano Hernandez), a black jazz musician. Rick saves up to buy a trumpet and learns to play under Art's tutelage, and by age 20 Rick is performing in a dance band that includes Smoke and torch singer Jo Jordon (Doris Day). He's quickly frustrated by the band's dull sound, however, and gets himself and Smoke fired. The two continue to play in cheap dives, broke but having fun, after which Rick ends up in New York City, where he finds Jo singing with a new band. Rick's brilliant playing soon makes him a sensation, but stardom brings trouble in the form of a rich, neurotic, beautiful, and controlling Amy North (Lauren Bacall), who both marries Rick and ruins him—although the film's ending suggest that he may be on his way back, with the help of the loyal Smoke and Jo. YOUNG MAN WITH A HORN suffers from excessive melodrama, but boasts several fine performances and plenty of enjoyable jazz. Douglas studied under trumpeter Larry Sullivan and learned how to "play" convincingly, although all his trumpeting is dubbed by Harry James, the film's musical adviser (some of Carmichael's piano was dubbed by Buddy Cole, and Jimmy Zito handled Hernandez's playing).

YOUNG MR. LINCOLN

1939 100m bw Biography/Political   ★★★★
Fox (U.S.)   /A

Henry Fonda (*Abraham Lincoln*), Alice Brady (*Abigail Clay*), Marjorie Weaver (*Mary Todd*), Arleen Whelan (*Hannah Clay*), Eddie Collins (*Efe Turner*), Pauline Moore (*Ann Rutledge*), Richard Cromwell (*Matt Clay*), Ward Bond (*John Palmer Cass*), Donald Meek (*John Felder*), Spencer Charters (*Judge Herbert A. Bell*)

p, Kenneth MacGowan; d, John Ford; w, Lamar Trotti; ph, Bert Glennon, Arthur Miller; ed, Walter Thompson; m, Alfred Newman; art d, Richard Day, Mark-Lee Kirk; cos, Royer

AAN Best Original Screenplay: Lamar Trotti

The early days of Abraham Lincoln get the full treatment in this film by Ford, who simultaneously makes Lincoln both a man and a myth. The film opens with a poem familiar to most: "If Nancy Hanks/came back as a ghost/seeking news/of what she loved most/She'd ask first/'Where's my son?/What's happened to Abe?/What's he done?'" This sets the tone for the rest of the film, in which these questions are answered, but only in the context of what Lincoln (played by Fonda) had done by 1837. The film's first scene has Fonda making a speech to a convention of the Whig party in 1832, in which the first words from his mouth are "You all know me." In that same year he talks with his girlfriend, Moore, by a riverside, which dissolves to the same riverside five years later, covered with ice. Moore is dead, and her grave is on the same spot where they had spoken. Fonda speaks to it and asks her to help him decide his future. He stands a stick up on the grave, holding it with his finger at the top, and tells her that if it falls on her grave, he'll go into the legal profession. It falls for the law, and soon we see Fonda practicing his first case, a dispute between two men. Fonda listens to both of them, then proposes a compromise. They both refuse that solution, so he threatens them: "Did you fellas ever hear 'bout the time I butted two heads together?" They acquiesce, and it is with great satisfaction that Fonda collects his fee. Following a fair in which Fonda serves as the pie judge, there is a murder during a fight involving the

two sons of an old friend, Brady, and two local roughnecks, of whom the survivor is Bond. Fonda takes on the boys' defense, first by stopping a lynch mob from killing the pair on the spot. He tries to learn from Brady which of her sons killed the victim, but she can't say. Bond indicates that it was the bigger of the two, though neither is especially larger than the other. The judge tries to convince Fonda that he is too inexperienced for a case of this importance and suggests that he let an established lawyer take on the defense, namely Milburn Stone, a noted trial lawyer and Fonda's rival for the hand of socialite Weaver. Fonda refuses, and in court he manages to uses the *Farmer's Almanac* to trap Bond into confessing to the crime himself. Fonda is triumphant, and Stone comes up to him and says he'll never underestimate him again. Fonda walks away in a rainstorm that just happened to come up that day of shooting, and as he is lost in the rain, the film dissolves to a picture of the statue in the Lincoln Memorial.

Ford was originally reluctant to take on the film. He had just made STAGECOACH and was in a position to pick and choose his work. Two plays had recently been on Broadway on the subject of Lincoln's early years, and Ford felt that the subject had been "worked to death." But when he read the Lamar Trotti script he changed his mind. Executive Producer Darryl F. Zanuck wanted rising actor Fonda to take on the title role, but Fonda was too much in awe of the character and he turned it down at first. But after talking to Ford, Fonda changed his mind and took the part, turning in a marvelous performance that simultaneously captures both the awkwardness of the young man and his promise. Unlike most of Ford's films after STAGECOACH, this was very much a studio project, and Ford knew he was going to move on to his next film almost immediately after finishing work on this, leaving control of the editing to others. Since Ford had already argued with Zanuck over the slow, elegiac pace Ford was taking with the material, the director ensured that the film would be cut the way he wanted by editing in the camera, setting up slow dissolves, and destroying the negatives of all the takes except the ones he wanted. Throughout the film Zanuck gave Ford a lot of input about how he thought the film should go, mostly suggesting it move faster. The story of the murder in the film was taken from Trotti's own experiences as a reporter in the South. There he had reported on a murder case in which one of two brothers was accused of killing a man. Their mother refused to tell which of them did it, so both were hanged. A superb motion picture, and one in which Ford's obsession with Americana and the forces and emotions that made this country what it is are plainly in view.

YOUNG WINSTON

1972 145m c Biography/Adventure/Political   ★★★
Highroad/Hugh French (U.K.)   PG

Simon Ward (*Winston Churchill/Sir Winston Churchill's Voice*), Peter Cellier (*Captain 35th Sikhs*), Ronald Hines (*Adjutant 35th Sikhs*), Dino Shafeek (*Sikh Soldier*), John Mills (*Gen. Herbert Kitchener*), Anne Bancroft (*Lady Jennie Churchill*), Russell Lewis (*Winston, Age 7*), Pat Heywood (*Mrs. Everest*), Robert Shaw (*Lord Randolph Churchill*), Laurence Naismith (*Lord Salisbury*)

p, Carl Foreman; d, Richard Attenborough; w, Carl Foreman (based on *My Early Life: A Roving Commission* by Sir Winston Churchill); ph, Gerry Turpin; ed, Kevin Connor; m, Alfred Ralston, Sir Edward Elgar; prod d, Geoffrey Drake, Don Ashton; art d, John Graysmark, William Hutchinson; fx, Cliff Richardson, Tom Howard, Charles Staffel; cos, Anthony Mendleson

AAN Best Adapted Screenplay: Carl Foreman; *AAN Best Art Direction:* Don Ashton, Geoffrey Drake, John Graysmark William Hutchinson, Peter James; *AAN Best Costume Design:* Anthony Mendleson

Winston Churchill's self-serving memoirs of his youthful adventures are brought to the screen by the current master (or at least the most frequent practitioner) of the large-scale bio-pic, Richard Attenborough. The film follows Churchill through childhood, school, and succesful efforts win fame in the Sudan and the Boer War, ending with his election to Parliament at the age of 26.

YOUNG WINSTON works as an action-packed adventure, with lots of rousing battle scenes and hairsbreadth escapes, but its attempt to penetrate the motivations of its hero is about as profound as a high school psychology text. Ward is convincing as Churchill, and the other performances, particularly that of Shaw, are of a high order. Attenborough's direction, in his debut feature, is fairly accomplished and even innovative—he experimented with "flashing" techniques here, exposing the film before shooting to get subtle color tints. Well-paced, but still very long at almost two and a half hours.

YOU'RE A BIG BOY NOW

1966 96m c Comedy/Drama ★★★
Seven Arts (U.S.) /X

Elizabeth Hartman (Barbara Darling), Geraldine Page (Margery Chanticleer), Julie Harris (Miss Thing), Peter Kastner (Bernard Chanticleer), Rip Torn (I.H. Chanticleer), Michael Dunn (Richard Mudd), Tony Bill (Raef), Karen Black (Amy), Dolph Sweet (Policeman Francis Graf), Michael O'Sullivan (Kurt Doughty)

p, Phil Feldman; d, Francis Ford Coppola; w, Francis Ford Coppola (based on the novel by David Benedictus); ph, Andrew Laszlo; ed, Aram Avakian; m, Robert Prince; art d, Vassele Fotopoulos; chor, Robert Tucker; cos, Theoni V. Aldredge

AAN Best Supporting Actress: Geraldine Page

YOU'RE A BIG BOY NOW is significant as an early example of the developing talent of one of the most important (if not the most important) American directors of the 1970s. Coppola scripted and directed this whimsical look at coming of age in the 1960s as part of his graduate thesis at UCLA. Though not his first film, it revealed a willingness to experiment with technique and themes that would continue throughout his career. As in both RUMBLE FISH and THE OUTSIDERS, made by Coppola nearly two decades later, his subject here is a teenager's passage into manhood. The tone in this film is much less serious, though, more appropriate for the 1960s, when a laid-back attitude toward drama in general was prevalent, and deep messages lurked beneath surfaces. But unlike the work of either Jean-Luc Godard or Richard Lester (both obvious influences on Coppola at this point in his career), YOU'RE A BIG BOY NOW fails to have much impact beyond its lightheartedness. It is as if Coppola were too concerned with creating a style to put much effort into the implications of his material. Kastner plays a young Long Islander given his first taste of what it's like to be on his own. His move to New York City has come at the behest of Torn, his father, who wants to get the boy away from his security-blanket existence with doting mother Page. Kastner moves into a boarding house run by Harris and discovers sex and drugs under the guidance of older and wiser Bill, with whom he works at the New York Public Library. Kastner is obsessed with discotheque dancer and actress Hartman in a big way, but his pursuit of her leaves him with an extremely bitter taste of romance. He eventually does discover something about love through his relationship with Black, the woman who has been waiting on the sidelines all along, acting as his friend while harboring a gigantic crush. Though YOU'RE A BIG BOY NOW has been criticized for being too whimsical, it offers a wide range of fascinating characters and situations that make for great entertainment. The soundtrack by the Lovin' Spoonful is also a delight. Like much of Coppola's early work, however, it presents his themes in a cliched manner, almost as if he has learned about human experience and emotions through the cinema instead of real life. That Coppola, an unknown just embarking on his career, was able to persuade so many established performers to appear in the film, is indicative of the organization skills and the ability to gain people's trust and respect that have made him such an outstanding director.

Z

Z

1969 127m c Political ★★★★
Reggane (France/Algeria) M/A

Yves Montand (The Deputy), Jean-Louis Trintignant (The Examining Magistrate), Irene Papas (Helene, the Deputy's Wife), Jacques Perrin (Photojournalist), Charles Denner (Manuel), Francois Perier (Public Prosecutor), Pierre Dux (The General), Julien Guiomar (The Colonel), Bernard Fresson (Matt), Renato Salvatori (Yago)

p, Jacques Perrin, Hamed Rachedi; d, Constantin Costa-Gavras; w, Constantin Costa-Gavras, Jorge Semprun (based on the novel by Vassili Vassilikos); ph, Raoul Coutard; ed, Francoise Bonnot; m, Mikis Theodorakis; art d, Jacques d'Ovidio

AAN Best Picture; AAN Best Director: Constantine Costa-Gavras; AAN Best Adapted Screenplay: Constantine Costa-Gavras, Jorge Semprun; AA Best Editing: Francoise Bonnot; AA Best Foreign Language Film:

A chilling, manipulative rollercoaster ride. Originally subtitled "The Anatomy of a Political Assassination," this intense political thriller is based on the real-life 1963 killing of Gregorios Lambrakis, a Greek liberal whose extreme popularity and advocacy of peace shook the stability of the government in power. Starring is Yves Montand, who, although referred to only as "the Deputy," is clearly Lambrakis. After his liberal organization, the Friends of Peace, loses a large meeting hall at the last moment, the Deputy is forced to find another venue. He appeals and is given a permit to hold the meeting in a small, 200-seat auditorium, although it is expected to draw over 4,000. During the meeting, the Deputy's supporters are taunted by a violent right-wing faction, while the police "protection" stands by passively. Later, the police do little to protect the Deputy from a truck that speeds by, from which one of the passengers ferociously clubs the Deputy in the head, killing him. In order to give the appearance of an investigation, the general in charge appoints an Examining Magistrate (Jean-Louis Trintignant), who is believed to be a pawn of the government, but soon surprises all by probing deep into a government conspiracy and cover-up.

Rather than appealing only to a politically minded audience, Z found a great deal of enthusiastic support from almost everyone who saw it. At the Cannes Film Festival it received a unanimous vote for the Jury Prize, with Trintignant receiving Best Actor honors. The Academy Awards also responded, with Oscars for Best Foreign Film and Best Editing (it was nominated for Best Picture as well). Z succeeds where so many political pictures have failed because of its concentration on the thriller aspects of the story. Borrowing heavily from American gangster/prison/anti-Facist melodrama conventions, Costa-Gavras' film contains many breathtaking, pressure-filled scenes that help pummel home the sometimes confusing politics. Rather than worrying about which right-wing general did what, the audience becomes wrapped up in whether or not a character will survive a beating, or be run down by a speeding car. Detractors complained that the film commercialized and simplified the Lambrakis incident and politics in general. Costa-Gavras responded: "That's the way it is in Greece. Black and White. No nuances." The glorious Irene Papas plays Montand's wife—she's an actress whose eyes speak volumes even when she's standing stock-still. The score is by Mikis Theodorakis—who was under arrest in Greece at the time. Z was filmed in Algeria, in French.

ZABRISKIE POINT

1970 112m c Drama ★★
MGM/Trianon (U.S.) R/15

Mark Frechette (Mark), Daria Halprin (Daria), Rod Taylor (Lee Allen), Paul Fix (Cafe Owner), G.D. Spradlin (Lee's Associate), Bill Garaway (Morty), Kathleen Cleaver (Kathleen)

p, Carlo Ponti; d, Michelangelo Antonioni; w, Michelangelo Antonioni, Fred Gardner, Sam Shepard, Tonino Guerra, Clare Peploe (based on a story by Michelangelo Antonioni); ph, Alfio Contini; ed, Franco Arcalli; prod d, Dean Tavoularis; fx, Earl McCoy; cos, Ray Summers

In his super-successful BLOW-UP, Antonioni made an attempt to understand the English youth movement of the 1960s. Here, in his first American film, Antonioni took his search for answers to the States. Unfortunately, with this picture the director falls into two traps: employing endless "anti-Establishment" cliches and saddling himself with the underwhelming talents of Mark Frechette. The picture opens in documentary style, with a meeting of college radicals discussing the meaning of revolution. Mark (Frechette), disgusted with the students' stagnant ideals, declares that he is ready to die—but not of boredom—and walks out. Identified as a cop killer during a campus riot, Mark flees to a nearby airfield, steals a small private plane, flies through Death Valley, and meets Daria (Daria Halprin), a pretty, pot-smoking, meditative secretary. It's not long before they are holding hands at

Zabriskie Point, a tourist spot marked by a small plaque explaining that a man named Zabriskie discovered mineral matter there. The psychedelic happenings plod along until the explosive, apocalyptic finale. On the basis of Antonioni's "art-house" following in the US, MGM decided to jump on the bandwagon and give the director carte blanche for this film. The result is a critical but relatively accurate portrait of America in the late 1960s, which, however, now seems horribly dated. Antonioni concentrates chiefly on the gaps between student radicals and the establishment, naturalism and plasticity, free-spirited individualism and the restraints of modern life. While Antonioni's visual sense is once again in top form, his "mind-expanding" hippie dialogue, as delivered by his amateur leads, is painful to experience. MGM hoped that a combination of art-house and hippie audiences would help return their $7 million investment. Instead the film was a box-office and critical bomb, surviving today as a nugget of the hippie culture.

ZANDY'S BRIDE

1974 116m c Western	★★½
Warner Bros. (U.S.)	PG/AA

Gene Hackman (*Zandy Allan*), Liv Ullmann (*Hannah Lund*), Eileen Heckart (*Ma Allan*), Harry Dean Stanton (*Songer*), Joe Santos (*Frank Gallo*), Frank Cady (*Pa Allan*), Sam Bottoms (*Mel Allan*), Susan Tyrrell (*Maria Cordova*), Bob Simpson (*Bill Pincus*), Fabian Gregory Cordova (*Paco*)

p, Harvey Matofsky; d, Jan Troell; w, Marc Norman (based on the novel *The Stranger* by Lillian Bos Ross); ph, Jordan Cronenweth; ed, Gordon Scott; m, Michael Franks; prod d, Albert Brenner; cos, Patricia Norris

A beautifully photographed, intimate little western shot in the Big Sur area of California that boasts some fine acting but really nothing more. Hackman stars as an ill-tempered rancher who decides to end his loneliness by sending off for a mail-order bride (Ullmann). When the woman arrives, she is shocked by Hackman's apparent cruelty and heartlessness toward her as he treats her like a slave. She decides to fight back against his tyranny, and the shock of someone standing up to him begins to arouse long-repressed feelings of tenderness and compassion in Hackman. By the end of the film, Hackman accepts Ullmann as an equal and demonstrates his ability to be a loving father when she bears his child. Despite the gorgeous scenery and strong performances, ZANDY'S BRIDE is a rather hollow film that suffers from lackadaisical scripting. There is not much plot here (and there is nothing wrong with that if the characters are interesting), and the people and their actions are cliched and predictable. There is no spontaneity; it all seems very cold and mannered. Hackman and Ullmann (with able support from Heckart, Stanton, and Bottoms) struggle to wring some life and meaning out of the material, and it is through their efforts that ZANDY'S BRIDE works at all. Directed by celebrated Swedish director Troell, whose films THE EMIGRANTS and THE NEW LAND were magnificent period pieces about Swedes settling in America during the 19th century, ZANDY'S BRIDE suffered because of his inability to adjust to American production methods. In Sweden, Troell worked with a close-knit crew of 15 and had complete access to the camera—even shooting scenes himself if he chose to. Warner Bros. gave the director a union crew of 100. The sheer number of these strangers intimidated the director and made him extremely nervous and self-conscious. He was also not allowed anywhere near the camera—union rules. In her book *Changing,* Ullmann relates how Troell and his actors sneaked a camera into the cabin and "rehearsed" while the director photographed the whole scene hand-holding the camera—finally able to feel as if he controlled the set. Problems aside, ZANDY'S BRIDE is beautiful to watch and at times an interesting look into frontier life.

ZAZIE
(ZAZIE DANS LE METRO)

1960 86m c Comedy	★★★½
Nouvelle Editions de Films (France)	/X

Catherine Demongeot (*Zazie*), Philippe Noiret (*Uncle Gabriel*), Hubert Deschamps (*Turnadot*), Antoine Roblot (*Charles*), Annie Fratellini (*Mado*), Carla Marlier (*Albertine*), Vittorio Caprioli (*Trouscaillon*), Yvonne Clech (*Mme. Mouaque*), Nicolas Bataille (*Fedor*), Jacques Dufilho (*Gridoux*)

p, Louis Malle; d, Louis Malle; w, Louis Malle, Jean-Paul Rappeneau (based on the book *Zazie dans le Metro* by Raymond Queneau); ph, Henri Raichi; ed, Kenout Peltier; m, Andre Pontin, Fiorenzo Carpi; art d, Bernard Evein; fx, Locafilms; cos, Marc Doelnitz

Demongeot is an 11-year-old nuisance who must spend a few days with her uncle, Noiret, in Paris when her mother goes off with a new lover. She wants nothing more than to ride the subway, but a strike by the Paris Metro workers prevents this. The foul-mouthed girl blames it on grownups but decides to have fun in spite of this setback. She takes Noiret on a mad chase through the town, and at one point he's forced to leap from the Eiffel Tower using a balloon as a parachute. Finally she is granted her wish when the strike ends, but Demongeot is tuckered out from all the loony goings on and ends up falling asleep on the way home. This is a great romp with some wonderfully wild moments. A fine early effort from the director of ATLANTIC CITY and MURMUR OF THE HEART.

ZELIG

1983 80m c/bw Comedy	★★★½
Orion (U.S.)	PG

Woody Allen (*Leonard Zelig*), Mia Farrow (*Dr. Eudora Fletcher*), John Buckwalter (*Dr. Sindell*), Marvin Chatinover (*Glandular Diagnosis Doctor*), Stanley Swerdlow (*Mexican Food Doctor*), Paul Nevens (*Dr. Birsky*), Howard Erskine (*Hypodermic Doctor*), George Hamlin (*Experimental Drugs Doctor*), Ralph Bell, Richard Whiting

p, Robert Greenhut; d, Woody Allen; w, Woody Allen; ph, Gordon Willis; ed, Susan E. Morse; m, Dick Hyman; prod d, Mel Bourne; art d, Speed Hopkins; fx, John Caglione Jr., Joel Hynek, Stuart Robinson, Richard Greenberg; chor, Danny Daniels; cos, Santo Loquasto; anim, Steven Plastrik

AAN Best Cinematography: Gordon Willis; *AAN Best Costume Design:* Santo Loquasto

ZELIG employs technical wizardry to create a memorable fable of cultural assimilation. Leonard Zelig (Woody Allen) is a minor celebrity of the Depression era whose abilities as a "human chameleon" astound the world. Desperate to be accepted by others, he goes to extraordinary lengths to become one of the crowd. This desire is realized, formally speaking, through a number of astonishing lab effects by which Allen's character is seamlessly blended with archival footage from the 1930s: he appears waiting in the on-deck circle as Babe Ruth is batting, among a crowd of Nazis cheering Hitler, and growing a beard to become a Hassidic rabbi. His case captures the imagination of America, as well as the attentions of a psychiatrist (Mia Farrow) who falls in love with him.

ZELIG's loving recreation of Depression-era pop culture is accomplished with amazing verisimilitude; the *faux*-documentary sequences are among the best since CITIZEN KANE. Allen's ongoing struggles with psychoanalysis and his Jewish identity—stridently literal preoccupations in most of his work—are for once rendered allegorically. The result is deeply satisfying.

ZELLY AND ME

1988 87m c Drama	★★★½
Cypress (U.S.)	PG/15

Alexandra Johnes (*Phoebe*), Isabella Rossellini (*Joan, "Zelly"*), Glynis Johns (*Co-Co*), Kaiulani Lee (*Nora*), David Lynch (*Willie*), Joe Morton (*Earl*), Courtney Vickery (*Dora*), Lindsay Dickon (*Kitty*), Jason McCall (*Alexander*), Aaron Boone (*David*)

p, Sue Jett, Tony Mark; d, Tina Rathborne; w, Tina Rathborne; ph, Mikael Salomon; ed, Cindy Kaplan Rooney; m, Pino Donaggio, Jeremiah Clarke; prod d, David Morong; cos, Kathleen Detoro

In this deceptively cuddly picture about the psychological violence inflicted by a grandmother on her granddaughter, Alexandra Johnes plays Phoebe, an orphaned eight-year-old who lives with her grandmother (Glynis Johns) on an immaculate Virginia estate. Phoebe is deeply attached to her French nanny, Joan, called "Zelly" (a childish version of "Mademoiselle"), played by Isabella Rossellini. Phoebe's favorite pastime is learning about St. Joan of Arc. The grandmother, a lonely, bereaved woman, tries to bind Phoebe to her by separating the youngster from anyone who might come between them. She gradually banishes the gardener for giving Phoebe a gift, Zelly for an imagined violation of trust, and the child's stuffed animals because they are close to Phoebe's heart. A gentle and spiritual film, ZELLY AND ME is directed with great grace. It is also a film of unrelenting psychological and spiritual cruelty. In addition to Tina Rathborne's fine direction and some excellent technical credits, ZELLY AND ME offers impeccable performances from Alexandra Johnes and Glynis Johns, and a superlative one from Isabella Rossellini.

ZERO FOR CONDUCT
(ZERO DE CONDUITE)
1933 44m bw Drama   ★★★★★
Gaumont/Franco Film/Aubert   (France)

Jean Daste, le nain Delfin, Robert Le Flem, Louis de Gonzague-Frick, Louis Lefevre, Gilbert Pluchon, Gerard de Bedarieux, Constantin Goldstein-Kehler

p, Jean Vigo; d, Jean Vigo; w, Jean Vigo; ph, Boris Kaufman; ed, Jean Vigo; m, Maurice Jaubert

One of the greatest films about children ever made and a haunting celebration of anarchic rebellion. The first fictional work from writer/director/scenarist/editor Jean Vigo, ZERO FOR CONDUCT was closely based on his own miserable experiences as a boarding-school pupil and influenced other screen classics of disaffected youth including Truffaut's THE 400 BLOWS and Lindsay Anderson's IF . . .

The plot follows the misadventures of a group of young students as they endure the absurdities and deprivations forced upon them by their petty, authoritarian teachers. After a confrontation in which one of the students repeats before the entire faculty the phrase with which he has rebuffed the sexual advances of a teacher (literally, "shit on you"), matters escalate into a full-scale dormitory rebellion. Beds are overturned and pillows ripped open, resulting in a rain of feathers which falls over everything—one of the most beautiful images in this, or any, film. Finally, locked in an attic for the duration of the school fete, the young rebels escape onto the roof and rain down a barrage of books, stones, and shoes onto a group of visiting dignitaries, inspiring the rest of the boys to revolt and take over the school.

Vigo, whose promising career was cut short by his death from septicemia at the age of 29, demonstrates a complete mastery of his art in ZERO, only the third film he had made. Despite occasionally poor acting (the cast was largely nonprofessional), several sequences stand out as near-perfect fusions of shot composition, editing, lighting, and dialogue. The "rain of feathers" sequence is justly celebrated; so is the scene in which three of the boys, after being ordered to stand still for two hours at the bedside of a supervisor, plead with him to allow one of them, who has developed a stomach ache, to visit the bathroom. Their repeated pleas become a kind of incantation which takes on a haunting, other-worldly quality.

ZERO was made for a mere 200,000 francs and shot by Vigo's friend Boris Kaufman, younger brother of Soviet "Kino-Eye" pioneer Dziga Vertov. It received a mixed reception on its initial 1933 release and was soon banned for fear it would instigate civil unrest. Rereleased in 1945, it has since been accepted as a landmark of world cinema.

ZIEGFELD FOLLIES
1945 110m c Musical   ★★★★
MGM   (U.S.)   /U

William Powell (The Great Ziegfeld), Fred Astaire, Lucille Ball, Judy Garland, Lena Horne, Esther Williams, Red Skelton, Gene Kelly, Fanny Brice, Edward Arnold

p, Arthur Freed; d, Vincente Minnelli, George Sidney, Charles Walters, Roy Del Ruth, Lemuel Ayers; w, E.Y. Harburg, Jack McGowan, Guy Bolton, Frank Sullivan, John Murray Anderson, Lemuel Ayers, Don Loper, Kay Thompson, Roger Edens, Hugh Martin, Ralph Blane, William Noble, Wilkie Mahoney, Cal Howard, Erik Charell, Max Liebman, Bill Schorr, Harry Crane, Lou Holtz, Eddie Cantor, Allen Boretz, Edgar Allan Woolf, Philip Rapp, Al Lewis, Joseph Schrank, Robert Alton, Eugene Loring, Robert Lewis, Charles Walters, James O'Hanlon, David Freedman, Joseph Erons, Irving Brecher, Samson Raphaelson, Everett Freeman, Devery Freeman; ph, George Folsey,

Charles Rosher, William Ferrari; ed, Albert Akst; art d, Cedric Gibbons, Jack Martin Smith, Merrill Pye, Lemuel Ayers; chor, Robert Alton; cos, Florence Bunin, Irene, Helen Rose

On his deathbed, a delirious Florenz Ziegfeld reportedly cried out stage directions ("Ready for the last finale! Great! The show looks good! The show looks good!") continually. ZIEGFELD FOLLIES takes its cue from there, and the film opens up with Ziegfeld (William Powell, reprising his role in THE GREAT ZIEGFELD) up in heaven, dreaming about a new show. A group of puppets (caricatures of some of his original Follies stars) entertain him, followed by Fred Astaire, Lucille Ball, and Cyd Charisse in the first of a whopping 13 musical and comic sequences featuring MGM's top stars (Astaire and Gene Kelly among them, dancing together for the first time in "The Babbitt and the Bromide"). The film was shot by several directors, starting with George Sidney, who was replaced by Vincente Minnelli, while Robert Lewis, Norman Taurog, Charles Walters, Roy Del Ruth, Merrill Pye, and Lemuel Ayres also lent uncredited hands. With so many big names in the cast, it had to be shot bit by bit, with the actors called off other productions and many writers paged from other projects. The film premiered with 19 sequences, clocking in at 273 minutes, too long for any sensible release, so several segments were cut, including a duet between Mickey Rooney and Judy Garland (who parodies Greer Garson in "A Great Lady Has an Interview") and some comic bits. The film eventually made over $5 million in theaters—deservedly, since ZIEGFELD FOLLIES is a marvel of music and dance as only MGM could do it.

ZIEGFELD GIRL
1941 131m bw Musical   ★★★½
MGM   (U.S.)   /A

James Stewart (Gilbert Young), Judy Garland (Susan Gallagher), Hedy Lamarr (Sandra Kolter), Lana Turner (Sheila Regan), Tony Martin (Frank Merton), Jackie Cooper (Jerry Regan), Ian Hunter (Geoffrey Collis), Charles Winninger (Pop Gallagher), Edward Everett Horton (Noble Sage), Paul Kelly (John Slayton)

p, Pandro S. Berman; d, Robert Z. Leonard; w, Marguerite Roberts, Sonya Levien (based on a story by William Anthony McGuire); ph, Ray June; ed, Blanche Sewell; m, Herbert Stothart; art d, Cedric Gibbons, Daniel B. Cathcart; chor, Busby Berkeley; cos, Adrian

This MGM extravaganza details the fortunes of Ziegfeld girls Susan Gallagher (Judy Garland), Sandra Kolter (Hedy Lamarr), and Sheila Regan (Lana Turner). Show business trouper Susan quits the vaudeville act run by her father (Charles Winninger) to further her Follies career, and soon falls in love with the brother (Jackie Cooper) of former elevator operator Sheila, another new Ziegfeld girl. Meanwhile, Sheila's head is turned by the glamor of it all, and she begins to hobnob with high society, especially Park Avenue socialite Geoffrey Collis (Ian Hunter). Left behind is truck driver Gilbert Young (James Stewart), who, in the hopes of winning back his wayward love, tries to make extra money as a bootlegger and winds up in prison. Sandra, the third Ziegfeld girl, finds life on the stage more eventful than life with her penniless violinist husband (Philip Dorn)—until she finally comes to her senses and realizes that love means more to her than show business. Eventually, Susan uses her success to renew interest in her father's career, while Sheila botches her life and career, becoming an alcoholic. For all the melodramatic goings on among the principals, the true stars of this entertaining film are, quite fittingly, the lavish, spectacular dance numbers, employing hundreds of Ziegfeld girls in glittering costumes in the best style of both Florenz Ziegfeld and Busby Berkeley.

ZORBA THE GREEK
(ZORBA)
1964 142m bw Drama   ★★★½
Fox/Cacoyannis-Rochley   (U.S./Greece)   /PG

Anthony Quinn (Alexis Zorba), Alan Bates (Basil), Irene Papas (The Widow), Lila Kedrova (Mme. Hortense), George Foundas (Mavrandoni), Eleni Anousaki (Lola), Sotiris Moustakas (Mimithos), Takis Emmanuel (Manolakas), Yorgo Voyagis (Pavlo), Anna Kyriakou (Soul)

p, Michael Cacoyannis; d, Michael Cacoyannis; w, Michael Cacoyannis (based on the novel by Nikos Kazantzakis); ph, Walter Lassally; ed, Michael Cacoyannis; m, Mikis Theodorakis; art d, Vassele Fotopoulos; cos, Anna Stavropoulou

AAN Best Picture; AAN Best Actor: Anthony Quinn; *AA Best Supporting Actress:* Lila Kedrova; *AAN Best Director:* Michael Cacoyannis; *AAN Best Adapted Screenplay:* Michael Cacoyannis; *AA Best Cinematography:* Walter Lassally; *AA Best Art Direction:* Vassilis Fotopoulos

As spritely and exuberant as a tank, but worth a watch. Although Quinn has often played earthy, force-of-nature characters, his title role in ZORBA THE GREEK was a career performance loved by both critics and audiences—so much, in fact, that he's been doing it ever since.

The film opens with Bates, a young English writer, arriving in Greece to collect his thoughts and discover his own identity. When he goes to Crete to work at a lignite mine, an inheritance from his native-Greek father, he is joined by Quinn, a lusty Greek peasant who also wants to work at the mine. The unusual duo move into a hotel run by Kedrova, a tattered French prostitute, former lover to four different admirals, and ex-cabaret dancer. Quinn begins wooing her and encourages Bates to show some attention to Papas, a beautiful widow much desired by the local male population. The mine is in need of some repairs, so the irrepressible Quinn cons a group of monks into letting him remove some lumber from a forest on a nearby mountain. Quinn devises a scheme to transport the lumber to the mine but must first obtain the necessary equipment. When Quinn ventures into the city, Kedrova helps Bates overcome his bashfulness, and the Englishman gathers up the courage to visit Papas. They make love, and rumors begin spreading about the island after Bates is seen leaving the house.

Through several upheavals, ZORBA boils down to the joyful dance that expresses Quinn's surpassingly positive philosophy—life may be painful, but it is beautiful nonetheless.

Quinn brings all his larger-than-life magic to his part—that of a character who is happy, devil-may-care, and zestfully mad. (When ZORBA THE GREEK was adapted into a spirited Broadway musical, "Zorba," for the 1968-1969 season, Quinn was chosen for the title role.) Bates, as the inhibited Englishman, is a fine contrast, never overshadowed by the enormity of Quinn's character as he learns about the forces of life. And both Kedrova and Papas are wonderful.

Despite its loose structure and excessive length, ZORBA THE GREEK has some marvelous moments. The film itself was somewhat revolutionary in its language and irreverent sense of humor, although these elements, controversial in 1964, have since become commonplace.

ZULU

1964   135m   c   Historical/War   ★★★★★
Diamond   (U.K.)   /PG

Stanley Baker *(Lt. John Chard)*, Jack Hawkins *(Rev. Otto Witt)*, Ulla Jacobsson *(Margareta Witt)*, James Booth *(Pvt. Henry Hook)*, Michael Caine *(Lt. Gonville Bromhead)*, Nigel Green *(Color Sgt. Bourne)*, Ivor Emmanuel *(Pvt. Owen)*, Paul Daneman *(Sgt. Maxfield)*, Glynn Edwards *(Cpl. Allen)*, Neil McCarthy *(Pvt. Thomas)*

p, Stanley Baker, Cy Endfield; d, Cy Endfield; w, John Prebble, Cy Endfield (based on a story by Prebble); ph, Stephen Dade; ed, John Jympson; m, John Barry; art d, Ernest Archer; cos, Arthur Newman

Set in 1879 in Natal, this magnificently staged, brilliantly acted film tells the story of the heroic defense by overwhelmingly outnumbered British troops of the tiny outpost Rorke's Drift. Having been warned by a pacifist missionary (Jack Hawkins) that a British army contingent has been massacred by Zulu warriors, Lt. John Chard (Stanley Baker, the film's producer) orders his troops to dig in, despite the pleas of Lt. Gonville Bromhead (Michael Caine), the blueblood second-in-command who wants to abandon the post and who feels that he, rather than Chard (an engineer), should be in charge. Rather than fleeing, however, the courageous Brits withstand attack after attack, night and day, from 4,000 Zulus, and eventually triumph through a combination of ingenuity, determination, and luck. This amazing film is devastatingly accurate in its depiction of the Rorke's Drift action, and is superbly directed by Cy Endfield, whose battle scenes are some of the most terrifying ever committed to film. Producer Baker, however, had a difficult time getting his Zulu extras to cooperate on the location shoot in Natal. None had ever seen a motion picture, and he couldn't make the chiefs understand what he wanted to do. Finally, Baker had an old western starring Gene Autry flown in and showed it to the Zulus, who, grasping the fictional game at hand, later cooperated and lent the battle scenes tremendous power. ZULU is dramatically narrated by Richard Burton, who points out that of the 1,344 Victoria Crosses awarded since 1856, 11 were given to the defenders at Rorke's Drift, an all-time record for one engagement.

ZYDECKO MULATTO

1983   187m   c   Documentary   ★★★★
Wild Entrepreneurs, Inc.   (U.S.)

Janet Fille *(Singer)*, Jacques Pallette *(Composer)*, S. Cohn *(Narrator)*, Antoine Boitano *(Chef Tony)*, The People of Fil-au-fond, LA

p, Radha Homay; d, Jacob Munch

This charming if obscure documentary limning the struggles of a small group of aspiring musicians from a village in the bayou garnered little attention at the time of its release in the early 80s. It was only with the increasing interest in Zydeco music in the late 80s that bootleg videocassettes began circulating in the entertainment community. Music/Food/Film critic Michael Goodwin, who did so much for various facets of Acadian culture in the 70s, championed Munch's work for years before turning his attention elsewhere. The film is still little known outside the professional community, where it has since become a well-established underground classic, as much for the story of its production as for its music. Munch, the Swiss critic and erstwhile filmmaker, struggled for years to raise the funding for the enterprise, relying on a dedicated crew who often worked without pay.

The result is a colorful canvas replete with meticulous detail, with all sorts of enjoyable nuances buried deep within the soundtrack or delicately sketched in the background, on the edges of the frame. Coming through strongly is the courage and humor of the small group of musicians, set against the multiethnic canvas of the community, who almost—but not quite—make it to the big time at the end of the lengthy film. It's as if Robert Altman and Richard Lester collaborated with Les Blank. Although the subject of the film is clearly the music, Munch often gets carried away with portraits of minor characters (often children), meticulous financial details of the Zydeco business, and food and gardening tips. (In the cassette version we saw, several recipes are included in the credits.) This fullness and variety are in large part responsible for the charm of the film, which was just slightly ahead of its time.

ALTERNATE TITLE INDEX

The main portion of this book lists films alphabetically according to the tile by which they were first released in the US. If you cannot find the movie you are looking for, please check this index to see if the work is listed under a different title. The column on the left contains: original foreign-language titles; British titles, where they differed from those used for US release; and alternative English-language titles.

ALTERNATE TITLE	U.S. TITLE
A BOUT DE SOUFFLE	BREATHLESS
A COR DO SEU DESTINO	COLOR OF DESTINY, THE
ABBOTT AND COSTELLO MEET THE GHOSTS	ABBOTT AND COSTELLO MEET FRANKENSTEIN
ABISMOS DE PASION	WUTHERING HEIGHTS
ACE, THE	GREAT SANTINI, THE
AFFAIR OF THE HEART, AN	BODY AND SOUL
AGE OF GOLD	L'AGE D'OR
AGUIRRE, DER ZORN GOTTES	AGUIRRE, THE WRATH OF GOD
AI NO CORRIDA	IN THE REALM OF THE SENSES
AKIBIYORI	LATE AUTUMN
AKIRA KUROSAWA'S DREAMS	DREAMS
ALEXANDER GRAHAM BELL	STORY OF ALEXANDER GRAHAM BELL, THE
ALICE IN DEN STADTEN	ALICE IN THE CITIES
ALL THAT MONEY CAN BUY	DEVIL AND DANIEL WEBSTER, THE
ALL THE MORNINGS OF THE WORLD	TOUS LES MATINS DU MONDE
AMORE A VENT'ANNI	LOVE AT TWENTY
AMOROUS GENERAL, THE	WALTZ OF THE TOREADORS
AND WOMAN. . . WAS CREATED	AND GOD CREATED WOMAN
ANGEL STREET	GASLIGHT
ANGELS AND THE PIRATES	ANGELS IN THE OUTFIELD
ANGST ESSEN SEELE AUF	ALI, FEAR EATS THE SOUL
ANIMAL HOUSE	NATIONAL LAMPOON'S ANIMAL HOUSE
ANNE AND MURIEL	TWO ENGLISH GIRLS
ANSIKTE MOT ANSIKTE	FACE TO FACE
ANSIKTET	MAGICIAN, THE
ANTONIA	ANTONIA'S LINE
APUR SANSAR	WORLD OF APU, THE
ATAME	TIE ME UP! TIE ME DOWN!
ATLANTIC CITY, U.S.A.	ATLANTIC CITY
ATOMIC ROCKETSHIP	FLASH GORDON
BA WANG BIE JI	FAREWELL, MY CONCUBINE
BABE, THE GALLANT PIG	BABE
BABETTE'S GASTEBUD	BABETTE'S FEAST
BACHELOR KNIGHT	BACHELOR AND THE BOBBY-SOXER, THE
BAD GIRLS, THE	LES BICHES
BAILIFF, THE	SANSHO THE BAILIFF
BAISERS VOLES	STOLEN KISSES
BAL NA VODI	HEY BABU RIBA
BALTHAZAR	AU HASARD, BALTHAZAR
BANK DETECTIVE, THE	BANK DICK, THE
BATTLE STRIPE	MEN, THE
BATTLING BELLHOP, THE	KID GALAHAD
BEAUTE VOLEE	STEALING BEAUTY
BEGGARS' OPERA	THREEPENNY OPERA, THE
BIAN ZHOU BIAN CHANG	LIFE ON A STRING
BIG CARNIVAL, THE	ACE IN THE HOLE
BIG HEART, THE	MIRACLE ON 34TH STREET
BIRDS OF A FEATHER	LA CAGE AUX FOLLES
BIRTHMARK	OMEN, THE
BIZALOM	CONFIDENCE

ALTERNATE TITLE	U.S. TITLE
DEVIL-DOLL, THE	DEVIL DOLL, THE
DIABOLO MENTHE	PEPPERMINT SODA
DIAMOND EARRINGS, THE	EARRINGS OF MADAME DE . . . , THE
DIARY OF MAJOR THOMPSON	FRENCH, THEY ARE A FUNNY RACE, THE
DIARY OF OHARU	LIFE OF OHARU, THE
DIE ANGST DES TORMANNS BEIM ELFMETER	GOALIE'S ANXIETY AT THE PENALTY KICK, THE
DIE BLECHTROMMEL	TIN DRUM, THE
DIE BLEIERNE ZEIT	MARIANNE AND JULIANE
DIE DREIGROSCHENOPER	THREEPENNY OPERA, THE
DIE EHE DER MARIA BRAUN	MARRIAGE OF MARIA BRAUN, THE
DIE FALSCHUNG	CIRCLE OF DECEIT
DIE REGENSCHIRME VON CHERBOURG	UMBRELLAS OF CHERBOURG, THE
DIE SEHNS UCHT DER VERONIKA VOSS	VERONIKA VOSS
DIE TAUSEND AUGEN DES DR. MABUSE	THOUSAND EYES OF DR. MABUSE, THE
DIE UNENDLICHE GESCHICHTE	NEVERENDING STORY, THE
DIE VERLORENE EHRE DER KATHARINA BLUM	LOST HONOR OF KATHARINA BLUM, THE
DIE XUE SHUANG XIONG	KILLER, THE
DIVORZIO ALL'ITALIANA	DIVORCE, ITALIAN STYLE
DOES, THE	LES BICHES
DON QUICHOTTE	DON QUIXOTE
DON-KIKHOT	DON QUIXOTE
DONA FLOR E SEUS DOIS MARIDOS	DONA FLOR AND HER TWO HUSBANDS
DONA HERLINDA Y SU HIJO	DONA HERLINDA AND HER SON
DONNA DI VITA	LOLA
DOOMED, LIVING	IKIRU
DOUBLE POSSESSION	GANJA AND HESS
DOUBLE, THE	KAGEMUSHA
DOWN WENT McGINTY	GREAT McGINTY, THE
DRACULA	HORROR OF DRACULA
DRACULA CERCA SANGUE DI VERGINE E. . . MORI DI SETE	ANDY WARHOL'S DRACULA
DRACULA VUOLE VIVERE: CERCA SANGUE DI VERGINA	ANDY WARHOL'S DRACULA
DREYFUS	DREYFUS CASE, THE
DRUM, THE	DRUMS
DU RIFIFI CHEZ DES HOMMES	RIFIFI
DUVAR	WALL, THE
E LA NAVE VA	AND THE SHIP SAILS ON
EIGHT ARMS TO HOLD YOU	HELP!
EL ANGEL EXTERMINADOR	EXTERMINATING ANGEL, THE
EL ESPIRITU DE LA COLMENA	SPIRIT OF THE BEEHIVE, THE
EN PASSION	PASSION OF ANNA, THE
ENEMIES OF THE PUBLIC	PUBLIC ENEMY, THE
ENIGMA OF KASPAR HAUSER, THE	EVERY MAN FOR HIMSELF AND GOD AGAINST ALL
ERNEST HEMINGWAY'S THE KILLERS	KILLERS, THE
ET DIEU CREA LA FEMME	AND GOD CREATED WOMAN
ETAT DE SIEGE	STATE OF SIEGE
EVERYBODY'S CHEERING	TAKE ME OUT TO THE BALL GAME
EXTASE	ECSTASY
EYE OF EVIL	THOUSAND EYES OF DR. MABUSE, THE
FACE OF FEAR	PEEPING TOM
FACE, THE	MAGICIAN, THE
FALL OF LOLA MONTES, THE	LOLA MONTES
FALL OF THE HOUSE OF USHER, THE	HOUSE OF USHER
FALSE WITNESS	CIRCLE OF DECEIT
FALSTAFF	CHIMES AT MIDNIGHT
FANNY OCH ALEXANDER	FANNY AND ALEXANDER
FAREWELL, MY LOVELY	MURDER, MY SWEET
FATHER'S ON A BUSINESS TRIP	WHEN FATHER WAS AWAY ON BUSINESS

ALTERNATE TITLE	U.S. TITLE
FEAR EATS THE SOUL	ALI, FEAR EATS THE SOUL
FEDERICO FELLINI'S 8 1/2	8 1/2
FIELDS OF HONOR	SHENANDOAH
FIENDS, THE	DIABOLIQUE
FIRST OF THE FEW, THE	SPITFIRE
FISTS IN THE POCKET	FIST IN HIS POCKET
FONTANE EFFI BRIEST	EFFI BRIEST
FOR A FISTFUL OF DOLLARS	FISTFUL OF DOLLARS, A
FORBIDDEN ALLIANCE	BARRETTS OF WIMPOLE STREET, THE
FORBIDDEN LOVE	FREAKS
FORBIN PROJECT, THE	COLOSSUS: THE FORBIN PROJECT
FOREVER IN LOVE	PRIDE OF THE MARINES
47 SAMURAI	CHUSHINGURA
FRANCESCO, GIULLARE DI DIO	FLOWERS OF ST. FRANCIS, THE
FRATERNALLY YOURS	SONS OF THE DESERT
FREEDOM FOR US	A NOUS LA LIBERTE
FRENCH ARE A FUNNY RACE	FRENCH, THEY ARE A FUNNY RACE, THE
GANG WAR	ODD MAN OUT
GERMAN SISTERS, THE	MARIANNE AND JULIANE
GESTAPO	NIGHT TRAIN TO MUNICH
GHARE BAIRE	HOME AND THE WORLD, THE
GION NO SHIMAI	SISTERS OF THE GION
GIRL WAS YOUNG, THE	YOUNG AND INNOCENT
GIRLFRIENDS, THE	LES BICHES
GIRLS HE LEFT BEHIND, THE	GANG'S ALL HERE, THE
GIRLS IN UNIFORM	MAEDCHEN IN UNIFORM
GIULIETTA DEGLI SPIRITI	JULIET OF THE SPIRITS
GOING APE	WHERE'S POPPA?
GOLDEN VIRGIN	STORY OF ESTHER COSTELLO, THE
GOOD MARRIAGE, A	LE BEAU MARIAGE
GOODBYE, CHILDREN	AU REVOIR, LES ENFANTS
GORGEOUS BIRD LIKE ME, A	SUCH A GORGEOUS KID LIKE ME
GOTTERDAMMERUNG	DAMNED, THE
GRAVE ROBBERS FROM OUTER SPACE	PLAN 9 FROM OUTER SPACE
GUNEY'S THE WALL	WALL, THE
GUNS IN THE AFTERNOON	RIDE THE HIGH COUNTRY
HAMP	KING AND COUNTRY
HANDLE WITH CARE	CITIZENS BAND
HANDS OF ORLAC, THE	MAD LOVE
HANDSOME SERGE	LE BEAU SERGE
HANOI HANNA—QUEEN OF CHINA	CHELSEA GIRLS, THE
HAPPY KNOWLEDGE	LE GAI SAVOIR
HARD DRIVER	LAST AMERICAN HERO, THE
HARDCORE LIFE, THE	HARDCORE
HATACHI NO KOI	LOVE AT TWENTY
HAUNTED AND THE HUNTED, THE	DEMENTIA 13
HEAD OVER HEELS	CHILLY SCENES OF WINTER
HEART IN WINTER, A	UN COEUR EN HIVER
HEAVEN AND HELL	HIGH AND LOW
HEIST, THE	$ (DOLLARS)
HENRY VIII	PRIVATE LIFE OF HENRY VIII, THE
HERE IS A MAN	DEVIL AND DANIEL WEBSTER, THE
HIM	EL
HITLER, EIN FILM AUS DEUTSCHLAND	OUR HITLER, A FILM FROM GERMANY
HOLLYWOOD COWBOY	HEARTS OF THE WEST
HOMBRE MIRANDO AL SUDESTE	MAN FACING SOUTHEAST
HOMELAND	HEIMAT
HONG GAOLIANG	RED SORGHUM
HOPALONG CASSIDY ENTERS	HOPALONG CASSIDY

ALTERNATE TITLE	U.S. TITLE
LE MUR	WALL, THE
LE NOTTI DI CABIRIA	NIGHTS OF CABIRIA
LE PASSAGER DE LA PLUIE	RIDER ON THE RAIN
LE PROCES	TRIAL, THE
LE RIDICULE	RIDICULE
LE ROI DE COEUR	KING OF HEARTS
LE ROMAN D'UN TRICHEUR	STORY OF A CHEAT, THE
LE SALAIRE DE LA PEUR	WAGES OF FEAR, THE
LE SOUFFLE AU COEUR	MURMUR OF THE HEART
LE TESTAMENT D'ORPHEE	TESTAMENT OF ORPHEUS, THE
LE TESTAMENT DU DR. MABUSE	TESTAMENT OF DR. MABUSE, THE
LE TRAIN	TRAIN, THE
LE VENT SOUFFLE OU IL VEUT	MAN ESCAPED, A
LE VIEIL HOMME ET L'ENFANT	TWO OF US, THE
LEARN, BABY, LEARN	LEARNING TREE, THE
LES AMANTS	LOVERS, THE
LES AMOURS DE TONI	TONI
LES CAMARADES	ORGANIZER, THE
LES CARNETS DU MAJOR THOMPSON	FRENCH, THEY ARE A FUNNY RACE, THE
LES COUSINS	COUSINS, THE
LES DEUX ANGLAISES ET LE CONTINENT	TWO ENGLISH GIRLS
LES DIABOLIQUES	DIABOLIQUE
LES ENFANTS DU PARADIS	CHILDREN OF PARADISE
LES JEUX INTERDITS	FORBIDDEN GAMES
LES NUITS DE LA PLEINE LUNE	FULL MOON IN PARIS
LES NUITS FAUVES	SAVAGE NIGHTS
LES PARAPLUIES DE CHERBOURG	UMBRELLAS OF CHERBOURG, THE
LES QUATRES CENTS COUPS	FOUR HUNDRED BLOWS, THE
LES SOMNAMBULES	MON ONCLE D'AMERIQUE
LES TROIS COURONNES DU MATELOT	THREE CROWNS OF THE SAILOR
LES VACANCES DE MONSIEUR HULOT	MR. HULOT'S HOLIDAY
LES VALSEUSES	GOING PLACES
LEST WE FORGET	HANGMEN ALSO DIE
LETYAT ZHURAVLI	CRANES ARE FLYING, THE
LIEBE MIT ZWANZIG	LOVE AT TWENTY
LIFE OF BRIAN	MONTY PYTHON'S LIFE OF BRIAN
LITTLE THEATER OF JEAN RENOIR, THE	LE PETIT THEATRE DE JEAN RENOIR
LO BALLO DA SOLA	STEALING BEAUTY
LO SCEICCO BIANCO	WHITE SHEIK, THE
LO STRANIERO	STRANGER, THE
LONELY HEARTS KILLERS, THE	HONEYMOON KILLERS, THE
LONELY WIFE, THE	CHARULATA
LOST ILLUSION, THE	FALLEN IDOL, THE
LOVE THE MAGICIAN	EL AMOR BRUJO
LOVELY TO LOOK AT	THIN ICE
LOYAL 47 RONIN, THE	CHUSHINGURA
LULLABY, THE	SIN OF MADELON CLAUDET, THE
M. HIRE	MONSIEUR HIRE
MA NUIT CHEZ MAUD	MY NIGHT AT MAUD'S
MAARAKAT ALGER	BATTLE OF ALGIERS, THE
MAD CAGE, THE	LA CAGE AUX FOLLES
MAD MAX II	ROAD WARRIOR, THE
MADAME DE . . .	EARRINGS OF MADAME DE . . . , THE
MAGNIFICENT SEVEN, THE	SEVEN SAMURAI, THE
MAN OF BRONZE	JIM THORPE—ALL AMERICAN
MAN WITH THE X-RAY EYES, THE	"X"—THE MAN WITH THE X-RAY EYES
MANNER	MEN. . .
MANON DES SOURCES	MANON OF THE SPRING

ALTERNATE TITLE	U.S. TITLE
PHANTOM OF TERROR, THE	BIRD WITH THE CRYSTAL PLUMAGE, THE
PO DEZJU	BEFORE THE RAIN
POE'S TALES OF TERROR	TALES OF TERROR
POOKIE	STERILE CUCKOO, THE
POPE ONDINE STORY, THE	CHELSEA GIRLS, THE
POPIOL I DIAMENT	ASHES AND DIAMONDS
POR UN PUNADO DE DOLARES	FISTFUL OF DOLLARS, A
POTE TIN KYRIAKI	NEVER ON SUNDAY
PRENOM: CARMEN	FIRST NAME: CARMEN
PREPAREZ VOS MOUCHOIRS	GET OUT YOUR HANDKERCHIEFS
PRIMA DELLA REVOLUTIONA	BEFORE THE REVOLUTION
PROCES DE JEANNE D'ARC	TRIAL OF JOAN OF ARC
PROFESSION: REPORTER	PASSENGER, THE
QIU JU DA GUANSI	STORY OF QIU JU, THE
QUAI DES BRUMES	PORT OF SHADOWS
QUATRE NUITS D'UN REVEUR	FOUR NIGHTS OF A DREAMER
QUE LA BETE MEURE	THIS MAN MUST DIE
QUOI DE NEUF, PUSSYCAT?	WHAT'S NEW, PUSSYCAT?
RAGE	RABID
RANSOM, THE	HIGH AND LOW
REBEL WITH A CAUSE	LONELINESS OF THE LONG DISTANCE RUNNER, THE
REDL EZREDES	COLONEL REDL
RELAZIONI PERICOLOSE	LES LIAISONS DANGEREUSES
RETOUR DE MARTIN GUERRE, LE	RETURN OF MARTIN GUERRE, THE
REVENGE OF MILADY, THE	FOUR MUSKETEERS, THE
REVOLT OF THE BOYARS, THE	IVAN THE TERRIBLE, PARTS I & II
RIGET	KINGDOM, THE
RISO AMARO	BITTER RICE
ROAD TO FRISCO	THEY DRIVE BY NIGHT
ROAD, THE	LA STRADA
ROBIN HOOD	ADVENTURES OF ROBIN HOOD, THE
ROBINSON CRUSOE	ADVENTURES OF ROBINSON CRUSOE, THE
ROCCO ED I SUOI FRATELLI	ROCCO AND HIS BROTHERS
ROCCO ET SES FRERES	ROCCO AND HIS BROTHERS
ROCKET SHIP	FLASH GORDON
ROMA	FELLINI'S ROMA
ROMA, CITTA APERTA	OPEN CITY
ROME, OPEN CITY	OPEN CITY
ROMEO AND JULIET	WILLIAM SHAKESPEARE'S ROMEO + JULIET
ROMMEL—DESERT FOX	DESERT FOX, THE
ROSE IN THE MUD, THE	BAD SLEEP WELL, THE
RUDYARD KIPLING'S JUNGLE BOOK	JUNGLE BOOK, THE
RUE CASES NEGRES	SUGAR CANE ALLEY
SABRINA FAIR	SABRINA
SACCO E VANZETTI	SACCO AND VANZETTI
SAFE	[SAFE]
SAGA OF THE ROAD, THE	PATHER PANCHALI
SAIKAKU ICHIDAI ONNA	LIFE OF OHARU, THE
SALERNO BEACHHEAD	WALK IN THE SUN, A
SALO	SALO, OR THE 120 DAYS OF SODOM
SALO, O LE 120 GIORNATE DI SODOMA	SALO, OR THE 120 DAYS OF SODOM
SANS MOBILE APPARENT	WITHOUT APPARENT MOTIVE
SANS TOIT NI LOI	VAGABOND
SANSHO DAYU	SANSHO THE BAILIFF
SATYRICON	FELLINI SATYRICON
SAUVE QUI PEUT—LA VIE	EVERY MAN FOR HIMSELF
SCARFACE, SHAME OF A NATION	SCARFACE
SCIUSCIA	SHOESHINE
SE PERMETTETE	LET'S TALK ABOUT WOMEN

ALTERNATE TITLE	U.S. TITLE
SE7EN	SEVEN
SECRET OF ANNA, THE	CRIA!
SEPT FOIS FEMME	WOMAN TIMES SEVEN
SETTE VOLTE DONNA	WOMAN TIMES SEVEN
SETTLERS, THE	NEW LAND, THE
SHADOW VERSUS THE THOUSAND EYES OF DR. MABUSE, THE	THOUSAND EYES OF DR. MABUSE, THE
SHADOW WARRIOR, THE	KAGEMUSHA
SHE GOT WHAT SHE ASKED FOR	YESTERDAY, TODAY, AND TOMORROW
SHE LET HIM CONTINUE	PRETTY POISON
SHERLOCK HOLMES	ADVENTURES OF SHERLOCK HOLMES, THE
SHICHININ NO SAMURAI	SEVEN SAMURAI, THE
SHOOT THE PIANIST	SHOOT THE PIANO PLAYER
SHOP ON HIGH STREET, THE	SHOP ON MAIN STREET, THE
SIERRA DE TERUEL	MAN'S HOPE
SILKEN SKIN	SOFT SKIN, THE
SIN OF HAROLD DIDDLEBOCK, THE	MAD WEDNESDAY
SINS OF LOLA MONTES, THE	LOLA MONTES
SKAMMEN	SHAME
SLOW MOTION	EVERY MAN FOR HIMSELF
SMULTRONSTALLET	WILD STRAWBERRIES
SOMMARNATTENS LEENDE	SMILES OF A SUMMER NIGHT
SON OF GREETINGS	HI, MOM!
SONG OF THE ROAD, THE	PATHER PANCHALI
SONS OF THE LEGION	SONS OF THE DESERT
SOUS LES TOITS DE PARIS	UNDER THE ROOFS OF PARIS
SPACE SOLDIERS	FLASH GORDON
SPACESHIP TO THE UNKNOWN	FLASH GORDON
SPECTER OF FREEDOM, THE	PHANTOM OF LIBERTY, THE
SPINAL TAP	THIS IS SPINAL TAP
SPIRIT OF THE PEOPLE	ABE LINCOLN IN ILLINOIS
SPIVS	VITELLONI
SPOORLOOS	VANISHING, THE
STORM WITHIN, THE	LES PARENTS TERRIBLES
STORY OF DR. EHRLICH'S MAGIC BULLET, THE	DR. EHRLICH'S MAGIC BULLET
STRANGE ADVENTURE OF DAVID GRAY, THE	VAMPYR
STRANGE INCIDENT	OX-BOW INCIDENT, THE
STRANGE JOURNEY	FANTASTIC VOYAGE
STRANGE ONES, THE	LES ENFANTS TERRIBLES
STRANGERS	I NEVER SANG FOR MY FATHER
STRIKERS, THE	ORGANIZER, THE
SUITABLE CASE FOR TREATMENT, A	MORGAN!
SUMMER MADNESS	SUMMERTIME
SUNA NO ONNA	WOMAN IN THE DUNES
SUPERCOP: POLICE STORY III	SUPERCOP
SWEPT AWAY	SWEPT AWAY. . . BY AN UNUSUAL DESTINY IN THE BLUE SEA OF AUGUST
SYMPHONY OF LOVE	ECSTASY
SZAMARKOHOGES	WHOOPING COUGH
T.P.A.	PRESIDENT'S ANALYST, THE
T2	TERMINATOR 2: JUDGMENT DAY
TALES OF A PALE AND MYSTERIOUS MOON AFTER THE RAIN	UGETSU MONOGATARI
TARZAN VERSUS I.B.M.	ALPHAVILLE
TEN LITTLE NIGGERS	AND THEN THERE WERE NONE
TENGOKU TO-JIGOKU	HIGH AND LOW
THAT THEY MAY LIVE	J'ACCUSE
THE BOAT	DAS BOOT
THE GRAIL	LANCELOT OF THE LAKE

INDEX OF DIRECTORS

The following index includes filmographies for notable directors whose films appear in this book. Titles reviewed in this guide are indicated by a bullet. In the case of directors whose careers date back to the silent era, listings include sound films only.

Benedek, Laslo
KISSING BANDIT, THE (48); PORT OF NEW YORK (49); •DEATH OF A SALESMAN (52); •WILD ONE, THE (53); BENGAL BRIGADE (54); KINDER MUTTER UND EIN GENERAL (55); AFFAIR IN HAVANA (57); MALAGA (59); NAMU, THE KILLER WHALE (66); DARING GAME (68); NIGHT VISITOR, THE (70); ASSAULT ON AGATHON (75)

Benjamin, Richard
•MY FAVORITE YEAR (82); CITY HEAT (84); RACING WITH THE MOON (84); MONEY PIT, THE (86); LITTLE NIKITA (88); MY STEPMOTHER IS AN ALIEN (88); DOWNTOWN (90); MERMAIDS (90); MADE IN AMERICA (93); MILK MONEY (94); MRS. WINTERBOURNE (96)

Bennett, Compton
•SEVENTH VEIL, THE (45); DAYBREAK (46); YEARS BETWEEN, THE (46); MY OWN TRUE LOVE (48); THAT FORSYTE WOMAN (49); •KING SOLOMON'S MINES (50); GLORY AT SEA (52); IT STARTED IN PARADISE (52); SO LITTLE TIME (52); DESPERATE MOMENT (53); AFTER THE BALL (57); CITY AFTER MIDNIGHT (57); MAILBAG ROBBERY (57); BEYOND THE CURTAIN (60)

Benton, Robert
•BAD COMPANY (72); •LATE SHOW, THE (77); •KRAMER VS. KRAMER (79); STILL OF THE NIGHT (82); •PLACES IN THE HEART (84); NADINE (87); •BILLY BATHGATE (91); •NOBODY'S FOOL (94)

Beresford, Bruce
ADVENTURES OF BARRY MCKENZIE, THE (72); BARRY MCKENZIE HOLDS HIS OWN (74); SIDE BY SIDE (75); •DON'S PARTY (76); GETTING OF WISDOM, THE (77); MONEY MOVERS (78); •BREAKER MORANT (80); CLUB, THE (80); FORTRESS (81) ; PUBERTY BLUES (81); •TENDER MERCIES (83); FRINGE DWELLERS, THE (84); KING DAVID (85); CRIMES OF THE HEART (86); ARIA (87); •DRIVING MISS DAISY (89); HER ALIBI (89); •BLACK ROBE (91); MISTER JOHNSON (91); RICH IN LOVE (93); GOOD MAN IN AFRICA, A (94); SILENT FALL (94); LAST DANCE (96); PARADISE ROAD (97)

Bergman, Andrew
SO FINE (81); •FRESHMAN, THE (90); •HONEYMOON IN VEGAS (92); IT COULD HAPPEN TO YOU (94); STRIPTEASE (96)

Bergman, Ingmar
CRISIS (45); IT RAINS ON OUR LOVE (46); NIGHT IS MY FUTURE (48); SHIP TO INDIA, A (47); PORT OF CALL (48); DEVIL'S WANTON, THE (49); THIRST (49); TO JOY (50); THIS CAN'T HAPPEN HERE (50); ILLICIT INTERLUDE (51); SECRETS OF WOMEN (52); MONIKA (53); SAWDUST AND TINSEL (53); NAKED NIGHT, THE (53); LESSON IN LOVE, A (54); DREAMS (55); •SMILES OF A SUMMER NIGHT (55); •SEVENTH SEAL, THE (57); •WILD STRAWBERRIES (57); BRINK OF LIFE (58); •MAGICIAN, THE (58); •VIRGIN SPRING, THE (59); DEVIL'S EYE, THE (60); THROUGH A GLASS DARKLY (61); WINTER LIGHT (62); SILENCE, THE (63); ALL THESE WOMEN (64); •PERSONA (66); STIMULANTIA (67); •HOUR OF THE WOLF, THE (68); •SHAME (68); •PASSION OF ANNA, THE (69); RITUAL, THE (69); FARO DOCUMENTARY, THE (70); TOUCH, THE (71); •CRIES AND WHISPERS (72); •SCENES FROM A MARRIAGE (73); MAGIC FLUTE, THE (74); •FACE TO FACE (76); SERPENT'S EGG, THE (77); AUTUMN SONATA (78); FARO 1979 (79); FROM THE LIFE OF THE MARIONETTES (80); •FANNY AND ALEXANDER (82); •AFTER THE REHEARSAL (84)

Berkeley, Busby
SHE HAD TO SAY YES (33); •FOOTLIGHT PARADE (33); BRIGHT LIGHTS (35); •GOLD DIGGERS OF 1935 (35); I LIVE FOR LOVE (35); STAGE STRUCK (36); GO-GETTER, THE (37); HOLLYWOOD HOTEL (37); COMET OVER BROADWAY (38); GARDEN OF THE MOON (38); MEN ARE SUCH FOOLS (38); •BABES IN ARMS (39); FAST AND FURIOUS (39); THEY MADE ME A CRIMINAL (39); FORTY LITTLE MOTHERS (40); •STRIKE UP THE BAND (40); BABES ON BROADWAY (41); BLONDE INSPIRATION (41); •FOR ME AND MY GAL (42); •GANG'S ALL HERE, THE (43); CINDERELLA JONES (46); •TAKE ME OUT TO THE BALL GAME (49)

Berri, Claude
LES BAISERS (64); LA CHANCE ET L'AMOUR (64); •TWO OF US, THE (67); MARRY ME! MARRY ME! (69); MAN WITH CONNECTIONS, THE (70); LE CINEMA DE PAPA (70); LE SEX SHOP (72); LE MALE DU SIECLE (75); FIRST TIME, THE (76); UN MOMENT D'EGAREMENT (77); I LOVE

YOU (80); LE MAITRE D'ECOLE (82); TCHAO PANTIN (83); •JEAN DE FLORETTE (86); •MANON OF THE SPRING (86); URANUS (91); GERMINAL (93); LUCIE AUBRAC (97)

Bertolucci, Bernardo
GRIM REAPER, THE (62); •BEFORE THE REVOLUTION (64); VANGELO '70 (67); PARTNER (68); SPIDER'S STRATAGEM, THE (70); •CONFORMIST, THE (70); •LAST TANGO IN PARIS (73); •1900 (76); LUNA (79); TRAGEDY OF A RIDICULOUS MAN, THE (81); •LAST EMPEROR, THE (87); SHELTERING SKY, THE (90); LITTLE BUDDHA (94); •STEALING BEAUTY (96)

Besson, Luc
LE DERNIER COMBAT (84); SUBWAY (85); BIG BLUE, THE (88); •LA FEMME NIKITA (90); ATLANTIS (91); PROFESSIONAL, THE (94); •FIFTH ELEMENT, THE (97)

Bigelow, Kathryn
SET-UP (78); LOVELESS, THE (82); •NEAR DARK (87); •BLUE STEEL (90); POINT BREAK (91); •STRANGE DAYS (95)

Blier, Bertrand
HITLER... CONNAIS PAS! (62); BREAKDOWN (67); •GOING PLACES (74); CALMOS (75); •GET OUT YOUR HANDKERCHIEFS (78); BUFFET FROID (79); BEAU PERE (81); MY BEST FRIEND'S GIRL (83); NOTRE HISTOIRE (84); MENAGE (86); TOO BEAUTIFUL FOR YOU (89); MERCI, LA VIE (91); 1, 2, 3 SOLEIL (93); MON HOMME (96)

Boetticher, Budd
MISSING JUROR, THE (44); ONE MYSTERIOUS NIGHT (44); ESCAPE IN THE FOG (45); GUY, A GAL, AND A PAL, A (45); YOUTH ON TRIAL (45); ASSIGNED TO DANGER (48); BEHIND LOCKED DOORS (48); BLACK MIDNIGHT (49); WOLF HUNTERS, THE (49); KILLER SHARK (50); BULLFIGHTER AND THE LADY (51); CIMARRON KID, THE (51); BRONCO BUSTER (52); HORIZONS WEST (52); RED BALL EXPRESS (52); BLADES OF THE MUSKETEERS (53); CITY BENEATH THE SEA (53); EAST OF SUMATRA (53); MAN FROM THE ALAMO, THE (53); SEMINOLE (53); WINGS OF THE HAWK (53); MAGNIFICENT MATADOR, THE (55); KILLER IS LOOSE, THE (56); SEVEN MEN FROM NOW (56); DECISION AT SUNDOWN (57); •TALL T, THE (57); BUCHANAN RIDES ALONE (58); RIDE LONESOME (59); WESTBOUND (59); •COMANCHE STATION (60); RISE AND FALL OF LEGS DIAMOND, THE (60); TIME FOR DYING, A (71)

Bogart, Paul
MARLOWE (69); HALLS OF ANGER (70); SKIN GAME (71); CANCEL MY RESERVATION (72); CLASS OF '44 (73); MR. RICCO (75); THREE SISTERS, THE (77); OH GOD! YOU DEVIL (84); •TORCH SONG TRILOGY (88)

Bogdanovich, Peter
VOYAGE TO THE PLANET OF PREHISTORIC WOMEN (66); •TARGETS (68); •LAST PICTURE SHOW, THE (71); •WHAT'S UP, DOC? (72); •PAPER MOON (73); DAISY MILLER (74); AT LONG LAST LOVE (75); NICKELODEON (76); •SAINT JACK (79); THEY ALL LAUGHED (81); MASK (85); ILLEGALLY YOURS (88); TEXASVILLE (90); NOISES OFF (92); THING CALLED LOVE, THE (93)

Boorman, John
HAVING A WILD WEEKEND (65); •POINT BLANK (67); HELL IN THE PACIFIC (68); LEO THE LAST (70); •DELIVERANCE (72); ZARDOZ (74); EXORCIST II: THE HERETIC (77); •EXCALIBUR (81); •EMERALD FOREST, THE (85); •HOPE AND GLORY (87); WHERE THE HEART IS (90); BEYOND RANGOON (95)

Borden, Lizzie
REGROUPING (76); BORN IN FLAMES (83); •WORKING GIRLS (86); LOVE CRIMES (92); EROTIQUE (94)

Borsos, Phillip
•GREY FOX, THE (82); MEAN SEASON, THE (85); ONE MAGIC CHRISTMAS (85); DR. BETHUNE (90); FAR FROM HOME: THE ADVENTURES OF YELLOW DOG (95)

Borzage, Frank
RIVER, THE (28); STREET ANGEL (28); LUCKY STAR (29); THEY HAD TO SEE PARIS (29); LILIOM (30); SONG O' MY HEART (30); BAD GIRL (31); DOCTORS' WIVES (31); YOUNG AS YOU FEEL (31); AFTER TOMORROW (32); •FAREWELL TO ARMS, A (32); YOUNG AMERICA (32); MAN'S CASTLE (33); SECRETS (33); FLIRTATION WALK (34); LITTLE MAN, WHAT NOW? (34); •NO GREATER GLORY (34); LIVING ON VELVET (35); SHIPMATES FOREVER (35); STRANDED (35); •DESIRE

(36); HEARTS DIVIDED (36); BIG CITY (37); GREEN LIGHT (37); HISTORY IS MADE AT NIGHT (37); MANNEQUIN (37); SHINING HOUR, THE (38); •THREE COMRADES (38); DISPUTED PASSAGE (39); FLIGHT COMMAND (40); I TAKE THIS WOMAN (40); MORTAL STORM, THE (40); STRANGE CARGO (40); SMILIN' THROUGH (41); VANISHING VIRGINIAN, THE (41); SEVEN SWEETHEARTS (42); HIS BUTLER'S SISTER (43); •STAGE DOOR CANTEEN (43); TILL WE MEET AGAIN (44); SPANISH MAIN, THE (45); I'VE ALWAYS LOVED YOU (46); MAGNIFICENT DOLL (46); THAT'S MY MAN (47); MOONRISE (48); CHINA DOLL (58); BIG FISHERMAN, THE (59); JOURNEY BENEATH THE DESERT (61)

Boulting, John
JOURNEY TOGETHER (45); •BRIGHTON ROCK (47); SEVEN DAYS TO NOON (50); •MAGIC BOX, THE (51); CREST OF THE WAVE (54); PRIVATE'S PROGRESS (56); LUCKY JIM (57); •I'M ALL RIGHT, JACK (59); RISK, THE (60); HEAVENS ABOVE! (63); ROTTEN TO THE CORE (65)

Boyle, Danny
•SHALLOW GRAVE (95); •TRAINSPOTTING (95)

Branagh, Kenneth
•HENRY V (89); •DEAD AGAIN (91); PETER'S FRIENDS (92); •MUCH ADO ABOUT NOTHING (93); •MARY SHELLEY'S FRANKENSTEIN (94); •MIDWINTER'S TALE, A (96); •HAMLET (96)

Bresson, Robert
ANGELS OF THE STREETS (43); LADIES OF THE PARK (45); •DIARY OF A COUNTRY PRIEST (50); •MAN ESCAPED, A (56); •PICKPOCKET (59); •TRIAL OF JOAN OF ARC (62); •AU HASARD, BALTHAZAR (66); MOUCHETTE (67); •GENTLE CREATURE, A (69); •FOUR NIGHTS OF A DREAMER (71); LANCELOT OF THE LAKE (74); •DEVIL PROBABLY, THE (77); •L'ARGENT (83)

Brest, Martin
HOT TOMORROWS (78); GOING IN STYLE (79); •BEVERLY HILLS COP (84); •MIDNIGHT RUN (88); •SCENT OF A WOMAN (92)

Brickman, Paul
•RISKY BUSINESS (83); MEN DON'T LEAVE (90)

Bridges, Alan
ACT OF MURDER (64); INVASION (65); LIE, THE (70); SHELLEY (72); •HIRELING, THE (73); OUT OF SEASON (75); SUMMER RAIN (76); AGE OF INNOCENCE (77); RETURN OF THE SOLDIER, THE (81); SHOOTING PARTY, THE (84); SECRET PLACES OF THE HEART (91)

Bridges, James
BABY MAKER, THE (70); •PAPER CHASE, THE (73); 9/30/55 (77); •CHINA SYNDROME, THE (79); •URBAN COWBOY (80); MIKE'S MURDER (84); PERFECT (85); BRIGHT LIGHTS, BIG CITY (88)

Brook, Peter
•BEGGAR'S OPERA, THE (52); MODERATO CANTABILE (60); •LORD OF THE FLIES (63); •MARAT/SADE (66); TELL ME LIES (68); KING LEAR (70); MEETINGS WITH REMARKABLE MEN (79); TRAGEDY OF CARMEN, THE (83); MAHABHARATA, THE (90)

Brooks, Albert
•REAL LIFE (79); •MODERN ROMANCE (81); •LOST IN AMERICA (85); DEFENDING YOUR LIFE (91); MOTHER (96)

Brooks, James L.
•TERMS OF ENDEARMENT (83); •BROADCAST NEWS (87); I'LL DO ANYTHING (94)

Brooks, Mel
•PRODUCERS, THE (67); •TWELVE CHAIRS, THE (70); •BLAZING SADDLES (74); •YOUNG FRANKENSTEIN (74); •SILENT MOVIE (76); •HIGH ANXIETY (77); HISTORY OF THE WORLD, PART 1 (81); •SPACEBALLS (87); LIFE STINKS (91); ROBIN HOOD: MEN IN TIGHTS (93); DRACULA: DEAD AND LOVING IT (95)

Brooks, Richard
CRISIS (50); LIGHT TOUCH, THE (51); DEADLINE—U.S.A. (52); BATTLE CIRCUS (53); TAKE THE HIGH GROUND (53); FLAME AND THE FLESH (54); LAST TIME I SAW PARIS, THE (54); •BLACKBOARD JUNGLE (55); •CATERED AFFAIR, THE (56); LAST HUNT, THE (56); SOMETHING OF VALUE (57); •BROTHERS KARAMAZOV, THE (58); •CAT ON A HOT TIN ROOF (58); •ELMER GANTRY (60); •SWEET BIRD OF YOUTH (62); •LORD JIM (65); PROFESSIONALS, THE (66); •IN COLD BLOOD (67); HAPPY ENDING, THE (69); •$ (DOLLARS) (71); BITE THE BULLET (75); •LOOKING FOR MR. GOODBAR (77); WRONG IS RIGHT (82); FEVER PITCH (85)

Brown, Clarence
WONDER OF WOMEN (29); •ANNA CHRISTIE (30); NAVY BLUES (30); ROMANCE (30); •FREE SOUL, A (31); INSPIRATION (31); POSSESSED (31); EMMA (32); LETTY LYNTON (32); SON-DAUGHTER, THE (32); LOOKING FORWARD (33); NIGHT FLIGHT (33); CHAINED (34); SADIE MCKEE (34); •AH, WILDERNESS! (35); •ANNA KARENINA (35); GORGEOUS HUSSY, THE (36); WIFE VS. SECRETARY (36); CONQUEST (37); OF HUMAN HEARTS (38); IDIOT'S DELIGHT (39); RAINS CAME, THE (39); •EDISON, THE MAN (40); COME LIVE WITH ME (41); THEY MET IN BOMBAY (41); HUMAN COMEDY, THE (43); •NATIONAL VELVET (44); •WHITE CLIFFS OF DOVER, THE (44); •YEARLING, THE (46); SONG OF LOVE (47); •INTRUDER IN THE DUST (49); TO PLEASE A LADY (50); •ANGELS IN THE OUTFIELD (51); IT'S A BIG COUNTRY (51); PLYMOUTH ADVENTURE (52); WHEN IN ROME (52)

Browning, Tod
OUTSIDE THE LAW (30); THIRTEENTH CHAIR, THE (30); •DRACULA (31); IRON MAN, THE (31); •FREAKS (32); FAST WORKERS (33); MARK OF THE VAMPIRE (35); •DEVIL DOLL, THE (36); MIRACLES FOR SALE (39)

Bunuel, Luis
•L'AGE D'OR (30); •LOS OLVIDADOS (50); DAUGHTER OF DECEIT (51); MEXICAN BUS RIDE (51); WOMAN WITHOUT LOVE, A (51); •ADVENTURES OF ROBINSON CRUSOE, THE (52); BRUTE, THE (52); •EL (52); •WUTHERING HEIGHTS (53); ILLUSION TRAVELS BY STREETCAR, THE (54); CRIMINAL LIFE OF ARCHIBALDO DE LA CRUZ, THE (55); DEATH IN THE GARDEN (56); NAZARIN (58); YOUNG ONE, THE (60); •VIRIDIANA (61); •EXTERMINATING ANGEL, THE (62); •DIARY OF A CHAMBERMAID (64); •BELLE DE JOUR (67); •MILKY WAY, THE (69); •TRISTANA (70); •DISCREET CHARM OF THE BOURGEOISIE, THE (72); •PHANTOM OF LIBERTY, THE (74); •THAT OBSCURE OBJECT OF DESIRE (77)

Burnett, Charles
•KILLER OF SHEEP (77); MY BROTHER'S WEDDING (83); •TO SLEEP WITH ANGER (90); GLASS SHIELD, THE (95)

Burton, Tim
•PEE-WEE'S BIG ADVENTURE (85); •BEETLEJUICE (88); •BATMAN (89); •EDWARD SCISSORHANDS (90); •BATMAN RETURNS (92); •ED WOOD (94); •MARS ATTACKS! (96)

Cacoyannis, Michaele
WINDFALL IN ATHENS (54); STELLA (55); GIRL IN BLACK, A (56); FINAL LIE, THE (58); OUR LAST SPRING (60); ELECTRA (60); WASTREL, THE (61); •ZORBA THE GREEK (64); DAY THE FISH CAME OUT, THE (67); TROJAN WOMEN, THE (71); STORY OF JACOB AND JOSEPH, THE (74); ATTILA '74 (74); IPHIGENIA (77); SWEET COUNTRY (87); ZOE (89); PANO KATO KE PLAGIOS (93); UP, DOWN AND SIDEWAYS (94)

Cameron, James
PIRANHA II: THE SPAWNING (81); •TERMINATOR, THE (84); •ALIENS (86); •ABYSS, THE (89); •TERMINATOR 2: JUDGMENT DAY (91); •TRUE LIES (94)

Cammell, Donald
•PERFORMANCE (70); DEMON SEED (77); WHITE OF THE EYE (87); WILD SIDE (96)

Campbell, Martin
SEX THIEF, THE (74); HER FAMILY JEWELS (75); CRIMINAL LAW (89); DEFENSELESS (91); CAST A DEADLY SPELL (91); NO ESCAPE (94); •GOLDENEYE (95)

Campion, Jane
TWO FRIENDS (86); •SWEETIE (89); •ANGEL AT MY TABLE, AN (90); •PIANO, THE (93); •PORTRAIT OF A LADY, THE (96)

Camus, Marcel
FUGITIVE IN SAIGON (57); •BLACK ORPHEUS (59); OS BANDEIRANTES (60); DRAGON SKY (62); LE CHANT DU MONDE (65); L'HOMME DE NEW YORK (67); VIVRE LA NUIT (68); LE MUR DE L'ATLANTIQUE (70); UN ETE SAUVAGE (70); OS PASTORIS DA NOITE (77)

Capra, Frank
TRAMP TRAMP TRAMP (26); STRONG MAN, THE (26); LONG PANTS (27); FOR THE LOVE OF MIKE (27); THAT CERTAIN THING (28); SAY IT WITH SABLES (28); SUBMARINE (28); POWER OF THE PRESS, THE (28); DONOVAN AFFAIR, THE (29); FLIGHT (29); YOUNGER GENERATION, THE (29); LADIES OF LEISURE (30); RAIN OR SHINE (30); DIRIGIBLE (31); •MIRACLE WOMAN, THE (31); PLATINUM BLONDE (31); •AMERI-

AWAY (44); •ENCHANTED COTTAGE, THE (45); •ANNA AND THE KING OF SIAM (46); DEAD RECKONING (47); NIGHT SONG (47); CAGED (50); COMPANY SHE KEEPS, THE (50); •RACKET, THE (51); GODDESS, THE (58); SCAVENGERS, THE (59); MATTER OF MORALS, A (61)

Cronenberg, David
STEREO (69); CRIMES OF THE FUTURE (70); THEY CAME FROM WITHIN (75); •RABID (77); FAST COMPANY (79); •BROOD, THE (79); •SCANNERS (81); •VIDEODROME (83); •DEAD ZONE, THE (83); •FLY, THE (86); •DEAD RINGERS (88); •NAKED LUNCH (91); M. BUTTERFLY (93); •CRASH (96)

Crowe, Cameron
•SAY ANYTHING (89); •SINGLES (92); •JERRY MAGUIRE (96)

Cukor, George
GRUMPY (30); •ROYAL FAMILY OF BROADWAY, THE (30); VIRTUOUS SIN, THE (30); GIRLS ABOUT TOWN (31); TARNISHED LADY (31); •BILL OF DIVORCEMENT, A (32); ONE HOUR WITH YOU (32); ROCKABYE (32); WHAT PRICE HOLLYWOOD? (32); •DINNER AT EIGHT (33); •LITTLE WOMEN (33); OUR BETTERS (33); •DAVID COPPERFIELD (35); NO MORE LADIES (35); •ROMEO AND JULIET (36); SYLVIA SCARLETT (36); •CAMILLE (37); •PRISONER OF ZENDA, THE (37); HOLIDAY (38); I MET MY LOVE AGAIN (38); •GONE WITH THE WIND (39); •WOMEN, THE (39); ZAZA (39); •PHILADELPHIA STORY, THE (40); SUSAN AND GOD (40); TWO-FACED WOMAN (41); WOMAN'S FACE, A (41); HER CARDBOARD LOVER (42); KEEPER OF THE FLAME (42); •GASLIGHT (44); WINGED VICTORY (44); DESIRE ME (47); •DOUBLE LIFE, A (47); •ADAM'S RIB (49); EDWARD, MY SON (49); LIFE OF HER OWN, A (50); •BORN YESTERDAY (51); MODEL AND THE MARRIAGE BROKER, THE (51); MARRYING KIND, THE (52); •PAT AND MIKE (52); ACTRESS, THE (53); •IT SHOULD HAPPEN TO YOU (54); •STAR IS BORN, A (54); BHOWANI JUNCTION (56); •LES GIRLS (57); WILD IS THE WIND (57); HELLER IN PINK TIGHTS (60); LET'S MAKE LOVE (60); SONG WITHOUT END (60); CHAPMAN REPORT, THE (62); •MY FAIR LADY (64); JUSTINE (69); TRAVELS WITH MY AUNT (72); BLUE BIRD, THE (76); RICH AND FAMOUS (81)

Curtiz, Michael
NOAH'S ARK (28); TENDERLOIN (28); GAMBLERS, THE (29); GLAD RAG DOLL, THE (29); HEARTS IN EXILE (29); MADONNA OF AVENUE A, THE (29); MAMMY (30); MATRIMONIAL BED, THE (30); UNDER A TEXAS MOON (30); BRIGHT LIGHTS (31); GOD'S GIFT TO WOMEN (31); MAD GENIUS, THE (31); RIVER'S END (31); SOLDIER'S PLAYTHING, A (31); CABIN IN THE COTTON, THE (32); •DOCTOR X (32); STRANGE LOVE OF MOL a CARLO, THE (32); FEMALE (33); GOODBYE AGAIN (33); •KENNEL MURDER CASE, THE (33); KEYHOLE, THE (33); •MYSTERY OF THE WAX MUSEUM, THE (33); PRIVATE DETECTIVE 62 (33); •20,000 YEARS IN SING SING (33); BRITISH AGENT (34); JIMMY THE GENT (34); KEY, THE (34); MANDALAY (34); BLACK FURY (35); •CAPTAIN BLOOD (35); CASE OF THE CURIOUS BRIDE, THE (35); FRONT PAGE WOMAN (35); LITTLE BIG SHOT (35); •CHARGE OF THE LIGHT BRIGADE, THE (36); WALKING DEAD, THE (36); •KID GALAHAD (37); MOUNTAIN JUSTICE (37); PERFECT SPECIMEN, THE (37); STOLEN HOLIDAY (37); •ADVENTURES OF ROBIN HOOD, THE (38); •ANGELS WITH DIRTY FACES (38); •FOUR DAUGHTERS (38); FOUR'S A CROWD (38); GOLD IS WHERE YOU FIND IT (38); DAUGHTERS COURAGEOUS (39); •DODGE CITY (39); FOUR WIVES (39); PRIVATE LIVES OF ELIZABETH AND ESSEX, THE (39); •SANTA FE TRAIL (40); •SEA HAWK, THE (40); VIRGINIA CITY (40); DIVE BOMBER (41); •SEA WOLF, THE (41); CAPTAINS OF THE CLOUDS (42); •CASABLANCA (42); •YANKEE DOODLE DANDY (42); MISSION TO MOSCOW (43); •THIS IS THE ARMY (43); JANIE (44); •PASSAGE TO MARSEILLE (44); •MILDRED PIERCE (45); ROUGHLY SPEAKING (45); NIGHT AND DAY (46); •LIFE WITH FATHER (47); UNSUSPECTED, THE (47); ROMANCE ON THE HIGH SEAS (48); FLAMINGO ROAD (49); LADY TAKES A SAILOR, THE (49); MY DREAM IS YOURS (49); BREAKING POINT, THE (50); BRIGHT LEAF (50); •YOUNG MAN WITH A HORN (50); FORCE OF ARMS (51); I'LL SEE YOU IN MY DREAMS (51); •JIM THORPE—ALL AMERICAN (51); STORY OF WILL ROGERS, THE (52); JAZZ SINGER, THE (53); TROUBLE ALONG THE WAY (53); BOY FROM OKLAHOMA, THE (54); EGYPTIAN, THE (54); •WHITE CHRISTMAS (54); WE'RE NO ANGELS (55); BEST THINGS IN LIFE ARE FREE, THE (56); SCARLET HOUR, THE (56); VAGABOND KING, THE (56); HELEN MORGAN STORY, THE (57); KING CREOLE (58); PROUD REBEL, THE (58); HANGMAN, THE (59); MAN IN THE NET,

THE (59); ADVENTURES OF HUCKLEBERRY FINN, THE (60); BREATH OF SCANDAL, A (60); COMANCHEROS, THE (61); FRANCIS OF ASSISI (61)

Da Costa, Morton
•AUNTIE MAME (58); •MUSIC MAN, THE (62); ISLAND OF LOVE (63)

Dahl, John
KILL ME AGAIN (90); •LAST SEDUCTION, THE (94); •RED ROCK WEST (94); UNFORGETTABLE (96)

Dante, Joe
•HOLLYWOOD BOULEVARD (76); PIRANHA (78); •HOWLING, THE (81); TWILIGHT ZONE—THE MOVIE (83); GREMLINS (84); EXPLORERS (85); AMAZON WOMEN ON THE MOON (87); INNERSPACE (87); 'BURBS, THE (89); •GREMLINS 2: THE NEW BATCH (90); •MATINEE (93)

Dassin, Jules
AFFAIRS OF MARTHA, THE (42); NAZI AGENT (42); REUNION IN FRANCE (42); YOUNG IDEAS (43); CANTERVILLE GHOST, THE (44); LETTER FOR EVIE, A (45); TWO SMART PEOPLE (46); •BRUTE FORCE (47); •NAKED CITY, THE (48); THIEVES' HIGHWAY (49); •NIGHT AND THE CITY (50); •RIFIFI (54); WHERE THE HOT WIND BLOWS (58); •NEVER ON SUNDAY (60); PHAEDRA (62); •TOPKAPI (64); 10:30 P.M. SUMMER (66); UPTIGHT (68); PROMISE AT DAWN (70); DREAM OF PASSION, A (78); CIRCLE OF TWO (80)

Daves, Delmer
DESTINATION TOKYO (44); •HOLLYWOOD CANTEEN (44); VERY THOUGHT OF YOU, THE (44); •PRIDE OF THE MARINES (45); •DARK PASSAGE (47); RED HOUSE, THE (47); TO THE VICTOR (48); KISS IN THE DARK, A (49); TASK FORCE (49); BROKEN ARROW (50); BIRD OF PARADISE (51); RETURN OF THE TEXAN (52); NEVER LET ME GO (53); TREASURE OF THE GOLDEN CONDOR (53); DEMETRIUS AND THE GLADIATORS (54); DRUM BEAT (54); JUBAL (56); LAST WAGON, THE (56); •3:10 TO YUMA (57); BADLANDERS, THE (58); COWBOY (58); KINGS GO FORTH (58); HANGING TREE, THE (59); SUMMER PLACE, A (59); PARRISH (61); SUSAN SLADE (61); ROME ADVENTURE (62); SPENCER'S MOUNTAIN (63); BATTLE OF THE VILLA FIORITA, THE (64); YOUNGBLOOD HAWKE (64)

Davies, Terence
CHILDREN (76); MADONNA AND CHILD (80); DEATH AND TRANSFIGURATION (83); •DISTANT VOICES, STILL LIVES (88); •LONG DAY CLOSES, THE (92); NEON BIBLE, THE (95)

Davis, Andrew
STONY ISLAND (78); FINAL TERROR, THE (83); CODE OF SILENCE (85); ABOVE THE LAW (88); PACKAGE, THE (89); •UNDER SIEGE (92); •FUGITIVE, THE (93); STEAL BIG, STEAL LITTLE (95); CHAIN REACTION (96)

Davis, Ossie
•COTTON COMES TO HARLEM (70); KONGI'S HARVEST (71); BLACK GIRL (72); GORDON'S WAR (73); COUNTDOWN AT KUSINI (76)

De Bont, Jan
•SPEED (94); •TWISTER (96); •SPEED 2: CRUISE CONTROL (97)

de Broca, Philippe
LOVE GAME, THE (60); JOKER, THE (61); FIVE DAY LOVERS, THE (61); SEVEN CAPITAL SINS (61); LES VEINARDS (62); CARTOUCHE (62); MALE COMPANION (64); •THAT MAN FROM RIO (64); UP TO HIS EARS (65); •KING OF HEARTS (66); OLDEST PROFESSION, THE (67); DEVIL BY THE TAIL, THE (69); GIVE HER THE MOON (70); TOUCH AND GO (71); CHERE LOUISE (72); MAGNIFICENT ONE, THE (73); INCORRIGIBLE (75); JULIE POT DE COLLE (77); DEAR DETECTIVE (77); JUPITER'S THIGH (79); LE CAVALEUR (79); PSY (81); AFRICAN, THE (83); LOUISIANE (84); GYPSY, THE (86); CHOUANS! (88); SCHEHERAZADE (90); LES CLES DU PARADIS (91)

De Palma, Brian
•GREETINGS (68); MURDER A LA MOD (68); WEDDING PARTY, THE (69); HI, MOM! (70); GET TO KNOW YOUR RABBIT (72); SISTERS (73); PHANTOM OF THE PARADISE (74); •CARRIE (76); OBSESSION (76); FURY, THE (78); HOME MOVIES (79); •DRESSED TO KILL (80); •BLOW OUT (81); •SCARFACE (83); BODY DOUBLE (84); WISE GUYS (86); •UNTOUCHABLES, THE (87); •CASUALTIES OF WAR (89); BONFIRE OF THE VANITIES, THE (90); RAISING CAIN (92); •CARLITO'S WAY (93); •MISSION: IMPOSSIBLE (96)

LUV (67); ALFRED THE GREAT (69); OLD DRACULA (73); NUDE BOMB, THE (80); CHARLIE CHAN AND THE CURSE OF THE DRAGON QUEEN (81); STEALING HEAVEN (88)

Donner, Richard
X-15 (61); SALT AND PEPPER (68); LOLA (69); •OMEN, THE (76); •SUPERMAN (78); INSIDE MOVES (80); TOY, THE (82); GOONIES, THE (85); •LADYHAWKE (85); •LETHAL WEAPON (87); SCROOGED (88); •LETHAL WEAPON 2 (89); LETHAL WEAPON 3 (92); RADIO FLYER (92); •MAVERICK (94); ASSASSINS (95)

Dorrie, Doris
FIRST WALTZ, THE (77); STRAIGHT THROUGH THE HEART (83); INSIDE THE WHALE (84); •MEN. . . (85); PARADISE (86); ME AND HIM (89); MONEY (89); HAPPY BIRTHDAY, TURKE! (92); NOBODY LOVES ME (94)

Dreyer, Carl-Theodor
•VAMPYR (32); •DAY OF WRATH (43); TWO PEOPLE (45); •ORDET (55); GERTRUD (64)

Duigan, John
FIRM MAN, THE (75); TRESPASSERS, THE (76); MOUTH TO MOUTH (78); DIMBOOLA (79); WINTER OF OUR DREAMS (81); FAR EAST (83); ONE NIGHT STAND (83); YEAR MY VOICE BROKE, THE (87); ROMERO (89); •FLIRTING (90); WIDE SARGASSO SEA (93); SIRENS (94); JOURNEY OF AUGUST KING, THE (95); LEADING MAN, THE (96)

Duke, Bill
RAGE IN HARLEM, A (91); •DEEP COVER (92); CEMETERY CLUB, THE (93); SISTER ACT 2: BACK IN THE HABIT (93); AMERICA'S DREAM (96)

Duvivier, Julien
DAVID GOLDER (30); LES CINQ GENTLEMEN MAUDITS (32); ALLO BERLIN? ICI PARIS! (32); POIL DE CAROTTE (32); LA VENUS DU COLLEGE (32); LA TETE D'UN HOMME (33); LA MACHINE A REFAIRE LA VIE (33); LE PETIT ROI (33); LA PAQUEBOT "TENACITY" (34); NAKED HEART, THE (34); ESCAPE FROM YESTERDAY (35); GOLGOTHA (35); GOLEM, THE (36); MAN OF THE HOUR, THE (36); THEY WERE FIVE (36); •PEPE LE MOKO (37); UN CARNET DE BAL (37); GREAT WALTZ, THE (38); •MARIE ANTOINETTE (38); END OF A DAY, THE (39); LA CHARRETTE FANTOME (39); LYDIA (41); •TALES OF MANHATTAN (42); HEART OF A NATION, THE (43); FLESH AND FANTASY (43); DESTINY (44); IMPOSTER, THE (44); PANIQUE (46); •ANNA KARENINA (47); SINNERS, THE (49); CAPTAIN BLACK JACK (50); LITTLE WORLD OF DON CAMILLO, THE (51); UNDER THE PARIS SKY (51); HOLIDAY FOR HENRIETTA (52); RETURN OF DON CAMILLO, THE (53); ON TRIAL (54); MARIANNE OF MY YOUTH (55); DEADLIER THAN THE MALE (56); MAN IN THE RAINCOAT, THE (57); POT-BOUILLE (57); FEMALE, THE (59); MARIE OCTOBRE (59); LA GRANDE VIE (60); BOULEVARD (60); BURNING COURT, THE (62); DEVIL AND THE TEN COMMANDMENTS, THE (62); HIGHWAY PICKUP (63); DIABOLICALLY YOURS (67)

Dwan, Allan
FROZEN JUSTICE (29); IRON MASK, THE (29); SOUTH SEA ROSE (29); WHAT A WIDOW! (30); CHANCES (31); MAN TO MAN (31); WICKED (31); HER FIRST AFFAIRE (32); WHILE PARIS SLEEPS (32); COUNSEL'S OPINION (33); I SPY (33); HOLLYWOOD PARTY (34); BLACK SHEEP (35); 15 MAIDEN LANE (36); HIGH TENSION (36); HUMAN CARGO (36); NAVY WIFE (36); SONG AND DANCE MAN, THE (36); HEIDI (37); ONE MILE FROM HEAVEN (37); THAT I MAY LIVE (37); WOMAN-WISE (37); JOSETTE (38); REBECCA OF SUNNYBROOK FARM (38); SUEZ (38); FRONTIER MARSHAL (39); GORILLA, THE (39); THREE MUSKETEERS, THE (39); SAILOR'S LADY (40); TRAIL OF THE VIGILANTES (40); YOUNG PEOPLE (40); LOOK WHO'S LAUGHING (41); RISE AND SHINE (41); FRIENDLY ENEMIES (42); HERE WE GO AGAIN (42); AROUND THE WORLD (43); ABROAD WITH TWO YANKS (44); UP IN MABEL'S ROOM (44); •BREWSTER'S MILLIONS (45); GETTING GERTIE'S GARTER (45); RENDEZVOUS WITH ANNIE (46); CALENDAR GIRL (47); DRIFTWOOD (47); NORTHWEST OUTPOST (47); ANGEL IN EXILE (48); INSIDE STORY, THE (48); •SANDS OF IWO JIMA (49); SURRENDER (50); BELLE LE GRAND (51); I DREAM OF JEANIE (52); MONTANA BELLE (52); WILD BLUE YONDER, THE (52); FLIGHT NURSE (53); SWEETHEARTS ON PARADE (53); WOMAN THEY ALMOST LYNCHED (53); CATTLE QUEEN OF MONTANA (54); PASSION (54); SILVER LODE (54); ESCAPE TO BURMA (55); PEARL OF THE SOUTH PACIFIC (55); TEN-

NESSEE'S PARTNER (55); HOLD BACK THE NIGHT (56); SLIGHTLY SCARLET (56); RESTLESS BREED, THE (57); RIVER'S EDGE, THE (57); ENCHANTED ISLAND (58); MOST DANGEROUS MAN ALIVE (61)

Eastwood, Clint
•PLAY MISTY FOR ME (71); BREEZY (73); •HIGH PLAINS DRIFTER (73); EIGER SANCTION, THE (75); •OUTLAW JOSEY WALES, THE (76); GAUNTLET, THE (77); BRONCO BILLY (80); FIREFOX (82); HONKY-TONK MAN (82); SUDDEN IMPACT (83); •PALE RIDER (85); •HEARTBREAK RIDGE (86); •BIRD (88); ROOKIE, THE (90); •WHITE HUNTER, BLACK HEART (90); •UNFORGIVEN (92); •PERFECT WORLD, A (93); •BRIDGES OF MADISON COUNTY, THE (95); ABSOLUTE POWER (97)

Edel, Uli
•LAST EXIT TO BROOKLYN (89); BODY OF EVIDENCE (93); TYSON (95); RASPUTIN (96)

Edwards, Blake
BRING YOUR SMILE ALONG (55); HE LAUGHED LAST (56); MISTER CORY (57); PERFECT FURLOUGH, THE (58); THIS HAPPY FEELING (58); •OPERATION PETTICOAT (59); HIGH TIME (60); •BREAKFAST AT TIFFANY'S (61); •DAYS OF WINE AND ROSES (62); EXPERIMENT IN TERROR (62); •PINK PANTHER, THE (64); •SHOT IN THE DARK, A (64); GREAT RACE, THE (65); WHAT DID YOU DO IN THE WAR, DADDY? (66); GUNN (67); PARTY, THE (68); DARLING LILI (70); WILD ROVERS (71); CAREY TREATMENT, THE (72); TAMARIND SEED, THE (74); •RETURN OF THE PINK PANTHER, THE (75); PINK PANTHER STRIKES AGAIN, THE (76); REVENGE OF THE PINK PANTHER (78); •10 (79); S.O.B. (81); TRAIL OF THE PINK PANTHER, THE (82); •VICTOR/VICTORIA (82); CURSE OF THE PINK PANTHER (83); MAN WHO LOVED WOMEN, THE (83); •MICKI & MAUDE (84); FINE MESS, A (86); THAT'S LIFE! (86); BLIND DATE (87); SUNSET (88); SKIN DEEP (89); SWITCH (91); BLAKE EDWARDS' SON OF THE PINK PANTHER (93)

Edzard, Christine
STORIES FROM A FLYING TRUNK (79); BIDDY (83); •LITTLE DORRIT (88); FOOL, THE (90); AS YOU LIKE IT (92)

Egoyan, Atom
HOWARD IN PARTICULAR (79); AFTER GRAD WITH DAD (80); PEEP SHOW (81); OPEN HOUSE (82); NEXT OF KIN (84); IN THIS CORNER (85); MEN: A PASSION PLAYGROUND (85); FAMILY VIEWING (87); FINAL TWIST, THE (87); LA BOITE A SOLEIL (88); LOOKING FOR NOTHING (88); SPEAKING PARTS (89); MONTREAL VU PAR. . . (91); ADJUSTER, THE (91); GROSS MISCONDUCT (92); CALENDAR (93); •EXOTICA (94)

Eisenstein, Sergei
•ALEXANDER NEVSKY (38); •IVAN THE TERRIBLE, PARTS I & II (58)

Elliott, Stephan
FRAUDS (93); •ADVENTURES OF PRISCILLA, QUEEN OF THE DESERT, THE (94)

Emmerich, Roland
NOAH'S ARK PRINCIPLE, THE (84); MAKING CONTACT/JOEY (85); GHOST CHASE (88); MOON 44 (91); UNIVERSAL SOLDIER (92); •STARGATE (94); •INDEPENDENCE DAY (96)

Enyedi, Ildiko
FLIRT (81); ROSENKAVALIER (81); NEW BOOKS (82); VIEWER, THE (85); INVASION (85); MOLE, THE (86); •MY 20TH CENTURY (89); WINTER WAR (91); MAGIC HUNTER (94)

Ephron, Nora
THIS IS MY LIFE (92); •SLEEPLESS IN SEATTLE (93); MIXED NUTS (94); •MICHAEL (96)

Erice, Victor
•SPIRIT OF THE BEEHIVE, THE (73); EL SUR (83); DREAM OF LIGHT (92)

Eustache, Jean
BAD COMPANY (67); •MOTHER AND THE WHORE, THE (73); MY LITTLE LOVES (75); DIRTY STORY, A (77)

Eyre, Richard
IMITATION GAME, THE (80); COUNTRY (81); LOOSE CONNECTIONS (83); •PLOUGHMAN'S LUNCH, THE (83); LAUGHTERHOUSE (84); PAST CARING (85); INSURANCE MAN, THE (85)

LIBERTY VALANCE, THE (62); DONOVAN'S REEF (63); •HOW THE WEST WAS WON (63); •CHEYENNE AUTUMN (64); YOUNG CASSIDY (65); SEVEN WOMEN (66)

Forman, Milos
BLACK PETER (64); •LOVES OF A BLONDE (65); •FIREMAN'S BALL, THE (67); •TAKING OFF (71); VISIONS OF EIGHT (73); •ONE FLEW OVER THE CUCKOO'S NEST (75); •HAIR (79); •RAGTIME (81); •AMADEUS (84); VALMONT (89); •PEOPLE VS. LARRY FLYNT, THE (96)

Forsyth, Bill
THAT SINKING FEELING (79); •GREGORY'S GIRL (81); •LOCAL HERO (83); •COMFORT AND JOY (84); •HOUSEKEEPING (87); BREAKING IN (89); BEING HUMAN (94)

Fosse, Bob
•SWEET CHARITY (69); •CABARET (72); •LENNY (74); •ALL THAT JAZZ (79); •STAR 80 (83)

Francis, Freddie
TWO AND TWO MAKE SIX (61); BRAIN, THE (62); •DAY OF THE TRIFFIDS, THE (63); NIGHTMARE (63); PARANOIAC (63); EVIL OF FRANKENSTEIN, THE (64); DR. TERROR'S HOUSE OF HORRORS (65); HYSTERIA (65); SKULL, THE (65); TRAITOR'S GATE (65); PSYCHOPATH, THE (66); DEADLY BEES, THE (67); THEY CAME FROM BEYOND SPACE (67); TORTURE GARDEN (67); DRACULA HAS RISEN FROM THE GRAVE (69); MUMSY, NANNY, SONNY, AND GIRLY (70); TROG (70); CREEPING FLESH, THE (72); TALES FROM THE CRYPT (72); CRAZE (73); TALES THAT WITNESS MADNESS (73); SON OF DRACULA (74); GHOUL, THE (75); DOCTOR AND THE DEVILS, THE (85); DARK TOWER (89)

Frank, Melvin
REFORMER AND THE REDHEAD, THE (50); CALLAWAY WENT THATAWAY (51); STRICTLY DISHONORABLE (51); ABOVE AND BEYOND (53); •KNOCK ON WOOD (54); •COURT JESTER, THE (56); THAT CERTAIN FEELING (56); JAYHAWKERS, THE (59); LI'L ABNER (59); FACTS OF LIFE, THE (60); STRANGE BEDFELLOWS (65); BUONA SERA, MRS. CAMPBELL (68); •TOUCH OF CLASS, A (73); PRISONER OF SECOND AVENUE, THE (75); DUCHESS AND THE DIRTWATER FOX, THE (76); LOST AND FOUND (79); WALK LIKE A MAN (87)

Frankenheimer, John
YOUNG STRANGER, THE (57); YOUNG SAVAGES, THE (61); ALL FALL DOWN (62); •BIRDMAN OF ALCATRAZ (62); •MANCHURIAN CANDIDATE, THE (62); •SEVEN DAYS IN MAY (64); •TRAIN, THE (65); •GRAND PRIX (66); •SECONDS (66); FIXER, THE (68); EXTRAORDINARY SEAMAN, THE (69); GYPSY MOTHS, THE (69); •I WALK THE LINE (70); HORSEMEN, THE (71); •ICEMAN COMETH, THE (73); IMPOSSIBLE OBJECT (73); 99 AND 44/100% DEAD (74); FRENCH CONNECTION II (75); •BLACK SUNDAY (77); PROPHECY (79); CHALLENGE, THE (82); RAINMAKER, THE (82); HOLCROFT COVENANT, THE (85); 52 PICK-UP (86); RIVIERA (87); DEAD-BANG (89); FOURTH WAR, THE (90); YEAR OF THE GUN (91); AGAINST THE WALL (94); BURNING SEASON, THE (94); ANDERSONVILLE (96); ISLAND OF DR. MOREAU, THE (96)

Franklin, Carl
NOWHERE TO RUN (89); EYE OF THE EAGLE II: INSIDE THE ENEMY (89); FULL FATHOM FIVE (90); •ONE FALSE MOVE (92); •DEVIL IN A BLUE DRESS (95)

Franklin, Sidney
DEVIL MAY CARE (29); LAST OF MRS. CHEYNEY, THE (29); LADY OF SCANDAL, THE (30); LADY'S MORALS, A (30); •GUARDSMAN, THE (31); •PRIVATE LIVES (31); •SMILIN' THROUGH (32); REUNION IN VIENNA (33); •BARRETTS OF WIMPOLE STREET, THE (34); DARK ANGEL, THE (35); •GOOD EARTH, THE (37); •BARRETTS OF WIMPOLE STREET, THE (56)

Frears, Stephen
•GUMSHOE (71)THREE MEN IN A BOAT (75); BLOODY KIDS (83); LOVING WALTER (83); SAIGON — YEAR OF THE CAT (83); •HIT, THE (84); •MY BEAUTIFUL LAUNDRETTE (85); SONG OF EXPERIENCE (86); MR. JOLLY LIVES NEXT DOOR (87); •PRICK UP YOUR EARS (87); •SAMMY AND ROSIE GET LAID (87); •DANGEROUS LIAISONS (88); •GRIFTERS, THE (90); HERO (92); •SNAPPER, THE (93); TYPICALLY BRITISH (95); MARY REILLY (96); VAN, THE (96)

Freund, Karl
•MUMMY, THE (32); MOONLIGHT AND PRETZELS (33); COUNTESS OF MONTE CRISTO, THE (34); GIFT OF GAB (34); I GIVE MY LOVE (34); MADAME SPY (34); UNCERTAIN LADY (34); •MAD LOVE (35)

Friedkin, William
GOOD TIMES (67); BIRTHDAY PARTY, THE (68); NIGHT THEY RAIDED MINSKY'S, THE (68); BOYS IN THE BAND, THE (70); •FRENCH CONNECTION, THE (71); •EXORCIST, THE (73); SORCERER (77); BRINK'S JOB, THE (78); CRUISING (80); DEAL OF THE CENTURY (83); •TO LIVE AND DIE IN L.A. (85); GUARDIAN, THE (90); RAMPAGE (92); BLUE CHIPS (94); JADE (95)

Fuller, Samuel
•I SHOT JESSE JAMES (49); BARON OF ARIZONA, THE (50); FIXED BAYONETS (51); •STEEL HELMET, THE (51); PARK ROW (52); •PICKUP ON SOUTH STREET (53); HELL AND HIGH WATER (54); HOUSE OF BAMBOO (55); CHINA GATE (57); FORTY GUNS (57); RUN OF THE ARROW (57); CRIMSON KIMONO, THE (59); VERBOTEN! (59); UNDERWORLD U.S.A. (61); MERRILL'S MARAUDERS (62); •SHOCK CORRIDOR (63); NAKED KISS, THE (64); SHARK! (70); •DEAD PIGEON ON BEETHOVEN STREET (72); •BIG RED ONE, THE (80); •WHITE DOG (82); THIEVES AFTER DARK (84); STREET OF NO RETURN (91)

Furie, Sidney J.
DANGEROUS AGE, A (57); BOYS, THE (61); DOCTOR BLOOD'S COFFIN (61); DURING ONE NIGHT (61); SNAKE WOMAN, THE (61); THREE ON A SPREE (61); WONDERFUL TO BE YOUNG! (61); •LEATHER BOYS, THE (63); SWINGER'S PARADISE (64); •IPCRESS FILE, THE (65); APPALOOSA, THE (66); NAKED RUNNER, THE (67); LAWYER, THE (69); LITTLE FAUSS AND BIG HALSY (70); •LADY SINGS THE BLUES (72); HIT! (73); SHEILA LEVINE IS DEAD AND LIVING IN NEW YORK (75); GABLE AND LOMBARD (76); BOYS IN COMPANY C, THE (78); ENTITY, THE (82); PURPLE HEARTS (84); IRON EAGLE (86); SUPERMAN IV: THE QUEST FOR PEACE (87); IRON EAGLE II (88); TAKING OF BEVERLY HILLS, THE (91); LADYBUGS (92); HOLLOW POINT (95); IRON EAGLE IV (96)

Gance, Abel
END OF THE WORLD, THE (30); MATER DOLOROSA (32); POLICHE (34); NAPOLEON BONAPARTE (34); LE ROMAN D'UN JEUNE HOMME PAUVRE (35); LUCREZIA BORGIA (35); QUEEN AND THE CARDINAL, THE (35); LIFE AND LOVES OF BEETHOVEN, THE (36); LE VOLEUR DE FEMMES (36); J'ACCUSE (39); LOUISE (39); FOUR FLIGHTS TO LOVE (40); LA VENUS AVEUGLE (41); LA CAPTAINE FRACASSE (43); LA TOUR DE NESLES (55); MAGIRAMA (56); AUSTERLITZ (59); CYRANO ET D'ARTAGNAN (63); BONAPARTE ET LA REVOLUTION (71)

Garnett, Tay
CELEBRITY (28); FLYING FOOL, THE (29); OH, YEAH! (29); SPIELER, THE (29); HER MAN (30); OFFICER O'BRIEN (30); BAD COMPANY (31); OKAY AMERICA (32); ONE WAY PASSAGE (32); PRESTIGE (32); DESTINATION UNKNOWN (33); S.O.S. ICEBERG (33); CHINA SEAS (35); SHE COULDN'T TAKE IT (35); PROFESSIONAL SOLDIER (36); LOVE IS NEWS (37); SLAVE SHIP (37); STAND-IN (37); JOY OF LIVING (38); TRADE WINDS (38); ETERNALLY YOURS (39); SEVEN SINNERS (40); SLIGHTLY HONORABLE (40); CHEERS FOR MISS BISHOP (41); MY FAVORITE SPY (42); BATAAN (43); CROSS OF LORRAINE, THE (43); MRS. PARKINGTON (44); SEE HERE, PRIVATE HARGROVE (44); VALLEY OF DECISION, THE (45); •POSTMAN ALWAYS RINGS TWICE, THE (46); WILD HARVEST (47); •CONNECTICUT YANKEE IN KING ARTHUR'S COURT, A (49); FIREBALL, THE (50); CAUSE FOR ALARM (51); SOLDIERS THREE (51); ONE MINUTE TO ZERO (52); MAIN STREET TO BROADWAY (53); BLACK KNIGHT, THE (54); NIGHT FIGHTERS, THE (60); CATTLE KING (63); DELTA FACTOR, THE (70); CHALLENGE TO BE FREE (76)

Gibson, Brian
BREAKING GLASS (80); POLTERGEIST II (86); •WHAT'S LOVE GOT TO DO WITH IT (93); JUROR, THE (96)

Gilbert, Lewis
LITTLE BALLERINA, THE (47); ONCE A SINNER (50); SCARLET THREAD (50); WALL OF DEATH (51); TIME GENTLEMEN PLEASE! (52); ALBERT, R.N. (53); HUNDRED HOUR HUNT (53); JOHNNY ON THE RUN (53); SLASHER, THE (53); GOOD DIE YOUNG, THE (54); SEA SHALL NOT HAVE THEM, THE (54); CAST A DARK SHADOW (55); •REACH FOR THE SKY (56); ADMIRABLE CRICHTON, THE (57); CARVE HER NAME

WITH PRIDE (58); CRY FROM THE STREETS, A (58); FERRY TO HONG KONG (58); LIGHT UP THE SKY (60); •SINK THE BISMARCK! (60); LOSS OF INNOCENCE (61); DAMN THE DEFIANT! (62); SEVENTH DAWN, THE (64); •ALFIE (66); •YOU ONLY LIVE TWICE (67); ADVENTURERS, THE (70); FRIENDS (71); PAUL AND MICHELLE (74); OPERATION DAY-BREAK (76); SEVEN NIGHTS IN JAPAN (76); •SPY WHO LOVED ME, THE (77); •MOONRAKER (79); •EDUCATING RITA (83); NOT QUITE JERUSALEM (85); SHIRLEY VALENTINE (89); STEPPING OUT (91); HAUNTED (95)

Gilliam, Terry
•MONTY PYTHON AND THE HOLY GRAIL (75); JABBERWOCKY (77); •TIME BANDITS (81); •BRAZIL (85); •ADVENTURES OF BARON MUN-CHAUSEN, THE (89); •FISHER KING, THE (91); •TWELVE MONKEYS

Glen, John
•FOR YOUR EYES ONLY (81); OCTOPUSSY (83); VIEW TO A KILL, A (85); •LIVING DAYLIGHTS, THE (87); •LICENCE TO KILL (89); ACES: IRON EAGLE III (92); CHRISTOPHER COLUMBUS: THE DISCOVERY (92)

Godard, Jean-Luc
•BREATHLESS (59); LE PETIT SOLDAT (60); •WOMAN IS A WOMAN, A (60); SEVEN CAPITAL SINS (61); ROGOPAG (62); •MY LIFE TO LIVE (62); •CONTEMPT (63); LES CARABINIERS (63); •BAND OF OUTSIDERS (64); BEAUTIFUL SWINDLERS, THE (64); •MARRIED WOMAN, THE (64); •ALPHAVILLE (65); •PIERROT LE FOU (65); •SIX IN PARIS (65); MADE IN U.S.A. (66); •MASCULINE FEMININE (66); •TWO OR THREE THINGS I KNOW ABOUT HER (66); FAR FROM VIETNAM (67); LA CHINOISE (67); LOVE AND ANGER (67); OLDEST PROFESSION, THE (67); •WEEK-END (67); •LE GAI SAVOIR (68); UN FILM COMME LES AUTRES (68); BRITISH SOUNDS (69); PRAVDA (69); ONE PLUS ONE (69); STRUGGLE IN ITALY (69); WIND FROM THE EAST (69); 'TIL VICTORY (70); VLADIMIR ET ROSA (70); 1 A.M. (71); LETTER TO JANE (72); •TOUT VA BIEN (72); COMMENT CA VA (75); ICI ET AILLEURS (75); •NUMBER TWO (75); •EVERY MAN FOR HIMSELF (80); PASSION (82); •FIRST NAME: CARMEN (83); DETECTIVE (85); •HAIL, MARY (85); GRAN-DEUR ET DECADENCE D'UN PETIT COMMERCE DE CINEMA (86); ARIA (87); •KING LEAR (87); SOIGNE TA DROITE (87); NOUVELLE VAGUE (90); GERMANY YEAR 90 NINE ZERO (91); CONTRE L'OUBLI (92); HELAS POUR MOI (93); JLG BY JLG (94); FOR EVER MOZART (96)

Gomez, Nick
•LAWS OF GRAVITY (92); NEW JERSEY DRIVE (95)

Gordon, Keith
•CHOCOLATE WAR, THE (88); •MIDNIGHT CLEAR, A (92); MOTHER NIGHT (96)

Gordon, Stuart
•RE-ANIMATOR (85); FROM BEYOND (86); DOLLS (87); ROBOT JOX (90); DAUGHTER OF DARKNESS (90); PIT AND THE PENDULUM, THE (91); FORTRESS (93); CASTLE FREAK (95)

Goretta, Claude
MADMAN, THE (70); WEDDING DAY, THE (71); •INVITATION, THE (73); WONDERFUL CROOK, THE (75); •LACEMAKER, THE (77); ROADS OF EXILE, THE (78); GIRL FROM LORRAINE, THE (80); BONHEUR TOI-MEME (80); DEATH OF MARIO RICCI, THE (83); ORPHEUS (85); SI LE SOLEIL NE REVENAIT PAS (87); LES ENNEMIS DE LA MAFIA (88); L'OMBRE (91); VISAGES SUISSES (91); VERDRIET VAN BELGIE, HET (94)

Gorris, Marleen
•QUESTION OF SILENCE, A (83); BROKEN MIRRORS (84); LAST IS-LAND, THE (90); •ANTONIA'S LINE (95)

Goulding, Edmund
TRESPASSER, THE (29); DEVIL'S HOLIDAY, THE (30); NIGHT ANGEL, THE (31); REACHING FOR THE MOON (31); BLONDIE OF THE FOLLIES (32); •GRAND HOTEL (32); RIPTIDE (34); FLAME WITHIN, THE (35); THAT CERTAIN WOMAN (37); •DAWN PATROL, THE (38); WHITE BAN-NERS (38); DARK VICTORY (39); OLD MAID, THE (39); WE ARE NOT ALONE (39); 'TIL WE MEET AGAIN (40); GREAT LIE, THE (41); CLAUDIA (43); CONSTANT NYMPH, THE (43); FOREVER AND A DAY (43); OF HUMAN BONDAGE (46); •RAZOR'S EDGE, THE (46); •NIGHT-MARE ALLEY (47); EVERYBODY DOES IT (49); MISTER 880 (50); WE'RE NOT MARRIED (52); DOWN AMONG THE SHELTERING PALMS (53); TEENAGE REBEL (56); MARDI GRAS (58)

Greenaway, Peter
FALLS, THE (80); •DRAUGHTSMAN'S CONTRACT, THE (82); ZED & TWO NOUGHTS, A (85); •BELLY OF AN ARCHITECT, THE (87); •DROWNING BY NUMBERS (87); •COOK, THE THIEF, HIS WIFE & HER LOVER, THE (89); •PROSPERO'S BOOKS (91); BABY OF MACON, THE (93); STAIRS 1 GENEVA, THE (94); •PILLOW BOOK, THE (97)

Griffith, D.W.
LADY OF THE PAVEMENTS (29); ABRAHAM LINCOLN (30); STRUG-GLE, THE (31); •SAN FRANCISCO (36); ONE MILLION B.C. (40)

Grosbard, Ulu
•SUBJECT WAS ROSES, THE (68); WHO IS HARRY KELLERMAN AND WHY IS HE SAYING THOSE TERRIBLE THINGS; ABOUT ME? (71); •STRAIGHT TIME (78); •TRUE CONFESSIONS (81); FALLING IN LOVE (84); •GEORGIA (95)

Guney, Yilmaz
HORSE, THE WOMAN, AND THE GUN, THE (66); BULLETS CANNOT PIERCE ME (67); MY NAME IS KERIM (67); NURI THE FLEA (68); BRIDE OF THE EARTH (68); HUNGRY WOLVES, THE (69); UGLY MAN, AN (69); HOPE (70); OSMAN THE WANDERER (70); SEVEN BASTARDS, THE (70); FUGITIVES, THE (71); WRONGDOERS, THE (71); EXAMPLE, THE (71); TOMORROW IS THE LAST DAY (71); HOPELESS ONES, THE (71); PAIN (71); ELEGY (71); FATHER, THE (71); FRIEND, THE (74); ANXIETY (74); POOR ONES, THE (75); HERD, THE (78); ENEMY, THE (79); •YOL (82); •WALL, THE (83)

Gutierrez Alea, Tomas
LITTLE RED RIDING HOOD (47); FAKIR, THE (47); EVERYDAY MIX-UP, AN (50); IL SOGNO DI GIOVANNI BASAIN (53); EL MEGANO (55); THIS LAND IS OURS (59); STORIES OF THE REVOLUTION (60); GENERAL ASSEMBLY (60); DEATH TO THE INVADER (61); TWELVE CHAIRS, THE (62); CUMBITE (66); •DEATH OF A BUREAUCRAT (66); MEMORIES OF UNDERDEVELOPMENT (68); CUBAN FIGHT AGAINST THE DEMONS, A (71); ART OF TOBACCO, THE (74); LAST SUPPER, THE (76); SURVI-VORS, THE (78); UP TO A CERTAIN POINT (84); LETTERS FROM THE PARK (88); WITH YOU IN THE DISTANCE (91); STRAWBERRY AND CHOCOLATE (93); GUANTANAMERA (95)

Hackford, Taylor
•IDOLMAKER, THE (80); •OFFICER AND A GENTLEMAN, AN (82); AGAINST ALL ODDS (84); WHITE NIGHTS (85); CHUCK BERRY: HAIL! HAIL! ROCK 'N' ROLL (87); EVERYBODY'S ALL-AMERICAN (88); BOUND BY HONOR (93); DOLORES CLAIBORNE (95)

Haines, Randa
•CHILDREN OF A LESSER GOD (86); DOCTOR, THE (91); WRESTLING ERNEST HEMINGWAY (93)

Hall, Peter
WORK IS A FOUR LETTER WORD (67); MIDSUMMER NIGHT'S DREAM, A (68); THREE INTO TWO WON'T GO (69); PERFECT FRIDAY (70); •HOMECOMING, THE (73); NEVER TALK TO STRANGERS (95)

Hallstrom, Lasse
LOVER AND HIS LASS, A (75); ABBA—THE MOVIE (77); FATHER TO BE (79); ROOSTER, THE (81); •MY LIFE AS A DOG (85); CHILDREN OF BULLERBY VILLAGE, THE (86); MORE ABOUT THE CHILDREN OF BULLERBY VILLAGE (87); ONCE AROUND (91); •WHAT'S EATING GILBERT GRAPE? (93); SOMETHING TO TALK ABOUT (95); CHILDREN OF NOISY VILLAGE, THE (96)

Hamer, Robert
•DEAD OF NIGHT (45); PINK STRING AND SEALING WAX (45); IT ALWAYS RAINS ON SUNDAY (47); •KIND HEARTS AND CORONETS (49); SPIDER AND THE FLY, THE (49); HIS EXCELLENCY (51); LONG MEMORY, THE (52); DETECTIVE, THE (54); TO PARIS WITH LOVE (54); SCAPEGOAT, THE (59); SCHOOL FOR SCOUNDRELS (60)

Hamilton, Guy
RINGER, THE (52); INTRUDER, THE (53); COLDITZ STORY, THE (54); INSPECTOR CALLS, AN (54); CHARLEY MOON (56); STOWAWAY GIRL (57); DEVIL'S DISCIPLE, THE (59); TOUCH OF LARCENY, A (59); BEST OF ENEMIES, THE (61); •GOLDFINGER (64); MAN IN THE MIDDLE (64); PARTY'S OVER, THE (65); •FUNERAL IN BERLIN (66); •BATTLE OF BRITAIN (69); •DIAMONDS ARE FOREVER (71); LIVE AND LET DIE (73); MAN WITH THE GOLDEN GUN, THE (74); FORCE 10 FROM NAVARONE (78); MIRROR CRACK'D, THE (80); EVIL UNDER THE SUN (82); REMO WILLIAMS: THE ADVENTURE BEGINS . . . (85)

Hampton, Christopher
•CARRINGTON (95); JOSEPH CONRAD'S THE SECRET AGENT (96)

Hancock, John
STICKY MY FINGERS. . . FLEET MY FEET (70); LET'S SCARE JESSICA TO DEATH (71); •BANG THE DRUM SLOWLY (73); BABY BLUE MARINE (76); CALIFORNIA DREAMING (79); WEEDS (87); •PRANCER (89)

Hanson, Curtis
AROUSERS, THE (70); LITTLE DRAGONS, THE (80); LOSIN' IT (83); BEDROOM WINDOW, THE (87); •BAD INFLUENCE (90); •HAND THAT ROCKS THE CRADLE, THE (92); RIVER WILD, THE (94)

Hare, David
•WETHERBY (85); PARIS BY NIGHT (88); •STRAPLESS (89); DESIGNATED MOURNER, THE (97)

Harlin, Renny
BORN AMERICAN (86); NIGHTMARE ON ELM STREET 4: THE DREAM MASTER, A (88); PRISON (88); ADVENTURES OF FORD FAIRLANE, THE (90); DIE HARD 2: DIE HARDER (90); •CLIFFHANGER (93); CUTTHROAT ISLAND (95); LONG KISS GOODNIGHT, THE (96)

Hartley, Hal
•UNBELIEVABLE TRUTH, THE (90); •TRUST (91); SIMPLE MEN (92); •AMATEUR (95); FLIRT (96)

Harvey, Anthony
DUTCHMAN (66); •LION IN WINTER, THE (68); THEY MIGHT BE GIANTS (71); ABDICATION, THE (74); EAGLE'S WING (79); PLAYERS (79); RICHARD'S THINGS (80); ULTIMATE SOLUTION OF GRACE QUIGLEY, THE (84)

Haskin, Byron
I WALK ALONE (48); MAN-EATER OF KUMAON (48); TOO LATE FOR TEARS (49); •TREASURE ISLAND (50); SILVER CITY (51); TARZAN'S PERIL (51); WARPATH (51); DENVER AND RIO GRANDE, THE (52); NAKED JUNGLE, THE (53); •WAR OF THE WORLDS, THE (53); HIS MAJESTY O'KEEFE (54); LONG JOHN SILVER (54); CONQUEST OF SPACE (55); BOSS, THE (56); FIRST TEXAN, THE (56); FROM THE EARTH TO THE MOON (58); LITTLE SAVAGE, THE (59); JET OVER THE ATLANTIC (60); SEPTEMBER STORM (60); ARMORED COMMAND (61); CAPTAIN SINDBAD (63); ROBINSON CRUSOE ON MARS (64); POWER, THE (68)

Hathaway, Henry
WILD HORSE MESA (32); HERITAGE OF THE DESERT (33); MAN OF THE FOREST (33); SUNSET PASS (33); TO THE LAST MAN (33); UNDER THE TONTO RIM (33); COME ON, MARINES (34); LAST ROUND-UP, THE (34); NOW AND FOREVER (34); THUNDERING HERD, THE (34); WITCHING HOUR, THE (34); •LIVES OF A BENGAL LANCER, THE (35); PETER IBBETSON (35); GO WEST, YOUNG MAN (36); •TRAIL OF THE LONESOME PINE, THE (36); SOULS AT SEA (37); SPAWN OF THE NORTH (38); REAL GLORY, THE (39); BRIGHAM YOUNG—FRONTIERSMAN (40); JOHNNY APOLLO (40); SHEPHERD OF THE HILLS, THE (41); SUNDOWN (41); CHINA GIRL (42); TEN GENTLEMEN FROM WEST POINT (42); HOME IN INDIANA (44); WING AND A PRAYER (44); •HOUSE ON 92ND STREET, THE (45); NOB HILL (45); DARK CORNER, THE (46); 13 RUE MADELEINE (46); •KISS OF DEATH (47); •CALL NORTHSIDE 777 (48); DOWN TO THE SEA IN SHIPS (49); BLACK ROSE, THE (50); •DESERT FOX, THE (51); FOURTEEN HOURS (51); RAWHIDE (51); YOU'RE IN THE NAVY NOW (51); DIPLOMATIC COURIER (52); O. HENRY'S FULL HOUSE (52); NIAGARA (53); WHITE WITCH DOCTOR (53); GARDEN OF EVIL (54); PRINCE VALIANT (54); RACERS, THE (55); BOTTOM OF THE BOTTLE, THE (56); 23 PACES TO BAKER STREET (56); LEGEND OF THE LOST (57); FROM HELL TO TEXAS (58); WOMAN OBSESSED (59); NORTH TO ALASKA (60); SEVEN THIEVES (60); •HOW THE WEST WAS WON (63); CIRCUS WORLD (64); OF HUMAN BONDAGE (64); SONS OF KATIE ELDER, THE (65); NEVADA SMITH (66); LAST SAFARI, THE (67); FIVE CARD STUD (68); •TRUE GRIT (69); •AIRPORT (70); RAID ON ROMMEL (71); SHOOT OUT (71); HANGUP (74)

Hatton, Maurice
•PRAISE MARX AND PASS THE AMMUNITION (70); LONG SHOT (81); NELLY'S VERSION (83)

Hauff, Reinhard
MATTHIAS KNEISSL (70); DIE VERROHUNG DES FRANZ BLUM (74); DER HAUPTDARSTELLER (77); ZUENDSCHNUERE (77); •KNIFE IN THE HEAD (78); SLOW ATTACK (81); DER MANN AUF DER MAUER (82); 10 TAGE IN CALCUTTA (84); STAMMHEIM (86); LINIE 1 (87); BLAUAUGIG (89)

Hawks, Howard
AIR CIRCUS, THE (28); •DAWN PATROL, THE (30); CRIMINAL CODE, THE (31); CROWD ROARS, THE (32); •SCARFACE (32); TIGER SHARK (32); TODAY WE LIVE (33); •TWENTIETH CENTURY (34); •VIVA VILLA! (34); BARBARY COAST (35); CEILING ZERO (35); COME AND GET IT (36); ROAD TO GLORY, THE (36); •BRINGING UP BABY (38); •ONLY ANGELS HAVE WINGS (39); •HIS GIRL FRIDAY (40); •BALL OF FIRE (41); •SERGEANT YORK (41); •AIR FORCE (43); •OUTLAW, THE (43); •TO HAVE AND HAVE NOT (44); •BIG SLEEP, THE (46); •RED RIVER (48); SONG IS BORN, A (48); I WAS A MALE WAR BRIDE (49); •THING, THE (51); BIG SKY, THE (52); MONKEY BUSINESS (52); O. HENRY'S FULL HOUSE (52); •GENTLEMEN PREFER BLONDES (53); LAND OF THE PHARAOHS (55); •RIO BRAVO (59); HATARI! (62); •MAN'S FAVORITE SPORT? (64); RED LINE 7000 (65); •EL DORADO (67); •RIO LOBO (70)

Haynes, Todd
SUPERSTAR: THE KAREN CARPENTER STORY (88); POISON (91); •[SAFE] (95)

Hecht, Ben
•CRIME WITHOUT PASSION (34); •SCOUNDREL, THE (35); ONCE IN A BLUE MOON (36); SOAK THE RICH (36); •ANGELS OVER BROADWAY (40); SPECTER OF THE ROSE (46); ACTORS AND SIN (52)

Heckerling, Amy
•FAST TIMES AT RIDGEMONT HIGH (82); JOHNNY DANGEROUSLY (84); NATIONAL LAMPOON'S EUROPEAN VACATION (85); •LOOK WHO'S TALKING (89); LOOK WHO'S TALKING TOO (90); •CLUELESS (95)

Heisler, Stuart
STRAIGHT FROM THE SHOULDER (36); •HURRICANE, THE (37); BISCUIT EATER, THE (40); AMONG THE LIVING (41); MONSTER AND THE GIRL, THE (41); •GLASS KEY, THE (42); REMARKABLE ANDREW, THE (42); ALONG CAME JONES (45); •BLUE SKIES (46); SMASH-UP, THE STORY OF A WOMAN (47); TOKYO JOE (49); TULSA (49); CHAIN LIGHTNING (50); DALLAS (50); STORM WARNING (50); VENDETTA (50); JOURNEY INTO LIGHT (51); ISLAND OF DESIRE (52); STAR, THE (53); BEACHHEAD (54); THIS IS MY LOVE (54); I DIED A THOUSAND TIMES (55); LONE RANGER, THE (55); BURNING HILLS, THE (56); HITLER (62)

Hellman, Monte
BEAST FROM THE HAUNTED CAVE (60); TERROR, THE (63); BACK DOOR TO HELL (64); FLIGHT TO FURY (66); RIDE IN THE WHIRLWIND (66); •SHOOTING, THE (71); •TWO-LANE BLACKTOP (71); BORN TO KILL (75); SHATTER (75); CHINA 9, LIBERTY 37 (78); IGUANA (88); SILENT NIGHT, DEADLY NIGHT 3: BETTER WATCH OUT! (89)

Henenlotter, Frank
•BASKET CASE (82); BRAIN DAMAGE (88); BASKET CASE 2 (90); •FRANKENHOOKER (90); BASKET CASE 3: THE PROGENY (92)

Henson, Jim
GREAT MUPPET CAPER, THE (81); •DARK CRYSTAL, THE (82); LABYRINTH (86)

Herek, Stephen
CRITTERS (86); •BILL & TED'S EXCELLENT ADVENTURE (89); DON'T TELL MOM THE BABYSITTER'S DEAD (91); MIGHTY DUCKS, THE (92); THREE MUSKETEERS, THE (93); •MR. HOLLAND'S OPUS (96); •101 DALMATIANS (96)

Herman, Mark
UNUSUAL GROUND FLOOR CONVERSATION (87); BLAME IT ON THE BELLBOY (92); •BRASSED OFF (96)

Herzog, Werner
HERAKLES (62); SIGNS OF LIFE (68); FATA MORGANA (69); BEHINDERTE ZUKUNFT (70); EVEN DWARVES STARTED SMALL (70); LAND OF SILENCE AND DARKNESS (71); •AGUIRRE, THE WRATH OF GOD (72); DIE GROSSE EKSTASE DES BILDSCHNITZERS STEINER (74); •EVERY MAN FOR HIMSELF AND GOD AGAINST ALL (75); HEART OF GLASS (76); HOW MUCH WOOD WOULD A WOODCHUCK CHUCK (76); MIT MIR WILL KEINER SPIELEN (76); LA SOUFRIERE (77);

STROSZEK (77); •NOSFERATU, THE VAMPIRE (79); WOYZEK (79); GLAUBE UND WAHRUNG (80); HUIE'S PREDIGT (80); •FITZCAR-RALDO (82); BALLAD OF THE LITTLE SOLDIER, THE (84); WHERE THE GREEN ANTS DREAM (84); GASHERBRUM — DER LEUCHTENDE BERG (85); COBRA VERDE (88); IT ISN'T EASY BEING GOD (89); HERDSMEN OF THE SUN (91); ECHOES FROM A SOMBER EMPIRE (90); LESSONS OF DARKNESS (92)

Hickox, Douglas
GIANT BEHEMOTH, THE (59); IT'S ALL OVER TOWN (63); •ENTER-TAINING MR. SLOANE (69); SITTING TARGET (72); •THEATRE OF BLOOD (73); BRANNIGAN (75); SKY RIDERS (76); ZULU DAWN (79); HOUND OF THE BASKERVILLES, THE (83)

Hicks, Scott
FREEDOM! (81); SEBASTIAN AND THE SPARROW (88); •SHINE (96)

Hill, George Roy
PERIOD OF ADJUSTMENT (62); TOYS IN THE ATTIC (63); •WORLD OF HENRY ORIENT, THE (64); HAWAII (66); THOROUGHLY MODERN MILLIE (67); •BUTCH CASSIDY AND THE SUNDANCE KID (69); SLAUGHTERHOUSE-FIVE (72); •STING, THE (73); GREAT WALDO PEP-PER, THE (75); •SLAP SHOT (77); LITTLE ROMANCE, A (79); •WORLD ACCORDING TO GARP, THE (82); LITTLE DRUMMER GIRL, THE (84); FUNNY FARM (88)

Hill, Walter
HARD TIMES (75); •DRIVER, THE (78); •WARRIORS, THE (79); •LONG RIDERS, THE (80); •SOUTHERN COMFORT (81); 48 HRS. (82); STREETS OF FIRE (84); BREWSTER'S MILLIONS (85); CROSSROADS (86); EX-TREME PREJUDICE (87); RED HEAT (88); JOHNNY HANDSOME (89); ANOTHER 48 HRS. (90); TRESPASS (92); GERONIMO: AN AMERICAN LEGEND (93); WILD BILL (95); LAST MAN STANDING (96)

Hiller, Arthur
CARELESS YEARS, THE (57); MIRACLE OF THE WHITE STALLIONS (63); WHEELER DEALERS, THE (63); AMERICANIZATION OF EMILY, THE (64); PENELOPE (66); PROMISE HER ANYTHING (66); TOBRUK (66); TIGER MAKES OUT, THE (67); POPI (69); •LOVE STORY (70); •OUT-OF-TOWNERS, THE (70); •HOSPITAL, THE (71); •PLAZA SUITE (71); MAN OF LA MANCHA (72); CRAZY WORLD OF JULIUS VROODER, THE (74); MAN IN THE GLASS BOOTH, THE (75); SILVER STREAK (76); W.C. FIELDS AND ME (76); IN-LAWS, THE (79); NIGHT-WING (79); AUTHOR! AUTHOR! (82); MAKING LOVE (82); ROMANTIC COMEDY (83); LONELY GUY, THE (84); TEACHERS (84); OUTRAGEOUS FORTUNE (87); SEE NO EVIL, HEAR NO EVIL (89); TAKING CARE OF BUSINESS (90); BABE, THE (92); MARRIED TO IT (93); CARPOOL (96)

Hitchcock, Alfred
•BLACKMAIL (29); JUNO AND THE PAYCOCK (30); •MURDER (30); SKIN GAME, THE (31); NUMBER SEVENTEEN (32); RICH AND STRANGE (32); STRAUSS'S GREAT WALTZ (33); •MAN WHO KNEW TOO MUCH, THE (34); •39 STEPS, THE (35); •SABOTAGE (36); •SECRET AGENT (36); •YOUNG AND INNOCENT (37); LADY VANISHES, THE (38); JAMAICA INN (39); •FOREIGN CORRESPONDENT (40); •REBECCA (40); MR. AND MRS. SMITH (41); •SUSPICION (41); •SABOTEUR (42); •SHADOW OF A DOUBT (43); •LIFEBOAT (44); •SPELLBOUND (45); •NOTORIOUS (46); PARADINE CASE, THE (47); •ROPE (48); UNDER CAPRICORN (49); •STAGE FRIGHT (50); •STRANGERS ON A TRAIN (51); I CONFESS (53); •DIAL M FOR MURDER (54); •REAR WINDOW (54); •TO CATCH A THIEF (55); •TROUBLE WITH HARRY, THE (55); •MAN WHO KNEW TOO MUCH, THE (56); •WRONG MAN, THE (56); •VERTIGO (58); •NORTH BY NORTHWEST (59); •PSYCHO (60); •BIRDS, THE (63); •MARNIE (64); TORN CURTAIN (66); •TOPAZ (69); •FRENZY (72); •FAM-ILY PLOT (76)

Holland, Agnieszka
EVENING AT ABDON'S (74); SUNDAY CHILDREN (76); SOMETHING FOR SOMETHING (77); SCREEN TEST (77); PROVINCIAL ACTORS (79); FEVER (80); WOMAN ALONE, A (82); ANGRY HARVEST (84); TO KILL A PRIEST (88); •EUROPA, EUROPA (91); OLIVIER, OLIVIER (92); •SE-CRET GARDEN, THE (93); TOTAL ECLIPSE (95)

Holland, Tom
•FRIGHT NIGHT (85); FATAL BEAUTY (87); CHILD'S PLAY (88); TEMP, THE (93); LANGOLIERS, THE (95); STEPHEN KING'S THINNER (96)

Hooper, Tobe
•TEXAS CHAINSAW MASSACRE, THE (74); EATEN ALIVE (76); FUN-HOUSE, THE (81); •POLTERGEIST (82); LIFEFORCE (85); INVADERS FROM MARS (86); TEXAS CHAINSAW MASSACRE PART 2, THE (86); SPONTANEOUS COMBUSTION (90); TOBE HOOPER'S NIGHT TER-RORS (94); MANGLER, THE (95)

Hopper, Dennis
•EASY RIDER (69); •LAST MOVIE, THE (71); OUT OF THE BLUE (82); •COLORS (88); HOT SPOT, THE (90); BACKTRACK (92); CHASERS (94)

Hou Hsiao-hsien
CUTE GIRLS (80); CHEERFUL WIND (81); GROWING UP (82); SAND-WICH MAN, THE (83); BOYS FROM FENGKUEI, THE (83); SUMMER AT GRANDPA'S, A (84); TIME TO LIVE AND A TIME TO DIE, A (85); DUST IN THE WIND (86); •DAUGHTER OF THE NILE (87); CITY OF SADNESS, A (89); PUPPETMASTER, THE (93); GOOD MEN, GOOD WOMEN (95)

Howard, Leslie
•PYGMALION (38); •PIMPERNEL SMITH (41); •SPITFIRE (42); GENTLE SEX, THE (43)

Howard, Ron
GRAND THEFT AUTO (77); NIGHT SHIFT (82); •SPLASH (84); •COCOON (85); GUNG HO (86); WILLOW (88); •PARENTHOOD (89); •BACKDRAFT (91); FAR AND AWAY (92); •PAPER, THE (94); •APOLLO 13 (95); •RAN-SOM (96)

Hudlin, Reginald
•HOUSE PARTY (90); BOOMERANG (92); COSMIC SLOP (94); GREAT WHITE HYPE, THE (96)

Hudson, Hugh
•CHARIOTS OF FIRE (81); •GREYSTOKE: THE LEGEND OF TARZAN, LORD OF THE APES (84); REVOLUTION (85); LOST ANGELS (89)

Hughes, Albert and Allen
•MENACE II SOCIETY (93); DEAD PRESIDENTS (95)

Hughes, John
•SIXTEEN CANDLES (84); •BREAKFAST CLUB, THE (85); WEIRD SCI-ENCE (85); •FERRIS BUELLER'S DAY OFF (86); •PLANES, TRAINS, AND AUTOMOBILES (87); SHE'S HAVING A BABY (88); •UNCLE BUCK (89); CURLY SUE (91)

Hunter, Tim
•TEX (82); SYLVESTER (85); •RIVER'S EDGE (87); PAINT IT BLACK (90); SAINT OF FORT WASHINGTON, THE (93)

Huston, John
•MALTESE FALCON, THE (41); ACROSS THE PACIFIC (42); IN THIS OUR LIFE (42); •KEY LARGO (48); •TREASURE OF THE SIERRA MADRE, THE (48); WE WERE STRANGERS (49); •ASPHALT JUNGLE, THE (50); •AFRICAN QUEEN, THE (51); •RED BADGE OF COURAGE, THE (51); •MOULIN ROUGE (52); •BEAT THE DEVIL (53); •MOBY DICK (56); HEAVEN KNOWS, MR. ALLISON (57); BARBARIAN AND THE GEISHA, THE (58); ROOTS OF HEAVEN, THE (58); UNFORGIVEN, THE (60); •MISFITS, THE (61); FREUD (62); LIST OF ADRIAN MESSENGER, THE (63); •NIGHT OF THE IGUANA, THE (64); BIBLE. . . IN THE BEGINNING, THE (66); •CASINO ROYALE (67); REFLECTIONS IN A GOLDEN EYE (67); SINFUL DAVEY (68); WALK WITH LOVE AND DEATH, A (69); KREMLIN LETTER, THE (70); •FAT CITY (72); LIFE AND TIMES OF JUDGE ROY BEAN, THE (72); MACKINTOSH MAN, THE (73); •MAN WHO WOULD BE KING, THE (75); •WISE BLOOD (79); PHOBIA (80); VICTORY (81); ANNIE (82); •UNDER THE VOLCANO (84); •PRIZZI'S HONOR (85); •DEAD, THE (87)

Hyams, Peter
BUSTING (74); OUR TIME (74); PEEPER (75); CAPRICORN ONE (78); HANOVER STREET (79); •OUTLAND (81); STAR CHAMBER, THE (83); 2010 (84); RUNNING SCARED (86); PRESIDIO, THE (88); NARROW MARGIN (90); STAY TUNED (92); TIMECOP (94); SUDDEN DEATH (95); RELIC, THE (97)

Hytner, Nicholas
•MADNESS OF KING GEORGE, THE (94); •CRUCIBLE, THE (96)

Ichaso, Leon
EL SUPER (79); •CROSSOVER DREAMS (85); FEAR INSIDE, THE (92); SUGAR HILL (94); ZOOMAN (95); BITTER SUGAR (96)

Imamura, Shohei
STOLEN DESIRE (58); LIGHTS OF NIGHT (58); ENDLESS DESIRE (58); MY SECOND BROTHER (59); FLESH IS HOT, THE (61); INSECT WOMAN, THE (64); UNHOLY DESIRE (64); PORNOGRAPHER, THE (66); MAN VANISHES, A (67); KURAGEJIMA—LEGENDS FROM A SOUTHERN ISLAND (68); HISTORY OF POSTWAR JAPAN AS TOLD BY A BAR HOSTESS (70); STILL IN SEARCH OF UNRETURNED SOLDIERS (71); REPORT ON TWO PEOPLE NAMED YOSHINOBU (75); KARAYUKI-SAN, THE MAKING OF A PROSTITUTE (75); VENGEANCE IS MINE (79); WHY NOT (81); •BALLAD OF NARAYAMA, THE (83); LORD OF THE BROTHELS, THE (87); •BLACK RAIN (89); UNAGI (97)

Irvin, John
DOGS OF WAR, THE (80); GHOST STORY (81); CHAMPIONS (83); •TURTLE DIARY (85); RAW DEAL (86); •HAMBURGER HILL (87); NEXT OF KIN (89); EMINENT DOMAIN (91); FREEFALL (94); WIDOWS' PEAK (94); MONTH BY THE LAKE, A (94); CITY OF INDUSTRY (97)

Itami, Juzo
•FUNERAL, THE (84); •TAMPOPO (86); •TAXING WOMAN, A (87); TAXING WOMAN'S RETURN, A (88); A-GE-MAN (90); MINBO - OR THE GENTLE ART OF JAPANESE EXTORTION (94); DIABYONIN (95)

Ivory, James
HOUSEHOLDER, THE (63); •SHAKESPEARE WALLAH (65); GURU, THE (69); BOMBAY TALKIE (70); SAVAGES (72); WILD PARTY, THE (75); ROSELAND (77); HULLABALOO OVER GEORGIE AND BONNIE'S PICTURES (78); EUROPEANS, THE (79); JANE AUSTEN IN MANHATTAN (80); QUARTET (81); •HEAT AND DUST (83); BOSTONIANS, THE (84); •ROOM WITH A VIEW, A (85); MAURICE (87); SLAVES OF NEW YORK (89); MR. AND MRS. BRIDGE (90); •HOWARDS END (92); •REMAINS OF THE DAY, THE (93); JEFFERSON IN PARIS (95); SURVIVING PICASSO (96)

Jackson, Mick
CHATTAHOOCHEE (90); •L.A. STORY (91); •BODYGUARD, THE (92); CLEAN SLATE (94); •VOLCANO (97)

Jackson, Peter
BAD TASTE (88); MEET THE FEEBLES (89); DEAD ALIVE (92); •HEAVENLY CREATURES (94); FRIGHTENERS, THE (96)

Jaeckin, Just
•EMMANUELLE (74); STORY OF O, THE (75); MADAME CLAUDE (77); LE DERNIER AMANT ROMANTIQUE (78); COLLECTIONS PREVEES (79); GIRLS (80); LADY CHATTERLEY'S LOVER (81); PERILS OF GWENDOLINE IN THE LAND OF THE YIK YAK, THE (84)

Jarman, Derek
SEBASTIANE (76); JUBILEE (78); TEMPEST, THE (79); IN THE SHADOW OF THE SUN (80); ANGELIC CONVERSATION, THE (85); •CARAVAGGIO (86); ARIA (87); LAST OF ENGLAND, THE (87); •WAR REQUIEM (89); GARDEN, THE (90); EDWARD II (91); WITTGENSTEIN (93); •BLUE (94)

Jarmusch, Jim
PERMANENT VACATION (82); •STRANGER THAN PARADISE (84); •DOWN BY LAW (86); •MYSTERY TRAIN (89); •NIGHT ON EARTH (92); •DEAD MAN (96)

Jeunet, Jean-Pierre
•DELICATESSEN (91); CITY OF LOST CHILDREN, THE (95)

Jewison, Norman
FORTY POUNDS OF TROUBLE (62); THRILL OF IT ALL, THE (63); SEND ME NO FLOWERS (64); ART OF LOVE, THE (65); •CINCINNATI KID, THE (65); RUSSIANS ARE COMING, THE RUSSIANS ARE COMING, THE (66); •IN THE HEAT OF THE NIGHT (67); •THOMAS CROWN AFFAIR, THE (68); GAILY, GAILY (69); •FIDDLER ON THE ROOF (71); JESUS CHRIST, SUPERSTAR (73); •ROLLERBALL (75); F.I.S.T. (78); . . . AND JUSTICE FOR ALL (79); BEST FRIENDS (82); •SOLDIER'S STORY, A (84); •AGNES OF GOD (85); •MOONSTRUCK (87); IN COUNTRY (89); OTHER PEOPLE'S MONEY (91); ONLY YOU (94); BOGUS (96)

Joffe, Roland
•KILLING FIELDS, THE (84); •MISSION, THE (86); FAT MAN AND LITTLE BOY (89); CITY OF JOY (92); SCARLET LETTER, THE (95)

Johnson, Nunnally
BLACK WIDOW (54); NIGHT PEOPLE (54); HOW TO BE VERY, VERY POPULAR (55); •MAN IN THE GRAY FLANNEL SUIT, THE (56); OH, MEN! OH, WOMEN! (57); •THREE FACES OF EVE, THE (57); MAN WHO UNDERSTOOD WOMEN, THE (59); ANGEL WORE RED, THE (60)

Johnston, Joe
•HONEY, I SHRUNK THE KIDS (89); ROCKETEER, THE (91); PAGEMASTER, THE (94); JUMANJI (95)

Jones, David
•BETRAYAL (82); •84 CHARING CROSS ROAD (87); •JACKNIFE (89); TRIAL, THE (93); IS THERE LIFE OUT THERE? (94)

Jones, Terry
•MONTY PYTHON AND THE HOLY GRAIL (75); •MONTY PYTHON'S LIFE OF BRIAN (79); •MONTY PYTHON'S THE MEANING OF LIFE (83); PERSONAL SERVICES (87); ERIK THE VIKING (89)

Jordan, Neil
•ANGEL (82); •COMPANY OF WOLVES, THE (84); •MONA LISA (86); HIGH SPIRITS (88); WE'RE NO ANGELS (89); MIRACLE, THE (91); •CRYING GAME, THE (92); •INTERVIEW WITH THE VAMPIRE (94); •MICHAEL COLLINS (96)

Kadar, Jan
KATYA (50); HIJACK (52); MUSIC FROM MARS (54); HOUSE AT THE TERMINUS (57); THREE WISHES (58); MAGIC LANTERN II (60); YOUTH (60); SPARTAKIADE (60); DEATH IS CALLED ENGELCHEN (63); ACCUSED, THE (64); •SHOP ON MAIN STREET, THE (65); ANGEL LEVINE, THE (70); ADRIFT (71); BLUE HOTEL, THE (73); CASE AGAINST MILLIGAN, THE (75); LIES MY FATHER TOLD ME (75); OTHER SIDE OF HELL, THE (78); FREEDOM ROAD (79)

Kalatozov, Mikhail
BLIND (30); SALT FOR SVANETIA (30); NAIL IN THE BOOT, A (32); MANHOOD (39); WINGS OF VICTORY (41); INVICIBLE (43); MOSCOW MUSIC-HALL (45); CONSPIRACY OF THE DOOMED (50); TRUE FRIENDS (54); FIRST ECHELON, THE (56); HOSTILE WIND, THE (56); WOMAN FROM WARSAW, THE (56); •CRANES ARE FLYING, THE (57); LETTER THAT WAS NEVER SENT, THE (60); I AM CUBA (66); RED TENT, THE (71)

Kanevski, Vitaly
•FREEZE—DIE—COME TO LIFE (90); SAMOSTOJATELNAJA SHIZN (92); WE, CHILDREN OF THE TWENTIETH CENTURY (94)

Kanin, Garson
MAN TO REMEMBER, A (38); NEXT TIME I MARRY (38); •BACHELOR MOTHER (39); GREAT MAN VOTES, THE (39); •MY FAVORITE WIFE (40); THEY KNEW WHAT THEY WANTED (40); TOM, DICK AND HARRY (41); SOME KIND OF A NUT (69); WHERE IT'S AT (69)

Kaplan, Jonathan
SLAMS, THE (73); STUDENT TEACHERS, THE (73); NIGHT CALL NURSES (74); TRUCK TURNER (74); WHITE LINE FEVER (75); MR. BILLION (77); •OVER THE EDGE (79); •HEART LIKE A WHEEL (83); PROJECT X (87); •ACCUSED, THE (88); IMMEDIATE FAMILY (89); LOVE FIELD (92); •UNLAWFUL ENTRY (92); BAD GIRLS (94)

Karlson, Phil
SCANDAL SHEET (31); WAVE, A WAC AND A MARINE, A (44); G.I. HONEYMOON (45); SHANGHAI COBRA, THE (45); THERE GOES KELLY (45); BEHIND THE MASK (46); BOWERY BOMBSHELL (46); DARK ALIBI (46); LIVE WIRES (46); MISSING LADY, THE (46); SWING PARADE OF 1946 (46); WIFE WANTED (46); BLACK GOLD (47); KILROY WAS HERE (47); LOUISIANA (47); ADVENTURES IN SILVERADO (48); LADIES OF THE CHORUS (48); THUNDERHOOF (48); BIG CAT, THE (49); DOWN MEMORY LANE (49); IROQUOIS TRAIL, THE (50); LORNA DOONE (51); MASK OF THE AVENGER (51); TEXAS RANGERS, THE (51); BRIGAND, THE (52); KANSAS CITY CONFIDENTIAL (52); 99 RIVER STREET (53); THEY RODE WEST (54); 5 AGAINST THE HOUSE (55); HELL'S ISLAND (55); PHENIX CITY STORY, THE (55); TIGHT SPOT (55); BROTHERS RICO, THE (57); GUNMAN'S WALK (58); HELL TO ETERNITY (60); KEY WITNESS (60); SECRET WAYS, THE (61); YOUNG DOCTORS, THE (61); KID GALAHAD (62); SCARFACE MOB, THE (62); RAMPAGE (63); SILENCERS, THE (66); TIME FOR KILLING, A (67); WRECKING CREW, THE (68); HORNET'S NEST (70); BEN (72); •WALKING TALL (73); FRAMED (75)

Kasdan, Lawrence
•BODY HEAT (81); •BIG CHILL, THE (83); •SILVERADO (85); •ACCIDENTAL TOURIST, THE (88); I LOVE YOU TO DEATH (90); •GRAND CANYON (91); WYATT EARP (94); FRENCH KISS (95)

Kassovitz, Mathieu
FIERROT LE POU (90); WHITE NIGHTMARE (91); ASSASSINS (92); CAFE AU LAIT/METISSE (93); •HATE (95); ASSASSINS (97)

Kaufman, Philip
GOLDSTEIN (64); FEARLESS FRANK (67); •GREAT NORTHFIELD, MIN-NESOTA RAID, THE (72); WHITE DAWN, THE (74); •INVASION OF THE BODY SNATCHERS (78); •WANDERERS, THE (79); •RIGHT STUFF, THE (83); •UNBEARABLE LIGHTNESS OF BEING, THE (88); •HENRY AND JUNE (90); •RISING SUN (93)

Kaurismaki, Aki
SAIMAA GESTURE, THE (81); CRIME AND PUNISHMENT (83); CALA-MARI UNION (85); ROCKY VI (86); SHADOWS IN PARADISE (86); HAMLET GETS BUSINESS (87); THRU THE WIRE (87); ARIEL (89); LENINGRAD COWBOYS GO AMERICA, THE (90); •MATCH FACTORY GIRL, THE (90); I HIRED A CONTRACT KILLER (90); LA VIE DE BO-HEME (92); THOSE WERE THE DAYS (92); TOTAL BALALAIKA SHOW, THE (93); THESE BOOTS (93); LENINGRAD COWBOYS MEET MOSES (94); TAKE CARE OF YOUR SCARF, TATIANA (94); DRIFTING CLOUDS (96)

Kazan, Elia
•TREE GROWS IN BROOKLYN, A (45); •BOOMERANG (47); •GENTLE-MAN'S AGREEMENT (47); SEA OF GRASS, THE (47); •PINKY (49); PANIC IN THE STREETS (50); •STREETCAR NAMED DESIRE, A (51); •VIVA ZAPATA! (52); MAN ON A TIGHTROPE (53); •ON THE WATER-FRONT (54); •EAST OF EDEN (55); BABY DOLL (56); •FACE IN THE CROWD, A (57); •WILD RIVER (60); •SPLENDOR IN THE GRASS (61); AMERICA, AMERICA (63); ARRANGEMENT, THE (69); VISITORS, THE (72); LAST TYCOON, THE (76)

Keighley, William
MATCH KING, THE (32); •FOOTLIGHT PARADE (33); LADIES THEY TALK ABOUT (33); BABBITT (34); BIG HEARTED HERBERT (34); DOC-TOR MONICA (34); EASY TO LOVE (34); JOURNAL OF A CRIME (34); KANSAS CITY PRINCESS (34); G-MEN (35); MARY JANE'S PA (35); RIGHT TO LIVE, THE (35); SPECIAL AGENT (35); STARS OVER BROAD-WAY (35); BULLETS OR BALLOTS (36); •GREEN PASTURES (36); SING-ING KID, THE (36); GOD'S COUNTRY AND THE WOMAN (37); •PRINCE AND THE PAUPER, THE (37); VARSITY SHOW (37); •ADVENTURES OF ROBIN HOOD, THE (38); BROTHER RAT (38); SECRETS OF AN ACTRESS (38); VALLEY OF THE GIANTS (38); EACH DAWN I DIE (39); YES, MY DARLING DAUGHTER (39); •FIGHTING 69TH, THE (40); NO TIME FOR COMEDY (40); TORRID ZONE (40); BRIDE CAME C.O.D., THE (41); FOUR MOTHERS (41); GEORGE WASHINGTON SLEPT HERE (42); •MAN WHO CAME TO DINNER, THE (42); HONEYMOON (47); STREET WITH NO NAME, THE (48); ROCKY MOUNTAIN (50); CLOSE TO MY HEART (51); MASTER OF BALLANTRAE, THE (53)

Kelly, Gene
•ON THE TOWN (49); •SINGIN' IN THE RAIN (52); •IT'S ALWAYS FAIR WEATHER (55); INVITATION TO THE DANCE (56); HAPPY ROAD, THE (57); TUNNEL OF LOVE, THE (58); GIGOT (62); GUIDE FOR THE MAR-RIED MAN, A (67); •HELLO, DOLLY! (69); CHEYENNE SOCIAL CLUB, THE (70)

Kershner, Irvin
STAKEOUT ON DOPE STREET (58); YOUNG CAPTIVES, THE (59); HOODLUM PRIEST, THE (61); FACE IN THE RAIN, A (63); •LUCK OF GINGER COFFEY, THE (64); FINE MADNESS, A (66); FLIM-FLAM MAN, THE (67); LOVING (70); UP THE SANDBOX (72); S*P*Y*S (74); RETURN OF A MAN CALLED HORSE, THE (76); EYES OF LAURA MARS (78); •EMPIRE STRIKES BACK, THE (80); •NEVER SAY NEVER AGAIN (83); ROBOCOP 2 (90)

Kieslowski, Krzysztof
PICTURE (69); WORKERS (72); FIRST LOVE (74); PERSONNEL (75); BIOGRAPHY (75); SCAR (76); POLITICS (76); HOSPITAL (77); CALM (77); SEEN BY THE NIGHT PORTER (78); STATION (78); CAMERA BUFF (79); TALKING HEADS (80); SHORT DAY'S WORK, A (82); NO END (84); BLIND CHANCE (82); DEKALOG (88); •SHORT FILM ABOUT KILLING, A (88); SHORT FILM ABOUT LOVE, A (88); CITY LIFE (90); •DOUBLE LIFE OF VERONIQUE, THE (91); •BLUE (93); •RED (94); •WHITE (94)

King, Henry
SHE GOES TO WAR (29); EYES OF THE WORLD, THE (30); HELL HARBOR (30); LIGHTNIN' (30); MERELY MARY ANN (31); OVER THE HILL (31); WOMAN IN ROOM 13, THE (32); I LOVED YOU WEDNESDAY (33); STATE FAIR (33); CAROLINA (34); MARIE GALANTE (34); ONE MORE SPRING (35); WAY DOWN EAST (35); COUNTRY DOCTOR, THE (36); LLOYDS OF LONDON (36); RAMONA (36); SEVENTH HEAVEN (37); •ALEXANDER'S RAGTIME BAND (38); •IN OLD CHICAGO (38); •JESSE JAMES (39); STANLEY AND LIVINGSTONE (39); CHAD HANNA (40); LITTLE OLD NEW YORK (40); MARYLAND (40); REMEMBER THE DAY (41); YANK IN THE R.A.F., A (41); •BLACK SWAN, THE (42); •SONG OF BERNADETTE, THE (43); •WILSON (44); BELL FOR ADANO, A (45); MARGIE (46); •CAPTAIN FROM CASTILE (47); DEEP WATERS (48); •PRINCE OF FOXES (49); •TWELVE O'CLOCK HIGH (49); •GUN-FIGHTER, THE (50); •DAVID AND BATHSHEBA (51); I'D CLIMB THE HIGHEST MOUNTAIN (51); O. HENRY'S FULL HOUSE (52); •SNOWS OF KILIMANJARO, THE (52); WAIT TILL THE SUN SHINES, NELLIE (52); KING OF THE KHYBER RIFLES (53); LOVE IS A MANY-SPLENDORED THING (55); UNTAMED (55); •CAROUSEL (56); •SUN ALSO RISES, THE (57); BRAVADOS, THE (58); BELOVED INFIDEL (59); THIS EARTH IS MINE (59); TENDER IS THE NIGHT (61)

Kinoshita, Keisuke
BLOSSOMING PORT, THE (43); ARMY (44); JUBILATION STREET (44); GIRL I LOVED, THE (46); MARRIAGE (47); YOTSUYA GHOST STORY, THE (49); BROKEN DRUM, THE (49); CARMEN COMES HOME (51); JAPANESE TRAGEDY, A (53); •TWENTY-FOUR EYES (54); TIMES OF JOY AND SORROW (57); CANDLE IN THE WIND (57); •BALLAD OF NARAYAMA (58); SNOW FLURRY (59); SPRING DREAMS (60); IMMOR-TAL LOVE (61); BALLAD OF A WORKMAN (62); NEW YEAR'S LOVE (62); SING YOUNG PEOPLE (63); SCENT OF INCENSE, THE (64); EYES, THE SEA AND A BALL (67); LOVE AND SEPARATION IN SRI LANKA (76); MY SON (79); PARENTS AWAKE! (80); LEAVING THESE CHIL-DREN BEHIND (83); BIG JOYS, SMALL SORROWS (86)

Kinugasa, Teinosuke
BEFORE DAWN (31); LOYAL FORTY SEVEN-RONIN, THE (32); TWO STONE LANTERNS (33); SWORD AND THE SUMO RING, THE (34); YUKINOJO'S DISGUISE (36); MISS SNAKE PRINCESS (40); ROSE OF THE SEA (45); FOUR LOVE STORIES (47); FACE OF A MURDERER, THE (50); SAGA OF THE GREAT BUDDAH (52); •GATE OF HELL (53); DUEL OF A SNOWY NIGHT (54); IT HAPPENED IN TOKYO (55); SYMPHONY OF LOVE (58); WHITE HERON, THE (58); LANTERN, THE (60); SOR-CERER, THE (63); LITTLE RUNAWAY, THE (67)

Kleiser, Randal
•GREASE (78); BLUE LAGOON, THE (80); SUMMER LOVERS (82); GRANDVIEW, U.S.A. (84); FLIGHT OF THE NAVIGATOR (86); BIG TOP PEE-WEE (88); GETTING IT RIGHT (89); WHITE FANG (91); HONEY, I BLEW UP THE KID (92); IT'S MY PARTY (96)

Klimov, Elem
WELCOME KOSTYA! (65); ADVENTURES OF A DENTIST (67); SPORT SPORT SPORT (71); RASPUTIN (81); FAREWELL (81); •COME AND SEE (85)

Klos, Elmar
HIJACK (52); MUSIC FROM MARS (54); HOUSE AT THE TERMINUS (57); THREE WISHES (58); MAGIC LANTERN II (60); YOUTH (60); SPAR-TAKIADE (60); DEATH IS CALLED ENGELCHEN (63); ACCUSED, THE (64); •SHOP ON MAIN STREET, THE (65)

Kloves, Steve
•FABULOUS BAKER BOYS, THE (89); FLESH AND BONE (93)

Kobayashi, Masaki
MY SON'S YOUTH (52); SINCERE HEART (53); ROOM WITH THICK WALLS (53); THREE LOVES (54); SOMEWHERE BENEATH THE WIDE SKY (54); BEAUTIFUL DAYS (55); FOUNTAINHEAD, THE (56); I'LL BUY YOU (56); BLACK RIVER (57); NO GREATER LOVE (59); ROAD TO ETERNITY (59); SOLDIER'S PRAYER, A (61); HARAKIRI (62); INHERI-TANCE, THE (62); •KWAIDAN (64); REBELLION (67); YOUTH OF JAPAN, THE (68); INN OF EVIL (71); FOSSILS (75); GLOWING AUTUMN (79); TOKYO TRIALS, THE (83); EMPTY TABLE, THE (85)

Konchalovsky, Andrei
FIRST TEACHER, THE (65); ASYA'S HAPPINESS (67); NEST OF GEN-TLEFOLK, A (69); UNCLE VANYA (71); ROMANCE FOR LOVERS (74); SIBERIADE (78); MARIA'S LOVERS (85); •RUNAWAY TRAIN (85); DUET FOR ONE (86); •SHY PEOPLE (88); TANGO AND CASH (89); HOMER & EDDIE (90); INNER CIRCLE, THE (91); KOUROTCHKA RIABA (94)

Korda, Alexander
HER PRIVATE LIFE (29); SQUALL, THE (29); LILIES OF THE FIELD (30); PRINCESS AND THE PLUMBER, THE (30); WOMEN EVERYWHERE (30); DIE MANNER UM LUCIE (31); •MARIUS (31); RESERVED FOR LADIES (32); WEDDING REHEARSAL (32); GIRL FROM MAXIM'S, THE

(33); •PRIVATE LIFE OF HENRY VIII, THE (33); PRIVATE LIFE OF DON JUAN, THE (34); •SCARLET PIMPERNEL, THE (35); •REMBRANDT (36); •THIEF OF BAGHDAD, THE (40); •THAT HAMILTON WOMAN (41); VACATION FROM MARRIAGE (45); IDEAL HUSBAND, AN (47)

Korda, Zoltan
MEN OF TOMORROW (32); FOR LOVE OR MONEY (33); SANDERS OF THE RIVER (35); FOREVER YOURS (36); ELEPHANT BOY (37); •DRUMS (38); •FOUR FEATHERS, THE (39); CONQUEST OF THE AIR (40); •THIEF OF BAGHDAD, THE (40); •JUNGLE BOOK, THE (42); SAHARA (43); COUNTER-ATTACK (45); MACOMBER AFFAIR, THE (47); WOMAN'S VENGEANCE, A (47); CRY, THE BELOVED COUNTRY (51); STORM OVER THE NILE (55)

Koster, Henry
•ONE HUNDRED MEN AND A GIRL (37); •THREE SMART GIRLS (37); AFFAIRS OF MAUPASSANT (38); RAGE OF PARIS, THE (38); FIRST LOVE (39); THREE SMART GIRLS GROW UP (39); SPRING PARADE (40); IT STARTED WITH EVE (41); BETWEEN US GIRLS (42); MUSIC FOR MILLIONS (44); TWO SISTERS FROM BOSTON (46); •BISHOP'S WIFE, THE (47); UNFINISHED DANCE, THE (47); LUCK OF THE IRISH, THE (48); COME TO THE STABLE (49); INSPECTOR GENERAL, THE (49); •HARVEY (50); MY BLUE HEAVEN (50); WABASH AVENUE (50); ELOPE-MENT (51); MR. BELVEDERE RINGS THE BELL (51); NO HIGHWAY IN THE SKY (51); MY COUSIN RACHEL (52); O. HENRY'S FULL HOUSE (52); STARS AND STRIPES FOREVER (52); •ROBE, THE (53); DESIREE (54); GOOD MORNING, MISS DOVE (55); MAN CALLED PETER, A (55); VIRGIN QUEEN, THE (55); D-DAY THE SIXTH OF JUNE (56); POWER AND THE PRIZE, THE (56); MY MAN GODFREY (57); FRAULEIN (58); NAKED MAJA, THE (59); STORY OF RUTH, THE (60); FLOWER DRUM SONG (61); MR. HOBBS TAKES A VACATION (62); TAKE HER, SHE'S MINE (63); DEAR BRIGITTE (65); SINGING NUN, THE (66)

Kotcheff, Ted
TIARA TAHITI (62); LIFE AT THE TOP (65); TWO GENTLEMEN SHAR-ING (69); OUTBACK (70); BILLY TWO HATS (73); •APPRENTICESHIP OF DUDDY KRAVITZ, THE (74); FUN WITH DICK AND JANE (77); WHO IS KILLING THE GREAT CHEFS OF EUROPE? (78); •NORTH DALLAS FORTY (79); FIRST BLOOD (82); SPLIT IMAGE (82); UNCOMMON VALOR (83); JOSHUA THEN AND NOW (85); SWITCHING CHANNELS (88); WEEKEND AT BERNIE'S (89); WINTER PEOPLE (89); FOLKS! (92); HIDDEN ASSASSIN (96)

Kozintsev, Gregory
ALONE (31); YOUTH OF MAXIM (35); RETURN OF MAXIM (37); NEW HORIZONS (39); BELINSKI (53); PLAIN PEOPLE (56); •DON QUIXOTE (57); HAMLET (64); KING LEAR (72)

Kramer, Stanley
NOT AS A STRANGER (55); PRIDE AND THE PASSION, THE (57); •DEFIANT ONES, THE (58); •ON THE BEACH (59); •INHERIT THE WIND (60); •JUDGMENT AT NUREMBERG (61); •IT'S A MAD, MAD, MAD, MAD WORLD (63); •SHIP OF FOOLS (65); •GUESS WHO'S COMING TO DINNER (67); SECRET OF SANTA VITTORIA, THE (69); R.P.M. (70); BLESS THE BEASTS AND CHILDREN (71); OKLAHOMA CRUDE (73); DOMINO PRINCIPLE, THE (77); RUNNER STUMBLES, THE (79)

Kubrick, Stanley
•FEAR AND DESIRE (53); •KILLER'S KISS (55); •KILLING, THE (56); •PATHS OF GLORY (57); •SPARTACUS (60); •LOLITA (62); •DR. STRAN-GELOVE: OR HOW I LEARNED TO STOP WORRYING AND; LOVE THE BOMB (63); •2001: A SPACE ODYSSEY (68); •CLOCKWORK ORANGE, A (71); •BARRY LYNDON (75); •SHINING, THE (80); •FULL METAL JACKET (87)

Kurosawa, Akira
•DRUNKEN ANGEL (48); •STRAY DOG (49); •RASHOMON (50); SCAN-DAL (50); IDIOT, THE (51); •IKIRU (52); •SEVEN SAMURAI, THE (54); I LIVE IN FEAR (55); LOWER DEPTHS, THE (57); •THRONE OF BLOOD (57); •HIDDEN FORTRESS, THE (58); •BAD SLEEP WELL, THE (60); •YOJIMBO (61); SANJURO (62); •HIGH AND LOW (63); RED BEARD (65); DODES 'KA-DEN (70); •DERSU UZALA (75); •KAGEMUSHA (80); •RAN (85); •DREAMS (90); RHAPSODY IN AUGUST (91); MADADAYO (93)

Kurys, Diane
•PEPPERMINT SODA (77); COCKTAIL MOLOTOV (80); •ENTRE NOUS (83); •MAN IN LOVE, A (87); •C'EST LA VIE (90); LOVE AFTER LOVE (94); SIX DAYS, SIX NIGHTS (94)

Kusturica, Emir
GUERNICA (76); DO YOU REMEMBER DOLLY BELL? (81); •WHEN FATHER WAS AWAY ON BUSINESS (85); •TIME OF THE GYPSIES (89); ARIZONA DREAM (93); UNDERGROUND (95)

Landis, John
SCHLOCK (73); •KENTUCKY FRIED MOVIE, THE (77); •NATIONAL LAMPOON'S ANIMAL HOUSE (78); •BLUES BROTHERS, THE (80); •AMERICAN WEREWOLF IN LONDON, AN (81); •TRADING PLACES (83); TWILIGHT ZONE—THE MOVIE (83); INTO THE NIGHT (85); SPIES LIKE US (85); THREE AMIGOS (86); AMAZON WOMEN ON THE MOON (87); •COMING TO AMERICA (88); OSCAR (91); INNOCENT BLOOD (92); BEVERLY HILLS COP III (94); STUPIDS, THE (96)

Lang, Fritz
•M (31); •TESTAMENT OF DR. MABUSE, THE (33); LILIOM (34); •FURY (36); •YOU ONLY LIVE ONCE (37); YOU AND ME (38); RETURN OF FRANK JAMES, THE (40); •MAN HUNT (41); •WESTERN UNION (41); MOONTIDE (42); •HANGMEN ALSO DIE (43); MINISTRY OF FEAR (45); •SCARLET STREET (45); •WOMAN IN THE WINDOW, THE (45); CLOAK AND DAGGER (46); SECRET BEYOND THE DOOR, THE (48); AMERI-CAN GUERILLA IN THE PHILIPPINES, AN (50); HOUSE BY THE RIVER (50); •CLASH BY NIGHT (52); •RANCHO NOTORIOUS (52); •BIG HEAT, THE (53); BLUE GARDENIA, THE (53); HUMAN DESIRE (54); MOON-FLEET (55); BEYOND A REASONABLE DOUBT (56); •WHILE THE CITY SLEEPS (56); JOURNEY TO THE LOST CITY/TIGER OF BENGAL (59); •THOUSAND EYES OF DR. MABUSE, THE (60)

Lang, Walter
BROTHERS (30); COCK O' THE WALK (30); COSTELLO CASE, THE (30); HELLO SISTER (30); COMMAND PERFORMANCE, THE (31); HELL BOUND (31); WOMEN GO ON FOREVER (31); MEET THE BARON (33); NO MORE ORCHIDS (33); WARRIOR'S HUSBAND, THE (33); MIGHTY BARNUM, THE (34); PARTY'S OVER, THE (34); WHOM THE GODS DESTROY (34); CARNIVAL (35); HOORAY FOR LOVE (35); LOVE BE-FORE BREAKFAST (36); SECOND HONEYMOON (37); WIFE, DOCTOR AND NURSE (37); BARONESS AND THE BUTLER, THE (38); I'LL GIVE A MILLION (38); LITTLE PRINCESS, THE (39); BLUE BIRD, THE (40); GREAT PROFILE, THE (40); STAR DUST (40); •TIN PAN ALLEY (40); MOON OVER MIAMI (41); WEEKEND IN HAVANA (41); MAGNIFICENT DOPE, THE (42); SONG OF THE ISLANDS (42); CONEY ISLAND (43); GREENWICH VILLAGE (44); •STATE FAIR (45); CLAUDIA AND DAVID (46); SENTIMENTAL JOURNEY (46); MOTHER WORE TIGHTS (47); •SITTING PRETTY (48); WHEN MY BABY SMILES AT ME (48); YOU'RE MY EVERYTHING (49); •CHEAPER BY THE DOZEN (50); JACKPOT, THE (50); ON THE RIVIERA (51); •WITH A SONG IN MY HEART (52); CALL ME MADAM (53); •THERE'S NO BUSINESS LIKE SHOW BUSINESS (54); •KING AND I, THE (56); DESK SET (57); BUT NOT FOR ME (59); CAN-CAN (60); MARRIAGE-GO-ROUND, THE (60); SNOW WHITE AND THE THREE STOOGES (61)

Lapine, James
•IMPROMPTU (90); LIFE WITH MIKEY (93)

Lean, David
•MAJOR BARBARA (41); •IN WHICH WE SERVE (42); •THIS HAPPY BREED (44); •BLITHE SPIRIT (45); •BRIEF ENCOUNTER (45); •GREAT EXPECTATIONS (46); •OLIVER TWIST (48); ONE WOMAN'S STORY (48); MADELEINE (49); BREAKING THE SOUND BARRIER (52); •HOB-SON'S CHOICE (54); •SUMMERTIME (55); •BRIDGE ON THE RIVER KWAI, THE (57); •LAWRENCE OF ARABIA (62); •DOCTOR ZHIVAGO (65); •RYAN'S DAUGHTER (70); •PASSAGE TO INDIA, A (84)

Leconte, Patrice
LES VECES ETAIENT FERMES DE L'INTERIEUR (75); LES BRONZES (78); LES BRONZES FONT DU SKI (79); VIENS CHEZ MOI J'HABITE CHEZ UNE COPINE (80); MA FEMME S'APPELLE REVIENS (82); CIR-CULEZ Y'A RIEN A VOIR (83); LES SPECIALISTES (85); TANDEM (87); •MONSIEUR HIRE (89); •HAIRDRESSER'S HUSBAND, THE (92); CON-TRE L'OUBLI (92); LE BATTEUR DU BOLERO (92); TANGO (93); YVONNE'S PERFUME (94); GRAND DUKES, THE (95); •RIDICULE (96)

Lee, Ang
PUSHING HANDS (91); •WEDDING BANQUET, THE (93); •EAT DRINK MAN WOMAN (94); •SENSE AND SENSIBILITY (95)

Lee, Rowland V.

DANGEROUS WOMAN, A (29); •MYSTERIOUS DR. FU MANCHU, THE (29); WOLF OF WALL STREET, THE (29); DERELICT (30); LADIES LOVE BRUTES (30); MAN FROM WYOMING, A (30); RETURN OF DR. FU MANCHU, THE (30); GUILTY GENERATION, THE (31); RULING VOICE, THE (31); OVERNIGHT (33); ZOO IN BUDAPEST (33); •COUNT OF MONTE CRISTO, THE (34); GAMBLING (34); I AM SUZANNE (34); CARDINAL RICHELIEU (35); THREE MUSKETEERS, THE (35); ONE RAINY AFTERNOON (36); •LOVE FROM A STRANGER (37); TOAST OF NEW YORK, THE (37); MOTHER CAREY'S CHICKENS (38); SERVICE DE LUXE (38); •SON OF FRANKENSTEIN (39); SUN NEVER SETS, THE (39); TOWER OF LONDON (39); SON OF MONTE CRISTO, THE (41); POWDER TOWN (42); BRIDGE OF SAN LUIS REY, THE (44); CAPTAIN KIDD (45)

Lee, Spike

•SHE'S GOTTA HAVE IT (86); SCHOOL DAZE (88); •DO THE RIGHT THING (89); MO' BETTER BLUES (90); JUNGLE FEVER (91); •MALCOLM X (92); •CROOKLYN (94); CLOCKERS (95); GIRL 6 (96); •GET ON THE BUS (96); FOUR LITTLE GIRLS (97)

Lehmann, Michael

•HEATHERS (89); HUDSON HAWK (91); MEET THE APPLEGATES (91); AIRHEADS (94); TRUTH ABOUT CATS AND DOGS, THE (96)

Leigh, Mike

BLEAK MOMENTS (71); HARD LABOUR (73); NUTS IN MAY (75); KISS OF DEATH, THE (77); WHO'S WHO (78); GROWN-UPS (80); HOME SWEET HOME (82); MEANTIME (83); FOUR DAYS IN JULY (84); •HIGH HOPES (88); •LIFE IS SWEET (91); •NAKED (93); •SECRETS & LIES (95)

Leisen, Mitchell

CRADLE SONG (33); •DEATH TAKES A HOLIDAY (34); MURDER AT THE VANITIES (34); BEHOLD MY WIFE (35); FOUR HOURS TO KILL (35); HANDS ACROSS THE TABLE (35); BIG BROADCAST OF 1937, THE (36); 13 HOURS BY AIR (36); BIG BROADCAST OF 1938, THE (37); •EASY LIVING (37); SWING HIGH, SWING LOW (37); ARTISTS AND MODELS ABROAD (38); MIDNIGHT (39); ARISE, MY LOVE (40); •REMEMBER THE NIGHT (40); •HOLD BACK THE DAWN (41); I WANTED WINGS (41); LADY IS WILLING, THE (42); TAKE A LETTER, DARLING (42); NO TIME FOR LOVE (43); FRENCHMAN'S CREEK (44); •LADY IN THE DARK (44); PRACTICALLY YOURS (44); KITTY (45); MASQUERADE IN MEXICO (45); •TO EACH HIS OWN (46); DREAM GIRL (47); GOLDEN EARRINGS (47); SUDDENLY IT'S SPRING (47); BRIDE OF VENGEANCE (49); SONG OF SURRENDER (49); CAPTAIN CAREY, U.S.A. (50); NO MAN OF HER OWN (50); DARLING, HOW COULD YOU! (51); MATING SEASON, THE (51); YOUNG MAN WITH IDEAS (52); TONIGHT WE SING (53); BEDEVILLED (55); GIRL MOST LIKELY, THE (57)

Lelouch, Claude

RIGHT OF MAN, THE (60); L'AMOUR AVEC DES SI (63); TO BE A CROOK (65); LES GRANDS MOMENTS (65); •MAN AND A WOMAN, A (66); LIVE FOR LIFE (67); LES GAULOISES BLEU (68); LIFE LOVE DEATH (69); LOVE IS A FUNNY THING (69); CROOK, THE (71); SMIC SMAC SMOC (71); MONEY MONEY MONEY (72); HAPPY NEW YEAR (73); AND NOW MY LOVE (75); CAT AND MOUSE (75); GOOD AND THE BAD, THE (76); SECOND CHANCE (76); ANOTHER MAN, ANOTHER CHANCE (77); ROBERT ET ROBERT (78); ADVENTURE FOR TWO, AN (79); BOLERO (81); EDITH AND MARCEL (83); VIE LA VIE (84); GOING AND COMING BACK (85); BANDITS (86); •MAN AND A WOMAN: 20 YEARS LATER, A (86); ITINERARY OF A SPOILED CHILD (88); THERE WERE DAYS AND MOONS (90); LA BELLE HISTOIRE (92); TOUT CA… POUR CA! (93); LES MISERABLES (95); HOMMES, FEMMES: MODE D'EMPLOI (96)

Leonard, Robert Z.

LADY OF CHANCE, A (28); MARIANNE (29); •DIVORCEE, THE (30); IN GAY MADRID (30); LET US BE GAY (30); BACHELOR FATHER, THE (31); FIVE AND TEN (31); IT'S A WISE CHILD (31); SUSAN LENOX: HER FALL AND RISE (31); LOVERS COURAGEOUS (32); STRANGE INTERLUDE (32); DANCING LADY (33); PEG O' MY HEART (33); OUTCAST LADY (34); AFTER OFFICE HOURS (35); ESCAPADE (35); •GREAT ZIEGFELD, THE (36); PICCADILLY JIM (36); FIREFLY, THE (37); •MAYTIME (37); GIRL OF THE GOLDEN WEST, THE (38); BROADWAY SERENADE (39); NEW MOON (40); •PRIDE AND PREJUDICE (40); THIRD FINGER, LEFT HAND (40); WHEN LADIES MEET (41); •ZIEGFELD GIRL (41); STAND BY FOR ACTION (42); WE WERE DANCING (42); MAN FROM DOWN UNDER, THE (43); MARRIAGE IS A PRIVATE AFFAIR (44); WEEKEND AT THE WALDORF (45); SECRET HEART, THE (46); CYNTHIA (47);

B.F.'S DAUGHTER (48); BRIBE, THE (49); IN THE GOOD OLD SUMMERTIME (49); DUCHESS OF IDAHO (50); GROUNDS FOR MARRIAGE (50); NANCY GOES TO RIO (50); TOO YOUNG TO KISS (51); EVERYTHING I HAVE IS YOURS (52); CLOWN, THE (53); GREAT DIAMOND ROBBERY, THE (53); HER TWELVE MEN (54); KING'S THIEF, THE (55); KELLY AND ME (57)

Leone, Sergio

COLOSSUS OF RHODES, THE (60); SODOM AND GOMORRAH (62); •FISTFUL OF DOLLARS, A (64); •FOR A FEW DOLLARS MORE (65); •GOOD, THE BAD, AND THE UGLY, THE (66); •ONCE UPON A TIME IN THE WEST (69); DUCK, YOU SUCKER (72); •ONCE UPON A TIME IN AMERICA (84)

LeRoy, Mervyn

BROADWAY BABIES (29); HOT STUFF (29); LITTLE JOHNNY JONES (30); NUMBERED MEN (30); PLAYING AROUND (30); SHOWGIRL IN HOLLYWOOD (30); TOP SPEED (30); BROADMINDED (31); FIVE STAR FINAL (31); GENTLEMAN'S FATE (31); •LITTLE CAESAR (31); LOCAL BOY MAKES GOOD (31); TONIGHT OR NEVER (31); TOO YOUNG TO MARRY (31); BIG CITY BLUES (32); HEART OF NEW YORK, THE (32); HIGH PRESSURE (32); •I AM A FUGITIVE FROM A CHAIN GANG (32); THREE ON A MATCH (32); TWO SECONDS (32); ELMER THE GREAT (33); •GOLD DIGGERS OF 1933 (33); HARD TO HANDLE (33); TUGBOAT ANNIE (33); WORLD CHANGES, THE (33); HAPPINESS AHEAD (34); HEAT LIGHTNING (34); HI, NELLIE! (34); I FOUND STELLA PARISH (35); OIL FOR THE LAMPS OF CHINA (35); PAGE MISS GLORY (35); SWEET ADELINE (35); •ANTHONY ADVERSE (36); THREE MEN ON A HORSE (36); KING AND THE CHORUS GIRL, THE (37); •THEY WON'T FORGET (37); FOOLS FOR SCANDAL (38); ESCAPE (40); •WATERLOO BRIDGE (40); BLOSSOMS IN THE DUST (41); UNHOLY PARTNERS (41); •JOHNNY EAGER (42); •RANDOM HARVEST (42); •MADAME CURIE (43); •THIRTY SECONDS OVER TOKYO (44); WITHOUT RESERVATIONS (46); DESIRE ME (47); HOMECOMING (48); ANY NUMBER CAN PLAY (49); EAST SIDE, WEST SIDE (49); LITTLE WOMEN (49); •QUO VADIS (51); LOVELY TO LOOK AT (52); MILLION DOLLAR MERMAID (52); LATIN LOVERS (53); ROSE MARIE (54); •MISTER ROBERTS (55); STRANGE LADY IN TOWN (55); BAD SEED, THE (56); TOWARD THE UNKNOWN (56); HOME BEFORE DARK (58); •NO TIME FOR SERGEANTS (58); FBI STORY, THE (59); WAKE ME WHEN IT'S OVER (60); DEVIL AT 4 O'CLOCK, THE (61); MAJORITY OF ONE, A (61); •GYPSY (62); MARY, MARY (63); MOMENT TO MOMENT (66)

Lester, Richard

•RING-A-DING RHYTHM (62); MOUSE ON THE MOON, THE (63); •HARD DAY'S NIGHT, A (64); •HELP! (65); •KNACK… AND HOW TO GET IT, THE (65); •FUNNY THING HAPPENED ON THE WAY TO THE FORUM, A (66); •HOW I WON THE WAR (67); •PETULIA (68); •BED SITTING ROOM, THE (69); •JUGGERNAUT (74); •THREE MUSKETEERS, THE (74); •FOUR MUSKETEERS, THE (75); •ROYAL FLASH (75); RITZ, THE (76); •ROBIN AND MARIAN (76); BUTCH AND SUNDANCE: THE EARLY DAYS (79); •CUBA (79); •SUPERMAN II (80); SUPERMAN III (83); FINDERS KEEPERS (84); GET BACK (91)

Levinson, Barry

•DINER (82); •NATURAL, THE (84); YOUNG SHERLOCK HOLMES (85); •GOOD MORNING, VIETNAM (87); •TIN MEN (87); •RAIN MAN (88); •AVALON (90); •BUGSY (91); TOYS (92); •DISCLOSURE (94); JIMMY HOLLYWOOD (94); SLEEPERS (96)

Lewis, Jerry

BELLBOY, THE (60); ERRAND BOY, THE (61); LADIES' MAN, THE (61); •NUTTY PROFESSOR, THE (63); PATSY, THE (64); FAMILY JEWELS, THE (65); THREE ON A COUCH (66); BIG MOUTH, THE (67); ONE MORE TIME (70); WHICH WAY TO THE FRONT? (70); HARDLY WORKING (81); SMORGASBORD (83)

Lewis, Joseph H.

COURAGE OF THE WEST (37); SINGING OUTLAW (37); BORDER WOLVES (38); LAST STAND, THE (38); SPY RING, THE (38); BLAZING SIX SHOOTERS (40); BOYS OF THE CITY (40); MAN FROM TUMBLEWEEDS, THE (40); RETURN OF WILD BILL, THE (40); TEXAS STAGECOACH (40); THAT GANG OF MINE (40); TWO-FISTED RANGERS (40); ARIZONA CYCLONE (41); CRIMINALS WITHIN (41); INVISIBLE GHOST, THE (41); PRIDE OF THE BOWERY (41); BOMBS OVER BURMA (42); BOSS OF HANGTOWN MESA (42); MAD DOCTOR OF MARKET STREET, THE (42); SECRETS OF A CO-ED (42); SILVER BULLET, THE (42); MINSTREL MAN (44); FALCON IN SAN FRANCISCO, THE (45); MY

Mandel, Robert
INDEPENDENCE DAY (83); •F/X (86); TOUCH AND GO (86); BIG SHOTS (87); SCHOOL TIES (92); SUBSTITUTE, THE (96)

Mandoki, Luis
GABY—A TRUE STORY (87); WHITE PALACE (90); BORN YESTERDAY (93); •WHEN A MAN LOVES A WOMAN (94)

Mankiewicz, Joseph L.
DRAGONWYCK (46); SOMEWHERE IN THE NIGHT (46); •GHOST AND MRS. MUIR, THE (47); LATE GEORGE APLEY, THE (47); ESCAPE (48); •LETTER TO THREE WIVES, A (48); HOUSE OF STRANGERS (49); •ALL ABOUT EVE (50); NO WAY OUT (50); •PEOPLE WILL TALK (51); •FIVE FINGERS (52); •JULIUS CAESAR (53); BAREFOOT CONTESSA, THE (54); GUYS AND DOLLS (55); QUIET AMERICAN, THE (58); SUDDENLY, LAST SUMMER (59); CLEOPATRA (63); HONEY POT, THE (67); THERE WAS A CROOKED MAN (70); •SLEUTH (72)

Mann, Anthony
DR. BROADWAY (42); MOONLIGHT IN HAVANA (42); NOBODY'S DARLING (43); MY BEST GAL (44); STRANGERS IN THE NIGHT (44); GREAT FLAMARION, THE (45); SING YOUR WAY HOME (45); TWO O'CLOCK COURAGE (45); BAMBOO BLONDE, THE (46); STRANGE IMPERSONATION (46); DESPERATE (47); RAILROADED (47); •T-MEN (47); •HE WALKED BY NIGHT (48); •RAW DEAL (48); BLACK BOOK, THE (49); BORDER INCIDENT (49); DEVIL'S DOORWAY (50); FURIES, THE (50); SIDE STREET (50); •WINCHESTER '73 (50); TALL TARGET, THE (51); BEND OF THE RIVER (52); •GLENN MILLER STORY, THE (53); •NAKED SPUR, THE (53); THUNDER BAY (53); FAR COUNTRY, THE (55); LAST FRONTIER, THE (55); MAN FROM LARAMIE, THE (55); •STRATEGIC AIR COMMAND (55); SERENADE (56); MEN IN WAR (57); TIN STAR, THE (57); GOD'S LITTLE ACRE (58); •MAN OF THE WEST (58); CIMARRON (60); •SPARTACUS (60); •EL CID (61); FALL OF THE ROMAN EMPIRE, THE (64); HEROES OF TELEMARK, THE (65); DANDY IN ASPIC, A (68)

Mann, Daniel
•COME BACK, LITTLE SHEBA (52); ABOUT MRS. LESLIE (54); •I'LL CRY TOMORROW (55); ROSE TATTOO, THE (55); •TEAHOUSE OF THE AUGUST MOON, THE (56); HOT SPELL (58); LAST ANGRY MAN, THE (59); •BUTTERFIELD 8 (60); MOUNTAIN ROAD, THE (60); ADA (61); FIVE FINGER EXERCISE (62); WHO'S GOT THE ACTION? (62); WHO'S BEEN SLEEPING IN MY BED? (63); JUDITH (65); OUR MAN FLINT (66); FOR LOVE OF IVY (68); DREAM OF KINGS, A (69); WILLARD (71); REVENGERS, THE (72); INTERVAL (73); MAURIE (73); JOURNEY INTO FEAR (74); LOST IN THE STARS (74); MATILDA (78)

Mann, Delbert
•MARTY (55); BACHELOR PARTY, THE (57); DESIRE UNDER THE ELMS (58); •SEPARATE TABLES (58); MIDDLE OF THE NIGHT (59); DARK AT THE TOP OF THE STAIRS, THE (60); LOVER COME BACK (61); OUTSIDER, THE (62); •THAT TOUCH OF MINK (62); GATHERING OF EAGLES, A (63); DEAR HEART (64); QUICK, BEFORE IT MELTS (64); MISTER BUDDWING (66); FITZWILLY (67); PINK JUNGLE, THE (68); DAVID COPPERFIELD (70); JANE EYRE (71); •KIDNAPPED (71); BIRCH INTERVAL (76); NIGHT CROSSING (82)

Mann, Michael
•THIEF (81); KEEP, THE (83); •MANHUNTER (86); •LAST OF THE MOHICANS, THE (92); •HEAT

Marquand, Richard
LEGACY, THE (78); EYE OF THE NEEDLE (81); •RETURN OF THE JEDI (83); UNTIL SEPTEMBER (84); •JAGGED EDGE (85); HEARTS OF FIRE (87)

Marshall, Garry
YOUNG DOCTORS IN LOVE (82); •FLAMINGO KID, THE (84); NOTHING IN COMMON (86); OVERBOARD (87); •BEACHES (88); •PRETTY WOMAN (90); FRANKIE AND JOHNNY (91); EXIT TO EDEN (94); DEAR GOD (96)

Marshall, Penny
JUMPIN' JACK FLASH (86); •BIG (88); AWAKENINGS (90); •LEAGUE OF THEIR OWN, A (92); RENAISSANCE MAN (94); PREACHER'S WIFE, THE (96)

Mate, Rudolph
IT HAD TO BE YOU (47); DARK PAST, THE (48); •D.O.A. (50); NO SAD SONGS FOR ME (50); UNION STATION (50); BRANDED (51); PRINCE WHO WAS A THIEF, THE (51); WHEN WORLDS COLLIDE (51); GREEN

GLOVE, THE (52); PAULA (52); SALLY AND SAINT ANNE (52); FORBIDDEN (53); MISSISSIPPI GAMBLER, THE (53); SECOND CHANCE (53); BLACK SHIELD OF FALWORTH, THE (54); SIEGE AT RED RIVER, THE (54); FAR HORIZONS, THE (55); VIOLENT MEN, THE (55); MIRACLE IN THE RAIN (56); PORT AFRIQUE (56); RAWHIDE YEARS, THE (56); THREE VIOLENT PEOPLE (56); DEEP SIX, THE (58); FOR THE FIRST TIME (59); SEVEN SEAS TO CALAIS (62); 300 SPARTANS, THE (62)

May, Elaine
NEW LEAF, A (71); •HEARTBREAK KID, THE (72); •MIKEY AND NICKY (76); •ISHTAR (87)

Mayo, Archie
MY MAN (28); ON TRIAL (28); STATE STREET SADIE (28); IS EVERYBODY HAPPY? (29); SACRED FLAME, THE (29); SAP, THE (29); SONNY BOY (29); COURAGE (30); DOORWAY TO HELL, THE (30); OH! SAILOR, BEHAVE! (30); VENGEANCE (30); WIDE OPEN (30); BOUGHT (31); ILLICIT (31); SVENGALI (31); EXPERT, THE (32); NIGHT AFTER NIGHT (32); STREET OF WOMEN (32); TWO AGAINST THE WORLD (32); UNDER EIGHTEEN (32); CONVENTION CITY (33); EVER IN MY HEART (33); LIFE OF JIMMY DOLAN, THE (33); MAYOR OF HELL, THE (33); DESIRABLE (34); GAMBLING LADY (34); MAN WITH TWO FACES, THE (34); BORDERTOWN (35); CASE OF THE LUCKY LEGS, THE (35); GO INTO YOUR DANCE (35); GIVE ME YOUR HEART (36); I MARRIED A DOCTOR (36); •PETRIFIED FOREST, THE (36); BLACK LEGION (37); CALL IT A DAY (37); IT'S LOVE I'M AFTER (37); ADVENTURES OF MARCO POLO, THE (38); YOUTH TAKES A FLING (38); THEY SHALL HAVE MUSIC (39); FOUR SONS (40); HOUSE ACROSS THE BAY, THE (40); •CHARLEY'S AUNT (41); CONFIRM OR DENY (41); GREAT AMERICAN BROADCAST, THE (41); MOONTIDE (42); ORCHESTRA WIVES (42); CRASH DIVE (43); SWEET AND LOWDOWN (44); ANGEL ON MY SHOULDER (46); NIGHT IN CASABLANCA, A (46)

Mazursky, Paul
•BOB & CAROL & TED & ALICE (69); ALEX IN WONDERLAND (70); •BLUME IN LOVE (73); •HARRY AND TONTO (74); •NEXT STOP, GREENWICH VILLAGE (76); UNMARRIED WOMAN, AN (78); WILLIE AND PHIL (80); TEMPEST (82); •MOSCOW ON THE HUDSON (84); •DOWN AND OUT IN BEVERLY HILLS (86); MOON OVER PARADOR (88); ENEMIES, A LOVE STORY (89); SCENES FROM A MALL (91); PICKLE, THE (93); FAITHFUL (96)

McBride, Jim
•DAVID HOLZMAN'S DIARY (68); HOT TIMES (74); •BREATHLESS (83); •BIG EASY, THE (87); GREAT BALLS OF FIRE (89); WRONG MAN, THE (93)

McCarey, Leo
SOPHOMORE, THE (29); LET'S GO NATIVE (30); PART TIME WIFE (30); RED HOT RHYTHM (30); WILD COMPANY (30); INDISCREET (31); •KID FROM SPAIN, THE (32); •DUCK SOUP (33); BELLE OF THE NINETIES (34); SIX OF A KIND (34); RUGGLES OF RED GAP (35); MILKY WAY, THE (36); •AWFUL TRUTH, THE (37); MAKE WAY FOR TOMORROW (37); •LOVE AFFAIR (39); ONCE UPON A HONEYMOON (42); •GOING MY WAY (44); •BELLS OF ST. MARY'S, THE (45); GOOD SAM (48); MY SON JOHN (52); AFFAIR TO REMEMBER, AN (57); RALLY 'ROUND THE FLAG, BOYS! (58); SATAN NEVER SLEEPS (62)

McLeod, Norman Z.
ALONG CAME YOUTH (31); •MONKEY BUSINESS (31); TOUCHDOWN (31); •HORSE FEATHERS (32); MIRACLE MAN, THE (32); ALICE IN WONDERLAND (33); LADY'S PROFESSION, A (33); MAMA LOVES PAPA (33); •IT'S A GIFT (34); MANY HAPPY RETURNS (34); MELODY IN SPRING (34); CORONADO (35); HERE COMES COOKIE (35); REDHEADS ON PARADE (35); EARLY TO BED (36); •PENNIES FROM HEAVEN (36); MIND YOUR OWN BUSINESS (37); •TOPPER (37); MERRILY WE LIVE (38); THERE GOES MY HEART (38); REMEMBER? (39); TOPPER TAKES A TRIP (39); LITTLE MEN (40); LADY BE GOOD (41); TRIAL OF MARY DUGAN, THE (41); JACKASS MAIL (42); PANAMA HATTIE (42); POWERS GIRL, THE (42); SWING SHIFT MAISIE (43); KID FROM BROOKLYN, THE (46); ROAD TO RIO (47); •SECRET LIFE OF WALTER MITTY, THE (47); ISN'T IT ROMANTIC? (48); PALEFACE, THE (48); LET'S DANCE (50); MY FAVORITE SPY (51); NEVER WAVE AT A WAC (52); CASANOVA'S BIG NIGHT (54); PUBLIC PIGEON NO. 1 (57)

McNaughton, John
•HENRY: PORTRAIT OF A SERIAL KILLER (89); BORROWER, THE (91); SEX, DRUGS, ROCK & ROLL (91); •MAD DOG AND GLORY (93); NORMAL LIFE (96)

McTiernan, John
NOMADS (85); •PREDATOR (87); •DIE HARD (88); •HUNT FOR RED OCTOBER, THE (90); MEDICINE MAN (92); •LAST ACTION HERO (93); •DIE HARD WITH A VENGEANCE (95)

Medak, Peter
NEGATIVES (68); DAY IN THE DEATH OF JOE EGG, A (72); •RULING CLASS, THE (72); ODD JOB, THE (78); CHANGELING, THE (79); ZORRO, THE GAY BLADE (81); MEN'S CLUB, THE (86); KRAYS, THE (90); LET HIM HAVE IT (91); PONTIAC MOON (94); ROMEO IS BLEEDING (94)

Melville, Jean-Pierre
LE SILENCE DE LA MER (49); •LES ENFANTS TERRIBLES (50); QUAND TU LIRA CETTE LETTRE (53); •BOB LE FLAMBEUR (55); DEUX HOMMES DANS MANHATTAN (59); LEON MORIN PRETRE (61); FINGERMAN, THE (62); MAGNET OF DOOM (62); SECOND BREATH (66); THE SAMURAI (67); GODSON, THE (67); L'ARMEE DES OMBRES (69); LE CERCLE ROUGE (70); COP, A (72)

Menzel, Jiri
PEARLS ON THE GROUND (65); •CLOSELY WATCHED TRAINS (66); CAPRICIOUS SUMMER (68); LARKS ON A STRING (69); WHO SEEKS A HANDFUL OF GOLD (75); SECLUSION NEAR A FOREST (76); MAGICIANS OF THE SILVER SCREEN (78); SHORT CUT (80); SNOWDROP FESTIVAL, THE (82); PRAGUE (85); MY SWEET LITTLE VILLAGE (85); KONEC STARYCH CASU (89); OPERA ZEBRACKA (91); LIFE AND EXTRAORDINARY ADVENTURES OF PRIVATE IVAN CHONKIN (95); FRANCISKA VASARNAPJAI (97)

Menzies, William Cameron
ALWAYS GOODBYE (31); SPIDER, THE (31); ALMOST MARRIED (32); CHANDU THE MAGICIAN (32); I LOVED YOU WEDNESDAY (33); WHARF ANGEL, THE (34); •THINGS TO COME (36); GREEN COCKATOO, THE (37); •THIEF OF BAGHDAD, THE (40); ADDRESS UNKNOWN (44); DRUMS IN THE DEEP SOUTH (51); WHIP HAND, THE (51); INVADERS FROM MARS (53); MAZE, THE (53)

Meyer, Nicholas
•TIME AFTER TIME (79); •STAR TREK II: THE WRATH OF KHAN (82); VOLUNTEERS (85); DECEIVERS, THE (88); COMPANY BUSINESS (91); STAR TREK VI: THE UNDISCOVERED COUNTRY (91)

Meyer, Russ
IMMORAL MR. TEAS, THE (59); THIS IS MY BODY (59); EVE AND THE HANDYMAN (60); NAKED CAMERA (60); EROTICA (61); IMMORAL WEST, THE (62); EUROPE IN THE RAW (63); HEAVENLY BODIES (63); LORNA (64); FANNY HILL: MEMOIRS OF A WOMAN OF PLEASURE (65); MUDHONEY (65); MOTORPSYCHO (65); ROPE OF FLESH (65); •FASTER, PUSSYCAT, KILL! KILL! (66); MONDO TOPLESS (66); GOOD MORNING. . . AND GOODBYE (67); COMMON-LAW-CABIN (67); FINDERS KEEPERS, LOVERS WEEPERS (68); VIXEN (68); •BEYOND THE VALLEY OF THE DOLLS (70); SEVEN MINUTES, THE (71); SWEET SUZY (73); SUPERVIXENS (75); UP! (76); BENEATH THE VALLEY OF THE ULTRAVIXENS (79)

Mikhalkov, Nikita
QUIET DAY AT THE END OF THE WAR, A (70); AT HOME AMONG STRANGERS (74); SLAVE OF LOVE, A (77); UNFINISHED PIECE FOR A MECHANICAL PIANO, AN (77); FIVE EVENINGS (79); OBLOMOV (80); FAMILY RELATIONS (82); WITHOUT WITNESSES (83); •DARK EYES (87); URGA (91); CLOSE TO EDEN (92); ANNA (94); BURNT BY THE SUN (94)

Milestone, Lewis
NEW YORK NIGHTS (29); •ALL QUIET ON THE WESTERN FRONT (30); •FRONT PAGE, THE (31); RAIN (32); HALLELUJAH, I'M A BUM (33); CAPTAIN HATES THE SEA, THE (34); PARIS IN SPRING (35); ANYTHING GOES (36); GENERAL DIED AT DAWN, THE (36); NIGHT OF NIGHTS, THE (39); •OF MICE AND MEN (39); LUCKY PARTNERS (40); MY LIFE WITH CAROLINE (41); EDGE OF DARKNESS (43); NORTH STAR, THE (43); PURPLE HEART, THE (44); •WALK IN THE SUN, A (45); •STRANGE LOVE OF MARTHA IVERS, THE (46); ARCH OF TRIUMPH (48); NO MINOR VICES (48); RED PONY, THE (49); HALLS OF MONTEZUMA (51);

KANGAROO (52); LES MISERABLES (52); MELBA (53); THEY WHO DARE (53); •PORK CHOP HILL (59); OCEAN'S ELEVEN (60); MUTINY ON THE BOUNTY (62)

Milius, John
DILLINGER (73); •WIND AND THE LION, THE (75); BIG WEDNESDAY (78); CONAN THE BARBARIAN (82); RED DAWN (84); FAREWELL TO THE KING (89); FLIGHT OF THE INTRUDER (91)

Miller, Claude
BEST WAY, THE (78); TELL HIM I LOVE HIM (77); INQUISITOR, THE (81); DEADLY CIRCUIT (83); IMPUDENT GIRL, AN; •LITTLE THIEF, THE (89); •ACCOMPANIST, THE (92); SMILE, THE (93); LES ENFANTS DE LUMIERE (95)

Miller, David
BILLY THE KID (41); FLYING TIGERS (42); SUNDAY PUNCH (42); LOVE HAPPY (49); TOP O' THE MORNING (49); OUR VERY OWN (50); SATURDAY'S HERO (51); SUDDEN FEAR (52); BEAUTIFUL STRANGER (54); DIANE (55); OPPOSITE SEX, THE (56); •STORY OF ESTHER COSTELLO, THE (57); HAPPY ANNIVERSARY (59); MIDNIGHT LACE (60); BACK STREET (61); •LONELY ARE THE BRAVE (62); CAPTAIN NEWMAN, M.D. (63); HAMMERHEAD (68); HAIL, HERO! (69); EXECUTIVE ACTION (73); BITTERSWEET LOVE (76)

Miller, George
•MAD MAX (79); •ROAD WARRIOR, THE (81); MAD MAX BEYOND THUNDERDOME (85); •WITCHES OF EASTWICK, THE (87); •LORENZO'S OIL (92)

Miller, George
•MAN FROM SNOWY RIVER, THE (82); AVIATOR, THE (85); GREAT ELEPHANT ESCAPE, THE (95); COOL CHANGE (86); LES PATTERSON SAVES THE WORLD (87); NEVERENDING STORY II: THE NEXT CHAPTER, THE (91); FROZEN ASSETS (92); OVER THE HILL (92); GROSS MISCONDUCT (94); ANDRE (94); ZEUS AND ROXANNE (97)

Minghella, Anthony
•TRULY, MADLY, DEEPLY (91); MR. WONDERFUL (93); •ENGLISH PATIENT, THE (96)

Minnelli, Vincente
•CABIN IN THE SKY (43); I DOOD IT (43); •MEET ME IN ST. LOUIS (44); •CLOCK, THE (45); YOLANDA AND THE THIEF (45); •ZIEGFELD FOLLIES (45); UNDERCURRENT (46); •PIRATE, THE (48); MADAME BOVARY (49); •FATHER OF THE BRIDE (50); •AMERICAN IN PARIS, AN (51); FATHER'S LITTLE DIVIDEND (51); •BAD AND THE BEAUTIFUL, THE (52); •BAND WAGON, THE (53); STORY OF THREE LOVES, THE (53); •BRIGADOON (54); LONG, LONG TRAILER, THE (54); COBWEB, THE (55); KISMET (55); •LUST FOR LIFE (56); •TEA AND SYMPATHY (56); DESIGNING WOMAN (57); •GIGI (58); RELUCTANT DEBUTANTE, THE (58); •SOME CAME RUNNING (59); •BELLS ARE RINGING (60); HOME FROM THE HILL (60); FOUR HORSEMEN OF THE APOCALYPSE, THE (62); TWO WEEKS IN ANOTHER TOWN (62); COURTSHIP OF EDDIE'S FATHER, THE (63); GOODBYE CHARLIE (64); SANDPIPER, THE (65); ON A CLEAR DAY YOU CAN SEE FOREVER (70); MATTER OF TIME, A (76)

Mizoguchi, Kenji
HOME TOWN (30); MISTRESS OF A FOREIGNER (30); AND YET THEY GO (31); MAN OF THE MOMENT, THE (32); DAWN OF MANCHURIA AND MONGOLIA, THE (32); WATER MAGICIAN, THE (33); GION FESTIVAL (33); JIMPU GROUP, THE (33); MOUNTAIN PASS OF LOVE AND HATE, THE (34); DOWNFALL OF OSEN (34); OYUKI THE VIRGIN (35); POPPY (35); OSAKA ELEGY (36); •SISTERS OF THE GION (36); STRAITS OF LOVE AND HATE, THE (37); AH, MY HOME TOWN (38); SONG OF THE CAMP, THE (38); STORY OF THE LAST CHRYSANTHEMUM, THE (39); WOMAN OF OSAKA, THE (40); LIFE OF AN ACTOR, THE (41); 47 RONIN, THE (PARTS I & II) (41); THREE GENERATIONS OF DANJURO (44); SWORDSMAN, THE (44); NOTED SWORD, THE (45); VICTORY SONG (45); VICTORY OF WOMEN, THE (46); UTAMARRO AND HIS FIVE WOMEN (46); LOVE OF SUMAKO THE ACTRESS, THE (47); WOMEN OF THE NIGHT (48); MY LOVE HAS BEEN BURNING (49); PICTURE OF MADAME YUKI, A (50); MISS OYU (51); LADY MUSASHINO (51); •LIFE OF OHARU, THE (52); GEISHA, A (53); •UGETSU MONOGATARI (53); •SANSHO THE BAILIFF (54); WOMAN IN THE RUMOR, THE (54); CRUCIFIED LOVERS, THE (54); EMPRESS YANG KWI-FEI, THE (55); TAIRA CLAN, THE (55); STREET OF SHAME (56)

Ophuls, Max

BARTERED BRIDE, THE (32); UNE HISTOIRE D'AMOUR (33); MAN STOLEN (34); DIVINE (35); TENDER ENEMY, THE (36); WERTHER (38); MAYERLING TO SARAJEVO (40); EXILE, THE (47); •LETTER FROM AN UNKNOWN WOMAN (48); CAUGHT (49); RECKLESS MOMENT, THE (49); •LA RONDE (50); VENDETTA (50); LE PLAISIR (52); •EARRINGS OF MADAME DE . . . , THE (53); •LOLA MONTES (55)

Oshima, Nagisa

TOWN OF LOVE AND HOPE, A (59); NAKED YOUTH (60); SUN'S BUR-IAL, THE (60); NIGHT AND FOG IN JAPAN (60); CATCH, THE (61); REVOLUTIONARY, THE (62); CHILD'S FIRST ADVENTURE, A (64); I'M HERE BELLET (64); PLEASURES OF THE FLESH, THE (66); VIOLENCE AT NOON (66); BAND OF NINJA (67); SING A SONG OF SEX (67); JAPANESE SUMMER: DOUBLE SUICIDE (67); DEATH BY HANGING (68); SINNER IN PARADISE, A (68); DIARY OF A SHINJUKU BURGLAR (69); BOY (69); HE DIED AFTER THE WAR (70); CEREMONY, THE (71); DEAR SUMMER SISTER (72); •IN THE REALM OF THE SENSES (76); EMPIRE OF PASSION (78); •MERRY CHRISTMAS, MR. LAWRENCE (83); MAX MON AMOUR (86); YUNBOGI NO NIKKI (86); KYOTO, MY MOTHER'S PLACE (91); 100 YEARS OF JAPANESE CINEMA (95)

Ouedraogo, Idrissa

POKO (81); LES ECUELLES (83); LES FUNERAILLES DU LARLE NAABA (84); ISSA LE TISSERAND (85); OUAGADOUGOU, OUAG DEUX ROUES (85); YAM DAABO (87); •YAABA (89); TILAI (90); KARIM NA SALA (91); OBI (91); SAMBA TRAORE (92); HEART'S CITY, THE (94); AFRICA, MY AFRICA (95); KINI & ADAMS (97)

Oz, Frank

•DARK CRYSTAL, THE (82); •MUPPETS TAKE MANHATTAN, THE (84); •LITTLE SHOP OF HORRORS (86); DIRTY ROTTEN SCOUNDRELS (88); WHAT ABOUT BOB? (91); HOUSESITTER (92); •INDIAN IN THE CUP-BOARD, THE (95)

Ozu, Yasujiro

INTRODUCTION TO MARRIAGE (30); WALK CHEERFULLY (30); I FLUNKED BUT. . . (30); THAT NIGHT'S WIFE (30); REVENGEFUL SPIRIT OF EROS, THE (30); LOST LUCK (30); YOUNG MISS (30); LADY AND THE BEARD, THE (31); BEAUTY'S SORROWS (31); TOKYO CHO-RUS (31); SPRING COMES WITH THE LADIES (32); I WAS BORN BUT. . . (32); WHERE ARE THE DREAMS OF YOUTH? (32); UNTIL THE DAY WE MEET AGAIN (32); WOMAN OF TOKYO (33); WOMEN ON THE FIRING LINE (33); PASSING FANCY (33); MOTHER SHOULD BE LOVED, A (34); STORY OF FLOATING WEEDS, A (34); INNOCENT MAID, AN (35); INN IN TOKYO, AN (35); COLLEGE IS A NICE PLACE (36); ONLY SON, THE (36); WHAT DID THE LADY FORGET? (37); TODA BROTHERS AND SISTERS, THE (41); THERE WAS A FATHER (42); RECORD OF A TENE-MENT GENTLEMAN, THE (47); HEN IN THE WIND, A (48); LATE SPRING (49); MUNEKATA SISTERS, THE (50); EARLY SUMMER (51); TEA AND RICE (52); •TOKYO STORY (53); EARLY SPRING (56); TOKYO TWILIGHT (57); EQUINOX FLOWER (58); FLOATING WEEDS (59); OHAYO (59); •LATE AUTUMN (60); EARLY AUTUMN (61); AN AUTUMN AFTERNOON (62)

Pabst, G.W.

•KAMERADSCHAFT (31); •THREEPENNY OPERA, THE (31); MISTRESS OF ATLANTIS, THE (32); •DON QUIXOTE (33); FROM TOP TO BOTTOM (33); MODERN HERO, A (34); STREET OF SHADOWS (37); SHANGHAI DRAMA, THE (38); JEUNES FILLES EN DETRESSE (39); KOMODIAN-TEN (41); PARACELSUS (43); DER FALL MOLANDER (45); TRIAL, THE (48); GEHEIMNISVOLLE TIEFEN (49); VOICE OF SILENCE, THE (52); COSE DA PAZZI (53); CONFESSION OF INA KAHR, THE (54); LAST TEN DAYS, THE (55); JACKBOOT MUTINY, THE (55); BALLERINA (56); DURCH DIE WALDER DURCH DIE AUEN (56)

Pagnol, Marcel

DIRECT AU COEUR (33); LE GENDRE DE MONSIEUR POIRIER (33); LEOPOLD LE BIEN-AIME (33); WAYS OF LOVE (34); LE VOYAGE DE MONSIEUR PERRICHON (34); L'ARTICLE 330 (34); ANGELE (34); MER-LUSSE (35); CIGALON (35); •CESAR (36); TOPAZE (36); HARVEST (37); HEARTBEAT (38); •BAKER'S WIFE, THE (38); WELL-DIGGER'S DAUGHTER, THE (41); LA BELLE MEUNIERE (48); WAYS OF LOVE (50); TOPAZE (51); MANON DES SOURCES (52); LETTERS FROM MY WIND-MILL (54); LE CURE DE CUCUGNAN (67)

Pakula, Alan J.

•STERILE CUCKOO, THE (69); •KLUTE (71); LOVE AND PAIN AND THE WHOLE DAMN THING (73); •PARALLAX VIEW, THE (74); •ALL THE PRESIDENT'S MEN (76); COMES A HORSEMAN (78); •STARTING OVER (79); ROLLOVER (81); •SOPHIE'S CHOICE (82); DREAM LOVER (86); •ORPHANS (87); SEE YOU IN THE MORNING (89); •PRESUMED INNO-CENT (90); CONSENTING ADULTS (92); •PELICAN BRIEF, THE (93); •DEVIL'S OWN, THE (97)

Pal, George

TOM THUMB (58); •TIME MACHINE, THE (60); ATLANTIS, THE LOST CONTINENT (61); WONDERFUL WORLD OF THE BROTHERS GRIMM, THE (62); •7 FACES OF DR. LAO (64)

Palcy, Euzhan

•SUGAR CANE ALLEY (83); •DRY WHITE SEASON, A (89); SIMEON (92)

Palmer, Tony

•TWO HUNDRED MOTELS (71); SPACE MOVIE, THE (79); WAGNER (83); TESTIMONY (87); CHILDREN, THE (90); ENGLAND, MY ENGLAND (95)

Parker, Alan

•BUGSY MALONE (76); •MIDNIGHT EXPRESS (78); •FAME (80); SHOOT THE MOON (82); •PINK FLOYD—THE WALL (82); •BIRDY (84); ANGEL HEART (87); •MISSISSIPPI BURNING (88); COME SEE THE PARADISE (90); •COMMITMENTS, THE (91); ROAD TO WELLVILLE, THE (94); •EVITA (97)

Parks, Sr., Gordon

•LEARNING TREE, THE (69); •SHAFT (71); SHAFT'S BIG SCORE! (72); SUPER COPS, THE (74); •LEADBELLY (76)

Parks, Jr., Gordon

•SUPERFLY (72); THOMASINE AND BUSHROD (74); THREE THE HARD WAY (74); AARON LOVES ANGELA (75)

Pasolini, Pier Paolo

ACCATTONE! (61); •MAMMA ROMA (62); •GOSPEL ACCORDING TO ST. MATTHEW, THE (64); HAWKS AND THE SPARROWS, THE (66); OEDIPUS REX (67); WITCHES, THE (67); •TEOREMA (68); VANGELO '70 (69); PORCILE (69); DECAMERON, THE (70); MEDEA (70); CANTER-BURY TALES, THE (71); ARABIAN NIGHTS (74); •SALO, OR THE 120 DAYS OF SODOM (75)

Pasquin, John

NIGHTMARE (91); •SANTA CLAUSE, THE (94); JUNGLE 2 JUNGLE (97)

Passer, Ivan

INTIMATE LIGHTING (66); BORN TO WIN (71); LAW AND DISORDER (74); CRIME AND PASSION (76); SILVER BEARS (78); •CUTTER'S WAY (81); CREATOR (85); HAUNTED SUMMER (88); COLORS OF LOVE, THE (92)

Pearce, Richard

HEARTLAND (80); THRESHOLD (81); •COUNTRY (84); NO MERCY (86); LONG WALK HOME, THE (91); LEAP OF FAITH (92); FAMILY THING, A (96)

Peckinpah, Sam

DEADLY COMPANIONS, THE (61); •RIDE THE HIGH COUNTRY (62); MAJOR DUNDEE (65); •WILD BUNCH, THE (69); •BALLAD OF CABLE HOGUE, THE (70); •STRAW DOGS (71); •GETAWAY, THE (72); •JUNIOR BONNER (72); •PAT GARRETT AND BILLY THE KID (73); •BRING ME THE HEAD OF ALFREDO GARCIA (74); KILLER ELITE, THE (75); •CROSS OF IRON (77); CONVOY (78); OSTERMAN WEEKEND, THE (83)

Penn, Arthur

•LEFT-HANDED GUN, THE (58); •MIRACLE WORKER, THE (62); MICKEY ONE (65); CHASE, THE (66); •BONNIE AND CLYDE (67); •ALICE'S RESTAURANT (69); •LITTLE BIG MAN (70); NIGHT MOVES (75); •MISSOURI BREAKS, THE (76); •FOUR FRIENDS (81); TARGET (85); DEAD OF WINTER (87); PENN & TELLER GET KILLED (89); INSIDE (96)

Perry, Frank

•DAVID AND LISA (62); LADYBUG, LADYBUG (63); •SWIMMER, THE (68); LAST SUMMER (69); TRUMAN CAPOTE'S TRILOGY (69); •DIARY OF A MAD HOUSEWIFE (70); DOC (71); PLAY IT AS IT LAYS (72); MAN ON A SWING (74); •RANCHO DELUXE (75); •MOMMIE DEAREST (81); MONSIGNOR (82); COMPROMISING POSITIONS (85); HELLO AGAIN (87)

GLASS MENAGERIE, THE (50); ANOTHER MAN'S POISON (51); FOREVER FEMALE (53); BAD FOR EACH OTHER (54); BRAVE ONE, THE (56); STRANGE INTRUDER (56); MARJORIE MORNINGSTAR (58); MIRACLE, THE (59); STORY OF JOSEPH AND HIS BRETHREN, THE (60); PONTIUS PILATE (64); CHRISTINE JORGENSEN STORY, THE (70); BORN AGAIN (78)

Rash, Steve
•BUDDY HOLLY STORY, THE (78); UNDER THE RAINBOW (81); CAN'T BUY ME LOVE (87); QUEENS LOGIC (91); SON-IN-LAW (93); EDDIE (96)

Ray, Nicholas
•THEY LIVE BY NIGHT (49); •KNOCK ON ANY DOOR (49); WOMAN'S SECRET, A (49); BORN TO BE BAD (50); •IN A LONELY PLACE (50); FLYING LEATHERNECKS (51); ON DANGEROUS GROUND (51); •RACKET, THE (51); •LUSTY MEN, THE (52); MACAO (52); •JOHNNY GUITAR (54); •REBEL WITHOUT A CAUSE (55); RUN FOR COVER (55); BIGGER THAN LIFE (56); HOT BLOOD (56); TRUE STORY OF JESSE JAMES, THE (57); BITTER VICTORY (58); PARTY GIRL (58); WIND ACROSS THE EVERGLADES (58); SAVAGE INNOCENTS, THE (59); •KING OF KINGS (61); 55 DAYS AT PEKING (63)

Ray, Satyajit
PATHER PANCHALI (55); •APARAJITO (56); PHILOSOPHER'S STONE, THE (57); •MUSIC ROOM, THE (58); •WORLD OF APU, THE (59); GODDESS, THE (60); TWO DAUGHTERS (61); KANCHENJUNGHA (62); EXPEDITION, THE (62); BIG CITY, THE (63); •CHARULATA (64); COWARD AND THE HOLY MAN, THE (65); NAYAK (66); CHIRIAKHANA (67); ADVENTURES OF GOOPY AND BAGHA, THE (69); DAYS AND NIGHTS IN THE FOREST (70); ADVERSARY, THE (71); SIMBADDHA (72); DISTANT THUNDER (73); GOLDEN FORTRESS, THE (74); MIDDLEMAN, THE (75); CHESS PLAYERS, THE (77); ELEPHANT GOD, THE (78); KINGDOM OF DIAMONDS, THE (80); SADGHATI (81); •HOME AND THE WORLD, THE (84); GANASHATRU (89); BRANCHES OF THE TREE (90); AGANTUK (92)

Redford, Robert
•ORDINARY PEOPLE (80); MILAGRO BEANFIELD WAR, THE (88); •RIVER RUNS THROUGH IT, A (92); •QUIZ SHOW (94)

Reed, Carol
IT HAPPENED IN PARIS (35); MEN OF THE SEA (35); LABURNUM GROVE (36); TALK OF THE DEVIL (37); WHO'S YOUR LADY FRIEND? (37); BANK HOLIDAY (38); CLIMBING HIGH (38); PENNY PARADISE (38); GIRL MUST LIVE, A (39); •STARS LOOK DOWN, THE (39); GIRL IN THE NEWS, THE (40); •NIGHT TRAIN TO MUNICH (40); REMARKABLE MR. KIPPS (41); YOUNG MR. PITT, THE (42); •WAY AHEAD, THE (44); •ODD MAN OUT (47); •FALLEN IDOL, THE (48); •THIRD MAN, THE (49); OUTCAST OF THE ISLANDS (51); MAN BETWEEN, THE (53); •KID FOR TWO FARTHINGS, A (55); •TRAPEZE (56); KEY, THE (58); •OUR MAN IN HAVANA (59); RUNNING MAN, THE (63); AGONY AND THE ECSTASY, THE (65); •OLIVER! (68); FLAP (70); PUBLIC EYE, THE (72)

Reiner, Carl
•ENTER LAUGHING (67); COMIC, THE (69); •WHERE'S POPPA? (70); OH, GOD! (77); ONE AND ONLY, THE (78); JERK, THE (79); •DEAD MEN DON'T WEAR PLAID (82); •MAN WITH TWO BRAINS, THE (83); •ALL OF ME (84); SUMMER RENTAL (85); SUMMER SCHOOL (87); BERT RIGBY, YOU'RE A FOOL (89); SIBLING RIVALRY (90); FATAL INSTINCT (93); THAT OLD FEELING (97)

Reiner, Rob
•THIS IS SPINAL TAP (84); •SURE THING, THE (85); •STAND BY ME (86); •PRINCESS BRIDE, THE (87); •WHEN HARRY MET SALLY. . . (89); •MISERY (90); •FEW GOOD MEN, A (92); NORTH (94); AMERICAN PRESIDENT, THE (95); GHOSTS OF MISSISSIPPI (96)

Reisz, Karel
•SATURDAY NIGHT AND SUNDAY MORNING (60); NIGHT MUST FALL (64); •MORGAN! (66); ISADORA (68); GAMBLER, THE (74); •WHO'LL STOP THE RAIN? (78); •FRENCH LIEUTENANT'S WOMAN, THE (81); SWEET DREAMS (85); EVERYBODY WINS (90)

Reitman, Ivan
FOXY LADY (71); CANNIBAL GIRLS (72); MEATBALLS (79); •STRIPES (81); •GHOSTBUSTERS (84); LEGAL EAGLES (86); TWINS (88); GHOSTBUSTERS II (89); KINDERGARTEN COP (90); •DAVE (93); JUNIOR (94); FATHERS' DAY (97)

Reitz, Edgar
LUST FOR LOVE (67); FUSSNOTEN (67); CADILLAC (69); GESCHICHTEN VOM KUBELKIND (70); KINO II (71); GOLDEN FLEECE, THE (71); DIE REISE NACH WIEN (73); MIDDLE OF THE ROAD IS A VERY DEAD END, THE (74); ZERO HOUR (76); GERMANY IN AUTUMN (78); TAILOR FROM ULM, THE (78); •HEIMAT (84); DAS SCHWEIGEN DES DICHTERS (86); DIE ZWEITE HEIMAT: LEAVING HOME (92); NIGHT OF THE FILM-MAKERS, THE (95)

Renoir, Jean
ON PURGE BEBE (31); LA CHIENNE (31); LA NUIT DE CARREFOUR (32); •BOUDU SAVED FROM DROWNING (32); CHOTARD ET COMPAGNIE (33); MADAME BOVARY (34); •TONI (35); •CRIME OF MONSIEUR LANGE, THE (71); DIE REISE NACH WIEN (73); PEOPLE OF FRANCE, THE (36); DAY IN THE COUNTRY, A (36); LOWER DEPTHS, THE (36); •GRAND ILLUSION (37); •LA BETE HUMAINE (38); LA MARSEILLAISE (38); •RULES OF THE GAME (39); SWAMP WATER (41); •THIS LAND IS MINE (43); •SOUTHERNER, THE (45); DIARY OF A CHAMBERMAID (46); WOMAN ON THE BEACH, THE (47); WAYS OF LOVE (50); •RIVER, THE (51); •GOLDEN COACH, THE (52); •FRENCH CANCAN (55); ELENA AND HER MEN (56); PICNIC ON THE GRASS (59); LE TESTAMENT DU DR. CORDELIER (61); ELUSIVE CORPORAL, THE (62); •LE PETIT THEATRE DE JEAN RENOIR (69)

Resnais, Alain
•HIROSHIMA, MON AMOUR (59); •LAST YEAR AT MARIENBAD (61); •MURIEL (63); •LA GUERRE EST FINIE (66); JE T'AIME, JE T'AIME (68); •STAVISKY (74); •PROVIDENCE (77); •MON ONCLE D'AMERIQUE (80); •LIFE IS A BED OF ROSES (83); L'AMOUR A MORT (84); •MELO (86); I WANT TO GO HOME (89); CONTRE L'OUBLI (92); SMOKING (93); NO SMOKING (93)

Reynolds, Kevin
FANDANGO (85); BEAST, THE (88); •ROBIN HOOD: PRINCE OF THIEVES (91); RAPA NUI (94); •WATERWORLD (95)

Richardson, Tony
•LOOK BACK IN ANGER (59); •ENTERTAINER, THE (60); SANCTUARY (61); •TASTE OF HONEY, A (61); •LONELINESS OF THE LONG DISTANCE RUNNER, THE (62); •TOM JONES (63); •LOVED ONE, THE (65); MADEMOISELLE (66); SAILOR FROM GIBRALTAR, THE (67); •CHARGE OF THE LIGHT BRIGADE, THE (68); LAUGHTER IN THE DARK (69); •HAMLET (69); NED KELLY (70); DELICATE BALANCE, A (73); DEAD CERT (73); JOSEPH ANDREWS (77); BORDER, THE (82); HOTEL NEW HAMPSHIRE, THE (84); •BLUE SKY (94)

Richert, William
•WINTER KILLS (79); AMERICAN SUCCESS COMPANY, THE (80); NIGHT IN THE LIFE OF JIMMY REARDON, A (88)

Richter, W.D.
•ADVENTURES OF BUCKAROO BANZAI: ACROSS THE 8TH DIMENSION, THE (84); LATE FOR DINNER (91)

Ritchie, Michael
•DOWNHILL RACER (69); •CANDIDATE, THE (72); •PRIME CUT (72); •SMILE (75); •BAD NEWS BEARS, THE (76); •SEMI-TOUGH (77); ALMOST PERFECT AFFAIR, AN (79); ISLAND, THE (80); SURVIVORS, THE (83); FLETCH (84); GOLDEN CHILD, THE (86); WILDCATS (86); COUCH TRIP, THE (88); FLETCH LIVES (89); DIGGSTOWN (92); COPS AND ROBBERSONS (94); SCOUT, THE (94)

Ritt, Martin
EDGE OF THE CITY (57); NO DOWN PAYMENT (57); LONG, HOT SUMMER, THE (58); BLACK ORCHID, THE (59); SOUND AND THE FURY, THE (59); FIVE BRANDED WOMEN (60); PARIS BLUES (61); ADVENTURES OF A YOUNG MAN (62); •HUD (63); OUTRAGE, THE (64); •SPY WHO CAME IN FROM THE COLD, THE (65); HOMBRE (67); BROTHERHOOD, THE (68); •GREAT WHITE HOPE, THE (70); MOLLY MAGUIRES, THE (70); PETE 'N' TILLIE (72); •SOUNDER (72); CONRACK (74); FRONT, THE (76); CASEY'S SHADOW (78); •NORMA RAE (79); BACK ROADS (81); •CROSS CREEK (83); MURPHY'S ROMANCE (85); NUTS (87); STANLEY AND IRIS (90)

Rivette, Jacques
•PARIS BELONGS TO US (60); NUN, THE (66); L'AMOUR FOU (68); OUT ONE OUT TWO (74); •CELINE AND JULIE GO BOATING (74); TWILIGHT (76); NORTHWEST (77); MERRY-GO-ROUND (80); PARIS S'EN VA (80); LE PONT DU NORD (82); LOVE ON THE GROUND (84); WUTHERING HEIGHTS (85); GANG OF FOUR, THE (89); LA BELLE NOISEUSE (91); JEANNE LA PUCELLE (94); UP/DOWN/FRAGILE (95)

Robbins, Tim
•BOB ROBERTS (92); •DEAD MAN WALKING (95)

Robert, Yves
WAR OF THE BUTTONS (62); MONKEY MONKEY (65); VERY HAPPY ALEXANDER (68); •TALL BLOND MAN WITH ONE BLACK SHOE, THE (72); SALUT L'ARTISTE (73); RETURN OF THE TALL BLOND MAN WITH ONE BLACK SHOE, THE (74); •PARDON MON AFFAIRE (77); NOUS IRONS TOUS AU PARADIS (78); LE JUMEAU (84); MY FATHER'S GLORY (90); MY MOTHER'S CASTLE (90); LA BAL DES CASSE-PIEDS (92); MONTPARNASSE—PONDICHERY (93)

Robinson, Bruce
•WITHNAIL & I (87); •HOW TO GET AHEAD IN ADVERTISING (89); JENNIFER EIGHT (92)

Robinson, Phil Alden
IN THE MOOD (87); •FIELD OF DREAMS (89); •SNEAKERS (92)

Robson, Mark
GHOST SHIP, THE (43); •SEVENTH VICTIM, THE (43); YOUTH RUNS WILD (44); ISLE OF THE DEAD (45); BEDLAM (46); •CHAMPION (49); •HOME OF THE BRAVE (49); MY FOOLISH HEART (49); ROUGHSHOD (49); EDGE OF DOOM (50); BRIGHT VICTORY (51); I WANT YOU (51); RETURN TO PARADISE (53); •BRIDGES AT TOKO-RI, THE (54); HELL BELOW ZERO (54); PHFFFT! (54); PRIZE OF GOLD, A (55); TRIAL (55); •HARDER THEY FALL, THE (56); LITTLE HUT, THE (57); •PEYTON PLACE (57); INN OF THE SIXTH HAPPINESS, THE (58); FROM THE TERRACE (60); NINE HOURS TO RAMA (63); PRIZE, THE (63); •VON RYAN'S EXPRESS (65); LOST COMMAND (66); •VALLEY OF THE DOLLS (67); DADDY'S GONE A-HUNTING (69); HAPPY BIRTHDAY, WANDA JUNE (71); LIMBO (72); EARTHQUAKE (74); AVALANCHE EXPRESS (79)

Rocha, Glauber
STORM, THE (62); BLACK GOD WHITE DEVIL (64); EARTH ENTRANCED (67); O CANCER (68); •ANTONIO DAS MORTES (69); LION HAS SEVEN HEADS, THE (70); SEVERED HEADS (71); CLARO! (75); AGE OF THE EARTH, THE (80)

Roddam, Franc
•QUADROPHENIA (79); LORDS OF DISCIPLINE, THE (83); BRIDE, THE (85); ARIA (87); WAR PARTY (89); K2 (92)

Rodriguez, Robert
•EL MARIACHI (93); FOUR ROOMS (95); DESPERADO (95); •FROM DUSK TILL DAWN (96)

Roeg, Nicolas
•PERFORMANCE (70); •WALKABOUT (71); •DON'T LOOK NOW (73); •MAN WHO FELL TO EARTH, THE (76); BAD TIMING: A SENSUAL OBSESSION (80); EUREKA (82); INSIGNIFICANCE (85); CASTAWAY (86); ARIA (87); TRACK 29 (88); •WITCHES, THE (90); SWEET BIRD OF YOUTH (90); COLD HEAVEN (92); HOTEL PARADISE (95); FULL BODY MASSAGE (96); TWO DEATHS (95)

Rohmer, Eric
SIGN OF LEO, THE (59); •SIX IN PARIS (65); LA BOULANGERE DE MONCEAUF (62); LA CARRIERE DE SUZANNE (63); •LA COLLECTION-NEUSE (67); •MY NIGHT AT MAUD'S (69); •CLAIRE'S KNEE (70); •CHLOE IN THE AFTERNOON (72); MARQUISE OF O..., THE (76); PERCEVAL (78); AVIATOR'S WIFE, THE (81); •LE BEAU MARIAGE (82); •PAULINE AT THE BEACH (83); •FULL MOON IN PARIS (84); SUMMER (86); FOUR ADVENTURES OF REINETTE AND MIRABELLE (87); BOY-FRIENDS AND GIRLFRIENDS (87); TALE OF SPRINGTIME, A (90); TALE OF WINTER, A (91); L'ARBRE, LE MAIRE ET LA MEDIATHEQUE (92); RENDEZVOUS IN PARIS (96); TALE OF SUMMER, A (96)

Romero, George
•NIGHT OF THE LIVING DEAD (68); THERE'S ALWAYS VANILLA (72); CRAZIES, THE (73); HUNGRY WIVES (73); •MARTIN (78); •DAWN OF THE DEAD (79); KNIGHTRIDERS (81); •CREEPSHOW (82); •DAY OF THE DEAD (85); MONKEY SHINES: AN EXPERIMENT IN FEAR (88); TWO EVIL EYES (90); DARK HALF, THE (93)

Rose, Bernard
PAPERHOUSE (88); CHICAGO JOE AND THE SHOWGIRL (90); •CANDY-MAN (92); IMMORTAL BELOVED (94); ANNA KARENINA (97)

Rosenberg, Stuart
MURDER, INC. (60); QUESTION 7 (61); •COOL HAND LUKE (67); APRIL FOOLS, THE (69); MOVE (70); WUSA (70); POCKET MONEY (72); LAUGHING POLICEMAN, THE (73); DROWNING POOL, THE (75); VOY-

AGE OF THE DAMNED (76); •AMITYVILLE HORROR, THE (79); LOVE AND BULLETS (79); •BRUBAKER (80); POPE OF GREENWICH VILLAGE, THE (84); LET'S GET HARRY (87); MY HEROES HAVE ALWAYS BEEN COWBOYS (91)

Rosi, Francesco
ANITA GARIBALDI (52); CHALLENGE, THE (58); I MAGLIARI (59); •SALVATORE GIULIANO (61); OVER THE CITY (63); MOMENT OF TRUTH, THE (65); MORE THAN A MIRACLE (67); UOMINI CONTRO (70); MATTEI AFFAIR, THE (72); RE: LUCKY LUCIANO (74); IL CONTESTO (75); ILLUSTRIOUS CORPSES (76); CHRIST STOPPED AT EBOLI (79); •THREE BROTHERS (80); •BIZET'S CARMEN (84); •CHRONICLE OF A DEATH FORETOLD (87); PALERMO CONNECTION, THE (90); TRUCE, THE (97)

Ross, Herbert
GOODBYE MR. CHIPS (69); OWL AND THE PUSSYCAT, THE (70); T.R. BASKIN (71); •PLAY IT AGAIN, SAM (72); •LAST OF SHEILA, THE (73); FUNNY LADY (75); •SUNSHINE BOYS, THE (75); •SEVEN-PER-CENT SOLUTION, THE (76); •GOODBYE GIRL, THE (77); •TURNING POINT, THE (77); •CALIFORNIA SUITE (78); NIJINSKY (80); •PENNIES FROM HEAVEN (81); I OUGHT TO BE IN PICTURES (82); MAX DUGAN RETURNS (83); FOOTLOOSE (84); PROTOCOL (84); DANCERS (87); SECRET OF MY SUCCESS, THE (87); •STEEL MAGNOLIAS (89); MY BLUE HEAVEN (90); TRUE COLORS (91); UNDERCOVER BLUES (93); BOYS ON THE SIDE (95)

Rossellini, Roberto
LA NAVA BIANCA (41); UNA PILOTA RITORNA (42); L'UOMO DELLA CROCE (43); DESIDERIO (43); •OPEN CITY (45); •PAISAN (46); GERMANY, YEAR ZERO (47); LA MACCHINA AMMAZZACATTIVI (48); STROMBOLI (49); •FLOWERS OF ST. FRANCIS, THE (50); WAYS OF LOVE (50); GREATEST LOVE, THE (51); SEVEN DEADLY SINS, THE (52); DOV'E LA LIBERTE? (53); STRANGERS, THE (53); FEAR (54); JOAN AT THE STAKE (54); INDIA (58); •GENERAL DELLA ROVERE (59); ERA NOTTE A ROMA (59); VIVA L'ITALIA (60); BETRAYER, THE (61); ANIMA NERA (62); ROGOPAG (62); •RISE OF LOUIS XIV, THE (66); SOCRATES (68); AUGUSTINE OF HIPPO (72); BLAISE PASCAL (75); YEAR ONE (75); MESSIAH, THE (78); AGE OF THE MEDICI, THE (79)

Rossen, Robert
•BODY AND SOUL (47); JOHNNY O'CLOCK (47); •ALL THE KING'S MEN (49); BRAVE BULLS, THE (51); MAMBO (54); ALEXANDER THE GREAT (56); ISLAND IN THE SUN (57); THEY CAME TO CORDURA (59); •HUSTLER, THE (61); LILITH (64)

Ruben, Joseph
SISTER-IN-LAW, THE (75); POM-POM GIRLS, THE (76); JOYRIDE (77); OUR WINNING SEASON (78); GORP (80); DREAMSCAPE (84); •STEPFATHER, THE (87); •TRUE BELIEVER (89); •SLEEPING WITH THE ENEMY (91); GOOD SON, THE (93); MONEY TRAIN (95)

Rudolph, Alan
BARN OF THE NAKED DEAD (76); •WELCOME TO L.A. (76); REMEMBER MY NAME (78); ROADIE (80); ENDANGERED SPECIES (82); •CHOOSE ME (84); SONGWRITER (84); •TROUBLE IN MIND (85); MADE IN HEAVEN (87); MODERNS, THE (88); LOVE AT LARGE (90); MORTAL THOUGHTS (91); EQUINOX (93); MRS. PARKER AND THE VICIOUS CIRCLE (94)

Ruiz, Raul
THREE SAD TIGERS (68); QUE HACER? (70); LA COLONIA PENAL (71); NADJE DIJO NADA (71); LA EXPROPRIOACION (72); EL REALISMO SOCIALISTA (73); PALOMILLA BLANCA (73); PALOMILLA BRAVA (73); DIALOGO DE EXILADOS (74); MENSCH VERSTREUT UND VERKEHRT (75); LA VOCATION SUSPENDUE (76); HYPOTHESIS OF THE STOLEN PAINTING, THE (78); DE GRANDS EVENEMENTS ET DES GENS ORDINAIRES (78); LE JEU DE L'OIE (80); TERRITORY, THE (81); ON TOP OF THE WHALE (82); •THREE CROWNS OF THE SAILOR (83); BERENICE (84); LA VILLE DES PIRATES (84); VOYAGE AUTOUR D'UNE MAIN (84); L'EVEILLE DU PONT DE L'ALMA (85); LES DESTINS DE MANCEL (85); REGIME SANS PAIN (86); MAMAMME (86); TREASURE ISLAND (86); RICHARD III (86); LIFE IS A DREAM (87); LA CHOUETTE AVEUGLE (87); LE PROFESSEUR TARANNE (87); TOUS LES NUAGES SONT DES HORLOGES (88); DERRIERE LE MUR (88); PALLA Y TALLA (89); GOLDEN BOAT, THE (90); LA TELENOVELLA ERRANTE (90); L'EXODE (90); DARK AT NOON (92); FADO MAJEUR ET MINEUR (94); THREE LIVES AND ONLY ONE DEATH (96)

Rush, Richard

TOO SOON TO LOVE (60); OF LOVE AND DESIRE (63); FICKLE FINGER OF FATE, THE (67); HELL'S ANGELS ON WHEELS (67); MAN CALLED DAGGER, A (67); THUNDER ALLEY (67); PSYCH-OUT (68); SAVAGE SEVEN, THE (68); •GETTING STRAIGHT (70); FREEBIE AND THE BEAN (74); •STUNT MAN, THE (80); COLOR OF NIGHT (94)

Russell, Charles

NIGHTMARE ON ELM STREET 3: DREAM WARRIORS, A (87); BLOB, THE (88); •MASK, THE (94); ERASER (96)

Russell, Ken

AMELIA AND THE ANGEL (58); FRENCH DRESSING (63); BILLION DOLLAR BRAIN (67); •WOMEN IN LOVE (69); DEVILS, THE (70); MUSIC LOVERS, THE (70); •BOY FRIEND, THE (71); SAVAGE MESSIAH (72); MAHLER (74); LISZTOMANIA (75); •TOMMY (75); VALENTINO (77); ALTERED STATES (80); CRIMES OF PASSION (84); ARIA (87); GOTHIC (87); LAIR OF THE WHITE WORM, THE (88); SALOME'S LAST DANCE (88); RAINBOW, THE (89); WHORE (91); LADY CHATTERLEY (93); INSATIABLE MRS. KIRSCH, THE (94)

Rydell, Mark

FOX, THE (67); REIVERS, THE (69); COWBOYS, THE (72); CINDERELLA LIBERTY (73); HARRY AND WALTER GO TO NEW YORK (76); •ROSE, THE (79); •ON GOLDEN POND (81); RIVER, THE (84); FOR THE BOYS (91); INTERSECTION (94)

Saks, Gene

•BAREFOOT IN THE PARK (67); •ODD COUPLE, THE (68); CACTUS FLOWER (69); LAST OF THE RED HOT LOVERS (72); MAME (74); BRIGHTON BEACH MEMOIRS (86); FINE ROMANCE, A (92)

Sandrich, Mark

TALK OF HOLLYWOOD, THE (29); AGGIE APPLEBY, MAKER OF MEN (33); MELODY CRUISE (33); COCKEYED CAVALIERS (34); •GAY DIVORCEE, THE (34); HIPS, HIPS, HOORAY (34); •TOP HAT (35); •FOLLOW THE FLEET (36); WOMAN REBELS, A (36); •SHALL WE DANCE (37); CAREFREE (38); MAN ABOUT TOWN (39); BUCK BENNY RIDES AGAIN (40); LOVE THY NEIGHBOR (40); SKYLARK (41); •HOLIDAY INN (42); •SO PROUDLY WE HAIL (43); HERE COME THE WAVES (44); I LOVE A SOLDIER (44)

Saura, Carlos

LA CUENCA (58); URCHINS, THE (60); LAMENT FOR A BANDIT (64); •HUNT, THE (66); PEPPERMINT FRAPPE (67); STRESS ES TRES TRES (68); HONEYCOMB, THE (69); GARDEN OF DELIGHTS, THE (70); ANNA AND THE WOLVES (73); COUSIN ANGELICA (74); •CRIA! (76); ELISA MY LIFE (77); BLINDFOLD (78); MAMA TURNS 100 (79); HURRY HURRY (81); SWEET HOURS (81); •BLOOD WEDDING (81); ANTONIETA (82); •CARMEN (83); STILTS, THE (84); •EL AMOR BRUJO (86); EL DORADO (88); DARK NIGHT, THE (89); AY, CARMELA! (90); SEVILLANAS (92); BARCELONA (92); DISPARA! (93); MARATHON (93); FLAMENCO (94); TAXI (96)

Sautet, Claude

BONJOUR SOURIRE (55); BIG RISK, THE (60); BACKFIRE (64); GUNS FOR THE DICTATOR (65); L'AMANTE (70); THINGS OF LIFE, THE (70); MAX ET LES FERRAILLEURS (70); •CESAR AND ROSALIE (72); VINCENT, FRANCOIS, PAUL... ET LES AUTRES (74); MADO (76); UN HISTOIRE SIMPLE (78); UN MAUVAIS FILS (80); GARCON! (83); FEW DAYS WITH ME, A (88); •UN COEUR EN HIVER (92); LES ENFANTS DE LUMIERE (95); NELLY AND M. ARNAUD (95)

Savoca, Nancy

•TRUE LOVE (89); DOGFIGHT (91); HOUSEHOLD SAINTS (93)

Sayles, John

•RETURN OF THE SECAUCUS SEVEN (80); BABY, IT'S YOU (83); •LIANNA (83); •BROTHER FROM ANOTHER PLANET, THE (84); •MATEWAN (87); •EIGHT MEN OUT (88); •CITY OF HOPE (91); •PASSION FISH (92); •SECRET OF ROAN INISH, THE (95); •LONE STAR (96)

Schaffner, Franklin J.

STRIPPER, THE (63); •BEST MAN, THE (64); WAR LORD, THE (65); DOUBLE MAN, THE (67); •PLANET OF THE APES (68); •PATTON (70); •NICHOLAS AND ALEXANDRA (71); PAPILLON (73); ISLANDS IN THE STREAM (77); •BOYS FROM BRAZIL, THE (78); SPHINX (81); YES, GIORGIO (82); WELCOME HOME (89); LIONHEART (90)

Schatzberg, Jerry

PUZZLE OF A DOWNFALL CHILD (70); PANIC IN NEEDLE PARK, THE (71); •SCARECROW (73); DANDY, THE ALL AMERICAN GIRL (76); SEDUCTION OF JOE TYNAN, THE (79); HONEYSUCKLE ROSE (80); MISUNDERSTOOD (84); NO SMALL AFFAIR (84); •STREET SMART (87); REUNION (89)

Schell, Maximilian

FIRST LOVE (70); •PEDESTRIAN, THE (74); END OF THE GAME (75); GESCHICHTEN AUS DEM WIENERWALD (78); MARLENE (86)

Schepisi, Fred

LIBIDO (73); DEVIL'S PLAYGROUND, THE (76); CHANT OF JIMMIE BLACKSMITH, THE (78); •BARBAROSA (82); ICEMAN (84); •PLENTY (85); •ROXANNE (87); •CRY IN THE DARK, A (88); RUSSIA HOUSE, THE (90); MR. BASEBALL (92); •SIX DEGREES OF SEPARATION (93); I.Q. (94); •FIERCE CREATURES (97)

Schlesinger, John

•KIND OF LOVING, A (62); •BILLY LIAR (63); •DARLING (65); •FAR FROM THE MADDING CROWD (67); •MIDNIGHT COWBOY (69); •SUNDAY, BLOODY SUNDAY (71); VISIONS OF EIGHT (73); •DAY OF THE LOCUST, THE (75); •MARATHON MAN (76); YANKS (79); HONKY TONK FREEWAY (81); ENGLISHMAN ABROAD, AN (83); •FALCON AND THE SNOWMAN, THE (85); BELIEVERS, THE (87); •MADAME SOUSATZKA (88); PACIFIC HEIGHTS (90); INNOCENT, THE (93); •COLD COMFORT FARM (95); EYE FOR AN EYE (96)

Schlondorff, Volker

YOUNG TORLESS (66); DEGREE OF MURDER, A (67); MICHAEL KOLHASS—DER REBELL (69); SUDDEN WEALTH OF THE POOR PEOPLE OF HALBFASS, THE (71); DIE MORAL DER RUTH HALBFASS (71); SUMMER LIGHTNING (72); UBERACHTUNG IN TIROL (72); GEORGINAS GRUNDE (74); •LOST HONOR OF KATHARINA BLUM, THE (75); COUP DE GRACE (76); NUR RUM SPASS NUR UM SPIEL: KALEIDOSKOP VALESKA GERT (77); GERMANY IN AUTUMN (78); •TIN DRUM, THE (79); DER KANDIDAT (80); •CIRCLE OF DECEIT (81); WAR AND PEACE (83); •SWANN IN LOVE (84); DEATH OF A SALESMAN (85); ODDS AND ENDS (87); HANDMAID'S TALE, THE (90); VOYAGER (91); OGRE, THE (96)

Schoedsack, Ernest B.

RANGO (31); •MOST DANGEROUS GAME, THE (32); BLIND ADVENTURE (33); •KING KONG (33); MONKEY'S PAW, THE (33); SON OF KONG (33); LONG LOST FATHER (34); LAST DAYS OF POMPEII, THE (35); OUTLAWS OF THE ORIENT (37); TROUBLE IN MOROCCO (37); DR. CYCLOPS (40); MIGHTY JOE YOUNG (49)

Schrader, Paul

•BLUE COLLAR (78); •HARDCORE (79); AMERICAN GIGOLO (80); CAT PEOPLE (82); •MISHIMA (85); LIGHT OF DAY (87); PATTY HEARST (88); •COMFORT OF STRANGERS, THE (91); LIGHT SLEEPER (92); WITCH HUNT (94); TOUCH (97)

Schroeder, Barbet

MORE (69); VALLEY, THE (72); IDI AMIN DADA (74); MAITRESSE (76); KOKO LE GORILLE QUI PARLE (78); LES TRICHEURS (84); CHARLES BUKOWSKI TAPES, THE (85); •BARFLY (87); •REVERSAL OF FORTUNE (90); •SINGLE WHITE FEMALE (92); •KISS OF DEATH (95); BEFORE AND AFTER (96)

Schumacher, Joel

INCREDIBLE SHRINKING WOMAN, THE (81); D.C. CAB (83); ST. ELMO'S FIRE (85); LOST BOYS, THE (87); COUSINS (89); FLATLINERS (90); DYING YOUNG (91); •FALLING DOWN (93); •CLIENT, THE (94); •BATMAN FOREVER (95); TIME TO KILL, A (96); •BATMAN & ROBIN (97)

Scola, Ettore

•LET'S TALK ABOUT WOMEN (64); ONE MILLION DOLLARS (65); THRILLING (66); DEVIL IN LOVE, THE (68); RIUSCIRANNO I NOSTRI EROI A TROVARE L'AMICO MISTERIOSAMENTE SCOMPARSO IN AFRICA? (68); IL COMMISSARIO PEPE (69); MOTIVE WAS JEALOUSY, THE (70); PIZZA TRIANGLE, THE (70); ROCCO PAPALEO (71); MOST WONDERFUL EVENING OF MY LIFE, THE (72); TREVICO-TORINO: VIAQQIO NEL FIAT-NAM (73); FESTIVAL DELL'UNITA (73); WE ALL LOVED EACH OTHER SO MUCH (75); CONFRONTO PARTECIPAZIONE UNITA (75); •DOWN AND DIRTY (76); SILENZIO E COMPLICITA (76); GOODNIGHT, LADIES AND GENTLEMEN (76); SPECIAL DAY, A (77); VIVA ITALIA! (77); PASSIONE D'AMORE (81); •LA NUIT DE VARENNES

Spheeris, Penelope

DECLINE OF WESTERN CIVILIZATION, THE (81); SUBURBIA (84); BOYS NEXT DOOR, THE (85); HOLLYWOOD VICE SQUAD (86); DUDES (88); DECLINE OF WESTERN CIVILIZATION II: THE METAL YEARS, THE (88); •WAYNE'S WORLD (92); BEVERLY HILLBILLIES, THE (93); LITTLE RASCALS, THE (94); BLACK SHEEP (96)

Spielberg, Steven

DUEL (73); •SUGARLAND EXPRESS, THE (74); •JAWS (75); •CLOSE ENCOUNTERS OF THE THIRD KIND (77); 1941 (79); •RAIDERS OF THE LOST ARK (81); •E.T. THE EXTRA-TERRESTRIAL (82); TWILIGHT ZONE—THE MOVIE (83); •INDIANA JONES AND THE TEMPLE OF DOOM (84); •COLOR PURPLE, THE (85); •EMPIRE OF THE SUN (87); ALWAYS (89); •INDIANA JONES AND THE LAST CRUSADE (89); •HOOK (91); •JURASSIC PARK (93); •SCHINDLER'S LIST (93); •LOST WORLD: JURASSIC PARK, THE (97)

Spottiswoode, Roger

TERROR TRAIN (80); PURSUIT OF D.B. COOPER, THE (81); •UNDER FIRE (83); BEST OF TIMES, THE (86); SHOOT TO KILL (88); TURNER & HOOCH (89); AIR AMERICA (90); STOP! OR MY MOM WILL SHOOT (92); HIROSHIMA (95)

Stahl, John M.

LADY SURRENDERS, A (30); SEED (31); •STRICTLY DISHONORABLE (31); BACK STREET (32); ONLY YESTERDAY (33); •IMITATION OF LIFE (34); MAGNIFICENT OBSESSION (35); PARNELL (37); LETTER OF INTRODUCTION (38); WHEN TOMORROW COMES (39); OUR WIFE (41); HOLY MATRIMONY (43); IMMORTAL SERGEANT, THE (43); EVE OF ST. MARK, THE (44); KEYS OF THE KINGDOM, THE (44); LEAVE HER TO HEAVEN (46); FOXES OF HARROW, THE (47); WALLS OF JERICHO, THE (48); FATHER WAS A FULLBACK (49); OH, YOU BEAUTIFUL DOLL (49)

Stevens, George

COHENS AND KELLYS IN TROUBLE, THE (33); BACHELOR BAIT (34); •ALICE ADAMS (35); ANNIE OAKLEY (35); KENTUCKY KERNELS (35); LADDIE (35); NITWITS, THE (35); •SWING TIME (36); DAMSEL IN DISTRESS, A (37); QUALITY STREET (37); VIVACIOUS LADY (38); •GUNGA DIN (39); VIGIL IN THE NIGHT (40); PENNY SERENADE (41); •TALK OF THE TOWN, THE (42); •WOMAN OF THE YEAR (42); MORE THE MERRIER, THE (43); •I REMEMBER MAMA (48); •PLACE IN THE SUN, A (51); SOMETHING TO LIVE FOR (52); •SHANE (53); •GIANT (56); •DIARY OF ANNE FRANK, THE (59); GREATEST STORY EVER TOLD, THE (65); ONLY GAME IN TOWN, THE (70)

Stevenson, Robert

HAPPY EVER AFTER (32); FALLING FOR YOU (33); LADY JANE GREY (36); MAN WHO LIVED AGAIN, THE (36); TWO OF US, THE (36); •KING SOLOMON'S MINES (37); NON-STOP NEW YORK (37); TO THE VICTOR (38); WARE CASE, THE (38); YOUNG MAN'S FANCY (39); RETURN TO YESTERDAY (40); TOM BROWN'S SCHOOL DAYS (40); •BACK STREET (41); JOAN OF PARIS (42); FOREVER AND A DAY (43); •JANE EYRE (44); DISHONORED LADY (47); TO THE ENDS OF THE EARTH (48); WALK SOFTLY, STRANGER (50); WOMAN ON PIER 13, THE (50); MY FORBIDDEN PAST (51); LAS VEGAS STORY, THE (52); JOHNNY TREMAIN (57); •OLD YELLER (57); •DARBY O'GILL AND THE LITTLE PEOPLE (59); KIDNAPPED (60); •ABSENT-MINDED PROFESSOR, THE (61); IN SEARCH OF THE CASTAWAYS (62); SON OF FLUBBER (63); •MARY POPPINS (64); MISADVENTURES OF MERLIN JONES, THE (64); MONKEY'S UNCLE, THE (65); THAT DARN CAT (65); GNOME-MOBILE, THE (67); BLACKBEARD'S GHOST (68); LOVE BUG, THE (68); •BEDKNOBS AND BROOMSTICKS (71); HERBIE RIDES AGAIN (74); ISLAND AT THE TOP OF THE WORLD, THE (74); ONE OF OUR DINOSAURS IS MISSING (75); SHAGGY D.A., THE (76)

Stiller, Ben

REALITY BITES (94); •CABLE GUY, THE (96)

Stillman, Whit

•METROPOLITAN (90); •BARCELONA (94)

Stone, Oliver

SEIZURE (74); HAND, THE (81); •PLATOON (86); •SALVADOR (86); •WALL STREET (87); TALK RADIO (88); •BORN ON THE FOURTH OF JULY (89); DOORS, THE (91); •JFK (91); HEAVEN AND EARTH (93); •NATURAL BORN KILLERS (94); •NIXON (95)

Streisand, Barbra

•YENTL (83); •PRINCE OF TIDES, THE (91); MIRROR HAS TWO FACES, THE (96)

Sturges, John

MAN WHO DARED, THE (46); SHADOWED (46); FOR THE LOVE OF RUSTY (47); KEEPER OF THE BEES (47); BEST MAN WINS, THE (48); SIGN OF THE RAM, THE (48); WALKING HILLS, THE (49); CAPTURE, THE (50); MAGNIFICENT YANKEE, THE (50); MYSTERY STREET (50); RIGHT CROSS (50); IT'S A BIG COUNTRY (51); KIND LADY (51); PEOPLE AGAINST O'HARA, THE (51); GIRL IN WHITE, THE (52); ESCAPE FROM FORT BRAVO (53); FAST COMPANY (53); JEOPARDY (53); •BAD DAY AT BLACK ROCK (55); SCARLET COAT, THE (55); UNDERWATER! (55); BACKLASH (56); •GUNFIGHT AT THE O.K. CORRAL (57); LAW AND JAKE WADE, THE (58); •OLD MAN AND THE SEA, THE (58); LAST TRAIN FROM GUN HILL (59); NEVER SO FEW (59); •MAGNIFICENT SEVEN, THE (60); BY LOVE POSSESSED (61); GIRL NAMED TAMIKO, A (62); SERGEANTS 3 (62); •GREAT ESCAPE, THE (63); HALLELUJAH TRAIL, THE (65); SATAN BUG, THE (65); HOUR OF THE GUN (67); ICE STATION ZEBRA (68); MAROONED (69); JOE KIDD (72); CHINO (73); MC Q (74); EAGLE HAS LANDED, THE (76)

Sturges, Preston

•CHRISTMAS IN JULY (40); •GREAT MCGINTY, THE (40); •LADY EVE, THE (41); •SULLIVAN'S TRAVELS (41); •PALM BEACH STORY, THE (42); GREAT MOMENT, THE (44); •HAIL THE CONQUERING HERO (44); •MIRACLE OF MORGAN'S CREEK, THE (44); •UNFAITHFULLY YOURS (48); BEAUTIFUL BLONDE FROM BASHFUL BEND, THE (49); •MAD WEDNESDAY (50); VENDETTA (50); •FRENCH, THEY ARE A FUNNY RACE, THE (55)

Svankmajer, Jan

KOSTNICE (70); JABBERWOCKY (71); MOZNOSTI DIALOGU (82); DO PIVNICE (83); KYVALDO, JAMA A NADEJE (83); •ALICE (88); LEONARDUV DENIK (880; ANIMATED SELF-PORTRAITS (89); MUZNE HRY (89); DARKNESS, LIGHT, DARKNESS (90); DEATH OF STALINISM IN BOHEMIA, THE (90); FOOD (93); FAUST (94); CONSPIRATORS OF PLEASURE (96)

Swaim, Bob

LA NUIT DE SAINT-GERMAIN DES PRES (77); •LA BALANCE (82); HALF MOON STREET (86); MASQUERADE (88); ATLANTIDE (92)

Swift, David

POLLYANNA (60); PARENT TRAP, THE (61); INTERNS, THE (62); LOVE IS A BALL (63); UNDER THE YUM YUM TREE (63); •GOOD NEIGHBOR SAM (64); •HOW TO SUCCEED IN BUSINESS WITHOUT REALLY TRYING (67)

Syberberg, Hans-Jurgen

LUDWIG—REQUIEM FUR EINEN JUNGFRAULICHEN KONIG (72); NACH MEINEM LETZTEN UMZUG (72); KARL MAY (74); WINIFRED WAGNER UND DIE GESCHICHTE DES HAUSES WAHNFRIED 1914-1975 (75); •OUR HITLER, A FILM FROM GERMANY (77); PARSIFAL (83); DIE NACHT (85)

Szabo, Istvan

AGE OF ILLUSIONS (64); FATHER (66); FILM ABOUT LOVE, A (70); 25 FIREMEN'S STREET (74); PREMIERE (76); TALES OF BUDAPEST (77); HUNGARIANS, THE (78); •CONFIDENCE (79); •MEPHISTO (81); •COLONEL REDL (84); HANUSSEN (88); OPERA EUROPA (90); MEETING VENUS (91); SWEET EMMA, DEAR BOBE (92)

Tamahori, Lee

•ONCE WERE WARRIORS (94); MULHOLLAND FALLS

Tanner, Alain

CHARLES, DEAD OR ALIVE (69); SALAMANDER, THE (71); RETURN FROM AFRICA (72); MIDDLE OF THE WORLD (74); •JONAH WHO WILL BE 25 IN THE YEAR 2000 (76); MESSIDOR (79); LIGHT YEARS AWAY (81); IN THE WHITE CITY (83); NO MAN'S LAND (85); FLAME IN MY HEART, A (87); LA VALLEE FANTOME (89); LA FEMME DE ROSE HILL (89); L'HOMME QUI A PERDU SOM OMBRE (92); DIARY OF LADY M (93); FOURBI (96); LES HOMMES DU PORT (96)

Tarantino, Quentin

•RESERVOIR DOGS (92); •PULP FICTION (94)

Tarkovsky, Andrei

VIOLIN AND ROLLER (60); •MY NAME IS IVAN (62); ANDREI ROUBLEV (66); •SOLARIS (72); MIRROR, THE (75); •STALKER (79); •NOSTALGHIA (83); •SACRIFICE, THE (86)

Tashlin, Frank
FIRST TIME, THE (52); •SON OF PALEFACE (52); MARRY ME AGAIN (53); SUSAN SLEPT HERE (54); ARTISTS AND MODELS (55); GIRL CAN'T HELP IT, THE (56); HOLLYWOOD OR BUST (56); LIEUTENANT WORE SKIRTS, THE (56); •WILL SUCCESS SPOIL ROCK HUNTER? (57); GEISHA BOY, THE (58); ROCK-A-BYE BABY (58); SAY ONE FOR ME (59); CINDERFELLA (60); BACHELOR FLAT (62); IT'S ONLY MONEY (62); MAN FROM THE DINERS' CLUB, THE (63); WHO'S MINDING THE STORE? (63); DISORDERLY ORDERLY, THE (64); ALPHABET MURDERS, THE (65); GLASS BOTTOM BOAT, THE (66); CAPRICE (67); PRIVATE NAVY OF SGT. O'FARRELL, THE (68)

Tati, Jacques
•JOUR DE FETE (49); •MR. HULOT'S HOLIDAY (53); •MY UNCLE (58); •PLAYTIME (67); •TRAFFIC (72); PARADE (74)

Tavernier, Bertrand
LA CHANCE ET L'AMOUR (64); LES BAISERS (65); •CLOCKMAKER, THE (73); LET JOY REIGN SUPREME (75); JUDGE AND THE ASSASSIN, THE (76); SPOILED CHILDREN (77); •DEATH WATCH (80); WEEK'S VACATION, A (80); •COUP DE TORCHON (81); PHILIPPE SOUPAULT (82); MISSISSIPPI BLUES (83); •SUNDAY IN THE COUNTRY, A (84); •ROUND MIDNIGHT (86); BEATRICE (88); DADDY NOSTALGIA (90); •LIFE AND NOTHING BUT (90); 50 ANS DE CINEMA AMERICAINE (91); UNDECLARED WAR, THE (91); L.627 (92); CONTRE L'OUBLI (92); D'ARTAGNAN'S DAUGHTER (94); LIVE BAIT (95); CAPTAIN CONAN (96)

Taviani, Paolo and Vittorio
SUBVERSIVES, THE (68); UNDER THE SIGN OF SCORPIO (69); SAN MICHELE AVEVA UN GALLO (72); ALLONSANFAN (74); •PADRE PADRONE (77); MEADOW, THE (79); •NIGHT OF THE SHOOTING STARS, THE (81); KAOS (84); GOOD MORNING, BABYLON (87); SUN ALSO SHINES AT NIGHT, THE (90); FIORILE (93); ELECTIVE AFFINITIES 96)

Techine, Andre
PAULINA S'EN VA (69); FRENCH PROVINCIAL (75); BAROCCO (77); BRONTE SISTERS, THE (79); HOTEL DES AMERIQUES (81); LA MATIOUETTE OU L'ARRIERE-PAYS (83); RENDEZ-VOUS (85); SCENE OF THE CRIME (86); LES INNOCENTS (87); J'EMBRASSE PAS (91); MA SAISON PREFEREE (93); •WILD REEDS (94); LES VOLEURS (96)

Temple, Julien
GREAT ROCK 'N' ROLL SWINDLE, THE (79); SECRET POLICEMAN'S OTHER BALL, THE (81); MANTRAP (84); •ABSOLUTE BEGINNERS (86); RUNNING OUT OF LUCK (86); ARIA (87); EARTH GIRLS ARE EASY (89); ROLLING STONES "AT THE MAX" (91); BULLET (95)

Teshigahara, Hiroshi
PITFALL, THE (61); •WOMAN IN THE DUNES (64); THAT TENDER AGE (64); FACE OF ANOTHER, THE (66); MAN WITHOUT A MAP, THE (68); SUMMER SOLDIERS (72); ANTONIO GAUDI (85); RIKYU (89); BASARA: PRINCESS GOS (92)

Tolkin, Michael
RAPTURE, THE (91); •NEW AGE, THE (94)

Tornatore, Giuseppe
PROFESSOR, THE (86); •CINEMA PARADISO (88); EVERYBODY'S FINE (90); ESPECIALLY ON SUNDAY (91); PURE FORMALITY, A (94); LO SCHERMO A TRE PUNTE (95); STAR MAKER, THE (95)

Tourneur, Jacques
NICK CARTER, MASTER DETECTIVE (39); THEY ALL COME OUT (39); PHANTOM RAIDERS (40); DOCTORS DON'T TELL (41); •CAT PEOPLE (42); •I WALKED WITH A ZOMBIE (43); LEOPARD MAN, THE (43); DAYS OF GLORY (44); EXPERIMENT PERILOUS (44); CANYON PASSAGE (46); •OUT OF THE PAST (47); BERLIN EXPRESS (48); EASY LIVING (49); FLAME AND THE ARROW, THE (50); STARS IN MY CROWN (50); ANNE OF THE INDIES (51); CIRCLE OF DANGER (51); WAY OF A GAUCHO (52); APPOINTMENT IN HONDURAS (53); STRANGER ON HORSEBACK (55); WICHITA (55); GREAT DAY IN THE MORNING (56); NIGHTFALL (56); CURSE OF THE DEMON (58); FEARMAKERS, THE (58); GIANT OF MARATHON, THE (59); TIMBUKTU (59); COMEDY OF HORRORS, THE (64); CITY UNDER THE SEA (65)

Towne, Robert
•PERSONAL BEST (82); TEQUILA SUNRISE (88)

Tran Anh Hung
SCENT OF GREEN PAPAYA, THE (93); •CYCLO (95)

Troell, Jan
HERE'S YOUR LIFE (66); WHO SAW HIM DIE? (68); •EMIGRANTS, THE (71); •NEW LAND, THE (72); •ZANDY'S BRIDE (74); BANG! (77); FLIGHT OF THE EAGLE, THE (78); HURRICANE (79); INGENJOR ANDREES LUFTFARD (82); SAGOLANDET (86); SWEDISH REQUIEM, A (91); HAMSUM (96)

Trueba, Fernando
OSCAR Y CARLOS (74); URCULO (77); EN LEGITIMA DEFENSA (78); EL LEON ENAMORADO (79); HOMENAGE A TROIS (79); OPERA PRIMA (80); MIENTRAS EL CUERPO AGUANTE (82); SAL GORDA (83); SE INFIEL Y NO MIRES CON QUIEN (85); YEAR OF AWAKENING, THE (86); TWISTED OBSESSION (90); •BELLE EPOQUE (92); TWO MUCH (95)

Truffaut, Francois
•FOUR HUNDRED BLOWS, THE (59); •SHOOT THE PIANO PLAYER (60); •JULES AND JIM (62); •LOVE AT TWENTY (62); •SOFT SKIN, THE (64); •FAHRENHEIT 451 (66); BRIDE WORE BLACK, THE (67); •STOLEN KISSES (68); •MISSISSIPPI MERMAID (69); •WILD CHILD, THE (69); •BED AND BOARD (70); •TWO ENGLISH GIRLS (71); •DAY FOR NIGHT (73); •SUCH A GORGEOUS KID LIKE ME (73); •STORY OF ADELE H., THE (75); •SMALL CHANGE (76); •MAN WHO LOVED WOMEN, THE (77); •GREEN ROOM, THE (78); •LOVE ON THE RUN (79); •LAST METRO, THE (80); •WOMAN NEXT DOOR, THE (81); •CONFIDENTIALLY YOURS (83)

Tsui Hark
BUTTERFLY MURDERS (79); DANGEROUS ENCOUNTERS OF THE THIRD KIND ; ALL THE WRONG CLUES. . . FOR THE RIGHT SOLUCTION (81); ACES GO PLACES III (84); •PEKING OPERA BLUES (86); CHINESE GHOST STORY (87); BETTER TOMORROW III, A (89); SWORDSMAN (90); CHINESE GHOST STORY II, A (90); •ONCE UPON A TIME IN CHINA (91); SWORDSMAN II (92); ONCE UPON A TIME IN CHINA II (92); DRAGON INN (92); KING OF CHESS (92); SWORDSMAN III (93); WICKED CITY, THE (93); GREEN SNAKE (94); LOVERS, THE (94); ONCE UPON A TIME IN CHINA III (94); ONCE UPON A TIME IN CHINA IV (94); LOVE IN THE TIME OF TWILIGHT (94); ONCE UPON A TIME IN CHINA V (94); CHINESE FEAST, THE (95); •DOUBLE TEAM (97)

Turteltaub, Jon
DRIVING ME CRAZY (91); 3 NINJAS (92); COOL RUNNINGS (93); •WHILE YOU WERE SLEEPING (95); PHENOMENON (96)

Ulmer, Edgar G.
DAMAGED LIVES (33); MR. BROADWAY (33); •BLACK CAT, THE (34); THUNDER OVER TEXAS (34); DAMAGED LIVES (37); GIRL FROM POLTAVA (37); GREEN FIELDS (37); SINGING BLACKSMITH (38); COSSACKS IN EXILE (39); TOMORROW WE LIVE (42); GIRLS IN CHAINS (43); ISLE OF FORGOTTEN SINS (43); MY SON, THE HERO (43); BLUEBEARD (44); JIVE JUNCTION (44); DETOUR (45); STRANGE ILLUSION (45); CLUB HAVANA (46); HER SISTER'S SECRET (46); STRANGE WOMAN, THE (46); CARNEGIE HALL (47); RUTHLESS (48); PIRATES OF CAPRI, THE (49); MAN FROM PLANET X, THE (51); ST. BENNY THE DIP (51); BABES IN BAGDAD (52); LOVES OF THREE QUEENS, THE (54); MURDER IS MY BEAT (55); NAKED DAWN, THE (55); DAUGHTER OF DR. JEKYLL (57); AMAZING TRANSPARENT MAN, THE (60); BEYOND THE TIME BARRIER (60); HANNIBAL (60); JOURNEY BENEATH THE DESERT (61); CAVERN, THE (66)

Underwood, Ron
•TREMORS (90); •CITY SLICKERS (91); HEART AND SOULS (93); SPEECHLESS (94)

Vadim, Roger
•AND GOD CREATED WOMAN (56); NO SUN IN VENICE (57); NIGHT HEAVEN FELL, THE (58); •LES LIAISONS DANGEREUSES (59); BLOOD AND ROSES (60); PLEASE, NOT NOW! (61); SEVEN CAPITAL SINS (61); LOVE ON A PILLOW (62); NUTTY, NAUGHTY CHATEAU (63); VICE AND VIRTUE (63); CIRCLE OF LOVE (64); GAME IS OVER, THE (66); BARBARELLA (68); SPIRITS OF THE DEAD (68); PRETTY MAIDS ALL IN A ROW (71); HELLE (72); MS. DON JUAN (73); CHARLOTTE (74); UN FEMME FIDELE (76); NIGHT GAMES (80); SURPRISE PARTY (83); COME BACK (83); AND GOD CREATED WOMAN (88); MAD LOVER, THE (91)

Van Dormael, Jaco
MAEDLI-LA-BRECHE (80); LES VOISINS (81); STADE (81); L'IMITATEUR (82); SORTIE DE SECOURS (83); E PERICOLOSO SPORGERSI (84); DE BOOT (85); •TOTO LE HEROS (91); EIGHTH DAY, THE (96)

Van Dyke, II, W.S.
WHITE SHADOWS IN THE SOUTH SEAS (28); PAGAN, THE (29); CUBAN LOVE SONG, THE (31); GUILTY HANDS (31); NEVER THE TWAIN SHALL MEET (31); TRADER HORN (31); NIGHT COURT (32); •TARZAN, THE APE MAN (32); PENTHOUSE (33); PRIZEFIGHTER AND THE LADY, THE (33); HIDE-OUT (34); LAUGHING BOY (34); •MANHATTAN MELODRAMA (34); •THIN MAN, THE (34); FORSAKING ALL OTHERS (35); I LIVE MY LIFE (35); •NAUGHTY MARIETTA (35); AFTER THE THIN MAN (36); DEVIL IS A SISSY, THE (36); HIS BROTHER'S WIFE (36); LOVE ON THE RUN (36); •ROSE MARIE (36); •SAN FRANCISCO (36); PERSONAL PROPERTY (37); •PRISONER OF ZENDA, THE (37); ROSALIE (37); THEY GAVE HIM A GUN (37); •MARIE ANTOINETTE (38); SWEETHEARTS (38); ANDY HARDY GETS SPRING FEVER (39); ANOTHER THIN MAN (39); IT'S A WONDERFUL WORLD (39); STAND UP AND FIGHT (39); BITTER SWEET (40); I LOVE YOU AGAIN (40); I TAKE THIS WOMAN (40); DR. KILDARE'S VICTORY (41); FEMININE TOUCH, THE (41); RAGE IN HEAVEN (41); SHADOW OF THE THIN MAN (41); CAIRO (42); I MARRIED AN ANGEL (42); JOURNEY FOR MARGARET (42)

Van Peebles, Melvin
SUNLIGHT (58); THREE PICKUP MEN FOR HERRICK (58); •STORY OF A THREE DAY PASS, THE (67); WATERMELON MAN (70); •SWEET SWEETBACK'S BAADASSSSS SONG (71); DON'T PLAY US CHEAP (72); IDENTITY CRISIS (91); VROOOM, VROOOM, VROOOM (94)

Van Sant, Gus
MALA NOCHE (85); •DRUGSTORE COWBOY (89); •MY OWN PRIVATE IDAHO (91); EVEN COWGIRLS GET THE BLUES (94); •TO DIE FOR (95)

Varda, Agnes
LA POINTE COURTE (54); RIVIERA: TODAY'S EDEN, THE (58); LES FIANCES DU PONT MACDONALD (61); •CLEO FROM 5 TO 7 (62); LE BONHEUR (65); LES CREATURES (66); LIONS LOVE (69); ONE SINGS, THE OTHER DOESN'T (77); •VAGABOND (85); KUNG FU MASTER (87); JACQUOT (91); A HUNDRED AND ONE NIGHTS (95); UNIVERSE OF JACQUES DEMY, THE (95)

Verhoeven, Paul
BUSINESS IS BUSINESS (71); TURKISH DELIGHT (73); CATHY TIPPEL (75); •SOLDIER OF ORANGE (77); FOURTH MAN, THE (79); •SPETTERS (80); FLESH AND BLOOD (85); •ROBOCOP (87); •TOTAL RECALL (90); •BASIC INSTINCT (92); •SHOWGIRLS (95)

Vidor, Charles
DOUBLE DOOR (34); SENSATION HUNTERS (34); ARIZONIAN, THE (35); STRANGERS ALL (35); HIS FAMILY TREE (36); MUSS 'EM UP (36); DOCTOR'S DIARY, A (37); GREAT GAMBINI (37); SHE'S NO LADY (37); BLIND ALLEY (39); ROMANCE OF THE REDWOODS (39); THOSE HIGH GREY WALLS (39); LADY IN QUESTION, THE (40); MY SON, MY SON! (40); LADIES IN RETIREMENT (41); NEW YORK TOWN (41); TUTTLES OF TAHITI, THE (42); DESPERADOES, THE (43); •COVER GIRL (44); TOGETHER AGAIN (44); OVER 21 (45); •SONG TO REMEMBER, A (45); •GILDA (46); LOVES OF CARMEN, THE (48); EDGE OF DOOM (50); IT'S A BIG COUNTRY (51); •HANS CHRISTIAN ANDERSEN (52); THUNDER IN THE EAST (53); RHAPSODY (54); •LOVE ME OR LEAVE ME (55); SWAN, THE (56); FAREWELL TO ARMS, A (57); JOKER IS WILD, THE (57); SONG WITHOUT END (60)

Vidor, King
•HALLELUJAH (29); BILLY THE KID (30); NOT SO DUMB (30); •CHAMP, THE (31); STREET SCENE (31); BIRD OF PARADISE (32); CYNARA (32); MASK OF FU MANCHU, THE (32); STRANGER'S RETURN, THE (33); •OUR DAILY BREAD (34); SO RED THE ROSE (35); WEDDING NIGHT, THE (35); TEXAS RANGERS, THE (36); •STELLA DALLAS (37); •CITADEL, THE (38); WIZARD OF OZ, THE (39); COMRADE X (40); •NORTHWEST PASSAGE (40); H.M. PULHAM, ESQ. (41); AMERICAN ROMANCE, AN (44); •DUEL IN THE SUN (46); ON OUR MERRY WAY (48); BEYOND THE FOREST (49); FOUNTAINHEAD, THE (49); LIGHTNING STRIKES TWICE (51); JAPANESE WAR BRIDE (52); RUBY GENTRY (52); MAN WITHOUT A STAR (55); •WAR AND PEACE (56); SOLOMON AND SHEBA (59)

Vigo, Jean
A PROPOS DE NICE (30); •ZERO FOR CONDUCT (33); •L'ATALANTE (34)

Visconti, Luchino
•OSSESSIONE (42); •LA TERRA TREMA (47); BELLISSIMA (51); WE THE WOMEN (53); SENSO (54); WHITE NIGHTS (57); •ROCCO AND HIS BROTHERS (60); •BOCCACCIO '70 (62); •LEOPARD, THE (63); SANDRA (65); •STRANGER, THE (67); WITCHES, THE (67); •DAMNED, THE (69); •DEATH IN VENICE (71); LUDWIG (72); CONVERSATION PIECE (75); INNOCENT, THE (76)

von Sternberg, Josef
THUNDERBOLT (29); •BLUE ANGEL, THE (30); •MOROCCO (30); AMERICAN TRAGEDY, AN (31); DISHONORED (31); •BLONDE VENUS (32); •SHANGHAI EXPRESS (32); •SCARLET EMPRESS, THE (34); CRIME AND PUNISHMENT (35); DEVIL IS A WOMAN, THE (35); KING STEPS OUT, THE (36); GREAT WALTZ, THE (38); SERGEANT MADDEN (39); I TAKE THIS WOMAN (40); SHANGHAI GESTURE, THE (41); MACAO (52); ANATAHAN (53); JET PILOT (57)

Von Trier, Lars
LIBERATION PICTURES (83); ELEMENT OF CRIME, THE (84); EPIDEMIC (87); MEDEA (88); ZENTROPA (91); KINGDOM, THE (94); •BREAKING THE WAVES (96)

von Trotta, Margarethe
•LOST HONOR OF KATHARINA BLUM, THE (75); SECOND AWAKENING OF CHRISTA KLAGES, THE (77); SISTERS, OR THE BALANCE OF HAPPINESS (79); •MARIANNE AND JULIANE (81); FRIENDS AND HUSBANDS (82); ROSA LUXEMBURG (85); FELIX (87); FEAR AND LOVE (88); THREE SISTERS, THE (90); AFRICAN WOMAN, THE (90); LONG SILENCE, THE (93); PROMISE, THE (95)

Wajda, Andrzej
GENERATION, A (54); •KANAL (56); •ASHES AND DIAMONDS (58); LOTNA (59); INNOCENT SORCERERS (60); SAMSON (61); FURY IS A WOMAN (62); •LOVE AT TWENTY (62); ASHES (65); GATES TO PARADISE (67); EVERYTHING FOR SALE (68); HUNTING FLIES (69); LANDSCAPE AFTER BATTLE (70); BIRCH-WOOD, THE (71); WEDDING, THE (72); PROMISED LAND (74); SHADOW LINE (76); •MAN OF MARBLE (77); WITHOUT ANESTHETIC (79); CONDUCTOR, THE (79); YOUNG GIRLS OF WILKO, THE (79); •MAN OF IRON (80); •DANTON (82); LOVE IN GERMANY, A (84); CHRONICLES OF LOVE AFFAIRS (86); POSSESSED, THE (87); KORCZAK (90)

Walsh, Raoul
COCK-EYED WORLD, THE (29); IN OLD ARIZONA (29); •BIG TRAIL, THE (30); HOT FOR PARIS (30); MAN WHO CAME BACK, THE (31); WOMEN OF ALL NATIONS (31); YELLOW TICKET, THE (31); ME AND MY GAL (32); WILD GIRL (32); BOWERY, THE (33); GOING HOLLYWOOD (33); SAILOR'S LUCK (33); BABY FACE HARRINGTON (35); EVERY NIGHT AT EIGHT (35); UNDER PRESSURE (35); BIG BROWN EYES (36); KLONDIKE ANNIE (36); SPENDTHRIFT (36); ARTISTS & MODELS (37); HITTING A NEW HIGH (37); WHEN THIEF MEETS THIEF (37); YOU'RE IN THE ARMY NOW (37); COLLEGE SWING (38); •ROARING TWENTIES, THE (39); ST. LOUIS BLUES (39); DARK COMMAND (40); •THEY DRIVE BY NIGHT (40); •HIGH SIERRA (41); MANPOWER (41); STRAWBERRY BLONDE, THE (41); DESPERATE JOURNEY (42); •GENTLEMAN JIM (42); •THEY DIED WITH THEIR BOOTS ON (42); BACKGROUND TO DANGER (43); NORTHERN PURSUIT (43); UNCERTAIN GLORY (44); HORN BLOWS AT MIDNIGHT, THE (45); •OBJECTIVE, BURMA! (45); SALTY O'ROURKE (45); MAN I LOVE, THE (45); CHEYENNE (47); •PURSUED (47); STALLION ROAD (47); FIGHTER SQUADRON (48); ONE SUNDAY AFTERNOON (48); SILVER RIVER (48); COLORADO TERRITORY (49); •WHITE HEAT (49); ALONG THE GREAT DIVIDE (51); •CAPTAIN HORATIO HORNBLOWER (51); DISTANT DRUMS (51); BLACKBEARD THE PIRATE (52); GLORY ALLEY (52); LAWLESS BREED, THE (52); •WORLD IN HIS ARMS, THE (52); GUN FURY (53); LION IS IN THE STREETS, A (53); SEA DEVILS (53); SASKATCHEWAN (54); BATTLE CRY (55); TALL MEN, THE (55); KING AND FOUR QUEENS, THE (56); REVOLT OF MAMIE STOVER, THE (56); BAND OF ANGELS (57); NAKED AND THE DEAD, THE (58); SHERIFF OF FRACTURED JAW, THE (58); PRIVATE'S AFFAIR, A (59); ESTHER AND THE KING (60); MARINES, LET'S GO! (61); DISTANT TRUMPET, A (64)

Walters, Charles
•ZIEGFELD FOLLIES (45); GOOD NEWS (47); •EASTER PARADE (48); •BARKLEYS OF BROADWAY, THE (49); SUMMER STOCK (50); TEXAS CARNIVAL (51); THREE GUYS NAMED MIKE (51); BELLE OF NEW YORK, THE (52); DANGEROUS WHEN WET (53); EASY TO LOVE (53); •LILI (53); TORCH SONG (53); GLASS SLIPPER, THE (55); TENDER TRAP, THE (55); •HIGH SOCIETY (56); DON'T GO NEAR THE WATER